Barr & Stroud

Seekers

The pursuit of improved optical and electro-optical systems is relentless at **Barr & Stroud**, the Defence Systems company of the Pilkington Group. New heights of technical achievement remain the constant goal.

Sharp eyes come into their own especially in the air. **Barr & Stroud** thermal imaging technology has brought a new clarity of vision to helicopters and fixed wing aircraft for navigation, reconnaissance and attack purposes. Helping them seek and find their prey swiftly and surely, by day or night, even in the worst conditions.

And the search for ever higher standards continues on land and at sea, as well as in the air. For a clearer view contact **Barr & Stroud** for all the details of air borne thermal imaging.

PILKINGTON

◄ **Optronics** ►

Barr & Stroud Limited
Caxton Street Anniesland Glasgow Scotland G13 1HZ
Telephone 041-954 9601 Telex 778114 Fax 041-954 2380

45⁰⁰

JANE'S ALL THE WORLD'S AIRCRAFT

FOUNDED IN 1909 BY FRED T. JANE

COMPILED AND EDITED BY
JOHN W R TAYLOR, FRAeS, FRHistS, AFAIAA
ASSISTANT EDITOR
KENNETH MUNSON, AMRAeS, ARHistS

1988-89

ISBN 0 7106-0867-5
JANE'S DEFENCE DATA
A principal activity of Jane's Information Group Limited
"Jane's" is a registered trade mark

In the USA and its dependencies
Jane's Information Group Inc, 1340 Braddock Place, Suite 300, PO Box 1436, Alexandria, Virginia 22313-2036, USA

Alphabetical list of Advertisers

A

AMX International
c/o Aeritalia SpA, Gruppo Velivoli da Combattimento,
Corso Marche 41, 10146 Turin, Italy .... *inside front cover*

Aermacchi SpA
Via San Vito 80, 21100 Varese, Italy .... [46]

Aerospatiale
Division Engins Tactiques, 2 rue Beranger,
92322 Chatillon Cedex, France .... [4] & [5]

Aerospatiale
37 Boulevard de Montmorency, 75016 Paris,
France .... [12] & [13]

AGUSTA Group
Via Caldera 21, 20153 Milan, Italy .... [8] & [9]

Allied Signal Aerospace Company
PO Box 92248, 9851 Sepulveda Boulavard,
CA 90009, USA .... *facing page 321*

AP Precision Hydraulics Ltd
PO Box 1, Shaw Road, Speke,
Liverpool L24 9JY, England .... [34]

Aviaexport
v/o 19 Ivan Frank Street, 121355 Moscow, USSR .... [42]

Azienda Autonoma Assistenza AL Volo
Via Salaria 716, 00199 Rome, Italy .... [21]

B

Barr & Stroud Ltd
Caxton Street, Anniesland, Glasgow GL13 1HZ,
Scotland .... *facing inside front cover*

C

Cardoen Industrias
Los Conquistadores 1700, Piso 28,
Santiago, Chile .... *back index section*

Central Engineering International Company
2930 Anthony Lane, Minneapolis,
Minnesota 55418, USA .... [3]

D

DAF Special Products B/V
PO Box 14, 5600 AA Eindhoven, The Netherlands .... [11]

E

Elettronica SpA
Via Tiburtina Km 13.700, 00131 Rome,
Italy .... *front endpaper IV*

Embraer Aircraft Corporation
Military Sales Division, Av Brig Faria Lima,
2170 Cx P 343, 12200 Sao Jose dos Campos,
Sao Poulo, Brazil .... [32]

F

FIAR SpA
Via Montefeltro 8, 20156 Milan, Italy .... [30]

FIAT Aviazione
Casella Postale 1389, Via Nizza 312,
10127 Turin, Italy .... [24] & [25]

Flight Refuelling Ltd
Brook Road, Leigh Park, Wimborne,
Dorset BH21 2BJ, England .... *bookmark*

FOM Aeromodell snc
Via E Romagna 184, 47033 Cattolica, Italy .... [23]

G

Goodyear Great Britain Ltd
Viscount Way, Heathrow Airport, London, Hounslow,
Middlesex, TW6 2JN, England .... [15]

H

Hughes Aircraft Company
PO Box 45066, Los Angeles, CA 90045-0066, USA .... [19]

I

Israel Military Industries
PO Box 1044, Ramat Hasharon 47100, Israel .... [34]

K

Kaman Aerospace Corporation
PO Box 2, Bloomfield, Connecticut
06002, USA .... *facing page 352*

L

Lake Aircraft
Kissemmee Airport, Kissimmee,
FL 32741, USA .... *facing page 353*

Lucas Aerospace Ltd
Brueton House, New Road, Solihull, West Midlands
B91 3TX, England .... [40]

M

Meteor Contruzioni Aeronautiche ed Elettronishe SpA
Via Nomentana 146, 00162 Rome, Italy .... [50]

McDonnell Douglas
PO Box 516, St. Louis, Missouri 63166, USA *facing page 320*

Motoren-und Turbinen-Union GmbH (MTU)
PO Box 50 06 40, D-8000 Munich 50,
Federal Republic of Germany .... [7]

O

Oficinas Gerais De Material Aeronautico (OGMA)
2615 Alverca, Portugal .... [27]

Omnipol Foreign Trade Corporation
Nekazanka 11, 112 21 Praha 1, Czechoslovakia .... [44]

P

Pilatus Aircraft Ltd
CH-6370 Stans, Switzerland .... [36]

Promavia SA
Chaussee de Fleurus 181, B-6200 Gosselies,
Belgium.. *back index section*

R

Rotorway Aircraft Inc
7411 West Galveston, Chandler, AZ 85226, USA.......... [23]

S

SECA
Aeroport du Bourget Zone Nord, BP 132,
93350 Le Bourget, France...................................... [3]

Selenia Industrie Elettronische Associte SpA
Defence Systems Division, Via Tiburtina Km 12.400,
00131 Rome, Italy .... [38]

SNECMA Group
2 boulevard Victor, 75724 Paris Cedex 15, France .... [27]

SNIA/BPD SpA
Corso Garibaldi 22, 00034 Colleferro Rome, Italy.......... [23]

T

Teledyne Continental Motors
Aircraft Products Division, PO Box 90,
Mobile, Alabama 36601, USA................... *facing page 353*

Thomson-CSF Aerospace Group
204 round Point du Pont de Sevres, 92516 Bologne,
BP 77 France... [17]

V

Vickers Instruments
Haxby Road, York YO3 7SD, England ..... *back index section*

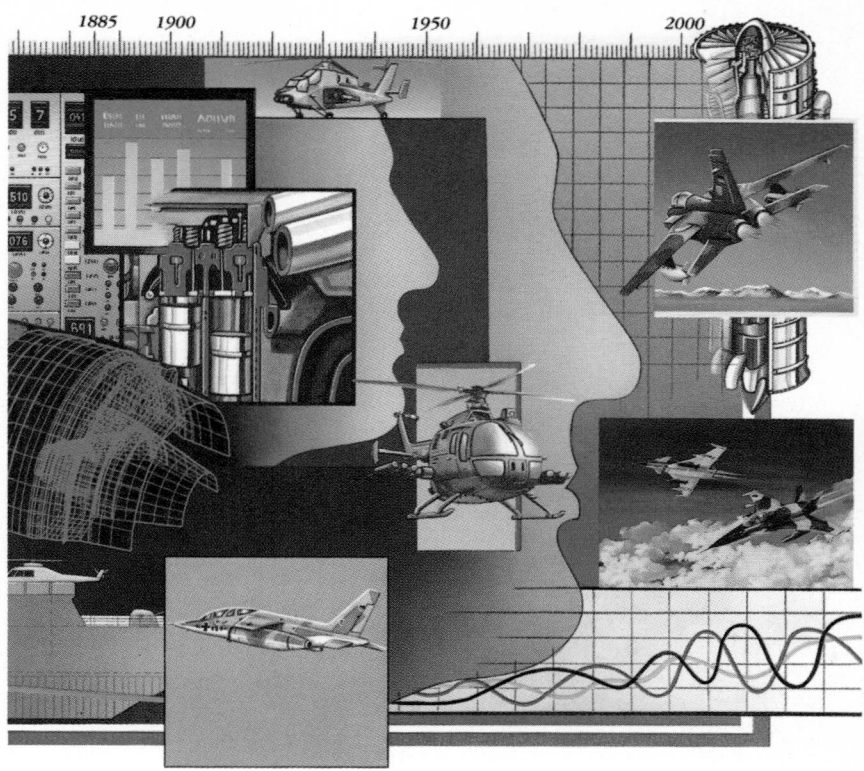

Many great names such as Benz, Daimler, Diesel and Maybach are closely associated with MTU's history. The origins of MTU Motoren- und Turbinen-Union in Munich and Friedrichshafen can be traced back to the beginning of motorization. **Ever since, MTU has been among the world's leaders when it comes to propulsion power on land, sea and in the air.** The MTU Group produces jet and turboshaft engines, industrial gas turbines, diesel engines, power transmissions, and electronic monitoring and control systems. Partnerships in advanced-technology aircraft engine development and production have been established with all internationally renowned manufacturers. MTU products are backed up by a worldwide marketing and service organization.

MTU Group members:

MTU München
MTU Friedrichshafen
MTU Maintenance GmbH
Aktiengesellschaft Kühnle,
Kopp & Kausch
L'Orange GmbH
MTU-Turbomeca GmbH
Sulzer-MTU Casting
Technology GmbH
Turbo-Union Ltd.
EUROJET Turbo GmbH
MTU of North America, Inc.
MTU Motores Diesel Ltda.
MTU Argentina S. A.
MTU Asia Pte. Ltd.
MTU Australia Pty. Ltd.

MTU Motoren- und Turbinen-Union
München GmbH
P.O.Box 500640 · D-8000 München 50
Telephone (089) 1489-1

8.6/86 Schellenberg, Ogilvy & Mather

Aero Engines for Airliners · Aero Engines for General Aviation and Commuter Aircraft · Aero Engines for Turboprops · Aero Engines for Helicopters · Aero Engines for Combat Aircraft · Components · Service- Piston Engines · Product Support

S 211. MISSION

"Mission training" means that the basic jet trainer S 211 Siai Marchetti has been designed and built to provide the best training for tomorrow's pilots.
Supercritical wing design, dive speed 400 knots/0.8 m.; rate of climb 4,200 ft/min.; service ceiling 40,000 feet; 0-0 type ejection seats.
The use of composite materials and the low specific consumption of its turbofan engine make the S 211 highly competitive.
Advancing pilots rapidly through the training syllabus at the highest possible skill level is considered maximum cost effectiveness. This is the mission the S 211 performs so well.
Furthermore, in the armed version, the S 211 can effectively be used for light ground attack missions.
The S 211 Siai Marchetti has a lot to teach.

GRUPPO

AGUSTA

Research and Aerospace Technology

TRAINING.

Classified list of advertisers

The companies advertising in this publication have informed us that
they are involved in the fields of manufacture indicated below:

Ac motors
Lucas Aerospace

Accelerometers
AGUSTA

Accessories
SECA

Accuracy equipment
Vickers Instruments

Actuators, electric
Lucas Aerospace
SECA
Thomson-CSF

Actuators, hydraulic
AP Precision Hydraulics
DAF Special Products
Thomson-CSF

Acoustic transducers
Aviaexport

Aerials, aircraft
AGUSTA

Aero-engine test plant
Aviaexport
Central Engineering International
SECA
SNECMA Group

Aero-engines
FIAT Aviazione
MTU
SECA
SNECMA Group

Aeronautical engineers and consultants
AGUSTA
Aviaexport
Industrias Cardoen
SECA

Aerosystems
Flight Refuelling
SECA

Aileron power control units
AP Precision Hydraulics

**Airborne acoustic & magnetic mine
countermeasures systems**
Aviaexport
SECA

Airborne surveillance drone systems
Aerospatiale
Aviaexport
Flight Refuelling
Selenia

Airborne video systems
Aviaexport
Thomson-CSF

Air compressors (cabin) & (engine starting)
Lucas Aerospace
SECA
Thomson-CSF

Air compressors for engine starting
Lucas Aerospace

Air conditioning equipment
Thomson-CSF

Air-control equipment for cabins
Thomson-CSF

Air cycle refrigeration packages
Aviaexport
Thomson-CSF

Air dust computer systems
AGUSTA
Aviaexport

Ailerons
SECA

Air traffic control equipment
FIAR
Hughes Aircraft Company
Selenia
Thomson-CSF

Aircraft, agricultural
AGUSTA
Aviaexport
Omnipol

Aircraft, agricultural (dusters & sprayers)
Aviaexport
Embraer Tucano
Pilatus Aircraft

Aircraft, ambulance
AGUSTA
Aviaexport
Embraer Tucano
Pilatus Aircraft
SECA

Aircraft, combat, light
Promavia

Aircraft, combat
AGUSTA
Aviaexport
Embraer/Aeritalia (AMX)
Kaman Aerospace Corporation
Promavia
Selenia

Aircraft, commercial
Aerospatiale
AGUSTA
Aviaexport
Embraer Tucano
Promavia
SECA

Aircraft, commercial trainers
Promavia

Aircraft, executive
AGUSTA
Aviaexport
Embraer Tucano
Promavia
SECA

Aircraft, integrated date systems
Aviaexport
Hughes Aircraft Company

Aircraft, military
Aerospatiale
Aermacchi
AGUSTA
Aviaexport
CASA
Embraer/Aeritalia (AMX)
Embraer Tucano
Kaman Aerospace Corporation
Pilatus Aircraft
Promavia
SECA
Selenia

Aircraft, naval
AGUSTA
Aviaexport
CASA
Kaman Aerospace Corporation
Promavia
SECA

Aircraft, private
AGUSTA
Aviaexport
Embraer Tucano
Promavia
SECA

Aircraft, radio controlled
AGUSTA
Aviaexport
Kaman Aerospace Corporation
Meteor

Aircraft, supersonic
Aviaexport

Aircraft training
Aermacchi
AGUSTA
Aviaexport
CASA
Embraer Tucano
Omnipol
Pilatus Aircraft
Promavia
SECA

Aircraft, transport
AGUSTA
CASA
Embraer Tucano
Kaman Aerospace Corporation
Omnipol
SECA

Aircraft, v/stol
Pilatus Aircraft

Aircraft canopies
Aviaexport
Lucas Aerospace

Aircraft construction
Aviaexport
Pilatus Aircraft

Aircraft developments
AGUSTA
Aviaexport
CASA
Embraer Tucano
Industrias Cardoen
Kaman Aerospace Corporation
Pilatus Aircraft

Aircraft escape systems
Aviaexport

Aircraft field operations & support
Kaman Aerospace Corporation
SECA
Vickers Instruments

Aircraft freight handling equipment
Aviaexport

Aircraft integrated data systems
Aviaexport
Hughes Aircraft Company
SECA

Aircraft mechanical handlers
Aviaexport
SECA

Aircraft modifications
Embraer Tucano
Kaman Aerospace Corporation

Aircraft product support
Aermacchi
AGUSTA
Embraer Tucano
Kaman Aerospace Corporation
Pilatus Aircraft
Vickers Instruments

Aircraft seats
Aerospatiale
SECA

Aircraft supersonic
Aviaexport
Selenia

Aircraft wire and cable
Hughes Aircraft Company
SECA

The specialist experience of DAF Trucks with high-quality means of transport forms the solid foundation of its independent DAF Special Products division. Its defence and aviation know-how has helped DAF Special parts. At present DAF Special Products assists in the development of the new NATO helicopters with a revolutionary crownwheel pinion transmission. DAF Special Products demonstrates its strength on the ground as well as in the air.

HIGH TECHNOLOGY IS OUR BUSINESS

achieve a place of its own in the world of technology. The construction of aircraft landing gear is a good example of what we are talking about.

DAF Special Products accepted this challenge and together with Menasco Inc. began building this essential part of the F-16, the by now almost legendary fighter plane.

DAF managed to produce the complete undercarriage in accordance with the very strict quality requirements. It proved to be a profitable operation, for DAF Special Products now uses the knowledge and experience it gained this way not only for other types of aircraft but also in the production of helicopter

Its knowledge and experience in the field of defence technology has found a logical sequel in the development and production of infantry vehicles, weapon systems, fuel systems and simulators.

You come across DAF Special Products in various national and international collaborative programs: as one of the industrial partners in a consortium, as project-managing organization, as a partner in joint development schemes (Fokker 50) or in joint production activities (Leopard), or as licensee (YPR 765, F-16).

Quality comes natural to DAF Special Products.

It is hardly surprising that on behalf of the NATO the Dutch Ministry of Defence was able to issue the AQAP-1 certificate to DAF Special Products: guarantee of optimum quality control from the design stage to the final inspection and maintenance.

DAF Special Products

DAF Special Products The Netherlands Tel.: +3140143056. Telex: 51970.

CLASSIFIED LIST OF ADVERTISERS

Airport ground handling equipment
Aviaexport

Airports planning
Aviaexport

Airspeed indications
Thomson-CSF

Air traffic control systems, civilian and military
Aviaexport
Hughes Aircraft Company
Selenia

Alternators
Lucas Aerospace
SECA
Thomson-CSF

Ammunition boosters
Aviaexport
SNIA/BPD
Thomson-CSF

Amplifiers
AGUSTA
Hughes Aircraft Company
SECA

Antennas, aircraft
Elettronica
SECA

Antennas
Elettronica
Selenia
SECA

Anti-skid systems
SNECMA Group

Asw
Aviaexport
Hughes Aircraft Company
Thomson-CSF

Automatic checkout systems
Aviaexport

Automatic digital data equipment
Aviaexport
Central Engineering International

Automatic pilot
SECA
Meteor

Automatic navigation equipment
Meteor

Automatic voltage & current regulators
Lucas Aerospace
SECA
Thomson-CSF

Auxiliary power plants
FIAT Aviazione
Lucas Aerospace
SNECMA Group

Avionic systems
FIAR
Hughes Aircraft Company
SECA
Selenia
Thomson-CSF

Bars, stainless steel & heat resisting steel
Aviaexport

Batteries
Aviaexport

Beacon equipment
SECA

Blades, gas turbine
SECA
SNECMA Group

Bomb racks
Aviaexport
Israel Military Industries

Bombs
Cardoen Industrias

Bombsights
Aviaexport
Thomson-CSF

Bonding jumpers bus bars
Aviaexport

Brake lining
Aviaexport
Goodyear Tyre & Rubber Company

Brakes for aircraft
Goodyear Tyre & Rubber Company
SNECMA Group

Cabin cooling (tropical airfield equipment)
Thomson-CSF

Cabin pressure control systems
Thomson-CSF

Cables, electric
Hughes Aircraft Company
SECA

Cables, rf
Hughes Aircraft Company

Canisters
Aviaexport
Israel Military Industries

Carbon fibre components
AGUSTA
Aviaexport

Coating, erosion resistant
Aviaexport
Goodyear Tyre & Rubber Company
SECA

Cockpit windows – heated & unheated
Lucas Aerospace

Combat command & control
Aviaexport
Hughes Aircraft Company
Thomson-CSF

Combustion systems (gas turbine)
Lucas Aerospace
SECA
SNECMA Group

Communications control systems
Hughes Aircraft Company

Components
AGUSTA
Kaman Aerospace Corporation
SECA

Composite structure
AGUSTA
Aviaexport
Israel Military Industries
Kaman Aerospace Corporation
Lucas Aerospace
SNECMA Group

Computers
AGUSTA
Aviaexport
Hughes Aircraft Company
Thomson-CSF

Computers, aerodynamic analogue & digital
Aviaexport
Selenia

Connectors, connector accessories
Hughes Aircraft Company
SECA

Constant speed drive test benches
Aviaexport
Lucas Aerospace

Control equipment for aircraft
AP Precision Hydraulics
SECA

Controls, cockpit
SECA

Controls, main engine fuel
Lucas Aerospace
SECA
SNECMA Group

Cooling compressors
SECA
Thomson-CSF

Cooling engines
Lucas Aerospace
SECA
Thomson-CSF

Couplings, self-sealing
AP Precision Hydraulics
Aviaexport
Kaman Aerospace Corporation
SECA

Cowlings
Aviaexport

Data links
Aviaexport
Hughes Aircraft Company

Data processing equipment
Aviaexport
Hughes Aircraft Company
SNECMA Group
Thomson-CSF

Data processing equipment for atc
Hughes Aircraft Company
Selenia
Thomson-CSF

Data transmission equipment
AGUSTA
Aviaexport
SNECMA Group

Dc generators
Lucas Aerospace
SECA
Thomson-CSF

Dc Motors
Lucas Aerospace
SECA
Thomson-CSF

Defence contractors
Aviaexport
Hughes Aircraft Company
Kaman Aerospace Corporation

Defence data handling & display
Aviaexport
Hughes Aircraft Company
Selenia
Thomson-CSF

De-icing equipment
Lucas Aerospace
SECA

Desktop aluminium
FOM Aeromodelli

Digital data links
Aviaexport

Direction finding equipment (triangulation)
AGUSTA
Aviaexport
Selenia

Display systems
Aviaexport
FIAR
Hughes Aircraft Company
Thomson-CSF

Displays, in cockpits
Aviaexport
FIAR
Hughes Aircraft Company
Selenia
Thomson-CSF

Doors
Aviaexport
SECA

Drive shafts
SECA

Drones
Aviaexport
Flight Refuelling
Israel Military Industries
Kaman Aerospace Corporation
Selenia

Earling warning systems
Aviaexport
Hughes Aircraft Company
Selenia

Ejection seats
Aviaexport
SNECMA Group

Electrical equipment
Aviaexport
Lucas Aerospace
SECA
Thomson-CSF

Electrical wiring assemblies
AGUSTA
Hughes Aircraft Company
Kaman Aerospace Corporation
SECA

Electro-hydraulic power packs
AP Precision Hydraulics
Lucas Aerospace

Electro-optical systems
AGUSTA
Aviaexport
FIAR
Hughes Aircraft Company
Selenia
Thomson-CSF
Vickers Instruments

Electro hydraulic power packs
AP Precision Hydraulics
Aviaexport
Thomson-CSF

Electronic countermeasures (ecm)
Aviaexport
Elettronica
Hughes Aircraft Company
Israel Military Industries
Selenia
Thomson-CSF

Electronic equipment
AGUSTA
Aviaexport
Hughes Aircraft Company
Lucas Aerospace
SECA
SNECMA Group
Thomson-CSF

Electronic flight controls
Aerospatiale
AGUSTA
Lucas Aerospace
Thomson-CSF

Electronic fuel control systems
Lucas Aerospace
SECA
SNECMA Group
Thomson-CSF

Electronic map systems
Aviaexport
Hughes Aircraft Company
Thomson-CSF

Electronic support measures (esm)
Aviaexport
Elettronica
Selenia
Thomson-CSF

Electronics & guidance
AGUSTA
Aviaexport
Thomson-CSF

Engine compressor cleaning rigs
SECA

Engine design and manufacture
Aviaexport
Motoren-und Turbinen-Union Munchen
SNECMA Group

Engine parts fabrication
Aviaexport
DAF Special Products
FIAT Aviazione
Motoren-un Turbinen-Union Munchen
SNECMA Group

Engine run-up facilities – mobile
Aviaexport
Motoren-und Turbinen-Union Munchen

Engine starting equipment
Christie Electric Corporation
FIAT Aviazione
Lucas Aerospace
Thomson-CSF

Engine testing equipment
Central Engineering
Motoren-und Turbinen-Union Munchen
SECA
SNECMA Group

Engines, aircraft
Aviaexport
Motoren-und Turbinen-Union Munchen
Omnipol
SECA
SNECMA Group
Teledyne Continental Motors

Engines, auxilliary
Lucas Aerospace

Engines, v/stol
Aviaexport

Environmental control systems
Aviaexport
Thomson-CSF

EW systems
Aviaexport
Elettronica
Hughes Aircraft Company
Selenia
Thomson-CSF

Experimental assemblies
Aviaexport

External crash survivable fuel tanks
Aviaexport
SECA

Fibre optic recorders
Aviaexport
EDO Corporation (Western Division)

Fibre optics
Aviaexport
Hughes Aircraft Company

Filters, air
AP Precision Hydraulics
SECA

Filters, electronic
SECA

Filters – fuel & oil
AP Precision Hydraulics
Flight Refuelling
SECA

Fire suppression systems
Hughes Aircraft Company
SECA
Thomson-CSF

Flight instrument test sets
AGUSTA
Hughes Aircraft Company
SECA
Thomson-CSF

Flow gauges
AGUSTA
SECA
Thomson-CSF

Flying controls
AGUSTA
AP Precision Hydraulics
Thomson-CSF

Forgings, steel
Israel Military Industries
SNECMA Group

Fuel control test benches
AGUSTA

Fuel flow proportioners
Flight Refuelling
Lucas Aerospace
SECA

Fuel pump test benches
SECA

Fuel pumps
Flight Refuelling
Lucas Aerospace
SECA
SNECMA Group
Thomson-CSF

Fuel sprayers
Lucas Aerospace
SECA

Fuel systems protection
SECA
Thomson-CSF

Fuel systems and refuelling equipment
Flight Refuelling
Israel Military Industries
SECA
Thomson-CSF

Fuel tank pressurisation equipment
Flight Refuelling
Thomson-CSF

Furnishings & aircraft cabins
SECA

Gas turbine starting systems
Lucas Aerospace
Thomson-CSF

Gas turbines
Aviaexport
FIAT Aviazione
Lucas Aerospace
SECA
SNECMA Group

Gas turbines, equipment & accessories
Aviaexport
SECA

Gauges
Aviaexport
SECA
Thomson-CSF

[14]

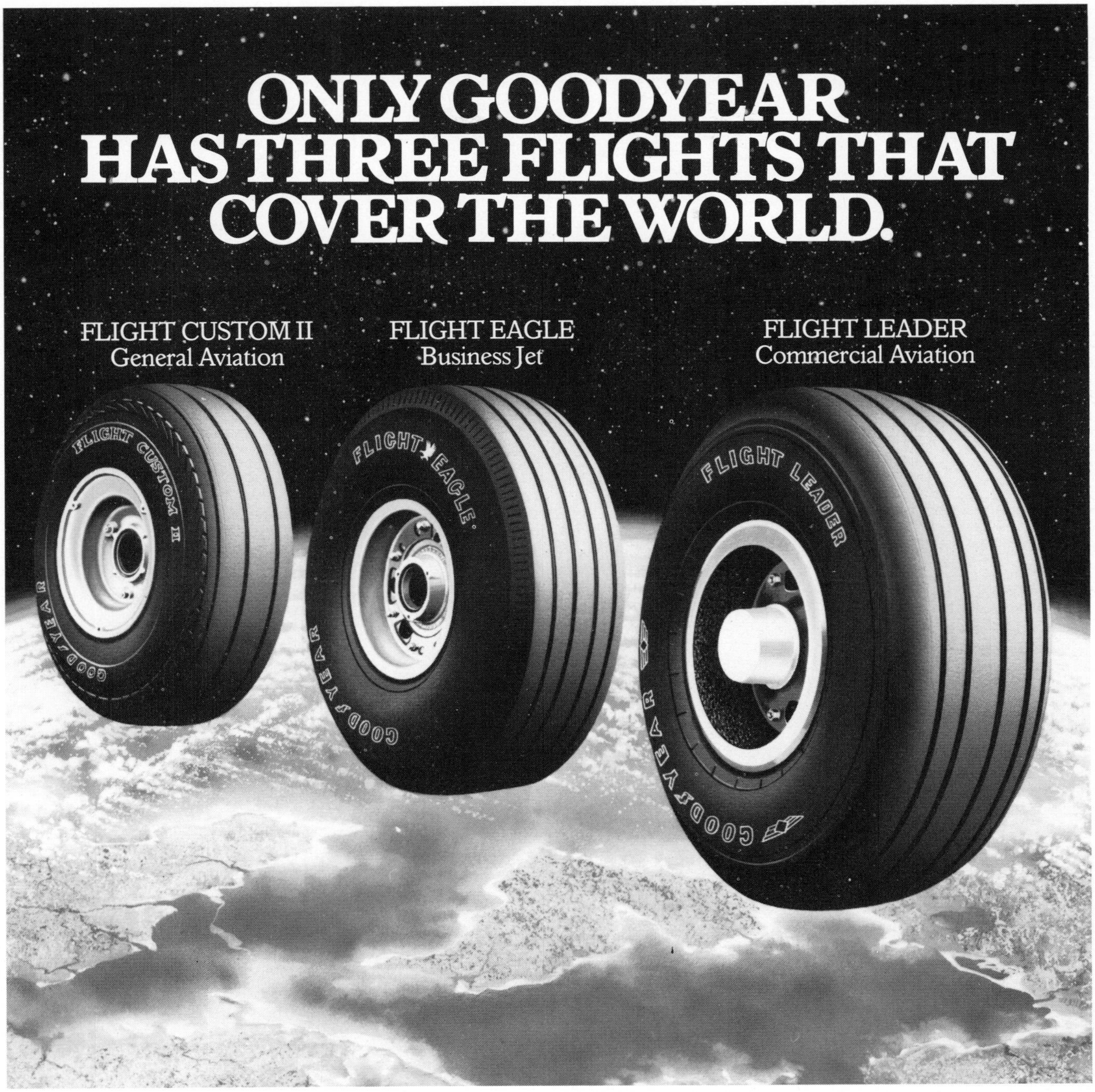

ONLY GOODYEAR HAS THREE FLIGHTS THAT COVER THE WORLD.

FLIGHT CUSTOM II
General Aviation

FLIGHT EAGLE
Business Jet

FLIGHT LEADER
Commercial Aviation

It makes no difference whether it's North or South America, Europe, Africa, Asia, or Australia. Because anywhere in the world that you'll find aircraft, you'll find Goodyear Aircraft tyres.

Only Goodyear produces aircraft tyres and retreads at 20 plants worldwide. And when you add worldwide availability to Goodyear's outstanding record of prompt supply and service, that's good news. Whether you manufacture airplanes, fly for fun, or fly for a living.

Flight Custom II for general aviation. Flight Eagle for business jets. Flight Leader for commercial aviation. Goodyear's three Flights that cover the world.

And whatever your aircraft, wherever your destination, they're ready whenever you need them.

For more information, please contact: The Goodyear Tyre and Rubber Company (Great Britain) Ltd., Aviation Products, Viscount Way, Heathrow Airport–London, Hounslow, Middlesex TW6 2JN. Tel: 01-759 1922.

GOODYEAR AVIATION PRODUCTS

Generators
Lucas Aerospace
SECA
Thomson-CSF

Ground support equipment
Aermacchi
AGUSTA
Hughes Aircraft Company
Israel Military Industries
Kaman Aerospace Corporation
Selenia
Vickers Instruments

Guided missile ground handling equipment
Hughes Aircraft Company
Selenia

Guided missiles
AGUSTA
Aerospatiale
Aviaexport
Hughes Aircraft Company
Selenia
SNIA/BPD
Thomson-CSF

**Harmonisation systems, weapons &
avionics**
Vickers Instruments

Heated windows
Lucas Aerospace

Heated winscreen controllers
Lucas Aerospace

Helicopter gun turrets
Aviaexport
Lucas Aerospace

Helicopter landing gears
AP Precision Hydraulics

Helicopter parts & components
AGUSTA
AP Precision Hydraulics
DAF Special Products
FIAT Aviazione
Kaman Aerospace Corporation

Helicopter stabilisation
Kaman Aerospace Corporation

**Helicopter surface-to-air refuelling
equipment**
AGUSTA
Aviaexport
Flight Refuelling

Helicopter support
AGUSTA
Aviaexport
Kaman Aerospace Corportion
Pilatus Aircraft
SECA

Helicopter training & support
AGUSTA
Aviaexport
Kaman Aerospace Corporation
Thomson-CSF

Helicopter winches
AGUSTA
Aviaexport
Kaman Aerospace Corporation
Thomson-CSF

Helicopter, ambulances
Aerospatiale
AGUSTA
Aviaexport
SECA

Helicopters, commercial-executive
Aerospatiale
AGUSTA
Aviaexport
Rotorway
SECA

Helicopters, military-naval
Aerospatiale
AGUSTA
Aviaexport
Kaman Aerospace Corporation
SECA

**High performance aircraft ejection and
stores release units**
Aviaexport
Israel Military Industries

High pressure couplings
AP Precision Hydraulics
Aviaexport
Kaman Aerospace Corporation

High-speed research cameras
AGUSTA
Aviaexport

Horizon sensors
EDO Corporation (Engineering Division)

Hud
Aviaexport
Hughes Aircraft Company
Selenia
Thomson-CSF

Hydraulic actuation systems
AP Precision Hydraulics
Lucas Aerospace
SNECMA Group
Thomson-CSF

Hydraulic control/systems
AP Precision Hydraulics
Flight Refuelling
Thomson-CSF

Hydraulic equipment
AP Precision Hydraulics
Thomson-CSF

Hydraulic pressure pumps
AP Precision Hydraulics
Lucas Aerospace
SNECMA Group
Thomson-CSF

Hydromechanical engine controls
Lucas Aerospace
SECA

Ignition exciters
Aviaexport
Lucas Aerospace
SECA

Inertial navigation & cockpit systems
SECA

Infared detectors
Aviaexport
Elettronica
Hughes Aircraft Company
Thomson-CSF

Information services
DMS

Infra-red materials
Aviaexport
Barr & Stroud
Hughes Aircraft Company

Infra-red systems
AGUSTA
Aviaexport
Barr & Stroud
Electtronica
FIAR
Hughes Aircraft Company
Selenia
Thomson-CSF

Instrument components
AGUSTA
SECA

Instruments, aircraft
AGUSTA
SECA
Thomson-CSF

Instruments, electronic
AGUSTA
SECA
Thomson-CSF

Instruments, navigational
AGUSTA
SECA
Thomson-CSF

Instruments – test equipment
AGUSTA
Israel Military Industries
SECA
Thomson-CSF
Vickers Instruments

Integrated marine navigation systems
Aviaexport
SECA

Integrated total pneumatic systems
Lucas Aerospace

Jet engine parts
FIAT Aviazione
Thomson-CSF
SECA
SNECMA Group

Jet engine test parts
Central Engineering International

Jet fuel starters
Lucas Aerospace

Jet propulsion engines
SNECMA Group

Jet trainer, military
Aermacchi
AGUSTA
Aviaexport
CASA
Promavia

Joining compound
Aviaexport
Goodyear Tyre & Rubber Company

Kevlat components
AGUSTA
Aviaexport
Israel Military Industries

Lamps, cockpit
Lucas Aerospace

Landing gear
AP Precision Hydraulics
DAF Special Products

Laser countermeasures
Aviaexport
FIAR
Thomson-CSF

Lasers
Aviaexport
FIAR
Hughes Aircraft Company
Kaman Aerospace Corporation
Selenia

Laser rangefinders
AGUSTA
Aviaexport
Barr & Stroud
FIAR
Selenia
Thomson-CSF

Lavatories & cabin liners
SECA

Lights, aircraft
SECA

Lights, landing
SECA

Lights, navigation
Omnipol
SECA

THOMSON-CSF
IS FLYING HIGH.

Thomson-CSF Aerospace Group. A team of 14,000 engineers and technicians specializing in every aspect of aerospace.

Starting with defense. Thomson-CSF is Europe's leading supplier of airborne radars and EW systems for fighter aircraft.

For pilots on combat missions our display systems and radar and laser missile guidance systems provide critical capabilities in ensuring the missions' success.

In the field of commercial aviation, we help ensure passenger comfort and safety with a broad line of instruments and sensors designed to monitor flight control, pressurization and the generation of electrical power.

For instructing and training aircrews we provide a wide range of simulators.

At the same time, down here on the ground, we've been busily applying the technology we've developed for aircraft to more down-to-earth fields such as nuclear plant and vehicle driving simulation – as well as to shipboard electronics.

Worldwide.

Over sixty-five percent of our revenues – totaling close over $ 1,500,000,000 in 1987 is generated internationally.

Our goal at Thomson-CSF Aerospace Group: to continue to bring together all the skills and resources that make Thomson-CSF a pillar of the European aerospace industry as we wing toward the 21st century.

AEROSPACE GROUP

122, avenue du Général Leclerc
92100 Boulogne-Billancourt - FRANCE
Tel.: (1) 46.84.71.71 - Telex: TCSF 204 780 F.

◆ THOMSON-CSF

THE BRAINPOWER.   THE WILLPOWER.   THE WINPOWER.

[18]

SCIENCE/SCOPE®

A new navigation system for the F/A-18 Hornet has begun flight tests prior to delivery to the U.S. Navy. The system, known as the Thermal Imaging Navigation Set (TINS) was developed by Hughes Aircraft Company based on its AN/AAQ-16 Night Vision System installed on U.S. Army helicopters. TINS, designated AN/AAR-50, relies on a thermal imaging sensor that provides pilots with a TV-like picture on a head-up display, making low-level flights possible at night or in adverse weather conditions. Production deliveries of the system are expected to begin in fall 1989.

Two new systems will allow the F-4F Phantom to retain air superiority well into the 21st century. The Federal Republic of Germany selected Hughes' Advanced Medium-Range Air-to-Air Missile (AMRAAM) and APG-65 radar to upgrade its Luftwaffe Phantoms, a more cost-effective solution than purchasing an entirely new aircraft. The APG-65 is a proven, highly reliable system designed for air-to-air and air-to-surface missions. AMRAAM, designed to work in conjunction with the APG-65, allows a single pilot to attack multiple targets in a single engagement and provides the freedom to launch-and-maneuver. MBB is integrating the radar, AMRAAM, and other improved avionics into the aircraft, and AEG is manufacturing the APG-65 in Germany. Hughes provides technical support to both MBB and AEG.

A new simulation demonstration lets U.S. Air Force pilots and air crews experience the hazards and difficulties in flight operations of large cargo aircraft in the vicinity of battle areas. The MAC-BARON simulation, developed by Hughes, creates the battle environment and duplicates the sensor and navigational information available to the aircrew. The crew must then "fly" the aircraft to avoid detection and engagement by enemy airborne interceptors. Among the simulation's attributes, MAC-BARON emphasizes the importance of situational awareness to potential airlifters.

A new cabin control system for Boeing's 747-400 jumbo jetliner uses all-digital technology to perform a wide range of passenger service functions previously unavailable. The Advanced Cabin Entertainment and Service System (ACESS), designated the APAX-140, extends the application of digital multiplexed techniques to such functions as cabin interphone, lighting, and advisory signs. Other features include an interactive, two-way capability that allows passengers to communicate back to a central computer for in-flight ordering of specific goods and services, and a self-test function that monitors and records faults while in flight. Hughes, supplying multiplexed passenger entertainment and service systems since 1970, designed and built ACESS for Boeing.

An infrared sensor system for the joint services' V-22 Osprey aircraft will help crews navigate and land in darkness and during periods of poor visibility. The Infrared Detection Set (IDS), developed by Hughes, senses small differences in radiated heat and provides a TV-like image of the surrounding area. The V-22, the first of the new tilt-rotor aircraft for the U.S. Armed Forces, is able to take off and land like a helicopter, but fly like a plane. Hughes will start flight testing the IDS in early 1989, with flight test support continuing through 1991.

For more information write to: P. O. Box 45068, Los Angeles, CA 90045-0068 USA

Subsidiary of GM Hughes Electronics

CLASSIFIED LIST OF ADVERTISERS

Repair & maintenance of aircraft
AGUSTA
Aviaexport
CASA
Kaman Aerospace Corporation
OGMA
Pilatus Aircraft
Promavia
SECA

Repair & overhaul of aero-engines
AGUSTA
Aviaexport
DAF Special Products
FIAT Aviazione
OGMA
Promavia
SECA
SNECMA Group

Repair of aircraft instruments
AGUSTA
Aviaexport
OGMA
SECA

Rocket engine test plant
Aviaexport
SNIA/BPD

Rocket propulsion
Aviaexport
SNECMA Group
SNIA/BPD

Rotary actuators
AP Precision Hydraulics
Lucas Aerospace

Rotor parts & components
DAF Special Products

RPV acoustic tracking and positioning systems
Aviaexport

RPV electronics
AGUSTA
Aviaexport
Flight Refuelling
Hughes Aircraft Company
Meteor
Thomson-CSF

RPV's
Aerospatiale
Aviaexport
Flight Refuelling
Israel Military Industries
Kaman Aerospace Corporation
Meteor
Selenia

Runway friction measuring equipment
Aviaexport

Satellite navigation and positioning gps receivers
Aviaexport
FIAR

Seals
SECA

Security systems
Aviaexport

Sensors & transducers
Hughes Aircraft Company
SNECMA
Thomson-CSF

Servo actuators
AP Precision Hydraulics
Lucas Aerospace
Thomson-CSF

Sheet metal work
AGUSTA
Aviaexport
Israel Military Industries
Lucas Aerospace
SECA

Simulators
AGUSTA
Omnipol
Thomson-CSF

Simulators, combat
Aviaexport
FIAR
Thomson-CSF

Sonar
Aviaexport
FIAR
Thomson-CSF

Space hardware recovery
Aviaexport
SNIA/BPD

Space launchers
Aerospatiale
Aviaexport
SNECMA
SNIA/BPD

Space satellites
Aerospatiale
Aviaexport
Hughes Aircraft Company
SNIA/BPD

Space systems
AGUSTA
Aviaexport
FIAR
Hughes Aircraft Company
SNIA/BPD

Spacecraft
Aviaexport
Hughes Aircraft Company

Space parts for us built aircraft
Aviaexport
Israel Military Industries
Kaman Aerospace Corporation

Staring systems, airborne
Lucas Aerospace

Static inverters
Lucas Aerospace
SECA
Thomson-CSF

Steering controls (hydraulic)
AP Precision Hydraulics
Thomson-CSF

Struts & trunnions
DAF Special Products

Surveillance systems
Barr & Stroud
Selenia
Thomson-CSF

Switches
Lucas Aerospace

Switchgear
Lucas Aerospace

Tachometers
SECA

Tactical radios
Aviaexport
Hughes Aircraft Company
Thomson-CSF

Targets, aerial
Aerospatiale
Aviaexport
Kaman Aerospace Corporation
Meteor
Promavia

Target towed bodies
Meteor

Target towing winches
Aviaexport
Flight Refuelling
Pilatus Aircraft

Technical publications
Aviaexport
Hughes Aircraft Company
Kaman Aerospace Corporation

Technical publications, special studies
Aviaexport
Kaman Aerospace Corporation

Telemetry equipment
AGUSTA
Aviaexport
Hughes Aircraft Company
Meteor
SNECMA Group

Temperature control equipment
Lucas Aerospace

Test equipment
Aermacchi
Central Engineering
Hughes Aircraft Company
Israel Military Industries
Kaman Aerospace Corporation
Vickers Instruments

Test equipment, radar, air data computer, fire-control systems, avionics etc
Kaman Aerospace
FIAR
Hughes Aircraft Company
Selenia
Thomson-CSF
Vickers Instruments

Test equipment airborne radio
Thomson-CSF

Test facilities
Central Engineering International
Israel Military Industries
SNECMA Group

Thermal imaging system
AGUSTA
Aviaexport
Barr & Stroud
FIAR
Hughes Aircraft Company
Selenia

Thrust reversers
Lucas Aerospace
SNECMA Group

Torsion springs
Aviaexport

Training & simulation
AGUSTA
Aviaexport
Hughes Aircraft Company
KHD
Pilatus Aircraft
Promavia
Thomson-CSF

Training devices
Aermacchi
AGUSTA
Hughes Aircraft Company
Kaman Aerospace Corporation
Thomson-CSF

Transfer of technology
AGUSTA
Aviaexport
Industrias Cardoen
Thomson-CSF

Troop transport
Aerospatiale

Tubes, stainless steel
Aviaexport

Turbofan engine
Motoren-und Turbinen-Union Munchen
SECA
SNECMA Group

Turboprop
Motoren-und Turbinen-Union Munchen

[20]

AIR TRAFFIC CONTROL ■
FLIGHT INSPECTION ■ AD-
VISORY AND ALERTING ■ AE-
RODROME WEATHER SERVICE
■ AERONAUTICAL INFORMA-
TION ■ AERONAUTICAL FIX-
ED AND MOBILE TELECOMMU-
NICATIONS ■ RADIONAVIGA-
TION AND BROADCASTING ■
PROFESSIONAL COURSES FOR
AIR TRAFFIC CONTROLLERS ■
ADVICES AND STUDIES ON ANY
MATTER RELATED TO AIR
TRAFFIC

AZIENDA AUTONOMA
ASSISTENZA AL VOLO

VIA SALARIA, 716 - 00199 ROMA - TEL. (06) 81661
TELEX 622680 - 624826 LIRW I - FAX (06) 8166.517

Turnkey project management
Aviaexport
Israel Military Industries

Tyres for aircraft
Goodyear (Great Britain)

Unmanned aircraft
Aermacchi
Meteor

Undercarriage gear, retractable
AP Precision Hydraulics
DAF Special Products
SNECMA Group

Valves
Flight Refuelling
Lucas Aerospace

Valves, control hydraulic
AP Precision Hydraulics
SECA
Thomson-CSF

Valves, non-return hydraulic
AP Precision Hydraulics
Thomson-CSF

Valves, relief hydraulic
AP Precision Hydraulics
SECA
Thomson-CSF

Voltage & current regulators
Lucas Aerospace
Thomson-CSF

Wheels for aircraft
Goodyear Tyre & Rubber Company
SECA
SNECMA Grou

Windscreens-electrically heated
Lucas Aerospace

Wind tunnel testing plant
Aviaexport

Wires & cables, all types
SECA

[23]

Our mark in the sky.

Our mark in the sea.

FIAT AVIAZIONE - AN OUTSTANDING, CONTINUING PRESENCE AT THE FOREFRONT OF AIRCRAFT AND MARINE ENGINE TECHNOLOGY

AEROENGINES

RB 199 FOR THE ALL-WEATHER TORNADO

SPEY M.K. 807 FOR THE AMX LIGHT TACTICAL FIGHTER

T64-P4D FOR THE G 222 TRANSPORT PLANE

V 2500 FOR SHORT-HAUL AIRCRAFT

PW 2037/PW2040 FOR MEDIUM-HAUL AIRCRAFT

PW 4000 AND CF6-80C2 FOR LONG-HAUL AIRCRAFT

ENGINES FOR HELICOPTERS

PT6B-36

T700-CT7

MECHANICAL COMPONENTS FOR HELICOPTERS

SA321 SUPERFRELON

SA330 PUMA

SA360/365 DAUPHIN

MARINE AND INDUSTRIAL TURBINES

LM 2500 IN THE 30,000 HP CLASS

LM 500 IN THE 6,000 HP CLASS

AUXILIARY UNIT POWER

FA 150 – ARGO

INDUSTRIAL GAS TURBINES

TG 16 - TG 20 - TG 50

AEROSPACE PROPULSION

CRYOGENIC LIQUID TURBOPUMPS

TRIM ROCKET ENGINES

WIND TURBINES

GAMMA 60

FIAT AVIAZIONE

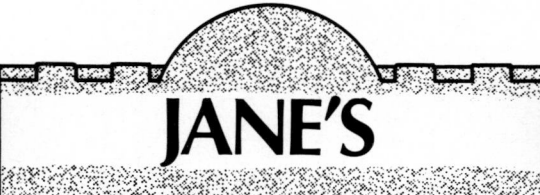

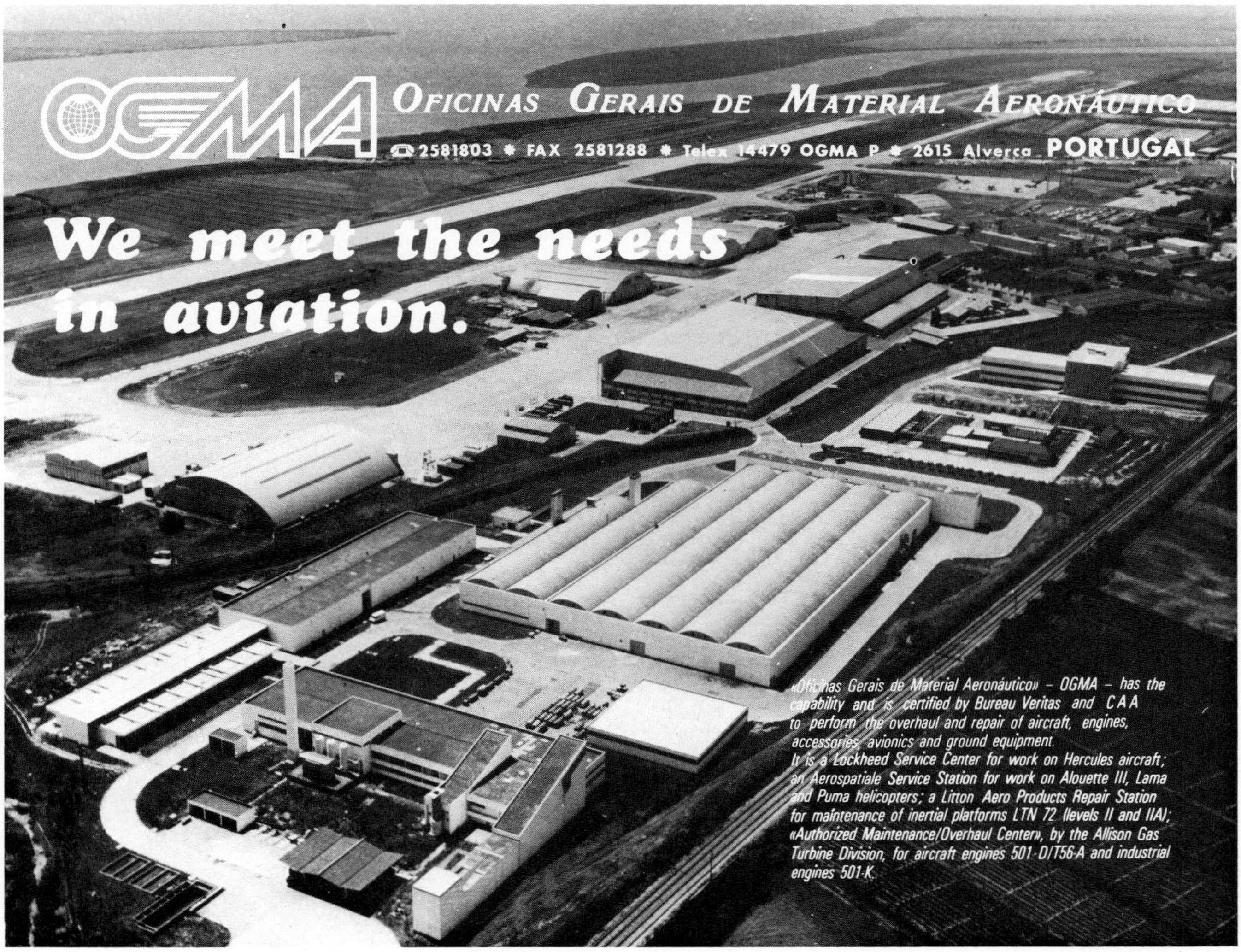

STEALTH FIGHTER 1988: An AV-8B Harrier II hides in the woods, close to the troops for whom it provides close support

JANE'S
ALL THE WORLD'S AIRCRAFT
1988-89

Jane's Information Group Limited, Sentinel House, 163 Brighton Road, Coulsdon, Surrey CR3 2NX, UK
Jane's Information Group Inc, 1340 Braddock Place, Suite 300, PO Box 1436, Alexandria, Virginia 22313-2036, USA

HIGHWAY TO TECHNOLOGY

SPACE SYSTEMS
ARTIFICIAL INTELLIGENCE
ENVIRONMENTAL SURVEILLANCE
ELECTRONIC SYSTEMS

Fabbrica Italiana
Apparecchiature Radioelettriche S.p.A.

Headquarters
Via Montedcsiro, 8 - 20156 Milan - Italy
Tel.: (02) 35790.1 - Telex: 331140 FIARMO I
Telefax: INFOTEC 6500 - Tel.: (02) 342030

CONTENTS

The Editor has been assisted in the compilation of this edition as follows:

Kenneth Munson   AIRCRAFT SECTION: ARGENTINA TO FINLAND, WEST GERMANY TO TURKEY; LIGHTER THAN AIR

Bill Gunston   GLOSSARY; AERO ENGINES

Paul Jackson   AIRCRAFT SECTION: FRANCE, UNITED KINGDOM

Mike Jerram   AIRCRAFT SECTION: UNITED STATES OF AMERICA

Michael Taylor   SPORT AIRCRAFT; SAILPLANES; HANG GLIDERS; METRIC CONVERSIONS

Foreword .... [33]
Glossary .... [43]
**Some first flights made between
1 June 1987 and 1 October 1988** .... [47]
Official Records .... [51]

Aircraft
Argentina 1
Australia 4
Belgium 8
Brazil 9
Canada 17
Chile 32
China (People's Republic) 34
Colombia 46
Czechoslovakia 47
Egypt 53
Ethiopia 53
Finland 54
France 55
Germany (Federal Republic) 86
Greece 97
Hungary 97
India 97
Indonesia 101
International Programmes 103
Iran 136
Israel 136
Italy 142
Japan 166
Korea (Republic) 173
Malaysia 174
Netherlands 174
New Zealand 178
Nigeria 179
Pakistan 179
Philippines 180
Poland 181
Portugal 196
Romania 196
Singapore 203
South Africa 203
Spain 205
Sweden 208
Switzerland 212
Taiwan 217
Thailand 218
Turkey 219

Union of Soviet Socialist Republics 220
United Kingdom 279
United States of America 319
Yugoslavia 498

Sport Aircraft
Australia 503
Belgium 507
Canada 507
China (People's Republic) 516
Finland 516
France 517
Germany (Federal Republic) 531
Israel 535
Italy 536
Luxembourg 539
Poland 540
South Africa 540
Sweden 540
Switzerland 542
Union of Soviet Socialist Republics 542
United Kingdom 543
United States of America 549

Sailplanes
Australia 617
Austria 617
Belgium 617
Brazil 618
China (People's Republic) 619
Czechoslovakia 620
France 621
Germany (Federal Republic) 624
Hungary 636
India 636
Poland 636
Romania 638
Sweden 640
Switzerland 640
Union of Soviet Socialist Republics 641
United Kingdom 642
United States of America 643
Yugoslavia 647

Hang Gliders 649

Lighter than Air: Airships
Australia 655
Canada 655
China (People's Republic) 656
France 657
Germany (Federal Republic) 657
Italy 658
Mexico 658
New Zealand 659
Union of Soviet Socialist Republics 659
United Kingdom 659
United States of America 663

Lighter than Air: Balloons 669

Aero-Engines
Australia 675
Austria 675
Belgium 676
Brazil 676
Canada 676
China (People's Republic) 680
Czechoslovakia 682
Egypt 683
France 683
Germany (Federal Republic) 688
India 691
International Programmes 691
Israel 696
Italy 696
Japan 698
Poland 699
Romania 702
Singapore 702
South Africa 702
Spain 702
Sweden 702
Turkey 702
Union of Soviet Socialist Republics 703
United Kingdom 710
United States of America 716
Yugoslavia 743

Addenda 745

Indexes 753

Jet-like training at turboprop costs.

Tucano

More than 500 Tucanos have been ordered in the last 3 years by Air Forces of countries like Great-Britain, Brazil, Egypt, Iraq to name but a few.

The Tucano is always the first choice when it comes to high training efficiency at low operating costs.

The Tucano is the only basic trainer designed from the outset around a turboprop engine with all-new airframe, cockpit and systems, simulating the environment and handling characteristics of a modern jet fighter.

The Tucano has the best all around visibility for both trainee and instructor, thanks to the single-piece canopy and staggered tandem seating arrangement.

The Tucano introduced the single-lever engine propeller control concept, that reduces transition time to pure jet aircraft, and ejection seats as standard equipment.

EMBRAER
CEILING UNLIMITED

FOREWORD

At the time when the Foreword to the last edition of this yearbook was written, few of its readers could have imagined that Soviet MiG-29 fighters would excite the crowds, and impress professionals, at the 1988 Farnborough Air Show in the United Kingdom. The politics of Mr Mikhail Gorbachev had already introduced the Russian words *glasnost* and *perestroika* (openness and restructuring) into everyday language, both east and west of the wall across central Europe that appeared increasingly anachronistic. But who would have dared to predict that 1988 would also see Soviet troops leaving Afghanistan, South African forces pulling out of Angola, and the eight-year war between Iran and Iraq ending in a ceasefire supervised by the United Nations?

The intermediate-range nuclear forces (INF) treaty was still four weeks from signature, and by no means assured, when that Foreword went to press. Only the two leaders who eventually signed the treaty might have asserted with conviction that the first batches of SS-20s and ground launched cruise missiles would be withdrawn, and destroyed publicly, by the Autumn of 1988.

Such events are recorded in *Jane's All the World's Aircraft* without any political or military motive. The content of this yearbook has been non-political and international for at least the last three decades. Its strong support for air power has been as the primary instrument for preventing, not waging war. Its Forewords have suggested consistently through the 1980s that nuclear inventories could be diminished drastically without prejudicing their crucial effectiveness as a deterrent, while acknowledging that nuclear weapons cannot yet be eliminated completely because nothing can ever be disinvented. Sufficient invulnerable, unstoppable, warheads must be retained, in equal numbers in East and West, to deter any nation from initiating a nuclear exchange, but far below the numbers required to fuel a Third World War.

Those who believe that signatures on a piece of paper are, by themselves, adequate to prevent the use of a particular type of weapon sometimes claim that inter-war agreements precluded the use of poison gas during the Second World War. They should tell that to the relatives of millions who died in Nazi gas chambers. Even if the Holocaust is viewed as a campaign of genocide separate from the military campaigns, the Gulf War of 1980-88 should have dispelled any remaining misapprehension that chemical warfare is part of a barbarous past.

Can we then have confidence that the INF treaty has made the world a safer place? The television viewer may breathe a sigh of relief on seeing film of Soviet and US missiles being burned and blown up; but these are only the vehicles for the parts that really matter. No 'mushroom' clouds spread rapidly over these carcases, for which we must be thankful; but it *does* raise the question of what is happening to the 436 US nuclear warheads, and more than 1,565 Soviet warheads, that were the key components of the missiles now being destroyed. Cynics expect them to be transferred to a new generation of air-launched cruise missiles, and other weapons, outside the scope of the INF treaty.

Even those who have faith in the goodwill, and instinct for national survival, of US and Soviet political leaders are uneasy in the knowledge that the United Kingdom—uncommitted by the INF treaty—is in the process of increasing the number of nuclear warheads carried by each of the Royal Navy's ballistic missile submarines by "about two and a half times" according to its Defence Secretary. Clearly, there is a long way to go before nuclear arsenals are reduced to a level that no longer forms an ever-present threat to the survival of life on our planet. Sadly, in an age when Western politics are governed by economics, it would be extremely costly to discard an existing or part-completed nuclear deterrent force and replace it with an effective non-nuclear force. Only when one considers a multi-nation alliance like NATO or the Warsaw Pact group as an entity, in which one nation might maintain the minimal nuclear deterrent force, and all contribute differing portions of the carefully planned and integrated conventional forces, does it become feasible as well as logical.

Has Russia got it right?

This brings us back to the MiG-29s that flew at Farnborough, and to the unexpected invitation for US Defense Secretary Frank C. Carlucci to inspect one of the Soviet Union's new Tupolev 'Blackjack' strategic bombers at Kubinka Air Base, near Moscow, on 2 August. Both occurrences can be regarded as products of *glasnost*. Never before had one of the Soviet Union's newest combat aircraft been displayed in public at a Western air show. Nor had any Western leader been taken on board a bomber so new that the first operational unit had formed only weeks or months earlier. However, the Soviet Union has never before been able to demonstrate so clearly that its designers and engineers are as capable as any in the world.

Close studies of the MiGs 'in the flesh', and of 'Blackjack' on video, revealed a standard of workmanship and finish light-years beyond that of Soviet jet fighters of the 1950s and 60s. It was encouraging to discover that no changes were necessary to the entry on the bomber that had been typeset for this edition of *Jane's All the World's Aircraft*, although the maximum take-off weight may be somewhat higher than expected, at 267,625 kg (590,000 lb). The estimated maximum wing sweep of 64° that appeared also in last year's edition seems to be 1° too low if reports of what Mr Carlucci saw in the cockpit at Kubinka are accurate.

On comparing our 1987 estimates of the size of the MiG-29 with an Aviaexport leaflet distributed at Farnborough, it was discovered that the wing span is a mere 14 cm (5½ in) less than we calculated, the length 12 cm (5 in) greater, and the wheelbase 7 cm (2¾ in) greater. We can only hope that all our estimates of the size of Soviet combat aircraft will prove to be accurate within the same margin of around one to three per cent. Our estimated take-off weight was exactly halfway between the official figures released this Summer for normal and maximum take-off weights.

Of course, it is now possible to add new facts to those known or estimated previously. 'Blackjack' can be seen to have a one-piece all-moving tail fin, which was not anticipated. Its six-wheel main landing gear bogies are similar in configuration to those of the Tu-154 airliner, its turned-up nose like that of 'Backfire C'. Each of its two massive bomb bays is large enough to house a rotary launcher for six AS-15 air-launched cruise missiles. Perhaps more significant is that Soviet Air Force General-Colonel Boris F Korolkov is reported to have told Mr Carlucci that 'Blackjack' can carry 12 short-range attack missiles (presumably similar in principle to the US XAGM-131A SRAM II) on each rotary launcher. This implies a low-altitude penetration role for 'Blackjack', which had been viewed previously as a high-altitude standoff cruise missile launcher.

Farnborough's MiG-29s provided equally thought-provoking proof of the extent of Soviet progress in military aviation technology. No comment was made in the aviation press when photographs of Soviet pilots published some months earlier, in *Soviet Military Review*, showed them wearing wide helmets with a row of holes across the forehead. These suggested some form of helmet sight, probably slaved to the infra-red search/track sensor that gives modern Soviet counter-air fighters a significant advantage over their Western counterparts. Only at Farnborough did it become known that the MiG-29's fire control system links its pilot's helmet with not only the IRS/T but a laser embodied in the same sensor and two radar modes. A Hughes Aircraft technician considered this to be up to eight years in advance of anything the USAF is likely to have in operational use.

It was fascinating to discover that what had been thought to be simply aerodynamic fences forward of the fins, on top of each wing, are also packed with countermeasures flares. Reference in this edition to flare packs carried in the landing gear fairings and on each side of the fuselage of Il-76 transports likewise indicates the seriousness with which the Soviet military regard the threat of missiles like Stinger which they encountered in Afghanistan.

It should be evident by now that the Soviet leadership appreciates

the importance of conventional air power, not merely as a substitute for the nuclear missiles that will be deactivated during the next decade, but now, in 1988. Unlike their Western counterparts, these people do not waste time debating whether or not they can afford IRS/Ts, helmet sights, and aircraft with the impressive short take-off capability demonstrated by the (albeit lightly loaded) MiG-29s at Farnborough. This is right thinking.

Has the West got it wrong?

It would be foolish to suggest that Soviet willingness to utilise the advanced concepts of their aerospace industry means that their aircraft outclass those of the West in every respect. The letter X painted on portions of the MiG-29's airframe, notably at the rear end (as one would expect), was said to indicate areas where groundcrew should not push or lean, because the skin is made of honeycomb or composites. So, as Mr Pyotr Balabuyev of Antonov told *Jane's* in Paris three years ago, Soviet designers are fully aware of the weightsaving qualities of such materials. On the other hand, it was surprising to discover that the MiG does not have fly-by-wire controls; and one had to look very hard to see, or even imagine, any sign of the 'stealth' or low-observables technology so beloved of the US military, Congress, and their civilian contractors.

At the time this Foreword is being written, the public knows nothing more factual about the reputed Lockheed 'RF-19 stealth fighter' than it knew a year ago or, for that matter, when first mention was made of such a project in *Jane's All the World's Aircraft 1977-78*, before the prototype is supposed to have flown. In contrast, this edition includes an official artist's impression of the Northrop B-2 'stealth bomber', which is expected to fly for the first time, in full view of cameras, before the end of this year. Why should one design be revealed and not the other?

No-one can doubt the superb capability of the US aerospace industry, or that of the research centres like NASA that feed it with every form of advanced technology. Nonetheless, remembering the history of earlier Northrop flying wings, the sight of such a revolutionary design, made of new materials and said to be controlled entirely by thrust vectoring, must inspire sincere prayers for the safety of those who will fly it. While hoping for its success, which would add a unique weapon to the forces required for maintenance of a worldwide balance of power, it is consoling to know that the USAF has its B-1Bs. Problems encountered with these variable-geometry bombers have given them a hard time in the US press during the past year; but few aeroplanes enjoy a trouble-free life when they first enter service.

Last year's Foreword caused considerable controversy in the USA by suggesting that America might be paying too high a price for the supposed benefits of 'stealth' technology, or trying too hard to pack its military aircraft with avionics that would be fine if they worked but would cause unacceptable low standards of readiness for action when they don't. Is there not merit still in simplicity? For example, can we learn nothing from the fact that the Harrier, with a single vectored-thrust engine providing lift, thrust and stability through 'puffer-jets', is the West's only completely successful V/STOL combat aircraft, despite vast sums spent on trying to perfect dozens of alternative techniques?

Such remarks do not reflect the efforts of an Englishman to promote a configuration developed within five miles of his home. The Harrier is the first-generation example of a concept that ought by now to be in its fourth or fifth, supersonic, generation in NATO air forces. This reflects no discredit on teams that designed aircraft like the French Rafale, European EFA and US ATF. All are, or will be, exquisite last-generation manifestations of the conventional fighter, with hints of next-generation advances. On a traditional English schoolboy's end-of-year report, they would earn the admonition "Could do better".

An air force for the 21st century

There is little point in discussing weapons to fight a nuclear Third World War. East and West already possess inventories of missiles capable of destroying all life on Earth. This will remain true if a future treaty eliminates 50 per cent of all long-range strategic ballistic missiles. So we must assume either that such weapons will never be used or that, if they are, there will be nobody left to say "I told you so!".

At the time this is being written, some wars appear to be ending; but truth is often different from what appears to be fact. When Soviet troops have been withdrawn from Afghanistan, they will leave behind an unresolved civil war. The Gulf ceasefire seems only to have left Iraq free to suppress the Kurdish population in the

Lockheed concept for a short take-off, vertical landing jet fighter for the 21st century, powered by a Rolls-Royce hybrid fan vectored-thrust engine

north of its own nation. Local wars, like family squabbles, will continue. Some will be minor and will end quickly. Others may be so lengthy and bloody that they threaten to grow into East-West confrontations although, thank God, this becomes increasingly unlikely.

So, what kind of air force will be effective and survivable in the 21st century?

There are two disparate answers to that question. One represents the traditional path. The other looks to the kind of 'wonder weapons' that Hitler demanded from his scientists and engineers in the Second World War. Elements of the latter approach that are currently discernible range from 'stealth' aircraft to the space weapons of America's Strategic Defense Initiative. If they are practicable, few of the weapons produced under the traditional programme would continue to be viable. If they are as illusory in the foreseeable future as were Hitler's 'wonder weapons' of half a century ago, the real cost could prove equally high. Whether or not this is a path worth following is a decision that must be faced by the US administration that will take over from President Reagan in 1989. Part of the price already being paid is recorded in this edition of *Jane's All the World's Aircraft*.

Upgrade programmes like that being applied to the USAF's KC-135 in-flight refuelling tankers are planned to extend the operational life of these aircraft "well beyond the year 2020". By the time they are retired, some KC-135s will be around 60 years old. Young US Air Force pilots may fly reskinned, re-engined tankers that were piloted in their shiny new days by their grandfathers. It may make sense to an economist, a politician, or an engineer who trusts a computer for all his decisions; but would any of the older generation of great designers such as Sydney Camm, Andrei Tupolev or Donald Douglas have considered it advisable? Even on terra firma the average 1988 motorist might prefer not to commute in a 1928 car with a new engine and strengthened chassis.

The traditional path is one that has to be favoured at the moment by China, although its comparatively young aviation industry is learning at an astonishing rate. Up to the present time, its air forces have been equipped largely with aircraft cloned or developed from Soviet designs of the 1950s and 60s. Beginning with a clean sheet of paper, its industry has now bypassed a generation or two of combat aircraft evolution by designing and building prototypes of the H-7 twin-turbofan attack aircraft, of which a one-twentieth scale model was displayed for the first time at Farnborough 1988.

In the same class as the Soviet Su-24 'Fencer', and almost certainly benefiting from deals with European and US high-technology manufacturers, the H-7 is one of the few types of conventional tactical combat aircraft that might still have a place in the skies of the 21st century. To do so, it will require to be kept in a hardened shelter, and possess a combat radius great enough to put it beyond the reach of most tactical surface-to-surface missiles. Even then, it must be built and equipped to survive in an environment packed with elaborate countermeasures, surface-to-air missiles, and airborne interceptors of unprecedented efficiency.

For years these Forewords have expressed a belief that, within minutes of the start of any future major confrontation, there would be no usable forward area runways, and no airborne warning and

SWISS PRECISION ON WINGS

PC-9 Advanced Turboprop Trainer

Some countries
train their pilots to higher standards;
they are the ones who
choose Pilatus trainers

[36]

control (AWACS) aircraft near enough to the forward edge of the battle area to be of any practical value.

In the absence of any sign of enthusiasm from the UK government to build on the achievements of the Harrier, it is good to learn that NASA and Lockheed are collaborating on design studies of aircraft that might take the vectored-thrust V/STOL concept into the 21st century. Nor should we overlook first reports of Yakovlev's Yak-41 successor to the rather tame Yak-38. From this type of aircraft, tilt-wing machines of the kind pioneered by the revolutionary Bell/Boeing V-22 Osprey, and the agile, heavily armed battlefield helicopter that will emerge eventually from the US Army's LHX formula, must stem the forward area combat aircraft of next century.

To help them to survive, there is evidence at last that military leaders are beginning to realise the potential of the UMA (unmanned aircraft) and RPV (remotely piloted vehicle). The Israel Defence Force needs no convincing of the value of these small, relatively inexpensive, decoys to deplete the necessarily limited resources of hostile missile defences in advance of strikes by piloted aircraft. If the UMAs carry warheads they cannot be ignored. If they have anti-radiation seekers, they may remove much of the threat to the aircraft that follow in their wake.

UMAs have become so important that they now justify their own *Jane's* book, and no longer appear in *Jane's All the World's Aircraft*. However, this edition contains details for the first time of another cost-effective move that might enable air forces to spend a larger proportion of their total budget on first-line aircraft in future.

During the past 30 years, many military and airline pilots have enhanced their flying skills, and logged many valuable hours of experience, by building and flying the kind of aircraft described in our Sport Aircraft pages. Air forces like that of Jordan have formed aerobatic display teams, using types like the Pitts Special which could be purchased by amateurs in kit form. As the standards of the kit-built aircraft steadily improved, and familiar professional designs like the Piper Cub and Stelio Frati's Falco became available in the form of plans and kits, air forces awakened to the fact that these types can be bought very economically, and assembled by relatively unskilled labour in a few hundred hours, after which they form perfectly adequate liaison aircraft and, in some cases, *ab initio* trainers.

So, this year, the diligent searcher for little publicised facts can discover that the Iranian Islamic Revolutionary Guards Corps' Fajr (Dawn) military prototype looks surprisingly like a kit-built Neico Lancair. Peru, it seems, hopes to establish an indigenous aviation industry on the basis of Light Aero Avid Flyer microlights, which will perform flying training and cropspraying duties in the insignia of the Peruvian Air Force. Nigeria's AIEP Air Beetle primary trainer, expected to enter production at Kaduna Airport for the Nigerian Air Force, with 60 per cent of the finance coming from Dornier GmbH of West Germany, is a variant of the US Van's RV-6 homebuilt. The Philippine Aircraft Company has placed an initial order for 36 Denney Kitfoxes, which it is assembling for tasks that include regular mail deliveries, on floats, between some of the nation's 7,000 islands.

These are just four examples of how kitbuilts, homebuilts and microlights, once dismissed as irrelevancies by the professional aircraft manufacturers, may fill the big gap left by dwindling sales of two-to-four-seat Cessnas, Beechcraft and Pipers. There are more sinister applications, such as the use of humble powered hang gliders by PLO insurgents to attack and kill Israeli soldiers within Israel. Perhaps next year it might be permissible to add something about the use by a famous military unit of powered parawings, of the sort that opened this year's Farnborough flying display on some days.

Airliners by the thousand!

The past year has been one of tremendous achievement for the commercial air transport sector, marred only by the intervention of those who rate the final figure on the balance sheet more highly than national wellbeing, and by two much publicised disasters that should never have happened and reflect no shortcomings in the aircraft concerned.

Fortunately, *Jane's All the World's Aircraft* is devoted to the vehicles in which people fly, not finance. So this Foreword will not become deeply involved in the kind of criticism which will lead to restructuring of Airbus Industrie in the 1990s and, on the other hand, led its management to point out that it is not unique in receiving subsidies from the governments that founded it. In any

Mockup of the Panorama Deck on a McDonnell Douglas MD-11

case, the sort of figures bandied around by economists have little meaning to the average citizen. He is unlikely to have seen, consciously, a million of anything. So, when he reads, for example, that Airbus expects world airlines to require 9,200 new aircraft with more than 150 seats, worth a total of $510 billion, by the year 2006, he is likely to register only the hope that when he and a hundred thousand others want to fly to places like Tenerife on holiday there will be enough aeroplanes to carry them. He is more concerned with the possible disruptive habits of Spanish air traffic controllers than with that figure of $510 billion, which is as impossible to imagine as the distance to Alpha Centauri in relation to his daily commuter train ride to town.

When he flies in an Airbus, does he worry that its construction might have added a few pence to his taxes? Even if he believes that no Airbus is likely to produce a profit until 1995, might he not consider it worthwhile in order to keep much of Europe's aerospace industry at work? At the very least, he would show interest in the fact that the products of the industry are so sound that — except as a result of the wrongful firing of a surface-to-air missile in a war zone — only three passengers had lost their life in an accident to an Airbus by the Autumn of 1988, and then, reportedly, through unforgivable pilot error.

Like the Concorde and Harrier, Airbus transports demonstrate that Europe's aviation engineers retain the capability of doing things that none of their foreign counterparts have proved capable of doing, anywhere in the world. This does not diminish in any respect the achievement of companies like Boeing, whose immense sales successes are but one measure of the quality of their products. However, bearing in mind that the first Airbus Industrie jetliner entered service a mere 14½ years ago, by which time Boeing had already celebrated the handover of its 2,500th commercial jet transport, its progress has been spectacular.

At that time, in May 1974, Airbus had received firm orders for a total of 21 aircraft for seven operators. By the beginning of August 1988, its order book stood at 806 A300s, A310s and A320s, of which 426 had been delivered to nearly 60 customers. These statistics tell only part of the story. With 486 orders, options and commitments received from 21 customers by March 1988, the A320 had won more orders by the time of its first delivery than any other airliner. Its success is so great that production of this model is scheduled to reach at least eight a month by mid-1990. Few people could have expected a European transport aircraft ever to be built at such a rate in peacetime. The underlying reasons for such success should be understood by European governments, and particularly by that of the UK, whose industry designed and supplies Airbus's highly advanced wings.

From the start, Airbus Industrie took advantage of every technical advance that would enhance the performance, safety and economy of its products without unacceptable risk. Sometimes it seemed to go too far, as when it opted for F-16 type sidestick controllers, instead of conventional sticks or yokes, on the flight deck of the A320. In the event, airline crews soon described it as a "pilot's aeroplane". Also new was the first computer-driven fly-by-wire control system standardised on a subsonic transport.

After fitting a carbonfibre fin to the A310-300 in Spring 1985, Airbus standardised it on the entire range of its transports. The A320 also has a carbonfibre tailplane. Based on Concorde experience, this contains a trim tank. By transferring fuel between

SELENIA.
A LEADER IN DEFENCE SYSTEMS

Today's lethal threats and the vast, rapidly increasing amounts of information that must be handled in the event of conflict, require modern integrated defence systems, with a high degree of survivability.

Over thirty years of active involvement in major defence projects, have given Selenia a profound understanding of the complex needs of such systems, as well as the capability to provide solutions through an in-depth systems approach.

Selenia's **Defence Systems Division** implements military systems on a turn-key basis, using its wide systems experience and its own products in the fields of C^3I, Surveillance, Missiles, Electronic Warfare, Avionics and Electron optics.

Selenia technology and products of today already meet tomorrow's defence requirements

RAGGRUPPAMENTO
SELENIA ELSAG

Defence Systems Division
Via Tiburtina km 12,400 - 00131 Rome, Italy
Telex: 613690 SELROM I - Phone: (06) 4360 2890

IRI GROUP

the tailplane and wings during flight, the aircraft's CG can be adjusted to produce a 1.5 per cent improvement in fuel burn. A further 1.5 per cent reduction is offered by the arrow-shape wingtip devices that reduce drag and wingtip turbulence.

All the experience gained in years of successful innovation will be embodied in the big new A330 and A340 which will enter service in 1992-93. So, provided timid politics and economics are not allowed to frustrate technical leadership, the future of Europe's commercial transport manufacturing industry should be assured well into next century.

On the other side of the Atlantic, McDonnell Douglas has bounced back strongly after seeming at one stage almost to be squeezed out of the market by the sales successes of Boeing and Airbus. During the 1988 Farnborough Show it announced its latest order, from Alitalia, for seven MD-82s, plus 20 options, which brought total commitments for the MD-80 series to 1,113. Whether or not one likes the term 'commitments', as opposed to firm orders or even options, it is a fact that these fine medium-range transports are proving so popular that anyone ordering new MD-80s at this time must be prepared to wait until 1992 before putting them into service.

This is not an isolated case of a huge backlog of orders being held by the three big manufacturers. Boeing, having sold more commercial transports in the first nine months of 1988 than in any previous full year, has a backlog of well over 1,000 aircraft to deliver, with plans to complete one every working day while the bonanza lasts. Airbus has a backlog of half that number. Even an airline choosing McDonnell Douglas's new MD-11, which has yet to fly, will need to queue for at least two years before taking delivery.

Like Airbus, McDonnell Douglas is not afraid to be innovative. It is offering a unique lower-deck cabin that will accommodate from 44 business class to 94 economy class passengers in a stretched version of the MD-11. A visit to the mockup at Long Beach showed it to be surprisingly roomy, with a magnificent view from sloping windows reminiscent of those in the passenger airships of the 1930s. A projected 'Super-Stretch' version of the aircraft, having this kind of 'Panorama deck', with total seating for 368 to 520 passengers on both decks and powered by three of Rolls-Royce's mighty RB211-524L turbofans, could provide healthy competition for the Boeing 747 and Airbus A330/340.

McDonnell Douglas's other major new programme, based on the propfan-powered MD-91/92, still has to convince potential customers that it is a good concept. Rolls-Royce engineers at Farnborough suggested that there is no case whatsoever for an unshrouded fan, but that a ducted ultra-high-bypass-ratio fan might evolve within 20 years if oil prices again rise. McDonnell Douglas's answer was probably "They would, wouldn't they?"

What effect the new generation of Soviet Il-96-300, Tu-204 and Il-114 airliners will have on the worldwide situation remains to be seen. With new-generation fuel-efficient engines like the big PS-90A replacing earlier 'gas-guzzlers', these aircraft promise entirely new standards of competition for Western types. So we should not read too much into the news that Airbus has made its first breakthrough into the Comecon market by selling three A310-300s to Interflug of East Germany.

SSTs and AGVs

Supersonics are still something apart. Despite the unexcelled safety record, and current operating profit, of the small Concorde fleet, most people still throw up their hands in horror, and mutter about economics and noise, whenever the subject of a successor is raised. But there *will* be a successor; never doubt that.

As long ago as the early 1970s, before Concorde itself entered scheduled service, and soon after the USA had spent $915,675,000 on the Boeing Model 2707 SST without even completing a prototype, *Jane's* asked a top design engineer at Douglas Long Beach what America's first practical SST would be like. The answer was: "It will probably have the same shape as Concorde, be made of the same materials, and fly at much the same speed. It will simply carry twice as many passengers". This was expected to make the whole programme viable.

Interestingly, the formula for a second-generation SST given by Boeing Executive Vice-President Philip Condit during a Farnborough 1988 press conference was: "My guess is that it will seat 250, fly at Mach 2 to 2.5 using conventional fuels, and have a range exceeding 5,000 nm". It appeared that the USA has changed its ideas very little in sixteen years.

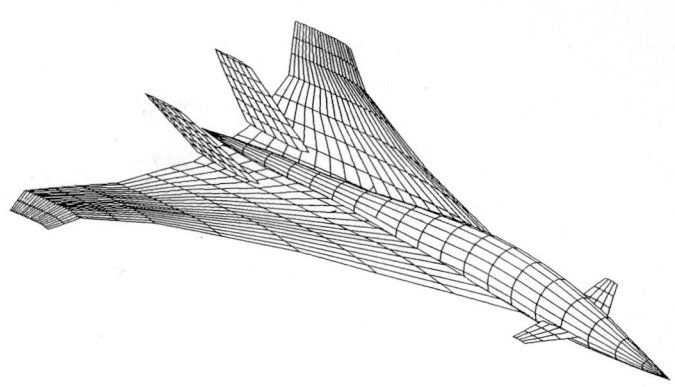

Computer aided design drawing of a Gulfstream Aerospace concept for a supersonic business transport

Those best placed to design and build the Super Concorde must be Aérospatiale and British Aerospace, who were responsible for the present version. But Her Majesty's Government is no more attracted to investing money in another SST than in financing a supersonic Harrier or the Hotol recoverable space launch vehicle that could prove one of the greatest revenue earners in aerospace history.

France, through Aérospatiale, has shown more awareness. It has not only produced design studies and exhibited models of the kind of Super Concorde that has been on everyone's mind for years; it has also displayed its concept of an AGV (*avion à très grande vitesse*) that could offer a speed of around Mach 4.7 by the year 2010. Aérospatiale will have to seek partners outside the UK, and should lose no time, as the Japanese Ministry of International Trade and Industry is expected to launch in 1989 two parallel projects for SSTs able to cruise at Mach 3 and Mach 5.

A more startling programme announced in 1988 is Gulfstream Aerospace Corporation's ambitious intention to develop a supersonic successor to its Gulfstream IV executive transport. As the company is a subsidiary of Chrysler, we should perhaps beg its pardon for referring to the G.IV as the "Rolls-Royce of business jets"; but the quality of this aircraft is certainly unrivalled. It holds the official FAI records for speed around the world both eastbound and westbound, and it is no coincidence that Gulfstream's Chairman, Mr Allen Paulson, personally took command of both circuits. He, more than any other aeroplane company head in the world, has the enthusiasm for flying needed to see such a project through to fruition.

If he finds the right partners and succeeds in producing an aircraft as good as the Gulfstream IV, the business man who 'has everything' will be able to whisk ten of his friends and colleagues between factories or golf courses 4,000 miles (6,400 km) apart at a speed of Mach 1.5 to Mach 2.0 in the early years of next century. Cost estimates are $1 billion over ten years for development and $30 to $50 million each for the Rolls-Royce powered production SSTs.

About this edition

Those familiar with the content of *Jane's All the World's Aircraft* over past decades will be accustomed to change. The 1959-60 edition contained only 557 pages in the body of the book, plus a two-page Preface, a few pages of historical material to mark 50 years of publication, and the indexes. The type size and illustrations were larger than they are now; so the volume of text was very much smaller. Nevertheless, it included 50 pages of 'Guided Missiles and Test Vehicles' that gave birth eventually to the much expanded and separate *Jane's Weapon Systems*. In the same way, later sections on 'Spaceflight' and 'Air Cushion Vehicles' inspired the yearbooks that have become *Jane's Spaceflight Directory* and *Jane's High-speed Marine Craft and Air Cushion Vehicles*.

This year the book has undergone further change. The aircraft covered formerly in the 'RPVs and Targets' section promise to become such important, multi-role components of all military services that they have been removed to form the basis of a new and more comprehensive reference work entitled *World Unmanned Aircraft*, compiled by Kenneth Munson and published by Jane's Defence Data.

Another new title which grew out of *Jane's All the World's Aircraft*, but has not resulted in deletions from this yearbook, is *Jane's World Combat Aircraft*, edited by Michael J H Taylor. This resulted from requests like that contained in a letter from one of Britain's Defence Attachés in Africa, saying: "I find it aggravating

that only aircraft currently in production are listed (in *Jane's All the World's Aircraft*). Especially here in Africa there is a great need for details of old aircraft". *Jane's World Combat Aircraft* gives such readers precisely what they need—current types described and illustrated in full *Jane's All the World's Aircraft* detail, plus all the earlier types like Skyhawks, Hunters, Mirage IIIs and Phantoms which are no longer to be found in current editions of this yearbook.

This year the entries on Air-Launched Missiles have been deleted and those who require data can find them in *Jane's Air Launched Weapons*, a new binder and subscription service. The former subsections on balloons and hang gliders are restricted to tables and company details, as this appears to be all that our readers require.

After considerable debate, it was decided to remove virtually all one-off homebuilts from the 'Sport Aircraft' section. Had this been done in Fred T. Jane's 1909 edition it would have eliminated almost all aeroplanes except the Voisin and Wright biplanes. However, aviation has changed utterly since then, and few of our professional readers are interested in one man's conversion of an agricultural aircraft into a representation of a First World War Junkers CL-1, or a Pitts Special that can take off and land inverted. What remains continues to list — so far as we know — all homebuilts, microlights and kitplanes that are now available in the form of plans, kits and ready to fly aircraft. This Foreword has already made reference to the growing adoption of such inexpensive aircraft for both military and civil tasks.

Finally, the previous lengthy listings of executives under the entries for major companies have been reduced generally to names of the chief executive officer, chief operating officer, and the persons responsible for design, marketing and public relations. These are the people whom our readers might wish to contact most frequently. The others can be found in one of our associated publications, the *Interavia ABC Aerospace Directory*.

The size of *Jane's All the World's Aircraft* has grown alarmingly through the years. As was noted in our 1984-85 edition, "Louis Blériot's Type XI monoplane had one of the most detailed entries (in 1909), totalling more than 100 words — as befitted the aircraft which had begun the whole history of practical flying when it flew across the English Channel on 25 July 1909. By 1939, the entry on the Spitfire fighter required over 400 words". Today, the 747 fills more than four pages, with well over 6,000 words, three half-tone illustrations and two three-view drawings. Long paragraphs devoted to systems, avionics and equipment were not dreamed of in 1909 or 1939, or even 1959; and the volume of specification data is a feature to be found in no other reference work.

By restricting the coverage of major sections of this year's book to professionally built aircraft, sport aircraft other than one-offs and trikes, sailplanes, airships and aero-engines, it has become possible to maintain the standards of completeness, accuracy and authenticity that are associated with *Jane's All the World's Aircraft* in every nation that builds and flies aeroplanes. Handling and transportability have been improved by switching to a lighter-weight, but not less costly, paper. Its matt finish and whiteness should also make the book easier to read.

As Editor, I should like to end this 1988-89 Foreword on a personal note. Compilation of this much changed edition imposed an exceptional workload on everyone associated with its writing and production. They could not have responded more admirably, or with greater loyalty to the publisher and myself.

Revision of the contents, involving for example an almost total re-write of the former 'Sport Aircraft' section, represented only the first stage of the task. The small editorial team also had to take in its stride a totally new production process, enabling *Jane's All the World's Aircraft* to be made available on database, and the only change of printer since the yearbook first appeared in 1909. Halfway through the production period, the entire publisher's office and the computer setting team moved to the new headquarters of Jane's Information Group in Coulsdon, Surrey, from the City of London and Portsmouth respectively. At the crucial page proof stage—with the members of the editorial team dispersed in Greater London, Surrey, Sussex, Essex and Lincolnshire, and the three-view artists in Kent and Somerset — a three-week postal strike left one key batch of 50 pages 'lost' in a stagnant sorting office.

Paul Jackson had joined the team, to become responsible for the French and UK aircraft sections, in time to help the others in coping with all this, in a year when it was planned to bring forward the book's publication date by one month. You, the reader, will now know whether or not this was achieved. Next year we hope to publish in October, and then to have the 1990-91 edition at the Farnborough Air Show in September. This will represent an optimum publication date, averting the panics of past years when the book was published during the two or three weeks before Christmas.

It is seldom appreciated how much is involved in producing an edition of *Jane's All the World's Aircraft*, in even a normal year. To ensure authenticity, every manufacturer whose products are listed in the book is invited to update his entire entry, and to supply highly detailed information on new products under development or currently available. The reply rate to this mailing is probably unique in aerospace publishing. This year, for example, only one builder of commercial transport aircraft outside the Soviet Union failed to respond — inevitably, perhaps, the one nearest to the publishing office! However, the replies come in a variety of languages and styles, and to very differing standards of completeness. It is the task of the editorial team to transform the raw material into the entries you see in the book, by analysing the facts and figures, and putting them into a consistent form, to an agreed and carefully monitored house style. No task could be more demanding, as our readers are professionals who would not tolerate inaccuracy.

Perhaps 50 per cent of new material is received each year from the manufacturers. The remainder is provided by the editorial team, comprising the Editor, Assistant Editor Kenneth Munson and Compilers Bill Gunston, Paul Jackson, Mike Jerram and Michael Taylor, whose individual responsibilities are listed on the Contents page at the front of this book.

Computer setting of the huge quantity of new copy was handled by Keith Faulkner and Ruth Simmance. All such material is submitted in manuscript, in six very varied writing styles. So, the prospect of checking the resulting computer printouts was viewed initially with trepidation. In fact, the quality proved to be immaculate, with hardly a literal to be seen. Eventually, it was considered a waste of precious time to check the setting before the pages had been made up. My sincere thanks go, therefore, to Keith and Ruth, and to Chrissie Richards, an old friend who returned after a number of years' absence to take charge of the production side of this edition at Jane's Defence Data.

Maurice Allward emerged from well-earned retirement to compile this year's indexes — a job for which his previous 27 years as a member of the editorial team proved invaluable. As in previous years, the new three-view drawings came from Dennis Punnett and Mike Keep, whose capabilities remain unmatched. News, facts and figures that would not appear in the book had we relied only on 'official' sources came from colleagues and friends including Delden Badcock in Australia; Neil A. Macdougall and David Godfrey in Canada; Wolfgang Wagner in West Germany; Roland Eichenberger and Dr Ulrich Haller in Switzerland; Tom DeFrank, Jay Miller and Nelson Fuller in the USA; Dipl Ing Andrzej Glass and Dipl Ing Jerzy Grzegorzewski in Poland; William Green and Gordon Swanborough of *Air International*, David Dorrell of *Air Pictorial*, James Gilbert of *Pilot*, and Arnold Nayler of *Airship* in the UK; and the editorial staffs of *Flight International* (UK); *Aviation Magazine International* and *Air et Cosmos* (France); FLYGvapenNYTT (Sweden); *Australian Aviation* and *Aircraft* (Australia), *Letectvi + Kosmonautika* (Czechoslovakia); and *Air Force Magazine* (Washington, DC), with whom we have now worked so happily for eighteen years through our bi-monthly *Jane's All the World's Aircraft* Supplements and other contributed features.

It is a pleasure to record again how much the completeness and attraction of this edition owes to the many photographers whose names are included in the captions to the illustrations they supplied. Just one more name, that of my wife Doris, completes the list of those whose never-failing help, in so many ways, made this new edition possible in a very challenging year.

Surbiton, September 1988   JWRT

Glossary

AAM Air-to-air missile.
AATH Automatic approach to hover.
AC Alternating current.
ACLS (1) Automatic carrier landing system; (2) Air cushion landing system.
ADAC Avion de décollage et attérrissage court (STOL).
ADAV Avion de décollage et attérrissage vertical (VTOL).
ADC (1) US Air Force Aerospace Defense Command (no longer active); (2) air data computer.
ADF Automatic direction finding (equipment).
ADG Accessory-drive generator.
ADI Attitude/director indicator.
aeroplane (N America, airplane) Heavier-than-air aircraft with propulsion and a wing that does not rotate in order to generate lift.
AEW Airborne early warning.
AFB Air Force Base (USA).
AFCS Automatic flight control system.
AFRP Aramid fibre reinforced plastics.
afterburning Temporarily augmenting the thrust of a turbofan or turbojet by burning additional fuel in the jetpipe.
AGREE Advisory Group on Reliability in Electronic Equipment.
Ah Ampère-hours.
AHRS Attitude/heading reference system.
AIDS Airborne integrated data system.
aircraft All man-made vehicles for off-surface navigation within the atmosphere, including helicopters and balloons.
airstair Retractable stairway built into aircraft.
ALCM Air-launched cruise missile.
AM Amplitude modulation.
anhedral Downward slope of wing seen from front, in direction from root to tip.
AP Ammonium perchlorate.
APFD Autopilot flight director.
aphelion The point in a solar (Sun-centred) orbit furthest from the Sun.
apogee The point in an Earth-centred orbit furthest from the Earth.
approach noise Measured 1 nm from downwind end of runway with aircraft passing overhead at 112.6 m (370 ft).
APS Aircraft prepared for service; a fully equipped weight.
APU Auxiliary power unit (part of aircraft).
ARINC Aeronautical Radio Inc, US company whose electronic box sizes (racking sizes) are the international standard.
ASE Automatic stabilisation equipment.
ASI Airspeed indicator.
ASIR Airspeed indicator reading.
ASM Air-to-surface missile.
aspect ratio Measure of wing (or other aerofoil) slenderness seen in plan view, usually defined as the square of the span divided by area.
ASPJ Advanced self-protection jammer.
AST Air Staff Target (UK).
ASV (1) Air-to-surface vessel; (2) Anti surface vessel.
ASW Anti-submarine warfare.
ATA Air Transport Association of America.
ATC Air traffic control.
ATR Airline transport radio, series of ARINC standard box sizes.
attack, angle of Angle at which airstream meets aerofoil (angle between mean chord and free-stream direction). Not to be confused with angle of incidence (which see).
augmented Boosted by afterburning.
autogyro Rotary-wing aircraft propelled by a propeller (or other thrusting device) and lifted by a freely running autorotating rotor.
AUW All-up weight (term meaning total weight of aircraft under defined conditions, or at specific time during flight). Not to be confused with MTOGW (which see).
avionics Aviation electronics, such as communications radio, radars, navigation systems and computers.
AVLF Airborne very low frequency.
AWACS Airborne warning and control system (aircraft).

bar Non-SI unit of pressure adopted by this yearbook pending wider acceptance of Pa. 1 bar = 10^5 Pa, and ISA pressure at S/L is 1,013.2 mb, or just over 1 bar.
bare weight Undefined term meaning unequipped empty weight.
basic operating weight MTOGW minus payload (thus, including crew, fuel and oil, bar stocks, cutlery etc).
BCAR British Civil Airworthiness Requirements.
Beta mode Propeller or rotor operating regime in which pilot has direct control of pitch.
BFO Beat-frequency oscillator.
BITE Built-in test equipment.
bladder tank Fuel (or other fluid) tank of flexible material.
bleed air Hot high-pressure air extracted from gas-turbine engine compressor or combustor and taken through valves and pipes to perform useful work such as driving machinery or anti-icing by heating surfaces.
blown flap Flap across which bleed air is discharged at high (often supersonic) speed to prevent flow-breakaway.
BOW Basic operating weight.
BPR Bypass ratio.
BRW Brake release weight, maximum permitted weight at start of T-O run.
BTU Non-SI unit of energy (British Thermal Unit) = 0.9478 J.
bulk cargo All cargo not packed in containers or on pallets.
bus Busbar, main terminal in electrical system to which battery or generator power is supplied.
bypass ratio Airflow through fan duct (not passing through core) divided by airflow through core.

CAA Civil Aviation Authority (UK).
CAB Civil Aeronautics Board (USA).
CAB Pt 298 Sets the commercial standards for non-certificated carriers, mainly commuter airlines.
cabin altitude Height above S/L at which ambient pressure is same as inside cabin.
CAM Cockpit-angle measure (crew field of view).
canards Foreplanes, fixed or controllable aerodynamic surfaces ahead of CG.
CAN 5 Committee on Aircraft Noise (ICAO) rules for new designs of aircraft.
CAR Civil Airworthiness Regulations.
CAS Calibrated airspeed, ASI calibrated to allow for air compressibility according to ISA S/L.
CBR California bearing ratio, measure of ability of airfield surface (paved or not) to support aircraft.
CBU Cluster bomb unit.
CCV Control configured vehicle.
CEAM Centre d'Expériences Aériennes Militaires.
CEAT Centre d'Essais Aéronautiques de Toulouse.
CEP Circular error probability (50/50 chance of hit being inside or outside) in bombing, missile attack or gunnery.
CEV Centre d'Essais en Vol.
CFRP Carbonfibre-reinforced plastics.
CG Centre of gravity.
chaff Thin slivers of radar-reflective material cut to length appropriate to wavelengths of hostile radars and scattered in clouds to protect friendly aircraft.
chord Distance from leading-edge to trailing-edge measured parallel to longitudinal axis.
CKD Component knocked down, for assembly elsewhere.
clean In flight configuration with landing gear, flaps, slats etc retracted.
'clean' Without any optional external stores.
c/n Construction (or constructor's) number.
COINS Computer operated instrument system.
comint communications intelligence.
composite material Made of two constituents, such as filaments or short whiskers plus adhesive.
CONUS Continental USA (ie, excluding Hawaii, etc).
convertible Transport aircraft able to be equipped to carry passengers or cargo.
core Gas generator portion of turbofan comprising compressor(s), combustion chamber and turbine(s).
C/R Counter-rotating (propellers).
CRT Cathode-ray tube.
CSAS Command and stability augmentation system (part of AFCS).
CSD Constant-speed drive (output shaft speed held steady, no matter how input may vary).
CSRL Common strategic rotary launchers (for ALCMs or SRAMs).

DADC Digital air data computer.
DADS Digital air data system.
daN Decanewtons (Newtons force × 10).
DARPA Defense Advanced Research Projects Agency.
dB Decibel.
DC Direct current.
DECU Digital engine control unit.
derated Engine restricted to power less than potential maximum (usually such engine is flat rated).
design weight Different authorities have different definitions; weight chosen as typical of mission but usually much less than MTOGW.
DF Direction finder, or direction finding.
DGAC Direction Générale à l'Aviation Civile.
dibber bomb Designed to cause maximum damage to concrete runways.
dihedral Upward slop of wing seen from front, in direction from root to tip.
DINS Digital inertial navigation system.
disposable load Sum of masses that can be loaded or unloaded, including payload, crew, usable fuel etc; MTOGW minus OWE.
DME Distance-measuring equipment; gives slant distance to a beacon directly ahead.
dog-tooth A step in the leading-edge of a plane resulting from an increase in chord. (See also saw-tooth.)
Doppler Short for Doppler radar — radar using fact that received frequency is a function of relative velocity between transmitter or reflecting surface and receiver.
double-slotted flap One having an auxiliary aerofoil ahead of main surface to increase maximum lift.
dP Maximum design differential pressure between pressurised cabin and ambient (outside atmosphere).
drone Pilotless aircraft, usually winged, following preset programme of manoeuvres.
DS Directionally solidified.

EAA Experimental Aircraft Association (divided into local branches called Chapters).
EAS Equivalent airspeed, RAS minus correction for compressibility.
ECCM Electronic counter-countermeasures.
ECM Electronic countermeasures.
EFIS Electronic flight instrument(ation) system, in which large multifunction CRT displays replace traditional instruments.
EGT Exhaust gas temperature, downstream of turbine(s).
ehp Equivalent horsepower, measure of propulsive power of turboprop made up of shp plus addition due to residual thrust from jet.
EICAS Engine indication (and) crew alerting system.
EIS Entry into service.
ekW Equivalent kilowatts, SI measure of propulsive power of turboprop (see ehp).
elevon Wing trailing-edge control surface combining functions of aileron and elevator.
elint electronics intelligence.
ELT Emergency locator transmitter, to help rescuers home on to a disabled or crashed aircraft.
EPA Environmental Protection Agency.
EPNdB Effective perceived noise decibel, SI unit of EPNL.
EPNL Effective perceived noise level, measure of noise effect on humans which takes account of sound intensity, frequency, character and duration, and response of human ear.
EPU Emergency power unit (part of aircraft, not used for propulsion).
ERP Effective radiated power.
ESA European Space Agency.
ESM (1) Electronic surveillance (or support) measures; (2) Electronic signal monitoring.
EVA Extra-vehicular activity, ie outside spacecraft.
EWSM Early-warning support measures.

FAA Federal Aviation Administration.
factored Multiplied by an agreed number to take account of extreme adverse conditions, errors, design deficiencies or other inaccuracies.
FADEC Full authority digital engine control.
FAI Fédération Aéronautique Internationale.
fail-operational System which continues to function after any single fault has occurred.
fail-safe Structure or system which survives failure (in case of system, may no longer function normally).
FAR Federal Aviation Regulations.
FAR Pt 23 Defines the airworthiness of private and airtaxi aeroplanes of 5,670 kg (12,500 lb) MTOGW and below.
FAR Pt 25 Defines the airworthiness of public transport aeroplanes exceeding 5,670 kg (12,500 lb) MTOGW.
FBW Fly by wire (which see).
FDS Flight director system.
feathering Setting propeller or similar blades at pitch aligned with slipstream to give resultant torque (not tending to turn shaft) and thus minimum drag.
FEBA Forward edge of battle area.
fence A chordwise projection on the surface of a wing, used to modify the distribution of pressure.
fenestron Helicopter tail rotor with many slender blades rotating in short duct.
ferry range Extreme safe range with zero payload.
FFAR Folding-fin (or free-flight) aircraft rocket.
FFVV Fédération Française de Vol à Voile (French gliding authority).
field length Measure of distance needed to land and/or take off; many different measures for particular purposes, each precisely defined.
flaperon Wing trailing-edge surface combining functions of flap and aileron.
flat-four Engine having four horizontally opposed cylinders; thus, flat-twin, flat-six etc.
flat rated Propulsion engine capable of giving full thrust or power for take-off up to high airfield height and/or high ambient temperature (thus, probably derated at S/L).
FLIR Forward-looking infra-red.

AFTER ALL — WE'RE

OMNIPOL

fly by wire Flight control system with electrical signalling (ie, without mechanical interconnection between cockpit flying controls and control surfaces).

FM Frequency modulation.

FMCS Flight management computer system.

FOL Forward operating location.

footprint A precisely delineated boundary on the surface, inside which the perceived noise of an aircraft exceeds a specified level during take-off and/or landing.

Fowler flap Moves initially aft to increase wing area and then also deflects down to increase drag.

free turbine Turbine mechanically independent of engine upstream, other than being connected by rotating bearings and the gas stream, and thus able to run at its own speed.

Frise aileron Most common manual aileron, with leading-edge that projects below wing to increase drag when aileron is raised.

FSW Forward-swept wing.

FY Fiscal year (1 July to 30 June in US government affairs).

g Acceleration due to mean Earth gravity, ie of a body in free fall.

gallons Non-SI measure; 1 Imp gal (UK) = 4.546 litres, 1 US gal = 3.785 litres.

GCI Ground-controlled interception.

geostationary Of an Earth satellite, rotating with the Earth and thus always overhead the same point. Corresponds to altitude above Earth's surface of about 35,800 km (22,245 miles).

geostationary orbit An Earth-centred orbit at a height above the Earth's surface of about 35,800 km (22,245 miles) and lying approximately in the plane of the equator. A satellite in such an orbit travelling eastwards will remain over the same point, rotating precisely with the Earth.

geosynchronous See geostationary.

GfK Glassfibre-reinforced plastics (German).

glide ratio Of a sailplane, distance travelled along track divided by height lost in still air.

glove In a swing-wing aeroplane with pivots well out from the centreline it is geometrically impossible to have one-piece pivoted wings because at zero sweep the inner ends would overlap; the answer is fixed inner leading portions called gloves.

GPU Ground power unit (not part of aircraft).

GPWS Ground-proximity warning system.

green aircraft Aircraft flyable but lacking furnishing and customer's choice of avionics.

gross wing area See wing area.

GRP Glassfibre-reinforced plastics.

GS Glideslope, of ILS.

GSE Ground-support equipment (such as special test gear, steps and servicing platforms).

GTS Gas-turbine starter (ie starter is miniature gas turbine).

gunship Helicopter designed for battlefield attack, normally with slim body carrying pilot and weapon operator only.

h Hour(s).

hardened Protected as far as possible against nuclear explosion.

hardpoint Reinforced part of aircraft to which external load can be attached, eg weapon or tank pylon.

helicopter Rotary-wing aircraft both lifted and propelled by one or more power-driven rotors turning about substantially vertical axes.

HF High frequency.

'hot and high' Adverse combination of airfield height and high ambient temperature, which lengthens required TOD.

hovering ceiling Ceiling of helicopter (corresponding to air density at which maximum rate of climb is zero), either IGE or OGE.

HP High pressure.

hp Horsepower.

HSI Horizontal situation indicator.

HUD Head-up display (bright numbers and symbols projected on pilot's windscreen and focussed on infinity so that pilot can simultaneously read display and look ahead).

HVAR High-velocity aircraft rocket.

Hz Hertz, cycles per second.

IAS Indicated airspeed, ASIR corrected for instrument error.

IATA International Air Transport Association.

ICAO International Civil Aviation Organization.

IFF Identification friend or foe.

IFR Instrument flight rules (ie, not VFR).

IGE In ground effect: helicopter performance with theoretical flat horizontal surface just below it.

ILS Instrument landing system.

IMC Instrument meteorological conditions, basically IFR.

IMK Increased manoeuvrability kit.

IMS Integrated multiplex system.

INAS Integrated nav/attack system.

incidence Strictly, the angle at which the wing is set in relation to the fore/aft axis. Wrongly used to mean angle of attack (which see).

inertial navigation Measuring all accelerations imparted to a vehicle and, by integrating these with respect to time, calculating speed at every instant (in all three planes) and by integrating a second time calculating total change of position in relation to starting point.

INS Inertial navigation system.

integral construction Machined from solid instead of assembled from separate parts.

integral tank Fuel or other liquid tank formed by sealing part of structure.

intercom Wired telephone system for communication within aircraft.

inverter Electric or electronic device for inverting (reversing polarity of) alternate waves in AC power to produce DC.

IP Intermediate pressure.

IR Infra-red.

IRAN Inspect and repair as necessary.

IRLS Infra-red linescan (builds TV-type picture showing cool regions as dark and hot regions as light).

IRS Inertial reference system.

ISA International Standard Atmosphere.

ISIS (1 Boeing Vertol) Integral spar inspection system; (2 Ferranti) integrated strike and interception sight.

ITE Involute throat and exit (rocket nozzle).

IVSI Instantaneous VSI.

J Joules, SI unit of energy.

JAR Joint Airworthiness Requirements, agreed by all major EEC countries (in 1988 JAR.25 was latest standard).

JASDF Japan Air Self-Defence force.

JATO Jet-assisted take-off (actually means rocket-assisted).

JCAB Japan Civil Airworthiness Board.

JDA Japan Defence Agency.

JGSDF Japan Ground Self-Defence Force.

JMSDF Japan Maritime Self-Defence Force.

JTIDS Joint Tactical Information Distribution System.

Kevlar Aramid fibre used as basis of high-strength composite material.

km/h Kilometres per hour.

kN Kilonewtons (the Newton is the SI unit of force; 1 lbf = 4.448 N).

knot 1 nm per hour.

Krüger flap Hinges down and then forward from below the leading-edge.

Küchemann tip Wing tip of curving planform intended to minimise drag at high subsonic speed.

kVA Kilovolt-ampères.

kW Kilowatt, SI measure of all forms of power (not just electrical).

LABS Low-altitude bombing system.

LANTIRN Low-altitude navigation targeting infra-red, night.

LARC Low-altitude ride control.

LBA Luftfahrtbundesamt (Federal German civil aviation authority).

lbf Pounds of thrust.

LCN Load classification number, measure of 'flotation' of aircraft landing gear linking aircraft weight, weight distribution, tyre numbers, pressures and disposition.

LDNS Laser Doppler navigation system.

LED Light-emitting diode.

LGSC Linear glideslope capture.

Lidar Light detection and ranging (laser counterpart of radar).

LITVC Liquid-injection thrust vector control.

LLTV Low-light TV (thus, LLLTV, low-light-level).

Load factor (1) percentage of max payload; (2) stress limit.

LOC Localiser.

localiser Element giving steering guidance in ILS.

loiter Flight for maximum endurance, such as supersonic fighter on patrol.

longerons Principal fore-and-aft structural members (eg, in fuselage).

Loran (Long Range Navigation) Family of hyperbolic navaids based on ground radio emissions.

lox Liquid oxygen.

LP Low pressure.

LRMTS Laser ranger and marked-target seeker.

m Metre(s), SI unit of length.

M or Mach number The ratio of the speed of a body to the speed of sound (1,116 ft; 340 m/sec in air at 15°C) under the same ambient conditions.

MAC US Air Force Military Airlift Command.

MAD Magnetic anomaly detector.

Madar Maintenance analysis, detection and recording.

Madge Microwave aircraft digital guidance equipment.

marker, marker beacon Ground beacon giving position guidance in ILS.

MASTACS Manoeuvrability augmentation system for tactical air combat simulation.

mb Millibars, bar × 10³.

MBR Marker-beacon receiver.

MEPU Monofuel emergency power unit.

METO Maximum except take-off.

MF Medium frequency.

mg Milligrammes, grammes × 10³.

MLS Microwave landing system.

MLW Maximum landing weight.

mm Millimetres, metres × 10³.

MMH Monomethyl hydrazine.

MMO Maximum permitted operating Mach number.

MNPS Minimum navigation performance specification.

monocoque Structure with strength in outer shell, devoid of internal bracing.

MoU Memorandum of understanding.

MPA Man-powered aircraft.

mph Miles per hour.

MRW Maximum ramp weight.

MTBF Mean time between failures.

MTI Moving-target indication.

MTOGW Maximum take-off gross weight (MRW minus taxi/run-up fuel).

MZFW Maximum zero-fuel weight.

NACA US National Advisory Committee for Aeronautics (now NASA).

Nadge NATO air defence ground environment.

NAS US Naval Air Station.

NASA National Aeronautics and Space Administration.

NASC US Naval Air Systems Command (also several other aerospace meanings).

NATC US Naval Air Training Command or Test Center (also several other aerospace meanings).

NBAA US National Business Aircraft Association.

NDB Non-directional beacon.

NH₄ClO₄ Ammonium perchlorate.

nm nautical mile, 1.8532 km, 1.15152 miles.

NOAA US National Oceanic and Atmospheric Administration.

NOE Nap-of-the-Earth (low flying in military aircraft, using natural cover of hills, trees, etc).

NOGS Night observation gunship.

NOS Night observation surveillance.

Ns Newton-second (1 N thrust applied for 1 second)

OBS Omni-bearing selector.

OCU Operational Conversion Unit.

OEI One engine inoperative.

OGE Out of ground effect; helicopter hovering, far above nearest surface.

Omega Long-range hyperbolic navaid.

OMI Omni-bearing magnetic indicator.

omni Generalised word meaning equal in all directions (as in omni-range, omni-flash beacon).

OTPI On-top position indicator (indicates overhead of submarine in ASW).

OUV Osker-Ursinus-Vereinigung (West German chapter of EAA).

OWE Operating weight empty, MTOGW minus payload, usable fuel and oil and other consumables.

PA system Public-address.

pallet (1) for freight, rigid platform for handling by forklift or conveyor; (2) for missile, mounting and electronics box outside aircraft.

payload Disposable load generating revenue (passengers, cargo, mail and other paid items), in military aircraft loosely used to mean total load carried of weapons, cargo or other mission equipment.

PD radar Pulse-Doppler.

penaids Penetration aids, such as jammers, chaff or decoys to help aircraft fly safely through hostile airspace.

perigee The point in an Earth-centred orbit nearest to the Earth.

perihelion The point in a solar (Sun-centred) orbit closest to the Sun.

PFA Popular Flying Association (UK).

PHI Position and heading (or homing) indicator.

plane A lifting surface (eg, wing, tailplane).

plug door Door larger than its frame in pressurized fuselage, either opening inwards or arranged to retract parts prior to opening outwards.

plume The region of hot air and gas emitted by a helicopter jetpipe.

pneumatic de-icing Covered with flexible surfaces alternately pumped up and deflated to throw off ice.

port Left side, looking forward.

power loading Aircraft weight (usually MTOGW) divided by total propulsive power or thrust at T-O.

pressure fuelling Fuelling via a leakproof connection through which fuel passes at high rate under pressure.

pressure ratio In gas-turbine engine, compressor delivery pressure divided by ambient pressure (in supersonic aircraft, divided by ram pressure downstream of inlet).

primary flight controls Those used to control trajectory of aircraft (thus, not trimmers, tabs, flaps, slats, airbrakes or lift dumpers etc).

propfan A family of new technology propellers characterised by multiple scimitar-shaped blades with thin sharp-edged profile. Single and contra-rotating examples promise to extend propeller efficiency up to about Mach 0.8.

pulse-Doppler Radar sending out pulses and measuring frequency-shift or returns from target(s).

pylon Structure linking aircraft to external load (engine nacelle, drop-tank, bomb etc). Also used in conventional sense in pylon racing.

AERMACCHI

MB-339C   A COMPLETE TRAINING SYSTEM

Nowadays, mission management techniques receive a great deal of emphasis in the training syllabus of a modern combat pilot.

To meet the demands arising from the adoption of such modern training philosophy it has become necessary to provide the student pilot with a cockpit environment as close as possible to that he will encounter in the most recent types of combat aircraft.

The MB-339C Digital Avionics, the latest development of the well known MB-339 advanced jet trainer, has been conceived expressly for this demanding task.

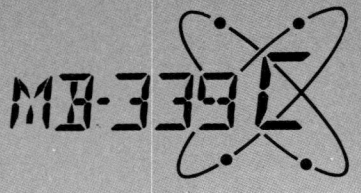

MB-339C Nav/Attack System Configuration:
Inertial Platform/Doppler Radar; Navigation Computer Head up Display/Weapons Aiming Computer, CRT Multifunction Display, Radar Altimeter, Laser Range Finder, Radar Warning System; Store Management System.

FOTOAERMACCHI

PUBBLIAERMACCHI

radius In terms of performance, the distance an aircraft can fly from base and return without intermediate landing.

RAE Royal Aircraft Establishment.

RAI Registro Aeronautica Italiano.

ram pressure Increased pressure in forward-facing aircraft inlet, generated by converting (relative) kinetic energy to pressure.

ramp weight Maximum weight at start of flight (MTOGW plus taxi/run-up fuel).

range Too many definitions to list, but essentially the distance an aircraft can fly (or is permitted to fly) with specified load and usually whilst making allowance for specified additional manoeuvres (diversions, stand-off, go-around etc).

RAS Rectified airspeed, IAS corrected for position error.

raster Generation of large-area display, eg TV screen, by close-spaced horizontal lines scanned either alternately or in sequence.

RATT Radio teletype.

redundant Provided with spare capacity or data channels and thus made to survive failures.

refanned Gas-turbine engine fitted with new fan of higher BPR.

rigid rotor Helicopter rotor without articulating hinges (eg, flapping hinge, drag hinge) but with pitch variation.

RLD Rijksluchtvaartdienst. Netherlands civil aviation department.

RMI Radio magnetic indicator (compass).

R/Nav Area navigation, navaid covering whole of local area instead of just crowded airways.

Rotor-kite Rotary-wing aircraft with no internal power, lifted by a freely running autorotating rotor and towed by an external vehicle.

roving Multiple-strands of fibre, as in a rope (but usually not twisted).

RPV Remotely piloted vehicle (pilot in other aircraft or on ground).

RSA Réseau du Sport de l'Air.

RVR Runway visual range.

s Second(s).

SAC US Air Force Strategic Air Command.

safe-life A term denoting that a component has proved by testing that it can be expected to continue to function safely for a precisely defined period before replacement.

salmon (French saumon) Streamlined fairings, usually at wingtip of sailplane, serving same function as endplate and acting also as tip-skid.

SAR (1) Search and rescue; (2) synthetic aperture radar.

SATS (1) Small airfield for tactical support; (2) Small Arms Target System.

saw-tooth Same as dog-tooth.

SCAS Stability and control augmentation system.

second-source Production of identical item by second factory or company.

semi-active Homing on to radiation reflected from target illuminated by radar or laser energy beamed from elsewhere.

service ceiling Usually height equivalent to air density at which maximum attainable rate of climb is 100 ft/min.

servo A device which acts as a relay, usually augmenting the pilot's efforts to move a control surface or the like.

SFAR Special Federal Aviation Regulation(s).

sfc Specific fuel consumption.

SGAC Secrétariat Général à l'Aviation Civile (now DGAC).

shaft Connection between gas turbine and compressor or other driven unit. Two-shaft engine has second shaft, rotating at different speed, surrounding the first (thus, HP surrounds inner LP or fan shaft).

Shoran Short range navigation (radio).

shp Shaft horsepower, measure of power transmitted via rotating shaft.

sideline noise EPNdB measure of aircraft landing and taking off, at point 0.25 nm (2- or 3-engined) or 0.35 nm (4-engined) from runway centreline.

SIF Selective identification facility.

sigint Signals intelligence.

signature Characteristic 'fingerprint' of all electromagnetic radiation (radar, IR etc).

single-shaft Gas-turbine in which all compressors and turbines are on common shaft rotating together.

S/L Sea Level.

SLAR Side-looking airborne radar.

snap-down Air-to-air interception of low-flying aircraft by AAM fired from fighter at a higher altitude.

soft target Not armoured or hardened.

specific fuel consumption Rate at which fuel is consumed divided by power or thrust developed, and thus a measure of engine efficiency. For jet engines (air-breathing, ie not rockets) unit is mg/Ns, milligrams per Newton-second; for shaft engines unit is µg/J, micrograms (millionths of a gram) per Joule (SI unit of work or energy).

specific impulse Measure of rocket engine efficiency; thrust divided by rate of fuel/oxidant consumption per second, the units for mass and force being the same so that the answer is expressed in seconds.

SPILS Stall protection and incidence-limiting system.

spool One complete axial compressor rotor; thus a two-shaft engine may have a fan plus an LP spool.

SSB Single-sideband (radio).

SSR Secondary surveillance radar.

st Static thrust.

stabiliser Fin (thus, horizontal stabiliser = tailplane).

stall strips Sharp-edged strips on wing leading-edge to induce stall at that point.

stalling speed TAS at which aircraft stalls at $1g$, ie wing lift suddenly collapses.

standard day ISA temperature and pressure.

starboard Right side, looking forward.

static inverter Solid-state inverter of alternating waveform (ie not rotary machine).

stick-pusher Stall-protection device that forces pilot's control column forward as stalling angle of attack is neared.

stick-shaker Stall-warning device that noisily shakes pilot's control column as stalling angle of attack is neared.

STOL Short take-off and landing. (Several definitions, stipulating allowable horizontal distance to clear screen height of 35 or 50 ft or various SI measures).

store Object carried as part of payload on external attachment (eg bomb, drop-tank).

strobe light High-intensity flashing beacon.

substrate The underlying layer on which something (such as a solar cell or integrated circuit) is made.

supercritical wing Wing of relatively deep, flat-topped profile generating lift right across upper surface instead of concentrated close behind leading edge.

sweepback Backwards inclination of wing or other aerofoil, seen from above, measured relative to fuselage or other reference axis, usually measured at quarter-chord (25%) or at leading-edge.

synchronous See geostationary.

synchronous satellite Geostationary.

t Tonne, 1 Megagram, 1,000 kg.

tabbed flap Fitted with narrow-chord tab along entire trailing-edge which deflects to greater angle than main surface.

tabs Small auxiliary surfaces hinged to trailing-edge of control surfaces for purposes of trimming, reducing hinge moment (force needed to operate main surface) or in other way assisting pilot.

TAC US Air Force Tactical Air Command.

Tacan Tactical air navigation, simple military navaid using ground beacons.

taileron Left and right tailplanes used as primary control surfaces in both pitch and roll.

tailplane Main horizontal tail surface, originally fixed and carrying hinged elevator(s) but today often a single 'slab' serving as control surface.

TANS Tactical air navigation system (Doppler-based computer, control and display unit).

TAS True airspeed, EAS corrected for density (often very large factor) appropriate to aircraft height.

TBO Time between overhauls.

t/c ratio Ratio of the thickness (aerodynamic depth) of a wing or other surface to its chord, both measured at the same place parallel to the fore-and-aft axis.

TET Turbine entry temperature (of the gas).

TFR Terrain-following radar (for low-level attack).

thickness Depth of wing or other aerofoil; maximum perpendicular distance between upper and lower surfaces.

T-O Take-off.

T-O noise EPNdB measure of aircraft taking off, at point directly under flight path 3.5 nm from brakes-release (regardless of altitude).

TOD Take-off distance.

TOGW Take-off gross weight (not necessarily MTOGW).

ton Imperial (long) ton = 1.016 t (Mg), US (short) ton = 0.9072 t.

track Distance between centres of contact areas of main landing wheels measured left/right across aircraft (with bogies, distance between centres of contact areas of each bogie).

transceiver Radio transmitter/receiver.

transfer orbit Orbit, or part of an orbit, linking two others at different heights around the same planetary body.

transponder Radio transmitter triggered automatically by a particular received signal.

TRU Transformer/rectifier unit.

TSFC Thrust specific fuel consumption of jet engine (turbojet, turbofan, ducted propfan or ramjet).

TSO Technical Standard Order (FAA).

turbofan Gas-turbine jet engine generating most thrust by a large-diameter cowled fan, with small part added by jet from core.

turbojet Simplest form of gas turbine comprising compressor, combustion chamber, turbine and propulsive nozzle.

turboprop Gas turbine in which as much energy as possible is taken from gas jet and used to drive reduction gearbox and propeller.

turboshaft Gas turbine in which as much energy as possible is taken from gas jet and used to drive high-speed shaft (which in turn drives external load such as helicopter gearbox).

TVC Thrust vector control (rocket).

TWT Travelling-wave tube.

tyre sizes In simplest form, first figure is rim diameter (in or mm) and second is rim width (in or mm). In more correct three-unit form, first figure is outside diameter, second is max width and third is wheel diameter.

UBE, Ubee Ultra bypass engine, alternative terminology (Boeing) for UDF.

UDF Unducted fan, one form of advanced propulsion system in which gas-turbine blading directly drives large fan (propfan) blades mounted around the outside of the engine pod.

UHF Ultra-high frequency.

unfactored Performance level expected of average pilot, in average aircraft, without additional safety factors.

usable fuel Total mass of fuel consumable in flight, usually 95-98 per cent of system capacity.

US gallon 0.83267 Imperial gallon.

variable-geometry Capable of grossly changing shape in flight, especially by varying sweep of wings.

VD Maximum permitted diving speed.

vernier Small thruster, usually a rocket, for final precise adjustment of a vehicle's trajectory and velocity.

VFR Visual flight rules.

VHF Very high frequency.

VLF Very low frequency.

VMO Maximum permitted operating flight speed (IAS, EAS or CAS must be specified).

VNE Never-exceed speed (aerodynamic or structural limit).

VOR VHF omni-directional range, ground navaid usable only when flying along predetermined airways.

VSI Vertical speed (climb/descent) indicator.

VTOL Vertical take-off and landing.

washout Inbuilt wing twist reducing angle of incidence towards the tip.

wheelbase Minimum distance from nosewheel or tailwheel (centre of contact area) to line joining main wheels (centres of contact areas).

wing area Total projected area of clean wing (no flaps, slats etc) including all control surfaces and area of fuselage bounded by leading- and trailing-edges projected to centre-line (inapplicable to slender-delta aircraft with extremely large leading-edge sweep angle). Sometimes called gross wing area; net area excludes projected areas of fuselage, nacelles, etc.

wing loading Aircraft weight (usually MTOGW) divided by wing area.

winglet Small auxiliary aerofoil, usually sharply upturned and often swept back, at tip of wing.

wire guidance Guidance of missile of RPV by signals transmitted through fine wire(s) linking it with operator.

zero-fuel weight MTOGW minus usable fuel and other consumables, in most aircraft imposing severest stress on wing.

zero/zero seat Ejection seat designed for use even at zero speed on ground.

ZFW Zero-fuel weight.

µg Microgrammes, grammes $\times 10^6$.

First Flights

Some first flights made during the period 1 June 1987 to 7 September 1988

JUNE 1987

1   Boeing E-6A Tacamo, first flight with full avionics (62782) (USA)
10   Boeing Helicopters Model 360 (N360BV) (USA)
18   Airbus A320, third aircraft (International)
24   E-Systems/Grob/Garrett Egrett-1 (D-FGEI) (International)
24   PZL Mielec M-26 01 Iskierka (SP-PIB) (Poland)
25   NASA/McDonnell Douglas HIDEC F-15 Eagle (NASA 287) (USA)
25   SSAKTB SL-2P research sailplane (Poland)
26   McDonnell Douglas/BAe AV-8B Harrier II, night attack version (162966) (International)

JULY 1987

1   Questair Venture homebuilt (N62V) (USA)
2   McDonnell Douglas MD-82, first assembled in China (USA/China)
2   McDonnell Douglas F-4F Phantom II, first flight with MBB VBW anti-tank weapon pod (Germany, Federal Republic)
7   Dassault-Breguet Atlantic 1, first modernised aircraft for Italian Air Force (France)
8   Airbus A320, fourth aircraft (International)
11   Lundy Graflite homebuilt (N870GF) (USA)
14   PZL Mielec M-24 Dromader Super (SP-PFA) (Poland)
16   Sequoia F.8L Falco homebuilt, 180 hp version (USA)
28   Wheeler Express homebuilt (N200EX) (USA)
30   Airship Industries Skyship 500 HL airship (G-SKSB) (UK)

AUGUST 1987

11   IAI/IAF (McDonnell Douglas F-4) Phantom 2000 (Israel)
11   Akaflieg Berlin B 12T sailplane (D-7612) (Germany, Federal Republic)
15   McDonnell Douglas MD-88 (USA)
18   McDonnell Douglas MD-80 UHB testbed, first flight with improved GE36 engine (USA)
21   Boeing 767 Airborne Optical Adjunct sensor test aircraft (N767BA) (USA)
25   Grumman A-6F Intruder II (162183) (USA)
31   Mitsubishi (Sikorsky) XSH-60J Seahawk (8202) (Japan/USA)

SEPTEMBER 1987

3   McDonnell Douglas F/A-18C Hornet, first production (USA)
4   Cranfield/BAe 748 Turbine Tanker (G-BNJK) (UK)
11   Sikorsky S-70A-9 Black Hawk, first for RAAF (A25-101) (USA)

OCTOBER 1987

5   Verilite Sunbird, Emdair CF-092B engine (N100VL) (USA)
6   Sikorsky VH-60A (183239) (USA)
9   EHI EH 101 (PP1/ZF641) (International)
9   Goodyear GZ-22 airship (N4A) (USA)
11   General Dynamics F-16C Fighting Falcon, first assembled by TAI in Turkey (USA/Turkey)

NOVEMBER 1987

13   Bell XV-15, first flight with Boeing advanced technology rotor blades (N703NA) (USA)
14   Grumman F-14A(Plus) Tomcat, first production (USA)
18   Schempp-Hirth Discus K sailplane (D-8111) (Germany, Federal Republic)
23   Grumman A-6F Intruder II, second aircraft (USA)
24   Grumman F-14A(Plus) Tomcat, first avionics testbed aircraft (USA)
26   EHI EH 101, second pre-production (PP2) (International)

DECEMBER 1987

2   Sikorsky S-72 X-wing RSRA, without X-wing (N741NA/NASA 741) (USA)
3   Valmet L-90 TP Redigo, second prototype (OH-VTM) (Finland)
4   Sikorsky S-70B-2 Seahawk, first for RAN (N7265H) (USA)
9   Airbus A300-600R (F-WWAU) (International)
11   Rolladen-Schneider LS7 sailplane (D-7737) (Germany, Federal Republic)
14   Schleicher ASW 24 sailplane (D-1124) (Germany, Federal Republic)
15   Westland Sea King HAS. Mk 6 (XZ581) (UK)
24   Skytek Maverick homebuilt (VH-JOX) (Australia)

16 April 1988: McDonnell Douglas/BAe T-45A Goshawk trainer for US Navy

11 May 1988: first production AMX multi-role combat aircraft

28 July 1988: Airbus A320 with IAE V2500 engines

[48]

DECEMBER 1987 *Cont.*
29 Beech/Scaled Composites Advanced Technology Tactical Transport scale prototype (N133SC) (USA)
30 Fokker 100, first production (HB-IVA) (Netherlands)

FEBRUARY 1988
11 Cirrus Design Cirrus VK30 homebuilt (N30VK) (USA)
12 Spacial MLA-32-A Toluca airship, inadvertent first flight (XB-RGP) (Mexico)
18 Schempp-Hirth Ventus CM powered sailplane (Germany, Federal Republic)
19 Boeing Model 737-400 (N73700) (USA)
22 IRGC Fajr (Iran)

MARCH 1988
5 ENAER T-35S Pillán (CC-PZB) (Chile)
17 Schempp-Hirth Nimbus 3DM powered sailplane (Germany, Federal Republic)
18 Akaflieg Braunschweig SB-13 sailplane (Germany, Federal Republic)
25 Boeing Model 737-400, second aircraft (USA)
25 Advanced Aviation Sierra sailplane (USA)

APRIL 1988
8 Lockheed P-3 AEW&C Blue Sentinel, first flight with full avionics (USA)
15 Tupolev Tu-155, first flight on liquid hydrogen fuel (SSSR-85035) (USSR)
16 McDonnell Douglas/BAe T-45A Goshawk (162787) (USA)
27 Fuji KM-2D, first production conversion (Japan)
29 Grob G 116 (D-EGRF) (Germany, Federal Republic)
29 Boeing Model 747-400 (N401PW) (USA)

MAY 1988
6 McDonnell Douglas F/A-18D Hornet, night attack prototype (USA)
7 Boeing Model 720B, testbed for IAE V2500 engine (USA)
11 AMX, first production (International)
11 Skyrider (Rider) BA-3 airship (N25FR) (USA)
27 Teledyne Ryan Model 410 (N53578) (USA)

JUNE 1988
8 Fokker 100, first flight with Tay 650 engines (PH-MKH) (Netherlands)
14 Schweizer Model 330 Sky Knight (N330TT) (USA)
27 Boeing Model 747-400, first with CF6-80C2 engines (USA)
28 Kawasaki T-4, first production (Japan)

JULY 1988
12 Beechcraft Cabin Class Twin (N143SC) (USA)
12 Valsan re-engined Boeing Model 727-200 (OY-SAS) (USA)
14 TBM 700 (F-WTBM) (International)
15 Boeing Model 757-200M Combi (USA)
19 LoPresti Piper Swiftfire (USA)
24 Arocet AT-9 (USA)
28 Airbus A320, first flight with IAE V2500 engines (F-WWAI) (International)
29 OMAC Laser 300, first production (N301L) (USA)

AUGUST 1988
2 NASA (Convair) F-106B with leading-edge vortex flaps (N816NA/NASA 816) (USA)
7 Conair Turbo Firecat (C-GHPU) (Canada)
17 Sikorsky HH-60H (USA)
18 Panavia Tornado ECR (International)
25 FFV BA-14 Starling (SE-KFV) (Sweden)

7 August 1988: Conair Turbo Firecat firefighting conversion of ASW Tracker

7 September 1988: McDonnell Douglas F-15 STOL manoeuvring technology demonstrator

SEPTEMBER 1988
7 McDonnell Douglas F-15 STOL manoeuvring technology demonstrator (71-290) (USA)

MIRACH. THE LEADER SYSTEM.

The Mirachs are a family of unmanned aircraft, designed and produced by Meteor, capable of carrying
out a wide range of missions, such
as: training (Mirach 70 and 100),
operational support and reconnaissance (Mirach 20 and 100) as well as
rescue and civil protection (Mirach
20) as sophisticated air vehicle within the framework of rescue arrangement in case of national emergencies.
Meteor Costruzioni Aeronautiche
ed Elettroniche S.p.A. - Via Nomentana, 146 - 00162 Rome (Italy).

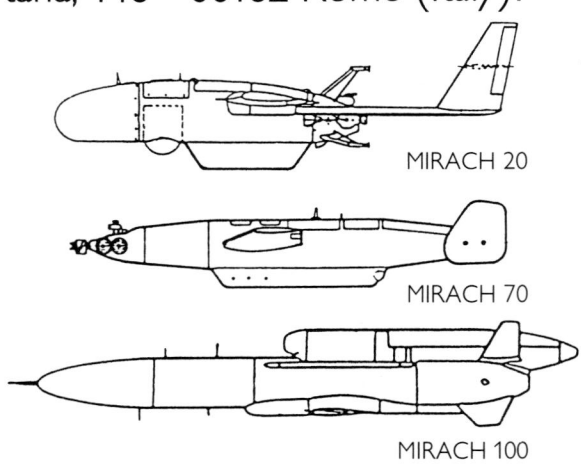

MIRACH 20

MIRACH 70

MIRACH 100

METEOR
Raggruppamento ◇ **AERITALIA**

IRI finmeccanica
COSTRUZIONI
AERONAUTICHE ed
ELETTRONICHE s.p.a.

Official Records

ABSOLUTE WORLD RECORDS

Three records are classed as Absolute World Records for balloons by the Fédération Aéronautique Internationale, as follows:

Duration (USA)
M. L. Anderson, B. L. Abruzzo and L. M. Newman in the gas balloon *Double Eagle II*, on 12-17 August 1978. 135 h 5 min 50 s.

Distance (USA)
B. L. Abruzzo, L. M. Newman, R. Aoki and R. Clark in the gas balloon *Double Eagle V*, from Nagashima, Japan, to Covello, California, USA, on 9-12 November 1981. 4,526.21 nm (8,382.54 km; 5,208.67 miles).

Altitude (USA)
Cdr M. D. Ross and Lt Cdr V. A. Prather in a gas balloon on 4 May 1961. 34,668 m (113,740 ft).

CLASS C

Seven records are classed as Absolute World Records for aeroplanes by the Fédération Aéronautique Internationale, as follows:

Distance in a straight line (USA), and **Distance in a closed circuit** (USA)
Dick Rutan and Jeana Yeager in the Voyager, on 14-23 December 1986. Circumnavigation of the World, starting and finishing at Edwards AFB, California. 21,712.816 nm (40,212.139 km; 24,986.664 miles).

Height (USSR)
Alexander Fedotov in an E-266M (MiG-25) on 31 August 1977. 37,650 m (123,523 ft).

Height in sustained horizontal flight (USA)
Captain Robert C. Helt and Major Larry A. Elliott (USAF) in a Lockheed SR-71A on 28 July 1976 at Beale AFB, California. 25,929.031 m (85,069 ft).

Height, after launch from a 'mother-plane' (USA)
Major R. White, USAF, in the North American X-15A-3 on 17 July 1962, at Edwards AFB, California. 95,935.99 m (314,750 ft).

Speed in a straight line (USA)
Captain Eldon W. Joersz and Major George T. Morgan Jr (USAF) in a Lockheed SR-71A on 28 July 1976 over a 15/25 km course at Beale AFB, California. 1,905.81 knots (3,529.56 km/h; 2,193.17 mph).

Speed in a closed circuit (USA)
Major Adolphus H. Bledsoe Jr and Major John T. Fuller (USAF) in a Lockheed SR-71A on 27 July 1976, over a 1,000 km closed circuit from Beale AFB, California. 1,818.154 knots (3,367.221 km/h; 2,092.294 mph).

CLASS K

Eight records are classed as Absolute World Records for manned spacecraft by the Fédération Aéronautique Internationale, as follows:

Endurance in Earth orbit (USSR)
Leonid Kizim, Vladimir Soloviev and Oleg Atkov on board Soyuz T-10/Salyut-7/Soyuz T-11, from 8 February to 2 October 1984. 236 days 22 h 49 min 4 s.

Altitude (USA)
F. Borman, J. A. Lovell and W. Anders in Apollo 8, on 21-27 December 1968. 203,925 nm (377,668.9 km; 234,673 miles).

Greatest mass lifted to altitude (USA)
F. Borman, J. A. Lovell and W. Anders in Apollo 8, on 21-27 December 1968. 127,980 kg (282,147 lb).

Distance in Earth orbit (USSR)
Anatoli Berezovoi and Valentin Lebedev on board Soyuz T-5/Salyut-7/Soyuz T-7, from 13 May to 10 December 1982, 76,025.908 nm (140,800,000 km; 87,489,056 miles).

Extravehicular duration in space (USSR)
Svetlana Savitskaya from Salyut-7, on 25 July 1984. 3 h 33 min 4 s.

Extravehicular duration on surface of moon or planet (USA)
Eugene A. Cernan, from the Apollo 17 lunar module *Challenger*, on 12, 13 and 14 December 1972, during mission of 7-19 December 1972. 21 h 31 min 44 s.

Number of astronauts remaining simultaneously outside spacecraft (USSR)
A. Eliseiev and E. Khrounov, from Soyuz 4 and 5, for 37 min on 14-18 January 1969. Two astronauts.

Accumulated time in spaceflight (USSR)
Valery Ryumin, on board Soyuz 25, Soyuz 32, Salyut 6, Soyuz 34, Soyuz 35 and Soyuz 37, a total of 361 days 21 h 31 min 55 s.

CLASS P

Four records are classed as Absolute World Records for aerospacecraft by the Fédération Aéronautique Internationale, as follows:

Duration (USA)
John W. Young and crew of five in the Space Shuttle Orbiter OV-102 *Columbia*, on 28 November-8 December 1983. 10 days 7 h 47 min 24 s.

Altitude (USA)
Robert L. Crippen and crew of four in the Space Shuttle Orbiter OV-099 *Challenger*, between 6 and 13 April 1984, 272.047 nm (503.830 km; 313.066 miles).

Greatest mass lifted to altitude (USA)
V. D. Brand in the Space Shuttle Orbiter OV-102 *Columbia*, on 11 November 1982, 106,882 kg (235,634 lb).

Distance (USA)
J. R. Lousma and C. G. Fullerton in the Space Shuttle Orbiter OV-102 *Columbia*, on 22-30 March 1982. 2,897,953 nm (5,367,009 km; 3,334,904 miles).

WORLD CLASS RECORDS

Following are details of some of the more important world class records confirmed by the FAI:

CLASS C, GROUP I (Aeroplanes with piston engines)
Distance in a straight line and **Distance in a closed circuit**
See Absolute World Records.

Height (Italy)
Mario Pezzi, in a Caproni Ca 161*bis*, on 22 October 1938. 17,083 m (56,046 ft).

Speed in a straight line (USA)
Frank Taylor in a modified North American P-51D Mustang, with 2,237 kW (3,000 hp) Rolls-Royce/Packard Merlin V-1650-9 engine, on 30 July 1983, over a 15/25 km course at Mojave, California. 449.31 knots (832.12 km/h; 517.06 mph).

CLASS C, GROUP II (Aeroplanes with turboprop engines)

Distance in a straight line (USA)
Lt Col E. L. Allison and crew in a Lockheed HC-130H Hercules, on 20 February 1972. 7,587.99 nm (14,052.95 km; 8,732.098 miles).

Distance in a closed circuit (USA)
Cdr Philip R. Hite and crew in a Lockheed RP-3D Orion, on 4 November 1972. 5,455.46 nm (10,103.51 km; 6,278.03 miles).

Height (USA)
Donald R. Wilson in an LTV Electrosystems L450F, on 27 March 1972, at Majors Field, Greenville, Texas. 15,549 m (51,014 ft).

Speed in a straight line (USA)
Cdr Donald H. Lilienthal and crew in a Lockheed P-3C Orion, over 15/25 km course on 27 January 1971. 435.26 knots (806.10 km/h; 500.89 mph).

Speed in a closed circuit (USSR)
Ivan Sukhomlin and crew in a Tupolev Tu-114, on 9 April 1960, carrying a 25,000 kg payload over a 5,000 km circuit. 473.66 knots (877.212 km/h; 545.07 mph).

CLASS C, GROUP III (Aeroplanes with jet engines)

Distance in a straight line (USA)
Major Clyde P. Evely, USAF, in a Boeing B-52H Stratofortress, on 10-11 January 1962, from Okinawa to Madrid, Spain. 10,890.27 nm (20,168.78 km; 12,532.3 miles).

Distance in a closed circuit (USSR)
Vladimir Terski and crew in an Antonov An-124, on 6-7 May 1987. Moscow-Astrakhan-Tashkent-Lake Baikal-Petropavlovsk-Chukot Peninsula-Murmansk-Zhdanov-Moscow. 10,880.625 nm (20,150.921 km; 12,521.201 miles).

Height, speed in straight line and **speed in 1,000 km closed circuit**
See Absolute World Records

Speed over a 3 km course at restricted altitude (USA)
Darryl Greenamyer in the modified Red Baron F-104RB Starfighter, on 24 October 1977, at Mud Lake, Tonopah, Nevada. 858.77 knots (1,590.45 km/h; 988.26 mph).

Speed in a 100 km closed circuit (USSR)
Alexander Fedotov in a Mikoyan E-266 (MiG-25) on 8 April 1973. 1,406.641 knots (2,605.1 km/h; 1,618.734 mph).

Speed in a 500 km closed circuit (USSR)
M. Komarov in a Mikoyan E-266 (MiG-25), on 5 October 1967, near Moscow. 1,609.88 knots (2,981.5 km/h; 1,852.62 mph).

Speed around the world (USA)
Brooke Knapp and crew in a Gulfstream III, on 13-15 February 1984, in 45 h 32 min 53 s. 445.64 knots (825.32 km/h; 512.83 mph).

Greatest payload lifted to a height of 2,000 m (USSR)
Vladimir Terski and crew in an Antonov An-124, near Moscow, on 26 July 1985. 171,219 kg (377,473 lb).

CLASS C.2, ALL GROUPS (Seaplanes)

Distance in a straight line (UK)
Capt D. C. T. Bennett and First Officer I. Harvey, in the Short-Mayo *Mercury*, on 6-8 October 1938, from Dundee, Scotland, to the Orange River, South Africa. 5,211.66 nm (9,652 km; 5,997.5 miles).

Height (USSR)
Georgi Buryanov and crew of two in a Beriev M-10, on 9 September 1961, over the Sea of Azov. 14,962 m (49,088 ft).

Speed in a straight line (USSR)
Nikolai Andrievsky and crew of two in a Beriev M-10, on 7 August 1961, at Joukovski-Petrovskoe, over a 15/25 km course. 492.44 knots (912 km/h; 566.69 mph).

CLASS D, GROUP I (Single-seat sailplanes)

Distance in a straight line (Germany, Federal Republic)
Hans W. Grosse in a Schleicher ASW 12, on 25 April 1972. 788.77 nm (1,460.8 km; 907.70 miles).

Height (USA)
Robert R. Harris in a Grob G 102, on 17 February 1986. 14,938 m (49,009 ft).

CLASS D, GROUP II (Two-seat sailplanes)

Distance in a straight line (New Zealand)
S. H. Georgeson and Helen Georgeson in a Schempp-Hirth Janus C, on 31 October 1982, from Alexandra to Gisborne, New Zealand. 536.59 nm (993.76 km; 617.49 miles).

Height (USA)
L. E. Edgar and H. E. Klieforth in a Pratt-Read sailplane, on 19 March 1952, at Bishop, California. 13,489 m (44,256 ft).

OFFICIAL RECORDS

CLASS E.1 (Helicopters)

Distance in a straight line (USA)
R. G. Ferry in a Hughes OH-6A, on 6-7 April 1966. 1,923.08 nm (3,561.55 km; 2,213 miles)

Height (France)
Jean Boulet in an Aérospatiale SA 315B Lama on 21 June 1972. 12,442 m (40,820 ft).

Speed in a straight line (UK)
Trevor Egginton in a Westland Lynx, on 11 August 1986, over a 15/25 km course. 216.45 knots (400.87 km/h; 249.09 mph).

Speed in a 100 km closed circuit (USSR)
Boris Galitsky and crew of five in a Mil Mi-6, on 26 August 1964, near Moscow. 183.67 knots (340.15 km/h; 211.36 mph).

Speed in a 500 km closed circuit (USA)
Thomas Doyle in a Sikorsky S-76A, at West Palm Beach, Florida, on 8 February 1982. 186.68 knots (345.74 km/h; 214.83 mph).

CLASS E.2 (Convertiplanes)

Height (USSR)
D. Efremov and crew of two, in the Kamov Ka-22 Vintokryl, on 24 November 1961 at Bykovo. 2,588 m (8,491 ft).

Speed in a straight line (USSR)
D. Efremov and crew of five, in the Kamov Ka-22 Vintokryl, on 7 October 1961, at Joukovski-Petrovskoe, over a 15/25 km course. 192.39 knots (356.3 km/h; 221.4 mph).

Speed in a 100 km closed circuit (New Zealand)
Sqd Ldr W. R. Gellatly and J. G. P. Morton, in the Fairey Rotodyne, on 5 January 1959, White Waltham-Wickham-Radley Bottom-Kintbury-White Waltham. 165.89 knots (307.22 km/h; 190.90 mph).

CLASS E.3 (Autogyros)

Height (UK)
Wing Cdr K. H. Wallis, in a Wallis WA-121/Mc, on 20 July 1982. 5,463.7 m (18,516 ft).

Distance in a straight line (UK)
Wing Cdr K. H. Wallis, in a Wallis WA-116/F, from Lydd Airport, Kent, to Wick, Scotland, on 28 September 1975. 472,092 nm (874.315 km; 543.274 miles).

Distance in a closed circuit (UK)
Wing Cdr K. H. Wallis, in a Wallis WA-116/F on 13 July 1974. 361.91 nm (670.26 km; 416.48 miles).
Awaiting confirmation is a new record of 541.44 nm (1,002.75 km; 623.08 miles) set by Wing Cdr Wallis in the WA-116/F/S on 5 August 1988.

Speed in a straight line (UK)
Wing Cdr K. H. Wallis, in a Wallis WA-116/F/S, over a 3 km course, on 18 September 1986. 104.5 knots (193.6 km/h; 120.3 mph).

SUB-CLASS C1a/o (Microlights)

Height (USA)
Richard J. Rowley, in a Mitchell U-2 Superwing, on 17 September 1983. 7,906.5 m (25,940 ft).

Distance in a straight line (USA)
Norman E. Howell, in a Quickie, on 9 April 1987. 674.69 nm (1,249.52 km; 776.42 miles).

Speed in a straight line (USA)
David Green, in a Monnett Moni, on 23 October 1985, over a 3 km course. 102.16 knots (189.21 km/h; 117.57 mph).

Wing Cdr K. H. Wallis in the WA-116/F/S in which he set a new closed circuit distance record for autogyros of 1,002.75 km (subject to confirmation), on 5 August 1988. The same flight set records for speed in 500 km and 1,000 km closed circuits, and for duration.

The Wallis WA-116/F/S weighed 331 kg (730 lb), complete with pilot and fuel, at the start of its 7 h 42 min flight on 5 August 1988. This Boeing 747-400 set a world record by taking off at a gross weight of 404,815 kg (892,450 lb) and climbing to a height of 2,000 m.

AIRCRAFT

ARGENTINA

AERO BOERO
AERO BOERO SA
Brasil y Alem, 2421 Morteros, Provincia de Córdoba
Telephone: Morteros (0562) 2121 and 2690
PRESIDENT: Hector A. Boero

Aero Boero's activities were seriously affected in 1979 by a tornado and floods, which damaged several aircraft including the AB 260 Ag prototype. The new factory opened in May 1981 was extended in 1987.

AERO BOERO 115 TRAINER
The original AB 115 was developed from the AB 95 (1969-70 *Jane's*). Thirty had been built by January 1983, including examples of the AB 115 BS ambulance version and the 112 kW (150 hp) AB 115/150, descriptions of which can be found in the 1983-84 edition.

In early 1988 Aero Boero was manufacturing and delivering 100 examples of a trainer version for Brazil and was negotiating a further substantial sale to the same customer.

TYPE: Two/three-seat light aircraft.
AIRFRAME: As described for AB 180, but with Dacron fabric covering and no tab on rudder.
POWER PLANT: One 86 kW (115 hp) Textron Lycoming O-235-C2A flat-four engine, driving a Sensenich 72-CK-0-50 two-blade fixed-pitch propeller with spinner. Two aluminium fuel tanks in wings, combined capacity 128 litres (33.9 US gallons; 28.2 Imp gallons). Refuelling point in top of each tank.
ACCOMMODATION: Pilot and one or two passengers in fully enclosed, heated and ventilated cabin.
ELECTRICAL SYSTEM: 40A alternator and 12V battery.
AVIONICS AND EQUIPMENT: Com/nav equipment, blind-flying instrumentation and landing lights optional.
DIMENSIONS, EXTERNAL, AND AREAS: As for AB 180, plus:
Propeller diameter   1.93 m (6 ft 4 in)
WEIGHTS AND LOADINGS:
Weight empty   510 kg (1,124 lb)
Max T-O weight   770 kg (1,698 lb)
Max wing loading   43.9 kg/m² (8.99 lb/sq ft)
Max power loading   8.9 kg/kW (14.77 lb/hp)
PERFORMANCE (at max T-O weight):
Never-exceed speed   118 knots (220 km/h; 136 mph)
Max cruising speed   91 knots (169 km/h; 105 mph)
Stalling speed, power off:
flaps up   41 knots (75 km/h; 47 mph)
flaps down   35 knots (64 km/h; 40 mph)
Max rate of climb at S/L   182 m (597 ft)/min
T-O run   100 m (330 ft)
T-O to, and landing from, 15 m (50 ft)   250 m (820 ft)
Landing run   80 m (265 ft)
Range with max fuel   664 nm (1,230 km; 765 miles)

AERO BOERO 180
The Aero Boero 180 is a higher-powered variant of the AB 150 (see 1983-84 *Jane's*). It has been built in four versions, as follows:

AB 180 RV. Standard version, flown for first time in October 1972. Externally identical to AB 150 RV.

AB 180 RVR. Glider towing version of AB 180 RV, to which it is generally similar except for a cabin rear window and provision of a towing hook. Production continued in 1987 for customers in Brazil (seven) and Argentina; further Brazilian sale anticipated in 1988.

AB 180 Ag. Agricultural version, certificated in Restricted category.

AB 180 SP. Biplane version of AB 180 Ag, with short span lower wings and enhanced payload/range capability. Prototype only. Details in earlier editions of *Jane's*.
TYPE: Single/three-seat light aircraft.
WINGS: Strut braced high-wing monoplane. Streamline section V bracing strut each side. Wing section NACA 23012 (modified). Dihedral 1° 45′. Incidence 3° at root (3° 30′ on 180 Ag), 1° at tip (2° on 180 Ag). Light alloy structure, including skins. Aluminium alloy flaps and ailerons. No tabs.
FUSELAGE: Welded steel tube structure (SAE 4130), covered with Ceconite.
TAIL UNIT: Wire braced welded steel tube structure, covered with Ceconite. Sweptback fin and rudder; non-swept fixed incidence tailplane with elevators. Ground adjustable tab on rudder; trim tab in port elevator.
LANDING GEAR: Non-retractable tailwheel type, with shock absorption by helicoidal springs inside fuselage. Mainwheels carried on faired-in V struts and half-axles. Mainwheels and tyres size 6.00-6; tailwheel tyre size 2.80-2.50. Hydraulic disc brakes on main units; tailwheel steerable and fully castoring.
POWER PLANT: One 134 kW (180 hp) Textron Lycoming O-360-A1A flat-four engine, driving a Sensenich 76-EM8 fixed-pitch or Hartzell HC-92ZK-8D constant-speed two-blade propeller with spinner. Fuel capacity (two aluminium wing tanks) 200 litres (53 US gallons; 44 Imp

Aero Boero 115 two/three-seat training and touring aircraft

Aero Boero 180 RVR glider towing aircraft

gallons); oil capacity 8 litres (2.1 US gallons; 1.75 Imp gallons).
ACCOMMODATION: Pilot and two passengers in 180 RV and RVR; pilot only in 180 Ag. Fully enclosed, heated and ventilated cabin. Cockpit rear window in 180 RVR.
EQUIPMENT: Glider towing hook in AB 180 RVR. Flush fitting underfuselage pod on AB 180 Ag, containing 320 litres (84.5 US gallons; 70.4 Imp gallons) of chemical; spraybars fitted along rear bar of V strut and horizontally below wings; electrically operated rotary atomisers (two each side) fitted to rear bar of V strut.
DIMENSIONS, EXTERNAL:
Wing span   10.90 m (35 ft 9 in)
Wing chord, constant   1.61 m (5 ft 3½ in)
Wing aspect ratio   6.8
Length overall   7.27 m (23 ft 10¼ in)
Height overall   2.10 m (6 ft 10½ in)
Wheel track   2.05 m (6 ft 8¾ in)
Wheelbase   5.10 m (16 ft 8¾ in)
AREAS:
Wings, gross   17.55 m² (188.9 sq ft)
Ailerons (total)   1.84 m² (19.81 sq ft)
Trailing-edge flaps (total)   1.94 m² (20.88 sq ft)
Fin   0.93 m² (10.01 sq ft)
Rudder   0.41 m² (4.41 sq ft)
Tailplane   1.40 m² (15.07 sq ft)
Elevators (total, incl tab)   0.97 m² (10.44 sq ft)
WEIGHTS AND LOADINGS (AB 180 RV):
Weight empty   550 kg (1,212 lb)
Max T-O weight   844 kg (1,860 lb)
Max wing loading   51.2 kg/m² (10.5 lb/sq ft)
Max power loading   6.29 kg/kW (10.34 lb/hp)
PERFORMANCE (AB 180 RV/RVR, at max T-O weight except where indicated):
Never-exceed speed   134 knots (249 km/h; 155 mph)
Max level speed at S/L:
180 RV   132 knots (245 km/h; 152 mph)
180 RVR   122 knots (225 km/h; 140 mph)
Max cruising speed at S/L:
180 RVR   108 knots (201 km/h; 125 mph)
Stalling speed, flaps down   40 knots (73 km/h; 45 mph)
Max rate of climb at S/L   360 m (1,180 ft)/min
Rate of climb (180 RVR):
with single-seat sailplane
more than 180 m (590 ft)/min
with two-seat sailplane   120 m (394 ft)/min

Prototype of the Aero Boero 260 Ag two-seat cropspraying aircraft

Time to 600 m (1,970 ft), 75% power, with Blanik two-seat sailplane (180 RVR)	3 min 10 s
Service ceiling	more than 7,000 m (22,965 ft)
T-O run	100 m (330 ft)
T-O to 15 m (50 ft), two persons	188 m (615 ft)
Landing from 15 m (50 ft)	160 m (525 ft)
Landing run	60 m (195 ft)
Range with max fuel	636 nm (1,180 km; 733 miles)

AERO BOERO 260 Ag

Work to achieve bilateral DNA/FAA certification of this two-seat agricultural aircraft under FAR Pt 23 was still in progress in 1987. Details of its early history can be found in previous editions of *Jane's*, and a description of it in its current form in the 1987-88 edition.

POWER PLANT: One 194 kW (260 hp) Textron Lycoming O-540-H2B5D flat-six engine, driving a two-blade propeller with spinner. Two aluminium fuel tanks in wings, combined capacity 200 litres (53 US gallons; 44 Imp gallons).

EQUIPMENT: Flush fitting internal tank forward of cockpit for chemical, capacity 600 litres (158.5 US gallons; 132 Imp gallons). Underwing rotary atomisers (two per wing).

DIMENSIONS, EXTERNAL:

Wing span	10.90 m (35 ft 9 in)
Length overall	7.30 m (23 ft 11½ in)
Height overall	2.04 m (6 ft 8¼ in)
Wheel track	2.30 m (7 ft 6½ in)
Wheelbase	5.10 m (16 ft 8¾ in)

WEIGHTS:

Weight empty	690 kg (1,521 lb)
Max T-O weight	1,350 kg (2,976 lb)

PERFORMANCE (at max T-O weight):

Never-exceed speed	135 knots (250 km/h; 155 mph)
Stalling speed, flaps down, engine idling	46 knots (85 km/h; 53 mph)
Max rate of climb at S/L	360 m (1,180 ft)/min
Service ceiling	5,600 m (18,375 ft)
Range with max fuel	432 nm (800 km; 497 miles)

CHINCUL
CHINCUL S.A.C.A.I.F.I.

25 de Mayo 489, 6° Piso, (1339) Buenos Aires
Telephone: 312 5458 and 5671/5
Telex: 22706 MACUB AR
WORKS: Calle Mendoza entre 6 y 7, (5400) San Juan, Pcia de San Juan; and at Avenida Diaz Velez 1034, (1702) Ciudadela, Pcia de Buenos Aires
PRESIDENT: José Maria Beraza
SALES DIRECTOR: Juan Pablo Beraza

This company, a wholly owned subsidiary of La Macarena SA, Piper's Argentine distributor, was formed in 1972 to assemble a range of Piper aircraft in Argentina with a gradually increasing degree of local manufacture. Some

Chincul products have incorporated more than 60 per cent local manufacture. The factory at San Juan has a covered area of 16,500 m² (177,600 sq ft) and a workforce of about 300 people, and had delivered more than 850 aircraft by May 1987. The Ciudadela plant produces jigs, dies and aircraft parts for production line embodiment and as spares. All Piper kits delivered to Chincul have for several years been for Phase 3 completion, involving the assembly and riveting of wings and control surfaces, manufacture of interiors, electrical harness, and other systems installation. Items of Argentine manufacture include batteries, upholstery, fabrics, tyres, engine instruments, fire extinguishers, and glassfibre components. Chincul also assembles a range of King avionics for its Piper product line.

Piper-designed aircraft produced by Chincul include the PA-18-105 (115 hp) Super Cub, PA-25-235 and -260 Pawnee, PA-36-300 and -375 Pawnee Brave, PA-28-161 Warrior II, PA-28-181 Archer II, PA-28RT-201 Arrow and Turbo Arrow IV, PA-28-236 Dakota, PA-32 Cherokee Lance/Saratoga/Turbo Saratoga, PA-31-350 Navajo Chieftain, PA-34-220T Seneca III, PA-31T Cheyenne I and II, and PA-42 Cheyenne III and 400. The company has developed its own tandem two-seat conversion of the Pawnee D agricultural aircraft, and a two-seat aerobatic military trainer based on the Cherokee Arrow, as described in the 1983-84 and earlier editions of *Jane's*.

Chincul built examples of the Piper Pawnee Brave 300 (left) and Archer II

FAMA
FÁBRICA ARGENTINA DE MATERIALES AEROESPACIALES

Avenida Fuerza Aérea Argentina Km 5½, 5103 Guarnición Aérea Córdoba
Telephone: 45011 to 45015
Telex: 51965 AMCOR AR
GENERAL DIRECTOR:
  Brigadier Roberto José Engroba
DIRECTOR OF RESEARCH AND DEVELOPMENT, AND PROGRAMME DIRECTOR, IA 63:
  Comodoro Alberto Héctor Lindow
COMMERCIAL MANAGER: H. Francisco Luciano
CHIEF OF PUBLIC RELATIONS: Mayor Luis V. Mazzeo

The original Fábrica Militar de Aviones (Military Aircraft Factory) came into operation on 10 October 1927 as a central organisation for aeronautical research and production in Argentina. After several changes of name (see 1987-88 and earlier *Jane's*), it reverted to its original title in 1968 as a component of the Area de Material Córdoba (AMC) division of the Argentine Air Force. The new title FAMA, a consequence of the joint agreement with Brazil for co-development of the CBA-123 transport aircraft (see under Embraer/FAMA in the International section), became effective at the end of 1987.

FAMA comprises two large divisions. The Instituto de Investigaciones Aeronáuticas y Espacial (IIAE) is responsible for the design of aircraft, and the design, manufacture and testing of rockets, sounding equipment and other equipment. FAMA itself controls the aircraft manufacturing facilities (Grupo Fabricación) situated in Córdoba, as well as the Centro de Ensayos en Vuelo (Flight Test Centre), to which all aircraft produced in Argentina are sent for certification tests. The laboratories, factories and other aeronautical division buildings occupy a total covered area of approx 253,000 m² (2,723,265 sq ft); the Area de Material Córdoba employs more than 3,500 persons, of whom about 2,300 are in the Grupo Fabricación.

Current products are the nationally designed Pucará counter-insurgency aircraft and the IA 63 Pampa basic and advanced jet trainer.

CBA-123

The former Embraer EMB-123 twin-turboprop regional transport aircraft became a joint Embraer/FAMA develop-

ment programme in May 1987, and is described under the latter heading in the International section.

FAMA IA 58 PUCARÁ

Four versions of this twin-turboprop light attack aircraft were built, as follows:

IA 58A. Initial (two-seat) production version. Total of 60 ordered originally for the Fuerza Aérea Argentina (FAA), which later ordered 48 more. Deliveries began in the Spring of 1976, and the last example was completed in 1986. Some early production aircraft have been converted to single-seat configuration, with extra fuselage fuel tank in place of rear seat; further similar conversions may be planned. Six IA 58As were delivered to the Fuerza Aérea Uruguaya, and a further 40 were made available for export in 1986, but no details of further sales have been received.

IA 58B. Prototype only (AX-05): details in 1982-83 *Jane's.*

IA 58C. Improved single-seat version (see separate entry).

IA 66. Prototype (AX-06) only: details in 1984-85 and earlier *Jane's.*

A full description of the IA 58A in its final production form can be found in the 1987-88 edition. The following is a shortened version of that description:

TYPE: Twin-turboprop close support, reconnaissance and counter-insurgency aircraft.

AIRFRAME: See 1987-88 *Jane's.*

POWER PLANT: Two 729 kW (978 shp) Turbomeca Astazou XVIG turboprops, each driving a Ratier-Forest 23LF-379 three-blade variable-pitch fully-feathering metal propeller with spinner. Fuel in two AMC (Area de Material Córdoba) fuselage tanks (combined capacity 772 litres; 204 US gallons; 170 Imp gallons) and one AMC self-sealing tank in each wing (combined capacity 508 litres; 134 US gallons; 111 Imp gallons). Overall usable internal capacity 1,280 litres (338 US gallons; 281 Imp gallons). Gravity refuelling point for all tanks on top of fuselage aft of cockpit. Fuel system includes two accumulator tanks, permitting up to 30 s of inverted flight. A long-range auxiliary tank, usable capacity 318 or 1,100 litres (84 or 290 US gallons; 70 or 242 Imp gallons) can be attached to the fuselage centreline pylon, and a 318 litre (84 US gallon; 70 Imp gallon) auxiliary tank on each underwing pylon. Possible external fuel loads are

Single-seat conversion of standard IA 58A Pucará

therefore 318, 636, 954, 1,100 or 1,736 litres (84, 168, 252, 290 or 458 US gallons; 70, 140, 210, 242 or 382 Imp gallons); max internal and external usable fuel capacity is 3,016 litres (796 US gallons; 663 Imp gallons).

ACCOMMODATION: Pilot and co-pilot in tandem on Martin-Baker AP06A zero/zero ejection seats beneath single AMC moulded Plexiglas canopy which is hinged at rear and opens upward. Rear (co-pilot) seat elevated 25 cm (10 in) above front seat. Rearview mirror for each crew member. Teleflex heated and bulletproof windscreen, with wiper. Armour plating in cockpit floor, resistant to 7.62 mm ground fire from 150 m (500 ft). Dual controls and blind-flying instrumentation standard. Cockpits heated and ventilated by mixture of engine bleed and external air.

SYSTEMS, AVIONICS AND EQUIPMENT: As detailed in 1987-88 *Jane's*.

ARMAMENT: Two 20 mm Hispano DCA-804 cannon, each with 270 rds, in underside of forward fuselage; and four 7.62 mm FN-Browning M2-30 machine-guns, each with 900 rds, in sides of fuselage abreast of cockpit. Alkan 115E ejector pylon on centreline beneath fuselage, capacity 1,000 kg (2,205 lb); Alkan 105E pylon, capacity 500 kg (1,102 lb), beneath each wing outboard of engine nacelle. Max external stores load with full internal fuel is 1,500 kg (3,307 lb), including gun and rocket pods, bombs, cluster bombs, incendiaries, mines, torpedoes, air-to-surface missiles, camera pod(s) or auxiliary fuel tank(s). Max external weapons load when carrying drop tanks on the fuselage or wing stations is 1,000 kg (2,205 lb). Typical loads can include twelve 125 kg bombs; seven launchers each with nineteen 2.75 in rockets; a 12.7, 20 or 30 mm gun pod and two 318 litre drop tanks; six 125 kg bombs and sixteen 5 in rockets; six launchers each with forty 74 mm cartridges, plus onboard ECM; twelve 250 lb napalm bombs; three 500 kg delayed action bombs; or two twin-7.62 mm machine-gun pods, plus three launchers each containing nineteen 2.75 in rockets. SFOM 83A3 reflector sight permits weapon release at any desired firing angle; optional Bendix AWE-1 programmer allows release in step or ripple modes of single weapons, pairs or salvos.

DIMENSIONS, EXTERNAL:

Wing span	14.50 m (47 ft 6⅞ in)
Length overall	14.253 m (46 ft 9⅛ in)
Fuselage: Max width	1.32 m (4 ft 4 in)
Max depth	1.95 m (6 ft 4¾ in)
Height overall	5.362 m (17 ft 7⅛ in)
Tailplane span	4.70 m (15 ft 5 in)
Wheel track (c/l of shock absorbers)	4.20 m (13 ft 9¼ in)
Wheelbase	3.885 m (12 ft 9 in)
Propeller diameter	2.59 m (8 ft 6 in)

DIMENSIONS, INTERNAL:

Cockpit: Length	2.85 m (9 ft 4¼ in)
Max width	0.81 m (2 ft 8 in)
Max height	1.25 m (4 ft 1¼ in)
Floor area	2.90 m^2 (31.2 sq ft)
Volume	2.74 m^3 (96.8 cu ft)

AREA:

Wings, gross	30.30 m^2 (326.1 sq ft)

WEIGHTS AND LOADINGS:

Weight empty, equipped	4,020 kg (8,862 lb)
Max fuel load: internal	1,000 kg (2,205 lb)
external	1,359 kg (2,997 lb)
Max external stores load	1,500 kg (3,307 lb)
Max T-O weight	6,800 kg (14,991 lb)
Max zero-fuel weight	4,546 kg (10,022 lb)
Max landing weight	5,600 kg (12,345 lb)
Max wing loading	224.4 kg/m^2 (45.97 lb/sq ft)
Max power loading	4.66 kg/kW (7.66 lb/shp)

PERFORMANCE (at AUW of 5,500 kg; 12,125 lb except where indicated):

Max critical Mach number at max T-O weight	0.77
Never-exceed speed at max T-O weight	Mach 0.63 (405 knots; 750 km/h; 466 mph)
Max level speed at 3,000 m (9,840 ft)	270 knots (500 km/h; 310 mph)
Max cruising speed at 6,000 m (19,680 ft)	259 knots (480 km/h; 298 mph)
Econ cruising speed	232 knots (430 km/h; 267 mph)
Max speed for landing gear extension (all weights)	150 knots (278 km/h; 172 mph)
Stalling speed, flaps and landing gear down, AUW of 4,790 kg (10,560 lb)	78 knots (143 km/h; 89 mph)
Max rate of climb at S/L	1,080 m (3,543 ft)/min
Service ceiling	10,000 m (32,800 ft)
Service ceiling, one engine out	6,000 m (19,680 ft)
T-O run	300 m (985 ft)
T-O to 15 m (50 ft)	705 m (2,313 ft)
Landing from 15 m (50 ft), landing weight of 5,100 kg (11,243 lb)	603 m (1,978 ft)
Landing run, landing weight as above	200 m (656 ft)

Attack radius at T-O weight of 6,500 kg (14,330 lb), 10% reserves of initial fuel:

with 1,500 kg (3,307 lb) of external weapons:

lo-lo-lo	121 nm (225 km; 140 miles)
lo-lo-hi	175 nm (325 km; 202 miles)
hi-lo-hi	189 nm (350 km; 217 miles)

with 1,200 kg (2,645 lb) of external weapons:

lo-lo-lo	216 nm (400 km; 248 miles)
lo-lo-hi	310 nm (575 km; 357 miles)
hi-lo-hi	350 nm (650 km; 404 miles)

with 800 kg (1,764 lb) of ordnance and 450 litres (119 US gallons; 99 Imp gallons) of external fuel:

lo-lo-lo	310 nm (575 km; 357 miles)
lo-lo-hi	445 nm (825 km; 512 miles)
hi-lo-hi	526 nm (975 km; 606 miles)
Ferry range at 5,485 m (18,000 ft) with max internal and external fuel	2,002 nm (3,710 km; 2,305 miles)
g limits	+6/−3

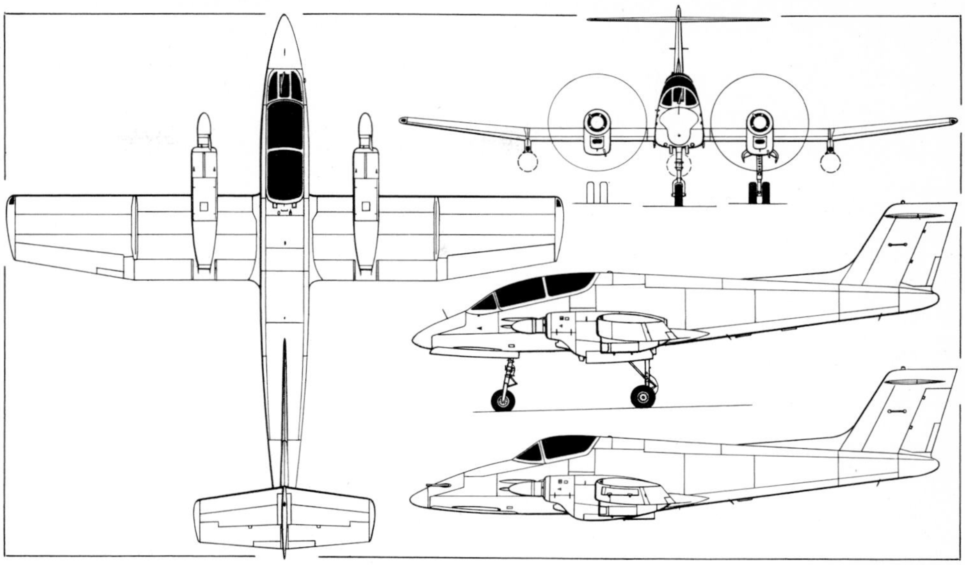

FAMA IA 58A Pucará two-seat close support and reconnaissance aircraft, with additional side view (bottom) of single-seat IA 58C *(Pilot Press)*

FAMA IA 58C PUCARA CHARLIE

This single-seat Pucará variant was flown for the first time on 30 December 1985. Its development, based on experience gained during the Falklands/Malvinas campaign of 1982, was intended to extend attack capability against such targets as helicopters and surface vessels, and to enable the Pucará also to carry out a low level air defence role.

The IA 58C programme, details of which can be found in the 1987-88 edition, is no longer in progress.

FAMA IA 63 PAMPA

To modernise its military pilot training system, the Fuerza Aérea Argentina initiated the IA 63 programme in 1979. The present configuration, powered by a single Garrett TFE731 turbofan, was selected from seven possible designs in early 1980. Detail definition was followed in early 1981 by the start of the development phase. Under contract to the Argentine government, Dornier GmbH of West Germany provided technical assistance during development, including manufacture of the wings and tailplanes for the prototypes and ground test airframes.

Two IA 63 airframes were allocated for static and fatigue testing. The first flying prototype (EX-01) flew on 6 October 1984. First flight of the second prototype took place on 7 August 1985; the third flew during the first half of 1986, and the first production aircraft was completed in October 1987. The first three were delivered to the FAA's IV Brigada Aérea in the Spring of 1988.

The FAA requirement is for 64 aircraft, primarily to replace about 35 Morane-Saulnier Paris III jet trainers. A further 40, for use as combat proficiency trainers, may be ordered later.

For weapons training, the IA 63 can be equipped with a 30 mm DEFA gun pod and underwing practice bombs. Development of an armed version for the weapons training and light close support role, probably with an uprated engine such as the 19.13 kN (4,300 lb st) TFE731-5, is under consideration.

TYPE: Single-engined basic and advanced jet trainer.

AIRFRAME: Incorporates integrated structures for high-load components such as wing spar box and main frames; numerically controlled, mechanically and chemically milled components; and the use of fibre composites.

WINGS: Cantilever shoulder-wing monoplane. Non-swept tapered wings are of Dornier DoA-7 advanced transonic section, with thickness/chord ratios of 14.5% at root, 12.5% at tip. Two-spar wing box forms integral fuel tank. Hydraulically actuated two-segment single-slotted Fowler trailing-edge flaps inboard of ailerons. Redundant primary controls, actuated hydraulically with assistance by Liebherr servo actuators. Stick forces simulated by artificial feel. Three-axis trim is operated electro-mechanically.

FUSELAGE: Conventional semi-monocoque structure. Hydraulically actuated door type airbrake on each side of upper rear fuselage.

TAIL UNIT: Sweptback fin and rudder; non-swept all-moving anhedral tailplane. Control surface actuation as for ailerons.

LANDING GEAR: Retractable tricycle type, developed and built by SHL of Israel, with hydraulic extension/retraction and emergency free-fall extension. Oleo-pneumatic shock absorbers. Single wheel and

First two prototypes of the IA 63 Pampa single-engined trainer flying alongside an IA 58A Pucará. EX-01 nearest camera is fitted with ventral gun pod and underwing stores

low-pressure tyre on each unit. Nosewheel retracts rearward, mainwheels inward into underside of engine air intake trunks. Braking system incorporates an anti-skid device; nosewheel steering is optional. Gear is designed for operation from unprepared surfaces.

POWER PLANT: One 15.57 kN (3,500 lb st) Garrett TFE731-2-2N turbofan, installed in rear fuselage, with twin lateral air intakes. Standard internal fuel capacity of 968 litres (255 US gallons; 213 Imp gallons) is contained in an integral wing tank of 550 litres (145 US gallons; 121 Imp gallons) and a 418 litre (110 US gallon; 92 Imp gallon) flexible fuselage tank with a negative g chamber. An additional 415 litres (109 US gallons; 91 Imp gallons) can be carried in auxiliary tanks installed inside the outer wing panels, to give a max internal capacity of 1,383 litres (364 US gallons; 304 Imp gallons). Single-point pressure refuelling system. Engine air intakes anti-iced by engine bleed air.

ACCOMMODATION: Instructor and student in tandem (instructor at rear, on elevated seat), on Stencel S-III-S3IA63 ejection seats (Martin-Baker on first prototype) operable also while aircraft is on ground. Ejection procedure can be pre-selected for separate single ejections, or for both seats to be fired from front or rear cockpit. Dual controls standard. One-piece wraparound windscreen. One-piece canopy, with internal screen, is hinged at rear and opens upward. Entire accommodation pressurised and air-conditioned.

SYSTEMS: AiResearch air-conditioning system, supplied by high or low pressure engine bleed air, also provides ram air for negative g system and canopy seal. Oxygen system supplied by lox converter. Two independent hydraulic systems, each at pressure of 207 bars (3,000 lb/sq in), supplied by engine driven pumps. Each system incorporates a bootstrap reservoir pressurised at 4 bars (58 lb/sq in). No. 1 system, with flow rate of 16 litres (4.2 US gallons; 3.5 Imp gallons)/min, actuates primary flight controls, airbrakes, landing gear and wheel brakes; No. 2 system, with flow rate of 8 litres (2.1 US gallons; 1.75 Imp gallons)/min, actuates primary flight controls, wing flaps, emergency and parking brakes, and (if fitted) nosewheel steering. A ram air turbine provides emergency hydraulic power for No. 2 system if pressure in this system drops below minimum. Primary electrical system (28V DC) supplied by an 11.5kW engine driven starter/generator; secondary supply (115/26V AC power at 400Hz) from two static inverters; onboard battery for engine starting.

AVIONICS: Standard avionics package comprises two redundant VHF com transceivers, intercom system, VOR/ILS with marker beacon receiver, DME, and ADF radio compass. Navigation system allows complete navigation/landing training under IFR conditions. Attitude and heading information provided by a three-gyro platform, with magnetic flux valve compass for additional heading reference.

ARMAMENT: No built-in weapons. Five attachments for external stores, with max pylon load of 400 kg (882 lb) on each inboard underwing station, 250 kg (551 lb) each on fuselage centreline and outboard underwing pair. With a 30 mm gun pod containing 145 rds on the fuselage station, typical underwing loads can include six Mk 81 bombs, two each Mk 81 and Mk 82 bombs, or one 7.62 mm twin-gun pod and one practice bomb/rocket training container. Gyrostabilised sighting system in front cockpit (optional in rear cockpit), with recorder in front sight. Weapon management system adequate for several different tactical configurations.

FAMA IA 63 Pampa two-seat basic and advanced jet trainer *(Pilot Press)*

DIMENSIONS, EXTERNAL:
Wing span	9.686 m (31 ft 9¼ in)
Wing aspect ratio	6.0
Length overall (excl pitot probe)	10.90 m (35 ft 9¼ in)
Height overall	4.29 m (14 ft 1 in)
Tailplane span	4.58 m (15 ft 0⅓ in)
Wheel track	2.66 m (8 ft 8¾ in)
Wheelbase	4.42 m (14 ft 6 in)

AREAS:
Wings, gross reference	15.63 m² (168.2 sq ft)
Vertical tail surfaces (total)	2.52 m² (27.13 sq ft)
Horizontal tail surfaces (total)	4.35 m² (46.82 sq ft)

WEIGHTS AND LOADINGS:
Weight empty	2,821 kg (6,219 lb)
Fuel load:	
wings (incl auxiliary tanks)	780 kg (1,719 lb)
fuselage	338 kg (745 lb)
Max underwing load with normal internal fuel	1,160 kg (2,557 lb)
Design gross weight	3,500 kg (7,716 lb)
T-O weight, 'clean' configuration:	
968 litres internal fuel	3,700 kg (8,157 lb)
1,383 litres internal fuel	3,800 kg (8,377 lb)
Max T-O weight with external stores	5,000 kg (11,023 lb)
Typical landing weight	3,500 kg (7,716 lb)
Wing loading:	
at 'clean' T-O weight:	
968 litres internal fuel	236.72 kg/m² (48.51 lb/sq ft)
1,383 litres internal fuel	243.12 kg/m² (49.82 lb/sq ft)
at max T-O weight with external stores	319.90 kg/m² (65.55 lb/sq ft)
Power loading:	
at 'clean' T-O weight:	
968 litres internal fuel	237.8 kg/kN (2.33 lb/lb st)
1,383 litres internal fuel	244.2 kg/kN (2.39 lb/lb st)

at max T-O weight with external stores	321.4 kg/kN (3.15 lb/lb st)

PERFORMANCE (ISA, at design gross weight with 50% normal fuel, except where indicated):
Max limiting Mach number at 9,500 m (31,170 ft)	0.81
Max level speed:	
at S/L	Mach 0.62 (407 knots; 755 km/h; 469 mph)
at 7,000 m (22,965 ft)	442 knots (819 km/h; 509 mph)
Max cruising speed at 4,000 m (13,125 ft)	403 knots (747 km/h; 464 mph)
Max rate of climb at S/L	1,813 m (5,950 ft)/min
Time to 11,000 m (36,000 ft)	10 min 54 s
Turn rate (max sustained) at 4,000 m (13,125 ft)	12.9°/s
Service ceiling	12,900 m (42,325 ft)
T-O run at T-O weight of 3,700 kg (8,157 lb)	450 m (1,477 ft)
T-O to 15 m (50 ft) at S/L, T-O weight of 3,700 kg (8,157 lb)	700 m (2,297 ft)
Landing from 15 m (50 ft), landing weight of 3,500 kg (7,716 lb)	850 m (2,789 ft)
Landing run at landing weight of 3,500 kg (7,716 lb)	430 m (1,411 ft)

Typical mission radius with 30 min reserves:
air-to-air gunnery (hi-hi), T-O weight of 3,950 kg (8,708 lb) with 250 kg (551 lb) external load, 5 min allowance for dogfight   237 nm (440 km; 273 miles)
air-to-ground (hi-lo-hi), T-O weight of 4,860 kg (10,714 lb) with 1,000 kg (2,205 lb) external load, 5 min allowance for weapon delivery
194 nm (360 km; 223 miles)
Range at 300 knots (556 km/h; 345 mph) at 4,000 m (13,125 ft):
968 litres internal fuel   540 nm (1,000 km; 621 miles)
1,383 litres internal fuel
809 nm (1,500 km; 932 miles)
Max endurance at 300 knots (556 km/h; 345 mph) at 4,000 m (13,125 ft), 1,383 litres internal fuel
3 h 48 min
g limit   +4.5 max sustained

AUSTRALIA

ASTA
AEROSPACE TECHNOLOGIES OF AUSTRALIA PTY LTD

Fishermen's Bend, Private Bag No. 4, Post Office, Port Melbourne, Victoria 3207
Telephone: (613) 647 3111
Telex: AA 34851 GAFAIR
Fax: (613) 646 4381
WORKS: Avalon Airfield, Beach Road, Lara, Victoria 3212
Telephone: Lara (6152) 82 2988
MANAGING DIRECTOR AND CHIEF EXECUTIVE OFFICER:
G. Stuart
GENERAL MANAGER:
P. Raphael (Design and Business Development)

It was announced in December 1986 that the former Government Aircraft Factories were to be reconstituted as a private enterprise organisation (though still government owned), under the new title Aerospace Technologies of Australia, and this change of name took effect on 1 July

1987. Formerly, the GAF were owned by the Australian government and operated by the Department of Defence. The functions of ASTA include the design, development, manufacture, assembly, maintenance and modification of aircraft, target drones and guided weapons. At Avalon airfield, subassembly of components, final assembly, modification, repair and test flying of jet and other aircraft are undertaken. The early 1988 workforce totalled about 1,500.

Current or recent activity includes manufacture of the Ikara anti-submarine missile and Jindivik target drone, and, under subcontract from HDH (which see), 40 per cent of the production work on the RAAF Pilatus PC-9/A programme. ASTA also produces in-spar wing ribs for the Boeing 757, Krueger flaps for the 747, wing flaps for the Fokker F28 Fellowship, and composite flaps and flap shrouds for the McDonnell Douglas F/A-18. It is responsible for final assembly of 73 of the 75 F/A-18

Hornets ordered for the RAAF. The first flight by an Australian assembled Hornet (an AF/A-18B) was made on 26 February 1985. ASTA is contracted to supply carbonfibre landing gear doors and floor support panels for the Airbus A330 and A340, and is to join with Aérospatiale (France) and CATIC (China) in developing a new light helicopter for Chinese and other markets.

ASTA NOMAD

Nomad production ended in late 1984 after completion of 170 aircraft; 157 of these had been sold by December 1986, including seven Searchmasters to the US Customs Service. The remaining 13 have since been acquired by the Australian Department of Defence for use by the Army (nine) and Air Force (four). Full details of the Nomad are given in the 1985-86 and previous editions. In May 1985, the N22B was recertificated as the N22C (see 1986-87 *Jane's*), with max T-O weight increased to 4,060 kg (8,950 lb).

AUSTRALIAN AUTOGYRO
THE AUSTRALIAN AUTOGYRO CO
29 Benning Avenue, Turramurra, Sydney, NSW 2074
Telephone: 449 9816
PROPRIETOR: E. R. Minty

AUSTRALIAN AUTOGYRO SKYHOOK

Development history of Mr Ted Minty's Skyhook 'mini-chopper' was recorded in the 1982-83 and earlier editions of *Jane's*. A basic 'open frame' model with 1,835 cc Volkswagen engine is in production as the **Mk I**; also available are a **Mk II** (unpainted, with enclosed body) and a

fully customised **Mk III**. Sales by 1 February 1988 included 18 Mk Is, two Mk IIIs, as well as numerous kits and components.

Existing features include the anatomically designed seat/fuel tank, mounted on rubber blocks at the keel/mast junction, which wraps around the mast to bring pilot and fuel load closer to the CG; an all-new joystick control mechanism to operate the rotor head and blades; and a Stromberg single side draught carburettor with automatically adjustable mixture control. The seat/tank can be fitted also to all versions of the Bensen autogyro (see US part of 1986-87 Sport Aircraft section). New glassfibre rotor blades and a more streamlined glassfibre fuselage shell are under development, and a Rotax engined version was expected to become available during 1988.

TYPE: Single-seat lightweight autogyro.

ROTOR SYSTEM: Two-blade rotor, with aluminium alloy Skyhook blades attached directly to a fully adjustable hub bar. Joystick control actuates two nylon encased 6.35 mm (¼ in) stainless steel push/pull cables to operate rotor head and blades.

FUSELAGE: Single keel to which are attached the landing gear, fuselage structure, seat, engine mounting frame, rotor mast and tail unit. Keel and rotor mast are of 5.1 cm (2 in) square section 6061-T6 aluminium alloy with radiused corners. The majority of structural attachments are clamped, rather than bolted or riveted, to reduce to a minimum the number of potential fracture locations in the airframe. Glassfibre fuselage shell on Mks II and III.

TAIL UNIT: Twin rudders, united by a dihedral tailplane attached to the keel. The upper ends of the rudders are braced by double V triangular frames of light alloy and chrome molybdenum steel tube. Rudders manufactured from marine quality aluminium, tailplane from 2024 aluminium sheet. Entire tail assembly operates as a single unit which swivels from side to side to provide directional stability and power-off manoeuvrability.

LANDING GEAR: Non-retractable type with small sprung tailwheel at rear end of keel. Fully sprung steerable nosewheel, linked to rudders. Mainwheels are ultra-lightweight 5 in nylon go-kart rims, each with a 4.00-5 tyre and tube. Disc brakes optional.

POWER PLANT: One 1.42 kN (320 lb st) 1,835 cc VW or 1.60 kN (360 lb st) 2,200 cc VW/Porsche engine (both ratings at 3,600 rpm), mounted on chrome molybdenum brackets attached to mast and keel, and driving a Skyhook two-blade fixed-pitch pusher propeller of Queensland maple. VW engine is now installed with computer designed camshaft for extra torque; Rotax engine to be offered later in 1988. Fuel contained in pilot's hollow seat, capacity 43 litres (11.4 US gallons; 9.5 Imp gallons) plus a reserve of 7 litres (1.8 US gallons; 1.5 Imp gallons).

ACCOMMODATION: Pilot only, in enclosed cockpit, on rotationally moulded super-strength cross-linked polyethylene seat/fuel tank located just forward of mast/keel junction, close to CG. Aircraft can be flown without

Australian Autogyro Co (Minty) Skyhook single-seat autogyro in Mk III production form

fuselage shell and Plexiglas windscreen enclosure if desired. Adjustable vents in fuselage nose provide ventilation when the aircraft is flown with the cockpit enclosed.

EQUIPMENT: Standard equipment includes cylinder head high temperature and low fuel warning lights.

DIMENSIONS, EXTERNAL:

Rotor diameter	7.01 m (23 ft 0 in)
Length overall	3.35 m (11 ft 0 in)
Height to top of rotor head	2.06 m (6 ft 9 in)
Height to top of cockpit canopy	1.42 m (4 ft 8 in)
Tailplane span (incl rudders)	0.86 m (2 ft 10 in)
Wheel track	1.68 m (5 ft 6 in)
Propeller diameter	1.35 m (4 ft 5 in)

AREA:

Rotor disc	38.6 m² (415.5 sq ft)

WEIGHTS:
Weight empty, excl rotor blades:

Mk I	121 kg (267 lb)
Mk III	147 kg (325 lb)
Max T-O weight	271 kg (597 lb)

PERFORMANCE:
Max level speed

	more than 87 knots (161 km/h; 100 mph)
Max rate of climb at S/L	305 m (1,000 ft)/min
T-O run (depending on headwind)	
	approx 122 m (400 ft)
Landing run (with disc brakes)	approx 5 m (15 ft)

Range with 43 litres (11.4 US gallons; 9.5 Imp gallons) fuel at constant 61 knots (113 km/h; 70 mph)
243 nm (450 km; 280 miles)

EAA
EAGLE AIRCRAFT AUSTRALIA
Clarence Industrial Estate, Cockburn Road, Henderson, WA 6166
Telephone: (09) 410 1077
MARKETING DIRECTOR: Deryck F. Graham Jr

EAA EAGLE X
Eagle Aircraft Australia is developing a new all-composite light aircraft known as the Eagle X. Although the prototype conforms to current Australian (ANO 101-25) experimental category regulations, the next three (pre-production) aircraft are dual control two-seaters and are intended to lead on to a production version that will be certificated to ANO 101-55, ie to a standard similar to that of the European JAR 22. The two-seat Eagle X was undergoing flight test in the Spring of 1988, but EAA declined to release a more detailed description until at least mid-1988, when positive data should have become available.

First photograph of the Eagle X TSP1 (two-seat prototype Number 1)

HDH
HAWKER DE HAVILLAND LTD (Member company of the Hawker Siddeley Group)
PO Box 30, 361 Milperra Road, Bankstown, NSW 2200
Telephone: (02) 772 8111
Telex: AA20719
Fax: (02) 771 2632
CHAIRMAN: B. S. Price
MANAGING DIRECTOR: J. B. Hattersley
TECHNICAL DIRECTOR: S. S. Schaetzel
COMMERCIAL DIRECTOR: P. A. Smith

Hawker de Havilland's main activity continues to be the provision of overhaul, modification and repair services to the Australian defence forces, and to a wide variety of other Australian and regional customers in some 25 nations. Manufacturing activity involves subcontract work for Aérospatiale, Boeing, British Aerospace, General Electric, Lockheed, McDonnell Douglas, Northrop and Pratt & Whitney. Its workforce numbered about 2,800 in mid-1987.

Under subcontract to Sikorsky Aircraft (USA), HDH is responsible for final assembly of 14 of the 16 S-70B-2 RAWS (role adaptable weapon system) Seahawk helicop-

ters currently being delivered to the Royal Australian Navy. Thirty-nine Sikorsky S-70A-9 Black Hawks for the RAAF are being assembled under a parallel programme.

During 1985 HDH acquired Commonwealth Aircraft Corporation Limited and Australian Aircraft Consortium Pty Limited, and in December 1985 HDH was nominated as prime contractor for Australian licence production, at its Trainer Division (formerly AAC), of the Pilatus PC-9/A trainers ordered by the RAAF.

TRAINER AIRCRAFT DIVISION

HDH (PILATUS) PC-9/A
The version of the PC-9 ordered for the RAAF is designated PC-9/A, differing from the standard Swiss built PC-9 (see Pilatus entry) in having Bendix EFIS instrumentation and a landing gear fitted with the low

pressure tyres of the PC-7 in order to give the PC-9/A grass field operating capability. The latter modification, involving the fitting of bulged mainwheel doors, was developed and fitted under an Australian contract, with no loss of aircraft performance.

The first of two Swiss built PC-9/As (A23-001) was delivered to the RAAF in the Summer of 1987, following its

first flight on 19 May. A further 17 are being completed by HDH from kits supplied by Pilatus, and HDH has begun production of the remaining 48 aircraft of the total Australian order for 67. The first three HDH assembled PC-9/As were handed over to the RAAF on 19 December 1987.

HAWKER DE HAVILLAND VICTORIA LTD (Subsidiary of Hawker de Havilland Ltd)
304 Lorimer Street, Port Melbourne, Victoria 3207
POSTAL ADDRESS: Box 779H, GPO Melbourne, Victoria 3001

Telephone: (03) 647 6111
Telex: AA 30721
Fax: (03) 646 3431

As Commonwealth Aircraft Corporation, HDH Victoria was formed in 1936, and became a wholly owned subsidiary of Hawker de Havilland Ltd on 1 July 1985. The change to its present title took effect on 1 July 1986. HDH Victoria has produced more than 1,750 military aircraft, over 2,500 aero engines, and is a major supplier of equipment and services to the Australian Defence Forces.

The company holds Dept of Aviation approval for civil aviation activities, and maintains a capability for initial design and engineering support of manufacturing and overhaul activities.

Major current programmes include manufacture of airframe components for the McDonnell Douglas F/A-18 Hornet (engine access doors, rear fairings and wing pylons) and HDH (Pilatus) PC-9/A (wings); assembly and testing of the General Electric F404 engine and manufacture of a range of components; life-of-type extension for RAAF Aermacchi MB-326H jet trainers; repair and overhaul, including life-of-type extension of RAAF Mirage major

airframe components; repair and overhaul of RAAF Atar 9C and Viper engines; components for General Electric CF6 engines, and Sikorsky S-70 gearboxes; and design of maintenance trainers for Sikorsky MH-53E helicopters. Details of the programme to install the AQS-901 sonics processor into Lockheed P-3 Orions of the RAAF were given in the 1986-87 *Jane's*.

SADLEIR
VTOL INDUSTRIES AUSTRALIA LTD
8th Floor, 160 St George's Terrace, Perth, WA 6000
Telephone: (619) 481 0524
Telex: ATEPS AA 94635
Fax: (619) 481 0287
MANAGING DIRECTOR: Kim V. Sadleir
CONSULTANTS:
  Don M. Devenish, MEngSc, MIEAust
  Graham Swannell, MIE, AMRAeS

SADLEIR AIR BEARING FAN
The Air Bearing Fan, devised by Mr Kim Sadleir, represents a radical new approach to VTOL technology design which is in an advanced R & D stage. Two test rigs have been constructed, with highly successful results. The first, designed to test an innovative control system, demonstrated a 20 per cent variation in lift. It was also found that the centre of pressure could be moved plus or minus 10 per cent of the fan diameter from the CG. The second rig, designed to explore the design of various air bearing shoes in static mode, resulted in a preliminary design for a dynamic air bearing shoe.

Construction has begun on a 2 m (6 ft 6¾ in) composite fan supported by air bearing shoes and powered by a motor vehicle engine. This rig will be static and should simulate loads of a real aircraft. By the end of 1988 it was anticipated that this fan unit would be placed in a 5 m (16 ft 4¾ in) delta-winged testbed, with the object of achieving controlled take-off, landing and hovering manoeuvres.

Applications for the technology include remotely piloted vehicles, model aircraft, light aircraft, subsonic and supersonic military applications, small commuter aircraft and business aircraft, with possible extensions to larger passenger-carrying aircraft.

Essentially, the ABF is a series of inlet and outlet stator vanes with a fixed-pitch fan. Each set of stator vanes performs separate control and functional requirements. The tips of the fan blades are joined by a solid rim which is supported by multiple air bearing shoes. This eliminates wingtip deflection, thus allowing the fan to sit inside

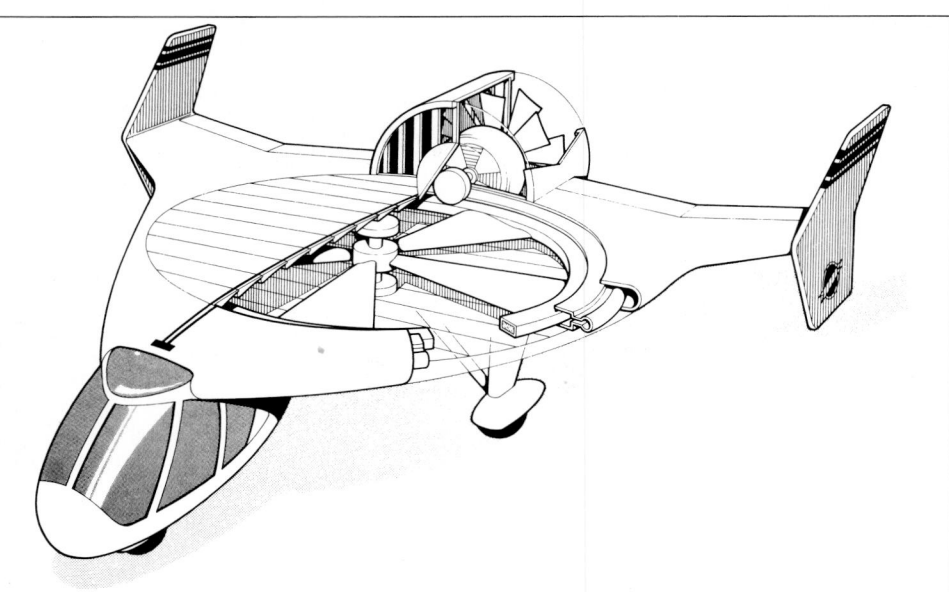

Cutaway artist's impression of the Sadleir Air Bearing Fan installed in a four-seat executive/commuter aircraft

conventional aerofoil sections. As the load is carried on the rim, substantial structural and weight benefits accrue.

Other advantages claimed for the concept are a better potential than helicopters for high-speed flight and unrestricted manoeuvrability; and better operating economics than a vectored thrust jet VTOL aircraft. Ability also to use conventional runway take-off and landing procedures would permit further improvement in overall economics and allow higher take-off weights with greater payloads. Typically, a 9.00 m (29 ft 6¼ in) span military ABF aircraft

powered by an 800 kW (1,073 shp) turboshaft would have a gross VTOL weight of 1,700 kg (3,748 lb), level speed of 240 knots (445 km/h; 276 mph), and range of 200 nm (370 km; 230 miles) with a 350 kg (771 lb) payload. The four-seat executive/commuter aircraft illustrated would be powered by a piston engine, have a 5.00 m (16 ft 4¾ in) fan in a 10.50 m (34 ft 5½ in) span wing, and cruise at 130-150 knots (241-278 km/h; 150-173 mph) over a useful range of 400 nm (741 km; 460 miles).

SEABIRD
SEABIRD AVIATION AUSTRALIA PTY LTD
PO Box 618, Pialba, Queensland 4655
Telephone: (071) 280222
Telex: AA 49648 MAMEX
Fax: (071) 223214
MANAGING DIRECTOR: Donald C. Adams
CHIEF DESIGN ENGINEER: C. W. Whitney

SEABIRD SB-4 SENTINEL
Unlike Seabird's other aircraft (see Sport Aircraft section of the 1986-87 *Jane's*), the Sentinel was designed to achieve full certification under FAR Pt 23 following its first flight, which was expected in 1988. Its primary application is for observation and reconnaissance, for which it offers a helicopter-like view from the cockpit and very good low-speed handling characteristics. A secondary role as a training or agricultural aircraft is also foreseen. Two prototypes and two production aircraft are being built initially.

TYPE: Two-seat observation and training light aircraft.
WINGS: Strut braced high-wing monoplane, with NACA 63₂-215 aerofoil section and constant chord except at tips. Dihedral 2° 30′ from roots. Incidence 4°. No sweepback. Aluminium alloy structure, with slotted

ailerons and trailing-edge slotted flaps. Single bracing strut each side.
FUSELAGE: Pod and boom structure, mainly of 4130 steel tube with a Kevlar non-load-bearing skin. Aluminium alloy semi-monocoque tailboom.
TAIL UNIT: Sweptback fin and horn balanced rudder; non-swept fixed incidence cantilever tailplane with one-piece horn balanced elevator. Construction similar to that of wings. Elevator trim tab.
LANDING GEAR: Non-retractable type, comprising Cleveland 5.00-5 mainwheels (6.00-6 optional) on cantilever spring steel legs plus a Maule tailwheel. Mainwheel tyre pressure 1.38 bars (20 lb/sq in); Cleveland disc brakes. Tailwheel has solid tyre. Alternative float gear to be developed.
POWER PLANT: One 67 kW (90 hp) Norton P 64 rotary or 52 kW (70 hp) Emdair CF092B four-stroke engine, pod mounted above and behind cabin and driving a Hoffman or MT two-blade fixed-pitch pusher propeller (wood or composite blades) via a 3:1 reduction gear. Fuel in two wing tanks, combined capacity 136 litres (36 US gallons; 30 Imp gallons), with single overwing refuelling point. Oil capacity 4.5 litres (1.2 US gallons; 1 Imp gallon).
ACCOMMODATION: Side by side seats for pilot and observer/ passenger in enclosed and extensively glazed cabin. Right hand seat is removable, and aircraft can be flown with both forward opening fully glazed doors removed. Space

for 22.7 kg (50 lb) of baggage aft of seats.
ELECTRICAL SYSTEM: 24V 35A alternator standard.
AVIONICS AND EQUIPMENT: VOR, ADF and dual VHF com. Wing hardpoints for external stores. Quick-change photo/survey modules or spraytank in place of right hand seat.

DIMENSIONS, EXTERNAL:	
Wing span	10.97 m (36 ft 0 in)
Wing chord, constant	1.22 m (4 ft 0 in)
Wing aspect ratio	9.6
Length overall	7.01 m (23 ft 0 in)
Fuselage: Max width	1.12 m (3 ft 8 in)
Height overall	1.83 m (6 ft 0 in)
Tailplane span	3.05 m (10 ft 0 in)
Wheel track	1.83 m (6 ft 0 in)
Propeller diameter	1.73 m (5 ft 8 in)
DIMENSIONS, INTERNAL:	
Cabin: Max length	1.83 m (6 ft 0 in)
Max width	1.09 m (3 ft 7 in)
Max height	1.12 m (3 ft 8 in)
Baggage compartment volume	0.23 m³ (8.0 cu ft)
AREA:	
Wings, gross	12.54 m² (135.0 sq ft)
WEIGHTS AND LOADINGS:	
Weight empty, equipped	295 kg (650 lb)
Max fuel	113 kg (250 lb)
Max T-O weight	545 kg (1,200 lb)
Max wing loading	43.35 kg/m² (8.88 lb/sq ft)
Max power loading	8.10 kg/kW (13.33 lb/hp)

PERFORMANCE (estimated at max T-O weight):

Never-exceed speed	127 knots (235 km/h; 146 mph)
Max level speed at 1,525 m (5,000 ft)	
	100 knots (185 km/h; 115 mph)
Max cruising speed at 1,525 m (5,000 ft)	
	90 knots (166 km/h; 103 mph)
Econ cruising speed at 1,525 m (5,000 ft)	
	85 knots (157 km/h; 98 mph)
Stalling speed, flaps down	35 knots (65 km/h; 40 mph)
Max rate of climb at S/L	244 m (800 ft)/min
Service ceiling	4,875 m (16,000 ft)
T-O and landing run	92 m (300 ft)
T-O to 15 m (50 ft)	305 m (1,000 ft)
Landing from 15 m (50 ft)	365 m (1,200 ft)
Min ground turning radius	12.2 m (40 ft 0 in)
Range, 45 min reserves:	
with max payload	600 nm (1,110 km; 690 miles)
with max fuel	800 nm (1,480 km; 920 miles)
g limits	+4.4/−2.2 (Utility category)

Model of the Seabird SB-4 Sentinel lightweight observation aircraft

TRANSAVIA

TRANSFIELD PTY LTD, TRANSAVIA DIVISION

73 Station Road, Seven Hills, NSW 2147
Telephone: 624 4400
Telex: AA 170300 TRANSAC
Fax: 624 7284
GENERAL MANAGER: John Corby
SALES MANAGER: Neil McDonald

Transavia, formed in 1964, is a division of Transfield Pty Ltd, one of Australia's largest construction companies.

TRANSAVIA SKYFARMER

The original PL-12 **Airtruk**, designed by Mr Luigi Pellarini for agricultural use and first flown on 22 April 1965, was type certificated on 10 February 1966. A general purpose version, the **PL-12-U** for passenger/cargo/aerial survey/cropspraying, flew in December 1970, and received certification in February 1971. Deliveries of production aircraft began in December 1966, and by early 1988 about 120 of all versions (including 18 assembled by Flight Engineers Ltd in New Zealand) had been sold for use in Australia, New Zealand, China, Denmark, Malaysia, South Africa, Taiwan, Thailand, the USA and Yugoslavia.

The **Skyfarmer T-300** (first flight July 1978) differs chiefly in having a Textron Lycoming IO-540 engine, and was followed in 1981 by an improved **Skyfarmer T-300A**. Significant changes in the latter include a larger upper-fuselage structure (providing a roomier cockpit and larger hopper throat), and new aerodynamically balanced ailerons, horn balanced elevators and electromechanical flaps to reduce pilot workload.

Five Skyfarmers provided to China in 1986 are of a **Skyfarmer T-400** version, powered by a Textron Lycoming IO-720 engine, for which FAA certification was being sought in 1987.

Details of the original PL-12 and PL-12-U can be found in earlier editions of *Jane's*. The following description applies to the Skyfarmer 300A, except where indicated:
TYPE: Single-engined agricultural aircraft.
WINGS: Strut braced sesquiplane. Wing section NACA 23012. Dihedral 1° 30′ on upper wings. Incidence (upper wings) 3° 30′, stub-wings 4°. Conventional all-metal structure, covered with Alclad sheet. All-metal trailing-edge flaps and ailerons, covered with ribbed Alclad sheet, and operated manually. Upper-wing fence on each side of each tailboom to ensure full aileron control, even below stalling speeds. Small stub-wings at base of fuselage, constructed on a 4130 steel leading-edge D box section welded to the integral hopper frame and braced to the upper wings by a V strut on each side.
FUSELAGE: Pod shaped structure comprising 4130 welded steel frame with stainless steel and 2024 Alclad covering. Hopper is integrally structured. Entire one-piece rear cabin is of glassfibre to eliminate corrosion and withstand hard wear and tear.
TAIL UNIT: Twin units, each comprising a fin, rudder and separate T tailplane with elevator, and each carried on a cantilever tapered tubular Alclad boom extending from the upper wings.
LANDING GEAR: Non-retractable tricycle type. Mainwheels carried on pivoted trailing legs supported by Transavia short stroke, heavy duty oleo-pneumatic shock absorbing suspension units. Port and starboard main units are interchangeable. Nosewheel carried on a heavy duty, long stroke straight oleo-suspension unit. All wheels and tyres same size (8.00-6); tyre pressure 1.72 bars (25 lb/sq in) (nose); 2.07 bars (30 lb/sq in) (main). Cleveland disc brakes with parking lock.
POWER PLANT: One 224 kW (300 hp) Textron Lycoming IO-540-K1A5 flat-six engine, driving a Hartzell three-blade constant-speed metal propeller with spinner (298

Transavia Skyfarmer T-300 agricultural aircraft (Textron Lycoming IO-540 engine)

kW; 400 hp IO-720-D1BD in Skyfarmer 400). Two upper-wing fuel tanks, total capacity 189 litres (50 US gallons; 41.5 Imp gallons). Optional long range installation of second tank in each upper mainplane (standard in T-400), increasing total usable capacity to 364 litres (96.2 US gallons; 80.1 Imp gallons). Refuelling point above upper wings. Oil capacity 11.4 litres (3 US gallons; 2.5 Imp gallons).
ACCOMMODATION: Single-seat cockpit, with door on starboard side. Two-seat cabin aft of chemical hopper/tank for carriage of ground crew, with door at rear of lower deck. Accommodation heated and ventilated.
SYSTEM: 24V electrical system standard, 12V optional.
AVIONICS AND EQUIPMENT: Optional VHF, HF, ADF, artificial horizon and directional gyro. Standard hopper aft of cockpit for 907 kg (2,000 lb) of dry chemical or 818 litres (216 US gallons; 180 Imp gallons) of liquid. Optional Powermist spray system, Transavia safety take-off weight (STOW) checking system, wire cutter, seed spreader attachment, and cockpit heater.

DIMENSIONS, EXTERNAL:

Upper wing span: 300A, 400	11.98 m (39 ft 3½ in)
Upper wing chord (300A):	
constant portion	1.76 m (5 ft 9¼ in)
at tip	1.27 m (4 ft 2 in)
Stub-wing span	4.93 m (16 ft 2 in)
Length overall: 300A	6.35 m (20 ft 10 in)
400	7.37 m (24 ft 2 in)
Length of fuselage: 300A	4.19 m (13 ft 9 in)
Height overall: 300A	2.79 m (9 ft 2 in)
400	2.87 m (9 ft 5 in)
Fuselage: Max width	0.97 m (3 ft 2 in)
Tailplane span (each)	2.13 m (7 ft 0 in)
Distance between tailplanes:	
300A, 400	3.48 m (11 ft 5 in)
Wheel track	2.44 m (8 ft 0 in)
Wheelbase	1.64 m (5 ft 4½ in)
Propeller diameter: 300A	2.13 m (7 ft 0 in)
400	2.18 m (7 ft 2 in)
Min propeller ground clearance: 300A	0.36 m (1 ft 2 in)
Passenger door: Height	0.97 m (3 ft 2 in)

DIMENSIONS, INTERNAL:

Rear passenger cabin: Length	1.83 m (6 ft 0 in)
Max width	0.97 m (3 ft 2 in)
Max height	2.03 m (6 ft 8 in)
Floor area	0.37 m² (4 sq ft)
Volume: Passenger cabin	0.85 m³ (30 cu ft)
Hopper: 300A, 400	1.05 m³ (37 cu ft)

AREAS:

Wings, gross: 300A	24.53 m² (264.0 sq ft)
400	26.76 m² (288.0 sq ft)

Ailerons, total	1.67 m² (18.0 sq ft)
Trailing-edge flaps, total	1.67 m² (18.0 sq ft)
Fins, total	1.30 m² (14.0 sq ft)
Rudders, total	0.56 m² (6.0 sq ft)
Tailplanes, total	2.60 m² (28.0 sq ft)
Elevators, total, incl tabs	1.30 m² (14.0 sq ft)

WEIGHTS AND LOADINGS:

Typical weight empty: 300A	1,017 kg (2,242 lb)
400	1,111 kg (2,450 lb)
Max T-O weight (agricultural category):	
300A	1,925 kg (4,244 lb)
400	2,227 kg (4,910 lb)
Max T-O weight (normal category):	
400	1,814 kg (4,000 lb)
Max landing weight: 300A	1,723 kg (3,800 lb)
Max wing loading: 300A	78.5 kg/m² (16.1 lb/sq ft)
400	83.2 kg/m² (17.0 lb/sq ft)
Max power loading: 300A	8.6 kg/kW (14.15 lb/hp)
400	7.5 kg/kW (12.28 lb/hp)

PERFORMANCE (at max agricultural T-O weight, ISA at S/L, except where indicated):

Never-exceed speed:	
300A	148 knots (274 km/h; 170 mph)
Max level speed:	
300A at 915 m (3,000 ft)	
	106 knots (196 km/h; 122 mph)
400	109 knots (202 km/h; 125 mph)
Max cruising speed (75% power):	
300A	102 knots (188 km/h; 117 mph)
400	103 knots (191 km/h; 118 mph)
Stalling speed, power on (300A):	
flaps up	47 knots (88 km/h; 55 mph)
flaps down	39 knots (73 km/h; 45 mph)
Stalling speed, power off (400):	
flaps up	52 knots (97 km/h; 60 mph)
flaps down	50 knots (93 km/h; 58 mph)
Max rate of climb at S/L: 300A	156 m (514 ft)/min
400	168 m (550 ft)/min
* Max light-weight rate of climb:	
300A	457 m (1,500 ft)/min
400	488 m (1,600 ft)/min
Service ceiling: 300A	3,810 m (12,500 ft)
* Light-weight service ceiling: 300A	6,890 m (22,600 ft)
T-O run: 300A	329 m (1,080 ft)
400	275 m (900 ft)
* Light-weight T-O run: 300A	77 m (252 ft)
400	72 m (234 ft)
* Light-weight landing run: 300A	82 m (270 ft)
400	78 m (255 ft)

* *Weight of empty aircraft plus pilot and 50 per cent standard fuel*

VTOL

VTOL AIRCRAFT PTY LTD

123 Marshall Street, Kotara Heights, NSW 2288
Telephone: (049) 43 5348
CHAIRMAN: Duan A. Phillips

VTOL PHILLICOPTER Mk 1

Design of the Phillicopter, by Mr D. A. Phillips and Mr P. Gerakiteys, began in 1962, and the prototype made its first flight in 1971. The original 108 kW (145 hp) O-200-C engine was later replaced by a Rolls-Royce Continental O-300 of the same power.

The Phillicopter was granted Australian type certification in mid-1984, and was exhibited in model form at the 1985 Paris Air Show with the news that Australian production was imminent and foreign licence manufacture was available. Construction of a modified pre-production Phillicopter, to which the following details apply, was continuing in 1988.
TYPE: Two-seat light helicopter.
ROTOR SYSTEM: Two-blade all-metal main rotor and two-blade tail rotor. New high-inertia stabilised main rotor system, installed on prototype in 1987, was still undergoing test in early 1988. Tail rotor has aluminium alloy blades. Main blades do not fold. Main rotor brake optional.

ROTOR DRIVE: Via steel gears in aluminium alloy boxes. Primary gearbox is right angled from engine to drive main rotor via secondary reduction gearbox. Integrated tail rotor gear drive to tail rotor gearbox. Main rotor/engine rpm ratio 1:5.67; tail rotor/engine rpm ratio 1:1.
FUSELAGE: Tubular steel skeletal frame, unclad at rear. Forward portion aluminium clad, with large Perspex 'goldfish bowl' canopy.
TAIL UNIT: Steel tube tail rotor guard, with small triangular underfin. Tailplane incidence ground-adjustable by jackscrews.
LANDING GEAR: Tubular skid type, incorporating ground handling wheels. Elastomeric and torsion leg shock absorption.
POWER PLANT: One 112 kW (150 hp) Textron Lycoming O-320 flat-six engine standard; 119 kW (160 hp) engine will be available optionally. Two fuel tanks, total capacity 91 litres (24 US gallons; 20 Imp gallons), are standard; optional 91 litre (24 US gallon; 20 Imp gallon) tank available for extended range. Refuelling point in each tank. Oil capacity 5.7 litres (1.5 US gallons; 1.25 Imp gallons).
ACCOMMODATION: Side by side seats for pilot and one student/passenger, with dual controls. Door on each side of cabin. Baggage space at base of rotor mast. Cabin ventilated; heating optional.

SYSTEM: 12V battery for engine starting, navigation lights and radio.
AVIONICS AND EQUIPMENT: To customer's requirements. Cargo hook or cropspraying equipment optional.

DIMENSIONS, EXTERNAL:

Main rotor diameter	7.77 m (25 ft 6 in)
Main rotor blade chord	0.203 m (8 in)
Tail rotor diameter	1.22 m (4 ft 0 in)
Distance between rotor centres	4.57 m (15 ft 0 in)
Length overall:	
both rotors turning	9.35 m (30 ft 8 in)
excl rotors	7.01 m (23 ft 0 in)
Height overall	2.69 m (8 ft 9 in)
Height to top of rotor head	2.59 m (8 ft 6 in)
Width overall, excl main rotor	1.83 m (6 ft 0 in)
Skid track	1.83 m (6 ft 0 in)
Crew/passenger doors (each):	
Height	0.76 m (2 ft 6 in)
Width	0.61 m (2 ft 0 in)
Height to sill	0.51 m (1 ft 8 in)

DIMENSIONS, INTERNAL:

Cabin: Length	1.22 m (4 ft 0 in)
Max width	1.17 m (3 ft 10 in)
Max height	1.07 m (3 ft 6 in)
Floor area	1.49 m² (16.0 sq ft)
Volume	1.59 m³ (56.0 cu ft)

AREAS:

Main rotor blades, each	0.74 m² (8.00 sq ft)
Tail rotor blades, each	0.124 m² (1.33 sq ft)
Main rotor disc	47.45 m² (510.7 sq ft)
Tail rotor disc	1.17 m² (12.57 sq ft)
Fin	0.25 m² (2.7 sq ft)
Tailplane	0.25 m² (2.7 sq ft)

WEIGHTS:

Weight empty	486 kg (1,070 lb)
Max payload	217 kg (480 lb)
Max fuel weight	64 kg (140 lb)
Max T-O and landing weight	703 kg (1,550 lb)

*PERFORMANCE (at max T-O weight):

Max level speed at S/L	100 knots (185 km/h; 115 mph)
Max cruising speed at S/L	
	90 knots (167 km/h; 104 mph)
Econ cruising speed at S/L	
	75 knots (139 km/h; 86 mph)
Max forward rate of climb at S/L	366 m (1,200 ft)/min
Vertical rate of climb at S/L	122 m (400 ft)/min
Service ceiling	4,880 m (16,000 ft)
Hovering ceiling OGE	2,440 m (8,000 ft)
Range with max fuel	400 nm (741 km; 460 miles)

*Prototype with 145 hp engine

VTOL LIFT ACTIVATOR DISC

Construction of an LAD prototype (see description and illustration in the 1987-88 edition) has been postponed due to work commitments on the Phillicopter.

VTOL Phillicopter Mk 1 with new (1987) high inertia stabilised rotor system

BELGIUM

PROMAVIA
PROMAVIA SA

Chaussée de Fleurus 181, B-6200 Gosselies-Aéroport
Telephone: 32 71 34 15 11
Telex: 51872 SQUAL B
Fax: 32 71 35 79 54
PRESIDENT: André L. Delhamende

Promavia SA was formed by a number of industrialists, investment companies and a bank, with offices and facilities at Charleroi-Gosselies Airport. Results of a market survey completed in 1983 confirmed the company's belief that a requirement existed for an 'all-through' jet trainer, built to a specification similar to that which led to the US Air Force's next generation trainer (NGT) programme. Promavia therefore initiated the Jet Squalus programme, commissioning Dott Ing Stelio Frati to undertake the aircraft's design and prototype construction. Substantial financial backing was obtained by Promavia from the Belgian government in 1985 to contribute towards prototype research and development.

Marketing and support of the production Jet Squalus, including training programmes, will be undertaken by Promavia; production will be undertaken by Sonaca (which see). Promavia has proposed the Jet Squalus as a possible USAF alternative to the Fairchild T-46A new generation trainer. For this purpose, Promavia has established contacts with US manufacturers in order to build examples for the US market.

PROMAVIA JET SQUALUS F1300 NGT

The Jet Squalus (Latin for 'shark') was designed to cover all stages of flying training, from ab initio to part of the advanced syllabus, and to be powered by a small, modern, fuel-efficient and quiet turbofan engine. A side by side seating arrangement was chosen for instructor and trainee, and the aircraft is provided with four underwing attachment points enabling it also to undertake weapons training or light tactical missions.

Two prototypes have been built, the first of which made its public debut as a static exhibit at the Farnborough International air show in September 1986. It made its first flight on 30 April 1987, and is powered by a Garrett TFE76 turbofan of the kind developed for the twin-engined T-46A. The second prototype (OO-SQA), displayed at the Paris Air Show in June 1987, is equipped with air-conditioning and anti-icing systems. Static, flutter and other testing of major components has been completed, as have drawings for the production version, which will be manufactured in Belgium by Sonaca.

In an announcement at the 1987 Paris Air Show, Promavia proposed the Jet Squalus as an air ward system (AWS) aircraft in addition to its primary NGT role. Four such versions were suggested:

AWS-MS/SAR. Maritime surveillance/search and rescue, with SLAR and VHF-FM com radio.

AWS-R. Reconnaissance, with photographic equipment and a VLF/Omega R/Nav system.

AWS-W. For bombing and gunnery training, police and border defence missions.

AWS-TT. For target towing.

In addition, a civil version for training airline pilots and pilots of business jets is being developed.

By December 1987 the first prototype had completed about 100 hours' flying, and a Belgian Air Force evaluation was scheduled for later that month.

The following description applies to the first prototype, except where indicated:

TYPE: Two-seat aircraft for pilot screening, primary, basic and part of advanced jet training.

AIRFRAME: Composite materials are used for fairings and some non-structural components; otherwise the aircraft is basically of metal construction throughout.

WINGS: Cantilever low-wing monoplane, with supercritical wing section (thickness/chord ratio 13%, constant). Dihedral 5° from roots. Incidence 1° at root, –1° 45' at tip. All-metal single-spar structure in light alloy with flush riveted stressed skin. Differentially operated all-metal Frise ailerons with servo-tabs, and hydraulically operated metal trailing-edge flaps.

FUSELAGE: All-metal semi-monocoque structure with press-formed light alloy frames, linked by stringers and stiffeners; flush riveted aluminium alloy skin. Hydraulically operated two-piece light alloy airbrake in lower central part of fuselage, in line with flaps. Avionics and equipment bay in nose. Large quick-disconnect panel in lower rear fuselage permits rapid engine access or removal.

TAIL UNIT: Cantilever all-metal structure with flush riveted skin. Sweptback fin and rudder (42° on fin leading-edge). Non-swept, fixed incidence tailplane. Trim tab in port elevator.

LANDING GEAR: Retractable tricycle type, with single wheel and oleo-pneumatic shock absorber on each unit. Mainwheels retract inward, nosewheel rearward. Hydraulic actuation, with built-in emergency system. Main gear of trailing-arm type. Nosewheel steerable 18° left and right. Mainwheels and tyres size 6.00-6, nosewheel 5.00-5.

POWER PLANT: One Garrett TFE76 turbofan mounted in rear fuselage of first prototype, rated currently at 5.92 kN (1,330 lb st); will be uprated to 6.67 kN (1,500 lb st). Alternative engine under consideration is an 8.01 kN (1,800 lb st) Williams International FJ44 turbofan. Semi-integral metal fuel tank in centre-fuselage, max usable capacity 720 litres (190 US gallons; 158 Imp gallons). Single gravity refuelling point on top of fuselage, aft of canopy. Electric fuel pump for engine starting and emergency use.

ACCOMMODATION: Two persons side by side in air-conditioned cockpit, on Martin-Baker Mk 11 lightweight ejection seats capable of operation at altitudes up to 12,200 m (40,000 ft) and at any speed between 60 and 400 knots (111-741 km/h; 69-461 mph), including ejection through canopy. One-piece framed canopy is hinged at rear and opens upward.

SYSTEMS: Environmental control system for cockpit air-conditioning. Hydraulic system (operating pressure 117 bars; 1,700 lb/sq in) for actuation of airbrake, landing gear and flaps. System incorporates electrically driven oil pump, with two air/oil accumulators (one for normal and one for emergency operation); separate standby system for emergency lowering of landing gear. Electrical system is 28V DC, using an engine driven starter/generator and

First prototype of the Promavia Jet Squalus next generation trainer

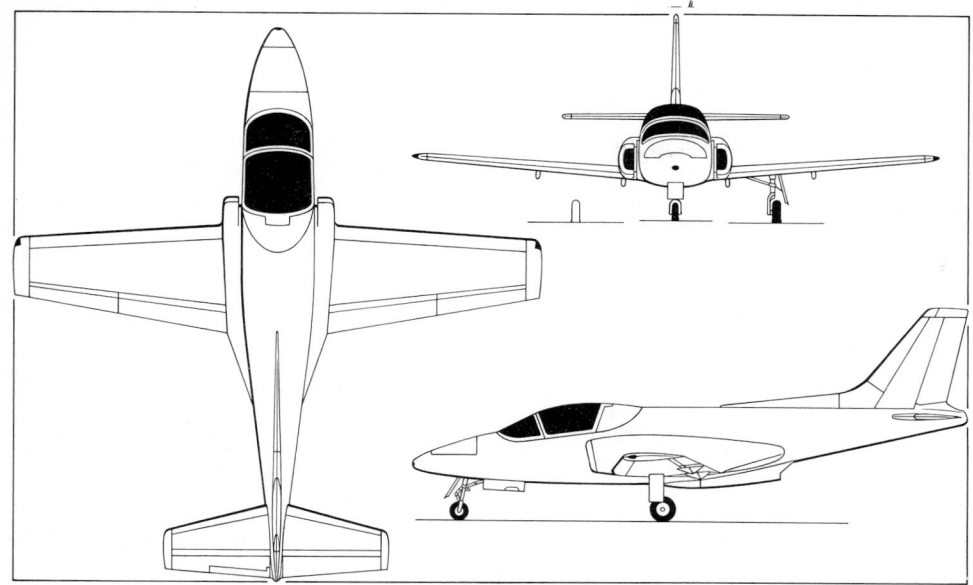

Promavia Jet Squalus F1300 NGT jet trainer *(Jane's/Mike Keep)*

nickel-cadmium or lead-acid battery. Negretti Aviation oxygen system.

AVIONICS AND EQUIPMENT: Include dual Collins Pro Line II EFIS avionics and radio equipment.

ARMAMENT: Four underwing attachment points for such weapons or other stores as 0.50 in/12.7 mm machine-gun pods, seven-round 2.75 in rocket launchers, practice bombs or auxiliary fuel tanks. Optionally, two 20 mm guns in underwing pods.

DIMENSIONS, EXTERNAL:

Wing span	9.04 m (29 ft 8 in)
Wing chord: at root	1.90 m (6 ft 2¾ in)
at tip	1.00 m (3 ft 3¼ in)
mean aerodynamic	1.575 m (5 ft 2 in)
Wing aspect ratio	6.0
Length of fuselage	9.36 m (30 ft 8½ in)
Height overall	3.60 m (11 ft 9¾ in)
Tailplane span	3.80 m (12 ft 5½ in)
Wheel track	3.59 m (11 ft 9¼ in)
Wheelbase	3.58 m (11 ft 9 in)

AREAS:

Wings, gross	13.58 m² (146.17 sq ft)
Ailerons (total)	1.122 m² (12.08 sq ft)
Trailing-edge flaps (total)	1.784 m² (19.20 sq ft)
Fin	1.256 m² (13.52 sq ft)
Rudder	0.782 m² (8.42 sq ft)
Tailplane	2.04 m² (22.00 sq ft)
Elevators (total, incl tab)	1.61 m² (17.33 sq ft)

WEIGHTS AND LOADINGS (A: standard engine, B: uprated engine):

Weight empty: A	1,300 kg (2,866 lb)
B	1,400 kg (3,086 lb)
Max external stores load	600 kg (1,323 lb)
Max T-O weight: A (Aerobatic)	2,000 kg (4,409 lb)
A (Normal), B	2,400 kg (5,291 lb)
Max wing loading:	
A (Aerobatic)	147.27 kg/m² (30.18 lb/sq ft)
A (Normal), B	176.73 kg/m² (36.21 lb/sq ft)
Max power loading:	
A (Aerobatic)	337.75 kg/kN (3.31 lb/lb st)
A (Normal), B (TFE76)	
	291.83 kg/kN (2.86 lb/lb st)
A (Normal), B (FJ44)	300.00 kg/kN (2.94 lb/lb st)

PERFORMANCE (estimated at max T-O weight, A and B as above):

Max permissible diving speed:	
A	380 knots (704 km/h; 437 mph)
Never-exceed speed in level flight:	
A	Mach 0.70 (345 knots; 638 km/h; 397 mph)
Max level speed at 4,265 m (14,000 ft):	
A	315 knots (584 km/h; 363 mph)
Normal operating speed:	
A	300 knots (556 km/h; 345 mph)
Max speed for landing gear extension:	
A	150 knots (278 km/h; 173 mph)
Max speed for flap extension (landing position):	
A	130 knots (241 km/h; 150 mph)
Stalling speed, flaps down:	
A	67 knots (124 km/h; 77 mph)
Max rate of climb at S/L: A	853 m (2,800 ft)/min
B	1,219 m (4,000 ft)/min
Service ceiling: A	11,280 m (37,000 ft)
B	12,800 m (42,000 ft)
Max operating ceiling: A	7,620 m (25,000 ft)
T-O run: A	335 m (1,100 ft)
T-O to 15 m (50 ft): A	396 m (1,300 ft)
Landing from 15 m (50 ft): A	427 m (1,400 ft)
Landing run: A	366 m (1,200 ft)
Ferry range at 6,100 m (20,000 ft), max internal fuel:	
A	1,000 nm (1,850 km; 1,150 miles)
g limits (A):	
	+2.8 sustained, at 3,050 m (10,000 ft)
	+7/−3.5 aerobatic

SABCA
SOCIÉTÉ ANONYME BELGE DE CONSTRUCTIONS AÉRONAUTIQUES

Chaussée de Haecht 1470, B-1130 Brussels
Telephone: Brussels (02) 2462 511
Telex: 21 237 SABCA B
Fax: (02) 2161570
CHAIRMAN: J. Groothaert
DIRECTOR/GENERAL MANAGER: J. Detemmerman
MARKETING MANAGER: J. E. Versmessen
OTHER WORKS: Aéroport de Gosselies-Charleroi, B-6200 Gosselies
Telephone: Charleroi (071) 35 01 70
Telex: 51 251 SABGO B

Founded in 1920, SABCA is the major aerospace company in Belgium. Since the Second World War, it has participated in various European aircraft programmes. At Haren, SABCA is manufacturing mainframe structures such as wings and nose sections, and other structural components and equipment, for the General Dynamics F-16; Dassault-Breguet/Dornier Alpha Jet; Dassault-Breguet Mirage III/5/F1 and Atlantic 1/Atlantique 2; Airbus A310; Fokker F27 and F28; Aérospatiale SA 330 Puma; Spacelab; and Ariane launchers. Servo controls are produced for the F-16 and the Ariane launchers.

At Gosselies, SABCA assembles and tests F-16s for Belgium and is also incorporating modifications to Belgian Air Force and USAFE F-16s.

SABCA's Electronic Division produces IFF components and aircraft electronic ground equipment, as well as maintaining Doppler equipment.

For many years SABCA has been responsible for the maintenance and overhaul of Belgian and other armed forces' military aircraft, their electronic components and accessories, as well as commercial fixed-wing aircraft and helicopters. It is currently integrating ECM devices in Belgian aircraft.

SABCA is a member of various European industrial consortia; Dassault-Breguet and Fokker have parity holdings in the company. The company's works occupy a total area of approx 82,000 m² (882,640 sq ft) and in early 1988 employed an average of 1,600 people.

SONACA
SOCIÉTÉ NATIONALE DE CONSTRUCTION AÉROSPATIALE SA

Parc Industriel, Route Nationale Cinq, B-6200 Gosselies
Telephone: Charleroi (071) 34 22 11
Telex: 51241
Fax: (071) 34 40 35
GENERAL MANAGER: J. Storrer
MANUFACTURING DIRECTOR: P. Wacquez
MARKETING AND PROGRAMMES DIRECTOR: E. Barthelemy
Sonaca SA, formerly Fairey SA (established in 1931), was

incorporated on 1 May 1978. Its capital is held 50% by public institutions and 50% by Belgian industry. Built on 20.25 ha (50 acres) of ground adjacent to Charleroi Airport, Sonaca's 67,500 m² (726,565 sq ft) facility employed 1,380 people in early 1988.

Sonaca participates in civil and military aviation manufacturing programmes, co-producing the General Dynamics F-16 (rear fuselage, vertical fin, dorsal fairing and final mating) and components (leading-edge moving surfaces) for the Airbus A310, A320 and, shortly,

A330/340. It supplies parts for various aircraft, including Aérospatiale and Westland helicopters, the Dassault-Breguet Atlantique 2, Lockheed C-130, Boeing 747SP, Saab 340 and Dassault-Breguet/Dornier Alpha Jet. Sonaca is also the designated industrial prime contractor for the Promavia Jet Squalus trainer (which see). The company designed and sells aircraft galley polycarbonate containers.

R & D resources include an IBM Cadam scientific data processing system. Structures made of composite materials are manufactured for the Hermes spacecraft programme.

BRAZIL

AEROTEC
AEROTEC S/A INDUSTRIA AERONÁUTICA

Caixa Postal 286, 12200 São José dos Campos, SP
Telephone: (123) 21 8011

AEROTEC A-135 TANGARÁ II

The original A-132 Tangará (see 1983-84 *Jane's*) was developed in the late 1970s as a potential replacement for the Brazilian Air Force's T-23 Uirapuru primary trainer, and made its first flight on 26 February 1981. It had completed its basic CTA flight test programme by Spring 1982, at which time it was reportedly planned to replace the 119 kW (160 hp) Textron Lycoming O-320-B2B flat-four with a 149 kW (200 hp) engine. Nothing more had been heard of this proposal until October 1986, when Aerotec exhibited a full size mockup of the A-135 Tangará II in São José dos Campos. Apart from the more powerful engine, major changes from the A-132 include wings of increased span and area, and relocation of the seats in tandem

Mockup of the proposed Aerotec A-135 Tangará II *(Mario B. M Vinagre)*

configuration under a single elongated bubble canopy.

The status of this project was still uncertain at the time of going to press. All known details were given in the 1987-88 *Jane's*.

POWER PLANT: One 149 kW (200 hp) Textron Lycoming AEIO-360-A1B6 flat-four engine, driving a three-blade constant-speed propeller with spinner. Fuel tank in each wing leading-edge, immediately outboard of root fillet.

ACCOMMODATION: Two fully adjustable seats in tandem under one-piece rearward sliding bubble canopy. One-piece wraparound windscreen. Dual controls standard. Baggage space aft of rear seat.

DIMENSION, EXTERNAL:	
Wing span	9.636 m (31 ft 7½ in)
Length overall	7.90 m (25 ft 11 in)
Height overall	2.70 m (8 ft 10¼ in)
AREA:	
Wings, gross	14.65 m² (157.7 sq ft)
WEIGHTS AND LOADINGS (Aerobatic category):	
Weight empty	660 kg (1,455 lb)
Max T-O weight	960 kg (2,116 lb)
Max wing loading	65.53 kg/m² (13.43 lb/sq ft)
Max power loading	6.44 kg/kW (10.58 lb/hp)
PERFORMANCE (estimated at max Aerobatic T-O weight):	
Max level speed	136 knots (252 km/h; 156 mph)

Max cruising speed	120 knots (222 km/h; 138 mph)
Econ cruising speed	110 knots (204 km/h; 127 mph)
Stalling speed: flaps up	55 knots (101 km/h; 63 mph)
flaps down	48 knots (89 km/h; 56 mph)
Max rate of climb at S/L	427 m (1,400 ft)/min
Service ceiling	6,100 m (20,000 ft)
T-O run	270 m (886 ft)
Landing run	160 m (525 ft)
Range with max fuel	432 nm (800 km; 497 miles)
Endurance with max fuel	4 h

CTA
CENTRO TÉCNICO AEROESPACIAL
PO Box 6001, 12225 São José dos Campos, SP
Telephone: (123) 21 1311
Telex: 0123 3393 CTAE BA
PROGRAMME MANAGER: Dilson Faria Pessoa

The CTA (see earlier editions of *Jane's*) is composed of five institutes. One of these, the IFI (Instituto de Fomento e Coordenação Industrial), co-ordinated the development of a re-engined version of the Neiva Paulistinha P-56, last described fully in the 1968-69 edition. Another CTA institute, the IPD (Instituto de Pesquisa e Desenvolvimento), made the aircraft modifications, bench tested the new engine, and performed a flight test programme which had totalled about 120 hours by February 1988.

CTA (NEIVA) PAULISTINHA 56
It is estimated that about 250 examples of Continental engined Paulistinhas are still operated in Brazil, and that these are affected by both high maintenance costs and a shortage of C65 and C90 engines. Since the aircraft still forms the main basic training equipment for many of Brazil's flying clubs, the IFI successfully investigated the feasibility of refitting them with the 59.5 kW (80 hp) IMAER (formerly Retimotor) TM 2000 EM1 engine (a dual ignition version of the TM 2000 M1 developed for the Aeromot Ximango motor glider), driving a Hoffmann HO-V 62 R/L 160 BT two-position (climb and cruise) propeller.

Results obtained from flight trials of the prototype (PP-HOT) have shown no loss of performance, and

CTA modified Paulistinha 56 prototype, with TM 2000 EM1 engine

improved fuel consumption, compared with the C90 engined Paulistinha.

PERFORMANCE:
Never-exceed speed	118 knots (220 km/h; 136 mph) IAS
Max level speed at S/L	73 knots (136 km/h; 84 mph)

Max cruising speed at S/L	72 knots (133 km/h; 82 mph)
Econ cruising speed at S/L	62 knots (114 km/h; 71 mph)
Stalling speed at S/L	35 knots (64 km/h; 40 mph)
Max rate of climb at S/L	152 m (500 ft)/min
Service ceiling	4,265 m (14,000 ft)

EMBRAER
EMPRESA BRASILEIRA DE AERONÁUTICA SA
Av Brig Faria Lima 2170, Caixa Postal 343, 12225 São José dos Campos, SP
Telephone: (123) 25 1711
Telex: (391) 1233589 EBAE BR
RIO OFFICE: Aeroporto Santos-Dumont, Sobreloja, Salão de Embarque No. 2, 20021 Rio de Janeiro, RJ
Telephone: (21) 262 6411
CHAIRMAN: Eng Ozires Silva
CHIEF EXECUTIVE OFFICER: Eng Ozilio Carlos da Silva
COMMERCIAL DIRECTOR: Heitor Fernandes Serra
MILITARY PROGRAMMES DIRECTOR:
Luiz Thomaz Carrilho Teixeira-Gomes
TECHNICAL DIRECTOR: Eng Guido Fontegalante Pessotti
PRESS RELATIONS: Antonio Augusto de Oliveira
US SUBSIDIARY:
Embraer Aircraft Corporation, 276 Southwest 34th Street, PO Box 21623, Fort Lauderdale, Florida 33335
Telephone: (305) 524 5755 and 5744
Telex: (230) 522318 EMBRAER FORT LAUDERDALE
PARIS OFFICE:
Embraer Aviation International, BP 74, Aéroport du Bourget, Zone d'Aviation d'Affaires, 93350 Le Bourget, France
Telephone: (4) 835 9420
Telex: 213498F EBAE PAR

Embraer was created on 19 August 1969, and came into operation on 2 January 1970. The Brazilian government owns 88.77% of the voting shares, 11.23% of the subscribed capital being held by private shareholders. Embraer had a workforce in January 1988 of 9,900 persons and a factory area of 333,225 m² (3,586,920 sq ft). By the end of 1987 Embraer had built a total of 3,773 aircraft.

Since August 1974, Embraer has had an agreement with Piper Aircraft Corporation to manufacture in Brazil the Seneca and Navajo Chieftain and (currently) three models of four- and six-passenger single-engined types. Production of the Navajo Chieftain has since ended. Since 1976, Embraer has manufactured components for the Northrop F-5E Tiger II combat aircraft. Agreements concluded in 1983-84 with Sikorsky provide for development of Embraer's capability to manufacture aircraft components in composite materials, initially for the S-70C helicopter, the EMB-120 Brasilia and the AMX attack aircraft. A 1987 agreement with McDonnell Douglas provides for the supply of 200 sets of wing flaps, in composites material, for the MD-11 airliner, with a further 100 sets on option. Embraer has in current production the EMB-110 Bandeirante, the EMB-120 Brasilia commuter transport,

Embraer EMB-110P1A Bandeirante in the insignia of the Angolan operator Gamek

and the EMB-312 Tucano military trainer. The AMX tactical fighter is produced jointly in partnership with Aeritalia and Aermacchi of Italy, and the CBA-123 commuter transport is being developed jointly with FAMA of Argentina. Manufacture of the EMB-201A Ipanema agricultural aircraft, and various Embraer licence produced versions of Piper single- and twin-engined light aircraft, is the responsibility of Neiva (which see), which became a subsidiary of Embraer in March 1980.

AMX
Details of this military aircraft programme with Aeritalia and Aermacchi are given in the International section.

EMBRAER EMB-110 BANDEIRANTE (PIONEER)
Brazilian Air Force designation: C-95
The Bandeirante twin-turboprop light transport was developed to a Brazilian Ministry of Aeronautics specification calling for a general purpose aircraft capable of carrying out transport, navigation training and aeromedical evacuation missions. The first of three EMB-100 prototypes (described in the 1970-71 *Jane's*) made its initial flight on 26 October 1968, followed by the first production EMB-110 Bandeirante (C-95/2133) on 9 August 1972. Following Brazilian certification to FAR Pt 23, the first three

Bandeirantes were delivered to the Brazilian Air Force on 9 February 1973.

Bandeirantes of various models have been sold to more than 80 operators in 36 countries worldwide. By 1 June 1988 the worldwide fleet of Bandeirantes had logged more than 4.2 million flying hours; at that time Embraer had delivered 469 Bandeirantes, of which 241 were for export. A further seven were due for delivery during 1988.

Details of models no longer in regular production can be found in the 1984-85 and previous editions of *Jane's*, and any of these can still be produced to special order. Principal models in current production are as follows:

EMB-110P1A. Updated version of P1 with 10° tailplane dihedral and other detail changes (listed in 1987-88 and earlier editions). First two delivered in December 1983 to Provincetown-Boston Airlines, USA. Replaced P1 as standard version from c/n 439 onwards; retrofits available for earlier P1s. Delivery of six to Brazilian Air Force (as **C-95C**), with Collins EFIS package, began in 1988.

EMB-110P1K. Military utility, cargo and paradropping version of P1 (Brazilian Air Force designation **C-95B**; 28 delivered). No tailplane dihedral.

EMB-110P1K SAR. Search and rescue version of P1K (Brazilian Air Force designation **SC-95B**), equipped for inland and overwater search, paradropping, and aeromedical evacuation. Max T-O weight 6,000 kg (13,230

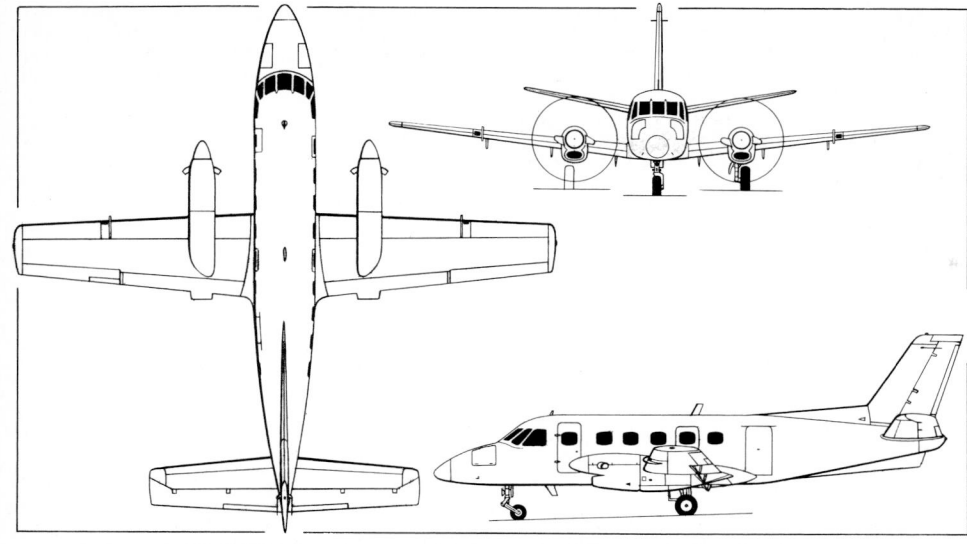

Embraer EMB-110P2A Bandeirante, with dihedral tailplane and other changes *(Pilot Press)*

lb). Accommodation for up to six stretchers plus seats for observers and space for inflatable dinghies and other rescue equipment. Two 'bubble' windows in each side of cabin. Independent oxygen system for medevac missions. Five ordered by Brazilian Air Force; operated by 2° Esquadrão of the 10° Grupo de Aviação at Campo Grande.

EMB-110P2A. Replaced former P2 (1984-85 *Jane's*) as third-level commuter transport version, carrying up to 21 passengers. Incorporates same changes as P1A. Detailed description applies mainly to this version.

EMB-110P1A/41 and EMB-110P2A/41. New versions of P1A and P2A, available from 1983, certificated under SFAR Pt 41 for a max T-O weight of 5,900 kg (13,010 lb). These versions replaced former P1/41 and P2/41. Power plant and dimensions unchanged. Available also as retrofit to existing P1/41 and P2/41 versions.

EMB-111. Maritime surveillance version, described separately.

The following description, except where indicated, applies to the standard production EMB-110P2A:

TYPE: Twin-turboprop general purpose transport.

WINGS: Cantilever low-wing monoplane. Wing section NACA 23016 (modified) at root, NACA 23012 (modified) at tip. Sweepback 0° 19′ 48″ at quarter-chord. Dihedral 7° at 28 per cent chord. Incidence 3°. All-metal two-spar structure, of 2024-T3 and -T4 aluminium alloy, with detachable glassfibre wingtips. Glassfibre wing/fuselage fairing. All-metal statically balanced Frise ailerons and double-slotted flaps. Trim tab in port aileron. De-icing system optional.

FUSELAGE: All-metal semi-monocoque structure of 2024-T3 aluminium alloy. Two upward hinged doors, one on each side of nose, provide access to avionics.

TAIL UNIT: Cantilever all-metal structure, with sweptback vertical surfaces and 10° tailplane dihedral. Glassfibre dorsal fin. Ventral fin. Trim tabs in rudder and port elevator; mass balance on elevator tab and duplicated control rods to elevator. De-icing system optional.

LANDING GEAR: Hydraulically retractable tricycle type, with single wheel and ERAM oleo-pneumatic (nitrogen) shock absorber on each unit. Main units retract into engine nacelles. Mainwheel tyre size 670 × 270-12 (10 ply rating), pressure 5.86-6.20 bars (85-90 lb/sq in). Steerable, forward retracting nosewheel unit has tyre size 6.50-8, pressure 4.27-4.69 bars (62-68 lb/sq in).

POWER PLANT: Two 559 kW (750 shp) Pratt & Whitney Canada PT6A-34 turboprops, each driving a Hartzell HC-B3TN-3C/T10178H-8R constant-speed three-blade metal propeller with autofeathering and full reverse-pitch capability. Four integral fuel tanks in wings, with total capacity of 1,720 litres (454 US gallons; 378 Imp gallons). Oil capacity 8.7 litres (2.3 US gallons; 1.9 Imp gallons). Gravity refuelling point on top of each wing. Optional de-icing system for engine air inlets and propellers.

ACCOMMODATION: Pilot and co-pilot side by side on flight deck. Seats for up to 21 passengers in main cabin of P2A, at 74 cm (29 in) pitch. P1A has quick-change cabin seating up to 18 persons. Crew/passenger door at front and passenger/baggage door at rear, both on port side; emergency exit over wing on each side, and opposite crew/passenger door on starboard side. Crew/passenger door can also be used as emergency exit. Cabin floor stressed for uniformly distributed loads of up to 488 kg/m² (100 lb/sq ft). Baggage compartment at rear of cabin. Flush type toilet in compartment at rear of cabin. Toilet/lavatory standard. Windscreen de-icing optional.

SYSTEMS: Air cycle air-conditioning system with cooling capacity of 25,000 BTU/h and engine bleed heating. Primary hydraulic system for actuation of landing gear, brakes, nosewheel steering and parking/emergency braking. Hydraulic power supply system basically comprises (a) reservoir with electric booster pump and 10 litre (2.6 US gallon; 2.2 Imp gallon) capacity; (b) two

engine driven, pressure compensated variable delivery pumps, with pump pressure of 207 bars (3,000 lb/sq in) and flow rate of 6.05 litres (1.6 US gallons; 1.33 Imp gallons)/min, mounted on engine accessory gearbox; (c) a 0.5 litre (0.13 US gallon; 0.11 Imp gallon) capacity pressure accumulator in the pressure line; and (d) hydraulic fluid conforming to MIL-H-5606. Emergency hydraulic system, for landing gear only, consists of handpump in cockpit with 103.5 bars (1,500 lb/sq in) pressure and max flow rate of 15 cc (0.915 cu in) per cycle. Electrical system utilises two starter/generators, giving 200A continuously or 300A for one minute, and one 24V 34Ah nickel-cadmium battery with two 250VA static inverters to supply 115/26V 400Hz AC power. External power receptacle on port side of forward fuselage. Oxygen system for crew and passengers (standard in P2A, optional in P1A), using oxygen cylinder in rear of fuselage with capacity of 3.3 m³ (115 cu ft) at 128 bars (1,850 lb/sq in) pressure.

AVIONICS AND EQUIPMENT: Collins Pro Line, Collins Microline and King Silver Crown II avionics packages available (see 1987-88 edition for detailed list). Other avionics options include Collins HF-200 SSB 20-channel HF transceiver; Bendix M4-D autopilot; King KA 52 autopilot adapter (necessary with King package); Collins AVR-101 cockpit voice recorder (mandatory for French certification); Dorne & Margolin DMELT-6 emergency locator transmitter system (mandatory for US, Canadian and French certification); encoding altimeter (IDC, Smiths or Jaeger); and weather radar (Bendix RDR-1200 or RDR-160).

DIMENSIONS, EXTERNAL:

Wing span	15.33 m (50 ft 3½ in)
Wing chord: at root	2.33 m (7 ft 7¾ in)
at tip	1.37 m (4 ft 6 in)
Wing aspect ratio	8.1
Length overall	15.10 m (49 ft 6½ in)
Length of fuselage	14.59 m (47 ft 10½ in)
Height overall	4.92 m (16 ft 1¾ in)
Fuselage: Max width	1.72 m (5 ft 7¾ in)
Tailplane span	7.54 m (24 ft 9 in)
Wheel track	4.94 m (16 ft 2½ in)
Wheelbase	5.10 m (16 ft 8¾ in)
Propeller diameter	2.36 m (7 ft 9 in)
Distance between propeller centres	4.80 m (15 ft 9 in)
Propeller ground clearance	0.276 m (10¾ in)
Passenger door (rear, port):	
Height	1.35 m (4 ft 5¼ in)
Width	0.85 m (2 ft 9½ in)
Crew/passenger door (fwd, port):	
Height	1.42 m (4 ft 8 in)
Width	0.63 m (2 ft 1 in)
Passenger and crew emergency exits (three, each):	
Height	0.80 m (2 ft 7½ in)
Width	0.63 m (2 ft 1 in)

DIMENSIONS, INTERNAL:

Cabin: Max length	9.53 m (31 ft 3¼ in)
Width	1.60 m (5 ft 3 in)
Height	1.60 m (5 ft 3 in)
Floor area	12.00 m² (129.2 sq ft)
Volume	20.4 m³ (720.4 cu ft)
Baggage compartment volume	2.0 m³ (70.6 cu ft)

AREAS:

Wings, gross	29.10 m² (313.23 sq ft)
Ailerons (total)	2.16 m² (23.25 sq ft)
Flaps (total)	4.90 m² (52.74 sq ft)
Fin, excl dorsal fin	3.81 m² (41.01 sq ft)
Dorsal fin	0.82 m² (8.83 sq ft)
Ventral fin	0.80 m² (8.61 sq ft)
Rudder, incl tab	1.69 m² (18.19 sq ft)
Tailplane	5.51 m² (59.31 sq ft)
Elevators, incl tabs	4.31 m² (46.39 sq ft)

WEIGHTS AND LOADINGS (A: P2A; B: P1A/41 and P2A/41; C: P1A in passenger configuration):

Weight empty, equipped: A	3,516 kg (7,751 lb)
B, commercial	3,590 kg (7,915 lb)
B, cargo	3,393 kg (7,480 lb)
Fuel weight: A, B, C	1,308 kg (2,883 lb)
Max payload: A	1,681 kg (3,706 lb)
B, commercial	1,561 kg (3,443 lb)
B, cargo	1,712 kg (3,774 lb)
C	1,633 kg (3,600 lb)
Max T-O weight: A	5,670 kg (12,500 lb)
B	5,900 kg (13,010 lb)
Max ramp weight: B	5,930 kg (13,073 lb)
Max landing weight: A	5,670 kg (12,500 lb)
B	5,700 kg (12,566 lb)
Max zero-fuel weight: A, B	5,450 kg (12,015 lb)
Max wing loading: A	195.52 kg/m² (40.04 lb/sq ft)
B	202.61 kg/m² (41.50 lb/sq ft)
Max power loading: A	5.07 kg/kW (8.33 lb/shp)
B	5.27 kg/kW (8.67 lb/shp)

PERFORMANCE (at max T-O weight, ISA, except where indicated. A: P2A; B: P1A/41 and P2A/41):

Max level speed at 2,440 m (8,000 ft):	
A	248 knots (460 km/h; 286 mph)
Max cruising speed at 2,440 m (8,000 ft):	
A	223 knots (413 km/h; 257 mph)
B	222 knots (411 km/h; 256 mph)
Econ cruising speed at 3,050 m (10,000 ft):	
A	181 knots (335 km/h; 208 mph)
B	184 knots (341 km/h; 212 mph)
Stalling speed at max landing weight:	
A	69 knots (128 km/h; 80 mph) CAS
Max rate of climb at S/L: A	545 m (1,788 ft)/min
B	500 m (1,640 ft)/min
Rate of climb at S/L, one engine out:	
A	131 m (430 ft)/min
B	113 m (370 ft)/min
Time to 3,050 m (10,000 ft): A	6 min
Time to 4,575 m (15,000 ft): A	10 min
Service ceiling: A	6,860 m (22,500 ft)
B	6,550 m (21,500 ft)
Service ceiling, one engine out:	
A	3,385 m (11,100 ft)
B	3,050 m (10,000 ft)
T-O run:	
A, FAR 23.135A	675 m (2,215 ft)
B, FAR 23.135/SFAR 41A	807 m (2,650 ft)
Landing run (non-factored) at max landing weight:	
A	850 m (2,790 ft)
B	868 m (2,850 ft)
Range with max fuel (long-range cruising speed, 45 min reserves): A	1,080 nm (2,001 km; 1,244 miles)
B	1,062 nm (1,964 km; 1,220 miles)

EMBRAER EMB-111
Brazilian Air Force designation: P-95

This land based maritime surveillance aircraft, based on the EMB-110 Bandeirante, was designed to meet specifications issued by the Comando Costeiro, the Brazilian Air Force's Coastal Command. Main external differences are the large nose radome, housing search radar, and the addition of wingtip fuel tanks.

The EMB-111 flew for the first time on 15 August 1977, and 12 were delivered to the Brazilian Air Force. Six were delivered to the Chilean Navy in 1978 and 1979. These aircraft have some mission equipment changes, including full de-icing system, and passive ECM antennae under the

Embraer EMB-111 maritime surveillance aircraft of the Brazilian Air Force

nose and at the tail. One EMB-111 was delivered in August 1981 to the Gabonese Air Force, and two were ordered in 1986 by the air force of Angola. Delivery dates for the Angolan pair were awaiting financial approval in 1988.

In December 1987, the Brazilian Air Force ordered a further ten EMB-111s, with deliveries to begin in October 1989. The new aircraft will be similar to those currently in service, except for structural improvements and updated avionics which include MEL Super Searcher radar and Thomson-CSF DR 2000A Mk II/Dalia 1000A Mk II ESM; Collins EFIS-74 electronic flight instrument system, ADI-84 and APS-65 autopilot; and a Canadian Marconi CMA 771 Mk III Omega navigation system. The earlier aircraft will be brought up to a similar standard.

A full description of the EMB-111 can be found in the 1985-86 and earlier editions of *Jane's*.

EMBRAER EMB-120 BRASILIA
Brazilian Air Force designation: C-97

Design of this twin-turboprop passenger and cargo transport started in September 1979. The first prototype (PT-ZBA) made its initial flight on 27 July 1983, the second (PT-ZBB) on 21 December 1983, and the third (PT-ZBC) on 9 May 1984. These aircraft were used for flight test and certification trials. Nos. 2 and 5 were static and fatigue test aircraft; No. 6 was a pre-series demonstration aircraft.

Certification by the Brazilian CTA was granted on 10 May 1985, and FAA (FAR Pt 25) type approval on 9 July 1985. Type certification by the British CAA, French DGAC and German LBA was granted in 1986. The first customer, Atlantic Southeast Airlines of the USA, received its first Brasilia at the Paris Air Show in June 1985. By 9 May 1988 firm orders totalled 153, with 142 more on option. By that date, a total of 75 had been delivered, including two **VC-97** VIP transports for the Brazilian Air Force, which has eight more **C-97**s on order. The first order for the corporate version was received from United Technologies Corporation (USA) in August 1985. Furnished for 18 passengers, it was delivered in September 1986. Scheduled production rate was three aircraft per month in 1987, rising to four per month in 1988.

From Brasilia c/n 120028, delivered to DLT in October 1986, composite materials equivalent to 10 per cent of the aircraft's basic empty weight have been used in the airframe, as noted in the following descriptive details:

TYPE: Twin-turboprop general purpose transport.

WINGS: Cantilever low-wing monoplane. Wing section NACA 23018 (modified) at root, NACA 23012 at tip. Dihedral 6° 30′ from roots at 66 per cent chord. Incidence 2°. Sweepback 0° at 66 per cent chord. Single continuous fail-safe structure, attached to underside of fuselage on three special frames. Main wing box has three spars (at 15, 28 and 66 per cent chord), ribs, stiffeners and skin. Spar caps machined from 2024 or 7050 aluminium alloy extrusions; skin panels are of 2024 or 7475 laminations, chemically milled. Leading-edges, wingtips and root fairings of Kevlar reinforced glassfibre. Hydraulically actuated electrically controlled double-slotted Fowler trailing-edge flap, of carbonfibre construction, inboard and outboard of each engine nacelle; small plain flap beneath each nacelle. No slats, slots, spoilers or airbrakes. Small fence on each outer wing between outboard flap and aileron. Internally balanced all-metal ailerons. Lateral trimming by tabs (two in starboard aileron, one in port aileron). Ailerons actuated by dual irreversible mechanical actuators operated manually by cable controls. Pneumatic boot de-icing of leading-edges, using engine bleed air.

FUSELAGE: Semi-monocoque pressurised structure, of circular cross-section throughout most of its length. Chemically milled skin, reinforced by extruded stiffeners; C

frames attached to skin by shear clips. Entire structure is of 2024, 7050 and 7475 aluminium alloys, and meets the damage tolerance requirements of FAR Pt 25 (Transport category) up to Amendment 25-54. Nosecone of Kevlar reinforced glassfibre; tailcone also of Kevlar reinforced glassfibre on aircraft without APU. Pressurised area contained within flat bulkhead forward of flight deck and spherical rear bulkhead aft of baggage compartment. Twin ventral strakes under rear fuselage.

TAIL UNIT: Cantilever T tail, of three-spar metal construction except for leading-edges and tips, which are of Kevlar reinforced glassfibre. Fixed incidence swept tailplane, with horn balanced elevators. Sweptback fin, with Kevlar reinforced glassfibre dorsal fin. Serially hinged two-segment rudder actuated hydraulically by Bertea CSD unit. Mechanically actuated trim tab in each half of elevator. Pneumatic boot de-icing of leading-edges, using engine bleed air.

LANDING GEAR: Retractable tricycle type, with Goodrich twin wheels and oleo-pneumatic shock absorber on each unit (main units 12 in, nose unit 8 in). Hydraulic actuation; all units retract forward (main units into engine nacelles). Hydraulically powered nosewheel steering. Goodyear tyres, size 24 × 7.25 in (main), 18 × 5.5 in (nose); pressure 6.90-7.58 bars (100-110 lb/sq in) on main units, 4.14-4.83 bars (60-70 lb/sq in) on nose unit. Goodrich carbon brakes standard (steel optional). Hydro Aire anti-skid system standard; autobrake optional.

POWER PLANT: Two Pratt & Whitney Canada PW118 turboprops, each rated at 1,342 kW (1,800 shp) for T-O and max continuous power, and driving a Hamilton Standard 14RF-9 four-blade constant-speed reversible-pitch fully-feathering propeller with glassfibre blades containing aluminium spars. Fuel in two-cell 1,670 litre (441 US gallon; 367.2 Imp gallon) integral tank in each wing; total capacity 3,340 litres (882 US gallons; 734.4 Imp gallons), of which 3,312 litres (875 US gallons; 728.6 Imp gallons) are usable. Single-point pressure refuelling (beneath outer starboard wing), plus gravity point in upper surface of each wing. Oil capacity 9 litres (2.4 US gallons; 2 Imp gallons).

ACCOMMODATION: Pilot and co-pilot on flight deck, with dual controls. Main cabin accommodates cabin attendant and 30 passengers in three-abreast seating at 79 cm (31 in) pitch, with overhead lockable baggage racks, in pressurised and air-conditioned environment. Passenger seats are made of carbonfibre and Kevlar, floor and partitions of carbonfibre and Nomex sandwich, side panels and ceiling of glassfibre/Kevlar/Nomex/ carbonfibre sandwich. Provisions for wardrobe, galley and toilet. Downward opening main passenger door, with airstairs, forward of wing on port side. Type II emergency exit on starboard side at rear. Overwing Type III emergency exit on each side. Pressurised baggage compartment aft of passenger cabin, with large door on port side. Also available with all-cargo interior; executive or military transport interior; or in mixed-traffic version with 24 or 26 passengers (toilet omitted in latter case), and 900 kg (1,984 lb) of cargo in enlarged rear baggage compartment.

SYSTEMS: AiResearch air-conditioning/pressurisation system (differential 0.48 bars; 7 lb/sq in), with dual packs of recirculation equipment. Duplicated hydraulic systems (pressure 207 bars; 3,000 lb/sq in), each powered by an engine driven pump, for landing gear, flap, rudder and brake actuation, and nosewheel steering. Emergency standby electric pumps on each system, plus single standby handpump, for landing gear extension. Main electrical power supplied by two 28V 400A DC starter/generators; two 28V 100A DC auxiliary brushless generators for secondary and/or emergency power; one 24V 40Ah nickel-cadmium battery for assisted starting and emergency power. Main and standby 450VA static inverters for 26/115V AC power at 400Hz. Single high-pressure (127.5 bars; 1,850 lb/sq in) oxygen cylinder for crew; individual chemical oxygen generators for passengers. Pneumatic de-icing for wing and tail leading-edges, and engine air intakes; electrically heated windscreens, propellers and pitot tubes; bleed air de-icing of engine air intakes. Optional Garrett GTCP36-150(A) APU in tailcone, for electrical and pneumatic power supply (fitted to second and third prototypes).

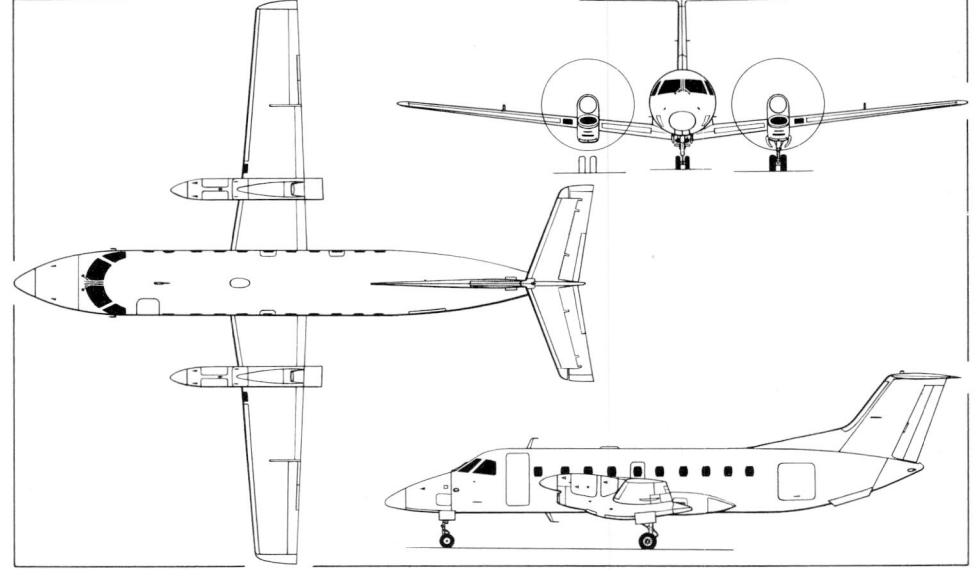

Embraer EMB-120 Brasilia twin-turboprop transport *(Pilot Press)*

Embraer EMB-120 Brasilia twin-turboprop passenger transport in the insignia of Air Littoral of France

First of two EMB-120s operated as VC-97 VIP transports by the Brazilian Air Force

AVIONICS: Collins Pro Line II digital avionics package includes as standard dual VHF-22 com transceivers, dual VIR-32 VHF nav receivers, one ADF-60A, one TDR-90 transponder, CLT-22/32/62/92 control heads, one DME-41, one WXR-270 weather radar, dual AHRS-85 digital strapdown AHRS, dual ADI-84, dual EHSI-74, dual RMI-36, one Dorne & Margolin DMELT-81 emergency locator transmitter, dual Avtech audio/interphones, Avtech PA and cabin interphone, Fairchild voice recorder, and IET standby attitude indicator. Optional avionics include third VHF com, second transponder and DME, WXR-300 weather radar, two EFIS-86 electronic flight instrument systems, one MFD-85 multi-function display, one or two J.E.T. RNS-8000 3D or Racal Avionics RN 5000 nav, one APS-65 digital autopilot, one or two FCS-65 digital flight directors, flight entertainment music, one or two Canadian Marconi CMA-771 Alpha VLF/Omega, one or two ALT-55 radio altimeters, altitude alerter/preselect, microwave landing system, ground proximity warning system, flight recorder, and Motorola Selcal. Second (Bendix) avionics package is available optionally. Other types of avionics, for special versions of the aircraft, as required for the missions concerned.

DIMENSIONS, EXTERNAL:

Wing span	19.78 m (64 ft 10¾ in)
Wing chord: at root	2.81 m (9 ft 2¾ in)
at tip	1.40 m (4 ft 7 in)
Wing aspect ratio	9.9
Length overall	20.00 m (65 ft 7½ in)
Length of fuselage	18.73 m (61 ft 5½ in)
Fuselage: Max diameter	2.28 m (7 ft 5¾ in)
Height overall	6.35 m (20 ft 10 in)
Elevator span	6.94 m (22 ft 9¼ in)
Wheel track (c/l of shock struts)	6.58 m (21 ft 7 in)
Wheelbase	6.97 m (22 ft 10½ in)
Propeller diameter	3.20 m (10 ft 6 in)
Propeller ground clearance (min)	0.48 m (1 ft 7 in)
Passenger door (fwd, port): Height	1.70 m (5 ft 7 in)
Width	0.774 m (2 ft 6½ in)
Height to sill	1.47 m (4 ft 10 in)
Cargo door (rear, port): Height	1.36 m (4 ft 5½ in)
Width	1.30 m (4 ft 3¼ in)
Height to sill	1.67 m (5 ft 5¾ in)
Emergency exit (rear, stbd): Height	1.37 m (4 ft 6 in)
Width	0.51 m (1 ft 8 in)
Height to sill	1.56 m (5 ft 1½ in)
Emergency exits (overwing, each):	
Height	0.91 m (3 ft 0 in)
Width	0.51 m (1 ft 8 in)
Emergency exits (flight deck side windows, each):	
Min height	0.48 m (1 ft 7 in)
Min width	0.51 m (1 ft 8 in)

DIMENSIONS, INTERNAL:

Cabin, excl flight deck and baggage compartment:

Length	9.35 m (30 ft 8 in)
Max width	2.10 m (6 ft 10¾ in)
Max height	1.76 m (5 ft 9¼ in)
Floor area	14.97 m² (161.14 sq ft)

Rear baggage compartment volume:

30-passenger version	6.40 m³ (226 cu ft)
all-cargo version	2.70 m³ (95 cu ft)
passenger/cargo version	11.00 m³ (388 cu ft)

Cabin, incl flight deck and baggage compartment:

Total volume	approx 41.8 m³ (1,476 cu ft)

Max available cabin volume (all-cargo version)
31.10 m³ (1,098 cu ft)

AREAS:

Wings, gross	39.43 m² (424.42 sq ft)
Ailerons (total)	2.88 m² (31.00 sq ft)
Trailing-edge flaps (total)	3.23 m² (34.77 sq ft)
Fin, incl dorsal fin	5.74 m² (61.78 sq ft)
Rudder	2.59 m² (27.88 sq ft)
Tailplane	6.10 m² (65.66 sq ft)
Elevator, incl tabs	3.90 m² (41.98 sq ft)

WEIGHTS AND LOADINGS:

Weight empty, equipped	7,070 kg (15,586 lb)
Max fuel	2,659 kg (5,862 lb)
Max payload	3,470 kg (7,650 lb)
Max T-O weight	11,500 kg (25,353 lb)
Max ramp weight	11,580 kg (25,529 lb)
Max landing weight	11,250 kg (24,802 lb)
Max zero-fuel weight	10,500 kg (23,148 lb)
Max wing loading	292 kg/m² (59.8 lb/sq ft)
Max power loading	4.29 kg/kW (7.04 lb/shp)

PERFORMANCE (at max T-O weight, ISA, except where indicated):

Max operating speed
272 knots (504 km/h; 313 mph) EAS

Max level speed at 6,100 m (20,000 ft)
328 knots (608 km/h; 378 mph)

Max cruising speed at 6,100 m (20,000 ft)
298 knots (552 km/h; 343 mph)

Long-range cruising speed at 7,620 m (25,000 ft)
260 knots (482 km/h; 299 mph)

Stalling speed, power off:
flaps up 117 knots (217 km/h; 135 mph) CAS
flaps down 87 knots (162 km/h; 100 mph) CAS

Max rate of climb at S/L 646 m (2,120 ft)/min

Rate of climb at S/L, one engine out 206 m (675 ft)/min

Service ceiling 9,085 m (29,800 ft)

Service ceiling, one engine out 5,240 m (17,200 ft)

FAR Pt 25 T-O field length 1,420 m (4,660 ft)

FAR Pt 135 landing field length, max landing weight at S/L 1,370 m (4,495 ft)

Min ground turning radius 15.76 m (51 ft 8½ in)

Range at 7,620 m (25,000 ft), reserves for 100 nm (185 km; 115 mile) diversion and 45 min hold:
with max (30) passenger payload (2,721 kg; 6,000 lb)
945 nm (1,750 km; 1,088 miles)
with max fuel and 1,920 kg (4,233 lb) payload (21 passengers) 1,610 nm (2,983 km; 1,854 miles)

OPERATIONAL NOISE LEVELS (FAR Pt 36, BCAR-N and ICAO Annex 16):

T-O	78.6 EPNdB
Approach	89.1 EPNdB
Sideline	76.8 EPNdB

EMBRAER/FAMA CBA-123

Details of this twin-turboprop airliner, which is being developed jointly by Embraer and FAMA of Argentina, can be found in the International section.

EMBRAER EMB-312 TUCANO (TOUCAN)
Brazilian Air Force designation: T-27

Design of the EMB-312, by a team under the leadership of Ing Joseph Kovacs, began in January 1978 as part of a programme to develop a new basic trainer for the Brazilian Air Force. On 6 December that year a contract was received from the Departamento de Pesquisas e Desenvolvimento (Department of Research and Development) of the Brazilian Ministry of Aeronautics, for two flying prototypes plus two other airframes for static and fatigue testing.

Characteristics of the EMB-312 include high manoeuvrability, short take-off and landing, the ability to operate from unprepared runways, and a high degree of stability. In addition to meeting the requirements of FAR Pt 23 Appendix A, the aircraft meets MIL and CAA Section K specifications. Its construction embodies such modern techniques as integral numerical control machining, chemical milling, and metal to metal bonding.

The first prototype (Brazilian Air Force serial number 1300) made its initial flight on 16 August 1980, and the second (1301) on 10 December 1980. A third prototype (PP-ZDK), embodying the modifications intended for production Tucanos, flew on 16 August 1982.

The EMB-312 is designated T-27 by the Brazilian Air Force, which in September 1986 received the last of 118 on order as replacements for the Cessna T-37C. Deliveries began on 29 September 1983, with the first six Tucanos going to the Esquadrilha da Fumaça (Smoke Squadron), the aerobatic team of the Brazilian Air Force, and two to the Air Force Academy. The FAB has options on a further 50 Tucanos.

The Egyptian government ordered 120 Tucanos: 40 for its own air force and 80 for Iraq, with options on 60 more, of which 20 would be for Iraq. Embraer built the first ten of these aircraft, which were ferried to Egypt in flyaway condition in 1984. Kits for the remaining 110 had been delivered by the end of 1987 to AOI in Egypt (which see), which is completing these aircraft under licence. By 1 January 1988 deliveries had also been made to the air forces of Argentina (21, of 30 on firm order), Honduras (12), Paraguay (six), Peru (20) and Venezuela (30). Tucano deliveries then totalled 349 out of 467 firm orders; options were held for a further 125. Production rate was four to five per month in 1987.

The version selected for the Royal Air Force (130), with British equipment and a more powerful 820 kW (1,100 shp) Garrett TPE331 engine, is being built by Short Brothers and is described under that company's entry in the UK section. The first Garrett engined prototype (PP-ZTC) made its first of six flights in Brazil on 14 February 1986. It was then dismantled and airfreighted to the UK for continued testing.

The following description applies to the standard Embraer version.

TYPE: Tandem two-seat basic trainer.

WINGS: Cantilever low-wing monoplane. Wing section NACA 63₂A-415 at root, NACA 63A-212 at tip. Dihedral 5° 30′ at 30% chord. Incidence 1° 25′. Geometric twist 2° 13′. Sweepback 0° 43′ 26″ at quarter-chord. Aluminium alloy two-spar torsion box structure of 2024-T3511 extrusions and 2024-T3 sheet. Single-slotted electrically actuated trailing-edge flaps of 2024-T3, supported on 4130 steel tracks. Frise constant chord balanced ailerons. Electromechanically actuated aileron trim.

FUSELAGE: Conventional semi-monocoque structure of 2024-T3 aluminium alloy.

TAIL UNIT: Cantilever all-metal structure, of similar construction to wings. Non-swept fin, with dorsal fin, and horn balanced rudder. Non-swept fixed incidence tailplane and balanced elevators. Small fillet forward of tailplane root on each side. Electromechanically actuated spring trim in rudder and port elevator.

LANDING GEAR: Hydraulically retractable tricycle type, with single wheel and Piper oleo-pneumatic shock absorber on each unit. Accumulator for emergency extension in the

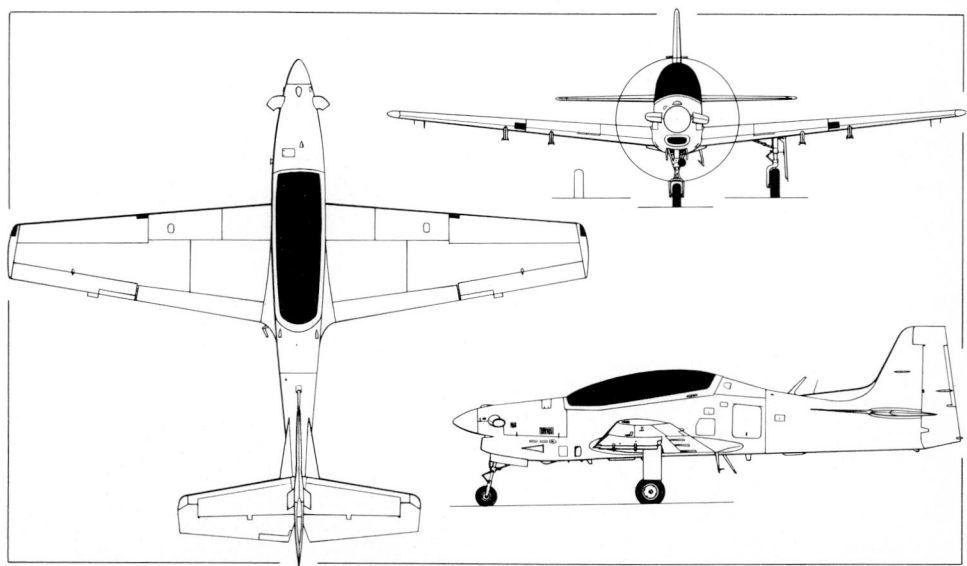

Embraer EMB-312 Tucano basic trainer (Pratt & Whitney Canada PT6A-25C turboprop) *(Pilot Press)*

Three of the six EMB-312 Tucano tandem two-seat trainers ordered by the Paraguayan Air Force

event of hydraulic system failure. Shimmy damper on nose unit. Rearward retracting steerable nose unit; main units retract inward into wings. Parker Hannifin 40-130 mainwheels, Oldi-DI-1.555-02-OL nosewheel. Tyre sizes 6.50-10 (Type III, 8-ply rating) on mainwheels, 5.00-5 (Type III, 6-ply rating) on nosewheel. Tyre pressures (plus or minus 0.21 bars; 3 lb/sq in in each case) are 5.17 bars (75 lb/sq in) on mainwheels, 4.48 bars (65 lb/sq in) on nosewheel. Parker Hannifin 30-95A hydraulic mainwheel brakes.

POWER PLANT: One 559 kW (750 shp) Pratt & Whitney Canada PT6A-25C turboprop, driving a Hartzell HC-B3TN-3C/T10178-8R three-blade constant-speed fully-feathering reversible-pitch propeller with spinner. Single-lever combined control for engine throttling and propeller pitch adjustment. Two integral fuel tanks in each wing, total capacity 694 litres (183.3 US gallons; 152.7 Imp gallons). Fuel tanks lined with anti-detonation plastics foam. Gravity refuelling point in each wing upper surface. Fuel system allows nominally for up to 30 s of inverted flight. (Aircraft was flown inverted for up to 10 min during testing.) Provision for two underwing ferry fuel tanks, total capacity 660 litres (174.4 US gallons; 145 Imp gallons).

ACCOMMODATION: Instructor and pupil in tandem, on Martin-Baker BR8LC lightweight ejection seats, in air-conditioned cockpit. One-piece fully transparent vacuum formed canopy, opening sideways to starboard, with internal and external jettison provisions. Rear seat elevated. Dual controls standard. Baggage compartment in rear fuselage, with access via door on port side. Cockpit heating and canopy demisting by engine bleed air.

SYSTEMS: Freon cycle air-conditioning system, with engine driven compressor. Single hydraulic system, consisting basically of (a) control unit, including reservoir with usable capacity of 1.9 litres (0.5 US gallon; 0.42 Imp gallon); (b) an engine driven pump with nominal pressure of 131 bars (1,900 lb/sq in) and nominal flow rate of 4.6 litres (1.22 US gallons; 1.01 Imp gallons)/min at 3,800 rpm; (c) landing gear and gear door actuators; (d) filter; (e) shutoff valve; and (f) hydraulic fluid to MIL-H-5606. Under normal operation, hydraulic system actuates landing gear extension/retraction and control of gear doors. Landing gear extension can be performed under emergency operation; emergency retraction may also be possible during landing and T-O with engine running. Reservoir and system are suitable for aerobatics. No pneumatic system. 28V DC electrical power provided by a 6kW starter/generator, 26Ah battery and, for 115V and 26V AC power at 400Hz, a 250VA inverter. Diluter-demand oxygen system conforms to MIL-C-5887 and is supplied individually to each occupant by six MS 21227 D2 type cylinders (total capacity approx 1,200 litres; 317 US gallons; 264 Imp gallons) at a pressure of 31 bars (450 lb/sq in).

AVIONICS AND EQUIPMENT: Standard avionics include two Collins VHF-20A transceivers; two Collins 387C-4 audio systems, one Embraer radio transferring system; Telephonics audio control panel; one Collins VIR-31A VOR/ILS/marker beacon receiver; one Collins TDR-90 ATC transponder; one Collins DME-40; one Collins PN-101 gyromagnetic compass; and one Collins ADF-60A. Landing light in each wing leading-edge; taxying lights on nosewheel unit.

ARMAMENT: Two hardpoints under each wing, each stressed for a max load of 250 kg (551 lb). Typical loads, on GB100-20-36B pylons, include two 0.30 in C2 machine-gun pods, each with 500 rds; four 25 lb Mk 76 practice bombs; four 250 lb Mk 81 general purpose bombs; or four LM-37/7A or LM-70/7 launchers, each

with seven rockets (Avibras SBAT-37 and SBAT-70 respectively). Fixed reflex-type gunsight.

DIMENSIONS, EXTERNAL:
Wing span	11.14 m (36 ft 6½ in)
Wing chord: at root	2.30 m (7 ft 6½ in)
at tip	1.07 m (3 ft 6⅛ in)
Wing aspect ratio	6.4
Length overall	9.86 m (32 ft 4¼ in)
Length of fuselage (excl rudder)	8.53 m (27 ft 11⅞ in)
Fuselage: Max width	1.00 m (3 ft 3¼ in)
Max depth	1.55 m (5 ft 1 in)
Height overall (static)	3.40 m (11 ft 1¾ in)
Tailplane span	4.66 m (15 ft 3½ in)
Wheel track	3.76 m (12 ft 4 in)
Wheelbase	3.16 m (10 ft 4½ in)
Propeller diameter	2.36 m (7 ft 9 in)
Propeller ground clearance (static)	0.33 m (1 ft 1 in)
Baggage compartment door:	
Height	0.60 m (1 ft 11⅝ in)
Width	0.54 m (1 ft 9¼ in)
Height to sill	1.25 m (4 ft 1¼ in)

DIMENSIONS, INTERNAL:
Cockpits: Combined length	2.90 m (9 ft 6⅛ in)
Max height	1.55 m (5 ft 1 in)
Max width	0.85 m (2 ft 9½ in)
Baggage compartment volume	0.17 m³ (6.0 cu ft)

AREAS:
Wings, gross	19.40 m² (208.82 sq ft)
Ailerons (total)	1.97 m² (21.20 sq ft)
Trailing-edge flaps (total)	2.58 m² (27.77 sq ft)
Fin, incl dorsal fin	2.29 m² (24.65 sq ft)
Rudder, incl tab	1.38 m² (14.85 sq ft)
Tailplane, incl fillets	4.77 m² (51.34 sq ft)
Elevators, incl tab	2.00 m² (21.53 sq ft)

WEIGHTS AND LOADINGS:
Basic weight empty	1,810 kg (3,991 lb)
Max internal fuel load (usable)	529 kg (1,166 lb)
Max external stores load	1,000 kg (2,205 lb)
Max T-O weight: 'clean'	2,550 kg (5,622 lb)
with external load	3,175 kg (7,000 lb)
Max ramp weight	3,195 kg (7,044 lb)
Max landing weight: 'clean'	2,800 kg (6,173 lb)
Max zero-fuel weight	2,050 kg (4,519 lb)

Max wing loading: 'clean'	131.4 kg/m² (26.92 lb/sq ft)
with external stores	163.7 kg/m² (33.52 lb/sq ft)
Max power loading: 'clean'	4.56 kg/kW (7.50 lb/shp)
with external stores	5.68 kg/kW (9.33 lb/shp)

PERFORMANCE (at max 'clean' T-O weight except where indicated):
Never-exceed speed	280 knots (519 km/h; 322 mph) EAS
Max level speed at 3,050 m (10,000 ft)	242 knots (448 km/h; 278 mph)
Max cruising speed at 3,050 m (10,000 ft)	222 knots (411 km/h; 255 mph)
Econ cruising speed at 3,050 m (10,000 ft)	172 knots (319 km/h; 198 mph)
Stalling speed, power off:	
flaps and landing gear up	72 knots (133 km/h; 83 mph) EAS
flaps and landing gear down	67 knots (124 km/h; 77 mph) EAS
Max rate of climb at S/L	680 m (2,231 ft)/min
Service ceiling	9,150 m (30,000 ft)
T-O run	380 m (1,250 ft)
T-O to 15 m (50 ft)	710 m (2,330 ft)
Landing from 15 m (50 ft)	605 m (1,985 ft)
Landing run	370 m (1,214 ft)
Range at 6,100 m (20,000 ft) with max fuel, 30 min reserves	995 nm (1,844 km; 1,145 miles)
Ferry range at 6,100 m (20,000 ft) with underwing tanks	1,797 nm (3,330 km; 2,069 miles)
Endurance on internal fuel at econ cruising speed at 6,100 m (20,000 ft), 30 min reserves	approx 5 h
g limits: fully Aerobatic category, at max 'clean' T-O weight	+6/-3
at max T-O weight with external stores	+4.4/-2.2

EMBRAER EMB-201A IPANEMA

The original version of this agricultural aircraft was designed to Brazilian Ministry of Agriculture specifications, and the EMB-200 prototype (PP-ZIP) made its first flight on 30 July 1970. A type certificate was granted on 14 December 1971.

Details of the EMB-200/200A (73 built), EMB-201 (200 built) and EMB-201R (three built) can be found in the 1977-78 and previous editions of *Jane's*. The current production version, first flown on 10 March 1977, is the EMB-201A, of which 324 had been sold by December 1987, bringing total Ipanema sales (all versions) to 600. Delivery of the 600th aircraft took place on 23 March 1988.

Manufacture of the EMB-201A was transferred to Embraer's Neiva subsidiary during the second half of 1981.

TYPE: Single-seat agricultural aircraft.

WINGS: Cantilever low-wing monoplane. Wing section NACA 23015 (modified), with cambered leading-edges. Dihedral 7° from roots. Incidence 3°. All-metal single-spar structure of 2024 aluminium alloy with all-metal Frise ailerons outboard and all-metal slotted flaps on trailing-edge, and detachable cambered leading-edges. No tabs. Cambered wingtips standard.

FUSELAGE: Rectangular section all-metal safe-life structure, of welded 4130 steel tube with removable skin panels of 2024 aluminium alloy. Structure is specially treated against chemical corrosion.

TAIL UNIT: Cantilever two-spar all-metal structure of 2024 aluminium alloy. Slight sweepback on fin and rudder. Fixed incidence tailplane. Trim tab in starboard elevator.

LANDING GEAR: Non-retractable main- and tailwheels, with oleo shock absorbers in main units. Tailwheel has tapered spring shock absorber. Mainwheels and tyres size 8.50-10. Tailwheel diameter 250 mm (10 in). Tyre pressures: main, 2.07-2.41 bars (30-35 lb/sq in); tailwheel, 3.79 bars (55 lb/sq in). Hydraulic disc brakes on mainwheels.

POWER PLANT: One 224 kW (300 hp) Textron Lycoming IO-540-K1J5D flat-six engine, driving a Hartzell two-blade constant-speed metal propeller with spinner.

Embraer Ipanema agricultural aircraft in cropdusting configuration

Integral fuel tanks in each wing leading-edge, with total capacity of 292 litres (77.1 US gallons; 64.2 Imp gallons). Refuelling point on top of each tank. Oil capacity 12 litres (3.2 US gallons; 2.6 Imp gallons).

ACCOMMODATION: Single horizontally/vertically adjustable seat in fully enclosed cabin with bottom-hinged window/door on each side. Ventilation system in cabin. Inertial shoulder harness standard.

SYSTEM: 28V DC electrical system supplied by a 24Ah BB639/U battery and a Bosch K.1 28V 35A alternator. Power receptacle for external battery (AN-2552-3A type) on port side of forward fuselage.

AVIONICS AND EQUIPMENT: Standard VFR avionics include 720-channel Collins VHF-251S transceiver and Collins RCR-650 ADF transceiver. Hopper for agricultural chemicals has capacity of 680 litres (179.6 US gallons; 149.5 Imp gallons) liquid or 750 kg (1,653 lb) dry. Dusting system below centre of fuselage. Spraybooms or Micronair atomisers aft of or above wing trailing-edges respectively.

DIMENSIONS, EXTERNAL:

Wing span	11.20 m (36 ft 9 in)
Wing chord (constant)	1.71 m (5 ft 7½ in)
Wing aspect ratio	6.3
Length overall (tail up)	7.43 m (24 ft 4½ in)
Height overall (tail down)	2.20 m (7 ft 2½ in)
Fuselage: Max width	0.93 m (3 ft 0½ in)
Tailplane span	3.66 m (12 ft 0 in)
Wheel track	2.20 m (7 ft 2½ in)
Wheelbase	5.20 m (17 ft 7¼ in)
Propeller diameter	2.20 m (7 ft 2½ in)

DIMENSIONS, INTERNAL:

Cockpit: Max length	1.20 m (3 ft 11¼ in)
Max width	0.85 m (2 ft 9½ in)
Max height	1.34 m (4 ft 4¾ in)

AREAS:

Wings, gross	19.94 m² (214.63 sq ft)
Ailerons (total)	1.60 m² (17.22 sq ft)
Trailing-edge flaps (total)	2.30 m² (24.76 sq ft)
Fin	0.58 m² (6.24 sq ft)
Rudder	0.63 m² (6.78 sq ft)
Tailplane	3.17 m² (34.12 sq ft)
Elevators (total, incl tab)	1.50 m² (16.15 sq ft)

WEIGHTS AND LOADINGS (N: Normal; R: Restricted category):

Weight empty: N, R	1,011 kg (2,229 lb)
Max payload: N, R	750 kg (1,653 lb)
Max T-O and landing weight: N	1,550 kg (3,417 lb)
R	1,800 kg (3,968 lb)
Max wing loading: N	77.75 kg/m² (15.92 lb/sq ft)
R	90.29 kg/m² (18.49 lb/sq ft)

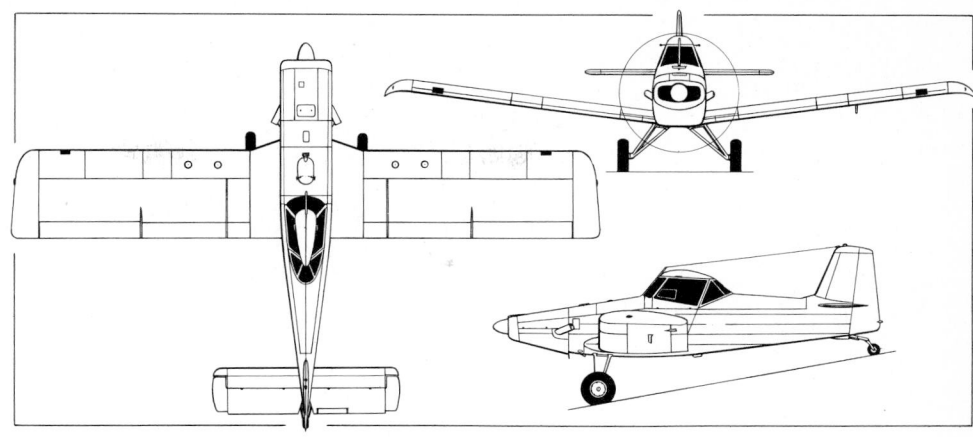

Embraer EMB-201A Ipanema single-seat agricultural aircraft *(Pilot Press)*

Max power loading: N	6.92 kg/kW (11.39 lb/hp)	
R	8.03 kg/kW (13.23 lb/hp)	

PERFORMANCE (at max T-O weight, 'clean' configuration, ISA):

Never-exceed speed:	
N	147 knots (272 km/h; 169 mph)
R	113 knots (209 km/h; 130 mph)
Max level speed at S/L:	
N	124 knots (230 km/h; 143 mph)
R	121 knots (225 km/h; 140 mph)
Max cruising speed (75% power) at 1,830 m (6,000 ft):	
N	115 knots (212 km/h; 132 mph)
R	110 knots (204 km/h; 127 mph)
Stalling speed, power off (N):	
flaps up	56 knots (103 km/h; 64 mph)
8° flap	54 knots (100 km/h; 62 mph)
30° flap	50 knots (92 km/h; 57 mph)
Stalling speed, power off (R):	
flaps up	60 knots (110 km/h; 68 mph)
8° flap	58 knots (107 km/h; 66 mph)
30° flap	53 knots (99 km/h; 61 mph)
Max rate of climb at S/L, 8° flap:	
N	283 m (930 ft)/min
R	201 m (660 ft)/min
Service ceiling, 8° flap: R	3,470 m (11,385 ft)
T-O run at S/L, 8° flap, asphalt runway:	
N	200 m (656 ft)
R	354 m (1,160 ft)

T-O to 15 m (50 ft), conditions as above:	
N	333 m (1,093 ft)
R	564 m (1,850 ft)
Landing from 15 m (50 ft) at S/L, 30° flap, asphalt runway: N	440 m (1,444 ft)
R	500 m (1,640 ft)
Landing run, conditions as above: N	153 m (502 ft)
R	170 m (558 ft)
Range at 1,830 m (6,000 ft), no reserves:	
N	506 nm (938 km; 583 miles)
R	474 nm (878 km; 545 miles)

EMBRAER-PIPER LIGHT AIRCRAFT PROGRAMME

Detailed descriptions of Piper aircraft built under licence by Embraer can be found in the US section of this and earlier editions of *Jane's*. Manufacture is undertaken by Embraer's subsidiary, Neiva. The following types were in production in 1988:

EMB-711ST Corisco Turbo. Piper PA-28RT-201T Turbo Arrow IV.

EMB-712 Tupi. Piper PA-28-181 Archer II.

EMB-720D Minuano. Piper PA-32-301 Saratoga.

EMB-810D Seneca III. Piper PA-34-220T Seneca III.

EMB-820C Navajo. Piper PA-31-350 Navajo Chieftain. Production phased out, but available aircraft are being converted to Schafer Comanchero 500B turboprop powered form, as the Neiva **NE-821 Carajá** (which see).

HELIBRAS
HELICÓPTEROS DO BRASIL S/A

Rua Projetada Um 200, Distrito Industrial, Caixa Postal 184, 37500 Itajubá, MG
Telephone: (35) 622 3366 and 622 2455
Telex: 031 2602 HLBR BR
PRESIDENT: Sérgio Murta Machado
COMMERCIAL ASST DIRECTOR: Lionel Albert Jean Paulhiac
PUBLIC RELATIONS: Mônica David

Formed in 1978 and owned jointly by Aérospatiale of France (45%) and (until 1987) the state government of Minas Gerais (55%), Helibras is engaged in the assembly (graduating to local manufacture) of Aérospatiale SA 315B Lama and AS 350B and B₁ Ecureuil single-engined helicopters, and the twin-engined AS 355F₂ Ecureuil. Of the total assembly hours per helicopter, approx 30 per cent involve the incorporation of locally manufactured items. The first assembly hall was officially inaugurated on 28 March 1980. The complete facility will extend over an area of 210,000 m² (2,260,420 sq ft), of which 9,000 m² (96,875 sq ft) is covered at present, with plans to extend this to 18,000 m² (193,750 sq ft) and increase the workforce accordingly. A total of 350 people was employed in 1987. During that year the Minas Gerais government gave up its holding in Helibras; the new major shareholder is the Brazilian armoured vehicle manufacturer Engesa.

It was announced in February 1988 that the Helibras/Aérospatiale/Engesa submission had won a Brazilian Army competition for 52 troop transport and reconnaissance/attack helicopters to form initial equipment of three new airmobile battalions. These will comprise 16 Esquilos and 36 SA 365K Dauphins, with some five per cent of Dauphin fabrication being undertaken by Helibras. Formal contract signing was completed on 24 June 1988, enabling the Esquilo deliveries to begin in the first quarter of 1989.

HELIBRAS HB 315B GAVIÃO

These are the Brazilian name and designation of the SA 315B Lama assembled by Helibras, the first of which was completed during the latter half of 1979. Production by early 1988 included seven for the Bolivian Air Force and one civil example for a customer in Chile.

HELIBRAS HB 350B, HB 350B1, HB 350L1 and HB 355F2 ESQUILO

All Brazilian models of the Ecureuil have the name Esquilo, the HB 350B and B1 corresponding to the French single-engined AS 350B and B₁ and the HB 355F2 to the twin-engined AS 355F₂. Deliveries began in 1979, and by early 1988 totalled more than 100 single-engined Esquilos

and six of the twin-engined version. These included 19 HB 350B/B1s and three HB 355F2s for the Brazilian Air Force (designations **CH-50**, **TH-50**, **CH-55** and **VH-55**), 19 for the Brazilian Navy (designation **UH-12**), and 56, including three HB 355F2s, for the Brazilian police and civilian customers. The Brazilian Navy Esquilos, which serve with the 1° Esquadrão de Helicópteros de Emprego General (squadron of general purpose helicopters), are equipped to carry two Avibrás LM-70/7 pods each containing seven SBAT 70 mm rockets, an FN twin 7.62 mm MAG machine-gun pod, and a door mounted MAG pedestal. Eight HB 350Bs have been sold to foreign civil customers in Argentina (one), Bolivia (four) and Venezuela (three), and five military examples to Paraguay (Air Force three, Navy two).

An aeromedical version of the Esquilo was launched in February 1984. Equipment includes an electrocardiograph, respirator, pacemaker, stretchers, battery operated incubator, oxygen and compressed air cylinders, first aid kit, and a four-way electrical socket for 115V AC (60Hz) and 12V DC power. Apart from the pilot, this version can carry a doctor, nurse and two stretcher patients.

As noted in the introductory copy, 16 of the Brazilian Army order for 52 helicopters will be Esquilos. These, known as HB 350L1s, are expected to be equipped with a 20 mm gun, anti-tank missiles and 2.75 in unguided rockets.

Left: An HB 350B Esquilo of the Paraguayan Air Force. Helibras production also includes the twin-engined HB 355F2 Esquilo, illustrated on the right, which has the FAB designation VH-55

IPE

INDÚSTRIA PARANAENSE DE ESTRUTURAS

Caixa Postal 7931, Rua J. Durski 357, 80.000 Curitiba, Paraná State

MANAGER: Eng J. C. Boscardin

Best known for its range of gliders (see Sailplanes section), the IPE is also developing a small training aircraft known as the IPE 04.

IPE 04

The IPE 04 is a two-seat training aircraft of wooden construction, development of which has been approved by the Brazilian government. Its appearance is illustrated in the accompanying three-view drawing; two prototypes were under construction in 1987, with 82 kW (110 hp) and 134 kW (180 hp) engine respectively.

DIMENSIONS, EXTERNAL:

Wing span	8.00 m (26 ft 3 in)
Length overall	6.80 m (22 ft 3½ in)
Height overall	2.30 m (7 ft 6½ in)

WEIGHTS (A: 110 hp, B: 180 hp):

Weight empty: A	550 kg (1,213 lb)
B	620 kg (1,367 lb)
Max T-O weight: A	920 kg (2,028 lb)
B	980 kg (2,160 lb)

PERFORMANCE (estimated):

Never-exceed speed:	
A, B	189 knots (350 km/h; 217 mph)
Max level speed: A	135 knots (250 km/h; 155 mph)

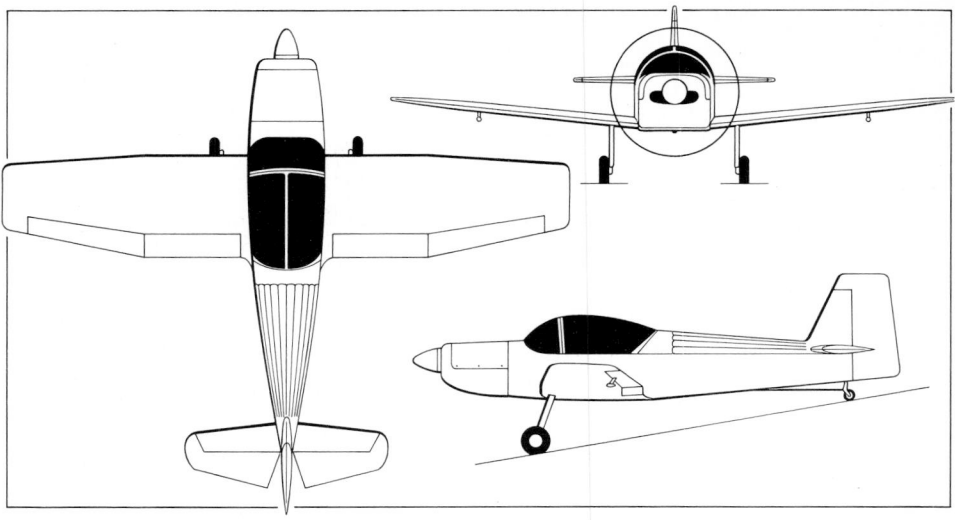

General arrangement of the IPE 04 two-seat trainer *(Jane's/Mike Keep)*

B	162 knots (300 km/h; 186 mph)
Max cruising speed: A	97 knots (180 km/h; 112 mph)
B	135 knots (250 km/h; 155 mph)
Stalling speed, flaps up: A	49 knots (90 km/h; 56 mph)

B	50 knots (92 km/h; 57 mph)
Stalling speed, flaps down:	
A	41 knots (75 km/h; 47 mph)
B	42 knots (78 km/h; 49 mph)

NEIVA

INDÚSTRIA AERONÁUTICA NEIVA S/A (Subsidiary of Embraer)

Rua Nossa Senhora de Fátima 360, Vila Antártica, Caixa Postal 10, 18600 Botucatu, SP

Telephone: (149) 22 1010

Telex: 0142 423 SOAN BR

PRESIDENT: Eng Antonio Garcia da Silveira

ENGINEERING MANAGER: Luíz Carlos Benetti

Neiva, which has a workforce of 516 and factory area of 23,515 m² (253,120 sq ft), was formed in 1954 and became a wholly owned subsidiary of Embraer on 10 March 1980. It participates in Embraer's general aviation programme,

being responsible for all production of the EMB-711ST Corisco Turbo, EMB-712 Tupi, EMB-720D Minuano and EMB-810D Seneca III. For many years Neiva has built fuselages for the Embraer Ipanema, and since 1981 has been entirely responsible for Ipanema engineering, manufacture and assembly. The 597th Ipanema, completed in November 1987, was the 2,000th aircraft to be produced at the Neiva facility. The company also produces subassemblies for the Embraer Tucano.

NEIVA NE-821 CARAJÁ

Responsibility for the EMB-820C was transferred to Neiva in mid-1983, and in 1984 four of the last five Embraer

assembled examples were converted to Comanchero 500B eight-seat executive configuration (see Schafer entry in US section), in which form they are designated NE-821 Carajá. The first Carajá made its initial flight on 9 March 1984, and deliveries began in November of that year. A total of 23 had been delivered by 1 January 1988. Brazilian certification covers the use of either PT6A-27 or PT6A-34 engines, flat rated in both cases at 410 kW (550 shp) and driving Hartzell three-blade constant-speed propellers with reverse pitch and automatic synchronisation. The most recent examples have been delivered with the -34 power plant. Usable fuel capacity is 1,314 litres (347 US gallons; 289 Imp gallons).

WEIGHTS:

Weight empty, equipped	2,300 kg (5,070 lb)
Max payload	784 kg (1,728 lb)
Max T-O weight	3,629 kg (8,000 lb)
Max ramp weight	3,651 kg (8,050 lb)
Max landing weight	3,447 kg (7,600 lb)
Max zero-fuel weight	3,084 kg (6,800 lb)

PERFORMANCE:

Max cruising speed at 3,050 m (10,000 ft), max T-O weight, ISA	232 knots (430 km/h; 267 mph)
Normal cruising speed	221 knots (410 km/h; 255 mph)
Econ cruising speed	174 knots (323 km/h; 200 mph)
Stalling speed	80 knots (148 km/h; 92 mph)
Max rate of climb at S/L	740 m (2,425 ft)/min
Rate of climb at S/L, one engine out	170 m (560 ft)/min
Max operating altitude	7,315 m (24,000 ft)
Service ceiling, one engine out	5,335 m (17,500 ft)
T-O to 15 m (50 ft)	540 m (1,772 ft)
Landing from 15 m (50 ft)	563 m (1,847 ft)
Max range, 45 min reserves	945 nm (1,750 km; 1,087 miles)

NE-821 Carajá, a Schafer Comanchero 500B built under licence by Neiva

---

SUPER ROTOR

M.M. SUPER ROTOR INDÚSTRIA AERONÁUTICA LTDA

Rua Itapeti 541, Tatuapé, 03324 São Paulo, SP

Telephone: (11) 295 8187

DIRECTOR: José Montalvá Perez

SUPER ROTOR AC-4 ANDORINHA

This all-Brazilian single-seat autogyro was designed in 1970, as a private venture, by Eng Altair Coelho. The prototype first flew in December 1972, being sold subsequently to Sr Francisco Mattos Jr, who introduced a number of modifications before obtaining Brazilian CTA certification in January 1985. It is produced in both ready to fly and kit forms. By early 1988 domestic and foreign orders for the AC-4, including kits, totalled 291.

TYPE: Single-seat autogyro.

ROTOR SYSTEM AND DRIVE: Single rotor, with two blades of NACA H-12 (modified) section, each attached to hub by ten bolts. Aluminium alloy blades (6061-T6 spars and 0.8 mm sheet skins), each with tab inset from tip. No blade folding or rotor brake. Engine power take-off for pre-spinning rotor before T-O.

FUSELAGE: Welded truss structure of SAE 1025 carbon steel tube, with nose fairing and windscreen.

TAIL UNIT: Fin and rudder only, latter with trim tab.

LANDING GEAR: Non-retractable unsprung tricycle type, with belt type mainwheel brakes and steerable nosewheel. Goodyear tyres, size 5.00-5 (main) and 3.50-5 (nose); pressure (all three tyres) 1.38 bars (20 lb/sq in). Streamline fairing on nosewheel.

POWER PLANT: One 63 kW (85 hp) modified VW 1600 motorcar engine, driving a two-blade wooden pusher propeller. Single aluminium fuel tank beneath engine, capacity 40 litres (10.5 US gallons; 8.8 Imp gallons). Oil capacity 3 litres (0.8 US gallon; 0.66 Imp gallon).

ACCOMMODATION: Single open seat for pilot.

EQUIPMENT: 7.5Ah battery.

DIMENSIONS, EXTERNAL:

Main rotor diameter	7.44 m (24 ft 5 in)
Main rotor blade chord	0.185 m (7.3 in)
Length overall, incl rotors	3.75 m (12 ft 3¾ in)
Height to top of rotor head	2.36 m (7 ft 9 in)
Width overall, excl main rotor	1.70 m (5 ft 7 in)
Wheel track	1.446 m (4 ft 9 in)
Propeller diameter	1.51 m (4 ft 11½ in)

AREAS:

Main rotor blades, each	0.63 m² (6.78 sq ft)
Main rotor disc	43.47 m² (467.9 sq ft)
Fin	0.21 m² (2.26 sq ft)
Rudder	0.36 m² (3.88 sq ft)

WEIGHTS AND LOADINGS:

Basic weight empty	190 kg (419 lb)
Max T-O weight	310 kg (683 lb)
Max disc loading	7.13 kg/m² (1.46 lb/sq ft)
Max power loading	4.92 kg/kW (8.04 lb/hp)

PERFORMANCE (at max T-O weight):

Never-exceed speed	97 knots (180 km/h; 112 mph)
Max level speed	86 knots (160 km/h; 99 mph)
Max cruising speed	70 knots (130 km/h; 81 mph)
Econ cruising speed	59 knots (110 km/h; 68 mph)
Max rate of climb at S/L	366 m (1,200 ft)/min

Service ceiling	3,660 m (12,000 ft)
T-O run	35 m (115 ft)
T-O to 15 m (50 ft)	100 m (328 ft)
Landing from 15 m (50 ft)	30 m (99 ft)
Landing run	10 m (33 ft)
Range with max fuel	243 nm (450 km; 280 miles)

SUPER ROTOR M-1 MONTALVÁ

Design of this two-seat development of the AC-4 started in June 1984, and it flew for the first time in March 1985. Production aircraft became available in the Summer of that year, and 50 (of which 41 had been ordered) had been completed by early 1988.

TYPE: Tandem two-seat autogyro.

ROTOR SYSTEM AND DRIVE: As described for AC-4, but rotor is of increased diameter.

AIRFRAME: As described for AC-4, except for longer fuselage and increased mainwheel tyre pressure of 1.72 bars (25 lb/sq in).

POWER PLANT: One 72 kW (97 hp) modified VW 1600 engine and 27 litre (7 US gallon; 6 Imp gallon) fuel tank; otherwise as described for AC-4.

ACCOMMODATION: Two open seats in tandem.

EQUIPMENT: 7.5Ah battery.

DIMENSIONS, EXTERNAL:

Main rotor diameter	8.14 m (26 ft 8½ in)
Main rotor blade chord	0.21 m (8¼ in)
Length overall, excl rotors	4.38 m (14 ft 4½ in)
Height to top of rotor head	2.68 m (8 ft 9½ in)
Width overall, excl main rotor	1.70 m (5 ft 7 in)

Wheel track	1.90 m (6 ft 3 in)
Propeller diameter	1.51 m (4 ft 11½ in)

AREAS:

Main rotor blades, each	0.77 m² (8.29 sq ft)
Main rotor disc	52.04 m² (560.2 sq ft)
Fin	0.21 m² (2.26 sq ft)
Rudder	0.36 m² (3.88 sq ft)

WEIGHTS AND LOADINGS:

Basic weight empty	194 kg (428 lb)
Max T-O weight	374 kg (825 lb)
Max disc loading	7.19 kg/m² (1.47 lb/sq ft)
Max power loading	5.19 kg/kW (8.50 lb/hp)

PERFORMANCE (at max T-O weight):

Never-exceed speed	97 knots (180 km/h; 112 mph)
Max level speed	75 knots (140 km/h; 87 mph)
Max cruising speed	65 knots (120 km/h; 75 mph)
Econ cruising speed	54 knots (100 km/h; 62 mph)
Max rate of climb at S/L	213 m (700 ft)/min
Service ceiling	3,660 m (12,000 ft)
T-O run	160 m (525 ft)
T-O to 15 m (50 ft)	250 m (820 ft)
Landing from 15 m (50 ft)	30 m (99 ft)
Landing run	10 m (33 ft)
Range with max fuel	118 nm (220 km; 136 miles)

Super Rotor M-1 Montalvá 1 two-seat autogyro

CANADA

AIRTECH
AIRTECH CANADA
Peterborough Municipal Airport, PO Box 415,
    Peterborough, Ontario K9J 6Z3
Telephone: (705) 743 9483
Telex: 06-962912
Fax: (705) 749 0841
PRESIDENT: John O'Dwyer
CHIEF ENGINEER: James C. Mewett
PRESS RELATIONS: Alison M. Mewett

Airtech specialises in retrofitting versions of the de Havilland Canada Otter and Beaver with more powerful Polish built engines that offer increased climb rates and considerably greater fuel economy, at lower power settings, than the original engines which they replace. It has also refitted a former Spanish Air Force C-47/DC-3 with ASz-62IR engines and Polish propellers in place of the original Pratt & Whitney R-1830s.

In 1986 Airtech flew a prototype of the Turbo Orlik trainer, further details of which can be found under the WSK-PZL Warszawa-Okecie heading in the Polish section.

AIRTECH CANADA DHC-3/1000 OTTER
Airtech Canada refitted eight de Havilland Canada DHC-3 Otters with Polish PZL-3S radial engines. Details of this DHC-3/PZL-3S version can be found in the 1983-84 *Jane's.*

Following the first flight of a prototype on 25 August 1983, the Otter conversion is now offered with a 746 kW (1,000 hp) Polish ASz-62IR engine instead of the 447 kW (600 hp) PZL-3S. Six of these conversions, designated DHC-3/1000, were flying in North and South America by February 1988, with a seventh being converted.

POWER PLANT: One 746 kW (1,000 hp) PZL Kalisz ASz-62IR nine-cylinder aircooled radial engine, driving a PZL Warszawa AW-2-30 four-blade constant-speed propeller.

Airtech Canada's DHC-3/1000 Otter conversion, powered by a PZL Kalisz ASz-62IR radial engine

Fuel capacity as for standard DHC-3; oil capacity 41 litres (10.8 US gallons; 9 Imp gallons).

WEIGHTS:

Weight empty, equipped	2,200 kg (4,850 lb)
Max T-O weight	3,628 kg (8,000 lb)

PERFORMANCE (at max T-O weight): As for standard DHC-3 except:

Never-exceed speed	157 knots (291 km/h; 181 mph)

Max level speed and max cruising speed at S/L

	125 knots (232 km/h; 144 mph)

Econ cruising speed at 1,525 m (5,000 ft)

	117 knots (217 km/h; 135 mph)

Max rate of climb at S/L:

at full rated power	552 m (1,810 ft)/min

at 602 kW (808 hp) max cruise power

	421 m (1,380 ft)/min
Service ceiling	5,945 m (19,500 ft)
T-O run	91 m (300 ft)
T-O to 15 m (50 ft)	182 m (600 ft)

Max range, allowances for 10 min warm-up, T-O, climb to 1,525 m (5,000 ft), and reserves for 45 min at cruise power   800 nm (1,482 km; 921 miles)

AIRTECH CANADA DHC-2/PZL-3S BEAVER
Airtech Canada introduced a conversion of the DHC-2 Beaver with the PZL-3S engine at the request of operators who wanted an increase in power to provide improved performance and safer operation from short airstrips. Four such conversions had been completed by February 1987, one in Canada, one in the USA and two in Peru. A fifth was due for completion in 1988.

POWER PLANT: One 447 kW (600 hp) PZL-3S seven-cylinder aircooled radial engine, driving a PZL US132000A four-blade constant-speed propeller. Fuel capacity 359 litres (95 US gallons; 79 Imp gallons), or 523 litres (138 US gallons; 115 Imp gallons) with auxiliary tank in each wingtip.

WEIGHTS:

Weight empty	1,419 kg (3,129 lb)
Useful load with full fuel	636 kg (1,402 lb)
Max T-O weight	2,313 kg (5,100 lb)

PERFORMANCE:

Normal operating speed and max cruising speed

	126 knots (233 km/h; 145 mph) IAS
Max rate of climb at S/L	488 m (1,600 ft)/min
T-O to 15 m (50 ft)	305 m (1,000 ft)

Airtech DHC-2 Beaver floatplane, converted to a Polish PZL-3S radial engine and four-blade propeller

AIRTECH CANADA DC-3/2000

In an attempt to prolong the useful life of the already long-lived DC-3, Airtech Canada successfully replaced the existing 895 kW (1,200 hp) Pratt & Whitney R-1830 engines of an ex-Spanish Air Force C-47, converted to a DC-3C, with 746 kW (1,000 hp) PZL ASz-62IR radials driving PZL AW-2 four-blade propellers modified by Airtech to provide full feathering capability. As the prototype DC-3/2000 (C-CJDM), it made its first flight on 6 March 1987. Flight testing was completed in 1987, indicating a lower single-engine climb performance than with the original engines. Airtech feels that the resultant decreased payload makes the 1,000 hp engine conversion commercially unviable, and plans to install a pair of 895 kW (1,200 hp) engines currently being developed by WSK-PZL Kalisz. Delivery of these engines, which would be externally identical to the ASz-62IR, was expected in late 1988.

Airtech believes that about 1,400 DC-3s are still flying.

AIRTECH CANADA/PZL TURBO ORLIK

The prototype Turbo Orlik (SP-RCC) is described under the PZL Warszawa-Okecie heading in the Polish section. It flew for the first time on 13 July 1986, but was lost in a crash, caused by pilot error, in January 1987. A second prototype was due to be completed by September 1988.

The re-engined DC-3/2000, which was flight tested in 1987

AVALON
AVALON AVIATION
(a Division of Powell Corporation)

5 Great North Road, Parry Sound, Ontario P2A 2N9
Telephone: (705) 378 2414

Telex: 068-75753
PRESIDENT: Frank D. Powell, QC
WORKS: Georgian Bay Airport, Parry Sound, Ontario

Powell Corporation was formed, as Georgian Bay Airways Ltd, in 1946, and has specialised subsequently in the aerial detection of forest fires and in firefighting support. In 1980 it acquired Avalon Aviation Ltd and its fleet of Canso water bombers, as part of a programme to expand its fire suppression activities.

Avalon currently operates eight Cansos, five Piper Aztecs and a Cessna Model 185 amphibian. One Canso is based at Oslo, operating under Norwegian government contract.

A description and illustration of Avalon's piston engined Canso water bomber conversion appeared in the 1982-83 *Jane's*, and Avalon delivered one of these aircraft to the US State of South Carolina in the Spring of 1987. Its proposed **Turbo-Canso**, a heavier duty water bomber with Rolls-Royce Dart turboprop engines, is still in the engineering study stage. Brief details can be found in the 1984-85 *Jane's*.

BELL
BELL HELICOPTER TEXTRON
(a Division of Textron Canada Ltd)

12800 rue de l'Avenir, St Janvier, Quebec J0N 1L0
Telephone: (514) 437 3400
PRESIDENT: James P. Schwalbe
EXECUTIVE VICE-PRESIDENT: Fred Hubbard
VICE-PRESIDENT, OPERATIONS: Jack Tarpley

On 7 October 1983 the Canadian government announced the signing of a memorandum of understanding under which Bell had been selected to establish a helicopter industry in Canada, the second largest user of helicopters outside the Soviet bloc. Construction began in 1984 of a new 34,560 m² (372,000 sq ft) facility at Mirabel, Quebec, some 32 km (20 miles) from Montreal. This plant opened in late 1985 and had a workforce of 650 people by early 1988.

US civil production of the Model 206B JetRanger and 206L LongRanger had been transferred to the Canadian factory by early 1987, and is being followed by the Model 212 (scheduled for mid-1988) and Model 412 (in January 1989). Product support for the Model 206 series is now also based in Canada.

The Model 400A/440 programme, described in the previous edition, has been suspended indefinitely.

BELL MODEL 206B JETRANGER III

In the Summer of 1977, Bell began delivery of the Model 206B JetRanger III, which subsequently replaced in production the lower-powered JetRanger II, of which 1,619 were delivered.

Power plant of the JetRanger III is the Allison 250-C20 turboshaft, installed with minimal modification of the original airframe to meet requests for higher performance under hot day/high altitude conditions. This enables Bell to offer modification kits to convert JetRanger IIs to JetRanger III standard.

Under a succession of major contracts, Beech Aircraft has produced airframes for all US built commercial and military versions of the JetRanger, the first airframe being delivered to Bell on 1 March 1968. This work, which involves manufacture of the fuselage, skid gear, tailboom, spars, stabiliser and two rear fairing assemblies, will gradually be taken over by the Canadian factory. Licence production of JetRangers is undertaken by Agusta in Italy (which see).

By January 1988, Bell and its licensees had manufactured well over 7,000 helicopters of the Model 206 series, more than 4,600 of them for commercial customers. Manufacture of the Model 206B was transferred to the Mirabel facility in 1986, the first Canadian built example being delivered on 20 December that year. About 60 JetRangers and LongRangers had been completed at Mirabel by early 1988, with combined production then at the rate of about seven aircraft a month.

TYPE: Turbine powered general purpose light helicopter.
ROTOR SYSTEM: Two-blade semi-rigid seesaw type main rotor, employing pre-coning and underslinging to ensure smooth operation. Blades are of standard Bell 'droop snoot' section. They have a D-shape aluminium spar, bonded aluminium alloy skin, honeycomb core and a

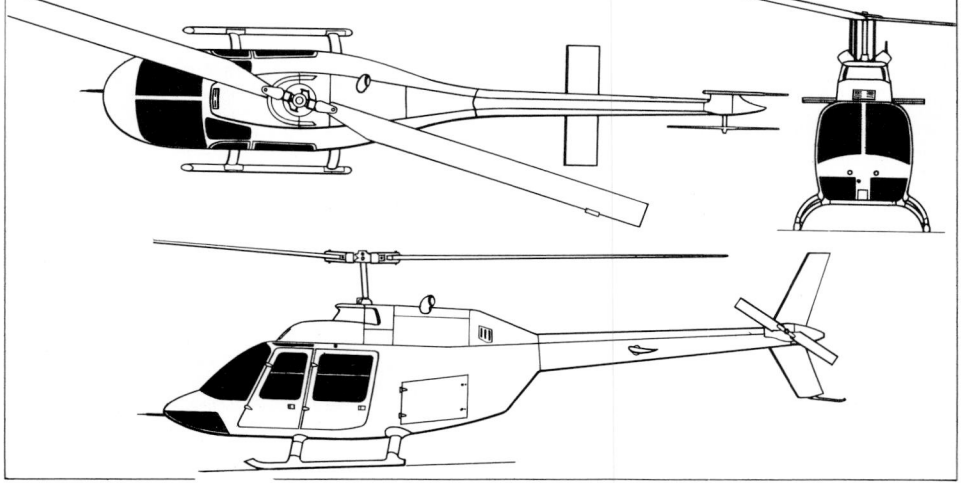

Bell 206B JetRanger III (Allison 250-C20J turboshaft) *(Pilot Press)*

trailing-edge extension. Each blade is connected to the head by means of a grip, pitch change bearings and a tension-torsion strap assembly. Two tail rotor blades have bonded aluminium skin but no core. Main rotor blades do not fold, but modification to permit manual folding is possible. Rotor brake available as optional kit.
ROTOR DRIVE: Rotors driven through tubular steel alloy shafts with spliced couplings. Initial drive from engine through 90° spiral bevel gear to single-stage planetary main gearbox. Shaft to tail rotor single-stage bevel gearbox. Freewheeling unit ensures that main rotor continues to drive tail rotor when engine is disengaged. Main rotor/engine rpm ratio 1 : 15; main rotor rpm 374-394. Tail rotor/engine rpm ratio 1 : 2.3.
FUSELAGE: Forward cabin section is made up of two aluminium alloy beams and 25 mm (1 in) thick aluminium honeycomb sandwich. Rotor, transmission and engine are supported by upper longitudinal beams. Upper and lower structures are interconnected by three fuselage bulkheads and a centrepost to form an integrated structure. Intermediate section is of aluminium alloy semi-monocoque construction. Aluminium monocoque tailboom.
TAIL UNIT: Fixed stabiliser of aluminium monocoque construction, with inverted aerofoil section. Fixed vertical tail fin in sweptback upper and ventral sections, of aluminium honeycomb with aluminium alloy skin.
LANDING GEAR: Aluminium alloy tubular skids bolted to extruded cross-tubes. Tubular steel skid on ventral fin to protect tail rotor in tail-down landing. Special high skid gear (0.25 m; 10 in greater ground clearance) available for use in areas with high brush. Pontoons or stowed floats, capable of in-flight inflation, available as optional kits.

POWER PLANT: One 313 kW (420 shp) Allison 250-C20J turboshaft, flat rated at 236 kW (317 shp). Rupture resistant fuel tank below and behind rear passenger seat, capacity 344 litres (91 US gallons; 75.75 Imp gallons). Refuelling point on starboard side of fuselage, aft of cabin. Oil capacity 5.2 litres (11 US pints; 9 Imp pints).
ACCOMMODATION: Two seats side by side in front and rear bench seat for three persons. Dual controls optional. Two forward hinged doors on each side, made of formed aluminium alloy with transparent panels (bulged on rear pair). Baggage compartment aft of rear seats, capacity 113 kg (250 lb), with external door on port side.
SYSTEMS: Hydraulic system, pressure 41.5 bars (600 lb/sq in), for cyclic, collective and directional controls. Maximum flow rate 7.57 litres (2 US gallons; 1.65 Imp gallons)/min. Open reservoir. Electrical supply from 150A starter/generator. One 24V 13Ah nickel-cadmium battery.
AVIONICS AND EQUIPMENT: Full range of avionics available in form of optional kits, including VHF communications and omni navigation kit, ADF, DME, R/Nav, transponder and intercom and speaker system. Standard equipment includes cabin fire extinguisher, first aid kit, door locks, night lighting, and dynamic flapping restraints. Optional items include clock, engine hour meter, turn and slip indicator, custom seating, internal litter kit, cabin heater, environmental control system, camera access door, high intensity night lights, engine fire detection system, and external cargo sling of 680 kg (1,500 lb) capacity.
DIMENSIONS, EXTERNAL:

Main rotor diameter	10.16 m (33 ft 4 in)
Tail rotor diameter	1.65 m (5 ft 5 in)
Main rotor blade chord	0.33 m (1 ft 1 in)

Distance between rotor centres	5.96 m (19 ft 6½ in)
Length: overall, rotors turning	11.82 m (38 ft 9½ in)
fuselage, incl tailskid	9.50 m (31 ft 2 in)
Height: over tail fin	2.54 m (8 ft 4 in)
overall	2.91 m (9 ft 6½ in)
Stabiliser span	1.97 m (6 ft 5¾ in)
Width over skids	1.92 m (6 ft 3½ in)

DIMENSIONS, INTERNAL:
Cabin: Length	2.13 m (7 ft 0 in)
Max width	1.27 m (4 ft 2 in)
Max height	1.28 m (4 ft 3 in)
Volume	1.13 m³ (40 cu ft)
Baggage compartment volume	0.45 m³ (16 cu ft)

AREAS:
Main rotor blades (total)	3.35 m² (36.1 sq ft)
Tail rotor blades (total)	0.22 m² (2.37 sq ft)
Main rotor disc	81.07 m² (872.7 sq ft)
Tail rotor disc	2.14 m² (23.04 sq ft)
Stabiliser	0.90 m² (9.65 sq ft)

WEIGHTS:
Weight empty, standard configuration	742 kg (1,635 lb)
Max T-O weight	1,451 kg (3,200 lb)

PERFORMANCE (at max T-O weight, ISA):
Never-exceed speed at S/L	122 knots (225 km/h; 140 mph)
Max cruising speed:	
at 1,525 m (5,000 ft)	116 knots (216 km/h; 134 mph)
at S/L	115 knots (214 km/h; 133 mph)
Max rate of climb at S/L	384 m (1,260 ft)/min
Vertical rate of climb at S/L	91 m (300 ft)/min
Service ceiling	4,115 m (13,500 ft)
Hovering ceiling: IGE	3,900 m (12,800 ft)
OGE	2,680 m (8,800 ft)
Range with max fuel and max payload:	
at S/L, no reserves	364 nm (674 km; 419 miles)
at 1,525 m (5,000 ft), no reserves	404 nm (748 km; 465 miles)

BELL MODEL 206L-3 LONGRANGER III

Announced on 25 September 1973, Bell's LongRanger was developed to satisfy a requirement for a turbine powered general purpose light helicopter in a size and performance range between the five-seat JetRanger II and 15-seat Model 205A-1. It incorporates Bell's Noda-Matic cabin suspension system, which gives a substantial reduction in rotor-induced vibration and results in a standard of comfort comparable with that of turboprop powered fixed-wing aircraft.

The current production **Model 206L-3 LongRanger III**, developed during 1981, has a 485 kW (650 shp) Allison 250-C30P engine with a max continuous rating of 415 kW (557 shp). The transmission is rated at 324 kW (435 shp) for take-off, with a continuous rating of 276 kW (370 shp). 340 kW (456 shp) transmission optional. Main rotor rpm is 394. Fuel capacity is 416 litres (110 US gallons; 91 Imp gallons).

Cabin volume of the LongRanger III is 2.35 m³ (83 cu ft), representing a considerable increase over that of the original JetRanger, and utility is enhanced by innovations that allow maximum use of this space. For example, the port forward passenger seat has a folding back to allow loading of a container measuring 2.44 × 0.91 × 0.30 m (8 × 3 × 1 ft), making possible the carriage of such items as survey equipment, skis, and long components that cannot be accommodated in any other light helicopter. Double doors on the port side of the cabin provide an opening 1.52 m (5 ft 0 in) wide, for easy straight-in loading of litter patients or utility cargo; in an ambulance or rescue role two litter patients and two ambulatory patients/attendants may be carried. With a crew of two, the standard cabin layout accommodates five passengers in two canted rearward facing seats and three forward facing seats. An optional executive cabin layout has four individual passenger seats.

Detail improvements first introduced in the LongRanger II include a redesigned rear cabin to provide 0.05 m (2 in) more headroom for passengers in aft cabin seats; new cowlings, firewall, engine mountings, and engine deck area structure; new freewheeling unit, input shaft, forward tail rotor driveshaft, and increased-thrust tail rotor; a rupture resistant fuel system; new engine oil system, oil tank, cooler, and transition duct; deletion of the water/alcohol system required formerly; and increased capacity 17Ah battery. Optional kits include emergency flotation gear, a 907 kg (2,000 lb) cargo hook, and an engine bleed air environmental control system.

Standard avionics fit of Collins MicroLine equipment includes dual nav/com, ADF, DME, transponder and marker beacon receiver. R/Nav, radio altimeter and encoding altimeter are optional. A Collins AP-107H autopilot can be fitted, to provide single-pilot IFR capability. A Sfena autopilot is also available, featuring automatic heading, altitude navigation, approach and basic stabilisation modes of operation. By January 1986 a total of more than 960 LongRangers had been delivered. They have proved particularly popular in an ambulance role, far outnumbering any other type in the fleet of more than 130 helicopters used by 112 US emergency medical service (EMS) centres at that time.

Canadian production of the LongRanger began in January 1987, deliveries beginning in May of that year.

The following details apply to the LongRanger III:

Canadian built JetRanger III operated by the French aerial photography company Caliop

DIMENSIONS, EXTERNAL:
Main rotor diameter	11.28 m (37 ft 0 in)
Tail rotor diameter	1.65 m (5 ft 5 in)
Length overall, both rotors turning	13.02 m (42 ft 8½ in)
Height: over tail fin	2.90 m (9 ft 6¼ in)
to top of rotor head	3.14 m (10 ft 3¾ in)
Fuselage: Max width	1.32 m (4 ft 4 in)
Stabiliser span	1.98 m (6 ft 6 in)

DIMENSION, INTERNAL:
Cabin volume	2.35 m³ (83 cu ft)

AREAS:
Main rotor disc	99.89 m² (1,075.2 sq ft)
Tail rotor disc	2.14 m² (23.04 sq ft)

WEIGHTS:
Weight empty, standard	998 kg (2,200 lb)
Max external load	907 kg (2,000 lb)
Max T-O weight: normal	1,882 kg (4,150 lb)
external load	1,927 kg (4,250 lb)

PERFORMANCE (at max normal T-O weight, ISA):
Never-exceed speed:	
at S/L	130 knots (241 km/h; 150 mph)
at 1,525 m (5,000 ft)	133 knots (246 km/h; 153 mph)
Max cruising speed at 1,525 m (5,000 ft)	110 knots (203 km/h; 126 mph)
Max rate of climb at S/L	408 m (1,340 ft)/min
Service ceiling at max cruise power	6,100 m (20,000 ft)
Hovering ceiling: IGE	5,030 m (16,500 ft)
OGE	1,645 m (5,400 ft)
Range, no reserves: at S/L	320 nm (592 km; 368 miles)
at 1,525 m (5,000 ft)	360 nm (666 km; 414 miles)

BELL MODEL 212 TWIN TWO-TWELVE
US military designation: UH-1N
Canadian military designation: CH-135

Bell announced on 1 May 1968 that the Canadian government had approved development of a twin-engined UH-1 helicopter to be powered by a Pratt & Whitney Canada PT6T-3 power plant. Subsequently, the Canadian government ordered 50 of these aircraft (designated CUH-1N) for the Canadian Armed Forces. Simultaneously, orders totalling 141 aircraft for the US services were announced, comprising 79 for the US Air Force, 40 for the US Navy and 22 for the US Marine Corps, all having the designation **UH-1N**. Subsequent orders covered the delivery of 159 more UH-1Ns to the US Navy and Marine Corps in 1973-78.

Initial deliveries to USAF began in 1970, when UH-1Ns joined UH-1Ps (modified UH-1Fs) in support of Special Operations Force counter-insurgency activities, psychological warfare and unconventional warfare operations worldwide. The Canadian aircraft (now designated **CH-135**) were delivered in 1971-72. Deliveries to the US Navy and US Marine Corps also began during 1971. Six were delivered to the air force of Bangladesh in early 1977, and the Argentine Air Force ordered eight in 1978. More recent deliveries of military Model 212s have been made to the Panamanian Air Force (two), Royal Thai Army (four) and Mexican Air Force (seven).

A commercial version, known as the Twin Two-Twelve, received FAA type certification with PT6T-3 power plant in October 1970, and FAA Transport Type Category A certification on 30 June 1971. The PT6T-3B engine was introduced in June 1980, offering improved single-engine performance and, consequently, additional safety margins.

The Twin Two-Twelve has been certificated for IFR operations by the FAA, UK's CAA, Norwegian DCA and Canadian DoT. Conversion from VFR to IFR configuration requires a new avionics package, new instrument panel and aircraft stabilisation controls. In June 1977, the Model 212 became the first helicopter FAA certificated for single-pilot IFR operations with fixed floats.

Deliveries of civil Model 212s have included nine to the People's Republic of China in 1979-81 (see 1987-88 and earlier *Jane's* for details) and four to the Japanese Maritime Safety Agency.

Production of the Model 212 continues, and was transferred to Bell's Canadian factory in mid-1988.

TYPE: Twin-turbine utility helicopter.
ROTOR SYSTEM: Two-blade all-metal semi-rigid main rotor with interchangeable blades, built up of extruded

Bell Model 212 twin-turbine helicopter of the Fuerza Aérea Panamena

aluminium spars and laminates. Stabilising bar above and at right angles to main rotor blades. Underslung feathering axis head. Two-blade all-metal tail rotor. Main rotor blades do not fold. Rotor brake optional.

ROTOR DRIVE: Shaft drive to both main and tail rotors.

FUSELAGE: Conventional all-metal semi-monocoque structure.

TAIL UNIT: Small fixed stabiliser on rear fuselage.

LANDING GEAR: Tubular skid type. Lock-on ground handling wheels, fixed floats and inflatable nylon float bags optional.

POWER PLANT: Pratt & Whitney Canada PT6T-3B Turbo Twin Pac, comprising two PT6 turboshafts coupled to a combining gearbox with a single output shaft. Producing 1,342 kW (1,800 shp), the Twin Pac is flat rated at 962 kW (1,290 shp) for T-O and 842 kW (1,130 shp) for continuous operation. In the event of an engine failure, the remaining engine can deliver 764 kW (1,025 shp) for 2.5 min, 723 kW (970 shp) for 30 min, or 596 kW (800 shp) continuously. Five interconnected rubber fuel cells, total usable capacity 814 litres (215 US gallons; 179 Imp gallons). Auxiliary fuel tanks optional, to provide a max total capacity of 1,495 litres (395 US gallons; 329 Imp gallons). Single-point refuelling on starboard side of cabin. Oil capacity 11.5 litres (3 US gallons; 2.5 Imp gallons) for engines, 8.5 litres (2.25 US gallons; 1.87 Imp gallons) for transmission.

ACCOMMODATION: Pilot and up to 14 passengers. In cargo configuration there is a total internal volume of 7.02 m³ (248 cu ft), including baggage space in tailboom. Exterior baggage compartment capacity 181 kg (400 lb). Forward door on each side of fuselage, opening forward. Two doors on each side of cabin; forward door hinged to open forward, rear door sliding aft. Accommodation heated and ventilated. Dual controls optional. AiResearch air-cycle environmental control unit available optionally.

SYSTEMS: Dual hydraulic systems, pressure 69 bars (1,000 lb/sq in), maximum flow rate 22.7 litres (6 US gallons; 5 Imp gallons)/min. Open reservoir. 28V DC electrical system supplied by two completely independent 30V 200A starter/generators. Secondary AC power supplied by two completely independent 250VA single-phase solid state inverters. A third inverter can acquire automatically the load of a failed inverter. 34Ah nickel-cadmium battery.

AVIONICS AND EQUIPMENT: Optional IFR avionics include dual King KTR 900A com transceivers; dual King KNR 660A VOR/LOC/RMI receivers; King KDF 800 ADF; King KMD 700A DME; King KXP 750A transponder; King KGM 690 marker beacon/glideslope receiver; dual Sperry Tarsyn-444 three-axis gyro units; stability control augmentation system; and an automatic flight control system. Flight director and weather radar optional. Other optional equipment includes a litter kit, cargo hook, cargo sling, rescue hoist, fixed float gear, emergency pop-out flotation gear and high skid gear.

DIMENSIONS, EXTERNAL:

Main rotor diameter (with tracking tips)	14.69 m (48 ft 2¼ in)
Tail rotor diameter	2.59 m (8 ft 6 in)
Main rotor blade chord	0.59 m (1 ft 11¼ in)
Tail rotor blade chord	0.292 m (11½ in)
Length:	
overall (main rotor fore and aft)	17.46 m (57 ft 3¼ in)
fuselage	12.92 m (42 ft 4¾ in)
Height: to top of rotor head	3.91 m (12 ft 10 in)
overall	4.53 m (14 ft 10¼ in)
Width: over skids	2.64 m (8 ft 8 in)
overall (main rotor fore and aft)	2.86 m (9 ft 4½ in)
Stabiliser span	2.86 m (9 ft 4½ in)
Rear sliding doors (each): Height	1.24 m (4 ft 1 in)
Width	1.88 m (6 ft 2 in)
Height to sill	0.76 m (2 ft 6 in)
Baggage compartment door: Height	0.53 m (1 ft 9 in)
Width	1.71 m (2 ft 4 in)
Emergency exits (centre cabin windows, each):	
Height	0.76 m (2 ft 6 in)
Width	0.97 m (3 ft 2 in)

DIMENSIONS, INTERNAL:

Cabin, excl flight deck: Length	2.34 m (7 ft 8 in)
Max width	2.44 m (8 ft 0 in)
Max height	1.24 m (4 ft 1 in)
Volume	6.23 m³ (220 cu ft)
Baggage compartment volume	0.78 m³ (28 cu ft)

AREAS:

Main rotor disc	173.90 m² (1,871.91 sq ft)
Tail rotor disc	5.27 m² (56.74 sq ft)

WEIGHTS:

VFR empty weight plus usable oil	2,720 kg (5,997 lb)
Max external load: 212	2,268 kg (5,000 lb)
UH-1N	1,814 kg (4,000 lb)
Max T-O weight and mission weight	5,080 kg (11,200 lb)

PERFORMANCE (at max T-O weight):

Never-exceed speed and max cruising speed at S/L	100 knots (185 km/h; 115 mph)
Max rate of climb at S/L	402 m (1,320 ft)/min
Service ceiling	3,960 m (13,000 ft)
Max altitude for T-O and landing	1,430 m (4,700 ft)
Hovering ceiling IGE	3,350 m (11,000 ft)

Bell Military 412SP with Lucas undernose gun turret

Max range with standard fuel at S/L, no reserves
227 nm (420 km; 261 miles)

BELL MODEL 412

Bell announced on 8 September 1978 its intention to develop this variant of the twin-turbine Model 212 with a four-blade main rotor of advanced design. The Model 412 is Bell's first production helicopter with a four-blade rotor, although the parent US company has flown many helicopters with multi-blade rotors for research purposes.

Introduction of the new rotor not only improved performance and reduced noise, but reduced vibration significantly without requiring a costly redesign of the fuselage structure to introduce nodal suspension. A pendulum absorber kit, to reduce internal vibration levels, became standard in mid-1984, and is available for retrofit to earlier Model 412s.

Two new fully certificated Model 212s were modified for the Model 412 development and certification programme. The first of these began its flight trials in early August 1979, and the second in December 1979. FAA type approval, in accordance with FAR Pt 29, for VFR operation was received on 9 January 1981, and IFR certification on 13 February 1981. The first delivery to a customer was made to ERA Helicopters of Anchorage, Alaska, on 18 January 1981; this operator has since acquired 11 more Model 412s, supplementing 16 Model 212s and 52 other Bell helicopters. Two Model 412s are operated by the Venezuelan Air Force, two by the Public Security Flying Wing of the Bahrain Defence Force, four by Sri Lanka's armed forces and two by the Nigerian Police Air Wing. By January 1988 a total of 145 Model 412s (all versions) had been delivered.

The latest commercial version is known as the **Model 412SP** (Special Performance), and features an increased max T-O weight, new interior seating options and a 55 per cent increase in standard fuel capacity.

The Indonesian aircraft industry (IPTN) is producing 100 Model 412SPs, with progressive increase of manufacturing content. Other orders for the SP have been received from the Republic of Honduras (10) and Royal Norwegian Air Force (18). Seventeen of the latter are being assembled by Helikopter Services A/S of Stavanger, using subassemblies and components supplied by Bell. The helicopters, delivery of which is scheduled for completion in September 1989, will replace Bell UH-1Bs with 339 Squadron at Bardufoss and 720 Squadron at Rygge.

In June 1986 Bell announced the **Military 412SP**, equipped with a 600 rds/min 0.50 in calibre machine-gun in a Lucas Aerospace undernose turret, guided by a Sperry Head Tracker helmet sight system similar to that used in the AH-1S. The installation carries 875 rounds of ammunition, weighs 188 kg (414 lb) including the helmet sight, and can be installed or removed in less than 30 minutes. The turret mounted gun can be fired through a 110° degree arc in azimuth, at a maximum elevation of 15° and a maximum depression of 45° to the horizontal. With the turret, the 412SP has a max level speed of 120 knots (222 km/h; 138 mph); in addition, it can be equipped with 19 air-to-ground rockets on each side of the aircraft.

Bell's Italian licensee, Agusta, has developed its own multi-role military version, known as the **Griffon**, capable of performing medical evacuation, armed tactical support, logistic transport, SAR and patrol missions. Details of the Griffon are given under the Agusta heading in the Italian section.

Model 412 production was due to be transferred to the Canadian factory in January 1989. The description of the Model 212 applies also to the Model 412SP, except as follows:

ROTOR SYSTEM: Four-blade flex-beam soft-in-plane advanced technology main rotor. Blades are of similar construction to those described for the Model 214ST, but are interchangeable and have lightning protection mesh moulded into the structure and provisions for inclusion of de-icing heater elements. New design main rotor head of steel and light alloy construction, with elastomeric bearings and dampers. Main rotor can be folded. Rotor brake standard. Two-blade tail rotor of all-metal construction. Main rotor rpm 314.

ROTOR DRIVE: As for Model 212, except for shorter main rotor mast. Transmission rating 1,044 kW (1,400 shp) for T-O, 846 kW (1,134 shp) max continuous.

POWER PLANT: Pratt & Whitney Canada PT6T-3B-1 Turbo Twin Pac, comprising two 671 kW (900 shp) turboshafts, rated to produce a total of 1,044 kW (1,400 shp) for take-off and 843 kW (1,130 shp) for continuous operation. In the event of an engine failure the remaining engine can deliver up to 764 kW (1,025 shp) for 2½ min, or 723 kW (970 shp) for 30 min. Seven interconnected rupture resistant fuel cells, with automatic shut-off valves (breakaway fittings), have a combined capacity of 1,249 litres (330 US gallons; 275 Imp gallons). Optional auxiliary fuel tanks provide a maximum total capacity of 1,870 litres (494 US gallons; 411 Imp gallons). Single-point refuelling on starboard side of cabin.

AVIONICS AND EQUIPMENT: Optional IFR avionics include King Gold Crown III equipment and dual Sperry automatic flight control systems. Optional equipment includes a cargo sling, rescue hoist, emergency pop-out flotation gear and high skid gear.

DIMENSIONS, EXTERNAL:

Main rotor diameter	14.02 m (46 ft 0 in)
Tail rotor diameter	2.59 m (8 ft 6 in)
Main rotor blade chord: at root	0.40 m (1 ft 3.9 in)
at tip	0.22 m (8½ in)
Tail rotor blade chord	0.29 m (11½ in)
Length: overall, rotors turning	17.07 m (56 ft 0 in)
fuselage, excl rotors	12.92 m (42 ft 4¾ in)
Height: to top of rotor head	3.29 m (10 ft 9½ in)
overall, tail rotor turning	4.32 m (14 ft 2¼ in)
Stabiliser span	2.86 m (9 ft 4½ in)
Width over skids	2.59 m (8 ft 6 in)
Door sizes	as Model 212

AREAS:

Main rotor disc	154.40 m² (1,661.9 sq ft)
Tail rotor disc	5.27 m² (56.75 sq ft)

WEIGHTS:

Weight empty with utility seating, plus usable oil	2,935 kg (6,470 lb)
Max T-O weight	5,397 kg (11,900 lb)

PERFORMANCE (at max T-O weight except where indicated):

Never-exceed speed at S/L	140 knots (259 km/h; 161 mph)
Max cruising speed at S/L	124 knots (230 km/h; 143 mph)
Max rate of climb at S/L	411 m (1,350 ft)/min
Service ceiling	4,970 m (16,300 ft)
Max altitude for T-O and landing	427 m (1,400 ft)
Hovering ceiling: IGE	2,805 m (9,200 ft)
OGE, AUW of 4,762 kg (10,500 lb)	2,805 m (9,200 ft)

Range with max payload, standard fuel, at 118 knots (219 km/h; 136 mph) at 3,200 m (10,500 ft), 30 min fuel reserves
375 nm (695 km; 432 miles)
Max range with standard fuel at S/L, no reserves
354 nm (656 km; 408 miles)

BELL MODEL 400A/440 TWINRANGER

This programme has been suspended indefinitely pending a market situation that would support an annual sales rate of 120 aircraft. A full description appeared in the 1987-88 *Jane's*.

BLACKHOLE

BLACKHOLE INVESTMENTS LTD

RR4, Kenilworth, Ontario N0G 2E0

PRESIDENT: Charles A. Miller

This company started small-scale production in 1986 of replicas of the 1930s-vintage Bücker Bü 131 Jungmann and Bü 133 Jungmeister, planning to build an initial batch of 14 aircraft of which 12 had been sold to US customers. No further information has been received.

BOEING CANADA

BOEING OF CANADA LTD
(de Havilland Division)

Garratt Boulevard, Downsview, Ontario M3K 1Y5

Telephone: (416) 633 7310

PRESIDENT: Ronald B. Woodard

VICE-PRESIDENTS:
John Thompson (Engineering)
Thomas E. Appleton (Marketing and Sales)

DIRECTOR. MARKETING: John Giraudy

MANAGER. PUBLIC RELATIONS: Colin S. Fisher

The de Havilland Aircraft of Canada Ltd was established in early 1928 as a subsidiary of The de Havilland Aircraft Co Ltd, and became subsequently a member of the Hawker Siddeley Group. On 26 June 1974 ownership was transferred to the Canadian government, continuing until 31 January 1986 when purchase was completed by The Boeing Company, and de Havilland Canada became a Division of Boeing of Canada Ltd. On 3 October 1986, handover of a Dash 8 Series 100 to Horizon Air marked the 7,000th aircraft produced by de Havilland Canada. Of this total, 3,791 were DHC designs.

Approximately 5,300 people were employed by the Division in 1987. Repair and overhaul services for the Buffalo, Twin Otter, Dash 7 and Dash 8, by a newly formed Aero Services organisation, were introduced in 1981. Production of the Buffalo ended in December 1986; that for the Twin Otter was scheduled to end in December 1988, and that for the Dash 7 in mid-1988.

DHC-5D BUFFALO

The twin-turboprop Buffalo, first flown on 9 April 1964, was developed from the piston engined DHC-4 Caribou. A total of 126 (all versions) was built before production ended in December 1986. Final production version was the DHC-5D, of which deliveries began in 1976. A full description of this version can be found in the 1984-85 and earlier editions of *Jane's*, and an abbreviated description in the 1986-87 edition.

DHC-6 TWIN OTTER SERIES 300

CAF designation: CC-138
US Army designation: UV-18A
USAF designation: UV-18B

The Twin Otter flew for the first time on 20 May 1965, and deliveries began in July 1966, shortly after the aircraft received FAA type approval. All Series are certificated to FAR 23 Pt 135, and the manufacturer's warranty was doubled in 1985 in recognition of the aircraft's 20 years of operation.

Four standard production versions have been built, of which the Series 100 (115 built), Series 200 (115 built) and Series 300S (six built) were described in the 1967-68, 1970-71 and 1976-77 *Jane's* respectively. The final production version is the Series 300, of which deliveries began in Spring 1969 with the 231st Twin Otter off the line.

Four Twin Otters were delivered and two more ordered during 1987, total deliveries by the Spring of 1988 reaching 834 for customers in more than 80 countries. Production was scheduled to end with the completion of c/n 844 in late 1988. Six of the final batch have been sold to Etty Aerospace of Toronto for resale or lease; the balance will be held in the Division's sales inventory. In Spring 1988 preliminary

discussions had been held for possible limited offshore production.

The Twin Otter has been described fully in the 1986-87 and many previous editions of *Jane's*; the following is an abbreviated version of that description.

TYPE: Twin-turboprop STOL transport.

AIRFRAME: As described in 1986-87 *Jane's*.

POWER PLANT: Two 462 kW (620 shp) Pratt & Whitney Canada PT6A-27 turboprops, each driving a Hartzell HC-B3TN-3DY three-blade reversible-pitch fully-feathering metal propeller with Beta control (zero-pitch propeller on floatplane). Two underfloor fuel tanks (eight cells), total capacity of 1,446 litres (382 US gallons; 318 Imp gallons). Refuelling point for each tank on port side of fuselage. Oil capacity 9.1 litres (2.4 US gallons; 2 Imp gallons) per engine. Optional electric de-icing system for propellers and air intakes.

ACCOMMODATION: Side by side seats for one or two pilots on flight deck, access to which is by a forward opening car type door on each side or via the passenger cabin. Dual controls standard. Windscreen demisting and defrosting standard. Cabin divided by bulkhead into main passenger or freight compartment and baggage compartment. Seats for up to 20 passengers in main cabin. Standard interior is 20-seat commuter layout, with Douglas track, carpets, double windows, individual air vents and reading lights, and airstair door. Optional layouts include 18- or 19-seat commuter versions, and 13/20-passenger utility version with foldaway seats and double cargo doors with ladder. Access to cabin by door on each side of rear fuselage; airstair door on the port side. Optional double door for cargo on port side instead of airstair door. Compartments in nose and aft of main cabin, each with upward hinged door on port side, for 136 kg (300 lb) and 227 kg (500 lb) of baggage respectively; rear baggage hold accessible from cabin in emergency. Emergency exits near front of cabin on each side. Heating of flight deck and passenger cabin by engine bleed air; ventilation via a ram air intake on the port side of the fuselage nose. Oxygen system for crew and passengers optional. Executive, survey or ambulance interiors can be fitted at customer's option. Tiedown cargo rings are installed as standard for the freighter role.

SYSTEMS, AVIONICS AND EQUIPMENT: See 1986-87 edition.

DIMENSIONS. EXTERNAL (landplane):

Wing span	19.81 m (65 ft 0 in)
Wing chord (constant)	1.98 m (6 ft 6 in)
Wing aspect ratio	10.1
Length overall	15.77 m (51 ft 9 in)
Height overall	5.94 m (19 ft 6 in)
Tailplane span	6.30 m (20 ft 8 in)
Wheel track	3.71 m (12 ft 2 in)
Wheelbase	4.53 m (14 ft 10½ in)
Propeller diameter	2.59 m (8 ft 6 in)
Passenger door (port): Height	1.27 m (4 ft 2 in)
Width	0.76 m (2 ft 6 in)
Height to sill	1.32 m (4 ft 4 in)
Passenger door (starboard):	
Height	1.15 m (3 ft 9½ in)
Width	0.77 m (2 ft 6¼ in)
Height to sill	1.32 m (4 ft 4 in)
Cargo double door (port, rear):	
Height	1.27 m (4 ft 2 in)

Width	1.42 m (4 ft 8 in)
Height to sill	1.32 m (4 ft 4 in)

DIMENSIONS. INTERNAL:

Cabin, excl flight deck, galley and baggage compartment:	
Length	5.64 m (18 ft 6 in)
Max width	1.61 m (5 ft 3¼ in)
Max height	1.50 m (4 ft 11 in)
Floor area	7.45 m² (80.2 sq ft)
Volume	10.87 m³ (384 cu ft)
Baggage compartment volume:	
nose	1.08 m³ (38 cu ft)
rear	2.49 m³ (88 cu ft)

AREA:

Wings, gross	39.02 m² (420.0 sq ft)

WEIGHTS:

Typical operating weight (20-seat commuter, incl 2 crew and 59 kg; 130 lb of avionics)	3,363 kg (7,415 lb)
Max payload for 100 nm (185 km; 115 miles)	1,941 kg (4,280 lb)
Max fuel weight	1,171 kg (2,583 lb)
Max T-O weight	5,670 kg (12,500 lb)
Max landing weight:	
wheels and skis	5,579 kg (12,300 lb)
floats	5,670 kg (12,500 lb)

PERFORMANCE (at max T-O weight, ISA):

Max cruising speed at 3,050 m (10,000 ft)	182 knots (338 km/h; 210 mph)
Stalling speed:	
flaps up	74 knots (138 km/h; 86 mph) EAS
flaps down	58 knots (108 km/h; 67 mph) EAS
Max rate of climb at S/L	488 m (1,600 ft)/min
Rate of climb at S/L, one engine out	104 m (340 ft)/min
Service ceiling	8,140 m (26,700 ft)
Service ceiling, one engine out	3,530 m (11,600 ft)
T-O run: STOL	213 m (700 ft)
CAR Pt 3	262 m (860 ft)
T-O to 15 m (50 ft): STOL	366 m (1,200 ft)
CAR Pt 3	457 m (1,500 ft)
Landing from 15 m (50 ft): STOL	320 m (1,050 ft)
CAR Pt 3	591 m (1,940 ft)
Landing run: STOL	157 m (515 ft)
CAR Pt 3	290 m (950 ft)
Range at long-range cruising speed with 1,134 kg (2,500 lb) payload	700 nm (1,297 km; 806 miles)

DHC-7 DASH 7

The Dash 7 quiet STOL airliner project was begun by de Havilland Canada in late 1972. Two pre-production aircraft were built, the first of these flying on 27 March and the second on 26 June 1975. The first production Dash 7 (C-GQIW, c/n 3), flew on 30 May 1977.

Certification by the Canadian Department of Transport to FAR 25 was received on 2 May 1977; STOL performance is approved under conventional FAR 25 and FAR 121 regulations. In addition, certification has been given for 7° 30′ glideslope and 10.7 m (35 ft) landing reference height adopted by the FAA for STOL aircraft. The first Dash 7 to enter service was c/n 4, with Rocky Mountain Airways (USA), on 3 February 1978.

One Dash 7 was delivered during 1987, and six more ordered. Deliveries totalled 108 by April 1988, to 35 customers in 22 countries, and production was scheduled to end in the middle of that year with completion of the 114th aircraft. The Dash 7 has been built in the following basic versions:

Series 100. Initial passenger version (**Series 101** in all-cargo form).

Series 150 (or all-cargo **Series 151**). Higher weight/greater fuel capacity version, introduced in 1986. Customers include Canadian government, which received one specially equipped non-standard ice reconnaissance example designated **Dash 7 IR** (see 1986-87 *Jane's*).

TYPE: Four-engined short/medium-range quiet STOL transport.

AIRFRAME: As described in 1987-88 *Jane's*.

POWER PLANT: Four Pratt & Whitney Canada PT6A-50 turboprops, each flat rated at 835 kW (1,120 shp) and driving a Hamilton Standard 24PF-305 constant-speed fully-feathering reversible-pitch four-blade propeller, with Beta control, of slow-turning type (1,320 rpm) to reduce noise level. Propeller blades are of GRP, with forged aluminium spars and foam cores. Fuel in two integral tanks in each wing, total standard capacity 5,652 litres (1,493 US gallons; 1,243 Imp gallons), increasable optionally to 9,940 litres (2,626 US gallons; 2,186 Imp gallons). Single pressure refuelling/defuelling point on underside of rear fuselage, aft of pressure dome. Pneumatic de-icing of engine air intakes; electric de-icing for propellers. Oil capacity 23 litres (6 US gallons; 5 Imp gallons).

ACCOMMODATION: Flight crew of two, plus one or two cabin attendants. Dual controls standard. Seats for 50

DHC-6 Twin Otter Series 300 twin-turboprop STOL transport

DHC-7 Dash 7 four-turboprop quiet STOL transport in the insignia of Ransome Airlines, USA

passengers at 81 cm (32 in) pitch standard, in pairs on each side of centre aisle, with generous provision for underseat carry-on baggage. Optional high-density seating for 54 passengers at 74 cm (29 in) pitch. Outward opening airstair door at rear on port side. Emergency exits on each side at front of cabin and on starboard side at rear. Baggage compartment in rear fuselage (capacity 998 kg; 2,200 lb), with external access on starboard side and internal access from cabin. Galley, coat rack and toilet at rear of cabin. Optional arrangements include movable bulkhead for mixed freight/passenger loads and (Srs 101/151) large forward freight door on port side. Up to five standard pallets can be accommodated in an all-cargo role. Quick change cargo handling system available optionally. Entire accommodation pressurised and air-conditioned.

SYSTEMS, AVIONICS AND EQUIPMENT: See 1987-88 *Jane's*.

DIMENSIONS, EXTERNAL:

Wing span	28.35 m (93 ft 0 in)
Length overall	24.54 m (80 ft 6 in)
Height overall	7.98 m (26 ft 2 in)
Tailplane span	9.45 m (31 ft 0 in)
Fuselage: Max diameter	2.79 m (9 ft 2 in)
Wheel track	7.16 m (23 ft 6 in)
Wheelbase	8.38 m (27 ft 6 in)
Propeller diameter	3.43 m (11 ft 3 in)
Passenger door (rear, port):	
Height	1.75 m (5 ft 9 in)
Width	0.76 m (2 ft 6 in)
Height to sill	1.12 m (3 ft 8 in)
Emergency exit doors (fwd, each):	
Height	0.91 m (3 ft 0 in)
Width	0.51 m (1 ft 8 in)
Height to sill	1.55 m (5 ft 1 in)
Emergency exit door (rear, stbd):	
Height	1.35 m (4 ft 5 in)
Width	0.61 m (2 ft 0 in)
Height to sill	1.09 m (3 ft 7 in)
Baggage hold door (rear, stbd):	
Height	1.02 m (3 ft 4 in)
Width	0.84 m (2 ft 9 in)
Height to sill	1.47 m (4 ft 10 in)
Cargo door (fwd, port, optional):	
Height	1.78 m (5 ft 10 in)
Width	2.31 m (7 ft 7 in)
Height to sill	approx 1.22 m (4 ft 0 in)

DIMENSIONS, INTERNAL:

Cabin, excl flight deck: Length	12.04 m (39 ft 6 in)
Max width	2.60 m (8 ft 6¼ in)
Floor width	2.13 m (7 ft 0 in)
Max height	1.94 m (6 ft 4½ in)
Height under wing	1.85 m (6 ft 1 in)
Volume	54.1 m³ (1,910 cu ft)
Baggage compartment (rear fuselage):	
Max length	2.30 m (7 ft 6½ in)
Volume	6.8 m³ (240 cu ft)

AREA:

Wings, gross	79.90 m² (860.0 sq ft)

WEIGHTS AND LOADINGS:

Operating weight empty: Srs 100	12,519 kg (27,600 lb)
Srs 150	12,528 kg (27,620 lb)
Max payload: Srs 100	5,171 kg (11,400 lb)
Srs 150	5,162 kg (11,380 lb)
Max fuel: standard:	
Srs 100, 150	4,606 kg (10,155 lb)
optional:	
Srs 100, 150	8,099 kg (17,855 lb)
Max T-O weight: Srs 100	19,958 kg (44,000 lb)
Srs 150	21,319 kg (47,000 lb)
Max zero-fuel weight:	
Srs 100, 150	17,690 kg (39,000 lb)
Max landing weight: Srs 100	19,050 kg (42,000 lb)
Srs 150	20,411 kg (45,000 lb)

One of the two CC-142 passenger/cargo transports delivered to the Canadian DND *(David Godfrey)*

Max cabin floor loading:	
Srs 100, 150	366.2 kg/m² (75 lb/sq ft)
Max wing loading:	
Srs 100	249.7 kg/m² (51.16 lb/sq ft)
Srs 150	266.7 kg/m² (54.65 lb/sq ft)
Max power loading:	
Srs 100	5.98 kg/kW (9.82 lb/shp)
Srs 150	6.38 kg/kW (10.49 lb/shp)

PERFORMANCE (Srs 100 at max T-O weight, FAR Pt 25, at S/L, ISA except where indicated):

Max cruising speed at 2,440 m (8,000 ft) at AUW of (18,597 kg (41,000 lb):

Srs 100	231 knots (428 km/h; 266 mph)
Srs 150	229 knots (424 km/h; 263 mph)

Max cruising speed at 4,575 m (15,000 ft) at AUW of (18,597 kg (41,000 lb)

  227 knots (420 km/h: 261 mph)

En route rate of climb, flaps and landing gear up:

4 engines, max climb power	366 m (1,200 ft)/min
3 engines, max continuous power	214 m (700 ft)/min

Service ceiling at AUW of 18,597 kg (41,000 lb):

4 engines, max climb power	6,370 m (20,900 ft)
3 engines, max continuous power	
	3,870 m (12,700 ft)

T-O field length: Srs 100	689 m (2,260 ft)
Srs 150	792 m (2,600 ft)
T-O field length at 3,050 m (10,000 ft), 15° flap	
	1,829 m (6,000 ft)

Landing field length at max landing weight:

Srs 100, 45° flap	595 m (1,950 ft)
Srs 150, 25° flap	959 m (3,145 ft)

Landing field length at 3,050 m (10,000 ft) at 18,915 kg (41,700 lb) landing weight, 45° flap 854 m (2,800 ft)

Runway LCN with 32 × 11.50-15 low-pressure tyres, rigid, 30 in relative stiffness 16.2

Range at 4,575 m (15,000 ft) with 50 passengers and baggage, at long-range cruising speed, IFR reserves:

  Srs 100   735 nm (1,362 km; 846 miles)

Max range at 4,575 m (15,000 ft) with standard fuel and 2,948 kg (6,500 lb) payload, long-range cruising speed:

  Srs 100   1,170 nm (2,168 km: 1,347 miles)

Range at max cruise power, IFR reserves:

Srs 150 (50 passengers)

  1,100 nm (2,038 km; 1,266 miles)

  Srs 150 (max)   2,528 nm (4,685 km; 2,911 miles)

OPERATIONAL NOISE LEVELS (FAR Pt 36 at S/L, ISA + 10°C, Srs 100 confirmed):

T-O	80.5 EPNdB
Approach on 3° glideslope	91.4 EPNdB
Sideline	82.8 EPNdB

DHC-8 DASH 8 SERIES 100

The first of four flying prototypes of the Dash 8 Series 100 (C-GDNK) made its first flight on 20 June 1983, followed by the second (C-GGMP) on 26 October and the third in November 1983. The fourth aircraft (first with production PW120 engines) was flying by early 1984, followed by the first Dash 8 with production interior in June. Certification by the Canadian DoT, to FAR Pts 25 and 36 and SFAR No. 27, was awarded on 28 September 1984, and FAA type approval before the end of that year. Certification has since been granted by Austria, West Germany and the UK. The first customer Dash 8, one of two Series 100s for NorOntair (c/n 6), was delivered on 23 October 1984, and entered service on 19 December that year.

The Series 100 is available with PW120A or PW121 engines (as **Model 102** and **Model 103** respectively), and in the following two basic versions:

Commuter. Standard local service version, to which the detailed description mainly applies. With full IFR fuel reserves for a 100 nm (185 km; 115 mile) diversion, plus 45 min at long-range cruising speed at 1,525 m (5,000 ft), this version has enough fuel to fly four 100 nm stages without refuelling, carrying a 3,102 kg (6,840 lb) payload of 36 passengers and their baggage.

Corporate. Marketed in North America exclusively by Innotech Aviation of Montreal, outside North America by Boeing, the corporate version has an extended range capability of up to 2,000 nm (3,706 km; 2,303 miles), plus IFR reserves, with a 544 kg (1,200 lb) payload. In a more typical mission it can carry 17 passengers and their baggage for up to 1,320 nm (2,446 km; 1,520 miles), with reserves, at a max cruising speed of 270 knots (500 km/h; 311 mph). An APU is standard in this version. Alternative layouts can include a single cabin with first class accommodation for about 24 passengers; the standard commuter interior is also available for corporate customers.

By 1 April 1988 a total of 154 firm orders had been received for the Series 100, of which 91 had been delivered. The production rate was scheduled to rise to five per month by the end of 1988 as Twin Otter and Dash 7 manufacture is phased out, and to seven per month by mid-1989.

The military **Dash 8M** and 'stretched' **Dash 8 Series 300** are described separately. The following description applies to the standard Dash 8 Series 100:

TYPE: Twin-turboprop quiet short-range transport.

WINGS: Cantilever high-wing monoplane, with constant chord centre-section and tapered outer panels. Thickness/chord ratio 18% at root, 13% at tip. Sweepback 3° 1′ 48″ at quarter-chord. Dihedral 2° 30′ on outer panels.

DHC-8 Dash 8 Series 100 twin-turboprop transport in the insignia of AirOntario *(David Godfrey)*

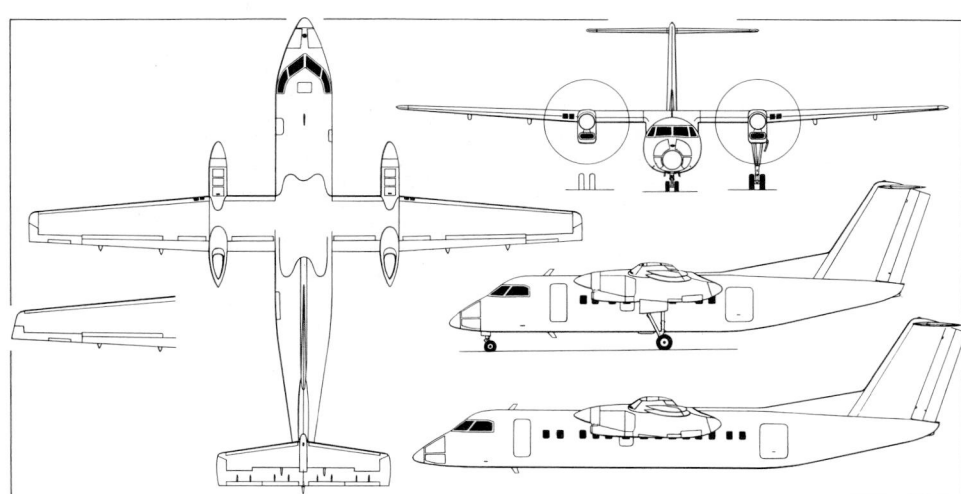

DHC-8 Dash 8 Series 100, with additional side view (bottom) and wingtip of Series 300 *(Pilot Press)*

Drooped inboard leading-edges. Tip to tip torsion box formed by front and rear spars, ribs and skin. Single-slotted Fowler trailing-edge flaps inboard and outboard of engine nacelles. Hydraulically actuated roll control spoilers/lift dumpers forward of each outer flap segment; independent ground spoiler/lift dumper inboard and outboard of each engine nacelle. Mechanically actuated balanced ailerons, with inset tabs. Small stall strip on each wing leading-edge outboard of engine. Pneumatic rubber boot de-icing of leading-edges. Composite materials used for construction of leading-edges, wingtip fairings, flap shrouds, flap trailing-edges and other components.

FUSELAGE: Conventional flush riveted semi-monocoque pressurised structure, of near-circular cross-section. Extensive use of adhesively bonded stringers and cutout reinforcements. Radome, nose bay, wing/fuselage fairings and tailcone of Kevlar and other composites.

TAIL UNIT: Cantilever T tailplane; full span horn balanced elevator, with tabs. Sweptback fin (integral with rear fuselage), large dorsal fin, and two-segment serially hinged hydraulically actuated rudder with yaw damper. Composites used in construction of dorsal fin, fin leading-edge, fin/tailplane fairings, tailplane leading-edges and elevator tips. Pneumatic rubber boot de-icing of tailplane leading-edges.

LANDING GEAR: Retractable tricycle type, by Dowty Equipment of Canada Ltd, with twin wheels on each unit. Steer by wire nose unit retracts forward, main units rearward into engine nacelles. Goodrich mainwheels and brakes; Hydro-Aire Mk 3 anti-skid system. Standard tyre pressures: main 7.93 bars (115 lb/sq in), nose 5.52 bars (80 lb/sq in). Low pressure tyres optional, pressure 4.48 bars (65 lb/sq in) on main units, 3.31 bars (40 lb/sq in) on nose unit. Wheel doors of Kevlar and other composites.

POWER PLANT: Two 1,491 kW (2,000 shp) Pratt & Whitney Canada PW120A turboprops in Model 102, each driving a Hamilton Standard 14SF-7 four-blade constant-speed fully-feathering propeller with reversible pitch. Model 103 has 1,603 kW (2,150 shp) PW121 engines. Propeller blades have a solid aluminium spar, glassfibre outer shell, nickel erosion sheath outboard, electric de-icing, and Beta control. Engine cowlings, produced by British Hovercraft Corporation, have lower panels, air intakes and rear panels of Kevlar/Nomex sandwich, aluminium side panels, and a titanium firewall. Standard fuel capacity (in-wing tanks) of 3,202 litres (846 US gallons; 704 Imp gallons); optional auxiliary tank system increases this maximum to 5,807 litres (1,534 US gallons; 1,277 Imp gallons). Pressure refuelling point in rear of starboard engine nacelle; overwing gravity point in each outer wing panel. Oil capacity 21 litres (5.5 US gallons; 4.6 Imp gallons) per engine.

ACCOMMODATION: Crew of two on flight deck, plus one attendant in cabin. Dual controls standard, although aircraft will be certificated for single-pilot operation. Standard commuter layout in main cabin provides four-abreast seating, with central aisle, for 36 passengers at 79 cm (31 in) pitch, plus buffet, toilet and large rear baggage compartment. Wardrobe at front of passenger cabin, in addition to overhead lockers and underseat stowage, provides additional carry-on capacity for passengers' baggage. Alternative 40-passenger, mixed passenger/cargo or corporate layouts available at customer's option. Movable bulkhead to facilitate conversion to mixed-traffic or all-cargo configuration. Port side airstair door at front provides access for crew as well as passengers; large inward opening port side door aft of wing for cargo loading. Emergency exit each side, in line with wing leading-edge, and opposite passenger door on starboard side. Entire accommodation pressurised and air-conditioned.

SYSTEMS: Air cycle air-conditioning system provides heating, cooling, ventilation and pressurisation (cabin max differential 0.38 bars; 5.5 lb/sq in). Normal hydraulic installation comprises two independent systems, each having an engine driven variable displacement pump and an electrically driven standby pump; accumulator and handpump for emergency use. Electrical system DC power provided by two starter/generators, two transformer-rectifier units, and two nickel-cadmium batteries. Variable frequency AC power provided by two engine driven AC generators and three static inverters. Ground power receptacles in port side of nose (DC) and rear of starboard nacelle (AC). De-icing system consists of pneumatic system plus electric heating. APU standard in corporate version.

AVIONICS AND EQUIPMENT: Standard factory installed avionics package includes King Gold Crown III com/nav (KTR 908 VHF com, KNR 634 VHF nav, KDF 806 ADF, KDM 706A DME and KXP 756 transponder), Sperry SPZ-800 dual-channel digital AFCS with integrated fail-operational flight director/autopilot system, dual digital air data system, electromechanical flight instruments, and Primus 800 colour weather radar; Sperry electronic flight instrumentation system (EFIS) optional on commuter, standard on corporate version. Avtech audio integrating system. Telephonics PA system. Simmonds fuel monitoring system.

DIMENSIONS, EXTERNAL:
Wing span	25.91 m (85 ft 0 in)
Wing aspect ratio	12.4
Length overall	22.25 m (73 ft 0 in)
Fuselage: Max diameter	2.69 m (8 ft 10 in)
Height overall	7.49 m (24 ft 7 in)
Elevator span	7.92 m (26 ft 0 in)
Wheel track (c/l of shock struts)	7.87 m (25 ft 10 in)
Wheelbase	7.95 m (26 ft 1 in)
Propeller diameter	3.96 m (13 ft 0 in)
Propeller ground clearance	0.94 m (3 ft 1 in)
Propeller/fuselage clearance	0.76 m (2 ft 6 in)
Passenger/crew door (fwd, port):	
Height	1.65 m (5 ft 5 in)
Width	0.76 m (2 ft 6 in)
Height to sill	1.09 m (3 ft 7 in)
Baggage door (rear, port):	
Height	1.52 m (5 ft 0 in)
Width	1.27 m (4 ft 2 in)
Height to sill	1.09 m (3 ft 7 in)

DIMENSIONS, INTERNAL:
Cabin: Length	9.17 m (30 ft 1 in)
Max width	2.49 m (8 ft 2 in)
Width at floor	2.03 m (6 ft 8 in)
Max height	1.88 m (6 ft 2 in)
Volume	36.8 m³ (1,300 cu ft)
Baggage compartment volume	8.5 m³ (300 cu ft)

AREAS:
Wings, gross	54.35 m² (585.0 sq ft)
Vertical tail surfaces (total)	14.12 m² (152.0 sq ft)
Horizontal tail surfaces (total)	13.94 m² (150.0 sq ft)

WEIGHTS AND LOADINGS:
Operating weight empty	9,979 kg (22,000 lb)
Max usable fuel: standard	2,576 kg (5,678 lb)
optional	4,646 kg (10,244 lb)
Max payload: passengers	4,082 kg (9,000 lb)
cargo	4,467 kg (9,849 lb)
Max ramp weight	15,785 kg (34,800 lb)
Max T-O weight	15,650 kg (34,500 lb)
Max landing weight	15,375 kg (33,900 lb)
Max zero-fuel weight	14,060 kg (31,000 lb)
Max wing loading	287.95 kg/m² (58.97 lb/sq ft)
Max power loading:	
Model 102	5.25 kg/kW (8.62 lb/shp)
Model 103	4.88 kg/kW (8.02 lb/shp)

PERFORMANCE (at max T-O weight except where indicated):
Max cruising speed at 13,834 kg (30,500 lb) AUW:	
at 4,575 m (15,000 ft)	
	268 knots (497 km/h; 308 mph)
at 6,100 m (20,000 ft)	
	266 knots (492 km/h; 305 mph)
Stalling speed, flaps down	
	72 knots (134 km/h; 83 mph)

The first Series 300 'stretched' version of the DHC Dash 8 during its initial flight on 15 May 1987

Max rate of climb at S/L	475 m (1,560 ft)/min
Rate of climb at S/L, one engine out	137 m (450 ft)/min
Certificated ceiling	7,620 m (25,000 ft)
Service ceiling, one engine out	4,575 m (15,000 ft)

FAR Pt 25 T-O field length at S/L, 15° flap:

ISA	960 m (3,150 ft)
ISA + 15°C	1,052 m (3,450 ft)

FAR Pt 25 landing field length, 35° flap, at max landing

weight	908 m (2,979 ft)

Range:

full passenger load	1,085 nm (2,010 km; 1,249 miles)
2,721 kg (6,000 lb) payload	
	1,190 nm (2,205 km; 1,370 miles)
max cargo payload	550 nm (1,019 km; 633 miles)

OPERATIONAL NOISE LEVELS (FAR Pt 36 Stage 3 and ICAO
Annex 16):

T-O	81 EPNdB
Sideline	86 EPNdB
Approach	95 EPNdB

DHC-8 DASH 8M
CAF designations: CC-142 and CT-142
US Air Force designation: E-9A

The Dash 8 is adaptable to a wide range of missions, and is currently in service or on order in a number of variants including military transport, flight calibration, missile range control and navigation training. Other potential missions include medevac, surveillance, search and rescue, early warning and ASW/ASV/maritime patrol.

Two Dash 8M-100s are in service with the Canadian Dept of Transport for airways calibration duties. The Canadian Dept of National Defence operates two as **CC-142** passenger/cargo transports, based at Lahr in West Germany, and is awaiting delivery of four others configured as **CT-142** navigation trainers with an extended nose. These DND aircraft have long-range fuel tanks, rough-field landing gear, high-strength floors and mission-related avionics. Two other Dash 8M-100s, delivered in Spring 1988, have been outfitted by Sierra Research in the USA to be operated by USAF as airborne platforms for patrols off Florida's Gulf Coast, with the designation **E-9A**. They are equipped as flying data links that can relay telemetry, voice communications and drone tracking data while simultaneously performing radar surveillance functions. Equipment includes a large, electronically steerable phased-array radar antenna in a starboard-side fuselage fairing, an AN/APS-128D sea surveillance radar in a ventral radome, and extensive internal avionics and electronics. These ten aircraft are included in the order total given for the Dash 8 Series 100.

Similar special mission versions of the Series 300 are available, notably a **300M ASW** with equipment that would include a nose mounted maritime surveillance radar, FLIR, MAD, ESM, inertial navigation system, sonobuoy processing equipment, a universal display and control system, and wing and fuselage weapon attachment points (see accompanying illustration).

DHC-8 DASH 8 SERIES 300

Announced in mid-1985, the Series 300 is a 'stretched' version of the Dash 8 Series 100 in which fore and aft plugs

Model of proposed Dash 8 Series 300M ASW

totalling 3.43 m (11 ft 3 in) in length are inserted in the fuselage to increase seating capacity to 50 (standard) or 56 passengers (optional) at a seat pitch of 79 cm (31 in). Other fuselage/cabin changes include a new rear service door on the starboard side, an additional wardrobe, larger lavatory, dual air-conditioning packs, and an optional Turbomach T-40 APU. Wing span is increased by tip extensions, and the Series 300 is powered by 1,775 kW (2,380 shp) PW123 engines installed in nacelles identical to those of the Series 100. The large rear cargo compartment of the Series 100, and its door, are retained, as are the standard and optional fuel capacities of the Series 100.

First flight of the Series 300 prototype (converted from the No. 1 Series 100 aircraft C-GDNK) took place on 15 May 1987. Initial deliveries are due to be made in the first quarter of 1989. Orders for the Series 300 totalled 27 by 1 April 1988, with a further 12 on option.

Planned future variants include a cargo or combi version with quick-change options, 2.36 × 1.78 m; 7 ft 9 in × 5 ft 10 in cargo door, and space for up to seven containers plus 454 kg; 1,000 lb of bulk cargo.

DIMENSIONS, EXTERNAL: As for Series 100 except:

Wing span	27.43 m (90 ft 0 in)
Wing aspect ratio	13.4
Length overall	25.68 m (84 ft 3 in)
Wheelbase	9.80 m (32 ft 2 in)

DIMENSIONS, INTERNAL: As for Series 100 except:

Cabin: Length	12.60 m (41 ft 4 in)
Volume	48.7 m³ (1,720 cu ft)
Baggage compartment volume	9.06 m³ (320 cu ft)

AREAS:

Wings, gross	56.21 m² (605.0 sq ft)
Tail surfaces	as for Series 100

WEIGHTS AND LOADINGS:

Operating weight empty	11,204 kg (24,700 lb)

Max usable fuel	as for Series 100
Max payload (passengers)	5,670 kg (12,500 lb)
Max T-O weight	18,642 kg (41,100 lb)
Max landing weight	18,144 kg (40,000 lb)
Max zero-fuel weight	16,873 kg (37,200 lb)
Max wing loading	331.65 kg/m² (67.93 lb/sq ft)
Max power loading	5.25 kg/kW (8.63 lb/shp)

PERFORMANCE (at max T-O weight except where indicated):

Max cruising speed at 13,834 kg (30,500 lb) AUW:	
at 4,575 m (15,000 ft)	286 knots (530 km/h; 329 mph)
at 6,100 m (20,000 ft)	283 knots (524 km/h; 326 mph)
Stalling speed, flaps down	77 knots (141 km/h; 88 mph)
Certificated ceiling	7,620 m (25,000 ft)
Service ceiling, one engine out	4,115 m (13,500 ft)

FAR Pt 25 T-O field length at S/L, 15° flap:

ISA	1,122 m (3,680 ft)
ISA + 15°C	1,220 m (4,000 ft)

FAR Pt 25 landing field length, 35° flap, at max landing

weight	1,122 m (3,680 ft)

Range:

full passenger load	890 nm (1,649 km; 1,025 miles)
2,721 kg (6,000 lb) payload	
	930 nm (1,723 km; 1,071 miles)

DHC-8 DASH 8 SERIES 400

In early 1988 Boeing Canada was continuing to evaluate market prospects for a further 3.05 m (10 ft) 'stretch' of the Dash 8 with a passenger capacity in the 64/70-seat range. New power plants, and cruising speeds in the region of 330 knots (611 km/h; 380 mph), could give the Series 400 broadly equal block times to the smaller jet transports on routes of up to 500 nm (926 km; 576 miles), with substantial reductions in available-seat-mile costs. Deliveries could begin in 1992-93 if a decision to go ahead was taken during 1988.

BRISTOL AEROSPACE
BRISTOL AEROSPACE LTD

PO Box 874, 660 Berry Street, Winnipeg, Manitoba R3C 2S4

Telephone: (204) 775 8331

Telex: 0757774

PRESIDENT: J. A. Bowden

NORTHROP CF-5A UPGRADE PROGRAMME

A major avionics upgrade programme is under way for the Canadian Forces' fleet of approx 50 CF-5A and CF-5D fighters and fighter/trainers, to enable these aircraft to serve in the capacity of pilot familiarisation and lead-in training for the service's CF-18 Hornets. As a part of this programme, Bristol Aerospace has awarded contracts to Ferranti Defence Systems of the UK to supply two

prototype HUDWACs (head-up displays and weapon aiming computers) for a flight test programme due to begin in the Spring of 1988, and to GEC Avionics for two prototype air data computers. Substantial production orders are expected to follow.

In May 1988 the company was also reported to have approached Northrop Corporation with a view to possibly acquiring rights to produce the F-5 and/or F-20 Tigershark.

CANADAIR
CANADAIR INC

Cartierville Airport, 1800 Laurentien Boulevard, St Laurent, Quebec H4R 1K2
POSTAL ADDRESS: PO Box 6087, Station 'A', Montreal, Quebec H3C 3G9
Telephone: (514) 744 1511
Telex: 05-826747
Fax: (514) 744 6586
PRESIDENT AND CHIEF EXECUTIVE OFFICER: Donald C. Lowe
EXECUTIVE VICE-PRESIDENT: Robert A. Wohl
PRESIDENT, MILITARY AIRCRAFT DIVISION:
   Laurent A. Bergeron
PRESIDENT, CHALLENGER DIVISION: L. Anthony Edwards
VICE-PRESIDENTS/GENERAL MANAGERS:
   Andreas Throner (CL-215)
   Vincent Ambrico (Manufacturing and Subcontracts Division)
PUBLIC RELATIONS: Catherine Chase

Canadair Challenger 601-3A, with 'glass cockpit' and upgraded turbofans

Canadair has manufactured more than 4,000 military and commercial aircraft since 1944. It has also been employed in the research, design, development and production of missile components, pilotless surveillance systems and a variety of non-aerospace products. It currently has three plants in the St Laurent complex at Cartierville Airport, and a fourth (being expanded in 1988) at Dorval International Airport, Montreal. Total covered floor space is 260,127 m² (2,800,000 sq ft), and total workforce at the beginning of 1988 was 5,500.

Canadair business was carried on between 1976 and 1986 by the Canadian government, which then sold the company to Bombardier Inc of Montreal. It became a wholly owned Bombardier subsidiary on 23 December 1986. Restructuring into a corporate group and four major business divisions (Challenger, CL-215, Military Aircraft and Manufacturing) took place in 1987. Military Aircraft Division amalgamates the company's unmanned airborne surveillance systems, the CF-18 system engineering support, and other military product support programmes. The Manufacturing Division brings together all fabrication and its supporting services, Challenger assembly and subcontract activities.

The Challenger entered production during 1978, with advanced design of a 'stretched' version starting in November 1987; manufacture of the fifth series of CL-215 tanker/utility amphibians (c/n 1081 onwards) continues, and a CL-215T turboprop version was announced in 1986. Major subcontracts concern outer wing boxes, wing stubs, rear fuselages, forward and aft radomes and main electrical load centres for US Navy and other Lockheed P-3C Orions and the CP-140 Aurora Canadian version of this aircraft; aluminium bulkheads, frames and other machined parts for the McDonnell Douglas F-15; nose barrel assemblies for the McDonnell Douglas F/A-18 Hornet; wing leading-edge components, ailerons and rear cargo doors for the Lockheed C-5B Galaxy transport programme; and rear fuselage sections for the Boeing 767. Engineering support for the CAF's CF-18 Hornet fleet is provided under a 1986 four-year contract by a team comprising Canadair, CAE Electronics (Montreal) and NWI (Edmonton), with Canadair as prime contractor. Production of aircraft spares, and the modification, repair and overhaul of aircraft, are also included in the current work programme.

CANADAIR CHALLENGER 600 and 601
CAF designation: CC-144

The first of three pre-production Challengers (C-GCGR-X, c/n 1001) made its first flight on 8 November 1978. The second flew on 17 March and the third on 14 July 1979. First flight by a production Challenger was made on 21 September 1979, and this joined the programme in October 1979.

The version with Textron Lycoming engines, known as the **Challenger 600**, received Canadian DoT type approval on 11 August 1980, and FAA certification on 7 November of that year. On 10 April 1982 the prototype of a second version was flown for the first time. Known as the **Challenger 601** (previously CL-601), this has General Electric engines and winglets. The first production 601 (C-GBUU) flew for the first time on 17 September 1982. Canadian DoT and FAA certification were awarded on 25 February and 11 March 1983 respectively, and customer deliveries began shortly afterwards. They totalled 163 (83 600s and 80 601s) by 7 April 1988, of which 62 Challenger 600s had been retrofitted with winglets, a modification certificated in 1984. One 600 specially equipped by Dornier of Germany for the Swiss Air-Ambulance service of Zurich is capable of providing intensive care for four stretcher patients on nonstop flights of more than 3,000 km (5,550 km; 3,450 miles) and can carry up to eight patients. No Model 600s are being produced at present, but this version remains available if sufficient orders are received.

The FAI has ratified 18 international records by Challengers for time to height, altitude without payload, and altitude in horizontal flight. Some have since been beaten.

A new version of the 601, with a 'glass cockpit' and upgraded engines, is designated **601-3A**. First flight was made on 28 September 1986; Canadian and US type certification were received on 21 and 30 April 1987 respectively. Category II certification was received five months later. The 601-3A incorporates four main improvements: CF34-3A engines, flat rated to 21°C, for better climb and hot day take-off performance; fully integrated digital flight guidance and flight management system; a power assisted passenger door; and twin landing lights mounted in the nose. First delivery, to TAG Aeronautics, was made on 6 May 1987, and 15 of this version had been delivered by 7 April 1988.

A long range option, to become available in the first quarter of 1989 on new production aircraft and for retrofit, will increase the range of the Challenger 601 to 3,600 nm (6,667 km; 4,142 miles) with NBAA IFR reserves. The modification will add 91 kg (200 lb) to the aircraft's empty weight. Max ramp weight will be increased to 20,300 kg (44,750 lb).

Several military variants have been ordered or are under development. The Canadian Dept of Transport has two 601s for flight inspection missions; the Dept of National Defence ordered seven 600s for electronic support and training with No. 414 Squadron, with an eighth for the Aeronautical Engineering and Test Establishment at Cold

Lake, Alberta, as a testbed for developing such future military applications as maritime reconnaissance. The DND's No. 412 Squadron has four 600s for government transport duties, and four 601s as VIP transports. All 16 DND aircraft have a Litton LTN-91 inertial navigation system. Other military versions have been ordered by the Royal Malaysian Air Force (two), West German Luftwaffe (seven 601s for special air missions), and the People's Republic of China (three 601s and two 601-3As as VIP transports). Some Luftwaffe 601s are configured as 12/16-passenger transports, one as a passenger/cargo combi, and one as an air ambulance.

The following description applies to the 601 and 601-3A, except where indicated otherwise:

TYPE: Twin-turbofan business, cargo and commuter transport.

WINGS: Cantilever low-wing monoplane, built in one piece. Advanced technology section (with winglets on Challenger 601; optional on 600). Thickness/chord ratio 14% at root, 12% at leading-edge sweep break and 10% at tip. Dihedral 2° 20'. Incidence 3° at root. Sweepback at quarter-chord 25°. Two-spar structure, primarily of aluminium alloy; spars covered with skin/stringer panels to form rigid torsion box. Two-section double-slotted trailing-edge flaps. Hydraulically powered aluminium plain ailerons. Inboard spoilers for descent control and ground lift dumping. No tabs. Thermal anti-icing of leading-edges by engine bleed air.

FUSELAGE: Aluminium alloy damage-tolerant semi-monocoque pressurised structure of circular cross-section. Employs chemically milled aluminium alloy skins with riveted frames and stringers, providing optimum strength characteristics while minimising aircraft weight.

TAIL UNIT: Cantilever multi-spar aluminium alloy T tail, with swept vertical and horizontal surfaces. All control surfaces hydraulically powered. Tailplane incidence adjusted by electric trim motor. No tabs.

LANDING GEAR: Hydraulically retractable tricycle type, with twin wheels and Dowty Rotol oleo-pneumatic shock absorber on each unit. Mainwheels retract inward into wing centre-section, nose unit forward. Nose unit steerable and self-centring. Mainwheels have Goodyear 26 × 6.65 tyres, pressure 15.38 bars (223 lb/sq in); nosewheels have Goodyear 18 × 4.4 tyres, pressure 10.0 bars (145 lb/sq in). Goodyear hydraulically operated multiple-disc carbon brakes with fully modulated anti-skid system.

POWER PLANT: Two 33.36 kN (7,500 lb st) Textron Lycoming ALF 502L-2 or L-3 turbofans in Challenger 600; General Electric CF34-1As in Challenger 601 or CF34-3A in 601-3A, each rated at 40.66 kN (9,140 lb st) with automatic power reserve, or 38.48 kN (8,650 lb st) without APR. One engine is pylon mounted on each side of rear fuselage, fitted with cascade type fan-air thrust reversers. Integral fuel tank in centre-section (capacity 2,839 litres; 750 US gallons; 624 Imp gallons), one in each wing (each 2,725 litres; 720 US gallons; 600 Imp gallons) and auxiliary tank beneath cabin floor; total capacity 9,278 litres (2,451 US gallons; 2,041 Imp gallons). Pressure and gravity fuelling and defuelling. Oil capacity 13.6 litres (3.6 US gallons; 3 Imp gallons).

ACCOMMODATION: Pilot and co-pilot side by side on flight deck with dual controls. Blind-flying instrumentation standard. Interiors are installed to customer's specifications. A maximum of 19 passenger seats is approved. Typical installations include toilet, buffet, bar and wardrobe. The baggage compartment, with its own loading door, is accessible in flight. Downward opening door on port side, forward of wing, from c/n 24 onwards. (Upward opening on earlier aircraft.) Door is power assisted on 601-3A. Overwing emergency exit on starboard side. Entire accommodation heated, ventilated and air-conditioned.

SYSTEMS: Sundstrand pressurisation and AiResearch air-conditioning systems, max pressure differential 0.64 bars (9.3 lb/sq in) in Challenger 600, 0.62 bars (9.0 lb/sq in) in Challenger 601 and 601-3A. Three independent hydraulic systems, each of 207 bars (3,000 lb/sq in). No. 1 system

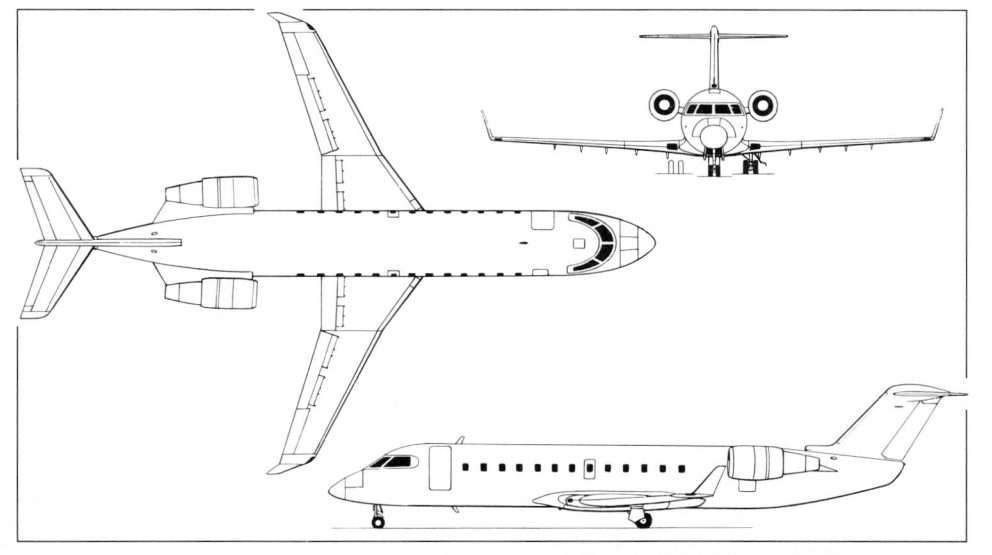

Canadair CL-601 RJ regional jet transport (two General Electric CF34-3A turbofans) *(Pilot Press)*

powers flight controls (via servo-actuators positioned by cables and pushrods); No. 2 system for flight controls and brakes; No. 3 system for flight controls, landing gear extension/retraction, brakes and nosewheel steering. Nos. 1 and 2 systems each powered by an engine driven pump, supplemented by an AC electric pump; No. 3 system by two AC pumps. Two 30kVA engine driven generators supply primary 115/200V three-phase AC electric power at 400Hz. Three transformer-rectifiers to convert AC power to 28V DC; one 43Ah nickel-cadmium battery. Alternative primary power provided by APU and an air driven generator, the latter being deployed automatically if the engine driven generators and APU are inoperative. Stall warning system, with stick shakers and stick pusher. Garrett GTCP-100E gas turbine APU (to be certificated for in-flight operation) for engine start, ground air-conditioning and other services. Electric anti-icing of windscreen, flight deck side windows and pitot heads; Sundstrand bleed air anti-icing of wings, tailplane, engine intake cowls and guide vanes. Gaseous oxygen system, pressure 124 bars (1,800 lb/sq in). Continuous-element fire detectors in each engine nacelle and APU; two-shot extinguishing system for engines, single-shot system for APU.

AVIONICS (except 601-3A): Standard avionics include dual Collins VHF-20A com, dual Collins VIR-30A VOR/ILS/marker beacon receiver, dual Sperry SPZ 600 flight directors, SPZ 600 autopilot with dual servos, dual TDR-90 transponders, dual DME (with HSI display), one ALT-55B radio altimeter, dual C-14 compasses, standby compass, one ADF-60, dual intercom system, comparator warning system, RCA Primus 400 weather radar, HF and other antennae. Provision, at customer's option, for HF com, third VHF com, second ADF, VLF nav, INS, GPWS, ELT, flight data recorder and cockpit voice recorder.

AVIONICS (601-3A): Sperry digital avionics include five-tube electronic flight instrument system (EFIS); single multi-function display (MFD); dual Honeywell laser inertial reference systems (LIRS); dual flight management systems; digital automatic flight control system, with dual channel fail-operational autopilot and flight director; Mach trim and auto trim; dual digital air data system; Sperry four-colour digital weather radar; radio altimeter; Collins Pro Line II nav/coms, including dual VHF com; dual VHF nav; dual DME; dual ATC transponders; dual ADF; dual HF com; cockpit voice recorder; standby instruments (artificial horizon, airspeed indicator and altimeter). Systems certificated for Cat. II operations. Space provisions for flight data recorder, ELT, VLF/Omega, GPWS, and full provisions for third LIRS.

DIMENSIONS, EXTERNAL:

Wing span: 600	18.85 m (61 ft 10 in)
601, over winglets	19.61 m (64 ft 4 in)
Wing chord: at fuselage c/l	4.89 m (16 ft 0½ in)
at tip	1.27 m (4 ft 1.9 in)
Wing aspect ratio: 600	7.4
601	8.5
Length overall	20.85 m (68 ft 5 in)
Fuselage: Max diameter	2.69 m (8 ft 10 in)
Height overall	6.30 m (20 ft 8 in)
Tailplane span	6.20 m (20 ft 4 in)
Wheel track (c/l of shock struts)	3.18 m (10 ft 5 in)
Wheelbase	7.99 m (26 ft 2½ in)
Passenger door (port, fwd): Height	1.78 m (5 ft 10 in)
Width	0.91 m (3 ft 0 in)
Height to sill	1.61 m (5 ft 3½ in)
Baggage door (port, rear): Height	0.84 m (2 ft 9 in)
Width	0.71 m (2 ft 4 in)
Height to sill	1.61 m (5 ft 3½ in)
Overwing emergency exit (stbd):	
Height	0.91 m (3 ft 0 in)
Width	0.51 m (1 ft 8 in)

DIMENSIONS, INTERNAL:

Cabin: Length, incl galley, toilet and baggage area, excl flight deck	8.61 m (28 ft 3 in)
Max width	2.49 m (8 ft 2 in)
Width at floor level	2.18 m (7 ft 2 in)
Max height	1.85 m (6 ft 1 in)
Floor area	18.77 m² (202 sq ft)
Volume	32.6 m³ (1,150 cu ft)

AREAS:

Wings, gross: 600	48.31 m² (520.0 sq ft)
Ailerons (total)	1.39 m² (15.0 sq ft)
Trailing-edge flaps (total)	7.80 m² (84.0 sq ft)
Fin	9.18 m² (98.8 sq ft)
Rudder	2.03 m² (21.9 sq ft)
Tailplane	6.45 m² (69.4 sq ft)
Elevators (total)	2.15 m² (23.1 sq ft)

WEIGHTS:

Manufacturer's weight empty:	
600	8,464 kg (18,660 lb)
601	9,049 kg (19,950 lb)
601-3A	9,292 kg (20,485 lb)
Typical operating weight empty:	
600	10,562 kg (23,285 lb)
601	11,151 kg (24,585 lb)
601-3A	11,197 kg (24,685 lb)
Max fuel: 600	6,754 kg (14,890 lb)
601, 601-3A	7,559 kg (16,665 lb)

Max payload: 600	2,365 kg (5,215 lb)
601	2,229 kg (4,915 lb)
601-3A	2,184 kg (4,815 lb)
Payload with max fuel: 600	1,395 kg (3,075 lb)
601	907 kg (2,000 lb)
601-3A	862 kg (1,900 lb)
Max T-O weight: 600	18,642 kg (41,100 lb)*
601, 601-3A	19,550 kg (43,100 lb)
Max ramp weight: 600	18,710 kg (41,250 lb)
601, 601-3A	19,618 kg (43,250 lb)
Max landing weight:	
600, 601, 601-3A	16,329 kg (36,000 lb)
Max zero-fuel weight: 600	12,927 kg (28,500 lb)
601	14,061 kg (31,000 lb)
601-3A	13,381 kg (29,500 lb)**
Max wing loading: 600	385.9 kg/m² (79.04 lb/sq ft)
601, 601-3A	404.7 kg/m² (82.88 lb/sq ft)
Max power loading: 600	279.41 kg/kN (2.74 lb/lb st)
601	254.03 kg/kN (2.49 lb/lb st)
601-3A	240.81 kg/kN (2.36 lb/lb st)

*18,710 kg (41,250 lb) with optional winglets
**14,061 kg (31,000 lb) available optionally

PERFORMANCE (at max T-O weight except where indicated):

Max cruising speed:	
600, 601, 601-3A	459 knots (851 km/h; 529 mph)
Normal cruising speed:	
600, 601, 601-3A	442 knots (819 km/h; 509 mph)
Long-range cruising speed:	
600	401 knots (743 km/h; 462 mph)
601, 601-3A	424 knots (786 km/h; 488 mph)
Time to initial cruise altitude: 600	25 min
601	21 min
601-3A	20 min
Max operating altitude (all)	12,500 m (41,000 ft)
Service ceiling, one engine out (all)	7,315 m (24,000 ft)
Balanced T-O field length (ISA at S/L):	
600	1,737 m (5,700 ft)
601, 601-3A	1,645 m (5,400 ft)
Landing distance at S/L at max landing weight:	
600, 601-3A	1,006 m (3,300 ft)
601	1,082 m (3,550 ft)
Min ground turning radius (all)	20.27 m (66 ft 6 in)
Range with max fuel and five passengers, NBAA IFR reserves (200 nm; 370 km; 230 mile alternate) at long-range cruising speed:	
600 (basic)	2,800 nm (5,186 km; 3,222 miles)
600 (with fuselage tank)	3,123 nm (5,784 km; 3,594 miles)
601	3,440 nm (6,371 km; 3,959 miles)
601-3A	3,430 nm (6,356 km; 3,950 miles)
Design g limit: 600	+2.7
601, 601-3A	+2.6

OPERATIONAL NOISE LEVELS (FAR Pt36):

T-O: 600	84.7 EPNdB
601	79.9 EPNdB
601-3A	79.4 EPNdB
Sideline: 600	89.5 EPNdB
601	84.8 EPNdB
601-3A	85.9 EPNdB
Approach: 600	91.6 EPNdB
601, 601-3A	89.4 EPNdB

CANADAIR CL-601 RJ REGIONAL JET

Canadair has received encouraging interest in a 'stretched' version of the Challenger 601, for which design studies began in Autumn 1986. This project officially entered a one-year full advanced design phase in November 1987.

Intended primarily for commuter and package express service operators, the Challenger CL-601 RJ (for regional jet) has fuselage extensions of 3.25 m (10 ft 8 in) forward of the wings and 2.84 m (9 ft 4 in) aft. This more than doubles the capacity of the 19-passenger Challenger 601, enabling the RJ to accommodate up to 48 people in its passenger form, while retaining a generous baggage capacity; or a maximum payload of 4,799 kg (10,580 lb) in all-cargo configuration. Emergency exits are increased to three: one overwing each side, plus one opposite the port side (forward) passenger door. To meet field length requirements for this class of aircraft, some modifications will also be made to the wings. The power plant of the Challenger 601-3A will be retained in the RJ.

TYPE: Twin-turbofan regional transport.

WINGS: Of generally similar planform to Challenger 601, but with some design and structural changes. Wing sections NACA 0010-64 (mod) at root, NACA 0008-64 (mod) at tip, with respective thickness/chord ratios of 13.3% and 10.0%. Dihedral 2° 20′. Incidence 3° 27′ 36″ at root. Sweepback at quarter-chord 24° 51′ 36″. Flap vanes of composite material. Spoilers increased to four on each wing, inner two each side functioning as ground spoilers, outer two comprising one proportional spoiler and a spoileron.

FUSELAGE: Generally as for Challenger except for increased length.

TAIL UNIT: As Challenger except for modified tailplane leading-edge.

LANDING GEAR: Hydraulically retractable tricycle type, with nosewheel unit generally as described for Challenger. Inward retracting main units each have Dowty floating piston type shock absorption, and 14 in wheels with 28 ×

9-14 Goodyear tyres, pressure 10.55 bars (153 lb/sq in). Steel multi-disc brakes and fully modulated anti-skid system.

POWER PLANT: Two General Electric CF34-3A turbofans, each rated at 41.0 kN (9,220 lb st) with APR. Fuel in two integral wing tanks, combined capacity 5,300 litres (1,400 US gallons; 1,166 Imp gallons). Pressure refuelling point in starboard leading-edge wingroot; two gravity points on each wing.

ACCOMMODATION: Pilot, co-pilot and one or two cabin attendants. Main cabin seats up to 48 people, four-abreast at 81 cm (32 in) pitch, with centre aisle. Downward opening passenger door at front, port side, with plug type outward opening forward exit/service door (Class I emergency exit) opposite on starboard side. Inward opening baggage door on port side at rear. Overwing emergency exit each side. Outward opening equipment bay door at rear, starboard side. Crew hatch in flight deck roof. Entire accommodation pressurised, including rear baggage compartment.

SYSTEMS: Generally as for Challenger.

AVIONICS: 650 weather radar, Collins Pro Line II radios, dual flight guidance system, dual AHRS, single flight management system, EFIS and MFD proposed as standard, with HF radio, dual/triple IRS, dual FMS and MLS as options.

DIMENSIONS, EXTERNAL: As for Challenger 601 except:

Wing span	21.44 m (70 ft 4 in)
Wing chord at root	5.37 m (17 ft 7.7 in)
Wing aspect ratio	9.5
Length overall	26.95 m (88 ft 5 in)
Length of fuselage	24.38 m (80 ft 0 in)
Wheelbase	11.32 m (37 ft 1½ in)

DIMENSIONS, INTERNAL:

Cabin: Length, incl galley and toilet, excl flight deck	14.71 m (48 ft 3 in)
Cross-section	as Challenger 601
Floor area	32.05 m² (345.0 sq ft)
Volume	56.27 m³ (1,987 cu ft)
Stowage volume:	
Main (rear) baggage compartment	9.23 m³ (326.0 cu ft)
Wardrobes/bins/underseat (total)	6.54 m³ (231.0 cu ft)

AREAS:

Wings, gross	48.31 m² (520.0 sq ft)
Ailerons (total)	1.93 m² (20.8 sq ft)
Trailing-edge flaps (total)	10.57 m² (113.8 sq ft)
Spoilers (total)	2.23 m² (24.0 sq ft)
Winglets (total)	1.38 m² (14.9 sq ft)
Fin	9.13 m² (98.3 sq ft)
Rudder	2.03 m² (21.9 sq ft)
Tailplane	11.15 m² (120.0 sq ft)
Elevators (total)	2.15 m² (23.1 sq ft)

WEIGHTS AND LOADINGS:

Operating weight empty	13,485 kg (29,730 lb)
Max payload (structural)	5,565 kg (12,270 lb)
Max fuel	4,441 kg (9,790 lb)
Max T-O weight	21,432 kg (47,250 lb)
Max ramp weight	21,545 kg (47,500 lb)
Max zero-fuel weight	19,051 kg (42,000 lb)
Max landing weight	20,185 kg (44,500 lb)
Max wing loading	443.8 kg/m² (90.9 lb/sq ft)
Max power loading	261.37 kg/kN (2.56 lb/lb st)

PERFORMANCE (estimated, at max T-O weight except where indicated):

Max operating speed	Mach 0.80 or 335 knots (621 km/h; 386 mph) CAS
Max cruising speed at 11,000 m (36,000 ft)	Mach 0.77
Long-range cruising speed at 11,000 m (36,000 ft)	Mach 0.74
Stalling speed, 45° flap	100 knots (185 km/h; 115 mph)
Max rate of climb at S/L	1,190 m (3,900 ft)/min
Max operating altitude	11,275 m (37,000 ft)
FAR T-O field length at S/L, ISA	1,585 m (5,200 ft)
FAR landing field length at S/L, ISA, at max landing weight	1,631 m (5,350 ft)
Range, at long-range cruising speed, FAR Pt 121 reserves: with max payload	981 nm (1,818 km; 1,130 miles)

OPERATIONAL NOISE LEVELS (estimated):

T-O	82.0 EPNdB
Approach	91.0 EPNdB
Sideline	86.0 EPNdB

CANADAIR CL-215

The Canadair CL-215 is a twin-engined amphibian, intended primarily for firefighting but adaptable to a wide variety of other duties. Operable from small airstrips, lakes, ocean bays etc, it made its first flight on 23 October 1967 and its first water take-off on 2 May 1968. Canadian DoT certification in the Utility and Restricted categories was obtained on 7 March 1969, followed by FAA certification in the Restricted category on 15 May of the same year.

By 1 March 1988 sales totalling 112 had been made to the governments of France (15); Greece (15); Italy (4); Spain (20); Thailand (2); Venezuela (2); Yugoslavia (5); and eight Canadian provinces (Alberta 4, Manitoba 5, Newfoundland 4, Northwest Territories 2, Ontario 9, Quebec 19, Saskatchewan 4 and Yukon 2). Deliveries totalled 105 by 1 January 1988, leaving seven to be delivered to Canadian provincial governments. Six export positions were available for sale during 1988. All aircraft are capable of firefighting and other roles: Spain has eight equipped for SAR and coastal patrol, and Thailand two; the Venezuelan pair are configured as passenger transport aircraft.

Production of the first 80 aircraft was completed in batches of 30, 20, 15 and 15. Details of the first and second can be found in the 1977-78 *Jane's*, and of the third in the 1979-80 edition. The current fifth series involves 45 aircraft, after which series production of the CL-215T (see next entry) will begin.

The firefighting installation consists of two internal tanks, two retractable probes and two drop doors, plus the associated operating systems. It attacks fires either: (a) with water or chemical retardants ground loaded at airports; or (b) with fresh or salt water scooped from a suitable body of water as the aircraft skims across the surface.

The aircraft carries a maximum water or retardant load of 5,346 litres (1,412 US gallons; 1,176 Imp gallons). The tanks can be ground filled in 2 min, or scoop filled in 10 s while the aircraft planes at 70 knots (130 km/h; 81 mph). Pickup distance in still air, from 15 m (50 ft) above the surface on approach to 15 m (50 ft) above the surface during climb-out, is 1,200 m (3,935 ft).

Single CL-215s have frequently made over 100 drops totalling more than 534,600 litres (141,230 US gallons; 117,600 Imp gallons) in one day. Full loads have been scooped from the Mediterranean in wave heights of up to 2 m (6 ft). In 1983 a Yugoslav CL-215 made 225 drops totalling 1,202,850 litres (317,760 US gallons; 264,590 Imp gallons) on fires in one day. Total drops by CL-215s had reached 660,000 by February 1988.

A lightweight integrated liquid spray system has also been certificated, and four have been purchased for the Yugoslav CL-215s. The system, which does not interfere with the primary role of firefighting, is available for retrofit. Uses include the application of oil dispersants and pesticides. Tests conducted at Canadair have shown that the CL-215 can be used to extinguish oil fires by airdropping a suitable foaming agent. Another type of foam agent, mixed on board the aircraft after scooping, has proved particularly effective against forest fires in field trials in France and Spain.

TYPE: Twin-engined multi-purpose amphibian.

WINGS: Cantilever high-wing monoplane. No dihedral. All-metal one-piece fail-safe structure, with front and rear spars at 16 and 49 per cent chord. Spars of conventional construction, with extruded caps and webs stiffened by vertical members. Aluminium alloy skin, with riveted spanwise extruded stringers, is supported at 762 mm (30 in) pitch by interspar ribs. Leading-edge consists of aluminium alloy skin attached to pressed nose-ribs and spanwise stringers. Hydraulically operated all-metal single-slotted flaps, supported by four external hinges on interspar ribs on each wing. Trim tab and geared tab in port aileron, rudder/aileron interconnect tab in starboard aileron. Detachable glassfibre wingtips.

FUSELAGE: All-metal single-step flying-boat hull of conventional fail-safe construction.

TAIL UNIT: Cantilever all-metal fail-safe structure with horizontal surfaces mounted midway up fin. Structure of aluminium alloy sheet, honeycomb panels, extrusions and fittings. Elevators and rudder fitted with dynamic balance, trim tab (port elevator only), spring tabs and geared tabs. Provision for de-icing of leading-edges.

LANDING GEAR: Hydraulically retractable tricycle type. Fully castoring, self-centring twin-wheel nose unit retracts rearward into hull and is fully enclosed by doors. Fifth series aircraft are fitted with nosewheel steering, and a retrofit kit will be made available for earlier aircraft. Main gear support structures retract into wells in sides of hull. A plate mounted on each main gear assembly encloses bottom of wheel well. Mainwheel tyre pressure 5.31 bars (77 lb/sq in); nosewheel tyre pressure 6.55 bars (95 lb/sq in). Hydraulic disc brakes. Non-retractable stabilising floats are each carried on a pylon cantilevered from wing box structure, with breakaway provision.

POWER PLANT: Two 1,566 kW (2,100 hp) Pratt & Whitney R-2800-CA3 eighteen-cylinder radial engines, each driving a Hamilton Standard Hydromatic constant-speed fully-feathering three-blade propeller, with 43E60 hub and type 6903A blades. Two fuel tanks, each of eight flexible cells, in wing spar box, with total usable capacity of 5,910 litres (1,561 US gallons; 1,300 Imp gallons). Gravity refuelling through two points above each tank. Oil in two tanks, with total capacity of 272.75 litres (72 US gallons; 60 Imp gallons), aft of engine firewalls.

ACCOMMODATION (water bomber version): Crew of two side by side on flight deck. Dual controls standard. Two 2,673 litre (706 US gallon; 588 Imp gallon) water tanks in main fuselage compartment, with retractable pickup probe in each side of hull bottom. Water drop door in each side of hull bottom. Flush doors on port side of fuselage forward and aft of wings. Emergency exit on starboard side aft of wing trailing-edge. Emergency hatch above starboard cockpit. Mooring hatch in upper surface of nose. Side facing canvas folding seats for eight people are located in the forward cabin area.

ACCOMMODATION (other roles): When configured for patrol and search and rescue missions, aircraft has additional stations for a flight engineer, navigator and two observers. Navigator's station, immediately behind flight deck, includes search radar display. Observers' stations in rear fuselage have sliding seats which can be positioned alongside blister windows. Toilet in rear of cabin; galley installed. Additional seats and/or stretchers available. In passenger transport configuration, up to 26 forward facing seats can be fitted in a fully furnished interior with toilet and galley. Cargo tiedown fittings for loads of up to 2,268 kg (5,000 lb). Provision for extra cabin windows, to a maximum of 14.

Canadair CL-215 of the Spanish Air Force *(Ivo Sturzenegger)*

SYSTEMS: Hydraulic system, pressure 207 bars (3,000 lb/sq in), utilises two engine driven pumps (max flow rate 45.5 litres; 12 US gallons; 10 Imp gallons/min) to actuate landing gear, flaps, water drop doors, pickup probes and wheel brakes. Unpressurised air/oil reservoir. Electrically driven third pump provides hydraulic power for emergency actuation of landing gear and brakes and closure of water doors. Electrical system includes two 400VA 115V 400Hz static inverters (800VA in SAR version), two 28V 200A DC engine driven generators, one 36Ah lead-acid battery, and one aircooled petrol engine driven 28V 200A generator GPU.

AVIONICS AND EQUIPMENT: Standard installation includes dual VHF transceivers, single VHF/FM com, dual VOR/ILS receivers, dual ADF, two marker beacon receivers, ATC transponder and ELT. Optional avionics include HF, DME and radio altimeter. A search radar is optional on the SAR version.

DIMENSIONS, EXTERNAL:

Wing span	28.60 m (93 ft 10 in)
Wing chord (constant)	3.54 m (11 ft 7½ in)
Wing aspect ratio	8.2
Length overall	19.82 m (65 ft 0¼ in)
Beam	2.59 m (8 ft 6 in)
Length/beam ratio	7.5
Height overall: on land	8.98 m (29 ft 5½ in)
on water	6.88 m (22 ft 7 in)
Draught: wheels up	1.12 m (3 ft 8 in)
wheels down	2.03 m (6 ft 8 in)
Tailplane span	10.97 m (36 ft 0 in)
Wheel track	5.28 m (17 ft 4 in)
Wheelbase	7.23 m (23 ft 9 in)
Propeller diameter	4.34 m (14 ft 3 in)
Forward door: Height*	1.37 m (4 ft 6 in)
Width	1.03 m (3 ft 4 in)
Height to sill	1.68 m (5 ft 6 in)
Rear door: Height	1.12 m (3 ft 8 in)
Width	1.03 m (3 ft 4 in)
Height to sill	1.83 m (6 ft 0 in)
Water drop door: Length	1.60 m (5 ft 3 in)
Width	0.81 m (2 ft 8 in)
Emergency exit: Height	0.91 m (3 ft 0 in)
Width	0.51 m (1 ft 8 in)

* *incl 25 cm (10 in) removable sill*

DIMENSIONS, INTERNAL:

Cabin, excl flight deck: Length	9.38 m (30 ft 9½ in)
Max width	2.39 m (7 ft 10 in)
Max height	1.90 m (6 ft 3 in)
Floor area	19.69 m^2 (212 sq ft)
Volume	35.59 m^3 (1,257 cu ft)

AREAS:

Wings, gross	100.33 m^2 (1,080.0 sq ft)
Ailerons (total)	8.05 m^2 (86.6 sq ft)
Flaps (total)	22.39 m^2 (241.0 sq ft)
Fin	11.22 m^2 (120.75 sq ft)
Rudder, incl tabs	6.02 m^2 (64.75 sq ft)
Tailplane	20.55 m^2 (221.2 sq ft)
Elevators (total, incl tabs)	7.88 m^2 (84.8 sq ft)

WEIGHTS AND LOADINGS:

Manufacturer's weight empty	12,220 kg (26,941 lb)
Typical operating weight empty	12,738 kg (28,082 lb)
Max fuel weight	4,245 kg (9,360 lb)
Max payload: Water bomber	5,443 kg (12,000 lb)
Utility version	3,864 kg (8,518 lb)
Max T-O weight (land)	19,731 kg (43,500 lb)
Max T-O weight (water)	17,100 kg (37,700 lb)
Max zero-fuel weight	18,143 kg (40,000 lb)
Max landing weight: on land	15,603 kg (34,400 lb)
on water	16,780 kg (37,000 lb)
Cabin floor loading	732 kg/m^2 (150 lb/sq ft)
Max wing loading	196.66 kg/m^2 (40.3 lb/sq ft)
Max power loading	6.23 kg/kW (10.36 lb/hp)

PERFORMANCE:

Cruising speed (max recommended power) at AUW of 18,595 kg (41,000 lb) at 3,050 m (10,000 ft)
157 knots (291 km/h; 181 mph)

Stalling speed, 15° flap, AUW of 19,731 kg (43,500 lb)
79 knots (145 km/h; 90 mph)

Stalling speed, 25° flap, AUW of 15,603 kg (34,400 lb), power off 66 knots (123 km/h; 76 mph)

Max rate of climb at S/L at AUW of 19,731 kg (43,500 lb) at max continuous power 305 m (1,000 ft)/min

Rate of climb at S/L, one engine out, at AUW of 17,100 kg (37,700 lb) at T-O power 75 m (245 ft)/min

T-O to 15 m (50 ft):
from land at AUW of 19,731 kg (43,500 lb)
811 m (2,660 ft)
from water at AUW of 17,100 kg (37,700 lb)
800 m (2,625 ft)

Landing from 15 m (50 ft):
on land at AUW of 15,603 kg (34,400 lb)
732 m (2,400 ft)
on water at AUW of 16,780 kg (37,000 lb)
835 m (2,740 ft)

Range with 1,587 kg (3,500 lb) payload:
at max cruise power
925 nm (1,714 km; 1,065 miles)
at long-range cruise power
1,130 nm (2,094 km; 1,301 miles)

CANADAIR CL-215T

In August 1986 Canadair announced its intention to develop a turboprop version of the CL-215. The CL-215T will become available in 1989, both as a new-build aircraft and in the form of retrofit kits for existing operators. Firefighting/aerial spraying are expected to account for some 44 per cent of CL-215T sales, but a larger share of the potential market is envisaged for various maritime, military or paramilitary versions (33 per cent, including surveillance, ASV/ASW coastal defence, SAR, and customs/immigration patrol), and for civil personnel or utility transport versions (23 per cent).

The CL-215T will, in essence, utilise the well proven basic airframe of the piston engined CL-215, with a number of improvements. These will include an upgraded and air-conditioned flight deck, a new fuel system with both pressure and gravity refuelling, nosewheel steering (on new-build aircraft only), wingtip endplates, and a four-tank drop system for firefighting missions. An extensive list of options will be available for specialised applications, including underwing hardpoints. Various military and commercial versions have been defined, including variants equipped with airborne radar and for night firefighting and maritime operations.

Starting on 7 December 1987, Canadair is modifying two CL-215s as CL-215T prototypes, with a first flight planned for December 1988, followed by certification in October 1989. Retrofit kits will become available first, in October 1989, followed by new-production CL-215Ts in February 1990. Three potential launch customers (France, Quebec and Spain) have been identified, and orders for "upwards of 24" aircraft are said to be required to substantiate a production commitment. Co-production or licence manufacture agreements are open for negotiation.

TYPE: Twin-turboprop multi-purpose amphibian.

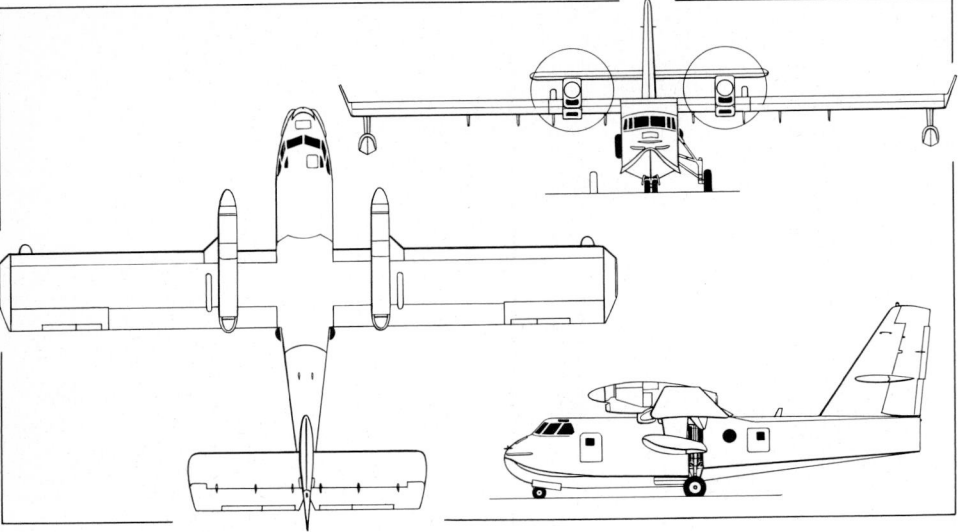

Canadair CL-215T twin-turboprop general purpose amphibian *(Pilot Press)*

AIRFRAME: As described for CL-215, except for new damage tolerant nacelles and metal wingtip endplates. Latter improve lateral stability and permit use of full engine ratings. Powered ailerons, with Jacottet actuators, standard on production aircraft. Steerable nosewheel unit standard on new-build aircraft.

POWER PLANT: Two 1,775 kW (2,380 shp) Pratt & Whitney Canada PW123AF turboprops, each driving a Hamilton Standard 14SF-17 four-blade constant-speed fully-feathering reversible-pitch propeller with spinner. Two fuel tanks, each of eight identical flexible cells, in wing spar box, with total usable capacity of 5,796 litres (1,531 US gallons; 1,275 Imp gallons). Single-point pressure refuelling (rear fuselage, starboard side), plus gravity point above each tank. Provision for carrying two 1,136 litre (300 US gallon; 250 Imp gallon) auxiliary fuel tanks on underwing pylons. Pneumatic/electric intake de-icing system.

ACCOMMODATION: Normal crew of two side by side on flight deck, with dual controls. Additional stations in maritime patrol/SAR versions for flight engineer, navigator and two observers. For water bomber cabin installation, see under 'Equipment' paragraph. With water tanks removed, transport configurations can include shuttle layout for 35 passenger seats plus toilet; or standard layout for 32 passengers plus toilet, galley and baggage area, both with seat pitch of 79 cm (31 in). Combi layout offers cargo at front, full firefighting capability, plus 11 seats at rear. Other quick-change interiors available for medevac (12 stretchers and two medical attendants), utility/paratroop (up to 14 foldup troop-type canvas seats in cabin, in two inward facing rows), all-cargo, or other special missions according to customer's requirements. Flush doors to main cabin on port side of fuselage forward and aft of wings. Emergency exit on starboard side aft of wing trailing-edge. Crew emergency

hatch in flight deck roof on starboard side. Mooring hatch in upper surface of nose. Large cargo loading door optional; provision for additional cabin windows.

SYSTEMS: Generally similar to those described for CL-215 except for Janitrol heater and Casey vapour cycle air-conditioning. Electrical system power supplied by two 28V DC 400A starter/generators and two 800VA static inverters, plus two 40Ah nickel-cadmium batteries instead of single lead-acid battery. Ice protection system optional.

AVIONICS: Assumed to be similar to those in CL-215. Stated options for CL-215T include autopilot, VLF/Omega nav system, search radar and colour weather radar.

EQUIPMENT (water bomber): Four integral water tanks in main fuselage compartment, near CG (combined capacity 6,132 litres; 1,620 US gallons; 1,350 Imp gallons), forward of which are eight inward facing seats. Hydraulically actuated scoop on each side, aft of hull step, fillable also on ground by hose adapter on each side of fuselage. Four independently openable water drop doors in hull bottom. Improved drop pattern and drop door sequencing compared with CL-215. Optional spray kit can be coupled with firefighting tanks for large scale spraying of oil dispersants and insecticides. In a typical mission profile, with a fire 100 nm (185 km; 115 miles) from the CL-215T's base, a water source 6 nm (11 km; 7 miles) from the fire, and 45 min fuel reserves, aircraft could make 35 water scoop and drop circuits before having to return to base to refuel. Water tanks can be scoop-filled completely (on smooth water in ISA conditions) in an on-water distance of only 564 m (1,850 ft); partial water loads can be scooped on smaller bodies of water. Minimum safe water depth for scooping operations is only 1.40 m (4 ft 7 in).

EQUIPMENT (other versions): Stretcher kits, passenger or troop seats, cargo tiedowns, searchlight, and other

equipment according to mission and customer requirements. Provision for two underwing pylon attachment points for auxiliary fuel tanks or other stores.

DIMENSIONS, EXTERNAL AND INTERNAL, AND AREAS:
As for CL-215 except:

Propeller diameter	3.97 m (13 ft 0¼ in)
Propeller/fuselage clearance	0.59 m (1 ft 11¼ in)
Propeller/water clearance	1.30 m (4 ft 3¼ in)
Propeller/ground clearance	2.77 m (9 ft 1 in)

WEIGHTS (A: water bomber; B: utility, land or water based):

Typical operating weight empty:	
A	11,975 kg (26,400 lb)
B	11,720 kg (25,840 lb)
Max internal fuel weight: A, B	4,649 kg (10,250 lb)
Max payload: A (disposable)	6,123 kg (13,500 lb)
B	4,790 kg (10,560 lb)
Max ramp weight: A (land)	19,890 kg (43,850 lb)
A (water), B	17,236 kg (38,000 lb)
Max T-O weight:	
A, production (land)	19,890 kg (43,850 lb)
A, retrofit (land)	19,731 kg (43,500 lb)
A (water), B (land and water)	17,100 kg (37,700 lb)
Max flying weight for water scooping:	
A	16,102 kg (35,500 lb)
Max flying weight after water scooping:	
A, new production	20,865 kg (46,000 lb)
A, retrofit	19,731 kg (43,500 lb)
Max landing weight:	
A, new production (land)	16,783 kg (37,000 lb)
A, retrofit (land)	15,603 kg (34,400 lb)
A, new production (water), B (water), and retrofit from c/n 1056	16,783 kg (37,000 lb)
A (water), B (water), retrofit c/n 1001-1055	15,603 kg (34,400 lb)
Max zero-fuel weight:	
A, new production	19,051 kg (42,000 lb)
A, retrofit	17,917 kg (39,500 lb)
B	16,511 kg (36,400 lb)

PERFORMANCE (estimated at weights shown):
Max cruising speed at 3,050 m (10,000 ft), AUW of 14,741 kg (32,500 lb)   208 knots (385 km/h; 240 mph)
Long-range cruising speed at 3,050 m (10,000 ft), AUW of 14,741 kg (32,500 lb)
174 knots (322 km/h; 200 mph)
Patrol speed at S/L, AUW of 15,876 kg (35,000 lb)
110 knots (204 km/h; 127 mph)
Stalling speed:
15° flap, AUW of 20,865 kg (46,000 lb)
77 knots (143 km/h; 89 mph) CAS
25° flap, AUW of 16,783 kg (37,000 lb)
66 knots (123 km/h; 76 mph) CAS
Max rate of climb at S/L, AUW of 20,865 kg (46,000 lb)
372 m (1,220 ft)/min
T-O distance at S/L, ISA:
land, AUW of 19,890 kg (43,850 lb)   703 m (2,307 ft)
water, AUW of 17,100 kg (37,700 lb)   677 m (2,220 ft)
Landing distance at S/L, ISA:
land, AUW of 16,783 kg (37,000 lb)   768 m (2,520 ft)
water, AUW of 16,783 kg (37,000 lb)   838 m (2,750 ft)
Scooping distance at S/L, ISA (incl safe clearance heights)   1,189 m (3,900 ft)
Ferry range with 884 kg (1,950 lb) payload
1,125 nm (2,085 km; 1,295 miles)
Design g limits (15° flap)   +3.25/−1

CONAIR
CONAIR AVIATION LTD

PO Box 220, Abbotsford, British Columbia V2S 4N9
Telephone: (604) 853 1171
Telex: 04-363529
Fax: (604) 853 9017
PRESIDENT: L. G. Kerr
DIRECTOR OF MARKETING: Barry DeBruyn, PEng
PUBLIC RELATIONS CO-ORDINATOR: Lorna Thomassen

Conair specialises in aerial control services such as forest fire control, oil spill control, insect control, forest fertilisation, and salmonid enhancement. The company also designs and manufactures many speciality aviation systems such as fire retardant delivery systems, dispersal equipment, and various spray systems. Among these are underbelly retardant tanks for a range of helicopters including the Bell 205 and 212 and Aérospatiale Ecureuil, Lama and Puma, and an 11,365 litre (3,002 US gallon; 2,500 Imp gallon) ventral retardant tank for a firefighting version of the Douglas DC-6B. Since 1978 Conair has undertaken 30 conversions of Grumman or Canadian built S-2 Tracker aircraft to Conair Firecat air tanker configuration, and planned to fly the first turboprop powered Turbo Firecat in mid-1988.

Orders due for delivery in 1988 included the first of two 7,560 litre (1,997 US gallon; 1,663 Imp gallon) modular spray systems for Lockheed C-130s, to be operated by the 356th Tactical Airlift Squadron of USAF; a prototype 15,000 litre (3,963 US gallon; 3,300 Imp gallon) eight-door delivery system for a firefighting version of the Shin Meiwa US-1 amphibian; one SA 330 and two AS 350 B₁ helitanker systems for the French Sécurité Civile; and a third AS 350B₁ system for Aérospatiale Helicopter Corporation of Grand Prairie, Texas. In addition to the C-130 spray system,

Conair produces similar modifications for the Douglas DC-6, Fokker F27 and Aeritalia G222.

In 1986 Conair was awarded a five-year contract to maintain and operate the four Canadair CL-215 water bombers of the Yukon and Northwest Territories. These aircraft are equipped with Conair foam injection systems.

CONAIR FIRECAT

The Firecat is converted from standard Grumman S-2A (S2F-1) or de Havilland Canada CS2F-1/2/3 Tracker aircraft for specialised fire control operation, and the aircraft so converted are part of the Conair fleet as well as being available for export. The Canadian type certificate for the S2F/CS2F was transferred to Conair from de Havilland Canada in 1984, and special purpose Canadian type approval A-107 was awarded for the Firecat on 1 January 1984.

A total of 30 Firecat conversions had been delivered by mid-1988, including 15 for Conair, 14 for the French government's Sécurité Civile and one for the government of Saskatchewan.

The Conair conversion includes raising the cabin floor by 20.3 cm (8 in) and installing a 3,296 litre (870 US gallon; 725 Imp gallon) retardant tank in the fuselage; modifying the landing gear by fitting larger wheels with low pressure tyres, for soft field operation; inspecting the wing spar caps for corrosion, and repairing or replacing them as necessary; removing 1,361 kg (3,000 lb) of military equipment; completely rewiring the aircraft; and rebuilding/updating the flight deck instrument panels. Options include a hydraulic or pneumatic system for discharging the retardant, and a microcomputer system to control the retardant drop pattern. The retardant tank has four compartments

which can be discharged in a single salvo, two two-door salvos, or four single-door drops. A 227 litre (60 US gallon; 50 Imp gallon) foam injection system is available for enhancing water drops.

POWER PLANT: Two 1,100 kW (1,475 hp) Wright 982C9HE2 (R-1820-82) Cyclone nine-cylinder aircooled radial engines, each driving a Hamilton Standard 43D51-355 three-blade constant-speed propeller. Total internal fuel capacity 1,968 litres (520 US gallons; 433 Imp gallons).

ACCOMMODATION: Minimum crew: one pilot.

WEIGHTS:

Operating weight empty	6,895 kg (15,200 lb)
Max payload	4,746 kg (10,464 lb)
Max fuel	1,418 kg (3,126 lb)
Max T-O weight	11,793 kg (26,000 lb)
Max landing weight	11,113 kg (24,500 lb)

PERFORMANCE (at max T-O weight):
Never-exceed speed   280 knots (519 km/h; 322 mph)
Max level speed at 1,220 m (4,000 ft)
244 knots (452 km/h; 281 mph)
Max cruising speed   220 knots (408 km/h; 253 mph)
Normal drop speed   120 knots (222 km/h; 138 mph)
Stalling speed, flaps down, power off
82 knots (152 km/h; 95 mph)
Max rate of climb at S/L   366 m (1,200 ft)/min
Rate of climb at S/L, one engine out
170 m (560 ft)/min
Service ceiling   6,860 m (22,500 ft)
Service ceiling, one engine out   4,115 m (13,500 ft)
T-O to 15 m (50 ft)   368 m (1,208 ft)
Landing from 15 m (50 ft)   549 m (1,800 ft)
Min field length   915 m (3,000 ft)
Endurance with max payload   4 h 30 min

CONAIR TURBO FIRECAT

This turboprop version of the Firecat, with P&WC PT6A-67AF engines (max cruise rating 761 kW; 1,020 shp) and a computer controlled dispersal system (with foam injection) for retardant, was developed in 1987 and was due to make its first flight in mid-1988. The Turbo Firecat programme is a joint one between Conair and IMP of Halifax, Nova Scotia.

The four-compartment tank is dimensionally similar to that of the Firecat, but is 4 kg (9 lb) heavier. In addition to 3,296 litres (870 US gallons; 725 Imp gallons) of normal retardant, the Turbo Firecat can carry 173 litres (46 US gallons; 38 Imp gallons) of foam concentrate.

WEIGHTS:

Operating weight empty	6,169 kg (13,600 lb)
Max T-O weight	11,793 kg (26,000 lb)

PERFORMANCE (estimated at max T-O weight):

Max cruising speed	220 knots (408 km/h; 253 mph)
Normal drop speed	120 knots (222 km/h; 138 mph)
T-O run	442 m (1,450 ft)
Endurance with max payload	5 h 6 min

CONAIR F27 FIREFIGHTER

Conair has modified a Fokker F27 Mk 600 commuter transport for firefighting roles, for which it received Canadian DoT type approval on 5 June 1986. The world's first turboprop conversion dedicated to forest fire suppression and resource protection, this aircraft has since undertaken firefighting contracts in British Columbia, France and Australia. A second F27 conversion was under way in 1987. Conair anticipates a world market for at least 30 such conversions, and plans to operate a fleet of six itself.

The extensive modification programme includes installation of a Conair designed and manufactured fire retardant delivery system which can carry 6,364 litres (1,681 US gallons; 1,400 Imp gallons) of long-term retardant. A 455 litre (120 US gallon; 100 Imp gallon) foam injection system is also available. The converted aircraft is readily adaptable to other functions such as transporting cargo and fire crews, infra-red fire detection and mapping, aerial survey, aerial spraying and pararescue operations. Unnecessary internal items such as cabin insulation, bulkheads, pressurisation equipment and galleys are deleted, modern avionics installed, and the eight-compartment retardant delivery system fitted ventrally as an integral part of the fuselage structure. The tank structure is blended to the fuselage with Kevlar fairings. The tank can be loaded at a rate of 1,514 litres (400 US gallons; 333 Imp gallons)/min. Door sequencing is computer controlled, and the entire vent system is integral with the modified fuselage floor so that the aircraft's cargo-carrying capabilities are retained. The aircraft is crewed by two pilots, and seating for 19 support crew members is retained, together with the large forward (port) freight door.

WEIGHTS:

Operating weight empty	10,646 kg (23,471 lb)
Max payload	6,731 kg (14,840 lb)
Max fuel	4,152 kg (9,153 lb)
Max T-O weight	20,411 kg (45,000 lb)
Max landing weight	18,143 kg (40,000 lb)

PERFORMANCE (at max T-O weight except where indicated):

Never-exceed speed	259 knots (480 km/h; 298 mph)
Max cruising speed	230 knots (426 km/h; 265 mph)
Normal drop speed	125 knots (232 km/h; 144 mph)
Min control speed	80 knots (149 km/h; 92 mph)
Stalling speed, flaps down, power off	
	77 knots (143 km/h; 89 mph)
Max rate of climb at S/L	366 m (1,200 ft)/min

Rate of climb at S/L, one engine out, AUW of 14,060 kg	
(31,000 lb)	177 m (580 ft)/min
Service ceiling	7,620 m (25,000 ft)
Service ceiling, one engine out, AUW of 14,060 kg	
(31,000 lb)	5,640 m (18,500 ft)
T-O to 10.7 m (35 ft)	1,600 m (5,250 ft)
Landing from 15 m (50 ft) at max landing weight	
	987 m (3,240 ft)
Min field length	1,525 m (5,000 ft)
Max endurance	3 h 24 min

Artist's impression of the Conair Turbo Firecat (two P&WC PT6A-67AF turboprops)

First Conair Firefighter conversion of the Fokker F27

CONAIR HELITANKERS

Conair has developed a growing number of helicopter-mounted fire control systems known as helitankers. Of semi-monocoque construction, the belly-mounted tanks feature individually operated, full length rigid doors which may be opened in various combinations over a wide range of airspeeds to permit variable retardant line lengths and drop concentrations. A self-loading hover-fill system allows the tank to be filled while the helicopter hovers above a remote water source, and an offload feature allows the water payload to be pumped to a portable ground reservoir for the use of ground-based firefighters. A foam injection system permits the fire suppressing qualities of a water payload to be greatly enhanced. A reversible pump allows single-point loading injection into the tank and single-point offloading.

Helitanker system sales to mid-1988 included seven Bell 205/212s to Frontier Helicopters (a Conair subsidiary) and five to the National Safety Council of Australia; four Aérospatiale AS 350B₁ Ecureuils to the French Sécurité Civile and one to Aérospatiale Helicopter Corporation in the USA; and three SA 315B Lamas to the Sécurité Civile. System capacities are 1,360 litres (359 US gallons; 299 Imp gallons) for the Bell 205/212; 900 litres (238 US gallons; 198 Imp gallons) for the Lama; and 800 litres (211 US gallons; 176 Imp gallons) for the Ecureuil. The Bell 205 and 212 helitankers are also offered with a rappelling system to deliver firefighters to remote fire sites.

Conair is building a 2,355 litre (622 US gallon; 517.5 Imp gallon) tank for the Aérospatiale SA 330 Puma for delivery to the Sécurité Civile in 1988. This system features an 800 litre (211 US gallon; 176 Imp gallon) two-door belly tank, and a 1,296 litre (342 US gallon; 285 Imp gallon) fuselage main tank with two internal doors for reloading the external tank via a 261 litre (69 US gallon; 57 Imp gallon) chute. Foam tank capacity is 173 litres (46 US gallons; 38 Imp gallons).

Conair 800 litre (211 US gallon; 176 Imp gallon) helitanker system on an AS 350B₁ Ecureuil

DE HAVILLAND CANADA — see Boeing Canada

HELICOP-JET
HELICOP-JET PROJECT MANAGEMENT

2 Complex Desjardins, Tour Est (Suite 3100), Montreal, Quebec H5B 1B3
Telephone: (514) 281 1850
Telex: 05-61075 or 05-25426
Fax: (514) 281 1997
PRESIDENT: Pierre Bergeron

Helicop-Jet Project Management was formed in France to progress towards series manufacture of the Helicop-Jet which was under development in France, by M Charles Déchaux, for many years.

HELICOP-JET

A full scale mockup of this 'cold-jet' tip-driven light helicopter, in its original configuration, was first exhibited at the Paris Air Show in June 1969. The initial prototype made its first flight in December 1976 at Issy-les-Moulineaux. It logged about 60 flying hours, powered by a 186 kW (250 hp) Turbomeca Palouste IV air generator, with

which it could lift only the pilot.

An improved 002 prototype (F-WZJO), with an Astazou engine, was displayed at Paris in June 1979. After preliminary ground testing it made its initial flight on 12 December 1984. It fulfilled its role as a demonstrator, and is now used for ground development and testing.

Helicop-Jet Project Management proposed to build a seven-seat pre-production prototype with an optimised two-blade rotor of composite materials and driven by either a Turbomeca TM 319 turbogenerator or a Pratt & Whitney Canada PW205 or Allison 250-C23 turboshaft. No further progress towards this version (see 1987-88 *Jane's*) has been reported.

The following description applies to the fully developed 002 prototype:

TYPE: Four-seat tip-driven light helicopter.
ROTOR SYSTEM: One four-blade main rotor; no anti-torque rotor. Blade section NACA 23018. Constant chord blades, each built around a hollow extruded spar and attached to the hub via a laminated torsion strap of

high-strength steel. Trailing-edge of each blade consists of a light alloy sheet box structure, bonded over ribs carried by a light spar. The laminated blade attachment straps permit pitch change and flapping without need for the usual blade bearings and stops. Compressed air from engine passes through a large-diameter non-rotating steel rotor mast, via a spherical bearing to the hollow spar of each blade and thence to the blade-tip nozzle. Rotor speed variable from 260-400 rpm, optimised at over 290 rpm.
FUSELAGE: Extensively glazed light alloy cabin made up basically of two roof sections of the Panhard B-24 motor car (lower one inverted), of which M Déchaux bought the tooling. Twin tailbooms of elliptical section.
TAIL UNIT: Variable incidence horizontal surface between tailbooms, which end in integral endplate fins. Central stainless steel rudder, working in jet efflux, for use particularly during hovering and low-speed flight.
LANDING GEAR: Tubular skid type, with attachments for two small ground handling wheels.
POWER PLANT: One Turbomeca Astazou IIIA turbogenerator, supplying compressed air for the tip-drive nozzles at an originally planned flow rate of 2.15 kg (4.75 lb)/s and pressure ratio of 3.5:1, and with a residual jet thrust of 20-40 kg (44-88 lb). Single internal fuel tank, capacity 250 litres (66 US gallons; 55 Imp gallons).
ACCOMMODATION: Seats for four persons in side by side pairs. Dual controls. Fully transparent forward hinged door on each side of cabin. Tinted glass optional.
EQUIPMENT: Optional equipment includes radio, intercom, night flying equipment, baggage compartment, winch, rescue and medical equipment and stretcher.

DIMENSIONS, EXTERNAL:
Rotor diameter	10.00 m (32 ft 10 in)
Rotor blade chord, constant	0.23 m (9 in)
Fuselage: Length	3.30 m (10 ft 10 in)
Max width	1.42 m (4 ft 8 in)
Height overall	2.85 m (9 ft 4¼ in)
Skid track	2.00 m (6 ft 6¾ in)

AREA:
Rotor disc	78.54 m² (845.4 sq ft)

WEIGHTS AND LOADING:
Weight empty	650 kg (1,433 lb)
Max T-O weight	1,030 kg (2,271 lb)
Max disc loading	13.11 kg/m² (2.69 lb/sq ft)

PERFORMANCE (demonstrated):
Max cruising speed	84 knots (155 km/h; 96 mph)

002 prototype of the Helicop-Jet tip-driven light helicopter

MBB
MBB HELICOPTER CANADA LIMITED
(Subsidiary of Messerschmitt-Bölkow-Blohm GmbH)

MARKETING OFFICE: Suite 910, 130 Albert Street, Ottawa, Ontario K1P 5G4
Telephone: (613) 232 1557
Telex: 053-4109
Fax: (613) 232 5454
VICE-PRESIDENT, MARKETING: E. James Grant
HEAD OFFICE: PO Box 250, 1100 Gilmore Road, Fort Erie, Ontario L2A 5M9
Telephone: (416) 871 7772
Telex: 061-5250
Fax: (416) 871 3320
PRESIDENT: Helge Wittholz

MBB Helicopter Canada Limited began operations as Canada's first helicopter manufacturer in April 1984. The company was established as a result of a contract between Messerschmitt-Bölkow-Blohm GmbH (MBB) of West Germany and the Federal and Ontario governments of Canada. In mid-1986, MBB Helicopter Canada opened a 7,897 m² (85,000 sq ft) manufacturing plant in Fort Erie, Ontario.

MBB Helicopter Canada Limited has the world product mandate for the manufacture in Canada of the BO 105 LS light twin-engined helicopter, designed for operations in areas of hot temperature and high altitudes and for outstanding single-engine performance. Technology and design authority for the BO 105 LS was transferred to Canada, where production began with the BO 105 LS A-3 version, powered by Allison 250-C28C engines. The first customer delivery was made in February 1987.

Currently, MBB Helicopter Canada is developing the BO 105 LS B-1 version, which will be powered by Pratt & Whitney Canada PW205B turboshafts.

MBB Helicopter Canada is responsible for sales and completion of all MBB helicopters in Canada, including the BO 105 CBS and the larger MBB/Kawasaki BK 117 (see International section). The Canadian Coast Guard has been a major customer for the BO 105 CBS, with a total fleet of 16, the last of which was delivered on 3 May 1988.

MBB BO 105 LS

This 'hot and high' version of the BO 105 (L for Lift and S for Stretch) combines the enlarged cabin of the CBS version with more powerful engines and an uprated transmission, permitting operation at a higher gross weight. It was first flown on 23 October 1981. Certification by the LBA was granted in July 1984, and extended in April 1985 to cover

'hot and high' take-offs and landings at altitudes up to 6,100 m (20,000 ft). It was extended again on 7 July 1986 to cover the A-3 version of the BO 105 LS, with FAA and Canadian DoT certification granted subsequently. Engine ground testing and first flight test for the BO 105 LS B-1 were scheduled for Spring and Summer 1988 respectively.

The description of the BO 105 CBS in the German section applies also to the BO 105 LS A-3, except as follows:
ROTOR DRIVE: Main transmission, type ZF-FS 112, is rated for independent restricted input of 310 kW (416 shp) per engine at T-O power or 294 kW (394 shp) per engine for max continuous operation; or a single-engine restricted input of 368 kW (493 shp) at max continuous power, or 410 kW (550 shp) for 2.5 min at T-O power.
POWER PLANT: Two Allison 250-C28C turboshafts, each rated at 410 kW (550 shp) for 2.5 min, and with 5 min T-O and max continuous power ratings of 373 kW (500 shp)

and 368 kW (493 shp) respectively. Fuel capacity as for CB/CBS. Oil capacity 5 litres (1.3 US gallons; 1.1 Imp gallons) per engine.
ACCOMMODATION: Pilot, and co-pilot or passenger, on two front seats; three or four passengers in main cabin. Cargo space behind rear seats, plus additional 20 kg (44 lb) in baggage compartment. Crew door and passengers' sliding door each side; clamshell rear cargo doors, removable for carriage of extra-long cargo. Cabin heating and air-conditioning available optionally.
SYSTEMS: As for BO 105 CBS, except stability augmentation system is standard, bleed air anti-icing optional.

WEIGHTS:
Weight empty, basic	1,382 kg (3,047 lb)
Fuel weight	456 kg (1,005 lb)
Max T-O weight	2,600 kg (5,732 lb)

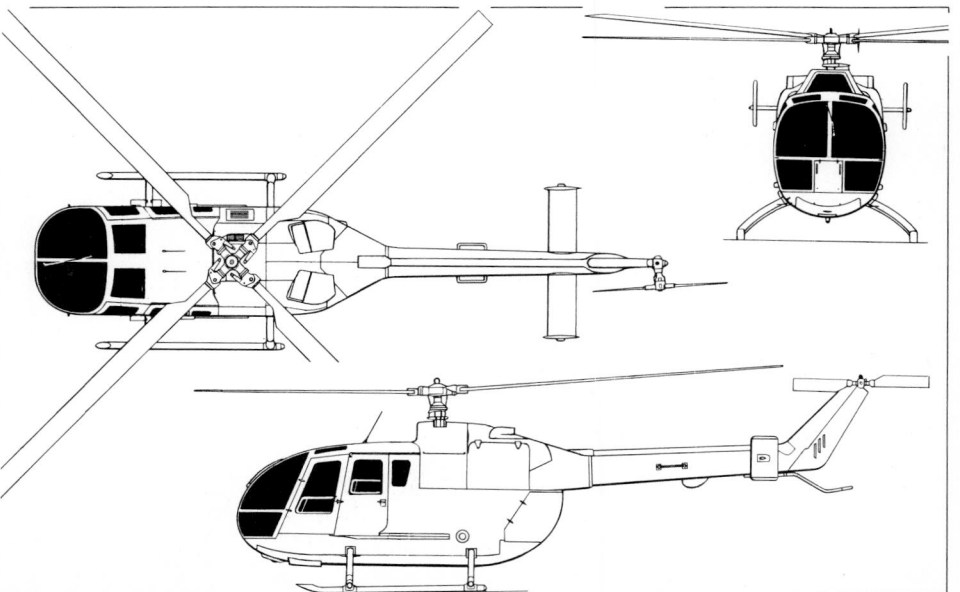

MBB Helicopter Canada Ltd BO 105 LS 'hot and high' helicopter (*Pilot Press*)

PERFORMANCE (at T-O weight of 2,400 kg; 5,291 lb, ISA,
except where indicated):
Never-exceed speed at S/L
                        145 knots (270 km/h; 167 mph)
Max cruising speed at S/L
                        131 knots (243 km/h; 151 mph)
Max rate of climb at S/L, AUW of 2,600 kg (5,732 lb)
                        546 m (1,790 ft)/min
Vertical rate of climb at S/L, AUW of 2,600 kg (5,732 lb)
                        229 m (750 ft)/min
Max operating altitude   6,100 m (20,000 ft)
Service ceiling, one engine out   1,768 m (5,800 ft)
Hovering ceiling: IGE   3,505 m (11,500 ft)
     OGE   2,255 m (7,400 ft)
Range at S/L, standard fuel, max internal payload, no
   reserves   278 nm (515 km; 320 miles)

**BO 105 LS A-3 operated by the US Drug
Enforcement Administration in Hawaii**

MODERN WING
MODERN WING AIRCRAFT LTD
Suite 102, 7880 Alderbridge Way, Richmond, British
Columbia V6X 2A5
PRESIDENT: John N. Hill

MODERN WING (DE HAVILLAND CANADA) DHC-2 BEAVER
At the Abbotsford Air Show in August 1986 Modern
Wing exhibited the first prototype of a modernised version
of the Beaver utility aircraft, and certification was expected
by the end of that year. The major change involved
replacing the Beaver's original constant chord wings with
redesigned, flush riveted wings having tapered outer panels,
modified wingtips and higher-lift flaps. Improvements were
also made to the fuselage to reduce drag, and increase
payload and speed.

The modifications increase max T-O weight from 2,358
kg (5,200 lb) to 2,721 kg (6,000 lb), and were expected to
offer increases of 5-10 per cent in cruising speed and
91.5-122 m (300-400 ft)/min in climb rate, coupled with
reductions of 30 per cent in T-O run, 20 per cent in landing
run, and 10-15 per cent in fuel consumption.

More than a thousand of the 1,692 Beavers built by de
Havilland Canada are still flying, and Modern Wing
estimated a sale of 150 sets of new wings in the first five years
of production, but no recent news of this venture has been
received.

NWI
NORTHWEST INDUSTRIES LIMITED (Subsidiary of CAE Industries Ltd)
PO Box 9864, Edmonton International Airport, Edmonton,
Alberta T5J 2T2
Telephone: (403) 955 6300
Telex: 037-41574
Fax: (403) 955 2181
PRESIDENT: L. H. Prokop
VICE-PRESIDENT AND GENERAL MANAGER: F. A. Maybee

NWI is one of Canada's largest aircraft maintenance,
repair, overhaul and modification centres for military
and commercial aircraft, including the Lockheed C-130
Hercules, Dassault Falcon, Lockheed T-33, Canadair
CL-41 (CT-114) and CF-104 Starfighter. In addition to its
major in-plant aircraft programmes, mobile repair parties
are stationed at CFBs Edmonton, Cold Lake and Bagotville
in support of the C-130 Hercules, CF-5 and CF-18 aircraft
of the Canadian Armed Forces. The manufacturing shops
produce structural, mechanical and electronic components
for its aircraft overhaul and modification programmes and,
under subcontract, for North America's principal aerospace
manufacturers.

In 1987 NWI completed a major structural upgrade of the
CAF's fleet of 22 Lockheed C-130E Hercules. This included
fitting new (Lockheed supplied) C-130H outer wings, new
auxiliary fuel cells, structural repairs to the fuselage and a
full repaint in camouflage colours. In addition, two new
C-130H-84 and two used C-130H-73 aircraft, purchased
by the CAF, required extensive avionics upgrading,
modification, repair and repaint to achieve commonality
with the remainder of the fleet. A progressive structural
inspection programme, begun in Autumn 1987, will result
in the complete CAF C-130 fleet being routed through NWI
over the ensuing three-year period. Depot level inspection,
repair and service life extension of 64 CAF T-33A Silver
Star jet trainers is providing a comprehensive structural,
mechanical and electrical upgrading of these aircraft. An
aircraft sampling inspection and repaint of ten CL-41
(CT-114) Tutor jet trainers, to assess their structural
condition and determine the need for a more in-depth depot
level inspection and rewiring programme, is continuing at
the Edmonton facility.

VENGA
VENGA AIRCRAFT INC
666 Sherbrooke Street West, Suite 700, Montreal, Quebec
H3A 1E7
Telephone: (514) 842 2724
Fax: (514) 849 8367
PRESIDENT: Graham Wells
VICE-PRESIDENT, MARKETING: Jay Lumiere

Venga Aircraft was incorporated in May 1985 to
develop, manufacture and market a new, all-composites
high-performance jet trainer known as the TG-10. The
company combines more than 20 years' experience in
developing composite aircraft prototypes and airframe
materials, by the Thunder group of Phoenix, Arizona,
USA, and Ecomcon (Empire Composite Consultants) of
Vancouver, Canada.

VENGA TG-10
An all-composites airframe and modular construction
are intended to give the TG-10 an estimated flying life of
about 10,000 hours, due to a considerable reduction in the
corrosion and fatigue problems associated with aircraft of
metal construction. Its configuration, broadly similar to
that of the Northrop F-5E and McDonnell Douglas
FA-18A, also incorporates low-observables design features
intended to improve its survivability. It will be repairable in
the field, using replacement major components and
quick-change engine modules, and will be operable from
roads, grass or unprepared airstrips, with mission capability
not only for its primary role as an 'all-through' trainer but
also, in single-seat form (with the rear cockpit module
removed), as a light ground attack aircraft.

Venga reports that it has received letters of interest from
five countries, involving approximately 160 aircraft.
Rollout of the TG-10 prototype has been rescheduled for
September 1988.

TYPE: Fully aerobatic two-seat 'all-through' jet trainer or
single-seat light attack aircraft.

AIRFRAME: Construction utilises a modular, all-composites
structure designed for ease of repair in the field, built
from pressure formed foam core laminates bonded
together into a single lightweight moulded unit. Materials
used are layers of aircraft grade glassfibre cloth bonded to
a core of PVC foam (Klégécel or Divinycell) in a vacuum
process using various resin matrices. Primary structure
built entirely of composites materials, with extensive use
of carbonfibre for high stress and other critical areas,
though use of carbonfibre reinforced aluminium alloy (eg
for main spars) is a customer option.

WINGS: Cantilever low-wing monoplane, with 2° 30′
dihedral from roots. Trailing-edge flaps are operated
electrically via Commercial Aircraft Products actuators.
Differentially operating ailerons, each with trim tab.

FUSELAGE: Modular structure (see 'Airframe' paragraph),
of similar general appearance to Northrop F-5E.
Electro-hydraulically actuated airbrake beneath fuselage.

TAIL UNIT: Low-set, sweptback tailplane with slight
anhedral. Twin non-swept, outward canted fins, with
inset rudders, forward of horizontal surfaces. Trim tabs
in elevator and each rudder.

LANDING GEAR: Retractable tricycle type, with electro-
hydraulic actuation; nosewheel retracts forward, mainwheels inward into fuselage. Wheel sizes 5.00-5 (nose),
6.00-10 (main). Nosewheel steerable through 30°. Mainwheels have hydraulic brakes and parking brake.

POWER PLANT: Prototype powered by one 13.01 kN (2,925 lb
st) General Electric J85-GE-5 turbojet; standard engine
for basic production version will be an 11.12 kN (2,500 lb
st) Pratt & Whitney Canada JT15D-4C turbofan, but
customer options will include General Electric CJ610 or
Rolls-Royce Viper 632 or 680 turbojets. Intakes are each
fitted with a large splitter plate, and are designed to
inhibit foreign object damage. Fuel system, designed to
permit fully aerobatic manoeuvres, comprises three
fuselage cells with total usable capacity of 1,223 litres (323
US gallons; 269 Imp gallons). A 265 litre (70 US gallon;
58 Imp gallon) drop tank can be carried on the fuselage
centreline station in the single-seat attack configuration.

ACCOMMODATION: Standard trainer has tandem accommodation for pupil (in front) and instructor on Stencel
zero/zero ejection seats under jettisonable bubble canopy,
with internal screen between cockpits. Seats are reclined,
adjustable horizontally and vertically, and can accommodate back-type parachutes. Dual controls standard,
except for switches for fuel pumps, weapon control panel

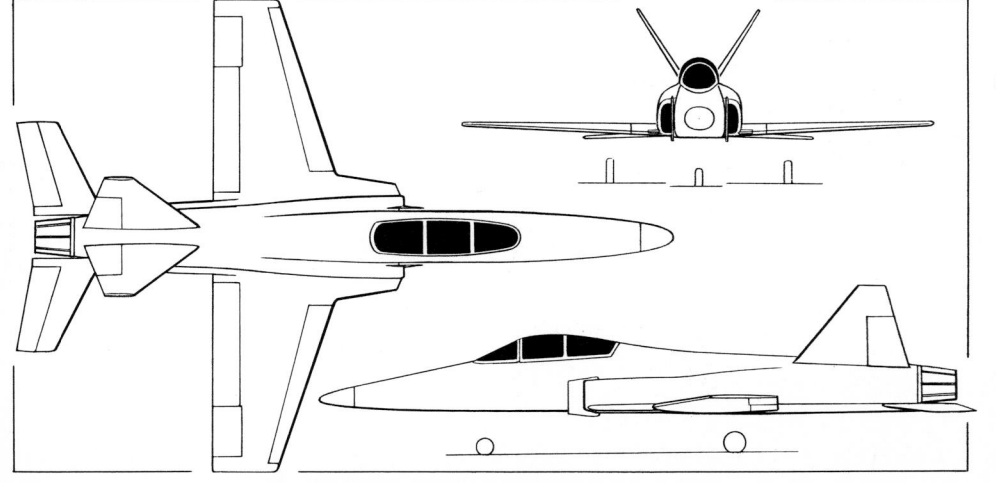

Venga TG-10 trainer/light attack aircraft *(Pilot Press)*

and parking brake; in lieu of these, rear panel has a full set of indicators for the weapons system, an override switch to prevent firing, and a parking brake indicator. Rail mounted rear seat and rear instrument panel module are easily removable to permit quick conversion to single-seat light attack configuration. Cockpit(s) fully air-conditioned, but not pressurised; latter may be offered later as a customer option.

SYSTEMS: 28V DC electrical system, powered by a standard starter/generator and Gates Energy Products lead-acid battery, with second battery for emergency backup. Power sources are coupled to three busbars in front cockpit (main, avionics, and emergency) containing trip-free circuit breakers. NATO type external ground power socket. Normalair-Garrett diluter demand oxygen system, capacity 225 litres (8 cu ft).

AVIONICS AND EQUIPMENT: Avionics include two VHF com, intercom, VOR/ILS/marker beacon receiver (front), VOR/LOC nav (rear), ADF, transponder, and DME. Full IFR capability, with electrically driven gyro instruments; main directional gyro is a King slaved type unit. Provision for HUD, radar altimeter, nose radar or other avionics to customer's requirements. Standard cockpit instrumentation and equipment includes ASI (two), VSI (two), encoding altimeter, standard altimeter, clock (two), horizon gyro (two), turn and slip indicator (two), accelerometer (two), angle of attack indicator, pictorial navigation indicator, magnetic compass (two), DME indicator (two), ADF information display (two), first aid kit, IFF transponder, fire extinguishing system, and internal/external lighting.

ARMAMENT: One centreline and four underwing hardpoints, each stressed for loads of up to 181.5 kg (400 lb), for weapons, fuel tank (centreline only), survival or rescue packs, or other stores, subject to a max external load of 845 kg (1,864 lb) in single-seat attack version. Weapons specified at present include up to three Portsmouth Aviation 7.62 mm FN gun pods with 450 rds/gun; up to three HMP 0.50 in Browning gun pods with 250 rds/gun; two GIAT 20 mm M621 gun pods with 150 rds/gun; various rocket launchers (Matra F2 with six 68 mm, Aerea AL 18-50 with eighteen 2 in, AL 8-70 with eight 2.75 in FFAR, AL 6-80 with six 81 mm, LAU-32 with seven 2.75 in FFAR, SNIA 2 in, Brandt 7 with seven 68 mm, or SURA-D 81 mm); SAMP 32 kg or 50 kg general purpose or 120 kg fragmentation bombs; 11 kg Mk 76 practice bombs; or a 70 mm automatic panoramic IRLS reconnaissance pod.

DIMENSIONS, EXTERNAL:
Wing span	8.23 m (27 ft 0 in)
Wing chord at root	2.29 m (7 ft 6 in)
Wing aspect ratio	5.4
Length overall	11.89 m (39 ft 0 in)
Fuselage: Max width	1.42 m (4 ft 8 in)
Height overall	4.04 m (13 ft 3 in)
Tailplane span	3.96 m (13 ft 0 in)
Wheel track	3.05 m (10 ft 0 in)

AREAS:
Wings, gross	12.54 m² (135.0 sq ft)
Trailing-edge flaps (total)	1.30 m² (14.0 sq ft)
Rudders (total, incl tabs)	1.11 m² (12.0 sq ft)

Tailplane	1.67 m² (18.0 sq ft)
Elevators (total, incl tab)	1.67 m² (18.0 sq ft)

WEIGHTS (A: two-seat trainer, B: single-seat attack):
Weight empty, equipped (incl unusable fuel):
A	1,288 kg (2,840 lb)
B	1,047 kg (2,308 lb)
Max usable internal fuel: A, B	908 kg (2,002 lb)
Max external stores load: A	277 kg (610 lb)
B	845 kg (1,864 lb)
Max T-O weight: A	2,645 kg (5,832 lb)
B (without external stores)	2,041 kg (4,500 lb)
B (with max external stores)	2,886 kg (6,364 lb)

PERFORMANCE (estimated: prototype with J85 engine at 2,645 kg; 5,832 lb max T-O weight):
Max level speed:
at S/L, ISA	485 knots (899 km/h; 558 mph)
at 9,150 m (30,000 ft), ISA	450 knots (834 km/h; 518 mph)
Stalling speed	78 knots (145 km/h; 90 mph)
Max rate of climb at S/L, ISA	2,134 m (7,000 ft)/min
Time to 9,150 m (30,000 ft)	7 min 12 s
T-O run at S/L, ISA	186 m (610 ft)
T-O to 15 m (50 ft) at S/L, ISA	402 m (1,320 ft)
Ground turning radius, all wheels rolling	6.10 m (20 ft 0 in)

Max range:
internal fuel only, 10% reserves	950 nm (1,760 km; 1,094 miles)
with c/l drop tank, no reserves	1,271 nm (2,355 km; 1,463 miles)
Max endurance at 9,150 m (30,000 ft)	2 h 30 min

CHILE

CARDOEN
INDUSTRIAS CARDOEN LTDA
WORKS: Planta Macul, Exequiel Fernandez 3397, Santiago
Fax: 2212678
CHIEF ENGINEER, CARDOEN 206L-III HELICOPTER:
Rene M. Gonzalez
HEADQUARTERS: Los Conquistadores 1700, Piso 28, Santiago

Telephone: (562) 231 3420
Telex: 340997 INCAR CK
Fax: (562) 231 6366

Cardoen has been well known for many years as a major manufacturer of weapons and other military equipment. Its current products include three sizes of cluster bomb (the 130

lb CB-60-K, 500 lb CB-250-K and 1,000 lb CB-500-K); standard 250/500/1,000/2,000 lb Mk 81/82/83/84 general purpose bombs; the 661 lb CFB 27-300 high fragmentation bomb; an anti-runway concrete-piercing bomb; and the Palloon low-altitude bomb retarding system. The company is currently developing an armed attack helicopter, based on the Bell 206L-III LongRanger. Further details of this programme were not available in early 1988.

ENAER
EMPRESA NACIONAL DE AERONÁUTICA DE CHILE
Avenida José Miguel Carrera 11087, Santiago
Telephone: 5582707, 5585296 and 5588960
Telex: 645115 ENAER CT
PRESIDENT: Caupolicán Boisset
COMMERCIAL MANAGER: Hernán Cárdenas

ENAER is a state owned company formed in 1984 from the IndAer industrial organisation set up by the Chilean Air Force in 1980. Aircraft manufacturing started in 1980 with the assembly of 27 Piper PA-28 Dakota light aircraft for Chilean Air Force and flying club use. With a 1988 workforce of about 1,900 people, ENAER's current activities are the design and production of aircraft and electronic warfare equipment.

ENAER's major current programmes are production of the T-35 Pillán trainer and T-36/A-36 Halcón (CASA C-101) jet trainer/attack aircraft, plus development of Chile's first lightplane of indigenous design, the Avion Liviano. It also undertakes upgrade programmes for the Chilean Air Force which include conversion of Beechcraft 99s for maritime surveillance (see 1987-88 *Jane's*), retrofitting FACh Hawker Hunters with a Caiquen II radar warning receiver system, and an airframe/avionics upgrade for the service's Mirage 50CNs.

ENAER T-35 PILLÁN (DEVIL)
Spanish Air Force designation: E.26 Tamiz
The Pillán is a tandem two-seat, fully aerobatic aircraft for basic, intermediate and instrument flying training. It is cleared to FAR Pt 23 (Aerobatic category) and military standards. Design was based on the Piper Cherokee series, utilising in particular many components of the PA-28 Dakota and PA-32 Saratoga.

Two prototypes were developed by Piper, the first of these making its initial flight on 6 March 1981 and the second at the end of that year. Three further aircraft were delivered by Piper as kits for assembly by ENAER: the first of these (FACh serial number 101) flew on 30 January 1982 and the third in September of that year. After replacement of the original all-moving tailplane by an electrically trimmable tailplane with a conventional elevator, increasing rudder mass balance, and deepening the canopy, series production began in September 1984.

The following versions have been announced:

T-35A. Primary trainer version for Chilean Air Force (60 ordered, including the three assembled from Piper kits). First flight 28 December 1984, first delivery (two aircraft) 31 July 1985.

T-35B. Instrument trainer version for Chilean Air Force (20 ordered), with more comprehensive instrumentation.

T-35C. Primary trainer version for Spanish Air Force (40), first flown on 12 May 1986. These have the Spanish

designation **E.26 Tamiz**, and were assembled by CASA (which see) from components supplied by ENAER. Kit deliveries to CASA began on 27 December 1985 and were completed in September 1987.

T-35D. Primary trainer version for Panamanian Air Force (four delivered in January 1988). Further six on option.

T-35S. Single-seat version, first flown (CC-PZB) on 5 March 1988 with IO-540-K1K5 piston engine; 313 kW (420 shp) Allison 250-B17 turboprop intended for production version.

T-35T Aucán. Turboprop version, listed separately. Prototype only; development suspended.

Pillán production was continuing at the rate of four per month in early 1988. Completion of the Chilean Air Force orders is due by early 1989.

The following description applies to the basic T-35A except where indicated:

TYPE: Two-seat fully aerobatic basic (T-35A/C/D) and instrument (T-35B) military trainer.

WINGS: Cantilever low-wing monoplane. Wing section NACA 65₂-415 on constant chord inboard panels, NACA 65₂-415 (modified) at tips. Dihedral 7°. Incidence 2° at root, -0° 30' at tip. Single-spar fail-safe structure of light alloy, steel and glassfibre, with components mainly from PA-28-236 Dakota (leading-edges) and PA-32R-301 Saratoga (trailing-edges) modified to shorter span. Slotted aluminium ailerons and electrically operated single-slotted trailing-edge flaps of riveted construction, identical to those of Saratoga. Electrically actuated trim tab in port aileron.

FUSELAGE: Semi-monocoque fail-safe structure of aluminium alloy frames and longerons, with riveted skin. Tailcone assembled from Cherokee components, modified to fit narrower fuselage. Two-piece engine cowling of GRP.

TAIL UNIT: Cantilever structure of light alloy with sweptback (38° 43') vertical surfaces, identical to those of Dakota except for heavier gauge skins, minor reinforcement of fin, and increased rudder mass balance. One-piece non-swept variable incidence tailplane, with electric trim and glassfibre tips. Full span mass balanced elevator. Tailplane incorporates some standard PA-28 and PA-31 (Navajo/Cheyenne) components; elevator is of all-new design. No tabs; rudder trimmed electrically.

LANDING GEAR: Hydraulically retractable tricycle type, with single wheel on each unit. Main gear legs and doors identical to those on PA-32R-301; nose gear assembled from PA-32R-301 and PA-28R-200 components. Main units retract inward, steerable nosewheel rearward. Piper oleo-pneumatic shock absorber in each unit. Emergency free-fall extension. Cleveland mainwheels and McCreary tyres size 6.00-6 (8 ply), nosewheel and tyre size 5.00-5 (6 ply). Tyre pressures: 2.62 bars (38 lb/sq in) on

ENAER T-35A Pillán trainer of the Chilean Air Force

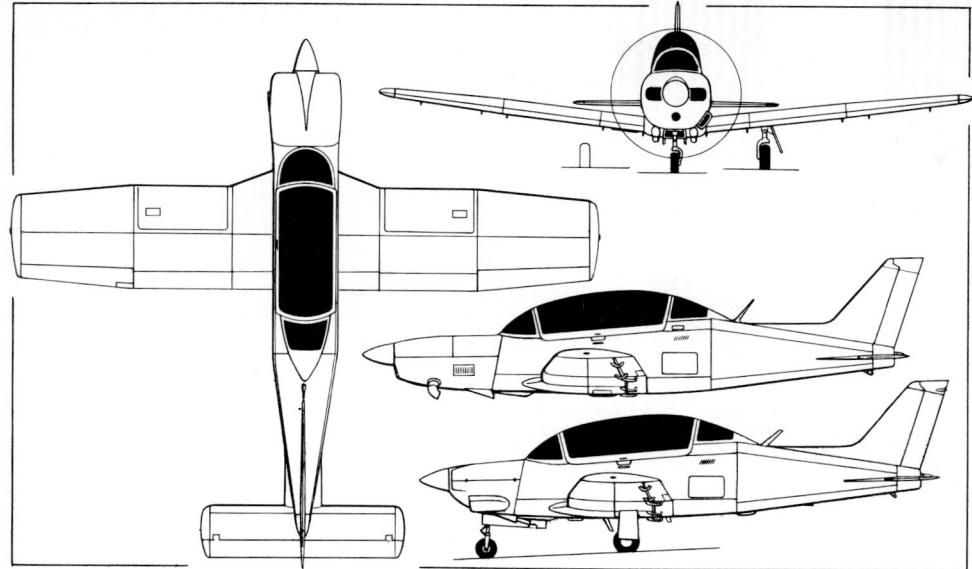

ENAER T-35 Pillán tandem two-seat basic/intermediate trainer *(Pilot Press)*

mainwheels, 2.41 bars (35 lb/sq in) on nosewheel. Single-disc aircooled hydraulic brake on each mainwheel. Parking brake.

POWER PLANT: One 224 kW (300 hp) Textron Lycoming IO-540-K1K5 flat-six engine, driving a Hartzell HC-C3YR-4BF/FC7663R three-blade constant-speed metal propeller with spinner. Fuel contained in two integral aluminium tanks in wing leading-edges, total capacity 291.5 litres (77 US gallons; 64.1 Imp gallons), of which 272.5 litres (72 US gallons; 60 Imp gallons) are usable. Overwing gravity refuelling point on each wing. Oil capacity 11.4 litres (3 US gallons; 2.5 Imp gallons). Fuel and oil systems permit unlimited inverted flight (up to 40 min flight tested).

ACCOMMODATION: Vertically adjustable seats for two persons, with seat belts and shoulder harnesses, in tandem beneath one-piece transparent jettisonable canopy which opens sideways to starboard. One-piece acrylic windscreen, and one-piece window in glassfibre fairing aft of canopy. Rear (instructor's) seat 22 cm (8⅔ in) higher than front seat. Dual controls standard. Baggage compartment aft of rear cockpit, with external access on port side. Accommodation heated, and canopy demisted, by engine bleed air. Ventilation system as for Piper Dakota.

SYSTEMS: Electrically operated hydraulic system, at 124 bars (1,800 lb/sq in) pressure for landing gear retraction and 44.8 bars (650 lb/sq in) for gear extension; separate system at 20.7 bars (300 lb/sq in) for wheel brakes. Electrical system is 24V DC, powered by a 28V 70A engine driven Prestolite alternator and 24V 10Ah battery, with an inverter for AC power at 400Hz to operate RMIs and attitude indicators. External power socket. No oxygen or de-icing provisions.

AVIONICS AND EQUIPMENT: (*T-35A*) Two Collins VHF-251 com transceivers, two Collins AMR-350 audio panels, one Clark Isocom, and one each Collins VIR-351 VOR, Collins ADF-650A and Collins TOR-950 IFF. (*T-35C*) One King KTR 908, two King KFS 598A control units, two King KMA 244 audio panels and two King KR 87 ADF. Blind-flying instrumentation and full IFR capability in T-35B.

DIMENSIONS, EXTERNAL:

Wing span	8.84 m (29 ft 0 in)
Wing chord: at root	1.88 m (6 ft 2 in)
at tip	1.26 m (4 ft 1½ in)
inboard (constant)	1.60 m (5 ft 3 in)
mean aerodynamic	1.55 m (5 ft 1 in)
Wing aspect ratio	5.7
Length overall	8.00 m (26 ft 3 in)
Height overall	2.64 m (8 ft 8 in)
Fuselage: Length	7.66 m (25 ft 1¾ in)
Max width	0.86 m (2 ft 9¾ in)
Max depth	1.56 m (5 ft 1¼ in)
Tailplane span	3.05 m (10 ft 0 in)
Wheel track	3.02 m (9 ft 11 in)
Wheelbase	2.09 m (6 ft 10¼ in)
Propeller diameter	1.93 m (6 ft 4 in)

DIMENSIONS, INTERNAL:

Cockpit: Length	3.24 m (10 ft 7½ in)
Max width	1.04 m (3 ft 5 in)
Max height	1.48 m (4 ft 10¼ in)

AREAS:

Wings, gross	13.69 m² (147.34 sq ft)
Ailerons (total)	1.135 m² (12.22 sq ft)
Trailing-edge flaps (total)	1.36 m² (14.64 sq ft)
Fin	0.69 m² (7.43 sq ft)
Rudder	0.38 m² (4.09 sq ft)
Tailplane	1.57 m² (16.90 sq ft)
Elevator	0.77 m² (8.29 sq ft)

WEIGHTS AND LOADINGS:

Weight empty, equipped	930 kg (2,050 lb)
Fuel	210 kg (462 lb)
Max aerobatic T-O weight	1,315 kg (2,900 lb)
Max T-O and landing weight	1,338 kg (2,950 lb)
Max wing loading	97.73 kg/m² (20.03 lb/sq ft)
Max power loading	5.98 kg/kW (9.83 lb/hp)

PERFORMANCE (at max T-O and landing weight, ISA):

Never-exceed speed	241 knots (446 km/h; 277 mph)
Max level speed at S/L	168 knots (311 km/h; 193 mph)
Cruising speed:	
75% power at 2,680 m (8,800 ft)	
	144 knots (266 km/h; 166 mph) IAS
55% power at 5,120 m (16,800 ft)	
	138 knots (255 km/h; 159 mph) IAS
Stalling speed: flaps up	67 knots (125 km/h; 78 mph)
flaps down	62 knots (115 km/h; 72 mph)
Max speed for flap extension	
	118 knots (218 km/h; 136 mph) IAS
Max speed for landing gear extension	
	138 knots (256 km/h; 159 mph) IAS
Approach speed over 15 m (50 ft) obstacle	
	80 knots (148 km/h; 92 mph)
Landing speed	65 knots (120 km/h; 75 mph)
Max rate of climb at S/L	465 m (1,525 ft)/min
Time to: 1,830 m (6,000 ft)	4 min 42 s
3,050 m (10,000 ft)	8 min 48 s
Service ceiling	5,840 m (19,160 ft)
Absolute ceiling	6,250 m (20,500 ft)
T-O run	287 m (940 ft)
T-O to 15 m (50 ft)	494 m (1,620 ft)
Landing from 15 m (50 ft)	509 m (1,670 ft)
Landing run	238 m (780 ft)
Min ground turning radius	6.20 m (20 ft 4 in)
Range with 45 min reserves:	
75% power at 2,440 m (8,000 ft)	
	590 nm (1,093 km; 679 miles)
55% power at 3,660 m (12,000 ft)	
	650 nm (1,204 km; 748 miles)
Range, no reserves:	
75% power at 2,440 m (8,000 ft)	
	680 nm (1,260 km; 783 miles)
55% power at 3,660 m (12,000 ft)	
	735 nm (1,362 km; 846 miles)
Endurance at S/L: 75% power	4 h 24 min
55% power	5 h 36 min
g limits	+6/−3

ENAER T-35T AUCÁN (BLITHE SPIRIT)

Design studies for a turboprop version of the Pillán were completed in 1985. Originally known as the Turbo Pillán, it is powered by a 313 kW (420 shp) Allison 250-B17D engine. A T-35TX prototype (CC-PZC), converted by Soloy, made its first flight (in the USA) on 12 February 1986. It had completed about 500 hours' flying by mid-1987, but the Aucán programme has now been suspended.

DIMENSIONS, EXTERNAL: As for Pillán except:

Length overall	8.35 m (27 ft 4¾ in)
Height overall	2.35 m (7 ft 8½ in)
Propeller diameter	1.99 m (6 ft 6½ in)

WEIGHTS AND LOADINGS: As for Pillán except:

Basic weight empty, equipped	943 kg (2,080 lb)
Max T-O and landing weight	1,360 kg (3,000 lb)
Max wing loading	99.4 kg/m² (20.36 lb/sq ft)
Max power loading	4.35 kg/kW (7.14 lb/shp)

PERFORMANCE:

Never-exceed speed	241 knots (446 km/h; 277 mph)
Max level speed	198 knots (366 km/h; 228 mph)
Max cruising speed	186 knots (344 km/h; 214 mph)
Stalling speed at S/L, flaps down, engine idling	
	62 knots (115 km/h; 72 mph)
Max rate of climb at S/L	676 m (2,220 ft)/min
Service ceiling	7,620 m (25,000 ft)
T-O run	252 m (825 ft)
T-O to 15 m (50 ft)	396 m (1,300 ft)

ENAER T-36/A-36 HALCÓN (HAWK)

In 1980 the Chilean Air Force (FACh) ordered 14 C-101 Aviojet trainers from CASA of Spain, the contract including a licence for local manufacture by ENAER in a progressive programme advancing from assembly of CASA built components to partial manufacture of major components in Chile. The first four were built in Spain as C-101BB-02s, then delivered to the FACh to serve as pattern aircraft in organising the production line. A further ten of this version were completed by ENAER.

Designated **T-36** Halcón by the FACh, the C-101BB-02 differs from the Spanish Air Force C-101EB in having a more powerful (16.46 kN; 3,700 lb st) Garrett TFE731-3 turbofan instead of the 15.57 kN (3,500 lb st) TFE731-2. Deliveries of the T-36, to the tactical school of the 1st Air Group of the FACh in northern Chile, began in late 1983.

During 1982 ENAER and CASA initiated a programme to develop an attack version of the C-101 with a higher thrust turbofan. Designated C-101CC-02 by CASA and **A-36** by the FACh, this flew for the first time in November 1983. Chile has ordered 23 of this version, to replace the Cessna A-37 in FACh service. The A-36 is powered by a TFE731-5 of 19.13 kN (4,300 lb st), with a military power reserve (MPR) system which allows the thrust to be increased to 20.91 kN (4,700 lb).

Four of the C-101CC-02s/A-36s from the follow-on order are Spanish built aircraft; the remaining 19, which are built by ENAER, are progressing towards phase 3A (Chilean manufacture of electrical and hydraulic systems and small subassemblies) and phase 4 (manufacture of front fuselage). ENAER is also continuing to develop an **A-36M** in naval strike configuration with underwing BAe Sea Eagle missiles.

ENAER MIRAGE 50 UPGRADE

With technical assistance from Israel Aircraft Industries, ENAER is upgrading the Chilean Air Force's 16 Dassault-Breguet Mirage 50CN fighters by fitting them with non-moving canard surfaces, an inertial navigation system, computerised head-up display, modified electrical, hydraulic and armament control systems, ENAER Caiquen III radar warning receiver and Eclipse chaff/flare dispensing system. The foreplanes have a different planform from those of the IAI Kfir. The first upgraded aircraft was displayed at the FIDA air show in March 1986.

ENAER AVION LIVIANO

Revealed in June 1987, the Avion Liviano (light aircraft) project was launched twelve months earlier to develop a small, inexpensive club aircraft, initially for domestic use

ENAER A-36 Halcón in Fuerza Aérea de Chile insignia

and later for export. Prototype construction began in February 1987. It has been designed for use also as a trainer, with full capability for aerobatic flying.

The first ENAER aircraft of all-Chilean design, the prototype was scheduled to make its initial flight in December 1988.

TYPE: Two-seat light aircraft.

WINGS: Cantilever low-wing monoplane. Wing section NACA 63_2-415. Dihedral 5° from roots. Incidence 3° at root, 0° 30′ at tip. Tapered, non-swept all-composites

structure (glassfibre/foam sandwich with carbonfibre spar caps). Plain trailing-edge flaps and plain ailerons also of glassfibre/foam sandwich construction.

FUSELAGE: All-composites stressed skin structure of glassfibre/foam sandwich, with four bulkheads.

TAIL UNIT: Conventional assembly, with swept vertical and non-swept horizontal surfaces, of similar construction to wings. Balanced elevators and rudder; trim tab in starboard elevator.

LANDING GEAR: Non-retractable tricycle type. Cantilever spring steel main units; steerable nose unit, with oleo-pneumatic shock absorber. Cleveland wheel and Goodyear 6-ply tyre on each unit; all three tyres size 5.00-5. Cleveland hydraulic mainwheel brakes.

POWER PLANT: One 85.75 kW (115 hp) Textron Lycoming O-235-N2C flat-four engine, driving a fixed-pitch propeller with spinner and two composites blades. Single fuel tank in fuselage, capacity 100 litres (26.4 US gallons; 22 Imp gallons), with refuelling point in fuselage side.

ACCOMMODATION: Seats for two persons side by side in fully enclosed cockpit. Two independent 'gull wing' doors, hinged on centreline to open upward. Cockpit heated and ventilated. Electric defrosting of windscreen.

SYSTEMS: Hydraulic system for brakes only. Electrical power supplied by 12V 70A alternator and 12V 35Ah battery.

AVIONICS AND EQUIPMENT: VFR flight and engine instrumentation, and VHF transceiver, are standard; IFR instrumentation optional.

DIMENSIONS, EXTERNAL:
Wing span	8.70 m (28 ft 6½ in)
Wing chord: at root	1.53 m (5 ft 0¼ in)
at tip	0.84 m (2 ft 9 in)
Wing aspect ratio	7.6
Length overall	6.89 m (22 ft 7¼ in)
Height overall	2.28 m (7 ft 5¾ in)
Tailplane span	3.00 m (9 ft 10 in)
Wheel track	2.54 m (8 ft 4 in)
Wheelbase	1.50 m (4 ft 11 in)
Propeller diameter	1.78 m (5 ft 10 in)

DIMENSIONS, INTERNAL:
Cockpit: Max width	1.16 m (3 ft 9½ in)

AREAS:
Wings, gross	10.01 m² (107.75 sq ft)
Ailerons (total)	0.44 m² (4.74 sq ft)
Trailing-edge flaps (total)	0.92 m² (9.90 sq ft)
Fin	0.88 m² (9.47 sq ft)
Rudder	0.34 m² (3.66 sq ft)
Tailplane	2.08 m² (22.39 sq ft)
Elevators (total)	0.76 m² (8.18 sq ft)

WEIGHTS AND LOADINGS:
Basic weight empty	446 kg (983 lb)
Max fuel	72 kg (159 lb)
Max T-O and landing weight	700 kg (1,543 lb)
Max wing loading	69.93 kg/m² (14.32 lb/sq ft)
Max power loading	8.16 kg/kW (13.42 lb/hp)

PERFORMANCE (estimated, at max T-O weight except where indicated):
Never-exceed speed	158 knots (292 km/h; 182 mph)
Max level speed at S/L	128 knots (237 km/h; 147 mph)
Max cruising speed, 75% power at 2,440 m (8,000 ft)	107 knots (198 km/h; 123 mph)
Stalling speed, power off:	
flaps up	54 knots (100 km/h; 62 mph)
flaps down	48 knots (89 km/h; 56 mph)
Max rate of climb at S/L	362 m (1,187 ft)/min
Service ceiling	4,270 m (14,000 ft)
T-O run	226 m (742 ft)
T-O to 15 m (50 ft)	308 m (1,010 ft)
Landing from 15 m (50 ft)	364 m (1,195 ft)
Landing run	160 m (525 ft)
Range with max fuel, 10% reserves	516 nm (955 km; 594 miles)
g limits	+4.4/−2.2

ENAER modified Mirage 50CN, with fixed foreplanes and upgraded avionics

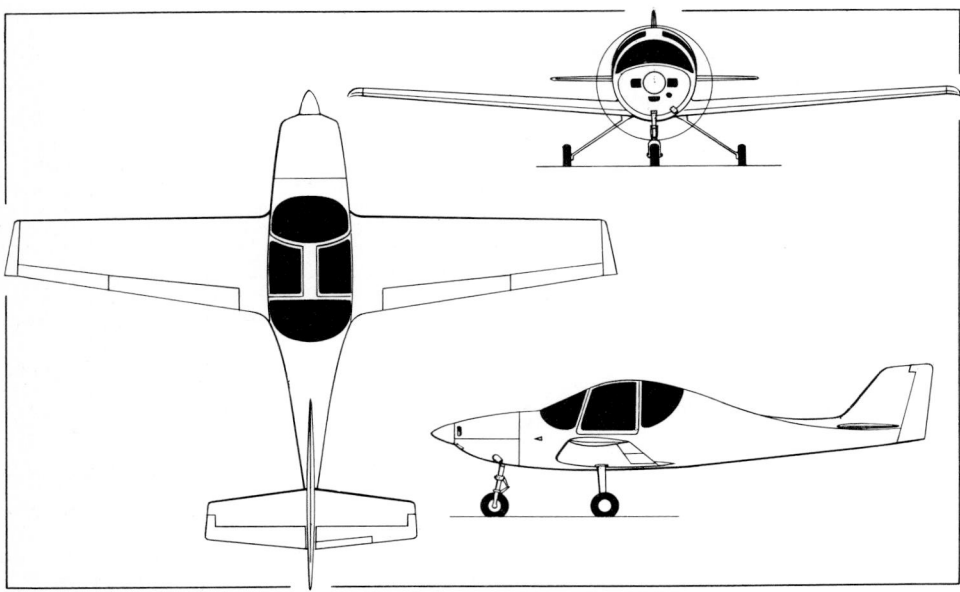

ENAER Avion Liviano two-seat light aircraft (*Pilot Press*)

CHINA
(PEOPLE'S REPUBLIC)

NATIONAL AIRCRAFT FACTORIES

Beijing, Chengdu, Guangzhou, Guizhou, Hanzhong, Harbin, Jingdezhen, Liyang, Nanchang, Shanghai, Shenyang, Shijiazhuang, Tianjin, Xian and elsewhere

INTERNATIONAL MARKETING:

CATIC (China National Aero-Technology Import and Export Corporation)

5 Liang Guo Chang Road, East City District (PO Box 1671), Beijing

Telephone: 44 5831

Telex: 22318 AEROT CN

PRESIDENT: Sun Zhaoqing

EXECUTIVE VICE-PRESIDENT: Tang Xiaoping

Chinese national aircraft factories function under the jurisdiction of the Ministry of Aviation Industry. There are design and development centres at Shenyang, Beijing, Harbin and elsewhere. Xian, Harbin and other Chinese factories also carry out subcontract work on the Airbus A300, ATR 42, BAe 146, Boeing 737 and 747, Canadair CL-215, McDonnell Douglas MD-80 and Shorts 360. Total workforce of the aerospace industry was estimated at 350,000 in 1984, although several aircraft factories are engaged also in manufacturing non-aerospace products.

Details of new military programmes remain speculative. The **J-9** fighter is now known to have been a 1970 project, by the No. 611 Design Bureau of the Ministry of Aviation Industry, for a Kfir-type single-engined delta-wing fighter with movable foreplanes. For reasons not yet known, it was

terminated in 1979. Persistent reports of a delta-wing J-10 and swept (or swing) wing J-12 under development, and possible Chinese production of the MiG-23 (as J-11), appear to have been answered by PLA Air Force spokesmen who told visiting US journalists in 1987 that swing-wing and delta-wing designs studied earlier "have not been pursued". On the other hand, prototypes of two new supersonic fighters were reportedly flown at Shenyang in 1987, and a new Spey 202 powered aircraft was expected to be flown at Xian during 1988.

Output of older fighters and bombers is now diminishing, with increasing emphasis being placed on the development of new aircraft making use of China's growing technological capability. The reduction of 1 million personnel in China's armed forces manpower is intended to make more funds available during the seventh Five-Year Plan (1986-90) for the purchase of modern weapons and technology, while at the same time shifting emphasis in the aviation industry towards a target of a 60-40 per cent bias in favour of civil aircraft production. As a further step in this direction, increased effort is being made to export Chinese built aircraft (particularly the F-7M, A-5C, Z-9, Y7-100, Y-8 and Y-12).

An outline of China's future plans for civil aircraft development was given in 1986 by the director of the Ministry of Aviation Industry's civil aircraft bureau, Mr Zhu Yu Li. In addition to continuing with production and new versions of the Y-7, Y-8 and Y-12, an international partner is being sought for a 30/40-passenger commuter

airliner programme (existing type or new design). A larger transport, designated MPC-75, is being undertaken by CATIC and the German company MBB (see MPC-75 entry in the International section). To follow the Y-8 a new, and possibly propfan/UDF powered, 150-passenger type is being explored.

Increasing attention is also being given to helicopter development, hitherto a rather neglected area. With the Z-5 out of production since 1979, the Z-6 programme also terminated and the Z-7 never identified, China's modern helicopter design and manufacturing expertise is restricted to development of the Z-8, a Chinese derivative of the Aérospatiale Super Frelon, and licence production of the same company's Dauphin as the Z-9. To extend this range, discussions took place with possible international collaborators concerning development of an 8,000 kg (17,635 lb) class multi-purpose transport helicopter, and an agreement was signed with Aérospatiale in 1987 for joint development of a small (2,500 kg; 5,500 lb class) type for agricultural and forestry work. The latter could also fulfil a current requirement for a small military helicopter. The PLA is said to need about 50 for anti-tank duties.

A model of an agricultural aircraft called the **Shennong-1** was displayed at an exhibition in Beijing in the Spring of 1986. Similar in appearance to the Air Tractor AT-400 (see US section), it was said to be proposed with either a piston or a turboprop engine. No other details were given, and no subsequent reference to this design has been seen.

CAC
CHENGDU AIRCRAFT CORPORATION
Chengdu, Sichuan
DEPUTY CHIEF ENGINEER: Wang Yingong

CAC (MIKOYAN) J-7
Chinese name: Jianjiji-7 (Fighter aircraft 7) or Jian-7
Westernised designations: F-7, F-7B and F-7M
NATO reporting name: Fishbed

The Chinese version of the Mikoyan MiG-21 day fighter was based originally on Soviet built MiG-21Fs ('Fishbed-Cs') delivered to China before the political break with the USSR in 1960. The task of copying the airframe, the Tumansky R-11 afterburning turbojet (built at Chengdu as the Wopen-7 or WP-7) and equipment was accomplished quickly, and the first J-7 made its initial flight in December 1964. The type began to enter service with the Air Force of the People's Liberation Army in 1965 and some 60-80 had been completed before production was halted in 1966 by the onset of the Cultural Revolution. It was resumed subsequently with a number of modifications, as detailed in the 1987-88 *Jane's*. Exports of early production J-7/F-7s were made to Albania and Tanzania.

At the beginning of the 1980s Chinese engineers undertook further modifications aimed at upgrading both handling qualities and combat performance of the aircraft. Major improvements in this version, designated **J-7 II** in China and **F-7B** for export, included use of a Wopen-7B engine, in which the afterburning thrust is increased by 9.8 kN (1,000 kg; 2,205 lb), the addition on the port side of a second 30 mm gun, and the ability to carry an 800 litre (211.3 US gallon; 176 Imp gallon) drop tank under the fuselage. The three-position, mechanically movable shock cone in the MiG-21F's nose intake, housing the range-only radar, was replaced by a more efficient no-step system permitting continuously variable positioning of the centrebody, similar to that introduced on the Soviet built 'Fishbed-E' in the mid-1960s. Introduction of a new zero-height/low-speed ejection seat was accompanied by a new cockpit canopy, hinged at the rear and opening upward, in place of the early pattern MiG-21 canopy hinged at the base of the windscreen. The tail braking parachute was transferred from under the rear fuselage to a 'bullet' fairing beneath the rudder.

Components and engines for the F-7 have been exported in some numbers to Egypt, which also ordered up to 160 complete aircraft for its own use (as advanced trainers) and for supply to Iraq. Some of these aircraft, and Egypt's Soviet supplied MiG-21MFs, have been retrofitted with an advanced head-up display and launchers for AIM-9P3/4 Sidewinder air-to-air missiles. In 1984 China introduced the improved **F-7M Airguard**, differing mainly in having more modern Western avionics which include a HUD-WAC (head-up display and weapon aiming computer) system instead of the optical sighting system, a more effective ranging radar, new air data computer and radar altimeter, new IFF, and more secure com radio. Other changes include a more efficient electrical power system to cater for the new avionics; two additional underwing stores points; ability to carry the newer and longer-range PL-7 air-to-air missile, which outwardly resembles the Matra Magic; a slightly different version of the Wopen-7B engine; and a relocated nose probe. The F-7M is in service with the PLA Air Force, and total exports of the F-7 (all models) have exceeded 500. Customer nations have included Egypt, Pakistan, Somalia and Sudan. Deliveries of 60 F-7Ms to Pakistan began in 1986, to replace Shenyang F-6s, and other countries reported to have received F-7s in 1986-87

F-7M Airguard Chinese built export version of the MiG-21 ('Fishbed') *(ATL)*

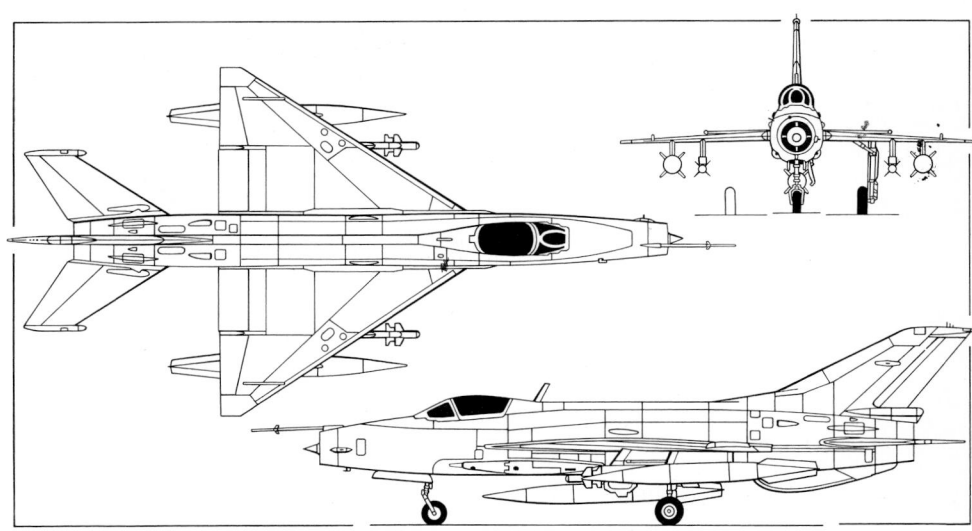

Chengdu F-7M Airguard single-seat fighter and close support aircraft *(Jane's/Mike Keep)*

include Iran (12-18, with a similar quantity on order) and Zimbabwe (48, to equip three squadrons). Chengdu production of the F-7M was reported to be about 20 aircraft per month, for domestic and foreign customers, in late 1987.

Current Soviet versions of the MiG-21 are fully described and illustrated in the USSR section of this edition. China has also developed its own two-seat training version, known as the **JJ-7** or **FT-7**; this is built at Guizhou by GAIGC and described under that company's entry. An all-weather **J-7 III**, possibly based on the MiG-21MF airframe, is reportedly being developed at Shenyang (which see); another variant under study, known as the **Sabre 2**, is being considered as a future collaborative programme between CAC and Grumman (USA), and is described separately.

The following description applies to the standard F-7B and F-7M:

TYPE: Single-seat day fighter and close support aircraft.
WINGS: As for standard MiG-21, with 57° sweepback on leading-edges, 2° anhedral, slotted flaps and balanced ailerons.
FUSELAGE: Generally as MiG-21F except for automatically operated, continuously adjustable shock cone in centre of nose intake. In F-7M, nose probe is relocated above intake, offset to starboard, as on Soviet built MiG-21PFM 'Fishbed-J'.
TAIL UNIT: All-swept surfaces, with all-moving tailplane, as for MiG-21.
LANDING GEAR: Inward retracting mainwheels, with 660 × 220 tyres and LS-16 disc brakes; forward retracting nosewheel, with 500 × 180 tyre and LS-15 double-acting brake. Tail braking parachute at base of vertical tail.
POWER PLANT: One Chengdu Wopen-7B turbojet in F-7B (43.15 kN/4,400 kg; 9,700 lb st dry, 59.82 kN/6,100 kg; 13,448 lb st with afterburning). Wopen-7B(BM) in F-7M has same ratings, but kerosene (instead of gasoline) starting. Total internal fuel capacity of 2,385 litres (630 US gallons; 524.5 Imp gallons), contained in six flexible tanks in fuselage and two integral tanks in each wing. Provision for carrying a 500 or 800 litre (132 or 211.3 US gallon; 110 or 176 Imp gallon) centreline drop tank, and/or a 500 litre drop tank on each outboard underwing pylon. Max possible internal/external fuel capacity 4,185 litres (1,105.6 US gallons; 920.5 Imp gallons).
ACCOMMODATION: Pilot only, on Chengdu Aircraft Corporation zero-height/low-speed ejection seat operable between 70 and 459 knots (130-850 km/h; 81-528 mph) IAS. One-piece canopy, hinged at rear to open upward.
SYSTEMS: Improved electrical system in F-7M, using three static (instead of four rotary) inverters, to cater for additional avionics. Jianghuai YX-3 oxygen system.
AVIONICS: *(F-7B)* Include CT-3 VHF com radio, WL-7 radio compass, Type 262 radio altimeter, XS-5A marker beacon receiver, Type 222 ranging radar, and Type 602 (Soviet 'Odd Rods' type) IFF transponder. *(F-7M)* GEC Avionics suite includes Type 956 HUDWAC, AD 3400 two-band UHF/VHF multi-function com system, Type 226 Skyranger ranging radar with ECCM, and an air data computer. Other avionics include Type 602 IFF transponder, Type 0101 HR A/2 radar altimeter, WL-7 radio compass, and XS-6A marker beacon receiver. The HUDWAC (head-up display and weapon aiming computer) provides the pilot with displays for instrument flying, with air-to-air and air-to-ground weapon delivery superimposed on the same area of view as the target. It can store 32 weapon parameter functions, allowing both current and future weapon variants to be accommodated. In air-to-air combat its four modes (missiles, conventional gunnery, snapshoot gunnery or dogfight status) allow for all eventualities. There are also two navigation

F-7B with centreline drop tank and underwing rocket pods *(CATIC)*

functions: approach mode, and a standby aiming reticle provided by the HUD.

ARMAMENT: *(F-7B)* Two 30 mm Type 30-1 belt-fed cannon, with 60 rds/gun, in fairings under front fuselage just forward of wingroot leading-edges. One hardpoint under each wing, each capable of carrying a PL-2 ('Atoll' type), PL-2A or similar infra-red homing air-to-air missile, a pod of eighteen 57 mm unguided rockets, or a bomb of up to 250 kg size (500 kg in max overload condition). SM-3A optical or AFS3A computing gunsight interfaced with ranging radar and angle of attack sideslip transmitter, with gun camera mounted on sighting head. *(F-7M)* Gunsight replaced by a GEC Avionics Type 956 HUDWAC. Outboard underwing pylons are 'wet' for the carriage of drop tanks. The centreline pylon is used for a drop tank only. Each inboard pylon is capable of carrying a PL-2, -2A, -5B or -7 air-to-air missile or, at customer's option, a Matra R.550 Magic; one pod of eighteen Type 57-2 (57 mm) air-to-air and air-to-ground rockets; one pod of seven Type 90-1 (90 mm) air-to-ground rockets; or a 50, 150, 250 or 500 kg bomb. Each outboard pylon can carry one of the above rocket pods, a 50 or 150 kg bomb, or a 500 litre drop tank.

DIMENSIONS, EXTERNAL:

Wing span	7.154 m (23 ft 5⅝ in)
Wing aspect ratio	2.2
Length overall:	
excl nose probe	13.945 m (45 ft 9 in)
incl nose probe	14.885 m (48 ft 10 in)
Height overall	4.103 m (13 ft 5½ in)
Tailplane span	3.74 m (12 ft 3¼ in)
Wheel track	2.692 m (8 ft 10 in)
Wheelbase	4.807 m (15 ft 9¼ in)

AREA:

Wings, gross	23.00 m² (247.6 sq ft)

WEIGHTS AND LOADINGS:

Weight empty: F-7B	5,145 kg (11,343 lb)
F-7M	5,275 kg (11,629 lb)
Normal max T-O weight with two PL-2 or PL-7 air-to-air missiles:	
F-7B	7,372 kg (16,252 lb)
F-7M	7,531 kg (16,603 lb)
Wing loading at normal max T-O weight:	
F-7B	320.52 kg/m² (65.68 lb/sq ft)
F-7M	327.43 kg/m² (67.10 lb/sq ft)
Power loading at normal max T-O weight:	
F-7B	123.3 kg/kN (1.21 lb/lb st)
F-7M	125.5 kg/kN (1.23 lb/lb st)

PERFORMANCE (at normal max T-O weight with two PL-2 or PL-7 air-to-air missiles, except where indicated):

Max level speed between 12,500 and 18,500 m (41,010-60,700 ft): F-7B, F-7M	Mach 2.05 (1,175 knots; 2,175 km/h; 1,350 mph)
Unstick speed: F-7B, F-7M	167-178 knots (310-330 km/h; 193-205 mph)
Touchdown speed: F-7B, F-7M	162-173 knots (300-320 km/h; 186-199 mph)
Max rate of climb at S/L:	
F-7B	9,000 m (29,527 ft)/min
F-7M	10,800 m (35,435 ft)/min
Acceleration from Mach 0.9 to 1.2 at 5,000 m (16,400 ft):	
F-7M	35 s
Max sustained turn rate:	
F-7M (Mach 0.7 at S/L)	14.7°/s
F-7M (Mach 0.8 at 5,000 m; 16,400 ft)	9.5°/s
Service ceiling: F-7B	18,800 m (61,680 ft)
F-7M	18,200 m (59,710 ft)
Absolute ceiling: F-7B	19,200 m (62,990 ft)
F-7M	18,700 m (61,350 ft)
T-O run: F-7B	800-1,000 m (2,625-3,280 ft)
F-7M	700-950 m (2,297-3,117 ft)

Comparative models illustrating differences between the F-7M (top) and the proposed Sabre II

Landing run with brake-chute:	
F-7B	800-1,000 m (2,625-3,280 ft)
F-7M	600-900 m (1,969-2,953 ft)

Typical mission profiles (F-7M):

Combat air patrol at 11,000 m (36,000 ft) with two air-to-air missiles and three 500 litre drop tanks, incl 5 min combat   45 min

Long range interception at 11,000 m (36,000 ft) at 351 nm (650 km; 404 miles) from base, incl Mach 1.5 dash and 5 min combat, stores as above

Hi-lo-hi interdiction radius, out and back at 11,000 m (36,000 ft), with three 500 litre drop tanks and two 150 kg bombs   324 nm (600 km; 373 miles)

Lo-lo-lo close air support radius with four rocket pods, no external tanks   200 nm (370 km; 230 miles)

Range:

F-7B, two PL-2 missiles only	647 nm (1,200 km; 745 miles)
F-7B, two PL-2s and one 800 litre drop tank	804 nm (1,490 km; 926 miles)
F-7M, two PL-7 missiles and three 500 litre drop tanks	939 nm (1,740 km; 1,081 miles)
F-7M, self-ferry with one 800 litre and two 500 litre drop tanks, no missiles	1,203 nm (2,230 km; 1,385 miles)

g limits: F-7B	+7
F-7M	+8

CAC/GRUMMAN SABRE II

In collaboration with Chengdu Aircraft Corporation, CATIC and the Pakistan Air Force, Grumman Corporation of the USA completed in August 1987 a five-month feasibility study for a re-engineered version of the Chengdu F-7M Airguard (see preceding entry). Under consideration to replace about 150 Chinese Shenyang F-6 (J-6) fighters of the Pakistan Air Force, the Sabre II would combine a new engine/avionics package with a much-modified front fuselage having a lengthened nose with 'solid' ogival nosecone, a new 'teardrop' cockpit canopy, and twin lateral air intakes instead of a single nose intake. Candidate engines under consideration include the General Electric F404 and Turbo-Union RB199. Possible avionics include a Westinghouse APG-66 radar, Singer Kearfott INS and GEC Avionics or other HUD.

Under the Grumman plan, the US company would initially manufacture the new forward fuselage, cockpit and intakes, and install the engine in a Chengdu-built modified rear fuselage; later in the programme, the Pakistan Aeronautical Complex at Kamra would become responsible for the nose section and eventually assemble the complete aircraft.

No firm decision to go ahead with the Sabre II had been announced at the time of going to press, but if it does proceed a 42 month FSED phase, with first flight after 24 months, is expected to lead to IOC in 1992-93.

CAMC
CHANGHE AIRCRAFT MANUFACTURING CORPORATION
Jingdezhen, Jiangxi

CAMC Z-8
Chinese name: Zhishengji-8 (Vertical take-off aircraft 8) or Zhi-8

This helicopter, based on the Aérospatiale SA 321JA Super Frelon, flew for the first time on 11 December 1985. It was developed jointly by the Changhe Aircraft Manufacturing Corporation and the China Helicopter Research and Design Bureau, both located at Jingdezhen. It is planned to complete a batch of ten Zhi-8s by 1990.

POWER PLANT: Three Wozhou-6 (WZ-6) turboshafts.

WEIGHT:

Max T-O weight	13,000 kg (28,660 lb)

PERFORMANCE:

Max level speed	162 knots (300 km/h; 186 mph)
Max range	324-432 nm (600-800 km; 373-497 miles)

First prototype of the Changhe Zhi-8 Chinese version of the Aérospatiale Super Frelon

GAIGC
GUIZHOU AVIATION INDUSTRY GROUP COMPANY
Guizhou

GAIGC JJ-7
Chinese name: Jianjiji Jiaolianji-7 or Jianjiao-7 (Fighter training aircraft 7)
Westernised designation: FT-7

First flown in July 1985, the JJ-7 or FT-7 is a tandem two-seat trainer version of the Chengdu J-7/F-7, generally similar outwardly to its Soviet counterpart, the MiG-21U (NATO 'Mongol-A'), and is said to be capable of providing most of the training necessary for the Shenyang J-8/F-8 fighter as well as the full syllabus for all versions of the J-7/F-7. Avionics and power plant are generally as described for the single-seat F-7M under the CAC heading.

Differences from the single-seat J-7 and MiG-21U include sideways opening (to starboard) twin canopies, the rear one fitted with a retractable periscope, twin ventral strakes of modified shape, and a removable saddleback fuel tank aft of the second cockpit. A 480 or 800 litre (127 or 211 US gallon; 105.5 or 176 Imp gallon) drop tank can be carried under the centre-fuselage, and there is a single underwing pylon each side for such stores as PL-2 or -2B air-to-air missiles, an HF-5A 18-round launcher for 57 mm rockets, or bombs of up to 250 kg size. The JJ-7 can also be fitted with a Type 23-3 twin-barrel 23 mm gun in an underbelly pack.

DIMENSIONS, EXTERNAL: As J-7 except:
Length overall, incl probe 14.874 m (48 ft 9½ in)
WEIGHTS:
Weight empty 5,330 kg (11,750 lb)
Internal fuel 1,891 kg (4,169 lb)

GAIGC JJ-7/FT-7 two-seat trainer version of the CAC J-7/ F-7 *(J. M. G. Gradidge)*

Normal max T-O weight with two PL-2 air-to-air missiles	7,590 kg (16,733 lb)	Service ceiling	17,300 m (56,760 ft)
		Absolute ceiling	17,700 m (58,070 ft)
Max T-O weight with two PL-2 missiles and one 800 litre drop tank	8,600 kg (18,960 lb)	T-O run	900-1,100 m (2,953-3,609 ft)

Normal max T-O weight with two PL-2 air-to-air missiles 7,590 kg (16,733 lb)
Max T-O weight with two PL-2 missiles and one 800 litre drop tank 8,600 kg (18,960 lb)
PERFORMANCE:
Max level speed as for J-7/F-7
Unstick speed 170-181 knots (315-335 km/h; 196-208 mph)
Touchdown speed 165-175 knots (305-325 km/h; 190-202 mph)

Service ceiling 17,300 m (56,760 ft)
Absolute ceiling 17,700 m (58,070 ft)
T-O run 900-1,100 m (2,953-3,609 ft)
Landing run with brake-chute and wheel braking 850-1,100 m (2,789-3,609 ft)
Range at 11,000 m (36,000 ft):
internal fuel only 545 nm (1,010 km; 627 miles)
with 800 litre drop tank 701 nm (1,300 km; 808 miles)
g limit with two PL-2B missiles +7

GOHL
GUANGZHOU ORLANDO HELICOPTERS LTD
Hoben, Jiahe, Guangzhou, Guangdong
Telephone: 627095

GUANGZHOU (ORLANDO) PANDA
Orlando Helicopter Airways (see US section) initiated a venture in 1985 in which its OHA-S-55 Bearcat is now being

assembled, and will later be part-built, in China, by a jointly owned company known as Guangzhou Orlando Helicopters Ltd. A 2,323 m² (25,000 sq ft) factory was built for the purpose at an airfield near the city of Guangzhou.

The 20-year contract, signed on 27 October 1985, provides for the initial assembly in China, from Orlando kits, of ten aircraft. Kits for five of these had been shipped to China by early 1988. Second and third stage batches of 20 and 30 aircraft respectively will include a proportion of

OHA-S-55T Challenger and/or Phoenix turbine powered versions, with 522 kW (700 shp) Textron Lycoming LTS 101-700A-3 engines. Chinese built OHA-S-55s are to be marketed, under the name Panda, by Orlando Helicopter Far East Ltd, based in Hong Kong. The contract also contains options for co-production of the Orlando modified S-58T Viking, and a 13-seat utility version of the Sikorsky S-76 powered by Turbomeca Arriel engines.

HAMC
HARBIN AIRCRAFT MANUFACTURING CORPORATION
PO Box 201, Harbin, Heilongjiang
Telephone: 62951
Telex: 87082 HAF CHN
PRESIDENT: Yang Shou Wen
VICE-PRESIDENT: Yang Yi Dian

Harbin had its origin in the plant of the Manshu Aeroplane Manufacturing Company, one of several aircraft and aero engine factories established in Manchukuo (Manchuria) by the Japanese in 1938. After the Communist regime came to power in mainland China in 1949 it was re-established and re-equipped with Soviet assistance, and in recent years has been responsible for production of the Soviet Ilyushin Il-28 jet bomber (Chinese designation H-5) and the nationally designed SH-5 amphibian and Y-11 and Y-12 agricultural and utility light twins. Details of the H-5 and Y-11 can be found in earlier editions of *Jane's*. Landing gear doors for the British Aerospace 146 are produced under a 1981 agreement with BAe, and doors and wing components for the Shorts 360.

Harbin is also the chief centre for helicopter production, which began with the Mil Mi-4 (Chinese Z-5; 1985-86 and earlier *Jane's*). It is currently responsible for the Aérospatiale Dauphin 2 (Z-9) manufacturing and assembly programme, and is producing components for China's Mil Mi-8s. The workforce numbers about 15,000.

Latest known Harbin product is the SH-5 (PS-5) maritime patrol amphibian.

HAMC SH-5
Chinese name: Shuishang Hongzhaji 5 (Maritime bomber 5) or Shuihong-5
Westernised designation: PS-5

First indications of the existence of this four-turboprop flying-boat amphibian came during a visit to China by US aerospace industry representatives in 1980, when two examples were reported to be under construction. The SH-5 was designed by the Seaplane Research and Design Bureau (No. 605) of the Ministry of Aviation Industry in Jingmen City, Hubei Province, but its development has been somewhat protracted. Design work began in 1969, the first prototype was rolled out in 1971, and the first flight was made on 3 April 1976. It is believed that three prototypes were completed, production not starting until about 1984. The aircraft's entry into PLA Navy service was announced by the *Liberation Army Daily* on 3 September 1986, following a demonstration to Premier Zhao Zhiyang on 30 August. At least four were then in service with a senior seaplane unit at Tuandao naval air station, Qingdao.

The SH-5 is intended for a wide range of maritime duties including anti-submarine and anti-surface-vessel warfare,

Two views of the HAMC SH-5 (PS-5) patrol and anti-submarine bomber amphibian, now in service with the Chinese Navy

patrol and surveillance, minelaying, search and rescue, and the carriage of bulk cargo. In several respects it bears a close resemblance to the Japanese Shin Meiwa US-1A. In particular, the hull shape, and the method of retracting the single mainwheels/twin nosewheels landing gear, show similarities to the US-1A, including the spray suppression strakes on each side of the nose and the fuselage-side slots almost in line with the propellers. The dihedral tailplane and twin oval fins and rudders clearly owe their configuration to the Soviet Beriev Be-12, although they are proportionately larger.

The Chinese are reportedly seeking an ASW and avionics upgrade for the SH-5, possibly similar to that now under way for the Dassault-Breguet Atlantique 2.

TYPE: Maritime patrol and anti-submarine bomber, surveillance, SAR and transport amphibian.

WINGS: All-metal cantilever high-wing monoplane. Constant chord centre-section; outer panels tapered, with anhedral outboard of outer engine nacelles. Non-retractable stabilising float, on N struts with twin I struts inboard, beneath each wing near tip. Spoiler forward of each outer flap segment. Trim tab in each aileron.

FUSELAGE: Unpressurised all-metal semi-monocoque hull, with high length/beam ratio and single-step planing

bottom. Curved spray suppression strakes along sides of nose; spray suppression slots in lower sides, aft of inboard propeller plane. Small water rudder at rear of hull. 'Thimble' radome on nose; MAD in extended tail 'sting'.

TAIL UNIT: High mounted dihedral tailplane, with oval endplate fins and rudders, mounted on fairing above rear fuselage. Trim tabs in each rudder and each elevator.

LANDING GEAR: Retractable tricycle type, with single mainwheels and twin-wheel nose unit. Oleo-pneumatic shock absorbers. Main units retract upward and rearward into wells in hull sides; nose unit retracts rearward.

POWER PLANT: Four 2,349 kW (3,150 ehp) Harbin WJ-5A-1 turboprops, each driving a four-blade propeller with spinner.

ACCOMMODATION: Standard eight-person crew includes a flight crew of five (pilot, co-pilot, navigator, flight engineer and radio operator), plus systems/equipment operators according to mission. Three freight compartments in front portion of hull. Mission crew cabin amidships, aft of which are two further compartments, one for communications and other electronic equipment and the rear one for specialised mission equipment. All compartments connected by corridor, with watertight doors aft of flight deck and between each compartment.

AVIONICS AND EQUIPMENT: Include inertial navigation system, air data computer, radio altimeter and radio compass.

ARMAMENT AND OPERATIONAL EQUIPMENT: Doppler search radar in 'thimble' radome forward of nose transparencies. Magnetic anomaly detector (MAD) in extended tail 'sting'. Four underwing hardpoints for C-101 sea skimming supersonic anti-shipping or other missiles (one on each inboard pylon), lightweight torpedoes (up to three on each outer pylon), or other stores. Depth charges, mines, bombs, sonobuoys, SAR gear or other mission equipment and stores in rear of hull, as required.

DIMENSIONS, EXTERNAL:

Wing span	36.00 m (118 ft 1¼ in)
Wing aspect ratio	9.0
Length overall	38.90 m (127 ft 7½ in)
Height overall	9.79 m (32 ft 1½ in)
* Span over tail-fins	11.40 m (37 ft 4¾ in)
* Wheel track	3.70 m (12 ft 1¾ in)
* Wheelbase	10.50 m (34 ft 5½ in)
* Propeller diameter	3.80 m (12 ft 5½ in)

* estimated

AREA:

Wings, gross	144.0 m² (1,550.0 sq ft)

WEIGHTS AND LOADINGS:

Weight empty, equipped:	
SAR and transport	less than 25,000 kg (55,115 lb)
ASW	26,500 kg (58,422 lb)
Fuel load (max)	16,500 kg (36,376 lb)
Max internal weapons load	6,000 kg (13,228 lb)
Max payload (bulk cargo)	10,000 kg (22,045 lb)
Normal T-O weight	36,000 kg (79,366 lb)
Max T-O weight	45,000 kg (99,208 lb)
Wing loading:	
at normal T-O weight	250.0 kg/m² (51.2 lb/sq ft)
at max T-O weight	312.5 kg/m² (64.0 lb/sq ft)
Power loading:	
at normal T-O weight	3.31 kg/kW (5.44 lb/ehp)
at max T-O weight	4.14 kg/kW (6.80 lb/ehp)

PERFORMANCE:

Max level speed	299 knots (555 km/h; 345 mph)
Max cruising speed	243 knots (450 km/h; 280 mph)
Min patrol speed	124 knots (230 km/h; 143 mph)
T-O speed (water)	87 knots (160 km/h; 100 mph)
Landing speed (water)	92 knots (170 km/h; 106 mph)
Service ceiling	7,000 m (22,965 ft)
T-O run (water)	548 m (1,798 ft)
Landing run (water)	240 m (788 ft)
Range with max fuel	2,563 nm (4,750 km; 2,951 miles)
Endurance (2 engines)	12 to 15 h

HAMC Y-12

Chinese name: Yunshuji-12 (Transport aircraft 12) or Yun-12

This STOL general purpose transport was developed in order to improve upon the modest payload/range capabilities of the piston engined nine/ten-seat Harbin Y-11 (see 1986-87 and earlier *Jane's*). It has a scaled-up airframe, the principal enlargement being that of the fuselage, which has an increased cross-section and is lengthened to enable up to 17 passengers to be carried in a commuter configuration. The wings, in addition to being greater in span, have a new aerofoil section intended to afford a 3 per cent increase in maximum speed and 10 per cent increase in rate of climb; they also incorporate additional fuel tanks in the wing spar box. Design and construction of the Y-12 are to FAR Pt 23 and Pt 135 (Annexe A) standards.

Three prototype **Y-12 Is** and about 30 production examples of this PT6A-11 engined version were built, the first flight taking place on 14 July 1982. Details of this version can be found in the 1987-88 and earlier *Jane's*.

Current version is the **Y-12 II**, which has higher rated PT6A-27 engines and no leading-edge slats. First flight of a Y-12 II took place on 16 August 1984. Domestic

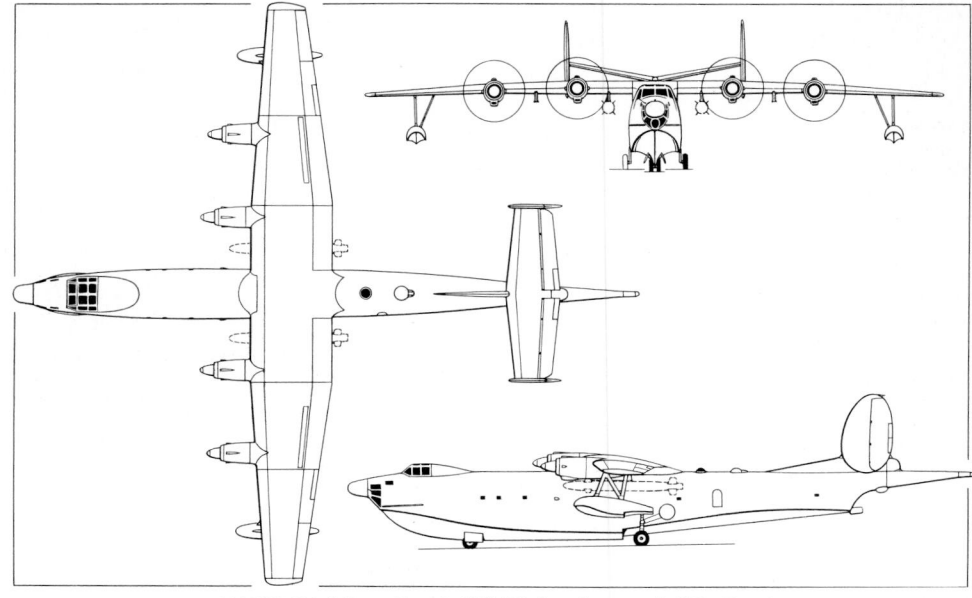

HAMC SH-5 (four Harbin WJ-5A-1 turboprops) *(Pilot Press)*

Harbin Y-12 II twin-turboprop utility transport with newly enlarged ventral fin *(Brian M. Service)*

certification was received in December 1985, and 35 production Y-12 IIs had been completed by 1 January 1988. First deliveries (of four, to the Sri Lanka government for patrol duties) were made in early 1987, and a further order from this customer was reported in late 1987. It was hoped to obtain international certification by the end of 1988, possibly with assistance from the British Civil Aviation Authority. A licence agreement for P&WC PT6 engines to be assembled in China was announced in May 1986, and kits for 300 engines have been ordered initially. China has a domestic requirement for more than 200 Y-12s, and the aircraft is available for export. Future plans include a 'stretched' version and one with a pressurised cabin.

The description applies to the current production version:

TYPE: Twin-turboprop STOL general purpose transport.

WINGS: Braced high-wing monoplane, with constant chord from root to tip. Wing section LS(1)-0417, with thickness/chord ratio of 17%. Anhedral 1° 41′. Incidence 4°. No sweep. Two-spar fail-safe structure, with aluminium alloy skin; Ziqiang-2 resin bonding on 70 per cent of structure and integral fuel tankage in wing spar box. All-metal drooping ailerons and electrically actuated two-section double-slotted flaps along full span of trailing-edges. Trim tab in starboard aileron. Type 29S-7D anti-icing of leading-edges. Small stub-wings at cabin floor level support the main landing gear units; bracing strut from each stub-wing out to approx one-third span.

FUSELAGE: Conventional semi-monocoque all-metal fail-safe structure of basically rectangular cross-section, swept upward at rear. Ziqiang-2 resin bonding on 40 per cent of structure.

TAIL UNIT: Cantilever non-swept metal structure, with low-set constant chord tailplane and large dorsal fin. Horn balanced rudder and elevators. Trim tab in rudder and each elevator. Ventral fin under tailcone. Type 29S-7D 5178 anti-icing of leading-edges.

LANDING GEAR: Non-retractable tricycle type, with oleo-pneumatic shock absorber in each unit. Single-wheel main units, attached to underside of stub-wings. Single steerable nosewheel. Mainwheel tyres size 640 × 230 mm, pressure 5.5 bars (80 lb/sq in); nosewheel tyre size 480 × 200 mm, pressure 3.5 bars (51 lb/sq in). Pneumatic brakes.

POWER PLANT: Two Pratt & Whitney Canada PT6A-27 turboprops, each flat rated at 507 kW (680 shp) and driving a Hartzell HC-B3TN-3B/T10173B-3 three-blade variable- and reversible-pitch propeller with spinner. All fuel in tanks in wing spar box, total capacity 1,616 litres (427 US gallons; 355.5 Imp gallons), with overwing gravity filling point each side.

ACCOMMODATION: Crew of two on flight deck, access to which is via a forward opening door on the port side. Four-way adjustable crew seats. Dual controls. Main cabin can accommodate up to 17 passengers in commuter configuration, in three-abreast layout (with aisle), at seat pitch of 79 cm (31 in). Alternative layouts for up to 16 parachutists, or an all-cargo configuration with 11 tiedown rings. Passenger/cargo double door on port side at rear, the rear half of which opens outward and the forward half inward; foldout steps in passenger entrance. Emergency exits on each side at front of cabin and opposite passenger door on starboard side at rear. Baggage compartments in nose and at rear of passenger cabin, for 100 kg (220 lb) and 260 kg (573 lb) respectively.

SYSTEM: R70-3WG environmental control system.

AVIONICS AND EQUIPMENT: Avionics include VHF-251 and HF-230 com radio, AUD-251H, ADF-650A radio compass, VIR-351 and Bendix 1400C weather radar. Standard instrumentation includes BK-450 airspeed indicator, BDP-1 artificial horizon, BG10-1A altimeter, ZGW-3G altitude indicator, ZHZ-4A radio magnetic heading indicator, BC10 rate of climb indicator, ZWH-1 outside air temperature indicator, and ZEY-1 flap position indicator; dual engine torquemeters, interturbine temperature indicators, gas generator tachometers, oil temperature and pressure indicators, and fuel pressure and quantity indicators; HSZ-2 clock; and XDH-10B warning light box.

EQUIPMENT: Hopper for 1,200 litres (317 US gallons; 264 Imp gallons) of dry or liquid chemical in agricultural version. Appropriate specialised equipment for fire-fighting, geophysical survey and other missions.

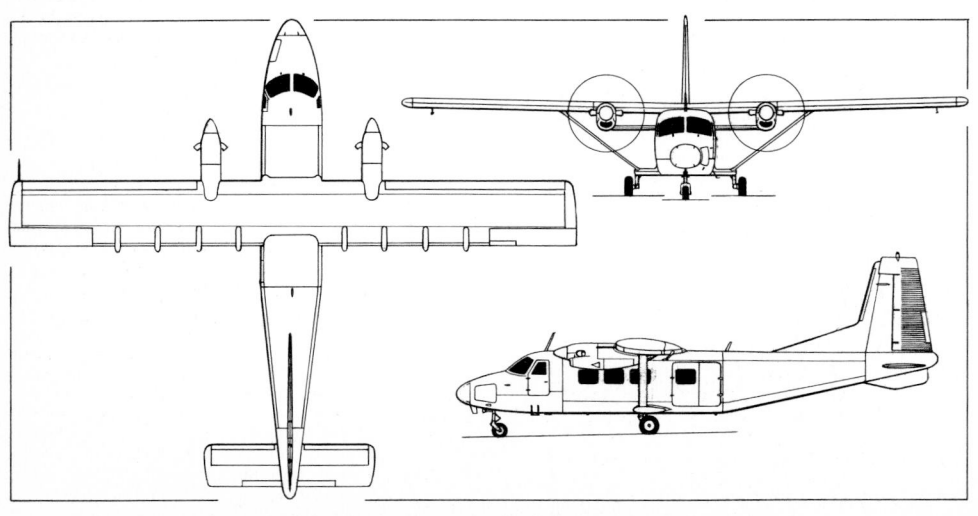

HAMC Y-12 II STOL general purpose transport *(Pilot Press)*

DIMENSIONS, EXTERNAL:
Wing span	17.235 m (56 ft 6½ in)
Wing chord, constant	2.00 m (6 ft 6¾ in)
Wing aspect ratio	8.7
Length overall	14.86 m (48 ft 9 in)
Height overall	5.575 m (18 ft 3½ in)
Elevator span	5.365 m (17 ft 7¼ in)
Wheel track	3.60 m (11 ft 9¾ in)
Wheelbase	4.698 m (15 ft 5 in)
Propeller diameter	2.49 m (8 ft 2 in)
Distance between propeller centres	
	4.937 m (16 ft 2⅜ in)
Fuselage/ground clearance	0.65 m (2 ft 1½ in)
Crew door: Height	1.35 m (4 ft 5¼ in)
Width	0.65 m (2 ft 1½in)
Passenger/cargo door: Height	1.38 m (4 ft 6¼ in)
Width (passenger door only)	0.65 m (2 ft 1½ in)
Width (double door)	1.45 m (4 ft 9 in)
Emergency exits (three, each):	
Height	0.68 m (2 ft 2¾ in)
Width	0.68 m (2 ft 2¾ in)
Baggage door (nose, port):	
Max height	0.56 m (1 ft 10 in)
Width	0.75 m (2 ft 5½ in)

DIMENSIONS, INTERNAL:
Cabin, excl flight deck and rear baggage compartment:	
Length	4.82 m (15 ft 9¾ in)
Max width	1.46 m (4 ft 9½ in)
Max height	1.70 m (5 ft 7 in)
Volume	12.9 m³ (455.5 cu ft)
Baggage compartment volume:	
nose	0.77 m³ (27.20 cu ft)
rear	1.89 m³ (66.75 cu ft)

AREAS:
Wings, gross	34.27 m² (368.88 sq ft)
Vertical tail surfaces (total)	5.064 m² (54.51 sq ft)
Horizontal tail surfaces (total)	7.024 m² (75.61 sq ft)

WEIGHTS AND LOADINGS:
Weight empty, equipped	2,840 kg (6,261 lb)
Operating weight empty	3,000 kg (6,614 lb)
Max fuel load	1,233 kg (2,718 lb)
Max payload	1,700 kg (3,748 lb)
T-O weight for agricultural operation	
	4,500 kg (9,921 lb)
Max T-O and landing weight	5,300 kg (11,684 lb)
Max ramp weight	5,330 kg (11,750 lb)
Max zero-fuel weight	4,700 kg (10,362 lb)
Max cabin floor loading (cargo)	
	750 kg/m² (153.7 lb/sq ft)
Max wing loading	145.9 kg/m² (29.90 lb/sq ft)
Max power loading	5.23 kg/kW (8.59 lb/shp)

PERFORMANCE (at max T-O weight, ISA):
Never-exceed speed at 3,000 m (9,840 ft)	
	177 knots (328 km/h; 204 mph)
Max cruising speed at 3,000 m (9,840 ft)	
	157 knots (292 km/h; 181 mph)
Econ cruising speed at 3,000 m (9,840 ft)	
	135 knots (250 km/h; 155 mph)
Max rate of climb at S/L	504 m (1,655 ft)/min
Rate of climb at S/L, one engine out	
	101 m (331 ft)/min
Service ceiling	7,000 m (22,960 ft)
Service ceiling, one engine out, 15 m (50 ft)/min rate of	
climb, max continuous power	3,000 m (9,840 ft)
T-O run, 15° flap	340 m (1,115 ft)
T-O to 15 m (50 ft), 15° flap	425 m (1,395 ft)
Landing from 15 m (50 ft), with braking and propeller	
reversal	500 m (1,640 ft)
Landing run with braking and propeller reversal	
	200 m (656 ft)

Min ground turning radius	16.75 m (54 ft 11½ in)
Range at 135 knots (250 km/h; 155 mph) at 3,000 m	
(9,840 ft) with max fuel, 45 min reserves	
	723 nm (1,340 km; 832 miles)
Endurance, conditions as above	5 h 12 min

HAMC H-5

Details of this Chinese version of the Soviet Ilyushin Il-28 can be found in the 1986-87 and earlier *Jane's*. It was reported in late 1987 that China had developed a firefighting version modified to carry a water load of approx 5,000 kg (11,025 lb).

HAMC Z-6

Further details of this early helicopter have emerged which amplify those in the 1986-87 *Jane's*. First flight took place in 1968, and more than 20 are said to have been built. The Z-6 appears to have been an attempt at a scaled-down, single-engined version of the Mil Mi-8, with a fuselage of similar configuration but accommodating only 12 passengers. The four-blade main rotor had a diameter of 21.00 m (68 ft 10¾ in); other data were as follows:

WEIGHTS:
Weight empty	4,820 kg (10,626 lb)
Max payload (cargo): internal	1,200 kg (2,645 lb)
external	1,100 kg (2,425 lb)
Max T-O weight	7,600 kg (16,755 lb)

PERFORMANCE:
Max level speed at 1,000 m (3,280 ft)	
	102 knots (190 km/h; 118 mph)
Range with max fuel	351 nm (651 km; 404 miles)

HAMC (AÉROSPATIALE) Z-9 HAITUN (DOLPHIN)
Chinese name: Zhishengji-9 (Vertical take-off aircraft 9) or Zhi-9

A licence agreement was signed on 2 July 1980 between Aérospatiale and the Chinese government for the former's SA 365N Dauphin 2 twin-turboshaft helicopter (which see) to be manufactured in China. The first (French built) example for China made its initial acceptance flight in the Beijing area on 6 February 1982. Production is now under way at Harbin, and is scheduled to run until 1989. Current examples, designated **Z-9A**, are to the upgraded standard of the SA 365N₁ French version, and have a substantial proportion of locally manufactured components.

The agreement is for an initial batch of 50, which are divided between civil and military duties. About 35 had

been completed by the Autumn of 1987, including at least nine for the Air Force and one for the Navy. Others are allocated to offshore oil rig support work, and some are configured as air ambulances accommodating four stretchers and two seats or two stretchers and five seats. The aircraft's Arriel IC and IC₁ turboshafts are produced in China as the WZ-8. Fuel capacity is 1,140 litres (301 US gallons; 251 Imp gallons).

An OADS (omnidirectional air data system) for the Z-9 was ordered from Pacer Systems Inc of the USA in the Summer of 1987. It has been reported that China is seeking a suitable magnetic anomaly detector for installation on naval versions of the Z-9.

The following Chinese figures have been published for the Z-9 and Z-9A:

WEIGHTS:
Weight empty, equipped: Z-9	1,975 kg (4,354 lb)
Z-9A	2,050 kg (4,519 lb)
Max payload: Z-9	1,863 kg (4,107 lb)
Z-9A	2,038 kg (4,493 lb)
Max load on cargo sling: Z-9, Z-9A	1,600 kg (3,527 lb)
Max T-O weight, internal or external load:	
Z-9	3,850 kg (8,488 lb)
Z-9A	4,100 kg (9,039 lb)

PERFORMANCE (at max T-O weight):
Max cruising speed at S/L:	
Z-9	158 knots (293 km/h; 182 mph)
Z-9A	154 knots (285 km/h; 177 mph)
Max vertical rate of climb at S/L:	
Z-9	252 m (827 ft)/min
Z-9A	246 m (805 ft)/min
Max forward rate of climb at S/L:	
Z-9	462 m (1,515 ft)/min
Z-9A	456 m (1,495 ft)/min
Service ceiling: Z-9	4,500 m (14,765 ft)
Z-9A	6,000 m (19,685 ft)
Hovering ceiling IGE: Z-9	1,950 m (6,400 ft)
Z-9A	2,600 m (8,530 ft)
Hovering ceiling OGE: Z-9	1,020 m (3,350 ft)
Z-9A	1,600 m (5,250 ft)
Max range at 140 knots (260 km/h; 161 mph) normal	
cruising speed, no reserves:	
standard tanks: Z-9	491 nm (910 km; 565 miles)
Z-9A	464 nm (860 km; 534 miles)
with 180 litre (47.5 US gallon; 39.6 Imp gallon)	
auxiliary tank:	
Z-9	572 nm (1,060 km; 658 miles)
Z-9A	539 nm (1,000 km; 621 miles)

HAMC Z-9A Haitun twin-turbine light helicopter *(CATIC)*

HMP
HUABEI MACHINERY PLANT
Shijiazhuang, Hebei

HMP (ANTONOV) Y-5
Chinese name: Yunshuji-5 (Transport aircraft 5) or Yun-5
NATO reporting name: Colt

The Antonov An-2 general purpose biplane was supplied to, and since 1957 has been built under licence in, China in considerable numbers (nearly 1,000). Its 746 kW (1,000 hp) Shvetsov ASh-62IR engine is built at Zhuzhou as the Huosai-5 or HS-5. The Y-5 was manufactured initially at Nanchang, and later at Harbin; small scale production was continuing, by HMP, in 1987.

The Y-5 continues to be used extensively both by the PLA

Air Force, which has about 300, and in a civil capacity, for agricultural (see 1982-83 *Jane's*) and general transport work. A turboprop version, with an engine rated at approx 1,380 kW (1,850 shp), is reported to be under development.

A description of the basic An-2 can be found under the WSK-PZL Mielec heading in the Polish section of this edition.

NAMC
NANCHANG AIRCRAFT MANUFACTURING COMPANY
PO Box 5001-506, Nanchang, Jiangxi
Telephone: 41112 3737
Telex: 95068 NAMC CN
Fax: 41112 2272
PRESIDENT: Wu Mingwang
INFORMATION: Feng Jinghua

Nanchang, previously responsible for licence production of the Yak-18A (Chinese designation CJ-5), continues to manufacture its own development of this aircraft (as the CJ-6 and Haiyan), and the Chinese Q-5 attack aircraft developed from the Shenyang J-6/MiG-19. Workforce in 1986-87 was more than 10,000.

NAMC Q-5
Chinese name: Qiangjiji-5 (Attack aircraft 5) or Qiang-5
Westernised designation: A-5
NATO reporting name: Fantan

Design of this twin-jet attack aircraft, derived from the J-6/MiG-19 produced in China, began in 1958, and the first flight was made on 5 June 1965. By 1978 production had almost ended, apart from making good attrition losses, but it was stepped up in about 1981 to meet export orders from Pakistan. This important Chinese aircraft continues in production, both for domestic use (**Q-5 III**) and, as the **A-5C**, for export. The total number in Chinese service in 1987-88 was thought to be in the region of 600, including up to 100 serving in an air defence role with the air arm of the PLA Navy.

Deliveries of an initial batch of 52 export A-5Cs to the Pakistan Air Force began in February 1983 and have been followed by others that may eventually provide a total of 140 to equip eight attack squadrons and an OCU. The first PAF units are No. 16 Squadron at Rafiqui Shorkot, No. 26 at Peshawar and No. 7 at Masroor.

The airframe of the Q-5 is based substantially on that of the J-6 (see 1982-83 *Jane's*), but with a number of significant changes. The main wing structure is basically unchanged, but the underwing spoilers are omitted and the flaps have undergone redesign. There are more extensive changes to the centre and front of the fuselage, which is nearly 25 per cent longer than that of the J-6. The purpose of these changes in the original **Q-5 I** was to make room for an internal weapons bay, but this area is no longer used for carrying weapons. Instead, fuselage fuel tank capacity has been increased by approx 70 per cent compared with that carried internally by the J-6. Cockpit canopy opening differs from that on the J-6, and the spine fairing behind it leads to a smaller dorsal fin and larger main fin. The 'solid' ogival nose provides sufficient room for an attack radar, although the metal-nosed aircraft in service so far do not carry this equipment, which would require relocation of the nose mounted pitot tube. It is, however, to be a feature of the improved **Q-5M/A-5M** now under development (see following entry).

The WP-6 power plant (uprated in the latest versions) is retained, but with twin lateral intakes instead of the single divided nose intake of the Soviet design. The A-5C/Q-5 III also has a relocated tail braking parachute installation similar to that on later production versions of the J-6. Like the J-6, the Q-5 has two wing mounted cannon (23 mm instead of 30 mm); these occupy the revised wingroot position outboard of the engine air intake trunks.

A design study has been carried out by FRL in the UK to equip the Q-5 as a receiver for in-flight refuelling, with a Xian H-6 bomber adapted to act as the tanker aircraft. Go-ahead approval for such a modification programme had not been given up to the Spring of 1988.

The following description applies to the current Q-5 III/A-5C, except where otherwise indicated:

TYPE: Single-seat close air support and ground attack aircraft, with capability also for air-to-air combat.

WINGS: Cantilever all-metal mid-wing monoplane, of low aspect ratio, with 4° anhedral from roots. Sweepback at quarter-chord 52° 30′. Multi-spar basic structure with ribs and stressed skin, essentially similar in construction to that of J-6/MiG-19 (see 1982-83 *Jane's*), with three-point attachment to fuselage. Deep, full chord boundary layer fence on each upper surface at mid span. Inboard of each fence is a hydraulically actuated Gouge flap, the inner end of which is angled to give a trailing-edge at right angles to side of fuselage. Hydraulically actuated internally balanced aileron outboard of each fence. Electrically operated inset trim tab at inboard end of port aileron.

FUSELAGE: Conventional all-metal structure of longerons, stringers and stressed skin, built in forward and rear portions which are detachable aft of wing trailing-edge to provide access to engines. Air intake on each side of fuselage, abreast of cockpit; twin jetpipes side by side at rear. Top and bottom 'pen nib' fairings aft of nozzles. Centre-fuselage is 'waisted' in accordance with area rule. Dorsal spine fairing between rear of cockpit and leading-edge of fin. Forward hinged, hydraulically actuated door type airbrake under centre of fuselage, forward of bomb attachment points. Shallow ventral strake under each jetpipe.

TAIL UNIT: Cantilever all-metal stressed skin structure, with sweepback on all surfaces; of generally similar configuration to that of J-6, but with taller main fin and smaller dorsal fin. Mechanically actuated mass balanced rudder, with electrically operated inset trim tab. One-piece hydraulically actuated all-moving tailplane, with anti-flutter weight projecting forward from each tip. Tail warning antenna in tip of fin.

LANDING GEAR: Hydraulically retractable wide-track tricycle type, with single wheel and oleo-pneumatic shock absorber on each unit. Main units retract inward into wings, non-steerable nosewheel forward into fuselage, rotating through 87° to lie flat in gear bay. Mainwheels have size 830 × 205 mm tubeless tyres, and pneumatic and plate brakes. Tail braking parachute, deployed when aircraft is 1 m (3.3 ft) above the ground, in bullet fairing at root of vertical tail trailing-edge beneath rudder (or in tailcone of early production Q-5 I).

POWER PLANT: Two Shenyang Wopen-6 (WP-6) turbojets (Chinese version of Tumansky/Mikulin R-9BF-811), each rated at 25.50 kN (5,732 lb st) dry and 31.87 kN (7,165 lb st) with afterburning, mounted side by side in

rear of fuselage. Improved Wopen-6A engines (see Q-5M entry for details) available optionally. Lateral air intake, with small splitter plate, for each engine. Hydraulically actuated nozzles. Internal fuel in three forward and two rear fuselage tanks with combined capacity of 3,720 litres (983 US gallons; 818.5 Imp gallons). Provision for carrying a 760 litre (201 US gallon; 167 Imp gallon) drop tank on each centre underwing pylon, to give max internal/external fuel capacity of 5,240 litres (1,384 US gallons; 1,153 Imp gallons). When centre wing stations are occupied by bombs, a 400 litre (105.7 US gallon; 88 Imp gallon) drop tank can be carried instead on each outboard underwing pylon.

ACCOMMODATION: Pilot only, under one-piece jettisonable canopy which is hinged at rear and opens upward. Downward view over nose, in level flight, is 13° 30′. Low-speed seat allows for safe ejection within speed range of 135-458 knots (250-850 km/h; 155-528 mph) at zero height or above. Aircraft in Pakistan service have been refitted with Martin-Baker PKD10 zero/zero seats. Armour plating in some areas of cockpit to protect pilot from anti-aircraft gunfire.

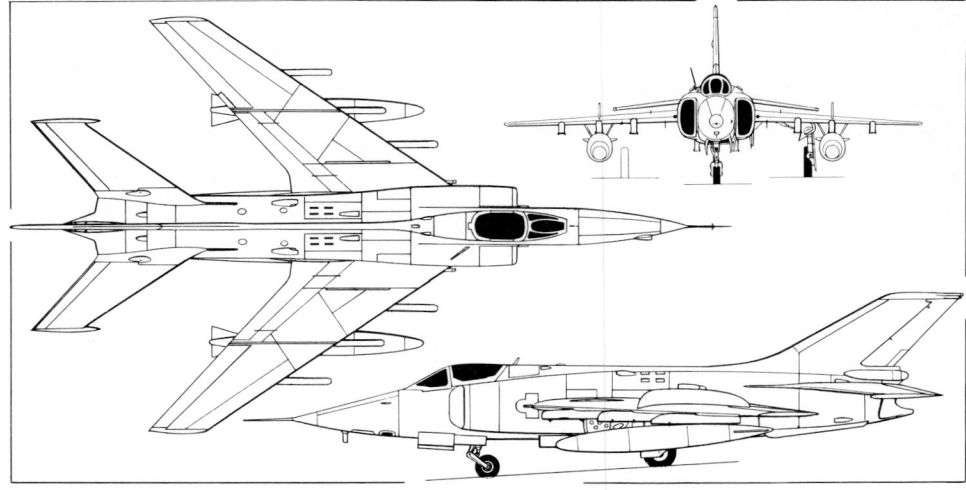

NAMC Q-5 III 'Fantan' single-seat twin-jet combat aircraft (*Pilot Press*)

Q-5 III with ECM pods on its centre underwing stations

SYSTEMS: Two independent hydraulic systems, each operating at pressure of 207 bars (3,000 lb/sq in). Primary system actuates landing gear extension and retraction, flaps, airbrake and afterburner nozzles; auxiliary system supplies power for aileron and all-moving tailplane boosters, and emergency actuation of main landing gear. Electrical system (28V DC) powered by two 6kW engine driven starter/generators, with two inverters for 115V single-phase and 36V three-phase AC power at 400Hz.

AVIONICS AND EQUIPMENT: Include CT-3 VHF com transceiver, WL-7 radio compass, WG-4 low altitude radio altimeter, LTC-2 horizon gyro, YD-3 IFF, Type 930 radar warning receiver and XS-6 marker beacon receiver. 'High Fix' type gun ranging radar on air defence version, in small 'teardrop' fairing on starboard side of nose. 'Odd Rods' type IFF aerials under nose on Q-5 I/A-5A replaced on Q-5 III/A-5C by a single blade antenna. Space provision in nose and centre-fuselage for additional or updated avionics, including an attack radar. Landing light under fuselage, forward of nosewheel bay and offset to port; taxying light on nosewheel leg.

ARMAMENT AND OPERATIONAL EQUIPMENT: Internal armament consists of one 23 mm cannon (Chinese 23-2), with 100 rds, in each wingroot. Ten attachment points normally for external stores: two pairs in tandem under centre of fuselage, and three under each wing (one inboard and two outboard of mainwheel leg). Fuselage stations can each carry a 250 kg bomb (Chinese 250-2, US Mk 82 or Snakeye, French Durandal, or similar). Inboard wing stations can carry 6 kg or 25 lb practice bombs, or a pod containing eight Chinese 57-1 (57 mm), seven 68 mm, or seven Chinese 90-1 (90 mm) rockets. Centre wing stations can carry a 500 kg or 750 lb bomb, a BL755 600 lb cluster bomb, a Chinese 250-2 (250 kg) bomb, a US Mk 82 or Snakeye, French Durandal, or similar. Normal bomb carrying capacity is 1,000 kg (2,205 lb), max capacity 2,000 kg (4,410 lb). Instead of bombs, the centre wing stations can each carry a 760 litre drop tank (see 'Power Plant' paragraph) or an ECM pod. The outboard wing stations can each be occupied by a 400 litre drop tank (when the larger tank is not carried on the centre wing station) or, with suitable modification, by air-to-air missiles such as the Chinese PL-2 ('Atoll' derivative), PL-2B, PL-7, AIM-9 Sidewinder and Matra R.550 Magic. Within the overall max T-O weight, all stores mentioned can be carried provided that CG shift remains within the allowable operating range of 31 to 39 per cent of mean aerodynamic chord, and more than 22 external stores configurations are possible. The aircraft carries an SH-1J or ABS1A optical sight for level and dive bombing, or for air-to-ground rocket launching. Aircraft in Chinese service can carry a single 5-20 kT nuclear bomb.

DIMENSIONS, EXTERNAL (Q-5 III):

Wing span	9.70 m (31 ft 10 in)
Wing chord (mean aerodynamic)	3.097 m (10 ft 2 in)
Wing aspect ratio	3.4
Length overall: incl nose probe	16.255 m (53 ft 4 in)
excl nose probe	15.415 m (50 ft 7 in)
Height overall	4.516 m (14 ft 9¾ in)
Wheel track	approx 4.70 m (15 ft 5 in)
Wheelbase	approx 4.00 m (13 ft 1½ in)

AREAS:

Wings, gross	27.95 m² (300.85 sq ft)
Vertical tail surfaces (total)	4.64 m² (49.94 sq ft)
Horizontal tail surfaces:	
movable	5.00 m² (53.82 sq ft)
total, incl projected fuselage area	
	8.62 m² (92.78 sq ft)

WEIGHTS AND LOADINGS:

Weight empty	6,494 kg (14,317 lb)
Fuel: max internal	2,883 kg (6,356 lb)
two 400 litre drop tanks	620 kg (1,367 lb)
two 760 litre drop tanks	1,178 kg (2,597 lb)
max internal/external	4,061 kg (8,953 lb)

Nanchang A-5C of Pakistan Air Force armed with Sidewinder missiles (*Denis Hughes*)

Max external stores load	2,000 kg (4,410 lb)
Max T-O weight: 'clean'	9,530 kg (21,010 lb)
with max external stores	12,000 kg (26,455 lb)
Max wing loading: 'clean'	341 kg/m² (69.9 lb/sq ft)
with max external stores	429 kg/m² (87.9 lb/sq ft)
Max power loading: 'clean'	149.5 kg/kN (1.47 lb/lb st)
with max external stores	188.3 kg/kN (1.85 lb/lb st)

PERFORMANCE (at max 'clean' T-O weight, with afterburning, except where indicated):

Max limiting Mach number (VNE)		Mach 1.5
Max level speed:		
at 11,000 m (36,000 ft)		
	Mach 1.12 (643 knots; 1,190 km/h; 740 mph)	
at S/L	653 knots (1,210 km/h; 752 mph)	
T-O speed:		
'clean', 15° flap	162 knots (300 km/h; 186 mph)	
with max external stores, 25° flap		
	178 knots (330 km/h; 205 mph)	
* Landing speed:		
25° flap, brake-chute deployed		
	150-165 knots (278-307 km/h; 172-191 mph)	
* Max rate of climb at 5,000 m (16,400 ft)		
	4,980-6,180 m (16,340-20,275 ft)/min	
Service ceiling	15,850 m (52,000 ft)	
T-O run:		
*'clean', 15° flap	700-750 m (2,300-2,460 ft)	
with max external stores, 25° flap		
	1,250 m (4,100 ft)	
Landing run:		
25° flap, brake-chute deployed	1,060 m (3,480 ft)	

Combat radius with max external stores, afterburners off:
lo-lo-lo (500 m; 1,640 ft)   216 nm (400 km; 248 miles)
hi-lo-hi (8,000/500/8,000 m; 26,250/1,640/26,250 ft)
324 nm (600 km; 373 miles)
Range at 11,000 m (36,000 ft) with max internal and external fuel, afterburners off
nearly 1,080 nm (2,000 km; 1,243 miles)
g limits:
with full load of bombs and/or drop tanks   5
with drop tanks empty   6.5
'clean'   7.5
* depending upon airfield altitude and temperature

NAMC Q-5M/A-5M

This improved version of the Q-5 III/A-5C is the subject of a 30-month development programme started in July 1986 between CATIC and Aeritalia to upgrade the aircraft's avionics by incorporating a new nav/attack system similar to that used in the AMX aircraft. The M (for Modified) version of the Q-5 will also have improved WP-6A turbojets with dry and afterburning ratings of 29.42 kN (6,614 lb st) and 36.78 kN (8,267 lb st) respectively. The changes are expected to increase empty weight by 140 kg (309 lb); external stores load and max T-O weight remain unchanged.

Two A-5M prototypes have been built in China, where flight testing was expected to be completed in 1988 by a joint Chinese and Italian team. Rollout of the first production example was scheduled for the end of that year, with deliveries to the PLA Air Force beginning in early 1989. The avionics upgrade and improved engines are expected to be available also as a retrofit kit for existing Q-5/A-5s.

The new nav/attack system is designed around two powerful central digital computers and a dual-redundant MIL-STD-1553B databus with plenty of growth potential. Other new sensors and equipment include a ranging radar, inertial navigation system, head-up display, air data computer, three-axis gyro package, radar warning receiver, attitude indicator, HSI, static inverters, mode controls, and an interface unit linking these with the aircraft's existing VHF com radio, radio altimeter, radio compass, marker beacon receiver, IFF and armament system. The number of external stores stations is increased to 12 by adding two more pylons beneath each outer wing, with some redistribution of the weapons carried on each wing station, and the PL-5 is added to the range of air-to-air missiles. External stores configurations are essentially the same as for the Q-5 III/A-5C.

WEIGHTS:

Weight empty	6,634 kg (14,625 lb)
Max external stores load	2,000 kg (4,410 lb)
Max T-O weight	12,000 kg (26,455 lb)

PERFORMANCE (estimated):
Max level speed:
at 11,000 m (36,000 ft)
Mach 1.2 (688 knots; 1,275 km/h; 792 mph)

at S/L	661 knots (1,225 km/h; 761 mph)	
Service ceiling	16,000 m (52,500 ft)	
T-O run with max external stores, 25° flap		
	1,200 m (3,937 ft)	

Combat radius with max external stores, ISA, 10% reserves:
lo-lo-lo   more than 162 nm (300 km; 186 miles)
hi-lo-hi   more than 216 nm (400 km; 248 miles)

NAMC L-8 KARAKORUM 8

A model of this tandem two-seat jet trainer was displayed at the 1987 Paris Air Show, where it was described as able to provide all basic flying training, plus parts of the primary and advanced training syllabi, with capability also for light air-to-ground close support. The accompanying illustrations should be regarded as provisional, since the L-8's design is still being refined. First flight is scheduled for early 1990.

The L-8 is being developed to PLA Air Force and Pakistan Air Force specifications, and has been named after the mountain range that links the two countries. Wind tunnel testing was completed in the Spring of 1988, and the programme reportedly will involve about 200 production aircraft. Cockpits will have Collins EFIS-86 avionics.

Leading details are as follows:
POWER PLANT: One 15.57 kN (3,500 lb st) Garrett TFE731-2A turbofan.
DIMENSIONS, EXTERNAL:

Wing span	9.63 m (31 ft 7¼ in)
Length overall (excl nose probe)	10.40 m (34 ft 1½ in)
Height overall	4.21 m (13 ft 9¾ in)

AREA:

Wings, gross	16.51 m² (177.7 sq ft)

WEIGHTS:

Internal fuel (fuselage)	780 kg (1,720 lb)
Drop tank fuel	388 kg (855 lb)
T-O weight 'clean'	3,500 kg (7,716 lb)
Max T-O weight	4,200 kg (9,259 lb)

PERFORMANCE (estimated, at 'clean' T-O weight except where indicated):

Max level speed at 7,620 m (25,000 ft)		
	432 knots (800 km/h; 497 mph)	
Unstick speed	103 knots (190 km/h; 118 mph)	
Landing speed	89 knots (165 km/h; 102 mph)	
Max rate of climb at S/L	1,600 m (5,249 ft)/min	
Service ceiling	13,000 m (42,650 ft)	
T-O and landing run	500 m (1,640 ft)	
Range with max fuel (incl drop tank)		
	1,241 nm (2,300 km; 1,429 miles)	
Max endurance (with drop tank)	4 h 30 min	

NAMC CJ-6
Chinese name: Chuji Jiaolianji-6 (Basic training aircraft 6) or Chujiao-6
Westernised designation: PT-6

Developed to replace the Yak-18A/CJ-5 (1980-81 *Jane's*) in the basic training role, the two-seat CJ-6 first flew in 1958 and entered production in 1961. More than 2,000 have been delivered, including exports to Albania, Bangladesh, Cambodia, Korea, Tanzania and Zambia.

Civil versions known as the **Haiyan** (see following entry) have been developed, and a six-seat utility version has been proposed. The details which follow apply to the standard CJ-6 basic trainer:
AIRFRAME: All-metal cantilever low-wing monoplane. Two-spar wings, with detachable, tapered and dihedralled outer panels. Retractable tricycle landing gear, with low-pressure mainwheel tyres, suitable for operation from grass strips.
POWER PLANT: One 213 kW (285 hp) Zhuzhou Huosai-6A nine-cylinder aircooled radial engine (Chinese version of Ivchenko/Vedeneyev AI-14RF), driving a J9-G1 two-blade variable-pitch propeller. Fuel capacity (two tanks) 100 litres (26.4 US gallons; 22 Imp gallons).
DIMENSIONS, EXTERNAL:

Wing span	10.18 m (33 ft 4¾ in)
Length overall	8.46 m (27 ft 9 in)
Height overall	3.25 m (10 ft 8 in)

WEIGHTS:

Weight empty	1,172 kg (2,584 lb)
Max fuel	110 kg (243 lb)
Max T-O weight	1,419 kg (3,128 lb)

PERFORMANCE:

Max level speed	155 knots (286 km/h; 178 mph)
Landing speed	62 knots (115 km/h; 72 mph)
Max rate of climb at S/L	380 m (1,248 ft)/min
Service ceiling	5,080 m (16,665 ft)
T-O run	280 m (920 ft)
Landing run	350 m (1,150 ft)
Endurance	3 h 36 min

NAMC HAIYAN (PETREL)

To meet a national requirement for a multi-purpose agricultural and forestry aircraft, the Nanchang Aircraft Manufacturing Company decided to undertake a conversion of its CJ-6 basic trainer (see preceding entry). Work on the conversion started in April 1985, and the **Haiyan A** prototype flew for the first time on 17 August that year.

Little change to the basic, proven airframe of the CJ-6 was necessary. To cater for the higher operating weights

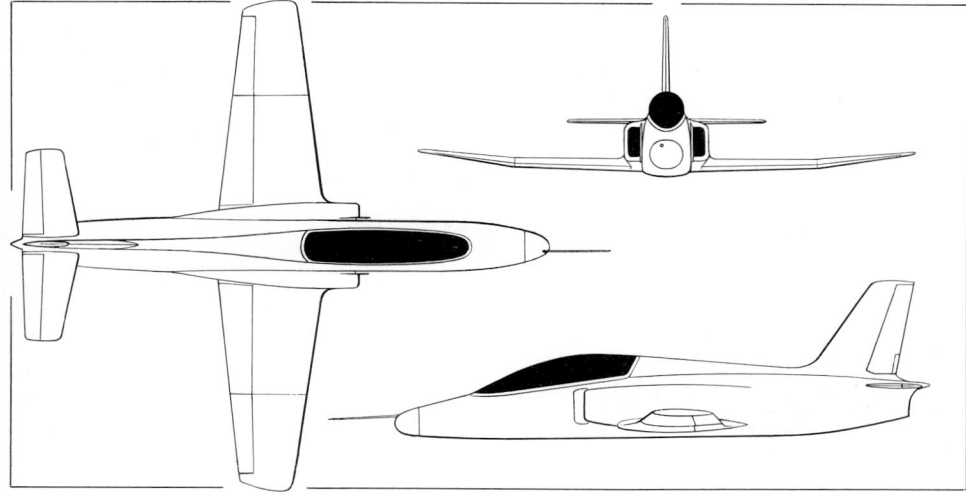

Model (*Paul Jackson photo*) **and provisional drawing** (*Pilot Press*) **of the Nanchang L-8 jet trainer**

involved, the Haiyan A was fitted with a more powerful (257 kW; 345 hp) version of the HS-6A engine and a new-design propeller. Removal of the rear seat allowed a 400 kg (882 lb) insecticide tank to be installed, and another 200 kg (441 lb) of chemical was accommodated in the leading-edge of the wing centre-section. Volumetric capacity in the rear cockpit, without removing the instrument panel, is sufficient to allow 800 kg (1,764 lb) to be carried in this location if desired. The dispersal system consists of four Type 751 underwing sprinkler heads, fed by a modified LB-4 fuel pump, and can be used for both low and ultra-low volume spraying.

Two production conversions are planned:

Haiyan B. Specialised agricultural and forestry version for cropspraying (dry or liquid pesticide or fertiliser), seed-sowing and forest firefighting.

Haiyan C. Patrol and observation version, with normal CJ-6 rear seat accommodation but having increased fuel capacity to extend endurance to over 6 hours. Suitable for forestry and fishery patrol, cartography, aerial photography, geological survey, coastal and border patrol, with appropriate equipment.

The following details apply to the Haiyan A prototype:
DIMENSIONS, EXTERNAL: As for CJ-6
WEIGHTS:

Weight empty	1,214 kg (2,676 lb)
Max T-O weight	2,035 kg (4,486 lb)

PERFORMANCE (at max T-O weight):

Max level speed	160 knots (297 km/h; 185 mph)
Normal operating speed	86 knots (160 km/h; 99 mph)
Operating height: max	6,250 m (20,500 ft)
min	1 m (3 ft)
T-O run	280 m (919 ft)
Landing run	350 m (1,148 ft)
Range	421 nm (780 km; 484 miles)
Endurance	4 h 11 min
Swath width	30 m (98 ft)

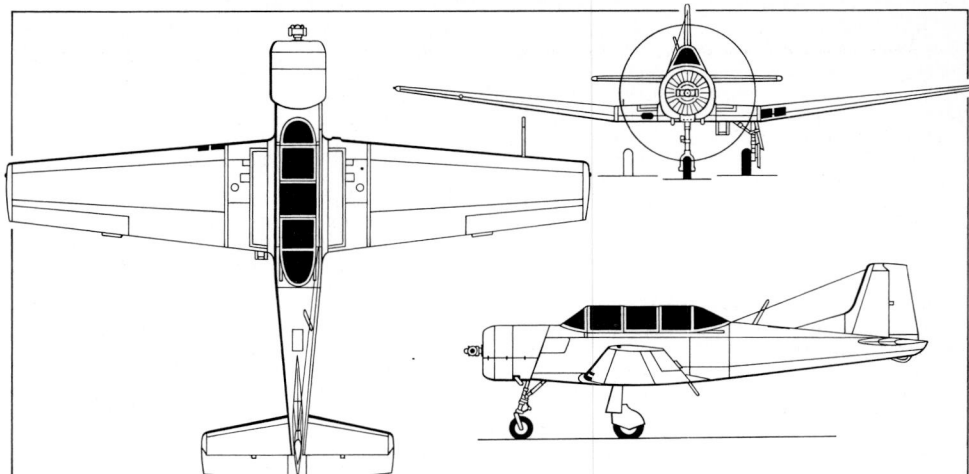

Three-view drawing *(Jane's/Mike Keep)* **and photograph of the NAMC Haiyan, developed from the Yak-18A**

SAC
SHENYANG AIRCRAFT COMPANY
PO Box 328, Shenyang, Liaoning
Telephone: 62680
Telex: 80018 SAC CN

SAC J-?
It was reported in late 1987 that flight testing had begun at Shenyang of prototypes of two new supersonic all-weather fighters, SAC having completed two flight test examples of each type. One may be the J-7 III referred to in the next entry; the other may be the "completely new" Mach 2 "training and combat" aircraft mentioned to US aviation journalists by PLA Air Force officials during a visit to Beijing in the Autumn of 1987. The latter, as yet undesignated, was described at that time as being a year or two away from becoming operational.

SAC J-7 III
Shenyang is understood to have finalised (in 1984) design of a J-7 III version of the CAC J-7/F-7 (which see), potentially as the 'low' component in an eventual 'high-low' mix with the J-8 II. The all-weather J-7 III is reported to resemble the MiG-21MF in outward appearance and possibly to carry some avionics of Western origin.

SAC J-8 II
Chinese name: Jianjiji-8 II (Fighter aircraft 8) or Jian-8 II
Westernised designation: F-8 II
NATO reporting name: Finback
Development of the J-8 began in the mid-1960s, the first **J-8 0** day fighter example being completed in 1969. Initially, it had a single air intake in the nose and appeared to follow closely the same design philosophy as the Soviet Mikoyan Ye-152A 'Flipper'. A description of it in the later, similarly configured all-weather form of 1981 (the **J-8 I**) appeared in the 1985-86 *Jane's*.

Only limited production of these early models (about 50 aircraft) was undertaken, but an improved **J-8 II** prototype with twin lateral air intakes made its first flight in early May 1984. Initial flight testing was said to have confirmed a considerable improvement in performance compared with the earlier models. The main purpose of the configuration change was twofold, the first being to provide a 'solid' nose with adequate accommodation for a fire control radar and the second to provide increased airflow for a more powerful engine installation, it being generally conceded that, with its original 59.82 kN (13,448 lb st) WP-7B engines, the J-8 I was underpowered.

Under an FMS (foreign military sales) programme known as Peace Pearl, USAF's Aeronautical Systems Division is sponsoring an avionics upgrade for the J-8 II. A contract was awarded to Grumman Aerospace Corporation on 5 August 1987, and is due for completion in January 1995. The initial requirement is for 50 shipsets, plus five spare kits, of an avionics suite comprising a fire control system, inertial navigation system, HUD, mission and air

Prototype J-8 II single-seat multi-role fighter *(CATIC)*

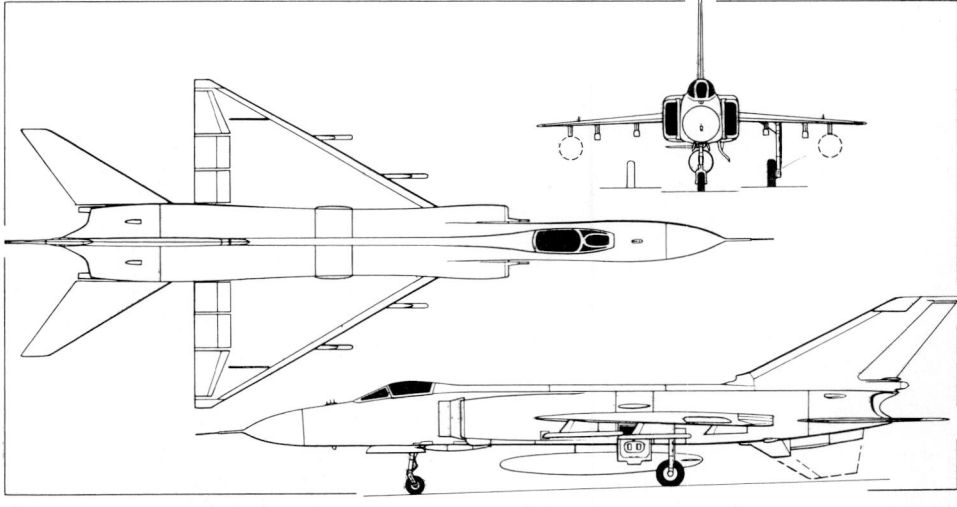

J-8 II version of the 'Finback' twin-jet air superiority fighter *(Pilot Press)*

data computers, and a databus. Under subcontract to Grumman, Westinghouse is developing the fire control system (modified AN/APG-66 radar, fire control computer, backup control and interface unit, CW illuminator, fire control software, variable-speed constant-frequency power generation system and logistics support), while Litton will supply the LN-39 INS. Two J-8 IIs are to be delivered to the USA in early 1989 for flight test (at Edwards AFB) at the end of that year followed by certification of the upgrade package, with kit deliveries scheduled for 1991-95. The

improved version is intended for service in Manchuria and along China's northern border with the USSR. The US avionics have been approved only for J-8 IIs for use within China, and other Western alternatives are being sought to enable the aircraft to be exported.

TYPE: Single-seat twin-engined air superiority fighter, with secondary ground attack capability.
WINGS: Cantilever mid-wing monoplane. Thin-section delta wings, with slight anhedral and 60° sweepback on leading-edges. Small fence on each upper surface near tip.

Two-segment single-slotted trailing-edge flaps on each wing inboard of aileron. Main wing structure is of aluminium alloy and high tensile steel. Control surfaces, which have hydraulically boosted actuation, are of aluminium honeycomb with skins of sheet aluminium.

FUSELAGE: Conventional semi-monocoque structure, 'waisted' between air intakes and tail section in accordance with area rule. Construction is mainly of aluminium alloy, with high tensile steel for main load-bearing members and titanium in high-temperature areas. Dielectric nosecone. Four door-type underfuselage airbrakes, one under each engine air intake trunk and one immediately aft of each mainwheel well. Spine fairing along top of fuselage from cockpit to fin, with small airscoop at foot of fin leading-edge. Additional airscoop at top of rear fuselage on each side, above tailplane.

TAIL UNIT: Cantilever sweptback all-metal surfaces, comprising broad chord fin and rudder and low-set all-moving tailplane; 60° sweepback on tailplane leading-edges. Ventral fin similar to that of MiG-23, main portion of which folds sideways to starboard during take-off and landing, to provide additional directional stability. Rudder and tailplane are of aluminium honeycomb, with sheet aluminium skins; actuation is hydraulically boosted. Dielectric panels at tip of main fin and on non-folding portion of ventral fin leading-edge.

LANDING GEAR: Hydraulically retractable tricycle type, with single wheel and oleo-pneumatic shock absorber on each unit. Nose unit retracts forward, main units inward into centre-fuselage; mainwheels turn to stow vertically inside fuselage, resulting in a slight overwing bulge. Brake-chute in bullet fairing at base of rudder.

POWER PLANT: Two Liyang Wopen-13A II turbojets (Chinese development of Tumansky R-13-300), each rated at 42.7 kN (9,590 lb st) dry and 65.9 kN (14,815 lb st) with afterburning, mounted side by side in rear fuselage with 'pen nib' fairing above and between exhaust nozzles. Lateral, non-swept air intakes, with automatically regulated ramp angle and large splitter plates similar in shape to those of MiG-23. Internal fuel capacity (four integral wing tanks plus fuselage tanks) approx 5,400 litres (1,426 US gallons; 1,188 Imp gallons). Provision for auxiliary fuel tanks on fuselage centreline and each outboard underwing pylon.

ACCOMMODATION: Pilot only, on ejection seat under one-piece canopy hinged at rear and opening upward. Cockpit pressurised, heated and air-conditioned.

SYSTEMS: Two simple air-cycle environmental control systems, one for cockpit heating and air-conditioning and one for radar cooling; cooling air bled from engine compressor. Two 207 bar (3,000 lb/sq in) independent hydraulic systems (main utility system plus one for flight control surfaces boost), powered by engine driven pumps. 28.5V DC primary electrical power from two 12kW engine driven starter/generators, with two 6kVA alternators for 115/200V three-phase AC at 400Hz.

AVIONICS AND OPERATIONAL EQUIPMENT: VHF/UHF and HF/SSB com radio, Tacan, radio compass, radar altimeter, marker beacon receiver, 'Odd Rods' type IFF, radar warning receiver and ECM. Autopilot for attitude and heading hold, altitude hold and stability augmentation. Existing fire control system comprises a mono-pulse radar, optical gyro gunsight and gun camera. Enlarged avionics bays in nose and fuselage provide room for modernised fire control system and other upgraded avionics now under development.

ARMAMENT: One 23 mm Type 23-3 twin-barrel cannon, with 200 rds, in underfuselage pack immediately aft of nosewheel door. Seven external stations (one under fuselage and three under each wing) for a variety of stores which can include PL-2B infra-red air-to-air missiles, PL-7 medium-range semi-active radar homing air-to-air missiles, 18-round pods of 57 mm Type 57-2 unguided air-to-air rockets, launchers for 90 mm air-to-surface rockets, bombs or (centreline and outboard underwing stations only) auxiliary fuel tanks.

DIMENSIONS, EXTERNAL:

Wing span	9.344 m (30 ft 7⅞ in)
Wing aspect ratio	2.1
Length overall, incl nose probe	21.59 m (70 ft 10 in)
Height overall	5.41 m (17 ft 9 in)
Wheel track	approx 3.80 m (12 ft 7 in)
Wheelbase	approx 7.25 m (23 ft 9½ in)

AREA:

Wings, gross	42.2 m² (454.2 sq ft)

WEIGHTS AND LOADINGS:

Weight empty	9,820 kg (21,649 lb)
Normal T-O weight	14,300 kg (31,526 lb)
Max T-O weight	17,800 kg (39,242 lb)
Wing loading:	
at normal T-O weight	338.9 kg/m² (69.4 lb/sq ft)
at max T-O weight	421.8 kg/m² (86.4 lb/sq ft)
Power loading:	
at normal T-O weight	110.5 kg/kN (1.08 lb/lb st)
at max T-O weight	137.5 kg/kN (1.35 lb/lb st)

PERFORMANCE:

Design max operating Mach number	2.2
Design max level speed	
	701 knots (1,300 km/h; 808 mph) IAS
Unstick speed	175 knots (325 km/h; 202 mph)
Landing speed	156 knots (290 km/h; 180 mph)
Max rate of climb at S/L	12,000 m (39,370 ft)/min
Acceleration from Mach 0.6 to 1.25 at 5,000 m	
(16,400 ft)	54 s
Service ceiling	20,000 m (65,620 ft)
T-O run, with afterburning	670 m (2,198 ft)
Landing run, brake-chute deployed	1,000 m (3,280 ft)
Combat radius	432 nm (800 km; 497 miles)
Max range	1,187 nm (2,200 km; 1,367 miles)
g limit in sustained turn at Mach 0.9 at 5,000 m	
(16,400 ft)	+4.83

SAIC

SHANGHAI AVIATION INDUSTRIAL CORPORATION

3115 Chang Zhong Lu, 8503 Shanghai
Telephone: 680793 or 680273
Telex: 33136 SHAIR CN
PRESIDENT: Jing Deyuan
VICE-PRESIDENT AND CHIEF ENGINEER: Tao Fakuan

SAIC (MCDONNELL DOUGLAS) MD-82

McDonnell Douglas Corporation announced on 11 January 1984 the signing of a letter of intent with SAIC on a co-production programme for 25 MD-82 jet transports.

Shanghai has produced well over 100 sets of landing gear doors for the MD-80 series under subcontract since 1979.

Details of this new programme were confirmed in an April 1985 announcement of the sale of 26 MD-82s to China, of which 25 are being assembled in Shanghai.

One Douglas built aircraft was delivered in October 1985, and assembly at Shanghai began in April 1986, during which month the second set of subassemblies was despatched from Long Beach. Complete major subassemblies were supplied by Douglas for the first three MD-82s to be assembled at Shanghai; thereafter, the Chinese industry will take a gradually increasing share in the manufacturing process for the remaining 22, producing its own landing gear doors, cargo doors and aileron supports from aircraft No. 7. Starting with the 20th aircraft, SAIC will produce tailplanes for both its own and Douglas built MD-82s. Of SAIC's total workforce of about 7,000, some 2,200 are engaged on the MD-82 programme.

Rollout of the first Chinese assembled MD-82 took place on 8 June 1987, with first flight following on 2 July. Delivery to the Shenyang branch of CAAC was made on the last day of that month, and the aircraft entered service with China Northeast Airlines on 4 August. This operator is to receive six of the first ten Chinese assembled MD-82s; the other four, beginning with the second aircraft (delivered in December 1987), are for China Eastern Airlines based at Shanghai. The third and fourth SAIC MD-82s were due for delivery in March and June 1988, with two more to follow by year-end. Peak production of eight a year is due to be reached in 1989, and completion of all 25 aircraft by 1991. The original option for a further 15 MD-82s has been allowed to lapse.

STAF

SHAANXI TRANSPORT AIRCRAFT FACTORY

Hanzhong, Shaanxi

STAF (ANTONOV) Y-8

Chinese name: Yunshuji-8 (Transport aircraft 8) or Yun-8

NATO reporting name: Cub

The Shaanxi Transport Aircraft Factory is building a Chinese version of the Antonov An-12BP four-turboprop civil/military transport aircraft. Soviet built An-12s have been in service (although not in large numbers) with the country's military services and the civil airline, CAAC, for several years. Redesign of the Chinese version was carried out at Xian, beginning in 1969, and the first Y-8 made its initial flight in 1974.

Outwardly, the Y-8 can be distinguished from the An-12 by its more pointed nose transparencies, which extend the overall length of the aircraft by approx 0.91 m (3 ft). The aircraft's 3,169 kW (4,250 ehp) engines, derived from the Ivchenko AI-20K, are produced at Shanghai under the Chinese designation Wojiang-6 or WJ-6.

The decision to put the Y-8 into production was taken in February 1980, and 26 (including one for static testing) had been completed by the Spring of 1986. At present, Y-8s are in use mainly for specialised long-range cargo flights to such places as Tibet and Hong Kong. The Y-8 is a major production priority programme for the 1986-90 period, including the development of a 100-passenger fully pressurised version: the current version has a small pressurised forward cabin for up to 14 passengers in addition to the five-man crew, but the rear cargo hold is unpressurised.

Meanwhile, in an attempt to upgrade the original avionics and equipment, the Canadian firm Litton has supplied items such as inertial navigation systems, Doppler and weather radars, radio compasses and transponders, and Sully (France) provided windscreen de-icing installations for two Y-8s. An in-flight refuelling tanker study for the Y-8 has been made by FRL of the UK.

On 4 September 1985 Beijing radio reported that the first maritime patrol version of the Y-8 had cleared its technical qualification tests that day. This aircraft (see accompanying photograph) has a large 'chin' radome housing the antenna for a Litton Canada APS-504(V)3 search radar. Other equipment includes dual Litton LTN-72R inertial navigation systems, a single LTN-211 Omega navigation system, and Collins radio sets. The maritime surveillance version is expected to be used for both naval patrol and civilian offshore duties such as fishery patrol, pollution

STAF Y-8 four-turboprop multi-purpose medium-range transport

monitoring, and support of the oil exploration industry.

A detailed description of the An-12BP can be found in the USSR section of the 1982-83 and earlier editions of *Jane's*. Chinese published details for the standard Y-8 transport are as follows:

ACCOMMODATION: Standard seating for crew of six and 96 passengers.

DIMENSIONS, EXTERNAL:

Wing span	38.00 m (124 ft 8 in)
Length overall	34.02 m (111 ft 7½ in)
Fuselage: Max diameter	4.10 m (13 ft 5½ in)
Height overall	11.16 m (36 ft 7½ in)
Rear loading hatch: Length	7.67 m (25 ft 2 in)
Width: min	2.16 m (7 ft 1 in)
max	3.10 m (10 ft 2 in)

DIMENSIONS, INTERNAL:

Cargo hold: Length	13.50 m (44 ft 3½ in)
Width: min	3.00 m (9 ft 10 in)
max	3.50 m (11 ft 5¾ in)
Height: min	2.40 m (7 ft 10½ in)
max	2.60 m (8 ft 6½ in)

AREA:

Wings, gross	121.86 m² (1,311.7 sq ft)

WEIGHTS:

Weight empty, equipped	35,500 kg (78,265 lb)
Max fuel load	22,909 kg (50,505 lb)
Max payload: concentrated	16,000 kg (35,275 lb)
distributed	20,000 kg (44,090 lb)
Max T-O weight	61,000 kg (134,480 lb)
Max landing weight	58,000 kg (127,870 lb)

Prototype maritime surveillance version of the Y-8

PERFORMANCE:

Max level speed at 7,000 m (22,965 ft)	
	357 knots (662 km/h; 411 mph)
Normal cruising speed	297 knots (550 km/h; 342 mph)
Max rate of climb at S/L, AUW of 51,000 kg	
(112,435 lb)	600 m (1,968 ft)/min

Service ceiling	10,400 m (34,120 ft)
T-O run	1,230 m (4,035 ft)
Landing run	1,100 m (3,609 ft)
Range with max fuel	3,030 nm (5,615 km; 3,490 miles)
Max endurance	10 h 40 min

XAC
XIAN AIRCRAFT COMPANY

PO Box 140, Xian, Shaanxi
Telephone: 61971 4137
Telex: 70101 XAC CN
Cables: 2401 Yanliang Shaanxi
PRESIDENT: Shao Guobin
VICE-PRESIDENT: Fu Baoxin
CHIEF DESIGN ENGINEER: Wang Suren

Established in 1958, the Xian aircraft factory has a covered area of some 400,000 m² (4,305,560 sq ft), with other major new facilities under construction in 1987. The 1987 workforce numbered about 12,000, of whom about 3,000 were engaged in aircraft production. Aircraft built at Xian include Chinese versions of the Soviet Tupolev Tu-16 bomber (Chinese designation H-6) and Antonov An-24 (Y-7/Y7-100). Xian Aero Engines (XAE) produces the Wopen-8 (RD-3M) turbojets for the Tu-16/H-6. Since 1980 XAC has manufactured glassfibre header tanks, water float pylons, ailerons and various doors for the Canadair CL-215 amphibian; other subcontract work since that time has included various components for the Airbus A300, Boeing 737 and 747, and ATR 42. It is expected to be the main Chinese centre for the proposed MBB/CATIC MPC-75 airliner (see International section). Design studies have been initiated for a 1990s twin-engined supersonic bomber (H-7?), possibly with Shenyang WS-6 turbofans, and Xian is also developing another new tandem two-seat military aircraft of which a mockup or prototype was under construction in 1985. The latter may be the reported Q-6 attack aircraft, said to be equipped with a 30 mm anti-tank gun.

XAC (TUPOLEV) H-6
Chinese name: Hongzhaji-6 (Bomber aircraft 6) or Hong-6
Westernised designation: B-6
NATO reporting name: Badger

First steps to assemble the Tupolev Tu-16 bomber (see USSR section) under licence in China were taken in 1958, but work was suspended in 1960 after the political break with the USSR. A production programme was reinstated some two years later, and the formidable task was undertaken of copying the design without Soviet assistance. Deliveries of the H-6 began in about 1968, and seven of the 26 nuclear devices tested at Lop Nur up to 1980 were airdropped from Tu-16/H-6s. Other weapons that can be carried by the H-6 include the C-ASM cruise missile and the C-601 air-launched derivative of the Soviet 'Styx'.

Production of this aircraft has been relatively slow, but it is continuing at a low rate (three or four per year), and the number in service with the PLA Air Force and Navy is now believed to be about 120, the current version being a naval one designated **H-6 IV** or **B-6D**. China is supplying spares for the Tu-16 bombers of the Egyptian Air Force, and the sale of four to Iraq was reported in mid-1987. The possibility remains that ECM, reconnaissance or other variants may be developed in the future. A probe and drogue aerial tanker design study for the H-6 has been carried out by FRL of the UK, followed by a memorandum of understanding in September 1986 for FRL to assist CATIC in converting a number of H-6s to the tanker role. This version, for which a go-ahead was still awaited in early 1988, would serve primarily as a refuelling tanker for the Q-5/A-5 attack aircraft; there are no plans at present for a receiver version of the H-6.

As with other Chinese developments of original Soviet designs, some local modifications have been noted: some

XAC H-6 strategic bomber, based on the Tupolev Tu-16, showing the modified 'chin' radome associated with C-601 missile carriage

B-6Ds carrying C-601 missiles, for example, have a bigger and cylindrical 'chin' fairing, presumably housing a Chinese variation of the original radar antenna, and other H-6/B-6s have no chin radome at all. One Tu-16/H-6 has been seen with fully circular air intakes, made possible by greater engine/fuselage clearance apparently to overcome intake boundary layer airflow problems. There have also been unconfirmed reports of a four-engined version.

Chinese data for the B-6D are as follows:

POWER PLANT: Two 93.17 kN (20,944 lb st) Xian Wopen-8 turbojets, derived from Mikulin RD-3M.

DIMENSIONS, EXTERNAL:

Wing span	34.189 m (112 ft 2 in)
Length overall	34.800 m (114 ft 2 in)
Height overall	10.355 m (33 ft 11¾ in)

WEIGHTS:

Weight empty	38,530 kg (84,944 lb)
Internal bomb load: normal	3,000 kg (6,614 lb)
max	9,000 kg (19,841 lb)
Two C-601 missiles	4,880 kg (10,758 lb)
Max T-O weight	75,800 kg (167,110 lb)
Max landing weight	55,000 kg (121,254 lb)

PERFORMANCE (with two underwing C-601 anti-shipping missiles):

Max cruising speed	424 knots (786 km/h; 488 mph)
T-O speed with full load	163 knots (302 km/h; 188 mph)
Normal landing speed	126 knots (233 km/h; 145 mph)
Max rate of climb at S/L	1,140 m (3,740 ft)/min
Service ceiling	12,000 m (39,370 ft)
T-O run with full load	2,100 m (6,890 ft)
Normal landing run	1,540 m (5,050 ft)
Combat radius	971 nm (1,800 km; 1,118 miles)
Max range	2,320 nm (4,300 km; 2,672 miles)
Max endurance	5 h 41 min

XAC (ANTONOV) Y-7 and Y7-100
Chinese name: Yunshuji-7 (Transport aircraft 7) or Yun-7
NATO reporting name: Coke

Civil and military examples of the Antonov An-24 twin-turboprop transport aircraft (40 of which were purchased from the USSR) have been in service with CAAC and the PLA Air Force since about 1970. A 'considerably improved' version of this 48/52-passenger aircraft, known as the **Y-7**, received its Chinese certificate of airworthiness

in 1980, following the completion of three prototypes plus two additional airframes for static and fatigue testing. The Y-7 is now in full production at Xian; its WJ-5A-1 engines (derived from the Ivchenko AI-24A) are manufactured at Harbin.

Public debut by a pre-production Y-7 took place on 17 April 1982, and production is believed to have started in 1983. First flight of a production Y-7 was announced on 1 February 1984, and the initial delivery to CAAC was made shortly afterwards. Scheduled passenger services began in April 1986. The PLA Naval Air Force operates one Y-7 in the transport role and another as a navigation trainer. Twenty of the initial Y-7 version were built, on one of which (B-3499) Hong Kong Aircraft Engineering Company (HAECO) undertook 'prototype' refurbishment in 1985. This programme called for a new three-person flight deck layout, all-new cabin interior with 52 reclining seats, windscreen de-icing, new HF/VHF communications, new navigation equipment, and installation of oxygen, air data and environmental control systems. The aircraft was also fitted with winglets which, by reducing induced drag by 4 per cent, are claimed to offer a 5 per cent reduction in fuel consumption. In this new form the aircraft meets BCAR standards, and is known as the **Y7-100**. The first production Y7-100 was flown in late 1986, and ten had been completed by the Autumn of 1987. The winglet modification is being applied to the original batch of Y-7s.

North American, British, French and German firms supplying equipment include Becker, Collins, Hamilton Standard, IDC, Lermer, Litton, Nordam, PTC, Puritan-Bennett, Sfena, Smiths, Sperry and Sundstrand. The contract with Nordam, which was responsible for the cabin interior redesign, included an option for 50 shipsets of floors, seats, lights and toilets. In the longer term, China estimates a requirement for at least 100 Y-7s by the year 1990, and plans an ongoing development programme intended to lead to a more fuel-efficient **Y7-200** in 1988, with a reduced-weight **Y7-300** and a rear-ramp cargo version appearing about a year later. Boeing Commercial Airplane Company is assisting in the weight reduction programme.

The following description is based on that of the An-24RV, modified where possible to refer to the Y-7 and Y7-100:

TYPE: Twin-turboprop short/medium-range transport.

XAC Y-7 (Chinese development of the Antonov An-24) after modification by HAECO of Hong Kong as the prototype Y7-100 *(HAECO)*

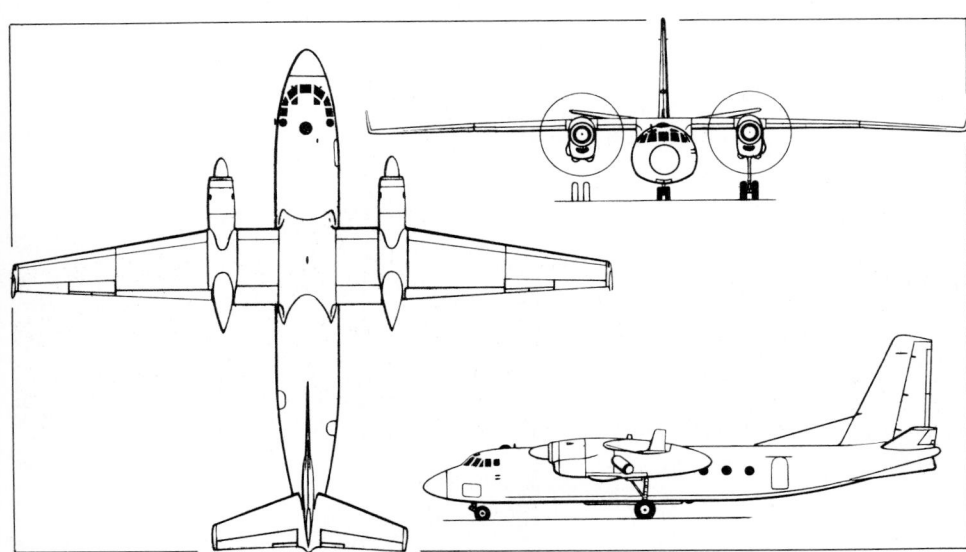

XAC Y7-100 current production version of this twin-turboprop transport aircraft *(Pilot Press)*

WINGS: Cantilever high-wing monoplane, with 2° 12′ 2″ anhedral on outer panels. Incidence 3°. Sweepback at quarter-chord on outer panels 6° 50′. All-metal two-spar structure, built in five sections: constant chord centre-section, two tapered inner wings and two tapered outer panels. Mass balanced servo-compensated ailerons, with large glassfibre trim tabs. Hydraulically operated Fowler flaps along entire wing trailing-edges inboard of un-powered ailerons; single-slotted flaps on centre-section, double-slotted outboard of nacelles. Servo tab and trim tab in each aileron. Winglet at each tip on Y7-100 (being retrofitted also on Y-7).

FUSELAGE: All-metal semi-monocoque structure in front, centre and rear portions, of bonded/welded construction.

TAIL UNIT: Cantilever all-metal structure, with single ventral fin. Tailplane dihedral 9°. All controls operated manually. Balance tab in each elevator, trim tab and spring tab in rudder.

LANDING GEAR (An-24RV): Retractable tricycle type with twin wheels on all units. Hydraulic actuation, with emergency gravity extension. All units retract forward. Mainwheels are size 900 × 300-370, tyre pressure 3.45-4.90 bars (50-71 lb/sq in); nosewheels size 700 × 250, tyre pressure 2.45-3.45 bars (35.5-50 lb/sq in). (Tyre pressures variable to cater for different types of runway.) Disc brakes on mainwheels; steerable and castoring nosewheel unit.

POWER PLANT: Two Harbin WJ-5A-1 turboprops, each rated at 2,080 kW (2,790 shp) for T-O and 1,976 kW (2,650 shp) at ISA + 23°C; four-blade constant-speed fully-feathering propellers with elongated spinners. Fuel in integral wing tanks immediately outboard of nacelles, and four bag-type tanks in centre-section, total capacity 5,550 litres (1,466 US gallons; 1,220 Imp gallons). Provision for four additional tanks in centre-section. Pressure refuelling point in starboard engine nacelle; gravity fuelling point above each tank. One 8.83 kN (1,985 lb st) Type RU 19-300 auxiliary turbojet (or Chinese equivalent ?) in starboard engine nacelle for engine starting, to improve take-off and in-flight performance, and to reduce stability and handling

problems if one turboprop engine fails in flight.

ACCOMMODATION: Crew of three (Y7-100) or five (Y-7) on flight deck, plus cabin attendant. Standard layout has four-abreast seating, with centre aisle, for 48 (Y-7) or 52 passengers (Y7-100) in air-conditioned, soundproofed (by Tracor) and pressurised cabin. Galley (by Lermer) and toilet at rear on starboard side. Baggage compartments forward and aft of passenger cabin, plus overhead stowage bins in cabin. Passenger door on port side, at rear of cabin, is of airstair type. Doors to forward and rear baggage compartments on starboard side. All doors open inward. Electric windscreen de-icing in Y7-100.

SYSTEMS: Hamilton Standard environmental control system in Y7-100 (cabin pressure differential in An-24RV is 0.29 bars; 4.27 lb/sq in). Main and emergency hydraulic systems, pressure 152 bars (2,200 lb/sq in), for landing gear actuation, nosewheel steering, flaps, brakes, wind-screen wipers and propeller feathering. Electrical system in An-24RV includes two 27V DC starter/generators, two alternators to provide 115V 400Hz AC supply, and two inverters for 36V 400Hz three-phase AC. Puritan-Bennett passenger oxygen system optional in Y7-100.

AVIONICS AND EQUIPMENT (Y7-100): Standard communications equipment comprises Collins 618M-3 dual VHF, Collins 628T-3 single HF, Becker audio selection and intercom, and Sundstrand AV-557C cockpit voice recorder. Standard navigation equipment comprises dual ADI-84A, dual EHSI-74 electronic HSI, dual RMI-36, FGS-65 flight guidance system, dual 51RV-4B VOR/ILS, dual DME-42, dual DF-206 ADF, 860F-4 radio altimeter, 621A-6A ATC transponder, 51Z-4 marker beacon receiver and CWC-80 instrument warning system, all by Collins; Litton LTN-211 VLF/Omega navigation system; Sperry MHRS dual compass system, dual attitude reference and Primus 90 colour weather radar; IDC air data system; Sundstrand UFDR flight data recorder; and KJ-6A autopilot. Gables control units. Other instrumentation by Gould, IDC, Sfena and Smiths.

DIMENSIONS, EXTERNAL:

Wing span: Y-7	29.20 m (95 ft 9½ in)
Y7-100 (over winglets)	29.637 m (97 ft 2¾ in)
Wing chord: at root	3.50 m (11 ft 5¾ in)
at tip	1.095 m (3 ft 7 in)
Wing aspect ratio	11.7
Length overall	23.708 m (77 ft 9½ in)
Height overall	8.553 m (28 ft 0¾ in)
Fuselage: Max width	2.90 m (9 ft 6¼ in)
Max depth	2.50 m (8 ft 2½ in)
Tailplane span	9.08 m (29 ft 9½ in)
Wheel track (c/l of shock struts)	7.90 m (25 ft 11 in)
Wheelbase	7.90 m (25 ft 11 in)
Passenger door (port, rear):	
Height	1.40 m (4 ft 7 in)
Width	0.75 m (2 ft 5½ in)
Height to sill	1.40 m (4 ft 7 in)
Baggage compartment door (starboard, fwd):	
Height	1.10 m (3 ft 7¼ in)
Width	1.20 m (3 ft 11¼ in)
Height to sill	1.30 m (4 ft 3 in)
Baggage compartment door (starboard, rear):	
Height	1.41 m (4 ft 7½ in)
Width	0.75 m (2 ft 5½ in)

DIMENSIONS, INTERNAL:

Cabin:	
Length, incl flight deck: Y-7	9.90 m (32 ft 5¾ in)
Y7-100	10.50 m (34 ft 5½ in)
Max width	2.80 m (9 ft 2¼ in)
Max height	1.90 m (6 ft 2¾ in)
Volume: Y7-100	56.0 m³ (1,978 cu ft)
Baggage compartment volume (Y7-100):	
fwd	4.50 m³ (159 cu ft)
rear	6.70 m³ (237 cu ft)

AREAS:

Wings, gross	74.98 m² (807.1 sq ft)
Vertical tail surfaces (total)	13.38 m² (144.0 sq ft)
Horizontal tail surfaces (total)	17.23 m² (185.5 sq ft)

WEIGHTS AND LOADINGS:

Operating weight empty: Y-7	14,235 kg (31,383 lb)
Y7-100	14,900 kg (32,849 lb)
Max fuel (both)	4,790 kg (10,560 lb)
Max payload: Y-7	4,700 kg (10,362 lb)
Y7-100	5,500 kg (12,125 lb)
Max T-O and landing weight (both)	21,800 kg (48,060 lb)
Max wing loading (both)	290.7 kg/m² (59.6 lb/sq ft)
Max power loading (both)	5.24 kg/kW (8.61 lb/shp)

PERFORMANCE (Y7-100 except where indicated):

Max level speed	279 knots (518 km/h; 322 mph)
Max cruising speed at 4,000 m (13,125 ft):	
Y-7	258 knots (478 km/h; 297 mph)
Y7-100	261 knots (484 km/h; 301 mph)
Econ cruising speed at 6,000 m (19,685 ft)	228 knots (423 km/h; 263 mph)
Max rate of climb at S/L	458 m (1,504 ft)/min
Service ceiling	8,750 m (28,700 ft)
Service ceiling, one engine out	3,900 m (12,800 ft)
T-O run at S/L, FAR Pt 25: ISA	1,248 m (4,095 ft)
ISA + 20°C	1,398 m (4,590 ft)
Landing run	620 m (2,035 ft)
Range:	
max (52-passenger) payload	491 nm (910 km; 565 miles)
max standard fuel	1,025 nm (1,900 km; 1,180 miles)
standard and auxiliary fuel	1,306 nm (2,420 km; 1,504 miles)

COLOMBIA

AERO MERCANTIL

AERO MERCANTIL SA

Carrera 3 No. 56-19, Apartado Aéreo 6781, Bogotá
Telephone: 211 8100
Telex: 044 581
Fax: 212 8952
PRESIDENT: James G. Leaver
PROJECTS MANAGER: Eric Leaver

Aero Mercantil has been associated with Piper Aircraft Corporation since 1952, first as a dealer and then as a distributor. Currently, it markets the aircraft produced by AICSA (see following entry) and provides the quality assurance at the latter's assembly plant. It is currently developing and building a prototype aircraft of its own design, known as the Gavilan.

AERO MERCANTIL GAVILAN

Construction of the Gavilan prototype began in March 1987, and first flight was planned for December 1988.
TYPE: Eight-seat light transport.
WINGS: Braced high-wing monoplane, with dihedral. Wing section NACA 4412. Incidence 1° 30′. Unswept, two-spar structure of 2024-T3 aluminium alloy, with constant chord and single-strut bracing each side. Piano hinged ailerons and offset hinged trailing-edge flaps also of 2024-T3. No tabs.
FUSELAGE: Mainframe of 4130N steel tube, with 2025-T3 aluminium alloy skin.
TAIL UNIT: Two-spar fin and fixed incidence tailplane; single tab on elevator. Entire structure of 2025-T3 aluminium alloy.

LANDING GEAR: Non-retractable tricycle type, with elastomeric shock absorption and single wheel on each unit. Tyre sizes 700 × 6-6 (main) and 600 × 6-6 (nose). Parker Hannifin mainwheel brakes.
POWER PLANT: One 261 kW (350 hp) Textron Lycoming TIO-540-W2A flat-six engine, driving a Hartzell propeller. Fuel tank in each wing, combined capacity 295 litres (78 US gallons; 65 Imp gallons); refuelling point in each tank. Oil capacity 11.4 litres (3 US gallons; 2.5 Imp gallons).
ACCOMMODATION: Pilot and co-pilot or one passenger at front. Three more pairs of seats to rear of these, middle row of which faces aft. Door at front on each side, plus larger cargo double door at rear on port side.
SYSTEMS: Pneumatic system, vacuum pump driven at 0.34 bars (5 lb/sq in). 12V 70A electrical system. Oxygen system optional.
AVIONICS: King KX 165 VHF/VOR and KR 87 ADF, and blind-flying instrumentation, are standard.

DIMENSIONS, EXTERNAL:
Wing span	12.19 m (40 ft 0 in)
Wing chord, constant	1.55 m (5 ft 1 in)
Wing aspect ratio	7.8
Length overall	9.22 m (30 ft 3 in)
Height overall	3.35 m (11 ft 0 in)
Tailplane span	3.10 m (10 ft 2 in)
Wheelbase	3.35 m (11 ft 0 in)
Propeller diameter	2.13 m (7 ft 0 in)
Propeller ground clearance	0.36 m (1 ft 2 in)
Crew/passenger doors (each): Height	0.91 m (3 ft 0 in)
Width	0.97 m (3 ft 2 in)
Height to sill	1.02 m (3 ft 4 in)

Cargo double door: Height	1.17 m (3 ft 10 in)
Width	1.02 m (3 ft 4 in)
Height to sill	1.02 m (3 ft 4 in)

DIMENSIONS, INTERNAL:
Cabin: Length	3.66 m (12 ft 0 in)
Max width	1.37 m (4 ft 6 in)
Max height	1.22 m (4 ft 0 in)
Floor area	5.02 m² (54.0 sq ft)

AREAS:
Wings, gross	18.95 m² (204.0 sq ft)
Horizontal tail surfaces (total)	5.57 m² (60.0 sq ft)

WEIGHTS AND LOADINGS:
Max fuel	106 kg (234 lb)
Max payload	862 kg (1,900 lb)
Max T-O and landing weight	1,905 kg (4,200 lb)
Max wing loading	100.6 kg/m² (20.6 lb/sq ft)
Max power loading	7.30 kg/kW (12.0 lb/hp)

PERFORMANCE (estimated, at max T-O weight):
Never-exceed speed	203 knots (376 km/h; 233 mph)
Max level speed at 5,500 m (18,000 ft)	145 knots (269 km/h; 167 mph)
Max cruising speed at 5,500 m (18,000 ft)	135 knots (250 km/h; 155 mph)
Stalling speed, 40° flap, engine idling	58 knots (108 km/h; 67 mph)
Max rate of climb at S/L	366 m (1,200 ft)/min
Service ceiling	7,620 m (25,000 ft)
T-O run	275 m (900 ft)
T-O to 15 m (50 ft)	475 m (1,500 ft)
Landing from 15 m (50 ft)	366 m (1,200 ft)
Range with max fuel, no reserves	580 nm (1,075 km; 668 miles)

AICSA

AERO INDUSTRIAL COLOMBIANA SA

Aeropuerto Guaymaral, Bogotá
GENERAL MANAGER: Francisco Restrepo

AICSA has been engaged in the assembly of Piper aircraft since 1968. The programme was initiated when the Colombian Air Force made it possible for the aircraft to be imported in kit form, enabling some locally produced materials and skilled local labour to be used in their completion. AICSA was created to assemble Pipers not only for Colombia but also for member countries of the Andean Pact, although in the event exports of Colombian assembled aircraft have been limited to Bolivia, Chile and Ecuador. Currently, through another subsidiary, the Colombian Air Force owns 51% of AICSA; the other major shareholder is the Instituto de Fomento Industrial (IFI), which is the industrial development agency of the Colombian government.

From 1968 to the end of 1985, AICSA assembled 492 Piper aircraft (275 single-engined and 217 twin-engined), as listed in the 1987-88 *Jane's*. No aircraft were built in 1986, but in 1987 AICSA completed 12 Seneca IIIs and one example each of the Cheyenne 400 and Turbo Saratoga.

Piper Seneca III assembled under licence by AICSA

AVIONES DE COLOMBIA

AVIONES DE COLOMBIA SA

Calle 26 No. 4A-45 Piso 8, Bogotá
Telephone: (282) 9648, 9668 and 9728
Telex: 45 220
WORKS: Aeropuerto Guaymaral, Apartado Aéreo 6876, Bogotá
Telephone: (671) 8211, 8488 and 8502
COMMERCIAL MANAGER: Rafael Urdaneta

This company, established in the 1950s and known formerly as Urdaneta y Galvez Ltda, has been a South American distributor for Cessna aircraft since 1961. In 1969 it began assembling and partly building selected Cessna types under licence (see 1981-82 and earlier editions of *Jane's*), and is now qualified to manufacture complete airframes. Facilities include 464.5 m² (5,000 sq ft) of office space in Bogotá, and 13,935 m² (150,000 sq ft) at Guaymaral, the general aviation airport for Bogotá.

On 31 January 1986 the company had a workforce of 150 persons, and had assembled a total of 1,017 Cessna aircraft, as listed in the 1987-88 *Jane's*. No later total has been received.

AVIONES DE COLOMBIA/CESSNA AGTRAINER

Illustrated in an accompanying photograph, the AgTrainer is modified by Aviones de Colombia from the Cessna Model 188 Ag Truck (1984-85 *Jane's*). The cabin is widened to accommodate two persons side by side, increasing the empty weight by approx 91 kg (200 lb). Flight characteristics remain unchanged. Two prototypes were flown (the first of them on 16 September 1976), and the first

prototype has since been operated by Aeroandes, a local cropspraying flying school.

Seven AgTrainers had been produced by early 1986, of which three were operating in Colombia, three in Central America and one in Ecuador.
TYPE: Two-seat agricultural monoplane.
WINGS: Braced low-wing monoplane, with single streamline section bracing strut each side. Wing section NACA 2412, modified. Dihedral 9°. Incidence 1° 30′ at root, −1° 30′ at tip. All-metal structure with NACA all-metal single-slotted flaps inboard of Frise all-metal ailerons. Aileron leading-edge gaps sealed. Wing fences immediately outboard of bracing strut attachments.
FUSELAGE: Rectangular section welded steel tube structure with removable metal skin panels forward of cabin. All-metal semi-monocoque rear fuselage.
TAIL UNIT: Cantilever all-metal structure. Fixed incidence tailplane. Trim tab in starboard elevator. Tailplane abrasion boots standard.
LANDING GEAR: Non-retractable tailwheel type. Land-O-Matic cantilever main legs of heavy duty spring steel. Tapered tubular tailwheel spring shock absorber. Mainwheel tyres size 22 × 8.00-8, 6-ply rating, pressure 2.41 bars (35 lb/sq in). Oversize tyres optional, size 8.50-10, 6-ply rating, pressure 1.72 bars (25 lb/sq in). Tailwheel tyre size 3.50-10, 4-ply rating, pressure 3.45-4.14 bars (50-60 lb/sq in). Steerable tailwheel. Hydraulic disc brakes and parking brake.
POWER PLANT: One 224 kW (300 hp) Continental IO-520-D flat-six engine, driving a McCauley three-blade constant-speed propeller. Fuel capacity 204 litres (54 US gallons; 45 Imp gallons). Oil capacity 11.4 litres (3 US gallons; 2.5

Imp gallons).
ACCOMMODATION: Side by side seats for two persons, in enclosed cabin with steel overturn structure. Combined window and door on each side, hinged at bottom. Ventilation standard. Air-conditioning, heating and windscreen defrosting optional.
SYSTEM: Electrical system powered by a 28V 60A alternator and 24V 12.75Ah battery as standard. 28V 95A alternator and 24V 15.5Ah heavy duty battery optional.
EQUIPMENT: Standard equipment includes a 1,060 litre (280 US gallon; 233 Imp gallon) hopper with shatter-resistant window, engine driven hydraulic spray system and manually controlled spray valve and gearbox without agitator, hopper side loading system on port side, pilot's four-way adjustable seat, control stick lock, wire cutters, cable deflector, navigation lights, tailcone lift handles, quick drain oil valve, remote fuel strainer drain control, and auxiliary fuel pump.

DIMENSIONS, EXTERNAL:
Wing span	12.70 m (41 ft 8 in)
Length overall	8.00 m (26 ft 3 in)
Height overall	2.44 m (8 ft 0 in)
Propeller diameter	2.03 m (6 ft 8 in)

DIMENSIONS, INTERNAL:
Cabin: Max width	1.09 m (3 ft 7 in)
Hopper volume	0.85 m³ (30.0 cu ft)

AREA:
Wings, gross	19.05 m² (205.0 sq ft)

WEIGHTS:
Weight empty:	
without dispersal equipment	1,017 kg (2,242 lb)
with dispersal equipment	1,099 kg (2,424 lb)

Max T-O weight:
Normal category   1,497 kg (3,300 lb)
Restricted category   1,905 kg (4,200 lb)
Max landing weight   1,497 kg (3,300 lb)
PERFORMANCE (at max T-O weight):
Max level speed at S/L   105 knots (195 km/h; 121 mph)
Max cruising speed (75% power) at 1,980 m (6,500 ft)
    98 knots (182 km/h; 113 mph)
Stalling speed, power off:
flaps up   53 knots (98 km/h; 61 mph) IAS
flaps down   50 knots (92 km/h; 57 mph) IAS
Max rate of climb at S/L   210 m (690 ft)/min
Service ceiling   3,385 m (11,100 ft)
T-O run   207 m (680 ft)
T-O to 15 m (50 ft)   332 m (1,090 ft)
Landing from 15 m (50 ft)   386 m (1,265 ft)
Landing run   128 m (420 ft)
Range, reserves for start, taxi, T-O and 45 min at 45%
power   256 nm (474 km; 295 miles)
Endurance, conditions as above   2 h 36 min

Aviones de Colombia/Cessna AgTrainer, a modified Cessna 188 Ag Truck

CZECHOSLOVAKIA

Central direction of the Czechoslovak aircraft industry is by a body known as the Generální Reditelstvi Aero—Ceskoslovenské Letecke Podniky (Trust Aero—Czechoslovak Aeronautical Works), Prague-Letnany, whose General Director is Josef Skarohlid.

About 29,000 people are employed by the Czechoslovak aircraft industry. Principal factories concerned with aircraft manufacture are the Aero Vodochody National Corporation, Let National Corporation and Zlin Aircraft Moravan National Corporation, whose current products appear under the appropriate headings in this section. Other Czechoslovak factories engaged in the production of aero engines and sailplanes are listed in the relevant sections of this edition.

Sales of all aircraft products outside Czechoslovakia are handled by the Omnipol Foreign Trade Corporation.

OMNIPOL
FOREIGN TRADE CORPORATION
Nekázanka 11, 112 21 Prague 1
Telephone: (02) 2140111

Telex: 121297 and 121299
GENERAL DIRECTOR: Ing Stanislav Fritzl
COMMERCIAL DIRECTOR: Ing František Háva
PUBLICITY MANAGER: Jan Boček

This concern handles the sales of products of the Czechoslovak aircraft industry outside Czechoslovakia and furnishes all information requested by customers with regard to export goods.

AERO
AERO VODOCHODY NÁRODNÍ PODNIK
(Aero Vodochody National Corporation)
250 70 Odolena Voda
Telephone: (2) 842551
Telex: 121169 AERO C
MANAGING DIRECTOR: Ing Václav Klouda
CHIEF DESIGNER: Ing Vlastimil Havelka
CHIEF PILOT: Antonin Saller

This factory was established on 1 July 1953. Aero's major product in 1963-74 was the L-29 Delfin jet basic and advanced trainer, of which approx 3,600 were built. It was superseded by the L-39.

AERO L-39 ALBATROS
The L-39 basic and advanced jet trainer was developed by a team led by Dipl Ing Jan Vlcek, working in close co-operation with the USSR, and flew for the first time on 4 November 1968. The prototypes (see earlier *Jane's*) were followed by ten pre-production aircraft from 1971, and series production started in late 1972, following official selection of the L-39 to succeed the L-29 Delfin (1974-75 *Jane's*) as the standard jet trainer for the air forces of the Soviet Union, Czechoslovakia and the German Democratic Republic. Service trials took place in 1973 in Czechoslovakia and the USSR, and by the Spring of 1974 the L-39 had begun to enter service with the Czechoslovak Air Force. Other recipients include Afghanistan (18), Algeria (16), Bulgaria (30), Cuba (30), Ethiopia (12), Iraq (80), Libya (170), Nigeria (10), Romania (35), Syria (100) and Vietnam (25).

Production totalled more than 1,900 by 1 January 1987, and was expected to continue for at least five more years, at the rate of 200 a year. The Albatros is used in Czechoslovakia for all pilot training, including that of helicopter pilots. On average, pupils solo after approx 14 hours' dual instruction on the L-39 C.

Official Czechoslovak designations for the L-39 are as follows:
L-39 C. Basic version, for basic and advanced flying training, to which the detailed description chiefly applies. Two underwing stations only. In service with the air forces of Afghanistan, Cuba, Czechoslovakia, Germany (Democratic Republic) and USSR. In production.

L-39 V. As basic L-39 C, but modified as single-seater for target towing (see 1987-88 and earlier editions). No longer in production.

L-39 Z0. Jet trainer with four underwing weapon stations (Z Zbrojní: armed) and reinforced wings. Prototype (X-09) first flown 25 August 1975. Export customers include the air forces of Iraq, Libya and Syria. In production.

L-39 ZA. Ground attack and reconnaissance version of L-39 Z0, with underfuselage gun pod and four underwing weapon stations; reinforced wings and landing gear. Prototypes (X-10 and X-11) first flown 1975-76. In service with the air forces of Czechoslovakia and Romania. In production.

L-39 MS. New advanced training version with improved airframe, more powerful engine (S/L static thrust 21.57 kN;

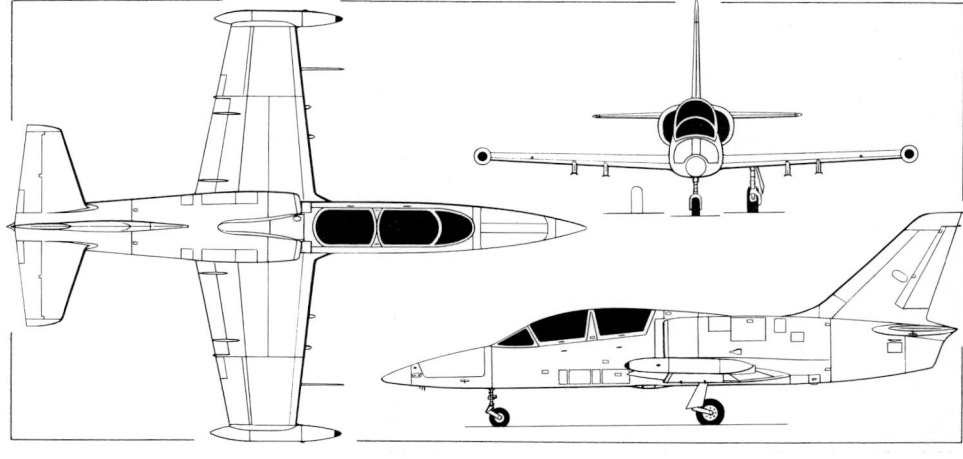

Aero L-39 Z0 Albatros two-seat basic and advanced jet trainer *(Pilot Press)*

4,850 lb) and upgraded avionics and equipment, including electronic displays. First flight with new engine 1986. Further details withheld until completion of test programme, which was continuing in early 1988.

The following description applies to the current production L-39 C basic version, except where indicated:
TYPE: Two-seat basic and advanced jet trainer; L-39 ZA also has ground attack and reconnaissance capability.

WINGS: Cantilever low-wing monoplane, with 2° 30′ dihedral from roots. Wing section NACA 64A012 mod. 5. Incidence 2°. Sweepback 6° 26′ on leading-edges, 1° 45′ at quarter-chord. One-piece all-metal stressed skin structure, with main spar and auxiliary spar; four-point attachment to fuselage. All-metal double-slotted trailing-edge flaps, operated by push/pull rods actuated by a single hydraulic jack. Flaps retract automatically when airspeed reaches 167 knots (310 km/h; 193 mph). Small fence above and below each trailing-edge between flap and aileron. Mass balanced ailerons, each with electrically operated servo tab; port tab, used also for trim, is operated by electromechanical actuator. Non-jettisonable wingtip fuel tanks, incorporating landing/taxying lights.

FUSELAGE: Metal semi-monocoque structure, built in two portions. Front portion consists of three sections, the first of which is a laminated glassfibre nosecone housing avionics, antennae, battery, compressed air and oxygen bottles and the nose landing gear. Next comes the pressurised compartment for the crew. The third section incorporates the fuel tanks, air intakes and the engine bay. The rear fuselage, carrying the tail unit, is attached by five bolts and can be removed quickly to provide access for engine installation and removal. Two airbrakes side by side under fuselage, just forward of wing leading-edge, actuated by single hydraulic jack; these are

lowered automatically as airspeed nears a maximum of Mach 0.8.

TAIL UNIT: Conventional all-metal cantilever structure, with sweepback on vertical surfaces. Variable incidence tailplane. Control surfaces actuated by pushrods. Electrically operated trim tab in each elevator; servo tab in rudder. Elevators deflect 30° up, 20° down; rudder 30° to right and left.

LANDING GEAR: Retractable tricycle type, with single wheel and oleo-pneumatic shock absorber on each unit. Gear is designed for a touchdown sink rate of 3.4 m (11.15 ft)/s at AUW of 4,600 kg (10,141 lb). Retraction/extension is operated hydraulically, with electrical control. All wheel well doors close automatically after wheels are lowered, to prevent ingress of dirt and debris. Mainwheels retract inward into wings (with automatic braking during retraction), nosewheel forward into fuselage. K24 mainwheels, fitted with Barum tubeless tyres size 610 × 215 mm (610 × 185 mm on early production aircraft), pressure 5.88 bars (85.34 lb/sq in). K25 castoring and self-centring nosewheel, fitted with Barum tubeless tyre size 450 × 165 mm (430 × 150 mm on early production aircraft), pressure 3.92 bars (56.89 lb/sq in). Hydraulic disc brakes and anti-skid units on mainwheels; shimmy damper on nosewheel leg. The L-39 is capable of operation from grass strips (with a bearing strength of 6 kg/cm²; 85 lb/sq in) at up to 4,600 kg (10,141 lb) T-O weight, or from unprepared runways. Landing gear of L-39 ZA reinforced to cater for higher operating weights.

POWER PLANT: One 16.87 kN (3,792 lb st) Ivchenko AI-25 TL turbofan mounted in rear fuselage, with semi-circular lateral air intake, fitted with splitter plate, on each side of fuselage above wing centre-section. Fuel in five rubber main bag tanks aft of cockpit, with combined capacity of 1,055 litres (279 US gallons; 232 Imp gallons), and two

100 litre (26.5 US gallon; 22 Imp gallon) non-jettisonable wingtip tanks. Total internal fuel capacity 1,255 litres (332 US gallons; 276 Imp gallons). Gravity refuelling points on top of fuselage and on each tip tank. Provision for two 350 litre (92.5 US gallon; 77 Imp gallon) drop tanks on inboard underwing pylons, increasing total overall fuel capacity to a maximum of 1,955 litres (517 US gallons; 430 Imp gallons). Fuel system permits up to 20 s of inverted flight.

ACCOMMODATION: Crew of two in tandem, on Czechoslovak VS-1-BRI rocket assisted ejection seats, operable at zero height and at speeds down to 81 knots (150 km/h; 94 mph), beneath individual transparent canopies which hinge sideways to starboard and are jettisonable. Rear seat elevated. One-piece windscreen hinges forward to provide access to front instrument panel. Internal transparency between cockpits. Dual controls standard.

SYSTEMS: Cabin pressurised (standard pressure differential 0.227 bars; 3.29 lb/sq in, max overpressure 0.29 bars; 4.20 lb/sq in) and air-conditioned, using engine bleed air and cooling unit. Air-conditioning system provides automatic temperature control from 10° to 25°C at ambient air temperatures from −55°C to +45°C. Main and standby interconnected hydraulic systems, the main system having a variable flow pump with an operating pressure of 147 bars (2,133 lb/sq in) for actuation of landing gear, flaps, airbrakes, ram air turbine and (at 34.3 bars; 500 lb/sq in pressure) wheel brakes. Emergency system, for all of above except airbrakes, incorporates three accumulators. Pneumatic canopy seals supplied by a 2 litre compressed air bottle in nose (pressure 147 bars; 2,133 lb/sq in). Electrical system (27V DC) is powered by a 7.5kVA engine driven generator. If primary generator fails, a V 910 ram air turbine is extended automatically into the airstream and generates up to 3kVA of emergency power for essential services. 12V 28Ah SAM 28 lead-acid battery for standby power and for APU starting. Two 800VA static inverters (the first for radio equipment, ice warning lights, engine vibration measurement and air-conditioning, the second for navigation and landing systems, IFF and air-to-air missiles) provide 115V single-phase AC power at 400Hz. A second circuit incorporates a 500VA rotary inverter and 40VA static inverter to provide 36V three-phase AC power, also at 400Hz. Saphir 5 APU and SV-25 turbine for engine starting. Air intakes and windscreen anti-iced by engine bleed air; normally, anti-icing is sensor-activated automatically, but a manual standby system is also provided. Six-bottle oxygen system for crew, pressure 147 bars (2,133 lb/sq in).

AVIONICS AND EQUIPMENT: Standard avionics include R-832 M two-band com radio (VHF 118-140MHz, UHF 220-389MHz); SPU-9 crew intercom; RKL-41 ADF (150-1,800kHz); RV-5 radar altimeter; MRP-56 P/S marker beacon receiver; SRO-2 IFF; and RSBN-5S navigation and landing system. VOR/ILS system available at customer's option. Landing and taxying light in forward end of each tip tank.

ARMAMENT (L-39 Z0 and ZA): Underfuselage pod on ZA only, below front cockpit, housing a single 23 mm Soviet GSh-23 two-barrelled cannon; ammunition for this gun (max 150 rds) is housed in fuselage, above gun pod. Gun/rocket firing and weapon release controls, including electrically controlled ASP-3 NMU-39 Z gyroscopic gunsight and FKP-2-2 gun camera, in front cockpit only (no FKP-2-2 in L-39 V). Z0 and ZA have four underwing hardpoints, the inboard pair each stressed for loads of up to 500 kg (1,102 lb) and the outer pair for loads of up to 250 kg (551 lb) each; max underwing stores load 1,100 kg (2,425 lb). Non-jettisonable pylons, each comprising a D3-57D stores rack. Typical underwing stores can include various combinations of bombs (two 500 kg, four 250 kg or six 100 kg); four UB-16-57 M pods each containing sixteen S-5 57 mm air-to-surface rockets; infra-red air-to-air missiles (outer pylons only); a five-camera day reconnaissance pod (port inboard pylon only); or (on inboard stations only) two 350 litre (92.5 US gallon; 77 Imp gallon) drop tanks.

Aero L-39 ZA version of the Albatros, in Czechoslovak Air Force insignia
(Václav Jukl, Letectví + Kosmonautika)

DIMENSIONS, EXTERNAL:

Wing span	9.46 m (31 ft 0½ in)
Wing chord (mean)	2.15 m (7 ft 0½ in)
Wing aspect ratio: geometric	4.4
incl tip tanks	5.2
Length overall	12.13 m (39 ft 9½ in)
Height overall	4.77 m (15 ft 7¾ in)
Tailplane span	4.40 m (14 ft 5 in)
Wheel track	2.44 m (8 ft 0 in)
Wheelbase	4.39 m (14 ft 4¾ in)

AREAS:

Wings, gross	18.80 m^2 (202.36 sq ft)
Ailerons (total)	1.23 m^2 (13.26 sq ft)
Trailing-edge flaps (total)	2.68 m^2 (28.89 sq ft)
Airbrakes (total)	0.50 m^2 (5.38 sq ft)
Vertical tail surfaces (total)	3.51 m^2 (37.78 sq ft)
Tailplane	3.93 m^2 (42.30 sq ft)
Elevators, incl tabs	1.14 m^2 (12.27 sq ft)

*WEIGHTS AND LOADINGS:

Weight empty, equipped: C	3,455 kg (7,617 lb)
Z0	3,480 kg (7,672 lb)
ZA	3,565 kg (7,859 lb)
Fuel load: fuselage tanks	824 kg (1,816 lb)
wingtip tanks	156 kg (344 lb)
Max external stores load: C	284 kg (626 lb)
Z0	1,150 kg (2,535 lb)
ZA	1,290 kg (2,844 lb)
T-O weight 'clean': C	4,525 kg (9,976 lb)
Z0	4,550 kg (10,031 lb)
ZA	4,635 kg (10,218 lb)
Max T-O weight: C	4,700 kg (10,362 lb)
Z0 and ZA	5,600 kg (12,346 lb)
Max wing loading: C	250.0 kg/m^2 (51.23 lb/sq ft)
Z0 and ZA	297.9 kg/m^2 (61.01 lb/sq ft)
Max power loading: C	278.6 kg/kN (2.73 lb/lb st)
Z0 and ZA	332.0 kg/kN (3.25 lb/lb st)

*PERFORMANCE (C at 'clean' T-O weight of 4,500 kg; 9,921 lb, Z0 and ZA at max T-O weight):

Max limiting Mach number	0.80
Max level speed at S/L:	
C	378 knots (700 km/h; 435 mph)
Z0 and ZA	329 knots (610 km/h; 379 mph)
Max level speed at 5,000 m (16,400 ft):	
C	405 knots (750 km/h; 466 mph)
Z0 and ZA	340 knots (630 km/h; 391 mph)
Stalling speed: C	90 knots (165 km/h; 103 mph)
Z0 and ZA	103 knots (190 km/h; 118 mph)
Max rate of climb at S/L: C	1,260 m (4,130 ft)/min
Z0 and ZA	810 m (2,657 ft)/min
Time to 5,000 m (16,400 ft): C	5 min
Z0 and ZA	10 min
Service ceiling: C	11,000 m (36,100 ft)
Z0 and ZA	7,500 m (24,600 ft)
T-O run (concrete): C	530 m (1,740 ft)
Z0 and ZA	970 m (3,182 ft)
Landing run (concrete): C	650 m (2,135 ft)
Z0 and ZA	800 m (2,625 ft)
Range at 7,000 m (22,975 ft):	
C, 980 kg (2,160 lb) max internal fuel	593 nm (1,100 km; 683 miles)
C, 1,524 kg (3,360 lb) max internal and external fuel	944 nm (1,750 km; 1,087 miles)
Endurance at 7,000 m (22,975 ft):	
C, max internal fuel as above	2 h 30 min
C, max internal/external fuel as above	3 h 50 min
g limits:	
operational, at 4,200 kg (9,259 lb) AUW	+8/−4
ultimate, at 4,200 kg (9,259 lb) AUW	+12
operational, at 5,500 kg (12,125 lb) AUW	+5.2/−2.6

* *A more detailed listing of weight and performance data for earlier versions can be found in the 1982-83 and previous editions*

LET

LET NÁRODNI PODNIK (Let National Corporation)

Uherské Hradiste-Kunovice
Telephone: 411111
Telex: 060387 and 060388
MANAGING DIRECTOR: Ing Stanislav Boura
TECHNICAL DIRECTOR: Ing Zdeněk Karásek
CHIEF DESIGNER: Ing Vlastimil Mertl

The Let plant at Kunovice was established in 1950, its early activities including licence production of the Soviet Yak-11 trainer under the Czechoslovak designation C-11. It is currently responsible for the L-410UVP-E light transport aircraft and development of the larger L-610. The factory also produces equipment for radar and computer technology.

LET L-410UVP-E TURBOLET

Details of the prototypes and initial L-410A, L-410AF and L-410M production versions of the Turbolet can be found in the 1980-81 and earlier editions of *Jane's*. Variants of these included the L-410AS (L-410A with Soviet avionics), the L-410MA (L-410M with M 601 B instead of M 601 A engines), and L-410MU (L-410MA with changes required by Aeroflot).

The L-410UVP, first flown on 1 November 1977, introduced a number of major changes (see previous editions for details). Developed to comply with Soviet NLGS-2 airworthiness regulations (similar to BCAR, class A), it became in 1980 the first non-USSR aircraft to receive a type certificate under these regulations. Stringent Aeroflot requirements included the ability to operate in temperatures ranging from −50°C to +45°C; systems were required to be survivable in temperatures as low as −60°C. Production of the UVP, in four models, ran from early 1979 until late 1985 and totalled 495.

A prototype of the improved L-410UVP-E (OK-120) was flown on 30 December 1984, and this entered production in 1985, replacing the UVP. It received NLGS-2 Soviet certification in March 1986, and Let had delivered 141 examples by 1 January 1988. In this version the rear fuselage is modified by moving the baggage and toilet compartments further aft, creating space for four additional seats without increasing overall length. The wings are reinforced to support two optional streamlined wingtip tanks, enabling range to be increased by more than 40 per cent. Maximum flap deflection is increased compared with the UVP, and the spoilers have two fixed deflection angles: 25° (for use in flight) and 72°. Power plant associated changes include a vacuum sintered oil cooler of new design, an oil-to-fuel heat exchanger on each engine firewall to avoid the need for fuel additives at low ambient temperatures, relocation of the engine fire extinguishing bottles under the port rear wing/fuselage fairing and, on the instrument panel, separate speed indicators for each engine and propeller. Cabin improvements include installation of portable oxygen equipment and an improved PA system; a fire extinguishing system is installed in the nose baggage compartment. The aircraft can be operated in temperatures ranging from −50°C to +50°C. Its design life is 20,000 flying hours or 20,000 landings.

Nearly 800 L-410s of all versions have been produced for civil and military use, the 500th aircraft for the USSR being delivered to Aeroflot in March 1985. Several hundred more are believed to be required by the Soviet Union.

The following description applies to the L-410UVP-E:

TYPE: Twin-turboprop general purpose light transport.

WINGS: Cantilever high-wing monoplane. Wing section NACA 63A418 at root, NACA 63A412 at tip. Dihedral 1° 45′. Incidence 2° at root, −0° 30′ at tip. No sweepback at front spar. Conventional all-metal two-spar torsion box structure, attached to fuselage by four-point mountings. Chemically machined skin with longitudinal reinforcement. Hydraulically actuated two-section double-slotted metal flaps. Spoiler forward of each flap. All-metal ailerons, forward of which are 'pop-up' bank control surfaces that come into operation automatically during single-engine operation and decrease the lift on the side of the running engine. Tab in port aileron. Kléber-Colombes pneumatic de-icing of leading-edges.

FUSELAGE: Conventional all-metal semi-monocoque spot welded and riveted structure, built in three main portions.

TAIL UNIT: Conventional cantilever structure, of all-metal construction except for elevators and rudder, which are fabric covered. Vertical tail surfaces sweptback 35°; shallow dorsal fin and deeper ventral fin. One-piece tailplane, with 7° dihedral from roots, mounted part-way up fin. Balance tab in rudder and each elevator. Kléber-Colombes pneumatic de-icing of leading-edges.

LANDING GEAR: Retractable tricycle type, with single wheel on each unit. Hydraulic retraction, nosewheel forward, mainwheels inward to lie flat in fairing on each side of

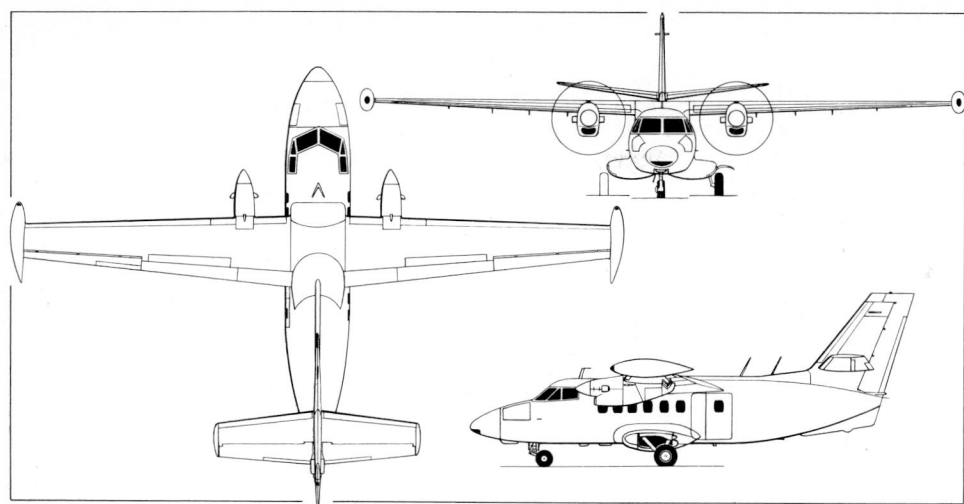

Let L-410UVP-E Turbolet twin-turboprop 19-passenger light transport (*Pilot Press*)

fuselage. Technometra Radotin oleo-pneumatic shock absorbers. Non-braking nosewheel, with servo-assisted steering, fitted with 548 × 221 mm (9.00-6) tubeless tyre, pressure 4.5 bars (65 lb/sq in). Nosewheel is also steerable by rudder pedals. Mainwheels fitted with 718 × 306 mm (12.50-10) tubeless tyres, pressure 4.5 bars (65 lb/sq in). All wheels manufactured by Moravan Otrokovice, tyres by Rudy Rijen, Gottwaldow. Moravan Otrokovice K38-3200.00 hydraulic disc brakes, parking brake and anti-skid units on mainwheels. Metal ski landing gear, with plastics undersurface, optional.

POWER PLANT: Two 559 kW (750 shp) Motorlet Walter M 601 E turboprops, each driving an Avia V 510 five-blade constant-speed reversible-pitch metal propeller with manual and automatic feathering and Beta control. At higher ambient temperatures, engine power can be increased to 603 kW (809 ehp) for short periods by water injection into compressor. De-icing for propeller blades (electrical) and lower intakes (bleed air); anti-icing flaps inside each nacelle. Eight bag fuel tanks in wings, total capacity 1,290 litres (341 US gallons; 284 Imp gallons), plus additional optional 200 litres (52.8 US gallons; 44 Imp gallons) of fuel in each wingtip tank. Fuel system operable after failure of electrical system. Total oil capacity (incl oil in cooler) 22 litres (5.8 US gallons; 4.8 Imp gallons). Water tank capacity (for injection into compressor) 11 litres (2.9 US gallons; 2.4 Imp gallons).

ACCOMMODATION: Crew of one or two on flight deck, with dual controls. Electric de-icing for windscreen. Standard accommodation in main cabin for 19 passengers, with pairs of adjustable seats on starboard side of aisle and single seats opposite, all at 76 cm (30 in) pitch. Baggage compartment (at rear, accessible from cabin), toilet and wardrobe standard. Cabin heated by engine bleed air. Alternative layouts include all-cargo; ambulance, accommodating six stretchers, five sitting patients and a medical attendant; accommodation for 18 parachutists and a dispatcher/instructor; firefighting configuration, carrying 16 firefighters and a pilot/observer. All-cargo version has protective floor covering, crash nets on each side of cabin, and tiedown provisions; floor is at truckbed height. Aircraft can also be equipped for aerial photography or for calibration of ground navigation aids. Double upward opening doors aft on port side, with stowable steps; right hand door serves as passenger entrance and exit. Both doors open for cargo loading, and can be removed for paratroop training missions. Rearward opening door, forward on starboard side, serves as emergency exit.

SYSTEMS: No APU, air-conditioning or pressurisation systems. Duplicated hydraulic systems, No. 1 system actuating landing gear, flaps, spoilers, automatic pitch trim surfaces, mainwheel brakes, nosewheel steering and windscreen wipers. No. 2 system for emergency landing gear extension, flap actuation and parking brake. 28V DC electrical system supplied by two 5.6kW starter/generators, connected for autonomous starting, plus two 25V 25Ah batteries for emergency power. Two input systems for AC power (three-phase 200V/115Hz, variable frequency), incorporating two 3.7kW alternators with alternator control unit. Port alternator provides for windscreen heating, starboard one for propeller blade de-icing. Two static inverters provide three-phase 36V/400Hz AC. Two 115V/400Hz inverters. One three-phase 36V/400Hz static inverter for standby horizon. Two portable oxygen breathing sets on flight deck and two in passenger cabin. Fire extinguishing system for engines and nose baggage compartment.

AVIONICS AND EQUIPMENT: Standard instrumentation provides for flight in IMC conditions, with all basic instruments duplicated and three artificial horizons. Communications include two VHF transceivers with a range of 65 nm (120 km; 75 miles) at 1,000 m (3,280 ft) altitude, passenger address system and crew intercom. Standard instruments include LUN 1205 horizon gyros,

rate of climb indicators, LUN 1215 turn and bank indicator, RMIs, gyro compasses, ILS/SP-50A instrument landing system with marker beacon receiver, dual ARK-22 ADF, A-037 radio altimeter, SO-69 SSR transponder with encoding altimeter, ASI with stall warning, magnetic compass, GMK-1GE VOR, and BUR-1-2G flight data recorder. Cockpit, instrument and passenger cabin lights, navigation lights, three landing lights in nose (each with two levels of light intensity), crew and cabin fire extinguishers, windscreen wipers, and alcohol spray for windscreen and wiper de-icing, are also standard. Weather radar and VZLU autopilot optional.

DIMENSIONS, EXTERNAL:

Wing span: over tip tanks	19.98 m (65 ft 6½ in)
excl tip tanks	19.48 m (63 ft 11 in)
Wing chord at root	2.534 m (8 ft 3¾ in)
Length overall	14.424 m (47 ft 4 in)
Fuselage: Max width	2.08 m (6 ft 10 in)
Max depth	2.10 m (6 ft 10¾ in)
Height overall	5.83 m (19 ft 1½ in)
Tailplane span	6.74 m (22 ft 1¼ in)
Wheel track	3.65 m (11 ft 11½ in)
Wheelbase	3.67 m (12 ft 0¼ in)
Propeller diameter	2.30 m (7 ft 6½ in)
Propeller ground clearance	1.26 m (4 ft 1½ in)
Distance between propeller centres	4.82 m (15 ft 9½ in)
Passenger/cargo door (port, rear):	
Height	1.46 m (4 ft 9½ in)
Width overall	1.25 m (4 ft 1¼ in)
Width (passenger door only)	0.80 m (2 ft 7½ in)
Height to sill	0.70 m (2 ft 3½ in)
Emergency exit door (stbd, fwd):	
Height	0.97 m (3 ft 2¼ in)
Width	0.66 m (2 ft 2 in)
Height to sill	0.80 m (2 ft 7½ in)

DIMENSIONS, INTERNAL:

Cabin, excl flight deck:	
Max width	1.95 m (6 ft 4¾ in)
Max height	1.66 m (5 ft 5¼ in)
Aisle width at 0.4 m (1 ft 3¾ in) above cabin floor	0.34 m (1 ft 1½ in)
Floor area	10.0 m² (107.6 sq ft)
Volume	17.9 m³ (632.1 cu ft)
Baggage compartment volume:	
nose	0.60 m³ (21.19 cu ft)
rear	0.77 m³ (27.19 cu ft)

AREAS:

Wings, gross	35.18 m² (378.67 sq ft)
Ailerons (total)	2.89 m² (31.11 sq ft)
Automatic bank control flaps (total)	0.49 m² (5.27 sq ft)

Trailing-edge flaps (total)	5.92 m² (63.72 sq ft)
Spoilers (total)	0.87 m² (9.36 sq ft)
Fin	4.49 m² (48.33 sq ft)
Rudder, incl tab	2.81 m² (30.25 sq ft)
Tailplane	6.41 m² (69.00 sq ft)
Elevators, incl tabs	3.15 m² (33.91 sq ft)

WEIGHTS AND LOADINGS:

Weight empty	3,985 kg (8,785 lb)
Operating weight empty, equipped	4,160 kg (9,171 lb)
Max fuel	1,300 kg (2,866 lb)
Max payload	1,615 kg (3,560 lb)
Max ramp weight	6,420 kg (14,154 lb)
Max T-O weight	6,400 kg (14,110 lb)
Max zero-fuel weight	5,775 kg (12,732 lb)
Max landing weight	6,200 kg (13,668 lb)
Max wing loading	181.9 kg/m² (37.26 lb/sq ft)
Max power loading	5.38 kg/kW (8.93 lb/ehp)

PERFORMANCE (at max T-O weight):

Never-exceed speed	192 knots (357 km/h; 222 mph) EAS
Max level speed at 4,200 m (13,780 ft)	168 knots (311 km/h; 193 mph) EAS
Max cruising speed at 4,200 m (13,780 ft)	205 knots (380 km/h; 236 mph)
Econ cruising speed at 4,200 m (13,780 ft)	197 knots (365 km/h; 227 mph)
Stalling speed:	
flaps up	84 knots (155 km/h; 97 mph) EAS
flaps down	66 knots (121 km/h; 76 mph) EAS
Max rate of climb at S/L	444 m (1,455 ft)/min
Rate of climb at S/L, one engine out	108 m (354 ft)/min
Service ceiling: practical	6,320 m (20,725 ft)
theoretical	7,050 m (23,125 ft)
Service ceiling, one engine out:	
practical	2,700 m (8,860 ft)
theoretical	3,980 m (13,050 ft)
T-O run	445 m (1,460 ft)
T-O to 10.7 m (35 ft)	685 m (2,250 ft)
Landing from 9 m (30 ft)	480 m (1,575 ft)
Landing run	240 m (787 ft)
Min ground turning radius	13.40 m (43 ft 11½ in)
Range at 4,200 m (13,780 ft), max cruising speed, 30 min reserves:	
with max payload	294 nm (546 km; 339 miles)
with max fuel and 885 kg (1,951 lb) payload	744 nm (1,380 km; 857 miles)

LET L-610

Intended for certification in 1990 under Soviet ENLG-S civil airworthiness requirements, the L-610 is designed for short-haul operations over stage lengths of 216-324 nm (400-600 km; 248-373 miles). It was scheduled to fly for the first time in the second half of 1988.

TYPE: Twin-turboprop transport aircraft.

WINGS: Cantilever high-wing monoplane. Wing sections MS(1)-0318D at root, MS(1)-0312 at tip, with respective thickness/chord ratios of 18.29% and 12%. Dihedral 2°. Incidence 3° 8′ 38.4″ at root, 0° at tip. Sweepback 1° at quarter-chord. All-metal fail-safe stressed skin structure, built of high grade aluminium alloys and high strength steel and incorporating sandwich panels. All-metal horn balanced ailerons and single-slotted Fowler trailing-edge flaps. Spoiler, of sandwich construction, forward of each outer flap segment. Electro-mechanically actuated trim tab in port aileron. Pneumatic de-icing of leading-edges.

FUSELAGE: Pressurised all-metal semi-monocoque structure, incorporating fail-safe principles. Central portion has a constant circular cross-section.

TAIL UNIT: All-metal structure, with sweptback fin and rudder and long dorsal fin. Non-swept tailplane and elevators mounted near top of fin. Trim tab and balance tab in rudder, trim tab and geared tab in each elevator. Pneumatic de-icing of leading-edges.

LANDING GEAR: Retractable tricycle type, with single wheel on each unit. Hydraulic actuation, mainwheels retracting inward to lie flat in fairing each side of fuselage, nosewheel retracting forward. Oleo-pneumatic shock absorber in each unit. Mainwheels are type XK

L-410UVP-E Turbolet twin-turboprop transport, with wingtip tanks and five-blade propellers

34-3000.00, with 1,050 × 390 × 480 mm tyres; type XR 25-1000.00 nosewheel has a 720 × 310 × 254 mm tyre. Hydraulic disc brakes and electronically controlled anti-skid units.

POWER PLANT: Two 1,358 kW (1,822 shp) Motorlet M 602 turboprops, each driving an Avia V-518 five-blade fully-feathering metal propeller with reversible pitch. Fuel in two integral wing tanks, combined capacity 3,500 litres (925 US gallons; 770 Imp gallons). Pressure refuelling point in fuselage, gravity points in wings. Oil capacity 30 litres (7.9 US gallons; 6.6 Imp gallons).

ACCOMMODATION: Crew of two on flight deck, plus one cabin attendant. Standard accommodation for 40 passengers, four-abreast at seat pitch of 75 cm (29.5 in). Aisle width 51 cm (20 in). Galley, two wardrobes, toilet, freight and baggage compartment, all located at rear of cabin. Passenger door at rear of fuselage, freight door at front, both opening outward on port side. Outward opening service door on starboard side, opposite passenger door, serving also as emergency exit; outward opening emergency exit beneath wing on each side. Entire accommodation pressurised and air-conditioned.

SYSTEMS: Bootstrap type air-conditioning system. Max operating cabin pressure differential 0.3 bars (4.35 lb/sq in). Duplicated hydraulic systems, operating at pressure of 210 bars (3,045 lb/sq in). APU for engine starting and auxiliary on-ground and in-flight power. Electrical system powered by two 115/200V 25kVA variable frequency AC generators, plus a third 8kVA 115/200V three-phase AC generator driven by APU. System also includes two 115V 400Hz inverters (each 1.5kVA), two 27V DC transformer-rectifiers (each 4.5kW), and a 25Ah nickel-cadmium battery for APU starting and auxiliary power supply. Portable oxygen equipment for crew and 10 per cent of passengers. Pneumatic de-icing of wing and tail unit leading-edges, engine inlets and oil cooler; electric de-icing of propeller blades, windscreen, pitot static system and horn balances.

AVIONICS AND EQUIPMENT: Equipped with dual 760-channel VHF com, single HF com (optional), intercom, cabin address system, weather radar, blind-flying instrumentation, dual ILS with two LOC/glideslope receivers and two marker beacon receivers, single or dual ADF, Doppler radar, navigation computer, dual compasses, single or dual radio altimeters, transponder, autopilot, voice recorder, flight recorder, and Cat. II approach aids.

DIMENSIONS, EXTERNAL:

Wing span	25.60 m (84 ft 0 in)
Wing chord: at root	2.917 m (9 ft 6⅞ in)
at tip	1.458 m (4 ft 9½ in)
Wing aspect ratio	11.7
Length overall	21.419 m (70 ft 3¼ in)
Fuselage: Length	20.533 m (67 ft 4⅜ in)
Max diameter	2.70 m (8 ft 10¼ in)
Distance between propeller centres	7.00 m (22 ft 11½ in)
Height overall	7.608 m (24 ft 11½ in)
Tailplane span	7.908 m (25 ft 11⅓ in)
Wheel track	4.59 m (15 ft 0¾ in)
Wheelbase	6.596 m (21 ft 7¾ in)
Propeller diameter	3.50 m (11 ft 5¾ in)
Propeller ground clearance	1.64 m (5 ft 4½ in)
Passenger door: Height	1.625 m (5 ft 4 in)
Width	0.76 m (2 ft 6 in)
Height to sill	1.448 m (4 ft 9 in)
Freight door: Height	1.30 m (4 ft 3¼ in)
Width	1.25 m (4 ft 1¼ in)
Height to sill	1.448 m (4 ft 9 in)
Service door: Height	1.286 m (4 ft 2⅔ in)
Width	0.61 m (2 ft 0 in)
Emergency exits (underwing, each):	
Height	0.915 m (3 ft 0 in)
Width	0.515 m (1 ft 8¼ in)

DIMENSIONS, INTERNAL:

Cabin: Length	11.10 m (36 ft 5 in)
Max width	2.54 m (8 ft 4 in)
Width at floor	2.02 m (6 ft 7½ in)
Max height	1.825 m (5 ft 11⅞ in)
Floor area	22.4 m² (241.1 sq ft)
Volume	44.1 m³ (1,557.4 cu ft)
Wardrobe volume (total)	1.0 m³ (35.3 cu ft)
Baggage/freight hold volume (total)	4.3 m³ (151.8 cu ft)

AREAS:

Wings, gross	56.0 m² (602.8 sq ft)
Ailerons (total)	3.27 m² (35.20 sq ft)
Trailing-edge flaps (total)	11.29 m² (121.52 sq ft)
Spoilers (total)	3.54 m² (38.10 sq ft)
Fin	8.30 m² (89.34 sq ft)
Rudder, incl tabs	5.54 m² (59.63 sq ft)
Tailplane	7.68 m² (82.67 sq ft)
Elevators (total, incl tabs)	5.82 m² (62.65 sq ft)

WEIGHTS AND LOADINGS:

Weight empty, equipped	8,730 kg (19,246 lb)
Operating weight empty	9,000 kg (19,841 lb)
Max fuel	2,650 kg (5,842 lb)
Max payload	3,800 kg (8,377 lb)
Max T-O weight	14,000 kg (30,865 lb)
Max ramp weight	14,040 kg (30,953 lb)
Max landing weight	13,500 kg (29,762 lb)
Max zero-fuel weight	12,800 kg (28,219 lb)
Max wing loading	250 kg/m² (51.2 lb/sq ft)
Max power loading	5.147 kg/kW (8.47 lb/shp)

PERFORMANCE (estimated at max T-O weight):

Never-exceed speed	216 knots (400 km/h; 248 mph) EAS
Max level and max cruising speed at 7,200 m (23,620 ft)	264 knots (490 km/h; 304 mph)
Long-range cruising speed at 7,200 m (23,620 ft)	220 knots (408 km/h; 253 mph)
Approach speed	92 knots (170 km/h; 106 mph)
Stalling speed:	
flaps up	93 knots (172 km/h; 107 mph) EAS
flaps down	75 knots (139 km/h; 87 mph) EAS
Max rate of climb at S/L	570 m (1,870 ft)/min
Rate of climb at S/L, one engine out	150 m (492 ft)/min
Service ceiling:	
theoretical	10,750 m (35,270 ft)
practical	10,250 m (33,630 ft)
Service ceiling, one engine out (30.5 m; 100 ft/min rate of climb):	
theoretical	4,750 m (15,585 ft)
practical	3,980 m (13,060 ft)
Min ground turning radius	18.33 m (60 ft 1¾ in)
T-O run	370 m (1,214 ft)
T-O to 10.7 m (35 ft)	613 m (2,011 ft)
Balanced T-O distance	752 m (2,467 ft)
Balanced T-O field length:	
hard runway	875 m (2,870 ft)
unpaved surface	1,030 m (3,380 ft)
Landing from 9 m (30 ft)	545 m (1,788 ft)
Landing run	340 m (1,115 ft)
Range, reserves for 45 min hold:	
with max payload	469 nm (870 km; 540 miles)
with max fuel	1,298 nm (2,406 km; 1,495 miles)

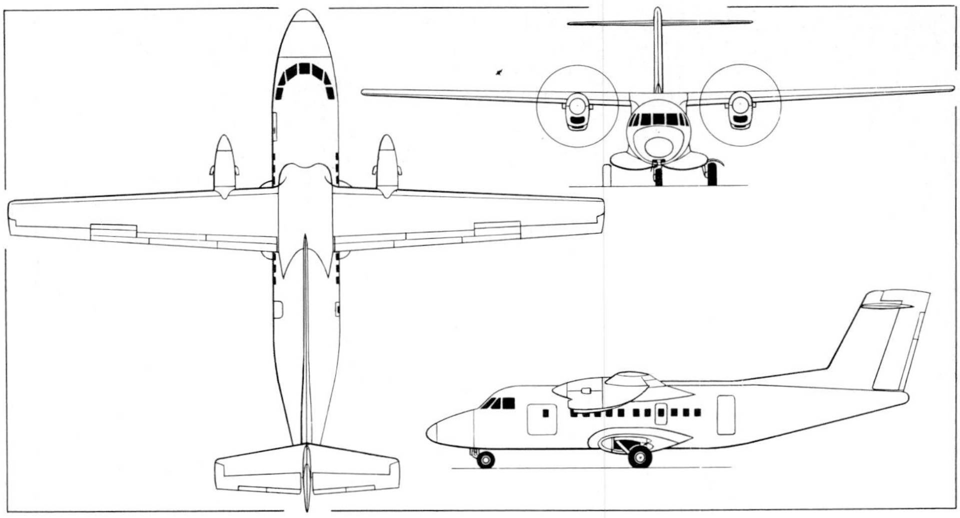

Let L-610 twin-turboprop 40-seat commuter transport *(Pilot Press)*

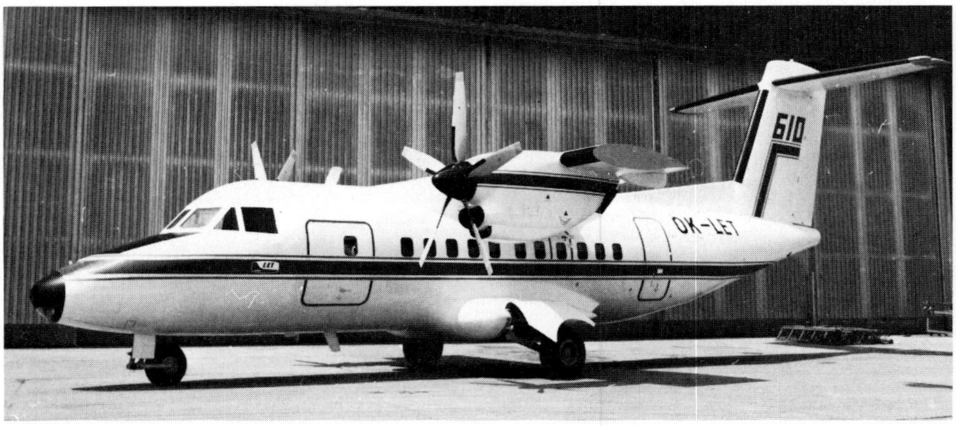

Full scale mockup of the Let L-610 (two Motorlet M 602 turboprops), the prototype of which was due to make its first flight in 1988

ZLIN

MORAVAN NÁRODNÍ PODNIK (Zlin Aircraft Moravan National Corporation)

76581 Otrokovice

Telephone: Gottwaldov 92 2041/44

Telex: Gottwaldov 067 240

MANAGING DIRECTOR: Ing Josef Panáček

CHIEF DESIGNER: Ing Vojtěch Vraj

VICE-DIRECTOR, SALES: František Mužný

The Moravan Company was formed on 18 September 1934 as Zlinská Letecká Akciová Spolecnost (Zlin Aviation Joint Stock Co) in Zlin, although manufacture of Zlin aircraft was actually started in 1933 by the Masarykova Letecká Liga (Masaryk League of Aviation). The factory was renamed Moravan after the Second World War. Moravan also manufactures items of aircraft equipment.

ZLIN 142

The Zlin 142 is employed for basic and advanced flying training, aerobatic flying and the training of aerobatic pilots, glider towing, and (when equipped with appropriate instrumentation) for night and IFR flying training. It is a progressive development of the Zlin 42 M (1980-81 *Jane's*), and first flew on 29 December 1978. In 1980 it received FAR Pt 23 certification in the Aerobatic, Utility and Normal categories, and production began in 1981. A total of 240 had been built by 1 January 1988. Exports have been made to Cuba, Germany (Democratic and Federal Republics), Hungary, Poland and Romania.

TYPE: Two-seat fully aerobatic (A), light training (U) and touring (N) aircraft.

WINGS: Cantilever low-wing monoplane. Wing section NACA $63_2416.5$. Dihedral 6° from roots. Sweepforward 4° 20′ at quarter-chord. All-metal structure with single main spar and auxiliary spar; skins (fluted on control surfaces) of aluminium plated duralumin sheet. All-metal slotted ailerons and flaps all have same dimensions. Mass balanced flaps and ailerons, operated mechanically by control rods. Ground adjustable tab on each aileron.

FUSELAGE: Engine cowlings of sheet metal. Centre-fuselage of welded steel tube truss construction, covered with laminated glassfibre panels. Rear fuselage is all-metal semi-monocoque structure.

TAIL UNIT: Cantilever all-metal structure with skins (fluted on control surfaces) of duralumin sheet. Control surfaces have partial mass and aerodynamic balance. Trim tabs on elevator and rudder. Rudder actuated by control cables, elevator by control rods.

LANDING GEAR: Non-retractable tricycle type, with nosewheel offset to port. Oleo-pneumatic nosewheel shock absorber. Mainwheels carried on flat spring steel legs. Nosewheel steered by rudder pedals. Mainwheels and Barum tyres size 420 × 150, pressure 1.90 bars (27.6

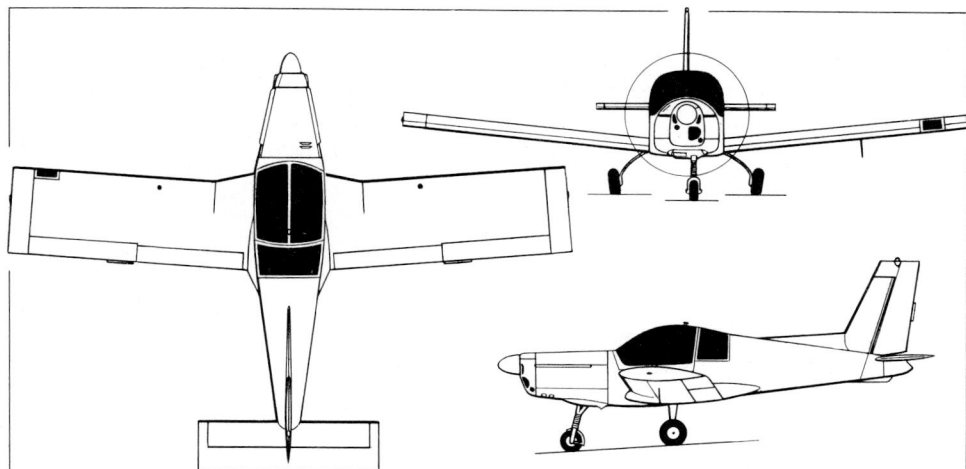

Photograph and three-view drawing *(Pilot Press)* **of the two-seat Zlin 142**

lb/sq in); nosewheel and Barum tyre size 350 × 135, pressure 2.50 bars (36.3 lb/sq in). Hydraulic disc brakes on mainwheels can be operated from either seat. Parking brake standard.

POWER PLANT: One 156.5 kW (210 hp) Avia M 337 AK inverted six-cylinder aircooled inline engine, with supercharger and low-pressure injection pump, driving a two-blade Avia V 500 A constant-speed metal propeller. Fuel tanks in each wing leading-edge, with combined capacity of 125 litres (33 US gallons; 27.5 Imp gallons). Normal category version has auxiliary 50 litre (13.2 US gallon; 11 Imp gallon) tank at each wingtip, increasing total fuel capacity to 225 litres (59.4 US gallons; 49.5 Imp gallons). Fuel and oil systems permit inverted flying for up to 3 min. Oil capacity 12 litres (3.2 US gallons; 2.6 Imp gallons).

ACCOMMODATION: Individual side by side seats for two persons, the main pilot's seat being to port. Both seats are adjustable and permit the use of back type parachutes. Baggage space aft of seats. Cabin and windscreen heating and ventilation standard. Forward sliding cockpit canopy. Dual controls standard.

SYSTEMS: Electrical system includes a 600W 27V engine driven generator and 24V 25Ah Teledyne battery. External power source can be used for starting the engine.

AVIONICS AND EQUIPMENT: VHF radio with IC (Mesit LUN 3524.20) and IFR instrumentation optional. Standard equipment includes cockpit, instrument and cabin lights; navigation lights; landing and taxying lights; and anti-collision light. Towing gear, for gliders of up to 500 kg (1,102 lb) weight, optional.

DIMENSIONS, EXTERNAL:

Wing span	9.16 m (30 ft 0½ in)
Wing aspect ratio	6.4
Wing chord (constant portion)	1.42 m (4 ft 8 in)
Length overall	7.33 m (24 ft 0½ in)
Height overall	2.75 m (9 ft 0¼ in)
Elevator span	2.904 m (9 ft 6⅓ in)
Wheel track	2.33 m (7 ft 7¾ in)
Wheelbase	1.66 m (5 ft 5¼ in)
Propeller diameter	2.00 m (6 ft 6¾ in)
Propeller ground clearance	0.40 m (1 ft 3¾ in)

DIMENSIONS, INTERNAL:

Cabin: Length	1.80 m (5 ft 10¾ in)
Max width	1.12 m (3 ft 8 in)
Max height	1.20 m (3 ft 11¼ in)
Baggage space	0.2 m³ (7.1 cu ft)

AREAS:

Wings, gross	13.15 m² (141.5 sq ft)

Ailerons (total)	1.408 m² (15.16 sq ft)
Trailing-edge flaps (total)	1.408 m² (15.16 sq ft)
Fin	0.54 m² (5.81 sq ft)
Rudder, incl tab	0.81 m² (8.72 sq ft)
Tailplane	1.23 m² (13.24 sq ft)
Elevator, incl tabs	1.36 m² (14.64 sq ft)

WEIGHTS AND LOADINGS (A: Aerobatic; U: Utility; N: Normal category):

Basic weight empty (all versions)	730 kg (1,609 lb)
Max T-O weight: A	970 kg (2,138 lb)
U	1,020 kg (2,248 lb)
N	1,090 kg (2,403 lb)
Max landing weight: A	970 kg (2,138 lb)
U	1,020 kg (2,248 lb)
N	1,050 kg (2,315 lb)
Max wing loading: A	73.76 kg/m² (15.11 lb/sq ft)
U	77.57 kg/m² (15.89 lb/sq ft)
N	82.89 kg/m² (16.98 lb/sq ft)

Max power loading: A		6.19 kg/kW (10.17 lb/hp)
U		6.51 kg/kW (10.69 lb/hp)
N		6.96 kg/kW (11.43 lb/hp)

PERFORMANCE (at max T-O weight):

Never-exceed speed (all versions)		179 knots (333 km/h; 206 mph) IAS
Max level speed at 500 m (1,640 ft):		
A, U		125 knots (231 km/h; 143 mph)
N		122 knots (227 km/h; 141 mph)
Max cruising speed at 500 m (1,640 ft):		
A, U		106 knots (197 km/h; 122 mph)
N		102 knots (190 km/h; 118 mph)
Econ cruising speed at 500 m (1,640 ft):		
A		97 knots (180 km/h; 112 mph)
Stalling speed, flaps up:		
A		56 knots (103 km/h; 64 mph) IAS
U		58 knots (107 km/h; 67 mph) IAS
N		60 knots (110 km/h; 69 mph) IAS
Stalling speed, T-O flap setting:		
A		54 knots (99 km/h; 62 mph) IAS
U		56 knots (102 km/h; 64 mph) IAS
N		57 knots (105 km/h; 66 mph) IAS
Stalling speed, flaps down:		
A		48 knots (88 km/h; 55 mph) IAS
U		50 knots (91 km/h; 57 mph) IAS
N		52 knots (95 km/h; 60 mph) IAS
Max rate of climb at S/L, ISA:		
A		330 m (1,082 ft)/min
U		306 m (1,004 ft)/min
N		264 m (866 ft)/min
Service ceiling: A		5,000 m (16,400 ft)
U		4,700 m (15,425 ft)
N		4,300 m (14,100 ft)
T-O run: A		220 m (722 ft)
T-O to 15 m (50 ft): A		440 m (1,444 ft)
U		475 m (1,560 ft)
N		540 m (1,772 ft)
Landing from 15 m (50 ft): A		400 m (1,313 ft)
U		425 m (1,395 ft)
N		460 m (1,510 ft)
Landing run: A		190 m (624 ft)
Range at max cruising speed:		
A, U		283 nm (525 km; 326 miles)
N		513 nm (950 km; 590 miles)
Max range: N	566 nm (1,050 km; 652 miles)	
g limits: A		+6/−3.5
U		+5/−3
N		+3.8/−1.5

ZLIN Z 50 L

Full details of the original **Z 50 L**, with 194 kW (260 hp) Textron Lycoming AEIO-540-D4B5 engine, can be found in the 1982-83 *Jane's*. Series production is continuing of the more powerful **Z 50 LS**, and of the **Z 50 LA**, which is a modified L with propeller pitch control and a propeller speed governor. The LS was flown for the first time on 29 June 1981, and in the following year received FAR Pt 23 certification in the Aerobatic and Normal categories. It won the European Aerobatic Championships in 1983 and the World Championships in 1984 and 1986; in 1985 it came 1st and 2nd in the European Championships, and won nine of the first 22 places. A total of 50 Z 50 L, LA and LS had been delivered by 1 January 1988.

The following description applies to the Z 50 LS:

TYPE: Single-seat aerobatic aircraft.

WINGS: Cantilever low-wing monoplane. Wing section NACA 0018 at root, NACA 0012 at tip. Dihedral 1° 7′ 24″. All-metal structure, with single continuous main spar, rear auxiliary spar, and aluminium-clad duralumin

Zlin Z 50 LS single-seat aerobatic light aircraft

skin. All-metal mass balanced ailerons, actuated by pushrods, occupy most of each trailing-edge. Ground adjustable tab on port outer aileron; automatic trim tab on each inboard aileron. No flaps. Provision for fitting wingtip fuel tanks for cross-country flights.

FUSELAGE: All-metal semi-monocoque structure with stressed duralumin skin.

TAIL UNIT: Conventional metal structure. Braced tailplane and fin duralumin covered, elevators and rudder fabric covered. One mechanically adjustable balance tab and one automatic trim tab on elevators; automatic balance tab on rudder. Elevators actuated by pushrods, rudder by cables.

LANDING GEAR: Non-retractable tailwheel type. Mainwheels carried on flat-spring titanium cantilever legs. Mechanical mainwheel brakes actuated by rudder pedals. Fully castoring tailwheel, with flat-spring shock absorption, has automatic locking device to maintain aircraft on a straight track during taxying, take-off and landing. Mainwheel tyres size 350 × 135 mm, pressure 2.5 bars (36 lb/sq in); tailwheel tyre size 200 × 80 mm, pressure 1.0 bar (14.5 lb/sq in). Mainwheel fairings optional.

POWER PLANT: One 224 kW (300 hp) Textron Lycoming AEIO-540-L1B5D flat-six engine, driving a Hoffmann HO-V123K-V/200AH three-blade constant-speed wooden propeller with spinner. Single main fuel tank in fuselage, aft of firewall, capacity 60 litres (15.9 US gallons; 13.2 Imp gallons). Auxiliary 50 litre (13.2 US gallon; 11 Imp gallon) tank can be attached to each wingtip for cross-country flights only. Fuel and oil systems designed for full aerobatic manoeuvres, including inverted flight. Oil capacity 12 litres (3.2 US gallons; 2.6 Imp gallons).

ACCOMMODATION: Single seat under fully transparent sideways opening (to starboard) bubble canopy, which can be jettisoned in an emergency. Seat and backrest are adjustable, and permit the use of a back type parachute. Cockpit ventilated by sliding panel in canopy.

SYSTEM: Electrical system includes an alternator as main power source and a Varley battery. External power socket in fuselage side for engine starting.

AVIONICS: VHF radio optional.

DIMENSIONS, EXTERNAL:

Wing span	8.58 m (28 ft 1¾ in)
Wing span over tip tanks	9.03 m (29 ft 7½ in)
Wing chord: at root	1.73 m (5 ft 8¼ in)
at tip	1.21 m (3 ft 11¾ in)
Wing aspect ratio	5.9
Length overall (tail up)	6.62 m (21 ft 8¾ in)
Height over tail (static)	2.075 m (6 ft 9¾ in)
Elevator span	3.44 m (11 ft 3½ in)
Wheel track	1.90 m (6 ft 2¾ in)
Wheelbase	5.05 m (16 ft 7 in)
Propeller diameter	2.00 m (6 ft 6¾ in)
Propeller ground clearance (tail up)	0.31 m (1 ft 0¼ in)

AREAS:

Wings, gross	12.50 m^2 (134.55 sq ft)
Ailerons (total)	2.80 m^2 (30.14 sq ft)
Fin	0.59 m^2 (6.35 sq ft)
Rudder, incl tab	0.81 m^2 (8.72 sq ft)
Tailplane	1.66 m^2 (17.87 sq ft)
Elevators (total, incl tabs)	1.20 m^2 (12.92 sq ft)

WEIGHTS AND LOADINGS (A: Aerobatic, N: Normal category):

Weight empty: A	600 kg (1,322 lb)
N	610 kg (1,345 lb)
Max T-O weight: A	760 kg (1,675 lb)
N	840 kg (1,852 lb)
Max wing loading: A	60.8 kg/m^2 (12.45 lb/sq ft)
N	67.2 kg/m^2 (13.76 lb/sq ft)
Max power loading: A	3.40 kg/kW (5.58 lb/hp)
N	3.75 kg/kW (6.17 lb/hp)

PERFORMANCE (at max Aerobatic T-O weight):

Never-exceed speed	181 knots (337 km/h; 209 mph) CAS
Max level speed at 500 m (1,640 ft), ISA	166 knots (308 km/h; 191 mph)
Max cruising speed at 500 m (1,640 ft), ISA	148 knots (275 km/h; 171 mph)
Stalling speed, engine idling	56 knots (103 km/h; 81 mph) CAS
Max rate of climb at S/L, ISA	840 m (2,755 ft)/min
Service ceiling, ISA	8,175 m (26,820 ft)
T-O run	150 m (492 ft)
T-O to 15 m (50 ft)	300 m (985 ft)
Landing from 15 m (50 ft)	530 m (1,740 ft)
Landing run	300 m (985 ft)
g limits: A	+8/−6
N	+3.8/−1.5

ZLIN Z 50 M

Intended as a successor to the Z 526AFS Akrobat (1975-76 *Jane's*), the Z 50 M has a longer and slimmer nose than the L series, accommodating a 134 kW (180 hp) Avia M 137 AZ six-cylinder inline engine driving an Avia V 503 A constant-speed propeller. First flight was expected in 1988, with certification due in 1989.

DIMENSIONS, EXTERNAL:

Wing span	8.58 m (28 ft 1¾ in)
Length overall	6.96 m (22 ft 10 in)

WEIGHTS:

Weight empty	560 kg (1,235 lb)
Max T-O weight	700 kg (1,543 lb)

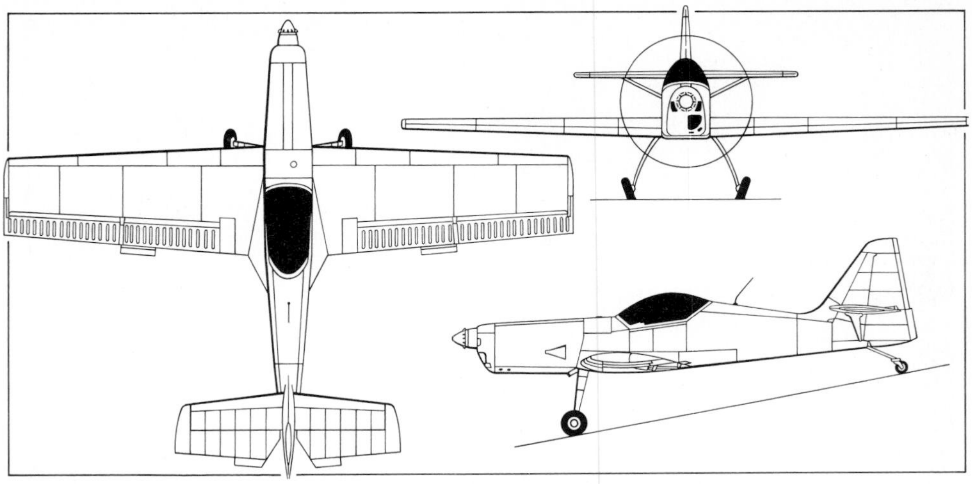

General arrangement of the new Zlin 50 M single-seat aerobatic aircraft *(Jane's/Mike Keep)*

PERFORMANCE (estimated):

Max level speed at 500 m (1,640 ft)	151 knots (280 km/h; 174 mph)
Max cruising speed at 500 m (1,640 ft)	137 knots (254 km/h; 158 mph)
Stalling speed	54 knots (100 km/h; 63 mph)
Max rate of climb at S/L	600 m (1,970 ft)/min
Service ceiling	7,000 m (22,975 ft)
T-O run	220 m (722 ft)
T-O to 15 m (50 ft)	370 m (1,214 ft)
Landing from 15 m (50 ft)	550 m (1,805 ft)
g limits	+7/−4.5

ZLIN Z 37T AGRO TURBO

The piston engined Z-37A Cmelák (Bumble-bee) agricultural aircraft, of which more than 700 were built by Let (651 plus 26 two-seaters) and Moravan, was last described in the 1976-77 *Jane's*. Let then built an XZ-37T prototype (OK-146) of a turboprop version, powered by a 515 kW (691 shp) Walter M 601 B engine, which flew for the first time on 6 September 1981. Brief details of this prototype appeared in the 1982-83 *Jane's*.

In 1982 Moravan began the design and construction of a lower powered turbine engined version known as the Z 37T. Two prototypes (OK-072 and OK-074) made their first flights on 12 July and 29 December 1983; a third was completed in 1985. Certification under BCAR Section K was received in 1984, followed by the start of series production in 1985. First delivery of a production aircraft, to Slov-Air for operational trials, was made in 1985, and 28 had been delivered to this operator by 1 January 1988.

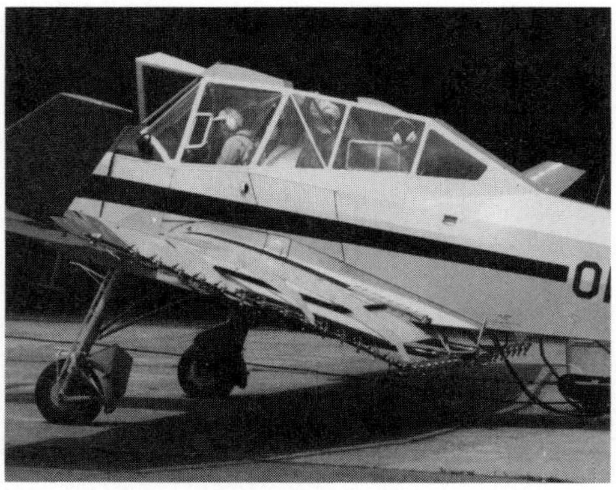

Close-up of Z 37T-2 tandem cockpits

A two-seat **Z 37T-2**, for training agricultural pilots, was certificated in 1986.

TYPE: Single/two-seat agricultural aircraft.

WINGS: Cantilever low-wing monoplane. Wing section NACA 33015 at root, NACA 44012A at tip. Dihedral 7° on outer panels only. Incidence 3° at root, 0° at tip. All-metal single-spar structure, with auxiliary rear spar, comprising centre-section, built integrally with fuselage, and two outer panels. Linen covered duralumin ailerons, each with ground adjustable tab. All-metal duralumin skinned double-slotted trailing-edge flaps. Leading-edge fixed slats. Outward canted winglet at each tip.

FUSELAGE: Welded steel tube structure, with part-metal, part-linen covering.

TAIL UNIT: Cantilever all-metal two-spar structure, with fabric covering on control surfaces. Elevator aerodynamically and mass balanced. Trim tabs in rudder and centre of elevator, latter controlled from cockpit.

LANDING GEAR: Non-retractable tailwheel type, with Technometra oleo-pneumatic mainwheel shock absorbers, Moravan light alloy wheels and Barum tyres. Steerable tailwheel. Mainwheel tyres size 556 × 163 × 254 mm, tailwheel tyre size 290 × 110 mm; pressure 3.45 bars (50 lb/sq in) on all units. Moravan hydraulic drum brakes on mainwheels.

POWER PLANT: One 365 kW (490 shp) Motorlet Walter M 601 Z turboprop, driving an Avia VJ7-508Z three-blade constant-speed propeller. Two metal fuel tanks in wing centre-section, combined capacity 350 litres (92.5 US gallons; 77 Imp gallons). Fuel can be transported to distant airstrips in four auxiliary tanks with a combined capacity of 500 litres (132 US gallons; 110 Imp gallons). Gravity refuelling point in top of each wing. Oil capacity 7 litres (1.8 US gallons; 1.5 Imp gallons). Air intake filter.

ACCOMMODATION: Pilot in enclosed cockpit, with forward opening window/door on starboard side. Auxiliary seat to rear for one passenger (mechanic or loader). Cockpit heated, and provided with filtered fresh air intake, contoured seat with headrest, rearview mirror and windscreen wiper and washer. Door can be jettisoned in an emergency. Two-seat training version available.

SYSTEMS: Pneumatic system of 50 bars (725 lb/sq in) pressure, reduced to 30 bars (435 lb/sq in) for agricultural equipment and flaps. Electrical power supplied by 28V 5.6kW DC starter/generator.

AVIONICS AND EQUIPMENT: LUN 3524 VHF radio standard. Hopper/tank capacity (max) 1,000 litres (264 US gallons; 220 Imp gallons) of liquid or 900 kg (1,984 lb) of dry chemical. Distribution system for both liquid and dry chemicals is operated pneumatically. Chemicals can be jettisoned in 5 s in emergency. Steel cable cutter on windscreen and each mainwheel leg; steel deflector cable

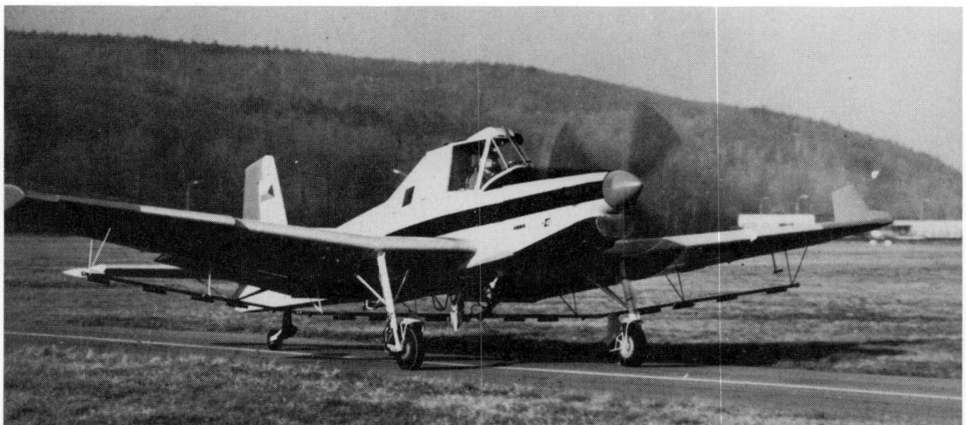

Zlin Z 37T Agro Turbo fitted with underwing spraybars

runs from tip of windscreen cable cutter to tip of fin. Windscreen washer and wiper standard. Other equipment includes gyro compass, clock, rearview mirror, second (mechanic's) seat, cockpit air-conditioning, ventilation and heating, and anti-collision light. Can be modified for firefighting role.

DIMENSIONS, EXTERNAL:
Wing span	13.63 m (44 ft 8½ in)
Wing chord: at root	2.39 m (7 ft 10 in)
at tip	1.224 m (4 ft 0¼ in)
Wing aspect ratio	7.0
Length overall (flying attitude)	10.46 m (34 ft 4 in)
Fuselage: Max width	1.70 m (5 ft 7 in)
Height overall	3.505 m (11 ft 6 in)
Elevator span	5.294 m (17 ft 4½ in)
Wheel track	3.30 m (10 ft 10 in)
Wheelbase	6.375 m (20 ft 11 in)
Propeller diameter	2.50 m (8 ft 2½ in)
Propeller ground clearance (min)	0.45 m (1 ft 5¾ in)

AREAS:
Wings, gross	26.69 m² (287.3 sq ft)
Ailerons (total)	2.428 m² (26.13 sq ft)
Trailing-edge flaps (total)	4.37 m² (47.04 sq ft)
Fin	1.185 m² (12.76 sq ft)
Rudder, incl tab	1.054 m² (11.35 sq ft)
Tailplane	2.776 m² (29.88 sq ft)
Elevator, incl tab	3.008 m² (32.38 sq ft)

WEIGHTS AND LOADINGS:
Weight empty with basic agricultural equipment	1,250 kg (2,756 lb)
Max payload	900 kg (1,984 lb)
Max fuel	280 kg (617 lb)
Max T-O weight: ferry flights	2,260 kg (4,982 lb)
agricultural, forestry and waterways work	2,525 kg (5,566 lb)
Max zero-fuel weight	2,250 kg (4,960 lb)
Max wing loading	89.9 kg/m² (18.41 lb/sq ft)
Max power loading	6.67 kg/kW (10.95 lb/shp)

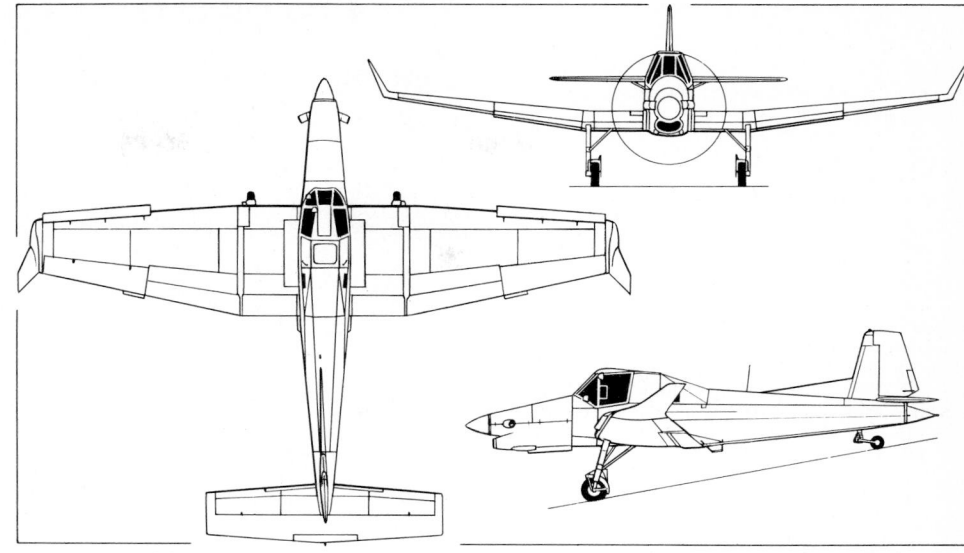

Zlin Z 37T Agro Turbo agricultural aircraft (Motorlet M 601 Z turboprop) *(Pilot Press)*

PERFORMANCE (at 2,525 kg; 5,566 lb max T-O weight):
Never-exceed speed	153 knots (285 km/h; 177 mph)
Max level speed at 500 m (1,640 ft)	118 knots (218 km/h; 135 mph)
Max cruising speed at 500 m (1,640 ft)	103 knots (190 km/h; 118 mph)
Working speed	78-89 knots (145-165 km/h; 90-103 mph)
Stalling speed:	
flaps up	48 knots (88 km/h; 55 mph)
flaps down	42 knots (77 km/h; 48 mph)
Max rate of climb at S/L	252 m (827 ft)/min
T-O run	265 m (870 ft)
T-O to 15 m (50 ft)	580 m (1,905 ft)
Landing from 15 m (50 ft)	720 m (2,365 ft)
Landing run	300 m (985 ft)
Range with max fuel	188 nm (350 km; 217 miles)
Swath width: granules	30 m (98 ft)
liquid	40 m (131 ft)
g limits	+3.2/−1.28

EGYPT

AOI
ARAB ORGANISATION FOR INDUSTRIALISATION
PO Box 770, Cairo
CHAIRMAN: Ahmed Zendou

Aircraft Factory (36), Helwan
CHAIRMAN: Ahmed Heiba

Engine Factory (135), Helwan
CHAIRMAN: Hassen El Gebali

Kader Factory (72), Heliopolis
SAKR Factory (333), Heliopolis
Avionics Factory

SUBSIDIARIES:
Arab American Vehicle Co (AAVCo)
Arab British Dynamics Co (ABDCo)
Arab British Engine Co (ABECo), Helwan
Arab British Helicopter Co (ABHCo)

The AOI was set up in November 1975 by Egypt, Saudi Arabia, Qatar and the United Arab Emirates, to provide the basis for an Arab military industry. The main centres of production are in the Cairo area, using and building upon the extensive facilities already existing.

Recently, the AOI has been engaged in several important aircraft, aero engine and other military programmes. It is organised into five divisions, which between them have a workforce of about 20,000 people, including approximately 3,000 employed in its four subsidiaries. Rockets, missiles and other weapons are produced by the SAKR Factory (except for the Swingfire programme, which is managed by ABDCo).

The main AOI centre is at Helwan, south of Cairo.

Embraer Tucano of the Iraqi Air Force Academy *(Ivo Sturzenegger)*

Helwan air base is the Egyptian Air Force centre for all major aircraft overhaul and maintenance, as well as its headquarters for maintenance and repair training. Nearby is a large industrial complex, the chief elements of which are an aircraft factory (No. 36) and an aero-engine factory (No. 135), with 3,000 and 3,500 employees respectively. Helwan also accommodates the Arab British Helicopter Company and Arab British Engine Company. By 'reverse engineering', ABECo has also manufactured components for, and overhauled, Soviet TV2-117A turboshaft engines for Egypt's Mil Mi-8 helicopter fleet.

Details of the AOI Gazelle and Alpha Jet programmes can be found in the 1986-87 *Jane's*. Other more recent aircraft and engine programmes are as follows:

Aérospatiale Super Puma. Protocol signed on 10 November 1983, providing for component manufacture (now in progress) and possible ultimate assembly.

Dassault-Breguet Falcon 50. Component manufacture.

Dassault-Breguet Mirage 2000. Egyptian Air Force has received 20 (French built), and has a further 20 on option. Some components for first batch are of Egyptian manufacture; first deliveries made in second half of 1986. Egyptian assembly (possibly from 27th aircraft onward) may be undertaken in second batch.

Embraer EMB-312 Tucano. October 1983 contract for 120 Tucanos (80 for Iraq, 40 for Egypt), of which first ten were delivered complete by Embraer. Remainder being assembled from Brazilian built kits; PT6A-25 engines for these aircraft also being assembled in Egypt. Deliveries of Egyptian assembled Tucanos to the Egyptian Air Force began with three aircraft in November 1985, and totalled 42 by 1 January 1987. Contract includes option for further 60 (Egypt 40, Iraq 20).

ETHIOPIA

EAL
ETHIOPIAN AIRLINES CORPORATION
PO Box 1755, Addis Ababa
Telephone: 182222
Telex: 21012 ETHAIR ADDIS
GENERAL MANAGER: Capt Mohammed Ahmed
DEPUTY GENERAL MANAGER (MARKETING):
Wolde Gabriel Tsehay

Under licence from Schweizer Aircraft Corporation in the USA (which see), Ethiopian Airlines is assembling for domestic use and eventual export the latter's **Ag-Cat Super B Turbine** agricultural aircraft. Initial output is at the rate of 12 aircraft a year, the first example (ET-AIY *Eshet*) having been rolled out on 20 December 1986. EAC has the sole rights to build, market and service this aircraft throughout the African continent with the exceptions of Algeria, Tunisia and South Africa.

First Ethiopian assembled example of the Schweizer Ag-Cat Super B Turbine

FINLAND

VALMET
VALMET AVIATION INDUSTRIES
35600 Halli
Telephone: (358) 42 8291
Telex: 28269 VALKU SF
Fax: (358) 42 829667
GENERAL MANAGER: Juhani Mäkinen
MARKETING: Per Falenius

Valmet Aviation Industries continues the traditions of Ilmailuvoimien Lentokonetehdas, established in 1921, and was formerly a part of the Valmet Oy Tampere factory group. It is the largest aircraft industry establishment in Finland. Since 1922, Valmet Aviation Industries and its predecessors have built 30 different types of aircraft, of which 18 have been of Finnish design. Valmet was responsible for assembly of the 12 Saab 35XS Drakens ordered by Finland in 1970 and 46 of the 50 BAe Hawk Mk 51 jet trainers and their Adour Mk 851 jet engines, purchased by the Finnish Air Force in December 1977.

Current activities include the overhaul and repair of military and civil aircraft, piston engines and instruments. The factory has a covered production area of approximately 18,000 m² (193,750 sq ft) and a workforce of 607 people. Linnavuori Works, at Siuro, is concerned primarily with the overhaul and repair of aircraft jet engines.

The latest aircraft of Finnish design to be built by Valmet is the L-90 TP Redigo turboprop primary and basic trainer.

An agreement to participate in licence production of derivatives of the Avtek 400 (see US section) was signed on 20 March 1985. These would include versions for such duties as surveillance, coastal patrol, geophysical research and liaison.

VALMET L-90 TP REDIGO
The L-90 TP is developed from, and is slightly larger than, the L-70 (1986-87 *Jane's*), from which it differs primarily in having a turboprop power plant, new wings and retractable landing gear. The first prototype (OH-VTP) made its initial flight on 1 July 1986. Valmet first flew the second prototype (OH-VTM) in early December 1987, powered by a 373 kW (500 shp) Turbomeca TP 319 turboprop, derated to 313 kW (420 shp), instead of the Allison 250 of the first prototype. This engine, and a West German (Becker) avionics fit, will be offered on production Redigos. With the TP 319, the Redigo has a more compact nose contour.

Suitable for primary and basic flying training, aerobatic training, night and instrument flight training, tactical training, observation and liaison missions, the Redigo is designed to fit a training system that can produce combat-ready pilots within minimum time and cost levels, students proceeding directly from the L-90 TP to a demanding advanced trainer such as the BAe Hawk used by the Finnish Air Force. Additional roles can include search and rescue, weapons training, photographic reconnaissance and target towing. An alternative wing, built of Kevlar and carbonfibre, has been successfully fatigue tested; its development is continuing.

Certification of the Redigo was expected to be awarded by the Summer of 1988.

TYPE: Two/four-seat multi-purpose military primary and basic training aircraft, designed to airworthiness requirements of FAR Pt 23 and BCAR Section K. Minimum fatigue life of 10,000 flight hours (fatigue spectrum MIL-A-8866B), and 30,000 landings in heavy military use.

WINGS: Cantilever low-wing monoplane of tapered planform, with forward-swept inboard leading-edges. Wing section NACA 63-218 (Mod B3) at root, NACA 63-412

Second prototype of the Valmet L-90 TP Redigo two/four-seat multi-stage military trainer

(mod B3) at tip. Dihedral 6° from roots. Incidence 3° at root; −3° washout at tip. Fail-safe structure comprising main spar, auxiliary spar, ribs and stringers, bolted to fuselage. Construction mainly of aluminium alloy, with riveted skin (fluted on flaps and ailerons). In-wing fuel tanks are of Valmet load bearing sandwich construction. Wingroot fairings are of CFRP, wingtips of glassfibre. All-metal single-slotted trailing-edge flaps, actuated electrically by screwjack. Ailerons, also all-metal, are of modified Frise type, mass balanced, and actuated by cables. Geared tab and spring tab in each aileron; starboard geared tab can be operated also as a trim tab.

FUSELAGE: Conventional aluminium alloy semi-monocoque fail-safe structure of frames and longerons, with riveted skin; CFRP and glassfibre used in tailcone and engine cowling panels.

TAIL UNIT: Cantilever aluminium alloy structure, with riveted skin (fluted on fin, rudder and elevators). CFRP dorsal fin. Fin and rudder sweptback; horizontal surfaces non-swept. Elevators and rudder horn balanced and cable operated. Geared tab in rudder and each elevator, all three operable also as trim tabs.

LANDING GEAR: AP Precision Hydraulics electro-hydraulically retractable tricycle type, with single wheel and oleo-pneumatic shock absorber on each unit. Nosewheel, which is centred by a spring, retracts rearward; main units retract inward into wings. Spring assisted lowering of all units in event of emergency. Mainwheel tyres size 17.5 × 6.3-6.0 in, pressure 3.79 bars (55 lb/sq in); nosewheel tyre size 14.2 × 4.95-5.0 in, pressure 3.45 bars (50 lb/sq in). Differential brakes on mainwheels. Parking brake.

POWER PLANT: One Allison 250-B17F turboprop (max power 373 kW; 500 shp), flat rated at 313 kW (420 shp), or a similarly rated Turbomeca TP 319 turboprop, each driving a Hartzell HC-B3TF-7A/T10173-15 three-blade constant-speed reversible-pitch propeller with spinner. Fuel in four wing tanks and a fuselage collector tank, total usable capacity 360 litres (95 US gallons; 79 Imp gallons). Collector tank of 15 litres (4 US gallons; 3.3 Imp gallons) serves as tank for up to 30 s of inverted flight.

Gravity refuelling point in top of each wing tank. Oil capacity 5.7 litres (1.5 US gallons; 1.25 Imp gallons). Anti-icing for engine air intake, spinner and propeller blades.

ACCOMMODATION: Instructor and pupil, side by side, beneath one-piece rearward sliding jettisonable canopy with steel tube turnover windscreen frame. Canopy can be locked in partially open position if required. Zero/zero rocket assisted escape system optional. Dual controls standard, but instructor's or pupil's control column can be removed if desired. Both front seats are adjustable longitudinally and for rake, and are fitted with five-point seat belts and inertia reel shoulder harnesses. Provision for two more seats at rear, with four-point harnesses, which can be removed to make room for up to 200 kg (440 lb) of baggage. As ambulance, can accommodate one stretcher patient, and a medical attendant or sitting patient, in addition to pilot. Accommodation heated and ventilated by heat exchanger, fresh air intake and mixer unit. Auxiliary fresh air intake in fin leading-edge. Air-conditioning system optional.

SYSTEMS: No hydraulic or pneumatic systems. Electrical system is 28V DC, powered normally by a 150A engine driven starter/generator, with a 23Ah nickel-cadmium battery for emergency supply and engine starting. Ground power receptacle. Emergency battery for main artificial horizon. Oxygen system available to customer's requirements.

AVIONICS AND EQUIPMENT: Dual controls and instrumentation for day and night VFR and IFR operation, including VHF com radios (two), ADF, DME, transponder, RMI, HSI, marker beacon receiver, standby compass, airspeed indicator, attitude indicator, altimeter, turn and bank indicator, vertical speed indicator, outside air temperature gauge, and clock. Twin landing lights in starboard wing leading-edge.

ARMAMENT AND OPERATIONAL EQUIPMENT: Six underwing attachments, each inner point stressed for 250 kg (551 lb) and the other four for 150 kg (331 lb) each; max external stores load 800 kg (1,764 lb). When flown solo, can carry six 100 kg bombs; two 250 kg bombs plus two 50 kg bombs and two flares; six pods each with eighteen 37 mm or six 68 mm rockets; two rocket pods, two gun pods (each with either two 7.62 mm and 2,000 rds or one 12.7 mm and 300 rds), and two flares; or up to four photographic, TV, radar or reconnaissance pods plus two flares. As two-seater, typical loads can include six to twelve anti-tank missiles; five liferafts or emergency packs and one searchlight pod; and photo and TV pods. Provision for reflector sight, internally mounted cameras (one long-focus or four short-focus), or for target towing with winch and hit counters.

DIMENSIONS, EXTERNAL:

Wing span	10.34 m (33 ft 11 in)
Wing chord: at root	1.83 m (6 ft 0 in)
mean aerodynamic	1.50 m (4 ft 11 in)
at tip	1.098 m (3 ft 7¼ in)
Wing aspect ratio	7.25
Length overall	7.90 m (25 ft 11 in)
Fuselage: Max width	1.22 m (4 ft 0 in)
Height overall	2.85 m (9 ft 4¼ in)
Elevator span	3.68 m (12 ft 1 in)
Wheel track	3.36 m (11 ft 0¼ in)
Wheelbase	2.13 m (7 ft 0 in)
Propeller diameter	2.19 m (7 ft 2¼ in)
Propeller ground clearance	0.29 m (11½ in)

DIMENSIONS, INTERNAL:

Cockpit: Length	1.81 m (5 ft 11¼ in)
Max width	1.14 m (3 ft 9 in)
Height (seat cushion to canopy)	1.02 m (3 ft 4¼ in)

Valmet L-90 TP Redigo turboprop powered development of the L-70 Miltrainer *(Pilot Press)*

Valmet L-70 Vinka two-seat trainers of the Finnish Air Force

ACCOMMODATION: Side by side seats for instructor and pupil in trainer version, with integral longitudinal central console which serves also to reinforce fuselage floor. Dual controls standard, but instructor's or pupil's control column can be removed if desired. Windscreen and one-piece rearward sliding fully transparent jettisonable canopy, with steel tube turnover frame. Canopy can be locked in partially open position if required. Provision for two more seats at rear, which can be removed to make room for additional baggage. Up to 280 kg (617 lb) of baggage or freight can be carried internally if aircraft is flown as a single-seater. As ambulance, can accommodate one stretcher patient and medical attendant in addition to pilot. Cockpit heated and ventilated.

ARMAMENT AND OPERATIONAL EQUIPMENT: Four underwing attachments, the inner pair each stressed for 150 kg (330.5 lb) and the outer pair for 100 kg (220 lb) each; max external load 300 kg (661 lb). Detailed loads listed in 1986-87 and earlier *Jane's*.

DIMENSIONS, EXTERNAL:

Wing span	9.63 m (31 ft 7¼ in)
Length overall	7.50 m (24 ft 7¼ in)
Height overall	3.31 m (10 ft 10¼ in)
Wheel track	2.30 m (7 ft 6½ in)
Wheelbase	1.61 m (5 ft 3½ in)
Propeller diameter	1.88 m (6 ft 2 in)

AREA:

Wings, gross	14.00 m² (150.70 sq ft)

WEIGHTS AND LOADINGS:

Operating weight empty, equipped	767 kg (1,691 lb)
Max payload with full fuel	380 kg (838 lb)
Max T-O weight: Aerobatic	1,040 kg (2,293 lb)
Utility	1,050 kg (2,315 lb)
Normal	1,250 kg (2,756 lb)
Max wing loading:	
Aerobatic	74.3 kg/m² (15.22 lb/sq ft)
Utility	75.0 kg/m² (15.36 lb/sq ft)
Normal	89.3 kg/m² (18.53 lb/sq ft)
Max power loading:	
Aerobatic	6.97 kg/kW (11.47 lb/hp)
Utility	7.04 kg/kW (11.58 lb/hp)
Normal	8.38 kg/kW (13.78 lb/hp)

PERFORMANCE (at AUW of 1,000 kg; 2,205 lb):

Never-exceed speed	193 knots (360 km/h; 223 mph)
Max level speed at S/L	127 knots (235 km/h; 146 mph)
Cruising speed (75% power) at 1,525 m (5,000 ft)	120 knots (222 km/h; 138 mph)
Stalling speed, power off:	
flaps up	53 knots (98 km/h; 61 mph)
flaps down	46 knots (85 km/h; 53 mph)
Max rate of climb at S/L	342 m (1,120 ft)/min
Service ceiling	5,000 m (16,400 ft)
T-O run	230 m (755 ft)
Landing run	175 m (575 ft)
Range with max fuel, no reserves	513 nm (950 km; 590 miles)
Endurance at S/L (65% power)	4 h 48 min
Max endurance, no reserves	6 h 12 min
g limits	+6/−3 (Aerobatic)
	+4.4/−2.02 (Utility)
	+3.3/−1.8 (Normal)

AREAS:

Wings, gross	14.75 m² (158.8 sq ft)
Ailerons (total, incl tabs)	1.98 m² (21.31 sq ft)
Trailing-edge flaps (total)	1.76 m² (18.94 sq ft)
Fin	0.97 m² (10.44 sq ft)
Rudder, incl tab	0.99 m² (10.66 sq ft)
Tailplane	1.56 m² (16.79 sq ft)
Elevators (total, incl tabs)	1.53 m² (16.47 sq ft)

WEIGHTS AND LOADINGS (A: Aerobatic category; U: Utility; N: Normal category):

Weight empty, equipped: A	890 kg (1,962 lb)
Max fuel	296 kg (652 lb)
External stores: max	800 kg (1,764 lb)
with max fuel	600 kg (1,323 lb)
Max T-O weight: A	1,350 kg (2,976 lb)
U	1,470 kg (3,241 lb)
U (with external stores)	1,900 kg (4,189 lb)
N	1,600 kg (3,527 lb)
Max wing loading: A	91.5 kg/m² (18.75 lb/sq ft)
U	99.7 kg/m² (20.42 lb/sq ft)
U (with external stores)	128.8 kg/m² (26.40 lb/sq ft)
N	108.5 kg/m² (22.23 lb/sq ft)
Max power loading: A	5.03 kg/kW (8.27 lb/shp)
U	5.48 kg/kW (9.00 lb/shp)
U (with external stores)	7.08 kg/kW (11.64 lb/shp)
N	5.96 kg/kW (9.80 lb/shp)

PERFORMANCE (at max Aerobatic T-O weight, ISA):

Max permissible speed in dive	280 knots (520 km/h; 323 mph)
Never-exceed speed	251 knots (465 km/h; 289 mph)
Max level speed at 1,525 m (5,000 ft)	181 knots (335 km/h; 208 mph)
Cruising speed (75% power) at 3,000 m (9,840 ft)	164 knots (305 km/h; 189 mph)
Max speed for flap extension	129 knots (240 km/h; 149 mph)
Stalling speed, engine idling:	
flaps up	57 knots (105 km/h; 65 mph)
10° flap	54 knots (100 km/h; 62 mph)
40° flap	50 knots (93 km/h; 58 mph)

Max rate of climb at S/L	588 m (1,929 ft)/min
Time to height: 3,000 m (9,840 ft)	5 min
5,000 m (16,400 ft)	11 min 30 s
Service ceiling (engine limited)	7,620 m (25,000 ft)
T-O run	195 m (640 ft)
T-O to 15 m (50 ft)	310 m (1,017 ft)
Landing from 15 m (50 ft)	360 m (1,181 ft)
Landing run (without propeller reversal)	210 m (689 ft)
Min ground turning radius	10.80 m (35 ft 5 in)
Range at 6,000 m (19,685 ft) with max internal fuel, 30 min reserves	approx 809 nm (1,500 km; 932 miles)
Endurance, conditions as above	more than 5 h
g limits	+7/−3.5 aerobatic
	+2.7 max sustained

VALMET L-70 MILTRAINER
Finnish Air Force name: Vinka

A development contract for the L-70 was placed with Valmet by the Finnish Air Force on 23 March 1973. The aircraft, which was originally designated Leko-70, an abbreviation of 'Lentokone', the Finnish word for 'aeroplane', first flew on 1 July 1975. It is named Vinka (a cold Arctic wind) by the Finnish Air Force, to whom 30 were delivered during 1980-82, as recorded in earlier editions of *Jane's*. As the L-70 Miltrainer, the aircraft continues to be available for export.

The following is an abbreviated version of the full description of this aircraft, which can be found in the 1986-87 and previous editions of *Jane's*:

TYPE: Two-seat training or two/four-seat touring aircraft.

POWER PLANT: One 149 kW (200 hp) Textron Lycoming AEIO-360-A1B6 flat-four engine, driving a Hartzell HC-C2YK-4F/FC × 7666A-2 two-blade constant-speed propeller with spinner. Christen-801 fuel and oil systems permit up to 1½ min of continuous inverted flight in Aerobatic category. Semi-integral bonded sandwich fuel tank in each wing root ahead of main spar; total capacity 170 litres (45 US gallons; 37.4 Imp gallons). Gravity fuelling point in top of each tank.

FRANCE

A.C.E.
A.C.E. INTERNATIONAL

MEMBER COMPANIES:

Avions Marcel Dassault-Breguet Aviation, BP 32, 92420 Vaucresson
Telephone: (1) 47 41 79 21

SNECMA, 2 boulevard Victor, 75724 Paris Cédex 15
Telephone: (1) 45 54 92 00

Thomson-CSF, 173 boulevard Hausmann, 75379 Paris Cédex 08
Telephone: (1) 45 61 96 00
Electronique Serge Dassault, 55 quai Carnot, BP 301, 92214 Saint-Cloud Cédex
Telephone: (1) 46 02 50 00
MANAGING DIRECTOR: Bruno Revellin-Falcoz

On 8 April 1987, the Chairmen of the four member companies listed signed documents creating the A.C.E. International Groupement d'Intérêt Economique. Its pur-

pose is to co-ordinate the launch of the future Avion de Combat Européen (A.C.E.) programme. The consortium is open to foreign companies interested in becoming members.

In addition to its own management bodies, the consortium will have a Technical Co-ordination Committee and a Finance and Contract Committee. As a first step, A.C.E. International is co-ordinating work undertaken by its member companies, with government authorities and military staff of concerned countries, to determine the common technical definition of the A.C.E.

AÉROSPATIALE
AÉROSPATIALE SNI

37 boulevard de Montmorency, 75781 Paris Cédex 16
Telephone: (1) 42 24 24 24
Telex: AISPA 620059 F
PRESIDENT AND CHIEF EXECUTIVE OFFICER:
Henri Martre
DIRECTOR OF INFORMATION AND COMMUNICATIONS:
Patrice Kreis
AIRCRAFT DIVISION
DIVISION MANAGER: Jacques Plenier
AIRBUS PROGRAMME DIRECTOR: Alain Bruneau
ATR 42 PROGRAMME DIRECTOR: Jean-Paul Perrais
COMMERCIAL DIRECTOR: Henri Paul Puel
WORKS AND FACILITIES:
Toulouse. PLANT MANAGER: Jean-Louis Fache
Nantes-Bouguenais. PLANT MANAGER: Daniel Huet
Saint-Nazaire. PLANT MANAGER: Jean-Marie Mir
Méaulte. PLANT MANAGER: Jean Mousson

HELICOPTER DIVISION
DIVISION MANAGER: Jean François Bigay
DIRECTOR OF RESEARCH AND DEVELOPMENT:
René Mouille
COMMERCIAL DIRECTOR: Lucien Lordereau
WORKS AND FACILITIES:
Marignane and La Courneuve. FACTORY DIRECTOR:
Paul Chandez
SUBSIDIARIES
Société Girondine d'Entretien et de Réparation de Matériel Aéronautique (SOGERMA)
Société de Construction d'Avions de Tourisme et d'Affaires (SOCATA)
Société d'Exploitation et de Constructions Aéronautiques (SECA)
Electronique Aérospatiale (EAS)
Société Charentaise d'Equipements Aéronautiques (SOCEA)
Aerospatiale Helicopter Corporation (USA)

Aérospatiale was formed on 1 January 1970, by decision of the French government, as a result of the merger of the former Sud-Aviation, Nord-Aviation and SEREB companies. It had a registered capital of 1,016,490,000 francs, facilities extending over a total area of 8,498,465 m² (91,477,475 sq ft), of which 2,005,674 m² (21,589,075 sq ft) is covered, and a staff (including subsidiary companies) of 38,800 persons on 1 January 1987. By December 1987 Aérospatiale had delivered 7,476 helicopters, of French design, excluding licenced production abroad, plus 328 assembled under licence.

In addition to the programmes of which details follow, Aérospatiale is a partner in the European Airbus programmes (see International section), and participates financially in Helibras (Brazil), Samaero (Singapore) and Maroc Aviation (Morocco). Its activities are devoted 32% to fixed-wing aircraft, 19.3% to helicopters, 32% to tactical missiles, 16.4% to ballistic missiles and space, and 0.3% to other work.

Aérospatiale Epsilon (Textron Lycoming AEIO-540-L1B5D engine)

AÉROSPATIALE EPSILON

First details of this tandem two-seat primary/basic trainer were released in September 1978. Purpose of the project was to meet a French Air Force requirement for a propeller driven aircraft for use in the initial stages of a more cost effective pilot training scheme than that then operated.

A development contract from the Air Force, for two prototypes and two ground test airframes, was announced by Aérospatiale in June 1979. The first prototype flew on 22 December that year, followed by the second prototype on 12 July 1980. On 6 January 1982, a manufacturing programme was approved, covering delivery of 150 Epsilons at the rate of 30 a year. Contracts for the first two production increments, each of 30 aircraft, were received on 5 March and 30 December 1982 respectively. The first production Epsilon flew on 29 June 1983; deliveries to the Centre d'Expériences Aériennes Militaires (CEAM) at Mont-de-Marsan began on 29 July 1983, and a total of 130 had been delivered to Groupement École 315 at Cognac/Chateaubernard by March 1988.

The Epsilon programme is handled by the Aircraft Division of Aérospatiale, as prime contractor responsible for the entire programme. Design and manufacture are subcontracted to Socata, the company's light aircraft subsidiary at Tarbes. In October 1987, an order was announced for 18 Epsilons for the Escola de Instrucão Elementar de Pilotagem (Esquadra 101) of the Portuguese Air Force at Ota. Delivery will begin in 1989 following

assembly by OGMA in Portugal.

An armed version is available to export customers, with four underwing hardpoints for a total 300 kg (661 lb) of external stores with pilot only, or 200 kg (441 lb) with crew of two. Empty weight of this version is 944 kg (2,081 lb), max T-O weight 1,400 kg (3,086 lb), and g limits +6/−3. An Epsilon armed with two twin 7.62 mm machine-gun pods could loiter for 30 min at low altitude over a combat area 170 nm (315 km; 195 miles) from its base. First export order, for three armed Epsilons, was placed by the Togolese Air Force in the Autumn of 1984. These aircraft (c/n 51, 55 and 59) were delivered in August 1986 and were followed by a single attrition replacement ordered in 1987.

The first prototype Epsilon is being used as testbed for the 335 kW (450 shp) TP 319 turboprop developed by Turbomeca from the TM 319 turboshaft. The engine is derated to 261 kW (350 shp) for this installation and drives a Ratier-Figeac propeller with three composites blades. First flight was made on 9 November 1985. An illustration can be found in the 1987-88 *Jane's.*

The following description applies to the basic version of the Epsilon, as operated by the French Air Force:
TYPE: Two-seat military primary/basic trainer.
WINGS: Cantilever low-wing monoplane. Wing section RA 1643 at root, RA 1243 at tip. Thickness/chord ratio 16% at root, 12% at tip. Dihedral 5°. Incidence 2°. All-metal light alloy structure, with single main spar and rear auxiliary spar, built in two panels attached directly to sides of fuselage. Press-formed ribs and heavy gauge skin

without stringers. Slightly upturned wingtips. Electrically actuated single-slotted flaps. Light alloy ailerons, with spring tabs.
FUSELAGE: Light alloy semi-monocoque structure of four longerons, frames and heavy gauge skin, without stringers.
TAIL UNIT: Cantilever single-spar light alloy structure. Fixed surfaces metal covered; elevators and rudder covered with polyester fabric. Fixed incidence tailplane, with dihedral. Balanced elevators and rudder, with spring tab in each elevator and ground adjustable tab on rudder. Shallow ventral fin.
LANDING GEAR: Electro-hydraulically retractable tricycle type, with single wheel on each unit. Inward retracting main units and rearward retracting castoring nosewheel. Mainwheel tyres size 380 × 150; nosewheel tyre size 330 × 130. Independent hydraulic single-disc brake on each mainwheel. Parking brake.
POWER PLANT: One 224 kW (300 hp) Textron Lycoming AEIO-540-L1B5D flat-six engine, driving a Hartzell HC-C2YR-4()F/FC 8475-6R two-blade constant-speed metal propeller, with spinner. Fuel in two wing leading-edge tanks, with total capacity of 210 litres (55.5 US gallons; 46 Imp gallons). Refuelling points on wing upper surface. Christen system to permit up to 2 min inverted flight.
ACCOMMODATION: Two seats in tandem, with rear seat raised by 70 mm (2.7 in). Rudder pedals are mechanically adjustable fore and aft. Two-component sliding Plexiglas canopy, with emergency jettison system, plus sideways hinged (to port) windscreen, providing access to instruments for servicing. Full dual controls. Baggage compartment aft of cabin, with door on port side.
SYSTEMS: Hydraulic systems for actuating landing gear and brakes. 28V electrical system includes engine driven alternator; battery for engine starting and emergency use; ground power socket in port side of rear fuselage. Cabin heated and ventilated. Windscreen demister.
AVIONICS AND EQUIPMENT: Standard installation includes blind-flying instrumentation, standby artificial horizon, VHF, UHF, automatic and manual VOR, transponder, ILS capability and Tacan.
ARMAMENT AND OPERATIONAL EQUIPMENT (not on French Air Force Epsilons): Four underwing hardpoints; outboard points each able to carry 80 kg (176 lb), inboard points 160 kg (352 lb). Alternative loads include two Matra CM pods each containing two 7.62 mm machine-guns, four Matra F2D launchers for six XF1 68 mm rockets, six Bavard F4B practice bombs, two 125 kg bombs, two Alkan 500 grenade launchers with 10 Lacroix rounds each, and four land or sea survival kit containers. Associated equipment includes Alkan 663 stores racks, SFOM 83A3 sight and Alkan E105C firing control box.

DIMENSIONS, EXTERNAL:
Wing span	7.92 m (25 ft 11¾ in)
Wing chord: at root	1.46 m (4 ft 9½ in)
at tip	0.92 m (3 ft 0¼ in)
Wing aspect ratio	7.0
Length overall	7.59 m (24 ft 10¾ in)
Height overall	2.66 m (8 ft 8¾ in)
Tailplane span	3.20 m (10 ft 6 in)
Wheel track	2.30 m (7 ft 6½ in)
Wheelbase	1.80 m (5 ft 10¾ in)
Propeller diameter	1.98 m (6 ft 6 in)
Propeller ground clearance	0.25 m (10 in)

AREAS:
Wings, gross	9.00 m² (96.9 sq ft)
Fin	1.02 m² (10.98 sq ft)
Tailplane	2.00 m² (21.53 sq ft)

WEIGHTS AND LOADINGS:
Weight empty, equipped	932 kg (2,055 lb)
Fuel weight	150 kg (330 lb)
Max T-O and landing weight	1,250 kg (2,755 lb)
Max wing loading	139 kg/m² (28.4 lb/sq ft)
Max power loading	5.58 kg/kW (9.18 lb/hp)

PERFORMANCE (at max T-O weight):
Never-exceed speed	281 knots (520 km/h; 323 mph)
Max level speed at S/L	204 knots (378 km/h; 236 mph)
Max cruising speed (75% power) at 1,830 m (6,000 ft)	193 knots (358 km/h; 222 mph)
Approach speed	80 knots (148 km/h; 92 mph)
Stalling speed, flaps and landing gear down, power off	62 knots (115 km/h; 72 mph)
Max rate of climb at S/L	564 m (1,850 ft)/min
Service ceiling	7,010 m (23,000 ft)
T-O run	410 m (1,345 ft)
T-O to 15 m (50 ft)	640 m (2,100 ft)
Landing from 15 m (50 ft)	440 m (1,444 ft)
Landing run	250 m (820 ft)
Endurance (65% power)	3 h 45 min
g limits	+6.7/−3.35

AÉROSPATIALE/MBB HAP and PAH-2/HAC

Details of this Franco-German anti-tank helicopter programme can be found under the Eurocopter heading in the International section.

AÉROSPATIALE/AERITALIA ATR 42/72

Details of the ATR 42/72 programme can be found in the International section.

Camouflaged Aérospatiale Epsilon demonstrator with underwing weapon pylons *(Paul Jackson)*

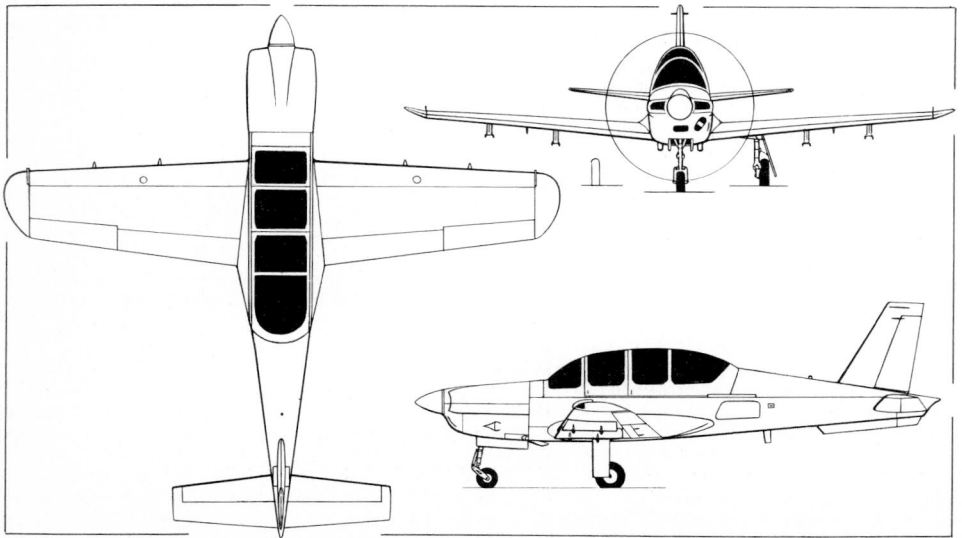

Aérospatiale Epsilon tandem two-seat primary/basic trainer *(Pilot Press)*

AÉROSPATIALE SA 315B LAMA
Indian Army name: Cheetah

Design of the SA 315B Lama began in late 1968, initially to meet a requirement of the Indian armed forces, and a prototype was flown for the first time on 17 March 1969. French certification was granted on 30 September 1970 and FAA Type Approval on 25 February 1972.

The Lama combines features of the Alouette II and III, having the airframe (with some reinforcement) of the former and the dynamic components, including the Artouste power plant and rotor system, of the SA 316 Alouette III.

During demonstration flights in the Himalayas in 1969 a Lama, carrying a crew of two and 140 kg (308 lb) of fuel, made the highest landings and take-offs ever recorded, at a height of 7,500 m (24,600 ft).

On 21 June 1972, a Lama set a helicopter absolute height record of 12,442 m (40,820 ft). The pilot was Jean Boulet, holder of the previous record in an SE 3150 Alouette.

The production Lama is capable of transporting an external load of 1,135 kg (2,500 lb) at an altitude of more than 2,500 m (8,200 ft). In an agricultural role, it can be fitted with spraybars and an underbelly tank of 1,135 litres (250 Imp gallons; 300 US gallons) capacity, developed jointly by Aérospatiale Helicopter Corporation and Simplex Manufacturing Company. The tank is equipped with an electrical emergency dump system.

A total of 401 Lamas had been sold and delivered for operation in 31 countries by 1 March 1988. In addition to manufacture by Aérospatiale, the SA 315B is produced under licence by HAL for the Indian Army, under the name Cheetah; and is assembled by Helibras in Brazil under the name Gavião.

TYPE: Turbine-driven general purpose helicopter.
ROTOR SYSTEM: Three-blade main and anti-torque rotors. Folding main rotor blades, of NACA 63A section and constant chord, on articulated hinges, with hydraulic drag hinge dampers. Each blade has aluminium alloy spar with steel cuff, aluminium alloy sheet skin, with stainless steel protective strips, and sandwich type Moltoprene block filling. Rotor brake standard. Tail rotor blades are hollow aluminium alloy aerofoils, with stainless steel leading-edge strip.
ROTOR DRIVE: Main rotor driven through planetary gearbox, with freewheel for autorotation. Take-off drive for tail rotor at lower end of main gearbox, from where a torque shaft runs to a small gearbox which supports the tail rotor and houses the pitch change mechanism. Steel alloy shafts. Cyclic and collective pitch controls are powered. Main rotor rpm 353. Tail rotor rpm 2,001.
FUSELAGE: Glazed cabin has light metal frame. Centre and rear fuselage have triangulated steel tube framework.
LANDING GEAR: Skid type, with removable wheels for ground manoeuvring. Pneumatic floats for normal operation from water, and emergency flotation gear, inflatable in the air, are available.
POWER PLANT: One 640 kW (858 shp) Turbomeca Artouste IIIB turboshaft, derated to 404 kW (542 shp). Fuel tank in fuselage centre-section, with capacity of 575 litres (152 US gallons; 126.5 Imp gallons), of which 573 litres (151.5 US gallons; 126 Imp gallons) are usable. Oil capacity 7 litres (1.85 US gallons; 1.55 Imp gallons).
ACCOMMODATION: Glazed cabin seats pilot and co-pilot or passenger side by side in front and three passengers behind. Jettisonable door on each side. Provision for external sling for loads of up to 1,135 kg (2,500 lb). Can be equipped for rescue (hoist capacity 160 kg; 352 lb), liaison, observation, training, agricultural, photographic and other duties. As an ambulance, can accommodate two stretchers and a medical attendant. Cabin heating optional.
SYSTEMS: Single hydraulic system. Electrical system includes engine starter/generator, 36Ah battery and external power socket. Oxygen system optional.

DIMENSIONS, EXTERNAL:
Main rotor diameter	11.02 m (36 ft 1¾ in)
Tail rotor diameter	1.91 m (6 ft 3¼ in)
Distance between rotor centres	6.435 m (21 ft 1½ in)
Main rotor blade chord (constant)	0.35 m (13.8 in)
Length overall, both rotors turning	12.91 m (42 ft 4¼ in)
Length of fuselage	10.23 m (33 ft 6¾ in)
Height overall	3.09 m (10 ft 1¾ in)
Skid track	2.38 m (7 ft 9¾ in)

DIMENSIONS, INTERNAL:
Cabin: Length	2.10 m (6 ft 10½ in)
Max width	1.40 m (4 ft 7 in)
Max height	1.28 m (4 ft 2¼ in)
Volume	3.10 m³ (109.5 cu ft)

AREAS:
Main rotor disc	95.38 m² (1,026.7 sq ft)
Tail rotor disc	2.87 m² (30.84 sq ft)

WEIGHTS:
Weight empty	1,021 kg (2,251 lb)
Max T-O weight: normal	1,950 kg (4,300 lb)
with externally slung cargo	2,300 kg (5,070 lb)

PERFORMANCE (A, at AUW of 1,950 kg; 4,300 lb. B, at AUW of 2,300 kg; 5,070 lb with slung load):
Never-exceed speed at S/L:		
A		113 knots (210 km/h; 130 mph)

Aérospatiale SA 315B Lama equipped for mountain rescue missions in Switzerland

Max cruising speed: A		103 knots (192 km/h; 119 mph)
B		65 knots (120 km/h; 75 mph)
Max rate of climb at S/L: A		330 m (1,080 ft)/min
B		234 m (768 ft)/min
Service ceiling: A		5,400 m (17,715 ft)
B		3,000 m (9,840 ft)
Hovering ceiling IGE: A		5,050 m (16,565 ft)
B		2,950 m (9,675 ft)
Hovering ceiling OGE: A		4,600 m (15,090 ft)
B		1,550 m (5,085 ft)
Range with max fuel: A		278 nm (515 km; 320 miles)

AÉROSPATIALE ALOUETTE III
The seven-seat Alouette III helicopter was produced by Aérospatiale in two major versions, details of which can be found in the 1981-82 and previous editions of *Jane's*:

SA 316B. Powered by 649 kW (870 shp) Turbomeca Artouste IIIB turboshaft, derated to 425 kW (570 shp). Prototype flew for first time on 28 February 1959.

SA 319B. Powered by 649 kW (870 shp) Turbomeca Astazou XIV turboshaft, derated to 447 kW (600 shp). Prototype completed in 1967.

A total of 1,455 Alouette IIIs had been delivered for civil and military operation in 74 countries by 1 May 1985. Production in France has ended, but manufacture of the SA 316B by ICA of Brasov, Romania, continued in 1988, under the designation IAR-316B. ICA has also developed a military gunship version of the Alouette III, known as the IAR-317 Airfox, which is described in the Romanian section of this edition. A further gunship development, the Atlas Alpha, was described briefly in the South African section of the 1987-88 *Jane's*. SA 316B production by HAL in India, as the Chetak, also continues.

AÉROSPATIALE SA 330 PUMA
The twin-engined SA 330 Puma was developed initially to meet a French Army requirement for a medium sized *hélicoptère de manoeuvre*, able to operate by day or night in all weathers and all climates. In 1967, the SA 330 was selected for the RAF Tactical Transport Programme, and was included in a three-type joint production agreement between Aérospatiale and Westland in the UK.

The first of two SA 330 prototypes flew on 15 April 1965, and the last of six pre-production models on 30 July 1968, followed in September 1968 by the first production aircraft.

Details of six early versions of the Puma can be found in the 1976-77 *Jane's*. The final French production versions were as follows:

SA 330J/L. Civil (J) and military (L) versions introduced in 1976 with main rotor blades of composite materials. Increased max T-O weight, including certification at 7,500 kg (16,535 lb) for cargo-sling mission. Last described fully in 1982-83 *Jane's*.

A total of 697 SA 330 Pumas had been sold by 1 February 1987, in 46 countries. ICA of Brasov, Romania (which see), began manufacture of an initial 100 SA 330H Pumas under licence in 1977, as IAR-330s, and is now the sole producer of this helicopter. Nurtanio of Indonesia (see IPTN) completed the assembly of 11 from knocked-down components in the second quarter of 1983 but, like the parent company, is now concentrating on manufacture of the Super Puma.

AÉROSPATIALE AS 332 SUPER PUMA
Swedish Air Force designation: Hkp 10
Brazilian Air Force designation: CH-34

The early history of the Super Puma, a list of its improved features compared with the original SA 330 Puma, and details of 1985 versions can be found in the 1985-86 edition of *Jane's*. The first prototype AS 332 Super Puma (F-WZJA) flew for the first time on 13 September 1978. The current versions of the Super Puma introduced in 1986, with uprated Turbomeca Makila IA1 engines, are as follows:

AS 332B₁. Military version. Standard fuselage, seating up to 21 troops and two crew. Cabin floor reinforced for loads of 1,500 kg/m² (307 lb/sq ft).

AS 332F₁. Naval version, with folding tail rotor pylon and deck landing assist device. Suitable for search and rescue, ASW and anti-ship roles.

AS 332L₁. Civil version, with cabin lengthened 0.76 m (2 ft 6 in) to seat crew of two and up to 24 passengers. Cabin has two additional windows. Fuel capacity increased.

AS 332M₁. As 332B₁, but with cabin lengthened 0.76 m (2 ft 6 in) to provide seats for 25 troops and a crew of two, with two additional windows. Fuel capacity increased.

Super Puma Mk II. This improved version is described separately.

The air component of the French Army (ALAT) has started to replace its current SA 330B Pumas with AS 332M₁ Super Pumas. An initial 30 AS 332M₁s are on order for the Army's Force d'Action Rapide, comprising six for 1988 delivery, followed by eight per year in 1989-91.

All Super Puma variants are certificated for IFR category A and B operation, to FAR Pt 29 standards. The first Super Puma (an AS 332L) equipped for operation to IFR Cat II standards was certificated by the DGAC on 7 July 1983 and delivered to Lufttransport of Norway in September 1983. Certification of this version for flight into known icing conditions was granted on 29 June 1983. Corresponding FAA certifications cover Cat II automatic approach, using a SFIM CDV 85 P4 four-axis flight director coupler, and flight into known icing conditions under FAR Pt 25 Appendix C.

Orders for 275 Super Pumas (plus six prototypes), for service in 31 countries, had been received by 1 March 1988; deliveries totalled 228 at that date. They include three for operation by the French Air Force on support duties at nuclear firing ranges in the Pacific; 22 for transport, SAR and other duties with the Singapore Air Force; 30 for maritime search and rescue (10), VIP transportation (2) and tactical transport duties (18) with the Spanish armed forces; six naval models, each armed with two Exocet missiles, for Kuwait; other military models for Abu Dhabi (8, incl 2 VIP), Argentina (up to 24), Brazil (8), Chile (3) and Oman (2 for Royal Flight); and 35 AS 332Ls for Bristow Helicopters, whose 19-passenger aircraft, serving offshore oil platforms, are known as **Tigers**. Special equipment on the Tigers includes foldable seats, large rear baggage compartment, in-flight music, public address system, automatic emergency door jettison, and large capacity liferafts. Subsequent orders include ten AS 332M₁s for delivery to the Swedish Air Force in 1988-90, for search and rescue duties; three for the Federal German border patrol service; 15 for the Brazilian Navy; three for the Swiss Air Force; four AS 332F₁s for the Chilean Navy; two AS 332L₁s for the Finnish border police; and 12 (some with Exocet missiles) for Saudi Arabia.

ASW version of Aérospatiale AS 332F₁ Super Puma armed with torpedoes

Deliveries of the Super Puma from French production began in mid-1981. IPTN of Indonesia (which see) is manufacturing several versions under licence, and 12 of the Spanish tactical transports are being assembled in Spain by CASA.

TYPE: Twin-turbine multi-role helicopter.

ROTOR SYSTEM: Four-blade main rotor, with a fully articulated hub and integral rotor brake. Each drag hinge is fitted with an elastomeric frequency adaptor. The blade cuffs, equipped with horns, are connected by link rods to the swashplate, which is actuated by three hydraulic twin-cylinder servo control units. Each of the moulded blades is made up of a glassfibre roving spar and a composite glassfibre and carbonfibre fabric skin, with Moltoprene filler. The leading-edge is covered with a titanium protective section. The tips are swept. Attachment of each blade to its sleeve by means of two quick-disconnect pins enables the blades to be folded back quickly by manual methods. The five-blade tail rotor has flapping hinges only, and is located on the starboard side of the tailboom. Optional de-icing system, with heating mat on leading-edge of each main and tail rotor blade.

ROTOR DRIVE: Mechanical shaft and gear drive. Modular main gearbox is fitted with two torquemeters and has two separate lubrication circuits. It is mounted on top of the cabin behind the engines, has two separate inputs from the engines and five reduction stages. The first stage drives, from each engine, an intermediate shaft directly driving the alternator and indirectly driving the two hydraulic pumps, with a further shaft drive to the ventilation fan. At the second stage the action of the two units becomes synchronised on a single main driveshaft by means of freewheeling spur gears. If one or both engines are stopped, this enables the drive gears to be rotated by the remaining turbine or the autorotating rotor, thus maintaining drive to the ancillary systems when the engines are stopped. Drive to the tail rotor is via shafting and an intermediate angle gearbox, terminating at a right-angle tail rotor gearbox. Turbine output 23,840 rpm; main rotor shaft 265 rpm, tail rotor shaft 1,278 rpm. The hydraulically controlled rotor brake, installed on the main gearbox, permits stopping of the rotor 15 s after engine shutdown.

FUSELAGE: Conventional all-metal semi-monocoque structure, embodying anti-crash features. Local use of titanium alloy under engine installation, which is outside the main fuselage shell. Monocoque tailboom supports the tail rotor on the starboard side and a horizontal stabiliser with fixed leading-edge slat (and optional pneumatic de-icing) on the port side. Large ventral fin. Optional folding tailboom for aircraft that serve on ships such as frigates.

LANDING GEAR: Retractable tricycle type, of Messier-Hispano-Bugatti high energy absorbing design. All units retract rearward hydraulically, mainwheels into sponsons on sides of fuselage. Dual-chamber oleo-pneumatic shock absorbers. Optional 'kneeling' capability for main units. Twin-wheel self-centring nose unit, tyre size 466 × 176, pressure 6.0 bars (85 lb/sq in). Single wheel on each main unit with tyre size 615 × 225-10 or 640 × 230-10, pressure 6.0 bars (85 lb/sq in). Hydraulic differential disc brakes, controlled by foot pedals. Lever operated parking brake. Emergency pop-out flotation units can be mounted on main landing gear fairings and forward fuselage.

POWER PLANT: Two Turbomeca Makila IA1 turboshafts, each with max contingency rating of 1,400 kW (1,877 shp) and max continuous rating of 1,184 kW (1,588 shp). Air intakes protected by a grille against ingestion of ice, snow and foreign objects; but Centrisep multi-purpose intake is necessary for flight into sandy areas. AS 332B₁ has five flexible fuel tanks under cabin floor, with total capacity of 1,560 litres (412 US gallons; 343 Imp gallons). AS 332L₁/M₁ have a basic fuel system of six flexible tanks with total capacity of 2,060 litres (544 US gallons; 453 Imp gallons). Provision for additional 1,900 litres (502 US gallons; 418 Imp gallons) in four auxiliary ferry tanks installed in cabin. Two external auxiliary tanks are available, with total capacity of 700 litres (185 US gallons; 154 Imp gallons). For long range missions (mainly offshore), special internal auxiliary and external tanks can be fitted to raise the total fuel capacity to 3,090 litres (816 US gallons; 680 Imp gallons) in AS 332L₁. This auxiliary tank fits in cargo sling well beneath cabin floor and is quickly removable to permit use of sling. Refuelling point on starboard side of cabin. Fuel system is designed to avoid fuel leakage following a crash, with flexible fuel lines and interconnections between tanks, self-sealing valves and automatic fuel pump shutdown in a crash. Options include a fuel dumping system, pressure refuelling, and crash resistant or self-sealing tanks.

ACCOMMODATION: One pilot (VFR) or two pilots side by side (IFR) on flight deck, with jump seat for third crew member or paratroop dispatcher. Ergonomic seat for pilot optional on AS 332L₁. Provision for composite light alloy/Kevlar armour for crew protection on military models. Door on each side of flight deck and internal doorway connecting flight deck to cabin. Dual controls, co-pilot instrumentation and crashworthy flight deck and cabin floors. Max accommodation for 21 passengers in AS 332B₁/F₁, 24 in AS 332L₁ and 25 in AS 332M₁. Variety of interiors available for VIP use, or for air ambulance duty carrying six stretchers and eleven seated casualties/attendants, or nine stretchers and three seated. Strengthened floor for cargo carrying, with lashing points. Jettisonable sliding door on each side of main cabin; or port side door with built-in steps and starboard side double door in VIP or airline configurations. Removable panel on underside of fuselage, at rear of main cabin, permits longer loads to be accommodated, and also serves as emergency exit. Removable door with integral steps for access to baggage racks optional. A hatch in the floor below the centreline of the main rotor is provided for carrying loads of up to 4,500 kg (9,920 lb) on an internally mounted cargo sling. A fixed or retractable rescue hoist (capacity 275 kg; 606 lb) can be mounted externally on the starboard side of the fuselage. Cabin and flight deck are heated, ventilated and soundproofed. Demisting, de-icing, washers and wipers for pilots' windscreens.

SYSTEMS: Two independent hydraulic systems, supplied by self-regulating pumps driven by the main gearbox. Each system supplies one set of servo unit chambers, the left-hand system supplying in addition the autopilot, landing gear, rotor brake and wheel brakes. Freewheels in main gearbox ensure that both systems remain in operation, for supplying the servo controls, if the engines are stopped in flight. Other hydraulically actuated systems can be operated on the ground from the main gearbox (when a special disconnect system is installed to permit running of port engine with rotors stationary), or by external power through the ground power receptacle. There is also an independent auxiliary system, fed through a handpump, which can be used in an emergency to lower the landing gear. Three-phase 200V AC electrical power supplied by two 20kVA 400Hz alternators, driven by the port side intermediate shaft from the main gearbox and available on the ground under the same conditions as the hydraulic ancillary systems. 28.5V DC power provided from the AC system by two transformer-rectifiers. Main aircraft battery used for self starting and emergency power in flight.

AVIONICS AND EQUIPMENT: Optional communications equipment includes VHF, UHF, tactical HF and HF/SSB radio installations and intercom system. Navigational equipment includes radio compass, radio altimeter, VLF Omega, Decca navigator and flight log, Doppler, and VOR/ILS with glidepath. SFIM 155 autopilot, with provision for coupling to self contained navigation and microwave landing systems. Full IFR instrumentation available optionally. Offshore models have nose mounted radar. The search and rescue version has nose mounted Bendix RDR 1400 or RCA Primus 500 search radar, Doppler, and Crouzet Nadir or Decca self contained navigation system, including navigation computer with SAR patterns, polar indicator, roller map display, hover indicator, route mileage indicator and ground speed and drift indicator. A SFIM CDV 155 autopilot coupler makes possible automatic nav track including search patterns, transitions and hover. A multifunction video display shows radar and route images, SAR patterns and hover indication. For naval ASW and ASV missions, aircraft can be fitted with nose mounted Thomson-CSF Varan radar, linked to a tactical table in the cabin, and an Alcatel/Thomson-Sintra HS 312 sonar station at the rear of the cabin.

ARMAMENT AND OPERATIONAL EQUIPMENT (optional): Typical alternatives for army/air force missions are one 20 mm gun, two 7.62 mm machine-guns, or two pods each containing twenty-two 68 mm rockets or nineteen 2.75 in rockets. Armament and equipment for naval missions includes two AM39 Exocet missiles, or two lightweight torpedoes and sonar, or MAD and sonobuoys.

DIMENSIONS, EXTERNAL:

Main rotor diameter	15.60 m (51 ft 2¼ in)
Tail rotor diameter	3.05 m (10 ft 0 in)
Main rotor blade chord	0.60 m (1 ft 11½ in)
Length overall, rotors turning	18.70 m (61 ft 4¼ in)
Length of fuselage, incl tail rotor:	
AS 332B₁/F₁	15.53 m (50 ft 11½ in)
AS 332L₁/M₁	16.29 m (53 ft 5½ in)
Width, blades folded:	
AS 332B₁/L₁/M₁	3.79 m (12 ft 5¼ in)
AS 332F₁	4.04 m (13 ft 3 in)
Height overall	4.92 m (16 ft 1¾ in)
Height, blades and tail pylon folded:	
AS 332F₁	4.80 m (15 ft 9 in)
Height to top of rotor head	4.60 m (15 ft 1¼ in)
Width overall, excl rotors	3.79 m (12 ft 5¼ in)
Wheel track	3.00 m (9 ft 10 in)
Wheelbase: AS 332B₁/F₁	4.49 m (14 ft 8¾ in)
AS 332L₁/M₁	5.28 m (17 ft 4 in)
Passenger cabin doors, each:	
Height	1.35 m (4 ft 5 in)
Width	1.30 m (4 ft 3¼ in)

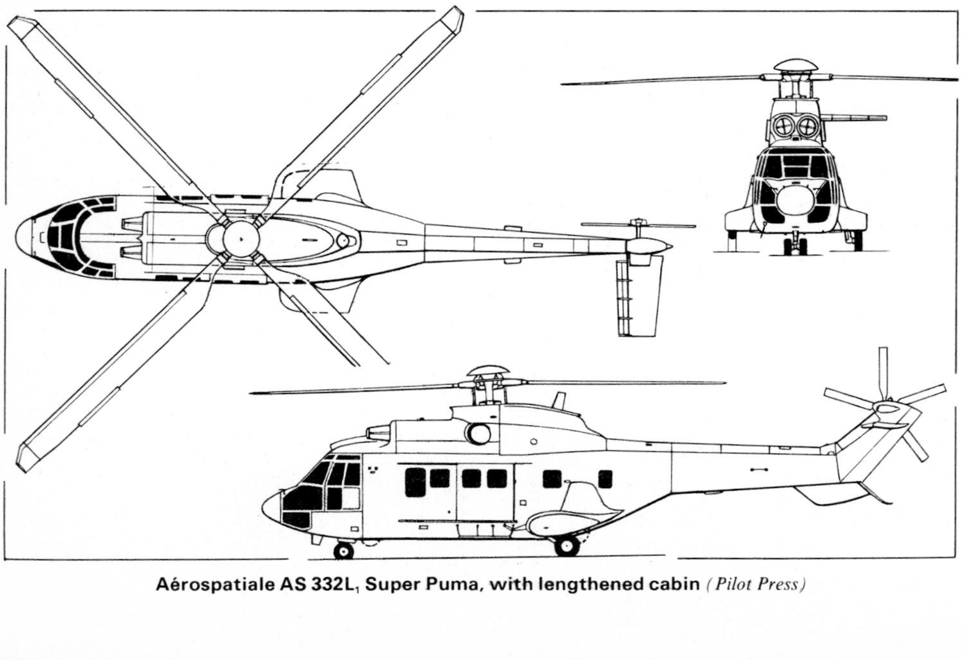

Aérospatiale AS 332L₁ Super Puma, with lengthened cabin *(Pilot Press)*

Floor hatch, rear of cabin:

Length	0.98 m (3 ft 2¾ in)
Width	0.70 m (2 ft 3½ in)

DIMENSIONS, INTERNAL:

Cabin: Length: AS 332B₁	6.05 m (19 ft 10½ in)
AS 332L₁/M₁	6.81 m (22 ft 4 in)
Max width	1.80 m (5 ft 11 in)
Max height	1.55 m (5 ft 1 in)
Floor area: AS 332B₁/F₁	7.80 m² (84 sq ft)
AS 332L₁/M₁	9.18 m² (98.8 sq ft)
Usable volume: AS 332B₁	11.40 m³ (403 cu ft)
AS 332L₁/M₁	13.30 m³ (469.5 cu ft)

AREAS:

Main rotor disc	191.1 m² (2,057.4 sq ft)
Tail rotor disc	7.31 m² (78.64 sq ft)

WEIGHTS:

Weight empty: AS 332B₁	4,290 kg (9,458 lb)
AS 332F₁	4,475 kg (9,866 lb)
AS 332L₁/M₁	4,420 kg (9,744 lb)
Max T-O weight:	
AS 332B₁/F₁/M₁, internal load	9,000 kg (19,841 lb)
AS 332L₁, internal load	8,600 kg (18,960 lb)
all versions, with slung load	9,350 kg (20,615 lb)

PERFORMANCE (at max T-O weight):

Never-exceed speed	150 knots (278 km/h; 172 mph)
Cruising speed at S/L:	
AS 332B₁/M₁	141 knots (262 km/h; 163 mph)
AS 332F₁	130 knots (240 km/h; 149 mph)
AS 332L₁	144 knots (266 km/h; 165 mph)
Max rate of climb at S/L:	
AS 332B₁/M₁	426 m (1,397 ft)/min
AS 332F₁	372 m (1,220 ft)/min
AS 332L₁	486 m (1,594 ft)/min
Service ceiling: AS 332L₁	4,600 m (15,090 ft)
AS 332B₁/F₁/M₁	4,100 m (13,450 ft)
Hovering ceiling IGE:	
AS 332B₁/F₁/M₁	2,700 m (8,860 ft)
AS 332L₁	3,100 m (10,170 ft)
Hovering ceiling OGE:	
AS 332B₁/F₁/M₁	1,600 m (5,250 ft)
AS 332L₁	2,300 m (7,545 ft)
Range at S/L, standard tanks, no reserves:	
AS 332B₁	334 nm (618 km; 384 miles)
AS 332F₁/L₁	470 nm (870 km; 540 miles)
AS 332M₁	455 nm (842 km; 523 miles)
Range at S/L with external (2 × 338 litre) and auxiliary (320 litre) tanks, no reserves:	
AS 332M₁	672 nm (1,245 km; 773 miles)

AÉROSPATIALE SUPER PUMA Mk II

This developed version of the Super Puma introduces a new main rotor which offers improved performance and economy without changes to the standard power plant of two Makila IA1 turboshafts, although the main transmission is upgraded to transmit increased power. Slightly longer main rotor blades with parabolic tips are fitted to a Spheriflex head, which is lighter and simpler than the current type. The rear fuselage is lengthened by 45 cm (1 ft 5¾ in), to provide adequate clearance between the new main rotor and the tail rotor. Range can be increased by installing two 250 litre (66 US gallon; 55 Imp gallon) optional fuel tanks in the main landing gear sponsons. A four-tube EFIS cockpit display and digital autopilot will be included.

Following testing of the Spheriflex head on a Puma, a Super Puma Mk II development vehicle flew for the first time on 6 February 1987. A definitive Super Puma Mk II prototype is due to fly early in 1991, and that model will be retained in production until a new 9-tonne helicopter is introduced in the next century. The Mk II will be the carrier vehicle for the Orchidée radar system, an aerodynamic

Aérospatiale AS 332L₁ Super Puma with lengthened cabin for 24 passengers

model of which began trials beneath an SA 330B Puma in 1986.

Orchidée (Observatoire Radar Cohérent Héliporté d'Investigation Des Eléments Ennemis) is a battlefield surveillance system, intended as a key system for co-ordinating the actions of all French ground forces by the mid-1990s. As can be seen in an accompanying illustration, the Orchidée scanner is carried on a rotating mount under the rear of the helicopter's cabin. When not in use it is retracted upward to stow transversely under the junction of the rear fuselage and tailboom. It is a high-performance Doppler radar, capable of detecting and pinpointing troops and vehicles up to 54 nm (100 km; 62 miles) behind enemy lines while the helicopter is 27 nm (50 km; 31 miles) inside friendly territory at an altitude of around 3,000 m (9,850 ft). Aérospatiale is industrial prime contractor for Orchidée, in conjunction with Laboratoire Central des Télécommunications, which supplies the radar and is responsible for the surveillance system. This is able to transmit data in real time to mobile ground stations built by Electronique Serge Dassault. Thomson-CSF and Matra are responsible for associated countermeasures.

DIMENSIONS, EXTERNAL:

Main rotor diameter	16.20 m (53 ft 1¾ in)

WEIGHT:

Max T-O weight: civil	9,000 kg (19,841 lb)
military	9,500 kg (20,945 lb)

AÉROSPATIALE SA 342 GAZELLE

The first prototype of the Gazelle (designated SA 340) made its first flight on 7 April 1967, powered by an Astazou III engine. Details of early versions of the helicopter can be found in the 1979-80 and 1984-85 Jane's. Versions currently available are as follows:

SA 342L₁. Current basic military version, with higher max T-O weight than earlier models. Powered by Astazou XIVM turboshaft with max rating of 640 kW (858 shp) and max continuous rating of 441 kW (592 shp).

SA 342M. For ALAT (French Army Light Aviation Corps). Differs from SA 342L₁ in having an ALAT instrument panel. Optional equipment specified as standard by ALAT includes SFIM PA 85G autopilot, Crouzet Nadir self-contained navigation system, Decca 80 Doppler and night flying equipment. An exhaust deflector remains optional. Order for first increment of planned total of 158 announced in December 1978, each armed with four Hot missiles and gyro stabilised sight for anti-tank warfare. Deliveries to the ALAT trials unit (GALSTA) began on 1 February 1980, and to an operational unit on 9 June 1980.

A two-stretcher ambulance configuration has received FAA supplemental type certification. No major modification is necessary to convert the aircraft to carry two patients longitudinally on the port side of the cabin, one above the other, leaving room for the pilot and a medical attendant in tandem on the starboard side. The dual spineboard arrangement weighs 27 kg (60 lb) and stows into the baggage compartment when not in use.

Under an Anglo-French agreement signed in 1967, Gazelles are produced jointly with Westland Helicopters Ltd; they have been assembled in Egypt, and built under licence in Yugoslavia. A total of 1,238 had been ordered from Aérospatiale and Westland for civil and military operation in 41 countries by 1 March 1988, of which 1,209

Orchidée battlefield surveillance radar extended in operational position under Puma test aircraft

had been delivered, plus some 200 built in Yugoslavia. Westland manufacture of complete Gazelles ended in March 1984 with the 294th example, of which 12 were for civilian use.

Military customers for the Gazelle include Abu Dhabi (12), Angola (seven), Burundi (three), Cameroon (four), Chad (one), China (eight), Cyprus (six), Egypt (90 including local assembly of 30), Ecuador (28), France (327), Gabon (five), Guinea Republic (one), Iraq (81), Ireland (two), Kenya (two), Kuwait (24), Lebanon (seven), Morocco (30), Rwanda (four), Qatar (16), Senegal (one), Syria (65), Trinidad and Tobago (two), United Kingdom (282) and Yugoslavia (21 French-built). Civilian sales total some 170.

TYPE: Five-seat light utility helicopter.

ROTOR SYSTEM: Three-blade semi-articulated main rotor and 13-blade shrouded fan anti-torque tail rotor (known as a 'fenestron' or 'fan-in-fin'). Rotor head and rotor mast form a single unit. The main rotor blades are of NACA 0012 section, attached to NAT hub by flapping hinges. There are no drag hinges. Each blade has a single leading-edge spar of plastics material reinforced with glassfibre, a laminated glass-fabric skin and honeycomb filler. Tail rotor blades are of die-forged light alloy, with articulation for pitch change only. Main rotor blades can be folded manually for stowage. Rotor brake standard.

ROTOR DRIVE: Main reduction gearbox forward of engine, which is mounted above the rear part of the cabin. Intermediate gearbox beneath engine, rear gearbox supporting the tail rotor. Main rotor/engine rpm ratio 387 : 6,334. Tail rotor/engine rpm ratio 5,918 : 6,334.

FUSELAGE: Cockpit structure is based on a welded light alloy frame which carries the windows and doors. This is mounted on a conventional semi-monocoque lower structure consisting of two longitudinal box sections connected by frames and bulkheads. Central section, which encloses the baggage hold and main fuel tank and supports the main reduction gearbox, is constructed of light alloy honeycomb sandwich panels. Rear section, which supports the engine and tailboom, is of similar construction. Honeycomb sandwich panels are also used for the cabin floors and transmission platform. Tailboom is of conventional sheet metal construction, as are the horizontal tail surfaces and the tail fin.

TAIL UNIT: Small horizontal stabiliser on tailboom, ahead of tail rotor fin.

LANDING GEAR: Steel tube skid type. Wheel can be fitted at rear of each skid for ground handling. Provision for alternative float or ski landing gear.

POWER PLANT: One Turbomeca Astazou XIVM turboshaft, installed above fuselage aft of cabin and rated at 640 kW (858 shp). Two standard fuel tanks in fuselage (one beneath baggage compartment) with total usable capacity of 545 litres (144 US gallons; 120 Imp gallons). Provision for 200 litre (53 US gallon; 44 Imp gallon) ferry tank inside rear cabin. Total possible usable fuel capacity 745 litres (197 US gallons; 164 Imp gallons). Refuelling point on starboard side of cabin. Oil capacity 14.6 litres (4 US gallons; 3.2 Imp gallons) for engine, 3.5 litres (0.9 US gallon; 0.77 Imp gallon) for gearbox.

ACCOMMODATION: Crew of one or two side by side in front of cabin, with bench seat to the rear for a further three persons. The bench seat can be folded into floor wells to leave a completely flat cargo floor. Access to baggage compartment via rear cabin bulkhead, or via optional door on starboard side. Cargo tiedown points in cabin floor. Forward opening car type door on each side of cabin, immediately behind which are rearward opening

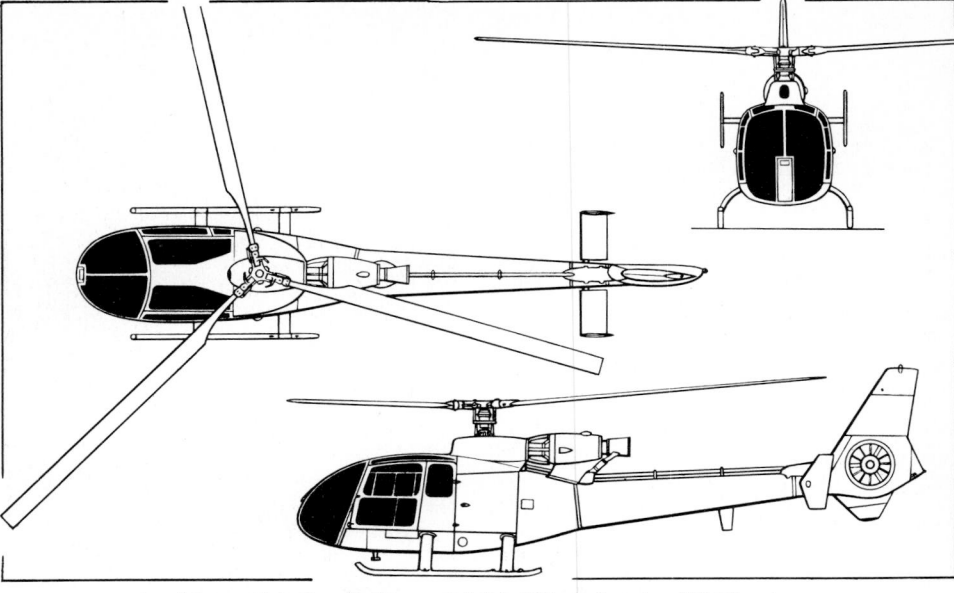

Aérospatiale Gazelle five-seat light utility helicopter *(Pilot Press)*

auxiliary cargo loading doors. Baggage compartment at rear of cabin. Ventilation standard. Dual controls optional.

SYSTEMS: Hydraulic system, pressure 40 bars (570 lb/sq in), serves three pitch change jacks for main rotor head and one for tail rotor. 28V DC electrical system supplied by 4kW engine driven generator and 40Ah battery. Optional 26V AC system, supplied by 0.5kVA alternator at 115/200V 400Hz.

AVIONICS AND EQUIPMENT: Optional communications equipment includes UHF, VHF, HF, intercom systems and homing aids. Optional navigation equipment includes radio compass, radio altimeter and VOR. Blind-flying instrumentation and autopilot optional. A variety of operational equipment can be fitted, according to role, including a 700 kg (1,540 lb) cargo sling, 135 kg (300 lb) rescue hoist, one or two stretchers (internally), or photographic and survey equipment.

ARMAMENT: Military loads can include two pods of Brandt 68 mm or FZ 2.75 in rockets, four or six Hot wire guided missiles with APX M397 gyro stabilised sight, two forward firing 7.62 mm machine-guns, or one GIAT M.621 20 mm gun on starboard side. Yugoslav SA 342Ls are fitted with dual-role carriers for a total of four AT-3 'Sagger' ATMs and two SA-7 'Grail' AAMs.

DIMENSIONS, EXTERNAL:

Main rotor diameter	10.50 m (34 ft 5½ in)
Tail rotor diameter	0.695 m (2 ft 3⅜ in)
Distance between rotor centres	5.85 m (19 ft 2¼ in)
Main rotor blade chord (constant)	0.30 m (11.8 in)
Length overall	11.97 m (39 ft 3⁵⁄₁₆ in)
Length of fuselage, incl tail rotor	
	9.53 m (31 ft 3³⁄₁₆ in)
Width, rotors folded	2.04 m (6 ft 8½ in)
Height to top of rotor head	2.72 m (8 ft 11⅛ in)
Height overall	3.19 m (10 ft 5½ in)
Skid track	2.015 m (6 ft 7⁵⁄₁₆ in)

Main cabin doors, each:	
Height	1.05 m (3 ft 4⁹⁄₁₆ in)
Width	1.00 m (3 ft 3¼ in)
Height to sill	0.63 m (2 ft 0¾ in)
Auxiliary cabin doors, each:	
Height	1.05 m (3 ft 4⁹⁄₁₆ in)
Width	0.48 m (1 ft 6¾ in)
Height to sill	0.63 m (2 ft 0¾ in)

DIMENSIONS, INTERNAL:

Cabin: Length	2.20 m (7 ft 2⁹⁄₁₆ in)
Max width	1.32 m (4 ft 4 in)
Max height	1.21 m (3 ft 11⅝ in)
Floor area	1.50 m² (16.1 sq ft)
Volume	1.80 m³ (63.7 cu ft)
Baggage hold volume	0.45 m³ (15.9 cu ft)

AREAS:

Main rotor blades, each	1.57 m² (16.9 sq ft)
Tail rotor blades, each	0.007 m² (0.075 sq ft)
Main rotor disc	86.59 m² (932.05 sq ft)
Tail rotor disc	0.37 m² (3.98 sq ft)
Fin	0.45 m² (4.84 sq ft)
Tailplane	1.80 m² (19.4 sq ft)

WEIGHTS AND LOADINGS:

Weight empty: 342L₁	990 kg (2,183 lb)
Max T-O and landing weight:	
342L₁	2,000 kg (4,410 lb)
342M	1,900 kg (4,188 lb)
Max disc loading: 342L₁	23.1 kg/m² (4.73 lb/sq ft)
342M	21.94 kg/m² (4.49 lb/sq ft)

PERFORMANCE (SA 342L₁ at max T-O weight):

Never-exceed speed at S/L	
	151 knots (280 km/h; 174 mph)
Max cruising speed at S/L	
	140 knots (260 km/h; 161 mph)
Max rate of climb at S/L	468 m (1,535 ft)/min
Service ceiling	4,100 m (13,450 ft)
Hovering ceiling: IGE	3,040 m (9,975 ft)
OGE	2,370 m (7,775 ft)
Range at S/L with standard fuel	
	383 nm (710 km; 440 miles)

AÉROSPATIALE AS 350 ECUREUIL/ASTAR
Brazilian Air Force designation: CH-50 Esquilo

Developed as a successor to the Alouette, the AS 350 Ecureuil (Squirrel) embodies Aérospatiale's Starflex type of main rotor hub, made of glassfibre, with elastomeric spherical stops and oleo-elastic frequency matchers. The first prototype (F-WVKH) flew on 27 June 1974, powered by a Textron Lycoming LTS 101 turboshaft. It was followed on 14 February 1975 by a second prototype (F-WVKI) with a Turbomeca Arriel turboshaft.

The Textron Lycoming powered version is marketed only in North America, as the **Astar**; and the Arriel powered **Ecureuil** is marketed throughout the rest of the world. Initial production of the latter included the basic AS 350B, with 478 kW (641 shp) Arriel 1B, for which French certification was received on 27 October 1977. Current production versions are as follows:

AS 350B₁ Ecureuil. With 510 kW (684 shp) Arriel 1D turboshaft; uprated transmission, with gearbox able to absorb max input of 440 kW (590 shp); and wide-chord, new section main and tail rotor blades developed originally for the Ecureuil 2/Twinstar. Certificated by DGAC on 9 January 1986.

On 14 May 1985 an AS 350B₁, at an AUW of 1,270 kg (2,800 lb) with a crew of two, set three official class E1c records by climbing to 3,000 m in 2 min 59.3 s, 6,000 m in 6 min 54.9 s, and 9,000 m in 13 min 51.5 s.

AS 350D Astar. Current Astar Mk III has 459 kW (615 shp) Textron Lycoming LTS 101-600A-3 turboshaft. Otherwise as AS 350B.

Aérospatiale SA 342L Gazelle armed with four AATCP Mistral anti-helicopter missile launchers

AS 350B Ecureuil water bomber refilling its water tank while hovering

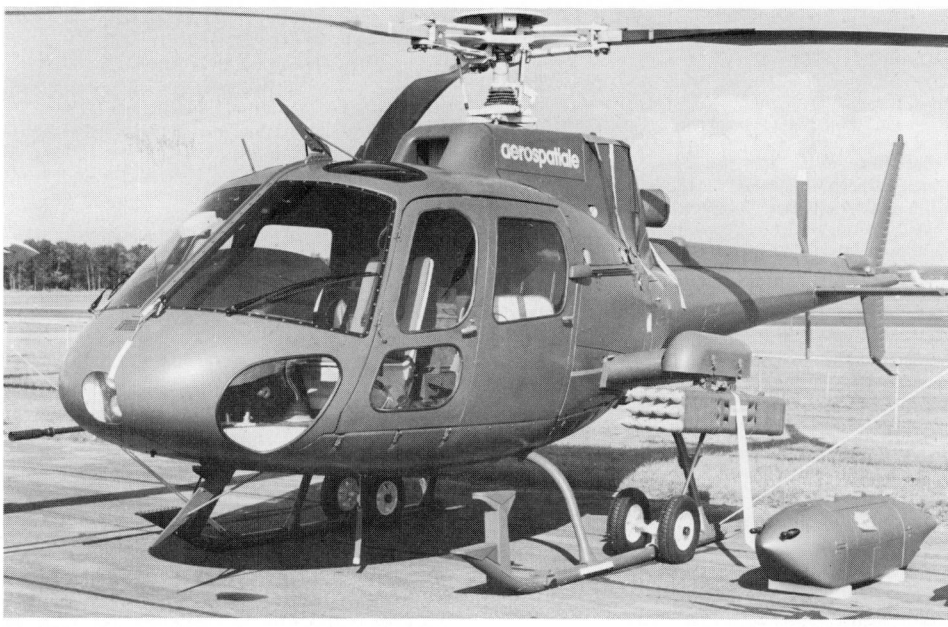

AS 350L₁ Ecureuil armed with 20 mm gun and rocket pack. Alternative twin-gun pod on ground
(Brian M. Service)

AS 350L₁, Ecureuil. Military version of AS 350B₁, with Arriel 1D turboshaft. Standard features include a taller landing gear, sliding doors, extended instrument panel and airframe reinforcement for axial armament. Provision for armoured seats. First flown in March 1985. Firing trials began in October 1985 and deliveries were in progress by Spring 1986.

Deliveries of the basic AS 350B began in March 1978. FAA certification of the original AS 350C Astar was obtained on 21 December 1977 and the first production delivery was made in April 1978. The AS 350C was superseded in 1978 by the AS 350D. By 1 March 1988 a total of 1,140 AS 350 Ecureuils and Astars had been ordered for service in 43 countries; 1,090 had been delivered. Customers include the Singapore armed forces, which have six, and the Australian government, which has taken delivery of 18 AS 350Bs for RAAF pilot training, liaison, search and rescue, and six more for survey and utility duties with the Royal Australian Navy. In mid-1987, the Danish Army ordered 12 AS 350L₁s, equipped with the Saab/Emerson Electric HeliTOW anti-tank missile system. Ecureuils are also produced under licence by Helibras of Brazil, with the name Esquilo.

During 1986, an AS 350B₁ Ecureuil with taller landing gear was fitted with a firefighting kit purchased from Conair of Canada, to test its effectiveness in dealing with forest fires in Southern France. The kit consists of a streamlined tank which can be refilled in 30 s through a snout while the helicopter hovers over a stretch of water. Five Ecureuils had been so equipped by mid-1988, as described and illustrated under the Conair entry.

Under a French government contract, Aérospatiale flew in 1986 an AS 350 fitted with a 'fenestron' shrouded tail rotor, but this is not expected to become a feature of production Ecureuils of the current series.

TYPE: Five/six-seat light general purpose helicopter.

ROTOR SYSTEM: Three-blade main rotor, with Starflex glassfibre hub in which the three conventional hinges for each blade are replaced by a single balljoint of rubber/steel sandwich construction, requiring no maintenance. Glassfibre blades, with stainless steel leading-edge sheath, produced by an entirely mechanised process. Symmetrical blade section on AS 350B; OA 209 section on wider-chord blades of AS 350B₁ and L₁. Two-blade tail rotor; each blade comprises a sheet metal skin around a glassfibre spar, the flexibility of which obviates the need for hinges.

ROTOR DRIVE: Simplified transmission, with single epicyclic main gear train. Tail rotor driveshaft coupling on engine.

FUSELAGE: Basic structure of light alloy pressings, with skin mainly of thermoformed plastics, including baggage compartment doors.

TAIL UNIT: Horizontal stabiliser, of inverted aerofoil section, mid mounted on tailboom. Sweptback fin, in two sections above and below tailboom.

LANDING GEAR: Steel tube skid type. Taller version standard on military aircraft. Emergency flotation gear optional.

POWER PLANT: One turboshaft (for type see individual model listings) mounted above fuselage to rear of cabin. Plastics fuel tanks (self sealing on AS 350L₁) with total capacity of 535 litres (141.3 US gallons; 117.7 Imp gallons).

ACCOMMODATION: Two individual bucket seats at front of cabin and two two-place bench seats are standard. In the alternative layout the two benches are replaced by three armchair seats. Optional ambulance layout described in detail in introductory notes. Large forward hinged door on each side of versions for civil use. Optional sliding door at rear of cabin on port side. (Sliding doors standard on military version.) Baggage compartment aft of cabin, with full-width upward hinged door on starboard side. Top of baggage compartment reinforced to provide platform on each side for inspecting and servicing rotor head.

SYSTEMS: Hydraulic system includes four single-body servo units, operating at 40 bars (570 lb/sq in) pressure, and accumulators to protect against a hydraulic power supply failure. Electrical system includes a 4.5kW engine driven starter/generator, a 16Ah 24V nickel-cadmium battery and a ground power receptacle connected to the busbar which distributes power to the electrical equipment. Cabin air-conditioning system optional.

AVIONICS AND EQUIPMENT: Optional com/nav radio equipment includes VHF/AM, ICS, VOR/LOC/glideslope, marker beacon indicator, radio compass, HF/SSB, transponder and DME. IFR instrumentation optional. Available equipment includes a SFIM PA 85E, Sperry HelCis or Collins APS-841H autopilot, a 907 kg (2,000 lb) cargo sling (1,160 kg; 2,557 lb for B₁ and L₁ versions), a 135 kg (297 lb) electric hoist, a TV camera for aerial filming, and a 735 litre (194 US gallon; 161 Imp gallon) Simplex agricultural spraytank and boom system.

ARMAMENT (AS 350L₁): Provision for wide range of weapons, including 20 mm GIAT M621 gun, FN Herstal TMP twin 7.62 mm machine-gun pods, Thomson Brandt 68.12 launchers for twelve 68 mm rockets, Forges de Zeebrugge launchers for seven 2.75 in rockets, and Saab/Emerson Electric HeliTOW anti-tank missile systems.

DIMENSIONS, EXTERNAL:

Main rotor diameter	10.69 m (35 ft 0¾ in)
Main rotor blade chord: AS 350B/D	300 mm (11.8 in)
AS 350B₁/L₁	350 mm (13.8 in)
Tail rotor diameter	1.86 m (6 ft 1¼ in)
Tail rotor blade chord: AS 350B/D	185 mm (7.28 in)
AS 350B₁/L₁	205 mm (8.07 in)
Length overall	12.94 m (42 ft 5½ in)
Length of fuselage, incl tail rotor	10.93 m (35 ft 10½ in)
Width of fuselage	1.80 m (5 ft 10¾ in)
Height overall: AS 350B/B₁/D	3.14 m (10 ft 3½ in)
AS 350L₁	3.34 m (10 ft 11½ in)
Skid track	2.17 m (7 ft 1½ in)

Cabin doors (civil versions, standard, each):

Height	1.15 m (3 ft 9¼ in)
Width	1.10 m (3 ft 7¼ in)

DIMENSIONS, INTERNAL:

Cabin: Length	2.42 m (7 ft 11¼ in)
Width at rear	1.65 m (5 ft 5 in)
Height	1.35 m (4 ft 5 in)
Baggage compartment volume	1.00 m³ (35.31 cu ft)

AREAS:

Main rotor disc	89.75 m² (966.1 sq ft)
Tail rotor disc	2.72 m² (29.25 sq ft)

WEIGHTS:

Weight empty: 350B	1,088 kg (2,398 lb)
350B₁	1,120 kg (2,469 lb)
350D	1,070 kg (2,359 lb)
350L₁	1,169 kg (2,577 lb)
Max T-O weight: normal: 350B/D	1,950 kg (4,300 lb)
350B₁/L₁	2,200 kg (4,850 lb)
with max slung load: 350B/D	2,100 kg (4,630 lb)
350B₁/L₁	2,450 kg (5,400 lb)

PERFORMANCE (at normal max T-O weight):

Never-exceed speed below 500 m (1,640 ft):

All versions	147 knots (272 km/h; 169 mph)

Max cruising speed at S/L:

350B	125 knots (232 km/h; 144 mph)
350B₁/D/L₁	124 knots (230 km/h; 143 mph)

Max rate of climb at S/L:

350B, 350D	480 m (1,575 ft)/min
350B₁/L₁	450 m (1,475 ft)/min
Service ceiling: 350B/D	4,575 m (15,000 ft)
350B₁/L₁	4,500 m (14,760 ft)
Hovering ceiling IGE: 350B	2,950 m (9,675 ft)
350B₁/L₁	2,870 m (9,415 ft)
350D	2,500 m (8,200 ft)
Hovering ceiling OGE: 350B	2,250 m (7,380 ft)
350B₁/L₁	1,920 m (6,300 ft)
350D	1,800 m (5,900 ft)

Range with max fuel at S/L, no reserves:

350B	378 nm (700 km; 435 miles)
350B₁/L₁	354 nm (655 km; 407 miles)
350D	410 nm (760 km; 472 miles)

AÉROSPATIALE AS 355 ECUREUIL 2/TWINSTAR
Brazilian Air Force designations: CH-55 and VH-55 Esquilo

The AS 355 is a twin-engined version of the AS 350 Ecureuil/Astar family. Many components, such as the main rotor mast and head, tail rotor hub, servo units, cabin and landing gear, are identical to those of the AS 350. The main and tail rotor blades are also identical to those of the current AS 350B₁/L₁ versions. Major changes apply to the power plant, transmission, fuel system and fuselage structure.

The first of two prototypes (F-WZLA) flew on 28 September 1979. Details of the AS 355E/F initial production versions, with Allison engines, can be found in the 1984-85 and earlier editions of *Jane's*.

From January 1984, the AS 355F was superseded by the **AS 355F₁**, incorporating three significant modifications. Addition of a laminated tab increased the tail rotor blade chord. The max power transmitted to the main gearbox was increased, by setting the torque limiter to 2 × 78% instead of 2 × 73%. Addition of a rotor overspeed alarm set to 410 rpm represented a complementary function of the normal alarm system. These changes permitted increased max T-O weight and payload.

A further increase in max T-O weight is offered by the **AS 355F₂**, which received DGAC certification on 10 December 1985. This version introduced a load compensator in the yaw channel and an extension of the CG limits.

The AS 355F₂ is intended primarily for the civil market, in particular for use by companies working in the oil industry. The Armée de l'Air is receiving 50 military models for surveillance of strategic military bases and other support duties, of which the last annual increment of six is scheduled for procurement in 1989. Following delivery by 1987 of ten Allison powered AS 355F₁s, the remaining 40 are following from 1988 in **AS 355N** guise with two Turbomeca TM 319 turboshafts. An Allison engined military version known as the **AS 355M₂** (embodying the improvements developed for the latest civil variants) is available to other customers. Provision for carrying Matra Mistral infra-red missiles was expected to be introduced on the Armée de l'Air aircraft as deliveries built up. Alternative weapon loads include rocket packs, an anti-tank missile installation and guns. The Brazilian Air Force has 11 AS 355Ms, of which eight with armament are designated **CH-55** and three VIP transports are designated **VH-55**. These are assembled by Helibras (which see).

By 1 March 1988, a total of 374 AS 355s had been ordered for service in 30 countries; 344 had been delivered. The version for the North American market is known as the **Twinstar**; aircraft marketed elsewhere are named **Ecureuil 2**.

The following details apply to the AS 355F₂ and M₂ versions:

TYPE: Twin-turbine light general purpose helicopter.

ROTOR SYSTEM: As for AS 350B₁/L₁.

ROTOR DRIVE: Single main gearbox, made up of three modules (coupling gearbox with freewheel, angle gearing with spiral bevel gears, and epicyclic gear train including five oscillating planetary gears). Power take-offs for the accessories and tail rotor.

FUSELAGE: Light alloy centre fuselage structure, with deep drawn sheet metal forms of simple geometric design. Cabin skin of thermoformed plastics. Tapered tailboom

of light alloy sheet wrapped and riveted around deep drawn sheet metal cylindrical frames.

TAIL UNIT AND LANDING GEAR: As for AS350B₁/L₁.

POWER PLANT: Two Allison 250-C20F turboshafts, each rated at 313 kW (420 shp) for take-off and 276 kW (370 shp) max continuous, mounted above fuselage to rear of cabin. (AS 355N has two Turbomeca TM 319 turboshafts, each rated at 340 kW; 456 shp for take-off and 295 kW; 395 shp max continuous.) Two structural fuel tanks, with total usable capacity of 730 litres (193 US gallons; 160 Imp gallons), in body structure.

ACCOMMODATION: As for AS 350B₁, except sliding doors are optional on both sides (standard on military aircraft), and there are three baggage holds with external doors.

SYSTEMS, AVIONICS AND EQUIPMENT: As for AS 350B₁/L₁, except that twin-body servo command units and a second electrical generator are standard. Options include a second VHF/AM, radio altimeter and casualty installations. Provisions for IFR instrumentation, and SFIM 85 T31 three-axis autopilot and CDV 85 T3 nav coupler.

ARMAMENT (AS 355M₂): Optional alternative weapons include Brandt or Forges de Zeebrugge rocket packs, Matra or FN machine-gun pods, a GIAT M621 20 mm gun, and Hot or TOW anti-tank missiles.

DIMENSIONS, EXTERNAL AND INTERNAL:
As for AS 350B₁/L₁

WEIGHTS:

Weight empty: 355F₂	1,305 kg (2,877 lb)
355M₂	1,360 kg (2,998 lb)
Max sling load: 355F₂/M₂	1,134 kg (2,500 lb)
Max T-O weight:	
355F₂/M₂, internal load	2,540 kg (5,600 lb)
355F₂/M₂, max slung load	2,600 kg (5,732 lb)

PERFORMANCE (AS 355F₂/M₂ at max T-O weight, ISA):

Never-exceed speed (structural limitation)	
	150 knots (278 km/h; 172 mph)
Max cruising speed at S/L	
	121 knots (224 km/h; 139 mph)
Max rate of climb at S/L	390 m (1,280 ft)/min
Service ceiling	3,400 m (11,150 ft)
Hovering ceiling: IGE	1,800 m (5,900 ft)
OGE	1,350 m (4,425 ft)
Range with max fuel at S/L, no reserves	
	380 nm (703 km; 437 miles)

Aérospatiale AS 355F₁ Ecureuil 2 twin-turbine five/six-seat light helicopter

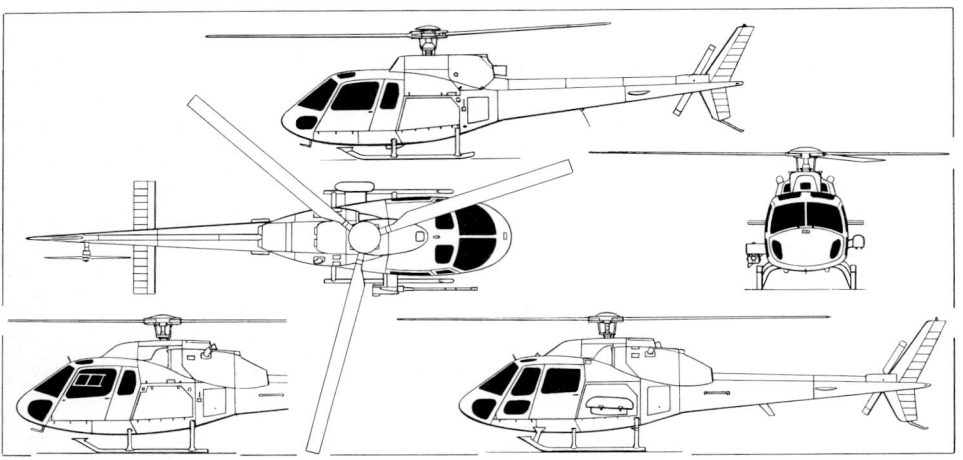

Aérospatiale AS 355M₂ Ecureuil 2, with additional side elevation (top) of single-engined AS 350 and scrap view of AS 355F₁ *(Pilot Press)*

AÉROSPATIALE SA 365F/AS.15TT DAUPHIN 2

On 13 October 1980, the government of Saudi Arabia placed in France orders for four frigates and associated naval equipment including 24 SA 365F Dauphin 2 helicopters, based on the SA 365N. The first four of these are equipped with an Omera ORB 32 radar for search and rescue duties. The remaining 20 are anti-ship helicopters, equipped with Thomson-CSF Agrion 15 radar, Aérospatiale AS.15TT all-weather air-to-surface missiles and Crouzet MAD, for operation from both shore bases and frigates. Subsequent orders include five for Ireland, equipped with Bendix RDR 1500 search radar, SFIM 155 autopilot, CDV 155 four-axis flight director/coupler, Crouzet Nadir Mk II nav computer, ESD Cina B Doppler, Crouzet ONS 200A long-distance nav system and five-screen EFIS instrumentation, for fishery surveillance and SAR from ship and shore bases. Irish Dauphins have no AS.15 capability, but may be fitted with other forms of light armament. Early in 1988, the French Navy ordered three SA 365Fs in SAR configuration for plane guard duties on board its two aircraft carriers. Four have been ordered by the Chilean Navy.

An SA 365N (c/n 5100) was modified to flight test the equipment and weapon systems of the SA 365F, and made its first flight in the new configuration on 22 February 1982. It was followed by the first production SA 365F (c/n 6014) on 2 July 1982, equipped as a search and rescue helicopter with arrester hook, search radar, searchlight, self-contained navigation system, automatic hover/transition coupler and rescue winch.

The anti-ship version carries the Agrion 15 radar on a roll-stabilised pivot mounting under its nose, to ensure a 360° field of sweep, a total of four AS.15TT missiles, in pairs on an outrigger on each side of the fuselage, and the MAD 'bird' on the port side of the rear fuselage. Range of the AS.15TT missile is greater than 8 nm (15 km; 9.3 miles). In addition to locating and attacking hostile warships, the SA 365F/AS.15TT can be utilised for coastal surveillance and ship escort duties, and to provide over-the-horizon target designation for long-range anti-ship missiles launched from ship or shore. An anti-submarine version is available, initially with MAD, sonobuoys and homing torpedoes, but with provision for Alcatel HS 12 sonar.

The SA 365F carries a normal crew of two, has provision for 10 passengers and is powered by two Turbomeca Arriel IM turboshafts, each rated at 522 kW (700 shp) for take-off and with a max continuous rating of 465 kW (624 shp). Standard fuel capacity of 1,145 litres (302.5 US gallons; 252 Imp gallons) can be augmented by a 180 litre (47.5 US gallon; 39.6 Imp gallon) auxiliary tank. Like the current SA 365N₁, it has a larger, carbonfibre 11-blade 'fenestron' to improve hovering performance, particularly in the most severe condition of hovering with the wind from three-quarters aft.

DIMENSIONS, EXTERNAL:
As for SA 365N₁, except:

Length overall, rotor turning	13.74 m (45 ft 1 in)
Length of fuselage	12.11 m (39 ft 8¾ in)
Width over missiles	4.20 m (13 ft 9½ in)

WEIGHTS:

Weight empty	2,205 kg (4,861 lb)
Max slung load	1,600 kg (3,527 lb)
Max T-O weight, internal or external load	
	4,100 kg (9,039 lb)

PERFORMANCE (at max T-O weight):

Never-exceed speed	160 knots (296 km/h; 184 mph)
Max cruising speed at S/L	
	154 knots (285 km/h; 177 mph)
Max rate of climb at S/L	390 m (1,280 ft)/min

20 mm gun installation on an AS 355M₂ military version of the Ecureuil 2

Aérospatiale SA 365F used by the Irish Air Corps for fishery surveillance, search and rescue *(Paul Duffy)*

Hovering ceiling: IGE   2,150 m (7,050 ft)
OGE   1,200 m (3,935 ft)
Range with max standard fuel at S/L
    467 nm (865 km; 537 miles)

AÉROSPATIALE SA 365N₁ DAUPHIN 2

The SA 365N₁ is the current production version of the civil Dauphin. Compared with the SA 365N, described in previous editions of *Jane's*, it has improved engines and a larger carbonfibre 'fenestron' tail rotor with eleven blades.

Orders for all versions of SA 365/366 totalled 385 for civil and military use in 38 countries by 1 March 1988; deliveries totalled 367 on that date. The totals included production in China (as the Harbin Z-9), as well as SA 366Gs for the US Coast Guard and SA 365F/AS.15TTs with special equipment for search and rescue, and for attacking surface ships. These last two variants are described separately.

A special aeromedical version of the SA 365N₁, with a flight crew of two, is available in two forms. An 'intensive care' layout is arranged to carry two patients, one on each side of the cabin on a standard NATO stretcher, with space between for the doctor's seat and medical equipment. One of the stretchers can be replaced by seats for two patients, if required. The alternative 'ambulance' configuration provides space for two stretchers on each side of the cabin, one above the other, plus room for the doctor; or a single pair of stretchers, with room for four seated persons on the other side, and a doctor. Stretchers are loaded through nose doors, with 180° opening, on both models. Those in the ambulance layout are fixed to the sides of the cabin, and the patients are carried on them on special mattresses.

The following structural description refers to the standard SA 365N₁, but is generally applicable to all versions:

TYPE: Twin-turbine commercial general purpose helicopter.
ROTOR SYSTEM: Four-blade main rotor. Blades attached by quick disconnect pins to Starflex glassfibre/carbonfibre hub, in which the three conventional hinges for each blade are replaced by a single balljoint of rubber/steel sandwich construction, requiring no maintenance. Blades of new OA 2 section, developed in collaboration with Onera: varying from OA 212 (thickness/chord ratio 12%) at root to OA 207 (7%) at tip, with 10° negative twist from root to tip. Each blade comprises two Z section carbonfibre spars and carbonfibre skin, a solid glassfibre-resin leading-edge covered with a stainless steel sheath, and Nomex honeycomb filling. Leading-edge of carbonfibre tip is swept back at 45°. Ground adjustable tab on trailing-edge of each blade towards tip. Blade chord extended outboard of tab to align with tab trailing-edge. Rotor brake standard. Eleven-blade 'fenestron' type of carbonfibre ducted fan anti-torque tail rotor.
ROTOR DRIVE: Mechanical shaft and gear drive. Transmission shaft from each engine extends forward, through freewheel, to helical and epicyclic reduction stages of main gearbox. Shaft to 'fenestron' driven off bottom of main rotor shaft. Main rotor rpm 350. 'Fenestron' rpm 3,665.
FUSELAGE: Semi-monocoque structure. Bottom structure and framework of front fuselage, primary machined frames fore and aft of the main gearbox platform and at the rear of the centre fuselage, floors under main gearbox and engines, cabin doors and fin are all of light alloy (AU4G). Nose and power plant fairings and fin tip of glassfibre/Nomex sandwich. Centre and rear fuselage assemblies, flight deck floor, roof, walls and bottom skins of fuel tanks of light alloy/Nomex sandwich.
TAIL UNIT: Horizontal stabiliser mid-set on rear fuselage, forward of 'fenestron'; swept endplate fins offset 10° to port. Construction of carbonfibre and Nomex/Rohacell sandwich.
LANDING GEAR: Hydraulically retractable tricycle type. Twin-wheel steerable and self-centring nose unit retracts rearward. Single wheel on each rearward retracting main unit, fully enclosed by doors of Kevlar/Nomex sandwich when retracted. All three units embody oleo-pneumatic shock absorber. Mainwheel tyres size 15 × 6.00, pressure 8.6 bars (125 lb/sq in); nosewheel tyres size 5.00-4, pressure 5.5 bars (80 lb/sq in). Hydraulic disc brakes.

POWER PLANT: Two Turbomeca Arriel IC1 turboshafts, each rated at 540 kW (724 shp) for T-O and 437 kW (586 shp) max continuous, side by side aft of main rotor driveshaft, with stainless steel firewall between them. Standard fuel in four tanks under cabin floor and a fifth tank in the bottom of the centre-fuselage; total capacity 1,135 litres (300 US gallons; 249.5 Imp gallons). Provision for auxiliary tank in baggage compartment, with capacity of 180 litres (47.5 US gallons; 39.5 Imp gallons); or ferry tank in place of rear seats in cabin, capacity 475 litres (125.5 US gallons; 104.5 Imp gallons). Refuelling point above landing gear door on port side. Oil capacity 14 litres (3.7 US gallons; 3 Imp gallons).
ACCOMMODATION: Standard accommodation for pilot and co-pilot or passenger in front, and two rows of four seats to rear. High density seating for one pilot and 13 passengers. VIP configurations for four to six persons in addition to pilot. Three forward opening doors on each side. Freight hold aft of cabin rear bulkhead, with door on starboard side. Cabin heated and ventilated.
SYSTEMS: Air-conditioning system optional. Duplicated hydraulic system, pressure 60 bars (870 lb/sq in). Electrical system includes two 4.8kW starter/generators, one 43Ah 24V battery and two 250VA 115V 400Hz inverters.
AVIONICS AND EQUIPMENT: Two-pilot IFR instrument panel and SFIM 155 duplex autopilot standard. Optional avionics include VHF and HF com/nav, VOR, ILS, ADF, transponder, DME, radar and self contained nav system. Optional equipment includes a SFIM CDV 85 nav coupler, a 1,600 kg (3,525 lb) capacity cargo sling, and 275 kg (606 lb) capacity hoist with 90 m (295 ft) cable length.

DIMENSIONS, EXTERNAL:
Main rotor diameter	11.94 m (39 ft 2 in)
Diameter of 'fenestron'	1.10 m (3 ft 7⁵⁄₁₆ in)
Main rotor blade chord: basic	0.385 m (1 ft 3¼ in)
outboard of tab	0.405 m (1 ft 4 in)
Length overall, rotor turning	13.88 m (45 ft 6½ in)
Length of fuselage	11.63 m (38 ft 1⅞ in)
Width, rotor blades folded	3.21 m (10 ft 6½ in)
Height to top of rotor head	3.52 m (11 ft 6½ in)
Height overall (tip of fin)	3.98 m (13 ft 0¾ in)
Wheel track	1.90 m (6 ft 2¾ in)
Wheelbase	3.61 m (11 ft 10¼ in)
Main cabin door (fwd, each side):	
Height	1.16 m (3 ft 9½ in)
Width	1.14 m (3 ft 9 in)
Main cabin door (rear, each side):	
Height	1.16 m (3 ft 9½ in)
Width	0.87 m (2 ft 10¼ in)

Baggage compartment door (stbd):
Height	0.51 m (1 ft 8 in)
Width	0.73 m (2 ft 4¾ in)

DIMENSIONS, INTERNAL:
Cabin: Length	2.30 m (7 ft 6½ in)
Max width	1.92 m (6 ft 3½ in)
Max height	1.40 m (4 ft 7 in)
Floor area	4.20 m² (45.20 sq ft)
Volume	5.00 m³ (176 cu ft)
Baggage compartment volume	1.00 m³ (35.3 cu ft)

AREAS:
Main rotor disc	111.9 m² (1,204.5 sq ft)
'Fenestron' disc	0.95 m² (10.23 sq ft)

WEIGHTS:
Weight empty, equipped	2,161 kg (4,764 lb)
Max T-O weight:	
internal or external load	4,100 kg (9,039 lb)

PERFORMANCE (at max T-O weight):
Never-exceed speed at S/L	160 knots (296 km/h; 184 mph)
Max cruising speed at S/L	153 knots (283 km/h; 176 mph)
Econ cruising speed at S/L	140 knots (260 km/h; 161 mph)
Max rate of climb at S/L	396 m (1,300 ft)/min
Service ceiling	3,600 m (11,810 ft)
Hovering ceiling: IGE	2,100 m (6,890 ft)
OGE	1,100 m (3,610 ft)
Max range with standard fuel at S/L	460 nm (852 km; 530 miles)
Endurance with standard fuel	4 h

AÉROSPATIALE SA 366 DAUPHIN 2
US Coast Guard designation: HH-65A Dolphin

At the 1979 Paris Air Show, Aérospatiale announced that it had won with this aircraft the competition for a helicopter to perform SRR (Short Range Recovery) duties from 18 shore bases, and from icebreakers and cutters, of the US Coast Guard. Current orders for the Coast Guard are for a total of 99 SA 366Gs, basically similar to the SA 365N but with engines and equipment of US manufacture accounting for about 60 per cent of the total cost of each aircraft.

The SA 366G (known to the Coast Guard as the HH-65A Dolphin) is powered by two Textron Lycoming LTS 101-750A-1 turboshafts, each rated at 507 kW (680 shp) and fitted with a Lucas SDS 300 full authority digital electronic control system. It normally carries a crew of three (pilot, co-pilot and aircrewman/hoist operator). Rockwell Collins is prime contractor for the advanced communications, navigation and all-weather search equipment. The communications package includes dual UHF/VHF transceivers and single UHF/FM and HF systems, plus a data link for automatic transmission of data, such as aircraft position, flight path, ground speed, wind and fuel state, to ship or shore base. A nose mounted Northrop See Hawk forward looking infra-red sensor aids rescue operations in bad weather, darkness or high seas. Important design features include the passive failure characteristics of the Dolphin's automatic flight control system, and an omnidirectional airspeed system able to provide information while the aircraft is hovering. Inflatable flotation bags are effective up to sea state 5.

The first SA 366G flew for the first time at Marignane on 23 July 1980. It was later shipped to Aerospatiale Helicopter Corporation in Texas for installation of avionics, and flight testing for FAA certification. DGAC certification was received on 20 July 1982. As on the SA 365F/M, the size of the tail fin and carbonfibre 'fenestron' is increased on the operational Coast Guard aircraft, designated **SA 366G-1**. The first was delivered on 19 November 1984, and about 50 had been accepted by 1 February 1987. The first life-saving medevac mission was completed on 20 September 1985. Aircraft covered by current USCG contracts will all be in service by the end of 1988. In 1985, the Israel Defence Force

Aérospatiale SA 365N₁ Dauphin 2 commercial helicopter in medical evacuation service

Aérospatiale HH-65A Dolphin (SA 366G-1) for the US Coast Guard

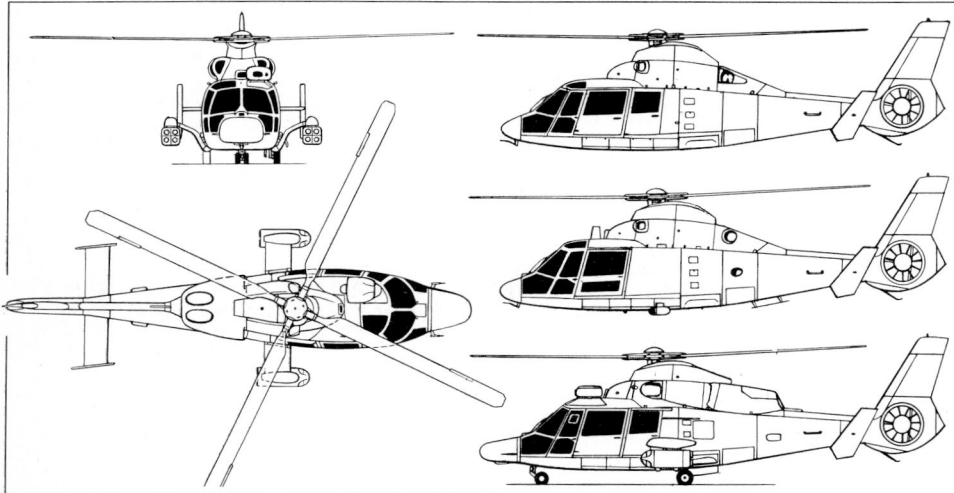

Aérospatiale SA 365M Panther, with added side views of HH-65A Dolphin (SA 366G-1) for US Coast Guard (centre) and SA 365N₁ Dauphin 2 (top) *(Pilot Press)*

Aérospatiale SA 365M Panther, armed with two 20 mm gun pods

Artist's impression of Hermes aerospacecraft placing a satellite in orbit

purchased two ex-USCG trials SA 366s for an 18-month evaluation. This was completed successfully in 1987 when a contract was placed with Aerospatiale Helicopter Corporation for 20 more to HH-65A standards, bought with FMS funds. Duties will include fire control, ASW and SAR duties from 'Sa'ar' missile boats.

WEIGHTS:
Weight empty, incl mission equipment	
	2,718 kg (5,992 lb)
Max T-O weight	4,050 kg (8,928 lb)

PERFORMANCE (at max T-O weight):
Never-exceed speed	175 knots (324 km/h; 201 mph)
Max cruising speed	139 knots (257 km/h; 160 mph)
Hovering ceiling: IGE	2,290 m (7,510 ft)
OGE	1,627 m (5,340 ft)
SRR range	166 nm (307 km; 191 miles)
Range with max passenger load	
	216 nm (400 km; 248 miles)
Range with max fuel	410 nm (760 km; 471 miles)
Endurance with max fuel	4 h

AÉROSPATIALE SA 365M PANTHER

This multi-role military development of the Dauphin 2 was first flown in prototype form (F-WZJV) on 29 February 1984. It has since undergone considerable refinement, and was first shown in production form, as the Panther, on 30 April 1986. Armament integration and firing trials were completed successfully in late 1986, and a second, improved prototype (F-ZVLO) was flown in April 1987. The Panther was expected to be available for delivery in 1988.

The airframe of the Panther is basically similar to that of the SA 365N₁, but with greater emphasis on survivability in combat areas. Composite materials are used exclusively for the dynamic components and for an increased (15 per cent) proportion of the fuselage structure. The crew seats are armoured, and similar protection will be extended to the flying control servos and engine controls of production Panthers. Other features include a cable cutter, self-sealing fuel tanks and redundant hydraulic circuits. Further development is expected to permit continued operation of the main transmission after total loss of lubricating oil.

Similar attention has been paid to crashworthiness. The crew seats will tolerate 15g. The entire basic airframe is designed to withstand an impact at a vertical speed of 7 m (23 ft)/s at max T-O weight; the fuel system is capable of withstanding a 14 m (46 ft)/s crash.

The Panther is powered by two Turbomeca TM 333-1M turboshafts, each rated at 681 kW (913 shp) for take-off and 560 kW (751 shp) continuous, and utilises the larger carbonfibre 'fenestron' of the SA 365F. To reduce IR signature, the airframe is finished in low IR reflecting paint, and the engine efflux is first mixed with cool ambient air and then ejected upward. Noise level is low, and radar signature is minimised by the aircraft's composite structure and special paints. Night operations are made practicable by adaptation of the cockpit to nap-of-the-earth flight using night vision goggles. Equipment can include a Thomson-CSF TMV 011 Sherloc radar warning receiver, IR jammer and chaff dispenser.

Two world helicopter records were established by the prototype Panther on 15 September 1987 when, at a weight of 2,774 kg (6,116 lb), it achieved an altitude of 3,000 m in 2 min 54 s and 6,000 m in 6 min 14 s.

As a high speed assault transport, the Panther will carry a crew of two and eight to ten troops over a radius of action of 215 nm (400 km; 248 miles), or 60 troops per hour over 11 nm (20 km; 12 miles). For close support missions of three-hour duration, the fuselage-side outriggers can each carry a pack of 22 Thomson-Brandt 68 mm rockets, a launcher for 19 Forges de Zeebrugge 2.75 in rockets or a 20 mm GIAT M621 gun pod with 180 rounds. Three-hour day or night anti-tank missions are possible, carrying four two-round packs of Hot anti-tank missiles with an associated Viviane roof mounted stabilised sight. Operations against fixed-wing aircraft or other helicopters are envisaged, using either 20 mm guns or four two-round packs of Matra Mistral infra-red homing air-to-air missiles. Secondary roles could include armed or unarmed reconnaissance, electronic warfare, target designation, aerial command post, search and rescue, casualty evacuation (four stretchers) and transport of up to 1,600 kg (3,525 lb) of external freight.

DIMENSIONS, EXTERNAL: As for SA 365F, except:
Length of fuselage	12.07 m (39 ft 7 in)
Height overall (tip of fin)	4.07 m (13 ft 4¼ in)

WEIGHTS:
Weight empty	2,300 kg (5,070 lb)
Max slung load	1,600 kg (3,527 lb)
Max T-O weight, internal or external load	
	4,100 kg (9,039 lb)

PERFORMANCE (at max T-O weight):
Never-exceed speed	160 knots (296 km/h; 184 mph)
Max cruising speed at S/L	
	148 knots (275 km/h; 171 mph)
Max rate of climb at S/L	480 m (1,575 ft)/min
Hovering ceiling: IGE	3,200 m (10,500 ft)
OGE	2,500 m (8,200 ft)
Range with max standard fuel at S/L	
	421 nm (780 km; 485 miles)

HERMES AEROSPACECRAFT

On 18 October 1985 it was announced that the French Centre National d'Études Spatiales (CNES) had appointed Aérospatiale as industrial prime contractor for the Hermes aerospacecraft programme. Aérospatiale will build two of the vehicles over a ten-year period. Dassault-Breguet will be responsible for the work required to achieve successful flight in the atmosphere.

The Hermes vehicle is envisaged as a delta-wing aircraft with winglets, able to carry four to six persons and up to three tonnes of payload. It will have an ejectable crew compartment, and a pressurised cargo compartment linked by an airlock tunnel to the rear docking port. The cargo compartment will be enclosed at the top by large sideways opening solar panels. Placed in low Earth orbit by an Ariane 5 launcher, Hermes' primary mission will be to service space stations. First flight is planned for 1997.

WEIGHTS:

Payload for 500 km (310 mile) circular Earth orbit inclined at 28.5°	3,000 kg (6,615 lb)
Fuel	1,500 kg (3,307 lb)
Max T-O weight	21,000 kg (46,300 lb)

CAGNY
RAYMOND DE CAGNY
5 square des Bégonias, 91370 Verrières le Buisson
Telephone: (1) 60 11 98 02

M de Cagny is developing a unique side by side three-seat light aircraft, which was first displayed in the form of a full scale mockup at the 1985 Paris Air Show.

CAGNY PERFORMANCE 2000
The design of this all-composites light aircraft was based on the results of a survey carried out among flying clubs in France and overseas. Answers to two of the questions showed a general preference for a Textron Lycoming engine and a three-seat cabin. M Cagny decided to place the three seats of his Performance 2000 side by side, so that the third occupant would share the excellent field of view of the pilots and, being aware of their actions during flying training, might be encouraged to become a pupil pilot.

Current high costs of flying training are expected to be reduced in the Performance 2000 by use of sturdy but lightweight composites, which offer a smooth surface finish, minimal maintenance requirements, easy replacement, and long service life. Positioning of the engine on the fin leading-edge reduces cabin noise, while the shrouded propeller eliminates danger for those around the aircraft on the ground.

First flight of the prototype Performance 2000 was scheduled to take place in January 1988. However, this was postponed, partly as the result of a re-design which transferred power plant from the leading edge of the fin (as shown in mockup form) to a pylon immediately to the rear of the cockpit. The former shrouded tractor propeller is replaced by an unshrouded pusher unit, but projected weights and performance are unchanged.

The description which follows applies to this first prototype. Studies are underway, in conjunction with the Teledyne Continental and Porsche companies, to select the most suitable power plant for production aircraft, preferably one able to use automobile gasoline or a fuel less costly than 100 octane low-lead brands.

TYPE: Three-seat light training aircraft.
WINGS: Cantilever mid-wing monoplane. Dihedral and sweepback constant from roots, except for inboard trailing-edges which are unswept. All-composites structure with slightly upswept tips. Inset aileron in each outer wing panel; trailing-edge flap in each inboard panel. Wings easily removable.
FUSELAGE: All-composites semi-monocoque structure of pod and boom form. Retractable steps.
TAIL UNIT: Cantilever all-composites structure, with sweepback on all surfaces. Easily removable tailplane,

Mockup of Cagny Performance 2000 three-seat trainer in original configuration *(Brian M. Service)*

mid-mounted on fin. Elevators and two-section rudder. Shallow ventral fin/bumper on each bottom edge of tailboom.
LANDING GEAR: Non-retractable tricycle type, with single wheel on each unit. Cantilever main units with composite spring legs. Disc brakes on mainwheels.
POWER PLANT: One 80 kW (108 hp) Textron Lycoming O-235 flat-four engine, mounted on a pylon immediately behind the cockpit, close to the CG. Provision for alternative engines. Two bladder type fuel cells in fuselage, in line with the wingroots, total capacity 75 litres (19.8 US gallons; 16.5 Imp gallons).
ACCOMMODATION: Three seats side by side in fully enclosed and soundproofed cabin. Seats of semi-reclining type. Baggage hold aft of seats. Access to cabin by means of a downward hinged door. Large wraparound windscreen and canopy, each in one piece. Cabin heated and ventilated.

DIMENSIONS, EXTERNAL:
Wing span	8.60 m (28 ft 2½ in)
Length overall	6.80 m (22 ft 3¾ in)
Height overall	2.80 m (9 ft 2¼ in)
Wheel track	1.80 m (5 ft 11 in)
Wheelbase	2.80 m (9 ft 2¼ in)

DIMENSIONS, INTERNAL:
Cabin: Length	1.80 m (5 ft 11 in)
Max width	1.54 m (5 ft 0½ in)
Max height	1.04 m (3 ft 5 in)

AREA:
Wings, gross	10.80 m² (116.3 sq ft)

WEIGHTS AND LOADINGS (estimated):
Weight empty	390 kg (860 lb)
Max baggage	20 kg (44 lb)
Max T-O weight	680 kg (1,500 lb)
Max wing loading	62.9 kg/m² (12.88 lb/sq ft)
Max power loading	8.50 kg/kW (13.9 lb/hp)

PERFORMANCE (estimated):
Max level speed	118 knots (220 km/h; 136 mph)
Cruising speed (75% power)	110 knots (205 km/h; 127 mph)
Stalling speed: flaps up	46 knots (85 km/h; 53 mph)
flaps down	38 knots (70 km/h; 44 mph)
Max rate of climb at S/L	210 m (690 ft)/min
Service ceiling	4,000 m (13,125 ft)
T-O run	350 m (1,150 ft)
Landing run	160 m (525 ft)
Range with max fuel	432 nm (800 km; 497 miles)

CENTRAIR
SA CENTRAIR
BP 44, Aérodrome, 36300 Le Blanc
Telephone: (54) 37 07 96
Telex: 750272 F

PRESIDENT/DIRECTOR GENERAL: Marc Ranjon
In addition to manufacturing sailplanes and sport aircraft, as described in the appropriate sections of this edition, Centrair designed the Sup'Air small business aircraft of advanced concept in collaboration with the École Nationale Supérieure de l'Aéronautique et de l'Espace of Toulouse (ENSAE). Construction of a prototype (as described in the 1987-88 *Jane's*) was abandoned in 1987.

DASSAULT-BREGUET
AVIONS MARCEL DASSAULT—BREGUET AVIATION
33 rue du Professeur Victor Pauchet, 92420 Vaucresson
POSTAL ADDRESS: BP 32, 92420 Vaucresson
Telephone: (1) 47 41 79 21
Telex: AMADAS 203944 F
PRESS INFORMATION OFFICE: 46 avenue Kléber, 75116 Paris
Telephone: (1) 47 27 61 19
Telex: AMDPARI 643758 F
WORKS: 92214 Saint-Cloud, 77000 Melun-Villaroche, 95100 Argenteuil, 92100 Boulogne/Seine, 78140 Vélizy-Villacoublay, 33610 Martignas, 33700 Bordeaux-Mérignac, 91120 Brétigny, 33630 Cazaux, 31770 Toulouse-Colomiers, 64600 Biarritz-Anglet, 64200 Biarritz-Parme, 13800 Istres, 74370 Argonay, 93350 Le Bourget, 59113 Lille-Seclin, 86000 Poitiers
CHAIRMAN AND CHIEF EXECUTIVE OFFICER: Serge Dassault
VICE-PRESIDENT, RESEARCH: Bruno Revellin-Falcoz
VICE-PRESIDENT, MILITARY EXPORTS: Paul-Emile Jaillard
VICE-PRESIDENT, CIVIL AIRCRAFT: Bernard Latreille
DIRECTOR, COMMUNICATIONS: Bernard Garrigou-Torchy

Avions Marcel Dassault—Breguet Aviation resulted from the merger in December 1971 of Avions Marcel Dassault with Breguet Aviation. In January 1979, 20 per cent of its stock was assigned to the French State, and in November 1981 the State shareholding was raised to 46 per cent. Due to a double voting right of some of its shares, the French State holds a majority control of the company.

Dassault-Breguet is engaged in the development and production of military and civil aircraft, flight control system components, maintenance and support equipment, and CAD/CAM software. Series production of its aircraft is undertaken under a widespread subcontracting programme, with final assembly and flight testing handled by the company. Its 17 separate works and facilities covered 600,000 m² (6,458,340 sq ft), with a total of about 14,700 employees, in January 1988.

Dassault-Breguet has established close links with the industries of other countries. The programme for the Atlantique maritime patrol aircraft associates manufacturers in Belgium, France, West Germany and Italy under the overall responsibility of their respective governments. In the same way the British and French governments are associated in the SEPECAT concern, formed to control the Dassault-Breguet/BAe Jaguar programme; and the West German and French governments are associated in the Dassault-Breguet/Dornier Alpha Jet programme. The A.C.E. International consortium has been formed to co-ordinate the launch programme for the future Avion de Combat Européen. Purchase of Mirage fighters by Belgium and Spain led to Belgian and Spanish participation in production of Dassault aircraft. Similarly, purchase of Mirage 2000 fighters by Greece and Egypt has led to co-production of components for this aircraft by the Hellenic Aerospace Industry and the AOI. Dassault-Breguet's Biarritz-Parme factory manufactures fuselages for Fokker.

DASSAULT-BREGUET MIRAGE III
The Mirage III was designed initially as a Mach 2 high altitude all-weather interceptor, capable also of performing ground support missions. Developed versions included a two-seat trainer, long range fighter-bomber and reconnaissance aircraft. A total of 1,410 Mirage III/5/50s of all types (incl 989 Mirage IIIs and radar-equipped Mirage 5s) was ordered and delivered for service in 20 countries, including licence production abroad. They were described fully in the 1985-86 and previous editions of *Jane's*.

DASSAULT-BREGUET MIRAGE 5
The Mirage 5 is a ground attack aircraft using the same airframe and engine as the Mirage III-E. A total of 404 was ordered and built, including Mirage 5-R reconnaissance variants and two-seat Mirage 5-Ds. A further 127 radar-equipped aircraft were built as Mirage 5s but retrospectively designated Mirage III. Details can be found in the 1985-86 and previous editions of *Jane's*.

DASSAULT-BREGUET MIRAGE 50
The Mirage 50 multi-mission fighter retains the basic airframe of the Mirage III/5 series, but is powered by the SNECMA Atar 9K-50 turbojet, as fitted in the Mirage F1.

Demonstration by Peruvian Mirages of flight refuelling system available for Mirage III/5/50 aircraft. The 'buddy' tanker is a Mirage 2000

This gives 70.6 kN (15,873 lb st) with afterburning, representing a thrust increase of between 17 and 23 per cent compared with standard Mirage III/5s.

The prototype Mirage 50 flew for the first time on 15 April 1979. First customer was the air force of Chile, which originally ordered 16, including eight converted from French Air Force Mirage 5Fs. Early in 1988, Venezuela ordered 12 Mirage 50s together with an upgrading programme to similar standards for its eight surviving Mirage III/5s. Further details can be found in the 1985-86 *Jane's*.

MIRAGE ADVANCED TECHNOLOGY UPDATE PROGRAMME

Since 1977, Dassault has been involved in programmes to update the navigation and attack systems, flight aids, radio com/nav, power plant and other features of in-service Mirage III/5/50 aircraft. In particular, several air forces have awarded Dassault contracts to install an inertial platform, digital computer, CRT head-up display, air-to-ground laser rangefinder and other equipment for improved navigational accuracy, easier target acquisition, and high bombing precision in the various CCIP (continuous computation of the impact point) or CCRP (continuous computation of the release point) modes, including standoff capability through the introduction of CCRP with initial point. Combat efficiency in the air-to-air gunnery mode is improved considerably by display of a highly accurate hot-line on the HUD.

All of these improvements are designed to decrease the pilot's task, so enhancing efficiency and survivability, in parallel with improved reliability. Modernisation programmes involving the Peruvian, Pakistani and part of the Egyptian Mirage 5 inventories were completed by the end of 1987 in the respective home countries. The intention has been, primarily, to add an inertial platform, digital computer and CRT head-up display. External fitments to Peruvian Mirage 5s include a refuelling probe (see below), a laser rangefinder and the two strakes beneath the lower forward fuselage previously applied only to two-seat Mirage 5Ds.

Another major improvement available for the Mirage III/5/50 series is a flight refuelling kit able to offer an increase of 30 to more than 100 per cent in radius of action. Already ordered by several air forces for their Mirage 5s, this system was demonstrated in flight before becoming generally available to Mirage operators in 1986. It involves lengthening the nose of the aircraft by 90 mm (3½ in) to accommodate system changes associated with a non-retractable probe on the starboard side, forward of the windscreen, and a single-point pressure refuelling port for both internal and external tanks. Overall refuelling can be accomplished at a rate of 1,000 litres (264 US gallons; 220 Imp gallons)/min. Turnround time between missions can be greatly reduced, at no cost in Mach 2 performance.

DASSAULT-BREGUET MIRAGE 3 NG and MIRAGE 50M

This new-generation (Nouvelle Génération) development of the Mirage III/5/50 series is based on the same well-proven airframe, but introduces features which give it much improved air combat performance and survivability in air-to-ground operations. It is powered, like the Mirage 50 and F1, by a SNECMA Atar 9K-50 turbojet, rated at 70.6 kN (15,873 lb st) with afterburning. New aerodynamic advances are evident in the added non-retractable swept-back foreplanes and highly-swept wingroot leading-edge extensions. It also features a fully fly by wire control system derived from that of the Mirage 2000, and can be equipped for in-flight refuelling.

The full range of Mirage update avionics is available for fitment to the **Mirage 3NG**, including reconnaissance pods as an alternative to the specialised camera nose. A prototype (converted from the first Mirage 50) first flew on 21 December 1982, but no orders for new or refurbished aircraft have been reported.

Dassault has assigned the broad designation **Mirage 50M** to aircraft updated with canards for improved air-to-air performance, and other changes, but not a fly by wire system. Options include zero/zero ejection seats; a liquid oxygen system; nosewheel steering; HUD video recorder; and various ECM, reconnaissance and laser targeting pods, several of which have been ordered by Mirage III/5/50 operators.

The following data, although referring to the Mirage 3NG, may be taken as broadly representative of the canard and Atar 9K-50 equipped first-generation Mirage.

DIMENSIONS, EXTERNAL:

Wing span	8.22 m (26 ft 11½ in)
Wing aspect ratio	1.9
Length overall	15.65 m (51 ft 4¼ in)
Height overall	4.50 m (14 ft 9 in)
Wheel track	3.15 m (10 ft 4 in)
Wheelbase	4.87 m (15 ft 11¾ in)

AREAS:

Wings, gross	35.00 m² (376.7 sq ft)
Foreplanes, total	1.00 m² (10.76 sq ft)

WEIGHTS:

T-O weight 'clean'	10,000 kg (22,050 lb)
Max T-O weight	14,700 kg (32,400 lb)

PERFORMANCE:

Max authorised Mach number in level flight	2.2
Max authorised speed in level flight	750 knots (1,390 km/h; 863 mph) IAS
Service ceiling at Mach 2	16,460 m (54,000 ft)

'Prototype' of the Advanced Technology Update Mirage 50M (*Paul Jackson*)

DASSAULT MIRAGE IV-P

Eighteen of the Mirage IV strategic bombers operated by the Commandement des Forces Aériennes Stratégiques (CFAS) of the French Air Force are assigned to carry the ASMP medium-range air-to-surface nuclear missile. Navigation and targeting capabilities are improved by installation of a Thomson-CSF Arcana pulse-Doppler radar (replacing DR-AA 8A) and dual inertial systems. Uprated EW equipment includes, typically, a Thomson-CSF TMV 015 Barem self-protection jamming pod on the port outboard underwing pylon and a Philips BOZ-100 chaff/flare pod on the starboard outer pylon, with external fuel tanks of 2,500 litres (660 US gallons; 550 Imp gallons) or optionally 1,650 litres (436 US gallons; 363 Imp gallons) on the inboard hardpoints. Radar warning receivers are also fitted, in the form of a Thomson-CSF Serval system.

The Mirage IV was last described in the 1969-70 *Jane's*. Modified aircraft, redesignated Mirage IV-P (for

Dassault Mirage IV-P strategic bomber carrying an ASMP test vehicle

pénétration), attained initial operational capability with Escadron de Bombardement 1/91 'Gascogne' at Mont-de-Marsan on 1 May 1986, followed by Escadron de Bombardement 2/91 'Marne' at St Dizier on 1 December 1986. A few aircraft are allocated to the OCU, CIFAS 328 'Aquitaine' at Bordeaux. The first had arrived at the French Air Force's Atelier Industriel de l'Air at Clermont Ferrand for conversion to IV-P on 30 May 1983 and the 18th was re-delivered on 9 December 1987, completing the original programme. However, one further IV-A is being converted to a IV-P as an attrition replacement.

DASSAULT-BREGUET MIRAGE F1
Spanish Air Force designation: C.14

Details of the early history of the Mirage F1 can be found in the 1977-78 *Jane's*. The prototype flew for the first time on 23 December 1966 and was followed by three pre-series aircraft.

The primary role of the single-seat Mirage **F1-C** production version, to which the detailed description applies, is that of all-weather interception at any altitude. It is equally suitable for visual ground attack missions, carrying a variety of external loads beneath the wings and fuselage. Other versions include the **F1-B** two-seat version of F1-C, the first of which made its first flight on 26 May 1976; the **F1-D** two-seat version of F1-E; the single-seat **F1-E** multi-role air superiority/ground attack/ reconnaissance version for export customers, with an inertial navigation system, nav/attack central computer, CRT head-up display, and a large inventory of external stores; and the single-seat **F1-R** (French Air Force **F1-CR**) day and night reconnaissance variant. Production of the F1-A ground attack version, with reduced equipment, a retractable flight refuelling probe and increased fuel, has been completed.

Many F1-Cs of the French Air Force were delivered or modified to **F1-C-200** standard by installation of an 8 cm (3.15 in) fuselage plug for a removable flight refuelling probe. Export customers who have F1s equipped with refuelling probes include Iraq, Libya, Morocco, South Africa and Spain.

By January 1988, a total of 731 Mirage F1s had been ordered, comprising 256 (incl 6 prototypes) for the French Air Force and 475 for service with the air forces of Ecuador (two F1-JE and 16 JA, equivalent to F1-B and E), Greece (40 F1-CG), Iraq (13 F1-BQ and 112 EQ), Jordan (two F1-BJ, 17 CJ and 17 EJ), Kuwait (six F1-BK and 27 CK), Libya (six F1-BD, 16 AD and 16 ED), Morocco (30 F1-CH and 20 EH), Qatar (two F1-DDA and 12 EDA), South Africa (32 F1-AZ and 16 CZ) and Spain (six F1-BE, 45 CE and 22 EE). A total of 694 had been delivered at 1 January 1988. The first production F1 flew on 15 February 1973 and was delivered officially to the French Air Force on 14 March 1973. The first unit to receive the F1 was the 30e Escadre at Reims, which became operational in early 1974. This now has three squadrons of F1-Cs; the 5e Escadre at Orange has two squadrons of F1-Cs and one of F1-Bs; the 12e Escadre at Cambrai has three squadrons of F1-Cs.

Deliveries of the F1-C series to the French Air Force totalled 168, made up of four prototypes, 81 F1-Cs and 83 F1-C-200s. Twenty two-seat F1-Bs began to equip the third squadron at Orange, as the F1 OCU, in June 1980; each aircraft is equipped with the same radar, weapon system and air-to-air missiles as the F1-C, but has no internal guns. Fuel capacity is reduced by 450 litres (119 US gallons; 99 Imp gallons); empty weight increased by 200 kg (441 lb); and the forward fuselage extended by 30 cm (11¾ in).

The French Air Force also purchased F1-CRs to re-equip the three squadrons of the 33e Escadre de Reconnaissance, at Strasbourg. These aircraft are designated **F1-CR-200** (having a fixed in-flight refuelling probe) and differ from the F1-C in being fitted with the IVMR model of Cyrano radar (with additional ground mapping, contour mapping, air-ground ranging and blind let-down modes), a Sagem Uliss 47 inertial platform and ESD 182 navigation computer. An SAT SCM2400 Super Cyclope infra-red linescan reconnaissance system replaces the starboard gun, and an undernose bay houses either a 75 mm Omera 40 panoramic camera or a 150 mm Omera 33 vertical camera. French aircraft have a secondary ground attack role and may also carry a centreline podded sensor in the form of a

Dassault-Breguet Mirage F1-CR-200 reconnaissance fighter *(Paul Jackson)*

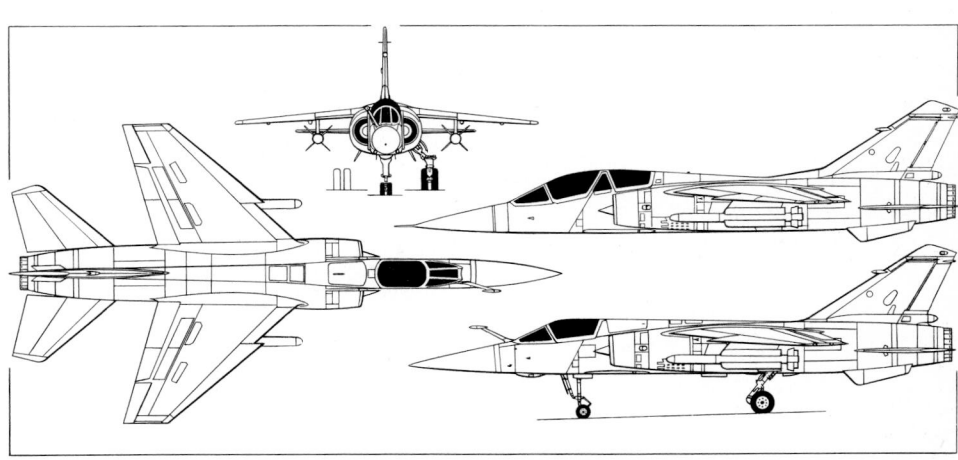

Dassault-Breguet Mirage F1-C-200 single-seat multi-mission fighter and attack aircraft *(Pilot Press)*

Thomson Raphaël TH SLAR or a Thomson-CSF Astac electronic reconnaissance system for detection of ground radars. Several types of sensor pod are available for fitment to export Mirage F1-Es. The first of two F1-CR-200 prototypes, converted from F1-C-200s, flew on 20 November 1981. Sixty-four (including the two prototypes) were ordered for the French Air Force. The first production F1-CR-200 flew on 10 November 1982, and the first squadron (2/33) became operational in July 1983. Deliveries were completed in 1987; four more were acquired in 1988. Consideration has been given to converting 60 F1-Cs for ground attack, with appropriate radar and other modifications, under the designation F1-T.

Export F1-Cs have a radar similar to Cyrano IV or IVM. Export F1-Es have radar similar to Cyrano IVMR but repackaged to save space. Mirage F1-EQ5s and EQ6s of the Iraqi Air Force are equipped to carry Exocet anti-ship missiles and laser guided weapons such as the AS.30L missile and Matra 400 kg laser guided bomb. They have Thomson-CSF Agave radar.

The Mirage F1 is produced by Dassault-Breguet in co-operation with the Belgian company SABCA, in which Dassault-Breguet has a parity interest, and CASA of Spain, which is building fuselage sections for all Mirage F1s ordered. Dassault-Breguet also has a technical and industrial co-operation agreement with the Armaments Development and Production Corporation of South Africa Ltd, whereby the latter company has rights to build the Mirage F1 under licence.

The following description applies to the F1-C-200 production version for the French Air Force, except where indicated:

TYPE: Single-seat multi-mission fighter and attack aircraft.

WINGS: Cantilever shoulder-wing monoplane. Anhedral from roots. Sweepback 47° 30′ on leading-edges, with extended chord on approximately the outer two-thirds of each wing. All-metal two-spar torsion box structure, making extensive use of mechanically or chemically milled components. Trailing-edge control surfaces of honeycomb sandwich construction, with carbonfibre aileron skin on current production aircraft. Entire leading-edge can be drooped hydraulically (manually for T-O and landing, automatic in combat). Two differentially operating double-slotted flaps and one aileron on each trailing-edge, actuated hydraulically by servo controls. Ailerons are compensated by trim devices incorporated in linkage. Two spoilers on each wing, ahead of flaps.

FUSELAGE: Conventional all-metal semi-monocoque structure. Titanium alloy is used for landing gear trunnions, engine firewall and certain other major structures. High tensile steel wing attachment points. Large hydraulically actuated door type airbrake in forward underside of each intake trunk.

TAIL UNIT: Cantilever all-metal structure, with sweepback on all surfaces. Single-spar fin. All-moving tailplane mid-set on fuselage, and actuated hydraulically by electric or manual control. Tailplane trailing-edge panels are of honeycomb sandwich construction. Auxiliary fin beneath each side of rear fuselage.

LANDING GEAR: Retractable tricycle type, by Messier-Hispano-Bugatti. Hydraulic retraction, nose unit rearward, main units upward into rear of intake trunk fairings. Twin wheels on each unit. Nose unit steerable and self centring. Oleo-pneumatic shock absorbers. Mainwheel tyres size 605 × 155, pressure 9-11 bars (130-160 lb/sq in). Nosewheel tyres size 360 × 135, pressure 7 bars (100 lb/sq in). Messier-Hispano-Bugatti brakes and anti-skid units. Brake parachute in bullet fairing at base of rudder.

POWER PLANT: One SNECMA Atar 9K-50 turbojet, rated at 70.6 kN (15,873 lb st) with afterburning. Movable semi-conical centrebody in each intake. Fuel in integral tanks in wings (combined capacity 375 litres; 99 US gallons; 82.5 Imp gallons), and three main tanks and one inverted-flight supply tank (combined capacity 3,925 litres; 1,037 US gallons; 863.5 Imp gallons) in fuselage. Total internal fuel capacity 4,300 litres (1,136 US gallons;

Dassault-Breguet Mirage F1-B two-seat combat trainer of the French Air Force

946 Imp gallons). Internal tanks able to be pressure refuelled completely in about 6 min. Provision for two jettisonable auxiliary fuel tanks (each 1,200 litres; 317 US gallons; 264 Imp gallons) to be carried on inboard wing pylons, plus a single tank of 2,200 litres (581 US gallons; 484 Imp gallons) capacity on the underfuselage station. Non-retractable, but removable, flight refuelling probe on starboard side of nose optional.

ACCOMMODATION: Single SEM Martin-Baker F1RM4 ejection seat for pilot, under rearward hinged canopy (SEM Martin-Baker F10M rocket seat in latest F1-Cs and in F1-E and F1-CR. Two Mk 10 seats with inter-seat sequence system in F1-B). Cockpit is air-conditioned, and is heated by warm air bled from engine which also heats the radar compartment and certain equipment compartments. Intertechnique liquid oxygen converter, miniature regulator and anti-g valve for pilot. No-delay through-the-canopy escape system, with pyrotechnic pre-fragmentation of canopy, on all versions.

SYSTEMS: Two independent hydraulic systems, pressure 207 bars (3,000 lb/sq in), for landing gear actuation, flaps and flying controls. Hydraulic flow rate 45 litres (12 US gallons; 10 Imp gallons)/min at nominal rate of 4,000 rpm. Electrical system includes two Auxilec 15kVA variable speed alternators, either of which can supply all functional and operational requirements. Emergency and standby power provided by SAFT Voltabloc 40Ah nickel-cadmium battery and ESD static converter. DC power provided by two transformer-rectifiers operating in conjunction with battery.

AVIONICS AND EQUIPMENT: Thomson-CSF Cyrano IV fire control radar in nose. Two UHF transceivers (one UHF/VHF), Socrat 6200 VOR/ILS with Socrat 5600 marker beacon receiver, LMT Tacan, LMT NR-AI-4-A IFF, remote setting interception system, three-axis generator, central air data computer, SFIM spherical indicator with ILS pointers, Crouzet Type 63 navigation indicator, SFENA 505 autopilot and CSF head-up display, with wide field of view double-converter. (Standard equipment on F-1E includes Sagem Uliss 47 INS, EMD 182 central digital computer for nav/attack computations, TH C8F VE-120C CRT head-up display, Crouzet air data computer and digital armament/nav control panels.)

ARMAMENT AND OPERATIONAL EQUIPMENT: Standard installed armament of two 30 mm DEFA 553 cannon, with 135 rds/gun, mounted in lower central fuselage. Two Alkan universal stores attachment pylons under each wing and one under centre-fuselage, plus provision for carrying one air-to-air missile at each wingtip. Max theoretical external combat load 6,300 kg (13,890 lb), comprising 2,100 kg (4,630 lb) on centreline pylon; 1,300 kg (2,866 lb) on each inner wing pylon; 550 kg (1,213 lb) on each outer wing pylon; 150 kg (331 lb) on each wingtip AAM rail (Matra 550 Magic or AIM-9 Sidewinder) and 100 kg (220 lb) of chaff/flare dispensers on each fuselage shoulder position. Practical max operational load is 4,000 kg (8,818 lb). Externally mounted weapons for interception role include Matra Super 530 air-to-air missiles under inboard wing pylons. For ground attack, typical loads may include one ARMAT anti-radar missile, or one AM39 Exocet anti-ship missile, or up to fourteen 250 kg bombs, thirty anti-runway bombs or 144 Thomson-Brandt rockets. Other possible external loads include auxiliary fuel tanks, a Thomson-CSF Atlis laser designator pod with AS.30L missiles or 400 kg laser guided bombs, air-to-surface missiles and sensor pods comprising a Thomson Raphaël SLAR, an Omera-Dassault Harold long-range oblique photographic unit (1,700 mm Omera 38), an Omera-Dassault COR2 multi-purpose pod (visual spectrum and IR linescan), a Thomson-CSF TMV 018 Syrel real-time optronic reconnaissance pod, a Dassault Nora real-time video pod and a Thomson-CSF Astac ground radar detector unit. A Thomson-CSF BF radar warning receiver is standard, and a range of jamming (Barracuda, Barem, Barrax) and chaff/flare (Phimat, Sycomor) pods may be fitted.

DIMENSIONS, EXTERNAL (F1-C):

Wing span: without missiles	8.40 m (27 ft 6¾ in)
over Magic missiles	approx 9.32 m (30 ft 6¾ in)
Length overall: F1-C	15.23 m (49 ft 11¾ in)
F1-C-200	15.30 m (50 ft 2½ in)
F1-B	15.53 m (50 ft 11½ in)
Height overall	4.50 m (14 ft 9 in)
Wheel track	2.50 m (8 ft 2½ in)
Wheelbase	5.00 m (16 ft 4¾ in)

AREA:

Wings, gross	25.00 m² (269.1 sq ft)

WEIGHTS AND LOADING (F1-C):

Weight empty	7,400 kg (16,314 lb)
T-O weight, 'clean'	10,900 kg (24,030 lb)
Max T-O weight	16,200 kg (35,715 lb)
Max wing loading	648 kg/m² (132.7 lb/sq ft)

PERFORMANCE (F1-C):

Max level speed: high altitude	Mach 2.2
low altitude	Mach 1.2
	(800 knots; 1,480 km/h; 920 mph EAS)
Approach speed	141 knots (260 km/h; 162 mph)
Landing speed	124 knots (230 km/h; 143 mph)
Max rate of climb at S/L (with afterburning)	
	12,780 m (41,930 ft)/min

Max rate of climb at high altitude (with afterburning)	
	14,580 m (47,835 ft)/min
Service ceiling	20,000 m (65,600 ft)
Stabilised supersonic ceiling	16,000 m (52,500 ft)
T-O run (AUW of 11,500 kg; 25,355 lb)	
	600 m (1,970 ft)
Landing run (AUW of 8,500 kg; 18,740 lb)	
	670 m (2,200 ft)

Combat radius:
hi-lo-hi at Mach 0.75/0.88, with fourteen 250 kg bombs and max internal fuel, with reserves
230 nm (425 km; 265 miles)
lo-lo-lo at 400-550 knots (740-1,020 km/h; 460-633 mph), with six 250 kg bombs and two external tanks, with reserves   325 nm (600 km; 374 miles)
lo-lo with one Exocet and two external tanks, with reserves and including missile flight path
378 nm (700 km; 435 miles)
hi-lo-hi at Mach 0.8/0.9, with two 250 kg bombs and three external tanks, with reserves
750 nm (1,390 km; 863 miles)
Combat air patrol endurance, with two Super 530 missiles and underbelly tank, with reserves, incl one attack at ceiling   2 h 15 min

DASSAULT-BREGUET MIRAGE 2000
Indian Air Force name: Vajra

The Mirage 2000 was selected on 18 December 1975 as the primary combat aircraft of the French Air Force from the mid-1980s. Under French government contract, it was developed initially as an interceptor and air superiority fighter, powered by a single SNECMA M53 turbofan and with Thomson-CSF RDM multi-mode Doppler radar. The Mirage 2000 is equally suitable for reconnaissance, close support, and low altitude attack missions in areas to the rear of a battlefield. Its early history has been outlined in previous editions of *Jane's*. On the basis of structural testing, the Mirage 2000 airframe was approved for a load factor of +9g and rate of roll of 270°/s in subsonic and supersonic flight, clean or with four air-to-air missiles.

A SNECMA M53-2 turbofan, rated at 83.4 kN (18,740 lb st), was fitted for early prototype testing, and was replaced in 1980 by the uprated M53-5 which also powers early production aircraft. Export aircraft have the more powerful M53-P2, which was introduced on French Air Force Mirage 2000Cs from No. 38 onwards in 1987 in conjunction with Thomson-CSF RDI pulse-Doppler radar.

The first production **Mirage 2000C** made its first flight on 20 November 1982 and deliveries began in 1983. The first production **Mirage 2000B** two-seat trainer flew on 7 October 1983. Escadron de Chasse (EC) 1/2 'Cigognes' is the first French Air Force unit to become operational, at

Dijon on 2 July 1984. EC 3/2 'Alsace' followed in 1986 and Escadron de Chasse et de Transformation (ECT) 2/2 'Côte d'Or', the OCU with Mirage 2000Bs and three 2000Cs, in early 1987. Eventually, Mirage 2000Cs will equip four wings (escadres), each with three interceptor squadrons. First unit to receive 2000Cs with RDI radar and M53-P2 engines, from July 1988, was the 5th Escadre de Chasse, at Orange, for EC 2/5 'Ile de France' and EC 3/5 'Comtat Venaissin'. The third squadron, EC 1/5 'Vendée', is retaining its Mirage F1-Cs during deployment to Djibouti. The designation **'2000DA'** (Défense Aérienne) is used loosely in collective reference to Mirage 2000Bs and Cs.

Following a mid-1979 go-ahead, the first of two prototypes of the **Mirage 2000N** two-seat low-altitude penetration version made its first flight on 3 February 1983; the second flew on 21 September 1983. Strengthened for flight at a typical 600 knots (1,110 km/h; 690 mph) at 60 m (200 ft) above the terrain, this version was intended basically as a vehicle for the ASMP medium-range air-to-surface nuclear missile, and has ESD Antilope V terrain following radar, two Sagem inertial platforms, improved TRT AHV-12 radio altimeter, Thomson-CSF colour CRT, an Omera vertical camera, special ECM and two Magic air-to-air missiles for self defence. Production deliveries began on 19 February 1987, and 36 were to be in service by 1988, when the 2000N was planned to become operational as a replacement for Mirage III-E and Jaguar nuclear attack aircraft. Two wings with a total of five tactical squadrons will receive this version, beginning with the 4th Escadre at Luxeuil, followed by the 7th at Toul.

Funding approved under the 1987 defence budget brought the total number of aircraft ordered to 204, comprising 107 Cs, 22 Bs and 75 Ns, but excluding the seven prototypes. Procurement is planned of 112 Mirage 2000Ns out of an eventual requirement of 300 to 400 Mirage 2000s of various versions for the French Air Force, and 1988 funding of a B, 16 Cs and 18 Ns is planned to include an initial 10 non-ASMP **2000N[1]** aircraft for conventional attack roles pending availability of the Rafale. By January 1988, nine Ns, 15 Bs and 37 Cs had been delivered to the French Air Force. Wings are manufactured at Martignas, fuselages at Argenteuil; final assembly and flight testing take place at Mérignac, from where 181 Mirage 2000s of all versions had been delivered to home and export customers by 1 January 1988.

Export customers for the Mirage 2000 comprise Abu Dhabi, Egypt, India, Peru and Greece. The Egyptians placed an initial firm contract for 20 (16 2000EM and 4 BM, all with M53-P2 engines) in January 1982. The first was delivered on 30 June 1986. India placed an initial order for 40 in October 1982 (36 2000H and 4 TH), the last of which were delivered in 1986. The four THs and 26 of the Hs had

Two-seat Dassault-Breguet Mirage 2000B of the French Air Force

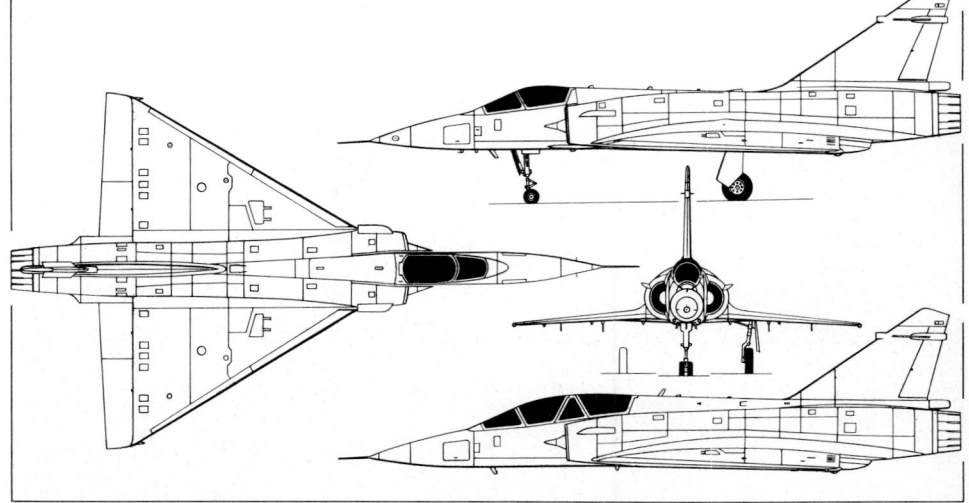

Dassault-Breguet Mirage 2000C, with added side view (bottom) of Mirage 2000N *(Pilot Press)*

M53-5 engines temporarily; the final 10 Hs were powered from the start by the M53-P2. First flight by a 2000H (KF-101) was made on 21 September 1984, followed in early 1985 by the first TH (KT-201). The first of two Indian squadrons (No. 7 *Battle Axe*) was formed at Gwalior AB on 29 June 1985, when the Mirage 2000 received the Indian name **Vajra** (Divine Thunder). A follow-on order for nine aircraft was signed in March 1986 and executed by late 1987 to complete No. 1 *Tigers* squadron. Peru ordered 26 aircraft in December 1982 (24 2000P and 2 DP), but reduced the total subsequently to 12. The first 2000DP was handed over on 7 June 1985 to begin pilot training in France. Abu Dhabi has ordered 36 (22 2000EAD, 8 RAD and 6 DAD); deliveries were due to begin in 1986 but were delayed for fitment of additional equipment. The RAD reconnaissance versions for this customer will be able to carry a COR 2 or Harold surveillance equipment pod; the second 18 for Abu Dhabi will be fitted with Elettronica (Italy) ECM, comprising ELT/158 threat warning receivers and ELT/558 self-protection jammers. Most recent customers are Greece, which in July 1985 ordered 40 (36 2000EGM and 4 BGM), the first of which was handed over on 21 March 1988; and Jordan, which ordered 20 in 1988.

Current models are the 2000C interceptor (and associated 2000B trainer); 2000E multi-role fighter (and 2000D trainer); and 2000N strike/attack model. A two-stage private venture update programme announced by Dassault in 1987 includes the **2000-3** with Rafale-type cockpit multifunction displays, flown in 1988. By 1990, addition of Thomson-CSF RDY radar and a new central processing unit will produce the **2000-5** or APSI (Advanced Pilot-System Interface) Mirage, which will also feature a Thomson-CSF VEH 3020 holographic HUD.

The following description applies to the single-seat Mirage 2000C, except where indicated:

TYPE: Single-seat interceptor, air superiority and multi-role fighter.

WINGS: Cantilever multi-spar low-wing monoplane of delta planform, with cambered profile. Leading-edge sweepback 58°. Large radius root fairings. Full span two-segment automatic leading-edge slats provide variable camber in combat, but are retracted during all phases of acceleration and low altitude cruise, to reduce drag. Two-section elevons, forming entire trailing-edge of each wing, have carbonfibre skin, with AG5 light alloy honeycomb core. Fly by wire control system for elevons and slats, with surfaces actuated by hydraulic servo units. No tabs. Retractable airbrake above and below each wing.

FUSELAGE: Conventional semi-monocoque structure, 'waisted' in accordance with area rule; of conventional all-metal construction except for glassfibre radome and carbonfibre/light alloy honeycomb panel over avionics compartment, immediately aft of canopy. Small fixed strake, with marked dihedral, near leading-edge of each air intake trunk.

TAIL UNIT: Cantilever fin and inset rudder only; latter actuated by fly by wire control system via hydraulic servo units. Much of fin skin and all rudder skin of boron/epoxy/carbon composites with a light alloy structure for the fin and light alloy honeycomb core for the rudder. Sweepback on fin leading-edge 53°. No tab.

LANDING GEAR: Retractable tricycle type by Messier-Hispano-Bugatti, with twin nosewheels, and single wheel on each main unit. Hydraulic retraction, nosewheels rearward, main units inward. Oleo-pneumatic shock absorbers. Electro-hydraulic nosewheel steering, through 45° to each side. Manual disconnect permits nosewheel unit to castor through 360° for ground towing. Light alloy wheels and tubeless tyres, size 360 × 135-6, pressure 8.0 bars (116 lb/sq in) on nosewheels, 750 × 230-15, pressure 15.0 bars (217 lb/sq in) on mainwheels. Messier-Hispano-Bugatti hydraulically actuated carbon composite disc brakes on mainwheels, with anti-skid units. Runway arrester gear standard. Brake-chute in canister above jet nozzle.

POWER PLANT: One SNECMA M53-P2 turbofan, rated at 64.3 kN (14,462 lb st) dry and 95.1 kN (21,385 lb st) with afterburning. Movable half-cone centrebody in each air

Dassault-Breguet Mirage 2000N, carrying an ASMP nuclear missile *(Brian M. Service)*

intake. Internal fuel capacity 4,000 litres (1,057 US gallons; 880 Imp gallons) in 2000C, 3,920 litres (1,035 US gallons; 862 Imp gallons) in 2000B. Provision for one jettisonable 1,300 litre (343 US gallon; 286 Imp gallon) fuel tank under centre of fuselage, and a 1,700 litre (449 US gallon; 374 Imp gallon) drop tank under each wing. Total internal/external fuel capacity 8,700 litres (2,298 US gallons; 1,914 Imp gallons) in 2000C, 8,620 litres (2,276 US gallons; 1,896 Imp gallons) in 2000B. Detachable flight refuelling probe forward of cockpit on starboard side. Drop tanks of 2,000 litres (528 US gallons; 440 Imp gallons) are available for the 2000N.

ACCOMMODATION: Pilot only in 2000C, on Martin-Baker F10Q zero/zero ejection seat, under transparent canopy, in air-conditioned and pressurised cockpit. Canopy hinged at rear to open upward.

SYSTEMS: ABG-Semca air-conditioning and pressurisation system. Two independent hydraulic systems, pressure 280 bars (4,000 lb/sq in), to actuate flying control servo units, landing gear and brakes. Hydraulic flow rate 110 litres (29 US gallons; 24 Imp gallons)/min. Electrical system includes two Auxilec 20110 aircooled 20kVA 400Hz constant frequency alternators, two Bronzavia DC transformers, a SAFT 40Ah battery and ATEI static inverter. Fly by wire flight control system. Eros oxygen system.

AVIONICS AND EQUIPMENT: Thomson-CSF RDM multi-mode radar or RDI pulse-Doppler radar, each with operating range of 54 nm (100 km; 62 miles). (Mirage 2000N has ESD/Thomson-CSF Antilope V terrain-following and ground mapping radar.) Sagem Uliss 52 inertial platform, ESD Type 2084 central digital computer and Digibus digital data bus, Thomson-CSF TMV-980 data display system (VE-130 head-up and VMC-180 head-down) (two head-down in 2000N), Sfena 605 autopilot, Thomson-CSF/ESD ECM with VCM-65 display (jammers on leading-edge of fin and in bullet fairing at base of rudder; chaff/flare dispenser under fuselage at wing trailing-edge), Matra Spirale passive countermeasures, LMT Deltac Tacan, LMT NRAI-7A IFF transponder, Socrat 8900 solid state VOR/ILS and IO-300-A marker beacon receiver, TRT radio altimeter (AHV-6 in 2000B and C, AHV-9 in export aircraft, AHV-12 in 2000N), TRT ERA 7000 V/UHF com transceiver, TRT ERA 7200 UHF or EAS secure voice com, Thomson-CSF Serval radar warning receiver (antennae at each wingtip and on trailing-edge of fin, near tip), Crouzet type 90 air data computer, and Thomson-CSF Atlis laser designator and marked target seeker (in pod on forward starboard underfuselage station). Omera vertical camera in 2000N.

ARMAMENT: Two 30 mm DEFA 554 guns in 2000C and 2000E (not fitted in B, D or N), with 125 rds/gun. Nine attachments for external stores, five under fuselage and two under each wing. Fuselage centreline and inboard wing stations each stressed for 1,800 kg (3,968 lb) loads; other four fuselage points for 400 kg (882 lb) each, and outboard wing points for 300 kg (661 lb) each. Typical interception weapons comprise two Matra Super 530D or (with RDM radar) 530F missiles (inboard) and two Matra 550 Magic or Magic 2 missiles (outboard) under wings. Alternatively, each of the four underwing hardpoints can carry a Magic. Primary weapon for 2000N is ASMP tactical nuclear missile. In an air-to-surface role, the Mirage 2000 can carry up to 6,300 kg (13,890 lb) of external stores, including eighteen Matra 250 kg retarded bombs or Thomson-Brandt BAP 100 anti-runway bombs; sixteen Durandal penetration bombs; one or two Matra BGL 1,000 kg laser guided bombs; five or six Matra Belouga cluster bombs or Thomson-Brandt BM 400 400 kg modular bombs; one Rafaut F2 practice bomb launcher; two Aérospatiale AS 30L, Matra Armat anti-radar, or Aérospatiale AM39 Exocet anti-ship, air-to-surface missiles; four Matra LR F4 rocket launchers, each with eighteen 68 mm rockets; two packs of 100 mm rockets; a Dassault-Breguet CC 630 gun pod, containing two 30 mm cannon and ammunition; a Dassault-Breguet COR 2 multi-camera pod or Dassault-Breguet AA-3-38 Harold long-range oblique photographic (Lorop) pod; a Thomson-CSF Atlis laser designator/marked target seeker pod; two Thomson-CSF DB 3141/3163 self-defence ECM pods; one Thomson-CSF Caiman offensive or intelligence ECM pod; or an Intertechnique 231-300 'buddy' type in-flight refuelling pod. Fuselage centreline and inboard underwing stations are 'wet' for carriage of jettisonable fuel tanks (see 'Power Plant' paragraph for details). For air defence weapon training, a Cubic Corpn AIS (airborne instrumentation subsystem) pod, externally resembling a Magic missile, can replace the Magic on its launch rail, enabling pilot to simulate a firing without carrying the actual missile.

DIMENSIONS, EXTERNAL:
Wing span	9.13 m (29 ft 11½ in)
Wing aspect ratio	2.03
Length overall: 2000C	14.36 m (47 ft 1¼ in)
2000B, N	14.55 m (47 ft 9 in)
Height overall: 2000C	5.20 m (17 ft 0¾ in)
2000B, N	5.15 m (16 ft 10¾ in)
Wheel track	3.40 m (11 ft 1¾ in)
Wheelbase	5.00 m (16 ft 4¾ in)

AREA:
Wings, gross	41.0 m² (441.3 sq ft)

WEIGHTS AND LOADING:
Weight empty: 2000C	7,500 kg (16,534 lb)
2000B	7,600 kg (16,755 lb)
Max internal fuel: 2000C	3,160 kg (6,967 lb)
2000B	3,095 kg (6,823 lb)
Max external fuel: 2000C	3,720 kg (8,201 lb)
2000B	3,715 kg (8,190 lb)
Max external stores load	6,300 kg (13,890 lb)
T-O weight 'clean': 2000C	10,860 kg (23,940 lb)
2000B	10,960 kg (24,165 lb)
Max T-O weight: 2000C and B	17,000 kg (37,480 lb)
Max wing loading:	
2000C and B	414.63 kg/m² (84.97 lb/sq ft)

PERFORMANCE (Mirage 2000C):
Max level speed	over Mach 2.2
Max continuous speed	Mach 2.2
	(800 knots; 1,482 km/h; 921 mph IAS)

Max speed at low altitude without afterburning, carrying eight 250 kg bombs and two Magic missiles

over 600 knots (1,110 km/h; 690 mph)

Min speed in stable flight

100 knots (185 km/h; 115 mph)

Dassault-Breguet Mirage 2000C, armed with Super 530 and Magic air-to-air missiles

Max rate of climb at S/L   17,060 m (56,000 ft)/min
Time to 15,000 m (49,200 ft) and Mach 2   4 min
Time from brake release to intercept target flying at
    Mach 3 at 24,400 m (80,000 ft)   less than 5 min
Service ceiling   18,000 m (59,000 ft)
Range: with four 250 kg bombs
              more than 800 nm (1,480 km; 920 miles)
    with two 1,700 litre drop tanks
              more than 1,000 nm (1,850 km; 1,150 miles)
    with one 1,300 litre and two 1,700 litre drop tanks
                   1,800 nm (3,335 km; 2,073 miles)
g limits: +9 normal
                                      +13.5 ultimate

DASSAULT-BREGUET MIRAGE 4000

The Mirage 4000 (originally Super Mirage 4000) prototype is a twin-turbofan scale-up of the Mirage 2000 that was designed to be suitable for interception as well as low altitude penetration attack at a considerable distance from its base. It flew for the first time on 9 March 1979 and was described fully in the 1984-85 *Jane's*.

In 1986 the Mirage 4000 resumed flying in support of the Rafale programme, with particular emphasis on evaluating the behaviour of a delta-canard aircraft in turbulent conditions.

DASSAULT-BREGUET SUPER ÉTENDARD

At the 1985 Paris Air Show, Dassault-Breguet announced its readiness to relaunch production of the Super Étendard against initial orders for about 40 aircraft. Changes by comparison with the original version would be limited to removal of equipment needed only for deck operations from aircraft carriers, and installation of new fire control and nav/attack systems. An example of the aircraft (ex-Aéronavale No. 37) in this form was exhibited at the 1987 Paris Air Show. High European labour costs were cited by Dassault as restricting sales potential, prompting a 1987 proposal to transfer production to IPTN of Indonesia as the result of interest from the Indonesian Air Force.

Production of the original, carrier-based, version of this single-seat transonic strike fighter for the navies of France (71 aircraft) and Argentina (14 aircraft) ended in 1983. However, in late 1986, the French Navy signed a contract to initiate study of a weapon system modernisation, including replacement of the existing Agave radar by ESD Anemone, a new SAGEM inertial platform and computer, a new head-up display and overall cockpit modernisation. The first modified aircraft is scheduled to be delivered in late 1991. Adaptation of the Super Étendard to carry the ASMP nuclear air-to-surface missile is nearing completion. So, while readers are referred to the 1982-83 and previous editions of *Jane's* for a full description of the Super Étendard in its carrier-based form, the following expanded entry on its current armament may be of continuing interest:

ARMAMENT AND OPERATIONAL EQUIPMENT: Two DEFA 30 mm guns, each with 125 rds, in bottom of engine air intake trunks. Underfuselage attachment for two 250 kg bombs, one 600 litre (158.5 US gallon; 132 Imp gallon) drop fuel tank, a flight refuelling 'buddy' pack or a reconnaissance pod. Four underwing hardpoints for four 250 kg or 400 kg bombs, two Matra Magic air-to-air missiles, or four rocket pods (each eighteen 68 mm rockets). The inner wing hardpoints can carry two 595 litre or 1,100 litre (157 or 290.5 US gallon; 131 or 242 Imp gallon) fuel tanks, or one AM39 Exocet anti-ship missile and one fuel tank. Standard weapons include AN52 nuclear bomb, 18 (optionally 27) BAP 100 concrete-piercing bombs, 18 (optionally 27) BAT 120 bombs, and one self defence jamming pod (plus, optionally, one chaff/flare pod).

DASSAULT-BREGUET RAFALE A (SQUALL)

Known initially as the ACX (advanced combat experimental), the **Rafale A** is an experimental prototype that was built to demonstrate technologies applicable to the tactical combat aircraft (ACT) needed to replace French Air Force Jaguars in the 1990s, and to the ship-based combat aircraft (ACM: avion de combat marine) proposed for deployment on the French Navy's nuclear powered aircraft carrier. The production versions will be known as **Rafale D** and **M** and are described separately.

Essential characteristics of the Rafale A were revealed in the early weeks of 1983, at the time of Dassault-Breguet's decision to build it. On the basis of an airframe with overall dimensions little greater than those of the Mirage 2000, the company set out to produce a multi-role aircraft able to destroy everything from supersonic fighters to a helicopter in an air-to-air role, and able to deliver at least 3,500 kg (7,715 lb) of modern weapons on targets up to 350 nm (650 km; 400 miles) from its base. The ability to carry, and fire in rapid succession, at least six air-to-air missiles was considered essential, together with the ability to launch electro-optically guided and advanced 'fire and forget' standoff air-to-surface weapons.

High manoeuvrability, high angle-of-attack flying capability under combat conditions, and optimum low-speed performance for short take-off and landing, were basic design aims. This led to choice of a compound-sweep delta wing, a large active canard foreplane mounted higher than the mainplane, twin engines, air intakes of new design in a

Dassault-Breguet Mirage 4000 twin-turbofan prototype combat aircraft

Dassault-Breguet Super Étendard in shore-based ground attack form *(Paul Jackson)*

semi-ventral position, and a single fin. To ensure a thrust-to-weight ratio far superior to one, it was decided to make extensive use of composites such as carbon and aramid fibres, and aluminium-lithium alloys, throughout the airframe, as well as the latest manufacturing techniques such as superplastic forming/diffusion bonding of titanium components.

Ergonomic cockpit studies suggested that the pilot's seat should be reclined at an angle of 30° to 40° during flight testing, and that equipment should include a side-stick controller, a wide angle holographic head-up display, an eye-level display collimated to infinity (avoiding the need to refocus from the HUD to the instrument panel), and lateral multi-function colour displays.

The digital fly by wire control system will embody automatic self-protection functions to prevent the aircraft from exceeding its limits at all times. Functional reconfiguration of the system in case of failure, and anti-turbulence functions, will be embodied. Provisions will be made for the introduction of fibre optics to enhance nuclear hardening, and of voice-activated controls and voice warning systems.

A full scale mockup of the original ACX design was exhibited at the 1983 Paris Air Show, and construction of the Rafale A began in March 1984. Compared with the mockup, it embodies a number of significant refinements. In particular, Dassault-Breguet was able to achieve improved flow into the engine air intakes, and greater efficiency at high angles of attack, by modifying the lower fuselage cross-section to a V shape, enabling it to dispense with centrebodies and other moving parts. The size of the fin was also greatly reduced.

Rafale A was rolled out of the Saint-Cloud assembly plant on 14 December 1985, and exceeded Mach 1.3 during its first test flight on 4 July 1986. Mach 1.8 was achieved during the sixth flight, by which time the aircraft had been subjected to load factors of +6g in supersonic flight and +8g in subsonic flight, and angles of attack up to 23°. After completion of 90 flights, on 13 January 1987, the aircraft's test instrumentation was updated. Subsequent performance measurements demonstrated a stabilised speed of Mach 2 at 13,000 m (42,650 ft). On 30 April 1987, the prototype performed successfully a series of carrier approaches to the

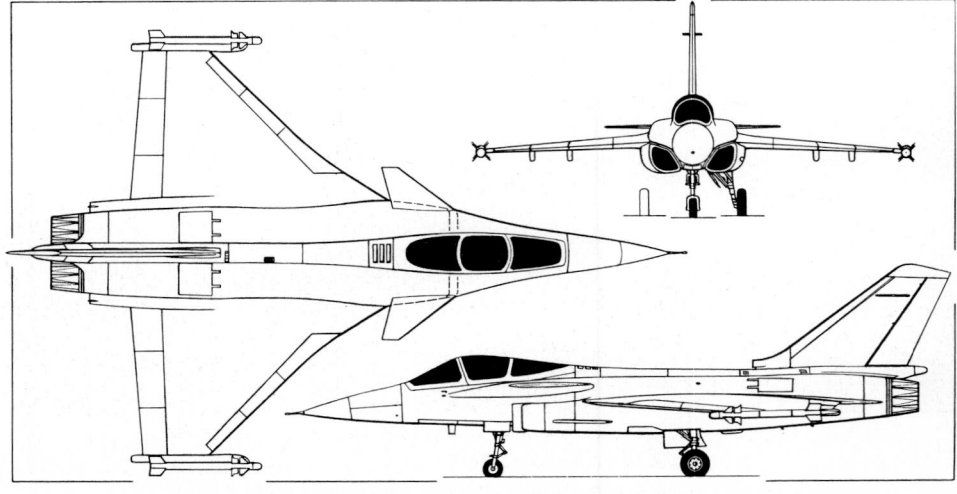

Dassault-Breguet Rafale A experimental combat aircraft *(Pilot Press)*

French Navy's aircraft carrier *Clémenceau*, without touchdown.

TYPE: Single-seat twin-engined experimental combat aircraft.

WINGS: Cantilever multi-spar mid-wing monoplane of compound delta planform. Most of wing components made from carbonfibre, including three-segment full-span elevons on each trailing-edge. Wing spar/fuselage attachment fittings of aluminium-lithium alloy. Elevons can be deflected identically or differentially. Full span three-segment leading-edge slats on each wing operate automatically with the elevons to alter wing camber and provide high lift. Slats made from titanium. Wingroot tip fairings of aramid fibre. All movable surfaces actuated by fly by wire control system, via hydraulic actuators.

FUSELAGE: Conventional semi-monocoque structure; 50 per cent carbonfibre, including entire front fuselage and dorsal spine fairings. Aramid fibre nosecone and jetpipe fairings. Most centre and rear fuselage skin panels of aluminium-lithium alloy. Wheel doors and engine doors of carbonfibre. Dorsal spine fairing from rear of canopy to jet nozzles. Forward hinged door type airbrake above engine duct on each side of fin leading-edge.

FOREPLANES: Shoulder-mounted active foreplanes of swept-back planform, actuated hydraulically by fly by wire control system. Made primarily of carbonfibre with honeycomb core and aramid fibre tips.

TAIL UNIT: Fin and inset rudder only, of sweptback form, made primarily of carbonfibre, with honeycomb core in rudder. Aramid fibre fin tip. Air intake in base of fin leading-edge. Rudder actuated hydraulically by fly by wire control system. No tabs.

LANDING GEAR: Hydraulically retractable tricycle type supplied by Messier-Hispano-Bugatti, with single wheel on each unit. Hydraulically steerable nosewheel. All wheels retract forward. Designed for impact at vertical speed of 4 m (13 ft)/s, without flare-out. Michelin radial tyres. Mainwheel tyres size 810 × 275-15, pressure 16.0 bars (232 lb/sq in). Nosewheel tyre size 550 × 200-10. Carbon brakes on all three wheels, controlled by fly by wire system. Brake-chute for emergency use in cylindrical container at base of rudder.

POWER PLANT: Two General Electric F404-GE-400 augmented turbofans, in 71.2 kN (16,000 lb st) class, mounted side by side in rear fuselage. (Port F404 to be replaced by trials SNECMA M88 Mk 2 in mid-1989.) Kidney shape plain air intakes, with splitter plates, mounted low on centre-fuselage. Integral tanks in fuselage and wings for more than 4,250 kg (9,370 lb) of fuel. Inboard underwing pylons able to carry two 2,000 litre (528 US gallon; 440 Imp gallon) drop tanks. Provision for flight refuelling.

ACCOMMODATION: Pilot only, on Martin-Baker Mk 10 zero/zero ejection seat, reclined at angle of 30-40°. One-piece blister windscreen/canopy, hinged to open sideways to starboard. HOTAS (hands on throttle and stick) controls, with sidestick controller on starboard console and small-travel throttle lever.

SYSTEMS: Bootstrap cockpit air-conditioning system. Dual hydraulic circuits, pressure 280 bars (4,000 lb/sq in), each with two Messier-Hispano-Bugatti pumps. Variable frequency electrical system, with two 30/40kVA Auxilec alternators. Triplex digital plus one dual analog fly by wire flight control system, integrated with engine controls and linked with weapons system. Eros oxygen system.

AVIONICS AND EQUIPMENT: Provision for more than 780 kg (1,720 lb) of avionics equipment and racks, including Thomson-CSF RDX lookdown/shootdown radar with acquisition range in 50 nm (92 km; 57 mile) class, able to track up to eight targets simultaneously, with automatic threat assessment and allocation of priority. (Radar and

Model of the first prototype (two-seat) Rafale D *(Paul Jackson)*

some other advanced equipment are not installed initially.) Sagem Uliss 52X INS. Digital CRT display of fuel, engine, hydraulic, electrical, oxygen and other systems information. Wide-angle diffractive optics HUD, collimated eye-level display and lateral multi-function colour displays by Thomson-CSF/SFENA. TRT com. SOCRAT VOR/ILS. Crouzet voice activated radio controls and voice alarm warning system. LMT IFF. Internal ECM suite.

ARMAMENT: One 30 mm DEFA 554 gun in side of port engine duct. Twelve external stores attachments: four under fuselage, four under wings, two at wingtips, and two below engine air intakes for sensors. Basic armament of four fuselage mounted Matra Mica medium-range air-to-air missiles and two wingtip mounted Matra Magic close-range air-to-air missiles for air defence role, with provision for four additional Micas under wings.

DIMENSIONS, EXTERNAL:

Wing span	11.2 m (36 ft 9 in)
Length overall	15.8 m (51 ft 10 in)
Wheel track	2.675 m (8 ft 9¼ in)
Wheelbase	5.185 m (17 ft 0¼ in)

AREA:

Wings, gross	47.0 m² (506.0 sq ft)

WEIGHTS:

Weight empty	9,400-9,500 kg (20,725-20,945 lb)
Combat weight, with 4 Mica and 2 Magic missiles	14,000 kg (30,865 lb)

PERFORMANCE (estimated):

Max level speed	Mach 2
	(800 knots; 1,480 km/h; 920 mph IAS)
Approach speed	under 120 knots (223 km/h; 138 mph)
T-O run: at 14,000 kg (30,865 lb) AUW	400 m (1,313 ft)
at 20,000 kg (44,100 lb) AUW	under 700 m (2,300 ft)
g limit	+9

DASSAULT-BREGUET RAFALE D and M

Rafale D is the planned production version of Rafale A, to replace French Air Force Mirage III-Es and Jaguars in the mid-1990s. It is intended to be slightly smaller overall than the Rafale A, although the general configuration will

be identical except for deletion of the air intake at the base of the tail fin. A two-seat trainer version is under development.

Rafale M is the naval counterpart, to replace French Navy Crusaders and Étendard IV-Ps. Differences by comparison with Rafale D include a reinforced main landing gear able to cope with rates of sink up to 6 m (19.7 ft)/s; a modified nose gear for nose gear catapult launch and possible use of a mini ski-jump T-O technique; and added arrester hook. Navalisation of the Rafale increases empty weight by 700 kg (1,543 lb).

French government approval for the Rafale D was announced in June 1987 and full-scale development authorised in January 1988. Two of a planned five prototypes were funded soon afterwards, comprising a two-seat Rafale D (first flight planned for early 1991) and a single-seat Rafale M. Three more single-seat aircraft, including one naval, will follow. Series production is due to begin in 1994, with the first of a planned 250 Rafale Ds being delivered to the Air Force on 1 July 1996. Deliveries of 80 Rafale Ms will start some two years later. Features of Rafale D are as follows:

POWER PLANT: Two SNECMA M88 turbofans, each rated at approx 50 kN (11,240 lb st) dry and 73.55 kN (16,534 lb st) with afterburning. Internal fuel capacity more than 4,000 kg (8,818 lb).

AVIONICS: Thomson-CSF RDX or ESD Antilope 50 (decision due late 1988) multi-function radar to permit terrain following/terrain avoidance/threat avoidance flight at low altitude, with simultaneous air-to-air search/track of multiple targets; and fire control of Mica and AMRAAM air-to-air missiles. Self protection integrated ECM. Communications via SINTAC/JTIDS. Autonomous navigation, supplemented by use of GPS/Navstar satellite systems.

DASSAULT-BREGUET/DORNIER ALPHA JET

Details of the Alpha Jet programme can be found in the International section of this edition.

DASSAULT-BREGUET/BAe JAGUAR

Details of the Jaguar programme can be found under 'SEPECAT' in the International section of this edition.

DASSAULT-BREGUET ATLANTIQUE 2 (ATL2)

The Atlantique 2, or ATL2 (formerly ANG—Atlantique Nouvelle Génération), is a twin-turboprop maritime patrol aircraft derived directly from the earlier Atlantic that was produced in 1964-73 for operation by the armed services of France (40, of which 3 were sold subsequently to Pakistan), the German Federal Republic (20, including 5 special-purpose elint/sigint aircraft), Italy (18) and the Netherlands (9, of which three survivors transferred to French Navy and three sold back to Dassault). Design definition of the ATL2 was initiated by the French government in July 1977, with the aim of providing a replacement for the first generation Atlantic (now known retrospectively as the Atlantic 1) during the period from 1988 to 1996. This led to launch of the development phase of the ATL2 programme in September 1978.

Two ATL2 prototypes were produced by modification of Atlantic 1 airframes. Work started in January 1979, and the first prototype flew for the first time in its new form on 8 May 1981, followed by the second on 26 March 1982. Series production was authorised on 24 May 1984 and the first production aircraft was scheduled to fly in October 1988, enabling deliveries to begin in 1989 and the first squadron

Dassault-Breguet Rafale A twin-engined experimental combat aircraft

to be formed at Lann Bihoué by the end of 1990. The French Navy requirement is for 42 aircraft, of which two were funded in 1985, followed by three in 1986, five in 1987 and six in 1988. The work is being shared by most members of the European SECBAT (Société d'Etude et de Construction du Breguet Atlantic) consortium that was responsible for the earlier programme, with some modification of the work-split to reflect varying national interests in the ATL2 aircraft. Companies involved, under Dassault-Breguet direction, are SABCA and Sonaca of Belgium, MBB and Dornier of Federal Germany, Aeritalia of Italy and Aérospatiale of France. The Tyne engines are being produced by SNECMA of France, Rolls-Royce of the UK, FN of Belgium and MTU of Federal Germany; and propellers by Ratier of France and British Aerospace.

Structural changes by comparison with the Atlantic 1 include use of a refined bonding technique, improved anti-corrosion protection, better sealing between skin panels, and design improvements offering longer fatigue life and more economical maintenance. These are intended to ensure increased serviceability, with at least 75 per cent of squadron aircraft permanently available for operations; readiness to take off within 30 minutes of an order to go; and an aircraft life of 30 years.

The basic mission performance requirements envisaged for the ATL2 are similar to those of the Atlantic 1: a high cruising speed to the operational area, quick descent from cruising altitude to patrol height, lengthy patrol endurance at low altitude, and a high degree of manoeuvrability at sea level. It is able to carry a wide variety of weapons and equipment for finding and attacking both submarines and surface targets in all weathers. In particular, its Thomson-CSF Iguane search radar can detect large ships at a range of 150-200 nm (275-370 km; 170-230 miles), and small targets such as submarine schnorkels over 'several dozen nautical miles' in rough seas.

Like the original Atlantic, the ATL2 is able to perform minelaying, logistic support, and passenger and freight transport missions. It could be adapted for advanced AEW duties, and is suitable for civilian tasks such as air/sea rescue and patrol of offshore fishing and oil interests.

TYPE: Twin-turboprop maritime patrol aircraft.

WINGS: Cantilever mid-wing monoplane, with streamlined ESM pods on tips. Wing section NACA 64 series. Dihedral 6° on outer panels only. Incidence 3°. Tapered planform, with 9° sweepback on leading-edge. All-metal three-spar fail-safe structure, with bonded light alloy honeycomb skin panels on torsion box and on main landing gear doors. Two conventional all-metal ailerons on each wing, actuated by SAMM twin-cylinder jacks. All-metal slotted flaps, with bonded light alloy honeycomb filling, in three segments on each wing, over 75 per cent of span. Three hinged spoilers on upper surface of each outer wing, forward of flaps. Metal airbrake above and below each wing. No trim tabs. Air Equipement/Kléber-Colombes pneumatic de-icing system on leading-edges.

FUSELAGE: All-metal 'double-bubble' fail-safe structure, with bonded honeycomb sandwich skin on pressurised central section of upper lobe, upward sliding weapons bay doors and nosewheel door. Large air intake and duct for air-conditioning system on each side of nose.

TAIL UNIT: Cantilever all-metal structure, with bonded honeycomb sandwich skin panels on torsion boxes. Slightly bulged housing for ESM antennae at top of fin leading-edge. Fixed incidence tailplane, with dihedral.

Control surfaces operated through SAMM twin-cylinder jacks. No trim tabs. Air Equipement/Kléber-Colombes pneumatic de-icing system on leading-edges.

LANDING GEAR: Retractable tricycle type, supplied by Messier-Hispano-Bugatti, with twin wheels on each unit. Hydraulic retraction, nosewheels rearward, main units forward into engine nacelles. Kléber-Colombes or Dunlop tyres; size 39 × 13-20 on mainwheels, pressure 12 bars (170 lb/sq in), 26 × 7.75-13 on nosewheels, pressure 6.5 bars (94 lb/sq in). New Messier-Hispano-Bugatti disc brakes with higher braking energy, and Modistop anti-skid units.

POWER PLANT: Two 4,549 kW (6,100 ehp) Rolls-Royce Tyne RTy.20 Mk 21 turboprops, each driving a four-blade Ratier/British Aerospace constant-speed metal propeller type PD 249/476/3 on prototypes. Four pressure-refuelled integral fuel tanks in wings, with total capacity of 23,120 litres (6,108 US gallons; 5,085 Imp gallons). Updated gauging system. Oil capacity 100 litres (26.5 US gallons; 22 Imp gallons).

ACCOMMODATION: Normal flight crew of 12, comprising observer in glazed nose; pilot, co-pilot and flight engineer on flight deck; a radio-navigator, ESM-ECM-MAD operator, radar-IFF operator, tactical co-ordinator and two acoustic sensor operators at stations on the starboard side of the tactical compartment; and two observers in beam positions at the rear. Provision for carrying relief crew, or 12 other personnel. Rest compartment, with eight seats, in centre fuselage, forward of crew room with tables and seats, galley, toilet and wardrobe. Primary access via extending airstair door in bottom of rear fuselage. Emergency exits above and below flight deck and on each side of fuselage, above wing trailing-edge.

SYSTEMS: Air-conditioning system supplied by two compressors driven by gearboxes. Heat exchangers and bootstrap system for cabin temperature control. Duplicated hydraulic system, pressure 186 bars (2,700 lb/sq in), to operate flying controls, landing gear, flaps, weapons bay doors and retractable radome. Hydraulic flow rate 17.85 litres (4.7 US gallons; 3.9 Imp gallons)/min. Three basic electrical systems: variable frequency three-phase

115/200V AC system, with two 60/80kVA Auxilec alternators and modernised control and protection equipment; fixed frequency three-phase 115/200V 400Hz AC system, with four 15kVA Auxilec Auxivar generators, two on each engine; 28V DC system, with four 6kW transformer-rectifiers supplied from the variable frequency AC system, and one 40Ah battery. One 60kVA emergency AC generator, driven at constant speed by APU. Individual oxygen bottles for emergency use. Electric anti-icing for engine air intake lips, propeller blades and spinners. Turbomeca/ABG/SEMCA Astadyne gas turbine APU for engine starting, emergency electrical supply, and air-conditioning on ground.

ARMAMENT, AVIONICS AND OPERATIONAL EQUIPMENT: Main weapons bay in unpressurised lower fuselage can accommodate all NATO standard bombs, depth charges, up to eight Mk 46 homing torpedoes, seven French Murène advanced torpedoes or two air-to-surface missiles (typical load comprises three torpedoes and one AM39 Exocet missile). Four underwing attachments for up to 3,500 kg (7,716 lb) of stores, including future air-to-surface and air-to-air missiles or pods. More than 100 sonobuoys, with Alkan pneumatic launcher, in compartment aft of weapons bay, where whole of upper and lower fuselage provides storage for sonobuoys and 160 smoke markers and flares. SAT/TRT Tango forward looking infra-red sensor in turret under nose. Thomson-CSF Iguane retractable radar immediately forward of weapons bay, with integrated LMT IFF interrogator and SECRE decoder. Omera 35 cameras in starboard side of nose and in bottom of rear fuselage. Crouzet MAD in lengthened tail sting. Thomson-CSF Arar 13A radar detector for ESM. Thomson-CSF Sadang system for processing active and passive acoustic detection data. A distributed data processing system around a databus, with a CIMSA Mitra 125X tactical computer (512K words memory), two ESD bus computers, two Sagem magnetic bubble mass memories and Thomson-CSF display subsystem. Other equipment includes IFF transponder and HF com by LMT, UHF AM/FM by Sintra, Tacan and DME by Thomson-CSF, VHF AM/FM com by Socrat, VOR/ILS by EAS, TRT radio altimeter, Collins MF radio compass, ADF, HSI and autopilot/flight director by SFENA, dual Sagem Uliss 53 inertial navigation systems coupled to a Navstar receiver, Sagem high-speed printer and terminal display, Crouzet navigation table and air data computer.

DIMENSIONS, EXTERNAL:

Wing span, incl wingtip pods	37.42 m (122 ft 9¼ in)
Wing aspect ratio	10.9
Length overall	31.62 m (103 ft 9 in)
Height overall	10.89 m (35 ft 8¾ in)
Fuselage: Max depth	4.00 m (13 ft 1½ in)
Tailplane span	12.31 m (40 ft 4½ in)
Wheel track (c/l of shock struts)	9.00 m (29 ft 6¼ in)
Wheelbase	9.40 m (30 ft 10 in)
Propeller diameter	4.88 m (16 ft 0 in)
Distance between propeller centres	
	9.00 m (29 ft 6¼ in)
Main weapons bay: Length	9.00 m (29 ft 6¼ in)
Width	2.10 m (6 ft 10¾ in)

DIMENSIONS, INTERNAL:

Cabin, incl rest compartment, galley, toilet, aft observers' stations: Length	18.50 m (60 ft 8½ in)
Max width	3.60 m (11 ft 9½ in)
Max height	2.00 m (6 ft 6¾ in)
Floor area	155 m² (1,668 sq ft)
Volume	92 m³ (3,250 cu ft)

AREAS:

Wings, gross	120.34 m² (1,295.3 sq ft)
Ailerons (total)	5.26 m² (56.62 sq ft)
Flaps (total)	26.42 m² (284.38 sq ft)
Spoilers (total)	1.66 m² (17.87 sq ft)
Vertical tail surfaces (total)	16.64 m² (179.11 sq ft)
Rudder	5.96 m² (64.15 sq ft)
Horizontal tail surfaces (total)	32.50 m² (349.83 sq ft)
Elevators	8.30 m² (89.34 sq ft)

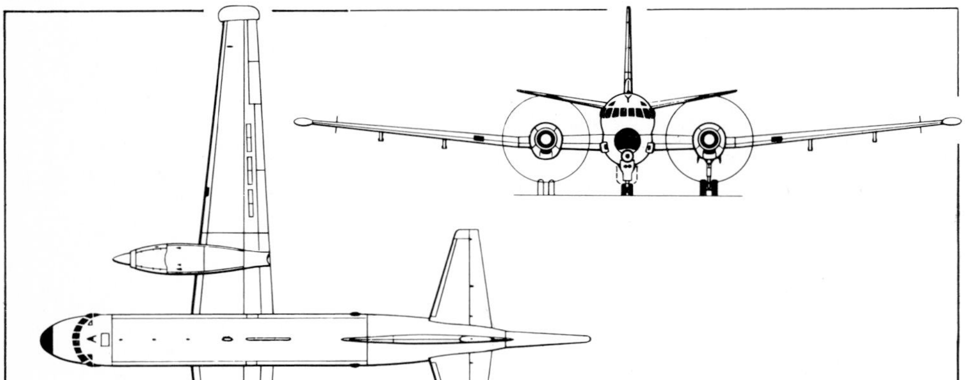

Second prototype Dassault-Breguet Atlantique 2 (ATL2) maritime patrol aircraft

Dassault-Breguet Atlantique 2 (ATL2) twin-turboprop maritime patrol aircraft *(Pilot Press)*

WEIGHTS AND LOADINGS:

Weight empty, equipped, standard mission	25,700 kg (56,659 lb)
Military load:	
ASW or ASSW mission	3,000 kg (6,600 lb)
Max fuel	18,500 kg (40,785 lb)
Standard mission T-O weight:	
ASW or ASSW mission	44,200 kg (97,440 lb)
combined ASW/ASSW mission	45,000 kg (99,200 lb)
Max T-O weight	46,200 kg (101,850 lb)
Max zero-fuel weight	32,500 kg (71,650 lb)
Normal design landing weight	36,000 kg (79,365 lb)
Max landing weight	46,000 kg (101,400 lb)
Max wing loading	385 kg/m² (78.96 lb/sq ft)
Max power loading	5.07 kg/kW (8.34 lb/ehp)

PERFORMANCE (with metal propellers, at T-O weight of 45,000 kg; 99,200 lb except where indicated):

Never-exceed speed	Mach 0.73
Max level speed at optimum height	350 knots (648 km/h; 402 mph)
Max level speed at S/L	320 knots (592 km/h; 368 mph)
Max cruising speed at 7,200 m (25,000 ft)	300 knots (555 km/h; 345 mph)
Normal patrol speed, S/L to 1,525 m (5,000 ft)	170 knots (315 km/h; 195 mph)
Stalling speed, flaps down	90 knots (167 km/h; 104 mph)
Max rate of climb at S/L:	
AUW of 30,000 kg (66,140 lb)	884 m (2,900 ft)/min
AUW of 40,000 kg (88,185 lb)	610 m (2,000 ft)/min
Rate of climb at S/L, one engine out:	
AUW of 30,000 kg (66,140 lb)	365 m (1,200 ft)/min
AUW of 40,000 kg (88,185 lb)	213 m (700 ft)/min
Service ceiling	9,145 m (30,000 ft)
Runway LCN at max T-O weight	60
T-O to 10.5 m (35 ft)	1,840 m (6,037 ft)
Landing from 15 m (50 ft)	1,500 m (4,922 ft)
170 knot turning radius at AUW of 40,000 kg (88,185 lb)	
at: 30° bank	1,380 m (4,530 ft)
45° bank	800 m (2,625 ft)
60° bank	460 m (1,510 ft)

Typical mission profiles, with reserves of 5% total fuel, 5% of fuel consumed and 20 min hold-off:

Anti-ship mission: T-O with max fuel and one AM39 missile; fly 1,800 nm (3,333 km; 2,071 miles) to target area; descend for two-hour search and attack at 90 m (300 ft); return to base

Anti-submarine mission: T-O at 44,300 kg (97,665 lb) AUW with 15,225 kg (33,565 lb) of fuel, four Mk 46 torpedoes, 78 sonobuoys, and a full load of markers and flares; cruise to search area at 290 knots (537 km/h; 333 mph) at 7,620 m (25,000 ft); descend for 8 h low altitude patrol at 600 nm (1,110 km; 690 miles) from base, or 5 h patrol at 1,000 nm (1,850 km; 1,150 miles) from base; return to base at 9,145 m (30,000 ft). Total mission time 12 h 31 min

Ferry range with max fuel	4,900 nm (9,075 km; 5,635 miles)
Max endurance	18 h

DASSAULT-BREGUET MYSTÈRE-FALCON 20-5

From the first quarter of 1989, operators of the Mystère-Falcon 20 will have the option of updating their aircraft to 20C-5, D-5, E-5 or F-5 standard, with Garrett TFE731-5AR turbofans of 20.02 kN (4,500 lb st). The 'Dash 5' package, marketed by Garrett General Aviation Services Division, comprises two Falcon 900 type engine nacelles, plus associated hydraulic pumps, starter/generators and pylons. Dee Howard target type thrust reversers are an optional extra.

Flight testing of two modified Falcon 20s was due to begin in September/October 1988, followed by certification in Spring 1989. Despite a slight weight penalty, compared with the original General Electric CF700s, the Falcon 20-5 will have 3% lower engine operating costs and performance gains including (20F-5) a 15 minute climb to 9,450 m (31,000 ft) with eight passengers and full fuel. Range of a Falcon 20F-5 with eight passengers and NBAA reserves at Mach 0.72 is estimated as 2,100 nm (3,892 km; 2,418 miles) compared with 1,430 nm (2,650 km; 1,646 miles) unmodified.

DASSAULT-BREGUET MYSTÈRE-FALCON 200

The Mystère-Falcon 200 is the latest in a family of twin-turbofan light transports based on the Mystère 20 design, which was first flown in prototype form on 4 May 1963. Production is undertaken jointly by Aérospatiale, which builds the fuselage and tail unit, and Dassault-Breguet's Mérignac works, which manufactures the wings and has responsibility for final assembly.

Manufacture of the Mystère-Falcon 200 began with aircraft c/n 401, first flown on 30 April 1980, concurrent with the production rundown of the earlier Mystère-Falcon 20F series, the last of which (c/n 486) came off the assembly line in late 1983. The model 200 had been introduced, originally as the Mystère-Falcon 20H, at the 1981 Paris Air Show, with Garrett turbofans in place of the F's General Electric CF700s, larger integral fuel tankage in the rear fuselage, redesigned wingroot fairings, automatic slat extension, and many important systems changes. Certification was achieved on 21 June 1981. Like the earlier Mystère-Falcon 20 series, it can be modified for specific duties, as follows:

Dassault-Breguet Mystère-Falcon 200 (two Garrett ATF 3-6A-4C turbofans)

Calibration: Ten Mystère-Falcons, in several different variants, have been delivered to the French DGAC, French Air Force, and authorities in Spain, Indonesia and Iran, for navaid calibration. Most are equipped with Dassault designed high/low level navigation facility calibration systems, some in the form of a removable console.

Airline crew training: Mystère-Falcon 20s have been used by Air France to train pilots for its jet airliners, with up to five aircraft being used simultaneously. Japan Air Lines also used three of this version.

Quick-change and cargo: A quick-change kit, consisting of an assembly of nets and supports, keeps the centre aisle free and allows direct access to nine freight compartments. Total usable volume of these compartments is 6.65 m³ (235 cu ft), and transformation from executive configuration to cargo configuration, or vice versa, takes less than one hour. A different specific cargo conversion was performed on 33 aircraft in the USA. For both versions the maximum zero-fuel weight of 9,980 kg (22,000 lb) allows a payload of up to 3,000 kg (6,615 lb).

Target towing: A Mystère-Falcon 20 is used by the French Air Force for target towing missions. It carries a Secapem target on an inboard hardpoint under each wing and a pod containing a winch and cable on each of two outboard hardpoints. Missions of up to 2 h duration can be flown, cruising at up to 300 knots (555 km/h; 345 mph) at 450 m (1,500 ft) or 270 knots (500 km/h; 310 mph) at 4,500 m (15,000 ft). The hardpoints (650 kg; 1,433 lb inboard, 750 kg; 1,650 lb outboard) can be used to carry alternative stores if required. Sixteen former Federal Express cargo aircraft operated by Flight Refuelling Ltd of the UK provide Royal Navy target facilities with equipment including an RM30A target winch, ALQ-167 radar jammer, BOZ-3 chaff dispenser, ALE-43 chaff/flare dispenser and ATRS-5 radar simulator, all mounted under the wings.

Aerial photography: This version has two ventral camera bays fitted with optical glass windows. It is operated for high altitude photography, survey and scientific research in several countries. The camera installation can be supplemented by a multispectral scanner and other scientific loads.

Systems trainer: Four aircraft fitted with the combat radar and navigation systems of various Mirage types are in service with the French Air Force for training its interceptor, strike and reconnaissance pilots.

Ambulance: Up to three stretchers can be accommodated, together with a large supply of oxygen and equipment for intensive care and monitoring of patients. Cabinets near the door are removed to facilitate the loading of stretchers.

Electronic warfare: Norway, Canada and Morocco have been followed by several other nations, including Pakistan, in operating Mystère-Falcon 20 aircraft modified for ECM duties such as radar and communications intelligence and jamming.

By the beginning of 1988, deliveries totalled 471 Mystère-Falcon 20s and 35 Mystère-Falcon 200s.

The following data apply to the standard Mystère-Falcon 200 executive transport:

TYPE: Twin-turbofan executive transport.

WINGS: Cantilever low-wing monoplane. Thickness/chord ratio varies from 10.5 to 8%. Dihedral 2°. Incidence 1° 30′. Sweepback at quarter-chord 30°. All-metal (copper bearing alloys) fail-safe torsion box structure with machined stressed skin. Ailerons are each operated by Dassault twin-body actuators, from dual hydraulic systems, with airspeed-slaved artificial feel. Non-slotted slats inboard of fence, and slotted slats outboard, on each wing, with automatic extension and retraction. Hydraulically actuated airbrakes forward of the hydraulically actuated two-section single-slotted flaps. Leading-edges anti-iced by engine bleed air.

FUSELAGE: All-metal semi-monocoque structure of circular cross-section, built on fail-safe principles.

TAIL UNIT: Cantilever all-metal structure, with electrically controlled variable incidence tailplane mounted halfway up fin. Elevators and rudder each actuated by twin hydraulic servos. No trim tabs.

LANDING GEAR: Retractable tricycle type, by Messier-Hispano-Bugatti, with twin wheels on all three units. Hydraulic retraction, main units inward, nosewheels forward. Oleo-pneumatic shock absorbers. Steerable and self centring nosewheels. Tyres size 26 × 6.6-14 on main units, 14.5 × 5.5-6 on nosewheels. Tyre pressure 11.5 bars (166 lb/sq in) on mainwheels, 10.4 bars (151 lb/sq in) on nosewheels. Goodyear disc brakes and anti-skid units.

POWER PLANT: Two Garrett ATF 3-6A-4C turbofans (each rated at 23.13 kN; 5,200 lb st). Optional thrust reversers are produced by Hurel-Dubois. Fuel in two integral tanks in wings and large integral tank in rear fuselage, with total capacity of 6,000 litres (1,585 US gallons; 1,320 Imp gallons).

ACCOMMODATION: Flight deck for crew of two, with airline type instrumentation. Jump seat and crew wardrobe. Airstair door, with handrail, on port side. On starboard side, opposite door, is a galley with oven and hot beverage containers. Main cabin normally seats nine passengers in three pairs of facing chairs, separated by tables, and an inward facing three-seat sofa, with a central 'trench' aisle. Alternative arrangement provides 12 compact seats at a pitch of 76 cm (30 in). Wardrobe immediately aft of door on port side. Externally serviced toilet compartment aft of main cabin on port side, with a baggage bay opposite on starboard side. Main heated, non-pressurised, baggage compartment in rear fuselage with external access on port side.

SYSTEMS: Duplicated air-conditioning and pressurisation system, supplied with air bled from both engines. Pressure differential 0.607 bars (8.8 lb/sq in). Cooling by bootstrap system. Two independent hydraulic systems, pressure 207 bars (3,000 lb/sq in), actuate primary flying controls, flaps, landing gear, wheel brakes, spoilers and nosewheel steering. No. 1 system is powered by one engine driven hydraulic pump and, in emergency, by a motor pump package driven by No. 2 system hydraulic pressure and by an electric standby pump. No. 2 system is powered by one engine driven hydraulic pump and, in emergency, by the electric standby pump. Hydraulic reservoir pressure 1.47 bars (21 lb/sq in). Electrical system includes a 9kW 28V DC starter/generator on each engine, three 750VA inverters and two 36Ah batteries. Solar T40 APU optional. Wing leading-edges and engine air inlets anti-iced with LP compressor bleed air. Windscreen, pitot and temperature probes anti-iced electrically.

AVIONICS AND EQUIPMENT: Collins FCS-80 flight control system standard, with dual Collins EFIS-86C electronic flight instrument system using colour CRTs. System includes four identical CRTs plus one multi-function display used for weather radar, navigation display or checklist. Standard avionics include duplicated VHF, VOR, ADF, DME and ATC transponder, one weather radar and one radio altimeter. Optional equipment includes HF, VLF/Omega navigation system and laser inertial reference system.

DIMENSIONS, EXTERNAL:

Wing span	16.32 m (53 ft 6½ in)
Wing chord (mean)	2.85 m (9 ft 4 in)
Wing aspect ratio	6.5
Length overall	17.15 m (56 ft 3 in)
Length of fuselage	15.55 m (51 ft 0 in)
Height overall	5.32 m (17 ft 5 in)
Fuselage diameter (max external)	2.05 m (6 ft 8¾ in)
Tailplane span	6.74 m (22 ft 1 in)
Wheel track	3.34 m (10 ft 11½ in)

Wheelbase	5.74 m (18 ft 10 in)
Passenger door: Height	1.52 m (5 ft 0 in)
Width	0.80 m (2 ft 7½ in)
Height to sill	1.09 m (3 ft 7 in)
Emergency exits (each side, over wing):	
Height	0.66 m (2 ft 2 in)
Width	0.48 m (1 ft 7 in)

DIMENSIONS, INTERNAL:

Cabin, incl fwd baggage space and rear toilet:	
Length	7.26 m (23 ft 10 in)
Max width	1.79 m (5 ft 10½ in)
Max height	1.70 m (5 ft 7 in)
Volume	20.0 m³ (700 cu ft)
Baggage space (cabin)	0.65 m³ (23 cu ft)
Baggage compartment (rear fuselage)	
	0.80 m³ (28.2 cu ft)

AREAS:

Wings, gross	41.00 m² (440 sq ft)
Horizontal tail surfaces (total)	11.30 m² (121.6 sq ft)
Vertical tail surfaces (total)	7.60 m² (81.8 sq ft)

WEIGHTS:

Weight empty, equipped	8,250 kg (18,190 lb)
Payload with max fuel	1,265 kg (2,790 lb)
Max fuel	4,845 kg (10,680 lb)
Max T-O and ramp weight	14,515 kg (32,000 lb)
Max zero-fuel weight	10,200 kg (22,500 lb)
Max landing weight	13,100 kg (28,800 lb)

PERFORMANCE:

Max operating Mach No.	0.865
Max operating speed:	
at S/L	350 knots (648 km/h; 402 mph) IAS
at 6,100 m (20,000 ft)	
	380 knots (704 km/h; 438 mph) IAS
Max cruising speed at 9,150 m (30,000 ft) at AUW of	
11,340 kg (25,000 lb)	
	470 knots (870 km/h; 541 mph)
Econ cruising speed at 12,500 m (41,000 ft)	
	420 knots (780 km/h; 485 mph)
Stalling speed	84 knots (156 km/h; 97 mph)
Service ceiling	13,715 m (45,000 ft)
FAR 25 balanced field length with 8 passengers and full	
fuel	1,420 m (4,660 ft)
FAR 121 landing distance with 8 passengers, FAR 121	
reserves	1,130 m (3,710 ft)
Range with max fuel and 8 passengers at long-range	
cruising speed, 45 min reserves	
	2,510 nm (4,650 km; 2,890 miles)

DASSAULT-BREGUET GARDIAN 2

The Gardian 2 is a Falcon 200 fitted with a Thomson-CSF Varan radar for maritime detection, a Crouzet Omega navigation system and four underwing hardpoints. With additional equipment, it can perform the following missions:

Target designation: This includes over-the-horizon targeting for maritime forces or coastal missile batteries; missile midcourse retargeting; control of surface operations; and strike guidance against surface ships or land objectives. Equipment includes a navigation table, UHF modem to transmit data, V/UHF DF, and IFF interrogator. Options include ESM, search windows, inertial platform, VHF/FM, HF and track-while-scan radar system.

AM39 Exocet attack: As well as two Exocet sea-skimming air-to-surface missiles, this requires an inertial platform, Omega/INS interface, AM39 interface and controls, and IFF interrogator. Options are track-while-scan, navigation table and ESM.

Electronic surveillance and countermeasures: This requires either Thomson-CSF DR 2000 ESM and navigation table, or an integrated system including a Thomson-CSF DR 4000 ESM, a computer, the Varan radar, an inertial platform and tactical visualisation elements from the Atlantique 2 system. Options include an IFF interrogator, AM39 installation, track-while-scan, countermeasures or decoy pods, elint equipment, HF/VHF/UHF comint equipment and V/UHF DF.

Target towing: As for Falcon 200.

In all cases, the cabin can be arranged to permit secondary transport missions.

Two Gardian 2s have been ordered by the Chilean Navy for maritime reconnaissance duties.

DASSAULT-BREGUET MYSTÈRE-FALCON 100

The Mystère-Falcon 100 is the latest version of the Mystère-Falcon 10 series, which it has replaced in production. Like its predecessors, it is a small executive 'jet' for five to eight passengers, with compound swept wings fitted with high-lift devices, and powered by Garrett TFE731-2 turbofans.

Details of the early history of the Mystère-Falcon 10 series can be found in the 1982-83 *Jane's*. By February 1988, a total of 216 Mystère-Falcon 10s and 100s had been delivered. Fuselages are provided by the Potez works at Aire-sur-Adour, which assembles components built by Sogerma, Socea and Socata. Wings come from CASA of Spain; tail units and nose assemblies from IAM of Italy; and many other components such as tail fins, doors and emergency exits from Latécoère's Toulouse works.

By comparison with the Mystère-Falcon 10, the model 100 has an increase of 225 kg (496 lb) in max T-O weight and

Dassault-Breguet Gardian 2 carrying two Exocet missiles, a Thomson-CSF Barem self-protection jamming pod and a Matra Sycomor chaff dispensing pod on underwing pylons *(Air Portraits)*

higher max ramp weight; a fourth cabin window on the starboard side, opposite the door; a larger heated, unpressurised rear baggage compartment; and a Collins five-CRT EFIS-85 instrument package.

In December 1986, the Falcon 100 was certificated by the DGAC for Cat II approaches in commercial operation.

Under a state sponsored research and development programme, Aérospatiale and Dassault-Breguet have manufactured a set of resin-impregnated carbonfibre wings for a Falcon 10 designated **V10F**. Dassault-Breguet made the port wing, Aérospatiale the starboard wing, retaining the aerodynamic form of the standard metal wings. The V10F (F-WVPR, c/n 5) flew for the first time on 21 May 1985 and received DGAC certification on 16 December 1985. It made a total of 40 test flights and built up flying hours subsequently as one of the aircraft in the charter fleet of Europe Falcon Service.

The following details apply to the standard production Mystère-Falcon 100:

TYPE: Twin-turbofan executive transport.

WINGS: Cantilever low-wing monoplane with increased sweepback on inboard leading-edges. All-metal torsion box structure, with leading-edge slats and double-slotted trailing-edge flaps and plain ailerons. Two-section spoilers above each wing, forward of flaps.

FUSELAGE: All-metal semi-monocoque structure, designed to fail-safe principles.

TAIL UNIT: Cantilever all-metal structure, similar to that of Falcon 200.

LANDING GEAR: Retractable tricycle type, manufactured by Messier-Hispano-Bugatti, with twin wheels on each main gear unit, single wheel on nose gear. Hydraulic retraction, main units inward, nosewheel forward. Oleo-pneumatic shock absorbers. Mainwheel tyres size 22 × 5.75 in, pressure 9.31 bars (135 lb/sq in). Nosewheel tyre size 18 × 5.75 in, pressure 6.55 bars (95 lb/sq in).

POWER PLANT: Two Garrett TFE731-2 turbofans (each 14.4 kN; 3,230 lb st), pod mounted on sides of rear fuselage.

Dassault-Breguet Mystère-Falcon 100 of Lyon-Air, equipped for operations to Cat II landing minima

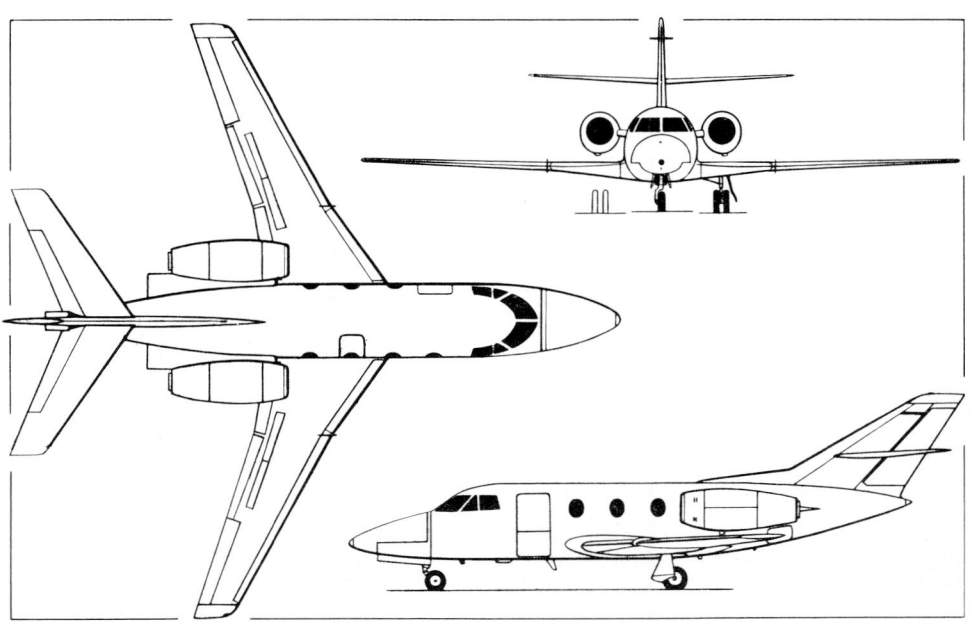

Dassault-Breguet Mystère-Falcon 100 four/eight-passenger executive transport *(Pilot Press)*

Thrust reversers optional. Fuel in two integral tanks in wings and two integral feeder tanks in rear fuselage, with total capacity of 3,340 litres (882 US gallons; 735 Imp gallons). Separate fuel system for each engine, with provision for cross-feeding. Pressure refuelling system.

ACCOMMODATION: Crew of two on flight deck, with dual controls and airline type instrumentation. Provision for third crew member on a jump seat. Seating arrangements differ from aircraft to aircraft in accordance with customer preference. All have a two/three-place sofa in the rear of the cabin, with further seats for a total of up to eight passengers. There is an internal baggage compartment behind the sofa, and a small galley and toilet forward of the passenger accommodation. Clamshell door at the front, on the port side, with built-in steps.

SYSTEMS: Duplicated air-conditioning and pressurisation systems supplied with air bled from both engines. Pressure differential 0.61 bars (8.8 lb/sq in). Two independent hydraulic systems, each of 207 bars (3,000 lb/sq in) pressure and with twin engine driven pumps and emergency electric pump, to actuate primary flight controls, flaps, landing gear, wheel brakes, spoilers, yaw damper and nosewheel steering. Plain hydraulic reservoir, pressurised at 1.47 bars (21 lb/sq in). 28V DC electrical system with a 9kW DC starter/generator on each engine, three 750VA 400Hz 115V inverters and two 23Ah batteries. Automatic emergency oxygen system.

AVIONICS AND EQUIPMENT: Standard avionics include Collins APS 80 autopilot and EFIS-85, ADC 80 air data computer and electrical instruments, dual VHF, VOR, DME, transponders, ADF and intercom systems, Collins weather radar, and radio altimeter. Optional avionics are a 718 U5M HF transceiver, Collins APS 85 autopilot and EFIS-86C, and Global GNS 500 flight management system and long-range navigation system.

DIMENSIONS, EXTERNAL:

Wing span	13.08 m (42 ft 11 in)
Wing chord (mean)	2.046 m (6 ft 8½ in)
Wing aspect ratio	7.1
Length overall	13.86 m (45 ft 5¾ in)
Length of fuselage	12.47 m (40 ft 11 in)
Height overall	4.61 m (15 ft 1½ in)
Tailplane span	5.82 m (19 ft 1 in)
Wheel track	2.86 m (9 ft 5 in)
Wheelbase	5.30 m (17 ft 4¾ in)
Passenger door: Height	1.47 m (4 ft 10 in)
Width	0.80 m (2 ft 7 in)
Height to sill	0.884 m (2 ft 10¾ in)
Emergency exit (stbd side, over wing):	
Height	0.914 m (3 ft 0 in)
Width	0.508 m (1 ft 8 in)

DIMENSIONS, INTERNAL:

Cabin, excl flight deck: Length	4.70 m (15 ft 5 in)
Max width	1.55 m (5 ft 1 in)
Max height	1.45 m (4 ft 9 in)
Volume	7.11 m³ (251 cu ft)
Baggage compartment volume:	
cabin	0.72 m³ (25.4 cu ft)
rear	0.81 m³ (28.6 cu ft)

AREAS:

Wings, gross	24.1 m² (259.4 sq ft)
Horizontal tail surfaces (total)	6.75 m² (72.65 sq ft)
Vertical tail surfaces (total)	4.54 m² (48.87 sq ft)

WEIGHTS:

Weight empty, equipped	5,055 kg (11,145 lb)
Max payload	1,305 kg (2,875 lb)
Payload with max fuel	840 kg (1,852 lb)
Max fuel	2,680 kg (5,910 lb)
Max T-O weight	8,755 kg (19,300 lb)
Max zero-fuel weight	6,540 kg (14,420 lb)
Max landing weight	8,000 kg (17,640 lb)

PERFORMANCE:

Never-exceed speed at S/L	
	350 knots (648 km/h; 402 mph)
Max operating Mach No.	0.87
Max cruise Mach No. at 10,670 m (35,000 ft)	0.84
Max cruising speed at 7,620 m (25,000 ft)	
	492 knots (912 km/h; 566 mph)
Approach speed	100 knots (185 km/h; 115 mph)
Operational ceiling (four passengers, full fuel)	
	13,715 m (45,000 ft)

FAR 25 balanced T-O field length with four passengers and fuel for a 1,000 nm (1,850 km; 1,150 mile) stage, 45 min reserves 960 m (3,150 ft)

FAR 25 balanced T-O field length, with four passengers and max fuel 1,325 m (4,350 ft)

FAR 121 landing field length, with four passengers and 45 min reserves 1,065 m (3,495 ft)

Range with four passengers and 45 min reserves 1,883 nm (3,490 km; 2,168 miles)

DASSAULT-BREGUET MYSTÈRE-FALCON 50

The Mystère-Falcon 50 three-turbofan executive transport has the same external fuselage cross-section as the Mystère-Falcon 200, but is an entirely new design, featuring area ruling and advanced wing aerodynamics. Normal layout is for a crew of two and eight or nine passengers, with provision for up to twelve passengers.

The original prototype (F-WAMD) flew for the first time on 7 November 1976, followed by a second prototype (F-WINR) on 18 February 1978 and the third (and sole pre-production) aircraft on 13 June 1978. DGAC certification was received on 27 February 1979, followed by FAA type approval on 7 March. Falcon 50 c/n 4, flown on 2 March 1979, was the first built on Dassault-Breguet's Mérignac assembly line and became Falcon Jet's US demonstrator. Deliveries began in July 1979 and totalled 179 aircraft, registered in 30 countries, by the beginning of 1988. Since delivery of the fifth aircraft to the Armée de l'Air's GLAM (Groupe de Liaisons Aériennes Ministérielles) in early 1980, for use by the President of the French Republic, Mystère-Falcon 50s have been purchased for state VIP transportation in Iraq, Jordan, Libya, Morocco, South Africa, Spain and Yugoslavia. Two supplied to the Italian Air Force are equipped for both VIP and air ambulance duties.

On 31 March 1979 a Falcon 50 set the current straight-line distance record for Class C1h (business aircraft of 12,000-16,000 kg AUW) in the USA, by flying 3,293.69 nm (6,099.91 km; 3,790.31 miles). Two current records in Class C1i (16,000-20,000 kg) were set in France on 24 April 1980, with a sustained level flight at 13,716 m (45,000 ft), which qualified also as the altitude record in this class.

Fuselages for the Mystère-Falcon 50 are produced at Aérospatiale's Saint-Nazaire works, wings at the Colomiers plant of Dassault-Breguet, tail units by Aérospatiale at Méaulte, and cowlings by Hurel-Dubois at Vélizy-Villacoublay.

TYPE: Three-turbofan executive transport.

WINGS: Cantilever low-wing monoplane, with compound leading-edge sweepback and optimised section. Each wing is attached to the central box structure by multiple bolts and forms an integral fuel tank. Full span leading-edge slats, of which the outboard sections are slotted. Double-slotted trailing-edge flaps and ailerons, latter with carbonfibre skin. Three-section two-position airbrakes on top surface of each wing.

FUSELAGE: All-metal semi-monocoque structure of circular cross-section, with aft baggage compartment included in pressure cell.

TAIL UNIT: Cantilever all-metal structure. Horizontal

surfaces, with anhedral, mounted partway up fin. Tailplane incidence adjustable by screwjack, driven by two electric motors controlled by 'normal' and 'emergency' controls located respectively on the control wheels and pedestal.

LANDING GEAR: Retractable tricycle type by Messier-Hispano-Bugatti, with twin wheels on each unit. Hydraulic retraction, main units inward, nosewheels forward. Mainwheel tyres size 26 × 6.6-14 in, pressure 14.34 bars (208 lb/sq in). Nosewheel tyres size 14.5 × 5.5-6 in, pressure 8.96 bars (130 lb/sq in). Four-disc brakes designed for 400 landings with normal energy braking.

POWER PLANT: Three Garrett TFE731-3 turbofans, each rated at 16.5 kN (3,700 lb st) for take-off. Two engines pod mounted on sides of rear fuselage, the third attached by two top mounts. Thrust reverser on centre engine. Fuel in wing and fuselage tanks, with total capacity of 8,765 litres (2,315 US gallons; 1,928 Imp gallons). Single point pressure fuelling.

ACCOMMODATION: Crew of two side by side on flight deck, with full dual controls and airline type instrumentation. Third seat to rear of co-pilot. Various cabin configurations available, based on two alternative toilet locations. An aft cabin toilet allows an eight/nine-passenger arrangement, with four chairs in forward cabin, facing each other in pairs, and a three-place sofa and two facing chairs in the rear cabin. A wardrobe, galley and crew toilet are located forward, in the entrance area. Alternatively, a forward toilet, facing the door, makes possible a lounge in the rear cabin, furnished with a four/five-place angle sofa and a chair. This rear lounge is separated from the forward cabin by either a wardrobe and refreshment/recreation console, or by two additional seats, raising the cabin accommodation to twelve persons. After removing forward cabin equipment (wardrobe and galley) and seats, the cabin will accommodate up to three stretchers, two doctors and medical equipment, or freight. The rear baggage compartment is pressurised and air-conditioned, and has a capacity of 1,000 kg (2,200 lb). Access is by a separate door on the port side.

SYSTEMS: Air-conditioning system utilises bleed air from all

Dassault-Breguet Mystère-Falcon 50 of the Yugoslav government *(Press Office Sturzenegger)*

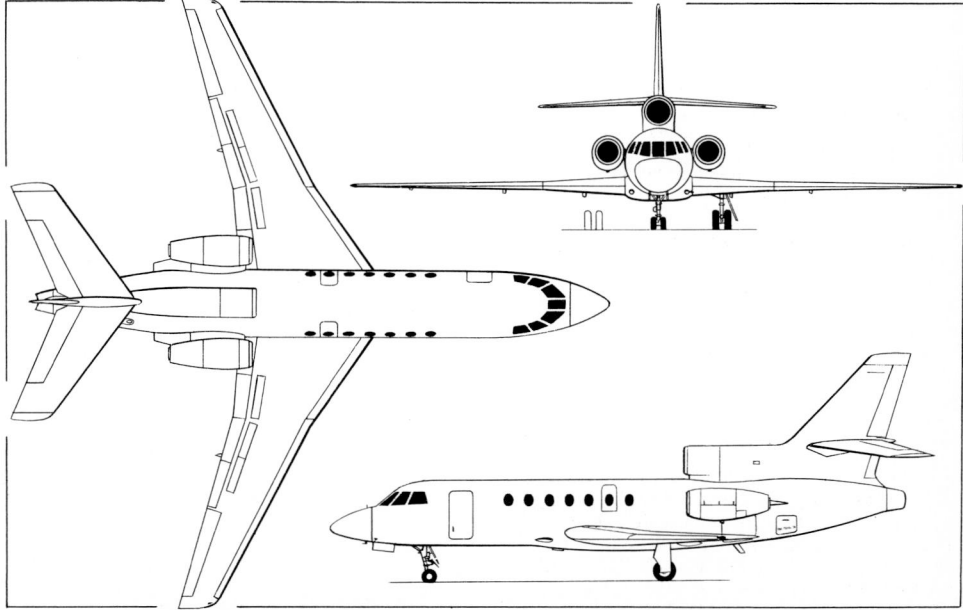

Dassault-Breguet Mystère-Falcon 50 long-range three-turbofan executive transport *(Pilot Press)*

Dassault-Breguet Mystère-Falcon 900 three-turbofan executive transport for up to 19 passengers

three engines. Max pressure differential 0.61 bars (8.8 lb/sq in). Pressurisation maintains a max cabin altitude of 2,440 m (8,000 ft) to a flight altitude of 13,700 m (45,000 ft). Two independent hydraulic systems, pressure 207 bars (3,000 lb/sq in), with three engine driven pumps and one emergency electric pump, actuate primary flying controls, flaps, slats, landing gear, wheel brakes, airbrakes and nosewheel steering. Plain reservoir, pressurised by bleed air at 1.47 bars (21 lb/sq in). 28V DC electrical system, with a 9kW 28V DC starter/generator on each engine and two 23Ah batteries. Automatic emergency oxygen system. Optional 9kW Garrett APU.

AVIONICS: Standard fit provides Collins FCS 80F autopilot in conjunction with dual five-CRT EFIS-85 system, ADC 80 air data computer, dual VHF, VOR, DME, ADF, transponders, radar altimeter and Honeywell Sperry Primus 400 weather radar. Main options provide for advanced symbology EFIS-86C, digital radio controllers used in conjunction with autotune FMS (Global GNS 1000 or UNS 1), Honeywell laser inertial systems, which may also replace gyro reference systems, and Omega. Installation of Collins digital avionics including APS-85 autopilot, EFIS-86, ADS-82, AHS-85 AHRS and Pro Line II com/nav/pulse makes possible certificated Cat II operation.

DIMENSIONS, EXTERNAL:

Wing span	18.86 m (61 ft 10½ in)
Wing chord (mean)	2.84 m (9 ft 3¾ in)
Wing aspect ratio	7.6
Length overall	18.52 m (60 ft 9¼ in)
Length of fuselage	17.66 m (57 ft 11 in)
Height overall	6.97 m (22 ft 10½ in)
Tailplane span	7.74 m (25 ft 4¾ in)
Wheel track	3.98 m (13 ft 0¾ in)
Wheelbase	7.24 m (23 ft 9 in)
Passenger door: Height	1.52 m (4 ft 11¾ in)
Width	0.80 m (2 ft 7½ in)
Height to sill	1.30 m (4 ft 3¼ in)
Emergency exits (each side, over wing):	
Height	0.92 m (3 ft 0¼ in)
Width	0.51 m (1 ft 8 in)

DIMENSIONS, INTERNAL:

Cabin, incl forward baggage space and rear toilet:	
Length	7.16 m (23 ft 6 in)
Max width	1.86 m (6 ft 1¼ in)
Max height	1.79 m (5 ft 10½ in)
Volume	20.15 m³ (711.6 cu ft)
Baggage space	0.75 m³ (26.5 cu ft)
Baggage compartment (rear)	2.55 m³ (90 cu ft)

AREAS:

Wings, gross	46.83 m² (504.1 sq ft)
Horizontal tail surfaces (total)	13.35 m² (143.7 sq ft)
Vertical tail surfaces (total)	9.82 m² (105.7 sq ft)

WEIGHTS:

Weight empty, equipped	9,150 kg (20,170 lb)
Max payload: normal	1,570 kg (3,461 lb)
optional	2,170 kg (4,784 lb)
Max fuel	7,040 kg (15,520 lb)
Max T-O and ramp weight:	
standard	17,600 kg (38,800 lb)
optional	18,500 kg (40,780 lb)
Max zero-fuel weight: standard	11,000 kg (24,250 lb)
optional	11,600 kg (25,570 lb)
Max landing weight	16,200 kg (35,715 lb)

PERFORMANCE:

Max operating Mach No.	0.86
Max operating speed:	
at S/L	350 knots (648 km/h; 402 mph) IAS
at 7,225 m (23,700 ft)	370 knots (685 km/h; 425 mph) IAS
Max cruising speed	Mach 0.82 or 475 knots (880 km/h; 546 mph)
Service ceiling	14,935 m (49,000 ft)
FAR 25 balanced field length with 8 passengers and fuel for 3,500 nm (6,480 km; 4,025 miles)	1,365 m (4,480 ft)
FAR 121 landing distance with 8 passengers and 45 min LR reserves	1,080 m (3,545 ft)
Range at Mach 0.75 with 8 passengers and 45 min LR reserves	3,500 nm (6,480 km; 4,025 miles)

DASSAULT-BREGUET GARDIAN 50

A maritime surveillance and environmental protection version of the Falcon 50 is offered by the manufacturer, equipped with Thomson-CSF Varan sea search radar, Crouzet Omega and a Sagem INS. Crew of three includes a radar operator located in the rear of the cabin, although the aircraft is otherwise able to undertake transport and air ambulance missions. Extras include a navigation table, search windows and a dropping hatch, and additional reconnaissance and electronic surveillance roles may be undertaken by fitment of appropriate external pods.

Data as Mystère-Falcon 50 except:

WEIGHTS:

Weight empty, equipped	11,640 kg (25,662 lb)

PERFORMANCE:

Balanced field length at max T-O weight	1,600 m (5,250 ft)
FAR 25 landing distance with 3 crew	1,050 m (3,445 ft)
Range at sea level with 3 crew and 5% +30 min reserves	3,448 nm (6,390 km; 3,970 miles)
Endurance at 7,620 m (25,000 ft), no reserves	10 h

DASSAULT-BREGUET MYSTÈRE-FALCON 900

On 27 May 1983, at the Paris Air Show, Dassault-Breguet announced a programme to develop an intercontinental three-turbofan executive transport to be known as the Mystère-Falcon 900. The prototype (F-WIDE *Spirit of Lafayette*) made its first flight on 21 September 1984. The second development aircraft (F-WFJC) flew on 30 August 1985. In the following month it made a nonstop flight of 4,305 nm (7,973 km; 4,954 miles) from Paris to Little Rock, Arkansas, USA, for demonstration at the NBAA Convention and at 30 other locations. The return transatlantic flight from Teterboro, New Jersey, to Istres, France, was made at Mach 0.84.

DGAC certification was received on 14 March 1986, and FAA type approval on 21 March. Deliveries began in December 1986. By 1 January 1988, 36 aircraft had been delivered, with 28 in service on all five continents and eight being outfitted by Falcon Jet Corporation at Little Rock, Arkansas, to customers' requirements.

In February 1987, a Mystère-Falcon 900 (c/n 10) set three class C1g records (subject to FAI homologation) by climbing to 9,000 m in 5 min 24.5 s, and to 15,000 m in 21 min 0.5 s, and by maintaining a height of 51,000 ft (15,545 m) in horizontal flight.

As can be seen in the accompanying illustrations, the Mystère-Falcon 900 is similar in configuration to the Mystère-Falcon 50, but with increased overall dimensions, notably a larger fuselage. Design and manufacturing

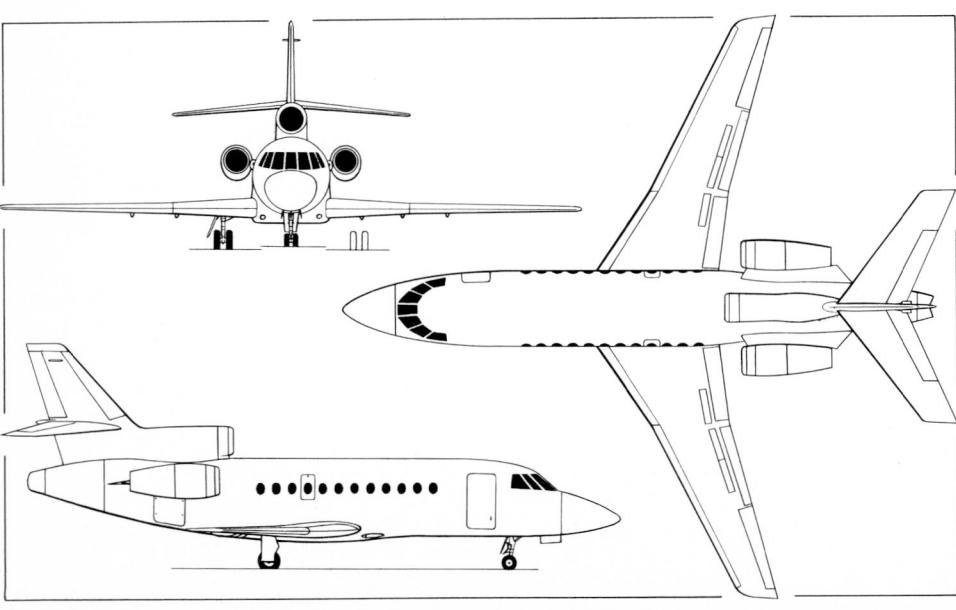

Dassault-Breguet Mystère-Falcon 900 (three Garrett TFE731-5AR-1C turbofans) *(Pilot Press)*

programmes are computer assisted, and extensive use is made of carbonfibre and aramid composite (Kevlar) materials. Certification is to FAR Pt 25 and 55 requirements, including qualification of the entire airframe to 'damage tolerance' standards. A secondary pressure bulkhead, while allowing in-flight access to the large baggage compartment at the rear, isolates the latter in the event of pressure loss. In a belly landing, the bottom fuselage fuel tanks would be protected by ventral skids and energy absorbing honeycomb pads which form an integral part of the fuselage structure.

The first two examples of a long-range maritime surveillance Falcon 900 were ordered by the Japan Maritime Safety Agency in September 1987, for delivery during 1989.

TYPE: Three-turbofan executive transport.
WINGS: Cantilever low-wing monoplane, with profile optimised for Mach 0.84 cruise. Dihedral 0° 30'. Sweepback at quarter-chord 29° inboard, 24° 30' on outer panels. Constructional details as Falcon 50.
FUSELAGE: All-metal semi-monocoque damage tolerant structure, with less riveting than in Falcon 50. Kevlar nosecone over radar. Kevlar fairing on each side of fuselage in area of wingroots.
TAIL UNIT: Cantilever structure, with horizontal surfaces mounted partway up fin at anhedral of 8°. All surfaces sweptback. Tailplane incidence adjustable by screwjack, driven by two electric motors controlled by 'normal' and 'emergency' controls located respectively on the pilots' control wheels and pedestal. All-metal construction, except for rear portion of fin below rudder, and tailcone, which are of Kevlar. Rudder and elevators operated hydraulically.
LANDING GEAR: Retractable tricycle type by Messier-Hispano-Bugatti, with twin wheels on each unit. Hydraulic retraction, main units inward, nosewheels forward. Oleo-pneumatic shock absorbers. Mainwheels fitted with Michelin radial tyres size 29 × 7.7-15, pressure 12.8 bars (183 lb/sq in). Nosewheel tyres size 17.5 × 5.75-8, pressure 9.8 bars (140 lb/sq in). Hydraulic nosewheel steering. MHB triple-disc carbon brakes and anti-skid system. Nosewheel doors of Kevlar; mainwheel doors of carbonfibre.
POWER PLANT: Three Garrett TFE731-5AR-1C turbofans, each rated at 20 kN (4,500 lb st). Thrust reverser on centre engine. Fuel in two integral tanks in wings, centre-section tank, and two tanks under floor of forward and rear fuselage. Total fuel capacity 10,735 litres (2,835 US gallons; 2,361 Imp gallons). Kevlar air intake trunk for centre engine, and rear cowling for side engines. Carbonfibre central cowling around all three engines.
ACCOMMODATION: Provision of a Type III emergency exit on the starboard side of the cabin permits a wide range of layouts for up to 19 passengers. The basic configuration has two crew side by side on the flight deck, with a jumpseat behind the pedestal. The flight deck is separated from the cabin by a door, with a crew wardrobe and baggage locker on either side. At the front of the main cabin, on the starboard side opposite the main cabin door, is a galley. The passenger area is divided into three

lounges. The forward zone has four armchairs in facing pairs, separated by two tables. The centre zone contains a four-place sofa on the port side, facing a longitudinal table. On the starboard side, a bar cabinet contains a foldaway longitudinal bench, allowing five to six persons to be seated around the table for dinner, while leaving the emergency exit clear. In the rear zone, an inward facing settee on the starboard side converts into a bed. On the port side, two armchairs are separated by a table. At the rear of the cabin, a door leads to the toilet compartment, on the starboard side, and a second structural plug door to the large rear baggage area. The baggage door is electrically actuated. Other interior configurations include Dreyfuss 'human engineered' designs in the USA and IDEI 'travel ergonomics' concepts in France. The Dreyfuss interior features patented seating and galley innovations. It includes a crew lavatory forward, a transverse table with four chairs and two stowable lateral seats in a central conference area, a sofa bed on the port side and an executive work station opposite. An alternative eight-passenger configuration has a bedroom at the rear and three personnel seats in the forward zone. A 15-passenger layout divides a VIP area at the rear from six (three-abreast) chairs forward. The 18-passenger scheme has four rows of three-abreast airline type seats forward, and a VIP lounge with two chairs and a settee aft. Many optional items, including stereo, video and hot running water, are available. Windscreens anti-iced electrically.
SYSTEMS: Air-conditioning system uses engine bleed air or air from Garrett GTCP36-150 APU installed in rear fuselage. Softair pressurisation system, with max differential of 0.64 bars (9.3 lb/sq in), maintains sea level cabin environment to a height of 7,620 m (25,000 ft), and a cabin equivalent of 2,440 m (8,000 ft) at 15,550 m (51,000 ft). Cold air supply is by a single oversize air cycle unit. Two independent hydraulic systems, pressure 207 bars (3,000 lb/sq in), with three engine driven pumps and one emergency electric pump, actuate primary flying controls, flaps, slats, landing gear retraction, wheel brakes, airbrakes, nosewheel steering and thrust reverser. Bootstrap hydraulic reservoirs. DC electrical system supplied by three 9kW 28V Auxilec starter/generators and two 23Ah batteries. Eros (SFIM/Intertechnique) oxygen system.
AVIONICS AND EQUIPMENT: Dual bi-directional Honeywell Sperry ASCB digital databus operating in conjunction with dual SPZ 800 flight director/autopilot and EFIS. Dual Honeywell Sperry FMZ 605 flight management system, associated with two AZ 810 air data computers and Honeywell laser gyro inertial platforms. Collins Pro Line II ARINC 429 series com/nav receivers. Honeywell Sperry Primus 800 colour radar.

DIMENSIONS, EXTERNAL:
Wing span	19.33 m (63 ft 5 in)
Wing chord: at root	4.08 m (13 ft 4¾ in)
at tip	1.12 m (3 ft 8 in)
Wing aspect ratio	7.6
Length overall	20.21 m (66 ft 3¾ in)
Fuselage: Max diameter	2.50 m (8 ft 2½ in)

Height overall	7.55 m (24 ft 9¼ in)
Tailplane span	7.74 m (25 ft 4¾ in)
Wheel track	4.45 m (14 ft 7¼ in)
Wheelbase	7.93 m (26 ft 0¼ in)
Passenger door: Height	1.72 m (5 ft 7¾ in)
Width	0.80 m (2 ft 7½ in)
Height to sill	1.79 m (5 ft 10½ in)
Emergency exit (overwing, stbd):	
Height	0.91 m (2 ft 11¾ in)
Width	0.53 m (1 ft 8¾ in)

DIMENSIONS, INTERNAL:
Cabin, excl flight deck, incl toilet and baggage compartments:
Length	11.90 m (39 ft 0½ in)
Max width	2.34 m (7 ft 8 in)
Width at floor	1.86 m (6 ft 1¼ in)
Max height	1.87 m (6 ft 1½ in)
Volume	35.79 m³ (1,264 cu ft)
Rear baggage compartment volume	
	3.60 m³ (127 cu ft)
Flight deck volume	3.75 m³ (132 cu ft)

AREAS:
Wings, gross	49.03 m² (527.75 sq ft)
Horizontal tail surfaces (total)	13.35 m² (143.7 sq ft)
Vertical tail surfaces (total)	9.82 m² (105.7 sq ft)

WEIGHTS:
Weight empty, equipped	10,170 kg (22,421 lb)
Operating weight empty	10,545 kg (23,248 lb)
Max payload	1,885 kg (4,155 lb)
Max fuel	8,690 kg (19,158 lb)
Max T-O weight	20,640 kg (45,500 lb)
Max landing weight	19,050 kg (42,000 lb)
Normal landing weight	12,250 kg (27,000 lb)
Max zero-fuel weight: standard	12,430 kg (27,400 lb)
optional	14,000 kg (30,865 lb)

PERFORMANCE (at AUW of 12,250 kg; 27,000 lb, except where indicated):
Max cruising speed	Mach 0.84
Econ cruising speed	Mach 0.75
Stalling speed: clean	101 knots (188 km/h; 117 mph)
landing configuration	79 knots (147 km/h; 91 mph)
Approach speed, eight passengers and fuel reserves	
	103 knots (191 km/h; 119 mph)
Max cruising height	15,550 m (51,000 ft)
Balanced T-O field length with full tanks, eight passengers and baggage	1,515 m (4,970 ft)
FAR 91 landing field length at AUW of 12,250 kg (27,000 lb)	700 m (2,300 ft)
Range with max payload, NBAA IFR reserves	
	3,460 nm (6,412 km; 3,984 miles)

Range at Mach 0.75 with max fuel and NBAA IFR reserves:
15 passengers	3,760 nm (6,968 km; 4,329 miles)
8 passengers	3,900 nm (7,227 km; 4,491 miles)

HERMES AEROSPACECRAFT

Dassault-Breguet is responsible for all work required to achieve successful re-entry atmospheric flight by the Hermes aerospacecraft, of which brief details can be found under the Aérospatiale entry in this section.

MICROJET

MICROJET SA (Member company of Groupe Creuzet)

Aérodrome de Marmande-Virazeil, 47200 Marmande
Telephone: (1) 47 41 79 21
Telex: 550 777
CHAIRMAN: Robert Creuzet

MICROJET 200 B

The early history of the Microjet programme was recorded in the 1984-85 and previous editions of *Jane's*.

Aim of the programme is to offer economies in military pilot training by use of very small high-performance jet aircraft with comparatively low initial and operating costs.

First flight of a pre-production aircraft (F-WDMT) took place on 19 May 1983. Together with the earlier, wooden, prototype, it then underwent technical evaluation by pilots of the CEV, but was lost while flying over the sea on 13 March 1985. The second pre-production Microjet (F-WDMX), manufactured entirely by Marmande Aéronautique, flew for the first time on 5 January 1985 and has special significance in that it is the first Microjet with

underwing hardpoints for expanded military applications. A third pre-production aircraft (also F-WDMT) flew for the first time on 4 November 1986. The fourth pre-production airframe will be used for static tests at the CEAT, Toulouse.

The following description applies to the planned initial production version of the Microjet 200 B. Take-off rating of each engine will be increased progressively to 1.80 kN (405 lb st), to improve performance and payload, with particular emphasis on the aircraft's potential in an anti-helicopter combat role.

TYPE: Two-seat lightweight training aircraft.
WINGS: Cantilever low-wing monoplane of tapered planform. Wing section RA 16.3c3. Thickness/chord ratio 16%. Dihedral 5° 2' constant from roots. Incidence 3°. Sweepback 0° at 30 per cent chord. Wings, Frise ailerons and electrically operated single-slotted trailing-edge flaps all of glassfibre/epoxy, with carbonfibre wing spars. Small airbrake forward of outer end of flap on upper surface of each wing. Ailerons embody adjustable artificial feel. Ground adjustable tab on starboard aileron.
FUSELAGE: Conventional light alloy semi-monocoque structure. NACA flush engine air intake on each side of fuselage aft of cockpit; exhaust through lateral jetpipes forward of tail unit.
TAIL UNIT: Cantilever V type, comprising interchangeable fixed surfaces and elevators of glassfibre/epoxy, with carbonfibre spars. Sweepback 26° at 50 per cent chord. Included angle 110°. Controllable tab at root end of each elevator. Shallow ventral fin.
LANDING GEAR: Retractable tricycle type, with single wheel on each unit. Electric retraction, nosewheel rearward, main units inward into fuselage. Manual emergency extension. All wheels fully enclosed by doors when retracted. Microjet oleo-pneumatic shock absorber in all three units. Nosewheel offset 149 mm (6 in) to starboard.

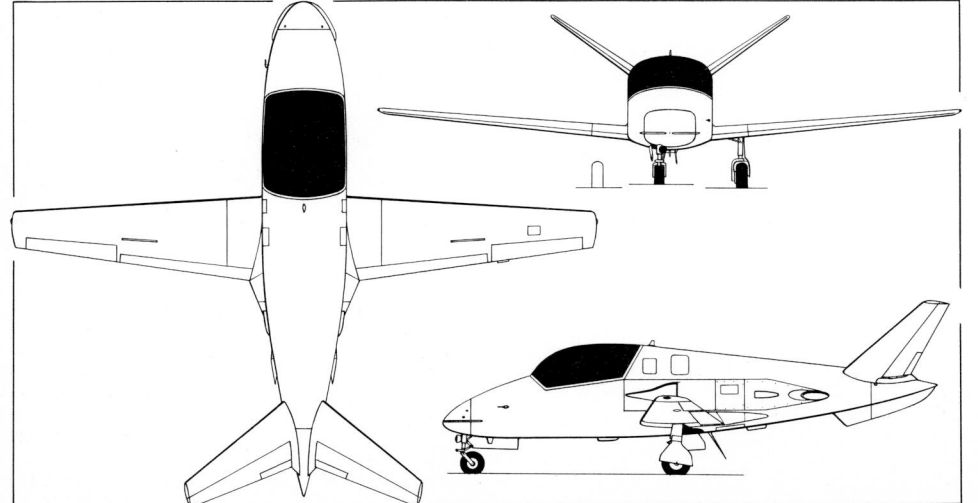

Microjet 200 B in production configuration *(Pilot Press)*

Second pre-production Microjet 200 B lightweight training aircraft *(Air Photo Supply)*

Goodyear wheels, tyres and two-disc hydraulic brakes. Mainwheel tyres size 386 × 172-150, pressure 4.2 bars (61 lb/sq in); nosewheel tyre size 361 × 120-125, pressure 1.8 bars (26 lb/sq in). Parking brake.

POWER PLANT: Two Microturbo TRS 18-1 turbojets, each rated at 1.30 kN (293 lb st) for normal operation, uprated automatically to the T-O rating of 1.45 kN (326 lb st) on surviving engine if the other should fail during take-off. Ratings will be increased to 1.60 kN (360 lb st) and 1.80 kN (405 lb st) respectively in TRS 18-2 form for series production aircraft. Fuel in two structural tanks behind cockpit and one in each wing, with total capacity of 440 litres (116 US gallons; 97 Imp gallons). Two refuelling points, aft of cockpit on each side. Total oil capacity 1.6 litres (0.42 US gallon; 0.35 Imp gallon).

ACCOMMODATION: Pilot and instructor on side by side adjustable seats, under one-piece rearward hinged jettisonable tinted transparent canopy. Starboard (instructor's) seat staggered 55 cm (1 ft 9¾ in) aft of port seat. Adjustable rudder pedals. Cockpit heated and ventilated by ram air and exhaust heat exchanger, but not pressurised.

SYSTEMS: Electrical system comprises two 1.6kW engine driven generators and a 15Ah nickel-cadmium battery which actuate the landing gear and flaps through non-reversible mechanical jacks. Gaseous oxygen supply for two crew for four hours, from one 1,400 litre (50 cu ft) bottle.

AVIONICS AND EQUIPMENT: Blind-flying instrumentation and avionics for IFR flight standard, including ADI, HSI and RMI. Typical installation would include VHF, VOR, ILS, DME, marker beacon receiver, transponder, ADF and intercom. Military version would have UHF, Tacan and IFF.

DIMENSIONS, EXTERNAL:

Wing span	7.56 m (24 ft 9¾ in)
Wing chord at root	0.85 m (2 ft 9½ in)
Wing aspect ratio	9.3
Length overall	6.665 m (21 ft 10½ in)
Length of fuselage	6.56 m (21 ft 6¼ in)
Width of fuselage	1.10 m (3 ft 7¼ in)
Height overall	2.42 m (7 ft 11¼ in)
Tailplane span	3.07 m (10 ft 1 in)
Wheel track	1.92 m (6 ft 3½ in)
Wheelbase	2.64 m (8 ft 8 in)

AREAS:

Wings, gross	6.12 m² (65.87 sq ft)
Ailerons (total)	0.446 m² (4.80 sq ft)
Trailing-edge flaps (total)	0.69 m² (7.43 sq ft)
Tail surfaces (total)	2.50 m² (26.91 sq ft)

WEIGHTS AND LOADINGS:

Weight empty	780 kg (1,719 lb)
Max fuel	340 kg (750 lb)
Max T-O weight: Aerobatic	1,140 kg (2,513 lb)
Utility	1,300 kg (2,866 lb)
Max ramp weight	1,300 kg (2,866 lb)
Max zero-fuel weight	960 kg (2,116 lb)
Max landing weight	1,280 kg (2,822 lb)
Max wing loading	212.4 kg/m² (43.5 lb/sq ft)
Max power loading	448 kg/kN (4.40 lb/lb st)

PERFORMANCE (at max T-O weight with 1.45 kN engines):

Never-exceed speed	300 knots (555 km/h; 345 mph)
Max level speed and max cruising speed at 5,500 m	
¹ (18,045 ft)	250 knots (463 km/h; 287 mph)
Econ cruising speed	210 knots (389 km/h; 241 mph)
Stalling speed, flaps down, engines idling	
	72 knots (134 km/h; 83 mph)
Max rate of climb at S/L	520 m (1,705 ft)/min
Rate of climb at S/L, one engine out	120 m (390 ft)/min
Service ceiling	9,150 m (30,000 ft)
Service ceiling, one engine out	3,050 m (10,000 ft)
T-O run	850 m (2,800 ft)
T-O to 15 m (50 ft)	1,180 m (3,870 ft)
Landing from 15 m (50 ft)	510 m (1,674 ft)
Landing run	390 m (1,280 ft)
Range with max internal fuel, 20 min hold	
	470 nm (870 km; 541 miles)
Max endurance	2 h
g limits:	+7/−3.5 Aerobatic
	+4/−1.8 Utility

MUDRY
AVIONS MUDRY et CIE
Aérodrome de Bernay, BP 47, 27300 Bernay
Telephone: 32 43 47 34
Telex: MUDRY 180 587 F
DIRECTOR: Auguste Mudry
Mudry Aviation Ltd
Dutchess County Airport, Wappingers Falls, NY 12590, USA
PRESIDENT: Daniel Heligoin

M Auguste Mudry established this company in 1958 in the works of the former Société Aéronautique Normande at Bernay, and operated it in parallel with his other aircraft manufacturing company, C.A.A.R.P. of Beynes (see 1977-78 *Jane's*). All activities of C.A.A.R.P. were subsequently combined with those of Avions A. Mudry, at Bernay, where employees totalled 50 at the beginning of 1987.

MUDRY CAP 10 B
Developed from the Piel Emeraude two-seat light aircraft (see Sport Aircraft section), via the prototype C.P. 100 aerobatic version built by C.A.A.R.P., the CAP 10 is designed for use as a training, touring or aerobatic aeroplane. The prototype was flown for the first time in August 1968, and certification of the CAP 10 was granted on 4 September 1970. Later production aircraft, with ventral fin and enlarged rudder, are designated **CAP 10 B**. Construction is to French AIR 2052 (CAR 3) Category A standards for aerobatic flying. FAA certification for day and night VFR operation was received in 1974.

A total of 225 CAP 10/10 Bs had been delivered to customers in 24 countries by January 1988, including 56 for the French Air Force and six for the French Navy. The Air Force aircraft are operated currently by EFIPN 307 (École de Formation Initiale du Personnel Navigant) at Avord and the École de l'Air at Salon de Provence. The Navy CAP 10s serve with 51 Escadrille de Servitude at Rochefort/Soubise. Overseas operators include the Mexican Air Force's flying training school, whose 20 aircraft are equipped almost to IFR standard, and the Royal Moroccan Air Force, which has two for its Green March aerobatic team. Ten CAP 10s were scheduled to be built in 1988.

To extend the potential market for the CAP 10, Mudry has produced the prototype of a version equipped for glider towing, under the designation **CAP 10 R** (for remorqueur).

TYPE: Two-seat aerobatic light aircraft.

WINGS: Cantilever low-wing monoplane. Wing section NACA 23012. Dihedral 5° from roots. Incidence 0°. No sweepback. All-spruce single-spar torsion box structure, with trellis ribs, rear auxiliary spar and okoumé plywood

CAP 10 B two-seat aerobatic light aircraft in Moroccan markings *(J. M. G. Gradidge)*

covering, with outer skin of polyester fabric. Inner section of each wing is rectangular in plan, outer section semi-elliptical. Wooden trailing-edge plain flaps and slotted ailerons.

FUSELAGE: Conventional spruce girder structure, built in two halves and joined by three main frames. Of basically rectangular section with rounded top decking. Polyester fabric covering. Forward section also has an inner plywood skin for added strength. Engine cowling panels of non-inflammable laminated plastics.

TAIL UNIT: Conventional cantilever structure. All-wood single-spar fin, integral with fuselage, and tailplane. All surfaces covered with both plywood and polyester fabric. Tailplane incidence adjustable on ground. Trim tab in each elevator. Automatic rudder trim. Small ventral fin.

LANDING GEAR: Non-retractable tailwheel type. Mainwheel legs of light alloy, with ERAM type 9 270 C oleo-pneumatic shock absorbers. Single wheel on each main unit, tyre size 380 × 150. Solid tailwheel tyre, size 6 × 200. Tailwheel is steerable by rudder linkage but can be disengaged for ground manoeuvring. Hydraulically actuated mainwheel disc brakes (controllable from port seat) and parking brake. Streamline fairings on mainwheels and legs.

POWER PLANT: One 134 kW (180 hp) Textron Lycoming AEIO-360-B2F flat-four engine, driving a Hoffmann two-blade fixed-pitch wooden propeller. Standard fuel tank of engine fireproof bulkhead, capacity 72 litres (19 US gallons; 16 Imp gallons). Optional auxiliary tank, capacity 75 litres (20 US gallons; 16.5 Imp gallons),

beneath baggage compartment. Fuel and oil systems modified to permit periods of inverted flying.

ACCOMMODATION: Side by side adjustable seats for two persons, with provision for back parachutes, under rearward sliding and jettisonable moulded transparent canopy. Special aerobatic shoulder harness standard. Space for 20 kg (44 lb) of baggage aft of seats in training and touring models.

SYSTEMS: Electrical system includes Delco-Rémy 40A engine driven alternator and SAFT 12V DC nickel-cadmium battery.

AVIONICS AND EQUIPMENT: CSF 262 12-channel VHF radio and g meter fitted. Optional equipment includes starboard brake pedals; Narco, Jolliet or Badin VHF; Narco VOR; radio compass; IFR instrumentation; navigation and landing lights; and heated pitot.

DIMENSIONS, EXTERNAL:

Wing span	8.06 m (26 ft 5¼ in)
Wing aspect ratio	6.0
Length overall	7.16 m (23 ft 6 in)
Height overall	2.55 m (8 ft 4½ in)
Tailplane span	2.90 m (9 ft 6 in)
Wheel track	2.06 m (6 ft 9 in)

DIMENSION, INTERNAL:

Cockpit: Max width	1.054 m (3 ft 5½ in)

AREAS:

Wings, gross	10.85 m² (116.79 sq ft)
Ailerons (total)	0.79 m² (8.50 sq ft)
Vertical tail surfaces (total)	1.32 m² (14.25 sq ft)
Horizontal tail surfaces (total)	1.86 m² (20.0 sq ft)

WEIGHTS (A: Aerobatic, U: Utility):

Weight empty, equipped: A, U		540 kg (1,190 lb)
Fuel load: A		54 kg (119 lb)
U		108 kg (238 lb)
Max T-O weight: A		760 kg (1,675 lb)
U		830 kg (1,829 lb)

PERFORMANCE (at max T-O weight):

Never-exceed speed	183 knots (340 km/h; 211 mph)
Max level speed at S/L	146 knots (270 km/h; 168 mph)
Max cruising speed (75% power)	
	135 knots (250 km/h; 155 mph)
Stalling speed:	
flaps up	54 knots (100 km/h; 62 mph) IAS
flaps down	46 knots (85 km/h; 53 mph) IAS
Max rate of climb at S/L	over 360 m (1,180 ft)/min
Service ceiling	5,000 m (16,400 ft)
T-O run	350 m (1,149 ft)
T-O to 15 m (50 ft)	450 m (1,477 ft)
Landing from 15 m (50 ft)	600 m (1,968 ft)
Landing run	360 m (1,182 ft)
Range with max fuel	647 nm (1,200 km; 745 miles)
g limits	+6/-4.5

MUDRY CAP 21

The CAP 21 is a single-seat aerobatic competition aircraft which retains the fuselage and tail unit of the earlier CAP 20LS-200, but has cantilever main landing gear legs and an entirely new wing, with a computer developed section, different planform and built by a new production method. This wing has improved the rate of roll to 180°/s at 135 knots (250 km/h; 155 mph) by comparison with the CAP 20L's 130°/s, and facilitates the execution of snap manoeuvres.

The prototype (F-WZCH) was displayed at the 1979 Paris Air Show. It flew for the first time on 23 June 1980, and work was started on a first batch of ten production CAP 21s, for customers in Belgium, Brazil, France and Italy. Deliveries began in May 1982, and Mudry began manufacture of a second series in 1983. By January 1988, a total of 39 CAP 20/21s had been delivered to 30 customers and a further five were under construction for 1988 delivery.

An earlier aircraft, registered in Italy (I-SIVM), has been retrofitted, easily and successfully, with a 194 kW (260 hp) engine by its Italian owner, Sig Sergio Dallan. Known as the CAP 21-260, the Italian aircraft embodies several other modifications, including a main wing spar which permits load factors of ±10g; larger wingroot fairings on both the leading- and trailing-edges; longer exhaust pipes which reduce noise; repositioned main landing gear legs with root fairings to reduce airflow disturbance at the wingroot leading-edge; a larger rudder; improved aileron control linkage; substitution of a one-piece canopy; movement of the pilot's seat further aft, and use of an inclined backrest to offset the effect on CG of a heavier power plant;

replacement of the standard 40 litre (10.5 US gallon; 8.8 Imp gallon) fuel tank with a 60 litre (15.8 US gallon; 13.2 Imp gallon) tank; and installation of a ferry tank under the pilot's seat.

The following details apply to the standard CAP 21 production aircraft:

TYPE: Single-seat aerobatic light aircraft.

WINGS: Cantilever low-wing monoplane. Wing section V16F. Thickness/chord ratio 16%. Dihedral 1° 30'. No twist. All-wood single-spar structure, with flaps. Automatic tab in each aileron to reduce stick forces.

FUSELAGE: Conventional all-wood structure, of basically triangular section with rounded top decking. Wood covering, except for laminated plastics engine cowling.

TAIL UNIT: Cantilever all-wood structure. Trim tab in each elevator.

LANDING GEAR: Non-retractable tailwheel type. Cantilever glassfibre main legs, with streamline fairings over wheels. Disc brakes.

POWER PLANT: One 149 kW (200 hp) Textron Lycoming AEIO-360-A1B flat-four engine, driving a two-blade Hartzell variable-pitch propeller. Fixed-pitch propeller optional. Normal fuel tank capacity 40 litres (10.5 US gallons; 8.8 Imp gallons). Max fuel capacity 75 litres (20 US gallons; 16.5 Imp gallons), with 15 litre (4 US gallon; 3.3 Imp gallon) gravity tank for inverted flying.

ACCOMMODATION: Single glassfibre seat under rearward sliding transparent canopy. Special aerobatic shoulder harness.

Prototype Mudry CAP 230 single-seat aerobatic aircraft *(M. J. Hooks)*

DIMENSIONS, EXTERNAL:

Wing span	8.08 m (26 ft 6 in)
Wing aspect ratio	7.0
Length overall	6.46 m (21 ft 2½ in)
Height overall	1.52 m (5 ft 0 in)

AREA:

Wings, gross	9.2 m² (99.0 sq ft)

WEIGHTS AND LOADINGS:

Weight empty	500 kg (1,103 lb)
Max T-O weight (Aerobatic)	620 kg (1,367 lb)
Max wing loading (Aerobatic)	
	67.4 kg/m² (13.8 lb/sq ft)
Max power loading (Aerobatic)	
	4.16 kg/kW (6.84 lb/hp)

PERFORMANCE:

Never-exceed speed	205 knots (380 km/h; 236 mph)
Max cruising speed (75% power)	
	143 knots (265 km/h; 165 mph)
Stalling speed	46 knots (85 km/h; 53 mph)
Max rate of climb at S/L	840 m (2,755 ft)/min
Endurance with max fuel	2 h
g limits	+6/-5

MUDRY CAP 230

The CAP 230 is a version of the CAP 21 powered by a 224 kW (300 hp) Textron Lycoming AEIO-540-L1 flat-six engine of the kind fitted to the Aérospatiale Epsilon. Its development was announced in January 1985, simultaneously with news of an initial order for four CAP 230s to equip the Royal Moroccan Air Force's aerobatic team. Four were ordered for the French Air Force's Équipe de Voltige Aérienne (EVA) at Salon de Provence, to replace the team's current CAP 20s. The first of these (actually prototype F-WZCH) was delivered on 13 June 1986 and in January 1988 remained the only aircraft supplied to a customer, despite a total of nine orders for three operators.

The following details apply to the prototype, which flew for the first time on 8 October 1985:

DIMENSIONS, EXTERNAL:

Wing span	8.08 m (26 ft 6 in)
Length overall	6.75 m (22 ft 1¾ in)
Height overall	1.80 m (5 ft 11 in)

WEIGHTS:

Weight empty	600 kg (1,323 lb)
Max T-O weight	720 kg (1,587 lb)

PERFORMANCE:

Never-exceed speed	215 knots (400 km/h; 248 mph)
Max cruising speed	172 knots (320 km/h; 198 mph)
Range with max fuel	405 nm (750 km; 466 miles)
g limits	±10

MUDRY CAP X

The CAP X is a side-by-side two-seat trainer, last described in the 1987-88 *Jane's*. A prototype and a pre-series aircraft were flown in 1982 and 1985 respectively, but production has been postponed indefinitely.

Mudry CAP 21 (Textron Lycoming AEIO-360-A1B engine) *(Air Photo Supply)*

REIMS AVIATION
REIMS AVIATION SA

Aérodrome de Reims-Prunay, BP 2745, 51062 Reims Cédex

Telephone: 26 06 96 55

Telex: REMAVIA 830754

PRESIDENT DIRECTOR-GENERAL AND PRODUCTION DIRECTOR: Jean Pichon

PUBLIC RELATIONS OFFICER: Paul Pierini

Reims Aviation is the successor to the former Société Nouvelle des Avions Max Holste, which had been founded in 1956. It has the right to manufacture under licence Cessna designs for sale in Europe, Africa and Asia; but the suspension of Cessna production of piston engined aircraft applies also to Reims Aviation. By 1 January 1988 Reims had assembled a total of 6,286 aircraft of all types, including 2,518 Reims-Cessna F150/152s and 2,496 F172s.

As an extension of its collaboration with Cessna, Reims Aviation developed and is manufacturing a twin-turboprop light transport aircraft known as the Reims-Cessna F 406.

Reims Aviation is a subcontractor to Dassault-Breguet in the Mystère-Falcon 100, 200, 50 and 900 programmes; and a subcontractor to Aérospatiale in the Transall and ATR 42 programmes and for miscellaneous parts. It had 510 employees in 1988. Its offices and factory at Reims-Prunay Airport have an area of 26,600 m² (286,325 sq ft).

REIMS-CESSNA F 406 CARAVAN II

It was announced in mid-1982 that, with financial support from the French government, Reims Aviation and Cessna were collaborating in the development of an unpressurised twin-turboprop transport known as the F 406 Caravan II. Intended for business and utility use, it is a variant of Cessna's 400 series of light twins. A prototype (F-WZLT), constructed by Reims Aviation, was exhibited

at the Paris Air Show prior to its first flight on 22 September 1983. Certification was achieved on 21 December 1984, and the F 406 is now being manufactured and marketed exclusively by Reims, using wings supplied by Cessna. Twenty-five production aircraft had been completed by the beginning of 1988, with deliveries stabilised at one aircraft each month.

The first production F 406 (F-GDRK) flew for the first time on 20 April 1985 and was to be used as Cessna's US demonstrator following FAA certification. Next to fly, on 3 May, was c/n 4 (F-ZBEO), one of two F 406s for the French Customs Service, equipped with full King Gold Crown IFR avionics, a Crouzet Nadir navigation computer and a Bendix 1500 radar with 360° scan in an underbelly radome. Two are operated by No. 3 GHL of the French Army at Rennes as target tugs, with underbelly tow equipment.

In 1987, flight testing began of a coastal surveillance and pollution detection version of the F 406. Primary sensors housed in a long underfuselage fairing are a Terma side-looking airborne radar (SLAR) and an SAT infra-red linescan. These are claimed to detect ships over a range of 40 nm (74 km; 46 miles) and oil spills up to about half that distance.

TYPE: Twin-turboprop light business and utility transport.

WINGS: Cantilever low-wing monoplane. Wing section NACA 23018 at root, NACA 23012 at tip. Dihedral 3° 30′ on wing centre-section, 4° 55′ on outer panels. Incidence 2° at root, −1° at construction tip. All-metal three-spar centre-section structure to meet SFAR 41C fail-safe requirements: two-spar structure for outer wing panels. Hydraulically operated Fowler trailing-edge flaps of light alloy construction. Plain ailerons of light alloy construction. Trim tab in port aileron. Goodrich pneumatic de-icing system optional.

FUSELAGE: All-metal semi-monocoque structure of light alloy.

TAIL UNIT: Cantilever all-metal two-spar structure, with horizontal surfaces mounted on sweptback fin. Fin offset 1° to port to counter torque of non-handed engines. Tailplane dihedral 9°. Goodrich pneumatic de-icing of leading-edges optional.

LANDING GEAR: Hydraulically retractable tricycle type with single wheel on each unit. Main units retract inward into wing, nosewheel rearward. Emergency extension by means of a 138 bar (2,000 lb/sq in) rechargeable nitrogen bottle. Cessna oleo-pneumatic shock absorbers. Main units of articulated (trailing link) type. Single-disc hydraulic brakes. Parking brake.

POWER PLANT: Two Pratt & Whitney Canada PT6A-112 turboprops (each 373 kW; 500 shp), driving McCauley 3GFR34C701/93KB-0 three-blade reversible-pitch and automatically feathering metal propellers. Fuel capacity 1,823 litres (481 US gallons; 401 Imp gallons).

ACCOMMODATION: Crew of two and up to 12 passengers, in pairs, facing forward, with centre aisle, except at rear of cabin in 12/14-seat versions. Alternative basic configurations for six VIP passengers in reclining seats in executive version, and for operation in mixed passenger/freight role. Executive version has a partition between cabin and flight deck, and toilet on starboard side at rear. Split main door immediately aft of wing, on port side, with built-in airstair in downward hinged lower portion. Optional cargo door forward of this door to provide single large opening. Overwing emergency exit on each side. Passenger seats removable for cargo carrying, or for conversion to ambulance, air photography, maritime surveillance and other specialised roles. Baggage compartments in nose, with three doors, at rear of cabin and in rear of each engine nacelle. Electric windscreen de-icing optional.

SYSTEMS: Freon air-conditioning system of 17,500 BTU capacity, plus engine bleed air and electric boost heating. Pressurisation system with max differential of 0.35 bars (5.0 lb/sq in). Electrical system includes a 28V 250A starter/generator on each engine and a 39Ah nickel-cadmium battery. Hydraulic system, pressure 120 bars (1,750 lb/sq in), for operation of landing gear. Separate hydraulic system for brakes.

AVIONICS AND EQUIPMENT: To customer's individual requirements. Provision for equipment to FAR Pt 135A standards, including full controls and instrumentation for co-pilot, IFR com/nav, Bendix RDS 82 weather radar and additional emergency exit.

DIMENSIONS, EXTERNAL:
Wing span	15.08 m (49 ft 5¾ in)
Wing aspect ratio	9.7
Length overall	11.89 m (39 ft 0 in)
Height overall	4.01 m (13 ft 2 in)
Tailplane span	5.87 m (19 ft 3 in)
Wheel track	4.28 m (14 ft 0½ in)
Wheelbase	3.81 m (12 ft 5⅞ in)
Propeller diameter	2.36 m (7 ft 9 in)
Cabin door: Height	1.27 m (4 ft 2 in)
Width	0.58 m (1 ft 10¾ in)
Cargo double door (optional):	
Total width	1.24 m (4 ft 1 in)

DIMENSIONS, INTERNAL:
Cabin (incl flight deck): Length	5.71 m (18 ft 8¾ in)
Max width	1.42 m (4 ft 8 in)
Max height	1.31 m (4 ft 3¼ in)
Min height (at rear)	1.21 m (3 ft 11½ in)
Width of aisle	0.29 m (11½ in)
Volume	8.64 m³ (305 cu ft)
Baggage compartment volume	2.22 m³ (78.5 cu ft)

AREA:
Wings, gross	23.50 m² (253 sq ft)

WEIGHTS:
Weight empty, equipped	2,283 kg (5,033 lb)
Max payload	1,563 kg (3,446 lb)
Max fuel	1,444 kg (3,183 lb)
Max ramp weight	4,280 kg (9,435 lb)
Max T-O and landing weight	4,246 kg (9,360 lb)
Max zero-fuel weight	3,856 kg (8,500 lb)

PERFORMANCE:
Max operating Mach No.	0.52
Max operating speed	
	229 knots (424 km/h; 263 mph) IAS

Reims-Cessna F 406 surveillance aircraft of the Douanes Françaises

Reims-Cessna F 406 target tug of the French Army

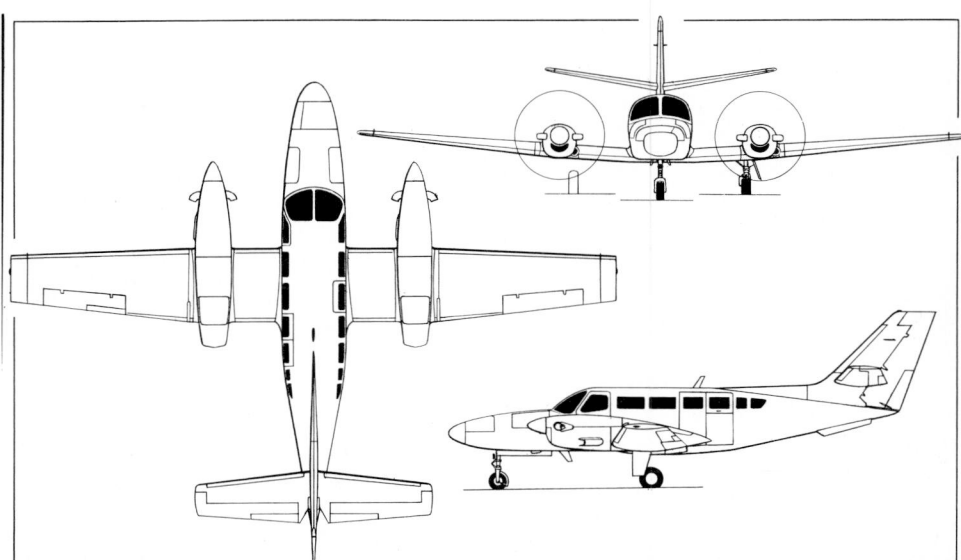

Reims-Cessna F 406 Caravan II light business and utility transport *(Pilot Press)*

Max cruising speed	246 knots (455 km/h; 283 mph)		Service ceiling	9,145 m (30,000 ft)
Econ cruising speed	200 knots (370 km/h; 230 mph)		Service ceiling, one engine out	4,935 m (16,200 ft)
Max rate of climb at S/L	564 m (1,850 ft)/min		T-O run	526 m (1,725 ft)
Rate of climb at S/L, one engine out	121 m (397 ft)/min		T-O to 15 m (50 ft)	803 m (2,635 ft)
Stalling speed:			Landing from 15 m (50 ft), without reverse pitch	
'clean'	94 knots (174 km/h; 108 mph) IAS			674 m (2,212 ft)
wheels and flaps down			Range with max fuel, at max cruising speed, 45 min	
	81 knots (150 km/h; 93 mph) IAS		reserves	1,153 nm (2,135 km; 1,327 miles)

ROBIN

AVIONS PIERRE ROBIN

BP 87, Aérodrome de Dijon Val-Suzon, Darois, 21121 Fontaine-les-Dijon Cédex
Telephone: 80 35 61 01
Telex: 350 818 Robin F

PRESIDENT DIRECTOR GENERAL: Pierre Robin
SALES MANAGER: Michel Pelletier
TECHNICAL DIRECTOR: Daniel Muller
PUBLIC RELATIONS: Jacques Bigenwald

This company was formed in October 1957 as Centre Est Aéronautique to design, manufacture and sell touring aircraft. In 1969 the name of the company was changed to Avions Pierre Robin. It was acquired by Aéronautique Service in mid-1988.

Since 1973, Avions Pierre Robin has manufactured the DR 400 series of wooden light aircraft, which represent highly refined developments of the company's earlier Jodel designs. A new variant, the Cadet, was introduced in 1987. Production of 'DR' aircraft of all designations and models totalled 2,207 by January 1988.

A total of 80 aircraft was delivered during 1987, made up of 51 DR 400s, seven R 3000s and 22 ATLs. They included 13 DR 400/180RP glider tugs ordered for delivery to Germany, Switzerland and Austria.

The company's works cover an area of about 11,500 m² (123,785 sq ft) and it employed 130 people in January 1988.

ROBIN DR 400/100 CADET

Deliveries began in 1987 (two aircraft) of a two-seat DR 400 based on the srs 120 Dauphin, but with rear seating removed and max weight reduced by 100 kg (220 lb). The 1988 refinements to the Dauphin (revised instrument panel and toe-operated brakes) are included in the current Cadet.

Data as DR 400/120, except:

TYPE: Two-seat training and touring aircraft.

WEIGHTS AND LOADINGS:

Useful load (incl baggage)	270 kg (595 lb)
Max T-O and landing weight	800 kg (1,764 lb)
Max wing loading	58.8 kg/m² (12.04 lb/sq ft)
Max power loading	9.58 kg/kW (15.75 lb/hp)

PERFORMANCE (at max T-O weight):

Max level speed at S/L	129 knots (239 km/h; 149 mph)
Max rate of climb at S/L	249 m (817 ft)/min
Service ceiling	5,030 m (16,500 ft)
T-O run	190 m (623 ft)
T-O to and landing from 15 m (50 ft)	425 m (1,395 ft)
Landing run	180 m (591 ft)
Range with standard fuel at 1,830 m (6,000 ft) and 116 knots (215 km/h; 133 mph) max cruising speed, no reserves	510 nm (945 km; 587 miles)

ROBIN DR 400/120 DAUPHIN

The prototype of this DR 400 series lightplane flew for the first time on 15 May 1972 and received DGAC certification during that month, followed by CAA certification in December 1972. The original version had a 93 kW (125 hp) engine and was manufactured as the DR 400/125 Petit Prince. It was superseded in 1975 by the DR 400/120 Petit Prince, with 88 kW (118 hp) engine, as described in the 1979-80 *Jane's*. The current version has a fine-pitch propeller, and entered production in 1979 as the Dauphin. Fourteen were built in 1987; the 1988 model introduced a redesigned instrument panel, toe brakes, an enlarged baggage compartment and additional windows.

TYPE: Three/four-seat light training and touring aircraft.

WINGS: Cantilever low-wing monoplane. Wing section NACA 23013.5 (modified). Centre-section has constant chord and no dihedral; outer wings have a dihedral of 14°. All-wood one-piece structure, with single box spar. Leading-edge plywood covered; Dacron covering overall. Wooden ailerons, covered with Dacron. Aluminium alloy flaps. Ailerons and flaps interchangeable port and starboard. Manually operated airbrake under spar outboard of landing gear on each side. Picketing ring under each wingtip.

FUSELAGE: Wooden semi-monocoque structure of basic rectangular section, plywood covered.

TAIL UNIT: Cantilever all-wood structure, covered with Dacron. Sweptback fin and rudder. All-moving one-piece horizontal surface, with tab.

LANDING GEAR: Non-retractable tricycle type, with oleo-pneumatic shock absorbers and hydraulically actuated disc brakes. All three wheels and tyres are size 380 × 150, pressure 1.57 bars (22.8 lb/sq in) on nose unit, 1.77 bars (25.6 lb/sq in) on main units. Nosewheel steerable via rudder bar. Fairings over all three legs and wheels. Tailskid with damper. Toe brakes and parking brake.

POWER PLANT: One 83.5 kW (112 hp) Textron Lycoming O-235-L2A flat-four engine, driving a Sensenich 72 CKS 6-0-56 two-blade fixed-pitch metal propeller, or Hoffmann two-blade fixed-pitch wooden propeller. Fuel tank in fuselage, usable capacity 100 litres (26.5 US gallons; 22 Imp gallons); optional 50 litre (13.2 US gallon; 11 Imp gallon) auxiliary tank. Oil capacity 5.7 litres (1.5 US gallons; 1.25 Imp gallons).

ACCOMMODATION: Enclosed cabin, with seats for three or four persons, in pairs, up to a max weight of 154 kg (340 lb) on front pair and 136 kg (300 lb), including baggage, at rear. Access via forward sliding jettisonable transparent canopy. Dual controls standard. Cabin heated and ventilated. Baggage compartment with internal access.

SYSTEMS AND EQUIPMENT: Standard equipment includes a 12V 50A alternator, 12V 32Ah battery, push-button starter, audible stall warning, and windscreen de-icing. Radio, blind-flying equipment, and navigation, landing and anti-collision lights, to customer's requirements.

DIMENSIONS, EXTERNAL:

Wing span	8.72 m (28 ft 7¼ in)
Wing chord:	
centre-section (constant)	1.71 m (5 ft 7½ in)
at tip	0.90 m (3 ft 0 in)
Wing aspect ratio	5.6
Length overall	6.96 m (22 ft 10 in)
Height overall	2.23 m (7 ft 3¾ in)
Tailplane span	3.20 m (10 ft 6 in)
Wheel track	2.60 m (8 ft 6¼ in)
Wheelbase	5.20 m (17 ft 0¾ in)
Propeller diameter	1.78 m (5 ft 10 in)

DIMENSIONS, INTERNAL:

Cabin: Length	1.62 m (5 ft 3¾ in)
Max width	1.10 m (3 ft 7¼ in)
Max height	1.23 m (4 ft 0½ in)
Baggage volume	0.39 m³ (13.75 cu ft)

AREAS:

Wings, gross	13.60 m² (146.39 sq ft)
Ailerons, total	1.15 m² (12.38 sq ft)
Flaps, total	0.70 m² (7.53 sq ft)
Fin	0.61 m² (6.57 sq ft)
Rudder	0.63 m² (6.78 sq ft)
Horizontal tail surfaces, total	2.88 m² (31.00 sq ft)

WEIGHTS AND LOADINGS:

Weight empty, equipped	530 kg (1,169 lb)
Max baggage	40 kg (88 lb)
Max T-O and landing weight	900 kg (1,984 lb)
Max wing loading	66.2 kg/m² (13.56 lb/sq ft)
Max power loading	10.78 kg/kW (17.71 lb/hp)

PERFORMANCE (at max T-O weight):

Never-exceed speed	166 knots (308 km/h; 191 mph)
Max level speed at S/L	130 knots (241 km/h; 150 mph)
Max cruising speed at 2,250 m (7,400 ft)	116 knots (215 km/h; 133 mph)
Econ cruising speed at 3,000 m (9,840 ft)	105 knots (195 km/h; 121 mph)
Stalling speed: flaps up	51 knots (94 km/h; 59 mph)
flaps down	45 knots (82 km/h; 51 mph)
Max rate of climb at S/L	183 m (600 ft)/min
Service ceiling	3,650 m (12,000 ft)
T-O run	235 m (771 ft)
T-O to 15 m (50 ft)	535 m (1,755 ft)
Landing from 15 m (50 ft)	460 m (1,510 ft)
Range with standard fuel at max cruising speed, no reserves	464 nm (860 km; 534 miles)

ROBIN DR 400/160 MAJOR

The first DR 400/160 flew on 29 June 1972. It was awarded DGAC certification on 6 September 1972, and CAA certification in December of the same year, and was manufactured as the Chevalier (see 1979-80 *Jane's*). The current version, with wingroot fuel tanks, a baggage hold door, a propeller of finer pitch and a new instrument panel based on experience with the Aiglon, has been in production since 1980 as the Major. A total of 105 had been built by January 1988, including three delivered during 1987.

TYPE: Four-seat light aircraft.

WINGS, FUSELAGE, TAIL UNIT, LANDING GEAR: Generally as for DR 400/120, but with external baggage door aft of cabin, in top of fuselage on port side.

POWER PLANT: One 119 kW (160 hp) Textron Lycoming O-320-D flat-four engine, driving a Sensenich two-blade metal fixed-pitch propeller. Fuel tank in fuselage, capacity 110 litres (29 US gallons; 24 Imp gallons), and two tanks in wingroot leading-edges, giving total capacity of 190 litres (50 US gallons; 41.75 Imp gallons), of which 182 litres (48 US gallons; 40 Imp gallons) are usable. Provision for auxiliary tank, raising total capacity to 240 litres (63.5 US gallons; 52.75 Imp gallons). Oil capacity 7.5 litres (2 US gallons; 1.6 Imp gallons).

ACCOMMODATION: Seating for four persons, on two side by side adjustable front seats (max load 154 kg; 340 lb total) and rear bench seat (max load 154 kg; 340 lb total). Forward sliding transparent canopy gives access to all seats. Up to 40 kg (88 lb) of baggage can be stowed aft of rear seats when four occupants are carried.

SYSTEMS AND EQUIPMENT: As for DR 400/120.

DIMENSIONS AND AREAS: As for DR 400/120, except:

Propeller diameter	1.83 m (6 ft 0 in)
Baggage door: Height	0.47 m (1 ft 6½ in)
Width	0.55 m (1 ft 9½ in)
Wing area	14.20 m² (152.8 sq ft)

WEIGHTS AND LOADINGS:

Weight empty, equipped	570 kg (1,257 lb)
Max T-O and landing weight	1,050 kg (2,315 lb)
Max wing loading	74.2 kg/m² (15.20 lb/sq ft)
Max power loading	8.82 kg/kW (14.47 lb/hp)

PERFORMANCE (at max T-O weight):

Never-exceed speed	166 knots (308 km/h; 191 mph)
Max level speed at S/L	146 knots (271 km/h; 168 mph)
Max cruising speed (75% power) at 2,440 m (8,000 ft)	132 knots (245 km/h; 152 mph)
Econ cruising speed (65% power) at 3,200 m (10,500 ft)	130 knots (241 km/h; 150 mph)
Stalling speed: flaps up	56 knots (103 km/h; 64 mph)
flaps down	50 knots (93 km/h; 58 mph)
Max rate of climb at S/L	255 m (836 ft)/min
Service ceiling	4,115 m (13,500 ft)
T-O run	300 m (985 ft)
T-O to 15 m (50 ft)	500 m (1,640 ft)
Landing from 15 m (50 ft)	545 m (1,788 ft)
Landing run	250 m (820 ft)
Range with standard fuel at econ cruising speed, 45 min reserves	693 nm (1,285 km; 798 miles)

ROBIN DR 400/180 RÉGENT

First flown on 27 March 1972, this most powerful, four/five-seat member of the wooden DR 400 series received DGAC certification on 10 May 1972, and CAA certification in December 1972. A total of 185 had been built by January 1988, including 11 delivered in 1987.

The DR 400/180 is generally similar to the DR 400/160 Major, except in the following details:

POWER PLANT: One 134 kW (180 hp) Textron Lycoming O-360-A flat-four engine. Fuel tankage as for DR 400/160.

ACCOMMODATION, SYSTEMS AND EQUIPMENT: Basically as for DR 400/160, but optional seating for three persons on rear bench seat. Baggage capacity 55 kg (121 lb).

DIMENSIONS AND AREAS: As for DR 400/160, except:

Propeller diameter	1.93 m (6 ft 4 in)

WEIGHTS AND LOADINGS:

Weight empty, equipped	600 kg (1,322 lb)
Max T-O and landing weight	1,100 kg (2,425 lb)
Max wing loading	77.7 kg/m² (15.91 lb/sq ft)
Max power loading	8.21 kg/kW (13.47 lb/hp)

PERFORMANCE (at max T-O weight):

Never-exceed speed	166 knots (308 km/h; 191 mph)
Max level speed at S/L	150 knots (278 km/h; 173 mph)
Max cruising speed (75% power) at 2,440 m (8,000 ft)	144 knots (267 km/h; 166 mph)
Econ cruising speed (60% power) at 3,660 m (12,000 ft)	134 knots (249 km/h; 155 mph)
Stalling speed: flaps up	57 knots (105 km/h; 65 mph)
flaps down	52 knots (95 km/h; 59 mph)
Max rate of climb at S/L	252 m (825 ft)/min
Service ceiling	4,720 m (15,475 ft)
T-O run	315 m (1,035 ft)
T-O to 15 m (50 ft)	610 m (2,000 ft)
Landing from 15 m (50 ft)	530 m (1,740 ft)
Landing run	249 m (817 ft)
Range with standard fuel at 65% power, no reserves	783 nm (1,450 km; 900 miles)

ROBIN DR 400/180R REMORQUEUR

The **DR 400/180R** is a member of the DR 400 range designed for use as a glider towing aircraft, although it can also be flown as a normal four-seat tourer. The prototype first flew on 6 November 1972 and received DGAC certification on the 28th of that month.

A new version, designated **DR 400/180RP** (prototype F-WEIQ, DR 400 c/n 999), has a Porsche PFM 3200 aircooled flat-six engine, with fan forced cooling and

Robin DR 400/120 Dauphin three/four-seat light aircraft *(Kenneth Munson)*

developing 158 kW (212 hp) at 5,300rpm. This aircraft had flown only four hours before being exhibited at the 1985 Paris Air Show, but had already demonstrated a rate of climb of 420 m (1,378 ft)/min at max T-O weight, and a cruising speed of 146 knots (270 km/h; 168 mph) at 75% power. It offers a range of 607 nm (1,125 km; 700 miles) at that speed, with a fuel consumption of 35 litres (9.25 US gallons; 7.7 Imp gallons)/h. At present the 'RP' is available only for export, and deliveries began to Austria, Germany and Switzerland during 1987. The DR 400/180RP was the first production aircraft with a Porsche engine to receive German certification. Remorqueur production totalled 234 by January 1988, including eight 180Rs and thirteen 180RPs delivered in 1987.

Specification details of the standard DR 400/180R are generally the same as for the DR 400/180 Régent, except for the following items:

FUSELAGE: No external baggage door. The baggage compartment is covered with transparent Plexiglas as an extension of the canopy, allowing optimum rearward view.

POWER PLANT: One 134 kW (180 hp) Textron Lycoming O-360-A flat-four engine, driving (for glider towing) a Sensenich 76 EM 8S5 058 or Hoffmann HO-27-HM-180/138 two-blade propeller. For touring, a Sensenich 76 EM 8S5 064 propeller of the same diameter is fitted. Fuel capacity as for DR 400/120.

DIMENSIONS AND AREAS: As for DR 400/120, except:
Propeller diameter	1.83 m (6 ft 0 in)

WEIGHTS AND LOADINGS:
Weight empty, equipped	560 kg (1,234 lb)
Max T-O and landing weight	1,000 kg (2,205 lb)
Max wing loading	73.5 kg/m² (15.05 lb/sq ft)
Max power loading	7.46 kg/kW (12.25 lb/hp)

PERFORMANCE (glider tug, at max T-O weight):
Never-exceed speed	166 knots (308 km/h; 191 mph)
Max level speed at S/L (70% power)	124 knots (230 km/h; 143 mph)
Max cruising speed at 2,440 m (8,000 ft)	124 knots (230 km/h; 143 mph)
Econ cruising speed (56% power) at 3,660 m (12,000 ft)	122 knots (226 km/h; 140 mph)
Stalling speed: flaps up	54 knots (99 km/h; 62 mph)
flaps down	47 knots (87 km/h; 54 mph)
Max rate of climb at S/L towing Bijave sailplane	210 m (690 ft)/min
Service ceiling	6,000 m (19,685 ft)
T-O run	205 m (673 ft)
T-O to 15 m (50 ft)	400 m (1,313 ft)
Landing from 15 m (50 ft)	470 m (1,542 ft)
Landing run	220 m (722 ft)
Range at econ cruising speed, max fuel, no reserves	444 nm (825 km; 512 miles)

Robin DR 400/180RP Remorqueur glider towing aircraft (Porsche PFM 3200 engine)

ROBIN R 3000 SERIES

Development of this series of all-metal light aircraft began in 1978, to replace types then in production. Two prototypes were built, with the designation R 3140. The first of these to fly, on 8 December 1980, had conventional unswept constant chord wings. The second, flown on 2 June 1981, introduced the tapered outer panels (later with upturned tips) that are now standard.

Marketing of R 3000s was assigned to the Socata division of Aérospatiale from 1 September 1983 until 1 February 1988, when Robin resumed responsibility. Deliveries totalled 32 by 1 January 1988, including five srs 120s and two srs 140s in 1987. No srs 120s were expected to be built in 1988, and thus of the ten projected versions listed in the 1983-84 *Jane's* only the R 3000/140 (formerly R 3140E) is currently in production. It was certificated by the DGAC on 13 October 1983.

Robin is investigating the practicability of replacing the present engines of the R 3000 series with engines based on the more modern and fuel-efficient 89-119 kW (120-160 hp) PRV six-cylinder engines built in France for Peugeot, Renault and Volvo motorcars. First aircraft to be fitted with a PRV engine was an R 3140, which flew for the first time in this form on 2 August 1983. The basic motorcar engine was adapted for aircraft use by the École Nationale des Ingénieurs de St-Etienne (ENISE) in collaboration with Robin. Initial test results were promising and a company

named Société France Aéromoteur has been established to produce an aviation certificated PRV engine.

The following details apply to the R 3000/140:

TYPE: Four-seat all-metal light aircraft.

WINGS: Cantilever low-wing monoplane, with upturned tips. Wing section NACA 43013.5 on constant chord inner wings, NACA 43010.5 at tip of each tapered outer panel. Dihedral 6° from roots. Incidence 3°. No sweep at quarter-chord. Conventional single-spar aluminium alloy structure. Entire trailing-edge of each constant chord panel comprises an electrically controlled slotted flap. Ailerons and flaps of aluminium alloy construction.

FUSELAGE: Conventional aluminium alloy semi-monocoque structure, except for quickly removable glassfibre engine cowling.

TAIL UNIT: Cantilever T tail of aluminium alloy construction, with dorsal fin. Elevator trim with anti-tabs.

LANDING GEAR: Non-retractable tricycle type. Nosewheel, steerable via rudder pedals, is self-centring and locks automatically after take-off. Robin long-stroke low pressure oleo-pneumatic shock absorbers. Mainwheel tyres size 380 × 150-6. Nosewheel tyre size 5.00-5. Cleveland disc brakes. Streamline polyester fairings on all three legs and wheels. Hydraulic disc brakes. Parking brake.

POWER PLANT: One 119.3 kW (160 hp) Textron Lycoming O-320-D2A flat-four engine, driving a Sensenich 74DMS5-2-64 two-blade fixed-pitch metal propeller. Two integral fuel tanks in wing leading-edges, with total capacity of 160 litres (42.25 US gallons; 35.2 Imp gallons) standard, or 200 litres (52.8 US gallons; 44 Imp gallons) optional. Oil capacity 7.5 litres (2 US gallons; 1.6 Imp gallons).

ACCOMMODATION: Four seats in pairs in enclosed cabin, with dual controls and brakes. Adjustable front seats, with inertia reel safety belts. Removable rear seats, with belts. Carpeted floor. Forward sliding jettisonable and tinted transparent canopy, with safety lock, accessible from both sides. Automatically retracting step on each side. Baggage capacity 40 kg (88 lb). Cabin heated and ventilated. Windscreen demister.

SYSTEM: Electrical system includes 12V 60A alternator and 12V 32Ah battery.

AVIONICS AND EQUIPMENT: Standard equipment includes hour meter, audible stall warning system and towbar. Three standards of optional avionics and equipment available. Series I includes horizon and directional gyros with vacuum pump, type 9100 electric turn co-ordinator, rate of climb indicator, C 2400 magnetic compass (exchange for standard C 2300), position lights and two beacons, anti-collision light and instrument panel lighting. Series II adds to Series I either Becker AR 2009/25 720-channel VHF, with NR 2029 VOR/LOC receiver and indicator; or King KX 155/08 nav/com with audio and KI 203 VOR indicator. Series III adds to Series II either a Becker ATC 2000 transponder and type 2079 ADF; or King KT 76 A transponder and KR 87 digital ADF.

DIMENSIONS, EXTERNAL:
Wing span	9.81 m (32 ft 2¼ in)
Wing chord: at root	1.72 m (5 ft 7¾ in)
at tip	0.655 m (2 ft 1¾ in)
Wing aspect ratio	6.6
Length overall	7.51 m (24 ft 7¾ in)
Height overall	2.66 m (8 ft 8¾ in)
Tailplane span	3.20 m (10 ft 6 in)
Wheel track	2.64 m (8 ft 8 in)
Wheelbase	1.74 m (5 ft 8½ in)
Propeller diameter	1.83 m (6 ft 0 in)
Propeller ground clearance	0.30 m (11¾ in)

DIMENSIONS, INTERNAL:
Cabin: Length	2.70 m (8 ft 10¼ in)
Max width	1.14 m (3 ft 8¾ in)
Max height	1.20 m (3 ft 11¼ in)

Photograph and three-view drawing (*Pilot Press*) **of Robin R 3000/140 four-seat light aircraft (Textron Lycoming O-320-D2A engine)**

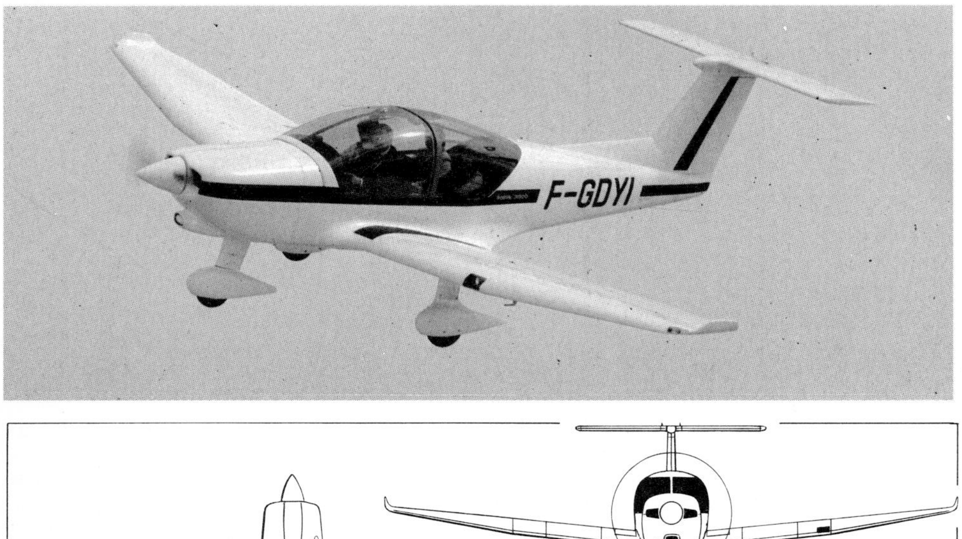

Robin ATL Club very light two-seat personal and club aircraft

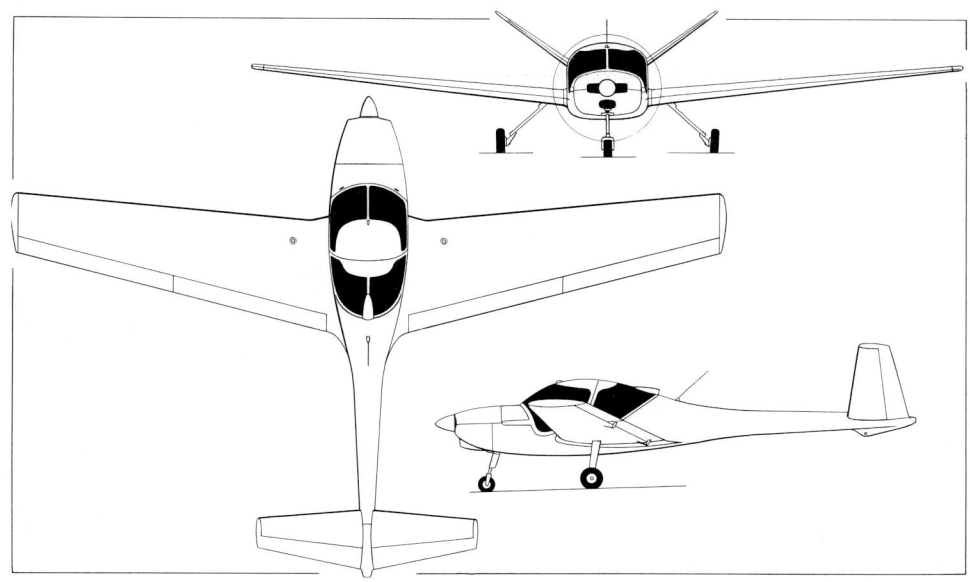

Robin ATL Club (JPX 4T 60A converted Volkswagen engine) *(Pilot Press)*

Floor area	2.60 m² (28.0 sq ft)
Volume (incl baggage space)	2.4 m³ (84.75 cu ft)
Baggage space	0.43 m³ (15.2 cu ft)

AREAS:

Wings, gross	14.47 m² (155.75 sq ft)
Ailerons (total)	1.32 m² (14.21 sq ft)
Trailing-edge flaps (total)	2.02 m² (21.74 sq ft)
Vertical tail surfaces (total)	1.30 m² (14.00 sq ft)
Horizontal tail surfaces (total)	2.44 m² (26.26 sq ft)

WEIGHTS AND LOADINGS:

Weight empty	600 kg (1,323 lb)
Max T-O and landing weight	1,050 kg (2,315 lb)
Max wing loading	72.6 kg/m² (14.86 lb/sq ft)
Max power loading	10.10 kg/kW (16.54 lb/hp)

PERFORMANCE (at max T-O weight):

Max level speed at S/L	135 knots (250 km/h; 155 mph)
Max cruising speed (75% power) at optimum height	130 knots (240 km/h; 149 mph)
Econ cruising speed (65% power)	119 knots (220 km/h; 136 mph)
Stalling speed, flaps down	47 knots (87 km/h; 54 mph)
Max rate of climb at S/L	258 m (846 ft)/min
Service ceiling	4,265 m (14,000 ft)
T-O run	280 m (920 ft)
T-O to 15 m (50 ft)	525 m (1,725 ft)
Landing from 15 m (50 ft)	490 m (1,610 ft)
Landing run	190 m (625 ft)

Range with max standard fuel, no reserves:

75% power	605 nm (1,120 km; 696 miles)
65% power	640 nm (1,185 km; 736 miles)

Range with max optional fuel, no reserves:

75% power	756 nm (1,400 km; 870 miles)
65% power	799 nm (1,480 km; 919 miles)

ROBIN ATL

In the first half of 1981, Avions Pierre Robin began design of the ATL (avion très léger) to meet the requirement of French flying clubs for a very lightweight two-seat monoplane that would, in the tradition of the veteran Jodel D.112, be economical to buy and to operate. The prototype (F-WFNA) flew initially, on 17 June 1983, with a 35 kW (47 hp) JPX PAL 1300 three-cylinder aircooled radial two-stroke engine. To speed certification, it was re-engined subsequently with a 41.5 kW (56 hp) JPX converted 1,835 cc Volkswagen motorcar engine, and a 2,050 cc version of this engine is the current standard power plant of production ATLs. The increased power plant weight necessitated sweeping the wings forward to maintain an acceptable CG.

A first order, for 30, was placed by the French National Aeronautical Federation (FNA) on 28 November 1983.

A second ATL flew for the first time on 7 December 1984. Deliveries began on 27 April 1985, when the Coulommiers Aero Club received a production ATL (F-WFNC). Twenty-five more were delivered (one to Australia) with an F-W registration and DGAC 'laissez-passer' before certification was received on 15 January 1986. All of these aircraft were called back to Dijon for modification to full certification standards and re-registration in F-G sequence.

By 20 March 1988, a total of 120 ATLs had been delivered and had logged more than 70,000 flying hours. The initial production model, to which the detailed description applies, is known as **ATL Club** in France and **Bijou** in the UK. The current **ATL Club Model 88** has a new propeller of smaller diameter, to increase ground clearance, improvements to the cabin, equipment and systems, and increased fuel capacity, giving a max range of 594 nm (1,100 km; 683 miles). Four Model 88s had been

delivered by January 1988, and this version is to be followed by the **ATL Voyage**, with 56 kW (75 hp) JPX 4T 75B and more extensive equipment for longer cross-country flights and night VFR flying; an **ATL 2+2** with a 74.5 kW (100 hp) JPX engine; and two four-seat versions with 2.5 litre and 3 litre turbocharged PRV engines. A version with a 59.6 kW (80 hp) Limbach four-cylinder engine has been developed especially for the German market.

The following data apply to the initial version of the ATL Club, except where indicated:

TYPE: Two-seat very light personal and club aircraft.

WINGS: Cantilever mid-wing monoplane. Wing section NACA 43015 modified. Dihedral 6° from roots. Incidence 3° at root, −1° at tip. Sweepforward at front spar 7° 30′. Conventional wood single-spar structure in two halves, with plywood covered leading-edge torsion box, light auxiliary rear spar, girder ribs and Dacron covering. Frise ailerons, actuated by cables, and electrically actuated flaps of light alloy along entire trailing-edges. No tabs.

FUSELAGE: Pod and boom configuration, made of glassfibre/Nomex honeycomb/epoxy sandwich.

TAIL UNIT: Cantilever V structure, with fixed surfaces of Dacron covered wood, and rod actuated light alloy control surfaces. Spring trim in elevator control.

LANDING GEAR: Non-retractable tricycle type. Cantilever main legs. Nosewheel has rubber shock absorption and is steerable via rudder pedals. Mainwheel tyres size 300-130, pressure 2.2 bars (32 lb/sq in); nosewheel tyre size 270-100, pressure 1.6 bars (23 lb/sq in). Hydraulic disc brakes on mainwheels. Parking brake. Wheel fairings optional.

POWER PLANT: One JPX 4T 60A (converted 2,050 cc Volkswagen) aircooled flat-four engine, rated at 48 kW (65 hp) and driving an EVRA two-blade wooden propeller. Fuel tank in each wingroot; total usable capacity 42 litres (11 US gallons; 9.25 Imp gallons).

ACCOMMODATION: Two glassfibre seats side by side under large canopy which hinges upward and forward. Dual controls, with adjustable rudder pedals, cabin heating and ventilation standard. All-transparent canopy optional.

SYSTEM: Electrical system includes 12V alternator and 12V 15Ah battery. Anti-collision, navigation, cabin and instrument lights optional.

AVIONICS AND EQUIPMENT: Optional avionics include 720 channel VHF transceiver, VOR, ADF and transponder. Standard equipment includes basic instruments, safety belts and tiedown rings. Optional items include horizon and directional gyros, rate of climb indicator, turn co-ordinator, outside air temperature gauge, hourmeter, exhaust gas temperature gauge, four-strap safety harness, tinted canopy, leather furnishing, faired main landing gear legs and canopy cover.

DIMENSIONS, EXTERNAL:

Wing span	10.25 m (33 ft 7½ in)
Wing mean aerodynamic chord	1.25 m (4 ft 1¼ in)
Wing aspect ratio	8.65
Length overall	6.72 m (22 ft 0½ in)
Height overall	2.00 m (6 ft 6¾ in)
Tailplane span	3.82 m (12 ft 6½ in)
Wheel track	3.00 m (9 ft 10 in)

AREA:

Wings, gross	12.15 m² (130.8 sq ft)

WEIGHTS AND LOADINGS (JPX 4T 60A engine):

Weight empty	360 kg (794 lb)
Max T-O weight	580 kg (1,278 lb)
Max wing loading	47.7 kg/m² (9.77 lb/sq ft)
Max power loading	12.1 kg/kW (19.7 lb/hp)

PERFORMANCE (A: ATL Club with JPX 4T 60A engine, B: estimated data for ATL Voyage, at max T-O weight):

Max level speed at S/L:	
A	100 knots (185 km/h; 115 mph)
B	111 knots (206 km/h; 128 mph)
Max cruising speed (75% power) at 2,440 m (8,000 ft):	
A	94 knots (175 km/h; 108 mph)
B	106 knots (196 km/h; 122 mph)
Econ cruising speed (50% power) at 2,440 m (8,000 ft):	
A	76 knots (142 km/h; 88 mph)
B	88 knots (163 km/h; 101 mph)
Stalling speed, flaps down:	
A	41 knots (75 km/h; 47 mph)
B	42 knots (77 km/h; 48 mph)
Max rate of climb at S/L: A	168 m (550 ft)/min
B	198 m (650 ft)/min
Service ceiling: A	3,960 m (13,000 ft)
B	4,420 m (14,500 ft)
T-O to 15 m (50 ft): A	420 m (1,378 ft)
B	400 m (1,313 ft)
Landing from 15 m (50 ft): A	380 m (1,247 ft)
B	390 m (1,280 ft)
Range with max fuel, at max cruising speed, no reserves:	
A	351 nm (650 km; 404 miles)
B	561 nm (1,040 km; 646 miles)
Range with max fuel at econ cruising speed, no reserves:	
A	426 nm (790 km; 490 miles)
B	702 nm (1,300 km; 807 miles)

SELLET-PELLETIER
SELLET-PELLETIER HÉLICOPTÈRE
c/o Lange SA, 35 rue de Naples, 75008 Paris
Telephone: 45 22 66 68
Telex: 640 627

M Christian Sellet and M Jacques Pelletier, engineers, are responsible for a small helicopter known as the Grillon 120, of which the single-seat prototype was exhibited in public for the first time at the 1985 Paris Air Show. This aircraft was designed and built by M Sellet. His partner is handling the administrative, commercial and public relations aspects of the project.

SELLET-PELLETIER GRILLON 120
The general appearance of the Grillon 120 (Cricket) is shown in an accompanying illustration. It was designed primarily to provide a means of training helicopter pilots at much reduced cost by comparison with other aircraft. Thus, although the prototype has been completed in single-seat form, production Grillons could have one or two seats, with single or dual controls.

Design of the Grillon began in August 1984; construction of the prototype started three months later. It was almost complete when exhibited at the Paris Air Show, and flew for the first time during 1986. Certification is expected by 1989.

TYPE: Prototype light helicopter.

ROTOR SYSTEM: Three-blade fully articulated main rotor and two-blade tail rotor. Boeing Helicopters blade section. Each main rotor blade has carbonfibre reinforced plastics skin (three laminations at 45°), polyurethane foam filler and steel weight adjustment bar in leading-edge. Carbonfibre tail rotor blades. Main rotor/engine rpm ratio 1:8.4. Tail rotor/engine rpm ratio 1:2.1.

FUSELAGE: Extensively glazed cabin pod, with aluminium alloy structure and minimal aluminium alloy skin. Tail rotor carried on aluminium alloy tube supported by mast structure at rear of cabin.

LANDING GEAR: Prototype was exhibited at 1985 Paris Air Show with a single Goodyear 10-A go-kart wheel on each unit of a non-retractable tricycle gear. The wheels, without brakes, were carried on aluminium alloy tube supports. Production aircraft are expected to have skid

landing gear, as installed on prototype for initial flight testing.

POWER PLANT: One 89.5 kW (120 hp) Mazda twin-rotor engine, mounted above cabin, forward of main rotor mast. Fuel tank under seat; capacity 50 litres (13.2 US gallons; 11 Imp gallons) on prototype, 100 litres (26.4 US gallons; 22 Imp gallons) planned for production aircraft. Oil capacity 6 litres (1.6 US gallons; 1.3 Imp gallons) for engine; 2 litres (0.53 US gallon; 0.44 Imp gallon) for main gearbox.

ACCOMMODATION: Prototype has single semi-reclining seat and conventional helicopter controls, comprising collective and cyclic sticks and rudder pedals. Provision for two seats, side by side, and dual controls in certificated version. Large fully transparent door panel on each side. Heater standard.

DIMENSIONS, EXTERNAL:

Main rotor diameter	5.00 m (16 ft 4¾ in)
Tail rotor diameter	1.03 m (3 ft 4½ in)
Distance between rotor centres	3.10 m (10 ft 2 in)
Main rotor blade chord	0.18 m (7 in)
Length overall, rotors turning	5.10 m (16 ft 9 in)
Length of fuselage, excl rotors	4.60 m (15 ft 1¼ in)
Width, excl rotors	1.40 m (4 ft 7¼ in)
Height to top of rotor head	2.30 m (7 ft 6½ in)
Height overall	2.35 m (7 ft 8½ in)

AREAS:

Main rotor blade (each)	0.32 m² (3.44 sq ft)
Tail rotor blade (each)	0.034 m² (0.366 sq ft)
Main rotor disc	19.63 m² (211.35 sq ft)
Tail rotor disc	0.83 m² (8.97 sq ft)

WEIGHTS:

Weight empty	270 kg (595 lb)
Max T-O weight	500 kg (1,102 lb)

PERFORMANCE (estimated):

Max level speed at S/L	108 knots (200 km/h; 124 mph)
Max cruising speed at S/L	89 knots (165 km/h; 102 mph)
Econ cruising speed at S/L	62 knots (115 km/h; 71 mph)
Max rate of climb at S/L	360 m (1,180 ft)/min
Service ceiling	3,500 m (11,500 ft)
Range: with max fuel	243 nm (450 km; 280 miles)
with max payload	191 nm (355 km; 220 miles)

Prototype of the Sellet-Pelletier Grillon 120 light helicopter

SOCATA
SOCIÉTÉ DE CONSTRUCTION D'AVIONS DE TOURISME ET D'AFFAIRES
(Subsidiary of Aérospatiale)
12 rue Pasteur, 92150 Surèsnes
Telephone: (1) 45 06 37 60
Telex: SOCATAS 614 549 F
WORKS AND AFTER-SALES SERVICE: Aérodrome de Tarbes-Ossun-Lourdes, BP 38, 65001 Tarbes Cédex
Telephone: 62 51 73 00
Telex: SOCATA 520 828 F
PRESIDENT AND DIRECTOR GENERAL: Pierre Gautier
TECHNICAL DIRECTOR: Denis Legrand
COMMERCIAL DIRECTOR: A. Aubry
MANAGER, PROMOTION AND COMMUNICATION:
   Gérard Maoui

This company, formed in 1966, is a subsidiary of Aérospatiale, responsible for producing all of the group's piston engined light aircraft. As well as those described in this entry, Socata manufactures the Aérospatiale Epsilon military primary/basic trainer, described under the Aérospatiale heading in this section.

Sales of the 'TB' series of light aircraft totalled 820 by January 1988, of which 784 had been delivered, and production was continuing at seven per month.

Socata also produces components for the A300 Airbus, ATR 42, Mystère-Falcon 100, 200 and 50 business aircraft, and Super Puma, Dauphin and Ecureuil helicopters. It is responsible for overhaul and repair of MS 760 Paris light jet aircraft.

Socata's works cover an area of 56,000 m² (602,775 sq ft), and employed a total of 950 people in 1987.

SOCATA R 235 GUERRIER
This armed version of the Rallye touring aircraft is no longer in production, the last of 14 having been delivered in November 1984. It remains available to special order, as described in the 1987-88 *Jane's.*

SOCATA TB 9 TAMPICO AND TB 10 TOBAGO
The prototype for this new series of all-metal light aircraft was the original TB 10 (F-WZJP), of which design was initiated by Socata's Research and Development Department in February 1975. Construction began in February 1976, and it made a 25 min first flight at Tarbes on 23 February 1977, powered by a 119 kW (160 hp) Textron Lycoming O-320-D2A engine. The second prototype of the TB 10 was fitted with a 134 kW (180 hp) Lycoming engine.

Current production versions are as follows:

TB 9 Tampico FP. Four-seater, with 119 kW (160 hp) Textron Lycoming O-320-D2A engine, Sensenich fixed-pitch propeller, fuel capacity of 158 litres (41.75 US gallons; 34.75 Imp gallons), and non-retractable landing

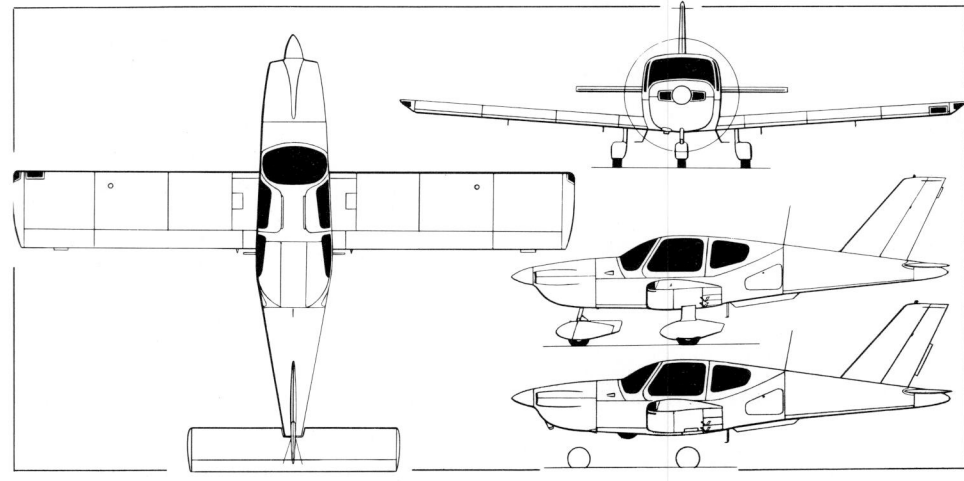

Socata Tobago, with additional side view (bottom) of Trinidad *(Pilot Press)*

gear. Options include 210 litre (55.5 US gallon; 46 Imp gallon) fuel tanks (replacing standard tanks). First flown on 9 March 1979 and received DGAC certification on 27 September 1979. Deliveries by April 1987 totalled 120.

TB 9 Tampico CS. As Tampico FP, but with Hartzell constant-speed propeller. Sales included in total under Tampico FP listing.

TB 10 Tobago. Four/five-seater, with 134 kW (180 hp) engine and non-retractable landing gear. DGAC certification received on 26 April 1979, followed by FAA approval on 27 November 1985. Sales by 1 January 1988 totalled 390, of which 364 had been delivered, some to customers in the USA. Eight are used by SFACT to provide flying training for French air traffic control officers.

The aerobatic TB 11 Tobago, listed in the 1983-84 *Jane's*, is not currently available. The more powerful **TB 20/21 Trinidad**, with retractable landing gear, is described separately.

The following description applies specifically to the TB 10 Tobago, but the Tampico is generally similar in basic construction.

TYPE: Four/five-seat all-metal light aircraft.

WINGS: Cantilever low-wing monoplane. Wing section RA 16.3C3. Thickness/chord ratio 16%. Dihedral 4° 30′ from roots. No incidence at root. No sweep. Conventional light alloy single-spar structure of constant chord, with glassfibre tips. Balanced ailerons and electrically actuated slotted flaps, of light alloy. Ground adjustable tabs.

FUSELAGE: Light alloy semi-monocoque structure. Shallow strake under each side of fuselage immediately aft of wing root fillet. Glassfibre engine cowlings.

TAIL UNIT: Cantilever all-metal type, with sweptback vertical surfaces and constant chord all-moving horizontal surfaces mounted at extreme tail, aft of rudder. Ground adjustable tab at top of rudder. Anti-tab in horizontal surfaces.

LANDING GEAR: Non-retractable tricycle type, with steerable nosewheel. Oleo-pneumatic shock absorber in all three units. Mainwheel tyres size 6.00-6, 6-ply rating, pressure 2.3 bars (33 lb/sq in). Glassfibre wheel fairings on all three units. Hydraulic disc brakes. Parking brake.

POWER PLANT: One 134 kW (180 hp) Textron Lycoming O-360-A1AD flat-four engine, driving a Hartzell two-blade constant-speed propeller with spinner. Two integral fuel tanks in wing leading-edges; total capacity 210 litres (55.5 US gallons; 46 Imp gallons), of which 204 litres (54 US gallons; 45 Imp gallons) are usable. Oil capacity 7.5 litres (2 US gallons; 1.6 Imp gallons).

ACCOMMODATION: Four/five seats in enclosed cabin, with dual controls. Adjustable front seats with inertia reel seat belts. Removable rear bench seat with safety belts. Sharply inclined low-drag windscreen. Access via upward hinged window/doors of glassfibre. Baggage compartment aft of cabin, with external door on port side. Cabin carpeted, soundproofed, heated and ventilated. Windscreen defrosting standard.

SYSTEMS: Electrical system includes 12V 60A alternator and 12V 32A battery, landing and navigation lights, four individual cabin lights and instrument panel lighting. Hydraulic system for wheel brakes only.

AVIONICS AND EQUIPMENT: Avionics to customer's specification. Current aircraft are equipped without extra charge with a basic nav pack that includes a rate of climb indicator, electric turn and bank indicator, horizontal and directional gyro, true airspeed indicator, EGT and outside air temperature indicator. Standard equipment includes armrests for all seats, map pockets, anti-glare visors, stall warning indicator, tiedown fittings and towbar.

DIMENSIONS, EXTERNAL (Tampico and Tobago):

Wing span	9.76 m (32 ft 0¼ in)
Wing chord (constant)	1.22 m (4 ft 0 in)
Wing aspect ratio	8.0
Length overall	7.63 m (25 ft 0½ in)
Height overall	3.20 m (10 ft 6 in)
Tailplane span	3.20 m (10 ft 6 in)
Wheelbase	1.96 m (6 ft 5 in)
Propeller diameter	1.88 m (6 ft 2 in)
Propeller ground clearance	0.10 m (4 in)
Cabin doors (each): Width	0.90 m (2 ft 11½ in)
Height	0.76 m (2 ft 6 in)
Baggage door: Width	0.64 m (2 ft 1¼ in)
Height	0.44 m (1 ft 5¼ in)

DIMENSIONS, INTERNAL (Tampico and Tobago):

Cabin: Length, firewall to rear bulkhead	2.53 m (8 ft 3½ in)
Length, panel to rear bulkhead	2.00 m (6 ft 6¾ in)
Max width, at rear seats	1.28 m (4 ft 2¼ in)
Max width, at front seats	1.15 m (3 ft 9¼ in)
Max height, floor to roof	1.12 m (3 ft 8 in)

AREAS:

Wings, gross	11.90 m² (128.1 sq ft)
Ailerons (total)	0.91 m² (9.80 sq ft)
Trailing-edge flaps (total)	3.72 m² (40.04 sq ft)
Fin	0.88 m² (9.47 sq ft)
Rudder	0.63 m² (6.78 sq ft)
Horizontal tail surfaces (total)	2.56 m² (27.56 sq ft)

WEIGHTS (A: Tampico FP, B: Tampico CS, C: Tobago):

Weight empty, with unusable fuel and oil:	
A	675 kg (1,488 lb)
B	685 kg (1,510 lb)
C	700 kg (1,543 lb)
Baggage: C	45 kg (100 lb)
Max T-O weight: A, B	1,060 kg (2,340 lb)
C	1,150 kg (2,535 lb)

PERFORMANCE (at max T-O weight, A, B and C as above):

Max level speed: A	122 knots (226 km/h; 140 mph)	
B	126 knots (234 km/h; 145 mph)	
C	133 knots (247 km/h; 153 mph)	
Max cruising speed (75% power):		
A, B	121 knots (225 km/h; 140 mph)	
C	127 knots (235 km/h; 146 mph)	
Econ cruising speed (65% power):		
A, B	108 knots (201 km/h; 125 mph)	
C	117 knots (217 km/h; 135 mph)	
Stalling speed, flaps up:		
A, B	58 knots (107 km/h; 67 mph)	
C	61 knots (112 km/h; 70 mph)	
Stalling speed, flaps down:		
A, B	48 knots (89 km/h; 56 mph)	
C	52 knots (97 km/h; 60 mph)	
Max rate of climb at S/L: A	201 m (660 ft)/min	
B	231 m (760 ft)/min	
C	240 m (790 ft)/min	
Service ceiling: A	3,810 m (12,500 ft)	
B	4,205 m (13,800 ft)	
C	3,960 m (13,000 ft)	
T-O run: A	355 m (1,165 ft)	
B	286 m (938 ft)	
C	325 m (1,066 ft)	
T-O to 15 m (50 ft): A	565 m (1,853 ft)	
B	426 m (1,398 ft)	
C	505 m (1,657 ft)	
Landing from 15 m (50 ft): A, B	405 m (1,329 ft)	
C	425 m (1,395 ft)	
Landing run: A, B, C	190 m (623 ft)	

Range with max standard fuel, allowances for T-O, climb, econ power cruise and descent, 45 min reserves:

A, B	496 nm (920 km; 571 miles)
C	653 nm (1,210 km; 752 miles)

Range with max optional fuel, conditions as above:

A, B	696 nm (1,290 km; 801 miles)

SOCATA TB 20/21 TRINIDAD

The Trinidad is a four/five-seat touring and IFR training aircraft, basically similar to the TB 10 Tobago (which see) but with a more powerful engine and retractable landing gear. The prototype (F-WDBA) flew for the first time, at Tarbes, on 14 November 1980. French certification was received on 18 December 1981, and the first production Trinidad (F-WDBB) was delivered on 23 March 1982. FAA type approval was obtained on 27 January 1984. Orders totalled 265 by 1 January 1988, including 42 for the SFACT for commercial airline pilot training. Others have been supplied to civilian aviation training centres in Australia, India (eight) and Tunisia. In March 1988, China ordered 28 for use at its Chengdu airline pilot training centre.

Socata TB 10 Tobago four/five-seat all-metal light aircraft

Socata TB 21 Trinidad TC, with retractable landing gear (G. Maoui)

There are two current versions of the Trinidad, as follows:

TB 20 Trinidad. Basic version with 186 kW (250 hp) Textron Lycoming IO-540-C4D5D engine.

TB 21 Trinidad TC. Turbocharged version, first flown on 24 August 1984, with 186 kW (250 hp) Textron Lycoming TIO-540-AB1AD engine and oxygen system. DGAC certification received on 23 May 1985, followed by FAA type approval on 5 March 1986. The first production Trinidad TC (F-GENI), displayed at the 1985 Paris Air Show, was the 500th aircraft of the TB 9/10/20/21 series produced by Socata.

The description of the Tobago applies also to both versions of the Trinidad, except as follows:

WINGS: Dihedral 6° 30′ from roots. Flap preselector standard.

TAIL UNIT: Span and chord of horizontal tail surfaces increased. Mechanical rudder trim standard.

LANDING GEAR: Hydraulically retractable tricycle type, with single wheel on each unit. Free fall emergency extension. Steerable nosewheel retracts rearward. Main units retract inward into fuselage. Hydraulic disc brakes. Parking brake.

POWER PLANT: One Textron Lycoming flat-six engine, as described in individual model listings, driving a Hartzell HC-C2YK-1BF/F8477-4 two-blade metal propeller. Fuel tanks in wings; total usable capacity 326 litres (86 US gallons; 71.75 Imp gallons). Oil capacity 12.6 litres (3.3 US gallons; 2.8 Imp gallons).

SYSTEMS: Self-contained electro-hydraulic system for landing gear actuation. Eros oxygen system is standard in TB 21.

EQUIPMENT: In addition to basic nav pack described in the Tampico/Tobago entry, current aircraft have as standard equipment a heated pitot, emergency static vent, cylinder head temperature gauge, emergency lighting systems, tinted windows and a storm window.

DIMENSIONS:

As for Tobago, except:

Length overall	7.71 m (25 ft 3½ in)
Height overall	2.85 m (9 ft 4¼ in)
Tailplane span	3.64 m (11 ft 11¼ in)
Wheelbase	1.91 m (6 ft 3¼ in)
Propeller diameter	2.03 m (6 ft 8 in)

AREAS:

As for Tobago, except:

Horizontal tail surfaces (total)	3.06 m² (32.94 sq ft)

WEIGHTS (A: TB 20, B: TB 21):

Weight empty: A	800 kg (1,763 lb)
B	844 kg (1,861 lb)
Max baggage: A, B	65 kg (143 lb)

Max T-O weight: A, B	1,400 kg (3,086 lb)

PERFORMANCE (at max T-O weight, A and B as above):

Max level speed: A	167 knots (310 km/h; 192 mph)
B at 4,575 m (15,000 ft)	200 knots (370 km/h; 230 mph)
Max cruising speed (75% power) at 2,440 m (8,000 ft):	
A	164 knots (303 km/h; 188 mph)
Best power cruising speed (75% power) at 7,620 m (25,000 ft): B	190 knots (352 km/h; 219 mph)
Econ cruising speed (65% power):	
A at 3,660 m (12,000 ft)	160 knots (296 km/h; 184 mph)
B at 7,620 m (25,000 ft)	170 knots (315 km/h; 195 mph)
Stalling speed: flaps up:	
A	64 knots (118 km/h; 74 mph)
B	66 knots (121 km/h; 75 mph)
flaps and wheels down:	
A	54 knots (99 km/h; 62 mph)
B	55 knots (101 km/h; 63 mph)
Rate of climb: A at S/L	384 m (1,260 ft)/min
B at 610 m (2,000 ft)	332 m (1,090 ft)/min
B at 5,180 m (17,000 ft)	244 m (800 ft)/min
Service ceiling: A	6,100 m (20,000 ft)
Certification ceiling: B	7,620 m (25,000 ft)
T-O run: A	295 m (968 ft)
B	330 m (1,083 ft)
T-O to 15 m (50 ft): A	479 m (1,572 ft)
B	540 m (1,772 ft)
Landing from 15 m (50 ft): A	530 m (1,739 ft)
B	540 m (1,772 ft)
Landing run: A	230 m (755 ft)

Range with max fuel, allowances for T-O, climb, cruise at best econ setting and descent, 45 min reserves:

A at 75% power at 2,135 m (7,000 ft)	885 nm (1,640 km; 1,019 miles)
A at 65% power at 3,050 m (10,000 ft)	963 nm (1,785 km; 1,109 miles)

Range with max fuel, no reserves:

B at 75% power at 7,620 m (25,000 ft)	890 nm (1,648 km; 1,024 miles)
B at 65% power at 7,620 m (25,000 ft)	1,030 nm (1,907 km; 1,185 miles)

Max ferry range at 6,100 m (20,000 ft):

A	1,158 nm (2,145 km; 1,332 miles)

TBM 700

This Socata/Mooney turboprop business aircraft is described under TBM Corporation in the International section.

GERMANY
(FEDERAL REPUBLIC)

CCE
COLANI/COMPOSITE ENGINEERING
Josef-Baumann-Strasse 29, 4630 Bochum 1
Telephone: (0234) 865346
Telex: 825 828 LEMAB D
Fax: (0234) 864125
HEAD OF DEVELOPMENT: Dipl-Ing Walter Schulze

COLANI CORMORAN CCE-208
Conceived by industrial designer Luigi Colani and sponsored by the Tohshin Company of Japan, the Cormoran is a four/five-seat light aircraft of which a prototype (D-EBCN) is being built by Composite Engineering in West Germany, for a planned first flight in 1988.

TYPE: Four/five-seat light aircraft.

WINGS: Cantilever mid-wing monoplane, of safe-life all-composites construction (carbon/aramid/glass fibres and foam sandwich). Newly developed Wortmann wing sections, with thickness/chord ratios of 18.8% at root and 16% at tip. No sweepback. Ailerons and electrically actuated trailing-edge Fowler flaps are of carbonfibre/sandwich construction.

FUSELAGE: Elliptical-section all-composites structure of carbon/aramid fibre and Nomex sandwich. Carbonfibre/sandwich airbrake under rear fuselage.

TAIL UNIT: Cantilever T tail, construction as for wings and fuselage. Elevators and rudder actuated by pushrods.

LANDING GEAR: Retractable tricycle type, with electric actuation; single wheel on each unit. Mainwheels retract inward, nosewheel forward. Mainwheels are carried on self-sprung cantilever carbon/glass fibre legs; nosewheel on a hydraulic oleo strut. Wheel sizes 6.00-6 (main) and 5.00-5 (nose), all three having Goodyear tyres. Composite Engineering hydraulic brakes on mainwheels.

POWER PLANT: One 164 kW (220 hp) normally aspirated Porsche PFM N 03 or turbocharged 182.7 kW (245 hp) PFM T 03 engine, installed in centre-fuselage with carbonfibre driveshaft to a Hoffmann three-blade constant-speed pusher propeller aft of tail unit. NACA type flush air inlet on top of fuselage. Fuel in two 378 litre (100 US gallon; 83.15 Imp gallon) integral wing tanks, giving total capacity of 756 litres (200 US gallons; 166.3 Imp gallons). Gravity refuelling point above each tank. Oil capacity 10 litres (2.6 US gallons; 2.2 Imp gallons).

ACCOMMODATION: Fully enclosed cabin seats pilot and one passenger in front, three more passengers at rear. Baggage space, with external access, aft of rear seats. Window/door on each side, forward of wing, hinged at centreline to open upward for access to all seats.

SYSTEMS: 24V electrical system (two 24V alternators) for landing gear and control surface actuation. Oxygen mask for each passenger in turbocharged version.

Mockup of the Colani/Composite Engineering Cormoran CCE-208

AVIONICS AND EQUIPMENT: Range of Becker or King avionics, to customer's requirements. Blind-flying instrumentation optional.

DIMENSIONS, EXTERNAL:
Wing span	11.80 m (38 ft 8½ in)
Wing aspect ratio	9.95
Length overall	8.60 m (28 ft 2½ in)
Height overall, propeller turning	3.60 m (11 ft 9¾ in)
Fuselage: Max diameter	1.38 m (4 ft 6⅓ in)
Tailplane span	4.50 m (14 ft 9¼ in)
Wheel track	3.00 m (9 ft 10 in)
Wheelbase	2.75 m (9 ft 0¼ in)
Propeller diameter	2.40 m (7 ft 10½ in)
Cabin doors (each): Height	1.00 m (3 ft 3¼ in)
Width	0.90 m (2 ft 11½ in)
Baggage door (rear): Height	0.60 m (1 ft 11½ in)
Width	0.55 m (1 ft 9¾ in)

DIMENSIONS, INTERNAL:
Cabin: Length	2.40 m (7 ft 10½ in)
Max width	1.28 m (4 ft 2½ in)
Max height	1.10 m (3 ft 7¼ in)
Baggage compartment volume	0.70 m³ (24.7 cu ft)

AREAS:
Wings, gross	14.00 m² (150.7 sq ft)
Horizontal tail surfaces (total)	3.00 m² (32.29 sq ft)

WEIGHTS AND LOADINGS (A: 220 hp, B: 245 hp):
Weight empty, standard: A	795 kg (1,753 lb)
B	825 kg (1,819 lb)
Max fuel: A, B	544 kg (1,199 lb)
Max payload	630 kg (1,389 lb)
Max T-O weight: A, B	1,500 kg (3,307 lb)
Max landing weight	1,425 kg (3,141 lb)
Max wing loading: A, B	107.1 kg/m² (21.94 lb/sq ft)
Max power loading: A	9.49 kg/kW (15.6 lb/hp)
B	8.21 kg/kW (13.5 lb/hp)

PERFORMANCE (estimated, at max T-O weight with T 03 Turbo engine):
Never-exceed speed	270 knots (500 km/h; 311 mph)
Max level speed at 5,490 m (18,000 ft)	240 knots (445 km/h; 276 mph)
Max cruising speed (84% power) at 5,490 m (18,000 ft)	225 knots (417 km/h; 259 mph)
Econ cruising speed (70% power) at 5,490 m (18,000 ft)	209 knots (387 km/h; 241 mph)
Stalling speed: flaps up	65 knots (121 km/h; 75 mph)
flaps down	55 knots (102 km/h; 64 mph)
Max rate of climb at S/L	393 m (1,290 ft)/min
Service ceiling	7,620 m (25,000 ft)
T-O to 15 m (50 ft)	453 m (1,486 ft)

Range:
at 2,440 m (8,000 ft) with four passengers and 100 kg (220 lb) of baggage, cruising at 188 knots (348 km/h; 216 mph) 1,477 nm (2,737 km; 1,701 miles)
at 3,660 m (12,000 ft) with one passenger only, cruising at 197 knots (365 km/h; 227 mph) 3,161 nm (5,858 km; 3,640 miles)

CLAUDIUS DORNIER
CLAUDIUS DORNIER SEASTAR
GmbH & Co KG
Werksflugplatz Oberpfaffenhofen, 8031 Wessling
Telephone: (08153) 4010
Telex: 5270288 CDS D
Fax: (08153) 3636
MANAGING DIRECTORS:
Dipl Kfm Conrado Dornier
Dipl Ing Hannes Lucas

The first product of this company, founded by the late Prof Dipl Ing Claudius Dornier Jr, is the Seastar utility amphibian, of which design was initiated in January 1982. The VT 01 first prototype (D-ICDS), described in the 1984-85 *Jane's*, made its first flight on 17 August 1984, but in mid-1985 was retired after being damaged. In October 1985 the company moved to Oberpfaffenhofen where, with an initial development team of ten people, work began on an improved version known as the CD2. In March 1988 the company's workforce numbered 100.

CLAUDIUS DORNIER SEASTAR CD2
The only portion of the VT 01 prototype to suffer serious damage was the strut braced metal wing, and this was replaced in the pre-series CD2 Seastar by a larger wing manufactured entirely from composite materials, with carbonfibre reinforcement in two spars that eliminates the need for strut bracing of the outer panels. Hull design was improved by a flatter planing bottom, enlarged cockpit, reprofiled nose and extended sponsons, and the original PT6A-11 turboprops were replaced by PT6A-112s driving four-blade instead of three-blade propellers. The virtually all-composites airframe thus offers both light weight and a high degree of corrosion resistance.

As a basic transport aircraft the Seastar provides accommodation for two pilots and up to 12 passengers. It is suitable for a variety of missions, including feeder transport from water bases to airports; missions for which helicopters would be restricted by range, economics or safety factors; search and rescue; law enforcement; air ambulance; and

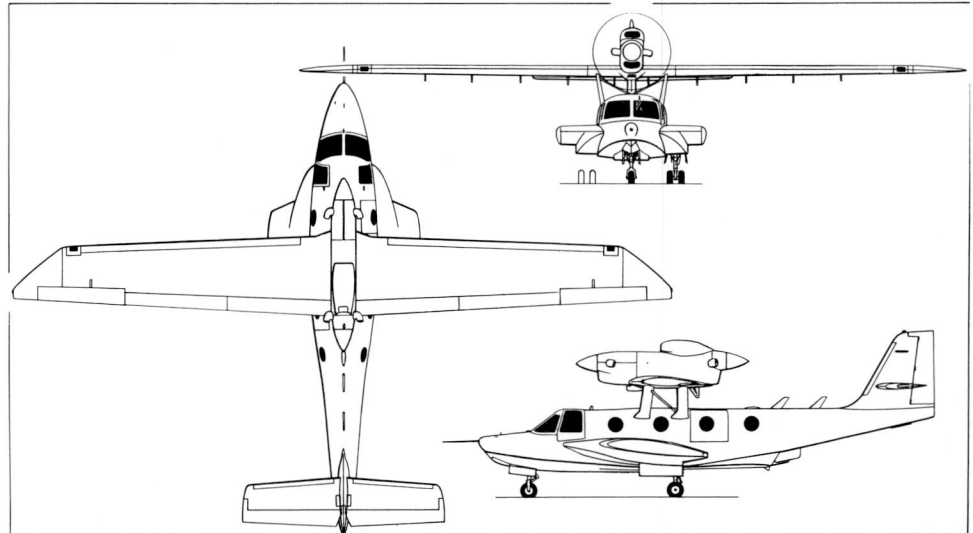

Claudius Dornier Seastar in its production form *(Pilot Press)*

civil or military special missions, accommodating four people over a range of 1,000 nm (1,850 km; 1,150 miles). Its ability to operate from land, water, snow or ice enables it to perform such roles as aerial surveillance, sightseeing and hunting tours, fire control and firefighting.

The first CD2 (also registered D-ICDS) made its first flight on 24 April 1987. Sea trials in the Baltic, off Kiel, were completed successfully later that year, and a second pre-production aircraft was due to fly in the Spring of 1988. It differs from D-ICDS only in having larger cabin windows and a fully furnished interior. Certification by the German LBA and FAA type approval under FAR Pt 23 are

scheduled for Autumn 1989, and initial deliveries for Summer 1990. By Spring 1988 the company held options for 20 Seastar CD2s, and letters of intent for another 13.

Changes planned for the production Seastar include 462 kW (620 shp) PT6A-135 engines, all three wing spars made of carbonfibre, and raked wingtips, increasing the wing area to 30.5 m² (328.3 sq ft). Useful load will be increased to 1,800 kg (3,968 lb) and max T-O weight to 4,600 kg (10,141 lb). Max cruising speed will be increased to 190 knots (352 km/h; 219 mph).

The following description applies to the pre-production CD2:

TYPE: Twin-turboprop utility amphibian.

WINGS: Cantilever parasol monoplane, with modified NACA 23015 aerofoil section. The high-lift wing has drooped outboard leading-edges. It is constructed of GRP with a foam core and is a three-spar structure, with carbonfibre reinforcement of the front and rear spars, fitted with single-slotted trailing-edge flaps and horn balanced ailerons.

HULL: Conventional unpressurised flying-boat hull, constructed almost entirely of glassfibre. Large chined sponson on each side.

TAIL UNIT: Conventional unit, constructed of glassfibre and incorporating a variable incidence tailplane. Horn balanced elevators and rudder, each with trim tab.

LANDING GEAR: Hydraulically retractable tricycle type, with twin wheels on each main unit and single nosewheel. All wheels size 6.00-6. Main units retract forward into hull sponsons, nose unit forward into bow.

POWER PLANT: Two 373 kW (500 shp) Pratt & Whitney Canada PT6A-112 turboprops, mounted in tandem above wing in continuous nacelle and driving one tractor and one pusher propeller. Each is a four-blade McCauley C-760 series constant-speed metal propeller with spinner. Fuel tank in each sponson, combined max usable capacity 1,869 litres (494 US gallons; 411 Imp gallons).

ACCOMMODATION: Max accommodation for two pilots and 12 passengers in four rows of three, at 81 cm (32 in) seat pitch, with single aisle. Dual controls standard. Alternative layouts for six executives in VIP seating, with a lavatory at rear of cabin and toilet in part of baggage compartment; or nine passengers, with lavatory and toilet optional. By utilising entire baggage compartment space, aircraft can accommodate six stretchers plus two attendants and medical equipment; or can be configured for all-cargo use with front and rear loading access, able to transport items up to 5.50 m (18 ft 0½ in) in length. Crew door on port side. Passenger doors at front of cabin on starboard side and at rear on port side; latter has an optional airstair incorporated in the adjacent sponson structure. Baggage compartment at rear of cabin, with external door on starboard side. All accommodation heated and ventilated; air-conditioning optional.

SYSTEMS: Hydraulic system for landing gear actuation. Electrical system. Pneumatic de-icing for wing and tail leading-edges and engine air intakes.

AVIONICS: Complete IFR installation standard.

DIMENSIONS, EXTERNAL:

Wing span	15.50 m (50 ft 10¼ in)
Wing chord, mean	1.89 m (6 ft 2½ in)
Wing aspect ratio	8.4
Width over sponsons	4.20 m (13 ft 9½ in)
Length overall	12.46 m (40 ft 10½ in)
Fuselage: Max width	1.90 m (6 ft 2¾ in)
Max depth	1.80 m (5 ft 10¾ in)
Height overall (on land)	4.60 m (15 ft 1 in)

Claudius Dornier Seastar CD2 amphibian (two P&WC PT6A-112 (turboprops)

Tailplane span	5.56 m (18 ft 3 in)
Wheel track	2.45 m (8 ft 0½ in)
Propeller diameter: front	2.40 m (7 ft 10½ in)
rear	2.35 m (7 ft 8½ in)
Crew door: Height	0.85 m (2 ft 9½ in)
Width	0.70 m (2 ft 3½ in)
Passenger door (fwd, stbd):	
Height	1.00 m (3 ft 3¼ in)
Width	0.80 m (2 ft 7½ in)
Passenger door (rear, port):	
Height	1.15 m (4 ft 11 in)
Width	0.95 m (3 ft 1½ in)
Baggage compartment door:	
Height	0.50 m (1 ft 7¾ in)
Width	0.90 m (2 ft 11½ in)

DIMENSIONS, INTERNAL:

Cabin, excl flight deck:	
Length: excl baggage compartment	5.00 m (16 ft 5 in)
incl baggage compartment	5.50 m (18 ft 0½ in)
Max width	1.68 m (5 ft 6 in)
Max height	1.45 m (4 ft 9 in)
Floor area: excl baggage compartment	
	6.30 m² (67.8 sq ft)
Volume: excl baggage compartment	
	8.30 m³ (293.1 cu ft)
Rear baggage compartment volume	
	1.70 m³ (60.0 cu ft)

AREAS:

Wings, gross	28.48 m² (306.6 sq ft)
Vertical tail surfaces (total)	3.15 m² (33.9 sq ft)
Horizontal tail surfaces (total)	6.32 m² (68.0 sq ft)

WEIGHTS AND LOADINGS:

Weight empty, equipped (standard)	2,400 kg (5,291 lb)
Max payload	1,460 kg (3,218 lb)
Max usable fuel	1,495 kg (3,296 lb)
Max T-O and landing weight	4,200 kg (9,259 lb)
Max wing loading	147.5 kg/m² (30.2 lb/sq ft)
Max power loading	5.63 kg/kW (9.26 lb/shp)

PERFORMANCE (preliminary, at max T-O weight):

Max cruising speed at 3,000 m (9,840 ft)	
	184 knots (341 km/h; 212 mph)
Stalling speed at S/L	62 knots (115 km/h; 72 mph)
Max rate of climb at S/L	480 m (1,575 ft)/min
Rate of climb at S/L, one engine out	150 m (492 ft)/min
Service ceiling	8,535 m (28,000 ft)
Service ceiling, one engine out	4,200 m (13,780 ft)
T-O distance (land or water)	410 m (1,345 ft)
T-O to 15 m (50 ft) on land or water	640 m (2,100 ft)
Landing from 15 m (50 ft) on land	480 m (1,575 ft)
Landing distance (land or water)	270 m (886 ft)
Range: with 12 passengers at max cruising speed, 10% reserves	300 nm (555 km; 345 miles)
with 454 kg (1,000 lb) payload	831 nm (1,541 km; 957 miles)
with max fuel	1,000 nm (1,850 km; 1,150 miles)
Max endurance: two engines	8 h
one engine	9 h 12 min

DORNIER
DORNIER GmbH

Postfach 1420, 7990 Friedrichshafen/Bodensee
Telephone: Immenstaad (07545) 81
Telex: 0734 209-0
WORKS:
Research and Development:
7990 Friedrichshafen/Bodensee
Production: Postfach 2160, Trimburgstrasse, 8000 Munich 66
AIRFIELD AND FLIGHT TEST CENTRE:
8031 Oberpfaffenhofen, near Munich
BONN OFFICE: Heussallee 2-10, 5300 Bonn
CHAIRMAN OF SUPERVISORY BOARD:
Edzard Reuter
CHAIRMAN OF MANAGING DIRECTORS:
Johann Schäffler
PUBLIC RELATIONS: Gerhard Patt
Postfach 2160, 8000 Munich 66
Telephone: (089) 87 153480
Telex: 52 35 43

Dornier GmbH, formerly Dornier-Metallbauten, was formed in 1922 by the late Professor Claude Dornier. It has operated as a GmbH since 22 December 1972. Of 9,500 employees in the Dornier group, approximately 43% are production staff, 32% in research and development, and 25% engaged in technical and logistic support. Daimler-Benz AG acquired a majority holding (65.5%) in Dornier GmbH in 1985; the remaining stock is held by Silvius Dornier and the State of Baden-Württemberg.

Member companies, in addition to Dornier GmbH, include Dornier-Reparaturwerft GmbH, at Oberpfaffenhofen (aircraft servicing and maintenance), Dornier System GmbH of Friedrichshafen (spaceflight, new technologies, electronics, management consultancy and contract research) and Dornier Medizintechnik GmbH of Munich.

The Dornier 228 twin-turboprop regional transport continues in production. Available in several versions, the 228 embodies Dornier's TNT advanced technology wing, which was embodied also in the proposed 30-seat Dornier 328.

Dornier is active in development of various types of RPV, and continues to develop and improve the Alpha Jet training/light attack aircraft, described in the International section, in partnership with Dassault-Breguet of France.

Dornier is participating, under subcontract from Deutsche Airbus GmbH, in the manufacturing and development programmes for the Airbus Industrie family of transport aircraft. It was responsible for integrating the operational avionics in the 18 Boeing E-3A Sentry AWACS aircraft acquired by NATO for use in Europe, and now conducts depot-level maintenance of these aircraft under NATO contract. Dornier-Reparaturwerft GmbH is prime contractor for planning and implementation of the NATO Trainer/Cargo Aircraft (TCA) programme, under which three Boeing 707-329Cs are being modified for E-3A pilot training and transport duties.

Dornier undertakes technical and logistic servicing of the Breguet Br 1150 Atlantic 1 aircraft operated by the Federal German Navy. It is also prime contractor for modernisation of the German Atlantics.

Dornier is one of the European aerospace companies defining and developing the multi-nation Eurofighter EFA (see International section).

DORNIER 128-6

A full description of the Dornier 128-6 has appeared in many previous editions of *Jane's*, most recently in the 1985-86 edition.

DORNIER 228

The design of the Dornier 228 complies with US FAR Pt 23 requirements, including Amendment 23, and Appendix A of FAR Pt 135. One prototype of each initial version was built; the first of these, the Dornier 228-100 (D-IFNS) made its first flight on 28 March 1981. The 228-200 (D-ICDO) flew for the first time on 9 May 1981. A static test airframe of the 228-200 was also completed.

British CAA and American FAA certification were granted on 17 April and 11 May 1984 respectively, followed by Australian certification on 11 October 1985; in addition, LBA certification has been accepted by the licensing authorities of Bhutan, Canada, India, Japan, Malaysia, Nigeria, Norway, Sweden and Taiwan.

Excluding Indian licence production, firm orders for the Dornier 228 (all versions) totalled 151, including 99 in commuter configuration, by 31 March 1988; deliveries at that time had reached 140.

The Dornier 228 is available in the following versions:

228-100. Basic version, with standard accommodation for 15 passengers in airline seats at 76 cm (30 in) pitch. German (LBA) certification awarded on 18 December 1981. Deliveries began in February 1982; entered service, with A/S Norving Flyservice in Norway, in late Summer of 1982. Suitable for a wide range of other duties, including freight or mixed cargo/passenger transport, executive travel, air taxi service, photogrammetry, airways calibration, training, ambulance or search and rescue operations, and paramilitary missions. Details of two 228-100s specially equipped for polar research were given in the 1986-87 *Jane's*. Two ordered for SAR and other special duties by Australia's National Safety Council in 1987 are being fitted with bubble windows each side of the cabin, a wide roller cabin door for SAR or firefighting operations, lightweight 360° Bendix radar, an Omega Loran system, 20-man liferaft, a launching chute in the rear fuselage for smoke or colour markers and flares, and provision for two stretchers.

228-101. Identical to 228-100 except for reinforced fuselage and different mainwheel tyres, to permit higher operating weights, and installation of engine fire extinguishing system to conform to SFAR Pt 4 lb. Introduced in 1984.

228-200. Lengthened fuselage, providing standard accommodation for 19 passengers at 76 cm (30 in) seat pitch and a larger rear baggage compartment, but otherwise generally similar to 228-100. Certificated by German LBA on 6 September 1982. One due for delivery to Japan's National Aerospace Laboratory in March 1988 has been specially equipped by AAR Oklahoma Inc, USA, for use as an in-flight simulator to evaluate aerodynamic and flight control system characteristics for future aircraft, including an automatic landing system for a future spaceplane.

228-201. Identical to 228-200 except for changes noted under 228-101. Introduced in 1984. One (98 + 78) evaluated by MFG 5 of the German Navy and by German Air Force during 1986-87. Two specially equipped -201s, delivered in 1985-86 to DFVLR for meteorological (remote sensing) and environmental forestry and pollution control work, have ventral camera/scanner apertures and numerous attachments for special sensors and other equipment under the wings and fuselage.

228-202. Designed to offer increases in payload/range performance, compared with 228-201, for only a slight difference in empty weight. Certificated by LBA and FAA in early September 1986; available from Autumn 1987.

228-203F. Freighter version, with higher payload and operating weights. Additional crew door on starboard side. Due to become available in Autumn 1987.

228-212. As -201, but with 6,100 kg (13,448 lb) landing weight, allowing increased payload on short route segments.

228 Maritime Patrol. Described separately.

On 29 November 1983 contracts were signed covering the transfer of technology in a progressive programme to manufacture versions of the Dornier 228 under licence in India, by Hindustan Aeronautics Ltd. A production run of about 150 aircraft is envisaged, for various Indian organisations and customers, and was prefaced by the delivery of five 228-201s to Vayudoot, the Indian regional airline, in 1984-85, and three 228-101s to the Indian Coast Guard in 1986-87. Meanwhile, Dornier began delivery of complete sets of aircraft assemblies to India in early 1985, and the first flight of an HAL assembled 228 was made on 31 January 1986. Further details of this licence programme can be found in the HAL entry in the Indian section.

TYPE: Twin-turboprop light transport.

WINGS: Cantilever high-wing monoplane, comprising two-spar rectangular centre-section and two tapered outer panels ending in raked tips. Dornier Do A-5 supercritical wing section. No dihedral or anhedral. Sweepback on leading-edge of outer panels 8°. Wing leading-edge and raked wingtips of glassfibre/Kevlar composites. Remainder of wing of light alloy construction. Fowler single-slotted trailing-edge flaps and ailerons of carbon-fibre composites. Ailerons can be drooped symmetrically to augment trailing-edge flaps, and are operated differentially to serve as conventional ailerons. Trim coupling of flaps and tailplane optional.

FUSELAGE: Conventional stressed skin unpressurised struc-ture of light alloy, built in five sections. Glassfibre nose- and tailcones.

TAIL UNIT: Cantilever all-metal structure, with rudder and horizontal surfaces partly Eonnex covered. All-moving tailplane, with horn balanced elevators. Trim tab in rudder.

LANDING GEAR: Retractable tricycle type, with single mainwheels and twin-wheel nose unit. Main units retract forward and inward into fairings built on to the lower fuselage. Hydraulically steerable nosewheels retract forward. Goodyear wheels and tyres, size 8.50-10 on mainwheels (12 ply rating on 228-100, 10 ply rating on 228-200); size 6.00-6, 6 ply rating, on nosewheels. Low pressure tyres optional. Goodyear brakes on mainwheels.

POWER PLANT: Two 533 kW (715 shp) Garrett TPE331-5-252D turboprops in -100/-101, each driving a Hartzell HC-B4TN-5ML/LT10574 four-blade constant-speed fully-feathering reversible-pitch metal propeller; -200 series have 578.7 kW (776 shp) version of same engine. Primary wing box forms an integral fuel tank with a total usable capacity of 2,386 litres (630 US gallons; 525 Imp gallons).

ACCOMMODATION: Crew of two, and standard accommo-dation in cabin for 15 or 19 passengers as described under model listings, or 21 or 25 seats respectively in troop transport configuration. Pilots' seats adjustable fore and aft. Individual seats down each side of the cabin with a central aisle. Flight deck door on port side (both sides on -203F). Combined two-section passenger and freight door, with integral steps, on port side of cabin at rear. One emergency exit on port side of cabin, two on starboard side (deleted on -203F). Baggage compartment at rear of cabin, accessible externally and from cabin. Enlarged baggage door optional. Additional baggage space in fuselage nose. Modular units for rapid changes of role.

SYSTEMS: Entire accommodation heated and ventilated. Air-conditioning system optional. Heating by engine bleed air. Hydraulic system, pressure 207 bars (3,000 lb/sq in), for landing gear, brakes and nosewheel steering. Handpump for emergency landing gear extension. Primary 28V DC electrical system, supplied by two 28V 250A engine driven starter/generators and two 24V 25Ah nickel-cadmium batteries. Two 350VA inverters supply 115/26V 400Hz AC system. APU optional. Air intake anti-icing standard. De-icing system optional for wing and tail unit leading-edges, windscreen and propellers.

AVIONICS AND EQUIPMENT: Instrumentation for IFR flight standard. Autopilot optional, to permit single-pilot IFR operation. Standard avionics include dual King KY 196 VHF com, KN 53 VOR/ILS and KN 72 VOR/LOC converters; single KMR 675 marker beacon receiver, KR 87 ADF and KT 76A transponder; Aeronetics 7137 RMI; two Sperry GH14B gyro horizons; two King KPI 552 HSIs; Becker audio selector and intercom. Standard equipment includes complete internal and external lighting, hand fire extinguisher, first aid kit, gust control locks and tiedown kit. Wide range of optional avionics and equipment available. Equipment for a version to support oil pollution location and dispersal is under development.

DIMENSIONS, EXTERNAL:

Wing span	16.97 m (55 ft 8 in)
Wing aspect ratio	9.0
Length overall: 100 series	15.04 m (49 ft 4⅛ in)
200 series	16.56 m (54 ft 4 in)
Height overall	4.86 m (15 ft 11½ in)
Tailplane span	6.45 m (21 ft 2 in)
Wheel track	3.30 m (10 ft 10 in)
Wheelbase: 100 series	5.53 m (18 ft 1¾ in)
200 series	6.29 m (20 ft 7½ in)
Propeller diameter	2.73 m (8 ft 11½ in)
Passenger door (port, rear):	
Height	1.34 m (4 ft 4¾ in)
Width	0.64 m (2 ft 1¼ in)
Height to sill	0.60 m (1 ft 11½ in)
Freight door (port, rear):	
Height	1.34 m (4 ft 4¾ in)
Width, incl passenger door	1.28 m (4 ft 2½ in)
Emergency exits (each): Height	0.66 m (2 ft 2 in)
Width	0.48 m (1 ft 7 in)

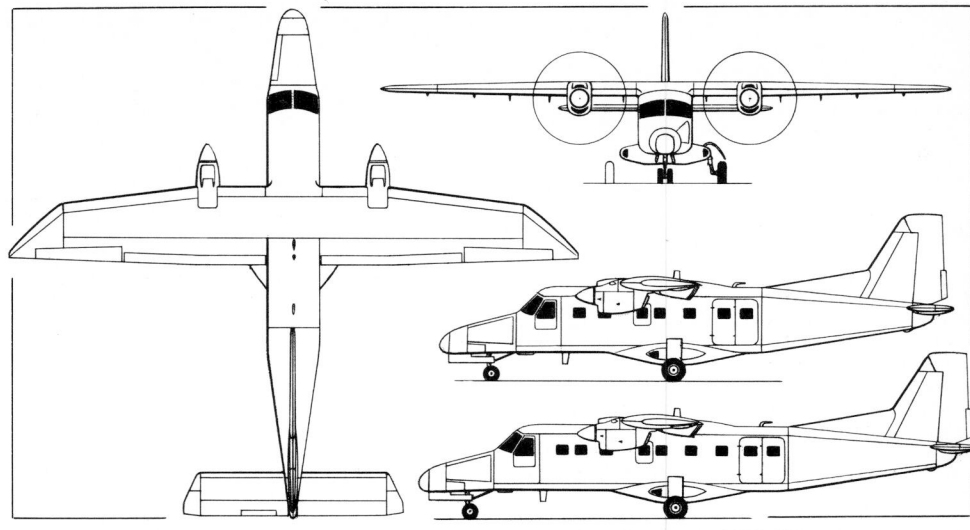

Dornier 228-100 light transport, with additional side view (bottom) of 228-200 (*Pilot Press*)

Dornier 228-101 twin-engined utility transport (two Garrett TPE331-5-252D turboprops)

Dornier 228-200 commuter transport in the insignia of Formosa Airlines of Taiwan

Baggage door (nose): Height	0.50 m (1 ft 7½ in)
Width	1.32 m (4 ft 4 in)
Standard baggage door (rear):	
Height	0.76 m (2 ft 6 in)
Width	0.54 m (1 ft 9¼ in)

DIMENSIONS, INTERNAL:

Cabin, excl flight deck and rear baggage compartment:	
Length: 100 series	6.33 m (20 ft 9 in)
200 series	7.08 m (23 ft 2¾ in)
Max width	1.346 m (4 ft 5 in)
Max height	1.55 m (5 ft 1 in)
Floor area: 100 series	8.50 m² (91.49 sq ft)
200 series	9.56 m² (102.9 sq ft)
Volume: 100 series	13.00 m³ (459.1 cu ft)
200 series	14.70 m³ (519.1 cu ft)
Rear baggage compartment volume:	
100 series, standard	1.20 m³ (42.4 cu ft)
100 series, optional; 200 series, standard	
	2.60 m³ (91.8 cu ft)
Nose baggage compartment volume	0.89 m³ (31.4 cu ft)
Cargo volume (203F):	
main cabin	13.20 m³ (466.1 cu ft)
nose	0.88 m³ (31.1 cu ft)
rear fuselage	2.25 m³ (79.5 cu ft)

AREAS:

Wings, gross	32.00 m² (344.3 sq ft)
Ailerons (total)	2.708 m² (29.15 sq ft)
Trailing-edge flaps (total)	5.872 m² (63.21 sq ft)
Fin, incl dorsal fin	4.50 m² (48.44 sq ft)
Rudder, incl tab	1.50 m² (16.15 sq ft)
Horizontal tail surfaces (total)	8.33 m² (89.66 sq ft)

WEIGHTS AND LOADINGS:

Weight empty, standard: 100	2,980 kg (6,570 lb)
101	2,990 kg (6,592 lb)
200	3,086 kg (6,803 lb)
201	3,096 kg (6,825 lb)
Operating weight empty: 100	3,413 kg (7,524 lb)
101	3,423 kg (7,546 lb)
200	3,547 kg (7,820 lb)
201	3,737 kg (8,238 lb)
202	3,698 kg (8,153 lb)
Max payload: 100	2,127 kg (4,689 lb)
101	2,117 kg (4,667 lb)
200	1,853 kg (4,085 lb)
201	1,903 kg (4,195 lb)
202	2,502 kg (5,516 lb)
203F	2,300 kg (5,070 lb)
Max ramp weight: 100, 200	5,730 kg (12,632 lb)
101, 201	6,010 kg (13,250 lb)
Max T-O weight: 100, 200	5,700 kg (12,566 lb)
101, 201	5,980 kg (13,183 lb)
202	6,200 kg (13,668 lb)
203F	6,500 kg (14,330 lb)
Max landing weight: 100, 101, 200	5,700 kg (12,566 lb)
201, 202	5,900 kg (13,007 lb)
212	6,100 kg (13,448 lb)
Max wing loading:	
100, 200	178.1 kg/m² (36.48 lb/sq ft)
101, 201	186.9 kg/m² (38.28 lb/sq ft)
202	193.7 kg/m² (39.67 lb/sq ft)
203F	203.1 kg/m² (41.60 lb/sq ft)
Max power loading:	
100, 200	5.35 kg/kW (8.79 lb/shp)
101, 201	5.17 kg/kW (8.49 lb/shp)
202	5.36 kg/kW (8.81 lb/shp)
203F	4.19 kg/kW (9.23 lb/shp)

PERFORMANCE (at max T-O weight, S/L, ISA, except where indicated):

Never-exceed speed (all)	
	255 knots (472 km/h; 293 mph) IAS
Max cruising speed at 3,050 m (10,000 ft) (all)	
	231 knots (428 km/h; 266 mph)
Max cruising speed at S/L (all)	
	199 knots (370 km/h; 230 mph)

Stalling speed, flaps up:	
100	79 knots (146 km/h; 91 mph) IAS
200	81 knots (150 km/h; 93 mph) IAS
Stalling speed, flaps down:	
100	63 knots (117 km/h; 73 mph) IAS
200	67 knots (124 km/h; 77 mph) IAS
Max rate of climb at S/L:	
100, 200	618 m (2,025 ft)/min
101, 201	582 m (1,910 ft)/min
202	546 m (1,790 ft)/min
Rate of climb at S/L, one engine out:	
100, 200	162 m (531 ft)/min
101, 201	138 m (450 ft)/min
202	150 m (490 ft)/min
Service ceiling, 30.5 m (100 ft)/min rate of climb:	
100, 200	9,020 m (29,600 ft)
101, 201	8,535 m (28,000 ft)
Service ceiling, one engine out, 30.5 m (100 ft)/min rate of climb: 100, 200	4,265 m (14,000 ft)
202	4,575 m (15,000 ft)
T-O run: 100	411 m (1,350 ft)
101	442 m (1,450 ft)
T-O to 15 m (50 ft): 100	564 m (1,850 ft)
101	592 m (1,945 ft)
200	750 m (2,461 ft)
201	625 m (2,050 ft)
202	686 m (2,250 ft)
Landing from 15 m (50 ft) at max landing weight:	
100	600 m (1,968 ft)
200	620 m (2,034 ft)
Range at 3,050 m (10,000 ft) with max passenger payload, max cruising speed:	
100	724 nm (1,343 km; 834 miles)
101	939 nm (1,740 km; 1,081 miles)
200	323 nm (600 km; 372 miles)
Max range at 3,050 m (10,000 ft) at econ cruising speed, reserves for 85 nm (157 km; 98 mile) diversion, 45 min hold and 15% fuel remaining:	
201	164 nm (305 km; 189 miles)
202	524 nm (972 km; 604 miles)
203F (max payload)	
	over 400 nm (741 km; 460 miles)
203F (1,360 kg; 3,000 lb) payload	
	over 1,200 nm (2,224 km; 1,380 miles)

DORNIER 228 MARITIME PATROL

Dornier has developed two specialised versions of the Dornier 228-100 for maritime patrol. Designated Version A and Version B, they are equipped for particular roles as follows:

Version A: Intended for surveillance of domestic and foreign fisheries; territorial tasks and activities of national safety relating to infiltration, prohibited border traffic and smuggling; and SAR. Ordered by Indian Coast Guard (three German built 228-101s, delivered in July 1986 (two) and July 1987, plus 33 by HAL, beginning in 1987). Primary surveillance sensor is an underfuselage MEL Marec 2 radar with 360° scan (to be replaced on 15 aircraft by Super Marec ordered in early 1987). The cabin is laid out to accommodate two observers, each with a forward facing seat adjacent to a bubble window at the forward end of the cabin; a radar operator's station is situated on the port side in a mid-cabin position. There are storage positions for a hand held camera and a crew liferaft. Two additional liferafts, each with capacity for 20 persons, are optional. There is a double entry door with airstair on the port side, just to the rear of the radar operator's position; a toilet towards the rear of the cabin on the starboard side; and, to its rear, storage and a deployment chute for marine markers, smoke floats and flares. Two 300A Lear Siegler starter/generators are standard to supply power for specialised equipment which, in addition to the Marec 2 radar, includes IR/UV linescan, high resolution optical equipment, underwing Micronair spraypods for oil spill/chemical pollution control, Global Navigation GNS-500A-3B VLF/Omega, Collins HF 220

HF com, Collins RT 1327/ARC VHF/AF-FM com, and Becker EB 3100 interphone. Additional equipment in the radar operator's console includes an airspeed indicator, altimeter and clock; Aeronetics Model 7137 RMI; VLF/Omega control unit; and a Becker ASI-3100 interphone. A Spectrol Sk-16 Nightscan steerable searchlight, mounted externally, is optional.

Version B: Intended for surveillance of coastal waters to locate oil spills, survey sea traffic and protect fisheries. Secondary tasks include the detection of other pollution and the support of SAR missions. No orders announced up to Spring 1988. Primary surveillance source would be an Ericsson/Swedish Space Corporation SLAR. Standard cabin layout for SLAR operator, adjacent to a bubble window on port side of cabin; an instrument console almost opposite SLAR operator on starboard side with, behind it, a desk and crew rest seat. Stowage for crew liferaft, and toilet as in Version A, but space behind it is available for installation of an optional Swedish Space Corporation SSP-1100 IR/UV scanner system. Other optional equipment includes Bendix RDR-1400 forward looking radar, Decca-Racal Mk 19 nav system with TANS, or Type 72 Doppler nav system with TANS, plus the additional equipment in the radar operator's console as detailed for Version A.

WEIGHTS (A: Version A; B: Version B):

Weight empty, standard:	
A, B	2,960 kg (6,526 lb)
Operating weight empty: A	3,935 kg (8,675 lb)
B	4,015 kg (8,852 lb)
Fuel weight: A, B	1,885 kg (4,155 lb)
Max T-O weight: A, B	5,980 kg (13,183 lb)
Typical zero-fuel weight:	
A, B	4,095 kg (9,028 lb)

PERFORMANCE (A and B at max T-O weight, ISA):

Average speed for max range	
	165 knots (305 km/h; 190 mph)
Average speed for max endurance	
	100 knots (185 km/h; 115 mph)
* Search time, max range cruise speed at 610 m (2,000 ft), search area adjacent to base	7 h 45 min
* Search time, max range cruise speed at 610 m (2,000 ft), search area 400 nm (740 km; 460 miles) from base	3 h 45 min
* Search time, max endurance cruise speed at 610 m (2,000 ft), search area adjacent to base	9 h 45 min
* Search time, max endurance cruise speed at 610 m (2,000 ft), search area 400 nm (740 km; 460 miles) from base	4 h 45 min
* Search time increased by approx 1 h 30 min if optional auxiliary fuel tank installed	

DORNIER 328

Development of this twin-turboprop regional transport was suspended in mid-1988. For details see 1987-88 *Jane's*.

ATLANTIC 1 MODERNISATION PROGRAMME

The Federal German Navy fleet of 20 Atlantic 1s entered service in 1965. Of these, 15 are allocated to ASW and long-range maritime reconnaissance, and these aircraft have been modernised by Dornier under a DM200 million programme to extend their capability into the mid-1990s. The original search radar is replaced by a new Texas Instruments system with digital cockpit display. A new Loral ESM system, installed in the wingtip pods, has increased frequency range, improved direction finding accuracy and automatic analysis. Passive underwater sonar detection is improved by means of an Emerson Electric 8-channel modification kit with increased frequency range and digital signal processing. A new Dornier sonobuoy launcher replaces the original rotary launcher; and all these improvements are backed up by replacing the former tape recorder with a new IRIG standard model, and adding a Litton LN-33 second navigation system with Decca updated inertial platform, primarily for tactical navigation.

EXTRA

EXTRA-FLUGZEUGBAU

Flugplatz Dinslaken, 4224 Hünxe
Telephone: (02858) 6851
MANAGING DIRECTOR: Walter Extra

EXTRA 230

This single-seat aerobatic monoplane was designed by Walter Extra for high performance competition work. First flight was made on 14 July 1983 by the second aircraft (D-EJNC), with the first (D-EKEW) following shortly after. The third Extra 230 (D-EHLE) was purchased by members of the Swiss national aerobatic team, and by March 1987 a total of 12 complete aircraft and two in kit form had been sold. No 1988 total was received.

TYPE: Single-seat aerobatic aircraft.

WINGS: Cantilever mid-wing monoplane. Tapered wings, with square-cut tips and thick trailing-edge. Root and tip aerofoil sections of MA 15S and MA 12S respectively, resulting in a wing with virtually no curvature except on leading-edge. Incidence 0°. Structure comprises a box spar of high strength Polish pine, with pine capstrips and 'solid' ribs, covered with Dacron fabric and doped with

US registered Extra 230 flown in the 1986 World Aerobatic Championships *(Austin J. Brown)*

an acrylic urethane paint. Long span ailerons (±26° deflection) occupy approx three-quarters of each trailing-edge. No flaps.

FUSELAGE: Steel tube mainframe, with aluminium alloy skin at front and on top-decking. Rear section covering similar to that of wings.

TAIL UNIT: Conventional wire braced structure of steel tube and bent sheet metal ribs; all parts fabric covered. Horn balanced rudder. Trim tab and servo tab in elevators. All control surfaces ±26° deflection.

LANDING GEAR: Non-retractable tailwheel type, with main-wheel units essentially similar to those of Christen Pitts Special, and Haigh steerable tailwheel. Mainwheel fairings optional.

POWER PLANT: One 149 kW (200 hp) Textron Lycoming AEIO-360-A1E flat-four engine (DeMars modification). Mühlbauer two-blade constant-speed propeller, with composites-skinned wooden blades, McCauley hub, and large spinner. 12V battery for electric engine starting. Fuel capacity 80 litres (21.1 US gallons; 17.5 Imp gallons).

ACCOMMODATION: Single seat, under one-piece canopy which opens sideways to starboard.

DIMENSIONS, EXTERNAL:
Wing span	7.40 m (24 ft 3⅓ in)
Length overall	5.82 m (19 ft 1¼ in)
Height overall	1.73 m (5 ft 8¼ in)

WEIGHTS:
Weight empty	440 kg (970 lb)
Max T-O weight	560 kg (1,234 lb)

PERFORMANCE:
Never-exceed speed	220 knots (407 km/h; 253 mph)
Max level speed	190 knots (352 km/h; 218 mph) IAS
Stalling speed	38 knots (71 km/h; 44 mph) IAS
Max rate of climb at S/L	900 m (2,950 ft)/min
Roll rate at 160 knots (296 km/h; 184 mph) IAS	200°/s
T-O run	50 m (164 ft)
Endurance with max fuel	2 h 30 min
g limits	±10

GROB
BURKHART GROB FLUGZEUGBAU
(Division of Grob-Werke GmbH & Co KG)
Postfach 150, 8948 Mindelheim
Telephone: (082) 68 411
Telex: 5 39 623

Grob was founded in 1972, employs about 180 people, and has built about 3,000 aircraft. In addition to the G 115 and 116 described in this entry, Grob manufactured the airframe of the high-altitude Egrett-1 described in the International section.

GROB G 115

The first prototype of this light aircraft made its initial flight in November 1985, powered by an O-235 engine with fixed-pitch propeller. The second prototype, which flew in the Spring of 1986, was similarly powered, but had a variable-pitch propeller, a taller fin and rudder and relocated tailplane. The latter version is now in production as the **G 115A**. The third prototype, first flown in 1986, represented the **G 115B**, having an uprated (O-320) engine.

The G 115A was certificated to FAR Pt 23 standards by the LBA on 31 March 1987 and by the British CAA in May 1988. Deliveries began in mid-1987 and totalled about 40, of 60 ordered, by May 1988. Most of those sold at that time were G 115As. The G 115B has glider towing capability.

TYPE: Two-seat light aircraft.

AIRFRAME: Cantilever low-wing monoplane with non-retractable tricycle landing gear (speed fairings on 160 hp version). Construction mainly of GRP.

POWER PLANT: One 85.8 kW (115 hp) Textron Lycoming O-235-H2C flat-four engine in G 115A, driving a two-blade fixed-pitch propeller with spinner; 86.5 kW (116 hp) O-235-P1 and variable-pitch propeller optional. One 112 kW (150 hp) Textron Lycoming O-320-E2A with v-p propeller in G 115B. Fuel capacity 100 litres (26.4 US gallons; 22 Imp gallons) in 115A/B.

ACCOMMODATION: Two seats side by side under one-piece rearward sliding framed canopy, with dual controls. Baggage space behind seats.

AVIONICS: To customer's requirements. Instrument panel will accommodate full IFR instrumentation.

DIMENSIONS, EXTERNAL:
Wing span	10.00 m (32 ft 9¾ in)
Wing aspect ratio	8.2
Length overall	7.36 m (24 ft 1¾ in)
Height overall: A	2.75 m (9 ft 0¼ in)
B	2.82 m (9 ft 3 in)

AREA:
Wings, gross	12.21 m² (131.4 sq ft)

WEIGHTS AND LOADINGS:
Basic weight empty: A	590 kg (1,301 lb)
B	620 kg (1,367 lb)
Fuel weight: A, B	72 kg (159 lb)
Max T-O weight: A, B	850 kg (1,874 lb)
Max wing loading: A, B	69.61 kg/m² (14.26 lb/sq ft)
Max power loading: A (115 hp)	9.91 kg/kW (16.30 lb/hp)
A (116 hp)	9.83 kg/kW (16.15 lb/hp)
B	8.04 kg/kW (13.23 lb/hp)

PERFORMANCE (at max T-O weight):
Max level speed: A	119 knots (220 km/h; 137 mph)
B	135 knots (250 km/h; 155 mph)
Cruising speed, 75% power:	
A	110 knots (205 km/h; 127 mph)
B	121 knots (225 km/h; 140 mph)
Stalling speed: A	45 knots (83 km/h; 52 mph)
B	47 knots (87 km/h; 54 mph)
Max rate of climb at S/L: A	210 m (689 ft)/min
B	305 m (1,000 ft)/min
T-O run: A	250 m (820 ft)
B	210 m (689 ft)
T-O to 15 m (50 ft): A	420 m (1,378 ft)
B	390 m (1,280 ft)
Range with max fuel (approx):	
A	540 nm (1,000 km; 621 miles)
B	394 nm (730 km; 453 miles)

GROB G 116

The G 116 is essentially a four-seat (2 + 2) version of the G 115, with a higher powered engine. First flight of the prototype (D-EGRF) took place on 29 April 1988, and certification is anticipated in Spring 1989.

Grob G 115B two-seat light aircraft *(Peter F. Selinger)*

Four-seat Grob G 116 (Textron Lycoming O-360 engine) *(Peter F. Selinger)*

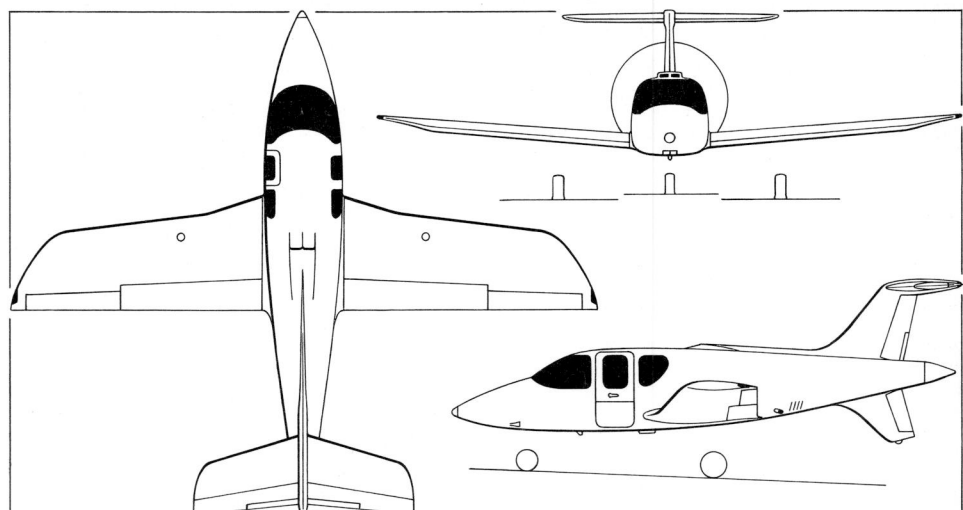

Grob GF 200 all-composites four-seat light aircraft *(Jane's / Mike Keep)*

POWER PLANT: One 134 kW (180 hp) Textron Lycoming O-360 flat-four engine, driving a three-blade propeller with spinner. Fuel capacity 200 litres (52.8 US gallons; 44 Imp gallons).

DIMENSIONS, EXTERNAL:
Wing span	11.00 m (36 ft 1 in)
Wing aspect ratio	7.8
Length overall	8.50 m (27 ft 10½ in)
Height overall	3.00 m (9 ft 10 in)

AREA:
Wings, gross	15.50 m² (166.8 sq ft)

WEIGHTS AND LOADINGS:
Weight empty	710 kg (1,565 lb)
Fuel weight	144 kg (317 lb)
Max T-O weight	1,198 kg (2,641 lb)
Max wing loading	77.3 kg/m² (15.83 lb/sq ft)
Max power loading	8.93 kg/kW (14.67 lb/hp)

PERFORMANCE (estimated, at max T-O weight):
Max level speed	154 knots (285 km/h; 177 mph)
Cruising speed, 75% power	137 knots (255 km/h; 158 mph)
Stalling speed	48 knots (88 km/h; 55 mph)
Max rate of climb at S/L	288 m (945 ft)/min
T-O run	265 m (869 ft)
T-O to 15 m (50 ft)	410 m (1,345 ft)
Range with max fuel	647 nm (1,200 km; 745 miles)

GROB GF 200

Grob announced this new four-seat all-composites high-performance aircraft in early 1988, displaying a full size mockup in May at the Hanover Air Show. First flight is planned for 1989, and the aircraft will have a pressurised cabin, a choice of Porsche PFM 3200 flat-six engines (164 kW; 220 hp normally aspirated N 03 or 182.7 kW; 245 hp turbocharged T 03), three-blade pusher propeller, and standard fuel capacity of 250 litres (66 US gallons; 55 Imp gallons) in integral wing tanks. Optional long-range tanks (combined capacity 340 litres; 90 US gallons; 74.8 Imp gallons) will be available for the turbocharged version.

General appearance of the GF 200 is shown in the accompanying three-view drawing.

DIMENSIONS, EXTERNAL:
- Wing span: 9.60 m (31 ft 6 in)
- Wing aspect ratio: 6.4
- Length overall: 8.25 m (27 ft 0¾ in)
- Height overall: 3.20 m (10 ft 6 in)

DIMENSIONS, INTERNAL:
- Cabin: Max width: 1.22 m (4 ft 0 in)
- Max height: 1.20 m (3 ft 11¼ in)

AREA:
- Wings, gross: 14.40 m² (155.0 sq ft)

WEIGHTS:
- Basic weight empty: 850 kg (1,874 lb)
- Max fuel weight: 180 kg (397 lb)
- Max T-O weight: 1,400 kg (3,086 lb)

PERFORMANCE (at max T-O weight, T 03 engine):
- Max level speed at 6,700 m (22,000 ft): 218 knots (404 km/h; 251 mph)
- Max cruising speed at 5,485 m (18,000 ft), 75% power: 195 knots (361 km/h; 224 mph)
- Econ cruising speed at 5,485 m (18,000 ft), 55% power: 175 knots (324 km/h; 201 mph)
- Max rate of climb at S/L: 396 m (1,300 ft)/min
- Service ceiling: 8,535 m (28,000 ft)
- T-O run: 290 m (950 ft)
- T-O to 15 m (50 ft): 450 m (1,476 ft)
- Landing from 15 m (50 ft): 480 m (1,575 ft)
- Landing run: 220 m (722 ft)
- Range at 5,485 m (18,000 ft), 75% power, with 340 litres of fuel: 1,274 nm (2,361 km; 1,467 miles)

GYROFLUG

GYROFLUG INGENIEURGESELLSCHAFT mbH

Flugplatz, 7947 Mengen
Telephone: (07572) 5081
Telex: 732 543 SCAV D
Fax: (07572) 1689

PRESIDENT AND MANAGING DIRECTOR: Dipl-Ing Justus Dornier

DIRECTOR, SALES AND MARKETING: Wolfgang Müller

CHIEF ENGINEER: Dipl-Ing Rudolf Voit-Nitschmann

Dipl-Ing Peter Krauss and Herr Jörg Elzenbeck built, and in April 1977 flew for the first time, the first Rutan VariEze two-seat homebuilt aircraft to be completed in Europe (D-EEEZ). They decided to develop, manufacture and market a similar aircraft, known as the Speed Canard, as a ready to fly, certificated production aircraft that would conform to the requirements of FAR Pt 23. In August 1978, with Dipl-Ing Wolfgang Schiller, they formed Gyroflug for this purpose. At the end of 1984 the company became a member of the Justus Dornier Group. In September 1987 Gyroflug moved to its present location in Mengen, where a new factory complex is being built. The 35 person workforce moved into its new production quarters in May 1988.

GYROFLUG SC 01 B SPEED CANARD

As well as being slightly larger overall than the Rutan VariEze, the Speed Canard differs in a number of important details, as noted in the 1987-88 *Jane's*. Wings and other GRP/CFRP components, manufactured initially by Glaser-Dirks, are now produced by Gyroflug.

Construction of the first prototype (D-EEEX, c/n A-1) began in late 1978, and this aircraft made its first flight on 2 December 1980. Initial test flights revealed the need for a number of design changes before it could be approved for series production. Of these, the principal one was the adoption of a new Eppler aerofoil section, claimed to give a 30 per cent reduction in drag, and a new 'first' flight with this modified wing was made by D-EEEX on 10 July 1981. A second airframe was completed for static testing, followed by a second flying prototype (D-EEEW, c/n A-3), which made its initial flight on 17 April 1983 and enabled the Speed Canard to receive German LBA type certification on 30 September that year.

Series production began with the fourth aircraft (D-EELZ, c/n S-4), and 20 examples of this initial version were built by September 1985 for customers in Germany (17), Switzerland (2), and Belgium (1). As built with the standard O-235 engine, they are designated **SC-01**; some examples have been retrofitted with the more powerful O-320 engine, in which form they are known as the **SC 01-160**. Their details can be found in the 1987-88 *Jane's*.

Beginning with c/n S-24, current production models are designated **SC 01 B** (O-235 engine) and **SC 01 B-160** (O-320 engine). These versions, which first flew in the Summer of 1985 and received LBA certification on 26 March 1986, have winglets of increased area, plus other minor improvements. A number of earlier Speed Canards have also been modified to the current B/B-160 standard. A **GT** version of the SC 01 B-160 was introduced in 1987; this has VFR avionics as standard.

The Speed Canard is certificated in West Germany, Switzerland, Scandjnavia and the Benelux countries. British, French and American certification was anticipated during the Summer of 1988. A total of 45 B/B-160s had been ordered by April 1988, at which time production (which is to order) was at the approximate rate of one per month.

Gyroflug SC 01 B-160 Speed Canard two-seat light aircraft

TYPE: Two-seat sporting aircraft.

WINGS: Cantilever mid-wing monoplane. Short-span centre-section strakes, sweptback approx 60° on leading-edges, without anhedral or dihedral. Main wings have an Eppler E793 aerofoil section, with thickness/chord ratio of 15.6%, anhedral angle of 5° 54', and 22° sweepback at quarter-chord. Single-spar structure of GRP and CFRP, without ribs. Each wingtip is upswept at nearly 90° to form a slightly outward canted NASA type winglet with inset rudder. Centrally located aileron in each wing trailing-edge. No flaps. No aileron or rudder tabs. Main wings are detachable for transportation and storage.

FOREPLANE: Narrow-chord cantilever structure, of Eppler E1231 aerofoil section, mounted high on nose. Balanced elevator, with fixed tab near inboard end, on each trailing-edge. Construction (GRP and CFRP) similar to that of wings.

FUSELAGE: Non-pressurised oval-section nacelle type, of GRP composites construction.

LANDING GEAR: Tricycle type, with fixed main units and electrically retractable nosewheel which is carried on a carbon/Kevlar strut moulded to conform to the outside contour of the fuselage, eliminating need for a fairing door. Main units, carried on cantilever self-sprung carbon/Kevlar struts, are fitted with Cleveland wheels (tyre size 5.00-5), Cleveland disc brakes, and speed fairings. The Scott nosewheel, which retracts rearward, is fitted with a size 10 × 3.5-4 tyre. Nosewheel strut is hinged to allow aircraft to be parked in a 'kneeling' position with only the wheel exposed.

POWER PLANT (SC 01 B): One 86.5 kW (116 hp) Textron Lycoming O-235-P2A flat-four engine, mounted in the rear fuselage and driving a Hoffmann HO-V113B-L/LD 150+2A three (composites)-blade variable-pitch pusher propeller with spinner. Fuel in two integral tanks (one in each wing centre-section strake) with combined capacity of 160 litres (42.3 US gallons; 35.2 Imp gallons). Oil capacity 6 litres (1.58 US gallons; 1.32 Imp gallons).

POWER PLANT (SC 01 B-160): One 119 kW (160 hp) Textron Lycoming O-320-D1A flat-four engine, driving an MT-Propeller (Mühlbauer) MTV-6-C/LD 152-07 three-blade variable-pitch propeller. Fuel capacity as for lower powered version. Oil capacity 8 litres (2.11 US gallons; 1.76 Imp gallons).

ACCOMMODATION: Pilot and passenger in tandem, on semi-reclining seats in individual cockpits. Side-stick controls. Separate one-piece moulded canopies, both opening sideways to starboard. Space for 15 kg (33 lb) of baggage aft of rear seat. Both cockpits heated and ventilated.

ELECTRICAL SYSTEM: Alternator to provide power to actuate nosewheel extension/retraction mechanism.

AVIONICS AND EQUIPMENT: To customer's requirements except for GT, which has VFR instrumentation as standard. Can be equipped to full IFR standard, including autopilot, two com/nav, ILS, ADF, artificial horizon, turn and bank indicator and heading gyro.

DIMENSIONS, EXTERNAL:
- Wing span: 7.77 m (25 ft 6 in)
- Foreplane span: 3.60 m (11 ft 9¾ in)
- Foreplane chord, constant: 0.34 m (1 ft 1¾ in)
- Wing aspect ratio: 7.7
- Foreplane aspect ratio: 10.6
- Length overall: 4.70 m (15 ft 5 in)
- Fuselage: Length: 4.40 m (14 ft 5¼ in)
  - Max width: 0.74 m (2 ft 5 in)
  - Max depth: 1.06 m (3 ft 5¾ in)
- Height overall: 1.81 m (5 ft 11¼ in)
- Wheel track: 1.66 m (5 ft 5¼ in)
- Wheelbase: 2.47 m (8 ft 1¼ in)
- Propeller diameter: 1.52 m (5 ft 0 in)
- Propeller ground clearance: 0.31 m (1 ft 0¼ in)

DIMENSIONS, INTERNAL:
- Cockpits: Max combined length: 2.80 m (9 ft 2¼ in)
  - Max width: 0.64 m (2 ft 1¼ in)
  - Max height: 0.99 m (3 ft 3 in)

AREAS:
- Wings, gross: 7.84 m² (84.39 sq ft)
- Foreplane, gross: 1.22 m² (13.13 sq ft)
- Ailerons (total): 0.376 m² (4.05 sq ft)
- Winglets (total): 2.20 m² (23.68 sq ft)
- Rudders (total): 0.168 m² (1.81 sq ft)
- Elevators (total, incl tabs): 0.33 m² (3.55 sq ft)

WEIGHTS AND LOADINGS (A: with O-235, B: with O-320 engine):
- Weight empty: A: 420 kg (926 lb)
  - B: 440 kg (970 lb)
- Max fuel: A, B: 115 kg (253 lb)
- Max payload with 100 litres (26.4 US gallons; 22 Imp gallons) fuel: A: 188 kg (414.5 lb)
  - B: 204 kg (450 lb)
- Max T-O weight: A: 680 kg (1,499 lb)
  - B: 715 kg (1,576 lb)
- Max landing weight: A, B: 680 kg (1,499 lb)
- Max wing/foreplane loading:
  - A: 75.05 kg/m² (15.38 lb/sq ft)
  - B: 78.92 kg/m² (16.16 lb/sq ft)
- Max power loading: A: 7.86 kg/kW (12.92 lb/hp)
  - B: 6.01 kg/kW (9.85 lb/hp)

PERFORMANCE (at max T-O weight, A and B as above):
- Never-exceed speed:
  - A, B: 197 knots (365 km/h; 226 mph) IAS
- Max level speed at S/L:
  - A: 146 knots (270 km/h; 168 mph)
  - B: 159 knots (295 km/h; 183 mph)
- Max cruising speed, 75% power:
  - A at 1,830 m (6,000 ft): 143 knots (265 km/h; 165 mph)
  - B at 2,135 m (7,000 ft): 154 knots (285 km/h; 177 mph) IAS
- Econ cruising speed, 65% power:
  - A at 3,050 m (10,000 ft): 138 knots (257 km/h; 160 mph)
  - B at 3,350 m (11,000 ft): 148 knots (275 km/h; 171 mph)
- Stalling speed: A, B: 57 knots (105 km/h; 66 mph) IAS
- Max rate of climb at S/L: A: 300 m (985 ft)/min
  - B: 396 m (1,300 ft)/min
- Service ceiling: A: 4,420 m (14,500 ft)
  - B: 5,640 m (18,500 ft)
- T-O run: A: 450 m (1,475 ft)
  - B: 350 m (1,150 ft)
- T-O to 15 m (50 ft): A: 700 m (2,300 ft)
  - B: 540 m (1,770 ft)
- Landing from 15 m (50 ft): A, B: 700 m (2,300 ft)
- Landing run: A, B: 300 m (985 ft)
- Range with max fuel, no reserves:
  - 55% power: A: 1,025 nm (1,900 km; 1,180 miles)
  - B: 815 nm (1,510 km; 938 miles)
- Range at S/L with max fuel, 45 min reserves:
  - 75% power: A: 728 nm (1,350 km; 839 miles)
  - B: 553 nm (1,025 km; 637 miles)
  - 45% power: A: 1,011 nm (1,875 km; 1,165 miles)
  - B: 715 nm (1,325 km; 823 miles)
- *g* limits: A: +4.4/−2.2
  - B: +3.8/−2.2

GYROFLUG E 400

Gyroflug announced brief details of this four/five-seat derivative of the Speed Canard in April 1987, originally under the project study designation E 401. Powered by a 182.7 kW (245 hp) Porsche turbocharged engine driving a three-blade pusher propeller, it will have a cruising speed (75% power) of more than 200 knots (370 km/h; 230 mph) at 6,100 m (20,000 ft) and a range of more than 1,079 nm (2,000 km; 1,242 miles). It is not planned to fly a prototype until 1992, with production starting in late 1994 or early 1995. Eventual configuration may differ from that illustrated in the 1987-88 *Jane's*.

HOFFMANN

WOLF HOFFMANN FLUGZEUGBAU KG

Sportflugplatz, 8870 Günzburg/Ulm
Telephone: (08221) 1417
Telex: 531625 HOFBG D
Fax: (08221) 32034
DIRECTOR: Dipl-Ing Wolf D. Hoffmann
Mr Hoffmann, designer of the Dimona motor glider (see Sailplanes section), is developing a two-seat light aircraft known as the H-40.

HOFFMANN H-40

Design and construction of the H-40 began in 1986. The prototype (D-EIOF) was exhibited at the Hanover Air Show in May 1988 and was expected to make its first flight shortly afterwards.
TYPE: Two-seat light aircraft.
WINGS: Cantilever low-wing monoplane. Wortmann FX-63-137 section. Dihedral 4°. Incidence 2°. Sweepforward 3° at quarter-chord. Single-spar glassfibre structure, with sandwich skin. Carbonfibre split flaps on trailing-edge; ailerons of glassfibre and carbonfibre. No tabs.
FUSELAGE: Glassfibre semi-monocoque structure, with sandwich tailboom.
TAIL UNIT: Cantilever T tail, of similar glassfibre/sandwich construction to wings. Fixed incidence tailplane. Trim tab in elevator.
LANDING GEAR: Non-retractable tricycle type, with steel plate spring shock absorption on main units. All units have Cleveland wheels and Goodyear tyres, size 380 × 150 (6.00-5) on main gear, 40-78 (5.00-5) on nose unit. Cleveland 30-5 mainwheel brakes.
POWER PLANT: One 71 kW (95 hp) Limbach L 2400 DB1 engine, driving a Mühlbauer MTV-1 two-blade fixed-pitch (optionally constant-speed) propeller with spinner. Fuel in two wing tanks, combined capacity 100 litres (26.4 US gallons; 22 Imp gallons). Overwing gravity refuelling.
ACCOMMODATION: Side by side seats for pilot and passenger. 'Gull wing' window/doors, hinged on centreline and opening upward.

Prototype Hoffmann H-40 (71 kW; 95 hp Limbach L 2400 DB1 engine) *(Peter F. Selinger)*

DIMENSIONS, EXTERNAL:
Wing span	10.84 m (35 ft 6¾ in)
Wing chord: at root	1.34 m (4 ft 4¾ in)
at tip	0.94 m (3 ft 1 in)
Wing aspect ratio	8.6
Length overall	6.99 m (22 ft 11¼ in)
Fuselage: Max width	1.20 m (3 ft 11¼ in)
Height overall	2.39 m (7 ft 10 in)
Tailplane span	3.00 m (9 ft 10 in)
Wheel track	2.00 m (6 ft 6¾ in)
Propeller diameter	1.60 m (5 ft 3 in)
Propeller ground clearance	0.20 m (8 in)

AREAS:
Wings, gross	13.62 m² (146.6 sq ft)
Ailerons (total)	0.912 m² (9.82 sq ft)
Trailing-edge flaps (total)	1.072 m² (11.54 sq ft)
Fin	1.17 m² (12.59 sq ft)
Rudder	0.47 m² (5.06 sq ft)
Tailplane	1.80 m² (19.38 sq ft)
Elevators (total)	0.54 m² (5.81 sq ft)

WEIGHTS AND LOADINGS:
Basic weight empty	530 kg (1,168 lb)
Max fuel weight	72 kg (159 lb)
Max T-O weight	800 kg (1,764 lb)
Max wing loading	58.74 kg/m² (12.03 lb/sq ft)
Max power loading	11.94 kg/kW (19.60 lb/hp)

PERFORMANCE (estimated, at max T-O weight):
Never-exceed speed	148 knots (275 km/h; 171 mph)
Max cruising speed	113 knots (210 km/h; 130 mph)
Stalling speed, power on, flaps down	42 knots (78 km/h; 49 mph)
Max rate of climb at S/L	240 m (787 ft)/min
Service ceiling	5,485 m (18,000 ft)
T-O run	180 m (590 ft)
T-O to and landing from 15 m (50 ft)	300 m (985 ft)
Range with max fuel	647 nm (1,200 km; 745 miles)

MBB

MESSERSCHMITT-BÖLKOW-BLOHM GmbH

Postfach 801109, 8000 Munich 80
Telephone: (089) 6000 0
Telex: 5287-310 MBB D
In May 1969 the former Messerschmitt-Bölkow GmbH and Hamburger Flugzeugbau GmbH (see 1968-69 *Jane's*) merged to form a new group known as Messerschmitt-Bölkow-Blohm GmbH. MBB acquired all shares of VFW on 1 January 1981. Current shareholders in MBB are Bayerisch-Hamburgische Beteiligungsgesellschaft mbH (35.28%), Fides Industrie-Beteiligungsgesellschaft mbH (20%), ABM Beteiligungsgesellschaft mbH (19.02%), BD Industrie-Beteiligungsgesellschaft mbH (10%), the State of Bavaria (7.02%), the Willy and Lilly Messerschmitt Foundation (7%), Dr-Ing h.c. Ludwig Bölkow (1%), and the Blohm family (0.68%). The MBB group employed approx 37,000 people in 1987.

HELICOPTER AND MILITARY AIRCRAFT GROUP
(Helicopter Division and Military Aircraft Division)
See this page
Helicopter activities of this Group include civil and military versions of the MBB BO 105 and MBB/Kawasaki BK 117, participation in the Eurocopter and NH 90 programmes (described in the International section), and the ALH programme in co-operation with Hindustan Aeronautics Ltd (see Indian section). Main centre for the BO 105 and BK 117 is MBB's Donauwörth factory. The Division also overhauls and repairs Sikorsky CH-53G and Westland Sea King Mk 41 helicopters in service with the West German armed forces, and is currently upgrading 22 German Navy Sea Kings with Ferranti Seaspray Mk 3 radar, a Ferranti Link II target data transformer, AEG ALR-69 radar warning receiver, Tracor M130 chaff/flare dispenser and four BAe Sea Skua missiles.
Major military aircraft activities of the Group involve the Panavia Tornado (see International section), for which MBB is the German prime contractor; modifications to improve the combat capability of Luftwaffe F-4F and RF-4E Phantoms; and participation in the European manufacturing programme for the General Dynamics F-16 combat aircraft.
The company has been engaged for a considerable time in intensive studies to define a new generation tactical fighter aircraft for the Luftwaffe and other European air forces in the 1990s (see Eurofighter entry in International section). In addition, it is conducting research and development programmes concerned with carbonfibre technology, and the creation of more simple, more reliable aircraft subsystems.

TRANSPORT AIRCRAFT GROUP
See page 94
MBB's Transport Aircraft Group, with 13,600 employees in six factories in northern Germany, is involved in manufacture and development for several international European collaborative programmes, including the Airbus A300/310/320 (68% of the group's workload), Fokker 100 (5%), Panavia Tornado (15%), and miscellaneous programmes. Maintenance and conversion work on Airbus and other aircraft, for customers throughout the world, is carried out at Lemwerder as part of MBB's product support activities. Airspares in Hamburg provides a worldwide 24 h spares service for the company. Spoilers and rudders of carbonfibre reinforced plastics (CFRP) are produced for Airbus aircraft, and the fin box for the A310, designed and manufactured by MBB, is currently the largest CFRP aircraft component made in Europe. The A320 is fitted with CFRP horizontal and vertical tail surfaces, which save 25 per cent in weight compared to metal equivalents and also minimise corrosion.

DEFENCE SYSTEMS GROUP
(Guided Missiles Division, Ballistic and Dispenser Systems Division, and Marine and Special Products Division)
GUIDED MISSILES DIVISION AND BALLISTIC & DISPENSER SYSTEMS DIVISION:
Postfach 801149, 8000 Munich 80
Telephone: (089) 6000 6056
Telex: 5287-0 MBB D
MARINE AND SPECIAL PRODUCTS DIVISION:
Postfach 107845, 2800 Bremen 1
Telephone: (0421) 538-1
Telex: 245821 MBB D
WORKS: Ottobrunn, Bremen, Kassel, Nabern/Teck and Schrobenhausen
Missile programmes on which the Defence Systems Group is engaged include those for the air-launched MBB Kormoran, Euromissile Hot and Aérospatiale/MBB ANS. Others include the surface-launched Hot, Milan, MLRS, Patriot, Roland and RAM. The Group also produces a special type of conventional weapon system, designated MW-1, which is carried by the Tornado.
Marine and Special Products Division is involved extensively in RPV development (KZO/Brevel, DAR and KDH), and in diversified MBB activities which include airborne subsystems, training systems and simulators, measuring and tracking systems, test and automation systems, and logistics.

SPACE SYSTEMS GROUP (MBB/ERNO)
Postfach 105909, 2800 Bremen 1
Telephone: (0421) 539 4348
Telex: 245548A ERNO D
Postfach 801169, 8000 Munich 80
Telephone: (089) 6000 3738
Telex: 5287-0 MBB D
WORKS: Bremen and Ottobrunn
Details of this Group's recent and current space programme activities can be found in the Spaceflight section of the 1983-84 and earlier editions of *Jane's*, and currently in *Jane's Spaceflight Directory*.

INDUSTRIAL PRODUCTS GROUP
Postfach 801109, 8000 Munich 80

ENERGY AND PROCESS TECHNOLOGY DIVISION
Postfach 801109, 8000 Munich 80

HELICOPTER AND MILITARY AIRCRAFT GROUP

Postfach 801160, 8000 Munich 80
Telephone: (089) 6000 6488/5711
Telex: 5287-071/074 MBB D
WORKS: Ottobrunn, Donauwörth, Augsburg, Manching, Laupheim and Speyer

PUBLIC RELATIONS:
Christina Gotzhein (Helicopter Division)
Wolfram Wolff (Military Aircraft Division)

MBB/KAWASAKI BK 117
MBB is building in conjunction with Kawasaki of Japan an 8/11-seat multi-purpose helicopter known as the BK 117. The main description of this aircraft can be found in the International section; details of the all-German military BK 117 M are given in this entry, after the description of the BO 105.

NTT BN-109
The BN-109 is a small four-seat helicopter being developed by MBB in collaboration with IPTN of Indonesia (see NTT entry in International section).

EUROCOPTER HAP and PAH-2/HAC
The programme for this Franco-German common anti-tank helicopter is described under the Eurocopter heading in the International section.

NH 90
This four-nation programme (NATO helicopter for the 1990s) is described under the NH 90 heading in the International section.

MBB BO 105
The first prototype of this light utility helicopter was fitted with an existing conventional rotor and two Allison

250-C18 turboshafts; subsequent aircraft, of which the first one flew on 16 February 1967, have had a rotor system based on a rigid titanium hub, with feathering hinges only, and hingeless flexible glassfibre blades.

Details of prototypes, early BO 105C and D production helicopters and special variants can be found in previous editions of *Jane's*. Production of 100 BO 105 M (VBH) and 212 BO 105 P (PAH-1) military versions for the Federal German Army ended in 1984, and details of these versions can be found in the 1985-86 edition. MBB is currently preparing for a PAH-1 upgrade programme that includes retrofit with Allison 250-C20R-3 engines, new rotor blades of improved aerofoil section, a Hot 2 missile system with digital guidance, and new lightweight launching system and suspension racks. Changes would allow a max T-O weight increase from 2,400 kg (5,291 lb) to 2,500 kg (5,511 lb), effectively increasing payload capacity by 135 kg (297.5 lb). This would permit either an increase in fuel load or integration of a Leitz/Eltro/MBB night vision system for the pilot and gunner. Upgrading of 209 in-service PAH-1s is to begin in 1990, with the night vision system and improved self-defence capability following in 1992.

BO 105s in use as military testbeds in early 1988 included one being used by MBB to flight test an AEG mast mounted radar system, and one being fitted by Lucas Aerospace in the UK with a bolt-on undernose turret that would permit off-axis firing of Stinger air-to-air missiles, controlled by a Ferranti helmet pointing system. Due to fly during 1988, the Lucas modification may be proposed as a possible upgrade for the German Army's VBH escort helicopters.

By 1 January 1988 more than 1,200 BO 105s of all models had been delivered, to 37 countries in five continents. All BO 105 component manufacture is now undertaken in Indonesia by IPTN (which see). Current models are as follows:

Swedish Army MBB BO 105 CB helicopter equipped with Saab-Emerson HeliTOW anti-tank system

BO 105 CB. Standard production version since 1975, with two Allison 250-C20B engines, operable in air temperatures ranging from –45° to +54°C. LBA certification received in November 1976. Details of specially equipped versions for the Mexican Navy (12) and Swedish Army (20) were given in the 1987-88 *Jane's*. The latter are being delivered at the rate of three per month (beginning on 22 September 1987) to FFV Aerotech in Sweden for weapons installation. In Spain, CASA assembled 57 of an initial 60 for the Spanish Army for armed reconnaissance (18), observation (14) and anti-tank missions (28), and is

currently assembling a further undisclosed number.

BO 105 CBS. Version with increased seating or cargo capacity in a 0.25 m (10 in) longer fuselage. Available in five-seat executive or six-seat high density configurations. Identified by small additional window aft of rear door on each side. Marketed in the USA, by MBB Helicopter Corporation, under the name **Twin Jet II**. Certificated in early 1983 by FAA for IFR operation in accordance with SFAR Pt 29-4, requiring two pilots, radar, Loran-C and a separate battery, but not a stability augmentation system, though SAS is available as an option. The Swedish Air Force has four BO 105 CBSs, equipped to IFR search and rescue configuration.

BO 105 LS. Now produced in Canada and described separately under MBB entry in Canadian section. Five pre-production models produced in Germany during 1984.

The description which follows applies to the BO 105 CB except where indicated:

TYPE: Five-seat light helicopter.

ROTOR SYSTEM: Four-blade main rotor, comprising rigid titanium head and GRP blades, with titanium anti-erosion strip forming leading-edge and vibration damper on each blade. MBB designed 'droop-snoot' blades of NACA 23012 asymmetrical section, having a specially designed trailing-edge giving improved control in pitching moment. Flexible tension/torsion blade retention, to take up centrifugal forces. Roller bearings for pitch change. Main rotor blade folding optional. Two-blade semi-rigid tail rotor; blades of GRP, with stainless steel anti-erosion strip on leading-edge. Main rotor rpm 424. Tail rotor rpm 2,220.

ROTOR DRIVE: Main transmission utilises two bevel gear input stages with freewheeling clutches and a spur collector gear stage. Planetary reduction gear; three auxiliary drives for accessories. Main transmission rated for twin-engine input of 257 kW (345 shp) per engine, or a single engine input of 283 kW (380 shp). Main rotor brake standard. Tail rotor gearbox on fin. Main rotor/engine rpm ratio 1 : 14.2. Tail rotor/engine rpm ratio 1 : 2.7.

FUSELAGE: Conventional light alloy semi-monocoque structure of pod and boom type. Glassfibre reinforced cowling over power plant. Titanium sheet engine deck.

TAIL UNIT: Horizontal stabiliser of conventional light alloy construction with small endplate fins.

LANDING GEAR: Skid type, with cross-tubes designed for energy absorption by plastic deformation in the event of a heavy landing. Inflatable emergency floats can be attached to skids.

POWER PLANT: Two 313 kW (420 shp) Allison 250-C20B turboshafts, each with a max continuous rating of 298 kW (400 shp). Bladder fuel tanks under cabin floor, capacity 580 litres (153.2 US gallons; 127.5 Imp gallons), of which 570 litres (150.6 US gallons; 125.3 Imp gallons) are usable. Fuelling point on port side of cabin. Auxiliary tanks in freight compartment available optionally. Oil capacity: engine 12 litres (3.2 US gallons; 2.6 Imp gallons), gearbox 11.6 litres (3.06 US gallons; 2.55 Imp gallons).

ACCOMMODATION: Pilot and co-pilot or passenger on individual longitudinally adjustable front seats with safety belts and automatic locking shoulder harnesses. Optional dual controls. Bench seat at rear for three persons, removable for cargo and stretcher carrying. Both cabin and cargo compartment have panelling, sound insulation and floor covering. Entire rear fuselage aft of seats and under power plant available as freight and baggage space, with access through two clamshell doors at rear. Two standard stretchers can be accommodated side by side in ambulance role. One forward opening hinged and jettisonable door and one sliding door on each side of cabin. Ram air and electrical ventilation system. Heating system optional.

SYSTEMS: Tandem fully redundant hydraulic system, pressure 103.5 bars (1,500 lb/sq in), for powered main rotor controls. System flow rate 6.2 litres (1.64 US gallons; 1.36

CBS version of the BO 105 operated by the Devon and Cornwall police in England

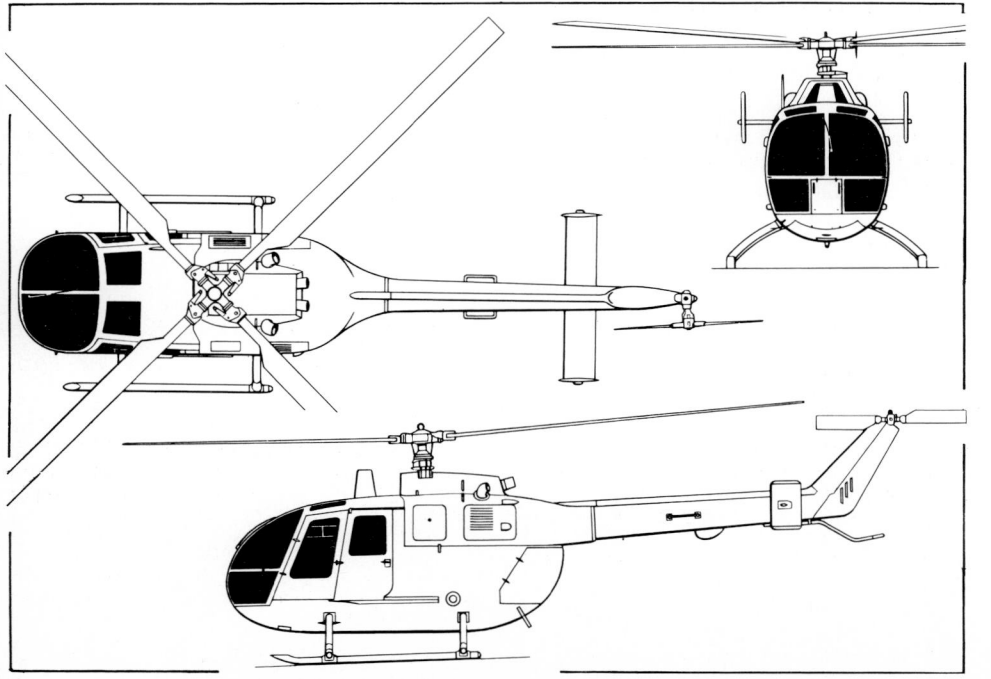

BO 105 CB five-seat light helicopter (two Allison 250-C20B turboshafts) *(Pilot Press)*

Imp gallons)/min. Bootstrap/oil reservoir, pressurised at 1.7 bars (25 lb/sq in). Electrical system powered by two 150A 28V DC starter/generators and a 24V 25Ah nickel-cadmium battery; external power socket.

AVIONICS AND EQUIPMENT: Standard equipment includes basic flight instruments, engine instruments, heated pitot, tiedown rings in cargo compartment, cabin and cargo compartment dome lights, position lights and collision warning lights. A wide range of optional avionics and equipment is available, including stability augmentation system, Doppler navigation, search radar, dual controls, heating system, windscreen wiper, rescue winch, landing light, searchlight, externally mounted loudspeaker, fuel dump valve, external load hook, settling protectors, snow skids, and main rotor blade folding. GEC Avionics AD 2780 Tacan in aircraft of Royal Netherlands Air Force. A completely equipped ambulance version is available.

ARMAMENT (military versions): Provision for a variety of alternative military loads, including six Hot or eight TOW anti-tank missiles and associated stabilised sight, or a Saab/Emerson HeliTOW installation. Qualification of Lucas Aerospace turret system for use on BO 105 and NBO-105 was under way in 1988. Turret mounts an FN gun and is aimed by a Ferranti helmet sight.

DIMENSIONS, EXTERNAL:
Main rotor diameter	9.84 m (32 ft 3½ in)
Tail rotor diameter	1.90 m (6 ft 2¾ in)
Main rotor blade chord	0.27 m (10⅝ in)
Tail rotor blade chord	0.18 m (7 in)
Distance between rotor centres	5.95 m (19 ft 6¼ in)
Length, incl main and tail rotors	11.86 m (38 ft 11 in)
Length, excl rotors: CB	8.56 m (28 ft 1 in)
CBS	8.81 m (28 ft 11 in)
Length of fuselage pod: CB	4.30 m (14 ft 1 in)
CBS	4.55 m (14 ft 11 in)
Height to top of main rotor head	3.00 m (9 ft 10 in)
Width over skids: unladen	2.53 m (8 ft 3½ in)
laden	2.58 m (8 ft 5½ in)
Rear loading doors: Height	0.64 m (2 ft 1 in)
Width	1.40 m (4 ft 7 in)

DIMENSIONS, INTERNAL:
Cabin, incl cargo compartment:	
Max width	1.40 m (4 ft 7 in)
Max height	1.25 m (4 ft 1 in)
Volume	4.80 m³ (169 cu ft)
Cargo compartment: Length	1.85 m (6 ft 0¾ in)
Max width	1.20 m (3 ft 11¼ in)
Max height	0.57 m (1 ft 10½ in)
Floor area	2.25 m² (24.2 sq ft)
Volume	1.30 m³ (45.9 cu ft)

AREAS:
Main rotor disc	76.05 m² (818.6 sq ft)
Tail rotor disc	2.835 m² (30.5 sq ft)

WEIGHTS AND LOADING:
Weight empty, basic: CB	1,276 kg (2,813 lb)
CBS	1,301 kg (2,868 lb)
Standard fuel (usable)	456 kg (1,005 lb)
Max fuel, incl auxiliary tanks	776 kg (1,710 lb)
Standard T-O weight	2,400 kg (5,291 lb)
Max T-O weight	2,500 kg (5,511 lb)
Max disc loading	32.9 kg/m² (6.74 lb/sq ft)

PERFORMANCE (A at 2,400 kg; 5,291 lb standard T-O weight, B at 2,500 kg; 5,511 lb max T-O weight):
Never-exceed speed at S/L:	
A	145 knots (270 km/h; 167 mph)
B	131 knots (242 km/h; 150 mph)
Max cruising speed at S/L:	
A, B	131 knots (242 km/h; 150 mph)
Best range speed at S/L:	
A, B	110 knots (204 km/h; 127 mph)
Max rate of climb at S/L, max continuous power:	
A	480 m (1,575 ft)/min
B	419 m (1,375 ft)/min
Vertical rate of climb at S/L, T-O power:	
A	183 m (600 ft)/min
B	91 m (300 ft)/min
Max operating altitude: A	5,180 m (17,000 ft)
B	3,050 m (10,000 ft)

Service ceiling, one engine out (30.5 m; 100 ft/min climb
reserve, T-O power): A	890 m (2,920 ft)

Hovering ceiling IGE, T-O power:
A	2,560 m (8,400 ft)
B	1,525 m (5,000 ft)

Hovering ceiling OGE, T-O power:
A	1,615 m (5,300 ft)
B	457 m (1,500 ft)

Range with standard fuel and max payload:
at S/L: A	310 nm (575 km; 357 miles)
B	307 nm (570 km; 354 miles)
at 1,525 m (5,000 ft): A	355 nm (657 km; 408 miles)
B	321 nm (596 km; 370 miles)

Ferry range with auxiliary tanks, no reserves:
at S/L: A	540 nm (1,000 km; 621 miles)
B	537 nm (995 km; 618 miles)
at 1,525 m (5,000 ft):	
A	600 nm (1,112 km; 691 miles)
B	550 nm (1,020 km; 634 miles)

Endurance with standard fuel and max payload, no reserves:
at S/L: A	3 h 30 min
B	3 h 24 min

MBB BK 117 M

Shown publicly for the first time at the 1985 Paris Air Show, this multi-role military version of the MBB/Kawasaki BK 117 (see International section) is a purely German development by MBB. The airframe and power plant are virtually unchanged from the commercial 117, except for a new high-skid landing gear to provide clearance for an underfuselage Lucas turret housing a 0.50 in or 12.7 mm Browning automatic machine-gun, with 450 rounds of ammunition, controlled by a helmet mounted sight. Typical weapons load is eight Hot 2 anti-tank missiles, mounted on outrigger pylons (four missiles each side of cabin), with which are associated a SFIM APX-M397 stabilised roof mounted sight and digital weapons control avionics. Provisions exist for a mast mounted sight of up to 120 kg (264 lb) weight, infra-red jamming and chaff/flare ECM, a Racal Prophet radar warning system, and a Racal RAMS 3000 Series avionics management system which uses a dual MIL-STD-1553B databus and multifunction cockpit displays. In this configuration the BK 117 M has an empty equipped weight of 2,560 kg (5,644 lb), carries a crew of two and 460 kg (1,014 lb) of fuel, for a max T-O weight of 3,200 kg (7,055 lb). Alternative ordnance can include TOW anti-tank missiles, air-to-air missiles, unguided rockets, machine-gun pods, fixed forward-firing cannon, or a doorway gunner's position with a 0.50 in machine-gun. The capacity to serve instead as an 11-troop or cargo transport helicopter is the same as for the commercial BK 117.

BK 117 M with twin 19-round launchers for unguided rockets

Market studies and customer reactions were still being evaluated by MBB in early 1988, and flight tests with various sights and weapons systems were continuing. No orders had been announced up to that time.

MBB BO 108

This new MBB helicopter, powered initially by Allison 250-C20R turboshafts, is in the same weight class as the BO 105 but will have a bearingless main rotor and a new-design tail rotor. Two prototypes are being built, with first flights expected to take place in 1988 (third quarter) and 1989 (mid-year). The following details were known at the time of closing for press.

TYPE: Four/five-seat light helicopter.

ROTOR SYSTEM AND DRIVE: Four-blade bearingless main rotor, with elastomeric damping. Blades of composites construction, with foam core; new aerofoil section, non-linear twist, and tapered transonic tips. Two-blade hingeless tail rotor with elastomeric bearings and composites blades, mounted on port side of tail pylon. Transmission system of new design, with two-stage reduction gearing.

AIRFRAME: Generally similar in appearance to BK 117, but with longer and more streamlined fuselage. Construction mainly of composites in cabin area, mixture of composites and metal elsewhere. Clamshell rear loading doors and outward opening cabin side doors. Twin sweptback endplate fins. Skid type landing gear.

POWER PLANT: Two 335.5 kW (450 shp) class Allison 250-C20R-3 turboshafts, mounted side by side above cabin. Large volume for fuel in underfloor tanks.

SYSTEM: Dual hydraulic systems.

DIMENSION, EXTERNAL:
Main rotor diameter	9.84 m (32 ft 3½ in)

PERFORMANCE OBJECTIVES:
Max cruising speed	148 knots (275 km/h; 171 mph)
Hovering ceiling OGE	3,000 m (9,850 ft)
Range with max fuel	388 nm (720 km; 447 miles)

MBB F-4F ICE PROGRAMME

Under a German Defence Ministry programme known as ICE (improved combat effectiveness), 110 Luftwaffe F-4F Phantom IIs, primarily those of fighter wings JG 71 and JG 74, are to be upgraded to give them a lookdown/shootdown capability against multiple targets. The programme, for which MBB is the prime contractor, was initiated in late 1983 and reached the end of the definition phase some two years later. It entered the full scale development phase in December 1986, with first test flight planned for Summer 1989; redelivery of 'production' ICE Phantoms is planned to begin in November 1991.

Main ingredient of this retrofit programme involves replacement of the existing Westinghouse APQ-120 radar with the all-digital multi-mode Hughes APG-65, built under licence in Germany by AEG. This advanced X band system has 30 air-to-air and air-to-ground modes, with a ten-target track-while-scan capability, of which eight can be displayed simultaneously. APG-65 subsystems include a low sidelobe planar array antenna, a 16-bit (256K) memory, and a radar data processor with advanced ECCM. Armament capability of the ICE Phantoms will be extended to include up to four Hughes AIM-120 (AMRAAM) air-to-air missiles. Other new avionics in the full ICE package are to include a new AEG radar control console, optimisation (by Hughes) of the cockpit display, installation of a new Litef digital fire control computer, Honeywell H-423 laser inertial platform, GEC Avionics CPU-143/A digital air data computer, new IFF system, a Frazer-Nash AMRAAM launcher, a MIL-1553B digital databus with advanced operational software, and improved resistance to electronic jamming and other countermeasures.

A further 40 Luftwaffe F-4Fs, serving in the fighter-bomber role with JaboGs 35 and 36, are to undergo partial update (databus, INS and ADC only, initially), with the option of a full ICE installation later. The first of these was to fly in the second quarter of 1988, and deliveries should begin in May 1990.

TRANSPORT AIRCRAFT GROUP
Postfach 950109, 2103 Hamburg 95
Telephone: (040) 7437 1
Telex: 21950-0 MBBH D
WORKS: Hamburg-Finkenwerder, Bremen, Einswarden, Varel, Lemwerder and Stade
PUBLIC RELATIONS: Josef Grendel

MBB VFW 614 ATTAS

A twin-turbofan VFW 614 transport (c/n G-017, D-ADAM) has been converted for use by the DFVLR research establishment in developing and evaluating future flight control concepts for civil air transports; the acronym ATTAS stands for advanced technologies testing aircraft system. Modifications include replacement of the original wing flaps with new area-increasing flaps split over their full length. Each comprises a one-piece forward segment and three rear DLC (direct lift control) segments, all actuated independently by a total of four actuators. Under computer

The MBB VFW 614 ATTAS fly by wire research aircraft

control, they can move at more than 100°/s to ±30°. Wing loading and aerodynamics can be changed instantly to represent the characteristics of almost any other type of aircraft programmed into the computer. The duplex fly by wire system, controlled by five onboard Rolm MSE 14 computers, operates via a high-speed fibre optics databus which controls 15 new Liebherr Aerotechnik electro-hydraulic actuators governing all movement of the elevators, rudder, ailerons, DLC flaps and landing flaps, as well as a digital engine control system. There is mechanical backup for control surface actuation in the event of FBW system failure. The flight deck is equipped with separate controls for the safety pilot (in the right hand seat) and the evaluating pilot, together with an artificial feel system for the latter. There are seats for a third crew member at the rear of the flight deck, and positions in the main cabin for a flight engineer and for flight test personnel as required, depending upon mission. The main cabin has control consoles for data

acquisition, processing and recording equipment, plus provisions for a wide range of nav/com installations. The galley service door is replaced by an in-flight-jettisonable door.

With these changes, the ATTAS made its first flight in February 1985, and after receiving LBA certification in the following September it was handed over to the DFVLR for installation of the central five-computer control system, cabin simulator, main cabin racks and consoles, new flight deck instrumentation, telemetry and other avionics.

The planned programme consists primarily of:

(1) Testing and evaluating the new concept for use within integrated digital flight control systems, including navigation and air traffic control, in particular using a microwave landing system and position-finding and navigation systems;

(2) Testing of flight and systems characteristics by in-flight simulation; and

(3) Study of aerodynamic questions, in particular in connection with the boundary layer and fast-moving flaps.

DFVLR flight testing of the fly by wire/fly by light equipment continued during 1987, together with a 40-flight programme of laminar airflow studies with a glassfibre 'glove' section fitted to one wing.

WEIGHT:
Max T-O weight	20,865 kg (46,000 lb)

PERFORMANCE:
Mach operating Mach number	0.63
Max cruising speed:	
at S/L	288 knots (534 km/h; 331 mph)
at 5,950 m (19,500 ft)	292 knots (541 km/h; 336 mph)
Max manoeuvring speed:	
1° flap	225 knots (417 km/h; 259 mph)
14° flap	200 knots (370 km/h; 230 mph)
Max operating altitude	9,140 m (30,000 ft)
Max endurance	approx 3 h 30 min

RFB
RHEIN-FLUGZEUGBAU GmbH
(Subsidiary of MBB)
Flugplatz (Postfach 408), 4050 Mönchengladbach 1
Telephone: (02161) 6820
Telex: 852 506
OTHER WORKS: Köln/Bonn, Lübeck-Blankensee, Dahlem and Hamburg
PRESIDENT: Dipl Ing Alfred Schneider
CHIEF DESIGNER: Hanno Fischer
MARKETING MANAGER: Bernard Doran

This company, founded in 1956, is an independent subsidiary of MBB. Its own two former subsidiaries, Sportavia-Pützer of Dahlem and Elektro-Mechanischer Fluggerätebau of Hamburg, became branches of RFB in 1981.

RFB specialises in the development and manufacture of airframe structural components, especially wings and fuselages made entirely of glassfibre reinforced plastics. Recent production has also included components and assemblies of light alloy, steel and GRP for aircraft in quantity production by other West German companies, as well as spare parts and ground equipment.

Under contract to the Federal German government, RFB services military aircraft, and provides target towing flights and other services with special aircraft. It has Luftfahrt-Bundesamt (LBA) approval as an organisation for aircraft development, manufacture, maintenance and overhaul. It also operates a factory certificated service centre for Piper, Partenavia and Mitsubishi aircraft, as well as for Bendix, Becker and King avionics. General servicing of other types of all-metal aircraft is undertaken.

In the aircraft propulsion field, RFB has been engaged for many years in developing specialised applications for ducted propellers, one of which led to the Fantrainer multi-purpose training aircraft.

RFB FANTRAINER 400 and 600

Early development history of the Fantrainer has been given in the 1987-88 and previous editions of *Jane's*. There are two versions: the **Fantrainer 400**, powered by an Allison 250-C20B turboshaft, and the **Fantrainer 600**, which has an Allison 250-C30. About 92 per cent of the airframe is common to the 400 and the 600.

The first German built production Fantrainer, a 600, flew for the first time on 12 August 1984. This aircraft and one prototype were allocated to the certification programme, and LBA type approval of the 600 was granted on 23 May 1985.

In August 1982 RFB received a contract covering the production of 31 Fantrainer 400s and 16 Fantrainer 600s for the Royal Thai Air Force. The first two aircraft were

RFB Fantrainer 600 two-seat primary and basic trainers of the Royal Thai Air Force

built in Germany and delivered to Thailand in October 1984; the remaining 45 were supplied in CKD form for assembly in Thailand by RTAF (which see), all kits having been delivered by RFB by early 1988. These aircraft are intended eventually to have all-metal wings designed and manufactured by RTAF: further details are given in the RTAF entry. The Fantrainer 600s began regular flight operations in January 1987, and all 16 have been completed and delivered for service. Assembly of Fantrainer 400s was under way in the early Spring of 1988. RTAF student pilots are now transferring directly from the Fantrainer to operational F-5 aircraft, without first being trained on a dedicated jet trainer.

One Fantrainer 400 and two 600s underwent evaluation by the Luftwaffe in 1985, as a result of which some modifications were recommended, including a revised instrument layout. The fan blades were also modified to have sweptback and slightly twisted tips, to reduce still further the already low noise level of the installation. First flight with the modified fan was made on 16 May 1986. The Fantrainer is being considered by the Luftwaffe as a possible replacement for its ageing Piaggio P.149Ds. RFB is also reportedly studying a possible **Fantrainer 1000** advanced trainer version with a 746 kW (1,000 shp) ducted fan.

The following description applies to the Fantrainer 400 and 600 as built by RFB:

TYPE: Two-seat primary and basic training aircraft (IFR).
WINGS: Cantilever mid-wing monoplane. Wing section Eppler 502. Thickness/chord ratio 15.7%. Dihedral 3°. No incidence. Sweepforward 2° 30′ at quarter-chord. Wings constructed of GRP and plastics tube sandwich. Conventional ailerons and electrically actuated trailing-edge split flaps. Trim tab in port aileron.

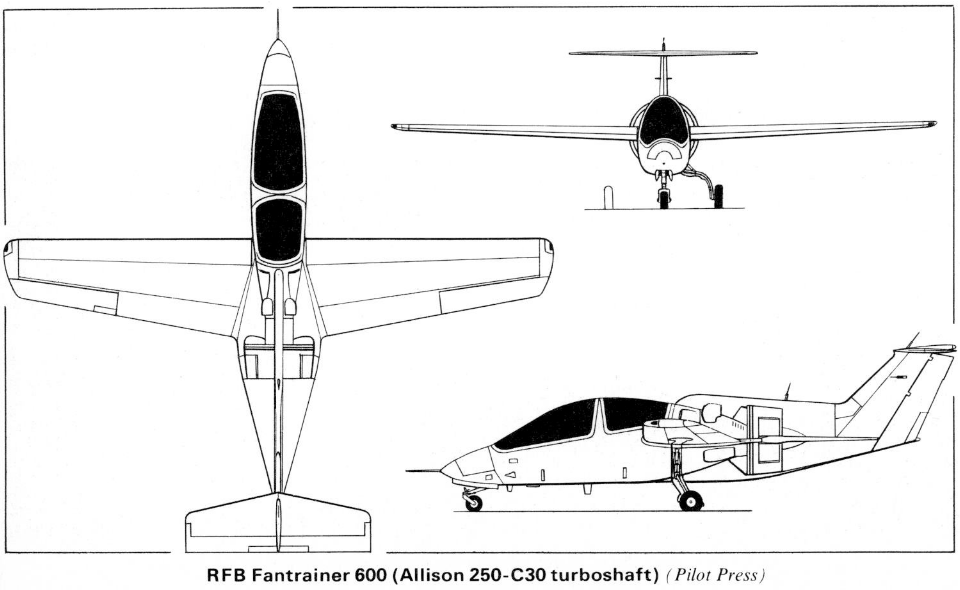

FUSELAGE: The load-carrying fail-safe structure of the forward and centre-fuselage is of light alloy, with non-load-bearing GRP skin, sections of which are removable for servicing purposes. Cruciform metal rear fuselage is connected to the centre-fuselage at three points. The integral fan duct is free of structural loads. Large airbrake on each side of fan duct, operation of which causes no lift or stability changes.

TAIL UNIT: All-metal T tail of light alloy, with conventional rudder and elevators. Trim tab in each elevator; rudder trim tab optional.

LANDING GEAR: Retractable tricycle type, with single wheel on each unit. Hydraulic actuation, with manual emergency extension. Fully castoring nosewheel retracts forward, main units inward and upward into wing roots. Steel tube legs, acting as torsional/bending springs. Cleveland mainwheels, size 15 × 6.00-6, tyre pressure 4.14 bars (60 lb/sq in). Goodyear nosewheel, size 5.00-5, tyre pressure 2.76 bars (40 lb/sq in). Cleveland wheel brakes.

POWER PLANT: One turboshaft, driving a Hoffmann five-blade constant-speed ducted fan. Fantrainer 400 has a 313 kW (420 shp) Allison 250-C20B, Fantrainer 600 a 485 kW (650 shp) Allison 250-C30. Air intakes above wing leading-edges. Four integral fuel tanks in wings, with combined capacity of 480 litres (127 US gallons; 105.5 Imp gallons). Refuelling points in wing upper surface. Provision to carry 440 litres (116 US gallons; 97 Imp gallons) of auxiliary fuel externally. Oil capacity 16 litres (4.2 US gallons; 3.5 Imp gallons).

ACCOMMODATION: Two seats in tandem cockpit, meeting US MIL specifications in terms of dimensions and layout. Rear (instructor's) seat elevated 8 cm (3 in). Seats and rudder pedals adjustable. Stencel Ranger zero/zero rocket assisted escape system standard; ejection seats optional. Fighter type side consoles. Canopy over each seat hinges sideways (to starboard) independently. Accommodation heated and ventilated.

SYSTEMS: Electrical system includes a starter/generator and battery. Hydraulic system for operation of landing gear and airbrakes.

DIMENSIONS, EXTERNAL:
Wing span	9.74 m (31 ft 11½ in)
Wing chord: at root	1.89 m (6 ft 2½ in)
at tip	1.02 m (3 ft 4 in)
Wing aspect ratio	6.8
Length overall: incl probe	9.48 m (31 ft 1¼ in)
excl probe	9.20 m (30 ft 2¼ in)
Height overall	3.16 m (10 ft 4½ in)
Tailplane span	3.59 m (11 ft 9½ in)
Wheel track	1.94 m (6 ft 4¼ in)
Wheelbase	3.89 m (12 ft 9 in)
Fan diameter	1.20 m (3 ft 11¼ in)

AREAS:
Wings, gross	14.00 m² (150.7 sq ft)
Ailerons (total)	1.68 m² (18.08 sq ft)
Trailing-edge flaps (total)	1.22 m² (13.13 sq ft)
Rudder, incl tab	0.87 m² (9.36 sq ft)
Tailplane	3.12 m² (33.58 sq ft)
Elevators, incl tabs	0.92 m² (9.90 sq ft)

RFB Fantrainer 600 (Allison 250-C30 turboshaft) *(Pilot Press)*

WEIGHTS AND LOADINGS (A: Aerobatic; U: Utility category):

Weight empty: 400: A, U	1,114 kg (2,456 lb)
600: A, U	1,160 kg (2,557 lb)
Fuel weight: A	176 kg (388 lb)
U, internal fuel only	384 kg (847 lb)
U, with drop tanks	736 kg (1,623 lb)
Max T-O weight: 400: A	1,600 kg (3,527 lb)
U	1,800 kg (3,968 lb)
600: A	1,600 kg (3,527 lb)
U	2,300 kg (5,070 lb)
Max landing weight: 600: A	1,600 kg (3,527 lb)
U	2,000 kg (4,409 lb)
Max wing loading: 400	128.6 kg/m² (26.34 lb/sq ft)
600	164.3 kg/m² (33.65 lb/sq ft)
Max power loading: 400	5.75 kg/kW (9.45 lb/shp)
600	4.74 kg/kW (7.80 lb/shp)

PERFORMANCE (at max Aerobatic T-O weight, S/L, ISA, except where indicated):

Max permissible diving speed:

400, 600	300 knots (555 km/h; 345 mph)
Max operating speed:	
400, 600	250 knots (463 km/h; 288 mph)
Max level speed:	
400 at 3,050 m (10,000 ft)	
	200 knots (370 km/h; 230 mph)
600 at 5,490 m (18,000 ft)	
	225 knots (417 km/h; 259 mph)
Cruising speed at 3,050 m (10,000 ft):	
400	175 knots (325 km/h; 201 mph)
600	200 knots (370 km/h; 230 mph)
Stalling speed at AUW of 1,800 kg (3,968 lb):	
400, 600	61 knots (113 km/h; 71 mph)
Max rate of climb at S/L: 400	472 m (1,550 ft)/min
600	914 m (3,000 ft)/min
Service ceiling: 400	6,100 m (20,000 ft)
600	7,620 m (25,000 ft)

T-O run: 400	280 m (920 ft)
600	250 m (820 ft)
Landing run: 400, 600	250 m (820 ft)
Range with max internal fuel, optimum cruising speed at 3,050 m (10,000 ft), 45 min reserves:	
400	640 nm (1,186 km; 737 miles)
600	560 nm (1,037 km; 645 miles)
Endurance, conditions as above: 400	4 h 36 min
600	4 h 6 min
Range with drop tanks, at 3,050 m (10,000 ft):	
600	1,250 nm (2,316 km; 1,439 miles)
Endurance, conditions as above:	
600	7 h 0 min
g limits (both): A	+6/−3
U	+4.4/−1.76

RUSCHMEYER

RUSCHMEYER LUFTFAHRTTECHNIK GmbH

Flugplatz, 4520 Melle 1
Telephone: (05422) 6566
Telex: 941 500 RULUF D
MANAGING DIRECTOR: Horst Ruschmeyer

RUSCHMEYER MF-85 P-RG

The MF-85 is a new all-composites four-seat light aircraft, the prototype of which (D-EEHE) was rolled out on 24 March 1988 and was due to fly at the end of May 1988. Eight had been ordered by the beginning of May. The P-RG designation indicates a Porsche engine and retractable landing gear, and the design conforms to FAR Pt 23 requirements in the Normal and Utility categories. A second (P-FG) prototype, with fixed gear, was expected to fly in late 1988, followed in March 1989 by the third prototype, which will be a PT-RG variant with a 183 kW (245 hp) PFM 3200 Turbo engine.

The following details apply to the first prototype MF-85 P-RG:

TYPE: Four-seat cabin monoplane.
AIRFRAME: Cantilever low-wing monoplane, with Wortmann wing aerofoil sections and sweptback vertical tail surfaces. Construction of carbon-/aramid-/glassfibre and Divinycell sandwich.
LANDING GEAR: Electro-hydraulically retractable tricycle type, main units retracting inward, nose unit rearward. Goodyear tyres. Tost hydraulic mainwheel brakes.
POWER PLANT: One 156 kW (212 hp) Porsche PFM 3200 N 01 flat-six engine, driving a Hoffmann three-blade composites propeller with spinner. Fuel capacity 200 litres (52.75 US gallons; 44 Imp gallons) standard, 400 litres (105.5 US gallons; 88 Imp gallons) optional.
ACCOMMODATION: Seats for pilot and three passengers in

Prototype Ruschmeyer MF-85 P-RG at the 1988 Hanover Air Show *(Peter F. Selinger)*

pairs in fully enclosed cabin, with space for up to 30 kg (66 lb) of baggage aft of seats. Two 'gull wing' window/doors, hinged on centreline to open upward.
AVIONICS: Becker avionics in prototype.
DIMENSIONS, EXTERNAL:

Wing span	9.50 m (31 ft 2 in)
Wing aspect ratio	7.0
Length overall	7.80 m (25 ft 7 in)
Height overall	2.75 m (9 ft 0¼ in)
Propeller diameter	2.00 m (6 ft 6¾ in)

DIMENSIONS, INTERNAL:

Cabin: Length	3.00 m (9 ft 10 in)
Max width	1.15 m (3 ft 9¼ in)
Max height	1.28 m (4 ft 2½ in)

AREA:

Wings, gross	12.94 m² (139.3 sq ft)

WEIGHTS:

Weight empty	700 kg (1,543 lb)
Standard fuel	144 kg (317.5 lb)
Max T-O weight	1,300 kg (2,866 lb)

PERFORMANCE (estimated):

Max cruising speed	185 knots (343 km/h; 213 mph)
Econ cruising speed (65% power)	
	150 knots (278 km/h; 173 mph)
Max rate of climb at S/L	488 m (1,600 ft)/min
T-O run at S/L	250 m (820 ft)
Landing run at S/L	220 m (722 ft)
Range, 30 min reserves:	
with standard fuel	863 nm (1,600 km; 994 miles)
with max optional fuel	
	1,726 nm (3,200 km; 1,988 miles)

VALENTIN

VALENTIN FLUGZEUGBAU GmbH

Flugplatzstrasse 18 (Postfach 26), 8728 Hassfurt
Telephone: (09521) 2041
MANAGING DIRECTOR: Dipl-Ing Bernard Valentin
HEAD OFFICE AND OTHER WORKS: Germanenstrasse 2 (Postfach 1165), 8901 Königsbrunn
Telephone: (08231) 4033/4

VALENTIN TAIFUN 11 S

A mockup of this '2+2' four-seater was displayed at Friedrichshafen in the Spring of 1987. First flight was said to be planned for Summer 1988.

TYPE: Four-seat light aircraft.
WINGS: Cantilever low-wing monoplane, with Horstmann-Quast HQ-38-1478 aerofoil section. One-piece box spar structure, incorporating integral fuel tanks, built of carbonfibre reinforced glassfibre/PVC sandwich. Conventional ailerons and trailing-edge flaps.
FUSELAGE: Semi-monocoque structure of glassfibre and PVC sandwich construction.
TAIL UNIT: Cantilever T tail, of similar construction to wings. Trim tab in elevator.
LANDING GEAR: Non-retractable tricycle type, with gas/elastomeric shock absorption. Steerable nosewheel, size 5.00-5; mainwheels size 380 × 150-5. Disc brakes on mainwheels.
POWER PLANT: One 85.75 kW (115 hp) Textron Lycoming O-235-H2C flat-four engine, driving a two-blade variable-pitch propeller with spinner. Fuel in two integral tanks in wings, total capacity 120 litres (31.7 US gallons; 26.4 Imp gallons).
ACCOMMODATION: Seats for four persons in '2+2' layout under one-piece canopy which is hinged at front and opens upward.
DIMENSIONS, EXTERNAL:

Wing span	11.60 m (38 ft 0¾ in)
Wing aspect ratio	9.8
Length overall	7.30 m (23 ft 11½ in)
Height overall	approx 2.10 m (6 ft 10¾ in)
Tailplane span	3.30 m (10 ft 10 in)

Mockup of the proposed four-seat Valentin Taifun 11 S *(Wolfgang Wagner)*

DIMENSIONS, INTERNAL:

Cabin: Max width	1.10 m (3 ft 7¼ in)
Max height	1.15 m (3 ft 9¼ in)

AREAS:

Wings, gross	13.72 m² (147.7 sq ft)
Vertical tail surfaces (total)	1.56 m² (16.79 sq ft)
Horizontal tail surfaces (total)	2.19 m² (23.57 sq ft)

WEIGHTS AND LOADINGS:

Weight empty	550 kg (1,212 lb)
Max T-O weight	900 kg (1,984 lb)
Max wing loading	65.6 kg/m² (13.44 lb/sq ft)
Max power loading	10.5 kg/kW (17.25 lb/hp)

PERFORMANCE (estimated at max T-O weight):

Never-exceed speed	162 knots (300 km/h; 186 mph)
Max cruising speed	129 knots (240 km/h; 149 mph)
Stalling speed	49 knots (90 km/h; 56 mph)
Max rate of climb at S/L	240 m (787 ft)/min
Range with max fuel	540 nm (1,000 km; 621 miles)

VALENTIN TAIFUN 12E

No news of the Taifun 12E has been received since mid-1985. All known details, and a photograph, can be found in the 1987-88 *Jane's*.

GREECE

HAI
HELLENIC AEROSPACE INDUSTRY LTD
Athens Tower, Messogion 2-4, 115 27 Athens
Telephone: (01) 77 99 678
Telex: 219528 HAI GR
WORKS: Tanagra, PO Box 23, 320 09 Schimatari
Telephone: (0262) 52000
Telex: 299372 HAI GR
CHAIRMAN AND MANAGING DIRECTOR:
 Prof Pan. Fotilas
DIRECTOR OF ENGINEERING, RESEARCH AND DEVELOPMENT:
 Th. Spathopoulos

MARKETING MANAGER: D. Sarlis
PUBLIC RELATIONS MANAGER: Spyros M. Xenos
 Hellenic Aerospace Industry is Greece's most techno-
logically developed industrial complex. It is owned 100% by
the Greek government, headed by a board of directors. A
total of 3,000 people was employed in 1988.
 HAI covers Greece's own needs for manufacture and
repair in both military and civil aviation fields, and is
proving its capability in the international market by
signing contracts with such customers as Dassault-Breguet,
SNECMA, Thomson-CSF, Dornier, Airbus Industrie,
USAFE, British Aerospace, the RAF, Aeritalia, Agusta,

General Dynamics and Jordan. These include production
of flaps for the BAe ATP, fuselage components for the
Agusta A 109A, and components for the Dassault Mirage
2000, Dornier 228, General Dynamics F-16 and Aeritalia
G222 aircraft, as well as for SNECMA M53 aero engines
and Thomson-CSF airborne radars.
 The HAI facility comprises an Aircraft Division, Engine
Division, Electronics/Avionics Division and Manufacturing
Division. The Directorate of Engineering, Research and
Development provides support, maintenance and modifi-
cation of equipment as well as production of new electronic
and aeronautical systems.

HUNGARY

GANZAVIA
GANZAVIA
Pongrácz út. 15, H-1101 Budapest
Telephone: (01) 570 828
Telex: 4 22 7951 H
TECHNICAL MANAGER: Eng Willy Simó

GANZAVIA GAK-22 DINO
 Displayed in model form at the June 1987 Paris Air Show,
the GAK-22 Dino is a small, side by side two-seat biplane
designed to FAR Pt 23 standards and suitable for training,
aerobatics, aerial photography, glider towing and (with 200
kg; 441 lb of spray chemicals) light agricultural duties. A
prototype was expected to fly in mid-1988.
 It was preceded by a proof-of-concept aircraft (HA-
XAD), which was illustrated in the 1987-88 *Jane's*.
 The following description applies to the full size
prototype:
TYPE: Two-seat light general purpose biplane.
WINGS: Negative-stagger biplane, with both wings fully
 cantilevered. Near full span flaperons, on lower wings
 only, are interconnected with elevator and pushrod
 operated (upward movement of elevator produces
 downward movement of flaperons). Wings and control
 surfaces are of corrosion resistant aluminium alloy.
FUSELAGE: Welded steel tube structure, duralumin covered
 at front and fabric covered at rear.
TAIL UNIT: Conventional configuration, of similar construction to wings. All controls pushrod operated.
LANDING GEAR: Non-retractable tricycle type, with Ka-26
 nosewheel and 300 × 125 tyre on each unit.
POWER PLANT: One 85.7 kW (115 hp) Textron Lycoming
 O-235-H2C flat-four engine in prototype, driving a
 two-blade fixed-pitch propeller with spinner. Fuel
 capacity 100 litres (26.4 US gallons; 22 Imp gallons).
ACCOMMODATION: Side by side adjustable seats for pilot and
 one passenger in fully enclosed glazed cockpit.
DIMENSIONS, EXTERNAL:
 Wing span (both)   7.60 m (24 ft 11¼ in)
 Wing chord, constant portion   1.00 m (3 ft 3¼ in)

Ganzavia GAK-22 Dino two-seat light biplane

Wing stagger	1.09 m (3 ft 7 in)	Fuel weight	80 kg (176 lb)
Length overall	6.40 m (21 ft 0 in)	Max T-O weight	650 kg (1,433 lb)
Fuselage: Max width	1.20 m (3 ft 11¼ in)	Max wing loading	46.3 kg/m² (9.49 lb/sq ft)
Height overall	2.60 m (8 ft 6½ in)	Max power loading	7.58 kg/kW (12.46 lb/hp)
Elevator span	2.80 m (9 ft 2¼ in)		
Wheel track	2.50 m (8 ft 2½ in)	PERFORMANCE (estimated, at max Aerobatic T-O weight):	
Wheelbase	1.60 m (5 ft 3 in)	Max level speed at S/L 100 knots (186 km/h; 116 mph)	
Propeller diameter	1.78 m (5 ft 10 in)	Max cruising speed at S/L 97 knots (180 km/h; 112 mph)	
AREA:		Stalling speed, flaps up 45 knots (83 km/h; 52 mph)	
Wings, gross	14.04 m² (151.13 sq ft)	Max rate of climb at S/L 282 m (925 ft)/min	
WEIGHTS AND LOADINGS (Aerobatic):		T-O run 230 m (755 ft)	
Weight empty, equipped	360 kg (794 lb)	Range with max fuel 378 nm (700 km; 435 miles)	

INDIA

HAL
HINDUSTAN AERONAUTICS LIMITED
CORPORATE OFFICE: Indian Express Building,Dr Ambedkar
 Veedhi, PO Box 5150, Bangalore 560 017
Telephone: 76901 (8 lines)
Telex: 845 266 HAL IN
CHAIRMAN: I. M. Chopra
MARKETING: 16/3 Ali Asker Road, Bangalore 560 052
CHIEF OF MARKETING: B. S. Jaswal
 Hindustan Aeronautics Limited (HAL) was formed on 1

October 1964, and has 12 Divisions (six at Bangalore and
one each at Nasik, Koraput, Hyderabad, Kanpur, Lucknow
and Korwa), plus a Design Complex. The total workforce is
about 42,000.
 Kanpur Division is producing the HPT-32 trainer and
assembles, under licence, the Dornier 228. Nasik and
Koraput Divisions are manufacturing airframes and
engines of the Soviet MiG-27 in collaboration with the
USSR. Hyderabad Division manufactures avionics for all
aircraft produced by HAL, as well as airport radars.

Lucknow Division is producing aircraft accessories under
licence from manufacturers in the UK, France and the
USSR, and Korwa manufactures inertial navigation
systems.
 In addition to its manufacturing programmes, major
design and development activities include the Light Combat
Aircraft (LCA) and Advanced Light Helicopter (ALH)
programmes. HAL is also studying proposals for an
Advanced Jet Trainer (AJT) to meet the requirements of the
Indian Air Force from the early 1990s.

BANGALORE COMPLEX
Post Bag 1785, Bangalore 560 017
Telephone: 561020 and 565201
Telex: 845 234
MANAGING DIRECTOR, DESIGN AND DEVELOPMENT:
 Prof K. Balaraman
GENERAL MANAGER, AIRCRAFT DIVISION:
 K. K. Ganapathy
GENERAL MANAGER, HELICOPTER DIVISION:
 K. N. Murthy

 The Bangalore Complex is subdivided into an Aircraft
Division, Helicopter Division, Engine Division, Overhaul
Division, Services Division, Foundry and Forge Division,
Flight Operations, and Design Complex. It is engaged in the
manufacture of the SEPECAT Jaguar International
combat aircraft and its Adour engine, and the Kiran Mk II
armed jet trainer. The Complex also undertakes repair and
overhaul of airframes, engines, and allied instruments and
accessories. A contract to supply up to 150 sets of tailplanes

for the British Aerospace ATP transport aircraft was signed
in May 1987.

HAL (SEPECAT) JAGUAR INTERNATIONAL
Indian Air Force name: Shamsher (Assault sword)
 The Bangalore Complex is producing SEPECAT Jaguar
International combat aircraft (see International section) for
the Indian Air Force. Current orders are for 76 aircraft:
45 assembled from European built components (now
completed) and 31 of virtually all-Indian manufacture. The
first Indian assembled Jaguar (JS136) made its initial flight
on 31 March 1982. The first example of indigenous
manufacture was completed in early 1988, and IAF Jaguar
Squadrons include Nos. 5 and 14. Jaguars assigned to
anti-shipping duty will have nose mounted Thomson-CSF
Agave radar, a Smiths Industries Darin nav/attack system,
and air-to-surface missiles. The first aircraft so modified
was reportedly flown in late 1987. Proposals have been put
to the Indian Parliament that a further 25-30 Jaguars should
be built when the present contract is completed in 1989.

LIGHT COMBAT AIRCRAFT
 The Indian government has confirmed a requirement for
an air superiority and light close air support aircraft for
service in the 1990s, known currently as the LCA (light
combat aircraft). A single-seat, single-engined delta-wing
aircraft, it will embody composite materials in its construction, and have a fly by wire flight control system, an Indian
multi-function radar, a ring laser gyro, digital databus and
engine controls, and a central weapons management
system. Empty and max T-O weights were originally
believed to be in the order of 6,000 kg (13,230 lb) and 10,500
kg (23,150 lb), but the latter has reportedly since risen to
12,500 kg (27,558 lb). An indigenous afterburning engine of
about 83.4 kN (18,740 lb st), designated GTX-35, entered
development by the Gas Turbine Research Establishment
at Bangalore, but General Electric F404-F2J3 turbofans
have been ordered to power the six prototypes until this is
ready. The original feasibility study has been completed, and
Dassault-Breguet of France was selected to provide
technological assistance to the Indian Aeronautical Development Authority (IADA) in the current project definition

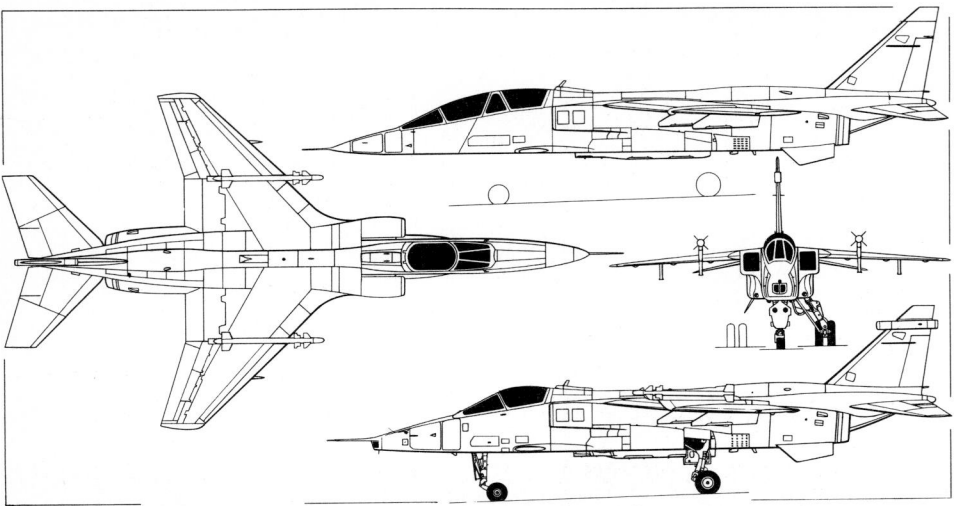

SEPECAT Jaguar International single-seat strike aircraft, as built by HAL, with additional side view (top) of two-seat version *(Pilot Press)*

stage, which began in the Spring of 1987. A first flight is not expected before the early 1990s. Production will be entrusted to HAL.

HAL HJT-16 KIRAN Mk II

This version of the Kiran, for armament training and counter-insurgency duties, was developed from the Mks I/IA (1982-83 *Jane's*) and first flew on 30 July 1976. A second prototype was flown in February 1979. Principal differences include improved weapon carrying capability, a more powerful engine, updated avionics and an improved hydraulic system. The Rolls-Royce Orpheus 701-01 turbojet, replacing the Viper engine of the Mks I/IA, gives the Kiran Mk II improved maximum speed, climb and manoeuvrability.

By mid-1985 HAL had delivered 16 of the 57 then on order, with others intended to follow at the rate of 18 a year. No subsequent information has been received.

TYPE: Two-seat jet trainer and light attack aircraft.
AIRFRAME: As described in 1987-88 and earlier *Jane's*.
POWER PLANT: One Rolls-Royce Orpheus 701-01 turbojet, derated to 18.68 kN (4,200 lb st). Internal fuel in flexible main saddle tank in fuselage, collector tank in wing centre-section, and two outboard integral wing tanks, with total capacity of 1,345 litres (355.3 US gallons; 295.5 Imp gallons). Provision for two underwing tanks with total capacity of 454 litres (120 US gallons; 100 Imp gallons). One refuelling point in each outer wing and two in fuselage. Oil capacity 11.4 litres (3 US gallons; 2.5 Imp gallons).
ACCOMMODATION: Crew of two side by side in air-conditioned and pressurised cockpit, on Martin-Baker H4HA zero-altitude fully automatic ejection seats. Clamshell type canopy, hinged at rear and opening upward. Dual controls and duplicated blind-flying instruments.
SYSTEMS, AVIONICS AND EQUIPMENT: See 1987-88 and earlier *Jane's*.
ARMAMENT: Two 7.62 mm machine-guns in nose, with 150 rds/gun; G90 gun camera, and Ferranti ISIS gunsights with Teledyne camera. Two pylons under each outer wing, each with an ejector release unit capable of carrying a 227 litre (60 US gallon; 50 Imp gallon) drop tank, a 250 kg bomb, a re-usable pod containing eighteen 68 mm SNEB rockets, or a CBLS-200 carrier with four 25 lb practice bombs.

DIMENSIONS, EXTERNAL:
Wing span	10.70 m (35 ft 1¼ in)
Wing aspect ratio	6.0
Length overall	10.60 m (34 ft 9½ in)
Height overall	3.635 m (11 ft 11 in)
Tailplane span	3.90 m (12 ft 9½ in)
Wheel track	2.42 m (7 ft 11 in)
Wheelbase	3.50 m (11 ft 6 in)

AREA:
Wings, gross	19.00 m² (204.5 sq ft)

WEIGHTS AND LOADING:
Weight empty, equipped	2,995 kg (6,603 lb)
Max fuel load	1,775 kg (3,913 lb)
Normal T-O weight 'clean'	4,250 kg (9,369 lb)
Max T-O weight	5,000 kg (11,023 lb)
Normal landing weight	4,300 kg (9,480 lb)
Max wing loading	263.1 kg/m² (53.9 lb/sq ft)

PERFORMANCE (at max T-O weight, ISA):
Never-exceed speed	421 knots (780 km/h; 484 mph)
Max level speed at S/L	363 knots (672 km/h; 418 mph)
Max cruising speed at 4,575 m (15,000 ft)	335 knots (621 km/h; 386 mph) IAS
Econ cruising speed at 4,575 m (15,000 ft)	225 knots (417 km/h; 259 mph) IAS
Stalling speed:	
flaps and landing gear up	100 knots (185 km/h; 115 mph) IAS

flaps and landing gear down
	85 knots (158 km/h; 98 mph) IAS
Max rate of climb at S/L	1,600 m (5,250 ft)/min
Service ceiling	12,000 m (39,375 ft)
T-O run	540 m (1,772 ft)
T-O to 15 m (50 ft)	730 m (2,395 ft)
Landing from 15 m (50 ft)	1,440 m (4,725 ft)
Range at 6,000 m (19,680 ft) with max internal fuel	397 nm (735 km; 457 miles)

HAL AJEET TRAINER

A description of the single-seat Ajeet (Invincible) lightweight fighter/ground attack aircraft last appeared in the 1982-83 *Jane's*. This tandem two-seat trainer version retains the four underwing hardpoints and full combat capability of the single-seater but has sections 0.70 m (2 ft 3½ in) long inserted in the fuselage fore and aft of the wings. Two of the single-seater's fuselage fuel tanks are deleted to make room for the second cockpit, although this can be offset by deleting the Aden cannon to make space for an additional 273 litres (72.1 US gallons; 60 Imp gallons) of internal fuel. In the latter event, provision is made for carrying a 7.62 mm gun pod on each of the inboard wing pylons.

The first prototype of the Ajeet Trainer made its initial flight on 20 September 1982, but was lost in an accident in December of that year. A second prototype (E2427) was flown on 7 September 1983, at which time the Indian Air Force had a stated requirement for 18 and the Indian Navy wanted twelve. Production of these was reportedly resumed in the Autumn of 1986. At about the same time British Aerospace announced the receipt of a contract for 16 SCR-300 flight data recorders for the Ajeet Trainer.

The following is the latest available description of the Ajeet Trainer:
TYPE: Tandem two-seat operational trainer.
WINGS: Cantilever shoulder-wing monoplane. Sweptback wings, of modified RAE 102 section. Thickness/chord ratio 8% at root and tip. Anhedral 5°. Incidence 0°. Sweepback 40° at quarter-chord. One-piece wing of two-spar thick-skin light alloy safe-life construction, fitting into recess in top of fuselage and secured by bolts at four points. Inboard ailerons, powered by Automotive Products hydraulic actuators, droop 22° to serve as flaps when the landing gear is lowered. Provision for alternative manual operation of ailerons. Ground adjustable tab on port aileron.
FUSELAGE: Light alloy semi-monocoque safe-life structure, with pressed frames and extruded stringers.
TAIL UNIT: Cantilever all-metal structure. Three-spar sweptback fin, integral with fuselage. One-piece three-spar variable incidence tailplane, powered by Lucas Aerospace hydraulic actuators. Rear portions of tailplane can be unlocked to perform as elevators; or locked to provide the functions of an all-moving tailplane. Ground adjustable tab on rudder. Electric datum trim.
LANDING GEAR: Retractable tricycle type, all units retracting rearward hydraulically into fuselage. Dowty Rotol oleo-pneumatic shock absorber struts. Wheel well fairings attached to individual landing gear units serve as airbrakes when landing gear is partly lowered, the relative movements of the airbrakes being so adjusted that no change of trim occurs at any speed. Dunlop mainwheel tyres size 542 × 146 × 279 mm, pressure 10.34 bars (150 lb/sq in); twin Dunlop nosewheel tyres, size 430 × 87 × 279 mm, pressure 5.65 bars (82 lb/sq in). Dunlop hydraulic disc brakes and Maxaret anti-skid units on mainwheels. GQ Mk 4 or Mk 6 brake-chute, diameter 2.29 m (7 ft 6 in), in fairing at base of fin.
POWER PLANT: One Rolls-Royce Orpheus 701-01AT non-afterburning turbojet, rated at 21.57 kN (4,850 lb st). Air

HAL Kiran Mk II armament training and counter-insurgency aircraft

Prototype of the tandem two-seat HAL Ajeet Trainer

intakes in sides of fuselage. Five flexible tanks in fuselage, and two 227 litre (60 US gallon; 50 Imp gallon) integral wing tanks. Total internal fuel capacity 900 litres (237.8 US gallons; 198 Imp gallons). Refuelling point in fuselage and one in each wing. Provision for two 136.5 litre (36 US gallon; 30 Imp gallon) underwing drop tanks. Oil capacity 5.1 litres (1.35 US gallons; 1.12 Imp gallons).

ACCOMMODATION: Instructor and pupil in tandem, on Martin-Baker GF4 zero-height/90 knot (167 km/h; 104 mph) lightweight ejection seats. Pressurised, heated and air-conditioned cockpits, with individual canopies which are hinged at rear and open upward.

SYSTEMS: HAL (Lucknow Divn) bootstrap type air-conditioning and Semca pressurisation system, max differential 0.25 bars (3.6 lb/sq in) above 13,100 m (43,000 ft). Hydraulic system of 207 bars (3,000 lb/sq in) pressure, with variable-delivery pump, for aileron, landing gear, mainwheel brake and tailplane actuation. No pneumatic system. 28V DC electrical system, with 5.1kW generator, 40Ah nickel-cadmium battery and 4Ah Globe standby battery. BOC gaseous oxygen system. No de-icing provisions or APU.

AVIONICS AND EQUIPMENT: V/UHF main and standby com radio; HAL ADF and Mk 10 IFF. Blind-flying instrumentation and dual controls standard.

ARMAMENT: Two 30 mm Aden Mk 4 cannon in air intake fairings, one on each side of fuselage. Ferranti ISIS gunsight (front cockpit only), Vinten gun camera and Teledyne recording camera. Each inboard underwing pylon capable of carrying a Type 122 practice rocket pod, one pod of 57 mm rockets, one cluster bomb, or one CBLS with four 25 lb practice bombs. With a 136.5 litre (36 US gallon; 30 Imp gallon) drop tank on each outboard pylon, a 250 kg bomb can be carried on each inboard attachment.

DIMENSIONS, EXTERNAL:

Wing span	6.731 m (22 ft 1 in)
Wing chord: at c/l	2.583 m (8 ft 5¾ in)
at tip	1.175 m (3 ft 10¼ in)
Wing aspect ratio	3.6
Length overall	10.45 m (34 ft 3½ in)
Length of fuselage	10.055 m (33 ft 0 in)
Fuselage: Max width	1.483 m (4 ft 10¼ in)
Height overall	2.575 m (8 ft 5½ in)
Tailplane span	2.845 m (9 ft 4 in)
Wheel track	1.552 m (5 ft 1¼ in)
Wheelbase	3.069 m (10 ft 0¾ in)

AREAS:

Wings, gross	12.646 m² (136.12 sq ft)
Ailerons/flaps (total)	1.230 m² (13.24 sq ft)
Fin	0.936 m² (10.08 sq ft)
Rudder, incl tab	0.206 m² (2.22 sq ft)
Tailplane	2.967 m² (31.94 sq ft)
Elevators (total)	0.540 m² (5.81 sq ft)

WEIGHTS AND LOADINGS:

Basic weight empty, incl crew	2,940 kg (6,482 lb)
Max internal fuel	703 kg (1,550 lb)
Max external stores	850 kg (1,874 lb)
Max T-O weight	4,536 kg (10,000 lb)
Max landing weight	3,330 kg (7,341 lb)
Max wing loading	358.7 kg/m² (73.47 lb/sq ft)
Max power loading	210.2 kg/kN (2.06 lb/lb st)

PERFORMANCE (at max T-O weight):

Never-exceed speed at S/L	
	661 knots (1,225 km/h; 761 mph)
Max level speed at S/L	
	577 knots (1,070 km/h; 665 mph)
Max cruising speed at 11,000 m (36,000 ft)	
	Mach 0.95 (540 knots; 1,000 km/h; 621 mph)
Econ cruising speed at 11,000 m (36,000 ft)	
	Mach 0.80 (459 knots; 850 km/h; 528 mph)
Stalling speed, ailerons/flaps down, engine idling	
	133 knots (246 km/h; 153 mph)
Max rate of climb at S/L	3,240 m (10,625 ft)/min
Service ceiling	14,000 m (45,925 ft)
Min ground turning radius	6.00 m (19 ft 8¼ in)
Runway LCN	5.5
T-O run	725 m (2,380 ft)
T-O to 15 m (50 ft)	1,130 m (3,705 ft)
Landing from 15 m (50 ft)	1,400 m (4,595 ft)
Landing run	900 m (2,955 ft)
Range with max internal fuel, 136.5 litres (36 US gallons; 30 Imp gallons) reserves	485 nm (900 km; 559 miles)

HAL (AÉROSPATIALE) SA 315B LAMA
Indian name: Cheetah

The last known details of HAL's Lama licence production were given in the 1987-88 *Jane's*. Indian production continues.

HAL (AÉROSPATIALE) SA 316B ALOUETTE III
Indian name: Chetak

The latest known details of the Indian Alouette manufacturing programme, which was continuing in 1988, can be found in the 1987-88 edition.

MBB/HAL ADVANCED LIGHT HELICOPTER

In July 1984, the Indian government and MBB signed a contract for the development of an advanced twin-turboshaft light helicopter (ALH), initially for Indian national requirements, which are said to be in the order of 200 for the armed forces and Coast Guard. Development of the ALH basic version will be by HAL of Bangalore with MBB collaboration. MBB is providing support during design, development and the necessary preparations for production of the helicopter in Bangalore.

The preliminary design phase started on 1 November 1984 and has been completed. Configuration has been 'frozen' (see accompanying drawing), and overall design of critical components has also been completed. Power plant will be two 746 kW (1,000 shp) Turbomeca TM 333 2B turboshafts. Maximum take-off weight is four to five tonnes (8,818-11,023 lb), with seating capacity for up to 14 persons (16 in high density configuration), including a crew of two; emphasis is on optimum 'hot and high' performance. Other details so far released are that the ALH will have an MBB four-blade all-composites FEL (fibre/elastomerics) bearingless main rotor with integrated drive system and Nardi actuators, fully retractable tricycle landing gear, and capability to carry sling loads. A civil version, and a variant with skid landing gear, are under consideration. Performance requirements are reported to include a sea level range of 216 nm (400 km; 248 miles), service ceiling of 6,000 m (19,685 ft) and hovering ceiling of 3,000 m (9,845 ft). A full scale engineering mockup was completed in 1987, and prototype first flight of the ALH is scheduled for mid-1989; production is expected to start in about 1992.

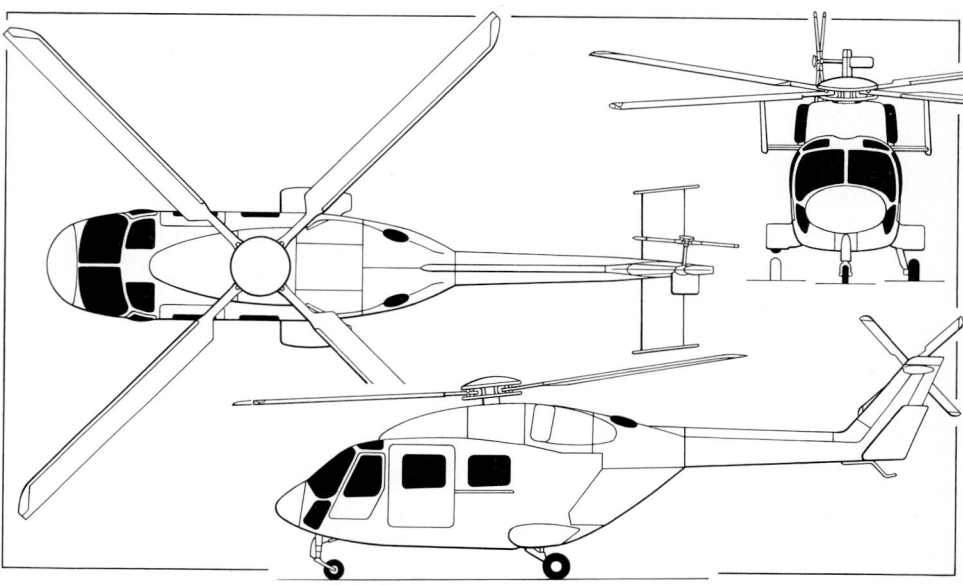

MBB/HAL Advanced Light Helicopter *(Jane's/Mike Keep)*

KANPUR DIVISION

PO Box 225, Kanpur 208 008
Telephone: 43071 to 43074
Telex: 325 243 HALK IN
GENERAL MANAGER: S. K. Ohri

HAL (DORNIER) 228

The Dornier 228 (see German section) was chosen in August 1983 to fulfil an Indian government LTA (light transport aircraft) requirement, resulting on 29 November that year in the signing of a contract for HAL to undertake licence assembly and manufacture of up to 150 of these twin-turboprop utility transports in a ten-year technology transfer programme. Kanpur Divison is responsible for the airframe, final assembly and flight testing; the HAL Engine Division at Bangalore manufactures the Garrett TPE331-5

turboprops; instrumentation and accessories are supplied by Lucknow Division; and Hyderabad Division provides various items of avionics including the colour weather radar and Omega navigation system. The Indian licence programme is based on a production rate of two Dornier 228s a month.

The 228, in several versions, will be used for a wide variety of civil and military duties in India, and while Kanpur Division was preparing for its manufacture a number of Dornier built aircraft were supplied to meet urgent Indian customer needs. Two 228-201s were delivered in November 1984 to the newly formed regional airline Vayudoot, which received a third in February 1985 and two more in November 1985. Two 228-101s (CG-752 and -753) were supplied to the Indian Coast Guard in July 1986, followed by a third in July 1987. Other early deliveries from Germany

included VT-EIX (c/n 7032), a VIP executive 228-101 to the Indian Oil and Natural Gas Commission in April 1985, and a 228-101 for the National Airport Authority, equipped for airfield calibration work with a flight inspection system that includes laser tracking equipment.

Meanwhile, in early 1985 Dornier began delivering complete shipsets of aircraft assemblies to HAL, and the first Kanpur assembled 228 made its initial flight on 31 January 1986. First deliveries from Kanpur, of five 228-201s for Vayudoot, were made in March 1986. The initial three Coast Guard 228-101s from Germany are being followed by 33 more from the Kanpur assembly line, the first of which were delivered in 1987. In service with No. 750 Squadron at Daman, they are used for a wide variety of coastal patrol, environmental control and anti-smuggling missions with equipment that includes a 360° MEL Marec 2 underfuselage search radar, Litton Omega navigation system, a Swedish infra-red/ultraviolet linescanner for pollution detection, search and rescue liferafts, a 1 million candlepower searchlight, side mounted loudhailer, marine markers, and provision for two Micronair underwing spraypods to combat oil spills and chemical pollution. The standard cabin door is replaced by a sliding door to permit airdropping of the 20-man liferaft. Normal crew comprises a pilot, co-pilot, radar operator and observer. The Marec 2 radar will eventually be replaced on 15 aircraft by Super Marec, ordered in 1987. Armament (optional) can include two 7.62 mm multi-barrel machine-guns and underwing air-to-surface missiles.

In Phase 2 of the manufacturing programme, more than 50 Dornier 228s are being built for the Indian Air Force, of which four had been delivered by the beginning of 1988. In various utility and logistic support roles they will eventually replace all of the IAF's Otters, Devons and remaining C-47s currently serving with Nos. 41 and 59 Squadrons.

HAL built Dornier 228-201 in the insignia of Vayudoot

HAL HPT-32 two-seat basic training aircraft in Indian Navy insignia

For maritime surveillance and anti-shipping tasks, the Indian Navy will also add specially equipped Dornier 228s to its shore based fixed-wing fleet. Twenty-four are reportedly required, and are expected to have anti-ship missile carrying capability.

HAL HPT-32

The HPT-32 is a fully aerobatic piston engined basic trainer, with side by side seats for instructor and pupil. It can be used for a wide range of ab initio training, including instrument, navigation, night flying and formation flying; for armed patrol; for observation, liaison or sport flying; or for weapon training, light strike duties, supply dropping, search and rescue, reconnaissance, or glider or target towing. The all-metal airframe is designed to FAR Pt 23.

The first prototype (X2157) made its initial flight on 6 January 1977. The third, flown on 31 July 1981, represented the production version, substantially lighter in weight and with aerodynamic refinements. By 31 March 1987 a total of 40 had been delivered to the Indian Air Force and eight to the Indian Navy. Production of a further 40, against anticipated IAF orders, was in progress in early 1988.

TYPE: Two-seat ab initio, aerobatic, night flying, instrument flying and navigation trainer.

WINGS: Cantilever low-wing monoplane. Wing section NACA 64A$_1$-212. Dihedral 5° from roots. Incidence 2° 30' at root. No sweepback. Light alloy safe-life wings, of tapered planform, with stressed skin. Light alloy plain ailerons and plain trailing-edge flaps. Balance tab in, and ground adjustable tab on, each aileron. Pitot static tube can be heated.

FUSELAGE: Semi-monocoque safe-life structure of light alloy, with stressed skin.

TAIL UNIT: Cantilever light alloy stressed skin structure, with sweptback vertical surfaces. One-piece elevator. Trim tabs in rudder and starboard half of elevator; balance tabs in rudder and port half of elevator.

LANDING GEAR: Non-retractable tricycle type, with HAL oleo-pneumatic shock absorber in each unit. Dunlop UK single mainwheels and nosewheel. Dunlop UK mainwheel tyres, size 446 × 151 × 166 mm, pressure 3.10 bars (45 lb/sq in); Dunlop India nosewheel tyre, size 361 × 126 × 127 mm, pressure 2.41 bars (35 lb/sq in). Dunlop UK aircooled hydraulic disc brakes on mainwheels.

POWER PLANT: One 194 kW (260 hp) Textron Lycoming AEIO-540-D4B5 flat-six engine, driving a Hartzell two-blade constant-speed metal propeller with spinner. Total of 220 litres (58.1 US gallons; 48.4 Imp gallons) of fuel in four flexible tanks (two in each wing), plus a 9 litre (2.4 US gallon; 2 Imp gallon) metal collector tank in fuselage. Total fuel capacity 229 litres (60.5 US gallons; 50.4 Imp gallons). Overwing refuelling points. Oil capacity 13.6 litres (3.6 US gallons; 3 Imp gallons).

ACCOMMODATION: Side by side seats for two persons under rearward sliding jettisonable framed canopy. Seats adjustable in height by 127 mm (5 in). Full dual controls, and adjustable rudder pedals, for instructor and pupil. Cockpits ventilated.

SYSTEMS: Hydraulic system for brakes only. Electrical system (28V DC earth return type) powered by 70A alternator, with SAFT 24V nickel-cadmium standby battery. No air-conditioning, pneumatic, de-icing or oxygen systems.

AVIONICS: HAL (Hyderabad Divn) COM-150 main UHF and COM-104A standby VHF com; directional gyro. No blind-flying instrumentation.

DIMENSIONS, EXTERNAL:

Wing span	9.50 m (31 ft 2 in)
Wing chord: at root	2.24 m (7 ft 4¼ in)
at tip	0.92 m (3 ft 0¼ in)
Wing aspect ratio	6.0
Length overall	7.72 m (25 ft 4 in)
Fuselage: Max width	1.25 m (4 ft 1¼ in)
Height overall	2.88 m (9 ft 5½ in)
Tailplane span	3.60 m (11 ft 9¾ in)
Wheel track	3.45 m (11 ft 4 in)
Wheelbase	2.10 m (6 ft 10¾ in)
Propeller diameter	2.03 m (6 ft 8 in)
Propeller ground clearance (static)	0.23 m (9 in)

AREAS:

Wings, gross	15.00 m² (161.5 sq ft)
Ailerons (total)	1.04 m² (11.19 sq ft)
Trailing-edge flaps (total)	1.82 m² (19.59 sq ft)
Vertical tail surfaces (above fuselage reference line)	2.06 m² (22.17 sq ft)
Rudder (aft of hinge line), incl tabs	0.869 m² (9.35 sq ft)
Tailplane	3.024 m² (32.55 sq ft)
Elevator (aft of hinge line), incl tabs	1.34 m² (14.42 sq ft)

WEIGHTS AND LOADINGS:

Basic weight empty	890 kg (1,962 lb)
Fuel and oil (guaranteed minimum)	164 kg (361 lb)
Max T-O and landing weight	1,250 kg (2,756 lb)
Max wing loading	83.33 kg/m² (17.07 lb/sq ft)
Max power loading	6.44 kg/kW (10.60 lb/hp)

PERFORMANCE (at max T-O weight, ISA):

Never-exceed speed (structural)	240 knots (445 km/h; 276 mph)
Max level speed at S/L	143 knots (265 km/h; 164 mph) IAS
Max cruising speed at 3,050 m (10,000 ft)	115 knots (213 km/h; 132 mph)
Econ cruising speed	95 knots (176 km/h; 109 mph)
Stalling speed, 20° flap, engine idling	60 knots (110 km/h; 69 mph)
Max rate of climb at S/L	335 m (1,100 ft)/min
Service ceiling	5,500 m (18,045 ft)
T-O run	345 m (1,132 ft)
T-O to 15 m (50 ft)	545 m (1,788 ft)
Landing from 15 m (50 ft)	487 m (1,598 ft)
Landing run	220 m (720 ft)
Min ground turning radius	6.50 m (21 ft 4 in)
Range at 3,050 m (10,000 ft) at econ cruise power	401 nm (744 km; 462 miles)
g limits	+6/–3

MiG COMPLEX

Ojhar Township Post Office, Nasik 422 207, Maharashtra
Telephone: 3396
Telex: 752 241
GENERAL MANAGER, NASIK DIVISION:
  H. K. L. Anand (ret'd)
CO-GENERAL MANAGER, NASIK DIVISION:
  C. S. Singhal
GENERAL MANAGER, KORAPUT DIVISION:
  Wg Cdr A. K. Sar

The MiG Complex was originally formed with the Nasik, Koraput and Hyderabad Divisions of HAL, which, under an agreement concluded in 1962, built respectively the airframes, power plants and avionics of MiG-21 series fighters under licence from the USSR. Indian production of MiG-21s was phased out in 1986-87, as production of the MiG-27M increased. Nasik had a workforce of 8,019 in September 1986. The Hyderabad Division is now a part of the Accessories Complex.

HAL (MIKOYAN) MiG-27M
Indian Air Force name: Bahadur (Valiant)
NATO reporting name: Flogger-J

Licence assembly of some 165 MiG-27Ms (see USSR section) began at HAL in 1984, and the first example assembled by HAL was rolled out in October of that year. These aircraft supplement Soviet built MiG-23s and MiG-27s already supplied to the Indian Air Force, and are the first MiG-27s to be assembled outside the USSR. From 1988-89, MiG-27Ms assembled at Nasik were expected to incorporate components manufactured in India. First IAF unit to receive Bahadurs was No. 32 ('Tiger Sharks') Squadron, the type being formally inducted into IAF service on 11 January 1986.

POWER PLANT: One Tumansky R-29B turbofan, rated at 78.65 kN (17,681 lb st) dry and 112.78 kN (25,353 lb st) with afterburning.

ARMAMENT: One Gatling type cannon and up to 3,000 kg (6,614 lb) of external stores which can include 500 kg bombs, 57 mm S-24 rockets, two 'Kerry' air-to-surface or four R-60 air-to-air missiles.

WEIGHT:

Max T-O weight	18,000 kg (39,685 lb)

PERFORMANCE:

T-O run at S/L	800 m (2,625 ft)
Combat radius (low level)	210 nm (390 km; 242 miles)
Ferry range	1,349 nm (2,500 km; 1,553 miles)

NAL
NATIONAL AERONAUTICAL LABORATORY
PO Bag 1779, Kodihalli, Bangalore 560017
Telephone: 573351/4
Telex: 279 NAL IN
DIRECTOR: Prof R. Narasimha

NAL LCRA

The LCRA (light canard research aircraft), which flew for the first time on 27 February 1987, is a specially instrumented Rutan Long-EZ used by the NAL as a vehicle for analysing canard configurations. It has an airframe of GRP/rigid plastics foam construction and is powered by an 80.5 kW (108 hp) piston engine driving a two-blade pusher propeller. Fuel capacity is 200 litres (53 US gallons; 44 Imp gallons).

The two-seat LCRA is the first in a series of experimental aircraft to be used by the NAL to gain experience in composites manufacturing techniques, and to flight test such areas as aerodynamics, structures, materials and control systems.

WEIGHT:

Max T-O weight	600 kg (1,323 lb)

PERFORMANCE:

Max level speed	189 knots (350 km/h; 217 mph)
Service ceiling	7,010 m (23,000 ft)
T-O and landing run	1,000 m (3,280 ft)
Range with max fuel	1,457 nm (2,700 km; 1,678 miles)

NAL BASIC TRAINER

In 1988 NAL was about to begin design of a basic trainer, using composites materials.

NARAS
NARAS AVIATION PVT LTD
  (Subsidiary of Naras Avionics Inc)
9 Kapaleswar Nagar, Neelankarai, Madras 600041
Telephone: 446841
PRESIDENT, NARAS AVIONICS INC: N. Narayanan
MANAGER, NARAS AVIATION: K. Shankar

Naras Aviation's parent company, Naras Avionics Inc of Miami, Florida, USA, has acquired the manufacturing and marketing rights for the former Brantly B-2B and Model 305 helicopters, which were last produced in the USA by Hynes Helicopter, as described in the 1987-88 *Jane's*. A Model 305 demonstrator was delivered by Naras Avionics to its Indian subsidiary in early 1988, and it is planned to manufacture both types at a factory in Tambaram, near Madras, offering them (as did Hynes) in both manned and remotely piloted versions. Turkish interest in possible licence assembly or manufacture of these aircraft, referred to in the 1987-88 edition, was reported to be continuing in late 1987.

NARAS (BRANTLY) B-2B
TYPE: Two-seat light helicopter.

ROTOR SYSTEM: Three-blade main rotor. Articulated inboard flapping hinges offset 0.07 m (2.67 in) from hub, and coincident flap and lag hinges offset 1.31 m (4 ft 3¾ in) from rotor head. Symmetrical blade section with 29% thickness/chord ratio on inboard portion; NACA 0012 section outboard of hinge. Blades are semi-rigid at hub and fully articulated at inboard/outboard junction (40 per cent blade span) to eliminate ground resonance.

Inboard portion of each blade is built around a steel spar, outboard portion has an extruded aluminium leading-edge spar and polyurethane core; aluminium skin is bonded to core and riveted to spar. Blades are attached to head by flapping links; they do not fold, but can be quickly separated at inboard/outboard junction for easy storage. A rotor brake is standard equipment. Two-blade all-metal anti-torque tail rotor.

ROTOR DRIVE: Through automatic centrifugal clutch and planetary reduction gears. Bevel gear take-off from main transmission with flexible coupling via intermediate and upper gearboxes to tail rotor driveshaft. Main rotor/engine rpm ratio 1 : 6.0. Tail rotor/engine rpm ratio 1 : 1.

FUSELAGE: Stressed skin all-metal structure with conical tail section and small fixed horizontal stabilisers. Tail rotor on swept-up boom extension.

LANDING GEAR: Alternative skid, wheel or float gear. Skid type has small retractable wheels for ground handling, fixed tailskid and four shock absorbers with rubber in compression. Inflatable pontoons, which attach to standard skids, are available to permit operation from water. Alternative non-retractable tricycle landing gear has oleo-pneumatic shock absorbers in all units, with single wheels on main units and twin castoring nosewheels. Goodyear tyres size 10 × 3½, pressure 2.07 bars (30 lb/sq in), on mainwheels; tyre pressure 1.93 bars (28 lb/sq in) on nosewheels. Goodyear mainwheel brakes.

POWER PLANT: One 134 kW (180 hp) Textron Lycoming IVO-360-A1A flat-four engine, mounted vertically, with dual fan cooling system. Rubber bag type fuel tank under engine, capacity 117 litres (31 US gallons; 25.8 Imp gallons). Refuelling point on port side of fuselage. Oil capacity 5.7 litres (1.5 US gallons; 1.25 Imp gallons).

ACCOMMODATION: Totally enclosed circular section cabin for two persons seated side by side. Forward hinged door on each side. Dual controls, cabin heater and demisting fan standard. Compartment for 22.7 kg (50 lb) baggage in forward end of tail section.

AVIONICS AND EQUIPMENT: Provision for all standard nav/com radios. Blind-flying instrumentation available as an option, but the Model B-2B is not certificated for instrument flight. Twin landing lights in nose.

DIMENSIONS, EXTERNAL:

Main rotor diameter	7.24 m (23 ft 9 in)
Main rotor blade chord: inboard	0.225 m (8.85 in)
outboard	0.203 m (8.0 in)
Tail rotor diameter	1.30 m (4 ft 3 in)
Length overall, rotors turning	8.53 m (28 ft 0 in)
Length of fuselage	6.62 m (21 ft 9 in)
Height overall	2.06 m (6 ft 9 in)
Skid track	1.73 m (5 ft 8¼ in)
Passenger doors (each): Height	0.79 m (2 ft 7 in)
Width	0.86 m (2 ft 9¾ in)
Baggage compartment door:	
Mean height	0.25 m (9¾ in)
Length	0.55 m (1 ft 9¾ in)

DIMENSIONS, INTERNAL:

Cabin: Length	1.83 m (6 ft 0 in)
Max width	1.19 m (3 ft 11 in)
Max height	0.99 m (3 ft 3 in)
Floor area	2.60 m² (28.0 sq ft)
Volume	2.78 m³ (98.0 cu ft)
Baggage compartment	0.17 m³ (6.0 cu ft)

AREAS:

Main rotor blades (each)	0.69 m² (7.42 sq ft)
Main rotor disc	41.16 m² (443 sq ft)
Tail rotor disc	1.32 m² (14.19 sq ft)

WEIGHTS AND LOADINGS:

Weight empty: with skids	463 kg (1,020 lb)
with floats	481 kg (1,060 lb)
Max T-O weight	757 kg (1,670 lb)
Max disc loading	18.40 kg/m² (3.77 lb/sq ft)
Max power loading	5.65 kg/kW (9.27 lb/hp)

PERFORMANCE (at max T-O weight):

Max level speed at S/L	87 knots (161 km/h; 100 mph)
Max cruising speed (75% power)	
	78 knots (145 km/h; 90 mph)
Max rate of climb at S/L	580 m (1,900 ft)/min
Service ceiling	3,290 m (10,800 ft)
Hovering ceiling IGE	2,040 m (6,700 ft)
Range with max fuel, with reserves	
	217 nm (400 km; 250 miles)

NARAS (BRANTLY) MODEL 305

The Model 305 is a five-seat helicopter of similar configuration to the B-2B, but larger in every respect. The

US built Brantly B-2B two-seat light helicopter *(Brian M. Service)*

Brantly Model 305, of the type to be produced by Naras Aviation

prototype flew for the first time in January 1964, and FAA type approval was received on 29 July 1965. The following description applies to the certificated passenger carrying version:

TYPE: Five-seat light helicopter.

ROTOR SYSTEM AND DRIVE: As described for B-2B, except rotor/engine rpm ratio 1:6.6.

FUSELAGE AND TAIL UNIT: As described for B-2B.

LANDING GEAR: Choice of skid, wheel or float gear. Skid type has four oleo struts, two on each side, and small retractable ground handling wheels. The wheel gear has single mainwheels and twin nosewheels, all with oleo-pneumatic shock absorbers. Goodyear mainwheels and tyres size 6.00-6, pressure 2.07 bars (30 lb/sq in); Goodyear nosewheels and tyres size 5.00-5, pressure 1.93 bars (28 lb/sq in). Goodyear single-disc hydraulic brakes on mainwheels.

POWER PLANT: One 227.4 kW (305 hp) Textron Lycoming IVO-540-B1A flat-six engine, mounted vertically, with dual cooling fans. One rubber fuel cell under engine, capacity 163 litres (43 US gallons; 35.8 Imp gallons). Refuelling point in port side of fuselage. Oil capacity 9.5 litres (2.5 US gallons; 2.1 Imp gallons).

ACCOMMODATION: Two individual seats side by side, with dual controls. Rear bench seat for three persons. Door on each side. Rear compartment for 113 kg (250 lb) of baggage, with downward hinged door on starboard side.

AVIONICS AND EQUIPMENT: King or Narco radio, to customer's specification. Blind-flying instrumentation is available, but helicopter is not certificated for instrument flight.

DIMENSIONS, EXTERNAL:

Main rotor diameter	8.74 m (28 ft 8 in)
Main rotor blade chord (constant)	0.254 m (10 in)
Tail rotor diameter	1.30 m (4 ft 3 in)

Length overall, rotors turning	10.03 m (32 ft 11 in)
Length of fuselage	7.44 m (24 ft 5 in)
Height overall	2.44 m (6 ft 0⅛ in)
Wheel track	2.10 m (6 ft 10¾ in)
Wheelbase	2.15 m (7 ft 0½ in)
Passenger doors (each): Height	0.82 m (2 ft 8⅛ in)
Width	1.02 m (3 ft 3⅞ in)
Baggage compartment door:	
Mean height	0.30 m (1 ft 0¼ in)
Width	0.69 m (2 ft 3 in)

DIMENSIONS, INTERNAL:

Cabin: Length	2.30 m (7 ft 6½ in)
Max width	1.39 m (4 ft 6¾ in)
Max height	1.22 m (4 ft 0½ in)
Baggage compartment	0.47 m³ (16.7 cu ft)

AREAS:

Main rotor blades (each)	0.09 m² (11.79 sq ft)
Tail rotor blades (each)	0.05 m² (0.50 sq ft)
Main rotor disc	59.96 m² (645.4 sq ft)
Tail rotor disc	1.32 m² (14.19 sq ft)

WEIGHTS AND LOADINGS:

Weight empty	816 kg (1,800 lb)
Max T-O and landing weight	1,315 kg (2,900 lb)
Max zero-fuel weight	1,224 kg (2,700 lb)
Max disc loading	21.92 kg/m² (4.49 lb/sq ft)
Max power loading	5.78 kg/kW (9.51 lb/hp)

PERFORMANCE (at max T-O weight):

Max level speed at S/L	
	104 knots (193 km/h; 120 mph)
Max cruising speed at S/L	
	96 knots (177 km/h; 110 mph)
Max rate of climb at S/L	297 m (975 ft)/min
Service ceiling	3,660 m (12,000 ft)
Hovering ceiling IGE	1,245 m (4,080 ft)
Range with max fuel and max payload, 15 min reserves	
	191 nm (354 km; 220 miles)

INDONESIA

IPTN
INDUSTRI PESAWAT TERBANG NUSANTARA (Nusantara Aircraft Industries Ltd)
PO Box 563, Jalan Pajajaran 154, Bandung
Telephone: (022) 611081/2
Telex: 28295 IPTN BD

HEAD OFFICE: PO Box 3752, 8 Jalan M.H. Thamrin, Jakarta
Telephone: (021) 322395 and 336651
Telex: 46141 ATP JAKARTA
PRESIDENT DIRECTOR: Prof Dr-Ing B. J. Habibie
DIRECTOR, COMMERCIAL AFFAIRS: Ir S. Paramajuda
CHIEF ENGINEER: Ir Budiarta Suradiningrat
PUBLIC RELATIONS MANAGER: Suripto Sugondo

This company was officially inaugurated as PT Industri Pesawat Terbang Nurtanio (Nurtanio Aircraft Industry Ltd) on 23 August 1976, when the government of Indonesia implemented a decision to centralise all existing facilities in the establishment of a single new aircraft industry. The original capital was provided by combining the assets of Pertamina's Advanced Technology and Aeronautical

Division with those of the former Nurtanio Aircraft Industry (LIPNUR: see 1977-78 *Jane's*). The present name of the company was adopted in late 1985. A weapons system division, located in Menang Tasikmalaya, West Java, develops and produces the weaponry fitted to aircraft built by the company for military customers.

IPTN is jointly responsible with CASA of Spain for development and production of the Airtech CN-235 (see International section), as well as continuing licence manufacture of the NC-212 Aviocar, NBO-105, NAS-332 Super Puma, NBell-412 and MBB/Kawasaki NBK-117, as described in the following entries. Major subcontracting includes the manufacture of components for the Boeing 767 and General Dynamics F-16. The company had a workforce of approx 13,000 employees in 1987, and occupies a 69 ha (170.5 acre) site with 365,000 m² (3,928,824 sq ft) of covered accommodation.

With MBB of West Germany, IPTN has set up a joint company known as NTT (New Transport Technologies), with its headquarters in Munich. Its first venture is a small helicopter (the BN-109). Launch of the international ATRA 90 transport aircraft programme, to which reference was made in the 1987-88 *Jane's*, is no longer considered to be justified.

In 1987-88 two Lockheed L-100-30 commercial Hercules cargo transports of Merpati Nusantara Airlines were modified (one by Lockheed, with IPTN technicians assisting, and one by IPTN under Lockheed supervision) to a 97-passenger configuration. The second of these was due for redelivery in June 1988.

AIRTECH (CASA/IPTN) CN-235

Details of this joint transport programme can be found under the Airtech heading in the International section.

IPTN N-260

The N-260 is a design concept for a 60/70-passenger medium-range STOL transport aircraft based on the CN-235 configuration and using as many components of that aircraft as possible. Provisional data are as follows:

DIMENSIONS, EXTERNAL:
Wing span	29.0 m (95 ft 2 in)
Length overall	26.0 m (85 ft 4 in)
Height overall	8.0 m (26 ft 3 in)
Tailplane span	11.0 m (36 ft 1 in)

WEIGHT:
Max T-O weight	20,000-23,000 kg (44,100-50,700 lb)

PERFORMANCE:
Max cruising speed at 2,440-3,050 m (8,000-10,000 ft)	
	180 knots (334 km/h; 207 mph)

IPTN (CASA) NC-212 AVIOCAR

The C-212 Aviocar twin-turboprop multi-purpose transport aircraft has been manufactured in Indonesia since 1976, under licence from CASA of Spain (which see). Indonesian built Aviocars have the designation NC-212.

Contracts were placed for 114 NC-212s, and IPTN built 29 NC-212-100 series Aviocars before switching production to the NC-212-200 version, of which 81 had been delivered by February 1987 for duties which include civil passenger and cargo carrying, LAPES airdropping (low altitude parachute extraction system), military transport, search and rescue, maritime patrol, medical evacuation, photographic, survey, and rainmaking. Domestic and foreign operators were listed in the 1985-86 *Jane's*.

IPTN N-228

Under this designation, IPTN is developing its own 'stretched' version of the NC-212 Aviocar to carry 28 passengers. Design max T-O weight is 9,500 kg (20,950 lb).

IPTN (MBB) NBO-105

The BO 105 helicopter has been manufactured in

IPTN NC-212-200 Aviocar twin-turboprop transport in Indonesian Air Force insignia

NAS-332 Super Puma assembled by IPTN

Indonesia since 1976, under licence from MBB (see German section). Indonesian designation is NBO-105.

By February 1987 a total of 100 NBO-105s had been delivered (of 142 then on order), and production was continuing with the **NBO-105 S**, which has a 25 cm (10 in) longer fuselage and optional radar. An armed version, designated **NBO-105MPDS** (multi-purpose delivery system), can be equipped with unguided rockets (50 mm to 81 mm calibre), machine-gun pods (single or twin 0.30 in or 0.50 in), reconnaissance pods or FLIR pods. Customers for the NBO-105 include the Indonesian Army, Navy and Police, Pelita Air Service, the Indonesian Forestry Department, Indonesian Immigration Department, Indonesian Search and Rescue Agency, Gudang Garam, Gunung Madu, and the Indonesian Civil Aviation Training Centre.

It was announced in February 1987 that MBB was to cease manufacture of BO 105 components and in future purchase them direct from IPTN for assembly in Germany to meet its own marketing requirements. This decision will require IPTN to produce the equivalent of 80-100 of these helicopters per year to cater for MBB sales of the aircraft, in addition to those produced to meet its own orders. Accordingly, MBB has licensed IPTN to produce the aircraft with 100 per cent Indonesian content.

IPTN (MBB/KAWASAKI) NBK-117

Under a contract signed with MBB in November 1982, IPTN is manufacturing the BK 117 helicopter (see International section) under licence. Indonesian aircraft, which have been ordered by government agencies and private operators, are designated NBK-117; three had been completed by 1 January 1987.

NTT BN-109

Under this designation, MBB and IPTN are developing a small four-seat helicopter. All known details are given under the NTT heading in the International section.

IPTN (AÉROSPATIALE) NAS-332 SUPER PUMA

IPTN began assembling the NSA 330J Puma in 1981, completing 11 before switching production to the AS 332 Super Puma in early 1983.

Rollout of the first IPTN assembled NAS-332 for Pelita Air Service took place on 22 April 1983. Ten had been completed by mid-1987. Two of these, delivered to the Indonesian Navy, are each equipped to carry a pair of AM39 Exocet anti-shipping missiles. One has been ordered by the Royal Malaysian Air Force, which has selected the NAS-332 to replace its Sikorsky S-61A-4 Nuri fleet.

IPTN (BELL) NBELL-412

A licence agreement for IPTN to manufacture the Bell Model 412 (see Canadian section) was signed in November 1982. It covers the partial manufacture and assembly of more than 100 Bell 412s, the first of which was flown for the first time in April 1986. Orders have been placed by the Indonesian armed forces and private operators. IPTN built aircraft, three of which had been completed by mid-1987, are designated NBell-412.

Indonesian Air Force NBO-105 helicopter, equipped for search and rescue duties

INTERNATIONAL PROGRAMMES

AÉROSPATIALE/ASTA/CATIC

Aérospatiale (France), ASTA (Australia) and CATIC (People's Republic of China) signed a protocol agreement in early 1988 covering the development and production of a new 2 to 2½ tonne light helicopter for civil and military applications. This was expected to be followed by a more detailed co-operation agreement defining the role requirements, development/production work sharing and marketing responsibilities.

AIRBUS

AIRBUS INDUSTRIE

1 Rond Point Maurice Bellonte, 31707 Blagnac Cédex, France
Telephone: (61) 93 33 33
Telex: AIRBU 530526 F
Fax: (61) 93 37 92
PARIS OFFICE: 12bis avenue Bosquet, 75007 Paris, France
Telephone: (33) 145 51 40 95
AIRFRAME PRIME CONTRACTORS:
  Aérospatiale, 37 boulevard de Montmorency, 75781 Paris Cédex 16, France
  Deutsche Airbus GmbH, 8000 Munich 81, Arabellastrasse 30, Postfach 810260, Federal Republic of Germany
  British Aerospace PLC, Richmond Road, Kingston upon Thames, Surrey KT2 5QS, England
  Construcciones Aeronauticas SA, Rey Francisco 4, Apartado 193, 28008 Madrid, Spain
PRESIDENT AND CHIEF EXECUTIVE OFFICER: Jean Pierson
EXECUTIVE VICE-PRESIDENT AND GENERAL MANAGER: Heribert Flosdorff
SENIOR VICE-PRESIDENT, COMMERCIAL: Stuart Iddles
PRESS RELATIONS MANAGER: David Velupillai

Airbus Industrie was set up in December 1970 as a Groupement d'Intérêt Economique to manage the development, manufacture, marketing and support of the A300 twin-engined large-capacity short/medium-range transport. This management now extends to the A300-600, A310, A320 and A340/A330 included in this entry. Airbus Industrie is responsible for all work on these programmes by the partner companies, made up of Aérospatiale of France, which has a 37.9% interest in Airbus Industrie, MBB (through Deutsche Airbus) of West Germany (37.9%), British Aerospace PLC (20%), and CASA of Spain (4.2%). Fokker (Netherlands) is an associate in the A300 and A310 programmes; and Belairbus (Belgium) in the programmes for the A310, A320 and A330/340. Among the major partners, a total workforce of 23,000 is engaged on Airbus Industrie programmes. Some of the Deutsche Airbus work on the A300/A310 is subcontracted to the Italian aerospace industry, and some BAe work to the Australian industry.

Large, fully equipped and inspected airframe sections are flown from their places of manufacture in Europe to the final assembly line in Toulouse on board Super Guppy outsize cargo aircraft. After assembly, painting in customers' colour scheme is usually carried out at Toulouse. Aircraft are then flown to Hamburg for installation of interior furnishings and cabin and cargo hold equipment before returning to Toulouse for final customer acceptance.

AIRBUS A300-600

The early history of the A300 programme has appeared in previous editions of *Jane's.*

The first A300, a B1 (F-WUAB, later F-OCAZ) made its first flight on 28 October 1972, and was followed by the second B1 (F-WUAC) on 5 February 1973. The B1 was described in detail in the 1971-72 *Jane's.* Detailed descriptions of the B2 and B4 series (248 built) can be found in the 1984-85 and earlier editions. A300B4 production ended in Autumn 1984.

The major production versions since early 1984 are:

A300-600. Advanced version of B4-200, first flown (F-WZLR) on 8 July 1983 and certificated (with JT9D-7R4H1 engines) on 9 March 1984. French certification for Category IIIB take-offs and landings awarded on 26 March 1985. Increased passenger and freight capacity.

Modifications include use of rear fuselage developed for A310, shorter by two frame pitches in unpressurised section than that of 100/200 series A300s, with three frame pitches extension of parallel section of fuselage to restore tail moment arm. Passenger capacity thus increased by two seat rows for increase in overall length equivalent to only one frame pitch. Other improvements include forward facing two-man cockpit with CRT displays, new digital avionics, new braking control system, and new APU.

An extensive weight reduction programme, including simplified systems and the use of composite materials for some secondary structural components, allows greater payload capacity with very little change in empty weight. Performance improvements, offering better payload/range capability and greater fuel economy, result from a comprehensive 'drag clean-up' programme.

First delivery (to Saudia) was made on 26 March 1984. September 1985 certification was obtained for the improved version (first flown on 20 March 1985) with CF6-80C2 engines, carbon brakes, wingtip fences and 'New World' cockpit. This version has been ordered by Thai Airways International (six), the Abu Dhabi Private Flight (one), Korean Air (five), LATUR of Mexico (one) and Lufthansa (seven); first delivery (to Thai Airways) was made on 26 September 1985.

A300-600R. Extended range version of -600 (formerly known as -600ER), first flown on 9 December 1987. European and FAA certification granted on 10 and 28 March 1988 respectively. Principal differences from the improved A300-600 are incorporation of tailplane trim tank (already in service on the A310-300) and increased max T-O weight. Deliveries began on 21 April 1988 to launch customer American Airlines, which has ordered 25. Other customers include Emirates (one), ILFC (four), Korean Air (two), LATUR (one) and Thai Airways International (two).

A300-600 Convertible. Convertible passenger/cargo version of the A300-600; described separately.

By 1 July 1988 orders for the A300-600 and -600R, including Convertibles, totalled 70, of which 38 had been delivered.

Aérospatiale is responsible for the entire nose section (including the flight deck), lower centre fuselage, two inboard spoilers on each wing, wing/body fairings and engine pylons, and for final assembly. MBB builds the forward fuselage between the flight deck and wing box, the upper centre fuselage, rear fuselage, vertical tail surfaces, tailcone, five outboard spoilers on each wing, and some cabin doors. British Aerospace has design responsibility for the wings, builds the wing fixed structures, and collaborates with Fokker, which is building the wingtips, leading-edge slats, ailerons, trailing-edge flaps, and main landing gear leg fairings. Wing assembly is done by MBB. CASA manufactures all horizontal tail surfaces, port and starboard forward passenger doors, mainwheel doors and nosewheel doors.

The following description applies to the A300-600, except where otherwise indicated:
TYPE: Large-capacity wide-bodied medium/long-range transport.
WINGS: Cantilever mid-wing monoplane. Thickness/chord ratio 10.5%. Sweepback 28° at quarter-chord. Primary two-spar box structure, integral with fuselage and incorporating fail-safe principles, built of high strength aluminium alloy except for spoilers and outer flap deflector doors (carbonfibre); flap track fairings and rear wing/body fairings (aramid fibre); and upper surface panels above mainwheel bays (glassfibre). All CFRP moving surfaces have aluminium or titanium trailing-edges. Third spar across inboard sections. Machined skin with open-sectioned stringers. Each wing has three-section metal leading-edge slats (no slat cutout over the engine pylon), and three cambered tabless metal flaps on trailing-edge; a Krueger flap on the leading-edge wingroot; and an all-speed metal aileron between inboard flap and outer pair. Seven spoilers on each wing, forward of flaps, all of which are used as lift dumpers. The five outboard spoilers are used for roll control; the five inboard spoilers are used as airbrakes. The flaps extend over 84 per cent of each half span, and increase the wing

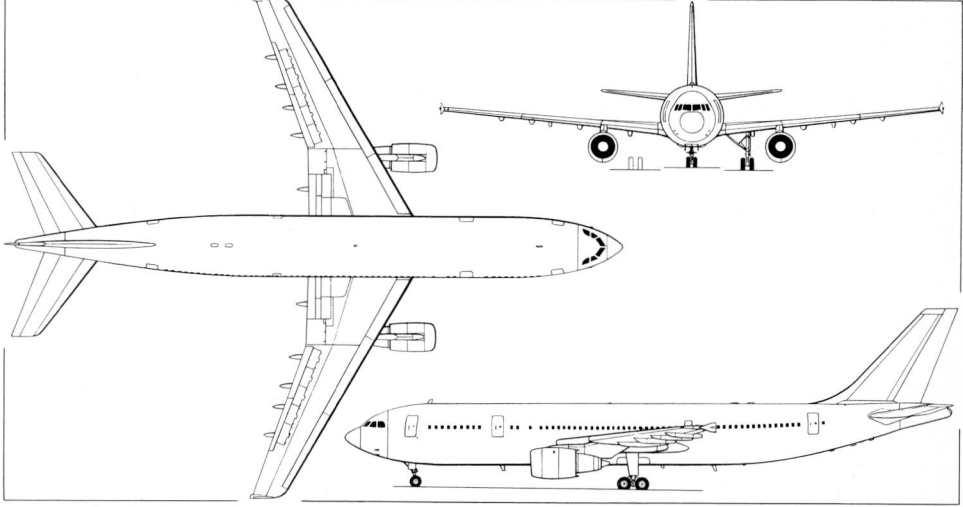

Airbus A300-600R wide-bodied medium-range transport (JT9D engines) *(Pilot Press)*

Airbus A300-600R twin-turbofan extended range transport for entry into service in 1988 with American Airlines

chord by 25 per cent when fully extended. The aileron is deflected downward automatically 9° 2′ on each side when the flaps are operated. Drive mechanisms for flaps and slats are similar to one another, each powered by twin motors driving ball screwjacks on each surface with built-in protection against asymmetric operation. Two slat positions for take-off and landing. Pre-selection of the spoiler/lift dump lever allows automatic extension of the lift dumpers on touchdown. Ailerons are fully powered by mechanically controlled hydraulic servos (three per surface); secondary control surfaces (spoilers, flaps and slats) fully hydraulically powered, with electrical control. Wingtip fences introduced 1985. Anti-icing of wing leading-edges, outboard of engines, is by engine bleed air.

FUSELAGE: Semi-monocoque pressurised structure of circular cross-section, with frames and open Z-section stringers. Built of damage-tolerant aluminium alloy, with steel or titanium for some major components; cooling air inlet fairings and radome of AFRP. Skin panels integrally machined in areas of high stress. Honeycomb panels or selected glassfibre laminates for secondary structures.

TAIL UNIT: Cantilever structure, with sweepback on all surfaces. Construction mainly of metal except for fin leading/trailing-edges, fin tip, fin/fuselage fairings, rudder, tailplane trailing-edge and elevator leading-edge panels, tailplane and elevator tips, and access panels to elevator actuator, which are made of GFRP (with CFRP in case of elevators and rudder). Fin box made of carbonfibre since mid-1987. Variable incidence tailplane is actuated by a fail-safe ball screwjack, driven by two independent hydraulic motors which are electrically controlled with an additional mechanical input. Elevators and rudder are fully powered by mechanically controlled hydraulic servos (three per surface). No anti-icing of leading-edges.

LANDING GEAR: Hydraulically retractable tricycle type, of Messier-Hispano-Bugatti design, with Messier-Hispano-Bugatti/Liebherr/Dowty shock absorbers and wheels standard. Twin-wheel nose unit retracts forward, main units inward into fuselage. Free-fall extension. Nosewheel doors and mainwheel leg fairing doors are of CFRP. Nose gear is structurally identical to B2/B4/A310; main gear is generally reinforced, with a new-design hinge arm and a new pitch damper hydraulic and electrical installation. Each four-wheel main unit comprises two tandem mounted bogies, interchangeable left with right. Standard bogie size is 927 × 1,397 mm (36½ × 55 in); wider bogie of 978 × 1,524 mm (38½ × 60 in) is optional. Mainwheel tyres size 49 × 17-20 (standard) or 49 × 19-20 (wide bogie), with respective pressures of 12.4 and 11.1 bars (180 and 161 lb/sq in). Nosewheel tyres size 40 × 14-16, pressure 9.4 bars (136 lb/sq in). Steering angles 65°/95°. Messier-Hispano-Bugatti/Liebherr/Dowty hydraulic disc brakes standard on all mainwheels. Normal braking powered by 'green' hydraulic system, controlled electrically through two master valves and monitored by a brake system control box to provide anti-skid protection. Standby braking (powered automatically by 'yellow' hydraulic system if normal 'green' system supply fails) controlled through a dual metering valve; anti-skid protection is ensured through same box as normal system, with emergency pressure supplied to brakes by accumulators charged from 'yellow' system. Automatic braking system optional. Duplex anti-skid units fitted, with a third standby hydraulic supply for wheel brakes. Bendix or Goodrich wheels and brakes available optionally.

POWER PLANT: Two turbofans in underwing pods. A300-600 was launched with the 249 kN (56,000 lb st) Pratt & Whitney JT9D-7R4H1 and is currently available with the 249 kN (56,000 lb st) Pratt & Whitney PW4156 or 262.4 kN (59,000 lb st) General Electric CF6-80C2A1. A300-600R is offered with the 273.6 kN (61,500 lb st) CF6-80C2A5 or 258 kN (58,000 lb st) PW4158. The CF6-80C2A5 and PW4158 are also available as options on the A300-600. Nacelles have CFRP cowling panels and are subcontracted to Rohr (California); pylon fairings are of AFRP. Fuel in two integral tanks in each wing, and fifth integral tank in wing centre-section, giving standard usable capacity of 62,000 litres (16,379 US gallons; 13,638 Imp gallons). Additional 6,150 litre (1,625 US gallon; 1,353 Imp gallon) fuel/trim tank in tailplane (-600R only) increases this total to 68,150 litres (18,004 US gallons; 14,991 Imp gallons). Optional extra fuel cell in aft cargo hold can increase totals to 69,200 litres (18,281 US gallons; 15,222 Imp gallons) in A300-600 or 75,350 litres (19,906 US gallons; 16,575 Imp gallons) in -600R. Two standard refuelling points beneath starboard wing; similar pair optional under port wing.

ACCOMMODATION: Crew of two on flight deck, plus two observers' seats. Passenger seating in main cabin in six, seven, eight or nine-abreast layout with two aisles. Typical mixed class layout has 267 seats (28 first class and 239 economy), six/eight abreast at 96/86 cm (38/34 in) seat pitch with one galley and two toilets forward, two galleys in mid-cabin, and one galley and four toilets at rear. Typical economy class layout for 289 passengers eight-abreast at 86 cm (34 in) pitch. Max capacity (subject to certification) 375 passengers. Closed overhead baggage lockers on each side (total capacity 10.48 m^3; 370 cu ft) and in double-sided central 'super-bin' installation (total capacity 14.50 m^3; 512 cu ft), giving 0.03 to 0.09 m^3 (1.2 to 3.2 cu ft) per passenger in typical economy layout. Two outward parallel-opening Type A plug type passenger doors ahead of wing on each side, and one on each side at rear. Type I emergency exit on each side aft of wing. Underfloor baggage/cargo holds fore and aft of wings, with doors on starboard side. Forward hold will accommodate twelve LD3 containers, or four 2.24 × 3.17 m (88 × 125 in) or, optionally, 2.43 × 3.17 m (96 × 125 in) pallets, or engine modules. Rear hold will accommodate ten LD3 containers. Additional bulk loading of freight provided for in an extreme rear compartment with usable volume of 17.3 m^3 (611 cu ft). Alternatively, the rear hold can be arranged optionally to carry eleven LD3 containers, with bulk cargo capacity reduced to 8.6 m^3 (303 cu ft). The bulk cargo compartment can be used for the transport of livestock. Entire accommodation is pressurised, including freight, baggage and avionics compartments.

SYSTEMS: Air supply for air-conditioning system taken from engine bleed and/or APU via two high pressure points. Conditioned air can also be supplied direct to cabin by two low pressure ground connections. Ram air inlet for fresh air ventilation when packs not in use. Pressure control system (max differential 0.574 bars; 8.32 lb/sq in) consists of two identical, independent, automatic systems (one active, one standby). Switchover from one to the other is automatic after each flight and in case of active system failure. In each system, pressure is controlled by two electric outflow valves, its function depending on pre-programmed cabin pressure altitude and rate of change of cabin pressure, aircraft altitude, and preselected landing airfield elevation. Automatic pre-pressurisation of cabin before take-off is provided, to prevent noticeable pressure fluctuation during take-off. Hydraulic system comprises three fully independent circuits, operating simultaneously. Each system includes a reservoir of the direct air/fluid contact type, pressurised at 3.5 bars (51 lb/sq in); fluid used is a fire resistant phosphate ester type. Nominal output flow of 136 litres (35.9 US gallons; 30 Imp gallons)/min is delivered at pressure of 207 bars (3,000 lb/sq in). 'Blue' and 'yellow' systems have one pump each, 'green' system has two pumps. The three circuits provide triplex power for primary flying controls; if any circuit fails, full control of the aircraft is retained without any necessity for action by the crew. All three circuits supply the ailerons, rudder and elevators; 'blue' circuit additionally supplies spoiler 7, spoiler/airbrake 4, airbrake 1, yaw damper and slats; 'green' circuit additionally supplies spoiler 6, flaps, Krueger flaps, slats, landing gear, wheel brakes, steering, tailplane trim, artificial feel, and roll/pitch/yaw autopilot; 'yellow' circuit additionally supplies spoiler 5, spoiler/airbrake 3, airbrake 2, flaps, wheel brakes, cargo doors, artificial feel, yaw damper, tailplane trim, and roll/pitch/yaw autopilot. Ram air turbine driven pump provides standby hydraulic power should both engines become inoperative. Main electrical power is supplied under normal flight conditions by two integrated drive generators, one on each engine. A third (auxiliary) generator, driven by the APU, can replace either of the main generators, having the same electromagnetic components but not the constant-speed drive. Each generator is rated at 90kVA, with overload ratings of 112.5kVA for 5 min and 150kVA for 5 s. The APU generator is driven at constant speed through a gearbox. Three unregulated transformer-rectifier units (TRUs) supply 28V DC power. Three 25Ah nickel-cadmium batteries are used for emergency supply and APU starting. Emergency electrical power taken from main aircraft batteries and an emergency static inverter, providing single-phase 115V 400Hz output for flight instruments, navigation, communications and lighting when power is not available from normal sources. Hot air anti-icing of engines, engine air intakes, and outer segments of leading-edge slats. Electrical heating for anti-icing flight deck front windscreens, demisting flight deck side windows, and for sensors, pitot probes and static ports, and waste water drain masts. Garrett GTCP 331-250F APU in tailcone, exhausting upward. The installation incorporates APU noise attenuation. Fire protection system is self-contained, and firewall panels protect main structure from an APU fire. APU provides bleed air to pneumatic system, and drives an auxiliary AC generator during ground and in-flight operation. APU drives a 90kVA oil spray cooled generator, and supplies bleed air for main engine start or air-conditioning system. For future deliveries of A300-600, APU has an improved relight capability, with starting capability throughout the flight envelope. Modular box system provides passenger oxygen to all installation areas. For new A300-600s and -600Rs, two optional modifications are offered for compliance with full extended-range operations (EROPS) requirements: a hydraulically driven fourth generator and an increased cargo hold fire suppression capability. EROPS kit is already qualified for aircraft with CF6-80C2 and JT9D-7R series engines, and was to be qualified from mid-1988 for those with PW4000 series.

AVIONICS AND EQUIPMENT: Standard communications avionics include two VHF sets, one HF, one Selcal system, interphone and passenger address systems, groundcrew call system, and voice recorder. Radio navigation avionics include two DME interrogators, two VOR receivers, two ATC transponders, one ADF, two marker beacon receivers, two ILS receivers, weather radar, and two radio altimeters. Full provisions for second weather radar and GPWS; space provisions for one or two HF, third VHF; structural provision for such future systems as a discrete address beacon system. Two Sperry digital air data computers standard. Most other avionics are to customer's requirements, only those related to the blind landing system (ILS and radio altimeter) being selected and supplied by the manufacturer. Six identical and interchangeable CRT electronic displays (four EFIS and two ECAM: electronic flight instrument system and electronic centralised aircraft monitor), plus digitalised electromechanical instruments with liquid crystal displays. The basic digital AFCS comprises a single flight control computer (FCC) for flight director and autopilot functions, a single thrust control computer (TCC) for speed and thrust control, and two flight augmentation computers (FACs) to provide yaw damping, electric pitch trim, and flight envelope monitoring and protection. Options include second FCC (for Cat III automatic landing); second TCC; two flight management computers (FMCs) and two control display units for full flight management system; windscreen guidance display by adding optical device in glareshield; and addition of delayed flap approach (DFA) to TCC for decelerated approach. Basic aircraft is also fitted with an ARINC 717 data recording system, comprising a digital flight data acquisition unit, digital flight data recorder, three-axis linear accelerometer, and flight data entry panel. An optional speed reference system with built-in windshear protection is available. Dual automatic landing system provides coupled approach and automatic landing facilities suitable for Category II operation.

DIMENSIONS, EXTERNAL:

Wing span	44.84 m (147 ft 1 in)
Wing aspect ratio	7.7
Length overall	54.08 m (177 ft 5 in)
Fuselage: Length	53.30 m (174 ft 10½ in)
Max diameter	5.64 m (18 ft 6 in)
Height overall	16.62 m (54 ft 6½ in)
Tailplane span	16.26 m (53 ft 4 in)
Wheel track	9.60 m (31 ft 6 in)
Wheelbase (c/l of shock absorbers)	18.60 m (61 ft 0 in)
Passengers doors (each): Height	1.93 m (6 ft 4 in)
Width	1.07 m (3 ft 6 in)
Height to sill: fwd	4.60 m (15 ft 1 in)
centre	4.80 m (15 ft 9 in)
rear	5.50 m (18 ft 0½ in)
Emergency exits (each): Height	1.60 m (5 ft 3 in)
Width	0.61 m (2 ft 0 in)
Height to sill	4.87 m (15 ft 10 in)
Underfloor cargo door (fwd):	
Height	1.71 m (5 ft 7½ in)
Width	2.69 m (8 ft 10 in)
Height to sill	3.07 m (10 ft 1 in)
Underfloor cargo door (rear):	
Height	1.71 m (5 ft 7½ in)
Width	1.81 m (5 ft 11¼ in)
Height to sill	3.41 m (11 ft 2¼ in)
Underfloor cargo door (extreme rear):	
Height (projected)	0.95 m (3 ft 1 in)
Width	0.95 m (3 ft 1 in)
Height to sill	3.56 m (11 ft 8 in)

DIMENSIONS, INTERNAL:

Cabin, excl flight deck:	
Length	40.21 m (131 ft 11 in)
Max width	5.28 m (17 ft 4 in)
Max height	2.54 m (8 ft 4 in)
Underfloor cargo hold:	
Length: fwd	10.60 m (34 ft 9¼ in)
rear	7.95 m (26 ft 1 in)
extreme rear	3.40 m (11 ft 2 in)
Max height	1.76 m (5 ft 9 in)
Max width	4.20 m (13 ft 9¼ in)
Underfloor cargo hold volume:	
fwd	75.1 m^3 (2,652 cu ft)
rear	55.0 m^3 (1,942 cu ft)
extreme rear	17.3 m^3 (611 cu ft)

AREAS:

Wings, gross	260.0 m^2 (2,798.6 sq ft)
Leading-edge slats (total)	30.30 m^2 (326.15 sq ft)
Krueger flaps (total)	1.115 m^2 (12.00 sq ft)
Trailing-edge flaps (total)	47.30 m^2 (509.13 sq ft)
All-speed ailerons (total)	7.06 m^2 (75.99 sq ft)
Spoilers (total)	5.396 m^2 (58.08 sq ft)
Airbrakes (total)	12.59 m^2 (135.52 sq ft)
Fin	45.20 m^2 (486.53 sq ft)
Rudder	13.57 m^2 (146.07 sq ft)
Horizontal tail surfaces (total)	64.0 m^2 (688.89 sq ft)

*WEIGHTS AND LOADINGS (A: CF6-80C2A1/A5 engines; B: PW4156/4158 engines, all in 289-seat configuration):

Manufacturer's weight empty:	
A (600)	78,260 kg (172,533 lb)
A (600R)	77,813 kg (171,548 lb)

B (600)   78,201 kg (172,403 lb)
B (600R)   77,728 kg (171,360 lb)
Operating weight empty:
A (600)   86,662 kg (191,057 lb)
A (600R)   86,246 kg (190,140 lb)
B (600)   86,614 kg (190,951 lb)
B (600R)   86,172 kg (189,976 lb)
Max payload (structural): A (600)   43,338 kg (95,544 lb)
A (600R)   43,754 kg (96,461 lb)
B (600)   43,386 kg (95,650 lb)
B (600R)   43,828 kg (96,624 lb)
Underfloor cargo capacity (A and B):
containerised   31,300 kg (69,005 lb)
bulk   2,800 kg (6,173 lb)
Max usable fuel:
600: standard   49,777 kg (109,740 lb)
with optional cargo hold tank
   55,556 kg (122,480 lb)
600R: standard   54,712 kg (120,620 lb)
with optional cargo hold tank
   58,604 kg (129,200 lb)
Max T-O weight (A and B):
600   165,000 kg (363,765 lb)
600R (standard)   170,500 kg (375,885 lb)
600R (option)   171,700 kg (378,535 lb)
Max ramp weight (A and B):
600   165,900 kg (365,745 lb)
600R (standard)   170,500 kg (375,885 lb)
600R (option)   172,600 kg (380,520 lb)
Max landing weight (A and B):
600   138,000 kg (304,240 lb)
600R (standard)   140,000 kg (308,645 lb)
Max zero-fuel weight (A and B):
600, 600R (standard)   130,000 kg (286,600 lb)
600R (with MTOGW option)   123,000 kg (271,170 lb)
Max wing loading: 600   635 kg/m² (130.0 lb/sq ft)
600R (standard)   656 kg/m² (134.4 lb/sq ft)
   * Production aircraft from 1988 onward. See 1987-88 and
previous editions for earlier versions
PERFORMANCE (at max T-O weight except where indicated:
A and B as for 'Weights'):
Max operating speed (V$_{MO}$) from S/L to 8,075 m (26,500
ft)   345 knots (639 km/h; 397 mph) CAS
Max operating Mach number (M$_{MO}$) above 8,075 m
(26,500 ft)   0.82
Max cruising speed at 7,620 m (25,000 ft)
   480 knots (890 km/h; 553 mph)
Typical high-speed cruise at 9,150 m (30,000 ft)
   Mach 0.82 (484 knots; 897 km/h; 557 mph)
Typical long-range cruising speed at 9,450 m (31,000
ft)   Mach 0.80 (472 knots; 875 km/h; 543 mph)
Approach speed: 600   134.5 knots (249 km/h; 155 mph)
600R   135.5 knots (251 km/h; 156 mph)
Max operating altitude   12,200 m (40,000 ft)
Min ground turning radius (wingtips)
   33.51 m (109 ft 11¼ in)
Runway ACN for flexible runway, category B:
standard bogie & tyres: 600   56
600R   59
600R (option)   60
optional bogie & tyres: 600   52
600R   55
600R (option)   56
T-O field length at S/L, ISA + 15°C:
600: A   2,384 m (7,820 ft)
B   2,332 m (7,650 ft)
600R: A (C2A5 engines)   2,451 m (8,040 ft)
B (PW4158 engines)   2,500 m (8,200 ft)
Landing field length: 600   1,536 m (5,040 ft)
600R   1,555 m (5,100 ft)
Range (1988 deliveries) at typical airline OWE and 267
passengers with baggage, reserves for 200 nm (370 km;
230 miles):
600: A   3,710 nm (6,875 km; 4,272 miles)
B   3,760 nm (6,968 km; 4,330 miles)
600R (standard fuel):
A   4,115 nm (7,626 km; 4,738 miles)
B   4,155 nm (7,700 km; 4,784 miles)
600R (MTOGW option and additional fuel):
A   4,320 nm (8,006 km; 4,974 miles)
B   4,380 nm (8,117 km; 5,043 miles)
OPERATIONAL NOISE LEVELS (A300-600, ICAO Annex 16,
Chapter 3):
T-O (flyover): A, B   91.3 EPNdB (96.2 limit)
T-O (sideline): A, B   97.1 EPNdB (99.8 limit)
Approach: A, B   99.1 EPNdB (103.3 limit)

AIRBUS A300-600 CONVERTIBLE

The Convertible is a version of the A300-600, with the same range of power plant options. Main differences are a large forward upper deck cargo door, a reinforced cabin floor, a smoke detection system in the main cabin, and an interior trim adaptable to the freighter role. The upper deck cargo door is on the opposite side to that of the forward underfloor hold, enabling loading or unloading to be carried out simultaneously at all positions. Three are operated by Kuwait Airways and one by the Private Flight of Abu Dhabi.

The A300-600 Convertible can be converted to passenger or mixed passenger/cargo configuration. Typical options include accommodation (in mainly eight-abreast seating)

for up to 297 passengers on the upper deck; or 145 passengers (seven/eight abreast) plus six 2.44 × 3.17 m (96 × 125 in) pallets; or 83 passengers plus nine 96 × 125 in pallets; up to twenty 2.24 × 3.17 m (88 × 125 in) pallets; or five 88 × 125 in plus nine 96 × 125 in pallets.

DIMENSIONS, EXTERNAL: As A300-600, plus:
Upper deck cargo door (fwd, port):
Height (projected)   2.57 m (8 ft 5¼ in)
Width   3.58 m (11 ft 9 in)
Height to sill   4.91 m (16 ft 1 in)
DIMENSIONS, INTERNAL:
Cabin upper deck usable for cargo:
Length   33.45 m (109 ft 9 in)
Min height   2.01 m (6 ft 7 in)
Max height   2.22 m (7 ft 3½ in)
Volume   192-203 m³ (6,780-7,169 cu ft)
WEIGHTS (basic. A: with JT9D-7R4H1 engines, B: with
CF6-80C2A1s):
Manufacturer's weight empty:
A, passenger mode   80,259 kg (176,940 lb)
B, passenger mode   80,578 kg (177,644 lb)
A, freight mode   81,258 kg (179,143 lb)
B, freight mode   81,577 kg (179,846 lb)
* Operating weight empty:
A, passenger mode   88,903 kg (195,997 lb)
B, passenger mode   89,222 kg (196,700 lb)
A, freight mode   82,286 kg (181,409 lb)
B, freight mode   82,605 kg (182,112 lb)
Max payload (structural):
A, passenger mode   41,097 kg (90,603 lb)
B, passenger mode   40,778 kg (89,900 lb)
A, freight mode   47,714 kg (105,191 lb)
B, freight mode   47,395 kg (104,488 lb)
Max T-O weight (A and B)   165,000 kg (363,765 lb)
Max landing weight (A and B)   138,000 kg (304,240 lb)
Max zero-fuel weight (A and B)   130,000 kg (286,600 lb)
*incl weight of underfloor cargo hold containers and pallets
PERFORMANCE:
Range with max (structural) payload, allowances for 30
min hold at 460 m (1,500 ft) and 200 nm (370 km; 230
mile) diversion   2,300 nm (4,262 km; 2,648 miles)

AIRBUS A310

The A310 was launched in July 1978. Compared with the A300B2/B4-100 and 200 series, the cabin is shorter by 11 frames and the overall fuselage by 13 frames. The cabin thus normally seats from 210 to 250 passengers, although the aircraft is certificated for up to 280 persons. The A310 retains the same fuselage cross-section as the A300, thus being able to carry standard LD3 containers two abreast, and/or standard pallets installed crosswise. Convertible and freighter versions are available.

The A310 also has new, advanced technology wings, of reduced span and area; new and smaller horizontal tail surfaces; common pylons able to support all types of General Electric and Pratt & Whitney engines offered; and landing gear modified to cater for these changes in size and weight. It features Airbus Industrie's advanced digital two-man flight deck.

Manufacturing breakdown of the A310 differs in minor respects from that of the A300. Aérospatiale builds the nose section (including flight deck), lower centre-fuselage and wing box, rear wing/body fairings, engine pylons and airbrakes, and is responsible for final assembly. MBB is responsible for the forward passenger cabin, upper centre-fuselage, rear fuselage and associated doors, tailcone, fin and rudder, flaps and spoilers; for wing assembly, and for commercial installation. BAe Chester produces the wing fixed structures. CASA's contribution includes the horizontal tail surfaces, nose-gear doors and mainwheel doors, and forward passenger doors. Fokker manufactures

the main landing gear leg doors, wingtips, all-speed ailerons and flap track fairings. The wing leading-edge slats and forward wing/fuselage fairings are produced by Belairbus.

The prototype A310 (F-WZLH) flew for the first time on 3 April 1982. Simultaneous French and German certification was awarded on 11 March 1983, UK certification in January 1984 and FAA type approval in early 1985. The first aircraft (for Lufthansa and Swissair) were handed over on 29 March 1983, entering service on 12 and 21 April respectively. Certification to JAR Category IIIA was awarded by the French and German authorities on 28 and 29 September 1983, and Category IIIB on 28 November 1984.

The following versions have been announced:
A310-200. Basic passenger version. Wingtip fences introduced as standard from Spring 1986 (first delivery: Thai Airways on 7 May).
A310-200C. Convertible version; first delivered to Martinair on 29 November 1984.
A310-200F. Freighter version.
A310-300. Extended-range version. First flown on 8 July 1985 with JT9D-7R4E engines; certificated with these engines on 5 December 1985 and delivered to launch customer Swissair on 17 December. Second member of Airbus family to introduce as standard the delta shaped wingtip fences (for drag reduction) developed by BAe and test flown in 1983 on an A310-200 testbed. Version with CF6-80C2 engines first flew on 6 September 1985, followed by certification and first delivery (to Air-India) in April 1986. Certificated with PW4152 engines and first delivered (to Pan American) in June 1987. Extra range is provided by an increased basic max T-O weight (150,000 kg; 330,695 lb) and greater fuel capacity. Higher max T-O weights optional. The standard extra fuel capacity is in the tailplane, which allows in-flight CG control for improved fuel efficiency; for extra long range, an ACT (additional centre tank) can be installed in part of the cargo hold. First customer for this version, certificated in November 1987, is Wardair of Canada; ILFC has ordered six.

By 8 July 1988 firm orders for 163 A310s had been received, of which 132 had been delivered.

TYPE: Large-capacity wide-bodied medium/extended-range transport.

WINGS: Cantilever mid-wing monoplane. Thickness/chord ratio 15.2% at root, 11.8% at kink in trailing-edge, and 10.8% at tip. Dihedral at trailing-edge 11° 8' (inboard) and 4° 3' (outboard). Incidence 5° 3' at root. Sweepback 28° at quarter-chord. Construction is mainly of high strength aluminium alloy except for outer shroud (structure in place of low-speed aileron), airbrakes, spoilers, leading-edge lower access panels and outer deflector doors (CFRP); flap track fairings, flap access doors and rear wing/body fairings (AFRP); and leading-edge top panels, panel aft of rear spar, upper surface skin panel above mainwheel bay, and forward wing/body fairings (GFRP). Wing box is two-spar multi-rib metal structure, with top and bottom load-carrying skins. Three-section leading-edge slats on each wing over almost full span, with no cutout over engine pylon; Krueger flap between inboard slat and wing root. Fowler trailing-edge flap on outboard section of each wing; vaned Fowler flap inboard. All-speed metal aileron between flaps on each wing. Electrically signalled spoilers for roll control. Two independent computer systems with different software provide redundancy and operational safety. Two airbrakes between root and engine, two airbrakes outboard of engine, and three spoilers outboard of outer airbrakes, on each wing; all 14 surfaces are used also as lift dumpers. Delta shaped wingtip fences standard from 1985. Outer slat leading-edges de-iced by engine bleed air.

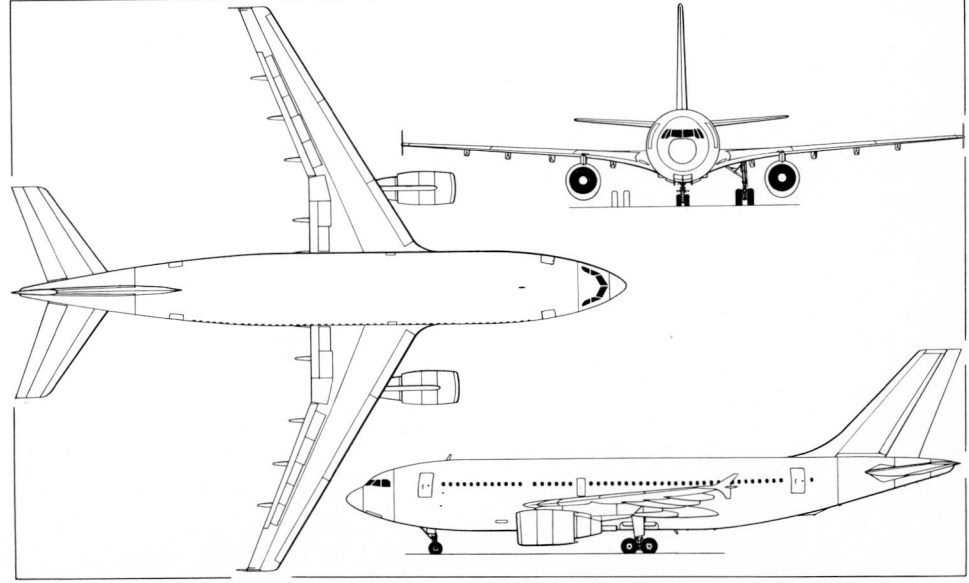

Airbus A310 medium/extended-range transport aircraft (*Pilot Press*)

Airbus A310-300 in the insignia of Wardair of Canada

FUSELAGE: Generally similar to A300B4, except for reduced length (see introductory copy), resulting in deletion of two passenger doors. Rear fuselage reprofiled and shortened between pressure bulkhead and tailcone. Construction generally as described for A300-600, with AFRP radome and cooling air inlet fairings, GFRP cover panel over glidescope antenna.

TAIL UNIT: Generally as described for A300-600, with CFRP fin box standard since Spring 1985. GFRP fin leading-/trailing-edges and fin tip. Metal tailplane, with GFRP tips, CFRP trailing-edge actuator access panel and AFRP trailing-edge panels. Rudder of CFRP and GFRP; CFRP elevators to be introduced in 1989.

LANDING GEAR: Hydraulically retractable tricycle type. Twin-wheel steerable nose unit (steering angle 65°/95°) as for A300. Main gear by Messier-Hispano-Bugatti, each bogie comprising two tandem mounted twin-wheel units. Retraction as for A300. Nosewheel doors and mainwheel leg fairing doors of CFRP. Undertail bumper beneath rear fuselage, to protect structure against excessive nose-up attitude during T-O and landing. Standard tyre sizes: main, 46 × 16-20, pressure 11.2 bars (163 lb/sq in); nose, 40 × 14-16, pressure 9.0 bars (131 lb/sq in). Two options for low-pressure tyres on main units: (1) size 49 × 17-20, pressure 9.8 bars (143 lb/sq in); (2) size 49 × 19-20, pressure 8.9 bars (129 lb/sq in). Messier-Hispano-Bugatti brakes and anti-skid units standard; Bendix type optional on A310-200. Carbon brakes standard from Spring 1986.

POWER PLANT: Currently ordered or available with the following turbofan engines:
Launched with two 213.5 kN (48,000 lb st) Pratt & Whitney JT9D-7R4D1; currently available with 222.4 kN (50,000 lb st) General Electric CF6-80C2A2, or Pratt & Whitney JT9D-7R4E1; or two 231.2 kN (52,000 lb st) Pratt & Whitney PW4152. CFRP cowling panels and AFRP pylon fairings. Total usable fuel capacity 55,000 litres (14,530 US gallons; 12,098 Imp gallons) in A310-200. Increased to 61,100 litres (16,141 US gallons; 13,440 Imp gallons) in A310-300, with additional fuel in tailplane trim tank. Further 7,200 litres (1,902 US gallons; 1,584 Imp gallons) can be carried by both versions in forward part of aft cargo hold. Two refuelling points, one beneath each wing outboard of engine.

ACCOMMODATION: Crew of two on flight deck. Provision for third and fourth crew seats. Cabin can be configured with six/seven/eight and nine-abreast seating. Typical two-class layout is for 218 passengers: 20 first class, six-abreast at 96.5 cm (38 in) seat pitch, plus 198 economy class mainly eight-abreast at 86 cm (34 in) pitch. Max capacity is for up to 280 passengers nine-abreast in high-density configuration at pitch of 76 cm (30 in). Standard layout has galley and toilet at forward end of cabin, plus larger galley and four toilets at rear. Depending upon customer requirements, a second toilet and galley can be added forward, and an additional galley aft. Toilets and galleys can be located at the forward end at the class divider position. Overhead baggage stowage as for A300, rising to 0.09 m³ (3.2 cu ft) per passenger in typical economy layout. Four passenger doors, one forward and one aft on each side. Type I emergency exit over wing on each side. Underfloor baggage/cargo holds fore and aft of wings, each with door on starboard side. Forward hold will accommodate eight LD3 containers or three 2.24 × 3.17 m (88 × 125 in) standard pallets. Rear hold will accommodate six LD3 containers, with an optional seventh LD3 or LD1 position.

SYSTEMS: Garrett GTCP 331-250 APU. Air-conditioning system, powered by compressed air from engines, APU, or a ground supply unit, comprises two separate packs; air is distributed to flight deck, three separate cabin zones, electrical and electronic equipment, avionics bay and bulk cargo compartment. Ventilation of forward cargo compartments optional. Pressurisation system has a max normal differential of 0.57 bars (8.25 lb/sq in). Air supply for wing ice protection, engine starting and thrust reverser system is bled from various stages of the engine

compressors, or supplied by the APU or a ground supply unit. Hydraulic system (three fully independent circuits operating at 207 bars; 3,000 lb/sq in: details as described for A300-600). Electrical system, similar to that of A300-600, consists of a three-phase 115/200V 400Hz constant frequency AC system and a 28V DC system. Two 90kVA engine driven brushless generators for normal single-channel operation, with automatic transfer of busbars in the event of a generator failure. Each has an overload rating of 135kVA for 5 min and 180kVA for 5 s. A third (identical) AC generator, directly driven at constant speed by the APU, can be used during ground operations, and also in flight to compensate for the loss of one or both engine driven generators. Current production A310s have APU with improved relight capability, which can be started and operated throughout the flight envelope. Any one generator can provide sufficient power to operate all equipment and systems necessary for an indefinite period of safe flight. DC power is generated via three 150A transformer-rectifiers. Three nickel-cadmium batteries are supplied. Flight crew oxygen system fed from rechargeable pressure bottle of 2,166 litres (76.5 cu ft) capacity. Standard options are a second 76.5 cu ft bottle, a 3,256 litre (115 cu ft) bottle, and an external filling connection. Emergency oxygen sets for passengers and cabin attendants. Anti-icing of outer wing leading-edge slats and engine air intakes by hot air bled from engines; and of pitot probes, static ports and plates, and sensors, by electric heating. For current production A310s, an EROPS (extended-range operations) modification kit, as for the A300-600, is available.

AVIONICS AND EQUIPMENT: Basic standard flight deck displays include flight guidance, navigation, configuration and engine management/monitoring information presented by electro-mechanical indicators, and an electronic centralised aircraft monitoring (ECAM) system unique to Airbus Industrie; warning information presented by conventional warning lights and on a master warning CRT; system information presented on a system CRT. Electronic flight instrument system comprises a CRT primary flight display, replacing the ADI and radio altimeter, and a CRT navigation display replacing the HSI and weather radar. The latter displays data from the flight management system (map mode, flight data display). A flight data recorder is also installed. Head-up display is optional. The basic aircraft is fitted with an AIDS (airborne integrated data system) providing a basic 80-parameter system (40 mandatory plus 40 additional) with an option to extend the system to 160 parameters. Standard com system includes HF radio (ARINC 719) (full provision); two VHF transceivers and space provision for a third (all to ARINC 716); Selcal system (ARINC 714); passenger address system (the amplifier conforming to ARINC 715); audio systems, comprising service interphone, audio integrating and flight interphone systems, and a ground crew call circuit. Digital navigation system, to ARINC 429 and ARINC 600, includes ADF (ARINC 712); two radio altimeters (ARINC 707); two DME (ARINC 709); two ATC transponders (ARINC 718); two VOR, one including marker beacon receiver (ARINC 711); weather radar (ARINC 708); two ILS (ARINC 710); and three AHRS (ARINC 705). Options include a second ADF; two or three IRS (ARINC 704); Omega system; and a second weather radar. The digital automatic flight control system (AFCS), in its basic definition, comprises a single flight control computer (FCC) for automatic flight control (to ARINC 701); a single thrust control computer (TCC) for speed and thrust control (to ARINC 703); and a duplicated flight augmentation computer (to ARINC 701). The flight management system (to ARINC 702) comprises a computer unit and control display unit. The FCC, functioning as autopilot, flight director and speed reference system, has the following basic modes: pitch hold, heading/roll altitude hold, altitude hold, altitude acquire, level change, vertical speed select and hold,

heading select, VOR, heading, take-off and go-around. The installation of a second FCC will provide Cat. III autolands. The TCC provides the following functions: permanent computation of N1 or EPR limits, autothrottle functions, throttle pusher with windshear protection, speed and angle of attack protection, and a test function. A delayed flap approach mode is available as an option.

DIMENSIONS, EXTERNAL:
Wing span	43.89 m (144 ft 0 in)
Wing chord: at root	8.38 m (27 ft 6 in)
at tip	2.18 m (7 ft 1¾ in)
Wing aspect ratio	8.8
Length overall	46.66 m (153 ft 1 in)
Length of fuselage	45.13 m (148 ft 0¾ in)
Fuselage: Max diameter	5.64 m (18 ft 6 in)
Height overall	15.80 m (51 ft 10 in)
Tailplane span	16.26 m (53 ft 4¼ in)
Wheel track	9.60 m (31 ft 6 in)
Wheelbase (c/l of shock absorbers)	15.21 m (49 ft 10¾ in)
Passenger door (fwd, port): Height	1.93 m (6 ft 4 in)
Width	1.07 m (3 ft 6 in)
Height to sill at OWE	4.54 m (14 ft 10¾ in)
Passenger door (rear, port): Height	1.93 m (6 ft 4 in)
Width	1.07 m (3 ft 6 in)
Height to sill at OWE	4.85 m (15 ft 11 in)
Servicing doors (fwd and rear, stbd)	as corresponding passenger doors
Upper deck cargo door (A310C/F)	as A300-600
Emergency exits (overwing, port and stbd, each):	
Height	1.39 m (4 ft 6¾ in)
Width	0.67 m (2 ft 2½ in)
Underfloor cargo door (fwd):	
Height	1.71 m (5 ft 7½ in)
Width	2.69 m (8 ft 10 in)
Height to sill at OWE	2.611 m (8 ft 6¾ in)
Underfloor cargo door (rear):	
Height	1.71 m (5 ft 7½ in)
Width	1.81 m (5 ft 11¼ in)
Height to sill at OWE	2.72 m (8 ft 11 in)
Underfloor cargo door (aft bulk hold):	
Height	0.95 m (3 ft 1½ in)
Width	0.95 m (3 ft 1½ in)
Height to sill at OWE	2.751 m (9 ft 0¼ in)

DIMENSIONS, INTERNAL:
Cabin, excl flight deck: Length	33.24 m (109 ft 0¾ in)
Max width	5.28 m (17 ft 4 in)
Max height	2.33 m (7 ft 7¾ in)
Volume	210.0 m³ (7,416.1 cu ft)
Fwd cargo hold: Length	7.63 m (25 ft 0½ in)
Max width	4.18 m (13 ft 8½ in)
Height	1.71 m (5 ft 7¼ in)
Volume	50.3 m³ (1,776.3 cu ft)
Rear cargo hold: Length	5.033 m (16 ft 6¼ in)
Max width	4.17 m (13 ft 8¼ in)
Height	1.67 m (5 ft 5¾ in)
Volume	34.5 m³ (1,218.4 cu ft)
Aft bulk hold: Volume	17.3 m³ (610.9 cu ft)
Total overall cargo volume	102.1 m³ (3,605.6 cu ft)

AREAS:
Wings, gross	219 m² (2,357.3 sq ft)
Leading-edge slats (total)	28.54 m² (307.20 sq ft)
Trailing-edge flaps (total)	36.68 m² (394.82 sq ft)
Ailerons (total)	6.86 m² (73.84 sq ft)
Spoilers (total)	7.36 m² (79.22 sq ft)
Airbrakes (total)	6.16 m² (66.31 sq ft)
Fin	45.20 m² (486.53 sq ft)
Rudder	13.57 m² (146.07 sq ft)
Tailplane	44.80 m² (482.22 sq ft)
Elevators (total)	19.20 m² (206.67 sq ft)

WEIGHTS (243-seat configuration. A: CF6-80C2A2 engines; B: PW4152s):
Manufacturer's weight empty:	
200: A	70,016 kg (154,360 lb)
B	69,957 kg (154,230 lb)
300: A	70,334 kg (155,060 lb)

Airbus A320 short/medium-range twin-turbofan commercial transport aircraft in British Airways livery

B	70,275 kg (154,930 lb)
Operating weight empty: 200: A	76,795 kg (169,304 lb)
B	76,516 kg (168,690 lb)
300: A	76,911 kg (169,560 lb)
B	76,861 kg (169,450 lb)
Max payload: 200: A	35,439 kg (78,130 lb)
B	35,484 kg (78,230 lb)
300: A	36,088 kg (79,560 lb)
B	36,137 kg (79,670 lb)
* Max fuel: 200	44,089 kg (97,200 lb)
300	49,029 kg (108,090 lb)
Max T-O weight: 200 (basic)	138,600 kg (305,560 lb)
200 (option)	142,000 kg (313,055 lb)
300 (basic)	150,000 kg (330,695 lb)
300 (options)	153,000 kg (337,305 lb)
	or 157,000 kg (346,125 lb)
Max landing weight: 200	122,000 kg (268,965 lb)
300	123,000 kg (271,170 lb)
options (200 and 300)	124,000 kg (273,375 lb)
Max zero-fuel weight: 200	112,000 kg (246,915 lb)
300	113,000 kg (249,120 lb)
options (200 and 300)	114,000 kg (251,330 lb)

optional additional tank in aft cargo hold adds 5,779 kg (12,740 lb) of fuel and increases OWE/reduces payload by 757 kg (1,670 lb)

PERFORMANCE (at max T-O weight for 243-seat configuration except where indicated; engines A and B as under 'Weights'):

Typical long-range cruising speed at 9,450-12,500 m (31,000-41,000 ft): A, B	Mach 0.80

Approach speed at max landing weight:

A, B	135 knots (250 km/h; 155 mph)

T-O field length at S/L, ISA + 15°C:

200: A	1,860 m (6,100 ft)
B	1,799 m (5,900 ft)
300: A	2,408 m (7,900 ft)
B	2,225 m (7,300 ft)

Landing field length at S/L, at max landing weight (200 and 300): A 1,479 m (4,850 ft)

B	1,555 m (5,100 ft)

Runway ACN for flexible runway, category B:

standard tyres: 200	43
300	49
optional tyres: 200	41
300	47

Range (1988 deliveries) at typical airline OWE with 218 passengers and baggage, international reserves for 200 nm (370 km; 230 mile) diversion:

200 at basic MTOGW:

A	3,610 nm (6,690 km; 4,157 miles)
B	3,650 nm (6,765 km; 4,205 miles)

200 at optional MTOGW:

A	3,910 nm (7,246 km; 4,502 miles)
B	3,960 nm (7,338 km; 4,560 miles)

300 at basic MTOGW:

A	4,440 nm (8,228 km; 5,113 miles)
B	4,480 nm (8,300 km; 5,160 miles)

300 at 157 tonne MTOGW and with additional fuel tank: A 4,900 nm (9,080 km; 5,642 miles)

B	4,950 nm (9,175 km; 5,700 miles)

OPERATIONAL NOISE LEVELS (ICAO Annex 16, Chapter 3):

T-O (flyover): 200	89.0 EPNdB (95.1 limit)
300	91.2 EPNdB (95.6 limit)
T-O (sideline): 200	96.1 EPNdB (99.1 limit)
300	96.3 EPNdB (99.4 limit)
Approach: 200, 300	98.6 EPNdB (102.7 limit)

AIRBUS A320

The A320 is an entirely new short/medium-range, single-aisle, twin-turbofan commercial transport aircraft, making optimum use of advanced design concepts, modern production techniques, new materials, advanced digital avionics, and efficient systems design. Among a number of technological 'firsts', it is the first subsonic commercial

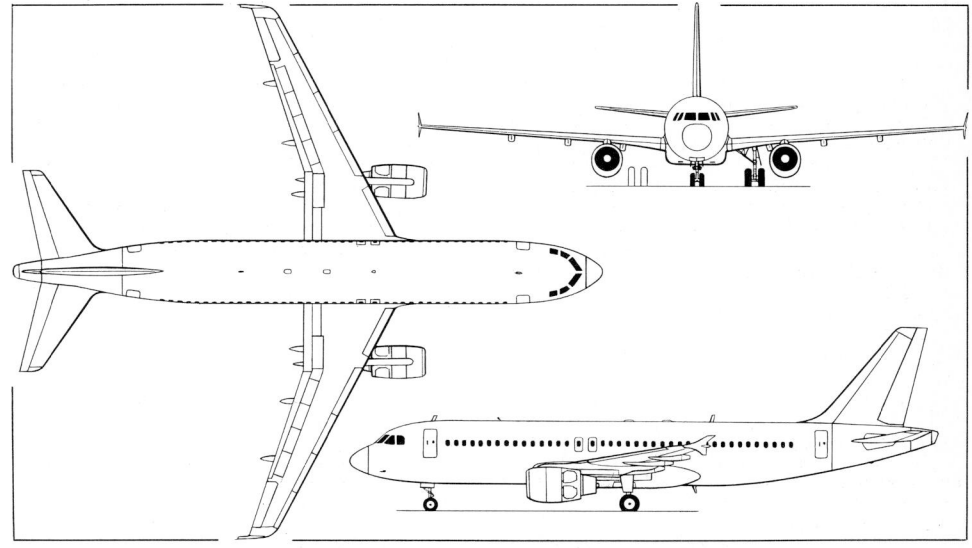

Airbus A320-200 twin-turbofan single-aisle 150/179-seat transport (*Pilot Press*)

aircraft to have fly by wire (FBW) control throughout normal flight; a centralised maintenance system; side-stick controls in the cockpit, in place of control columns; and composites materials for major elements of primary structure, including the fin and horizontal tailplane. Wing design incorporates the latest advances in technology (including a gust load alleviation system), as well as experience from the wing of the A310, and the A320 offers significant commonality with other Airbus Industrie aircraft where this is cost-effective.

Compared with existing single-aisle aircraft, the fuselage cross-section is significantly increased, permitting the use of wider triple seats to provide higher standards of passenger comfort; five-abreast business class seating provides a standard equal to that offered as first class on major competitive aircraft. In addition, the wider aisle permits quicker turnrounds. Overhead stowage space is superior to that available on existing aircraft of similar capacity, and provides ample carry-on baggage space; best use of the underseat space for baggage is provided by improved seat design and optimised positioning of the seat rails. The fuselage double-bubble cross-section provides increased baggage/cargo hold volume and working height, and the ability to carry containers derived from the standard interline LD3 type. As the base is the same as that of the LD3, all existing wide-body aircraft and ground handling equipment can accept these containers without modification.

Full go-ahead to develop and build the A320 was confirmed on 2 March 1984. The **A320-100** (21 ordered) was offered originally (see 1987-88 *Jane's*), but was replaced from Autumn 1988 by the **A320-200**, which has wingtip fences, a wing centre-section fuel tank and higher max T-O weight. Convertible and all-freight versions, with a large upper deck cargo door, are being considered.

Four aircraft were used in the flight test programme, the first of which (F-WWAI) made its first flight on 22 February 1987, followed by the others on 27 April, 18 June and 8 July 1987; one static test and one fatigue test airframe were also completed. European (UK, French, German and Dutch) JAA certification with CFM56-5 engines, for two-crew operation, was achieved on 26 February 1988. First deliveries, initially to Air France and British Airways (previously British Caledonian), took place on 28 and 31 March 1988 respectively. Certification with IAE V2500 engines is due in the Spring of 1989, following the first flight

(by the No. 1 aircraft) on 28 July 1988. In September 1988 the No. 2 aircraft was due to resume flight testing after replacement of the twin-wheel main landing gear units by four-wheel bogies, suitable for operation from low-strength runways.

Aérospatiale is building the entire front fuselage (forward of the wing leading-edge), cabin rear doors, nosewheel doors, the centre wing box and engine pylons, and is responsible for final assembly. The centre and rear fuselage, tailcone, wing flaps, fin, rudder, and commercial furnishing are undertaken by MBB. British Aerospace builds the main wings, including ailerons, airbrakes, spoilers and wingtips, and the main landing gear leg fairings. Belairbus produces the leading-edge slats. CASA is responsible for the tailplane, elevators, mainwheel doors, and sheet metal work for parts of the rear fuselage.

Firm orders for the A320 (-100 and -200) totalled 336 by 29 July 1988, from 23 operators.

TYPE: Twin-turbofan short/medium-range transport.

WINGS: Cantilever low/mid-wing monoplane, with 5° 6′ 36″ dihedral and 25° sweepback at quarter-chord. Five-segment leading-edge slats (one inboard and four outboard of engine pylon) over almost full span. These and most of fixed portion of wing are of aluminium alloy construction. CFRP materials are used for the fixed leading/trailing-edge bottom access panels and deflectors, trailing-edge flaps, flap track fairings, spoilers and ailerons. Spoilers, in five segments on each wing, are located forward of the flaps. The four outer spoilers are used in roll, the three middle ones as speed brakes, and all five for lift dumping. Ailerons, spoilers, flaps and slats are controlled electrically by the fly by wire control system, acting via hydraulic actuators. Slat and flap controls manufactured by Liebherr and Lucas.

FUSELAGE: Semi-monocoque pressurised structure, of 'double bubble' cross-section. Construction generally as described for A310, but belly fairing skins are of AFRP.

TAIL UNIT: Cantilever structure, with sweepback on all surfaces (35° on fin, 28° on tailplane) and 6° dihedral on tailplane. Entire fin and tailplane are fabricated from CFRP, except for fin leading-edge and fin/fuselage fairing (GFRP); rudder and elevators are of CFRP. Elevators are controlled and tailplane trimmed electrically, with hydraulic actuation, by the FBW system; if elevator control is lost through electrical failure, the tailplane can be trimmed mechanically to act as a backup pitch control surface. Rudder provides directional control by conventional mechanical means if ailerons are lost due to FBW system failure. Electric rudder trim.

LANDING GEAR: Hydraulically retractable tricycle type, with twin wheels and oleo-pneumatic shock absorber on each unit. Dowty main units retract inward into wing/body fairing; steerable Messier-Hispano-Bugatti nose unit retracts forward. Nosewheel doors, main gear leg fairing doors and mainwheel doors are of CFRP. Radial tyres, size 45 × 16-R20 on main units and 30 × 8.8-15 on nose unit, are standard. Size 49 × 19-R20 radial tyres with 36 × 11 bogie, or conventional crossply tyres (46 × 16-20 or 49 × 19-20) with 36 × 11-XX bogie, are optional on main units; size 32 × 11.5-15 tyres optional for nose unit. Carbon brakes standard.

POWER PLANT: Two 104.5-111.2 kN (23,500-25,000 lb st) class CFM International CFM56-5-A1 turbofans for first aircraft delivery in Spring 1988, or 111.2 kN (25,000 lb st) IAE V2500-A1 engines for first aircraft delivery in Spring 1989. Rohr Industries nacelles and thrust reversers for both types of engine. Dual-channel FADEC (full authority digital engine control) system on each engine standard. Standard fuel capacity in wing and wing centre-section tanks is 23,432 litres (6,190 US gallons; 5,154 Imp gallons); or 15,590 litres (4,118 US gallons; 3,429 Imp gallons) without centre-section tank. Composites materials used in construction of engine cowlings and pylon fairings.

ACCOMMODATION: Standard crew of two on flight deck, with one (optionally two) forward facing folding seats for additional crew members; seats for four cabin attendants. Seating for up to 179 passengers, depending upon layout, with locations at front and rear of cabin for galley(s) and toilet(s). Typical two-class layout would have 12 seats four-abreast at 91.5 cm (36 in) pitch in 'super first' and 138 six-abreast at 81 cm (32 in) pitch economy class; or 152 six-abreast seats (84 business + 68 economy) at 86 and 78 cm (34 and 31 in) pitch respectively. Single class economy layout could offer 164 seats at 81 cm (32 in) pitch, or up to 179 in high-density configuration. Passenger doors at front and rear of cabin on port side, forward one having optional integral airstairs; service door opposite each of these on starboard side. Two overwing emergency exits each side. Forward and rear underfloor baggage/cargo holds, plus overhead lockers; with 164 seats, overhead stowage space per seat is 0.056 m^3 (2.0 cu ft). Mechanised cargo loading system will allow up to seven LD3-46 containers to be carried in freight holds (three forward and four aft).

SYSTEMS: The A320 is the first subsonic commercial aircraft to be equipped for fly by wire (FBW) control throughout the entire normal flight regime, and the first to have a side-stick controller (one for each pilot) instead of a control column and hand wheel. The Thomson-CSF/Sfena digital FBW system features five main computers and operates, via hydraulic jacks, all primary and secondary flight controls, except for the rudder and tailplane trim. The pilot's pitch and roll commands are applied through the side-stick controller via two different types of computer. These have a redundant architecture to provide safety levels at least as high as those of the mechanical systems they replace. The Thomson-CSF/Sfena flight control system incorporates flight envelope protection features to a degree that cannot be achieved with conventional mechanical control systems, and the systems's computers will not allow the aircraft's structural and aerodynamic limitations to be exceeded: even if the pilot pushes the side-stick fully forward, it is impossible to go beyond the aircraft's maximum design speed. Similarly, the A320 has angle of attack protection: if the pilot pulls the side-stick fully back, he will just achieve maximum lift from the wing and no more, and therefore cannot stall the aircraft. Other systems include Liebherr/ABG-Semca air-conditioning, Hamilton Standard/Nord-Micro pressurisation, hydraulic, Sundstrand electrical system, and a new and more efficient Garrett APU. Primary electrical system is powered by two Sundstrand 90kVA constant frequency generators, providing 115/200V three-phase AC at 400Hz. A third generator of the same type, directly driven at constant speed by the APU, can be used during ground operations and, if required, during flight.

AVIONICS: Fully equipped digital avionics fit, to ARINC 700 series specification, including advanced digital automatic flight control and flight management systems. AFCS integrates functions of Sfena autopilot and Honeywell FMS. Each pilot has two Thomson-CSF/VDO electronic flight instrumentation system (EFIS) displays: a primary flight display and a navigation display. Primary flight display is first on an airliner to incorporate speed, altitude and heading. Between these two pairs of displays are two Thomson-CSF/VDO electronic centralised aircraft monitor (ECAM) displays unique to Airbus Industrie and developed from the ECAM systems on the A310 and A300-600. The larger size of the A320 displays allows the upper one to incorporate engine performance and warnings. The lower display carries warning and system synoptic diagrams. Honeywell air data and inertial reference system.

DIMENSIONS, EXTERNAL:

Wing span	33.91 m (111 ft 3 in)
Wing aspect ratio	9.4
Length overall	37.57 m (123 ft 3 in)
Fuselage: Max width	3.95 m (12 ft 11½ in)
Max depth	4.14 m (13 ft 7 in)
Height overall	11.80 m (38 ft 8½ in)
Tailplane span	12.45 m (40 ft 10 in)
Wheel track (c/l of shock struts)	7.59 m (24 ft 11 in)
Wheelbase	12.63 m (41 ft 5 in)
Passenger doors (port, fwd and rear), each:	
Height	1.85 m (6 ft 1 in)
Width	0.81 m (2 ft 8 in)
Height to sill	3.415 m (11 ft 2½ in)
Service doors (stbd, fwd and rear), each:	
Height	1.85 m (6 ft 1 in)
Width	0.81 m (2 ft 8 in)
Height to sill	3.415 m (11 ft 2½ in)
Overwing emergency exits (two port and two stbd), each:	
Height	1.02 m (3 ft 4¼ in)
Width	0.51 m (1 ft 8 in)
Underfloor baggage/cargo hold doors (stbd, fwd and rear), each: Height	1.249 m (4 ft 1¼ in)
Width	1.82 m (5 ft 11½ in)

DIMENSIONS, INTERNAL:

Cabin: Max width	3.696 m (12 ft 1½ in)
Max height	2.22 m (7 ft 4 in)
Baggage/cargo hold volume:	
front	13.28 m^3 (469 cu ft)
rear	25.48 m^3 (900 cu ft)

AREAS:

Wings, gross	122.4 m^2 (1,317.5 sq ft)
Leading-edge slats (total)	12.64 m^2 (136.1 sq ft)
Trailing-edge flaps (total)	21.10 m^2 (227.1 sq ft)
Ailerons (total)	2.74 m^2 (29.49 sq ft)
Spoilers (total)	8.64 m^2 (93.00 sq ft)
Airbrakes (total)	2.35 m^2 (25.30 sq ft)
Vertical tail surfaces (total)	21.5 m^2 (231.4 sq ft)
Horizontal tail surfaces (total)	31.0 m^2 (333.7 sq ft)

WEIGHTS AND LOADINGS (A: CFM56-5-A1 engines, B: V2500-A1s):

Operating weight empty: 100	38,201 kg (84,220 lb)
200: A	39,777 kg (87,693 lb)
B	40,150 kg (88,515 lb)
Max payload: 100	18,801 kg (41,450 lb)
200: A	20,723 kg (45,686 lb)
B	20,350 kg (44,864 lb)
Max fuel: 100	12,517 kg (27,595 lb)
200	18,812 kg (41,473 lb)
Max T-O weight: 100	68,000 kg (149,915 lb)
200	73,500 kg (162,040 lb)
Max landing weight: 100	63,000 kg (138,890 lb)
200	64,500 kg (142,200 lb)
Max zero-fuel weight: 100	57,000 kg (125,665 lb)
200	60,500 kg (133,380 lb)
Max wing loading: 100	555.5 kg/m^2 (113.8 lb/sq ft)
200	600.5 kg/m^2 (123.0 lb/sq ft)

PERFORMANCE (estimated, at max T-O weight except where indicated; engines A and B as for 'Weights'):

T-O distance at S/L, ISA + 15°C:	
100	1,707 m (5,600 ft)
200: A	2,058 m (6,750 ft)
B	2,180 m (7,150 ft)
Landing distance at max landing weight:	
200: A and B	1,540 m (5,050 ft)
Runway ACN (flexible runway, category B):	
diabolo, standard 45 × 16-R20 tyres: 100	36
200	40
bogie option, 36 × 11-R16 or -16 tyres: 100	20
200	22
Range with 150-seat two-class layout, typical international reserves and 200 nm (370 km; 230 mile) diversion:	
200: A	2,870 nm (5,318 km; 3,305 miles)
B	2,840 nm (5,263 km; 3,270 miles)

OPERATIONAL NOISE LEVELS (ICAO Annex 16, Chapter 3):

T-O (flyover): 100	85.7 EPNdB (90.1 limit)
200	88.2 EPNdB (91.3 limit)
T-O (sideline): 100	94.6 EPNdB (96.3 limit)
200	94.4 EPNdB (96.7 limit)
Approach: 100, 200	96.6 EPNdB (100.1 limit)

AIRBUS A340 and A330

Airbus Industrie launched the A340 and A330 as a combined programme on 5 June 1987, at which time it had 130 commitments (89 A340s and 41 A330s) from ten customers—Lufthansa, Air France, Northwest, Air Inter, Thai Airways International, UTA, International Lease Finance Corporation, Royal Jordanian, TAP-Air Portugal and Sabena. Firm orders for 12 A330s and 71 A340s had been received by 1 June 1988, with options for a further 29 A330s and 37 A340s.

The four-engined A340-300 will launch the programme, with first flight of the first development aircraft planned for April 1991, to be followed in October 1991 by the first extended-range A340-200, and in June 1992 by the first example of the twin-engined A330. Lufthansa and UTA will be the first to take delivery of the A340, in May 1992. The first to receive the A330 will be Thai Airways International and Air Inter, in September 1993.

In launching the A340/A330 as a single programme, Airbus Industrie is capitalising on commonality (an identical wing, cockpit and tail unit and the same basic fuselage) to create aircraft for different markets. This approach is made possible by the similar size and shape of the two aircraft, which differ mainly in the number of engines and engine-related systems. In addition, the A340 and A330 have much in common with the present range of Airbus aircraft: both will employ existing wide-body fuselage cross-sections, the A310/A300-600 fin, and advanced versions of the A320 cockpit and systems.

In addition to sharing basic airframe components and systems, the A340 and A330 will incorporate technological advances introduced in the A320, such as fly by wire flight control and state of the art avionics design with multi-function cockpit displays. Work sharing will be along lines similar to those for the A310 and A300-600, with percentages similar to those held in the consortium. Aérospatiale will thus be responsible for the cockpit, engine pylons, part of the centre-fuselage, and final assembly; British Aerospace (with Textron Aerostructures, USA, as subcontractor) for the wings; Deutsche Airbus (through MBB) for the bulk of the fuselage, fin and interior; and CASA for the tailplane. Belairbus of Belgium will make the wing leading-edge slats and slat tracks. As with the rest of the Airbus family, final assembly will be carried out in Toulouse.

The following versions have been announced:

A340-300. Four-engined long-range version, carrying up to 375 passengers (standard) or 440 (optional) and powered initially by CFM56-5C-2 turbofans, a more powerful and efficient version of the engine fitted on the A320. Due to enter service in May 1992.

A340-300 Combi. Passenger/freight version of A340-300; described separately.

A340-200. Longer-range version of A340-300, with same initial power plant and shorter fuselage. Exit-limited seating capacities as for A340-300. Due to enter service in August 1992.

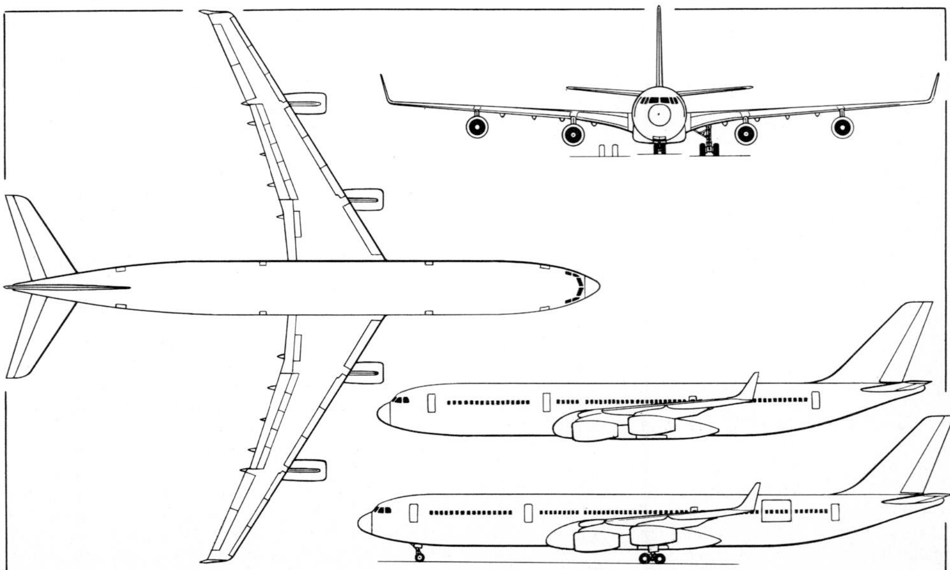

Airbus A340-300 four-turbofan long-range transport, with additional side view (top) of A340-200
(Pilot Press)

A330. Twin-engined, medium/long-range version, with
CF6-80C2 turbofans initially and seating capacities as for
A340. Fuselage longer than A340-200, but slightly shorter
than A340-300. Alternative power plants will include
Rolls-Royce RB211-524L and Pratt & Whitney PW4000.
Due to enter service in September 1993.
TYPE: Large-capacity wide-bodied medium- and long-range
transport.
WINGS: Of new design (by BAe), some 40 per cent larger than
those of A300-600, with 30° sweepback and 2.74 m (9 ft)
wingtip devices. Movable surfaces comprise seven-
segment leading-edge slats, two-segment trailing-edge
flaps, two-segment ailerons, single airbrake (forward of
inboard flap) and five-segment spoilers (forward of
outboard flap) on each wing. Wing is virtually identical
for A340 and A330, but A340 is strengthened in area of
outboard engine pylon with appropriate modification of
leading-edge slats 4 and 5. Main three-spar wing box
structure, and leading/trailing-edge ribs and fittings, are
of aluminium alloy, and Al-Li is under consideration for
some secondary structures. Approx 11 per cent (by
weight) will be of CFRP, AFRP or GFRP, including
outer flap pair, ailerons, spoilers, flap track fairings, all
leading/trailing-edge fixed surface panels, and (possibly)
wingtip devices. Slat support structures are of steel or
titanium; flap supports are of aluminium alloy with
titanium elements.
FUSELAGE: Is of existing Airbus wide-body cross-section,
and of generally similar construction to that of A310 and
A300-600, but with new centre-section to accept the new
wing. Common fuselage for all three current versions,
except in overall length, with A340-300 the longest, A330
two frames shorter and A340-200 six frames shorter than
A330.
TAIL UNIT: Common to all versions; utilises same carbonfibre
vertical fin as A300-600 and A310. New tailplane includes
trim tank and features outer main boxes of carbonfibre
bridged by centre-section of aluminium alloy.
LANDING GEAR: Main (four-wheel bogie) and twin-wheel
nose units identical on all versions. A340 has additional
twin-wheel auxiliary unit on fuselage centreline
amidships.
POWER PLANT (A330): Launched with two 291.4 kN (65,500
lb st) General Electric CF6-80C2 turbofans. Alternative
engines, using a common pylon and mount, will include
developments of the Pratt & Whitney PW4000 and
Rolls-Royce RB211-524L series. Fuel capacity 93,500
litres (24,700 US gallons; 20,568 Imp gallons).
POWER PLANT (A340): Four 138.8 kN (31,200 lb st)
CFM56-5C-2 turbofans initially. Max fuel capacity (-200
and -300) 135,000 litres (35,664 US gallons; 29,697 Imp
gallons).
ACCOMMODATION: Crew of two on flight deck (all versions).
Passenger seating typically six-abreast in first class,
seven-abreast in business class and eight-breast in
economy (nine-abreast optional), all with twin aisles.
Two-class configurations seat 335 passengers in A340-
300, 303 in A340-200 and 328 in A330. More typically, a
three-class layout would seat 295 in A340-300 and 262 in
the A340-200. Underfloor cargo holds have capacity for
up to 32 LD3 containers or 11 standard 2.24 × 3.17 m (88
× 125 in) pallets in A340-300, 26 LD3s or 9 pallets in
A340-200, and 30 LD3s and 11 pallets in A330. Both
front and rear cargo holds have doors wide enough to
accept 2.44 × 3.17 m (96 × 125 in) pallets. In addition,
all models have a 19.68 m³ (695 cu ft) bulk cargo hold aft
of the rear cargo hold.
DIMENSIONS, EXTERNAL:
Wing span (all versions)   58.65 m (192 ft 5 in)

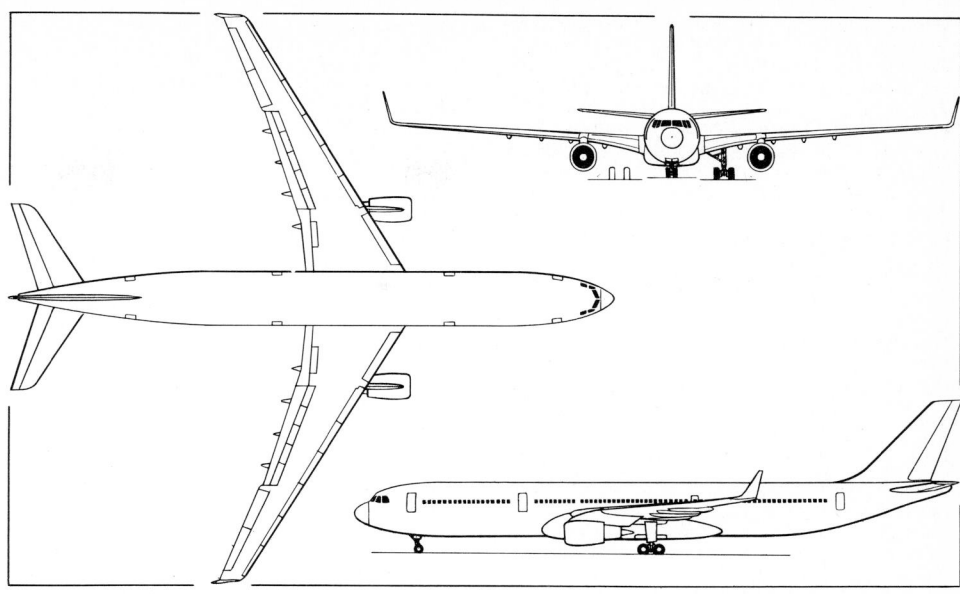

Airbus A330 twin-turbofan transport, launched as a joint programme with the A340 *(Pilot Press)*

Wing aspect ratio (all versions)	9.5
Wing sweepback (all versions)	30°
Length overall: A330	62.56 m (205 ft 3 in)
A340-200	59.39 m (194 ft 10 in)
A340-300	63.65 m (208 ft 10 in)
Fuselage: Max diameter (all versions)	5.64 m (18 ft 6 in)
Height overall (all versions)	16.74 m (54 ft 11 in)
Wheel track (all versions)	10.49 m (34 ft 5 in)

AREA:
Wings, gross (all versions)	361.6 m² (3,892.0 sq ft)

WEIGHTS:
Typical airline operating weight empty:
A330	115,300 kg (254,200 lb)
A340-200	121,700 kg (268,300 lb)
A340-300	125,500 kg (276,680 lb)
Max payload: A330	45,700 kg (100,750 lb)
A340-200	47,300 kg (104,280 lb)
A340-300	45,400 kg (100,100 lb)
Max T-O weight: A330	208,000 kg (458,560 lb)
A340-200, -300	251,000 kg (553,360 lb)
Max landing weight: A330	171,000 kg (376,990 lb)
A340-200	181,000 kg (399,040 lb)
A340-300	183,000 kg (403,445 lb)
Max zero-fuel weight: A330	161,000 kg (354,945 lb)
A340-200	169,000 kg (372,580 lb)
A340-300	171,000 kg (376,990 lb)

PERFORMANCE (estimated):
Max operating speed	Mach 0.84 to 0.86
Typical operating speed	Mach 0.82

Range at typical OWE, with allowances for 200 nm (370
km; 230 mile) diversion and international reserves:
330 with 328 passengers and baggage
4,850 nm (9,000 km; 5,585 miles)
330 with 328 passengers and 16,200 kg (35,715 lb) of
cargo   3,280 nm (6,080 km; 3,780 miles)
340-200 with 262 passengers and baggage
7,450 nm (13,806 km; 8,579 miles)
340-200 with 262 passengers and 24,550 kg (54,123 lb)
of cargo   5,200 nm (9,636 km; 5,988 miles)
340-300 with 295 passengers and baggage
6,650 nm (12,325 km; 7,655 miles)
340-300 with 295 passengers and 17,650 kg (38,911 lb)
of cargo   5,100 nm (9,451 km; 5,873 miles)

AIRBUS A340-300 COMBI

Launch and future customers for the Airbus A340 are
being offered an A340-300 Combi, typically carrying 194
passengers (in a three-class layout) and six 2.44 × 3.18 m
(96 × 125 in) freight pallets on the main deck. The
A340-300 Combi features a large port-side cargo door in the
rear fuselage, with a clear opening on to a main deck flat
floor (the rear part of the floor slopes upward very slightly
in the standard aircraft). It thus has the ability to carry the
same pallets and containers as other wide-body combis,
freighters and convertibles, allowing the 'interlining' of
freight between different aircraft types. In addition, the
A340-300 Combi can accommodate even larger cargo, such
as the outsize AMA container or an assembled large
turbofan.
Customers for the A340-300 Combi will also be able to
obtain a kit to replace one, two or all of the main deck pallet
positions by seats, giving them the added flexibility of
additional layouts.
DIMENSIONS, EXTERNAL:
Cargo door: Height	2.57 m (8 ft 5 in)
Width	3.58 m (11 ft 9 in)

WEIGHTS:
Max T-O weight	251,000 kg (553,400 lb)
Max landing weight	186,000 kg (410,000 lb)
Max zero-fuel weight	178,000 kg (392,400 lb)

PERFORMANCE (estimated):
Range with 194 passengers and 33,700 kg (74,400 lb) of
freight (six pallets)   4,600 nm (8,525 km; 5,297 miles)

AIRTECH
AIRCRAFT TECHNOLOGY INDUSTRIES
PRESIDENT: Prof Dr-Ing B. J. Habibie (IPTN)
VICE-PRESIDENT: Javier Alvarez Vara (CASA)
PARTICIPATING COMPANIES:
Construcciones Aeronauticas SA, Rey Francisco
4, Apartado 193, 28008 Madrid, Spain
Telephone: (91) 247 2500
Telex: 27418 CASA E
IPTN (Industri Pesawat Terbang Nusantara), PO
Box 563, Jalan Pajajaran 154, Bandung, Indonesia
Telephone: (022) 611081/2
Telex: 28295 IPTN BD
Airtech is a joint company formed by CASA and IPTN to
develop a twin-turboprop transport known as the CN-235.
Design and production is shared 50-50 between the
two companies.

AIRTECH (CASA/IPTN) CN-235 SERIES 100
Preliminary design of the CN-235 was initiated in
January 1980, and prototype construction in May 1981.
Two prototypes were built, one in each country (ECT-100
and PK-XNC), plus static and fatigue test airframes.
Simultaneous rollouts were made on 10 September 1983,
and first flights took place on 11 November (CASA) and 30
December 1983 (IPTN).

The first production CN-235 made its initial flight on 19
August 1986. Spanish and Indonesian certification was
received on 20 June 1986, and FAA type approval to FAR
Pts 25 and 121 on 3 December that year. First delivery, of an
IPTN aircraft to Merpati Nusantara Airlines, was made on
15 December 1986; the first two CN-235s from the CASA
assembly line, equipped as VIP transports for the Royal
Saudi Air Force, were handed over on 4 February 1987,
with two more (in **CN-235 M** military transport
configuration) following in April 1987. Commercial operation, by the first Merpati aircraft, began on 1 March 1988.
Firm orders for the CN-235 totalled 114 by 1 March 1988
(57 civil and 57 military). Twenty-two of these are
for Spanish regional airlines, including four for Binter
Canarias; four are for Saudi Arabia, two for the Botswana
Defence Force and one for the Panamanian Air Force. The
other 85 are for Indonesian customers (Deraya 11, Merpati
14, Pelita 10, Indonesian Air Force 32, and Indonesian
Navy 18, including six in ASW/maritime patrol configuration). The Chilean Air Force has decided in principle to
order six CN-235 Ms. CASA markets the aircraft in the
Americas and Europe, IPTN in Asia, with other markets
shared as appropriate.
CASA builds the wing centre-section, inboard flaps,
forward and centre fuselage and engine nacelles; the outer
wings, outboard flaps, ailerons, rear fuselage and tail unit
are built by IPTN. Numerical control machinery is used
extensively in the CN-235's manufacture. Design has been
optimised for short-haul operations, enabling the CN-235

to fly four 100 nm (185 km; 115 mile) stage lengths, with
reserves, before needing to refuel, and to operate from either
paved runways or unprepared strips.
Initial production CN-235s have General Electric
CT7-7A engines, as described in previous editions of *Jane's*,
and are designated **Series 10**. The following description
applies to the **Series 100** version, with CT7-9C engines in
new composites nacelles, which replaced it in production in
1988:
TYPE: Twin-turboprop commuter and utility transport.
WINGS: Cantilever high-wing monoplane. NACA 65₃-218
wing section. Constant chord centre-section, without
dihedral; 3° dihedral on tapered outer panels. Incidence
3°. Sweepback 3° 51′ 36″ at quarter-chord on outer
panels. Three main assemblies each consist of a machined
fail-safe box structure of aluminium/copper alloy, with
main spars at 15 and 55 per cent chord, plus leading- and
trailing-edge structures. Inboard flaps on centre-section,
outboard flap segments and ailerons on outer panels.
Fail-safe attachment of centre-section to top of fuselage;
large wing/fuselage fairing, made of composites. Chemically milled skins. Leading-edges each made up of a false
spar, ribs and skin panels. Flap segments each have a
machined aluminium spar, two sheet metal ribs of
aluminium/zinc alloy, and leading/trailing-edges of
glassfibre laminates with honeycomb core. Inboard and
outboard pairs are interchangeable port/starboard.
Flaps are single-slotted and actuated hydraulically by
Dowty Rotol irreversible jacks. Ailerons, of similar

construction to flaps, are statically and dynamically balanced and have duplicated flight controls. Mechanically operated servo tab and electrically actuated trim tab in each aileron. Raked wingtips are of glassfibre. Pneumatic boot anti-icing of outer leading-edges.

FUSELAGE: Conventional fail-safe pressurised semi-monocoque structure (including baggage compartment), built mainly of aluminium/copper and aluminium/zinc alloy longerons, frames, stringers and skin panels. Flattened circular cross-section, upswept at rear. Glass-fibre nose radome, reinforced with glassfibre/Nomex honeycomb/glassfibre sandwich, forward of front pressure bulkhead. Forward pressurised section includes flight deck and bulkhead at front of passenger cabin. Central (passenger cabin) section is 19 frames long, at 508 mm (20 in) pitch. Rear fuselage, 15 frames long, includes rear cargo ramp and door, baggage compartment, and the tailcone, which incorporates the rear pressure bulkhead. Composite fairings on fuselage sides house some equipment and systems, in addition to retracted main landing gear.

TAIL UNIT: Sweptback fin and statically and dynamically balanced rudder, large dorsal fin, two small honeycomb ventral fins, and non-swept fixed incidence tailplane with statically and dynamically balanced elevators. Main fin and tailplane boxes are two-spar aluminium/copper alloy structures, with detachable leading-edges and glassfibre tips. Rudder and elevators have glassfibre skin, Nomex honeycomb core, and leading-edge vortex generators. Rudder and elevators actuated mechanically. Mechanically operated servo tab and electrically actuated trim tab in rudder and starboard elevator; trim tab only in port elevator. Pneumatic boot anti-icing of fin and tailplane leading-edges.

LANDING GEAR: Messier-Hispano-Bugatti retractable tricycle type with levered suspension, suitable for operation from semi-prepared runways. Electrically controlled hydraulic extension/retraction, with mechanical backup for emergency extension. Oleo-pneumatic shock absorber in each unit. Each main unit comprises two wheels in tandem, retracting rearward into fairing on side of fuselage. Mainwheels semi-exposed when retracted. Single steerable nosewheel retracts forward into unpressurised bay under flight deck. Dunlop 28 × 9.00-12 (12 ply rating) tubeless mainwheel tyres standard, pressure 5.17 bars (75 lb/sq in) on civil version, 5.58 bars (81 lb/sq in) on military version; low pressure mainwheel tyres optional, size 11.00-12/10, pressure 3.45 bars (50 lb/sq in). Dunlop 24 × 7.7 (10/12 ply rating) tubeless nosewheel tyre, pressure 5.65 bars (82 lb/sq in) on civil version, 6.07 bars (88 lb/sq in) on military version. Dunlop hydraulic differential disc brakes; Dunlop anti-skid units on main gear.

POWER PLANT: Two General Electric CT7-9C turboprops, each flat rated at 1,305 kW (1,750 shp) (S/L, to 41°C) for take-off and 1,394.5 kW (1,870 shp) up to 31°C with automatic power reserve. Hamilton Standard 14-RF21 four-blade constant-speed propellers, with full feathering and reverse-pitch capability. Blades are of glassfibre, with metal spar and urethane foam core. Lightweight low-drag composites nacelles. Fuel in two 1,042 litre (275 US gallon; 229 Imp gallon) integral main tanks in wing centre-section and two 1,592 litre (421 US gallon; 350

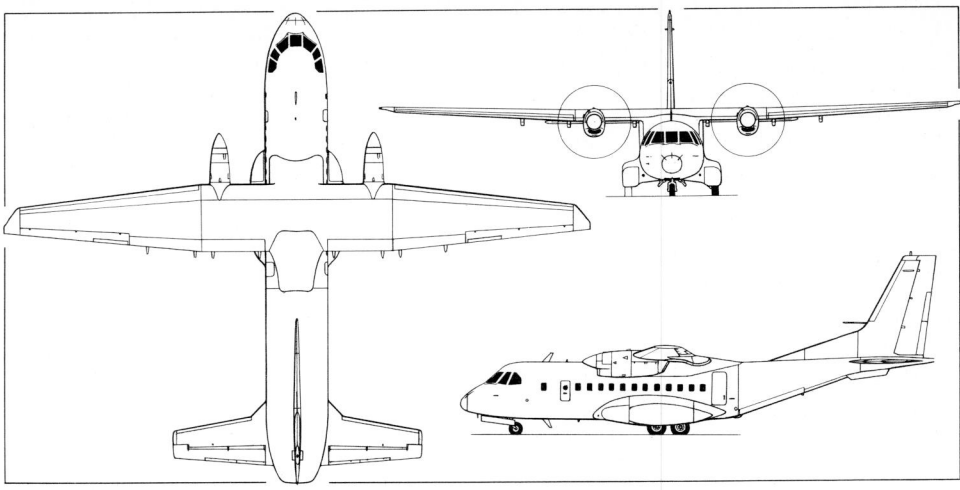

Airtech (CASA/IPTN) CN-235 twin-turboprop commuter transport *(Pilot Press)*

Imp gallon) integral outer-wing auxiliary tanks; total fuel capacity 5,268 litres (1,392 US gallons; 1,158 Imp gallons), of which 5,128 litres (1,355 US gallons; 1,128 Imp gallons) are usable. Single pressure refuelling point in starboard main landing gear fairing; gravity filling point in top of each tank. Propeller braking permits engine to be used as an on-ground APU. Oil capacity 13.97 litres (3.69 US gallons; 3.07 Imp gallons).

ACCOMMODATION: Crew of two on flight deck, plus cabin attendant (civil version) or third crew member (military version). Accommodation in commuter version for up to 45 passengers in four-abreast seating, at 76 cm (30 in) pitch, with 22 seats each side of central aisle. Toilet, galley and overhead luggage bins standard. Pressurised baggage compartment at rear of cabin, aft of movable bulkhead; additional stowage in rear ramp area and in overhead lockers. Can also be equipped as mixed passenger/cargo combi (eg, 19 passengers and two LD3 containers), or for all-cargo operation, with roller loading system, carrying four standard LD3 containers, five LD2s, or two 2.24 × 3.18 m (88 × 125 in) and one 2.24 × 2.03 m (88 × 80 in) pallets; or for military duties, carrying up to 48 troops or 46 paratroops. Other options include layouts for aeromedical (24 stretchers and four medical attendants), ASW/maritime patrol (with 360° search radar and Exocet missiles or Mk 46 torpedoes), electronic warfare, geophysical survey or aerial photographic duties. Main passenger door, outward and forward opening with integral stairs, aft of wing on port side, serving also as a Type I emergency exit. Type III emergency exit facing this door on starboard side. Crew/service downward opening door (forward, starboard) has built-in stairs, and serves also as a Type I emergency exit, or as passenger door in combi version; a second Type III exit is provided, opposite this door, on the port side. Wide ventral door/cargo ramp in underside of upswept rear fuselage, for loading of bulky cargo. Accommodation fully air-conditioned and pressurised.

SYSTEMS: Hamilton Standard air-conditioning system, using engine compressor bleed air. AiResearch electropneumatic pressurisation system (max differential 0.25 bars; 3.6 lb/sq in) giving cabin environment of 2,440 m (8,000 ft) up to operating altitude of 5,485 m (18,000 ft). Hydraulic system, operating at nominal pressure of 207 bars (3,000 lb/sq in), comprises two engine driven, variable displacement axial electric pumps, a self pressurising standby mechanical pump, and a modular unit incorporating connectors, filters and valves; system is employed for actuation of wing flaps, landing gear extension/retraction, wheel brakes, emergency and parking brakes, nosewheel steering, cargo ramp and door, and propeller braking. Accumulator for backup braking system. No pneumatic system. 28V DC primary electrical system powered by two 400A Auxilec engine driven starter/generators, with two 24V 37Ah nickel-cadmium batteries for engine starting and 30 min (minimum) emergency power for essential services. Constant frequency single-phase AC power (115/26V) provided at 400Hz by three 600VA static inverters (two for normal operation plus one standby); two three-phase engine driven alternators for 115/200V variable frequency AC power. Fixed oxygen installation for crew of three (single cylinder at 124 bars; 1,800 lb/sq in pressure); three portable units and individual masks for passengers. Pneumatic boot anti-icing of wing (outboard of engine nacelles), fin and tailplane leading-edges. Electric anti-icing of propellers, engine air intakes, flight deck windscreen, pitot tubes and angle of attack indicators. No APU: starboard engine, with propeller braking, can be used to fulfil this function. Hand type fire extinguishers on flight deck (one) and in passenger cabin (two); smoke detector in baggage compartment. Engine fire detection and extinguishing system.

AVIONICS AND EQUIPMENT: Standard avionics include two Collins VHF-22B com radios, one Avtech DADS crew interphone, one Collins TDR-90 ATC transponder, two

Spanish built Airtech (CASA/IPTN) CN-235 M Series 10 military transport aircraft, in Royal Saudi Air Force insignia

Collins VIR-32 VOR/ILS/marker beacon receivers, one Collins DME-42, one Collins ADF-60A, one Collins WXR-300 weather radar, two Collins 332D-11T vertical gyros, two Collins MCS-65 directional gyros, two Collins ADI-85A, two Collins HSI-85, two Collins RMI-36, one Collins APS-65 autopilot/flight director, one Collins ALT-55B radio altimeter, one Fairchild/Teledyne flight data recorder, one Fairchild A-100A cockpit voice recorder, one Avtech PACIS PA system, two Collins 345A-7 rate of turn sensors, one Sfena H-301 APM standby attitude director indicator, one Dorne & Margolin ELT 8-1 emergency locator transmitter, and one Sundstrand Mk II GPWS. Collins EFIS-85 five-tube CRT system optional. Other options include Collins EFIS-85B; second TDR-90, DME-42 and ADF-60A; plus Collins HF-230 com radio, Collins RNS-325 radar nav, Litton LTN-72R inertial nav or Global GNS-500A Omega navigation system. Navigation lights, anti-collision strobe lights, 600W landing light in front end of each main landing gear fairing, taxi lights, ice inspection lights, emergency door lights, flight deck and flight deck emergency lights, cabin and baggage compartment lights, individual passenger reading lights, and instrument panel white lighting, are all standard.

ARMAMENT (military version): Three attachment points under each wing. Indonesian Navy ASW version can be fitted with two AM39 Exocet anti-shipping missiles.

DIMENSIONS, EXTERNAL:

Wing span	25.81 m (84 ft 8 in)
Wing chord: at root	3.00 m (9 ft 10 in)
at tip	1.20 m (3 ft 11¼ in)
Wing aspect ratio	11.3
Length overall	21.353 m (70 ft 0¾ in)
Length of fuselage	20.90 m (68 ft 7 in)
Fuselage: Max width	2.90 m (9 ft 6 in)
Max depth	2.615 m (8 ft 7 in)
Height overall	8.177 m (26 ft 10 in)
Tailplane span	11.00 m (36 ft 1 in)
Wheel track (c/l of mainwheels)	3.90 m (12 ft 9½ in)
Wheelbase	6.919 m (22 ft 8½ in)
Propeller diameter	3.35 m (11 ft 0 in)
Propeller ground clearance	1.66 m (5 ft 5¼ in)
Distance between propeller centres	7.00 m (22 ft 11½ in)
Passenger door (port, rear), paratroop door (stbd, rear) and service door (stbd, fwd): Height	1.70 m (5 ft 7 in)
Width	0.73 m (2 ft 4¾ in)
Height to sill	1.22 m (4 ft 0 in)
Ventral upper door (rear): Length	2.366 m (7 ft 9¼ in)
Width	2.349 m (7 ft 8½ in)
Height to sill	1.22 m (4 ft 0 in)
Ventral ramp/door (rear): Length	3.042 m (9 ft 11¾ in)
Width	2.349 m (7 ft 8½ in)
Height to sill	1.22 m (4 ft 0 in)
Type III emergency exits (port, fwd, and stbd, rear): Height	0.91 m (3 ft 0 in)
Width	0.51 m (1 ft 8 in)

DIMENSIONS, INTERNAL:

Cabin, excl flight deck: Length	9.65 m (31 ft 8 in)
Max width	2.70 m (8 ft 10½ in)
Width at floor	2.366 m (7 ft 9 in)
Max height	1.88 m (6 ft 2 in)
Floor area	22.822 m^2 (245.65 sq ft)
Volume	43.24 m^3 (1,527.0 cu ft)
Baggage compartment volume: ramp	5.30 m^3 (187.2 cu ft)
overhead bins	1.68 m^3 (59.3 cu ft)

AREAS:

Wings, gross	59.10 m^2 (636.1 sq ft)
Ailerons (total, incl tabs)	3.07 m^2 (33.06 sq ft)
Trailing-edge flaps (total)	10.87 m^2 (117.0 sq ft)
Fin, incl dorsal fin	11.38 m^2 (122.49 sq ft)
Rudder, incl tabs	3.32 m^2 (35.74 sq ft)
Tailplane	21.20 m^2 (228.2 sq ft)
Elevators (total, incl tabs)	6.17 m^2 (66.41 sq ft)

WEIGHTS AND LOADINGS:

Operating weight empty: passenger version	9,400 kg (20,725 lb)
cargo and military versions	8,600 kg (18,960 lb)
Max fuel	4,230 kg (9,325 lb)
Max payload: passenger version	4,200 kg (9,260 lb)
cargo and military versions	5,000 kg (11,025 lb)
Max weapon load (CN-235 M)	3,500 kg (7,716 lb)
Max T-O weight	15,100 kg (33,290 lb)
Max landing weight	15,050 kg (33,180 lb)
Max zero-fuel weight	13,600 kg (29,980 lb)
Cabin floor loading: cargo and military versions	1,504 kg/m^2 (308.0 lb/sq ft)
Max wing loading	255.5 kg/m^2 (52.36 lb/sq ft)
Max power loading without APR	5.78 kg/kW (9.51 lb/shp)

PERFORMANCE (civil versions at max T-O weight, ISA, except where indicated):

Max operating speed at S/L	240 knots (445 km/h; 276 mph) IAS
Max cruising speed at 4,575 m (15,000 ft)	244 knots (452 km/h; 280 mph)
Stalling speed at S/L: flaps up	100 knots (186 km/h; 116 mph) IAS
flaps down	84 knots (156 km/h; 97 mph) IAS
Max rate of climb at S/L	465 m (1,527 ft)/min
Rate of climb at S/L, one engine out	128 m (420 ft)/min
Service ceiling	8,110 m (26,600 ft)
Service ceiling, one engine out	4,550 m (14,925 ft)
T-O run	554 m (1,818 ft)
T-O to 10.7 m (35 ft) at S/L	687 m (2,254 ft)
Landing from 15 m (50 ft) at S/L	585 m (1,920 ft)
Min ground turning radius	18.98 m (62 ft 3¼ in)
Range at 5,485 m (18,000 ft), reserves for 87 nm (161 km; 100 mile) diversion and 45 min hold: with max payload	208 nm (385 km; 239 miles)
with max fuel	2,110 nm (3,910 km; 2,429 miles)

OPERATIONAL NOISE LEVELS (civil versions):

T-O	84.0 EPNdB
Approach	87.0 EPNdB
Sideline	86.0 EPNdB

PERFORMANCE (CN-235 M at max T-O weight, ISA, except where indicated):

As for civil versions except:

Max rate of climb at S/L	579 m (1,900 ft)/min
Rate of climb at S/L, one engine out	156 m (512 ft)/min
Service ceiling	7,620 m (25,000 ft)
Service ceiling, one engine out	4,665 m (15,300 ft)
T-O to 15 m (50 ft)	732 m (2,400 ft)
Landing from 15 m (50 ft)	772 m (2,530 ft)
Landing run, with propeller reversal	286 m (939 ft)
Range at 6,100 m (20,000 ft), long-range cruising speed, reserves for 45 min hold: with max payload	669 nm (1,240 km; 770 miles)
with 2,400 kg (5,291 lb) payload	2,304 nm (4,270 km; 2,653 miles)

AMX

AMX INTERNATIONAL

Aldwych House, Aldwych, London WC2B 4JP, England
Telex: 25660
PRESIDENT: Ing Giandomenico Cantele (Aeritalia)
PARTICIPATING COMPANIES:

Aeritalia (Combat Aircraft Group), Corso Marche 41, 10146 Turin, Italy
Telephone: (011) 33321
Telex: 221076 AERITOR

Aermacchi SpA, Via Sanvito Silvestro 80 (Casella Postale 246), 21100 Varese, Italy
Telephone: (0332) 254111
Telex: 380070 AERMAC I

Embraer (Empresa Brasileira de Aeronáutica SA), Av Brig Faria Lima 2170, Caixa Postal 343, 12200 São José dos Campos, SP, Brazil
Telephone: (0123) 251000
Telex: 1233589 EBAE BR

AMX

Brazilian Air Force designation: A-1

The AMX is the outcome of an Italian Air Force specification drawn up in 1977 for a small tactical fighter-bomber, optimised for direct air reconnaissance and weapons support of friendly ground and naval forces but capable also, when required, of carrying out missions which would otherwise require use of both the Tornado and F-104S. The early background to the AMX programme has been described in the 1987-88 and previous editions of *Jane's*.

In March 1980, soon after completion of the definition phase by Aeritalia and Aermacchi, the Brazilian government confirmed its intention of taking part in the programme, and four months later Embraer became an industrial partner of the two Italian manufacturers. The development phase, initiated in January 1981, was followed by a production phase agreement signed in the late Spring of 1987.

Seven prototypes were built (three by Aeritalia, two each by Aermacchi and Embraer), plus one airframe (by Aeritalia at Turin) for static testing. In addition, selected components for fatigue testing were completed by each of the three manufacturers. The Aeritalia-assembled A01 first prototype made its initial flight on 15 May 1984. First Brazilian assembled (YA-1) prototype to fly, on 16 October 1985, was A04, and the final prototype (Embraer's A06) made its initial flight on 16 December 1986. Further details of the prototypes can be found in the 1987-88 and earlier editions. In all, the prototypes had accumulated about 1,000 hours, in more than 800 flights, by January 1988.

Close-up of interchangeable reconnaissance pallet on Brazilian YA-1 AMX prototype A04

Based on present stated requirements for the air forces of Italy and Brazil, series production of the AMX is expected to continue until 1994. Manufacture of the first 30 production aircraft (21 for Italy and nine for Brazil) began on schedule in July 1986, and the first of these was rolled out at Turin on 29 March 1988, making its first flight on 11 May. Deliveries were expected to begin to the Italian Air Force in June 1988 and the Brazilian Air Force in May 1989. The work split gives Aeritalia, the programme leader, 46.7 per cent (fuselage centre-section, nose radome, fin and rudder, elevators, flaps, ailerons and spoilers); Aermacchi has 23.6 per cent (forward fuselage, including gun and avionics integration, canopy and tailcone); and Embraer 29.7 per cent (air intakes, wings, wing leading-edge slats, tailplane, wing pylons, external fuel tanks and reconnaissance pallets). There is single source component manufacture only, but there are final assembly lines in both Italy and Brazil.

The series production phase is expected to involve 266 single-seat AMXs (187 for the Aeronautica Militare Italiana and 79 for the Força Aérea Brasileira) and 51 two-seaters (37 for Italy and 14 for Brazil). In the Italian Air Force the AMX is intended to take over duties performed at present by the G91R, the G91Y interdictor, and the F-104G and S Starfighter. The close air support and interdiction tasks will be undertaken fully by the AMX, while counter-air duties will be shared with the longer-range Tornado; the 187 aircraft to be ordered will be sufficient to equip eight squadrons.

The Brazilian Air Force aircraft differ primarily in avionics and weapon delivery systems, and have two internally mounted 30 mm cannon instead of the single multi-barrel 20 mm weapon of the Italian version.

The AMX will be capable of carrying out missions at high subsonic speed and very low altitude, by day and night, in poor visibility, and if necessary from bases with poorly equipped or partially damaged runways. Basic requirements included good take-off and landing performance, good penetration capability, and a proven, in-production power plant requiring a minimum of adaptation to the AMX airframe. The primary flying control surfaces have manual reversion, to provide a fly-home capability even if both of the two independent hydraulic systems become inoperative.

Work on the tandem two-seat version of the AMX began in mid-1986, and one Brazilian and two Italian prototypes are expected to be completed. The first of these, under construction in Italy, is due to fly in June 1989. The two-seat version is envisaged both as an operational trainer and, with suitable specialist equipment, for such roles as electronic warfare or maritime attack. The second cockpit will occupy the area vacated by the forward fuselage fuel tank, with virtually no significant change to the remainder of the airframe. Embraer is undertaking design of the dual controls, canopy, and integration of the Ferranti rear cockpit HUD monitor; and redesign of the environmental control and oxygen systems.

The following description applies to the single-seat AMX:

TYPE: Single-seat close air support, battlefield interdiction and reconnaissance aircraft, with secondary capability for offensive counter-air.

WINGS: Cantilever shoulder-wing monoplane, with sweepback of 31° on leading-edges, 27° 30′ at quarter chord, and thickness/chord ratio of 12%. Three-spar torsion box structure, machined from solid aluminium alloy with integrally stiffened skins. Three-point attachment of each wing to fuselage main frames. Leading-edge slats (two segments each side) over most of span, and two-segment double-slotted Fowler flaps over approx two-thirds of each trailing-edge, are operated electrically and actuated hydraulically. Forward of each pair of flaps is a pair of hydraulically actuated spoilers, deployed separately in inboard and outboard pairs. These are controlled electronically by Aeritalia/GEC Avionics flight control computer, and serve also as airbrakes/lift dumpers. Hydraulically actuated ailerons, with manual reversion. No tabs.

FUSELAGE: Conventional semi-monocoque oval-section structure, built chiefly of aluminium alloy. Forward section incorporates main avionics and equipment bays, airborne systems, gun(s), nose landing gear and cockpit; central section includes engine air intake ducts, main landing gear and engine bay. Extreme rear fuselage, complete with tailplane, detachable for access to engine.

TAIL UNIT: Sweptback fin (of carbonfibre) and rudder. Variable incidence tailplane, mid-mounted on fuselage. Tailplane and rudder movement controlled electronically by Aeritalia/GEC Avionics flight control computer.

Hydraulically actuated carbonfibre elevators, with manual reversion. No elevator or rudder tabs.

LANDING GEAR: Hydraulically retractable tricycle type, of Messier-Hispano-Bugatti levered suspension design, built in Italy by Magnaghi (nose unit) and ERAM (main units). Single wheel and oleo-pneumatic shock absorber on each unit. Nose unit retracts forward; main units retract forward and inward, turning through approx 90° to lie almost flat in underside of engine air intake trunks. Nosewheel is hydraulically steerable (60° to left and right), self-centring, and fitted with anti-shimmy device. Mainwheel tyres size 670 × 210-12, pressure 9.65 bars (140 lb/sq in); nosewheel tyre size 18 × 5.5-8, pressure 10.7 bars (155 lb/sq in). Hydraulic brakes and anti-skid system. No brake-chute. Prototypes fitted with runway arrester hook.

POWER PLANT: One 49.1 kN (11,030 lb st) Rolls-Royce Spey Mk 807 non-afterburning turbofan, built under licence in Italy by Fiat, Piaggio and Alfa Romeo Avio, in association with Companhia Eletro-Mecânica (CELMA) in Brazil. Fuel in compartmented fuselage tank and two integral wing tanks with combined capacity of 3,555 litres (939 US gallons; 782 Imp gallons). Auxiliary underwing fuel tanks of up to 1,000 litres (264 US gallons; 220 Imp gallons) capacity can be carried on each of the inboard underwing pylons, and up to 500 litres (132 US gallons; 110 Imp gallons) on each of the outboard pylons. Single-point pressure or gravity refuelling of internal and external tanks. Provision for in-flight refuelling.

ACCOMMODATION: Pilot only, on Martin-Baker Mk 10L zero/zero ejection seat; 18° downward view over nose. One-piece wraparound windscreen; one-piece hinged canopy, opening sideways to starboard. Cockpit pressurised and air-conditioned. Tandem two-seat combat trainer/special missions version under development.

SYSTEMS: Microtecnica environmental control system (ECS) provides air-conditioning of cockpit, avionics and reconnaissance pallets, cockpit pressurisation, air intake and inlet guide vane anti-icing, windscreen demisting, and anti-g systems. Duplicated redundant hydraulic systems, driven by engine gearbox, operate at pressure of 207 bars (3,000 lb/sq in) for actuation of primary flight control system, flaps, spoilers, landing gear, wheel brakes, anti-skid system, nosewheel steering and gun operation. Primary electrical system AC power (115/200V at fixed frequency of 400Hz) supplied by two 30kVA IDG generators, with two transformer-rectifier units for conversion to 28V DC; 36Ah nickel-cadmium battery for emergency use, to provide power for essential systems in the event of primary and secondary electrical system failure. Aeroeletrônica (Brazil) external power control unit. Fiat FA 150 Argo APU for engine starting. An APU driven electrical generator for ground operation is planned. Liquid oxygen system.

AVIONICS AND EQUIPMENT: Avionics and equipment are divided into six main subsystems: (1) UHF and VHF com, and IFF; (2) navigation (Litton Italia inertial system, with Tacan and standby AHRS, for Italian Air Force; VOR/ILS for Brazil); (3) Litton computer based weapons aiming and delivery, incorporating an Elta/FIAR range-only radar and OMI/Selenia stores management system; (4) digital data display (OMI/Selenia head-up, multi-function head-down, and

Brazilian prototype of the AMX single-seat close support aircraft

weapons/nav); (5) data processing, with Microtecnica digital air data computer; and (6) Elettronica active and passive ECM, including fin mounted radar warning receiver. The ranging radar in Italian AMXs, known as Pointer, is an I/J band set modified from the Elta (Israel) EL/M-2001B and built in Italy by FIAR. Brazilian aircraft will have a Technasa/SMA SCP-01 radar. Ferranti MED 2067 video monitor display in rear cockpit of two-seater, for use as HUD monitor by instructor/navigator. Modular design and space provisions within the aircraft permit retrofitting of alternative avionics systems if and when required. All avionics/equipment packages are pallet mounted and positioned to allow rapid access.

ARMAMENT AND OPERATIONAL EQUIPMENT: One M61A1 multi-barrel 20 mm cannon, with 350 rds, in port side of lower forward fuselage (one 30 mm DEFA 554 cannon on each side in aircraft for Brazilian Air Force). Single twin-pylon stores attachment point under fuselage, on centreline, plus two attachments under each wing, and wingtip rails for two AIM-9L Sidewinder or similar infra-red air-to-air missiles (MAA-1 Piranha on Brazilian aircraft). Fuselage and inboard underwing hardpoints each stressed for loads of up to 907 kg (2,000 lb), outboard underwing points for 454 kg (1,000 lb) each. Total external stores load 3,800 kg (8,377 lb). Attack weapons can include free-fall or retarded Mk 82/83/84 bombs, cluster bombs, air-to-surface missiles (including area denial, anti-radiation and anti-shipping weapons), electro-optical precision guided munitions, and rocket launchers. For reconnaissance missions, any one of three interchangeable Aeroeletrônica (Brazil) pallet mounted photographic systems (panoramic, TV and photogrammetric) can be carried, installed internally in forward fuselage; an external infra-red/optronics pod can be carried on the centreline pylon. Each of these systems is fully compatible with the aircraft, and will not affect

operational capability; the aircraft will therefore be able to carry out reconnaissance missions without effect upon its normal navigation/attack and self defence capabilities. Camera bay is in lower starboard side of fuselage, forward of mainwheel bay.

DIMENSIONS, EXTERNAL:

Wing span:	
excl wingtip missiles and rails	8.874 m (29 ft 1½ in)
over missiles	10.00 m (32 ft 9¾ in)
Wing aspect ratio	3.75
Wing taper ratio	0.5
Length overall	13.575 m (44 ft 6½ in)
Length of fuselage	12.55 m (41 ft 2 in)
Height overall	4.576 m (15 ft 0¼ in)
Tailplane span	approx 5.20 m (17 ft 0¾ in)
Wheel track	2.15 m (7 ft 0¾ in)
Wheelbase	4.74 m (15 ft 6½ in)

AREAS:

Wings, gross	21.00 m² (226.04 sq ft)
Ailerons (total)	0.88 m² (9.47 sq ft)
Trailing-edge flaps (total)	7.36 m² (79.22 sq ft)
Leading-edge slats (total)	2.066 m² (22.24 sq ft)
Spoilers (total)	2.80 m² (30.14 sq ft)
Fin (exposed)	3.389 m² (36.48 sq ft)
Rudder	0.835 m² (8.99 sq ft)
Tailplane (total exposed)	5.815 m² (62.59 sq ft)
Elevators (total)	0.632 m² (6.80 sq ft)

WEIGHTS AND LOADINGS:

Operational weight empty	6,700 kg (14,770 lb)
Max fuel weight: internal	2,790 kg (6,150 lb)
external	1,732 kg (3,818 lb)
Max external stores load	3,800 kg (8,377 lb)
T-O weight 'clean'	9,600 kg (21,164 lb)
Typical mission T-O weight	10,750 kg (23,700 lb)
Max T-O weight	12,500 kg (27,558 lb)
Normal landing weight	7,000 kg (15,432 lb)
Combat wing loading ('clean')	385 kg/m² (78.9 lb/sq ft)
Max wing loading	595.2 kg/m² (122.0 lb/sq ft)
Max power loading	254.77 kg/kN (2.5 lb/lb st)

PERFORMANCE (A: at 10,750 kg; 23,700 lb mission T-O weight, B: at max T-O weight, ISA in both cases):

Max level and max cruising speed	Mach 0.86
Max rate of climb at S/L: A	3,840 m (12,600 ft)/min
Service ceiling	13,000 m (42,650 ft)
T-O run at S/L: A	750 m (2,461 ft)
B	950 m (3,120 ft)
T-O to 15 m (50 ft) at S/L: B	1,525 m (5,000 ft)
Landing run at S/L: A	732 m (2,400 ft)
Min ground turning radius: A, B	11.00 m (36 ft 1 in)

Attack radius, with allowance for 5 min combat over target and 10% fuel reserves:

A with 907 kg (2,000 lb) of external stores:

hi-lo-hi	480 nm (890 km; 550 miles)
lo-lo-lo	300 nm (555 km; 345 miles)

B with 2,720 kg (6,000 lb) of external stores:

hi-lo-hi	280 nm (520 km; 320 miles)
lo-lo-lo	200 nm (370 km; 230 miles)

Ferry range with two 1,000 litre (264 US gallon; 220 Imp gallon) drop tanks, 10% reserves:

A	1,700 nm (3,150 km; 1,957 miles)
g limits	+8/-4

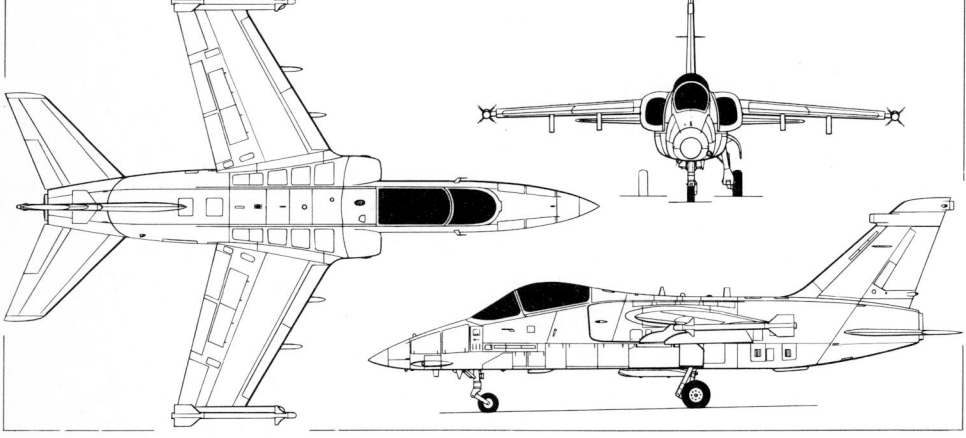

Aeritalia/Aermacchi/Embraer AMX, in production for the air forces of Italy and Brazil (*Pilot Press*)

ATR
AVIONS DE TRANSPORT RÉGIONAL

316 route de Bayonne (BP 31107), 31060 Toulouse Cédex 03, France
Telephone: (61) 93 55 55
Telex: 531 546 F
CHAIRMAN AND CHIEF EXECUTIVE OFFICER (alternate):
  Henri Martre (Aérospatiale)
  Fausto Cereti (Aeritalia)
EXECUTIVE VICE-PRESIDENT: Gérard Hibon (Aérospatiale)
VICE-PRESIDENT, SALES ENGINEERING:
  P. Lebouc
COMMERCIAL MANAGER: Henri-Paul Puel

Launch of the initial ATR 42 programme, by Aérospatiale (France) and Aeritalia (Italy), was confirmed on 4 November 1981 by setting up a Groupement d'Intérêt Economique (pooling of common economic interest) to manage the programme. This GIE was formally established on 5 February 1982. ATR corresponds to the initial letters of the French and Italian words for 'regional transport aircraft', and 42 to the seating capacity of the basic aircraft.

ATR 42

The ATR 42 is a twin-turboprop transport designed to FAR Pt 25 and European Joint Airworthiness Requirement JAR 25 for the certification of transport aircraft. Choice of the Pratt & Whitney Canada PW120 turboprop as the

Aérospatiale/Aeritalia ATR 42 short-haul commuter transport in the insignia of Aero Trasporti Italiani, an Alitalia subsidiary

aircraft's original power plant was announced on 8 June 1981.

Aeritalia is responsible for the entire fuselage, including the tail unit and installation of the landing gear; and for the hydraulic, air-conditioning and pressurisation systems. Aérospatiale undertakes design and construction of the wings; layout of the flight deck and cabin; and is also responsible for power plant, electrical system, flight controls and de-icing system installation, and for final assembly and flight testing of the civil passenger versions. Aeritalia will assemble and flight test any cargo/military variants with a rear loading ramp.

Two development aircraft were built, plus airframes for static and fatigue test. First flight was made by F-WEGA on 16 August 1984, with the second aircraft (F-WEGB) following on 31 October 1984. The first production aircraft (F-WEGC) made its initial flight on 30 April 1985. French DGAC certification of the ATR 42-200 and -300 to JAR 25 was granted on 24 September 1985, with concurrent type approval by the Italian RAI. FAA certification (FAR Pt 25) followed on 25 October 1985 and German LBA approval on 12 February 1988. Deliveries began on 2 December 1985 with the fourth aircraft (to Air Littoral), and services with this airline began seven days later.

By 1 August 1988, a total of 149 orders and 63 options had been received for the ATR 42, of which 98 had been delivered.

Initial production is centred on the **ATR 42-300** which has an increased maximum take-off weight and payload/range capability by comparison with the prototypes. The following variants have been or are being studied:

ATR 42 F. Commercial freighter version, capable of carrying 3,800 kg (8,377 lb) or 42 passengers over 1,250 nm (2,316 km; 1,439 miles). Modified interior, reinforced cabin floor, port side flight-openable cargo/airdrop door.

ATM 42 L. Military freighter version, with large forward cargo door. Described separately.

SAR 42. Search and rescue/maritime surveillance version for public utility missions, with 4 hour search endurance at 600 nm (1,112 km; 691 miles) from base. Search radar, survival equipment, ship or shore communications link.

ATR 72. 'Stretched' version, launched in mid-1985. Described separately.

The following description applies to the standard ATR 42-300:

TYPE: Twin-turboprop regional transport aircraft.
WINGS: Cantilever high-wing monoplane. Aérospatiale RA-XXX-43 wing section, derived from NACA 43 series, with thickness/chord ratio of 18% at root and 13% at tip. Constant chord centre-section and tapered outer panels. Dihedral 2° 30′ and sweepback 3° 6′ at quarter-chord on outer panels. Incidence 2° at root. Two-spar fail-safe wings, constructed mainly of aluminium alloys, with leading-edges of Kevlar/Nomex sandwich, and skin panels of Kevlar/Nomex with carbon reinforcement on upper surface aft of rear spar. Two-segment double-slotted single-rotation flaps, each segment with a Ratier-Figeac hydraulic actuator, on each trailing-edge. Spoiler forward of outer end of each outer flap segment. Ailerons actuated mechanically by cables and push/pull rods; no servos. Flaps and ailerons of carbonfibre/Nomex and carbon/epoxy construction respectively, with alu-

minium frames and spars. Electrically actuated automatic trim tab in each aileron. Kléber-Colombes pneumatic de-icing of leading-edges outboard of engine nacelles.
FUSELAGE: Conventional semi-monocoque fail-safe structure mainly of light alloy unit construction, employing main and secondary frames and longitudinally disposed skin panels. Nosecone, tailcone, wing/body fairings, nosewheel doors and main landing gear fairings of Kevlar/Nomex sandwich. Crew, passenger and baggage/cargo compartments pressurised.
TAIL UNIT: Cantilever structure, with sweptback vertical surfaces (attached to rearmost fuselage frame) and non-swept horizontal surfaces. Fixed incidence tailplane mounted near tip of fin. Fin and tailplane construction mainly of aluminium alloys, with dorsal fin of Kevlar/Nomex and glassfibre/Nomex sandwich. Mechanically actuated mass balanced rudder and elevators, of carbonfibre/Nomex sandwich construction. Electrically actuated automatic trim tab in rudder and each elevator. Kléber-Colombes pneumatic de-icing of tailplane leading-edges.
LANDING GEAR: Hydraulically retractable tricycle type, of Messier-Hispano-Bugatti/Magnaghi/Nardi trailing-arm design, with twin wheels and oleo-pneumatic shock absorber on each unit. Nose unit retracts forward, main units inward into fuselage and large underfuselage fairing. Goodyear multi-disc brakes and Hydro-Aire anti-skid units on main gear. No brake cooling. Goodyear mainwheels and tubeless tyres, size 32 × 8.8-10PR, pressure 7.17 bars (104 lb/sq in). Low pressure tyres optional. Goodyear nosewheels and tubeless tyres, size 450 × 190-5TL, pressure 4.14 bars (60 lb/sq in).
POWER PLANT: Two Pratt & Whitney Canada PW120 turboprops, each flat rated at 1,342 kW (1,800 shp) and driving a Hamilton Standard 14SF four-blade constant-speed fully-feathering and reversible-pitch propeller with spinner. Blades have metal spars and

glassfibre/polyurethane skins. Two PW121 turboprops, each flat rated at 1,454 kW (1,950 shp), optional. Fuel in two integral tanks formed by wing spar box, total capacity 5,700 litres (1,506 US gallons; 1,254 Imp gallons). Single pressure refuelling point in starboard wing leading-edge. Gravity refuelling points in wing upper surface. Oil capacity 40 litres (10.6 US gallons; 8.8 Imp gallons). Cowlings of carbonfibre/Nomex and Kevlar/Nomex sandwich, reinforced with carbonfibre in nose and underside.
ACCOMMODATION: Crew of two on flight deck, with optional third seat for observer. Seating for 42 passengers at 81 cm (32 in) pitch; or 46, 48 or 50 passengers at 76 cm (30 in) pitch, in four-abreast layout with central aisle. Passenger door, with integral steps, at rear of cabin on port side. Main baggage/cargo compartment between flight deck and passenger cabin, with access from inside cabin and separate loading door on port side. Rear baggage/cargo compartment, toilet, galley, wardrobe, and seat for cabin attendant, aft of passenger cabin, with service door on starboard side. Additional baggage space provided by overhead bins and underseat stowage. Entire accommodation, including baggage/cargo compartments, pressurised and air-conditioned. Passenger/cargo version (42 passengers or five LD3 containers) fitted with ball transfer plates aft, roller tracks, and anti-crash net at front of cabin. Emergency escape hatch for crew in roof of flight deck. Emergency exit via rear passenger and service doors, and by additional exits on each side at front of cabin.
SYSTEMS: AiResearch air-conditioning and Softair pressurisation systems, utilising engine bleed air. Pressurisation system (nominal differential 0.41 bars; 6.0 lb/sq in) provides cabin altitude of 2,000 m (6,560 ft) at flight altitudes of up to 7,620 m (25,000 ft), and a sea level cabin environment at flight levels up to 4,025 m (13,200 ft). Two independent hydraulic systems, each at system pressure

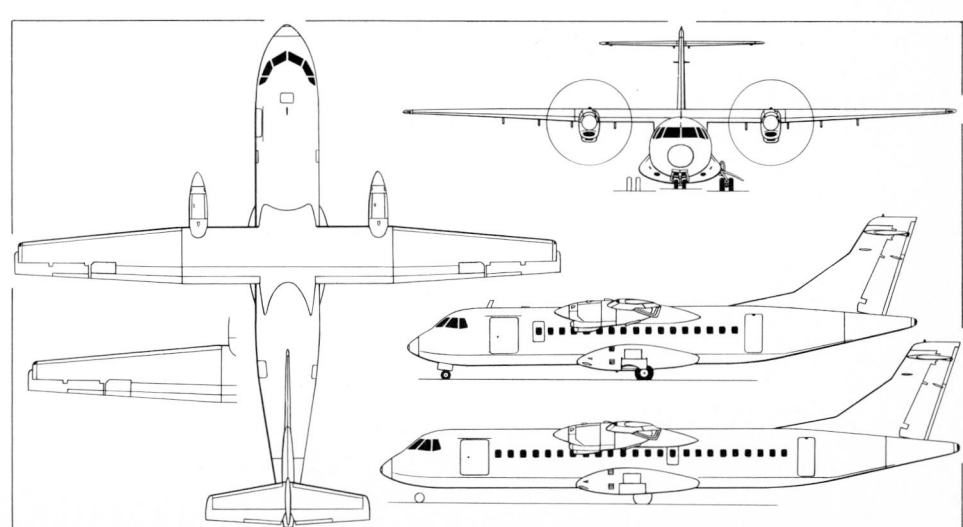

Aérospatiale/Aeritalia ATR 42 twin-turboprop regional transport aircraft, with added side view (bottom) and extended outer wing of ATR 72 *(Pilot Press)*

of 207 bars (3,000 lb/sq in), driven by an electrically operated Abex pump and separated by an interconnecting valve controlled from the flight deck. System flow rate 7.9 litres (2.09 US gallons; 1.74 Imp gallons)/min. One system actuates wing flaps, spoilers, propeller braking, emergency wheel braking and nosewheel steering; second system for landing gear and normal braking system. Kléber-Colombes pneumatic system for de-icing of outer wing leading-edges, tailplane leading-edges and engine air intakes. Main electrical system is 28V DC, supplied by two Auxilec 12kW engine driven starter/generators and two nickel-cadmium batteries (27Ah and 16Ah) with two solid state static inverters for 115/26V single-phase AC supply, and a third (standby) inverter for 115V only. A 115/200V three-phase supply from two 20kVA frequency-wild engine driven alternators is used for anti-icing of windscreen, flight deck side windows, stall warning and airspeed indicator pitots, pitot tubes, propeller blades and control surface horns. Eros/Puritan oxygen system. No APU.

AVIONICS: King Gold Crown III com/nav equipment standard, Collins Pro Line II optional. Other standard avionics include Sperry DFZ-600 autopilot/flight director, Sperry P-800 weather radar, dual Sperry AZ-800 digital air data computers and dual AH-600 attitude/heading reference systems with ASCB (avionics standard communication bus), GPWS, radio altimeter, and digital flight deck recorder. EDZ-820 electronic flight instrumentation system (R/Nav, microwave landing system, Omega nav and HF com) optional. Standard avionics package includes two VHF, two VOR/ILS/marker beacon receivers, radio compass, radio altimeter, DME, ATC transponder, cockpit voice recorder, intercom, PA system, and equipment to FAR Pt 121.

DIMENSIONS, EXTERNAL:

Wing span	24.57 m (80 ft 7½ in)
Wing chord: at root	2.57 m (8 ft 5¼ in)
at tip	1.41 m (4 ft 7½ in)
Wing aspect ratio	11.08
Length overall	22.67 m (74 ft 4½ in)
Fuselage: Max width	2.865 m (9 ft 4½ in)
Height overall	7.586 m (24 ft 10¾ in)
Elevator span	7.31 m (23 ft 11¾ in)
Wheel track (c/l of shock struts)	4.10 m (13 ft 5½ in)
Wheelbase	8.78 m (28 ft 9¾ in)
Propeller diameter	3.96 m (13 ft 0 in)
Distance between propeller centres	8.10 m (26 ft 7 in)
Propeller/fuselage clearance	0.82 m (2 ft 8¼ in)
Propeller ground clearance	1.20 m (3 ft 11¼ in)
Passenger door (rear, port): Height	1.75 m (5 ft 9 in)
Width	0.75 m (2 ft 5½ in)
Height to sill (at OWE)	1.375 m (4 ft 6¼ in)
Service door (rear, stbd): Height	1.22 m (4 ft 0 in)
Width	0.61 m (2 ft 0 in)
Height to sill	1.375 m (4 ft 6¼ in)
Cargo/baggage door (fwd, port):	
Height	1.52 m (5 ft 0 in)
Width	1.275 m (4 ft 2¼ in)
Height to sill (at OWE)	1.15 m (3 ft 9¼ in)
Emergency exits (fwd, each): Height	0.91 m (3 ft 0 in)
Width	0.51 m (1 ft 8 in)
Crew emergency hatch (flight deck roof):	
Length	0.51 m (1 ft 8 in)
Width	0.483 m (1 ft 7 in)

DIMENSIONS, INTERNAL:

Cabin:	
Length (excl flight deck, incl toilet and baggage compartments)	13.85 m (45 ft 5¼ in)
Max width	2.57 m (8 ft 5¼ in)
Max width at floor	2.263 m (7 ft 5⅛ in)
Max height	1.91 m (6 ft 3¼ in)
Floor area	31.0 m² (333.7 sq ft)
Volume	58.0 m³ (2,048.25 cu ft)
Baggage/cargo compartment volume:	
front (max)	6.2 m³ (219 cu ft)
front (50 passengers)	3.5 m³ (123.6 cu ft)
rear (max)	2.9 m³ (102.4 cu ft)
overhead bins	1.5 m³ (53 cu ft)

AREAS:

Wings, gross	54.5 m² (586.6 sq ft)
Ailerons (total)	3.12 m² (33.58 sq ft)
Flaps (total)	11.00 m² (118.40 sq ft)
Spoilers (total)	1.12 m² (12.06 sq ft)
Fin, excl dorsal fin	8.48 m² (91.28 sq ft)
Rudder, incl tab	4.00 m² (43.05 sq ft)
Tailplane	7.81 m² (84.07 sq ft)
Elevators (total, incl tabs)	3.92 m² (42.19 sq ft)

WEIGHTS AND LOADINGS:

Operating weight empty (incl FAR 121 equipment)	10,285 kg (22,674 lb)
Max fuel weight	4,500 kg (9,920 lb)
Max payload	4,915 kg (10,835 lb)
Max T-O weight	16,700 kg (36,817 lb)
Max ramp weight	16,720 kg (36,860 lb)
Max zero-fuel weight	15,200 kg (33,510 lb)
Max landing weight	16,400 kg (36,156 lb)

Loading a large jet engine via the forward cargo door of a full scale mockup of the ATM 42 L

Max wing loading	306.4 kg/m² (62.79 lb/sq ft)
Max power loading	6.22 kg/kW (10.23 lb/shp)

PERFORMANCE (at max T-O weight, to FAR Pt 25, incl Amendment 42, ISA, except where indicated):

Never-exceed speed
Mach 0.55 (250 knots; 463 km/h; 287 mph CAS)

Max cruising speed at 5,180 m (17,000 ft)
267 knots (495 km/h; 307 mph)

Econ cruising speed at 7,620 m (25,000 ft)
243 knots (450 km/h; 279 mph)

Stalling speed: flaps up 104 knots (193 km/h; 120 mph)
30° flap 81 knots (151 km/h; 94 mph)

Max rate of climb at S/L, AUW of 15,000 kg (33,069 lb)
640 m (2,100 ft)/min

Rate of climb at S/L, one engine out, AUW as above
191 m (625 ft)/min

Max operating altitude 7,620 m (25,000 ft)

Service ceiling, one engine out, at 97% of max T-O weight, ISA + 10°C 2,515 m (8,250 ft)

FAR Pt 25 T-O balanced field length:
at S/L 1,090 m (3,576 ft)
at 915 m (3,000 ft), ISA + 10°C 1,300 m (4,265 ft)

FAR Pt 25 landing field length at S/L at max landing weight 1,030 m (3,380 ft)

Runway LCN at max T-O weight:
rigid pavement, 200 cm radius of relative stiffness:
standard tyres 19
low pressure tyres 16
76 cm flexible pavement, standard tyres 20
83 cm flexible pavement, low pressure tyres 16

Min ground turning radius 17.08 m (56 ft 0½ in)

Max range with 46 passengers, reserves for 87 nm (161 km; 100 mile) diversion and 45 min hold
1,050 nm (1,946 km; 1,209 miles)

Range with max fuel, reserves as above:
max cruising speed 2,420 nm (4,481 km; 2,785 miles)
long-range cruising speed
2,700 nm (5,003 km; 3,109 miles)

Block time for 200 nm (370 km; 230 mile) stage length at max cruising speed at 6,100 m (20,000 ft), IFR reserves 58 min

Block fuel for above 469 kg (1,034 lb)

OPERATIONAL NOISE CHARACTERISTICS:

Take-off	83.1 EPNdB
Approach	96.7 EPNdB
Sideline	83.7 EPNdB

ATM 42 L

The ATM 42 L (M for military, L for lateral door) troop and cargo transport version of the ATR 42 was proposed by Aérospatiale in late 1986 as a replacement for the French Air Force's ageing fleet of Nord 2501 Noratlases. The main feature of this version is an upward hinged cargo door, 2.95 m (9 ft 8¼ in) wide by 1.75 m (5 ft 9 in) high, in the front of the fuselage on the port side, large enough to permit direct loading of jeeps or Peugeot P4D vehicles, three 2.24 × 2.74 m (88 × 108 in) freight pallets, or five LD3 containers. With the aid of a retractable threshold extension even the largest (Atar or M53) aero engines in service with the Armée de l'Air could be loaded via this door, which is considered less expensive, lighter in weight, and less drag-producing than a rear-loading ramp/door. The cabin floor, reinforced for loads of up to 800 kg/m² (164 lb/sq ft), would be equipped with loading rails or a ball type roller loading system. In other missions, the ATM 42 L would be able to carry, in two inward facing seat rows, up to 38 fully armed troops or 44 paratroops under training; 27 stretchers and four medical personnel; or 52 people in standard passenger seats. Paradropping would be accomplished via a 0.90 m × 1.75 m (2 ft 11½ in × 5 ft 9 in) door on each side at the rear. Performance would be substantially similar to that of the standard ATR 42, with ranges varying from 540 nm (1,000 km; 621 miles) with a max payload of 5,375 kg (11,850 lb) to 2,158 nm (4,000 km; 2,485 miles) carrying a 2,900 kg (6,393 lb) payload.

The French Air Force, which has also been evaluating the Airtech CN-235, has a reported requirement for about 25 of the type chosen. An **ATR 42 L** civil version is being offered to air freight operators.

ATR 72

Go-ahead for this 'stretched' version of the ATR 42 was announced at the 1985 Paris Air Show. Powered by 1,790 kW (2,400 shp) PW124/2 engines with Hamilton Standard 14SF-11 four-blade propellers, it has a greater wing span and area, and the lengthened fuselage can accommodate 66-74 passengers. The pressure refuelling point is in the starboard main landing gear fairing. The new wings outboard of the engines have front and rear spars and top and bottom panels of carbonfibre. Customers have a choice of passenger or cargo door at front on the port side. Two development aircraft are being built.

First flight was scheduled for October 1988, with deliveries starting in August 1989. The launch customer is Finnair, which ordered five with another three on option. Orders and options totalled 23 + 33 by 1 August 1988.

WINGS: Generally as described for ATR 42 except for increased span, and wing spar box of new outer panels (with 2° 18′ sweepback at quarter-chord) manufactured from carbonfibre/epoxy.

FUSELAGE: As ATR 42, but of increased length.

TAIL UNIT: As ATR 42.

LANDING GEAR: Main units of improved type, fitted with Dunlop mainwheels and structural carbon brakes. Mainwheel tyres size 34 × 10 R-16, pressure 7.86 bars (114 lb/sq in). Nose gear as ATR 42.

ACCOMMODATION: Crew of two on flight deck. Cabin seating for 64, 66, 70 or (high density) 74 passengers, at respective seat pitches of 81/79/76/76 cm (32/31/30/30 in), plus cabin attendant's seat. Single baggage compartment at rear of cabin; one or two at front, depending on seating layout and type of port forward door fitted. This can be a passenger or cargo door, with a service door opposite on starboard side. Second passenger door at rear of cabin, also with service door opposite. Two emergency exits (one each side); both rear doors also serve as emergency exits. All doors are of plug type. Passenger cabin equipped with folding tables on seats, individual air outlets and reading lights, and increased-capacity air-conditioning system.

AVIONICS AND EQUIPMENT: Flight deck equipment and layout generally as for ATR 42. Additions/improvements include engine monitoring mini-aids, and fuel repeater on refuelling panel.

DIMENSIONS, EXTERNAL: As ATR 42 except:

Wing span	27.05 m (88 ft 9 in)
Wing chord at tip	1.59 m (5 ft 2½ in)
Wing aspect ratio	12.0
Length overall	27.166 m (89 ft 1½ in)
Height overall	7.65 m (25 ft 1¼ in)
Wheelbase	10.79 m (35 ft 5 in)
Passenger door (fwd, port): Height	1.75 m (5 ft 9 in)

Width	0.82 m (2 ft 8¼ in)			
Height to sill	1.12 m (3 ft 8 in)			

Alternative cargo door (fwd, port):
Height   1.52 m (5 ft 0 in)
Width   1.275 m (4 ft 2½ in)
Height to sill   1.12 m (3 ft 8 in)

DIMENSIONS, INTERNAL:
Cabin:
Length (excl flight deck, incl toilet and baggage compartments)   19.21 m (63 ft 0¼ in)
Cross-section   as for ATR 42
Floor area   41.7 m² (449 sq ft)
Volume   76.0 m³ (2,684 cu ft)

Baggage volume (total, incl overhead bins and stowage):
74 pass, front pass door   8.60 m³ (304 cu ft)
70 pass, front pass door   11.85 m³ (418 cu ft)
66 pass, front pass door   11.70 m³ (413 cu ft)
66 pass, front cargo door   13.20 m³ (466 cu ft)
64 pass, front pass door   12.00 m³ (424 cu ft)

AREAS: As ATR 42 except:
Wings, gross   61.0 m² (656.6 sq ft)

Ailerons (total)   3.75 m² (40.36 sq ft)
Flaps (total)   12.28 m² (132.18 sq ft)
Spoilers (total)   1.34 m² (14.42 sq ft)

WEIGHTS AND LOADINGS (A: basic, B: optional):
Operating weight empty:
A, B   12,200 kg (26,896 lb)
Max fuel weight: A, B   5,000 kg (11,023 lb)
Max payload:
A   7,150 kg (15,763 lb)
B   7,500 kg (16,535 lb)
Max T-O weight: A   19,990 kg (44,070 lb)
B   21,500 kg (47,400 lb)
Max ramp weight: A   20,020 kg (44,136 lb)
B   21,530 kg (47,465 lb)
Max zero-fuel weight: A   19,350 kg (42,660 lb)
B   19,700 kg (43,430 lb)
Max landing weight: A   19,900 kg (43,872 lb)
B   21,350 kg (47,068 lb)
Max wing loading: A   327.7 kg/m² (67.12 lb/sq ft)
B   352.5 kg/m² (72.20 lb/sq ft)
Max power loading: A   5.58 kg/kW (9.18 lb/shp)
B   6.01 kg/kW (9.88 lb/shp)

PERFORMANCE (estimated, at max basic T-O weight except where indicated):
Max cruising speed at 7,620 m (25,000 ft):
A   286 knots (530 km/h; 329 mph)
B   284 knots (526 km/h; 327 mph)
Econ cruising speed at 7,620 m (25,000 ft)
    248 knots (460 km/h; 286 mph)
Max operating altitude   7,620 m (25,000 ft)
Service ceiling, one engine out, at 97% MTOGW and
ISA + 10°C: A   3,550 m (11,650 ft)
B   2,850 m (9,350 ft)
T-O balanced field length at S/L, ISA: A
    1,270 m (4,167 ft)
B   1,525 m (5,000 ft)
Landing field length at S/L, ISA: A   1,010 m (3,314 ft)
B   1,065 m (3,495 ft)
Min ground turning radius   19.76 m (64 ft 10 in)
Still air range at max optional T-O weight (ISA), reserves for 87 nm (161 km; 100 mile) diversion and 45 min continued cruise:
max optional payload 645 nm (1,195 km; 742 miles)
66 passengers   1,440 nm (2,666 km; 1,657 miles)
max fuel and zero payload
    2,370 nm (4,389 km; 2,727 miles)

DASSAULT-BREGUET/DORNIER

AIRFRAME PRIME CONTRACTORS:
Avions Marcel Dassault-Breguet Aviation, 27 rue du Professeur Victor Pauchet, BP 32, 92420 Vaucresson, France
Telephone: (1) 741 79 21
Telex: AMADAS 203944 F
Dornier GmbH, Postfach 2160, 8000 Munich 66, Federal Republic of Germany
Telephone: (089) 87 15 3480
Telex: 52 35 43

On 22 July 1969 the French and Federal German governments announced a joint requirement for a new subsonic basic/advanced training and light attack aircraft to enter service with their armed forces in the 1970s. The Alpha Jet was selected in 1970 to meet this requirement, and production was authorised in March 1975. Dassault-Breguet was named as main contractor and Dornier as industrial collaborator, the total workload being shared primarily between the two groups.

Dassault-Breguet/Dornier Alpha Jet 2, with uprated Larzac engines and Sagem inertial nav/attack system

DASSAULT-BREGUET/DORNIER ALPHA JET

All initial production Alpha Jets had essentially identical structure, power plant, landing gear and standard equipment. For all aircraft, the outer wings, tail unit, rear fuselage, landing gear doors and cold-flow exhaust are manufactured in West Germany; the forward and centre fuselage (with integrated wing centre-section) are manufactured in France. Fuselage nosecones and wing flaps are manufactured in Belgium by SABCA. The power plant prime contractors are Turbomeca and SNECMA in France, and MTU and KHD in West Germany; and, for the landing gear, Messier-Hispano-Bugatti in France and Liebherr Aero Technik in West Germany.

The Alpha Jet made its first flight, at Istres, on 26 October 1973. Details of the four prototypes can be found in the 1978-79 and earlier editions of *Jane's*, and of Dornier's DSFC and TST national experimental programmes in the 1982-83 edition. Existing prototypes continue to be used as testbeds for various programmes, including armament testing, a CFRP wing, and development of the Larzac 04-C20 engine.

There are six versions of the Alpha Jet, as follows:
Advanced trainer/light attack version (formerly Alpha Jet E). Ordered for the air forces of France (176), Belgium (33), Egypt (30, designated **MS1**), Ivory Coast (7), Morocco (24), Nigeria (24), Qatar (6) and Togo (6). Those

for Nigeria are from German assembly line, others from French production; 26 of Egyptian MS1s assembled in Egypt by AOI (which see). First production aircraft (E1 for French Air Force) flown on 4 November 1977; those for Armée de l'Air (delivered in 1978-85) are currently in service with Groupement-École 314 at Tours (58); the Patrouille de France (18) at Salon de Provence; three at Mont-de-Marsan; and 40 with the 8e Escadre de Transformation at Cazaux. Aircraft for Belgian Air Force, assembled by SABCA and delivered in 1978-80, serve with Nos. 7, 9 and 11 Squadrons.

Close support version (formerly Alpha Jet A). Ordered for Federal German Luftwaffe (175). First flown (A1) on 12 April 1978. Delivered in 1979-83 for JaboGs 41, 43 and 49 (51 aircraft each) and the Luftwaffe base at Beja in Portugal (18) for weapons training; these are earmarked to form an additional combat unit (JaboG 44) in the event of an emergency. An update programme for the armament and avionics of Luftwaffe Alpha Jets, due to be implemented in 1989-92, will include improved instruments, navigation and air data sensors; a stall warning indicator; improved wheel/tyre/brake cooling; a three-axis damping system; and provision for two AIM-9L Sidewinder missiles and a jettisonable gun pod. Under a separate programme, these aircraft are being refitted with Larzac 04-C20 engines.

Alternative close support version, developed by Dassault-Breguet and first flown on 9 April 1982. Equipped with new nav/attack system which includes inertial platform, head-up display, laser rangefinder in modified nosecone, and radar altimeter. Ordered by Egypt (15, including 11 co-produced by AOI) and Cameroun (7). Egyptian Air Force version is designated **MS2**.

Alpha Jet 2 (formerly NGEA: Nouvelle Génération pour l'Ecole et l'Appui). Improved attack version, incorporating nav/attack system developed for MS2; uprated Larzac 04-C20 engines; capability of carrying Magic 2 air-to-air missiles, plus auxiliary fuel tanks of up to 625 litres (165 US gallons; 137.5 Imp gallons) on inboard underwing stations and 450 litres (119 US gallons; 99 Imp gallons) on inboard or outboard stations. No orders announced up to Spring 1988.

Lancier. Extended capability version, derived from Alpha Jet 2, for day/night attack, anti-shipping strike, airspace denial and self defence, and anti-helicopter missions. Incorporates fully tested core systems of Alpha Jet 2 (inertial platform and multiplex databus); added capabilities (a FLIR system providing a thermal image on the head-up display, Thomson-CSF/ESD Agave or Anémone multi-function radar in a lengthened nose and a CP 2084 computer with corresponding extension of capability); wider variety of weapons including anti-ship all-weather missiles, laser guided bombs and missiles; internal passive and active ECM; and greater external fuel capacity. No orders announced up to Spring 1988.

Alpha Jet 3. Advanced training system version fitted with state of the art cockpit controls and displays such as CRT raster HUD combined with collimated head-level

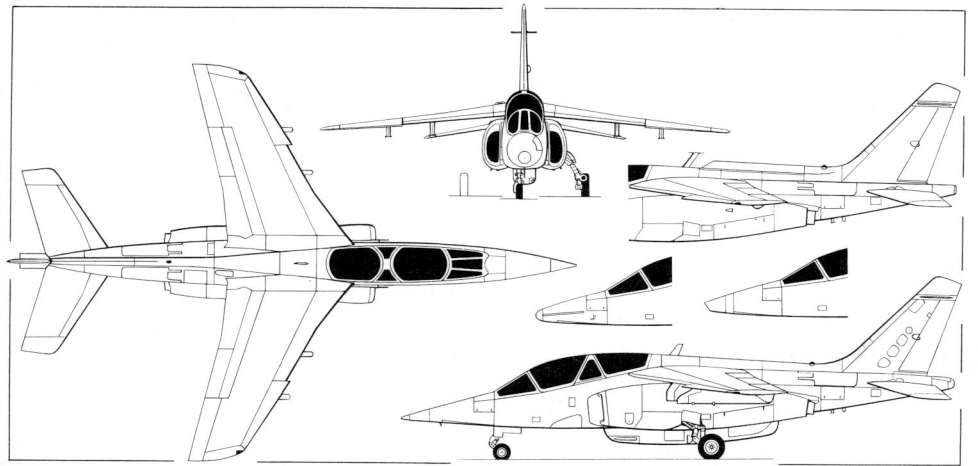

Alpha Jet close support version, with scrap views showing noses of advanced trainer/light attack version (centre left) and MS2 (centre right), plus rear fuselage with dorsal fin antenna fairing
(Pilot Press)

MBB VBW anti-tank weapon pod, currently under development for West German Alpha Jets and F-4F Phantoms

display, rear cockpit TV monitor, and lateral multi-function displays and multi-function keyboards in each cockpit. Proposed for training in the use of nav/attack systems of future combat aircraft, including training in the operation of such sensors as radar, FLIR, laser and ECM systems. No orders announced up to Spring 1988.

By May 1988, 510 of the 512 Alpha Jets then on order had been delivered.

TYPE: Tandem two-seat basic, low-altitude and advanced jet trainer and close support and battlefield reconnaissance aircraft.

WINGS: Cantilever shoulder-wing monoplane, with 6° anhedral from roots. Thickness/chord ratio 10.2% at root, 8.6% at tip. Sweepback 28° at quarter-chord. All-metal numerically or chemically milled structure, consisting of two main wing panels bolted to a centre frame. Extended chord on outer wings. Hydraulically actuated Fowler slotted flaps on each trailing-edge. Ailerons actuated by double-body irreversible hydraulic servo, with trimmable artificial feel system.

FUSELAGE: All-metal semi-monocoque structure, numerically or chemically milled, of basically oval cross-section. Built in three sections: nose (including cockpit), centre-section (including engine air intake trunks and main landing gear housings) and rear (including engine mounts and tail assembly). Narrow strake on each side of nose of aircraft with no nav/attack system. Pointed nose, with pitot probe, on Luftwaffe version. Electrically controlled, hydraulically actuated airbrake on each side of rear upper fuselage, of carbonfibre reinforced epoxy resin.

TAIL UNIT: Cantilever type, of similar construction to wings, with 45° sweepback on fin leading-edge and 30° on tailplane leading-edge. Dorsal spine fairing between cockpit and fin. Aircraft equipped with radio compass have a long, narrow strake above the dorsal spine fairing to house the antenna for this equipment. All-flying tailplane, with trimmable and IAS-controlled artificial feel system. Glassfibre fin tip and tailplane tips. Double-body irreversible hydraulic servo-actuated rudder, with trimmable artificial feel system. Yaw damper on close support versions. A rudder and tailplane of CFRP have been developed and flight tested.

LANDING GEAR: Forward retracting tricycle type, of Messier-Hispano-Bugatti/Liebherr design. All units retract hydraulically, main units into underside of engine air intake trunks. Single wheel and low-pressure tyre (approx 4 bars; 58 lb/sq in at normal T-O weight) on each unit. Tyre sizes 615 × 255-10 on main units, 380 × 150-4 on nose unit. Steel disc brakes and anti-skid units on main gear (Minispad or Modistop). Emergency braking system. Hydraulic nosewheel steering and arrester hook on close support version. Nosewheel offset to starboard to permit ground firing from gun pod.

POWER PLANT: Standard installation of two SNECMA/Turbomeca Larzac 04-C6 turbofans, each rated at 13.24 kN (2,976 lb st), mounted on sides of fuselage. Alternative option (on any Alpha Jet) for 14.12 kN (3,175 lb st) Larzac 04-C20 turbofans, which are retrofitted to Luftwaffe aircraft and are standard on the Alpha Jet 2. Splitter plate in front of each intake. Fuel in two integral tanks in outer wings, one in centre-section and three fuselage tanks. Internal fuel capacity 1,900 litres (502 US gallons; 418 Imp gallons) or 2,040 litres (539 US gallons; 449 Imp gallons). Provision for 310 or 450 litre (82 or 119 US gallon; 68 or 99 Imp gallon) capacity drop tank on each outer wing pylon, plus (on Alpha Jet 2) a 450 or 625 litre (119 or 165 US gallon; 99 or 137.5 Imp gallon) tank on each inboard wing pylon. Pressure refuelling standard for all tanks, including drop tanks. Gravity system for fuselage tanks and drop tanks. Pressure refuelling point near starboard engine air intake. Fuel system incorporates provision for inverted flying.

ACCOMMODATION: Two persons in tandem, in pressurised cockpit under individual upward opening canopies. Dual controls standard. Rear seat (for instructor in trainer versions) is elevated. French trainer versions fitted with Martin-Baker AJRM4 ejection seats, operable (including ejection through canopy) at zero height and speeds down to 90 knots (167 km/h; 104 mph). Martin-Baker B10N zero/zero seats in aircraft for Belgium, F10N in those for Egypt and Qatar. Aircraft for West Germany fitted with licence built (by MBB) Stencel S-III-S3AJ zero/zero ejection seats. Baggage compartment in tailcone, with door on starboard side.

SYSTEMS: Cockpit air-conditioning and demisting system. Cabin pressure differential 0.30 bars (4.3 lb/sq in). Two independent and redundant hydraulic systems, each 207 bars (3,000 lb/sq in), with engine driven pumps (emergency electric pump on one circuit), for actuating control surfaces, landing gear, brakes, flaps, airbrakes, and (when fitted) nosewheel steering. Pneumatic system, for cockpit pressurisation and air-conditioning, occupants' pressure suits and fuel tank pressurisation, is supplied by compressed air from engines. Main electric power supplied by two 28V 9kW starter/generators, one on each engine. Circuit includes a 36Ah nickel-cadmium battery for self-starting and two static inverters for supplying 115V AC power at 400Hz to auxiliary systems. External ground DC power receptacle in port engine air intake trunk. Hydraulic and electrical systems can be sustained by either engine in the event of the other engine becoming inoperative. De-icing by electric heater mats. Oxygen mask for each occupant, supplied by lox converter of 10 litres (2.6 US gallons; 2.2 Imp gallons) capacity. Emergency gaseous oxygen bottle for each occupant.

AVIONICS AND EQUIPMENT: Large avionics bays in rear fuselage, containing most of the radio and navigation equipment. Standard avionics, according to version, include V/UHF and VHF or UHF transceivers, IFF/SIF, VOR/ILS/marker beacon receiver, Tacan, radio compass, gyro platform and intercom. Landing light on starboard mainwheel leg, taxying light on port leg. Avionics of basic French and German Air Force versions as listed in 1987-88 and earlier *Jane's*, except that IFF/SIF is Thomson-CSF NRAI 4A. Alpha Jet 2 has Sagem Uliss 81 inertial platform (replacing SFIM 550) and Una 81 nav/attack unit, Thomson-CSF VE 110C head-up display with film or video camera (VEM 130 in Lancier), Thomson-CSF TMV 630 laser rangefinder, TRT AHV 9 radar altimeter and ESD Digibus digital multiplexed avionics databus.

ARMAMENT AND OPERATIONAL EQUIPMENT: More than 75 different basic weapon configurations for training and tactical air support missions have been qualified for Alpha Jet users. For armament training and close support, the Alpha Jet can be equipped with an underfuselage jettisonable pod containing a 30 mm DEFA or 27 mm Mauser cannon with 150 rds; or an underfuselage pylon for one 250 kg bomb, one 400 kg modular bomb, or a target towing system. Provision also for two hardpoints under each wing, with non-jettisonable adaptor pylons. On these can be carried M155 launchers for eighteen 68 mm rockets; HE or retarded bombs of 125, 250 or 400 kg; 625 lb cluster dispensers; 690 or 825 lb special purpose tanks; practice launchers for bombs or rockets; Dassault-Breguet CC-420 underwing 30 mm gun pods, each with 180 rds; or two 310, 450 or 625 litre (82, 119 or 165 US gallon; 68, 99 or 137.5 Imp gallon) drop tanks (see Power Plant paragraph). Provision for air-to-air or air-to-surface missiles such as Sidewinder, Magic or Maverick, or reconnaissance pod. Total load for all five stations more than 2,500 kg (5,510 lb). Dassault-Breguet CEM-1 (combined external multistore) carriers can be attached to inboard underwing pylons, permitting simultaneous carriage of mixed fuel/bomb/rocket loads, including six rockets and four practice bombs, or eighteen rockets with one 500 lb bomb, or six penetration bombs, or grenades or other stores. A special version of the CEM-1 allows carriage of a reconnaissance pod containing four cameras (three Omera 61 cameras and an Omera 40 panoramic camera) and a decoy launcher. Luftwaffe aircraft equipped with ML Aviation twin stores carriers, CBLS 200 practice bomb and rocket launcher carriers, and ejector release units. Fire control system for air-to-air or air-to-ground firing, dive bombing and low-level bombing. Firing by trainee pilot (in front seat) is governed by a safety interlock system controlled by the instructor, which energises the forward station trigger circuit and illuminates a fire clearance indicator in the trainee's cockpit. Thomson-CSF 902 sight and film or video gun camera in French version; Kaiser/VDO KM 808 sight and gun camera in West German attack version.

DIMENSIONS, EXTERNAL:

Wing span	9.11 m (29 ft 10¾ in)
Wing aspect ratio	4.8
Length overall: trainer	11.75 m (38 ft 6½ in)
close support version, incl probe	13.23 m (43 ft 5 in)
Height overall (at normal T-O weight)	4.19 m (13 ft 9 in)
Tailplane span	4.33 m (14 ft 2½ in)
Wheel track	2.71 m (8 ft 10¾ in)
Wheelbase	4.72 m (15 ft 5¾ in)

AREAS:

Wings, gross	17.50 m² (188.4 sq ft)
Ailerons (total)	1.04 m² (11.19 sq ft)
Trailing-edge flaps (total)	2.86 m² (30.78 sq ft)
Airbrakes (total)	0.74 m² (7.97 sq ft)
Fin	2.97 m² (31.97 sq ft)
Rudder	0.62 m² (6.67 sq ft)
Horizontal tail surfaces (total)	3.94 m² (42.41 sq ft)

WEIGHTS:

Weight empty, equipped:	
trainer	3,345 kg (7,374 lb)
close support version	3,515 kg (7,749 lb)
Fuel (internal)	1,520 kg (3,351 lb)
	or 1,630 kg (3,593 lb)
Fuel (external)	500 kg (1,102 lb)
	or 720 kg (1,587 lb)
	or 1,440 kg (3,174 lb)
Max external load	more than 2,500 kg (5,510 lb)
Normal T-O weight:	
trainer, 'clean'	5,000 kg (11,023 lb)
Max T-O weight:	
with external stores	8,000 kg (17,637 lb)

PERFORMANCE (at normal 'clean' T-O weight, except where indicated):

Max level speed at 10,000 m (32,800 ft):	
Larzac 04-C6	Mach 0.85
Larzac 04-C20	Mach 0.86
Max level speed at S/L:	
Larzac 04-C6	540 knots (1,000 km/h; 621 mph)
Larzac 04-C20	560 knots (1,038 km/h; 645 mph)
Max speed for flap and landing gear extension	200 knots (370 km/h; 230 mph)
Approach speed	110 knots (204 km/h; 127 mph)
Landing speed at normal landing weight	92 knots (170 km/h; 106 mph)
Stalling speed: flaps and landing gear up	116 knots (216 km/h; 134 mph)
flaps and landing gear down	90 knots (167 km/h; 104 mph)
Max rate of climb at S/L	3,660 m (12,000 ft)/min
Rate of climb at S/L, one engine out, at 4,782 kg (10,542 lb) AUW, in landing configuration	330 m (1,085 ft)/min
Time to 9,150 m (30,000 ft)	less than 7 min
Service ceiling	14,630 m (48,000 ft)
T-O run: Larzac 04-C6	370 m (1,215 ft)
Larzac 04-C20	320 m (1,050 ft)
Landing run at usual landing weight	approx 500 m (1,640 ft)
Low altitude radius of action (trainer):	
'clean', max internal fuel	291 nm (540 km; 335 miles)
with external tanks	361 nm (670 km; 416 miles)
High altitude radius of action (trainer), reserves of 15% internal fuel:	
'clean', max internal fuel	664 nm (1,230 km; 764 miles)
with external tanks	782 nm (1,450 km; 901 miles)
Lo-lo-lo mission radius (close support version), incl combat at max continuous thrust and 54 nm (100 km; 62 mile) dash:	
with belly gun pod and underwing weapons	210 nm (390 km; 242 miles)
with belly gun pod, underwing weapons and external tanks	340 nm (630 km; 391 miles)
Hi-lo-hi mission radius (close support version), incl combat at max continuous thrust and 54 nm (100 km; 62 mile) dash:	
with belly gun pod and underwing weapons	315 nm (583 km; 363 miles)
with belly gun pod, underwing weapons and external tanks	580 nm (1,075 km; 668 miles)
Ferry range (internal fuel and four 450 litre external tanks)	more than 2,160 nm (4,000 km; 2,485 miles)
Endurance (internal fuel only):	
low altitude	more than 2 h 30 min
high altitude	more than 3 h 30 min
g limits	+12/-6.4 ultimate

EGRETT

PARTICIPATING COMPANIES:

E-Systems Inc, PO Box 660248, 6250 LBJ Freeway, Dallas, Texas 75266-0248, USA
Telephone: (214) 661 1000
Telex: 703365

Burkhart Grob Flugzeugbau, Postfach 150, 8948 Mindelheim, Federal Republic of Germany
Telephone: (08268) 411
Telex: 539623

Garrett Turbine Engine Company, Sky Harbor Airport, 111 South 34th Street (PO Box 5217), Phoenix, Arizona 85010, USA
Telephone: (602) 231 1000
Telex: 667337

EGRETT-1

Described as being "adaptable to a broad spectrum of market requirements", the Egrett-1 surveillance and relay aircraft derives its name from those of the three companies collaborating in its development. The first announcement of its existence, in April 1987, revealed that overall design of the aircraft had been formulated by the Greenville Division of E-Systems Inc, the project's programme leader. Detail airframe design, and prototype construction, were undertaken by Grob TFE of West Germany; Garrett Turbine Engine Company provided the aircraft's turboprop engine. Systems integration, related to individual customers' mission requirements, is the responsibility of E-Systems.

The prototype Egrett-1 (D-FGEI) made its first flight on 24 June 1987, at Manching in West Germany, in the hands

of NASA test pilot Einar Enevoldson. At the end of the following month the flight test programme was described as yielding "very positive results", and was scheduled to continue for several more months. Assistance in this area is being provided by Messerschmitt-Bölkow-Blohm (MBB).

E-Systems, describing the Egrett-1 as "essentially a re-usable communications satellite" able to offer "the near-continuous coverage of high-altitude, geosynchronous orbits", claims that it could provide outstanding opportunities for radio communication spanning vast areas of the Earth's surface, such a capability having been the basic objective behind its design and creation. Its capacious fuselage — very large for a single-seater — and long-span, high aspect ratio wings, clearly place it in the HALE (high altitude, long endurance) category, and extensive use of radio- and radar-transparent materials in its construction contribute considerably to its ability to act as a platform for data communications equipment, or for systems transmitting and receiving radio waves from different frequency bands. The lower part of the fuselage, which is designed specifically so that it is not involved in the structural integrity of the aircraft, can accept a variety of payloads according to individual customer requirements. These can be mounted in removable canoe- or bathtub-shaped ventral panniers to facilitate straightforward installation, servicing and removal; large doors provide easy access to all installed equipment.

Civil communications roles envisaged for the Egrett-1 include — but are not limited to — airborne communications relay, pollution and other disaster detection and reporting, search and rescue, scientific missions such as geophysical survey, and public service or entertainment broadcasting. The aircraft's high-altitude capability facilitates the relay of radio transmissions over considerable distances, including transmission into mountainous areas. Additional on-station endurance can be provided by installing optional auxiliary internal fuel tanks. Equipped with a microwave relay payload (eg, two computer-pointed antennae, a receiver and a power amplifier, transmitting broadband signals over long distances), the Egrett-1 could provide quick response in emergency situations where other long-term communications facilities might become overloaded. Public service and other broadcasts could be relayed in real time to provide, for example, quick-reaction support for law enforcement agencies or instantaneous direct news coverage of international events. In another application, one or more Egrett-1s could be deployed carrying payload packages to establish a radio based data communications network over a very large area.

The very few official announcements about the Egrett-1 programme have referred only to civil applications, but the fact that even such elementary data as basic overall dimensions remain classified has served only to confirm that the aircraft is foreseen as at least equally suitable for covert military roles such as tactical reconnaissance or surveillance and sigint/elint collection, and it is widely believed that both the West German Luftwaffe and USAF have expressed interest in its military potential. The Luftwaffe, whose Erprobungsstelle 61 test centre is located at Manching, had

Prototype E-Systems/Grob/Garrett Egrett-1 high-altitude surveillance aircraft

substantial 1986 funding for the first phase of a programme known as Luftgestütztes Erfassungs- und Auswertesystem (airborne data gathering and evaluation system) and is reported to be considering the possibility of acquiring up to 20 of these aircraft for service in the mid-1990s. A prototype elint system was expected to be ordered during 1988.

Pending the release of official data the dimensions, weight and performance figures that follow should be regarded as provisional:

TYPE: Multi-purpose high-altitude surveillance and relay aircraft.

AIRFRAME: Cantilever mid-wing monoplane, constructed largely of glassfibre, carbonfibre and Kevlar composites. Split flaps on wing inboard trailing-edges. Large, deep fuselage, underside of which is upswept at rear. Very tall, angular fin and rudder, latter with inset trim tab. Low-set tailplane and elevators.

LANDING GEAR: Tricycle type, with single wheel on each unit. Nose unit retracts rearward; main units on prototype are fixed in the down position, but on production aircraft are intended to retract rearward into underwing pods.

POWER PLANT: One Garrett TPE331-14 turboprop, flat rated at 731 kW (980 shp), driving a four-blade propeller with spinner.

ACCOMMODATION: Prototype has accommodation for pilot only, but large fairing aft of present pressurised cockpit appears to offer ample space for a second crew member such as a systems operator.

DIMENSIONS, EXTERNAL (estimated):

Wing span	28.80 m (94 ft 6 in)
Wing aspect ratio	19.8
Length overall	10.36 m (34 ft 0 in)
Height overall	5.64 m (18 ft 6 in)
Wheel track	4.80 m (15 ft 9 in)
Wheelbase	3.66 m (12 ft 0 in)
Propeller diameter	2.74 m (9 ft 0 in)

AREA (estimated):

Wings, gross	41.8 m² (450 sq ft)

WEIGHT (estimated):

Max T-O weight	5,670 kg (12,500 lb)

PERFORMANCE (estimated):

Max level speed	280-310 knots (519-574 km/h; 322-357 mph)
Econ cruising speed	155-185 knots (287-343 km/h; 178-213 mph)
Normal operating altitude	14,935-17,985 m (49,000-59,000 ft)
Endurance at 17,070 m (56,000 ft)	10-12 h

EHI

EH INDUSTRIES LIMITED

500 Chiswick High Road, London W4 5RG, England
Telephone: 01 995 8221
Telex: 291600 EHILON
CHAIRMAN: Dott R. Teti
MANAGING DIRECTOR: G. Bologna
MARKETING DIRECTOR: V. Floridia
PARTICIPATING COMPANIES:

Agusta SpA, Via Caldera 21, 20153 Milan, Italy
Telephone: (02) 452751
Telex: 333280 AGUMI I
Westland Helicopters Ltd, Yeovil, Somerset BA20 2YB, England
Telephone: (0935) 75222
Telex: 46277

EH Industries was formed in June 1980 by Westland Helicopters and Agusta to undertake the joint development of a new anti-submarine warfare helicopter, for which the Royal Navy and Italian Navy both have a requirement. Such a programme was initiated by Westland in the UK in 1977 in response to Naval Staff Requirement 6646, leading to the WG 34 helicopter described under that company's heading in the 1979-80 *Jane's*. Following extensive market research and project definition, it was established that civil and military requirements were compatible with the naval requirements.

British and Italian government approval for the nine-month project definition phase was given on 12 June 1981, and full programme go-ahead was announced by the two governments on 25 January 1984. A formal contract for full development of the naval version was signed on 7 March 1984. The programme is being handled on behalf of both governments by the British Ministry of Defence. Technical responsibility rests with Westland Helicopters and Agusta, each of which has a 50% interest in EHI. Westland has design leadership for the commercial version, and Agusta for the rear loading military/utility version; the naval version is being developed jointly by the two companies for their respective navies and export customers.

EH INDUSTRIES EH 101

In the Spring of 1977 the British MoD (Navy) completed a series of feasibility studies for a new ASW helicopter, and examined what sensors and performance standards it would require. Westland's WG 34 design, marginally smaller than the Sea King but with substantially more disposable load capability, was selected by the MoD (Navy) for development in the late Summer of 1978. The Italian Navy, although it would place more emphasis on shore-based than shipboard operation, has a requirement broadly similar to that of the Royal Navy, and in 1980 Westland and Agusta decided to combine forces in a joint design, the EH 101, to

meet the requirements of both services. Subsequent market research indicated that commercial payload/range and military tactical transport/logistics requirements for a medium sized helicopter were also compatible with the basic airframe design requirements of the naval version, and it was decided to develop all three variants, based on a common aircraft. Development of the EH 101 is now proceeding, and the commercial version is expected to enter service in 1991, followed shortly afterwards by the naval and military variants.

Nine pre-production aircraft, numbered PP1 to PP9, are planned; in addition, an 'iron bird' airframe is being used in Italy for ground tests. Aircraft PP1 (ZF641) made its initial flight at Yeovil on 9 October 1987, and PP2 flew at Cascina Costa on 26 November 1987. These two aircraft are being used for basic development. PP3 will be used to speed the award of civil certification, planned for 1991. Aircraft PP4 (ZF644) will be used for development of a basic naval variant; PP5 (ZF649) and PP6 will be devoted to development of the Royal Navy and Italian Navy versions. PP7 will be allocated to developing a rear ramp variant; PP8 and PP9 will be used for reliability proving and as demonstrators for the commercial and utility versions. Metal for the first two aircraft was first cut in March 1985, and all nine are expected to fly within about two years of the first flight. First deliveries of the commercial version are

planned for 1991, followed by deliveries to both navies. Aircraft will be produced by single source manufacture of components, with a final assembly line in each country. Major design responsibilities at present include Westland for the front fuselage, cabin, cockpit and main rotor blades; Agusta for the rear fuselage, tail, rotor head and drive system, hydraulic system and part of the electrical system.

The airframe, power plant, rotor and transmission systems, flight controls and utility systems are common to all three variants. The design philosophy is to provide significant improvements in performance, integrity, availability, operating cost, and crew/passenger acceptability. Design features include the use of three engines, providing higher power margins; fail-safe, damage-tolerant airframe structure and rotating components; greater system redundancy; and onboard monitoring of the engines, transmission, avionics and utility systems.

The **naval EH 101** is designed for fully autonomous all-weather operations, and will operate from land bases, large and small vessels (including merchant ships), and oil rigs. It is specifically designed for operation from a 3,500 tonne frigate, and its physical dimensions are designed for compatibility with frigate hangar size. It will be capable of launch and recovery from a frigate in sea state 6, with the ship on any heading and in wind speeds, from any direction, of up to 50 knots (93 km/h; 57 mph). It will have the greater

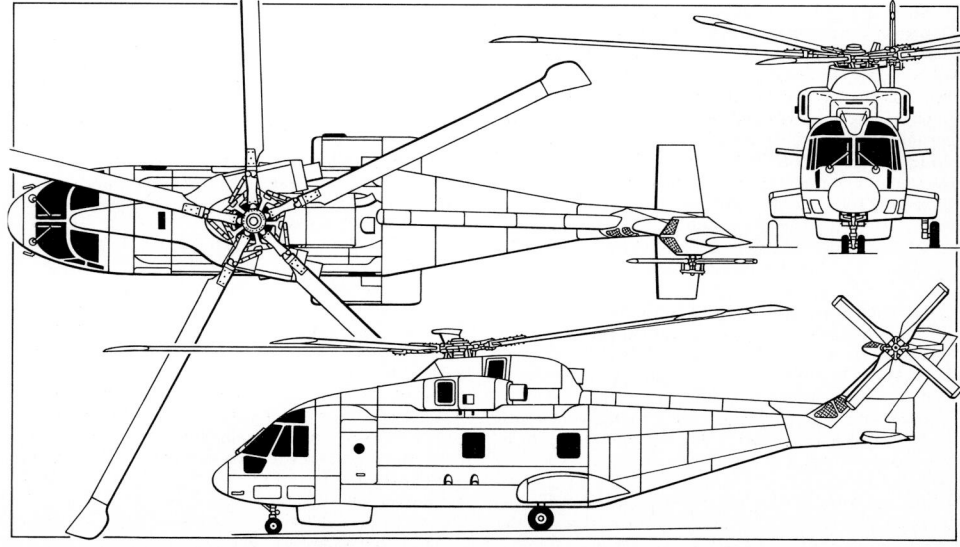

Basic naval ASW version of the EH 101 multi-role helicopter *(Jane's/Mike Keep)*

PP1, the first pre-production EH 101, which made its first flight at Yeovil in October 1987

endurance and carrying capacity necessary to meet the expanding maritime tactical requirements of the 1990s, with the ability to operate distantly for up to 5 hours with all the new technology detection equipment and weaponry currently under development.

Primary roles of the maritime version will be anti-submarine warfare, anti-ship surveillance and tracking, anti-surface-vessel, amphibious operations, and search and rescue. Other roles include airborne early warning, vertical replenishment, and electronic countermeasures (deception, jamming and missile seduction). For the Royal Navy, the EH 101 has been specified as equipment for its Type 23 general purpose frigates; it has also been announced that the helicopter will operate from 'Invincible' class aircraft carriers, Royal Fleet Auxiliaries and other ships, as well as from land bases. Initial orders will comprise 50 for the Royal Navy and 38 for the Italian Navy.

After eliminating the only other contender (the Aérospatiale Super Puma), which did not comply with all of its requirements, the Canadian government confirmed in August 1987 its selection of the EH 101 to meet the Canadian Navy's **NSA** (new shipborne aircraft) need for a Sea King replacement. In April 1988 it awarded a contract to define the EH 101 to meet the exact specifications of the NSA programme. Canada is expected eventually to buy between 30 and 50 EH 101s, and EHI is joined in the contract definition phase by four Canadian companies (Bell Helicopter Canada, Canadian Marconi, the IMP Group and Paramax Electronics), plus Sikorsky Aircraft of the USA.

Intended to operate from patrol frigates and destroyers as a fully autonomous weapons system, the Canadian Navy EH 101 will have three to four times the capability of the service's present CH-124A Sea Kings when it enters service in the mid-1990s. Bell Canada will assemble and flight test the Canadian version; Paramax will have prime responsibility for mission systems integration, assisted by Canadian Marconi and Sikorsky; IMP will provide long-term integrated support for the helicopter once it has entered service. To co-ordinate the international team and manage the Canadian programme, EHI has formed a new, Ottawa-based company known as EH Industries (Canada) Inc.

The **commercial variant**, based on the common aircraft but with detail design tailored to meet civil requirements, will offer a range of 500 nm (926 km; 576 miles), with full IFR reserves, carrying 30 passengers and their baggage. The three-engine configuration gives the EH 101 a Category A VTO performance, capable of offshore and oil rig operations or scheduled flights into inner cities at high all-up weights under the more rigorous civil operating rules of the future. It will be operated by a crew of two, with provision for a cabin attendant, and will offer airline standards of comfort with stand-up headroom, airline style seating, overhead baggage storage, full environmental control, passenger entertainment, plus a toilet and galley. It will also be available, if required, with a large rear-loading ramp.

The **military variant**, in a tactical transport or logistic configuration, will incorporate a rear-loading ramp for vehicles and cargo, and will be able to airlift a load of almost 6 tons. Alternatively, up to 35 combat equipped and seated troops can be carried. Initially, 25 of this version are to be ordered for the Royal Air Force. A **civil/utility version** will also be available to commercial operators requiring a rear-loading facility.

TYPE: Multi-role helicopter.

ROTOR SYSTEM: Five-blade main rotor, hub of which is designed on multiple load path concept, incorporating fail-safe principles, and is formed from composite materials surrounding a metal core. Blades, also of composites construction, have an advanced aerofoil section, special high-speed tips resulting from British Experimental Rotor Programme (BERP), and are attached to hub by multi-path loading including elastomeric bearings. Naval version has fully automatic power folding of main rotor blades (optional on other versions) and tail rotor pylon, with manual system for emergency backup. Electric de-icing of main and tail rotor blades (Lucas Spraymat system) standard on naval version, optional on other versions. Four-blade tail rotor, mounted on port side of tail rotor pylon.

ROTOR DRIVE: Front drive directly into main gearbox from all three engines, with all gears straddle mounted for greater rigidity. Transmission has 45 min 'run-dry' capability.

FUSELAGE AND TAIL UNIT: Main fuselage is an aluminium alloy stressed skin structure. Composites are used where cost-effective in parts of complex shape such as forward fuselage, windscreen structure, entire tail-fin and tailplane, and upper fuselage cowling panels. Main fuselage panels are of bonded honeycomb. Fuselage is divided into four major modules, with front and centre fuselage common to all three variants. Modified rear fuselage and slimmer tailboom on military version, to accommodate rear-loading ramp/door in underside. Tailcone and tail rotor pylon of composite construction; on naval version, this folds forward and downward so that starboard half of tailplane passes underneath rear fuselage.

LANDING GEAR: Hydraulically retractable tricycle type, with single mainwheels and steerable twin-wheel nose unit, designed and manufactured by AP Precision Hydraulics in association with Officine Meccaniche Aeronautiche. Main units retract into fairings on sides of fuselage. Goodrich wheels, tyres and brakes. A twin-mainwheel gear is under evaluation for the military and civil variants.

POWER PLANT: Three General Electric T700-GE-401A turboshafts in naval variant, rated at 1,278 kW (1,714 shp) max contingency, 1,254 kW (1,682 shp) intermediate and 1,071 kW (1,437 shp) max continuous at S/L, ISA. Engines for naval variant will be assembled by Alfa Romeo Avio and Fiat. Commercial and military variants powered by three General Electric CT7-6 turboshafts (CT7-6A in PP3) with ratings of 1,432 kW (1,920 shp) max and intermediate contingency, 1,230 kW (1,649 shp) max continuous. A possible alternative engine is the Rolls-Royce Turbomeca RTM 322, with max contingency and intermediate contingency ratings of 1,724 kW (2,312 shp) and 1,566 kW (2,100 shp) respectively. Computerised fuel management system. Pressure refuelling point on starboard side; three gravity positions on port side. Dunlop electric anti-icing of engine air intakes, which are of Kevlar reinforced with aero-web honeycomb.

ACCOMMODATION: One or two pilots on flight deck (naval version will be capable of single-pilot operation, commercial variant will be certificated for two-pilot operation). ASW version will normally also carry observer and acoustic systems operator. Martin-Baker crew seats in naval version, able to withstand 10.7 m (35 ft)/s impact. Socea or Ipeco crew seats in commercial variant. Commercial version able to accommodate 30 passengers, four abreast at approx seat pitch of 76 cm (30 in), plus cabin attendant, with toilet, galley and baggage facilities (including overhead bins). Military variant can accommodate up to 35 combat equipped troops or equivalent cargo. Main passenger door/emergency exit at front on port side with additional emergency exits on starboard side and on each side of cabin at rear, above main landing gear sponson. Large sliding door at mid-cabin position on starboard side, with inset emergency exit. Commercial variant has baggage bay aft of cabin, with external access via door on port side. Cargo loading ramp/door at rear of cabin on utility version. Cabin floor loading 976 kg/m² (200 lb/sq ft) on PP1.

SYSTEMS: Hamilton Standard/Microtecnica environmental control systems. Dual redundant integrated hydraulic system, pressurised by three Vickers pumps each supplying fluid at 207 bars (3,000 lb/sq in) nominal working pressure, with flow rates of 55, 59 and 60 litres (14.5, 15.6 and 15.9 US gallons; 12.1, 13.0 and 13.2 Imp gallons)/min respectively. Hydraulic system reservoirs are of the piston load pressurised type, with a nominal pressure of 0.97 bars (14 lb/sq in). Primary electrical system is 115/200V three-phase AC, powered by two Lucas brushless, oilspray-cooled 45kVA generators (90kVA if Lucas Spraymat blade ice protection system fitted), with one driven by main gearbox and the other by accessory gearbox, plus a third, separately driven standby alternator. APU for main engine air-starting, and to provide electric power, plus air for ECS, without running main engines or using external power supplies. Fire detection and suppression systems by Graviner and Walter Kidde respectively. BAJ Ltd four-float emergency flotation system.

AVIONICS: Integrated avionics system of naval and military variants based on two MIL-STD-1553B multiplex databuses that link the basic aircraft management, avionics and mission systems. Integrated avionics system of commercial variant based on ARINC 429 data transfer bus. On naval variant, main processing element of the management system is a dual redundant aircraft management computer, which carries out navigation, control and display management, performance computation and health and usage monitoring of the principal systems (engines, drive systems, avionics and utilities); it also controls the basic bus. On civil variant, dual redundant management system provides performance calculations and health and usage monitoring of the principal systems (as for naval variant); a flight management system providing R/Nav and navigation management is optional. Smiths Industries/OMI dual redundant digital AFCS is standard, providing fail-operational autostabilisation and four-axis autopilot modes (auto hover, auto transitions to/from hover standard on naval variants, optional on commercial and military variants). AFCS sensors on naval variant include British Aerospace LINS 300 ring laser gyro inertial reference unit (IRU) and Litton Italia LISA-4000 strapdown AHRS; IRU also provides self-contained navigation, with Racal Doppler 91E velocity sensor; Navstar global positioning system is optional. AFCS sensors on commercial variant include two Litton Italia LISA-4000 strapdown AHRS. Advanced flight deck incorporates standard Smiths Industries/OMI electronic instrument system (EIS) providing colour flight instrument, navigation and power systems displays. Other avionics on naval variants include Plessey/Elettronica PA 5015 I-band radar altimeters, GEC Avionics low airspeed sensing and air data system, MEL pilot's mission display unit, Selenia/Racal cabin mission display unit, and Selenia/Ferranti aircraft management computer. On commercial variant, standard avionics include Penny and Giles air data system, Racal intercom system, optional Collins or King/Bendix communications and navigation systems, optional Sperry or Bendix weather radar.

ARMAMENT AND OPERATIONAL EQUIPMENT (naval and military utility versions): Naval version able to carry up to four homing torpedoes (probably Marconi Sting Ray in RN version) or other weapons. ASW version will have 360° search radar (Ferranti Blue Kestrel in RN aircraft) in a 'chin' radome, plus dipping sonar, two sonobuoy dispensers, advanced sonobuoy processing equipment, Racal ESM and an external rescue hoist. GEC Avionics AQS-903 ASW system and Fairey Hydraulics deck lock have been selected for Royal Navy aircraft. ASST (anti-ship surveillance and tracking) version will carry equipment for tactical surveillance and OTH (over the horizon) targeting, to locate and relay to a co-operating frigate the position of a target vessel, and for midcourse guidance of the frigate's missiles. On missions involving the patrol of an exclusive economic zone it can also, with suitable radar, monitor every hour all surface contacts within an area of 77,700 km² (30,000 sq miles); can patrol an EEZ 400 × 200 nm (740 × 370 km; 460 × 230 miles) twice in one sortie; and can effect boarding and inspection of surface vessels during fishery protection and anti-smuggling missions. ASV version is designed to carry air-to-surface missiles and other weapons, for use as appropriate, from strikes against major units using sea-skimming anti-ship missiles to small-arms deterrence of smugglers. Various duties in amphibious operations could include personnel/stores transportation, casualty evacuation, surveillance over the beachhead, and logistic support. The military tactical transport or logistic support variant can seat up to 35 troops; alternatively, palleted internal loads or external slung loads up to a total of 5,443 kg (12,000 lb) can be carried. Armament and self-protection systems are optional.

DIMENSIONS, EXTERNAL:

Main rotor diameter 18.59 m (61 ft 0 in)

Tail rotor diameter	4.01 m (13 ft 2 in)	commercial/utility variant	6.50 m (21 ft 4 in)	B (30 passengers plus baggage)	2,721 kg (6,000 lb)

Tail rotor diameter   4.01 m (13 ft 2 in)
Length:
  overall, both rotors turning   22.81 m (74 ft 10 in)
  main rotor and tail pylon folded (naval variant)
           16.00 m (52 ft 6 in)
Width: excl main rotor   4.52 m (14 ft 10 in)
  main rotor and tail pylon folded (naval variant)
           5.49 m (18 ft 0 in)
Height: overall, both rotors turning   6.65 m (21 ft 10 in)

  main rotor and tail pylon folded (naval variant)
           5.21 m (17 ft 1 in)
Passenger door (fwd, port):
  Height   1.70 m (5 ft 7 in)
  Width   0.97 m (3 ft 2 in)
Sliding cargo door (mid-cabin, stbd):
  Height   1.63 m (5 ft 4 in)
  Width   1.83 m (6 ft 0 in)
Baggage compartment door (rear, port, commercial variant):
  Height   1.63 m (5 ft 4 in)
  Width   0.79 m (2 ft 7 in)
Rear-loading ramp/door (rear, military/utility variant):
  Height   1.80 m (5 ft 11 in)
  Width   2.11 m (6 ft 11 in)
DIMENSIONS, INTERNAL:
Cabin:
  Length: naval variant   7.09 m (23 ft 3 in)

commercial/utility variant   6.50 m (21 ft 4 in)
Max width   2.49 m (8 ft 2 in)
Width at floor   2.39 m (7 ft 10 in)
Max height   1.83 m (6 ft 0 in)
Volume: naval variant   29.0 m³ (1,024 cu ft)
  commercial variant   27.5 m³ (970 cu ft)
Baggage compartment volume (commercial variant)
           3.82 m³ (135 cu ft)
AREAS:
Main rotor disc   271.51 m² (2,922.5 sq ft)
Tail rotor disc   12.65 m² (136.2 sq ft)
WEIGHTS (A: naval variant, B: commercial variant, C: military/utility variant):
Basic weight empty (estimated): A   7,121 kg (15,700 lb)
  B   6,967 kg (15,360 lb)
  C   7,284 kg (16,060 lb)
Operating weight empty (estimated):
  A   9,298 kg (20,500 lb)
  B (IFR, offshore equipped)   8,718 kg (19,220 lb)
  C   8,618 kg (19,000 lb)
Max fuel weight (four internal tanks, total):
  A   3,438 kg (7,580 lb)
  B, C   3,370 kg (7,430 lb)
Max fuel weight with optional auxiliary tank:
  A   4,298 kg (9,475 lb)
  B, C   4,213 kg (9,288 lb)
Disposable load/payload:
  A (four torpedoes)   960 kg (2,116 lb)

B (30 passengers plus baggage)   2,721 kg (6,000 lb)
C (35 combat equipped troops)   4,309 kg (9,500 lb)
Max T-O weight: A   13,000 kg (28,660 lb)
     or 13,530 kg (29,830 lb)
  B, C   14,288 kg (31,500 lb)

PERFORMANCE (estimated):
Never-exceed speed
       167 knots (309 km/h; 192 mph) EAS
Average cruising speed   160 knots (296 km/h; 184 mph)
Best range cruising speed
       140 knots (259 km/h; 161 mph)
Best endurance speed   90 knots (167 km/h; 104 mph)
Range (B, estimated):
  standard fuel, offshore IFR equipped, with reserves, 30 passengers   500 nm (926 km; 576 miles)
  auxiliary fuel, offshore IFR equipped, with reserves, 30 passengers   625 nm (1,158 km; 720 miles)
  with zero T-O distance (Category A rules)
       330 nm (611 km; 380 miles)
Ferry range:
  B (standard fuel, IFR equipped, with reserves)
       630 nm (1,167 km; 725 miles)
  B (auxiliary fuel, IFR equipped, with reserves)
       800 nm (1,482 km; 921 miles)
  C (standard fuel plus internal auxiliary tanks)
       1,130 nm (2,094 km; 1,301 miles)

EMBRAER/FAMA

PARTICIPATING COMPANIES:

Empresa Brasileira de Aeronáutica SA, Caixa Postal 343, 12225 São José dos Campos, SP, Brazil
Telephone: (0123) 25 1711
Telex: 12 33589 EBAE BR
Fábrica Argentina de Materiales Aeroespaciales, Avenida Fuerza Aérea Argentina Km 5½, 5103 Córdoba, Argentina
Telephone: 45011
Telex: AMCOR AR 51965

Following a co-operation agreement with the Fábrica Militar de Aviones (FMA) of Argentina, signed in January 1986, Embraer revealed in April 1986 provisional details of a proposed new commuter and business transport then known as the EMB-123. Details of the early stages of the design were given in the Addenda to the 1986-87 *Jane's*.

On 21 May 1987 Embraer formally joined forces with FMA (now FAMA) to develop and produce the aircraft as a fully international programme. As a result, it is now known as the CBA-123 (for Co-operation Brazil-Argentina).

EMBRAER/FAMA CBA-123

Due to make its first flight in December 1989, the CBA-123 utilises a shortened version of the Embraer EMB-120 Brasilia fuselage, and will share with that aircraft approximately 60 per cent commonality of components, including almost the same flight deck, as well as common maintenance and cabin and crew procedures. Combined with a new supercritical wing, a T tail, and two rear mounted propfans with scimitar propeller blades, the CBA-123 is expected to offer an optimum combination of fuel efficiency and speed, as well as an extremely smooth and quiet ride. Certification will be to FAR/JAR Pt 25 (Transport Category), with noise certification to FAR Pt 36 (ICAO Annex 16). The programme will be divided two-thirds to Embraer, one-third to FAMA, with assembly lines in both countries. FAMA will manufacture the front section of the centre-fuselage, sections 1 and 2 of the rear fuselage (including the dorsal fin and ventral fin), tailcone, vertical fin, fin/tailplane junction fairings, tailplane, elevators and engine pylons. Embraer will be responsible for the remainder of the airframe structure. The first two prototypes will be built in Brazil and the third in Argentina.

The CBA-123 is expected to enter service in June 1991, replacing such types as the EMB-110 Bandeirante, and the Brazilian and Argentine governments have announced their intention to support its launch with the purchase of 36 aircraft each, for military and executive transport or corporate use.

TYPE: Twin-propfan regional and corporate transport aircraft.

AIRFRAME (general): Extensive use of chemical milling and 7000 series aluminium alloys.

WINGS: Cantilever low-wing monoplane. High aspect ratio wings with taper increased on inboard portions by extending chord and sweeping trailing-edges forward. Aerofoil section Embraer EA 160316 at root, EA 160313 at tip (thickness/chord ratios 16% and 13%). Dihedral 3°. Incidence 2° at root, 0° at tip. Sweepback 4° 8' at quarter-chord. Basic damage-tolerant structure of riveted aluminium alloy, with composites leading-edges. Three-segment, mechanically actuated double-slotted Fowler flaps and single electrically actuated aileron (aerodynamically sealed internally) on each trailing-edge. Hydraulically actuated two-segment ground spoilers forward of inboard flaps. Ailerons, flaps and spoilers all of composites construction. Pneumatic inflatable anti-icing boots on leading-edges.

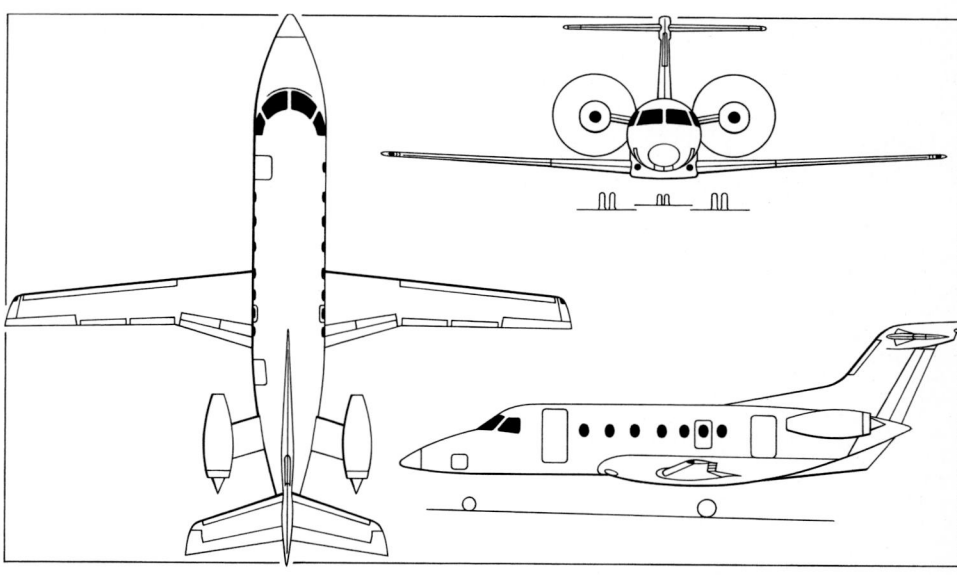

Embraer/FAMA CBA-123 twin-propfan transport under development by Brazil and Argentina
(Jane's/Mike Keep)

FUSELAGE: Pressurised semi-monocoque damage-tolerant structure of circular cross-section; generally as for EMB-120 Brasilia (which see), but of reduced length. Basic structure is of riveted aluminium alloy, with composites fairings.

TAIL UNIT: Broad chord sweptback fin, with dorsal fin, and electrically actuated tandem dual rudders. Sweptback, electrically actuated variable incidence tailplane with mechanically actuated balanced elevators. Riveted aluminium alloy tailplane and fin, with composites leading-edges; all-composites rudders and elevators. Pneumatic inflatable anti-icing boots on leading-edges. Ventral fin beneath rear fuselage, to protect propellers during take-off rotation.

LANDING GEAR: Hydraulically retractable tricycle type, with twin wheels and oleo-pneumatic shock absorber on each unit. Mainwheels retract inward into wing/underfuselage fairing; nose unit retracts forward. Emergency free-fall extension capability. Electrically actuated nosewheel steering. Mainwheel tyres size 22 × 6.75-10, pressure 7.24 bars (105 lb/sq in); nosewheel tyres size 16 × 4.1-8, pressure 5.17 bars (75 lb/sq in). Hydraulic carbon brakes with anti-skid provision. Backup braking system for use if one hydraulic system fails. Mechanical emergency and parking brake systems. High flotation tyres optional.

POWER PLANT: Two 969 kW (1,300 shp) class Garrett TPF351-20 propfans, each driving a slow-turning constant-speed pusher propeller with reversible pitch, autofeathering, synchrophasing, and six scimitar blades. Engines are pylon mounted at rear of fuselage, and have a cruise/climb rating of 746 kW (1,000 shp). Fuel in integral wing tanks and auxiliary tank with combined capacity of 2,612 litres (690 US gallons; 574.5 Imp gallons). Single-point underwing pressure fuelling/defuelling, and two overwing gravity points. Oil capacity 9.5 litres (2.5 US gallons; 2.1 Imp gallons) per engine. Pneumatic inflatable de-icing boots on pylon leading-edges and engine air inlets.

ACCOMMODATION: Crew of two on flight deck, with dual controls; optional seat to rear for observer. Standard commuter cabin layout for 19 passengers, in five rows of three and a final four-seat row, at 79 cm (31 in) pitch. Wardrobe, toilet, galley, jump seat, and seat for cabin attendant at front of cabin. Underseat and overhead bin stowage for carry-on baggage; main baggage/cargo compartment aft of rear row of seats. Executive interiors, to customer's requirements, available optionally. Plug type passenger door and baggage door on port side, at front and rear of cabin respectively. Plug type passenger emergency exit above wing on each side; flight deck side windows serve as emergency exits for crew. Entire accommodation pressurised and air-conditioned. Electric anti-icing of windscreens.

SYSTEMS: Dual air-conditioning and pressurisation systems (max differential 0.56 bars; 8.2 lb/sq in), giving a S/L cabin atmosphere up to 6,400 m (21,000 ft) and a 2,440 m (8,000 ft) environment at altitudes up to 12,200 m (40,000 ft). Two independent hydraulic systems (each 207 bars; 3,000 lb/sq in). Primary electrical power supply is 28V DC, provided by two 400A engine driven starter/generators and two nickel-cadmium batteries. Additional 400A starter/generator driven by APU. Two solid state inverters for 115V and 26V single-phase AC power at 400Hz. Digital fly by wire system provides electric signalling of flap and rudder actuation. High pressure (127.5 bars; 1,850 lb/sq in) gaseous oxygen system for crew and passengers. Garrett APU for air-conditioning and electrical power generation.

AVIONICS: Generally similar to those for EMB-120 Brasilia. Standard basic EFIS/EICAS fit will include two VHF com, audio distribution system, two VHF nav (VOR/ILS/marker beacon receiver), DME, colour weather radar, ADF, two ATC transponders with altitude encoders, two EADI, multifunction display system, two AHRS, two RMI, standby attitude indicator, standby magnetic compass, ELT, PA system, cabin interphone and dual autopilots. Options include GPWS, flight data recorder, Selcal, MLS and FMS.

DIMENSIONS, EXTERNAL:	
Wing span	17.72 m (58 ft 1½ in)
Wing chord: at root	2.50 m (8 ft 2½ in)
at tip	0.99 m (3 ft 3 in)
Wing aspect ratio	11.6
Length overall	17.75 m (58 ft 2¾ in)
Fuselage: Length	16.21 m (53 ft 2¼ in)
Max diameter	2.28 m (7 ft 5¾ in)
Height overall	6.32 m (20 ft 8¾ in)
Elevator span	6.31 m (20 ft 8½ in)
Wheel track (c/l of shock struts)	3.56 m (11 ft 8¼ in)
Propeller diameter	2.59 m (8 ft 6 in)
Propeller ground clearance: min	1.48 m (4 ft 10¼ in)
max	1.64 m (5 ft 4½ in)
Distance between propeller centres	4.36 m (14 ft 3¾ in)
Passenger door (fwd, port): Height	1.70 m (5 ft 7 in)
Width	0.77 m (2 ft 6¼ in)
Baggage door (rear, port): Height	1.36 m (4 ft 5½ in)
Width	1.30 m (4 ft 3¼ in)
Emergency exits (two, each):	
Height	0.92 m (3 ft 0¼ in)
Width	0.51 m (1 ft 8 in)

DIMENSIONS, INTERNAL:	
Cabin: Length	6.46 m (21 ft 2¼ in)
Max width	2.10 m (7 ft 3 in)
Max height	1.76 m (5 ft 9¼ in)
AREAS:	
Wings, gross	27.0 m² (290.6 sq ft)
Ailerons (total)	1.10 m² (11.84 sq ft)
Trailing-edge flaps (total)	4.70 m² (50.59 sq ft)
Spoilers (total)	1.50 m² (16.15 sq ft)
Fin	1.33 m² (14.32 sq ft)
Rudder	1.79 m² (19.27 sq ft)
Tailplane	8.00 m² (86.11 sq ft)
Elevators (total)	2.40 m² (25.83 sq ft)
WEIGHTS:	
Basic operating weight empty	5,640 kg (12,434 lb)
Max fuel weight	1,980 kg (4,365 lb)
Max payload	2,160 kg (4,762 lb)
Max T-O weight	8,500 kg (18,739 lb)
Max ramp weight	8,540 kg (18,827 lb)
Max zero-fuel weight	7,800 kg (17,196 lb)
Max landing weight	8,350 kg (18,408 lb)

PERFORMANCE (estimated):	
Max cruising speed at 9,150 m (30,000 ft)	
	350 knots (648 km/h; 403 mph)
Max rate of climb at S/L	823 m (2,700 ft)/min
Rate of climb at S/L, one engine out	
	232 m (760 ft)/min
Service ceiling	12,190 m (40,000 ft)
Service ceiling, one engine out	8,535 m (28,000 ft)
T-O to 15 m (50 ft):	
FAR 25 at S/L, ISA	1,080 m (3,545 ft)
at 1,525 m (5,000 ft), ISA + 20°C	1,600 m (5,250 ft)
Landing from 15 m (50 ft):	
FAR 135 at S/L, ISA	1,030 m (3,380 ft)
at 1,525 m (5,000 ft), ISA + 20°C	1,180 m (3,872 ft)
Min ground turning radius	10.04 m (32 ft 11 in)
Range (ISA), reserves for 100 nm (185 km; 115 mile) diversion and 45 min hold:	
with 19 passengers	754 nm (1,397 km; 868 miles)
with max fuel	1,900 nm (3,521 km; 2,188 miles)

EUROCOPTER

Eurocopter GIE
2-20 avenue Marcel Cachin, 93126 La Courneuve, France
Telephone: (1) 48 38 91 78
Telex: ECOPTER 232 743 F

Eurocopter GmbH
Gustav Heinemann Ring 135, 8000 Munich 83, Federal Republic of Germany
Telephone: (089) 600 9000
Fax: (089) 600 90050

CHIEF EXECUTIVE OFFICER (both Eurocopter companies):
Frank Dorn

PARTICIPATING COMPANIES:
Messerschmitt-Bölkow-Blohm GmbH, Helicopter and Military Aircraft Group, Postfach 801160, 8000 Munich 80, Federal Republic of Germany
Telephone: (089) 6000 3444
Telex; 5287 710/740 MBB D

Aérospatiale, 37 boulevard de Montmorency, 75781 Paris Cédex 16, France
Telephone: (1) 42 24 24 24
Telex; AISPA 620059 F

Following approval of a Franco-German co-operation programme on the basis of industry proposals, the defence ministers of West Germany and France signed on 13 November 1987 an amendment to their 1984 memorandum of understanding covering the development of a new anti-tank helicopter for service with their two armies in the 1990s. Leadership and work is being shared between MBB and Aérospatiale.

Eurocopter GIE is the instrument of co-operation in the field of helicopters between Aérospatiale and MBB. For the purpose of managing the Franco/German battlefield helicopter programme, Eurocopter GmbH was established in Munich on 18 September 1985 as a wholly owned subsidiary of Eurocopter GIE in Paris. Executive authority for the battlefield helicopter programme is the Bundesamt für Wehrtechnik und Beschaffung (German federal defence technology and procurement agency).

Estimated costs for the three variants originally proposed (see 1986-87 *Jane's*) caused the programme to be temporarily halted in mid-1986 pending a reappraisal of requirements and aircraft specifications. It was re-launched in March 1987 on the basis of an anti-tank version common to both countries, plus an HAP version for France, and full scale development was approved on 8 December 1987.

EUROCOPTER HAP and PAH-2/HAC
The HAP and PAH-2/HAC programme, which is intended to provide 427 aircraft for the two countries, utilises a single basic helicopter design, from which the following versions will be developed:

HAP (Hélicoptère d'Appui Protection). Escort and fire support version for French Army, for delivery from 1997. Armed with a 30 mm GIAT AM-30781 automatic cannon in undernose turret, with 150-450 rds of ammunition. Releasable weapons, mounted on stub-wings, comprise four Matra Mistral infra-red air-to-air missiles and two pods each with twenty-two 68 mm SNEB rockets. Roof mounted TV, FLIR, laser rangefinder and direct-optics sensors.

PAH-2 (Panzerabwehr-Hubschrauber, 2nd generation). Variant of the common anti-tank version for West German Army, for delivery from 1998. Underwing pylons for up to eight Hot 2/3 anti-tank missiles (inboard) and four Stinger 2 air-to-air missiles for self-defence (outboard). Mast mounted TV/FLIR/tracker/laser rangefinder sighting system for gunner; nose mounted FLIR viewing system for pilot. Will have later, as alternative to Hot, the capability to carry up to eight Euromissile DG Trigat long-range 'fire and forget' infra-red homing anti-tank missiles.

HAC (Hélicoptère Anti-Char). Anti-tank variant for French Army, for delivery from 1998. Wing pylons for up to eight Hot 2/3 or Trigat missiles inboard and four Matra

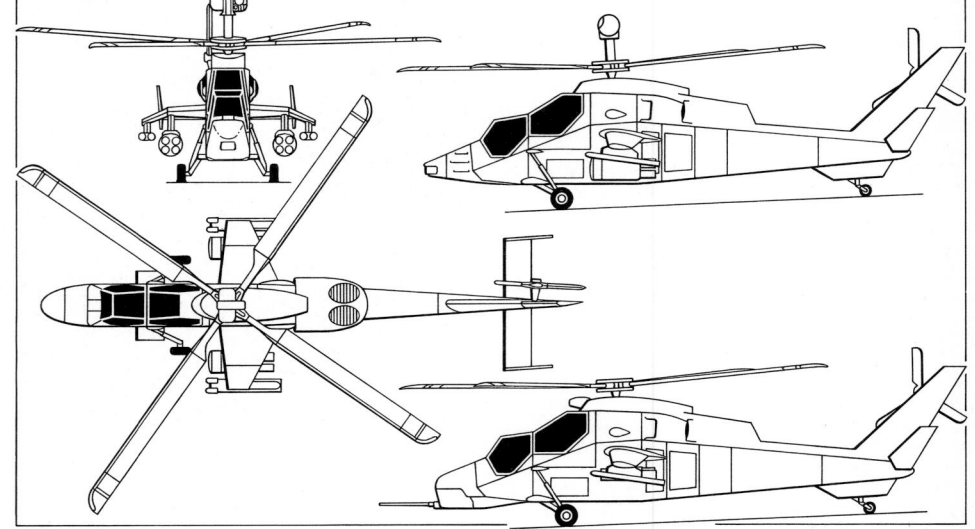

Eurocopter PAH-2/HAC anti-tank helicopter, with additional side view (bottom) of HAP escort and support version *(Jane's/Mike Keep)*

Mistral air-to-air missiles outboard. Mast mounted sight and pilot FLIR system similar to PAH-2.

Five development aircraft are to be built, including three unarmed aerodynamic prototypes (PT1, 2 and 3) to flight test the common basic airframe and systems. First flight is expected to take place in 1991, with PT2 flying for the first time in 1992 and the remaining prototypes at six-monthly intervals thereafter. PT2 and PT3 will be avionics testbeds, PT4 will be completed in HAP configuration, and PT5 as a PAH-2/HAC prototype. After their initial flight testing is completed, PT2 and PT3 will be retrofitted to HAP and PAH-2/HAC standard respectively, to carry out some of the weapon trials programme.

The agreed work sharing gives Aérospatiale responsibility for the tail rotor, centre-fuselage (including engine installation), transmission, fuel and electrical systems, aerodynamics, weight control, maintainability, reliability and survivability. MBB is responsible for the front and rear fuselage (including cockpits), main rotor, hydraulic and flight control systems, prototype assembly, flight performance, flight characteristics, stress, vibration testing, and simulation. Jointly staffed teams will be based at Marignane for flight testing the basic helicopter, updating the avionics fit during trials, and testing the HAP version; and at Ottobrunn for basic avionics, the Euromep mission equipment (armament) package, and weapons system integration.

Requirements have been estimated at 212 PAH-2s for Germany, 75 HAPs and 140 HACs for France.

TYPE: Twin-engined anti-tank and ground support helicopter.

ROTOR SYSTEM AND DRIVE: Four-blade semi-rigid main rotor, with composite blades; no flapping or lead-lag hinges; two elastomeric pitch bearings per blade. Rotor head consists of two fibre composite starplates bolted together with a titanium spacer, a configuration which permits almost unrestricted installation of a mast mounted sight. Main features are a compact, robust construction, low aerodynamic drag, a very small number of parts, and ease of maintenance. Development of new DM blade aerofoil sections and geometries promises performance improvements of about 10 per cent over most present-day systems, and will provide the agility needed in typical anti-tank missions, ie in extreme nap-of-the-earth flights. Three-blade Aérospatiale Spheriflex composite tail rotor, mounted on starboard side, has OA asymmetrical aerofoil blade section.

Principal features of main transmission are separate load paths, high run-dry capability (up to 30 min), compatibility with the mast mounted sight, and ability to withstand 12.5 mm hits.

WINGS, FUSELAGE AND TAIL UNIT: Conventional semi-monocoque metal and composites structures, meeting criteria for safety, crash resistance (to MIL-STD-1290 standards), and damage tolerance (survivable against hits from weapons of up to 23 mm calibre). Centre-fuselage built mainly of metal sandwich; rear portion, cockpit area and wings mainly of carbonfibre, with glassfibre or Kevlar fairings. Stub wings, with anhedral on outer panels, for releasable weapons. Sweptback fin/tail rotor pylon and underfin; horizontal stabiliser, with sweptback endplate auxiliary fins.

LANDING GEAR: Non-retractable tailwheel type, with single wheel on each unit. Designed to absorb impacts of up to 6 m (20 ft)/s.

POWER PLANT: Two 957 kW (1,284 shp) MTU/Rolls-Royce/Turbomeca MTM 390 turboshafts, mounted side by side above centre-fuselage. Infra-red exhaust suppressors, using ram air. Self-sealing crashworthy fuel tanks, with explosion suppression.

ACCOMMODATION: Crew of two in tandem, with pilot in front and weapons system operator at rear. Armoured, impact-absorbing seats. Stepped cockpits, with flat-plate transparencies.

SYSTEMS: Redundant hydraulic, electrical and fuel systems.

AVIONICS: Essential characteristics will be common to both French and German versions, and European in origin. Flight controls are mechanical, comprising duplex primary hydraulic servocontrols (controlled by autopilot and trim), and duplex main hydraulic servocontrols to generate control loads towards rotors. Support is provided by a redundant, four-axis duplex AFCS with stabilisation and autopilot functions. Systems architecture is based on a dual digital databus. Via two central computers with symbol generation, information for pilot and gunner is shown on multiple displays in cockpit. Essential flight data for pilot are also displayed by backup conventional instruments. Navigation subsystem consists of two identical strapdown units together with such sensors as ASI, Doppler radar, radar altimeter and magnetic sensor. Subsystem conducts functions of autonomous navigation as well as flight path computation, and supplies data necessary for AFCS and mission equipment packages. An integrated radar/laser warning subsystem will be installed to recognise, identify and classify specific threats. Provisions are made for comprehensive additional active ECM. *Anti-tank mission* equipment package, based on a MIL-STD-1553B redundant databus, comprises visionic system with gunner's sight, pilot's night vision system and combined helmet mounted sight and display, plus armament according to variant. Mast mounted sight, controlled by gunner, is a multi-sensor system with optical and infra-red channels and various fields of view. Visionic system is stabilised, includes tracker for single and multiple targets, a laser rangefinder, and cockpit display. Advanced technologies such as IR charge coupled devices will ensure high performance. Nose mounted piloting IR sensor (pilot's vision system, or PVS) image is displayed and steered via

helmet sight display; in the event of PVS loss, switchover can be made to a redundant IR image of the gunner's sight. Mission equipment of HAP *escort/combat support version* is also based on MIL-STD-1553B redundant databus, which interconnects firing control and redundant bus management computer, gunner's sight, HUD, gun turret, rockets, air-to-air missiles, pilot's and gunner's helmet sights, and pilot's and gunner's armament control unit. Between all three versions some equipment (eg com radios, sand filters) will vary according to individual operator's specifications.

ARMAMENT: As listed under model descriptions.

DIMENSIONS, EXTERNAL:

Main rotor diameter	13.00 m (42 ft 7¾ in)
Tail rotor diameter	2.70 m (8 ft 10¼ in)

Wheel track	2.40 m (7 ft 10½ in)
AREAS:	
Main rotor disc	132.7 m² (1,428.7 sq ft)
Tail rotor disc	5.72 m² (61.63 sq ft)
WEIGHTS:	
Basic weight empty	3,300 kg (7,275 lb)
Mission T-O weight	
	5,400 to 5,800 kg (11,905 to 12,787 lb)
Max overload T-O weight	6,000 kg (13,227 lb)
PERFORMANCE (estimated, at AUW of 5,400 kg; 11,905 lb):	
Cruising speed	
	135-151 knots (250-280 km/h; 155-174 mph)
Max rate of climb at S/L	more than 600 m (1,970 ft)/min
Hovering ceiling OGE	more than 2,000 m (6,560 ft)
Endurance, incl 20 min reserves	2 h 48 min

EUROFAR
EUROPEAN FUTURE ADVANCED ROTORCRAFT

Six European aerospace companies (Aérospatiale, MBB, Agusta, Aeritalia, CASA and Westland) signed an accord in September 1986 to collaborate in a preliminary study phase to develop a European tilt-rotor convertiplane, initially for civil applications. Funding of the three-year study (1987-90) is being provided in the approximate ratio of 75 per cent from the Eureka European technology research programme, which voted £31.5 million to the project in September 1987, and 25 per cent from the participating companies. Of the latter, the major share will be borne by Aérospatiale (France), MBB (Germany) and Agusta/Aeritalia (Italy), with substantially smaller contributions from CASA (Spain) and Westland (UK).

Early parameters for the Eurofar aircraft envisage a twin-engined, 30-passenger design in the 10,000 kg (22,046 lb) gross weight class, with a cruising speed of 313 knots (580 km/h; 360 mph) and a range of 539 nm (1,000 km; 621 miles). Various power plant options are being studied, with a selection expected by the end of 1988.

Artist's impression of a possible Eurofar civil tilt-rotor aircraft for the mid-1990s

EUROFIGHTER
EUROFIGHTER JAGDFLUGZEUG GmbH

Arabellastrasse 16 (Postfach 860366), 8000 Munich 86, Federal Republic of Germany
Telephone: (089) 928030
Telex: 5213908 or 5213744
Fax: (089) 92803260
CHAIRMAN (1986-88): Dr Carl-Peter Fichtmüller (MBB)
MANAGING DIRECTOR: F. G. Willox (BAe)
MARKETING: H. A. Merriman (BAe)
PUBLICITY EXECUTIVE: U. Kruse (MBB)
PUBLIC RELATIONS: Eduardo Sanchez Ulloa (CASA)

EUROPEAN FIGHTER AIRCRAFT (EFA/JF-90)

The chiefs of air staff of France, West Germany, Italy, Spain and the UK issued in December 1983 an outline staff target for a new combat aircraft to enter service with all five air forces in the mid-1990s. France withdrew in July 1985, participation by the remaining four countries then being set at 33% each for the UK and Germany, 21% for Italy and 13% for Spain. National design teams from MBB (with Dornier as co-contractor), Aeritalia, CASA and British Aerospace are collaborating in developing and harmonising individual national requirements, incorporating some of the design aspects and technology from the BAe EAP programme (see UK section). The initial feasibility study, launched in July 1984, was followed by the project definition phase. In June 1986 Eurofighter GmbH, with headquarters in Munich, was formed to manage the EFA programme. Eurojet Turbo GmbH was formed shortly afterwards to manage the engine programme.

The project definition stage was completed in September 1986. This phase was followed by a definition refinement and risk reduction stage, which lasted until the end of 1987. In September of that year the four air staffs issued European Staff Requirement-Development (ESR-D), featuring the military requirements of the EFA in further detail. At the same time, industry delivered all necessary technical and economic data to the four governments for go-ahead negotiations. The full scale development phase was initiated by the signing of a three-nation agreement on 16 May 1988 (with Spain to follow), and this is scheduled to lead to a first flight in 1991, the start of series production in 1993 and initial deliveries in 1996. Eight prototypes are expected to be built, with flight testing in all four countries. This programme is being supervised by an international office known as NEFMA (NATO European Fighter Management Agency) independent of, but co-located with, the NAMMA agency for the Panavia Tornado, based in Munich.

Artist's impression of the EFA (European Fighter Aircraft), of which full scale development began in 1988

The EFA will be configured primarily for the air defence role, but with a secondary capability for air-to-surface attack. Nearly 800 aircraft are expected to be required by the partner nations, in the approximate ratio of 250 for Germany, 165 for Italy, 100 for Spain and 250 for Great Britain; a proportion of two-seat trainer versions (probably about 100) would be included in these totals. Export orders are also anticipated. The agreed workshare gives BAe

responsibility for design and manufacture of the front fuselage and foreplanes; MBB (teamed with Dornier) will produce the centre-fuselage and fin; Aeritalia and CASA will build the rear fuselage; and wing production will be shared between Aeritalia, CASA and BAe, without any duplication of tooling. There will be a final assembly line at each of the four airframe companies.

TYPE: Single-seat, extremely agile STOL-capable fighter, optimised for air-to-air roles, with secondary ground attack capability.

AIRFRAME: Will incorporate low detectability technologies, and a substantial proportion will be built of composites materials, in conjunction with new lightweight metal alloys, using advanced manufacturing techniques such as superplastic forming and diffusion bonding.

WINGS AND FOREPLANES: Cantilever low-mounted delta-wing monoplane of low aspect ratio, with 53° sweepback on leading-edges, inboard and outboard 'flaperons' on trailing-edges. All-moving foreplanes mid-mounted on nose, in line with windscreen. Wings and foreplanes, including flaperons, built mainly of CFC (carbonfibre composites) materials, except for use of Al-Li (aluminium-lithium) alloys for foreplane leading/trailing-edges and two-segment slats on main wing leading-edges. Pitch control via foreplanes and flaperons, using advanced active control technology to provide artificial longitudinal stability (aircraft is otherwise aerodynamically unstable). Al-Li ECM pod at each wingtip.

FUSELAGE: Conventional semi-monocoque, built largely of CFC except for glassfibre nose radome, magnesium canopy surround, Al-Li wing/body fairing and intake cowling, and titanium in exhaust nozzle area. Dorsal spine aft of cockpit incorporates airbrake.

TAIL UNIT: Vertical surfaces only, comprising sweptback Al-Li/CFC fin (with GRP tip) and Al-Li inset rudder.

LANDING GEAR: Retractable tricycle type. Single-wheel main units retract inward into fuselage, steerable nosewheel unit forward.

POWER PLANT: Early EFA prototypes will each be powered by two Turbo-Union RB199-122 afterburning turbofans. Later prototypes and the production aircraft will be powered by two Eurojet EJ200 advanced technology turbofans (90 kN; 20,250 lb thrust class with afterburning), mounted side by side in rear fuselage with ventral intakes. Prototype EJ200 due to make first run, at MTU in Germany, in October 1988. Provision for external fuel tanks and in-flight refuelling.

ENGINE AIR INTAKES: Side by side intakes in underfuselage box, each having a fixed upper wedge/ramp and a variable-position lower cowl lip (vari-cowl).

SYSTEMS: Full authority four-channel ACT (active control technology) fly by wire flight control system, combined with mission adaptive configuring and the aircraft's artificial longitudinal instability, will provide the EFA with the required 'carefree' handling, gust alleviation and high sustained manoeuvrability throughout the flight envelope. Pitch control effected via foreplane/elevators ACT to provide artificial longitudinal stability; yaw control via rudder. The quadruplex AFCS, which will operate through a NATO standard databus, is intended to ensure that pilot cannot exceed aircraft's flying limits. Utilities systems controlled by microcomputer.

AVIONICS: Primary sensor will be a multi-mode pulse-Doppler radar with an interception range of 50-80 nm (92.5-148 km; 57.5-92 miles), able to acquire at least 85 per cent of probable targets (including eight targets simultaneously), and to direct lookdown/shootdown and snap-up weapons against them. Other radar requirements include velocity and single-target search, track-while-scan and range-while-scan, target priority processing, automatic weapons selection, and recommended combat tactics display. In attack mode, it will have capability for ground mapping/ranging and terrain avoidance, but not terrain following. Candidates include MSD 2000, an adaptation of the Hughes Aircraft APG-65, with Marconi Defence Systems (UK) and AEG (Germany); and an all-new radar known as ECR 90 by Ferranti (UK), Fiar (Italy) and Inisel (Spain). Radar will form part of a comprehensive avionics suite which also includes extensive communications, and an advanced integrated defensive aids support system (DASS). A team comprising Ceselsa (Spain), Ferranti, Honeywell Sondertechnik (Germany) and Litton Italia has proposed a ring laser gyro based INS called Eurolins. All avionics, flight control and utilities control systems will be integrated through NATO standard databus highways with appropriate redundancy levels and full use of microprocessors. Special attention has been given to reducing pilot

workload. New cockpit techniques will simplify flying the aircraft safely and effectively to the limits of the flight envelope while monitoring and managing the aircraft and its operational systems, and detecting/identifying/attacking desired targets while remaining safe from enemy defences. This will be achieved through a high level of system integration and automation, together with three large multi-function colour displays.

ARMAMENT: Interceptor will have an internally mounted cannon, plus a mix of AIM-120 AMRAAM and short-range (AIM-132 ASRAAM or Sidewinder) air-to-air missiles carried externally, four of the former being mounted in tandem pairs in a semi-recessed underfuselage installation similar to that of the ADV Tornado. The short-range missiles are carried on underwing pylons. The EFA will, if necessary, be able to carry a considerable overload of air-to-air weapons. For secondary role air-to-surface weapons, and/or auxiliary fuel tanks, it will have a total of 15 external attachment points.

DIMENSIONS, EXTERNAL:

Wing span	10.50 m (34 ft 5½ in)
Wing aspect ratio	2.205
Length overall	approx 14.50 m (47 ft 7 in)

AREA:

Wings, gross	50.0 m² (538.2 sq ft)

WEIGHTS (approx):

Weight empty	9,750 kg (21,495 lb)
Internal fuel load	4,000 kg (8,818 lb)
External stores load (weapons and/or fuel)	4,500 kg (9,920 lb)
Max T-O weight	17,000 kg (37,480 lb)

DESIGN PERFORMANCE:

Max level speed	more than Mach 1.8

T-O and landing distance with full internal fuel and two AMRAAM plus two ASRAAM or Sidewinder missiles, ISA + 15°C   500 m (1,640 ft)

Combat radius (estimated)   250-300 nm (463-556 km; 288-345 miles)

g limits with full internal fuel and two AMRAAM missiles   +9/−3

FIMA
FUTURE INTERNATIONAL MILITARY/CIVIL AIRLIFTER

FIMA is the acronym for a study group set up in December 1982 to work towards development of a late-1990s replacement for the Lockheed C-130 Hercules and Transall C-160 transport aircraft with increased payload capacity, enhanced performance and reduced operating costs.

The original study group of Aérospatiale, British Aerospace, Lockheed Corporation and MBB was joined on 3 December 1987 by CASA and Aeritalia, when these six companies signed a memorandum of understanding to carry out preliminary studies for an aircraft that would satisfy a common NATO/European requirement. It was hoped to formulate an outline European Staff Target by late 1988/early 1989. Additional roles for the FIMA may also include long-range maritime patrol, aerial refuelling tanker, airborne command post and AEW.

As individual requirements are clarified, the FIMA is emerging as a high-wing aircraft with four 11,930 kW (16,000 shp) class propfan engines, a T tail, rough-field landing gear, a cargo hold at least 4 m (13.12 ft) wide, a rear loading ramp, and a max T-O weight in the order of 72,575 kg (160,000 lb). Joint needs of the six nations are estimated at 700-1,000 aircraft, with plans for one production line in Europe and one in the USA. First flight is planned for about 1998, with deliveries beginning two years later, assuming a 1993 start for the full scale engineering development phase.

Artist's impression of the six-nation FIMA military/civil transport

JEH

JOINT EUROPEAN HELICOPTER Srl

Via Sicilia 43, 00187 Rome, Italy
Telephone: (06) 49801
Telex: 614398

Following industrial agreements between Agusta, CASA, Fokker and Westland, JEH was formed on 4 September 1986 to manage the multi-national programme to produce a third-generation multi-role light attack helicopter known as Tonal, based on the Agusta A 129 Mangusta. Shareholdings are 38% each to Agusta and Westland, 19% to Fokker and 5% to CASA.

JEH A 129 LAH TONAL

The Tonal programme came into being to meet the requirements of the Italian, British, Dutch and Spanish armed forces for an advanced multi-role combat helicopter for the late 1990s. Named after an ancient Aztec deity, Tonal will have a structure based on that of the Mangusta (see Italian section), but with equipment and weapons systems to give it anti-tank, scout and anti-helicopter capability. Primary armament will comprise third-generation anti-tank and air-to-air weapons, but a wide range of other ordnance, including guns and rockets, will also be deployable. Designed to be operable at night and in adverse weather, the Tonal is planned to enter service in 1997. At present, a joint Anglo-Italian Staff Target is forming the basis of a two-year feasibility and cost definition study which began on 1 June 1987, and a detailed description would therefore be premature. Reported requirements of the four partner nations are: Italy 90, UK 125, Netherlands 50 and Spain 40. A modified A 129 will be used to demonstrate the new configuration.

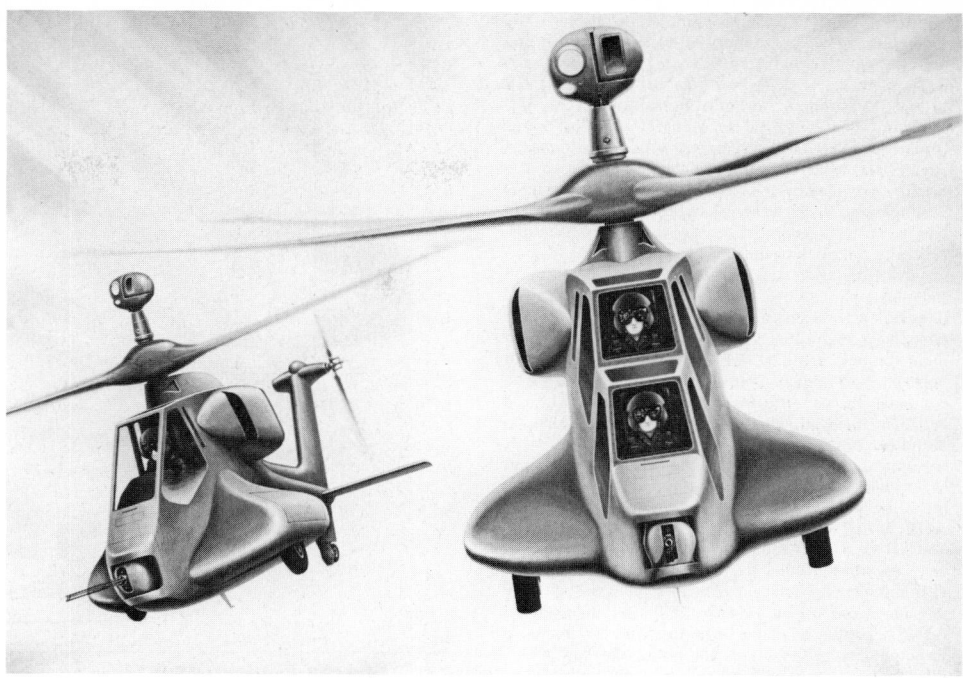

Agusta artist's 1987 impression of the JEH Tonal light attack helicopter

MBB/KAWASAKI

AIRFRAME PRIME CONTRACTORS:
Messerschmitt-Bölkow-Blohm GmbH (Helicopter and Military Aircraft Group), Postfach 801160, 8000 Munich 80, Federal Republic of Germany
Telephone: (089) 6000 6488
Telex: 5287-071/074 MBB D
Kawasaki Heavy Industries Ltd, World Trade Center Building, 4-1 Hamamatsu-cho 2-chome, Minato-ku, Tokyo, Japan
Telephone: (03) 435 2971
Telex: 242 4371 KAWAJU J

MBB/KAWASAKI BK 117 B-1

MBB and Kawasaki agreed on 25 February 1977 to develop jointly a multi-purpose helicopter known as the BK 117. This aircraft has a number of components and accessories interchangeable with those of the MBB BO 105, from which aircraft the principle of the hydraulic boost system is also adapted. The transmission is based on that developed by Kawasaki for its earlier KH-7 design.

The BK 117 is manufactured by the single source method, each company producing the components which it has developed, which are then exchanged. There are two final assembly lines, one at Donauwörth and one at Gifu. MBB is responsible for production of the main and tail rotor systems, tailboom and tail unit, skid landing gear, hydraulic system, engine firewall and cowlings, power-amplified controls and systems integration; Kawasaki is responsible for the fuselage, transmission, fuel and electrical systems, and standard items of equipment. An agreement was signed with MBB in November 1982 whereby IPTN of Indonesia (which see) is licensed to manufacture the BK 117, as the **NBK-117**.

Four prototypes (first flight 13 June 1979) and one pre-production BK 117 (first flight 6 March 1981) were built, as described in earlier editions of *Jane's*. The first production BK 117 to fly was a Kawasaki-built aircraft (JQ1001), which flew for the first time on 24 December 1981. The first MBB production aircraft flew on 23 April 1982. German LBA type certification was granted on 9 December 1982, followed by Japanese certification on 17 December 1982. Certification is to FAR Pt 29, Category A and B, including Amendments 29-1 to 29-16. FAA certification was granted on 29 March 1983.

Customer deliveries began in early 1983, the initial production model being known as the **BK 117 A-1** (described in the 1984-85 *Jane's*). On 15 March 1985 the LBA certificated the **BK 117 A-3** with max T-O weight increased from 2,850 kg (6,283 lb) to 3,200 kg (7,055 lb), and from January 1987 a **BK 117 A-4** model (certificated by the LBA on 29 July 1986 and JCAB on 29 August 1986) became available. The A-3 introduced an enlarged tail rotor with twisted blades; the A-4, with an increased transmission limit at T-O power, improved tail rotor head and (on German built examples) more internal fuel, offered enhanced performance. Details of the A-3 and A-4 can be found in the 1987-88 *Jane's*.

A new **BK 117 B-1** series was certificated in 1987 by the LBA (on 10 December) and FAA (11 December). This has LTS 101-750B-1 engines, enabling it to hover OGE, in ISA conditions, at a 427 m (1,400 ft) higher altitude than the A-4, with 140 kg (309 lb) more payload; and hover IGE with

BK 117 in EMS (emergency medical service) configuration for a hospital in the USA

the same payload increase at altitudes increased by 457 mm (1,500 ft) (ISA) and 549 m (1,800 ft) (ISA + 20°C). All production BK 117s are now to B-1 standard.

On behalf of, and subsidised by, the German Federal Ministry of Defence, MBB is developing an entire BK 117 airframe of fibre reinforced composite materials in a 3½ year research programme.

Kawasaki had delivered 14 BK 117s by mid-1987, and MBB 139 by the end of that year. The following description applies to the BK 117 B-1, except where stated otherwise:

TYPE: Twin-turbine multi-purpose helicopter.

ROTOR SYSTEM: Four-blade 'System Bölkow' rigid main rotor; head almost identical to that of BO 105; main rotor blades similar to those of BO 105, but larger. Two-blade teetering tail rotor. Main rotor has a titanium head, to which are attached hingeless, fail-safe GRP blades of NACA 23012/23010 (modified) section with a stainless steel anti-erosion strip on each leading-edge. Optional folding of two blades of main rotor. Main rotor rpm: 383. Two-blade semi-rigid (teetering) tail rotor, mounted on port side of vertical fin and rotating clockwise when viewed from that side. Blades are of GRP, with high impact resistance and MBB-S102E performance/noise-optimised section. Tail rotor rpm: 2,169.

ROTOR DRIVE: Each engine has separate drive input into Kawasaki KB 03 main transmission via single bevel gear and collector. Transmission rated at 736 kW (986 shp) for twin-engine take-off and 632 kW (848 shp) for max continuous operation; and, for single-engine operation, at 442 kW (592 shp) for 2½ min, 404 kW (542 shp) for 30 min, and 368 kW (493 shp) max continuous. Auxiliary drives for accessories. Dual redundant lubrication system.

FUSELAGE: Of typical pod shaped configuration, comprising flight deck, cabin, cargo compartment and engine deck. Main structural components are of semi-monocoque riveted aluminium alloy with single curvature sheets and bonded aluminium sandwich panels. Secondary components are compound curvature shells with sandwich panels and Kevlar skins. Floor extends throughout cockpit, cabin and cargo compartment at same level. Engine deck forms roof of cargo compartment and, adjacent to engine bays, is of titanium to serve as a firewall.

TAIL UNIT: Semi-monocoque tailboom, of tapered conical section, attached integrally to engine deck at forward end. Rear end, which is detachable, carries main fin/tail rotor support, and horizontal stabiliser with endplate fins set at an offset angle.

LANDING GEAR: Non-retractable tubular skid type, of aluminium construction. Skids are detachable from cross-tubes. Ground handling wheels standard. Emergency flotation gear, settling protectors and snow skids available optionally.

POWER PLANT: Two Textron Lycoming LTS 101-750B-1 turboshafts, each rated at 442 kW (592 shp) for 30 min for take-off and 410 kW (550 shp) max continuous power. Fuel in four flexible bladder tanks (forward and aft main tanks, with two supply tanks between), in compartments under cabin floor. Two independent fuel feed systems for the engines and a common main fuel tank. Total standard fuel capacity (A-4 and B-1), 708 litres (187 US gallons; 155.7 Imp gallons). A 200 litre (53 US gallon; 44 Imp gallon) auxiliary tank is available optionally, raising total capacity to 908 litres (240 US gallons; 199.7 Imp gallons).

ACCOMMODATION: Pilot and up to six (executive version) or seven passengers (standard version). High-density layouts available for up to ten passengers in addition to pilot. Provision for two-pilot operation at customer's option. Jettisonable forward hinged door on each side of cockpit, pilot's door having an openable window. Jettisonable rearward sliding passenger door on each side of cabin, lockable in open position. Fixed steps on each side. Two hinged, clamshell doors at rear of cabin, providing access to cargo compartment. Rear cabin window on each side. Aircraft can be equipped, according to mission, for offshore, medical evacuation (one or two stretchers side by side and up to six attendants), firefighting, search and rescue, law enforcement, cargo transport or other operations.

SYSTEMS: Ram air and electrical ventilation system. Fully redundant tandem hydraulic boost system (one operating and one standby), pressure 103.5 bars (1,500 lb/sq in), for flight controls. System flow rate 8.1 litres (2.14 US gallons; 1.78 Imp gallons)/min. Bootstrap/oil reservoir, pressure 1.7 bars (25 lb/sq in). Main DC electrical power from two 150A 28V starter/generators (one on each engine) and a 24V 25Ah nickel-cadmium battery. AC power is provided by an inverter; a second AC inverter is available optionally. Emergency busbar provides direct battery power to essential services in event of a double generator failure. External DC power receptacle.

AVIONICS AND EQUIPMENT: Basic aircraft has instrumentation for single-pilot VFR operation, including airspeed indicator with electrically heated pitot tube and static ports, encoding altimeter, instantaneous vertical speed indicator, 4 in artificial horizon, 3 in standby artificial horizon, gyro magnetic heading system, HSI, magnetic compass, ambient air thermometer, and clock. (The 4 in and 3 in artificial horizons and HSI are optional on Kawasaki built aircraft.) Dual controls and dual VFR instrumentation available optionally. Com/nav and other avionics available to customer's requirements, including VHF-AM/FM, UHF and HF transceivers, ADF, nav, R/Nav, Loran, Decca, VLF/Omega, LDNS and AHRS systems, radar altimeter, ATC/IFF transponder, encoding altimeter, DME, multi-mode radar, IFR instrumentation packages, and pitch/roll stability augmentation system. Sperry SPZ-7100 dual digital AFCS to become available from Autumn 1988. Standard basic equipment includes rotor brake and yaw CSAS (both optional only on Kawasaki aircraft), annunciator panel, master caution light, rotor rpm/engine fail warning control unit, fuel quantity indicator and low level sensor, outside air temperature indicator, engine and transmission oil pressure and temperature indicators, two exhaust temperature indicators, dual torque indicator, triple tachometer, two NI tachometers, mast moment indicator, instrument panel lights, cockpit/cabin/cargo compartment dome lights, utility lights, emergency exit lights, position lights, anti-collision warning light, retractable landing light, portable flashlight, ground handling wheels, pilot's and co-pilot's windscreen wipers, floor covering, interior panelling and sound insulation, ashtrays, map/document case, tiedown rings in cabin and cargo compartment, engine compartment fire warning indicator, engine fire extinguishing system, portable fire extinguisher, first aid kit, and single colour exterior paint scheme. Optional equipment includes high-density seating arrangement, bleed air heating system, long-range fuel tank, emergency flotation gear, settling protectors, snow skids, main rotor blade folding kit, non-retractable landing light, dual pilot operation kit, stretcher installation, external cargo hook, rescue hoist, SX 16 remotely controlled searchlight, external loudspeaker, and sand filter. Special optional equipment, including special mission kits for rescue, law enforcement and VIP transport, available at customer's request.

DIMENSIONS, EXTERNAL:

Main rotor diameter	11.00 m (36 ft 1 in)
Tail rotor diameter	1.956 m (6 ft 5 in)
Main rotor blade chord	0.32 m (1 ft 0½ in)
Length overall, main and tail rotors turning	13.00 m (42 ft 8 in)
Length of fuselage, tail rotor blades vertical	9.91 m (32 ft 6¼ in)
Fuselage: Max width	1.60 m (5 ft 3 in)
Height overall, main and tail rotors turning	3.85 m (12 ft 7½ in)

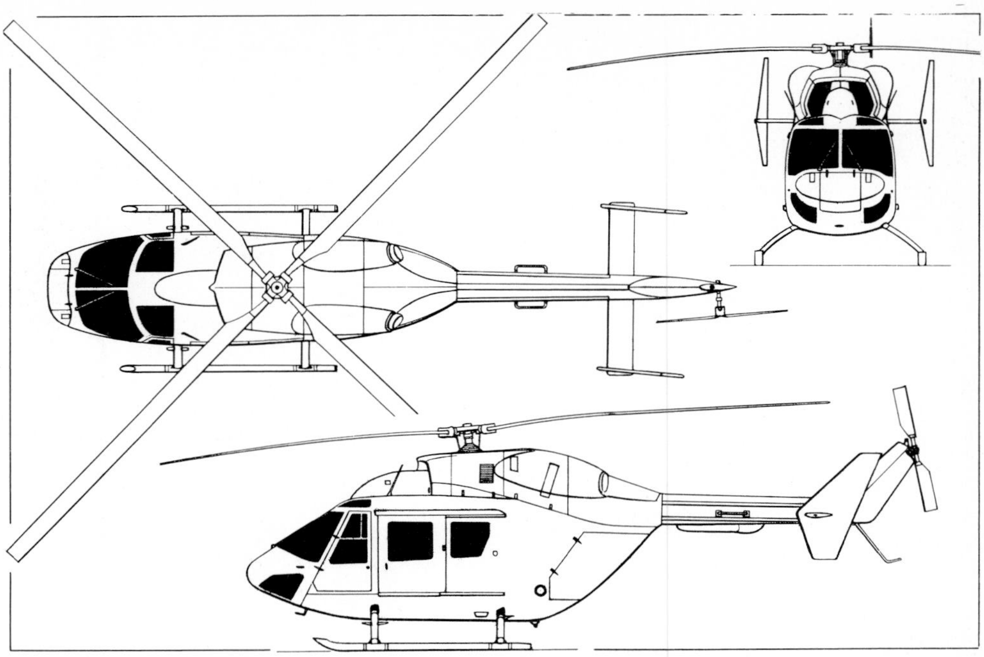

MBB/Kawasaki BK 117 twin-turboshaft multi-purpose helicopter (*Pilot Press*)

Height to top of main rotor head	3.36 m (11 ft 0¼ in)
Tailplane span (over endplate fins)	2.70 m (8 ft 10¼ in)
Tail rotor ground clearance	1.90 m (6 ft 2¾ in)
Width over skids	2.50 m (8 ft 2½ in)

DIMENSIONS, INTERNAL:
Combined cabin and cargo compartment:

Max length	3.02 m (9 ft 11 in)
Width: max	1.49 m (4 ft 10½ in)
min	1.21 m (3 ft 11½ in)
Height: max	1.28 m (4 ft 2½ in)
min	0.99 m (3 ft 3 in)
Useful floor area	3.70 m² (39.83 sq ft)
Volume	5.00 m³ (176.6 cu ft)

AREAS:

Main rotor blades (each)	1.76 m² (18.94 sq ft)
Tail rotor blades (each)	0.0975 m² (1.05 sq ft)
Main rotor disc	95.03 m² (1,022.9 sq ft)
Tail rotor disc	3.00 m² (32.24 sq ft)

WEIGHTS:

Basic weight empty: A-4	1,705 kg (3,759 lb)
B-1	1,727 kg (3,807 lb)
Fuel: standard usable:	
Japanese A-4	478 kg (1,054 lb)
German A-4 and B-1	558 kg (1,230 lb)
incl auxiliary tank:	
Japanese A-4	638 kg (1,407 lb)
German A-4 and B-1	718 kg (1,583 lb)
Max T-O weight (A-4 and B-1):	
internal and external payload	3,200 kg (7,055 lb)

*PERFORMANCE (B-1 at ISA; A at gross weight of 2,800 kg; 6,173 lb, B at 3,000 kg; 6,614 lb, C at 3,200 kg; 7,055 lb):

Never-exceed speed at S/L:	
A, B, C	150 knots (278 km/h; 172 mph)
Max cruising speed at S/L:	
A	137 knots (254 km/h; 158 mph)
B	135 knots (250 km/h; 155 mph)
C	134 knots (248 km/h; 154 mph)
Max forward rate of climb at S/L:	
A	714 m (2,345 ft)/min
B	660 m (2,165 ft)/min
C	582 m (1,910 ft)/min
Max certificated operating altitude:	
A, B	4,575 m (15,000 ft)
C	3,050 m (10,000 ft)
Service ceiling, one engine out, 46 m (150 ft)/min climb	
reserve: A	3,110 m (10,200 ft)
B	2,440 m (8,000 ft)
C	1,770 m (5,800 ft)
Hovering ceiling IGE (zero wind):	
A	4,205 m (13,800 ft)
B	3,565 m (11,700 ft)
C	2,925 m (9,600 ft)
Hovering ceiling IGE (17 knot; 32 km/h; 20 mph crosswind): A	2,865 m (9,400 ft)
B	2,195 m (7,200 ft)
C	1,495 m (4,900 ft)
Hovering ceiling OGE: A	3,625 m (11,900 ft)
B	2,955 m (9,700 ft)
C	2,285 m (7,500 ft)
Range at S/L with standard fuel, no reserves:	
A	315 nm (585 km; 363 miles)
B	313 nm (580 km; 360 miles)
C	307 nm (570 km; 354 miles)
Ferry range at S/L with auxiliary fuel, no reserves:	
A	408 nm (756 km; 469 miles)
B	404 nm (750 km; 466 miles)
C	399 nm (740 km; 460 miles)
Endurance at S/L, standard fuel, no reserves:	
A	3 h 15 min
B	3 h 12 min
C	3 h 6 min

*Data are for German built aircraft: those for Japanese models vary slightly

MCDONNELL DOUGLAS/BAe

AIRFRAME PRIME CONTRACTORS:

McDonnell Douglas Corporation, Box 516, St Louis, Missouri 63166, USA
Telephone: (314) 234 7019
Telex: 234 4857 MCDL DGLS STZ
British Aerospace PLC, Richmond Road, Kingston upon Thames, Surrey KT2 5QS, England
Telephone: 01 546 7741
Telex: 23726

VICE-PRESIDENT AND GENERAL MANAGER, AV-8:
Roger H. Mathews (McDonnell Aircraft Co)
PROGRAMME MANAGER, T45TS:
Sterling D. Stalford (Douglas Aircraft Co)

MCDONNELL DOUGLAS/BRITISH AEROSPACE HARRIER II

US Marine Corps designations: AV-8B and TAV-8B
RAF designation: Harrier GR. Mk 5

The early background to the Harrier II programme has been given in several previous editions of *Jane's*. After McDonnell Douglas and BAe (then Hawker Siddeley) joined forces in the current collaborative programme, two AV-8As were modified as YAV-8B aerodynamic prototypes

by McDonnell Douglas and the USMC, these flying for the first time on 9 November 1978 and 19 February 1979. Four full scale development AV-8Bs were then built, the first of these making its initial flight on 5 November 1981. Two other airframes were built for structural and fatigue testing. The decision to commit the AV-8B to production was announced on 24 August 1981, and the first 12 (pilot production) aircraft were ordered in FY 1982. Compared with the Harrier GR. Mk 3/AV-8A (see under BAe in UK section), features of the AV-8B include the use of graphite epoxy (carbonfibre) composite materials for the wings, and parts of the fuselage and tail unit; adoption of a supercritical wing section; addition of lift improvement devices (LIDs) comprising fuselage mounted or under-gun-pod strakes and a retractable fence panel forward of the pods, to augment lift for vertical take-off; larger wing trailing-edge flaps and drooped ailerons; redesigned forward fuselage and cockpit; redesigned engine air intakes to provide more VTO/STO thrust and more efficient cruise; two additional wing stores stations; and the Hughes Angle Rate Bombing Set. Wing outriggers are relocated at mid-span to provide better ground manoeuvring capability, and leading-edge root extensions (LERX) add considerably to the instantaneous turn rate. Combined with an expanded thrust vectoring envelope, the LERX also enhance air combat capability. The landing gear is strengthened to cater for higher operating weights and greater external stores loads made possible by these changes.

Work split on the airframe for the AV-8B (including those for Spain) is 60 per cent to McDonnell Douglas and 40 per cent to British Aerospace; the GR.Mk 5 work split is 50 per cent to each manufacturer. On any future third party orders McDonnell Douglas will make 50 per cent of the aircraft deliveries and British Aerospace 50 per cent. Each manufacturer is responsible for the systems in those parts of the airframe which are its concern, and for their installation. British Aerospace provides the complete reaction control system for all aircraft in the programme, and undertakes final assembly of aircraft for the RAF. McDonnell Douglas assembles the aircraft for the USMC and Spain. Planned peak production rates are four US and two UK aircraft per month.

Pratt & Whitney manufactures up to 25 per cent by value of the engines for the USMC aircraft; Rolls-Royce builds the remainder. Current production engine is the F402-RR-406A (Pegasus Mk 105), an improved version of the Pegasus 11 with new features designed to offer substantially increased engine life and reduced peacetime operating costs. It also features a digital engine control system (DECS), developed by Dowty and Smiths Industries, which was installed in the first TAV-8B in October 1986, and in production AV-8Bs beginning in March 1987.

The following variants of the Harrier II have been announced:

AV-8B. Single-seat close support version for US Marine Corps, which has a requirement for 295. First of 12 pilot production aircraft first flown on 29 August 1983; subsequent contracts placed in FYs 1983 to 1988 inclusive for a further 192 aircraft (21, 27, 32, 46, 42 and 24), including TAV-8Bs (see next paragraph), with 24 included in FY 1989 request. Deliveries to USMC began on 12 January 1984. Intended to re-equip three fleet operational AV-8A/C squadrons, one training squadron and five A-4 Skyhawk squadrons, and already operated (Spring 1988) by VMA-223, -231, -331, -513 and -542, and training squadron VMAT-203, with a sixth operational squadron due to form at MCAS Yuma, Arizona, in late 1988 or early 1989. First operational squadron (VMA-331) was commissioned on 30 January 1985 at MCAS Cherry Point, North Carolina, achieving IOC in August 1985. Total of 104 (including TAV-8Bs) delivered to USMC by 1 February 1988. A programme to develop a **night attack** version of the AV-8B was announced by McDonnell Douglas in November 1984, and a USMC prototype of this version flew for the first time on 26 June 1987. New systems include a nose mounted FLIR sensor, Smiths Industries colour head-down displays, a wide field of view HUD, Honeywell digital map system, displays, and pilot's night vision goggles. First production night attack AV-8B due for delivery to USMC in September 1988. Aircraft delivered from 1990 intended to have both night attack capability and an uprated F402-RR-408 (Pegasus 11-61) engine of approx 13.34 kN (3,000 lb) greater thrust.

TAV-8B. Two-seat operational trainer version for USMC, which has a requirement for 28. BAe is major subcontractor for this version, which first flew (BuAer No. 162747) on 21 October 1986. Total of 18 ordered in FYs 1985-1988 (2, 7, 6 and 3), deliveries (to VMAT-203) beginning in August 1987. Three more included in FY 1989 budget request. Longer forward fuselage and 0.43 m (1 ft 5 in) taller vertical tail than AV-8B, with two cockpits in tandem, and only two underwing stores stations. For weapons training, can carry six Mk 76 practice bombs, two LAU-68 rocket launchers or two 1,135 litre (300 US gallon; 250 Imp gallon) external fuel tanks.

EAV-8B. US designation of single-seat export (FMS) version for Spanish Navy, to supplement its carrier based AV-8A Matadors; assembled by McDonnell Douglas. Twelve ordered, first three of which were handed over on 6 October 1987. Deliveries completed. Will eventually be based on new aircraft carrier *Principe de Asturias*.

Harrier GR. Mk 5. Single-seat close support and reconnaissance version for Royal Air Force. Two development aircraft (ZD318 and ZD319), first flown on 30 April and 31 July 1985, plus fatigue test airframe to clear aircraft for central European low-level operating environment. First of initial production order for 60 (ZD324) was delivered to RAF on 1 July 1987, first unit being No. 233 OCU at Wittering. Due to equip Nos. 1, 3 and 4 Squadrons by 1991. Follow-on contract for additional 34 aircraft announced in April 1988: these will be built from outset to 'GR. Mk 7' standard (see next paragraph), with GEC Avionics FLIR, new Smiths HUD/HDD, and cockpit displays compatible with night vision goggles. When these 34 have been completed, first 41 production GR. 5s will be retrofitted to this standard, followed by Nos. 42-60 (which meanwhile will have been completed to an interim specification).

Harrier GR. Mk 7. Unofficial designation for RAF two-seat night attack version, being developed under a programme known as Nightbird, initiated in Spring 1987 by refitting a Harrier T. Mk 4, on loan to the RAE at Bedford, with an integrated avionics suite from Ferranti Defence Systems. The new nav/attack equipment includes two FD 4512 HUDs and a HUDWAC, an upgraded digital INS unit, projected digital colour map display, high-resolution head-down TV-type raster display in each cockpit, and video recording facilities, and is compatible with the aircraft's nose mounted FLIR sensor. 'Production' Nightbird Harrier IIs, planned to begin deliveries in early 1990, will be undertaken as a GR. Mk 5 retrofit programme, requiring an enhanced (ACCS 2500) Computing Devices mission computer, and a multi-purpose colour display with a separate GEC Avionics DCMU video map generator.

Prototype of the US night attack version of the AV-8B Harrier II

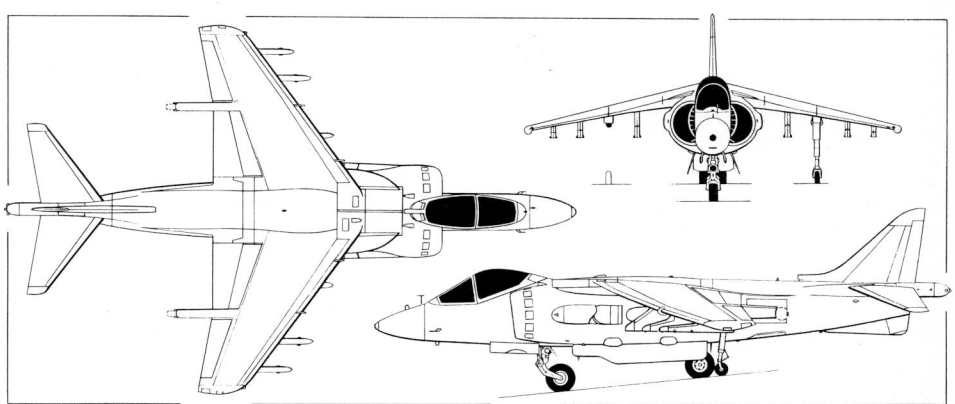

McDonnell Douglas/BAe AV-8B Harrier II V/STOL close support aircraft *(Pilot Press)*

McDonnell Douglas TAV-8B two-seat training version of the Harrier II

The following description applies to the production AV-8B and the Harrier GR. Mk 5:

TYPE: Single-seat V/STOL close support, night attack and (RAF only) reconnaissance aircraft.

WINGS: Cantilever shoulder-wing monoplane. Low aspect ratio sweptback wings, with non-swept inboard trailing-edges and curved leading-edge root extensions (LERX). Span and area increased by approx 20 per cent and 14.5 per cent respectively compared with Harrier GR. Mk 3/AV-8A. Supercritical aerofoil section, with thickness/chord ratio of 11.5% at root, 7.5% at tip. Leading-edge sweep 10° less than that of GR. Mk 3/AV-8A. Marked anhedral. One-piece structure, of mixed construction, with extensive use of graphite epoxy (carbonfibre) and other composite materials in the main multi-spar torsion box, ribs, skins, flaps, ailerons, LERX, and outrigger pods and fairings. Leading-edges (reinforced against bird strikes on GR. Mk 5) and wingtips of aluminium alloy. Wide chord single-slotted trailing-edge flaps, with flap slot closure doors. Drooping ailerons, actuated by Fairey hydraulic jacks. Jet reaction control valve at each wingtip. All wing manufacture and assembly by McDonnell Douglas.

FUSELAGE: Conventional semi-monocoque safe-life structure of frames and stringers, generally similar to that of GR. 3 and AV-8A, but longer, due to provision of a new forward fuselage built largely of graphite epoxy composite material and a lengthened rear fuselage. Centre and rear fuselage mainly of aluminium alloy, except for forward and rear underfuselage heatshields, and small area immediately forward of the windscreen, which are of titanium. Lift augmenting underfuselage devices consist of a fixed strake on each of the two ventral gun packs, plus a retractable fence between forward edges of gun packs, just aft of forward main landing gear unit. During VTOL modes the 'box' formed by these surfaces, which are made of composite materials, traps the cushion of air bounced off the ground by the engine exhaust, providing sufficient additional lift to enable the aircraft to take off vertically at a gross weight equal to its maximum hovering gross weight. Access to engine accessories through top of fuselage, immediately ahead of wing. Large forward hinged airbrake beneath fuselage, aft of rear main landing gear bay. Jet reaction control valves in nose and tailcone. McDonnell Douglas is responsible for manufacture of all forward and forward centre-fuselages, including nosecones, air intakes, heatshields, engine access doors, and forward fuel tanks; and for the underfuselage fences and strakes. British

McDonnell Douglas/BAe Harrier GR. Mk 5, with nose modified to carry an infra-red reconnaissance sensor

Aerospace builds, for all aircraft, the rear centre and rear fuselages, including blast and heatshields, centre and rear fuel tanks, dorsal air intakes, and tail bullets. Fuselage assembly is by McDonnell Douglas for USMC and Spain and by BAe for RAF aircraft.

TAIL UNIT: One-piece variable incidence tailplane, with marked anhedral, differing in planform from that of AV-8A in having constant sweep on leading-edges and reduced sweep on trailing-edges. Tailplane is built mainly of graphite epoxy, with aluminium alloy tips and leading-edges, and is operated by Fairey tandem irreversible hydraulic jacks. Aluminium alloy fin, with dielectric tip; manually operated graphite epoxy composite rudder. Dorsal airscoop, at base of fin, for equipment bay cooling system. Ventral fin under rear fuselage. Fins and rudders for all aircraft, and tailplanes for RAF aircraft, built by BAe; tailplanes for USMC and Spanish aircraft built by McDonnell Douglas.

LANDING GEAR: Retractable bicycle type of Dowty Rotol design, permitting operation from rough unprepared surfaces of very low CBR (California Bearing Ratio). Hydraulic actuation, with nitrogen bottle for emergency extension. Single steerable nosewheel retracts forward, twin coupled mainwheels rearward, into fuselage. Small outrigger units, at approx mid span between flaps and ailerons, retract rearward into streamline pods. Telescopic oleo-pneumatic main and outrigger gear; levered suspension nosewheel leg. Dunlop wheels, tyres, multi-disc carbon brakes and anti-skid system. Mainwheel tyres (size 26.0 × 7.75-13.00) and nosewheel tyre (size 26.0 × 8.75-11) all have pressure of 8.62 bars (125 lb/sq in). Outrigger tyres are size 13.5 × 6.00-4.00, pressure 10.34 bars (150 lb/sq in). McDonnell Douglas responsible for entire landing gear system.

POWER PLANT: One 95.42 kN (21,450 lb st) Rolls-Royce F402-RR-406A (Pegasus 11) vectored thrust turbofan in AV-8B; one 96.75 kN (21,750 lb st) Pegasus Mk 105 in Harrier GR. Mk 5; Mk 152-42 in EAV-8B. Redundant digital engine control system (DECS), with mechanical backup, standard from March 1987. Zero-scarf front nozzles. Air intakes have an elliptical lip shape, leading-edges reinforced against bird strikes, and a single row of auxiliary intake doors. Integral fuel tanks in wings; total internal fuel capacity (fuselage and wing tanks) 4,163 litres (1,100 US gallons; 915 Imp gallons). Retractable in-flight refuelling probe. Each of the four inner underwing stations capable of carrying a 1,135 litre (300 US gallon; 250 Imp gallon) auxiliary fuel tank.

ACCOMMODATION: Pilot only, on zero/zero ejection seat (Stencel for USMC, Martin-Baker for RAF), in pressurised, heated and air-conditioned cockpit. AV-8B cockpit raised approx 30.5 cm (12 in) by comparison with AV-8A/YAV-8B, with redesigned one-piece wraparound windscreen (thicker on RAF aircraft than on those for USMC) and rearward sliding bubble canopy, to improve all-round field of view. Windscreen de-icing. Windscreens and canopies for all aircraft manufactured by McDonnell Douglas.

SYSTEMS: No. 1 hydraulic system has a flow rate of 43 litres (11.4 US gallons; 9.5 Imp gallons)/min; flow rate of No. 2 system is 26.5 litres (7.0 US gallons; 5.8 Imp gallons)/min. Reservoirs are nitrogen pressurised at 2.76-5.52 bars (40-80 lb/sq in). Other systems include Westinghouse variable speed constant frequency (VSCF) solid state electrical system, Lucas Mk 4 gas turbine starter/APU, Clifton Precision onboard oxygen generating system (OBOGS), and Graviner Firewire fire detection system.

AVIONICS AND EQUIPMENT: Include dual Collins RT-1250A/ARC U/VHF com (GEC Avionics AD3500 ECM-resistant U/VHF-AM/FM in GR. Mk 5), R-1379B/ARA-63 all-weather landing receiver, RT-1159A/ARN-118 Tacan, RT-1015A/APN-194(V) radar altimeter, Honeywell CV-3736/A com/nav/identification data converter, Bendix RT-1157/APX-100 IFF (Cossor IFF 4760 transponder in GR. Mk 5), Litton AN/ASN-130A inertial navigation system (Ferranti FIN 1075 in GR. Mk 5), AiResearch CP-1471/A digital air data computer, Smiths Industries SU-128/A dual combining glass head-up display and CP-1450/A display computer, IP-1318/A CRT Kaiser digital display indicator, and (RAF aircraft only) Ferranti moving map display. Litton AN/ALR-67(V)2 fore/aft looking radar warning receiver, and Goodyear AN/ALE-39 flare/chaff dispenser (in lower rear fuselage) (Tracor AN/ALE-40 in GR. Mk 5). Primary weapon delivery sensor system for AV-8B and GR.Mk 5 is the Hughes Aircraft AN/ASB-19(V)2 or (V)3 Angle Rate Bombing Set, mounted in the nose and comprising a dual-mode (TV and laser) target seeker/tracker. System functions in conjunction with Control Data Corporation CP-1429/AYK-14(V) mission computer (Computing Devices ACCS 2000 in GR. Mk 5), the Lear Siegler AN/AYQ-13 stores management system, the display computer, the head-up display, and the digital display indicator. Flight controls that interface with the reaction control system are provided by the Honeywell AN/ASW-46(V)2 stability augmentation and attitude hold system currently being updated to the high AOA capable configuration. RAF aircraft have an accident data recorder. Backup standby mechanical instrumentation includes airspeed indicator, altimeter, angle of attack indicator, attitude indicator, cabin pressure altitude indicator, clock, flap position indicator, horizontal situation indicator, standby compass, turn and slip indicator, and vertical speed indicator. Other equipment includes anti-collision, approach, formation, in-flight refuelling, landing gear position, auxiliary exterior lights, and console, instrument panel and other internal lighting.

ARMAMENT AND OPERATIONAL EQUIPMENT: Two underfuselage packs, mounting on the port side a five-barrel 25 mm cannon based on the General Electric GAU-12/U, and a 300 round container on the starboard side, in the AV-8B; or two 25 mm Royal Ordnance Factories cannon with 200 rds (derived from the 30 mm Aden) in the GR. Mk 5. Single 562 kg (1,240 lb) stores mount on fuselage centreline, between gun packs. Three stores stations under each wing on AV-8B, stressed for loads of up to 1,048 kg (2,310 lb) inboard, 635 kg (1,400 lb) on the intermediate stations, and 286 kg (630 lb) outboard. The four inner wing stations are 'wet', permitting the carriage of auxiliary fuel tanks. Including fuel, stores, weapons and ammunition, and water injection for the engine, the maximum useful load for vertical take-off is approximately 3,062 kg (6,750 lb), and for short take-off more than 7,710 kg (17,000 lb). Typical weapons include two or four AIM-9L Sidewinder, Magic or AGM-65E Maverick missiles; up to sixteen 500 lb general purpose bombs, 12 cluster bombs, ten Paveway laser guided bombs, eight fire bombs, ten rocket pods, or (in addition to the underfuselage gun packs) two underwing gun pods. Chaff/flare dispenser housings under fuselage. ML Aviation BRU-36/A bomb release units standard on all versions. Provision for AN/ALQ-164 defensive ECM pod on centreline pylon. RAF aircraft have two additional underwing weapon stations, for Sidewinder air-to-air missiles, ahead of the outrigger wheel fairings; a Marconi Defence Systems Zeus internal ECM system comprising an advanced radar warning receiver, and a multi-mode jammer with a Northrop RF transmitter; and provision for a nose mounted infra-red reconnaissance sensor.

DIMENSIONS, EXTERNAL:

Wing span	9.25 m (30 ft 4 in)
Wing aspect ratio	4.0
Length overall (flying attitude):	
AV-8B	14.12 m (46 ft 4 in)
TAV-8B	15.32 m (50 ft 3 in)
Height overall	3.55 m (11 ft 7¾ in)
Tailplane span	4.24 m (13 ft 11 in)
Outrigger wheel track	5.18 m (17 ft 0 in)

AREAS:

Wings, excl LERX, gross	21.37 m² (230 sq ft)
LERX (total)	0.81 m² (8.7 sq ft)
Ailerons (total)	1.15 m² (12.4 sq ft)
Trailing-edge flaps (total)	2.88 m² (31.0 sq ft)
Ventral fixed strakes (total)	0.51 m² (5.5 sq ft)
Ventral retractable fence (LIDs)	0.24 m² (2.6 sq ft)
Ventral airbrake	0.42 m² (4.5 sq ft)
Fin	2.47 m² (26.6 sq ft)
Rudder, excl tab	0.49 m² (5.3 sq ft)
Tailplane	4.51 m² (48.5 sq ft)

WEIGHTS (single-seaters, except where indicated):

Operating weight empty (incl pilot and unused fuel):	
AV-8B	5,936 kg (13,086 lb)
GR. Mk 5	6,343 kg (13,984 lb)
TAV-8B	6,451 kg (14,223 lb)
Max fuel: internal only	3,519 kg (7,759 lb)
internal and external	7,180 kg (15,829 lb)
Max external stores	4,173 kg (9,200 lb)
Basic flight design gross weight for 7*g* operation	10,410 kg (22,950 lb)
Max T-O weight:	
405 m (1,330 ft) STO	14,061 kg (31,000 lb)
S/L VTO, ISA	8,595 kg (18,950 lb)
S/L VTO, 32°C	8,142 kg (17,950 lb)
Design max landing weight	11,340 kg (25,000 lb)
Max vertical landing weight	8,459 kg (18,650 lb)

PERFORMANCE:

Max Mach number in level flight:	
at S/L	0.87 (575 knots; 1,065 km/h; 661 mph)
at altitude	0.91
STOL T-O run at max T-O weight:	
ISA	405 m (1,330 ft)
32°C	518 m (1,700 ft)
Operational radius with external loads shown:	
short T-O (366 m; 1,200 ft), twelve Mk 82 Snakeye bombs, internal fuel, 1 h loiter	90 nm (167 km; 103 miles)
hi-lo-hi, short T-O (366 m; 1,200 ft), seven Mk 82 Snakeye bombs, external fuel tanks, no loiter (payload of 1,814 kg; 4,000 lb)	480 nm (889 km; 553 miles)
deck launch intercept mission, two AIM-9 missiles and two external fuel tanks	627 nm (1,162 km; 722 miles)
Unrefuelled ferry range, with four 300 US gallon external tanks:	
tanks retained	1,750 nm (3,243 km; 2,015 miles)
tanks dropped	2,100 nm (3,891 km; 2,418 miles)
Combat air patrol endurance at 100 nm (185 km; 115 miles) from base	3 h
g limits	+7/–3

MCDONNELL DOUGLAS/BRITISH AEROSPACE HARRIER II PLUS

Plans for a further upgrade of the basic Harrier design took a significant step forward at the 1987 Paris Air Show, when the two partners announced their intention to develop a version powered by a 111.2 kN (25,000 lb) thrust class Pegasus 11-61 (F402-RR-408) engine and fitted with a Hughes APG-65 or Ferranti Blue Vixen pulse-Doppler radar. Such a version would be able to deploy AMRAAM or other BVR (beyond visual range) missiles in the air defence role, or Sea Eagle or Harpoon sea skimming missiles in anti-shipping configuration. Initial deliveries of the F402-RR-408 are to begin in 1990 for the lead customer, the USMC. Modification kits will also be available for conversion of current engines.

MCDONNELL DOUGLAS/BRITISH AEROSPACE T-45A

US Navy designation: T-45A Goshawk

On 18 November 1981 the British Aerospace Hawk (see UK section) was selected, out of six designs considered, as winner of the US Navy's VTXTS competition for an undergraduate jet pilot trainer, in which role it is to replace the T-2C Buckeye and TA-4J Skyhawk. The complete VTXTS system, since renamed T45TS (T-45 Training System), consists of modified Hawk aircraft (designated T-45A Goshawk) together with academic materials, flight simulators, computer aided training devices, a training integration system, and contractor operated logistics support.

The original plan for the US Navy to acquire an initial 54 'dry' (land based) T-45Bs followed by 253 carrier-capable 'wet' T-45As was amended in FY 1984 to eliminate the interim B model in favour of an 'all-wet' fleet of T-45As, and current plans are to acquire a total of 300 production examples of this version. To meet USN specifications, the T-45A has new main and nose landing gear, an arrester hook, and airframe strengthening to enable it to operate from aircraft carriers. The nose gear is twin-wheel, has a catapult launch bar/nosewheel tow, is steerable, and requires a slightly deeper nose contour to accommodate it when retracted. Two smaller fuselage-side airbrakes replace the single large underfuselage airbrake of the standard Hawk. The latter's twin ventral strakes are replaced by a single ventral surface, which is used also as a fairing for the arrester hook. Avionics and cockpit displays are modified for carrier-compatible operations, and weapons delivery capability for advanced training is incorporated. Douglas Aircraft Company manufactures the front fuselage at Long

US Navy T-45A Goshawk derivative of the BAe Hawk taking off for its first flight

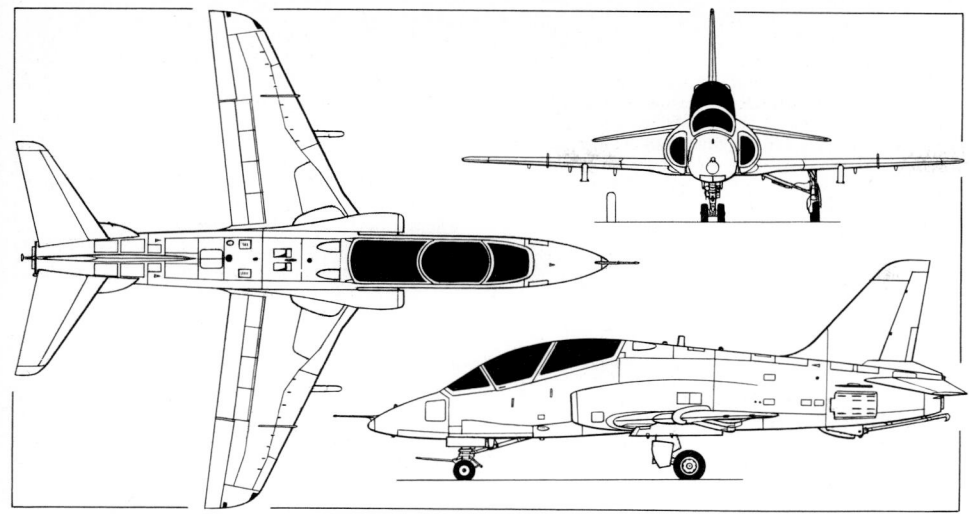

McDonnell Douglas/BAe T-45A Goshawk tandem two-seat trainer for the US Navy *(Pilot Press)*

Beach, California, where the two flying pre-production Goshawks were assembled; final assembly and flight testing of production T-45As will be undertaken at US Air Force Plant 42, Palmdale, California. British Aerospace is principal T-45A subcontractor, its Kingston, Brough, Samlesbury and Hamble factories being responsible for the wings, centre and rear fuselage, tail surfaces, windscreen, canopy and flight controls. Rolls-Royce (Derby) supplies the Adour turbofan engines; Honeywell manufactures the flight simulators at Reston, Virginia.

The T45TS programme entered the full scale engineering development (FSED) phase in October 1984, and a contract fixing prices for the first three production lots (including 60 T-45A aircraft and 15 flight simulators during FYs 1988-90) was signed on 16 May 1986. Twelve production T-45As are included in the FY 1988 Lot 1 contract, awarded on 26 January 1988. The FY 1989 budget included $517 million for 24 more Goshawks and associated equipment. Production deliveries are due to begin in October 1989, and production is scheduled to reach a peak of 48 a year in 1993, with completion of all 302 aircraft in 1997.

Drop tests of a non-flying airframe began in early 1988, and a second airframe, for fatigue testing, is being completed at BAe's Brough factory. The first of the two pre-production T-45As (BuAer number 162787), construction of which had started in February 1986, was rolled out at Long Beach on 16 March 1988. It made its first flight on 16 April, and was due to be joined in the 19-month test programme by the second example in June 1988. Main flight testing will be conducted from the McDonnell Douglas facility in Yuma, Arizona, and the US Naval Air Test Center at Patuxent River, Maryland.

The T45TS is scheduled to become operational initially, with the first 12 Goshawks and their associated equipment, in the fourth quarter of 1990 at Kingsville Naval Air Station, Texas. The system will eventually be based also at NAS Chase Field, Texas, and NAS Meridian, Mississippi. The complete programme will involve 300 production aircraft, 32 flight simulators, 49 computer aided instructional devices, four training integration system mainframes and 200 terminals, as well as academic materials, to allow the training of up to 600 pilots a year. Introduction of the Goshawk system is expected to meet the USN's training

requirements with 42 per cent fewer aircraft than at present, 25 per cent fewer flight hours, and 46 per cent fewer personnel, as well as saving up to 182 million litres (48 million US gallons; 40 million Imp gallons) of fuel per year.

TYPE: Two-seat basic and advanced jet trainer.

WINGS: Similar to BAe Hawk, but redesigned and strengthened to accommodate modified main landing gear. Increased aileron travel compared with standard Hawk, and trailing-edge flaps have full span flap vanes.

FUSELAGE: Similar to BAe Hawk, but with large metal airbrake on each side of rear fuselage aft of wing, actuated by Dowty hydraulic jacks. Deeper and wider nose, to accommodate modified nosewheel unit. Under-fuselage arrester hook, deployable 20° to each side of longitudinal axis.

TAIL UNIT: Similar to BAe Hawk, but with single ventral fin/fairing at arrester hook attachment point. Forward of each tailplane leading-edge root is a small curved horizontal surface (US Navy 'smurf', or side mounted unit root fin) to eliminate pitch-down during low-speed flaps-down/gear-up manoeuvres.

LANDING GEAR: Wide-track hydraulically retractable tricycle type, stressed for vertical landing forces of up to 7.32 m (24 ft)/s. Single wheel and long-stroke oleo (increased from 28 cm; 11 in of standard Hawk to 48 cm; 19 in) on each main unit; twin-wheel steerable nose unit. Articulated main gear, by AP Precision Hydraulics, is of levered suspension (trailing arm) type with a folding side-stay. Cleveland Pneumatic nose gear, with Sterer steering system. Main units retract inward into wing, forward of front spar; nose unit retracts forward. All wheel doors are sequenced to close after gear lowering; inboard mainwheel doors are bulged to accommodate larger trailing arm and tyres. Goodrich wheels, tyres and brakes. Mainwheel tyres size 24 × 7.7-10, pressure 20.69 bars (300 lb/sq in); 16 in diameter nosewheels have size 19 × 5.25-10 tyres, pressure 22.06 bars (320 lb/sq in). Hydraulic multi-disc mainwheel brakes with Dunlop adaptive anti-skid system.

POWER PLANT: One 24.24 kN (5,450 lb st) Rolls-Royce Turbomeca F405-RR-400L (Adour Mk 861-49) non-afterburning turbofan. Air intakes and engine starting as described for BAe Hawk. Fuel system similar to BAe

Hawk, but with revision for carrier operation. Capacities are 840 litres (222 US gallons; 185 Imp gallons) in fuselage bag tank and 863 litres (228 US gallons; 190 Imp gallons) in integral wing tank, giving total internal capacity of 1,703 litres (450 US gallons; 375 Imp gallons). Provision for carrying one 591 litre (156 US gallon; 130 Imp gallon) drop tank on each underwing pylon.

ACCOMMODATION: Similar to BAe Hawk, except that ejection seats are of Martin-Baker Mk 14 NACES (Navy aircrew common ejection seat) zero/zero rocket assisted type.

SYSTEMS: Air-conditioning and pressurisation systems, using engine bleed air. Duplicated hydraulic systems, each 207 bars (3,000 lb/sq in), for actuation of control jacks, flaps, airbrakes, landing gear, arrester hook and anti-skid wheel brakes. No. 1 system has a flow rate of 36.4 litres (9.6 US gallons; 8.0 Imp gallons)/min, No. 2 system a rate of 22.7 litres (6.0 US gallons; 5.0 Imp gallons)/min. Reservoirs are nitrogen pressurised at 2.75-5.5 bars (40-80 lb/sq in). Hydraulic accumulator for emergency operation of wheel brakes. Pop-up Dowty Rotol ram air turbine in upper rear fuselage provides emergency hydraulic power for flying controls in the event of an engine or No. 2 pump failure. No pneumatic system. DC electrical power from single brushless generator, with two static inverters to provide AC power and two batteries for standby power. Onboard oxygen generating system (OBOGS).

AVIONICS: AN/ARN-182 UHF/VHF com radios and AN/ARN-194 VOR/ILS by Rockwell Collins, Honeywell AN/APN-194 radio altimeter, Bendix APX-100 IFF, Sierra AN/ARN-136A Tacan, US Navy AN/USN-2 standard attitude and heading reference system (SAHRS), Smiths Industries Mini-HUD (front cockpit), Racal Acoustics avionics/com management system, GEC Avionics yaw damper computer, Electro Dynamics airborne data recorder.

ARMAMENT: No built-in armament. Single pylon under each wing for carriage of practice multiple bomb rack or auxiliary fuel tank. Provision also for carrying single stores pod on fuselage centreline. CAI Industries gunsight in rear cockpit.

DIMENSIONS: As for two-seat BAe Hawk except:
Length: overall, incl nose probe	11.97 m (39 ft 3⅛ in)
fuselage	10.89 m (35 ft 9 in)
Height overall	4.09 m (13 ft 5 in)
Wheel track (c/l of shock struts)	3.90 m (12 ft 9½ in)
Wheelbase	4.29 m (14 ft 1 in)

AREAS: As for BAe Hawk except:
Airbrakes (total)	0.79 m² (8.55 sq ft)

WEIGHTS:
Weight empty	4,261 kg (9,394 lb)
Internal fuel	1,312 kg (2,893 lb)
Max T-O weight	5,787 kg (12,758 lb)

PERFORMANCE (estimated at max T-O weight):
Design limit diving speed at 1,000 m (3,280 ft)	
	610 knots (1,130 km/h; 702 mph)
Max Mach number in dive	1.2
Max level speed at 2,440 m (8,000 ft)	
	538 knots (997 km/h; 620 mph)
Max level Mach number at 9.150 m (30,000 ft)	0.85
Max rate of climb at S/L	2,128 m (6,982 ft)/min
Time to 9,150 m (30,000 ft), 'clean'	7 min 12 s
Service ceiling	12,875 m (42,250 ft)
T-O to 15 m (50 ft)	1,141 m (3,744 ft)
Landing from 15 m (50 ft)	1,189 m (3,900 ft)
Ferry range, internal fuel only	
	1,000 nm (1,850 km; 1,150 miles)
g limits	+7.33/-3

MPC-75
MPC-75 GmbH

PARTICIPATING COMPANIES:

Messerschmitt-Bölkow-Blohm (Transport Aircraft Group), Postfach 950109, 2103 Hamburg 95, Federal Republic of Germany
Telephone: (040) 7437 1
Telex: 21950-0 MBBH D

China National Aero-Technology Import and Export Corporation, 5 Liang Guo Chang Road, East City District (PO Box 1671), Beijing, People's Republic of China
Telephone: 44 5831
Telex: 22318 AEROT CN

MBB/CATIC MPC 75

MBB and CATIC signed a memorandum of understanding on 3 October 1985 to explore together the possible development of a 60/85-seat regional transport aircraft. On 6 June 1986 the partnership was taken a stage further with the signing of an agreement to set up a joint office in Hamburg tasked with pursuing the feasibility study and co-ordinating contacts with potential customers and equipment suppliers. The same day, MBB also signed an MoU with General Electric, under which the German and US companies will explore the advantages of powering such an aircraft with two unducted fan (UDF) engines. In May

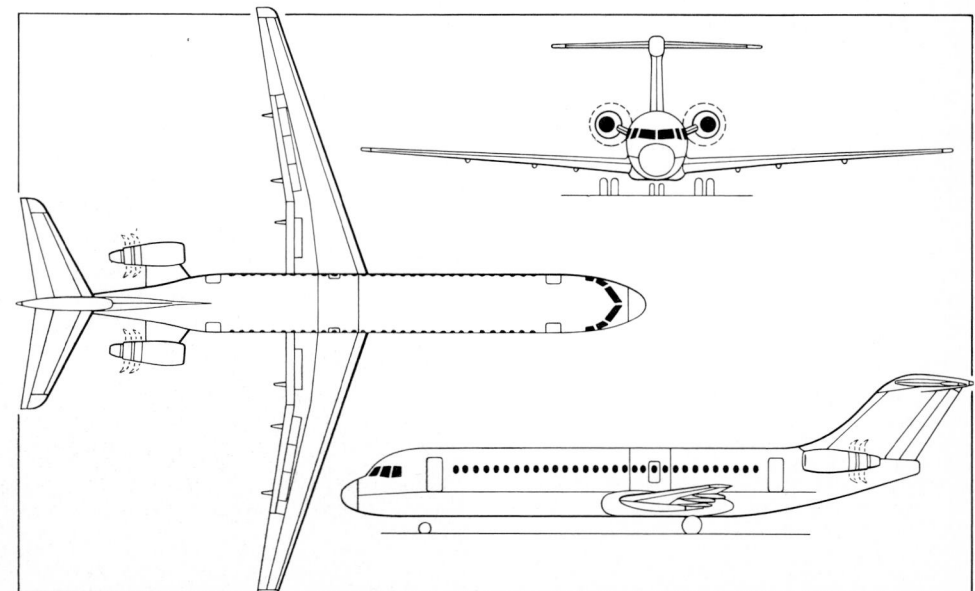

Provisional drawing of the MBB/CATIC MPC 75 twin-propfan 80-seat transport *(Jane's/Mike Keep)*

1988 an MoU was signed by MBB and Allison, to explore possibilities of a version powered by a derivative of that company's T406 propfan. In the same month, MBB and CATIC set up a separate company in Hamburg, MPC-75 GmbH, to manage the complete programme.

MBB is programme leader; the Chinese industrial partner is the Xian Aircraft Company. First flight is envisaged for late 1994, with series production beginning in 1996.

The following data, and the accompanying three-view drawing, reflect the MPC 75 as envisaged in mid-1988:

POWER PLANT: Two General Electric UDF or Allison UHB propfan engines, pylon mounted on sides of rear fuselage.

ACCOMMODATION: Typical mixed class layout for 69 passengers, with nine seats three-abreast at 91 cm (36 in) and 60 four-abreast at 81 cm (32 in) pitch; or 76 in an all-economy layout; or up to 84 in single-class high-density configuration. Seats for three cabin attendants. Galley and toilet at front of cabin, second galley and toilet at rear, and wardrobes amidships.

DIMENSIONS, EXTERNAL:

Wing span	28.594 m (93 ft 9¾ in)
Wing aspect ratio	10.9
Length overall	32.046 m (105 ft 1¾ in)
Height overall	7.55 m (24 ft 9¼ in)

AREA:

Wings, gross	75.0 m² (807.3 sq ft)

WEIGHTS:

Operating weight empty	18,825 kg (41,502 lb)
Max T-O weight	30,000 kg (66,140 lb)

PERFORMANCE (estimated):

Max operating Mach number at 10,670 m (35,000 ft)	0.75
Max operating altitude (152 m; 500 ft/min rate of climb, Mach 0.70)	10,970 m (36,000 ft)
T-O run (S/L, ISA) at max T-O weight	1,585 m (5,200 ft)
Landing run (S/L) at typical landing weight	1,250 m (4,100 ft)
Range with 76 passengers, with reserves	1,500 nm (2,780 km; 1,727 miles)

NH 90

PROGRAMME GENERAL CO-ORDINATOR: Gilbert Beziac (Aérospatiale), BP 13, 13725 Marignane Cédex, France
Telephone: (42) 85 61 95
Telex: AISPA 410975 F

Following a September 1985 memorandum of understanding signed by the defence ministers of France, UK, Germany, Italy and Netherlands, a 14-month feasibility/pre-definition study was established, from which a new helicopter was proposed for the armed services of these countries, known as the NH 90 (NATO Helicopter for the '90s). British participation was terminated by the UK government in April 1987.

One manufacturer from each country (Aérospatiale, MBB, Agusta and Fokker) make up the present industrial group, which has established a common basic configuration for the two major versions: an **NFH 90** (NATO frigate helicopter) for ASW, surface attack and SAR duties, and a land based tactical transport, SAR and special missions version known as the **TTH 90**. Estimated total requirements by the armed forces of the participating nations are 200 and 400 respectively; this total could be doubled if civil and export potential is realised. A multi-national team manages the NH 90 programme, with Aérospatiale as general co-ordinator.

The initial design phase was approved in December 1986, and a second MoU signed in September 1987 governs the definition of the complete weapons system; this was due to be completed in June 1988. First flight is envisaged for mid-1992, with initial deliveries following in 1996.

The leading technology features of the helicopter have been defined as: mission weights between 7,500 and 8,500 kg (16,535-18,739 lb), according to version; twin 1,566 kW (2,100 shp) Rolls-Royce Turbomeca RTM 322-01/2 or 1,506 kW (2,020 shp) General Electric CT7-6 turboshafts; four-blade main and tail rotors, utilising composite blades of advanced aerofoil sections and tip planform; titanium main rotor hub with elastomeric bearings; a bearingless tail rotor; cabin space for 20 commandos, or a 2 ton tactical vehicle loaded via a rear ramp, with a high level of composites utilised in the fuselage structure; retractable crashworthy tricycle landing gear; automatic folding of main rotor blades and tail pylon in naval version; quadruplex fly by wire controls, with multi-cycle blade pitch control to minimise vibration; an APU; modern avionics with dual MIL-1553B digital databus; instrument panel with multi-function colour CRT displays; design features for low vulnerability and detectability; reduced maintenance requirements; and all-weather, day/night operability within temperature range of −40°C to +50°C.

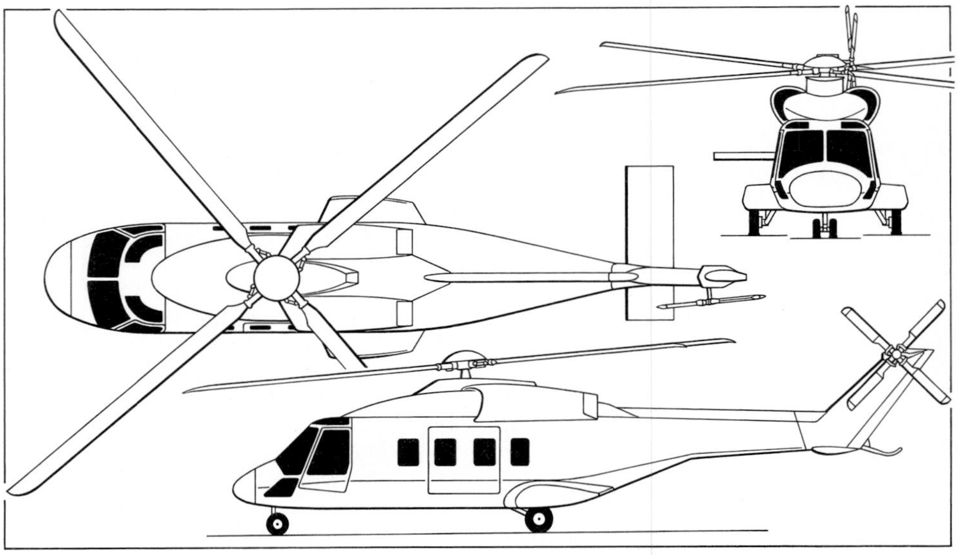

Provisional three-view of NFH 90 NATO frigate helicopter *(Jane's/Mike Keep)*

The naval variant will offer autonomy in ASW, ASV and anti-air warfare support operations, and will be designed for an all-weather, severe ship-motion environment. The payload capacity will meet a wide range of national requirements for such additional duties as vertical replenishment, SAR and personnel transport. The army/air force variant will offer a defensive weapons suite and low pilot workload.

The following data are provisional:

DIMENSIONS, EXTERNAL:

Main rotor diameter	16.00 m (52 ft 6 in)
Tail rotor diameter	3.20 m (10 ft 6 in)
Length overall, rotors turning	19.40 m (63 ft 7¾ in)
Length of fuselage, tail rotor static	16.00 m (52 ft 6 in)
Length folded: NFH	13.20 m (43 ft 3¾ in)
Height folded: NFH	4.05 m (13 ft 3½ in)
Wheel track	3.20 m (10 ft 6 in)
Wheelbase	6.03 m (19 ft 9½ in)

DIMENSIONS, INTERNAL:

Cabin: Length, excl rear ramp	3.80 m (12 ft 5¾ in)
Max width	2.12 m (6 ft 11½ in)
Max height	1.55 m (5 ft 1 in)
Volume	11.80 m³ (416.7 cu ft)

WEIGHTS:

Weight empty (basic)	approx 4,000 kg (8,818 lb)
Payload: TTH	2,000 kg (4,409 lb)
Max T-O weight: TTH	8,000 kg (17,637 lb)
NFH	8,500 kg (18,739 lb)

PERFORMANCE (estimated):

Max level speed: both	160 knots (297 km/h; 184 mph)
Max cruising speed: both	140 knots (259 km/h; 161 mph)
Max vertical rate of climb at S/L, ISA, AUW of 8,000 kg (17,637 lb)	462 m (1,515 ft)/min
Hovering ceiling OGE (ISA + 20°C)	3,500 m (11,485 ft)
Range (TTH): standard fuel	540 nm (1,000 km; 620 miles)
with auxiliary tanks	755 nm (1,400 km; 870 miles)
Endurance: NFH	approx 4 h
TTH	approx 2 h 30 min

NTT

NEW TRANSPORT TECHNOLOGIES LTD

Postfach 801304, 8000 Munich 80, Federal Republic of Germany
Telephone: (089) 6000 3444
Telex: 5287-740 MBB D

It was announced in April 1984 that MBB (West Germany) and IPTN (Indonesia) had signed an agreement to carry out a market development study (still in progress in 1988) for a small, four-seat light helicopter to be known as the BN-109. A joint company, NTT, with headquarters in Munich, was set up, in which MBB and IPTN each hold 50 per cent of the shares.

NTT BN-109

The BN-109 is being designed for a variety of roles which include light transport, surveillance, search and rescue, casualty evacuation, police patrol and training. It will have an advanced three-blade main and two-blade tail rotor system, and will be powered by an engine in the 230-260 kW (308-348 hp) range. Certification will be under FAR Pt 27.

The following provisional data have been released:

TYPE: Four-seat multi-purpose light helicopter.

ROTOR SYSTEM AND DRIVE: Three-blade main and two-blade tail rotor, turning at 473 and 2,865 rpm respectively. Three-stage main gearbox. Mechanical controls, without hydraulics. Main rotor/engine rpm ratio 16.9:1.

AIRFRAME: Of conventional pod and boom configuration (see accompanying illustration), with skid landing gear. Two hinged doors on each side of cabin.

POWER PLANT: One Porsche motorcar engine (TAG modification), derated to 230 kW (308 hp), or an Allison

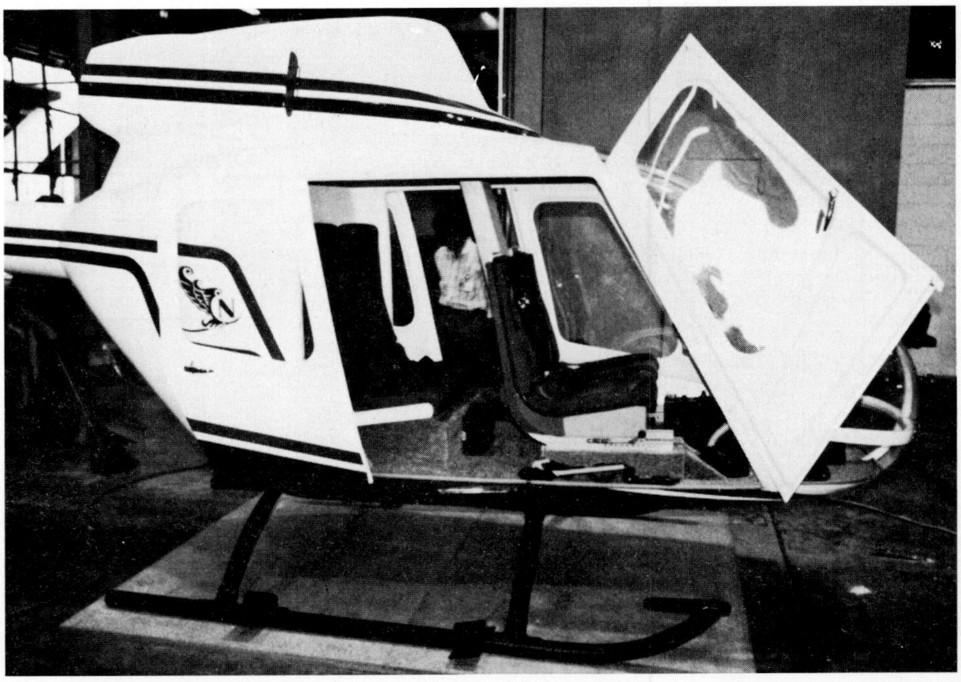

Full size mockup of the proposed NTT BN-109, displayed by IPTN at Jakarta in August 1985

turboshaft of 260 kW (348 shp). (Engine studies still in progress in 1988.) Fuel tank under cabin floor.

ACCOMMODATION: Cabin space for pilot, three passengers and up to 30 kg (66 lb) of baggage.

DIMENSIONS, EXTERNAL:

Main rotor diameter	8.40 m (27 ft 6¾ in)
Main rotor blade chord	0.27 m (10.6 in)
Tail rotor diameter	1.40 m (4 ft 7 in)

Length overall, excl rotors	7.41 m (24 ft 3¾ in)
Fuselage: Max width	1.15 m (3 ft 9¼ in)

AREAS:

Main rotor disc	55.42 m² (596.5 sq ft)
Tail rotor disc	1.54 m² (16.57 sq ft)

WEIGHTS:

Weight empty	640 kg (1,411 lb)

Fuel weight	190 kg (419 lb)
Max T-O weight	1,200 kg (2,645 lb)

PERFORMANCE (estimated):

Max cruising speed at S/L	108 knots (200 km/h; 124 mph)
Hovering ceiling OGE (ISA + 25°C)	2,500 m (8,200 ft)
Range with max fuel	264 nm (490 km; 304 miles)

PANAVIA

PANAVIA AIRCRAFT GmbH

8 Munich 86, Postfach 860629, Arabellastrasse 16, Federal Republic of Germany

Telephone: (089) 92171
Telex: 05 29 825

Panavia was formed on 26 March 1969 to design, develop and produce an all-weather combat aircraft for the air forces of the United Kingdom, the Federal Republic of Germany and Italy, and the Federal German Navy. The name Tornado for this aircraft was adopted officially in March 1976. This programme is one of the largest European industrial programmes ever undertaken. The three component companies of Panavia are British Aerospace PLC (42.5% participation), MBB (42.5%) and Aeritalia (15%).

The Federal German, British and Italian governments set up a joint organisation known as NAMMO (NATO MRCA Management and production Organisation). This has its executive agency NAMMA (NATO MRCA Management Agency) in the same building as Panavia, in Munich.

On 29 July 1976 the three governments signed a memorandum of understanding for the production of 809 Tornados, which are being manufactured under six successive contracts for a total of 805 aircraft, plus four pre-series Tornados brought up to production standard. Subsequent contracts have increased the total of production aircraft to 937, of which more than 700 had been delivered by May 1988.

PANAVIA TORNADO IDS

RAF designation: Tornado GR. Mk 1

The Tornado is intended to fulfil six major requirements, some of which are shared by more than one of the partners. These are: close air support/battlefield interdiction; interdiction/counter air strike; air superiority; interception/air defence; naval strike; and reconnaissance. Design was completed in August 1972. Nine flying prototypes were built—four in the UK, three in West Germany and two in Italy. The first prototype made its initial flight in West Germany on 14 August 1974. Details of the prototypes can be found in the 1978-79 and earlier editions of *Jane's*, and of the six pre-series Tornados in the 1980-81 and earlier editions. The first British production Tornado made its initial flight on 10 July 1979, the first West German on 27 July 1979, and the first Italian on 25 September 1981.

The total of 937 production Tornados ordered by Spring 1988 comprises 705 of the IDS (interdictor strike) version for the air forces of Great Britain (228), West Germany (211), Italy (99), Jordan (8) and Saudi Arabia (48), and for the West German Navy (111); 35 of the ECR (electronic combat and reconnaissance) version, described separately, for the German Air Force; and 197 examples of the ADV (air defence variant, also described separately) for the RAF (165), Saudi Arabia (24) and Oman (8). In addition, four of the early IDS pre-series batch are being brought up to production standard (one for Great Britain, two for Germany, one for Italy). Of the aircraft for Great Britain, West Germany and Italy, 163 will be dual control trainers with full operational capability. Export deliveries to other

Trials installation of sensors for the RAF's Tornado reconnaissance system: windows for sidelooking IR in sides of fuselage, and linescan aperture beneath

countries began in March 1986 with the first four IDS aircraft for Saudi Arabia.

The Tri-national Tornado Training Establishment (TTTE) at RAF Cottesmore received 50 Tornados in 1981-82. Weapons training is carried out at Tornado Weapons Conversion Units (TWCU) at RAF Honington (UK) and JaboG 38 at Jever (West Germany), and by the 154° Gruppo of the Italian Air Force at Brescia-Ghedi.

The RAF's planned total of 229 Tornados of the GR. Mk 1 interdictor/strike version includes at least 48 trainers. Squadron deliveries began on 6 January 1982 to No. IX Squadron at RAF Honington, Suffolk, which became Strike Command's first operational Tornado squadron on 1 June 1982. It now also equips Nos. 27 and 617 at Marham (UK), Nos. XV, 16 and 20 at Laarbruch (West Germany), and Nos. 14, 17 and 31 at Brüggen (Germany). No. IX transferred to Brüggen in October 1986 to become the seventh Tornado GR. Mk 1 strike/attack squadron with RAF Germany; the eighth RAFG Tornado squadron, a reconnaissance squadron due to form in late 1988, is No. 2 at Laarbruch. The RAF camera-less reconnaissance version of Tornado is identifiable by a small underbelly blister fairing, immediately behind the laser rangefinder pod, containing a BAe sideways looking infra-red (SLIR) system, BAe Linescan 4000 infra-red surveillance system and Computing Devices Company signal processing and video recording system. In 1984, RAF GR. Mk 1s based in West Germany began to be modified to carry tactical nuclear weapons; they are also the first RAF Tornados to be equipped with the Hunting JP 233 anti-airfield weapon. In 1985, an initial technology demonstration was completed by an RAF Tornado equipped with BAe's Terprom (terrain profile matching) self-contained navigation system, and a contract was awarded to GEC Avionics for a night vision FLIR system for the GR. Mk 1. The FLIR sensor is installed in the undernose fairing used currently to house a laser rangefinder.

Luftwaffe IDS Tornados equipped eight squadrons by the Summer of 1988: two each with JaboG 31 at Nörvenich, JaboG 32 at Lechfeld, JaboG 33 at Büchel and JaboG 34 at Memmingen. Those for the Federal German Navy are equipped for strike missions against sea and coastal targets, and for reconnaissance. Two squadrons of IDS Tornados are in service with Marinefliegergeschwader 1 at Jagel, and two with MFG 2 at Eggebeck.

The 100 Italian Air Force Tornados (99 production aircraft plus the No. 14 pre-series Tornado brought up to production standard) include 54 to replace F/RF-104G aircraft in the air superiority, ground attack and reconnaissance roles. Of the remainder, 34 will be kept in reserve and 12 equipped as dual control trainers. First unit was the 154° Gruppo (Squadron) of 6° Stormo (Wing) at Brescia-Ghedi, which received its first Tornados in August 1982. By 1988 the Kormoran anti-shipping 156° Gruppo (36° Stormo) at Gioia del Colle (Bari), and the 155° Gruppo at Ghedi, had also been equipped.

By 1988, RAF Squadrons Nos. IX, 27 and 617 were SACEUR declared, RAF Germany Squadrons Nos. XV and 16 were strike declared, and the six squadrons at German MFG. 1 and JaboGs 31, 32 and 33 were NATO assigned. The first operational batch of MW-1 weapons systems had been delivered to JaboG 31; and German Tornados had been cleared for in-flight refuelling by USAF KC-10A and KC-135 tanker aircraft.

Integration of HARM, ALARM, Kormoran 1/2 and Maverick missiles was continuing in 1988, including integration of a common missile control unit. Radar improvement and MW-1 weapon dispenser flight trials were also continuing, and an enhanced flight control system has entered flight test. Testing of the digital engine control unit (DECU) has been completed.

The following details apply to the basic IDS production version:

TYPE: Twin-engined all-weather multi-purpose combat aircraft.

WINGS: Cantilever shoulder-wing monoplane. All-metal wings, of variable geometry, the outer panels having a leading-edge sweep of 25° in the fully forward position and 67° when fully swept. Fixed inboard portions have a leading-edge sweep of 60°. Wing carry-through box is of electron-beam-welded titanium alloy; majority of remaining wing structure is of aluminium alloy, with integrally stiffened skin. There is a Krueger flap on the leading-edge of each wing glove box. The wings each pivot hydraulically, on Teflon plated bearings, from a point in the centre-section just outboard of the fuselage. The root of the outer wing mates with the pivot pin through attachment members made of titanium alloy and fixed to the upper and lower light alloy panels of the outer wing box, and a so-called 'round rib', also of titanium alloy, transmitting the normal aerodynamic force. Sweep actuators are of the ballscrew type, with hydraulic motor drive. In the event of wing sweep failure, the aircraft can land safely with the wings fully swept. High-lift devices on the outer wings include full span leading-edge slats (three sections on each side), full span double-slotted fixed-vane trailing-edge flaps (four sections each side), and spoilers (two on upper surface on each side). Spoilers give

Two Panavia Tornado IDS aircraft of the Royal Saudi Air Force

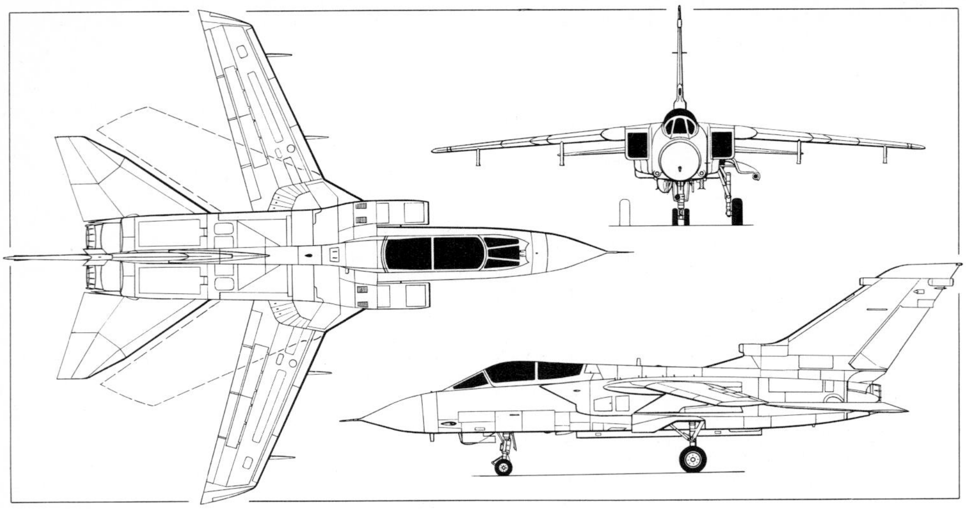

Panavia Tornado IDS multi-role combat aircraft *(Pilot Press)*

augmented roll control at unswept and intermediate wing positions at low speed, and also act as lift dumpers after touchdown. All flying control surfaces actuated by electrically controlled tandem hydraulic jacks. No ailerons. Entire outer wings, including control surfaces, are Italian built, Aeritalia having prime responsibility for final assembly and production, assisted by Aermacchi, Aeronavali Venezia, Piaggio, Saca and SIAI-Marchetti as subcontractors. Microtecnica (Italy) is prime subcontractor for the wing sweep system.

FUSELAGE: Conventional all-metal semi-monocoque structure, mainly of aluminium alloy, built in three main sections. MBB is prime contractor for the centre fuselage section, including the engine air intake ducts and wing centre-section box and pivot mechanism. This task includes responsibility for the surface interface between the movable wing and the fixed portion, to ensure both a smooth and slender external contour and proper sealing against aerodynamic pressure over a range of wing sweep positions. The design uses fibre reinforced plastics in these areas, and an elastic seal between the outer wings and the fuselage sides. Responsibility for the front fuselage, including both cockpits, and for the rear fuselage, including the engine installation, is undertaken by BAe (Warton). Radar-transparent nosecone by AEG-Telefunken, assisted by Aeritalia and BAe, hinges sideways to starboard to provide access to ground mapping and terrain following radar antennae. Slice of fuselage immediately aft of nosecone also hinges sideways to starboard, to provide access to forward avionics bay and/or rear of radar. Door type airbrake on each side at top of rear fuselage.

TAIL UNIT: Cantilever all-metal structure, consisting of single sweptback two-spar fin and rudder, and low-set all-moving horizontal surfaces ('tailerons') which operate together for pitch control and differentially for roll control, assisted by use of the wing spoilers when the wings are not fully swept. Rudder and tailerons actuated by electrically controlled tandem hydraulic jacks. Passive ECM antenna fairing near top of fin. Ram air intake for heat exchanger at base of fin. Entire tail unit is the responsibility of BAe. Four tailerons of carbonfibre composite, 17 per cent lighter than the standard metal ones, have been developed by MBB and BAe. Two were for structural and fatigue testing; the other pair began flight testing on prototype P07 on 8 November 1982.

LANDING GEAR: Hydraulically retractable tricycle type, with forward retracting twin-wheel steerable nose unit. Single-wheel main units retract forward and upward into centre section of fuselage. Emergency extension system, using nitrogen gas pressure. Development and manufacture of the complete landing gear and associated hydraulics is headed by Dowty Rotol (UK). Dunlop aluminium alloy wheels, hydraulic multi-disc brakes and low-pressure tyres (to permit operation from soft, semi-prepared surfaces) and Goodyear anti-skid units. Mainwheel tyres size 30 × 11.50-14.5, Type VIII (24 or 26 ply); nosewheel tyres size 18 × 5.5, Type VIII (12 ply). Runway arrester hook beneath rear of fuselage.

POWER PLANT: Two Turbo-Union RB199-34R Mk 101 turbofans in initial production aircraft, each rated at more than 40.0 kN (9,000 lb st) dry and more than 71.2 kN (16,000 lb st) with afterburning, fitted with bucket type thrust reversers and installed in rear fuselage with downward opening doors for servicing and engine change. Mk 103 engines, offering approx 5 per cent more thrust, introduced on to production line from engine number 761 in May 1983; 100 modification kits ordered by RAF in 1983 to upgrade a number of Mk 101 engined aircraft to Mk 103 standard. (This retrofit continuing in 1988.) All integral fuel in multi-cell Uniroyal self-sealing integral fuselage tanks and/or wing box tanks, all fitted with press-in fuel sampling and water drain plugs, and all refuelled from a single-point NATO connector. Capacity of these tanks totals approx 6,090 litres (1,610 US gallons; 1,340 Imp gallons). Additional 551 litre (145.5 US gallon; 121 Imp gallon) tank in fin (on RAF aircraft only). Detachable and retractable in-flight refuelling probe can be mounted on starboard side of fuselage, adjacent to cockpit. System also designed to accept a buddy-to-buddy refuelling pack (at present used only by Federal German Navy). Provision for one or two drop tanks to be carried beneath fuselage (1,500 litres; 396 US gallons; 330 Imp gallons) and single tanks on the shoulder pylons and inboard underwing pylons (1,500 or 2,250 litres; 396 or 594 US gallons; 330 or 495 Imp gallons). Dowty Fuel Systems/Lucas/Microtecnica afterburning fuel control system. AEG-Telefunken intake de-icing system.

ACCOMMODATION: Crew of two on tandem Martin-Baker Mk 10A zero/zero ejection seats under Kopperschmidt/AIT one-piece canopy, which is hinged at rear and opens upward. Flat centre armoured windscreen panel and curved side panels, built by Lucas Aerospace, incorporate Sierracote electrically conductive heating film for windscreen anti-icing and demisting. Canopy (and windscreen in emergency) demisted by engine bleed air. Windscreen is hinged at front and can be opened forward and upward, allowing access to back of pilot's instrument panel. Seats provide safe escape at zero altitude and at speeds from zero up to 630 knots (1,166 km/h; 725 mph) IAS.

SYSTEMS: Cockpit air-conditioned and pressurised (max differential 0.36 bars; 5.25 lb/sq in) by Normalair-Garrett conventional air cycle system (with bootstrap cold air unit) using engine bleed air with ram air precooler, Marston intercooler, and Teddington temperature control system. Nordmicro/BAe/Microtecnica air intake control system, and Dowty Boulton Paul/Liebherr Aerotechnik engine intake ramp control actuators. Two independent hydraulic systems, each of 276 bars (4,000 lb/sq in pressure), are supplied from two separate, independently driven Vickers pumps, each mounted on an engine accessory gearbox. Each system is supplied from a separate bootstrap type reservoir. Systems provide fully duplicated power for primary flight control system, tailerons, rudder, flaps, slats, wing sweep, pitch Q-feel system, and refuelling probe. Left system also supplies power for Krueger flaps, inboard spoilers, port air intake ramps, canopy, and wheel brakes; right system for airbrakes, outboard spoilers, starboard air intake ramps, landing gear, nosewheel steering, and radar stabilisation and scanning. Main system includes Dowty accumulators and Teves power pack. Fairey Hydraulics system for actuation of spoilers, rudder and taileron control. Provision for reversion to single-engine drive of both systems, via a mechanical cross-connection between the two engine auxiliary gearboxes, in the event of a single engine failure. In the event of a double engine flameout, an emergency pump in No. 1 system has sufficient duration for re-entry into the engine cold relight boundary. Flying control circuits are protected from loss of fluid due to leaks in other circuits by isolating valves which shut off the utility circuits if the reservoir contents drop below a predetermined safety limit level. Electrical system consists of a 115/200V AC three-phase 400Hz constant frequency subsystem and a 28V DC subsystem. Power is generated by two automatically controlled oil-cooled brushless AC generators integrated with a constant speed drive unit and driven by the engines via an accessory gearbox. Normally, each engine drives its own accessory gearbox, but provision is also made for either engine to drive the opposite gearbox through a cross-drive system. In the event of a generator failure, the remaining unit can supply the total aircraft load. Both gearboxes and generators can be driven by APU when aircraft is on ground. The generators supply two main AC busbars and an AC essential busbar. DC power is provided from two fan-cooled TRUs (power being derived from the main AC system), these feeding power to two main DC busbars, one essential DC busbar and a battery busbar. Either TRU can supply total aircraft DC load. A fifth DC busbar is provided for maintenance purposes only. Battery is a rechargeable nickel-cadmium type, and provides power for basic flightline servicing and for starting APU. In the event of main electrical system or double TRU failure, it is connected automatically to the essential services busbar to supply essential electrical loads. Normalair-Garrett/Draegerwerk/OMI demand type oxygen system, using a 10 litre (2.6 US gallon; 2.2 Imp gallon) lox converter. Emergency oxygen system installed on each seat. KHD accessory drive gearboxes and Rotax/Lucas/Siemens integrated drive generator. GEC Avionics flow metering system. Eichweber fuel gauging system and Flight Refuelling flexible couplings. Graviner fire detection and extinguishing systems. Rotax contactors. Smiths engine speed and temperature indicators.

AVIONICS AND EQUIPMENT: Communications equipment includes Plessey PTR 1721 (UK and Italy) or Rohde und Schwarz (West Germany) UHF/VHF transceiver; AEG-Telefunken UHF/ADF (UK and West Germany only); SIT/Siemens emergency UHF with Rohde und Schwarz switch; BAe HF/SSB aerial tuning unit; Rohde und Schwarz (UK and West Germany) or Montedel (Italy) HF/SSB radio; Ultra communications control system; GEC Avionics central suppression unit (CSU); Epsylon voice recorder; Chelton UHF communications and landing system aerials.

Primary self-contained nav/attack system includes Texas Instruments multi-mode forward looking ground mapping radar; Ferranti FIN 1010 three-axis digital inertial navigation system (DINS) and combined radar display; Decca Type 72 Doppler radar system, with Kalman filtering of the Doppler and inertial inputs for extreme navigational accuracy; Microtecnica air data computer; Litef Spirit 3 central digital computer (64K initially, 128K on current production aircraft); Aeritalia radio/radar altimeter; Smiths/Teldix/OMI electronic head-up display with Davall camera; Ferranti nose mounted laser rangefinder and marked target seeker; GEC Avionics TV tabular display, produced in partnership with AEG and Selenia; Astronautics (USA) bearing distance and heading indicator and contour map display. Defensive equipment includes Siemens (West Germany) or Cossor SSR-3100 (UK and Saudi Arabia) IFF transponder; and Elettronica ARI 23284 radar warning receiver (being replaced in GR. Mk 1 from 1987 by MSDS Hermes RHWR).

Flight control system includes a GEC Avionics/Bodenseewerk triplex command stability augmentation system (CSAS), incorporating fly by wire and autostabilisation; GEC Avionics/Aeritalia autopilot and flight director (APFD), using two self-monitoring digital computers; GEC Avionics triplex transducer unit (TTU), with analog computing and sensor channels; GEC Avionics terrain following E-scope (TFE), produced in partnership with Selenia; Fairey/GEC Avionics quadruplex electro-hydraulic actuator; and Microtecnica air data set. The APFD provides preselected attitude, heading or barometric height hold, heading and track acquisition, and Mach number or airspeed hold with autothrottle. Flight director operates in parallel with, and can be used as backup for, the autopilot, as a duplex digital system with an extensive range of modes. Automatic approach, terrain following and radio height-holding modes are also available. Other instrumentation includes Smiths horizontal situation indicator, vertical speed indicator and standby altimeter; Lital standby attitude and heading reference system; SEL (with Setac) or (in UK aircraft) GEC Avionics AD2770 (without Setac) Tacan; Cossor CILS 75/76 ILS; Bodenseewerk attitude director indicator; Dornier System flight data recorder.

Overall responsibility for the avionics rests with Panavia, with EASAMS (UK) as the avionics prime contractor, and ESG (Germany) and SIA (Italy) as subcontractors.

ARMAMENT: Fixed armament comprises two 27 mm IWKA-Mauser cannon, one in each side of the lower forward fuselage, with 180 rds/gun. Other armament varies according to version, with emphasis on the ability to carry a wide range of advanced weapons. A GEC Avionics/Selenia stores management system is fitted; Sandall Mace 355 and 762 mm (14 and 30 in) ejector release units, and ML Aviation CBLS 200 practice bomb carriers, are standard. The battlefield interdiction version is capable of carrying weapons for 'hard' or 'soft' targets. Weapons are carried on seven fuselage and wing hardpoints: one centreline pylon fitted with a single ejection release unit (ERU), two fuselage shoulder pylons each with three ERUs, and, under each wing, one inboard and one outboard pylon each with a single ERU. For German Navy and Italian Air Force Tornados, MBB has developed (first flight 14 April 1981) a multi-sensor reconnaissance pod to be carried on the centreline pylon. Some RAF Tornados are being fitted with infra-red cameras in ammunition bay. Among the weapons already specified for, or suitable for carriage by, the IDS Tornado are the Sidewinder and Aspide air-to-air, and ALARM or HARM anti-radiation missiles; JP 233 low-altitude

Kormoran air-to-surface missiles; napalm; BL755 Mks 1 and 2 600 lb cluster bombs; MW-1 munitions dispenser; Mk 83 or other 1,000 lb bombs; 'smart' or retarded bombs; BLU-1B 750 lb fire bombs; Matra 250 kg ballistic and retarded bombs; Lepus flare bombs; LAU-51A and LR-25 rocket launchers; Marconi Skyshadow (jamming/deception) and BOZ 100 or 107 (chaff/flare) ECM pods on GR.1, AEG Cerberus II or III jammer pods on German aircraft; AN/AVQ-23 Pave Spike pods; data link pods; and chaff/flare dispensers. External fuel tanks (see 'Power Plant' paragraph) can also be carried.

DIMENSIONS, EXTERNAL:
- Wing span: fully spread — 13.91 m (45 ft 7½ in)
  - fully swept — 8.60 m (28 ft 2½ in)
- Length overall — 16.72 m (54 ft 10¼ in)
- Height overall — 5.95 m (19 ft 6¼ in)
- Tailplane span — 6.80 m (22 ft 3½ in)
- Wheel track — 3.10 m (10 ft 2 in)
- Wheelbase — 6.20 m (20 ft 4 in)

WEIGHTS:
- Weight empty, equipped — 14,091 kg (31,065 lb)
- Fuel (approx):
  - internal: wing/fuselage tanks — 4,862 kg (10,720 lb)
  - fin tank (RAF only) — 440 kg (970 lb)
  - drop tanks (each): 1,500 litre — 1,197 kg (2,640 lb)
  - 2,250 litre — 1,796 kg (3,960 lb)
- Nominal max weapon load — approx 9,000 kg (19,840 lb)
- Max T-O weight:
  - 'clean', full internal fuel — 20,411 kg (45,000 lb)
  - with external stores — approx 27,215 kg (60,000 lb)

PERFORMANCE:
- Max Mach number in level flight at altitude, 'clean' — 2.2
- Max level speed, 'clean' — above 800 knots (1,480 km/h; 920 mph) IAS
- Max level speed with external stores — Mach 0.92 (600 knots; 1,112 km/h; 691 mph)
- Landing speed — approx 115 knots (213 km/h; 132 mph)
- Time to 9,150 m (30,000 ft) from brake release — less than 2 min
- Automatic terrain following — down to 61 m (200 ft)
- Required runway length — less than 900 m (2,950 ft)
- Landing run — 370 m (1,215 ft)
- Max 360° rapid roll clearance with full lateral control — 4*g*
- Radius of action with heavy weapons load, hi-lo-lo-hi — 750 nm (1,390 km; 863 miles)
- Ferry range — approx 2,100 nm (3,890 km; 2,420 miles)
- *g* limit — +7.5

TORNADO MID-LIFE IMPROVEMENT PROGRAMME

In order to retain effective mission capability and survivability in the face of the increased threat in the 1990s and beyond, a mid-life improvement programme is currently being developed by the Tornado air arms and industry. It will confer more accurate navigation for 'blind' attacks, improved sortie generation capability, increased range for better target coverage, increased target acquisition capability, reduced penetration altitude, covert operation, improved electronic self-defence, improved threat suppression, and greater reliability and maintainability.

The first avionics upgrade modifications are already incorporated in the sixth Tornado production batch. They include a MIL-1553B databus, upgraded radar warning equipment and active ECM, an improved missile control unit, a 128K main computer, and integration of the Texas Instruments HARM anti-radar guided missile. HARM is already in service with German Navy Tornados.

PANAVIA TORNADO ECR

The Federal German Luftwaffe has selected an ECR (electronic combat and reconnaissance) version of the IDS Tornado to replace tactical reconnaissance aircraft already in operation and to complement or supersede such NATO airborne electronic warfare types as the 'Wild Weasel' F-4G Phantom. Development of this version was authorised in June 1986.

Retaining its air-to-surface role, except for the removal of the two 27 mm guns, the ECR Tornado is intended for standoff reconnaissance and border control, reconnaissance via image-forming and electronic means, electronic support, and employment of anti-radar guided missiles. For this purpose, it is to be equipped with a direction-finding system for ground-based radar installations (emitter locator); a Honeywell/Sondertechnik infra-red linescanner system, FLIR, onboard systems for processing, storing and transmitting reconnaissance data; and advanced tactical displays for the pilot and weapons officer. The external load stations on fuselage and wings may be used in ECR or fighter-bomber missions, or a combination of both.

The ECR version will normally be configured to carry two HARMs, two AIM-9L Sidewinders, an active ECM pod, chaff/flare dispenser pod, and two 1,500 litre (396 US gallon; 330 Imp gallon) underwing fuel tanks. A Mk 105 version of the RB199 engine will provide some 10 per cent more thrust than the Mk 103 in current IDS aircraft.

The seventh Tornado production contract, signed on 10 June 1986, included an order for 35 Tornado ECRs for the Luftwaffe, deliveries of which are due to be made to 4/JaboG 32 and 2/JaboG 38 in 1989-91. Pre-production Tornado P16 and one other IDS aircraft were converted for initial ECR flight trials, which began on schedule at Manching in 1988. Italy has expressed interest in acquiring about 15 ECR Tornados, either as retrofits or as new-production aircraft.

PANAVIA TORNADO ADV

RAF designations: Tornado F. Mks 2, 2A and 3

A possible air defence role for the Tornado was considered by the RAF when the interdictor/strike (IDS) programme was inaugurated in 1968, and studies leading to an air defence variant (ADV) were given impetus in 1971, when the Ministry of Defence issued Air Staff Target (AST) 395 covering the development of an interceptor with an advanced technology radar and Sky Flash air-to-air missiles. Changes from the IDS Tornado were to be minimal, and costs kept as low as possible. Full scale development was authorised on 4 March 1976, and the RAF ordered 165 of this long-range interceptor model, in its total procurement of 394 Tornados, to re-equip two former Lightning squadrons and three Phantom squadrons, as well as two new squadrons and an OCU.

The ADV is being procured primarily for air defence of the UK and to protect the northern and western approaches of NATO. Equipped with a tactical display that can cover the entire North Sea, it also fulfils the RAF's commitments to provide long-range air defence of Britain's maritime forces, over a wide UK defence region extending from the Atlantic approaches to the Baltic and from Iceland to the English Channel; and to contribute towards air defence in the Central Region of Europe.

Two main airframe modifications distinguish the ADV from the IDS version. The principal one is an increase in fuselage length forward of the front cockpit, to accommodate the longer radome of the GEC Avionics AI-24 Foxhunter radar, and a small 'stretch' aft of the rear cockpit to allow the four Sky Flash missiles to be carried in two tandem pairs. The other is that the fixed inboard portions of the wings are extended forward at the leading-edges (sweep angle 67° instead of 60°), to give increased chord and compensate for the shift in the CG. These changes also benefit performance by reducing drag, especially at supersonic speed, compared with the IDS version. Extension of the fuselage provides additional space for avionics and for an additional 10 per cent of internal fuel. Other changes include deletion of one of the two IWKA-Mauser 27 mm cannon; and only the two inboard underwing pylons are used on the RAF's ADVs.

Two versions of the ADV have been produced for the Royal Air Force:

Tornado F. Mk 2. First 18 production aircraft, with RB199 Mk 103 engines. These aircraft, the last of which was delivered on 9 October 1985, are scheduled to be returned to BAe in the early 1990s and largely upgraded to F. 3 standard except for the Mk 104 engines, which could not be retrofitted without structural alterations to the rear fuselage. After upgrading, these F. 2s will be redesignated **F. Mk 2A**.

Tornado F. Mk 3. Major production version, with RB199 Mk 104 engines with extended nozzles, increased reheat combat thrust, and Lucas DECU 500 digital engine control unit; a ram air turbine, radar-dedicated cold air unit, and internally mounted retractable in-flight refuelling probe; added head-down display for the pilot, and a displayed data video recorder for the navigator instead of the original wet-film head-down display recorder; a second Ferranti 1010 INS platform; a new Cossor IFF interrogator; a Singer-Kearfott data link system (when development is completed); new cockpit displays and redesigned symbology, together with an increase in computer storage capacity. The F. Mk 3 also introduced automatic wing sweep (AWS) and automatic manoeuvre device system (AMDS).

Although possessing some 80 per cent commonality with the IDS version, the Tornado ADV is sufficiently different for the initial production contract to include funding for three prototypes of the fighter version. These made their first flights on 27 October 1979, 18 July 1980 and 18 November 1980. Flight development in 1987 concentrated on continuing guided firing trials of the Sky Flash and Sidewinder air-to-air missiles, and BAe flight trials of an F. 3 fitted with the Singer-Kearfott/Collins/GEC Avionics JTIDS jamming-resistant communications system.

The first two production F. Mk 2s (RAF serial numbers ZD899/900), which are conversion trainers, made their initial flights on 12 April and 5 March 1984 respectively. They were followed on 5 November 1984 by the first two aircraft for No. 229 Operational Conversion Unit at RAF Coningsby, Lincolnshire. The first F. Mk 3 (ZE154) made its initial flight on 20 November 1985. No. 229 OCU ('shadow' identity: No. 65 Squadron) received its first F. Mk 3 (ZE159) on 28 July 1986, and on 31 December that year was declared operational. No. 29 Squadron (Coningsby) became operational with the F. Mk 3 on 1 November 1987. No. 5 Squadron (Coningsby) and No. 11 (Leeming) were due to do so in May and November 1988 respectively. They will be followed by Nos. 43 and 111 (both at Leuchars) in November 1989 and May 1990, and by two new (as yet undesignated) squadrons at Leeming in May 1989 and November 1990.

The first unrefuelled transatlantic crossing by a British fighter was made on 24 September 1987 by a Tornado F. Mk 3 (c/n AS11) crewed by BAe Warton's Deputy Chief Test Pilot, Peter Gordon-Johnson, and Tornado ADV Project Navigator Les Hurst. Returning to the UK after tropical trials in Arizona, it covered some 2,200 nm (4,075 km; 2,530 miles) from Goose Bay, Canada, to Warton in 4 h 45 min. It carried two 2,250 litre (594 US gallon; 495 Imp gallon) and two 1,500 litre (396 US gallon; 330 Imp gallon) external fuel tanks, and armament of four Sky Flash missiles as well as the standard 27 mm gun.

Approximately 90 ADV Tornados had been delivered by the Spring of 1988, of which 14 F. Mk 2s and eight F. Mk 3s were then held in store, with a further ten F. Mk 3s scheduled for storage later in the year. Export orders were received in 1985 from the air forces of Oman (eight) and Saudi Arabia (24).

From 1990, a new data processor will be available to give the final standard of the F. Mk 3's Foxhunter radar considerably more capability than the earlier versions. In particular, more automation will be provided for the radar functions, to improve close combat capability. Modification kits will bring up to the new standard radars already in service.

TYPE: Twin-engined all-weather air defence interceptor.

WINGS: Similar to IDS version except that fixed inboard portions also have a leading-edge sweep of 67° and the Krueger leading-edge flaps are deleted. F. Mk 3 fitted with automatic wing sweep (AWS) and automatic manoeuvre device system (AMDS). With AWS, four different wing sweeps can be scheduled (25° at speeds up to Mach 0.73, 45° from there up to Mach 0.88, 58° up to Mach 0.95, and 67° above Mach 0.95), enabling specific excess power at transonic speeds and turning capability at subsonic speeds to be maximised. Buffet-free handling

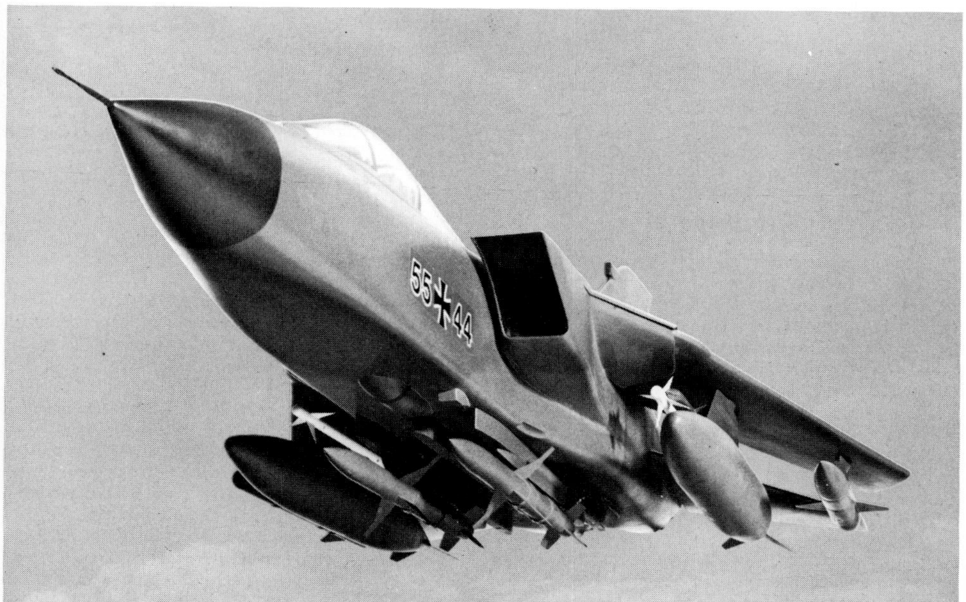

MBB model of Luftwaffe Tornado in ECR configuration, with two HARM anti-radiation missiles under the fuselage, two Sidewinders and two drop tanks (underwing, inboard), and chaff/flare dispenser (port) and AECM (starboard) pods under the outer wings

Panavia Tornado F. Mk 3 of No. 29 Squadron, Royal Air Force *(Flt Lt T. Paxton, RAF)*

can be maintained, to the limits defined by the SPILS, by use of the AMDS, which schedules with wing incidence to deploy either flaps and slats at 25° sweep angle or slats only at 45° sweep. Beyond 45°, both flaps and slats are scheduled 'in'.

FUSELAGE: Generally as for IDS version, but lengthened forward of front cockpit and aft of rear cockpit. Nosecone hinged in two places, providing access to front and rear of Foxhunter radar.

TAIL UNIT: As IDS version. On F. Mk 3, with extended afterburner nozzles, base of rudder is recontoured to clear the repositioned thrust reversers, and tailerons to clear the revised rear fuselage outline.

LANDING GEAR: As IDS version. Nosewheel steering augmentation system to minimise 'wander' on landing.

POWER PLANT: Two Turbo-Union RB199-34R Mk 103 afterburning turbofans in F. Mk 2/2A; F. Mk 3 has Mk 104 engines with 360 mm (14 in) extension to afterburner nozzles to increase reheat thrust. Compared with Mk 101 engine in early production IDS Tornados, the Mk 103 increases both dry and reheat thrust by 5 to 10 per cent; reheat combat thrust of the Mk 104 engine is increased by 7 per cent compared with that of the Mk 103. Fuselage fuel capacity (incl fin tank) approx 7,250 litres (1,915 US gallons; 1,595 Imp gallons). Internally mounted, fully retractable in-flight refuelling probe in port side of nose, adjacent to cockpit. Provision for drop tanks of 1,500 or 2,250 litres (396 or 594 US gallons; 330 or 495 Imp gallons) capacity to be carried on the shoulder pylons and underwing pylons.

ACCOMMODATION: As for IDS version.

SYSTEMS: Generally as described for IDS version, with the addition of a radar-dedicated cold air unit to cool the Foxhunter radar, and a pop-up ram air turbine to assist

recovery in the event of engine flameout at high altitude in a zoom climb.

AVIONICS AND EQUIPMENT: Among those in the IDS Tornado which are retained in the ADV are the communications equipment (Plessey VHF/UHF transceiver, SIT/Siemens emergency UHF, Rohde und Schwarz HF/SSB, Ultra communications control system and Epsylon cockpit voice recorder); GEC Avionics triplex fly by wire command stability augmentation system and autopilot/ flight director system (modified for increased roll rate and reduced pitch stick forces); Litef Spirit 3 central digital computer (with capacity increased from 64K to 128K) and data transmission system; Smiths electronic head-up and navigator's head-down display; Ferranti FIN 1010 inertial navigation system (to which is added a second 1010 to monitor the head-up display); GEC Avionics Tacan; Cossor ILS; and Cossor IFF transponder. Those deleted include the Texas Instruments nose radar, Decca 72 Doppler radar with terrain following, Ferranti laser rangefinder and marked target seeker, and Lital standby attitude and heading reference system.

Nose-mounted GEC Avionics AI-24 Foxhunter multimode track-while-scan pulse-Doppler radar with FMICW (frequency modulated interrupted continuous wave), with which is integrated a new Cossor IFF-3500 interrogator and a radar signal processor to suppress ground clutter. This system is intended to enable the aircraft to detect targets more than 100 nm (185 km; 115 miles) away, and to track several targets simultaneously. A ground mapping mode for navigation backup is available. Ferranti is subcontractor for the Foxhunter transmitter and aerial scanning mechanism. A pilot's head-down display is added, a Ferranti displayed data video recorder (DDVR) replaces the navigator's wet-film

display recorder, and an MSDS Hermes modular radar homing and warning receiver (RHWR) is added. Head-up/head-down displays are on front instrument panel only, radar control and data link presentations on rear panel only; both panels have weapon control and RHWR displays. A Ferranti FH 31A AC driven 3 in horizon gyro in the rear cockpit, in addition to providing an attitude display for the navigator, feeds pitch and roll signals to other avionics systems in the aircraft in certain modes. Analog electronic engine control unit on F. Mk 2 replaced by Lucas digital unit (DECU 500) on F. Mk 3. ESM (electronic surveillance measures) and ECCM are standard; a Singer-Kearfott ECM-resistant data link system, interoperable with other NATO systems, is under development for installation later. Because of its comprehensive avionics the Tornado ADV can contribute significantly to the transfer of vital information over the entire tactical area and can, if necessary, partially fulfil the roles of both AEW and ground based radar.

ARMAMENT AND OPERATIONAL EQUIPMENT: Fixed armament of one 27 mm IWKA-Mauser cannon in starboard side of lower forward fuselage. Four BAe Sky Flash semi-active radar homing medium-range air-to-air missiles semi-recessed under the centre-fuselage, carried on internally mounted Frazer-Nash launchers; one (F. Mk 2/2A) or two (on F. Mk 3) European built NWC AIM-9L Sidewinder infra-red homing short-range air-to-air missiles on each underwing station. Smiths Industries/ Computing Devices Company missile management system (MMS), which also controls tank jettison, has provision for pilot override, optimised for visual attack. The Sky Flash missiles, each fitted with an MSDS monopulse seeker head, can engage targets at high altitude or down to 75 m (250 ft), in the face of heavy ECM, and at standoff ranges of more than 25 nm (46 km; 29 miles). Release system permits the missile to be fired over the Tornado's full flight envelope. For the future, the ADV will be able to carry, instead of Sky Flash and Sidewinder, up to six Hughes AIM-20 AMRAAM medium-range and four BAe/Bodenseewerk ASRAAM short-range air-to-air missiles; studies are being undertaken for a 1553B multiplex digital databus associated with these weapons.

DIMENSIONS, EXTERNAL: As for IDS version, except:
Length overall	18.082 m (59 ft 3⅞ in)

WEIGHTS (approx):
Operational weight empty	14,500 kg (31,970 lb)
Fuel (approx):	
internal: wing/fuselage tanks	5,348 kg (11,790 lb)
fin tank	as for IDS version
drop tanks	as for IDS version
Max external fuel	5,806 kg (12,800 lb)
Nominal max weapon load	8,500 kg (18,740 lb)
Max T-O weight	27,986 kg (61,700 lb)

PERFORMANCE:
Max Mach number in level flight at altitude, 'clean'	2.2
Max level speed, 'clean'	
	800 knots (1,480 km/h; 920 mph) IAS
Rotation speed, depending on AUW	
	145-160 knots (269-297 km/h; 167-184 mph)
Normal touchdown speed	
	115 knots (213 km/h; 132 mph)
Demonstrated roll rate at 750 knots (1,390 km/h; 864 mph) and up to 4g	180°/s
Operational ceiling	approx 21,335 m (70,000 ft)

T-O run:
with normal weapon and fuel load	760 m (2,500 ft)
ferry configuration (four 1,500 litre drop tanks and full weapon load)	approx 1,525 m (5,000 ft)
T-O to 15 m (50 ft)	under 915 m (3,000 ft)
Landing from 15 m (50 ft)	approx 610 m (2,000 ft)
Landing run with thrust reversal	370 m (1,215 ft)

Intercept radius:
supersonic	more than 300 nm (556 km; 345 miles)
subsonic	more than 1,000 nm (1,853 km; 1,151 miles)

Endurance
2 h combat air patrol at 300-400 nm (555-740 km; 345-460 miles) from base, incl time for interception and 10 min combat

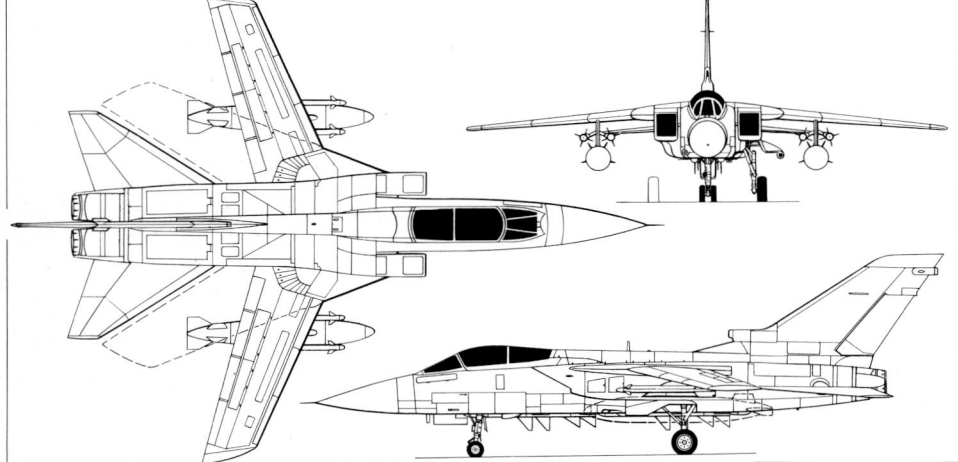

Panavia Tornado F. Mk 3, with lengthened afterburner nozzles *(Pilot Press)*

ROCKWELL INTERNATIONAL/MBB

PARTICIPATING COMPANIES:
Rockwell International Corporation (North American Aircraft Operations), 100 North Sepulveda Boulevard, El Segundo, California 90245, USA
Telephone: (213) 647 1000
Messerschmitt-Bölkow-Blohm GmbH, Postfach 801109, 8000 Munich 80, Federal Republic of Germany
Telephone: (089) 6000 0

ROCKWELL INTERNATIONAL/MBB X-31A EFM

The X-31A is the first US 'X' series experimental aircraft to be developed jointly with another country. Known also by the programme title EFM (Enhanced Fighter

Maneuverability), it was one of the first NATO co-operative efforts to be launched under the Nunn-Quayle research and development initiative, with a Phase 1 feasibility study which began in November 1984. This showed that close-in combat may continue to be necessary for future fighter aircraft, and that enhanced manoeuvring capabilities could lead to significant exchange ratio advantages. The X-31A programme is, therefore, intended to produce an aircraft that will break the so-called stall barrier, to allow close-in aerial combat beyond normal stall angles of attack.

The US Defense Advanced Research Projects Agency (DARPA), acting through US Naval Air Systems Command, is working with the German Federal Ministry of Defence to manage the X-31A development programme. An international memorandum of agreement was signed between the two countries in May 1986, and work on the year-long Phase 2 (vehicle preliminary design) started four months later. In the USA, Rockwell International has primary responsibility for the aircraft's configuration,

aerodynamics and construction, while Messerschmitt-Bölkow-Blohm (MBB) in Germany will develop the control systems and thrust vectoring design. General Electric is propulsion subcontractor, and its Aerospace Business Group will assist in cockpit development.

The X-31A design will integrate several technologies to expand the manoeuvring flight envelope, including vectored thrust, integrated control systems, and aircrew assistance. These advanced concepts are expected to enable extremely rapid target acquisition and fuselage pointing for addressing future low-speed, transonic and supersonic engagements. Earlier programmes such as the Rockwell HiMAT RPRV and MBB's TKF-90 are expected to contribute much useful data to the X-31A's design and development. As envisaged at the mid-point of Phase 2, the X-31A will be a single-engined aircraft with a cranked-delta wing and canard surfaces, powered by a non-afterburning General Electric F404-GE-400 turbofan, rated at approx 47.2 kN (10,600 lb st). Wing leading-edge sweep will be 56° 36' inboard and 45° outboard; thickness/chord ratio will be 5.5%. Configuration refinement and wind tunnel testing are being undertaken at Rockwell's facilities in southern California and at NASA's Langley Research Center in Virginia. Control system work is being carried out by MBB at Ottobrunn, and each company has on-site personnel at the other's facilities to ensure close co-ordination of all effort.

Two X-31A prototypes are being built under the 18-month Phase 3. These will be assembled by Rockwell, with MBB providing a number of major components and subassemblies including the CFRP wings. Under the one-year Phase 4, flight testing is expected to begin in late 1989, initially at the Rockwell facilities and then at the Naval Air Test Center at Patuxent River, Maryland. The flight test programme will involve an international team of pilots from Rockwell, MBB, the US Navy and the Federal German Luftwaffe. Funding between Rockwell and MBB is expected to be split approximately 80/20 per cent.

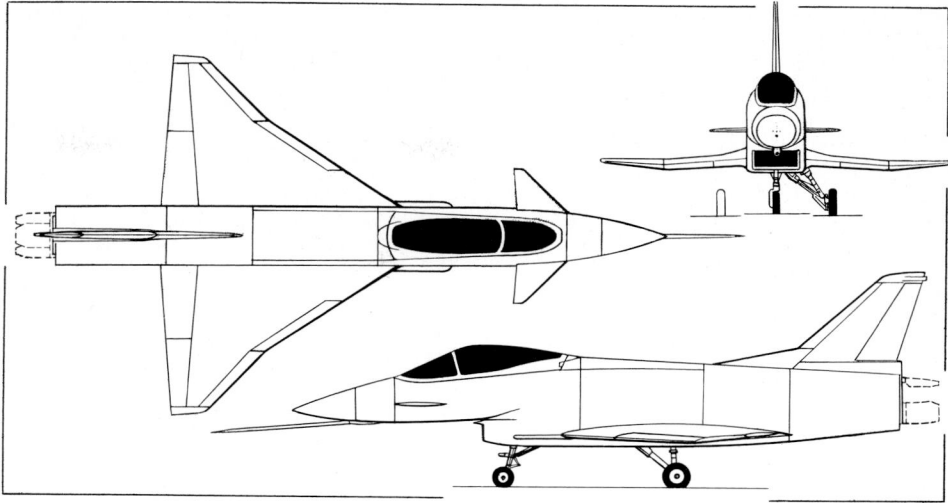

Rockwell International/MBB X-31A EFM experimental aircraft *(Pilot Press)*

DIMENSIONS, EXTERNAL (provisional):

Wing span	7.26 m (23 ft 10 in)
Wing aspect ratio	2.5
Foreplane span	2.64 m (8 ft 8 in)
Length overall, excl nose probe	13.21 m (43 ft 4 in)
Height overall	4.44 m (14 ft 7 in)
Wheel track	2.31 m (7 ft 7 in)
Wheelbase	3.54 m (11 ft 7¼ in)

AREAS (provisional):

Wings, gross	21.02 m² (226.3 sq ft)
Foreplanes, gross	2.19 m² (23.6 sq ft)
Vertical tail surfaces, total	3.49 m² (37.6 sq ft)

WEIGHTS (provisional):

Weight empty	4,632 kg (10,212 lb)
Fuel weight	1,497 kg (3,300 lb)
Mission T-O weight	5,366 kg (11,830 lb)
Max T-O weight	6,335 kg (13,968 lb)

PERFORMANCE (estimated):

Max level speed at 10,670 m (35,000 ft)	Mach 0.9
g limits	+9/−4

SEPECAT
SOCIÉTÉ EUROPÉENNE DE PRODUCTION DE L'AVION E.C.A.T.

AIRFRAME COMPANIES:
British Aerospace PLC, Richmond Road, Kingston upon Thames, Surrey KT2 5QS, England
Telephone: 01 546 7741
Avions Marcel Dassault-Breguet Aviation, BP 32, 92420 Vaucresson, France
Telephone: 741 79 21
PRESIDENT: I. R. Yates (BAe)
VICE-PRESIDENT: P. E. Jaillard (Dassault-Breguet)
PUBLIC RELATIONS: G. B. Hill (BAe)

This Anglo-French company was formed in May 1966 by Breguet Aviation and British Aircraft Corporation, to design and produce the Jaguar supersonic strike fighter/trainer.

Two-seat Jaguar International in the insignia of the Nigerian Air Force

SEPECAT JAGUAR INTERNATIONAL

Anglo-French production of the Jaguar and Jaguar International amounted to 497 aircraft for the Royal Air Force (203), Armée de l'Air (200), Ecuador (12), India (40), Nigeria (18) and Oman (24), as detailed in the 1987-88 and previous editions of *Jane's*. RAF Jaguars have since been re-engined with uprated Adour Mk 104 turbofans, equivalent to the Mk 804 which powered early Jaguar Internationals; all operational RAF Jaguars have been refitted with a Ferranti FIN 1064 INS, in place of the original GEC-Marconi NAVWASS.

Jaguar International is the export version, first flown on 19 August 1976. It has Adour Mk 804 or Mk 811 engines, which give improved combat performance with substantially enhanced manoeuvrability and acceleration in the low-level speed range. Other customer options include overwing pylons compatible with Matra R.550 Magic or similar dogfight missiles; a multi-purpose radar such as the Thomson-CSF Agave; up to four anti-shipping weapons such as Sea Eagle, Harpoon, Exocet and Kormoran on the underwing and underfuselage hardpoints; and night sensors such as low light level TV. Major servicing of the second batch of 12 Omani Jaguar Internationals, which includes fitment of a Ferranti FIN 1064 inertial navigation system, had been half completed by the beginning of 1988. BAe Jaguar activities also continue in the further development (major servicing and modification) of aircraft in service with the RAF, Ecuador and Nigeria.

Deliveries to India of 40 British built Jaguar Internationals with Adour Mk 804 engines were completed in 1982. A further 45 (with Mk 811 engines) have been assembled in India from European built components, and are now being followed by full manufacture of 31 additional aircraft under licence by Hindustan Aeronautics Ltd, Bangalore. Further details of this programme can be found under the HAL heading in the Indian section.
TYPE: Single-seat tactical support aircraft and two-seat operational or advanced trainer.
AIRFRAME: As described in 1985-86 and earlier *Jane's*.
POWER PLANT: Two Rolls-Royce Turboméca Adour Mk 804 turbofans, rated at 23.7 kN (5,320 lb st) dry and 35.75 kN (8,040 lb st) with afterburning, in aircraft for Ecuador, India (first 40) and Oman (first 12). Adour Mk 811, rated at 24.6 kN (5,520 lb st) dry and 37.4 kN (8,400 lb st) with afterburning, in remaining aircraft for India, second 12 for Oman and those for Nigeria. Fixed geometry air intake on each side of fuselage aft of cockpit. Fuel in six tanks, one in each wing and four in fuselage. Total internal fuel capacity 4,200 litres (1,110 US gallons; 924 Imp gallons). Armour protection for critical fuel system components. Provision for carrying three auxiliary drop tanks, each of 1,200 litres (317 US gallons; 264 Imp gallons) capacity, on fuselage and inboard wing pylons. Provision for in-flight refuelling, with retractable probe forward of cockpit on starboard side.
ACCOMMODATION (trainer): Crew of two in tandem on Martin-Baker 9B Mk II zero/zero ejection seats. Individual rearward hinged canopies. Rear seat 38 cm (15 in) higher than front seat. Windscreen bulletproof against 7.5 mm rifle fire.
ACCOMMODATION (single-seater): Enclosed cockpit for pilot, with rearward hinged canopy and Martin-Baker E9B (Ecuador), O9B (Oman) or IN9B (India) ejection seat as in two-seaters. Bulletproof windscreen, as in two-seat version.
SYSTEMS: As detailed in 1985-86 *Jane's*.
AVIONICS AND OPERATIONAL EQUIPMENT: Differ according to individual customer requirements; details are generally still classified, but first 40 for India have a Smiths head-up display similar to that in RAF Jaguars. Indian assembled Jaguars have a raster cursive head-up display, Sagem inertial navigation and weapon aiming system, and a Ferranti COMED 2045 combined map and electronic display.
ARMAMENT: Two 30 mm Aden or DEFA 553 cannon in lower fuselage aft of cockpit in single-seater; single Aden gun on port side in two-seater. One stores attachment on fuselage centreline and two under each wing. Centreline and inboard wing points can each carry up to 1,134 kg (2,500 lb) of weapons, outboard underwing points up to 567 kg (1,250 lb) each. Maximum external stores load, including overwing loads, 4,763 kg (10,500 lb). Typical alternative loads include one Martel AS.37 anti-radar missile and two 1,200 litre (317 US gallon; 264 Imp gallon) drop tanks; eight 1,000 lb bombs; various combinations of free-fall and retarded bombs, Hunting BL755 or Belouga cluster bombs, Matra R.550 Magic missiles and air-to-surface rockets, including the 68 mm SNEB rocket; a reconnaissance camera pack; or two drop tanks. Jaguar International can also carry two Matra Magic air-to-air missiles on overwing pylons; aircraft for Oman carry two AIM-9P Sidewinders on outboard underwing pylons.
DIMENSIONS, EXTERNAL:

Wing span	8.69 m (28 ft 6 in)
Length overall, incl probe:	
single-seat	16.83 m (55 ft 2½ in)
two-seat	17.53 m (57 ft 6¼ in)
Height overall	4.89 m (16 ft 0½ in)
Wheel track	2.41 m (7 ft 11 in)
Wheelbase	5.69 m (18 ft 8 in)

AREA:

Wings, gross	24.18 m² (260.27 sq ft)

WEIGHTS AND LOADINGS:

Typical weight empty	7,000 kg (15,432 lb)
Normal T-O weight (single-seater, with full internal fuel and ammunition for built-in cannon)	10,954 kg (24,149 lb)
Max T-O weight with external stores	15,700 kg (34,612 lb)
Max wing loading	649.3 kg/m² (133 lb/sq ft)
Max power loading:	
Adour Mk 804	219.6 kg/kN (2.15 lb/lb st)
Adour Mk 811	209.9 kg/kN (2.06 lb/lb st)

PERFORMANCE:

Max level speed at S/L	Mach 1.1 (729 knots; 1,350 km/h; 840 mph)
Max level speed at 11,000 m (36,000 ft)	Mach 1.6 (917 knots; 1,699 km/h; 1,056 mph)
Landing speed	115 knots (213 km/h; 132 mph)
T-O run: 'clean'	565 m (1,855 ft)
with four 1,000 lb bombs	880 m (2,890 ft)
with eight 1,000 lb bombs	1,250 m (4,100 ft)
T-O to 15 m (50 ft) with typical tactical load	940 m (3,085 ft)
Landing from 15 m (50 ft) with typical tactical load	785 m (2,575 ft)
Landing run:	
normal weight, with brake-chute	470 m (1,540 ft)
normal weight, without brake-chute	680 m (2,230 ft)
overload weight, with brake-chute	670 m (2,200 ft)
Typical attack radius, internal fuel only:	
hi-lo-hi	460 nm (852 km; 530 miles)
lo-lo-lo	290 nm (537 km; 334 miles)
Typical attack radius with external fuel:	
hi-lo-hi	760 nm (1,408 km; 875 miles)
lo-lo-lo	495 nm (917 km; 570 miles)
Ferry range with external fuel	1,902 nm (3,524 km; 2,190 miles)
g limits	+8.6/+12 ultimate

SOKO/CNIAR

PARTICIPANTS:

Sour Vazduhoplovna Industrija SOKO, 88000
Mostar, Yugoslavia
Telephone: (088) 22121 and 21970
Telex: 46 180 and 46 181 YU SOKOMO
**Centrul National al Industriei Aeronautice
Române,** 39 Bulevardul Aerogarii, Sector 1, Buch-
arest, Romania
Telephone: 50 27 14
Telex: 11648 AEROM

SOKO J-22 ORAO (EAGLE)/CNIAR IAR-93

This twin-jet close support and ground attack aircraft
was developed to meet a joint requirement of the air forces
of Romania and Yugoslavia. In the latter country it is
known as the J-22 Orao (Eagle); in Romania it is known as
the IAR-93. The joint programme is known as 'Yurom'
(from *Yugoslavia-Romania*).

The Orao/IAR-93 was designed jointly by Yugoslav and
Romanian engineers. Design began in 1970, and single-seat
prototypes were started simultaneously in the two countries
in 1972. A first flight in each country was made on 31
October 1974. SOKO and CNIAR each then completed a
two-seat prototype, these making simultaneous first flights
on 29 January 1977. In that year construction began in each
country of a pre-production batch of 15 aircraft, the first of
these making their initial flights in 1978. The IAR-93, which
is built by IAv Craiova, entered the series production phase
in 1979, and the Orao about a year later.

The following production versions have been announced:

IAR-93A. Romanian version with non-afterburning
Viper Mk 632 turbojet engines, first flown in 1981. Twenty
ordered for Romanian Air Force. Total includes single- and
two-seat versions, the latter having almost the same
operational capabilities despite a 0.41 m (1 ft 4¼ in) longer
front fuselage.

IAR-93B. Romanian version with Viper Mk 633 engines
and licence built afterburners. Total of 165 said to be
ordered by Romanian Air Force, including two-seaters.
First flight of production version made in 1985.

Orao 1. Yugoslav non-afterburning equivalent of
IAR-93A, produced both as single-seat tactical reconnaissance aircraft and two-seat operational conversion trainer.

Orao 2. Yugoslav afterburning version, in production as
single-seat attack aircraft. First flight (aircraft serial
number 25101) 20 October 1983. Increased external stores
load. Fuel system and capacities differ slightly from other
versions.

TYPE: Single-seat close support, ground attack and tactical
reconnaissance aircraft, with secondary capability as low
level interceptor. Combat capable two-seat versions used
also for advanced flying and weapon training.

WINGS: Cantilever shoulder-wing monoplane, of NACA
65A-008 (modified) section and low aspect ratio.
Anhedral 3° 30′ from roots. Incidence 0°. Sweepback 35°
at quarter-chord and approx 43° on outer leading-edges.
Inboard leading-edges extended forward (sweepback
approx 70°) on production single- and two-seaters, but
not on prototypes or pre-production aircraft. Two-spar
structure of aluminium alloy, with ribs, stringers and
partially machined skin. Wing spar box forms integral
fuel tanks on IAR-93B/Orao 2; IAR-93A/Orao 1 have
rubber fuel cells, forward of which are sandwich panels.
Hydraulically actuated (EEMCO system) two-segment
aluminium alloy leading-edge slats. Two small boundary
layer fences on upper surface of each wing. Hydraulically
operated wide chord plain ailerons and semi-Fowler
trailing-edge flaps, all of aluminium alloy; ailerons have
Dowty servo-actuators. No tabs.

FUSELAGE: Conventional all-metal, partially fail-safe semi-
monocoque structure of aluminium alloy. Hydraulically
actuated door type perforated airbrake under fuselage on
each side, forward of mainwheel bays. Narrow strake on
each side of nose (not on prototypes). Dorsal spine fairing

Single-seat SOKO Orao 2 attack aircraft of the Yugoslav Air Force

Romanian two-seat IAR-93A, showing the wing leading-edge root extensions and absence of ventral fins

houses circuits, systems and flight controls. 'Pen nib'
fairing above exhaust nozzles. Rear portion of fuselage is
detachable to facilitate access for engine maintenance
and removal.

TAIL UNIT: Cantilever all-metal structure, with sweepback
on all surfaces. Low-set all-moving tailplane. Small
dorsal fin. Auxiliary ventral fin on each side beneath rear
fuselage (single-seat production versions). Conventional
stressed skin construction, of aluminium alloy on
development aircraft and early production versions;
current aircraft have honeycomb rudder and tailplane.
Development and early production aircraft have anti-
flutter weights on tailplane tips; these are deleted on
definitive production models. Tailplane and rudder
controlled by Dowty Boulton Paul servo-actuators. Trim
tab in rudder on prototypes, deleted on pre-production
and production models.

LANDING GEAR: Hydraulically retractable tricycle type
of Messier-Hispano-Bugatti design, with single-wheel
hydraulically steerable nose unit and twin-wheel main
units. All units retract forward into fuselage. Two-stage
oleo-pneumatic shock absorber in each unit. Mainwheels
and tubeless tyres on all versions are size 615 × 225 ×
254 mm, pressure 5.2 bars (75.4 lb/sq in). Nosewheel and
tubeless tyre are size 551 × 250 × 152.4 mm, pressure 3.1
bars (45.0 lb/sq in), on IAR-93A/Orao 1; and size 451 ×
190 × 127 mm, pressure 3.8 bars (55.1 lb/sq in), on
afterburning versions. Hydraulic disc brakes on each
mainwheel unit, and electrically operated anti-skid

system. Bullet fairing at base of rudder contains a
hydraulically deployed 4.2 m (13 ft 9½ in) diameter
braking parachute.

POWER PLANT (non-afterburning versions): Two 17.79 kN
(4,000 lb st) Turbomecanica/ORAO (licence built
Rolls-Royce) Viper Mk 632-41R turbojets, mounted side
by side in rear fuselage; air intake on each side of fuselage,
below cockpit canopy. Fuel normally in seven fuselage
tanks and two collector tanks, with combined capacity of
2,480 litres (655 US gallons; 545.5 Imp gallons), and two
235 litre (62 US gallon; 51.75 Imp gallon) wing tanks,
giving total internal fuel capacity of 2,950 litres (779 US
gallons; 649 Imp gallons). Orao 2 has six fuselage and two
collector tanks, with two fuselage and both wing tanks
enlarged, giving total internal capacity of 3,100 litres (819
US gallons; 682 Imp gallons). Provision for carrying
three 540 litre (142.7 US gallon; 119 Imp gallon) auxiliary
fuel tanks, one on underfuselage stores attachment and
one inboard under each wing. Pressure refuelling point in
fuselage; gravity refuelling points in fuselage and each
external tank.

POWER PLANT (afterburning versions): Two Turbomecanica/
ORAO (licence built Rolls-Royce) Viper Mk 633-41
turbojets, each rated at 17.79 kN (4,000 lb st) dry and
22.24 kN (5,000 lb st) with afterburning.

ACCOMMODATION: Single-seat or tandem two-seat cockpit(s),
with Martin-Baker zero/zero seat for each occupant
(RU10J in IAR-93, YU10J in Orao), capable of ejection
through canopy. Canopy of single-seat IAR-93A and
Orao 1/2 is hinged at rear and actuated electrically to
open upward; single-seat IAR-93B, and all two-seaters,
have manually operated canopies opening sideways to
starboard. All accommodation pressurised, heated and
air-conditioned. Dual controls in two-seat versions.

SYSTEMS: Bootstrap type environmental control system for
cockpit pressurisation (max differential 0.214 bars; 3.1
lb/sq in), air-conditioning, and windscreen de-icing/
demisting. Two independent hydraulic systems, each of
207 bars (3,000 lb/sq in) pressure, for actuation of
leading-edge slats, trailing-edge flaps, ailerons, tailplane,
rudder, airbrakes, landing gear extension/retraction,
mainwheel brakes, nosewheel steering, brake-chute,
and afterburner nozzles. No pneumatic system. Main
electrical system is 28V DC, supplied by two Lucas
BC-0107 9kW engine driven starter/generators through
two voltage regulators and a switching system, and a
36Ah battery; two 700VA static inverters for AC power
at 400Hz. Oxygen system for crew.

AVIONICS AND EQUIPMENT: Standard avionics include VHF/
UHF air-to-air and air-to-ground com radio (20W
transmission power); gyro unit (British Aerospace
SGP500 twin-gyro platform in Orao), radio altimeter,
radio compass and marker beacon receiver; IFF; and
GEC Avionics three-axis stability augmentation system,
incorporating a basic bank/attitude hold autopilot and

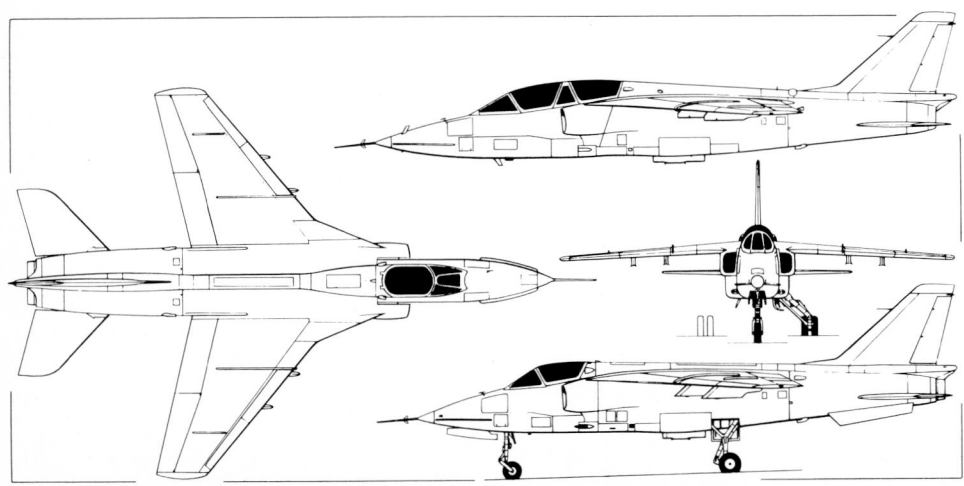

Single-seat IAR-93B close support/ground attack aircraft, with additional side view (top) of two-seat version of the IAR-93A (*Pilot Press*)

emergency wings-level facility. Orao 1 and 2 also have Collins VIR-30 VOR/ILS and Collins DME-40; Orao 2 fitted with Iskra SO-1 radar warning receiver. Landing light under nose, forward of nosewheel bay; taxying light on nosewheel shock strut.

ARMAMENT (IAR-93 and Orao 1): Two 23 mm GSh-23L twin-barrel cannon in lower front fuselage, below engine air intakes, with 200 rds/gun. Gun camera and Ferranti D282 gyro gunsight. Five external stores stations, of which the inboard underwing pair and the fuselage centreline station are each stressed for loads up to 500 kg (1,102 lb); outboard underwing stations stressed for up to 300 kg (661 lb) each, giving a max external stores load of 1,500 kg (3,307 lb). Typical weapon loads can include two or three 500 kg bombs; four or five 250 kg bombs; four multiple carriers each with three 100 kg or 50 kg bombs; two such multiple carriers plus two L-57-16MD launchers each with sixteen 57 mm rockets; four L-57-16MD launchers; four launchers each with two 122 mm, one 128 mm or one 240 mm rocket (122 and 240 mm not used on Orao); a GSh-23L cannon pod with four L-57-16MD rocket launchers; four 160 kg KPT-150 or similar munition dispensers; or (Romanian aircraft only) four L-57-32 launchers each with thirty-two 57 mm rockets. Centreline and inboard underwing points are each plumbed to carry a 540 litre (142.7 US gallon; 119 Imp gallon) drop tank; centreline point also capable of carrying a camera or infra-red reconnaissance pod or (not yet available for Orao) a night illumination pod.

ARMAMENT (Orao 2): Guns, gun camera, drop tanks and centreline camera or infra-red reconnaissance pod as for Orao 1. Thomson-CSF VE-120T head-up display. All four wing stations stressed for 500 kg (1,102 lb), and fuselage station for 800 kg (1,763 lb), giving a max external stores capacity of 2,800 kg (6,173 lb). Typical weapon loads include five 50 kg, 100 kg, 250 kg or 500 kg bombs; four multiple carriers for a total of twelve 50 or 100 kg or eight 250 kg bombs; four PLAB-340 napalm bombs (each 360 kg; 794 lb); five BL755 bomblet dispensers, each on four multiple carriers; sixteen BRZ-127 5 in HVAR rockets; four pods of L-57-16MD or L-128-04 (4 × 128 mm) rockets, or eight pods on multiple carriers; five 500 kg AM-500 sea mines; or two launch rails for AGM-65B Maverick or Yugoslav

developed Grom air-to-surface missiles. The 100 kg and 250 kg bombs can be parachute retarded. Chaff and IR decoy launch pods (up to three per aircraft) can also be carried.

DIMENSIONS, EXTERNAL:
Wing span	9.62 m (31 ft 6¾ in)
Wing chord: at root	4.20 m (13 ft 9⅜ in)
at tip	1.40 m (4 ft 7⅛ in)
Wing aspect ratio	3.6
Length overall, incl probe:	
single-seater	14.90 m (48 ft 10⅝ in)
two-seater	15.38 m (50 ft 5½ in)
Length of fuselage:	
single-seater	13.96 m (45 ft 9⅝ in)
two-seater	14.44 m (47 ft 4½ in)
Fuselage: Max width	1.68 m (5 ft 6⅛ in)
Height overall	4.45 m (14 ft 7¼ in)
Tailplane span	4.72 m (15 ft 5⅞ in)
Wheel track (c/l of shock struts)	2.50 m (8 ft 2½ in)
Wheelbase: single-seater	5.42 m (17 ft 9⅜ in)
two-seater	approx 6.50 m (21 ft 4 in)

AREAS:
Wings, gross	26.00 m² (279.86 sq ft)
Ailerons (total)	1.92 m² (20.67 sq ft)
Trailing-edge flaps (total)	3.13 m² (33.69 sq ft)
Leading-edge slats (total)	1.56 m² (16.79 sq ft)
Fin	2.67 m² (28.74 sq ft)
Rudder, incl tab	0.88 m² (9.47 sq ft)
Tailplane	7.62 m² (82.02 sq ft)

WEIGHTS AND LOADINGS (A: IAR-93A, B: IAR-93B, C: Orao 2):
Weight empty, equipped: A	6,150 kg (13,558 lb)
B	5,700 kg (12,566 lb)
C	5,750 kg (12,676 lb)
Max internal fuel: A	2,457 kg (5,416 lb)
B	2,450 kg (5,401 lb)
C	2,450 kg (5,401 lb)
Max external stores load: A	1,500 kg (3,307 lb)
B, C	2,800 kg (6,173 lb)
Basic operating weight: A	8,826 kg (19,458 lb)
B	8,400 kg (18,519 lb)
Max T-O weight: A	10,326 kg (22,765 lb)
B	11,200 kg (24,692 lb)
C	11,250 kg (24,800 lb)

Max landing weight: A	8,826 kg (19,458 lb)
B	9,360 kg (20,635 lb)
Max wing loading: A	397 kg/m² (81.3 lb/sq ft)
B	430.7 kg/m² (88.3 lb/sq ft)
Max power loading: A	289.8 kg/kN (2.84 lb/lb st)
B	251.8 kg/kN (2.47 lb/lb st)

PERFORMANCE (A at max T-O weight; B and C at 8,450 kg; 18,629 lb T-O weight):
Max level speed at S/L:	
A	577 knots (1,070 km/h; 665 mph)
B, C	626 knots (1,160 km/h; 721 mph)
Max cruising speed at 7,000 m (22,965 ft):	
A	394 knots (730 km/h; 453 mph)
Stalling speed at S/L: A	130 knots (241 km/h; 150 mph)
B, C	148 knots (274 km/h; 171 mph)
Max rate of climb at S/L: A	2,040 m (6,693 ft)/min
B, C	4,200 m (13,780 ft)/min
Service ceiling: A	10,500 m (34,450 ft)
B, C	13,500 m (44,300 ft)
Min ground turning radius	7.00 m (22 ft 11½ in)
T-O run: A	1,500 m (4,921 ft)
B, C	500 m (1,640 ft)
T-O to 15 m (50 ft): A	1,600 m (5,249 ft)
B, C	820 m (2,690 ft)
Landing from 15 m (50 ft): A	1,650 m (5,413 ft)
B, C	1,500 m (4,920 ft)
Landing run: A	720 m (2,362 ft)
B, C	1,050 m (3,445 ft)

Landing run with brake chute: A, B, C 670 m (2,200 ft)

Mission radius, B, C:
lo-lo-lo with four rocket launchers, 5 min over target
140 nm (260 km; 161 miles)
hi-hi-hi patrol with three 500 kg (1,102 lb) auxiliary fuel tanks, 45 min over target
205 nm (380 km; 236 miles)
lo-lo-hi with two rocket launchers, six 100 kg bombs and one 500 kg auxiliary fuel tank, 10 min over target
243 nm (450 km; 280 miles)
hi-hi-hi with four 250 kg bombs and one 500 kg auxiliary fuel tank, 5 min over target
286 nm (530 km; 329 miles)

g limits: A, B, C +8/-4.2

TBM
TBM CORPORATION
PARTICIPATING COMPANIES:

Socata (Aérospatiale-Aviation Générale), 12 rue Pasteur, 92150 Surèsnes, France
Telephone: 45 06 37 60
Telex: 614549
Fax: 45 06 71 76

Mooney Aircraft, PO Box 72, Kerrville, Texas 78029-0072, USA
Telephone: (512) 257 5112
Telex: 62913770
Fax: (512) 257 4635

Valmet Aviation Industries, 35600 Halli, Finland
Telephone: (358) 42 8291
Telex: 28269 VALKU SF
Fax: (358) 42 829667

TBM 700
The TBM 700, launched on 12 June 1987, is a pressurised single-engined business aircraft being developed by TBM Corporation, an association created jointly by Socata and Mooney, with one-third of its development cost being funded by a loan from the French government. Socata has full responsibility for technical development of the aircraft, including prototype manufacture and certification. Valmet joined the programme in June 1988.

Three prototypes are being built, the first of which (F-WTBM) made its initial flight on 14 July 1988. Certification under FAR Pt 23 (for one- or two-pilot operation) is expected to be followed by initial deliveries in early 1990. Orders for four TBM 700s had been reported by July 1988. Socata will build the forward fuselage, Mooney the rear fuselage and wings, and Valmet the tail unit.

TYPE: Six/eight-seat pressurised business aircraft.

WINGS: Cantilever low-wing monoplane, with dihedral from roots. Wing section Aérospatiale RA 1643 at root. Cambered leading-edges of laser drilled titanium. Two-spar wing torsion box, with light alloy skin, forms integral fuel tanks. Scaled-down 'ATR' single-slotted flaps, of Nomex honeycomb, occupy 71 per cent of each trailing-edge. Spoiler (forward of each flap at outer end) and aileron on each wing for roll control. Trim tab in port aileron. De-icing of leading-edges optional.

FUSELAGE: Conventional stressed skin structure, mainly of light alloy construction except for Nomex honeycomb cowling.

TAIL UNIT: Sweptback fin (with dorsal fin) and balanced rudder; non-swept variable incidence tailplane (of

Prototype of the TBM 700 six/eight-seat turboprop pressurised business aircraft

Nomex honeycomb) with balanced elevators. Trim tab in rudder.

LANDING GEAR: Inward retracting main units of trailing-link type; rearward retracting nosewheel.

POWER PLANT: One 522 kW (700 shp) Pratt & Whitney Canada PT6A-40/1 turboprop, driving a four-blade propeller with spinner. Propeller de-icing optional. Fuel in integral tank in each wing, combined capacity 1,130 litres (298.5 US gallons; 248.5 Imp gallons).

ACCOMMODATION: Seats for one or two pilots at front. Four seats in club layout aft of these, with centre aisle, or six seats in high-density layout. Single door on port side aft of wing; overwing emergency exit on starboard side. Cabin pressurised to 0.43 bars (6.2 lb/sq in). Individual emergency oxygen mask for each passenger. Baggage compartment at rear of cabin, with internal access only; additional compartment in nose, between engine and firewall, with external access via door on port side.

AVIONICS AND EQUIPMENT: Wide range of standard equipment to customer's requirements, including IFR instrumentation. Options include EFIS, GPS navigation system, weather radar, and de-icing for wing leading-edges and propeller blades.

DIMENSIONS, EXTERNAL:
Wing span	12.16 m (39 ft 10¾ in)
Length overall	10.43 m (34 ft 2½ in)
Height overall	3.99 m (13 ft 1 in)
Tailplane span	4.88 m (16 ft 0 in)

DIMENSIONS, INTERNAL:
Cabin: Length	4.10 m (13 ft 5½ in)
Max width	1.25 m (4 ft 1¼ in)

WEIGHTS:
Weight empty	1,492 kg (3,289 lb)
Baggage (two compartments, total)	60 kg (132 lb)
* Max T-O weight	2,672 kg (5,891 lb)
* Max ramp weight	2,687 kg (5,924 lb)

* *incl 50 kg (110 lb) of optional equipment*

PERFORMANCE (estimated: A at AUW of 2,500 kg; 5,511 lb, B at max T-O weight):
Max cruising speed at 7,620 m (25,000 ft):	
A	300 knots (555 km/h; 345 mph)
Max rate of climb at S/L: A	702 m (2,303 ft)/min

Range (B):
at 299 knots (555 km/h; 345 mph), 45 min reserves:
6 persons and 850 litres (224.5 US gallons; 187 Imp gallons) fuel 1,149 nm (2,130 km; 1,323 miles)
3 persons and max fuel
1,548 nm (2,870 km; 1,783 miles)
at 248 knots (460 km/h; 286 mph) at 9,150 m (30,000 ft), 45 min reserves:
6 persons and 850 litres fuel
1,403 nm (2,600 km; 1,615 miles)
3 persons and max fuel
1,996 nm (3,700 km; 2,299 miles)

TRANSALL
ARBEITSGEMEINSCHAFT TRANSALL
AIRFRAME COMPANIES:
Aérospatiale, 37 boulevard de Montmorency, 75781
  Paris Cédex 16, France
Telephone: (1) 42 24 24 24
Telex: AISPA 620059 F
MBB, Postfach 950109, 2103 Hamburg 95, Federal
  Republic of Germany
Telephone: (040) 7437 1
Telex: 21950 0 MBBH D

TRANSALL C-160 (Second Series)
Production of the original C-160 twin-turboprop transport for France (50), Germany (90), South Africa (9) and Turkey (20) ended in 1972. A second series was authorised in 1977 to meet additional requirements; these aircraft embody updated avionics, and extended range resulting from a reinforced wing with an optional additional fuel tank in the centre-section.

First flight of a second-series aircraft took place on 9 April 1981. The French Air Force ordered 25 (increased to 29 in 1982), deliveries of which were completed in mid-1985. Ten of these have in-flight refuelling equipment (hose reel and drogue type) in the port main landing gear fairing to permit their operation as tankers; five others incorporate provisions for this equipment and are capable of rapid adaptation to the tanker role. Eight are standard transports, four are in **Astarté** communications relay configuration, and two are equipped as **Gabriel** elint/ESM aircraft, as

Transall C-160 Astarté communications relay and flight refuelling tanker/receiver of the French Air
Force *(Avio Data)*

described in the 1987-88 *Jane's*. All 29 have a 4.00 m (13 ft 2 in) receiver boom mounted above and behind the flight deck. They are capable of refuelling carrier based aircraft of the French Navy, as well as French Air Force combat aircraft. In addition to the French order, six second-series Transalls were delivered to the Indonesian government.

Production of the second series ended in 1985; a detailed

description can be found in the 1985-86 *Jane's*, with a shortened account in the 1986-87 edition. Conversion kits or modifications are available for firefighting and anti-pollution missions (with a 12 ton liquid dropping capability), and for aeromedical duties. Modifications concerning self-protection devices and updated avionics are being studied.

IRAN

ISLAMIC REVOLUTIONARY GUARDS
CORPS (Air Industries division)
Tehran

IRGC FAJR (DAWN)
The first flight of this side by side two-seat light aircraft was announced in Tehran on 22 February 1988, together with the statement that it "could be used for military purposes" and was to be put into full scale production shortly afterwards. It is assumed that it will be used for primary training and, possibly, in a liaison or reconnaissance role.

Although claimed to be of Iranian design and manufacture, the Fajr is, to judge from its appearance, a Neico Lancair homebuilt of US origin (see description in Sport Aircraft section). It may embody some local modifications, but no details of the aircraft had been released at the time of going to press.

Prototype of the IRGC Fajr two-seat light aircraft *(IRNA)*

ISRAEL

IAI
ISRAEL AIRCRAFT INDUSTRIES LTD
Ben-Gurion International Airport, Israel 70100
Telephone: (03) 971 3111
Telex: ISRAVIA 381014, 381033 and 381002
Fax: (03) 971 3131 and 971 2290
PRESIDENT AND CHIEF EXECUTIVE OFFICER: M. Keret
CORPORATE EXECUTIVE VICE-PRESIDENTS:
  A. Ostrinsky
  Dr M. Dvir
VICE-PRESIDENT, MARKETING: D. Onn
DIRECTOR OF CORPORATE COMMUNICATIONS: D. Suslik
FOREIGN PRESS AND CORPORATE ADVERTISING MANAGER:
  F. P. Hermann (Dept 9003)

This company was established in 1953 as Bedek Aviation. The change of name to Israel Aircraft Industries was made on 1 April 1967, and the number of Divisions was reduced in February 1988 from five to four: Aircraft, Electronics, Technologies, and Bedek Aviation. Corporate headquarters provides overall guidance and support of these Divisions, and supports the service and marketing activities of several overseas subsidiaries. IAI covered space totalled 680,000 m² (7.32 million sq ft) at the end of March 1988, and the total workforce numbered about 17,000. The company is licensed by the Israel Civil Aviation Administration, US Federal Aviation Administration, British Civil Aviation Authority and the Israeli Air Force, among others, as an approved repair station and maintenance organisation.

In addition to aircraft of its own design (see Aircraft Division subsection), IAI markets a wide range of in-house

developed airframe systems and avionics; and service, upgrading and retrofit packages, encompassing civil and military fixed-wing and rotating-wing aircraft. Several of these are described under the Bedek Aviation Division heading, and utilise many electronic and optronic equipments (hardware and software) of IAI design and manufacture. Additional corporate activities involve space technology, 'smart' missiles and other ordnance, seaborne and ground equipment, and a wide range of component production and processing capability.

Aircraft Division
  Follows this entry
Bedek Aviation Division
  Follows Aircraft Division entry
Electronics Division
PO Box 105, Yahud Industrial Zone, Israel 56000
Telephone: (03) 717450
Telex: ISRAVIA 341450
Fax: (03) 536 5205
GENERAL MANAGER: M. Ortasse

The Electronics Division is now IAI's largest Division, with a 1988 workforce of 6,700 housed in 150,000 m² (1,614,585 sq ft) of covered accommodation. Operating plants of the Division are Elta Electronic Industries (a wholly owned subsidiary of IAI), MBT Weapon Systems, Tamam Precision Instruments, and MLM System Engineering and Integration. Division capability covers electronic and electro-optical systems and components, space technologies (including those applicable to an SDI environment), and manufacture/marketing of a wide range of military and civil hardware and software products and services.

Technologies Division
PO Box 190, Lod Industrial Zone 711101
Telephone: (08) 239111
Telex: SHLD IL 381520
Fax: (08) 222792
GENERAL MANAGER: Y. Shapira

This Division is the parent facility to five separate plants: SHL (Servo Hydraulics Lod), Ramta Structures and Systems, MATA Helicopters, Golan Industries, and Teud Technical Publications. SHL designs, develops and manufactures hydraulic system components, hydraulic flight control servo-systems, landing gears and brake systems; and produces air actuated chucks, miniature gears, clutches and brakes. Among others, its products equip the IAI Lavi/B-3, Kfir, Arava, Westwind and Astra, and IDF Sikorsky Black Hawk helicopters; manufacturing approvals are held from Boeing, Dornier, General Dynamics and General Electric, among others. Ramta undertakes metal and advanced composites fabrication for the F-4 Phantom, F-16 Fighting Falcon, E-2C Hawkeye, Lavi/B-3, Kfir, Westwind and Astra, as well as manufacturing ground vehicles and patrol boats. MATA repairs, reconfigures and remanufactures helicopter structures and components, and produces equipment and systems for rotating-wing aircraft. Golan designs and manufactures aircraft crew and passenger seats (including crashworthy seats for the Bell/Boeing V-22 Osprey), aircraft wheels and cockpit controls. Teud produces multi-language technical manuals, catalogues and checklists in hard copy, microfiche, microfilm or computer database form.

AIRCRAFT DIVISION

Ben-Gurion International Airport, Israel 70100
Telephone: (03) 9711415
Telex: ISRAVIA 381014 and 381033
Fax: (03) 971 3131 and 971 2290
GENERAL MANAGER: Dr M. Dvir

Newly established in February 1988, the Aircraft Division consists of five autonomous plants: military aircraft, civil aircraft, unmanned aerial vehicles (UAVs), manufacturing and subcontracting, and engineering services. The military aircraft plant is currently engaged in completing the B-3 third prototype Lavi as an advanced combat technology demonstrator; designing and integrating upgrades of the Kfir; and proposals for developing and manufacturing, with overseas partners, customer-specified advanced combat aircraft such as the supersonic multi-mission Nammer. Civil aircraft activity includes production of the Astra business aircraft, product support for the IAI Arava and Westwind (now out of production), and development of future non-military airframes. Multi-mission UAVs (see RPVs and Targets section of the 1987-88 *Jane's*) are marketed by Mazlat Ltd, a joint venture of IAI and Tadiran. The manufacturing and subcontracting plant produces structures and components for domestic and foreign customers. Engineering services include analysis, design, development, integration and testing of platforms and systems for domestic and international military and civil aerospace communities.

IAI LAVI (YOUNG LION)

The Lavi was conceived and designed to serve the Israeli Air Force in the close air support and interdiction roles, with a secondary capability for air-to-air self-defence to and from the target. Design characteristics included close-coupled delta main wings and canard surfaces, approx 22 per cent of the structure, by weight, being built of composite materials.

The Lavi received programme go-ahead in February 1980, and full scale development started in October 1982. Five flight development aircraft were planned, including two-seaters, plus a static test article. First flight of prototype B-1 took place on 31 December 1986, the second (B-2) making its initial flight on 30 March 1987. The programme envisaged production of at least 300 aircraft, including about 60 combat-capable two-seat operational trainers, but political and financial difficulties resulted in the programme being terminated by the Israeli government on 30 August 1987.

By mid-June 1987, in more than 60 test flights, the first two prototypes had flown at speeds up to Mach 1.07 and angles of attack up to 23° at a minimum speed of 110 knots (204 km/h; 127 mph). First air-to-air refuelling from an A-4 Skyhawk tanker had also been accomplished successfully.

Although series production of the prototype-qualified Lavi airframe has been discontinued, validation of the effort is continuing through the construction of a **B-3** two-seat technology demonstrator which is scheduled to make its first flight in early 1989.

In the absence of specific details of the B-3, the following description of the B-1/B-2 single-seat prototypes is retained:

TYPE: Single-seat close air support and interdiction aircraft, with secondary capability for air defence.

WINGS AND FOREPLANES: Cantilever low-wing monoplane. Close coupled 'swept delta' main wings (54° on leading-edges), plus all-moving foreplanes of similar planform. Leading-edge flaps over outer half of each wing. Inboard and outboard elevon on each trailing-edge. Substructure and skins of carbonfibre. Wings designed, developed and produced by Grumman Aerospace Corporation.

FUSELAGE: Conventional semi-monocoque structure, 'waisted' in accordance with area rule and incorporating composite materials as well as metal.

TAIL UNIT: Sweptback fin and rudder; Grumman built carbonfibre fins. No horizontal tail surfaces.

LANDING GEAR: SHL retractable tricycle type, with hydraulic actuation. Single wheel on each unit. Main units each have oleo-pneumatic shock absorber; two air chambers in nosewheel shock absorber. Steerable nosewheel retracts rearward, rotating through 90°; main units retract inward. Goodyear wheels, tyres and brakes. Golan Industries runway arrester hook.

POWER PLANT: One 91.7 kN (20,620 lb st) Pratt & Whitney PW1120 afterburning turbojet. Ventral single-shock intake based on that of General Dynamics F-16. Max fuel capacity 3,330 litres (880 US gallons; 732 Imp gallons) in integral wing tanks, plus 5,095 litres (1,346 US gallons; 1,121 Imp gallons) externally.

ACCOMMODATION: Pilot only, on ejection seat, under 'teardrop' cockpit canopy.

SYSTEMS: AiResearch environmental control system for air-conditioning, pressurisation and engine bleed air control. Pneudraulics bootstrap type hydraulic system, pressure 207 bars (3,000 lb/sq in), with Abex pumps. Electrical system powered by Sundstrand 60kVA integrated drive generator, for single-channel AC power at 400Hz. SAFT main and Marathon standby battery. AiResearch EPU and Garrett secondary power system.

AVIONICS: Electronic warfare self-protection system, by Elta Electronics, to provide rapid threat identification (IFF) and flexible response (ECM). This computer-based, fully automatic system uses active and passive countermeasures, including internal and externally podded power-managed noise and deception jammers. Elbit Computers Ltd was prime contractor for the integrated display system, which includes a Hughes Aircraft wide angle holographic head-up display, three multi-function displays (two monochrome and one colour), display computers, and communications controller. Pilot can operate most systems through a single El-Op up-front control. Lear Siegler/MBT quadruple-redundant digital fly by wire flight control system, with stability augmentation, MBT control unit and Moog servo-actuators. No mechanical backup. Sundstrand actuation system, with geared rotary actuators, for leading-edge flaps. Cockpit designed to minimise pilot workload in high *g* and dense threat environment, and full HOTAS (hands on throttle and stick) operation. Elta EL/M-2035 multi-mode pulse-Doppler radar, incorporating automatic target acquisition and track-while-scan in the air-to-air mode, and beam-sharpened ground mapping/terrain avoidance and sea search in the air-to-surface mode. The radar's coherent transmitter and stable multi-channel receiver ensures reliable lookdown performance over a broad band of frequencies, as well as high resolution mapping. Elta programmable signal processor, backed by a network of distributed, embedded computers, provides optimum allocation of computer power and considerable flexibility for algorithm updating and system growth. Advanced versions of Elbit ACE-4 mission computer (128K memory) and SMS-86 stores management systems, both compatible with MIL-STD-1553B databus; SMS-86 capable of managing both conventional and 'smart' weapons and sensors. Elta ARC-740 fully computerised onboard UHF com radio system, Elisra radar warning receiver and Astronautics air data computer. Tamam TINS 1700 advanced inertial navigation system.

ARMAMENT: Internally mounted 30 mm cannon, with helmet sight. Four underwing hardpoints for air-to-surface missiles, bombs, rockets and other stores; inboard pair 'wet' for carriage of auxiliary fuel tanks. Seven underfuselage stores attachments (three tandem pairs plus one on centreline). Infra-red air-to-air missile at each wingtip.

DIMENSIONS, EXTERNAL:
- Wing span: 8.78 m (28 ft 9⅔ in)
- Length overall: 14.57 m (47 ft 9⅔ in)
- Height overall: 4.78 m (15 ft 8¼ in)
- Wheel track: 2.31 m (7 ft 7 in)
- Wheelbase: 3.86 m (12 ft 8 in)

AREA:
- Wings, gross: 33.05 m² (355.75 sq ft)

WEIGHTS AND LOADING:
- Max fuel: internal: 2,721 kg (6,000 lb)
- external: 4,164 kg (9,180 lb)
- Max ordnance (excl air-to-air missiles): 2,721 kg (6,000 lb)
- Max external load: 7,257 kg (16,000 lb)
- T-O weight: basic: 9,990 kg (22,024 lb)
- max: 19,277 kg (42,500 lb)
- Max wing loading: 523 kg/m² (107 lb/sq ft)
- Combat thrust/weight ratio: 1.07

PERFORMANCE (estimated):
- Max level speed above 11,000 m (36,000 ft): Mach 1.8 or 800 knots (1,482 km/h; 921 mph) CAS
- Low-altitude penetration speed:
  - two infra-red missiles and eight 750 lb M117 bombs: 538 knots (997 km/h; 619 mph)
  - two infra-red missiles and two 2,000 lb Mk 84 bombs: 597 knots (1,106 km/h; 687 mph)
- Air turning rate at Mach 0.8 at 4,575 m (15,000 ft):
  - sustained: 13.2°/s
  - max: 24.3°/s
- T-O run: approx 305 m (1,000 ft)
- Combat radius:
  - air-to-ground, lo-lo-lo: 600 nm (1,112 km; 691 miles)
  - air-to-ground, hi-lo-hi with two Mk 84 or six Mk 82 bombs: 1,150 nm (2,131 km; 1,324 miles)
  - air-to-air, combat air patrol: 1,000 nm (1,853 km; 1,151 miles)
- *g* limit: +9

First (B-1) prototype of the IAI Lavi multi-role combat aircraft

IAI KFIR (LION CUB)

US Navy and Marine Corps designation: F-21A

A prototype of the Kfir (a modified Nesher airframe adapted to the J79 engine) was first flown in June 1973, following almost three years of flight tests of this engine in a Mirage III-B. Existence of the Kfir was made public on 14 April 1975, when the first production example was displayed at Ben-Gurion Airport.

The Kfir utilises a basic airframe similar to that of the Dassault Mirage 5, the main changes being a shorter but larger-diameter rear fuselage, to accommodate the J79 engine; an enlarged and flattened undersurface to the forward portion of the fuselage; introduction of four small fuselage airscoops, plus a larger dorsal airscoop in place of the triangular dorsal fin, to provide cooling air for the afterburner; and a strengthened landing gear, with longer-stroke oleos. Internal changes include a redesigned cockpit layout, addition of Israeli built avionics, and revised fuel tankage compared with the Mirage 5.

A total of 212 Kfirs was built, in the following versions:

C1. Initial production version: 27 built, originally equipping two Israeli Air Force squadrons (first combat mission 1977). Most examples later retrofitted to interim C2 standard with small canards; all except two were leased to US Navy and US Marine Corps as F-21A 'aggressor' aircraft (which see).

C2. Modified and major production version, first flown in 1974. Changes included sweptback, detachable foreplanes on engine intake trunks, small strake each side of nose, and extended chord outer wings to improve airfield and combat performance. Late-production examples had lengthened nose to accommodate larger EL/M-2001B radar. Total of 185 built, of which (according to Defence Minister Yitzhak Rabin in 1987) 95 were then "no longer in Israeli Air Force service"; these are assumed to include 12 supplied to Ecuador. Most other IAF C2s upgraded to C7 standard. Further details in 1983-84 *Jane's*.

TC2. Tandem two-seat operational trainer version of C2, with drooped and lengthened nose; first flown in February 1981. Included in total given for C2. Further details in 1983-84 *Jane's*.

C7. Upgraded conversion of C2, with 'combat plus' increase in engine thrust and improved avionics, delivered to Israeli Air Force from Summer 1983. Other features include new HOTAS (hands on throttle and stick) cockpit installation and two additional external stores stations. US State Department approval was given in 1988 for the export of 10 to Colombia.

TC7. Designation of TC2 when upgraded to C7 standard. Two to be exported to Colombia with the C7s mentioned above.

F-21A. Two versions leased to US Navy (12) and Marine Corps (13) as 'aggressor' trainers. Those for USN, leased from 1985-88, served with Squadron VF-43 at NAS Oceana, Virginia, and were of C1 configuration with small canards. They were due for reconfiguration and return to Israel in 1988. USMC aircraft, based at MCAS Yuma, Arizona, are to similar airframe configuration; they were leased from August 1987 and are in service with VMFT-401 until September 1989.

Production is understood to have ended, although tooling reportedly remains in place and the line could be reopened at short notice if required. The following description applies to the Kfir-C7 except where indicated otherwise:

TYPE: Single-seat strike, ground attack and fighter aircraft.

AIRFRAME: See 1987-88 and earlier *Jane's*.

POWER PLANT: One General Electric J79-J1E turbojet (modified GE-17) in C7, with variable area nozzle, rated at 52.89 kN (11,890 lb st) dry and 83.41 kN (18,750 lb st) with afterburning. Engine in F-21A, without 'combat

plus' modification, is rated at 53.0 kN (11,915 lb st) dry and 79.6 kN (17,900 lb st) with afterburning. Adjustable half-cone centrebody in each air intake. Internal fuel in five fuselage and four integral wing tanks. Total internal capacity 3,243 litres (857 US gallons; 713.4 Imp gallons) in C7, 3,443 litres (910 US gallons; 757 Imp gallons) in F-21A. Refuelling point on top of fuselage, above forward upper tank. Wet points for the carriage of one drop tank beneath each wing (inboard), and one under fuselage; these tanks may be of 500, 600, 825, 1,300 or 1,700 litres (132, 158.5, 218, 343.5 or 449 US gallons; 110, 132, 181.5, 286 or 374 Imp gallons) capacity; max external fuel capacity 4,700 litres (1,242 US gallons; 1,034 Imp gallons) for C7, 3,900 litres (1,030 US gallons; 858 Imp gallons) for F-21A. Provision for boom/receptacle or probe/drogue in-flight refuelling system, and for single-point pressure refuelling.

ACCOMMODATION: Pilot only, on Martin-Baker IL10P zero/zero ejection seat, under rearward hinged upward opening canopy. Cockpit pressurised, heated and air-conditioned. Two seats in tandem in TC7.

SYSTEMS: See 1987-88 *Jane's*.

AVIONICS AND EQUIPMENT: Compared with C2 (see 1987-88 *Jane's*), C7 differs in having an improved HOTAS (hands on throttle and stick) cockpit installation, facilitated by avionics which include a WDNS-341 weapons delivery and navigation system as standard, an Elbit System 82 computerised stores management and release system, video subsystems, 'smart weapons' delivery capability, and updated electronic warfare systems. The EL-2001 ranging radar is replaced by an Elta EL/M-2001B, but the C7 can also mount Elta's EL/M-2021 advanced pulse-Doppler fire control radar, with lookup/lookdown capability, Doppler beam-sharpened mapping, terrain avoidance/following and sea search modes.

ARMAMENT: Fixed armament of one IAI built 30 mm DEFA 552 cannon in underside of each engine air intake (140 rds/gun). Nine hardpoints (five under fuselage and two under each wing) for external weapons, ECM pods or drop tanks. For interception duties, one Sidewinder, Python 3 or Shafrir 2 infra-red homing air-to-air missile can be carried under each outer wing. Ground attack version can carry a 3,000 lb M118 bomb, two 800 or 1,000 lb bombs, up to four 500 lb bombs, or a Shrike, Maverick or GBU-15 air-to-surface weapon under the fuselage, and two 1,000 lb or six 500 lb bombs (conventional, 'smart' or 'concrete dibber' type) under the wings. Alternative weapons can include Mk 82/83/84 and M117/118 bombs; CBU-24/49 and TAL-1/2 cluster bombs; LAU-3A/10A/32A rocket launchers; napalm, flares, chaff, Elta EL-L8202 ECM and other podded systems.

IAI Kfirs supplied to US Marine Corps as F-21A 'aggressor' aircraft

IAI Kfir-C7 multi-mission combat aircraft, armed with Shafrir air-to-air missiles

DIMENSIONS, EXTERNAL:

Wing span	8.22 m (26 ft 11½ in)
Wing chord at root	8.04 m (26 ft 4½ in)
Wing aspect ratio	1.9
Foreplane span	3.73 m (12 ft 3 in)
Length overall, incl probe: C7	15.65 m (51 ft 4¼ in)
TC7	16.36 m (53 ft 8 in)
Height overall	4.55 m (14 ft 11¼ in)
Wheel track	3.20 m (10 ft 6 in)
Wheelbase: C7	4.87 m (15 ft 11¾ in)
TC7	4.50 m (14 ft 9 in)

AREAS:

Wings, gross	34.8 m² (374.6 sq ft)
Foreplanes (total)	1.66 m² (17.87 sq ft)

WEIGHTS AND LOADING:

Weight empty (interceptor, estimated)	
	7,285 kg (16,060 lb)
Max usable fuel: internal: C7	2,572 kg (5,670 lb)
F-21A	2,715 kg (5,985 lb)
external: C7	3,727 kg (8,217 lb)
F-21A	3,075 kg (6,780 lb)

Max external stores: C7	6,085 kg (13,415 lb)
F-21A	4,310 kg (9,502 lb)
Typical combat weight: C7	
interceptor, 50% internal fuel, two Shafrir missiles	
	9,390 kg (20,700 lb)
interceptor, two 500 litre drop tanks, two Shafrir missiles	11,603 kg (25,580 lb)
combat air patrol, three 1,300 litre drop tanks, two Shafrir missiles	14,270 kg (31,460 lb)
ground attack, two 1,300 litre drop tanks, seven 500 lb bombs, two Shafrir missiles	14,670 kg (32,340 lb)
Typical combat weight: F-21A	9,014 kg (19,872 lb)
Max 'clean' T-O weight: C7	10,415 kg (22,961 lb)
F-21A	10,390 kg (22,906 lb)
Max T-O weight: C7	16,500 kg (36,376 lb)
F-21A	14,700 kg (32,408 lb)
Wing/foreplane loading at 9,390 kg (20,700 lb) combat weight	257.5 kg/m² (52.8 lb/sq ft)

Thrust/weight ratio at 9,390 kg (20,700 lb) combat weight	0.91

PERFORMANCE (C7 except where indicated):

Max level speed above 11,000 m (36,000 ft)
over Mach 2.3 (1,317 knots; 2,440 km/h; 1,516 mph)
Max sustained level speed at height, 'clean'   Mach 2.0
Max level speed at S/L, 'clean'
750 knots (1,389 km/h; 863 mph)
Max rate of climb at S/L   14,000 m (45,930 ft)/min
Time to 15,240 m (50,000 ft), full internal fuel, two Shafrir missiles   5 min 10 s
Height attainable in zoom climb   22,860 m (75,000 ft)
Stabilised ceiling (combat configuration):
C7   17,680 m (58,000 ft)
F-21A   15,240 m (50,000 ft)
Turn performance (C7) at 4,575 m (15,000 ft), combat weight of 9,390 kg (20,700 lb):
turn rate: sustained   9.6°/s
instantaneous   18.9°/s
turn radius: sustained   1,326 m (4,350 ft)
instantaneous   671 m (2,200 ft)
T-O run at max T-O weight   1,450 m (4,750 ft)
Landing from 15 m (50 ft) at 11,566 kg (25,500 lb) landing weight   1,555 m (5,100 ft)
Landing run at 11,566 kg (25,500 lb) landing weight
1,280 m (4,200 ft)

*Combat radius, 20 min fuel reserves:
high-altitude interception, one 825 litre and two 1,300 litre drop tanks, two Shafrir missiles
419 nm (776 km; 482 miles)
combat air patrol, one 1,300 litre and two 1,700 litre drop tanks, two Shafrir missiles, incl 60 min loiter
476 nm (882 km; 548 miles)
ground attack, hi-lo-hi, two 800 lb and two 500 lb bombs, two Shafrir missiles, one 1,300 litre and two 1,700 litre drop tanks
640 nm (1,186 km; 737 miles)
Ferry range:
three 1,300 litre drop tanks
1,614 nm (2,991 km; 1,858 miles)
one 1,300 litre and two 1,700 litre drop tanks
1,744 nm (3,232 km; 2,008 miles)
g limit: C7   +7.5
F-21A   +8

*Can be increased by 30 per cent with in-flight refuelling

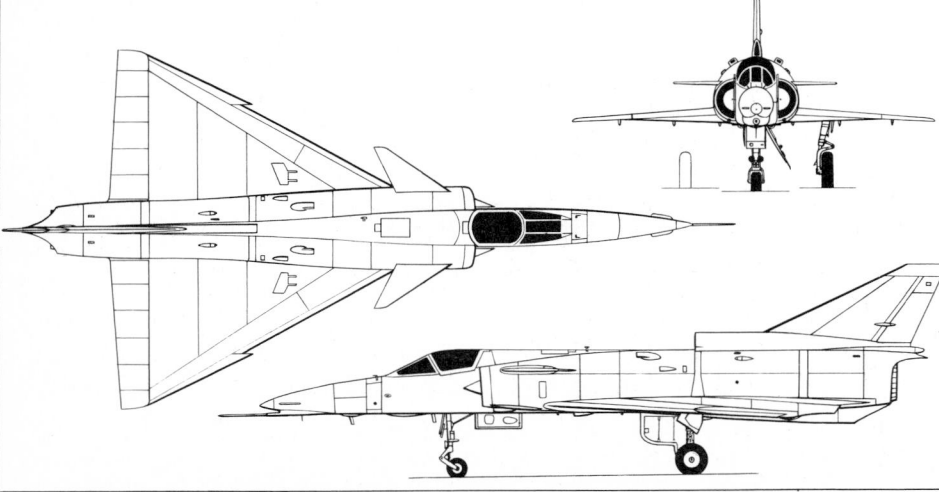

IAI Kfir-C7 (General Electric J79-J1E afterburning turbojet) *(Pilot Press)*

IAI NAMMER (TIGER)

In addition to the Mirage III/5 upgrade programmes described under the Bedek Aviation Division, IAI has proposed the Nammer as a joint venture to be developed with one or more international partners.

Externally, the Nammer can be identified by a longer nose than the Mirage or single-seat Kfir, fitment of Kfir type canard surfaces on the engine air intake trunks, an additional fuselage plug aft of the cockpit, and a 'clean' fin without the large dorsal airscoop of the Kfir. Like current Kfirs, it would be equipped with a contemporary weapon delivery and navigation system, HOTAS cockpit controls, and a related stores management and release system. There are two internally mounted 30 mm cannon, with 140 rds/gun, plus nine external wing and fuselage stations for weapons, drop tanks and other stores (similar to those listed for the Kfir, including capability for launching 'smart' weapons). Elta EL/M-2032 lookup/lookdown pulse-Doppler multi-mode fire control radar would be standard; a radar warning system with information presented on the tactical display, automatic chaff/flare dispensers, and jamming system, would be optional. UHF/VHF com and radio navigation systems would be to customer's requirements.

POWER PLANT: One General Electric/Flygmotor F404/RM12 turbofan, rated at 55.6 kN (12,500 lb) dry and 80.7 kN (18,140 lb st) with afterburning. (See under 'Weights' for fuel load.) In-flight and single-point ground pressure refuelling standard.

DIMENSIONS, EXTERNAL, AND AREAS: As listed for Kfir-C7 except:

Length overall	16.00 m (52 ft 6 in)
Wheel track	3.10 m (10 ft 2 in)

WEIGHTS:

Max fuel: internal	2,994 kg (6,600 lb)
external	3,719 kg (8,200 lb)
Max external stores	6,260 kg (13,800 lb)
T-O weight 'clean'	10,251 kg (22,600 lb)
Typical combat weight	9,049 kg (19,950 lb)
Max T-O weight with external stores	16,511 kg (36,400 lb)

PERFORMANCE (estimated at 9,049 kg; 19,950 lb combat weight except where indicated):

Max level speed:

at S/L	750 knots (1,390 km/h; 863 mph)
at altitude	Mach 2.2
Stabilised ceiling	17,680 m (58,000 ft)

Max instantaneous turn rate at 4,575 m (15,000 ft) 21°/s

Combat radius (tanks dropped when empty):

interceptor, one 1,300 litre tank and four IR air-to-air missiles, out and back at 12,200 m (40,000 ft) at Mach 1.8, incl 2 min combat
250 nm (463 km; 288 miles)

combat air patrol at 9,150 m (30,000 ft) at Mach 0.85, one 1,300 litre and two 1,700 litre tanks and four IR air-to-air missiles, incl 60 min loiter and 2 min combat
746 nm (1,382 km; 859 miles)

ground attack (hi-lo-lo-hi) at 544 knots (1,008 km/h; 626 mph) approach speed, two 1,700 litre tanks, two Mk 82 bombs and two IR air-to-air missiles
537 nm (995 km; 618 miles)

ground attack (lo-lo-lo-hi) at 535 knots (991 km/h; 616 mph) approach speed, one 1,300 and two 1,700 litre tanks, four CBU-58 cluster bombs and two IR air-to-air missiles
573 nm (1,062 km; 660 miles)

g limit +9

IAI ARAVA

The first of two prototypes of this light STOL transport made its initial flight on 27 November 1969. The Arava was first certificated as a civil aircraft, by the FAA in April 1972. This version, designated IAI 101, did not go into production, but formed the basis for the initial production Arava 102 (civil) and 201 (military) transport versions. The Arava 202 was a modified military version with a longer fuselage, winglets, and increased fuel capacity.

More than 90 Aravas had been delivered by mid-1987, most of these being military 201s and the majority of military and civil sales being to customers in Latin America. In 1984 the Israeli Air Force began to replace its Douglas C-47s in the main transport and trainer roles with a mixture of Arava 201s and 202s.

Production of the Arava has now ended, although a few unsold aircraft remained available in the Spring of 1988. In addition to the normal passenger and/or cargo configurations, the Arava can be outfitted as a low-cost electronic warfare platform, as illustrated and detailed in the following abbreviated description. A fully detailed description of the Arava can be found in the 1987-88 and many earlier editions of Jane's.

The following description applies to the Arava 201:

TYPE: Twin-turboprop STOL light military transport.

AIRFRAME: See 1987-88 and earlier Jane's.

POWER PLANT: Two 559 kW (750 shp) Pratt & Whitney Canada PT6A-34 turboprops, each driving a Hartzell HC-B3TN three-blade hydraulically actuated fully-feathering reversible-pitch metal propeller. Electric de-icing of propellers optional. Two integral fuel tanks in each wing, with total usable capacity of 1,665 litres (440 US gallons; 366 Imp gallons). Four overwing refuelling points. Optional pressure refuelling point behind fuselage/strut fairing. Two optional cabin mounted

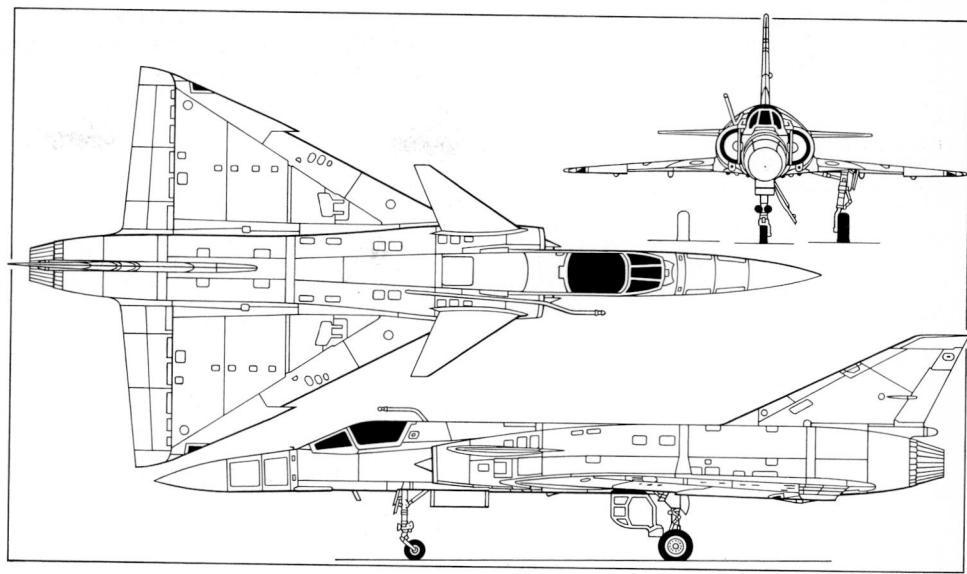

IAI Nammer upgraded version of the Mirage III and 5 *(Jane's/Mike Keep)*

tanks, each of 1,022 litres (270 US gallons; 225 Imp gallons), for self-ferry flights.

ACCOMMODATION: Crew of one or two on flight deck, with door on starboard side. Arava 201 can accommodate 24 fully equipped troops, or 16 paratroops and 2 dispatchers. Outward opening door at rear of cabin, opposite which, at floor level, is an emergency exit/baggage door on the starboard side. Fuselage tailcone is hinged to swing sideways through more than 90° to provide unrestricted access to main cabin. Alternative interior configurations available for ambulance role (10 stretchers and 2 medical attendants); as all-freight transport carrying (typically) a jeep mounted recoil-less rifle and its four-man crew; as an electronic warfare platform (see 'Avionics' paragraph); or as a maritime patrol aircraft fitted with search radar and other special equipment. Emergency exit on each side, forward of wing leading-edge.

SYSTEMS AND AVIONICS: See 1987-88 and earlier Jane's.

AVIONICS (electronic warfare versions): Arava can be modified to accept a variety of EW systems for comint, elint and jamming missions, to suit individual customer requirements. Equipment can be customer furnished, or from IAI or other manufacturers' product lines. Elint operator station would include omni antennae, spinning D/F antenna, a 0.5-18GHz elint receiver (manual, sweeping or computer controlled), signal analyser, signal recorder, data processor and intercom. Omni antennae, signal recorder and intercom also form part of comint operator station, together with 20-500MHz receivers (manual, computer controlled or preset) and a 20-500MHz instant direction finder. Jamming station equipment includes directional antennae, 20-400W spot and band jammers, plus manual and automatic jamming controls. Options on all EW versions include secure voice com, data processing computer, and multi-purpose display. Typical IAI installations could include Elta EL/L-8310 manually operated elint/ESM (electronic intelligence/surveillance) system (L-8311 or L-8312 systems optional); Elta EL/K-7010 jamming system;

plus 60kVA auxiliary generator to provide necessary additional electrical power. See also accompanying photograph.

ARMAMENT: Optional 0.50 in Browning machine-gun pack on each side of fuselage, above a pylon for a pod containing six 82 mm rockets. Rearward firing machine-gun optional. Librascope gunsight.

DIMENSIONS, EXTERNAL (201):

Wing span	20.96 m (68 ft 9 in)
Length overall	13.03 m (42 ft 9 in)
Height overall	5.21 m (17 ft 1 in)
Wheel track	4.01 m (13 ft 2 in)
Wheelbase	4.62 m (15 ft 2 in)
Propeller diameter	2.59 m (8 ft 6 in)

DIMENSIONS, INTERNAL (201):

Cabin, excl flight deck and hinged tailcone:

Length	3.87 m (12 ft 8 in)
Max width	2.33 m (7 ft 8 in)
Max height	1.75 m (5 ft 9 in)
Floor area	7.16 m² (77.07 sq ft)
Volume	12.7 m³ (449.2 cu ft)
Baggage compartment volume	2.60 m³ (91.8 cu ft)
Tailcone volume	3.20 m³ (113 cu ft)

AREA (201):

Wings, gross	43.68 m² (470.2 sq ft)

WEIGHTS AND LOADINGS (201):

Basic operating weight empty	3,999 kg (8,816 lb)
Max payload	2,313 kg (5,100 lb)
Max T-O and landing weight	6,804 kg (15,000 lb)
Max zero-fuel weight	6,350 kg (14,000 lb)
Max wing loading	155.8 kg/m² (31.90 lb/sq ft)
Max power loading	6.09 kg/kW (10.00 lb/shp)

PERFORMANCE (201 at max T-O weight):

Never-exceed speed	215 knots (397 km/h; 247 mph)
Max level speed at 3,050 m (10,000 ft)	176 knots (326 km/h; 203 mph)
Max cruising speed at 3,050 m (10,000 ft)	172 knots (319 km/h; 198 mph)

Electronic warfare versions of the Arava have been completed in various configurations. This one is equipped with an Elta EL/L-8310 elint system, the canister shaped antenna for which can be seen below the first cabin window. In flight, this is lowered to an underfuselage position where it can rotate through 360° to detect radar threat signals from any direction. An alternative EW configuration, with numerous blade antennae sprouting from the wings, tailbooms and flight deck roof, was illustrated in the 1985-86 edition

Econ cruising speed at 3,050 m (10,000 ft)
168 knots (311 km/h; 193 mph)
Stalling speed: flaps up   75 knots (140 km/h; 87 mph)
flaps down   62 knots (115 km/h; 72 mph)
Max rate of climb at S/L   393 m (1,290 ft)/min
Service ceiling   7,620 m (25,000 ft)
STOL T-O run   293 m (960 ft)
STOL T-O to 15 m (50 ft)   463 m (1,520 ft)
STOL landing from 15 m (50 ft)   469 m (1,540 ft)
STOL landing run   250 m (820 ft)
Range with max payload, 45 min reserves
140 nm (259 km; 161 miles)
Max range with 1,587 kg (3,500 lb) payload, 45 min
reserves   540 nm (1,000 km; 622 miles)

IAI 1124A WESTWIND 2

The Westwind had its origins in the Jet Commander designed in the USA and flown for the first time on 27 January 1963. Production was transferred in 1968 to Israel Aircraft Industries, which continued to develop and market successively improved versions. Details of the 186 early model Jet Commander/Commodore Jet/1123 Westwind executive aircraft, with General Electric CJ610 turbojet engines, built by Aero Commander in the USA (150) and IAI (36), have appeared in previous editions of *Jane's*.

In 1975, from aircraft c/n 187, the Garrett TFE731 turbofan became the standard power plant. Initial version with this engine was the 1124 Westwind (53 built), described in detail in the 1978-79 *Jane's*. This was followed in 1978 (from c/n 240) by the improved 1124 Westwind I: a description of this version, and its Sea Scan maritime patrol (1124N) variant, can be found in the 1986-87 edition.

Final version, described in the 1987-88 *Jane's*, was the 1124A Westwind 2, first flown on 24 April 1979. This introduced a new modified 'Sigma' wing of IAI section, NASA type winglets above the tip tanks, flat (instead of 'trenched') cabin floor, increased seated headroom, airline type flushing toilet, relocated overhead passenger service units, and other improvements. More than 50 were delivered.

Deliveries of turbofan powered Westwinds (all versions) totalled approximately 250 by mid-1987, but all Westwind production has now ended, although the aircraft remains available for lease from West Lease Corporation in the USA.

IAI 1125 ASTRA

Known originally as the 1125 Westwind, the Astra was developed as a more fuel-efficient, environmentally acceptable aircraft in the Westwind mould, featuring an improved standard of passenger comfort. In effect, only the tail unit and engine nacelles remain virtually unchanged

from the Westwind airframe. The major difference is in the wings, which have a new-design aerofoil section, are sweptback, and are mounted low on the fuselage. Whereas the Westwind's mid-mounted wings pass through the rear of the passenger cabin, those of the Astra pass beneath the cabin floor, so avoiding interruption of the available internal space. This relocation results in a deeper fuselage profile, allowing 25 cm (8 in) more cabin headroom than in the Westwind 2. The cabin is nearly 0.61 m (2 ft) longer and 5 cm (2 in) wider than in the Westwind, but otherwise the fuselage is little changed structurally except for a 50.8 cm (20 in) longer nose providing more space for avionics. The Sigma 2 wing section, a computer-assisted improvement by IAI of the Sigma 1 section employed in the Westwind 2, was designed to provide more efficient high-subsonic cruising flight over long ranges, with reduced operating costs. Construction makes wider use than the Westwind of composite materials, notably for the control surfaces.

Construction of two flying prototypes began in April 1982. The second of these (4X-WIN, c/n 4002) was the first to fly, on 19 March 1984, being followed by c/n 4001 (4X-WIA) in August 1984. The third airframe was used for static and fatigue testing. First flight by a production Astra (4X-CUA) was made on 20 March 1985, and FAA certification to FAR Pts 25 and 36 was received on 29 August of that year. First delivery, to a US customer, was made on 30 June 1986.

As from January 1988, at which time the production rate was one per month, marketing has been undertaken by a newly formed IAI subsidiary in the USA known as Astra-Jet Corporation, and product support for the Westwind/Astra family by Atlantic Aviation.

TYPE: Twin-turbofan business transport.

WINGS: Cantilever low-wing monoplane, with sweptback leading-edges (34° inboard, 25° on outer panels) and outboard trailing-edges. Thin, high-efficiency Sigma 2 aerofoil section, of IAI design. One-piece two-spar fail-safe structure, mainly of aluminium alloys, incorporates machined ribs and wing skin panels and is attached to underfuselage by four main and five secondary frames. Wing/fuselage fairings are of Kevlar, wingtips and inboard leading-edges of Kevlar and Nomex. Automatic leading-edge slats (outboard), interconnected with trailing-edge flaps; both flaps and slats are actuated electrically. Hydraulically actuated spoilers/lift dumpers forward of flaps. Ailerons, of Kevlar and honeycomb reinforced glassfibre, are hydraulically powered and pushrod operated. Pneumatic de-icing of leading-edge slats.

FUSELAGE: Metal semi-monocoque structure, mainly of aluminium alloy frames and chemically milled skins, with steel alloys or titanium in high stress or high temperature

areas. Kevlar reinforced upward opening panel over nose avionics bay. Glassfibre tailcone fairing. Flight deck windows of laminated polycarbonate.

TAIL UNIT: Cantilever all-sweptback structure, mainly of metal construction, with three-spar fin box and two-spar electrically actuated variable incidence tailplane. Fin and tailplane tips of glassfibre; small glassfibre ram air inlet at base of fin. Elevators and rudder operated manually via pushrods. Geared tab in rudder; electric trim for elevators, linked to flap operation. Pneumatic de-icing of tailplane leading-edges.

LANDING GEAR: SHL hydraulically retractable tricycle type, with oleo-pneumatic shock absorber and twin wheels on each unit. Mainwheels retract inward, nosewheels forward. Kevlar nosewheel doors. Tyre sizes 23 × 7 in (main), 16 × 4.4 in (nose). Hydraulic extension, retraction and nosewheel steering; hydraulic multi-disc anti-skid mainwheel brakes. Compressed nitrogen cylinder provides additional power source for emergency extension.

POWER PLANT: Two 16.23 kN (3,650 lb st) Garrett TFE731-3A-200G turbofans, with Grumman hydraulically actuated thrust reversers, pod-mounted in Grumman nacelle on each side of rear fuselage. Kevlar reinforced nacelle doors and panels. Thermal anti-icing of intakes. Standard fuel contained in integral tank in wing centre-section, two outer-wing tanks, and upper and lower tanks in centre-fuselage (combined usable capacity 4,910 litres; 1,297 US gallons; 1,080 Imp gallons). Additional fuel can be carried in a 378.5 litre (100 US gallon; 83.3 Imp gallon) tank in forward area of baggage compartment. Single pressure refuelling point in lower starboard side of fuselage aft of wing. Gravity points in tops of fuselage and outer-wing tanks.

ACCOMMODATION: Crew of two on flight deck. Dual controls standard. Sliding door between flight deck and cabin. Standard accommodation in pressurised cabin for six persons, two in forward facing seats at front and four in 'club' layout; galley in mid-cabin (port side), coat closet forward (stbd), toilet at rear. All six seats are individually adjustable fore and aft, laterally, and can be swivelled or reclined; all are fitted with armrests and headrests. Two wall mounted foldaway tables between 'club' seat pairs. Coat closet houses stereo tape deck. Maximum accommodation for nine passengers. Plug type airstair door at front on port side; emergency exit over wing on each side. Heated baggage compartment aft of passenger cabin, with external access. Cabin soundproofing improved compared with Westwind 2.

SYSTEMS: AiResearch environmental control system, using engine bleed air, with normal pressure differential of 0.615 bars (8.9 lb/sq in). Two independent hydraulic systems, each at pressure of 207 bars (3,000 lb/sq in). Primary system is operated by two engine driven pumps for actuation of brakes, anti-skid, landing gear, nosewheel steering, spoilers/lift dumpers and ailerons. Backup system, operated by electrically driven pump, provides power for emergency/parking brake, ailerons and thrust reversers. Electrical system comprises two 300A 28V DC engine driven starter/generators, with two 1kVA single-phase solid state inverters operating in unison to supply single-phase 115V AC power at 400Hz and 26V AC power for aircraft instruments. Two 24V nickel-cadmium batteries for engine starting and to permit operation of essential flight instruments and emergency equipment. 28V DC external power receptacle standard. Oxygen system for crew (pressure demand) and passengers (drop-down masks) supplied by single 1.35 m³ (48 cu ft) cylinder.

AVIONICS AND EQUIPMENT: Standard avionics suite comprises Collins EFIS-85A(1) five-tube electronic flight instrumentation system, dual FCS-80 flight director systems, dual VHF-22A com, dual VIR-32 nav, APS-80 autopilot, ADS-80 air data system, VNI-80D vertical nav system, Collins FMS-90 or Global GNS-1000 flight management system, dual DME-42, ADF-60A, dual RMI-36, dual C-14 compass systems, dual TDR-90 transponders, ALT-50A radio altimeter, Baker dual audio systems, and WXT-250A colour weather radar. A two-bottle freon type engine fire extinguishing system is standard. Standard equipment includes electric windscreen wipers, electric (warm air) windscreen demisting, cockpit and cabin fire extinguishers, axe, first aid kit, wing ice inspection lights, landing light in each wingroot, taxying light inboard of each mainwheel door, navigation and strobe lights at wingtips and tailcone, rotating beacons under fuselage and on top of fin, and wing/tailplane static wicks.

DIMENSIONS, EXTERNAL:

Wing span	16.05 m (52 ft 8 in)
Wing aspect ratio	8.8
Length overall	16.94 m (55 ft 7 in)
Fuselage: Max width	1.57 m (5 ft 2 in)
Max depth	1.905 m (6 ft 3 in)
Height overall	5.54 m (18 ft 2 in)
Tailplane span	6.40 m (21 ft 0 in)
Wheel track (c/l of shock struts)	2.77 m (9 ft 1 in)
Wheelbase	7.34 m (24 ft 1 in)
Passenger door (fwd, port): Height	1.37 m (4 ft 6 in)
Width	0.66 m (2 ft 2 in)

IAI Astra twin-turbofan business transport

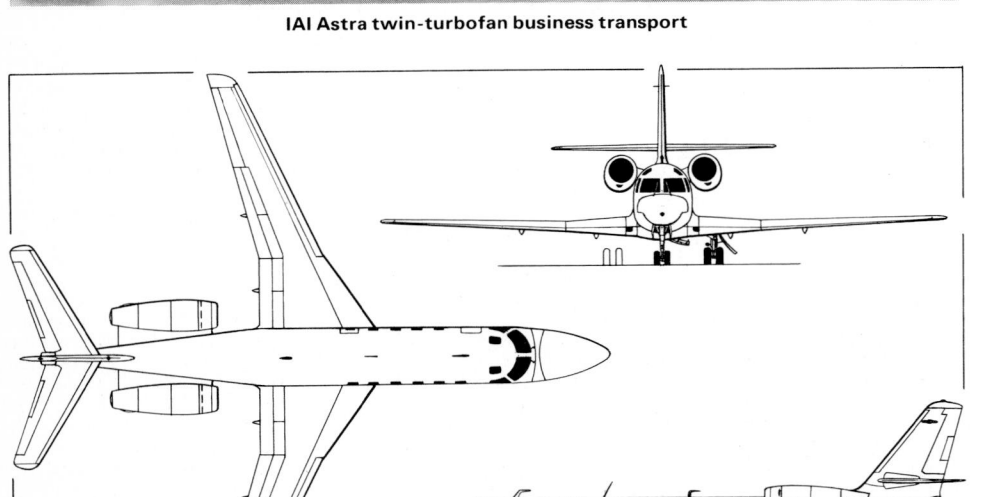

IAI 1125 Astra business transport (two Garrett TFE731-3A-200G turbofans) *(Pilot Press)*

Overwing emergency exits (each):	
Height	0.69 m (2 ft 3 in)
Width	0.48 m (1 ft 7 in)

DIMENSIONS, INTERNAL:

Cabin: Length: incl flight deck	6.86 m (22 ft 6 in)
excl flight deck	5.23 m (17 ft 2 in)
Max width	1.45 m (4 ft 9 in)
Max height	1.70 m (5 ft 7 in)
Baggage compartment volume	1.56 m³ (55 cu ft)

AREA:

Wings, gross	29.40 m² (316.6 sq ft)

WEIGHTS (A: without/B: with, long-range fuel tanks):

Basic operating weight empty, incl crew (typical):	
A	5,747 kg (12,670 lb)
B	5,801 kg (12,790 lb)
Max usable fuel: A	3,942 kg (8,692 lb)
B	4,248 kg (9,365 lb)
Fuel with max payload: A, B	3,470 kg (7,650 lb)

Max payload: A	1,510 kg (3,330 lb)
B	1,465 kg (3,230 lb)
Payload with max fuel: A	1,080 kg (2,380 lb)
B	730 kg (1,610 lb)
Max ramp weight: A, B	10,727 kg (23,650 lb)
Max T-O weight: A, B	10,659 kg (23,500 lb)
Max landing weight: A, B	9,389 kg (20,700 lb)
Max zero-fuel weight: A, B	7,257 kg (16,000 lb)

PERFORMANCE (at max T-O weight ISA except where indicated):

Max cruising speed at 10,670 m (35,000 ft), AUW of 7,257 kg (16,000 lb)	
	465 knots (862 km/h; 535 mph)
Max operating speed	
	Mach 0.855 or 360 knots (667 km/h; 414 mph)
Stalling speed at max landing weight:	
flaps and gear up	111 knots (206 km/h; 128 mph)
flaps and gear down	92 knots (171 km/h; 106 mph)

Max rate of climb at S/L	1,085 m (3,560 ft)/min
Rate of climb at S/L, one engine out	
	335 m (1,100 ft)/min
Max certificated altitude	13,715 m (45,000 ft)
Service ceiling, one engine out	5,485 m (18,000 ft)
FAR 25 T-O balanced field length at S/L at 10,296 kg (22,700 lb) T-O weight	1,518 m (4,980 ft)
FAR 25 landing field length at S/L at max landing weight	806 m (2,645 ft)
Range with long-range tanks and 4 passengers, 45 min reserves:	
at Mach 0.80	2,510 nm (4,651 km; 2,890 miles)
at Mach 0.72	3,110 nm (5,763 km; 3,581 miles)

OPERATIONAL NOISE LEVELS (FAR Pt 36 at max T-O weight, estimated):

T-O	88 EPNdB
Approach	92 EPNdB
Sideline	88 EPNdB

BEDEK AVIATION DIVISION

Ben-Gurion International Airport, Israel 70100
Telephone: (03) 9711240
Telex: ISRAVIA 381014 and 381033
Fax: (03) 971 3131 and 971 2290
GENERAL MANAGER: I. Geva (Brig-Gen Ret'd)

Bedek Aviation Division is internationally approved as a single-site civil and military airframe, power plant, systems and accessory service and upgrading centre. It has four operating plants (aircraft services and infrastructure, aircraft maintenance and upgrading, engine maintenance, and components maintenance) which, with the division headquarters, have a workforce of 3,400 housed in 110,000 m² (1,184,030 sq ft) of covered space. Bedek performs most of IAI's military and civil upgrading and retrofit programmes, current examples including the Phantom 2000 and Super Phantom programmes described in this entry and modification of a number of large transport aircraft to passenger/cargo, tanker, EW and reconnaissance mission configurations. Additional ongoing work includes the turnaround inspection, overhaul, repair, retrofit, outfitting and testing of more than 30 types of aircraft. Among these are various models of Boeing 707/727/737/747/767, McDonnell Douglas DC-8/DC-9/DC-10 and Lockheed C-130; combat aircraft that can be handled include the A-4 Skyhawk, F-4 Phantom, F-15 Eagle, F-16 Fighting Falcon and Mirage III. Power plants processed encompass 30 types of civil and military piston, turboprop, turbojet and turbofan engine and their components, including the JT3D, JT8D, JT9D, F100, J79, Atar 9C, TFE731, T56, PT6, C-250, T53 and T64. More than 10,000 types of accessories and instruments are serviced. The division provides total technical support to several international operators, and holds warranty and/or approved service centre appointments from domestic and foreign air regulatory agencies, air arms and a large number of leading aerospace manufacturers. Bedek is approved as a repair and overhaul agency by most major civil aviation authorities such as the FAA (USA), CAA (UK) and LBA (West Germany); these approvals cover aircraft, engine and accessory services.

IAI COMBAT AIRCRAFT UPGRADING

IAI's Bedek Aviation Division is currently offering a number of upgrade possibilities for existing combat aircraft such as the Dassault Mirage, McDonnell Douglas A-4 Skyhawk and F-4 Phantom; they are also available for other types such as the Northrop F-5 and the MiG family. Modular modernisation packages include new avionics such as a computerised digital weapon delivery and navigation system (WDNS) with multiple weapon delivery in air-to-air and air-to-ground modes and navigation data for up to 40 waypoints; a stores management and release system (SMRS), integrated with the WDNS, for both conventional and 'smart' weapons; various active and passive self-protection (ECM) systems such as podded or internally mounted jammers, radar warning, and flare/chaff dispensers; customised new digital ADI, HSI and ADC systems; and airframe and/or engine modifications and refits.

Typical programmes include the following:

Mirage III/5. Basic airframe modifications consist of the installation of Kfir type foreplanes and landing gear, the former permitting either a substantial reduction (305-457 m; 1,000-1,500 ft) in T-O run or a 907 kg (2,000 lb) increase in T-O gross weight, and the latter an increase in max T-O weight to 16,330 kg (36,000 lb). The foreplanes also offer a marked improvement in air turning radius (from 1,036 m; 3,400 ft to 610 m; 2,000 ft at 4,575 m; 15,000 ft altitude); improved sustained turn, a vastly extended usable angle of attack and low-speed envelope; and much improved handling qualities. By reducing air loads on the wings and fuselage, they extend the fatigue life of the airframe. An additional fuselage fuel tank can be installed aft of the cockpit, and a Kfir type nose provides additional space for avionics such as control and stability augmentation systems. Other avionics include a radar warning system, with omnidirectional threat analysis and cockpit display, and a WDNS-391 fully inertial weapon delivery and navigation system with head-up operation in all air-to-surface and air-to-air modes. Martin-Baker Mk 10 ejection

Three-point refuelling of A-4 Skyhawks by an IAI converted Boeing 707 tanker

Israeli Air Force Phantoms refuelling from a C-130 Hercules tanker converted by IAI's Bedek Aviation Division

seats are another option, and missiles or ECM pods can be carried on reinforced wingtip stations. Two or four additional external stores stations are provided, and flare/chaff dispensers can be installed under the rear fuselage.

IAI is also offering two other concurrent remanufacturing/upgrading options for Mirage III and 5 airframes:

Option 1 involves replacement of the existing power plant with a General Electric/Flygmotor F404/RM12 turbofan (55.6 kN; 12,500 lb st dry, 80.7 kN; 18,140 lb st with afterburning), permitting a shorter interception reaction time, better air combat performance, enhanced payload/range capability and improved fleet serviceability. In addition to providing some 30 per cent more thrust and up to 20 per cent better sfc, this re-engining saves some 453.5 kg (1,000 lb) in the aircraft's weight and enables it to carry an additional 544 kg (1,200 lb) of internal fuel. Max T-O weight is increased by 2,721 kg (6,000 lb).

Option 2 offers integration of the Elta EL/M-2011 or M-2032 lightweight fire control radar, conferring the following performance benefits: a coherent pulse-Doppler radar with low and medium PRFs; lookup/lookdown capability; target tracking by monopulse technique and tracking filter; ability to track low-altitude targets in heavy clutter; full utilisation of the launch envelopes and slaving capability of advanced missiles; all air target information presented on head-up display; improved air-to-ground ranging; extensive built-in testing and calibration; adaptability to other avionics systems; and growth potential through all-software-controlled LRUs and a MIL-STD-1553B interface.

Skyhawk. Major airframe improvements (already applied to Israeli Air Force A-4s) include a life extension overhaul, replacement of all wiring, provision of dual disc brakes on the mainwheels, a steerable nosewheel, addition of wing spoilers, an extra hardpoint under each wing, extension of the tailpipe (to change the heat signature and make the tailpipe more survivable and easier to repair), and addition of a brake-chute in a fairing beneath the rear

fuselage. The wingroot cannon are of increased calibre (30 mm instead of 20 mm), and a modern WDNS is installed. Additional space for lighter-weight avionics is made available in an extended nose compartment and in the 'saddleback' hump aft of the cockpit. Flare and chaff dispensers can be installed under the rear fuselage, forward of the brake-chute fairing. Bedek also offers a modification programme to convert single-seat A-4s into two-seat dual control trainers.

Phantom 2000. This programme is at present aimed specifically at Israeli Air Force F-4s, the major objectives being to extend service life, enhance mission capability, improve flight safety, and improve reliability and maintainability. These are being achieved by structural modifications, complete rewiring, and upgrading the avionics. A similar programme is available to other F-4 operators.

Three or four Phantom 2000 prototypes are being completed by the Israeli Air Force, the first of which flew for the first time on 11 August 1987. They are being strengthened structurally (reinforced skins and fuel cells in fuselage and wings), to improve flight safety and fatigue life and to extend their service life well into the next century. The aircraft are completely rewired, using fewer harnesses, simplified routing, and new generation hardware, and are equipped with 1553B dual redundant digital databuses. Hydraulic lines are selectively replaced and rerouted, built-in test features added, and the number of line-replaceable units reduced. Small strakes above the intake flanks improve stability and manoeuvrability, and cockpit comfort and instrument layout embody the latest human engineering data. Canards (not specified for the IAF programme) and a conformal underfuselage fuel tank are optional.

More important, the IAF Phantom 2000s are being given a new, advanced and fully integrated avionics suite, the major items of which are a Norden/UTC multi-mode high-resolution radar (first test flown in the USA in May 1988; not fitted in first prototype), Elop (Kaiser licence) wide-angle diffractive-optics head-up display, Elbit multi-function CRT displays for both crew members, a computerised WDNS, HOTAS (hands on throttle and stick) systems selection, Orbit integrated com and com/nav systems, and improved electronic warfare and self-protection (ECM) systems. Elbit Computers Ltd is overall integrator for the avionics refit, the core of which is a data processor derived from the company's ACE-3 currently fitted to all IAF F-16C/Ds. 'Production' conversions of IAF aircraft to Phantom 2000 standard will be undertaken by Bedek Aviation Division.

Super Phantom. First step in this programme was taken in 1986, when an IAF F-4E (serial number 334) was refitted with a 60.3 kN (13,550 lb st) Pratt & Whitney PW1120 turbojet (91.7 kN; 20,620 lb st with afterburning) in place of one of its J79s, for use as an engine testbed in the Lavi development programme. It flew for the first time in this form on 30 July 1986, subsequently having the other J79 similarly replaced and flying for the first time with two PW1120s on 24 April 1987. Structural changes include modifying the air inlet ducts; new engine attachment points; new or modified engine bay doors; new airframe mounted gearbox with integrated drive generators and automatic throttle system; modified bleed management and air-conditioning ducting system; modified fuel and hydraulic systems; and an engine control/airframe interface.

By mid-1987 flight test results with this Super Phantom demonstrator (all in 'clean' condition and at speeds of Mach 0.98 or below) had indicated significant performance improvements over the J79 powered F-4. Take-off distance is reduced by 21 per cent, from 1,006 m (3,300 ft) to 793 m (2,600 ft); sustained turn rate improved by 15 per cent (232° instead of 206° in a 40 s turn at Mach 0.9 at 9,150 m; 30,000 ft); rate of climb increased by 33 per cent; acceleration improved by 17 per cent; and penetration speed-with-load capability increased from 545 knots (1,010 km/h; 627 mph) with a 2,154 kg (4,750 lb) bomb load to 595 knots (1,102 km/h; 685 mph) with a 4,082 kg (9,000 lb) load. Other advantages of the PW1120 installation include a decrease in aircraft basic gross weight, and lower specific fuel consumption.

For IAF F-4s, only the Phantom 2000 stage had been authorised at the time of going to press. Super Phantom re-engineering, previously considered too costly for the IAF, may be reviewed following cancellation of the Lavi programme, but meanwhile is offered by IAI to other F-4 operators worldwide.

IAI (Bedek) Super Phantom demonstrator, re-engined with PW1120 turbojets

IAI AMIT FOUGA

Israeli Air Force name: Tzukit (Thrush)

The AMIT Fouga (Advanced Multi-mission Improved Trainer) was engineered by the Bedek Aviation Division of IAI to Israeli Air Force requirements, to remain as the standard IAF trainer during the 1980s. It is, in effect, completely rebuilt and modernised, and is a dedicated trainer with all armament removed, although it retains capability for patrol and aerial photographic missions.

Two prototypes were flight tested in 1981, and deliveries to the IAF (reportedly of 80 aircraft) were completed in 1986. Details of the modifications were given in the 1986-87 *Jane's*. The upgrade programme is available for other operators of this aircraft.

IAI HEAVY TRANSPORT CONVERSIONS

Bedek Aviation Division has carried out, or can offer, a variety of configuration conversions for large transport aircraft, including the following:

Boeing 707/720. Bedek has refurbished and resold numerous Boeing 707s and 720s, often after conversion from passenger to cargo, sigint, hose or boom refuelling tanker or other configurations, and several of these have been recorded in previous editions of *Jane's*. A sigint/tanker conversion with wingtip refuelling pods and Elta EL/L-8300 sigint system was illustrated in the 1987-88 edition. Also available is an AEW version mounting an Elta Electronics Phalcon solid state L band radar with six conformal phased array antennae: two on each side of the fuselage, one in an enlarged nose and one under the tail. In addition to the radar, the Phalcon system incorporates a sophisticated monopulse IFF, wide-range ESM system and a comint data processing system for tactical situation display.

Modifications involved in the tanker conversion include local reinforcement of the outer wings, supports for additional fuel tanks where applicable, and fuselage reinforcement for the boom support point or tail reel hose exit; an additional hydraulic system to power the fuel pumps and boom or tail reel; adaptation of the fuel supply system to the tanker role; electrical system changes to add external illumination, refuelling system controls, boom operator's station with 3-D optronic viewing system, and director lights for pilots of receiver aircraft; and avionics to individual customer requirements.

WEIGHTS (707-320C tanker, approx):

Operational weight empty	65,770 kg (145,000 lb)
*Internal fuel weight	72,575 kg (160,000 lb)
**Additional fuel weight	up to 13,605 kg (30,000 lb)
Tanker T-O weight	151,950 kg (335,000 lb)

**90,300 litres (23,855 US gallons; 19,863 Imp gallons)*
***17,034 litres (4,500 US gallons; 3,747 Imp gallons)*

Boeing 747-100 and -200 Combi. Bedek Aviation announced at the 1987 Paris Air Show that it was converting a Boeing 747-100 to prototype Combi configuration, for certification in 1988. Changes include installing a 3.05 × 3.40 m (10 ft 0 in × 11 ft 2 in) upward opening main deck cargo door aft of the wing on the port side, with local reinforcement of the fuselage; reinforcing the cabin floor to increase load carrying capacity; installing a fully powered ball mat/roller cargo handling system and restraint system, and a bulkhead between the passenger and cargo compartments; and interior modifications adapted to selected passenger/cargo combinations. Basic configuration options to be offered are (1) all-cargo, with up to 29 main deck standard pallets or containers; (2) Combi, with passengers at front and 7-13 pallets aft; and (3) all-passenger, with interior layout to customer's specification. Versions to accommodate non-standard containers, and similar conversions of the Model 747-200, can be made available optionally.

WEIGHTS (747-100 Combi, estimated):

Operational weight empty	148,325 kg (327,000 lb)
Max payload	98,883 kg (218,000 lb)
Max T-O weight	334,750 kg (738,000 lb)
Max landing weight	265,350 kg (585,000 lb)
Max zero-fuel weight	247,435 kg (545,500 lb)

Lockheed C-130/L-100 Hercules. Bedek Aviation has already accomplished several successful conversions of C-130 series aircraft to such configurations as in-flight refuelling tanker and sigint platform, with appropriate airframe modifications and avionics refits. Operational configurations currently being offered for any C-130B to C-130H variant, or their L-100 commercial counterparts, include: (1) probe and drogue aerial refuelling tanker, with transfer fuel in an 11,356 litre (3,000 US gallon; 2,498 Imp gallon) cargo compartment tank plus two underwing fuel pods; (2) maritime surface patrol and ASW, with appropriate surveillance, acoustic, MAD, armament or stores management systems, and operator stations; (3) C^3I and electronic warfare platform, with comint, elint, communications and EW systems to customer's requirements; (4) search and rescue, with a rescue kit, flare storage/launcher and operator station on a logistic pallet installed on the rear loading ramp; (5) emergency assistance, with an insulated cabin mounted on a logistic pallet for ambulance or 'flying hospital' missions or in a firefighting configuration with up to 11,356 litres (3,000 US gallons; 2,498 Imp gallons) of water and retardant in pallet mounted tanks in the cargo hold; and (6) VIP, 65-seat passenger or passenger/cargo combi transport, with full airliner type seating, galley and toilet facilities, pallet-mounted in an air-conditioned environment.

WEIGHTS (C-130H tanker, approx):

Operational weight empty	35,380 kg (78,000 lb)
*Internal fuel weight	29,030 kg (64,000 lb)
**Additional fuel weight	10,885 kg (24,000 lb)
Tanker T-O weight	75,295 kg (166,000 lb)
Max overload T-O weight	79,380 kg (175,000 lb)

**36,643 litres (9,860 US gallons; 8,060 Imp gallons)*
***13,627 litres (3,600 US gallons; 2,997 Imp gallons)*

ITALY

AERITALIA

AERITALIA—SOCIETÀ AEROSPAZIALE ITALIANA p.A.

Piazzale Vincenzo Tecchio 51A (Casella Postale 3065), 80125 Naples
Telephone: (081) 7252111
Telex: N. 710370 AERIT
PRESIDENT: Ing Roberto Mannu
DEPUTY CHAIRMAN AND MANAGING DIRECTOR:
Ing Fausto Cereti
GENERAL MANAGER: Dott Michele Crosio
PRESS RELATIONS MANAGER: Dott Alfredo Mingione

Aeritalia is a joint stock company formed on 12 November 1969 by an equal shareholding of Fiat and IRI-Finmeccanica, to combine Fiat's aerospace activities (except those which concerned aero engines) with those of Aerfer and Salmoiraghi of the Finmeccanica group. It became fully operational under that title on 1 January 1972. On 28 September 1976 IRI-Finmeccanica purchased the Aeritalia stock owned by Fiat, thus acquiring complete control of the company's stock capital. In the Summer of 1981 Aeritalia acquired shareholdings of 100% in Aeronavali Venezia, 60% in Partenavia, and 50% in Meteor. A 25% holding in Aeronautica Macchi was acquired in 1983; in 1988 it acquired a 31% holding in Rinaldo Piaggio (which see), a percentage share in FAMA of Argentina, and 40% in Dee Howard (see US section). Meteor is now 100% owned by Aeritalia. The combined Aeritalia workforce is approx 14,500.

Organisation is based upon a centralised general management and seven operational groups, as listed in this entry.

COMBAT AIRCRAFT GROUP

HEADQUARTERS AND TURIN WORKS: Corso Marche 41, 10146 Turin
Telephone: (011) 33321
Telex: N. 221076 (AERITOR)
GENERAL MANAGER: Ing Giandomenico Cantele
CASELLE WORKS: Turin Airport, 10100 Turin
Telephone: (011) 991362
Telex: 210095

The Turin area factories are responsible for work on the AMX combat aircraft; outer (movable) wings, final assembly and flight testing of the Panavia Tornado; definition, design and development of the Eurofighter European fighter aircraft, in partnership with other European companies; space vehicles; carbonfibre ailerons and rudders for the Boeing 767; and an improved weapons system for the F-104S. Other activities include extensive research in various fields of aerodynamics and advanced technologies, and the repair, overhaul and maintenance of aircraft.

TRANSPORT AIRCRAFT GROUP

HEADQUARTERS AND NAPLES AREA WORKS: Viale dell'Aeronautica, 80038 Pomigliano d'Arco, Naples
Telephone: (081) 8451111
Telex: N. 710082 and 710522 (AERITPOM)
GENERAL MANAGER: Ing Amedeo Caporaletti
CAPODICHINO WORKS: Via del Riposo alla Doganella, Aeroporto di Capodichino, 80144 Naples
Telephone: (081) 7817111
Telex: N. 710356
CASORIA WORKS: Strada Statale 87 km 8.7, 80026 Casoria
Telephone: (081) 7583222
FOGGIA WORKS: Zona ASI, Localita Incoronata
Telephone: (0881) 38951
Telex: 810213

Principal activities in the Naples area comprise construction of the complete series of fuselage structural panels and moving surfaces for the McDonnell Douglas MD-80; fuselage upper panels and vertical tail surfaces for the DC-10 commercial airliner and KC-10A aerial tanker; engine support pylons for the Boeing 747; nosecones, wing leading-edge slats, spoilers, trailing-edge flaps, elevators and fins for the Boeing 767; fuselages, outboard ailerons, spoilers and fins, assembly and flight testing of the Aeritalia G222; and manufacture of the complete fuselage and tail unit of the ATR 42 regional transport.

The Foggia Works is dedicated mainly to the manufacture of structural components in carbonfibre, aramid fibre and other composite materials.

AVIONICS SYSTEMS AND EQUIPMENT GROUP

HEADQUARTERS AND CASELLE WORKS: 10072 Caselle, Turin
Telephone: (011) 991362
Telex: AITCEA 210086

GENERAL MANAGER: Ing Carlo Scaglia
NERVIANO WORKS: Viale Europa, 20014 Nerviano, Milan
Telephone: (0331) 587330
Telex: AITNER 330675

Activities of this Group include research, development, production and integration of avionic systems and aircraft subsystems, ranging from nav/attack to computing and defensive aids.

SPACE SYSTEMS GROUP
HEADQUARTERS AND TURIN WORKS: Corso Marche 41, 10146 Turin
Telephone: (011) 33321
Telex: 221235
GENERAL MANAGER: Ing Ernesto Vallerani

This Group is a full partner in international programmes of the European Space Agency (ESA), and is involved in national programmes sponsored by the Ministry for Scientific Research and the National Research Council (CNR).

OVERHAUL, MODIFICATION, MAINTENANCE AND GENERAL AVIATION GROUP
HEADQUARTERS: Via Cupa Principe 102, 80144 Naples
Telephone: (081) 7817111
Telex: 722089
EXECUTIVE DIRECTORS:
Ing Nino D'Angelo
Ing Carlo Rosini
VENICE WORKS: Via Triestina 214, 30030 Tessera, Venice
Telephone: (041) 964044
Telex: 410446
CAPODICHINO WORKS: Via del Riposo alla Doganella, Capodichino, 80144 Naples
Telephone: (081) 7817111
CASELLE WORKS: Caselle Turin Airport, 10072 Caselle, Turin
Telephone: (011) 991362
Telex: 220411
CASORIA WORKS: Via Cava, 80026 Casoria
Telephone: (081) 7596311
Telex: 720199 PARTNA I

This Group is responsible for full product support of aircraft built by Aeritalia; overhaul and conversion, through Officine Aeronavali Venezia's factory, of aircraft not manufactured by Aeritalia; and support services, such as training of crew members and technicians, and field service, required by Aeritalia customers. On 1 September 1986 it also took over activities of the former General Aviation Group, centred upon the Partenavia plant at Casoria. Design and production activities in the latter field are undertaken by Partenavia, under which heading descriptions of current aircraft can be found.

RPVs and MISSILES GROUP
HEADQUARTERS: Piazzale Tecchio 51A, 80125 Naples
Telephone: (081) 7252111
Telex: 710370 AERIT I

ALFA ROMEO AVIO
HEAD OFFICE: Viale dell'Aeronautica, 80038 Pomigliano d'Arco, Naples
Telephone: (081) 8430111
Telex: 710082 AITPOM I
See Aero Engines section

EUROFIGHTER
Aeritalia is collaborating in the design of this new generation fighter, details of which can be found in the International section.

AMX
A description and illustration of this joint Italian-Brazilian attack aircraft programme, involving Aeritalia, Aermacchi and Embraer, can be found in the International section.

ATR 42/72
Aeritalia is an equal partner with Aérospatiale of France in developing these new regional transport aircraft, descriptions and illustrations of which appear under the ATR heading in the International section.

TORNADO
Aeritalia has a 15% participation in the manufacturing programme for the Panavia Tornado (see International section), being responsible for the radomes, the entire outer wings, including control surfaces, and the final assembly of aircraft for the Italian Air Force.

AERITALIA G222
Early history of the Aeritalia (originally Fiat) G222, the first prototype of which made its initial flight on 18 July 1970, can be found in the 1987-88 and previous editions of *Jane's.*

Several major Italian airframe companies have been involved in the construction programme, including Aermacchi (outer wings); Piaggio (wing centre-section); SIAI-Marchetti (tail unit); CIRSEA (landing gear); and IAM (miscellaneous airframe components). Wing flaps are contributed by Hellenic Aerospace Industries. Fuselages are built by Aeritalia's Transport Aircraft Group, in the Pomigliano d'Arco Works near Naples; final assembly takes place at the Capodichino Works, Naples.

The following versions have been built:

G222. Standard military transport, to which the detailed description mainly applies. The first of 44 G222s for the Italian Air Force (30 standard transports, eight G222SAA, four G222RM and two G222GE) flew on 23 December 1975, and deliveries began on 21 April 1978. Six quick-change kits, produced by Aeritalia, are held by the Italian Air Force for in-the-field conversions to the aeromedical configuration. Other customers included the Argentine Army (three), Dubai Air Force (one), Nigerian

Air Force (five), Somali Air Force (two), and the Venezuelan Army (two) and Air Force (six). Five have been ordered by the Italian Ministry for Civil Defence, to create a rapid-intervention squadron for firefighting, aeromedical evacuation, and airlift of supplies to earthquake and other disaster areas.

G222RM. Flight inspection (radiomisure) version, specially equipped for in-flight calibration of ground radio navigation and communication facilities as detailed in 1987-88 and earlier editions. Four delivered to Italian Air Force in 1983-84.

G222SAA. Firefighting version (Sistema Aeronautico Antincendio), with specially designed modular dispersal system for water or retardant (see 'Equipment' paragraph later). Eight delivered to Italian Air Force, which has used them extensively and successfully in many parts of Italy.

G222T. Version with Rolls-Royce Tyne turboprops, larger-diameter propellers and higher operating weights; details in 1986-87 *Jane's.* Twenty built, including two in VIP transport configuration, for Libyan Arab Air Force.

G222VS (Versione Speciale). Electronic warfare version, first flown on 9 March 1978. Carrying a pilot, co-pilot and up to ten systems operators, it has a modified cabin fitted with racks and consoles for detection, signal processing and data recording equipment, and an electrical system providing up to 40 kW of power for its operation. Externally distinguishable by small 'thimble' radome beneath the nose and a larger 'doughnut' radome on top of the tail fin. Two ordered by Italian Air Force, of which the first was delivered in 1983; in service with the 71° Gruppo Guerra Elettronica at Pratica di Mare. IAF designation is **G222GE** (Guerra Elettronica). Dimensions, weights and performance similar to those of the standard troop transport.

Of the total of 88 G222s ordered (all versions), all had reportedly been delivered by the end of 1986. Production was reportedly continuing in 1987, although no new orders had been announced up to the Spring of 1988.

Aeritalia has made studies for possible further versions of the G222. These include a version for **maritime patrol** and possible **ASW/ASV** missions, a **launch aircraft for RPVs**, and a G222 **air tanker**, for in-flight refuelling of either two or one combat aircraft, capable (with minimum modifications to the basic transport) of transferring up to 5,000 kg (11,023 lb) of fuel. The prototype of a **marine oil spill control** version, with an easily installed and removed tank holding 6,000 litres (1,585 US gallons; 1,320 Imp gallons) of oil dispersant, was demonstrated at the 1986

Farnborough Air Show and illustrated in the 1986-87 *Jane's.* No recent news of any of these variants has been received.

The following abbreviated description applies to the standard G222 transport version, except where indicated. A full description can be found in the 1987-88 and many earlier editions.

TYPE: Twin-turboprop general purpose transport aircraft.
AIRFRAME: As described in 1987-88 *Jane's.*
POWER PLANT (except G222T): Two Fiat built General Electric T64-GE-P4D turboprops, each flat rated at 2,535 kW (3,400 shp) at ISA + 25°C and driving a Hamilton Standard 63E60-27 three-blade variable- and reversible-pitch propeller with spinner. Fuel in integral tanks: two in the outer wings, combined capacity 6,800 litres (1,796 US gallons; 1,495 Imp gallons), and two centre-section tanks, combined capacity 5,200 litres (1,374 US gallons; 1,143 Imp gallons), with cross-feed provision to either engine. Total overall fuel capacity 12,000 litres (3,170 US gallons; 2,638 Imp gallons).
ACCOMMODATION: Normal crew of three (two pilots and radio operator/flight engineer) on flight deck. Provision for loadmaster or jumpmaster when required. Standard troop transport version has 32 foldaway sidewall seats and 21 stowable seats for 53 fully equipped troops, and carries also two 20-man life rafts stowed in the wing/fuselage fairing and a single 9-man life raft in the cargo compartment. Paratroop transport version can carry up to 40 fully equipped paratroops, and is fitted with the 32 sidewall seats and life rafts as in the troop transport version, plus eight stowable seats, door jump platforms and static lines. Five-person VIP lounge plus seats for 16 other passengers in VIP transport version. Cargo transport version can accept standard pallets of up to 2.24 m (88 in) wide, and can carry up to 9,000 kg (19,840 lb) of freight. Provision is made for 135 cargo tiedown points, on a 51 cm (20 in) square NATO standard grid, and a 1,500 kg (3,306 lb) capacity cargo hoist. Typical Italian military equipment loads can include two CL-52 light trucks; one CL-52 with a 105 mm L4 howitzer or one-ton trailer; Fiat AR-59 Campagnola reconnaissance vehicle with 106 mm recoilless gun or 250 kg (550 lb) trailer; or five standard A-22 freight pallets. In the aeromedical role the G222 can accommodate 36 stretchers and four medical attendants. A second toilet can be installed, and provision can be made to increase the water supply and to install electrical points and hooks for medical treatment bottles. In this version,

G222RM and Cessna Citation II modified by Aeritalia for flight inspection duties

the cabin oxygen system is available to all stretcher positions. Crew door is forward of cabin on port side. Passenger doors, at front and rear of main cabin on starboard side and at rear on port side, can be used also as emergency exits. Two emergency hatches in cabin roof, forward and aft of wing carry-through structure. Hydraulically operated rear loading ramp and upward opening door in underside of upswept rear fuselage, which can be opened in flight for airdrop operations. In cargo version, five pallets of up to 1,000 kg (2,205 lb) each can be airdropped from rear opening, or a single pallet of up to 5,000 kg (11,023 lb). Paratroop jumps can be made either from this opening or from the rear side doors. Windscreens and quarter-light panels are de-iced and demisted electrically. Wipers and screen wash for both windscreens. Entire accommodation pressurised and air-conditioned.

SYSTEMS: See 1987-88 and earlier *Jane's*.

AVIONICS AND EQUIPMENT: Standard communications equipment includes 3,500-channel UHF, two 1,360-channel VHF-AM, 920-channel VHF-FM, 28,000-channel HF/SSB, crew intercom and PA system. Navigation equipment includes Omega system, with TAS computer, autopilot, flight director, two compasses, and two vertical gyros; and an integrated ground based system incorporating two VOR, marker beacon receiver, two ILS, ADF, two Tacan or DME, and horizontal situation indicator. Other avionics include Meteo weather radar, with secondary terrain mapping mode; radar altimeter; and IFF/ATC transponder including altitude reporting. Provision for head-up display. Landing light on nosewheel leg.

EQUIPMENT (G222SAA): Modular palletised firefighting pack can be installed in under two hours without any modification to the basic transport aircraft. The module consists of a 6,000 litre (1,585 US gallon; 1,320 Imp gallon) tank and four pressurised air containers to activate the pneumatic actuators and discharge the retardant through the rear ramp/door opening via two nozzles. Length of area covered averages 300 m (985 ft).

DIMENSIONS, EXTERNAL:
Wing span	28.70 m (94 ft 2 in)
Wing aspect ratio	10.0
Length overall	22.70 m (74 ft 5½ in)
Height overall	9.80 m (32 ft 1¾ in)
Fuselage: Max diameter	3.55 m (11 ft 7¾ in)
Tailplane span	12.40 m (40 ft 8¼ in)
Wheel track	3.668 m (12 ft 0½ in)
Wheelbase (to c/l of main units)	6.23 m (20 ft 5¼ in)
Propeller diameter	4.42 m (14 ft 6 in)
Rear-loading ramp/door: Width	2.45 m (8 ft 0½ in)
Height	2.25 m (7 ft 4½ in)

DIMENSIONS, INTERNAL:
Main cabin: Length	8.58 m (28 ft 1¾ in)
Width	2.45 m (8 ft 0½ in)
Height	2.25 m (7 ft 4½ in)
Floor area: excl ramp	21.00 m² (226.0 sq ft)
incl ramp	25.68 m² (276.4 sq ft)
Volume	58.0 m³ (2,048 cu ft)

AREA:
Wings, gross	82.00 m² (882.6 sq ft)

WEIGHTS AND LOADINGS (standard version except where indicated):
Weight empty	14,590 kg (32,165 lb)
Weight empty, equipped	15,400 kg (33,950 lb)
Operating weight empty (standard and SAA)	15,700 kg (34,610 lb)
Max payload (cargo)	9,000 kg (19,840 lb)
Equipment module (SAA)	2,200 kg (4,850 lb)
Retardant (SAA)	6,800 kg (14,990 lb)
Max fuel load	9,400 kg (20,725 lb)
Fuel (SAA)	3,330 kg (7,340 lb)
Max T-O weight (standard and SAA)	28,000 kg (61,730 lb)
Max landing weight (standard and SAA)	26,500 kg (58,420 lb)
Max zero-fuel weight	24,400 kg (53,790 lb)
Max cargo floor loading	750 kg/m² (155 lb/sq ft)
Max wing loading	341.5 kg/m² (69.9 lb/sq ft)
Max power loading	5.52 kg/kW (9.08 lb/shp)

PERFORMANCE (standard transport, at max T-O weight except where indicated):
Max level speed at 4,575 m (15,000 ft)
291 knots (540 km/h; 336 mph)
Long-range cruising speed at 6,000 m (19,680 ft)
237 knots (439 km/h; 273 mph)
Airdrop speed (paratroops or cargo)
110-140 knots (204-259 km/h; 127-161 mph) IAS
Drop speed (G222SAA, T-O configuration)
120 knots (222 km/h; 138 mph)
Stalling speed, flaps and landing gear down
84 knots (155 km/h; 97 mph)
Time to 4,500 m (14,760 ft) 8 min 35 s
Max rate of climb at S/L 520 m (1,705 ft)/min
Rate of climb at S/L, one engine out 125 m (410 ft)/min
Service ceiling 7,620 m (25,000 ft)
Service ceiling, one engine out 5,000 m (16,400 ft)
Optimum height above ground during drop (G222SAA)
50-100 m (165-330 ft)
T-O run 662 m (2,172 ft)
T-O to 15 m (50 ft) 1,000 m (3,280 ft)

Aeritalia G222 twin-turboprop general purpose military transport aircraft *(Pilot Press)*

Aeritalia F-104S ASA with upgraded weapons systems, carrying two Sidewinder air-to-air missiles and two drop tanks *(Avio Data)*

Landing from 15 m (50 ft) 775 m (2,543 ft)
Landing run at max landing weight 545 m (1,788 ft)
Accelerate/stop distance 1,200 m (3,937 ft)
Range:
with max payload, at optimum cruising speed and height 740 nm (1,371 km; 852 miles)
with 36 stretchers and 4 medical attendants
1,349 nm (2,500 km; 1,553 miles)
with max retardant load (SAA)
540 nm (1,000 km; 621 miles)
Ferry range with max fuel
2,500 nm (4,633 km; 2,879 miles)
g limit +2.5

AERITALIA (LOCKHEED) F-104S ASA

Aeritalia production of the F-104S ended in March 1979 after the manufacture of 246 aircraft, including 40 for the Turkish Air Force. Development was initiated in 1982 of a weapons system updating programme for 160 of the Italian Air Force's F-104Ss, to increase their capability in the interception and interdiction/strike roles.

Known as ASA (Aggiornamento Sistemi d'Arma), this programme includes improved air-to-air self-defence and interception capability by the introduction of a Fiar R21G/M1 Setter lookdown/shootdown radar; advanced ECM; improved IFF and altitude reporting system; improved electrical power generation and distribution system; improved weapons delivery (armament computer and time delay unit); and a new automatic pitch control computer. Weapons include Aspide 1A medium-range and AIM-9L Sidewinder short-range air-to-air missiles.

An F-104S ASA demonstrator began flight testing in March 1985. Delivery of the first ASA aircraft to the Italian Air Force took place on 19 November 1986.

AERITALIA DC-8 FREIGHTER CONVERSION

Under a US programme launched in 1976, McDonnell Douglas converted 20 DC-8 passenger transports into specialised freighters, as recorded in the 1987-88 and earlier editions of *Jane's*. Since 1982 responsibility for the DC-8 freighter conversion programme has been held by Aeritalia's wholly owned subsidiary, Officine Aeronavali Venezia SpA, which delivered its first conversion, one of two DC-8-63Fs for Air Canada, in February 1986. Three further DC-8-63Fs were then produced for United Parcel Service of the USA, followed on 10 December 1987 by the first of 13 DC-8-71Fs that are being produced for UPS under a three-year programme.

Modification includes removal of passenger installations and fitting a production freighter seven-track floor, and a 2.16 × 3.56 m (85 × 140 in) main deck cargo door. Cabin windows are replaced by metal plugs, and a cargo loading system is installed. The aircraft are then recertificated at a new max T-O weight of 161,025 kg (355,000 lb). Conversion to turbofan power is optional for turbojet models.

AERITALIA ATLANTIC 1 MODERNISATION

The navigation, radar, sonar dropping and intercom systems of 18 Italian Air Force Breguet Atlantic 1 maritime patrol aircraft are being upgraded under a contract awarded to the European SECBAT consortium. The 'prototype' upgrade (c/n 80) was carried out by Dassault-Breguet in France, this aircraft making its first flight in the new configuration on 7 July 1987 and returning to service in March 1988. Aeritalia's Aeronavali Venezia facility is updating the remainder, the first of which (c/n 83) was due to be redelivered in August 1988. Programme completion is scheduled for October 1992.

Freighter conversion of a McDonnell Douglas DC-8 Super Sixty, carried out by Aeronavali Venezia

AERONAUTICA MACCHI

AERONAUTICA MACCHI SpA

Via Don Tornatore 6, 21100 Varese
Telephone: (0332) 287700
Telex: 380070
CHAIRMAN: Dott Fabrizio Foresio

The original Macchi company was founded in 1913 in Varese, and its first aeroplane was built in that year. On 1 January 1981 the Aeronautica Macchi group reorganised its structure, transforming itself into a holding company and transferring all of its operating activities to a newly formed, wholly owned company known as Aermacchi SpA. The group includes, besides Aermacchi SpA, the subsidiary companies SICAMB (airframe and equipment manufacturing, including licence production of Martin-Baker ejection seats), OMG (precision machining), and Vega (electronic data processing). A 25% holding in Aeronautica Macchi was acquired by Aeritalia in 1983.

AERMACCHI

AERMACCHI SpA (Subsidiary of Aeronautica Macchi SpA)

Via Sanvito Silvestro 80, CP 246, 21100 Varese
Telephone: (0332) 254111
Telex: 380070 AERMAC I
Fax: (0332) 254555
CHAIRMAN: Dott Fabrizio Foresio
MANAGING DIRECTOR: Dott Ing Ermanno Bazzocchi
GENERAL MANAGER: Dott Ing Giulio Cesare Valdonio
DEPUTY GENERAL MANAGERS:
Dott Ing Giovanni Cattaneo (Commercial)
Dott Ing Alberto Notari (Technical)
PUBLIC RELATIONS MANAGER: Franca Grandi

Aermacchi is the aircraft manufacturing company of the Aeronautica Macchi group. Its plants at Venegono airfield occupy a total area of 270,000 m² (2,906,260 sq ft), including 33,000 m² (355,210 sq ft) of covered space; the flight test centre has covered space of 5,100 m² (54,900 sq ft) in a total area of 28,000 m² (301,390 sq ft). Total workforce at the beginning of 1988 was approximately 2,500.

The MB-339A two-seat trainer is in series production for the Italian Air Force and for export. A single-seat version, the MB-339K, is also available. Other activities include the manufacture of wings for the Aeritalia G222 transport and underwing pylons for the Panavia Tornado. Aermacchi is also active in the field of aerospace ground equipment, with a complete line of hydraulic, electric and pneumatic ground carts for servicing civil and military aircraft.

AMX

Aermacchi is teamed with Aeritalia and Embraer in the AMX combat aircraft programme (see International section) for the Italian and Brazilian air forces.

AERMACCHI MB-339A

The first of two MB-339X prototypes (MM588) was flown for the first time on 12 August 1976. The second aircraft (MM589), which made its first flight on 20 May 1977, was built to pre-production standard; the third airframe was used for static and fatigue testing. The first production aircraft made its initial flight on 20 July 1978, and the first of an initial series of 51 aircraft for the Italian Air Force were handed over for pre-service trials on 8 August 1979. In addition to MB-339A trainers for the 61° Brigata Aerea at Lecce, this series included four **MB-339RM** (radiomisure) calibration aircraft delivered to 8° Gruppo Sorveglianza Elettronica of the 14° Stormo Radiomisure at Pratica de Mare from 16 February 1981, and fifteen **MB-339PAN**s (Pattuglia Acrobatica Nazionale) delivered to the Italian Air Force aerobatic team, the Frecce Tricolori, which began using the type on 27 April 1982. The PAN aircraft have the wingtip tanks deleted (to facilitate formation keeping) and a smoke generating system installed, but are otherwise similar to the standard MB-339A. At least two more MB-339As have since been converted to MB-339PAN standard to offset attrition. The last of 101 MB-339As for the Italian Air Force was delivered in 1987. Except for the RM and PAN aircraft, they are camouflaged and are available for use as an emergency close air support force.

Ten MB-339As were delivered to the Argentine Navy in 1980, 16 to the Peruvian Air Force in 1981-82, 12 to the Royal Malaysian Air Force in 1983-84, two to Dubai in 1984, and 12 to Nigeria in 1985. In 1987 three more were delivered to Dubai, plus a batch to the Ghana Air Force.

TYPE: Two-seat basic and advanced trainer and ground attack aircraft.

AIRFRAME: Structural design criteria based on MIL-A-8860A; 8g limit load factor in 'clean' configuration. Cockpit designed for 40,000 pressurisation cycles. Service life requirement 12,000 flying hours and 24,000 landings in the training role. Entire structure specially treated to prevent corrosion.

WINGS: Cantilever low/mid-wing monoplane. Wing section NACA 64A-114 (mod) at centreline, NACA 64A-212 (mod) at tip. Leading-edge swept back 11° 18′. Sweepback at quarter-chord 8° 29′. All-metal stressed skin structure, with single main spar and auxiliary rear spar, built in two portions and bolted to fuselage. Skin stiffened by spanwise stringers, closely spaced ribs, and false ribs. Wingtip tanks permanently attached. Single fence on each wing at approx two-thirds span. Servo powered ailerons embody 'Irving' type aerodynamic balance provisions, and are statically balanced along their entire span. Balance tabs facilitate reversion to manual operation in the event of servo failure. Hydraulically actuated single-slotted flaps, operated by push/pull rods.

FUSELAGE: All-metal semi-monocoque structure, built in two main portions: forward (nose to engine mounting

Aermacchi MB-339A of the Ghana Air Force

bulkhead), and rear (engine bulkhead to tailcone). Forward portion built of C section frames, four C section spars, longitudinal L section stringers, and skin panels. Rear section manufactured entirely from aluminium alloy except for firewall and most of tailcone, which are of stainless steel; four-bolt attachment to forward fuselage to facilitate access to engine. Hydraulically actuated, electrically controlled airbrake under centre of fuselage, just forward of CG.

TAIL UNIT: Cantilever all-metal structure, of similar construction to wings. Slightly sweptback vertical surfaces. Rudder and elevators are statically balanced, each having an electrically actuated dual-purpose balance and trim tab. Two auxiliary fins under rear fuselage.

LANDING GEAR: Hydraulically retractable tricycle type, with oleo-pneumatic shock absorbers; suitable for operation from semi-prepared runways. Nosewheel retracts forward, main units outward into wings. Hydraulically steerable nosewheel. Low-pressure mainwheel tubeless tyres size 545 × 175-10 (12 ply rating); nosewheel tubeless tyre size 380 × 150-4 (6 ply rating). Emergency extension system. Hydraulic disc brakes with anti-skid system.

POWER PLANT: One Rolls-Royce Viper Mk 632-43 turbojet, rated at 17.8 kN (4,000 lb st). Engines built in Italy under Rolls-Royce licence; final assembly by Piaggio. Fuel in two-cell rubber fuselage tank, capacity 781 litres (206 US gallons; 172 Imp gallons), and two integral wingtip tanks, combined capacity 632 litres (167 US gallons; 139 Imp gallons). Total internal capacity 1,413 litres (373 US gallons; 311 Imp gallons) usable. Single-point pressure refuelling receptacle in port side of fuselage, below wing trailing-edge. Gravity refuelling points on top of fuselage and each tip tank. Provision for two drop tanks, each of 325 litres (86 US gallons; 71.5 Imp gallons) usable capacity, on centre underwing stations. Anti-icing system for engine air intakes.

ACCOMMODATION: Crew of two in tandem, on Martin-Baker IT10F zero/zero ejection seats in pressurised cockpit. Rear seat elevated 32.5 cm (12¾ in). Rearview mirror for each occupant. Two-piece moulded transparent canopy, opening sideways to starboard.

SYSTEMS: Pressurisation system max differential 0.24 bars (3.5 lb/sq in). Bootstrap type air-conditioning system, which also provides air for windscreen and canopy demisting. Hydraulic system, pressure 172.5 bars (2,500 lb/sq in), for actuation of flaps, aileron servos, airbrake, landing gear, wheel brakes and nosewheel steering. Backup system for wheel brakes and emergency extension of landing gear. Main electrical DC power from one 28V 9kW engine driven starter/generator and one 28V 6kW secondary generator. Two 24V 22Ah nickel-cadmium batteries for engine starting. Fixed frequency 115/26V AC power from two 600VA single phase static inverters. External power receptacle. Low pressure demand type oxygen system, operating at 28 bars (400 lb/sq in).

AVIONICS AND EQUIPMENT: Typical avionics installation includes Collins AN/ARC-159(V)-2, or Magnavox AN/ARC-150(V), or Magnavox AN/ARC-164(V) UHF transceiver; Collins AN/ARC-186(V) VHF/AM and FM transceiver; Collins ICS-200 interphone; Collins AN/ARN-118(V) Tacan or King KDM 706A DME; Collins 51RV-4B or Bendix RNA-34A VOR/ILS and MKI-3 marker beacon receiver; Collins DF-206 ADF; GEC Avionics AD-620C computerised area and dead reckoning navigation system; and Bendix AN/APX-100(V) or Italtel SIT 421A IFF. Standard instrumentation includes ARU-2B/A attitude director indicator, AQU-6/A HSI, Sperry AS-339 attitude and heading reference system, AG-5 standby attitude indicator, and flight director system. Retractable landing light beneath port wing; taxying light on nosewheel leg.

ARMAMENT AND OPERATIONAL EQUIPMENT: Up to 1,815 kg (4,000 lb) of external stores can be carried on six underwing hardpoints, the inner four of which are stressed for loads of up to 454 kg (1,000 lb) each and the outer two for up to 340 kg (750 lb) each. Provisions are made, on the two inner stations, for the installation of two Macchi gun pods, each containing either a 30 mm DEFA 553 cannon with 120 rds, or a 12.7 mm AN/M-3 machine-gun with 350 rds. Other typical loads can include two Matra 550 Magic or AIM-9 Sidewinder air-to-air missiles on the two outer stations; four 1,000 lb or six 750 lb bombs; six SUU-11A/A 7.62 mm Minigun pods with 1,500 rds/pod; six Matra 155 launchers, each for eighteen 68 mm rockets; six Matra F-2 practice launchers, each for six 68 mm rockets; six LAU-68/A or LAU-32G launchers, each for seven 2.75 in rockets; six Aerea AL-25-50 or AL-18-50 launchers, each with twenty-five or eighteen 50 mm rockets respectively; six Aerea AL-12-80 launchers, each with twelve 81 mm rockets; four LAU-10/A launchers, each with four 5 in Zuni rockets; four Thomson-Brandt 100-4 launchers, each with four 100 mm Thomson-Brandt rockets; six Aerea BRD bomb/rocket dispensers; six Aermacchi 11B29-003 bomb/flare dispensers; six Thomson-Brandt 14-3-M2 adaptors, each with six 100 mm anti-runway bombs or 120 mm tactical support bombs; or two 325 litre (86 US gallon; 71.5 Imp gallon) drop tanks; or a photographic pod with four 70 mm Vinten cameras; or a single underwing Elettronica ECM pod, combined with a flare/chaff dispenser, onboard RHAW receiver and indicators. Provision for Aeritalia 8.105.924 fixed reflector sight or Saab RGS 2 gyroscopic gunsight; a gunsight can also be installed in rear cockpit, to enable instructor to evaluate manoeuvres performed by student pilot. All gunsights can be equipped with fully automatic Teledyne TSC 116-2 gun camera. Provision for towing type A-6B (1.83 × 9.14 m; 6 × 30 ft) aerial banner target; tow attachment point on inner surface of ventral airbrake.

DIMENSIONS, EXTERNAL:

Wing span over tip tanks	10.858 m (35 ft 7½ in)
Wing aspect ratio	6.1
Length overall	10.972 m (36 ft 0 in)
Height overall	3.994 m (13 ft 1¼ in)
Elevator span	4.08 m (13 ft 4¾ in)
Wheel track	2.483 m (8 ft 1¾ in)
Wheelbase	4.369 m (14 ft 4 in)

AREAS:

Wings, gross	19.30 m² (207.74 sq ft)
Ailerons (total)	1.328 m² (14.29 sq ft)
Trailing-edge flaps (total)	2.21 m² (23.79 sq ft)
Airbrake	0.68 m² (7.32 sq ft)
Fin	2.37 m² (25.51 sq ft)
Rudder, incl tab	0.61 m² (6.57 sq ft)
Tailplane	3.38 m² (36.38 sq ft)
Elevators (total, incl tabs)	0.979 m² (10.54 sq ft)

WEIGHTS AND LOADING:

Weight empty, equipped	3,125 kg (6,889 lb)
Basic operating weight empty	3,136 kg (6,913 lb)
Fuel load (internal, usable)	1,100 kg (2,425 lb)

T-O weight, 'clean'   4,400 kg (9,700 lb)
Typical T-O weights with armament indicated:
A: four Mk 82 bombs and two drop tanks
    5,895 kg (13,000 lb)
B: six Mk 82 bombs   5,895 kg (13,000 lb)
C: two Macchi 30 mm gun pods, two LR-25-0 rocket
    launchers and two drop tanks   5,808 kg (12,805 lb)
D: four LR-25-0 launchers and two drop tanks
    5,642 kg (12,440 lb)
E: six LR-25-0 launchers   5,323 kg (11,735 lb)
Max T-O weight with external stores
    5,895 kg (13,000 lb)
Wing loading (50 per cent fuel)
    205 kg/m² (42.00 lb/sq ft)
PERFORMANCE (at 'clean' T-O weight, ISA, except where
indicated):
IAS limit/Mach limit
    Mach 0.85 (500 knots; 926 km/h; 575 mph)
Max level speed at S/L
    485 knots (898 km/h; 558 mph) IAS
Max level speed at 9,150 m (30,000 ft)
    Mach 0.77 (441 knots; 817 km/h; 508 mph)
Max speed for landing gear extension
    175 knots (324 km/h; 201 mph) IAS
T-O speed   100 knots (185 km/h; 115 mph)
Approach speed over 15 m (50 ft) obstacle
    98 knots (182 km/h; 113 mph) IAS
Landing speed   89 knots (165 km/h; 103 mph) IAS
Stalling speed   80 knots (149 km/h; 93 mph)
Max rate of climb at S/L   2,010 m (6,595 ft)/min
Time to 9,150 m (30,000 ft)   7 min 6 s
Service ceiling (30.5 m; 100 ft/min rate of climb)
    14,630 m (48,000 ft)
Min ground turning radius   8.45 m (27 ft 8¾ in)
T-O run at S/L: 'clean' T-O weight   465 m (1,525 ft)
   max T-O weight   915 m (3,000 ft)
Landing run at S/L, ISA   415 m (1,362 ft)
Max range without drop tanks
    950 nm (1,760 km; 1,094 miles)
Max ferry range with two underwing drop tanks, 10%
   reserves   1,140 nm (2,110 km; 1,310 miles)
Max endurance without drop tanks   2 h 50 min
Max endurance at 7,620 m (25,000 ft) with two
   underwing drop tanks, 10% reserves   3 h 45 min
g limits   +8/−4
PERFORMANCE (armed configuration, at T-O weights given
earlier):
Radius of action, hi-lo-hi (no run-in or run-out):
   A   320 nm (593 km; 368 miles)
   B   212 nm (393 km; 244 miles)
   C   275 nm (510 km; 317 miles)
   D   305 nm (565 km; 351 miles)
   E   165 nm (306 km; 190 miles)
Radius of action, lo-lo-lo (no run-in or run-out):
   A   200 nm (371 km; 230 miles)
   B   146 nm (271 km; 168 miles)
   C   190 nm (352 km; 219 miles)
   D   193 nm (358 km; 222 miles)
   E   123 nm (228 km; 142 miles)

AERMACCHI MB-339B and C

Aermacchi introduced two new two-seat variants of the
MB-339 in 1985, both powered by the Viper 680 engine.
Details are as follows:

MB-339B. Advanced jet trainer, with enhanced light
close air support capability compared with MB-339A. Fuel
capacity increased by use of enlarged wingtip tanks. No
orders announced up to early 1988.

MB-339C. Improved trainer/close air support version,
with digital nav/attack system and other advanced avionics.
Engine and enlarged wingtip tanks as MB-339B. Modified
nose shape. Intended for effective pilot training in modern
mission management techniques. Design and development
began in 1982-83; prototype (I-AMDA) flew for the first
time on 17 December 1985; flight testing passed the
215-flight mark in December 1987 and a decision to begin
production of an initial batch of 20 was taken in January
1988, in anticipation of the first orders. Completion of the
first production aircraft was planned for Autumn 1988.
Meanwhile, qualification of specific weapons is continuing,
with the AIM-9L Sidewinder and AGM-65D Maverick
scheduled for integration by the Summer of 1989. The
description of the MB-339A applies also to the two new
models except for the following details:
POWER PLANT (B and C): One 19.57 kN (4,400 lb st)
Rolls-Royce Viper Mk 680-43 turbojet. Fuselage fuel
capacity as for MB-339A, but capacity of each integral
tip tank increased to 500 litres (132 US gallons; 110 Imp
gallons), giving total usable capacity of 1,781 litres (470
US gallons; 392 Imp gallons). Provision retained for two
325 litre (86 US gallon; 71.5 Imp gallon) drop tanks on
centre underwing stations.
AVIONICS AND EQUIPMENT (C): Typical avionics installation
includes Collins AN/ARN-118(V) type RT-1159/A
Tacan or King KDM 706A DME; Collins 51RV-4B
VOR/ILS and MKI-3 marker beacon receiver; Collins
ADF-6A ADF/LF; Collins DF-301E VHF/UHF ADF
(optional); GEC Avionics AD-660 Doppler radar
integrated with a Litton LR-80 inertial platform; GEC
Avionics 620K navigation computer; Kaiser Sabre
head-up display/weapons aiming computer; Aeritalia

Prototype MB-339C, equipped with Viper 680 engine and a digital nav/attack system

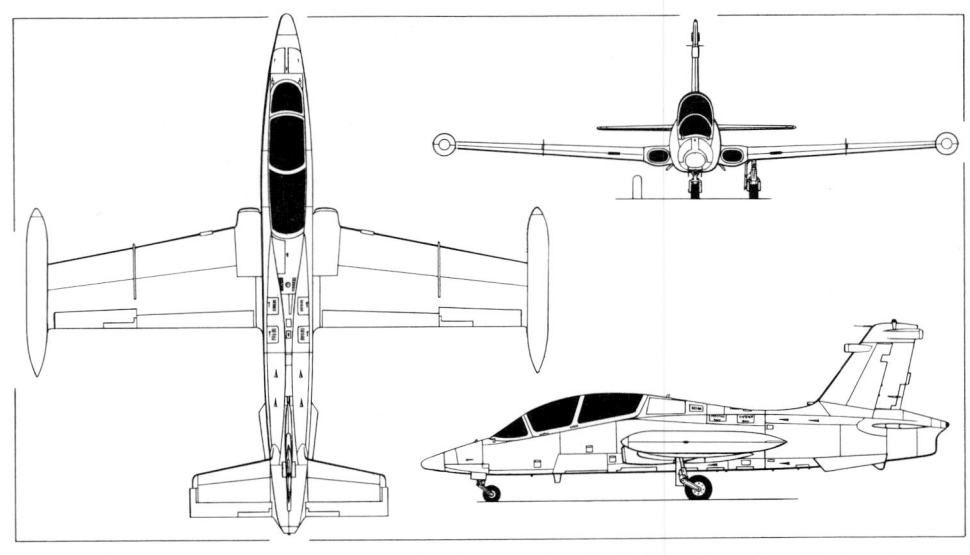
Aermacchi MB-339C, showing revised nose and vertical tail configuration (*Pilot Press*)

CRT multifunction display; Aeritalia/Honeywell
HG7505 radar altimeter; Fiar P 0702 laser rangefinder;
ELT-156 radar warning system; Logic stores manage-
ment system; Bendix AN/APX-100 IFF; Astronautics
ARU-50/A attitude director indicator; Astronautics
AQU-13 HSI; Fairchild Weston video camera; HOTAS
(hands on throttle and stick) controls; Tracor AN/ALE-
40 chaff/flare dispensers; and Elettronica ELT-555 active
ECM pod.
ARMAMENT (B): Loads on six underwing hardpoints as for
MB-339A. The aircraft is cleared for operation with
rockets of 50 mm (SNIA), 68 mm, 81 mm (SNORA), 100
mm (Thomson-Brandt), 2.75 in and 5 in calibre, and with
500 lb Mk 82 and R bombs, 100 mm Thomson-Brandt
runway demolition bombs, 120 mm close air support
bombs, 250 lb Expal BPR bombs, 500 lb Matra bombs,
and air-to-air infra-red missiles (AIM-9L and Matra
Magic).
ARMAMENT (C): Nav/attack system makes possible the
employment of air-to-air infra-red missiles (AIM-9L and
Matra Magic), AGM-65 Maverick air-to-ground missiles
and Marte Mk II sea skimming anti-ship missiles.
DIMENSIONS, EXTERNAL: As for MB-339A except:
Wing span over tip tanks: B, C   11.22 m (36 ft 9¾ in)
Length overall: C   11.24 m (36 ft 10½ in)
WEIGHTS (B):
Weight empty, equipped   3,310 kg (7,297 lb)
Max internal fuel (usable)   1,388 kg (3,060 lb)
T-O weight (training configuration)
    4,635 kg (10,218 lb)
Max T-O weight with external stores
    6,350 kg (14,000 lb)
PERFORMANCE (B at training configuration T-O weight,
ISA):
Max level speed at S/L   487 knots (902 km/h; 560 mph)
Max rate of climb at S/L   2,225 m (7,300 ft)/min
Time to 9,150 m (30,000 ft)   6 min 42 s
Combat radius with four 500 lb Mk 82 bombs, internal
   fuel only: lo-lo-lo   170 nm (315 km; 196 miles)
    hi-lo-hi   270 nm (500 km; 311 miles)
Max range:
   without drop tanks   1,060 nm (1,965 km; 1,221 miles)
   ferry, with two underwing drop tanks, 10% reserves
    1,187 nm (2,200 km; 1,367 miles)
Max endurance: without drop tanks   3 h 15 min
   with two underwing drop tanks, 10% reserves
    3 h 55 min

AERMACCHI MB-339D

Aermacchi confirmed in early 1988 that it was studying a
twin-engined MB-339, with two overwing mounted P&WC

JT15D turbofans, as a possible candidate to meet a USAF
primary trainer requirement.

AERMACCHI MB-339K

The MBB-339K (Aermacchi has dropped the original
name Veltro 2) is a single-seat development of the
MB-339A, optimised for the roles of light close air support
and operational training. The private venture prototype
(I-BITE) flew for the first time on 30 May 1980, powered by
a 17.8 kN (4,000 lb st) Viper Mk 632 engine. The airframe of
the MB-339A is retained, except for a new forward fuselage
with redesigned single-seat cockpit, internally mounted
cannon armament, auxiliary fuselage fuel tank and enlarged
wingtip tanks. The other major changes concern the power
plant, and the avionics and equipment relevant to the
different roles of the single-seater. Production aircraft
would have a Viper Mk 680 engine.

The following description applies to the basic MB-339K;
operational capability can, at customer's option, be
extended by adopting such additional features as a head-up
display, cockpit TV display, ECM, and other improved
avionics. (For further details of these, see Aermacchi
MB-339C entry.)

No orders had been announced by early 1988.
TYPE: Single-seat ground attack aircraft and operational
trainer.
AIRFRAME: As described in 1986-87 and earlier *Jane's*.
POWER PLANT: One 19.57 kN (4,400 lb st) Rolls-Royce Viper
Mk 680 turbojet. Fuel in one fuselage tank, consisting of
three rubber cells with a total capacity of 1,030 litres (272
US gallons; 226.5 Imp gallons), and two constant section
integral wingtip tanks with a combined capacity of 1,020
litres (269.5 US gallons; 224.5 Imp gallons). Total usable
internal fuel capacity 2,050 litres (541.5 US gallons; 451
Imp gallons).
ACCOMMODATION: Pilot only, on Martin-Baker IT10LK
zero/zero ejection seat in pressurised cockpit. Rearview
mirror standard. One-piece moulded transparent canopy,
opening sideways to starboard.
SYSTEMS, AVIONICS AND EQUIPMENT: See 1986-87 *Jane's*.
ARMAMENT AND OPERATIONAL EQUIPMENT: Two 30 mm
DEFA cannon, with 120 rds/gun, mounted internally in
lower forward fuselage, with external fairings. Firing rate
1,200 rds/min. Loads on six underwing hardpoints
generally as for MB-339A. Aircraft is cleared for
operation with rockets of 50 mm (SNIA), 68 mm, 81 mm
(SNORA), 100 mm (Thomson-Brandt), 2.75 in and 5 in
calibre, and with 500 lb Mk 82 and R bombs, 100 mm
Thomson-Brandt special runway demolition bombs, 120
mm close air support bombs, 250 lb Expal BPR bombs

and 500 lb Matra bombs. Elettronica ELT555 airborne deception jamming and warning pod can be carried underwing. Under study are two additional 30 mm guns in pods and a Sidewinder missile installation. Saab-Scania RGS 2 gunsight, with gyro lead computer; gunsight can be equipped with a fully automatic Teledyne TSC 116-2 gun camera. Provision for towing type A-6B (1.83 × 9.14 m; 6 × 30 ft) aerial banner target.

DIMENSIONS, EXTERNAL: As for MB-339A except:

Wing span over tip tanks	11.22 m (36 ft 9¾ in)
Length overall	10.85 m (35 ft 7 in)

AREAS: As for MB-339A

WEIGHTS:

Weight empty, equipped	3,245 kg (7,154 lb)
Fuel load (internal, usable, with circular-section tip tanks)	1,582 kg (3,488 lb)
Max external stores load	1,935 kg (4,266 lb)
T-O weight 'clean', incl ammunition for internal guns	5,050 kg (11,133 lb)
Max T-O weight with external stores	6,350 kg (14,000 lb)

PERFORMANCE (with full gun ammunition load):

Max limiting Mach number	0.85
Never-exceed speed	500 knots (927 km/h; 575 mph)
Max level speed at S/L	486 knots (900 km/h; 560 mph) IAS

Aermacchi MB-339K light close air support aircraft, developed from the two-seat MB-339A

Landing speed	95 knots (176 km/h; 109 mph) IAS	Landing run	450 m (1,475 ft)
Max rate of climb at S/L	2,400 m (7,875 ft)/min	Combat radius with two 30 mm cannon (125 rds/gun)	
Service ceiling	14,000 m (46,000 ft)	and four 500 lb Mk 82 bombs (total military load 1,088	
T-O run: 'clean'	580 m (1,900 ft)	kg; 2,400 lb): lo-lo-lo	205 nm (380 km; 236 miles)
at max T-O weight of 6,350 kg (14,000 lb)		hi-lo-hi	340 nm (630 km; 391 miles)
	910 m (2,985 ft)	g limits	+8/−4

AGUSTA

AGUSTA SpA

21017 Cascina Costa di Samarate (VA)
Telephone: (0331) 229111
Telex: 332569 AGUCA I
OFFICES:
Via Caldera 21, 20153 Milan
Telephone: (02) 452751
Telex: 333280 AGUMI I
Fax: (02) 3498729
Via Abruzzi 11, 00187 Rome
Telephone: (06) 49801
Telex: 614398 AGURO I
Via Sicilia 43, 00187 Rome
Telephone: (06) 49801
Telex: 614398 AGURO I
PRESIDENT AND CHIEF EXECUTIVE OFFICER:
Dott Raffaello Teti
MANAGING DIRECTOR: Dott Domenico Tatangelo
SENIOR VICE-PRESIDENTS:
Dott Ing Arnaldo Antichi
Dott Giuseppe Di Girolamo
Formed originally in 1977, the Agusta Group (see 1980-81 *Jane's*) completely reorganised its structure from 1 January 1981 under a new holding company known as Agusta SpA. It is part of the Italian public holding agency EFIM, and has three main divisions employing nearly 10,000 people in 12 factories in various parts of Italy.

DIVISIONE ELICOTTERI (Helicopter Division)
MANAGING DIRECTOR: Dott Ing Bruno Lovera
Costruzioni Aeronautiche Giovanni Agusta SpA
See following entry
EM (Elicotteri Meridionali SpA)
See page 155
EH Industries Ltd (50% holding), London, England
See International section
EH Industries Inc, Wilmington, Delaware, USA
EH Industries Inc, Ottawa, Canada
Joint European Helicopter
See International section
BredaNardi Costruzioni Aeronautiche SpA
See page 160
DIVISIONE AEROPLANI (Aircraft Division)
MANAGING DIRECTOR: Dott Ing Ferruccio Tommasi
SIAI-Marchetti SpA
See pages 155-159
Industria Aeronautica Meridionale SpA
Contrada Santa Teresa Pinti, 72100 Brindisi (aircraft co-production, and overhaul of aircraft and helicopters)
Telephone: (0831) 8911
Telex: 860026 IAMBR I
Caproni Vizzola Costruzioni Aeronautiche SpA
See pages 159-160

DIVISIONE SISTEMI ED ATTIVITÀ VARIE (Diversified Activities and Systems Division)
MANAGING DIRECTOR: Dott Ing Giuseppe Bertolazzi
Agusta Sistemi SpA
Via Isonzo 33, 21049 Tradate
Telephone: (0331) 843569 or 842143
Telex: 333893 OPTRA I
OMI (Ottico Meccanica Italiana SpA)
Via della Vasca Navale 79/81, 00145 Rome
Telephone: (06) 55421
Telex: 610137 SAROMI I
OMICA (OMI Corporation of America)
1319 Powhatan Street, Alexandria, Virginia 22314, USA
Telephone: (730) 549 4064
Telex: 809141 OMICA ALE
FOMB (Fonderie ed Officine Meccaniche di Benevento SpA)
Contrada Ponte Valentino, 82100 Benevento
Telephone: (0824) 43477
Telex: 710667 FOMBEN I
MV (Meccanica Verghera SpA)
Viale Adriatico 50, 21010 Verghera di Samarate (product support for MV Agusta motorcycles)
Telephone: (0331) 228200

COSTRUZIONI AERONAUTICHE GIOVANNI AGUSTA SpA

21017 Cascina Costa di Samarate (VA)
Telephone: (0331) 229111
Telex: 332569 AGUCA I
COMMERCIAL OFFICES:
Via Caldera 21, 20153 Milan
Telephone: (02) 452751
Telex: 333280 AGUMI I
PRESIDENT AND CHIEF EXECUTIVE OFFICER:
Dott Raffaello Teti
GENERAL MANAGER: Dott Ing Michele Ferraioli
The original Agusta company, established in 1907 by Giovanni Agusta, built many experimental and production aircraft before the Second World War. In 1952 Agusta acquired a licence to manufacture the Bell Model 47 helicopter, and the first Agusta built Model 47G made its initial flight on 22 May 1954.
In addition to the A 109A and A 129 of its own design, Agusta is currently producing under licence the Bell Models 206, 212 and 412, and the Sikorsky S-61A, SH-3H and HH-3F (S-61R). Agusta is now the sole production source of these Sikorsky aircraft. It has developed its own AS-61N1 short-fuselage derivative of the civil Sikorsky S-61N, produces under licence the Boeing CH-47C Chinook helicopter, and is collaborating with Westland Helicopters of the UK in developing the EH 101 three-turboshaft helicopter (see under EHI in the International section).
Other international programmes in which Agusta participates are the Eurofar tilt-rotor project, the JEH Tonal (derived from the A129) and the NH 90. Details of these also appear in the International section.

AGUSTA A 109A Mk II
The first of three A 109 flying prototypes flew for the first time on 4 August 1971. RAI and FAA certification for VFR operation was announced on 1 June 1975, and deliveries of the original A 109A production version started in early 1976. Certification for IFR single-pilot operation was obtained on 20 January 1977. Certification has also been granted in Australia, Canada, France, West Germany,

Agusta A 109A Mk II general purpose helicopter in 'wide-body' configuration

Japan, Mexico, New Zealand, the Philippines, Sweden, Switzerland, the UK and Venezuela. Brazilian certification was in progress in early 1988. Approximately 150 of this initial version, described in the 1981-82 *Jane's*, were built.
Deliveries of the uprated A 109A Mk II began in September 1981. This has an increase in transmission rating, a new tail rotor driveshaft, increased tail rotor blade life and reliability, new self-damping engine mounts, integral-design oil coolers and blowers, a structurally redesigned tailboom, higher-pressure hydraulic system, improved avionics and instrument layout, and a removable floor in the baggage compartment. It is also available in a utility version with less sophisticated interior and instrumentation. Under a 1983 agreement, Hellenic Aerospace Industries (see Greek section) was continuing to produce major fuselage components for 77 Mk IIs during 1988.
In 1985 Agusta introduced a 'wide-bodied' version of the Mk II, with a more roomy and comfortable cabin created by modifying the shape of the underfloor fuel tanks and using bulged fuselage side panels similar to those of the medevac version. These changes do not affect either the basic structure or aerodynamic characteristics of the helicopter.
Agusta had delivered about 180 A 109A Mk IIs by early 1988, of which about 100 were wide-body, VIP or

medevac versions (see 'Accommodation' paragraph) sold to customers in the USA. One VIP 'wide-body' was delivered to the President of Italy, for whom it is operated by the 31° Stormo of the Italian Air Force.
The following description applies to the standard A 109A Mk II:
TYPE: Twin-engined general purpose helicopter.
ROTOR SYSTEM: Fully articulated four-blade single main rotor and port side two-blade semi-rigid delta-hinged tail rotor. Main rotor blades have an NACA 23011.3/13006 'droop snoot' aerofoil section, with thickness/chord ratios of 11.3% at root and 6% at tip, and are attached to hub by tension/torsion straps. They are of aluminium alloy bonded construction, with a honeycomb core, have swept tips, stainless steel tip caps and leading-edge strips, and are protected against corrosion. A manual blade folding capability and rotor brake are optional. Tail rotor blades are of aluminium alloy, bonded at the trailing-edge, with a Nomex honeycomb core and stainless steel leading-edge strip.
ROTOR DRIVE: Main transmission assembly housed in fairing above passenger cabin, driving main rotor through a coupling gearbox and 90° two-stage (15.62:1) main reduction gearbox. Take-off drive from coupling gearbox drives tail rotor via an output shaft and tail rotor

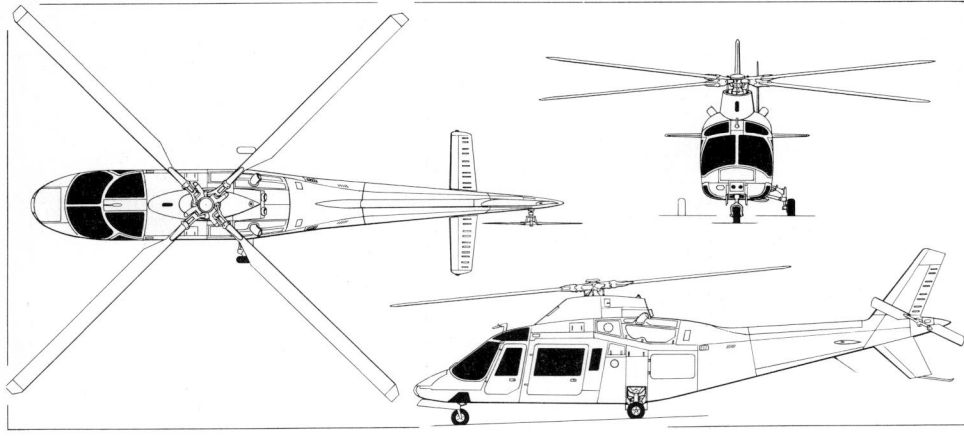

Agusta A 109A Mk II twin-engined general purpose helicopter *(Pilot Press)*

gearbox. Transmission ratings 552 kW (740 shp) for take-off and max continuous twin-engined operation, with max contingency rating of 607 kW (814 shp) for 6 s. Ratings for single-engined operation are 336 kW (450 shp) for take-off (5 min limit), 313 kW (420 shp) max continuous, and 336 kW (450 shp) max contingency for 10 s. Main rotor/engine rpm ratio 1:15.62; tail rotor/engine rpm ratio 1:2.80.

FUSELAGE AND TAIL UNIT: Pod and boom type, built in four main sections: nose, cockpit, passenger cabin and tailboom. Sweptback vertical fins (above and below tailboom). Non-swept elevator, mid-mounted on tailboom forward of fins, is linked to collective pitch control.

LANDING GEAR: Retractable tricycle type, with oleo-pneumatic shock absorber in each unit. Single main-wheels and castoring (45° each side of centre), self-centring nosewheel. Hydraulic retraction, nosewheel forward, mainwheels upward into fuselage. Hydraulic emergency extension and locking. Magnaghi disc brakes on mainwheels. All tyres are of Kléber-Colombes tubeless type, and of same size (650 × 6) and pressure (5.9 bars; 85 lb/sq in). Tailskid under ventral fin. Emergency pop-out flotation gear and fixed snow skis optional.

POWER PLANT: Two Allison 250-C20B turboshafts (each 313 kW; 420 shp for 5 min for T-O, 298 kW; 400 shp max continuous power, 276 kW; 370 shp max cruise power, derated to 258 kW; 346 shp for twin-engine operation), mounted side by side in upper rear fuselage and separated from passenger cabin and from each other by firewalls. Two bladder fuel tanks in lower rear fuselage, combined capacity 560 litres (148 US gallons; 123 Imp gallons), of which 550 litres (145.3 US gallons; 121 Imp gallons) are usable. Refuelling point in each side of fuselage, near top of each tank. Oil capacity 7.7 litres (2.0 US gallons; 1.7 Imp gallons) for each engine and 12 litres (3.2 US gallons; 2.6 Imp gallons) for transmission. Provision for internal auxiliary tank containing up to 170 litres (44.9 US gallons; 37.4 Imp gallons) of fuel.

ACCOMMODATION: Crew of one or two on flight deck, with pilot seated on right. Dual controls optional. Main cabin seats up to six passengers on three forward or rearward facing seats in centre, plus three forward facing seats at rear. A seventh passenger can be carried in lieu of second crew member. Four/five-seat VIP layout available, with refreshment and music centre. Forward opening crew door and passenger door on each side. Large space at rear of cabin for up to 150 kg (331 lb) of baggage, with access via forward opening door on port side. Centre row of seats removable to permit use as freight transport. Medevac version can accommodate one stretcher installed crosswise (by replacing standard doors with 'bubble' doors), and complete medical equipment including oxygen cylinders (enough for three hours' use), oxygen/air-oxygen respirator with flowmeter humidifier, ECG with monitoring equipment, and equipment for intensive care. A quick-change emergency medical service (EMS) unit is available which enables the standard transport configuration to be changed to air ambulance layout within a few minutes. The EMS configuration accommodates a pilot and three medical attendants, a longitudinally placed stretcher, and a cardio-circulatory and respiratory intensive care system. A second stretcher patient can be carried if necessary. In a cargo role, external freight can be transported on a CG hook. Sliding doors can be installed for rescue missions.

SYSTEMS: Two identical independent Magnaghi hydraulic systems, pressure 107 bars (1,550 lb/sq in), supply dual flight servo-controls and provide emergency power in the event of engine failure. A utility system connected to No. 2 servo-hydraulic system provides power to actuate landing gear, wheel and rotor braking, nosewheel locking, and emergency backup. 28V DC electrical system, using two 30V 150A engine driven starter/generators, and one 24V 13Ah nickel-cadmium battery (22Ah heavy duty battery on IFR version). Single phase AC power at 400Hz supplied by two 115/26V 250VA solid state static inverters. Third inverter as emergency backup on IFR version. External power receptacle. Engine anti-icing system, using engine bleed air.

AVIONICS: Standard instrumentation, plus Collins avionics for VFR or IFR operation, to customer's requirements, including VHF-20A VHF-AM com (dual in IFR version), AG-06 intercom, VIR-31A VOR/ILS with VOR/LOC, glideslope and marker beacon receiver, TDR-90 ATC transponder, ADF-60A and DME-40. Optional avionics include Sperry AA-300 radio altimeter with LGSC, Helcis II flight director and autotrim, AFCS, pilot's navigation instruments, co-pilot's flight and navigation instruments, standby attitude indicator, two-or three-axis autopilot, Bendix/FIAR RDR-1500 or Sperry Primus 300SL weather radar, and Loran or Omega navigation system, depending on requirement.

EQUIPMENT: Depending upon mission, may include internal cargo platform, external cargo sling, externally mounted rescue hoist, first aid kit, stretchers, Chadwick water bomber container for 208 or 584 litres (55 or 154.2 US gallons; 45.75 or 128.5 Imp gallons) of water or fire retardant, or equipment for exploration, thermal mapping, survey, or powerline control duties.

DIMENSIONS, EXTERNAL:

Main rotor diameter	11.00 m (36 ft 1 in)
Tail rotor diameter	2.03 m (6 ft 8 in)
Length overall, rotors turning	13.05 m (42 ft 9¾ in)
Fuselage: Length	10.706 m (35 ft 1½ in)
Max width (except 'wide-body')	1.42 m (4 ft 8 in)
Height over tail fin	3.30 m (10 ft 10 in)
Elevator span	2.88 m (9 ft 5½ in)
Width over mainwheels	2.45 m (8 ft 0½ in)
Wheelbase	3.535 m (11 ft 7¼ in)
Passenger doors (each): Height	1.06 m (3 ft 5¾ in)
Width	1.15 m (3 ft 9¼ in)
Height to sill	0.65 m (2 ft 1½ in)
Baggage door (port, rear): Height	0.51 m (1 ft 8 in)
Width	1.00 m (3 ft 3¼ in)

DIMENSIONS, INTERNAL:

Cabin, excl flight deck: Length	1.63 m (5 ft 4¼ in)
Max width	1.32 m (4 ft 4 in)
Max height	1.28 m (4 ft 2½ in)
Volume	2.82 m³ (100 cu ft)
Baggage compartment volume	0.52 m³ (18.4 cu ft)

AREAS:

Main rotor blades (each)	1.84 m² (19.8 sq ft)
Tail rotor blades (each)	0.203 m² (2.185 sq ft)
Main rotor disc	95.03 m² (1,022.9 sq ft)
Tail rotor disc	3.24 m² (34.87 sq ft)

WEIGHTS AND LOADINGS:

Basic weight empty, equipped:	
standard	1,418 kg (3,126 lb)
offshore oil support (IFR)	1,604 kg (3,536 lb)
ambulance (IFR)	1,647 kg (3,631 lb)
firefighting	1,596 kg (3,518 lb)
Max external slung load	907 kg (2,000 lb)
Max baggage	150 kg (331 lb)
Typical T-O weight:	
offshore oil support (IFR)	2,596 kg (5,723 lb)
ambulance (IFR)	2,409 kg (5,311 lb)
Max certificated T-O weight	2,600 kg (5,732 lb)

Max disc loading	27.4 kg/m² (5.60 lb/sq ft)
Max power loading	4.15 kg/kW (6.82 lb/shp)

PERFORMANCE (S/L, ISA, except where indicated. A: AUW of 2,250 kg; 4,960 lb, B: AUW of 2,450 kg; 5,400 lb, C: AUW of 2,600 kg; 5,732 lb):

Never-exceed speed:	
A, B, C	168 knots (311 km/h; 193 mph)
Max cruising speed: A	154 knots (285 km/h; 177 mph)
B, C	150 knots (278 km/h; 172 mph)
Econ cruising speed:	
A, B, C	126 knots (233 km/h; 145 mph)
Max rate of climb at S/L: A	643 m (2,110 ft)/min
B	555 m (1,820 ft)/min
C	503 m (1,650 ft)/min
Rate of climb at S/L, one engine out:	
A	152 m (500 ft)/min
B	108 m (355 ft)/min
C	78 m (255 ft)/min
Service ceiling, 30.5 m (100 ft)/min rate of climb, at max continuous power: A, B	4,575 m (15,000 ft)
C	4,450 m (14,600 ft)
Service ceiling, one engine out, 30.5 m (100 ft)/min rate of climb, at max continuous power:	
C	1,675 m (5,500 ft)
Hovering ceiling IGE: A	3,750 m (12,300 ft)
B	2,985 m (9,800 ft)
C	2,410 m (7,900 ft)
Hovering ceiling OGE: A	2,880 m (9,450 ft)
B	2,072 m (6,800 ft)
C	1,493 m (4,900 ft)
Range with max standard fuel, no reserves:	
A	350 nm (648 km; 402 miles)
B	341 nm (631 km; 392 miles)
C	332 nm (615 km; 382 miles)
Endurance with max fuel, no reserves: A	3 h 12 min
B	3 h 2 min
C	2 h 57 min

AGUSTA A 109A Mk II (MILITARY, NAVAL and POLICE VERSIONS)

Several non-commercial versions of the A 109A have been developed by Agusta. In general, their configuration, structure and power plant are similar to those of the standard civil versions, although specially modified versions can be made available if required. Features of some or all military and naval versions include, as standard, dual controls and instrumentation; rotor brake; tail rotor control magnetic brake; sliding doors; environmental control system; emergency flotation gear; armoured seats; heavy duty battery; particle separator; external cargo hook; multi-purpose universal supports for external stores; rescue hoist; and high-load cargo floor. The naval versions, specially configured for shipboard compatibility, can be equipped with four-axis AFCS, radar altimeter, internal auxiliary fuel tanks, non-retractable landing gear, search radar, anchorage points for deck lashings, and an automatic navigation system.

The principal military, naval and other non-commercial versions were listed in some detail in the 1984-85 *Jane's*. The following is an abbreviated description:

Aerial scout. Can be armed with a flexibly mounted 7.62 mm or 12.7 mm machine-gun, with stabilised sight, plus two XM157 launchers (each with seven 2.75 in rockets). Normal crew of three.

Light attack against tanks and other hard-point targets. Has been demonstrated with Hughes M65 TOW system incorporating undernose telescopic sight unit, plus four or eight TOW missiles. Normal crew of two. Argentine Army has adapted its A 109As to carry Mathogo anti-tank missiles.

Light attack against soft-point targets. Various combinations of armament include a pintle mounted 7.62 mm machine-gun in each doorway; a flexible, remotely controlled externally mounted 7.62 mm gun; twin trainable, remotely controlled externally mounted 7.62 mm guns; two external machine-gun pods; or two gun pods and two rocket launchers. Normal crew of two.

Command and control. For target designation and direction of helicopter attack force. Can be armed with combination of rockets and flexible machine-guns, as described in preceding paragraph.

Agusta A 109A Mk II in EMS (emergency medical service) operation

Utility. For up to seven troops; two stretcher patients and two medical attendants; externally mounted rescue hoist; or underfuselage hook for slung load.

Mirach. Version carrying two Mirach 100 RPVs for battlefield surveillance, reconnaissance, target acquisition, elint, ECM, attack on ground or naval targets, and enemy defence saturation or decoy.

ESM/ECM. Electronic warfare version, for military and naval use. Available with passive ESM only, plus weapon systems if required; and with passive ESM plus modularised active ECM (jamming), plus any required weapons. Provision for chaff dispenser to be mounted on tailboom.

Naval. Primary naval missions are anti-surface vessel, electronic warfare, standoff missile guidance, reconnaissance, and anti-submarine classification. Secondary capabilities for search and rescue, troop transportation, ambulance, flying crane, coastguard patrol, and inter-ship liaison duties. Configurations for electronic warfare and utility roles generally similar to those described in preceding 'Utility' and 'ESM/ECM' paragraphs. For the ASW role, specialised equipment includes MAD, one or two homing torpedoes and six marine markers. For the ASV role the naval A 109A carries a high performance long-range search radar with high discrimination in rough sea conditions. The surface attack is performed with air-to-surface wire-guided missiles. For the TG-2 (standoff missile guidance) mission, the helicopter is equipped with a special system to control and guide a ship-launched Otomat missile. For armed patrol, the naval A 109A is equipped with a search radar and armament to customer's requirements. The coastguard patrol configuration includes a search radar, a special installation for external high efficiency loudspeakers, and a searchlight.

Police and other patrol duties. For patrol (including armed patrol) and surveillance, search and rescue, fire-fighting, and similar utility missions. Principal SAR equipment includes search radar, rescue hoist, stretcher/first aid kits, radar altimeter, skis or emergency flotation gear, AFCS, and flare/smoke grenades. For aerial patrol it can include 360° radar, automatic stability control system, external loudspeakers, FLIR, pollution monitoring equipment, system for spraying chemical retardants, and other items depending upon requirements of mission.

ROTOR DRIVE: As for civil A 109A Mk II, except for twin-engined max contingency rating of 638 kW (856 shp) and 5 min single-engined T-O rating of 313 kW (420 shp).

TYPICAL WEIGHTS (military Mk II):

Basic weight empty	1,418 kg (3,126 lb)
Weight empty, equipped: utility	1,560 kg (3,439 lb)
ESM/ECM	1,627 kg (3,587 lb)
ambulance	1,630 kg (3,594 lb)
scout, attack, air defence	1,650 kg (3,638 lb)
anti-tank	1,790 kg (3,946 lb)
Armament/equipment/payload:	
ambulance (1 medical attendant)	80 kg (176 lb)
air defence (8 missiles)	150 kg (331 lb)
anti-tank (8 missiles)	196 kg (432 lb)
ESM/ECM (radar warning, deception jammer, noise jammer, ESM equipment)	270 kg (595 lb)
scout (2 podded 12.7 mm and 2 pintle mounted 7.62 mm machine-guns)	287 kg (633 lb)
attack (2 podded 12.7 mm machine-guns and 14 rockets in pods)	344 kg (758 lb)
utility (7 equipped troops)	630 kg (1,389 lb)
T-O weight: ambulance	2,330 kg (5,136 lb)
air defence	2,500 kg (5,512 lb)
scout, attack, anti-tank, Mirach, ESM/ECM, utility (max T-O weight)	2,600 kg (5,732 lb)

PERFORMANCE (S/L, ISA, except where indicated. A: AUW of 2,250 kg; 4,960 lb, B: AUW of 2,450 kg; 5,400 lb, C: AUW of 2,600 kg; 5,732 lb): As civil Mk II except:

Max cruising speed: A	155 knots (287 km/h; 178 mph)
B	150 knots (278 km/h; 173 mph)
C	147 knots (272 km/h; 169 mph)
Econ cruising speed: A	126 knots (233 km/h; 145 mph)
B	125 knots (232 km/h; 144 mph)
C	124 knots (230 km/h; 143 mph)
Max rate of climb at S/L: A	640 m (2,100 ft)/min

Service ceiling, 30.5 m (100 ft)/min rate of climb, at max continuous power: A 5,485 m (18,000 ft)
B 4,575 m (15,000 ft)
C 4,450 m (14,600 ft)

Range with max standard fuel, no reserves:
A 320 nm (593 km; 368 miles)
B 310 nm (574 km; 357 miles)
C 300 nm (556 km; 345 miles)

Range with max standard fuel, 10 min reserves:
Mirach 360 nm (667 km; 414 miles)

Endurance with max standard fuel, no reserves:
A 3 h 43 min
B 3 h 30 min
C 3 h 15 min

Endurance with max standard fuel, 10 min reserves:
Mirach 4 h 30 min

AGUSTA A 109 EOA

Twenty-four examples of this new version of the A 109 have been ordered by the Italian Army as advanced observation helicopters. Deliveries were due to begin in early 1988 and to be completed by mid-year.

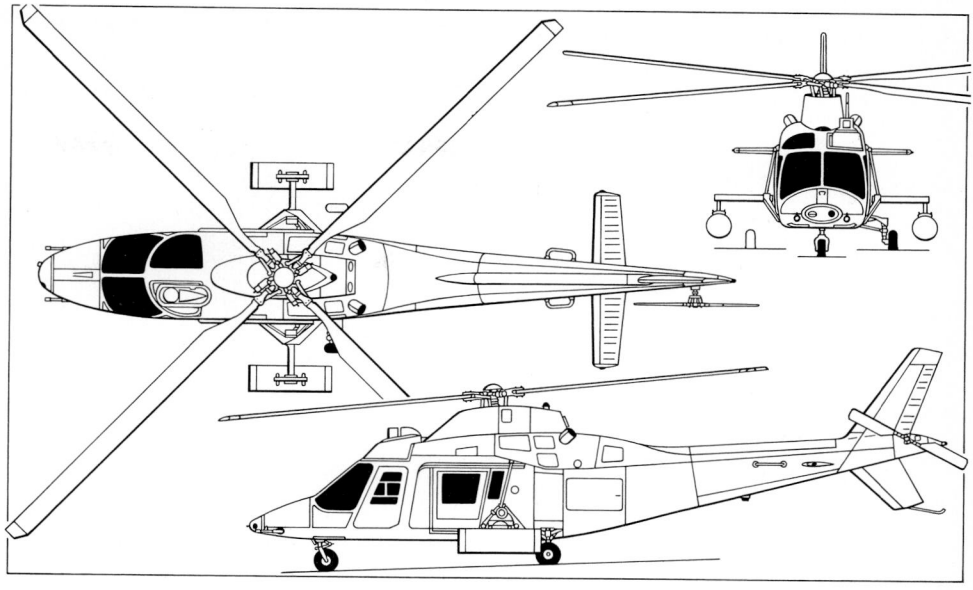

Agusta A 109 EOA, with uprated engines and transmission, non-retractable landing gear and other changes *(Jane's/Mike Keep)*

The EOA has the lengthened nose and fixed, raised landing gear of the A 109K (see following entry), but is powered by uprated Allison 250-C20R engines, offering better 'hot and high' performance than the -C20Bs in the standard A 109A Mk II. Other features include sliding cabin doors, crashworthy fuel tanks, a wide range of armament options, and electronic warfare equipment.

TYPE: Twin-engined observation and support helicopter.

ROTOR SYSTEM AND DRIVE: As described for standard A 109A Mk II. Main rotor brake standard, blade folding optional. Main transmission ratings 589/335.5 kW (790/450 shp) for twin- and single-engined operation respectively.

FUSELAGE AND TAIL UNIT: Generally as for A 109A Mk II, with lengthened nose of A 109K.

LANDING GEAR: Tricycle type, as described for A 109A Mk II, but non-retractable and higher, offering greater energy absorption.

POWER PLANT: Two 335.5 kW (450 shp) Allison 250-C20R/1 turboshafts. Two semi-self-sealing fuel tanks under rear passenger seats, capacities as for A 109A Mk II. Oil capacity also unchanged.

ACCOMMODATION: One or two pilots, with ergonomically designed instrument panel fully equipped for IFR/IMC conditions, and seats armoured to withstand 7.62 mm hits from 90 m (295 ft) away. Main cabin seats six or seven troops, with sliding door on each side.

SYSTEMS: Hydraulic and electrical systems as for standard A 109A Mk II.

AVIONICS AND EQUIPMENT: Wide range of available avionics includes VHF-AM, VHF-FM, UHF and HF com, homing, ADF, VOR/ILS/glideslope, DME, Tacan, autonomous (Doppler) or VLF Omega navigation, IFF, radar altimeter, weather radar, ELT, and intercom (three stations). Cockpit has space provisions for dedicated displays/control panels, and compatibility with optional night vision goggles. Optional auxiliary equipment can include external loudspeaker, windscreen wipers, bleed air heater, environmental control unit, stretcher installation, air ambulance kit, cargo platform kit (floor loading 500 kg/m²; 102.5 lb/sq ft), 900 kg (1,984 lb) capacity external cargo hook, rearview mirror, 200 kg (441 lb) rescue hoist, smoke/flare launcher, snow skis, emergency floats, oxygen system, and locator type or high-intensity searchlight.

ARMAMENT AND OPERATIONAL EQUIPMENT: One pintle mounted 7.62 mm machine-gun in cabin and one 12.7 mm at door gunner's position. External armament can include single or twin 7.62 mm gun pod, 12.7 mm gun pods with 250 rds/gun, 70 mm/2.75 in twelve-round rocket launchers, combined rocket launcher (four 2.75 in) and 12.7 mm gun pod with 250 rds, TOW anti-tank or Stinger air-to-air missiles, and RPVs. Stowable

roof-mounted collimator sight; Sfim gyro stabilised sight; FLIR; APX 334-25 sight; chaff/flare dispenser; and laser and radar warning receivers.

DIMENSIONS, EXTERNAL AND INTERNAL, AND AREAS:
As for A 109A Mk II except:
Length of fuselage, excl rotors 11.446 m (37 ft 6⅔ in)

WEIGHTS:
Weight empty, equipped 1,500 kg (3,307 lb)
Max T-O weight 2,720 kg (5,996 lb)

PERFORMANCE (at max T-O weight):
Never-exceed speed 150 knots (278 km/h; 172 mph)
Max cruising speed at 915 m (3,000 ft)
136 knots (252 km/h; 156 mph)
Max rate of climb at S/L 518 m (1,700 ft)/min
Service ceiling 4,575 m (15,000 ft)
Hovering ceiling: IGE 3,200 m (10,500 ft)
OGE 2,290 m (7,500 ft)
Range with max fuel 332 nm (615 km; 382 miles)

AGUSTA A 109K

This multi-role 'hot and high' military variant of the A 109A Mk II is powered by two 538 kW (722 shp) Turbomeca Arriel IK turboshafts (instead of the A 109's usual 313 kW; 420 shp Allisons). It flew for the first time in April 1983.

Designed for operation by a pilot and gunner in its primary combat role, the production A 109K is intended to have an uprated transmission, a new main rotor hub made of composites, elastomeric bearings, composites blades with a hard surface coating that is resistant to abrasion by sand and hard dust, a new tail rotor of Wortmann blade section, a longer nose to house additional avionics, and a taller and non-retractable high shock absorption wheeled landing gear.

The second prototype, which began flying in March 1984, was fully representative of the planned production version. No orders had been announced up to mid-1988. Differences by comparison with the standard A 109A Mk II are as follows:

TYPE: Twin-engined multi-role helicopter.

ROTOR SYSTEM AND DRIVE: Composites main rotor blades and hub, with elastomeric bearings, and special blade surface coating, for greater corrosion/abrasion resistance. New tail rotor of slightly reduced diameter, with high-efficiency Wortmann aerofoil section and stainless steel skins. Main transmission uprated to 671 kW (900 shp) for take-off and max continuous twin-engined operation. Ratings for single-engined operation are 492 kW (660 shp) for 2.5 minutes, and 373 kW (500 shp) max continuous.

FUSELAGE: Nose lengthened by 40 cm (15¾ in) and fitted with an upward hinged door on each side, for access to avionics. Provision for ECM or other sensors on nose.

Agusta A 109K multi-role 'hot and high' variant of the A 109A Mk II

LANDING GEAR: Non-retractable tricycle type, giving increased clearance between fuselage and ground. Changes restricted to replacement of nose leg actuator by a fixed strut, and replacement of each main leg actuator by a fixed strut and a V support frame.

POWER PLANT: Two Turbomeca Arriel IK turboshafts, each rated at 538 kW (722 shp) for 2.5 minutes, 522 kW (700 shp) for take-off (5 minutes) and 436 kW (585 shp) max cruise power. Engine particle separator added. Standard fuel capacity 700 litres (185 US gallons; 154 Imp gallons). Self-sealing fuel tanks optional.

ACCOMMODATION: Normal crew of two for combat missions, comprising pilot (on right) and gunner. Smaller instrument panel to improve forward view. Up to six passengers in cabin of utility version.

SYSTEMS: Lighter-weight hydraulic and electrical systems. 28V DC electrical system supplied by two 160A starter/generators, with 27Ah nickel-cadmium battery and external power socket. Three-phase AC power at 400Hz supplied by 6kVA 115V engine driven alternator and single-phase AC by a 250VA solid state inverter. Second alternator optional.

AVIONICS: Basic installation comprises dual UHF/VHF AM-FM, Collins AN/ARN-126 VOR/LOC/ILS, Collins ADF-60, AG-06 intercom, SIT 421 IFF transponder, Sperry three-axis AFCS and AN/ASN-75 nav compass system.

ARMAMENT AND OPERATIONAL EQUIPMENT (optional): Total of four stores attachments, two on each side of cabin, on outriggers. Typical loads include two 7.62 mm or 12.7 mm gun pods, rocket launchers, or up to eight TOW anti-armour missiles (with roof mounted sight), plus a 7.62 or 12.7 mm side-firing gun in cabin. Chaff/flare dispenser, and radar and laser warning systems, optional.

DIMENSIONS, EXTERNAL:
Tail rotor diameter	2.00 m (6 ft 6¾ in)
Length of fuselage	11.106 m (36 ft 5¼ in)

AREA:
Tail rotor disc	3.143 m² (33.83 sq ft)

WEIGHTS AND LOADINGS:
Weight empty	1,595 kg (3,517 lb)
Max T-O weight	2,850 kg (6,283 lb)
Max disc loading	30.0 kg/m² (6.15 lb/sq ft)
Max power loading	2.64 kg/kW (4.34 lb/shp)

PERFORMANCE (at max T-O weight except where indicated):
*Max level speed at S/L, 'clean':	
ISA	138 knots (255 km/h; 159 mph)
ISA + 20°C	140 knots (259 km/h; 161 mph)
*Max cruising speed at S/L, at average weight, 'clean':	
ISA	141 knots (261 km/h; 162 mph)
ISA + 20°C	144 knots (266 km/h; 166 mph)
**Econ cruising speed at S/L, at average weight, 'clean':	
ISA	128 knots (237 km/h; 147 mph)
ISA + 20°C	131 knots (243 km/h; 151 mph)
Max rate of climb at S/L: ISA	530 m (1,740 ft)/min
ISA + 20°C	509 m (1,670 ft)/min
Rate of climb at S/L, one engine out:	
ISA or ISA + 20°C	167 m (550 ft)/min
Service ceiling:	
ISA or ISA + 20°C	6,100 m (20,000 ft)
Service ceiling, one engine out: ISA	2,770 m (9,100 ft)
ISA + 20°C	1,950 m (6,400 ft)
Hovering ceiling IGE at average weight, 'clean':	
ISA	5,640 m (18,500 ft)
ISA + 20°C	4,970 m (16,300 ft)
Hovering ceiling OGE at average weight, 'clean':	
ISA	3,350 m (11,000 ft)
ISA + 20°C	2,680 m (8,800 ft)
Max range at S/L, 'clean':	
ISA	290 nm (537 km; 333 miles)
ISA + 20°C	284 nm (526 km; 326 miles)

*reduced by 9 knots (17 km/h; 11 mph) with two gun pods fitted

**reduced by 6 knots (11 km/h; 7 mph) with two gun pods fitted

AGUSTA A 129 MANGUSTA (MONGOOSE)

The Italian Army first made known its requirements for a light anti-armour helicopter in 1972, and the selected A 129 design received Italian Army go-ahead in March 1978, undergoing several changes of configuration before reaching its final form in 1980. The first A 129 (MM 590/E.I. 901) made an official first flight on 15 September 1983, following two earlier 'unofficial' flights of which the first took place on 11 September. First flights of the second and third prototypes took place on 1 July and 5 October 1984; the fourth was flown on 27 May 1985, and the fifth on 1 March 1986.

Initially, the A 129 is intended for service with the Italian Army, primarily for specialised attack against armoured targets with anti-tank or area suppression weapons, and will have full night/bad weather combat capability. It is also suitable for advanced scouting and other roles.

Approval has been given for an initial production batch of 60 A 129s, to equip two Italian Army Aviation operational squadrons. A requirement exists for an additional 30 aircraft, plus reserves, to equip a third operational squadron. Manufacture of the first 15 Mangustas for the Italian Army began in mid-1986, and five of these were due to be ready for deliveries to start in mid-1988. By mid-1989, when the first 15 should have entered service,

Agusta A 129 attack helicopter for the Italian Army

production is expected to be at the rate of three a month. The Dutch Army is negotiating a first batch of 20 Mangustas.

TYPE: Light anti-tank, attack and advanced scout helicopter.

ROTOR SYSTEM: Fully articulated four-blade main rotor and two-blade semi-rigid delta-hinged tail rotor, each with elastomeric bearings and low-noise tips (various tip designs evaluated before production). Main rotor blades, which have a very low vibration level, each consist of a carbonfibre and Kevlar spar, Nomex honeycomb leading- and trailing-edge, stainless steel leading-edge abrasion strip, frangible tip, and skin of composite materials. They are designed to have a ballistic tolerance against hits from 12.7 mm ammunition, but are expected also to have considerable tolerance against 23 mm hits. The hub has the same ballistic tolerance; all mechanical linkages and moving parts are housed inside the rotor mast to eliminate foreign object damage, decrease icing problems, and reduce radar signature. There are no lubricated bearings in the rotor head. Tail rotor blades are also of composite materials, with a stainless steel leading-edge, and are tolerant to 12.7 mm hits.

ROTOR DRIVE: Transmission rating 969 kW (1,300 shp) (two engines), 704 kW (944 shp) for single-engined operation, with emergency rating of 759 kW (1,018 shp); power input into transmission is at 27,000 rpm. All driveshafts, components and couplings ballistically tolerant to 12.7 mm hits. Main transmission has integral independent oil cooling system; intermediate and tail rotor gearboxes are grease lubricated. Transmission and gearboxes are designed to continue to operate safely for at least 30 min without oil (45 min already demonstrated). Accessory gearbox forward of main transmission. In normal operation, accessories are driven by main gear train, but on ground they can be engaged by a pilot actuated clutch which connects No. 1 engine to the accessory section without engaging the rotors. Rotor brake fitted, to stop rotors quickly while the two engines run at ground idle, one driving the accessories.

WINGS: Cantilever mid mounted stub wings, built of composite materials, aft of rear cockpit in plane of main rotor mast.

FUSELAGE: Conventional semi-monocoque structure of aluminium alloy longerons and frames. Honeycomb panels in centre-fuselage and fuel tank areas. Composite materials, making up 45 per cent of total fuselage weight

(excluding engine) and 16.1 per cent of total empty weight, are used for nosecone, tailboom, tail rotor pylon, engine nacelles, canopy frame and maintenance panels. Total 'wetted' surface area of airframe (excl blades and hub) is 50 m² (538.2 sq ft), of which 35 m² (376.7 sq ft) (70 per cent) are of composite materials. Small and narrow frontal area. Rollover bulkhead in nose and rollover bar in forward fuselage for crew protection; armour protection for vital areas of power plant. Overall infra-red-absorbing paint finish. Airframe has a ballistic tolerance against 12.7 mm armour-piercing ammunition, and meets the crashworthiness standards of MIL-STD-1290 (vertical velocity changes of up to 11.2 m; 36.75 ft/s and longitudinal changes of up to 13.1 m; 43 ft/s).

TAIL UNIT: Sweptback main fin, with tail rotor mounted near top on port side. Small underfin, serving also as mount for tailwheel. Tailplane mid-mounted on tailboom in line with fin leading-edge. All tail surfaces built of composite materials.

LANDING GEAR: Non-retractable tailwheel type, with single wheel on each unit. Hydraulic shock strut in each main unit. Gear designed to withstand hard landings at descent rates in excess of 10 m (32.8 ft)/s.

POWER PLANT: Two Rolls-Royce Gem 2 Mk 1004D turboshafts, each with a max continuous rating of 615 kW (825 shp) for normal twin-engined operation; intermediate contingency rating of 657 kW (881 shp) for 1 h; max contingency rating of 704 kW (944 shp) for 2½ min; and an emergency rating (S/L, ISA) of 759 kW (1,018 shp) for 20 s. Production engines licence built in Italy by Piaggio. Two separate fuel systems, with crossfeed capability; interchangeable self-sealing and crash resistant tanks, self-sealing lines, and digital fuel feed control. Tanks can be foam-filled for fire protection. Single-point pressure refuelling. Infra-red exhaust suppression system and low engine noise levels. Separate independent lubrication oil cooling system for each engine. Provision for auxiliary (self-ferry) fuel tanks on inboard underwing stations.

ACCOMMODATION: Pilot and co-pilot/gunner in separate cockpits in tandem. Elevated rear (pilot's) cockpit. External crew field of view exceeds MIL-STD-850B. Each cockpit has a flat plate low-glint canopy with upward hinged door panels on starboard side, blow-out side panel for exit in emergency, and armoured crashworthy seat.

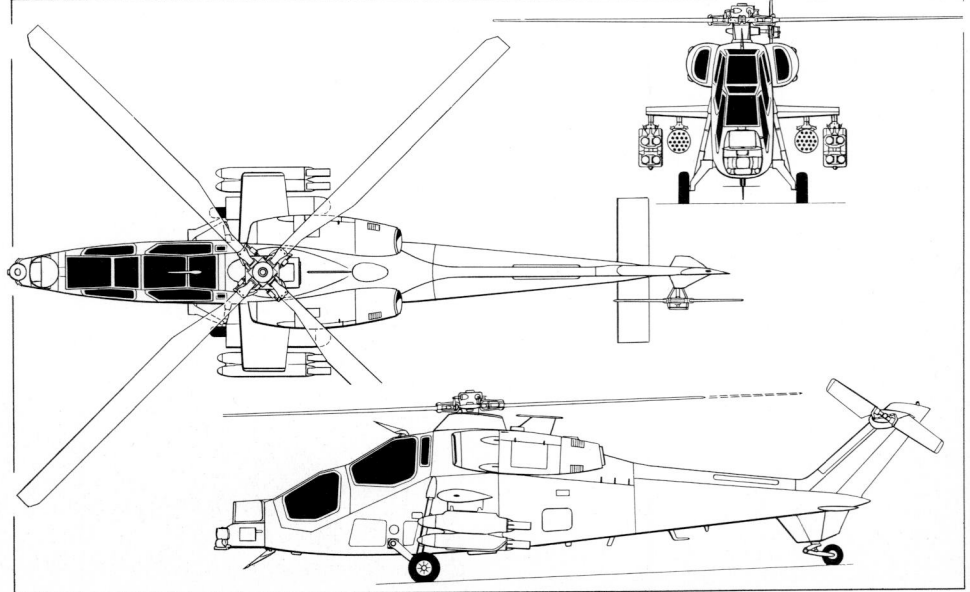

Agusta A 129 light anti-tank, attack and advanced scout helicopter *(Pilot Press)*

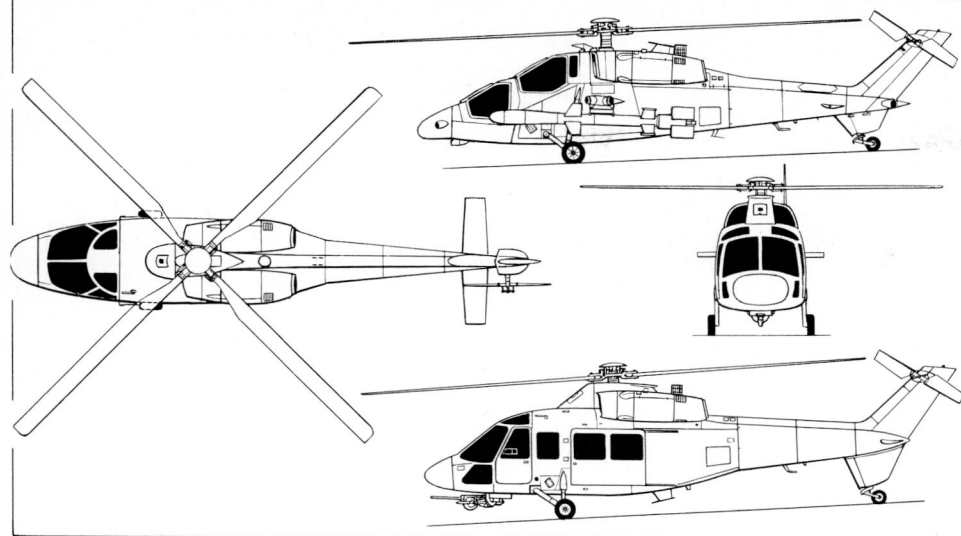

Three-view drawing of the proposed LBH battlefield support version of the Agusta A 129, with additional side view (top) of the projected naval version *(Pilot Press)*

SYSTEMS: Hydraulic system includes three main circuits dedicated to flight controls and two independent circuits for rotor and wheel braking. Main system operates at pressure of 207 bars (3,000 lb/sq in) and is fed by three independent power groups, two integrated and driven mechanically by the main transmission, the third integrated and driven by the tail rotor gearbox. Dual actuators are provided for main and tail rotor flight controls. Hydraulic system flow rate 23.6 litres (6.2 US gallons; 5.2 Imp gallons)/min in each main group. Spring type reservoirs, pressurised at 0.39 bars (5.6 lb/sq in). Electrical system includes fly by wire backup for mechanical control system. Full automatic stabilisation equipment, integrated with computerised IMS central management system. Automatic fire extinguishing system.

AVIONICS AND OPERATIONAL EQUIPMENT: All main functions of helicopter are handled and monitored by a fully integrated digital multiplex system (IMS), which controls com, nav, flight director, autopilot, fly by wire, transmission and engine condition monitoring, fuel/hydraulic/electrical systems monitoring, aircraft performance, caution and warning systems, and rocket fire control. IMS is managed by two redundant central computers, each capable of operating system independently. They are backed by two interface units which pick up outputs from sensors and avionic equipment and transfer them, via a system of redundant 1553B databuses, to main computers for real-time processing. Processed information is presented to pilot and co-pilot/gunner on separate graphic/alphanumeric head-down multi-function displays (MFDs) with standard multi-function keyboards for easy access to information, including area navigation and synthetic waypoint map, weapons status and selection, radio tuning and mode selection, caution and warning, and display of aircraft performance. IMS computer can store up to 100 waypoints, or up to ten flight plans with ten waypoints each, and 100 pre-set frequencies for HF, VHF and UHF radio management. Navigation is controlled by navigation computer of IMS coupled to a Doppler radar and radar altimeter. Synthetic map presentation of waypoints, target areas and dangerous areas is shown on pilot's or co-pilot's MFD.

The A 129 has full day/night operational capability, with equipment designed to give both crew members a view outside helicopter irrespective of light conditions. A pilot's night vision system allows nap-of-the-earth (NOE) flight by night, a picture of world outside being generated by Honeywell mini-FLIR sensor mounted on a Ferranti steerable platform at nose of aircraft and presented to pilot through monocle of his Honeywell integrated helmet and display sighting system (IHADSS), to which it is slaved. Symbology containing information required for flight is superimposed onto image, giving a true head-up reference. Co-pilot/gunner is also equipped with IHADSS. For night anti-tank engagements, TOW target acquisition and missile guidance unit will be augmented by a FLIR. This vision equipment can also be used during daylight, especially the integrated helmet sight, which provides automatic weapon aiming and reduces reaction time against unexpected targets. An omnidirectional air data system is also installed.

As requested by Italian Army, A 129 has provision to install a mast mounted sight (MMS) for target acquisition, TOW missile tracking, laser ranging, laser designation (eg for Hellfire launch), and automatic laser tracking of targets designated by other air or ground lasers. An MMS would give A 129 greater flexibility and survivability by allowing it to aim and fire from behind trees or other terrain features. Feasibility studies for an MMS have been carried out successfully.

Active and passive self-protection systems (ECCM and ECM) standard on Italian Army A 129. Passive electronic warfare systems include a radar warning receiver, and a laser warning receiver, which can detect enemy radars or lasers locked on to helicopter and signal them to crew for evasive action or appropriate use of active countermeasures. Latter can include radar and infra-red jammers, and a chaff/flare dispenser. Infra-red sensors will also be available.

ARMAMENT: Four underwing attachments, inner pair stressed for loads of up to 300 kg (661 lb) each, outer pair (at wingtips) also for 300 kg each. All stations incorporate articulation which allows pylon to be elevated 2° and depressed 10° from armament datum line. They are aligned with the aircraft automatically, with no need for boresighting. Initial armament of up to eight TOW wire guided anti-tank missiles (two, three or four in pod suspended from each wingtip station), with Saab/Emerson HeliTOW launch system and full TOW 2 capability; with these can be carried, on the inboard stations, either two 7.62, 12.7 or 20 mm gun pods, or two launchers each for seven air-to-surface rockets. For general attack missions, rocket launchers can be carried on all four stations (two nineteen-tube plus two seven-tube). Alternatively, is able to carry six Hellfire anti-tank missiles (three beneath each wingtip); eight Hot missiles; AIM-9L Sidewinder, Matra Mistral or Stinger air-to-air missiles for aerial combat; two gun pods plus two nineteen-tube rocket launchers; or grenade launchers. A 'chin' turret for a 0.50 in or 12.7 mm gun may be mounted under the nose.

DIMENSIONS, EXTERNAL:

Main rotor diameter	11.90 m (39 ft 0½ in)
Tail rotor diameter	2.24 m (7 ft 4¼ in)
Wing span	3.20 m (10 ft 6 in)
Width over TOW pods	3.60 m (11 ft 9¾ in)
Length overall, both rotors turning	
	14.29 m (46 ft 10½ in)
Fuselage: Length	12.275 m (40 ft 3¼ in)
Max width	0.95 m (3 ft 1½ in)
Height:	
over tail fin, tail rotor horizontal	2.65 m (8 ft 8¼ in)
tail rotor turning	3.315 m (10 ft 10½ in)
Height to top of rotor head	3.35 m (11 ft 0 in)
Tailplane span	3.00 m (9 ft 10 in)
Wheel track	2.20 m (7 ft 3½ in)
Wheelbase	6.955 m (22 ft 9¾ in)

AREAS:

Main rotor disc	111.2 m² (1,196.95 sq ft)
Tail rotor disc	3.94 m² (42.42 sq ft)

WEIGHTS AND LOADINGS:

Weight empty, equipped	2,529 kg (5,575 lb)
Max internal fuel load	750 kg (1,653 lb)
Max external weapons load	1,200 kg (2,645 lb)
Max T-O weight	4,100 kg (9,039 lb)
Max disc loading	33.3 kg/m² (6.8 lb/sq ft)
Max power loading	3.05 kg/kW (5.0 lb/shp)

PERFORMANCE:

At mission T-O weight of 3,700 kg (8,157 lb), at 2,000 m (6,560 ft), ISA + 20°C, except where indicated, the A 129 is designed to meet the following performance requirements:

Dash speed	170 knots (315 km/h; 196 mph)
Max level speed at S/L	140 knots (259 km/h; 161 mph)
Max rate of climb at S/L	655 m (2,150 ft)/min
Hovering ceiling: IGE	3,750 m (12,300 ft)
OGE	3,015 m (9,900 ft)

Basic 2 h 30 min mission profile with 8 TOW and 20 min fuel reserves:

Fly 54 nm (100 km; 62 miles) to battle area, mainly in NOE mode, 90 min loiter (incl 45 min hovering), and return to base

Max endurance, no reserves	3 h 0 min
g limit	+3.5

AGUSTA A 129 (DEVELOPED VERSIONS)

Three variants of the A 129 are being studied by Agusta, which released first details at the 1985 Paris Air Show. The first of these, now named **Tonal**, is described under the JEH heading in the International section.

Second proposed version is a ship or shore based **naval** development for anti-shipping and maritime support roles, with nose mounted radar, Elettronica ESM antennae at nose and tail and at the tips of the stub wings, a chaff dispenser on the starboard side behind the tailplane, and an armament of two Marte Mk 2 or four Sea Skua missiles in the anti-shipping role or Mavericks, TOWs or rocket pods for maritime support.

The third proposal is for an **LBH** (light battlefield helicopter) tactical support version which would combine the Mangusta's rotor system, power plant and landing gear with an entirely new and larger fuselage having side by side crew seating and a cabin able to accommodate a ten-man assault squad, or six stretchers and two medical attendants. Provisions would be made for a 'chin' mounted gun turret, a 272 kg (600 lb) capacity rescue hoist, side looking airborne radar, and gun or rocket pods.

AGUSTA-BELL 205

The Agusta-Bell 205 multi-purpose helicopter corresponds to the UH-1D/UH-1H versions described under the Bell heading in the US section. Agusta had built approx 600 AB 205s by early 1988, for the Italian armed forces and customers in many other countries. The production line has now been halted, except for support spares. Brief details of the AB 205 can be found in the 1987-88 and many earlier editions of *Jane's*.

AGUSTA-BELL 206B JETRANGER III

The JetRanger has been manufactured under licence from Bell since the end of 1967; deliveries began in 1972 of the Agusta-Bell 206B JetRanger II, and of the JetRanger III at the end of 1978. A description of the JetRanger III appears under the Bell entry in the Canadian section. Approx 1,000 JetRangers have been built by Agusta, and production is expected to continue at least until 1990.

AGUSTA-BELL 212

The Agusta-Bell 212 is a twin-engined utility transport helicopter generally similar to the Bell Model 212 Twin Two-Twelve described in the Canadian section.

Recent customers for the AB 212 have included the Italian Air Force, with an order for 35 equipped for the SAR role, and the Italian Police. Production is planned to continue until at least 1992.

The AB 212ASW naval version is described separately.

DIMENSIONS, EXTERNAL: As Bell Model 212 except:

Main rotor diameter	14.63 m (48 ft 0 in)
Length overall, rotors turning	17.40 m (57 ft 1 in)

Italian Police Agusta-Bell 212 utility helicopter, with 360° TV camera in spherical pod *(Avio Data)*

AREA:
Main rotor disc   168.1 m² (1,809.5 sq ft)
WEIGHTS: As Bell Model 212 except:
Weight empty (standard)   2,630 kg (5,800 lb)
PERFORMANCE (at AUW of 4,536 kg; 10,000 lb, ISA):
Cruising speed at S/L   110 knots (204 km/h; 127 mph)
Max rate of climb at S/L   567 m (1,860 ft)/min
Service ceiling   5,180 m (17,000 ft)
Hovering ceiling: IGE   3,960 m (13,000 ft)
OGE   3,050 m (10,000 ft)
Max range at 1,525 m (5,000 ft) with standard fuel, no
reserves:
on two engines   267 nm (494 km; 307 miles)
on one engine   318 nm (589 km; 366 miles)

AGUSTA-BELL 212ASW

The AB 212ASW is an extensively modified version of the AB 212, intended primarily for anti-submarine search and attack missions, and for attacks on surface vessels, but suitable also for search and rescue and utility roles. The current SAR version has such additional features as a hydraulically operated external hoist and a four-channel Sperry autopilot. The 212ASW benefits from considerable naval operational experience gained with the single-engined AB 204AS, and can operate from the same small ship decks. More than 100 are in service with the Italian and other navies; the most recent customers have included the navies of Greece (12, including some in electronic warfare configuration), Iraq (5), Turkey (12 in both ASW and ASV configurations) and Venezuela (6).

Apart from local strengthening and the provision of deck mooring equipment, the airframe structure remains essentially similar to that of the commercial Model 212 and military UH-1N, described under the Bell entries in the Canadian and US sections respectively. Main differences from the civil Agusta-Bell 212 are as follows:

TYPE: Twin-engined anti-submarine and anti-surface-vessel helicopter.

POWER PLANT: One Pratt & Whitney Canada PT6T-6 Turbo Twin Pac, rated at 1,398 kW (1,875 shp). Protection against salt water corrosion. Provision for one internal or two external auxiliary fuel tanks.

ACCOMMODATION: Normal crew of three or four. Volume of cabin is 6.1 m³ (215 cu ft), with floor area of 5.0 m² (54 sq ft). With sonar installed, volume is reduced to 5.1 m³ (180 cu ft). Can accommodate two pilots and seven passengers; or two pilots, four stretcher patients and attendant. Single sliding door, with jettisonable emergency exit panel, on each side.

SYSTEMS: Standard duplicated hydraulic systems for flight controls, as in AB 212. The hydraulic system operates the automatic flight control system. Self-contained hydraulic system for operation of sonar, rescue hoist and other utilities. Electrical system capacity increased to cater for higher power demand (28V DC, and three phase 200/115V or single phase 26V AC at 400Hz); the two standard generators are integrated with a 20kVA alternator.

AVIONICS AND EQUIPMENT: Complete instrumentation for day and night sea operation in all weathers. Avionics installed are UHF transceiver, HF transceiver, and Agusta AG-03-M intercom, for communications; ADF, Tacan and homing UHF, for navigation assistance; radar altimeter, Doppler radar, ASW navigation computer, and automatic flight control system with General Electric SR-3 gyro platform, Sperry four-axis autopilot with AATH (automatic approach to hover) mode for automatic navigation; IFF/SIF transponder; search radar and radar transponder; data link; and Bendix AN/AQS-13B/F sonar for ASW search.

ARMAMENT AND OPERATIONAL EQUIPMENT: Weapons may consist of two Motofides 244 AS or two Mk 44/46 homing torpedoes, or two Marte Mk 2 or Sea Skua type air-to-surface missiles. Rescue hoist, capacity 272 kg (600 lb), standard. Provisions for auxiliary installations such as a 2,270 kg (5,000 lb) capacity cargo sling, inflatable emergency pontoons, internal and external auxiliary fuel tanks, according to mission.

ASW MISSION: Basic sensor system for ASW search and attack is a Bendix AN/AQS-13B/F low-frequency variable depth sonar, with a max operating depth of 137 m (450 ft). Automatic navigation system permits positioning of helicopter over any desired 'dip' point of a complex search pattern. Position of helicopter, computed by automatic navigation system, is integrated with sonar target information in radar tactical display where both surface and underwater tactical situations can be continuously monitored. Additional navigation and tactical information provided by UHF direction finding equipment, from an A/A mode-capable Tacan and a radar transponder. Automatic flight control system (AFCS) integrates basic automatic stabilisation equipment with signal output from radar altimeter, Doppler radar, sonar cable angle signals, and outputs from dry cable transducer. Effectiveness of this system results in hands-off flight from cruise condition to sonar hover in all weathers and under rough sea conditions. Specially designed cockpit display shows pilots all flight parameters for each phase of ASW operation. Attack mission is carried out with two homing torpedoes, or with depth charges.

Agusta-Bell 212ASW in the insignia of the Italian Navy

ASV MISSION: For this mission AB 212ASW carries a Ferranti Seaspray long-range search radar, with very efficient scanner design and installation possessing high discrimination in rough sea conditions. Provisions made to permit incorporation of future radar system developments. Automatic navigation systems and search radar are integrated to permit continuously updated picture of tactical situation. Provisions also incorporated for installation of the most advanced ECM systems (Selenia or Elettronica is system most commonly used). Surface attack is performed with air-to-surface missiles of the Marte Mk 2 or Sea Skua type.

STANDOFF MISSILE GUIDANCE MISSION: In this mission the AB 212ASW, with special equipment, can provide midcourse passive guidance for the ship launched Otomat 2 surface-to-surface missile. Equipment includes an SMA/APS series 360° search radar and a TG-2 real-time target data transmission system for guidance of the missile.

DIMENSIONS, EXTERNAL: As AB 212, except:
Max width: with torpedoes   3.95 m (12 ft 11½ in)
with missiles   4.17 m (13 ft 8¼ in)
WEIGHTS (A: ASW mission with Mk 46 torpedoes; B: ASV mission with AS.12 missiles; C: search and rescue mission; all at S/L, ISA):
Weight empty, equipped:
A, B, C   3,420 kg (7,540 lb)
Crew of three: A, B, C   240 kg (529 lb)
Mission equipment:
A (two Mk 46 torpedoes)   490 kg (1,080 lb)
B (AS.12 installation and XM-58 sight)
     180 kg (396 lb)
C (rescue hoist)   40 kg (89 lb)
Full fuel (normal tanks)   1,021 kg (2,250 lb)
Auxiliary external tanks   32 kg (70 lb)
Auxiliary fuel   356 kg (785 lb)
Mission T-O weight: A   5,070 kg (11,176 lb)
B   4,973 kg (10,961 lb)
C   4,937 kg (10,883 lb)
PERFORMANCE (at max T-O weight except where indicated, ISA):
Never-exceed speed   130 knots (240 km/h; 150 mph)
Max level speed at S/L   106 knots (196 km/h; 122 mph)
Max cruising speed with armament
     100 knots (185 km/h; 115 mph)
Max rate of climb at S/L: A   396 m (1,300 ft)/min
Rate of climb at S/L, one engine out:
A   61 m (200 ft)/min
Hovering ceiling IGE: A   3,200 m (10,500 ft)
Hovering ceiling OGE:
A at AUW of 4,763 kg (10,500 lb)   396 m (1,300 ft)

Search endurance (A) with 50% at 90 knots (167 km/h; 103 mph) cruise and 50% hovering OGE, 10% reserve fuel   3 h 12 min
Search range (B) with 10% reserve fuel
     332 nm (615 km; 382 miles)
Endurance (B), no reserves   4 h 7 min
Endurance (C) at 90 knots (167 km/h; 103 mph) search speed   5 h 4 min
Max range with auxiliary tanks, 100 knots (185 km/h; 115 mph) cruise at S/L, 15% reserves
     360 nm (667 km; 414 miles)
Max endurance with auxiliary tanks, no reserves
     5 h 0 min

AGUSTA-BELL 412 SP and GRIFFON

The first Bell prototype of the Model 412 was flown for the first time in August 1979, and customer deliveries began in January 1981. Licence production by Agusta was initiated later that year, and civil versions for a variety of applications are now available from the Italian manufacturer. They now include a dedicated version for offshore work equipped with 'pop-out' inflatable pontoons, Bendix weather radar, a Spectrolab searchlight and special avionics. An EMS (emergency medical service) version has also been certificated. A description of the basic civil Model 412 SP can be found under the Bell entry in the Canadian section of this edition.

Agusta has also developed its own multi-purpose military version of the helicopter, known as the **Griffon**, for such applications as direct fire support, area suppression, scouting and reconnaissance, air defence, assault transport, combat equipment transport, and battlefield support. Special features include high-energy-absorbing landing gear, energy attenuating seats for crew and troops (the former also armour protected), and crash resistant self-sealing fuel tanks. Other survivability options can include passive (radar and laser warning, and missile detection) and active (ECM, radar jammer and decoy) systems, and a variety of ordnance can be carried. The Griffon is capable of performing medevac, tactical support, logistic transport, maritime surveillance, pollution monitoring, search and rescue, and patrol duties, and of being used effectively against surface ships, tanks and other armoured vehicles.

A version for SAR, maritime surveillance and pollution monitoring is under development for the Italian forces, equipped with an integrated 360° roof mounted search radar, FLIR, TV, four-axis autopilot and special navigation system. First deliveries are due in 1989.

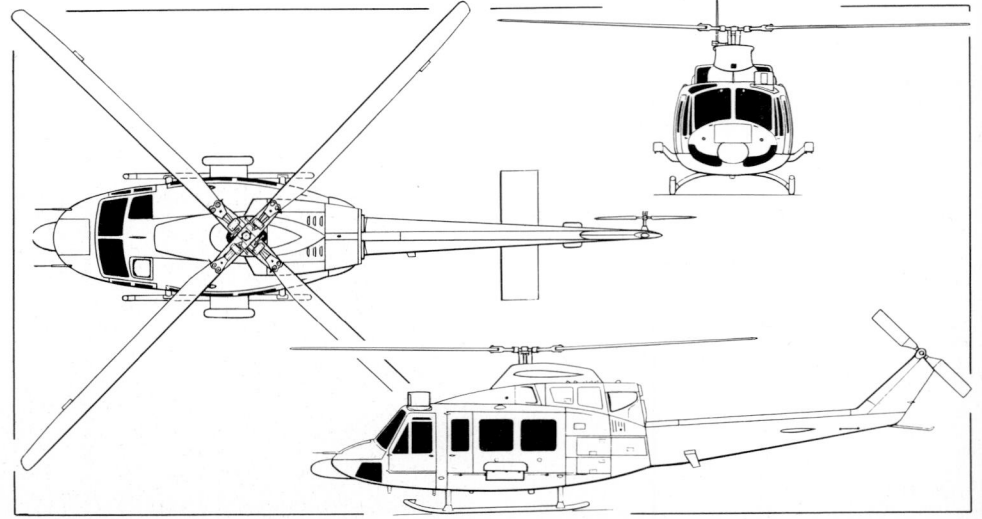

Agusta-Bell Griffon military helicopter, derived from the Bell Model 412 *(Pilot Press)*

A prototype of the Griffon was flown for the first time in August 1982. Deliveries began in January 1983, and 75 civil and military AB 412 SPs had been sold by 1 January 1988. Customers in Italy include the Army, Carabinieri and Special Civil Protection fleet; others include the Zimbabwe Air Force (10), Ugandan Army, and Finnish coastguard (2). The Griffon differs from the standard civil Model 412 SP in the following respects:

TYPE: Multi-purpose military helicopter.

AIRFRAME: Reinforced impact-absorbing landing gear and armour protection in selected areas.

POWER PLANT: One 1,342 kW (1,800 shp) Pratt & Whitney Canada PT6T-3B Turbo Twin Pac (single-engine ratings 764 kW; 1,025 shp for 2½ min and 723 kW; 970 shp for 30 min), as in civil Model 412. IR emission reduction devices optional. Fuel system and capacity as for Model 412 (1,250 litres; 330 US gallons; 275 Imp gallons). Single-point refuelling. Two 76 or 341 litre (20 or 90 US gallon; 16.7 or 75 Imp gallon) auxiliary fuel tanks optional.

ACCOMMODATION: One or two pilots on flight deck, on energy-absorbing, armour protected seats. Fourteen crash-attenuating troop seats in main cabin in personnel transport roles, six patients and two medical attendants in ambulance version, or up to 1,814 kg (4,000 lb) of cargo or other equipment. Space for 181 kg (400 lb) of baggage in tailboom. Total of 51 fittings in cabin floor for attachment of seats, stretchers, internal hoist or other special equipment.

SYSTEMS: Generally as for Bell 212/412. Electrical system supplied by two independent 30V 200A DC starter/generators (derated to 150A) and 34Ah nickel-cadmium battery, with three 250VA single-phase solid state inverters or a 10 kVA alternator for AC power.

AVIONICS AND EQUIPMENT: Typical avionics can include UHF/VHF (FM-AM) and HF secure voice com, ADF, VHF/UHF-DF, radar altimeter, IFF, DME, Tacan, VOR, navigation system, radar, Doppler radar, and four-axis AFCS. Optional avionics include AN/APR-39 radar warning receiver, laser warning receiver and pulse-Doppler radar missile detector system for passive warning of threats; active countermeasures options include AN/ALQ-144 ECM set, AN/ALQ-136 radar jammer, and chaff/flare dispenser. A 272 kg (600 lb) capacity external rescue hoist can be fitted for search and rescue mission, and an external hook for cargo, battlefield support and other duties. Other optional equipment includes auxiliary fuel tanks, emergency floats, rotor brake, heavy duty heater, heated windscreen, loudspeakers and searchlight, depending upon mission.

ARMAMENT: Wide variety of external weapon options for the Griffon includes a swivelling turret for a 12.7 mm gun, two 25 mm Oerlikon cannon, four or eight TOW anti-tank missiles, two launchers each with nineteen 2.75 in SNORA or twelve 81 mm rockets, 12.7 mm machine-guns (in pods or door mounted), four air-to-air or air defence suppression missiles, or, for attacking surface vessels, four Sea Skua or similar air-to-surface missiles.

WEIGHTS:

Weight empty, equipped (standard configuration)
2,841 kg (6,263 lb)
Max T-O weight 5,400 kg (11,905 lb)

PERFORMANCE (at max T-O weight, ISA):

Never-exceed speed at S/L	
	140 knots (259 km/h; 161 mph)
Cruising speed: at S/L	122 knots (226 km/h; 140 mph)
at 1,500 m (4,920 ft)	125 knots (232 km/h; 144 mph)
at 3,000 m (9,840 ft)	123 knots (228 km/h; 142 mph)
Max rate of climb at S/L	438 m (1,437 ft)/min
Rate of climb at S/L, one engine out	168 m (551 ft)/min
Service ceiling, 30.5 m (100 ft)/min climb rate	
	5,180 m (17,000 ft)
Service ceiling, one engine out, 30.5 m (100 ft)/min climb rate	
	2,320 m (7,610 ft)
Hovering ceiling: IGE	1,250 m (4,100 ft)
OGE	670 m (2,200 ft)

Range with max standard fuel at appropriate cruising speed (see above), no reserves:

at S/L	354 nm (656 km; 407 miles)
at 1,500 m (4,920 ft)	402 nm (745 km; 463 miles)
at 3,000 m (9,840 ft)	434 nm (804 km; 500 miles)
Max endurance: at S/L	3 h 36 min
at 1,500 m (4,920 ft)	4 h 12 min

AGUSTA-SIKORSKY AS-61 and ASH-3H

Agusta licence manufacture of the Sikorsky S-61 and SH-3D Sea King started in 1967, and deliveries of anti-submarine ASH-3Ds to the Italian Navy began in 1969. Additional orders have since been placed, both for the Italian armed forces and for other navies, including recently those of Brazil (four) and Argentina (four). Models currently in production are the utility **AS-61**, the **SH-3D/TS** (Trasporto Speciale) VIP transport, and the upgraded **SH-3H** multi-role naval version.

Apart from some local strengthening, uprated engines and an improved horizontal tail surface, the Agusta built airframe remains essentially similar to that of the Sikorsky built SH-3D/H (see 1982-83 Jane's), of which production has ended. The Agusta SH-3H is capable of operation in the roles of anti-submarine search, classification and strike;

Agusta-Bell AB 412 SP Griffon multi-role military helicopter

anti-surface-vessel (ASV); anti-surface-missile defence (ASMD); electronic warfare (EW); tactical troop lift; search and rescue (SAR); vertical replenishment; and casualty evacuation.

In mid-1987, an SH-3 became the first airborne testbed for the BAe/Bendix HELRAS long-range high resolution dipping sonar intended for naval versions of the Anglo-Italian EH 101 Sea King replacement helicopter.

The following description applies to the ASH-3H:

TYPE: Twin-engined amphibious all-weather naval helicopter.

ROTOR SYSTEM: Five-blade main and tail rotors. All-metal fully articulated oil lubricated main rotor. Flanged cuffs on blades bolted to matching flanges on all-steel rotor head. Main rotor blades are interchangeable and are provided with an automatic folding system. Rotor brake standard. All-metal tail rotor.

ROTOR DRIVE: Both engines drive through freewheel units and rotor brake to main gearbox. Steel driveshafts. Tail rotor shaft driven through intermediate and tail gearboxes. Accessories driven by power take-off on tail rotor shaft. Main rotor/engine rpm ratio 1 : 93.43. Tail rotor/engine rpm ratio 1 : 16.7.

FUSELAGE: Single-step boat hull of all-metal semi-monocoque construction. Tail section folds to reduce stowage requirements.

TAIL SURFACE: Fixed strut braced stabiliser on starboard side of tail section.

LANDING GEAR: Amphibious. Land gear consists of two twin-wheel main units, which are retracted rearward hydraulically into stabilising floats, and non-retractable tailwheel. Oleo-pneumatic shock absorbers. Mainwheels and tubeless tyres size 6.50-10 type III, pressure 4.83 bars (70 lb/sq in). Tailwheel and tyre size 6.00-6. Hydraulic disc brakes. Boat hull and pop-out flotation bags in stabilising floats permit emergency operation from water.

POWER PLANT: Two 1,118 kW (1,500 shp) General Electric T58-GE-100 turboshafts, mounted side by side above the cabin. An optional anti-ice/sand shield can be provided. Fuel in underfloor bag tanks with a total capacity of 3,180 litres (840 US gallons; 699 Imp gallons). Internal auxiliary fuel tank may be fitted for long-range ferry purposes. Pressure and gravity refuelling points.

ACCOMMODATION: Crew of four in ASW role (pilot, co-pilot and two sonar operators); accommodation for up to 31 paratroops in troop lift role, 15 stretchers and a medical attendant in casualty evacuation configuration, and up to 25 survivors in SAR role. Dual controls. Crew door at rear of flight deck on port side. Large loading door at rear of cabin on starboard side.

SYSTEMS: Three main hydraulic systems. Primary and auxiliary systems operate main rotor control. Utility system for landing gear, winches and blade folding,

pressure 207 bars (3,000 lb/sq in). Electrical system includes two 20kVA 200V three phase 400Hz engine driven generators, a 26V single phase AC supply fed from the aircraft's 22Ah nickel-cadmium battery through an inverter, and DC power provided as a secondary system from two 200A transformer-rectifier units.

ARMAMENT AND OPERATIONAL EQUIPMENT (ASW/ASV roles): As equipped for these roles the ASH-3H is a fully integrated all-weather weapons system, capable of operating independently of surface vessels, and has the following equipment and weapons to achieve this task: low-frequency 360° depth AQS-18/AQS-13F sonar; Doppler radar and ASW automatic navigation system; SMA/APS-707 radar with one or two transceivers, with 'chin' radome for 360° coverage; radio altimeter; AFCS; marine markers and smoke floats; two or four homing torpedoes (A 244 AS, Mk 44 or Mk 46); or four depth charges. The AFCS provides three-axis stabilisation in pilot-controlled manoeuvres, attitude hold, heading hold and height hold in cruising flight; controlled transition manoeuvres to and from hover; automatic height control and plan position control in the hover; and trim facility. According to the threat, the Agusta SH-3H can be equipped with medium-range (four AS.12 air-to-surface wire-guided) missiles or long-range (two Marte Mk 2 or Exocet AM39/Harpoon type) anti-shipping missiles. The SMA/APS-707 radar has been specially designed to operate in a dense electronic emission environment and has a special interface to draw out target data to feed the computer for the long-range missiles. Provisions are also incorporated for the installation of MAD and advanced EW systems.

OPERATIONAL EQUIPMENT (Search and rescue and transport roles): Search radar, and variable speed hydraulic rescue hoist of 272 kg (600 lb) capacity mounted above starboard side cargo door.

DIMENSIONS, EXTERNAL:

Main rotor diameter	18.90 m (62 ft 0 in)
Main rotor blade chord	0.46 m (1 ft 6¼ in)
Tail rotor diameter	3.23 m (10 ft 7 in)
Distance between rotor centres	11.10 m (36 ft 5 in)
Length overall, both rotors turning	
	21.91 m (71 ft 10.7 in)
Length of fuselage	16.69 m (54 ft 9 in)
Length, main rotor and tail pylon folded	
	14.40 m (47 ft 3 in)
Width (over sponsons), rotors folded	4.98 m (16 ft 4 in)
Height to top of rotor head	4.74 m (15 ft 6½ in)
Height overall, main rotor and tail pylon folded	
	4.93 m (16 ft 2 in)
Height overall, tail rotor turning	5.23 m (17 ft 2 in)
Wheel track	3.96 m (13 ft 0 in)
Wheelbase	7.18 m (23 ft 6½ in)

Agusta-Sikorsky ASH-3H ASW helicopter of the Italian Navy (*Press Office Sturzenegger*)

Crew door (fwd, port): Height	1.68 m (5 ft 6 in)
Width	0.91 m (3 ft 0 in)
Height to sill	1.14 m (3 ft 9 in)
Main cabin door (stbd): Height	1.52 m (5 ft 0 in)
Width	1.73 m (5 ft 8 in)
Height to sill	1.14 m (3 ft 9 in)

AREAS:

Main rotor blades (each)	4.14 m² (44.54 sq ft)
Tail rotor blades (each)	0.22 m² (2.38 sq ft)
Main rotor disc	280.5 m² (3,019 sq ft)
Tail rotor disc	8.20 m² (88.30 sq ft)
Stabiliser	1.86 m² (20.00 sq ft)

WEIGHTS:

Internal load capacity (cargo)	2,720 kg (6,000 lb)
Max external load capacity (with low response sling)	3,630 kg (8,000 lb)
Max T-O weight	9,525 kg (21,000 lb)

PERFORMANCE (at max T-O weight):

Never-exceed speed	144 knots (267 km/h; 165 mph)
Typical cruising speed	120 knots (222 km/h; 138 mph)
Max rate of climb at S/L	670 m (2,200 ft)/min
Service ceiling	3,720 m (12,200 ft)
Hovering ceiling: IGE	2,500 m (8,200 ft)
OGE	1,130 m (3,700 ft)
Range with 31 troops	314 nm (582 km; 362 miles)
Range with max standard fuel	630 nm (1,166 km; 725 miles)

AGUSTA-SIKORSKY AS-61N1 SILVER

Manufacture by Sikorsky of the S-61L and S-61N commercial helicopters ended in 1980, after completion of 13 of the former model and 123 of the latter. Production rights to the S-61N were acquired by Agusta, which has developed a modified version, designated AS-61N1 Silver. Greater range and slightly less seating capacity than the standard S-61N account for the two principal differences in the AS-61N1. The fuselage is shortened by 1.27 m (4 ft 2 in),

reducing maximum seating capacity from 30 passengers to 28, and internal fuel capacity is increased to 3,482 litres (920 US gallons; 766 Imp gallons). The Silver is tailored primarily to carry 24 passengers over distances of up to 550 nm (1,019 km; 633 miles). Initially, the standard S-61N power plant of two 1,119 kW (1,500 shp) General Electric CT58-140-1/2 turboshafts is retained.

The prototype flew for the first time on 25 July 1984. Italian RAI certification was received in 1987 and FAA certification was expected in early 1988. Three more Silvers, configured for offshore oil rig support, are under construction. The first of these was expected to be completed in June 1988.

DIMENSIONS, EXTERNAL:

Main rotor diameter	18.90 m (62 ft 0 in)
Length of fuselage	17.97 m (58 ft 11½ in)
Height over tail rotor	5.24 m (17 ft 2¼ in)
Width over sponsons	5.82 m (19 ft 1⅓ in)

DIMENSIONS, INTERNAL:

Cabin, excl flight deck: Length	8.26 m (27 ft 1⅛ in)
Baggage compartment volume	2.26 m³ (80 cu ft)

AREA:

Main rotor disc	280.5 m² (3,019 sq ft)

WEIGHTS:

Max useful load (offshore configuration)	3,560 kg (7,850 lb)
Max T-O weight: internal payload	9,525 kg (21,000 lb)
with slung load	10,205 kg (22,500 lb)

PERFORMANCE (A at average gross weight of 8,618 kg; 19,000 lb, B at 9,525 kg; 21,000 lb, C at 9,979 kg; 22,000 lb):

Never-exceed speed at S/L:

A	131 knots (242 km/h; 151 mph) IAS
B	115 knots (213 km/h; 132 mph) IAS
C	103 knots (191 km/h; 118 mph) IAS

Cruising speed at S/L:

A	121 knots (224 km/h; 139 mph) IAS

Max rate of climb at S/L, max continuous power:

A	396 m (1,300 ft)/min
B	320 m (1,050 ft)/min

Hovering ceiling IGE:

A	2,135 m (7,000 ft)
B	1,130 m (3,700 ft)
C	335 m (1,100 ft)

Range at S/L, 3,482 litres (920 US gallons; 766 Imp gallons) of fuel, incl 30 min reserves at cruising speed:

A	553 nm (1,025 km; 637 miles)
B	526 nm (974 km; 605 miles)

AGUSTA-SIKORSKY AS-61R (HH-3F)

Agusta began production of this multi-purpose search and rescue helicopter in 1974, and deliveries began in 1976. Twenty were built initially for the Italian Air Force, and production of a further 15 for the same customer was continuing in early 1988. These have updated avionics, which will be retrofitted to the original production series.

TYPE: Twin-engined amphibious helicopter.

ROTOR SYSTEM: Five-blade fully articulated main rotor of all-metal construction. Flanged cuffs on blades bolted to matching flanges on rotor head. Control by rotating and stationary swashplates. Blades do not fold. Rotor brake standard. Conventional tail rotor with five aluminium blades.

ROTOR DRIVE: Twin turbines drive through freewheeling units and rotor brake to main gearbox. Steel driveshafts. Tail rotor shaft driven through intermediate gearbox and tail gearbox. Main rotor/engine rpm ratio 1 : 93.43. Tail rotor/engine rpm ratio 1 : 16.7.

FUSELAGE: All-metal semi-monocoque structure of pod and boom type. Cabin of basic square section.

TAIL SURFACE: Strut braced horizontal stabiliser on starboard side of tail rotor pylon.

LANDING GEAR: Hydraulically retractable tricycle type, with twin wheels on each unit. Mainwheels retract forward into sponsons, each of which provides 2,176 kg (4,797 lb) of buoyancy and, with boat hull, permits amphibious operation. Oleo-pneumatic shock absorbers. All wheels and tyres tubeless Type III rib, size 22.1 × 6.50-10, pressure 6.55 bars (95 lb/sq in). Hydraulic disc brakes.

POWER PLANT: Two 1,118 kW (1,500 shp) General Electric T58-GE-100 turboshafts, mounted side by side above cabin, immediately forward of main transmission. Fuel in four bladder tanks beneath cabin floor, with total capacity of 4,225 litres (1,116 US gallons; 929 Imp gallons), of which 4,183 litres (1,105 US gallons; 920 Imp gallons) are usable. Provisions for removable internal auxiliary fuel tanks. Refuelling point on port side of fuselage. Total oil capacity 26.5 litres (7 US gallons; 5.8 Imp gallons).

ACCOMMODATION: Crew of two side by side on flight deck, with dual controls. Provision for flight engineer or attendant. Accommodation in SAR configuration for 10 passenger seats and six stretchers; utility version can accommodate up to 26 troops on foldable, safety belt-equipped seats, 15 stretchers plus two medical attendants, or cargo. Jettisonable sliding door on starboard side at front of cabin. Internal door between cabin and flight deck. Hydraulically operated rear loading ramp, in two hinged sections, giving opening with minimum width of 1.73 m (5 ft 8 in) and headroom of up to 2.21 m (7 ft 3 in). Ramp can be operated when helicopter is on the water. Reinforced (41 kg/m²; 200 lb/sq ft loading) cargo floor in utility version.

SYSTEMS: Primary and auxiliary hydraulic systems, pressure 103.5 bars (1,500 lb/sq in), for flying control servos. Utility hydraulic system, pressure 207 bars (3,000 lb/sq in), for landing gear, rear ramp and winches. Pneumatic system, pressure 207 bars (3,000 lb/sq in), for emergency blow-down landing gear extension. Electrical system includes 24V 22Ah battery, two 20kVA 115V AC generators and one 300A DC generator. APU standard.

EQUIPMENT: SAR version has comprehensive avionics suite for that role (including search/nav radar, Loran, FLIR and nav computer), plus 272 kg (600 lb) capacity rescue hoist, Nightsun searchlight, detachable rescue platform for use when afloat, auxiliary flotation system, loudhailer set, and sea anchor. Equipment for utility missions can include low response external cargo sling.

DIMENSIONS, EXTERNAL:

Main rotor diameter	18.90 m (62 ft 0 in)
Main rotor blade chord	0.46 m (1 ft 6¼ in)
Tail rotor diameter	3.15 m (10 ft 4 in)
Distance between rotor centres	11.22 m (36 ft 10 in)
Length overall, excl radome	22.25 m (73 ft 0 in)
Length of fuselage	17.45 m (57 ft 3 in)
Width over landing gear	4.82 m (15 ft 10 in)
Height to top of rotor head	4.90 m (16 ft 1 in)
Height overall	5.51 m (18 ft 1 in)
Wheel track	4.06 m (13 ft 4 in)
Wheelbase	5.21 m (17 ft 1 in)
Cabin door (fwd, stbd): Height	1.65 m (5 ft 4¾ in)
Width	1.22 m (4 ft 0 in)
Height to sill	1.27 m (4 ft 2 in)
Rear ramp: Length	4.29 m (14 ft 1 in)
Width	1.85 m (6 ft 1 in)

DIMENSIONS, INTERNAL:

Cabin (excl flight deck): Length	7.89 m (25 ft 10½ in)
Max width	1.98 m (6 ft 6 in)
Max height	1.91 m (6 ft 3 in)

Agusta-Sikorsky AS-61N1 Silver (two General Electric CT58-140-1/2 turboshafts)

Agusta-Sikorsky HH-3F (AS-61R) search and rescue helicopter of the Italian Air Force

| Floor area | approx 15.16 m² (168 sq ft) |
| Volume | approx 29.73 m³ (1,050 cu ft) |

AREAS:

Main rotor blades (each)	3.71 m² (39.9 sq ft)
Tail rotor blades (each)	0.22 m² (2.35 sq ft)
Main rotor disc	280.5 m² (3,019 sq ft)
Tail rotor disc	7.80 m² (83.9 sq ft)
Stabiliser	2.51 m² (27.0 sq ft)

WEIGHTS:

Weight empty	6,010 kg (13,255 lb)
Max cargo payload: internal	2,270 kg (5,000 lb)
external	3,628 kg (8,000 lb)
Normal T-O weight	9,635 kg (21,247 lb)
Max T-O weight	10,000 kg (22,050 lb)

PERFORMANCE (at normal T-O weight except where indicated):

Max level speed at S/L:

| normal T-O weight | 141 knots (261 km/h; 162 mph) |
| max T-O weight | 138 knots (255 km/h; 159 mph) |

Cruising speed at S/L, AUW of 9,072 kg (20,000 lb), ISA + 20°C:

for best range	130 knots (241 km/h; 150 mph)
for best endurance	75 knots (139 km/h; 86 mph)
Max rate of climb at S/L	408 m (1,340 ft)/min
Service ceiling: normal T-O weight	3,385 m (11,100 ft)
Hovering ceiling IGE	2,195 m (7,200 ft)
Min ground turning radius	11.29 m (37 ft 0½ in)

| Runway LCN at max T-O weight | approx 4.75 |

Typical mission profiles (ISA + 20°C):

SAR: Loiter for 5 h in search area 50 nm (92 km; 57 miles) from base, hover for 30 min to rescue survivors, return to base and land, 10% fuel remaining

Utility: Fly 240 nm (445 km; 276 miles) from base, pick up 24 fully equipped troops and return to base, landing with 272 kg (600 lb) of fuel remaining

| Range with max standard fuel, no reserves | 770 nm (1,427 km; 886 miles) |
| Endurance with max standard fuel, no reserves | 8 h |

EM (ELICOTTERI MERIDIONALI SpA)

Via Giovanni Agusta 1, 03100 Frosinone
Telephone: (0775) 82801
Telex: 611377 ELMEF I
PRESIDENT: Dott Raffaello Teti
GENERAL MANAGER: Dott Ing Alberto Armeni

This company was formed with assistance from Agusta and began to operate in October 1967. In 1968 EM acquired rights to the co-production, marketing and servicing of the Boeing CH-47C Chinook transport helicopter for customers in Italy and certain foreign countries. Italian production of the CH-47C airframe is undertaken by SIAI-Marchetti.

EM, whose works occupy a total area of more than 300,000 m² (3,229,170 sq ft), participates in the manufacturing programmes for the Agusta A 109A Mk II and A 129, Agusta-Bell 206B and 212, and Agusta-Sikorsky SH-3H helicopters. It has complete facilities for overhaul, repair and field assistance. EM is the designated overhaul organisation for all types of Italian Army helicopter, and is also distributor in Italy for Allison 250 turboshaft engines.

A new factory, completed in August 1983 at Anagni, has a total area of 218,000 m² (2,346,550 sq ft), including 18,000 m² (193,750 sq ft) of covered space, devoted to production of composite materials, especially rotor blades and other structures for helicopters.

EM (BOEING) CH-47C CHINOOK

Italian manufacture of the CH-47C began in the Spring of 1970, initially to meet an order for Italian Army Aviation. By 1 January 1988 sales totalled 165, customers including the armed forces of Egypt (15), Greece (10), Italy (32), Libya (20) and Morocco (9). Only 68 of the 95 ordered in 1977-78 by the Imperial Iranian government were delivered (54 before February 1979 and 14 later). Of the remaining 27, the Egyptian order accounted for 15, and 11 others were taken on charge by the US Army, which allocated them to the Pennsylvania Army National Guard.

Agusta developed, jointly with Hosp Ital SpA (a division of Cogefar) of Milan, an **ESFC** (emergency surgery flying centre) version of the Chinook for use as a mobile hospital.

Italian built Boeing CH-47C of the Italian Army

Details of the ESFC can be found in the 1983-84 *Jane's*. One was delivered to the Italian Army in 1987.

The Italian Army's entire fleet of Chinooks is being overhauled at the rate of three a year by Meridionali, which redelivered the first of 23 then-operational aircraft in March 1986. These aircraft are used for a wide range of duties, one important role being that of firefighting, in which configuration they can be equipped with a 5,000 litre (1,321 US gallon; 1,100 Imp gallon) metal tank for retardant.

Meridionali is also currently producing a further ten aircraft, designated **CH-47C Plus**, for operation by the Italian Army on behalf of the Civil Protection Agency. Four of these had been delivered by 1 January 1988. Simultaneously with this additional production, an upgrading programme is taking place, to fit the earlier aircraft with new Textron Lycoming T55-L-712E engines, composite rotor blades and a more advanced transmission system. Max T-O weight is increased to 22,680 kg (50,000 lb).

SIAI-MARCHETTI SpA
(Subsidiary of Agusta SpA)

Via Indipendenza 2, 21018 Sesto Calende (VA)
Telephone: (0331) 924421
Telex: 332601 SIAIAV I
PRESIDENT: Dott Raffaello Teti
MANAGING DIRECTOR: Ing Armando Romboli
AERODROME AND MAIN WORKS: Vergiate (Varese)
OTHER WORKS: Sesto Calende (Varese) and Malpensa

Founded in 1915, SIAI-Marchetti produced a wide range of military and civil landplanes and flying-boats up to the end of the Second World War. Its current products include piston, turboprop and turbofan powered trainers and the SF.600 utility transport. Since the 1970s it has also been engaged in the co-production with Agusta of licence built Boeing CH-47C, Bell 204/205/212/412, and Sikorsky S-61A, SH-3D/H and HH-3F helicopters.

SIAI-Marchetti undertakes the overhaul and repair of various types of aircraft (notably the C-130 Hercules, DHC-5 Buffalo and Cessna Citation II). It participates in national or multi-national programmes, producing parts for the Aeritalia G222, Panavia Tornado, AMX, Airbus A310, Dassault-Breguet Falcon 100 and Atlantique 2.

The company's works at Sesto Calende, Vergiate and Malpensa total 1,370,267 m² (14,749,416 sq ft) in area, of which 119,494 m² (1,286,221 sq ft) are covered, and employed nearly 2,000 people in 1988.

SIAI-MARCHETTI SF.260

The prototype for the SF.260 series, known as the F.250, was designed by Dott Ing Stelio Frati and built by Aviamilano. Flown for the first time on 15 July 1964, it was powered by a 186.5 kW (250 hp) Textron Lycoming engine and was certificated for aerobatic flying. A description appeared in the 1965-66 *Jane's*.

The version developed initially, for civil production, was manufactured, at first under licence from Aviamilano, by SIAI-Marchetti, and is designated SF.260. It received FAA type approval on 1 April 1966. Subsequently SIAI-Marchetti became the official holder of the type

SIAI-Marchetti SF.260M of the Italian Air Force (*Avio Data*)

certificate and of all manufacturing rights in the SF.260.

Descriptions of the civil SF.260A and SF.260B can be found in the 1980-81 and earlier editions of *Jane's*, and of the SF.260C in the 1985-86 edition. Current models are as follows:

SF.260D. Improved and updated civil version, replacing SF.260C, with aerodynamic and structural improvements developed for military SF.260M. Certificated by RAI on 14 December 1985 and by FAA in October 1986.

SF.260M. Two/three-seat military trainer, developed from civil SF.260A and first flown on 10 October 1970. Introduced a number of important structural and aerodynamic improvements, many of which were subsequently applied to later models. Meets requirements for basic flying training; instrument flying; aerobatics, including deliberate spinning and recovery; night flying; navigation flying; and formation flying. Detailed customer list in 1984-85 and earlier editions of *Jane's*.

SF.260W Warrior. Trainer/tactical support version of SF.260M, first flown (I-SJAV) in May 1972. Two or four underwing pylons, for up to 300 kg (661 lb) of external stores, and cockpit stores selection panel. Able to undertake a wide variety of roles, including low-level strike; forward air control; forward air support; armed reconnaissance; and liaison. Also meets same requirements as SF.260M for use as a trainer. Customers as listed in 1984-85 and earlier *Jane's*. One aircraft (described in 1980-81 and earlier editions) completed as **SF.260SW Sea Warrior** surveillance/SAR/supply version.

SF.260TP. Turboprop powered development. Described separately.

By early 1988 more than 800 SF.260s of all models had been delivered, mainly for export, and production of the piston engined models was continuing. Military trainer variants are operated by more than 20 armed forces worldwide.

The following description is generally applicable to all piston engined models unless otherwise stated:

TYPE: Two/three-seat fully aerobatic military light aircraft.

WINGS: Cantilever low-wing monoplane. Wing section NACA 64_1-212 (modified) at root, NACA 64_1-210 (modified) at tip. Dihedral 6° 20′ from roots (5° on SF.260D). Incidence 2° 45′ at root, 0° at tip. No sweepback. All-metal light alloy safe-life structure, with single main spar and auxiliary rear spar, built in two portions bolted together at centreline and attached to fuselage by six bolts. Press-formed ribs, with dimpled stiffening holes. Skin, which is butt joined and flush riveted, stiffened by stringers between main and rear spars. Differentially operating Frise light alloy mass balanced ailerons, and electrically actuated light alloy single-slotted flaps. Flaps operated by torque tube and mechanical linkage, ailerons by pushrods and cables. Servo tab in each aileron.

FUSELAGE: Semi-monocoque safe-life structure of frames, stringers and flush riveted skin, exclusively of light alloy except for welded steel tube engine mounting, glassfibre front panel of engine cowling, stainless steel firewall and detachable glassfibre tailcone.

TAIL UNIT: Cantilever light alloy safe-life structure, with sweptback vertical surfaces, fixed incidence tailplane and one-piece elevator. Two-spar fin and one-piece tailplane, bolted to fuselage; single-spar elevator, statically and aerodynamically balanced, and balanced rudder. Rudder and elevator operated by cables. Controllable trim tab in starboard half of elevator; ground adjustable tab on rudder.

LANDING GEAR: Electrically retractable tricycle type, with manual emergency actuation. Inward retracting main gear, of trailing arm type, and rearward retracting nose unit, each embodying Magnaghi oleo-pneumatic shock absorber (type 2/22028 in main units). Each welded steel tube main leg is hinged to the main and rear spars. Nose unit is of leg and fork type, with coaxial shock absorber and torque strut. Cleveland P/N 3080A mainwheels, with size 6.00-6 tube and tyre (6-ply rating), pressure 2.45 bars (35.5 lb/sq in). Cleveland P/N 40-77A nosewheel, with size 5.00-5 tube and tyre (6-ply rating), pressure 1.96 bars (28.4 lb/sq in). Cleveland P/N 3000-500 independent hydraulic single-disc brake and parking brake on each mainwheel. Nosewheel steering (20° to left or right) is operated directly by the rudder pedals, to which it is linked by pushrods. Up-lock secures main gear in retracted position during flight; anti-retraction system prevents main gear from retracting whenever strut is compressed by weight of aircraft.

POWER PLANT: One 194 kW (260 hp) Textron Lycoming O-540-E4A5 flat-six engine, driving a Hartzell HC-C2YK-1BF/8477-8R two-blade constant-speed metal propeller with spinner. AEIO-540-D4A5 engine available optionally. Fuel in two light alloy tanks in wings, capacity of each 49.5 litres (13.1 US gallons; 10.9 Imp gallons); and two permanent wingtip tanks, capacity of each 72 litres (19 US gallons; 15.85 Imp gallons). Total internal fuel capacity 243 litres (64.2 US gallons; 53.5 Imp gallons), of which 235 litres (62.1 US gallons; 51.7 Imp gallons) are usable. Individual refuelling point on top of each tank. In addition, SF.260W may be fitted with two 80 litre (21.1 US gallon; 17.5 Imp gallon) auxiliary tanks on underwing pylons. Oil capacity (all models) 11.4 litres (3.0 US gallons; 2.5 Imp gallons).

ACCOMMODATION (SF.260D): Three seats in enclosed cockpit, two side by side in front, one at rear. Two children with a combined weight not exceeding 113 kg (250 lb) may occupy rear seat. One-piece fully transparent rearward sliding Plexiglas canopy, with rubber cord canopy release. Baggage compartment, capacity 40 kg (88 lb), behind rear seat. Cabin carpeted, heated and ventilated; walls thermally insulated and soundproofed by a glassfibre lining. Slots at base of windscreen admit air for windscreen defrosting.

ACCOMMODATION (SF.260M; W similar): Side by side front seats (for instructor and pupil in SF.260M), with third seat centrally at rear. Front seats individually adjustable fore and aft, with forward folding backs and provision for back type parachute packs. Dual controls standard. All three seats equipped with lap belts and shoulder harnesses. Baggage compartment aft of rear seat. Upper portion of canopy tinted. Emergency canopy release handle for each front seat occupant. Steel tube windscreen frame for protection in the event of an overturn.

SYSTEMS (SF.260M; other models generally similar): Hydraulic equipment for mainwheel brakes only. No pneumatic system. 24V DC electrical system of single-conductor negative earth type, including 70A Prestolite engine mounted alternator/rectifier and 24V 24Ah Varley battery, for engine starting, flap and landing gear actuation, fuel booster pumps, electronics and lighting. Sealed battery compartment in rear of fuselage on port side. Connection of an external power source automatically disconnects the battery. Heating system for carburettor air intake. Emergency electrical system for extending landing gear if normal electrical actuation fails; provision for mechanical extension in the event of total electrical failure. Cabin heating, and windscreen de-icing and demisting, by heat exchanger using engine exhaust air. Additional manually controlled warm air outlets for general cabin heating. Oxygen system optional.

AVIONICS AND EQUIPMENT (SF.260M; W generally similar): Basic instrumentation and military equipment to customer's requirements. Blind-flying instrumentation and communications equipment optional: typical selection includes dual Collins 20B VHF com; Collins VIR-31A VHF nav; Collins ADF-60A; Collins TDR-90 ATC transponder; Collins PN-101 compass; ID-90-000 RMI; and Gemelli AG04-1 intercom. Landing light in nose, below spinner. Instrument panel can be slid rearward to provide access to rear of instruments.

ARMAMENT (SF.260W): Two or four underwing hardpoints, able to carry external stores on NATO standard pylons up to a maximum of 300 kg (661 lb) when flown as a single-seater. Typical alternative loads can include one or two SIAI gun pods, each with one or two 7.62 mm FN machine-guns and 500 rds; two Aerea AL-8-70 launchers each with eight 2.75 in rockets; two LAU-32 launchers each with seven 2.75 in rockets; two Aerea AL-18-50 launchers each with eighteen 2 in rockets; two Aerea AL-8-68 launchers each with eight 68 mm rockets; two Aerea AL-6-80 launchers each with six 81 mm rockets; two LUU-2/B parachute flares; two SAMP EU 32 125 kg general purpose bombs or EU 13 120 kg fragmentation bombs; two SAMP EU 70 50 kg general purpose bombs; Mk 76 11 kg practice bombs; two cartridge throwers for 70 mm multi-purpose cartridges, F 725 flares, or F 130 smoke cartridges; one or two photo-reconnaissance pods with two 70 mm automatic cameras; two supply containers; or two 80 litre (21.1 US gallon; 17.5 Imp gallon) auxiliary fuel tanks.

DIMENSIONS, EXTERNAL:

Wing span over tip tanks	8.35 m (27 ft 4¾ in)
Wing chord: at root	1.60 m (5 ft 3 in)
mean aerodynamic	1.325 m (4 ft 4¼ in)
at tip	0.784 m (2 ft 6⅞ in)
Wing aspect ratio (excl tip tanks)	6.3
Wing taper ratio	2.2
Length overall	7.10 m (23 ft 3½ in)
Fuselage: Max width	1.10 m (3 ft 7¼ in)
Max depth	1.042 m (3 ft 5 in)
Height overall	2.41 m (7 ft 11 in)
Elevator span	3.01 m (9 ft 10½ in)
Wheel track	2.274 m (7 ft 5½ in)
Wheelbase	1.66 m (5 ft 5¼ in)
Propeller diameter	1.93 m (6 ft 4 in)
Propeller ground clearance	0.32 m (1 ft 0½ in)

DIMENSIONS, INTERNAL:

Cabin: Length	1.66 m (5 ft 5¼ in)
Max width	1.00 m (3 ft 3¼ in)
Height (seat cushion to canopy)	0.98 m (3 ft 2½ in)
Volume	1.50 m³ (53 cu ft)
Baggage compartment volume	0.18 m³ (6.36 cu ft)

AREAS:

Wings, gross	10.10 m² (108.70 sq ft)
Ailerons (total, incl tabs)	0.762 m² (8.20 sq ft)
Trailing-edge flaps (total)	1.18 m² (12.70 sq ft)
Fin	0.76 m² (8.18 sq ft)
Dorsal fin	0.16 m² (1.72 sq ft)
Rudder, incl tab	0.60 m² (6.46 sq ft)
Tailplane	1.46 m² (15.70 sq ft)
Elevator, incl tab	0.96 m² (10.30 sq ft)

WEIGHTS AND LOADINGS:

Manufacturer's basic weight empty:	
M	755 kg (1,664 lb)
W	770 kg (1,697 lb)
Weight empty, equipped: D	755 kg (1,664 lb)
M	815 kg (1,797 lb)
W	830 kg (1,830 lb)
Fuel:	
in-wing and wingtip tanks (all versions)	169 kg (372.5 lb)
underwing tanks (W only)	114 kg (251.5 lb)
Typical mission weights:	
M, trainer ('clean')	1,140 kg (2,513 lb)
W, two 47 kg (103.5 lb) machine-gun pods and full internal fuel	1,163 kg (2,564 lb)
W, one Alkan 500B cartridge thrower, one two-camera reconnaissance pod and full internal fuel	1,182 kg (2,605 lb)
W, trainer with 94 kg (207 lb) external stores	1,249 kg (2,753 lb)
W, self-ferry with two 80 litre (21.1 US gallon; 17.5 Imp gallon) underwing tanks	1,285 kg (2,833 lb)
W, two 125 kg bombs and 150 kg (331 lb) internal fuel	1,300 kg (2,866 lb)
W, two AL-8-70 rocket launchers and 160 kg (353 lb) internal fuel	1,300 kg (2,866 lb)
Max T-O weight: D, M, Aerobatic	1,100 kg (2,425 lb)
D, Utility	1,100 kg (2,425 lb)
M, Utility	1,200 kg (2,645 lb)
W, max permitted	1,300 kg (2,866 lb)
Max wing loading: D	109 kg/m² (22.4 lb/sq ft)
M	119 kg/m² (24.4 lb/sq ft)
W	129 kg/m² (26.4 lb/sq ft)
Max power loading: D	5.68 kg/kW (9.33 lb/hp)
M	6.19 kg/kW (10.17 lb/hp)
W	6.70 kg/kW (11.01 lb/hp)

PERFORMANCE (C at AUW of 1,102 kg; 2,430 lb, M at AUW of 1,200 kg; 2,645 lb, W at 1,300 kg; 2,866 lb, except where indicated):

Never-exceed speed:	
D, M	235 knots (436 km/h; 271 mph)
Max level speed at S/L:	
D	187 knots (347 km/h; 215 mph)
M	180 knots (333 km/h; 207 mph)
W	165 knots (305 km/h; 190 mph)
Max cruising speed (75% power):	
D at 3,050 m (10,000 ft)	178 knots (330 km/h; 205 mph)
M at 1,500 m (4,925 ft)	162 knots (300 km/h; 186 mph)
W at 1,500 m (4,925 ft)	152 knots (281 km/h; 175 mph)
Stalling speed, flaps and landing gear up:	
M	74 knots (137 km/h; 86 mph)
W	88 knots (163 km/h; 102 mph)
Stalling speed, flaps and landing gear down:	
D	60 knots (111 km/h; 70 mph)
M	68 knots (126 km/h; 79 mph)
W	72 knots (134 km/h; 83 mph)
Max rate of climb at S/L: D	546 m (1,791 ft)/min
M	457 m (1,500 ft)/min
W	381 m (1,250 ft)/min
Time to 1,500 m (4,925 ft): M	4 min 0 s
W	6 min 20 s
Time to 2,300 m (7,550 ft): M	6 min 50 s
W	10 min 20 s
Time to 3,000 m (9,850 ft): M	10 min 0 s
W	18 min 40 s
Service ceiling: D	5,790 m (19,000 ft)
M	4,665 m (15,300 ft)
W	4,480 m (14,700 ft)
T-O run at S/L: D	480 m (1,575 ft)
M	384 m (1,260 ft)
T-O to 15 m (50 ft) at S/L: M	606 m (1,988 ft)
W	825 m (2,707 ft)
Landing from 15 m (50 ft) at S/L: D	445 m (1,460 ft)
M	539 m (1,768 ft)
W	645 m (2,116 ft)
Landing run at S/L: D, M	345 m (1,132 ft)
Operational radius:	
W, 6 h 25 min single-seat armed patrol mission at 1,163 kg (2,564 lb) AUW, incl 5 h 35 min over operating area, 20 kg (44 lb) fuel reserves	50 nm (92 km; 57 miles)
W, 3 h 38 min single-seat strike mission, incl two 5 min loiters over separate en-route target areas, 20 kg (44 lb) fuel reserves	250 nm (463 km; 287 miles)
W, 4 h 54 min single-seat strike mission, incl 5 min over target area, 20 kg (44 lb) fuel reserves	300 nm (556 km; 345 miles)
W, 4 h 30 min single-seat photo-reconnaissance mission at 1,182 kg (2,605 lb) AUW, incl three 1 h loiters over separate en-route operating areas, 20 kg (44 lb) fuel reserves	150 nm (278 km; 172 miles)
W, 6 h 3 min two-seat self-ferry mission with two 80 litre (21.1 US gallon; 17.5 Imp gallon) underwing tanks, at 1,285 kg (2,833 lb) AUW, 30 kg (66 lb) fuel reserves	926 nm (1,716 km; 1,066 miles)
Range with max fuel:	
D (two-seat)	805 nm (1,490 km; 925 miles)
M (two-seat)	890 nm (1,650 km; 1,025 miles)
g limits (M):	
at max Aerobatic T-O weight	+6/−3
at max Utility T-O weight without external load	+4.4/−2.2

SIAI-MARCHETTI SF.260TP

First flown in July 1980, the SF.260TP is a turboprop powered development of the SF.260M/W, the airframe remaining virtually unchanged aft of the firewall except for substitution of an inset rudder trim tab and provision of an automatic fuel feed system.

More than 60 SF.260TPs have been ordered by military customers.

AIRFRAME: As SF.260M/W, except for increased overall length and provision of trim tab in rudder.

POWER PLANT: One Allison 250-B17D turboprop, flat rated at 261 kW (350 shp) and driving a Hartzell HC-B3TF-7A/T10173-25R three-blade constant-speed fully-feathering and reversible-pitch propeller with spinner. Fuel capacity as for SF.260M/W; automatic fuel feed system. Oil capacity 7 litres (1.8 US gallons; 1.5 Imp gallons).

ACCOMMODATION, SYSTEMS, AVIONICS AND EQUIPMENT: Generally as for SF.260.

DIMENSIONS, EXTERNAL AND INTERNAL, AND AREAS:

As for SF.260 except:	
Length overall	7.40 m (24 ft 3¼ in)

WEIGHTS AND LOADINGS: As for SF.260M/W except:

Weight empty, equipped	750 kg (1,654 lb)
Max power loading: trainer	4.60 kg/kW (7.56 lb/shp)
Warrior	4.98 kg/kW (8.19 lb/shp)

PERFORMANCE (at trainer Utility T-O weight of 1,200 kg; 2,645 lb, ISA):

Never-exceed speed	236 knots (437 km/h; 271 mph)
Max level speed at 3,050 m (10,000 ft)	228 knots (422 km/h; 262 mph)

Max cruising speed at 2,440 m (8,000 ft)
216 knots (400 km/h; 248 mph)
Econ cruising speed at 4,575 m (15,000 ft)
170 knots (315 km/h; 195 mph)
Stalling speed at S/L, flaps down, power off
68 knots (126 km/h; 79 mph)
Max rate of climb at S/L   661 m (2,170 ft)/min
Service ceiling   7,500 m (24,600 ft)
T-O run   298 m (978 ft)
T-O to 15 m (50 ft)   467 m (1,532 ft)
Landing from 15 m (50 ft)   533 m (1,749 ft)
Landing run, without reverse pitch 307 m (1,007 ft)
Range at 4,575 m (15,000 ft) with max fuel, 30 min
reserves   512 nm (949 km; 589 miles)

SIAI-MARCHETTI S.211

This lightweight, low-cost basic trainer and light attack aircraft was first revealed in the form of a model at the Paris Air Show in May/June 1977. Two flying prototypes were built initially, and the first of these (I-SITF) made its initial flight on 10 April 1981.

Deliveries of production S.211s began in November 1984, and 40 have been ordered, of which 34 had been delivered by January 1988. Customers include the air forces of Singapore (30) and Haiti (4). The first six S.211s for Singapore were delivered in component knocked-down form for reassembly; subsequent aircraft were built by SAMCO, a subsidiary of Singapore Aircraft Industries (SAI, which see).

Features of the S.211 are its safe stalling and spinning characteristics, and the very low airframe weight, made possible by the fact that some 61 per cent of the external surfaces are made from composite materials.

In order to improve the S.211's operational capabilities a special nav/attack version, equipped with an OMI/Litton lightweight head-up display and Omega navigation computer, is under development. Joint development, with SAI, of a lengthened version of the S.211 was announced at the Paris Air Show in June 1987. No further details of either programme were available at the time of closing for press.

The following description applies to the standard production S.211:

TYPE: Two-seat basic trainer and light attack aircraft.

WINGS: Cantilever shoulder-wing monoplane, with super-critical section developed by computer with the assistance of the US universities of New York and Kansas. Thickness/chord ratio 15% at root, 13% at tip. Incidence 2° 13′ at root, −1° 17′ at tip. Anhedral 2° from roots. Sweepback 15° 30′ at quarter-chord. Two-spar metal torsion box structure, forming integral fuel tank; attached to fuselage by four bolts. Upper and lower skins each formed by two one-piece panels joined along centreline and to the spars. Hydraulically actuated ailerons, with electric trim, and large area electrically actuated Fowler flaps, on trailing-edges.

FUSELAGE: Conventional metal and glassfibre semi-monocoque structure. Hydraulically actuated airbrake under centre-fuselage. Equipment bay in nose. Large quick-disconnect panel at rear, for rapid engine access or removal.

TAIL UNIT: Cantilever metal structure. Sweptback fin; horn balanced rudder with electrically operated trim tab; electrically actuated variable incidence tailplane has sweptback leading-edge. Horn balanced elevators, with servo tab.

LANDING GEAR: Hydraulically retractable tricycle type, of Messier-Hispano-Bugatti/Magnaghi design. Oleo-pneumatic shock absorber in each unit. All units retract forward into fuselage (main units turning through 90° to lie flat in undersides of engine air intake trunks).

SIAI-Marchetti SF.260TP (Allison 250-B17D turboprop)

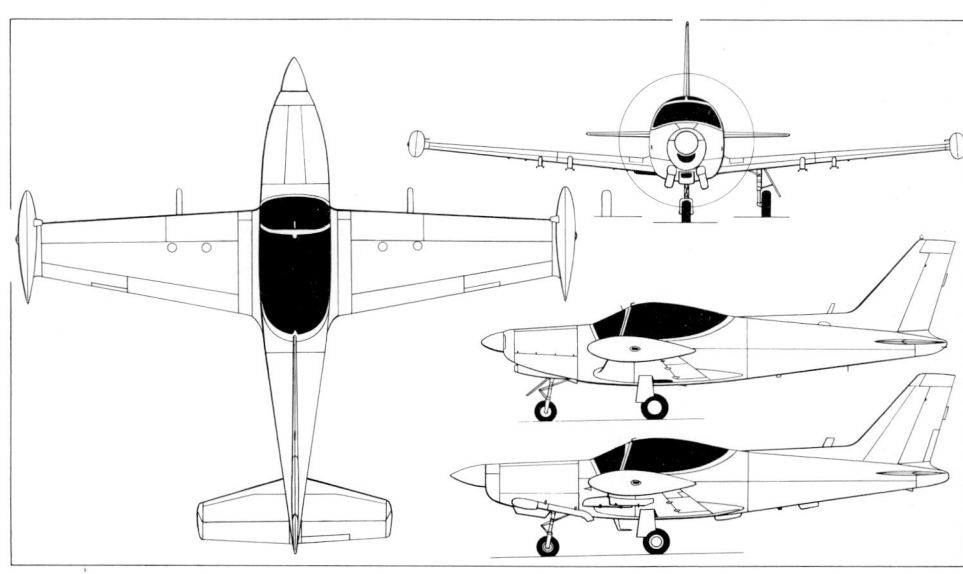

SIAI-Marchetti SF.260TP turboprop trainer, with additional side view (centre) of piston engined SF.260M *(Pilot Press)*

Nosewheel steerable 18° left and right. Mainwheels size 6.50-8; nosewheel size 5.00-5 with water deflecting tyre. Designed for sink rate of 4 m (13 ft)/s. Wheel brakes actuated hydraulically, independently of main hydraulic system. Provision for emergency free-fall extension.

POWER PLANT: One 11.12 kN (2,500 lb st) Pratt & Whitney Canada JT15D-4D non-afterburning turbofan, with electronic fuel control, mounted in rear of fuselage; lateral intake each side of fuselage, with splitter plate.

Fuel in 650 litre (171.5 US gallon; 143 Imp gallon) integral wing tank and 150 litre (39.5 US gallon; 33 Imp gallon) fuselage tank; total capacity 800 litres (211 US gallons; 176 Imp gallons). Single gravity refuelling point in top surface of starboard wing. Electric fuel pump for engine starting and emergency use. Fuel and oil systems permit inverted flight. Provision for two 270 litre (71.3 US gallon; 59.4 Imp gallon) drop tanks on inboard underwing stores points. Oil capacity 10 kg (22 lb).

ACCOMMODATION: Seats for two persons in tandem in pressurised and air-conditioned cockpit under one-piece framed canopy opening sideways to starboard: pupil in front, instructor on rear seat elevated 28 cm (11 in). Internal transparent screen between seats. Martin-Baker Mk 10 lightweight zero/zero ejection seats for both occupants.

SYSTEMS: Environmental control system for cockpit pressurisation and air-conditioning, using engine bleed air for heating, freon vapour for cooling. Max pressure differential 0.24 bars (3.5 lb/sq in). Hydraulic system, pressure 207 bars (3,000 lb/sq in), for actuation of airbrake, landing gear, freon compressor and aileron boost, and independent actuation of wheel brakes. Primary electrical system is 28V DC, using an engine driven starter/generator; nickel-cadmium battery; two static inverters supply AC power for instruments and avionics. External power receptacle in port side of lower fuselage aft of wing. Demand type main oxygen system, at 124 bars (1,800 lb/sq in) pressure, sufficient to supply both occupants for 4 hours, plus bottles for emergency oxygen supply.

AVIONICS AND EQUIPMENT: Standard avionics fit includes two V/UHF com, ADF, VOR/ILS and DME or Tacan, IFF or ATC, ICS, AHRS, HSI and AI, with full dual controls and handover. Provision for dual gyro stabilised gunsight system with miniaturised video recording or film camera. Additional provisions for R/Nav, radar altimeter, Doppler radar, head-up display, radar warning system and ECM.

SIAI-Marchetti S.211s of the Republic of Singapore Air Force

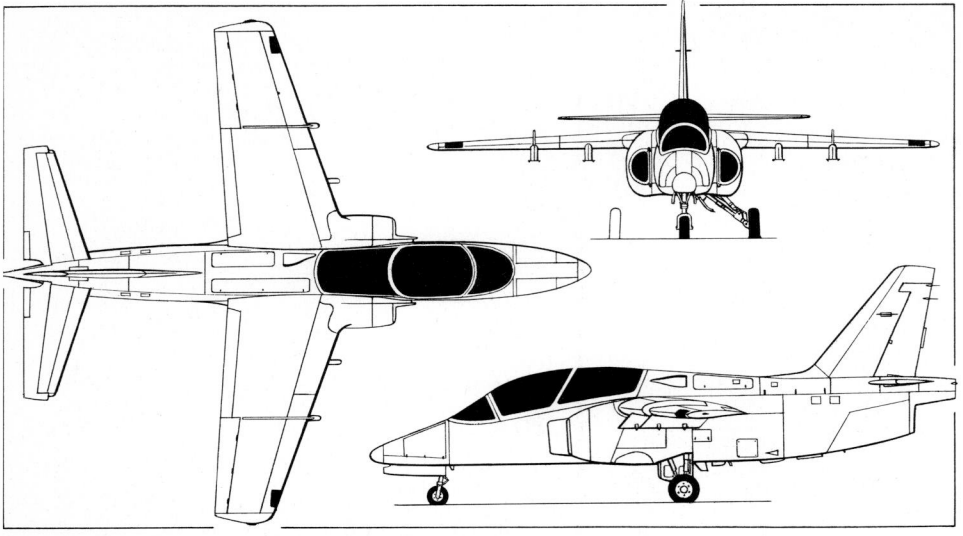

SIAI-Marchetti S.211 basic trainer and light attack aircraft *(Pilot Press)*

ARMAMENT: Four underwing hardpoints, stressed for loads of up to 330 kg (727.5 lb) inboard, 165 kg (364 lb) outboard; max external load 660 kg (1,455 lb). Typical loads can include four single- or twin-gun 7.62 mm machine-gun pods, four 12.7 mm gun pods, or (inboard only) two 20 mm gun pods; four AL-18-50 (18 × 50 mm), Matra F2 (6 × 68 mm), LAU-32 (7 × 2.75 in), or AL-6-80 (6 × 81 mm) rocket launchers, or (inboard only) two Matra 155 (18 × 68 mm), SNORA RWK-020 (12 × 81 mm) or 100 mm rocket launchers; four bombs or practice bombs of up to 150 kg size, or (inboard only) two bombs or napalm containers of up to 300 kg; four 74 mm cartridge throwers; or (inboard only) two photo-reconnaissance pods each with four cameras and infra-red linescan; or (inboard only) two 270 litre (71.3 US gallon; 59.4 Imp gallon) auxiliary fuel tanks. Ferranti ISIS D-211 optical weapon aiming system optional (fitted in aircraft for Haiti).

DIMENSIONS, EXTERNAL:

Wing span	8.43 m (27 ft 8 in)
Wing chord: at root	2.151 m (7 ft 0¾ in)
mean aerodynamic	1.646 m (5 ft 4¾ in)
at tip	1.00 m (3 ft 3¼ in)
Wing aspect ratio	5.1
Length overall	9.31 m (30 ft 6½ in)
Height overall	3.80 m (12 ft 5½ in)
Tailplane span	3.96 m (13 ft 0 in)
Wheel track	2.29 m (7 ft 6 in)
Wheelbase	4.02 m (13 ft 2¼ in)

AREAS:

Wings, gross	12.60 m² (135.63 sq ft)
Airbrake	0.42 m² (4.52 sq ft)
Vertical tail surfaces (total)	2.01 m² (21.64 sq ft)
Horizontal tail surfaces (total)	3.378 m² (36.36 sq ft)

WEIGHTS:

Weight empty, equipped	1,850 kg (4,078 lb)
Max usable fuel: internal	622 kg (1,371 lb)
external	390 kg (860 lb)
Max T-O weight: trainer, 'clean'	2,750 kg (6,063 lb)
armed version	3,150 kg (6,944 lb)

PERFORMANCE (at T-O weight of 2,500 kg; 5,511 lb except where indicated):

Never-exceed speed	
	Mach 0.80 (400 knots; 740 km/h; 460 mph EAS)
Max cruising speed at 7,620 m (25,000 ft)	
	360 knots (667 km/h; 414 mph)
Rotation speed	90 knots (167 km/h; 104 mph)
Stalling speed, flaps down	74 knots (138 km/h; 86 mph)
Max rate of climb at S/L	1,280 m (4,200 ft)/min
Time to 6,100 m (20,000 ft)	6 min 12 s
Service ceiling	12,200 m (40,000 ft)
T-O run (S/L, ISA)	390 m (1,280 ft)
T-O to 15 m (50 ft)	512 m (1,680 ft)
Landing from 15 m (50 ft)	705 m (2,313 ft)
Landing run (S/L, ISA)	361 m (1,185 ft)
Min air turning radius at S/L	less than 305 m (1,000 ft)

Typical attack radius with four rocket launchers, AUW of 3,150 kg (6,944 lb):

hi-lo-hi, out and back at 265 knots (491 km/h; 305 mph) at 9,150 m (30,000 ft), 2 h 50 min mission (incl 5 min over target), 60 kg (132 lb) of fuel remaining
  300 nm (556 km; 345 miles)

lo-lo-lo, out and back at 250 knots (463 km/h; 288 mph) at less than 305 m (1,000 ft), 1 h 5 min mission (incl 5 min over target), 60 kg (132 lb) of fuel remaining
  125 nm (231 km; 144 miles)

Max range on internal fuel, 30 min reserves	
	900 nm (1,668 km; 1,036 miles)

Ferry range (AUW of 3,150 kg; 6,944 lb, max internal and external fuel) at 270 knots (500 km/h; 311 mph) at 9,150 m (30,000 ft), 90 kg (198 lb) of fuel remaining
  1,340 nm (2,483 km; 1,543 miles)

Endurance, 30 min reserves	3 h 50 min

Sustained g limit at 4,575 m (15,000 ft)	3.4
g limits:	+6/–3 'clean'
	+5/–2.5 with external stores

SIAI-MARCHETTI SF.600TP CANGURO (KANGAROO)

The prototype F.600 Canguro (I-CANG), built by General Avia and then powered by 261 kW (350 hp) Textron Lycoming TIO-540-J flat-six piston engines, made its first flight on 30 December 1978. This aircraft was described under the General Avia heading in the 1979-80 *Jane's*.

The basic production aircraft is now offered with Allison 250-B17C turboprops and non-retractable landing gear; major options include retractable landing gear and a swing-tail rear fuselage. A version with 335 kW (450 shp) Allison 250-B17F engines is under development. The aircraft can be adapted for a variety of roles which include passenger or cargo transport, paratroop transport, air ambulance, maritime surveillance, electronic intelligence, and agricultural duties. The retractable gear version is considered especially suitable for a maritime surveillance role, equipped with an underfuselage radome and other appropriate avionics and equipment.

Certification by the RAI was received in the Spring of 1987. An initial production batch of nine aircraft has been started, and the first three of these, for the Rome based air taxi operator Sun Line, were delivered in April 1988.

TYPE: Twin-turboprop passenger, cargo, ambulance and general utility transport.

WINGS: Cantilever high-wing monoplane. Wing section NASA GAW-1, with 17% thickness/chord ratio. Dihedral 2°. Incidence (constant) 1° 30'. All-metal riveted structure in aluminium alloy, with stressed skin. Centre-section has main spar and two auxiliary spars; outboard of engines, wings have two spars. All-metal ailerons and electrically operated double-slotted flaps. Electrically operated trim tab in port aileron.

FUSELAGE: Aluminium alloy semi-monocoque structure of frames, stringers, bulkheads and stressed skin. Swing-tail rear fuselage available optionally.

TAIL UNIT: Cantilever all-metal stressed skin structure. Trim tabs in rudder (actuated mechanically) and each elevator (electrically/mechanically operated). Small dorsal fin.

LANDING GEAR: Choice of retractable or non-retractable tricycle gear, of trailing arm type, with oleo-pneumatic shock absorber in each unit. Twin-wheel main units, mounted on small stub-wings attached to fuselage floor; single steerable nose unit. Mainwheels and tyres size 7.00-6, pressure 2.90 bars (42 lb/sq in); nosewheel and tyre size 6.00-6. Hydraulic disc brakes on main units.

POWER PLANT: Two 313 kW (420 shp) Allison 250-B17C turboprops in current production version, each driving a Hartzell three-blade constant-speed fully-feathering reversible-pitch propeller. Uprated version with Allison 250-B17Fs under development. Fuel in four identical outer-wing tanks, total capacity 1,100 litres (290.6 US gallons; 242 Imp gallons). Self-sealing tanks optional on military versions. Provision for underwing tanks, total capacity 600 litres (158.5 US gallons; 132 Imp gallons). Oil capacity 11.4 litres (3.0 US gallons; 2.5 Imp gallons).

ACCOMMODATION: Pilot and co-pilot or passenger on flight deck. Dual controls standard. Cabin accommodates up to nine passengers at 100 cm (40 in) seat pitch (2-2-2-2-1); six passengers in VIP version, with reclining seats, folding tables, bar and toilet; or 10 paratroops on inward facing seats; or two stretcher patients and two medical attendants; or freight. Baggage compartment at rear of cabin in standard passenger version; in centre of cabin, opposite toilet, in VIP version; rear compartment used to store folding passenger seats when converted for cargo use. Forward door on port side for crew. Wider, sliding door at rear on port side for passenger and freight loading and paratroop dropping, with smaller emergency door opposite this on starboard side. Cargo version can accept three 1.30 × 1.15 × 1.07 m (51 × 45 × 42 in) containers, or two of size 2.20 × 1.15 × 1.07 m (87 × 45 × 42 in).

SYSTEMS: Standard cabin heating/defrosting system uses engine bleed air; ventilation is provided by ram air; freon air-conditioning system optional. Primary electrical system is 28V DC, powered by two 150A engine driven starter/generators, with a 24V 22Ah nickel-cadmium battery for independent engine starting and emergencies. AC power, 115V at 400Hz, is provided when required by a static inverter. Pneumatic de-icing system for wings and tail unit, and electric de-icing of propellers, are optional.

AVIONICS: Wide range of IFR com/nav avionics available, to customer's requirements. Typical installation includes VHF, UHF and HF com, ADF, VOR/LOC/ILS, DME and ATC transponder. Options include Omega nav system, weather radar, three-axis autopilot and flight director.

EQUIPMENT: Can be equipped for target towing, with floor mounted winch, 2,000 m (6,560 ft) of cable, electric power unit (100A/28V DC), and miss-distance indicator system; with undertail hook for towing one or more gliders; with one or two Wild or Zeiss type photogrammetric automatic cameras (plus additional avionics at customer's option); with equipment for in-flight inspection and calibration of ground radio/navigation aids; or with appropriate sensors and radar warning receiver. Other specialised applications include agricultural duties (single underfuselage tank, plus bubble type and additional lower windows in pilot's door, windscreen and nose-gear wire cutters, ceiling mounted airscoop, and anti-corrosion paint finish). The maritime surveillance version can be equipped with nose mounted search and navigation radar, underfuselage side/down-looking surveillance radar, belly mounted panoramic camera and forward looking oblique camera, FLIR or low light level TV camera under fuselage, Omega-VLF area navigation system, advanced compass system, periscopic sextant, bubble side windows for observers, and a searchlight.

DIMENSIONS, EXTERNAL:

Wing span	15.00 m (49 ft 2½ in)
Wing chord, constant	1.60 m (5 ft 3 in)
Wing aspect ratio	9.4
Length overall	12.15 m (39 ft 10½ in)

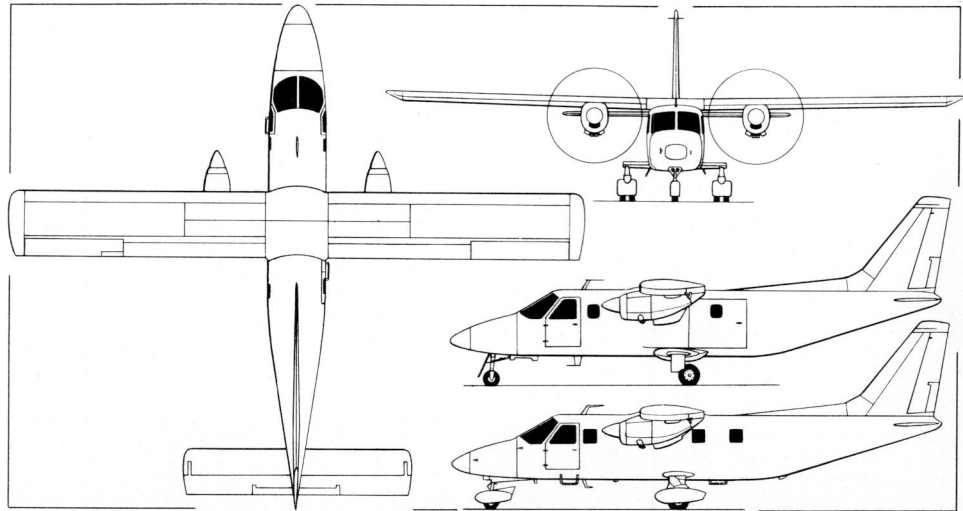

Basic SIAI-Marchetti SF.600TP, with additional side view (centre) of version with retractable landing gear *(Pilot Press)*

Height overall	4.60 m (15 ft 1 in)
Tailplane span	5.89 m (19 ft 4 in)
Wheel track	2.40 m (7 ft 10½ in)
Wheelbase	4.88 m (16 ft 0 in)
Propeller diameter	2.29 m (7 ft 6 in)
Crew door (fwd, port): Height	1.14 m (3 ft 9 in)
Width	0.86 m (2 ft 10 in)
Height to sill	0.90 m (2 ft 11½ in)
Cargo door (rear, port):	
Height	1.13 m (3 ft 8½ in)
Width	1.49 m (4 ft 10¾ in)
Height to sill	0.90 m (2 ft 11½ in)

DIMENSIONS, INTERNAL:

Cabin, excl flight deck: Length	5.05 m (16 ft 6¾ in)
Width	1.23 m (4 ft 0½ in)
Height	1.27 m (4 ft 2 in)
Floor area	6.0 m² (64.6 sq ft)
Volume	7.90 m³ (279 cu ft)

AREAS:

Wings, gross	24.00 m² (258.3 sq ft)
Fin	1.69 m² (18.19 sq ft)
Rudder	1.35 m² (14.53 sq ft)
Tailplane	3.68 m² (39.61 sq ft)
Elevators (total)	2.76 m² (29.71 sq ft)

WEIGHTS AND LOADINGS:

Weight empty (standard utility version)	1,875 kg (4,133 lb)
Max T-O weight	3,400 kg (7,495 lb)
Max cargo floor loading	400 kg/m² (81.93 lb/sq ft)
Max wing loading	141.7 kg/m² (29.0 lb/sq ft)
Max power loading	5.43 kg/kW (8.92 lb/shp)

PERFORMANCE (at max T-O weight, ISA):

Max cruising speed at 1,525 m (5,000 ft)	165 knots (306 km/h; 190 mph)
Cruising speed (75% power) at 3,050 m (10,000 ft)	155 knots (287 km/h; 178 mph)
Stalling speed, flaps down	59 knots (109 km/h; 68 mph)
Max rate of climb at S/L	451 m (1,480 ft)/min
Rate of climb at S/L, one engine out	152 m (500 ft)/min
Service ceiling	7,315 m (24,000 ft)

SIAI-Marchetti SF.600TP in standard form with non-retractable landing gear

Service ceiling, one engine out	3,050 m (10,000 ft)	Landing run: without propeller reversal	280 m (920 ft)
T-O run	287 m (940 ft)	with propeller reversal	204 m (670 ft)
T-O to 15 m (50 ft)	408 m (1,340 ft)	Range at 3,050 m (10,000 ft), 10% reserves:	
Landing from 15 m (50 ft):		with max payload	324 nm (600 km; 372 miles)
without propeller reversal	479 m (1,570 ft)	with max fuel and 500 kg (1,102 lb) payload	
with propeller reversal	396 m (1,300 ft)		853 nm (1,580 km; 981 miles)

CAPRONI VIZZOLA COSTRUZIONI AERONAUTICHE SpA
(Subsidiary of Agusta SpA)

Via Per Tornavento 15, 21019 Somma Lombardo
Telephone: (0331) 230 826
Telex: 332554 CAVIZ I
Fax: (0331) 230622
GENERAL MANAGER: Ing Marcello Puppi

The Caproni company, formed in 1910, is the oldest Italian aircraft manufacturer. Its works at Vizzola Ticino have approx 30,000 m² (322,917 sq ft) of covered space, and are equipped to manufacture complete structural subassemblies for helicopters and medium-sized fixed-wing aircraft. Caproni Vizzola also produces ground support equipment for General Electric T64/CT64, J79, J85 and CF6 and Turbo Union RB199 turbojet and turbofan engines.

A 100% holding in Caproni Vizzola was acquired by Agusta in 1983.

CAPRONI VIZZOLA C22J VENTURA

The C22J is a two-seat lightweight training aircraft, developed by Caproni Vizzola as a private venture. A prototype (I-CAVJ), powered by 1.0 kN (220 lb st) TRS 18-046 engines, made its first flight on 21 July 1980.

Intended primarily for student pilot screening, basic and proficiency training, the C22J is also suitable for ECM evaluation, ground and air navaid calibration, ecological survey and high-speed liaison. It can be converted easily for photographic survey duties, or for use as an RPV.

The first pre-series C22J (I-GIAC) made its initial flight on 17 February 1983, and differs from the prototype in having shorter span wings, with tip tanks, and more powerful TRS 18-1 engines. RAI certification under FAR Pt 23 was nearing completion in the Spring of 1988.

The following description applies to the intended production version:

TYPE: Two-seat basic training aircraft.

WINGS: Cantilever shoulder-wing monoplane. Constant chord wings, of Wortmann FX-67K-170 section. Dihedral 2°. Incidence 1° 9′. No sweepback. Single-spar structure, built as two panels and joined on centreline, with aluminium alloy skin and extruded leading-edge. Electrically actuated trailing-edge plain flaps can be set in any position throughout their full range of movement. Flaps operate in conjunction with aluminium alloy airbrakes/spoilers, of which there is one in upper surface of each wing, forward of flap. Airbrakes are opened manually, but move with flaps to provide balanced control. Aerodynamically balanced ailerons operate differentially and are drooped to provide additional flap area. All movable surfaces of extruded aluminium alloy, operated by push/pull rods. No tabs.

FUSELAGE: Tadpole shaped structure, designed as a laminar lifting body. Primary load-bearing keel and wing spar pickup cross-structure is of light alloy, inside moulded glassfibre shell. NACA type flush engine air inlet of glassfibre in top of fuselage, aft of cockpits. Tailboom is of light alloy.

TAIL UNIT: Cantilever T tail, with light alloy stressed skin tailplane. Full span balanced elevator is a chemically milled extrusion, and has spring trim, actuated by Industria electrical system located in fin. All-metal two-spar stressed skin fin, bolted to tailboom. All control surfaces operated by push/pull rods. No tabs. Rudder pedals adjustable in flight.

LANDING GEAR: Retractable tricycle type, actuated electrically with manual backup. All units retract forward into fuselage. Cantilever sprung main legs, of glassfibre epoxy; rubber-in-torsion shock absorption on nose unit. Cleveland mainwheels, with Goodyear size 5.00-5 tyres (6 ply rating), pressure 3.0 bars (43.5 lb/sq in). Tost nosewheel, with Dunlop tyre size 260 × 85 mm (4 ply rating), pressure 5.0 bars (72.5 lb/sq in). Cleveland independent hydraulic disc brakes on mainwheels. Steerable nosewheel, linked to rudder pedals. Safety lock for up and down positions. Electrical warning system.

POWER PLANT: Two Microturbo TRS 18-1 turbojets, each rated at 1.45 kN (326 lb st) for take-off and 1.28 kN (288 lb st) max continuous, mounted side by side in fuselage aft of cockpits. Integral fuel tank in each wing leading-edge, combined capacity 290 litres (76.6 US gallons; 64 Imp gallons), and two 70 litre (18.5 US gallon; 15.5 Imp gallon) wingtip tanks. Total fuel capacity 430 litres (113.6 US gallons; 95 Imp gallons). Fuel system incorporates fuselage collector tank which permits inverted flight. Refuelling point at each wingtip. Provision for two 112 litre (29.6 US gallon; 24.5 Imp gallon) underwing drop tanks. Oil capacity 0.8 litre (1.7 US pints; 1.4 Imp pints).

ACCOMMODATION: Seats for two persons side by side under jettisonable canopy hinged at rear and opening upward.

Caproni Vizzola C22J Ventura, equipped as standard with wingtip tanks

Seats are semi-supine. Dual controls on production version. Single instrument panel and centre console, eliminating need for dual instruments and avionics. Cockpit heated, ventilated and demisted.

SYSTEMS: Hydraulic system for mainwheel brakes only. No pneumatic system. Electrical system is 28V DC, incorporating two Microturbo 1.3kW starter/generators and a 24V 18Ah lead-acid battery. Cockpit ventilation and demisting by heat exchangers on jetpipes. Demand type low-pressure oxygen system, capacity 6.7 litres (0.24 cu ft), for each occupant.

AVIONICS AND EQUIPMENT: Avionics bay in top of fuselage, aft of cockpits. Collins Micro Line nav/com radio, Pro Line flight director, navigation, landing and anti-collision lights, standard.

ARMAMENT: Provision for two standard NATO underwing pylons, for a wide range of stores for gunnery/weapon training, photographic reconnaissance and target towing missions. Typical loads include one drop tank and one three-camera pod; two drop tanks; two 7.62 mm gun pods and 500 rds of ammunition; two Simpres AL-18-50 pods with eighteen 2 in rockets; four SAMP EU70 50 kg general purpose bombs; four Mk 70 11 kg or M38-A2 50 kg practice bombs; or two Dornier DATS 1 50 kg towed targets.

DIMENSIONS, EXTERNAL:

Wing span	9.20 m (30 ft 2¼ in)
Wing chord, constant	0.90 m (2 ft 11½ in)
Wing aspect ratio	11.1
Length overall	6.26 m (20 ft 6½ in)
Fuselage: Max width	1.228 m (4 ft 0½ in)
Height overall	1.88 m (6 ft 2 in)
Tailplane span	2.66 m (8 ft 8¾ in)

Wheel track	1.81 m (5 ft 11¼ in)
Wheelbase	1.81 m (5 ft 11¼ in)
AREAS:	
Wings, gross	7.65 m² (82.35 sq ft)
Ailerons (total)	0.718 m² (7.73 sq ft)
Trailing-edge flaps (total)	0.824 m² (8.87 sq ft)
Airbrakes/spoilers (total)	0.572 m² (6.16 sq ft)
Fin	0.808 m² (8.70 sq ft)
Rudder	0.225 m² (2.42 sq ft)
Tailplane	1.40 m² (15.07 sq ft)
Elevator	0.338 m² (3.64 sq ft)
WEIGHTS AND LOADING:	
Weight empty	738 kg (1,627 lb)
Max internal fuel	360 kg (794 lb)
Max external stores	250 kg (551 lb)
Max T-O and landing weight	1,255 kg (2,767 lb)
Max wing loading	164.0 kg/m² (33.59 lb/sq ft)

PERFORMANCE (at max T-O weight):

Max permissible diving speed	325 knots (602 km/h; 374 mph)
Max operating speed	300 knots (556 km/h; 345 mph)
Max cruising speed at S/L	260 knots (482 km/h; 299 mph)
Max design manoeuvring speed	228 knots (422 km/h; 262 mph)
Max diving speed with airbrakes fully deployed	214 knots (396 km/h; 246 mph)
Econ cruising speed at 3,050 m (10,000 ft)	175 knots (324 km/h; 202 mph)
Max speed for landing gear extension	140 knots (259 km/h; 161 mph)
Stalling speed, flaps down, power off	74 knots (137 km/h; 85 mph) EAS

Max rate of climb at S/L	600 m (1,970 ft)/min
Rate of climb at S/L, one engine out	177 m (580 ft)/min
Time to climb to 5,000 m (16,400 ft)	10 min
Max operating altitude	7,620 m (25,000 ft)
Service ceiling	10,000 m (32,800 ft)
Service ceiling, one engine out	5,500 m (18,045 ft)
T-O run at S/L, ISA, zero wind	650 m (2,133 ft)
T-O to 15 m (50 ft), conditions as above	880 m (2,887 ft)
T-O to 15 m (50 ft) at 1,500 m (4,920 ft), ISA, zero wind	1,000 m (3,280 ft)
Max range with wingtip tanks	700 nm (1,296 km; 805 miles)
Max endurance	3 h
g limits	+7/−3.5

BREDANARDI COSTRUZIONI AERONAUTICHE SpA (Subsidiary of Agusta SpA)

Monteprandone (AP), Casella Postale 108, 63039 San Benedetto del Tronto (Ascoli Piceno)
Telephone: (0735) 801721
Telex: 560165 BRENAR I
PRESIDENT: Dott Raffaello Teti

BredaNardi continues to produce, under licence from their US manufacturers, the NH-300C and NH-500D and E light helicopters. Descriptions of the Model 500 series can be found under the McDonnell Douglas Helicopters heading in the US section of this edition, and of the Model 300C under the Schweizer heading. Under a recent agreement with MDHC, BredaNardi is now also licensed to manufacture, and to sell in central Europe, the McDonnell Douglas Model 530F.

Sales continue for agricultural work (mainly of the NH-300C) and training. In recent years they have included 20 NH-300s to the Greek Air Force flying school, and 50 NH-500Es to the Italian Air Force for training duties.

NH-500D built by BredaNardi

AVIOLIGHT

Naples

This new company was formed on 29 February 1988 by Partenavia (which see), Avio Interiors of Latina, and the Naples based company Tecnam owned by the Pascale brothers. Its initial function will be to undertake production of the (originally Partenavia) P.86 Mosquito; it will also assume responsibility for other existing single-engined Partenavia aircraft, enabling the latter company to concentrate entirely on its twin-engined range.

AVIOLIGHT P.86 MOSQUITO

Powered by an Italian KFM 112M flat-four engine of 44.7 kW (60 hp), the prototype of this lightweight two-seater was built by Partenavia and flew for the first time on 27 April 1986. Production Mosquitos, to which the detailed description applies, are intended to have a more powerful engine, and to conform with FAR Pt 23 Utility category standards. An initial series of 100 is being produced for the Aero Club d'Italia.

TYPE: Two-seat light aircraft.
WINGS: High-wing monoplane, with single streamline section bracing strut each side. Constant chord non-swept wings, of NACA 63A-416 (modified) section, with 1° 30′ dihedral and 3° incidence. Two-spar torsion box structure of 2024-T3 aluminium alloy, with trailing-edge split flaps and plain ailerons. No tabs.
FUSELAGE: Semi-monocoque forward fuselage and tubular tailboom, all of aluminium alloy.
TAIL UNIT: Cantilever all-metal stressed skin structure of 2024-T3 aluminium alloy, with front and rear channel section spars. Fixed incidence tailplane, mounted above tailboom on short pylon. Endplate fins and rudders. No rudder tabs; trim tab in centre of elevator.
LANDING GEAR: Non-retractable tricycle type, with Partenavia leaf spring shock absorption. McCreary wheel size 5.00-5, and tyre size 360 × 120-165 mm (5 ply), on each unit; tyre pressures 1.72 bars (25 lb/sq in) on main gear, 1.03 bars (15 lb/sq in) on nose unit. Cleveland 30-18 brakes.
POWER PLANT: One 56 kW (75 hp) Limbach L 2000 flat-four engine, driving a Hoffmann two-blade fixed-pitch propeller with spinner. Single integral fuel tank in wings, capacity 70 litres (18.5 US gallons; 15.4 Imp gallons). Refuelling point in inboard section of starboard wing. Oil capacity 2.5 litres (0.66 US gallon; 0.55 Imp gallon).
ACCOMMODATION: Side by side seats for pilot and one passenger, with baggage space behind seats. Upward opening door, with window, on each side of cabin. Cabin ventilated via ram air intake in wing leading-edge.
AVIONICS: King or Collins VHF com/nav radio, ADF and ATC transponder at customer's option.

First prototype P.86 Mosquito two-seat light aircraft, as originally flown with KFM engine

DIMENSIONS, EXTERNAL:

Wing span	10.00 m (32 ft 9¾ in)
Wing chord, constant	1.25 m (4 ft 1¼ in)
Wing aspect ratio	8.0
Length overall	6.775 m (22 ft 2¾ in)
Fuselage: Max width	1.22 m (4 ft 0 in)
Height overall	1.923 m (6 ft 3¾ in)
Tailplane span	2.80 m (9 ft 2¼ in)
Wheel track	2.00 m (6 ft 6¾ in)
Wheelbase	1.567 m (5 ft 1½ in)
Propeller diameter	1.65 m (5 ft 5 in)
Propeller ground clearance	0.325 m (1 ft 0¾ in)
Cabin doors (each): Height	0.90 m (2 ft 11½ in)
Max width	0.60 m (1 ft 11½ in)
Height to sill	0.975 m (3 ft 2½ in)

DIMENSIONS, INTERNAL:

Cabin: Length	0.90 m (2 ft 11½ in)
Max width	1.00 m (3 ft 3¼ in)
Max height	1.00 m (3 ft 3¼ in)
Floor area	0.86 m² (9.26 sq ft)
Volume	0.82 m³ (28.96 cu ft)
Baggage compartment: Volume	0.42 m³ (14.83 cu ft)

AREAS:

Wings, gross	12.50 m² (135.2 sq ft)
Ailerons (total)	1.028 m² (11.07 sq ft)
Rudders (total)	0.61 m² (6.57 sq ft)
Tailplane	1.34 m² (14.42 sq ft)
Elevator	0.80 m² (8.61 sq ft)

WEIGHTS AND LOADINGS:

Basic weight empty	320 kg (705 lb)
Max fuel weight	50 kg (110 lb)
Max T-O and landing weight	540 kg (1,190 lb)
Max wing loading	43.2 kg/m² (8.85 lb/sq ft)
Max power loading	9.66 kg/kW (15.87 lb/hp)

PERFORMANCE (estimated, at max T-O weight):

Never-exceed speed	150 knots (278 km/h; 172 mph)
Max level speed at S/L	97 knots (180 km/h; 112 mph)
Max cruising speed at S/L	86 knots (160 km/h; 99 mph)
Econ cruising speed at S/L	80 knots (148 km/h; 92 mph)
Stalling speed: flaps up	41 knots (76 km/h; 47 mph)
flaps down	36 knots (67 km/h; 42 mph)
Max rate of climb at S/L	235 m (770 ft)/min
Service ceiling	3,995 m (13,100 ft)
T-O run	149 m (490 ft)
T-O to 15 m (50 ft)	311 m (1,020 ft)
Landing from 15 m (50 ft)	120 m (395 ft)
Range with max fuel at econ cruising speed, allowances for start, taxi, T-O and 30 min reserves	340 nm (630 km; 391 miles)

GENERAL AVIA

GENERAL AVIA COSTRUZIONI AERONAUTICHE SRL

Via Trieste 22-24, 20096 Pioltello, Milan
Telephone: (02) 9266774
Fax: (02) 92160395
TECHNICAL DIRECTOR: Dott Ing Stelio Frati
TECHNICAL: Dr Ing Giancarlo Monti
PUBLIC RELATIONS: Carla Bielli

Dott Ing Stelio Frati is well known for the many successful light aircraft which, as a freelance designer, he has developed since 1950. These have included the Procaer F15 Picchio and the F.250, now manufactured by SIAI-Marchetti as the SF.260; and the F.20 Pegaso, described in the 1981-82 *Jane's.* General Avia developed and built the prototype of the Canguro transport aircraft described under the Agusta (SIAI-Marchetti) heading in this section. In 1983 it developed for SIAI-Marchetti a retractable landing gear version of the Canguro.

In 1988, as a private venture, General Avia was manufacturing a large section of the fuselage of a 19-passenger twin-turbofan commuter transport, known as the F.3500 Sparviero, to define the interior configuration. An early three-view and specification of this aircraft can be found in the 1985-86 *Jane's.*

GENERAL AVIA F.20 TP CONDOR

Developed from the F.20 Pegaso six-seat light business twin (1981-82 *Jane's*), the Condor is a four-seat turboprop powered aircraft intended for such military applications as weapon training, long-range maritime surveillance, search and rescue, anti-armour, and ground attack. It can be equipped with two stores pylons under each wing, the outer one on each side being capable of carrying a 300 litre (79.25 US gallon; 66 Imp gallon) auxiliary fuel tank.

The prototype (I-GEAC) flew for the first time on 7 May 1983, and shortly afterwards was granted a special airworthiness certificate, enabling it to appear at the Paris Air Show later that month. The programme for full certification was delayed in order to give priority to the Promavia Jet Squalus programme (see Belgian section).
TYPE: Twin-turboprop general purpose military aircraft.
AIRFRAME: As described in 1987-88 *Jane's.*
POWER PLANT: Two 298 kW (400 shp) Allison 250-B17B turboprops, each driving a Hartzell HC-B3TF-7A/T10173-21R three-blade propeller with spinner. Total internal fuel capacity 600 litres (158.5 US gallons; 132

Prototype General Avia F.20 TP Condor (two Allison 250-B17B turboprops) *(Avio Data)*

Imp gallons); provision for a further 600 litres to be carried in two underwing auxiliary tanks. Oil capacity 16 litres (4.2 US gallons; 3.5 Imp gallons).
ACCOMMODATION: Normal seating for four persons, including pilot, in two pairs under rearward sliding moulded transparent canopy. Space for baggage in rear fuselage and rear of each engine nacelle. Cabin heated, ventilated, and soundproofed with glass-wool insulation.
DIMENSIONS, EXTERNAL:

Wing span over tip tanks	10.34 m (33 ft 11 in)
Wing chord: at root	1.65 m (5 ft 5 in)
at tip	1.50 m (4 ft 11 in)
Wing aspect ratio	6.7
Length overall	8.925 m (29 ft 3¼ in)
Height overall	3.50 m (11 ft 5¾ in)
Wheel track	3.50 m (11 ft 5¾ in)
Wheelbase	2.40 m (7 ft 10½ in)
Propeller diameter	2.03 m (6 ft 8 in)

DIMENSIONS, INTERNAL:

Cabin: Max length	3.66 m (12 ft 0 in)
Max width	1.17 m (3 ft 10 in)
Max height	1.13 m (3 ft 8½ in)

AREA:

Wings, gross	16.02 m² (172.4 sq ft)

WEIGHTS AND LOADINGS (A: without external stores; B: with external stores):

Weight empty, equipped: A		1,400 kg (3,086 lb)
Max T-O and landing weight: A		2,400 kg (5,291 lb)
B		2,700 kg (5,952 lb)
Max wing loading: A	149.8 kg/m² (30.68 lb/sq ft)	
B	168.5 kg/m² (34.51 lb/sq ft)	
Max power loading: A	4.03 kg/kW (6.61 lb/shp)	
B	4.53 kg/kW (7.44 lb/shp)	

PERFORMANCE (at max T-O weight, without external stores except where indicated):

Never-exceed speed	280 knots (519 km/h; 322 mph)
Max level speed at S/L	248 knots (460 km/h; 286 mph)
Max cruising speed (75% power) at 3,050 m (10,000 ft)	234 knots (435 km/h; 270 mph)
Econ cruising speed (60% power) at 3,050 m (10,000 ft)	210 knots (390 km/h; 242 mph)
Stalling speed, flaps down	70 knots (130 km/h; 81 mph)
Max rate of climb at S/L	900 m (2,950 ft)/min
Rate of climb at S/L, one engine out	300 m (985 ft)/min
Service ceiling	8,500 m (27,900 ft)
Service ceiling, one engine out	3,600 m (11,800 ft)
T-O run: without external stores	180 m (590 ft)
with external stores	220 m (720 ft)
Landing run	260 m (853 ft)
Combat radius with 900 kg (1,984 lb) of external stores	216 nm (400 km; 248 miles)

Range:

without external stores	836 nm (1,550 km; 963 miles)
with external stores	1,673 nm (3,100 km; 1,926 miles)

PARTENAVIA

PARTENAVIA COSTRUZIONI AERONAUTICHE SpA

Via G. Pascoli 7, 80026 Casoria (Naples)
Telephone: (081) 7596311
Telex: 720199 PARTNA I
PRESIDENT: Gen Fulvio Ristori
GENERAL MANAGER AND EXECUTIVE DIRECTOR:
Ing Carlo Rosini
TECHNICAL MANAGER: Ing C. A. D'Amato
PRESS RELATIONS: Mrs F. Ridolfi

This company was founded in 1957 and has since built a series of light aircraft designed by its founder, Prof Ing Luigi Pascale. It came under the control of Aeritalia, through the latter's General Aviation Group, in July 1981.

Since 1974 Partenavia has occupied a 12,000 m² (129,165 sq ft) facility on Capodichino Airport, Naples, where it is concentrating on production of the P.68C and P.68C-TC twin-engined seven-seat light aircraft, a derivative known as the Observer, and the turboprop powered Viator.

PARTENAVIA P.68

The original P.68, designed by Prof Ing Luigi Pascale in 1968, was described in the 1975-76 *Jane's.* From it was developed the P.68B Victor twin-engined light transport, which entered production in the Spring of 1974. Details of the P.68B, P.68C-R, P.68 floatplane/amphibian and P.68R can be found in the 1980-81 and earlier editions of *Jane's.*

The following versions are currently in production:
P.68C. Improved version of P.68B, with lengthened nose, increased fuel capacity, and several internal changes. Detailed description applies primarily to this version (also known formerly as the Victor), which superseded the P.68B (1979-80 *Jane's*) in late 1979.

P.68C-TC. Similar to P.68C, but powered currently by Textron Lycoming TIO-360-A1C6D turbocharged engines with fuel injection. Certificated in June 1980. In production; 43 delivered by beginning of 1988. Available as landplane or with twin amphibious floats. (Latter version first flown from land and water on 26 and 27 June 1985 respectively.)

P.68 Observer. Special observation version; described separately.

By the beginning of 1988 Partenavia had delivered approx 400 aircraft of the P.68 series, most of them for export to operators in more than 20 countries.
TYPE: Six/seven-seat light transport and trainer.
WINGS: Cantilever high-wing monoplane. Wing section NACA 63-3,515. Dihedral 1°. Incidence 1° 30′. No sweepback. Stressed skin two-spar torsion box structure of aluminium alloy. All-metal ailerons and electrically

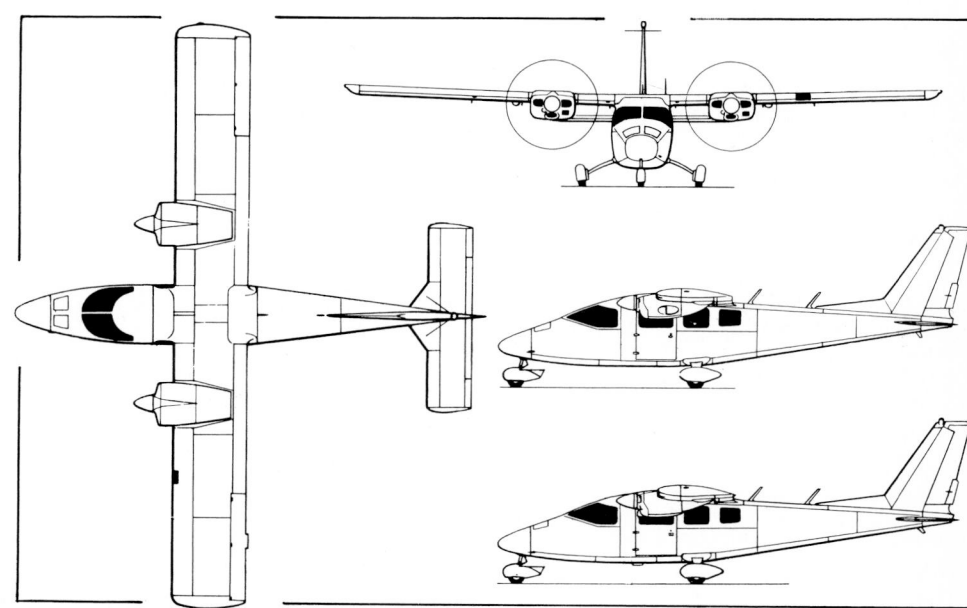
Partenavia P.68C, with additional side view (centre) of P.68C-TC *(Pilot Press)*

operated single-slotted trailing-edge flaps. Hoerner GRP wingtips. No tabs.
FUSELAGE: Conventional all-metal semi-monocoque structure of frames and longerons, with four main longerons and stressed skin covering. Fuselage/wing intersection mainly of GRP.
TAIL UNIT: Cantilever stressed skin metal structure. All-moving tailplane, in two symmetrical halves joined by steel cross-tube and of constant chord except for increase at leading-edge roots. Balance tab in tailplane trailing-edge, over 80 per cent of span. Sweptback fin and rudder, with small dorsal fin. Trim tab in rudder.
LANDING GEAR: Non-retractable tricycle type, with steerable nosewheel. Cantilever spring steel main legs. Oleo-pneumatic shock absorber on nosewheel. Cleveland mainwheels, type 40-96, with Pirelli eight-ply tyres size 6.00-6. Goodyear six-ply nosewheel tyre, size 5.00-5. Cleveland type 30-61 hydraulic disc brakes. Parking brake. Streamline wheel fairings standard. C-TC version

available optionally with De Vore PK twin-float gear having retractable ground wheels.
POWER PLANT (P.68C): Two 149 kW (200 hp) Textron Lycoming IO-360-A1B6 flat-four engines, each driving a Hartzell HC-C2YK-2C/C-7666A-4 two-blade constant-speed fully-feathering propeller with spinner. Integral fuel tank in each wing, total capacity 538 litres (142 US gallons; 118 Imp gallons), of which 520 litres (137 US gallons; 114 Imp gallons) are usable. Refuelling point above each wing. Oil capacity 15 litres (4 US gallons; 3.3 Imp gallons).
ACCOMMODATION: Seating for seven persons in cabin, including pilot, in two rows of two seats and a rear bench seat for three persons. A 'club' seating arrangement is available optionally, having the two middle seats facing rearward with a folding table between them and the bench seat. Front seats are of the adjustable sliding type. Access to all seats via large forward opening car type door on port side at front of cabin. Up to 181 kg (400 lb) of

Partenavia P.68C-TC six/seven-seat light aircraft *(Avio Data)*

baggage can be carried in compartment aft of rear bench seat. Access to baggage compartment from inside cabin, or via large forward hinged door on starboard side at rear, which serves also as emergency exit. Two stretchers or other loads can be carried when all passenger seats are removed. Dual controls, cabin heating, ventilation and soundproofing standard.

SYSTEMS: Electrical power supplied by two 24V 70A alternators and a 24V 17Ah battery. No hydraulic system. Goodrich pneumatic de-icing system optional.

AVIONICS AND EQUIPMENT (P.68C): Wide range of Collins Micro Line or King Silver Crown avionics, and Edo-Aire Mitchell Century III autopilot, to customer's requirements. Provision for SunAir ASB 100 HF radio. Standard equipment includes airspeed indicator, gyro horizon, directional gyro, two cylinder head temperature gauges, clock, exhaust gas temperature gauge, outside air temperature gauge, rate of climb indicator, sensitive altimeter, electric turn rate indicator, inertia reel shoulder harness for pilot and co-pilot, stall warning system, four upholstered seats with back pockets, and one bench seat with folding back (with safety belts on all seats), cabin fire extinguisher, six individual fresh air outlets and six floor warm air vents, windscreen defrosters, cabin soundproofing, annunciator panel warning lights, two map lights, individual reading lights, individual instrument panel floodlights with rheostat, anti-collision strobe light, two landing/taxying lights, navigation lights, anti-static kit, external power receptacle, oil coolers with thermostatic control, quick drain fuel and oil valves, and towbar. Optional equipment includes Janitrol 45,000 BTU combustion heater, wing and tail pneumatic de-icing system, electrothermal propeller de-icing system, 0.46 × 0.58 m (18 × 23 in) floor panel for photogrammetric camera, including periscope sight hatch, second airspeed indicator, second gyro horizon, chronometer, second altimeter, pilot's and co-pilot's vertically adjustable seats, alcohol windscreen de-icing, heated stall warning indicator, all-leather interior, forced ventilation blower, ice light and second oil cooler.

DIMENSIONS, EXTERNAL:
Wing span	12.00 m (39 ft 4½ in)
Wing chord (constant)	1.55 m (5 ft 1 in)
Wing aspect ratio	7.7
Length overall	9.55 m (31 ft 4 in)
Height overall	3.40 m (11 ft 1¾ in)
Tailplane span	3.90 m (12 ft 9½ in)
Wheel track	2.40 m (7 ft 10½ in)
Wheelbase	3.50 m (11 ft 5¾ in)
Propeller diameter	1.88 m (6 ft 2 in)
Distance between propeller centres	4.10 m (13 ft 5½ in)
Baggage door, stbd: Height	0.80 m (2 ft 7½ in)
Width	0.80 m (2 ft 7½ in)

DIMENSIONS, INTERNAL:
Cabin: Length	3.58 m (11 ft 9 in)
Max width	1.16 m (3 ft 9½ in)
Max height	1.20 m (3 ft 11¼ in)
Baggage space	0.56 m³ (20 cu ft)

AREAS:
Wings, gross	18.60 m² (200.2 sq ft)
Ailerons (total)	1.79 m² (19.27 sq ft)
Trailing-edge flaps (total)	2.37 m² (25.51 sq ft)
Fin	1.59 m² (17.11 sq ft)
Rudder, incl tab	0.44 m² (4.74 sq ft)
Tailplane, incl tab	4.41 m² (47.47 sq ft)

WEIGHTS AND LOADINGS:
Weight empty: C	1,230 kg (2,711 lb)
C-TC	1,300 kg (2,866 lb)
*Max T-O weight: C, C-TC	1,990 kg (4,387 lb)
Max landing weight: C, C-TC	1,890 kg (4,166 lb)
Max wing loading: C, C-TC	107 kg/m² (21.9 lb/sq ft)
Max power loading: C	6.68 kg/kW (10.97 lb/hp)
C-TC	6.36 kg/kW (10.45 lb/hp)

C-TC amphibian 317 kg (700 lb) heavier

PERFORMANCE (at max T-O weight):
Max level speed:
C at S/L	174 knots (322 km/h; 200 mph)

C-TC at 5,335 m (17,500 ft)	195 knots (361 km/h; 224 mph)

Max cruising speed (75% power):
C at 2,290 m (7,500 ft)	166 knots (307 km/h; 191 mph)
C-TC at 6,100 m (20,000 ft)	183 knots (339 km/h; 211 mph)
C-TC at 3,660 m (12,000 ft)	172 knots (318 km/h; 198 mph)

Cruising speed (65% power):
C at 3,350 m (11,000 ft)	161 knots (298 km/h; 185 mph)
C-TC at 3,050 m (10,000 ft)	158 knots (293 km/h; 182 mph)

Cruising speed (55% power):
C at 3,660 m (12,000 ft)	150 knots (278 km/h; 173 mph)
C-TC at 3,050 m (10,000 ft)	147 knots (272 km/h; 169 mph)

Stalling speed, flaps up:
C, C-TC	65 knots (120 km/h; 75 mph)

Stalling speed, flaps down:
C, C-TC	58 knots (106 km/h; 66 mph)

Max rate of climb at S/L: C	457 m (1,500 ft)/min
C-TC	472 m (1,550 ft)/min

Rate of climb at S/L, one engine out:
C	82 m (270 ft)/min
C-TC	88 m (290 ft)/min
Service ceiling: C	5,850 m (19,200 ft)
C-TC	7,620 m (25,000 ft)
Service ceiling, one engine out: C	2,100 m (6,900 ft)
C-TC	4,420 m (14,500 ft)
T-O run: C, C-TC	230 m (755 ft)

T-O to 15 m (50 ft): C | 396 m (1,300 ft)
C-TC	385 m (1,263 ft)
Landing from 15 m (50 ft): C, C-TC	488 m (1,600 ft)
Landing run: C, C-TC	215 m (705 ft)
Accelerate/stop distance: C	473 m (1,550 ft)
C-TC	510 m (1,673 ft)

Optimum cruising range (C), 45 min reserves:
75% power at 2,290 m (7,500 ft)
1,050 nm (1,945 km; 1,209 miles)
65% power at 3,350 m (11,000 ft)
1,140 nm (2,112 km; 1,312 miles)
55% power at 3,660 m (12,000 ft)
1,210 nm (2,242 km; 1,393 miles)

Optimum cruising range (C-TC) at 3,660 m (12,000 ft), 45 min reserves:
75% power	775 nm (1,436 km; 892 miles)
65% power	940 nm (1,742 km; 1,082 miles)
55% power	1,020 nm (1,890 km; 1,175 miles)

Range with max fuel (C-TC):
65% power at 6,400 m (21,000 ft)
1,100 nm (2,037 km; 1,266 miles)

PARTENAVIA P.68 OBSERVER

Developed originally in collaboration with Sportavia-Pützer of West Germany, the Observer has a forward and downward view for the crew equal to that of a helicopter. The Plexiglas nose, cockpit and associated structure were designed by Sportavia-Pützer; the prototype (D-GERD) was constructed at that company's Dahlemer-Binz factory, and first flew on 20 February 1976.

With its good low-speed handling characteristics, the Observer is considered to be capable of performing many roles allocated normally to helicopters. It is intended particularly for patrol and observation operations.

The first Partenavia built Observer was flown in the Spring of 1980, and certification was obtained in June of that year. Improvements were made subsequently to the flight deck and instrument panel. By the beginning of 1988 a total of 34 Observers had been ordered, for customers in Africa, Australia, western Europe, and North and South America. Twelve of these were for the Italian Police, with delivery to be completed during 1988.

DIMENSIONS, EXTERNAL: As P.68C except:
Length overall	9.35 m (30 ft 8 in)
Wheelbase	3.80 m (12 ft 5½ in)

WEIGHTS AND LOADINGS:
Weight empty	1,280 kg (2,822 lb)
Max T-O weight	1,960 kg (4,321 lb)
Max wing loading	105.3 kg/m² (21.58 lb/sq ft)
Max power loading	6.58 kg/kW (10.80 lb/hp)

PERFORMANCE (at max T-O weight):
Max level speed at S/L	174 knots (322 km/h; 200 mph)

Cruising speed:
75% power at 2,285 m (7,500 ft)
165 knots (306 km/h; 190 mph)
65% power at 3,350 m (11,000 ft)
160 knots (296 km/h; 184 mph)
55% power at 3,660 m (12,000 ft)
149 knots (276 km/h; 171 mph)
Stalling speed: flaps up	64 knots (118 km/h; 74 mph)
flaps down	56 knots (101 km/h; 64 mph)
Max rate of climb at S/L	488 m (1,600 ft)/min
Rate of climb at S/L, one engine out	98 m (320 ft)/min
Service ceiling	6,100 m (20,000 ft)
Service ceiling, one engine out	2,375 m (7,800 ft)
T-O run	229 m (750 ft)
T-O to 15 m (50 ft)	387 m (1,270 ft)
Landing from 15 m (50 ft)	479 m (1,570 ft)
Landing run	210 m (690 ft)
Accelerate/stop distance	473 m (1,550 ft)

Optimum cruising range, 45 min reserves:
75% power at 2,285 m (7,500 ft)
1,060 nm (1,964 km; 1,220 miles)
65% power at 3,350 m (11,000 ft)
1,140 nm (2,112 km; 1,312 miles)
55% power at 3,660 m (12,000 ft)
1,200 nm (2,224 km; 1,382 miles)

PARTENAVIA AP 68TP-300 SPARTACUS

The basic version of this eight/nine-seat turboprop derivative of the P.68 was developed by Partenavia in a joint programme with Aeritalia, receiving RAI certification on 8 June 1981. In the years that followed, as recorded in previous editions of *Jane's*, Partenavia introduced important modifications of its own which resulted in the current model that was certificated by the RAI in December 1983.

By early 1988 a total of 11 Spartacus was in operation across the world, but production had been suspended because of the prevailing market situation. A full description and illustrations of the Spartacus can be found in the 1987-88 *Jane's*.

Italian Police Observer equipped with Electronique Aérospatiale ATAL television surveillance system

PARTENAVIA AP 68TP-600 VIATOR (WAYFARER)

The first retractable landing gear version of the Spartacus (I-RAIZ, c/n 6) made its initial flight in early July 1984. It was followed on 29 March 1985 by a prototype of the Viator (I-RAIL, previously known as the Spartacus 10), which has a longer fuselage than the fixed-gear AP 68TP-300, seating two additional passengers.

Six Viators had been ordered by Spring 1988, of which three had been delivered: one to Aeritalia, for photogrammetric and other duties, one to Transavio, and one to a customer in Sierra Leone. The next three, for British, Italian and African customers, were due to be delivered later that year.

TYPE: Twin-turboprop general purpose transport.

WINGS: As described for P.68C Victor. Trim tab in starboard aileron. Goodrich pneumatic boot de-icing of leading-edges optional.

FUSELAGE: Similar to P.68C, but slightly longer.

TAIL UNIT: Vertical surfaces similar to P.68C, but of increased chord. Fixed incidence tailplane with separate elevators; geared tab in port elevator. Pneumatic boot de-icing of leading-edges.

LANDING GEAR: Retractable tricycle type, with electrically controlled hydraulic actuation. Oleo-pneumatic shock absorber in each unit. Nosewheel retracts forward, mainwheels inward into fuselage fairing. Cleveland wheels, sizes 40-77B (nose) and 40-163EA (main), with McCreary 8-ply tyres, sizes 6.50-8 (main) and 6.00-6 (nose). Mainwheel tyre pressure 4.83 bars (70 lb/sq in). Cleveland disc brakes. No anti-skid units.

POWER PLANT: Two Allison 250-B17C turboprops, each flat rated at 244.5 kW (328 shp) for T-O and max continuous operation. Hartzell HC-B3TF-7A/T10173B-21R three-blade constant-speed fully-feathering reversible-pitch metal propellers with spinners. Fuel in two 380 litre (100.4 US gallon; 83.6 Imp gallon) tanks in wings and a 40 litre (10.6 US gallon; 8.8 Imp gallon) tank in each engine nacelle. Total capacity 840 litres (222 US gallons; 185 Imp gallons). Two 100 litre (26.4 US gallon; 22 Imp gallon) underwing tanks optional. Refuelling point at each wingtip. Oil capacity 11.4 litres (3.0 US gallons; 2.5 Imp gallons) per engine.

ACCOMMODATION: Standard club seating for pilot and nine passengers, in five rows of two seats (second and fourth rows rearward facing). Forward opening door on starboard side of flight deck, and for second/third row passengers on port side at centre of cabin. Double door (starboard, rear) provides access for rear seat passengers, and to 181 kg (400 lb) capacity baggage compartment aft of rear seats, and serves also as an emergency exit. With all passenger seats removed and special kits installed, up to 12 parachutists, or two stretcher patients plus two medical attendants, can be carried in cabin. Dual controls, and cabin heating, ventilation and soundproofing, are standard. Hot air for cabin heating and windscreen de-icing is provided by heat exchangers installed on both turbine cases.

SYSTEMS: Primary electrical power supplied by two 150A 28V DC starter/generators and two voltage regulators. In the event of primary electrical failure, power is supplied by a 24V 29Ah lead-acid battery (self-sufficient for engine starting), and an inverter for 115/26V AC power. Electric de-icing of engine air intakes, propellers, pitot and stall detector; and pneumatic boot de-icing of wing leading-edges, are standard. Oxygen system optional.

AVIONICS: King Silver Crown IFR package standard. Typical installations include HF com, DME, weather radar (Honeywell or Bendix), autopilot, and Narco ELT.

DIMENSIONS, EXTERNAL:

Wing span	12.00 m (39 ft 4½ in)
Wing chord, constant	1.55 m (5 ft 1 in)
Wing aspect ratio	7.7
Length overall	10.85 m (35 ft 7¼ in)
Fuselage: Length	9.66 m (31 ft 8¼ in)
Max width	1.20 m (3 ft 11¼ in)
Height overall	3.64 m (11 ft 11¼ in)
Tailplane span	4.01 m (13 ft 2 in)
Wheel track	2.167 m (7 ft 1¼ in)
Wheelbase	3.51 m (11 ft 6¼ in)
Propeller diameter	2.03 m (6 ft 8 in)

Partenavia Viator, a 'stretched' version of the Spartacus with retractable landing gear

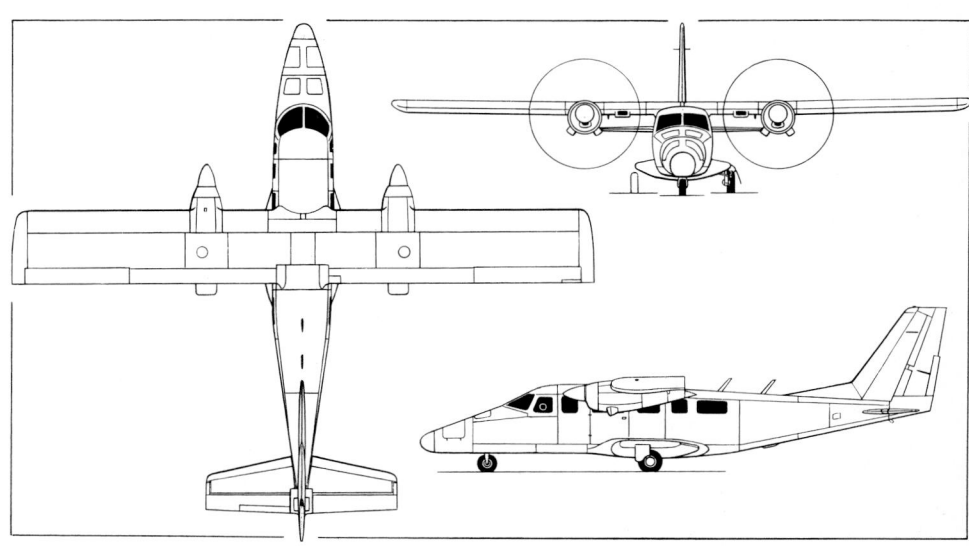

Partenavia Viator ten-seat twin-turboprop light transport *(Pilot Press)*

Propeller ground clearance	0.725 m (2 ft 4½ in)		Max payload	910 kg (2,006 lb)
Distance between propeller centres			Max T-O and landing weight	2,850 kg (6,283 lb)
	4.03 m (13 ft 2¾ in)		Max ramp weight	2,875 kg (6,338 lb)
Passenger door (port): Height	1.03 m (3 ft 4½ in)		Max zero-fuel weight	2,550 kg (5,622 lb)
Width	0.80 m (2 ft 7½ in)		Max wing loading	153.23 kg/m² (31.38 lb/sq ft)
Height to sill	0.79 m (2 ft 7 in)		Max power loading	5.83 kg/kW (9.58 lb/shp)
Passenger/emergency door (stbd):			PERFORMANCE (at max T-O weight):	
Height (mean)	0.91 m (2 ft 11½ in)		Max operating speed	
Width	1.10 m (3 ft 7¼ in)			200 knots (370 km/h; 230 mph) IAS
Height to sill	0.79 m (2 ft 7 in)		Max level and max cruising speed at 3,660 m (12,000 ft)	
DIMENSIONS, INTERNAL:				220 knots (408 km/h; 253 mph)
Cabin, excl flight deck and baggage compartment:			Econ cruising speed at 3,660 m (12,000 ft)	
Length	3.60 m (11 ft 9¾ in)			170 knots (315 km/h; 196 mph)
Max width	1.12 m (3 ft 8 in)		Stalling speed, power off:	
Max height	1.20 m (3 ft 11¼ in)		flaps up	81 knots (151 km/h; 94 mph)
Floor area	4.00 m² (43.06 sq ft)		flaps down	70 knots (130 km/h; 81 mph)
Volume	4.70 m³ (165.98 cu ft)		Max rate of climb at S/L	589 m (1,932 ft)/min
Baggage compartment volume	0.65 m³ (22.95 cu ft)		Rate of climb at S/L, one engine out	131 m (430 ft)/min
AREAS:			Max operating altitude	7,620 m (25,000 ft)
Wings, gross	18.60 m² (200.2 sq ft)		Service ceiling, one engine out	3,355 m (11,000 ft)
Ailerons (total)	1.76 m² (18.94 sq ft)		T-O run	275 m (900 ft)
Trailing-edge flaps (total)	2.42 m² (26.05 sq ft)		T-O to 15 m (50 ft)	460 m (1,510 ft)
Fin	2.90 m² (31.22 sq ft)		Landing from 15 m (50 ft)	500 m (1,640 ft)
Rudder, incl tab	1.64 m² (17.65 sq ft)		Landing run	250 m (820 ft)
Tailplane	3.76 m² (40.47 sq ft)		Min ground turning radius	10.36 m (34 ft 0 in)
Elevators (total)	1.30 m² (13.99 sq ft)		Range at long-range power, allowances for start, taxi,	
WEIGHTS AND LOADINGS:			take-off, descent, and 45 min reserves:	
Basic weight empty	1,640 kg (3,615 lb)		with max payload	445 nm (824 km; 512 miles)
Max fuel load (usable)	680 kg (1,499 lb)		with max fuel	860 nm (1,594 km; 990 miles)

PIAGGIO

INDUSTRIE AERONAUTICHE E MECCANICHE RINALDO PIAGGIO SpA

Via R. Piaggio, 17024 Finale Ligure (SV)
Telephone: (019) 69701
Telex: 226874 AERPIA I
BRANCH OFFICE: Via A. Gramsci 34, Rome
OTHER WORKS: Genoa-Sestri
CHAIRMAN AND MANAGING DIRECTOR:
Dott Rinaldo Piaggio
DIRECTOR OF INTERNATIONAL PROGRAMMES:
Ing Bruno Mori
TECHNICAL DIRECTOR: Ing Alessandro Mazzoni
MARKETING DIRECTOR: Commander G. B. Pizzinato

The original Piaggio company began the construction of aeroplanes in its Genoa-Sestri plant in 1916, and later in the Finale Ligure works. The present company was formed on

29 February 1964, and has since operated as an independent concern. It employs about 1,700 people in three production divisions and has a total covered works area (Genoa-Sestri and Finale Ligure) of approx 100,000 m² (1,076,390 sq ft). In addition to aircraft of its own design, Piaggio is producing components for the Aeritalia G222, Panavia Tornado, Boeing 767 and McDonnell Douglas DC-10. Aeritalia (which see) acquired a 31% holding in Piaggio in 1988.

The activities of the Aero-Engine Division are described in the appropriate section of this edition.

R. PIAGGIO P.180 AVANTI

First details of this new turboprop powered business aircraft were announced in October 1983, all research and development leading to the present design having been started by Piaggio in 1979. Gates Learjet became a partner

in 1983, but withdrew for economic reasons on 13 January 1986. All of Gates' tooling, together with the forward fuselages of the first three development aircraft (two flying prototypes and one for static tests), were transferred to Piaggio.

Construction began in late 1984, and the first Avanti (I-PJAV) made its first flight on 23 September 1986. First flight of the second aircraft (I-PJAR) took place on 14 May 1987, and RAI/FAA certification to FAR Pt 23 was planned for late 1988, followed by first deliveries in late 1989. Piaggio has begun to build an initial production batch of 12 aircraft, from subassemblies produced both in the USA (at a former Gates Learjet factory) and in Italy. Final assembly is at Genoa.

Major design features are the adoption of a 'three lifting surfaces' concept, to reduce cruise drag and fuel consumption, and placement of the engines aft of the rear

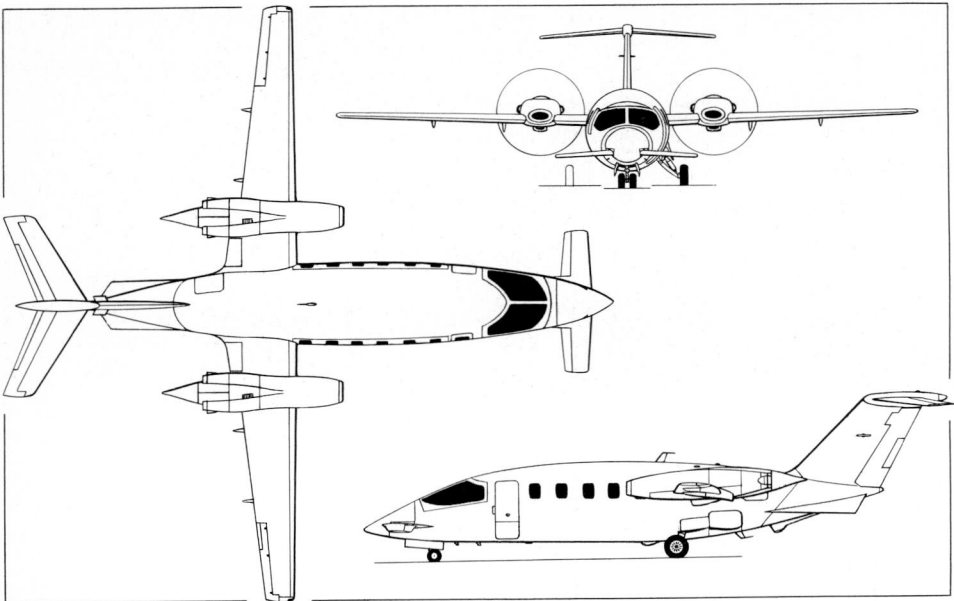

Piaggio P.180 Avanti twin-turboprop corporate transport *(Pilot Press)*

pressure bulkhead to minimise engine noise levels in the cabin. Primary lifting surface is the main wing, which is situated just above the mid position (to avoid drag-inducing bulges in the circular-section fuselage) and, by virtue of the 'pusher' engine installation, has an unbroken leading-edge except for the nacelle inlets. The second lifting surface is the horizontal T tailplane and elevator, which provides orthodox control from a conventional location. The third is the foreplane, which serves as a forward wing rather than a traditional canard surface, by producing a positive component of lift which not only assists the main wing in supporting the aircraft but allows the latter to be reduced in size, thereby also reducing cruise drag and fuel consumption. In assembly, fuselage skins are stretch-formed in unusually large panels to minimise seams, maintaining precise contour tolerances to ten one-thousandths of an inch. Structural members are then shaped to conform exactly to the skin, rather than the conventional reverse.

While most of the Avanti is of conventional metal construction, the nosecone, tailcone, tail unit, engine nacelles, wing moving surfaces and landing gear doors are built of composite materials: graphite/epoxy (carbonfibre) in areas of high stress and Kevlar/epoxy elsewhere. Most of these parts of the airframe—48 components in all, representing about 18 per cent of the aircraft's operating weight empty—are manufactured under subcontract by Sikorsky Aircraft. Wing moving surfaces and foreplane (including flaps) are Italian built, and front fuselages for the first 12 production Avantis are US built.

TYPE: Twin-turboprop corporate transport.

WINGS: Cantilever non-swept mid-wing monoplane, tapered on leading- and trailing-edges. Piaggio PE 1491 G (modified) section at root, PE 1332 G section at tip; thickness/chord ratio 13%. Dihedral 2° from roots. Incidence 0°. Sweep 0° at 15 per cent chord. Integrally machined skins and spars of aluminium alloy; main spar forms an integral fail-safe structural unit with rear pressure bulkhead and main landing gear. Trailing-edge flaps (outboard of engine nacelles), balanced ailerons and wingtips are of all-composite construction. Flaps are actuated electrically, as is trim tab in starboard aileron. Hot air anti-icing of outboard leading-edges.

FOREPLANE: All-composite fail-safe fixed incidence (+3°) foreplane at tip of nose, with 5° anhedral, fitted with electrically actuated all-composite single-slotted auxiliary trailing-edge flaps. Piaggio PE 1300 G aerofoil section, thickness/chord ratio 13%, and 0° sweep at 50 per cent chord. Electric anti-icing of leading-edges. Auxiliary flaps do not control the aircraft in pitch, but are primarily to assist lift, being coupled with the main wing flaps and deflecting with them to offset changes in trim.

FUSELAGE: Circular-section pressurised fail-safe structure of mainly metal construction (machined and bonded aluminium alloy), with rear pressure bulkhead in line with wing main spar. Nosecone, tailcone, baggage door and landing gear doors are built of composite materials. Two small metal ventral fins under tailcone.

TAIL UNIT: All-sweptback, all-composite T tail, with variable incidence, 5° anhedral tailplane and balanced elevators and rudder. Trim tab in rudder and each elevator. No tail unit anti-icing.

LANDING GEAR: Dowty Rotol hydraulically retractable tricycle type, with single-wheel main units and steerable, self-centring twin-wheel nose unit. Main units retract rearward into sides of fuselage; nose unit retracts forward. Dowty hydraulic shock absorbers. Tyre sizes 6.50-10 (main) and 5.00-4 (nose). Multi-disc carbon brakes.

POWER PLANT: Two 634 kW (850 shp) (flat rated) Pratt & Whitney Canada PT6A-66 turboprops, each mounted above the wing in an all-composite nacelle and driving a counter-rotating Hartzell five-blade constant-speed fully-feathering reversible-pitch pusher propeller with metal spinner. Propeller blades de-iced by engine exhaust. Fuel in two fuselage tanks totalling 700 litres (185 US gallons; 154 Imp gallons) and two 450 litre (119 US gallon; 99 Imp gallon) wing tanks; total fuel capacity 1,600 litres (423 US gallons; 352 Imp gallons). Single pressure refuelling point in lower centre-fuselage. Dual gravity refuelling points in upper part of fuselage.

ACCOMMODATION: Crew of one or two on flight deck. Seating in main cabin for five to nine passengers, with galley, fully enclosed toilet and coat storage area. Passenger seats are armchair type, which can be reclined, tracked and swivelled, and locked at any angle. Hardwood trimmed foldaway tables can be extended between facing club seats. Rectangular cabin windows, including one emergency exit at front on starboard side. Indirect lighting behind each window ring, plus individual overhead reading lights. Passenger airstair door at front on port side. Baggage compartment aft of rear pressure bulkhead, with door immediately aft of wing on port side. Entire accommodation pressurised and air-conditioned.

SYSTEMS: AiResearch bleed air environmental control system, with max pressure differential of 0.62 bars (9.0 lb/sq in). Single hydraulic system, driven by electric motor, with handpump for emergency backup. Electrical system powered by two starter/generators and a 25V 38Ah nickel-cadmium battery. Hot air anti-icing of main wing outer leading-edges; electric anti-icing for foreplane and windscreen.

AVIONICS AND EQUIPMENT: Standard com/nav equipment (Collins Pro Line or other, to customer's requirements).

Collins APS-65 digital autopilot systems. Blind-flying instrumentation standard. Landing and taxying lights on nosewheel leg.

DIMENSIONS, EXTERNAL:

Wing span	13.84 m (45 ft 5 in)
Foreplane span	3.28 m (10 ft 9¼ in)
Wing chord: at root	1.79 m (5 ft 10½ in)
at tip	0.63 m (2 ft 0¾ in)
Foreplane chord: at root	0.79 m (2 ft 7 in)
at tip	0.55 m (1 ft 9⅔ in)
Wing aspect ratio	11.8
Foreplane aspect ratio	4.9
Length overall	14.17 m (46 ft 5¾ in)
Fuselage: Length	12.53 m (41 ft 1¼ in)
Max width	1.95 m (6 ft 4¾ in)
Height overall	3.90 m (12 ft 9½ in)
Tailplane span	4.18 m (13 ft 8¾ in)
Wheel track	2.84 m (9 ft 4 in)
Wheelbase	5.79 m (19 ft 0 in)
Propeller diameter	2.16 m (7 ft 1 in)
Propeller ground clearance	0.78 m (2 ft 6⅔ in)
Distance between propeller centres	4.13 m (13 ft 6½ in)
Passenger door (fwd, port): Height	1.30 m (4 ft 3¼ in)
Width	0.61 m (2 ft 0 in)
Height to sill	0.58 m (1 ft 10¾ in)
Baggage door (rear, port): Height	0.64 m (2 ft 1¼ in)
Width	0.70 m (2 ft 3½ in)
Height to sill	1.38 m (4 ft 6½ in)
Emergency exit (stbd): Height	0.67 m (2 ft 2¼ in)
Width	0.48 m (1 ft 7 in)

DIMENSIONS, INTERNAL:

Cabin: Length	6.00 m (19 ft 8¼ in)
Max width	1.83 m (6 ft 0 in)
Max height	1.75 m (5 ft 9 in)
Volume	10.48 m³ (370 cu ft)
Baggage compartment volume	1.19 m³ (42 cu ft)

AREAS:

Wings, gross	15.76 m² (169.64 sq ft)
Ailerons (total, incl tab)	0.66 m² (7.10 sq ft)
Trailing-edge flaps (total)	1.60 m² (17.23 sq ft)
Foreplane	1.61 m² (17.30 sq ft)
Foreplane flaps (total)	0.585 m² (6.30 sq ft)
Fin	3.68 m² (39.62 sq ft)
Rudder, incl tab	1.05 m² (11.30 sq ft)
Tailplane	2.485 m² (26.75 sq ft)
Elevators (total, incl tabs)	1.35 m² (14.52 sq ft)

WEIGHTS AND LOADINGS:

Weight empty, equipped	3,039 kg (6,700 lb)
Operating weight empty	3,130 kg (6,900 lb)
Max fuel load	1,224 kg (2,700 lb)
Max payload	907 kg (2,000 lb)
Payload with max fuel	453 kg (1,000 lb)
Max T-O weight	4,767 kg (10,510 lb)
Max ramp weight	4,808 kg (10,600 lb)
Max landing weight	4,529 kg (9,985 lb)
Max wing loading	302.3 kg/m² (61.95 lb/sq ft)
Max power loading	4.0 kg/kW (6.57 lb/shp)

PERFORMANCE (preliminary, pending certification, at max T-O weight except where indicated):

Max operating Mach number	0.67
Max operating speed	
	300 knots (556 km/h; 345 mph) IAS
Max level and max cruising speed at 8,230 m (27,000 ft)	
	400 knots (740 km/h; 460 mph)
Econ cruising speed at 12,500 m (41,000 ft)	
	320 knots (593 km/h; 368 mph)
Stalling speed, power off:	
flaps and landing gear up	
	100 knots (185 km/h; 115 mph) CAS

Second prototype of the six/ten-passenger Avanti executive transport

flaps and landing gear down
82 knots (152 km/h; 95 mph) CAS
Max rate of climb at S/L 1,112 m (3,650 ft)/min
Rate of climb at S/L, one engine out
381 m (1,250 ft)/min
Service ceiling 12,495 m (41,000 ft)
Service ceiling, one engine out 9,750 m (32,000 ft)
T-O to 15 m (50 ft) 762 m (2,500 ft)
Landing from 15 m (50 ft) at max landing weight
759 m (2,490 ft)
Range with 4 passengers, NBAA reserves, at 320 knots (593 km/h; 368 mph) 1,800 nm (3,335 km; 2,072 miles)

R. PIAGGIO P.166-DL3

The P.166 has been produced in several basic versions, of which the original piston engined P.166 was described in the 1963-64 *Jane's*; the P.166M, P.166B Portofino and P.166C in the 1971-72 *Jane's*; the P.166S in the 1974-75 *Jane's*; and the P.166-DL2 in the 1978-79 *Jane's*.

Current version is the turboprop powered P.166-DL3, which flew for the first time on 3 July 1976 and received FAA and RAI certification in 1978. It can be configured and equipped for a wide variety of duties, including executive transport (EXC); transport and dropping of up to ten paratroops (PAR); air ambulance for two stretchers and two medical attendants (AMB); multi-engine aircrew training (MTR); light tactical transport (LTT); armed military counter-insurgency, field support, and search and rescue (AML); maritime reconnaissance (MAR); environmental control and geophysical survey (ECS); aerophotogrammetry (APH); and aerial firefighting (AFF). Piaggio is currently building a second batch of four P.166-DL3s for the Italian Ministry of Merchant Marine, in P.166-DL3SEM form, as maritime and ecological patrol aircraft. They are equipped for a variety of surveillance, reconnaissance and search and rescue duties. Four earlier aircraft were delivered in 1987, and deliveries of this second batch began in March 1988.

Maritime patrol version of R. Piaggio P.166-DL3 *(Avio Data)*

TYPE: Twin-turboprop light transport.

WINGS: Shoulder gull-wing cantilever monoplane. NACA 230 wing section. Dihedral 21° 30′ on inner portion, 2° 30′ on outer wings. Incidence 2° 43′ at root. Sweepback 7° 30′ at quarter-chord. Aluminium alloy flush riveted torsion box structure, with single main spar and auxiliary rear spar. All-metal slotted ailerons, with geared and trim tab in starboard aileron. All-metal hydraulically actuated slotted flaps. Rubber boot leading-edge de-icing optional.

FUSELAGE: Aluminium alloy flush riveted semi-monocoque structure of frames and L section extruded stringers: no longerons.

TAIL UNIT: Cantilever aluminium alloy structure, with flush riveted smooth skin on fixed surfaces and beaded skin on control surfaces. Rudder and elevators statically and dynamically balanced. Geared and trim tabs in elevators; trim tab in rudder. Rubber boot leading-edge de-icing of fin and tailplane optional.

LANDING GEAR: Retractable tricycle type. Magnaghi oleo-pneumatic shock absorbers in all units. Hydraulic actuation. Nosewheel retracts rearward, main units upward. Goodyear 24 × 7.7 mainwheels with size 8.50-10 tyres, pressure 3.79 bars (55 lb/sq in). Goodyear steerable and self-centring nosewheel with size 6.00-6 tyre, pressure 2.90 bars (42 lb/sq in). Goodyear or Magnaghi hydraulic brakes.

POWER PLANT: Two Textron Lycoming LTP 101-700 turboprops, each flat rated at 447.5 kW (600 shp) and driving a Hartzell HC-B3TN-3DL/LT10282-9.5 three-blade constant-speed fully-feathering metal pusher propeller. Fuel in two 212 litre (56 US gallon; 46.5 Imp gallon) outer-wing main tanks, two 323 litre (85.3 US gallon; 71 Imp gallon) wingtip tanks, and a 118 litre (31.2 US gallon; 26 Imp gallon) fuselage collector tank; total standard internal fuel capacity 1,188 litres (313.8 US gallons; 261 Imp gallons). Auxiliary fuel system available optionally, comprising a 236 litre (62.3 US gallon; 52 Imp gallon) fuselage tank, transfer pump and controls; with this installed, total usable fuel capacity is increased to 1,424 litres (376.2 US gallons; 313 Imp gallons). Gravity refuelling points in each main tank and tip tank. Provision for two 177 or 284 litre (46.8 or 75.0 US gallon; 39 or 62.5 Imp gallon) underwing drop tanks. Air intakes and propeller blades de-iced by engine exhaust.

ACCOMMODATION: Crew of two on raised flight deck, with dual controls. Aft of flight deck, accommodation consists of a passenger cabin, utility compartment and baggage compartment. Access to flight deck is via passenger/cargo double door on port side, forward of wing, or via individual crew door on each side of flight deck. External access to baggage compartment via port side door aft of wing. Passenger cabin extends from rear of flight deck to bulkhead at wing main spar; fitting of passenger carrying, cargo or other interiors is facilitated by two continuous rails on cabin floor, permitting considerable flexibility in standard or customised interior layouts. Standard seating for eight passengers, with individual lighting, ventilation and oxygen controls. Flight deck can be separated from passenger cabin by a screen. Door in bulkhead at rear of cabin provides access to utility compartment, in which can be fitted a toilet, bar, or mission equipment for certain roles. Entire accommodation is heated, ventilated and soundproofed. Emergency exit forward of wing on starboard side. Windscreen hot-air demisting standard. Windscreen wipers, washers and methanol spray de-icing optional.

SYSTEMS: Hydraulic system, pressure 127 bars (1,840 lb/sq in), for landing gear, flap and brake actuation, nosewheel steering and lock, and (on APH version) actuation of ventral door. Handpump for emergency extension of landing gear. Standard electrical system is 28V DC, supplied by two engine driven starter/generators and a nickel-cadmium battery. External power receptacle. Static or rotary inverters, to supply AC power for avionics and instruments, available optionally. Oxygen system.

AVIONICS AND EQUIPMENT (DL3SEM): UHF-AM, VHF-AM, VHF-FM, encrypted HF and HF/SSB com radios; navigation system includes ONI-7000 Loran-C, Sierra AN/ARN-136A Tacan, Collins VOR-31A VOR/ILS, Collins MC-103 radio compass, direction finder, IFF transponder and radar altimeter. Search and surveillance equipment includes Fiar/Bendix RDR 1500 360° radar with dual CRT colour displays; MSP-Daedalus AA 2000 infra-red/ultraviolet linescanning system; 2500 A FLIR system; two 70 mm Vinten 618 aerial cameras (one vertical, one side-looking); and a 3 million candlepower ORC Locator II searchlight under the port wing.

AVIONICS AND EQUIPMENT (general): Standard avionics packages available to individual customer's requirements: minimum recommended package includes two VHF com, two VHF nav (VOR/ILS), ADF, ATC transponder, compass system and intercom. Optional avionics include radar, autopilot, navigation system and synthesiser type HF radio. Quickly interchangeable individual seats of various types, bench seat, divan or stretchers for EXC, PAR, AMB, MTR and LTT versions; strengthened floor in LTT. Four underwing pylons standard on AML, for ordnance, supply containers and auxiliary fuel tanks. Four pylons and integrated search/detection/identification/plotting and reporting system on MAR. Magnetometer, multiscanner, multiple-head camera and associated equipment in ECS version. Two cameras, associated equipment, and ventral sliding doors in APH, with option for four underwing pylons. Internal removable water/extinguisher container and rapid charge/discharge system for AFF.

DIMENSIONS, EXTERNAL:
Wing span: without tip tanks 13.51 m (44 ft 4 in)
with tip tanks 14.69 m (48 ft 2½ in)
Wing chord: at root 2.40 m (7 ft 10½ in)
at tip 1.15 m (3 ft 9¼ in)
Wing aspect ratio 7.3
Length overall 11.88 m (39 ft 0 in)
Height overall 5.00 m (16 ft 5 in)
Tailplane span 5.10 m (16 ft 9 in)
Wheel track 2.66 m (8 ft 9 in)
Wheelbase 4.71 m (15 ft 5½ in)
Propeller diameter 2.36 m (7 ft 9 in)
Cabin door: Height 1.38 m (4 ft 6 in)
Width 1.28 m (4 ft 2 in)

DIMENSIONS, INTERNAL:
Cabin, incl flight deck: Length 3.20 m (10 ft 6 in)
Max width 1.57 m (5 ft 2 in)
Max height 1.76 m (5 ft 9 in)
Floor area 5.14 m² (55.3 sq ft)
Volume 6.63 m³ (234.1 cu ft)
Utility compartment: Length 0.65 m (2 ft 1½ in)
Max width 1.52 m (5 ft 0 in)
Max height 1.70 m (5 ft 7 in)
Volume 2.27 m³ (80.2 cu ft)
Baggage compartment volume 1.80 m³ (63.6 cu ft)

AREAS:
Wings, gross 26.56 m² (285.9 sq ft)
Ailerons (total) 1.95 m² (21.00 sq ft)
Trailing-edge flaps (total) 2.38 m² (25.60 sq ft)
Fin 1.62 m² (17.44 sq ft)
Rudder, incl tab 1.23 m² (13.24 sq ft)
Tailplane 3.50 m² (37.67 sq ft)
Elevators, incl tabs 1.29 m² (13.88 sq ft)

WEIGHTS AND LOADINGS:
Weight empty, equipped 2,650 kg (5,842 lb)
Max fuel 1,139 kg (2,511 lb)
Max payload 1,073 kg (2,365 lb)
Max T-O weight 4,300 kg (9,480 lb)
Max ramp weight 4,320 kg (9,524 lb)
Max zero-fuel weight 3,800 kg (8,377 lb)
Max landing weight 3,800 kg (8,377 lb)
Max wing loading 162 kg/m² (33.2 lb/sq ft)
Max power loading 4.81 kg/kW (7.9 lb/shp)

PERFORMANCE (at max T-O weight except where indicated):
Never-exceed speed
220 knots (407 km/h; 253 mph) CAS
Max level and max cruising speed at 3,050 m (10,000 ft)
215 knots (400 km/h; 248 mph)
Econ cruising speed at 3,660 m (12,000 ft)
162 knots (300 km/h; 186 mph)
Stalling speed:
flaps and landing gear up
86 knots (160 km/h; 99 mph) CAS
flaps and landing gear down
75 knots (139 km/h; 87 mph) CAS
Max rate of climb at S/L 670 m (2,200 ft)/min
Rate of climb at S/L, one engine out 177 m (580 ft)/min
Service ceiling 8,535 m (28,000 ft)
Service ceiling, one engine out 4,270 m (14,000 ft)
T-O to 15 m (50 ft) 665 m (2,180 ft)
Landing from 15 m (50 ft) at max landing weight
457 m (1,500 ft)
Range, VFR:
with max payload 750 nm (1,390 km; 863 miles)
with max fuel 1,125 nm (2,084 km; 1,295 miles)

STELUX

STELUX AIRCRAFT CORPORATION
(Division of Spartaria)

Via Jacopo Crescini 82c, 35100 Padova
Telex: Post Office 430005 PPPD I
CHIEF EXECUTIVE OFFICER: Dipl Spartaco Trevisan
HONORARY PRESIDENT: Dott Ing Sergio Stefanutti, Via Giovanni Severano 33, 0179 Rome
Telephone: (06) 425057
PRESS RELATIONS: Dott Raffaella Tursini (Padova)

This company is building the prototype of a two-seat glider towing aircraft known as the Trenzo. Its designer is Ing Sergio Stefanutti, well known for his pioneering work in 'tail-first' configurations featuring a nose mounted foreplane with positive incidence and a rear mounted main wing with zero incidence. Elevators of symmetrical section are mounted independently below and behind the trailing-edge of the foreplane. This configuration was first tested in 1938 on the small SS.2 and SS.3 lightplanes built by Stabilimento Costruzioni Aeronautiche of Guidonia. Evaluation of these led to the Ambrosini SS.4, the world's first all-metal 'canard' fighter, which first flew in May 1939.

STELUX 3esse3 TRENZO

Design of the Trenzo was started in 1979, in response to a request by Dipl Spartaco Trevisan on behalf of the Centro Nazionale di Volo a Vela at Rieti. Ing Sergio Stefanutti proposed a design of canard configuration, which has Italian RAI approval, and Mr S. Trevisan was responsible for completion of a one-quarter scale solid mockup. Work on a full size prototype, designed to FAR Pt 23, was initiated in September 1985, and was continuing in early 1988.

TYPE: Tandem two-seat light aircraft.

WINGS: Rear-mounted mid-wings of NACA 23012 aerofoil section, with tapered leading-edge and non-swept trailing-edge, have 0° incidence and approx 5° dihedral. Wings, ailerons and endplate fins/winglets are of CFRP.

FOREPLANES: Cantilever CFRP fixed foreplanes, of NACA 64₂-415 section and near-delta planform, at extreme tip of nose, set at 3° incidence with approx 5° anhedral. Elevator (NACA 0009 section; 0° dihedral) below and behind each foreplane trailing-edge.

FUSELAGE: Oval-section semi-monocoque of laminated wood construction, with three main longerons.

LANDING GEAR: Tricycle type, with fully retractable nosewheel and semi-retractable mainwheels. Hydraulic actuation. Cleveland wheels, with tyres size 6.00-6 (main) and 5.00-5 (nose) and Parker disc brakes. Van Sickle (USA) shock absorbers. Mainwheels retract upward into underwing 'trouser' fairings, nosewheel rearward. Inset rudder in rear of each fairing, split vertically to function also as airbrake.

POWER PLANT: One 59.7 kW (80 hp) Limbach L 2000 EI3 or 86.5 kW (116 hp) Textron Lycoming O-235-N2A flat-four engine, mounted at rear of fuselage and driving a Hamilton Standard pusher propeller. Fuel in two fuselage tanks between second cockpit and engine.

ACCOMMODATION: Seats for two persons in tandem under individual framed canopies which open sideways to starboard. Cockpits ventilated.

DIMENSIONS, EXTERNAL (A: Limbach, B: Textron Lycoming engine):

Wing span	10.50 m (34 ft 5½ in)
Wing chord: at root	1.90 m (6 ft 2¾ in)
at tip	0.60 m (1 ft 11½ in)
Foreplane span	4.00 m (13 ft 1½ in)
Length overall: A	6.85 m (22 ft 5¾ in)
B	7.10 m (23 ft 3½ in)
Fuselage: Length	6.50 m (21 ft 4 in)
Max width	0.70 m (2 ft 3½ in)
Wheel track	3.00 m (9 ft 10 in)
Propeller diameter: A	1.60 m (5 ft 3 in)
Propeller ground clearance: A	0.45 m (1 ft 5¾ in)

AREAS:

Wings, gross	18.70 m² (201.3 sq ft)
Foreplane, gross, incl elevators	5.00 m² (53.82 sq ft)
Fins/winglets (total)	2.80 m² (30.14 sq ft)

WEIGHTS AND LOADINGS:

Max T-O weight: A		750 kg (1,653 lb)
B		940 kg (2,072 lb)
Max wing loading: A		40.1 kg/m² (8.22 lb/sq ft)
B		50.3 kg/m² (10.30 lb/sq ft)

PERFORMANCE: No details available until aircraft has flown

Quarter-scale mockup of the Stefanutti (Stelux) Trenzo two-seat light aircraft

JAPAN

FUJI
FUJI HEAVY INDUSTRIES LTD (Fuji Jukogyo Kabushiki Kaisha)

Subaru Building, 7-2, 1-chome, Nishi-shinjuku, Shinjuku-ku, Tokyo
Telephone: (03) 347 2515
Telex: 0 232 2268
PRESIDENT: Toshihiro Tajima
UTSUNOMIYA MANUFACTURING DIVISION: 1-11, Yonan 1-chome, Utsunomiya, Tochigi 320
Telephone: (0286) 58 1111

Aircraft Division
GENERAL MANAGERS:
Yasumasa Honda (Managing Director)
Tsutou Ono (Commercial Business)
Masayuki Hara (Marketing and Sales, Defence Programmes)

Utsunomiya Manufacturing Division
GENERAL MANAGERS:
Akitoshi Nagao (Managing Director, and Gen Manager of Aircraft Plant)
Takeshi Makino (Aircraft Engineering Division)

Fuji Heavy Industries, established on 15 July 1953, is a successor to the Nakajima company, which was established in 1917 and built 25,935 aircraft up to the end of the Second World War.

The present Utsunomiya Manufacturing Division (Aircraft and Rolling Stock Plants) occupies a site of 510,094 m² (5,490,600 sq ft) including a floor area of 182,623 m² (1,965,735 sq ft) and in 1988 employed 2,257 people.

Details of Fuji production of the Cessna L-19E Bird Dog, Beechcraft Mentor, and several modified versions of the Mentor designated LM-1 Nikko, LM-2, KM, KM-2, KM-2B and TL-1, have appeared in previous editions of *Jane's*. The KM-2D, a turboprop version of the KM-2, is described in this entry.

Fuji is currently producing the Bell Model 204/205 series and AH-1S HueyCobra helicopters, as described in this entry. It is building wing main assemblies for JMSDF Lockheed P-3C Orions (see Kawasaki entry), and main landing gear doors and some titanium airframe parts for Japanese built McDonnell Douglas F-15J fighters (see Mitsubishi entry). Commercial aircraft components are produced for the Boeing 747 (spoilers, inboard and outboard ailerons), Boeing 767 (wing/body fairings and main landing gear doors), McDonnell Douglas MD-11 (outboard ailerons) and Fokker 50 (rudder and elevators). Those for the 767 and MD-11 are designed by Fuji, and manufactured from advanced composite materials.

FUJI KM-2D
In 1984 Fuji refitted a company owned KM-2 with an Allison 250-B17D turboprop in place of the Textron Lycoming IGSO-480 piston engine. First flight in KM-2D

form took place on 28 June 1984, and JCAB certification (Aerobatic and Utility categories) was gained in February 1985.

In March 1987 Fuji received an initial JMSDF contract to modify the current fleet of 32 KM-2s to turboprop power. First flight of a 'production' KM-2D was made on 27 April 1988, with deliveries of the first three due to begin in the following August. Three more were ordered in FY 1988.

The KM-2B tandem two-seat trainer was last described in full in the 1981-82 *Jane's*; the prototype KM-2D (see accompanying photograph) has the four-seat cabin of the original KM-2, which was described in the 1969-70 edition.

The production KM-2D, compared with the prototype, incorporates improvements in cabin structure and equipment. Other main differences are as follows:

POWER PLANT: One Allison 250-B17D turboprop, flat rated at 261 kW (350 shp), driving a Hartzell HC-B3TF-7A/T10173-18 three-blade propeller. Total fuel capacity 266 litres (70 US gallons; 58.3 Imp gallons), comprising one 95 litre (25 US gallon; 20.8 Imp gallon) and one 38 litre (10 US gallon; 8.3 Imp gallon) tank in each wing. Oil capacity 10 litres (2.7 US gallons; 2.25 Imp gallons).

SYSTEM: Electrical system (30V DC) powered by 150A starter/generator and a 24V 22Ah nickel-cadmium battery.

AVIONICS: King VHF, VOR, ADF, ATC transponder and DME.

DIMENSIONS, EXTERNAL:

Wing span	10.04 m (32 ft 11¼ in)
Length overall	8.43 m (27 ft 8 in)
Height overall	2.96 m (9 ft 8½ in)
Propeller diameter	2.12 m (6 ft 11½ in)

AREAS: As for KM-2 except:

Fin	2.00 m² (21.53 sq ft)
Rudder, incl tab	0.66 m² (7.10 sq ft)

WEIGHTS AND PERFORMANCE:
No details received

FUJI-BELL 204B-2 and UH-1H
Japanese designation: HU-1H
Fuji is manufacturing Bell Model 204B-2 and UH-1H helicopters under sublicence from Mitsui and Co Ltd, Bell's Japanese licensee, following the completion of 34 commercial 204Bs between 1962 and 1973.

Fuji developed the higher powered Model 204B-2 in October 1973. Powered by a 1,044 kW (1,400 shp) Kawasaki built Textron Lycoming KT5313B turboshaft, it has the same basic airframe and dynamic components as the 204B, but has a tractor tail rotor. The first example of this version was delivered in early 1974, and 20 had been built by March 1988.

Following the delivery of 90 HU-1Bs (Japanese military version of the 204B) to the Japan Ground Self-Defence Force by early 1973, Fuji production continued with the

Fuji KM-2D prototype conversion of KM-2 to turboprop power

Fuji built AH-1S HueyCobra for the JGSDF

AREAS:	
Main rotor disc	168.1 m² (1,809.5 sq ft)
Tail rotor disc	5.27 m² (56.75 sq ft)
WEIGHTS AND LOADINGS:	
Weight empty: 204B-2	2,177 kg (4,800 lb)
HU-1H	2,390 kg (5,270 lb)
Max T-O weight:	
204B-2, internal load	3,855 kg (8,500 lb)
204B-2, external load	4,309 kg (9,500 lb)
HU-1H	4,309 kg (9,500 lb)
Max disc loading	25.6 kg/m² (5.25 lb/sq ft)
Max power loading	4.13 kg/kW (6.78 lb/shp)
PERFORMANCE (at max T-O weight):	
Max level and max cruising speed	
	110 knots (204 km/h; 127 mph)
Max rate of climb at S/L: 204B-2	591 m (1,940 ft)/min
HU-1H	488 m (1,600 ft)/min
Service ceiling: 204B-2	5,790 m (19,000 ft)
HU-1H	3,840 m (12,600 ft)
Hovering ceiling IGE: 204B-2	4,635 m (15,200 ft)
HU-1H	4,145 m (13,600 ft)
Hovering ceiling OGE: 204B-2	3,200 m (10,500 ft)
HU-1H	335 m (1,100 ft)
Range at S/L: 204B-2	207 nm (383 km; 238 miles)
HU-1H	252 nm (467 km; 290 miles)

FUJI-BELL AH-1S

In FY 1982 Fuji was selected as prime contractor for a licence manufacturing programme for Bell AH-1S HueyCobra anti-armour helicopters for the JGSDF; Kawasaki is delivering the T53-K-703 engines for these aircraft. The JGSDF had previously purchased two Bell built examples in 1977 and 1978 for operational evaluation.

The first Fuji built AH-1S made its initial flight on 2 July 1984. Current JGSDF plans are to purchase 73 AH-1S. These will equip four anti-tank helicopter squadrons, with a surplus to provide attrition replacements and aircraft for training. Orders have so far been placed for 46 aircraft, of which 38 were due to be delivered by the end of FY 1988. The first squadron is based at Obihiro on Hokkaido, and the second at Hachinoe.

UH-1H (military version of the Bell 205 and known in Japan as the HU-1H), of which the first example flew for the first time on 17 July 1973; 107 had been ordered for the JGSDF by March 1988, and a further eight were approved in the FY 1988 budget.

The Fuji-Bell HU-1H has the same airframe and dynamic components as the Bell built UH-1H (see US section) but has a tractor tail rotor and 1,044 kW (1,400 shp) Kawasaki built Textron Lycoming T53-K-13B engine.

The following details apply to the standard Fuji-Bell 204B-2 and HU-1H:

DIMENSIONS, EXTERNAL:

Main rotor diameter	14.63 m (48 ft 0 in)
Tail rotor diameter	2.59 m (8 ft 6 in)
Length overall, tail rotor turning:	
204B-2	13.61 m (44 ft 8 in)
HU-1H	13.67 m (44 ft 10 in)
Length of fuselage: 204B-2	12.31 m (40 ft 4¾ in)
HU-1H	12.37 m (40 ft 7 in)
Height overall, tail rotor turning	4.42 m (14 ft 6 in)
Height to top of rotor head:	
204B-2	3.18 m (10 ft 5¼ in)
HU-1H	3.98 m (13 ft 0¾ in)
Max width over landing skids:	
204B-2	2.64 m (8 ft 8 in)
HU-1H	2.60 m (8 ft 6½ in)
Tailplane span	2.84 m (9 ft 4 in)

KAWASAKI

KAWASAKI JUKOGYO KABUSHIKI KAISHA
(Kawasaki Heavy Industries Ltd)
1-18 Nakamachi-Dori, 2-chome, Chuo-ku, Kobe
TOKYO AND AIRCRAFT GROUP OFFICE: World Trade Center Building, 4-1, Hamamatsu-cho 2-chome, Minato-ku, Tokyo
Telephone: (03) 435 2971
Telex: 242-4371 KAWAJU J
PRESIDENT: Hiroshi Ohba
EXECUTIVE VICE-PRESIDENT: Masahiko Iwata
Aircraft Group
MANAGING DIRECTOR AND SENIOR GENERAL MANAGER:
Kanji Sonoda
WORKS: Gifu

Kawasaki Aircraft Co amalgamated with Kawasaki Dockyard Co and Kawasaki Rolling Stock Mfg Co to form Kawasaki Heavy Industries Ltd on 1 April 1969. The Aircraft Group employs some 3,900 people. Kawasaki has a 25% holding in Nippi (which see).

In addition to extensive overhaul work, Kawasaki has built many US aircraft under licence since 1955, as detailed in earlier *Jane's*. From the Lockheed P2V-7 (P-2H) Neptune it developed the P-2J anti-submarine aircraft (see 1978-79 *Jane's*), two of which have since been converted to UP-2J configuration with equipment for target towing, ECM training and drone launch operations (see illustration in 1985-86 *Jane's*). Two others have been converted as UP-2J(E) electronic intelligence (elint) aircraft, equipped with HLR-105 and HLR-106 systems. All four serve with No. 81 Squadron (3rd Fleet Air Wing) at Iwakuni.

Kawasaki is developing, as prime contractor, the T-4 intermediate jet trainer to succeed the Lockheed T-33A and Fuji T-1. The company has developed, jointly with MBB of West Germany, the BK 117 twin-engined multi-purpose helicopter described in the International section. Kawasaki has exclusive rights to produce and develop the former Boeing 107 Model II helicopter. McDonnell Douglas MD 500 series light helicopters are being manufactured under a licence agreement concluded in October 1967. By 1 April 1988 a total of 156 KV107 series helicopters had been delivered, and 261 MD 500s to government and commercial operators in Japan. The company is now co-producing Boeing CH-47 Chinooks for the Japanese armed forces.

Kawasaki is a subcontractor to Mitsubishi (which see) for rear fuselages, wings and tail units of the McDonnell Douglas F-15J and DJ Eagles being licence built in Japan; is subcontracted to build forward and mid fuselage sections, and wing ribs, for the Boeing 767 jet transport; and has been nominated by the JASDF as prime contractor for maintenance and support of its Grumman E-2C Hawkeye AEW and Lockheed C-130 Hercules transport aircraft.

Kawasaki is prime contractor for Japanese assembly of engines for Fuji built Bell AH-1S gunship helicopters. Its aero engine activities are described in the appropriate section of this edition.

Lockheed P-3C Orion for the JMSDF, assembled by Kawasaki

KAWASAKI C-1 MODIFICATIONS

The National Aerospace Laboratory has built an experimental quiet STOL aircraft known as the **Asuka**, utilising the airframe of a C-1. Details are given under the NAL heading in this edition; the standard C-1 transport was described in the 1981-82 *Jane's*. Another JASDF C-1 was used as a flying testbed for the XF3 turbofan for the Kawasaki T-4, and to flight test the FJR710 high bypass turbofan which powers the Asuka.

Kawasaki modified the 21st production C-1 (JASDF 78-1021) for use as an ECM training aircraft. Known as the **EC-1**, it first flew on 3 December 1984 and was described and illustrated in the 1987-88 *Jane's*.

KAWASAKI (LOCKHEED) P-3C ORION

Kawasaki is prime contractor for licence production of the Lockheed P-3C/Update II Orion, 100 of which are to be purchased by the JMSDF. Of these, 78 had been ordered up to and including FY 1988. The first three (US built) P-3Cs were handed over to the JMSDF in April 1981. The next four were assembled by Kawasaki from knocked-down assemblies; the first of these made its initial flight on 17 March 1982, and was delivered on 26 May that year to Fleet Squadron 51 at Atsugi Air Base. The remaining 71 are being built almost entirely in Japan, and 40 had been delivered by 31 March 1988. Two squadrons, each with eight aircraft, are based at Atsugi. The third and fourth P-3C squadrons, at Hachinoe, were equipped in 1985-86. Remaining aircraft will include at least one (ordered in FY 1988) equipped as an EP-3C electronic surveillance version. Kawasaki is responsible for building the centre-fuselages, and for final assembly and flight testing. Participants in the programme include Fuji, Mitsubishi, Nippi and Shin Meiwa for the airframe, and IHI for the engines.

KAWASAKI T-4

Kawasaki was named by the Japan Defence Agency on 4 September 1981 as the prime contractor to develop a new intermediate trainer to replace Lockheed T-33As and Fuji T-1A/Bs in service with the JASDF. The designation XT-4 was allocated officially to the type during its development.

Current plans call for procurement of about 200 production T-4s, for pilot training, liaison and other duties. Funding was approved in the FY 1983 and 1984 defence budgets to procure four flying prototypes. The first 12 production aircraft were approved in the FY 1986 defence budget, and the next 20 in FY 1987.

The T-4 is based on Kawasaki's KA-851 design, by an engineering team led by Mr Kohki Isozaki. Mitsubishi (centre fuselage and engine air intakes) and Fuji (rear fuselage, wings and tail unit) each have a 30 per cent share in the production programme. Kawasaki, as prime contractor, builds the forward fuselage, and is responsible for final assembly and flight test.

The T-4 was required to have high subsonic manoeuvrability, and to be able to carry high external loads under the wings and fuselage. Basic design studies were completed in October 1982, and prototype construction began in April 1984. The first XT-4 (56-5601) made its first flight on 29 July 1985, and all four prototypes were delivered between December 1985 and July 1986, preceded by static and fatigue test aircraft. Production began in FY 1986, and the first production T-4 made its initial flight on 28 June 1988. Deliveries of the first 12 aircraft were due to begin in September and be completed by the end of March 1989. They will enter service with the JASDF training wing at Hamamatsu, near Tokyo.

TYPE: Tandem two-seat intermediate jet trainer and liaison aircraft.

WINGS: Cantilever mid-wing monoplane. Supercritical

aerofoil section, with thickness/chord ratios of 10.3% (root) and 7.3% (tip). Anhedral 7° from roots. Incidence 0°. Sweepback at quarter-chord 27° 30′. Extended chord on outer panels, giving a 'dog-tooth' leading-edge. Main structure of aluminium alloy, with slow crack growth characteristics. Double-slotted trailing-edge flaps of aluminium alloy with AFRP trailing-edges. Ailerons of plain hinged type, made of CFRP and fitted with Teijin hydraulically powered actuators. No tabs.

FUSELAGE: Conventional semi-monocoque structure (frames and longerons), mainly of aluminium alloy with minimum use of titanium in critical areas. Slow crack growth characteristics. CFRP airbrake on each side at rear.

TAIL UNIT: Cantilever structure, with sweepback on all surfaces. Fin and rudder are made of CFRP; all-moving anhedral tailplane is of aluminium alloy except for CFRP trailing-edge. Rudder and tailplane powered hydraulically via Mitsubishi servo actuators.

LANDING GEAR: Hydraulically retractable tricycle type, with Sumitomo oleo-pneumatic shock absorber in each unit. Single-wheel main units retract forward and inward; steerable nosewheel retracts forward. Bendix (Kayaba) mainwheels, tyre size 22 × 5.5-13.8, pressure 19.31 bars (280 lb/sq in); Bendix (Kayaba) nosewheel, tyre size 18 × 4.4-11.6, pressure 12.76 bars (185 lb/sq in). Bendix (Kayaba) carbon brakes and Hydro-Aire (Sumitomo) anti-skid units on mainwheels.

POWER PLANT: Two 16.32 kN (3,670 lb st) Ishikawajima-Harima F3-IHI-30 turbofans, mounted side by side in centre-fuselage. Internal fuel in two 401.25 litre (106 US gallon; 88.3 Imp gallon) wing tanks and two Japanese built Goodyear rubber bag tanks in fuselage, one of 776 litres (205 US gallons; 170.7 Imp gallons) and one of 662.5 litres (175 US gallons; 145.7 Imp gallons). Total internal capacity 2,241 litres (592 US gallons; 493 Imp gallons). Single pressure refuelling point in outer wall of port engine air intake. Provision to carry one 450 litre (119 US gallon; 99 Imp gallon) Shin Meiwa drop tank on each underwing pylon. Oil capacity 5 litres (1.3 US gallons; 1.1 Imp gallons).

ACCOMMODATION: Crew of two in tandem in pressurised and air-conditioned cockpit with wraparound windscreen and one-piece sideways (to starboard) opening canopy. Dual controls standard; rear (instructor's) seat elevated 27 cm (10.6 in). Stencel SIIIS-3ER ejection seats and Teledyne McCormick Selph canopy severance system, licence built by Daicel Chemical Industries. Baggage compartment in centre of fuselage, with external access via door on port side.

SYSTEMS: Shimadzu bootstrap type air-conditioning and pressurisation system (max differential 0.28 bars; 4.0 lb/sq in). Two independent hydraulic systems (one each for flight controls and utilities), each operating at 207 bars (3,000 lb/sq in) and each with separate air/fluid reservoir pressurised at 3.45 bars (50 lb/sq in). Flow rate of each hydraulic system 45 litres (12 US gallons; 10 Imp gallons)/min. No pneumatic system. Electrical system powered by two 9kW Shinko engine driven starter/generators. Tokyo Aircraft Instruments onboard oxygen generating system.

AVIONICS AND EQUIPMENT: Mitsubishi Electric J/ARC-53 UHF com, Nagano J/AIC-3 intercom, Nippon Electric J/ARN-66 Tacan, Toyo Communication (Teledyne Electronics) J/APX-106 SIF, Japan Aviation Electronics (Honeywell) J/ASN-3 AHRS, Tokyo Keiki (Sperry) J/ASK-1 air data computer, Shimadzu (Kaiser) J/AVQ-1 HUD, and Tokyo Aircraft Instrument J/ASH-3 VGH recorder.

ARMAMENT: No built-in armament. Two Nippi pylons under each wing for carriage of drop tanks (see 'Power Plant' paragraph); one Nippi pylon under fuselage, on which can be carried target towing equipment, an ECM/chaff dispenser or an air sampling pod. In weapons training role, can carry three or four 500 lb practice bombs, and has structural provision for outer wing mounted air-to-air missiles.

DIMENSIONS, EXTERNAL:

Wing span	9.94 m (32 ft 7½ in)
Wing chord: at root	3.11 m (10 ft 2½ in)
at tip	1.12 m (3 ft 8 in)
Wing aspect ratio	4.7
Length overall	13.00 m (42 ft 8 in)
Length of fuselage	11.96 m (39 ft 3 in)
Height overall	4.60 m (15 ft 1¼ in)
Tailplane span	4.40 m (14 ft 5¼ in)
Wheel track	3.20 m (10 ft 6 in)
Wheelbase	5.10 m (16 ft 9 in)

DIMENSIONS, INTERNAL:

Cockpit: Length	3.20 m (10 ft 6 in)
Max width	0.69 m (2 ft 3 in)
Max height	1.40 m (4 ft 7¼ in)

AREAS:

Wings, gross	21.00 m² (226.05 sq ft)
Ailerons (total)	1.51 m² (16.25 sq ft)
Trailing-edge flaps (total)	2.93 m² (31.54 sq ft)
Fin	3.78 m² (40.69 sq ft)
Rudder	0.91 m² (9.80 sq ft)
Tailplane	6.04 m² (65.02 sq ft)

WEIGHTS:

Weight empty	3,700 kg (8,157 lb)
T-O weight, 'clean'	5,500 kg (12,125 lb)

First and third prototype Kawasaki XT-4 twin-turbofan intermediate trainers

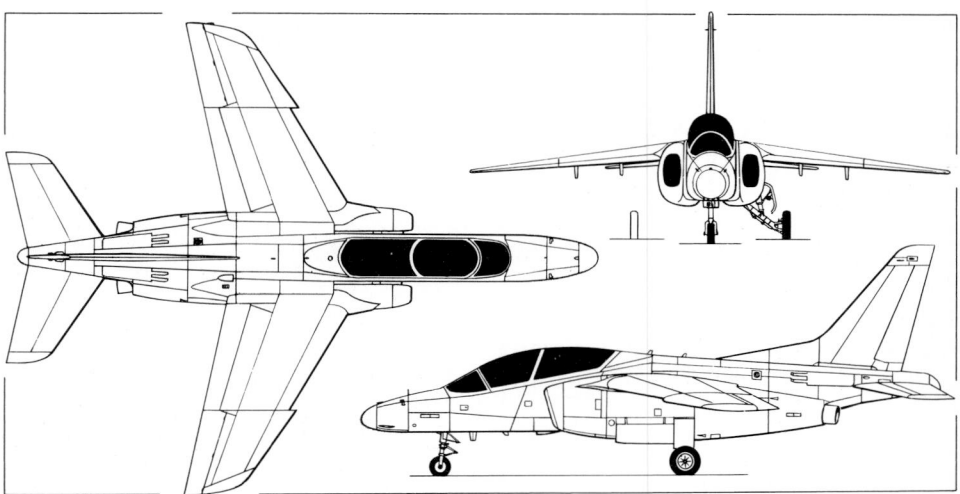
Kawasaki T-4 trainer (two Ishikawajima-Harima F3-IHI-30 turbofans) *(Pilot Press)*

Camouflaged Kawasaki KV107IIA-4 of the JGSDF, with extended-range fuel tanks on fuselage sides

Max design T-O weight	7,500 kg (16,535 lb)

PERFORMANCE (in 'clean' configuration. A: at weight of 4,700 kg; 10,361 lb with 50% fuel; B: at T-O weight of 5,500 kg; 12,125 lb):

Max level speed: A	Mach 0.9
Max level speed at S/L:	
A	560 knots (1,038 km/h; 645 mph)
Cruising speed: B	Mach 0.75
Stalling speed: A	90 knots (167 km/h; 104 mph)
Max rate of climb at S/L: B	3,050 m (10,000 ft)/min
Service ceiling: B	15,240 m (50,000 ft)
T-O run, 35°C: B	549 m (1,800 ft)
Landing run: B	670 m (2,200 ft)
Min ground turning radius	9.45 m (31 ft 0 in)
Range (B) at Mach 0.75 cruising speed:	
internal fuel only	700 nm (1,297 km; 806 miles)
with two 450 litre drop tanks	
	900 nm (1,668 km; 1,036 miles)
g limits	+7.33/−3

KAWASAKI KV107IIA

Kawasaki has exclusive rights to manufacture and sell the Boeing 107 Model II helicopter. The first KV107 to be produced by Kawasaki under this licence agreement flew for the first time in May 1962, and FAA type approval for this initial version was granted in November 1965. Details of the initial production KV107II models have been given in the 1984-85 and earlier editions of *Jane's*. Those for the Swedish Navy are to be retrofitted with more powerful Rolls-Royce Gnome H.1400-I (instead of H.1200) turboshafts, which will enable them to operate at a higher all-up weight.

The KV107IIA, introduced in 1968, has uprated turboshafts for improved performance during VTOL and in 'hot and high' conditions. A prototype, converted from a standard KV107II-2, first flew on 3 April 1968. Type approval was granted by the JCAB on 26 September 1968 and by the FAA on 15 January 1969.

Since then, several versions of the KV107IIA have been

produced, including the **A-2** (two built), **A-3** (seven for MCM: mine countermeasures duties with the JMSDF), **A-4** (18 as tactical transports for the JGSDF), **A-17** (one for Japanese Metropolitan Police), and a series of special missions **A-SM-1/-2/-3/-4** versions (16 in all) for Saudi Arabia. Details of these, which remain available, can be found in the 1987-88 and earlier editions of *Jane's*. Production in 1988 was centred on the following version:

KV107IIA-5. Long-range search and rescue helicopter for JASDF. Total of 31 delivered by early 1988; four more approved in FY 1988. Extended-range fuel tank each side of fuselage, making total capacity 3,785 litres (1,000 US gallons; 833 Imp gallons). Extensive nav/com equipment, four searchlights, domed observation window and rescue hoist. Twenty-seven aircraft have a Kawasaki/Boeing automatic flight control system.

A total of 156 KV107IIs and IIAs (all versions) had been delivered by 1 April 1988. The description which follows applies to the commercial KV107IIA-2, except where indicated:

TYPE: Twin-engined transport helicopter.

ROTOR SYSTEM: Two three-blade rotors in tandem, rotating in opposite directions. Each blade is made up of a steel D spar to which is bonded a trailing-edge box constructed of aluminium ribs and glassfibre or aluminium skin.

ROTOR DRIVE: Power is transmitted from each engine through individually-overrunning clutches into the rear transmission, which combines the engine outputs, thereby providing a single power output to the interconnecting shaft which enables both rotors to be driven by either engine.

FUSELAGE: Basically square-section semi-monocoque structure built primarily of high strength bare and Alclad aluminium alloy. Transverse bulkheads and built-up frames support transmission, power plant and landing gear. Loading ramp forms undersurface of upswept rear fuselage on utility and military models. Baggage container replaces ramp on A-2 airliner version. Fuselage is sealed to permit operation from water.

LANDING GEAR: Non-retractable tricycle type, with twin wheels on all three units. Oleo-pneumatic shock absorbers. Tubeless tyres, size 18 × 5.5, pressure 10.34 bars (150 lb/sq in), on all wheels. Disc brakes. Wheel/ski gear optional.

POWER PLANT: Two 1,044 kW (1,400 shp) General Electric CT58-140-1 or Ishikawajima-Harima CT58-IHI-140-1 turboshafts (max continuous rating 932 kW; 1,250 shp), mounted side by side at base of rear rotor pylon. Fuel tanks in sponsons, capacity 1,324 litres (350 US gallons; 291 Imp gallons) standard. Extended range fuel tank on each side of fuselage of KV107IIA-4/5, increasing total capacity to 3,785 litres (1,000 US gallons; 833 Imp gallons). Other versions have provision for 632 litre (167 US gallon; 139 Imp gallon) auxiliary tank or 3,929 litre (1,038 US gallon; 864 Imp gallon) extended range tank in cabin.

ACCOMMODATION: Standard accommodation for two pilots, stewardess and 25 passengers in airliner version. Seats in eight rows, in pairs on port side and single seats on starboard side (two pairs at rear of cabin) with central aisle. Airliner fitted with parcel rack and a rollout baggage container, with capacity of approximately 680 kg (1,500 lb), located in underside of rear fuselage. Ramp of utility model is power operated on the ground or in flight and can be removed or left open to permit carriage of extra-long cargo.

AVIONICS AND EQUIPMENT: Standard avionics include stability augmentation system (SAS) and automatic speed trim system (AST). Optional avionics include automatic stabilisation equipment (ASE); automatic flight control system (AFCS); Doppler radar; radio altimeter; HF, VHF and UHF radio; ADF; VOR/ILS; Tacan; compass system; attitude director indicator system; and intercom system.

DIMENSIONS, EXTERNAL:

Rotor diameter (each)	15.24 m (50 ft 0 in)
Length overall, both rotors turning	25.40 m (83 ft 4 in)
Length of fuselage	13.59 m (44 ft 7 in)
Height to top of rear rotor head	5.13 m (16 ft 10 in)
Wheel track (c/l of shock struts)	3.94 m (12 ft 11 in)
Width over mainwheels	4.42 m (14 ft 6 in)
Wheelbase	7.59 m (24 ft 11 in)
Passenger door (fwd): Height	1.60 m (5 ft 3 in)
Width	0.91 m (3 ft 0 in)

DIMENSIONS, INTERNAL:
Cabin, excl flight deck:

Length	7.37 m (24 ft 2 in)
Normal width	1.83 m (6 ft 0 in)
Max width	2.01 m (6 ft 7 in)
Max height	1.83 m (6 ft 0 in)

Kawasaki built Boeing CH-47J Chinook in JGSDF camouflage

Kawasaki (McDonnell Douglas) OH-6D light helicopter of the JGSDF

Floor area	13.47 m² (145 sq ft)
Volume (usable)	24.5 m³ (865 cu ft)

AREAS:

Rotor blades (each)	3.48 m² (37.50 sq ft)
Rotor discs (total)	364.6 m² (3,925 sq ft)

WEIGHTS AND LOADINGS:

Weight empty, equipped	5,250 kg (11,576 lb)
Max payload (at 8,618 kg; 19,000 lb T-O and landing weight)	3,172 kg (6,993 lb)

Fuel weight:

standard sponson tanks	1,032 kg (2,275 lb)
auxiliary tank	493 kg (1,087 lb)
extended range tank	3,061 kg (6,748 lb)
Max T-O and landing weight	8,618 kg (19,000 lb)
	or 9,706 kg (21,400 lb)

Cabin floor loading (cargo):

standard	976 kg/m² (200 lb/sq ft)
optional	1,464 kg/m² (300 lb/sq ft)
Max disc loading	23.6 kg/m² (4.84 lb/sq ft)
Max power loading	4.62 kg/kW (7.6 lb/shp)

PERFORMANCE (KV107IIA-2 at 8,618 kg; 19,000 lb AUW):

Never-exceed speed	146 knots (270 km/h; 168 mph)
Max speed at S/L, normal rated power	137 knots (254 km/h; 158 mph)
Cruising speed at 1,525 m (5,000 ft)	130 knots (241 km/h; 150 mph)
Max rate of climb at S/L	625 m (2,050 ft)/min
Max vertical rate of climb at S/L	381 m (1,250 ft)/min
Service ceiling	5,180 m (17,000 ft)
Service ceiling, one engine out	1,740 m (5,700 ft)
Hovering ceiling: IGE	3,565 m (11,700 ft)
OGE	2,680 m (8,800 ft)
Min landing area: Length	38 m (126 ft)
Width	23 m (75 ft)
T-O to 15 m (50 ft)	131 m (430 ft)
Landing from 15 m (50 ft), one engine out	84 m (275 ft)

Range: standard fuel	192 nm (357 km; 222 miles)
max fuel	592 nm (1,097 km; 682 miles)

KAWASAKI (BOEING) CH-47 CHINOOK
JASDF/JGSDF designation: CH-47J

The FY 1984 defence budget approved the purchase of three Boeing CH-47 Chinook helicopters: two for the JGSDF and one for the JASDF, which have eventual requirements for 39 and 15 respectively. The first two aircraft, delivered in Spring 1986, were US built, the third was delivered in CKD (component knocked down) form for assembly in Japan. Kawasaki has been granted a licence for local manufacture of Chinooks ordered for the Japanese services; the Japanese version is generally similar to the CH-47D, and is designated CH-47J. The first CH-47Js for the JGSDF and JASDF were delivered in late 1986, and deliveries totalled five and two respectively by 31 March 1988. The FY 1988 budget provided for four more for the JGSDF and three for the JASDF.

KAWASAKI (MCDONNELL DOUGLAS) MODEL 500D
JGSDF/JMSDF designation: OH-6D

The first Model 369D (500D) built by Kawasaki under licence from Hughes (now McDonnell Douglas) Helicopters was flown for the first time on 2 December 1977; JCAB Normal category certification was awarded on 20 April 1978. Nine Model 500Ds had been delivered for civil operation in Japan by March 1988. The JGSDF has ordered 89 as OH-6Ds, 77 of which had been delivered by the end of March 1988; purchase of a further 11 approved for FY 1988. The OH-6D was also selected by the JMSDF to replace its Bell 47G-2As in the training role. Five had been delivered by 1 January 1986, and two more have been ordered.

MITSUBISHI
MITSUBISHI JUKOGYO KABUSHIKI KAISHA
(Mitsubishi Heavy Industries Ltd)
5-1, Marunouchi 2-chome, Chiyoda-ku, Tokyo 100
Telephone: (03) 212 3111
Telex: J22282 and J22443

NAGOYA AIRCRAFT WORKS: 10, Oye-cho, Minato-ku, Nagoya 455

PRESIDENT: Yotaro Iida

EXECUTIVE VICE-PRESIDENTS:
Riichiro Kuroki
Toshio Sakashita

MANAGING DIRECTOR, AND GENERAL MANAGER OF AIRCRAFT AND SPECIAL VEHICLE HEADQUARTERS:
Takaaki Yamada

GENERAL MANAGER, AIRCRAFT DEPARTMENT:
Mitsuo Tomita

Mitsubishi began the production of aircraft in 1921, and manufactured 18,000 aircraft of approximately 100 different types prior to 1945, as well as 52,000 engines in the 1,000-2,500 hp range. The present Komaki South plant was built in 1952 and, together with the Oye and Komaki North plants, was later consolidated as Nagoya Aircraft Works, with a combined floor area of 552,463 m² (5,946,666 sq ft).

Mitsubishi was prime contractor for the T-2 supersonic trainer and F-1 close support combat aircraft for the JASDF, with Fuji, Nippi and Shin Meiwa as principal subcontractors. It is currently producing forward and rear fuselages for JMSDF Lockheed P-3C Orions, under subcontract to Kawasaki (which see). Other subcontract work includes manufacture of rear passenger cabin sections of the Boeing 767 jet transport. Part of this work is, in turn, subcontracted by Mitsubishi to Shin Meiwa. Mitsubishi also manufactures tailcones for the McDonnell Douglas DC-10 and MD-11, and wing trailing-edges for the MD-80 series of transports.

The MU-300 Diamond I and IA (see MAI entry in the US section of the 1985-86 *Jane's*) were developed into the MU-300-10 Diamond II, acquired by Beech Aircraft Corporation (which see) in 1987 and since developed further as the Beechjet executive transport. Mitsubishi supplied major assemblies to Beech for the latter in 1987-88.

Mitsubishi's aero engine activities are described in the appropriate section of this edition.

MITSUBISHI F-4EJKai

In co-operation with Kawasaki as subcontractor, Mitsubishi was the JDA's prime contractor in producing F-4EJ Phantom tactical fighters for the JASDF, under licence from McDonnell Douglas Corporation. The last of 140 F-4EJs was delivered to the JASDF on 20 May 1981; Mitsubishi is engaged currently in a major programme to update F-4EJ equipment and weapon systems. The prototype F-4EJKai (07-8431) was first flown on 17 July 1984 and delivered on the following 13 December. It has a Westinghouse AN/APG-66J fire control system, advanced avionics which include a Litton LN-39 INS, head-up display, and J/APR-4Kai radar warning receiver, lookdown/shootdown capability with AIM-7E/F Sparrows or AIM-9P/L Sidewinders, and can carry two ASM-1 anti-shipping missiles. Current plans are to convert 100 of the JASDF's remaining F-4EJs to F-4EJKai configuration and another 17 to RF-4EJ reconnaissance-fighters. A prototype RF-4EJ conversion, equipped with a Thomson-CSF reconnaissance pod and TRT radio altimeter, is expected to be modified in 1989 and begin flight testing in 1991.

MITSUBISHI (MCDONNELL DOUGLAS) F-15J and F-15DJ EAGLE

By 1990 the Japan Defence Agency plans to procure a total of 187 McDonnell Douglas F-15 Eagles, including 14 US built aircraft (two single-seat F-15Js and 12 two-seat F-15DJs). The two US built F-15Js were followed by eight assembled in Japan from US supplied knocked-down assemblies. First aircraft of the latter batch flew on 26 August 1981 and was delivered on 11 December that year. A total of 148 F-15J/DJs had been funded up to FY 1987; approx 100 had been delivered by the Spring of 1988.

First JASDF F-15 squadron was No. 202 (5th Air Wing) at Nyutabaru, which was activated in December 1982 with 20 F-15J/DJs. Other units now equipped are No. 201 and No. 203 Squadron of the 2nd Air Wing at Chitose, Hokkaido; No. 204 (7th Air Wing, at Hyakuri); and Nos. 205 and 303 (6th Air Wing, Komatsu). Mitsubishi is building the forward and centre-fuselages, and is responsible for final assembly and flight testing. Participants in the programme include Fuji (landing gear doors), Kawasaki (wings and tail assembly), Nippi (pylons and missile launchers), Shin Meiwa (drop tanks), Sumitomo (landing gear), and IHI (engines). The J/ALQ-8 ECM and radar warning systems of all these aircraft are of Japanese design and manufacture.

MITSUBISHI T-2

The T-2, the first supersonic aircraft developed by the Japanese aircraft industry, is a twin-engined two-seat jet trainer designed to meet the requirements of the JASDF. It flew for the first time on 20 July 1971.

Production orders were placed for 92 T-2s (28 **T-2** advanced trainers, 62 **T-2A** combat trainers, plus two development aircraft for the F-1 close support fighter version). All 90 T-2/2As had been delivered by 31 March 1988, to the 4th Air Wing at Matsushima. In 1982, the JASDF's Blue Impulse aerobatic team received six of these T-2As in place of its F-86F Sabres. Mitsubishi converted one T-2 as a CCV (control configured vehicle), as described in the 1986-87 and earlier editions of *Jane's*.

A full description of the standard production T-2/2A can be found in the 1987-88 and earlier editions of *Jane's*.

TYPE: Two-seat supersonic jet trainer.

AIRFRAME: See 1987-88 and earlier editions.

POWER PLANT: Two Ishikawajima-Harima TF40-IHI-801A (Rolls-Royce Turbomeca Adour Mk 801A) turbofans, each rated at 22.75 kN (5,115 lb st) dry and 32.49 kN (7,305 lb st) with afterburning, mounted side by side in centre of fuselage. Fixed geometry air intake, with auxiliary 'blow-in' intake doors, on each side of fuselage aft of rear cockpit. Fuel in seven fuselage tanks with total capacity of 3,823 litres (1,010 US gallons; 841 Imp

Mitsubishi F-15J Eagle of 204 Sqn, 7th Air Wing, Japan Air Self-Defence Force *(Katsumi Hinata)*

Mitsubishi T-2 tandem-seat advanced trainer from Hyakuri Air Base *(Katsumi Hinata)*

Mitsubishi F-1 single-seat close support fighters of the JASDF

gallons). Pressure refuelling point in starboard side of fuselage, forward of mainwheel bay. Three 821 litre (217 US gallon; 180 Imp gallon) auxiliary fuel tanks can be carried beneath the wings and fuselage.

ACCOMMODATION: Crew of two in tandem on Daiseru built Weber ES-7J zero/zero ejection seats in pressurised and air-conditioned cockpits, separated by windscreen. Rear seat elevated 28 cm (11 in) above front seat. Individual manually operated rearward hinged jettisonable canopies.

SYSTEMS AND AVIONICS: See 1987-88 *Jane's*.

ARMAMENT (combat trainer version): One Vulcan JM61 multi-barrel 20 mm cannon in lower fuselage, aft of cockpit on port side. Attachment point on underfuselage centreline and two under each wing for drop tanks or other stores. Wingtip attachments for air-to-air missiles.

DIMENSIONS, EXTERNAL:
Wing span	7.88 m (25 ft 10¼ in)
Length overall, incl probe	17.86 m (58 ft 7 in)
Length of fuselage	17.31 m (56 ft 9½ in)
Height overall	4.39 m (14 ft 5 in)
Wheel track	2.82 m (9 ft 3 in)
Wheelbase	5.72 m (18 ft 9 in)

AREA:
Wings, gross	21.17 m² (227.9 sq ft)

WEIGHTS:
Operational weight empty	6,307 kg (13,905 lb)
Max T-O weight	12,800 kg (28,219 lb)

PERFORMANCE (in 'clean' configuration):
Max level speed	Mach 1.6
Max rate of climb at S/L	10,670 m (35,000 ft)/min
Service ceiling	15,240 m (50,000 ft)
T-O run	610 m (2,000 ft)

MITSUBISHI F-1

The F-1 is a single-seat close air support fighter developed from the T-2 supersonic trainer, and was first flown on 3 June 1975.

Production orders were placed for 77 F-1s, the last of which was delivered on 9 March 1987. They serve with the 3rd Squadron of the 3rd Air Wing at Misawa and with two squadrons of the 8th Air Wing at Tsuiki.

TYPE: Single-seat close support fighter.

AIRFRAME, POWER PLANT AND SYSTEMS: Generally similar to T-2, but with the rear cockpit area modified as avionics compartment for bombing computer, inertial navigation system and radar warning system.

AVIONICS AND EQUIPMENT: See 1987-88 *Jane's*.

ARMAMENT: Single JM61 multi-barrel 20 mm cannon. One underfuselage and four underwing hardpoints, as in T-2, with detachable multiple ejector racks. Primary weapon is the Mitsubishi ASM-1 air-to-surface missile, of which two can be carried on underwing stations. Bombs of 500 or 750 lb can be carried on all five external stations, up to a maximum weight of 2,721 kg (twelve 500 lb bombs). Infra-red and laser guidance systems for free-fall 500 and

750 lb bombs were reported to be under development by the JASDF in 1983-84. The four underwing stations can each be used for rocket pods such as the JLAU-3A (with nineteen 70 mm), RL-7 (seven 70 mm) and RL-4 (four 125 mm). For air-to-air combat the F-1 can carry up to four AIM-9 Sidewinder missiles, one at each wingtip and one on each of the outboard underwing hardpoints. For long-range missions, the F-1 can carry up to three auxiliary fuel tanks (see 'Power Plant' paragraph for the T-2).

DIMENSIONS AND AREAS: As for T-2

WEIGHTS:

Operational weight empty	6,358 kg (14,017 lb)
Max T-O weight	13,700 kg (30,203 lb)

PERFORMANCE:

Generally similar to T-2 'clean', except for:	
T-O run at max T-O weight	1,280 m (4,200 ft)

MITSUBISHI (SIKORSKY) S-61

Mitsubishi holds licence agreements to manufacture the Sikorsky S-61, S-61B (HSS-2/2A/2B) and S-61A helicopters. Between 1 April 1987 and 31 March 1988 Mitsubishi delivered ten HSS-2Bs (for ASW) and one S-61A to the JMSDF. By the latter date it had delivered to the JMSDF, for ASW and rescue, 141 helicopters of the HSS-2 series and 13 S-61As, out of a total order for 167 HSS-2/2A/2B/S-61As. Seventeen HSS-2Bs and one S-61A were approved in the FY 1987 budget and are due for delivery by March 1990. Production will then be transferred to the SH-60J.

MITSUBISHI (SIKORSKY) SH-60J and HH-60J

Detailed design work on this developed version of the Sikorsky SH-60B Seahawk anti-submarine helicopter, to meet the specific requirements of the JMSDF, was funded under the FY 1983 budget. Japanese avionics and equipment, including ring laser gyro AHRS, data link, tactical data processing and automatic flight management systems, will be integrated by the Technical Research and Development Institute of the Japan Defence Agency. The first of two prototype XSH-60Js, based on imported airframes, flew for the first time on 31 August 1987. The JMSDF has a requirement for 80-100 SH-60Js, the first 12 of which were funded in FY 1988.

Mitsubishi will also be prime contractor for the licence assembly of 40 Sikorsky HH-60J helicopters to be procured for search and rescue duties with the JASDF, replacing the Kawasaki KV107II A-5 in this role from FY 1990. The first three HH-60Js were funded in FY 1988.

Mitsubishi built Sikorsky HSS-2B of the JMSDF

Second prototype Mitsubishi (Sikorsky) XSH-60J anti-submarine helicopter

NAL

NATIONAL AEROSPACE LABORATORY

7-44-1 Jindaijihigashi-machi, Chofu City, Tokyo 182
Telephone: (0422) 47 5911
DIRECTOR-GENERAL: Hideo Nagasu
DEPUTY DIRECTOR-GENERAL: Dr Kazuyuki Takeuchi

The National Aerospace Laboratory (NAL) is a government establishment responsible for research and development in the field of aeronautical and space sciences. Since 1962 it has extended its activity in the field of V/STOL techniques.

NAL ASUKA

The NAL is currently engaged in a 12-year programme to develop a large experimental quiet STOL transport aircraft. This is based upon the airframe of the Kawasaki C-1 tactical transport, with the following modifications: replacement of the two Pratt & Whitney JT8D engines by four MITI/NAL FJR710/600S high bypass ratio turbofans, installed above and far ahead of the wing leading-edges in nacelles with upper surface blowing (USB); installation of wing leading-edge and aileron boundary layer control systems; replacement of the existing inboard flaps by USB flaps; structural strengthening of the fuselage and landing gear; and installation of a digital stability and control augmentation system.

Modification began in 1979, and the aircraft (JQ8501) was named Asuka (after an ancient capital city of Japan) before making its first flight on 28 October 1985. Data obtained from the flight test programme will, it is hoped, enable NAL to develop, in co-operation with the Japanese aerospace industry, a commercial STOL transport aircraft able to operate from 800 m (2,625 ft) runways with 150 passengers. In its first STOL landing, on 23 March 1988, the prototype required a landing run of only 439 m (1,440 ft).

A full description of the Asuka, and a three-view drawing, were published in the 1986-87 *Jane's*. The following is a shortened version:

TYPE: Four-turbofan experimental 'quiet STOL' transport.

WINGS: Cantilever high-wing monoplane. Aerofoil sections YX-12641-M-097MOD at root, YX-1135-N-2000MOD at tip, with respective thickness/chord ratios of 12% and 11%. Wings have 20° sweepback at quarter-chord, with slightly increased leading-edge sweep on the inboard portions. Anhedral 5° 30' from centre-section. Incidence 4°. Two-spar fail-safe basic structure of aluminium alloy; upper surface of inner panels covered with thermal shielding panels of glass-polyimide honeycomb sandwich. Major elements of powered high lift device (PHLD)

system are the fore and main USB flaps, aft of the engine nacelles, which are manufactured from titanium and aluminium alloys and glass-polyimide FRP. They are actuated by two independent Kayaba hydraulic actuators on each wing, the inner one powered by No. 2 and the outer by No. 3 hydraulic system. Outboard of the USB flaps the C-1's outer quadruple-slotted flaps and drooping ailerons are retained, as are the four spoilers and three of the four sections of leading-edge slats. All these surfaces are actuated hydraulically, with actuators by Sumitomo (screwjacks), Mitsubishi, Teijin and Shimazu (screwjacks) respectively. Slotted flaps, ailerons, spoilers and slats are all of aluminium alloy construction. BLC flow of engine bleed air is directed over USB flaps and ailerons by vortex generators forward of these surfaces on top of wing.

FUSELAGE, TAIL UNIT AND LANDING GEAR: See 1986-87 edition.

POWER PLANT: Four 47.07 kN (10,582 lb st) MITI/NAL FJR710/600S turbofans, mounted in nacelles above and forward of wing centre-section. Six integral wing fuel tanks with total capacity of 15,414 litres (4,072 US gallons; 3,391 Imp gallons). Single pressure refuelling point for all tanks, plus overwing gravity refuelling point for each tank. Oil capacity 117 litres (31 US gallons; 25.7 Imp gallons). Air intakes have aluminium alloy acoustic panels.

ACCOMMODATION: Crew of three, comprising pilot, co-pilot and flight engineer. Accommodation in main cabin for up to seven technical personnel to monitor test equipment and instrumentation. Escape hatch in flight deck roof on starboard side. Flight deck and main cabin pressurised and air-conditioned by engine bleed air. Access to flight deck via downward opening door, with built-in stairs, on port side of forward fuselage. Emergency exit on each side of fuselage, aft of wing trailing-edge.

SYSTEMS: Pressurisation and air-conditioning systems utilise middle-stage engine bleed air at pressure of 6.21 bars (90 lb/sq in). No APU. Three independent hydraulic systems, each 207 bars (3,000 lb/sq in). No. 1 system actuates elevators, tailplane, rudder, starboard aileron, outboard spoilers, and signal actuators (output actuators of stability and control augmentation system); No. 2 actuates elevators, rudder, port aileron, inboard spoilers, signal actuators, slats, outboard flaps, USB flap inboard actuators, landing gear, nosewheel steering and brakes; No. 3 system actuates both ailerons, signal actuators, slats (alternate), outboard flaps (alternate), USB flap outboard actuators, and emergency brakes. Leading-edge and aileron BLC, and engine intake anti-icing system, utilise final stage engine bleed air at pressure of 11.72 bars (170 lb/sq in). Electrical power supplied by four engine driven 40kVA AC generators. DC power is obtained from AC source through a transformer-rectifier. Three

National Aerospace Laboratory Asuka QSTOL research aircraft

24V 34Ah nickel-cadmium batteries for emergency DC power. Three 30V 7.8Ah nickel-cadmium batteries for IRU and SCAS backup DC power. Liquid oxygen converter (capacity 5 litres; 1.3 US gallons; 1.1 Imp gallons) for flight crew; seven portable gaseous oxygen bottles for occupants of main cabin.

AVIONICS AND EQUIPMENT: Avionics include radio altimeter, VHF and UHF radio, ADF, marker beacon receiver, VOR/ILS, Tacan, ATC transponder, triple IRS and flight director system. Special equipment includes telemetry, radar transponder, and stability and control augmentation system (SCAS).

DIMENSIONS, EXTERNAL:
Wing span	30.60 m (100 ft 4¾ in)
Length overall	33.154 m (108 ft 9¼ in)
Height overall	10.175 m (33 ft 4½ in)
Wheel track (c/l of shock struts)	4.40 m (14 ft 5¼ in)
Wheelbase	9.33 m (30 ft 7¼ in)

AREAS:
Wings, gross	120.50 m² (1,297.0 sq ft)
Ailerons (total)	4.76 m² (51.24 sq ft)
Trailing-edge flaps (total): USB	12.70 m² (136.70 sq ft)
outboard	10.58 m² (113.88 sq ft)
Leading-edge slats (total)	9.23 m² (99.35 sq ft)
Spoilers (total)	4.30 m² (46.28 sq ft)

Fin	22.77 m² (245.09 sq ft)
Rudder, incl tabs	6.88 m² (74.06 sq ft)
Tailplane, incl slat	30.10 m² (323.99 sq ft)
Elevators (total, incl tabs)	7.60 m² (81.81 sq ft)

WEIGHTS AND LOADING:
Weight empty	32,372 kg (71,368 lb)
Max fuel weight	12,628 kg (27,840 lb)
Max T-O weight: STOL	38,700 kg (85,320 lb)
CTOL	45,000 kg (99,210 lb)
Max ramp weight	45,000 kg (99,210 lb)
Max zero-fuel weight	35,150 kg (77,490 lb)
Max wing loading	373.4 kg/m² (76.5 lb/sq ft)

PERFORMANCE (at max T-O weight except where indicated):
Never-exceed speed	320 knots (593 km/h; 368 mph) CAS
Max cruising speed	260 knots (482 km/h; 299 mph) CAS

Stalling speed at S/L, ISA, landing configuration, at landing weight of 36,860 kg (81,260 lb)
49 knots (91 km/h; 57 mph) CAS
Service ceiling, ISA, AUW of 38,700 kg (85,320 lb)
8,535 m (28,000 ft)
Min ground turning radius	26.70 m (87 ft 7¼ in)
STOL T-O to 15 m (50 ft)	823 m (2,700 ft)
STOL landing from 15 m (50 ft)	853 m (2,800 ft)

Range with max fuel, CTOL max T-O weight of 45,000 kg (99,210 lb)   720 nm (1,334 km; 829 miles)
OPERATIONAL NOISE LEVELS:
T-O, at 3.5 nm (6.5 km; 4 miles) from start of T-O run
93.8 EPNdB
Approach, at 1.0 nm (1.8 km; 1.1 miles) from landing threshold on 6° glideslope   100.6 EPNdB
Sideline, at 0.35 nm (0.65 km; 0.4 mile) from runway c/l   87.1 EPNdB

NAL SPACEPLANE STUDIES

The NAL is assisting in the study programme for a possible future Japanese space shuttle, and has tunnel tested a number of alternative configurations since about 1982. In March 1988 it was due to receive a Dornier 228-200 to be used for simulation of the final approach and landing phases of an eventual spaceplane. This aircraft will be equipped with a special work station from which its flight characteristics can be changed and controlled by computers. Gliding tests of two spaceplane models (with 1.5 m; 4 ft 11 in wing spans and each weighing only 100 kg; 220 lb) were carried out over the Sea of Japan in October 1987 by the Institute of Space and Astronautical Science, after air launch from a helicopter.

NIPPI

NIHON HIKOKI KABUSHIKI KAISHA (Japan Aircraft Manufacturing Co Ltd)

3175 Showa-machi, Kanazawa-ku, Yokohama 236
Telephone: (045) 773 5111
Telex: (3822) 267 NIPPI J
OTHER WORKS: Atsugi
PRESIDENT: Teruaki Yamada
PUBLIC RELATIONS MANAGER: Atsumasa Kubota

Nippi's Yokohama plant has a floor area of 56,885 m² (612,325 sq ft) and employs about 825 persons. The Atsugi plant, which employs about 660 persons, has a floor area of 39,280 m² (422,820 sq ft). Kawasaki has a 25% holding in Nippi.

The Atsugi plant is engaged chiefly in the overhaul, repair and maintenance of various types of aircraft and helicopters, including those of the Japan Defence Agency and Maritime Safety Agency, and carrier based aircraft of the US Navy. The Yokohama plant manufactures in-spar ribs for the Boeing 767; components and assemblies for the Mitsubishi T-2, F-1, F-15J (pylons and launchers), Kawasaki built P-3C (engine nacelles), and Shin Meiwa US-1A; airframe and dynamic components for the Kawasaki KV107; dynamic components for the Fuji-Bell HU-1H and Kawasaki-McDonnell Douglas OH-6D; body structures for Japanese satellites; tail units for Japanese built rocket vehicles; and targets for the Japan Defence Agency.

SHIN MEIWA

SHIN MEIWA INDUSTRY CO LTD

Nippon Building, 6-2, Otemachi 2-chome, Chiyoda-ku, Tokyo 100
Telephone: (03) 245 6611
Telex: 222 2431 SMIC T J
Fax: (03) 245 6616
HEAD OFFICE: 1-5-25, Kosone-Cho, Nishinomiya-Shi, Hyogo-Ken
Telephone: (0798) 47 0331
Telex: 5644493
WORKS (AIRCRAFT DIVISION):
Konan and Tokushima
PRESIDENT: Shinji Tamagawa
EXECUTIVE MANAGING DIRECTOR, AND GENERAL MANAGER, AIRCRAFT DIVISION: Yukio Koya
SALES MANAGER AND PUBLIC RELATIONS:
Junpei Matsuo (Tokyo Office)

The former Kawanishi Aircraft Company became Shin Meiwa in 1949 and established itself as a major overhaul centre for Japanese and US military and commercial aircraft.

Shin Meiwa's principal current activities concern production of the US-1A medium-range STOL search and rescue amphibian for the JMSDF, and overhaul work on flying-boats and amphibians. It manufactured drop tanks for the Kawasaki XT-4 trainer prototypes, and by December 1987 had modified two Learjet 36As into U-36A naval fleet training support aircraft for the JMSDF.

Shin Meiwa also produces components for other aircraft, including underwing drop tanks for the Mitsubishi T-2 and F-1 and Mitsubishi built McDonnell Douglas F-15J Eagles; nose and tail cones, ailerons and trailing-edge flaps for Kawasaki built examples of the Lockheed P-3C; wing and tail engine pylons for the McDonnell Douglas MD-11, under subcontract to Rohr Industries Inc; and components for the Boeing 767, under subcontract to Mitsubishi.

SHIN MEIWA SS-2A
JMSDF designation: US-1A

The **US-1** (manufacturer's designation SS-2A) is an amphibious adaptation of the PS-1 (SS-2) flying-boat (1980-81 *Jane's*), configured for search and rescue duties with the JMSDF. Details of the US-1, which first flew on 16 October 1974, can be found in the 1985-86 and earlier editions of *Jane's*.

The first US-1 was delivered on 5 March 1975, and ten are now in service with No. 71 SAR Squadron of the JMSDF, based at Iwakuni and Atsugi. The seventh and subsequent aircraft are fitted with T64-IHI-10J turboprops, offering a 14 per cent increase in power available for take-off, and are designated **US-1A**. The earlier aircraft are being retrofitted with these engines.

Following the 1976 modification of a PS-1 to firefighting configuration, with a 7,348 kg (16,200 lb) capacity water tank in the centre-fuselage aft of the step, a similar experimental conversion has been made more recently using a US-1A with a tank capacity increased to more than 13,608 kg (30,000 lb). The installation was developed by Conair of Canada (which see).

To make possible very low landing and take-off speeds, the US-1/-1A have both a boundary layer control system and extensive flaps for propeller slipstream deflection. Control and stability in low-speed flight are enhanced by 'blowing' the rudder, flaps and elevators, and by use of an automatic flight control system controlling the elevators, rudder and outboard flaps.

The following data apply to the US-1A:

TYPE: Four-turboprop STOL air/sea rescue amphibian.
WINGS: Cantilever high-wing monoplane. Conventional all-metal two-spar structure with rectangular centre-section and tapered outer panels. High-lift devices include outboard leading-edge slats extending over nearly 17 per cent of the span and large outer and inner blown trailing-edge flaps deflecting 60° and 80° respectively. Outboard flaps can be linked with ailerons. Two spoilers in front of outer flap on each wing. Hydraulically powered ailerons, with 'feel' trim. Leading-edge de-icing boots.
FUSELAGE: All-metal semi-monocoque hull, with high length/beam ratio. V shaped single-step planing bottom,

Shin Meiwa US-1A air/sea rescue amphibian (four Ishikawajima/General Electric T64-IHI-10J turboprops)

with curved spray suppression strakes along sides of nose and spray suppressor slots in lower fuselage sides aft of inboard propeller line. Double-deck interior.

TAIL UNIT: Cantilever all-metal T tail. Large dorsal fin. Tailplane has inverted slats and de-icing boots on leading-edge. Rudder and elevators are hydraulically powered, fitted with 'feel' trim, and blown by BLC system. Tab in each elevator.

LANDING GEAR: Flying-boat hull, plus hydraulically retractable Sumitomo tricycle landing gear with twin wheels on all units. Steerable nose unit. Oleo-pneumatic shock absorbers. Main units, which retract rearward into fairings on hull sides, have size 40 × 14-22 (Type VII) tyres, pressure 7.79 bars (113 lb/sq in). Nosewheel tyres size 25 × 6.75-18 (Type VII), pressure 20.69 bars (300 lb/sq in). Three-rotor hydraulic disc brakes. No anti-skid units.

POWER PLANT: Four 2,605 kW (3,493 ehp) Ishikawajima built General Electric T64-IHI-10J turboprops, each driving a Sumitomo built Hamilton Standard 63E60-27 three-blade constant-speed reversible-pitch propeller. Fuel in five wing tanks, with total usable capacity of 11,640 litres (3,075 US gallons; 2,560.5 Imp gallons) and two fuselage tanks (10,849 litres; 2,866 US gallons; 2,386.5 Imp gallons); total usable capacity 22,489 litres (5,941 US gallons; 4,947 Imp gallons). Pressure refuelling point on port side, near bow hatch. Oil capacity 152 litres (40.2 US gallons; 33.4 Imp gallons). The aircraft can be refuelled on open sea, either from a surface vessel or from another US-1/-1A fitted with detachable at-sea refuelling equipment.

ACCOMMODATION: Crew of three on flight deck (pilot, co-pilot and flight engineer), plus navigator/radio operator's seat in main cabin. Latter can accommodate up to 20 seated survivors or 12 stretchers, one auxiliary seat and two observers' seats. Sliding rescue door on port side of fuselage, aft of wing.

SYSTEMS: Cabin air-conditioning system. Two independent hydraulic systems, each 207 bars (3,000 lb/sq in). No. 1 system actuates ailerons, outboard flaps, spoilers, elevators, rudder and control surface 'feel'; No. 2 system actuates ailerons, inboard and outboard flaps, wing leading-edge slats, elevators, rudder, landing gear extension/retraction and lock/unlock, nosewheel steering, mainwheel brakes and windscreen wipers. Emergency system, also of 207 bars (3,000 lb/sq in), driven by 24V DC motor, for actuation of inboard flaps, landing gear extension/retraction and lock/unlock, and mainwheel brakes. Oxygen system for all crew and stretcher stations. Garrett GTCP85-131J APU provides power for starting main engines and shaft power for 40kVA emergency AC generator. BLC system includes a C-2 compressor, driven by a 1,014 kW (1,360 shp) Ishikawajima built General Electric T58-IHI-10-M2 gas turbine, housed in the upper centre portion of the fuselage, which delivers compressed air at 14 kg (30.9 lb)/s and pressure of 1.86 bars (27 lb/sq in) for ducting to inner and outer flaps, rudder and elevators. Electrical system includes 115/200V three-phase 400Hz constant frequency AC and three transformer-rectifiers to provide 28V DC. Two 40kVA AC generators, driven by Nos. 2 and 3 main engines. Emergency 40kVA AC generator driven by APU. 24V emergency DC power from two 34Ah nickel-cadmium batteries. Anti-icing, air-conditioning, fire detection and extinguishing systems standard.

AVIONICS AND EQUIPMENT: HIC-3 interphone, HRC-107 HF, N-CU-58/HRC antenna coupler, HGC-102 teletypewriter, HRC-106 radio, HRC-110 radio, HRN-101 ADF, AN/ARA-50 UHF/DF, HRN-105 Tacan, HRN-104 Loran, HRA-4 Loran signal processor, HRN-106 ILS marker beacon receiver, AN/APN-171 (N2) radio

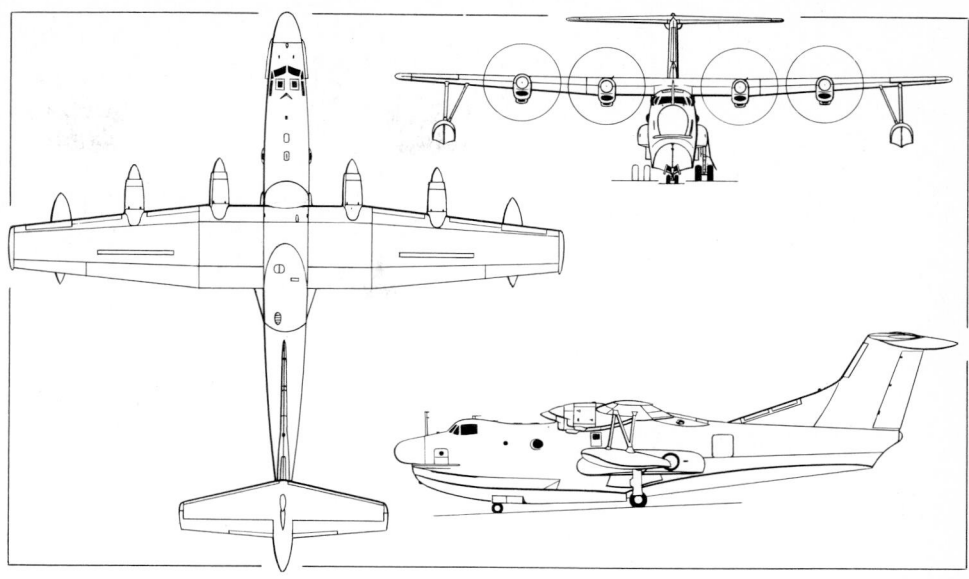

Shin Meiwa US-1A search and rescue amphibian, developed from the PS-1 *(Pilot Press)*

altimeter, HPN-101B wave height meter, AN/APN-187C Doppler radar, AN/AYK-2 navigation computer, A/A24G-9 TAS transmitter, N-PT-3 dead reckoning plotting board, N-OA-35/HSA tactical plotter group, AN/APS-80N search radar, AN/APA-125N indicator group, AN/APX-68N IFF transponder, RRC-15 emergency transmitter and N-ID-66/HRN BDHI. Sea anchor in nose compartment.

OPERATIONAL EQUIPMENT: Marker launcher, 10 marine markers, 6 green markers, 2 droppable message cylinders, 10 float lights, pyrotechnic pistol, parachute flares, 2 flare storage boxes, binoculars, 2 rescue equipment kits, 2 droppable liferaft containers, rescue equipment launcher, lifeline pistol, lifeline, 3 lifebuoys, loudspeaker, hoist unit, rescue platform, lifeboat with outboard motor, camera, and 12 stretchers. Stretchers can be replaced by troop seats.

DIMENSIONS, EXTERNAL:

Wing span	33.15 m (108 ft 9 in)
Wing chord: at root	5.00 m (16 ft 4¾ in)
at tip	2.39 m (7 ft 10 in)
Wing aspect ratio	8.1
Length overall	33.46 m (109 ft 9¼ in)
Height overall	9.95 m (32 ft 7¾ in)
Tailplane span	12.36 m (40 ft 8½ in)
Wheel track	3.56 m (11 ft 8¼ in)
Wheelbase	8.33 m (27 ft 4 in)
Propeller diameter	4.42 m (14 ft 6 in)
Rescue hatch, (port side, rear fuselage):	
Height	1.58 m (5 ft 2¼ in)
Width	1.46 m (4 ft 9½ in)

AREAS:

Wings, gross	135.82 m² (1,462.0 sq ft)
Ailerons (total)	6.40 m² (68.90 sq ft)
Inner flaps (total)	9.40 m² (101.18 sq ft)
Outer flaps (total)	14.20 m² (152.85 sq ft)
Leading-edge slats (total)	2.64 m² (28.42 sq ft)
Spoilers (total)	2.10 m² (22.60 sq ft)
Fin	17.56 m² (189.0 sq ft)
Dorsal fin	6.32 m² (68.03 sq ft)
Rudder	7.01 m² (75.50 sq ft)

Tailplane	23.04 m² (248.0 sq ft)
Elevators, incl tab	8.78 m² (94.50 sq ft)

WEIGHTS AND LOADINGS (search and rescue):

Manufacturer's weight empty	23,300 kg (51,367 lb)
Weight empty, equipped	25,500 kg (56,218 lb)
Usable fuel: JP-4	17,518 kg (38,620 lb)
JP-5	18,397 kg (40,560 lb)
Max oversea operating weight	36,000 kg (79,365 lb)
Max T-O weight: from water	43,000 kg (94,800 lb)
from land	45,000 kg (99,200 lb)
Max wing loading	331.4 kg/m² (67.9 lb/sq ft)
Max power loading	4.32 kg/kW (7.10 lb/ehp)

PERFORMANCE (US-1A search and rescue, at max T-O weight from land, except where indicated):

Max level speed	276 knots (511 km/h; 318 mph)
Max level speed at 3,050 m (10,000 ft), AUW of 36,000 kg	
(79,365 lb)	282 knots (522 km/h; 325 mph)
Cruising speed at 3,050 m (10,000 ft)	
	230 knots (426 km/h; 265 mph)
Max rate of climb at S/L	488 m (1,600 ft)/min
Max rate of climb at S/L, AUW of 36,000 kg (79,365 lb)	
	713 m (2,340 ft)/min
Service ceiling	7,195 m (23,600 ft)
Service ceiling, AUW of 36,000 kg (79,365 lb)	
	8,655 m (28,400 ft)
T-O to 15 m (50 ft) on land, 30° flap, BLC on (ISA)	
	655 m (2,150 ft)
T-O distance on water, AUW of 43,000 kg (94,800 lb), 40° flap, BLC on (ISA)	555 m (1,820 ft)
Landing from 15 m (50 ft) on land, AUW of 36,000 kg (79,365 lb), 40° flap, BLC on, with reverse pitch (ISA)	
	810 m (2,655 ft)
Landing distance on water, AUW of 36,000 kg (79,365 lb), 60° flap, BLC on (ISA)	220 m (722 ft)
Min ground turning radius:	
self-powered	21.20 m (69 ft 6¾ in)
towed	18.80 m (61 ft 8¼ in)
Runway LCN requirement at AUW of 43,000 kg (94,800 lb)	42
Max range at 230 knots (426 km/h; 265 mph) at 3,050 m (10,000 ft)	2,060 nm (3,817 km; 2,372 miles)

KOREA
(REPUBLIC)

KA
KOREAN AIR
KAL Building, CPO Box 864, 41-3 Seosomun-Dong, Chung-Ku, Seoul
Telephone: (02) 751 7114
Telex: KALHO K 27526
CHAIRMAN AND CHIEF EXECUTIVE OFFICER: C. H. Cho
PRESIDENT: C. K. Cho
Aerospace Division
Marine Center Building 18FL, 118-2Ga Namdaemun-Ro, Chung-Ku, Seoul
Telephone: (02) 771 66
Telex: KALHO K 27526 (SELDBKE)
Fax: (02) 756 7926
SENIOR VICE-PRESIDENT: J. M. Kim
VICE-PRESIDENT, MARKETING AND SALES: J. K. Lee

Aerospace Division, one of several divisions of Korean Air, was established in 1976 to manufacture and develop aircraft. It is now a leading aircraft manufacturer in Korea. In 1988 the Aerospace Division occupied a 64.75 ha (160 acre) site at Kim Hae, including a floor area of 130,065 m²

KA built Chegoong-Ho (Northrop F-5F) of the Republic of Korea Air Force

(1.4 million sq ft), and had a workforce of about 1,600 people.

Since 1978, Korean Air has carried out the complete overhaul of Republic of Korea Air Force aircraft. Programmed depot maintenance of US military aircraft in the Pacific area, under US government contract, began in 1979 and has included structural repair of F-4 Phantom IIs, systems modifications for the F-16 Fighting Falcon, MSIP upgrading of the F-15 Eagle and overhaul of C-130 Hercules transports. KA plans a major expansion in its co-production and subcontract programmes, and was to begin deliveries in 1988 of wingtip extensions and flap track fairings for the Boeing 747 and fuselage components for the McDonnell Douglas MD-11.

As a part of the Korean aircraft industry development programme from 1988, Korean Air is engaged in developing a basic trainer designed by its own staff, and a modified **Model 520MK** light helicopter, derived from the Model 500, in association with McDonnell Douglas.

KA (NORTHROP) F-5E TIGER II and F-5F
RoKAF name (F-5F): Chegoong-Ho (Air Master)
In 1981 KA began licence assembly of 68 Northrop F-5E Tiger IIs and F-5F combat trainers (48 and 20 respectively), ordered for the Republic of Korea Air Force. The first of these (an F-5F) made its initial flight in the Autumn of 1982, and the last was delivered to the RoKAF on 28 October 1986. Under an offset agreement with Northrop, KA also supplied F-5E/F bonded components to the US manufacturer between April 1985 and December 1986.

KA (MCDONNELL DOUGLAS) MODELS 500 and 530
Korean Air has manufactured the McDonnell Douglas (originally Hughes) Models 500D and 500MD under

McDonnell Douglas 500MD armed Scout helicopter built by Korean Air

licence from the US manufacturer since 1976, as described in earlier editions of *Jane's*. More than 450 of these two models had been delivered by late 1987. A new offset agreement was signed in 1984, under which KA has supplied McDonnell Douglas Helicopter Co with major

fuselage assemblies for the commercial Models 500E and 530F. More than 200 shipsets of these two models had been delivered to the USA by early 1988. Descriptions of the 500E and 530F can be found in the US section.

KBHC
KOREA BELL HELICOPTER COMPANY
Yesan

PRESIDENT: Kyu S. Rim

KBHC is a joint venture corporation between Bell Helicopter Textron (see US section) and Korea Technologies Corporation (KTC), a subsidiary of United Industries International that has represented Bell Helicopter and other US companies in Korea for many years. KBHC is already

licensed to repair, overhaul and modify Bell types, and to manufacture some components. Facilities are located at Yesan, south of Seoul. Plans include repair work for military and civil helicopters operating in Korea and the Pacific Rim area.

MALAYSIA

AIM
AEROSPACE INDUSTRIES OF MALAYSIA
PRESIDENT: Datuk Mohamed Taib

AIM was formed in January 1985 as part of the

Malaysian government's policy to develop an aerospace manufacturing capability. In January 1987 it signed a memorandum of understanding with British Aerospace under which BAe's Civil Aircraft Division will assist AIM, through an AIM subsidiary, to manufacture and supply

components for various BAe civil aircraft. The agreement also provides for BAe to assist with management, technical and supervisory expertise and appropriate training. No further details had been revealed at the time of closing for press.

NETHERLANDS

FOKKER
NV KONINKLIJKE NEDERLANDSE VLIEGTUIGFABRIEK FOKKER
CORPORATE CENTRE: PO Box 12222, 1100 AE Amsterdam-Zuidoost
Telephone: (020) 5649111
Telex: 11526 FMHS NL
Fax: (020) 5647015
CHAIRMAN: F. Swarttouw
MARKET COMMUNICATIONS MANAGER: Wim Bakker
OPERATING COMPANIES:
Fokker Aircraft BV, PO Box 12222, 1100 AE Amsterdam-Zuidoost
Telephone: (020) 5649111
Telex: 10687 FHK NL
Fax: (020) 5647015
PRESIDENT: R. J. van Duinen
EXECUTIVE VICE-PRESIDENT, MARKETING AND SALES:
F. M. van der Jagt
EXECUTIVE VICE-PRESIDENT, ENGINEERING:
F. Holwerda
Fokker Aircraft Services BV, PO Box 3, 4630 AA Hoogerheide
Fokker Space and Systems BV, PO Box 12222, 1100 AE Amsterdam-Zuidoost
Fokker Special Products BV, PO Box 59, 7900 AB Hoogeveen
Aircraft Financing and Trading BV, PO Box 12222, 1100 AE Amsterdam-Zuidoost
Avio-Diepen BV, PO Box 5952, 2280 HZ Rijswijk
Royal Netherlands Aircraft Factories NV Fokker, founded by Anthony Fokker in 1919, forms the main aircraft industry in the Netherlands, employing some 11,500 people. Under a new company structure which became effective on 1 January 1987, Fokker comprises a corporate centre and six operating companies.

Fokker has an important share in the European manufacturing programme for the General Dynamics F-16 fighter, being responsible for component production and assembly of F-16s for the Netherlands (213) and Denmark

(12). Seventy-two F-16s for Norway were delivered between January 1980 and June 1984 (see earlier editions of *Jane's*). Deliveries to the RNethAF began in June 1979, following the first flight by a Dutch assembled F-16 (J-259) on 3 May 1979. Deliveries totalled 163 to the RNethAF by 1 January 1988, and one to the Royal Danish Air Force. Altogether, Fokker is producing 1,286 centre-fuselages, 1,248 wing moving surfaces, 1,005 main landing gear doors, 518 main landing gear legs, 262 horizontal stabilisers, 658 rudders and 597 fin leading-edges (for Fokker's own assembly line, as well as for a similar line in Belgium and for General Dynamics, which manufactures F-16s for the USAF and for 'third nation' sales). Fokker-built F-16s for the RNethAF are being fitted with brake-chute housings in an extended fin root fairing. The first new aircraft so fitted was delivered to No. 315 Squadron on 30 June 1987; older aircraft will be modified later.

Some 5,400 people are employed at the Schiphol plant, Amsterdam, which accommodates the Fokker 50 and 100 and F-16 assembly lines and test flying facilities, and builds wing moving surfaces for Airbus Industrie. Also at Schiphol are the design offices, spare parts stores, research and development department, numerically controlled milling department, metal bonding department, electronics division, space division and scientific and administrative computer facilities.

The Drechtsteden plant, formed by the integrated production facilities at Dordrecht and Papendrecht, employs approx 2,000 people. Most of these are engaged on detail production and component assembly for the Fokker 50 and 100, F-16, Airbus A300/A310 and Shorts 330/360 and Sherpa; other work includes the manufacture of specialised products.

At Ypenburg the installation of F-16 centre-fuselages is carried out by a workforce of 700 people. Composite material components for the Fokker 50, Fokker 100, Shorts 330/360/Sherpa and Airbus A300/A310, and radomes and fairings for the Westland Lynx helicopter, are manufactured at Ypenburg.

Woensdrecht (Fokker Aircraft Services BV), which has a current workforce of about 800, specialises in maintenance,

overhaul, repair and modification of civil and military aircraft. Component production for the Patriot missile began in mid-1985. Also at Woensdrecht the ELMO division, with a workforce of approx 550, produces electrical and electronic systems and cable harnesses.

Hoogeveen (Fokker Special Products BV) is engaged in all activities relating to industrial products such as licence programmes, shelters, missile launchers, pylons and fuel tanks. It employs about 500 people.

FOKKER 50
On 24 November 1983, to mark the 25th anniversary in airline service of the F27 Friendship, Fokker announced follow-on developments of both the F27 and the F28 Fellowship, to be known respectively as the Fokker 50 and Fokker 100. Both aircraft build on successfully proven airframes, but with significant design and structural changes, allied to more efficient (and more fuel-efficient) power plants, increased use of composite materials, greater passenger comfort and convenience, advanced digital avionics, and improved airport handling characteristics. In consequence, more than 80 per cent of the component parts of the Fokker 50 are new or modified by comparison with those of the F27.

The two prototypes utilised modified F27 fuselages rather than the redesigned fuselage of the production aircraft. The first of them (PH-OSO) flew for the first time on 28 December 1985, and the second (PH-OSI) on 30 April 1986; the first production Fokker 50 (PH-DMO) flew on 13 February 1987, and certification was granted by the Dutch RLD on 15 May 1987.

In the production aircraft, differences from the F27 include new-technology engines, in redesigned nacelles, with six-blade propellers; use of carbon, aramid and glassfibre composites in such areas as the wings, tailplane, fin, radome, engine nacelles and propellers; passenger door relocated at the front of the aircraft, and the large cargo door deleted; more windows in the passenger cabin; pneumatic system replaced by a hydraulic system; and a cruising speed some 12 per cent higher than that of the F27. Seating range is 46-58, with 50 as standard, but the cabin

Fokker 50 twin-turboprop transport (two Pratt & Whitney Canada PW125B engines) in the insignia of Ansett of Australia

offers considerable flexibility for other layouts, including ample accommodation for baggage and freight. The production programme is shared with Dassault-Breguet (centre and rear fuselage sections), Fuji (rudder and elevators), MBB (wing trailing-edges/control surfaces, tailcone and dorsal fin), and Sabca (outer wing skins and wingtips).

Firm orders for 84 Fokker 50s had been received by 3 June 1988, from Ansett of Australia (15), Austrian Airlines (4), Busy Bee of Norway (5), Corsair of USA (7), DLT of West Germany (7), Kenya Airways (2), Luxair (3), Maersk Air of Denmark (8), MAS of Malaysia (9), SAS (20) and Sudan Airways (4). Deliveries (to DLT) began on 7 August 1987 and totalled 17 by 1 June 1988.

TYPE: Twin-turboprop short-haul transport.

WINGS: Cantilever high-wing monoplane. Wing section NACA 64_4-421 (modified) at root, NACA 64_2-415 (modified) at tip. Outer panels have 2° 30′ dihedral and 2° washout. Incidence 3° 30′. No sweepback. All-metal riveted and metal-bonded two-spar stressed skin primary structure, consisting of centre-section and two detachable outer wings. Detachable AFRP leading-edges with rubber boot de-icers. Trailing-edge skins are of composite material, supported by ribs of composite or metal construction. Single-slotted all-metal trailing-edge flaps (two segments per wing, divided by engine nacelle), operated by spindle/drive-nut. Flaps are actuated hydraulically, with electrical backup system, and are mechanically interconnected. Aileron structure is formed by bonded skin/stringer assemblies riveted to front, centre and rear spars and ribs, with leading-edges of composite material. Ailerons are actuated mechanically via cables. Each has an inboard spring tab and outboard geared/balance tab; starboard balance tab serves also as an electrically operated trim tab. Horn balance, known as Foklet, of metal reinforced composites, at each wingtip to increase lateral stability at low airspeeds.

FUSELAGE: All-metal stressed skin primary structure, built to fail-safe principles, with cylindrical portions metal bonded and conical part riveted. Pressurised between rear bulkhead of nosewheel compartment and circular pressure bulkhead aft of baggage compartment. Nosecone, fairings, nosewheel doors, access doors and cabin floor are of composite materials.

TAIL UNIT: Cantilever fin and fixed incidence tailplane of all-metal primary construction. Leading-edges are made of composites and have integral pneumatic de-icing boots; part of dorsal fin also of composite material. Elevators and rudder (both built by Fuji in Japan) are cable actuated. Elevators are mechanically interconnected, with trim tab in starboard elevator. Rudder is provided with a trim tab, geared balance tab and horn balance.

LANDING GEAR: Retractable tricycle type of Dowty Rotol manufacture, with twin wheels on all units. Main units are attached to wings, retracting rearward hydraulically into rear extension of engine nacelle; nosewheels retract

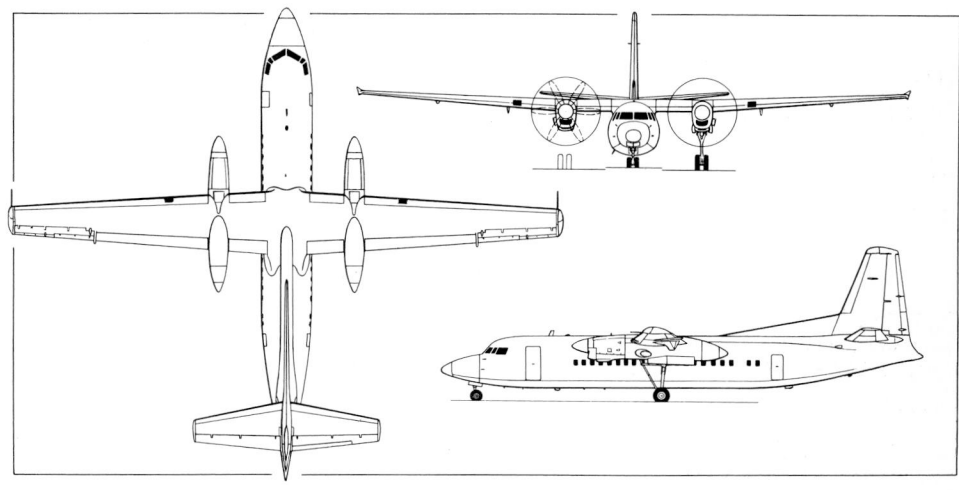

Fokker 50 twin-turboprop short-haul transport *(Pilot Press)*

forward. Long-stroke oleo-pneumatic shock absorber in each unit (single-stage on nose unit, double-acting on main units). Goodyear wheels and tyres on all units. Standard main unit tyres are size 34 × 10.75-R16, with pressure of 5.86 bars (85 lb/sq in); size 37 × 11.75-16 low-pressure tyres (4.00 bars; 58 lb/sq in) are optional. Nosewheel tyres are size 24 × 7.7-10, with pressure of 3.10 bars (45 lb/sq in). Goodyear hydraulic brakes, incorporating anti-skid system. Hydraulic nosewheel steering (± 73°); free-castoring angle of ± 130° available for towing.

POWER PLANT: Two 1,864 kW (2,500 shp) Pratt & Whitney Canada PW125B turboprops, each driving a Dowty Rotol six-blade propeller with spinner. Propellers have all-composite blades and Beta control. Lucas Aerospace 8.2 kW (11 hp) electric motor for engine starting. Composite materials used in construction of engine air intakes and nacelle cowlings. Fuel in two integral tanks located between the two spars of the central spar box outboard of the engine nacelle, with total standard capacity of 5,136 litres (1,357 US gallons; 1,130 Imp gallons). Single-point pressure refuelling and overwing gravity points. Engine air intakes, propeller blades and spinners de-iced electrically.

ACCOMMODATION: Crew of two on flight deck, plus two cabin attendants. Standard commuter layout seats 50 passengers, four-abreast with central aisle, at 81 cm (32 in) pitch. Alternative layouts include 46 business class passengers at 86 cm (34 in) pitch, 54 tourist class at 76 cm (30 in), or 58 in high-density arrangement, also at 76 cm

(30 in). All layouts mentioned have overhead stowage bins and forward and rear main baggage/cargo compartments as standard, with toilet and wardrobe areas forward and galley at rear of cabin. Downward opening airstair door at front on port side; service door at rear on same side; baggage/cargo door opposite each of these on starboard side. All four doors serve also as Type I emergency exits. Entire accommodation pressurised and air-conditioned. Windscreens anti-iced electrically, flight deck side windows demisted by hot air.

SYSTEMS: Hamilton Standard air-conditioning system. AiResearch digital cabin pressure control system. Max pressure differential 0.38 bars (5.46 lb/sq in). Hydraulic system, operating at 207 bars (3,000 lb/sq in) pressure via two engine driven Abex pumps, for landing gear actuation, brakes, nosewheel steering and flap drive. Pneumatic de-icing of wing, fin and tailplane leading-edges, using engine bleed air. Primary electrical system powered by a Sundstrand 30/40kVA integrated drive generator mounted on propeller gearbox of each engine, supplying 115/200V three-phase AC at 400Hz, with two 300A transformer-rectifiers and two 43Ah nickel-cadmium batteries for 28V DC power. Optional third (30/40kVA) generator driven by APU. External power socket. APU optional (in rear cone of starboard engine nacelle), for additional electrical power and bleed air for air-conditioning.

AVIONICS: Flight deck has dual Sperry EDZ-806 electronic flight instrument system (EFIS) with CRT displays for primary flight and navigation information, and space provisions for a central multifunction display. Standard avionics include Sperry SPZ-600 AFCS with Cat. I landing; Sperry FZ-500 dual flight director systems; dual Bendix Series III VHF com; single Bendix Series III ADF and DME (latter including frequency hold facility); Bendix Series III ATC transponder; Sperry Primus P-650 weather radar with dual presentation on EFIS; dual Bendix Series III VHF nav with VOR, ILS and marker beacon receiver; TRT AHV-530A (ARINC 552A) radio altimeter with dual presentation on EFIS; dual Litton LTR 81.01 AHRS; Sundstrand Mk II GPWS (ARINC 549); Sperry AZ-800 air data computer; Fairchild A100 (ARINC 557) cockpit voice recorder; Collins 346-2B (ARINC 560) PA system; Sundstrand 980-4100 DXUS (ARINC 573) flight data recorder, incl underwater locator beacon; and Teledyne Model 70-275 flight data acquisition unit. Full provisions for Cat. II landing on AFCS, single Collins 628T-2A HF com to ARINC 559A2 and second ADF; space provisions for second DME, second ATC transponder, Omega/VLF nav system, and Dorne & Margolin ELT.

DIMENSIONS, EXTERNAL:

Wing span	29.00 m (95 ft 1¾ in)
Wing chord: at root	3.464 m (11 ft 4½ in)
at tip	1.40 m (4 ft 7 in)
Wing aspect ratio	12.0
Length overall	25.247 m (82 ft 10 in)
Fuselage: Max width	2.70 m (8 ft 10¼ in)
Height overall (static)	8.317 m (27 ft 3½ in)
Tailplane span	9.746 m (31 ft 11¾ in)
Wheel track	7.20 m (23 ft 7½ in)
Wheelbase	9.70 m (31 ft 10 in)
Propeller diameter	3.66 m (12 ft 0 in)
Propeller ground clearance	1.162 m (3 ft 9¾ in)
Propeller/fuselage clearance	0.593 m (1 ft 11¼ in)
Passenger door (fwd, port): Height	1.78 m (5 ft 10 in)
Width	0.76 m (2 ft 6 in)
Service door (rear, port) and cargo door (fwd, stbd), each:	
Height	1.27 m (4 ft 2 in)
Width	0.61 m (2 ft 0 in)
Cargo door (rear, stbd): Height	1.27 m (4 ft 2 in)
Width	0.86 m (2 ft 9¾ in)

DIMENSIONS, INTERNAL:

Cabin, excl flight deck: Length	15.96 m (52 ft 4 in)
Width at floor	2.11 m (6 ft 11 in)
Max width	2.50 m (8 ft 2½ in)
Max height	1.96 m (6 ft 5¼ in)
Floor area (excl toilet)	30.2 m² (325.0 sq ft)
Baggage/cargo volume (standard commuter version):	
main compartments	7.38 m³ (260.6 cu ft)
wardrobe compartment	0.82 m³ (29 cu ft)
overhead bins	2.22 m³ (78.4 cu ft)

AREA:

Wings, gross	70.0 m² (753.5 sq ft)

WEIGHTS:

Typical operating weight empty	12,649 kg (27,886 lb)
Max fuel load	4,123 kg (9,090 lb)
Max payload	5,951 kg (13,120 lb)
Max ramp weight: standard	19,100 kg (42,110 lb)
optional	20,820 kg (45,900 lb)
Max T-O weight: standard	18,990 kg (41,865 lb)
optional	20,820 kg (45,900 lb)
Max landing weight: standard	18,990 kg (41,865 lb)
optional	19,730 kg (43,500 lb)
Max zero-fuel weight	18,600 kg (41,000 lb)

PERFORMANCE:

Max operating Mach number	0.507
Typical cruising speed	282 knots (522 km/h; 325 mph)
Typical climb speed	
	200 knots (370 km/h; 230 mph) CAS
Typical descent speed	
	227 knots (420 km/h; 261 mph) CAS
Max operating altitude	7,620 m (25,000 ft)
Service ceiling, one engine out, AUW of 18,250 kg (40,234 lb), ISA	4,300 m (14,100 ft)
Min ground turning radius	18.07 m (59 ft 3½ in)

Runway LCN (51 cm; 20 in flexible pavement), 34 × 10.75-R16 tyres at 5.86 bars (85 lb/sq in):

AUW of 19,050 kg (42,000 lb)	16.9
AUW of 20,820 kg (45,900 lb)	18.4

T-O field length at S/L, ISA, 15° flap:

standard MTOW	1,050 m (3,450 ft)
optional MTOW	1,355 m (4,450 ft)

Landing field length at S/L, ISA, 35° flap:

standard MLW	1,090 m (3,575 ft)
optional MLW	1,130 m (3,710 ft)

Range with 50 passengers and baggage, reserves for 45 min continued cruise at long-range speed and 87 nm (161 km; 100 mile) diversion:

at standard MTOW:

high-speed procedure	579 nm (1,073 km; 666 miles)
min fuel procedure	628 nm (1,163 km; 723 miles)

at optional MTOW:

high-speed procedure

    1,465 nm (2,715 km; 1,687 miles)

min fuel procedure

    1,588 nm (2,943 km; 1,828 miles)

OPERATIONAL NOISE LEVELS:

T-O	79.4 EPNdB
Approach	96.8 EPNdB
Sideline	85.2 EPNdB

Artist's impression of Fokker Maritime Enforcer Mk 2 armed surveillance and ASW aircraft

FOKKER 50 MARITIME AND SURVEILLANCE VERSIONS

The following maritime and surveillance variants of the Fokker 50 are available:

Maritime Mk 2. Basic unarmed maritime patrol version, for duties which include coastal surveillance, search and rescue, and environmental control. Crew of up to six persons.

Maritime Enforcer Mk 2. Similar to Maritime Mk 2, but equipped for armed surveillance, anti-submarine and anti-shipping warfare, with enhanced avionics and provisions for carrying external stores (armament chosen and installed by operator).

Sentinel Mk 2. Border surveillance and standoff reconnaissance version. Primary sensor is a Motorola AN/APS-135(V) side looking airborne radar (SLAR), mounted in an underfuselage pod. Equipped with Doppler moving target indication, this can detect large targets at up to 80 nm (148 km; 92 miles) distant, or smaller targets at up to 48 nm (90 km; 56 miles). Onboard data processing via colour CRT display. Standoff photography with Litton/Itek KA-102 long-range oblique photography (Lorop) system, or a Vinten pod containing 70 mm vertical and oblique cameras or an infra-red linescan. Options include an automatic computerised comint (communications intelligence) system to intercept, record and analyse radio signals in the 20-1,000MHz frequency band.

King Bird Mk 2. AEW version, with Thorn EMI Skymaster surveillance radar in retractable ventral radome. Capability includes pulse-Doppler search and acquisition modes (for all aircraft within a 120 nm; 222 km; 138 mile radius). ESM to detect and identify radar-emitting targets within surveillance area.

The following description applies specifically to the Maritime Enforcer Mk 2, Sentinel Mk 2 and King Bird Mk 2, based on the Fokker 50 airframe:

TYPE: Twin-turboprop maritime patrol aircraft.

WINGS, FUSELAGE AND TAIL UNIT: As described for Fokker 50, except that airframe is heavily treated with anti-corrosive measures.

LANDING GEAR: As described for Fokker 50, but with mainwheel tyre pressures of 5.52 bars (80 lb/sq in) standard, or 4.50 bars (65 lb/sq in) for low pressure tyres. Nosewheel tyre pressure increased to 3.80 bars (55 lb/sq in).

POWER PLANT: As for Fokker 50, plus additional centre-wing fuel tank of 2,310 litres (610 US gallons; 508 Imp gallons) capacity, and two 938 litre (248 US gallon; 206.5 Imp gallon) tanks on underwing pylons, giving overall total fuel capacity of 9,322 litres (2,463 US gallons; 2,051 Imp gallons). Methyl bromide fire extinguishing system, with flame detectors.

ACCOMMODATION: Crew of two on flight deck, with folding seat for third crew member if required. Main cabin of Maritime Mk 2 fitted out as tactical compartment (for two to four operators), containing advanced avionics, galley, toilet and crew rest area. Maritime Enforcer accommodates crew of seven including two pilots: tactical co-ordinator (Tacco) responsible for off-airways navigation and overall efforts of mission crew; acoustic sensor operator (ASO) to handle active and passive sonobuoys, acoustic receivers and processor display system; non-acoustic sensor operator (NASO) controlling search radar and electronic surveillance subsystem; and two observers. Bubble windows for observers at rear of main cabin. Rear cabin door is openable in flight. Standard cargo door at front on port side, with sill at truckbed height. Cargo holds forward and aft of main cabin.

SYSTEMS: Generally as described for Fokker 50, except that oxygen system includes individual supply for each tactical crew member.

AVIONICS AND EQUIPMENT: Com/nav equipment comprises

AN/ARC-190(V) HF transceivers, two Bendix VCS-40 VHF transceivers, Collins AN/ARC-182 VHF/UHF transceiver (three in Enforcer), interphone, crew address system, two Litton LTN-92 inertial navigation systems, air data computer, Bendix DFS-43 radio compass, two TRT AHV-530 radio altimeters, Collins DF-301E VHF/UHF direction finder, two Bendix VNS-41 VOR/ILS/marker beacon receivers, Sperry ADZ-80 EFIS, Teledyne AN/APX-101 IFF transponder, dual Sperry SPZ-600 AFCS, weather radar, low altitude warning system, and Tacan.

OPERATIONAL EQUIPMENT (Maritime Mk 2 and Maritime Enforcer Mk 2): Both versions fitted with Litton 360° search radar in ventral radome: AN/APS-140(V) or AN/APS-504(V)5. Additional mission equipment in Enforcer Mk 2 includes GEC Avionics central tactical computer and display system, radar detection and display system, on-top position indicator/receiver, dual sonobuoy signal receivers, GEC Avionics AQS 902 (LAPADS) sonar, and sonobuoy processing system. Both passive and active sonobuoys are carried (up to 40 of SSQ-36, SSQ-41B or SSQ-47B type, up to 120 smaller buoys, or a mixture of both sizes), and launched from the internal stores area in the rear of the cabin. General Instrument AN/ALR-66(V)3 electronic surveillance and monitoring equipment to detect radar transmissions, which can be classified and recorded and their bearings transferred to the tactical display. Infra-red detection system (IRDS). MAD. A data link with available ground or shipborne systems can be provided.

ARMAMENT (Maritime Enforcer Mk 2): Fokker installs Alkan stores management system and provisions for armament; weapon mix and purchase is up to customer. Two 907 kg (2,000 lb) stores attachments on the fuselage and three under each wing (capacities 295 kg; 650 lb inboard, 680 kg; 1,500 lb in centre, and 113 kg; 250 lb outboard). Typical ASW armament can include two or four Mk 44, Mk 46, Sting Ray or A244/S torpedoes and/or depth bombs. For anti-shipping warfare, two AM39 Exocet, AGM-65F Maverick, AGM-84A Harpoon, Sea Skua, Sea Eagle or similar air-to-surface missiles can be carried. Auxiliary fuel tanks can be carried on the central underwing pylons.

DIMENSIONS: As for Fokker 50

WEIGHTS AND LOADINGS (A: Maritime Enforcer Mk 2, B: Maritime Mk 2, C: Sentinel Mk 2, D: King Bird Mk 2):

Operating weight empty: A	13,314 kg (29,352 lb)
B (typical)	14,796 kg (32,620 lb)
C	14,515 kg (32,000 lb)
D	15,422 kg (34,000 lb)
Max fuel (incl pylon tanks): A	7,257 kg (16,000 lb)
B	7,511 kg (16,560 lb)
C	7,484 kg (16,500 lb)
D	5,978 kg (13,180 lb)
Normal T-O weight: all	20,820 kg (45,900 lb)
Max T-O weight: all	21,545 kg (47,500 lb)
Emergency overload T-O weight:	
B	22,680 kg (50,000 lb)
Max landing weight: all	19,730 kg (43,500 lb)
Max zero-fuel weight: all	18,144 kg (40,000 lb)
Max wing loading: all	291.6 kg/m² (59.75 lb/sq ft)
Max power loading: all	6.39 kg/kW (10.5 lb/shp)

PERFORMANCE (at normal T-O weight except where indicated):

Normal cruising speed	259 knots (480 km/h; 298 mph)
Typical search speed at 610 m (2,000 ft)	
	150 knots (277 km/h; 172 mph)
Service ceiling: all	7,620 m (25,000 ft)
Service ceiling, one engine out: A	3,565 m (11,700 ft)

Runway LCN (42 per cent tyre deflection) at 15,875 kg (35,000 lb) AUW: A:

rigid pavement, L 76.2 cm (30 in)	10.4
flexible pavement, h 25.4 cm (10 in)	11.4

Fokker 100 twin-turbofan short/medium-range transport in the insignia of launch customer Swissair

flexible pavement, h 12.7 cm (5 in)   9.0
Runway LCN (42 per cent tyre deflection) at 20,410 kg
(45,000 lb) AUW: A:
     rigid pavement, L 76.2 cm (30 in)   16.0
     flexible pavement, h 25.4 cm (10 in)   14.8
     flexible pavement, h 12.7 cm (5 in)   12.0
Runway CBR, unpaved soil, h 25.4 cm (10 in), 3,000
passes: A:
     AUW of 15,875 kg (35,000 lb)   6.2%
     AUW of 20,410 kg (45,000 lb)   7.8%
T-O run at S/L, AUW of 21,320 kg (47,000 lb):
     ISA   1,525 m (5,000 ft)
     ISA + 20°C   1,700 m (5,575 ft)
Landing distance (unfactored, ISA at S/L), landing
weight of 18,990 kg (41,866 lb)   762 m (2,500 ft)
Max radius of action with 1,814 kg (4,000 lb) mission
load   1,200 nm (2,224 km; 1,382 miles)
Max range, no reserves
     3,680 nm (6,820 km; 4,237 miles)
Max endurance, reserves for 30 min hold, 5% fuel
remaining   14 h 42 min

FOKKER 100

Announced simultaneously with the Fokker 50, the Fokker 100 is derived from the F28 Mk 4000, which it has superseded on the production line. It has a longer fuselage, extended and much redesigned wings, Rolls-Royce Tay turbofans, a completely new CRT flight deck and cabin interior, and extensively modernised systems. The first prototype (PH-MKH) made its initial flight on 30 November 1986, and a second (PH-MKC) joined the flight test and certification programme on 25 February 1987, followed by the first series production aircraft (for an undisclosed customer) on 25 September 1987.

The Fokker 100 complies with the Stage 3 noise requirements of FAR Pt 36, and RLD certification to JAR Pt 25 was received on 20 November 1987, followed by Cat. III autoland certification in June 1988. The first aircraft for Swissair made its initial flight on 30 December 1987, and was delivered on 29 February 1988. Certification of a version with uprated Tay Mk 650 engines and increased design weights, flown for the first time on PH-MKH on 8 June 1988, was scheduled for September 1988; first deliveries of this version will be to USAir in early 1989. Other options in this version include a new passenger door, large cargo doors, upper deck avionics and a polished outer skin.

The Fokker 100 is being produced in collaboration with MBB (large fuselage sections and tail section) and Shorts (wings); Grumman is subcontractor for the engine nacelles and thrust reversers. An agreement for IPTN of Indonesia to supply milled and wing and tail components was announced in June 1988.

By March 1988 firm orders for 87 Fokker 100s had been placed by Swissair (8), KLM (10), USAir (20), ILFC (8), GPA-Fokker 100 Ltd (40) and an unnamed customer (1), with another 91 on option. Eight of the ILFC aircraft will be leased to East-West Airlines (3), Inter-Canadian Airways (4) and Air Gabon (1).

TYPE: Twin-turbofan short/medium-haul transport.
WINGS: Cantilever low-wing monoplane. Fokker designed,

advanced transonic wing sections, which offer substantially improved aerodynamic efficiency, especially at high speeds. Thickness/chord ratio up to 12.3% on inner panels, 9.6% at tip. Dihedral 2° 30'. Sweepback at quarter-chord 17° 24'. Light alloy torsion box structure, comprising two-spar centre-section (integral with fuselage) and two outer panels with two main spars and auxiliary front spar. Fail-safe construction. Lower skin of outer wings made of three planks. Taper rolled top skin. Forged ribs in centre-section, built-up ribs in outer panels. Light alloy leading-edges, with hot air de-icing. Irreversible hydraulically operated ailerons. In the third mode, both ailerons are driven manually via servo tabs. Hydraulically operated double-slotted Fowler flaps with electrical alternative extension. Five-panel, hydraulically operated lift dumpers in front of flaps on each wing. Flaps and ailerons are of carbonfibre, spoilers and aileron servo tabs of aluminium alloy.

FUSELAGE: Circular-section semi-monocoque light alloy fail-safe structure, made up of skin panels with bonded Z-stringers. Bonded double plates at door and window cutouts. Quickly detachable sandwich floor panels (carbonfibre and glassfibre with Nomex core). Hydraulically operated petal airbrakes form rear end of fuselage. AFRP wing/fuselage fairing panels.

TAIL UNIT: Cantilever light alloy T structure, with hydraulically actuated variable incidence tailplane. Third mode is electric operation. Hydraulically boosted elevators, with manual backup. Hydraulically operated rudders, with manual third mode. Fin constructed from honeycomb sandwich skin panels in conjunction with multiple spars; dorsal fin of aramid fibre. Light alloy elevator, carbonfibre rudder. Hot air de-icing of tailplane leading-edge.

LANDING GEAR: Hydraulically retractable tricycle type, with twin wheels on each unit. Main units retract inward into

wing/body fairing; nosewheel retracts forward. Dowty Rotol shock absorber in each unit. Goodyear tyres, size H40 × 14-19 on main units (pressure 8.96 bars; 130 lb/sq in), size 24 × 7.7-10 (pressure 5.86 bars; 85 lb/sq in) on nose unit. Goodyear multiple-disc carbon brakes, with anti-skid system. Steerable nose unit (effective angle ±76°).

POWER PLANT: Two 61.6 kN (13,850 lb st) Rolls-Royce Tay Mk 620-15 turbofans initially, fitted with thrust reversers and pylon mounted on sides of rear fuselage. Nacelles manufactured from composite materials. Option in 1989 of 67.2 kN (15,100 lb st) Tay Mk 650-15 turbofans. Fuel in 4,870 litre (1,286.5 US gallon; 1,071 Imp gallon) main tank in each wing and 3,300 litre (872 US gallon; 726 Imp gallon) tank (seven flexible cells) in wing centre-section, giving total standard internal capacity of 13,040 litres (3,445 US gallons; 2,868 Imp gallons). Option for 1,550 litre (409.5 US gallon; 341 Imp gallon) auxiliary tank in wing leading-edge. Refuelling point under starboard wing, near wing/fuselage belly fairing. Oil capacity (two engines) 23 kg (51 lb).

ACCOMMODATION: Crew of two on flight deck; two cabin attendants. Standard accommodation for 107 passengers, in five-abreast seating (3+2) at 81 cm (32 in) pitch. Optional layouts include 12 first class seats (four-abreast) at 91 cm (36 in) pitch plus 85 economy class (five-abreast) at 32 in; 55 business class at 86 cm (34 in) plus 50 economy class, all five-abreast; or 119 tourist class passengers at 74 cm (29 in) pitch. Reduced galley and stowage space in 119 seat layout. Standard layout includes two galleys, two toilets, two wardrobes, two other stowage/wardrobe compartments, and carry-on baggage compartment. Outward opening passenger door at front of cabin on port side, with outward opening service/emergency door opposite on starboard side. Optional auxiliary service door on port side near rear galley. Two overwing

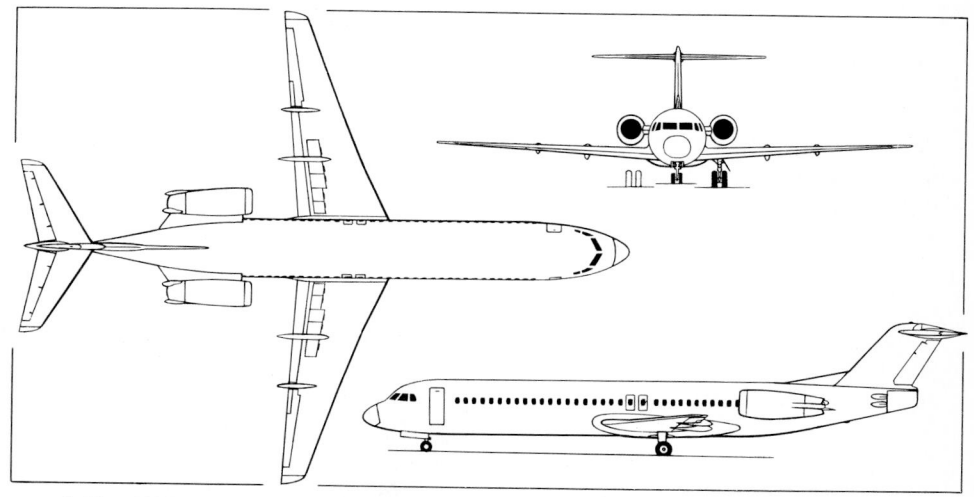

Fokker 100 'stretched' development of the F28 (two Rolls-Royce Tay turbofans) *(Pilot Press)*

emergency exits (inward opening plug type) each side. Two underfloor baggage/cargo holds (one forward of wing, one aft), with three downward opening doors on starboard side. Option for three identical large, upward opening cargo doors. Entire accommodation air-conditioned.

SYSTEMS: AiResearch air-conditioning and pressurisation system. Two fully independent hydraulic systems for actuation of flight control surfaces, landing gear, brakes and nosewheel steering. AiResearch pneumatic system. Sundstrand integrated drive generator electrical supply system. Oxygen system for flight crew and passengers. AiResearch thermal anti-icing system for wings and tail unit. Electric anti-icing of flight deck windows, pitot tubes, static vents, angle of attack vanes and ice detector probe. Garrett GTCP 36-150R APU.

AVIONICS: Standard avionics include dual VHF com (to ARINC 716), PA system (ARINC 715), audio management system, ATC transponder (ARINC 718), triple AHRS (ARINC 705), dual radio altimeters (ARINC 707), dual VOR with marker beacon receiver (ARINC 711), dual ILS (ARINC 710), dual ADF (ARINC 712), dual DME (ARINC 709), Collins EFIS electronic display systems: primary flight display (PFD) and navigation display (ND) for each pilot, and multi-function display system (MFDS), consisting of two CRTs on centre instrument panel. EFIS and MFDS display units are identical in size. Dual digital air data systems (ARINC 706) with computer driven instruments, weather radar (ARINC 708 on ND), dual advanced flight management systems (AFMS) plus full flight regime autothrottle system, and Collins digital automatic flight control and augmentation system (AFCAS) for Cat. IIIA automatic landing. (Cat. IIIB autoland certification anticipated in September 1988.) Optional avionics include single or dual HF com (ARINC 719), third VHF com, Selcal (ARINC 714), second ATC, third ILS, third radio altimeter, music reproducer, ACARS, aircraft integrated data system, and Cat. IIIB autoland capability.

DIMENSIONS, EXTERNAL:

Wing span	28.08 m (92 ft 1½ in)
Wing chord: at root	5.28 m (17 ft 4 in)
at tip	1.26 m (4 ft 1½ in)
Wing aspect ratio	8.4
Length overall	35.53 m (116 ft 6¾ in)
Fuselage: Length	32.50 m (106 ft 7½ in)
Max diameter	3.30 m (10 ft 10 in)
Height overall	8.50 m (27 ft 10½ in)
Tailplane span	10.04 m (32 ft 11¼ in)
Wheel track (c/l of shock struts)	5.04 m (16 ft 6½ in)
Wheelbase	14.01 m (45 ft 11½ in)
Passenger door (fwd, port): Height	2.21 m (7 ft 3 in)
Width	0.86 m (2 ft 9¾ in)
Service door (fwd, stbd): Height	1.28 m (4 ft 2½ in)
Width	0.61 m (2 ft 0 in)

Cargo compartment doors (fwd and rear, stbd):

Height (each)	0.95 m (3 ft 1½ in)
Width (each)	0.90 m (2 ft 11½ in)
Height to sill (MTOW):	
fwd door at front	1.31 m (4 ft 3½ in)
fwd door at rear	1.37 m (4 ft 6 in)
rear door	1.46 m (4 ft 9½ in)

Overwing emergency exits (four, each):

Height	0.91 m (3 ft 0 in)
Width	0.51 m (1 ft 8 in)

DIMENSIONS, INTERNAL:

Cabin, excl flight deck: Length	21.19 m (69 ft 6¼ in)
Max length of seating area	18.80 m (61 ft 8¼ in)
Max width	3.10 m (10 ft 2 in)
Width at floor	2.90 m (9 ft 6¼ in)
Max height	2.01 m (6 ft 7¼ in)
Max floor area	58.48 m² (629.5 sq ft)
Max volume	107.58 m³ (3,799 cu ft)
Overhead stowage bins (total)	5.23 m³ (184.7 cu ft)
Additional baggage space (total)	3.17 m³ (112.0 cu ft)
Underfloor compartment volume:	
fwd	9.8 m³ (346 cu ft)
rear	7.36 m³ (260 cu ft)

AREAS:

Wings, gross	93.5 m² (1,006.4 sq ft)
Ailerons (total)	3.528 m² (37.98 sq ft)
Trailing-edge flaps (total)	17.00 m² (182.99 sq ft)
Lift dumpers (total)	5.27 m² (56.73 sq ft)
Rudder	2.30 m² (24.76 sq ft)
Elevators (total)	7.92 m² (85.25 sq ft)
Airbrakes (total)	1.81 m² (19.48 sq ft)

WEIGHTS (A: basic, B: optional):

Typical operating weight empty (107 passengers)	24,355 kg (53,695 lb)
Max payload (weight-limited)	12,385 kg (27,305 lb)
Max ramp weight: A	43,320 kg (95,500 lb)
B	44,680 kg (98,500 lb)
Max T-O weight: A	43,090 kg (95,000 lb)
B	44,450 kg (98,000 lb)
Max landing weight	39,915 kg (88,000 lb)
Max zero-fuel weight	36,740 kg (81,000 lb)

PERFORMANCE (at basic max T-O weight, Tay 620-15 engines, except where indicated):

Max operating Mach number	0.77
Max operating speed at 7,375 m (24,200 ft)	452 knots (837 km/h; 520 mph)
Approach speed at max landing weight	131 knots (243 km/h; 151 mph)
Service ceiling	10,670 m (35,000 ft)
FAR T-O field length at S/L, ISA: Tay 620-15 engines	1,990 m (6,530 ft)
Tay 650-15 engines	1,747 m (5,730 ft)
FAR landing field length at max landing weight (S/L, ISA)	1,360 m (4,460 ft)

Range with 107 passengers and baggage:
at basic max T-O weight, Tay 620-15 engines
1,305 nm (2,418 km; 1,502 miles)
at optional max T-O weight with auxiliary fuel tank, Tay 650-15 engines
1,535 nm (2,844 km; 1,767 miles)

OPERATIONAL NOISE LEVELS (FAR Pt 36 and ICAO Annex 16, Tay 620-15 engines):

Flyover	83.4 EPNdB
Approach	93.4 EPNdB
Sideline	89.3 EPNdB

NEW ZEALAND

AERO TRADER
AERO TRADER LTD
1 Cracroft Street, Devonport, Auckland 9
MANAGING DIRECTOR: A. Water

Mr Water of Aero Trader is building a prototype two-seat training/touring aircraft, intended to obtain FAA certification under FAR Pt 25 Appendix A. The fuselage and landing gear had been completed by early 1987, at which time further work on the glassfibre wings was in progress and the engine was awaited from Germany. No subsequent news has been received.

PAC
PACIFIC AEROSPACE CORPORATION LIMITED
Private Bag, Hamilton Airport, Hamilton
Telephone: (071) 436 144
Telex: NZ 21242 PACORP
Fax: (071) 436 134
CHIEF EXECUTIVE: A. Hyde
CHIEF DESIGNER: R. J. Guest
SALES MANAGER: R. Geer

The former New Zealand Aerospace Industries Ltd was reconstituted on 1 July 1982 as Pacific Aerospace Corporation Ltd. PAC maintains full spares support for the Airtrainer CT4A/CT4B, Fletcher FU24-950 series and PAC Cresco. It is continuing to market the FU24-954, Cresco, and new CT4C/CR/D variants of the Airtrainer CT4B.

Lockheed Corporation has a 24.9% holding in Pacific Aerospace Corporation.

PAC FLETCHER FU24-954
The US built FU24 prototype flew in July 1954, followed by the first production aircraft five months later, as recorded in earlier editions of *Jane's*. Type certification was granted on 22 July 1955. All manufacturing and sales rights were transferred to New Zealand in 1964, and by April 1986 a total of 292 Fletcher FU24 series aircraft had been completed, including 56 for export to Australia, Bangladesh, Dubai, Iraq, Pakistan, Thailand, Uruguay and the USA. Six were ordered by the Thailand Ministry of Agriculture in early 1988, and marketing and support are continuing.

A full description of the current standard production version, the FU24-954, can be found in the 1985-86 *Jane's*. The following is an abbreviated version of that entry:

TYPE: Agricultural and general purpose aircraft.
AIRFRAME: See 1985-86 *Jane's*.
POWER PLANT: One 298 kW (400 hp) Textron Lycoming IO-720-A1A or A1B flat-eight engine, driving a Hartzell HC-C3YR-1R/847SR three-blade constant-speed variable-pitch metal propeller with spinner. Fuel tanks in wing leading-edges; total usable capacity 254 litres (67 US gallons; 55.8 Imp gallons) normal, 481 litres (127 US gallons; 105.75 Imp gallons) with optional long-range tanks.
ACCOMMODATION (agricultural models): Enclosed cockpit for pilot and one passenger on side by side seats under rearward sliding canopy. Cockpit reinforced for overturn/crash protection. Large port side cargo door. Optional features include additional cargo floor area and dual controls.
ACCOMMODATION (utility models): Enclosed cabin for pilot and up to seven passengers or equivalent freight. Dual controls optional. Rearward sliding hood over front two seats. Large passenger/cargo door on port side.
AGRICULTURAL EQUIPMENT: Glassfibre hopper aft of cockpit, capacity 1,211 litres (320 US gallons; 266 Imp gallons) of liquid, 1,066 kg (2,350 lb) of dry chemicals. Hopper outlets for spreading of solids (fertiliser, dry ice, poison bait etc). Transland Swathmaster for topdressing, seeding and high-volume spraying. Transland Boommaster for liquid spraying with booms, nozzles, fan driven pump etc for low- and high-volume spraying. Micronair spraying equipment with electrically or fan driven pump, varied control systems, side loading valve for liquids, and special adaptor plate for interchangeability of equipment.
OPTIONAL EQUIPMENT (all models): Full blind-flying instrumentation with ADF, VHF, VOR and DME. Full dual controls; dual mainwheels and brakes, wheel and leg fairings; long-range fuel tanks; cabin heating and air-conditioning systems; metric instrumentation.

PAC Cresco 08-600 (Textron Lycoming LTP 101-700A-1A turboprop)

DIMENSIONS, EXTERNAL:

Wing span	12.81 m (42 ft 0 in)
Length overall	9.70 m (31 ft 10 in)
Height overall	2.84 m (9 ft 4 in)
Wheel track	3.71 m (12 ft 2 in)
Wheelbase	2.28 m (7 ft 6 in)
Propeller diameter	2.18 m (7 ft 2 in)

DIMENSIONS, INTERNAL:

Cabin: Length	3.18 m (10 ft 5 in)
Max width	1.22 m (4 ft 0 in)
Max height	1.27 m (4 ft 2 in)
Floor area	3.87 m² (41.7 sq ft)
Volume aft of hopper	3.37 m³ (119.0 cu ft)
Hopper volume	1.22 m³ (43.0 cu ft)

AREA:

Wings, gross	27.31 m² (294.0 sq ft)

WEIGHTS:

Weight empty, equipped	1,188 kg (2,620 lb)
Max payload (agricultural)	1,052 kg (2,320 lb)
Normal max T-O weight	2,204 kg (4,860 lb)
Max agricultural T-O weight	2,463 kg (5,430 lb)

PERFORMANCE (at Normal max T-O weight):

Never-exceed speed	143 knots (265 km/h; 165 mph)
Max level speed at S/L	126 knots (233 km/h; 145 mph)

Max cruising speed (75% power)
113 knots (209 km/h; 130 mph)
Operating speed for spraying (75% power)
90-115 knots (167-212 km/h; 104-132 mph)
Stalling speed:
flaps up   55 knots (102 km/h; 64 mph)
flaps down   49 knots (91 km/h; 57 mph)
Max rate of climb at S/L   280 m (920 ft)/min
Service ceiling   4,875 m (16,000 ft)
T-O run   244 m (800 ft)
T-O to 15 m (50 ft)   372 m (1,220 ft)
Landing from 15 m (50 ft)   390 m (1,280 ft)
Landing run   207 m (680 ft)
Swath width (agricultural models):
oily   23 m (75 ft)
aqueous   21.3-24.4 m (70-80 ft)
dust   7.6-15.2 m (25-50 ft)
Range with max normal fuel, 45 min reserves
383 nm (709 km; 441 miles)

PAC CRESCO 08-600

Design of this turboprop development of the FU24 began in 1977, and the prototype (ZK-LTP) first flew on 28 February 1979. The Cresco has many components interchangeable with the FU24-954, and its name is Latin for 'I grow'. The first production Cresco was flown in early 1980, and the type entered service in January 1982. Five, all for domestic customers, had been built by April 1986. Production, as with the FU24-954, was then at a standstill, but the aircraft continues to be actively marketed and supported.

The description of the FU24-954 applies also to the Cresco, except in the following respects:

TYPE: Turboprop powered agricultural and general purpose aircraft.
AIRFRAME: See 1986-87 *Jane's*.
POWER PLANT: One Textron Lycoming LTP 101-700A-1A turboprop, flat rated at 447 kW (600 shp) and driving a Hartzell HC-B3TN-3D/T10282 three-blade constant-speed metal propeller with spinner. Four fuel tanks in wing centre-section, total capacity 545.5 litres (144 US gallons; 120 Imp gallons). Two refuelling points in upper surface of each wing. Oil capacity 5.5 litres (1.4 US gallons; 1.2 Imp gallons). Chin mounted engine air intake, fitted with Centrisep filter panel.
ACCOMMODATION: Pilot only, or crew of two side by side, under rearward sliding bulged cockpit hood. Tinted windscreen and canopy side panels standard. Dual controls available optionally. Large forward hinged door, with window, aft of wing on port side. Generous cargo space immediately aft of hopper. Cockpit ventilated; heating system optional.
SYSTEMS: See 1986-87 *Jane's*.
AVIONICS: See 1986-87 *Jane's*.
AGRICULTURAL EQUIPMENT: Generally similar to FU24-954, except for substantially larger hopper, increasing capacity to 1,779 litres (470 US gallons; 391 Imp gallons) of liquid or 1,860 kg (4,100 lb) of dry chemical. Range of dispersal systems available to customer's requirements, from ultra-high-volume solids dispersal to ultra-low-volume spray.

DIMENSIONS, EXTERNAL:
Wing span   12.81 m (42 ft 0 in)
Length overall   11.07 m (36 ft 4 in)
Height overall   3.63 m (11 ft 10¾ in)
Wheelbase   2.77 m (9 ft 1¼ in)
Propeller diameter   2.59 m (8 ft 6 in)
Cargo door (port): Height   0.94 m (3 ft 1 in)
Width   0.94 m (3 ft 1 in)
Height to sill   0.91 m (3 ft 0 in)
DIMENSIONS, INTERNAL:
Cargo compartment volume (aft of hopper)
3.40 m³ (120.0 cu ft)
Hopper volume   1.77 m³ (62.5 cu ft)

AREA:
Wings, gross   27.31 m² (294.0 sq ft)
WEIGHTS:
Weight empty, equipped   1,270 kg (2,800 lb)
Max disposable load (Agricultural, incl fuel)
1,828 kg (4,030 lb)
Max fuel load   435 kg (960 lb)
Max T-O weight: Normal   2,925 kg (6,450 lb)
Agricultural   3,175 kg (7,000 lb)
Max landing weight   2,925 kg (6,450 lb)
PERFORMANCE (at max Normal T-O weight, ISA, except where indicated):
Never-exceed speed   177 knots (328 km/h; 204 mph)
Max level speed at S/L   148 knots (274 km/h; 170 mph)
Max cruising speed (75% power)
135 knots (250 km/h; 155 mph)
Stalling speed at 2,767 kg (6,100 lb) AUW, flaps down, power off   52 knots (97 km/h; 60 mph)
Max rate of climb at S/L   379 m (1,245 ft)/min
Absolute ceiling   5,485 m (18,000 ft)
T-O to 15 m (50 ft)   436 m (1,430 ft)
Landing from 15 m (50 ft)   500 m (1,640 ft)
Range at 3,175 kg (7,000 lb) MTOGW with standard fuel, no reserves   460 nm (852 km; 529 miles)

PAC AIRTRAINER CT4C, CR and D

The CT4 Airtrainer was a New Zealand redesign of the Australian Victa Airtourer and first flew in prototype form on 23 February 1972. A total of 94 production CT4A and CT4B Airtrainers was built by PAC, for the air forces of Australia (51), New Zealand (19) and Thailand (24), plus one for Ware Engineering of Thailand, before production ceased in 1977.

PAC is now offering three new variants, as follows:
CT4C. With 313 kW (420 shp) Allison 250-B17 turboprop replacing the 157 kW (210 hp) Continental IO-360-H flat-six piston engine of the CT4A/B. Non-retractable landing gear. Overall length increased to 7.15 m (23 ft 5½ in).
CT4CR. As CT4C, but with retractable landing gear.
CT4D. With non-retractable landing gear and 210 kW (282 hp) Textron Lycoming TIO-360-X66 flat-four turbocharged piston engine. Length as for CT4A/B.
TYPE: Two/three-seat fully aerobatic light training aircraft.
WINGS: Cantilever low-wing monoplane. Wing section NACA 23012 (modified) at root, NACA 4412 (modified) at tip. Dihedral 6° 45' at chord line. Incidence 3° at root, 0° at tip. Root chord increased by forward sweep of the inboard leading-edges. Single main spar light alloy stressed skin structure, with glassfibre wingtips that are detachable to permit optional wingtip fuel tanks to be fitted. Single-slotted electrically actuated flap and aerodynamically balanced bottom-hinged aileron on each trailing-edge, of light alloy construction with fluted skins. No tabs.
FUSELAGE: All-metal stressed skin semi-monocoque structure. Glassfibre engine cowling.
TAIL UNIT: Cantilever light alloy structure, with some aerodynamic balance. One-piece elevator, statically balanced. Ground adjustable tab on rudder. Rudder controlled by rod and cable linkage, elevator by rod and mechanical linkage. Electrically actuated trim control for rudder and elevator.
LANDING GEAR: Tricycle type, retractable on CT4CR, non-retractable on CT4C and CT4D. Non-retractable gear has cantilever spring steel main legs, and steerable nosewheel carried on telescopic strut and oleo shock absorber. Main units fitted with Dunlop Australia wheels and tubeless tyres size 6.00-6; nosewheel fitted with tubeless tyre size 5.00-5. Dunlop Australia single-disc toe operated hydraulic brakes, with hand operated parking lock. Landing gear designed to shear before any excess impact loading is transmitted to wing, to minimise structural damage in the event of a crash landing.

POWER PLANT: As given in individual model listings. CT4A/B each have a total standard fuel capacity of 204.5 litres (54 US gallons; 45 Imp gallons). Wingtip tanks, each of 77 litres (20.5 US gallons; 17 Imp gallons) capacity, available optionally.
ACCOMMODATION: Two seats side by side under hinged, fully transparent Perspex canopy. Space to rear for optional third seat or 52 kg (115 lb) of baggage or equipment. Dual controls standard.
DIMENSIONS, EXTERNAL (CT4A/B):
Wing span   7.92 m (26 ft 0 in)
Wing chord: at root   2.17 m (7 ft 1¼ in)
at tip   0.98 m (3 ft 2½ in)
Wing aspect ratio   5.25
Length overall   7.06 m (23 ft 2 in)
Height overall   2.59 m (8 ft 6 in)
Fuselage: Max width   1.12 m (3 ft 8 in)
Max depth   1.40 m (4 ft 7¼ in)
Tailplane span   3.61 m (11 ft 10 in)
Wheel track   2.97 m (9 ft 9 in)
Wheelbase   1.71 m (5 ft 7⅜ in)
DIMENSIONS, INTERNAL (CT4A/B):
Cabin: Length   2.74 m (9 ft 0 in)
Max width   1.08 m (3 ft 6½ in)
Max height   1.35 m (4 ft 5 in)
AREAS (CT4A/B):
Wings, gross   11.98 m² (129.0 sq ft)
Ailerons (total)   1.07 m² (11.56 sq ft)
Flaps (total)   2.10 m² (22.60 sq ft)
Fin   0.60 m² (6.43 sq ft)
Rudder, incl tab   0.58 m² (6.26 sq ft)
Tailplane   1.43 m² (15.40 sq ft)
Elevator   1.26 m² (13.60 sq ft)
WEIGHT (CT4C/CR/D):
Max T-O weight (all)   1,202 kg (2,650 lb)
PERFORMANCE (estimated: C and CR at AUW of 1,111 kg; 2,450 lb, D at 1,134 kg; 2,500 lb AUW):
Max level speed at S/L: C
205 knots (380 km/h; 236 mph)
CR   234 knots (434 km/h; 269 mph)
D   156 knots (289 km/h; 179 mph)
Max level speed at 3,050 m (10,000 ft):
C   208 knots (385 km/h; 239 mph)
CR   240 knots (445 km/h; 276 mph)
D   170 knots (315 km/h; 196 mph)
Max level speed at 6,100 m (20,000 ft):
C   195 knots (361 km/h; 224 mph)
CR   228 knots (422 km/h; 262 mph)
D   188 knots (348 km/h; 216 mph)
Stalling speed at S/L:
flaps up: C, CR   57 knots (106 km/h; 66 mph)
D   58 knots (108 km/h; 67 mph)
flaps down: C, CR, D   44 knots (82 km/h; 51 mph)
Max rate of climb at S/L, ISA:
C   843 m (2,765 ft)/min
CR   930 m (3,050 ft)/min
D   406 m (1,330 ft)/min
Service ceiling: CR   5,455 m (17,900 ft)
T-O run at S/L, ISA:
C, CR   117 m (384 ft)
D   197 m (647 ft)
T-O to 15 m (50 ft) at S/L, ISA:
C, CR   206 m (675 ft)
D   333 m (1,092 ft)
Landing run: CR   156 m (510 ft)
Range with max fuel (75% power), ISA, no reserves:
at S/L: C   464 nm (860 km; 534 miles)
CR   529 nm (980 km; 609 miles)
D   562 nm (1,041 km; 647 miles)
at 3,050 m (10,000 ft): C 624 nm (1,156 km; 718 miles)
CR   724 nm (1,342 km; 834 miles)
D   632 nm (1,171 km; 728 miles)

NIGERIA

AIEP
AERONAUTICAL INDUSTRIAL ENGINEERING AND PROJECT MANAGEMENT CO LTD
General Aviation Service Centre, PO Box 5662, Kaduna Airport
Telephone: 217573

COMMERCIAL MANAGER: H. Preissler

AIEP AIR BEETLE

AIEP, in which Dornier GmbH of West Germany has a 60% holding, has begun assembling a prototype of this ab initio trainer, which was expected to make its first flight in

the Summer of 1988. Powered by a 134 kW (180 hp) Textron Lycoming flat-four engine, the Air Beetle is a variant of the US Van's RV-6 homebuilt (see Sport Aircraft section), reportedly differing only in being fitted with toe operated brakes for both occupants. If flight testing is successful, the Air Beetle is expected to enter production to supplement the Nigerian Air Force's BAe Bulldog trainers.

PAKISTAN

PAC
PAKISTAN AERONAUTICAL COMPLEX
Kamra, District Attock
WORKS: F-6 Rebuild Factory, Mirage Rebuild Factory, and Aircraft Manufacturing Factory (all at Kamra)
Telephone: (051) 580260/3
Telex: 5601 PAC KAMRA PK

DIRECTOR GENERAL:
Air Vice-Marshal Farooq Umar

MANAGING DIRECTORS:
Air Cdre Akbar Mehdi (MRF)
Air Cdre Noor Ilahi Siddiqi (AMF)
Air Cdre Mozammil Saeed (F-6RF)

Located approximately midway between Islamabad and Peshawar, the Pakistan Aeronautical Complex is an organ of the Pakistan Ministry of Defence. It is collaborating with NAMC in China (which see) in developing a new jet trainer known as the Karakorum 8, and was discussing in early 1988, with one French and two US manufacturers, the possible licence assembly of a light armed utility helicopter.

The **Mirage Rebuild Factory** (MRF) at Kamra, opened in 1978, can accomplish complete overhaul of Mirage III/5 aircraft, Atar 9C turbojets, and associated components and accessories, and has a current capacity of eight aircraft and over 30 engines per year. It has recently undertaken the overhaul of third country (UAE) Mirage III/5s and their engines. In 1988 it was being upgraded to enable it to overhaul the Pratt & Whitney F100-PW-200 turbofan. The MRF has a site area of some 810,000 m² (8,715,000 sq ft) and a workforce of nearly 1,700.

The **Aircraft Manufacturing Factory** came into operation in mid-1981, as licence production centre for the Saab Safari/Supporter two/three-seat light aircraft, which has the Pakistani name Mushshak (Urdu for 'proficient'). Progressive assembly of the first 90 of these aircraft began in 1976 from semi-knocked-down and completely knocked-down kits, and it is now being manufactured at Kamra from raw materials. By early 1988 about 150 examples of the Mushshak were in service with various units of the Pakistan Army and Air Force, with output continuing at the rate of 15 a year. In mid-1986 work began on installing a more powerful 156.6 kW (210 hp) Teledyne Continental TIO-360-MB engine, resulting in a considerable increase in performance. Production tooling was in hand in early 1988 for modifying additional aircraft, with series production expected to begin in December 1988 after US certification to FAR Pt 23. At least 100 of the uprated version are said to be required.

Major facilities at the AMF include equipment to manufacture all GRP components of the Mushshak. Engines, instruments, electrical equipment and radios are imported, but almost all other items are manufactured locally.

The **F-6 Rebuild Factory**, or F-6RF, was established in 1980 for the primary purpose of overhauling the Pakistan Air Force's Chinese Shenyang F-6 aircraft and their airframe accessories. It is authorised to manufacture about 4,000 spares items for that aircraft, and also produces the 1,140 litre (301 US gallon; 250 Imp gallon) auxiliary fuel tanks fitted to the F-6. Current capacity (1986-87) was for 24 aircraft a year. Engines for the F-6 are rebuilt at Faisal, a Pakistan Air Force base near Karachi. The F-6RF possesses modern technical facilities for various engineering processes such as surface treatment, heat treatment, forging, casting, non-destructive testing, and other machine tools required to manufacture items from raw materials. The F-6RF has now begun overhaul of Pakistan Air Force FT-5s, FT-6s and A-5Cs. In due course it is expected to assume responsibility for Chinese F/FT-7 aircraft in PAF service.

PAC (AMF) MUSHSHAK

TYPE: Two/three-seat training and observation light aircraft.
WINGS: Braced shoulder-wing monoplane with single strut each side. Thickness/chord ratio 10%. Dihedral 1° 30'. All-metal structure, sweptforward 5° from roots. Mass balanced all-metal ailerons. Electrically operated all-metal plain sealed flaps. Servo tab in starboard aileron.
FUSELAGE: Metal box structure. Glassfibre tailcone, engine cowling panels and wing strut/landing gear attachment fairings.
TAIL UNIT: Cantilever metal structure comprising swept fin and rudder and one-piece mass balanced horizontal 'stabilator' with large anti-servo and trimming tab. Glassfibre fin tip. Trim tab in rudder.
LANDING GEAR: Non-retractable tricycle type. Cantilever

Pakistan Air Force Mushshak (Saab Safari/Supporter), built under licence by PAC *(Denis Hughes)*

composite spring main legs. Goodyear 6.00-6 mainwheels and 5.00-5 steerable nosewheel. Cleveland disc brakes on main units.
POWER PLANT: One 149 kW (200 hp) Textron Lycoming IO-360-A1B6 flat-four engine, driving a Hartzell HC-C2YK-4F/FC7666A-2 two-blade constant-speed metal propeller with spinner. Version with 156.6 kW (210 hp) Teledyne Continental TIO-360-MB engine under development. Two integral wing fuel tanks, total capacity 190 litres (50.2 US gallons; 41.8 Imp gallons). Oil capacity 7.5 litres (2.0 US gallons; 1.6 Imp gallons). From 10-20 s inverted flight (limited by oil system) permitted.
ACCOMMODATION: Side by side adjustable seats, with provision for back type or seat type parachutes, for two persons beneath fully transparent upward hinged canopy. Dual controls standard. Space aft of seats for 100 kg (220 lb) of baggage (with external access on port side) or, optionally, a rearward facing third seat. Upward hinged door, with window, beneath wing on port side. Cabin heated and ventilated.
SYSTEM: 28V 50A DC electrical system.
AVIONICS AND EQUIPMENT: Provision for full blind-flying instrumentation and radio. Landing light in nose.
ARMAMENT: Provision for six underwing attachment points, the inner two stressed to carry up to 150 kg (330 lb) each and the outer four up to 100 kg (220 lb) each. Possible armament loads include two 7.62 mm machine-gun pods, two pods each with seven 75 mm air-to-surface rockets, four pods each with seven 68 mm rockets, eighteen 75 mm rockets, or six wire guided anti-tank missiles.

DIMENSIONS, EXTERNAL:
Wing span	8.85 m (29 ft 0½ in)
Wing chord (outer panels, constant)	1.36 m (4 ft 5½ in)
Length overall	7.00 m (22 ft 11½ in)
Height overall	2.60 m (8 ft 6½ in)
Tailplane span	2.80 m (9 ft 2¼ in)
Wheel track	2.30 m (7 ft 6½ in)
Wheelbase	1.59 m (5 ft 2¾ in)
Propeller diameter	1.88 m (6 ft 2 in)
Cabin door (port): Height	0.78 m (2 ft 6¾ in)
Width	0.52 m (1 ft 8½ in)

DIMENSIONS, INTERNAL:
Cabin: Max width	1.10 m (3 ft 7¼ in)
Max height (from seat cushion)	1.00 m (3 ft 3¼ in)

AREAS:
Wings, gross	11.90 m² (128.1 sq ft)
Ailerons (total)	0.98 m² (10.55 sq ft)
Flaps (total)	1.55 m² (16.68 sq ft)
Fin	0.77 m² (8.29 sq ft)
Rudder, incl tab	0.73 m² (7.86 sq ft)
Horizontal tail surfaces (total)	2.10 m² (22.6 sq ft)

WEIGHTS (200 hp engine):
Weight empty, equipped	646 kg (1,424 lb)
Max T-O weight: Normal	1,200 kg (2,645 lb)
Utility	1,125 kg (2,480 lb)
Aerobatic	900 kg (1,984 lb)

PERFORMANCE (at max T-O weight, Utility category, with 200 hp engine):
Never-exceed speed	197 knots (365 km/h; 227 mph)
Max level speed at S/L	127 knots (236 km/h; 146 mph)
Cruising speed	112 knots (208 km/h; 129 mph)
Stalling speed, flaps down, power off	58 knots (107 km/h; 67 mph)
Max rate of climb at S/L	246 m (807 ft)/min
Time to 1,830 m (6,000 ft)	9 min 18 s
Service ceiling	4,100 m (13,450 ft)
T-O run	205 m (673 ft)
T-O to 15 m (50 ft)	385 m (1,263 ft)
Landing from 15 m (50 ft)	390 m (1,280 ft)
Landing run	155 m (509 ft)
Max endurance (65% power) at S/L, 10% reserves	5 h 10 min
g limits:	+4.4/–1.76 Utility
	+6/–3 Aerobatic

PHILIPPINES

PAC
PHILIPPINE AIRCRAFT COMPANY
c/o Western Pacific Aviation Corporation, PO Box 7633, Airport Airmail Exchange, Pasay City, Metro Manila
PRESIDENT: Rolando P. Moscardon

It was announced in November 1987 that PAC had concluded an agreement with Denney Aerocraft of the USA (see Sport Aircraft section) to manufacture, market and support the latter company's Kitfox two-seat single-engined homebuilt aircraft in the Western Pacific area (excluding Australia, New Zealand and Hawaii). A total of 36 Kitfoxes is on order for use by provincial government agencies in the Philippines, and kits for the first two had been delivered to PAC by early 1988. PAC name for the aircraft is **Skyfox**.

PADC
PHILIPPINE AEROSPACE DEVELOPMENT CORPORATION
MIA Road, Pasay, Metro Manila
POSTAL ADDRESS: PO Box 7395, Airmail Exchange Office, MIA 3120
Telephone: 832 27 41 to 49
Telex: 66019 PADC PN
PRESIDENT: Oscar M. Alejandro
EXECUTIVE VICE-PRESIDENT: Jose L. Bustamante
MARKETING DIRECTOR: Antonio S. Duarte

SUBSIDIARY:
Philippine Helicopter Services Inc (PHSI) (maintenance and overhaul of BO 105 and Bell helicopters; overhaul and repair of Hughes/McDonnell Douglas helicopter blades; and repair of Zahnradfabrik Friedrichshafen AG products).

PADC is a government owned corporation established in 1973 to undertake business and development projects in the aviation and aerospace industry in the Philippines. It is engaged in the assembly and manufacture of **BO 105** helicopters and **Islander** light transport aircraft, under 1974 licence agreements with MBB of West Germany and Pilatus Britten-Norman of the UK respectively. By early 1987, PADC had assembled 44 BO 105s and 63 Islanders (including 22 Islanders for the Philippine Air Force), and had manufactured the GRP components for both types of aircraft. No 1988 totals were received.

PADC is also engaged in the maintenance and overhaul of lightweight aircraft, parts and components, and the sale of aircraft/engine related accessories and spare parts. It is the appointed area service centre for the Islander, Cessna (Caravan I/II, Conquest and Citation) and Piper light aircraft, King com/nav equipment, and Allison 250 series turboprops. It is also an authorised customer service facility of Bell Helicopter Asia (Pte) Ltd, providing maintenance, repair, overhaul and spare parts to owners and operators of Bell Model 204, 205 and 214 series helicopters.

POLAND

PZL

ZRZESZENIE WYTWÓRCÓW SPRZETU LOTNICZEGO I SILNIKOWEGO PZL (Association of Aircraft and Engine Industry)

ul. Miodowa 5, 00-251 Warszawa
Telephone: Warszawa 279985
Telex: 814281
PRESIDENT: Ing Eugeniusz Olko, MSc
DIRECTOR: Ing Jan Stojanowicz, MSc

The manufacture of aircraft in Poland began in 1910. In 1928 an industrial syndicate was established, grouping the existing aircraft factories into the Panstwowe Zaklady Lotnicze (State Aviation Works) to produce aircraft to meet domestic and export needs. Since then the Polish aircraft industry has designed and built several tens of thousands of aircraft, helicopters and gliders of various types, as well as of aero engines and equipment.

Until 1981 the aviation industry was organised under control of the ZPLS-PZL (Aircraft and Engine Industry Union). In 1982 (see earlier editions of this annual) its activities came under the control of the Bureau of Ministers Plenipotentiary for the Aircraft and Engine Industry, and it

is currently organised as the Zrzeszenie Wytwórców Sprzetu Lotniczego i Silnikowego PZL (Association of Aircraft and Engine Industry), managed by a council representing all factories which are members of the Association. Production plants within the Association are self-dependent.

Other members of the Association include the BTNU (Biuro Techniczne Nowych Uruchomień: Engineering Office for the Implementation of New Projects), and the PPT (Przedsiebiorstwo Projektowo-Technologiczne: Design and Production Methods Enterprise). The Instytut Lotnictwa (which see) is also a member of the Association.

The Polish aviation industry currently comprises 27 factories, scientific and development units, technical and commercial organisations, which between them employ about 90,000 qualified workers. Its work has a broad base which includes research, design, development, manufacture, foreign trade, agricultural aviation services, and technical support for its own products operated by other countries.

Production by the Polish aviation industry relies substantially on aircraft, engines and equipment of its own design, as well as on co-operation and co-production with leading foreign aircraft manufacturers in both the East and the West. These programmes currently include the

multi-purpose PZL-104 Wilga, the PZL-106 Kruk and M-18 Dromader agricultural aircraft; wing and tail component assembly for the Soviet Il-86 wide-bodied transport; the PZL-110 Koliber and M-20 Mewa light multi-purpose, training and sporting aircraft; local service transports such as the An-2 and An-28; the Mi-2, Kania and Sokól multi-purpose helicopters; sailplanes (see SZD entry in that section); piston, turbojet and turboprop engines (see PZL entries in the Aero Engines section); and aircraft military equipment, propellers, and ground equipment for agricultural aircraft and helicopters.

The export sales of all Polish aviation products are handled by:

Pezetel Foreign Trade Enterprise Co Ltd

Aleja Stanów Zjednoczonych 61, PO Box 6, 00-991 Warszawa 44
Telephone: (022) 10 80 01
Telex: 814651 PZL PL
DIRECTOR AND GENERAL MANAGER:
Jerzy Krezlewicz, MA
MANAGER OF AVIATION DEPARTMENT: Kazimierz Niepsuj
MANAGER OF PUBLICITY DEPARTMENT:
Ing Wojciech Kowalczyk

IL

INSTYTUT LOTNICTWA (Aviation Institute)

Al. Krakowska 110/114, 02-256 Warszawa-Okecie
Telephone: 460011 and 460993
Telex: 813537
GENERAL MANAGER: Ing Marian Pitat
CHIEF CONSULTANT FOR SCIENTIFIC AND TECHNICAL
CO-OPERATION: Dipl Eng Jerzy Grzegorzewski, MScEng

Founded in 1926, the Instytut Lotnictwa is directly subordinate to the Ministry of Heavy and Machine Building Industry and is responsible for all research and development work in the Polish aviation industry. It conducts scientific research, including the investigation of problems associated with low-speed and high-speed aerodynamics, static and fatigue tests, development and testing of aero engines, flight instruments, space science instrumentation, and other equipment, flight tests, and materials technology. It is also responsible for the construction of aircraft and aero engines, the latest such programme being the I-22 two-seat jet trainer.

PZL I-22 IRYD (IRIDIUM)

Pictures of this new jet trainer and light attack aircraft first appeared in a Polish television programme in October 1986, and it was identified by the designation I-22 a few weeks later, although the prototype had made its first flight as long ago as 3 March 1985.

The I-22 was designed at the Instytut Lotnictwa by a team led by chief designer Dr Eng Alfred Baron. They were assisted by the Ośrodek Badawczo-Rozwojowy Sprzetu Komunikacyjnego (Communications Equipment Research and Development Centre) at Mielec, where the prototypes were built, and various other Polish aviation industry establishments. The aircraft has been flown by a number of industry and air force pilots, and the flight test programme was continuing in 1988.

Evidently intended as a successor to the PZL Mielec TS-11 Iskra, the I-22 has been designed to cover the full spectrum of pilot, navigation, air combat, reconnaissance and ground attack training, with day/night and bad-weather capability. This versatility, coupled with the ability to operate from unprepared airstrips and carry a useful variety of ordnance, enables the I-22 also to fulfil the role of light close support aircraft. To this end, the airframe is designed to be tolerant of battle damage, capable of quick and inexpensive repair, and is stressed to a standard that will permit later the use of more powerful engines (one designated K-15 is reportedly under development) and the carriage of a greater weapons load, without jeopardising permissible load factors. Service life of the I-22 has been calculated on the basis of 2,500 flying hours or 10,000 take-offs and landings.

TYPE: Two-seat advanced jet trainer, reconnaissance and light close support aircraft.

WINGS: Cantilever high-wing monoplane, with 18° sweep-back on leading-edges, non-swept trailing-edges, and 4° 30′ anhedral from roots. Two-spar all-metal stressed skin structure, built as one unit with centre and inboard portions forming integral fuel tanks. Laminar flow aerofoil section, with multi-stage geometric and aerodynamic twist. All-metal mass balanced ailerons, actuated by pushrods with hydraulic boost. All-metal single-slotted trailing-edge flaps deflect hydraulically (20° for take-off, 40° for landing), with auxiliary pneumatic system for emergency deflection in the event of hydraulic failure.

FUSELAGE: Conventional oval-section all-metal semi-monocoque structure of frames and longerons, with aluminium alloy skin. Door type airbrake on each side beneath centre-fuselage, actuated hydraulically.

Three-view drawing *(Pilot Press)* **and photographs** *(Lech Zielaskowski)* **of the PZL I-22 tandem-seat advanced trainer, reconnaissance and ground attack aircraft**

TAIL UNIT: Conventional all-metal structure, with sweepback on all surfaces. Curved fillet at base of fin. Variable incidence tailplane, mid-mounted on fuselage tailcone, is actuated hydraulically; will have slight anhedral on production version. Mass balanced elevators and rudder, actuated by pushrods. Ground adjustable tab on rudder.

LANDING GEAR: Retractable tricycle type, with single wheel and low pressure tubeless tyre on each unit. Hydraulic extension and retraction: nose unit retracts forward, main units upward into engine nacelles. Auxiliary pneumatic system for lowering gear in an emergency. Oleo-pneumatic shock absorber in each unit. Hydraulic disc brakes on mainwheels; auxiliary mainwheel parking brake serves also as emergency brake. Braking parachute in fuselage tailcone. Small tail bumper under rear of fuselage.

POWER PLANT: Two 10.79 kN (2,425 lb st) PZL Rzeszów SO-3W22 non-afterburning turbojets, pod mounted on lower sides of centre-fuselage. Fuel in three integral wing tanks (combined capacity 1,180 litres; 312 US gallons; 259.5 Imp gallons) and two fuselage tanks (combined capacity 1,360 litres; 359 US gallons; 299 Imp gallons), to give total internal capacity of 2,540 litres (671 US gallons; 558.5 Imp gallons). Provision for one 400 litre (106 US gallon; 88 Imp gallon) auxiliary tank to be carried under each wing. Fuel system permits up to 30 s of inverted flight. Single-point pressure refuelling (at front of port engine nacelle), plus gravity filling point for each tank. Air intakes anti-iced by engine bleed air.

ACCOMMODATION: Pressurised, heated and air-conditioned cockpit, with tandem seating for pupil (in front) and instructor; rear seat elevated 400 mm (15¾ in). For solo flying, pilot occupies front seat. Back-type parachute, oxygen bottle and emergency pack for both occupants. Individual framed canopies, each hinged at rear and opening upward pneumatically. Rearview mirror in front cockpit. VS-1 rocket assisted ejection seats, fitted with canopy breakers, can be operated at zero altitude and at speeds down to 81 knots (150 km/h; 93 mph). Dual controls standard; front cockpit equipped for IFR flying. Windscreen anti-iced by electric heating, supplemented by alcohol spray. Remaining transparencies anti-iced and demisted by hot engine bleed air.

SYSTEMS: Cockpits pressurised and air-conditioned by engine bleed air. Air from air-conditioning system also used to pressurise crew's g suits. Main hydraulic system, nominal pressure 210 bars (3,045 lb/sq in), actuates landing gear extension and retraction, wing flaps, airbrakes, tailplane incidence, brake-chute deployment, differential braking of mainwheels, and parking/ emergency brake. Auxiliary hydraulic system for aileron control boost. Pneumatic system comprises three separate circuits, each with a nitrogen bottle pressurised at 150 bars (2,175 lb/sq in): one powers emergency extension of wing flaps for landing, one the emergency extension of the landing gear; the third is for canopy opening, closing and sealing, windscreen fluid de-icing system, and hydraulic reservoir pressurisation. All three bottles charged simultaneously through a common nozzle. Electrical system, powered by two 9kW DC starter/generators, supplies 115V single-phase AC (via two 1kVA static converters) and 36V three-phase AC (via 500VA electro-mechanical converters), both at 400Hz; two 24V batteries provide DC power in the event of a double failure. Each AC voltage is supplied by one main converter and one standby, the latter automatically assuming full load if a main converter fails. Engine fire detection and extinguishing system (two freon bottles in rear fuselage). Electronic control system for gun firing and weapon release.

AVIONICS AND EQUIPMENT: Avionics bays in nose and under floor of rear cockpit. Avionics include VHF and UHF multi-channel com radio; ADF; radar altimeter for low level flying; marker beacon receiver; ILS; IFF; and audio-visual radar warning system. Blind-flying instrumentation. Flight data recorder in dorsal fin fillet.

ARMAMENT: One 23 mm GSh-23L twin-barrel cannon in underfuselage pack, with up to 200 rds (50 rds normally carried for training missions), plus gyro gunsight and nose mounted gun camera. Four underwing attachments, each stressed for load of up to 500 kg (1,102 lb), for bombs, guided or unguided rockets, or (inboard stations only) auxiliary fuel tanks.

DIMENSIONS, EXTERNAL:

Wing span	9.60 m (31 ft 6 in)
Wing aspect ratio	4.6
Length overall	13.22 m (43 ft 4½ in)
Height overall	4.30 m (14 ft 1¼ in)
Wheel track	2.71 m (8 ft 10¾ in)
Wheelbase	4.90 m (16 ft 1 in)

AREAS:

Wings, gross	19.92 m² (214.4 sq ft)
Ailerons (total)	1.362 m² (14.66 sq ft)
Trailing-edge flaps (total)	3.36 m² (36.17 sq ft)
Airbrakes (total)	0.60 m² (6.46 sq ft)
Fin	2.72 m² (29.28 sq ft)
Rudder, incl tab	0.957 m² (10.30 sq ft)
Tailplane	3.14 m² (33.80 sq ft)
Elevators (total)	1.694 m² (18.23 sq ft)

WEIGHTS AND LOADINGS:

Operational weight empty	3,962 kg (8,735 lb)
Max fuel weight: internal	2,120 kg (4,674 lb)
external:	640 kg (1,411 lb)
Max external stores load	1,200 kg (2,645 lb)
Max T-O weight	7,493 kg (16,519 lb)
Max wing loading	376.15 kg/m² (77.08 lb/sq ft)
Max power loading	694.6 kg/kN (6.81 lb/lb st)

PERFORMANCE:

Max Mach number	0.85
Max level speed at S/L, ISA	494 knots (915 km/h; 568 mph)
Max cruising speed at altitude	499 knots (924 km/h; 574 mph)
Max rate of climb at S/L, ISA	2,220 m (7,283 ft)/min
Service ceiling	12,600 m (41,340 ft)
T-O run	770 m (2,525 ft)
T-O to 15 m (50 ft)	1,020 m (3,350 ft)
Landing from 15 m (50 ft)	950 m (3,115 ft)
Landing run	330 m (1,085 ft)
Range with max internal fuel	901 nm (1,670 km; 1,037 miles)
g limits ('clean')	+8/−4

WSK-PZL KROSNO
WYTWÓRNIA SPRZETU KOMUNIKACYJNEGO-PZL KROSNO (Transport Equipment Manufacturing Centre, Krosno)
38-400 Krosno n. Wislokiem

Telephone: 229 11
Telex: 065247 or 065263
GENERAL MANAGER: Ing Jan Czerniecki

PZL KROSNO KR-02
First flown in late 1982, the KR-02 is a very small aerobatic aircraft powered by a 45 kW (60 hp) PZL-F flat-twin engine. Flight testing was suspended in order to give priority to the Puchatek glider (see Sailplanes section), and had not been resumed by early 1988. All known details of the KR-02 can be found in the 1987-88 edition.

WSK-PZL MIELEC
WYTWÓRNIA SPRZETU KOMUNIKACYJ-NEGO-PZL MIELEC (Transport Equipment Manufacturing Centre, Mielec)
ul. Ludowego Wojska Polskiego 3, 39-300 Mielec
Telephone: Mielec 7010
Telex: 0632293 C WSK PL
GENERAL MANAGER: Tadeusz Ryczaj, MSc
COMMERCIAL DIRECTOR: Marian Krzemień, MSc
PRESS RELATIONS OFFICER: Manfred Sieroń

Largest and best equipped aircraft factory in Poland, the PZL factory at Mielec was founded in 1938, and had produced more than 13,500 aircraft by 1 January 1988. In current production are the An-2 general utility biplane, the An-28 twin-turboprop light general purpose transport, the Dromader series of agricultural aircraft and the twin-engined M-20 Mewa executive and ambulance aircraft. Production of the TS-11 Iskra jet trainer ended in 1987 after 23 years. In 1977 Mielec began to manufacture components, including fins, tailplanes, engine pylons, and wing slats and flaps, for the Ilyushin Il-86 Soviet wide-bodied transport. By 1 January 1988 Mielec had completed 223 shipsets of these Il-86 components.

PZL MIELEC (ANTONOV) An-2 ANTEK
NATO reporting name: Colt
The prototype of the An-2, designed to a specification of the Ministry of Agriculture and Forestry of the USSR, made its first flight on 31 August 1947. In 1948 the aircraft went into production in the USSR as the An-2, with a 746 kW (1,000 hp) ASh-62 engine.

By 1960, more than 5,000 An-2s had been built in the Soviet Union, as fully described in previous editions of *Jane's*. Licence rights were granted to China, where the first locally produced An-2 was completed in December 1957, as the Yunshuji-5 or Y-5. Limited production continues in China.

Since 1960, apart from a few dozen Soviet built An-2Ms (1971-72 *Jane's*), continued production of the An-2 has been primarily the responsibility of PZL Mielec, the original licence arrangement providing for two basic versions: the An-2T transport and An-2R agricultural version. The first Polish built An-2 was flown on 23 October 1960. Mielec has since built more than 11,200 An-2s for domestic use and for export to the USSR (more than 10,600), Bulgaria, Czechoslovakia, Egypt, France, the German Democratic Republic, Hungary, North Korea, Mongolia, Netherlands, Romania, Sudan, Tunisia and Yugoslavia. They include approx 7,500 An-2Rs.

Polish built versions have different designations from those built in the USSR. They include the An-2 Geofiz; An-2LW; An-2P, PK, P-Photo and PR; An-2R; An-2S; An-2T, TD and TP. Further details of these can be found in the 1983-84 and earlier editions of *Jane's*.

The following details apply to the PZL Mielec An-2P:

TYPE: Single-engined general purpose biplane.

WINGS: Unequal span single-bay biplane. Wing section RPS 14% (constant). Dihedral, both wings, approx 2° 48'. All-metal two-spar structure, fabric covered aft of front spar. I type interplane struts. Differential ailerons and full span automatic leading-edge slots on upper wings, slotted trailing-edge flaps on both upper and lower wings. Flaps operated electrically, ailerons mechanically by cables and push/pull rods. Electrically operated trim tab in port aileron.

PZL Mielec (Antonov) An-2R aircraft with spraygear stowed *(Peter J. Bish)*

FUSELAGE: All-metal stressed skin semi-monocoque structure of circular section forward of cabin, rectangular in the cabin section and oval in the tail section.

TAIL UNIT: Braced metal structure. Fin integral with rear fuselage. Fabric covered tailplane. Elevators and rudder operated mechanically by cables and push/pull rods. Electrically operated trim tab in rudder and port elevator.

LANDING GEAR: Non-retractable split axle type, with long stroke oleo shock absorbers. Mainwheel tyres size 800 × 260 mm, pressure 2.25 bars (32.7 lb/sq in). Pneumatic shoe brakes on main units. Fully castoring and self-centring PZL Krosno tailwheel, size 470 × 210, with electro-pneumatic lock. For rough field operation the oleo-pneumatic shock absorbers can be charged from a compressed air cylinder installed in the rear fuselage. Interchangeable ski landing gear available optionally.

POWER PLANT: One 746 kW (1,000 hp) PZL Kalisz ASz-62IR nine-cylinder radial aircooled engine, driving an AW-2 four-blade variable-pitch metal propeller. Six fuel tanks in upper wings, with total capacity of 1,200 litres (317 US gallons; 264 Imp gallons). Oil capacity 120 litres (31.7 US gallons; 26.4 Imp gallons).

ACCOMMODATION: Crew of two on flight deck, with access via passenger cabin. Standard accommodation for 12 passengers, in four rows of three with centre aisle. Two foldable seats for children in aisle between first and second rows, and infant's cradle at front of cabin on starboard side. Toilet at rear of cabin on starboard side. Overhead racks for up to 160 kg (352 lb) of baggage, with space for coats and additional 40 kg (88 lb) of baggage between rear pair of seats and toilet. Emergency exit on starboard side at rear. Walls of cabin are lined with glass-wool mats and inner facing of plywood to reduce internal noise level. Cabin floor is carpeted. Cabin heating and starboard windscreen de-icing by engine bleed air; port and centre windscreens are electrically de-iced. Cabin ventilation by ram air intakes on underside of top wings.

SYSTEMS: Compressed air cylinder, of 8 litres (0.28 cu ft) capacity, for pneumatic charging of shock absorbers and operation of tailwheel lock at 49 bars (711 lb/sq in) pressure and operation of mainwheel brakes at 9.80 bars (142 lb/sq in). Contents of cylinder are maintained by AK-50 P engine driven compressor, with AD-50 automatic relief device to prevent overpressure. DC electrical system is supplied with basic 27V power (and 36V or 115V where required) by an engine driven generator and a storage battery. CO_2 fire extinguishing system with automatic fire detector.

AVIONICS AND EQUIPMENT: Dual controls and blind-flying instrumentation standard. R-842 HF and RS-6102 or Baklan-5 VHF lightweight radio transceivers, RW-UM radio altimeter, ARK-9 radio compass, MRP-56P marker beacon receiver, GIK-1 gyro compass, GPK-48 gyroscopic direction indicator and SPU-7 intercom.

DIMENSIONS, EXTERNAL:
Wing span: upper	18.18 m (59 ft 7¾ in)
lower	14.24 m (46 ft 8½ in)
Wing chord (constant): upper	2.45 m (8 ft 0½ in)
lower	2.00 m (6 ft 6¾ in)
Wing aspect ratio: upper	7.6
lower	7.1
Wing gap	2.17 m (7 ft 1½ in)
Length overall: tail up	12.74 m (41 ft 9½ in)
tail down	12.40 m (40 ft 8¼ in)
Height overall: tail up	6.10 m (20 ft 0 in)
tail down	4.01 m (13 ft 2 in)
Tailplane span	7.20 m (23 ft 7½ in)
Wheel track	3.36 m (11 ft 0¼ in)
Wheelbase	8.19 m (26 ft 10½ in)
Propeller diameter	3.60 m (11 ft 9¾ in)
Propeller ground clearance	0.69 m (2 ft 3¼ in)
Cargo door (port): Mean height	1.55 m (5 ft 1 in)
Mean width	1.39 m (4 ft 6¾ in)
Emergency exit (stbd, rear): Height	0.65 m (2 ft 1½ in)
Width	0.51 m (1 ft 8 in)

DIMENSIONS, INTERNAL:
Cargo compartment: Length	4.10 m (13 ft 5½ in)
Max width	1.60 m (5 ft 3 in)
Max height	1.80 m (5 ft 11 in)

AREAS:
Wings, gross: upper	43.54 m² (468.7 sq ft)
lower	27.98 m² (301.2 sq ft)
Ailerons (total)	5.90 m² (63.5 sq ft)
Trailing-edge flaps (total)	9.60 m² (103 sq ft)
Fin	3.20 m² (34.4 sq ft)
Rudder, incl tab	2.65 m² (28.52 sq ft)
Tailplane	7.56 m² (81.4 sq ft)
Elevators (total, incl tab)	4.72 m² (50.81 sq ft)

WEIGHTS AND LOADINGS:
Weight empty	3,450 kg (7,605 lb)
Max T-O weight	5,500 kg (12,125 lb)
Max landing weight	5,250 kg (11,574 lb)
Max wing loading	76.82 kg/m² (15.7 lb/sq ft)
Max power loading	7.38 kg/kW (12.13 lb/hp)

PERFORMANCE (at AUW of 5,250 kg; 11,574 lb):
Max level speed at 1,750 m (5,740 ft)	139 knots (258 km/h; 160 mph)
Econ cruising speed	100 knots (185 km/h; 115 mph)
Min flying speed	49 knots (90 km/h; 56 mph)
T-O speed	43 knots (80 km/h; 50 mph)
Landing speed	46 knots (85 km/h; 53 mph)
Max rate of climb at S/L	210 m (689 ft)/min
Service ceiling	4,400 m (14,425 ft)
Time to 4,400 m (14,425 ft)	30 min
T-O run: hard runway	150 m (492 ft)
grass	170 m (558 ft)
T-O to 15 m (50 ft): hard runway	475 m (1,558 ft)
grass	495 m (1,624 ft)
Landing from 15 m (50 ft): hard runway	427 m (1,401 ft)
grass	432 m (1,417 ft)
Landing run: hard runway	170 m (558 ft)
grass	185 m (607 ft)
Range at 1,000 m (3,280 ft) with 500 kg (1,102 lb) payload	485 nm (900 km; 560 miles)

PZL MIELEC (ANTONOV) An-28
NATO reporting name: Cash

The prototype of this enlarged turboprop version of the piston-engined An-14 light general purpose transport

(SSSR-1968), initially designated An-14M, flew for the first time in the USSR in September 1969, powered by two 604 kW (810 shp) Isotov TVD-850 turboprop engines. It was described in the Soviet section of the 1974-75 and previous editions of *Jane's*; differences from the original An-14, and subsequent design changes, have been recorded in the 1983-84 and earlier editions.

Official Soviet flight testing was completed in 1972, and the production designation An-28 was allocated during 1973. The first pre-production An-28 (SSSR-19723) originally retained the same engines as the prototype, but in April 1975 (re-registered SSSR-19753) it flew for the first time with 716 kW (960 shp) Glushenkov TVD-10 turboprops, which are installed also in production An-28s.

The Antonov bureau developed the An-28 for service on Aeroflot's shortest routes, particularly those operated by An-2s into places relatively inaccessible to other fixed-wing types. Turboprops make possible full-payload operation under high temperature conditions and in mountainous regions; and the An-28 is suitable for carrying passengers, cargo and mail, for scientific expeditions, geological survey, forest fire patrol, air ambulance or rescue operations, and parachute training.

The An-28 will not stall, even with the control column held in the extreme rearward position, because of the action of its automatic slots. If an engine fails, the upper surface spoiler forward of the aileron on the opposite wing is opened automatically; as a result, the wing bearing the 'dead' engine drops only 12° in 5 s instead of the 30° that it would drop through loss of lift without the action of the Antonov patented spoiler. The fixed tailplane slat, also patented, improves handling during a high angle of attack climbout. Under icing conditions, if the normal anti-icing system fails, ice collects on the slat rather than the tailplane, to retain controllability.

Series production of the An-28 was entrusted to PZL Mielec in 1978, and a temporary type certificate, under Soviet NLGS-2 regulations, was awarded on 4 October that year to the second Soviet built pre-production aircraft (originally SSSR-19754, later SSSR-48105).

Polish manufacture began with an initial batch of 15 aircraft, and 42 had been completed by the beginning of 1988. First flight by a Polish built An-28 (SSSR-28800) was made on 22 July 1984, and the following description applies to this version, which received its full Soviet type certificate on 7 February 1986:

TYPE: Twin-turboprop short-range passenger transport.

WINGS: Braced high-wing monoplane, with single streamline section bracing strut each side. Wing section TsAGI P-II-14 (thickness/chord ratio 14%). Constant chord, non-swept no-dihedral centre-section, set at 4° incidence; tapered outer panels have 2° dihedral, negative incidence

and 2° sweepback at quarter-chord. Conventional two-spar all-duralumin torsion box structure, with steel attachment fittings. Duralumin automatic leading-edge slats over full span of outer panels. Entire trailing-edges hinged, the single-slotted mass and aerodynamically balanced ailerons being designed to droop with the large, two-segment double-slotted flaps. Unpowered ailerons and hydraulically actuated flaps are of duralumin, with fabric and CFRP skins respectively; port aileron has a CFRP trim tab. Slab type spoiler, also of CFRP, forward of each aileron and each outer flap segment at 75 per cent chord. Thermal anti-icing of wing leading-edges by engine bleed air. Short stub-wing extends from each side of the lower fuselage, carrying the main landing gear unit and providing lower attachment for the wing bracing strut.

FUSELAGE: Conventional all-metal semi-monocoque non-pressurised structure. Underside of rear fuselage upswept and incorporating clamshell doors for passenger and cargo loading.

TAIL UNIT: Cantilever all-metal structure. Twin fins and rudders, mounted vertically on an inverted-aerofoil, no-dihedral fixed incidence tailplane. Fixed leading-edge slat under full span of tailplane leading-edge. Electrically actuated trim tab in each rudder and each elevator; main controls are unpowered. Thermal (engine bleed air) anti-icing of tailplane and fin leading-edges.

LANDING GEAR: Non-retractable tricycle type, with single Soviet built wheel and PZL oleo-pneumatic shock absorber on each unit. Main units have wide tread balloon tyres of Soviet manufacture, size 720 × 320 mm, pressure 3.5 bars (51 lb/sq in), and are mounted on small stub-wings which curve forward and downward at front to serve as mudguards. Steerable (50° left and right) and self-centring nosewheel, with size 595 × 185 × 280 mm Stomil (Poland) tyre, pressure 3.5 bars (51 lb/sq in). Soviet multi-disc hydraulic brakes on main units, and Soviet inertial anti-skid units.

POWER PLANT: Two 716 kW (960 shp) PZL Rzeszów TVD-10B turboprops, each driving an AW-24AN three-blade automatic propeller with full feathering and reversible-pitch capability. Two centre-section and two outer-wing integral fuel tanks in wing spar boxes, with total capacity of 1,960 litres (518 US gallons; 431 Imp gallons). Refuelling point on each tank. Oil capacity 16 litres (4.2 US gallons; 3.5 Imp gallons) per engine. Air intakes lined with epoxy laminate and anti-iced by engine bleed air; propellers, spinners and pitot heads anti-iced electrically.

ACCOMMODATION: Pilot and co-pilot on flight deck, which has bulged side windows and electric anti-icing for windscreens, and is separated from main cabin by a

Polish built Antonov An-28 light general purpose transport (two PZL Rzeszow TVD-10B turboprops) *(Lech Zielaskowski)*

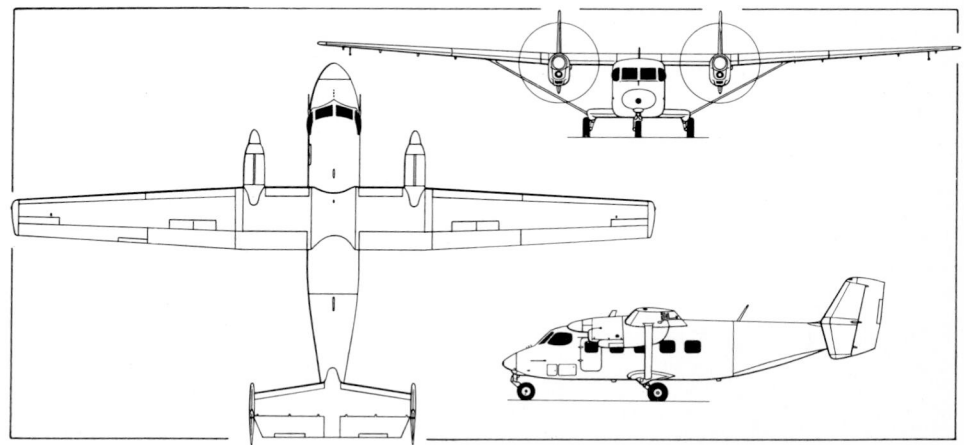

Antonov An-28 passenger transport, produced in Poland by WSK-PZL Mielec *(Pilot Press)*

bulkhead with connecting door. Dual controls standard. Jettisonable emergency door at front on each side. Standard cabin layout of passenger version has seats for 17 people, with six single seats on port side, one single seat and five double seats on starboard side of aisle, at 72 cm (28 in) pitch. Aisle width 34.5 cm (13.5 in). Five passenger windows in each side of cabin. Seats fold back against walls when aircraft is operated as a freighter or in mixed passenger/cargo role, the seat attachments providing cargo tiedown points. Hoist of 500 kg (1,102 lb) capacity able to deposit cargo in forward part of cabin. Entire cabin heated, ventilated and soundproofed. Outward/downward opening clamshell double door, under upswept rear fuselage, for passenger and cargo loading. Emergency exit at rear of cabin on each side.

SYSTEMS: No air-conditioning, pressurisation or pneumatic systems. Hydraulic system for flap and spoiler actuation, mainwheel brakes and nosewheel steering, with emergency backup system for spoiler extension and mainwheel braking. Primary electrical system is three-phase AC, with two engine driven alternators providing 200/115V power for heating systems, engine vibration monitoring, fuel pump, radio, recorders, and instrument lights. Transformer-rectifiers on this system provide 36V AC power for pressure gauges, artificial horizon, navigation and recording equipment, and 27V DC for control systems and signalling, internal and external lighting, firefighting system, propeller pitch control and feathering, radio, and engine starting and monitoring systems. In emergency, 36V AC can be provided by a static inverter and 27V DC by two 25Ah batteries. Thermal (engine bleed air) anti-icing of outer-wing, fin and tailplane leading-edges. Electric anti-icing of flight deck windscreens, propellers, spinners and pitot heads. Oxygen system (for crew plus two passengers) optional. No APU.

AVIONICS: Standard avionics include Baklan-5 (USSR) VHF com radio, R-855UM (USSR) VHF emergency locator transmitter, ARK-15 radio compass, MRP-66 marker beacon receiver, RW-5 or A-037 radio altimeter, Grebien-1 navigation unit, BUR-1-2A flight recorder, and SGU-6 intercom. Blind-flying instrumentation standard.

DIMENSIONS, EXTERNAL:
Wing span	22.063 m (72 ft 4½ in)
Wing chord: at root	2.20 m (7 ft 2½ in)
mean aerodynamic	1.886 m (6 ft 2¼ in)
at tip	1.10 m (3 ft 7¼ in)
Wing aspect ratio	12.25
Length overall	13.10 m (42 ft 11¾ in)
Fuselage: Length	12.68 m (41 ft 7¼ in)
Max width	1.90 m (6 ft 2¾ in)
Max depth	2.14 m (7 ft 0¼ in)
Height overall	4.90 m (16 ft 1 in)
Tailplane span	5.14 m (16 ft 10¼ in)
Wheel track	3.405 m (11 ft 2 in)
Wheelbase	4.354 m (14 ft 3½ in)
Propeller diameter	2.80 m (9 ft 2¼ in)
Propeller ground clearance	1.25 m (4 ft 1¼ in)
Distance between propeller centres	5.20 m (17 ft 0¾ in)
Rear clamshell doors: Length	2.40 m (7 ft 10½ in)
Total width: at top	1.00 m (3 ft 3¼ in)
at sill	1.40 m (4 ft 7 in)
Emergency exits (rear, each): Height	0.91 m (3 ft 0 in)
Width	0.51 m (1 ft 8 in)

DIMENSIONS, INTERNAL:
Cabin, excl flight deck: Length	5.26 m (17 ft 3 in)
Max width	1.74 m (5 ft 8½ in)
Max height	1.60 m (5 ft 3 in)
Floor area	approx 7.5 m² (80.73 sq ft)
Volume	approx 14.0 m³ (494.4 cu ft)

AREAS:
Wings, gross	39.72 m² (427.5 sq ft)
Ailerons (total)	4.33 m² (46.61 sq ft)
Trailing-edge flaps (total)	7.986 m² (85.96 sq ft)
Spoilers (total)	1.667 m² (17.94 sq ft)
Fins (total)	10.00 m² (107.64 sq ft)
Rudders (total, incl tabs)	4.00 m² (43.06 sq ft)
Tailplane	8.85 m² (95.26 sq ft)
Elevators (total, incl tabs)	2.56 m² (27.56 sq ft)

WEIGHTS AND LOADINGS:
Weight empty, equipped	3,900 kg (8,598 lb)
Max fuel load	1,529 kg (3,371 lb)
Max payload	2,000 kg (4,409 lb)
Max T-O and landing weight	6,500 kg (14,330 lb)
Normal wing loading	153.5 kg/m² (31.5 lb/sq ft)
Max power loading	4.64 kg/kW (7.62 lb/shp)

PERFORMANCE (at max T-O weight):
Never-exceed speed	210 knots (390 km/h; 242 mph)
Max level and max cruising speed at 3,000 m (9,850 ft)	189 knots (350 km/h; 217 mph)
Econ cruising speed at 3,000 m (9,850 ft)	181 knots (335 km/h; 208 mph)
Lift-off speed	73 knots (135 km/h; 84 mph)
Approach speed	70 knots (130 km/h; 81 mph)
Landing speed, flaps down	76 knots (140 km/h; 87 mph)
Max rate of climb at S/L	500 m (1,640 ft)/min
Rate of climb at S/L, one engine out	210 m (689 ft)/min
Service ceiling	above 6,000 m (19,685 ft)
Min ground turning radius	16.00 m (52 ft 6 in)
T-O run	260 m (853 ft)
T-O to 10.7 m (35 ft)	360 m (1,180 ft)
Landing from 15 m (50 ft)	315 m (1,035 ft)
Landing run	170 m (558 ft)

Range:
max payload, no reserves	302 nm (560 km; 348 miles)
max fuel and 1,000 kg (2,205 lb) payload, 30 min reserves	736 nm (1,365 km; 848 miles)
g limit	+3

PZL MIELEC TS-11 ISKRA-BIS (SPARK)

Designed in 1957, the TS-11 Iskra two-seat jet trainer flew for the first time on 5 February 1960 and entered quantity production in 1963. Handover of the first Iskra to the Polish Air Force took place in March 1963, and the aircraft entered service in 1964.

Early production Iskras were powered by a 7.66 kN (1,720 lb st) HO-10 Polish designed axial flow turbojet. The intended power plant, the more powerful 9.81 kN (2,205 lb st) SO-1, was introduced from 1967 and the modified but similarly rated SO-3 in 1969. The Iskra-Bis DF final production variant has the uprated SO-3W.

About 500 Iskras had been built by mid-1979. Production was then halted until 1982, when manufacture was resumed. It ended in 1987, the final overall total built being 550. Details of the earlier versions can be found in the 1981-82 and previous editions of *Jane's*; the Iskra-Bis DF was last described in the 1987-88 edition.

PZL MIELEC M-18 DROMADER (DROMEDARY)

Although superficially similar to the PZL Warszawa-Okecie PZL-106 Kruk (which see), the Dromader is an entirely different and much larger agricultural aircraft, and is designed to meet the requirements of FAR Pt 23. Particular attention was paid in the design to pilot safety, and all parts of the structure exposed to contact with chemicals are treated with polyurethane or epoxy enamels, or manufactured from stainless steel. Chief designer is Mr Józef Oleksiak.

The M-18 was first flown on 27 August 1976, and a second prototype flew on 2 October 1976. They were followed by ten pre-series aircraft, of which eight were used for operating trials, two of them spraying and dusting cotton in Egypt during the Summer of 1978, prior to the award of a Polish type certificate on 27 September 1978. The Dromader has also been certificated in Canada, Czechoslovakia, France, the German Democratic Republic,

the USA and Yugoslavia. Any M-18 can be converted to the firefighting role, a prototype for this version having flown for the first time on 11 November 1978.

Series production began in 1979, and a total of 408 production M-18s and M-18As had been built by the beginning of 1988, of which 90 per cent were for export. The two-seat **M-18A** is described separately. Customers include operators in Bulgaria, Canada, Chile, Cuba, Czechoslovakia, the German Democratic Republic, Greece (30 for firefighting), Hungary, Iran, Morocco, Nicaragua, Poland, Swaziland, Trinidad, Turkey, the USA, Venezuela and Yugoslavia. In addition, Melex USA (which see), a US subsidiary of Pezetel, is developing a turboprop version with an 895 kW (1,200 shp) Pratt & Whitney Canada PT6A-45AG engine and Hartzell propeller, known as the **T45 Turbine Dromader**. An amphibious water bomber floatplane version is also under consideration.

The following description refers to the current standard M-18 agricultural version:

TYPE: Single-seat agricultural aircraft.

WINGS: Cantilever all-metal low-wing monoplane, of constant chord, with 1° 25′ dihedral on centre-section and 6° on outer panels. Wing sections NACA 4416 at root, NACA 4412 at end of centre-section, and NACA 4412 on outer panels. Incidence 3°. Single steel capped duralumin spar. All-metal two-section trailing-edge slotted flaps, actuated hydraulically. All-metal slotted ailerons, mass and aerodynamically balanced, actuated by pushrods. Trim tab in each aileron.

FUSELAGE: All-metal structure. Main frame, of helium-arc welded chrome-molybdenum steel tube, oiled internally against corrosion. Duralumin side panels, detachable for airframe inspection and cleaning. Fixed stainless steel bottom covering.

TAIL UNIT: All-metal structure, with braced tailplane. Corrugated skin. Aerodynamically and mass balanced rudder and elevators. Elevator actuated by pushrods; rudder by cables. Trim tab on rudder and each elevator.

LANDING GEAR: Non-retractable tailwheel type. Oleopneumatic shock absorber in each unit. Main units have tyres size 800 × 260 mm, and are fitted with hydraulic disc brakes, parking brake and wire cutters. Fully castoring tailwheel, lockable for take-off and landing, with size 380 × 150 mm tyre.

POWER PLANT: One 746 kW (1,000 hp) PZL Kalisz ASz-62IR nine-cylinder radial aircooled supercharged engine, driving a PZL Warszawa AW-2-30 four-blade constant-speed aluminium propeller. Integral fuel tank in each

PZL Mielec M-18 Dromader (ASz-62IR radial engine) *(Lech Zielaskowski)*

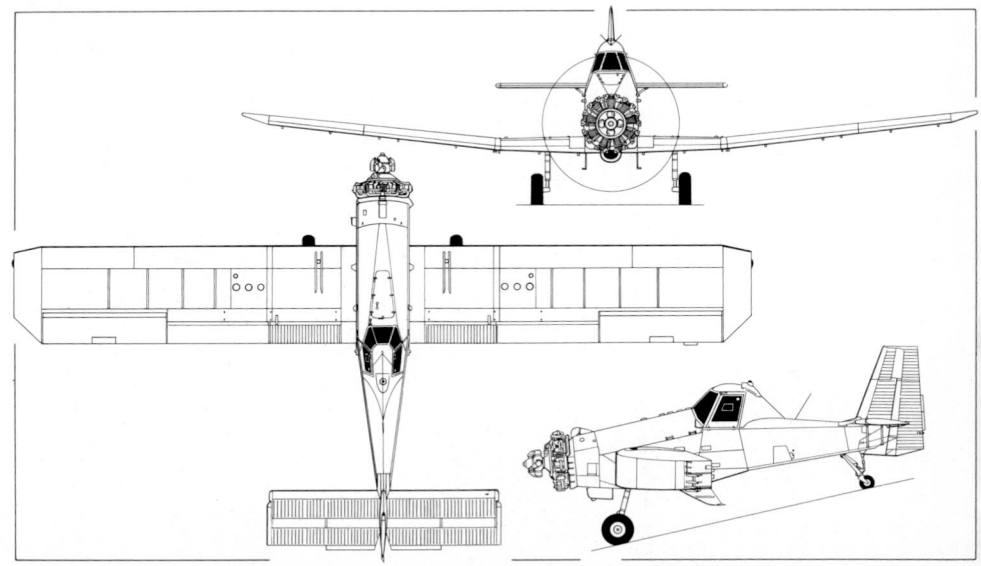

PZL Mielec M-18 Dromader single-seat agricultural aircraft *(Pilot Press)*

outer wing panel, combined usable capacity 400 or 712
litres (105.7 or 188 US gallons; 88 or 156.6 Imp gallons).
Gravity feed header tank in fuselage.

ACCOMMODATION: Single adjustable seat in fully enclosed,
sealed and ventilated cockpit which is stressed to
withstand 40*g* impact. Glassfibre cockpit roof and
rear fairing. Adjustable shoulder type safety harness.
Adjustable rudder pedals. Baggage compartment aft of
seat. Quick-opening door on each side; port door
jettisonable.

SYSTEMS: Hydraulic system, pressure 98-137 bars
(1,421-1,987 lb/sq in), for flap actuation, disc brakes and
dispersal system. Electrical system powered by 28.5V
100A generator, with 24V 25Ah nickel-cadmium battery
and overvoltage protection relay.

AVIONICS AND EQUIPMENT: RS6102 (Polish built), King KX
175B or KY 195B com transceiver, KI 201C nav receiver,
VOR-OBS indicator, gyro compass, radio compass, stall
warning, landing lights, taxi light and night working light
optional. Navigation lights, cockpit light, instrument
panel lights, and two rotating beacons standard. Built-in
jacking and tiedown points in wings and rear fuselage;
towing lugs on main landing gear. Cockpit fire extinguisher and first aid kit.

AGRICULTURAL AND OTHER EQUIPMENT: Glassfibre epoxy
hopper, with stainless steel tube bracing, forward of
cockpit; capacity 2,500 litres (660 US gallons; 550 Imp
gallons) of liquid or 1,350 kg (2,976 lb) of dry chemical
(1,850 kg; 4,078 lb under CAM 8 conditions). Deflector
cable from cabin roof to fin. The M-18 can be fitted
optionally with several different types of agricultural and
firefighting systems, as follows: spray system with 54/96
nozzles on spraybooms; dusting system with standard,
large or extra large spreader; atomising system with six
atomisers; water bombing installation; and fire-bombing
installation with foaming agents. Aerial application roles
can include seeding, fertilising, weed or pest control,
defoliation, forest and bush firefighting, and patrol
flights. Special wingtip lights permit agricultural flights at
night, and the aircraft can operate in both temperate and
tropical climates.

DIMENSIONS, EXTERNAL:

Wing span	17.70 m (58 ft 0¾ in)
Wing chord, constant	2.286 m (7 ft 6 in)
Wing aspect ratio	7.8
Length overall	9.47 m (31 ft 1 in)
Height over tail fin	3.70 m (12 ft 1¾ in)
Height overall (flying attitude)	4.60 m (15 ft 1 in)
Tailplane span	5.60 m (18 ft 4½ in)
Wheel track	3.48 m (11 ft 5 in)
Propeller diameter	3.30 m (10 ft 10 in)
Propeller ground clearance (tail up)	0.23 m (9 in)

AREAS:

Wings, gross	40.00 m² (430.5 sq ft)
Ailerons (total)	3.84 m² (41.33 sq ft)
Trailing-edge flaps (total)	5.69 m² (61.25 sq ft)
Vertical tail surfaces (total)	2.65 m² (28.5 sq ft)
Horizontal tail surfaces (total)	6.50 m² (70.0 sq ft)

WEIGHTS AND LOADINGS:

Basic weight empty	2,610 kg (5,754 lb)
Weight empty, equipped	
	2,670-2,760 kg (5,886-6,085 lb)
Payload: FAR 23	1,050-1,350 kg (2,315-2,976 lb)
CAM 8	1,550-1,850 kg (3,417-4,078 lb)
Max T-O weight: FAR 23	4,200 kg (9,259 lb)
CAM 8	4,700 kg (10,362 lb)
Max landing weight	4,200 kg (9,259 lb)
Max wing loading (FAR 23)	
	105.0 kg/m² (21.51 lb/sq ft)
Max power loading (FAR 23)	5.63 kg/kW (9.26 lb/hp)

M-18A Dromader for Slov-Air of Czechoslovakia, with four underwing self-filling fuel tanks

PERFORMANCE (at 4,200 kg; 9,259 lb T-O weight, ISA.
A: without agricultural equipment; B: with spreader
equipment):

Never-exceed speed: A	151 knots (280 km/h; 174 mph)
Max level speed: A	138 knots (256 km/h; 159 mph)
B	128 knots (237 km/h; 147 mph)
Cruising speed at S/L:	
A	110 knots (205 km/h; 127 mph)
B	102 knots (190 km/h; 118 mph)
Normal operating speed:	
A	124 knots (230 km/h; 143 mph)
B	108 knots (200 km/h; 124 mph)
Stalling speed, power off, flaps up:	
A, B	65 knots (119 km/h; 74 mph)
Stalling speed, power off, flaps down:	
A, B	59 knots (109 km/h; 68 mph)
Max rate of climb at S/L: A	414 m (1,360 ft)/min
B	340 m (1,115 ft)/min
Service ceiling: A	6,500 m (21,325 ft)
T-O run: A	180-200 m (590-656 ft)
B	210-245 m (689-805 ft)
Landing run: A, B	260-300 m (853-984 ft)
Max range, no reserves:	
A, 400 litres (105.7 US gallons; 88 Imp gallons) fuel	
	291 nm (540 km; 335 miles)
A, 712 litres (188 US gallons; 156.6 Imp gallons) fuel	
	523 nm (970 km; 602 miles)
g limits: FAR 23	+3.4/-1.4
CAM 8	+3/-1.2

PZL MIELEC M-18A DROMADER

Until 1983 the M-18 was produced only as a single-seater;
the M-18A was designed for operators requiring to
transport a ground mechanic/loader to provisional airstrips.
An additional cabin is located behind the cockpit and
separated from it by a wall. The cabin is equipped with a
rigid seat, with protective padding and safety belt, a
port-side jettisonable door, windows (port and starboard),
fire extinguisher, and ventilation valve. Communication
with the pilot is provided via a window in the dividing wall,
and by intercom.

A supplementary Polish type certificate was awarded to
the M-18A on 14 February 1984, and a total of 114
production M-18As had been built by the beginning of
1988. The US FAA type certificate for the M-18 was
extended to the M-18A in September 1987.

All other data are as for the M-18 except:

WEIGHTS:

Basic weight empty	2,690 kg (5,930 lb)
Weight empty, equipped	
	2,750-2,860 kg (6,063-6,305 lb)

PZL MIELEC M-20 MEWA (GULL)

The M-20 Mewa six/seven-seat twin-engined aircraft is
the Polish version of the Piper PA-34-200T Seneca II,
developed under an agreement made with Piper Aircraft
Corporation in 1977. It is designed for passenger transport,
training, liaison and ambulance duties, and is certificated to
FAR Pt 23. The Mewa can be operated from concrete
runways or grass strips, and differs chiefly from the US built
Seneca in being powered by Polish built PZL-F engines.

Adaptation of the PA-34-200T Seneca II airframe to
accept this power plant occupied the first half of 1978, and
the first Polish prototype made its initial flight on 25 July
1979. The Mewa has been produced in three versions, any of
which can be configured for passenger carrying or as an air
ambulance. Details of the M-20 00 (four built in 1979-80)
and M-20 01 (five built in 1983-84) can be found in the
1987-88 and earlier *Jane's*. Current version is:

M-20 02. Polish equipment and 27.5V electrical system.
Fifth M-20 01 rebuilt in 1985, flying for the first time on 10
October that year.

Design of the PZL-F engine installation, and develop-
ment of the Mewa, were conducted by a team led by Mr
Krzysztof Piwek. Production of the Mewa is to be resumed
after the manufacture of PZL-F engines is started at
the Dębica factory, to meet a Polish Ministry of Health and
Welfare order for 40 aircraft. In the meantime it is being
offered (and marketed in the western world by Aircraft
International of Ford, near Salisbury, Wiltshire SP4 6DJ,
England) with a power plant of 164 kW (220 hp) Teledyne
Continental TSIO/LTSIO-360-KB turbocharged engines.

The following details apply to the M-20 02 with PZL-F
engines:

TYPE: Six/seven-seat executive and ambulance aircraft.

WINGS: Cantilever low-wing monoplane. NACA 65₂-415
section constant chord wings, with 7° dihedral from roots
and 2° incidence. Leading-edges sweptforward at root.
Safe-life stressed skin structure of aluminium alloy,
including the Frise ailerons and single-slotted trailing-
edge flaps. Optional pneumatic anti-icing of leading-
edges.

FUSELAGE: Semi-monocoque safe-life structure of aluminium alloy.

TAIL UNIT: Cantilever type, of similar construction to wings,
with sweptback vertical and non-swept horizontal
surfaces. Rudder is aerodynamically and mass balanced,
and fitted with an anti-servo tab. Slab type all-moving
tailplane, with trim tab. Pneumatic anti-icing of fin and
tailplane leading-edges optional.

LANDING GEAR: Hydraulically retractable tricycle type, with
single wheel and oleo strut on each unit. Mainwheels
retract inward into wings, nosewheel forward. Size 6.00-6
wheels on all three units, tyre pressures 3.79 bars (55 lb/sq
in) on main units, 2.76 bars (40 lb/sq in) on nose unit.
Emergency gravity extension. PZL Hydral disc brakes;
parking brake.

POWER PLANT: Two 153 kW (205 hp) PZL-F 6A-350C1L/R
counter-rotating flat-six engines, each driving a PZL
Warszawa-Okęcie US 134 three-blade constant-speed
propeller with spinner and (optionally) electric blade
de-icing. Two 92.75 litre (24.5 US gallon; 20.4 Imp
gallon) fuel tanks in each wing leading-edge; total
standard fuel capacity 371 litres (98 US gallons; 81.6 Imp
gallons). Optional auxiliary tank in each leading-edge can
increase this total to 484.5 litres (128 US gallons; 106.6
Imp gallons). Oil capacity 10 litres (2.64 US gallons; 2.2
Imp gallons) per engine.

ACCOMMODATION: Passenger version seats one or two pilots
plus five or four passengers, with optional seventh seat.
Baggage space aft of rear seats. Ambulance version can
carry one stretcher patient, two medical attendants and
one other person in addition to the pilot. The stretcher
rack replaces the right hand centre seat and, like the seat,
can be quickly and easily removed. The rack has special

PZL Mielec M-20 Mewa, a version of the Piper Seneca II with PZL-F engines

guides which can be connected to the door threshold to facilitate stretcher loading; they can be folded back when the stretcher is on board and locked. There are hooks in the cabin ceiling for suspending a transfusion set, and the aircraft carries an oxygen installation for the patient. The doctor's seat (centre, left) has an earphone and microphone, enabling him to contact the ground for assistance if required, and there is a nurse's seat at the rear. A modified electrical system permits an incubator to be installed.

SYSTEMS: Two independent hydraulic systems, one operating at 154 bars (2,233 lb/sq in) for landing gear extension/retraction and the other at 103.5 bars (1,500 lb/sq in) for wheel braking. Electrical system powered by two 24V 55A alternators and a 24V 25Ah battery. Pneumatic anti-icing system optional.

AVIONICS: Multi-channel VOR/LOC radio and blind-flying instrumentation standard. Radio rangefinder, radio marker, radio compass and three-axis autopilot optional. Polish ARL 1601 ADF, CG 121 slaved gyro, RS 6102 VHF com transceiver, MRF-66 marker transceiver and SSA-1 audio control panel.

DIMENSIONS, EXTERNAL:

Wing span	11.86 m (38 ft 11 in)
Wing chord: at root	1.88 m (6 ft 2 in)
at tip	1.60 m (5 ft 3 in)
Wing aspect ratio	7.3
Length overall	8.72 m (28 ft 7¼ in)
Height overall	3.02 m (9 ft 11 in)
Tailplane span	4.13 m (13 ft 6½ in)
Wheel track	3.37 m (11 ft 0¾ in)
Wheelbase	2.13 m (7 ft 0 in)
Propeller diameter	1.93 m (6 ft 4 in)

DIMENSIONS, INTERNAL:

Cabin: Length	3.17 m (10 ft 4¾ in)
Max width	1.24 m (4 ft 0¾ in)
Max height	1.07 m (3 ft 6¼ in)
Volume	5.53 m³ (195.3 cu ft)

AREAS:

Wings, gross	19.18 m² (206.5 sq ft)
Ailerons (total)	1.17 m² (12.59 sq ft)
Trailing-edge flaps (total)	1.94 m² (20.88 sq ft)
Fin	1.96 m² (21.10 sq ft)
Rudder	0.89 m² (9.58 sq ft)
Tailplane, incl tab	3.60 m² (38.75 sq ft)

WEIGHTS AND LOADINGS:

Weight empty (standard)	1,290 kg (2,844 lb)
Max T-O weight	2,070 kg (4,563 lb)
Max landing weight	1,970 kg (4,343 lb)
Max zero-fuel weight	1,810 kg (3,990 lb)
Max wing loading	107.9 kg/m² (22.10 lb/sq ft)
Max power loading	6.86 kg/kW (11.13 lb/hp)

PERFORMANCE (at max T-O weight):

Never-exceed speed	194 knots (360 km/h; 223 mph)
Max level speed at 1,500 m (4,920 ft)	148 knots (275 km/h; 171 mph)
Econ cruising speed at 1,500 m (4,920 ft)	140 knots (260 km/h; 162 mph)
Stalling speed, flaps down	59 knots (108 km/h; 68 mph)
Max rate of climb at S/L	384 m (1,260 ft)/min
Service ceiling	4,000 m (13,125 ft)
T-O to 15 m (50 ft)	460 m (1,510 ft)
Landing from 15 m (50 ft)	655 m (2,150 ft)
Range, 45 min reserves:	
with max standard fuel	550 nm (1,020 km; 634 miles)
with max standard and auxiliary fuel	734 nm (1,360 km; 845 miles)

PZL MIELEC M-21 DROMADER MINI

This reduced capacity version of the Dromader was developed in response to a need expressed by many users of the M-18 for a smaller version, with a less powerful engine and reduced chemical load. Such a version, it was felt, would form part of a mixed fleet, providing greater flexibility and improved operating costs. As a result, the Research and Development Centre for Transport Industry (Osrodek Badawczo-Rozwojowy Sprzetu Komunikacyjnego) at WSK Mielec began design work on the M-21 in January 1980. Chief designer is Mr Jarosław Rumszewicz.

PZL Mielec M-21 Dromader Mini agricultural aircraft

PZL Mielec M-24 Dromader Super agricultural aircraft (*Lech Zielaskowski*)

Construction of two flying prototypes and static testing of the airframe started in August 1981, and the first prototype (SP-PDM) flew for the first time on 18 June 1982, powered by a PZL-3S engine. First flight of the same aircraft with a PZL-3SR engine was made on 20 October 1983. The second prototype, also with the -3SR engine, made its initial flight on 21 March 1985, gaining a provisional type certificate effective until June 1986 (subsequently extended to June 1987).

Some 70 per cent of parts are common to both the M-18 and M-21, among them the outer wing panels (including flaps and ailerons); rear fuselage (including cockpit and tailwheel); mainwheels and brakes; upper surface of hopper, including hood; parts of the fuel, oil, hydraulic and electrical systems; and some of the agricultural equipment. New to the M-21 are the PZL-3SR engine and its propeller, wing centre-section, enlarged tail surfaces, main landing gear legs, lower part of hopper, and forward fuselage. Some standard subassemblies are, however, used in the new assemblies.

AIRFRAME: Generally similar to M-18, but main landing gear is of split-axle type with oleo-pneumatic shock absorbers.

POWER PLANT: One 447 kW (600 hp) PZL-3SR seven-cylinder aircooled radial engine, driving a US 133 000 four-blade propeller. Fuel capacity as for M-18; oil capacity 75 litres (19.8 US gallons; 16.5 Imp gallons).

SYSTEMS: Hydraulic system pressure 153 bars (2,220 lb/sq in). Electrical system powered by 1.5kW alternator and 18Ah battery.

AVIONICS: RS 6201 Unimor VHF com transceiver.

DIMENSIONS, EXTERNAL:

Wing span	14.51 m (47 ft 7¼ in)
Wing aspect ratio	6.5
Length overall	9.48 m (31 ft 1¼ in)
Height overall	3.11 m (10 ft 2½ in)
Tailplane span	5.60 m (18 ft 4½ in)
Wheel track	2.70 m (8 ft 10¼ in)
Wheelbase	5.86 m (19 ft 2¾ in)
Propeller diameter	3.10 m (10 ft 2 in)
Propeller ground clearance	0.30 m (11¾ in)

AREAS:

Wings, gross	32.60 m² (350.9 sq ft)
Ailerons (total)	3.84 m² (41.33 sq ft)
Trailing-edge flaps (total)	2.78 m² (29.92 sq ft)
Fin	1.80 m² (19.38 sq ft)
Rudder, incl tab	1.44 m² (15.50 sq ft)
Tailplane	3.86 m² (41.55 sq ft)
Elevators (total, incl tabs)	3.42 m² (36.81 sq ft)

WEIGHTS AND LOADINGS:

Basic weight empty	2,060 kg (4,541 lb)
Weight empty, equipped	2,120-2,200 kg (4,674-4,850 lb)
Payload: FAR 23	900 kg (1,984 lb)
FAR 21.25	1,200 kg (2,645 lb)
Max T-O and landing weight:	
FAR 23	3,300 kg (7,275 lb)
FAR 21.25	3,600 kg (7,936 lb)
Max wing loading: FAR 23	101.2 kg/m² (20.73 lb/sq ft)
FAR 21.25	110.4 kg/m² (22.62 lb/sq ft)
Max power loading: FAR 23	7.38 kg/kW (12.12 lb/hp)
FAR 21.25	8.05 kg/kW (13.23 lb/hp)

PERFORMANCE (at 3,300 kg; 7,275 lb T-O weight, ISA):

Never-exceed speed	145 knots (270 km/h; 167 mph)
Max level speed	113 knots (210 km/h; 130 mph)
Normal operating speed	84-97 knots (155-180 km/h; 97-112 mph)
Stalling speed, power off:	
flaps up	65 knots (120 km/h; 75 mph)
flaps down	59 knots (108 km/h; 67 mph)
Max rate of climb at S/L	300 m (985 ft)/min
Service ceiling	4,000 m (13,125 ft)
T-O to 15 m (50 ft)	590 m (1,936 ft)
Landing from 15 m (50 ft)	550 m (1,805 ft)
Landing run	270 m (886 ft)
Range with max fuel, no reserves	324 nm (600 km; 373 miles)
Endurance, 30 min reserves	3 h
g limits	+3.5/-1.4

PZL MIELEC M-24 DROMADER SUPER

Three prototypes of the M-24 are being built, including one for static testing. The first aircraft (SP-PFA) made its initial flight on 14 July 1987, powered by a 746 kW (1,000 hp) ASz-62IR radial engine. Hopper capacity has been increased to 2,700 litres (713 US gallons; 594 Imp gallons) or 1,800 kg (3,968 lb), and other features include wings increased in span and having a new aerofoil section. Chief designer is Mr Józef Oleksiak. A turboprop version is also planned.

DIMENSIONS, EXTERNAL:

Wing span	19.90 m (65 ft 3½ in)
Length overall	10.80 m (35 ft 5¼ in)
Height overall	4.30 m (14 ft 1¼ in)

AREA:

Wings, gross	45.00 m² (484.4 sq ft)

WEIGHTS:

Weight empty	2,870 kg (6,327 lb)
Max T-O weight	5,000 kg (11,023 lb)

PERFORMANCE:

Max cruising speed	119 knots (220 km/h; 137 mph)
Stalling speed, flaps down	59 knots (110 km/h; 68 mph)
Max rate of climb at S/L: 'clean'	300 m (984 ft)/min
with agricultural equipment	180 m (590 ft)/min
Service ceiling	4,000 m (13,125 ft)
T-O to 15 m (50 ft)	340 m (1,116 ft)
Landing from 15 m (50 ft)	470 m (1,542 ft)
Range: standard	971 nm (1,800 km; 1,118 miles)
self-ferry	1,888 nm (3,500 km; 2,175 miles)
g limits	+3.5/-1.4

PZL MIELEC M-26 ISKIERKA (LITTLE SPARK)

The Iskierka is a single-piston-engined aircraft, designed to FAR Pt 23 and intended for civil pilot training and pilot selection for military training. Selected parts and assemblies of the M-20 Mewa were used in the design of the wings, tail unit, landing gear, power plant, and electrical and power systems. Chief designer is Mr Krzysztof Piwek.

The Iskierka is being developed with two different engines, as the **M-26 00** with a PZL-F engine and **M-26 01** with a Textron Lycoming AEIO-540. The first prototype (SP-PIA), with a PZL-F, made its initial flight on 15 July 1986; first flight of the Textron Lycoming powered M-26 01 (SP-PIB) took place on 24 June 1987.

TYPE: Tandem two-seat training aircraft.

WINGS: Cantilever low-wing monoplane. NACA 65_2-415 section constant chord wings, with 7° dihedral from roots and 2° incidence. Sweptforward leading-edges at root. Safe-life stressed skin structure of aluminium alloy, including the Frise ailerons and single-slotted trailing-edge flaps. No spoilers, airbrakes or tabs.

FUSELAGE: Semi-monocoque safe-life structure of aluminium alloy.

TAIL UNIT: Conventional cantilever type, of similar construction to wings, with sweptback vertical and non-swept horizontal surfaces. Fixed incidence tailplane. Trim tab in starboard elevator.

LANDING GEAR: Retractable tricycle type, actuated hydraulically, with single wheel and oleo strut on each unit. Mainwheels retract inward into wings, nosewheel rearward. Size 6.00-6 wheels on all three units; tyre pressures 3.43 bars (50 lb/sq in) on main units, 2.16 bars (31 lb/sq in) on nose unit. PZL Hydral hydraulic disc brakes on mainwheels. Parking brake.

POWER PLANT (M-26 00): One 153 kW (205 hp) PZL-F 6A-350CA flat-six engine, driving a PZL Warszawa-Okecie US 142 three-blade variable-pitch propeller with pointed spinner, or a two-blade Hartzell BHC-C2YF-2CKUF variable-pitch propeller. One 92 litre (24.3 US gallon; 20.2 Imp gallon) fuel tank in each wing leading-edge, plus a 9 litre (2.4 US gallon; 2.0 Imp gallon) fuselage tank, to give total capacity of 193 litres (51 US gallons; 42.4 Imp gallons). Gravity fuelling point in top of each wing tank. Oil capacity 10 litres (2.6 US gallons; 2.2 Imp gallons).

POWER PLANT (M-26 01): One 224 kW (300 hp) Textron Lycoming AEIO-540-L1B5D flat-six engine, driving a Hoffmann HO-V123K-V/200AH-10 three-blade variable-pitch propeller. Second tank in each wing. Total fuel capacity 377 litres (99.6 US gallons; 82.8 Imp gallons). Gravity fuelling point in top of each outer wing tank. Oil capacity 15 litres (4.0 US gallons; 3.3 Imp gallons).

ACCOMMODATION: Tandem seats for pupil (in front) and instructor, under framed canopy which opens sideways to starboard. Rear seat is elevated. Baggage compartment aft of rear seat. Both cockpits heated and ventilated.

SYSTEMS: Two independent hydraulic systems, one operating at 154 bars (2,233 lb/sq in) for landing gear extension/retraction and the other at 103 bars (1,494 lb/sq in) for wheel braking. DC electrical power supplied by a 24V alternator (50A in M-26 00, 100A in M-26 01) and a 25Ah battery.

AVIONICS AND EQUIPMENT: Polish made ARL 1601 ADF system, CG 121 slaved gyro system, RS 6102 VHF com transceiver, SSA-1 audio control panel, and ORS-2M marker beacon receiver standard. Landing light in port wing leading-edge.

DIMENSIONS, EXTERNAL:

Wing span	8.60 m (28 ft 2½ in)
Wing chord: at root	1.88 m (6 ft 2 in)
at tip	1.60 m (5 ft 3 in)
Wing aspect ratio	5.3
Length overall	8.30 m (27 ft 2¾ in)
Height overall	2.96 m (9 ft 8½ in)
Tailplane span	3.80 m (12 ft 5½ in)
Wheel track	2.93 m (9 ft 7¼ in)
Wheelbase	1.93 m (6 ft 4 in)
Propeller diameter	1.90 m (6 ft 2¾ in)

DIMENSIONS, INTERNAL:

Cockpits: Total length	2.91 m (9 ft 6½ in)
Max width	0.88 m (2 ft 10½ in)
Max height	1.30 m (4 ft 3¼ in)

AREAS:

Wings, gross	14.00 m² (150.7 sq ft)

Prototype PZL Mielec M-26 00 Iskierka (153 kW; 205 hp PZL-F 6A-350CA engine)

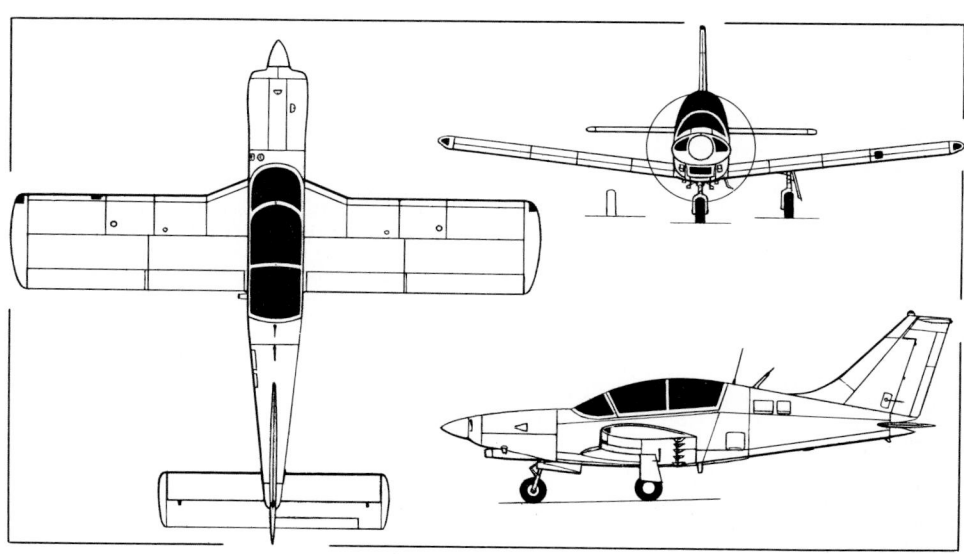

PZL Mielec M-26 Iskierka tandem two-seat primary trainer *(Pilot Press)*

Ailerons (total)	1.17 m² (12.59 sq ft)
Trailing-edge flaps (total)	1.06 m² (11.41 sq ft)
Fin	1.96 m² (21.10 sq ft)
Rudder	0.89 m² (9.58 sq ft)
Tailplane	3.30 m² (35.52 sq ft)
Elevators (total, incl tab)	1.15 m² (12.38 sq ft)

WEIGHTS AND LOADINGS (A: M-26 00, B: M-26 01):

Weight empty: A	850 kg (1,874 lb)
B	940 kg (2,072 lb)
Max fuel weight: A	139 kg (306 lb)
B	271 kg (597 lb)
Max T-O and landing weight: A	1,200 kg (2,645 lb)
B	1,400 kg (3,086 lb)
Max wing loading: A	85.7 kg/m² (17.56 lb/sq ft)
B	100.0 kg/m² (20.5 lb/sq ft)
Max power loading: A	7.86 kg/kW (12.91 lb/hp)
B	6.26 kg/kW (10.29 lb/hp)

PERFORMANCE (estimated, at max T-O weight, A and B as above):

Never-exceed speed:		
A, B		215 knots (400 km/h; 248 mph)
Max level speed at S/L:		
A		143 knots (265 km/h; 165 mph)
B		183 knots (340 km/h; 211 mph)
Stalling speed, flaps down:		
A		53 knots (98 km/h; 61 mph)
B		60 knots (110 km/h; 69 mph)
Max rate of climb at S/L: A		240 m (787 ft)/min
B		480 m (1,575 ft)/min
T-O to 15 m (50 ft): A		450 m (1,476 ft)
B		570 m (1,870 ft)
Landing from 15 m (50 ft): A		430 m (1,411 ft)
B		540 m (1,772 ft)
Range with max fuel, 30 min reserves:		
A		507 nm (940 km; 584 miles)
B		874 nm (1,620 km; 1,006 miles)
g limits: A		+6/-3
B at 1,100 kg (2,425 lb) AUW		+7/-3.5
B at max T-O weight		+4/-1.72

WSK-PZL SWIDNIK
WYTWÓRNIA SPRZETU KOMUNIKACYJ-NEGO lm. ZYGMUNTA PULAWSKIEGO-PZL SWIDNIK (Zygmunt Pulawski Transport Equipment Manufacturing Centre, Swidnik)

21-045 Swidnik k/Lublina
Telephone: Lublin 12061, 12071, 13061 and 13071
Telex: 0642301 WSK PL
GENERAL MANAGER: Andrzej Zeh, MScEng
DIRECTOR OF RESEARCH AND DEVELOPMENT, AND CHIEF DESIGNER: Stanisław Kaminski, MScEng
SALES MANAGER: Jan Widz, MSc
PRESS RELATIONS: Jerzy Jurak, MSc

The factory at Swidnik was established in 1951 and was engaged initially in manufacturing components for the LiM-1 (MiG-15) jet fighter. In 1955, Swidnik began licence production of the Soviet designed Mi-1 helicopter, 1,700 of which were built under the designation SM-1, followed by 450 examples of the Swidnik developed SM-2. A design office was formed at the factory to work on

variants and developments of the basic SM-1 design and on original projects such as the SM-4 Latka.

In September 1957, the Swidnik works was named after the famous pre-war PZL designer Zygmunt Pulawski, and currently employs about 10,000 people. Production is concentrated at present on various developments of the Soviet designed Mil Mi-2 turbine powered helicopter, and manufacture of wing and tailplane slats for the PZL Mielec (Antonov) An-28.

Swidnik, together with other PZL factories at Mielec and Kalisz, is manufacturing components for the Soviet Ilyushin Il-86 wide-bodied airliner.

PZL SWIDNIK (MIL) Mi-2
NATO reporting name: Hoplite

The Mil Mi-2, first flown in September 1961, was designed in the USSR by the Mikhail L. Mil bureau. It retains the basic configuration of Mil's earlier Mi-1 helicopter, but has a larger cabin and, instead of a single piston engine, has two Isotov turboshafts mounted side by side above the cabin.

Armed version of the PZL Swidnik Mi-2, with four pylon mounted 'Sagger' air-to-surface missiles

Development of the two Mi-2 prototypes continued in the USSR until the helicopter had completed its initial State trials programme of flying. Then, in accordance with an agreement signed in January 1964, further development, production and marketing of the Mi-2 were assigned exclusively to the Polish aircraft industry, which flew its own first example of the Mi-2 on 4 November 1965.

Series production began in 1965, and Swidnik has since built more than 5,000 for various civil and military operators; the majority of these have been exported. Among the operators of the Mi-2 are the air forces of Bulgaria, Czechoslovakia, East Germany, Hungary, Iraq, North Korea, Libya, Poland, Syria and the USSR, and civil operators in European and various developing countries. Production of the Mi-2B (see separate entry) accounts for "a few per cent" of the overall total.

During the course of production the Mi-2 has undergone continuous improvement and upgrading, with versions for new applications being developed to meet specific customers' requirements. A full list of these can be found in the 1984-85 and earlier *Jane's*; the principal versions being produced in 1988 were as follows:

(a) Convertible passenger/cargo transport;
(b) Ambulance and rescue versions (Mi-2R);
(c) Agricultural version, for dusting or conventional and ultra-low-volume spraying. In service in Bulgaria, Czechoslovakia, Egypt, Iraq, Poland and USSR;
(d) Freighter version, with external cargo sling and electric hoist;
(e) Training version;
(f) Aerial photography versions, able to carry photo-graphic, photogrammetric, thermal imaging or TV cameras for oblique or vertical pictures;
(g) Armed versions.

The following details apply specifically to the basic Mi-2, except where indicated.

TYPE: Twin-turbine general purpose light helicopter.

ROTOR SYSTEM: Three-blade main rotor fitted with hydraulic blade vibration dampers. All-metal blades, of NACA 230-12M section. Flapping, drag and pitch hinges on each blade. Main rotor blades and those of two-blade tail rotor each consist of an extruded duralumin spar with bonded honeycomb trailing-edge pockets. Anti-flutter weights on leading-edges, balancing plates on trailing-edges. Hydraulic boosters for longitudinal, lateral and collective pitch controls. Coil spring counterbalance mechanism in main and tail rotor systems. Pitch change centrifugal loads on tail rotor carried by ribbon type steel torsion elements. Rotors do not fold. Electric blade de-icing system for main and tail rotors. Rotor brake fitted.

ROTOR DRIVE: Main rotor shaft driven via gearbox on each engine; three-stage WR-2 main gearbox, intermediate gearbox and tail rotor gearbox. Main rotor/engine rpm ratio 1 : 24.6; tail rotor/engine rpm ratio 1 : 4.16. Main gearbox provides drive for auxiliary systems and take-off for rotor brake. Freewheel units permit disengagement of a failed engine and also autorotation.

FUSELAGE: Conventional semi-monocoque structure of pod and boom type, made up of three main assemblies: the nose (including cockpit), central section, and tailboom. Construction is of sheet duralumin, bonded and spot welded or riveted to longerons and frames. Main load bearing joints are of steel alloy.

TAIL UNIT: Variable incidence horizontal stabiliser controlled by collective pitch lever.

LANDING GEAR: Non-retractable tricycle type, plus tailskid. Twin-wheel nose unit. Single wheel on each main unit. Oleo-pneumatic shock absorbers in all units, including tailskid. Main shock absorbers designed to cope with both normal operating loads and possible ground resonance. Mainwheel tyres size 600 × 180, pressure 4.41 bars (64 lb/sq in). Nosewheel tyres size 400 × 125, pressure 3.45 bars (50 lb/sq in). Pneumatic brakes on mainwheels. Metal ski landing gear optional.

POWER PLANT: Two 298 kW (400 shp) Polish built Isotov GTD-350 turboshafts, mounted side by side above cabin. Fuel in single rubber tank, capacity 600 litres (158.5 US gallons; 131 Imp gallons), under cabin floor. Provision for carrying a 238 litre (63 US gallon; 52.4 Imp gallon) external tank on each side of cabin. Refuelling point in starboard side of fuselage. Oil capacity 25 litres (6.6 US gallons; 5.4 Imp gallons). Engine air intake de-icing by engine bleed air.

ACCOMMODATION: Normal accommodation for one pilot on flight deck (port side). Seats for up to eight passengers in air-conditioned cabin, comprising back to back bench seats for three persons each, with two optional extra starboard side seats at the rear, one behind the other. All passenger seats are removable for carrying up to 700 kg (1,543 lb) of internal freight. Access to cabin via forward hinged doors on each side at front of cabin and aft on port side. Pilot's sliding window jettisonable in emergency. Ambulance version has accommodation for four stretchers and a medical attendant, or two stretchers and two sitting casualties. Side by side seats and dual controls in pilot training version. Cabin heating, ventilation and air-conditioning standard. Electric de-icing of windscreen.

Wheel-ski equipped PZL Swidnik (Mil) Mi-2R rescue helicopter *(Lech Zielaskowski)*

SYSTEMS: Cabin heating, by engine bleed air, and ventilation; heat exchangers warm atmospheric air for ventilation system during cold weather. Hydraulic system, pressure 65 bars (940 lb/sq in), for cyclic and collective pitch control boosters. Hydraulic fluid flow rate 7.5 litres (1.98 US gallons; 1.65 Imp gallons)/min. Vented reservoir, with gravity feed. Pneumatic system, pressure 49 bars (710 lb/sq in), for mainwheel brakes. AC electrical system, with two STG-3 3kW engine driven starter/generators and 208V 16kVA three-phase alternator. 24V DC system, with two 28Ah lead-acid batteries.

AVIONICS AND EQUIPMENT: Standard equipment includes two transceivers (MF/HF), gyro compass, radio compass, radio altimeter, intercom system and blind-flying panel. Electrically operated wiper for pilot's windscreen. Fire extinguishing system, for engine bays and main gearbox compartment, is generally similar to, but simpler than, the freon system fitted to the Soviet Mil Mi-8, and can be actuated automatically or manually.

OPERATIONAL EQUIPMENT: Agricultural version carries a hopper on each side of the fuselage (total capacity 1,000 litres; 264 US gallons; 220 Imp gallons of liquid or 750 kg; 1,650 lb of dry chemical) and either a spraybar to the rear of the cabin on each side or a distributor for dry chemicals under each hopper. Swath width covered by the spraying version is 40-45 m (130-150 ft). As a search and rescue aircraft, an electric hoist, capacity 120 kg (264 lb), is fitted. In the freight role an underfuselage hook can be fitted for suspended loads of up to 800 kg (1,763 lb). Nose and tail warning radar fitted to some military versions.

ARMAMENT: Some Mi-2s of the Polish Air Force are equipped with rocket pods or 'Sagger' air-to-surface missiles mounted on pylons on each side of the cabin.

DIMENSIONS, EXTERNAL:
Main rotor diameter	14.50 m (47 ft 6⅞ in)
Main rotor blade chord (constant, each)	
	0.40 m (1 ft 3¾ in)
Tail rotor diameter	2.70 m (8 ft 10¼ in)
Length overall, rotors turning	17.42 m (57 ft 2 in)
Length of fuselage	11.40 m (37 ft 4¾ in)
Height to top of rotor head	3.75 m (12 ft 3½ in)
Stabiliser span	1.85 m (6 ft 0¾ in)
Wheel track	3.05 m (10 ft 0 in)
Wheelbase	2.71 m (8 ft 10¾ in)
Tail rotor ground clearance	1.59 m (5 ft 2¾ in)
Cabin door (port, rear): Height	1.065 m (3 ft 5¾ in)
Width	1.115 m (3 ft 8 in)
Cabin door (stbd, front): Height	1.11 m (3 ft 7¾ in)
Width	0.75 m (2 ft 5½ in)
Cabin door (port, front): Height	1.11 m (3 ft 7¾ in)
Width	0.78 m (2 ft 6¾ in)

DIMENSIONS, INTERNAL:
Cabin:	
Length: incl flight deck	4.07 m (13 ft 4¼ in)
excl flight deck	2.27 m (7 ft 5½ in)
Mean width	1.20 m (3 ft 11¼ in)
Mean height	1.40 m (4 ft 7 in)

AREAS:
Main rotor blades (each)	2.40 m² (25.83 sq ft)
Tail rotor blades (each)	0.22 m² (2.37 sq ft)
Main rotor disc	166.4 m² (1,791.11 sq ft)
Tail rotor disc	5.73 m² (61.68 sq ft)
Horizontal stabiliser	0.70 m² (7.53 sq ft)

WEIGHTS AND LOADING:
Weight empty, equipped:	
passenger version	2,402 kg (5,295 lb)

cargo version	2,372 kg (5,229 lb)
ambulance version	2,410 kg (5,313 lb)
agricultural version	2,372 kg (5,229 lb)
Basic operating weight empty:	
single-pilot versions	2,365 kg (5,213 lb)
dual control version	2,424 kg (5,344 lb)
Max payload, excl pilot, oil and fuel	800 kg (1,763 lb)
Normal T-O weight (and max T-O weight of agricultural version)	3,550 kg (7,826 lb)
Max T-O weight (special versions)	3,700 kg (8,157 lb)
Max disc loading	22.4 kg/m² (4.6 lb/sq ft)

PERFORMANCE (at 3,550 kg; 7,826 lb T-O weight):
Never-exceed speed at 500 m (1,640 ft):	
agricultural version	84 knots (155 km/h; 96 mph)
other versions	113 knots (210 km/h; 130 mph)
Max cruising speed at 500 m (1,640 ft):	
agricultural version (without agricultural equipment)	102 knots (190 km/h; 118 mph)
other versions	108 knots (200 km/h; 124 mph)
Max level speed with agricultural equipment	84 knots (155 km/h; 96 mph)
Econ cruising speed at 500 m (1,640 ft):	
for max range	102 knots (190 km/h; 118 mph)
for max endurance	54 knots (100 km/h; 62 mph)
Max rate of climb at S/L	270 m (885 ft)/min
Time to 1,000 m (3,280 ft)	5 min 30 s
Time to 4,000 m (13,125 ft)	26 min 0 s
Service ceiling	4,000 m (13,125 ft)
Hovering ceiling: IGE	approx 2,000 m (6,560 ft)
OGE	approx 1,000 m (3,280 ft)
Min landing area	30 × 30 m (100 × 100 ft)
Range at 500 m (1,640 ft):	
max payload, 5% fuel reserves	91 nm (170 km; 105 miles)
max internal fuel, no reserves	237 nm (440 km; 273 miles)
max internal and auxiliary fuel, 30 min reserves	313 nm (580 km; 360 miles)
max internal and auxiliary fuel, no reserves	430 nm (797 km; 495 miles)
Endurance at 500 m (1,640 ft), no reserves:	
max internal fuel	2 h 45 min
max internal and auxiliary fuel	5 h 0 min
Endurance (agricultural version), 5% reserves:	
spraying	40 min
dusting	50 min

PZL SWIDNIK Mi-2B

The PZL Mi-2B differs from the Mi-2 in having a different electrical system and more modern navigation aids. It has been manufactured in the same versions (except agricultural) as the Mi-2, and has the same flight performance. Empty equipped weights are 2,300 kg (5,070 lb) for the passenger version and 2,293 kg (5,055 lb) for the cargo version; T-O weight remains unchanged at 3,550 kg (7,826 lb). Rotor blade de-icing is not available on the Mi-2B.

PZL SWIDNIK KANIA/KITTY HAWK

In collaboration with Allison in the USA, PZL Swidnik developed the Kania or Kitty Hawk, powered by two Allison 250-C20B turboshaft engines. Two examples were converted from Mi-2 airframes, and the first of these (SP-PSA) made its initial flight on 3 June 1979.

Certification of the Kania was carried out in two stages. The first took place in 1979-81 and resulted, on 1 October 1981, in a supplementary type certificate to that of the Mi-2.

The second stage, concerning a considerably improved **Kania Model 1** version, was carried out during 1982-86 under the leadership of Stanisław I. Markisz. Improvements included, among others, redesigned cockpit and cabin layout, engine and flight controls, engine and transmission cowlings. On 21 February 1986 this version of the Kania was granted a separate type certificate as an FAR Pt 29 (Transport Category B) day and night SVFR multi-purpose utility helicopter with Category A engine isolation. Deliveries began in June 1987.

The Kania Model 1 is offered in a number of versions and configurations. These include passenger transport (with standard, executive or customised interiors), cargo transport (internal or slung load), agricultural (LV and ULV spraying, spreading and dusting), medical evacuation, training, rescue, and aerial surveillance.

TYPE: Twin-turboshaft multi-purpose light helicopter.

ROTOR SYSTEM: Three-blade fully articulated main rotor and two-blade seesaw tail rotor. Glassfibre/epoxy blades on both rotors. Three hydraulic boosters for longitudinal, lateral and collective pitch control augmentation. Electric de-icing of main and tail rotor blades (incl icing and 'system out' warnings) optional.

ROTOR DRIVE: Transmission includes main rotor, intermediate and tail rotor gearboxes, each with individual lubrication system. Main gearbox equipped with free-wheel units, oil cooling system, oil temperature and pressure gauges and switches, tacho-generator with low and high rpm warning, air compressor, and a spare power pad of 19.1 kW (25.6 shp) at 8,000 rpm. Steel engine driveshafts, each with two crowned tooth couplings. Tail rotor driveshaft of duralumin tube, with similar crowned tooth couplings and anti-friction bearings.

FUSELAGE AND TAIL UNIT: Conventional semi-monocoque fuselage and circular-section tailboom. Glassfibre/epoxy horizontal stabiliser at end of tailboom. Hoist and cargo sling attachment points standard.

LANDING GEAR: Non-retractable tricycle type, plus tailskid. Twin-wheel castoring and self-centring nose unit; single wheel on each main unit. Pneumatic brakes on mainwheels.

POWER PLANT: Two Allison 250-C20B turboshafts, mounted side by side above cabin; each rated at 313 kW (420 shp) for T-O, 30 min twin-engine emergency power and one engine out max continuous power, and 276 kW (370 shp) for normal cruise. Automatic and manual torque sharing control systems standard. Two separate fuel boost systems, each with fuel filter bypass switch, fuel pressure gauge and switch, connected by crossfeed. Standard usable fuel capacity of 600 litres (158.5 US gallons; 131 Imp gallons), with provision for additional 423 litres usable (111.75 US gallons; 93 Imp gallons) in optional auxiliary tanks. Fuel quantity gauge and fuel reserve warning. Two separate oil systems, each with oil cooling, temperature and pressure gauges, oil filter bypass pop-up and chip warning. Each engine equipped with starter/generator, engine fuel pump effective for cruise after both boost pumps out, N1 and N2 tacho-generators, TOT gauge and switch, start counter, and 'engine out' warning. Dual engine inlet anti-icing standard. Each engine compartment equipped with fire detection system and with automatic and manual fire extinguishing systems.

ACCOMMODATION: Pilot (port side), and co-pilot or passenger, on adjustable and removable front seats, each fitted with safety belt. Dual controls optional. Accommodation for up to eight more persons, on two three-person bench seats and a single or double seat at rear of cabin, all with safety belts. Seats removable for carriage of cargo (up to 1,200 kg; 2,645 lb), two or four stretchers plus medical attendants, agricultural or other specialised equipment. Access to cabin via jettisonable door on each side at front (port door of sliding type) and larger passenger/cargo door at rear on port side. Pilot's windscreen wiper standard, co-pilot's optional. Cargo and stretcher tiedown points in cabin floor. Cabin soundproofing and ventilation standard; heating, carpets, double pane windows, pilot's heated windscreen, all optional. Baggage compartment at rear of cabin. Cockpit and cabin lighting standard.

SYSTEMS: Hydraulic system, with pressure gauge and switch, standard. Compressed air system, with accumulator and system gauges, standard. Ventilation standard, with individually controllable fresh air outlets; Casey cabin heaters optional, with individual control of hot air flow and central control of overall cabin air temperature. DC electrical system based on two 28V 150A starter/generators and a 25Ah nickel-cadmium battery, with ground power receptacle. Ground/battery power, battery overtemperature and 'generator out' warnings standard. A 16kVA AC generator and/or 115V 250A static inverter are optional; this AC system is equipped with AC generator and AC 115V warnings. Dual fire detection and extinguishing systems for engines standard.

AVIONICS AND EQUIPMENT: Primary instrumentation includes attitude, altitude, airspeed, turn and slip, and rate of climb indicators; magnetic compass and gyro compass; HSI; clock; VHF com transceiver; and full range of power plant and systems control, monitoring and warning instruments. Optional radio-navigation avionics include digital ADF, R/Nav (VOR 1), audio panel, VOR/LOC/glideslope converter, transponder with or without altitude encoder, marker beacon receiver, DME, second VHF com transceiver, VOR 2 receiver, HF com transceiver, and radar altimeter. Standard equipment includes dual anti-collision lights, navigation lights, portable fire extinguisher, tool kit and first aid kit. Fluorescent tube cabin lighting and/or individual lights optional.

PZL Swidnik Kania Model 1 twin-turboshaft light helicopter *(Lech Zielaskowski)*

OPERATIONAL EQUIPMENT: According to mission, the Kania can be equipped with an 800 kg (1,763 lb) capacity stabilised cargo sling; 120 kg (265 lb) capacity hoist (275 kg; 606 lb hoist under test in 1986); stretchers and casualty care equipment; or equipment for a variety of agricultural duties.

DIMENSIONS, EXTERNAL:

Main rotor diameter	14.558 m (47 ft 9¼ in)
Tail rotor diameter	2.70 m (8 ft 10¼ in)
Length overall, rotors turning	17.47 m (57 ft 3¾ in)
Length of fuselage	12.03 m (39 ft 5½ in)
Height to top of rotor head	3.75 m (12 ft 3½ in)
Stabiliser span	1.84 m (6 ft 0½ in)
Wheel track	3.05 m (10 ft 0 in)
Wheelbase	2.71 m (8 ft 10¾ in)

DIMENSIONS, INTERNAL:

Cabin: Length, incl flight deck	4.07 m (13 ft 4¼ in)
Max width	1.50 m (4 ft 11 in)
Max height	1.62 m (5 ft 3¾ in)
Floor area	5.68 m² (61.1 sq ft)
Volume	7.76 m³ (274.0 cu ft)
Baggage compartment volume	0.45 m³ (15.89 cu ft)

AREAS:

Main rotor disc	166.50 m² (1,792.2 sq ft)
Tail rotor disc	5.725 m² (61.6 sq ft)

WEIGHTS:

Basic weight empty	2,000 kg (4,409 lb)
Normal T-O weight	3,350 kg (7,385 lb)
Max T-O weight	3,550 kg (7,826 lb)
Max load in cabin	1,200 kg (2,645 lb)
Max cargo sling load	800 kg (1,763 lb)
Max agricultural chemical load	1,000 kg (2,205 lb)
Max load in baggage compartment	100 kg (220 lb)

PERFORMANCE ('clean' aircraft at S/L, ISA, zero wind, at normal T-O weight):

Max cruising speed	116 knots (215 km/h; 134 mph)
Econ cruising speed	102 knots (190 km/h; 118 mph)
Max rate of climb (T-O power)	525 m (1,725 ft)/min
Rate of climb, one engine out	61 m (200 ft)/min
Service ceiling	4,000 m (13,125 ft)
Hovering ceiling: IGE	2,500 m (8,200 ft)
OGE	1,375 m (4,510 ft)
Range at econ cruising speed:	
standard fuel, 30 min reserves	232 nm (430 km; 267 miles)
standard fuel, no reserves	266 nm (493 km; 306 miles)
max fuel, 30 min reserves	432 nm (800 km; 497 miles)
max fuel, no reserves	466 nm (863 km; 536 miles)

PZL SWIDNIK W-3 SOKÓL (FALCON)

Development of this all-new Polish helicopter took place in the second half of the 1970s, and the first flight was made on 16 November 1979 by one of five prototypes, which subsequently underwent a wide range of tiedown tests. The remaining prototypes were completed embodying changes made as a result of these tests, the manufacturer's flight trials being resumed on 6 May 1982 by the second aircraft (SP-PSB). Certification trials with two other aircraft have been carried out in a wide range of operating conditions, including heavy icing conditions and extreme temperatures of -60°C and +50°C. Certification to Soviet NLGW regulations was due to be completed by the end of 1988. The design team was headed by Stanislav Kaminski. Larger than the Mi-2/Kania, the Sokól accommodates a crew of two, and 12 passengers or a maximum 2,100 kg (4,630 lb) of internal cargo.

The Sokól is intended to become Swidnik's major production programme during the 1990s.

TYPE: Twin-turboshaft medium weight multi-purpose helicopter.

ROTOR SYSTEM: Four-blade fully articulated main rotor and three-blade tail rotor. Main rotor has a pendular Salomon type vibration absorber, providing smooth flight and low vibration levels. Blades of both rotors constructed of laminated glassfibre impregnated with epoxy resin. Main rotor blades have tapered tips. Three hydraulic boosters for longitudinal, lateral and collective pitch control of main rotor, and one booster for tail rotor control. Blade anti-icing by electrically heated elements. Rotor brake fitted.

ROTOR DRIVE: Transmission driven via main rotor, intermediate and tail rotor gearboxes. Tail rotor driveshaft of duralumin tube with splined couplings.

FUSELAGE AND TAIL UNIT: Light alloy semi-monocoque structure, with circular section semi-monocoque tailboom. Fin integral with tailboom structure and fitted with glassfibre trailing-edge panels. Horizontal stabiliser, under end of tailboom, has a single continuous spar, is built up of laminated glassfibre impregnated with epoxy resin, and is not interconnected with the main rotor control system.

LANDING GEAR: Non-retractable tricycle type, plus tailskid beneath tailboom. Twin-wheel castoring nose unit; single wheel on each main unit. Oleo-pneumatic shock absorber in each unit. Mainwheel tyres size 500 × 250 mm; nosewheel tyres size 400 × 150 mm. Pneumatic disc brakes on mainwheels. Metal ski landing gear optional.

POWER PLANT: Two PZL-10W turboshafts (Polish developed helicopter version of Glushenkov TVD-10), each with rating of 662 kW (888 shp) for T-O and 30 min OEI, and emergency ratings of 735 kW (986 shp) and 845.5 kW (1,134 shp) for 8 min and 2½ min OEI respectively. Particle separators on engine intakes, and inlet de-icing, are standard. Power plant is equipped with advanced electronic fuel control system for maintaining rotor speed at pilot-selected value amounting to ±5 per cent of normal rpm, and also for torque sharing as well as for supervising engine limits during start-up and normal or OEI operation. Engines and main rotor gearbox are mounted on a bed frame, eliminating any drive misalignment due to deformations of the fuselage structure. Bladder fuel tanks beneath cabin floor, with combined capacity of 1,700 litres (449 US gallons; 374 Imp gallons). Auxiliary tank, capacity 1,100 litres (290.5 US gallons; 242 Imp gallons), optional.

ACCOMMODATION: Pilot (port side), and co-pilot or flight engineer, side by side on flight deck, on adjustable seats with safety belts. Dual controls and dual flight instrumentation optional. Accommodation for 12 passengers in main cabin. Seats removable for carriage of internal cargo. Ambulance version will carry four stretcher cases and a medical attendant. Baggage space at rear of cabin. Door on each side of flight deck; large sliding door for passenger and/or cargo loading on port side at forward end of cabin; second sliding door at rear of cabin on starboard side. Optically flat windscreens, improving view and enabling wipers to sweep a large area. Accommodation soundproofed, heated (by engine bleed air) and ventilated.

SYSTEMS: Two independent hydraulic systems, working pressure 90 bars (1,300 lb/sq in), for controlling main and tail rotors, unlocking collective pitch control lever, and feeding damper of directional steering system. Flow rate 11 litres (2.9 US gallons; 2.4 Imp gallons)/min in each system. Vented gravity feed reservoir, at atmospheric

First production PZL Swidnik W-3 Sokól (two PZL-10W turboshafts), used briefly during final stages of flight test programme *(Lech Zielaskowski)*

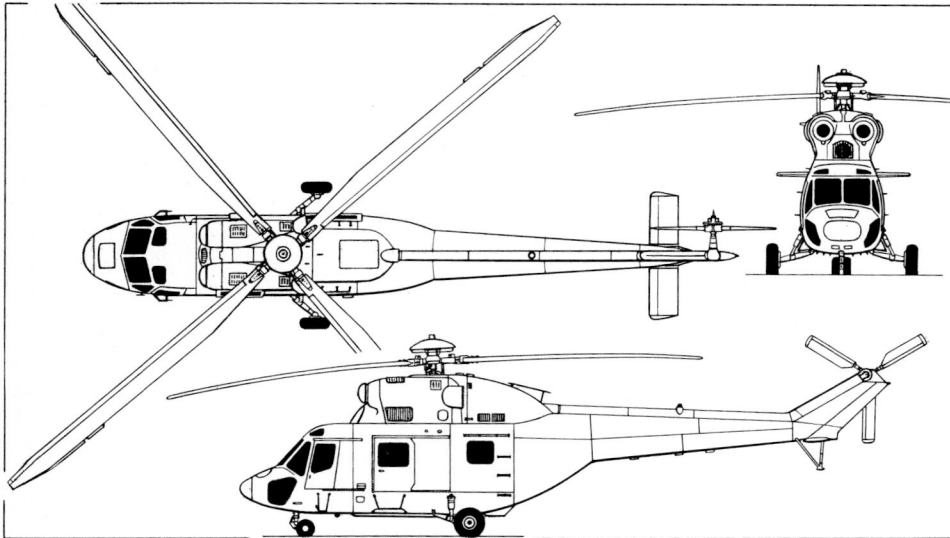

PZL Swidnik W-3 Sokól twin-turboshaft helicopter *(Pilot Press)*

Prototype of the PZL Swidnik SW-4 four/five-seat light helicopter *(Lech Zielaskowski)*

pressure. Pneumatic system for actuating hydraulic mainwheel brakes. Electrical system providing both AC and DC power. Fire detection/extinguishing system. Air-conditioning and oxygen systems optional. Neutral gas system optional, for inhibiting fuel vapour explosion.

AVIONICS AND EQUIPMENT: Standard IFR nav/com avionics permit adverse weather operation by day or night. Weather radar optional. Stability augmentation system standard. Cargo version equipped with 2,100 kg (4,630 lb) capacity external hook and 150 kg (331 lb) capacity rescue hoist; 300 kg (661 lb) capacity hoist to become available.

DIMENSIONS, EXTERNAL:
Main rotor diameter	15.70 m (51 ft 6 in)
Tail rotor diameter	3.03 m (9 ft 11¼ in)
Length overall, rotors turning	18.85 m (61 ft 10⅛ in)
Length of fuselage	14.21 m (46 ft 7½ in)
Height to top of rotor head	4.12 m (13 ft 6¼ in)
Stabiliser span	3.45 m (11 ft 3¾ in)
Wheel track	3.40 m (11 ft 2 in)
Wheelbase	3.55 m (11 ft 7¾ in)
Passenger/cargo doors:	
Height (each):	1.20 m (3 ft 11¼ in)
Width: port	0.95 m (3 ft 1½ in)
starboard	1.25 m (4 ft 1¼ in)

DIMENSIONS, INTERNAL:
Cabin: Length	3.20 m (10 ft 6 in)
Max width	1.55 m (5 ft 1 in)
Max height	1.40 m (4 ft 7 in)

AREAS:
Main rotor disc	193.6 m² (2,083.8 sq ft)
Tail rotor disc	7.2 m² (77.6 sq ft)

WEIGHTS:
Minimum basic weight empty	3,300 kg (7,275 lb)
Basic operating weight empty (multi-purpose versions)	
	3,630 kg (8,002 lb)
Max payload, internal or external	2,100 kg (4,630 lb)
Normal T-O weight	6,100 kg (13,448 lb)
Max T-O weight	6,400 kg (14,110 lb)

PERFORMANCE (at normal T-O weight at 500 m; 1,640 ft, ISA, except where indicated):
Never-exceed speed	145 knots (270 km/h; 167 mph)
Max level speed	138 knots (255 km/h; 158 mph)
Max cruising speed	127 knots (235 km/h; 146 mph)
Econ cruising speed	119 knots (220 km/h; 137 mph)
Max rate of climb at S/L	510 m (1,673 ft)/min
Rate of climb at S/L, one engine out:	
at 30 min rating	30 m (100 ft)/min
at 8 min emergency rating	96 m (315 ft)/min
at 2½ min emergency rating	186 m (610 ft)/min
Service ceiling:	
at normal T-O weight	5,100 m (16,725 ft)
at T-O weight below normal	
	up to 6,000 m (19,680 ft)
Service ceiling, one engine out:	
at 30 min rating	500 m (1,640 ft)
at 8 min emergency rating	1,800 m (5,905 ft)
at 2½ min emergency rating	
	approx 2,300 m (7,545 ft)
Hovering ceiling: IGE	3,000 m (9,845 ft)
OGE	2,100 m (6,890 ft)
Range:	
standard fuel, 5% reserves	
	367 nm (680 km; 422 miles)
standard fuel, no reserves	
	386 nm (715 km; 444 miles)
with auxiliary fuel, 5% reserves	
	626 nm (1,160 km; 721 miles)
with auxiliary fuel, no reserves	
	661 nm (1,225 km; 761 miles)
Endurance:	
standard fuel, 5% reserves	3 h 50 min
standard fuel, no reserves	4 h 5 min
with auxiliary fuel, 5% reserves	6 h 41 min
with auxiliary fuel, no reserves	7 h 5 min

PZL SWIDNIK SW-4
Development of this 4/5-seat single-engined multi-purpose light helicopter began in 1985. Its general appearance is shown in the accompanying photograph.

WSK-PZL WARSZAWA-OKECIE
WYTWÓRNIA SPRZETU KOMUNIKACYJNEGO-PZL WARSZAWA-OKECIE (Transport Equipment Manufacturing Centre, Warsaw-Okecie)

Al. Krakowska 110/114, 02-256 Warszawa-Okecie
Telephone: Warszawa 461173 and 460031
Telex: 814649
GENERAL MANAGER: Jerzy Milczarek, Eng MSc
EXPORT MANAGER: Paweł F. Dabkowski
PRESS AND PUBLIC RELATIONS: Z. Pęsko

The Okecie factory, founded in 1928, is responsible for light aircraft development and production, and for the design and manufacture of associated agricultural equipment for its own aircraft and for those built at other factories in the Polish aviation industry.

PZL-104 WILGA (ORIOLE) 35 and 80
The PZL-104 Wilga is a light general purpose aircraft for a wide variety of general aviation and flying club duties. The prototype Wilga 1 flew for the first time on 24 April 1962. This aircraft, and other early models, were described in the 1968-69 *Jane's*.

Production of the improved Wilga 35 and Wilga 32 began in 1968, and both received a Polish type certificate on 31 March 1969; the Wilga 32 was described in the 1974-75 *Jane's*, and its Indonesian built modified version, the Lipnur Gelatik, in the 1975-76 edition.

The aircraft is currently manufactured in two basic versions: the **Wilga 35** (first flight 28 July 1967), which meets the requirements of British BCAR regulations, and the **Wilga 80** (first flown on 30 May 1979), which conforms to US FAR Pt 23 requirements. The latter has the carburettor air intake located further aft. Aeroclub versions (Wilga 35A and 80A) are fitted with a glider towing hook;

Wilgas with agricultural equipment are designated 35R and 80R, and aircraft with twin Airtech (Canada) LAP-3000 floats are known as Wilga 35H and 80H.

Examples of the Wilga have been sold to customers in Austria, Belgium, Bulgaria, Canada, Cuba, Czechoslovakia, Denmark, Egypt, Germany (Democratic Republic), Germany (Federal Republic), Hungary, Indonesia, Italy, North Korea, Poland, Romania, Spain, Sweden, Switzerland, Turkey, the UK, the USA, the USSR (more than 300), Venezuela and Yugoslavia.

Total sales of the Wilga (all versions) had reached 860 by 1 January 1988.

The following description applies to the Wilga 35 and 80, except where a specific version is indicated:
TYPE: Single-engined general purpose aircraft.
WINGS: Cantilever high-wing monoplane. Wing section NACA 2415. Dihedral 1°. All-metal single-spar structure, with leading-edge torsion box and beaded metal skin.

Each wing attached to fuselage by three bolts, two at spar and one at forward fitting. All-metal aerodynamically and mass balanced slotted ailerons, with beaded metal skin. Ailerons can be drooped to supplement flaps during landing. Manually operated all-metal slotted flaps with beaded metal skin. Fixed metal slat on leading-edge along full span of wing and over fuselage. Tab on starboard aileron.

FUSELAGE: All-metal semi-monocoque structure in two portions, riveted together. Forward section incorporates main wing spar carry-through structure. Rear section is in the form of a tailcone. Beaded metal skin. Floor in cabin is of metal sandwich construction, with a paper honeycomb core, covered with foam rubber.

TAIL UNIT: Braced all-metal structure, with sweptback vertical surfaces. Stressed skin single-spar tailplane attached to fuselage by a single centre fitting and supported by a single aluminium alloy strut on each side. Stressed skin two-spar fin structure of semi-monocoque construction. Rudder and one-piece elevator are aerodynamically horn balanced and mass balanced. Trim tab at centre of elevator trailing-edge.

LANDING GEAR: Non-retractable tailwheel type. Semi-cantilever main legs, of rocker type, have oleo-pneumatic shock absorbers. Low-pressure tyres size 500 × 200 mm on mainwheels. Hydraulic brakes. Steerable tailwheel, tyre size 255 × 110 mm, carried on rocker frame with oleo-pneumatic shock absorber. Metal ski landing gear, and Airtech Canada LAP-3000 twin-float landing gear, optional.

POWER PLANT: One 194 kW (260 hp) PZL AI-14RA nine-cylinder supercharged radial aircooled engine (AI-14RA-KAF in Wilga 80), driving a PZL US-122000 two-blade constant-speed wooden propeller. Two removable fuel tanks in each wing, with total capacity of 195 litres (51.5 US gallons; 43 Imp gallons). Refuelling point on each side of fuselage, at junction with wing. Oil capacity 16 litres (4.2 US gallons; 3.5 Imp gallons).

ACCOMMODATION: Passenger version accommodates pilot and three passengers, in pairs, with adjustable front seats. Baggage compartment aft of seats, capacity 35 kg (77 lb). Upward opening door on each side of cabin, jettisonable in emergency. In the parachute training version the starboard door is removed and replaced by two tubular uprights with a central connecting strap, and the starboard front seat is rearward facing. Jumps are facilitated by a step on the starboard side and by a parachute hitch. A controllable towing hook can be attached to the tail landing gear permitting the Wilga, in this role, to tow a single glider of up to 650 kg (1,433 lb) weight or two or three gliders with a total combined weight of 1,125 kg (2,480 lb).

SYSTEMS: Hydraulic system pressure 39 bars (570 lb/sq in). Engine starting is effected pneumatically by a built-in system of 7 litres (0.25 cu ft) capacity with a pressure of 49 bars (710 lb/sq in). Electrical system powered by DC generator and 24V 10Ah battery.

AVIONICS AND EQUIPMENT: Standard avionics and equipment include VHF transceiver and blind-flying instrumentation. Optional avionics and equipment include RS-6102 (of Polish design), R-860 II, R860 IIM, King KY 195 or Bendix radio; and ARL-1601 VHF, ARK-9, King KR 85 or Bendix AV-200 ADF, GB-1 gyro compass, K2-715 airspeed and altitude recorder, sun visors, exhaust silencer and windscreen wiper.

DIMENSIONS, EXTERNAL:

Wing span: 35	11.12 m (36 ft 5¾ in)
80	11.13 m (36 ft 6¼ in)
Wing chord (constant)	1.40 m (4 ft 7¼ in)
Wing aspect ratio	8.0
Length overall: 35	8.10 m (26 ft 6¾ in)
80	8.03 m (26 ft 4¼ in)
Height overall	2.96 m (9 ft 8½ in)
Tailplane span	3.70 m (12 ft 1¾ in)
Wheel track	2.75 m (9 ft 0¼ in)
Wheelbase	6.70 m (21 ft 11¾ in)
Propeller diameter	2.65 m (8 ft 8 in)
Passenger doors (each): Height	1.00 m (3 ft 3¼ in)
Width	1.50 m (4 ft 11 in)

DIMENSIONS, INTERNAL:

Cabin: Length	2.20 m (7 ft 2½ in)
Max width	1.20 m (3 ft 10 in)
Max height	1.50 m (4 ft 11 in)
Floor area	2.20 m² (23.8 sq ft)
Volume	2.40 m³ (85 cu ft)
Baggage compartment	0.50 m³ (17.5 cu ft)

AREAS:

Wings, gross	15.50 m² (166.8 sq ft)
Ailerons (total)	1.57 m² (16.90 sq ft)
Trailing-edge flaps (total)	1.97 m² (21.20 sq ft)
Fin	0.97 m² (10.44 sq ft)
Rudder	0.92 m² (9.90 sq ft)
Tailplane	3.16 m² (34.01 sq ft)
Elevator, incl tab	1.92 m² (20.67 sq ft)

WEIGHTS AND LOADINGS (Wilga 35A and 80):

Weight empty, equipped	870 kg (1,918 lb)
Max T-O and landing weight	1,300 kg (2,866 lb)
Max wing loading	83.9 kg/m² (17.18 lb/sq ft)
Max power loading	6.70 kg/kW (11.02 lb/hp)

PERFORMANCE (Wilga 35A, at max T-O weight):

Never-exceed speed	150 knots (279 km/h; 173 mph)

Italian registered PZL-104 Wilga 80 (PZL AI-14RA-KAF engine) *(Avio Data)*

Max level speed	105 knots (194 km/h; 120 mph)
Cruising speed (75% power)	85 knots (157 km/h; 97 mph)
Cruising speed for max range	74 knots (137 km/h; 85 mph)
Stalling speed: flaps up	35 knots (65 km/h; 41 mph)
flaps down	30 knots (56 km/h; 35 mph)
Max rate of climb at S/L	276 m (905 ft)/min
Time to 1,000 m (3,280 ft)	3 min
Service ceiling	4,040 m (13,250 ft)
T-O run (grass)	121 m (397 ft)
Landing run	106 m (348 ft)
Range with max fuel, 30 min reserves	275 nm (510 km; 317 miles)

PZL-105

Although referred to at first as the Wilga 88, the PZL-105 is an entirely new design that is being developed as a successor to the widely used Wilga 35/80 series, and is scheduled to fly for the first time in 1989.

Intended to maintain the versatility of the Wilga, the PZL-105 will have a choice of power plants and landing gears, and will be suitable for such duties as light passenger or cargo transport, sport flying and aero club use, glider towing, parachute training, air ambulance, patrol or geophysical survey, and agricultural use. It will be capable of operation from unprepared airstrips, and is to be certificated to FAR Pt 23 (Amendments 1-28) in the Normal category.

General appearance of the PZL-105 is shown in the accompanying three-view drawing. Principal details are as follows:

TYPE: Single-engined general purpose aircraft.

WINGS: All-metal high-wing monoplane, with wing section similar to NASA GA(W)-1. Single bracing strut on each side. Single-slotted Fowler trailing-edge flaps and flaperons, actuated electrically. Construction generally similar to that of Wilga.

FUSELAGE: Conventional all-metal semi-monocoque structure.

TAIL UNIT: All-metal structure comprising sweptback fin and rudder, with small dorsal fin, and low-set non-swept tailplane and elevators. Raked tips on fin and tailplane.

Trim tab on port elevator; ground adjustable tab on rudder.

LANDING GEAR: Non-retractable type, with single mainwheels on cantilever self-sprung legs and a steerable tailwheel with oleo-pneumatic shock absorption. Low pressure tyres and hydraulic disc brakes on mainwheels. May also be fitted with floats, skis (with snow brakes) or wheel/skis.

POWER PLANT: Initial choice of one 209 kW (280 hp) PZL AI-14RD (with electric starting) or similarly rated AI-14RDP (with pneumatic starting) nine-cylinder aircooled radial engine, driving a two-blade constant-speed propeller with spinner. Provision for later use of 268.5 kW (360 hp) Vedeneyev M-14P radial. Fuel in integral tanks in wings, total capacity 270 litres (71.3 US gallons; 59.4 Imp gallons).

ACCOMMODATION: Fully enclosed cabin, with large door on each side, for up to six persons (including pilot and optional second pilot), in three rows of two.

DIMENSIONS, EXTERNAL:

Wing span	12.70 m (41 ft 8 in)
Wing aspect ratio	9.5
Length overall	8.60 m (28 ft 2½ in)
Height overall	2.80 m (9 ft 2¼ in)
Wheel track	3.10 m (10 ft 2 in)
Cabin door: Height	1.10 m (3 ft 7¼ in)
Width	1.60 m (5 ft 3 in)

DIMENSIONS, INTERNAL:

Cabin: Length	2.80 m (9 ft 2¼ in)
Max width	1.10 m (3 ft 7¼ in)
Max height	1.20 m (3 ft 11¼ in)

AREA:

Wings, gross	16.90 m² (181.9 sq ft)

WEIGHTS AND LOADINGS:

Standard weight empty, equipped	955 kg (2,105 lb)
Max T-O weight	1,670 kg (3,682 lb)
Max wing loading	98.8 kg/m² (20.24 lb/sq ft)
Max power loading	8.0 kg/kW (13.15 lb/hp)

PERFORMANCE (estimated. A: at 1,160 kg; 2,557 lb AUW, B: at 1,650 kg; 3,637 lb, rest at max T-O weight):

Never-exceed speed	160 knots (296 km/h; 184 mph)
Max level speed	135 knots (250 km/h; 155 mph)
Max cruising speed (134 kW; 180 hp)	116 knots (216 km/h; 134 mph)
Econ cruising speed (107.5 kW; 144 hp)	102 knots (190 km/h; 118 mph)

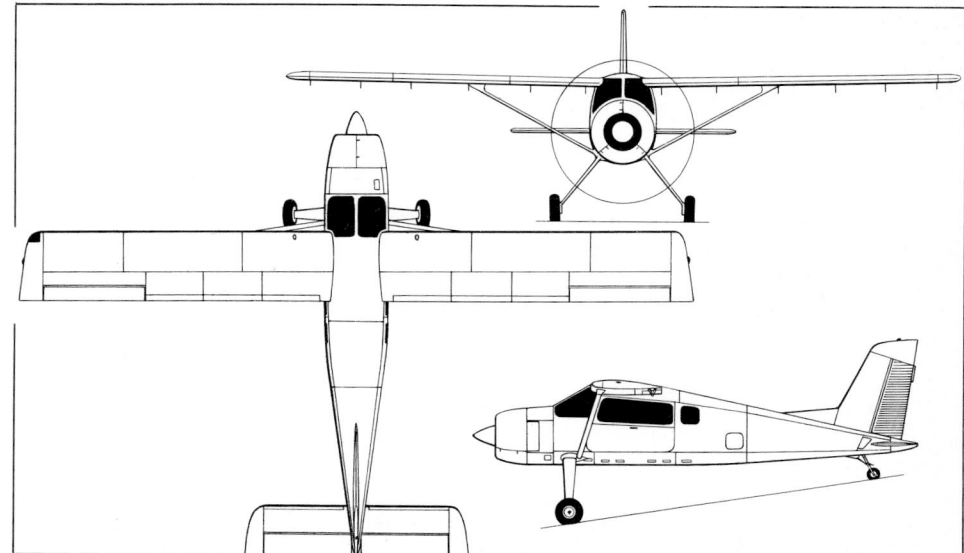

PZL Warszawa-Okecie PZL-105 six-seat general utility aircraft *(Pilot Press)*

Stalling speed: A	44 knots (80 km/h; 50 mph)
B	52 knots (95 km/h; 59 mph)
Max rate of climb at S/L: A	522 m (1,712 ft)/min
B	318 m (1,043 ft)/min
T-O run: A	42 m (138 ft)
B	111 m (365 ft)
T-O to 15 m (50 ft): A	117 m (384 ft)
B	218 m (716 ft)
Landing from 15 m (50 ft): A	168 m (552 ft)
B	201 m (660 ft)
Landing run: A	66 m (217 ft)
B	94 m (309 ft)
Range with max fuel:	
at max cruising speed	533 nm (989 km; 614 miles)
at econ cruising speed	625 nm (1,159 km; 720 miles)
g limits	+3.8/−1.52

PZL-106B KRUK (RAVEN)

The PZL-106 was designed in early 1972 by a team led by Andrzej Frydrychewicz. The first prototype (SP-PAS) flew for the first time on 17 April 1973, powered by a 298 kW (400 hp) Textron Lycoming IO-720 engine. It was followed in October of that year by a second Textron Lycoming engined prototype (SP-PBG) and, from October 1974, by four prototypes fitted with the 441 kW (592 hp) PZL-3S radial engine that powers the PZL-106A and B. Production versions also have a low-mounted tailplane instead of the earlier T tail, and a greater chemical load in a larger hopper. Manufacture of some 600 aircraft for the member countries of the CMEA (Council for Mutual Economic Aid) is anticipated. A total of more than 180 (all versions) had been built by January 1988, including 44 PZL-106As produced between 1976-81. Details of the PZL-106A, and of the AR and AT prototypes, can be found in the 1985-86 and earlier editions of *Jane's*.

The following versions of the Kruk were current in 1987-88:

PZL-106AS. To increase the performance of PZL-106A Kruks operated by Pezetel in Egypt and the Sudan, PZL Warszawa-Okecie adapted the design to take a 746 kW (1,000 hp) PZL (Shvetsov) ASz-62IR nine-cylinder radial engine instead of the standard 441 kW (592 hp) PZL-3S. The prototype of this version (SP-PBD) flew for the first time on 19 August 1981. First ten re-engined in 1982; 44 converted by early 1987. Hopper load reduced to 750 kg (1,653 lb) initially, due to heavier engine. Re-certificated in July 1983 for operation at higher (Restricted) max T-O weight of 3,600 kg (7,936 lb). New-production aircraft with this engine are to PZL-106BS standard (which see).

PZL-106B. Prototypes for improved series, having redesigned wings with a new aerofoil section, increased span and area, trailing-edge flaps, and shortened V bracing struts. First prototype (SP-PKW) flew for the first time on 15 May 1981. Two further prototypes made their first flights in July and September 1981. Weights and performance data in 1985-86 and earlier *Jane's*.

PZL-106BR. Version with geared PZL-3SR engine; first flown on 8 July 1983. Tested also with wingtip vanes (three at each tip). Total of 47 built by 1 January 1988.

PZL-106BS. The prototype (SP-PBK) of this uprated version of the Kruk, with a PZL (Shvetsov) ASz-62IR radial engine, flew for the first time on 8 March 1982. Total of 14 built by 1 January 1988. For Restricted category operation, with higher max T-O weight and increased load of chemical.

PZL-106BT Turbo-Kruk. Turboprop version; described separately.

The following description applies generally to the piston engined PZL-106B series, except where a specific version is indicated:

TYPE: Single-engined agricultural aircraft. Structure is corrosion resistant, and is additionally protected by an external finish of polyurethane enamel.

Prototype PZL-106BT, first version of the Kruk with a Czechoslovak turboprop (*Lech Zielaskowski*)

WINGS: Braced low-wing monoplane with upward cambered tips. NACA 2415 wing section throughout span. Dihedral 4° from roots. Incidence 6° 6′. Sweepback 1° at quarter-chord. All-metal two-spar duralumin structure, of constant chord. Metal and polyester fabric covering. Glassfibre wingtips, with upswept undersurfaces. Full span four-segment fixed leading-edge slats on each wing, of glassfibre sandwich construction with foam core. Slotted ailerons of duralumin, with polyester fabric covering. Trailing-edge flaps of similar construction. Ground adjustable tab on each aileron initially; aircraft from tenth production batch onward have electrically actuated trim tab in port aileron. Duralumin streamline section V bracing struts, with jury struts.

FUSELAGE: Welded steel tube structure, protected by several coats of polyurethane enamel and covered with quickly removable panels of light alloy and GRP. Steel tube structure can be pressure tested for crack detection.

TAIL UNIT: Conventional duralumin structure, initially with single tailplane bracing strut each side; two struts each side from ninth production batch onward. Fixed surfaces metal covered; rudder and mass balanced elevators are polyester fabric covered. Trim tab in port elevator, automatic tab on rudder.

LANDING GEAR: Non-retractable tailwheel type, with oleo-pneumatic shock absorber in each unit. Mainwheels, with low-pressure tyres size 800 × 260 mm, each carried on side V and half-axle. Mainwheel tyre pressure 2.0 bars (29 lb/sq in). Pneumatically operated hydraulic disc brakes on mainwheels. Parking brake. Steerable tailwheel, with tubeless tyre size 350 × 135 mm, pressure 2.5 bars (36.25 lb/sq in).

POWER PLANT: *(PZL-106BR):* One 448 kW (600 hp) PZL-3SR seven-cylinder radial aircooled geared and supercharged engine, driving a PZL US-133000 four-blade constant-speed metal propeller. *(PZL-106BS):* One 746 kW (1,000 hp) PZL (Shvetsov) ASz-62IR nine-cylinder radial aircooled engine and AW-2-30 propeller. Fuel in two integral wing tanks, total capacity 560 litres (148 US gallons; 123 Imp gallons); can be increased to total of 950 litres (251 US gallons; 209 Imp gallons) by using hopper as auxiliary fuel tank. Gravity refuelling point on each wing; semi-pressurised refuelling point on starboard side of fuselage. Oil capacity 54 litres (14.3 US gallons; 11.9 Imp gallons) max in BR, 67 litres (17.7 US gallons; 14.7 Imp gallons) in BS. Carburettor air filter fitted.

ACCOMMODATION: Single vertically adjustable seat in enclosed, ventilated and heated cockpit with steel tube overturn structure. Provision for instructor's cockpit with basic dual controls, forward of main cockpit and offset to starboard, for training of pilots in agricultural

duties. Optional rearward facing second seat (for mechanic) to rear. Jettisonable window/door on each side of cabin. Pilot's seat and seat belt designed to resist 40g impact.

SYSTEMS: Pneumatic system, rated at 49 bars (710 lb/sq in), for brakes and agricultural equipment. Electrical power, from 3kW 27.5V DC generator and 24V 15Ah battery, for engine starting, pneumatic system control, aircraft lights, instruments, VHF transceiver and semi-pressurised refuelling. Cockpit air-conditioning system optional.

EQUIPMENT: VHF com transceiver standard. Easily removable non-corroding (GRP) hopper/tank, forward of cockpit, can carry more than 1,000 kg (2,205 lb) (see under 'Weights and Loadings' paragraph) of dry or liquid chemical, and has a maximum capacity of 1,400 litres (370 US gallons; 308 Imp gallons). Turnround time, with full load of chemical, is in the order of 28 s. The hopper has a quick-dump system that can release 1,000 kg of chemical in 5 s or less. A pneumatically operated intake for the loading of dry chemicals is optional. Distribution system for liquid chemical (jets or atomisers) is powered by a fan driven centrifugal pump. A precise and reliable dispersal system, with positive on/off action for dry chemicals, gives effective swath widths of 30-35 m (100-115 ft). For ferry purposes, hopper can be used to carry additional fuel instead of chemical. When the Kruk is converted into a two-seat trainer (see 'Accommodation' paragraph), standard hopper can be replaced easily by a special container with reduced capacity tank for liquid chemical. Steel cable cutter on windscreen and each mainwheel leg; steel deflector cable runs from top of windscreen cable cutter to tip of fin. Windscreen washer and wiper standard. Other equipment includes 720-channel ultra short wave transceiver (optional), artificial horizon, gyro compass, engine hour meter, clock, rearview mirror, second (mechanic's) seat (optional), cockpit air-conditioning (optional), cockpit heating and ventilation, landing light, anti-collision light, and night working lights (optional).

DIMENSIONS, EXTERNAL:

Wing span	14.90 m (48 ft 10½ in)
Wing chord, constant	2.16 m (7 ft 1 in)
Wing aspect ratio	6.9
Length overall: BR	9.25 m (30 ft 4½ in)
BS	9.34 m (30 ft 7¾ in)
Height overall	3.32 m (10 ft 10¾ in)
Tailplane span	5.77 m (18 ft 11¼ in)
Wheel track	3.10 m (10 ft 2¼ in)
Wheelbase	7.41 m (24 ft 3¾ in)
Propeller diameter: BR	3.10 m (10 ft 2 in)
BS	3.30 m (10 ft 10 in)
Propeller ground clearance (tail up)	0.39 m (1 ft 3¼ in)
Crew doors (each): Height	0.91 m (2 ft 11¾ in)
Width	1.06 m (3 ft 5¾ in)
Baggage door: Height	0.70 m (2 ft 3½ in)
Width	0.60 m (1 ft 11¾ in)

DIMENSIONS, INTERNAL:

Cabin: Length	1.37 m (4 ft 6 in)
Max width	1.25 m (4 ft 1¼ in)
Max height	1.30 m (4 ft 3¼ in)
Floor area	1.12 m² (12.05 sq ft)
Rear cockpit/baggage compartment:	
Length	1.40 m (4 ft 7 in)
Width	1.00 m (3 ft 3¼ in)
Depth	0.60 m (1 ft 11¾ in)

AREAS:

Wings, gross	31.69 m² (341.1 sq ft)
Ailerons (total)	2.46 m² (26.50 sq ft)
Fin	1.26 m² (13.56 sq ft)
Rudder, incl tab	1.62 m² (17.44 sq ft)
Tailplane	3.34 m² (35.95 sq ft)
Elevators, incl tab	4.22 m² (45.42 sq ft)

WEIGHTS AND LOADINGS:

Weight empty, equipped: BR	1,790 kg (3,946 lb)
BS	2,080 kg (4,585 lb)
Max chemical payload: BR	1,300 kg (2,866 lb)
BS	1,150 kg (2,535 lb)
Max T-O and landing weight: BR, BS	3,000 kg (6,614 lb)
BR (Restricted category)	3,450 kg (7,606 lb)

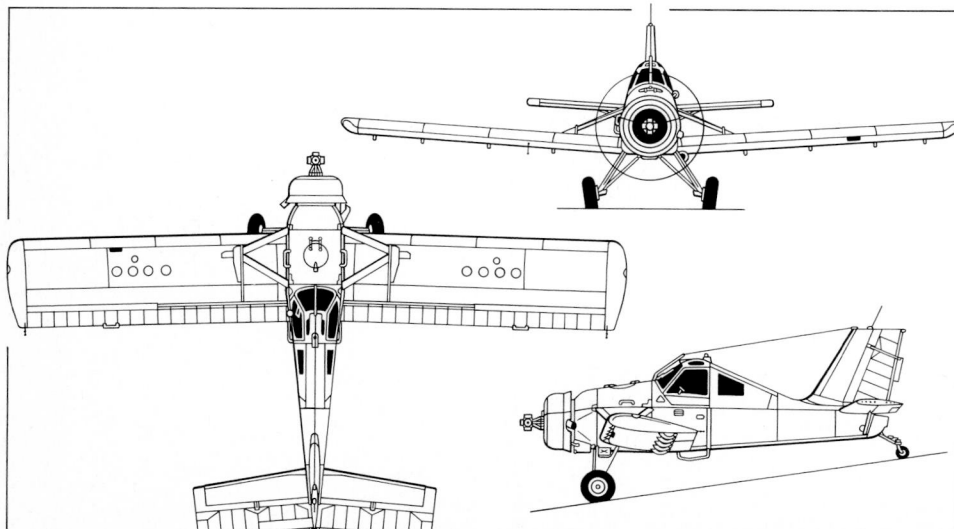

PZL-106BR Kruk single-seat agricultural aircraft (*Jane's/Mike Keep*)

BS (Restricted category)	3,500 kg (7,716 lb)

Max wing loading (Restricted category):
BR	108.86 kg/m² (22.30 lb/sq ft)
BS	110.44 kg/m² (22.62 lb/sq ft)

Max power loading (Restricted category):
BR	7.70 kg/kW (12.68 lb/hp)
BS	4.69 kg/kW (7.72 lb/hp)

PERFORMANCE (at max T-O weight):
Never-exceed speed:	
all	145 knots (270 km/h; 167 mph)
Max level speed at S/L:	
BR, BS	116 knots (215 km/h; 134 mph)
Operating speed with max chemical load:	
BR	81-86 knots (150-160 km/h; 93-99 mph)
BS	86 knots (160 km/h; 99 mph)
Stalling speed at S/L:	
BR, BS	54 knots (100 km/h; 62 mph)
Max rate of climb at S/L (with agricultural equipment):	
BR	228 m (748 ft)/min
BS	372 m (1,220 ft)/min
T-O run (with agricultural equipment):	
BR	250 m (820 ft)
BS	120 m (394 ft)
Landing run (with agricultural equipment):	
BR, BS	200 m (656 ft)
Range with max standard fuel:	
BR, BS	485 nm (900 km; 559 miles)

PZL-106BT TURBO-KRUK

This turboprop version of the Kruk was flown for the first time (prototype SP-PAA) on 18 September 1985. It has increased wing sweep, a taller fin, and carries a larger load of chemical. Production has started, and one series built aircraft had been completed by 1 January 1988.

Differences from the piston engined Kruk are as follows:
AIRFRAME: Wing sweepback 6° at quarter-chord. Dihedral 6°. Taller fin.
POWER PLANT: One 544 kW (730 shp) Walter M 601 D turboprop, driving an Avia V 508 D three-blade propeller with spinner.

DIMENSIONS, EXTERNAL:
Wing span	15.00 m (49 ft 2½ in)
Wing chord, constant	2.16 m (7 ft 1 in)
Wing aspect ratio	7.1
Length overall	10.24 m (33 ft 7¼ in)
Height overall	3.82 m (12 ft 6½ in)
Propeller diameter	2.50 m (8 ft 2½ in)

AREAS:
Wings, gross	31.69 m² (341.1 sq ft)
Fin	1.82 m² (19.59 sq ft)

WEIGHTS AND LOADINGS:
Weight empty, equipped	1,680 kg (3,704 lb)
Max chemical payload	1,300 kg (2,866 lb)
Max T-O weight	3,500 kg (7,716 lb)
Max landing weight	3,000 kg (6,614 lb)
Max wing loading	110.44 kg/m² (22.62 lb/sq ft)
Max power loading	6.07 kg/kW (9.97 lb/shp)

PERFORMANCE (at max T-O weight):
Never-exceed speed	145 knots (270 km/h; 167 mph)
Max level speed at S/L:	
without agricultural equipment	
	135 knots (250 km/h; 155 mph)
with agricultural equipment	
	116 knots (215 km/h; 134 mph)
Operating speed with max chemical load	
	81-92 knots (150-170 km/h; 93-106 mph)
Stalling speed at S/L	49 knots (90 km/h; 56 mph)
Max rate of climb at S/L (with agricultural equipment)	360 m (1,180 ft)/min
T-O run (with agricultural equipment)	230 m (755 ft)

PZL-110 Koliber Series II, Polish built version of the Socata Rallye 100 ST *(Lech Zielaskowski)*

Landing run (with agricultural equipment)	
	130 m (427 ft)
Range with max standard fuel	
	485 nm (900 km; 559 miles)

PZL-140 GĄSIOR (GANDER)

The Gąsior, design of which was started in 1984, has been proposed as a specialised firefighting and cropspraying aircraft combining the qualities and several airframe parts of the PZL Mielec An-2 and Warszawa-Okecie PZL-106 Kruk. Construction of a prototype is not expected before 1990.

If approved, the PZL-140 would combine the power plant, cabin module, rear fuselage, tailplane and tailwheel of the PZL-106BT Turbo-Kruk, with the propeller and main landing gear of the An-2. Thus the only major new structure required would be the forward fuselage, which would form an integral tank or hopper for water, retardant or agricultural chemical. This would have two or four internal chambers with a total volume of 3.4 m³ (120.1 cu ft), permitting a max payload of 3,000 kg (6,614 lb) to be carried.

Versions of the PZL-140 with a new (895 kW; 1,200 hp) variant of the ASz-62 radial engine, or an 895 kW (1,200 shp) TVD-20 turboprop, have also been projected. General appearance of the aircraft is shown in an accompanying drawing.

DIMENSIONS, EXTERNAL:
Wing span (lower)	14.67 m (48 ft 1½ in)
Length overall	10.72 m (35 ft 2 in)
Height overall	5.04 m (16 ft 6½ in)

AREA:
Wings, gross	60.5 m² (651.2 sq ft)

WEIGHTS AND LOADINGS (746 kW; 1,000 hp ASz-62 engine):
Standard weight empty, equipped	2,340 kg (5,159 lb)
Max T-O weight: Normal category	5,250 kg (11,574 lb)
Restricted category	5,700 kg (12,566 lb)
Wing loading (Normal cat)	86.8 kg/m² (17.78 lb/sq ft)
Power loading (Normal cat)	7.04 kg/kW (11.57 lb/hp)

PERFORMANCE (estimated at max Normal T-O weight, 746 kW; 1,000 hp ASz-62):
Never-exceed speed	145 knots (270 km/h; 167 mph)
Normal operating speed	129 knots (240 km/h; 149 mph)
Stalling speed, power off:	
flaps up	59 knots (109 km/h; 68 mph)
flaps down	53 knots (98 km/h; 61 mph)
Max rate of climb at S/L	210 m (689 ft)/min

Service ceiling	3,600 m (11,800 ft)
T-O to 15 m (50 ft): grass	750 m (2,461 ft)
concrete	690 m (2,264 ft)
Landing from 15 m (50 ft): grass	410 m (1,346 ft)
concrete	660 m (2,166 ft)
Normal range, no reserves	270 nm (500 km; 310 miles)
Max ferry range, with fuel in hopper	
	1,888 nm (3,500 km; 2,175 miles)
g limits:	+3/-1 Restricted
	+3.26/-1.3 Normal

PZL-110 KOLIBER (HUMMING-BIRD)

Under this designation, PZL Warszawa-Okecie is producing under licence a two/four-seat version of the Socata Rallye 100 ST, the lowest powered model in the Rallye light aircraft family. The first PZL-110, modified to receive an 86.5 kW (116 hp) PZL-F (Franklin) engine, made its initial flight on 18 April 1978.

The first production PZL-110 was flown on 8 May 1979, and ten Series I aircraft were built during that year. A Polish type certificate was awarded on 24 August 1979.

Although suitable for touring and liaison duties, the Koliber is intended primarily for basic and refresher flying training. Series II production aircraft (built 1983-84) are approved for limited aerobatics, and are for use mainly by Polish aeroclubs. Twenty-five have been delivered to Polish aero clubs since 1984. Production of Series III (45 aircraft) is awaiting availability of PZL-F 4A-235-B31 engines.

An agricultural version, with hopper capacity for 100 kg (220 lb) of liquid chemical, is under study. The following description applies to the Series II production version:
TYPE: Two/three-seat light aircraft.
WINGS: Cantilever low-wing monoplane. Wing section NACA 63A416 (modified). Dihedral 7°. Incidence 4°. All-metal single-spar structure. Wide chord slotted ailerons. Full span automatic leading-edge slats. Long span electrically actuated trailing-edge slotted flaps. Ailerons and flaps have corrugated metal skin. Ground adjustable aileron tabs. No anti-icing.
FUSELAGE: All-metal semi-monocoque structure.
TAIL UNIT: Cantilever all-metal structure, with corrugated skin on mass balanced control surfaces. Fixed incidence tailplane. One controllable tab on elevator; ground adjustable tab on rudder.
LANDING GEAR: Non-retractable tricycle type, with oleo-pneumatic shock absorption. Castoring nosewheel. Hydraulic disc brakes.
POWER PLANT: One 86.5 kW (116 hp) PZL-F 4A-235B1 flat-four engine, driving a PZL US 135 two-blade fixed-pitch propeller. Fuel in two metal tanks in wings, with total capacity of 95 litres (25 US gallons; 20.9 Imp gallons). Refuelling points above wings. Oil capacity 6 litres (1.6 US gallons; 1.3 Imp gallons).
ACCOMMODATION: Two side by side seats, plus bench seat at rear, under large rearward sliding canopy. Dual controls. Heating and ventilation standard.
SYSTEMS AND EQUIPMENT: 12V electrical system, with alternator and 18Ah battery. Equipment optional for Series I and standard for Series II and III includes VHF transceiver, ADF, electrically powered gyro attitude indicator, turn and bank indicator, and directional gyro. Equipment for the training role includes pupil's window blinds for instrument training, front seat backrests suitable for use with back type parachutes, safety belts, and accelerometers.

DIMENSIONS, EXTERNAL:
Wing span	9.74 m (31 ft 11½ in)
Wing chord, constant	1.30 m (4 ft 3 in)
Wing aspect ratio	7.5
Length overall	7.15 m (23 ft 5½ in)
Height overall	2.80 m (9 ft 2¼ in)
Tailplane span	3.67 m (12 ft 0½ in)
Wheel track	2.01 m (6 ft 7¼ in)
Wheelbase	1.71 m (5 ft 7¼ in)
Propeller diameter	1.78 m (5 ft 10 in)

AREAS:
Wings, gross	12.66 m² (136.3 sq ft)

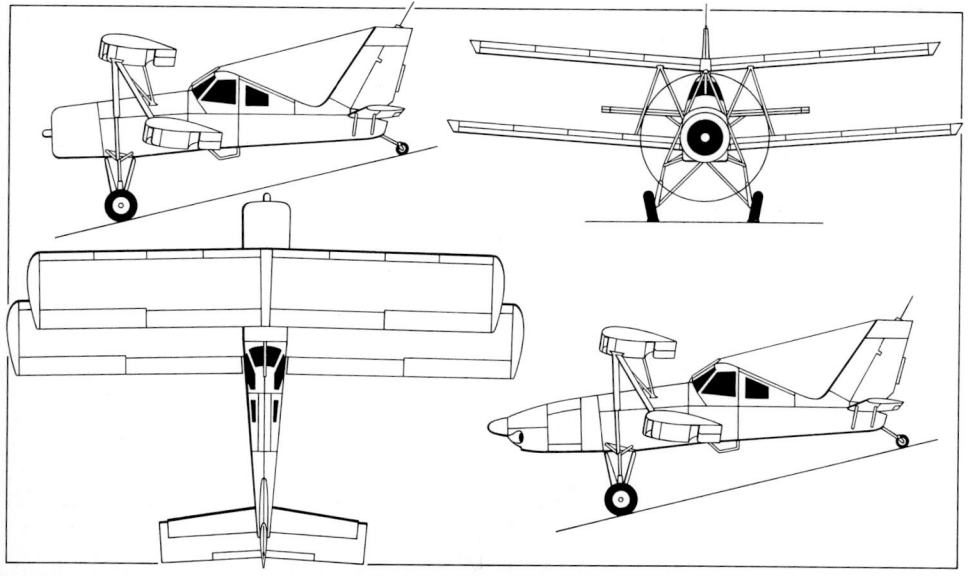

The proposed PZL-140 Gąsior firefighting/agricultural biplane, with additional side view of the PZL-140T Gąsior Turbo *(Jane's/Mike Keep)*

Ailerons (total)	1.56 m² (16.79 sq ft)
Trailing-edge flaps (total)	2.40 m² (25.83 sq ft)
Vertical tail surfaces (total)	1.74 m² (18.73 sq ft)
Horizontal tail surfaces (total)	3.48 m² (37.50 sq ft)

WEIGHTS AND LOADINGS:

Weight empty, equipped	535 kg (1,179 lb)
Max T-O weight: Utility	770 kg (1,697 lb)
Normal	820 kg (1,808 lb)
Max wing loading: Utility	60.82 kg/m² (12.46 lb/sq ft)
Normal	64.77 kg/m² (13.27 lb/sq ft)
Max power loading: Utility	8.90 kg/kW (14.63 lb/hp)
Normal	9.49 kg/kW (15.59 lb/hp)

PERFORMANCE (at 770 kg; 1,697 lb Utility max T-O weight):

Never-exceed speed	145 knots (270 km/h; 167 mph)
Max level speed at S/L	102 knots (190 km/h; 118 mph)
Max cruising speed at S/L	92 knots (170 km/h; 106 mph)
Stalling speed: flaps up	48 knots (89 km/h; 56 mph)
flaps down	41 knots (76 km/h; 48 mph)
Max rate of climb at S/L	180 m (590 ft)/min
Service ceiling	3,500 m (11,480 ft)
T-O run at S/L	155 m (509 ft)
T-O to 15 m (50 ft) at S/L	380 m (1,247 ft)
Landing from 15 m (50 ft) at S/L	275 m (902 ft)
Landing run at S/L	110 m (361 ft)
Range at 500 m (1,640 ft) with max fuel, no reserves	394 nm (730 km; 453 miles)

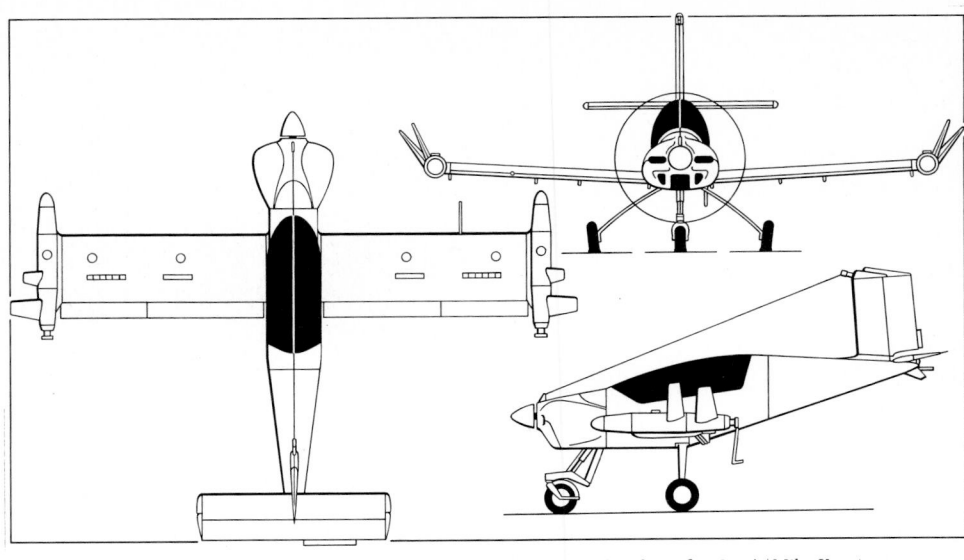

PZL-126 Mrówka agricultural and general purpose light aircraft *(Jane's/Mike Keep)*

PZL-126 MRÓWKA (ANT)

Design of this very small agricultural aircraft, and of an innovatory new airborne spraying system, was initiated in the late 1970s by Dipl Eng Andrzej Słocinski of PZL Warszawa-Okecie, who remains in charge of the Mrówka programme today. Its propeller, rear fuselage and parts of the landing gear were built by students of the factory's training college. Preliminary design was completed in late 1982 and initial detail design work in the second quarter of 1983, but original plans for a first flight in 1985 were revised pending a reappraisal of the project. One reason for this was the unavailability at that time of production PZL-F (Franklin) engines; it was also felt that the proposed use of many components from other existing production Polish aircraft might not be as satisfactory as was thought, and that more effort should be expended in perfecting the new agricultural equipment. However, by the Autumn of 1985 the project was sufficiently advanced for a full size mockup to be built and exhibited at the Olsztyn agricultural aviation exhibition. Construction of three prototypes has now begun, and the first of these was due to fly in mid-1988.

As now configured, the PZL-126 design meets the requirements of FAR Pt 23 (USA) and BCAR Section K (UK). It can be dismantled quickly for long-distance transportation in the cabin of an An-2 biplane, or can be towed on its own landing gear by a light all-terrain vehicle. Landing gear is normally of tricycle type, with a 'taildragger' gear available optionally. Another option to be tested on the prototypes is a wing with full span flaps, airbrakes and spoilers, instead of the basic slotted flaps plus flaperons system. The dedicated agricultural spray system is in the form of vaned and pressurised wingtip pods of chemical, attached by quick-fastening locks to facilitate rapid replacement of empty pods by full ones. A special retractable device for spreading biological agents is installed in the fuselage underside aft of the cockpit. (Further details of individual dispersal systems are given in the 'Equipment' paragraph.)

The primary use intended for the Mrówka is as an economical small aircraft for use on farms and smallholdings, but it is considered suitable also for patrol and liaison missions (eg for detecting/controlling forest fires, identification of diseased vegetation, and monitoring areas of polluted land and water).

TYPE: Single-seat light agricultural and ecological support aircraft.

WINGS: Cantilever low-wing monoplane, of constant chord and NASA GA(W)-1 wing section. Single-spar metal structure, with trailing-edge single-slotted flaps inboard and flaperons outboard. Some components of glassfibre/epoxy construction. Alternative wings with full span flaps, airbrakes and spoilers also to be tested.

FUSELAGE: Conventional metal semi-monocoque structure, built in two portions. Some elements constructed of glassfibre/epoxy composite material.

TAIL UNIT: Cantilever all-metal structure, comprising rectangular fin and rudder and low-set tailplane with one-piece elevator. Trim tab on starboard half of elevator; ground adjustable tab on rudder.

LANDING GEAR: Non-retractable tricycle gear standard. Cantilever self-sprung mainwheel legs; shock absorber in nosewheel unit. Mainwheels fitted with differential hydraulic disc brakes. Tailwheel configuration optional.

POWER PLANT: One 44.7 kW (60 hp) PZL-F 2A-120-C1 flat-twin engine, driving a two-blade fixed-pitch wooden propeller with spinner. (Interchangeable propellers for agricultural flying or patrol mission.) Integral fuel tanks in wing torsion box.

ACCOMMODATION: Single adjustable reclining seat under one-piece moulded canopy. Seat and canopy taken from SZD-51 Junior sailplane.

SYSTEMS: Hydraulic system for mainwheel brakes only; 12V DC electrical system.

Full size mockup of the PZL-126 Mrówka, showing the underfuselage spreader extended and spraypods at the wingtips

AVIONICS: VFR instrumentation standard, plus 720-channel UHF com and 10-channel radio telephone.

EQUIPMENT: Dedicated system for spraying with low volume liquid chemicals (pyrethroids) consists of a 25 litre (6.6 US gallon; 5.5 Imp gallon) pod at each wingtip. Spraying is controlled electrically by a push-button on the throttle lever and effected by dispersing the liquid under pressure via an atomiser at the rear of each pod. An area of 25 ha (61.8 acres) can be covered with one pair of full pods. Biological agents, such as the eggs of the Trichogramma wasp, are carried in capsules in a paper tape wound on a reel which is housed in the lower fuselage behind the cockpit and extended through an openable hatch in the floor. One spreader holds a 3 kg (6.6 lb) package of eggs, on four reels, and at a drop rate of four capsules every 50 m (164 ft) can cover an area of 800 ha (1,977 acres) on a single loading. Like the spray system, the spreader's actuation is electrical, by means of a push-button on the throttle lever. Other equipment can include cameras and first aid appliances.

DIMENSIONS, EXTERNAL:

Wing span (excl spraypods)	5.00 m (16 ft 4¾ in)
Length overall	4.66 m (15 ft 3½ in)
Height overall	2.53 m (8 ft 3¾ in)

WEIGHTS:

Weight empty (without agricultural equipment)	230 kg (507 lb)
Max T-O and landing weight	375 kg (827 lb)

PERFORMANCE (estimated):

Operating speed:	
agricultural mission	65-86 knots (120-160 km/h; 74-99 mph)
patrol mission	65-108 knots (120-200 km/h; 74-124 mph)
Stalling speed (depending on equipment)	41-46 knots (76-84 km/h; 48-53 mph)
Max rate of climb at S/L at max T-O weight	186 m (610 ft)/min
T-O run	142 m (466 ft)
T-O to 15 m (50 ft)	282 m (926 ft)
Swath width (spraying)	13 m (43 ft)
Endurance (patrol mission)	6 h

PZL-130 ORLIK (SPOTTED EAGLET)

The Orlik is being developed for the training of future military and civilian pilots. It is intended to be used for a wide range of duties, including preselection training, basic handling, aerobatics, instrument flying, navigation training, formation flying, aerial combat training, air gunnery and ground attack, reconnaissance and target acquisition, and target towing. Cockpit instruments and displays are installed in modular units similar to those of modern combat aircraft, to permit quick changes of avionics and equipment and enable the Orlik to perform as a 'flying operational simulator' for jet powered military aircraft.

Initial proposals for the PZL-130 were prepared in 1980, and detail design began in the Autumn of 1981 under the leadership of Mr Andrzej Frydrychewicz. Prototype construction started in the Spring of 1983. Two prototypes began flight testing in 1984: SP-PCA (c/n 002) on 12 October and SP-PCC on 29 December, followed by SP-PCB on 12 January 1985; a static test aircraft was also completed. The Orlik was designed and built to FAR Pt 23 standards and was certificated in two categories (Utility and Aerobatic) in early 1988. Construction of pre-production aircraft started in 1986. A turboprop powered **Turbo Orlik** prototype (described separately) was flown in mid-1986; future plans also include a version with extended wingtips, increasing span to 9.00 m (29 ft 6⅓ in).

The following description applies to the piston engined prototypes:

TYPE: Tandem two-seat primary, basic and multi-purpose trainer.

WINGS: Cantilever low-wing monoplane. Wing section NACA 64$_2$215 (modified). Dihedral 5° from roots. Incidence 0° at root, −3° at tip. One-piece all-metal (light alloy) multi-spar box structure. Torsion box, stiffened by riveted omega formers, forms integral fuel tanks. Trailing-edge skin panels are stiffened by L formers, electrically spot welded. Tapered planform, with raked tips of glassfibre/epoxy. Leading-edges are detachable. All-metal constant chord three-position single-slotted trailing-edge flaps, actuated electrically. Frise differential ailerons are also all-metal and of constant chord, aerodynamically and mass balanced, and actuated mechanically via pushrods and torque tube in fuselage. Electrically actuated trim tab on port aileron. Provision for anti-icing system in leading-edges.

FUSELAGE: All-metal (light alloy) unpressurised semi-monocoque structure, with skin panels stiffened by electrically spot welded L formers.

TAIL UNIT: Cantilever light alloy structure, with sweptback vertical and non-swept horizontal surfaces. Fin integral with rear fuselage. Curved dorsal fin; shallow ventral strake under fuselage tailcone. One-piece two-spar fixed incidence tailplane. Elevators aerodynamically and mass balanced, controlled by rods and cables; electrically actuated trim tab on port elevator. Aerodynamically and mass balanced rudder, also with electrically actuated trim tab, is cable controlled.

LANDING GEAR: Pneumatically retractable type, all three units retracting into fuselage (mainwheels inward, nosewheel rearward). PZL Warszawa-Okecie oleo-pneumatic shock absorber in each unit (nosewheel on semi-fork with shimmy damper and centring device). Low pressure tubeless tyres (2.0 bars; 29 lb/sq in in all three), size 500 × 200 mm (main) and 400 × 140 mm (nose). Differential disc brakes, operated pneumatically. Parking brake. No anti-skid units.

POWER PLANT: One 246 kW (330 hp) Vedeneyev M-14Pm (m = modified, without reduction gear) nine-cylinder radial aircooled engine, driving a PZL US 142 three-blade constant-speed metal propeller with pointed spinner. Four integral fuel tanks (two of 110 litres; 29 US gallons; 24.2 Imp gallons and two of 100 litres; 26.5 US gallons; 22.0 Imp gallons capacity) in wing torsion box, plus a 9 litre (2.5 US gallon; 2.0 Imp gallon) collector tank in fuselage; total usable internal fuel capacity 420 litres (111 US gallons; 92.4 Imp gallons). Overwing refuelling point for each wing tank. No provision for external fuel tanks. Oil capacity 18 litres (4.75 US gallons; 4.0 Imp gallons). Fuel and oil systems adapted for aerobatics, including up to 30 s of inverted flight. Electrically adjustable exhaust flaps for engine cooling air.

ACCOMMODATION: Tandem seating for pupil and instructor under one-piece canopy, which opens sideways to starboard. Rear (instructor's) seat slightly elevated. Both seats are adjustable electrically, can accommodate back type and seat type parachutes, and are fitted with seat belts/harnesses. Full dual controls standard; rudder pedals are adjustable (three positions). Windscreen and canopy frames are of glassfibre/epoxy; windscreen is removable, canopy jettisonable. Cockpits heated (electric heater with blower) and ventilated. Baggage compartment aft of rear seat.

SYSTEMS: Two independent pneumatic systems, each at 50 bars (725 lb/sq in) pressure: main system for engine starting, landing gear extension/retraction, and wheel braking/steering; emergency system for all of these except landing gear retraction. External source connector. No hydraulic system. Electrical power (24V DC) supplied by 3kW generator and 18Ah battery; system includes voltage regulator with overvoltage relay, and external DC power socket. Provision for anti-icing of wing leading-edges.

AVIONICS AND EQUIPMENT: RS-6102 720-channel UHF com and ARL-1601 ADF are standard; nav, VOR/ILS, transponder and radio altimeter are optional. First aid kit and fire extinguisher.

ARMAMENT: No installed armament. Four underwing pylons for practice bombs, gun and rocket pods or other weapon training stores. Provision for gunsight, gun camera and armament control system.

DIMENSIONS, EXTERNAL:

Wing span	8.00 m (26 ft 3 in)
Wing chord: at root	2.00 m (6 ft 6¾ in)
mean aerodynamic	1.62 m (5 ft 3¾ in)
Wing aspect ratio	5.2
Length overall	8.45 m (27 ft 8¾ in)
Fuselage: Max width	0.90 m (2 ft 11½ in)
Height overall	3.53 m (11 ft 7 in)
Tailplane span	3.50 m (11 ft 5¾ in)
Wheel track	3.10 m (10 ft 2 in)
Wheelbase	2.22 m (7 ft 3½ in)
Propeller diameter	1.93 m (6 ft 4 in)
Propeller ground clearance	0.30 m (11¾ in)

DIMENSIONS, INTERNAL:

Cockpits: Length	2.95 m (9 ft 8¼ in)
Baggage compartment volume	0.17 m³ (6.0 cu ft)

AREAS:

Wings, gross	12.28 m² (132.2 sq ft)
Ailerons (total, incl tab)	1.38 m² (14.85 sq ft)

Third flying prototype of the PZL-130 Orlik tandem two-seat trainer *(Lech Zielaskowski)*

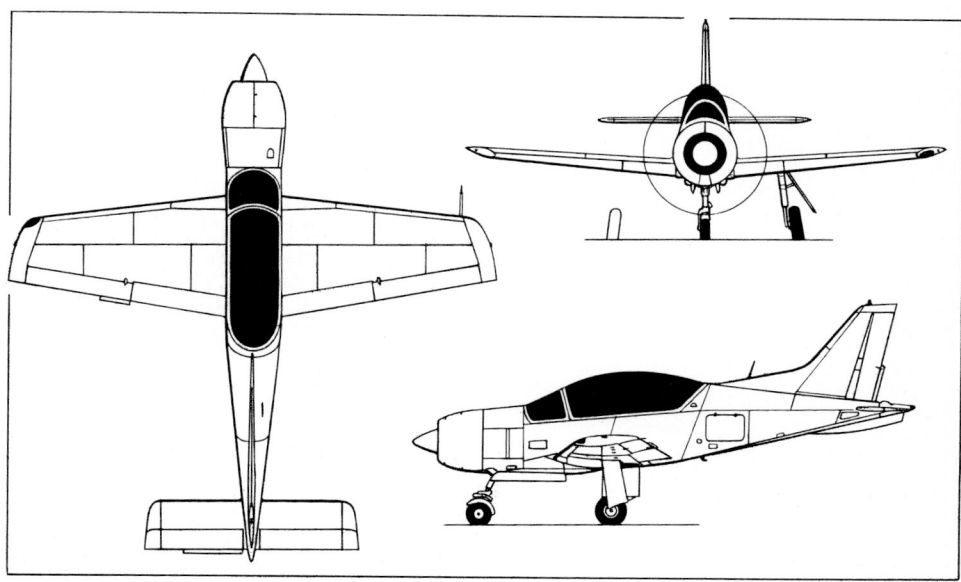

PZL-130 Orlik (Vedeneyev M-14Pm engine) *(Pilot Press)*

Trailing-edge flaps (total)	1.37 m² (14.75 sq ft)
Fin, incl dorsal fin	1.20 m² (12.92 sq ft)
Rudder, incl tab	0.65 m² (6.97 sq ft)
Tailplane	1.81 m² (19.48 sq ft)
Elevators (total, incl tab)	0.94 m² (10.12 sq ft)

WEIGHTS AND LOADINGS (A: Aerobatic, U: Utility):

Weight empty, equipped, standard	1,147 kg (2,529 lb)
Max usable fuel	305 kg (672 lb)
Max T-O and landing weight: A	1,450 kg (3,196 lb)
U	1,600 kg (3,527 lb)
Max wing loading: A	118.08 kg/m² (24.20 lb/sq ft)
U	130.29 kg/m² (26.70 lb/sq ft)
Max power loading: A	5.90 kg/kW (9.69 lb/hp)
U	6.50 kg/kW (10.69 lb/hp)

PERFORMANCE (S/L, at max Aerobatic T-O weight except where indicated):

Never-exceed speed	234 knots (434 km/h; 269 mph)
Max level speed	183 knots (340 km/h; 211 mph)
Max cruising speed (75% power)	156 knots (290 km/h; 180 mph)
Stalling speed, power off:	
flaps up: A	72 knots (132 km/h; 82 mph)
U	74 knots (137 km/h; 85 mph)
flaps down: A	65 knots (119 km/h; 74 mph)
U	68 knots (125 km/h; 78 mph)
Max rate of climb at S/L	420 m (1,378 ft)/min
Service ceiling	4,270 m (14,000 ft)
T-O run	340 m (1,115 ft)
T-O to 15 m (50 ft)	650 m (2,133 ft)
Landing from 15 m (50 ft)	590 m (1,936 ft)
Landing run	250 m (821 ft)

Range with max fuel, no reserves:

A at 124 knots (230 km/h; 143 mph)	764 nm (1,416 km; 880 miles)
U at 92 knots (170 km/h; 105 mph)	688 nm (1,276 km; 793 miles)

Endurance with max fuel, no reserves, speeds as above:

A	6 h 6 min
U	7 h 25 min
g limits:	+6/−3 at Aerobatic T-O weight
	+4.4/−1.76 at max T-O weight

PZL TURBO ORLIK

This turboprop version of the Orlik, intended for the export market, was designed in 1985 by Mr Andrzej Frydrychewicz, the chief designer of WSK-PZL Warszawa-Okecie, in collaboration with the Canadian company Airtech Canada (which see). In January 1986 work began to convert the third PZL-130 (SP-PCC) to take a Pratt & Whitney Canada PT6A-25A engine. Changes were made to the landing gear, internal systems (including replacement of the two pneumatic systems by a single hydraulic system), avionics and instrumentation. The dorsal fin was also enlarged.

This aircraft made its first flight as the Turbo Orlik prototype on 13 July 1986, piloted by Mr Jerzy Wojnar. Subsequent test flying was undertaken by Canadian test pilot B. Hartman and by Mr Bogdan Wolski, the president of Airtech Canada. The Turbo Orlik received a provisional type certificate under FAR Pt 23 in January 1987, but later that month, while being demonstrated by Mr Wolski to a representative of the Colombian Air Force, the aircraft and

The Turbo Orlik first prototype on a flight test in Canada

both occupants were lost. A second prototype is being converted to complete the certification programme.

WINGS, FUSELAGE, TAIL UNIT: As for Orlik, except for fuselage adaptation to turboprop engine, and enlargement of dorsal fin.

LANDING GEAR: As described for Orlik, but with hydraulic extension/retraction and braking.

POWER PLANT: One 410 kW (550 shp) Pratt & Whitney Canada PT6A-25A turboprop, driving a Hartzell HC-B3TN-3B/T10173K-11R three-blade constant-speed metal propeller with feathering and reverse pitch. Propeller blades de-iced electrically. Internal fuel capacity as for Orlik; provision for two 150 litre (39.6 US gallon; 33 Imp gallon) auxiliary tanks on underwing stations.

ACCOMMODATION: As for Orlik.

SYSTEMS: Hydraulic system added for landing gear actuation. Pneumatic systems deleted. Electrical power (115V/400Hz) supplied by 6kW Lear Siegler starter/generator and two 24V 15Ah nickel-cadmium batteries, with three-phase 36V/400Hz AC converters. External DC power socket. Oxygen bottles and crew masks.

AVIONICS: King VHF and UHF com, intercom and ADF.

ARMAMENT: As described for Orlik. Four underwing hardpoints, stressed for 200 kg (441 lb) each inboard, 160 kg (353 lb) each outboard.

DIMENSIONS, EXTERNAL AND INTERNAL, AND AREAS:
As for Orlik except:
Length overall	8.68 m (28 ft 5¾ in)
Propeller diameter	2.29 m (7 ft 6 in)

DESIGN WEIGHTS AND LOADINGS (A: Aerobatic, U: Utility):
Weight empty, equipped, standard	1,150 kg (2,535 lb)
Max usable fuel (internal)	366 kg (807 lb)
Max T-O and landing weight: A	1,580 kg (3,483 lb)
U (no stores)	1,750 kg (3,858 lb)
U (with external stores)	2,155 kg (4,751 lb)
Max wing loading: A	128.66 kg/m² (26.35 lb/sq ft)
U (no stores)	142.51 kg/m² (29.19 lb/sq ft)
U (with external stores)	175.49 kg/m² (35.94 lb/sq ft)
Max power loading: A	3.85 kg/kW (6.33 lb/shp)
U (no stores)	4.27 kg/kW (7.01 lb/shp)
U (with external stores)	5.26 kg/kW (8.64 lb/shp)

DESIGN PERFORMANCE (at max Aerobatic T-O weight except where indicated):
Max permissible diving speed	302 knots (560 km/h; 347 mph)

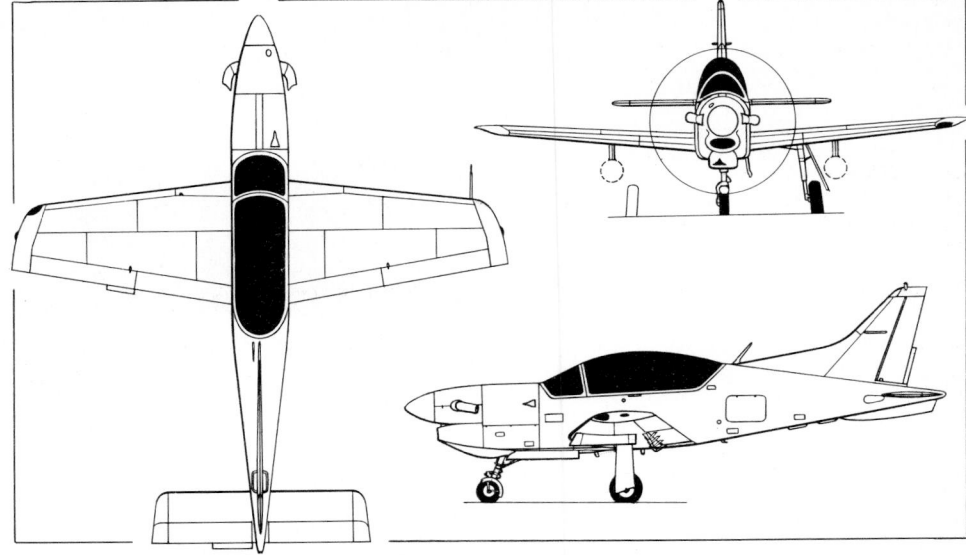

PZL Warszawa-Okecie/Airtech Canada Turbo Orlik (*Pilot Press*)

Max level speed at 4,575 m (15,000 ft)	269 knots (499 km/h; 310 mph)
Max cruising speed at S/L	236 knots (438 km/h; 272 mph)
Stalling speed, power off:	
flaps up, landing gear down	78 knots (144 km/h; 90 mph)
flaps and landing gear down:	
A	63 knots (115 km/h; 72 mph)
U (no stores)	66 knots (122 km/h; 76 mph)
U (with external stores)	73 knots (135 km/h; 84 mph)
Max rate of climb at S/L	954 m (3,130 ft)/min
Service ceiling	10,060 m (33,000 ft)
T-O run	250 m (821 ft)
T-O to 15 m (50 ft)	410 m (1,345 ft)
Landing from 15 m (50 ft)	570 m (1,870 ft)
Landing run	370 m (1,214 ft)

Range with max internal fuel, AUW of 1,600 kg (3,527 lb):
U at 248 knots (460 km/h; 286 mph)	603 nm (1,117 km; 694 miles)
U at 140 knots (260 km/h; 161 mph)	694 nm (1,287 km; 800 miles)

Endurance with max internal fuel, AUW as above:
U at 248 knots (460 km/h; 286 mph)	2 h 26 min
U at 140 knots (260 km/h; 161 mph)	4 h 57 min

Range with max internal and external fuel, AUW of 1,977 kg (4,358 lb):
U at 245 knots (454 km/h; 282 mph)	1,166 nm (2,161 km; 1,343 miles)
U at 147 knots (272 km/h; 169 mph)	1,198 nm (2,220 km; 1,397 miles)

Endurance with max internal and external fuel, AUW as above:
U at 245 knots (454 km/h; 282 mph)	4 h 46 min
U at 147 knots (272 km/h; 169 mph)	8 h 10 min
g limits	as for Orlik

PORTUGAL

OGMA
OFICINAS GERAIS DE MATERIAL AERONÁUTICO (General Aeronautical Material Workshops)

2615 Alverca
Telephone: (1) 258 1000, 1293, 1979 and 2368
Telex: 14479 OGMA P
Fax: (1) 258 1288
DIRECTOR:
Lt-Gen Eng Rui do Carmo da Conceição Espadinha
DEPUTY DIRECTOR AND COMMERCIAL MANAGER:
Maj-Gen A. Leitão
PRODUCTION MANAGER: Col C. A. Silva Lopes

OGMA, founded in 1918, is the department of the Portuguese Air Force responsible for maintenance and repair, at depot level, of its aircraft, avionics, engines, ground communications and radar equipment, and can undertake similar work for civil or military national or foreign customers. OGMA has a total covered area of 116,000 m² (1,248,612 sq ft), and a workforce of approx 2,500 people.

Under a contract signed in 1959, OGMA undertakes IRAN, refurbishing and rehabilitation, periodic inspection and emergency maintenance and crash repair of US Air Force and US Navy aircraft. For Aérospatiale of France, OGMA has manufactured main and tail rotor structures for the SA 315B Lama and some components for other helicopters. As indicated in the French section, it is undertaking licence assembly of 18 Aérospatiale Epsilon trainers ordered by the Portuguese Air Force. Deliveries are due to begin in 1989.

OGMA's engine repair and maintenance facility, with a covered area of 28,000 m² (301,390 sq ft), overhauls military and commercial turbojets and turbofans (up to 146.8 kN; 33,000 lb st), and turboprop and turboshaft engines of up to 5,667 kW (7,600 shp). In addition to two fully computerised test cells, this facility is equipped with plasma spray, two vacuum furnaces, complete cleaning and electroplating facilities, non-destructive testing, shot-peening and other specific equipment. Besides work for the Portuguese Air Force, OGMA also overhauls, under contract, Artouste III and Turmo IV turboshaft engines for Turbomeca of France; and, as a maintenance/overhaul centre for Allison, T56 engines and gearboxes for the USAF and other customers.

OGMA performs major maintenance on C-130/L-100 Hercules transport aircraft as a Lockheed Service Center, and on Alouette III, Puma and Ecureuil helicopters as an Aérospatiale Station-Service.

The Avionics Division has premises covering an area of approx 6,400 m² (68,900 sq ft), fully equipped to the latest demands in the field of maintenance for new generation avionics, communications systems, test equipment and calibration laboratories. OGMA is licensed by Litton Systems of Canada to carry out level 2 and 2A maintenance on LTN-72 INS equipment, and is currently doing work for that company.

ROMANIA

CNIAR
CENTRUL NATIONAL AL INDUSTRIEI AERONAUTICE ROMÂNE (National Centre of the Romanian Aeronautical Industry)

39 Bulevardul Aerogarii, Sector 1, Bucharest
Telephone: 50 27 14
Telex: 11648 AEROM
DIRECTOR GENERAL: Dipl Eng Ion Petroaica
COMMERCIAL DIRECTOR: Dipl Eng Vasile Racovitan

Romania has had a tradition of aviation since the earliest days of flying, dating from the first monoplane built in France in early 1906 by the Romanian engineer Traian Vuia. Since then the Romanian aircraft industry (IAR) has produced some 90 different types of landplane, including helicopters (of which 80 were Romanian designed), and about 40 different types of sailplane. The foundations for the present industry were laid at Brasov in 1926, and details of its history from then until the late 1960s can be found in the 1983-84 and earlier editions of *Jane's*.

The industry was reorganised in 1968, and its activities are now undertaken, within the Ministry of Machine Building Industry, by the CNIAR. The two main aircraft factories are the ICA at Brasov and IAv Bucuresti. The latter was enlarged in the late 1970s to cater for the Rombac 1-11 manufacturing programme. A third factory, IAv Bacau, builds the Soviet Yak-52 under licence and manufactures various components for the IAR-823 and IAR-316B. Romanian versions of the SOKO/CNIAR Orao/IAR-93 (see International section) are manufactured at IAv Craiova, which is also developing the indigenous IAR-99 Soim jet trainer. Viper 632 and 633 engines for the IAR-93, Spey 512-14DW engines for the Rombac 1-11, and Turmo IV CA engines for the IAR-330 (Puma) helicopter, are built by the Turbomecanica Enterprise in Bucharest.

Aerofina Bucharest is a dedicated factory for avionics and airborne equipment; forgings and castings for the aviation industry are manufactured at IMRA (Intreprinderea Metalurgica Romana Pentru Aeronautica), also in Bucharest.

Exports and imports of aircraft and aero engines are the responsibility of the CNA (see next entry), formed in 1979; avionics and electronic equipment sales are dealt with by Electronum and Electroexportimport. Aeronautical research and development are undertaken by INCREST (formerly IMFCA), the Aerospace Research and Design Institute at Bucharest. INCREST also designs and manufactures aerospace equipment, including anti-skid brakes, engine stands, fuel monitoring equipment, intercoms and various aviation raw materials. The flight test centre is the CIIAR (Centrul de încercari in zbor) at Craiova.

CNA

CENTRUL NATIONAL AERONAUTIC
(Intreprindere de Comert Exterior)
(National Centre for Aeronautical Foreign Trade)

Bulevardul Dacia 13, Casuta Postala 22-149, R-70185 Bucharest
Telephone: 12 08 78
Telex: 10660 CNAER

DIRECTOR GENERAL: Dipl Eng Aurel Adăscălitei
PUBLICITY: Dipl Ec Eugenia Irina Boros

IAv BACAU

INTREPRINDEREA DE AVIOANE BACAU
(Bacau Aircraft Enterprise)

Bacau
DIRECTOR GENERAL: Dipl Eng Eugen Pascariu

This factory, originally an aircraft repair centre known as URA (later IRA), now manufactures hydraulic, pneumatic, air-conditioning, fuel system and landing gear components for the Rombac 1-11 jet transport, the IAR-823 light aircraft and IAR-316B helicopter, and the IAR-93 close support fighter. It is building under licence the Soviet Yakovlev Yak-52 two-seat trainer, and is expected to manufacture the single-seat Yak-53 (see Soviet section).

IAv BACAU (YAKOVLEV) Yak-52

Announced in late 1978, the Yak-52 is a tandem-cockpit variant of the Yak-50, with unchanged span and length, but with a semi-retractable tricycle landing gear to reduce damage in a wheels-up landing. It is a replacement for the Yak-18, and made its first flight less than a year after design was started. Production was entrusted to the Romanian aircraft industry, under the Comecon (Council for Mutual Economic Assistance) programme.

Manufacture began at Bacau in 1979, and the aircraft is in series production; it does not have an IAR designation number. IAv Bacau delivered its 1,000th Yak-52 in 1987, and production was continuing in 1988.

TYPE: Tandem two-seat piston engined primary trainer.

WINGS: Cantilever low-wing monoplane of single-spar stressed skin all-metal construction. Clark YN wing section, with thickness/chord ratio of 14.5% at root, 9% at tip. Dihedral 2° from roots. Incidence 2°. No sweepback; each wing comprises a single straight-tapered panel, attached directly to the side of the fuselage. Fabric covered slotted ailerons. Light alloy trailing-edge split flaps. Ground adjustable tab on each aileron.

FUSELAGE: Conventional light alloy semi-monocoque structure.

TAIL UNIT: Cantilever light alloy structure. Fin and fixed incidence tailplane metal covered; control surfaces fabric covered. Horn balanced rudder, with ground adjustable tab. Mass balanced elevators. Controllable tab in port elevator.

LANDING GEAR: Semi-retractable tricycle type, with single wheel on each unit. Pneumatic actuation, nosewheel retracting rearward, main units forward. All three wheels remain fully exposed to airflow, against the undersurface of the fuselage and wings respectively, to offer greater safety in the event of a wheels-up emergency landing. Oleo-pneumatic shock absorbers. Mainwheel tyre size 500 × 150; nosewheel tyre size 400 × 150. Tyre pressure (all units) 3.0 bars (43 lb/sq in). Pneumatic brakes. Skis

can be fitted in place of wheels for Winter operations, permissible at temperatures down to –42°C.

POWER PLANT: One 268 kW (360 hp) Vedeneyev M-14P nine-cylinder aircooled radial, driving a two-blade variable-pitch propeller type V-530TA-D35, without spinner. Louvres in front of cowling to regulate cooling. Two-part cowling, split on horizontal centreline. Two fuel tanks, in wingroots forward of spar, each with capacity of 61 litres (16.1 US gallons; 13.5 Imp gallons). Collector tank in fuselage of 5.5 litres (1.45 US gallons; 1.25 Imp gallons) capacity supplies engine during inverted flight. Total internal fuel capacity 122 litres (32.2 US gallons; 27 Imp gallons). Oil capacity 22.5 litres (5.9 US gallons; 5 Imp gallons).

ACCOMMODATION: Tandem seats for pupil and instructor (at rear) under long 'glasshouse' canopy, with separate rearward sliding hood over each seat. Seats and dual flying controls are adjustable. Sides of cockpit have a soft synthetic lining. Heating and ventilation standard.

SYSTEMS: No hydraulic system. Independent main and emergency pneumatic systems, pressure 50 bars (725 lb/sq in), for flap actuation, landing gear actuation, engine starting, and wheel brake control. Pneumatic systems supplied by two compressed air bottles, mounted behind rear seat and recharged in flight by an AK-50T compressor. GSR-3000M 28.5V engine driven generator and (in port wing) 25V Varley battery for DC electric power; two static inverters in fuselage for 36V AC power at 400Hz.

AVIONICS AND EQUIPMENT: Dual engine and flying instruments. Equipment includes GMK-1A gyro compass, ARK-15M automatic radio compass, Baklan-5 VHF com and SPU-9 intercom. Oxygen system optional.

DIMENSIONS, EXTERNAL:
Wing span	9.30 m (30 ft 6¼ in)
Wing chord: at root	1.997 m (6 ft 6¾ in)
at tip	1.082 m (3 ft 6½ in)
Wing aspect ratio	5.8
Length overall	7.745 m (25 ft 5 in)
Fuselage: Max width	0.90 m (2 ft 11½ in)
Height overall	2.70 m (8 ft 10¼ in)
Tailplane span	3.16 m (10 ft 4½ in)
Wheel track	2.715 m (8 ft 10¾ in)
Wheelbase	1.86 m (6 ft 1¼ in)
Propeller diameter	2.40 m (7 ft 10½ in)
Propeller ground clearance	0.36 m (1 ft 2¼ in)

DIMENSIONS, INTERNAL:
Cockpit: Max width	0.736 m (2 ft 5 in)
Max height	1.12 m (3 ft 8 in)

AREAS:
Wings, gross	15.00 m² (161.5 sq ft)
Ailerons (total)	1.98 m² (21.31 sq ft)
Trailing-edge flaps (total)	1.03 m² (11.09 sq ft)
Fin	0.609 m² (6.55 sq ft)
Rudder	0.871 m² (9.37 sq ft)
Tailplane	1.325 m² (14.26 sq ft)
Elevators (total, incl tab)	1.535 m² (16.52 sq ft)

WEIGHTS AND LOADINGS:
Weight empty	1,000 kg (2,205 lb)
Max fuel load	100 kg (220 lb)
Max T-O weight	1,290 kg (2,844 lb)
Max wing loading	86.0 kg/m² (17.61 lb/sq ft)
Max power loading	4.80 kg/kW (7.90 lb/hp)

PERFORMANCE:
Never-exceed speed	194 knots (360 km/h; 223 mph)
Max level speed at 500 m (1,640 ft)	162 knots (300 km/h; 186 mph)
Max cruising speed at 1,000 m (3,280 ft)	145 knots (270 km/h; 167 mph)
Econ cruising speed at 1,000 m (3,280 ft)	102 knots (190 km/h; 118 mph)
Stalling speed: flaps up	60 knots (110 km/h; 69 mph)
flaps down:	
power on	54-57 knots (100-105 km/h; 62-66 mph)
engine idling	46-49 knots (85-90 km/h; 53-56 mph)
Max rate of climb at S/L	420 m (1,378 ft)/min
Service ceiling: without oxygen	4,000 m (13,125 ft)
with oxygen	6,000 m (19,685 ft)
Min ground turning radius	6.22 m (20 ft 5 in)
T-O run	170 m (558 ft)
Landing run	300 m (984 ft)
Range with max fuel	297 nm (550 km; 341 miles)
Endurance with max fuel	2 h 50 min
g limits	+7/–5

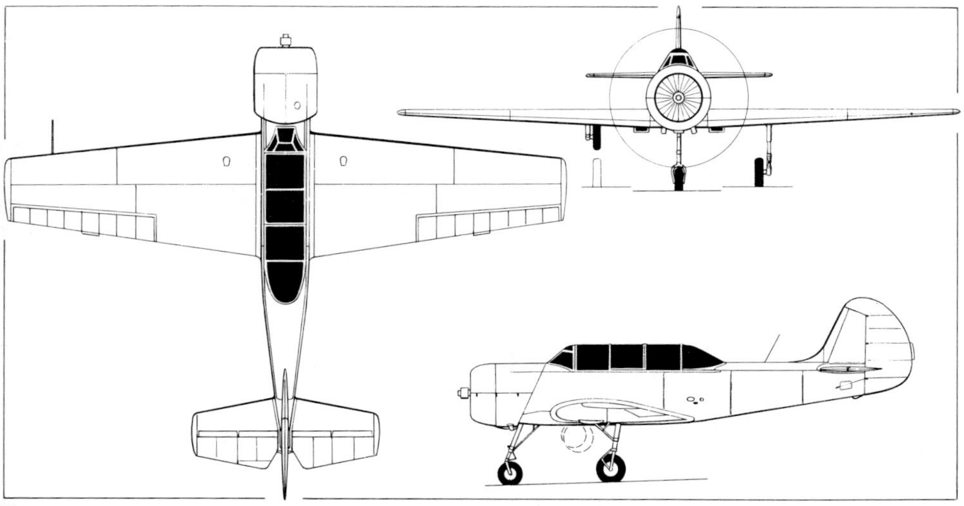

Yakovlev Yak-52 primary trainer, of which more than 1,000 have been built in Romania by IAv Bacau

Yakovlev Yak-52 tandem two-seat primary trainer *(Pilot Press)*

IAv BUCURESTI

INTREPRINDEREA DE AVIOANE BUCURESTI (Bucharest Aircraft Enterprise)

44 Bulevardul Ficusului, Baneasa Airport, Bucharest
Telephone: Bucharest 336260
DIRECTOR GENERAL: Dipl Eng Teodor Zanfirescu
CHIEF ENGINEER: Dipl Eng Mirica Dimitrescu

IAv Bucuresti's predecessor, IRMA, was formed in 1959 from part of the former URMV-3 at Brasov (see 1979-80 and earlier editions of *Jane's*). The present title was adopted in 1980. The factory is currently responsible for

manufacture of the BAe One-Eleven (components and complete aircraft) and the Pilatus Britten-Norman Islander. It specialises in the repair and overhaul of various large and small aircraft; is agent and repair centre for Textron Lycoming engines; and manufactures aircraft equipment.

IAv BUCURESTI ROMBAC 1-11 (BAe ONE-ELEVEN)

IAv Bucuresti is the Romanian prime contractor for the licence manufacture of BAe One-Eleven twin-turbofan transports, under the Romanian designation Rombac 1-11.

A corresponding programme provides for Romanian manufacture of the Rolls-Royce Spey engines. Details of British production of the One-Eleven can be found in the 1974-75 and 1981-82 *Jane's*.

Industrial transfer to the Romanian aircraft industry, preceded in 1981-82 by delivery of a BAe built Srs 487 freighter and two Srs 525/1s, was completed in 1986 and the first flight by a Romanian assembled Srs 560 (YR-BRA) was made on 18 September 1982. This aircraft was handed over to Tarom, the Romanian state airline, on 24 December 1982, and entered service in January 1983. Of the initial batch of 22 to be built in Romania, six had been completed

Romanian assembled Rombac 1-11-561 RC of Ryanair (two Rolls-Royce Spey Mk 512-14DW turbofans) *(Paul R. Duffy)*

by 1 January 1987, and four more were due for completion by the end of that year.

Romanian versions are designated as follows:

Series 495. Combines standard fuselage and accommodation of British built Series 400 with wings and power plant of Series 560 and a modified landing gear system, using low-pressure tyres, to permit operation from secondary low-pressure runways with poorer grade surfaces. Two on order in 1987.

Series 560. Derived from British built Series 300/400, this version has a lengthened fuselage (2.54 m; 100 in fwd of wing, 1.57 m; 62 in aft) which accommodates up to 109 passengers. Wingtip extensions increase span by 1.52 m (5 ft). Main landing gear strengthened and heavier wing planks used to cater for increased AUW.

In collaboration with foreign companies and interested operators, Romania plans to undertake a Tay powered updated version of the Rombac 1-11.

The following description applies to the currently available Series 495 and 560:

TYPE: Twin-turbofan short/medium-range transport.

WINGS: Cantilever low-wing monoplane. Modified NACA cambered wing section. Thickness/chord ratio 12½% at root, 11% at tip. Dihedral 2°. Incidence 2° 30′. Sweepback 20° at quarter-chord. All-metal structure of copper based aluminium alloy, built on fail-safe principles. Three-shear-web torsion box with integrally machined skin/stringer panels. Ailerons of Redux bonded light alloy honeycomb, manually operated through servo tabs. Port servo tab used for trimming. Hydraulically operated light alloy Fowler flaps. Light alloy spoiler/airbrakes on upper surface of wing, operated hydraulically. Hydraulically actuated lift dumpers, inboard of spoilers. Flaps on Series 495 have a glassfibre coating. Thermal de-icing of wing leading-edges with engine bleed air.

FUSELAGE: Conventional circular-section all-metal fail-safe structure with continuous frames and stringers. Skin made from copper based aluminium alloy.

TAIL UNIT: Cantilever all-metal fail-safe structure, with variable incidence T tailplane, controlled through duplicated hydraulic units. Fin integral with rear fuselage. Elevators and rudder actuated hydraulically through tandem jacks. Leading-edges of fin and tailplane de-iced by engine bleed air.

LANDING GEAR: Retractable tricycle type, with twin wheels on each unit. Hydraulic retraction, nose unit forward, main units inward. Oleo-pneumatic shock absorbers. Hydraulic nosewheel steering. Wheels have tubeless tyres, 5-plate heavy duty hydraulic disc brakes, and anti-skid units. Mainwheel tyres size 40 × 12 on Srs 560, pressure 11.03 bars (160 lb/sq in); size 44 × 16 on Srs 495, pressure 5.72 bars (83 lb/sq in). Nosewheel tyres size 24 × 7.25 on Srs 560, pressure 7.58 bars (110 lb/sq in); size 24 × 7.7 on Srs 495, pressure 7.24 bars (105 lb/sq in).

POWER PLANT: Two Rolls-Royce Spey Mk 512-14DW turbofans, each rated at 55.8 kN (12,550 lb st), pod-mounted on sides of rear fuselage. Fuel in integral wing tanks with usable capacity of 10,160 litres (2,684 US gallons; 2,235 Imp gallons) and centre-section tank of 3,968 litres (1,048 US gallons; 873 Imp gallons) usable capacity; total usable fuel 14,129 litres (3,732 US gallons; 3,108 Imp gallons). Executive versions can be fitted with auxiliary fuel tanks of up to 5,791 litres (1,530 US gallons; 1,274 Imp gallons) usable capacity. Pressure refuelling point in fuselage forward of wing on starboard side. Provision for gravity refuelling. Oil capacity (total engine oil) 13.66 litres (3.6 US gallons; 3 Imp gallons) per engine. Engine hush kits standard.

ACCOMMODATION (Srs 495): Crew of two on flight deck and up to 89 passengers in main cabin. Single class or mixed class layout, with movable divider bulkhead to permit any first/tourist ratio. Typical mixed class layout has 16 first class (four abreast) and 49 tourist (five abreast) seats. Galley units normally at front on starboard side. Coat

space available on port side aft of flight deck. Ventral entrance with hydraulically operated airstair. Forward passenger door on port side incorporates optional power operated airstair. Galley service door forward on starboard side. Overwing emergency exit on each side. Two baggage and freight holds under floor, fore and aft of wings, with doors on starboard side. Upward opening forward freight door available at customer's option. Entire accommodation air-conditioned.

ACCOMMODATION (Srs 560): Crew of two on flight deck and up to 109 passengers in main cabin. Two overwing emergency exits on each side. One toilet on each side of cabin at rear. Otherwise generally similar to Srs 495.

SYSTEMS: Fully duplicated air-conditioning and pressurisation systems. Air bled from engine compressors through heat exchangers. Max pressure differential 0.52 bars (7.5 lb/sq in). Hydraulic system, pressure 207 bars (3,000 lb/sq in), operates flaps, spoilers, rudder, elevators, tailplane, landing gear, brakes, nosewheel steering, ventral and forward airstairs and windscreen wipers. No pneumatic system. Electrical system utilises two 30kVA AC generators, driven by constant speed drive and starter units, plus a similar generator mounted on the APU and shaft driven. Gas turbine APU in tailcone to provide ground electric power, air-conditioning and engine starting, also some system checkout capability. APU is run during take-off to eliminate performance penalty of bleeding engine air for cabin air-conditioning.

AVIONICS AND EQUIPMENT: Communications and navigation avionics generally to customers' requirements. Typical installation includes dual VHF com to ARINC 546, dual VHF nav to ARINC 547A, including glideslope receivers, marker beacon receiver, flight/service interphone system, ADF, ATC transponder to ARINC 532D, DME, weather radar. Compass system and flight director system (dual) are also installed. Autopilot system. Provision on the Srs 560 for additional equipment, including automatic throttle control, for low weather minima operation.

DIMENSIONS, EXTERNAL:

Wing span	28.50 m (93 ft 6 in)
Wing chord: at root	5.00 m (16 ft 5 in)
at tip	1.61 m (5 ft 5 in)
Wing aspect ratio	8.5
Length overall: Srs 495	28.50 m (93 ft 6 in)
Srs 560	32.61 m (107 ft 0 in)
Length of fuselage: Srs 495	25.55 m (83 ft 10 in)
Srs 560	29.67 m (97 ft 4 in)
Height overall	7.47 m (24 ft 6 in)
Tailplane span	8.99 m (29 ft 6 in)
Wheel track	4.34 m (14 ft 3 in)
Wheelbase: Srs 495	10.08 m (33 ft 1 in)
Srs 560	12.62 m (41 ft 5 in)
Passenger door (fwd, port): Height	1.73 m (5 ft 8 in)
Width	0.84 m (2 ft 9 in)
Height to sill	2.08 m (6 ft 10 in)
Ventral entrance, bulkhead door:	
Height	1.83 m (6 ft 0 in)
Width	0.66 m (2 ft 2 in)
Height to sill	2.08 m (6 ft 10 in)
Freight door (fwd, starboard):	
Height (projected)	0.79 m (2 ft 7 in)
Width	0.91 m (3 ft 0 in)
Height to sill	1.04 m (3 ft 5 in)
Freight door (rear, starboard):	
Height (projected)	0.71 m (2 ft 4 in)
Width	0.91 m (3 ft 0 in)
Height to sill	1.17 m (3 ft 10 in)
Freight door, main deck (optional, fwd, Srs 495):	
Height	1.85 m (6 ft 1 in)
Width	3.05 m (10 ft 0 in)
Galley service door (fwd, starboard):	
Height (projected)	1.22 m (4 ft 0 in)
Width	0.69 m (2 ft 3 in)
Height to sill	2.08 m (6 ft 10 in)

DIMENSIONS, INTERNAL (Srs 495):

Cabin, excl flight deck: Length	17.32 m (56 ft 10 in)
Max width	3.15 m (10 ft 4 in)
Max height	1.98 m (6 ft 6 in)
Floor area	approx 47.4 m² (510 sq ft)
Freight hold: fwd	10.02 m³ (354 cu ft)
rear	4.42 m³ (156 cu ft)

DIMENSIONS, INTERNAL (Srs 560):

Cabin, excl flight deck: Length	21.44 m (70 ft 4 in)
Total floor area	approx 59.5 m² (640 sq ft)
Freight holds (total volume)	19.45 m³ (687 cu ft)

AREAS (Srs 495, 560):

Wings, gross	95.78 m² (1,031.0 sq ft)
Ailerons (total)	2.86 m² (30.8 sq ft)
Flaps (total)	16.26 m² (175.0 sq ft)
Spoilers (total)	2.30 m² (24.8 sq ft)
Vertical tail surfaces (total)	10.91 m² (117.4 sq ft)
Rudder, incl tab	3.05 m² (32.8 sq ft)
Horizontal tail surfaces (total)	23.97 m² (258.0 sq ft)
Elevators, incl tab	6.54 m² (70.4 sq ft)

WEIGHTS AND LOADINGS:

Operating weight empty, typical:	
Srs 495 (89 seats)	23,286 kg (51,339 lb)
Srs 560 (109 seats)	25,267 kg (55,704 lb)
Max payload, typical: Srs 495	10,733 kg (23,661 lb)
Srs 560	11,474 kg (25,296 lb)
Max T-O weight:	
Srs 495: standard	41,730 kg (92,000 lb)
optional	44,680 kg (98,500 lb)
Srs 560: standard	45,200 kg (99,650 lb)
optional	47,400 kg (104,500 lb)
Max ramp weight:	
Srs 495: standard	41,955 kg (92,500 lb)
optional	44,905 kg (99,000 lb)
Srs 560: standard	45,450 kg (100,200 lb)
optional	47,625 kg (105,000 lb)
Max landing weight:	
Srs 495: standard	38,100 kg (84,000 lb)
optional	39,465 kg (87,000 lb)
Srs 560	39,465 kg (87,000 lb)
Max zero-fuel weight:	
Srs 495: standard	33,110 kg (73,000 lb)
optional	34,020 kg (75,000 lb)
Srs 560	36,740 kg (81,000 lb)
Max wing loading: Srs 495	466.3 kg/m² (95.5 lb/sq ft)
Srs 560	495.1 kg/m² (101.4 lb/sq ft)
Max power loading: Srs 495	400.2 kg/kN (3.92 lb/lb st)
Srs 560	424.5 kg/kN (4.16 lb/lb st)

PERFORMANCE (at standard max T-O weights):

Design diving speed (S/L)	410 knots (760 km/h; 472 mph) EAS
Max level and max cruising speed at 6,400 m (21,000 ft)	470 knots (870 km/h; 541 mph)
Econ cruising speed at 10,670 m (35,000 ft)	410 knots (760 km/h; 472 mph)
Stalling speed (landing flap setting, at standard max landing weight):	
Srs 495	98 knots (182 km/h; 113 mph) EAS
Srs 560	100 knots (186 km/h; 115 mph) EAS
Rate of climb at S/L at 300 knots (555 km/h; 345 mph)	
EAS: Srs 495	786 m (2,580 ft)/min
Srs 560	722 m (2,370 ft)/min
Max cruising height	10,670 m (35,000 ft)
Min ground turning radius (to outer wingtip):	
Srs 495	15.24 m (50 ft 0 in)
Srs 560	17.07 m (56 ft 0 in)
Runway LCN, rigid pavement (130): Srs 495	32
Srs 560	53
T-O run at S/L, ISA: Srs 495	1,676 m (5,500 ft)
Srs 560	1,981 m (6,500 ft)
Balanced T-O to 10.7 m (35 ft) at S/L, ISA:	
Srs 495	1,798 m (5,900 ft)
Srs 560	2,225 m (7,300 ft)
Landing distance (BCAR) at S/L, ISA, at standard max landing weight: Srs 495	1,440 m (4,725 ft)

Srs 560   1,455 m (4,775 ft)

Max still air range, ISA, with reserves for 200 nm (370 km; 230 mile) diversion and 45 min hold:

Srs 495   1,933 nm (3,582 km; 2,226 miles)
Srs 560   1,897 nm (3,515 km; 2,184 miles)

Still air range with typical capacity payload, ISA, reserves as above:

Srs 495 at 44,680 kg (98,500 lb)
       1,454 nm (2,694 km; 1,674 miles)

Srs 560 at 47,400 kg (104,500 lb)
       1,327 nm (2,459 km; 1,528 miles)

Srs 495 executive aircraft with additional 5,602 litres (1,479 US gallons; 1,232 Imp gallons) fuel and ten passengers   2,875 nm (5,325 km; 3,308 miles)

IAv BUCURESTI (PILATUS BRITTEN-NORMAN) ISLANDER

The Pilatus Britten-Norman Islander (see UK section)

has been manufactured under licence in Romania, originally by IRMA, for many years. The first Romanian built example flew for the first time at Baneasa Airport, Bucharest, on 4 August 1969, and the initial commitment to build 215 Islanders was completed in 1976. A total of 415 had been delivered to Pilatus Britten-Norman by 30 June 1988.

IAv CRAIOVA
INTREPRINDEREA DE AVIOANE CRAIOVA (Craiova Aircraft Enterprise)

Craiova

DIRECTOR GENERAL: Dipl Eng Dumitru Geantă

This factory is responsible for Romanian manufacture of the IAR-93 close support and ground attack aircraft and operational trainer described under the SOKO/CNIAR heading in the International section. Craiova's latest product is the IAR-99 Soim jet trainer.

IAR-99 SOIM (HAWK)

The existence of this new Romanian designed advanced jet trainer/light ground attack aircraft first became known during the 1983 Paris Air Show. It was designed and built at Craiova, and is powered by a version of the non-afterburning Rolls-Royce Viper Mk 632 turbojet installed in the IAR-93A. First flight was made in December 1985.

TYPE: Tandem two-seat advanced jet trainer and light ground attack aircraft.

WINGS: Cantilever low-wing monoplane, with non-swept tapered leading- and trailing-edges and approx 3° dihedral from roots. Trim tab in each aileron.

FUSELAGE: Conventional all-metal semi-monocoque structure, of oval cross-section.

TAIL UNIT: Sweptback fin, with dorsal fin, and balanced rudder. Non-swept, no-dihedral tailplane, mounted above tailpipe, with balanced elevators. Trim tab in rudder and each elevator.

LANDING GEAR: Retractable tricycle type, with single wheel and oleo-pneumatic shock absorber on each unit. Mainwheels retract inward, nosewheel forward, all wheels being fully enclosed by doors when retracted. Landing light in port wingroot leading-edge.

POWER PLANT: One 17.8 kN (4,000 lb st) Rolls-Royce Viper Mk 632-41 turbojet, mounted in rear fuselage. Lateral air intake, with splitter plate, on each side of fuselage abreast of rear cockpit.

ACCOMMODATION: Crew of two in tandem, with elevated rear seat. One-piece wraparound windscreen; single framed canopy over both seats.

ARMAMENT: Four underwing attachments for weapons and other stores.

DIMENSIONS, EXTERNAL:

Wing span	10.16 m (33 ft 4 in)
Wing chord: at root	2.305 m (7 ft 6¾ in)
at tip	1.30 m (4 ft 3¼ in)
Wing aspect ratio	5.5
Length overall	11.009 m (36 ft 1½ in)
Height overall	3.898 m (12 ft 9½ in)

Tailplane span	4.20 m (13 ft 9½ in)
Wheel track	2.69 m (8 ft 10 in)
Wheelbase	4.38 m (14 ft 4½ in)

AREAS:

Wings, gross	18.71 m² (201.4 sq ft)
Ailerons (total)	1.567 m² (16.87 sq ft)
Trailing-edge flaps (total)	2.54 m² (27.34 sq ft)
Fin	1.919 m² (20.66 sq ft)
Rudder	0.629 m² (6.77 sq ft)
Tailplane	4.515 m² (48.60 sq ft)
Elevators (total)	1.30 m² (13.99 sq ft)

WEIGHTS AND LOADINGS:

Basic weight empty	3,364 kg (7,416 lb)
Max fuel weight: internal	1,080 kg (2,381 lb)
external	360 kg (794 lb)
Max T-O weight	5,641 kg (12,436 lb)
Max landing weight	3,985 kg (8,785 lb)
Max wing loading	301.5 kg/m² (61.75 lb/sq ft)
Max power loading	317.1 kg/kN (3.11 lb/lb st)

PERFORMANCE (at max T-O weight except where indicated):

Never-exceed speed	Mach 0.76
Max level speed at S/L	458 knots (850 km/h; 528 mph)
*Max rate of climb at S/L	2,190 m (7,185 ft)/min
Service ceiling	12,600 m (41,350 ft)
Min air turning radius	330 m (1,083 ft)
*T-O run	660 m (2,165 ft)
T-O to 15 m (50 ft)	725 m (2,378 ft)
‡Landing from 15 m (50 ft)	1,015 m (3,330 ft)
‡Landing run	725 m (2,378 ft)

*at AUW of 4,400 kg (9,700 lb)
‡at AUW of 3,370 kg (7,430 lb)

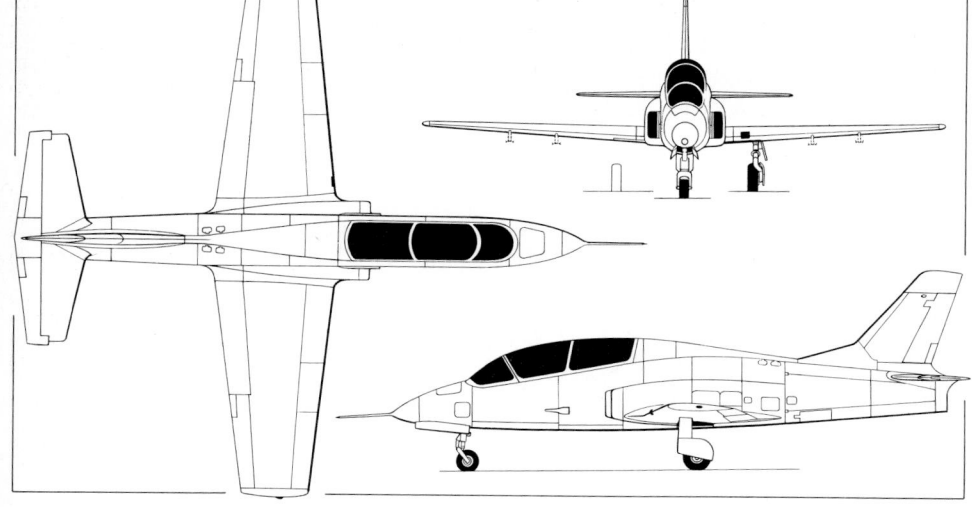

Romania's new advanced jet trainer, the IAR-99 Soim (*Pilot Press drawing*)

ICA
INTREPRINDEREA DE CONSTRUCTII AERONAUTICE (Aeronautical Construction Enterprise)

Casuta Postala 198, 2200 Brasov

Telephone: 92114037

Telex: 61 266

ICA, created in 1968, continues the work begun in 1926 by IAR-Brasov and undertaken in 1950-59 as URMV-3 Brasov. Today, it manufactures most types of Romanian designed light aircraft, plus Alouette III and Puma helicopters under licence from Aérospatiale of France (as the IAR-316B and IAR-330 respectively); is converting Ka-26 helicopters to Ka-126s on behalf of the USSR; and produces the IS-28/29 series of Romanian sailplanes and motor gliders. It also produces aircraft components and equipment.

ICA IAR-28MA

The IAR-28MA side by side two-seat light aircraft was derived from the IS-28M2 motor glider, with which it shares a common fuselage, tail unit and flying controls. It has a new-design wing, fitted with split flaps and ailerons, and is powered by a 60 kW (80 hp) Limbach L2000 EOI flat-four engine driving a Hoffmann HO-V-62R two-blade variable-pitch propeller with spinner.

An initial batch of ten, for training duties with the Romanian Air Force, was delivered in 1984, and production was continuing in the Spring of 1985, the latest date for which information has been received. Further details, and an illustration, can be found in the 1987-88 *Jane's*.

ICA IAR-823

Design of the IAR-823 two/five-seat training and touring light aircraft was started in May 1970, and the prototype made its first flight in July 1973. Construction and testing were in compliance with FAR Pt 23, and the aircraft is certificated for Aerobatic, Utility and Normal category operation. The first production aircraft flew in 1974, and 87 had been delivered to the Romanian Air Force and Romanian flying clubs by the Summer of 1982, the latest date for which a figure has been supplied. Production was continuing in 1985, but no indication of its status has been received since then.

As a two-seater, the IAR-823 is fully aerobatic and is intended for training duties. With a rear bench seat for up to three more persons it is suitable as an executive, taxi or touring aircraft. Provision is made for two underwing pylons for the carriage of drop tanks or practice weapons.

A full description of the IAR-823 was given in the 1987-88 and many previous editions of *Jane's*.

TYPE: Two/five-seat cabin monoplane.

AIRFRAME: See 1987-88 and earlier *Jane's*.

POWER PLANT: One 216 kW (290 hp) Textron Lycoming IO-540-G1D5 flat-six engine, driving a Hartzell HC-92WK-1D/W 9350-4.6 two-blade constant-speed metal propeller. Fuel in four integral wing tanks, total capacity 360 litres (95 US gallons; 79 Imp gallons). Provision for two 70 litre (18.5 US gallon; 15.4 Imp gallon) drop tanks on underwing pylons.

ACCOMMODATION: Fully enclosed cabin, seating two persons side by side on individual adjustable front seats, with removable bench seat at rear for up to three more people. Dual controls standard in training version, optional in other versions. Upward hinged window/door (optionally

jettisonable) on each side of cabin, which is sound-proofed, heated and ventilated. Compartment at rear of cabin for up to 40 kg (88 lb) of baggage. Equipment and layout can be varied for use as air taxi, executive or freight transport, ambulance, liaison or photographic aircraft.

SYSTEMS AND AVIONICS: See 1987-88 and earlier *Jane's*.

DIMENSIONS, EXTERNAL:

Wing span	10.00 m (32 ft 9¾ in)
Length overall	8.315 m (27 ft 3½ in)
Height overall	2.86 m (9 ft 4¾ in)
Wheel track	2.48 m (8 ft 1¾ in)
Wheelbase	1.86 m (6 ft 1¼ in)
Propeller diameter	2.23 m (7 ft 4 in)

AREA:

Wings, gross	15.00 m² (161.5 sq ft)

WEIGHTS (A: Aerobatic; U: Utility; N: Normal category):

Weight empty: A	910 kg (2,006 lb)
U	930 kg (2,050 lb)
N	950 kg (2,094 lb)
Max T-O weight: A	1,190 kg (2,623 lb)
U	1,380 kg (3,042 lb)
N	1,500 kg (3,307 lb)

PERFORMANCE (A: at Aerobatic max T-O weight, B: at AUW of 1,400 kg; 3,086 lb):

Never-exceed speed: B	215 knots (400 km/h; 248 mph)

Max level speed at S/L:

A, B	162 knots (300 km/h; 186 mph)

Max cruising speed (75% power):

A at S/L	154 knots (285 km/h; 177 mph)
B at 1,750 m (5,750 ft)	
	162 knots (300 km/h; 186 mph)

Econ cruising speed (60% power):

A at S/L	140 knots (260 km/h; 162 mph)

B at 3,050 m (10,000 ft)

	156 knots (290 km/h; 180 mph)
Stalling speed: flaps up: A	61 knots (112 km/h; 70 mph)
B	63 knots (115 km/h; 72 mph)
flaps down, power off:	
A	55 knots (102 km/h; 64 mph)
B	49 knots (90 km/h; 56 mph)
Max rate of climb at S/L: A, B	420 m (1,380 ft)/min
Service ceiling: A, B	5,600 m (18,375 ft)
T-O run: A, B	160 m (525 ft)
T-O to 15 m (50 ft): A, B	300 m (984 ft)
Landing from 15 m (50 ft): A, B	250 m (820 ft)
Landing run: A, B	200 m (656 ft)
Range with max fuel: A	701 nm (1,300 km; 807 miles)
B, according to mission and payload, 1 h reserves	
	431-970 nm (800-1,800 km; 497-1,118 miles)
Endurance, according to mission and payload	3-6 h
g limits	+6/−3

ICA IAR-825TP TRIUMF

The IAR-825TP is a turboprop powered tandem-seat aircraft developed to FAR Pt 23 standards as an economical multi-role trainer for the Romanian Air Force. The prototype (YR-IGB) flew for the first time on 12 June 1982, with a 507 kW (680 shp) P&WC PT6A-15AG engine. Series production with a more powerful engine, as described under 'Power Plant', was due to begin in 1986, though no confirmation of this has been received.

The IAR-825 has some features in common with the IAR-823, utilising essentially the same wings, which have metal skinned flaps and ailerons and are strengthened for the carriage of practice weapons in the armament training role. Fuselage, landing gear and tail unit are of new design.

TYPE: Turboprop powered military trainer.

WINGS: Cantilever low-wing monoplane. Wing section NACA 23012 (modified). Dihedral 7° from roots. Incidence 3° at root, 1° at tip. Conventional all-metal structure, with single main spar and rear auxiliary spar; three-point attachment to fuselage. Riveted spars, ribs and skin of corrosion-proof aluminium alloy. Leading-edges riveted, and sealed to ribs and main spar to form main torsion box and integral fuel tanks. Electrically actuated all-metal single-slotted flaps and all-metal Frise slotted ailerons. Ground adjustable tab on each aileron.

FUSELAGE: Conventional metal semi-monocoque structure. Small bumper under tailcone.

TAIL UNIT: Cantilever metal structure. Two-spar duralumin covered sweptback fin and non-swept tailplane; horn balanced rudder and elevators. Electrically actuated automatic trim tab in each elevator; controllable tab in rudder.

LANDING GEAR: Retractable tricycle type, with steerable nosewheel. Electric retraction, main units inward, nose unit rearward. Emergency manual actuation. Oleo-pneumatic shock absorbers. Mainwheel tyres size 500 × 180 mm, nosewheel tyre 355 × 150 mm. Independent hydraulic mainwheel brakes. Shimmy damper on nose unit.

POWER PLANT: One 559 kW (750 shp) Pratt & Whitney Canada PT6A-25C turboprop, driving a Hartzell HC-B3TN-3/T10173-13R three-blade constant-speed reversible-pitch metal propeller. Wings incorporate four integral fuel tanks, as in IAR-823. Two streamlined auxiliary tanks above wingtips optional.

ACCOMMODATION: Seats for two persons in tandem, under one-piece framed canopy which opens sideways to starboard. Dual controls standard.

DIMENSIONS, EXTERNAL:
Wing span, excl tip tanks	10.00 m (32 ft 9¾ in)
Wing aspect ratio	6.7
Length overall	8.99 m (29 ft 6 in)
Height overall	3.20 m (10 ft 6 in)
Wheel track	2.45 m (8 ft 0½ in)

DIMENSIONS, INTERNAL:
Cockpit: Max length	2.65 m (8 ft 8¼ in)
Max width	0.87 m (2 ft 10¼ in)

AREA:
Wings, gross	15.00 m² (161.5 sq ft)

IAR-823 two/five-seat light aircraft

IAR-827A single/two-seat agricultural aircraft

WEIGHTS (A: Aerobatic, U: Utility category):
Weight empty	1,250 kg (2,756 lb)
Max T-O weight: A	1,700 kg (3,748 lb)
U	2,300 kg (5,070 lb)

PERFORMANCE (at Aerobatic max T-O weight, PT6A-15AG engine):
Never-exceed speed	296 knots (550 km/h; 341 mph)
Max level speed at 4,000 m (13,125 ft)	
	254 knots (470 km/h; 292 mph)
Max cruising speed at 4,000 m (13,125 ft)	
	237 knots (440 km/h; 273 mph)
Stalling speed, flaps down, power off	
	57 knots (105 km/h; 66 mph)
Max rate of climb at S/L	960 m (3,150 ft)/min
Service ceiling	9,000 m (29,525 ft)
T-O to 15 m (50 ft)	250 m (820 ft)
Landing from 15 m (50 ft)	300 m (985 ft)
Range with max fuel, 30 min reserves	
	755 nm (1,400 km; 870 miles)
Endurance, conditions as above	3 h
g limits	+6/−3

ICA IAR-827A

The development history of this single/two-seat agricultural monoplane has appeared in many previous editions of *Jane's*. It first flew, with a flat-eight engine, in 1976, and was certificated, with a more powerful radial engine, in 1979. The two prototypes and five pre-series aircraft were built by IAv Bucuresti.

Series manufacture by ICA Brasov began in late 1981, and an initial batch of 15 was completed. No subsequent information has been received.

AIRFRAME: See 1987-88 and earlier *Jane's*.

POWER PLANT: One 447 kW (600 hp) PZL-3S seven-cylinder radial aircooled engine, driving a PZL US-132000/A four-blade constant-speed metal propeller. Fuel tank in each wing leading-edge, each of 230 litres (60.8 US gallons; 50.5 Imp gallons) capacity.

ACCOMMODATION: Side by side seats for pilot and mechanic in fully enclosed cockpit, with window/door on each side. Dual controls and emergency door jettison optional. Seat height and rudder pedals adjustable. Crash pylon in fairing aft of seats. Heated and ventilated cockpit is sealed and slightly pressurised to exclude dust.

EQUIPMENT: Glassfibre hopper in forward fuselage, with a volume of 1.23 m³ (43.44 cu ft). Hopper stressed for loads of up to 1,000 kg (2,205 lb), but normal max load is 900 kg (1,984 lb) of dry or 1,200 litres (317 US gallons; 264 Imp gallons) of liquid chemical. Hopper has a jettison system.

DIMENSIONS, EXTERNAL:
Wing span	14.00 m (45 ft 11¼ in)
Length overall	8.80 m (28 ft 10½ in)
Height overall	2.60 m (8 ft 6½ in)
Wheel track	3.42 m (11 ft 2¾ in)
Wheelbase	6.20 m (20 ft 4 in)
Propeller diameter	2.62 m (8 ft 7 in)

AREA:
Wings, gross	29.40 m² (316.46 sq ft)

WEIGHTS:
Weight empty, with agricultural equipment	
	1,660 kg (3,660 lb)
Max T-O weight	2,800 kg (6,173 lb)

PERFORMANCE (with agricultural equipment, at max T-O weight):
Max level speed	113 knots (210 km/h; 130 mph)
Cruising speed	104 knots (193 km/h; 120 mph)
Operating speed range	
	78-97 knots (145-180 km/h; 90-112 mph)
Stalling speed, 10° flap, power off	
	60 knots (110 km/h; 69 mph)
Max rate of climb at S/L	210 m (690 ft)/min
Service ceiling	4,500 m (14,775 ft)
T-O run	100 m (328 ft)
T-O to 15 m (50 ft)	550 m (1,805 ft)
Landing run	150 m (492 ft)
Range with max fuel	350 nm (650 km; 404 miles)
Endurance (agricultural operations)	1 h 30 min
Max endurance	2 h 30 min

ICA IAR-828TP

The original IAR-827 prototype (YR-MGA) was retrofitted with a 533 kW (715 shp) Pratt & Whitney Canada PT6A-15AG turboprop and Hartzell HC-B3TN-3/T10282R propeller. Known then as the **IAR-827TP**, it flew for the first time on 7 September 1981. Hopper load under

Prototype of the ICA Brasov IAR-825TP Triumf tandem-seat military trainer

FAR Pt 23 is 1,100 kg (2,425 lb); under CAM 8 regulations, this can be increased to 1,500 kg (3,307 lb).

Flight testing of this aircraft, by then redesignated **IAR-828TP**, was continuing towards certification in the Spring of 1985. No recent indication of programme status has been received. All known details have been given in the 1987-88 and earlier editions of *Jane's*.

ICA IAR-831 PELICAN

The Pelican, the prototype of which (YR-IGA) made its first public appearance at the 1983 Paris Air Show, is essentially a combination of the IAR-825TP airframe with the piston engine power plant of the IAR-823. No indication of its development status has been given by ICA. All known details, and a photograph, can be found in the 1987-88 and earlier *Jane's*.

ICA (AÉROSPATIALE) IAR-316B ALOUETTE III

ICA and Aérospatiale concluded an agreement in 1971 for manufacture in Romania of SA 316B Alouette III helicopters. Production totalled more than 185 by the Spring of 1985, the latest date for which details have been received. Romanian built components have also been supplied for French built Alouette IIIs.

The first French built SA 316B made its initial flight on 27 June 1968, and deliveries began in 1970. The sale of Alouette IIIs to India, Romania and Switzerland included licence agreements for manufacture of the aircraft in those countries, the quantities involved being 250, 180 and 60 respectively. Production continues in India and Romania.

TYPE: Turbine driven general purpose helicopter.

ROTOR SYSTEM: Three-blade main and anti-torque rotors. All-metal main rotor blades, of constant chord, on articulated hinges, with hydraulic drag-hinge dampers. Main rotor brake and blade folding standard.

ROTOR DRIVE: Main rotor driven through planetary gearbox, with freewheel for autorotation. Take-off drive for tail rotor at lower end of main gearbox, from where a torque shaft runs to a small gearbox which supports the tail rotor and houses the pitch change mechanism. Cyclic and collective pitch controls are powered.

FUSELAGE: Welded steel tube centre-section, carrying the cabin at the front and a semi-monocoque tailboom.

TAIL UNIT: Cantilever all-metal fixed tailplane, with twin endplate fins, mounted on tailboom.

LANDING GEAR: Non-retractable tricycle type, manufactured under Messier-Hispano-Bugatti licence. Hydraulic shock absorption. Nosewheel is fully castoring. Provision for skis or emergency pontoon landing gear.

POWER PLANT: One 649 kW (870 shp) Turboméca Artouste IIIB turboshaft, derated to 410 kW (550 shp) for max continuous operation. Fuel in single tank in fuselage centre-section, with capacity of 575 litres (152 US gallons; 126.5 Imp gallons), of which 573 litres (151 US gallons; 126 Imp gallons) are usable.

ACCOMMODATION: Normal accommodation for pilot and six persons, with three seats in front and a four-person folding seat at the rear of the cabin. Two baggage holds in centre-section, on each side of the welded structure and enclosed by the centre-section fairings. Provision for carrying two stretchers athwartships at rear of cabin, and two other persons, in addition to pilot. All passenger seats removable to enable aircraft to be used for freight carrying. Can also be adapted for cropspraying or aerial survey roles. Provision for external sling for loads of up to 750 kg (1,650 lb). One forward opening door on each side, immediately in front of two rearward sliding doors. Dual controls and cabin heating optional.

OPERATIONAL EQUIPMENT (military version): In the assault role, the Alouette III can be equipped with a wide range of weapons. A 7.62 mm machine-gun (with 1,000 rds) can be mounted athwartships on a tripod behind the pilot's seat, firing to starboard, either through a small window in the sliding door or through the open doorway with the door locked open. The rear seat is removed to allow the

IAR-828TP prototype, with spraybars under wings

gun mounting to be installed. In this configuration, max accommodation is for pilot, co-pilot, gunner and one passenger, although normally only the pilot and gunner would be carried. Alternatively, a 20 mm cannon (with 480 rds) can be carried on an open turret-type mounting on the port side of the cabin. For this installation all seats except that of the pilot are removed, as is the port side cabin door, and the crew consists of pilot and gunner. Instead of these guns, the Alouette III can be equipped with two or four wire-guided missiles on external jettisonable launching rails, a gyro-stabilised sight, or 68 mm rocket pods.

DIMENSIONS, EXTERNAL:
Main rotor diameter	11.02 m (36 ft 1¾ in)
Main rotor blade chord (each)	0.35 m (13.8 in)
Tail rotor diameter	1.912 m (6 ft 3¼ in)
Spraybar span (agricultural version)	
	10.00 m (32 ft 9¾ in)
Length overall, rotors turning	12.84 m (42 ft 1½ in)
Length of fuselage, tail rotor turning	
	10.17 m (33 ft 4½ in)
Width overall, blades folded	2.60 m (8 ft 6¼ in)
Height to top of rotor head	2.97 m (9 ft 9 in)
Wheel track	2.602 m (8 ft 6½ in)

AREAS:
Main rotor disc	95.38 m² (1,026.6 sq ft)
Tail rotor disc	2.87 m² (30.9 sq ft)

WEIGHTS:
Weight empty: standard version	1,050 kg (2,315 lb)
agricultural version	1,300 kg (2,866 lb)
Max payload (agricultural version)	685 kg (1,510 lb)
Max T-O weight	2,200 kg (4,850 lb)

PERFORMANCE (standard version at max T-O weight, except where indicated):
Never-exceed speed at S/L	
	113 knots (210 km/h; 130 mph)
Max cruising speed at S/L	
	100 knots (185 km/h; 115 mph)
Operating speed (agricultural version)	
	32-76 knots (60-140 km/h; 37-87 mph)
Max rate of climb at S/L	260 m (850 ft)/min
Service ceiling	3,200 m (10,500 ft)
Hovering ceiling: IGE	2,850 m (9,350 ft)
OGE	1,500 m (4,920 ft)
Range with max fuel at S/L	
	267 nm (495 km; 307 miles)
Range at optimum altitude	
	290 nm (540 km; 335 miles)
Swath width (agricultural version)	30-40 m (98-131 ft)

ICA IAR-317 AIRFOX

Exhibited publicly for the first time at the 1985 Paris Air Show, the IAR-317 first prototype had then accumulated about 100 hours of flying since it first flew in April 1984.

The prototype was modified from an IAR-316B Alouette III. The Airfox was intended primarily as a light ground attack, training and military liaison helicopter for the Romanian armed forces, although there has been no confirmation either of the completion of additional prototypes (scheduled for 1985) or of the start of production. The modifications occur mainly ahead of the main rotor mast, the new cabin contours being considerably slimmer with tandem seating for a crew of two, the rear cockpit being elevated to improve the pilot's field of view. In the combat version, armour protection is provided for crew seats and fuel tank, toughened material is used in the cockpit transparencies, and attachments are provided for up to six external weapons.

TYPE: Tandem two-seat light attack and training helicopter.

ROTOR SYSTEM AND DRIVE: Generally as described for Alouette III. Rotor brake and main rotor blade folding standard.

FUSELAGE AND TAIL UNIT: Similar to Alouette III except for modified front section of fuselage (of duralumin) and glassfibre tail surfaces.

LANDING GEAR: Similar to Alouette, but has steerable nosewheel with optional locking device. Metal ski gear, floats and emergency flotation gear optional.

POWER PLANT: One 640 kW (858 shp) Turboméca Artouste IIIB turboshaft, as in Alouette III. Standard usable fuel capacity 573 litres (151 US gallons; 126 Imp gallons); one or two auxiliary fuel tanks optional, each of 125 litres (33 US gallons; 27.5 Imp gallons) capacity.

ACCOMMODATION: Crew of two in tandem, with elevated rear (pilot's) cockpit. Seats are of bucket type, adjustable vertically and horizontally, removable, and armoured in combat versions. Windscreens and lower portions of side window/doors are flat-plate and of toughened material; forward and rear window/doors on each side can be jettisoned for escape in an emergency. Dual controls standard. Both cockpits heated and ventilated; air-conditioning is optional.

SYSTEM: Electrical system (28.5V DC) supplied by 4kW starter/generator and a 40Ah nickel-cadmium battery. Ground power receptacle.

AVIONICS AND EQUIPMENT: Standard avionics include TR-800A VHF nav, AHV-6 radio altimeter, radio compass, marker beacon receiver, intercom, and pilot's gyro horizon, directional gyro and sideslip indicator. Pilot's main and secondary panels include altimeter, airspeed indicator, VSI, magnetic compass, tachometer, voltmeter, collective pitch indicator, temperature indicator, fuel gauge, oil pressure and temperature indicator, outside air temperature indicator, and clock. Pilot's main instruments (altimeter, airspeed indicator, variometer and collective pitch indicator) are repeated on co-pilot's panel; option also for co-pilot's gyro horizon and directional gyro. Standard equipment includes gunsight,

ICA built IAR-316B Alouette III (left) and IAR-330L Puma helicopters

roof mounted missile sight, position lights, anti-collision light, pilot's instrument failure warning lights, instrument and panel lights, windscreen heating/demisting, windscreen wiper, retractable landing light, rotor brake, alternative static source, mission selector and cockpit fire extinguisher. Optional equipment includes agricultural spraygear, external cargo sling, rescue sling seat, 175 kg (386 lb) capacity rescue hoist, deck-lock harpoon, fuel quick drain, sand filter and flares.

ARMAMENT: Fixed armament of two 7.62 mm machine-guns, one on each side of lower front fuselage. Load carrying beam aft of rear cockpit, with two (optionally three) weapon attachment points on each side. Typical stores loads, up to a maximum of 750 kg (1,653 lb), can include four rocket launchers (each with four or twelve 57 mm rockets), four twin-gun machine-gun pods, four 50 kg or 100 kg bombs, or '2 + 2' combinations of these weapons; four cartridge launchers or flare pods; four air-to-surface missiles; or six small 'Sagger' type anti-tank missiles. Naval weapons and stores can also be carried. RAD weapon aiming system, with PKV gyrostabilised sight, in front cockpit.

DIMENSIONS, EXTERNAL: As for Alouette III except:

Length overall, main rotor blades folded	
	10.845 m (35 ft 7 in)
Length of fuselage	9.80 m (32 ft 1¾ in)

WEIGHTS:

Weight empty	1,150 kg (2,535 lb)
Max usable fuel: standard	453 kg (998 lb)
auxiliary tanks (two, total)	200 kg (441 lb)
Max T-O and landing weight	2,200 kg (4,850 lb)

PERFORMANCE (prototype: A at 1,700 kg; 3,748 lb gross weight, B at max T-O weight, no external stores, both in ISA zero wind conditions):

Never-exceed speed, and max level speed* at S/L:	
A, B	118 knots (220 km/h; 136 mph)
*Max cruising speed at S/L:	
A	108 knots (200 km/h; 124 mph)
B	102 knots (190 km/h; 118 mph)
Max rate of climb at S/L: A	510 m (1,673 ft)/min
B	270 m (886 ft)/min
Service ceiling: A	6,300 m (20,670 ft)
B	3,200 m (10,500 ft)
Hovering ceiling IGE: A	5,950 m (19,520 ft)
B	2,850 m (9,350 ft)
Hovering ceiling OGE: A	5,600 m (18,375 ft)
B	1,500 m (4,920 ft)
*Max range at S/L:	
with standard fuel: A	294 nm (545 km; 338 miles)
B	283 nm (525 km; 326 miles)
with auxiliary tanks: A	469 nm (870 km; 540 miles)
B	437 nm (810 km; 503 miles)

*Reduced by 10% with external stores

ICA (AÉROSPATIALE) IAR-330L PUMA

An agreement for licence production of the Aérospatiale SA 330 Puma in Romania was concluded in 1977, an initial quantity of 100 being involved. A total of 112 had been delivered by Spring 1985, most of them (and most Alouette IIIs) reportedly to the Romanian Air Force. No later total has been supplied.

ICA (KAMOV) Ka-126
NATO reporting name: Hoodlum-B

Work on a turboshaft version of the Kamov Ka-26 began in 1981, and a photograph published in that year depicted an early mockup apparently identical to the piston engined version except for the substitution of a very small (and still unidentified), closely cowled turboshaft on each side of the cabin roof. A photograph of this version appeared in the 1986-87 *Jane's*.

Subsequently, however, it was decided to adopt a single 537 kW (720 shp) TVD-100 turboshaft, installed centrally under a smooth fairing above the cabin. A ground test vehicle was completed in early 1986, and a prototype Ka-126 (SSSR-01963) flew for the first time later that year. It had been announced in 1985 that conversion of Ka-26s to Ka-126 standard would be undertaken by ICA Brasov in Romania, and this work began in 1987. A large proportion of the approx 600 Ka-26s produced by the Kamov bureau in the USSR are expected to undergo conversion, which will confer upon them a significant increase in payload, endurance and range capability, and the opportunity for greater year-round utilisation. The Ka-126 will be able to hover with full load at 1,000 m (3,280 ft), whereas the Ka-26 can do so only at sea level.

DIMENSIONS, EXTERNAL:

Rotor diameter (each)	13.00 m (42 ft 7¾ in)
Length of fuselage	7.755 m (25 ft 5¼ in)
Height to top of rotor head	4.155 m (13 ft 7½ in)
Span over tail-fins	3.224 m (10 ft 7 in)
Wheel track (mainwheels)	2.56 m (8 ft 4¾ in)
Wheelbase	3.479 m (11 ft 5 in)

WEIGHTS:

Max payload	1,000 kg (2,205 lb)
Max T-O weight	3,250 kg (7,165 lb)

PERFORMANCE:

Max level speed	97 knots (180 km/h; 112 mph)
Cruising speed	86 knots (160 km/h; 99 mph)
Max range	324 nm (600 km; 373 miles)
Endurance	4 h 40 min

First prototype of the IAR-317 Airfox gunship helicopter *(Brian M. Service)*

First conversion of a Ka-26 to 'production' standard Ka-126 (copied from *Krilya Rodini*)

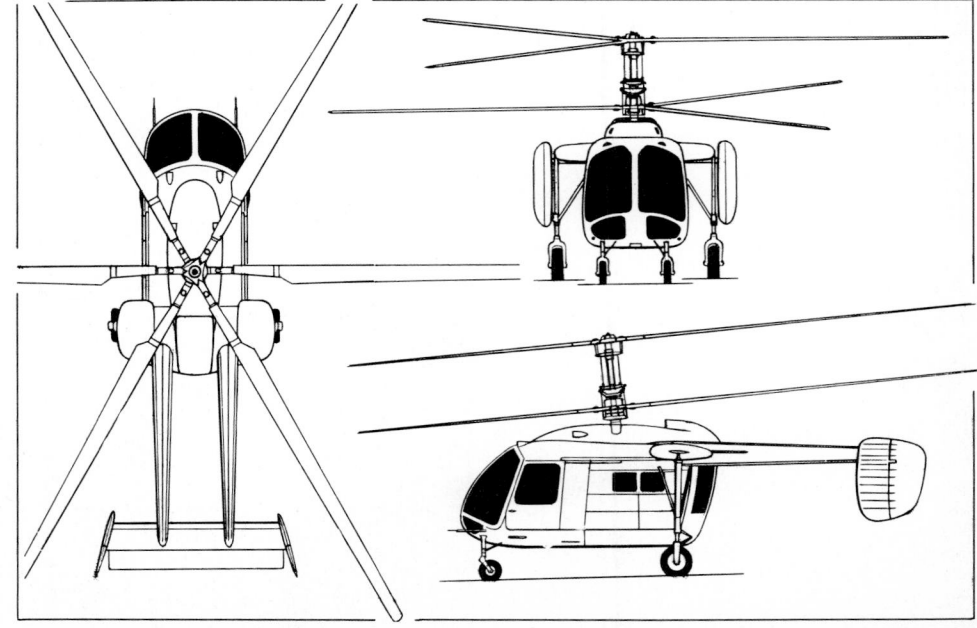

Kamov Ka-126 single-turboshaft helicopter, being converted in Romania by ICA Brasov *(Pilot Press)*

SINGAPORE

SAI

SINGAPORE AIRCRAFT INDUSTRIES PTE LTD

No. 3 Lim Teck Kim Road, 09-01 STC Building, Singapore 0208
Telephone: (65) 225 7977
Telex: RS 43255 SAIMKG
Fax: (65) 225 7661
MANAGING DIRECTOR: Quek Poh Huat
MARKETING EXECUTIVE: Mrs Suzanna Chua
    The SAI Group consists of six subsidiaries, as follows:

Singapore Aerospace Maintenance Co Pte Ltd (SAMCO), Building 454, West Camp, Seletar Air Base, Singapore 2879
Telephone: 481 5955
Telex: RS 25507 SAMAIR
Fax: (65) 4820245
GENERAL MANAGER: Richard Liao
    Maintenance, modification, repair and servicing of civil and military aircraft and helicopters.

Singapore Aero-Components Overhaul Pte Ltd (SACO), SAI Building, 540 Airport Road, Singapore 1953
Telephone: 287 2222
Telex: RS 34100 SACOMP
Fax: (65) 2809713
GENERAL MANAGER: Foo Hee Liat
    Service, maintenance, overhaul and repair of civil and military aircraft components and equipment. Authorised service centre for Bendix, Rockwell Collins, J.E.T., Lear Siegler, King Radio, AIM, Smiths Industries and SFENA.

Singapore Aerospace Manufacturing Pte Ltd (SAM), 503 Airport Road, Singapore 1953
Telephone: 284 6255
Telex: RS 38126 SAMPL
Fax: (65) 2880965
GENERAL MANAGER: Cheng Fook Choon
    Manufacture of engine blades, aircraft external fuel tanks and bomb racks, and aircraft spares and components.

Singapore Aero-Engine Overhaul Pte Ltd (SAEOL), 501 Airport Road, Singapore 1953
Telephone: 285 1111
Telex: RS 33268 SAEOL
Fax: (65) 2823010
GENERAL MANAGER: Chong Kok Pan
    Overhaul and repair of Pratt & Whitney, Rolls-Royce, Curtiss-Wright, Allison, General Electric and Textron Lycoming civil and military aero engines.

Singapore Electronic and Engineering Pte Ltd (SEEL), No. 24 Street 65, Ang Mo Kio Industrial Park 3, Singapore 2056
Telephone: 495 3555
Telex: RS 21901 SEELSIN
Fax: (65) 4553613

SIAI-Marchetti S.211 in Republic of Singapore Air Force insignia

GENERAL MANAGER: Lye Hoeng Fai
    Life cycle support for military and industrial electronic instruments, equipment and systems, covering system design, installation, maintenance, overhaul and upgrading.

Singapore Aerospace Warehousing and Supplies Pte Ltd (SAWS), SAWS Building, 540 Airport Road, Singapore 1953
Telephone: 287 2033
Telex: RS 56128 SAWS
Fax: (65) 2841167
GENERAL MANAGER: Wong Peng Hock
    Supply of wide range of aircraft spares to international and air force customers, as well as to support the SAI Group's ongoing maintenance and overhaul activities.

    SAI was formed in early 1982 as a government owned industrial group under control of the Ministry of Defence's Sheng-Li Holding Company Pte Ltd. It has a combined workforce of more than 2,600, in six subsidiaries, the largest of which are SAMCO and SEEL.
    SAMCO was formed in 1975, initially to maintain and overhaul aircraft of the Republic of Singapore Air Force (RSAF), and began operating in April 1976, on both fixed-wing aircraft and helicopters. Major programmes undertaken since that time have included rebuilding, refurbishing and A-4 to TA-4 conversion of Skyhawk aircraft for the RSAF and other air forces, and depot level maintenance, overhaul, repair and refurbishment of many types of aircraft including the C-130 Hercules, F-5E/F Tiger

II, Hunter, Strikemaster, and several models of Bell and Aérospatiale helicopters. Most of this work has been carried out at Seletar, but a new 15,000 m² (161,450 sq ft) factory at Paya Lebar was opened in October 1983.
    SAI's other subsidiaries have a substantial capability in the fields of aircraft and engine overhaul, maintenance and repair, component and equipment manufacture for civil and military aircraft and aero engines, external stores equipment, and defence avionics.
    In late 1983, SAI began evaluating potential aircraft licence assembly and manufacturing programmes, which led to the assembly, from 1985, of 30 SIAI-Marchetti S.211 jet trainers (which see) for the RSAF, using kits supplied by the Italian manufacturer. It also assembled 17 of the 22 Super Pumas ordered from Aérospatiale by the RSAF. In due course, SAI is expected to be involved in production programmes for aircraft selected to replace the RSAF's Hunters and Strikemasters.

SAI A-4S-1 SUPER SKYHAWK

    Under a programme initiated in May 1985 SAI converted two McDonnell Douglas A-4S Skyhawks (serial numbers 919 and 946) to prototype A-4S-1 configuration by replacing the existing 37.4 kN (8,400 lb st) Wright J65-W-20 turbojet with a 48.9 kN (11,000 lb st) General Electric F404-GE-100D non-afterburning turbofan. First flight was made on 19 September 1986, and by the end of 1987 the two prototypes had made nearly 80 test flights, totalling more than 200 hours. No quantified performance data have been received, but according to SAI the effect of the re-engining programme is to increase dash speed by 15 per cent, initial climb rate by 35 per cent and acceleration by 40 per cent compared with the A-4S, with appreciable improvements also in take-off run and in-flight turning rate.
    Redesign to accept the F404 engine was assisted by Grumman and General Electric, using SAI's CAD/CAM equipment, and includes the addition of an engine accessory drive gearbox, gas turbine engine starting, and a small airscoop on the outside of the port air intake trunk. The tailcone is also modified, and a more heat-resistant jetpipe fitted. A go-ahead for the 'production' conversion of some 50 RSAF A-4S Skyhawks was given in 1987, and the programme is expected to run for about three years; deliveries of the engines for these were reported to have begun by early 1988. The aircraft are also to undergo an avionics upgrade, involving principally a new Ferranti nav/attack system, a digital databus, and the ability to carry Maverick air-to-surface missiles.

Prototype SAI conversion of an A-4S Skyhawk to A-4S-1 configuration

---

SOUTH AFRICA

ATLAS

ATLAS AIRCRAFT CORPORATION OF SOUTH AFRICA (PTY) LIMITED

PO Box 11, Atlas Road, 1620 Kempton Park, Transvaal
Telephone: (011) 927 9111
Telex: 742403
GENERAL MANAGER: G. W. Ward
    Atlas Aircraft Corporation, which was founded in 1963, built two versions of the Impala (MB-326) under licence from Aermacchi. These programmes have now been completed.
    Atlas continues to manufacture, under licence, components for Dassault Mirage F1-AZ and -CZ multi-purpose combat aircraft currently in service with Nos. 1 and 3 Squadrons respectively of the South African Air Force. It also undertakes maintenance and overhaul of SAAF aircraft. The company has developed the Cheetah combat

Cheetah DZ two-seat multi-role fighter developed by Atlas from the Mirage III

aircraft for the SAAF, by modifying and upgrading the radar and other avionics of the service's Mirage IIIs. It has also developed a light attack helicopter, the Alpha XH-1 (see 1986-87 *Jane's*), based on the French Alouette III, and the larger XTP-1, adapted from the SA 330 Puma.

ATLAS CHEETAH

The South African Air Force has given the name Cheetah to a redesigned and upgraded version of its Mirage IIIs now undergoing modification by Atlas Aircraft Corporation. The new name, justified by the extensive changes, commemorates the fact that South Africa's first Mirage IIIs entered service, in March 1963, with the SAAF's No. 2 'Cheetah' Squadron.

Unveiled on 16 July 1986 and declared operational by the SAAF in Summer 1987, the Cheetah's configuration is very similar to that of the Israel Aircraft Industries Kfir-TC7 (1987-88 *Jane's*), although official South African statements imply that no outside assistance was given in its design.

South Africa received its Mirage IIIs between 1963 and the mid-1970s, and the majority of them remain in service. No. 2 Squadron at Hoedspruit in the Eastern Transvaal operates a mixture of the single-seat Mirage III-CZ, two-seat III-BZ trainer and reconnaissance III-RZ/R2Z models, while No. 85 Combat Flying School at Pietersburg flies mainly the III-EZ single-seater and III-DZ/-D2Z two-seat combat trainer versions. Most of these are powered by 60.8 kN (13,670 lb st) Snecma Atar 9C afterburning turbojets, but the later D2Z and R2Z have the higher rated (70.6 kN; 15,873 lb st) Atar 9K50. In the mid-1970s Atlas acquired a licence to manufacture the latter engine, which also powers the SAAF's Mirage F1s, and refit with the 9K50 is probably an ingredient of the Cheetah modification.

According to the SAAF, the Cheetah programme includes new performance levels, and the replacement of many structural components and upgrading of flight systems, about 50 per cent of the existing airframe being reconstructed and equipped with the latest navigation and weapons systems. The Cheetah chosen for the July 1986 rollout was a two-seat III-D2Z (SAAF serial number 845), and exhibited many outward similarities to the TC2/TC7 two-seat versions of the Kfir, including the sweptback, intake mounted fixed foreplanes, small nose side-strakes and 'dog-tooth' wing leading-edges. The nose extension appears to be shorter than that of the Kfir TC, and has rather more droop, but is large enough to accommodate a multi-mode radar. Beneath the nose mounted pitot probe are box and blister shaped fairings which suggest the presence of such equipment as a Doppler or terrain following radar and an infra-red seeker. Retention of the Atar engine is confirmed by absence of the Kfir's large dorsal airscoop (for its bigger, heavier J79 engine) and also of the smaller, rearmost pair of overfuselage airscoops of the Israeli aircraft. Cheetah 845 also retains the upward opening framed canopy of the two-seat Mirage. The underfuselage arrester hook fairing is retained, but the ILS aerials have been removed from the fin, which now carries what appears to be a radar warning receiver fairing. The small wing fences are the first seen on a Mirage III/5 airframe.

Sum total of the changes may be expected to confer upon the Cheetah the same kind of performance benefits as those claimed for the Kfir, namely improvements in dogfighting agility, especially in instantaneous and sustained turn rates (19°/s and 9.5°/s respectively in the case of the Kfir); handling and control at higher angles of attack; gust response, especially at low level; and take-off and landing distances. Other general performance figures are likely to remain similar to those of the Mirage III.

In addition to the pair of built-in 30 mm DEFA cannon, recent armament of SAAF Mirage IIIs has consisted primarily of Matra R.550 Magic or AIM-9 Sidewinder air-to-air missiles, medium-range Matra R.530 missiles, Matra JL-100 combined fuel/missile pods, and Nord AS 30 air-to-surface missiles. The Magic has already begun to be replaced by the domestic Armscor V3B infra-red homing missile, and it has been stated officially that all weaponry for the Cheetah is totally of South African origin. The Cheetah has been seen with an external load of eight 500 lb bombs, two V3B missiles and two underwing drop tanks. The V3C version of the missile is now believed to be in production.

ATLAS XTP-1

This modified version of the SA 330 Puma represents the second stage of South African progress, begun with the Alpha programme in 1981 (see 1986-87 *Jane's*), towards an armed helicopter based on indigenous design and manufacture. At its unveiling in Pretoria on 30 April 1987,

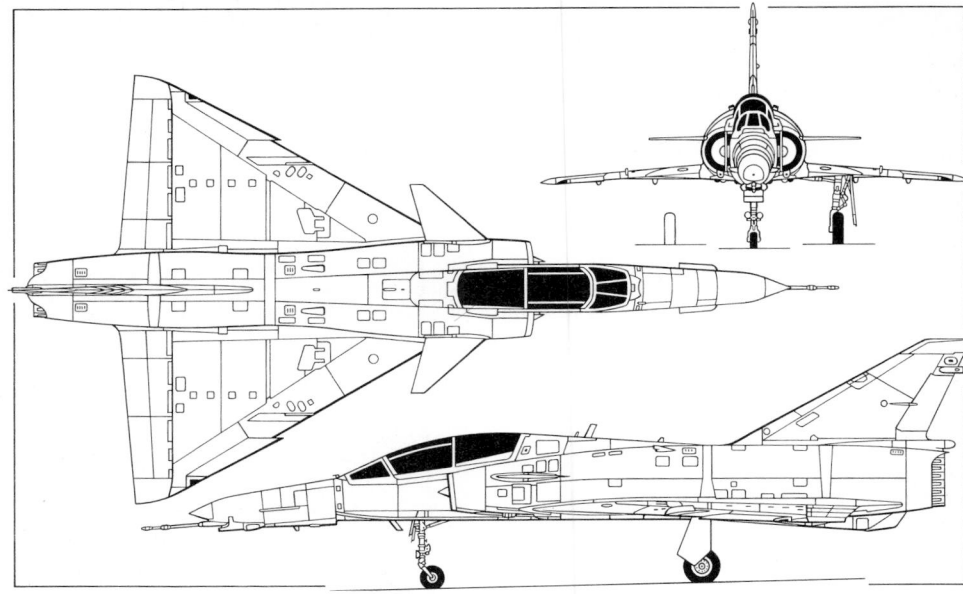

Atlas Cheetah multi-role fighter, a redesigned and upgraded Mirage III *(Jane's/Mike Keep)*

Atlas XTP-1 experimental armed helicopter, based on an SA 330 Puma

emphasis was laid on South Africa's existing ability to manufacture locally such items as gearboxes, engine hot sections and rotor blades, and to develop such items as fuel tanks, armoured crew seats, tyres, acrylic floor panels, transparencies, plastics and composites which it cannot purchase from abroad.

Major airframe changes to the XTP-1 (experimental test platform) include extended engine intake filters, horizontal stabiliser and ventral fin similar to those of the Super Puma, and the addition of stub wings mid-mounted on the cabin sides. Each wing is fitted with a pair of articulated pylons capable of carrying 18-round pods of 68 mm unguided rockets. A ventral turret mounts a computer controlled 20 mm GA-1 cannon (rate of fire 650 rds/min), aimed by helmet sight, and a 1,000-round magazine. The South

African Air Force has a fleet of approximately 50 Pumas.

According to unconfirmed press reports in mid-1988, a 'production' prototype was then well into its flight programme, and exhibited several additional changes. These included a redesigned front fuselage, with two cockpits in tandem, and replacement of the standard tricycle landing gear of the Puma with non-retractable single mainwheels and a 'tailwheel' beneath the rear of the cabin. The sliding side doors are deleted, enabling the stub wings to pass through the centre of the cabin, and the underfuselage GA-1 gun turret is relocated in a 'chin' position. In its production form, the gunship Puma is reportedly named **Beta**, and may be intended to enter service in 1989-90.

CAI
COMPOSITE AIRCRAFT INDUSTRIES
PO Box 4356, Pretoria 0001
PRESIDENT: J. Israel Harris

Mr Harris, an aeronautical engineer, businessman and former Israeli Air Force transport pilot, formed CAI to design, develop and market a new business aircraft known

as the SE-86. No news of the venture has been received since it was announced in March 1986. All known details were given in the 1987-88 *Jane's*.

SPAIN

AISA

AERONAUTICA INDUSTRIAL SA

Cuatro Vientos (Carretera del Aeroclub CarabanchelAlto),
Apartado 27.094, Madrid 28044
Telephone: (1) 208 13 40
Telex: E MADRID 48972
PRESIDENT: J. A. Pérez-Nievas
GENERAL MANAGER: Carlos Herraiz
DESIGN MANAGER: Rafael Moreno
PRESS RELATIONS: Enrique Gutierrez

This company was founded in 1923, assuming its present
title in 1935. Its design office has, since the Second World
War, been responsible for several liaison, training and
sporting aircraft for the Spanish Air Force and aeroclub
flying schools. The Cuatro Vientos factory has a covered
area of 8,000 m² (86,110 sq ft) and employs about 200
people.

AISA is engaged in repair and general overhaul of US
aircraft, in particular the Beechcraft B55 Baron and F33
Bonanza aircraft operated by the Spanish Air Force and the
National School of Aeronautics. It is also engaged in the
repair and overhaul of Bell 47, 204, 205, 206 and 212, and
Boeing CH-47 helicopters, and their dynamic components,
for the Spanish Army, Navy and Air Force and civilian
operators. As a subcontractor to Messier-Hispano-Bugatti,
it is producing landing gear shock absorbers and hydraulic
actuators for the Dassault Mirage F1 and 2000 and Falcon
series, Dassault-Breguet/Dornier Alpha Jet, and other
European aviation programmes. Under subcontract to
CASA, it produces structural components for the C-212
Aviocar and Airbus programmes; and, in offset programmes, helicopter structures and hydraulic components
for Aérospatiale and Agusta. AISA is also involved in the
Eurofighter EFA programme, participating in hydraulic
and fuel component design, the missile launcher and the
ejector release unit.

CASA

CONSTRUCCIONES AERONAUTICAS SA

Rey Francisco 4, Apartado 193, 28008 Madrid
Telephone: (1) 247 25 00
Telex: 27418 CASA E
Fax: (341) 248 88 85
WORKS: Getafe, Ajalvir, Tablada, San Pablo, San Fernando
and Cádiz
PRESIDENT AND CHAIRMAN OF THE BOARD:
Javier Alvarez Vara
MANAGING DIRECTOR: Luis Escudero
PUBLIC RELATIONS AND PRESS MANAGER:
José de Sanmillán

This company was formed on 3 March 1923 and has since
manufactured many aircraft and helicopters of foreign
design, recent examples including the Northrop F-5 fighter.
It assembled 57 MBB BO 105 helicopters ordered by the
Spanish Army, and delivered 24 armed BO 105s to the air
force of Iraq. Output of BO 105s continued with a further 32
aircraft in 1984, followed more recently by others for the
Spanish Guardia Civil and Customs Surveillance Service.
CASA also produces glassfibre doors and some rotor head
components for the BO 105 production line. Under a 1984
agreement CASA is producing tailcones, tail rotor pylons
and horizontal stabilisers for Sikorsky S-70 helicopters. The
agreement allows also for final assembly and flight testing
of S-70s purchased by the Spanish armed forces, and
development of additional helicopter collaboration. The
company is assembling six of the 12 Aérospatiale AS 332B₁
Super Pumas ordered for the Spanish Army, and in 1987
installed Thorn EMI Searchwater AEW radars in three
Spanish Navy Sikorsky SH-3D helicopters.

CASA's own Project Office has designed several aircraft
under contract to the Spanish Air Ministry, including the
current C-212 Aviocar transport and C-101 Aviojet jet
trainer. Production of the Series 200 version of the Aviocar
has ended, being replaced by the new Series 300 as the
current standard model. There is also a C-212 licence
assembly line in Indonesia (see IPTN entry in Indonesian
section). As described in the International section, CASA is
collaborating with IPTN in producing the Airtech CN-235
transport aircraft.

Under contract to Dassault-Breguet (which see), CASA
builds centre fuselages for the Mirage F1; it produces a
variety of F/A-18 components for McDonnell Douglas and
Northrop. As a full member (4.2%) of Airbus Industrie (see
International section), it manufactures horizontal tail
surfaces, landing gear doors and forward passenger doors
for the Airbus A300/310/320 family of wide-bodied
transport aircraft, and a fuselage section of the A320. It also
manufactures glassfibre honeycomb components, including
underwing fillets for McDonnell Douglas DC-10s, outboard flaps for the Boeing 757, and components for the
MD-80 series and Canadair CL-215.

CASA undertakes maintenance and modernisation work
for the Spanish Air Force and Navy, and for the US Air
Force in Europe. Its principal current activities of this kind
concern maintenance and specific modifications to the
McDonnell Douglas F-15, and overhaul and maintenance
of McDonnell Douglas F-4 and BAe Matador (Harrier)
combat aircraft and Bell 47G, 204 and 205 helicopters.

CASA has six factories, employing approx 10,200 people
in 1988, and has a total covered area of 270,000 m²
(2,906,253 sq ft). Majority shareholder is the INI (Instituto
Nacional de Industria); others include Northrop Corporation of the USA (13%) and MBB of the German Federal
Republic (11%).

AIRTECH (CASA-IPTN) CN-235

Details of this programme can be found in the
International section.

CASA C-212 SERIES 300 AVIOCAR

The original C-212-5 Series 100 Aviocar (1981-82 and
earlier *Jane's*), of which 135 examples (including ten
development aircraft) were built by CASA and 29 under
licence by Nurtanio (IPTN) in Indonesia, was followed in
1979 by the improved Srs 200 with more powerful
TPE331-10 engines and increased max T-O weight. Details
of the latter version can be found in the 1987-88 *Jane's*.
Production of the Series 200 has now also ended. It is
replaced by the Series 300, with further improvements, as
the current standard model.

CASA C-212 Series 200 maritime patrol Aviocar of the Venezuelan Navy *(Ivo Sturzenegger)*

CASA C-212 Series 300 Aviocar, now the standard production version *(Pilot Press)*

The C-212 is certificated under FAR Pt 25, can be
operated under FAR Pt 121 and Pt 135 conditions, and is
well within the noise requirements of FAR Pt 36. By
February 1988 total sales of the Aviocar (all versions) had
reached 413 (203 civil and 210 military), of which more than
400 had been delivered by CASA and IPTN, with
production continuing. Recent orders include five for the
French Air Force and three for the Panamanian Air Force.

Maritime patrol and elint/ECM versions of the Aviocar
are described separately. The following description applies
to the Series 300 transport:
TYPE: Twin-turboprop STOL utility transport.
WINGS: Cantilever high-wing monoplane. Wing section
NACA 65₃-218. Incidence 2° 30'. No dihedral or
sweepback on main wings, but wingtips have 45°
dihedral. All-metal light alloy fail-safe structure. Light
alloy ailerons and double-slotted trailing-edge flaps.
Trim tab in port aileron. Pneumatic de-icing of
leading-edges (rubber boots and engine bleed air).
FUSELAGE: Semi-monocoque non-pressurised fail-safe
structure of light alloy construction. New nose section,
compared with Srs 200, providing additional volume for
baggage (civil) or avionics (special mission versions).
TAIL UNIT: Cantilever two-spar all-metal structure, with
dorsal fin. Fixed incidence tailplane, mid mounted on
rear of fuselage. Trim tab in rudder and each elevator.
Pneumatic de-icing of leading-edges (rubber boots and
engine bleed air).
LANDING GEAR: Non-retractable tricycle type, with single
mainwheels and single steerable nosewheel. CASA
oleo-pneumatic shock absorbers. Goodyear wheels and
tyres, main units size 11.00-12 Type III (10-ply rating),
nose unit size 24-7.7 Type VII (8-ply rating). Tyre
pressure 3.86 bars (56 lb/sq in) on main units, 3.72 bars
(54 lb/sq in) on nose unit. Goodyear hydraulic disc brakes
on mainwheels. No brake cooling. Anti-skid system
optional.
POWER PLANT: Two Garrett TPE331-10R-513C turboprops,
each flat rated at 671 kW (900 shp) and equipped with an
automatic power reserve (APR) system providing 690
kW (925 shp) in the event of one engine failing during
take-off. Dowty Rotol R-334/4-82-F/13 four-blade
constant-speed fully-feathering reversible-pitch propellers. Fuel in four integral wing tanks, with total capacity
of 2,040 litres (539 US gallons; 449 Imp gallons), of which
2,000 litres (528 US gallons; 440 Imp gallons) are usable.
Gravity refuelling point above each tank. Single pressure
refuelling point in starboard wing leading-edge. Additional fuel can be carried in one 1,000 litre or two 750
litre (264 or 198 US gallon; 220 or 165 Imp gallon)
optional ferry tanks inside cabin, and/or two 500 litre
(132 US gallon; 110 Imp gallon) auxiliary underwing
tanks. Oil capacity 4.5 litres (1.2 US gallons; 1.0 Imp
gallon) per engine.
ACCOMMODATION: Crew of two on flight deck; cabin
attendant in civil version. For troop transport role, main
cabin can be fitted with 25 inward facing seats along
cabin walls, to accommodate 24 paratroops with an
instructor/jumpmaster; or seats for 25 fully equipped
troops. As an ambulance, cabin is normally equipped to
carry 12 stretcher patients and four medical attendants.
As a freighter, up to 2,700 kg (5,952 lb) of cargo can be

Series 300 version of the C-212 Aviocar in the insignia of the Colombian operator SATENA

carried in main cabin, including two LD1, LD727/DC-8 or three LD3 containers, or light vehicles. Cargo system, which is certificated to FAR Pt 25, includes roller loading/unloading system and 9g barrier net. Photographic version is equipped with two Wild RC-10A vertical cameras and a darkroom. Navigation training version has individual desks/consoles for instructor and five pupils, in two rows, with appropriate instrument installations. Civil passenger transport version has standard seating for up to 26 persons in mainly three-abreast layout at 72 cm (28.5 in) pitch, with provision for quick change to all-cargo or mixed passenger/cargo interior. Toilet, galley and 400 kg (882 lb) capacity baggage compartment standard, plus additional 1 m³ (35 cu ft) in nose bay. VIP transport version can be furnished to customer's requirements. Forward and outward opening door on port side immediately aft of flight deck; forward/outward opening passenger door on port side aft of wing; inward opening emergency exit opposite each door on starboard side. Additional emergency exit in roof of forward main cabin. A two-section underfuselage loading ramp/door aft of main cabin is openable in flight for discharge of paratroops or cargo, and can be fitted with optional external wheels for door protection during ground manoeuvring. Interior of rear loading door can be used for additional baggage stowage in civil version. Entire accommodation heated and ventilated; air-conditioning optional.

SYSTEMS: Freon cycle or (on special mission versions) engine bleed air air-conditioning system optional. Hydraulic system, operating at a service pressure of 138 bars (2,000 lb/sq in), provides power via an electric pump to actuate mainwheel brakes, flaps, nosewheel steering and rear cargo ramp/door. Handpump for standby hydraulic power in case of electrical failure or other emergency. Electrical system is supplied by two 9kW starter/generators, three batteries and three static converters. Pneumatic boot de-icing of wing and tail unit leading-edges; electric de-icing of propellers and windscreens. Oxygen system for crew (incl cabin attendant); two portable oxygen cylinders for passenger supply. Engine and cabin fire protection systems.

AVIONICS AND EQUIPMENT: Standard avionics include King or Collins VHF com, VOR/ILS, ADF, DME, ATC transponder, radio altimeter, intercom (with Gables control) and PA system; King directional gyro; Sperry flight director; and Bendix weather radar. Blind-flying instrumentation standard. Optional avionics include second King or Collins ADF and transponder; Collins HF com; Collins flight director; Global Omega nav; Sperry autopilot; Sperry weather radar; Martech emergency radio beacon; and Fairchild flight data and cockpit voice recorders.

ARMAMENT (military versions, optional): Two machine-gun pods or two rocket launchers, or one launcher and one gun pod, on hardpoints on fuselage sides (capacity 250 kg; 551 lb each).

DIMENSIONS, EXTERNAL:
Wing span	20.28 m (66 ft 6½ in)
Wing chord: at root	2.50 m (8 ft 2½ in)
at tip	1.25 m (4 ft 1¼ in)
Wing aspect ratio	10.0
Length overall	16.20 m (53 ft 1¾ in)
Fuselage: Max width	2.30 m (7 ft 6½ in)
Height overall	6.30 m (20 ft 8 in)
Tailplane span	8.40 m (27 ft 6¾ in)
Wheel track	3.10 m (10 ft 2 in)
Wheelbase	5.55 m (18 ft 2½ in)
Propeller diameter	2.74 m (9 ft 0 in)

Propeller ground clearance (min)	1.32 m (4 ft 4 in)
Distance between propeller centres	5.30 m (17 ft 4¾ in)
Passenger door (port, rear):	
Max height	1.58 m (5 ft 2¼ in)
Max width	0.70 m (2 ft 3½ in)
Crew and servicing door (port, fwd):	
Max height	1.10 m (3 ft 7¼ in)
Max width	0.58 m (1 ft 10¾ in)
Rear loading door: Max length	3.66 m (12 ft 0 in)
Max width	1.70 m (5 ft 7 in)
Max height	1.80 m (5 ft 11 in)
Emergency exit (stbd, fwd): Height	1.10 m (3 ft 7¼ in)
Width	0.58 m (1 ft 10¾ in)
Emergency exit (stbd, rear): Height	0.94 m (3 ft 1 in)
Width	0.55 m (1 ft 9¾ in)

DIMENSIONS, INTERNAL:
Cabin (excl flight deck and rear loading door):	
Length	6.50 m (21 ft 4 in)
Max width	2.10 m (6 ft 10¾ in)
Max height	1.80 m (5 ft 11 in)
Floor area	12.21 m² (131.4 sq ft)
Volume	23.0 m³ (812.2 cu ft)
Cabin: volume incl flight deck and rear loading door	27.0 m³ (953.5 cu ft)
Baggage compartment volume	2.9 m³ (102.4 cu ft)

AREAS:
Wings, gross	41.0 m² (441.33 sq ft)
Ailerons (total, incl tab)	3.75 m² (40.36 sq ft)
Trailing-edge flaps (total)	7.47 m² (80.41 sq ft)
Fin, incl dorsal fin	6.27 m² (67.49 sq ft)
Rudder, incl tab	2.05 m² (22.07 sq ft)
Tailplane	12.57 m² (135.31 sq ft)
Elevators, incl tabs	3.56 m² (38.32 sq ft)

WEIGHTS AND LOADINGS:
Manufacturer's weight empty	3,780 kg (8,333 lb)
Weight empty, equipped (cargo)	4,400 kg (9,700 lb)
Max payload (cargo)	2,700 kg (5,952 lb)
Max fuel: standard	1,600 kg (3,527 lb)
with underwing auxiliary tanks	2,400 kg (5,291 lb)
Max T-O weight: standard	7,700 kg (16,975 lb)
military version	8,000 kg (17,637 lb)
Max ramp weight	7,750 kg (17,085 lb)
Max landing weight	7,450 kg (16,424 lb)
Max zero-fuel weight	7,100 kg (15,653 lb)
Max cabin floor loading	732 kg/m² (150 lb/sq ft)
Max wing loading: standard	187.8 kg/m² (38.46 lb/sq ft)
Max power loading: standard	5.74 kg/kW (9.43 lb/shp)

PERFORMANCE (at max T-O weight. A: passenger version, B: freighter, C: military version at 8,000 kg; 17,637 lb MTOGW):
Max operating speed (VMO):	
A, B, C	200 knots (370 km/h; 230 mph)
Max cruising speed at 3,050 m (10,000 ft):	
A, B, C	191 knots (354 km/h; 220 mph)
Econ cruising speed at 3,050 m (10,000 ft):	
A, B, C	162 knots (300 km/h; 186 mph)
Stalling speed in T-O configuration:	
A, B, C	78 knots (145 km/h; 90 mph)
Max rate of climb at S/L: A, B, C	497 m (1,630 ft)/min
Rate of climb at S/L, one engine out:	
A, B, C	95 m (312 ft)/min
Service ceiling: A, B, C	7,925 m (26,000 ft)
Service ceiling, one engine out:	
A, B, C	3,380 m (11,100 ft)
T-O run: A, B	668 m (2,192 ft)
C	340 m (1,115 ft)
T-O to 15 m (50 ft): A, B	782 m (2,566 ft)
C	560 m (1,837 ft)
Landing from 15 m (50 ft) without propeller reversal:	
A, B	519 m (1,703 ft)

Landing run: A, B	269 m (883 ft)
Range at 3,050 m (10,000 ft), ISA, no reserves:	
A with max payload	321 nm (594 km; 369 miles)
B with max fuel	875 nm (1,620 km; 1,007 miles)
Range at econ cruising speed, no reserves:	
A with max payload	350 nm (648 km; 403 miles)
B with max fuel	978 nm (1,811 km; 1,125 miles)

CASA C-212 AVIOCAR (ASW and MARITIME PATROL VERSIONS)
Swedish Navy designation: Tp89

For service with the Spanish Air Force, and for several foreign countries, CASA has developed versions of the C-212 equipped for anti-submarine and maritime patrol duties. Nine Srs 100/200s were ordered by the Spanish Air Force for SAR duties, three by the Spanish Ministry of Finance, one ASW version by the Swedish Navy, two for maritime patrol (with a SLAR and IR/UV search equipment) by the Swedish Coastguard, four for maritime patrol by the Venezuelan Navy, ten for maritime patrol by the Mexican Navy, two by Sudan and one by the Uruguayan Air Force. All these versions are available also for the Series 300.

The principal external differences from the transport version are the addition of a nose radome and the appearance of various antennae on the fuselage and tail fin. Two fuselage hardpoints are provided for the carriage of torpedoes, rocket pods or other weapons.

TYPE: Twin-turboprop ASW and maritime patrol aircraft.

AIRFRAME: Generally similar to standard C-212 except for addition of nose radome and various external antennae.

POWER PLANT: As for standard C-212. Auxiliary fuel tanks, total capacity 1,400 litres (370 US gallons; 308 Imp gallons).

ACCOMMODATION (ASW version): Pilot and co-pilot on flight deck, with OTPI and additional central console for radar repeater; control for radio navigation, Doppler, DME, ADF, UHF/DF, Omega and VOR/ILS; weapons delivery controls; and intervalometer for rockets. Avionics rack on port side, aft of pilot, for com/nav equipment; second rack on starboard side, aft of co-pilot, contains avionics for mission equipment (radar, sonobuoys, MAD and ESM). Immediately aft of the latter rack, along the starboard side of the cabin, are three control consoles for the mission crew members. The first console has the radar control and display, ESM control and display, and intercom switch control. The second has the tactical display and control, MAD recorder and control, and intercom switch (ICS). The rearmost of the three incorporates intercom switch, sonobuoy receiver control unit, acoustic control panel, and acoustic control and display units.

ACCOMMODATION (maritime patrol version): Pilot and co-pilot on flight deck, with central console for radar repeater; control for radio navigation, Doppler, DME, ADF, UHF/DF, Omega, VOR/ILS and searchlight. Avionics rack on port side, aft of pilot, for com/nav and radar equipment. On starboard side of cabin is a console for the radar operator that incorporates radar PPI and ICS controls. Posts for two observers at rear of cabin.

AVIONICS: Communications equipment includes two HF and two VHF transceivers, single UHF, and interphone. Navigation equipment includes automatic flight control system, flight director, VOR/ILS (including VOR/LOC), glideslope and marker beacon receiver, DME, two ADF, UHF/DF, radar altimeter, Doppler radar, VLF/Omega, autopilot and compass.

OPERATIONAL EQUIPMENT (ASW version): Underfuselage search radar with 360° scan, electronic support measures

(ESM), sonobuoy processing system (SPS), OTPI, MAD, tactical processing system (TPS), IFF/SIF transponder, sonobuoy and smoke marker launcher, torpedoes, rockets and other weapons.

OPERATIONAL EQUIPMENT (maritime patrol version): Nose mounted AN/APS-128 100kW search radar with 270° scan, searchlight, FLIR (optional), smoke markers and camera.

ARMAMENT: Includes option to carry torpedoes such as Mk 46 and Sting Ray, and air-to-surface missiles such as Sea Skua and AS 15TT.

CASA C-212 AVIOCAR (ELINT/ECM VERSION)

A version of the Aviocar for electronic intelligence and electronic countermeasures duties entered development in 1981, at which time four had been ordered by an export customer. Two more have since been ordered by an undisclosed customer, and two C-212s already delivered to the Portuguese Air Force have been modified retrospectively for elint/ECM duties. This version is also available for the Series 300.

The elint/ECM version carries equipment for automatic signal interception, classification and identification in dense signal environments, data from which enable a map to be drawn plotting the position and characteristics of hostile radars. Emitters for the jamming part of the mission are also carried.

CASA C-101 AVIOJET

Spanish Air Force designation: E.25 Mirlo (Blackbird)

Chilean Air Force designations: T-36 and A-36 Halcón

The first of four prototypes of this basic and advanced military jet trainer made its initial flight on 27 June 1977. MBB (West Germany) and Northrop (USA) collaborated in the design, the latter providing design assistance with the inlets and the 'Norcasa' wing section. The C-101 is built on modular lines, with ample space within the airframe for equipment for any training mission likely to be required.

The C-101 is fully aerobatic, and can carry out such additional duties as ground attack, reconnaissance, escort, weapons training, electronic countermeasures (ECM), and photographic missions. Manufacture is entirely by CASA except for the nosewheel unit, which is produced in the UK by Dowty Rotol. Wings and main landing gear units are built at Getafe and fuselages at Seville. Aircraft for Chile are assembled and partially manufactured locally by ENAER (which see). Spanish production started at the beginning of 1978, and the first production aircraft made its initial flight on 8 November 1979.

The following versions have been announced:

C-101EB. Initial production trainer version for Spanish Air Force, with 15.57 kN (3,500 lb st) TFE731-2-2J engine. Total of 88 delivered from 17 March 1980; now in service with one squadron of the Academia General del Aire at San Javier and two squadrons of the Grupo de Escuelas at Matacán. Described in 1983-84 Jane's.

C-101BB. Armed export version, with 16.46 kN (3,700 lb st) TFE731-3-1J engine, ordered by air forces of Chile (14 BB-02) and Honduras (four BB-03, similar except for avionics, with options on eight more). All BB-02s except first four are for licence assembly and partial local manufacture in Chile (see ENAER entry in Chilean section), which has options on 23 more. Known as **T-36 Halcón** (Hawk) in Chilean service.

C-101CC. Light attack version, with more powerful TFE731-5-1J engine (normal rating 19.13 kN; 4,300 lb st, military power reserve (MPR) rating 20.91 kN; 4,700 lb st), and other modifications. First of two prototypes flown on 16 November 1983. Twenty-three **CC-02** ordered by Chile, including 19 for assembly and partial manufacture by ENAER as **A-36 Halcón**, and 16 **CC-04** ordered by Royal Jordanian Air Force.

CASA C-101CC-04 Aviojet of the Royal Jordanian Air Force (Ivo Sturzenegger)

C-101DD. Enhanced training version, announced in 1984 and flown for the first time on 20 May 1985. Additional avionics include Ferranti head-up display, weapon aiming computer and inertial AHRS, and GEC Avionics AD 6601 Doppler velocity sensor. Power plant as for C-101CC. No orders announced up to mid-1988.

The following description applies to the standard C-101CC except where indicated:

TYPE: Tandem two-seat basic and advanced trainer and light tactical aircraft.

WINGS: Cantilever low-wing monoplane. Wing section Norcasa 15, thickness/chord ratio 15%. Dihedral 5°. Incidence 1°. Sweepback at quarter-chord 1° 53'. All-metal (aluminium alloy) three-spar fail-safe stressed-skin structure, with six-bolt attachment to fuselage. Plain ailerons and slotted trailing-edge flaps, of glassfibre/honeycomb sandwich construction. Flap track guides of titanium. Ailerons actuated hydraulically, with electrically actuated artificial spring feel and manual backup. Ground adjustable tab on port aileron.

FUSELAGE: All-metal semi-monocoque fail-safe structure. Hydraulically operated aluminium honeycomb airbrake under centre of fuselage.

TAIL UNIT: Cantilever all-metal structure, with electrically actuated variable incidence tailplane. Aluminium honeycomb rudder and elevators, actuated manually via push/pull rods. Electrically actuated trim tab in rudder. Twin ventral strakes under jetpipe on armed versions.

LANDING GEAR: Hydraulically retractable tricycle type, with single wheel and oleo-pneumatic shock absorber on each unit. Forward retracting Dowty Rotol nose unit, with non-steerable nosewheel and chined tubeless tyre size 457 × 146 (18 × 5.75-8). Inward retracting mainwheels with tubeless tyres size 622 × 216 (24.5 × 8.5-10) and hydraulically actuated multi-disc brakes.

POWER PLANT: One Garrett TFE731 non-afterburning turbofan (see model listings for details), with lateral intake on each side of fuselage abreast of second cockpit. Fuel in one 1,155 litre (305 US gallon; 254 Imp) fuselage bag tank, one 575 litre (152 US gallon; 126.5 Imp gallon) integral tank in wing centre-section, and two outer wing integral tanks, for ferry missions, each of 342 litres (90.4 US gallons; 75.25 Imp gallons). Total internal fuel capacity 1,730 litres (457 US gallons; 380.5 Imp gallons) normal, 2,414 litres (637.8 US gallons; 531 Imp gallons) maximum, of which 1,667 litres (440 US gallons; 367 Imp gallons) and 2,337 litres (617 US gallons; 514 Imp gallons), respectively, are usable. Fuel system permits up to 30 s of inverted flight. Pressure refuelling point beneath port air intake; gravity fuelling point for each tank. No provision for external fuel tanks. Oil capacity 8.5 litres (2.2 US gallons; 1.8 Imp gallons).

ACCOMMODATION: Crew of two in tandem, on Martin-Baker Mk 10L zero/zero ejection seats, under individual canopies which open sideways to starboard and are separated by internal screen. Rear (instructor's) seat elevated 32.5 cm (12¾ in). Cockpit pressurised and air-conditioned by engine bleed air. Dual controls standard.

SYSTEMS: Hamilton Standard three-wheel bootstrap type air-conditioning and pressurisation system, differential 0.28 bars (4.07 lb/sq in), using engine bleed air. Single hydraulic system, pressure 207 bars (3,000 lb/sq in), for landing gear, ailerons, flaps, airbrake, anti-skid units and wheel brakes. Backup system comprising compressed nitrogen bottle for landing gear extension and accumulator for aileron boosters and emergency braking. Pneumatic system for air-conditioning, pressurisation and canopy seal. Electrical system includes 28V 9kW DC starter/generator, two 700VA static inverters for 115/26V single phase AC power, and two 24V 23Ah nickel-cadmium batteries for emergency DC power and engine starting. High pressure gaseous oxygen system.

AVIONICS AND EQUIPMENT: C-101EB and BB as listed in earlier Jane's. Standard C-101CC equipped with Magnavox AN/ARC-164 UHF com, Collins 21B VHF com, Collins VIR-31A VOR/ILS, Collins DME-40, Collins ADF-60, Andrea AN/AIC-18 interphone, Teledyne/CASA AN/APX-101 IFF/SIF, Sperry ZC-222 flight director, Sperry AS-339 gyro platform, ADI-500C, RD-550A HSI, Avimo RGS2 gunsight (front and rear cockpit), and CASA SCAR-81 armament control system. Wide range of alternative avionics and equipment available for export versions, including a Maverick pod, and (in the DD), a Ferranti FD4503 head-up display and weapon aiming computer, Ferranti FIN 1100 AHRS, General Instrument AN/ALR-66 radar warning receiver, GEC Avionics AD 6601-12 Doppler velocity sensor, TRT AHV-8 radio altimeter, Collins AN/ARC-182(V) UHF/VHF-AM/FM com, Ferranti FD 5000 video camera, Vinten Vicon 78 chaff and flare dispenser and Ferranti FD2062 rear seat monitor.

ARMAMENT AND OPERATIONAL EQUIPMENT: Large bay below rear cockpit suitable for quick-change packages, including a 30 mm DEFA 553 cannon pod with 130 rds, a twin 12.7 mm Browning M3 machine-gun pod with 220 rds/gun, reconnaissance camera, ECM package or laser designator. Six underwing hardpoints, capacities 500 kg (1,102 lb) inboard, 375 kg (827 lb) centre and 250 kg (551 lb) outboard; total external stores load 2,250 kg (4,960 lb). Typical armament can include one 30 mm cannon with up to 130 rds, or two 12.7 mm guns, in the fuselage; and four LAU-10 pods of 5 in rockets, six 250 kg BR250 bombs, four LAU-3/A rocket launchers, four 125 kg BR125 bombs and two LAU-3/A launchers, two AGM-65 Maverick missiles, or four BIN200 napalm bombs.

DIMENSIONS, EXTERNAL:
Wing span	10.60 m (34 ft 9⅜ in)
Wing chord: at c/l	2.36 m (7 ft 9 in)
at tip	1.41 m (4 ft 7½ in)
Wing aspect ratio	5.6

CASA C-101CC Aviojet light attack aircraft (Pilot Press)

Length overall	12.50 m (41 ft 0 in)
Height overall	4.25 m (13 ft 11¼ in)
Tailplane span	4.32 m (14 ft 2 in)
Wheel track (c/l of shock struts)	3.18 m (10 ft 5¼ in)
Wheelbase	4.77 m (15 ft 7¾ in)

AREAS:

Wings, gross	20.00 m² (215.3 sq ft)
Ailerons (total)	1.18 m² (12.70 sq ft)
Trailing-edge flaps (total)	2.50 m² (26.91 sq ft)
Fin	2.10 m² (22.60 sq ft)
Rudder	1.10 m² (11.84 sq ft)
Tailplane	3.44 m² (37.03 sq ft)
Elevators	1.00 m² (10.76 sq ft)

WEIGHTS AND LOADINGS:

Weight empty, equipped	3,500 kg (7,716 lb)
Max fuel weight: usable	1,822 kg (4,017 lb)
total	1,882 kg (4,149 lb)
Max external stores load	2,250 kg (4,960 lb)
T-O weight:	
trainer, 'clean': BB, CC	4,850 kg (10,692 lb)
DD	4,570 kg (10,075 lb)
ground attack: BB	5,600 kg (12,345 lb)
CC, DD	6,300 kg (13,890 lb)
Max landing weight:	
3.66 m (12 ft)/s sink rate	4,700 kg (10,361 lb)
3.05 m (10 ft)/s sink rate	5,400 kg (11,905 lb)
Wing loading:	
trainer, 'clean': BB, CC	242.5 kg/m² (46.69 lb/sq ft)
DD	228.5 kg/m² (46.82 lb/sq ft)
ground attack: BB	280.0 kg/m² (57.38 lb/sq ft)
CC, DD	315.0 kg/m² (64.55 lb/sq ft)
Power loading:	
trainer, 'clean': BB	294.9 kg/kN (2.89 lb/lb st)
CC (normal)	254.1 kg/kN (2.49 lb/lb st)
CC (with MPR)	231.6 kg/kN (2.27 lb/lb st)
DD (normal)	238.8 kg/kN (2.34 lb/lb st)
DD (with MPR)	218.4 kg/kN (2.14 lb/lb st)
ground attack: BB	340.8 kg/kN (3.34 lb/lb st)
CC, DD (normal)	329.6 kg/kN (3.23 lb/lb st)
CC, DD (with MPR)	301.0 kg/kN (2.95 lb/lb st)

PERFORMANCE (C-101BB at 4,400 kg; 9,700 lb AUW, C-101CC and DD at 4,500 kg; 9,921 lb):

Max limiting Mach No. (all)	Mach 0.80
Never-exceed speed (all)	
	450 knots (834 km/h; 518 mph) IAS
Max level speed at S/L:	
BB	373 knots (691 km/h; 430 mph)
CC	415 knots (769 km/h; 478 mph)
Max level speed at height:	
BB at 7,620 m (25,000 ft)	
	430 knots (797 km/h; 495 mph)
CC and DD at 6,100 m (20,000 ft)	
	435 knots (806 km/h; 501 mph)
CC and DD at 4,575 m (15,000 ft) with MPR	
	450 knots (834 km/h; 518 mph)
Econ cruising speed at 9,145 m (30,000 ft) (all)	
	Mach 0.60 (354 knots; 656 km/h; 407 mph)
Unstick speed (all)	115 knots (213 km/h; 132 mph)
Touchdown speed (all)	95 knots (176 km/h; 109 mph)
Stalling speed (all):	
flaps up	99 knots (183 km/h; 114 mph) IAS
flaps down	88 knots (164 km/h; 102 mph) IAS
Max rate of climb at S/L: BB	1,152 m (3,780 ft)/min
CC and DD (normal)	1,494 m (4,900 ft)/min
CC and DD (with MPR)	1,859 m (6,100 ft)/min
Time to 7,620 m (25,000 ft): BB	8 min 30 s
CC, DD	6 min 30 s
Service ceiling: BB	12,200 m (40,000 ft)
CC, DD	12,800 m (42,000 ft)
T-O run: BB	630 m (2,065 ft)
CC, DD	560 m (1,835 ft)
T-O to 15 m (50 ft): BB	850 m (2,790 ft)
CC, DD	750 m (2,460 ft)
Landing from 15 m (50 ft) (all)	800 m (2,625 ft)
Landing run (all)	480 m (1,575 ft)

Typical interdiction radius (lo-lo-lo) with four 250 kg bombs and 30 mm gun:
CC and DD, 3 min over target, 30 min reserves
280 nm (519 km; 322 miles)
Typical close air support radius (lo-lo-lo):

CC and DD with four 19 × 2.75 in rocket launchers and 30 mm gun, 50 min loiter over battle area, 8 min over target, 30 min reserves
200 nm (370 km; 230 miles)
CC and DD, load as above plus two 125 kg bombs, 30 min loiter, 10 min attack (MPR thrust) and 7% reserves
170 nm (315 km; 196 miles)
CC and DD with two Maverick missiles and 30 mm gun, 8 min over target, 30 min reserves
325 nm (602 km; 374 miles)
Typical ECM radius:
BB and CC, 3 h 15 min loiter over target, 30 min reserves
330 nm (611 km; 380 miles)
Typical photo-reconnaissance radius (hi-lo-lo):
BB and CC, 30 min reserves
520 nm (964 km; 599 miles)
Armed patrol, no underwing stores, 100 nm (185 km; 115 mile) transit from base to patrol area:
BB, CC and DD with one 30 mm or two 12.7 mm guns, 45 min reserves
3 h 30 min at 200 knots (370 km/h; 230 mph) at S/L
Ferry range (all), 30 min reserves
2,000 nm (3,706 km; 2,303 miles)
Typical training mission endurance (all):
two 1 h 10 min general handling missions, incl aerobatics, with 20 min reserves after second mission
Max endurance (all) 7 h
g limits (all):
at 4,800 kg (10,582 lb) AUW +7.5/−3.9
at 6,300 kg (13,890 lb) AUW +5.5/−1

CASA E.26 TAMIZ

Under a reciprocal agreement with ENAER of Chile (which see), CASA is assembling 40 T-35C Pillán trainers (generally similar to the T-35A) ordered for the Spanish Air Force in 1984, from kits supplied by ENAER. These are known as the E.26 Tamiz in Spanish Air Force service: the literal translation of this name is 'sieve' in English, indicating their function of sifting or grading trainee pilots.

SWEDEN

SAAB-SCANIA
SAAB-SCANIA AKTIEBOLAG
S-581 88 Linköping
Telephone: 46 13 18 00 02
Telex: 50040 SAABLG S
PRESIDENT: Georg Karnsund
EXECUTIVE VICE-PRESIDENT: Harald Schröder
Saab Aircraft Division
Telephone: 46 13 18 00 02
GENERAL MANAGER: Christer Skogsborg
DIRECTOR OF COMMERCIAL AIRCRAFT SECTOR:
Thure Svensson
DIRECTOR OF MILITARY AIRCRAFT SECTOR:
Tommy Ivarsson
PUBLIC AFFAIRS MANAGER: Rolf Erichs
WORKS: Linköping, Malmö, Ödeshog, Norrköping and Kramfors
SAAB 340 MARKETING:
Saab Aircraft International Ltd, Leworth House, 14-16 Sheet Street, Windsor, Berkshire SL4 1BG, England
Telephone: (0753) 859991
Telex: 847 815 SFIWIN G
Fax: 753 858884
VICE-PRESIDENT, PUBLIC RELATIONS AND PROMOTIONAL SERVICES: Mike Savage
Saab Aircraft of America Inc, 200 Fairbrook Drive, Herndon, Virginia 22070, USA

Telephone: (703) 478 9720
Fax: (703) 478 9727

The original Svenska Aeroplan AB was founded at Trollhättan in 1937 for the production of military aircraft. In 1939 this company was amalgamated with the Aircraft Division (ASJA) of the Svenska Järnvägsverkstäderna rolling stock factory in Linköping, where the main aerospace factory is now located. The company's name was changed to Saab Aktiebolag in May 1965. During 1968 Saab merged with Scania-Vabis, to strengthen the two companies' position in automotive products. Malmö Flygindustri (MFI) was acquired in the same year.

Saab-Scania has more than 49,000 employees, organised in three operating divisions and two major subsidiaries (Saab-Scania Combitech and Saab-Scania Enertech). Of these, nearly 6,500 are employed by the Saab Aircraft Division, including 5,500 at Linköping.

Saab-Scania's current aerospace activities include production of the JA 37 Viggen and Saab 340A, and development of the Saab JAS 39 Gripen multi-role combat aircraft. Since 1949 the company has delivered more than 2,000 military jet aircraft and more than 1,500 piston engined aircraft. Since 1962, it has had a dealership for McDonnell Douglas (Hughes) helicopters in Scandinavia and Finland. Since 1978, it has manufactured inboard wing flaps and vanes for the McDonnell Douglas MD-80 series, and now also produces composite spoilers for the

MD-82/83; it is currently manufacturing tailplanes, elevators, rudders, ailerons and spoilers for the British Aerospace 146. A 25,000 m² (269,100 sq ft) factory at Linköping, for final assembly of the Saab 340A, was completed in July 1982; an extension to this facility, to accommodate also the wing and tail unit production, was inaugurated on 26 June 1986.

In the electronics field, current production items include computer systems, autopilots, fire control and bombing systems for piloted aircraft, and electronics for guided missiles. Spaceborne computers, optronic fire control systems and field artillery computer systems are also under development and in production.

SAAB 340A
First details of this twin-turboprop transport aircraft (then known as the Saab-Fairchild SF 340A) were announced in January 1980, and the project definition phase was completed in September 1980, when agreement was reached for a full go-ahead on joint design, development, production and marketing programmes. Complete control of the programme passed to Saab-Scania in November 1985, with Fairchild remaining as a subcontractor until 1987, when SF was dropped from the designation.

The first of three prototype SF 340s (SE-ISF) made its first flight on 25 January 1983. The fourth (first production) 340A (SE-E04) flew for the first time on 5 March 1984, and Swedish type certification was awarded on 30 May 1984. The certification, which is to both FAR and JAR 25 standards, was ratified by nine other European countries and the US FAA on 29 June 1984.

First delivery, of the fifth aircraft, was to Crossair of Switzerland, with whom the 340A entered scheduled service on 14 June 1984; the sixth aircraft was delivered in July to Comair, the first US customer, and entered service in August 1984. The first corporate 340A was delivered, to Mellon Bank of Pittsburgh, Pennsylvania, in November 1985. Engine power rating was increased from 1,215 kW (1,630 shp) to 1,294 kW (1,735 shp) from mid-1985, and aircraft already delivered were modified to the new standard, with propellers of increased diameter. All aircraft built from mid-1988 (c/n 121 onward) have an improved cabin with newly designed ceiling and side panels, enlarged overhead storage bins, improved airflow system, a more efficient dropout oxygen system, new overhead passenger service unit, and improved toilet. The new interior, manufactured and installed by Metair Aircraft of the UK, meets the higher FAA standard for fire resistance which will become mandatory in August 1990.

By 12 July 1988 firm orders totalled 137 (including five corporate), of which more than half were from US customers; the remainder were from operators in Europe, Australia, Taiwan and South America. A total of 117 Saab 340As had been delivered by 22 June 1988.
TYPE: Twin-turboprop transport aircraft.

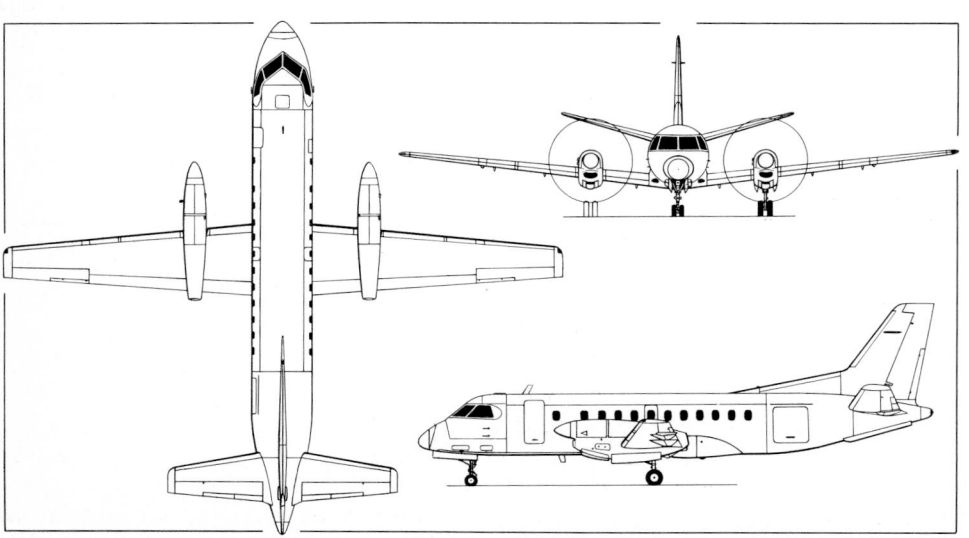

Saab 340A airliner (two General Electric CT7-5A2 turboprops) *(Pilot Press)*

Saab 340A twin-turboprop transport in the insignia of Kendell Airlines of Australia *(Norman Pealing)*

WINGS: Cantilever low-wing monoplane. Basic wing section NASA MS(1)-0313 with thickness/chord ratios of 16% and 12% at root and tip respectively. Dihedral 7° from roots. Incidence 2° at root. Sweepback 3° 36′ at quarter-chord. Tapered two-spar wings embodying fail-safe principles. Stringers and skins of 2024/7075 aluminium alloy. Wing-root/fuselage fairings of Kevlar sandwich. Hydraulically actuated single-slotted trailing-edge flaps with aluminium alloy spars, honeycomb panels faced with aluminium sheet, and leading/trailing-edges of Kevlar. Ailerons have Kevlar skins and glassfibre leading-edges. Electrically operated geared/trim tab in each aileron. Pneumatic boot de-icing of leading-edges.

FUSELAGE: Conventional fail-safe/safe-life semi-monocoque pressurised metal structure, of circular cross-section. Built in three portions: nose (incl flight deck), passenger compartment, and tail section (incorporating baggage compartment). All doors of aluminium honeycomb. Nosecone of Kevlar; cabin floor of carbonfibre sandwich.

TAIL UNIT: Cantilever structure, with sweptback vertical and non-swept horizontal surfaces, the latter having marked dihedral. Fin integral with fuselage. Construction similar to that of wings, with tailplane and fin of aluminium honeycomb. Rudder and elevators have Kevlar skins and glassfibre leading-edges. Geared/trim tab in each elevator; spring/trim tab in rudder. Pneumatic boot de-icing of fin and tailplane leading-edges.

LANDING GEAR: Retractable tricycle type, of AP Precision Hydraulics design and manufacture, with twin Goodyear wheels and oleo-pneumatic shock absorber on each unit. Hydraulic actuation. All units retract forward, main units into engine nacelles. Mainwheel doors of Kevlar sandwich. Hydraulically steerable nose unit (60° to both left and right), with shimmy damper. Mainwheel tyres size 24 × 7.7-10, pressure 6.89 bars (100 lb/sq in); nosewheel tyres size 18 × 6.0-6, pressure 3.79 bars (55 lb/sq in). Independent Goodyear carbon hydraulic disc brakes on main units, with anti-skid control.

POWER PLANT: Two General Electric CT7-5A2 turboprops, each rated at 1,294 kW (1,735 shp). Dowty Rotol four-blade slow-turning constant-speed propellers, with full autofeathering and reverse pitch capability, each with spinner and glassfibre/polyurethane foam/carbonfibre moulded blades. Fuel in integral tank in each outer wing; total capacity 3,220 litres (850.5 US gallons; 708 Imp gallons). Single-point pressure refuelling inlet in starboard outer wing panel. Overwing gravity refuelling point in each wing.

ACCOMMODATION: Two pilots and provision for observer on flight deck; attendant's seat (forward, port) in passenger cabin. Main cabin accommodates up to 35 passengers, in eleven rows of three, with aisle, and two rearward facing seats on starboard side at front. One rearward facing seat can be replaced by an optional galley module or baggage/wardrobe module; the two modules can replace both seats. Seat pitch 76 cm (30 in). Standard provision for galley, wardrobe or storage module on port side at front of cabin, regardless of installations on starboard side. Movable bulkhead aft of last row of seats. Toilet at front or rear of cabin. Aircraft can be converted quickly to various passenger/freight combinations (eg, 15 passengers and 1,814 kg; 4,000 lb of cargo). A corporate/executive version is also available. Passenger door (plug type) at front of cabin on port side, with separate airstair. Type II emergency exit opposite this on starboard side, and over wing on each side. Overhead crew escape hatch in flight deck roof. Baggage space under each passenger seat; overhead storage bins. Main baggage/cargo compartment aft of passenger cabin, with large plug type door on port side. Entire accommodation pressurised, including baggage compartment.

SYSTEMS: Hamilton Standard environmental control system (max pressure differential 0.48 bars; 7.0 lb/sq in) maintains a S/L cabin environment up to an altitude of

3,660 m (12,000 ft) and a 1,525 m (5,000 ft) environment up to the max cruising altitude of 7,620 m (25,000 ft). Single on-demand hydraulic system, operating between 138 and 207 bars (2,000-3,000 lb/sq in), for actuation of landing gear, wheel and propeller braking, nosewheel steering and wing flaps. System is powered by single 28V DC electric motor driven pump, rated delivery 9.5 litres (2.5 US gallons; 2.1 Imp gallons)/min. Self-pressurising main reservoir with 5.08 litres (0.18 cu ft) capacity, operating at pressure of 1.79-2.69 bars (26-39 lb/sq in). Hydraulic backup via four accumulators and pilot operated handpump, working via an emergency reservoir of 2.5 litres (0.09 cu ft) capacity. Electrical power supplied by two 28V 400A DC engine driven starter/generators, each connected to a separate busbar. Variable frequency 115/200V for heating circuits provided by two 26kVA AC generators; single-phase 115V and 26V AC at 400Hz for avionics provided by static inverters. Two 27Ah nickel-cadmium batteries for ground power and engine starting; standby 5Ah lead-acid battery for emergency use. External power receptacle. Pneumatic boot de-icing of wing and tail unit leading-edges, using engine bleed air. Flight deck windows have electric anti-icing and electrically driven windscreen wipers. Electric anti-icing is provided also for engine air intakes, propellers and pitot heads. Demisting by means of air-conditioning system. Plug-in connections for oxygen masks. Kidde engine fire detection system. Duncan/Garrett GTCP 36-150W APU kit certificated for installation as optional extra, to provide standby and emergency electrical power, main engine starting assistance, ground pre-heating and pre-cooling, and other power support functions.

AVIONICS AND EQUIPMENT: Standard avionics include all equipment required for FAR Pt 121 operations. The aircraft is equipped with King Gold Crown III or Collins Pro Line II com/nav radios, and a Collins integrated digital flight guidance and autopilot system (FGAS) consisting of attitude and heading reference units, electronic (CRT) flight display units, fail-passive autopilot/flight director system, colour weather radar, air data system with servo instruments, and radio altimeter. Lucas Aerospace electroluminescent flight deck instrument panel array. Dowty Electronics microprocessor-based flight deck central warning system. Rosemount pitot static tubes, total temperature sensors and stall warning system. Provision for additional avionics to customer's requirements. Landing light in each wing leading-edge.

DIMENSIONS, EXTERNAL:

Wing span	21.44 m (70 ft 4 in)
Wing chord: at root	2.837 m (9 ft 3.7 in)
at tip	1.0645 m (3 ft 5.9 in)
Wing aspect ratio	11.0
Length overall	19.72 m (64 ft 8½ in)
Fuselage: Max diameter	2.31 m (7 ft 7 in)
Height overall	6.86 m (22 ft 6 in)
Tailplane span	8.67 m (28 ft 5¼ in)
Wheel track	6.71 m (22 ft 0 in)
Wheelbase	7.14 m (23 ft 5 in)
Propeller diameter: initially	3.20 m (10 ft 6 in)
current	3.35 m (11 ft 0 in)
Propeller ground clearance	0.58 m (1 ft 11 in)
Distance between propeller centres	6.71 m (22 ft 0 in)
Passenger door: Height	1.60 m (5 ft 3 in)
Width	0.66 m (2 ft 2 in)
Height to sill	1.63 m (5 ft 4 in)
Cargo door: Height	1.30 m (4 ft 3¼ in)
Width	1.35 m (4 ft 5 in)
Height to sill	1.68 m (5 ft 6¼ in)
Emergency exit (fwd, stbd): Height	1.32 m (4 ft 4 in)
Width	0.51 m (1 ft 8 in)
Emergency exits (overwing, each):	
Height	0.91 m (3 ft 0 in)
Width	0.51 m (1 ft 8 in)

DIMENSIONS, INTERNAL:
Cabin, excl flight deck, incl toilet and galley:

Length	10.39 m (34 ft 1 in)
Max width	2.16 m (7 ft 1 in)
Width at floor	1.70 m (5 ft 7 in)
Max height	1.83 m (6 ft 0 in)
Volume	33.5 m³ (1,183.0 cu ft)
Baggage/cargo compartment volume	
	6.8 m³ (240.0 cu ft)

AREAS:

Wings, gross	41.81 m² (450.0 sq ft)
Ailerons (total)	2.12 m² (22.84 sq ft)
Trailing-edge flaps (total)	8.07 m² (86.84 sq ft)
Fin, incl dorsal fin	10.53 m² (113.38 sq ft)
Rudder, incl tab	2.76 m² (29.71 sq ft)
Tailplane	13.30 m² (143.16 sq ft)
Elevators (total, incl tabs)	3.29 m² (35.40 sq ft)

WEIGHTS AND LOADINGS:

Typical operating weight empty	7,899 kg (17,415 lb)
Max payload (weight limited)	3,668 kg (8,087 lb)
Max fuel load	2,581 kg (5,690 lb)
Max ramp weight	12,383 kg (27,300 lb)
Max T-O weight	12,700 kg (28,000 lb)
Max landing weight	12,020 kg (26,500 lb)
Max zero-fuel weight	11,567 kg (25,500 lb)
Max wing loading	303.75 kg/m² (62.22 lb/sq ft)
Max power loading	4.91 kg/kW (8.07 lb/shp)

PERFORMANCE (at max T-O weight, ISA, except where indicated):

Max operating speed (V$_{MO}$)	
	250 knots (463 km/h; 288 mph) IAS
Max operating Mach No. (M$_{MO}$)	0.5
Max cruising speed at 4,575 m (15,000 ft), AUW of	
11,793 kg (26,000 lb)	272 knots (504 km/h; 313 mph)
Best range cruising speed at 7,620 m (25,000 ft)	
	250 knots (463 km/h; 288 mph)
Stalling speed: 0° flap	104 knots (193 km/h; 120 mph)
T-O flap setting	93 knots (173 km/h; 107 mph)
approach flap setting	87 knots (162 km/h; 101 mph)
landing flap setting	82 knots (152 km/h; 95 mph)
Max rate of climb at S/L	548 m (1,800 ft)/min
Rate of climb at S/L, one engine out	167 m (550 ft)/min
Service ceiling	7,620 m (25,000 ft)
Service ceiling, one engine out (net)	3,960 m (13,000 ft)
FAR Pt 25 required T-O field length:	
at S/L	1,212 m (3,975 ft)
at S/L, ISA + 15°C	1,295 m (4,250 ft)
at 1,525 m (5,000 ft)	1,509 m (4,950 ft)
at 1,525 m (5,000 ft), ISA + 15°C	1,935 m (6,350 ft)
FAR Pt 25 landing field length at max landing weight:	
at S/L	1,180 m (3,870 ft)
at 1,525 m (5,000 ft)	1,335 m (4,380 ft)
Min ground turning radius	15.85 m (52 ft 0 in)
Runway LCN: flexible pavement	8
rigid pavement	10

Range with 35 passengers and baggage, reserves for 45 min hold at 1,525 m (5,000 ft) and 100 nm (185 km; 115 mile) diversion:
at max cruising speed   570 nm (1,056 km; 656 miles)
at long-range cruising speed
     630 nm (1,167 km; 725 miles)
Range with 30 passengers, reserves as above:
at max cruising speed   845 nm (1,566 km; 973 miles)
at long-range cruising speed
     940 nm (1,742 km; 1,082 miles)

OPERATIONAL NOISE LEVELS (FAR Pt 36 and ICAO Annex 16):

T-O (with cutback)	85.7 EPNdB
Sideline	87.6 EPNdB
Approach	89.6 EPNdB

SAAB 340B

In late 1987 Saab announced go-ahead for this new 'hot and high' version of the 340, to be powered by 1,394 kW (1,870 shp) CT7-9B turboprops and certificated in the

Spring of 1989. The 340B, to be produced in parallel with the 340A, will have the same payload capacity, but increased operating weights and an 800 nm (1,482 km; 921 mile) range with max payload. It will also have an extended-span tailplane which, together with the new engines, had already been flight tested in the second prototype (SE-ISA) at the time of the announcement. No further details had been received at the time of going to press.

WEIGHTS:

Max T-O weight	12,927 kg (28,500 lb)
Max landing weight	12,700 kg (28,000 lb)
Max zero-fuel weight	11,793 kg (26,000 lb)

SAAB JAS 39 GRIPEN (GRIFFIN)

The Swedish government approved funding for project definition and initial development of this Viggen replacement in June 1980. Known as the JAS 39 (Jakt/Attack/Spaning: fighter/attack/reconnaissance), it is a multi-role combat aircraft to replace, successively, the AJ/SH/SF/JA 37 versions of the Viggen and all remaining Swedish Air Force J 35 Drakens. A similar financial commitment was made by Industri Gruppen JAS, a Swedish aerospace industry group formed in 1980 by Saab-Scania, Volvo Flygmotor, Ericsson Radio Systems and FFV Aerotech.

On 3 June 1981 the group submitted to the Swedish Defence Materiel Administration (FMV) its initial proposals for an aircraft to meet the JAS requirement. Power plant is a modified version of the General Electric F404J afterburning turbofan offering higher thrust and having a strengthened front fan to meet Swedish bird strike requirements. The engine is developed and produced, as the RM12, in collaboration with Volvo Flygmotor.

Of similar aerodynamic configuration to the Viggen, with delta wings and close-coupled all-moving foreplanes, the Gripen has an airframe of which some 30 per cent is manufactured from CFRP, permitting weight savings of up to 25 per cent and enabling the normal T-O weight to be kept down to approx 8,000 kg (17,635 lb). Like the Viggen, the JAS 39 will be adapted to the specific Swedish defence profile, using 800 m (2,625 ft) V-90 airstrips and similar lengths of ordinary roads as air bases. It will require only simple maintenance, with turnround service handled mainly by conscripts.

The FMV evaluated the Swedish industry proposals against aircraft from other countries, and recommended adoption of the Saab design. The programme approved by the Swedish government on 6 May 1982 covers the development and procurement of 140 aircraft by the year 2000, and a contract for the first 30 was signed on 30 June 1982. On 14 September 1982 a JA 37 Viggen testbed aircraft made its first flight equipped with the triplex fly by wire flight control system intended for the JAS 39. With a second Viggen as testbed for avionics and weapons systems, this test and development programme was continuing in 1988. Overall programme go-ahead was confirmed in the Spring of 1983, and prototype construction began in 1984.

Five prototypes of the Gripen are being built, the first of which was rolled out on 26 April 1987 but was not due to make its first flight until the fourth quarter of 1988. The first and second aircraft were undergoing ground tests in early 1988. Early prototypes will be used for aerodynamic and performance testing, the later ones for trials of the avionics, weapons and other systems. The first three and a half sets of carbonfibre wings were manufactured for Saab by British Aerospace, but for all subsequent aircraft Saab is responsible for all CFRP components including the wings, canards, fin, and major (eg engine and landing gear) doors.

Although no Swedish Air Force requirement was originally declared for a two-seat version of the Gripen, Saab has completed a design study for a JAS 39B with an approx 0.50 m (1 ft 7¾ in) fuselage plug inserted to accommodate a second cockpit in tandem. A decision on procurement of the two-seater was anticipated during 1988.

Deliveries of the JAS 39 are scheduled to begin in 1991, permitting entry into service in 1992.

The following description applies to the single-seat prototypes:

TYPE: Single-seat all-weather, all-altitude fighter, attack and reconnaissance aircraft.

AIRFRAME: Close-coupled canard configuration, with extensive use of CFRP composites in its fail-safe construction. Cropped delta main wings, mid-mounted on fuselage, with leading-edge 'dog-tooth'; inboard and outboard elevons on trailing-edges. Sweptback all-moving foreplanes, mounted on upper sides of engine air intake trunks. Leading-edge sweepback approx 43° on canards, 45° on main wings. Fin and rudder; no horizontal tail surfaces. AP Precision Hydraulics retractable tricycle landing gear, single mainwheels retracting hydraulically forward into fuselage; steerable twin-wheel nose unit retracts rearward, turning through 90° to lie flat in underside of fuselage. Goodyear wheels, tyres, carbon disc brakes and anti-skid units. Nosewheel braking. Entire gear designed for high rate of sink.

POWER PLANT: One General Electric/Volvo Flygmotor RM12 (F404J) turbofan, rated initially at approx 53.4 kN (12,000 lb st) dry and 80.5 kN (18,100 lb st) with afterburning. Wedge-shape intakes, each with splitter plate. Fuel in self-sealing main tank and collector tank in

Prototype of the Saab JAS 39 Gripen multi-role air defence and attack aircraft

fuselage. Active control of CG location provided by Intertechnique fuel management system.

ACCOMMODATION: Pilot only, on Martin-Baker S10LS zero/zero ejection seat under 'teardrop' canopy. Canopy and one-piece wraparound windscreen by Lucas Aerospace. Design study for two-seat version, if required, has been carried out.

SYSTEMS: BAe environmental control system for cockpit air-conditioning, cockpit pressurisation and cooling of avionics. Hughes-Treitler heat exchanger. Two main Dowty Rotol hydraulic systems and one auxiliary system, with Abex pumps. Sundstrand main electrical power generating system (40kVA constant speed, constant frequency at 400Hz) comprises an integrated drive generator, generator control unit and current transformer assembly. Lear Siegler triple-redundant digital fly by wire flight control system, with Moog hydraulic servo-actuators for primary flight control surfaces, Lucas Aerospace rotary actuators ('geared hinges') for leading-edge flaps, and Saab Combitech aircraft motion sensors and throttle actuator subsystem. Single-channel analog backup system in the event of main FBW system failure. Lucas Aerospace auxiliary and emergency power system, comprising a gearbox mounted turbine, hydraulic pump and a 10kVA AC generator, to provide emergency electric and hydraulic power in the event of an engine or main generator failure. In emergency role, the turbine is driven by engine bleed or APU air; if this is not available the stored energy mode, using pressurised oxygen and methanol, is selected automatically. Microturbo TGA 15 APU and DA 15 air turbine starter for engine starting, cooling air and emergency electric power.

AVIONICS: Bofors Aerotronics AMR 345 VHF/UHF-AM/FM com transceiver. Honeywell laser inertial navigation system. Ericsson EP 17 electronic display system in cockpit, using one Hughes Aircraft wide-angle head-up display for weapon aiming, and three programmable Ericsson head-down CRT displays, with a Ferranti FD 5040 video camera, plus a minimum of conventional analog instruments for backup purposes only. The head-up display, using advanced diffraction optics, will present a combination of symbology and video images within the pilot's line of sight. Left hand (flight data) head-down display normally replaces all conventional flight instruments. Central display shows a computer generated map of the area surrounding the aircraft (indicating land, lakes, rivers, roads, population centres, and obstacles to low-level flying), on which tactical information is superimposed. Right hand CRT is a multi-sensor display showing information on targets acquired by the video camera, radar and FLIR. An Ericsson SDS 80 computing system, incorporating more than 30 microcomputers, controls the aircraft's central air data computer, radar, electronic displays, fuel management, hydraulic, environmental control and other systems, and allows for multi-mode use and

flexibility for further development. A BAe three-axis strapdown magnetometer provides standby heading information.

OPERATIONAL EQUIPMENT: Ericsson/Ferranti PS-05/A multi-mode pulse-Doppler target search and acquisition (lookdown/shootdown) system, comprising a nose mounted radar of 1kW output and (depending on mission) a pod mounted forward-looking infra-red sensor or a laser rangefinder pod. For fighter missions, this system provides fast target acquisition at long range; search and multi-target track-while-scan; quick-scanning and lock-on at short ranges; and automatic fire control for missiles and cannon. In the attack and reconnaissance roles its operating functions are search against sea and ground targets; ground and sea target track-while-scan; mapping, with normal and high resolution; fire control for missiles and other attack weapons; and obstacle avoidance and navigation. The pulse-Doppler radar is only some 60 per cent of the size of current Swedish fighter radars but has three times the number of functions, is designed to detect targets over land and water, at all altitudes and at longer ranges, and will have improved resistance to hostile ECM. It is the basic part of the system for attack and reconnaissance missions. The FLIR pod, carried externally under the starboard engine air intake trunk, forward of the wing leading-edge, is used for attack and reconnaissance missions at night, providing a 'heat picture' of the target on the right hand head-down CRT. A radar warning receiver fairing is mounted near the tip of the fin. The JAS 39 will also carry advanced ECM, both built-in and externally.

ARMAMENT: Internally mounted 27 mm Mauser BK27 automatic cannon in fuselage. External attachment for FLIR pod under starboard intake (see preceding paragraph). Six other external hardpoints (two under each wing and one at each wingtip). These stations can carry short and medium range air-to-air missiles such as RB71 (Sky Flash), RB74 (AIM-9L Sidewinder) or AMRAAM; air-to-surface missiles such as Maverick; anti-shipping missiles such as Saab RBS 15F; conventional or retarded bombs; air-to-surface rockets; or cluster bomb dispensers. MBB is contracted to develop for the Gripen a submunitions dispenser based on its MDS but capable of launch from the aircraft to glide towards its target before releasing its bomblets on command. Other external stores can include a laser rangefinder pod or a day/night reconnaissance pod.

DIMENSIONS, EXTERNAL (approx):

Wing span	8.00 m (26 ft 3 in)
Length overall	14.10 m (46 ft 3 in)
Height overall	4.70 m (15 ft 5 in)
Wheel track	2.60 m (8 ft 6½ in)
Wheelbase	5.30 m (17 ft 4¾ in)

WEIGHT:

Normal max T-O weight	approx 8,000 kg (17,635 lb)

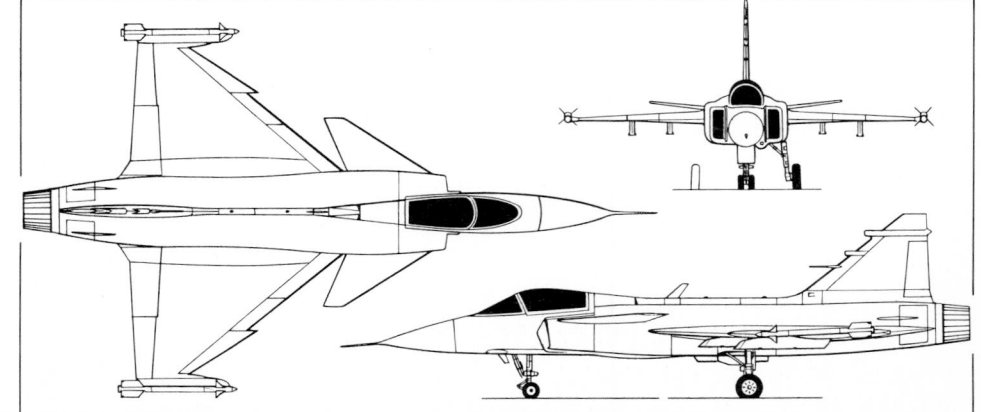

Saab JAS 39 Gripen multi-role combat aircraft for the Swedish Air Force (*Pilot Press*)

Saab JA 37 Viggens of F13 Wing, Swedish Air Force, in current blue-grey finish

PERFORMANCE:

Max level speed	supersonic at all altitudes
T-O and landing strip length	approx 800 m (2,625 ft)
g limit	+9

SAAB JA 37 VIGGEN (THUNDERBOLT)

The Saab 37 Viggen multi-mission combat aircraft has been produced to fulfil the primary roles of attack, interception, reconnaissance and training. Its STOL characteristics enable it to operate from narrow runways of about 500 m (1,640 ft) length. By early 1988 Viggens (all versions) equipped 15 of the planned total of 17 Swedish Air Force squadrons.

The first of seven prototypes flew for the first time on 8 February 1967, and by April 1969 all six single-seat prototypes were flying. The seventh was the prototype for the two-seat Sk37 operational trainer.

Production deliveries of the AJ 37, SF 37, SH 37 and Sk37 versions totalled 180. Details of these, and of the Saab 37X proposed export version, can be found in the 1980-81 and earlier editions of *Jane's*. The following version continues in production:

JA 37. Single-seat interceptor, with more powerful Volvo Flygmotor RM8B engine. Improved performance, and secondary capability for attack missions. Four elevon hydraulic actuators under each wing, instead of three as on other versions, and a modified, taller tail fin similar to that of the Sk37. Total of 149 ordered, to re-equip eight Draken fighter squadrons of the Swedish Air Force: two squadrons each of Wings F4, F16 and F21, and one each of F13 and F17. First flight by a production JA 37 (c/n 301) was made on 4 November 1977. Deliveries, to the second squadron of F13 Wing at Norrköping, began in 1979, and the 100th JA 37 was delivered on 20 August 1985. About 120 had been delivered by mid-1987. Improvements added since the JA 37's entry into service include new generation AIM-9L Sidewinder missiles, effective also against head-on targets, and an aircraft-to-aircraft communications system known as fighter link which makes possible efficient liaison between aircraft, even at night and in IMC conditions, regardless of their relative positions. Production is due to end in 1990.

TYPE: Single-seat all-weather multi-purpose combat aircraft.

WINGS: Tandem arrangement of delta foreplane, with trailing-edge flaps, and a rear mounted delta main wing with two-section hydraulically actuated powered elevons on each trailing-edge, which can be operated differentially or in unison. Main wing has compound sweep on leading-edge. Outer sections have extended leading-edge. Extensive use of metal bonded honeycomb panels for wing control surfaces, foreplane flaps and main landing gear doors.

FUSELAGE: Conventional all-metal semi-monocoque structure, using light metal forgings and heat resistant plastics bonding. Local use of titanium for engine firewall and other selected areas. Four plate type airbrakes, one on each side and two below fuselage. Metal bonded honeycomb construction is used to a large extent. Quick-release handle permits nosecone to be pulled forward on tracks to give access to radar compartment.

TAIL UNIT: Vertical surfaces only, comprising main fin and powered rudder, supplemented by a small ventral fin. Rudder of metal bonded honeycomb construction. The main fin can be folded downward to port. More than 20 fins for JA 37s are being made of composite materials, to gain experience in preparation for the JAS 39 programme. Deliveries of these began in 1986.

LANDING GEAR: Retractable tricycle type of Saab origin, built by Motala Verkstad and designed for a max rate of sink of 5 m (16.4 ft)/s. Power steerable twin-wheel nose unit retracts forward. Each main unit has two mainwheels in tandem and retracts inward into main wing and fuselage. Main oleos shorten during retraction. Nosewheel tyres size 18 × 5.5, pressure 10.7 bars (155 lb/sq in). Mainwheel tyres size 26 × 6.6, pressure 14.8 bars (215 lb/sq in). Goodyear wheels and brakes. Dunlop anti-skid system.

POWER PLANT: One Volvo Flygmotor RM8B (supersonic development of the Pratt & Whitney JT8D-22) turbofan, fitted with a Swedish developed afterburner and thrust reverser. This engine is rated at 72.1 kN (16,203 lb st) dry and 125 kN (28,108 lb st) with afterburning. Thrust reverser doors are actuated automatically by compression of the oleo as the nose gear strikes the runway, the thrust being deflected forward via three annular slots in the ejector wall. The ejector is normally kept open at subsonic speeds to reduce fuselage base drag; at supersonic speeds, with the intake closed, the ejector serves as a supersonic nozzle. Fuel is contained in one tank in each wing, a saddle tank over the engine, one tank in each side of the fuselage, and one aft of the cockpit. Electrically powered pumps deliver fuel to the engine from the central fuselage tank, which is kept filled continuously from the peripheral tanks. Pressure refuelling point beneath starboard wing. Provision for jettisonable external auxiliary tank on underfuselage centreline pylon.

ACCOMMODATION: Pilot only, on Saab-Scania fully adjustable rocket assisted zero/zero ejection seat beneath rearward hinged clamshell canopy. Cockpit pressurisation, heating and air-conditioning by engine bleed air, via Delaney Gallay heat exchangers, cooling turbines and water separator. Birdproof windscreen.

SYSTEMS: Two independent hydraulic systems, each of 207 bars (3,000 lb/sq in) pressure, each with engine driven pump; bootstrap reservoir; auxiliary electrically operated standby pump for emergency use. Three-phase AC electrical system supplies 210/115V 400Hz power via a Westinghouse 75kVA liquid-cooled brushless generator, which also provides 28V DC power via 24V nickel-cadmium batteries and rectifier. Emergency standby power from 6kVA turbogenerator, which is extended automatically into the airstream in the event of a power failure. External power receptacle on port side of fuselage. Graviner fire detection system.

AVIONICS AND FLIGHT EQUIPMENT: Altogether, about 50 avionics units, with a total weight of approx 600 kg (1,323 lb), are installed in the Viggen. Flight equipment includes an automatic speed control system, a Smiths electronic head-up display, Bofors Aerotronics aircraft attitude instruments, radio and fighter link equipment, Singer-Kearfott SKC-2037 central digital computer, Garrett LD-5 digital air data computer, Singer-Kearfott KT-70L inertial measuring equipment, Honeywell/Saab-Scania SA07 digital automatic flight control system, Honeywell radar altimeter, Decca Doppler Type 72 navigation equipment, SATT radar warning system, Ericsson radar display system and electronic countermeasures, and AIL Tactical Instrument Landing System (TILS), a microwave scanning beam landing guidance system. Most avionics equipment is connected to the central digital computer, which is programmed to check out and monitor these systems both on the ground and during flight. Ram air intake on underfuselage centreline, for cooling avionics compartment.

ARMAMENT AND OPERATIONAL EQUIPMENT: Permanent underbelly pack, offset to port side of centreline, containing one 30 mm Oerlikon KCA long-range cannon with 150 rounds, a muzzle velocity of 1,050 m (3,445 ft)/s, a rate of fire of 1,350 rds/min, and a projectile weight of 0.36 kg (0.79 lb). Improved fire control equipment. This gun installation permits retention of the three underfuselage stores attachment points, in addition to the four underwing hardpoints. Advanced target search and acquisition system, based on a high performance long-range Ericsson PS-46/A pulse-Doppler radar which is unaffected by variations of weather and altitude. This radar is not disturbed by ground clutter, and is highly resistant to ECM. Armament can include two BAe Sky Flash (Swedish designation RB71) and six AIM-9L Sidewinder (RB74) air-to-air missiles. For air-to-surface attack, a total of twenty-four 135 mm rockets can be carried in four pods.

DIMENSIONS, EXTERNAL:

Main wing span	10.60 m (34 ft 9¼ in)
Main wing aspect ratio	2.4
Foreplane span	5.45 m (17 ft 10½ in)
Length overall (incl probe)	16.40 m (53 ft 9¾ in)
Length of fuselage	15.58 m (51 ft 1½ in)
Height overall	5.90 m (19 ft 4¼ in)
Height overall, main fin folded	4.00 m (13 ft 1½ in)
Wheel track	4.76 m (15 ft 7½ in)
Wheelbase (c/l of shock absorbers)	5.69 m (18 ft 8 in)

AREAS:

Main wings, gross	46.00 m² (495.1 sq ft)
Foreplanes, outside fuselage	6.20 m² (66.74 sq ft)

WEIGHTS (approx):

T-O weight: 'clean'	15,000 kg (33,070 lb)
with normal armament	17,000 kg (37,478 lb)

PERFORMANCE:

Max level speed: at high altitude	above Mach 2
at 100 m (300 ft)	Mach 1.2
Approach speed:	approx 119 knots (220 km/h; 137 mph)
Time to 10,000 m (32,800 ft) from brakes off, with afterburning	less than 1 min 40 s
T-O run	approx 400 m (1,310 ft)
Landing run	approx 500 m (1,640 ft)
Required landing field length:	
conventional landing	1,000 m (3,280 ft)
no-flare landing	500 m (1,640 ft)
Tactical radius with external armament:	
hi-lo-hi	over 540 nm (1,000 km; 620 miles)
lo-lo-lo	over 270 nm (500 km; 310 miles)

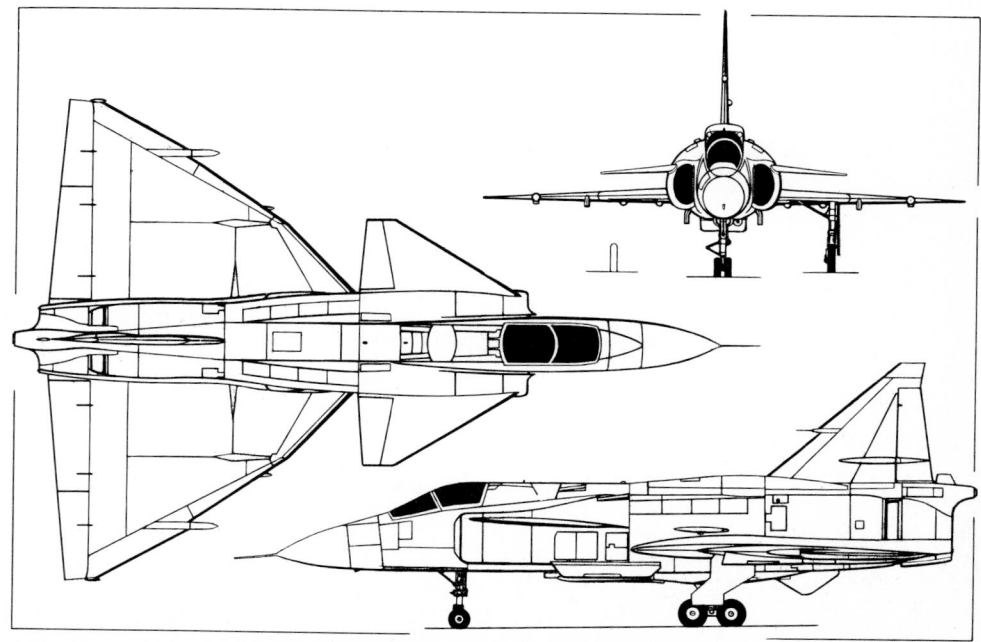

Saab JA 37 Viggen single-seat interceptor *(Pilot Press)*

SAAB J 32E LANSEN

Details of this extensively modified electronic warfare and countermeasures version of the Lansen were released in 1985 and published in the 1986-87 and 1987-88 editions of *Jane's*. All conversions have been completed.

SAAB 35 DRAKEN (DRAGON)

Under the revised designation **J 35J** (previously J 35F Mod or J 35F-Ny: new), about 50 J 35F Draken fighters of F10 Wing of the Swedish Air Force, based near Ängelholm in southern Sweden, are being updated to extend their service life until the end of the 1990s, when they will be replaced by the JAS 39 Gripen. Saab Aircraft Division is responsible for their modification and redelivery, with FFV Aerotech as subcontractor.

The modification programme is an extensive one. Two additional inboard underwing weapons pylons are fitted, enabling the J 35J to operate with four external fuel tanks and two air-to-air missiles, or four missiles and two fuel tanks. Modifications are being made to operation of the automatic gun and the electronics in the weapons system, and the J 35J will be given a modified radar and IFF transponder with considerably enhanced performance and reliability. The infra-red target seeker associated with the missile armament is being upgraded. An altitude warning system and transponder are added, and instrument changes include a new horizon system.

Aircraft selected for modification are transferred to FFV in Linköping, where they are split into front and rear fuselage sections. The rear portion remains at FFV, while the front portion is taken to Saab. When all installations are complete, the two portions are reunited at FFV. The first two upgraded aircraft were handed over to the Swedish Air Force on 3 March 1987, and all are due to be redelivered by the end of 1989. The three squadrons of F10 Wing will be the only units operating this version of the Draken.

The Saab/FFV team is also engaged currently in another extensive Draken modification programme, resulting from an Austrian government order of 21 May 1985 for 24 of these aircraft for the Austrian Air Force. These aircraft, which are designated Saab **35OE**, are modified from former Swedish Air Force J 35Ds, the work involved amounting to 20,000 man-hours per aircraft. The first Draken for Austria was handed over on 25 June 1987, and all 24 were due to be delivered before the end of 1988.

The J 35D and F were last described fully in the 1969-70 *Jane's*.

Additional underwing stores pylons identify this J 35J Draken fighter of F10 Wing

SAAB 105

Saab Aircraft Division received a government contract in late 1987 to modify 135 Saab 105 trainer/light attack aircraft (Swedish Air Force designation Sk60) to prolong their life beyond the year 2000. The programme will include modifying the wing spars, and is due for completion in 1991.

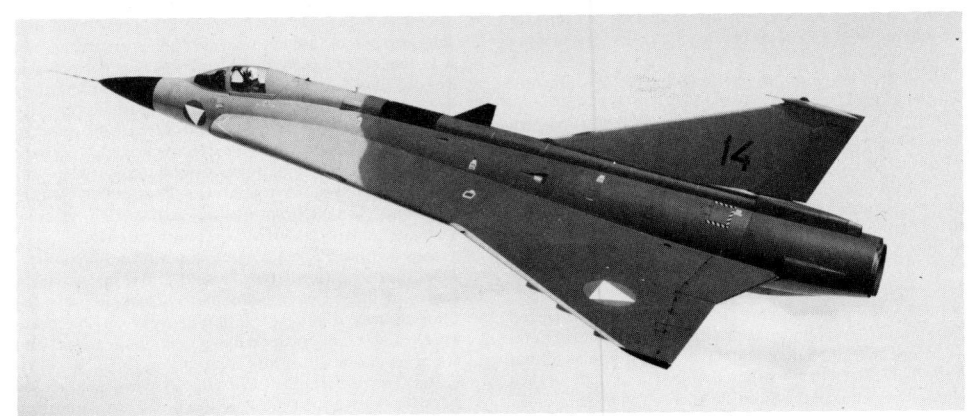

Saab 35OE (modified J 35D) Draken for the Austrian Air Force

SACAB

SCANDINAVIAN AIRCRAFT CONSTRUCTION AB

PO Box 43, S-23032 Malmö-Sturup
Telephone: (0) 40 500220
Telex: 8305192
PRESIDENT: Peter Ahrens

SACAB was formed in 1984 by Mr Peter Ahrens. His Puerto Rico based Ahrens Aircraft Corporation built four

prototypes of a square-fuselage turboprop transport known as the AR-404 before ceasing operations in 1982; this aircraft has been described in previous editions of *Jane's*.

SACAB KM-180

A full scale fuselage mockup of the KM-180 was com-pleted in 1985, and in early 1986 construction was under way of a flying prototype and static test airframe. First flight was then anticipated in December 1986.

No information has been received from SACAB since early 1986, and the KM-180 project certificate was cancelled by the Swedish Board of Civil Aviation in late 1987.

A description and illustration of the KM-180 can be found in the 1987-88 *Jane's*.

SWITZERLAND

DÄTWYLER

MDC MAX DÄTWYLER AG

Flugplatz, CH-3368 Bleienbach-Langenthal
Telephone: (063) 283 111
Telex: 982626 MDC CH
PRESIDENT OF THE BOARD: Max Dätwyler

Dätwyler has specialised for many years in the repair and modification of light aircraft. It has also manufactured components for the Pilatus Porter/Turbo-Porter STOL transport aircraft and B4-PC11 sailplane, and for the Dassault Mercure jet transport. Its latest design is the MD-3 Swiss Trainer.

DÄTWYLER MD-3 SWISS TRAINER

Dätwyler announced preliminary details of the Swiss Trainer in the late 1960s, and a description appeared in the 1974-75 *Jane's*. Since then considerable effort has been made to make the design genuinely modular, to facilitate manufacture by possible licensees in countries without a developed aircraft industry. In particular the ailerons, two-segment flaps, elevators and rudder constitute nine control surfaces which are all basically identical and interchangeable. The same is true of the tailplane halves and fin; fin and tailplane tips; wing leading-edge sections (four per aircraft); and the central inner and outer portions of the wings.

The MD-3-160 prototype (HB-HOH) made its first flight, with Mr Dätwyler at the controls, on 12 August 1983. Development test flying was continuing in 1988 and it was hoped to gain FAR Pt 23 certification later that year.

Two versions of the Swiss Trainer are planned, as follows:
MD-3-115. Two-seat primary training version, powered by an 82 kW (110 hp) Textron Lycoming O-235-N2A flat-four engine. Not yet flown; to become available after certification of MD-3-160.
MD-3-160. With more powerful Textron Lycoming O-320-D2A engine; particularly suitable for aerobatics and glider towing. Prototype is of this version.

The following description applies to the MD-3-160:
TYPE: Two-seat primary training aircraft.
WINGS: Cantilever mid-wing monoplane. Wing section NACA 64,15414 (modified). Thickness/chord ratio 14%. Dihedral 5° 30′. Incidence 2°. No sweepback. All-metal structure, with single main spar, consisting of five modules of which the largest measures 3.45 × 0.67 × 0.21 m (136 × 26.4 × 8.3 in). All-metal electrically operated two-segment flaps, and single-slotted mass balanced ailerons. Flap, aileron, rudder and elevator segments identical.
FUSELAGE: Mainly metal semi-monocoque structure, with glassfibre fairings and cowling. Tailboom detachable from fuselage aft of wing.

TAIL UNIT: Sweptback horizontal and vertical surfaces of all-metal two-spar construction, assembled from three equal modules. Dorsal fin. Mass balanced rudder and elevators, identical with aileron and flap modules. Trim tab in elevator.
LANDING GEAR: Non-retractable tricycle type with steerable nosewheel. Main-gear legs are cantilever steel struts, descending at 45° from fuselage main bulkhead. Nose gear fitted with oleo-pneumatic shock absorber. Cleveland 6.00-6 mainwheels and 5.00-5 nosewheel. Tyre pressure 2.41 bars (35 lb/sq in) on all units. Independent hydraulically operated Cleveland disc brake on each mainwheel. Speed fairings on all three wheels.
POWER PLANT: One 119 kW (160 hp) Textron Lycoming O-320-D2A flat-four engine, driving a McCauley 1-C160-F6M-7462 two-blade fixed-pitch metal propeller with spinner. Exhaust system can optionally be extended full length under fuselage to extreme rear of tailcone, exhaust gases being emitted through a narrow slot running along the pipe. (Aircraft meets noise requirements with short or long exhaust.) Integral fuel tank in each wing: total capacity 140 litres (36 US gallons; 30 Imp gallons). Refuelling point in top of each tank. Oil capacity 7.6 litres (2 US gallons; 1.7 Imp gallons).
ACCOMMODATION: Side by side adjustable seats for pilot and one passenger. Five-point fixed seat belts. Forward

sliding canopy. Space behind seats for 50 kg (110 lb) of baggage. Dual controls, cabin ventilation and heating standard.

SYSTEMS: Hydraulic system for brakes only. 28V 60A engine driven alternator and 24V 30Ah battery provide electrical power for engine starting, lighting, instruments and com/nav equipment.

AVIONICS AND EQUIPMENT: Provision for VHF radio, VOR, ADF, transponder or other special equipment at customer's option. Equipment for glider towing optional.

DIMENSIONS, EXTERNAL:

Wing span	10.00 m (32 ft 9¾ in)
Wing chord, constant	1.50 m (4 ft 11 in)
Wing aspect ratio	6.7
Length overall	6.98 m (22 ft 10¾ in)
Height overall	2.92 m (9 ft 7 in)
Tailplane span	3.00 m (9 ft 10 in)
Wheel track	2.00 m (6 ft 6¾ in)
Wheelbase	1.56 m (5 ft 1½ in)
Propeller diameter	1.88 m (6 ft 2 in)

DIMENSIONS, INTERNAL:

Cabin, from firewall to rear bulkhead:

Length	1.30 m (4 ft 3¼ in)
Max width	1.12 m (3 ft 8 in)
Max height	1.08 m (3 ft 6½ in)

AREAS:

Wings, gross	15.00 m² (161.5 sq ft)
Ailerons (total)	1.22 m² (13.13 sq ft)
Trailing-edge flaps (total)	1.96 m² (21.10 sq ft)
Vertical tail surfaces (total)	1.44 m² (15.50 sq ft)
Rudder	0.51 m² (5.49 sq ft)
Horizontal tail surfaces (total)	2.56 m² (27.56 sq ft)
Elevators (total)	1.04 m² (11.19 sq ft)

WEIGHTS AND LOADINGS (A: Aerobatic, U: Utility):

Weight empty	633 kg (1,395 lb)

Prototype Dätwyler MD-3-160 Swiss Trainer

Max T-O and landing weight: A		840 kg (1,852 lb)
U		920 kg (2,028 lb)
Max wing loading: A		56.0 kg/m² (11.47 lb/sq ft)
U		61.3 kg/m² (12.56 lb/sq ft)
Max power loading: A		7.06 kg/kW (11.58 lb/hp)
U		7.73 kg/kW (12.68 lb/hp)

PERFORMANCE (at T-O weight of 815 kg; 1,796 lb):

Never-exceed speed	169 knots (313 km/h; 195 mph)
Max manoeuvring speed	
	133 knots (246 km/h; 153 mph)
Max cruising speed (75% power) at 1,525 m (5,000 ft)	
	124 knots (230 km/h; 143 mph)

Econ cruising speed (66% power) at 1,525 m (5,000 ft)	
	117 knots (217 km/h; 135 mph)
Stalling speed, engine idling:	
flaps up	56 knots (104 km/h; 65 mph)
flaps down	46 knots (85 km/h; 53 mph)
Max rate of climb at S/L	420 m (1,378 ft)/min
Max rate of climb (75% power) towing 365 kg (805 lb)	
sailplane	104 m (341 ft)/min
T-O run	108 m (354 ft)
Landing run	130 m (426 ft)
Range with max fuel, no reserves	
	588 nm (1,090 km; 677 miles)

FFA

FFA FLUGZEUGWERKE ALTENRHEIN AG

CH-9423 Altenrhein
Telephone: (071) 43 01 11
Telex: 88 29 06 FFA CH
Fax: (071) 42 11 54
PRESIDENT: Oskar Ronner
CHIEF ENGINEER: Dipl Ing P. Spalinger
SALES MANAGER, MARKETING: Peter Hohl

This company had its origin in AG für Dornier Flugzeuge, the Swiss branch of the West German Dornier company. In 1948 it became an entirely Swiss company named FFA (Flug- und Fahrzeugwerke AG). In January 1987 the complete aviation activity was sold to the Justus Dornier group in Zurich, and the present company name took effect on 1 June 1987.

Current activities, besides production of the AS 202 Bravo, consist of subcontracting for various aircraft manufacturers throughout the world, and licence production of components for Swiss built Northrop F-5E/F Tiger IIs. Overhaul, servicing and maintenance for the Swiss Air Force and for general aviation are also done at Altenrhein. FFA has about 900 employees, approximately one-quarter of whom are engaged in aviation activities.

FFA AS 202/18A BRAVO

Following an agreement concluded with SIAI-Marchetti of Italy, FFA undertook production of the AS 202 Bravo light trainer and sporting aircraft.

The Swiss assembled AS 202/15 prototype (HB-HEA) flew for the first time on 7 March 1969. The Italian built second prototype flew on 7 May 1969. The third aircraft (HB-HEC) made its first flight on 16 June 1969, and the first production aircraft on 22 December 1971. The AS 202/15 (34 built: 1981-82 *Jane's*) and AS 202/26A (prototype only: 1985-86 and earlier editions) are no longer available.

The following version remained available in 1988:

AS 202/18A. Two/three-seat aerobatic version. First flew (HB-HEY) on 22 August 1974. Swiss certification granted on 12 December 1975; FAA certification awarded on 17 December 1976. Deliveries totalled 121 by early 1986

(no 1987 or 1988 figures received). Variants include the A2 (higher max T-O/landing weight, extended canopy, electric trim), A3 (as A2 but with mechanical trim and 24V electrical system) and A4 (as A2 but with CAA approved special instrumentation).

A total of approximately 180 Bravos had been sold by January 1988, in Switzerland and to foreign customers as listed in the 1987-88 and earlier *Jane's*. The 11 AS 202/18A4s for the BAe Flying College are known by the name **Wren**, and the College has a further 11 on order.

The following description applies to the AS 202/18A:

TYPE: Two/three-seat light aircraft.

WINGS: Cantilever low-wing monoplane. Wing section NACA 63_2618 (modified) at centreline, 63_2415 at tip. Thickness/chord ratio 17.63% at root, 15% at tip. Dihedral 5° 43′ from roots. Incidence 3°. Sweepback at quarter-chord 0° 40′. Conventional aluminium single-spar fail-safe structure, with riveted honeycomb laminate skin. Aluminium single-slotted flaps and single-slotted ailerons. Ground adjustable tab on each aileron.

FUSELAGE: Conventional aluminium semi-monocoque fail-safe structure, with engine cowling and several fairings of glassfibre.

TAIL UNIT: Cantilever aluminium single-spar structure with sweptback vertical surfaces. Rudder mass balanced, with provision for anti-collision beacon. Fixed incidence tailplane. Two-piece elevator with full span electrically actuated trim tab on starboard half. Electrically actuated tab on rudder of current 202/18A4.

LANDING GEAR: Non-retractable tricycle type, with steerable nosewheel. Rubber cushioned shock absorber struts of SIAI-Marchetti design. Mainwheel tyres size 6.00-6; nosewheel tyre size 5.00-5. Tyre pressure (all units) 2.41 bars (35 lb/sq in). Independent hydraulically operated disc brake on each mainwheel.

POWER PLANT: One 134 kW (180 hp) Textron Lycoming AEIO-360-B1F flat-four engine, driving a Hartzell HC-C2YK-1BF/F7666A-2 two-blade constant-speed propeller with spinner. Hoffmann three-blade propeller optional. Two wing leading-edge rubber fuel tanks with total capacity of 170 litres (44.9 US gallons; 37.4 Imp

gallons). Refuelling point above each wing. Starboard tank has additional flexible fuel intake for aerobatics. Christen 801 fully aerobatic oil system, capacity 7.6 litres (2 US gallons; 1.6 Imp gallons).

ACCOMMODATION: Seats for two persons side by side, in Aerobatic versions, under rearward sliding jettisonable transparent canopy. Space at rear in Utility versions for a third seat or 100 kg (220 lb) of baggage. Dual controls, cabin ventilation and heating standard.

SYSTEMS: Hydraulic system for brake actuation. One 12V 60A engine driven alternator (24V in A3) and one 25Ah battery provide electrical power for engine starting, lighting, instruments, communications and navigation installations. 28V electrical system optional.

AVIONICS AND EQUIPMENT: Provision for VHF radio, VOR, ADF, Nav-O-Matic 200A autopilot, blind-flying instrumentation or other special equipment at customer's option. Clutch and release mechanism for glider towing optional.

DIMENSIONS, EXTERNAL:

Wing span	9.75 m (31 ft 11¾ in)
Wing chord: at root	1.88 m (6 ft 2 in)
at tip	1.16 m (3 ft 9½ in)
Wing aspect ratio	6.5
Length overall	7.50 m (24 ft 7¼ in)
Length of fuselage	7.15 m (23 ft 5½ in)
Height overall	2.81 m (9 ft 2¾ in)
Tailplane span	3.67 m (12 ft 0½ in)
Wheel track	2.25 m (7 ft 4½ in)
Wheelbase	1.78 m (5 ft 10 in)
Propeller diameter	1.88 m (6 ft 2 in)
Propeller ground clearance	0.31 m (1 ft 0¼ in)

DIMENSIONS, INTERNAL:

Cabin: Max length	2.15 m (7 ft 0½ in)
Max width	1.00 m (3 ft 4 in)
Max height	1.10 m (3 ft 7¼ in)
Floor area	2.15 m² (23.14 sq ft)

AREAS:

Wings, gross	13.86 m² (149.2 sq ft)
Ailerons (total)	1.09 m² (11.7 sq ft)
Trailing-edge flaps (total)	1.49 m² (16.04 sq ft)
Fin	0.45 m² (4.84 sq ft)
Rudder, incl tab	0.94 m² (10.12 sq ft)
Tailplane	1.88 m² (20.24 sq ft)
Elevators, incl tab	0.76 m² (8.18 sq ft)

WEIGHTS AND LOADINGS:

Weight empty, equipped	710 kg (1,565 lb)
Max useful load (incl fuel): Aerobatic	177 kg (390 lb)
Utility	248 kg (546 lb)
Max T-O and landing weight:	
Aerobatic: A/A1	950 kg (2,094 lb)
A2/A3/A4	980 kg (2,160 lb)
Utility: current 18A models	1,080 kg (2,380 lb)
Max wing loading: Utility	75.8 kg/m² (15.52 lb/sq ft)
Max power loading: Utility	7.84 kg/kW (12.86 lb/hp)

PERFORMANCE (Utility category at max T-O weight):

Never-exceed speed	173 knots (320 km/h; 199 mph)
Max level speed at S/L	
	130 knots (241 km/h; 150 mph)
Max cruising speed (75% power) at 2,440 m (8,000 ft)	
	122 knots (226 km/h; 141 mph)
Econ cruising speed (55% power) at 3,050 m (10,000 ft)	
	109 knots (203 km/h; 126 mph)

FFA AS 202/18A4 Wren of the BAe Flying College at Prestwick, Scotland

Stalling speed, engine idling:

flaps up	62 knots (115 km/h; 71 mph)
flaps down	49 knots (90 km/h; 56 mph)
Max rate of climb at S/L	244 m (800 ft)/min
Service ceiling	5,180 m (17,000 ft)
T-O run at S/L	215 m (705 ft)
T-O to 15 m (50 ft) at S/L	415 m (1,360 ft)
Landing from 15 m (50 ft)	465 m (1,525 ft)
Landing run	210 m (690 ft)

Range with max fuel, no reserves

615 nm (1,140 km; 707 miles)

Max endurance	5 h 30 min
g limits	$+6/-3$

FFA-2000

On 25 April 1988 FFA announced the receipt of a contract from Swissair for eight trainers "of advanced design", designated FFA-2000, to replace the airline's flying school Piaggio P.149s which have been in service for 25 years. Development of the new trainer began in 1987, and design assistance was given by the Swiss ALR group (see 1987-88 *Jane's*); deliveries of the eight aircraft are planned for 1991. No other details were given in the announcement, but it has been reported that the FFA-2000 will feature composites construction and will be a four-seater powered by a 149-186 kW (200-250 hp) engine, possibly of Porsche manufacture.

PILATUS

PILATUS FLUGZEUGWERKE AG

CH-6370 Stans, near Lucerne
Telephone: (041) 63 61 11
Telex: 866202 PIL CH
Fax: (041) 613351
CHAIRMAN AND GENERAL MANAGER:
  W. Gubler
DIRECTOR, MARKETING AND SALES: Ulrich Wenger
  Pilatus Flugzeugwerke AG was formed in December 1939; details of its early history can be found in previous editions of *Jane's*. It is part of the Oerlikon-Bührle Group. Current products are the PC-6 Turbo-Porter, the PC-7 Turbo-Trainer and PC-9.
  On 24 January 1979 Pilatus purchased the assets of Britten-Norman (Bembridge) Ltd of the UK, which has operated since then under the name Pilatus Britten-Norman Ltd (which see) as a subsidiary of Pilatus Aircraft Ltd.

PILATUS PC-6 TURBO-PORTER
US Army designation: UV-20A Chiricahua

The PC-6 is a single-engined multi-purpose utility aircraft, with STOL characteristics permitting operation from unprepared strips under harsh environmental and terrain conditions. It can be converted rapidly from a freighter to a passenger transport, and adapted for a great number of missions, including supply dropping, search and rescue, ambulance, aerial survey and photography, parachuting, cropspraying, water bombing, rainmaking and glider or target towing. The PC-6 can operate from soft ground, snow, glacier or water.

The first piston engined prototype made its first flight on 4 May 1959, and details of piston engined production models can be found in contemporary editions of *Jane's*. The early PC-6/A, A1, A2, B, B1, B2 and C2-H2 Turbo-Porters, with various turboprop power plants, were last described in the 1974-75 edition, and the B2-H2 in editions up to and including 1986-87. The B1 and B2 can be fitted with an air inlet filter for operation in desert conditions and for agricultural applications.

Current version since 1985 is the **PC-6/B2-H4**, in which for CAR.3 operations (commercial operations with fare paying passengers) the maximum take-off weight is increased by 600 kg (1,323 lb), resulting in a payload increase of up to 570 kg (1,257 lb) compared with previous models. This was achieved by improving the aerodynamic efficiency of the wings with new tip fairings, enlarging the dorsal fin, installing uprated mainwheel shock absorbers and a new tailwheel assembly, and a slight strengthening of the airframe. While the H4 modification can be retrofitted to all existing PC-6/B2-H2 models equipped with electrically operated longitudinal trim, all new-production Porters since mid-1985 have been of the H4 version. By early 1988 approx 20 H4s were flying, including about 12 converted from H2s.

By that date more than 470 PC-6 aircraft, of all models, had been delivered (including US licence manufacture), and were operating in more than 50 countries. Military operators include the air forces of Angola, Argentina, Australia, Austria, Bolivia, Burma, Chad, Ecuador, Iran, Oman, Peru, Sudan, Switzerland and Thailand, and the US Army.

Approx 40 Turbo-Porters (all H2 or earlier series) have been completed in agricultural configuration: these are in service in Indonesia, Sudan, Switzerland, Thailand and Zaïre. For liquid spraying, a stainless steel tank (capacity 1,330 litres; 351.5 US gallons; 292.5 Imp gallons) is installed behind the two front seats, and 46- or 62-nozzle spraybooms are fitted beneath the wings. In this configuration the aircraft can cover a swath width of 45 m (148 ft). An ultra-low-volume system, using four to six atomisers or two to six Micronairs, is also available, permitting increase in swath width up to 400 m (1,310 ft).

For dusting with granulated materials, the lower part of the standard tank can be replaced by a discharge and dispersal door permitting coverage of a swath width of up to 20 m (66 ft). A Transland spreader can be fitted for dust application (swath up to 30 m; 100 ft). Effective swath width of these versions is 13-40 m (43-131 ft), the optimum being approx 20 m (66 ft).

Both versions are fitted with small doors in the fuselage sides, giving access to the tank/hopper for servicing, removal or replenishment, and two single seats or a bench seat for three persons can be installed aft of the tank. Optional items include an engine air intake screen and a loading door for chemical in the top of the fuselage.

The structural description which follows is applicable to the standard B2-H4 version:
TYPE: Single-engined STOL utility transport.

Pilatus PC-6/B2-H4 Turbo-Porter in the insignia of Tyrolean Jet Service of Austria

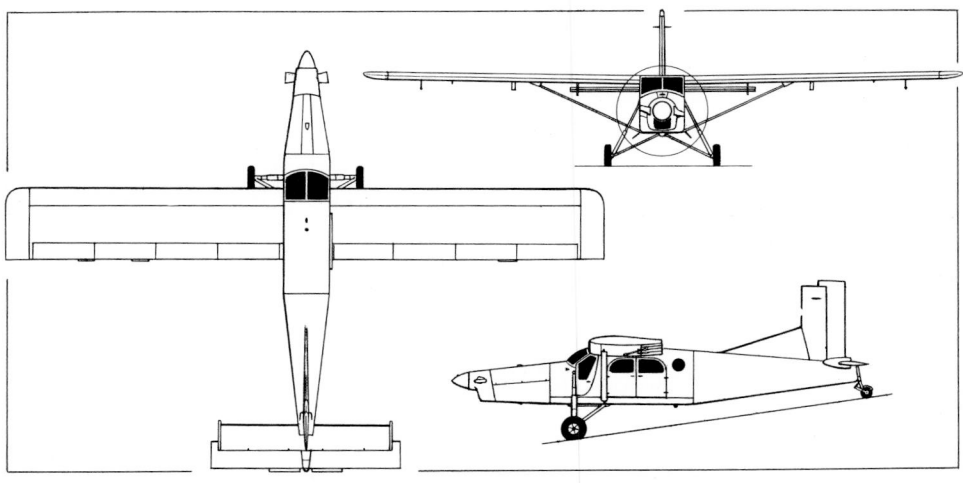

Pilatus PC-6/B2-H4 Turbo-Porter, the standard version since 1985 (*Pilot Press*)

WINGS: Braced high-wing monoplane, with single streamline-section bracing strut each side. Wing section NACA 64-514 (constant). Dihedral 1°. Incidence 2°. Single-spar all-metal structure, with span-increasing tip fairings. Entire trailing-edge hinged, inner sections consisting of electrically operated all-metal double-slotted flaps and outer sections of all-metal single-slotted ailerons. No airbrakes or de-icing equipment.
FUSELAGE: All-metal semi-monocoque structure.
TAIL UNIT: Cantilever all-metal structure. Variable incidence tailplane. Flettner tabs on elevator. Enlarged dorsal fin.
LANDING GEAR: Non-retractable tailwheel type. Oleo shock absorbers of Pilatus design in all units. Steerable/lockable tailwheel. Goodyear Type II mainwheels and GA 284 tyres size 24 × 7 or 7.50 × 10 (pressure 2.21 bars; 32 lb/sq in); oversize Goodyear Type III wheels and tyres optional, size 11.0 × 12, pressure 0.88 bars (12.8 lb/sq in). Goodyear tailwheel with size 5.00-4 tyre. Goodyear disc brakes. Pilatus wheel/ski gear optional.
POWER PLANT: One 507 kW (680 shp) Pratt & Whitney Canada PT6A-27 turboprop (flat rated at 410 kW; 550 shp at S/L), driving a Hartzell HC-B3TN-3D/T-10178 C or CH, or T10173 C or CH constant-speed fully-feathering reversible-pitch propeller with Beta mode control. Standard fuel in integral wing tanks, usable capacity 644 litres (170 US gallons; 142 Imp gallons). Two underwing auxiliary tanks, each of 245 litres (65 US gallons; 54 Imp gallons), available optionally. Oil capacity 12.5 litres (3.3 US gallons; 2.75 Imp gallons).
ACCOMMODATION: Cabin has pilot's seat forward on port side, with one passenger seat alongside, and is normally fitted with six quickly removable seats, in pairs, to the rear of these for additional passengers. Up to 11 persons, including the pilot, can be carried in 2-3-3-3 high density layout; or up to ten parachutists, who can be dropped from heights of up to 7,620 m (25,000 ft); or two stretchers plus three attendants in ambulance configuration. Floor is level, flush with door sill, and is provided with seat rails. Forward opening door beside each front seat. Large rearward sliding door on starboard side of main cabin. Port side sliding door optional. Double doors, without central pillar, on port side. Hatch in floor 0.58 × 0.90 m (1 ft 10¾ in × 2 ft 11½ in), openable from inside cabin, for aerial camera or for supply dropping. Hatch in cabin rear wall 0.50 × 0.80 m

(1 ft 7 in × 2 ft 7 in) permits stowage of six passenger seats or accommodation of freight items up to 5.0 m (16 ft 5 in) in length. Walls lined with lightweight soundproofing and heat insulation material. Adjustable heating and ventilation systems provided. Dual controls optional.
SYSTEMS: Cabin heated by engine bleed air. Scott 8500 oxygen system optional. 200A 30V starter/generator and 24V 34Ah (optionally 40Ah) nickel-cadmium battery.
EQUIPMENT: Generally to customer's requirements, but can include stretchers for ambulance role, aerial photography and survey gear, agricultural equipment (see earlier paragraphs) or an 800 litre (211 US gallon; 176 Imp gallon) water tank in cabin, with quick release system, for firefighting role. The 1,330 litre agricultural tank can also be used in the firebombing role.

DIMENSIONS, EXTERNAL:

Wing span	15.87 m (52 ft 0¾ in)
Wing chord, constant	1.90 m (6 ft 3 in)
Wing aspect ratio	8.4
Length overall	11.00 m (36 ft 1 in)
Height overall (tail down)	3.20 m (10 ft 6 in)
Elevator span	5.12 m (16 ft 9½ in)
Wheel track	3.00 m (9 ft 10 in)
Wheelbase	7.87 m (25 ft 10 in)
Propeller diameter	2.56 m (8 ft 5 in)
Cabin double door (port) and sliding door (starboard):	
Max height	1.04 m (3 ft 5 in)
Width	1.58 m (5 ft 2¼ in)

DIMENSIONS, INTERNAL:
Cabin, from back of pilot's seat to rear wall:

Length	2.30 m (7 ft 6½ in)
Max width	1.16 m (3 ft 9½ in)
Max height (at front)	1.28 m (4 ft 2½ in)
Height at rear wall	1.18 m (3 ft 10½ in)
Floor area	2.67 m² (28.6 sq ft)
Volume	3.28 m³ (107 cu ft)

AREAS:

Wings, gross	30.15 m² (324.5 sq ft)
Ailerons (total)	3.83 m² (41.2 sq ft)
Flaps (total)	3.76 m² (40.5 sq ft)
Fin	1.70 m² (18.3 sq ft)
Rudder, incl tab	0.96 m² (10.3 sq ft)
Tailplane	4.03 m² (43.4 sq ft)
Elevator, incl tab	2.11 m² (22.7 sq ft)

WEIGHTS AND LOADINGS:

Weight empty, equipped	1,270 kg (2,800 lb)
Max fuel weight: internal	508 kg (1,120 lb)
underwing	392 kg (864 lb)
Max payload:	
with reduced internal fuel	1,130 kg (2,491 lb)
with max internal fuel	1,062 kg (2,341 lb)
with max internal and underwing fuel	
	571 kg (1,259 lb)
Max T-O weight, Normal (CAR 3):	
wheels (standard)	2,800 kg (6,173 lb)
skis	2,600 kg (5,732 lb)
Max landing weight: wheels	2,660 kg (5,864 lb)
skis	2,600 kg (5,732 lb)
Max cabin floor loading	488 kg/m² (100 lb/sq ft)
Max wing loading (Normal):	
wheels	92.87 kg/m² (19.03 lb/sq ft)
skis	86.23 kg/m² (17.67 lb/sq ft)
Max power loading (Normal):	
wheels	6.83 kg/kW (11.22 lb/shp)
skis	5.13 kg/kW (8.43 lb/shp)

PERFORMANCE (at max T-O weight, ISA, Normal category):

Never-exceed speed 151 knots (280 km/h; 174 mph) IAS	
Econ cruising speed at 3,050 m (10,000 ft)	
	115 knots (213 km/h; 132 mph)
Stalling speed, power off, flaps down	
	52 knots (96 km/h; 60 mph)
Max rate of climb at S/L	287 m (941 ft)/min
Max operating altitude	7,620 m (25,000 ft)
T-O run at S/L	197 m (646 ft)
Landing run at S/L	127 m (417 ft)
Max range at 115 knots (213 km/h; 132 mph) at 3,050 m	
(10,000 ft), no reserves:	
with max payload	394 nm (730 km; 453 miles)
with max internal fuel	500 nm (926 km; 576 miles)
with max internal and underwing fuel	
	870 nm (1,612 km; 1,002 miles)
g limits	+3.72/−1.5

PILATUS PC-7 TURBO-TRAINER
Swiss Air Force designation: PC-7/CH

The PC-7 Turbo-Trainer is a fully aerobatic two-seat training aircraft, powered by a 410 kW (550 shp) Pratt & Whitney Canada PT6A-25A turboprop. It can be used for basic, transition and aerobatic training, and, with suitable equipment installed, for IFR and tactical training. It received FAA certification to FAR Pt 23 on 12 August 1983, and also meets the requirements of a selected group of US military specifications (Trainer category). As a single-seater, it is flown from the front seat. The PC-7 also holds type certificates in the Aerobatic and Utility categories from the Swiss Federal Office for Civil Aviation (5 December 1978/6 April 1979) and the French DGAC (16 May 1983).

The first production PC-7 was flown on 18 August 1978, and deliveries began in December of that year. Sales totalled more than 390 by 1 March 1988, of which more than 370 had been delivered. Customers include the air forces of Abu Dhabi (24), Angola (18), Austria (16), Bolivia (36), Burma (17), Chile (10 for Navy), Guatemala (12), Iran (35), Iraq (52), Malaysia (44), Mexico (75), Switzerland (40) and undisclosed countries; other customers include CIPRA of France (2), Swissair (1), Contraves (1) and three US private owners (1 each). From the 1987 air show season the French Patrouille Martini formation display team has flown three PC-7s, equipped with smoke generator pods.

The PC-7 is available with new, lightweight Mk CH 15A ejection seats developed in collaboration with Martin-Baker. These offer safe escape for both occupants at speeds between 60 knots on the runway and 300 knots in the air (111-556 km/h; 69-345 mph), and at altitudes up to 6,700 m (22,000 ft).

TYPE: Single-engined single/two-seat training aircraft.

WINGS: Cantilever low-wing monoplane. Wing section NACA 64₂A-415 at root, NACA 64₁A-612 at tip. Dihedral 7° on outer panels. Sweepback 1° at quarter-chord. One-piece all-metal single-spar structure, with auxiliary spar, ribs and stringer-reinforced skin. Constant chord centre-section and tapered outer panels. Alclad aluminium alloy (2022 or 2024) skin, reinforced by stringers. Some fairings of GRP. Mass balanced ailerons; trailing-edge split flaps, extending under fuselage. Flaps actuated electrically, ailerons mechanically by pushrods. Trim tab in port aileron.

FUSELAGE: All-metal semi-monocoque structure, with stringers, bulkheads and aluminium alloy skin. Some fairings of GRP.

TAIL UNIT: Cantilever all-metal structure, of similar construction to wings. Dorsal fin; small ventral fin under tailcone. Forward strakes on inboard leading-edges of tailplane. Trim tab in starboard half of elevator; anti-servo tab in rudder. All control surfaces mass balanced and cable operated.

LANDING GEAR: Electrically actuated retractable tricycle type, with emergency manual extension. Mainwheels retract inward, nosewheel rearward. Oleo-pneumatic shock absorber in each unit. Castoring nosewheel, with shimmy dampers. Goodrich mainwheels and tyres, size 6.50-8, pressure 4.5 bars (65 lb/sq in). Goodrich nosewheel and tyre, size 6.00-6, pressure 2.75 bars (40

PC-7 Turbo-Trainers in the colourful markings of the Fuerza Aérea Boliviano

lb/sq in). No mainwheel doors. Goodrich hydraulic disc brakes on mainwheels. Parking brake.

POWER PLANT: One 485 kW (650 shp) Pratt & Whitney Canada PT6A-25A turboprop, flat rated at 410 kW (550 shp at S/L), driving a Hartzell HC-B3TN-2/T10173C-8 three-blade constant-speed fully-feathering propeller with spinner. Fuel in integral tanks in outer wing leading-edges, total usable capacity 474 litres (125 US gallons; 104 Imp gallons). Overwing refuelling point on each tank. Engine oil system permits up to 30 s of inverted flight. Provision for two 152 or 240 litre (40 or 63.5 US gallon; 33.5 or 52.75 Imp gallon) underwing drop tanks. Oil capacity 16 litres (4.2 US gallons; 3.5 Imp gallons).

ACCOMMODATION: Adjustable seats for two persons in tandem (instructor at rear), beneath rearward sliding jettisonable Plexiglas canopy. Martin-Baker Mk 15 lightweight ejection seats available optionally. Dual controls standard. Cockpits ventilated and heated by engine bleed air, which can also be used for windscreen de-icing. Space for 25 kg (55 lb) of baggage aft of seats, with external access.

SYSTEMS: Freon air-conditioning and oxygen systems standard. Hydraulic system for mainwheel brakes only. No pneumatic system. 28V DC operational electrical system, incorporating Lear Siegler 30V 200A starter/generator and Marathon 36Ah or 42Ah nickel-cadmium battery; two static inverters for AC power supply. Ground power receptacle in port side of rear fuselage. Goodrich propeller electric de-icing system optional.

AVIONICS AND EQUIPMENT: Basic flight and navigation instrumentation in both cockpits, except for magnetic compass (front cockpit only). Additional nav and com equipment to customer's requirements. Other optional equipment includes instrument flying hood to screen pupil from rear cockpit during IFR training. Landing/taxiing light standard on each mainwheel leg.

DIMENSIONS, EXTERNAL:

Wing span	10.40 m (34 ft 1 in)
Wing chord: mean aerodynamic	1.64 m (5 ft 5 in)
mean geometric	1.60 m (5 ft 3 in)
Wing aspect ratio	6.5
Length overall	9.78 m (32 ft 1 in)
Height overall	3.21 m (10 ft 6 in)
Tailplane span	3.40 m (11 ft 2 in)
Wheel track	2.60 m (8 ft 6 in)
Wheelbase	2.32 m (7 ft 7 in)
Propeller diameter	2.36 m (7 ft 9 in)

AREAS:

Wings, gross	16.60 m² (179.0 sq ft)
Ailerons (total)	1.621 m² (17.45 sq ft)
Trailing-edge flaps (total)	2.035 m² (21.90 sq ft)
Fin, incl dorsal fin	1.062 m² (11.43 sq ft)
Rudder, incl tab	0.959 m² (10.32 sq ft)
Tailplane	1.783 m² (19.19 sq ft)
Elevators, incl tab	1.395 m² (15.02 sq ft)

WEIGHTS AND LOADINGS:

Basic weight empty	1,330 kg (2,932 lb)
Max T-O weight: Aerobatic	1,900 kg (4,188 lb)
Utility	2,700 kg (5,952 lb)
Max ramp weight: Utility	2,711 kg (5,976 lb)
Max landing weight:	
Aerobatic (military specification)	1,804 kg (3,977 lb)
Aerobatic (FAR Pt 23)	1,900 kg (4,188 lb)
Utility	2,565 kg (5,655 lb)
Max zero-fuel weight	1,664 kg (3,668 lb)
Max wing loading:	
Aerobatic	114.5 kg/m² (23.44 lb/sq ft)
Utility	162.7 kg/m² (33.31 lb/sq ft)
Max power loading:	
Aerobatic	4.63 kg/kW (7.61 lb/shp)
Utility	6.59 kg/kW (10.82 lb/shp)

PERFORMANCE (at max T-O weight, ISA, except where indicated. A: Aerobatic category, B: Utility category):

Never-exceed speed:	
A, B	270 knots (500 km/h; 310 mph) EAS
Max operating speed:	
A, B	270 knots (500 km/h; 310 mph) EAS
Max cruising speed at 6,100 m (20,000 ft):	
A	222 knots (412 km/h; 256 mph)
B	196 knots (364 km/h; 226 mph)
Econ cruising speed at 6,100 m (20,000 ft):	
A	171 knots (317 km/h; 197 mph)
B	165 knots (305 km/h; 190 mph)
Manoeuvring speed:	
A	175 knots (325 km/h; 202 mph) EAS
B	181 knots (335 km/h; 208 mph) EAS
Max speed with flaps and landing gear down:	
A, B	135 knots (250 km/h; 155 mph) EAS
Stalling speed, flaps and landing gear up, power off:	
A	71 knots (131 km/h; 82 mph) EAS
B	83 knots (154 km/h; 96 mph) EAS
Stalling speed, flaps and landing gear down, power off:	
A	64 knots (119 km/h; 74 mph) EAS
B	74 knots (138 km/h; 86 mph) EAS
Max rate of climb at S/L: A	655 m (2,150 ft)/min
B	364 m (1,195 ft)/min
Time to 5,000 m (16,400 ft): A	9 min
B	17 min
Max operating altitude	7,620 m (25,000 ft)
Service ceiling: A	10,060 m (33,000 ft)
B	7,925 m (26,000 ft)
T-O run at S/L: A	240 m (787 ft)
B	780 m (2,560 ft)
T-O to 15 m (50 ft) at S/L: A	400 m (1,312 ft)
B	1,180 m (3,870 ft)

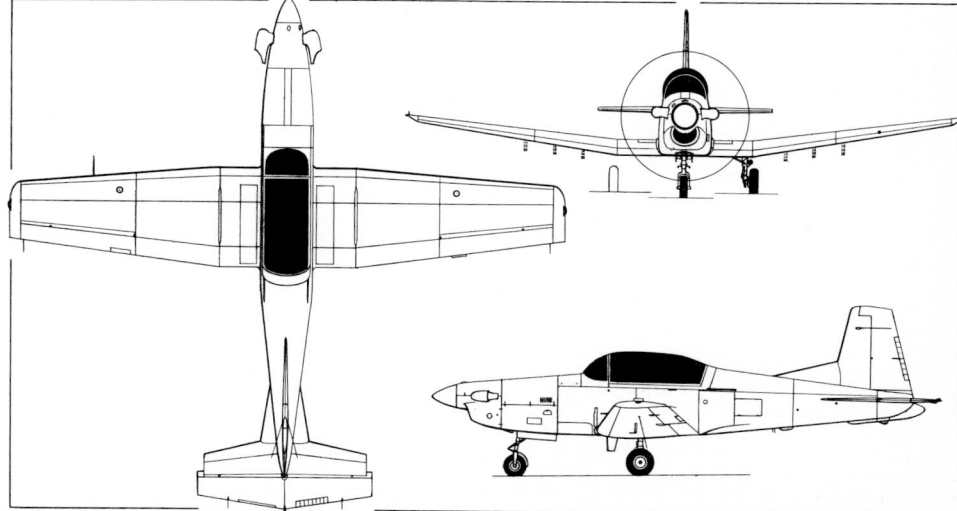

Pilatus PC-7 Turbo-Trainer (Pratt & Whitney Canada PT6A-25A turboprop) *(Pilot Press)*

Landing from 15 m (50 ft) at S/L at max landing weight:
A	510 m (1,675 ft)
B	800 m (2,625 ft)

Landing run at S/L at max landing weight:
A	295 m (968 ft)
B	505 m (1,655 ft)

Max range at cruise power at 5,000 m (16,400 ft), 5% fuel plus 20 min reserves:
A	647 nm (1,200 km; 745 miles)
B	1,420 nm (2,630 km; 1,634 miles)

Endurance at 6,100 m (20,000 ft), with reserves:
A, at max speed	3 h 0 min
A, for max range	4 h 22 min
B, at max speed	2 h 36 min
B, for max range	3 h 45 min
g limits: A	+6/−3
B	+4.5/−2.25

PILATUS PC-9

Design of the PC-9, as an advanced, high performance turboprop trainer suitable for all aspects from basic through to advanced flying, began in May 1982. Despite an external similarity to the PC-7, it has only about 10 per cent structural commonality with that aircraft, differences including a more powerful engine, 'stepped' tandem cockpits with ejection seats, a ventral airbrake, modified wing profiles and tips, new ailerons, a longer dorsal fin, mainwheel doors, and larger wheels with high pressure tyres. The PC-9 complies with FAR Pt 23 (Amendments 1-28), plus special conditions as specified by the Swiss Federal Office for Civil Aviation, in both the Aerobatic and Utility categories, and also complies with selected parts of US military specifications.

Flight testing of major components, and aerodynamic optimisation of the new design, were completed during 1982-83 on a PC-7 technology demonstration aircraft, and were followed by two pre-production PC-9s (HB-HPA, first flight 7 May 1984, and HB-HPB, first flown on 20 July 1984). The second of these was more fully representative of the production version. Aerobatic category certification was obtained on 19 September 1985.

First customer for the PC-9 was the Union of Burma Air Force, which ordered four. It was followed by the Royal Saudi Air Force, which ordered 30 on 26 September 1985. The first of these was handed over to the RSAF on 15 December 1986, and 12 had been delivered by mid-1987. On 16 December 1985 the Australian Defence Minister announced his government's decision to order PC-9s for the RAAF, and a contract for 67 aircraft, to be co-produced by Hawker de Havilland and ASTA, was signed on 10 July 1986. The Australian version is designated **PC-9/A**. For the Australian order, Pilatus supplied two complete aircraft in 1987; these are being followed by six in kit form (first kit delivered 27 February 1987), and major components for a further 11; the remaining 48 are being built by HDH and ASTA. The two Swiss built aircraft, and the first two assembled in Australia, were handed over to the RAAF on 14 December 1987. Total orders include approx 25 more PC-9s from two undisclosed customers (one of them reportedly Angola, for four, the other Iraq).

TYPE: Single/two-seat training aircraft.

WINGS: Cantilever low-wing monoplane. Wing section PIL15M825 at root, PIL12M850 at tip. Dihedral 7° from centre-section. Incidence 1° at root, washout −2° at tip. Sweepback 1° at quarter-chord. One-piece all-metal single-spar primary structure with auxiliary spar, ribs, and stringer-reinforced skin. Constant chord centre-section and tapered outer panels. Alclad aluminium alloy

Pilatus PC-9 single/two-seat trainer of the Royal Saudi Air Force

(2024) skin, reinforced by stringers; some fairings of GRP. Mass balanced plain ailerons; trailing-edge split flaps extending under fuselage with plate type airbrake at centre. Flaps and airbrake actuated hydraulically, ailerons mechanically by pushrods. Aileron trim is by an electrically actuated, variable load centring spring on the control column.

FUSELAGE: All-metal semi-monocoque structure with stringers, bulkheads and aluminium alloy skin. Some fairings of GRP.

TAIL UNIT: Cantilever all-metal structure with mass balanced cable operated rudder and elevator. Trim tab in starboard half of elevator, and trim/anti-balance tab in rudder, both mass balanced and electrically actuated.

LANDING GEAR: Retractable tricycle type, with hydraulic actuation in both normal and emergency modes. Mainwheels retract inward into wing centre-section, nosewheel rearward; all units enclosed by doors when retracted. Oleo-pneumatic shock absorber in each leg unit. Hydraulically actuated nosewheel steering. Goodrich wheels and tyres, with Goodrich multi-piston hydraulic disc brakes on mainwheels. RAAF version has low pressure tyres for grass field operation. Parking brake.

POWER PLANT: One 857 kW (1,150 shp) Pratt & Whitney Canada PT6A-62 turboprop, flat rated at 708 kW (950 shp), driving a Hartzell HC-D4N-ZA/09512A four-blade constant-speed fully-feathering propeller with spinner. Fuel in two integral tanks in wing leading-edges, total usable capacity 535 litres (141.3 US gallons; 117.7 Imp gallons). Overwing refuelling point on each side. Fuel system includes a 12 litre (3.2 US gallon; 2.6 Imp gallon) aerobatics tank in fuselage, forward of front cockpit, which permits up to 60 s of inverted flight. Provision for two 154 or 248 litre (40.7 or 65.5 US gallon; 33.9 or 54.5 Imp gallon) drop tanks on the centre underwing attachment points. Total oil capacity 16 litres (4.2 US gallons; 3.5 Imp gallons).

ACCOMMODATION: Two Martin-Baker Mk CH 11A adjustable ejection seats, each with integrated personal survival pack and fighter-standard pilot equipment. Stepped tandem arrangement with rear seat elevated 15 cm (6.3 in). Seats operable, through canopy, at zero height and speeds down to 60 knots (112 km/h; 70 mph). Anti-g system optional. One-piece acrylic Perspex windscreen; one-piece framed canopy, incorporating rollover bar, opens sideways to starboard. Dual controls standard. Cockpit heating, ventilation and canopy demisting standard. Space for 25 kg (55 lb) of baggage aft of seats, with external access.

SYSTEMS: AiResearch environmental control system, using air cycle and engine bleed air, for cockpit heating/ventilation and canopy demisting. Fairey Systems hydraulic system, pressure 207 bars (3,000 lb/sq in), for actuation of landing gear, mainwheel doors, nosewheel steering, flaps and airbrake; system max flow rate 18.8 litres (4.97 US gallons; 4.14 Imp gallons)/min. Bootstrap oil/oil reservoir, pressurised at 3.45-207 bars (50-3,000 lb/sq in). Oil/nitrogen accumulator, also charged to 207 bars (3,000 lb/sq in), provides emergency hydraulic power for flaps and landing gear. Primary electrical system (28V DC operational, 24V nominal) powered by a Lear Siegler 30V 200A starter/generator and a 24V 40Ah battery; two static inverters supply 115/26V AC power at 400Hz. Ground power receptacle provided. Electric anti-icing of pitot tube, static ports and AOA transmitter standard; electric de-icing of propeller blades optional. Diluter demand oxygen system, selected and controlled individually from a panel in each cockpit.

AVIONICS AND EQUIPMENT: Both cockpits fully instrumented to standard customer specifications, with Kratos computer operated instrument system (COINS). RAAF aircraft are equipped with Bendix EFIS (see below) as standard. Single or dual system VHF, UHF and/or HF to customer's requirements. Audio integrating system controls audio services from com, nav and interphone systems. Customer-specified equipment provides flight environmental, attitude and direction data, and ground-transmitted position determining information. Retractable 250W landing/taxiing light in each main landing gear leg bay. Optional equipment includes Bendix CRT displays (electronic ADI and HSI, standard on PC-9/A), J.E.T. head-up displays, encoding altimeter, emergency locator transmitter, propeller electric de-icing, and underwing drop tanks.

DIMENSIONS, EXTERNAL:
Wing span	10.124 m (33 ft 2½ in)
Wing chord: mean aerodynamic	1.65 m (5 ft 5 in)
mean geometric	1.61 m (5 ft 3½ in)
Wing aspect ratio	6.3
Length overall	10.175 m (33 ft 4¾ in)
Height overall	3.26 m (10 ft 8⅓ in)
Wheel track	2.54 m (8 ft 4 in)
Propeller diameter	2.44 m (8 ft 0 in)

AREAS:
Wings, gross	16.29 m² (175.3 sq ft)
Ailerons (total)	1.57 m² (16.90 sq ft)
Trailing-edge flaps (total)	1.77 m² (19.05 sq ft)
Airbrake	0.30 m² (3.23 sq ft)
Fin	0.86 m² (9.26 sq ft)
Rudder, incl tab	0.90 m² (9.69 sq ft)
Tailplane	1.80 m² (19.38 sq ft)
Elevator, incl tab	1.60 m² (17.22 sq ft)

WEIGHTS AND LOADINGS (A: Aerobatic, U: Utility):
Basic weight empty	1,685 kg (3,715 lb)
Max T-O weight: A	2,250 kg (4,960 lb)
U	3,200 kg (7,055 lb)
Max ramp weight: A	2,260 kg (4,982 lb)
U	3,210 kg (7,077 lb)
Max landing weight: A	2,250 kg (4,960 lb)
U	3,100 kg (6,834 lb)

Pilatus PC-9 basic/advanced trainer (Pratt & Whitney Canada PT6A-62 turboprop) *(Pilot Press)*

Max zero-fuel weight: A	1,900 kg (4,188 lb)
Max wing loading: A	138.1 kg/m² (28.3 lb/sq ft)
U	196.4 kg/m² (40.2 lb/sq ft)
Max power loading: A	3.18 kg/kW (5.22 lb/shp)
U	4.52 kg/kW (7.42 lb/shp)

PERFORMANCE (at appropriate max T-O weight, ISA, propeller speed 2,000 rpm):

Max permissible diving speed: A, U	
	Mach 0.73 (360 knots; 667 km/h; 414 mph EAS)
Max operating speed: A, U	
	Mach 0.68 (320 knots; 593 km/h; 368 mph EAS)
Max level speed:	
A at S/L	270 knots (500 km/h; 311 mph)
A at 6,100 m (20,000 ft)	
	300 knots (556 km/h; 345 mph)
Manoeuvring speed:	
A	210 knots (389 km/h; 242 mph) EAS

U	200 knots (370 km/h; 230 mph) EAS
Max speed with flaps and/or landing gear down:	
A and U	150 knots (278 km/h; 172 mph) EAS
Stalling speed, engine idling:	
A, flaps and landing gear up	
	79 knots (147 km/h; 91 mph) EAS
U, flaps and landing gear up	
	93 knots (172 km/h; 107 mph) EAS
A, flaps and landing gear down	
	70 knots (130 km/h; 81 mph) EAS
U, flaps and landing gear down	
	86 knots (159 km/h; 99 mph) EAS
Max rate of climb at S/L: A	1,250 m (4,100 ft)/min
Time to 4,575 m (15,000 ft): A	4 min 30 s
Max operating altitude	7,620 m (25,000 ft)
Service ceiling	12,200 m (40,000 ft)
T-O run at S/L: A	227 m (745 ft)

T-O to 15 m (50 ft) at S/L: A	372 m (1,220 ft)
Landing from 15 m (50 ft) at S/L: A	538 m (1,765 ft)
Landing run at S/L:	
A (normal braking action)	417 m (1,368 ft)
Max range at cruise power at 7,620 m (25,000 ft), 5% fuel plus 20 min reserves	887 nm (1,642 km; 1,020 miles)
Endurance (typical mission power settings)	
	2 sorties of 1 h duration plus 20 min reserves
g limits: A	+7/−3.5
U	+4.5/−2.25

PILATUS PC-12

Pilatus is developing a new 12-seat turboprop transport under the designation PC-12. No other details had been revealed at the time of going to press.

SWISS FEDERAL AIRCRAFT FACTORY (F+W)

EIDGENÖSSISCHES FLUGZEUGWERK— FABRIQUE FÉDÉRALE D'AVIONS— FABBRICA FEDERALE D'AEROPLANI

CH-6032 Emmen
Telephone: (041) 59 41 11
Telex: 868 505 FWE CH
Fax: (041) 55 25 88
MANAGING DIRECTOR: Hansjürg Kobelt

F+W is the Swiss government's official aircraft establishment for research, development, production, maintenance and modification of military aircraft and guided missile systems. It employs about 800 people in its works at Emmen, which cover 140,000 m² (1,506,946 sq ft). Research and development are divided among four departments: aerodynamics and thermodynamics, with appropriate test facilities which include four wind tunnels for speeds of up to Mach 4-5, test cells for piston engines and turbojets (with or without afterburners), all equipped with computerised data acquisition and processing; structural and systems engineering for aircraft, helicopters and space hardware, with a speciality in fatigue analysis and testing of entire aircraft structures; electronics and missile systems, covering all system aspects of aircraft and helicopter avionics, missiles and RPVs; and prototype fabrication, flight test, instrumentation, and system and environmental testing.

The production department covers the whole field of production capabilities, from mechanical and sheet metal parts to composite parts and subassemblies (including leading-edge slats for the McDonnell Douglas MD-80 series and wingtips for the Airbus A320); electronics, electrical, electro-mechanical and electro-optical subassemblies; final assembly of missiles, missile systems, aircraft and helicopters. Recent major activities have included licence manufacture of aircraft, helicopters and missile systems, and fabrication of all shrouds for the Ariane and Titan 3 space launchers (designed by F+W with Contraves as main contractor).

F+W is general contractor for full licence production of the MDAC Dragon missile, completed a similar programme for the Rapier missile in 1987, and began one for the TOW anti-tank missile in 1986. Missiles are assembled and tested at F+W and delivered to the Swiss government.

F+W conducts wind tunnel tests for foreign aircraft manufacturers, ground transportation developers and users, and for the building industry. It develops and integrates internal stores and performs other modification work on military aircraft, including, currently, adding

Swiss Air Force Mirage III-S evaluation aircraft, modified by F+W with nose strakes and fixed foreplane surfaces *(Swiss Air Force)*

canard surfaces to Swiss Air Force Mirages. Subsonic wind tunnel tests have been made, and appropriate models built, of the Hermes spacecraft. F+W developed the low-level dispenser bombing system now integrated on Swiss Air Force Hunter and Tiger II aircraft. This system utilises aerodynamically retarded bomblets, carried in underwing pods and ejected by ram air. Integration on other types of aircraft is under way.

F+W proprietary products include acoustic systems for failure and flight envelope warning; all-electronic linear angle of attack and g indicators; scoring indicators for air-to-air or ground-to-air shooting, with a microcomputer based ground station; multi-component strain gauge balances for testing purposes, covering forces from a few hundred grammes to several tons; water separators for aircraft conditioning; and POHWARO hot water rockets. (Details of these rockets can be found in the 1977-78 *Jane's*.) Co-operative development led to the Farner KZD 85 target drone described in the RPVs & Targets section of the 1987-88 *Jane's*, and F+W has since developed the air vehicle and catapult launcher of a new reconnaissance/aerial survey mini-RPV system known as the Ranger. Services are also offered for environmental testing, especially on F+W's own designed and proven test installation for high-shock long-duration tests.

F+W MIRAGE IMPROVEMENT PROGRAMME

The Swiss government approved funding in 1985 to retrofit Mirage III aircraft of the Swiss Air Force, which currently has 52 of these aircraft (30 III-S, 18 III-RS, two III-BS and two III-DS) in its inventory. Main ingredients of this programme are the fitting of non-moving canard surfaces just aft of the engine air intakes, and addition of a very slim strake on each side of the extreme nose, the former to improve manoeuvrability and low-speed handling and eliminate buffeting, the latter to increase stability in yaw near the upper limit of the flight envelope.

Other improvements include new audible warning and visual angle of attack monitoring systems, to alert the pilot when approaching limits of the flight envelope; substitution of Martin-Baker Mk 4 ejection seats in place of the present Mk 6 seats; addition of infra-red and passive/active ECM; provision of more powerful VHF radios; wing refurbishing; ability to carry two underwing 500 litre (132 US gallon; 110 Imp gallon) drop tanks and a 730 litre (193 US gallon; 160.5 Imp gallon) centreline tank; mounting of improved blast deflectors for the two internal guns, to allow firing at high angles of attack; and a new camouflage paint scheme. The retrofit programme is planned to continue until 1990.

TAIWAN

AIDC

AERO INDUSTRY DEVELOPMENT CENTER

PO Box 8676, Taichung, Taiwan 40722
Telephone: (04) 2523051 and 2523052
Telex: 51140 AIDC
OTHER WORKS: Kang-Shan
DIRECTOR: Dr Hsichun M. Hua
DEPUTY DIRECTOR, RESEARCH AND ENGINEERING: Dr Shih-sen Wang

The AIDC was established on 1 March 1969 as a successor to the Bureau of Aircraft Industry (BAI), which was formed in 1946 in Nanjing and moved to Taiwan in 1948. AIDC now employs more than 4,500 people, and is a subsidiary of the Chung Shan Institute of Science and Technology.

Between 1969 and 1976, the AIDC produced in Taiwan 118 Bell UH-1H (Bell Model 205) helicopters under licence for the Chinese Nationalist Army. From 1968 to 1974 it built a PL-1A prototype and 55 PL-1B Chienshou trainers (1975-76 *Jane's*), based on the US Pazmany PL-1, for the Nationalist Air Force. From 1974 to 1986 the AIDC was engaged in licence building 248 Northrop F-5E Tiger II tactical fighter aircraft (see 1986-87 *Jane's*) and 36 two-seat F-5Fs for the Chinese Nationalist Air Force.

The AIDC designed and produced the T-CH-1 turboprop basic trainer for the Chinese Nationalist Air Force, and has

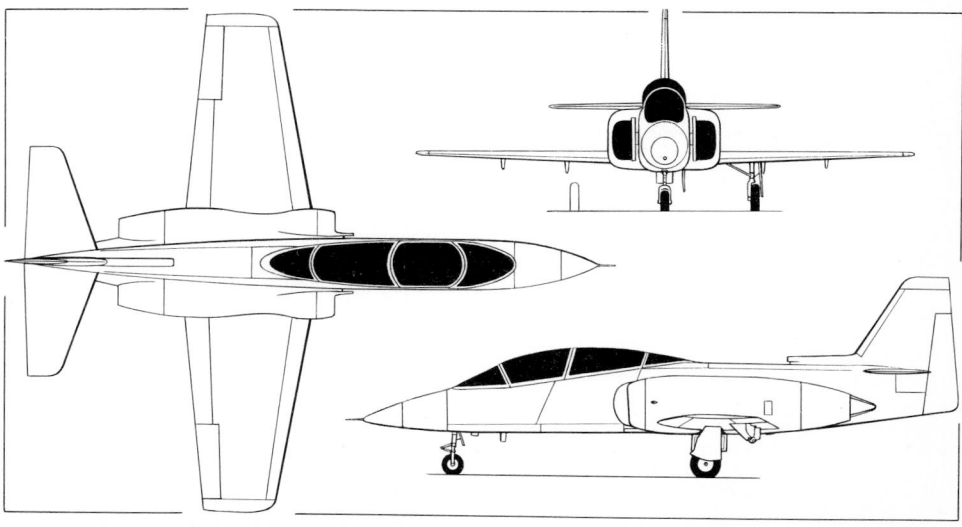

AIDC AT-3 twin-turbofan military basic and advanced trainer *(Pilot Press)*

AIDC AT-3 tandem two-seat trainer (two Garrett TFE731 turbofans)

since developed and put into production the twin-turbofan AT-3.

AIDC FIGHTER

Design definition is continuing of a supersonic light-weight air defence fighter to replace the Lockheed F-104 and Northrop F-5E in Chinese Nationalist Air Force service in the 1990s. The programme is expected to lead to an aircraft with similar performance characteristics to the Northrop F-20A Tigershark, the sale of which to Taiwan was forbidden by the US government. US technological assistance in developing an indigenous fighter is not, however, subject to the same restrictions, and AIDC is reported to have received such assistance from General Dynamics (airframe), Garrett (power plant), General Electric (APG-67 multi-mode radar) and Lear Siegler (avionics), the fighter being likely to be powered by two 37.14 kN (8,350 lb st) ITEC (Garrett/AIDC) TFE1042 afterburning turbofans. First flight is tentatively planned for 1989.

AIDC AT-3

In July 1975, AIDC was awarded a contract to design and develop prototypes of a new basic and advanced military jet training aircraft, designated XAT-3. Construction of two prototypes (0801 and 0802) began in January 1978, and these flew for the first time on 16 September 1980 and 30 October 1981 respectively. Following receipt of a contract for 60 production aircraft, AIDC began the manufacture of these, under the CAF designation AT-3, in March 1982. The first production aircraft (0803) made its initial flight on 6 February 1984. Deliveries began in the following month, and 44 had been delivered by the beginning of 1988.

According to 1988 press reports which AIDC declines to confirm, the AT-3 has the CNAF name Tsu-Chiang; and a single-seat A-3 version named Lui-Meng is now also in production. The single-seater was said to have a max external stores load of 2,721 kg (6,000 lb), including Sidewinder air-to-air missiles on wingtip launch rails, and to be intended for both ground attack and maritime strike roles.

The following description applies to the standard production AT-3:

TYPE: Tandem two-seat twin-turbofan military trainer.

WINGS: Cantilever low-wing monoplane of supercritical section. Thickness/chord ratio 10%. Dihedral 0° 46'. Incidence 1° 30'. Sweepback at quarter-chord 7° 20'. One-piece carry-through wing, with a machined torsion box, attached to fuselage by six bolts. Multi-spar light alloy structure, with heavy plate machined skin. Hydraulically powered light alloy honeycomb sealed-gap ailerons. Electrically operated light alloy single-slotted trailing-edge flaps. No anti-icing system.

FUSELAGE: Light alloy semi-monocoque basic structure, with steel, magnesium and graphite/epoxy used in certain areas. Built in three sections: forward fuselage, including cockpit; centre fuselage, including nacelles; and rear fuselage, including vertical and horizontal tail assembly. Two electrically controlled hydraulically actuated air-brakes, of laminated graphite/epoxy construction, mounted on fuselage undersurface forward of mainwheel wells. Fail-safe structure in pressurised cockpit section.

TAIL UNIT: Cantilever all-metal structure, integral with rear fuselage. One-piece all-moving tailplane; incidence varied by tandem hydraulic actuator. Dual hydraulic actuators for rudder, with yaw stability augmentation. No trim tabs.

LANDING GEAR: Hydraulically retractable tricycle type, with single wheel on each unit. Main units retract inward into fuselage, nosewheel forward. Oleo-pneumatic shock absorber in each unit. Two-position extending nose leg increases static angle of attack by 3° 30', to reduce T-O run, and is shortened automatically during retraction. Emergency extension by gravity. Mainwheels and tyres size 24 × 8.00-13, pressure 8.96 bars (130 lb/sq in). Hydraulically steerable nose unit, with wheel and tyre size 18 × 6.50-8, pressure 5.51 bars (80 lb/sq in). All-metal multi-disc brakes.

POWER PLANT: Two Garrett TFE731-2-2L non-afterburning turbofans (each 15.57 kN; 3,500 lb st), installed in nacelle on each side of fuselage. Inclined ram air intakes, each with splitter plate, abreast of rear cockpit. Engine starting by onboard battery or ground power. All fuel carried in fuselage, in two equal-size rubber impregnated nylon bladder tanks, with combined capacity of 1,630 litres (430.6 US gallons; 358.5 Imp gallons). Two independent fuel systems, one for each engine, with crossfeed to allow fuel from either or both systems to be fed to either or both engines. Pressure fuelling point forward of, and below, port air intake for internal and external tanks. A 568 litre (150 US gallon; 125 Imp gallon) auxiliary drop tank can be carried on each inboard underwing pylon. Oil capacity 5.7 litres (1.5 US gallons; 1.25 Imp gallons) total, 1.9 litres (0.5 US gallon; 0.42 Imp gallon) usable. Fire warning and extinguishing systems for each engine bay.

ACCOMMODATION: Crew of two in tandem on zero/zero ejection (through canopy) seats, under individual manu-ally operated canopies which open sideways to starboard. Crew separated by internal windscreen. Independent miniature detonation cord (MDC) system to break each canopy for ground and in-flight emergency egress. MDC can be operated from outside cockpit on ground. Rear seat elevated 30 cm (12 in). Dual controls standard.

SYSTEMS: AiResearch bootstrap air cycle environmental control system, for cockpit air-conditioning and pressur-isation (max differential 0.34 bars; 5 lb/sq in), canopy seal, demisting, and pressurisation of g suits, hydraulic reservoirs and external fuel tanks. Two independent hydraulic systems, pressure 207 bars (3,000 lb/sq in), with engine driven pumps (flow rate 34.4 litres; 9.09 US gallons; 7.57 Imp gallons/min). Air type reservoir, pressurised at 2.41 bars (35 lb/sq in). Flight control hydraulic system provides power only for operation of primary flying control surfaces. Utility system serves primary flying control surfaces, landing gear, landing gear doors, airbrakes, wheel brakes, nosewheel steering, and stability augmentation system. Primary electrical power supplied by two 28V 12kW DC starter/generators, one on each engine. One 40Ah nickel-cadmium battery for engine starting. Two static inverters supply AC power at 400Hz. External DC power socket on starboard side of centre fuselage. Hydraulic and electrical systems can be sustained by either engine. Liquid oxygen system,

capacity 5 litres (1.3 US gallons; 1.1 Imp gallons), for crew.

AVIONICS AND EQUIPMENT: Most radio and nav equipment located in large avionics bays in forward fuselage. Standard avionics include UHF com, intercom, IFF/SIF, Tacan, panel mounted VOR/ILS/marker beacon indi-cator, attitude and heading reference system and angle of attack system, plus full blind-flying instrumentation. Wide range of optional avionics available.

ARMAMENT AND OPERATIONAL EQUIPMENT: Manually adjust-able gunsight and camera in forward cockpit, for armament training. Large weapons bay beneath rear cockpit can house variety of stores, including quick-change semi-recessed machine-gun packs. Disposable weapons can be carried on a centreline pylon (stressed for 907 kg; 2,000 lb load), two inboard underwing pylons (each 635 kg; 1,400 lb and capable of accepting triple ejector racks), two outboard underwing pylons (each 272 kg; 600 lb), and wingtip launch rails (each of 91 kg; 200 lb capacity), subject to a max external stores load of 2,721 kg (6,000 lb). Weapons that can be carried include GP, SE, cluster and fire bombs; SUU-25A/A, -25C/A and -25E/A flare dispensers; LAU-3/A, -3A/A, -3B/A, -10/A, -10A/A, -60/A, -68A/A and -68B/A rocket launchers; wingtip infra-red air-to-air missiles; and rocket pods, practice bombs, and bomb or rocket training dispensers. The aircraft can also be equipped with an A/A37U-15TTS aerial target system, carried on the centreline and outboard pylons.

DIMENSIONS, EXTERNAL:

Wing span	10.46 m (34 ft 3¾ in)
Wing chord: at root	2.80 m (9 ft 2¼ in)
at tip	1.40 m (4 ft 7 in)
Wing aspect ratio	5.0
Length overall, incl nose probe	12.90 m (42 ft 4 in)
Height overall	4.36 m (14 ft 3¾ in)
Tailplane span	4.83 m (15 ft 10¼ in)
Wheel track	3.96 m (13 ft 0 in)
Wheelbase	5.49 m (18 ft 0 in)

AREAS:

Wings, gross	21.93 m² (236.05 sq ft)
Ailerons (total)	1.33 m² (14.32 sq ft)
Trailing-edge flaps (total)	2.53 m² (27.23 sq ft)
Fin	3.45 m² (37.14 sq ft)
Rudder	1.15 m² (12.38 sq ft)
Tailplane	5.02 m² (54.04 sq ft)

WEIGHTS AND LOADINGS:

Weight empty, equipped	3,855 kg (8,500 lb)
Max fuel: internal	1,270 kg (2,800 lb)
external	884 kg (1,950 lb)
Max external stores load	2,721 kg (6,000 lb)
Normal T-O weight:	
trainer, 'clean'	5,216 kg (11,500 lb)
Max T-O weight with external stores	
	7,938 kg (17,500 lb)
Max landing weight	7,360 kg (16,225 lb)
Max wing loading	362 kg/m² (74.14 lb/sq ft)
Max power loading	254.9 kg/kN (2.5 lb/lb st)

PERFORMANCE (at max T-O weight):

Max limiting Mach No.	1.05
Max level speed:	
at S/L	485 knots (898 km/h; 558 mph)
at 11,000 m (36,000 ft)	
	Mach 0.85 (488 knots; 904 km/h; 562 mph)
Max cruising speed at 11,000 m (36,000 ft)	
	Mach 0.83 (476 knots; 882 km/h; 548 mph)
Stalling speed:	
flaps and landing gear up	
	100 knots (185 km/h; 115 mph)
flaps and landing gear down	
	90 knots (167 km/h; 104 mph)
Max rate of climb at S/L	3,078 m (10,100 ft)/min
Service ceiling	14,625 m (48,000 ft)
T-O run	458 m (1,500 ft)
T-O to 15 m (50 ft)	671 m (2,200 ft)
Landing from 15 m (50 ft)	945 m (3,100 ft)
Landing run	671 m (2,200 ft)
Range with max internal fuel	
	1,230 nm (2,279 km; 1,416 miles)
Endurance with max internal fuel	3 h 12 min

THAILAND

IAC
INTERNATIONAL AIRCRAFT COMPANY LTD
DIRECTOR: Danai Phasatanan

At the beginning of 1988 IAC was seeking Thai government financial support to set up a domestic assembly line for the US RotorWay Exec two-seat light helicopter (which see) at the factory of the Siam International Co. At

that time it had already imported five Execs in CKD kit form, and had completed assembly of two of them for delivery to the Thai Police Aviation Division.

RTAF (SWDC)
ROYAL THAI AIR FORCE (Science and Weapon Systems Development Centre)
Office of Aeronautical Engineering, c/o Directorate of Aeronautical Engineering (DAE), No. 1 Pradipath Street, Dusit, Bangkok 10300
Telephone: 2412885
DIRECTOR OF SWDC: Air Marshal Vichai Karnchanapa
DIRECTOR OF DAE: Air Marshal Banyat Wongthongsuk

CHIEF DESIGNER: Gp Capt Preecha Wannabhoom
The Office of Aeronautical Engineering was set up in 1975, and has been responsible for all subsequent design activity. Its most ambitious product to date, the RTAF-5 turboprop trainer and FAC aircraft, was designed and built entirely in Thailand and made its first flight on 5 October 1984.

A full description of the prototype appeared in the 1986-87 and earlier editions.

RTAF (RFB) FANTRAINER 400 and 600
In 1986, under its co-production programme with RFB of West Germany (which see), RTAF began the design and manufacture of all-metal wings for 45 of the 47 Fantrainers ordered by the Royal Thai Air Force. These are identical to, and interchangeable with, the GRP wings of German built Fantrainers, and are provided with two hardpoints under

each wing; 19 pairs of metal wings had been completed by early 1988.

The description of the Fantrainer in the German section applies also to the RTAF aircraft except as follows:

WINGS: Cantilever mid-wing monoplane. All-metal stressed skin structure, with two-spar wing box forming integral fuel tank in each wing, attached to fuselage by bolts. Corrugated skins at wingroots, over mainwheel bays.

WEIGHT (600, Aerobatic category):

Weight empty	1,180 kg (2,601 lb)
Max internal fuel	310 kg (683 lb)
Max T-O weight	1,680 kg (3,703 lb)

PERFORMANCE (600 at max Aerobatic T-O weight):

Max level speed	240 knots (445 km/h; 276 mph) IAS
Cruising speed (70% power) at 915 m (3,000 ft)	
	186 knots (344 km/h; 214 mph) IAS
Approach speed	75 knots (139 km/h; 87 mph) IAS
Endurance	2 h 48 min

RTAF metal winged Fantrainer 600 prototype

TURKEY

TAI
TUSAS AEROSPACE INDUSTRIES INC
(Tusaş Havacilik Ve Uzay Sanayĩi As)

PO Box 18, 06690 Kavaklidere, Ankara
Telephone: (904) 3242140
Telex: 44640 TAIA TR
Fax: (904) 3244807
MANAGING DIRECTOR: J. R. Jones

TAI is a majority owned Turkish company made up of Turkish (51%) and American (49%) partners and was formed on 15 May 1984. The major shareholders are Turkish Aircraft Industries Inc (49%) and General Dynamics (42%); other shareholders are General Electric (7%), the Turkish Armed Forces Foundation (1.9%) and the Turkish Air League (0.1%).

For the first seven years of operation, four of the top management positions are filled by General Dynamics executives. General Dynamics is also training over 300

Turkish employees at its Fort Worth facility and another 300 at TAI's Training Centre at Mürted. As part of its investment, General Dynamics is providing all shop machinery, plus $15 million in cash for the purchase of new machine tools. Total investment by the two American partners is $67 million, with $70 million being contributed by the Turkish shareholders. The Turkish partners contributed the land and are providing the cash to construct all buildings. This large facility has over 92,903 m² (1,000,000 sq ft) of covered area, the main assembly building being 62,525 m² (673,000 sq ft). Other buildings include chemical processing, flight line, fuel station, heating centre, water purification and administrative areas. A 1,000-apartment complex is also being constructed, including a shopping centre, hospital and school. This will open in mid-1989.

By the end of 1987 TAI had completed over 95 per cent of its construction work, giving it the resources to assemble

and deliver fighter type aircraft, manufacture fuselage and wing components, machine close tolerance aluminium, steel and titanium parts, manufacture hydraulic tubes, fuel lines, harness boards, floor base tooling, and apply fixtures. It will also have a modern numerical control machine centre and one of the most up to date computer capabilities in the world. The company had more than 900 employees by the end of 1987, and this figure will expand to 2,000 by 1990.

TAI is under contract to General Dynamics to assemble and deliver 152 of the 160 F-16C and D aircraft ordered by the Turkish Air Force (the Peace Onyx programme), and to fabricate and assemble rear and centre fuselages and wings of F-16 aircraft for the United States Air Force. The first F-16C (86-0068) was delivered to the Turkish Air Force on 30 November 1987. In early 1988 a total of 12 aircraft was on the assembly line or in flight status, and all work was continuing to schedule.

UNION OF SOVIET SOCIALIST REPUBLICS

ANTONOV
OLEG K. ANTONOV DESIGN BUREAU
GENERAL DESIGNER: Pyotr Vasilyevich Balabuyev

This design bureau, based at Kiev, is named after its founder, Oleg Konstantinovich Antonov who, after establishing his reputation with a series of successful glider and sailplane designs, became one of the Soviet Union's leading designers of transport aircraft, particularly those types intended for short field operation. He died on 4 April 1984, at the age of 78.

ANTONOV An-2
NATO reporting name: Colt

Following manufacture of the An-2M specialised agricultural version of this large single-engined biplane, in the mid-sixties, production of the An-2 came to an end at Kiev in the Soviet Union. Details of the various versions that were built can be found in the 1971-72 *Jane's*.

Several versions of the An-2 continued in production under licence in Poland in 1988 (see WSK-PZL Mielec entry). Others have been built at Harbin and elsewhere, in China, under the Chinese designation Y-5.

ANTONOV An-3

It was first reported in the Spring of 1972 that the Antonov design bureau was engaged on design studies for a turboprop development of the An-2 biplane (see WSK-PZL Mielec in Polish section). Designated An-3, the aircraft was intended specifically for agricultural duties and was then expected to compete with the Polish turbofan engined WSK-Mielec M-15 as the next generation agricultural aircraft for use throughout the countries of eastern Europe and the Soviet Union.

At the 1979 Paris Air Show, Mr Oleg Antonov emphasised his continued interest in agricultural aircraft, and confirmed that a prototype of the An-3 had been produced by retrofitting an An-2 with a Glushenkov turboprop, driving a slow turning large-diameter three-blade propeller optimised for an aircraft operating speed of 75-97 knots (140-180 km/h; 87-112 mph). He added that an important feature was the ability of the turboprop to ensure adequate cockpit air-conditioning, with clean air at 18-20°C, during operation in ambient temperatures of 40-45°C.

A photograph of the An-3 prototype (SSSR-30576) under test was released to the East European press in 1979 and was reproduced in the 1982-83 and previous editions of *Jane's*. The production standard aircraft shown in an accompanying illustration differs externally from the standard An-2 in having a longer and slimmer nose, housing a 1,081 kW (1,450 shp) Glushenkov TVD-20 turboprop, and short plugs inserted immediately fore and aft of the wings to lengthen the fuselage. The cockpit is further forward, and is sealed and air-conditioned. Instrumentation, electrical and fuel systems are all new, and the former multi-panelled starboard cockpit windows are replaced by a single large blister window. When equipped for agricultural duties, access to the cockpit is via a small door on the port side. When the aircraft is to be used only for transport duties, this door is omitted and access is via the main cabin door and through the airtight door leading from the cabin to the flight deck.

The An-3 can be equipped for either dusting or spraying. The chemical spraytank has a capacity of 2,200 litres (581 US gallons; 484 Imp gallons), representing an increase of more than 50 per cent over that of the An-2; the cost of spraying each hectare of land is reduced by 25 to 30 per cent. A total of 1,200 litres (317 US gallons; 264 Imp gallons) of fuel is carried in six tanks in the upper wings.

State trials of the An-3 were conducted with renewed urgency in 1982-83, under the project leadership of Mr V. J. Zadrozhnyi, following rejection of the M-15 in the Soviet Union. At their conclusion, a plant in Kiev was assigned the task of converting piston engined An-2s to An-3 standard, using some fuselage components produced by WSK-PZL Mielec. A repair plant for An-3s will be operated at Bulharsk.

Six payload-to-height records were set by an An-3 in 1985. On 12 December, piloted by Vladimir Lysenko, it lifted a record 2,583 kg (5,694 lb) to 2,000 m and set two further Class C1f records by climbing to 6,100 m (20,013 ft) with a payload of 2,000 kg, qualifying also for the record with 1,000 kg. On the following day, piloted by Sergei Gorbik, it lifted 2,375 kg (5,236 lb) to 2,000 m and set two further Class C1e records for 1,000 and 2,000 kg lifted to 6,150 m (20,177 ft).

DIMENSIONS, EXTERNAL: As for An-2, except:
Length overall 14.33 m (47 ft 0 in)
WEIGHT:
Max T-O weight 5,800 kg (12,787 lb)
PERFORMANCE:
Normal cruising speed 97 knots (180 km/h; 112 mph)
Rate of climb at S/L with max payload
240 m (785 ft)/min

ANTONOV An-3M

Details of this much changed proposed agricultural version of the An-3 can be found under the heading of its

Antonov An-3 agricultural biplane (Glushenkov TVD-20 turboprop)

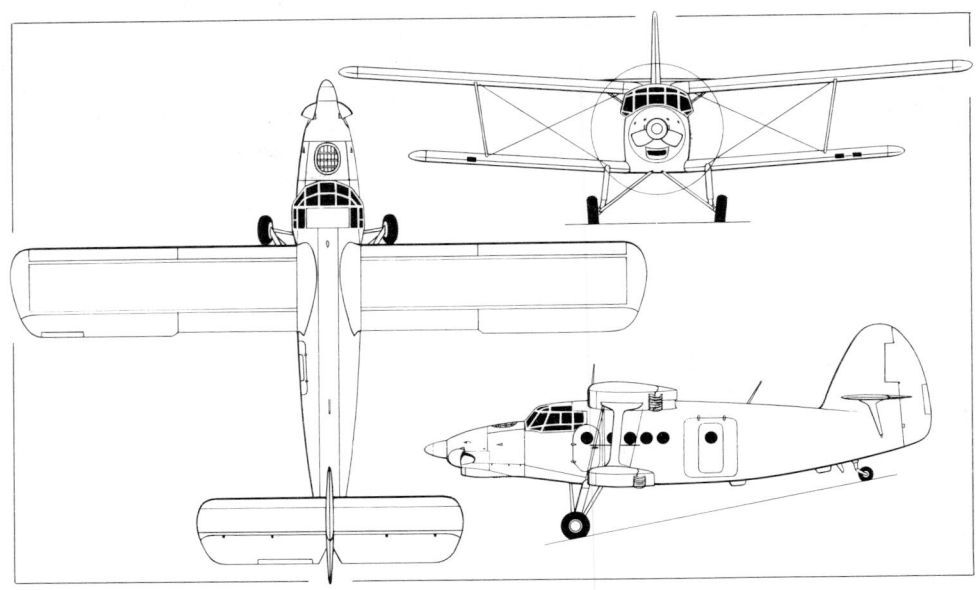
Antonov An-3 turboprop agricultural aircraft, with original flight deck side windows (*Pilot Press*)

ECM version of the Antonov An-12 ('Cub-C'), operated temporarily in Egyptian Air Force insignia

design organisation, WSK-PZL Warszawa-Okecie, in the Polish section of the 1986-87 *Jane's*.

ANTONOV An-12
NATO reporting name: Cub

More than 900 An-12 freighters were built for military and civil use before production ended in the Soviet Union in 1973. Versions in service with the Soviet air forces, and identified by NATO reporting names, are as follows:

Cub. Entered service as standard Soviet paratroop and freight transport in 1959. Replacement with Il-76s has been under way since 1974, but about 150 'Cubs', designated **An-12BP** in the USSR, continue to equip Military Transport Aviation (VTA) units located primarily along the southern and far eastern periphery of the Soviet Union, with 200 more serving in Soviet air armies and air forces of military districts and groups of forces. Another 200 An-12s and Il-76s are operated nominally by Aeroflot, forming an immediately available reserve military transport force.

An-12s are also operated by the air forces of Algeria, China, Czechoslovakia, Ethiopia, India, Iraq, Malagasy Republic, Poland and Yugoslavia. Civil An-12s serve with CAAC (China), Balkan Air and Air Guinée, as well as Aeroflot. 'Cub' has a tail gunner's position. In the refined commercial production version, first demonstrated at the 1965 Paris Air Show, the turret is removed and replaced by a streamline fairing.

China is building, at the Hanzhong factory near Xian, its own version of the An-12BP. Known as the **STAF Y-8**, this is listed in the Chinese section, together with a specialised maritime surveillance version of the Y-8.

Cub-A. Electronic intelligence (elint) version. Generally similar to basic 'Cub' but with blade aerials on front fuselage, aft of flight deck, and other changes.

Cub-B. Conversion of 'Cub' transport for elint duties with Soviet Naval Air Force. Examples photographed over international waters by the crews of Swedish and Norwegian combat aircraft each had two additional blister fairings

Electronic intelligence version of the Antonov An-12 known to NATO as 'Cub-B', with investigating F-104G of Royal Norwegian Air Force

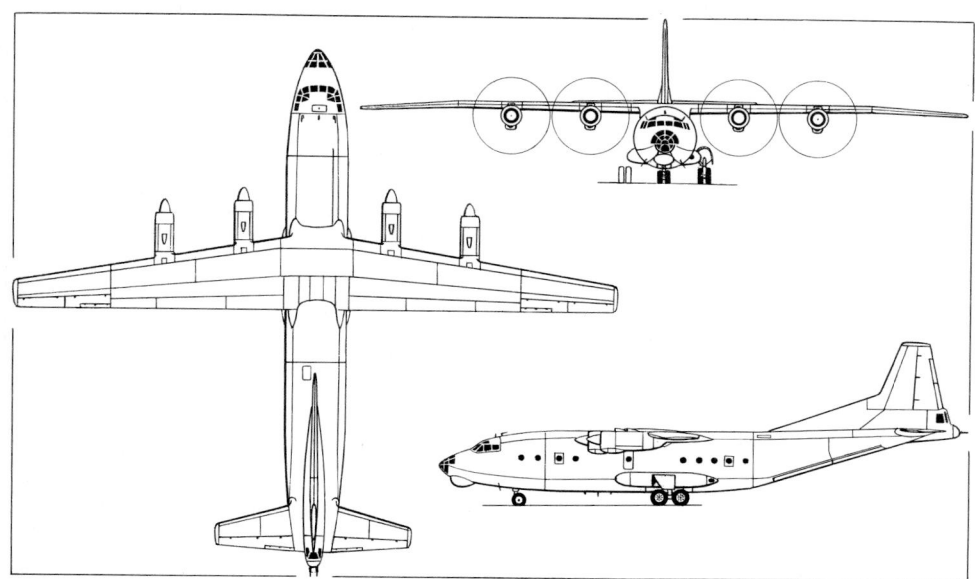

Antonov An-12BP ('Cub') four-turboprop general purpose military transport aircraft *(Pilot Press)*

Wing aspect ratio	11.85
Length overall	33.10 m (108 ft 7¼ in)
Height overall	10.53 m (34 ft 6½ in)
Tailplane span	12.20 m (40 ft 0¼ in)
Wheel track	5.42 m (17 ft 9½ in)
Wheelbase	10.82 m (35 ft 6 in)
Propeller diameter	4.50 m (14 ft 9 in)
Rear loading hatch: Length	7.70 m (25 ft 3 in)
Width	2.95 m (9 ft 8 in)
DIMENSIONS, INTERNAL:	
Cargo hold: Length	13.50 m (44 ft 3½ in)
Max width	3.50 m (11 ft 5¾ in)
Max height	2.60 m (8 ft 6¼ in)
Volume	97.2 m³ (3,432.6 cu ft)
AREA:	
Wings, gross	121.70 m² (1,310 sq ft)
WEIGHTS:	
Weight empty	28,000 kg (61,730 lb)
Max payload	20,000 kg (44,090 lb)
Normal T-O weight	55,100 kg (121,475 lb)
Max T-O weight	61,000 kg (134,480 lb)
PERFORMANCE:	
Max level speed	419 knots (777 km/h; 482 mph)
Max cruising speed	361 knots (670 km/h; 416 mph)
Min flying speed	88 knots (163 km/h; 101 mph)
Landing speed	108 knots (200 km/h; 124 mph)
Max rate of climb at S/L	600 m (1,970 ft)/min
Service ceiling	10,200 m (33,500 ft)
T-O run	700 m (2,300 ft)
Landing run	500 m (1,640 ft)
Range:	
with max payload	1,942 nm (3,600 km; 2,236 miles)
with max fuel	3,075 nm (5,700 km; 3,540 miles)

under forward and centre fuselage, plus other antennae. About 10 produced.

Cub-C. ECM variant carrying several tons of electrical generation, distribution and control gear in cabin, and palletised jammers for at least five wavebands faired into belly, plus ECM dispensers. Glazed nose and undernose radar of transport retained. An ogival 'solid' fuselage tailcone, housing electronic equipment, is fitted in place of the usual gun position.

Cub-D. This further variant of the An-12 reflects the huge efforts being made by the Soviet Union to ensure effective handling of every conceivable ECM task. Equipment differs from that of 'Cub-C', to handle different active countermeasures duties. Up to 25 'Cub-C and D' aircraft are believed to serve with the Soviet Navy.

In addition to these operational variants, An-12s have been modified extensively as testbeds for advanced avionics. Illustrations of such aircraft can be found in the 1986-87 and previous editions of *Jane's*.

The following abbreviated details apply to the standard Soviet built military An-12BP transport. A full description can be found in the 1979-80 *Jane's*.

TYPE: Four-engined cargo transport.
POWER PLANT: Four 2,983 kW (4,000 ehp) Ivchenko AI-20K turboprops, driving AV-68 four-blade reversible-pitch propellers. All fuel in 22 bag tanks in wings, total normal capacity 13,900 litres (3,672 US gallons; 3,058 Imp gallons). Max capacity 18,100 litres (4,781 US gallons; 3,981 Imp gallons).
ACCOMMODATION: Pilot and co-pilot side by side on flight deck. Engineer's station on starboard side, behind co-pilot. Radio operator in well behind pilot, facing outward. Navigator in glazed nose compartment. Rear gunner in tail turret. Crew door on port side forward of wing. No integral rear loading ramp. Access to freight hold via large door under upswept rear fuselage, comprising two longitudinal halves which can be hinged upward inside cabin to provide access for direct loading

of freight from trucks. Undersurface of fuselage aft of this door is formed by a further, rear-hinged, door which retracts upward into fuselage to facilitate loading and unloading. Equipped to carry 90 troops or 60 paratroops, all of whom can be despatched in under one minute, with rear door panels folded upward.
ARMAMENT: Two 23 mm NR-23 guns in tail turret.
DIMENSIONS, EXTERNAL:

Wing span	38.00 m (124 ft 8 in)
Wing chord (mean)	3.452 m (11 ft 4 in)

ANTONOV An-22 ANTHEUS
NATO reporting name: Cock

The prototype of this very large transport aircraft flew for the first time on 27 February 1965. About 55 production An-22s remain in service with the Soviet air forces and Aeroflot, which uses the aircraft primarily for military

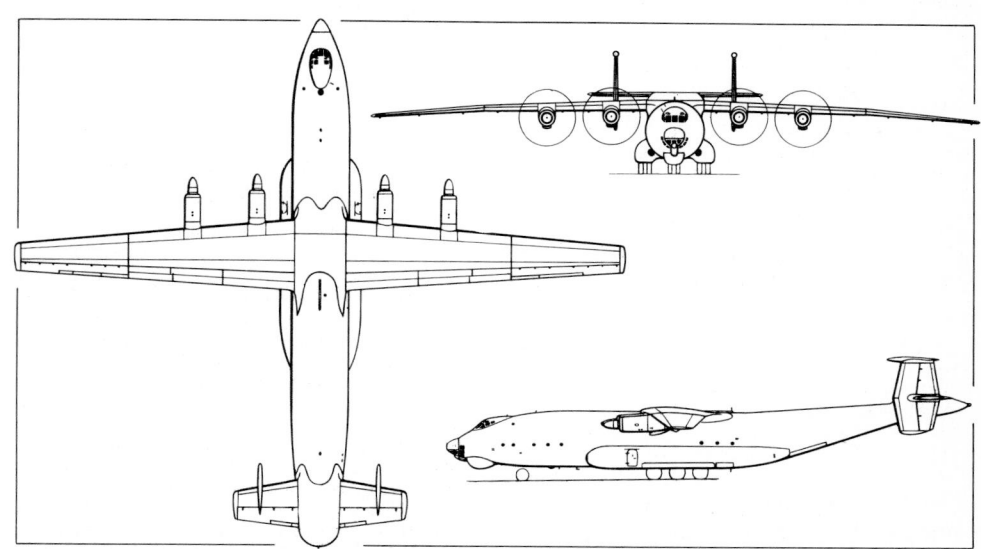

Antonov An-22 Antheus long-range heavy transport aircraft *(Pilot Press)*

Antonov An-22 Antheus long-range heavy transport aircraft (four Kuznetsov NK-12MA turboprops) *(Tass)*

support duties. Deliveries were completed during 1974, but the diminishing force of An-22s provided the only Soviet transports capable of airlifting tanks as large as the T-62, pending the introduction into service of the An-124 (NATO 'Condor'). A structural description can be found in the 1982-83 and earlier editions.

One An-22 has been adapted to deliver the wings of production An-124 transports non-stop over the 1,693 nm (3,136 km; 1,949 mile) route from Tashkent, where they are built, to the assembly plant in Kiev. Each port or starboard wing is carried on a mount above the centre-section, in such a way that flexing of the An-22 in flight is not transmitted to the An-124 wing structure. Addition of a small central tail fin was the only modification needed to preserve the handling qualities of the An-22 when carrying a wing in this manner.

TYPE: Long-range heavy turboprop transport.

POWER PLANT: Four 11,186 kW (15,000 shp) Kuznetsov NK-12MA turboprops, each driving a pair of four-blade contra-rotating propellers.

ACCOMMODATION: Crew of five or six. Navigator's station in nose. Cabin for 28-29 passengers aft of flight deck, separated from main cabin by bulkhead containing two doors. Uninterrupted main cabin, with reinforced titanium floor, tiedown fittings and rear loading ramp. When ramp lowers, a large door which forms the underside of the rear fuselage retracts upward inside fuselage to permit easy loading of tall vehicles. Rails in roof of cabin for four travelling gantries continue rearward on underside of this door. Two winches, used in conjunction with the gantries, each have a capacity of 2,500 kg (5,500 lb). Door in each landing gear fairing, forward of wheels, for crew and passengers.

DIMENSIONS, EXTERNAL:
Wing span	64.40 m (211 ft 4 in)
Length overall	approx 57.92 m (190 ft 0 in)
Height overall	12.53 m (41 ft 1½ in)
Propeller diameter	6.20 m (20 ft 4 in)

DIMENSIONS, INTERNAL:
Main cabin: Length	33.0 m (108 ft 3 in)
Max width	4.4 m (14 ft 5 in)
Max height	4.4 m (14 ft 5 in)

AREA:
Wings, gross	345 m² (3,713 sq ft)

WEIGHTS:
Weight empty, equipped	114,000 kg (251,325 lb)
Max payload	80,000 kg (176,350 lb)
Max fuel	43,000 kg (94,800 lb)
Max T-O weight	250,000 kg (551,160 lb)

PERFORMANCE:
Max level speed	399 knots (740 km/h; 460 mph)
T-O run	1,300 m (4,260 ft)
Landing run	800 m (2,620 ft)
Range with max fuel and 45,000 kg (99,200 lb) payload	5,905 nm (10,950 km; 6,800 miles)
Range with max payload	2,692 nm (5,000 km; 3,100 miles)

ANTONOV An-24
NATO reporting name: Coke

Production of the An-24 in the Soviet Union ended in 1978, after about 1,100 had been delivered. A version known as the **Y-7** (which see) continues in production at Xian in China.

ANTONOV An-26
NATO reporting name: Curl

First displayed in public at the 1969 Paris Air Show, the An-26 is generally similar to the earlier An-24RT specialised freighter, with an auxiliary turbojet in the starboard engine nacelle, but has more powerful AI-24T turboprop engines and a completely redesigned rear fuselage of the 'beaver-tail' type. This embodies Oleg Antonov's special type of loading ramp, which forms the underside of the rear fuselage when retracted, in the usual way, but can be slid forward under the rear of the cabin to facilitate direct loading, or when the cargo is to be airdropped.

There are two versions:

An-26. Original version, with electrically/manually operated conveyor built in flush with cabin floor to facilitate movement of freight.

An-26B. Improved version, announced in 1981. Equipped to carry three standard freight pallets, each 2.438 m (8 ft) long, 1.46 m (4 ft 9½ in) wide and 1.60 m (5 ft 3 in) high, with a total weight of 5,500 kg (12,125 lb). Rollgangs on floor, mechanism to move the pallets, and moorings, enable two men to load and unload all three pallets in 30

min. Rollgangs can be stowed against sides of cabin.

Although intended primarily for cargo carrying, the An-26 can be adapted easily for passenger, ambulance or paratroop transport duties. It has been exported to at least 27 Warsaw Pact and other foreign air forces. Examples operated by Angolan government forces are reported to have been used for bombing missions, and one of the Mozambique An-26s has been photographed with a bomb rack on the fuselage below each wingroot trailing-edge. Aeroflot has more than 200, which are available to supplement the military An-26s assigned to air commands in Soviet regiments and squadrons. Others have been supplied to Cubana, Aerocaribbean of Cuba, Syrianair and Tarom of Romania. The Chinese built **Y-14** version is described in the Addenda.

TYPE: Twin-turboprop pressurised short-haul transport.

WINGS: Cantilever high-wing monoplane, with 2° anhedral on outer panels. Incidence 3°. Sweepback at quarter-chord on outer panels 6° 50′; at leading-edge 9° 41′. Conventional all-metal two-spar structure, with ribs and stringers, built in five sections: centre-section, two inner wings and two detachable outer wings. Wing skin is attached by electrical spot welding. Mass balanced servo compensated ailerons, with large trim tabs of glassfibre construction. Hydraulically operated, tracked and slotted TsAGI flaps along entire wing trailing-edges inboard of unpowered ailerons; single-slotted flaps on centre-section, double-slotted outboard of nacelles. Servo tab and electrically operated trim tab in each aileron. Bleed-air thermal de-icing system.

FUSELAGE: Semi-monocoque aluminium alloy structure in front, centre and rear portions, of bonded/welded construction. Skin on lower portion of fuselage is made of 'bimetal' (duralumin-titanium) sheet for protection during operations from unpaved airfields. Blister on each side forward of rear loading ramp, carrying tracks to enable ramp to slide forward under fuselage.

TAIL UNIT: Cantilever all-metal structure, with large dorsal fin, ventral fin strake on each side of rear ramp. 9° dihedral on tailplane. All controls manually operated. Manually operated trim tab in each elevator. Electrically operated combined trim/servo tab in rudder. All leading-edges incorporate bleed-air thermal de-icing system.

Antonov An-26 transport of the Hungarian Air Force in landing configuration *(Press Office Sturzenegger)*

LANDING GEAR: Hydraulically retractable tricycle type, with twin wheels on each unit. Emergency extension by gravity. All units retract forward. Shock absorbers of oleo-nitrogen type on main units; nitrogen-pneumatic type on nose unit. Mainwheel tyres size 1,050 × 400, pressure 5.9 bars (85 lb/sq in). Nosewheel tyres size 700 × 250, pressure 3.9 bars (57 lb/sq in). Mainwheels fitted with hydraulic disc brakes and anti-skid units. Nosewheels can be steered hydraulically through 45° each side while taxying and are controllable through ±10° during take-off and landing.

POWER PLANT: Two 2,103 kW (2,820 ehp) Ivchenko AI-24VT turboprops, each driving a four-blade constant-speed fully-feathering propeller. Electric de-icing system for propeller blades and hubs; hot air system for engine air intakes. One 7.85 kN (1,765 lb st) RU 19A-300 auxiliary turbojet in starboard nacelle for use, as required, at take-off, during climb and in level flight, and for self-contained starting of main engines. Two independent but interconnected fuel systems, with 5,500 kg (12,125 lb) of fuel, contained in integral tanks in inner wings and ten bag tanks in centre-section. Pressure refuelling socket in starboard engine nacelle. Gravity fuelling point above each tank area. Carbon dioxide inert gas system to create fireproof condition inside fuel tanks.

ACCOMMODATION: Basic crew of five (pilot, co-pilot, radio operator, flight engineer and navigator), with station at rear of cabin on starboard side for loading supervisor or load dispatcher. Optional domed observation window for navigator on port side of flight deck. Electric de-icing system for windscreens. Toilet on port side aft of flight deck; crew door, small galley and oxygen bottle stowage on starboard side. Emergency escape hatch in door immediately aft of flight deck. Large downward hinged rear ramp/door, hinged to an anchorage mounted on tracks running forward under the blister fairings. This enables ramp/door to slide forward under fuselage for direct loading on to cabin floor or for airdropping of freight. When doing so, its rear is supported by the pivoted swinging arm on each side which also raises and lowers door in the alternative fixed-hinge mode. Door can be locked in any intermediate position. Electrically powered mobile winch, capacity 2,000 kg (4,409 lb), hoists crates through rear entrance and runs on a rail in the cabin ceiling to position payload in cabin. Electrically and manually operated conveyor, capacity 4,500 kg (9,920 lb), built-in flush with cabin floor of original An-26, facilitates loading and airdropping of freight. An-26B has removable rollgangs, mechanism for moving pallets inside hold, and moorings (see introductory notes). Both versions can accommodate a variety of motor vehicles, including GAZ-69 and UAZ-469 military vehicles, or cargo items up to 1.50 m (59 in) high by 2.10 m (82.6 in) wide. Height of rear edge of cargo door surround above the cabin floor is 1.50 m (4 ft 11 in). Cabin is pressurised and air-conditioned, and can be fitted with a row of tip-up seats along each wall to accommodate a total of 38 to 40 persons. Conversion to troop transport role, or to an ambulance for 24 stretcher patients and a medical attendant, takes 20 to 30 min in the field.

SYSTEMS: Air-conditioning system uses hot air tapped from the 10th compressor stage of each engine, with a heat exchanger and turbocooler in each nacelle. Cabin pressure differential 0.29 bars (4.27 lb/sq in). Main and emergency hydraulic systems, pressure 151.7 bars (2,200 lb/sq in), for landing gear retraction, nosewheel steering, flaps, brakes, windscreen wipers, propeller feathering and operation of cargo ramp and emergency escape doors. Handpump to operate doors only and build up pressure in main system. Electrical system includes two 27V DC starter/generators on engines, a standby generator on the auxiliary turbojet, and three storage batteries for emergency use. Two engine driven alternators provide 115V 400Hz single-phase AC supply, with standby inverter. Basic source of 36V 400Hz three-phase AC supply is two inverters, with standby transformer. Permanent oxygen system for pilot, installed equipment for other crew members and three portable bottles for personnel in cargo hold.

AVIONICS AND EQUIPMENT: Standard com/nav avionics comprise two VHF transceivers, HF, intercom, two ADF, radio altimeter, glidepath receiver, glideslope receiver, marker beacon receiver, weather/navigation radar, directional gyro and flight recorder. Optional equipment includes a flight director system, astrocompass and autopilot. Standard operational equipment includes parachute static line attachments and retraction devices, tiedowns, jack to support ramp sill, flight deck curtains, sun visors and windscreen wipers. Optional items include OPB-1R sight for pinpoint dropping of freight, medical equipment, and liquid heating system.

DIMENSIONS, EXTERNAL:

Wing span	29.20 m (95 ft 9½ in)
Wing aspect ratio	11.7
Length overall	23.80 m (78 ft 1 in)
Height overall	8.575 m (28 ft 1½ in)
Width of fuselage	2.90 m (9 ft 6 in)
Depth of fuselage	2.50 m (8 ft 2½ in)
Tailplane span	9.973 m (32 ft 8¾ in)
Wheel track (c/l shock struts)	7.90 m (25 ft 11 in)
Wheelbase	7.651 m (25 ft 1¼ in)

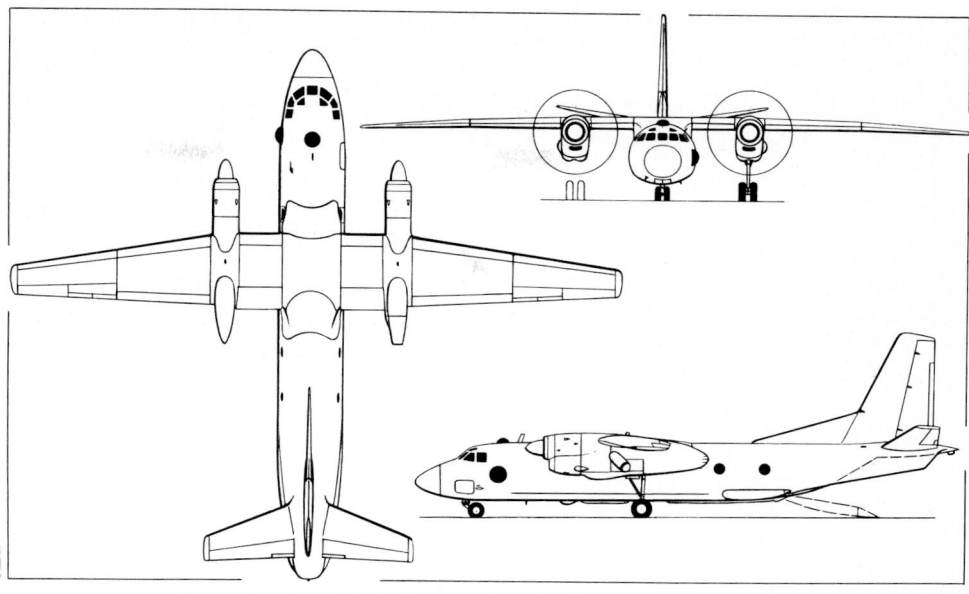

Antonov An-26 twin-turboprop short-haul transport *(Pilot Press)*

Propeller diameter	3.90 m (12 ft 9½ in)
Propeller ground clearance	1.227 m (4 ft 0¼ in)
Crew door (stbd, front): Height	1.40 m (4 ft 7 in)
Width	0.60 m (1 ft 11¾ in)
Height to sill	1.47 m (4 ft 9¾ in)
Loading hatch (rear): Length	3.40 m (11 ft 1¾ in)
Width at front	2.40 m (7 ft 10½ in)
Width at rear	2.00 m (6 ft 6¾ in)
Height to sill	1.47 m (4 ft 9¾ in)
Height to top edge of hatchway	3.014 m (9 ft 10¾ in)
Emergency exit (in floor at front):	
Length	1.02 m (3 ft 4¼ in)
Width	0.70 m (2 ft 3½ in)
Emergency exit (top): Diameter	0.65 m (2 ft 1½ in)
Emergency exits (one each side of hold):	
Height	0.60 m (1 ft 11¾ in)
Width	0.50 m (1 ft 7½ in)

DIMENSIONS, INTERNAL:

Cargo hold: Length of floor	11.50 m (37 ft 8¾ in)
Width of floor	2.40 m (7 ft 10½ in)
Max height	1.91 m (6 ft 3 in)

AREAS:

Wings, gross	74.98 m² (807.1 sq ft)
Horizontal tail surfaces (total)	19.83 m² (213.45 sq ft)
Vertical tail surfaces (total, incl dorsal fin)	15.85 m² (170.61 sq ft)

WEIGHTS:

Weight empty	15,020 kg (33,113 lb)
Normal payload	4,500 kg (9,920 lb)
Max payload	5,500 kg (12,125 lb)
Normal T-O and landing weight	23,000 kg (50,706 lb)
Max T-O and landing weight	24,000 kg (52,911 lb)

PERFORMANCE (at normal T-O weight):

Cruising speed at 6,000 m (19,675 ft)	237 knots (440 km/h; 273 mph)
T-O speed	108 knots (200 km/h; 124 mph) CAS
Landing speed	102 knots (190 km/h; 118 mph) CAS
Max rate of climb at S/L	480 m (1,575 ft)/min
Service ceiling	7,500 m (24,600 ft)
T-O run, on concrete	780 m (2,559 ft)
T-O to 15 m (50 ft)	1,240 m (4,068 ft)
Landing from 15 m (50 ft)	1,740 m (5,709 ft)
Landing run, on concrete	730 m (2,395 ft)

Min ground turning radius	22.3 m (73 ft 2 in)
Range, no reserves:	
with max payload	594 nm (1,100 km; 683 miles)
with max fuel	1,376 nm (2,550 km; 1,584 miles)

ANTONOV An-28
NATO reporting name: Cash

Responsibility for An-28 production has been allocated to the WSK-PZL Mielec works in Poland (see Polish section).

ANTONOV An-30
NATO reporting name: Clank

The An-30 aerial survey aeroplane was developed from the An-24RT and An-26 twin-turboprop transports, to which it is generally similar. The major modifications are made to the nose, which is extensively glazed to give the navigator a wide field of view, and to the flight deck, which is raised to provide access to the navigator's compartment. There are fewer windows in the main cabin, which contains a darkroom and film storage cupboard, as well as survey cameras and a control desk. Other amenities include a toilet, buffet and crew rest area with armchairs and couches. All accommodation is pressurised and air-conditioned.

Photography can be automatic or semi-automatic if required, but two photographer/surveyors are normally carried, in addition to a flight crew of five (pilot, co-pilot, flight engineer, radio operator and navigator).

For the primary task of air photography for map-making, the An-30 is equipped with large survey cameras. These are mounted in the cabin above glazed apertures, of which there are five, each covered by a door. A crew photographer uncovers the apertures, as required, by remote control from his desk in the aircraft.

Standard equipment includes radio topographic distance measuring equipment and a radio altimeter, with recording units. The pre-programmed flight path of the aircraft over the area to be photographed is fed into an onboard computer, controlled from the navigator's station, which maintains the correct speed, altitude and direction of flight throughout the mission. The cartographic An-30 has an AFA-41/7.5 wide-angle camera, in a TAU-M gyro-stabilised mounting, over No. 1 aperture; and an A54/50-

Antonov An-30 aerial survey development of the An-24 twin-turboprop transport *(Air Portraits)*

Antonov An-32/AI-20DM of the Indian Air Force, by which it is known as the Sutlej *(Franz Knuchel)*

FK long focal length camera over No. 3 aperture, each mounted vertically. Two further A54/50-FK cameras take oblique photographs at 28° to the vertical, port and starboard, through Nos. 4 and 5 apertures, and an SU-5 lightmeter is positioned over No. 2 window. One photogrammetric version has a vertically mounted AFA-41/7.5 camera in a TAU-M mount and an AFA-41/10 or AFA-41/20 camera in a fixed vertical mount. Another has the same installation without the gyroscopic mounting. A fourth variation offers an AFA-41/7.5 and an AFA-42/20, both in fixed mountings.

If required, the cameras can be replaced by other kinds of survey equipment, such as those used for mineral prospecting or for microwave radiometer survey, which measures the heat emission of land and ocean to obtain data on ocean surface characteristics, sea and lake ice, snow cover, flooding, seasonal vegetation changes, and soil types.

The power plant comprises two 2,103 kW (2,820 ehp) Ivchenko AI-24VT turboprops, with water injection, each driving an AV-72T four-blade constant-speed fully-feathering and reversible-pitch propeller. Main engines are supplemented by a 7.85 kN (1,765 lb st) RU 19A-300 auxiliary turbojet in the rear of the starboard engine nacelle. The latter is used for engine starting, and for take-off, climb and cruise power in the event of failure of one of the primary engines. Max fuel capacity is 6,200 litres (1,638 US gallons; 1,364 Imp gallons).

The An-30 can be converted into a transport aircraft by placing cover plates over the camera apertures. It retains the standard An-24 cabin door, on the port side of the fuselage at the rear, together with the standard forward freight compartment door on the starboard side and the load hoisting/conveying system. A version designated **An-30M** has been mentioned in the Soviet press, equipped for 'cloud seeding' to protect vulnerable areas from heavy rainfall.

The prototype An-30 flew for the first time in 1974. Operators include Balkan Bulgarian Airlines, CAAC of China and the Romanian Air Force, which has three. At least ten have been reported in Aeroflot markings.

DIMENSIONS, EXTERNAL:
Wing span	29.20 m (95 ft 9½ in)
Wing aspect ratio	11.4
Length overall	24.26 m (79 ft 7 in)
Height overall	8.32 m (27 ft 3½ in)
Tailplane span	9.09 m (29 ft 10 in)
Fuselage, nominal diameter	2.90 m (9 ft 6¼ in)
Wheel track (c/l of oleos)	7.90 m (25 ft 11 in)
Wheelbase	7.65 m (25 ft 1¼ in)
Propeller diameter	3.90 m (12 ft 9½ in)
Propeller ground clearance	1.20 m (3 ft 11¼ in)

AREAS:
Wings, gross	74.98 m² (807.1 sq ft)
Horizontal tail surfaces (total)	17.23 m² (185.46 sq ft)
Vertical tail surfaces (total, incl dorsal fin)	
	15.85 m² (170.61 sq ft)

WEIGHTS:
Basic operating weight	15,590 kg (34,370 lb)
Weight of aerial photography equipment	
	650 kg (1,433 lb)
Max T-O and landing weight	23,000 kg (50,706 lb)

PERFORMANCE:
Max level speed	291 knots (540 km/h; 335 mph)
Cruising speed at 6,000 m (19,685 ft)	
	232 knots (430 km/h; 267 mph)
Landing speed	95 knots (175 km/h; 109 mph)
Service ceiling:	
with APU operating	8,300 m (27,230 ft)
without APU	7,300 m (23,950 ft)
T-O run on concrete	710 m (2,330 ft)
Landing run on concrete	670 m (2,198 ft)
Range with max fuel, no reserves	
	1,420 nm (2,630 km; 1,634 miles)

ANTONOV An-32
NATO reporting name: Cline
Indian Air Force name: Sutlej

This pressurised short/medium-range transport, of which first details were released in May 1977, is a developed version of the An-26, with a generally similar airframe, except for having triple-slotted trailing-edge flaps outboard of the nacelles, automatic leading-edge slats, much enlarged ventral fins and a full span slotted tailplane. Improvements have also been made to the landing gear retraction mechanism, the de-icing and air conditioning systems, the electrical system and engine starting. In all, about 40 per cent of the subsystems, installations and units have been changed.

Two versions are available, differing only in the type of Ivchenko AI-20M turboprop fitted, as follows:

An-32/AI-20M. With two AI-20M engines, each rated at 3,128 kW (4,195 ehp) and driving a four-blade propeller, for operation in moderate climatic conditions.

An-32/AI-20DM. With two AI-20DM Series 5 engines, each rated at 3,812 kW (5,112 ehp), for operation under high temperature conditions, or from high altitude airfields.

The large increase in power compared with the An-26 is intended specifically to improve take-off performance, service ceiling and payload. Thus, the 'hot and high' version with AI-20DM engines is able to operate from airfields 4,000-4,500 m (13,125-14,750 ft) above sea level in an ambient temperature of ISA+ 25°C, and can transport 3 tonnes of freight over a 594 nm (1,100 km; 683 mile) stage length, with fuel reserves. The overwing location of the engines requires nacelles of considerable depth, as the main landing gear units continue to retract into the underwing portions. The nacelles terminated at mid-chord above the wing on the prototype, but extend beyond the trailing-edge on production An-32s.

Low pressure tyres (of the same sizes as those on the An-26) permit operation from unpaved strips. Maximum tyre pressure is 3.9 bars (57 lb/sq in) on the nosewheels and 5.9 bars (85 lb/sq in) on the mainwheels. All shock absorbers are of the oleo-nitrogen type. The high position of the engines reduces the possibility of stone or debris ingestion. A TG-16M APU, housed in the rear of the starboard landing gear fairing, helps to make the An-32 independent of ground servicing equipment by providing onboard engine starting capability at airfields up to 4,500 m (14,750 ft) above sea level.

A rear loading hatch and forward-sliding ramp/door, similar to those of the An-26, are retained, as well as a hoist with increased capacity of 3,000 kg (6,615 lb), to facilitate handling of the maximum payload of more than 6 tonnes of freight on 12 pallets. Cargo or vehicles can be airdropped by parachute, including extraction of large loads by drag parachute, with the aid of removable roller conveyors and guide rails on the floor of the hold. The air-conditioned and pressurised accommodation enables alternative payloads to include 50 passengers or 42 parachutists and a jumpmaster, on a row of tip-up seats along each cabin wall, or 24 stretcher patients and up to three medical personnel; the normal crew of three comprises pilot, co-pilot and navigator, with provision for a flight engineer.

Designed life of the airframe is 20,000 flying hours, 15,000 landings or 15 years; that of the AI-20M engine is 20,000 hours, of the AI-20DM 3,000 hours.

The prototype An-32 was exhibited at the 1977 Paris Air Show. No photographs have yet identified production aircraft in Soviet air force service, but India began taking delivery of 118 of the version with AI-20DM engines (named **Sutlej** after a Punjabi river) in 1984. Peru has 15, which have been seen with four racks for bombs, two on each side of the fuselage below the wings. Other orders are understood to have been received from Cape Verde, Sao Tome and Principe, and Tanzania.

The ability of the An-32 to lift heavy payloads at high altitudes was demonstrated by flights which set 14 official records for Group II (turboprop) aircraft in the Autumn of 1985. A climb to 11,760 m (38,583 ft) on 25 October set payload to height records with payloads of 1,000 and 2,000 kg in Classes C1 and C1j. On 5 November, further records in these Classes were set by a climb to 11,230 m (36,844 ft) with a 5,000 kg payload. A Class C1j height record of 12,010 m (39,403 ft) was set on 24 October, and a Class C1j record of 11,530 m (37,828 ft) for sustained height in horizontal flight on 21 October. Six records in Class C1k were for a climb to 10,940 m (35,892 ft) on 24 October; a sustained height of 10,420 m (34,186 ft) in horizontal flight on 21 October; climbs to 11,120 m (36,483 ft) with 1,000 kg payload and to 10,890 m (35,728 ft) with 2,000 kg on 28 October, and to 10,510 m (34,482 ft) with 5,000 kg on 4

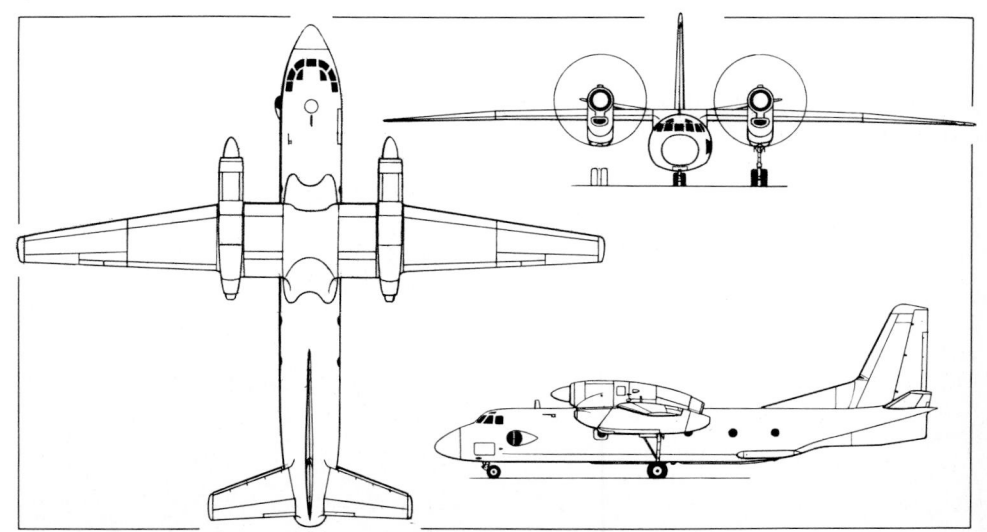

Antonov An-32 short/medium-range transport (two Ivchenko AI-20DM turboprops) *(Pilot Press)*

November; and a record payload of 7,256 kg (15,996 lb) lifted to 2,000 m on 4 November. The flights, near Kiev, were made by various two-man teams of test pilots Alexander Tkachenko, Vladimir Lysenko, Petr Kiritchuk, Yuri Kurlin and Georgi Pobol.

DIMENSIONS, EXTERNAL:
As for An-26, except:

Length overall	23.78 m (78 ft 0¼ in)
Height overall	8.75 m (28 ft 8½ in)
Tailplane span	10.23 m (33 ft 6¾ in)
Propeller diameter: AI-20M	4.50 m (14 ft 9 in)
AI-20DM	4.70 m (15 ft 5 in)
Propeller ground clearance	1.55 m (5 ft 1 in)

DIMENSIONS, INTERNAL:

Cargo hold: Length	15.68 m (51 ft 5¼ in)
Max width	2.78 m (9 ft 1¼ in)
Max height	1.84 m (6 ft 0½ in)
Volume	66.0 m³ (2,330 cu ft)

AREAS:

Wings, gross	74.98 m² (807.1 sq ft)
Ailerons (total)	6.12 m² (65.88 sq ft)
Flaps (total)	15.00 m² (161.46 sq ft)
Horizontal tail surfaces (total)	20.30 m² (218.5 sq ft)
Vertical tail surfaces (total, incl dorsal fin)	17.22 m² (185.36 sq ft)

WEIGHTS:

Weight empty	16,800 kg (37,038 lb)
Weight empty, equipped	17,308 kg (38,158 lb)
Max payload	6,700 kg (14,770 lb)
Max fuel	5,445 kg (12,004 lb)
Max fuel with max payload	2,267 kg (4,998 lb)
Max ramp weight	27,250 kg (60,075 lb)
Max T-O weight	27,000 kg (59,525 lb)
Max landing weight	25,000 kg (55,115 lb)

PERFORMANCE (AI-20DM engines):

Max cruising speed	286 knots (530 km/h; 329 mph)
Econ cruising speed	254 knots (470 km/h; 292 mph)
Landing speed	100 knots (185 km/h; 115 mph)
Optimum cruising height	8,000 m (26,250 ft)
Service ceiling	9,500 m (31,165 ft)
Service ceiling, one engine out	4,800 m (15,750 ft)
T-O run on concrete	760 m (2,495 ft)
T-O to 15 m (50 ft)	1,200 m (3,940 ft)
Landing run	470 m (1,542 ft)
Range, no reserves:	
with max payload	1,080 nm (2,000 km; 1,242 miles)
with 3,700 kg (8,157 lb) payload	1,350 nm (2,500 km; 1,553 miles)

ANTONOV An-72 and An-74
NATO reporting name: Coaler

Two prototypes of the An-72 twin-turbofan STOL transport were built, plus a third airframe for static testing. Photographs of one of these aircraft (SSSR-19774) were released by the Soviet Tass news agency shortly after the first flight of an An-72 on 22 December 1977. Details and photographs of the prototypes have appeared in previous editions of *Jane's*. In its current series production form, the An-72 airframe is identical to that of the An-74, with extended wing span, lengthened fuselage and other refinements. These basic configurations are identified by the following NATO reporting names:

Coaler-A. An-72 prototypes, with constant taper on short-span outer wing panels, and short fuselage. Wing span 25.83 m (84 ft 9 in), length overall 26.576 m (87 ft 2¼ in). Described fully in 1986-87 *Jane's*, together with details of many records set by 'Coaler-A'.

Coaler-B. Production **An-74**, with redesigned outer wings and lengthened fuselage, as described in detail. Flight

crew of four, more advanced navigation aids, including inertial navigation system, and provision for wheel/ski landing gear for polar operations. Distinguishable from 'Coaler-C' by larger radome that does not follow curve of fuselage undersurface. Scheduled for certification in 1988.

Coaler-C. Production **An-72** light STOL transport for military or civil operation. Crew of two on flight deck. Less extensive navigation equipment. Conventional landing gear. Otherwise identical with 'Coaler-B'.

Design features of 'Coaler-C' make it uniquely suited to its primary role, as a STOL replacement for the turboprop An-26, with the emphasis on freight carrying. Its low pressure tyres and multi-wheel landing gear enable it to operate from unprepared airfields, or from surfaces covered with ice or snow; and the high-set engines avoid problems caused by foreign object ingestion. The exhaust efflux is ejected over the upper surface of the wing and down over very large multi-slotted flaps. By taking advantage of the so-called 'Coanda effect', which causes the airflow to 'attach to' the extended flaps, a considerable increase in lift can be achieved. 'Coaler-C', like 'Coaler-B', has a ramp/door of the kind fitted to the An-26, which can be hinged down conventionally to allow wheeled or tracked vehicles to be driven into the hold or, alternatively, can slide forward under the fuselage to permit direct loading from a truck.

Particular care was taken to ensure easy handling in the air. 'Coaler-C's' Doppler based automatic navigation system, linked to an onboard computer, is pre-programmed before take-off on a push-button panel to the right of the large cockpit map display. Failure warning panels above the windscreen display red lights for critical failures, yellow lights for non-critical failures, to minimise the time that needs to be spent on monitoring instruments and equipment.

First details of the An-74 were given in February 1984, when the Soviet newspaper *Pravda* referred to it as a new transport intended for operation in the Arctic and Antarctic regions. The report stated that, unlike the Il-18D turboprop transports used to carry men and equipment between Leningrad and the Antarctic base of Molodejnaya, the An-74 can have a wheel-ski landing gear for operation on

snow and ice landing strips. It was described as an all-weather aircraft, equipped with the latest available radio navigation aids, and with de-icing equipment on the wings, tail unit and engine air intakes. In the Polar regions, its duties will include assistance in setting up scientific stations on Arctic ice floes, airdropping supplies to motorised trans-Antarctic expeditions, and reconnaissance to observe changes in the icefields. First demonstration of its capabilities was given on 14 March 1986, when an An-74 touched down alongside the Arctic drifting research station Severny Polus 27 (North Pole 27) and pulled up within 300 m (985 ft), to lift to safety 27 men whose 900 m (2,950 ft) runway had been split into two sections as the icefield broke up.

Examples of 'Coaler' have been seen in military camouflage. An AEW&C version is flying and has received the NATO reporting name 'Madcap' (see separate entry).

The following details apply to 'Coaler-B and C', as described in publicity brochures from Aviaexport:

TYPE: Twin-turbofan light STOL transport.

WINGS: Cantilever high-wing monoplane, with 17° sweep-back on leading-edge. Straight trailing-edge on inner panels. Tapered outer panels have modest trailing-edge sweepback. Multi-spar structure. Short constant chord centre-section, without dihedral or anhedral, mounted above fuselage to avoid encroaching on internal space. Approx 10° anhedral on outer panels. Wing upper surface blowing requires engines to be mounted above and forward of wings, to exhaust over upper surface. Aft of nacelles, wing skin, spoilers and flaps made of titanium. Hydraulically actuated full span leading-edge flaps outboard of nacelles, embodying thermal anti-icing. Wide span trailing-edge flaps, double-slotted in exhaust efflux, triple-slotted between nacelles and outer wing panels. Normal T-O flap setting 25-30°; max deflection 60°. Four-section spoilers forward of triple-slotted flaps on each side; two outer sections on each side raised before landing, remainder opened automatically on touchdown by sensors actuated by weight on main landing gear. Conventional mechanically actuated ailerons inset on outer wing panels. Two tabs in port aileron, one in starboard aileron.

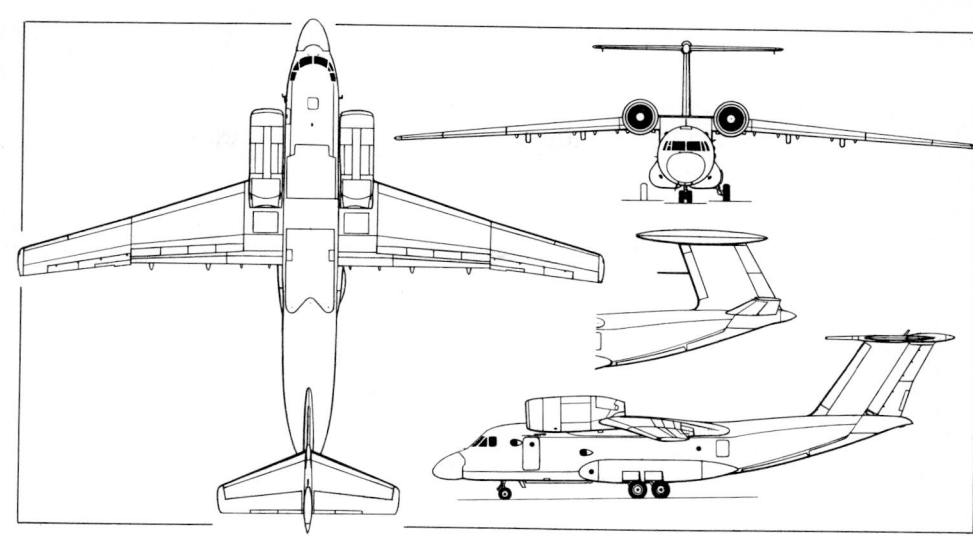

Antonov An-74 ('Coaler-B') STOL transport, with scrap view of 'Madcap' rotodome *(Pilot Press)*

Antonov An-74 ('Coaler-B') twin-turbofan STOL transport *(Paul Jackson)*

FUSELAGE: Conventional all-metal semi-monocoque structure of circular cross-section. Underside of upswept rear fuselage formed by ramp/door, which can hinge downward conventionally or slide forward under fuselage to permit direct loading of hold from truck. Underfuselage fairing panel aft of ramp drops and moves backward slightly to release ramp.

TAIL UNIT: Cantilever all-metal T tail, with wide chord sweptback vertical surfaces and fixed-incidence tailplane. Double-hinged rudder, with tab in lower portion of two-section aft panel. During normal flight only the lower rear segment is used. Both rear segments are used during low-speed flight. The forward segment is actuated automatically to offset thrust asymmetry. Tailplane leading-edge sweep slightly greater than that of wings, with straight trailing-edge on horn balanced and mechanically actuated, aerodynamically balanced elevators. Two tabs in each elevator. Inverted leading-edge slat on tailplane linked to wing flaps. Leading-edges of fin and tailplane, including slat, are de-iced by engine bleed air. Tapered fairing forward of fin/tailplane junction, blending into large ogival rear fairing.

LANDING GEAR: Hydraulically retractable tricycle type, made primarily of titanium. Twin wheels on rearward retracting steerable nose unit. Each main unit comprises two trailing-arm legs in tandem, each with a single wheel, retracting inward through 90° so that wheels lie horizontally in bottom of large fairings, outside fuselage pressure cell. Oleo-pneumatic shock absorber in each unit. Low pressure tyres, size 720 × 310 on nosewheels, 1050 × 400 on mainwheels. Hydraulic disc brakes. Telescopic strut is hinged downward, from rear of each side fairing, to support fuselage during direct loading of hold with ramp/door under fuselage.

POWER PLANT: Two Lotarev D-36 high bypass ratio turbofans, each rated at 63.74 kN (14,330 lb st). Integral fuel tanks between spars of outer wings. Thrust reversers standard.

ACCOMMODATION: Pilot and co-pilot/navigator side by side on very roomy flight deck of An-72; pilot, co-pilot, navigator and flight engineer in An-74. Heated windows. Two windscreen wipers. Flight deck and cabin pressurised and air-conditioned. Main cabin designed primarily for freight, but An-72 has folding seats for 32 passengers along side walls and provision for carrying 24 casualties and attendant in ambulance configuration. An-74 is able to carry eight mission staff in combi role, in two rows of seats, with tables, and with two bunks installed, one on each side of cabin aft of seats. Bulged observation windows on port side for navigator and hydrologist. Provision for wardrobe and galley. Movable bulkhead between passenger and freight compartments, with provision for up to 1,500 kg (3,307 lb) of freight in rear compartment. Freight can be airdropped. Large downward hinged and forward sliding rear ramp/door for loading trucks and tracked vehicles, and for direct loading of hold from trucks, as described under An-26 entry. Removable mobile winch, capacity 2,500 kg (5,511 lb), assists loading of containers up to 1.90 × 2.44 × 1.46 m (6 ft 3 in × 8 ft × 4 ft 9½ in) in size, pallets 1.90 × 2.42 × 1.46 m (6 ft 3 in × 7 ft 11 in × 4 ft 9½ in) in size, and other bulky items. Cargo straps and nets are stowed in lockers on each side of hold when not in use. Provision for building roller conveyors into floor. Main crew and passenger door at front of cabin on port side. Small emergency exit and servicing door at rear of cabin on starboard side.

An-74 after touchdown, with thrust reversers erected and flaps extended
(Paul Jackson)

SYSTEMS: Air-conditioning system provides comfortable environment to altitude of 10,000 m (32,800 ft), with independent temperature control in flight deck and main cabin areas. It can be used to refrigerate main cabin when perishable goods are carried. Hydraulic system for actuating landing gear, flaps, ailerons, variable incidence tailplane and ramp. Electrical system powers auxiliary systems, flight deck equipment, lighting and mobile hoist. Thermal de-icing system for leading-edges of wings and tail unit, engine air intakes and cockpit windows.

AVIONICS AND EQUIPMENT: HF com, VHF com/nav, ADF. Large radome over navigation/weather radar in nose. Doppler based automatic navigation system, with map display on flight deck. 'Odd Rods' IFF standard. An-74 has enhanced avionics, including INS. Provision for APU in starboard landing gear fairing. This can be used to heat the cabin; and, under cold ambient conditions, servicing personnel can gain access to major electric, hydraulic and air-conditioning components without stepping outside.

DIMENSIONS, EXTERNAL:
Wing span	31.89 m (104 ft 7½ in)
Length overall	28.07 m (92 ft 1¼ in)
Height overall	8.75 m (28 ft 8½ in)

DIMENSIONS, INTERNAL:
Cabin: Length	10.50 m (34 ft 5¼ in)
Width at floor level	2.15 m (7 ft 0½ in)
Height	2.20 m (7 ft 2½ in)

WEIGHTS:
Max payload: Normal	10,000 kg (22,045 lb)
Max T-O weight, from 1,800 m (5,905 ft) runway	34,500 kg (76,060 lb)

PERFORMANCE:
Max level speed	380 knots (705 km/h; 438 mph)
Normal cruising speed at 8,000-10,000 m (26,250-32,800 ft)	297 knots (550 km/h; 342 mph)
Approach speed	97 knots (180 km/h; 112 mph)
Service ceiling	10,000 m (32,800 ft)
Range: with max payload	620 nm (1,150 km; 715 miles)
with 1,500 kg (3,307 lb) payload and 2 h reserves	2,268 nm (4,200 km; 2,610 miles)

ANTONOV An-74 VARIANT
NATO reporting name: Madcap

A photograph taken during a visit to the Antonov OKB by Mr Gorbachev shows, in the background, the much modified tail of an An-74 bearing the serial number SSSR-780151. This has a large, sweptforward fin and rudder, at the top of which is mounted an AEW&C rotodome (see accompanying illustration). It can be assumed that this aircraft bears the same relationship to the Ilyushin 'Mainstay' as does the Grumman E-2C Hawkeye to the Boeing E-3 Sentry, with similar potential for export to selected customers. Production is likely to be at an early stage, with a few aircraft completed.

ANTONOV An-124
NATO reporting name: Condor

The An-124 has the NATO reporting name 'Condor'. This is appropriate, as condors are the largest flying birds and the An-124 is the largest aircraft currently flying, in terms of wing span, with the heaviest max take-off weight of any aeroplane yet built.

The prototype (SSSR-680125) was flown for the first time on 26 December 1982 by the Antonov bureau's chief test pilot, Vladimir Terski. He also commanded the second prototype (SSSR-82002 *Ruslan*, named after the giant hero of Russian folklore immortalised by Pushkin) when it was exhibited in public for the first time at the Paris Air Show in May/June 1985. The number of aircraft flown had increased to ten (including two prototypes) by the time SSSR-82009 was exhibited at the 1987 Paris Air Show. Operational flying was said to have started in January 1986 when units of a US/Canadian Euclid 154 tonne dumper truck were transported for use by Yakut diamond miners. Deliveries to VTA's heavy-lift military units, to replace the An-22, began in 1987.

Except for having a low mounted tailplane, the general configuration of the An-124 is similar to that of its US counterpart, the Lockheed C-5 Galaxy. It has an upward hinged visor type nose, and rear fuselage ramp/door, for simultaneous front and rear loading/unloading. Advanced features include a 100 per cent fly-by-wire control system, titanium floor throughout the main hold, and 5,500 kg (12,125 lb) of composites, making up more than 1,500 m² (16,150 sq ft) of its surface area and giving a weight saving of more than 2,000 kg (4,410 lb). The 24-wheel landing gear enables the An-124 to operate from unprepared fields, hard packed snow and ice covered swampland. Steerable nose- and mainwheels enable it to turn on a 45 m (148 ft) wide runway. Payloads range from the largest Soviet battle tanks to complete missile systems, Siberian oil well equipment and earth movers.

No major changes had to be made when progressing from prototypes to production. Development involved building 3,500 individual subassemblies for testing in laboratories throughout the USSR, and 18,000 hours of wind tunnel testing. The An-124 is approved for 8,000 operating cycles. Planned production rate is eight to ten aircraft a year.

Manufacture and assembly of the An-124 are centred in Antonov's headquarters works at Kiev. The wings are built in Tashkent, from where each port or starboard wing is ferried in one piece to Kiev above the fuselage of a specially adapted An-22 transport aircraft.

On 26 July 1985, an An-124 lifted a payload of 171,219 kg (377,473 lb) to a height of 10,750 m (35,269 ft). This exceeded by 53 per cent the previous official record for maximum payload lifted to 2,000 m, set by a Lockheed C-5A Galaxy, and also qualified for a total of 20 other FAI approved records with payloads from 75,000 to 170,000 kg. The pilot was Vladimir Terski, with Alexander Galunenko as co-pilot.

On 6-7 May 1987, a closed circuit distance record was set by an An-124 which covered a distance of 10,880.625 nm (20,150.921 km; 12,521.201 miles) in a time of 25 h 30 min, landing with a small amount of fuel remaining in its tanks. The route was from Moscow to Astrakhan, Tashkent, Lake Baikal, Petropavlovsk, Chukot Peninsula, Murmansk, Zhdanov and back to Moscow.

TYPE: Long-range heavy-lift freight transport.

WINGS: Cantilever shoulder-wing monoplane, of supercritical section, with anhedral. Sweepback approx 35° on inboard leading-edge, 32° over most of span. Conventional light alloy construction, with one-piece root-to-tip upper surface extruded skin panel on each wing. Strip of carbonfibre skin panels on undersurface forward of trailing-edge control surfaces. Glassfibre wingtips. Each wing has two-section aileron, three-section single-slotted Fowler flaps, and six-section full-span leading-edge flaps. Small slot in outer part of two inner flap segments on each side, to optimise aerodynamics. Front and rear portions of each flap guide

Mr Gorbachev's visit to the Antonov OKB produced the first illustration of an AEW&C version of the An-74 (background), known to NATO as 'Madcap'

Antonov An-124 heavy freight transport, with landing gear extended *(Brian M. Service)*

Nose of the An-124 opens upward around the flight deck *(Anna T. Hogg)*

World's largest transport aircraft, the Antonov An-124 (NATO 'Condor') *(Brian M. Service)*

fairing made of glassfibre; centre portion of carbonfibre. Eight spoilers on upper surface of each wing, forward of trailing-edge flaps. No fences, vortex generators, or tabs. All moving surfaces hydraulically operated, with hydraulic flutter dampers on ailerons. Bleed air anti-icing of wing leading-edges.

FUSELAGE: Conventional semi-monocoque light alloy structure of basic double-bubble form. Hard chine between sides and shallow-section bottom surface. Central frames each made up of four large forgings. Visor type nose door and rear ramp/door described under 'Accommodation' heading. Fairings over intersection of fuselage lobes, in line with wing, from rear of flight deck to plane of fin leading-edge, made primarily of glassfibre with central, and lower underwing, portions of carbonfibre. Other carbonfibre components include nose and main landing gear doors, some service doors, and clamshell doors aft of rear loading ramp. Glassfibre components include most of bottom skin panels forming underfuselage blister fairing between main landing gear legs, plus nosecone and tailcone. All control runs and other services are channelled along roof of fuselage.

TAIL UNIT: Cantilever all-metal structure, except for glassfibre tips of fixed incidence tailplane and strip of carbonfibre skin panels forward of each control surface. Rudder and each elevator in two sections, without tabs. Control surfaces hydraulically operated, with hydraulic

flutter dampers. Fence at mid-point on fin leading-edge. Electro-impulse de-icing of fin and tailplane leading-edges.

LANDING GEAR: Hydraulically retractable nosewheel type. Nose gear comprises two independent forward retracting and steerable twin-wheel units, side by side. Each main gear comprises five independent inward retracting twin-wheel units, of which the front two units on each side are steerable. Each mainwheel bogie is enclosed by separate upper and lower doors when retracted. Nosewheel doors and lower mainwheel doors close when gear is extended. All wheel doors are of carbonfibre. Main gear bogies can be retracted individually for repair or wheel change. Mainwheel tyres size 1270 × 510. Nosewheel tyres size 1120 × 450. Aircraft can 'kneel', by retracting nosewheels and settling on two extendable 'feet', giving floor of hold a 3.5° slope to assist loading and unloading. Rear of cargo hold can be lowered by compressing main gear oleos. Carbon brakes are normally toe operated, via rudder pedals. For severe braking, pedals are depressed by both toes and heels.

POWER PLANT: Four Lotarev D-18T turbofans, each rated at 229.5 kN (51,590 lb st). Thrust reversers standard. Engine cowlings of glassfibre; pylons have carbonfibre skin at rear end. All fuel in ten integral tanks in wings.

ACCOMMODATION: All crew and passenger accommodation on upper deck; freight and/or vehicles on lower deck. Flight crew of six, in pairs, on flight deck, with place for loadmaster in lobby area. Pilot and co-pilot on fully adjustable seats, which rotate for improved access. Two flight engineers, on wall-facing seats on starboard side, have complete control of master fuel cocks, detailed systems instruments, and digital integrated data system with CRT monitor. Behind pilot are the navigator and communications specialist, also on wall-facing seats. Between flight deck and wing carry-through structure, on port side, are toilets, washing facilities, galley, equipment compartment, and two cabins for total of up to six relief crew, with table and facing bench seats convertible into bunks. Aft of wing carry-through is a passenger cabin for up to 88 persons. Hatches in upper deck provide access to the wing and tail unit for maintenance in places where workstands may not be available. Flight deck and passenger cabin are each accessible from cargo hold by means of an hydraulically folding ladder, operated automatically with manual override. Rearward sliding and jettisonable window on each side of flight deck. Primary access to flight deck via airstair door, with ladder extension, forward of wing on port side. Smaller door forward of this and slightly higher. Door from main hold aft of wing on starboard side. Upper deck doors at rear of flight deck on starboard side and at rear of passenger cabin on each side. Emergency exit from upper deck aft of wing on each side. Hydraulically operated visor type upward hinged nose takes 7 min to open fully, with simultaneous extension of folding nose loading ramp. When open, nose is steadied by reinforcing arms against wind gusts. No hydraulic, electrical or other system lines are broken when nose is open. Radar wiring passes through hollow tube in hinge. Hydraulically operated rear loading doors take 3 min to open, with simultaneous extension of three-part folding ramp. This can be locked in intermediate position for direct loading from truck or loading galley. Aft of ramp, centre panel of fuselage undersurface hinges upward; clamshell door to each side opens downward. Completely unobstructed lower deck freight hold has titanium floor, attached 'mobilely' to lower fuselage structure to accommodate changes of temperature, with rollgangs and retractable attachments for cargo tiedowns. A narrow catwalk along each sidewall facilitates access to, and mobility past, loaded freight. No personnel are carried on lower deck in flight, because of low pressurisation of hold. Two electric travelling cranes in roof of hold, each with two lifting points, offer total lifting capacity of 20,000 kg (44,100 lb). Two winches can each pull a 3,000 kg (6,614 lb) load.

SYSTEMS: Entire interior of aircraft is pressurised and air-conditioned. Max pressure differential 0.55 bars (7.8 lb/sq in) on upper deck, 0.25 bars (3.55 lb/sq in) on lower deck. Four independent hydraulic systems. Quadruple redundant fly-by-wire flight control system, with mechanical emergency fifth channel to hydraulic control servos. Special secondary bus electrical system. Landing lights under nose and at front of each main landing gear fairing. APU in rear of each landing gear fairing is used for engine starting, and can be operated in the air or on the ground to open loading doors for airdrop from rear or normal ground loading/unloading, as well as for supplying electric, hydraulic and air-conditioning systems.

AVIONICS AND EQUIPMENT: Comprehensive but conventional flight deck equipment, including automatic flight control system control panel at top of glareshield, weather radar screen and moving map display forward of throttle and thrust reverse levers on centre console. No electronic flight displays. Dual attitude indicator/flight director and HSIs, and vertical tape engine instruments. Two

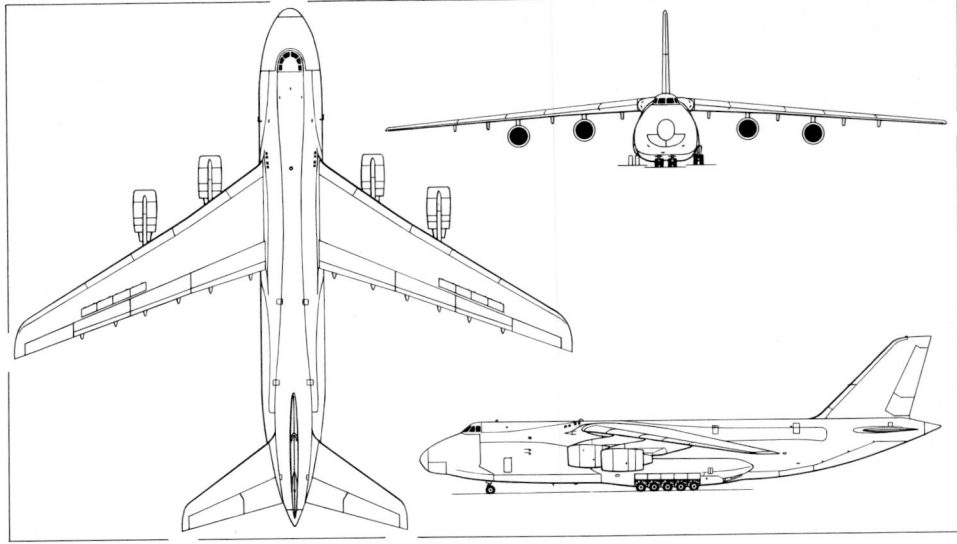

Antonov An-124 (four Lotarev D-18T turbofans) *(Pilot Press)*

dielectric areas of nose visor enclose forward looking weather radar and downward looking ground mapping/ navigation radar. Hemispherical dielectric fairing above centre fuselage for satellite navigation receiver. Quadruple INS, plus Loran and Omega. Small two-face mirror, of V form, enables pilots to adjust their seating position until their eyes are reflected in the appropriate mirror, which ensures an optimum field of view from the flight deck.

DIMENSIONS, EXTERNAL:
Wing span	73.30 m (240 ft 5¾ in)
Length overall	69.10 m (226 ft 8½ in)
Height overall	20.78 m (68 ft 2¼ in)

DIMENSIONS, INTERNAL:
Cargo hold: Length	36.0 m (118 ft 1¼ in)
Max width	6.4 m (21 ft 0 in)
Max height	4.4 m (14 ft 5¼ in)

AREA:
Wings, gross	628.0 m² (6,760.0 sq ft)

WEIGHTS:
Max payload	150,000 kg (330,693 lb)
Max fuel	230,000 kg (507,063 lb)
Max T-O weight	405,000 kg (892,872 lb)

PERFORMANCE:
Max cruising speed	467 knots (865 km/h; 537 mph)

Normal cruising speed at 10,000-12,000 m (32,800-39,370 ft) 432-459 knots (800-850 km/h; 497-528 mph)

Approach speed
124-140 knots (230-260 km/h; 143-162 mph)

T-O balanced field length at max T-O weight
3,000 m (9,850 ft)

Landing run at max landing weight   800 m (2,625 ft)

Range:
with max payload	2,430 nm (4,500 km; 2,795 miles)
with max fuel	8,900 nm (16,500 km; 10,250 miles)

OPERATIONAL NOISE LEVELS:
Stated to meet ICAO requirements

BERIEV

This design bureau is named after Georgi Mikhailovich Beriev, whose death at the age of 77 was reported in July 1979. Based at Taganrog, it has been the centre for all Soviet seaplane development since 1945.

BERIEV Be-12 (M-12) TCHAIKA (SEAGULL)
NATO reporting name: Mail

This twin-turboprop medium-range anti-submarine and maritime reconnaissance amphibian flew for the first time in 1960 and made its initial public appearance in the 1961 Aviation Day flypast at Tushino Airport, Moscow. Subsequently, during the period 23-27 October 1964, it established six international height records in Class C3 Group II. Data submitted in respect of these records

revealed that the designation of the aircraft was M-12 (changed subsequently to Be-12) and the power plant two 4,000 shp Ivchenko AI-20D turboprops. The aircraft was also, clearly, able to lift a payload of around 10 tons under record conditions.

The 1964 records have never been bettered. Subsequent record attempts ensured that the Be-12 retains 20 FAI records listed in Class C3 Group II for turboprop amphibians, and all 22 current records in Class C2 Group II, for turboprop flying-boats. All of these records have been listed in previous editions of *Jane's*. Some of the more important ones are included among the Official Records listed on an early page of this edition. Two further records were set by Nikolai Shlikov and Sergei Tyukavkin (pilot and co-pilot respectively), for distance in a straight line, in 1983. They covered a distance of 2,647.634 km (1,645.163 miles) between Morskoy and Sukhoputny on 30 October to

claim the class C3/II record. On the following day, they covered an identical distance between Severny and Morskoy to claim the class C2/II record.

Production started in 1964, and when three Be-12s took part in the 1967 air display at Domodedovo, the commentator said that the unit to which they belonged was "one of those serving where the country's military air force began", implying that the aircraft were then in operational service. Be-12s have subsequently formed standard equipment at coastal air bases of the Soviet Northern and Black Sea Fleets, for anti-submarine and surveillance duties out to some 200 nm (370 km; 230 miles) from shore, and were operational for a period from bases in Egypt, in Egyptian insignia. Production is believed to have totalled 100, of which about 95 remain in service.

TYPE: Twin-turboprop anti-submarine and maritime patrol amphibian.

Beriev Be-12 Tchaika anti-submarine and maritime patrol amphibian flying-boat of the Soviet Naval Air Force

WINGS: Cantilever high-wing monoplane of sharply cranked configuration to raise propellers clear of water. Unswept constant chord centre-section; tapered outer panels. All-metal two-spar structure. Hydraulically boosted ailerons actuated by pushrods. Two electrically operated tabs in each aileron. Hydraulically actuated trailing-edge flaps in two sections on each wing, from aileron to centre-section (passing under engine) and on centre-section.

FUSELAGE: Single-step all-metal semi-monocoque hull of high length to beam ratio. Two long strakes, one above the other, on each side of front fuselage to prevent spray from enveloping the propellers at take-off.

TAIL UNIT: All-metal structure. Considerable dihedral on two-spar tailplane, which has two endplate fins and horn balanced rudders at tips. Control surfaces actuated by pushrods, with hydraulic boost. Electrically operated trim tab in each elevator and each rudder.

LANDING GEAR: Hydraulically retractable tailwheel type, comprising single-wheel main units which retract upward through 180° to lie flush within sides of hull, and a rearward retracting steerable tailwheel. Oleo-pneumatic mainwheel shock absorbers. Except for top of each mainwheel, all units are fully enclosed by doors when retracted. Non-retractable wingtip floats.

POWER PLANT: Two Ivchenko AI-20D turboprops, each rated at 3,124 kW (4,190 ehp) and driving an AV-681 four-blade variable-pitch propeller. Metal cowlings open downward in halves, permitting their use as servicing platforms. Fuel tanks, between spars in wings and in fuselage, with total capacity of approx 11,000 litres (2,905 US gallons; 2,420 Imp gallons).

ACCOMMODATION: Crew of five on flight deck. Glazed navigation and observation station in nose. Astrodome observation station in top of rear fuselage. Side hatches in rear fuselage permit loading while afloat.

SYSTEMS: Hydraulic system actuates flaps and landing gear. Two engine driven generators power 28V DC electrical system.

AVIONICS AND EQUIPMENT: No details available of com/nav systems or IFF. Radome above nose glazing. MAD (magnetic anomaly detection) 'sting' extends rearward from tail. APU exhausts through aperture in port side of rear fuselage.

ARMAMENT: Internal weapons bay in bottom of hull aft of step. One large and one smaller external stores pylon under each outer wing panel, for torpedoes, depth charges, mines and other stores.

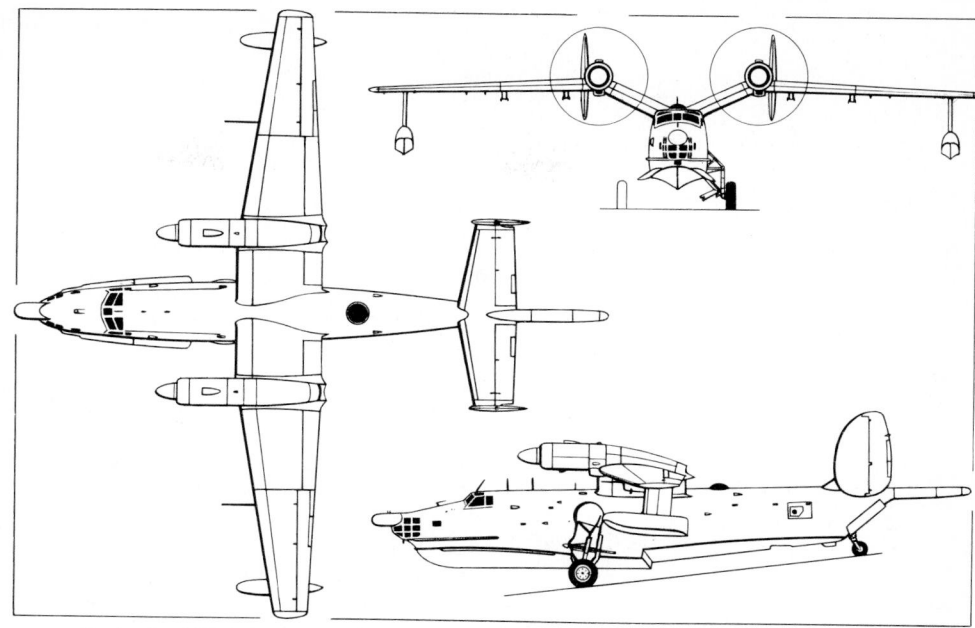

Beriev Be-12 Tchaika twin-turboprop maritime reconnaissance amphibian (*Pilot Press*)

DIMENSIONS, EXTERNAL:

Wing span	29.71 m (97 ft 5¾ in)
Wing aspect ratio	8.4
Length overall	30.17 m (99 ft 0 in)
Height overall	7.00 m (22 ft 11½ in)
Propeller diameter	4.85 m (16 ft 0 in)

AREA:

Wings, gross	105 m² (1,130 sq ft)

WEIGHTS:

Max operational load	10,000 kg (22,045 lb)
Max T-O weight	31,000 kg (68,345 lb)

PERFORMANCE:

Max level speed	328 knots (608 km/h; 378 mph)
Normal operating speed	
	172 knots (320 km/h; 199 mph)

Rate of climb at S/L	912 m (2,990 ft)/min
Service ceiling	11,280 m (37,000 ft)
Range with max fuel	4,050 nm (7,500 km; 4,660 miles)

NEW BERIEV FLYING BOAT

In a statement in Spring 1988, Rear Adm William O. Studeman, US director of naval intelligence, said that the Soviet Union is developing a seaplane, with the provisional Western designation 'Tag-D', which has a possible ASW/surveillance/minelaying role. No details are available, but the designation implies that it was identified at Taganrog, where the Beriev OKB is centred. No clues have been given to the 'Tag-A, B and C' types that must have been identified earlier.

ILYUSHIN

DESIGN BUREAU HEADQUARTERS: Moscow Central Airport, Khodinka, Moscow

GENERAL DESIGNER: Genrikh V. Novozhilov

This design bureau is named after its former leader, Sergei Vladimirovich Ilyushin, who died on 9 February 1977 at the age of 83. Aircraft designed by Ilyushin and still in service include the Il-14 piston engined light transport and four-turboprop Il-18 transport, of which details have been given in earlier editions of *Jane's*, and the Il-28 twin-jet bomber, produced also in China (see 1986-87 edition). More recent types from the Ilyushin bureau are as follows:

ILYUSHIN Il-18

The **Il-18DORR** conversion of an Il-18 airliner was first mentioned in the Soviet press in 1986. It was described as a long-range ocean fishery reconnaissance aircraft. No details are known.

Another variant of the Il-18D, shown in an accompanying illustration, is SSSR-75442, said to be one of four similar aircraft operated by the Soviet Meteorological Institute. It was photographed at Shannon, Ireland, en route to Havana, Cuba. Note the many protrusions and canisters.

ILYUSHIN Il-20
NATO reporting name: Coot-A

The Il-18 prototype flew for the first time on 4 July 1957 and production models entered service with Aeroflot in 1959. Production exceeded 700 aircraft, of which more than 100 were exported for use by commercial airlines; a few were delivered for military and government use, usually as VIP transports. Those still in civilian and military use include former passenger carrying Il-18s converted into freighters for Aeroflot by Factory 402 at Moscow/Bykovo. Modifications include installation of a freight door 3.50 m (11 ft 6 in) wide in the rear fuselage and a strengthened cabin floor.

An anti-submarine derivative, the **Il-38** (NATO reporting name 'May'), is in service and is described separately. Another military variant of the Il-18, seen for the first time in 1978, is the **Il-20** elint/reconnaissance aircraft, known to NATO as **Coot-A** and shown in accompanying illustrations. In this case, the airframe appears to be basically unchanged by comparison with the transport. It carries under its fuselage a container about 10.25 m long and 1.15 m deep (33 ft 7½ in × 3 ft 9 in), which is assumed to house side looking radar. There is a further container, about 4.4 m long and 0.88 m deep (14 ft 5 in × 2 ft 10½ in), on each side of the forward fuselage, containing a door over a camera or other sensor. Numerous other antennae and blisters can be seen, about eight of them on the undersurface

Variant of Il-18D described as a meteorological aircraft (*David O'Mahoney*)

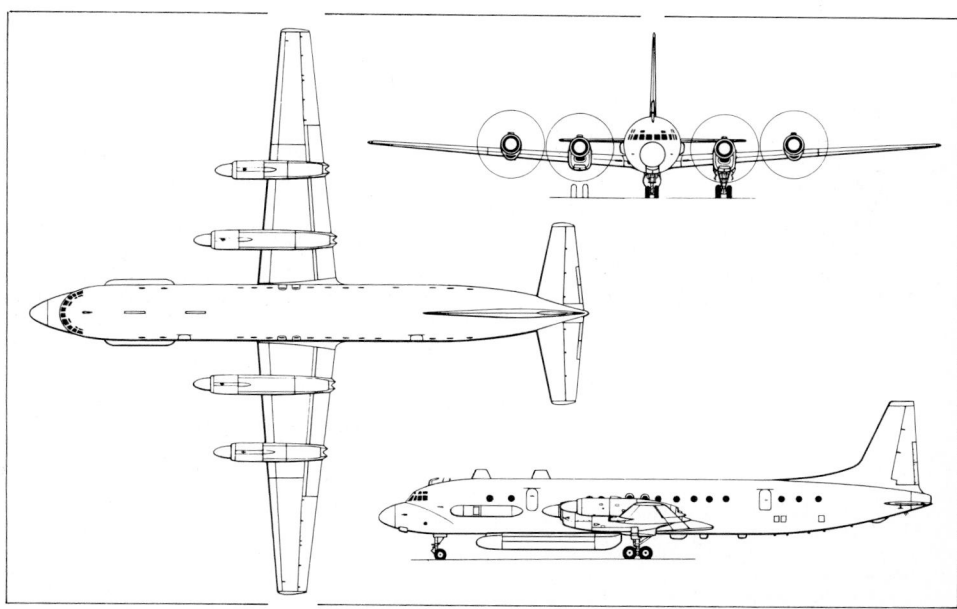

Ilyushin Il-20 (NATO 'Coot-A') elint/reconnaissance development of the Il-18 airliner (*Pilot Press*)

Ilyushin Il-20 (NATO 'Coot-A') electronic intelligence (elint) and reconnaissance aircraft *(Swedish Air Force, via FLYGvapenNYTT)*

of the centre and rear fuselage, with two large plates projecting above the forward fuselage. A brief reference to a further variant of the Il-18, designated Il-22, appears after this entry.

A detailed description of the commercial airliner versions of the Il-18 can be found in the 1979-80 and earlier editions of *Jane's*. The following abbreviated details of the Il-18D are retained as an indication of likely features of the military Il-20:

POWER PLANT: Four 3,169 kW (4,250 ehp) Ivchenko AI-20M turboprops, each driving an AV-68I four-blade reversible-pitch propeller. Ten flexible fuel tanks in inboard panel of each wing and integral tank in outboard panel, with a total capacity of 23,700 litres (6,261 US gallons; 5,213 Imp gallons). Some Il-18 airliners have additional bag tanks in centre-section, giving a total capacity of 30,000 litres (7,925 US gallons; 6,600 Imp gallons).

DIMENSIONS, EXTERNAL:

Wing span	37.42 m (122 ft 9¼ in)
Wing chord: at root	5.61 m (18 ft 5 in)
at tip	1.87 m (6 ft 2 in)
Wing aspect ratio	10
Length overall	35.9 m (117 ft 9 in)
Height overall	10.17 m (33 ft 4 in)
Tailplane span	11.80 m (38 ft 8½ in)
Wheel track	9.00 m (29 ft 6 in)
Wheelbase	12.78 m (41 ft 10 in)
Propeller diameter	4.50 m (14 ft 9 in)
Cabin doors (each): Height	1.40 m (4 ft 7 in)
Width	0.76 m (2 ft 6 in)
Height to sill	2.90 m (9 ft 6 in)

DIMENSIONS, INTERNAL:

Flight deck: Volume	9.36 m³ (330 cu ft)
Cabin, excl flight deck:	
Length	approx 24.0 m (79 ft 0 in)
Max width	3.23 m (10 ft 7 in)
Max height	2.00 m (6 ft 6¾ in)
Volume	238 m³ (8,405 cu ft)

AREA:

Wings, gross	140 m² (1,507 sq ft)

WEIGHTS (Il-18D airliner):

Max payload	13,500 kg (29,750 lb)
Max T-O weight	64,000 kg (141,100 lb)

PERFORMANCE (Il-18D airliner, at max T-O weight):

Max cruising speed	364 knots (675 km/h; 419 mph)
Econ cruising speed	337 knots (625 km/h; 388 mph)
Operating height	8,000-10,000 m (26,250-32,800 ft)
T-O run	1,300 m (4,265 ft)
Landing run	850 m (2,790 ft)
Range, 1 h reserves:	
with max fuel	3,508 nm (6,500 km; 4,040 miles)
with max payload	1,997 nm (3,700 km; 2,300 miles)

ILYUSHIN Il-22
NATO reporting name: Coot-B

A substantial number of Il-22 airborne command post adaptations of the Il-18 transport is operational with Soviet air forces. No details are available, but it would be logical to expect a variety of external fairings and antennae. NATO reporting name for these aircraft is 'Coot-B'.

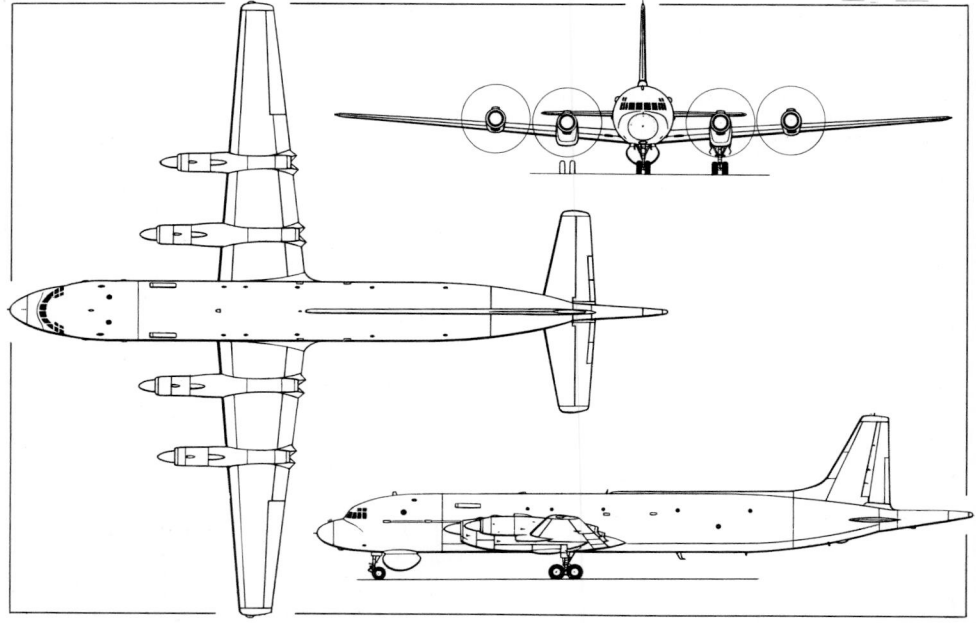

Ilyushin Il-38 anti-submarine/maritime patrol derivative of the Il-18 airliner *(Pilot Press)*

ILYUSHIN Il-38
NATO reporting name: May

The airframe of this intermediate-range shore-based anti-submarine/maritime patrol aircraft was developed from that of the Il-18 airliner in the same way that the US Navy's P-3 Orion was based on the Lockheed Electra transport. The fuselage is lengthened, and the complete wing assembly is much farther forward than on the Il-18, to cater for the effect on the CG position of internal equipment and stores.

Il-38s of the Soviet Naval Air Force are encountered frequently over the Baltic and North Atlantic. A treaty of friendship and co-operation signed with the People's Democratic Republic of Yemen permits patrols over the Red Sea, Gulf of Aden, Arabian Sea and Indian Ocean from a base in that country. Other Il-38s are deployed periodically to Libya and Syria.

In 1975, the Indian Navy ordered an initial batch of three refurbished ex-Soviet Navy Il-38s, which equip INAS 315 at Dabolim, Goa. About 59 are believed to be operational with Soviet naval units.

TYPE: Four-turboprop maritime patrol aircraft.

WINGS: Cantilever low-wing monoplane. Dihedral 3° from roots. Mean thickness/chord ratio 14%. All-metal structure. Three spars in centre-section, two in outer wings. All-metal ailerons are mass and aerodynamically balanced, and fitted with electrically actuated trim tabs. Flying controls cable actuated. Hydraulically actuated double-slotted flaps. Electro-thermal de-icing.

FUSELAGE: Circular-section all-metal semi-monocoque structure of fail-safe type, with rip stop doublers around

window cutouts, door frames and the more heavily loaded skin panels.

TAIL UNIT: Cantilever all-metal structure. Electrically actuated trim tabs in rudder and elevators. Additional spring tab in rudder. Flying controls cable actuated and power assisted. Electro-thermal de-icing.

LANDING GEAR: Retractable tricycle type, strengthened by comparison with that of Il-18. Hydraulic actuation. Four-wheel bogie main units, with 930 mm × 305 mm tyres and hydraulic brakes. Steerable (45° each way) twin nosewheel unit, with 700 mm × 250 mm tyres. Hydraulic brakes and nosewheel steering. Pneumatic emergency braking.

POWER PLANT: Four Ivchenko AI-20M turboprops, each rated at 3,169 kW (4,250 shp), driving AV-68I four-blade reversible-pitch metal propellers. Multiple bag type fuel tanks in centre-section and in inboard panel of each wing, and integral tank in outboard panel, with a total capacity of 30,000 litres (7,925 US gallons; 6,600 Imp gallons). Pressure fuelling through four international standard connections in inner nacelles. Provision for overwing fuelling. Oil capacity 58.5 litres (15.45 US gallons; 12.85 Imp gallons) per engine. Engines started electrically.

ACCOMMODATION: Pilot and co-pilot side by side on flight deck, with dual controls; flight engineer to rear. Number of operational crew believed to be nine, but unconfirmed. Flight deck is separated from main cabin by a pressure bulkhead to reduce hazards following sudden decompression of either. Main cabin has few windows and contains search equipment, electronic equipment and crew stations appropriate to role. Door is on

Ilyushin Il-38 anti-submarine/maritime patrol aircraft (four Ivchenko AI-20M turboprops) *(Royal Norwegian Air Force)*

starboard side at rear of cabin (location of Il-18 service door).

SYSTEMS: Cabin pressurised to max differential of 0.49 bars (7.1 lb/sq in). Electrical system includes eight engine driven generators for 28V DC and 115V 400Hz AC supply. Hydraulic system, pressure 207 bars (3,000 lb/sq in), for landing gear retraction, nosewheel steering, brakes, elevator and rudder actuators, flaps, weapon bay doors and radar antennae.

AVIONICS AND EQUIPMENT: Navigation/weather radar in nose. Search radar in undernose radome. MAD tail 'sting'. Automatic navigation equipment, radio compasses and radio altimeter probably similar to those of Il-18.

ARMAMENT: Two weapons/stores bays forward and aft of wing carry-through structure on most aircraft, to accommodate a variety of attack weapons and sonobuoys.

DIMENSIONS, EXTERNAL:

As listed under Il-20 entry, except:

Length overall	39.60 m (129 ft 10 in)
Height overall	10.16 m (33 ft 4 in)

WEIGHTS:

Weight empty	36,000 kg (79,367 lb)
Max T-O weight	63,500 kg (140,000 lb)

PERFORMANCE:

Max level speed at 6,400 m (21,000 ft)	
	390 knots (722 km/h; 448 mph)
Max cruising speed at 8,230 m (27,000 ft)	
	330 knots (611 km/h; 380 mph)
Patrol speed at 600 m (2,000 ft)	
	216 knots (400 km/h; 248 mph)
Min flying speed	103 knots (190 km/h; 118 mph)
T-O run	1,300 m (4,265 ft)
Landing run with reverse thrust	850 m (2,790 ft)
Range with max fuel	3,887 nm (7,200 km; 4,473 miles)
Patrol endurance with max fuel	12 h

ILYUSHIN Il-62
NATO reporting name: Classic

Brief details of the early history of this rear-engined four-turbofan long-range airliner can be found in the 1982-83 *Jane's*. The standard Kuznetsov engines were not ready in time for the first flight of the first prototype, which took place in January 1963 with four 73.55 kN (16,535 lb st) Lyulka AL-7 engines installed. Aeroflot introduced the Il-62 on to its Moscow-Montreal service on 15 September 1967, as a replacement for the Tu-114. Production is reported to have totalled nearly 250, of which 75 were exported, including developed Il-62M/MKs (described separately). Current operators of Il-62s and Il-62M/MKs include Aeroflot (about 150), Choson Minhang of North Korea, CSA Czechoslovak Airlines (11), Cubana (10), Interflug of East Germany (14), Polish Airlines LOT (8), TAAG Angola Airlines (2), Tarom of Romania (5) and the Czechoslovak government for VIP operation.

TYPE: Four-turbofan long-range airliner.

WINGS: Cantilever low-wing monoplane. Sweepback 32° 30′ at quarter-chord. Extended chord leading-edge on outer two-thirds of each wing. All-metal structure, with four spars inboard, two at tip. Removable leading-edge. Each wing fitted with three-section manually operated ailerons, electrically actuated slotted flaps and two hydraulically operated spoiler sections forward of flaps. Trim tab and spring loaded servo tab in each centre aileron, spring loaded servo tab in each inner aileron. Hot air anti-icing of leading-edges.

FUSELAGE: Conventional all-metal semi-monocoque structure. Frames are duralumin stampings and pressings. Integrally pressed skin panels at highly stressed areas. Floors are sandwich panels with foam plastics filler. Nosecone hinges upward for access to radar.

TAIL UNIT: Cantilever all-metal structure, with electrically actuated variable incidence T tailplane. All surfaces sweptback. Manually operated rudder, fitted with yaw damper, trim tab and spring servo tab. Manually operated elevators have two automatic trim tabs and two manual trim tabs. Hot air leading-edge anti-icing system.

LANDING GEAR: Hydraulically retractable tricycle type. Forward retracting twin-wheel steerable nose unit. Emergency extension by gravity. Oleo-nitrogen shock absorber in each unit. Each main unit carries a four-wheel bogie and retracts inward into wing roots. Mainwheel tyres size 1450 × 450, pressure 9.31 bars (135 lb/sq in). Nosewheel tyres size 930 × 305, pressure 7.86 bars (114 lb/sq in). Hydraulic disc brake and inertia type electric anti-skid unit on each mainwheel, supplemented by large tail parachute. Parking brakes. Hydraulic twin-wheel strut is extended downward to support rear fuselage during loading and unloading.

POWER PLANT: Four Kuznetsov NK-8-4 turbofans, each rated at 103 kN (23,150 lb st), mounted in horizontal pairs on each side of rear fuselage. Thrust reverser on each outboard engine. Hot air anti-icing system for engine intakes. Automatically controlled fuel system, with seven integral tanks, three in wing centre-section, two in each outer panel. Each engine has its own independent fuel system, with cross-feed. Total fuel capacity 100,000 litres (26,417 US gallons; 21,998 Imp gallons). Four standard international underwing pressure refuelling points. Eight gravity refuelling sockets. Total oil capacity 204 litres (54 US gallons; 45 Imp gallons).

ACCOMMODATION: Crew of five (two pilots, navigator, radio operator and flight engineer) on flight deck. Provision for two supernumerary pilot/navigators. Basic two-cabin layout, and galley, toilet and wardrobe facilities, are unchanged in the three main versions, only the width and pitch of the seats being varied. In the 186-passenger version, there are 72 seats in the forward cabin and 114 in the rear cabin, all six-abreast and all at a seat pitch of 86 cm (34 in). In the 168-seat configuration, increased pitch reduces capacity to 66 in the forward cabin and 102 in the rear cabin. The 114-passenger version has 45 seats in the forward cabin and 69 in the rear cabin, all five-abreast, except for four-abreast rear row by door. A first class/de luxe version for 85 passengers is available, with 45 seats in forward cabin and 40 four-abreast sleeperette chairs with footrests in rear cabin. Passenger doors forward of front cabin and between cabins on port side. Total of five toilets, opposite forward door, between cabins (starboard) and aft of rear cabin (both sides). Electrically powered galley/pantry amidships and wardrobes in each version. Pressurised baggage and freight compartments under cabin floor, forward and aft of wing. Unpressurised baggage/cargo compartment at extreme rear of fuselage. All compartments have tiedown fittings and rails in floor, and removable nets to restrain cargo.

SYSTEMS: Air-conditioning and pressurisation system maintains sea level conditions up to 7,000 m (23,000 ft) and gives equivalent of 2,100 m (6,900 ft) at 13,000 m (42,600 ft). Pressure differential 0.62 bars (9.0 lb/sq in). Hydraulic system, pressure 207 bars (3,000 lb/sq in), for landing gear retraction, nosewheel steering, brakes, spoilers and windscreen wipers. Emergency hydraulic system, powered by electric motor, for nosewheel steering, mainwheel extension and spoiler control. Three-phase 200/115V AC electrical supply from four 40kVA engine driven generators (optional 27V DC system with eight 18kW engine driven generators). Four transformer-rectifiers and four batteries for DC supply. Electric windscreen de-icing. TA-6 APU in tailcone.

AVIONICS: Standard avionics include two-channel autopilot, navigation computer, air data system, HF and UHF radio, VOR/ILS, RMI, Doppler, radio altimeter and weather radar. Polyot automatic flight control system optional.

DIMENSIONS, EXTERNAL:

Wing span	43.20 m (141 ft 9 in)
Length overall	53.12 m (174 ft 3½ in)
Length of fuselage	49.00 m (160 ft 9 in)
Height overall	12.35 m (40 ft 6¼ in)
Tailplane span	12.23 m (40 ft 1½ in)
Fuselage height	4.10 m (13 ft 5½ in)
Fuselage width	3.75 m (12 ft 3½ in)
Wheel track	6.80 m (22 ft 3½ in)
Wheelbase	24.49 m (80 ft 4½ in)
Passenger doors (each): Height	1.83 m (6 ft 0 in)
Width	0.86 m (2 ft 9¾ in)
Height to sill	3.55 m (11 ft 8 in)
Emergency exit (galley service) door:	
Height	1.38 m (4 ft 6¼ in)
Width	0.61 m (2 ft 0 in)
Emergency exits (overwing):	
Height	0.91 m (2 ft 11¾ in)
Width	0.51 m (1 ft 8 in)
Front cargo hold door: Height	1.31 m (4 ft 3½ in)
Width	1.26 m (4 ft 1½ in)
Height to sill	1.90 m (6 ft 3 in)
Second cargo hold door: Height	1.00 m (3 ft 3¼ in)
Width	1.26 m (4 ft 1½ in)
Height to sill	1.90 m (6 ft 3 in)
Third cargo hold door: Height	0.70 m (2 ft 3½ in)
Width	0.70 m (2 ft 3½ in)
Height to sill	2.26 m (7 ft 5 in)
Rear cargo hold door: Height	1.15 m (3 ft 9 in)
Width	1.07 m (3 ft 6 in)
Height to sill	3.68 m (12 ft 0¾ in)

DIMENSIONS, INTERNAL:

Cabin: Max height	2.12 m (6 ft 11½ in)
Max width	3.49 m (11 ft 5¼ in)
Volume	163 m³ (5,756 cu ft)
Total volume of pressure cell	396 m³ (13,985 cu ft)
Cargo hold volume: Front	22.7 m³ (801 cu ft)
Second	12.6 m³ (445 cu ft)
Third	6.9 m³ (243 cu ft)
Rear	5.8 m³ (205 cu ft)

AREAS:

Wings, gross	279.55 m² (3,009 sq ft)
Ailerons (total)	16.25 m² (174.9 sq ft)
Spoilers (total)	9.54 m² (102.7 sq ft)
Flaps (total)	43.48 m² (468.0 sq ft)
Horizontal tail surfaces (total)	40.00 m² (430.5 sq ft)
Vertical tail surfaces (total)	35.60 m² (383.2 sq ft)

WEIGHTS AND LOADING:

Weight empty	66,400 kg (146,390 lb)
Operating weight empty	69,400 kg (153,000 lb)
Max payload	23,000 kg (50,700 lb)
Max fuel	83,325 kg (183,700 lb)
Max ramp weight	167,000 kg (368,000 lb)
Max T-O weight	162,000 kg (357,150 lb)
Max landing weight	105,000 kg (231,500 lb)
Max zero-fuel weight	93,500 kg (206,130 lb)
Max wing loading	572 kg/m² (117.2 lb/sq ft)

PERFORMANCE (at max T-O weight):

Normal cruising speed	
	442-486 knots (820-900 km/h; 509-560 mph)
Normal cruising height	
	10,000-12,000 m (33,000-39,400 ft)
Landing speed	
	119-129 knots (220-240 km/h; 137-149 mph)
Max rate of climb at S/L	1,080 m (3,540 ft)/min
FAR T-O field length:	
ISA at S/L	3,250 m (10,660 ft)
ISA + 20°C at S/L	3,915 m (12,840 ft)
FAR landing field length:	
ISA at S/L	2,800 m (9,185 ft)
ISA + 20°C at S/L	2,950 m (9,680 ft)

Range: with max payload, 66,700 kg (147,050 lb) fuel, 1 h
   fuel reserves   3,612 nm (6,700 km; 4,160 miles)
   with 80,000 kg (176,370 lb) fuel and 10,000 kg
   (22,045 lb) payload, 1 h fuel reserves
                          4,963 nm (9,200 km; 5,715 miles)

ILYUSHIN Il-62M/MK
NATO reporting name: Classic

First displayed publicly at the 1971 Paris Air Show, the
Il-62M is a developed version of the Il-62, with no
dimensional changes to the airframe. It is fitted with more
powerful turbofans, of a different type, with clamshell
thrust reversers on the outboard engine of each pair,
offering a lower approach speed and improved airflow over
the rear of the nacelles. An additional fuel tank is installed in
the tail fin, contributing (with the improved specific fuel
consumption of the engines) to the longer range of this
version.

Revised layout of the flight deck equipment, and
improved navigation and radio communications equipment, are features of the Il-62M. Control wheels of different
design allow the pilots a better field of view, and the
aircraft's automatic flight control system permits automatic
landings in ICAO Category II conditions, with planned
extension to Category III. The wing spoilers of this version
can be utilised differentially to enhance roll control.

Additional emergency and rescue equipment is installed
on the Il-62M. Unlike the Il-62, it has a containerised
baggage and freight system, with mechanised loading and
unloading.

The Il-62M exhibited in Paris in 1971 and 1973 was the
prototype (SSSR-86673). Production models entered service
on Aeroflot's Moscow-Havana route in 1974 and took over
progressively all of the airline's very long distance services.

A variant announced in 1978 is the **Il-62MK**, still
dimensionally unchanged and with the same power plant as
the Il-62M, but with strengthened wings, wider main
landing gear bogies, lower-pressure tyres, improved brakes,
and revised spoilers which deploy automatically at
touchdown. Max T-O weight is increased to 167,000 kg
(368,170 lb) and max landing weight to 110,000 kg (242,500
lb), permitting the carriage of up to 195 passengers. To
ensure adequate cabin service with so many passengers, the
interior was redesigned to permit the more efficient use of
service trolleys. It has a 'wide-body look', with enclosed
overhead baggage racks and indirect lighting. Range with
max fuel and 10,000 kg (22,045 lb) payload is 5,180 nm
(9,600 km; 5,965 miles). Max payload is 25,000 kg (55,115
lb).

In 1985, the Il-62M and Il-62MK were being updated by
improvements to the navigation system, based on a new
triplex INS, and by changes to the turbofans and pods to
reduce noise and air pollution.

The basic structural description of the Il-62 applies also
to the Il-62M. The main innovations are as follows:

POWER PLANT: Four Soloviev D-30KU turbofans, each rated
at 107.9 kN (24,250 lb st), mounted in horizontal pairs on
each side of rear fuselage. Clamshell thrust reverser on
each outboard engine. Remainder of power plant
basically as for Il-62, but additional fuel tank in tail fin,
giving total capacity of 105,300 litres (27,817 US gallons;
23,162 Imp gallons).

ACCOMMODATION: Alternative configurations for up to 174
economy class, 168 tourist class or 140 mixed class
passengers. In the basic tourist class version there are two
toilets opposite the forward door, on the starboard side,
aft of the flight deck. The forward cabin contains 66 seats,
all six-abreast in threes with centre aisle. Galley/pantry,

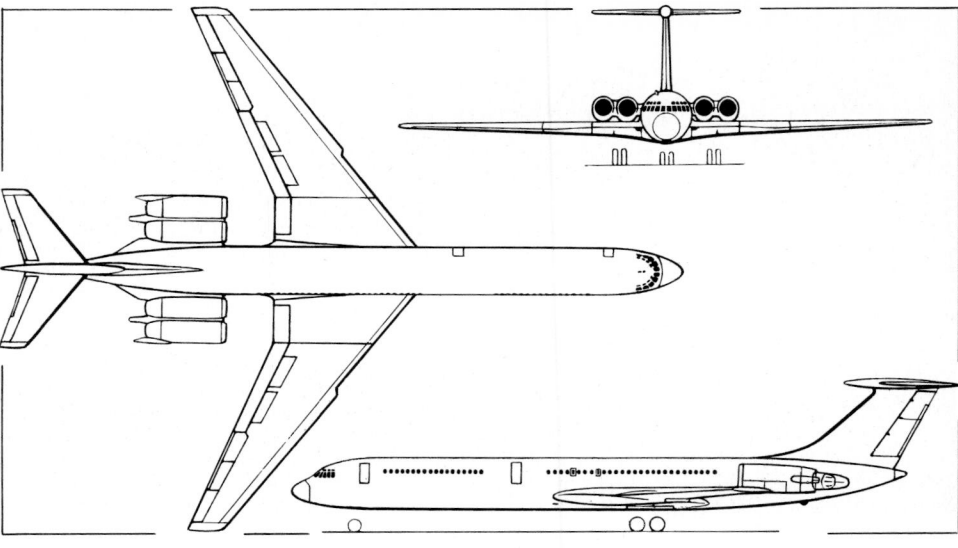

Ilyushin Il-62M (NATO 'Classic') long-range four-turbofan transport *(Pilot Press)*

coat stowage and toilet amidships. Rear cabin contains
102 seats, six-abreast in threes with centre aisle. Two
toilets and wardrobe to rear of this cabin. Doors as on
Il-62. Two emergency exits on each side, over wing.
Forward underfloor baggage and freight hold accommodates nine containers, each weighing approximately 45 kg
(100 lb) empty and with a capacity of 600 kg (1,322 lb)
and 1.6 m³ (56.5 cu ft). Rear hold accommodates five
similar containers. Two compartments for non-
containerised cargo. Total baggage and freight capacity
48 m³ (1,695 cu ft)

SYSTEMS AND EQUIPMENT: See introductory notes.

AVIONICS: Duplicated SAU-1T automatic flight control
system provides for automatic control from a height of
200 m (660 ft) after take-off to a height of 30 m (100 ft) on
the approach to land; DISS-013 Doppler indicator and
NV-PB-1 navigation computer; TKS-P course sensing
system; TsGV-10P vertical master gyros; SVS-PN-15 air
data system; Kurs-MP-2 radio navigation system,
utilising VOR, ILS or SP-50 beacons; GROZA radar;
SD-67 DME; ARK-15 ADF; RV-5 radio altimeter;
SO-70 IFF transponder; MIKRON 2-24MHz HF radio;
LANDASH 118-135MHz VHF radio; VESHANIE
public address and in-flight entertainment system.

DIMENSIONS AND AREAS:
Same as for Il-62

WEIGHTS (Il-62M):
Max payload	23,000 kg (50,700 lb)
Max T-O weight	165,000 kg (363,760 lb)
Max landing weight	105,000 kg (231,500 lb)
Max zero-fuel weight	94,600 kg (208,550 lb)

PERFORMANCE (Il-62M, at max T-O weight):
Normal cruising speed
                 442-486 knots (820-900 km/h; 509-560 mph)
Normal cruising height
                 10,000-12,000 m (33,000-39,400 ft)
Balanced T-O distance (ISA, S/L)   3,300 m (10,830 ft)
Landing run (ISA, S/L)   2,500 m (8,200 ft)
Range: with max payload, with 5,100 kg (11,240 lb) fuel
   reserves   4,210 nm (7,800 km; 4,846 miles)

with 10,000 kg (22,045 lb) payload, with reserves   5,400 nm (10,000 km; 6,215 miles)

ILYUSHIN Il-76
NATO reporting name: Candid
Indian Air Force name: Gajaraj

Towards the end of the 1960s, the Ilyushin design bureau,
under the leadership of Mr G. V. Novozhilov, began design
of a heavy transport to replace the turboprop An-12.
Nominal task for the aircraft was to transport 40 tonnes of
freight for a distance of 2,700 nm (5,000 km; 3,100 miles) in
less than six hours. It had to be capable of operation from
short unprepared airstrips, in the most difficult weather
conditions experienced in Siberia, the north of the Soviet
Union and the Far East, while being much simpler to service
and able to fly much faster than the An-12.

The prototype of the new transport, known as the Il-76
(SSSR-86712), flew for the first time on 25 March 1971 and
made its public debut at the 29th Salon de l'Aéronautique
et de l'Espace in Paris in May 1971. Test flying continued
until 1975, when the Il-76 entered series production.
Subsequent operation in the most difficult weather and
ground conditions of Central and Eastern Siberia revealed
operating costs more than 25 per cent lower per tonne/km
than for the An-12. This suggested that the Il-76 would be
competitive with river transport, even during Summer
months.

It was clear from the start that the Il-76 had considerable
potential as a military transport. Evaluation by the Soviet
Air Force had reached an advanced stage by 1974, when an
official film depicted Il-76s with twin-gun rear turrets in use
as vehicles for Soviet airborne troops, presumably with a
development squadron.

Since that time, development of the Il-76 has continued,
and the following major production versions can now be
identified:

Il-76 (Candid-A). Initial basic production version.

Il-76T (Candid-A). Developed version, with additional
fuel tankage in wing centre-section, above fuselage, and
heavier payload. No armament.

Ilyushin Il-62M long-range airliner (four Soloviev D-30KU turbofans) of CSA Czechoslovak Airlines *(Letectvi + Kosmonautika/Václav Jukl)*

Ilyushin Il-76MD freight transport (four Soloviev D-30KP-1 turbofans) in Aeroflot insignia *(Anton Wettstein)*

Il-76M (Candid-B). As Il-76T, but for military use, with rear gun turret containing two 23 mm NR-23 guns, and small ECM fairings between centre windows at front of navigator's compartment, on each side of front fuselage, and on each side of rear fuselage. Packs of ninety-six 50 mm IRCM flares in landing gear fairings and/or on sides of rear fuselage of Soviet aircraft operating into combat areas. Turret and ECM not always fitted on export Il-76Ms. Up to 140 troops or 125 paratroops can be carried as an alternative to freight.

Il-76TD (Candid-A). Unarmed version, generally similar to Il-76T. First identified in November 1982, when an example registered SSSR-76467 passed through Shannon Airport in Ireland. Fully operational from July 1983, this version has Soloviev D-30KP-1 engines which maintain full power up to ISA + 23°C against ISA + 15°C for earlier models. Max T-O weight and payload are increased. An increase of 10,000 kg (22,046 lb) in max fuel capacity provides an increase of 648 nm (1,200 km; 745 miles) in range with max fuel.

One Il-76TD has been equipped to transport members of Soviet Antarctic expeditions between Maputo in Mozambique and Molodozhnaya Station in Antarctica. The hold has been soundproofed and contains seats, a buffet kitchen, toilet and working facilities. Baggage is carried in containers. On its first proving flight from Moscow, via Leningrad, Larnaca, Djibuti and Maputo to Molodozhnaya and Novolazarevskaya stations, this aircraft carried 94 passengers and 14,000 kg (30,865 lb) of scientific equipment and other cargo. The final stage from Maputo was flown on 25 February 1986, replacing the Il-18D used on the service for five years.

Il-76MD (Candid-B). Military version, generally similar to Il-76M but with same improvements as Il-76TD.

By Spring 1988, about 360 military Il-76s and Il-76M/MDs had been delivered to first-line squadrons of the Soviet Transport Aviation force, as An-12 replacements, from the assembly plant at Tashkent. Other customers for the military version include the air forces of Iraq, Czechoslovakia and Poland. India has 24, which are known by the Indian Air Force name of **Gajaraj**.

India is reported to be considering the conversion of some of its standard Il-76s for AEW duties. A specialised AEW&C version of the Il-76, known to NATO as 'Mainstay', is described separately, as is a flight refuelling tanker version known as 'Midas'.

Aeroflot has more than 120 Il-76s, including Il-76Ts and Il-76Ms, which form an immediately available military reserve. At least 75 civil and military Il-76s have been exported. Of these, Iraqi Airways has received a total of at least 24 Il-76Ts and Il-76Ms (one has been shot down), which are operated on behalf of the military services; Jamahiriyan Air Transport of Libya has 19 Il-76Ts; Syrianair has two Il-76Ms and two Il-76Ts; Bakhtar Afghan Airlines had one Il-76 on loan from Aeroflot in 1986. The guns are removed from the rear turret of Il-76Ms in airline service, and the first of at least two Il-76MDs delivered to Cubana, in November 1984, had no tail turret.

In July 1975, the Il-76 set a total of 25 officially recognised records for speed and altitude with payload. Details can be found in the 1981-82 *Jane's*. Some of them have since been beaten by an Il-86, a B-1B and an An-124.

In specialised roles, Il-76s have served as a testbed for the power plant of the Il-86 and an experimental propfan, and as aircraft in which Soviet cosmonauts have been able to experience several tens of seconds of weightlessness during training.

Production was continuing at the rate of more than 50 aircraft a year in 1988. The following description applies to the Il-76T:

TYPE: Four-turbofan medium/long-range freight transport.

WINGS: Cantilever monoplane, mounted above fuselage to leave interior unobstructed, and with constant anhedral from junction with centre-section on each side. Sweepback 25° at quarter-chord. All-metal five-piece structure,

comprising centre-section, two inner panels carrying engines, and two outer panels. Leading-edge sweepback constant. Trailing-edge sweep increases outboard of joint between each inner and outer panel. Multi-spar fail-safe construction. Centre-section integral with fuselage. Mass balanced ailerons, with balance/trim tabs. Two-section triple-slotted flaps over approx 75 per cent of each semi-span, from wing root to inboard edge of aileron. Eight upper surface spoilers forward of flaps on each wing, four on each inner and outer wing panel. Leading-edge slats over almost entire span, two on each inner panel, three on each outer panel.

FUSELAGE: All-metal semi-monocoque fail-safe structure of basically circular section. Underside of upswept rear fuselage made up of two outward hinged clamshell doors, upward hinged panel between these doors, and downward hinged loading ramp.

TAIL UNIT: Cantilever all-metal structure, with variable incidence T tailplane. All surfaces sweptback. All control surfaces aerodynamically balanced. Tabs in rudder and each elevator.

LANDING GEAR: Hydraulically retractable tricycle type, designed for operation from prepared and unprepared runways. Nose unit made up of two pairs of wheels, side by side, with central oleo. Main gear on each side is made up of two units in tandem, each unit with four wheels on a single axle. Low-pressure tyres size 1,300 × 480 on mainwheels, 1,100 × 330 on nosewheels. Nosewheels retract forward. Main units retract inward into two large ventral fairings under fuselage, with an additional large fairing on each side of lower fuselage over actuating gear. During retraction mainwheel axles rotate around leg, so that wheels stow with axles parallel to fuselage axis (ie: wheels remain vertical but at 90° to direction of flight). All doors on wheel wells close when gear is down, to prevent fouling of legs by snow, ice, mud, etc. Oleo-pneumatic shock absorbers. Tyre pressure can be varied in flight from 2.5 to 5 bars (36-73 lb/sq in) to suit different landing strip conditions. Hydraulic brakes on mainwheels.

POWER PLANT: Four Soloviev D-30KP turbofans, each rated at 117.7 kN (26,455 lb st), in individual underwing pods. Each pod is carried on a large forward-inclined pylon and is fitted with a clamshell thrust reverser. Integral fuel tanks between spars of inner and outer wing panels. Total fuel capacity reported to be 81,830 litres (21,617 US gallons; 18,000 Imp gallons).

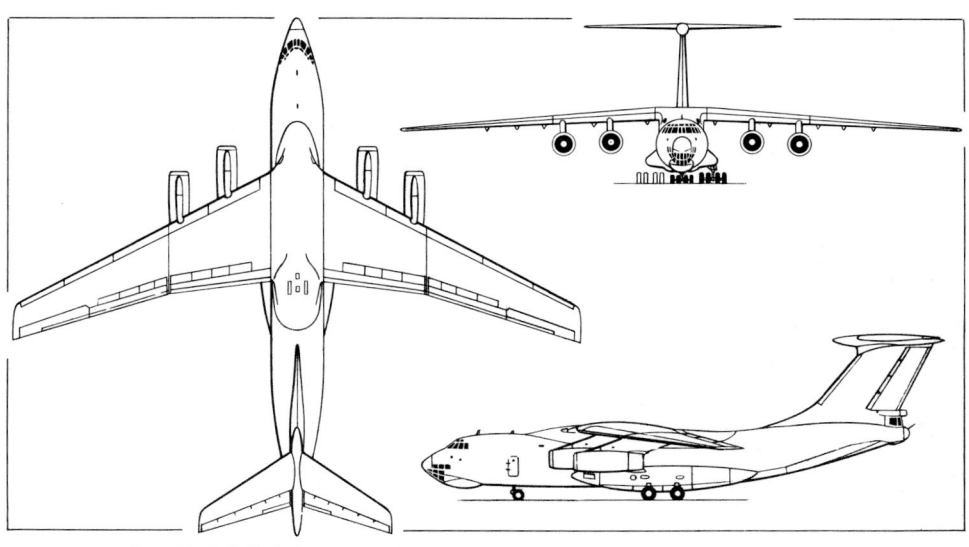

Ilyushin Il-76MD four-turbofan heavy freight carrying transport *(Pilot Press)*

ACCOMMODATION: Crew of seven, including two freight handlers. Conventional side by side seating for pilot and co-pilot on spacious flight deck. Station for navigator below flight deck in glazed nose. Forward hinged door on each side of fuselage forward of wing. Two windows on each side of hold serve as emergency exits. Hold has reinforced floor of titanium alloys, with folding roller conveyors, and is loaded via rear ramp. Entire accommodation is pressurised, and advanced mechanical handling systems are provided for containerised and other freight, which can include standard ISO containers, each 12 m (39 ft 4½ in) long, building machinery, heavy crawlers and mobile cranes. Typical loads include six containers measuring either 2.99 × 2.44 × 2.44 m (9 ft 9¾ in × 8 ft × 8 ft) or 2.99 × 2.44 × 1.90 m (9 ft 9¾ in × 8 ft × 6 ft 2¾ in) and with loaded weights of 5,670 kg (12,500 lb) or 5,000 kg (11,025 lb) respectively; or twelve containers measuring 1.46 × 2.44 × 1.90 m (4 ft 9¼ in × 8 ft × 6 ft 2¾ in) and each weighing 2,500 kg (5,511 lb) loaded; or six pallets measuring 2.99 × 2.44 m (9 ft 9¾ in × 8 ft) and each weighing 5,670 kg (12,500 lb); or twelve pallets measuring 1.46 × 2.44 m (4 ft 9¼ in × 8 ft) and each weighing 2,500 kg (5,511 lb). Quick configuration changes can be made by the use of modules, each able to accommodate 30 passengers in four-abreast seating, litter patients and medical attendants, or cargo. Three such modules can be carried, each approx 6.10 m (20 ft) long, 2.44 m (8 ft) wide and 2.44 m (8 ft) high. They are loaded through the rear doors by means of two overhead travelling cranes, and are secured to the cabin floor with cargo restraints. Cranes can utilise two hoists, each with capacity of 3,000 kg (6,615 lb), or four hoists, each with capacity of 2,500 kg (5,511 lb). Ramp can be used as additional hoist, with capacity of up to 30,000 kg (66,140 lb) to facilitate loading of large vehicles and those with caterpillar tracks. Pilot's and co-pilot's windscreens can each be fitted with two wipers, top and bottom.

SYSTEMS: Hydraulic system includes servo motors and motors to drive the flaps, slats, landing gear and its doors, ramp, rear fuselage clamshell doors and load hoists. Flying control boosters are supplied by electric pumps and are independent of the central hydraulic supply. Manual control is possible after booster failure. Electrical system includes engine driven generators, auxiliary generators driven by an APU, DC converters and batteries. It powers the pumps for the flying control system boosters, radio and avionics, and lighting systems.

AVIONICS AND EQUIPMENT: Full equipment for all-weather operation by day and night, including a computer for automatic flight control and automatic landing approach. Large meteorological and ground mapping radar in undernose radome. APU in port side landing gear fairing for engine starting and to supply all aircraft systems on ground, making aircraft independent of ground facilities.

DIMENSIONS, EXTERNAL:

Wing span	50.50 m (165 ft 8 in)
Wing aspect ratio	8.5
Length overall	46.59 m (152 ft 10¼ in)
Height overall	14.76 m (48 ft 5 in)
Rear loading aperture: Width	3.40 m (11 ft 1¾ in)
Height	3.45 m (11 ft 4 in)

DIMENSIONS, INTERNAL:

Cabin: Length: excl ramp	20.00 m (65 ft 7½ in)
incl ramp	24.50 m (80 ft 4½ in)
Width	3.40 m (11 ft 1¾ in)
Height	3.46 m (11 ft 4¼ in)
Volume	235.3 m³ (8,310 cu ft)

AREA:

Wings, gross	300.0 m² (3,229.2 sq ft)

WEIGHTS AND LOADINGS (A: Il-76T, B: Il-76TD):

Max payload: A	40,000 kg (88,185 lb)
B	48,000 kg (105,820 lb)
Max T-O weight: A	170,000 kg (374,785 lb)
B	190,000 kg (418,875 lb)
Permissible axle load (vehicles):	
A	7,500-11,000 kg (16,535-24,250 lb)
Permissible floor loading:	
A	1,450-3,100 kg/m² (297-635 lb/sq ft)
Max wing loading: A	566.7 kg/m² (116.05 lb/sq ft)
B	633.3 kg/m² (129.72 lb/sq ft)
Max power loading: A	361.1 kg/kN (3.54 lb/lb st)
B	403.6 kg/kN (3.95 lb/lb st)

PERFORMANCE (Il-76T):

Max level speed	459 knots (850 km/h; 528 mph)
Cruising speed	405-432 knots (750-800 km/h; 466-497 mph)
T-O speed	114 knots (210 km/h; 131 mph)
Approach and landing speed	119-130 knots (220-240 km/h; 137-149 mph)
Normal cruising height	9,000-12,000 m (29,500-39,370 ft)
Absolute ceiling	approx 15,500 m (50,850 ft)
T-O run	850 m (2,790 ft)
Landing run	450 m (1,475 ft)
Nominal range with 40,000 kg (88,185 lb) payload	2,700 nm (5,000 km; 3,100 miles)
Max range, with reserves	3,617 nm (6,700 km; 4,163 miles)

ILYUSHIN Il-76 (AEW&C)
NATO reporting name: Mainstay

Development of this AEW&C (airborne early warning and control) version of the Il-76 began in the 1970s as a replacement for the Tu-126s operated by the Soviet Voyska PVO home defence force and tactical air forces. Known to NATO as 'Mainstay', it has a conventionally located rotating 'saucer' radome, lengthened fuselage forward of the wings, a flight refuelling probe, a new IFF system and comprehensive ECM equipment. It provides the Soviet forces with the capability to detect and track aircraft and cruise missiles flying at low altitude over land and water and could be used to help direct fighter operations over European and Asian battlefields as well as to enhance air surveillance and defence of the USSR. More than 12 'Mainstays' are operational, and a production rate of at least five aircraft a year is expected. They are intended to operate primarily with the Soviet air forces' new-generation MiG-29, MiG-31 and Sukhoi Su-27 counter-air fighters.

'Mainstay', the AEW&C version of the Il-76 (333 Squadron, Royal Norwegian Air Force)

The starboard underwing pod of an Il-76 'Midas' tanker is visible under the nose of a Tupolev 'Blackjack' bomber

ILYUSHIN Il-76 FLIGHT REFUELLING TANKER
NATO reporting name: Midas

In the mid-1970s the Ilyushin OKB began development of a probe-and-drogue flight refuelling tanker version of the Il-76, known to NATO as 'Midas', to replace the modified Myasishchev M-4 ('Bison') aircraft which have served previously in this role. The first operational 'Midas' unit entered service in 1987, in support of both tactical and strategic combat aircraft. It is a three-point tanker, with refuelling pods under the outer wings and a hose-reel in the rear fuselage.

ILYUSHIN Il-86
NATO reporting name: Camber

The early history of this four-turbofan wide-bodied passenger transport was outlined in the 1982-83 and previous editions of *Jane's*. Construction of two prototypes was started in 1974. On 22 December 1976, piloted by Hero of the Soviet Union A. Kuznetsov, the first of these (SSSR-86000) made a first flight of about 40 min after taking off in 1,700 m (5,575 ft) from a 1,820 m (5,970 ft)

runway at the old Moscow Central Airport of Khodinka, where the Ilyushin Bureau has its headquarters, to the official flight test centre.

Aircraft SSSR-86002, which flew for the first time at Voronezh on 24 October 1977, was described as the first production Il-86. Aeroflot took delivery of its first Il-86 (SSSR-86004) on 24 September 1979, and scheduled services began on 26 December 1980. First international service operated by Il-86 was Moscow-East Berlin, from 3 July 1981. It is intended to produce a total of more than 100 Il-86s by 1995, of which approximately 60 had entered service in mid-1988. To remedy deficiencies in designed performance, the prototype of a new version with Soloviev PS-90A (D-90) high bypass ratio turbofans, each rated at approximately 157 kN (35,300 lb st), is scheduled to fly for the first time in 1990.

On 22 September 1981, an Il-86 piloted by G. Volokhov averaged 526.6 knots (975.3 km/h; 606 mph) over a 2,000 km closed circuit, carrying a payload of 65,000 kg. This flight set seven records, for payloads from 35,000 to 65,000 kg. Two days later, the same pilot averaged 519.4 knots (962 km/h; 597.8 mph) over 1,000 km, setting 11 records for payloads from 30,000 to 80,000 kg.

For production aircraft, wing slats, pylons to carry the engine pods, the tail fin and tailplane are being manufactured in Poland by PZL Mielec. Final assembly is centred at Voronezh. The airframe is believed to be designed for 40,000 flying hours or 20,000 landings.

The following description applies to the initial production Il-86:

TYPE: Four-turbofan wide-bodied passenger transport.

WINGS: Cantilever monoplane of all-metal construction (fixed surfaces made at Voronezh). Wings mounted in low-mid position on fuselage. Dihedral from roots. Sweepback 35° at quarter-chord. Three spars in inner wings, two in each outer panel. Large double-slotted trailing-edge flaps, in two sections along entire span of each wing inboard of aileron. Multi-section spoilers and airbrakes in top surface, forward of all four flap sections. Full span leading-edge slats, with small cutaway to clear each inboard engine pylon. Shallow fence on top surface in line with each pylon.

FUSELAGE: Conventional semi-monocoque light alloy pressurised structure of circular cross section. Floors of main and lower decks of honeycomb and carbonfibre reinforced plastics.

TAIL UNIT: Conventional sweptback cantilever structure, with tailplane dihedral. Variable incidence tailplane. Each control surface in two sections.

LANDING GEAR: Retractable four-unit type. Forward retracting steerable twin-wheel nose unit, and three four-wheel bogie main units. Two of the latter retract

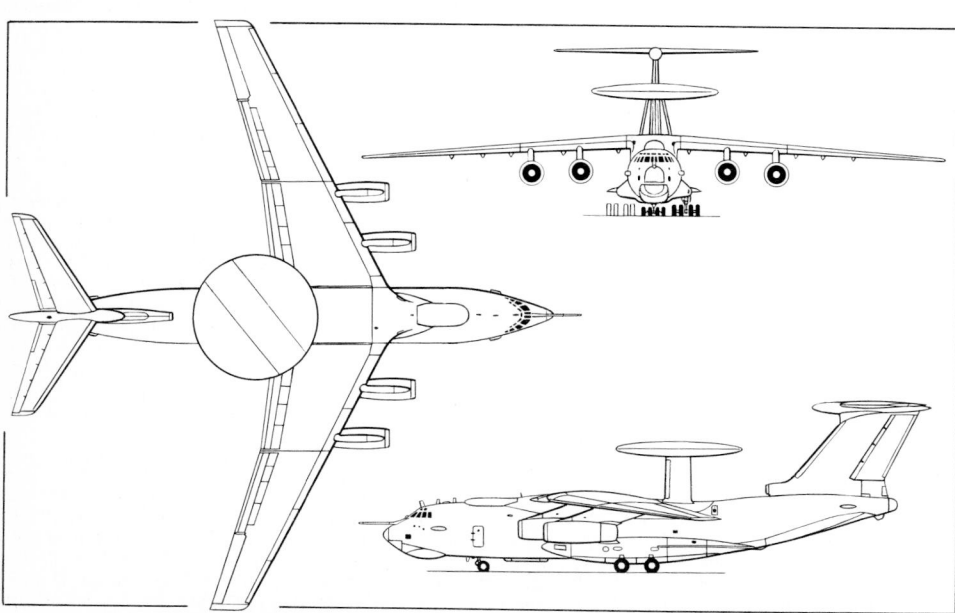

AEW&C version of Ilyushin Il-76, known to NATO as 'Mainstay' (Pilot Press)

Ilyushin Il-86 wide-bodied transport (four Kuznetsov NK-86 turbofans) in Aeroflot markings *(Martin Fricke)*

inward into the wingroot fairings; the third unit is mounted centrally under the fuselage, slightly forward of the others, and retracts forward. (Main landing gear made at Kuibyshev.) Mainwheel tyres size 1300 × 480; nosewheel tyres size 1120 × 450.

POWER PLANT: Four Kuznetsov NK-86 turbofans, each rated at 127.5 kN (28,660 lb st), mounted on pylons forward of wing leading-edges. Engines fitted with combined thrust reversers/noise attenuators. Integral fuel tanks in wings, capacity 70,000-80,000 litres (18,492-21,133 US gallons; 15,398-17,597 Imp gallons).

ACCOMMODATION: Standard flight crew comprises two pilots and a flight engineer, with provision for a navigator if required. Flight engineer's seat normally faces to starboard, aft of co-pilot, but can pivot to central forward-facing position to enable the engineer to operate the throttles. Upper deck, on which all seats are located, is divided into three separate cabins by wardrobes, a serving area connected by elevator to the lower deck galley, and cabin staff accommodation, with a total of eight toilets at front (2) and rear (6) of the aircraft. Cabins feature unusually large windows, indirect lighting in walls and in ceiling panels, and enclosed baggage lockers at top of side walls. Preponderance of metal and natural fibre materials rather than plastics throughout cabins to enhance safety in an emergency. Up to 350 passengers in basic nine-abreast seating throughout, with two aisles, each 55 cm (21.6 in) wide. Suggested mixed class alternative layout provides for 28 passengers six-abreast in the front cabin, and 206 passengers eight-abreast in the other two cabins. Passengers enter via three airstair doors (made in Kharkov), which hinge down from the port side of the lower deck. One of these doors is forward of the wing; the others are aft of the wing. Four further doors at upper deck level on each side, for emergency use (using dual inflatable escape slides) and for use at airports where the utilisation of high level boarding steps or bridges is preferred. Coats and hand baggage are stowed on the lower deck before passengers climb one of three fixed staircases to the main deck. (A version of the Il-86 is available without the lower deck airstair doors and staircases, reducing operating weight empty by 3,000 kg; 6,610 lb and permitting installation of 25 more seats on upper deck.) Cargo holds on the lower deck are designed to accommodate heavy or registered baggage and freight in 8 standard LD3 containers, or 16 LD3 containers if some of the carry-on baggage racks are omitted. Access is via upward hinged doors forward of the starboard wing root leading-edge and at the side of the rear hold. Containers can be loaded and unloaded by means of a self-propelled truck with built-in roller conveyor. Films can be shown in flight, and there is a choice of 12 tape recorded audio programmes. A bar-buffet can be provided on the lower deck in place of the baggage and freight accommodation in the forward vestibule.

SYSTEMS: Four completely self-contained hydraulic systems, each operated by one of the engines, for actuation of flying control surfaces, tailplane variable incidence, spoilers, airbrakes, slats, flaps, landing gear, nosewheel steering, wheel brakes, anti-skid system, and upper level doors when passenger gangways are used. No provision for manual operation of primary flying control surfaces after failure of powered systems. All hot pipelines of air-conditioning system, and all fuel supply lines, outside pressure cell. Primary 200/155V 400Hz AC electrical system, powered by four 40kVA engine driven generators. Secondary 36V three-phase AC and 27V DC systems. Five accumulators and static transformer. Smoke detection system, with sensors in baggage, freight and equipment stowage areas. Pulse generating de-icing

system consuming 500 times less energy than a conventional hot air or electrical system. APU in tailcone.

AVIONICS: All avionics equipment located within pressurised part of fuselage. Flight control and nav systems provide for automatic climb to the selected height, control of the rate of climb and automatic descent, and permit automatic landing in ICAO Cat IIIA conditions. Pre-programmable Doppler nav system with readout display screen on flight deck, on which microfilmed maps can be projected. Position of aircraft is indicated by cursor, driven by system computer. Nav system is updated automatically by inputs from VOR or VOR/DME radio beacons.

DIMENSIONS, EXTERNAL:

Wing span	48.06 m (157 ft 8¼ in)
Length overall	59.54 m (195 ft 4 in)
Length of fuselage	56.10 m (184 ft 0¾ in)
Diameter of fuselage	6.08 m (19 ft 11½ in)
Height overall	15.81 m (51 ft 10½ in)
Tailplane span	20.57 m (67 ft 6 in)
Wheel track (c/l of outer shock struts)	
	11.15 m (36 ft 7 in)
Wheelbase	21.34 m (70 ft 0 in)

DIMENSIONS, INTERNAL:

Main cabins: Height	2.61 m (8 ft 7 in)
Max width	approx 5.70 m (18 ft 8½ in)

AREA:

Wings, gross	320 m² (3,444 sq ft)

WEIGHTS:

Max payload	42,000 kg (92,600 lb)
Max fuel	86,000 kg (189,600 lb)
Max T-O weight (dependent on size and type of runway)	190,000-208,000 kg (418,875-458,560 lb)
Max landing weight	175,000 kg (385,800 lb)

PERFORMANCE (designed):
Normal cruising speed at 9,000-11,000 m (30,000-36,000 ft) 486-512 knots (900-950 km/h; 559-590 mph)
Approach speed
130-141 knots (240-260 km/h; 149-162 mph)
Field length for T-O and landing
2,300-2,600 m (7,550-8,530 ft)
* Range: with 40,000 kg (88,185 lb) payload
1,944 nm (3,600 km; 2,235 miles)

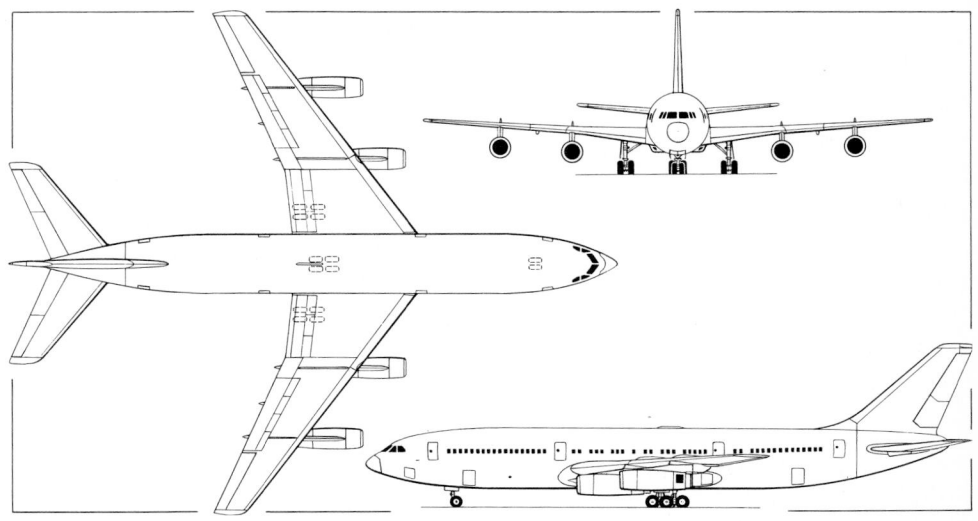

Ilyushin Il-86 four-turbofan wide-bodied passenger transport *(Pilot Press)*

* with max fuel 2,480 nm (4,600 km; 2,858 miles)
* *Reports suggest that these design ranges are not being achieved. The East German airline Interflug quotes a max range of 1,350 nm (2,500 km; 1,550 miles) in its sales literature*

ILYUSHIN Il-96-300

The longer-range derivative of the Il-86, to which reference was first made in the 1982-83 *Jane's*, is now designated Il-96-300. It bears a superficial resemblance to the Il-86 but is, in fact, a new design. Advanced structural materials and state of the art technology are intended to make practicable a service life of 60,000 hours and 12,000 landings. The power plant will comprise four Soloviev PS-90A (D-90A) high bypass ratio turbofans, each rated at about 157 kN (35,300 lb st).

The entirely new wings of the Il-96 will have a supercritical section, winglets, an increased span compared with those of the Il-86 and reduced sweepback of 30° at quarter-chord. The control surfaces are enlarged, to improve stability after an engine failure. The two-deck fuselage will be basically unchanged in form, with lighter and more comfortable seats for 235 to 300 passengers, eight or nine abreast, with two aisles, each 55 cm (21.65 in) wide.

The basic all-tourist class layout has two cabins for 66 and 234 passengers respectively, nine-abreast at 87 cm (34.25 in) seat pitch, separated by a buffet counter and lifts from the galley on the lower deck. There are two toilets and a wardrobe at the front, six more toilets, a rack for cabin staff's belongings and seats for cabin staff at the rear. Seats recline, and are provided with individual tables, ventilation, earphones and attendant call button. Indirect lighting is standard.

The 235-seat mixed class version will have a front cabin for 22 first class passengers, six abreast in pairs, at 102 cm (40 in) seat pitch; a centre cabin with 40 business class seats, eight abreast at 90 cm (35.4 in) seat pitch; and a rear cabin for 173 tourist class passengers, basically nine abreast at 87 cm (34.25 in) seat pitch.

Unlike the Il-86, the Il-96-300 passenger cabin will be entered through doors on the upper deck, three on each side, at the front and rear and forward of the wings. The lower deck will have a front cargo compartment for six

LD3 containers, a central compartment aft of the wing for ten containers, and a tapering compartment for general cargo at the rear. Three doors on the starboard side will provide separate access to each compartment. The galley and lifts will be located between the front cargo compartment and the wing.

The crew will consist of two pilots and a flight engineer, plus ten to twelve cabin attendants. On the flight deck, conventional standby instruments will be retained, but primary flight information will be presented on dual twin-screen colour CRTs, fed by triplex INS, a satellite navigation system and other sensors. Triplex flight control and flight management systems, together with a head-up display, will permit fully automatic en-route control and operations in ICAO Category IIIA minima. Duplex engine and systems monitoring and failure warning systems will feed in-flight information to both the flight engineer's station and monitors on the ground. Another electronic system will provide real-time automatic weight and CG situation data.

The Il-96 is designed to conform with ICAO Chapter 3 Supplement 16 noise requirements. First flight was expected to be made before the end of 1988, to be followed by manufacture of 60-70 production Il-96-300s during the period of the Soviet 1990-95 five-year plan. CSA of Czechoslovakia has stated its intention to operate Il-96-300s.

Brief details of a reported twin-engined version of the Il-96 are given in a separate entry.

DIMENSIONS, EXTERNAL:
Wing span	57.66 m (189 ft 2 in)
Wing aspect ratio	9.5
Length overall	55.35 m (181 ft 7¼ in)
Length of fuselage	51.15 m (167 ft 9¾ in)
Diameter of fuselage	6.08 m (19 ft 11½ in)
Height overall	17.57 m (57 ft 7¾ in)
Wheel track	10.40 m (34 ft 1½ in)

Cargo compartment doors (front and centre):
Height	1.825 m (5 ft 11¾ in)
Width	1.78 m (5 ft 10 in)
Galley door: Height	1.20 m (3 ft 11¼ in)
Width	0.80 m (2 ft 7½ in)

AREA:
Wings, gross	350.0 m² (3,767.4 sq ft)

WEIGHTS:
Basic operating weight	117,000 kg (257,940 lb)
Max payload	40,000 kg (88,185 lb)
Max T-O weight	216,000 kg (476,200 lb)
Max landing weight	175,000 kg (385,810 lb)

PERFORMANCE (estimated):
Normal cruising speed at 10,100-12,100 m (33,135-39,700 ft)
459-486 knots (850-900 km/h; 528-559 mph)
Approach speed	140 knots (260 km/h; 162 mph)
Balanced T-O runway length	2,600 m (8,530 ft)
Balanced landing runway length	1,980 m (6,500 ft)

Range, with reserves:
with max payload   4,050 nm (7,500 km; 4,660 miles)
with 30,000 kg (66,140 lb) payload
4,860 nm (9,000 km; 5,590 miles)
with 15,000 kg (33,070 lb) payload
5,940 nm (11,000 km; 6,835 miles)

ILYUSHIN Il-96 (Twin-engined version)

In early 1988, it was reported that the Ilyushin OKB is developing a twin-engined version of the Il-96, powered by Lotarev D-18 turbofans, each rated at between 275 and 314 kN (61,750-70,500 lb st). Like the West European Airbus A330 and A340, the twin-engined and four-engined variants of the Il-96 would use substantially the same wings.

ILYUSHIN Il-114

The Il-114 is the smallest of the new generation of transport aircraft that will be developed and produced jointly by various Comecon nations and Yugoslavia for operation at the turn of the century. Intended to replace aircraft in the class of the An-24, it is being designed for short-haul and feeder services from both paved and grass

Models of Il-96-300 (top) and Il-114 displayed at 1987 Paris Air Show *(Air Portraits)*

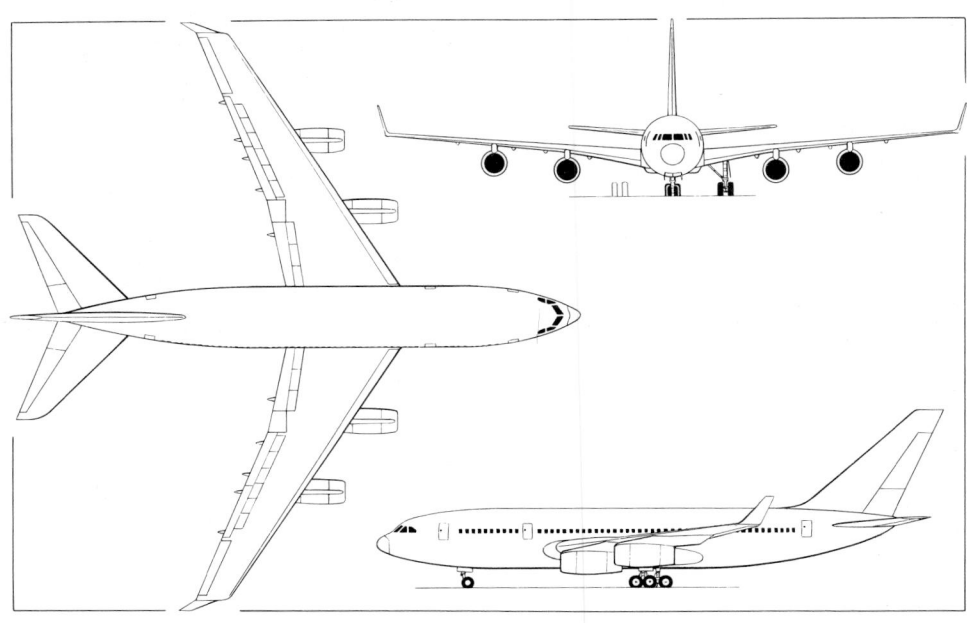

Ilyushin Il-96-300 four-turbofan long-range transport *(Pilot Press)*

surfaces. Equipment will be to the latest standards for ICAO Category I and II operations. Service life is intended to be 30,000 hours and 30,000 landings.

The prototype Il-114 is scheduled to fly for the first time during the Spring of 1989. Using up to three assembly lines, it is planned to manufacture some 500 production aircraft during the period of the Soviet 1990-95 five-year plan.

TYPE: Twin-turboprop short-range passenger and freight transport.

WINGS: Cantilever low-wing monoplane. Dihedral from roots. Conventional all-metal structure. Double-slotted flaps, inboard and outboard of engine nacelle, and aileron occupy entire trailing-edge of each wing. Airbrake forward of each flap section. Two tabs in each aileron.

FUSELAGE: Conventional metal semi-monocoque structure of circular section.

TAIL UNIT: Conventional cantilever metal structure, with sweptback vertical surfaces. Two tabs in rudder; one in each elevator.

LANDING GEAR: Retractable tricycle type, with twin wheels on each unit, manufactured by WSK-PZL Krosno. Hydraulic retraction, with emergency extension by gravity. Oleo-pneumatic shock absorber in each unit. Nosewheels steerable ±55°. Brakes on mainwheels. All wheel doors remain closed except during retraction or extension of the landing gear.

POWER PLANT: Two 1,864 kW (2,500 shp) Isotov TV7-117 turboprops, each driving a six-blade WSK-PZL Warszawa-Okecie propeller with spinner.

ACCOMMODATION: Flight crew of two, plus stewardess. Emergency exit window on each side of flight deck. Four abreast seats for 60 passengers in main cabin, at 75 cm (29.5 in) seat pitch, with central aisle 40 cm (15.75 in) wide. Airstair type passenger door at front of cabin on port side. Galley, cloakroom and toilet at rear, with emergency escape slide by service door on starboard side. Type III emergency exit over each wing. Baggage hold door at front of cabin on starboard side. Further baggage compartment to rear of cabin. Optional large carry-on baggage shelves in lobby by main door at front of cabin.

AVIONICS: Digital avionics for automatic or manual control by day or night, including automatic approach and landing in limiting weather conditions (ICAO Category I and II).

DIMENSIONS, EXTERNAL:
Wing span	30.00 m (98 ft 5¼ in)
Length overall	25.46 m (83 ft 6½ in)
Diameter of fuselage	2.86 m (9 ft 4½ in)
Height overall	8.60 m (28 ft 2½ in)
Wheel track	8.20 m (26 ft 11 in)
Propeller diameter	3.60 m (11 ft 9¾ in)
Propeller ground clearance	0.62 m (2 ft 0½ in)
Propeller fuselage clearance	0.90 m (2 ft 11½ in)
Passenger door: Height	1.75 m (5 ft 9 in)
Width	0.86 m (2 ft 9¾ in)

Artist's impression of Ilyushin Il-114 twin-turboprop airliner *(Jane's/Mike Keep)*

Service door (rear): Height	1.40 m (4 ft 7¼ in)			
Width	0.86 m (2 ft 9¾ in)			
Emergency exit (each): Height	0.91 m (2 ft 11¾ in)			
Width	0.51 m (1 ft 8 in)			

WEIGHTS:
Operating weight empty	13,000 kg (28,660 lb)
Max payload	6,000 kg (13,227 lb)
Max T-O weight	20,250 kg (44,640 lb)

PERFORMANCE (estimated):
Max cruising speed	270 knots (500 km/h; 310 mph)
Approach speed	97-102 knots (180-190 km/h; 112-118 mph)
Optimum cruising height	6,000-8,000 m (19,685-26,250 ft)
Balanced field length: paved	1,400 m (4,600 ft)
unpaved	1,650 m (5,415 ft)

Landing run	1,250 m (4,100 ft)

Range, with reserves:
with 5,400 kg (11,905 lb) payload	540 nm (1,000 km; 621 miles)
with 3,500 kg (7,715 lb) payload	1,538 nm (2,850 km; 1,770 miles)

KAMOV

CHIEF OF DESIGN BUREAU: S. V. Mikheyev

This design bureau continues the work of Nikolai I. Kamov, a leading designer of rotating wing aircraft since the late 1920s, who died on 24 November 1973, aged 71.

KAMOV Ka-25
NATO reporting name: Hormone

The prototype of this military helicopter took part in the Soviet Aviation Day flypast over Tushino Airport, Moscow, in July 1961. About 460 production Ka-25s were built in 1966-75, of which little more than 100 remain operational with the Soviet Navy. Others are in first-line service in India, Syria, Vietnam and Yugoslavia.

As well as serving as an anti-submarine and missile support aircraft, the Ka-25 fulfils other military roles. Three versions are identified by NATO reporting names:

Hormone-A. Basic ship-based anti-submarine version, operated from a variety of Soviet Navy ships, including missile frigates, cruisers, the helicopter carriers *Moskva* and *Leningrad*, and carrier/cruisers of the 'Kiev' class. A major shortcoming is said to be lack of night and all-weather sonar dipping capability. Being replaced progressively by Ka-27 ('Helix-A').

Hormone-B. Special electronics variant, able to provide over-the-horizon target acquisition for long-range cruise missiles launched from ships. These include SS-N-3B (NATO 'Shaddock') missiles launched from 'Kresta I' cruisers; SS-N-12 ('Sandbox') missiles from 'Kiev' class carrier/cruisers and 'Slava' class cruisers; SS-N-19 missiles from the battle cruisers *Kirov* and *Frunze*; and SS-N-22 missiles from destroyers of the 'Sovremenny' class. 'Kiev' and 'Kirov' class ships each carry three 'Hormone-Bs', the other classes one each. Larger undernose radome with more spherical undersurface than that of 'Hormone-A'. Cylindrical radome under rear of cabin. Data link equipment.

Hormone-C. Utility and search and rescue model, generally similar to 'Hormone-A' but with inessential operational equipment and weapons removed. This version sometimes has a yagi aerial mounted on the nose.

TYPE: Twin-turbine anti-submarine, missile support and general purpose helicopter.

ROTOR SYSTEM: Two three-blade coaxial contra-rotating rotors. Automatic blade folding.

FUSELAGE: Conventional all-metal semi-monocoque structure of pod and boom type.

TAIL UNIT: Cantilever all-metal structure, with central fin, ventral fin and twin endplate fins and rudders which are toed inward.

LANDING GEAR: Four-wheel type. Oleo-pneumatic shock absorbers. Nosewheels are smaller than mainwheels and are of castoring type. Each wheel can be enclosed in an inflatable pontoon surmounted by inflation bottles to provide flotation in event of an emergency alighting on water. All four legs are pivoted to retract upward, so that the wheels can be moved to a position where they offer least interference to signals from the nose radar.

POWER PLANT: Two 671 kW (900 shp) Glushenkov GTD-3F turboshafts, mounted side by side above cabin, forward of rotor driveshaft, on early aircraft. Later aircraft have

Kamov Ka-25 ('Hormone-A') anti-submarine helicopter in Yugoslav service *(Ivo Sturzenegger)*

738 kW (990 shp) GTD-3BM turboshafts. Independent fuel supply to each engine. Provision for carrying external fuel tank on each side of cabin.

ACCOMMODATION: Pilot and co-pilot side by side on flight deck, with rearward sliding door on each side. Entry to main cabin is via a rearward sliding door to rear of main landing gear on port side. Cabin accommodates two or three systems operators in ASW role, but is large enough to contain 12 folding seats for passengers.

AVIONICS AND EQUIPMENT: Equipment available for all versions includes autopilot, navigational system, radio compass, radio communications installations, lighting system for all-weather operation by day or night, and hoist mounted above cabin door. IFF antennae (NATO 'Odd Rods') above nose and alongside central tail fin. Dipping sonar housed in compartment at rear of main cabin, immediately forward of tailboom, and search radar in an undernose radome (diameter 1.25 m; 4 ft 1 in) on anti-submarine version, which can have a canister of sonobuoys mounted externally aft of the starboard main landing gear. Some aircraft have a blister fairing over equipment mounted at the base of the centre tail fin; most have a cylindrical housing for ESM above the tailboom, with a shallow blister fairing to the rear of the cylindrical

housing. Provision for a camera pod on port side of cabin.

ARMAMENT: Doors under the fuselage of some aircraft enclose a weapons bay for two 450 mm (18 in) ASW torpedoes, nuclear depth charges and other stores.

DIMENSIONS, EXTERNAL:
Rotor diameter (each)	15.74 m (51 ft 7¾ in)
Length of fuselage	9.75 m (32 ft 0 in)
Height to top of rotor head	5.37 m (17 ft 7½ in)
Width over tail-fins	3.76 m (12 ft 4 in)
Wheel track: front	1.41 m (4 ft 7½ in)
rear	3.52 m (11 ft 6½ in)
Cabin door: Height	1.10 m (3 ft 7¼ in)
Width	1.20 m (3 ft 11¼ in)

DIMENSIONS, INTERNAL:
Cabin, excl flight deck:
Length	3.95 m (12 ft 11½ in)
Max width	1.50 m (4 ft 11 in)
Max height	1.25 m (4 ft 1¼ in)

WEIGHTS:
Weight empty	4,765 kg (10,505 lb)
Max T-O weight	7,500 kg (16,535 lb)

PERFORMANCE:
Max level speed	113 knots (209 km/h; 130 mph)
Normal cruising speed	104 knots (193 km/h; 120 mph)
Service ceiling	3,350 m (11,000 ft)

Range, with reserves:
with standard fuel	217 nm (400 km; 250 miles)
with external tanks	351 nm (650 km; 405 miles)

KAMOV Ka-26
NATO reporting name: Hoodlum-A

The Ka-26 (NATO 'Hoodlum-A') first flew in prototype form in 1965 and entered service as an agricultural aircraft in the Soviet Union in 1970, being used primarily over orchards and vineyards. It is used widely on Aeroflot's air ambulance services and is suitable for many other applications, including cargo and passenger transport, aerial survey, forest firefighting, mineral prospecting, pipeline construction, laying transmission lines, and a number of military duties, including search and rescue (for detailed descriptions of variants see 1986-87 and earlier editions).

More than 600 Ka-26s were produced by 1977. They were delivered for civilian service in 15 countries; military operators include the air forces of Bulgaria and Hungary. Some are now being converted to turbine powered Ka-126 ('Hoodlum-B') standard by ICA Brasov (see Romanian section).

Abbreviated details of the Ka-26 follow. A full description can be found in the 1987-88 and previous editions of *Jane's*.

Ka-25 ('Hormone-B') with wheels retracted to prevent interference with signals from nose radar

TYPE: Twin-engined general purpose light helicopter.
POWER PLANT: Two 242.5 kW (325 hp) Vedeneyev M-14V-26 aircooled radial piston engines, mounted in pods on short stub wings at top of fuselage.
ACCOMMODATION: Fully enclosed cabin, with door on each side, fitted out normally for operation by single pilot; second seat and dual controls optional. Cabin warmed and demisted by air from combustion heater, which also heats passenger compartment when fitted. Air filter on nose of agricultural version. The space aft of the cabin, between the main landing gear units and under the rotor transmission, is able to accommodate a variety of interchangeable payloads. For agricultural work, a chemical hopper (capacity 900 kg; 1,985 lb) and dust spreader or spraybars are fitted in this position, on the aircraft's centre of gravity. This equipment is quickly removable and can be replaced by a cargo/passenger pod accommodating four or six persons, with provision for a seventh passenger beside the pilot; or two stretcher patients, two seated casualties and a medical attendant in ambulance role. Alternatively, the Ka-26 can be operated with either an open platform for hauling freight or a hook for slinging bulky loads at the end of a cable or in a cargo net.

DIMENSIONS, EXTERNAL:

Rotor diameter (each)	13.00 m (42 ft 8 in)
Vertical separation between rotors	1.17 m (3 ft 10 in)
Length of fuselage	7.75 m (25 ft 5 in)
Height overall	4.05 m (13 ft 3½ in)
Width over engine pods	3.64 m (11 ft 11½ in)
Width over agricultural spraybars	11.20 m (36 ft 9 in)
Tailplane span	4.60 m (15 ft 1 in)
Wheel track: mainwheels	2.42 m (7 ft 11½ in)
nosewheels	0.90 m (2 ft 11½ in)
Wheelbase	3.48 m (11 ft 5 in)
Passenger pod door: Height	1.40 m (4 ft 7 in)
Width	1.25 m (4 ft 1¼ in)

DIMENSIONS, INTERNAL:

Passenger pod:	
Length, floor level	1.83 m (6 ft 0 in)
Width, floor level	1.25 m (4 ft 1¼ in)
Headroom	1.40 m (4 ft 7 in)

WEIGHTS:

Operating weight, empty: stripped	1,950 kg (4,300 lb)
cargo/platform	2,085 kg (4,597 lb)
cargo/hook	2,050 kg (4,519 lb)
passenger	2,100 kg (4,630 lb)
agricultural	2,216 kg (4,885 lb)
Fuel weight: transport	360 kg (794 lb)
other versions	100 kg (220 lb)
Payload: transport	900 kg (1,985 lb)
agricultural duster	1,065 kg (2,348 lb)
agricultural sprayer	900 kg (1,985 lb)
with cargo platform	1,065 kg (2,348 lb)
flying crane	1,100 kg (2,425 lb)
Normal T-O weight: transport	3,076 kg (6,780 lb)
agricultural	2,980 kg (6,570 lb)
Max T-O weight: all versions	3,250 kg (7,165 lb)

PERFORMANCE (at max T-O weight):

Max level speed	91 knots (170 km/h; 105 mph)
Max cruising speed	81 knots (150 km/h; 93 mph)
Econ cruising speed	49-59 knots (90-110 km/h; 56-68 mph)
Agricultural operating speed range	16-62 knots (30-115 km/h; 19-71 mph)
Service ceiling	3,000 m (9,840 ft)
Service ceiling, one engine out	500 m (1,640 ft)
Hovering ceiling at AUW of 3,000 kg (6,615 lb):	
IGE	1,300 m (4,265 ft)
OGE	800 m (2,625 ft)
Range with 7 passengers, 30 min fuel reserves	215 nm (400 km; 248 miles)
Max range with auxiliary tanks	647 nm (1,200 km; 745 miles)
Endurance at econ cruising speed	3 h 42 min

KAMOV Ka-27
NATO reporting name: Helix-A, B and D

Ka-27 is the Soviet designation for military versions of the helicopter known as the Ka-32 in its civil forms. The basic airframe, power plant, systems and equipment of the Ka-27 and Ka-32 are identical. Furnishings, avionics and mission equipment vary accordingly to role.

First reference to a military version of this helicopter appeared in the 1981 document on *Soviet Military Power* published by the US Department of Defense, which referred to "Hormone variant" helicopters that could be carried in a telescoping hangar on the new 'Sovremenny' class of Soviet guided missile destroyers, for ASW missions. Photographs of such helicopters were released to the technical press after two of them had been seen on the stern platform of the *Udaloy*, first of a new class of Soviet ASW guided missile destroyers, during exercises in the Baltic in September 1981. The US Department of Defense referred to the ASW helicopter as Ka-27 in 1982. At least 16 were observed on board the 'Kiev' class carrier/cruiser *Novorossiysk* during its maiden deployment in 1983, since when the replacement of 'Hormone-As' with Ka-27s has continued at a rapid pace.

Four versions have been identified by unclassified NATO reporting names:

Kamov Ka-26 fitted with a freight platform, in service in Hungary

'Helix-B' infantry assault version of Kamov Ka-27 on the *Ivan Rogov* *(Marine Nationale, Paris)*

Kamov Ka-28 anti-submarine helicopter (NATO 'Helix-A') in Yugoslav service *(Ivo Sturzenegger)*

Helix-A. Basic ASW version. Probable crew of three. Operational since 1982. More than 60 in Soviet Naval Aviation service in 1988. Eight ordered for Indian Navy. (See also separate entry on Ka-28.)

'Helix-A' follows closely the configuration of 'Hormone' but has a longer and more capacious fuselage pod, no central tail fin, and different undernose radome. The overall dimensions of the two aircraft are generally similar, enabling 'Helix' to be stowed on board ship in hangars and via deck lifts built for its predecessor.

Helix-B. Sea-based combat version for amphibious assault duties. Assigned initially to the Northern and Pacific Fleets in 1985, and photographed on board the *Ivan Rogov* in the Mediterranean in 1987. Primary functions are delivery of precision-guided weapons and target designation. Faceted panels around nose, and undernose fairings, for sensors and specialised equipment. Two pylons on each side of cabin for rocket packs and other stores.

Helix-C. Civil versions. See Ka-32 entry.

Helix-D. Search and rescue and plane guard helicopter, first seen on the *Novorossiysk*. Features include an external fuel tank on each side of the cabin, as on the civil Ka-32 'Helix-C', and a winch beside the port cabin door.

The general description of the Ka-32 (which see) applies also to the Ka-27. The IFF (NATO 'Odd Rods'), radar warning antennae and directional ESM radomes fitted to Ka-32T prototype SSSR-31000 are standard on the Ka-27. The rectangular containers on each side of the bottom centre fuselage of 'Helix-A and D' house emergency flotation bags. Clamshell doors at the rear of the fuselage pod cover the compartment from which a dipping sonar is deployed. Sonobuoys are carried internally. Torpedoes and other stores are carried in the ventral weapons bay.

KAMOV Ka-28

First identified publicly at an air show in Yugoslavia in May 1988, the Ka-28 is an export version of the Ka-27 ('Helix-A') ASW helicopter. An accompanying placard described the power plant as two 1,618 kW (2,170 shp) TV3-117BK turboshafts. A total of 3,680 kg (8,113 lb) of fuel was stated to be carried in 12 tanks.

The Ka-28 appears to be outwardly identical to the Ka-27. Its max level speed was quoted as 135 knots (250 km/h; 155 mph) at an AUW of 10,700 kg (23,590 lb), with a max cruising speed of 124-129 knots (230-240 km/h; 143-149 mph) and max rate of climb of 750 m (2,460 ft)/min at S/L.

KAMOV Ka-32
NATO reporting name: Helix-C

It was announced in early 1981 that a new civilian helicopter, designed under the leadership of Mr S. V. Mikheyev and known as the Ka-32, was to be put on display in the permanent Exhibition of Achievements of the National Economy (VDNKL) in Moscow. Primary applications for the aircraft were said to be surveillance, search and rescue, by day and night in all weathers, from ships that would include the atomic powered icebreakers *Lenin*, *Sibir*, *Arktika* and *Rossiya*.

The Ka-32 was not identified officially until the first prototype (SSSR-04173) was exhibited in public with other Soviet and Polish aircraft at Minsk Airport, in late 1981, during the fourth CMEA scientific/technical conference on the use of aircraft in the national economy. As expected, it proved to be a demilitarised counterpart to the Ka-27 (NATO 'Helix-A') naval helicopter already observed on the Soviet ASW guided missile destroyer *Udaloy*, and was given the NATO reporting name **Helix-C**. Major applications of the civil Ka-32 shown at Minsk were said to be for construction/assembly and flying crane duties, and it carried a truck as a slung load during the flying display. It was claimed to be able to lift up to 5,000 kg (11,023 lb) as an external slung load, and to have a range of 100 nm (185 km; 115 miles) with such a load.

A detailed appraisal of the Ka-32 became possible in June 1985, when a prototype of the utility version (SSSR-31000), converted from an ASW Ka-27, was exhibited at the Paris Air Show. Its designer explained that there are two civil versions:

Ka-32T. As displayed in Paris. Basic transport and flying crane, with limited avionics. Duties include transport of internal and external freight, and passengers, along airways and over local routes.

Ka-32S (maritime). Equipped with more comprehensive avionics, including undernose radar, for operation to full IMC standards from icebreakers in adverse weather conditions and over terrain devoid of landmarks. Duties include ice patrol, unloading and loading ships, support of offshore drilling rigs, and maritime search and rescue.

According to Mr Mikheyev, the Ka-32 was conceived as a completely autonomous 'compact truck', able to stow in much the same space as the Ka-25 with its rotors folded, despite its much greater power and capability, and able to operate independently of ground support equipment. Titanium and composite materials are used extensively throughout the airframe, with particular emphasis on resistance to corrosion. Special attention was also paid to ease of handling, with a single pilot. Yaw control is by differential collective pitch applied through the rudder pedals. A 'mix' in the collective control system maintains constant total rotor thrust during turns, to reduce the pilot's workload when landing on a pitching deck, and to simplify transition into hover and landing. The twin rudders are intended mainly to improve control in autorotation, but are effective in co-ordinating turns in normal cruising flight. Being a 'workhorse' the helicopter is not designed for negative *g* loading.

Flight can be maintained on one engine at maximum take-off weight. The effectiveness of the automatic control system is illustrated by an accompanying photograph of a Ka-32S in flight. Both crew doors are open, to show that there is nobody on the flight deck; the crew can be seen in the rear doorway of the main cabin.

Flying alternately as pilot and co-pilot, two women instructors from the Yegoryevsk flying club, near Moscow, set a number of officially confirmed feminine records in the Ka-32 that was exhibited at the Paris Air Show in 1985.

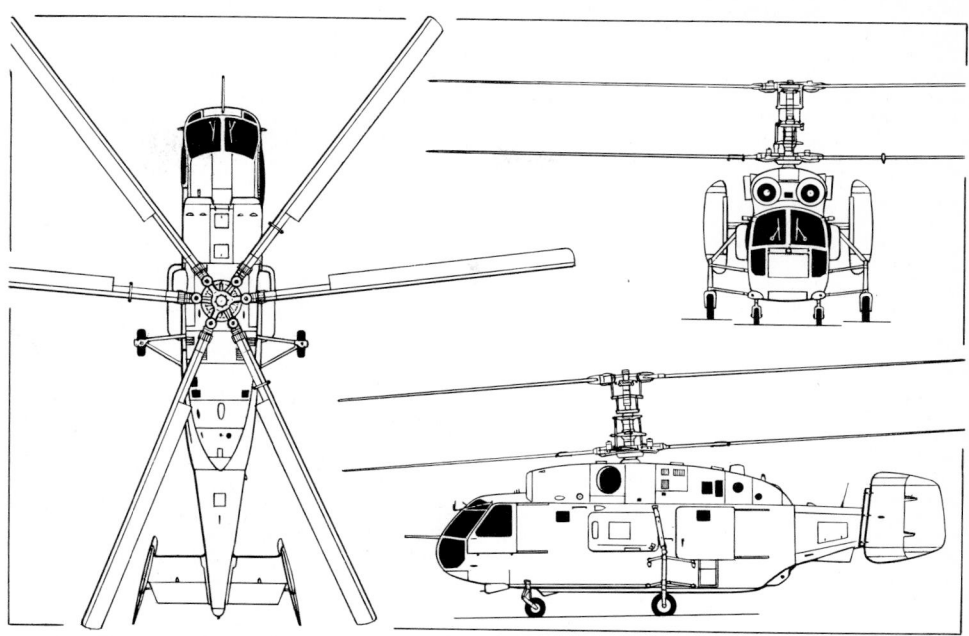

Kamov Ka-32T ('Helix-C') utility helicopter (two Isotov TV3-117V turboshafts) *(Pilot Press)*

Kamov Ka-32S ('Helix-C') under automatic control, with no crew on flight deck

Nadezhda Yeremina piloted the helicopter to set a time to height record by climbing to 3,000 m in 2 min 11.1 s on 12 May 1983. On the previous day Tatyana Zuyeva, flying as pilot, had climbed to 6,000 m in 4 min 46.5 s and set a record of 6,552 m for sustained height in level flight. The time to height records had been held previously by a Mil A-10 (Mi-24 'Hind'). Take-off weight of the Ka-32 was 7,251 kg (15,986 lb) on 11 May and 7,156 kg (15,776 lb) on 12 May. On 29 January 1985 Miss Zuyeva was pilot on a flight which set a women's height record of 8,250 m (27,067 ft) in a Ka-32, and raised the sustained height record to 8,215 m (26,952 ft). Miss Yeremina piloted the Ka-32 to 7,305 m (23,966 ft) with a 1,000 kg payload, and to 6,400 m (20,997 ft) with 2,000 kg on the same day.

The description which follows applies specifically to the Ka-32T displayed at the 1985 Paris Air Show, but is generally applicable also to the Ka-32S and the military Ka-27:

TYPE: Twin-turbine utility helicopter.

ROTOR SYSTEM: Two fully articulated three-blade coaxial contra-rotating rotors. Blades of all-composites construction, with carbonfibre and glassfibre main spars, pockets (13 per blade) of a material similar to Kevlar, and a filler similar to Nomex. As in all Soviet helicopters, blades have a non-symmetrical aerofoil section. Each blade is fitted with a ground adjustable tab. The three lower blades each carry an adjustable vibration damper, comprising two dependent weights, mounted on the root section, and there are further vibration dampers in the fuselage. Tip light on each blade of upper rotor. Blades fold manually outboard of all control mechanisms, to a folded width within the track of the main landing gear. Electrothermal de-icing of the entire profiled portion of each blade, operating at all times when engines are running. Heat generated by rotor head prevents icing of droop stops. Main rotor hub is 50 per cent titanium/50 per cent steel. Rotor brake standard.

FUSELAGE: Conventional all-metal semi-monocoque structure of pod and boom type, making extensive use of titanium for primary components. Tailcone of composites material. Lower fuselage sealed for flotation.

TAIL UNIT: Braced structure, comprising fixed incidence tailplane, elevators, twin endplate fins and rudders, with aluminium alloy structure and composite skins. Single bracing strut under each side of tailplane. Fins toe inward

approx 25°. Fixed leading-edge slat on each fin prevents airflow over fin stalling in crosswinds or at high yaw angles.

LANDING GEAR: Four-wheel type. Oleo-pneumatic shock absorbers. Nosewheels are smaller than mainwheels and of castoring type. Rear legs are pivoted on some versions, to retract upward about their wishbone supports so that the wheels can be moved to a position where they offer least interference to emissions from the undernose radar. Mainwheel tyres size 600 × 180. Nosewheel tyres size 400 × 150.

POWER PLANT: Two 1,660 kW (2,225 shp) Isotov TV3-117V turboshafts, with automatic synchronisation system, mounted side by side above cabin, forward of rotor driveshaft. Main gearbox brake standard. Oil cooler fan aft of gearbox. Electrothermal intake anti-icing. Cowlings hinge downward for use as maintenance platforms. All standard fuel in tanks under cabin floor and inside container on each side of centre fuselage. Provision for auxiliary tanks in cabin. Refuelling point behind small forward hinged door on port side, where bottom of tailboom meets rear of cabin. APU in rear of engine bay fairing on starboard side, for engine starting and to power all essential hydraulic and electrical services on the ground, eliminating need for GPU.

ACCOMMODATION: Pilot and navigator side by side on large air-conditioned flight deck, in fully adjustable seats. Rearward sliding jettisonable door with blister window on each side. Seat behind navigator, on starboard side, for observer, loadmaster or rescue hoist operator. Electric windscreen anti-icing. Direct access to cabin from flight deck. Heated and ventilated main cabin can accommodate freight or 16 passengers, on three folding seats at rear, six along port sidewall and seven along starboard sidewall. Lifejackets under seats. Fittings to carry stretchers. No provisions for toilet or galley. Pyramid structure can be fitted on floor beneath rotor driveshaft to prevent swinging of external cargo sling loads. Rearward sliding door aft of main landing gear on port side, with steps below. Emergency exit door opposite. Door to avionics compartment on port side of tailboom.

SYSTEMS: Dual hydraulically powered flight control systems without manual reversion. Spring stick trim.

AVIONICS AND EQUIPMENT: Include electro-mechanical flight director controlled from autopilot panel, Doppler hover indicator, two HSI and air data computer. Autopilot is capable of providing automatic approach and hover on predetermined course, using Doppler. Radar altimeter. Doppler box under tailboom. Doors at rear of fuel tank bay provide access to small compartment for auxiliary fuel, or liferafts which eject during descent in emergency, by command from flight deck. Container on each side of fuselage, under external fuel containers, for emergency flotation bags (not fitted to prototype shown in Paris). Rescue hoist, capacity 300 kg (661 lb), can be installed between top of door opening and landing gear. Optional external load sling, with automatic release and integral load weighing and stabilisation systems. Equipment on prototype (not necessarily standard on production Ka-32s) included IFF, two radar warning antennae above tailplane, and two ESM radomes above rear fuselage and tail.

DIMENSIONS, EXTERNAL:

Rotor diameter (each)	15.90 m (52 ft 2 in)
Length overall: excl rotors	11.30 m (37 ft 1 in)
rotors folded	12.25 m (40 ft 2¼ in)
Width, rotors folded	4.00 m (13 ft 1½ in)
Height to top of rotor head	5.40 m (17 ft 8½ in)
Wheel track: mainwheels	3.50 m (11 ft 6 in)
nosewheels	1.40 m (4 ft 7 in)
Wheelbase	3.02 m (9 ft 11 in)
Cabin door: Height	approx 1.20 m (3 ft 11¼ in)
Width	approx 1.20 m (3 ft 11¼ in)

DIMENSIONS, INTERNAL:

Cabin: Length	4.52 m (14 ft 10 in)
Max width	1.30 m (4 ft 3 in)
Max height	1.32 m (4 ft 4 in)

WEIGHTS:

Max payload: internal	4,000 kg (8,818 lb)
external	5,000 kg (11,023 lb)
Normal T-O weight	11,000 kg (24,250 lb)
Max flight weight with slung load	12,600 kg (27,775 lb)

PERFORMANCE (at AUW of 11,000 kg; 24,250 lb):

Max level speed	135 knots (250 km/h; 155 mph)
Max cruising speed	124 knots (230 km/h; 143 mph)
Service ceiling at normal T-O weight	
	6,000 m (19,685 ft)
Hovering ceiling OGE	3,500 m (11,480 ft)
Range with max fuel	432 nm (800 km; 497 miles)
Endurance with max fuel	4 h 30 min

KAMOV Ka-126
NATO reporting name: Hoodlum-B

Responsibility for converting piston engined Ka-26 helicopters to turbine powered Ka-126 standard has been allocated to ICA Brasov (see Romanian section).

KAMOV Ka-
NATO reporting name: Hokum

It became known in Summer 1984 that the Kamov bureau had begun flight testing a new combat helicopter that has the NATO reporting name 'Hokum'. The accompanying artist's impression, produced for the 1987 edition of the US Department of Defense's *Soviet Military*

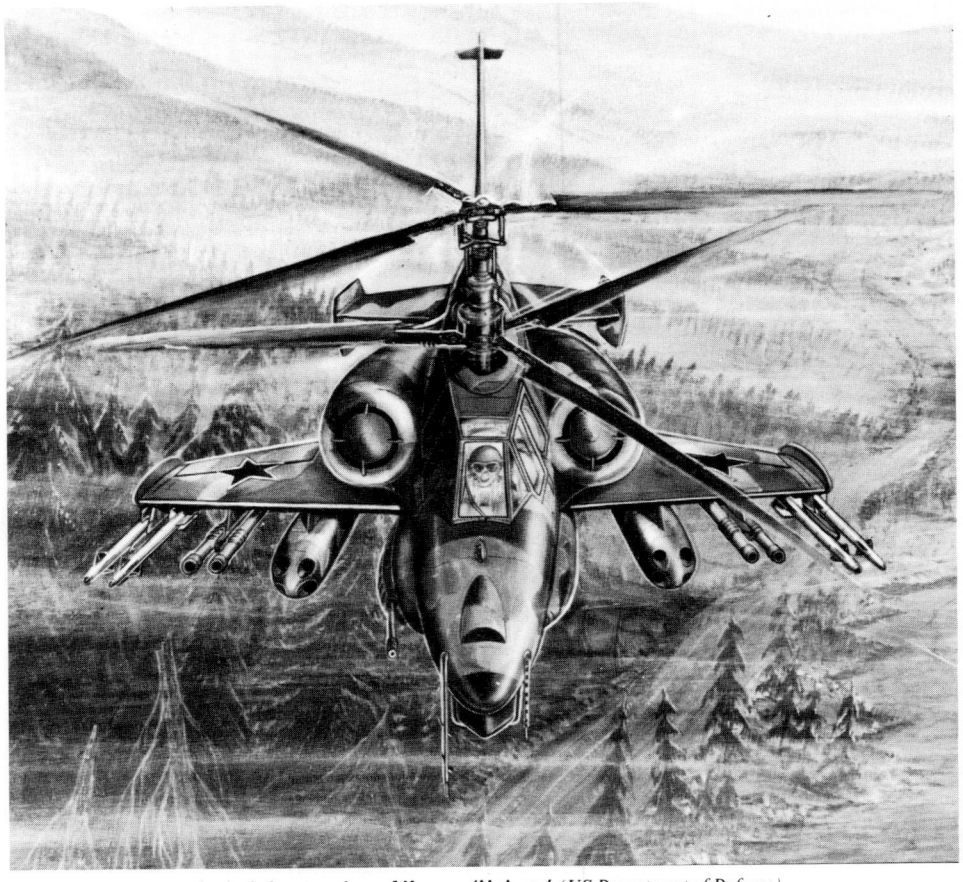

Artist's impression of Kamov 'Hokum' *(US Department of Defense)*

Power document, is believed to be accurate in all general detail. 'Hokum' can be seen to have co-axial contra-rotating and widely separated three-blade rotors, with swept blade tips; a streamlined fuselage with a tapered nose like that of a jet attack aircraft, with pitot, transducer to provide data for a fire control computer, and undernose sensor pack; and a retractable landing gear. DoD states that this helicopter has not been observed carrying anti-tank guided weapons. Instead, it is thought to have a primary air-to-air role (an assessment that is not universally accepted), with an armament of air-to-air missiles and a rapid-fire gun for employment as a low-level helicopter intercept system by day and night and in adverse weather conditions. Like other combat helicopters, 'Hokum' has a crew of two, in tandem, with elevated rear seat. Survivability is enhanced by use of infra-red suppressors, infra-red decoy dispensers and armour.

In 1987, 'Hokum' was still at the development stage, with only a few prototypes involved in flight and structural testing. If it enters production, the DoD expects that "Hokum will give the Soviets a significant rotary-wing air superiority capability. The system has no current Western counterpart".

DIMENSIONS, EXTERNAL:

Rotor diameter (each)	14.0 m (45 ft 10 in)
Length overall, excl nose probe and gun	
	13.5 m (44 ft 3½ in)
Height overall	5.4 m (17 ft 8 in)

WEIGHT (estimated):

Max T-O weight	7,500 kg (16,500 lb)

PERFORMANCE (estimated):

Max level speed	189 knots (350 km/h; 217 mph)
Combat radius	135 nm (250 km; 155 miles)

MiG

GENERAL DESIGNER IN CHARGE OF BUREAU:
Rostislav A. Belyakov

Colonel-General Artem I. Mikoyan, who died on 9 December 1970 at the age of 65, was head of the design bureau responsible for the MiG series of fighter aircraft from 1940. With Mikhail I. Gurevich (1893-1976), a mathematician, he collaborated in the design of the first really modern Soviet jet fighter, the MiG-15, which began to enter squadron service in numbers in 1949.

The MiG-17, a progressive development of the MiG-15, was first observed in Soviet squadrons in 1953 or 1954, and was followed into service by the supersonic MiG-19, which appeared in 1955 and has been manufactured also in large numbers in China (which see).

All available details of aircraft designed subsequently by the Mikoyan bureau that are currently in service, in production or known to be under development follow:

MIKOYAN MiG-21
NATO reporting names: Fishbed and Mongol

MiG-21s continue to be flown by about 37 air forces worldwide, but replacement with later fighters has left fewer than 500 in first-line units of the Soviet tactical air forces, including 65 of the reconnaissance models known to NATO as 'Fishbed-H'. Early MiG-21F/PF/PFM variants (NATO 'Fishbed-C/D/F') still serve with various Warsaw Pact and Soviet-supplied air forces; details of their individual features can be found in the 1985-86 and earlier editions of *Jane's*. The major versions currently deployed with Soviet air forces of the military districts (MDs) and groups of forces, and variants of these basic versions, are as follows:

MiG-21PFMA (Fishbed-J). Multi-role version with Tumansky R-11-300 turbojet, rated at 38.25 kN (8,598 lb st) dry and 60.8 kN (13,668 lb) with afterburning, improved radar (NATO 'Jay Bird'), and four underwing pylons instead of two. Deepened dorsal spine fairing above

fuselage contains additional tankage. Two outboard pylons carry either fuel tanks or radar-homing 'Advanced Atoll' missiles to supplement infra-red K-13As on inboard pylons and GSh-23 twin-barrel 23 mm gun. Zero-speed, zero-altitude ejection seat.

MiG-21R. Generally similar to MiG-21PFMA, but belly gun replaced by a pack of three reconnaissance cameras mounted on a side-hinged (to starboard) door which protrudes from underfuselage, immediately aft of nosewheel leg. Operated by Egyptian Air Force.

MiG-21R (Fishbed-H). Tactical reconnaissance ver-

sion, basically similar to MiG-21PFMA. Equipment includes an external pod for forward facing or oblique cameras, or elint sensors, on fuselage centreline pylon. Suppressed ECM antenna at mid-point on dorsal spine and optional radar warning receivers in wingtip fairings.

MiG-21MF (Fishbed-J). Generally similar to MiG-21PFMA but with a Tumansky R-13-300 turbojet, lighter in weight and with higher performance ratings. Debris deflector beneath each suction relief door forward of wingroot. Entered service with Soviet air forces in 1969.

MiG-21M. Export variant of MiG-21MF. Generally

MiG-21bis ('Fishbed-N') armed with two radar homing 'Atolls' outboard and two 'Aphids' inboard

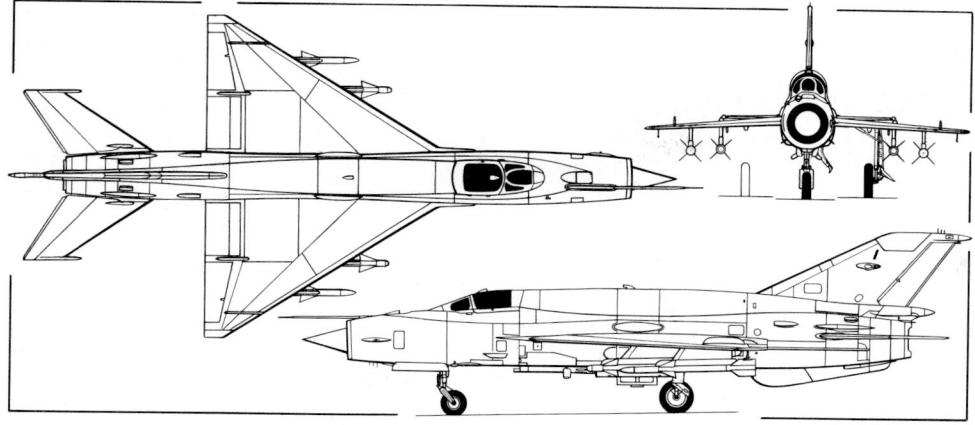

Mikoyan MiG-21SMB ('Fishbed-K') single-seat multi-role fighter *(Pilot Press)*

similar to MiG-21PFMA, but with R-11F2S-300 engine. Superseded MiG-21FL on Hindustan Aeronautics production line in India, with IAF designation Type 96. First Indian built MiG-21M handed over officially to IAF on 14 February 1973; HAL production ended 1981.

MiG-21RF (Fishbed-H). Tactical reconnaissance version of MiG-21MF. Equipment as for MiG-21R.

MiG-21SMB (Fishbed-K). Similar to MiG-21MF, but deep dorsal spine extends rearward as far as brake parachute housing, to provide maximum fuel tankage and optimum aerodynamic form. Deliveries reported to have begun in 1971.

MiG-21bis (Fishbed-L). Third generation multi-role air combat/ground attack version, with Tumansky R-25-300 turbojet, rated at 73.6 kN (16,535 lb st) with afterburning, updated avionics and generally improved construction standards. Wider and deeper dorsal fairing than MiG-21MF. Max fuel capacity of seven internal self-sealing tanks increased to 2,900 litres (766 US gallons; 638 Imp gallons).

MiG-21bis (Fishbed-N). Advanced version of 'Fishbed-L' with further improved avionics, indicated by 'Swift Rod' ILS antennae under nose and on fin tip. Empty weight reported to be 6,000 kg (13,225 lb), 'clean' T-O weight 8,500 kg (18,740 lb). Rate of climb at AUW of 6,800 kg (15,000 lb), with 50% fuel and two 'Atoll' missiles, is 17,700 m (58,000 ft)/min. Carries two radar homing 'Atolls' outboard, two 'Aphids' inboard. Produced also by HAL in India from 1980 to 1987.

MiG-21U (Mongol). Two-seat training versions. Initial version, 'Mongol-A', is generally similar to the MiG-21F but has two cockpits in tandem with sideways hinged (to starboard) double canopy, larger mainwheels and tyres of MiG-21PF, one-piece forward airbrake, and pitot boom repositioned above intake. Cannon armament is deleted. Later models, 'Mongol-B', have the broader-chord vertical tail surfaces and under-rudder brake parachute housing of the later operational variants, with a deeper dorsal spine and no dorsal fin fillet.

MiG-21US (Mongol-B). Similar to later MiG-21U but with provision for SPS flap-blowing, and retractable periscope for instructor in rear seat. Max internal fuel capacity 2,400 litres (634 US gallons; 528 Imp gallons).

MiG-21UM (Mongol-B). Two-seat trainer counterpart of MiG-21MF with R-13 turbojet and four underwing stores pylons.

In addition to these Soviet developed versions, the Chinese aircraft industry (which see) is producing fighters based on the MiG-21, under the designation **J-7/F-7**.

The following details refer to the MiG-21MF ('Fishbed-J'):

TYPE: Single-seat multi-role fighter.

WINGS: Cantilever mid-wing monoplane of clipped delta planform, with 2° anhedral from roots. TsAGI section; thickness/chord ratio 5% at root, 4.2% at tip. No leading-edge camber. Sweepback on leading-edges 57°. Small pointed fairing on each side of fuselage forward of wingroot leading-edge. Small boundary layer fence above each wing near tip. All-metal structure, with two primary spars and one auxiliary spar. Inset ailerons, hydraulically boosted. Large 'blown' plain trailing-edge flaps, actuated hydraulically.

FUSELAGE: Circular section all-metal semi-monocoque structure. Ram air intake in nose, with three-position movable centrebody. Forward hinged door in top of nose gives access to avionics. Large dorsal spine fairing along top of fuselage from canopy to fin, housing control pushrods, avionics, single-point refuelling cap and fuel tank. Forward hinged door type airbrake on each side of underfuselage below wing leading-edge. A further forward hinged airbrake under fuselage forward of ventral fin. All airbrakes actuated hydraulically. Blister fairings above and below wing on each side to accommodate mainwheels when retracted.

TAIL UNIT: Cantilever all-metal structure, with all surfaces sharply swept. Conventional fin and hydraulically boosted rudder. Hydraulically boosted one-piece all-moving horizontal surface, mass balanced at tips, with two gearing ratios for use at varying combinations of altitude and airspeed. Tailplane trim switch on control column. No trim tabs. Single large ventral fin.

LANDING GEAR: Hydraulically retractable tricycle type, with single wheel on each unit; all units housed in fuselage when retracted. Forward retracting non-steerable nosewheel unit, tyre size 500 × 180; inward retracting mainwheels which turn to stow vertically inside fuselage. Size 800 × 200 tyres on mainwheels, inflated to approximately 7.93 bars (115 lb/sq in), ruling out normal operation from grass runways. Pneumatic disc brakes on all three wheels, supplied from compressed air bottles. Steering by differential mainwheel braking. Wheel doors remain open when legs are extended. Brake parachute housed inside acorn fairing at base of rudder.

POWER PLANT: One Tumansky R-13-300 turbojet, rated at 40 kN (9,000 lb st) dry and 64.73 kN (14,550 lb st) with afterburning. Fuel tanks in fuselage, and two integral tanks in each wing, with total capacity of 2,600 litres (687 US gallons; 572 Imp gallons), of which approx 1,800 litres (475 US gallons; 396 Imp gallons) are usable within CG limits at low speed. Provision for carrying one finned external fuel tank, capacity 490 litres (130 US gallons; 108 Imp gallons) or 800 litres (211 US gallons; 176 Imp gallons), on underfuselage pylon and two 490 litre drop tanks on outboard underwing pylons. Two jettisonable solid propellant JATO rockets can be fitted under rear fuselage, aft of wheel doors.

ACCOMMODATION: Pilot only, on zero/zero ejection seat with spring loaded arm at top which ensures that seat cannot be operated unless hood is closed. Canopy is sideways hinged, to starboard, and is surmounted by a small rearview mirror. Flat bulletproof windscreen. Cabin air-conditioned. Armour plating forward and aft of cockpit.

SYSTEMS: Duplicated hydraulic system, supplied by engine driven pump, with backup by battery powered electric pump, and emergency electric tailplane trim and manual operation of flying controls. Autostabilisation in pitch and roll only.

AVIONICS AND EQUIPMENT: Search and track radar (NATO 'Jay Bird') in intake centrebody, with search range of 10.8 nm (20 km; 12.5 miles). Other standard avionics include VOR, ARK automatic radio-compass, IFF and Sirena 3 radar warning system with an indicator marked in 45° sectors in front of and behind the aircraft. Gyro gunsight maintains precision up to 2.75g. Automatic ranging can be fed into gunsight. Full blind-flying instrumentation, with attitude and heading indicators driven by remote central gyro platform.

ARMAMENT: One twin-barrel 23 mm GSh-23 gun, with 200 rounds, in belly pack. Four underwing pylons for weapons or drop tanks. Typical loads for interceptor role include two K-13A 'Atoll' air-to-air missiles on inner pylons and two radar homing 'Advanced Atolls' or two UV-16-57 rocket packs (each sixteen 57 mm rockets) on outer pylons; four K-13As/'Advanced Atolls'; or two drop tanks and two K-13As or 'Advanced Atolls'. Typical loads for ground attack role are four UV-16-57 rocket packs; two 500 kg and two 250 kg bombs; or four S-24 240 mm air-to-surface rockets.

DIMENSIONS, EXTERNAL (MiG-21MF):

Wing span	7.15 m (23 ft 5½ in)
Length, incl pitot boom	15.76 m (51 ft 8½ in)
Fuselage length, intake lip to jetpipe nozzle	
	12.30 m (40 ft 4¼ in)
Height overall	4.00 m (14 ft 9 in)
Tailplane span	3.70 m (12 ft 8 in)
Wheel track	2.69 m (8 ft 10 in)
Wheelbase	4.81 m (15 ft 9½ in)

AREA:

Wings, gross	23.0 m² (247.0 sq ft)

WEIGHTS (MiG-21MF):

Weight empty	5,843 kg (12,882 lb)
T-O weight:	
with four K-13A missiles	8,200 kg (18,078 lb)
with two K-13A missiles and two 490 litre (130 US gallon; 108 Imp gallon) drop tanks	
	8,950 kg (19,730 lb)
with two K-13As and three drop tanks	
	9,400 kg (20,725 lb)
Max T-O weight	9,800 kg (21,605 lb)

PERFORMANCE (MiG-21MF):

Max level speed above 11,000 m (36,000 ft)	
Mach 2.05 (1,175 knots; 2,175 km/h; 1,353 mph)	
Max level speed at low altitude	
Mach 1.06 (701 knots; 1,300 km/h; 807 mph)	
Landing speed	146 knots (270 km/h; 168 mph)
Design ceiling	18,000 m (59,050 ft)
Practical ceiling	about 15,250 m (50,000 ft)
T-O run at normal AUW	800 m (2,625 ft)
Landing run	550 m (1,805 ft)
Combat radius (hi-lo-hi):	
with four 250 kg bombs, internal fuel	
	200 nm (370 km; 230 miles)
with two 250 kg bombs and drop tanks	
	400 nm (740 km; 460 miles)
Range, internal fuel only	593 nm (1,100 km; 683 miles)
Ferry range, with three external tanks	
	971 nm (1,800 km; 1,118 miles)

PERFORMANCE (MiG-21US, 'clean'):

Max level speed above 12,200 m (40,000 ft)	
Mach 2.02 (1,159 knots; 2,150 km/h; 1,335 mph)	
Max level speed at S/L	
Mach 1.06 (701 knots; 1,300 km/h; 807 mph)	
Max rate of climb at S/L	6,400 m (21,000 ft)/min
Rate of climb at 11,000 m (36,000 ft)	
	3,050 m (10,000 ft)/min
Time to 1,500 m (4,920 ft)	20 s
Turn rate at 4,570 m (15,000 ft):	
instantaneous (Mach 0.5)	11.1°/s
instantaneous (Mach 0.9)	13.4°/s
sustained (Mach 0.9)	7.5°/s
T-O run	700 m (2,297 ft)

MIKOYAN MiG-23
NATO reporting names: Flogger-A, B, C, E, F, G, H and K

The Ye-23IG prototype of this variable geometry (izmenyaemaya geometriya; IG) air combat fighter was displayed in public for the first time on 9 July 1967, during the Aviation Day flypast at Domodedovo Airport, Moscow, soon after its first flight. Pre-series aircraft were delivered to the Soviet Air Force in 1970, followed by initial series production MiG-23 interceptors in 1973. Subsequently, the MiG-23 and related MiG-27 superseded the MiG-21 progressively as primary equipment of the Soviet tactical air forces and Voyska PVO home defence interceptor force. MiG-23s are flown by all of the Warsaw Pact air forces, and have been exported to twelve other air forces. Production ended in the mid-1980s.

US press reports suggest that former Egyptian operated MiG-23s are being flown by the US Air Force from an air base in the western USA, alongside MiG-21s, for realistic air-to-air combat training of USAF and allied pilots. At

MiG-21RF ('Fishbed-H') tactical reconnaissance aircraft of the Polish Air Force
(Swedish Air Force, via FLYGvapenNYTT)

least four others were presented to China in a technology transfer deal.

There have been twelve versions of the MiG-23:

MiG-23 (Flogger-A). Ye-23IG prototype shown at Domodedovo on 9 July 1967. One Lyulka AL-7F-1 afterburning turbojet, rated at 98.1 kN (22,046 lb st). Illustrated in 1973-74 and preceding editions of *Jane's*.

MiG-23S (Flogger-A). Pre-production version, with AL-7F-1 engine.

MiG-23SM (Flogger-A). As MiG-23S, but with four APU-13 pylons for external stores added under engine air intake ducts and fixed inboard wing panels.

MiG-23U. Tandem two-seat training counterpart of MiG-23S.

MiG-23M (Flogger-B). First series production version. Single-seat air combat fighter with Tumansky R-27 turbojet, rated at 68.65 kN (15,430 lb st) dry and 100.0 kN (22,485 lb st) with afterburning. Wings moved forward about 61 cm (2 ft) to compensate for lighter engine, increasing gap between wing and tailplane. Length of rear fuselage reduced; size of dorsal fin increased; wing chord increased on movable panels, giving large dogtooth.

MiG-23MF (Flogger-B). Improved version of MiG-23M, with more powerful R-29 engine and uprated equipment, including J band radar (NATO 'High Lark'), Sirena 3 radar warning system, Doppler, and a small infra-red search/track pod under the cockpit. The first Soviet aircraft with a demonstrated ability to track and engage targets flying below its own altitude. Standard version for Soviet air forces from about 1975, and for other Warsaw Pact air forces from 1978.

MiG-23UM (Flogger-C). Tandem two-seat version suitable for both operational training and combat use. Individual canopy over each seat. Rear seat slightly higher than forward seat, with retractable periscopic sight for occupant. Dorsal spine fairing of increased depth aft of rear canopy. Otherwise identical to MiG-23M with R-27 turbojet. In service with Soviet and Warsaw Pact air forces and those of other countries, including Angola, Cuba, Egypt, India and Libya.

MiG-23MS (Flogger-E). Export version of 'Flogger-B', equipped to a lower standard. Smaller radar (NATO 'Jay Bird': search range 15 nm; 29 km; 18 miles, tracking range 10 nm; 19 km; 12 miles) in shorter nose radome. No infra-red sensor or Doppler navigation equipment. Armed with 'Atoll' missiles and GSh-23 gun. In service in Angola, Algeria, Cuba, Iraq, North Korea and Libya.

MiG-23BN (Flogger-F). Export single-seat fighter-bomber. Has the nose shape, laser rangefinder, raised seat, cockpit external armour plate and larger, low pressure tyres of Soviet air forces' MiG-27 ('Flogger-D'), but retains the power plant, variable geometry intakes and GSh-23 twin-barrel gun of the MiG-23MF interceptor. Provision for AS-7 'Kerry' missiles. Supplied to Algerian, Cuban, Egyptian, Ethiopian, Iraqi, Libyan, Syrian and Vietnamese air forces.

MiG-23ML (Flogger-G). First identified when six aircraft from Kubinka air base made goodwill visits to Finland and France in the Summer of 1978. Basically similar to MiG-23MF version of 'Flogger-B', but with a much smaller dorsal fin. The radar is lighter in weight, and the undernose sensor pod on some aircraft is of new design. Standard Soviet operational variant, also exported to Czechoslovakia, the German Democratic Republic and Syria.

MiG-23BN (Flogger-H). As 'Flogger-F' but with small radar warning receiver fairing on each side at bottom of fuselage, immediately forward of nosewheel doors. Operated by Bulgarian, Czechoslovak and Polish air forces. Total of 80 delivered to Indian Air Force in 1980-82 to re-equip Nos. 10, 220 and 221 Squadrons. Has also been used by Soviet air forces.

MiG-23 (Flogger-K). Development of 'Flogger-G', identified by dogtooth notch at junction of wing glove leading-edge and intake trunk on each side, to generate vortices to improve stability in yaw at high angles of attack. This compensates for use of smaller ventral folding fin and small 'Flogger-G' type dorsal fin. New IFF antenna forward of windscreen. AA-11 (NATO 'Archer') close-range air-to-air missiles on fuselage pylons. Pivoting weapon pylons under outer wings. Operational units include a 14-aircraft squadron based at Cam Ranh Bay, Vietnam.

About 420 'Flogger-B/G/K' interceptors serve with the Soviet strategic air defence interceptor force, and a further 1,570 in tactical air force regiments.

The following description refers specifically to the single-seat MiG-23ML ('Flogger-G') as supplied to the Soviet air forces:

TYPE: Single-seat variable geometry air combat fighter.

WINGS: Cantilever shoulder-wing monoplane of conventional light alloy construction, with front and rear main spars and auxiliary centre spar. Sweepback of main panels variable in flight or on the ground by manual control, at 16°, 45° or 72°. Two hydraulic wing sweep motors driven separately by main and booster systems. If one system fails, wing sweep system remains effective at 50 per cent normal angular velocity. Extended chord (dogtooth) on outer panels visible when wings are swept. Fixed triangular inboard panels, with leading-edges swept at 72°. Welded steel pivot box

MiG-23MF 'Flogger-B' single-seat variable geometry fighter of the Soviet Air Force armed with two AA-7 'Apex' and two AA-8 'Aphid' air-to-air missiles *(Swedish Air Force, via FLYGvapenNYTT)*

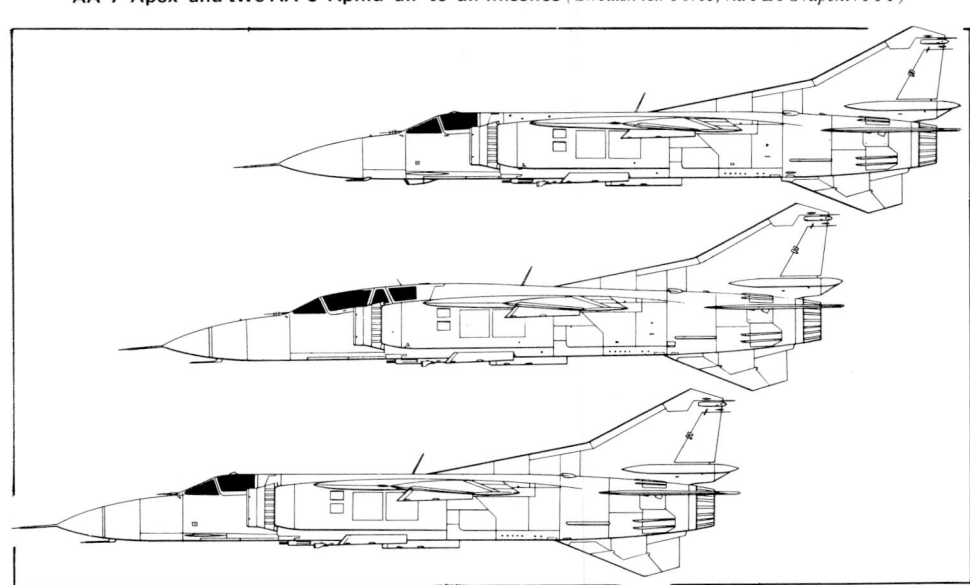

Top to bottom: Side views of the 'Flogger-B', 'Flogger-C' and 'Flogger-E' variants of the MiG-23 series *(Pilot Press)*

The two-seat MiG-23UM, identical to the early MiG-23M except for second cockpit

'Flogger-H' can be distinguished from 'Flogger-F' by the avionics pods near the nosewheel doors, and from the MiG-27 ('Flogger-D') by its variable geometry intakes *(Letectvi + Kosmonautika)*

carry-through structure. Full span hydraulically actuated trailing-edge single-slotted flaps, each in three sections, permitting independent actuation of outboard sections when wings are fully swept. No ailerons. Two-section hydraulically actuated upper surface spoilers/lift dumpers, forward of mid and inner flap sections on each side, operate differentially in conjunction with horizontal tail surfaces (except when disengaged at 72° sweep), and collectively for improved runway adherence and braking

after touchdown. Hydraulically actuated leading-edge flap on outboard two-thirds of each main (variable geometry) panel, coupled to trailing-edge flaps.

FUSELAGE: Conventional semi-monocoque structure of basic circular section; flattened on each side of cockpit, forward of lateral air intake trunks which blend into circular shape of rear fuselage. Large flat splitter plate, with boundary layer bleeds, forms inboard face of each intake. Two small rectangular suction relief doors in each trunk, under inboard wing leading-edge. Perforations under rear fuselage, aft of mainwheel bays, are pressure relief vents. Four hydraulically actuated door type airbrakes, mounted two on each side of rear fuselage above and below horizontal tail surface. Rear fuselage detachable between wing and tailplane for engine servicing.

TAIL UNIT: Hydraulically actuated all-moving horizontal surfaces, swept back at 57° on leading-edge, operate both differentially and symmetrically to provide aileron and elevator function respectively. Conventional fin, swept back at 65° on leading-edge, with inset rudder. Fin and forward portion of each horizontal surface of conventional light alloy construction with spars and ribs. Rudder and rear of each horizontal surface have honeycomb core. Ground adjustable tab on each horizontal surface at inboard trailing-edge. Large ventral fin in two portions. Lower portion is hinged to fold to starboard when landing gear is extended, to increase ground clearance.

LANDING GEAR: Hydraulically retractable tricycle type, with single wheel on each main unit and steerable twin-wheel nose unit. Main units retract inward into rear of air intake trunks. Main fairings to enclose these units are attached to legs. Small inboard fairing for each wheel bay hinged to fuselage belly. Nose unit, fitted with small mudguard over each wheel, retracts rearward. Mainwheels fitted with brakes and anti-skid units. Brake parachute, area 21 m² (226 sq ft), housed in cylindrical fairing at base of rudder with split conic doors.

POWER PLANT: One Tumansky R-29B turbojet, rated at up to 122 kN (27,500 lb st) with max afterburning in aircraft for Soviet Air Force. Water injection system, capacity 28 litres (7.4 US gallons; 6.15 Imp gallons). Four fuel tanks in fuselage, aft of cockpit, and two in wings. Max internal fuel capacity 5,750 litres (1,519 US gallons; 1,265 Imp gallons). Variable geometry air intakes and variable nozzle. Provision for carrying jettisonable external fuel tank, capacity 800 litres (211 US gallons; 176 Imp gallons), on underfuselage centreline pylon, and two more under fixed wing panels. Two additional external tanks of same capacity may be carried on non-swivelling pylons under outer wings for ferry flights, with wings in fully forward position. Attachment for assisted take-off rocket on each side of fuselage aft of landing gear.

ACCOMMODATION: Pilot only, on zero/zero ejection seat in air-conditioned and pressurised cockpit, under small hydraulically actuated rearward hinged canopy. Bullet-proof windscreen. Small electrically heated rearview mirror on top of canopy.

AVIONICS AND EQUIPMENT: J band radar dish (NATO 'High Lark': search range 46 nm; 85 km; 53 miles, tracking range 29 nm; 54 km; 34 miles) behind dielectric nosecone. ILS antennae (NATO 'Swift Rod') under radome and at tip of fin trailing-edge; suppressed UHF antennae form tip of fin and forward fixed portion of ventral fin; yaw vane above fuselage aft of radome; angle of attack sensor on port side. SRO-2 (NATO 'Odd Rods') IFF antenna immediately forward of windscreen. Undernose infra-red sensor pod, Sirena 3 radar warning system, and Doppler equipment standard on Soviet Air Force version. Sirena 3 antennae in horns at inboard leading-edge of each outer wing and below ILS antenna on fin. Retractable landing/taxying light under each engine air intake.

ARMAMENT: One 23 mm GSh-23L twin-barrel gun in fuselage belly pack, with large flash eliminator around muzzles. One pylon under centre-fuselage, one under each engine air intake duct, and one under each fixed inboard wing panel, for rocket packs, air-to-air missiles or other external stores. Use of twin launchers under air intake ducts permits carriage of four R-60 ('Aphid') missiles, plus two R-23 ('Apex') on underwing pylons.

DIMENSIONS, EXTERNAL:

Wing span: fully spread	13.95 m (45 ft 9 in)
fully swept	7.77 m (25 ft 6 in)
Length overall: excl nose probe	15.88 m (52 ft 1¼ in)
incl nose probe	16.71 m (54 ft 10 in)
Height overall	4.82 m (15 ft 9¾ in)

AREA:

Wings, gross: spread	31.3 m² (336.9 sq ft)
swept	34.6 m² (372.4 sq ft)

WEIGHTS:

Weight empty	10,200 kg (22,485 lb)
Max external weapon load	3,000 kg (6,615 lb)
T-O weight	16,100-18,900 kg (35,495-41,670 lb)

PERFORMANCE:

Max level speed: at height, with weapons	Mach 2.35
at S/L	Mach 1.2
Service ceiling	18,000 m (59,055 ft)
T-O run	900 m (2,950 ft)
Landing run	1,600 m (5,250 ft)
Combat radius	
	485-700 nm (900-1,300 km; 560-805 miles)

MIKOYAN MiG-27
NATO reporting names: Flogger-D and J
Indian Air Force name: Bahadur

Although the single-seat ground attack aircraft known to NATO as 'Flogger-D/J' have many airframe features in common with the MiG-23, they differ in important respects and are designated MiG-27. Their use of fixed air intakes and a two-position (on/off) afterburner nozzle is consistent

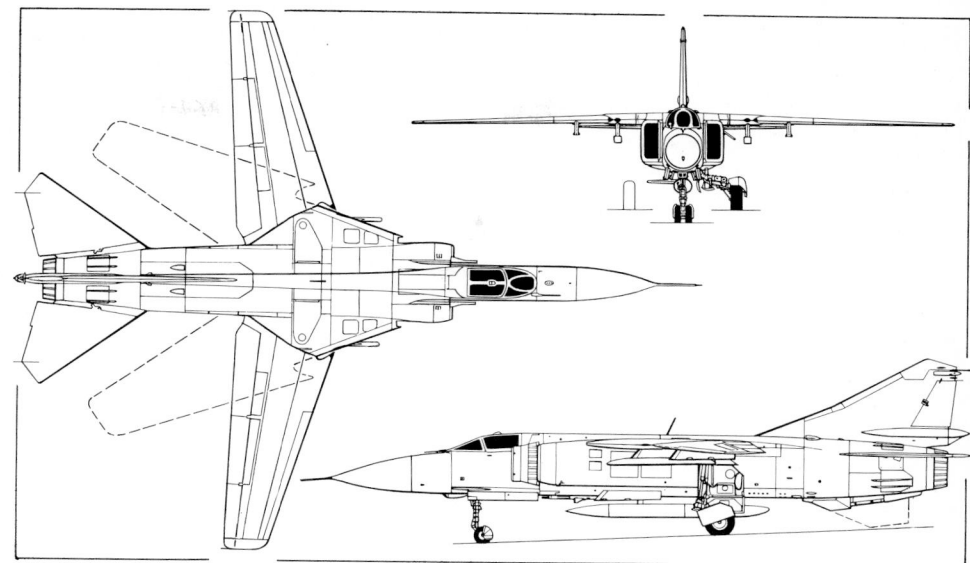

'Flogger-K' version of the MiG-23 interceptor (*Pilot Press*)

Notches in wing gloves identify the MiG-23 'Flogger-K' (*US Navy*)

MiG-27 ('Flogger-D') landing, with wings extended and ventral fin folded (*Flug Revue*)

with the primary requirement of transonic speed at low altitude. Two versions are operational in Soviet tactical air force regiments:

Flogger-D. Initial version for Soviet tactical air forces, introduced in second half of the 1970s. Forward portion of fuselage completely redesigned by comparison with interceptor versions of MiG-23. Instead of having an ogival radome, 'Flogger-D' nose is sharply tapered in side elevation, with a radar ranging antenna and a small sloping

window covering a laser rangefinder. Doppler navigation radar in nose. Additional armour on flat sides of cockpit. Seat and canopy raised to improve view from cockpit. Wider, low-pressure mainwheel tyres. Six-barrel 30 mm Gatling type underbelly gun replaces GSh-23 of interceptor. Bomb/JATO rack under each side of rear fuselage in addition to five pylons for external stores, including tactical nuclear weapons and the air-to-surface missiles known to NATO as AS-7 'Kerry', AS-10 'Karen', AS-12 'Kegler' and

AS-14 'Kedge'. Typical external load comprises six 500 kg bombs and two 800 litre (211 US gallon; 176 Imp gallon) jettisonable fuel tanks. Bullet shape antenna above each glove pylon, associated with missile guidance. Radar warning receiver blister on each side of front fuselage, ahead of nosewheel bay.

Flogger-J. Identified in 1981. New nose shape, with lip at top and blister fairing below. Enhanced electro-optical sensors, probably with rearward laser designation capability for laser guided bomb delivery. Bullet shape antennae above wingroot glove pylons and external armour on sides of cockpit deleted. Wingroot leading-edge extensions added (see illustrations). Armament includes two gun pods on underwing pylons, with gun barrels that can be depressed for attacking ground targets. **MiG-27M** export version is being built under licence by HAL in India as the Bahadur (Valiant) (see Indian section).

About 830 'Flogger-Ds' and 'Js' are deployed with the Soviet tactical air forces, plus at least one squadron with the East German Air Force. The somewhat similar aircraft known to NATO as 'Flogger-F and H' are members of the MiG-23 series, with variable geometry intakes and a GSh-23 twin-barrel gun, although having the nose shape, raised seat and larger, low pressure tyres of 'Flogger-D'. Both versions have been operated by Soviet units; but the 'F' and 'H' are basically export counterparts of 'Flogger-D', with lower standards of equipment and performance, and are described under the MiG-23 entry. Production of the 'F' and 'H' was completed in the mid-1980s.

The following data are estimated for the MiG-27 'Flogger-D':

POWER PLANT: Generally similar to MiG-23MF, but R-29-300 engine rated at 78.45 kN (17,635 lb st) dry and 112.8 kN (25,350 lb st) with max afterburning.

DIMENSIONS, EXTERNAL: As MiG-23, plus:

Wing aspect ratio (spread)	7.45
Length overall	16.00 m (52 ft 6 in)
Tailplane span	5.75 m (18 ft 10¼ in)

AREA:

Horizontal tail surfaces	6.88 m² (74.06 sq ft)

WEIGHTS:

Max external load	4,500 kg (9,920 lb)
Max T-O weight, 'clean'	15,500 kg (34,170 lb)
Max T-O weight	20,100 kg (44,313 lb)

PERFORMANCE (estimated):

Max level speed: at height	Mach 1.7
at S/L	Mach 1.1
Service ceiling	16,000 m (52,500 ft)

T-O to 15 m (50 ft) at AUW of 15,700 kg (34,600 lb)
    800 m (2,625 ft)
Combat radius, with underbelly fuel tank, four 500 kg bombs and two 'Atoll' missiles, lo-lo-lo
    210 nm (390 km; 240 miles)
Max ferry range with three external tanks
    1,350 nm (2,500 km; 1,550 miles)

MIKOYAN MiG-25
NATO reporting name: Foxbat

Still the fastest combat aircraft identified in squadron service, and holder of the absolute height record for aeroplanes, the MiG-25 was designed nearly 30 years ago to counter the threat of the B-70 Mach 3 strategic bomber then under development for the US Air Force. Its early history has been described in previous editions of *Jane's*. Emphasis was placed on high-speed, high-altitude capability and a radar/missile fit that would permit attack over a considerable range; manoeuvrability was less important. Despite the subsequent NATO switch to low-level operations, about 300 MiG-25s continue to equip the Soviet strategic interceptor force; a further 105 interceptors and 195 reconnaissance MiG-25s serve with the tactical air forces. Others fly in the national markings of Algeria, India, Iraq, Libya and Syria. Production was completed in the mid-1980s. Six versions have been identified:

MiG-25 (Foxbat-A). Basic interceptor, designed to attack high-flying targets, with large radar (NATO 'Fox Fire') in nose and armed with four air-to-air missiles on underwing attachments. Production cut back in 1977-78, reflecting new emphasis on interception of low flying targets. Most 'Foxbat-As' in service in the Soviet Union, and some operated by the Libyan Arab Air Force, have

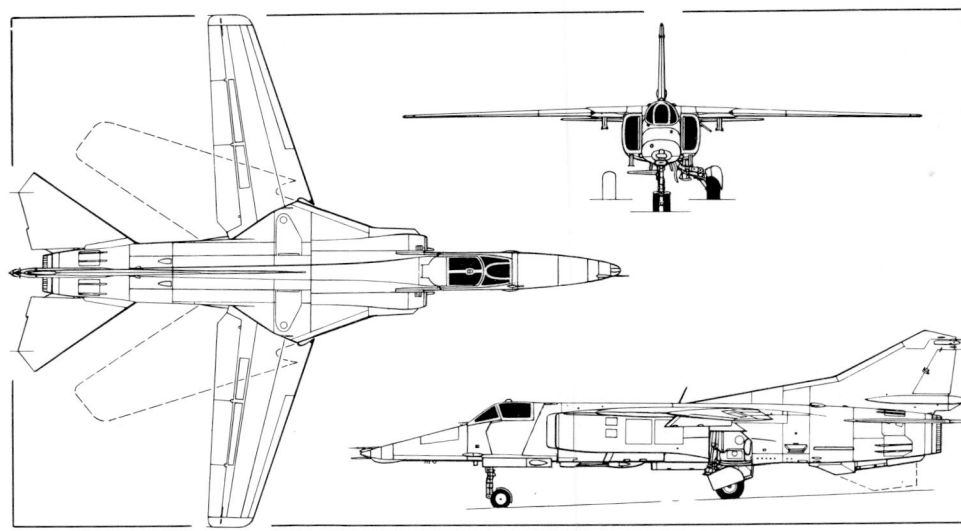

MiG-27 ('Flogger-J') single-seat ground attack aircraft *(Pilot Press)*

Comparison of this photograph of a MiG-27 'Flogger-J' with that of a 'Flogger-D' shows the restyled nose, absence of bullet shape antennae on the wing gloves, addition of wingroot leading-edge extensions and depressed barrel of gun in port underwing pod

This photograph shows clearly the tandem cockpits in the nose of the MiG-25U ('Foxbat-C')

been converted to 'Foxbat-E' standard. 'Foxbat-As' remain operational in Algeria, Iraq and Syria.

MiG-25R (Foxbat-B). Basic reconnaissance version, with five camera windows and various flush dielectric panels aft of very small dielectric nosecap for radar. Equipment believed to include Doppler navigation system and side looking airborne radar (SLAR). No armament. Slightly reduced span. Wing leading-edge sweep constant from root to tip. Operated by Soviet tactical air forces, and in Algeria, India, Libya and Syria.

MiG-25U (Foxbat-C). Trainer, of which first photographs were published towards the end of 1975. Generally similar to operational versions, but with new nose, containing separate cockpit with individual canopy, forward of standard cockpit and at a lower level. No search radar or reconnaissance sensors in nose. In service with air forces of Soviet Union and India (two).

MiG-25R (Foxbat-D). Generally similar to 'Foxbat-B', but with larger SLAR (side looking airborne radar) dielectric panel, further aft on side of nose, and no cameras. Operated by Soviet Air Force and in Libya.

MiG-25M (Foxbat-E). Converted 'Foxbat-A' with changes to radar and equipment to provide limited lookdown/shootdown capability comparable with that of 'Flogger-B'. Undernose sensor pod. Engines uprated to 137.3 kN (30,865 lb st). Developed via aircraft known as the **Ye-266M**, which set three time-to-height records in 1975 and also holds the absolute height record of 37,650 m (123,524 ft).

MiG-25 (Foxbat-F). First illustrated in the Soviet press in 1986, this 'Wild Weasel' type of defence suppression aircraft can launch AS-11 (NATO 'Kilter') anti-radiation missiles against surface-to-air missile sites from long stand-off ranges. Airframe generally similar to 'Foxbat' interceptors, but with dielectric panel aft of radome on port side (possibly both sides) of front fuselage. Entering service in 1988.

The following description applies to the MiG-25 ('Foxbat-A') interceptor except where indicated:
TYPE: Single-seat interceptor.

The reconnaissance version of the MiG-25 known to NATO as 'Foxbat'-B' in service with the Libyan Arab Air Force. Note the camera-carrying nose and dielectric panel *(US Navy)*

First illustration of what could be a 'Foxbat-F' defence suppression version of the MiG-25 (copied from *Krasnaya Zvezda*)

MiG-25M ('Foxbat-E') interceptor of the Libyan Arab Air Force, armed with 'Acrid' and 'Aphid' air-to-air missiles (*US Navy*)

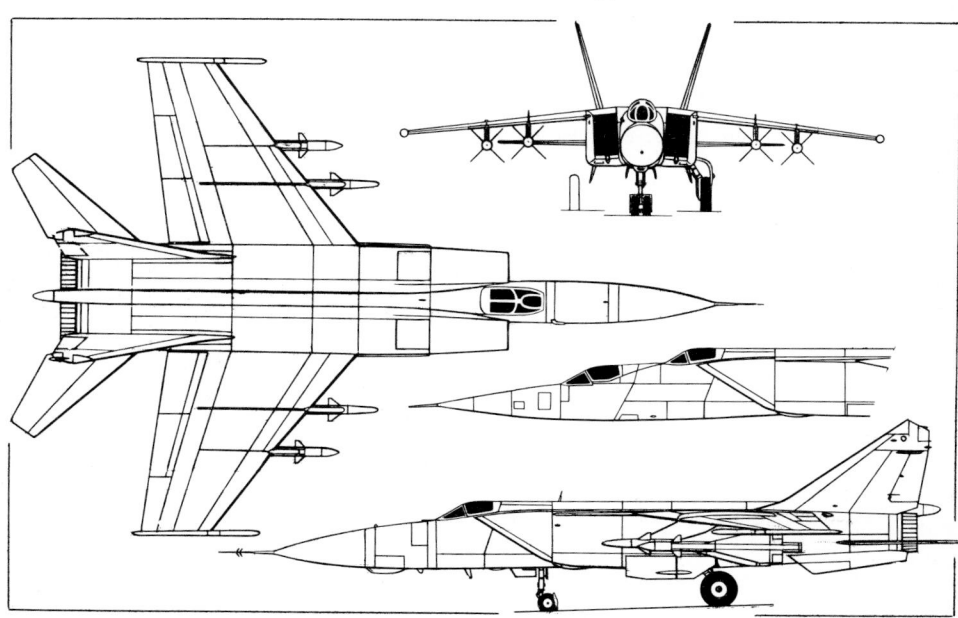

Mikoyan MiG-25M single-seat fighter (NATO 'Foxbat-E'), with scrap view of front fuselage of two-seat MiG-25U (*Pilot Press*)

WINGS: Cantilever high-wing monoplane. Anhedral 4° from roots. Sweepback on leading-edge approx 40° inboard, 38° outboard of each outer missile attachment. Sweepback at quarter-chord 32°. Wing structure basically of arc-welded nickel steel, with titanium leading-edge. Upper surface fence in line with each inboard weapon attachment; shorter shallow fence in line with each outer attachment. Long anti-flutter body (max diameter 30 cm; 11.8 in) at each wingtip, housing light alloy avionics. Light alloy aileron at centre of each semi-span, with simple light alloy flap on inboard 37 per cent of trailing-edge. No other movable wing surfaces.

FUSELAGE: Basic fuselage is quite slim, but is blended into the rectangular air intake trunks, which have wedge inlets. Inner walls of intakes are curved at top and do not run parallel with outer walls; a hinged panel forms the lower lip of each intake, enabling intake area to be varied electronically. Airbrake beneath jetpipes, between ventral fins. Structure mainly of arc-welded nickel steel.

TAIL UNIT: Cantilever structure comprising twin outward canted fins with inset rudders, and all-moving horizontal surfaces. All surfaces sweptback (tailplane 50°, fins 60°), without tabs. Main structures of arc-welded nickel steel, with titanium leading-edges and light alloy rear sections. Two outward canted ventral fins, with retractable sprung tailskids. Large areas of each main and ventral fin form flush antennae.

LANDING GEAR: Retractable tricycle type. Single wheel, with high pressure tyre of 1.20 m (47.25 in) diameter, on each forward retracting main unit. Wheel stows vertically between air intake duct and outer skin of each trunk. Twin-wheel forward retracting nose unit. Twin brake-chutes in fairing above and between jet nozzles.

POWER PLANT: Two Tumansky R-31 (R-266) single-shaft turbojets, each rated at 91.18 kN (20,500 lb st) dry, and 120 kN (27,010 lb st) with afterburning. Water-methanol injection standard. Fuel in two structural tanks in fuselage, between cockpit and engine bay, in saddle tanks around intake ducts, and in integral tank in each wing, filling almost the entire volume inboard of outer fence. Total fuel capacity approx 14,000 kg (30,865 lb) or 17,410 litres (4,600 US gallons; 3,830 Imp gallons).

ACCOMMODATION: Pilot only, on KM-1 zero-height, 80 knot (150 km/h; 93 mph) ejection seat similar to that fitted to some versions of MiG-21. Canopy hinged to open sideways, to starboard.

AVIONICS AND EQUIPMENT: Main fire control radar (NATO 'Fox Fire': range believed to be 45 nm; 85 km; 52 miles) in nose, forward of avionics compartment housing navigation radar. SRZO-2 (NATO 'Odd Rods') IFF and SOD-57M ATC/SIF, with antennae in starboard fin tip. Sirena 3 360° radar warning system with receivers in centre of each wingtip anti-flutter body and starboard fin tip. Unidentified ECCM, decoys and jammers. RSB-70/RPS HF, RSIU-5 VHF, R-831 UHF communications equipment, SP-50 (NATO 'Swift Rod') ILS, MRP-56P marker beacon receiver and ARK-15 radio compass. Retractable landing light under front of each intake trunk.

ARMAMENT: Air-to-air missiles on four underwing attachments. These may comprise one infra-red and one radar homing example of the missile known to NATO as 'Acrid' under each wing. Alternatively, one 'Apex' and a pair of 'Archers' or 'Aphids' can be carried under each wing. Backup optical weapon sight.

DIMENSIONS, EXTERNAL:
Wing span: 'Foxbat-A'	13.95 m (45 ft 9 in)
'Foxbat-B'	13.40 m (44 ft 0 in)
Wing aspect ratio: 'Foxbat-A'	3.4
Length overall	23.82 m (78 ft 1¾ in)
Length of fuselage	19.40 m (63 ft 7¾ in)
Height overall	6.10 m (20 ft 0¼ in)

AREA:
Wings, gross: 'Foxbat-A'	56.83 m² (611.7 sq ft)

WEIGHTS (estimated):
Basic operating weight, empty:	
'Foxbat-A'	at least 20,000 kg (44,100 lb)
'Foxbat-B'	19,600 kg (43,200 lb)
Max T-O weight: 'Foxbat-A'	37,425 kg (82,500 lb)
'Foxbat-B'	33,400 kg (73,635 lb)

PERFORMANCE (estimated):
Max level speed at height:	
'Foxbat-B', 'clean'	Mach 3.2
Never-exceed combat speed: 'Foxbat-A', with four 'Acrid' missiles and 50% fuel	Mach 2.83
Max level speed at low altitude: 'Foxbat-A', with four 'Acrid' missiles and 50% fuel	Mach 0.85
Landing speed:	
'Foxbat-A'	146 knots (270 km/h; 168 mph)
Max rate of climb at S/L:	
'Foxbat-A'	12,480 m (40,950 ft)/min
Time to 11,000 m (36,000 ft) with afterburning:	
'Foxbat-A'	2 min 30 s
Service ceiling: 'Foxbat-A'	24,400 m (80,000 ft)
'Foxbat-B, D'	27,000 m (88,580 ft)
T-O run: 'Foxbat-A'	1,380 m (4,525 ft)
Landing run: 'Foxbat-A'	2,180 m (7,150 ft)

Normal operational radius:	
'Foxbat-A'	610 nm (1,130 km; 700 miles)
'Foxbat-B, D'	485 nm (900 km; 560 miles)
Max combat radius, econ power:	
'Foxbat-A'	780 nm (1,450 km; 900 miles)

MIKOYAN MiG-29
NATO reporting name: Fulcrum
Indian Air Force name: Baaz (Eagle)

Operational since early 1985, the MiG-29 is a twin-engined combat aircraft comparable in size to the US F/A-18 Hornet. A large pulse Doppler lookdown/shootdown radar gives it day and night all-weather operating capability against low-flying targets, as well as freedom from the outmoded ground control interception techniques that formerly restricted Soviet air defence effectiveness. Like other new Soviet air superiority fighters, it has an infra-red search/track sensor, mounted inside a transparent dome in front of the windscreen, offset to starboard. It is replacing MiG-21s, Su-15s and some MiG-23s in Soviet service.

References to this fighter first appeared in the Western press in 1979, after a prototype had been identified on photographs taken over Ramenskoye flight test centre by a US reconnaissance satellite. NATO allocated the reporting

Later production version of MiG-29 armed with 'Alamo-A' and 'Aphid' missiles (*Swedish Air Force*)

name 'Fulcrum' when it became clear that the MiG was intended as a production aircraft.

From the start, it was plain that 'Fulcrum' represented a concerted effort by the Soviet Union to close the technology gap with the West. Its sustained turn rate is much improved over earlier Soviet fighters, and thrust-to-weight ratio is better than 1. Although intended primarily as a single-seat counter-air fighter, it is likely to have a full dual-role air combat/attack capability, and a combat capable two-seater, lacking only the radar of the single-seater, is also in production and service.

The only NATO reporting names that could be recorded in Summer 1988 were as follows:

Fulcrum-A. Basic operational single-seat version, of which four variants may be identified as follows:

1. The original single-seat production version, with two ventral tail fins similar to those of the Sukhoi Su-27. (Illustrated in 1987-88 *Jane's*.)

2. First version displayed in public, when a detachment of six from Kubinka air base made a goodwill visit to Finland on 1 July 1986. Instead of ventral fins, this variant has its dorsal fins extended forward as overwing fences.

3. Differs from second variant in having extended-chord rudders.

4. As preceding variant, but with more deeply curved fuselage aft of the cockpit, almost certainly providing additional fuel tankage.

Fulcrum-B. Combat trainer with second seat in front of the normal cockpit, under a continuous framed canopy. Nose radar replaced by radar rangefinder. Periscope above canopy. Underwing stores pylons retained.

Production is centred at a factory in Moscow. About 450 MiG-29s are operational with air forces of the Soviet military districts and groups of forces stationed in East Germany, Hungary, and in the Soviet Union west of the Urals. Export deliveries of an initial quantity of 44 MiG-29s ordered by India (40 single-seat, four two-seat) had been completed by mid-1987. Others have been delivered to East Germany, North Korea, Syria and Yugoslavia. Reported potential operators include the air force of Zimbabwe.

A unique feature of the MiG-29, first observed during the 1986 goodwill visit to Finland, is that as the nosewheel makes contact with the runway during landing, doors are triggered to blank off the underslung engine air intakes. This technique was adopted by the aircraft's designers to overcome problems caused by ingestion of stones, snow, slush, ice and foreign objects into the engine ducts during take-off and landing on the kind of runways used by Warsaw Pact front-line air forces, especially in Winter. When the intake trunks are closed, engine air is taken in through a series of lateral louvres in the upper surface of the aircraft's deep wingroot leading-edge extensions.

There was nothing on the MiG-29s in Finland to suggest that the Soviet Union is yet equipping its counter-air fighters to refuel in flight. Also, although the MiG-29 has a high-set cockpit, giving its pilot a reasonable forward view over the sloping nose, he lacks the all-round field of view offered to the pilots of western fighters such as the F-15 and F-16 through 360° low-sill canopies. Nor can the bulky head-up display, IR sensor, and large wing leading-edge extensions be helpful in this respect.

Comparison of the general configurations of the MiG-29 'Fulcrum' and Su-27 'Flanker' prompts the thought that some authority, perhaps the TsAGI Central Aerodynamics and Hydrodynamics Institute, may be exerting a considerable influence on current design concepts. The Sukhoi fighter maintains the tradition of being larger than the MiG, but the two designs are strikingly similar in most respects, even in such detail as current tail fin location and the manner in which the mainwheels retract into the wingroots.

The following description applies specifically to the later production 'Fulcrum-A', but is generally similar for other versions, except as already noted:

TYPE: All-weather counter-air fighter, with attack capability.
WINGS: Cantilever low-wing monoplane. Leading-edge sweepback approx 42° on outer wings, with very large ogival root extensions. Anhedral approx 2°. Leading-edge manoeuvring flaps over full span except for tips. Plain flap and aileron on trailing-edge of each wing. No tabs.
FUSELAGE: Semi-monocoque all-metal structure, sharply tapered and downswept aft of flat-sided cockpit area, with ogival dielectric nosecone. (More deeply curved fuselage aft of cockpit on some aircraft, containing additional fuel tankage.)
TAIL UNIT: Cantilever structure, comprising twin fins, small inset rudders, and all-moving horizontal surfaces, all carried on slim booms alongside engine nacelles. Vertical surfaces sweptback at approx 40° and canted outward at 7°, each with dorsal fin that extends forward as an overwing fence. Horizontal surfaces sweptback at approx 50°. No tabs.
LANDING GEAR: Retractable tricycle type, with single wheel on each main unit and twin nosewheels. Mainwheels retract forward into wingroots, turning through 90° to lie flat above leg. Nosewheels, on trailing-link oleo, retract rearward between engine air intakes. Mainwheel tyre size 770 × 200; nosewheel tyre size 530 × 100. Container for cruciform brake-chute recessed in centre of boat-tail between engine nozzles.
POWER PLANT: Two Tumansky R-33D turbofans, each rated at 50 kN (11,240 lb st) dry and 81.4 kN (18,300 lb st) with

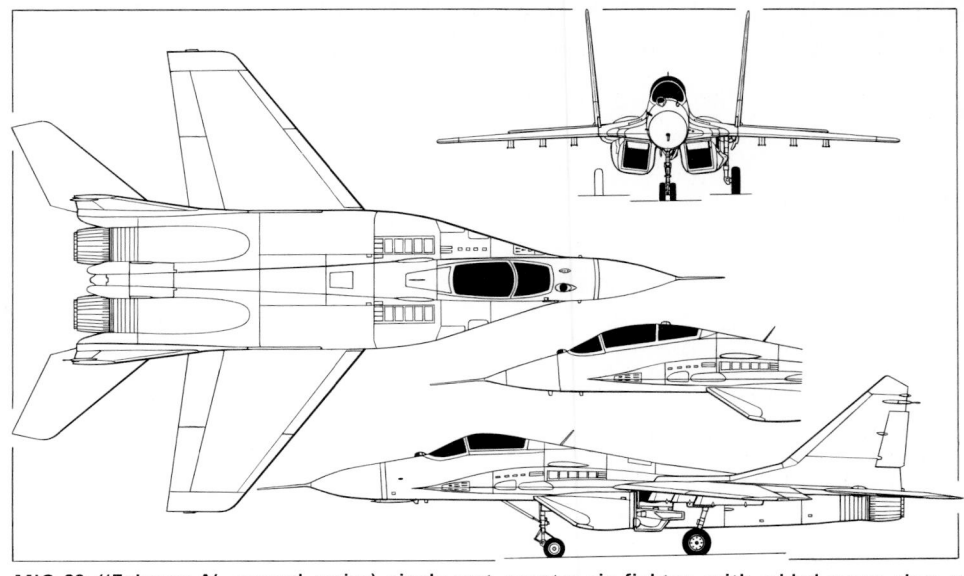

MiG-29 ('Fulcrum-A', second series) single-seat counter-air fighter, with added scrap view of 'Fulcrum-B' two-seat combat trainer *(Pilot Press)*

MiG-29 'Fulcrum-B' two-seat combat trainer of the Indian Air Force *(courtesy Air International)*

Two MiG-29s (NATO 'Fulcrum-A') of the Yugoslav Air Force

MiG-29 taking off from Kuopio-Rissala air base, Finland *(Press Association)*

afterburning. Engine ducts are canted at approx 9° and have wedge intakes, sweptback at approx 35°, under wingroot leading-edge extensions. Doors inside each intake close the duct while the nosewheels are in contact with the runway, to prevent ingestion of foreign objects, ice, or snow. Air is then fed to each engine through louvres in top of wingroot leading-edge extension. Attachment for a single (non-conformal) external fuel tank under fuselage, between ducts.

ACCOMMODATION: Pilot only, on zero/zero ejection seat, under rearward hinged transparent blister canopy in high-set cockpit. Sharply inclined one-piece curved windscreen.

SYSTEM: Hydraulically actuated flying controls. No fly-by-wire system.

ARMAMENT AND OPERATIONAL EQUIPMENT: Six medium-range radar homing AA-10 (NATO 'Alamo-A') and/or close-range AA-11 ('Archer') air-to-air missiles, on three pylons under each wing. Provision for carrying AA-9 ('Amos') and AA-8 ('Aphid') missiles. Able to carry bombs and 57 mm, 80 mm and 240 mm rockets in attack role. One 30 mm gun in port wingroot leading-edge extension. Equipment includes pulse Doppler engagement radar, IR sensor, laser rangefinder, SRZO-2 (NATO 'Odd Rods') IFF, Sirena-3 360° radar warning system, head-up display and helmet mounted sight.

DIMENSIONS, EXTERNAL:
Wing span	11.36 m (37 ft 3¼ in)
Wing chord: on centreline	5.60 m (18 ft 4½ in)
at tip	1.27 m (4 ft 2 in)
Length overall, incl nose probe	17.32 m (56 ft 10 in)
Height overall	4.73 m (15 ft 6¼ in)
Tailplane span	7.78 m (25 ft 6¼ in)
Wheel track	3.10 m (10 ft 2 in)
Wheelbase	3.67 m (12 ft 0½ in)

AREA:
Wings, gross	35.20 m² (378.9 sq ft)

WEIGHTS (approx):
Operating weight empty	8,175 kg (18,025 lb)
Normal T-O weight (interceptor)	15,000 kg (33,065 lb)
Max T-O weight	18,000 kg (39,700 lb)

PERFORMANCE:
Max level speed: at height	Mach 2.3 (1,320 knots; 2,440 km/h; 1,520 mph)
at S/L	Mach 1.06 (700 knots; 1,300 km/h; 805 mph)
Max rate of climb at S/L	19,800 m (65,000 ft)/min
Service ceiling	17,000 m (56,000 ft)
T-O run	240 m (790 ft)
Landing run	600 m (1,970 ft)
Max range approx	1,130 nm (2,100 km; 1,300 miles)

MIKOYAN MiG-31
NATO reporting name: Foxhound

Evidence that the Mikoyan design team was developing an improved interceptor based on the MiG-25 (NATO 'Foxbat') came first from Lt Viktor Belenko, the Soviet pilot who defected to Japan in a 'Foxbat-A' in September 1976. He said that the airframe of the new fighter was strengthened to permit supersonic flight at low altitude; more powerful engines were fitted, each giving 137.3 kN (30,865 lb st) with afterburning; the avionics were improved; and fuselage mountings had been added to enable the aircraft to carry six air-to-air missiles.

In mid-1982 it became known that NATO had allocated the reporting name 'Foxhound' to what the technical press referred to as 'Super Foxbat' and which was subsequently identified as the MiG-31. A three-view was displayed publicly for the first time in September of the following year, during briefings at the annual AFA Convention in Washington, DC, enabling the aircraft to be illustrated in the Addenda to the 1983-84 *Jane's*. The drawing showed significant new features, including tandem seating for a two-man crew, much enlarged engine air intakes, rearward extension of the jet nozzles, and wingroot leading-edge extensions on wings that were little changed in size and shape from those of the MiG-25. Its general accuracy was confirmed in the Autumn of 1985 when the pilot of an F-16 of the Royal Norwegian Air Force intercepted and photographed a MiG-31 off the coast of eastern Finnmark in northern Norway.

The MiG-31's large pulse-Doppler radar is said to embody technology found in the Hughes AN/APG-65 digital radar fitted in the US Navy's F/A-18 Hornet, providing true lookdown/shootdown and multiple target engagement capability for the first time in a Soviet interceptor. Other equipment includes active counter-measures dispensers, and an infra-red search/track sensor.

Delivery of MiG-31s to Voyska PVO air defence regiments had begun by early 1983, and more than 160 are now operational, deployed from the Arkhangelsk area near the USSR's western borders to Dolinsk on Sakhalin Island, north of Japan. Production is centred at the Gorkiy airframe plant.

The detailed description which follows must be regarded as provisional. Although it is likely, it is not yet possible to confirm that the arc-welded nickel steel structure of the MiG-25 has been retained on what has to be seen as a new design. The better heat resistant characteristics of steel are not essential at the reduced maximum speed of the MiG-31; but a switch to light alloy construction would have required extensive redesign of such well proven features as the basic wing structure, as well as major manufacturing changes. It

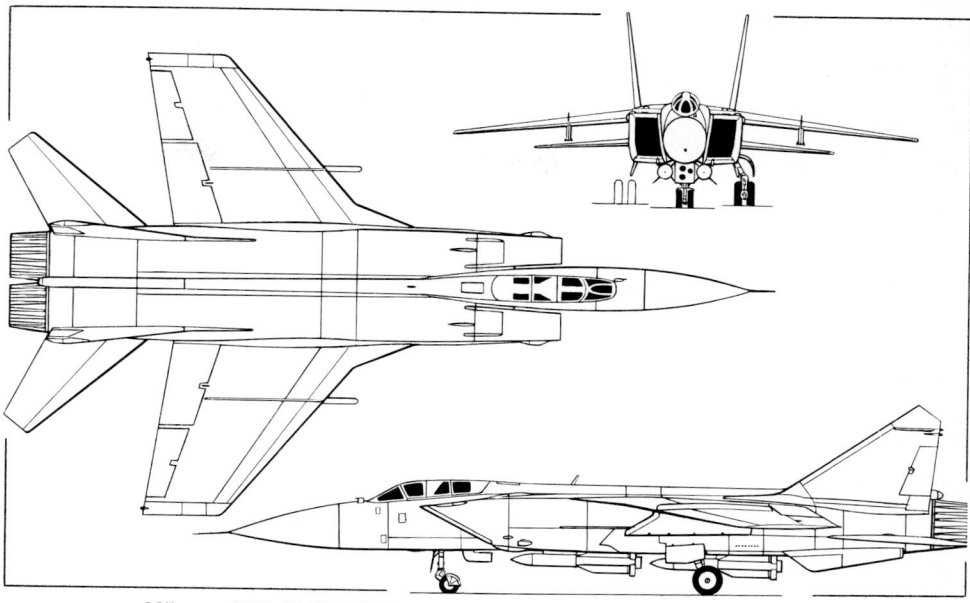

Mikoyan MiG-31 (NATO 'Foxhound') all-weather interceptor (*Pilot Press*)

Two views of the MiG-31 photographed by a Royal Norwegian Air Force pilot in Autumn 1985

MiG-31 all-weather interceptor, showing steerable mainwheels

is doubtful that these would have been considered worthwhile.

TYPE: Two-seat all-weather interceptor.

WINGS: Cantilever high-wing monoplane. Anhedral 4° from roots. Sweepback on leading-edge approx 40°, at quarter-chord 32°, with small sharply-swept wingroot extensions. Upper surface fence in line with each inboard weapon pylon. Aileron and flap on each wing, of greater span than those of MiG-25. No wingtip fairings or mountings.

FUSELAGE: Basic fuselage is slim, but is blended into wide rectangular air intake trunks, which have wedge inlets. Inner wall of each inlet is curved and does not run parallel with outer wall. Hinged panel forms lower lip of each inlet, and there is a large door towards the forward part of each top surface.

TAIL UNIT: Twin outward canted fins, with inset rudders, and all-moving one-piece horizontal surfaces. All surfaces sharply sweptback, without tabs. Two outward canted ventral fins. Large areas of each main and ventral fin form flush antennae. Aerodynamic fairings between base of each fin and engine duct, extending well forward of leading-edge.

LANDING GEAR: Retractable tricycle type. Twin steerable wheels on each main unit, retracting forward into air intake trunk. Rearward retracting twin nosewheel unit with mudguard.

POWER PLANT: Two Tumansky turbojets, each reportedly rated at 137.3 kN (30,865 lb st) with afterburning. Fuel tankage probably similar to that of MiG-25, which has two structural tanks in fuselage, between cockpit and engine bay, saddle tanks around intake ducts, and integral tank in each wing, filling almost the entire volume inboard of outer stores pylon, with total capacity of approx 17,410 litres (4,600 US gallons; 3,830 Imp gallons). Provision for two large external fuel tanks on outer underwing pylons.

ACCOMMODATION: Pilot and weapon systems operator in tandem. Canopy has only limited side glazing for rear cockpit and blends into shallow dorsal spine fairing which extends to forward edge of jet nozzles.

AVIONICS AND EQUIPMENT: Main fire control radar of pulse-Doppler lookdown/shootdown type in nose, with reported search range of 165 nm (305 km; 190 miles) and tracking range of 145 nm (270 km; 167 miles). Infra-red sensor in bottom of front fuselage. Radar warning receivers, active IR and electronic countermeasures.

ARMAMENT: Aircraft seen to date each had four AA-9 (NATO 'Amos') semi-active radar homing long-range air-to-air missiles in pairs under fuselage, and twin mounts for AA-8 ('Aphid') air-to-air missiles on one large pylon under each wing. These pylons plus outer underwing pylons (not yet observed) can probably increase the number of AA-9s carried by MiG-31 to reported total of eight.

DIMENSIONS, EXTERNAL (estimated):
Wing span 14.00 m (45 ft 11¼ in)
Length of fuselage, nosecone tip to end of jetpipe
21.50 m (70 ft 6½ in)

WEIGHTS (estimated):
Weight empty 21,825 kg (48,115 lb)
Max T-O weight 41,150 kg (90,725 lb)

PERFORMANCE (estimated):
Max level speed at height Mach 2.4
(1,375 knots; 2,550 km/h; 1,585 mph)
Max combat radius 1,135 nm (2,100 km; 1,305 miles)

MIL

GENERAL DESIGNER IN CHARGE OF BUREAU:
Marat N. Tishchenko

Mikhail L. Mil was connected with Soviet gyroplane and helicopter development from at least 1930 until his death on 31 January 1970. His original Mi-l, which was designed in 1949, first flown in 1950 and introduced into squadron service in 1951, was the first helicopter to enter series production in the Soviet Union. Current products of the design bureau named after him are as follows:

MIL Mi-2 (V-2)
NATO reporting name: Hoplite
Built exclusively in Poland and described under Polish aircraft industry entry for WSK-PZL Swidnik. About 675 serve with Soviet military ground forces.

MIL Mi-6
NATO reporting name: Hook
Announced in the Autumn of 1957, the Mi-6 was then the world's largest helicopter. From it were developed the Mi-10 and Mi-10K flying crane helicopters, and its dynamic components were used in duplicated form on the V-12 (Mi-12) of 1967, which remains the largest helicopter yet flown anywhere in the world.

Five Mi-6s are reported to have been built for development testing, followed by an initial pre-series of 30 and subsequent manufacture of more than 800 for military and civil use. About 450 serve currently with Soviet ground forces. Others serve with the Algerian, Iraqi, Peruvian and Vietnamese air forces and the Peruvian Army air force. A full structural description can be found in the 1983-84 and previous editions of *Jane's*.

TYPE: Heavy transport helicopter.

POWER PLANT: Two 4,101 kW (5,500 shp) Soloviev D-25V (TV-2BM) turboshafts, mounted side by side above cabin, forward of main rotor shaft. Eleven internal fuel tanks, with total capacity of 6,315 kg (13,922 lb), and two external tanks, on each side of cabin, with total capacity of 3,490 kg (7,695 lb). Provision for two additional ferry tanks inside cabin, with total capacity of 3,490 kg (7,695 lb).

ACCOMMODATION: Crew of five, consisting of two pilots, navigator, flight engineer and radio operator. Four jettisonable doors and overhead hatch on flight deck.

Electro-thermal anti-icing system for glazing of flight deck and navigator's compartment. Equipped normally for cargo operation, with easily removable tip-up seats along side walls. When these seats are supplemented by additional seats installed in centre of cabin, 65-90 passengers can be carried, with cargo or baggage in the aisles. Normal military seating is for 70 combat equipped troops. As an air ambulance, 41 stretcher cases and two medical attendants on tip-up seats can be carried. One of attendant's stations is provided with intercom to flight deck, and provision is made for portable oxygen installations for the patients. Cabin floor is stressed for loadings of 2,000 kg/m² (410 lb/sq ft), with provision for cargo tiedown rings. Rear clamshell doors and ramps are operated hydraulically. Standard equipment includes an electric winch of 800 kg (1,765 lb) capacity and pulley block system. Central hatch in cabin floor for cargo sling system for bulky loads. Three jettisonable doors, fore and aft of main landing gear on port side and aft of landing gear on starboard side.

AVIONICS AND EQUIPMENT: Standard equipment includes VHF and HF communications radio, intercom, radio altimeter, radio compass, three-channel autopilot, marker beacon receiver, directional gyro and full all-weather instrumentation.

ARMAMENT: Some military Mi-6s are fitted with a 12.7 mm machine-gun in the fuselage nose.

DIMENSIONS, EXTERNAL:
Main rotor diameter 35.00 m (114 ft 10 in)
Tail rotor diameter 6.30 m (20 ft 8 in)
Length overall, rotors turning 41.74 m (136 ft 11½ in)
Length of fuselage, excl nose gun and tail rotor
33.18 m (108 ft 10½ in)
Height overall 9.86 m (32 ft 4 in)
Wing span 15.30 m (50 ft 2½ in)
Wheel track 7.50 m (24 ft 7¼ in)
Wheelbase 9.09 m (29 ft 9¾ in)
Rear loading doors: Height 2.70 m (8 ft 10¼ in)
Width 2.65 m (8 ft 8¼ in)
Passenger doors:
Height: front door 1.70 m (5 ft 7 in)
rear doors 1.61 m (5 ft 3½ in)
Width 0.80 m (2 ft 7½ in)
Sill height: front door 1.40 m (4 ft 7¼ in)
rear doors 1.30 m (4 ft 3¼ in)

Central hatch in floor
1.44 m (4 ft 9 in) × 1.93 m (6 ft 4 in)
DIMENSIONS, INTERNAL:
Cabin: Length 12.00 m (39 ft 4½ in)
Max width 2.65 m (8 ft 8¼ in)
Max height: at front 2.01 m (6 ft 7 in)
at rear 2.50 m (8 ft 2½ in)
Cabin volume 80 m³ (2,825 cu ft)
WEIGHTS:
Weight empty 27,240 kg (60,055 lb)
Max internal payload 12,000 kg (26,450 lb)
Max slung cargo 8,000 kg (17,637 lb)
Fuel load: internal 6,315 kg (13,922 lb)
with external tanks 9,805 kg (21,617 lb)
Max T-O weight with slung cargo at altitudes under
1,000 m (3,280 ft) 38,400 kg (84,657 lb)
Normal T-O weight 40,500 kg (89,285 lb)
Max T-O weight for VTO 42,500 kg (93,700 lb)
PERFORMANCE (at max T-O weight for VTO):
Max level speed 162 knots (300 km/h; 186 mph)
Max cruising speed 135 knots (250 km/h; 155 mph)
Service ceiling 4,500 m (14,750 ft)
Range with 8,000 kg (17,637 lb) payload
334 nm (620 km; 385 miles)
Range with external tanks and 4,500 kg (9,920 lb)
payload 540 nm (1,000 km; 621 miles)
Max ferry range (tanks in cabin)
781 nm (1,450 km; 900 miles)

MIL Mi-8 (V-8)
NATO reporting name: Hip
Shown in public for the first time during the 1961 Soviet Aviation Day display, the original Mi-8 prototype (NATO Hip-A) had a single 2,013 kW (2,700 shp) Soloviev turboshaft and four-blade main rotor. When fitted with the five-blade rotor that became standard on subsequent aircraft, it was redesignated Hip-B. The second prototype, which flew for the first time on 17 September 1962, introduced the now-standard Isotov twin-turbine power plant and became Hip-C to NATO in both civil and military forms.

There are three civil transport versions, identified by large square cabin windows, as follows:

Mi-8. Passenger version, with standard seating for 28-32 persons in main cabin.

Mil Mi-6 heavy general purpose helicopter (two Soloviev D-25V turboshafts) of the Soviet air forces *(Letectvi + Kosmonautika/Václav Jukl)*

'Hip-D' has additional antennae as well as the canisters to which reference is made in the accompanying copy. It has an airborne communications role

'Hip-K' communications jamming variant of the Mi-8

Mi-8T. General utility version, equipped normally to carry internal or external freight, but able to accommodate 24 tip-up passenger seats along the cabin walls.

Mi-8 Salon. De luxe version. Main cabin is furnished normally for eleven passengers, with an eight-place couch facing inward on the port side, and two chairs and a swivelling seat on the starboard side. There is a table on the starboard side. An air-to-ground radio telephone and removable ventilation fans are standard equipment. Forward of the main cabin is a compartment for a hostess, with buffet and crew wardrobe. Aft of the main cabin are a toilet (port) and passenger wardrobe (starboard), to each side of the entrance. An alternative nine-passenger layout is available. The Mi-8 Salon has a max T-O weight of 10,400 kg (22,928 lb) and range of 205 nm (380 km; 236 miles) with 30 min fuel reserve. In other respects it is similar to the standard Mi-8.

Military versions, with small circular cabin windows, are identified by the following NATO reporting names:

Hip-C. Standard equipment of Soviet army support forces. Twin-rack for stores on each side of cabin, able to carry total of 128 × 57 mm rockets in four packs, or other weapons.

Hip-D. For airborne communications role. Generally similar to 'Hip-C' but with canisters of rectangular section on outer stores racks and added antennae.

Hip-E. Improved version of 'Hip-C'. One flexibly mounted 12.7 mm machine-gun in nose. Triple stores rack on each side of cabin, able to carry up to six suspended packs, plus four 'Swatter' anti-tank missiles (semi-automatic command to line of sight) on rails above racks. About 170 in service with Soviet ground forces.

Hip-F. Export counterpart of 'Hip-E'. Missile armament changed to six 'Saggers' (manual command to line of sight).

Hip-G. Airborne communications version with rearward inclined antennae projecting from rear of cabin and from undersurface of tailboom, aft of box for Doppler radar.

Hip-H. See separate entry on Mi-17. Some Mi-8s being updated to this standard.

Hip-J. Additional small boxes on sides of fuselage, fore and aft of main landing gear legs, identify this ECM version.

Hip-K. Communications jamming ECM version with large antenna array on each side of cabin, of the kind seen previously on the Mi-4 ('Hound-C'). No Doppler radar box under tailboom.

More than 10,000 Soviet built Mi-8s and uprated Mi-17s (described separately) have been delivered for military and civil use from two plants in Kazan and Ulan Ude. Component production of the Mi-8 has also taken place at Harbin in China. An estimated total of 1,950 Mi-8s and Mi-17s support Soviet armies in the field. Many others are operated by Soviet air forces, and military Mi-8s have been supplied to at least 39 other air forces, as listed in previous editions of *Jane's*.

Production is now concentrated on versions of the uprated Mi-17, except for the commercial Salon and export variants which remain available.

TYPE: Twin-engined transport helicopter.

ROTOR SYSTEM: Five-blade main rotor and three-blade tail rotor. Transmission comprises a type VR-8 two-stage planetary main reduction gearbox giving main rotor shaft/engine rpm ratio of 0.016 : 1, intermediate and tail gearboxes, main rotor brake and drives off the main gearbox for the tail rotor, fan, AC generator, hydraulic pumps and tachometer generators. Main rotor shaft inclined forward at 4° 30' from vertical. All-metal main rotor blades of basic NACA 230 section; solidity 0.0777. Each main blade is made up of an extruded light alloy spar carrying the blade root fitting, 21 trailing-edge pockets and the blade tip. Pockets are honeycomb filled. Main rotor blades are fitted with balance tabs, embody a spar failure warning system, and are interchangeable. Their drag and flapping hinges are a few inches apart, and they are carried on a machined spider. Control system utilises irreversible hydraulic boosters. Main rotor collective pitch control is interlocked to throttle controls. All-metal tail rotor blades, each made up of a spar and honeycomb filled trailing-edge. Automatically controlled electro-thermal de-icing system on all blades. In an emergency, the rotor blades of the Mi-8 and intermediate and tail gearboxes are interchangeable with those of the piston-engined Mi-4, although this prevents use of the de-icing system.

FUSELAGE: Conventional all-metal semi-monocoque structure of pod and boom type.

TAIL UNIT: Tail rotor support acts as small vertical stabiliser. Horizontal stabiliser near end of tailboom.

LANDING GEAR: Non-retractable tricycle type, with steerable twin-wheel nose unit, which is locked in flight, and single wheel on each main unit. All units embody oleo-pneumatic (gas) shock absorbers. Mainwheel tyres size 865 × 280; nosewheel tyres size 595 × 185. Pneumatic brakes on mainwheels. Pneumatic system can also recharge tyres in the field, using air stored in main landing gear struts. Optional mainwheel fairings.

Mil Mi-8 ('Hip-C') military helicopter of the Hungarian Air Force. This differs from the commercial versions in having circular cabin windows, and weapon carriers on outriggers *(Peter J. Bish)*

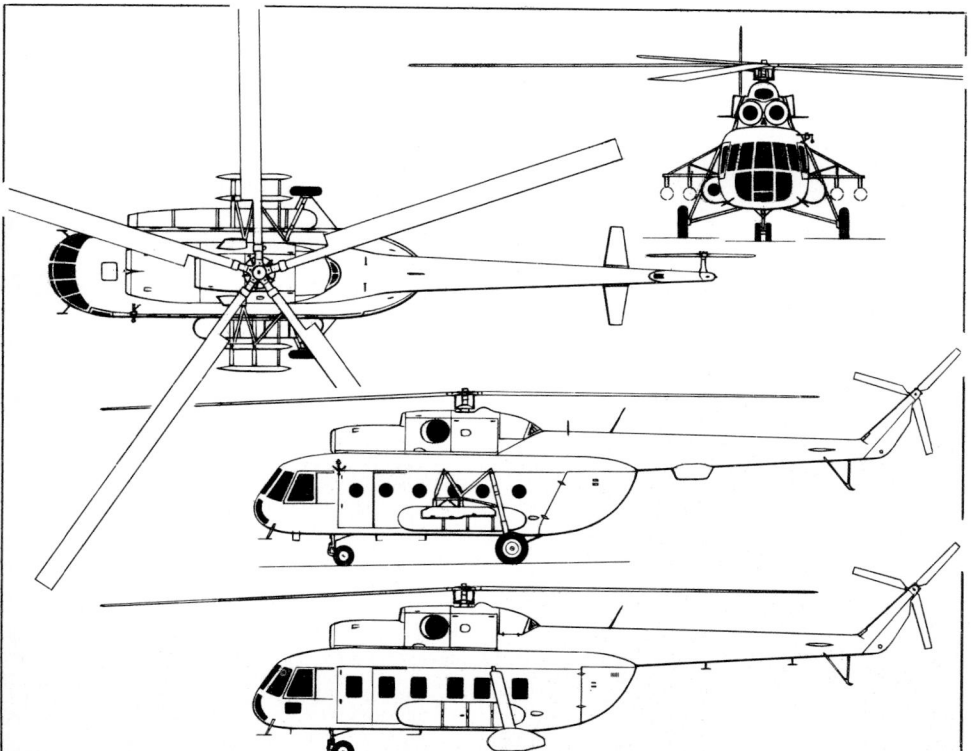

'Hip-C' military version of Mil Mi-8 twin-turbine helicopter, with additional side view (bottom) of commercial version *(Pilot Press)*

'Hip-J' ECM variant of the Mi-8

POWER PLANT: Two 1,267 kW (1,700 shp) Isotov TV2-117A turboshafts. Main rotor speed governed automatically, with manual override. Single flexible internal fuel tank, capacity 445 litres (117.5 US gallons; 98 Imp gallons), and two external tanks, one each side of cabin, with capacity of 745 litres (197 US gallons; 164 Imp gallons) in the port tank and 680 litres (179.5 US gallons; 149.5 Imp gallons) in the starboard tank. Total standard fuel capacity 1,870 litres (494 US gallons; 411.5 Imp gallons). Provision for carrying one or two additional ferry tanks in cabin, raising max total capacity to 3,700 litres (977 US gallons; 814 Imp gallons). Fairing over starboard external tank houses optional cabin air-conditioning equipment at front. Engine cowling side panels form maintenance platforms when open, with access via hatch on flight deck. Engine air intake de-icing standard. Total oil capacity 60 kg (132 lb).

ACCOMMODATION: Two pilots side by side on flight deck, with provision for a flight engineer's station. Windscreen de-icing standard. Basic passenger version is furnished with 28 four-abreast track mounted tip-up seats at a pitch of 72-75 cm (28-29.5 in), with a centre aisle 32 cm (12.5 in) wide, a wardrobe and baggage compartment; or 32 seats without wardrobe. Seats and bulkheads of basic version are quickly removable for cargo carrying. Mi-8T and standard military versions have cargo tiedown rings in floor, a winch of 200 kg (440 lb) capacity and pulley block system to facilitate the loading of heavy freight, an external cargo sling system (capacity 3,000 kg; 6,614 lb), and 24 tip-up seats along the side walls of the cabin. All versions can be converted for air ambulance duties, with accommodation for 12 stretchers and a tip-up seat for a medical attendant. The large windows on each side of the flight deck slide rearward. The sliding, jettisonable main passenger door is at the front of the cabin on the port side. An electrically operated rescue hoist (capacity 150 kg; 330 lb) can be installed at this doorway. The rear of the cabin is made up of clamshell freight loading doors, which are smaller on the commercial versions, with a downward hinged passenger airstair door inset centrally at the rear. Hook-on ramps are used for vehicle loading.

SYSTEMS: Standard heating system can be replaced by full air-conditioning system. Two independent hydraulic systems, each with own pump; operating pressure 44-64 bars (640-925 lb/sq in). DC electrical supply from two 27V 18kW starter/generators and six 28Ah storage batteries. AC supply for de-icing system and some

radio equipment supplied by 208/115/36/7.5V 400Hz generator, with 36V three-phase standby system. Provision for oxygen system for crew and, in ambulance version, for patients. Freon fire extinguishing system in power plant bays and service fuel tank compartments, actuated automatically or manually. Two portable fire extinguishers for use in cabin.

AVIONICS AND EQUIPMENT: Standard equipment includes a type R-842 HF transceiver with frequency range of 2 to 8MHz and range of up to 540 nm (1,000 km; 620 miles), type R-860 VHF transceiver operating on 118 to 135.9MHz over ranges of up to 54 nm (100 km; 62 miles), intercom, radio telephone, type ARK-9 automatic radio compass, type RV-3 radio altimeter with 'dangerous height' warning, and four-axis autopilot to give yaw, roll and pitch stabilisation under any flight conditions, stabilisation of altitude in level flight or hover, and stabilisation of pre-set flying speed, navigation equipment and instrumentation for all-weather flying by day and night, including two gyro horizons, two airspeed indicators, two main rotor speed indicators, turn indicator, two altimeters, two rate of climb indicators, magnetic compass, radio altimeter, radio compass and astrocompass for Polar flying. Doppler radar in box under forward part of tailboom. Military versions can be fitted with infra-red suppressors and infra-red decoy dispensers.

ARMAMENT: See individual model descriptions of military versions.

DIMENSIONS, EXTERNAL:
Main rotor diameter	21.29 m (69 ft 10¼ in)
Tail rotor diameter	3.91 m (12 ft 9⅞ in)
Distance between rotor centres	12.65 m (41 ft 6 in)
Length overall, rotors turning	25.24 m (82 ft 9¾ in)
Length of fuselage, excl tail rotor	18.17 m (59 ft 7⅜ in)
Width of fuselage	2.50 m (8 ft 2½ in)
Height overall	5.65 m (18 ft 6½ in)
Wheel track	4.50 m (14 ft 9 in)
Wheelbase	4.26 m (13 ft 11¾ in)
Fwd passenger door: Height	1.41 m (4 ft 7¼ in)
Width	0.82 m (2 ft 8¼ in)
Rear passenger door: Height	1.70 m (5 ft 7 in)
Width	0.84 m (2 ft 9 in)
Rear cargo door: Height	1.82 m (5 ft 11½ in)
Width	2.34 m (7 ft 8¼ in)

DIMENSIONS, INTERNAL:
Passenger cabin: Length	6.36 m (20 ft 10¼ in)
Width	2.34 m (7 ft 8¼ in)
Height	1.80 m (5 ft 10¾ in)
Cargo hold (freighter):	
Length at floor	5.34 m (17 ft 6¼ in)
Width	2.34 m (7 ft 8¼ in)
Height	1.80 m (5 ft 10¾ in)
Volume	approx 23 m³ (812 cu ft)

AREA:
Main rotor disc	356 m² (3,832 sq ft)

WEIGHTS:
Weight empty:	
civil passenger version	6,799 kg (14,990 lb)
civil cargo version	6,624 kg (14,603 lb)
military versions (typical)	7,260 kg (16,007 lb)
Max payload: internal	4,000 kg (8,820 lb)
external	3,000 kg (6,614 lb)
Fuel: standard tanks	1,450 kg (3,197 lb)
with 2 auxiliary tanks	2,870 kg (6,327 lb)
Normal T-O weight	11,100 kg (24,470 lb)
T-O weight with 28 passengers, each with 15 kg (33 lb) of baggage	11,570 kg (25,508 lb)
T-O weight with 2,500 kg (5,510 lb) of slung cargo	11,428 kg (25,195 lb)
Max T-O weight for VTO	12,000 kg (26,455 lb)

PERFORMANCE:
Max level speed at 1,000 m (3,280 ft):	
normal AUW	140 knots (260 km/h; 161 mph)
Max level speed at S/L:	
normal AUW	135 knots (250 km/h; 155 mph)
max AUW	124 knots (230 km/h; 142 mph)
with 2,500 kg (5,510 lb) of slung cargo	97 knots (180 km/h; 112 mph)
Max cruising speed:	
normal AUW	122 knots (225 km/h; 140 mph)
max AUW	97 knots (180 km/h; 112 mph)
Service ceiling	4,500 m (14,760 ft)
Hovering ceiling at normal AUW:	
IGE	1,900 m (6,235 ft)
OGE	800 m (2,625 ft)
Ranges:	
cargo version at 1,000 m (3,280 ft), with standard fuel, 5% reserves:	
normal AUW	251 nm (465 km; 289 miles)
max AUW	240 nm (445 km; 276 miles)
with 28 passengers at 1,000 m (3,280 ft), with 20 min fuel reserves	270 nm (500 km; 311 miles)
ferry range of cargo version, with auxiliary fuel, 5% reserves	647 nm (1,200 km; 745 miles)

MIL Mi-10 and Mi-10K
NATO reporting name: Harke

There have been two versions of this flying crane development of the Mi-6:

Harke-A. This original version, designated **Mi-10** or **V-10**, was demonstrated at the 1961 Soviet Aviation Day display at Tushino, having flown for the first time in the previous year. Above the line of the cabin windows the Mi-6 and Mi-10 were almost identical, but the depth of the fuselage was reduced considerably on the Mi-10, and the tailboom was deepened so that the flattened undersurface ran unbroken to the tail. The Mi-10 also lacked the fixed wings of the Mi-6, and was fitted with a tall long-stroke quadricycle landing gear, with wheel track exceeding 6.0 m (19 ft 8 in) and clearance under the fuselage of 3.75 m (12 ft 3½ in) with the aircraft fully loaded. This enabled the Mi-10 to taxi over a load it was to carry and to accommodate loads as bulky as a prefabricated building.

Harke-B. This developed version, known as the **Mi-10K**, was displayed in public for the first time, in Moscow, on 26 March 1966. It embodied a number of important design changes, most apparent of which were a reduction in the height of the landing gear and a more slender tail rotor support structure.

The Mi-10K can be operated by a crew of only two pilots. This is made possible by provision of an additional cockpit gondola under the front fuselage, with full flying controls and a rearward facing seat. By occupying this seat, one of the pilots can control the aircraft in hovering flight and, at the same time, have an unrestricted view of cargo loading, unloading and hoisting, which are also under his control.

In the Mi-10K, the maximum slung payload was initially 11,000 kg (24,250 lb) but was expected to be increased to 14,000 kg (30,865 lb) by using Soloviev D-25VF turboshafts, uprated to 4,847 kW (6,500 shp) each.

A detailed description of the original Mi-10 can be found in the 1982-83 and earlier editions of *Jane's*. A total of about 55 of both versions had been delivered by 1977, when production was resumed briefly, at a modest rate, after a six-year break. Most production helicopters are thought to be Mi-10Ks, to which the following data apply. A more extensive description can be found in the 1983-84 and previous editions of *Jane's*.

TYPE: Heavy flying-crane helicopter.

POWER PLANT: Two 4,101 kW (5,500 shp) Soloviev D-25V turboshafts in early production aircraft, mounted side by side above cabin, forward of main rotor driveshaft. Fuel capacity, in standard internal and two external tanks, on sides of cabin, 9,000 litres (2,377 US gallons; 1,980 Imp gallons). Provision for ferry tanks in cabin.

Mil Mi-10K (NATO 'Harke-B') preparing to lift a 10-tonne sheet steel drum to the top of a tower at the Sinarski pipe works in Kamensk-Uralskii *(Tass)*

ACCOMMODATION: Two pilots on flight deck, which has bulged side windows to provide an improved downward view. Flight deck is heated and ventilated and has provision for oxygen equipment. Additional cockpit gondola under front fuselage (see introductory notes). Crew door is immediately aft of flight deck on port side. Main cabin can be used for freight and/or passengers, 28 tip-up seats being installed along the side walls. Freight is loaded into this cabin through a door on the starboard side, aft of the rear landing gear struts, with the aid of a boom and 200 kg (440 lb) capacity electric winch. External sling gear standard, with hatch in the cabin floor, directly beneath main rotor shaft.

DIMENSIONS, EXTERNAL:

Main rotor diameter	35.00 m (114 ft 10 in)
Tail rotor diameter	6.30 m (20 ft 8 in)
Length overall, rotors turning	41.89 m (137 ft 5½ in)
Length of fuselage	32.86 m (107 ft 9¾ in)
Height overall	7.80 m (25 ft 7 in)
Wheel track (c/l of shock struts)	5.00 m (16 ft 4¾ in)
Wheelbase	8.74 m (28 ft 8 in)
Freight loading door: Height	1.56 m (5 ft 1½ in)
Width	1.26 m (4 ft 1½ in)
Height to sill	1.82 m (5 ft 11½ in)
Cabin floor hatch: Diameter	1.00 m (3 ft 3¼ in)

DIMENSIONS, INTERNAL:

Cabin: Length	14.04 m (46 ft 0¾ in)
Width	2.50 m (8 ft 2½ in)
Height	1.68 m (5 ft 6 in)
Volume	approx 60 m³ (2,120 cu ft)

WEIGHTS:

Weight empty	24,680 kg (54,410 lb)
Max fuel load with ferry tanks in cabin	8,670 kg (19,114 lb)
Max T-O weight with slung cargo	38,000 kg (83,775 lb)

PERFORMANCE:

Cruising speed, empty	135 knots (250 km/h; 155 mph)
Max cruising speed with slung load	109 knots (202 km/h; 125 mph)
Service ceiling	3,000 m (9,850 ft)
Ferry range with auxiliary fuel	428 nm (795 km; 494 miles)

MIL Mi-14 (V-14)
NATO reporting name: Haze

The Mi-14 shore-based amphibious helicopter flew for the first time in 1973. Overall dimensions, power plant and dynamic components are generally similar to those of the Mi-17, reflecting parallel development from the Mi-8 airframe. New features include a boat hull planing bottom on the fuselage, a sponson on each side at the rear, and a small float under the tailboom, to confer a degree of amphibious capability. The fully retractable landing gear comprises two single-wheel nose units and two twin-wheel main units. There is a Doppler radar box under the forward part of the tailboom.

Three versions may be identified by NATO reporting names, as follows:

Haze-A. Basic ASW version, with crew of four or five. Operational anti-submarine equipment can be seen to include a large undernose radome, a retractable sonar unit housed in the starboard rear of the planing bottom, forward of what appear to be two sonobuoy or signal flare chutes, and a towed magnetic anomaly detection (MAD) 'bird' stowed against the rear of the fuselage pod. Weapons include torpedoes and depth charges, carried in an enclosed bay in the bottom of the hull. About 100 operational with Soviet forces.

Haze-B. Mine countermeasures version, with fuselage strake and pod on starboard side of cabin, and no MAD. Two additional equipment boxes under the tailboom, to each side of the Doppler container. About 10 in service with

The search and rescue version of the Mi-14 ('Haze-C') in Polish service *(courtesy of Helicopter International)*

Mil Mi-14 anti-submarine helicopter ('Haze-A') in East German service
(Swedish Air Force, via FLYGvapenNYTT)

Soviet Navy; others with the East German and Polish services.

Haze-C. Search and rescue version in service in Soviet Union and Poland. Fuselage strake and pod as on 'Haze-B'. Double-width sliding door at front of cabin on port side, with retractable rescue hoist. Searchlight on each side of nose.

Three Mi-14s have been exported to Bulgaria, four to Cuba, twelve to Libya, at least four to Poland, six to Romania, eight to the German Democratic Republic and an unknown quantity to North Korea. Production continues.

DIMENSIONS, EXTERNAL:

Main rotor diameter	21.29 m (69 ft 10¼ in)
Length overall, rotors turning	25.30 m (83 ft 0 in)
Height overall	6.90 m (22 ft 7¾ in)

WEIGHT:

Max T-O weight	13,000 kg (28,660 lb)

PERFORMANCE:

Max level speed	124 knots (230 km/h; 143 mph)
Max cruising speed	108 knots (200 km/h; 124 mph)
Range with max fuel	500 nm (925 km; 575 miles)

MIL Mi-17
NATO reporting name: Hip-H

First displayed in public at the 1981 Paris Air Show, the Mi-17 combines the airframe of the Mi-8 with the uprated power plant that is used also in the Mi-14 and Mi-24. The basic civil and military version is known to NATO as 'Hip-H'. Many are operational side by side with Mi-8s in the Soviet armed forces, and with combat units in Afghanistan and Central America. They have the same armament options as the older aircraft, supplemented by 23 mm GSh-23 gun packs, and with external armour plate on the sides of the cockpit. Export deliveries include 16 to Cuba in 1983, and others subsequently to Angola, India, Nicaragua, North Korea and Peru. Mi-8s can be updated to Mi-17 standard.

The general description of the Mi-8 applies also to the Mi-17, except that the tail rotor is on the port side of the vertical stabiliser. Externally, the new power plant can be identified by the shorter nacelles, the air intakes extending forward only to the mid-point of the door on the port side at the front of the cabin. Also new is the small orifice on each side forward of the jetpipe. Take-off rating of each of the two Isotov TV3-117MT turboshafts is 1,417 kW (1,900 shp), which offers a considerable improvement in performance compared with the Mi-8. Correct rotor speed is maintained automatically by a system that also synchronises the output of the two engines. Should one engine stop, the output of the other is increased automatically to a contingency rating of 1,640 kW (2,200 shp), enabling the flight to continue. An APU is carried to start the turboshafts pneumatically, and the engine air intakes are fitted with deflectors to prevent the ingestion of sand, dust or foreign objects at unprepared landing sites.

Cabin configuration and payloads are unchanged by comparison with the Mi-8; but the civilian Mi-17 is

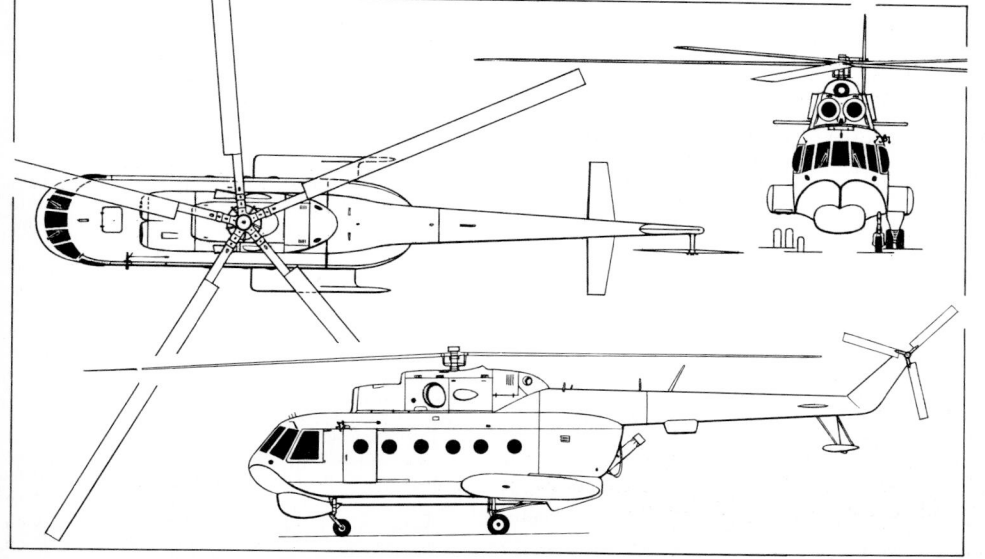

Mil Mi-14 (V-14) ASW helicopter (NATO 'Haze-A') *(Pilot Press)*

described by Aviaexport as essentially a cargo carrying helicopter, with secondary passenger transport role.

An illustration in the 1987-88 *Jane's* showed an Mi-17 used to patrol the border between East and West Germany. Features include rocket pods, a decoy flare dispenser under the tailboom, and domed and cylindrical covers replacing the two front cabin windows.

DIMENSIONS, EXTERNAL AND INTERNAL:

As for Mi-8, except:

Distance between rotor centres	12.661 m (41 ft 6½ in)
Length overall, rotors turning	25.352 m (83 ft 2 in)
Length of fuselage, excl tail rotor	
	18.424 m (60 ft 5⅜ in)
Height to top of main rotor head	4.755 m (15 ft 7¼ in)
Wheel track	4.510 m (14 ft 9½ in)
Wheelbase	4.281 m (14 ft 0½ in)

WEIGHTS:

Weight empty, equipped	7,100 kg (15,653 lb)
Max payload: internal	4,000 kg (8,820 lb)
external, on sling	3,000 kg (6,614 lb)
Normal T-O weight	11,100 kg (24,470 lb)
Max T-O weight	13,000 kg (28,660 lb)

PERFORMANCE (A at normal T-O weight; B at max T-O weight):

Max level speed: B	135 knots (250 km/h; 155 mph)
Max cruising speed: B	129 knots (240 km/h; 149 mph)
Service ceiling: A	5,000 m (16,400 ft)
B	3,600 m (11,800 ft)
Hovering ceiling OGE: A	1,760 m (5,775 ft)
Range with max standard fuel, 5% reserves:	
A	267 nm (495 km; 307 miles)
B	251 nm (465 km; 289 miles)
Range with auxiliary fuel:	
A	513 nm (950 km; 590 miles)

MIL Mi-24
NATO reporting name: Hind

This assault helicopter was known to exist for two years before photographs became available to the technical press in 1974. The two versions shown in those first photographs (known to NATO as 'Hind-A and B') each carried a crew of three (with pilot and co-pilot side by side) and were designed to deliver a squad of eight combat-equipped troops into a battle area. They had attachments under their auxiliary wings for a variety of ordnance with which to clear a path past any tanks, anti-aircraft guns or other obstructions encountered on the way, and to keep down the heads of enemy troops in the drop zone.

At least two units of approximate squadron strength were based at Parchim and Stendal, northwest and west of Berlin, near the border with West Germany, by the Spring of 1974. Experience gained in training exercises soon led to a major change in tactics. Today, the Mi-24 is regarded as not only an effective anti-tank weapon, but capable itself of functioning as a high-speed nap-of-the-earth 'tank', and of destroying opposing helicopters in air-to-air combat. Other duties include escort of troop carrying Mi-8/17s and ground attack.

To exploit the Mi-24's potential, the Mil bureau first increased performance by replacing the original Isotov TV2-117 turboshafts with more powerful TV3-117s, at the same time transferring the tail rotor from the starboard to the port side of the tail fin. The front fuselage was then redesigned to give priority to the gunship role, with a two-man crew of weapon operator and pilot in tandem individual cockpits, while retaining the original transport capability. To reduce vulnerability to ground fire, steel and titanium were substituted for aluminium in critical components, and glassfibre skinned rotor blades replaced the original metal blade pocket design. The gunship (beginning with the version known to NATO as 'Hind-D') then superseded the original versions in production. As a result of combat experience in Afghanistan, infra-red

Mil Mi-17 ('Hip-H') of the Czechoslovak Air Force *(Letectvi + Kosmonautika/Václav Jukl)*

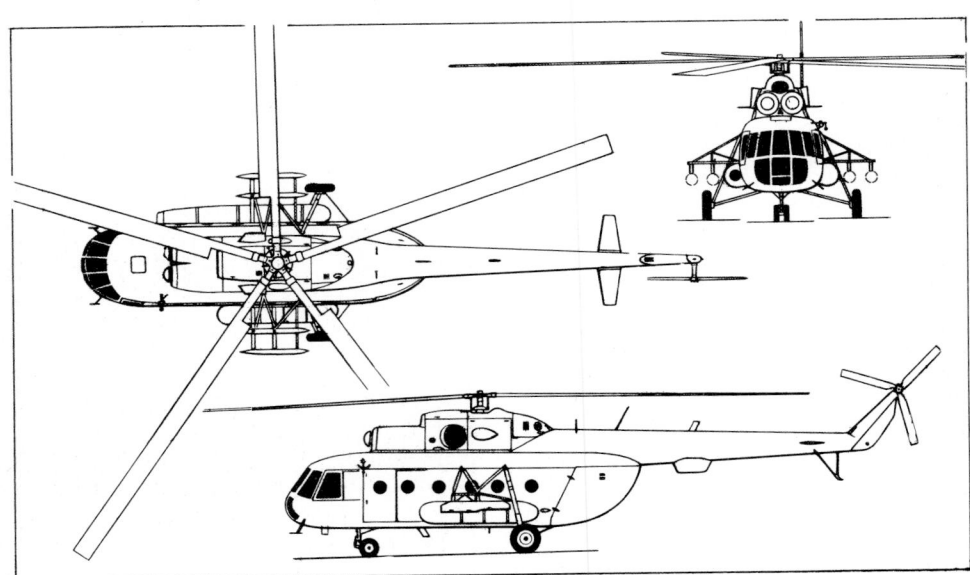

Mi-17 military general purpose helicopter, with external stores carriers *(Pilot Press)*

jammers, infra-red suppressors and decoy dispensers were added, and armour increased.

Except for the crew accommodation, the basic airframe, power plant and transmission system appear to be common to all current versions of the Mi-24, with differences in armament, operational equipment and tail rotor location. Major variants of which details may be published are known by the following NATO reporting names:

Hind-A. Armed assault helicopter, with large enclosed flight deck for crew of three, comprising pilot, co-pilot/gunner and ground engineer, and places for up to eight fully equipped troops in main cabin. Access to flight deck via large rearward sliding blistered transparent panel which

forms the aft flight deck window on the port side, and a large upward hinged window forward of this. Auxiliary wings, with considerable anhedral, carry total of four underwing pylons for UV-32 rocket pods, special bombs, or other stores, and rails for four AT-2 (NATO 'Swatter') anti-tank missiles under endplate pylons at wingtips. One 12.7 mm single-barrel DShK machine-gun in nose, slaved to undernose sighting system. Camera at top of port inner underwing pylon. Anti-torque rotor, originally on starboard side of offset tail pylon, repositioned to port side when original TV2-117 engines were replaced by TV3-117s on later and converted aircraft.

Hind-B. Similar to 'Hind-A' except that auxiliary wings have neither anhedral nor dihedral, and carry only the two inboard weapon stations on each side. This version preceded 'Hind-A' but was not built in large numbers.

Hind-C. Training version. Generally similar to late model 'Hind-A' but without nose gun and undernose blister fairing, and no missile rails at wingtips.

Hind-D. Basically similar to late model 'Hind-A', with TV3-117 engines and tail rotor on port side, but with completely new and heavily armoured accommodation for weapon operator and pilot, in tandem, forward of the engine inlets and above the fuselage floor for primary gunship role. Flight mechanic carried in main cabin. Transport capability retained. Undernose Gatling type 12.7 mm machine-gun provides air-to-air as well as air-to-surface capability. Extended nosewheel leg to increase ground clearance of sensor pack; nosewheels semi-exposed when retracted. Weapons, equipment and other details listed in aircraft structural description.

Hind-E. As 'Hind-D', for Soviet armed forces, but with modified wingtip launchers and four underwing pylons for a total of up to twelve AT-6 (NATO 'Spiral') radio guided tube-launched anti-tank missiles in pairs, and enlarged undernose missile guidance pod on port side. AA-8 ('Aphid') air-to-air missiles can be carried on underwing pylons.

Hind-F. First shown in service with Soviet forces in photographs published in 1982. Generally similar to 'Hind-E' but with the nose gun turret replaced by a

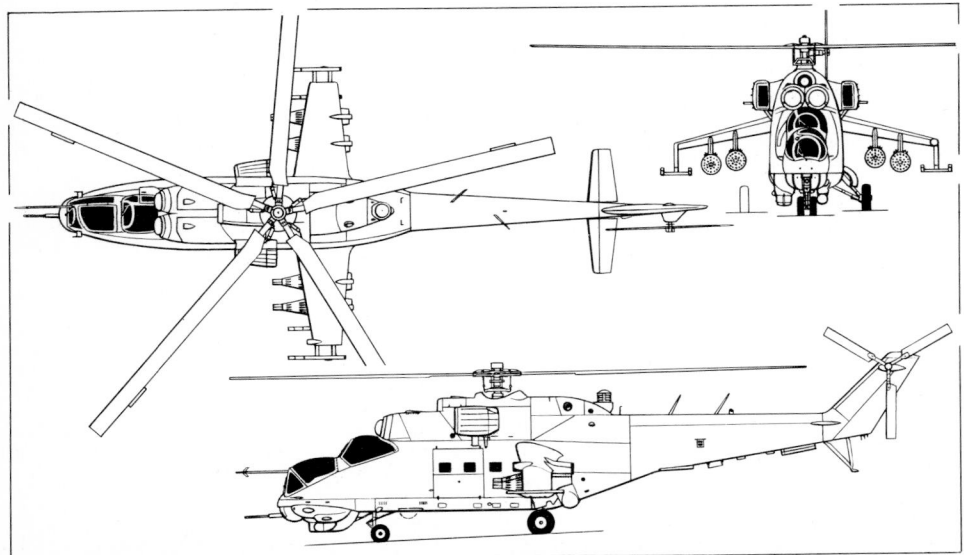

Mil Mi-24 gunship known to NATO as 'Hind-D', showing exhaust IR suppressor boxes *(Pilot Press)*

twin-barrel 30 mm gun mounted inside a semi-cylindrical pack on the starboard side of the fuselage, and the bottom of the nose smoothly faired above and forward of sensors.

Hind-G. First identified at Chernobyl, after the accident at a nuclear power station, this version lacks the usual undernose electro-optical and RF guidance packs for anti-tank missiles. Instead of wingtip weapon attachments, it has unidentified 'clutching hand' mechanisms which are probably associated with radiation sampling, on lengthened pylons. Other features include a lozenge shape housing with cylindrical insert under the port side of the cabin, a bubble window on the starboard side, and a plate of triangular shape mounted in the tailskid. Small numbers of 'Hind-Gs' are deployed individually throughout the Soviet ground forces.

Deliveries of all models are known to exceed 2,300, from plants in Arsenyev and Rostov, but production is now reducing from a long-maintained rate of more than 15 a month. At Soviet army level, there are some 20 helicopter attack regiments, each with up to 60 Mi-8/17s and Mi-24s, more than half of them deployed opposite NATO forces. At division level, helicopter detachments are expanding to squadrons. Other operators include the Warsaw Pact air forces of Bulgaria, Czechoslovakia, East Germany, Hungary and Poland. Export deliveries, mostly of the gunship version, have been made to Afghanistan, Algeria (including 'Hind-As'), Angola, Cuba, India, Iraq, Libya, Mozambique, Nicaragua, North Korea, Vietnam (including uprated 'Hind-As') and South Yemen. Some of these are designated **Mi-25** (see separate entry).

The following details apply to the 'Hind-D' gunship version:

TYPE: Gunship helicopter, with transport capability.

ROTOR SYSTEM: Dynamic components developed from those of Mi-8. Five-blade constant-chord main rotor, of NACA 230 blade section, and three-blade tail rotor; latter on port side of offset tail fin. Main rotor blades, with titanium spars, glassfibre skin and honeycomb core, on forged and machined steel head, with conventional flapping, drag and pitch change articulation. Blade spars nitrogen pressurised for crack detection. Hydraulic lead/lag dampers. Balance tab and electric leading-edge de-icing on each blade. Main rotor brake standard. Aluminium alloy tail rotor blades.

FUSELAGE: Conventional all-metal semi-monocoque structure of pod and boom type. Forward portion, above shallow floor structure, embodies integral side armour.

AUXILIARY WINGS: All-metal cantilever shoulder wings of tapered planform, with about 16° anhedral and 20° incidence. No movable surfaces. Wings contribute about 25 per cent of total lift in cruising flight.

TAIL UNIT: Swept fin, offset at 3°, serves also as tail rotor pylon. Variable incidence horizontal stabiliser at base of fin.

LANDING GEAR: Tricycle type, with rearward retracting steerable twin-wheel nose unit, and single-wheel main units with oleo-pneumatic shock absorbers and low pressure tyres. Main units retract rearward and inward into the aft end of the fuselage pod, turning through 90° to stow almost vertically, discwise to the longitudinal axis of the fuselage, under prominent blister fairings. Tubular tripod skid assembly, with shock strut, protects tail rotor in a tail-down take-off or landing.

POWER PLANT: Two Isotov TV3-117 turboshafts, each with max rating of 1,640 kW (2,200 shp), mounted side by side above the cabin, with their output shafts driving rearward to the main rotor shaft through a combining gearbox. Main fuel tank in fuselage to rear of cabin, with bag tanks under cabin floor. Internal fuel capacity of 1,500 kg (3,307 lb) can be supplemented by 1,000 kg (2,205 lb) auxiliary tank in cabin. Provision for carrying (instead of auxiliary tank) up to four external fuel tanks, each with estimated capacity of 300 kg (661 lb), on two inner pylons under each wing. Optional deflectors and separators for foreign objects and dust in air intakes; and infra-red suppression exhaust mixer boxes over exhaust ducts. APU mounted transversely inside fairing aft of rotor head.

ACCOMMODATION: Pilot (at rear) and weapon operator on armoured seats in tandem cockpits under individual canopies. Flight mechanic in cabin. Front canopy hinged to open sideways, to starboard; footstep under starboard side of fuselage for access to pilot's rearward hinged door. Rear seat raised to give pilot an unobstructed forward view. Anti-fragment shield between cockpits. Main cabin can accommodate eight persons on folding seats, or four stretchers. At front of passenger cabin on each side is a door, divided horizontally into two sections which are hinged to open upward and downward respectively, with integral step on lower portion. Optically flat bulletproof glass windscreen, with wiper, for each crew member. Cockpits heated and ventilated.

SYSTEMS: Dual electrical system, with three generators. Stability augmentation system. Electro-thermal de-icing system for main and tail rotor blades. Cabin heating and ventilation systems.

AVIONICS AND EQUIPMENT: Include VHF and UHF radio, autopilot, radar altimeter, blind-flying instrumentation, and ADF navigation system with map display. Retractable landing/taxying light under nose. Navigation lights. Anti-collision light above tailboom. Air data sensor

'Hind-A', first major production version of the Mil Mi-24 with original starboard side tail rotor

Mil Mi-24 ('Hind-D') of the Polish Air Force, fitted with full range of infra-red and electronic countermeasures *(Robert Senkowski)*

Mil Mi-24 'Hind-F', with twin-barrel cannon in place of earlier nose turret

boom forward of top starboard corner of bulletproof windscreen at extreme nose. Undernose pods for electro-optics and RF missile guidance. Gun camera on port wingtip. Many small antennae and blisters, including IFF (NATO 'Odd Rods') and radar warning antennae. Infra-red jammer in 'flower pot' container above forward end of tailboom; decoy flare dispenser under tailboom forward of tailskid assembly.

ARMAMENT: One remotely controlled four-barrel Gatling type 12.7 mm machine-gun in undernose turret with range of movement in azimuth and elevation, and slaved to undernose sighting system. Rails for four AT-2 'Swatter' anti-tank missiles under endplate pylons at wingtips. Four underwing pylons for UV-32-57 rocket pods (each thirty-two S-5 type 57 mm rockets), pods each containing twenty 80 mm rockets, UPK-23 pods each containing twin 23 mm guns, up to 1,500 kg (3,300 lb)

of chemical or conventional bombs, PFM-1 mine dispensers, or other stores. Helicopter can be landed to instal reload weapons carried in cabin. PKV reflector gunsight for pilot. Provisions for firing AK-47 guns from cabin windows.

DIMENSIONS, EXTERNAL (estimated):
Main rotor diameter	17.00 m (55 ft 9 in)
Tail rotor diameter	3.90 m (12 ft 9½ in)
Length overall:	
excl rotors and gun	17.50 m (57 ft 5 in)
rotors turning	21.50 m (70 ft 6½ in)
Height overall: rotors turning	6.50 m (21 ft 4 in)

WEIGHTS (estimated):
Weight empty	8,400 kg (18,520 lb)
Max external weapons	1,500 kg (3,300 lb)
Normal T-O weight	11,000 kg (24,250 lb)

'Hind-G' version of Mi-24 with 'clutching hand' wingtip fittings *(copied from Soviet Military Review)*

PERFORMANCE ('Hind-D'):

Max level speed	167 knots (310 km/h; 192 mph)
Max cruising speed	159 knots (295 km/h; 183 mph)
Max rate of climb at S/L	750 m (2,460 ft)/min
Service ceiling	4,500 m (14,750 ft)
Hovering ceiling OGE	2,200 m (7,200 ft)
Combat radius:	
with max military load	86 nm (160 km; 99 miles)
with two external fuel tanks	
	121 nm (224 km; 139 miles)
with four external fuel tanks	
	155 nm (288 km; 179 miles)
Range with max internal fuel	
	405 nm (750 km; 466 miles)

MIL Mi-25
NATO reporting name: Hind

Some export variants of the Mi-24 ('Hind-D'), including those for Angola, India and Peru, are reportedly designated Mi-25. Such a change presumably signifies different equipment standards.

MIL Mi-26
NATO reporting name: Halo

Design of the Mi-26 heavy lift helicopter began in the early 1970s to meet the requirement for an aircraft of greater capability than the Mi-6 and Mi-10, for day and night operation in all weathers. Except for the four-engined twin-rotor Mi-12 (see 1977-78 *Jane's*), which did not progress beyond prototype testing, it is the heaviest helicopter yet flown anywhere in the world. Its rotor diameter is smaller than that of the Mi-6 and Mi-10, but this is offset by the fact that the Mi-26 is the first helicopter to operate successfully with an eight-blade main rotor.

It has obvious military applications, with a payload and cargo hold very similar in size to those of a Lockheed C-130 Hercules. To meet also Soviet Ministry of Civil Aviation requirements, for operation in Siberia and northern swamp and tundra areas of the USSR, emphasis had to be placed on reliability, especially when operating into unprepared landing sites. According to Mr Marat Tishchenko, General Designer in charge of the Mil Bureau, this (plus, no doubt, the need to ensure torsional stiffness) explains why the main rotor blades have conventional steel spars.

Use of titanium for the rotor hub helped the Mil Bureau to meet the official requirement of an empty weight only 50 per cent of the aircraft's maximum permissible take-off weight. A further contribution to weight saving resulted from the decision to design the main gearbox in-house. The end product offers an impressive power to weight ratio, despite the need to absorb an unprecedented input from two Lotarev D-136 turboshafts. Nor does the Mi-26 need auxiliary wings, like the Mi-6, to achieve its required payload/range performance.

The prototype Mi-26 flew for the first time on 14 December 1977, and its D-136 engines had amassed more than 13,000 hours of running on the test-bench and in the air by the time of the 1981 Paris Air Show. The Mi-26 (SSSR-06141) exhibited at the Show was stated to be one of several prototypes or pre-production examples then flying. The Mi-26 began in-field evaluation, probably with a single air force development squadron, in early 1983 and was fully

operational by 1985. More than 50 are in service. The first export order, for ten, was placed by India, and the first two of these were delivered in June 1986.

During three days in February 1982, the Mi-26 set five world helicopter payload-to-height records, exceeding records established previously by the Sikorsky CH-54B Skycrane and Mil Mi-12. On 2 February, piloted by G. P. Karapetyan, it lifted a 10,000 kg payload to 6,400 m (20,997 ft). On 3 February, piloted by G. V. Alfeurov, it lifted a payload of 25,000 kg to 4,100 m (13,451 ft), and lifted a total mass of 56,768.8 kg (125,153.8 lb) to a height of 2,000 m. On 4 February, it lifted a payload of 15,000 kg to 5,600 m (18,373 ft), piloted by S. V. Petrov; and 20,000 kg to 4,600 m (15,092 ft), piloted by A. P. Kholoupov.

TYPE: Twin-turboshaft heavy transport helicopter.
ROTOR SYSTEM: Eight-blade constant-chord main rotor, with flapping and drag hinges, droop stops and hydraulic drag dampers; no elastomeric bearings or hinges. Five-blade constant-chord tail rotor, mounted on starboard side of tail fin. Each main rotor blade consists of a one-piece tubular steel spar and 26 glassfibre aerofoil shape full chord pockets, 'Nomex'-filled with ribs and stiffeners and non-removable titanium leading-edge abrasion strip. Blades have moderate twist, taper in thickness towards tip, and are attached to small forged titanium head of unconventional design. Ground adjustable tab on trailing-edge of each blade. Hydraulically powered cyclic and collective pitch controls actuated by small parallel jacks, with redundant autopilot and stability augmentation system inputs. Tail rotor blades made of glassfibre, attached to forged titanium head. Leading-edge of main and tail rotor blades heated electrically for anti-icing. Main rotor rpm 132.
ROTOR DRIVE: Conventional transmission. Tail rotor shaft runs inside roof of cabin. Main gearbox type VR-26, rated at 14,914 kW (20,000 hp), is fan cooled, with air intake above rear of engine cowlings.
FUSELAGE: Conventional all-metal riveted semi-monocoque structure of pod and boom type, with clamshell rear loading doors and ramp. Flattened undersurface to tailboom. Engine bay made of titanium for fire protection.
TAIL UNIT: Sweptback vertical stabiliser, carrying tail rotor, is offset to port. Ground adjustable variable incidence horizontal stabiliser mounted on leading-edge of vertical stabiliser, a short distance above the tailboom. Both components are of all-metal construction.
LANDING GEAR: Non-retractable tricycle type, with twin wheels on each unit. Steerable nosewheels. Mainwheel tyres size 1,120 × 450. Retractable tailskid at end of tailboom to permit unrestricted approach to rear cargo doors. Length of main legs can be adjusted hydraulically to facilitate loading through rear doors and to permit landing on varying surfaces. A device on the main gear indicates take-off weight to flight engineer at lift-off, on panel on shelf to rear of his seat.
POWER PLANT: Two 8,380 kW (11,240 shp) Lotarev D-136 free-turbine turboshafts, mounted side by side above cabin, forward of main rotor driveshaft. Air intakes designed to prevent foreign object ingestion, and provided with both electrical and bleed air anti-icing systems. Above and behind is a central oil cooler intake. System for synchronising the output of the engines and maintaining constant rotor rpm. If one engine fails, output of the other is increased to maximum automatically. Independent fuel system for each engine. Fuel in eight underfloor rubber tanks, feeding into two header tanks above engines, which permit gravity feed for a period in emergencies. Max fuel capacity 12,000 litres (3,170 US gallons; 2,640 Imp gallons). Two large panels on each side of main rotor mast fairing, aft of engine exhaust outlet, hinge downward as work platforms.
ACCOMMODATION: Crew of five on flight deck, consisting of pilot (on port side) and co-pilot side by side, with navigator's seat between pilots, and seats for flight engineer and loadmaster to rear. Four-seat passenger compartment aft of flight deck. Loads that can be accommodated in hold include two airborne infantry combat vehicles and a standard 20,000 kg (44,100 lb) ISO container. About 20 tip-up seats along each side wall of hold. Max military seating for about 85 combat equipped

Mil Mi-26 heavy lift helicopter (two Lotarev D-136 turboshafts) in Soviet military service

troops. Heated windscreen, with wipers. Four large blistered side windows on flight deck. Forward pair swing open slightly outward and rearward. Downward hinged doors, with integral airstairs, at front of hold on port side, and on each side of hold aft of main landing gear units. Hold is loaded via a downward hinged lower door, with integral folding ramp, and two clamshell upper doors which form rear wall of hold when closed. Doors are opened and closed hydraulically, with backup handpump for emergency use. Two electric hoists on overhead rails, each with capacity of 2,500 kg (5,511 lb), enable loads to be transported along cabin. Winch for hauling loads, capacity 500 kg (1,100 lb). Roller conveyor in floor and load lashing points throughout hold. Flight deck and hold fully air-conditioned.

SYSTEMS: Two hydraulic systems, operating pressure 207 bars (3,000 lb/sq in). (Much higher pressure than usual for Soviet helicopters, reflected by small size of jacks for rotor head controls.) 28V DC electrical system. APU under flight deck, with intake louvres (forming fuselage skin when closed) and exhaust on starboard side, for engine starting and to supply hydraulic, electrical and air-conditioning systems on ground. Only flight deck pressurised. Four-axis autostabilisation.

AVIONICS AND EQUIPMENT: All items necessary for day and night operations in all weathers are standard, including weather radar in the hinged (to starboard) nosecone, Doppler, map display, HSI, and automatic hover system. Com/nav equipment generally similar to that of Yak-42. Hatch for load sling in bottom of fuselage, in line with main rotor shaft, enabling sling cable to be attached to internal winching gear. Closed circuit TV cameras to observe slung payloads. Operational equipment on military version includes infra-red jammers and suppressors, and infra-red decoy dispensers.

DIMENSIONS, EXTERNAL:

Main rotor diameter	32.00 m (105 ft 0 in)
Tail rotor diameter	7.61 m (24 ft 11½ in)
Length overall, rotors turning	40.025 m (131 ft 3¾ in)
Length of fuselage, excl tail rotor	33.727 m (110 ft 8 in)
Height to top of rotor head	8.145 m (26 ft 8¾ in)
Width over mainwheels	8.15 m (26 ft 9 in)
Wheel track	7.17 m (23 ft 6¼ in)
Wheelbase	8.95 m (29 ft 4½ in)

DIMENSIONS, INTERNAL:

Freight hold:	
Length: ramp trailed	15.00 m (49 ft 2½ in)
excl ramp	12.00 m (39 ft 4¼ in)
Width	3.25 m (10 ft 8 in)
Height	2.95-3.17 m (9 ft 8 in to 10 ft 4¾ in)
Volume	121 m³ (4,273 cu ft)

AREA:

Main rotor disc	804.25 m² (8,657 sq ft)

WEIGHTS AND LOADINGS:

Weight empty	28,200 kg (62,170 lb)
Max payload, internal or external	20,000 kg (44,090 lb)
Normal T-O weight	49,500 kg (109,125 lb)
Max T-O weight	56,000 kg (123,450 lb)
Max rotor disc loading	69.6 kg/m² (14.26 lb/sq ft)
Max power loading	3.34 kg/kW (5.49 lb/shp)

PERFORMANCE:

Max level speed	159 knots (295 km/h; 183 mph)
Normal cruising speed	137 knots (255 km/h; 158 mph)
Service ceiling	4,600 m (15,100 ft)
Hovering ceiling OGE, ISA	1,800 m (5,900 ft)
Range with max internal fuel at max T-O weight, 5% reserves	432 nm (800 km; 497 miles)

MIL Mi-28
NATO reporting name: Havoc

The existence of this Soviet combat helicopter, known to NATO as 'Havoc', was confirmed in the 1984 edition of *Soviet Military Power*, published by the US Department of Defense. The 1985 edition contained the first detailed artist's impression of the Mi-28, which is reproduced in this entry, and the 1987 edition suggested that 'Havoc' might become operational during that year. There is, however, little reason to believe that it has yet emerged from the prototype development stage.

The DoD states that the Mi-28 was probably conceived to meet the threat presented by NATO weapons using thermal imaging systems. Its existence prompted abandonment of the US Army's Sergeant York mobile anti-aircraft gun in 1985. The gun had proved effective over ranges of no more than 4 km, and Defense Secretary Caspar Weinberger commented: "A helicopter that can stand off at six kilometres and fire lethal fire into troops manoeuvring or taking part in combat requires a defence system that can do the same".

Elimination of transport capability in the Mi-28, by comparison with the Mi-24, should ensure much improved agility and survivability, as the result of a greatly reduced cross-section (almost certainly smaller than suggested by the DoD drawing). The following details should be regarded as provisional:

TYPE: Twin-engined ground attack helicopter.

ROTOR SYSTEM: Five-blade main rotor and three-blade tail rotor of new design. Tail rotor mounted on starboard side of tail fin, possibly at tip of small horizontal stabiliser.

WINGS: Cantilever mid-mounted wings of low aspect ratio, with sweptback leading-edge. No movable surfaces.

Unloading armoured vehicles from a military Mil Mi-26

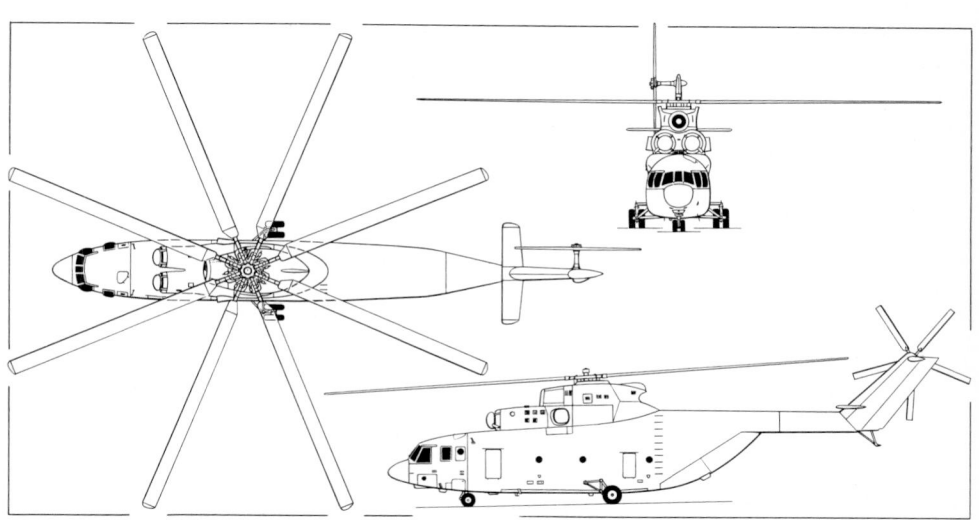

Mil Mi-26, first helicopter to operate successfully with an eight-blade main rotor *(Pilot Press)*

Artist's impression of Mil Mi-28 combat helicopters *(US Department of Defense)*

FUSELAGE: Conventional all-metal semi-monocoque structure, embodying integral armour around cockpit area.

TAIL UNIT: Sweptback fin with small horizontal stabiliser at tip.

LANDING GEAR: Non-retractable tailwheel type, with single wheel on each unit. Mainwheels carried on side Vs, embodying shock absorbers.

POWER PLANT: Two unidentified turboshafts, possibly related to TV3-117 engines of Mi-24, in pods mounted above each wingroot. Upward deflected jetpipes. Deflectors for dust and foreign objects forward of air intakes.

ACCOMMODATION: Co-pilot/gunner in front cockpit; pilot behind, on elevated seat. Flat, non-glint transparencies. Electro-optics pod, similar to that of US AH-64 Apache, under nose, probably enclosing low light level TV and/or laser designator and marked target seeker.

ARMAMENT AND OPERATIONAL EQUIPMENT: Heavy calibre gun in undernose turret, and up to 16 anti-tank guided missiles. These and other external stores, including rocket packs and tube-launched air-to-air/air-to-ground guided missiles, are carried on underwing and wingtip pylons. Radar in small radome on nose. Undernose electro-optics pod probably encloses low-light-level TV and/or laser designator and marked target seeker. Infra-red suppressors and infra-red decoy dispensers fitted.

DIMENSIONS, EXTERNAL (estimated):

Main rotor diameter	17.00 m (55 ft 9 in)
Length overall, excl rotors	17.40 m (57 ft 1 in)

WEIGHT (estimated):

Max T-O weight	8,000 kg (17,635 lb)

PERFORMANCE (estimated):

Max level speed	162 knots (300 km/h; 186 mph)
Combat radius	130 nm (240 km; 149 miles)

MIL Mi-34
NATO reporting name: Hermit

Exhibited in public for the first time at the 1987 Paris Air Show, the Mi-34 (NATO 'Hermit') is a lightweight two/four-seat helicopter intended primarily for pilot training and international competition flying. Like the Polish PZL-Swidnik SW-4, it is offered as a replacement for DOSAAF's veteran Mi-1 helicopter trainers; but, whereas the SW-4 is turboshaft powered, the Mi-34 has a Vedeneyev piston engine of the same basic type as that fitted in DOSAAF's current family of Yakovlev fixed-wing training aircraft and Kamov Ka-26 helicopters. Other applications for which the Mi-34 is suited include light utility, observation and liaison duties, and border patrol.

Two prototypes and a structure test airframe had been completed by mid-1987. The first flight took place in 1986 and certification was expected by mid-1988. A decision on whether or not the Mi-34 will be produced under the next five-year plan is scheduled to be made in 1988-89. If it is ordered, manufacture is likely to be centred at WSK-PZL Swidnik in Poland.

TYPE: Light general purpose helicopter.

ROTOR SYSTEM: Semi-articulated four-blade main rotor, with flapping and cyclic pitch hinges but with natural flexing in the lead/lag plane. Blades are made of glassfibre with carbonfibre reinforcement, and are attached by flexible steel straps to a head similar to that of the McDonnell Douglas (Hughes) MD 500. Two-blade tail rotor of similar composites construction, on starboard side of tailboom.

FUSELAGE: Simple riveted light alloy structure of pod and boom configuration.

TAIL UNIT: Sweptback fin, mid-mounted on port side of tailcone, with small constant chord unswept T tailplane.

LANDING GEAR: Conventional non-retractable skids on arched support tubes. Small tailskid to protect tail rotor.

POWER PLANT: One 242 kW (325 hp) Vedeneyev M-14V-26 nine-cylinder radial aircooled engine mounted sideways in the centre-fuselage. Fuel consumption 45 kg (99 lb)/hour.

ACCOMMODATION: Normally one or two pilots, side by side, in enclosed cabin, with optional dual controls. Rear of cabin contains low bench seat, available for two passengers and offering a flat floor for cargo carrying. Forward hinged door on each side of flight deck and on each side of rear cabin.

DIMENSIONS, EXTERNAL:

Main rotor diameter	10.00 m (32 ft 9¾ in)
Tail rotor diameter	1.48 m (4 ft 10¼ in)
Length of fuselage	8.71 m (28 ft 7 in)
Width of fuselage	1.42 m (4 ft 8 in)
Skid track	2.06 m (6 ft 9¼ in)

WEIGHTS:

Normal loaded weight, training mission	
	1,020 kg (2,249 lb)
Max T-O weight	1,250 kg (2,755 lb)

PERFORMANCE (at T-O weight of 1,020 kg; 2,249 lb, except where indicated):

Max level speed	113 knots (210 km/h; 130 mph)
Max cruising speed	97 knots (180 km/h; 112 mph)
Service ceiling	4,500 m (14,765 ft)
Hovering ceiling	1,500 m (4,920 ft)
Range at max T-O weight:	
with 165 kg (364 lb) payload	
	97 nm (180 km; 112 miles)
with 90 kg (198 lb) payload	
	243 nm (450 km; 280 miles)
g limits at AUW of 1,020 kg (2,249 lb) and speeds of 27-81 knots (50-150 km/h; 31-93 mph)	+2.5/-0.5

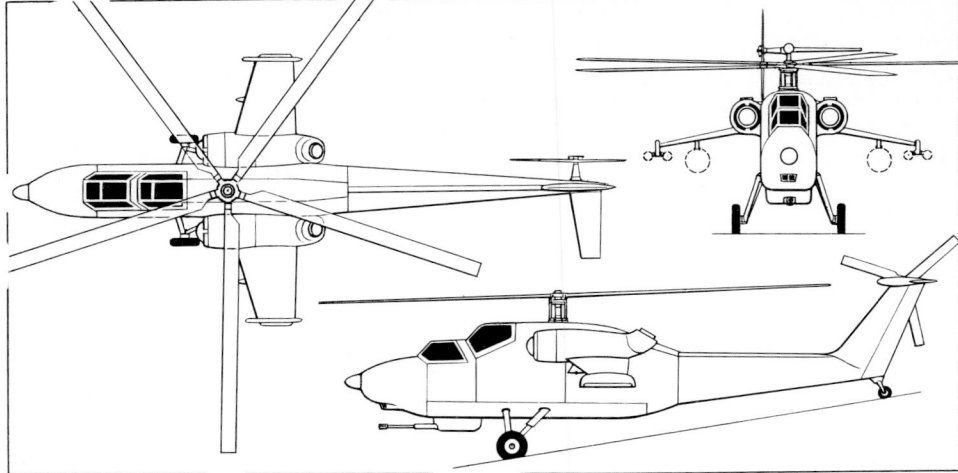

Mil Mi-28 combat helicopter (two turboshaft engines) *(Pilot Press, provisional)*

First prototype of the Mil Mi-34 (Vedeneyev M-14V-26 engine)

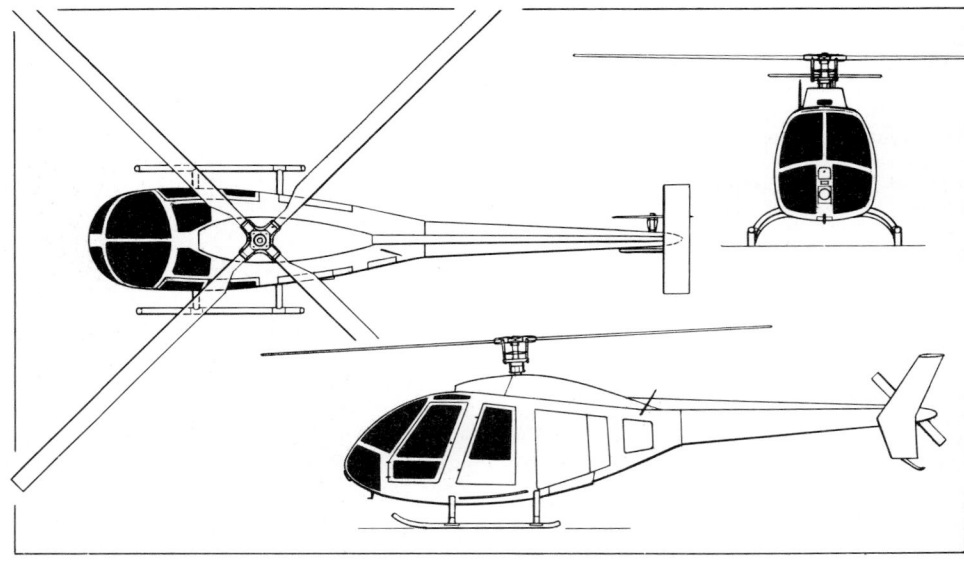

Mil Mi-34 two/four-seat training and competition helicopter *(Pilot Press)*

MYASISHCHEV

This design bureau was formed in 1951, under the leadership of Professor Vladimir Mikhailovich Myasishchev, who died on 14 October 1978, at the age of 76. Its first product was the four-jet M-4 bomber (known in the West by the reporting name of 'Bison') which remains in service as a strategic bomber, maritime reconnaissance aircraft and flight refuelling tanker.

MYASISHCHEV M-4
NATO reporting name: Bison

Three major production versions of this four-jet aircraft were identified by NATO reporting names, as follows:

Bison-A. The Soviet Union's first operational four-jet strategic bomber, carrying free fall weapons only. Design began in 1951 and the prototype was displayed over Moscow on 1 May 1954. Comparable with early versions of Boeing B-52 Stratofortress, it was powered by four 85.3 kN

(19,180 lb st) Mikulin AM-3D turbojets, buried in wing-roots. Defensive armament of eight 23 mm NR-23 cannon in twin-gun turrets in tail, above fuselage forward of wing and under fuselage fore and aft of three weapons bays.

Bison-B. Maritime reconnaissance version, described in 1979-80 *Jane's*. Few remain.

Bison-C. Improved maritime reconnaissance version, described in 1979-80 *Jane's*. Few remain.

About 45 of these aircraft were available in October 1986,

15 with the Moscow air army as bombers for maritime and Eurasian missions and 30 as probe-and-drogue flight refuelling tankers for the 'Backfire/Bear/Bison/Blinder' attack force. Pending replacement, other 'Bisons' had been phased out of service and placed in storage.

One M-4 has been adapted to carry on its back the large Soviet space shuttle orbiter vehicle. Most apparent change is replacement of the standard sweptback vertical tail surfaces by twin endplate fins and rudders of rectangular shape. In 1987, preparations were under way for the first landing test of the orbiter after mid-air separation from the M-4 carrier.

DIMENSIONS, EXTERNAL ('Bison-A'):
Wing span 50.48 m (165 ft 7½ in)
Length overall 47.20 m (154 ft 10 in)
Tailplane span 15.00 m (49 ft 2½ in)
WEIGHT ('Bison-A'):
Max T-O weight 158,750 kg (350,000 lb)
PERFORMANCE ('Bison-A', estimated):
Max level speed at 11,000 m (36,000 ft)
538 knots (998 km/h: 620 mph)
Service ceiling 13,700 m (45,000 ft)
Max unrefuelled combat radius
3,025 nm (5,600 km; 3,480 miles)
Range at 450 knots (835 km/h; 520 mph) with more than 5,450 kg (12,000 lb) of bombs
4,320 nm (8,000 km; 4,970 miles)

Artist's impression of M-4 ('Bison-C') adapted to carry the large Soviet space shuttle orbiter *(US Department of Defense)*

Myasishchev M-4 ('Bison-B') maritime reconnaissance aircraft *(Royal Air Force)*

SUKHOI

CHIEF DESIGNER OF SUKHOI BUREAU: J. A. Ivanov

This design bureau is named after Pavel Osipovich Sukhoi, who headed it from 1953 until his death in September 1975. It remains one of the two primary Soviet centres for fighter and attack aircraft development.

SUKHOI Su-7B
NATO reporting names: Fitter-A and Moujik

The Su-7B single-seat ground attack fighter has been almost phased out of service in the Soviet air forces, but remains operational in some Warsaw Pact and non-European air forces. Full details and illustrations can be found in the 1985-86 and previous editions of *Jane's*.

SUKHOI Su-15
NATO reporting name: Flagon

Details of the initial versions of this twin-jet delta-wing interceptor can be found in the 1983-84 and previous editions of *Jane's*. Some US sources claim that the late-model 'Flagons' still in first-line service are designated Su-21, but the US Department of Defense continues to refer to them by the original designation of Su-15. About 240 remain in home defence units, with another 260 in tactical units, in three versions, as follows:

Flagon-E. Single-seat interceptor. Longer-span wings than those of earlier 'Flagon-A, C and D', with compound sweep. Tumansky R-13F-300 turbojets, each rated at 64.73 kN (14,550 lb st), and additional fuel, giving increased speed and range. Uprated avionics (NATO 'Twin Scan' replacing 'Skip Spin' radar). Major production version, operational since second half of 1973.

Flagon-F. Last known production version. Ogival nose radome instead of conical type of earlier variants. Generally similar to 'Flagon-E', but with uprated engines.

Flagon-G. Two-seat training version of 'Flagon-F', with probable combat capability. Individual rearward hinged canopy over each seat. Periscope fitted above rear canopy for enhanced forward view. Overall length unchanged.

The following details apply to 'Flagon-F':
TYPE: Single-seat twin-jet all-weather interceptor.
WINGS: Cantilever mid-wing monoplane. Basic wings are of simple delta form, similar to those of earlier Su-11, but with new and extended outer panels. Sweepback 60° on

'Flagon-F' twin-jet interceptor, armed with 'Anab' missiles and gun pods *(Swedish Coast Guard/Air Patrol)*

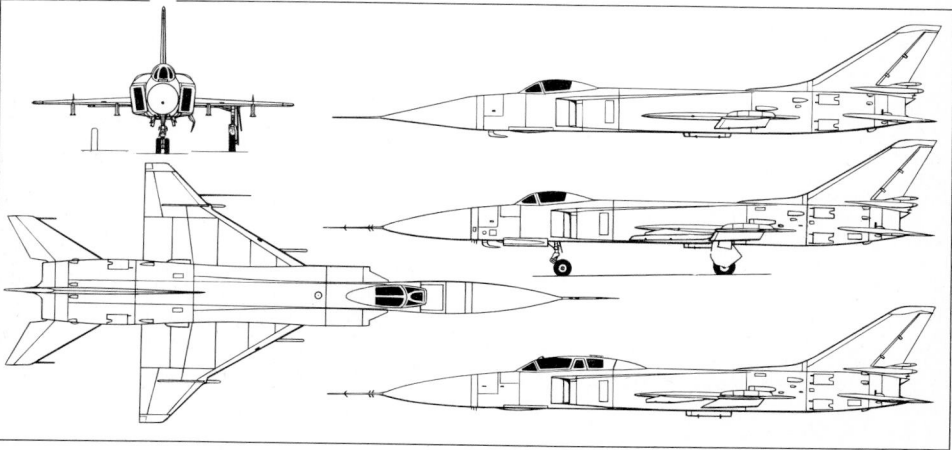

Sukhoi Su-15 ('Flagon-F') single-seat twin-jet all-weather interceptor, with additional side elevations of 'Flagon-E' (top) and 'Flagon-G' (bottom) *(Pilot Press)*

inner wings, 47° on outer panels. No dihedral or anhedral. All-metal structure. Single boundary layer fence above each wing at approx 70 per cent span. Large-chord plain flap extends from inboard end of aileron to fuselage on each side.

FUSELAGE: Cockpit section is basically circular with large ogival dielectric nosecone. Centre-fuselage is faired into rectangular section air intake ducts. Two door type airbrakes at top and bottom on each side of rear fuselage, forward of tailplane.

TAIL UNIT: Cantilever all-metal structure, with 60° leading-edge sweepback on all surfaces. All-moving tailplane, with anhedral, mounted slightly below mid position and fitted with anti-flutter bodies near tips. Conventional rudder. No trim tabs.

LANDING GEAR: Tricycle type, with single wheel on each main unit and twin nosewheels, all on levered-suspension legs. Mainwheels retract inward into wings and intake ducts; nosewheels retract forward, with blistered doors. Nosewheels steerable. Container for brake-chute between base of rudder and tailpipe.

POWER PLANT: Two turbojets, with variable area nozzles, mounted side by side in rear fuselage. These are reported to be Tumansky R-13F2-300s, each rated at 70.6 kN (15,875 lb st) with afterburning. Ram air intakes, with variable ramps on splitter plates, embodying vertical slots for boundary layer control. Blow-in auxiliary inlets between main intake and wing leading-edge in side of each duct. Fuel tanks in centre-fuselage and wings.

ACCOMMODATION: Single zero/zero ejection seat in enclosed cockpit, with rearward sliding blister canopy. Rearview mirror above canopy of some aircraft.

ARMAMENT: Two pylons for external stores under each wing. Normal armament comprises one radar homing and one infra-red homing air-to-air missile (NATO 'Anab') on outboard pylons, and an infra-red homing close-range missile ('Aphid') on each inboard pylon. Side by side pylons under centre-fuselage for weapons, including GSh-23L 23 mm gun pods, or external fuel tanks.

AVIONICS AND EQUIPMENT: Large I-band radar (NATO 'Twin Scan') in nose, SOD-57M ATC/SIF nav system, SRO-2 (NATO 'Odd Rods') IFF, Sirena 3 radar warning system.

DIMENSIONS, EXTERNAL (estimated):
Wing span	9.15 m (30 ft 0 in)
Length overall	21.33 m (70 ft 0 in)
Height overall	5.10 m (16 ft 8½ in)

WEIGHTS (estimated):
Weight empty	11,000 kg (24,250 lb)
Max T-O weight	18,000 kg (39,680 lb)

PERFORMANCE (estimated):
Max level speed above 11,000 m (36,000 ft): with external stores	Mach 2.1
Time to 11,000 m (36,000 ft)	2 min 30 s
Service ceiling	20,000 m (65,600 ft)
Combat radius	390 nm (725 km; 450 miles)

SUKHOI Su-17, Su-20 and Su-22
NATO reporting names: Fitter-C, D, E, F, G, H, J and K

The early history of this variable geometry fighter series, developed from the sweptwing Su-7 (NATO 'Fitter-A'), has been described in previous editions of *Jane's*. About 1,060 are deployed currently by Soviet tactical air forces, 75 more by Soviet Naval Aviation units assigned to anti-shipping strike and amphibious support roles in the Baltic Sea area, and a further Naval unit of indeterminate size in the Pacific theatre. All aircraft of this type in Soviet service are designated Su-17. Differences between the various versions are as follows:

Su-17 (Fitter-C). Basic single-seat attack aircraft for Soviet tactical air forces, with Lyulka AL-21F-3 turbojet and eight stores pylons. Manual wing sweep control. Additional wing fence on fixed centre-section each side. Curved dorsal fin between tail fin and dorsal spine fairing. Operational since 1971, in relatively small numbers. Serves also with Soviet Navy.

Su-17M (S-32M, Fitter-D). Generally similar to 'Fitter-C', but forward fuselage lengthened by about 0.25 m (10 in). Added undernose electronics pod for Doppler navigation radar. Laser rangefinder in intake centrebody.

Su-17UM (U-32, Fitter-E). Tandem two-seat trainer for Soviet air forces. Generally similar to 'Fitter-D', without electronics pod, but entire fuselage forward of wing drooped slightly to improve pilot's view. Deepened dorsal spine fairing, almost certainly to provide additional fuel tankage. Port wingroot gun deleted.

Su-17 (Fitter-G). Two-seat trainer variant of 'Fitter-H', with combat capability. Deepened dorsal spine fairing and drooped front fuselage like 'Fitter-E'. Taller vertical tail surfaces. Shallow ventral fin (removable). Starboard gun only. Laser rangefinder fitted in intake centrebody.

Su-17 (Fitter-H). Improved single-seater for Soviet air forces. Basically as 'Fitter-D', but with wide and deep dorsal fairing aft of canopy, like 'Fitter-E/G'. Doppler navigation radar fitted internally in deepened undersurface of nose. Taller fin like 'Fitter-G'. Removable ventral fin. Retains both wingroot guns. About 165 'Fitter-H/Ks' are equipped for tactical reconnaissance duties. Equipment includes, typically, an underfuselage pod containing sensors, and an active ECM pod under the port wing fixed centre-section, plus two external fuel tanks.

'Flagon-G' tandem two-seat combat trainer based on the 'Flagon-F' interceptor

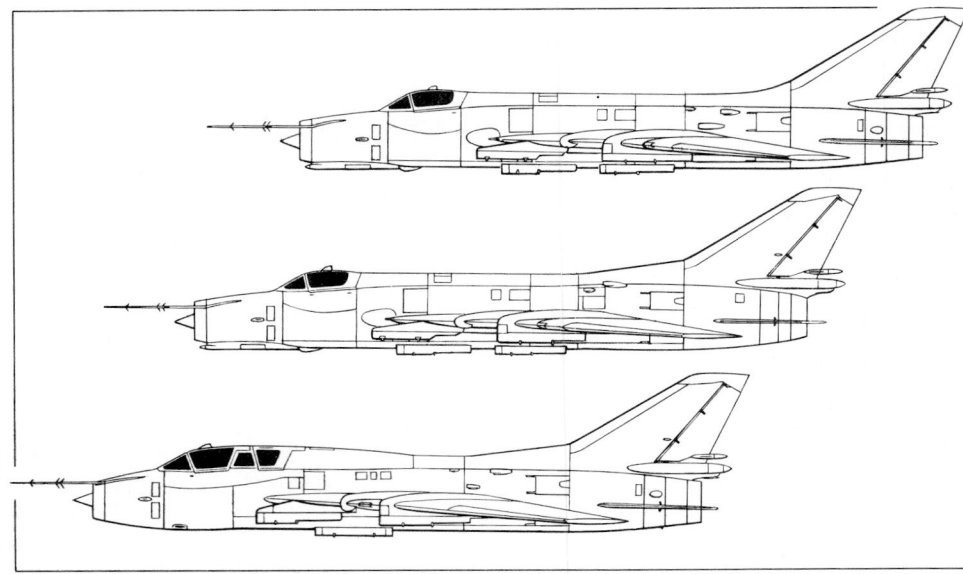

Top to bottom: The versions of the Su-17/20/22 series known to NATO as 'Fitter-D', 'Fitter-F' and 'Fitter-E' respectively. Tumansky powered versions can be identified by more bulged rear fuselage and single air intake by dorsal fin *(Pilot Press)*

Single-seat Su-17 ('Fitter-H') of Soviet Air Force, armed with underbelly rocket pods, 'Atoll' air-to-air missiles, and two AS-7 ('Kerry') air-to-surface missiles

A bulged rear fuselage and undernose electronics pod distinguish this Su-22 'Fitter-F' of the Libyan Arab Air Force *(US Navy)*

Su-17 (Fitter-K). Latest single-seat version for Soviet air forces, identified in 1984. Dorsal fin embodies small cooling air intake at front. Also in service with Polish Air Force.

It was deduced for some years that certain export versions of the variable geometry 'Fitter' series had different engines from the Su-17 variants listed above. 'Fitter-C/D/E/G/H/K' operated by the Soviet and some other air forces have a rear fuselage of basically constant diameter and are powered by a Lyulka turbojet. Versions exported to Angola, Libya, Peru, Syria, Vietnam, and North and South Yemen were seen to have a more bulged rear fuselage, now known to house a Tumansky R-29BS-300 turbojet, as fitted in the MiG-27, with rearranged external air ducts, and a shorter plain metal shroud terminating the rear fuselage. This change of power plant, and/or variations in equipment standard, is covered by the following changes to the Soviet type designation:

Su-20 (Su-17MK, S-32MK, Fitter-C). Generally similar to Soviet air forces' 'Fitter-C', with Lyulka engine, but with reduced equipment standard. Supplied to Algeria, Czechoslovakia, Egypt, Iraq and Poland. Two former Egyptian aircraft were acquired by Federal German Luftwaffe for evaluation during 1985 by Erprobungsstelle 61 at Manching.

Su-22 (Fitter-F). Export counterpart of 'Fitter-D', with slightly modified undernose electronics pod. Tumansky R-29B turbojet, rated at 112.8 kN (25,350 lb st) with afterburning, in increased diameter rear fuselage. Gun in each wingroot. Weapons include 'Atoll' air-to-air missiles. Aircraft supplied to Peru had Sirena 2 limited coverage radar warning receiver, virtually no navigation aids, and IFF incompatible with that nation's SA-3 (NATO 'Goa') surface-to-air missiles. Some basic US-supplied avionics fitted subsequently.

Su-22 (Fitter-G). Export counterpart of Su-17 'Fitter-G', with R-29B engine.

Su-22 (Fitter-J). Generally similar to 'Fitter-H' but with Tumansky engine. Internal fuel tankage 6,270 litres (1,656 US gallons; 1,379 Imp gallons). More angular dorsal fin. 'Atoll' air-to-air missiles. Supplied to Libya and Peru.

Production of the variable geometry 'Fitter' series has been reduced drastically in recent years. The following description applies to the Su-17 ('Fitter-C'):

TYPE: Single-seat ground attack fighter.

WINGS: Cantilever mid-wing monoplane, with wide span fixed centre-section and manually operated variable geometry outer panels, with min sweep angle of 28° and max sweep angle of approx 62°. Slight sweepback on trailing-edge of area-increasing centre-section flaps. Outboard of these flaps, centre-section trailing-edge is swept to align with trailing-edge of outer panels when they are fully swept. Full span leading-edge slats on movable panels. Trailing-edge of each movable panel made up of a slotted flap, operable only when the wings are spread, and a slotted aileron operable at all times. Large main fence on each side, at junction of fixed and movable panels, is square-cut at front and incorporates attachments for external stores. Shorter fence above centre-section on each side, inboard of main fence.

FUSELAGE: Conventional all-metal semi-monocoque structure of circular section. Large dorsal spine fairing along top of fuselage, from canopy to fin. Ram air intake in nose, with variable shock-cone centrebody. Four door type airbrakes, at top and bottom on each side of rear fuselage, forward of tailplane. Pitot on port side of nose; transducer to provide pitch and yaw data for fire control computer and antennae on starboard side.

TAIL UNIT: Cantilever all-metal structure, with sweepback on all surfaces. All-moving horizontal surfaces, with anti-flutter body projecting forward on each side near tip. Conventional rudder. No tabs.

LANDING GEAR: Retractable tricycle type, with single wheel on each unit. Nosewheel retracts forward, requiring blistered door to enclose it. Main units retract inward into centre-section. Container for twin brake-chutes between base of rudder and tailpipe.

POWER PLANT: One Lyulka AL-21F-3 turbojet, rated at 76.5 kN (17,200 lb st) dry and 110 kN (24,700 lb st) with afterburning. Fuel capacity increased to 4,550 litres (1,202 US gallons; 1,000 Imp gallons) by added tankage in dorsal spine fairing. Provision for carrying up to four 800 litre (211 US gallon; 176 Imp gallon) drop tanks on outboard wing pylons and under fuselage. When underfuselage tanks are carried, only the two inboard wing pylons may be used for ordnance, to a total weight of 1,000 kg (2,204 lb). Two solid propellant rocket units can be attached to rear fuselage to shorten T-O run.

ACCOMMODATION: Pilot only, on ejection seat, under rearward hinged transparent canopy. Rearview mirror above canopy.

AVIONICS AND EQUIPMENT: SRD-5M (NATO 'High Fix') I-band ranging radar in intake centrebody; ASP-5ND fire control system; Sirena 3 radar warning system providing 360° coverage, with antennae in slim cylindrical housing above brake-chute container and in each centre-section leading-edge, between fences; SRO-2M IFF; SOD-57M ATC/SIF, with transponder housing beneath brake-chute container; and RSIU-5/R-831 VHF/UHF.

Sukhoi Su-17 ('Fitter-K') of Polish Air Force, with four flare/chaff dispensers visible beside its dorsal spine

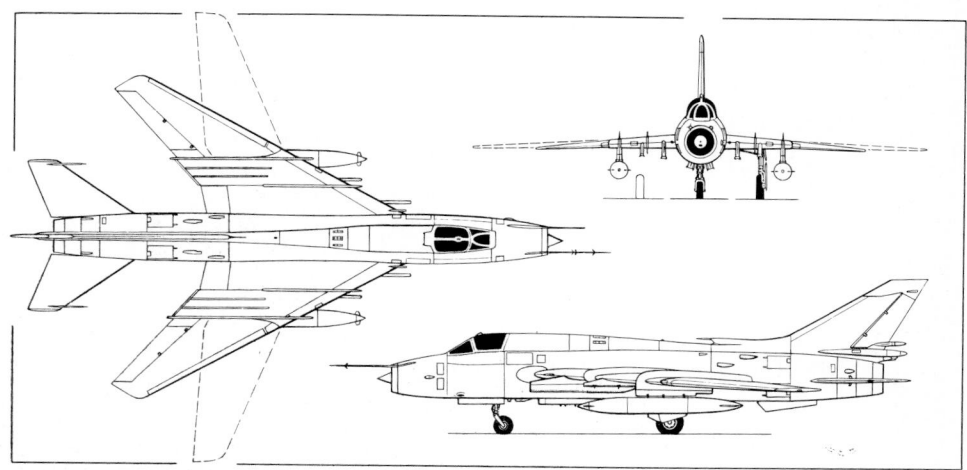
'Fitter-K', latest single-seat version of the Sukhoi Su-17 series *(Pilot Press)*

ARMAMENT: Two 30 mm NR-30 guns, each with 70 rds, in wingroot leading-edges. Total of eight weapon pylons (two tandem pairs under fuselage, one under each centre-section leading-edge, one under each main wing fence) for more than 3,175 kg (7,000 lb) of bombs, including nuclear weapons, rocket pods and guided missiles such as the air-to-surface AS-7 (NATO 'Kerry').

DIMENSIONS, EXTERNAL:
Wing span: fully spread	13.80 m (45 ft 3 in)
fully swept	10.00 m (32 ft 10 in)
Wing aspect ratio: fully spread	4.8
fully swept	2.7
Length overall, incl probes	18.75 m (61 ft 6¼ in)
Fuselage length	15.40 m (50 ft 6¼ in)
Height overall	5.00 m (16 ft 5 in)

AREAS (estimated):
Wings, gross: fully spread	40.0 m² (430.0 sq ft)
fully swept	37.0 m² (398.0 sq ft)

WEIGHTS (estimated):
Weight empty	10,000 kg (22,046 lb)
Max internal fuel	3,700 kg (8,157 lb)
T-O weight, 'clean'	14,000 kg (30,865 lb)
Max T-O weight	17,700 kg (39,020 lb)

PERFORMANCE (estimated for 'clean' aircraft, 60% internal fuel, except where indicated):
Max level speed: at height	Mach 2.09
	(1,200 knots; 2,220 km/h; 1,380 mph)
at S/L	Mach 1.05
	(693 knots; 1,285 km/h; 798 mph)
Touchdown speed	143 knots (265 km/h; 165 mph)
Max rate of climb at S/L	13,800 m (45,275 ft)/min
Service ceiling	18,000 m (59,050 ft)

T-O run at AUW of 17,000 kg (37,478 lb) 1,000 m (3,280 ft)
T-O to 15 m (50 ft) at AUW of 17,000 kg (37,478 lb) 1,400 m (4,600 ft)
Landing run 600 m (1,970 ft)
Combat radius with 2,000 kg (4,409 lb) external stores, incl fuel: hi-lo-hi 370 nm (685 km; 425 miles)
lo-lo-lo 240 nm (445 km; 275 miles)

SUKHOI Su-24
NATO reporting name: Fencer

Recognised since the mid-1970s as the best deep-interdiction aircraft in the Soviet tactical inventory, the Su-24 has twice the combat radius of the Su-17 while carrying a comparable weapon load. Its ability to carry a wide range of air-to-surface missiles provides defence suppression and some hard-target kill potential. A new long-range navigation system and electro-optical weapons delivery systems enable the Su-24 to penetrate hostile airspace at night or during poor weather with great precision and then deliver ordnance within 55 m (180 ft) of its target.

The Su-24 is smaller and lighter than the USAF's F-111, with three-position variable-geometry wings carrying the first pivoting pylons that were seen on a Soviet aircraft. It entered squadron service in December 1974 as a replacement for the Yak-28 (NATO 'Brewer'). More than 800 are now operational, including 500 assigned to strategic missions with the Legnica and Vinnitsa air armies, at least one squadron with the Baltic Fleet air force for maritime reconnaissance, and the remainder with air forces of the

Sukhoi Su-24 ('Fencer-C') two-seat attack aircraft *(Swedish Air Force)*

military districts and groups of forces. Five versions can be identified by NATO reporting names:

Fencer-A. Identifiable by rectangular rear fuselage box enclosing jet nozzles.

Fencer-B. Rear fuselage box around jet nozzles has deeply dished bottom skin between nozzles. Larger brake-chute housing.

Fencer-C. Introduced in 1981. Important equipment changes. Multiple fitting on nose instead of former simple probe. Triangular fairing forward of each fixed wingroot, on side of air intake (presumably housing ECM equipment of the kind seen on the fuselage sides, forward of the nosewheel doors, of ground attack MiG-23/27 'Floggers') and also on each side of fin, near tip.

Fencer-D. Introduced in 1983, with added probe-and-drogue flight refuelling capability. Slightly longer nose (approx 0.75 m; 2 ft 6 in) forward of windscreen; chord of lower part of tail fin extended, giving kinked leading-edge; large overwing fences integral with extended wingroot glove pylons, probably for AS-14 (NATO 'Kedge') missiles in class of US Maverick; undernose aerials deleted; blister, probably for electro-optical sensor, added aft of nosewheel bay; and single long noseprobe.

Fencer-E. About 65 of these reconnaissance variants of 'Fencer-D', retaining the ability to carry air-to-surface missiles, are operational with tactical air force and naval units. Deliveries to the Baltic Fleet, to replace Tu-16s, began in Summer 1985.

In addition, an electronic warfare version, to replace the 'Brewer-E' model of the Yak-28, was undergoing systems development in 1988.

The following details apply specifically to 'Fencer-C' but are generally applicable to all versions:

TYPE: Two-seat variable geometry attack aircraft.

WINGS: Cantilever shoulder-wing monoplane, each wing comprising a triangular fixed glove box and three-position pivoted outer panel of all-metal construction. Slight anhedral from roots. Leading-edge sweepback on outer panels estimated at 16° fully forward, and 68° fully swept, with an intermediate sweep angle of 45°. Full span leading-edge slats and almost full span two-section double-slotted trailing-edge flaps on the outer panels. Differential spoilers forward of flaps for roll control at low speeds and for use as lift dumpers on landing.

FUSELAGE: Conventional all-metal semi-monocoque structure of slab-sided rectangular section, with integral engine air intake trunks. Splitter plate and outer lip of each intake are inclined slightly downward. Variable intake ramps. Airbrake under each side of centre-fuselage, curved to follow shape of underbelly fairing.

TAIL UNIT: Cantilever all-metal structure, comprising single sweptback fin with inset rudder, and all-moving horizontal surfaces which operate together for pitch control and differentially for roll control, assisted by use of the wing spoilers when the wings are not fully swept. Two slightly splayed ventral fins, one each side of fuselage undersurface.

LANDING GEAR: Retractable tricycle type, with twin wheels on each unit. Main units retract forward and inward into air intake duct fairings; nose unit retracts rearward. Trailing link type of shock absorbers in main units and low pressure tyres for operation from semi-prepared fields. Mudguard on nosewheels.

POWER PLANT: Two afterburning engines side by side in rear fuselage. These are believed to be related to the Lyulka AL-21F turbojet, as fitted in Su-17. Internal fuel capacity, estimated at 13,000 litres (3,434 US gallons; 2,860 Imp gallons), can be supplemented by four large external tanks on wing and glove pylons.

ACCOMMODATION: Crew of two (pilot and weapon systems officer) side by side on ejection seats.

AVIONICS: Latest photographs show a small avionics pod at top of engine air intake duct on each side, immediately aft

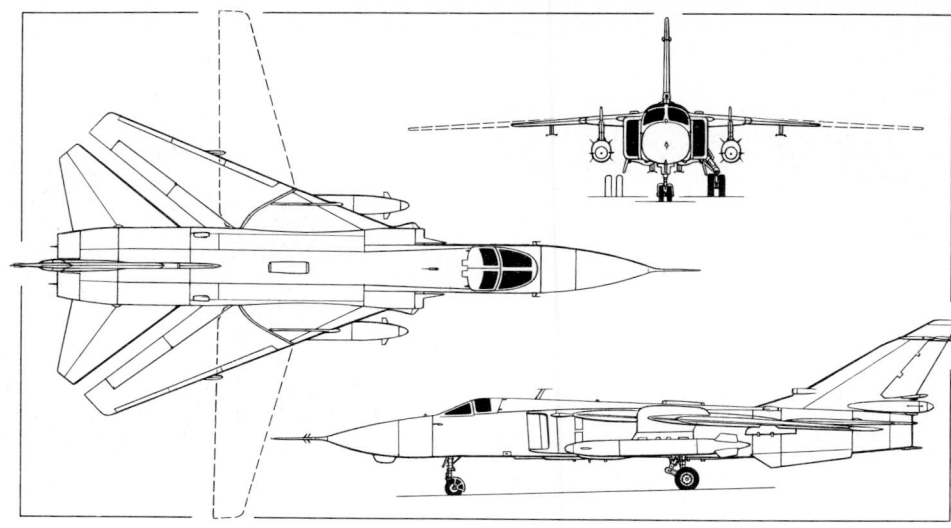

Sukhoi Su-24 ('Fencer-D') variable geometry attack aircraft *(Pilot Press)*

Sukhoi Su-24 ('Fencer-D') with wings fully spread and landing gear extended *(US Department of Defense)*

of lip, and on each side of fin. These pods appear similar to those immediately forward of the nosewheel bay of ground attack versions of the MiG-23/27.

ARMAMENT: Eight pylons under fuselage, each wingroot glove and outer wings for approx 11,000 kg (24,250 lb) of guided and unguided air-to-surface weapons, including nuclear weapons, missiles such as AS-7 (NATO 'Kerry'), AS-10 ('Karen'), AS-11 ('Kilter'), AS-12 ('Kegler'), AS-13 ('Kingbolt') and AS-14 ('Kedge'), or external fuel tanks. Two pivoting underwing pylons were the first of their kind observed on a Soviet aircraft. No internal weapons bay. One six-barrel 30 mm Gatling type gun inside fairing on starboard side of fuselage undersurface. Unidentified fairing on other side.

DIMENSIONS, EXTERNAL (estimated):

Wing span: spread	17.50 m (57 ft 5 in)
swept	10.50 m (34 ft 5½ in)
Length overall, excl probe	21.29 m (69 ft 10 in)
Height overall	6.00 m (19 ft 8¼ in)
Wheel track	4.00 m (13 ft 1½ in)

WEIGHTS (estimated):

Weight empty, equipped	19,000 kg (41,885 lb)
Max T-O weight	41,000 kg (90,390 lb)

PERFORMANCE (estimated):

Max speed, 'clean': at height	Mach 2.18
at S/L	Mach 1.2
Service ceiling	16,500 m (54,135 ft)
Combat radius:	
lo-lo-lo	over 174 nm (322 km; 200 miles)
lo-lo-hi with 2,500 kg (5,500 lb) weapons	
	515 nm (950 km; 590 miles)
hi-lo-hi, with 3,000 kg (6,615 lb) weapons and two	
external tanks	700 nm (1,300 km; 805 miles)

SUKHOI Su-25
NATO reporting name: Frogfoot

When first observed by satellite at Ramenskoye flight test centre in 1977, this Soviet counterpart to the US Air Force's A-10 Thunderbolt II single-seat attack aircraft was given the provisional US designation Ram-J. The NATO reporting name 'Frogfoot' was released in 1982, when a trials unit was sent to Afghanistan to support Soviet ground forces fighting in mountain terrain, and the Su-25 attained full operational capability in 1984. The emphasis during operational use in Afghanistan is said to have been on techniques for co-ordinating low level close support by fixed wing aircraft and Mi-24 helicopter gunships. About 210 Su-25s were operational with Soviet forces by October 1986, plus one squadron (named 'Ostrava') serving with the Czechoslovak Air Force. Others have been exported to Iraq. Production is centred at the Tbilisi airframe plant.

TYPE: Single-seat close support aircraft.

WINGS: Cantilever shoulder-wing monoplane. Anhedral from roots. Approx 20° sweepback. Entire trailing-edge occupied by hydraulically actuated ailerons and double-slotted two-section flaps. Multiple tabs in each aileron. Full span leading-edge slats in two segments on each wing. Extended chord leading-edge 'dogtooth' on outer 50 per cent of each wing. Pods at wingtips each split at rear to form airbrakes which project above and below wing when extended, like those of Grumman A-6 Intruder. Retractable landing light in base of each pod, aft of dielectric nosecap for ECM. Small landing light glareshield under each pod.

FUSELAGE: Conventional semi-monocoque structure, with flat armoured sides around cockpit. Pitot on port side of nose; transducer to provide data for fire control computer on starboard side.

TAIL UNIT: Conventional cantilever structure. Variable incidence tailplane, with slight dihedral. Hydraulically actuated two-section inset rudder. Tabs in lower rudder segment and each elevator.

LANDING GEAR: Hydraulically retractable tricycle type. Mainwheels retract to lie horizontally in bottom of engine air intake trunks. Single wheel with low-pressure

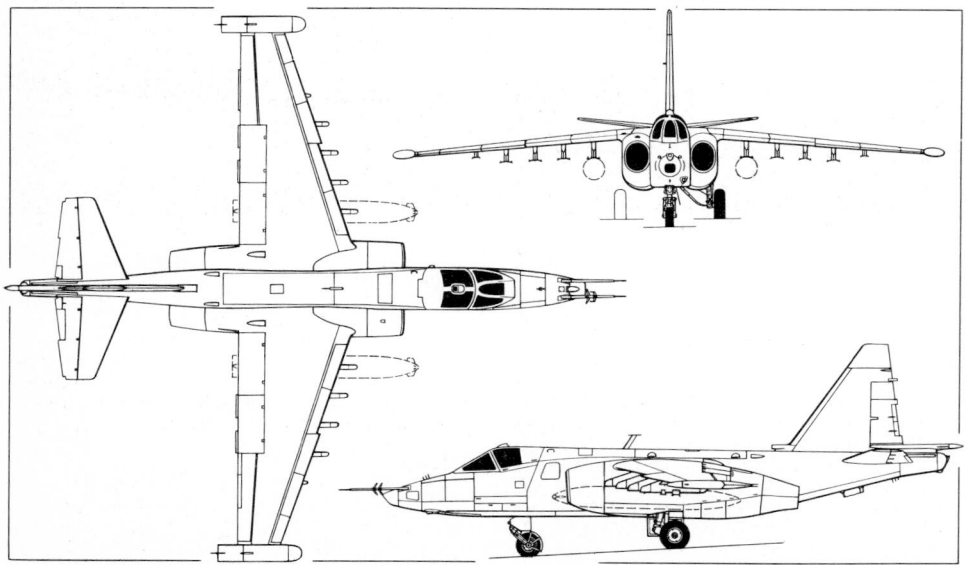

Sukhoi Su-25 single-seat close support aircraft *(Pilot Press)*

This photograph of an Su-25 shows the wingtip airbrakes open *(Letectvi + Kosmonautika)*

tyre on each levered suspension unit. Mudguard on forward retracting steerable nosewheel. Twin cruciform brake-chutes housed in tailcone.

POWER PLANT: Two non-afterburning Tumansky R-13-300 turbojets in long nacelles at wingroots, each rated at 41.5 kN (9,340 lb st). Fuel tanks in fuselage between cockpit and wing front spar, and between rear spar and fin leading-edge, and in wing centre-section. Provision for external fuel tank on each inboard underwing pylon.

ACCOMMODATION: Single ejection seat under sideways hinged (to starboard) canopy, with small rearview mirror on top. Flat bulletproof windscreen.

AVIONICS: SRO-2 (NATO 'Odd Rods') IFF antennae forward of windscreen and under tail. Sirena 3 radar warning system antenna above fuselage tailcone.

ARMAMENT AND OPERATIONAL EQUIPMENT: One twin-barrel 30 mm gun in bottom of front fuselage on port side. Eight large pylons under wings for estimated 4,500 kg (9,920 lb) of air-to-ground weapons, including 57 mm and 80 mm rockets and 500 kg incendiary, anti-personnel and chemical cluster bombs. Two small outboard pylons for 'Atoll' or 'Aphid' air-to-air self-defence missiles. Laser rangefinder and marked target seeker under flat sloping window in nose. Chaff/flare dispenser in tailcone. Strike camera in top of nosecone.

DIMENSIONS, EXTERNAL:
Wing span	14.30 m (46 ft 11 in)
Length overall	15.40 m (50 ft 6¾ in)
Height	4.80 m (15 ft 9 in)

AREA:
Wings, gross	33.7 m² (362.75 sq ft)

WEIGHTS:
Weight empty	9,500 kg (20,950 lb)
Max T-O weight	18,120-19,200 kg (39,950-42,330 lb)

PERFORMANCE (estimated):
Max level speed	Mach 0.8
	(530 knots; 980 km/h; 608 mph)

Combat radius, hi-lo-hi, with 2,000 kg (4,410 lb) air-to-ground weapons and two external fuel tanks
300 nm (556 km; 345 miles)

SUKHOI Su-26M

Among Soviet aircraft that participated in the World Aerobatic Championships in Hungary, in August 1984, were two examples of the hitherto unknown Sukhoi Su-26, which had flown for the first time in June of that year. Brief details of this initial version can be found in the 1985-86 *Jane's*. The three examples that gained both the men's and women's team prizes at the 1986 World Aerobatic Championships in the UK (c/n 06, 07 and 08) were modified Su-26Ms, identified by a sharp-cornered (rather than rounded) rudder and reduced fuselage side glazing. The following description applies to these aircraft:

TYPE: Single-seat aerobatic competition aircraft.

WINGS: Cantilever mid-wing monoplane of tapered planform. Specially developed symmetrical wing section, variable along span; slightly concave in region of ailerons to increase their effectiveness; leading-edge somewhat sharper than usual to make aircraft more responsive to control surface movement. Thickness/chord ratio 18% at root, 12% at tip. No dihedral, incidence or sweep at quarter-chord. One-piece two-spar stressed skin structure, without ribs, covered with three-lamination glassfibre/epoxy (GFRP). Foam filled front box spar with carbonfibre reinforced plastics (CFRP) booms and wound glassfibre webs. Channel section rear spar of CFRP. Outer 67% of each wing trailing-edge formed by plain aileron with CFRP box spar, GFRP skin and foam filling. Each aileron, actuated by pushrods, has ground adjustable tab on trailing-edge and two suspended triangular balance tabs. No flaps.

FUSELAGE: Oval-section, with basic welded truss structure of VNS-2 high strength stainless steel tubing. Lower nose section of truss removable to facilitate detachment of wings. Three-lamination GFRP skin panels, with duralumin reinforcement, are all quickly removable for access to interior. Light alloy engine cowlings.

TAIL UNIT: Conventional cantilever fin and tailplane of similar construction to wings. Horn balanced rudder and elevators of similar construction to ailerons and each with ground adjustable tab. Elevators actuated by pushrods, rudder by cable.

LANDING GEAR: Non-retractable tailwheel type. Arched cantilever mainwheel legs of titanium alloy. Mainwheels

The above three photographs of Sukhoi Su-25 combat aircraft of the Czechoslovak Air Force are reproduced by courtesy of *Letectvi + Kosmonautika (Václav Jukl)*

size 350 × 135 mm, with hydraulic disc brakes. Sprung steerable tailwheel connected to rudder.

POWER PLANT: One 268 kW (360 hp) Vedeneyev M-14P nine-cylinder radial engine, driving a three-blade Hoffmann variable-pitch metal propeller. Optional V-530TA-D35 two-blade variable-pitch propeller. Steel tube engine mounting. Fuel in glassfibre lined foam plastics tank bonded into each wingroot section between spars; total capacity 130 litres (34.3 US gallons; 28.6 Imp gallons). Port wing tank only is used in competition; starboard tank supplements it for ferry flights. Oil capacity 22.6 litres (6 US gallons; 5 Imp gallons). Fuel and oil systems adapted for inverted flight.

ACCOMMODATION: One-piece pilot's seat of GFRP, inclined at 45° and designed for use with PLP-60 back-pack parachute. Sideways hinged (to starboard) jettisonable canopy. Safety harness anchored to fuselage structure.

SYSTEM: Electrical system of 24/28V, with 3kW generator, batteries and external supply socket.

AVIONICS: Briz VHF radio.

DIMENSIONS, EXTERNAL:
Wing span	7.80 m (25 ft 7 in)
Wing chord: at root	1.95 m (6 ft 4¾ in)
at tip	1.10 m (3 ft 7¼ in)
Wing aspect ratio	5.6
Length overall	6.90 m (22 ft 7¾ in)

Sukhoi Su-26M (c/n 09) aerobatic competition aircraft (*Paul Jackson*)

This close-up of the Su-27 shows its airbrake extended (*Royal Norwegian Air Force*)

Height overall	2.78 m (9 ft 1½ in)
Tailplane span	2.95 m (9 ft 8¼ in)
Wheel track	2.20 m (7 ft 2½ in)
Wheelbase	5.05 m (16 ft 6¾ in)
Propeller diameter	2.40 m (7 ft 10½ in)
AREAS:	
Wings, gross	11.90 m² (128.1 sq ft)
Ailerons (total)	1.18 m² (12.70 sq ft)
Fin	0.34 m² (3.66 sq ft)
Rudder	0.89 m² (9.58 sq ft)
Tailplane	1.10 m² (11.84 sq ft)
Elevators (total)	1.53 m² (16.47 sq ft)
WEIGHT:	
Normal competition T-O weight	720 kg (1,587 lb)
Max T-O weight	800 kg (1,763 lb)
PERFORMANCE:	
Never-exceed speed	243 knots (450 km/h; 280 mph)
Max level speed	189 knots (350 km/h; 217 mph)
Normal cruising speed	140 knots (260 km/h; 161 mph)
T-O speed	70 knots (130 km/h; 81 mph)
Landing speed	65 knots (120 km/h; 75 mph)
Max rate of climb at S/L	1,080 m (3,540 ft)/min
Rate of roll	more than 360°/s
T-O and landing run	100 m (328 ft)
Ferry range at 1,000 m (3,280 ft)	
	432 nm (800 km; 497 miles)
g limits	+11/−9

SUKHOI Su-27
NATO reporting name: Flanker

Responsibility for the larger of the Soviet air forces' two new-generation single-seat fighters, equivalent to the USAF's F-15 Eagle, was assigned to the Sukhoi design bureau. Its general configuration is similar to that of the smaller MiG-29, suggesting that the two aircraft evolved from a common research programme by a central authority, such as the famous TsAGI Central Aerodynamics and Hydrodynamics Institute. Versions identified to date by NATO reporting names are as follows:

Flanker-A. Prototypes, which began flight tests in 1977, as illustrated in the 1985-86 *Jane's*. Curved wingtips, and tail fins mounted centrally above each engine housing.

Flanker-B. Production version, with square wingtips carrying launchers for air-to-air missiles, tail fins located outboard of engine housings, extended tailcone, and other changes.

Flanker-B variant 2. First mentioned in Spring 1988 by Rear Adm William O. Studeman, US director of naval intelligence, as a variant of the standard 'Flanker-B' that could be intended for operation from the Soviet Navy's large new aircraft carrier by 1992. No details of modifications yet available.

It can be assumed that a tandem two-seat trainer version of 'Flanker', with combat capability, also exists.

Following deployment to the Kola Peninsula, in the far northern Murmansk region of the Soviet Union, in 1986, first photographs of the operational version were taken by the crew of a Lockheed P-3B of No. 333 Squadron, Royal Norwegian Air Force. Two Su-27s were launched to identify the P-3B, each armed with six AA-10 air-to-air missiles of three different models.

Like the MiG-29, the Su-27 is described by the US Department of Defense as a supersonic all-weather counter-air fighter, with lookdown/shootdown weapon systems and beyond-visual-range air-to-air missiles, and with a possible secondary ground attack role. The Su-27's range, thrust-to-weight ratio and manoeuvrability are all said to be improved by comparison with earlier Soviet fighters. Its large pulse Doppler radar and heavy armament should give it formidable potential against low flying aircraft and cruise missiles, particularly when it is deployed in partnership with the new Soviet AEW&C aircraft, based on the Il-76 transport and known to NATO as 'Mainstay'. DoD estimates suggest a combat radius as great as that of the Tupolev Tu-28P 'Fiddler', which is overdue for replacement, making the Su-27 capable of escorting missile armed bombers and deep penetration ground attack aircraft on sorties against the UK and western Europe.

The DoD estimated that by October 1986 only five 'Flankers' had attained operational capability with the Voyska PVO, plus a further ten with the Soviet tactical forces. The total had increased to about 100 operational aircraft by the beginning of 1988.

Series production is centred in a plant at Komsomolsk, Khabarovsk territory. With the MiG-31, the Su-27 is expected to replace many of the MiG-21, MiG-23/27, Su-15 and MiG-25 aircraft in the 17 tactical air forces assigned to Soviet military districts and groups of forces. It will also form the exclusive equipment of fighter components of the Legnica and Vinnitsa air armies, with the primary task of providing escort for Su-24 strike missions.

The fighter designated **P-42** by the Soviet Union is a specially prepared version of the Su-27. Flown by Viktor Georgiyevich Pugachev, a test pilot assigned to the Sukhoi design bureau, it set a record by climbing to 3,000 m in 25.373 seconds on 27 October 1986, beating by two seconds the previous record set by the F-15 *Streak Eagle*. On 15 November the same pilot claimed another record by taking the P-42 to 6,000 m in 37.050 seconds. On 10 March 1987 N. F. Sadovnikov flew the P-42 to 9,000 m in 44.176 seconds and to 12,000 m in 55.542 seconds. Data submitted with the claim for the November record gave the power plant as two R-32 turbofans, each rated at 133.25 kN (29,955 lb st) with afterburning, and the take-off weight as 14,110 kg (31,110 lb).

The following details apply to the standard 'Flanker-B':

TYPE: Single-seat all-weather counter-air fighter, with secondary ground attack capability.

WINGS: Cantilever mid-wing monoplane. Basic wing sweepback approx 40° on leading-edge, with long and smoothly curved leading-edge root extensions. Anhedral approx 2° 30′. Full span leading-edge manoeuvring flaps. Flap and aileron on trailing-edge of each wing.

FUSELAGE: Semi-monocoque all-metal structure of basically circular section, sloping down sharply aft of canopy. Cockpit high-set behind drooped nose. Large ogival dielectric nosecone. Long rectangular blast panel forward of gun on starboard side, above wingroot extension. Large forward hinged door type airbrake in top of centre-fuselage.

TAIL UNIT: Cantilever structure, comprising uncanted twin fins and rudders, mounted on narrow decks outboard of engine housings, and all-moving horizontal surfaces, all sharply sweptback. Fins have extensions beneath decks to form parallel but widely separated ventral fins.

LANDING GEAR: Retractable tricycle type, with single wheel on each unit. Mainwheels retract forward into wingroots. Nosewheel, with mudguard, retracts rearward. Brake-chute housed in fuselage tailcone.

POWER PLANT: Probably two Tumansky R-32 turbofans, each rated at 133.25 kN (29,955 lb st) with afterburning. Large auxiliary air intake louvres in bottom of each engine duct near primary wedge intake. Two rows of small vertical louvres in each side wall of wedge.

ACCOMMODATION: Pilot only, under large rearward opening transparent blister canopy, with low sill.

AVIONICS AND EQUIPMENT: Track-while-scan pulse Doppler radar (antenna diameter approx 1.0 m; 3 ft 4 in) with reported search range of 130 nm (240 km; 150 miles) and tracking range of 100 nm (185 km; 115 miles). Head-up display. Infra-red search/track sensor in transparent

First photograph of Sukhoi Su-27 ('Flanker-B') taken from a P-3B of No. 333 Squadron, Royal Norwegian Air Force

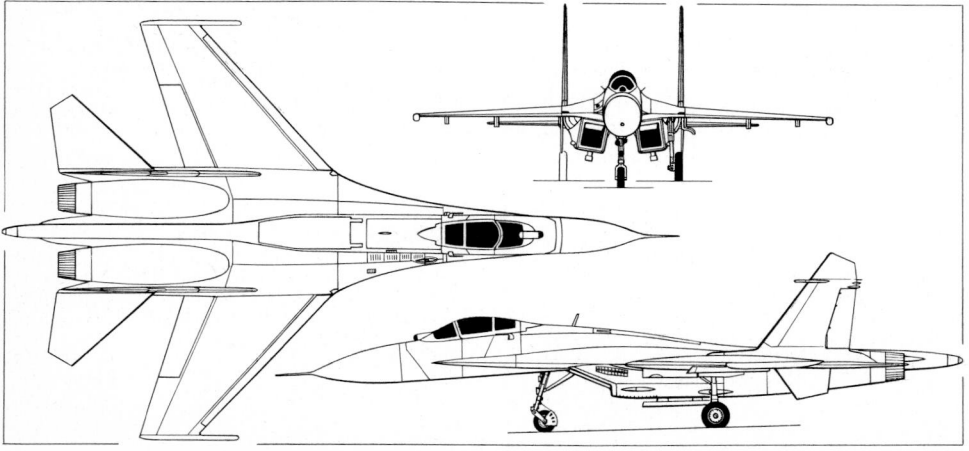

Sukhoi Su-27 twin-turbofan all-weather counter-air fighter (*Pilot Press*)

housing forward of windscreen. Sirena-3 (or later) 360° radar warning receivers, outboard of each bottom air intake lip and at tail.

ARMAMENT: One 30 mm gun in starboard wingroot extension. Up to ten air-to-air missiles, on tandem pylons under fuselage between engine ducts, beneath each duct, under each centre-wing and outer-wing, and at each wingtip. Aircraft illustrated has two short-burn semi-active radar homing AA-10A missiles (NATO 'Alamo-A') in tandem under fuselage; two short-burn infra-red homing AA-10B ('Alamo-B') missiles on the centre-wing pylons; and a long-burn semi-active radar homing AA-10C ('Alamo-C') beneath each engine duct. The four outer pylons are unoccupied, but are believed to carry either AA-11 ('Archer') or AA-8 ('Aphid') close-range infra-red missiles. Likely ability to carry up to 6,000 kg (13,225 lb) of external stores (e.g. twelve 500 kg bombs) for secondary attack role.

DIMENSIONS, EXTERNAL (estimated):

Wing span	14.70 m (48 ft 2¾ in)
Length overall, excl nose probe	21.60 m (70 ft 10½ in)
Height overall	5.50 m (18 ft 0 in)
Tailplane span	9.90 m (32 ft 6 in)
Distance between fin tips	4.30 m (14 ft 1¼ in)
Fuselage: Max width	1.50 m (4 ft 11 in)
Wheel track	4.40 m (14 ft 5¼ in)
Wheelbase	6.70 m (22 ft 0 in)

WEIGHT (estimated):
Max T-O weight   20,000-27,200 kg (44,000-60,000 lb)

PERFORMANCE (estimated):
Max level speed: at height
    Mach 2.0 (1,150 knots; 2,120 km/h; 1,320 mph)
    at S/L   Mach 1.1 (725 knots; 1,345 km/h; 835 mph)
Combat radius   810 nm (1,500 km; 930 miles)

Sukhoi Su-27 taxying at its base in the Kola Peninsula

TUPOLEV

CHIEF DESIGNERS: Dr Alexei A. Tupolev, L. L. Selyakov and Dmitry Markov

DEPUTY CHIEF OF BUREAU: Andrei Kandolov

Andrei Tupolev, born in 1888, was a leading figure in the Central Aero-Hydrodynamic Institute (TsAGI) in Moscow from the time when it was founded, in 1929, until his death on 23 December 1972. Current chief designers of the bureau which bears his name include his son, Dr Alexei A. Tupolev. The bureau has doubled in size during the past decade.

TUPOLEV Tu-16
NATO reporting name: Badger

The prototype of this intermediate-range bomber, which had the Tupolev design bureau designation Tu-88, was flown for the first time by N. Rybko in Winter 1951-52. The original strategic bomber version entered series production as the Tu-16 in 1953, and made its first major public appearance on 1 May 1954. About 2,000 were delivered to the medium-range bomber force and to Soviet Naval Aviation. An estimated 270 remain operational, mostly with the Smolensk and Irkutsk air armies, equipped to carry both nuclear and conventional weapons. The bombers are supported by 20 Tu-16 in-flight refuelling tankers and about 115 of various versions equipped for ECM duties and strategic reconnaissance. Soviet Naval Aviation has about 120 attack models of 'Badger', plus 70 tankers and up to 80 reconnaissance and ECM models.

Early production Tu-16s had AM-3 turbojet engines. These were replaced in later aircraft by improved RD-3M (AM-3M) engines, which increased maximum speeds by up to 54 knots (100 km/h; 62 mph), and range with max fuel to 3,885 nm (7,200 km; 4,470 miles). Eleven versions of the Tu-16 have been identified by unclassified NATO reporting names, as follows:

Badger-A. Basic strategic jet bomber, able to carry nuclear or conventional free-fall weapons. Glazed nose,

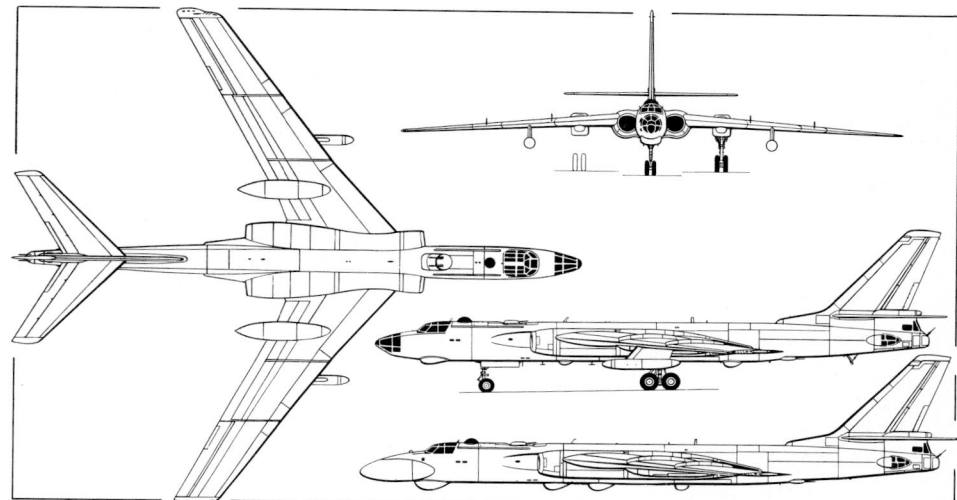

Tupolev Tu-16, in the form known to NATO as 'Badger-F', with additional side view (bottom) of 'Badger-D' (*Pilot Press*)

with small undernose radome. Defensive armament of seven 23 mm guns. Some equipped as flight refuelling tankers, using a unique wingtip-to-wingtip transfer technique to refuel other Tu-16s, or a probe-and-drogue system to refuel Tu-22s. Operational with Chinese Air Force, and production continues in China under the designation Xian **H-6** (see Chinese section).

Badger-B. Similar to 'Badger-A' but equipped originally to carry two turbojet powered aeroplane type anti-shipping missiles (NATO 'Kennel') underwing. Superseded by 'Badger-G'.

Badger-C. Anti-shipping version, first seen at 1961 Soviet Aviation Day display. Large air-to-surface winged missile (NATO 'Kipper') carried in recess under fuselage (**Badger-C Mod** carries 'Kingfish' on underwing pylons). Wide nose radome (NATO 'Puff Ball'), in place of glazing and nose gun of 'Badger-A'. No provision for free-fall bombs. About 120 operational with Soviet Northern, Baltic, Black Sea and Pacific Fleets.

Badger-D. Maritime/electronic reconnaissance version. Nose similar to that of 'Badger-C'. Larger undernose radome; three radomes in tandem under bomb bays.

Latest form of Tu-16 'Badger' flight refuelling tanker, photographed over the Baltic Sea (*Swedish Air Force*)

Badger-E. Photographic and electronic reconnaissance version. Similar to 'Badger-A' but with cameras in bomb bay and two additional radomes under fuselage, larger one aft.

Badger-F. Basically similar to 'Badger-E' but with electronic intelligence pod on a pylon under each wing. No radomes under centre-fuselage.

Badger-G. Converted from 'Badger-B' with underwing pylons for two rocket-powered air-to-surface missiles (NATO 'Kelt') which can be carried over a range greater than 1,735 nm (3,220 km; 2,000 miles). Free-fall bombing capability retained. Majority serve with anti-shipping squadrons of Soviet Naval Air Force. A few were transferred to Iraq.

A Soviet Navy Tu-16, probably a 'Badger-G', is shown in an accompanying illustration with an ECM nose thimble of the kind seen beneath the in-flight refuelling probe of 'Bear-G'. It can be assumed that it also carries further pods like those of 'Bear-G' on its centre or rear fuselage.

Badger-G modified. Specially equipped to carry 'Kingfish' air-to-surface missile under each wing; first observed in mid-1981. Large radome, presumably associated with missile operation, under centre-fuselage, replacing chin radome. Device mounted externally on glazed nose might help to ensure correct attitude of Tu-16 during missile launch. Operational with Soviet Northern, Black Sea and Pacific Fleets.

Badger-H. Stand-off or escort ECM aircraft, with primary function of chaff dispensing to protect missile carrying strike force. The dispensers, with a total capacity of up to 9,075 kg (20,000 lb) of chaff, are located in the weapons bay area. Hatch aft of weapons bay. Two teardrop radomes, fore and aft of weapons bay. Two blade antennae aft of weapons bay. Glazed nose and chin radome.

Badger-J. Specialised ECM jamming/elint aircraft to protect strike force, with some equipment located in a canoe shape radome protruding from inside the weapons bay and surrounded by heat exchangers and exhaust ports. Anti-radar noise jammers operate in A to I bands inclusive. Glazed nose as 'Badger-A'. Some aircraft (as illustrated) have large flat-plate antennae at wingtips.

Badger-K. Electronic reconnaissance variant, with nose as 'Badger-A'. Two teardrop radomes, inside and forward of weapons bay; four small pods on centreline in front of rear radome.

Maritime reconnaissance versions of 'Badger' make regular flights over units of the US Navy and other NATO naval forces at sea in the Atlantic, Pacific and elsewhere. They also make electronic intelligence (elint) sorties around the coastlines of NATO and other countries. Ten strike and six tanker and ECM variants of 'Badger' are deployed to Cam Ranh Bay, the former US Navy base in Vietnam.

TYPE: Twin-jet medium bomber and maritime reconnaissance/attack aircraft.

WINGS: Cantilever high mid-wing monoplane, with marked anhedral and with 35° of leading-edge sweep on outer panels; 42° sweep on inboard panels. Thickness/chord ratio 12½%. Two-spar light alloy structure, with two fences on each wing. Entire trailing-edge made up of slotted flaps (max deflection 35°) and mass balanced ailerons, each with trim tab. Heavy engine nacelles form root fairings. Versions equipped for in-flight refuelling have modified wingtips (see illustration of 'Badger-J').

FUSELAGE: All-metal semi-monocoque structure of oval cross-section, made in five sections. The nose section houses the navigator's pressure cabin with double-glazed nose panels in a magnesium alloy frame, the pilots' pressure cabin, the forward gunner's cabin, and radar equipment. The second and fourth sections house the aircraft's fuel tanks, with the weapon compartment between them; the tail section contains a pressure cabin for the radio operator and rear gunner. Skin panels made of 3 mm light alloy sheet.

TAIL UNIT: Cantilever all-metal structure, with 42° leading-edge sweepback on all surfaces. Trim tabs in rudder and each elevator.

LANDING GEAR: Retractable tricycle type. Twin-wheel nose unit retracts rearward. Main four-wheel bogies retract into housings projecting beyond the wing trailing-edge.

POWER PLANT: Early Tu-16s have two Mikulin AM-3 turbojets, each rated at 85.8 kN (19,285 lb st) at sea level. Later aircraft fitted with RD-3M (AM-3M) turbojets, each rated at 93.19 kN (20,950 lb st). Engines semi-recessed into sides of fuselage. Divided air intake ducts: main duct passes through wing torque box between spars; secondary duct passes under wing to feed into primary airflow in front of engine. Engines separated from wings and fuselage by firewalls. Jetpipes inclined outward 3° to shield fuselage from effects of exhaust gases. Fuel in wing and fuselage tanks, with total capacity of approx 45,450 litres (12,000 US gallons; 10,000 Imp gallons). Provision for underwing auxiliary fuel tanks and for flight refuelling. Tu-16 tankers trail hose from starboard wingtip; receiving equipment is in port wingtip extension.

ACCOMMODATION: Normal crew of six, with two pilots side by side on flight deck. Navigator, on seat with armoured sides and base, in glazed nose of all versions except 'Badger-C and D'. Manned tail position plus lateral observation blisters in rear fuselage under tailplane.

AS-5 'Kelt' air-to-surface missile under the port wing of a Tu-16 'Badger-G'
(Swedish Air Force, via FLYGvapenNYTT)

'Badger-J' ECM jamming version of Tu-16 *(Swedish Air Force)*

Entry via two hatches in bottom of fuselage, in front and rear structural sections.

AVIONICS AND EQUIPMENT: Radio and radar aids probably include HF and VHF R/T equipment, as well as IFF and a radio compass and radio altimeter. Other equipment differs according to role.

ARMAMENT: Forward dorsal and rear ventral barbettes each containing two 23 mm NR-23 guns. Two similar guns in tail position controlled by an automatic gun ranging radar set. Seventh, fixed, gun on starboard side of nose of versions with nose glazing. Bomb load of up to 9,000 kg (19,800 lb) delivered from weapons bay 6.5 m (21 ft) long in standard bomber, under control of navigator. Naval versions can carry air-to-surface winged standoff missiles.

DIMENSIONS, EXTERNAL ('Badger-G'):

Wing span	32.93 m (108 ft 0½ in)
Length overall	36.25 m (118 ft 11¼ in)
Height overall	14.00 m (45 ft 11¼ in)
Basic diameter of fuselage	2.50 m (8 ft 2½ in)
Tailplane span	11.75 m (38 ft 6½ in)
Wheel track	9.775 m (32 ft 0¾ in)

AREA:

Wings, gross	164.65 m² (1,772.3 sq ft)

WEIGHTS ('Badger-G'):

Weight empty, equipped	37,200 kg (82,000 lb)
Normal T-O weight	75,000 kg (165,350 lb)

PERFORMANCE ('Badger-G', at max T-O weight):

Max level speed at 6,000 m (19,700 ft)	
	535 knots (992 km/h; 616 mph)
Service ceiling	12,300 m (40,350 ft)
Range with 3,790 kg (8,360 lb) bomb load	
	3,200 nm (5,925 km; 3,680 miles)
Max unrefuelled combat radius	
	1,700 nm (3,150 km; 1,955 miles)

TUPOLEV Tu-95 and Tu-142
NATO reporting name: Bear

Although the first prototype of Andrei Tupolev's large four-turboprop 'Bear' was flown in the Summer of 1954, most of the 160 'Bears' now flying with the Soviet air armies are of the recently upgraded 'Bear-G' or new-production 'Bear-H' missile-carrying versions. In its *Soviet Military Power* document, the US Department of Defense warns that 'Bear-H' and the new 'Blackjack' give the Soviet air forces the capability to attack the USA with hundreds of difficult-to-detect, hard-target-kill AS-15 'Kent' cruise missiles. Similarly, most of the 80 Soviet Naval Aviation 'Bears' are of the 'F' model, which differs so greatly from earlier versions that its designation was changed from **Tu-95** to **Tu-142**. High performance is not the only factor that has kept this aircraft in continuous production for 34 years, to balance attrition and introduce new versions. Equally important has been its ability to accommodate extensive avionics and the largest air-to-surface missiles and radars yet carried by combat aircraft. Some of the 'Bears', including missile armed 'Gs', have been reassigned to a theatre role, and conduct regular combat training exercises

'Bear-G' has two large pylons under the wingroots on which to carry 'Kitchen' missiles (UK Ministry of Defence)

Deep flight deck glazing and new undernose antennae are features of the 'Bear-H' cruise missile carrier (UK Ministry of Defence)

against naval and land targets in the northern Pacific region.

'Bears' deployed regularly to staging bases in Cuba and Angola are capable of covering the North and South Atlantic from the Mediterranean approaches westward to the US east coast, and southward to the Cape of Good Hope. They are encountered frequently off the US east coast during transits between Murmansk and Cuba, and during elint missions from Cuba. 'Bear-Hs' from Dolon air base in the central USSR also carry out simulated attack and training missions against the USA and Canada. Eight 'Bears' are stationed permanently at Cam Ranh in Vietnam.

The nine versions identified by NATO reporting names are as follows:

Bear-A. Basic Tu-95 strategic bomber, first shown in Aviation Day display at Tushino in July 1955. Internal stowage for two nuclear or a variety of conventional free-fall weapons. Fitted with chin radar, and defensive armament comprising three pairs of 23 mm cannon in remotely controlled rear dorsal and ventral barbettes and manned tail turret. Two glazed blisters on rear fuselage, under tailplane, are used for sighting by the gunner controlling all these weapons. The dorsal and ventral barbettes can also be controlled from a station aft of the flight deck. Max range with 11,340 kg (25,000 lb) bomb load is 8,000 nm (14,800 km; 9,200 miles). Few remain in service.

Bear-B. First seen in 1961 Aviation Day flypast. Generally similar to 'Bear-A' but able to carry a large air-to-surface aeroplane type missile (NATO reporting name 'Kangaroo') under fuselage, with associated radar (NATO 'Crown Drum') in wide undernose radome, replacing the original glazing. Defensive armament retained. A few 'Bear-Bs' operate in maritime reconnaissance role, with flight refuelling nose-probe and, sometimes, an elint blister fairing on the starboard side of the rear fuselage. Some carry a pointed canister under each wing, for air sampling.

Bear-C. Third Tu-95 strike version, able to carry 'Kangaroo'; first observed near NATO naval forces in September 1964. Generally similar to 'Bear-B' but with an elint blister fairing on *both* sides of rear fuselage. Refuelling probe standard. Has been observed with a faired tail housing special equipment, like that first seen on a 'Bear-D' and illustrated on a 'Bear-G'.

Bear-D. Identified in August 1967, this maritime reconnaissance version of the Tu-95 has a glazed nose, an undernose radar (NATO 'Short Horn'), a large underbelly radome for I band surface search radar (NATO 'Big Bulge'), an elint fairing on each side of the rear fuselage like 'Bear-C', a nose refuelling probe, and a variety of blisters and antennae, including a streamlined fairing on each tailplane tip. The housing for I band tail warning radar above the tail turret is much larger than on previous versions. Tasks include pinpointing of maritime targets for missile launch crews on board ships and aircraft which are themselves too distant to ensure precise missile aiming and guidance. 'Bear-D' carries no offensive weapons. About 15 operational.

A 'Bear-D' was the first version seen, in 1978, with the normal tail turret and associated radome replaced by a faired tail housing special equipment. A similar tail is now fitted to 'Bear-G'.

Bear-E. Reconnaissance version of Tu-95, basically similar to 'Bear-A' but with refuelling probe and rear fuselage elint fairings as on 'Bear-C'. Six camera windows in bomb bay, in pairs in line with the wing flaps, with a seventh window to the rear on the starboard side. Few only.

Bear-F. Anti-submarine aircraft. First of the Tu-142 series of extensively redesigned 'Bears', with more highly cambered wings and longer fuselage forward of the wings. Deployed initially by the Soviet Naval air force in 1970, since when several variants have been seen. Re-entered production in the mid-1980s. Originally, 'Bear-F' had enlarged and lengthened fairings aft of its inboard engine

nacelles, and undernose radar. The main underfuselage J band radar housing is considerably farther forward than on 'Bear-D' and smaller in size; there are no large blister fairings under and on the sides of the rear fuselage; and the nosewheel doors are bulged prominently, suggesting the use of larger or low pressure tyres. 'Bear-F' has two stores bays for sonobuoys, torpedoes and nuclear depth charges in its rear fuselage, one of them replacing the usual rear ventral gun turret and leaving the tail turret as the sole defensive gun position. The variants of 'Bear-F' are identified as follows:

Mod 1: As original 'Bear-F' but reverted to standard size nacelles. Chin mounted J band radar deleted. Fewer protrusions.

Mod 2 (Tu-142M): Fuselage nose lengthened by 23 cm (9 in) and roof of flight deck raised. Angle of refuelling probe lowered by 4°.

Mod 3: MAD boom added to fin tip. Fairings at tips of tailplane deleted. Rear stores bay lengthened and made less wide.

Mod 4: Chin radar reinstated. Self-protection ECM thimble radome on nose, plus other fairings. Entered service with the air force of the Soviet Northern Fleet in 1985.

Most of approximately 60 'Bear-Fs' in service are to Mod 3 or Mod 4 standard.

In early 1988, Indian Navy Squadron INAS 312 took delivery of five ex-Soviet Navy 'Bear-Fs' for maritime reconnaissance from its base in Goa.

'Bear-H' has a new fin tip fairing
(UK Ministry of Defence)

Bear-G. Tu-95, generally similar to 'Bear-B/C' but reconfigured for elint missions and to carry two AS-4 ('Kitchen') supersonic air-to-surface missiles instead of one AS-3 ('Kangaroo'), on a large pylon under each wingroot. Features include an ECM thimble under the in-flight refuelling probe, a streamlined ECM pod on each side at the bottom of both the centre and rear fuselage, and a 'solid' tailcone, containing special equipment, similar in shape to that on some 'Bear-Ds'. More than 45 in service, all with the Irkutsk air army.

Bear-H. New production version, based on the Tu-142 type airframe of 'Bear-F' but with a shorter fuselage, of the same length as 'Bear-B/C'. Equipped to carry long-range cruise missiles, including the AS-15 (NATO 'Kent'). Aircraft observed up to mid-1988 had only an internal (rotary?) launcher for six of these ALCMs, but pylon mountings for four more can be attached under each wingroot. Built at Kuybyshev, 'Bear-H' achieved initial operational capability in 1984 and more than 70 had been built by Spring 1988. Features include a larger and deeper radome built into the nose and a small fin-tip fairing. There are no elint blister fairings on the sides of the rear fuselage and the ventral gun turret is deleted. Some aircraft have only a single twin-barrel gun, instead of the usual pair, in the tail turret.

Bear-J. Identified in 1986, this is the Soviet equivalent of the US Navy's E-6A and EC-130Q Tacamo aircraft, equipped with VLF communications avionics to maintain an on-station/all-ocean link between national command authorities and nuclear missile armed submarines under most operating conditions. Operational in comparatively small numbers by 1988, with the Soviet Northern and Pacific Fleets, it appears to use a modified Tu-142 'Bear-F' airframe.

TYPE: Four-turboprop long-range bomber and maritime reconnaissance aircraft.

WINGS: Cantilever mid-wing monoplane. Slight anhedral. Sweepback 37° at quarter-chord on inner panels, 35° at quarter-chord on outer panels. All-metal structure, with four spars in inboard panels, three spars outboard. All-metal three-segment hydraulically powered ailerons and two-segment Fowler flaps on each wing. Trim tab in each inboard aileron segment. Spoilers in top surface of wing forward of inboard end of ailerons. Three boundary layer fences on top surface of each wing. Thermal anti-icing system in leading-edges.

FUSELAGE: All-metal semi-monocoque structure of circular section, containing three pressurised compartments. Those forward and aft of the weapons bay are linked by a crawlway tunnel. The tail gunner's compartment is not accessible from the other compartments.

TAIL UNIT: Cantilever all-metal structure, with sweepback on all surfaces. Adjustable tailplane incidence. Hydrauli-

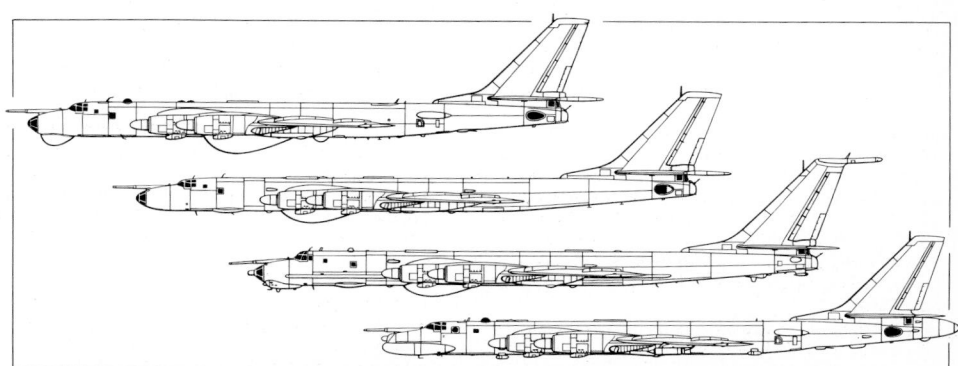

Top to bottom: Tu-95 'Bear-D', Tu-142 'Bear-F' Mod 1, Tu-142M 'Bear-F' Mod 4, Tu-95 'Bear-G'
(Pilot Press)

The Tu-95 'Bear-G' is a reconfigured 'Bear-B or C' equipped to carry 'Kitchen' missiles (*UK Ministry of Defence*)

cally powered rudder and elevators. Trim tabs in rudder and each elevator. Thermal anti-icing system in tailplane leading-edge.

LANDING GEAR: Hydraulically retractable tricycle type. Main units consist of four-wheel bogies, with tyres of approx 1.50 m (5 ft) diameter and hydraulic internal expanding brakes. Twin wheels on nose unit. All units retract rearward, main units into nacelles built on to wing trailing-edge. Retractable tail bumper consisting of two small wheels. Braking parachute may be used to reduce landing run.

POWER PLANT: Four Kuznetsov NK-12MV turboprops, each with max rating of 11,033 kW (14,795 ehp) and driving eight-blade contra-rotating reversible-pitch Type AV-60N propellers. Fuel in wing tanks, with normal capacity of 95,000 litres (25,100 US gallons; 20,900 Imp gallons).

ACCOMMODATION AND ARMAMENT: See notes applicable to individual versions and under 'Fuselage'.

OPERATIONAL EQUIPMENT ('Bear-D'): Large I band radar (NATO 'Big Bulge') in blister fairing under centre-fuselage, for reconnaissance and to provide data on potential targets for anti-shipping aircraft or surface vessels. In latter mode, PPI presentation is data linked to missile launch station. Four-PRF range J band circular and sector scan navigation radar (NATO 'Short Horn'). I band tail warning radar (originally NATO 'Bee Hind'; later 'Box Tail') in housing at base of rudder.

DIMENSIONS, EXTERNAL ('Bear-F', approx):
Wing span	51.10 m (167 ft 8 in)
Length overall	49.50 m (162 ft 5 in)
Height overall	12.12 m (39 ft 9 in)

WEIGHT ('Bear-F', estimated):
Max T-O weight	188,000 kg (414,470 lb)

PERFORMANCE:
Max level speed at 7,620 m (25,000 ft)
　　　　　500 knots (925 km/h; 575 mph)
Over-target speed at 12,500 m (41,000 ft)
　　　　　450 knots (833 km/h; 518 mph)
Max unrefuelled combat radius
　　　　　4,475 nm (8,285 km; 5,150 miles)

TUPOLEV Tu-126
NATO reporting name: Moss

An officially released Soviet documentary film, shown in the West in 1968, included sequences depicting a military version of the Tu-114 four-turboprop transport (see 1972-73 *Jane's*), carrying above its fuselage a rotating 'saucer' type early warning radar (NATO 'Flap Jack') with a diameter of about 11 m (36 ft). This was a logical development, as the Tu-114 had a fuselage of larger diameter than the military Tu-95, and could accommodate

Tupolev Tu-95 (NATO 'Bear-D') maritime reconnaissance aircraft

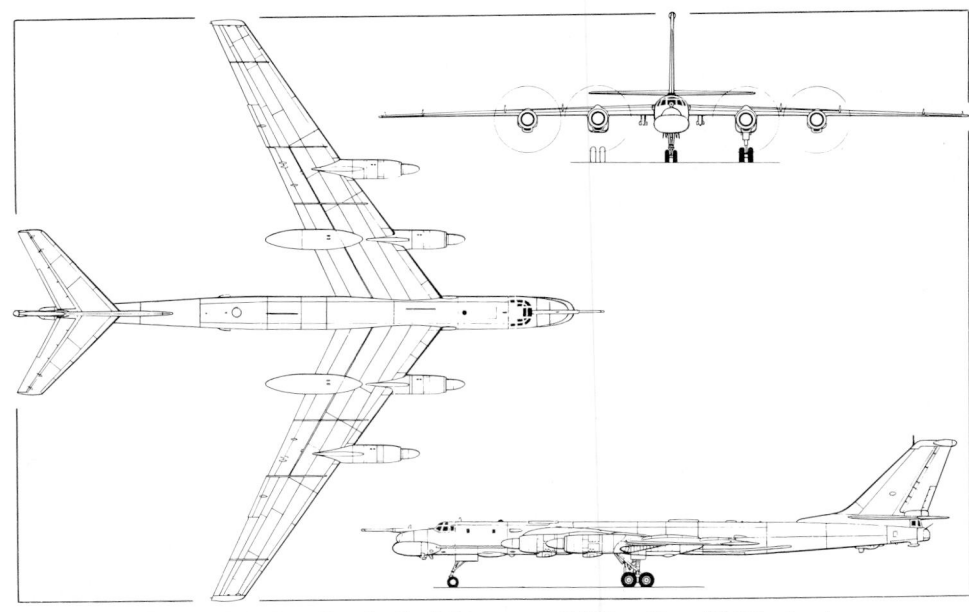

The version of the Tupolev Tu-142 known to NATO as 'Bear-H' (*Pilot Press*)

Tupolev Tu-142 ('Bear-F Mod 3') of the Soviet Naval Air Force with MAD 'sting' at the tip of its tail fin (*UK Ministry of Defence*)

The Tu-126 airborne early warning and control system aircraft, known to NATO as 'Moss'

more easily the extensive avionic equipment and crew of 12 required by what was soon confirmed as the Soviet air forces' first generation airborne early warning and control system aircraft, with the designation Tu-126. It proved to have also wings similar to those of the Tu-114, with extended chord trailing-edge flaps, rather than the 'straight' trailing-edge of the Tu-95. The interior of the fuselage is fully air-conditioned. Few cabin windows are installed.

The general appearance of the Tu-126, which has the NATO reporting name 'Moss', is shown in the accompanying illustrations. It can be seen to have a flight refuelling nose-probe, ventral tail fin and numerous additional antennae and blisters for electronic equipment, including streamlined fairings and associated dielectric panels on the sides of the rear fuselage as on the Tu-95 'Bear-C/D'. The power plant comprises four 11,033 kW (14,795 ehp) Kuznetsov NK-12MV turboprops. Wing fuel tanks have a capacity of 60,800 kg (134,040 lb).

The Tu-126 is intended to work in conjunction with advanced interceptors. After locating incoming low-level strike aircraft, it would ideally direct towards them fighters armed with 'snapdown' air-to-air missiles able to be fired from a cruising height of 6,100 m (20,000 ft) or higher. It has a further, obvious application in assisting strike aircraft to elude enemy interceptors picked up by its radar.

About seven Tu-126s are operational with the Soviet air defence forces. They are said, by US defence experts, to have demonstrated some effectiveness in overwater exercises but to be ineffective over land.

DIMENSIONS, EXTERNAL:

Wing span	51.20 m (168 ft 0 in)
Wing aspect ratio	8.42
Length overall	55.20 m (181 ft 1 in)
Fuselage diameter	3.70 m (12 ft 1½ in)
Height overall	16.05 m (52 ft 8 in)
Wheel track	13.70 m (44 ft 11½ in)
Propeller diameter	5.60 m (18 ft 4½ in)

AREA:

Wings, gross	311.1 m² (3,349 sq ft)

WEIGHT (estimated):

Max T-O weight	170,000 kg (374,785 lb)

PERFORMANCE:

Max level speed	459 knots (850 km/h; 528 mph)
Normal operating speed	
	351 knots (650 km/h; 404 mph)
Max range without flight refuelling	
	6,775 nm (12,550 km; 7,800 miles)

TUPOLEV Tu-22
NATO reporting name: Blinder

First shown publicly in the 1961 Aviation Day flypast over Moscow, the Tu-22 was the first operational Soviet bomber capable of supersonic performance for short periods. Of the ten examples which took part in that display, only one carried visible weapons, in the form of an

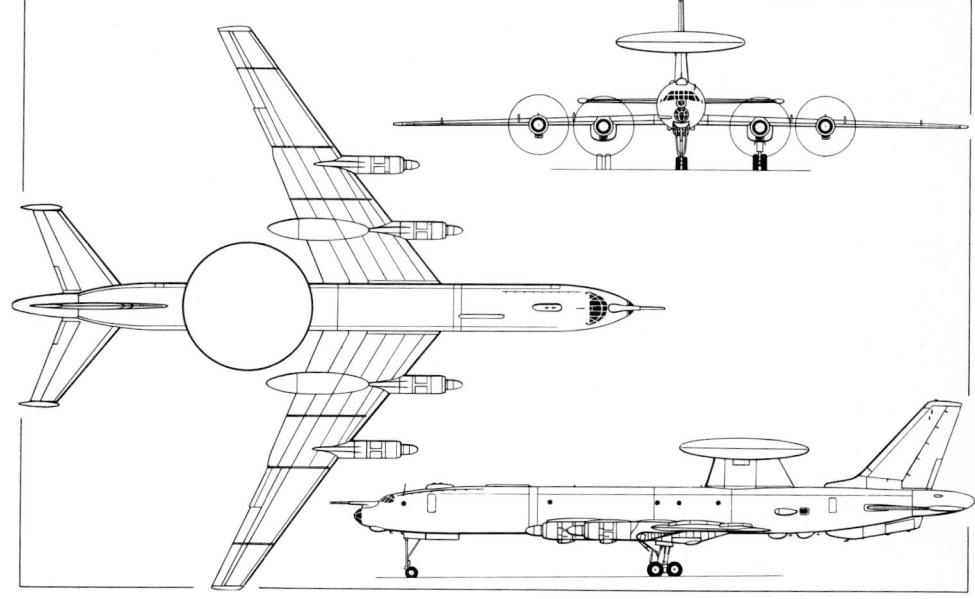

Tupolev Tu-126 (four Kuznetsov NK-12MV turboprops) *(Pilot Press)*

air-to-surface missile (NATO reporting name 'Kitchen'), some 11 m (36 ft) long, semi-submerged in the underside of its fuselage. This aircraft had also a wider nose radome.

A total of 22 Tu-22s took part in the 1967 display at Domodedovo. Most carried 'Kitchen' missiles; all had a partially retractable nose refuelling probe and the wide radome seen on the single missile-armed aircraft in 1961.

About 250 Tu-22s were built, in four versions, as follows:

Blinder-A. Basic reconnaissance bomber, with fuselage weapons bay for free-fall nuclear and conventional bombs. 'Blinder-A' entered limited service.

Blinder-B. Generally similar to 'Blinder-A' but equipped to carry air-to-surface nuclear missile (NATO reporting name 'Kitchen') recessed in weapons bay. Larger radar and partially retractable flight refuelling probe on nose.

Blinder-C. Maritime reconnaissance version, with six camera windows in weapons bay doors. Flight refuelling probe like 'Blinder-B'. Modifications to nosecone, dielectric panels, etc, on some aircraft suggest electronic intelligence role or equipment for electronic countermeasures (ECM) duties. About 60 delivered, for operation primarily over sea approaches to the Soviet Union, from bases in the Southern Ukraine and Estonia.

Blinder-D. Training version. Cockpit for instructor in raised position aft of standard flight deck, with stepped-up canopy. In service in the Soviet Union and Libya.

About 120 'Blinder-As' and 'Blinder-Bs' remain operational with medium-range units of the Smolensk and Irkutsk air armies. Most are used now for support roles, such as ECM jamming, plus 15 equipped for reconnaissance. The Soviet Naval Air Force has about 50, of which 20 are equipped for maritime reconnaissance and ECM duties. The Libyan and Iraqi Air Forces each have a few Tu-22s.

The following details apply to 'Blinder-A and B' but are generally applicable to all versions except as noted under model descriptions.

TYPE: Twin-jet supersonic bomber and maritime patrol aircraft.

WINGS: Cantilever mid-wing monoplane. Constant slight anhedral from roots. Sweepback approx 45° on leading-edge outboard of fence and 50° inboard of fence, increasing to acute sweep at roots. Conventional all-metal structure. Fully powered two-section ailerons, with tab in each inboard section. Flaps inboard and outboard of wheel pod on each wing trailing-edge.

FUSELAGE: All-metal semi-monocoque structure of circular section, with area rule 'waisting' at wingroots.

TAIL UNIT: Cantilever all-metal structure, with sweepback on all surfaces. Fully powered all-moving horizontal surfaces at bottom of fuselage. Aerodynamically balanced rudder, with inset tab.

LANDING GEAR: Retractable tricycle type. Wide track four-wheel bogie main units retract rearward into pods built on to wing trailing-edges. Oleo-pneumatic shock absorbers. Main legs designed to swing rearward for additional cushioning during taxying and landing on rough runways. Twin-wheel nose unit retracts rearward. Small retractable skid to protect rear fuselage in tail-down landing or take-off. Twin brake-chutes standard.

POWER PLANT: Two Koliesov VD-7 turbojets, each rated at 137.5 kN (30,900 lb st) with afterburning, mounted in pods above rear fuselage, on each side of tail fin. Lip of each intake is in the form of a ring which can be translated forward by jacks for take-off. Air entering ram intake is then supplemented by air ingested through annular slot between ring and main body of pod. Jetpipes have convergent-divergent nozzle inside outer fairing. Semi-retractable flight refuelling probe on nose of 'Blinder-B',

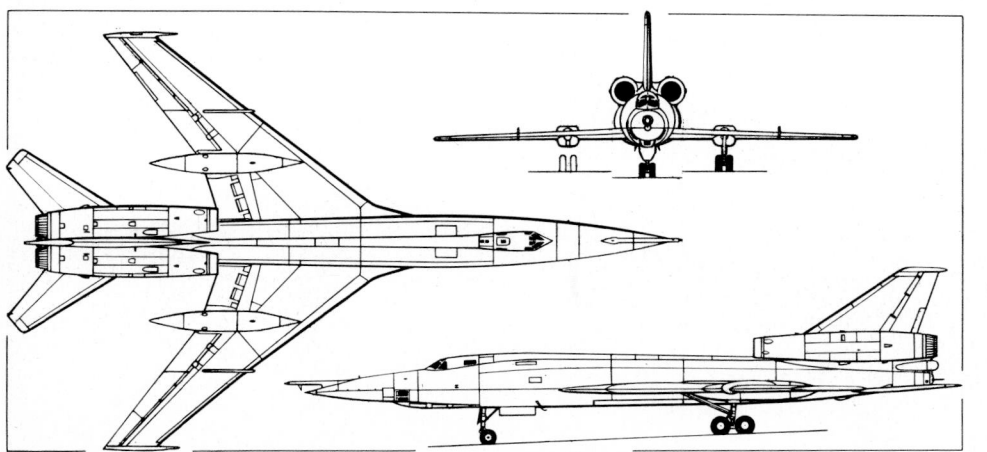

Tupolev Tu-22 twin-jet supersonic bomber ('Blinder-A') *(Pilot Press)*

Tupolev Tu-22 photographed from an investigating interceptor of the Swedish Air Force *(via FLYGvapenNYTT)*

with triangular guard underneath to prevent drogue damaging nosecone.

ACCOMMODATION: Crew of three in tandem. Row of windows in bottom of fuselage, aft of nose radome, at navigator/systems operator's station. Pilot has upward ejection seat; other crew members have downward ejection seats.

ARMAMENT AND OPERATIONAL EQUIPMENT: Weapons bay in centre-fuselage, with double-fold doors on 'Blinder-A'. Special doors with panels shaped to accommodate recessed 'Kitchen' missile on 'Blinder-B'. Single 23 mm NR-23 gun in radar directed tail turret, beneath 'Bee Hind' tail warning radar antenna. Radar in nose. Chaff/flare countermeasures dispensers and bombing assessment cameras carried in rear of wheel pods of some aircraft.

DIMENSIONS, EXTERNAL (estimated):
Wing span	23.75 m (78 ft 0 in)
Length overall	40.53 m (132 ft 11½ in)
Height overall	10.67 m (35 ft 0 in)

WEIGHT (estimated):
Max T-O weight	83,900 kg (185,000 lb)

PERFORMANCE (estimated):
Max level speed at 12,200 m (40,000 ft)
Mach 1.4 (800 knots; 1,480 km/h; 920 mph)
Service ceiling   18,300 m (60,000 ft)
Max unrefuelled combat radius
1,565 nm (2,900 km; 1,800 miles)

TUPOLEV Tu-26 (Tu-22M)
NATO reporting name: Backfire

NATO first acknowledged the existence of a Soviet variable geometry medium bomber in the Autumn of 1969. A prototype was observed in July 1970, on the ground near the manufacturing plant at Kazan in western Russia, and was confirmed subsequently as a twin-engined design by the Tupolev Bureau. At least two prototypes were built, and

flight testing is believed to have started in 1971. Up to twelve pre-production models followed, for development testing, weapons trials and evaluation, by the beginning of 1973. Soviet delegates referred to the type as the **Tu-22M** during the SALT 2 treaty talks, but the current designation is believed to be **Tu-26**. The NATO reporting name allocated to the aircraft is 'Backfire'.

By 1987, three versions of the Tu-26/Tu-22M had been identified by NATO reporting names:

Backfire-A. Initial version. Slightly inclined lateral air intakes. Large landing gear fairing pods on the wing trailing-edges. Believed to have equipped only one squadron.

Backfire-B. Initial series production version, with increased wing span and landing gear fairing pods eliminated except for shallow underwing fairings, no longer protruding beyond the trailing-edge. Inward retracting main landing gear units. During the abortive SALT 2 treaty

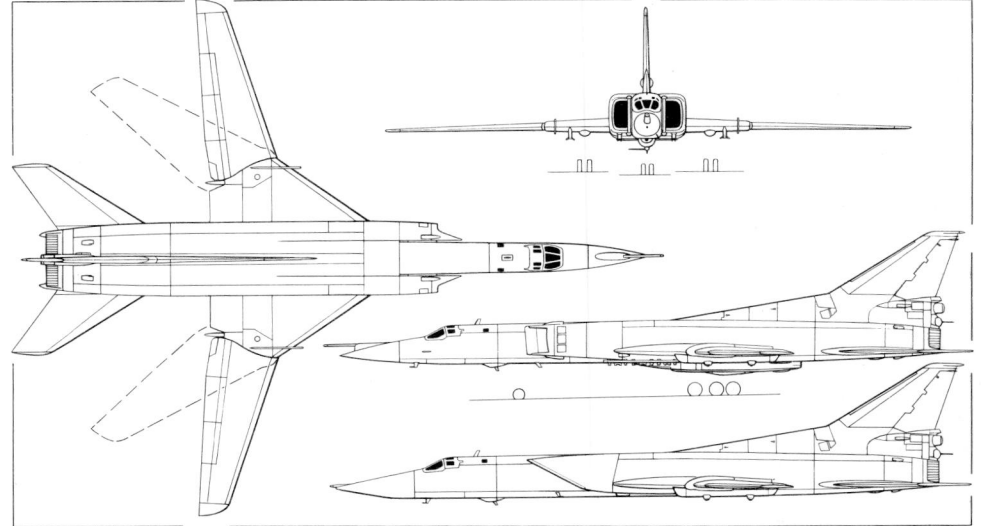

Tupolev Tu-26 (NATO 'Backfire-B') bomber and maritime reconnaissance/attack aircraft, with additional side view (bottom) of 'Backfire-C' *(Pilot Press)*

'Backfire-B' version of the Tupolev Tu-26 with wings spread, photographed from an interceptor of the Swedish Air Force
(via FLYGvapenNYTT)

negotiations, 'Backfire-Bs' were seen with the standard flight refuelling nose probe removed, although the housing remained. This was assumed to stress Soviet assertions that the aircraft are intended for peripheral/theatre operations rather than long-range strategic use, and were therefore exempt from the restrictions that would have been imposed on intercontinental bombers by the treaty. Initial armament was normally a single 'Kitchen' missile semi-recessed under fuselage. Current aircraft have a rack for a 'Kitchen' under each fixed wing centre-section panel, although fuselage mount is retained. External stores racks seen frequently under engine air intake trunks. Two GSh-23 twin-barrel 23 mm guns in tail mounting, initially beneath ogival radome, later with drum-shape radome of larger diameter.

Backfire-C. This advanced production version with wedge type engine air intakes, like those of the MiG-25, was first reported in the 1980-81 *Jane's*. The accompanying illustrations became available in 1987, by which time this version was operational in large numbers, in both long-range bomber and maritime roles, having entered service with the Black Sea Fleet air force in 1985. Upturned nosecone with small pod at tip. No visible flight refuelling probe. Single GSh-23 twin-barrel 23 mm gun, with barrels one above the other, in aerodynamically improved tail mounting, beneath large drum-shape radome.

'Backfire-B and C' are capable of performing nuclear strike, conventional attack, anti-ship and reconnaissance missions. Low-level penetration features make them more survivable than previous Soviet bombers, and they have adequate range to be employed against the contiguous United States on high-altitude subsonic missions, although such a flight profile would make them far more vulnerable. Their low altitude supersonic dash capability makes them formidable weapons with which to support military operations in Europe and Asia.

About 320 'Backfire-Bs and Cs' were in service in early 1988. Two-thirds of them oppose NATO in Europe and over the Atlantic, with the others in the far east of the Soviet Union. The latter are observed frequently over the Sea of Japan, and at least 30 of them are reportedly drawn from the 140 'Backfire-Bs and Cs' deployed in a maritime role by Soviet Naval Aviation.

It is expected that the 'Backfire' strategic/maritime force will be maintained eventually at a total of at least 400 aircraft. Production appears to be limited to the average rate of 30 aircraft a year that was specified by the unratified SALT 2 agreement. 'Backfires' have been used for development launches of new generation Soviet cruise missiles, but are not expected to become designated AS-15 carriers.

The following details refer specifically to 'Backfire-B':

TYPE: Twin-engined medium bomber and maritime recon-naissance/attack aircraft.

WINGS: Cantilever low mid-wing monoplane, made up of a large span fixed centre-section and two variable geometry outer panels. No anhedral or dihedral, but wing section is so thin that considerable flexing of the outer panels takes place in flight. Leading-edge fence towards tip of centre-section on each side. Each outer wing panel is fitted with a full span leading-edge slat, aileron, and three-section slotted trailing-edge flaps aft of spoilers/lift dumpers. Wing sweep is believed to be variable from fully spread (20°) to fully swept (65°).

FUSELAGE: Forward of wings, fuselage is basically circular with large ogival dielectric nosecone. Centre-fuselage is faired into rectangular section air intake trunks, each fitted with a large splitter plate and assumed to embody complex variable geometry ramps. No external area rule 'waisting' of these trunks.

TAIL UNIT: Cantilever structure, with sweepback on all surfaces. All-moving horizontal surfaces; conventional inset rudder.

LANDING GEAR: Retractable tricycle type. Each mainwheel bogie comprises three unequally spaced pairs of wheels in

Wedge type air intakes and missile racks under the fixed wing panels are features of 'Backfire-C'

tandem, which pivot inward from the vestigial fairing under the centre-section into the bottom of the fuselage.

POWER PLANT: Two turbofans with afterburners, mounted side by side in the rear fuselage. Reported to be uprated versions of the Kuznetsov NK-144 engines (each 196.1 kN; 44,090 lb st) that were developed for Tupolev's Tu-144 supersonic transport. Fuel tankage is believed to include integral tanks in the entire fixed portion of the wings and much of the centre-fuselage above the weapon bay. Removable flight refuelling nose probe; after one observed refuelling, a 'Backfire' prototype remained airborne for a further 10 h.

ACCOMMODATION: Pilot and co-pilot side by side on flight deck, under upward opening 'gull-wing' doors hinged on centreline. Two crew members further aft, as indicated by position of windows between flight deck and air intakes.

AVIONICS AND EQUIPMENT: Large bombing and navigation radar (NATO 'Down Beat') inside dielectric nosecone. Radar (NATO 'Bee Hind') for tail turret, above guns. Fairing with flat glazed front panel under front fuselage is believed to be for a video camera to provide visual assistance for weapon aiming.

ARMAMENT: Primary armament of two 'Kitchen' air-to-surface missiles, carried under the fixed centre-section panel of each wing, or a single 'Kitchen' semi-recessed in the underside of the centre-fuselage. Multiple racks for twelve 500 kg bombs sometimes fitted under air intake trunks. Alternative weapon loads include up to 12,000 kg (26,450 lb) of conventional bombs, carried internally. US reports have suggested that the Soviet Union is developing decoy missiles to assist penetration of advanced defence systems, in addition to very advanced ECM and ECCM. Two GSh-23 twin-barrel 23 mm guns, with barrels side by side horizontally, in radar directed tail mounting.

DIMENSIONS, EXTERNAL (estimated):

Wing span: fully spread	34.30 m (112 ft 6½ in)
fully swept	23.40 m (76 ft 9¼ in)
Length overall	39.60 m (129 ft 11 in)
Height overall	10.80 m (35 ft 5¼ in)

WEIGHTS:

Nominal weapon load	12,000 kg (26,450 lb)
Max T-O weight	130,000 kg (286,600 lb)

PERFORMANCE (estimated):

Max level speed at high altitude	Mach 2.0
Max level speed at low altitude	Mach 0.9
Max unrefuelled combat radius	
	2,160 nm (4,000 km; 2,485 miles)

NEW TUPOLEV BOMBER
NATO reporting name: Blackjack

First photographs of the Tupolev strategic bomber known to NATO as 'Blackjack' became available officially after US Defense Secretary Frank Carlucci was invited to inspect an example at Kubinka air base, near Moscow, on 2 August 1988. Earlier, it was known that eleven 'Blackjacks' had been completed by January 1988, and the first operational regiment was expected to form later that year at Dolon air base in the central USSR.

B-1B and 10 per cent longer than a B-52, with a higher supersonic speed than the B-1B and a similar combat radius. It is in no way a simple scale-up of 'Backfire'. Common features include low mounted variable geometry wings, and large vertical tail surfaces with a massive dorsal fin; but 'Blackjack's' horizontal tail surfaces are mounted higher, at the intersection of the dorsal fin and main fin. The fixed root panel of each wing seems to be long and very sharply swept. Sweepback on the outer panels is about 20° fully spread and 64° fully swept. The engine installation appears to resemble that of the now-retired Tu-144 supersonic airliner rather than 'Backfire'. Although the two bombers are designed for a similar subsonic cruise/high subsonic attack profile, it is unlikely that they are powered by similar engines. The housings on 'Blackjack' appear to be too small to accommodate engines related to the NK-144. Nor would 'Blackjack' need four engines of such high power.

The Soviet Union is expected to build a production series of at least 100 in a new complex added to the huge Kazan airframe plant, with deliveries reaching significant numbers by the end of this decade or the early 1990s. 'Blackjack's' primary weapons will be the AS-15 'Kent' air-launched cruise missile and the newer supersonic AS-X-19 missile, each with a range of 1,620 nm (3,000 km; 1,850 miles); but it will have provision for carrying bombs or a mix of ALCMs, short-range missiles and bombs, providing capability for both standoff and penetration missions.

DIMENSIONS, EXTERNAL (estimated):

Wing span: fully spread	55.70 m (182 ft 9 in)
fully swept	33.75 m (110 ft)
Length overall	54.00 m (177 ft)
Height overall	12.80 m (42 ft)

WEIGHTS (initial estimates):

Max weapon load	16,330 kg (36,000 lb)
Max T-O weight	250,000 kg (551,150 lb)

PERFORMANCE (estimated):

Max level speed at high altitude	Mach 2.0
Max unrefuelled combat radius	
	3,940 nm (7,300 km; 4,535 miles)

This head-on view shows clearly the new wedge intakes of 'Backfire-C'

TUPOLEV Tu-28P/Tu-128
NATO reporting name: Fiddler

Largest purpose-designed interceptor yet put into squadron service, this supersonic twin-jet aircraft was seen for the first time at Tushino in July 1961, with a large delta wing air-to-air missile (NATO 'Ash') mounted under each wing. It is thought to have the service designation Tu-28P (US Department of Defense has used Tu-128); its NATO reporting name is 'Fiddler'.

The Tu-28P carries a crew of two in tandem. It is powered by two afterburning turbojets, each estimated to have a max rating of about 120.1 kN (27,000 lb st). The first two aircraft seen in 1961 (**'Fiddler-A'**) were each fitted with two ventral fins. These were missing on the three Tu-28Ps (**'Fiddler-B'**) which flew past at Domodedovo in July 1967, as was the large bulged fairing fitted under the fuselage in 1961. 'Fiddler-B' proved to be the production configured version, with an armament double that seen in 1961, each aircraft being equipped to carry two 'Ash' missiles under each wing, one usually of the radar homing type and the other of the infra-red homing type.

Fewer than 80 'Fiddler-Bs' are thought to remain in service with the Soviet Union's Voyska PVO home defence fighter force, plus 20 with tactical air forces.

DIMENSIONS, EXTERNAL (estimated):
Wing span 18.10 m (59 ft 4½ in)
Length overall 27.20 m (89 ft 3 in)
WEIGHT (estimated):
Max T-O weight 45,000 kg (100,000 lb)
PERFORMANCE (estimated):
Max level speed at 11,000 m (36,000 ft) Mach 1.65
(950 knots; 1,760 km/h; 1,090 mph)
Service ceiling 20,000 m (65,620 ft)
Combat radius with max internal fuel
810 nm (1,500 km; 930 miles)

TUPOLEV Tu-154M
NATO reporting name: Careless

The basic three-engined **Tu-154**, announced in the Spring of 1966, was developed to replace the Tu-104, Il-18 and An-10 transport aircraft on Aeroflot's medium/long stage lengths of up to 3,240 nm (6,000 km; 3,725 miles). The first of six prototype and pre-production models flew for the first time on 4 October 1968. Regular passenger services began on 9 February 1972.

The Tu-154 was superseded in production successively by the **Tu-154A**, **Tu-154B** and **Tu-154B-2**, with uprated turbofans and many other refinements. Production of all four versions exceeded 600, of which more than 500 were delivered to Aeroflot and a total of 90 others to Balkan Bulgarian Airlines, Cubana, Malév and Tarom. Full descriptions of these aircraft can be found in the 1985-86 and previous editions of *Jane's*.

Following the development of the Tu-154B-2, the Tupolev Bureau decided that further improvement of the type would be impossible without more radical changes to the basic airframe and a switch to more modern engines. This led to development of the **Tu-154M**.

As the first step, a standard production Tu-154B-2 (SSSR-85317) was returned to the factory, where the original Kuznetsov NK-8-2U turbofans were removed. Soloviev D-30KU turbofans, as used on the Il-62M, were installed in their place, with the thrust rating of each engine (designated D-30KU-154-II in production form) reduced. The engine nacelles mounted on each side of the rear fuselage were developments of those fitted to the Il-62M, with the same type of clamshell thrust reverser on the engines they carried. To accommodate the centre engine, the TA-92 APU had to be transferred from its former position over the tail nozzle to the fuselage, and the air intake had to be enlarged. Flight testing began in 1982.

In its new configuration, as the prototype Tu-154M, SSSR-85317 had a redesigned tailplane; the slats were made smaller and the area of the spoilers was increased. The original three-crew flight deck and cabin layout for 169 passengers were retained, but the production Tu-154M offers alternative configurations for up to 180 economy class passengers. An executive version is available; and it is possible to remove all seats and utilise any version of the aircraft to carry light freight.

Production is centred in Kuybyshev, from where Aeroflot took delivery of its first two Tu-154Ms on 27 December 1984. Other customers include Balkan Bulgarian Airlines, CAAC of China, Cubana, LOT Polish Airlines (10) and Syrianair (4). CSA of Czechoslovakia has stated its intention to order seven. The Tu-154M is designed for a service life of 30,000 hours and 15,000 landings over a 15 year period.

TYPE: Three-turbofan medium-range transport aircraft.
WINGS: Cantilever low-wing monoplane. Sweepback 35° at quarter-chord. Anhedral on outer panels. Geometric twist along span. Conventional all-metal riveted three-spar structure, centre spar extending to just outboard of inner edge of aileron in each wing. Hydraulically actuated ailerons, double-slotted flaps and four-section spoilers forward of flaps on each wing. Electrically actuated slats on outer 80 per cent of each wing leading-edge. Tab in each aileron. Hot air anti-icing of wing leading-edge. Slats electrically heated.
FUSELAGE: Conventional all-metal semi-monocoque fail-safe structure of circular section. Single pressure cell,

Tupolev Tu-28P taking off, with underwing armament of two 'Ash' missiles

First photographs of the Tupolev strategic bomber known NATO as 'Blackjack'

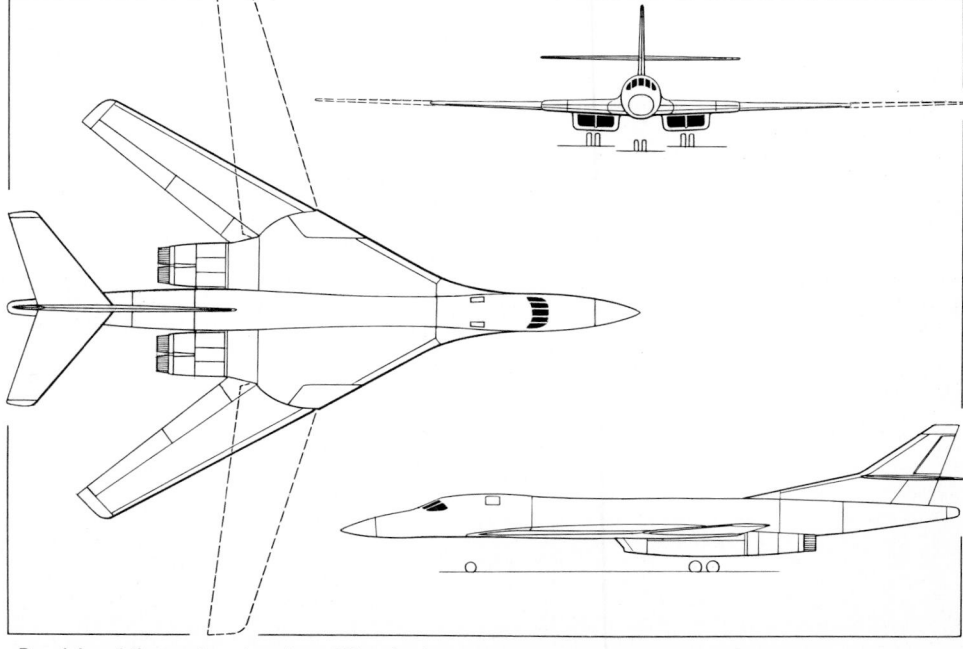
Provisional three-view drawing of Tupolev's new strategic bomber (NATO 'Blackjack') *(Pilot Press)*

Tupolev Tu-154M medium-range airliner (three Soloviev D-30KU-154-II turbofans) in service with CSA Czechoslovak Airlines *(Anton Wettstein)*

containing flight deck and two cabins separated by service compartments.

TAIL UNIT: Cantilever all-metal structure, with electrically actuated variable incidence T tailplane. Rudder and elevators of honeycomb sandwich construction. Sweepback of 40° at quarter-chord on horizontal surfaces, 45° on leading-edge of vertical surfaces. Control surfaces hydraulically actuated by irreversible servo controls. Tab in each elevator. Leading-edges of fin and tailplane and engine air intake anti-iced by hot air.

LANDING GEAR: Retractable tricycle type. Hydraulic actuation. Main units retract rearward into fairings on wing trailing-edge. Each consists of a bogie made up of three pairs of wheels in tandem. Rearward retracting anti-shimmy twin-wheel nose unit, steerable through ±63°. Disc brakes and anti-skid units on mainwheels.

POWER PLANT: Three Soloviev D-30KU-154-II turbofans, each rated at 103 kN (23,150 lb st), one in pod on each side of rear fuselage and one inside extreme rear of fuselage. Two lateral engines fitted with clamshell thrust reversers. Integral fuel tanks in wings: four tanks in centre-section and two in outer wings. For reasons of trim, all fuel is fed to a collector tank in the centre-section and thence to engines. Single-point refuelling. APU in rear fuselage.

ACCOMMODATION: Crew of three on flight deck, comprising two pilots and flight engineer, with provisions for navigator and five cabin staff. Alternative configurations for 180 economy class passengers, 164 tourist class with hot meal service, or 154 tourist/economy plus a separate first class cabin seating 8 to 24 persons. Mainly six-abreast seating with centre aisle. Washable non-flammable materials used for all interior furnishing. Fully enclosed luggage containers. Toilet, galley and wardrobe installations to customer's requirements. Executive and light cargo configurations available. Passenger doors are forward of the front cabin and between cabins on port side, with emergency and service doors opposite. All four doors open outward. Six emergency exits: two overwing and one immediately forward of engine nacelle on each side. Two pressurised baggage holds under floor of cabin, with two inward opening doors. Smaller unpressurised hold under rear of cabin.

SYSTEMS: Air-conditioning system pressure differential 0.58 bars (8.4 lb/sq in). Three independent hydraulic systems, working pressure 207 bars (3,000 lb/sq in), powered by engine driven pumps. Nos 2 and 3 systems each have additional electric backup pump. Systems actuate landing gear retraction and extension, nosewheel steering, and operation of ailerons, rudder, elevators, flaps and spoilers. Three-phase 200/115V 400Hz AC electrical system supplied by three 40kVA alternators. Additional 36V 400Hz AC and 27V DC systems and four storage batteries. Engine fire extinguishing system in each nacelle. Smoke detectors in baggage holds.

AVIONICS: Avionics meet ICAO standards for Cat II weather minima and include updated navigation system with triplex INS. Automatic flight control system operates throughout flight except during take-off to 400 m (1,312 ft) and landing from 30 m (100 ft). Automatic go-round and automatic speed control provided by autothrottle down to 10 m (33 ft) on landing. Weather radar, transponder, Doppler, dual HF and VHF com and emergency VHF, cockpit voice recorder and GPWS standard.

DIMENSIONS, EXTERNAL:

Wing span	37.55 m (123 ft 2½ in)
Length overall	47.90 m (157 ft 1¾ in)
Height overall	11.40 m (37 ft 4¾ in)
Diameter of fuselage	3.80 m (12 ft 5½ in)
Tailplane span	13.40 m (43 ft 11½ in)
Wheel track	11.50 m (37 ft 9 in)
Wheelbase	18.92 m (62 ft 1 in)
Passenger doors (each): Height	1.73 m (5 ft 7 in)

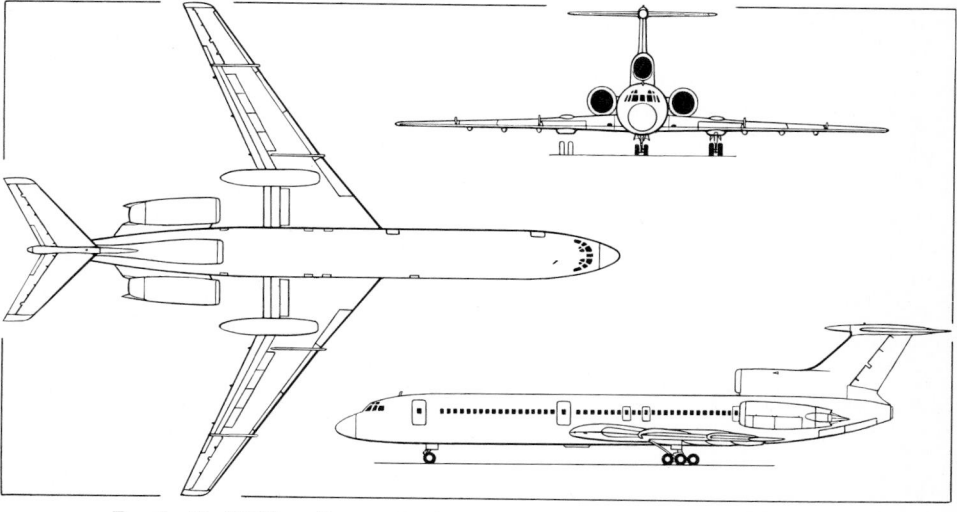

Tupolev Tu-154M medium-range three-turbofan transport aircraft *(Pilot Press)*

Width	0.80 m (2 ft 7½ in)
Height to sill	3.10 m (10 ft 2 in)
Servicing door: Height	1.28 m (4 ft 2½ in)
Width	0.61 m (2 ft 0 in)
Emergency door: Height	1.28 m (4 ft 2½ in)
Width	0.64 m (2 ft 1¼ in)
Emergency exits (each): Height	0.90 m (2 ft 11½ in)
Width	0.48 m (1 ft 7 in)
Main baggage hold doors (each):	
Height	1.20 m (3 ft 11¼ in)
Width	1.35 m (4 ft 5 in)
Height to sill	1.80 m (5 ft 11 in)
Rear (unpressurised) hold:	
Height	0.90 m (2 ft 11½ in)
Width	1.10 m (3 ft 7¼ in)
Height to sill	2.20 m (7 ft 2½ in)
DIMENSIONS, INTERNAL:	
Cabin: Width	3.58 m (11 ft 9 in)
Height	2.02 m (6 ft 7½ in)
Volume	163.2 m³ (5,763 cu ft)
Main baggage holds: front	21.5 m³ (759 cu ft)
rear	16.5 m³ (582 cu ft)
Rear underfloor hold	5.0 m³ (176 cu ft)
AREAS:	
Wings, gross	201.45 m² (2,169 sq ft)
Horizontal tail surfaces	42.20 m² (454.24 sq ft)
WEIGHTS:	
Basic operating weight empty	55,300 kg (121,915 lb)
Max payload	18,000 kg (39,680 lb)
Max fuel	39,750 kg (87,633 lb)
Max T-O weight	100,000 kg (220,460 lb)
Max landing weight	80,000 kg (176,370 lb)
PERFORMANCE:	
Max cruising speed	513 knots (950 km/h; 590 mph)
Max cruising height	11,900 m (39,000 ft)
Range:	
with max payload	2,019 nm (3,740 km; 2,324 miles)
with max fuel and 5,450 kg (12,015 lb) payload	
	3,563 nm (6,600 km; 4,100 miles)

TUPOLEV Tu-154C

This freight carrying version of the Tu-154 was announced in the Autumn of 1982. It is being offered primarily as a conversion of the Tu-154B, with an unobstructed cargo volume of 72 m³ (2,542 cu ft) in the main cabin. A freight door 2.80 m (9 ft 2¼ in) wide and 1.87 m (6 ft 1½ in) high is installed in the port side of the cabin, forward of the wing, with a ball mat inside and roller tracks the full length of the floor of the cabin. Typical loads include nine standard international pallets measuring 2.24 × 2.74 m (88 × 108 in), plus additional freight in the standard underfloor baggage holds which have a volume of 38 m³ (1,341 cu ft). Nominal range of the Tu-154C, with 20,000 kg (44,100 lb) of cargo, is 1,565 nm (2,900 km; 1,800 miles).

TUPOLEV Tu-155

The first flight of an aeroplane fuelled with liquid hydrogen was made by the Tu-155 (SSSR-85035) on 15 April 1988. As can be seen in an accompanying illustration, the Tu-155 is basically a Tu-154 three-turbofan transport that has been converted into a testbed for evaluating the viability of cryogenic fuels. The standard centre engine has been replaced by a Kuznetsov NK-88, probably based on the NK-8 turbofans fitted to early Tu-154A/Bs. A large tank to cater for the greatly increased fuel mass is installed

This photograph of the tail of the Tu-155 testbed shows external fuel ducting for the NK-88 centre engine *(Tass)*

in the rear of the cabin. Ducting visible on the starboard side of the rear fuselage is assumed to pipe the cryogenic fuel from this tank to the centre engine.

More than 30 special systems had to be developed to ensure safe storage and handling of the fuel. In particular, refrigeration and insulation systems were essential to maintain the fuel at extremely low temperature, calling for new materials and special vacuum-tight welding techniques.

In addition to liquid hydrogen, the NK-88 engine is designed to operate on liquefied natural gas, and flights using this alternative fuel were expected to be made later in 1988. The long-term advantage of liquid hydrogen is that it can, in theory, be produced in unlimited quantities from water, although current production costs are high. Also, it is claimed to offer major reductions in the harmful ecological effects of aircraft on the atmosphere.

TUPOLEV Tu-204

It was announced in 1983 that the Tupolev Bureau was developing a new medium-range transport aircraft, designated Tu-204, to replace the Tu-154. Preliminary details became available in Spring 1985. The prototype was scheduled to fly in Autumn 1988.

The Tu-204 will be a low-wing monoplane, with two Soloviev PS-90A (D-90A) turbofans of the type specified for the four-engined Il-96-300, pylon mounted in underwing pods. They will each be rated at 157 kN (35,300 lb st). The high aspect ratio wings will have a supercritical section; control will be fly by wire. The fuselage, of elliptical cross-section, will accommodate 170-214 passengers six-abreast. Two-crew operation will be permitted, but there will be provision for a flight engineer if required. New metals and composites will be used in the airframe; new generation equipment will include a dual EFIS with three colour CRT displays for each pilot, a triplex automatic approach and landing system permitting operation in ICAO Category III minima, and a head-up display. Noise levels will meet ICAO Chapter 3 Supplement 16 requirements.

The Tu-204 is being designed for a service life of 45,000 flight hours and 30,000 landings. It is planned to produce 80-90 production aircraft for Aeroflot during the period of the 1990-95 Soviet five-year plan. Other operators will include CSA of Czechoslovakia.

DIMENSIONS, EXTERNAL:
Wing span over winglets	42.00 m (137 ft 9½ in)
Length overall	45.00 m (147 ft 7¾ in)
Fuselage: Max depth	4.08 m (13 ft 4¾ in)
Max width	3.80 m (12 ft 5½ in)

DIMENSION, INTERNAL:
Cabin: Height	2.20 m (7 ft 2½ in)

WEIGHTS:
Weight empty	56,600 kg (124,780 lb)
Max payload	21,000-22,000 kg (46,300-48,500 lb)
Max T-O weight	93,500 kg (206,130 lb)

PERFORMANCE (estimated):
Max level speed	486 knots (900 km/h; 559 mph)

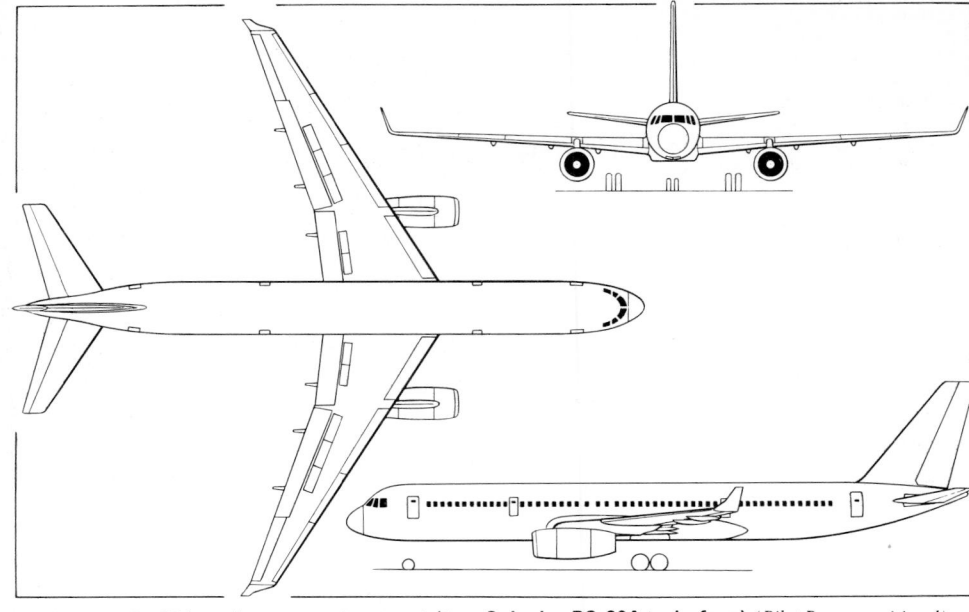

Tupolev Tu-204 medium-range transport (two Soloviev PS-90A turbofans) *(Pilot Press, provisional)*

Artist's impression of the twin-turbofan Tupolev Tu-204, under development to replace the Tu-154
(Jane's/Mike Keep)

Cruising speed at 11,000-12,000 m (36,100-39,375 ft)		
437-459 knots (810-850 km/h; 503-528 mph)		
Landing speed	135 knots (250 km/h; 155 mph)	
T-O balanced field length	2,500 m (8,200 ft)	
Range:		
with max payload	1,295 nm (2,400 km; 1,490 miles)	

with 17,500 kg (38,580 lb) payload
1,890 nm (3,500 km; 2,175 miles)
with 13,500 kg (29,760 lb) payload
2,480 nm (4,600 km; 2,855 miles)

YAKOVLEV

GENERAL DESIGNER IN CHARGE OF BUREAU:
Alexander Sergeivich Yakovlev

Alexander Yakovlev is one of the most versatile Soviet designers, and products of his design bureau have ranged from transonic long-range fighters to the Yak-24 tandem-rotor helicopter, an operational VTOL carrier based fighter and a variety of training and transport aircraft. Types in current production and service are described hereafter.

YAKOVLEV Yak-18T

The first prototype of this extensively redesigned cabin version of the Yak-18 trainer flew for the first time in Summer 1967. It was powered, like the Yak-18A and -18PM, with a 224 kW (300 hp) Ivchenko AI-14RF nine-cylinder radial engine, driving a two-blade variable-pitch propeller, but this was superseded by a more powerful M-14P radial engine when the Yak-18T was ordered into full production at Smolensk. Details of the development programme can be found in the 1982-83 and earlier editions of *Jane's*.

By 1974 it was possible to train the complete intake of 100 pupil pilots at Sasov flying school on the new aircraft. Now, as the standard basic trainer at Aeroflot schools, the Yak-18T is used for circuits, instrument training and navigation training, and as a flying classroom for an instructor and three pupils. Only one pupil accompanies the instructor on aerobatic flights.

Second version to enter service, as a successor to the Yak-12, was the Yak-18T ambulance, with accommodation for a stretcher patient on the starboard side of the cabin and a medical attendant behind the pilot. Other current versions include a light communications transport for four persons, in pairs; and a freighter with the three passenger seats removed to enable cargo to be carried beside and behind the pilot and in the baggage compartment.

Designer responsible for this variant of the Yak-18 was Mr Yuri Yankievich.

Yakovlev Yak-18T ambulance aircraft (Vedeneyev M-14P engine)

TYPE: Four-seat multi-purpose light aircraft.

WINGS: Cantilever low-wing monoplane, in three sections: a constant chord centre-section, integral with the fuselage, and two tapered outer panels. Wing section Clark YH, with thickness/chord ratio of 14.5% at root and 9.3% at tip. Dihedral on outer panels only. Two-spar light alloy construction. Light alloy covering on centre-section and on leading-edges of outer panels; inboard 25% of outer panels covered with light alloy, remainder with fabric. Slotted ailerons of light alloy construction, each hinged at three points and partly fabric covered. Light alloy split flap across entire span of centre-section, actuated by two pneumatic servo motors. Fixed step at port wingroot trailing-edge, with corrugated upper surface walkway to door on each side. Ailerons operated by pushrods. Ground adjustable tab on each aileron.

FUSELAGE: Conventional light alloy semi-monocoque structure, of basically square section. Skin on rear fuselage spot welded to frames and stringers.

TAIL UNIT: Braced light alloy structure, with wire bracing above tailplane and wire and strut bracing below. All surfaces fabric covered. Control surfaces operated by both pushrods and cables. Controllable trim tab in each elevator.

LANDING GEAR: Fully retractable tricycle type, with single wheel on each unit. Pneumatic retraction, nosewheel rearward, main units inward into centre-section. No mainwheel doors. Oleo-nitrogen shock absorbers. Castoring but non-steerable self-centring nosewheel with shimmy damper. Mainwheel tyres size 500 × 150; nosewheel tyre size 400 × 150. Differential pneumatic brakes on mainwheels, with override button on instructor's control wheel.

POWER PLANT: One 269 kW (360 hp) Vedeneyev M-14P nine-cylinder aircooled radial engine, driving a two-blade variable-pitch metal propeller, without spinner. Louvres in front of cowling to regulate cooling. Two-part cowling, split on horizontal centreline. Fuel tank in each wingroot, combined capacity 208 litres (55 US gallons; 45.75 Imp gallons).

ACCOMMODATION: Car type cabin, seating four persons in pairs. Large forward hinged door on each side, jettisonable in emergency. Provision for upholstered or parachute type front seats. Rear bench seat removable for freight carrying. Ambulance configuration available, for pilot, stretcher patient and medical attendant. Large baggage compartment aft of rear seat, with external access on port side. Stretcher of ambulance version is loaded via baggage door. Cabin furnishings of non-inflammable synthetic materials. Dual control wheels. Glareshield above panel. Heating and ventilation standard.

SYSTEMS: Pneumatic system for actuating landing gear and flaps. Electrical system includes instrument panel red lighting, navigation and landing lights, and anti-collision beacon at top of fin.

AVIONICS AND EQUIPMENT: Standard equipment includes UHF radio, intercom, radio compass, radio altimeter and flight recorder.

DIMENSIONS, EXTERNAL:
Wing span	11.16 m (36 ft 7¼ in)
Length overall	8.35 m (27 ft 4¾ in)

AREA:
Wings, gross	18.75 m² (201.8 sq ft)

WEIGHTS AND LOADINGS (A, with instructor and one pupil; B, with instructor and three pupils):
Max payload: A	306 kg (675 lb)
B	436 kg (960 lb)
Max T-O weight: A	1,500 kg (3,307 lb)
B	1,650 kg (3,637 lb)
Max wing loading: A	80 kg/m² (16.4 lb/sq ft)
B	88 kg/m² (18.0 lb/sq ft)
Max power loading: A	5.59 kg/kW (11.0 lb/hp)
B	6.15 kg/kW (12.1 lb/hp)

PERFORMANCE (at max T-O weight: A, with instructor and one pupil; B, with instructor and three pupils):
Max level speed:	
A, B	159 knots (295 km/h; 183 mph)
Max cruising speed: B	135 knots (250 km/h; 155 mph)
Max rate of climb at S/L: B	300 m (985 ft)/min
Service ceiling: A, B	5,500 m (18,000 ft)
T-O run: A	330 m (1,085 ft)
B	400 m (1,315 ft)
Landing run: A	400 m (1,315 ft)
B	500 m (1,640 ft)
Range with max fuel, with reserves:	
A	350 nm (650 km; 403 miles)
B	485 nm (900 km; 560 miles)

YAKOVLEV Yak-28
NATO reporting names: Brewer, Firebar and Maestro

First seen in considerable numbers in the 1961 Soviet Aviation Day flypast were three successors to the Yak-25/27 series (see 1971-72 *Jane's*), described by the

Version of the Yak-28 known to NATO as 'Brewer-D' *(Flug Revue)*

commentator as supersonic multi-purpose aircraft and identified subsequently by the designation Yak-28. Brief details of the two-seat tactical attack versions known to NATO as 'Brewer-A, B and C' can be found in earlier editions of *Jane's*. Versions still operational are as follows:

Brewer-D. Reconnaissance version, with cameras or other sensors, including side looking airborne radar, in bomb bay. Two-seater, with pilot under blister canopy and navigator in glazed nose. Blister radome under fuselage forward of wings.

Brewer-E. First Soviet operational ECM escort aircraft, deployed in 1970. Active ECM pack built into bomb bay, from which it projects in cylindrical form. No radome under front fuselage, but many additional antennae and fairings. Attachment under each outer wing, outboard of external fuel tank, for a rocket pod, chaff dispenser or anti-radiation missile.

US official sources estimate that about 195 Brewer-Ds and Es remain in service for tactical reconnaissance and ECM, and 102 for strategic reconnaissance and ECM.

Firebar. Tandem two-seat all-weather fighter. No internal weapons bay. Armament comprises one 'Anab' air-to-air missile under each wing. Identified as **Yak-28P** (Perekhvatchik; interceptor), the suffix 'P' indicating that the design had been *adapted* for the fighter role. Longer dielectric nosecone fitted retrospectively on many Yak-28Ps in squadron service does not indicate any increase in radar capability or aircraft performance. About 65 Yak-28P 'Firebars' continue to operate with the Soviet Voyska PVO home defence interceptor force and 20 with the tactical forces.

Maestro (Yak-28U). Trainer version of 'Firebar'. Normal cockpit layout replaced by two individual single-seat cockpits in tandem, each with its own canopy. Front canopy sideways hinged to starboard; rear canopy rearward sliding.

The airframe of the Yak-28 has been described in previous editions of *Jane's*. The following details apply specifically to the Yak-28P:

POWER PLANT: Two afterburning turbojets, related to Tumansky R-11 fitted to some versions of MiG-21, with rating of 58.35 kN (13,120 lb st). A pointed external fuel tank can be carried under the leading-edge of each wing, outboard of the engine nacelle.

ACCOMMODATION: Crew of two in tandem on ejection seats in pressurised cabin under long rearward sliding transparent blister canopy.

ARMAMENT: Two pylons under each outer wing. Normal armament comprises two air-to-air missiles (NATO 'Anab'), with alternative infra-red or semi-active radar homing heads.

DIMENSIONS, EXTERNAL (estimated):
Wing span	12.95 m (42 ft 6 in)
Length overall: Yak-28P (long nose)	
	23.00 m (75 ft 5½ in)
Height overall	3.95 m (12 ft 11½ in)

WEIGHT (estimated):
Max T-O weight: Yak-28P	20,000 kg (44,000 lb)

PERFORMANCE (Yak-28P, estimated):
Max level speed at 10,670 m (35,000 ft)	
	Mach 1.88 (1,080 knots; 2,000 km/h; 1,240 mph)
Cruising speed	496 knots (920 km/h; 571 mph)
Service ceiling	16,750 m (55,000 ft)
Max combat radius	500 nm (925 km; 575 miles)

YAKOVLEV Yak-36MP/Yak-38
NATO reporting name: Forger

Known originally as the **Yak-36MP** (*Morskoy Palubnyi*: maritime carrier-borne), the **Yak-38** is the V/STOL combat aircraft deployed by a Soviet Navy development squadron on the *Kiev*, the first of its class of four 40,000 ton carrier/cruisers to put to sea in 1976, and subsequently on its sister ships, the *Minsk, Novorossiysk* and *Baku*. Experimental operation from specially configured Ro/Ro ships has also been reported. The Yak-38 remains the only operational jet combat aircraft that shares the V/STOL capability of the Harrier, but requires three engines, rather than one, to make this possible. Two versions have been observed, as follows:

Forger-A. Basic single-seat combat aircraft, utilising a mixture of vectored thrust and direct jet lift. Prototype was completed in 1971 and production began in 1975. Twelve appear to be operational on each ship, in addition to 'Forger-Bs' and about 19 Kamov Ka-25 or Ka-27 anti-submarine and missile targeting helicopters. Primary operational roles assumed to be reconnaissance, strikes against small ships, and fleet defence against shadowing maritime reconnaissance aircraft.

Forger-B. Two-seat trainer, of which two are deployed on each carrier/cruiser. Second cockpit forward of normal cockpit, with ejection seat at a lower level, under a continuous transparent canopy. To compensate for the longer nose, a 'plug' is inserted in the fuselage aft of the wing, lengthening the constant-section portion without requiring modification of the tapering rear fuselage assembly. In other respects this version appears to be identical to 'Forger-A', but has no ranging radar or weapon pylons.

Observers of deck flying by 'Forger-As' report that the aircraft appear to be extremely stable during take-off and landing. Initially, take-off was always made vertically, with the vectored thrust nozzles up to 10° forward of vertical. This was followed by a smooth conversion about 5 to 6 m (15-20 ft) above the deck, achieved by lowering the aircraft's nose about 5° below the horizon and maintaining this attitude until the aircraft had accelerated to 30-40 knots (55-75 km/h; 35-46 mph). At this speed, a 5° nose-up

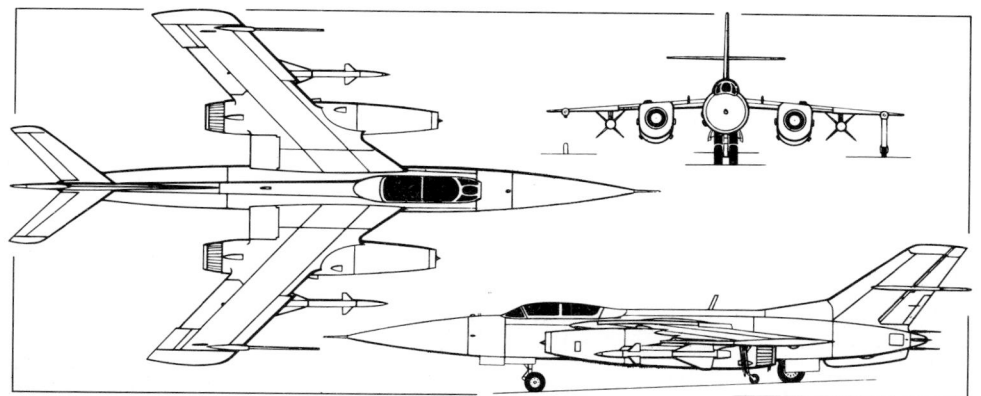

The long-nose version of the Yakovlev Yak-28P two-seat all-weather fighter ('Firebar') *(Pilot Press)*

Yak-28P ('Firebar') fitted with original short radome and carrying two 'Anab' missiles *(Flug Revue)*

Yakovlev Yak-38 (NATO 'Forger-A') V/STOL combat aircraft on the carrier/cruiser *Novorossiysk.* **Note the underwing gun and rocket pods** (*Royal Navy*)

The two-seat training version of the Yak-38 ('Forger-B')

attitude was assumed, and the accelerating transition was continued by vectoring aft the nozzles of the propulsion engine.

This VTO technique has been superseded by a STOL type of take-off, with a short forward run, made possible by an automatic control system which ensures "that the lift engines are brought into use, and the thrust vectoring rear nozzles rotated, at the optimum point in the take-off run". STOL take-off can be assumed to offer improved payload/range capability.

Landing procedure begins with a gradual descent from far astern, with the last 400 m (1,300 ft) flown essentially level, about 30 m (100 ft) above the water. The aircraft crosses the ship's stern with about a 5 knot (10 km/h; 6 mph) closure rate, 10-14 m (35-45 ft) above the flight deck, then flares gently to a hover and descends vertically. Precise landings are ensured by the automatic control system, perhaps in association with laser devices lining each side of the rear deck.

Development has been continuous throughout the period since the Yak-38 was first seen on the *Kiev*. Some early 'Forger-As' lacked the now standard auxiliary intake doors aft of each engine air intake. A fence has been added on each side of the hinged door above the liftjets, extending back to a station in line with the wingroot leading-edge, presumably to prevent ingestion of reflected exhaust efflux. Production is thought to have totalled some 75 aircraft by October 1986; the rate is said to have been reduced drastically since then.

The following description applies to the single-seat 'Forger-A':

TYPE: Ship based V/STOL combat aircraft.

WINGS: Cantilever mid-wing monoplane, of very small area. Thickness/chord ratio estimated at 6% or less. Constant anhedral from roots. Sweepback on leading-edge approx 45°. Conventional light alloy structure. Each wing comprises two all-metal panels of approx equal span, of which the outer panel folds vertically upward for stowage on board ship. Inboard panel has unswept trailing-edge, occupied by a large single-slotted Fowler flap. Outer panel has a slightly sweptback trailing-edge, occupied almost entirely by an aileron with setback hinges and inset trim tab. No leading-edge flaps or slats. Jet reaction control valve with upper and lower slots in each wingtip.

FUSELAGE: Conventional semi-monocoque light alloy structure of oval cross-section. Integral engine air intake ducts, with boundary layer splitter plates and downward inclined lips forward of rear edge of transparent cockpit canopy. Row of small blow-in auxiliary intake doors a short distance aft of each intake. Rearward hinged door over liftjets, immediately aft of canopy, with 16 spring loaded louvres. Location of corresponding side-hinged underfuselage doors conforms with forward tilt of lift engines. Positions of these doors are controlled automatically during take-off and landing as part of control system. Fence on each side of door above liftjets. Small fence aft of each door beneath liftjets. Yaw reaction control nozzle to each side of small tailcone. No reaction control system in nose.

TAIL UNIT: Conventional light alloy structure, with sweepback on all surfaces and considerable tailplane anhedral. Rudder and each elevator have setback hinges and trim tab. Air intake at front of long duct extending forward from base of fin, to cool avionics bay in rear fuselage.

LANDING GEAR: Retractable tricycle type. Single wheel on each unit, with legs of trailing link type with oleo-pneumatic shock absorption. Nose unit retracts

rearward, main units forward into fuselage. Small bumper under upward curving rear fuselage.

POWER PLANT: Primary power plant is a Lyulka AL-21 turbojet (approx 80 kN; 17,985 lb st), mounted in the centre-fuselage and exhausting through a single pair of vectoring side nozzles aft of the wings. No afterburner is fitted. Two Koliesov liftjets (each 35 kN; 7,875 lb st) in tandem immediately aft of cockpit, inclined forward at 13° from vertical, exhausting downward, and used also to adjust pitch and trim. Fuel tanks in fuselage, forward and aft of main engine. Drop tanks, each estimated to have capacity of 600 litres (158 US gallons; 132 Imp gallons), can be carried on underwing pylons.

ACCOMMODATION: Pilot only, on zero-speed/zero-height ejection seat, under sideways hinged (to starboard) transparent canopy. Electronic system ejects pilot automatically if aircraft height and descent rate are sensed to indicate an emergency. Armoured glass windscreen.

AVIONICS: Ranging radar in nose. IFF (NATO 'Odd Rods') antennae forward of windscreen. Other avionics in rear fuselage. Fully automatic control system for use during take-off and landing, to ensure synchronisation of engine functioning, aerodynamic control operation, jet reaction nozzle operation, stabilisation and guidance.

ARMAMENT: No installed armament. Two pylons under fixed panel of each wing for 2,600-3,600 kg (5,730-7,935 lb) of external stores, including gun pods each containing a 23 mm twin-barrel GSh-23 cannon, rocket packs, bombs weighing up to 500 kg each, short-range air-to-surface missiles (NATO 'Kerry'), armour-piercing anti-ship missiles, air-to-air missiles ('Aphid') and auxiliary fuel tanks.

DIMENSIONS, EXTERNAL (estimated):

Wing span	7.32 m (24 ft 0 in)
Width, wings folded	4.88 m (16 ft 0 in)
Length overall: 'Forger-A'	15.50 m (50 ft 10¼ in)
'Forger-B'	17.68 m (58 ft 0 in)
Height overall	4.37 m (14 ft 4 in)
Tailplane span	3.81 m (12 ft 6 in)
Wheel track	2.90 m (9 ft 6 in)
Wheelbase	5.50 m (18 ft 0 in)

AREA (estimated):

Wings, gross	18.5 m² (199 sq ft)

WEIGHTS (estimated):

Basic operating weight, incl pilot(s):	
'Forger-A'	7,485 kg (16,500 lb)
'Forger-B'	8,390 kg (18,500 lb)
Max T-O weight	11,700 kg (25,795 lb)

PERFORMANCE ('Forger-A', estimated, at max T-O weight):

Max level speed at height	
	Mach 0.95 (545 knots; 1,009 km/h; 627 mph)
Max level speed at S/L	
	Mach 0.8 (528 knots; 978 km/h; 608 mph)
Max rate of climb at S/L	4,500 m (14,750 ft)/min
Service ceiling	12,000 m (39,375 ft)
Combat radius:	
with air-to-air missiles and external tanks, 75 min on station	100 nm (185 km; 115 miles)
with max weapons, lo-lo-lo	130 nm (240 km; 150 miles)
with max weapons, hi-lo-hi	200 nm (370 km; 230 miles)

YAKOVLEV Yak-41

First reference to this second-generation V/STOL fighter/attack aircraft was made by Rear Adm William O. Studeman, US director of naval intelligence, in Spring 1988. It is assumed to be an evolutionary development of the Yak-38, almost certainly with a similar liftjet/vectored thrust multi-engine power plant, although the possibility of a single vectored-thrust turbofan, designed under the leadership of Eng Khatchaturov, on the lines of the Rolls-Royce Pegasus, has been suggested. Other features probably include the now conventional twin-fin configuration, a nose radar installation, and supersonic capability. It is likely to be compatible with the ski-jump launch ramp reportedly embodied at the bow of the large Soviet Navy carrier currently fitting out at Nikolayev.

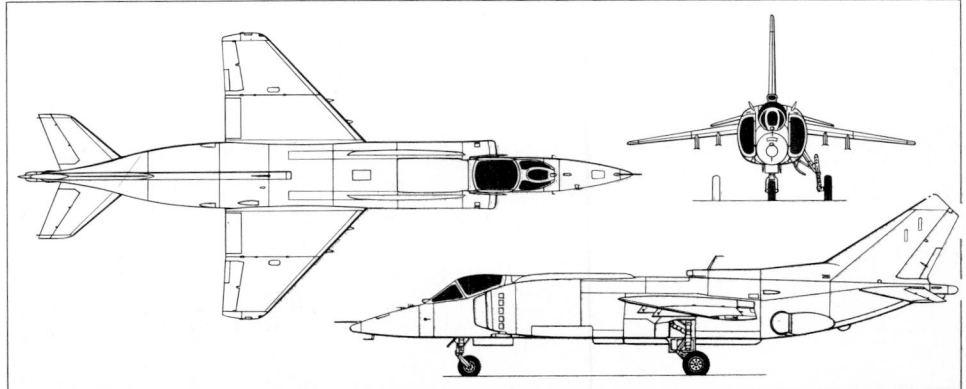

Yakovlev Yak-38 single-seat V/STOL carrier based combat aircraft (NATO 'Forger-A') (*Pilot Press*)

YAKOVLEV Yak-42
NATO reporting name: Clobber

On the basis of experience with the Yak-40, the Yakovlev Design Bureau developed for Aeroflot this larger civil airliner with a similar three-engined layout. According to Alexander Yakovlev, the basic design objectives were simple construction, reliability in operation, economy, and the ability to operate in remote areas with widely differing climatic conditions. Up to 2,000 aircraft in this category are needed, for use particularly on feederline services extending north and south from the main east-west trans-Siberian trunk routes.

Three prototypes of the Yak-42 were ordered initially. The first of these (SSSR-1974) flew for the first time on 7 March 1975, with a wing sweepback of 11°, and was furnished as a 100-passenger local service version with carry-on baggage and coat stowage fore and aft of the cabin. The second prototype (SSSR-1975) had 23° of wing sweep, and cabin windows which extended further forward and rearward on each side, indicating that it was representative of the 120-seat version with three more rows of seats and no carry-on baggage areas. The third prototype (SSSR-1976; re-registered subsequently as SSSR-42303) differed from the second only in detail, having hot air de-icing on the tail surfaces as well as the wings; fairing discs over the mainwheels and longer leg fairings to improve airflow over the doorless main landing gear when retracted; and movement further forward of the overwing emergency exits.

It was made known that a decision on the degree of wing sweep to be standardised for production aircraft would be taken after simultaneous evaluation of the prototypes, in terms of high speed cruise, economy and low speed handling characteristics. The 23° wing showed itself superior, and aircraft No. SSSR-42303, exhibited at the 1977 Paris Salon, was generally typical of the first series of 200 production Yak-42s, which are being built at Smolensk to replace Tu-134s currently in Aeroflot service. Further changes introduced on production aircraft include the use of four-wheel main landing gear bogies instead of the twin-wheel units fitted to the prototypes.

The Yak-42 entered scheduled passenger service with Aeroflot in late 1980, operating first over the Moscow-Krasnodar route. Ten aircraft had been flown by mid-1981, and it was hoped to complete 20 more by the end of the year. A first export order, for seven, had been placed by Aviogenex of Yugoslavia.

An accident in 1982 is reported to have led to withdrawal of the Yak-42 from Aeroflot service until October 1984. It then began to re-enter service, starting with the Saratov-Leningrad and Moscow-Bykovo routes.

On 29 January 1981, a Yak-42 piloted by Valentin Mukhin set a record in FAI Class C1m (T-O weight 45,000-55,000 kg) by lifting a load of 20,186 kg (44,502 lb) to a height of 2,000 m (6,562 ft). In subsequent flights, the aircraft climbed to 3,000 m in 2 min 37.3 s, 6,000 m in 5 min 11.4 s, and 9,000 m in 9 min 31.1 s to claim Class C11 (35,000-45,000 kg) records; and to 3,000 m in 3 min 5.9 s, 6,000 m in 6 min 26.9 s, and 9,000 m in 11 min 48.2 s to claim Class C1m records. On 14-15 December 1981, a Yak-42 with Valentin Mukhin as pilot in command set a Class C1m straight line distance record of 3,317.94 nm (6,144.82 km; 3,818.21 miles) between Sheremetievo (Moscow) and Khabarovsk.

The Yak-42 is intended to use all three engines at cruise power during flight. It can, however, continue take-off after the failure of any one engine, and can maintain level cruising flight on a single engine.

Design is in accordance with the latest airworthiness standards of the Soviet civil authorities and US FAR 25 requirements. Special care has been taken during design to ensure that the D-36 engines conform with national and international limits on smoke and noise; and the Yak-42 is intended to operate in temperatures ranging from −50°C to +50°C. An APU is standard, for engine starting and ground services, making the aircraft independent of airport equipment. Airframe design life is 30,000 flying hours or 30,000 landings in 15 years. Engine life is 18,000 operating hours with two major overhauls.

The following details refer to the Yak-42 in its current production form, as exhibited at the 1985 Paris Air Show. Wing span is increased by 48 cm (1 ft 7 in) and max T-O weight by 500 kg (1,102 lb) by comparison with early aircraft.

TYPE: Three-turbofan short/medium-range passenger transport.

WINGS: Cantilever low-wing monoplane, consisting of a centre-section and two outer panels. No dihedral or anhedral. Sweepback 23° at quarter-chord. All-metal two-spar torsion box structure. Two-section aileron on each wing, with servo tab on inner section and trim tab on outer section. Two-section single-slotted trailing-edge flaps on each wing. Three-section spoilers forward of outer flaps. Full span leading-edge flaps. Ailerons and flaps actuated hydraulically.

FUSELAGE: All-metal riveted, bonded and welded semi-monocoque structure, of basic circular section, blending into an oval section rear fuselage.

TAIL UNIT: Cantilever all-metal T tail structure, with sweepback on all surfaces. One-piece tailplane; incidence variable from 4° upward to 8° downward. Trim tab in each elevator. Trim tab and spring servo tab in rudder. Control surfaces actuated hydraulically.

LANDING GEAR: Hydraulically retractable tricycle heavy-duty type. Four-wheel bogie main units retract inward into flattened fuselage undersurface. Twin nosewheels retract forward. Hydraulic backup system for extension only. Emergency extension by gravity. Oleo-nitrogen shock absorbers. Steerable nose unit of levered suspension type. Low pressure tyres; size 930 × 305 on nosewheels. Hydraulic disc brakes on mainwheels. Nosewheel brakes to stop wheel rotation after take-off.

POWER PLANT: Three Lotarev D-36 three-shaft turbofans, each rated at 63.74 kN (14,330 lb st). Centre engine, mounted inside rear fuselage, has S-duct air intake. Outboard engines are mounted in pod on each side of rear fuselage. No thrust reversers. Integral fuel tanks between spars in wings, capacity approx 23,175 litres (6,120 US gallons; 5,100 Imp gallons). APU standard, for engine starting, and for power and air-conditioning supply on ground and, if necessary, in flight.

ACCOMMODATION: Crew of two side by side on flight deck, with provision for flight engineer if required, and two or three cabin attendants. Single passenger cabin, with total of 120 seats in six-abreast rows, at pitch of 75 cm (29.5 in), with centre aisle, 45 cm (17.7 in) wide, in high-density configuration. Alternative 104-passenger (96 tourist, 8 first class) local service configuration, with carry-on baggage and coat stowage compartments fore and aft of cabin. Main airstair door hinges down from undersurface of rear fuselage. Second door forward of cabin on port side, with integral airstairs. Service door opposite. Galley and crew coat stowage between flight deck and front vestibule. Passenger coat stowage and toilet between vestibule and cabin. Second coat stowage and toilet at rear of cabin. Two underfloor holds for cargo, mail and baggage in nets or standard containers, loaded through a door on the starboard side, forward of wing. Chain-drive handling system for containers built into cabin floor. Forward hold accommodates six containers, each with capacity of 2.2 m³ (77.7 cu ft); rear hold takes three similar containers. Provision for convertible passenger/cargo interior, with enlarged loading door on port side of front fuselage. Two emergency exits overwing on each side. All passenger and crew accommodation pressurised and air-conditioned, and furnished with non-inflammable materials.

AVIONICS AND EQUIPMENT: Flight and navigation equipment for operation by day and night under adverse weather conditions, with landings on concrete or unpaved runways in ICAO Category II weather minima down to 40 m (131 ft) visibility at 300 m (985 ft). Type SAU-42 automatic flight control system and area navigation system standard.

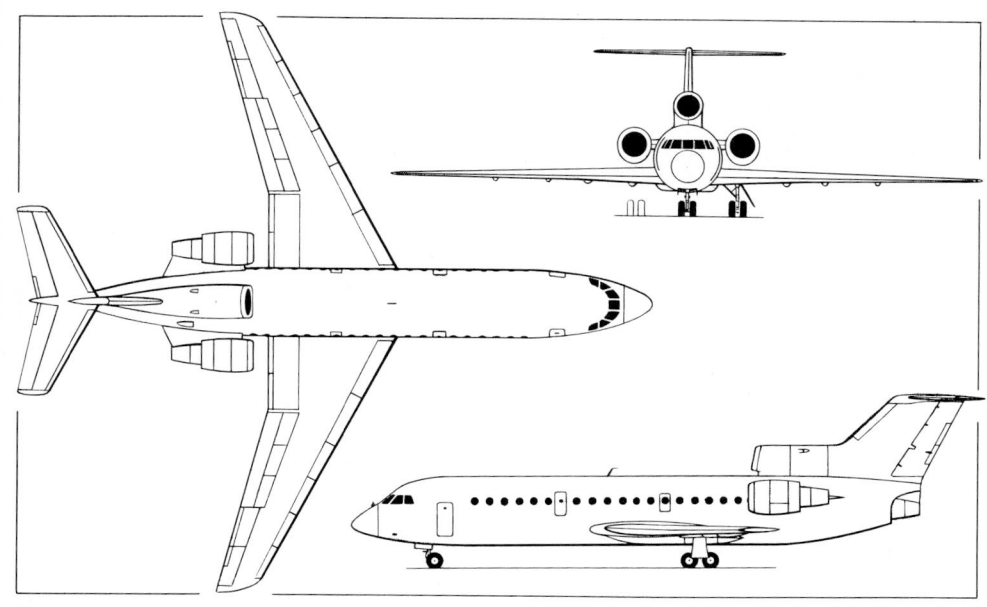

Yakovlev Yak-42 three-turbofan short/medium-range passenger transport *(Pilot Press)*

Yakovlev Yak-42 short/medium-range transport (three Lotarev D-36 turbofans) *(Brian M. Service)*

DIMENSIONS, EXTERNAL:

Wing span	34.88 m (114 ft 5¼ in)
Wing aspect ratio	8.11
Length overall	36.38 m (119 ft 4¼ in)
Fuselage diameter	3.80 m (12 ft 5½ in)
Height overall	9.83 m (32 ft 3 in)
Tailplane span	10.80 m (35 ft 5 in)
Wheel track	5.63 m (18 ft 5¾ in)
Wheelbase	14.78 m (48 ft 6 in)
Passenger door (fwd):	
Height	1.81 m (5 ft 11¼ in)
Width	0.83 m (2 ft 8½ in)
Passenger entrance (rear): Height	1.78 m (5 ft 10 in)
Width	0.81 m (2 ft 7¾ in)
Cargo door (convertible version):	
Height	2.025 m (6 ft 7¾ in)
Width	3.23 m (10 ft 7 in)
Baggage/cargo hold door: Height	1.35 m (4 ft 5 in)
Width	1.145 m (3 ft 9 in)
Height to sill	1.45 m (4 ft 9 in)

DIMENSIONS, INTERNAL:

Cabin: Length	19.89 m (65 ft 3 in)
Max width	3.60 m (11 ft 9¾ in)
Max height	2.08 m (6 ft 9¾ in)
Forward baggage compartment volume (100-seater)	
	19.8 m³ (700 cu ft)
Rear baggage compartment volume (100-seater)	
	9.5 m³ (335 cu ft)

AREAS:

Wings, gross	150 m² (1,615 sq ft)
Horizontal tail surfaces (total)	27.60 m² (297.1 sq ft)
Vertical tail surfaces (total)	23.29 m² (250.7 sq ft)

WEIGHTS:

Weight empty, equipped:	
104 seats	34,555 kg (76,180 lb)
120 seats	34,580 kg (76,236 lb)
Max payload	12,800 kg (28,220 lb)
Max fuel	18,500 kg (40,785 lb)
Max T-O weight	56,500 kg (124,560 lb)
Max landing weight	50,500 kg (111,333 lb)

PERFORMANCE:

Max cruising speed at 7,620 m (25,000 ft)	
	437 knots (810 km/h; 503 mph)
Econ cruising speed	400 knots (740 km/h; 460 mph)
T-O speed	119 knots (220 km/h; 137 mph) IAS
Approach speed	114 knots (210 km/h; 131 mph) IAS
Max cruising height	9,600 m (31,500 ft)
T-O balanced field length	2,200 m (7,220 ft)
Landing from 15 m (50 ft)	1,100 m (3,610 ft)
Range at econ cruising speed, with 3,000 kg (6,615 lb) fuel reserves:	
with max payload	702 nm (1,300 km; 807 miles)
with 120 passengers (10,800 kg; 23,810 lb payload)	
	1,025 nm (1,900 km; 1,180 miles)
with 104 passengers (9,360 kg; 20,635 lb payload)	
	1,240 nm (2,300 km; 1,430 miles)
with max fuel	2,105 nm (3,900 km; 2,423 miles)

YAKOVLEV Yak-42M

This stretched version of the Yak-42 was scheduled to enter service with Aeroflot in 1987. The fuselage is lengthened by 4.50 m (14 ft 9 in), to accommodate 156 to 168 passengers. The original D-36 engines are replaced by three Lotarev D-436 turbofans, each rated at 73.6 kN (16,550 lb st). Navigation equipment is also upgraded.

WEIGHT:

Max T-O weight	66,000 kg (145,505 lb)

PERFORMANCE (estimated):

Balanced T-O field length:	
at 62,000 kg (136,685 lb) AUW	1,800 m (5,900 ft)
at max T-O weight	2,300 m (7,550 ft)
Range:	
with 16,000 kg (35,275 lb) payload	
	1,350 nm (2,500 km; 1,550 miles)
with 10,000 kg (22,050 lb) payload	
	2,025 nm (3,750 km; 2,330 miles)
Range with max fuel, with reserves	
	2,160 nm (4,000 km; 2,485 miles)

YAKOVLEV Yak-50

First reference to this aircraft came in a Novosti Press Agency bulletin on 30 June 1975, which stated that tests of a

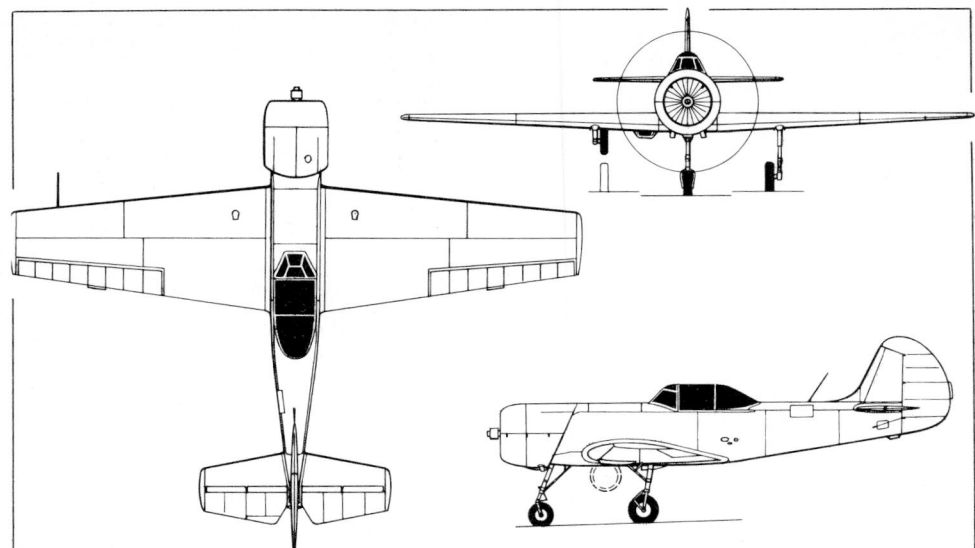

Yakovlev Yak-53 (Vedeneyev M-14P radial engine) *(Pilot Press)*

new Yakovlev sporting aircraft, designated Yak-50, had been carried out near Arsenyev in the Soviet Far East. Mr Nikolai Sazykin, director of the Progress Engineering Works in which all Yakovlev sporting aircraft are assembled, was quoted as saying that the Yak-50 was intended to participate in the 1976 world aerobatic championships. Test pilot Anatoly Sergeyev stated only that it was more advanced than the familiar Yak-18 training and aerobatic monoplane, with a more powerful engine, better manoeuvrability, a speed of over 215 knots (400 km/h; 248 mph) in a dive, and the ability to perform all aerobatics with its landing gear retracted or extended.

When six Yak-50s participated in the 1976 world aerobatic championships at Kiev, their evolution from the Yak-18 was apparent, but with significant changes. Basic configuration is little different from that of the single-seat Yak-18PS, with tailwheel type landing gear. This was deliberate, to keep the handling characteristics of the two types as similar as possible. However, overall dimensions are reduced; control surface hinge lines have been moved to keep control forces light; and overall structural strength has been increased by switching entirely to metal covering. In particular, the fuselage is now semi-monocoque instead of steel tube with fabric covering to the rear of the cockpit. Designers responsible for these and other changes were Sergei Yakovlev (son of Alexander Yakovlev) and Yuri Yankievich.

The wings dispense with the Yak-18's centre-section, have 2° dihedral and 2° incidence, and retain an asymmetric section. To ensure a high power/weight ratio in a relatively large aerobatic aircraft, the power plant is a 268 kW (360 hp) Vedeneyev (Ivchenko) M-14P aircooled radial piston engine, driving a V-530TA-D35 two-blade variable-pitch propeller, instead of the 224 kW (300 hp) Ivchenko AI-14RF of the Yak-18PS. Mainwheel tyre size is 500 × 150, tailwheel tyre size 200 × 80. The main fuel tank, capacity 55 litres (14.5 US gallons; 12 Imp gallons), is aft of the engine firewall, the electrical system battery behind the pilot's seat. A Zyablik radio transceiver is standard.

Observers at the 1976 world championships at Kiev reported that the Yak-50s performed the all-important Aresti manoeuvres with precision, their primary short-coming being excessive directional stability. Yak-50s flown by V. Letsko and I. Egorov finished first and second in the men's competition. Others came fifth, seventh and ninth, to win the team prize. First five places in the women's championship were taken by Yak-50s.

DIMENSIONS, EXTERNAL:

Wing span	9.50 m (31 ft 2 in)
Length overall	7.676 m (25 ft 2¼ in)
Tailplane span	3.16 m (10 ft 4½ in)
Wheel track	2.00 m (6 ft 6¾ in)

Wheelbase	5.10 m (16 ft 8¾ in)
Propeller diameter	2.40 m (7 ft 10½ in)

AREAS:

Wings, gross	15.00 m² (161.5 sq ft)
Ailerons (total)	1.95 m² (21.00 sq ft)
Vertical tail surfaces (total)	1.48 m² (15.93 sq ft)
Horizontal tail surfaces (total)	2.86 m² (30.78 sq ft)

WEIGHTS AND LOADINGS:

Weight empty, equipped	765 kg (1,686 lb)
Max T-O weight	900 kg (1,984 lb)
Max wing loading	60 kg/m² (12.29 lb/sq ft)
Max power loading	3.36 kg/kW (5.51 lb/hp)

PERFORMANCE:

Never-exceed speed	226 knots (420 km/h; 261 mph)
Max level speed	173 knots (320 km/h; 199 mph)
T-O speed	65 knots (120 km/h; 75 mph)
Rate of climb at S/L	960 m (3,150 ft)/min
Service ceiling	5,500 m (18,045 ft)
T-O run	200 m (657 ft)
Landing run	250 m (820 ft)
Max range at 1,000 m (3,280 ft), with 120 litres (31.7 US gallons; 26.4 Imp gallons) auxiliary fuel, reserve of 10 litres (2.6 US gallons; 2.2 Imp gallons)	
	267 nm (495 km; 307 miles)
Endurance at 500 m (1,640 ft) with 52 litres (13.7 US gallons; 11.4 Imp gallons) auxiliary fuel, reserve of 10 litres (2.6 US gallons; 2.2 Imp gallons)	48 min
g limits	+9/−6

YAKOVLEV Yak-52

Production of this tandem two-seat piston engined primary trainer was entrusted to the Romanian aircraft industry (which see), under the Comecon (Council for Mutual Economic Assistance) programme.

YAKOVLEV Yak-53

The Yak-53 is a single-seat fully aerobatic version of the Yak-52 two-seat primary trainer (see Romanian section). It retains the latter's pneumatically operated semi-retractable tricycle landing gear, but lacks the spring loaded controls of the Yak-52 and is stripped of non-essential equipment such as a radio compass and direction finder to enhance its agility. Power plant is a 268 kW (360 hp) Vedeneyev M-14P nine-cylinder aircooled radial piston engine, driving a two-blade variable-pitch propeller. Fuel capacity is 130 litres (34 US gallons; 28.5 Imp gallons), in two tanks forward of the main spar in the inner wings. The pilot sits under a rearward sliding canopy.

The Yak-53 is intended as a 'long life' aerobatic trainer, whereas the Yak-50 is a maximum-performance high g aircraft supplied exclusively to State Co-operatives. Production of the Yak-53 has started at the Progress Factory of the Soviet State Aviation Industry at Arsenyev, and is expected to be undertaken eventually by IAv Bacau in Romania, under licence.

DIMENSIONS, EXTERNAL:

Wing span	9.50 m (31 ft 2 in)
Length overall	7.68 m (25 ft 2¼ in)
Height overall	2.95 m (9 ft 8¼ in)
Propeller diameter	2.40 m (7 ft 10½ in)

AREA:

Wings, gross	15.00 m² (161.5 sq ft)

WEIGHTS:

Weight empty	900 kg (1,985 lb)
Max T-O weight	1,060 kg (2,337 lb)

PERFORMANCE:

Max permissible speed in dive	
	194 knots (360 km/h; 223 mph)
Max level speed	162 knots (300 km/h; 186 mph)
Cruising speed	124 knots (230 km/h; 143 mph)
Stalling speed	62 knots (115 km/h; 72 mph)

Yakovlev Yak-50 single-seat aerobatic and sporting aircraft

Max rate of climb at S/L	900 m (2,950 ft)/min
T-O run	150 m (492 ft)
Landing run	250 m (820 ft)
Endurance with max fuel	50 min

YAKOVLEV Yak-55

When a prototype of this Yakovlev single-seat competitive aerobatics monoplane made a surprise appearance at the 11th World Aerobatic Championships at Spitzerberg, Austria, in August 1982, it was described as the latest in the Yak-18/50 series. It is, however, smaller and almost entirely new, as can be seen in the accompanying illustrations.

Construction of the Yak-55 is all-metal, with mid-mounted cantilever wings, originally of 18% t/c NACA 23 section and with a low aspect ratio. In-flight structural failures compelled redesign, and Yak-55s entered for the 1984 World Aerobatic Championships had new and stronger tapered wings of thinner section. Incidence and dihedral appear to be nil. All control surfaces are horn balanced; the only tabs appear to be on the inboard trailing-edge of the almost full span ailerons. The tail unit is unbraced, the tailwheel steerable, and the small mainwheels are carried on bowed cantilever spring steel legs. The blister canopy is rearward sliding. Power plant is a 268 kW (360 hp) Vedeneyev M-14P nine-cylinder aircooled radial engine, driving a two-blade controllable-pitch propeller. Wing fuel tanks, capacity 120 litres (31.5 US gallons; 26 Imp gallons).

DIMENSIONS, EXTERNAL:

Wing span	8.20 m (26 ft 10¾ in)
Length overall	7.48 m (24 ft 6½ in)
Height	2.30 m (7 ft 6½ in)

AREA:

Wings, gross	14.30 m² (153.9 sq ft)

WEIGHTS:

Weight empty	640 kg (1,411 lb)
Max T-O weight	840 kg (1,852 lb)

PERFORMANCE:

Max level speed	173 knots (320 km/h; 199 mph)
Cruising speed	140 knots (260 km/h; 161 mph)
Max rate of climb at S/L	960 m (3,150 ft)/min
T-O run	150 m (492 ft)
Landing run	200 m (656 ft)
g limits	+9/−6

Yakovlev Yak-53 single-seat fully aerobatic light aircraft

Yakovlev's aerobatic Yak-55 (Vedeneyev M-14P engine) *(Flight International)*

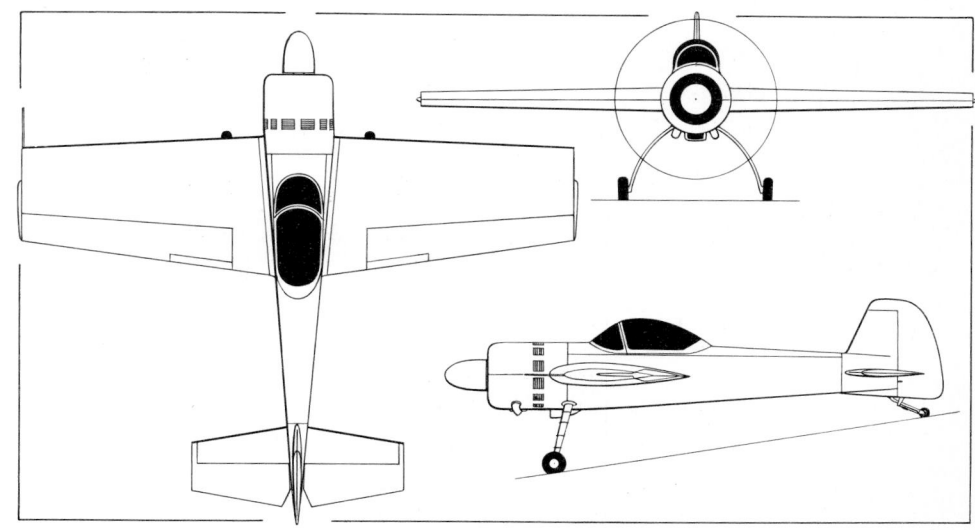

Yakovlev Yak-55 single-seat aircraft for competitive aerobatics *(Pilot Press)*

AIRCRAFT OF UNKNOWN DESIGN

ASF. The ASF (air-superiority fighter) is an offensive counter-air fighter that the Soviet Union is believed to be developing for initial operational capability in the late 1990s. Its manoeuvring capabilities will be significantly greater than those of the MiG-29 and Su-27.

CAF. The Soviet Union is developing in parallel with the ASF a new defensive counter-air fighter (CAF) with comparable manoeuvring capabilities. First flight is expected to take place by the mid-1990s, to permit an IOC before the end of the decade.

Ram-M. Among aircraft observed at Ramenskoye flight test centre, and allocated a provisional 'Ram' designation, is a high-altitude reconnaissance aircraft in the class of the USAF's Lockheed TR-1. Few details are known except that it has twin tail fins. It was first reported in mid-1982.

Tilt-rotor aircraft. The 1987 edition of the US Department of Defense's *Soviet Military Power* document suggested that the Soviet Union is pursuing development of tilt-rotor aircraft, most likely for use as troop carriers. This was to be expected in view of the US Bell/Boeing V-22 Osprey programme and the success of the Bell XV-15 tilt-rotor research aircraft. The objective of the Soviet effort must be to provide higher-performance and more versatile replacements for such helicopters as the Mi-8/17 (NATO 'Hip') and Mi-24 ('Hind') in the 1990s.

SOVIET AEROSPACECRAFT

REUSABLE SPACE PLANE

The Soviet spacecraft designated Cosmos 1374, launched from Kapustin Yar on 3 June 1982, was believed to be a small scale unmanned flight test version of a 're-usable space plane'. Weighing about 900 kg (2,000 lb), it was dispatched on its flight of just over one orbit by a standard Soviet launcher based on the SS-5 (NATO 'Skean') intermediate range ballistic missile. After successful re-entry into the atmosphere, it was recovered from the Indian Ocean.

Cosmos 1445 was also recovered from the Indian Ocean, on 16 March 1983, after a flight of one orbit. On this occasion the recovery operation was photographed from a Royal Australian Air Force Orion aircraft. The resulting pictures, one of which is reproduced on the next page, show a slender delta winged and finned vehicle, similar to the USAF/Boeing X-20 Dyna-Soar project of the early 1960s (see 1962-63 *Jane's*). Cosmos 1517, launched on 27

December 1983, was the third test of the subscale shuttle. This vehicle was recovered from the Black Sea, as was Cosmos 1614 at the end of the fourth test flight on 19 December 1984. Similar flights have continued, possibly including Cosmos 1871 and 1873, launched on 1 August and 28 August 1987 respectively. Each vehicle weighed about 10,000 kg (22,045 lb), suggesting 'boilerplate' mockups of the full scale space plane. It is considered that the fully developed vehicle could be used for military reconnaissance, crew transport to space stations, satellite repair and maintenance, satellite interception and/or destruction, and space station defence.

An accompanying drawing, from the US Department of Defense, suggests that the full scale 're-usable space plane' will have a wing span of about 9.4 m (30 ft 9 in) and length of 16.25 m (53 ft 3 in), including motors. Its SL-16 launcher, used for Cosmos 1871 and 1873, is capable of inserting a payload of more than 15,000 kg (33,000 lb) into a 185 km (115 mile) orbit.

SOVIET SHUTTLE ORBITER

Information and artist's impressions published in the 1987 edition of the Department of Defense's *Soviet Military Power* document suggest that the Soviet Union also has in the final stages of development a manned orbiter almost as large as NASA's Space Shuttle Orbiter and with a very similar configuration for both the vehicle and its Energiya (SL-X-17) launcher (large external tank, strap-on boosters and a piggy-back orbiter). The assembled launch vehicle is shown as being 65 m (213 ft) tall, compared with 56 m (184 ft) for the US Shuttle. Significant differences are said to be the use of liquid propellants for the strap-on boosters, and location of the liquid hydrogen main engines on the external tank rather than on the orbiter itself. Payload capability of the system is estimated as 30,000 kg (66,135 lb) into a 185 km (115 mile) orbit. Glide tests of the orbiter were expected to begin during 1988; but operational manned launches are unlikely to start before 1990. (See also Myasishchev entry in this section.)

Artist's impression of Soviet space shuttle orbiter on its launch ramp *(US Department of Defense)*

Soviet subscale re-usable space plane, designated Cosmos 1445, recovered from the Indian Ocean *(Australian Department of Defence)*

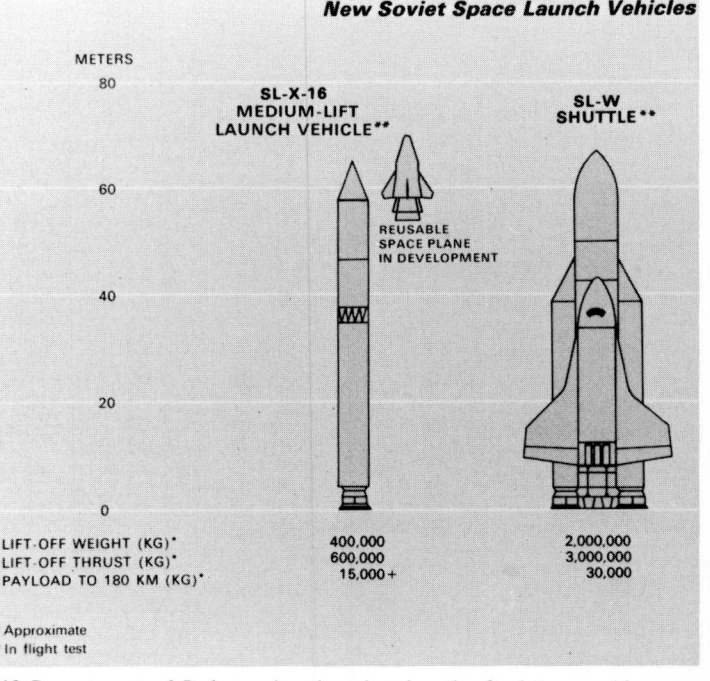

New Soviet Space Launch Vehicles

METERS	SL-X-16 MEDIUM-LIFT LAUNCH VEHICLE**	SL-W SHUTTLE**
80		
60	REUSABLE SPACE PLANE IN DEVELOPMENT	
40		
20		
0		
LIFT-OFF WEIGHT (KG)*	400,000	2,000,000
LIFT-OFF THRUST (KG)*	600,000	3,000,000
PAYLOAD TO 180 KM (KG)*	15,000+	30,000

* Approximate
** In flight test

US Department of Defense drawing showing the Soviet re-usable space plane and space shuttle orbiter, now under development

UNITED KINGDOM

ARV

ISLAND AIRCRAFT LTD
(Subsidiary of Taurus Aviation Ltd)

Isle of Wight Airport, Sandown, Isle of Wight PO36 9PJ
Telephone: 0983 406124
Telex: 86267 ARV SAN
Fax: 0983 405903
CHAIRMAN: C. Passmore
MANAGING DIRECTOR: C. Wald
CHIEF DESIGNER: J. N. Morton, BA
CHIEF ENGINEER: N. J. Sibley, BSc, MRAeS

Island Aircraft (formerly ARV Aviation) was formed in 1984 to design and produce the two-seat Super2 light aircraft, powered by a British aero-engine developed by Hewland Engineering Ltd. The objective was to produce an aircraft with both low initial and very low maintenance costs, leading to relatively low costs per flying hour. The ability to operate from European grass strips was also an important objective. Use is made of superplastically formed aluminium alloy pressings to save weight and to reduce manufacturing costs. The Super2 is designed to British Civil Aviation Airworthiness Requirements, Section K.

ARV-1 SUPER2

The prototype Super2 (G-OARV) flew for the first time on 11 March 1985, piloted by Mr Hugh Kendall, and was followed by two further trials/demonstrator aircraft. Before certification was obtained, in July 1986, the first five production aircraft were supplied in kit form, 65 per cent complete, for completion by home builders under the auspices of the Popular Flying Association. Subsequent deliveries, of completed aircraft, began with G-BMSJ (c/n 010) which went to the Airbourne School of Flying at Sandown, Isle of Wight. Planned production of eight aircraft per month by the end of 1987 was thwarted by power plant and financial problems, manufacture being temporarily suspended until these were rectified. Following a management buyout, 26 Super2s had been delivered by August 1988, including prototypes, demonstrators and five kits.

Potential developments include a semi-aerobatic version and a version for photographic duties.

TYPE: Two-seat light cabin monoplane.
WINGS: Braced shoulder-wing monoplane with single streamline bracing strut each side. Wing section NACA 2415 (modified). Single-spar wing, of aluminium alloy construction, cold bonded and flush riveted, is swept forward 5° 6′ to optimise the CG and the structural merits of a single uncompromised main bulkhead carrying the wings, bracing struts, controls, seats, fuel tank and main landing gear. Mass balanced ailerons operated by torque tube through leading-edge of manually operated plain flaps. Wings readily detachable for road transportation by light trailer.
FUSELAGE: Rear fuselage of aluminium alloy construction, cold bonded and flush riveted, with single curvature skinning. Forward of the main bulkhead the structure is conventional double beam carrying the firewall, nose landing gear and engine. Between the firewall and the main bulkhead, the fuselage is skinned by four panels, superplastically formed in Supral 220/150 aluminium alloy.
TAIL UNIT: Conventional aluminium alloy structure, cold bonded and flush riveted, with three-spar fixed surfaces and single-spar mass balanced control surfaces. Trim tab on elevator.
LANDING GEAR: Non-retractable tricycle type. Cantilever main legs of tapered steel leaf spring. All three wheels size 3.50 × 6.0, with tyres size 13 × 4.00-6, pressure 1.72 bars (25 lb/sq in). Hydraulic disc brakes. Nose leg of leading link design, with rubber in tension springing, with damping by an adjustable Spax gas filled shock absorber. Wheels and brakes made by ARV.
POWER PLANT: One 57.4 kW (77 hp) Hewland Engineering AE 75 three-cylinder, 750 cc liquid cooled inline two-stroke engine, driving a two-blade, fixed-pitch Hoffmann propeller through 2.7:1 reduction gearing. Electronically variable ignition timing. Serck aluminium radiator in recessed duct in rear fuselage. Fuel capacity 55 litres (14.4 US gallons; 12 Imp gallons) in single fuselage tank. Refuelling point in top of fuselage.
ACCOMMODATION: Enclosed cabin seating two side by side. The shoulder location of the wing with forward sweep,

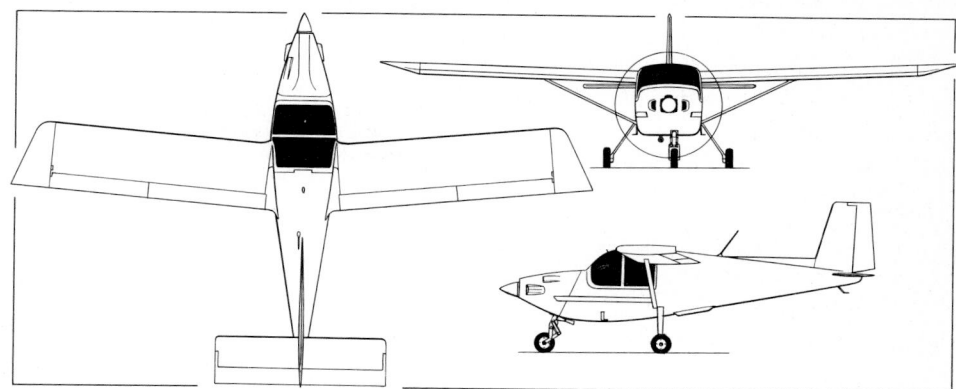

Photograph *(Air Photo Supply)* **and three-view drawing** *(Pilot Press)* **of the Island Aircraft ARV-1 Super2 two-seat monoplane (Hewland Engineering AE 75 engine)**

the low panel line and the close cowling of the small engine combine to provide an optimum view from the cabin, particularly in turns. Seats are adjustable for height, and fold to reveal baggage compartment. Additional storage space under the seats. Rearward hinged canopy is one-piece Perspex moulding with GRP frame. Dual flying controls standard.
SYSTEMS: Wheel disc brakes operated hydraulically. Electrical system includes 11A or 15A alternator.
AVIONICS AND EQUIPMENT: Standard equipment includes three basic flight instruments plus engine instruments. Optional vacuum instruments driven by dual venturis mounted under the front fuselage. Radio equipment to customers' requirements.

DIMENSIONS, EXTERNAL:
Wing span	8.69 m (28 ft 6 in)
Width, wings folded	2.54 m (8 ft 4 in)
Wing aspect ratio	8.8
Length overall	5.49 m (18 ft 0 in)
Height overall	2.31 m (7 ft 7 in)
Tailplane span	2.54 m (8 ft 4 in)
Wheel track	1.83 m (6 ft 0 in)
Wheelbase	1.74 m (5 ft 8½ in)
Propeller diameter	1.60 m (5 ft 3 in)
Propeller ground clearance	0.23 m (9 in)

DIMENSIONS, INTERNAL:
Cabin: Length	1.27 m (4 ft 2 in)
Max width	0.99 m (3 ft 3 in)
Max height	1.09 m (3 ft 7 in)

AREAS:
Wings, gross	8.59 m² (92.5 sq ft)
Ailerons (total)	0.60 m² (6.5 sq ft)
Trailing-edge flaps (total)	0.89 m (9.6 sq ft)
Fin	0.59 m² (6.4 sq ft)
Rudder	0.26 m² (2.8 sq ft)
Tailplane	1.23 m² (13.2 sq ft)
Elevators, incl tabs	0.55 m² (5.9 sq ft)

WEIGHTS AND LOADINGS:
Weight empty, equipped	306 kg (675 lb)
Max fuel weight	37 kg (80 lb)
Max T-O and landing weight	499 kg (1,100 lb)
Max wing loading	58.1 kg/m² (11.9 lb/sq ft)
Max power loading	8.9 kg/kW (14.7 lb/hp)

PERFORMANCE (at max T-O weight):
Never-exceed speed	126 knots (232 km/h; 149 mph)
Max level speed at 610 m (2,000 ft)	103 knots (190 km/h; 118 mph)
Max cruising speed at 610 m (2,000 ft)	93 knots (171 km/h; 107 mph)
Econ cruising speed at 610 m (2,000 ft)	83 knots (153 km/h; 95 mph)
Stalling speed, power off:	
flaps up	54 knots (99 km/h; 62 mph)
flaps down	48 knots (88 km/h; 55 mph)
Rate of climb at S/L	189 m (620 ft)/min
T-O to 15 m (50 ft)	712 m (2,336 ft)
Landing distance, from 15 m (50 ft)	470 m (1,540 ft)
Range with max fuel	270 nm (500 km; 311 miles)

BAe

BRITISH AEROSPACE PLC

HEADQUARTERS: 11 Strand, London WC2N 5JT
Telephone: 01 930 1020
Telex: 919221
Fax: 01 839 4774
and Brooklands Road, Weybridge, Surrey KT13 0SJ
Telephone: 0932 853444
Telex: 27111

CHAIRMAN: Professor Roland Smith, BA, MSc, PhD (Econ)
CHIEF EXECUTIVE: Admiral Sir Raymond Lygo, KCB, RN (Retd)
DEPUTY CHIEF EXECUTIVE, ENGINEERING:
 I. R. Yates, CBE, BEng, FEng, FRAeS, FIMechE
MARKETING DIRECTOR: R. H. Evans
EXECUTIVE VICE-PRESIDENT, CIVIL MARKETING OPERATIONS:
 B. G. Thomas
EXECUTIVE VICE-PRESIDENT, DEFENCE MARKETING:
 M. J. Turner, BA, ACIS
DIRECTOR OF PUBLIC AFFAIRS: Don McClen
PRESS RELATIONS MANAGER (Weybridge): Alan Piper

The history of British Aerospace has been recorded in detail in previous editions of *Jane's.* The company, employing 93,000 people in the UK and overseas, is again planning changes to its management structure, early in 1989, by devolving some of the business operations to its Divisions and Subsidiary Companies. The Military Aircraft and Dynamics Divisions, are to become subsidiary companies. Together with Royal Ordnance they will become part of a separate Defence services organisation under a common Chairman. Likewise Civil Aircraft Division will become a separate company, as will Space and Communications Division.

British Aerospace has the following principal overseas subsidiaries: British Aerospace Australia Ltd, British Aerospace Inc, and British Scandinavian Aviation AB; and the following UK subsidiaries: Royal Ordnance PLC, British Aerospace (Insurance) Ltd, British Aerospace (Insurance Brokers) Ltd, and British Aerospace (Pension Fund Trustees) Ltd.

Associated companies include SEPECAT (formed in May 1966 by BAC and Breguet Aviation to control the development and production of the Jaguar tactical strike fighter and trainer), Panavia Aircraft GmbH (formed in March 1969 by BAC, MBB and Aeritalia to manage the development and production of the Tornado all-weather combat aircraft), Eurofighter Jagdflugzeug GmbH, Dulles International Aeroservices Inc (formed in 1976 by BAC (USA) Inc and Rolls-Royce Inc to supply customers in North America with spares and engineering support), BBG GmbH (formed with Bodenseewerk to develop and produce the ASRAAM missile), Arab-British Dynamics Co (inaugurated in 1977 by BAC Guided Weapons Division and the Egyptian government to manufacture the Swingfire missile in Egypt), and British Aerospace Simulation Ltd.

British Aerospace is a 20% partner in the Airbus Industrie international consortium, with a 20% stake in the A300, A300-600 and A310 civil transports, a 26% stake in the A320 programme, and a 25% stake in the A330/A340 programme. British Aerospace is a partner in Euromissile Dynamics Group (EMDG), formed with MBB and Aérospatiale for the development and production of anti-tank missiles.

CIVIL AIRCRAFT DIVISION

HATFIELD: Hatfield, Hertfordshire AL10 9TL
Telephone: 07072 62345
Telex: 22411
CIVIL MARKETING OPERATIONS CENTRE: PO Box 35, Stevenage, Hertfordhire SG1 2DG
Telephone: 07072 68123
Telex: 826 876
Fax: 07072 61696
BRISTOL: Filton House, Bristol BS99 7AR
Telephone: 0272 693831
Telex: 44163
CHADDERTON: Chadderton Works, Greengate, Middleton, Manchester M24 1SA
Telephone: 061 681 2020
Telex: 667015
CHESTER: Broughton, near Chester, Clwyd CH4 0DR
Telephone: 0244 535333
Telex: 61201

PRESTWICK: Prestwick Airport, Ayrshire KA9 2RW
Telephone: 0292 79888
Telex: 77432
WOODFORD: Woodford Aerodrome, Chester Road, Woodford, Cheshire CK7 1QR
Telephone: 061 439 5050
Telex: 668939/667545
MANAGING DIRECTOR, CIVIL AIRCRAFT DIVISION:
   S. Gillibrand, MSc, CEng, FRAeS
DIVISIONAL TECHNICAL DIRECTOR:
   J. B. Scott-Wilson, MA, FRAeS
SENIOR VICE-PRESIDENT, MARKETING DEVELOPMENT:
   Dennis Little
DIVISIONAL PUBLIC RELATIONS MANAGER: D. A. Dorman
PUBLIC RELATIONS MANAGER, HATFIELD: M. V. Brown
PUBLIC RELATIONS OFFICER, CHESTER: Ms K. Roden
PUBLIC RELATIONS MANAGER, PRESTWICK: Ms C. Lang
PUBLIC RELATIONS MANAGER, AIRBUS: H. Berry
PUBLIC RELATIONS MANAGER, MANCHESTER: H. Holmes

PUBLIC RELATIONS MANAGER, FILTON: Mrs P. Telling

Civil Aircraft Division, centred at Hatfield, is responsible for design, development, production, marketing and support of the BAe 146 regional jet airliner, the BAe 125 business jet, the Jetstream 31 airliner, corporate and executive aircraft, the BAe 748 turboprop transport and the Advanced Turboprop (ATP) transport. The Division is also responsible for the Rombac 1-11 licence manufacturing programme with Romania; design, development and production of wings for all European Airbus transport aircraft; VC10 conversion to the air to air refuelling role for the Royal Air Force; and F-111 maintenance under USAF contract. The Division also supplies civil aircraft design, development, research, support, modification and refurbishing services. All marketing, sales and support activities are centred at the Civil Marketing Operations Centre at Stevenage.

MILITARY AIRCRAFT DIVISION

BROUGH: Brough, North Humberside HU15 1EQ
Telephone: 0482 667121
Telex: 52634 BAEBRO G
DUNSFOLD: Dunsfold Aerodrome, Godalming, Surrey, GU8 4BS
Telephone: 0483 272121
Telex: 859475 BAEDUN G
HAMBLE: Kings Avenue, Hamble, Hampshire SO3 5NF
Telephone: 0703 453371
Telex: 47543 BAEHAM G
KINGSTON: Richmond Road, Kingston upon Thames, Surrey KT2 5QS
Telephone: 01 546 7741
Telex: 23726 BAEKIN G
PRESTON: Strand Road, Preston, Lancs PR1 8UD
Telephone: 0772 54722
Telex: 67616 BAEP G
SAMLESBURY: Samlesbury Aerodrome, Balderstone, Lancs BB2 7LF
Telephone: 025 481 2371
Telex: 63435 BAES G
WARTON: Warton Aerodrome, Preston, Lancashire PR4 1AX

Telephone: 0772 633333
Telex: 67627 BAEWAA G
MANAGING DIRECTOR, MILITARY AIRCRAFT DIVISION:
   N. V. Barber, BA, MSc, FRAeS
DIVISIONAL TECHNICAL DIRECTOR:
   B. Young, BSc (Hons), FRAeS
PUBLIC RELATIONS MANAGER, BROUGH: E. Barker
PUBLIC RELATIONS MANAGER, KINGSTON: J. W. Coombs
PUBLIC RELATIONS MANAGER, WARTON:
   G. B. Hill, MBE, MBIM

During 1988, the Military Aircraft Division transferred its headquarters from Weybridge to Warton, resulting in closure of the former site. It is also intended to terminate flying at Samlesbury, while retaining the manufacturing facility.

Main activities of this Division include the development, in partnership with West Germany, Italy and Spain, of the European Fighter Aircraft (EFA); design and development of the Experimental Aircraft Programme (EAP) technology demonstrator; design, development, production and support, with MBB and Aeritalia, of the Panavia Tornado; design, development, production and support of the V/STOL Harrier and Sea Harrier and, with McDonnell Douglas, of the AV-8B/GR. Mk 5 Harrier for the USMC and RAF, respectively, and the T-45A Goshawk for the US Navy; design, development, production and support of the Hawk strike/advanced jet trainer and Hawk 200 single-seat lightweight fighter.

In addition to major contracts for the update of RAF Phantom and Buccaneer aircraft, the Division was responsible for joint design and manufacture, with Saab-Scania, of carbonfibre wings for JAS 39 Gripen prototypes. It undertakes conversion programmes for the Canberra bomber, and makes major contributions to the BAe 146, and Airbus family of airliners. Full product support services are provided for earlier aircraft still in service throughout the world.

The company's defence support services business is centred in the Military Aircraft Division, which additionally offers overseas and specialist training facilities covering a wide range of technical and management courses.

The Division has established a residential Flying College at Prestwick which trains future British Airways pilots, and cadets from other airlines, to Commercial Pilots Licence and Instrument Rating standard. The College began operations in November 1987 and was officially opened in May 1988, at which time it had received seven of 11 FFA AS.202 Wrens on order; 19 of 28 Piper Warriors; and one of nine Piper Seneca IIIs.

DYNAMICS DIVISION

Formed on 1 January 1988, Dynamics Division incorporates the former Air Weapons Division (Hatfield and Lostock); Army Weapons Division (Stevenage); and Naval and Electronic Systems Division (Bristol, Bracknell, Plymouth and Weymouth). Details of missiles and weapon systems will be found in the appropriate *Jane's* yearbooks; brief specifications of air-launched missiles are included in this volume.

SPACE AND COMMUNICATIONS DIVISION

STEVENAGE: Argyle Way, Stevenage, Hertfordshire SG1 2AS
Telephone: 0438 313456
Telex: 82130/82197
BRISTOL: PO Box No. 5, Filton, Bristol BS12 7QW
Telephone: 0272 693831
Telex: 449452

MANAGING DIRECTOR: J. A. Holt, MSc, BSc, CEng, MRAeS
PUBLIC RELATIONS MANAGER: J. Humby

The Space and Communications Division is responsible for the Skynet 4 UK military communications satellite programme, civil communications satellites, and pallets for the US Space Shuttle, as described in *Jane's Spaceflight Directory*. The Division is also responsible for development of the unmanned re-usable single-stage Hotol space transport, of which brief details are given in this section of *All the World's Aircraft*.

BAe JETSTREAM 31

Development of this current version of the Jetstream was launched by British Aerospace on 5 December 1978. A development aircraft (G-JSSD), converted from a Jetstream 1 built by Handley Page, flew for the first time on 28 March 1980. Full production go-ahead was given in January 1982, and the first production Jetstream 31 (G-TALL) made its first flight on 18 March 1982. On 29 June 1982 the Jetstream 31 was certificated to BCAR Section D in the UK. US certification under SFAR 41C followed on 30 November 1982. German (LBA) certification was gained in July 1983, Australian (DOA) certification in February 1984, Swedish (BCA) in December 1984, Dutch (RLD) in January 1985 and Canadian (TC) in May 1987. First deliveries, to customers in Germany and the UK, took place in December 1982, and the 100th delivery was made on 25 June 1986. Orders reached 226 by 4 August 1988, deliveries having totalled 54 in 1987, compared with 46 in 1986.

The following versions have been announced:

Airliner. Designed to carry 18/19 passengers. Able to operate up to 680 nm (1,260 km; 783 miles) stage length, without refuelling, with 18 passengers, baggage and full IFR reserves.

Corporate. Executive version, designed for eight to ten passengers, and able to carry nine passengers and baggage for 1,050 nm (1,945 km; 1,208 miles) with full IFR reserves. Typical interior has six fully reclining and swivelling chairs, a three-place divan, galley for hot and cold meal service, cocktail cabinet, wardrobe and washroom/toilet.

Executive Shuttle. Intended for the large company, shuttling its personnel between factories, or for the business charter market. With typical layout for 12 passengers, this version has a range of 1,050 nm (1,945 km; 1,208 miles) with full IFR reserves.

Special Role. Intended for various specialist applications such as military communications, casualty evacuation, multi-engine training, cargo operations, airfield calibration, resources survey and protection. A patrol version, designated **Jetstream 31EZ**, is available for operation in exclusive economic zones (ie offshore patrol and surveillance), with underbelly 360° scan radar, increased fuel, observation windows and searchlight. Two aircraft, specially equipped with Tornado IDS avionics, were delivered to the Royal Saudi Air Force in November 1987 for navigator training.

Jetstream Super 31. Announced at the 1987 Paris Air Show, this version has more powerful Garrett TPE331-12 engines, flat rated to 760 kW (1,020 shp) at temperatures up to 26°C. Described separately.

Jetstream T. Mk 3. Training version, in service with the Royal Navy. Eyebrow windows above flight deck windscreen to improve all-round view. Interior fitted with two observer training consoles with radar indicator, TANS computer and Doppler. Racal ASR 360 search radar mounted under the fuselage. Four ordered in April 1984, for operation by No. 750 Naval Air Squadron based at Culdrose, Cornwall, for helicopter observer training. All delivered by October 1986.

As part of the continuing programme of aircraft improvements, increases in design weights and engine ratings have been achieved. A quick change (QC) facility allows conversion from 18-seat to 12/10-seat layouts in just over one hour. An underfuselage baggage pod provides

BAe Jetstream 31 light transport of Ontario Express, trading as Canadian Partner, flying over Niagara Falls

stowage for an extra six cases and additional soft luggage. A water methanol injection system has been developed for 'hot and high' conditions, and the Jetstream 31 has been cleared for use from unsealed runways.

TYPE: Light commuter/executive transport.

WINGS: Cantilever low-wing monoplane. Wing section NACA 63A418 at root, NACA 63A412 at tip. Dihedral 7° from roots. Incidence 2° at root, 0° at tip. Sweepback 0° 34′ at quarter-chord. Aluminium alloy fail-safe structure. Aluminium alloy manually operated Frise ailerons. Hydraulically operated aluminium alloy double-slotted flaps. No slats or leading-edge flaps. Trim tab in each aileron. Goodrich rubber boot de-icing system for leading-edges.

FUSELAGE: Conventional aluminium alloy semi-monocoque fail-safe structure, with chemically milled skin panels. Fully pressurised.

TAIL UNIT: Cantilever two-spar aluminium alloy structure. Fixed incidence tailplane. Manually operated control surfaces. Trim tabs in rudder and each elevator. Goodrich rubber boot de-icing system for leading-edges.

LANDING GEAR: Retractable tricycle type, with nosewheel steering. Hydraulic retraction, mainwheels inward into wings, twin nosewheels forward. British Aerospace oleo-pneumatic shock absorbers in all units. Dunlop wheels and tyres: mainwheel tyres size 28 × 9.00-12, pressure 3.93 bars (57 lb/sq in); nosewheel tyres size 6.00-6, pressure 2.34 bars (34 lb/sq in). Anti-skid units.

POWER PLANT: Two 701 kW (940 shp) Garrett TPE331-10UG turboprops, each driving a Dowty Rotol four-blade variable- and reversible-pitch fully-feathering metal propeller. Fuel in integral tank in each wing, total capacity 1,718 litres (454 US gallons; 378 Imp gallons). Refuelling point on top of each outer wing. Water methanol injection optional.

ACCOMMODATION: Two seats side by side on flight deck, with provision for dual controls, though aircraft can be approved (subject to local regulations) for single pilot operation. Main cabin can be furnished in commuter layout for up to 19 passengers at 76/79 cm (30/31 in) pitch, or with executive interior for 8/10 passengers, but optional layouts are available, including a QC (quick change) option enabling an operator to change from an 18-seat layout to 12-seat executive configuration in around 1¼ hours. Downward opening passenger door, with integral airstairs, at rear of cabin on port side. Emergency exit over wing on starboard side. Baggage compartment in rear of cabin, aft of main door. Entire accommodation pressurised, heated, ventilated and air-conditioned. Toilet standard; galley and bar optional. Jetstream completion is by Field Aircraft.

SYSTEMS: Air-conditioning system with cabin pressurisation at max differential of 0.38 bars (5.5 lb/sq in), providing a 2,440 m (8,000 ft) cabin altitude at 7,620 m (25,000 ft). Single hydraulic system, pressure 138 bars (2,000 lb/sq in), with two engine driven pumps, each capable of supplying 20.7 litres (5.46 US gallons; 4.55 Imp gallons)/min. One pump is capable of supplying all hydraulic systems. Combined air/oil reservoir, pressurised to 1.24 bars (18 lb/sq in), for main and emergency supply, for actuation of flaps, landing gear, brakes and nosewheel steering. APU optional.

Royal Saudi Air Force Jetstream flying classroom for Tornado navigator training

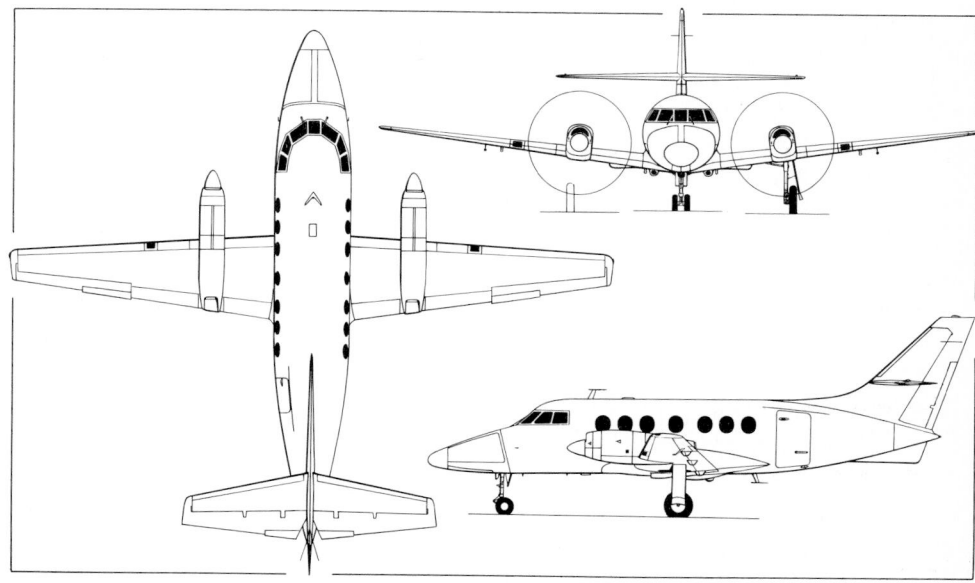

BAe Jetstream 31 twin-turboprop commuter/executive light transport *(Pilot Press)*

DIMENSIONS, EXTERNAL:

Wing span	15.85 m (52 ft 0 in)	Tailplane span	6.60 m (21 ft 8 in)
Wing chord: at root	2.19 m (7 ft 2½ in)	Wheel track	5.94 m (19 ft 6 in)
at tip	0.80 m (2 ft 7¼ in)	Wheelbase	4.60 m (15 ft 1 in)
Wing aspect ratio	10.0	Propeller diameter	2.69 m (8 ft 10 in)
Length overall	14.37 m (47 ft 1½ in)	Passenger door: Height	1.42 m (4 ft 8 in)
Length of fuselage	13.40 m (43 ft 11½ in)	Width	0.86 m (2 ft 10 in)
Height overall	5.32 m (17 ft 5½ in)	Emergency exit: Height	0.91 m (3 ft 0 in)
Fuselage: Max diameter	1.98 m (6 ft 6 in)	Width	0.56 m (1 ft 10 in)

DIMENSIONS, INTERNAL:

Cabin, excl flight deck: Length	7.39 m (24 ft 3 in)
Max width	1.85 m (6 ft 1 in)
Max height	1.80 m (5 ft 11 in)
Floor area	8.35 m² (90 sq ft)
Volume (trimmed aircraft)	16.92 m³ (598 cu ft)

Baggage compartment volume:

Airliner	2.13-2.74 m³ (75.2-96.7 cu ft)
Corporate	1.34-1.48 m³ (47.2-52.2 cu ft)
Baggage pod (optional)	1.39 m³ (49 cu ft)

AREAS:

Wings, gross	25.20 m² (271.3 sq ft)
Ailerons, aft of hinge line (total)	1.52 m² (16.4 sq ft)
Trailing-edge flaps (total)	3.25 m² (35.0 sq ft)
Vertical tail surfaces (total)	7.72 m² (83.1 sq ft)
Horizontal tail surfaces (total)	7.80 m² (84.0 sq ft)

WEIGHTS AND LOADINGS:

Operating weight empty	4,360 kg (9,613 lb)
Max fuel	1,372 kg (3,024 lb)
Max payload	1,805 kg (3,980 lb)
Max T-O weight: standard	6,950 kg (15,322 lb)
US domestic	6,900 kg (15,212 lb)
Max ramp weight	7,000 kg (15,432 lb)
Max landing weight	6,600 kg (14,550 lb)
Max zero-fuel weight	6,300 kg (13,889 lb)
Max wing loading	275.8 kg/m² (56.5 lb/sq ft)
Max power loading	4.96 kg/kW (8.15 lb/shp)

PERFORMANCE (at max T-O weight, except where stated):

Max cruising speed at max cruise power at 4,570 m (15,000 ft)	263 knots (488 km/h; 303 mph)
Econ cruising speed at 7,620 m (25,000 ft)	230 knots (426 km/h; 264 mph)
Stalling speed, flaps down	86 knots (159 km/h; 99 mph)
Max rate of climb at S/L	635 m (2,080 ft)/min
Rate of climb at S/L, one engine out	119 m (390 ft)/min
Certificated ceiling	7,620 m (25,000 ft)
Service ceiling, one engine out	3,660 m (12,000 ft)
T-O field length: BCAR Section D	1,440 m (4,724 ft)
T-O to 15 m (50 ft): SFAR 41C	975 m (3,200 ft)
Landing field length, at max landing weight:	
BCAR Section D	1,235 m (4,052 ft)
SFAR 41C/FAR 135	1,165 m (3,820 ft)
Accelerate/stop distance:	
SFAR 41C	1,362 m (4,470 ft)
Range	see individual model listings

BAe JETSTREAM SUPER 31

British Aerospace announced the Jetstream Super 31 at the 1987 Paris Air Show. This version provides significant improvements in performance and passenger comfort, and wider flexibility for regional and interline operations. These benefits derive from introduction of more powerful Garrett TPE331-12 turboprops, flat rated to give 760 kW (1,020 shp) at temperatures up to 26°C. The new power plant gives an 8 per cent power improvement at temperatures up to 20°C and, resulting from the flat rated characteristics, as much as 18 per cent power improvement at high altitude.

The Super 31 will be certificated in the FAA's 19-seat Commuter category, formulated under FAR Pts 23-24. It will also be certificated by the CAA under the International Public Transport Category of BCAR Section D. First order, for 15 by Wings West of the USA, was announced on 13 October 1987. These aircraft are included in the total of sales under the Jetstream 31 entry.

The description of the Jetstream 31 applies also to the Jetstream Super 31 except as follows:

WINGS: Structure simplified and lightened. Changes allow more fuel to be carried.

POWER PLANT: Two 760 kW (1,020 shp) Garrett TPE331-12 turboprops. Automatic power reserve (APR) optional. Fuel load increased by 58.5 kg (129 lb).

ACCOMMODATION: Cabin styling revised, with new sidewash lighting. Cabin furnishing panels re-contoured to give increased cabin height, width and side floor area. Cabin noise reduced by use of a smaller number of panels, isolator mountings and triple window panes.

WEIGHTS:

Operating weight empty	4,415 kg (9,733 lb)
Max T-O weight	7,350 kg (16,204 lb)
Max landing weight	7,080 kg (15,609 lb)
Max zero-fuel weight	6,500 kg (14,330 lb)

PERFORMANCE:

Max cruising speed	232 knots (430 km/h; 267 mph) CAS
Range with IFR reserves:	
19 passengers	700 nm (1,296 km; 805 miles)
18 passengers, flight attendant and galley	600 nm (1,111 km; 690 miles)

BAe JETSTREAM 41

A stretched version of the Jetstream 31, carrying 24-27 passengers, is under consideration by BAe. No launch decision has been made.

BAe 125 SERIES 800

US Air Force designation: C-29A

The prototype (G-BKTF) of this advanced version of the BAe 125 made a 3 h 8 min first flight on 26 May 1983, during which it climbed to its max operating altitude of 13,100 m (43,000 ft). Like the earlier turbojet and turbofan powered

versions of the 125, of which a total of 573 were sold, it is primarily a twin-engined business aircraft but can be used in a wide variety of other civil and military roles, including communications, air ambulance, airways inspection and airline crew training. The **Series 800A** is built by BAe's Civil Aircraft Division for the North American market, **Series 800B** for the rest of the world. Type certification was obtained on 4 May 1984 and the Certificate of Airworthiness, Public Transport Category, on 30 May 1984.

By August 1988, Series 800 sales totalled 127; and 700 BAe 125s of all models had been ordered by operators in 40 countries. Deliveries during the past year included two to REGA Swiss Air Ambulance for aeromedical use, with provision for two stretchers and a comprehensive suite of intensive care equipment.

The US Air Force has ordered six Series 800 aircraft equipped with LTV Sierra flight inspection equipment, to perform its combat flight inspection and navigation (C-FIN) mission, as replacements for its CT-39A and C-140A calibration fleet. The USAF designation of these aircraft is **C-29A**. In May 1988, BAe joined forces with Rockwell International to promote the C-29 in the USAF's Tanker Transport Training System competition for up to 200 lead-in trainers for prospective heavy-jet pilots. If successful in the mid-1989 decision, the C-29 would be assembled at Palmdale, California.

Airframe improvements compared with the Series 700 include a curved windscreen, sequenced nosewheel doors, extended fin leading-edge, larger ventral fuel tank, and an increased wing span which reduces induced drag, improves aerodynamic efficiency and accommodates additional fuel. The outboard 3.05 m (10 ft) of each wing was redesigned.

Garrett TFE731-5R-1H turbofans are fitted to improve airfield/climb performance and to increase both maximum speed and range. The interior was also redesigned. Increased headroom was achieved by relocating oxygen dropout units to the sidewall panels. Increased width resulted from sculpturing the sidewall panels around the fuselage frames, giving an extra 12.2 cm (4.8 in) at shoulder height. The flight deck incorporates a Collins EFIS-85 five-tube electronic flight instrument system, with a centrally mounted multi-function display which can show flight plans and checklists.

TYPE: Twin-turbofan business transport aircraft.

WINGS: Cantilever low-wing monoplane. BAe wing sections. Thickness/chord ratio 14% at root, 8.35% at tip. Dihedral 2°. Incidence 2° 5′ 42″ at root, –3° 5′ 49″ at tip. Sweepback 20° at quarter-chord. Wings built in one piece and dished to pass under fuselage, to which they are attached by four vertical links, a side link and a drag spigot. All-metal two-spar fail-safe structure, with partial centre spar of approx two-thirds span, sealed to form integral fuel tankage which is divided into two compartments by centreline rib. Skins are single-piece units on each of the upper and lower semi-spans. Detachable leading-edges. Mass balanced ailerons, operated manually by cable linkage. Each aileron has a servo action geared tab; port tab trimmed manually via screwjack. Large four-position double-slotted flaps, actuated hydraulically via a screwjack on each flap. Mechanically operated hydraulic cutout prevents asymmetric operation of the flaps. Airbrakes above and below each wing, forming part of flap shrouds, provide lift dumping facility during landing, and have interconnected controls to prevent asymmetric operation. TKS liquid system, using porous stainless steel leading-edge panels, for de-icing or anti-icing.

FUSELAGE: All-metal semi-monocoque fail-safe structure, making extensive use of Redux bonding. Constant circular cross-section over much of its length.

TAIL UNIT: Cantilever all-metal structure, with fixed incidence tailplane mounted on fin. Small fairings on tailplane undersurface to eliminate turbulence around elevator hinge cutouts. Extended dorsal fin, enclosing air-conditioning intake duct. Control surfaces operated manually via cable linkage. Geared tabs in rudder and each elevator. TKS liquid de-icing or anti-icing of tailplane leading-edges.

LANDING GEAR: Retractable tricycle type, with twin wheels on each unit. Hydraulic retraction; nosewheels forward, mainwheels inward into wings. Oleo-pneumatic shock absorbers. Fully castoring nose unit, steerable 45° to port and starboard. Dunlop mainwheels and 12-ply tubeless

Artist's impression of C-29A C-FIN version of the BAe 125 Series 800 for the US Air Force

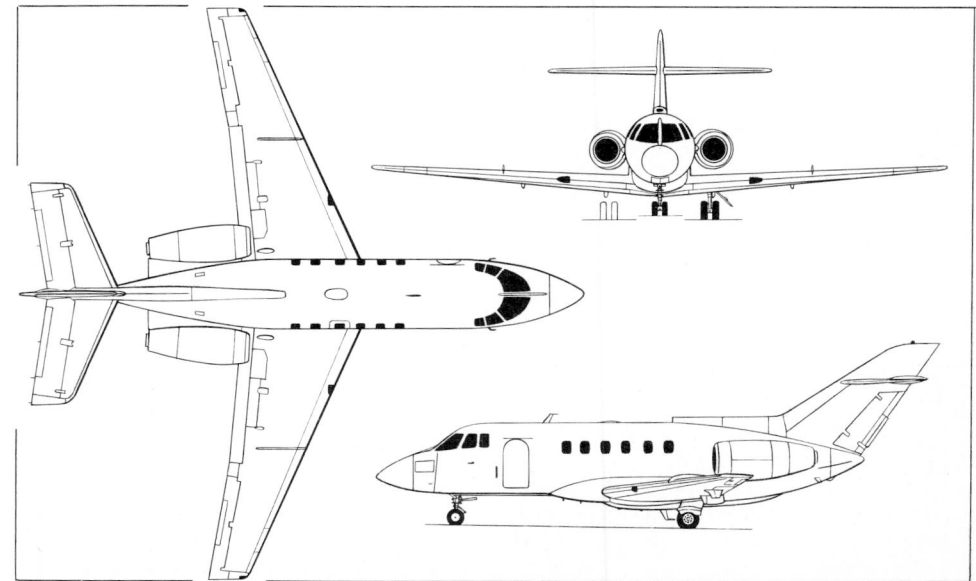

BAe 125 Series 800 (two Garrett TFE731-5R-1H turbofans) *(Pilot Press)*

BAe 125 Series 800 operated by REGA Swiss Air Ambulance *(Anton Wettstein)*

tyres, size 23 × 7-12. Dunlop nosewheels and 6-ply tubeless tyres, size 18 × 4.25-10. Dunlop triple-disc hydraulic brakes with Maxaret anti-skid units on all mainwheels.

POWER PLANT: Two 19.13 kN (4,300 lb st) Garrett TFE731-5R-1H turbofans, pod mounted on sides of rear fuselage, in pods designed and manufactured by Grumman Aerospace. Optional thrust reversers developed by Dee Howard Company. Engine intake anti-icing by engine bleed air. Integral fuel tanks in wings, with combined capacity of 4,820 litres (1,273 US gallons; 1,060 Imp gallons). Rear underfuselage tank of 854 litres (226 US gallons; 188 Imp gallons) capacity, giving total capacity of 5,674 litres (1,499 US gallons; 1,248 Imp gallons). Single pressure refuelling point at rear of ventral tank. Overwing refuelling point near each wingtip.

ACCOMMODATION: Crew of two on flight deck, which is fully soundproofed, insulated and air-conditioned. Dual controls standard. Seat for third crew member. Standard executive layout has forward and rear baggage compartments, forward galley, wardrobe and toilet at rear. Individual recessed lights, air louvres and oxygen masks above each passenger position. Cabin styling offers the operator a choice of interchangeable furnishing units to suit individual requirements, with up to 14 seats. The wide seats swivel through 180°, are adjustable fore, aft and sideways, and can be reclined and used as a bed. Primary configuration from mid-1987 is an open plan layout, with the traditional 'club four' seating moved to the rear of the cabin, the partial bulkhead at the front removed and the galley relocated behind the enlarged forward baggage area. Accommodation in the forward cabin comprises two individual swivelling chairs and a three-place settee. Outward opening door at front on port side, with integral airstairs. Emergency exit over wing on starboard side. Electric windscreen anti-icing. Optional heated baggage pannier in place of the rear underfuselage fuel tank.

SYSTEMS: AiResearch air-conditioning and pressurisation system. Max cabin differential 0.59 bars (8.55 lb/sq in). Oxygen system standard, with dropout masks for passengers. Hydraulic system, pressure 186-207 bars (2,700-3,000 lb/sq in), for operation of landing gear, mainwheel doors, flaps, spoilers, nosewheel steering, mainwheel brakes and anti-skid units. Two accumulators, pressurised by engine bleed air, one for main system pressure, the other providing emergency hydraulic power for wheel brakes in case of main system failure. Independent auxiliary system for lowering landing gear and flaps in the event of a main system failure. DC electrical system utilises two 30V 12kW engine driven starter/generators and two 24V 23Ah nickel-cadmium batteries. A 24V 4Ah battery provides separate power for standby instruments. AC electrical system includes two 1.25kVA static inverters, providing 115V 400Hz single-phase supplies, one 250VA standby static inverter for avionics, and two engine driven 208V 7.4kVA frequency-wild alternators for windscreen anti-icing. Ground power receptacle on starboard side at rear of fuselage for 28V external DC supply. Garrett GTCP-30-92 auxiliary power unit. Engine ice protection system supplied by engine bleed air. Graviner triple FD Firewire fire warning system and two BCF engine fire extinguishers. Stall warning system indicates approach to the stall, and an identification system operates a stick pusher to initiate a nose down pitching movement if the approach to the stall exceeds a predetermined rate.

AVIONICS AND EQUIPMENT: Digital avionics have been introduced and received FAA Cat II certification in 1987. Standard avionics include dual Collins VHF-22A com transceivers, Collins 628T-3 HF com transceiver, dual Collins VIR-32 VHF nav receivers with marker beacon indicator, dual Collins ADF-60B, dual Collins AHS-85 attitude and heading reference systems, dual Collins DME-42 DME, dual Collins TDR-90 ATC transponders, Collins WXR-300 weather radar, dual Collins ADS-82 air data systems, Collins APS-85 autopilot, dual Collins

EFIS-85B-2 electronic flight instrument systems, Collins ALT-55B radio altimeter, Baker M1045 audio system, Global GNS-1000 flight management system, Pioneer KE-8300 stereo tape and FM/AM radio.

DIMENSIONS, EXTERNAL:

Wing span	15.66 m (51 ft 4½ in)
Wing chord (mean)	2.29 m (7 ft 6¼ in)
Wing aspect ratio	7.06
Length overall	15.60 m (51 ft 2 in)
Height overall	5.36 m (17 ft 7 in)
Fuselage: Max diameter	1.93 m (6 ft 4 in)
Tailplane span	6.10 m (20 ft 0 in)
Wheel track (c/l of shock absorbers)	2.79 m (9 ft 2 in)
Wheelbase	6.41 m (21 ft 0½ in)
Passenger door (fwd, port):	
Height	1.30 m (4 ft 3 in)
Width	0.69 m (2 ft 3 in)
Height to sill	1.07 m (3 ft 6 in)
Emergency exit (overwing, stbd):	
Height	0.91 m (3 ft 0 in)
Width	0.51 m (1 ft 8 in)

DIMENSIONS, INTERNAL:

Cabin (excl flight deck): Length	6.50 m (21 ft 4 in)
Max width	1.83 m (6 ft 0 in)
Max height	1.75 m (5 ft 9 in)
Floor area	5.11 m² (55.0 sq ft)
Volume	17.10 m³ (604.0 cu ft)
Baggage compartments:	
forward	0.74 m³ (26.0 cu ft)
rear	0.74 m³ (26.0 cu ft)
pannier (optional)	0.79 m³ (28.0 cu ft)

AREAS:

Wings, gross	34.75 m² (374 sq ft)
Ailerons (total)	2.05 m² (22.1 sq ft)
Spoilers: upper (total)	0.74 m² (8.0 sq ft)
lower (total)	0.46 m² (5.0 sq ft)
Trailing-edge flaps (total)	4.83 m² (52.0 sq ft)
Fin (excl dorsal fin)	6.43 m² (69.2 sq ft)
Rudder	1.32 m² (14.2 sq ft)
Horizontal tail surfaces (total)	9.29 m² (100.0 sq ft)

WEIGHTS AND LOADING:

Basic weight	6,676 kg (14,720 lb)
Typical operating weight empty	6,858 kg (15,120 lb)
Max payload	1,088 kg (2,400 lb)
Max ramp weight	12,480 kg (27,520 lb)
Max T-O weight	12,430 kg (27,400 lb)
Max zero-fuel weight	7,950 kg (17,520 lb)
Max landing weight	10,590 kg (23,350 lb)
Max wing loading	357.69 kg/m² (73.26 lb/sq ft)

PERFORMANCE:

Never-exceed speed	Mach 0.87
Max level speed and max cruising speed at 8,840 m (29,000 ft)	456 knots (845 km/h; 525 mph)
Econ cruising speed at 11,900-13,100 m (39,000-43,000 ft)	400 knots (741 km/h; 461 mph)
Stalling speed in landing configuration at typical landing weight	92 knots (170 km/h; 106 mph)
Max rate of climb at S/L	945 m (3,100 ft)/min
Time to 10,670 m (35,000 ft)	19 min
Service ceiling	13,100 m (43,000 ft)
T-O balanced field length at max T-O weight	1,713 m (5,620 ft)
Landing from 15 m (50 ft) at typical landing weight (6 passengers and baggage)	1,372 m (4,500 ft)
Range with max payload	2,870 nm (5,318 km; 3,305 miles)
Range with max fuel, NBAA VFR reserves	3,000 nm (5,560 km; 3,454 miles)

BAe SUPER 748

Design of the original version of this short/medium range turboprop airliner started in January 1959, as the Avro 748. The first prototype flew on 24 June 1960, followed by a second on 10 April 1961. Initial UK production models were the 748 Series 1 (18 built), Series 2 (including two Andover CC.Mk 2s for The Queen's Flight and for Air Support Command), Series 2A and 2B. These were superseded by the Super 748, production of which ceased in 1988. A description appears in the 1986-87 *Jane's*, together with brief details of the 748 Military Transport with a large freight door.

Sales of all Series, including 31 Andover C. Mk 1s for the RAF (see 1968-69 *Jane's*) and licence manufacture of 89 in India, totalled 382 by May 1988, when the last two 748s were nearing completion before delivery to Taiwan.

BAe ATP

British Aerospace announced its intention to develop an advanced turboprop (ATP) regional transport aircraft, to succeed the Super 748, on 1 March 1984. The prototype ATP (G-MATP) flew for the first time on 6 August 1986. A second aircraft (G-BMYM) followed on 20 February 1987, in the markings of the first domestic customer, British Midland Airways. Certification, under the European Joint Airworthiness Regulations (JAR 25) was achieved in March 1988 after 1,290 hours of flying with three aircraft. Revenue-earning services (with British Midland) began on 9 May 1988. By August 1988 orders had been placed by Airlines of Britain (British Midland, Loganair and Manx Airlines) for eight (plus two options), British Airways (8 + 8), LIAT (2 + 2), and LAR of Portugal (3 + 1). Avline Trading Corporation of Toronto, Canada, has an option on five ATPs. Production in 1988 was planned to total 12 aircraft, increasing in 1989 to 18.

The ATP retains the same cabin cross section as the Super 748 but has a longer fuselage. Standard accommodation is for 64 passengers at a seat pitch of 79 cm (31 in), but various layouts are available for 60 to 72 passengers. There are separate forward and rear passenger doors, with integral airstairs at the forward door, and separate forward and rear baggage doors. The sill height of the forward passenger door allows the ATP to use jetways at regional airports. Sound measurements taken during take-off and landing have shown the ATP to be between 2 and 7 EPNdB quieter than any other airliner in its class.

Several military variants of the ATP have been proposed by BAe, including an AEW aircraft with Thorn EMI Skymaster radars in nose and tail radomes; an anti-submarine/anti-surface vessel adaptation having six weapons pylons, a sonobuoy launcher, GEC Avionics AQS-902 sonics processing equipment, MAD, ESM, Litton APS-504(V)5 surveillance radar, FLIR, and twin INS platforms; and a freighter with a shortened front fuselage and Andover C. Mk 1 rear-loading ramp, capable of transporting 7,257 kg (16,000 lb) of freight or 48 troops.

TYPE: Twin-turboprop regional transport aircraft.

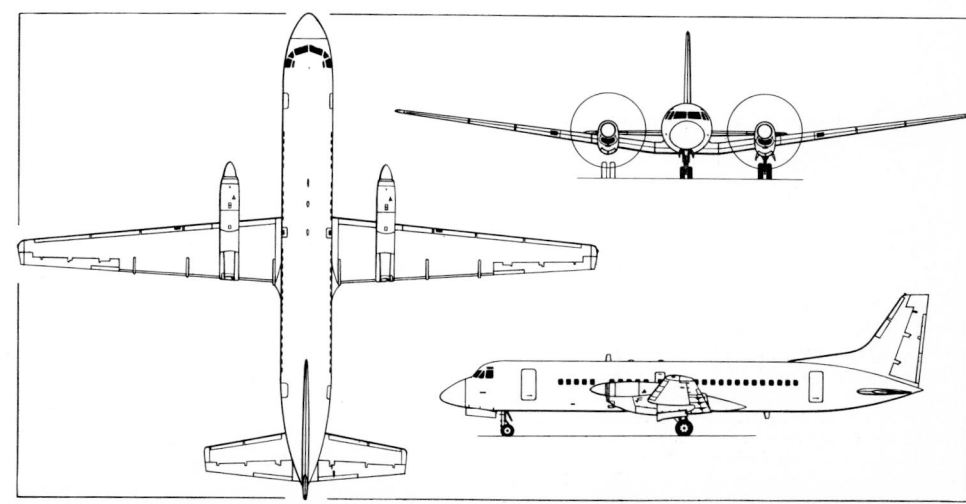

Three-view drawing of the twin-turboprop BAe ATP transport *(Pilot Press)*

BAe ATP regional transport aircraft (two Pratt & Whitney Canada PW126 turboprops) in the livery of British Midland Airways

WINGS: Cantilever low-wing monoplane, with dihedral from centre-section. All-metal two-spar fail-safe structure, generally similar to that of BAe 748. Wing spars do not intrude into passenger cabin. Horn balanced ailerons; Fowler trailing-edge flaps (manufactured by HAI, Greece); geared tab in each aileron. Pneumatic boot de-icing of leading-edges outboard of engine nacelles.

FUSELAGE: All-metal circular section semi-monocoque fail-safe structure, generally similar to BAe 748 but lengthened by 5.03 m (16 ft 6 in).

TAIL UNIT: Cantilever all-metal structure, with slightly swept vertical and non-swept horizontal surfaces. Power assisted rudder. Trim tab in each elevator; trim and spring tabs in rudder. Pneumatic boot de-icing of fin and tailplane leading-edges.

LANDING GEAR: Retractable tricycle type, of Dowty Rotol design, with twin-wheel main units and twin-wheel steerable nose unit. All units retract forward, main units into bottom of engine nacelles. Oleo-pneumatic shock absorbers. Mainwheels fitted with 34 × 11.75-14 tubeless tyres. Nosewheels fitted with 22 × 6.75-10 tubeless tyres. Mainwheels have fusible plugs operating at 199°C. All wheels have 'roll on rim' capability. Dunlop carbon brakes and Maxaret anti-skid units on mainwheels. Inner and outer brakes on each leg supplied from two hydraulically independent systems via engine driven pump or standby DC pump.

POWER PLANT: Two 1,978 kW (2,653 shp) Pratt & Whitney Canada PW126 (JAR) or 1,790 kW (2,400 shp) PW124A (FAA) turboprops. BAe/Hamilton Standard slow-turning propellers, each having six blades of advanced aerodynamic profile and lightweight composite construction. Fuel in two integral wing tanks, with combined capacity of 6,364 litres (1,681 US gallons; 1,400 Imp gallons). Single pressure refuelling point under starboard outer wing.

ACCOMMODATION: Crew of two on flight deck; two cabin attendants. Main cabin has standard pressurised accommodation for 64 passengers, at seat pitch of 79 cm (31 in), in four abreast layout with central aisle. Alternative layouts provide 60 to 72 seats. Galley at rear of cabin on starboard side, toilet forward on port side. Separate passenger doors at front (with airstairs) and rear of cabin on port side. Compartment for carry-on baggage on port side of cabin, forward of front row of seats. Two baggage/freight compartments, one forward on starboard side and one aft of main cabin, both with external access. Overhead lockers above passenger seats. Forward cabin bulkhead can be moved on seat rails to permit flexibility for multi-sector or mixed passenger/cargo operations.

SYSTEMS: Hamilton Standard environmental control system with twin ECS packs offering sub-zero delivery temperature capability. Automatic pressurisation system, giving altitude equivalent to 2,440 m (8,000 ft) at 7,620 m (25,000 ft). Pressure differential 0.38 bars (5.5 lb/sq in). Each engine drives an Abex variable delivery hydraulic pump providing hydraulic power at a regulated pressure of 172 bars (2,500 lb/sq in) for landing gear actuation, nosewheel steering, brakes and airstairs. Auxiliary hydraulic power is supplied from a separate DC pump and reservoir for emergency operation of the landing gear and brakes. The system also provides hydraulic pressure for servicing when the engines are not running. Main system has a flow rate of 41 litres (11 US gallons; 9 Imp gallons)/min controlled to 169 bars (2,450 lb/sq in);

emergency system has a flow rate of 2.25 litres (0.6 US gallons; 0.5 Imp gallon)/min controlled to 145 bars (2,100 lb/sq in). Air/oil reservoirs pressurised to 1.25 bars (18 lb/sq in). Electrical power provided by Lucas 200V 30/45KVa variable frequency alternators, mounted on each engine. 28V DC subsystem from either two TRUs or two 35Ah nickel-cadmium batteries. Second subsystem provides 1.5KVa 200/115V constant frequency power from two static inverters. Garrett Model GTCP36-150 APU for air-conditioning on the ground, and electrical power for battery charging, engine starting assist and other tasks.

AVIONICS AND EQUIPMENT: Digital avionics system using ARINC 429 data transmission, Smiths SDS-201 four-tube EFIS, Bendix avionics. Twin VHF com, twin VHF nav, scanning DME with additional frequency under R/Nav control, ADF, ATC transponder, CVR, FDR and digital GPWS. Bendix RDS-86 colour weather radar, with checklist facility, can display weather on EFIS nav display. Built-in test and recording facility. Dual AFCS, each with Litton LTR 81-01 AHRS and Smiths digital DADS, for Cat II ILS capability. Options include second DME, second ADF, second transponder, R/Nav, MLS and single HF.

DIMENSIONS, EXTERNAL:

Wing span	30.63 m (100 ft 6 in)
Length overall	26.00 m (85 ft 4 in)
Height overall	7.14 m (23 ft 5 in)
Wheel track	8.46 m (27 ft 9 in)
Wheelbase	9.70 m (31 ft 9¾ in)
Propeller diameter	4.19 m (13 ft 9 in)
Propeller/fuselage clearance	0.80 m (2 ft 7½ in)
Passenger doors: Height	1.73 m (5 ft 8 in)
Width	0.71 m (2 ft 4 in)
Height to sill: fwd door	2.09 m (6 ft 10 in)
rear door	1.71 m (5 ft 7½ in)

DIMENSIONS, INTERNAL:

Cabin: Length	19.20 m (63 ft 0 in)
Max width	2.49 m (8 ft 2 in)
Max height	1.92 m (6 ft 4 in)
Volume	75.1 m³ (2,652 cu ft)

Baggage/freight compartment volume (64 seats):

Forward hold	4.39 m³ (155 cu ft)
Rear hold	5.10 m³ (180 cu ft)
Carry-on stowage	6.60 m³ (233 cu ft)

WEIGHTS:

Operating weight empty	13,595 kg (29,970 lb)
Max fuel	5,080 kg (11,200 lb)
Max payload	6,726 kg (14,830 lb)
Max ramp weight	22,997 kg (50,700 lb)
Max T-O weight	22,930 kg (50,550 lb)
Max landing weight	22,250 kg (49,050 lb)
Max zero-fuel weight	21,000 kg (46,300 lb)

PERFORMANCE (provisional):

Cruising speed at AUW of 19,051 kg (42,000 lb) at 4,575 m (15,000 ft)   268 knots (496 km/h; 308 mph)

T-O field length:

at max T-O weight   1,539 m (5,050 ft)

for 150 nm (278 km; 173 mile) sector, 64 passengers, reserves for 100 nm (185 km; 115 miles) diversion, plus 45 min hold at 3,050 m (10,000 ft)
1,097 m (3,600 ft)

Landing field length at max landing weight
1,097 m (3,600 ft)

Range, with reserves for 100 nm (185 km; 115 mile) diversion and 45 min hold at 3,050 m (10,000 ft):

with max payload	575 nm (1,065 km; 662 miles)
with 64 passengers (5,806 kg; 12,800 lb)	
	985 nm (1,825 km; 1,134 miles)
with max fuel and 3,778 kg (8,330 lb) payload	
	1,860 nm (3,444 km; 2,140 miles)
Ferry range	2,198 nm (4,070 km; 2,529 miles)

BAe 146
RAF designation: BAe 146 CC. Mk 2

In August 1973, the former Hawker Siddeley Aviation announced that it was to produce with government support a four-turbofan quiet operating transport aircraft known as the HS 146. Within a few months economic problems in the UK halted this programme, but research and design continued on a limited basis. With the absorption of Hawker Siddeley Aviation into British Aerospace in April 1977, BAe continued to provide limited funding to allow the manufacture of assembly jigs, systems test rigs, and continuing design and wind tunnel testing. On 10 July 1978, the British Aerospace Board's decision to give the 146 programme a full go-ahead was approved by the government. Production of what is now known as the BAe 146 is undertaken in several BAe factories, including Brough (fin and flaps), Filton (centre fuselage), Manchester (rear fuselage), Hamble (flap track fairings), and Prestwick (engine pylons). Hatfield builds the front fuselage and flight deck, and initially was responsible for all final assembly and flight testing.

In March 1987 British Aerospace announced that production of the BAe 146 was to be increased to 40 aircraft a year by 1990. To help achieve this increase, a second final assembly line for the aircraft has been established at the BAe factory at Woodford, near Manchester. Woodford was scheduled to manufacture four 146s in 1988, with a progressive build-up thereafter and a total of 100 over six years. The first of these flew on 16 May 1988.

Under risk sharing agreements, Textron Aerostructures (USA) manufactures wings for the BAe 146 and Saab-Scania (Sweden) the tailplanes and all movable control surfaces.

The following versions of the BAe 146 are available:

Series 100. Designed to operate from short or semi-prepared airstrips with minimal ground facilities, with a normal seating capacity of 82-93. Rollout of the Series 100 prototype (G-SSSH) took place on 20 May 1981, and first flight was made on 3 September 1981. The second Series 100 (G-SSHH) flew on 25 January 1982, followed by the third (G-SSCH) on 2 April 1982. Type certification was obtained on 4 February 1983 and Transport category CAA certification of the Series 100 was obtained on 20 May 1983, with the first delivery, to Dan-Air, on 21 May 1983, and first scheduled operation on 27 May. Thicker skin on centre fuselage of later production aircraft will permit increased T-O weight if required. Two are operated by The Queen's Flight under the designation BAe 146 CC. Mk 2.

Series 200. For operation from paved runways only, with seating capacity of 82-112. Fuselage lengthened by five frame pitches (2.39 m; 7 ft 10 in). Increased maximum T-O weight and zero-fuel weight. Underfloor cargo volume increased by 35 per cent. The first Series 200 (G-WISC) flew on 1 August 1982 and received type certification on 4 February 1983. The first production Series 200 (N601AW) was delivered to Air Wisconsin in June 1983, and operated its first scheduled service on 27 June, following receipt of FAA certification of Series 100 and 200.

BAe 146 Series 200 four-turbofan transport in the insignia of Air UK

Series 300. Development of the Series 100, with length increased by inserting a forward fuselage plug of 2.46 m (8 ft 1 in) and rear plug of 2.34 m (7 ft 8 in). This enables 100 passengers to be carried in greatly increased comfort, in a five-abreast business class layout, with ample wardrobe and galley space. Wings and power plant unchanged. Thicker skin on centre-fuselage permits increased T-O weight of 43,090 kg (95,000 lb). Aerodynamic prototype (G-LUXE) was produced by conversion of the original Series 100 prototype (G-SSSH) and was flown for the first time in its new form on 1 May 1987. First production Series 300 was scheduled to fly in Summer 1988, with certification in September and delivery in October of that year. In May 1987, Air Wisconsin became the launch customer by changing from Series 200 to 300 five of the aircraft it had ordered in September 1986.

Series 350. Proposed freighter development of the Series 300 with the fuselage lengthened by insertion of another plug of around 1.5 m (5 ft), to permit the carriage of eight or nine standard freight pallets. Power plant and max payload weight unchanged.

146-QT Quiet Trader. Freighter versions. Cabin volume allows the 146-200 freighter to carry six standard 2.74 × 2.24 m (108 × 88 in) pallets, with space for an extra half pallet, or up to nine standard LD3 containers. Minor modifications to the standard floor make possible a maximum freight payload of 11,022 kg (24,300 lb), and the floor stressing permits a maximum individual pallet load of 2,721 kg (6,000 lb). Later versions, making use of further structural developments, will enable payloads of up to 12,973 kg (28,600 lb) to be carried.

The freight door is located in the rear fuselage, allowing normal passenger facilities to be retained at the front of the cabin for use in a Combi configuration; the rear passenger door is retained separately.

The first freighter conversion, a Series 200 aircraft (N146FT), was undertaken in the USA by Hayes International Corporation's Dothan, Alabama Division, which was responsible for the design, manufacture and installation of the door, the freight handling equipment, internal structure reinforcements and furnishings. After conversion this aircraft (then N146QT) was purchased by TNT, the Australian-origin transportation group, and (re-registered G-TNTA) entered service on 5 May 1987. In June 1987 TNT and BAe reached agreements covering a long term commitment for the acquisition of up to 72 BAe 146-QTs over the following five years. A substantial number of these will be used for the TNT freight network; the balance of the aircraft will be available for sale or lease through Ansett Worldwide Aviation Services. Firm orders by TNT had increased to eight by mid-1988. Ansett has ordered two.

Statesman. British Aerospace offers Statesman executive versions of Series 100 and 200 aircraft. The cabin area available allows flexibility of interior design. Staterooms, staff quarters, additional galley and wardrobe space can be provided. The first BAe 146 Statesman was delivered in mid-1986 for use in the Far East.

During the 1987 Paris Air Show, British Aerospace announced brief details of the following military developments of the BAe 146, any of which could be fitted with a flight refuelling probe above the flight deck:

BAe 146STA (Small Tactical Airlifter). Derived from the BAe 146-QT Quiet Trader freighter, the 146STA is offered as a versatile military airlifter with a 7,620 kg

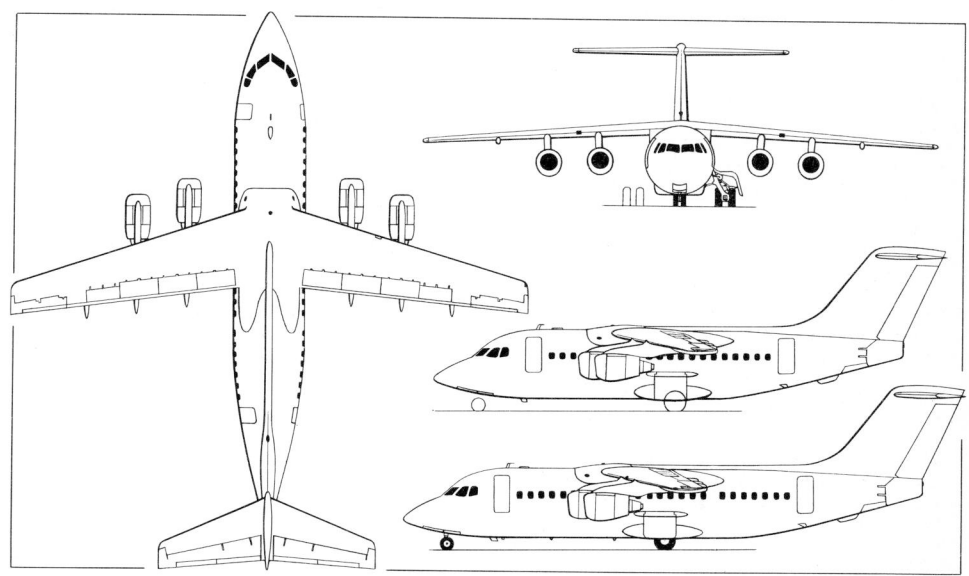

BAe 146 Series 200, with additional side view (centre right) of Series 100 (*Pilot Press*)

BAe 146-QT Quiet Traders, with freight door, in the livery of TNT

(16,800 lb) payload, forward field capability and low life cycle costs. The 146STA features a 4.44 m (14 ft 7 in) wide main deck cargo door in the port side of the rear fuselage. This offers maximum flexibility in load handling, allowing vehicles to be embarked as well as field guns or more conventional palletised loads. Roller tracks can be fitted to existing seat rails to facilitate movement of pallets weighing up to 2,720 kg (6,000 lb). A sliding door set within the main cargo door, and an inward opening door on the starboard side, permit paradropping. Up to 60 fully equipped paratroops can be carried, using side facing seats. The port side sliding door can also be opened in flight to a maximum

Prototype BAe 146 Series 300 four-turbofan transport

width of 1.52 m (5 ft 0 in), which permits standard military pallets to be dropped. Six pallets can be carried on purpose designed guiderails for rapid airdrop. Variations to the 146STA's transport role extend to dedicated military VIP versions and casualty evacuation, carrying up to 24 stretcher cases.

BAe 146MSL (Military Side Loader). Militarised version of the existing 146-QT Quiet Trader freighter, equipped with the standard upward opening 3.33 m (10 ft 11 in) wide side door.

BAe 146M. (Military Tanker). Underwing flight refuelling pods give this aircraft a dual-point aerial refuelling capability.

BAe 246M (Military Rear Loader). More advanced development, with large hydraulically operated rear loading ramp doors allied to a lowered main deck floor, capable of accepting larger and heavier payloads. The main landing gear would be redesigned to a tandem configuration housed in fuselage sponsons.

Orders totalled 26 Srs 100s, 77 Srs 200s, five Srs 300s and ten Srs 200-QTs by 29 June 1988, at which time 90 had been delivered.

The following description applies to the commercial Series 100, 200 and 300, except where indicated otherwise:

TYPE: Four-turbofan short range transport aircraft.

WINGS: Cantilever high-wing monoplane. British Aerospace high lift aerofoil section. Thickness/chord ratio 15.3% adjacent to fuselage, 12.2% at tip. Anhedral 3° at trailing-edge. Incidence 3° 6' at fuselage side, 0° at tip. Sweepback 15° at quarter-chord. All-metal fail-safe structure of light alloy with machined skins, integrally machined spars and ribs. Single-section hydraulically actuated tabbed Fowler flaps of light alloy, spanning 78 per cent of each wing trailing-edge, with Dowty Rotol actuators. Mechanically actuated balanced ailerons. Hydraulically operated roll spoiler outboard of three lift dumpers on each wing. Trim and servo tab in each aileron. No leading-edge lift devices. Hot air anti-icing of leading-edges.

FUSELAGE: All-metal fail-safe pressurised semi-monocoque structure. Strengthened centre section developed initially for the Series 300 will be standard on all future 146-100s.

Flight deck and tailcone areas free of stringers. Remainder of structure has 'top hat' stringers bonded to skins above keel area. Z section stringers 'wet' assembled with bonding agent and riveted to skin in keel area. Chemically etched skins of light alloy. Petal airbrakes form tailcone when closed.

TAIL UNIT: Cantilever sweptback T tail, of all-metal construction. Chemically etched light alloy skins bonded to 'top hat' section stringers. Fixed incidence tailplane. Manually operated balanced elevators, each with trim and servo tab. Powered rudder. Hot air anti-icing of tailplane leading-edges.

LANDING GEAR: Hydraulically retractable tricycle type, of Dowty Rotol design, with twin Dunlop wheels on each unit. Main units retract inward into fairings on fuselage sides; steerable nose unit retracts forward. Oleo-pneumatic shock absorbers with wheels mounted on trailing axle. Simple telescopic nosewheel strut. Mainwheel tyres size 12.50-16 Type III, pressure (Series 100) 8.42 bars (122 lb/sq in). Nosewheel tyres size 7.50-10 Type III, pressure (Series 100) 7.80 bars (113 lb/sq in). Low pressure tyres optional. Dunlop multi-disc carbon brakes operated by duplicated hydraulic systems. Anti-skid units in both primary and secondary brake systems.

POWER PLANT: Four Textron Lycoming ALF 502R-5 turbofans, each rated at 31.0 kN (6,970 lb st), installed in pylon mounted underwing pods. No reverse thrust. Fuel in two integral wing tanks and integral centre-section tank (the latter with a vented and drained sealing diaphragm above passenger cabin), having a combined capacity of 11,728 litres (3,098 US gallons; 2,580 Imp gallons). Optional auxiliary tanks in wingroot fairings, with combined capacity of 1,173 litres (310 US gallons; 258 Imp gallons), giving total capacity of 12,901 litres (3,408 US gallons; 2,838 Imp gallons). Single-point pressure refuelling, with coupling situated in starboard wing outboard of outer engine.

ACCOMMODATION: Crew of two pilots on flight deck, and two or three cabin staff. Optional observer's seat. Series 100 has accommodation in main cabin for 82 passengers with six-abreast seating at 84 cm (33 in) pitch, and up to 93 seats six-abreast at 74 cm (29 in) pitch. Series 200 has max

capacity for 112 passengers with six-abreast seating at 74 cm (29 in) pitch. Series 300 has standard accommodation in a slightly wider cabin interior for 100 passengers, with five-abreast seating at 79 cm (31 in) pitch. Various alternative layouts for mixed passenger/freight configurations. All seating layouts have two toilets and a forward galley as standard. Series 300 has wardrobe at front of cabin on starboard side. One outward opening passenger door forward and one aft on port side of cabin. Built-in airstairs optional. Servicing doors, one forward and one aft, on starboard side of cabin. Freight and baggage holds under cabin floor. All accommodation air-conditioned. Windscreen electrical anti-icing and demisting standard. Rain repellent system optional.

SYSTEMS: BAe/Normalair-Garrett cabin air-conditioning and pressurisation system, using engine bleed air. Electro-pneumatic pressurisation control with discharge valves at fore and aft of cabin. Max differential 0.45 bars (6.5 lb/sq in). Hydraulic system, duplicated for essential services, for landing gear, flaps, rudder, roll and lift spoilers, airbrakes, nosewheel steering, brakes and auxiliary fuel pumps; pressure 207 bars (3,000 lb/sq in). Electrical system powered by two 40kVA integrated-drive alternators to feed 115/200V 3-phase 400Hz primary systems. 28V DC power supplied by transformer-rectifier in each channel. Hydraulically powered emergency electrical power unit. Garrett GTCP 36-100M APU for ground air-conditioning and electrical power generation. High pressure gaseous oxygen system, pressure 124 bars (1,800 lb/sq in). Stall warning and identification system, comprising stick shaker (warning) and stick force (identification) elements, providing soft and hard corrective stick forces at the approach of stall conditions. Series 100: stick force soft with flaps up; Series 200: force soft above 185 knots (343 km/h; 213 mph) regardless of configuration.

AVIONICS: Smiths SEP 10 automatic flight control and flight guidance system incorporates a simplex Cat I autopilot with a flight director display and separate attitude reference for each pilot. Addition of extra equipment and wiring permits coupled approaches to Cat II minima. Standard ARINC interface with radio nav system allows choice of radio equipment. Basic avionics include dual VHF com, audio system, passenger address system, cockpit voice recorder, dual compass systems, dual ADIs with separate attitude reference driven by single computer, marker beacon receiver, weather radar, dual radio altimeters, ground proximity warning system, dual DME, dual ATC transponders, dual VHF nav and dual ADF. Dowty-UEL flight deck warning system. Optional avionics include third VHF com, area navigation system, Selcal, tape reproducer, and single or dual HF com.

DIMENSIONS, EXTERNAL:

Wing span, incl static dischargers	26.34 m (86 ft 5 in)

Note: Static discharger extends 6.3 cm (2½ in) from each wingtip

Wing aspect ratio	8.97
Length overall: Series 100	26.20 m (85 ft 11½ in)
Series 200	28.60 m (93 ft 10 in)
Series 300	30.99 m (101 ft 8¼ in)

Note: Static dischargers on elevator extend length of all series by 18.4 cm (7¼ in)

Height overall	8.61 m (28 ft 3 in)
Fuselage diameter	3.56 m (11 ft 8 in)
Tailplane span	11.09 m (36 ft 5 in)
Wheel track	4.72 m (15 ft 6 in)
Wheelbase: Series 100	10.09 m (33 ft 1½ in)
Series 200	11.20 m (36 ft 9 in)
Series 300	12.52 m (41 ft 1 in)

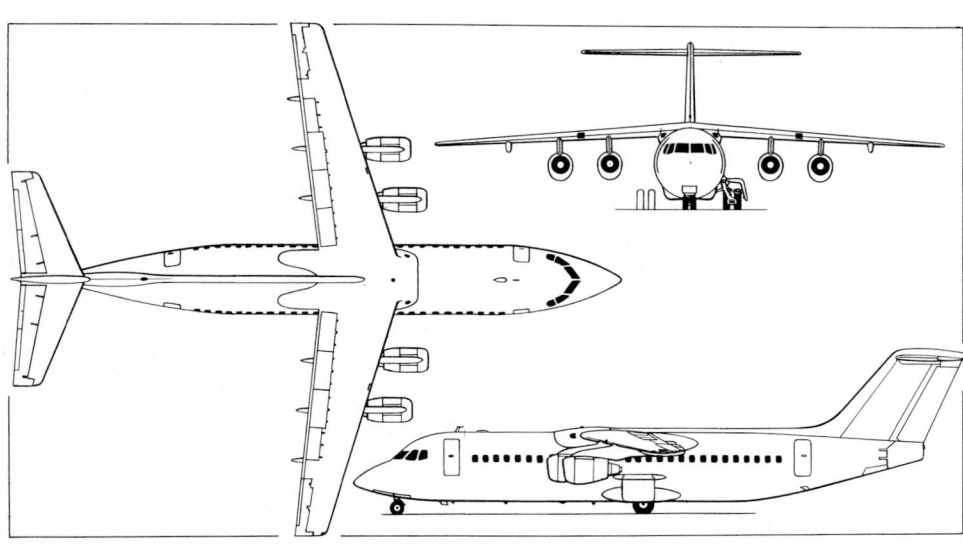

BAe 146 Series 300, the 'stretched' version of this short range transport *(Pilot Press)*

Passenger doors (port, fwd and rear):
Height 1.83 m (6 ft 0 in)
Width 0.85 m (2 ft 9½ in)
Height to sill: fwd 1.88 m (6 ft 2 in)
rear 1.98 m (6 ft 6 in)
Servicing doors (stbd, fwd and rear):
Height 1.47 m (4 ft 10 in)
Width 0.85 m (2 ft 9½ in)
Height to sill: fwd 1.88 m (6 ft 2 in)
rear 1.98 m (6 ft 6 in)
Underfloor freight hold door (stbd, fwd):
Height 1.09 m (3 ft 7 in)
Width 1.35 m (4 ft 5 in)
Height to sill 0.78 m (2 ft 7 in)
Underfloor freight hold door (stbd, rear):
Height 1.04 m (3 ft 5 in)
Width 0.91 m (3 ft 0 in)
Height to sill 0.90 m (2 ft 11½ in)
Freight door (Freighter versions):
Height 1.93 m (6 ft 4 in)
Width: Series 100 2.92 m (9 ft 7 in)
Series 200 3.33 m (10 ft 11 in)
Height to sill 1.93 m (6 ft 4 in)

DIMENSIONS, INTERNAL:
Cabin (excl flight deck, incl galley and toilets):
Length: Series 100 15.42 m (50 ft 7 in)
Series 200 17.81 m (58 ft 5 in)
Series 300 20.20 m (66 ft 3¼ in)
Max width: Series 100, 200 3.38 m (11 ft 1 in)
Series 300 3.42 m (11 ft 2½ in)
Max height 2.02 m (6 ft 7½ in)
Freight cabin, 146 Series 200-QT:
Cargo floor: Length 16.08 m (52 ft 9 in)
Width 3.23 m (10 ft 7 in)
Volume: pallets/igloos 60.3 m³ (2,145 cu ft)
LD3 containers 42.66 m³ (1,422 cu ft)
Baggage/freight holds, underfloor:
Series 100 13.7 m³ (479 cu ft)
Series 200 18.3 m³ (645 cu ft)
Series 300 22.31 m³ (788 cu ft)

AREAS:
Wings, gross 77.30 m² (832 sq ft)
Ailerons (total) 3.62 m² (39 sq ft)
Trailing-edge flaps (total) 19.51 m² (210 sq ft)
Spoilers (total) 10.03 m² (108 sq ft)
Fin 15.51 m² (167 sq ft)
Rudder 5.30 m² (57 sq ft)
Tailplane 15.61 m² (168 sq ft)
Elevators, incl tabs 10.03 m² (108 sq ft)

WEIGHTS AND LOADINGS:
Typical operating weight empty:
Series 100 22,226 kg (49,000 lb)
Series 200 22,861 kg (50,400 lb)
Series 200-QT 22,317 kg (49,200 lb)
Series 300 24,494 kg (54,000 lb)
Max payload: Series 100 8,845 kg (19,500 lb)
Series 200 10,478 kg (23,100 lb)
Series 200-QT 11,022 kg (24,300 lb)
Max fuel weight:
Series 100, 200 standard 9,362 kg (20,640 lb)
Series 100, 200, optional 10,298 kg (22,704 lb)
Max T-O weight:
Series 100 38,102 kg (84,000 lb)
Series 200, 300 (initial) 42,184 kg (93,000 lb)
Max ramp weight:
Series 100 38,329 kg (84,500 lb)
Series 200, 300 (initial) 42,410 kg (93,500 lb)
Max zero-fuel weight:
Series 100 31,071 kg (68,500 lb)
Series 200 33,339 kg (73,500 lb)
Series 300 34,246 kg (75,500 lb)
Max landing weight:
Series 100 35,153 kg (77,500 lb)
Series 200 36,741 kg (81,000 lb)
Series 300 37,648 kg (83,000 lb)
Max wing loading:
Series 100 493.0 kg/m² (101.0 lb/sq ft)
Series 200, 300 (initial) 545.7 kg/m² (111.8 lb/sq ft)
Max power loading:
Series 100, standard 307.3 kg/kN (3.01 lb/lb st)
Series 200, 300 (initial) 340.2 kg/kN (3.34 lb/lb st)

PERFORMANCE (at max standard T-O weight, except where indicated):
Max operating Mach No: Series 100 and 200 0.70
Max operating speed:
Series 100 300 knots (555 km/h; 345 mph) CAS
Series 200, 300 295 knots (546 km/h; 339 mph) CAS
Econ cruising speed at 9,145 m (30,000 ft):
all Series 383 knots (709 km/h; 440 mph)
Stalling speed, 30° flap:
Series 100 97 knots (180 km/h; 112 mph) EAS
Series 200, 300 102 knots (189 km/h; 118 mph) EAS
Stalling speed, 33° flap, at max landing weight:
Series 100 89 knots (165 km/h; 103 mph) EAS
Series 200, 300 92 knots (170 km/h; 106 mph) EAS
T-O to 11 m (35 ft), S/L, ISA:
Series 100 1,219 m (4,000 ft)
Series 200, 300 1,509 m (4,950 ft)
FAR landing distance from 15 m (50 ft), S/L, ISA, at max landing weight: Series 100 1,067 m (3,500 ft)

Series 200 1,103 m (3,620 ft)
Series 300 1,228 m (4,030 ft)
Range with standard fuel, incl 86 kg (190 lb) fuel for ground manoeuvres, plus fuel for 150 nm (278 km; 173 mile) diversion and 45 min hold at 1,525 m (5,000 ft):
Series 100 1,672 nm (3,096 km; 1,924 miles)
Series 200 1,476 nm (2,733 km; 1,698 miles)
Series 300 1,520 nm (2,817 km; 1,748 miles)
Range with max payload, allowances as above:
Series 100 935 nm (1,733 km; 1,077 miles)
Series 200 1,176 nm (2,179 km; 1,355 miles)
Series 200-QT 1,200 nm (2,223 km; 1,381 miles)
Series 300 1,090 nm (2,020 km; 1,253 miles)
OPERATIONAL NOISE LEVELS (FAR Pt 36-12, certificated):
T-O: Series 100 83.0 EPNdB
Series 200 86.1 EPNdB
Approach: Series 100 95.6 EPNdB
Series 200 96.0 EPNdB
Sideline: Series 100 87.5 EPNdB
Series 200 87.2 EPNdB

BAC ONE-ELEVEN

In February 1987 British Aerospace announced that the Dee Howard programme to re-engine the BAC One-Eleven airliner with Rolls-Royce Tay turbofan engines (see Dee Howard in the USA section) had been extended from the original plan for Executive 400 Series aircraft to cover the airliner variants, including the 500 and 475 Series. The agreement also covers potentially the Romanian One-Eleven licensed production programme. Under the arrangement, British Aerospace retains design authority for the One-Eleven.

BUCCANEER

It was announced in February 1985 that British Aerospace had been appointed prime contractor for a programme to update Buccaneer S.2Bs in service with the Royal Air Force, to improve the avionics, armaments and electronic countermeasures to meet Air Staff Requirement 1012.

A major element of the programme is the installation of a Ferranti FIN 1063 inertial navigation system. This is a derivative of the FIN 1064 which equips RAF SEPECAT Jaguars, minus the weapon aiming system. Ferranti will also update the Airpass III (Blue Parrot) attack radar, and Marconi Defence Systems is updating the radar warning/ESM suite to Guardian Series 200 standard. Tracor AN/ALE-40 chaff/flare dispensers and Plessey radios are also being fitted.

The aircraft are being updated for further service in the maritime role, armed with BAe Sea Eagle and the TV guided Martel anti-ship missiles. Complementary with the avionics update is a full-scale fatigue test intended to extend the airframe life for many years. The update programme involves 42 of the RAF's Buccaneers. Apart from the first aircraft (XW529, re-worked at Brough in 1985-86) updating is being undertaken by BAe at Woodford, from where ten were re-delivered in 1987.

PHANTOM

British Aerospace has a contract to design and manufacture new outer wings for the RAF's fleet of Phantom aircraft. The work is being undertaken mainly by its Military Aircraft Division at Brough, the design authority for UK Phantoms, with some of the activity at BAe Hamble; 75 sets have been ordered.

The requirement is to design an outer wing to a new structural standard, which will embody accumulated knowledge gained from many years of structural support of the Phantom aircraft and test data from the full scale fatigue test specimen. The need to re-wing the aircraft arises from an escalation of problems with the current outer wings, resulting basically from the loads experienced during realistic operational training manoeuvres. Delivery of the

new outer wings began in 1988 and forms a major element in a plan to extend the service life of the Phantom well into the 1990s.

STRIKEMASTER

The Strikemaster COIN aircraft and basic jet trainer was last described in the 1981-82 edition of *Jane's*. Ten aircraft, several of them existing only as sets of components, then remained to be sold, of which three Mk 90s were delivered to Sudan in November 1983. One further aircraft was supplied to Oman in 1986 and the final six went to Ecuador in 1988. Production thus totalled 151, comprising sales to Saudi Arabia (47), Oman (25), Kuwait (12), Kenya (six), South Yemen (four), Singapore (16), New Zealand (16), Sudan (three) and Ecuador (22). Nine surviving Kuwaiti aircraft were re-purchased by BAe in 1986 and sold to Botswana in 1988.

BAe HAWK (TWO-SEAT VERSIONS)
RAF designation: Hawk T. Mk 1
US Navy designation: T-45 Goshawk

After examining designs submitted by BAC and Hawker Siddeley to meet an RAF requirement for a basic and advanced jet trainer, the Ministry of Defence announced in October 1971 that the Hawker Siddeley P1182 had been selected to meet this requirement. Selection of a non-afterburning version of the Rolls-Royce Turbomeca Adour to power the aircraft was announced on 2 March 1972, and later in the same month the Ministry of Defence confirmed an order for 176 HS P1182s, which were given the RAF name of Hawk T. Mk 1. These were to consist of one pre-production aircraft (XX154), which first flew on 21 August 1974, and 175 production Hawks.

There were no separate prototypes; instead, the first five production aircraft were allocated to the development programme. The first two production Hawks (XX162 and 163) were delivered to No. 4 Flying Training School (which includes the Central Flying School's Hawk detachment) at RAF Valley on 4 November 1976, and this basic version now serves also with Nos. 1 and 2 Tactical Weapons Units at Brawdy, Wales, and Chivenor, Devon, and with the RAF's premier aerobatic team, the Red Arrows, at Scampton.

The Hawk is fully aerobatic. It replaced the Gnat Trainer and Hunter in RAF service for advanced flying training, and for radio, navigation and weapons training, and has since been adapted for point defence and limited air superiority duties. The design is capable of other operational roles, and has been developed through a succession of variants into a single-seat combat version, as follows:

Hawk T. Mk 1. Basic two-seater for RAF flying and weapon training. Adour 151-01 (-02 in Red Arrows aircraft) non-afterburning turbofan, rated at 23.13 kN (5,200 lb st). Two 'dry' underwing hardpoints. Underbelly 30 mm gun pack. Simple weapon sight on Nos. 1/2 TWU aircraft. Three-position flaps.

Hawk T. Mk 1A. Under a contract of January 1983, 88 Hawks of Nos. 1/2 TWUs and the Red Arrows were wired for carriage of an AIM-9L Sidewinder air-to-air missile on the inboard wing pylons and optional activation of the previously unused outer-wing hardpoints. The last conversion was re-delivered on 30 May 1986. A force of 72 Hawk T. Mk 1As is declared to NATO for point defence and participation in the RAF's Mixed Fighter Force, in which they would accompany radar-equipped Phantoms and Tornado ADVs on medium-range air defence sorties.

A two-part programme of wing replacement for the majority of RAF Hawks is due to begin in 1989, involving an initial 85 aircraft which will be modified by BAe. Work on a further 59 aircraft will be put out to tender, for completion by the mid-1990s.

Hawk 50 series. Initial export version, with Adour 851 turbofan, rated at 23.75 kN (5,340 lb st). Max operating weight increased by 30 per cent. Max disposable load

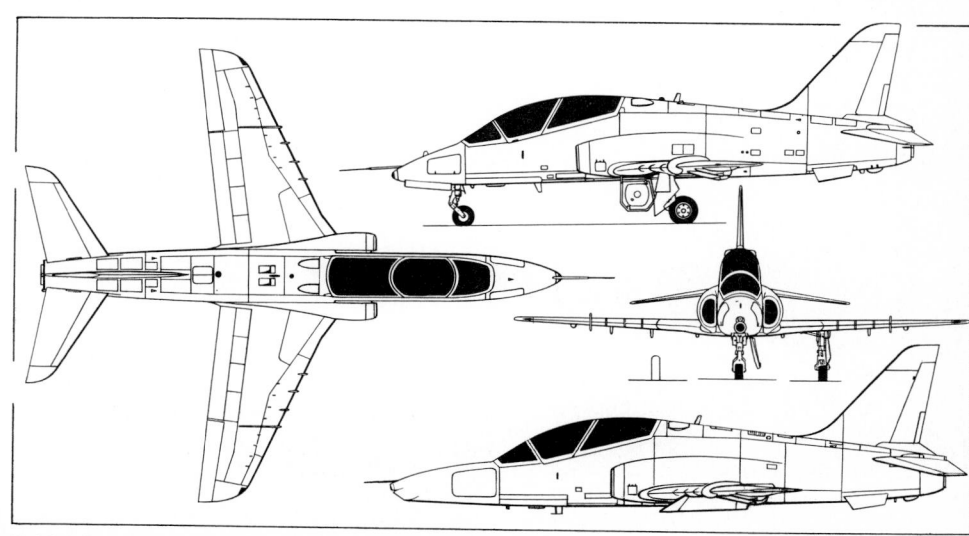

British Aerospace Hawk 60 series two-seat jet trainer, with additional side view (bottom) of Hawk 100 series *(Pilot Press)*

increased by 70 per cent. Max range increased by 30 per cent. Revised tailcone shape to improve directional stability at high speed. Larger nose equipment bay. Two additional weapon pylons underwing. All four wing stations configured for single or twin store carriage; each pylon cleared to carry 515 kg (1,135 lb). 'Wet' inboard pylons for 455 litre (120 US gallon; 100 Imp gallon) fuel tanks. Improved nav/com. Improved cockpit, with angle of attack indication, fully aerobatic twin gyro AHRS, slim seat head boxes and weapon control panel. Optional brake-chute. Suitable for ground attack in day VMC, and armed reconnaissance with camera/sensor pod. Sold to Finland (50 **Mk 51** to replace Fouga Magisters). Construction of components for 46 aircraft, and final assembly, undertaken in Finland by Valmet); Kenya (12 **Mk 52**); and Indonesia (20 **Mk 53** ground attack/trainers). Deliveries between December 1980 and October 1985.

Hawk 60 series. Development of the 50 series with Adour 861 turbofan, rated at 25.35 kN (5,700 lb st). Wing changes, including leading-edge devices and four-position flaps to improve lift capability. Low-friction nose leg, strengthened wheels and tyres, and adaptive anti-skid system. Drop tanks of 592 or 864 litre (156 or 228 US gallon; 130 or 190 Imp gallon) capacity. Provision for Sidewinder or Magic air-to-air missiles. Max operating weight increased by further 17 per cent compared with Mk 50 series, disposable load by 33 per cent and range by 30 per cent. Improved field performance, acceleration, rate of climb and turn rate. Sold to Zimbabwe (eight **Mk 60**), Dubai (nine **Mk 61**), Abu Dhabi (16 **Mk 63**), Kuwait (12 **Mk 64**), Saudi Arabia (30 **Mk 65**) and Switzerland (20 **Mk 66**). First deliveries were made (Mk 60) in July 1982. All except the first of the Mk 66s will be assembled by F + W at Emmen in Switzerland, with delivery from 1990.

T-45A Goshawk. In November 1981 the Hawk was selected, out of six designs, in the US Navy's VTXTS competition for an undergraduate jet pilot trainer, and is scheduled to replace the T-2C Buckeye and TA-4J Skyhawk. The US Navy's requirement is for 302 Hawks, designated T-45A Goshawk, with a limited armament capability and compatible with carrier deck operation. McDonnell Douglas is prime contractor to the US Navy for the programme, with British Aerospace as principal subcontractor for the airframe and Honeywell (Sperry) as principal subcontractor for simulators. Adour Mk 861-49 engine rated at 24.24 kN (5,450 lb st). Further details can be found under the McDonnell Douglas/BAe entry in the International section.

Hawk 100 series. To exploit the Hawk's five-pylon capability for carrying external stores, BAe announced this enhanced ground attack development of the 60 series in mid-1982. Still basically a two-seater, but likely to carry only a pilot on combat missions, the 100 series will be powered by a 26.0 kN (5,845 lb st) Adour Mk 871 engine. It will have a MIL-STD-1553B databus integrating Singer Kearfott SKN 2416 inertial navigation unit of the type used on the F-16, an advanced Smiths Industries head-up display/weapon aiming computer (HUD/WAC), and new air data sensor package, with optional laser ranging and FLIR; improved weapons management system allowing pre-selection during flight and displaying weapon status; manual or automatic weapon release; passive warning radar; HOTAS (hands on throttle and stick) controls; full colour multi-purpose CRT display in each cockpit; and provision for carrying an ECM pod.

Max external load will be increased to 3,265 kg (7,200 lb); T-O run reduced by typically 20 per cent and landing run by 15 per cent; max ferry range increased by over 50 per cent with two 864 litre (228 US gallon; 190 Imp gallon) external tanks; and hi-lo-hi combat radius improved to 660 nm (1,222 km; 759 miles) with two 1,000 lb bombs or 275 nm (509 km; 316 miles) with seven 1,000 lb bombs. In a combat air patrol mission, the Hawk Series 100 will be able to loiter for 3½ h on station, 140 nm (260 km; 160 miles) from its base, armed with two Sidewinder type missiles and its 30 mm gun. An aerodynamic prototype of the 100 series (converted from company demonstrator G-HAWK/ZA101) flew on 1 October 1987, featuring an extended nose with forward-facing optical flats for the FLIR and laser rangefinder.

Hawk 200 series. Single-seat multi-role combat version. Described separately.

The following description applies to current UK production Hawks for export:

TYPE: Two-seat basic and advanced jet trainer, with capability for air defence and ground attack roles.

WINGS: Cantilever low-wing monoplane. Thickness/chord ratio 10.9% at root, 9% at tip. Dihedral 2°. Sweepback 26° on leading-edge, 21° 30′ at quarter-chord. One-piece aluminium alloy wing, with six-bolt attachment to fuselage, employing a machined spars-and-skin torsion box (two main spars, auxiliary spar, ribs and machined skins with integral stringers), the greater part of which forms an integral fuel tank. Hydraulically activated double-slotted flaps. Ailerons, operated by AP Precision Hydraulics tandem actuators, are of honeycomb-filled aluminium alloy. No tabs. Small fence, of composites material, on leading-edge of each wing, at approximately two-thirds span.

FUSELAGE: Conventional aluminium alloy structure of frames and stringers, cut out to accept the one-piece wing. Large airbrake under rear fuselage, aft of wing.

TAIL UNIT: Cantilever all-metal structure, with sweepback on all surfaces. One-piece all-moving power operated (via push/pull rods) anhedral tailplane, with AP Precision Hydraulics tandem hydraulic actuators. Manually operated rudder, with electrically actuated trim tab. Two small ventral fins.

LANDING GEAR: Wide track hydraulically retractable tricycle type, with single wheel on each unit. AP Precision Hydraulics oleos and jacks. Main units retract inward into wing, ahead of front spar; castoring nosewheel retracts forward. Dunlop mainwheels, brakes and tyres size 6.50-10, pressure 9.86 bars (143 lb/sq in). Nosewheel and tyre size 4.4-16, pressure 8.27 bars (120 lb/sq in). Tail bumper fairing under rear fuselage. Anti-skid wheel brakes. Tail braking parachute, diameter 2.64 m (8 ft 8 in), on Mks 52/53 and all 60 series aircraft.

POWER PLANT: One Rolls-Royce Turbomeca Adour non-afterburning turbofan, as described under individual series entries. Air intake on each side of fuselage, forward of wing leading-edge. Engine starting by Microturbo integral gas turbine starter. Fuel in one fuselage bag tank of 868 litres (229 US gallons; 191 Imp gallons) capacity and integral wing tank of 836 litres (221 US gallons; 184 Imp gallons) capacity; total fuel capacity 1,704 litres (450 US gallons; 375 Imp gallons). Pressure refuelling point near front of port engine air intake trunk; gravity point on top of fuselage. Provision for carrying one 455, 592 or 864 litre (120, 156 or 228 US gallon; 100, 130 or 190 Imp gallon) drop tank on each inboard underwing pylon, according to series.

ACCOMMODATION: Crew of two in tandem under one-piece fully transparent acrylic canopy, opening sideways to starboard. Fixed front windscreen and separate internal windscreen in front of rear cockpit. Improved front windscreen fitted retrospectively to RAF Hawks, able to withstand a 1 kg (2.2 lb) bird at 528 knots (978 km/h; 607 mph). Rear seat elevated. Martin-Baker Mk 10B zero/zero rocket assisted ejection seats, with MDC (miniature detonating cord) system to break canopy before seats eject. The MDC can also be operated from outside the cockpit for ground rescue. Dual controls standard. Entire accommodation pressurised, heated and air-conditioned.

SYSTEMS: BAe cockpit air-conditioning and pressurisation systems, using engine bleed air. Two hydraulic systems; flow rate: System 1, 36.4 litres (9.6 US gallons; 8 Imp gallons)/min; System 2, 22.7 litres (6 US gallons; 5 Imp gallons)/min. Systems pressure 207 bars (3,000 lb/sq in), for actuation of control jacks, flaps, airbrake, landing gear and anti-skid wheel brakes. Compressed nitrogen accumulators provide emergency power for flaps and landing gear at a pressure of 2.75 to 5.5 bars (40 to 80 lb/sq in). Hydraulic accumulator for emergency operation of wheel brakes. Pop-up Dowty Rotol ram air turbine in upper rear fuselage provides emergency hydraulic power for flying controls in the event of an engine or No. 2 pump failure. No pneumatic system. DC electrical power from single brushless generator, with two static inverters to provide AC power and two batteries for standby power. Gaseous oxygen system for crew.

AVIONICS AND EQUIPMENT: The RAF standard of flight instruments includes Ferranti gyros and inverter, two Sperry Gyroscope RAI-4 4 in remote attitude indicators and a magnetic detector unit, and Louis Newmark compass system. Radio and navigation equipment includes Sylvania UHF and VHF, Cossor CAT.7000 Tacan, Cossor ILS with CILS.75/76 localiser/glideslope receiver and marker receiver, and IFF/SSR (Cossor 2720 Mk 10A IFF in aircraft for Finland).

ARMAMENT AND OPERATIONAL EQUIPMENT: Ferranti F.195 weapon sight and camera recorder in each cockpit of about 90 RAF and all 50 and 60 series aircraft. (Saab RGS2 sighting system in aircraft for Finland.) Underfuselage centreline mounted 30 mm Aden Mk 4 cannon with 120 rounds (VKT 12.7 mm machine-gun beneath Finnish aircraft), and two or four hardpoints underwing, according to series. Provision for pylon in place of the ventral gun pack. In RAF training roles the normal max external load is about 680 kg (1,500 lb), but the uprated Hawk has demonstrated its ability to carry a total external load of 3,084 kg (6,800 lb). Typical weapon loadings on 60 series include a 30 mm or 12.7 mm centreline gun pod and four packs each containing eighteen 68 mm rockets; a centreline reconnaissance pod and four packs each containing twelve 81 mm rockets; seven 1,000 lb free fall or retarded bombs; four launchers each containing four 100 mm rockets; nine 250 lb or 250 kg bombs; thirty-six 80 lb runway denial or tactical strike bombs; five 600 lb cluster bombs; four Sidewinder/Magic air-to-air missiles; four CBLS 100/200 carriers each containing four practice bombs and four rockets; or two 592 litre (156 US gallon; 130 Imp gallon, drop tanks and two Maverick air-to-surface missiles. A configuration demonstrated at the 1983 Paris Air Show included a Sea Eagle anti-ship missile on the centreline pylon, plus two Sidewinder missiles and two 864 litre (228 US gallon; 190 Imp gallon) drop tanks underwing.

DIMENSIONS, EXTERNAL:

Wing span	9.39 m (30 ft 9¾ in)
Wing chord: at root	2.65 m (8 ft 8¼ in)
at tip	0.90 m (2 ft 11½ in)
Wing aspect ratio	5.3
Length overall: excl probe: Mk 1, 50 and 60 srs	11.17 m (36 ft 7¾ in)
100 srs	11.68 m (38 ft 4 in)
incl probe	11.86 m (38 ft 11 in)
Height overall: Mk 1, 50 and 60 srs	3.99 m (13 ft 1¼ in)
100 srs	4.16 m (13 ft 8 in)
Tailplane span	4.39 m (14 ft 4¾ in)
Wheel track	3.47 m (11 ft 5 in)

AREAS:

Wings, gross	16.69 m^2 (179.6 sq ft)
Ailerons (total)	1.05 m^2 (11.30 sq ft)
Trailing-edge flaps (total)	2.50 m^2 (26.91 sq ft)
Airbrake	0.53 m^2 (5.70 sq ft)
Fin: Mk 1, 50 and 60 srs	2.51 m^2 (27.02 sq ft)
100 srs	2.61 m^2 (28.10 sq ft)
Rudder, incl tab	0.58 m^2 (6.24 sq ft)
Tailplane	4.33 m^2 (46.61 sq ft)

WEIGHTS:

Weight empty: 60 series	3,635 kg (8,015 lb)
100 series	3,855 kg (8,500 lb)
T-O weight:	
60 series trainer, 'clean'	5,150 kg (11,350 lb)
Max T-O weight: T. Mk 1	5,700 kg (12,566 lb)
50 series	7,350 kg (16,200 lb)
60, 100 series	8,570 kg (18,890 lb)
Max landing weight: T. Mk 1	4,649 kg (10,250 lb)
60 series	7,650 kg (16,865 lb)

PERFORMANCE:

Max speed in dive at height	575 knots (1,065 km/h; 661 mph)
Max Mach number in dive	1.2
Max level speed:	
50 series	535 knots (990 km/h; 615 mph)
60, 100 series	560 knots (1,037 km/h; 644 mph)
Max level speed Mach number	0.88
Max rate of climb at S/L	3,600 m (11,800 ft)/min
Time to 9,145 m (30,000 ft), 'clean'	6 min 6 s
Service ceiling	15,250 m (50,000 ft)
T-O run	550 m (1,800 ft)
Landing run	488 m (1,600 ft)
Combat radius:	
with 2,268 kg (5,000 lb) weapon load	538 nm (998 km; 620 miles)
with 908 kg (2,000 lb) weapon load	781 nm (1,448 km; 900 miles)
Ferry range 'clean'	1,313 nm (2,433 km; 1,510 miles)
Ferry range, 60 series, with two 864 litre (190 Imp gallon) drop tanks	2,200 nm (4,075 km; 2,530 miles)
Endurance, 100 nm (185 km; 115 miles) from base	approx 4 h 0 min
g limits	+8/−4

BAe's Hawk demonstrator, modified to the aerodynamic shape of the Hawk 100 series

BAe HAWK 200 SERIES (SINGLE-SEATER)

On 20 June 1984, British Aerospace announced its intention to build as a private venture a demonstrator single-seat combat version of the Hawk, and this aircraft (ZG200) flew for the first time on 19 May 1986. It was lost, through no aircraft fault, on 2 July 1986, and has been replaced by the first pre-production Hawk 200 (ZH200), which flew for the first time on 24 April 1987.

Except for its taller fin, the Hawk 200 is virtually identical with the current production two-seater aft of the cockpit, giving 80 per cent airframe commonality. The avionics fit, which is similar to that of the Hawk 100 series, enables a radar, or FLIR and laser rangefinder, to be carried. Built-in twin-cannon armament frees the centreline pylon for other stores, including a 592 litre (156 US gallon; 130 Imp gallon) external fuel tank. Each of the four underwing pylons is capable of carrying 907 kg (2,000 lb), within the max external load of 3,084 kg (6,800 lb). The wide range of missions that such capability permits include:

Airspace denial. Carrying two Sidewinder type missiles and two 864 litre (228 US gallon; 190 Imp gallon) drop tanks, the Hawk 200 could loiter for 3.5 hours on station at 9,150 m (30,000 ft), 100 nm (185 km; 115 miles) from base; or for one hour on station 550 nm (1,018 km; 633 miles) from base. Max intercept radius is 720 nm (1,333 km; 828 miles).

Close air support. Five 1,000 lb and four 500 lb bombs could be delivered with precision up to 104 nm (192 km; 120 miles) from base in a lo-lo mission.

Battlefield interdiction. In a hi-lo-hi operation, the Hawk 200 has a radius of action of 579 nm (1,072 km; 666 miles), with a 1,360 kg (3,000 lb) military load.

Long-range photo reconnaissance. A wide area of search is made possible by the mission range of 1,723 nm (3,190 km; 1,982 miles) offered by two external tanks, carried with a pod containing cameras and infra-red linescan. A rapid role change could then permit follow-up attack by the same aircraft. Lo-lo radius by day or night is 510 nm (945 km; 586 miles).

Long-range deployment. Ferry range with two 864 litre (228 US gallon; 190 Imp gallon) and one 592 litre (156 US gallon; 130 Imp gallon) external tanks is 1,950 nm (3,610 km; 2,244 miles), unrefuelled and with 864 litre tanks retained. Reserves would allow 10 min over destination at 150 m (500 ft).

Anti-shipping strike. Armed with a Sea Eagle sea skimming anti-ship missile, and carrying two 864 litre (228 US gallon; 190 Imp gallon) tanks, the Hawk 200 could attack a ship 800 nm (1,480 km; 920 miles) from base, and return with 10 per cent fuel reserves. This puts ships almost anywhere in the North Atlantic within range of the Hawk from shore bases. Weapon release could be beyond the target's radar envelope.

Three standards of equipment are envisaged, depending on the customer's mission requirements, as follows:

Day operation. The most simple equipment fit would comprise a gyro stabilised attack sight and attitude heading reference system, with navigation by radio aids. Navigation and weapon aiming capabilities could be extended by adding an inertial navigation system, head-up display and weapon aiming computer. Other options are HOTAS controls, laser rangefinder, IFF, radar warning receiver.

Night operation. With a FLIR and laser rangefinder mounted in a modified nosecone, the Hawk 200 could carry out precision ground attacks and tactical reconnaissance by day and night.

All-weather operation. Installation of an advanced multi-mode radar, with an antenna diameter of up to 61 cm (24 in), such as the Westinghouse APG-66, would add all-weather target acquisition and navigational fixing capabilities. Weapons like the anti-shipping Sea Eagle and air-to-air Sky Flash could also be employed.

Sixty Hawk 200s have been ordered by Saudi Arabia. Changes by comparison with the two-seat Hawk are as follows:

BAe Hawk Mk 65 advanced trainers of the Royal Saudi Air Force

BAe pre-production Hawk 200 single-seat multi-role combat aircraft

TYPE: Single-seat multi-role combat aircraft.

WINGS: As Hawk two-seater, except for detail modifications to leading-edge aerofoil section and fence configuration.

FUSELAGE: Modified to single-seat configuration. Unchanged design concept and criteria.

LANDING GEAR: Mainwheel tyres size 559 × 165-279, pressure 16.2 bars (235 lb/sq in). Nosewheel tyre size 457 × 140-203, pressure 7.24 bars (105 lb/sq in). Optional single Tornado-type nosewheel for increased T-O weight.

POWER PLANT: One Rolls-Royce Turbomeca Adour Mk 871 non-afterburning turbofan, with uninstalled rating of 26.0 kN (5,845 lb st).

ACCOMMODATION: Pilot only, on Martin-Baker Type 10L ejection seat, under side-hinged (to starboard) canopy.

SYSTEMS: Fairey Hydraulics yaw control system added, comprising rudder actuator and servo control system, incorporating an autostabiliser computer.

ARMAMENT: One or two internally mounted 25 mm Aden guns (with 100 rds each) beneath cockpit floor. Ferranti ISIS sight or Smiths head-up display optional.

DIMENSIONS, EXTERNAL:

As Hawk two-seater, except:

Length overall	11.38 m (37 ft 4 in)
Height overall	4.16 m (13 ft 8 in)
Wheelbase	3.298 m (10 ft 10 in)

AREAS:

As Hawk two-seater, except:

Fin	2.61 m² (28.10 sq ft)

WEIGHTS:

Weight empty	4,128 kg (9,100 lb)
Max fuel: internal	1,360 kg (3,000 lb)
internal + three drop tanks	3,210 kg (7,080 lb)
Max weapon load	3,500 kg (7,700 lb)
Max T-O weight	9,101 kg (20,065 lb)

PERFORMANCE (estimated; no external stores or role equipment unless stated):

Never-exceed speed at height	Mach 1.2 (575 knots; 1,065 km/h; 661 mph)
Max level speed at S/L	560 knots (1,037 km/h; 644 mph)
Max cruising speed at S/L	550 knots (1,019 km/h; 633 mph)
Econ cruising speed at 12,500 m (41,000 ft)	430 knots (796 km/h; 495 mph)
Stalling speed, flaps down	106 knots (197 km/h; 122 mph) IAS
Max rate of climb at S/L	3,508 m (11,510 ft)/min
Service ceiling	15,250 m (50,000 ft)
Runway LCN: flexible pavement	15
rigid pavement	10
T-O run with max weapon load	1,585 m (5,200 ft)

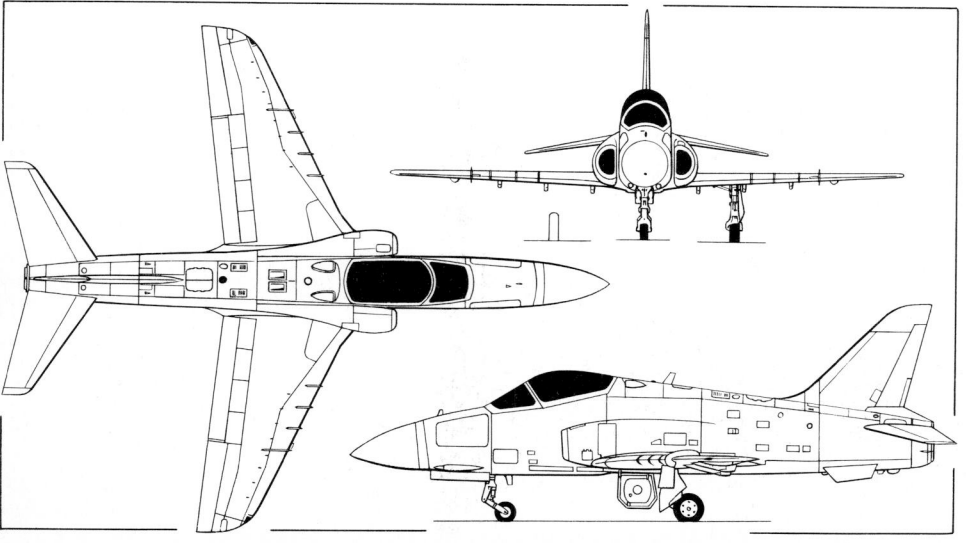

Three-view drawing of the single-seat Hawk 200 series *(Pilot Press)*

T-O to 15 m (50 ft) with max weapon load
                                      2,134 m (7,000 ft)
Landing from 15 m (50 ft) at landing weight of 4,550 kg
  g(10,030 lb): with brake-chute   854 m (2,800 ft)
  without brake-chute   1,250 m (4,100 ft)
Radius of action, hi-lo-lo-hi with three Sea Eagle
  anti-ship missiles and two 592 litre (156 US gallon; 130
  Imp gallon) drop tanks
                        333 nm (617 km; 383 miles)
Range:
  with internal fuel only   482 nm (892 km; 554 miles)
  with internal fuel plus three drop tanks
                  1,950 nm (3,610 km; 2,244 miles)
g limits   +8/-4

BAe HARRIER

RAF designations: Harrier GR. Mk 3 and T. Mk 4/4A

USMC designations: AV-8A (Mk 50) and TAV-8A (Mk 54)

Spanish Navy designation: Matador (AV-8S and TAV-8S)

The Harrier was the world's first operational fixed-wing V/STOL strike fighter. The first of six single-seat prototypes (XV276) flew for the first time on 31 August 1966; the following versions have since been built:

Harrier GR. Mk 1, 1A and 3. Single-seat close support and tactical reconnaissance versions for the RAF. First production GR. Mk 1 (XV738) flew on 28 December 1967. Deliveries made initially to Harrier Conversion Team (now No. 233 Operational Conversion Unit) at RAF Wittering, beginning with XV744 on 9 April 1969, and to No. 1 Squadron, formed at the same base on 18 July 1969. Delivered subsequently to Nos. 3, 4 and (temporarily) 20 Squadrons in West Germany. These aircraft were designated Harrier GR. Mk 1 when fitted initially with Pegasus 101 engines. When retrofitted subsequently with the Pegasus 102 they were redesignated GR. Mk 1A. Aircraft now in service have Pegasus 103 engines and are designated GR. Mk 3. A total of 118 production GR. 1/3s was built for the Royal Air Force up to 1987, excluding prototypes. Fourteen of them took part in the Falklands campaign in 1982, as described in the 1984-85 and previous editions of *Jane's*.

A prototype Harrier GR. Mk 3 (XV281), piloted by Sqn Ldr Bernard Scott, established three international time-to-height records after VTO, in Class H for jet-lift aircraft, on 12 January 1987. The Harrier reached 3,000 m in 39.48 s, 6,000 m in 60.65 s and 9,000 m in 1 min 26.66 s; and also attained an altitude of 15,499 m (50,850 ft), thereby exceeding Class H records set in 1971 by Sqn Ldr Tom L. Lecky-Thompson in a Harrier GR. Mk 1A.

Harrier T. Mk 2, 2A, 4, 4A and 6, and Harrier T. Mk 4RN. Two-seat versions, retaining the full combat capability of the single-seater in terms of equipment fit and weapon carriage. There is a large degree of commonality in structure and system components, ground support equipment and flight and ground crew training. Differences include a longer nose section forward of the wing leading-edge, with two cockpits in tandem; a tailcone approx 1.83 m (6 ft) longer than that of the single-seat model; and enlarged fin surfaces. The two-seat Harrier can be used operationally with the rear seat and compensating tail ballast removed, thus minimising the weight penalty over its single-seat counterpart. First of two development aircraft (XW174) flew on 24 April 1969, and the first of 25 production aircraft for the RAF (XW264) on 3 October 1969. The two-seater entered RAF service in July 1970, and the last aircraft (also the final first-generation Harrier for the RAF) was delivered on 2 October 1987.

BAe Harrier T. Mk 4RN of No. 899 Naval Air Squadron *(Alex Hay Porteous)*

BAe Harrier GR. Mk 3 of the Royal Air Force

The RAF Harrier T. Mk 2, like the GR. Mk 1, was powered originally by the Pegasus 101 engine. The designations T. Mk 2A and T. Mk 4 apply to aircraft retrofitted with, respectively, the Pegasus 102 and 103. The T. Mk 4A reverts to the original pointed nose, without LRMTS, to make it lighter for training duties with No. 233 OCU at RAF Wittering. One further T. Mk 4A (XZ455) was funded by the Royal Navy, but operated by the RAF. Genuine Royal Navy two-seaters are designated Harrier T. Mk 4RN; three were delivered, of which one was lost in 1985. Two-seat Harrier production for the UK thus totalled 31, including prototypes. It is expected that some RAF T. Mk 4s will be converted to T. Mk 6 standard, with night vision equipment for training pilots of GR. Mk 5s fitted eventually with FLIR sensors and possibly redesignated GR. Mk 7.

Harrier GR. Mk 5. Initial designation of 96 AV-8B Harrier IIs ordered for the RAF. This version, which is being produced jointly for the US Marine Corps, the RAF and the Spanish Navy, is described under the McDonnell Douglas/BAe heading in the International section. The first GR. Mk 5 delivery to the RAF (ZD323) took place at Wittering on 29 May 1987.

Harrier Mk 50 (USMC designation AV-8A/C). Single-seat close support and tactical reconnaissance version for the US Marine Corps, last described fully in the 1987-88 *Jane's*. The last of 102 single-seat AV-8A/Cs was withdrawn from front-line duties in 1987, and replacement of eight two-seat **TAV-8As** (Harrier Mk 54s) by TAV-8Bs was in progress.

Eleven AV-8As and two TAV-8As were ordered for the Spanish Navy, by whom they are known as **Matadors** and designated **AV-8S** and **TAV-8S** respectively. The first batch of six Spanish AV-8s are Mk 50 aircraft; the second batch of five are **Mk 55** aircraft; the TAV-8Ss are Mk 54s. Mks 50 and 54 aircraft were purchased via the USA. They equip the 8 Escuadrilla of the Spanish Navy at Rota, Cadiz, operating from the aircraft carrier *Dedalo* and its replacement ASW carrier, the *Principe de Asturias*. Like the AV-8As of the USMC, the Matador has a Sidewinder capability, but no nose-mounted LRMTS.

Harrier Mk 52. One aircraft built as a demonstrator using BAe and equipment suppliers' private funding. It is similar to the Harrier T. Mk 4, and is fitted with a Pegasus 103 engine; in recognition of its status as the first civil registered jet V/STOL aircraft in the UK, it was granted the civil registration G-VTOL. First flight was made on 16 September 1971, with a Pegasus 102 fitted initially.

Harrier T. Mk 60. Two-seat operational trainer version for Indian Navy. T. Mk 4A configuration, but with complete Sea Harrier avionics except for Blue Fox radar. Four ordered. Deliveries to India began in March 1984.

Sea Harrier FRS. Mks 1 and 51. Versions for Royal Navy and Indian Navy. Described separately.

Technical details as for Sea Harrier, except:

TYPE: V/STOL close support and reconnaissance aircraft.

LANDING GEAR: GR. Mk 3 tyre pressures 6.21 bars (90 lb/sq in) on nose and main units, 6.55 bars (95 lb/sq in) on outriggers. T. Mk 4 tyre pressures 6.90 bars (100 lb/sq in) on nose unit, 6.55 bars (95 lb/sq in) on main and outrigger units.

POWER PLANT: One Rolls-Royce Pegasus Mk 103 vectored thrust turbofan (95.6 kN; 21,500 lb st).

ACCOMMODATION: Crew of one (Mk 3) or two (Mk 4) on Martin-Baker Mk 9D zero/zero rocket ejection seat(s).

SYSTEMS: Ram air turbine removed from RAF and USMC Harriers in late 1970s.

AVIONICS AND EQUIPMENT: Plessey U/VHF, Ultra standby UHF, GEC Avionics AD 2770 Tacan and Cossor IFF, Ferranti FE 541 inertial navigation and attack system (INAS), with Sperry C2G compass, Smiths electronic

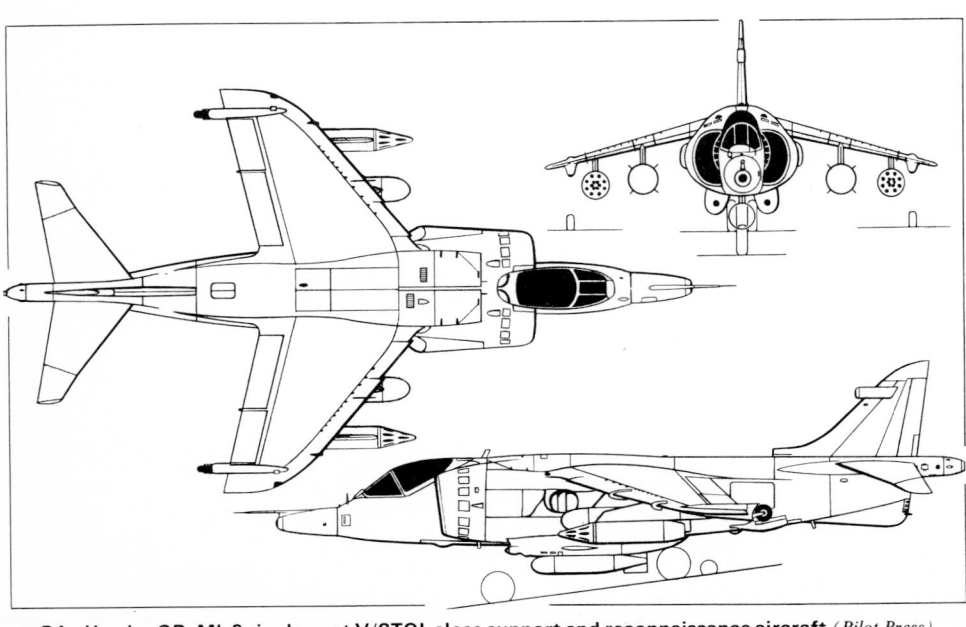

BAe Harrier GR. Mk 3 single-seat V/STOL close support and reconnaissance aircraft *(Pilot Press)*

head-up display of flight information, and air data computer. Marconi ARI.18223 radar warning receiver. The weapon aiming computer provides a general solution for manual or automatic release of free fall and retarded bombs, and for the aiming of rockets and guns, in dive and straight-pass attacks over a wide range of flight conditions and very considerable freedom of manoeuvre in elevation. Communications equipment ranges through VHF in the 100-156MHz band to UHF in the 220-400MHz band. Ferranti Type 106 laser ranger and marked target seeker (LRMTS) retrofitted to all RAF single-seat and some two-seat Harriers.

ARMAMENT AND OPERATIONAL EQUIPMENT: In addition to its fixed reconnaissance camera, the Mk 3 can also carry a five-camera reconnaissance pod on the underfuselage pylon. A typical combat load comprises a pair of 30 mm Aden gun pods with 150 rounds each, combat tank or a 1,000 lb bomb on each of the inboard underwing pylons, and a Hunting BL755 cluster bomb on each outboard underwing pylon. A Sidewinder installation is provided in the AV-8A and Matador versions (and retrospectively on some GR. Mk 3s), to give the aircraft an effective air-to-air capability in conjunction with the two 30 mm Aden guns. A Tracor AN/ALE-40 chaff/flare dispenser is fitted in the lower rear fuselage of some GR. Mk 3s.

DIMENSIONS, EXTERNAL:

Wing span: combat	7.70 m (25 ft 3 in)
ferry	9.04 m (29 ft 8 in)
Wing chord: at root	3.56 m (11 ft 8 in)
at tip	1.26 m (4 ft 1½ in)
Wing aspect ratio: combat	3.175
ferry	4.08
Length overall: single-seat	13.89 m (45 ft 7 in)
single-seat (laser nose)	14.27 m (46 ft 10 in)
two-seat (laser nose)	17.50 m (57 ft 5 in)
Height overall: single-seat	3.63 m (11 ft 11 in)
two-seat	4.17 m (13 ft 8 in)
Tailplane span	4.24 m (13 ft 11 in)
Outrigger wheel track	6.76 m (22 ft 2 in)
Wheelbase, nosewheel to mainwheels	approx 3.45 m (11 ft 4 in)

AREAS:

Wings, gross: combat	18.68 m² (201.1 sq ft)
ferry	20.1 m² (216 sq ft)
Ailerons (total)	0.98 m² (10.5 sq ft)
Trailing-edge flaps (total)	1.29 m² (13.9 sq ft)
Fin (excl ventral fin): single-seat	2.40 m² (25.8 sq ft)
two-seat	3.57 m² (38.4 sq ft)
Rudder, incl tab	0.49 m² (5.3 sq ft)
Tailplane	4.41 m² (47.5 sq ft)

WEIGHTS AND LOADING:

Basic operating weight, empty:	
GR. Mk 3	6,140 kg (13,535 lb)
T. Mk 4	6,850 kg (15,100 lb)
Internal fuel	2,295 kg (5,060 lb)
Max T-O weight:	
single-seat	11,430 kg (25,200 lb)
two-seat	11,880 kg (26,200 lb)
Max wing loading (single-seat)	610 kg/m² (125 lb/sq ft)

PERFORMANCE:

Max level speed at S/L	635 knots (1,176 km/h; 730 mph)
Max Mach number in a dive at height	1.3
Time to 12,200 m (40,000 ft) from vertical T-O	2 min 23 s
Service ceiling	15,600 m (51,200 ft)
T-O run: with 2,270 kg (5,000 lb) payload at max T-O weight	approx 305 m (1,000 ft)
Range: hi-lo-hi with 1,995 kg (4,400 lb) payload	360 nm (666 km; 414 miles)
lo-lo with 1,995 kg (4,400 lb) payload	200 nm (370 km; 230 miles)
Ferry range	1,850 nm (3,425 km; 2,129 miles)
Range with one in-flight refuelling	more than 3,000 nm (5,560 km; 3,455 miles)
Endurance:	
combat air patrol 100 nm (185 km; 115 miles) from base	1 h 30 min
with one in-flight refuelling	more than 7 h
g limits	+7.8/-4.2

BAe SEA HARRIER
RN designation: FRS. Mk 1/2
Indian Navy designation: FRS. Mk 51

On 15 May 1975, the British government announced its decision to proceed with full development of a maritime version of the Harrier, subsequently designated **Sea Harrier FRS. Mk 1**. The first Sea Harrier to fly (XZ450) made its first flight on 20 August 1978, and the first for the Royal Navy (XZ451) was handed over on 18 June 1979. The first Sea Harrier ship trials were carried out on board HMS *Hermes* during November 1979.

The initial Royal Navy order was for three development aircraft (XZ438-440). Successive production orders for 21 (XZ450-460, XZ491-500), 10, 14 and 9 had taken the total to 57 by September 1984. All were built as Mk 1s, including the final nine delivered from November 1987 onwards. The Naval Intensive Flying Trials Unit for the Sea Harrier (No. 700A Squadron) was commissioned at RNAS Yeovilton on 19 September 1979. It became subsequently the normally shore based No. 899 HQ squadron, with eight aircraft. Front line units, each nominally with five aircraft, but

Artist's impression of Sea Harrier FRS. Mk 2s embodying mid-life update

BAe Sea Harrier FRS. Mk 1 of the Royal Navy, armed with Sidewinder missiles

intended to increase to eight, are Nos. 800 and 801 Squadrons, able to operate from the anti-submarine cruisers HMS *Invincible, Illustrious* and *Ark Royal*. Six similar Sea Harriers, designated **FRS. Mk 51**, ordered by the Indian Navy are in service with No. 300 (White Tiger) Squadron and operate from INS *Vikrant*, having been handed over from January 1983 and delivered (after training of pilots in the UK) from December 1983. Three standard, non-navalised T. Mk 4N two-seaters were delivered to the Royal Navy for land based training, and two T. Mk 60s to the Indian Navy. In November 1985 the Indian Government ordered 10 additional FRS Mk 51 Sea Harriers and one more T. Mk 60 two-seat trainer. A letter of intent to purchase seven more FRS Mk 51s and one Mk 60 was issued in September 1986, to equip the former HMS *Hermes* which was transferred to the Indian Navy as the INS *Viraat*.

Following proposals by Lt Cdr D. R. Taylor, RN, tests were carried out successfully in 1977 with a 'ski-jump' launching ramp designed to boost the short take-off performance of vectored thrust aircraft. This technique makes possible substantial benefits in Harrier operation both at sea and ashore, and is a feature of Royal Navy ships in which Sea Harriers are based. A 7° ski-jump ramp is fitted to HMS *Invincible* and HMS *Illustrious*; that in HMS *Ark Royal* is more steeply angled, at 12°, permitting an increase of 1,135 kg (2,500 lb) in launch weight for the same T-O run, or a 50-60 per cent reduction in T-O run for the same weight. Two earlier ships are to be modified to have 12° ramps.

Major changes compared with the Harriers in service with the RAF, Spanish Navy and US Marine Corps comprise the elimination of magnesium components, introduction of a raised cockpit, revised operational avionics, and installation of multi-mode Ferranti radar in a redesigned nose that folds to port for carrier stowage. Known by the name Blue Fox, this radar is a derivative of the frequency agile Seaspray radar fitted in the Royal Navy Lynx helicopter, but embodies changes to suit its different role, with air-to-air intercept and air-to-surface modes of operation.

The Royal Navy's Sea Harrier FRS. Mk 1 has a Rolls-Royce Pegasus 104 vectored thrust turbofan, with the same rating as the Pegasus 103 fitted to current RAF Harriers. The two variants differ little in design, except that the Pegasus 104 incorporates additional anti-corrosion features and has the capability to generate more electrical power.

The Sea Harrier FRS. Mk 1 was intended to operate at approximately the same weights as the GR. Mk 3, and to lift

a full military load with a 152 m (500 ft) flat deck run into an overdeck wind of 30 knots (55.5 km/h; 34.5 mph). It was first used operationally during the Falkland Islands campaign in 1982, from HMS *Hermes* and *Invincible*, when a total of 28 Sea Harriers flew 2,376 sorties. They destroyed 22 enemy aircraft in air-to-air combat without loss. Four Sea Harriers were lost in accidents and two to ground fire.

In January 1985 the UK Ministry of Defence awarded a contract to British Aerospace for the project definition phase of a mid-life update of Royal Navy Sea Harriers, of which 34 had been delivered by that time, with 23 more on order. The upgraded Sea Harriers are designated **FRS. Mk 2**.

Following modifications to two trials aircraft at Dunsfold, operational Sea Harrier FRS. Mk 1s will be returned to BAe at Brough between 1991 and 1994 for conversion.

Externally, the Mk 2 will differ from the Mk 1 in having role change wingtip extensions that will increase the span by 61 cm (2 ft); a less pointed nose radome; a longer rear fuselage, resulting from insertion of a 35 cm (1 ft 1¾ in) plug aft of the wing trailing-edge; and revisions of the antennae and external stores.

Installation of Ferranti Blue Vixen pulse-Doppler radar, instead of the original Blue Fox, will give the Sea Harrier FRS. Mk 2 all-weather lookdown/shootdown capability, with inherent track-while-scan, multiple target engagement, greatly increased missile launch range, enhanced surface target acquisition, and improved ECCM performance. In addition to the wide range of weapons with which the current operational Sea Harrier is compatible, the FRS. Mk 2 will be equipped to carry the new air-to-air AIM-120 AMRAAM.

Improved systems will be built around a MIL 1553B databus. This uses a dual redundant data highway, allowing computerised time sharing of information processed in the databus control and interface unit.

Redesign of the cockpit and addition of a JTIDS terminal will allow presentation of the total fleet defence picture, radar picture, threat data, target priority, and navigational information on dual multi-purpose displays. All time-critical weapon systems controls will be positioned on the up-front control panel, or on the throttle and stick.

Operational efficiency will be improved by the ergonomic integration of additional switches as part of the control column and throttle handle functions. HOTAS (hands on throttle and stick) controls will provide simultaneous control of the aircraft, radar, and weapons systems without the need to operate separate controls and switches.

The Sea Harrier FRS. Mk 2 will retain two external stores

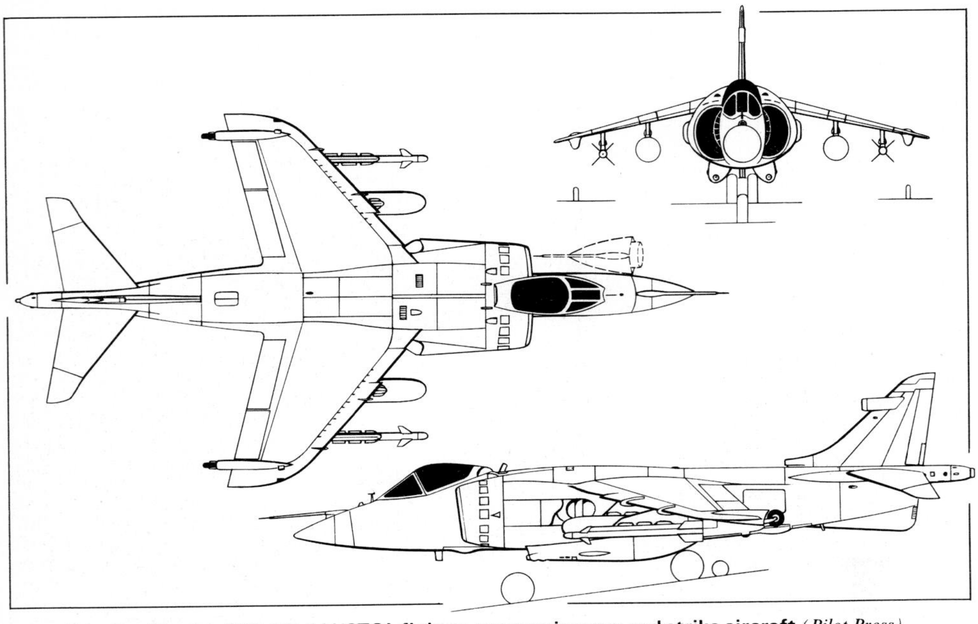

BAe Sea Harrier FRS. Mk 1 V/STOL fighter, reconnaissance and strike aircraft *(Pilot Press)*

pylons under each wing, an underbelly centreline pylon, and mountings under the fuselage for two 30 mm Aden or new 25 mm gun packs, or AMRAAM missile pylons. Two 455 or 864 litre (120 or 228 US gallon; 100 or 190 Imp gallon) combat drop tanks, or 1,500 litre (396 US gallon; 330 Imp gallon) ferry tanks, can be carried on the inboard underwing pylons. Alternative loadings include five free-fall or retarded 1,000 lb bombs, five cluster bombs, six Matra 115/116 packs of 68 mm rockets, eight Bofors Lepus flares, four Sidewinder, Magic or AMRAAM air-to-air missiles, two Sea Eagle air-to-surface missiles, or two ALARM anti-radiation missiles. Other standard weapons with which the aircraft will be compatible include 250, 500, and 1,000 lb LDGP free-fall bombs, 250 and 500 lb Snakeye retarded bombs, LAU-10A, LAU-68A and LAU-69A rocket launchers, Mk 77 fire bombs, APAM cluster/Mk 7 dispensers, Rockeye II cluster/Mk 7 dispensers, and PMBR practice bomb racks.

The description of the GR. Mk 3 applies also to the FRS. Mk 1, except as follows:

TYPE: V/STOL fighter, reconnaissance and strike aircraft.

WINGS: Cantilever shoulder-wing monoplane. Wing section of BAe (HS) design. Thickness/chord ratio 10% at root, 5% at tip. Anhedral 12°. Incidence 1° 45′. Sweepback at quarter-chord 34°. One-piece aluminium alloy three-spar safe-life structure with integrally machined skins, manufactured by Brough factory of BAe, with six-point attachment to fuselage. Plain ailerons and flaps, of bonded aluminium alloy honeycomb construction. Ailerons irreversibly operated by Fairey tandem hydraulic jacks. Jet reaction control valve built into front of each outrigger wheel fairing. Entire wing unit removable to provide access to engine. For ferry missions, the normal 'combat' wingtips can be replaced by bolt-on extended tips to increase ferry range.

FUSELAGE: Conventional semi-monocoque safe-life structure of frames and stringers, mainly of aluminium alloy, but with titanium skins at rear and some titanium adjacent to engine and in other special areas. Access to power plant through top of fuselage, ahead of wing. Jet reaction control valves in nose and tailcone. Large forward hinged airbrake under fuselage, aft of mainwheel well.

TAIL UNIT: One-piece variable incidence tailplane, with 15° of anhedral, irreversibly operated by Fairey tandem hydraulic jack. Rudder and trailing-edge of tailplane are of bonded aluminium honeycomb construction. Rudder is operated manually. Trim tab in rudder. Ventral fin under rear fuselage. Fin tip carries suppressed VHF aerial.

LANDING GEAR: Retractable bicycle type of Dowty Rotol manufacture, permitting operation from rough unprepared surfaces of CBR as low as 3 to 5 per cent. Hydraulic actuation, with nitrogen bottle for emergency extension of landing gear. Single steerable nosewheel retracts forward, twin coupled mainwheels rearward, into fuselage. Small outrigger units retract rearward into fairings slightly inboard of wingtips. Nosewheel leg is of levered suspension Liquid Spring type. Dowty Rotol telescopic oleo-pneumatic main and outrigger gear. Dunlop wheels and tyres, size 26.00 × 8.75-11 (nose unit), 27.00 × 7.74-13 (main units) and 13.50 × 6.4 (outriggers). Dunlop multi-disc brakes and Dunlop-Hytrol adaptive anti-skid system.

POWER PLANT: One Rolls-Royce Pegasus Mk 104 vectored thrust turbofan (95.6 kN; 21,500 lb st), with four exhaust nozzles of the two-vane cascade type, rotatable through 98.5° from fully aft position. Engine bleed air from HP compressor used for jet reaction control system and to power duplicated air motor for nozzle actuation. The low drag intake cowls each have eight automatic suction relief doors aft of the leading-edge to improve intake efficiency by providing extra air for the engine at low forward or zero speeds. A 227 litre (60 US gallon; 50 Imp gallon) tank supplies demineralised water for thrust restoration in high ambient temperatures for STO, VTO and vertical landings. Fuel in five integral tanks in fuselage and two in wings, with total capacity of approx 2,865 litres (757 US gallons; 630 Imp gallons). This can be supplemented by two 455 litre (120 US gallon; 100 Imp gallon) jettisonable combat tanks, or two 864 litre (228 US gallon; 190 Imp gallon) tanks, or two 1,500 litre (396 US gallon; 330 Imp gallon) ferry tanks on the inboard wing pylons. Ground refuelling point in port rear nozzle fairing. Provision for in-flight refuelling probe above the port intake cowl.

ACCOMMODATION: Crew of one on Martin-Baker Mk 10H zero/zero rocket ejection seat which operates through the miniature detonating cord equipped canopy of the pressurised, heated and air-conditioned cockpit. Sea Harrier seat raised 28 cm (11 in) compared with Harrier. Manually operated canopy, rearward sliding on single-seat, sideways opening (to starboard) on two-seat versions. Birdproof windscreen, with hydraulically actuated wiper. Windscreen washing system.

SYSTEMS: Three-axis limited authority autostabiliser for V/STOL flight. Pressurisation system of BAe design, with Normalair-Garrett and Delaney Gallay major components; max pressure differential 0.24 bars (3.5 lb/sq in). Two hydraulic systems; flow rate: System 1, 36 litres (9.6 US gallons; 8 Imp gallons)/min; System 2, 23 litres (6 US gallons; 5 Imp gallons)/min. Systems, pressure 207 bars (3,000 lb/sq in), actuate Fairey flying control and general services and a retractable ram air turbine inside top of rear fuselage, driving a small hydraulic pump for emergency power. Hydraulic reservoirs nitrogen pressurised at 2.75 to 5.5 bars (40 to 80 lb/sq in). AC electrical system with transformer-rectifiers to provide required DC supply. Two 15 kVA generators. Two 28V 25Ah batteries, one of which energises a 24V motor to start Lucas gas turbine starter/APU. This unit drives a 6kVA auxiliary alternator for ground readiness servicing and standby. Normalair-Garrett liquid oxygen system of 4.5 litres (1.2 US gallons; 1 Imp gallon) capacity. Bootstrap cooling unit for equipment bay, with intake at base of dorsal fin. Autopilot function on Fairey Hydraulics, giving throughput to aileron and tailplane power controls as well as to three-axis autostabs. British Oxygen liquid oxygen system of 4.5 litres (1.2 US gallons; 1 Imp gallon) capacity in Royal Navy aircraft; those for Indian Navy have gaseous oxygen system. Lucas Mk 2 GTS/APU.

AVIONICS AND EQUIPMENT: Nose mounted Ferranti Blue Fox multi-mode radar, with TV raster daylight viewing tube which conveys flight information, as well as radar data, to pilot. New and larger Smiths electronic head-up display and 20,000 word digital weapon aiming computer. Autopilot, radar altimeter and Decca Doppler 72 radar. Ferranti self aligning attitude and heading reference platform and digital navigation computer. Radio navaids include UHF homing, GEC Avionics AD 2770 Tacan with offset facility and I band transponder. Radio com by multi-channel Plessey PTR 377 U/VHF, with VHF standby via D 403M transceiver. Passive electronic surveillance and warning of external radar illumination by receiver with forward and rear hemisphere antennae in fin and tailcone respectively.

ARMAMENT AND OPERATIONAL EQUIPMENT: Optically flat panel in nose, on port side, for F.95 oblique camera, which is carried as standard. A cockpit voice recorder with in-flight playback facility supplements the reconnaissance cameras, and facilitates rapid debriefing and mission evaluation. No built-in armament. Combat load is carried on four underwing and one underfuselage pylons, all with ML ejector release units. The inboard wing points and the fuselage point are stressed for loads of up to 910 kg (2,000 lb) each, and the outboard underwing pair for loads of up to 295 kg (650 lb) each; the two strake fairings under the fuselage can each be replaced by a 30 mm Aden gun pod and ammunition. The aircraft is cleared for operations with a maximum external load exceeding 2,270 kg (5,000 lb), and has flown with a weapon load of 3,630 kg (8,000 lb). It is able to carry 30 mm guns, bombs, rockets and flares of UK and US designs. Sea Harrier has standard addition of four AIM-9 Sidewinder missiles on the outboard underwing pylons (Matra Magic instead of Sidewinder on Indian Navy aircraft), and provision for two air-to-surface missiles of Sea Eagle or Harpoon type.

DIMENSIONS, EXTERNAL: As GR. Mk 3 except:

Wing span: FRS. Mk 1	7.70 m (25 ft 3 in)
FRS. Mk 2	8.31 m (27 ft 3 in)
Length overall: FRS. Mk 1	14.50 m (47 ft 7 in)
FRS. Mk 2	14.10 m (46 ft 3 in)
Length overall, nose folded:	
FRS. Mk 1	12.73 m (41 ft 9 in)
FRS. Mk 2	13.16 m (43 ft 2 in)
Height overall	3.71 m (12 ft 2 in)

WEIGHTS (FRS. Mk 1):

Operating weight empty	6,374 kg (14,052 lb)
Max fuel: internal	2,295 kg (5,060 lb)
external	2,404 kg (5,300 lb)
Max weapon load: STO	3,630 kg (8,000 lb)
VTO	2,270 kg (5,000 lb)
Max T-O weight	11,880 kg (26,200 lb)

PERFORMANCE (FRS. Mk 1):

Max Mach No. at high altitude 1.25

Max level speed at low altitude
above 640 knots (1,185 km/h; 736 mph) EAS

Typical cruising speed:
high altitude, for well over 1 h on internal fuel
above Mach 0.8

low altitude
350-450 knots (650-833 km/h; 404-518 mph), with rapid acceleration to
600 knots (1,110 km/h; 690 mph)

STO run at max T-O weight, without 'ski-jump'
approx 305 m (1,000 ft)

Time from alarm to 30 nm (55 km; 35 miles) combat area under 6 min

High altitude intercept radius, with 3 min combat and reserves for VL 400 nm (750 km; 460 miles)

Strike radius 250 nm (463 km; 288 miles)

g limits +7.8/−4.2

COMBAT PROFILES (FRS. Mk 2, from carrier fitted with a 12° ski-jump ramp, at ISA + 15°C and with a 20 knot; 37 km/h; 23 mph wind over the deck):

Combat air patrol: Up to 1½ hours on station at a radius of 100 nm (185 km; 115 miles), carrying four AMRAAMs, or two AMRAAMs and two 30 mm guns, plus two 864 litre (228 US gallon; 190 Imp gallon) combat drop tanks.

Reconnaissance: Low-level cover of 28,000 nm² (96,000 km²; 37,065 sq miles) at a radius of 525 nm (970 km; 600 miles) from the carrier, with outward and return flights at medium/high level, carrying two 30 mm guns and two 864 litre (228 US gallon; 190 Imp gallon) combat drop tanks. Overall flight time 1 h 45 min.

Surface attack (hi-lo-hi): Radius of action to missile launch 200 nm (370 km; 230 miles), carrying two Sea Eagle missiles and two 30 mm guns.

Take-off deck run for the above missions is 137 m, 107 m and 92 m (450 ft, 350 ft and 300 ft) respectively, with vertical landing.

Interception: A typical deck-launched interception could be performed against a Mach 0.9 target at a radius of 116 nm (215 km; 133 miles), or a Mach 1.3 target at 95 nm (175 km; 109 miles), after initial radar detection of the approaching target at a range of 230 nm (425 km; 265 miles), with the Sea Harrier at 2 min alert status, carrying two AMRAAM missiles.

BAe EAP

British Aerospace exhibited at the 1982 Farnborough Air Show, and again at the 1983 Paris Air Show, a full scale mockup of what was then known as the Agile Combat Aircraft (**ACA**). It represented the result of several years of private venture research and development by BAe, with industry support from Rolls-Royce, Dowty, Ferranti, Lucas, GEC Avionics and Smiths Industries, at a total estimated cost of £25 million by mid-1983. MBB of Germany and Aeritalia of Italy had also contributed to the project.

No government support for the ACA was forthcoming but, at the 1982 Farnborough show, the UK government announced that it would make a financial contribution to an experimental aircraft programme (**EAP**) technology demonstrator based on the ACA design. The aims of the programme were to bring together a specific range of new and advanced technologies being developed by BAe and other aerospace manufacturers in Europe.

On 26 May 1983, BAe announced that a contract had been signed with the Ministry of Defence for the design, development and construction of a single demonstrator aircraft which would be used to prove advanced technological features, including advanced aerodynamics; active control technology for unstable aircraft; a digital databus system; advanced electronic cockpit; and advanced structural design including the extensive use of carbonfibre composites.

The EAP demonstrator was funded by the UK Ministry of Defence, BAe, its industrial partners and equipment suppliers in Britain, Italy and West Germany. The co-bonded wings were designed and manufactured by BAe and Aeritalia.

With the UK committed to participation in the international programme for a European fighter aircraft (Eurofighter, see International section), the relevance of the EAP is that it is designed to represent a weapon system that would meet a generally similar requirement. During its first flight, on 8 August 1986, the EAP demonstrator (ZF534) accelerated to Mach 1.1 at 9,150 m (30,000 ft). It made public appearances at the Farnborough Air Show in 1986 and, following installation of new flight controls and an anti-spin parachute, at the Paris Air Show in 1987. By 1 February 1988, the EAP had completed 128 flights and expanded the flight envelope to above Mach 1.6 (650 knots; 1,200 km/h; 750 mph CAS).

Development work conducted with the EAP has contributed to the Eurofighter EFA programme. Work in direct support of EFA and other research activities were continuing in 1988.

TYPE: Advanced technology demonstrator aircraft.

WINGS: Main wing aerofoil section varies from root to tip. Multi-spar carbonfibre composite co-bonded construction. Spars bonded to bottom skin; top skin bolted to spar flanges. Foreplanes of carbonfibre composite construction. Aerodynamic configuration provides high negative stability. The aluminium alloy leading-edge flaps and aluminium/lithium alloy skinned trailing-edge flight surfaces, and the foreplanes, are operated by a GEC Avionics computer controlled active control system, using quadruplex full authority digital fly by wire technology developed in the Jaguar ACT programme. Liebherr/Magnaghi/Dowty Boulton Paul actuators on the foreplanes, rudder and inboard/outboard flaperon control surfaces are operated via a pilot's stick sensor assembly (PSSA) which uses spring damping and viscous loading to give the required stick resistance, to allow full and accurate movement of the stick in relation to aircraft speed and attitude. No reversionary mechanical or electrical signalling to flight control actuators.

FUSELAGE: Front fuselage is of semi-monocoque construction, with light alloy structure and carbonfibre composites side skins, cockpit floor and some belly skins. Engine air inlet duct of conventional aluminium alloy construction. Hinged forward lower lip. Centre and rear fuselage of conventional metal construction, using Tornado technology and components. Centre keel member of superplastic formed/diffusion bonded titanium, with a conventionally fabricated titanium structure, to save weight and space.

TAIL UNIT: Cantilever all-metal structure, consisting of single sweptback two-spar fin and rudder, essentially the same as those fitted to the Tornado.

LANDING GEAR: Hydraulically operated tricycle type, with single wheel on each unit. Rearward retracting steerable nose unit. Operation of the forward retracting Dowty Rotol main landing gear involves rotary movement about the leg of each wheel during retraction and lowering, to facilitate compact stowage and positive locking when the gear is fully down. Carbonfibre wheel brakes. Brake parachute housed between rudder and jet nozzle.

POWER PLANT: Two Turbo-Union RB199-34R Mk 104D turbofans, as fitted to the Tornado F. Mk 3, but with thrust reversers removed, rated in the 40.0 kN (9,000 lb st) class dry and 75.5 kN (17,000 lb st) class with afterburning. Installed in rear fuselage with downward opening doors for servicing and engine change. Lucas

BAe EAP advanced technology demonstrator photographed during handling trials

DECU 500 full authority digital engine control system, developed in conjunction with Rolls-Royce. Fuel is carried integrally in the wings and in 14 tanks in the fuselage.

ACCOMMODATION: Pilot only, on specially-developed Martin-Baker Mk 10LX zero/zero ejection seat, in pressurised cockpit embodying advanced processor-controlled avionics and utilities management and control systems designed to reduce substantially the pilot's workload. Equipment includes three colour multi-function display CRTs supplied by Smiths Industries, and an advanced GEC Avionics head-up display embodying holographic optics, and an additional raster (TV-like) display for night flying. Processor-controlled cockpit lighting system adjusts lighting levels automatically throughout ambient lighting spectrum.

SYSTEMS: Environmental control system utilises engine bleed air piped inside fuselage spine fairing to a precooler and intercooler in systems/avionics bay aft of cockpit. Hot air is mixed with cold ram air taken in above engine intake splitter plate. Exhaust is ejected through duct above wingroot on each side of fuselage. Hydraulic system for actuating flying control surfaces and airbrakes, landing gear retraction and extension, nosewheel steering, anti-skid braking and air intake lip actuation. Lucas/ Rotax secondary power system, with electric starter/ generators. Liquid oxygen system. Comprehensive fire detection and extinguishing systems.

AVIONICS AND EQUIPMENT: Racal Acoustics RA 800 series digital audio control system (IDACS). GEC Avionics AD 3400 VHF/UHF multimode radio. GEC Avionics AD 2780 Tacan system. GEC Avionics television sensor in cockpit records what the pilot sees during flight. Ferranti FIN 1070 inertial navigation system and BAe SCR 300E flight data recorder. Major avionics units mounted in an innovative avionics equipment module in the front fuselage behind the cockpit. Information supplied to VDO cockpit multi-function displays by 1553B databus highways, replacing great lengths of multicored conventional wiring.

DIMENSIONS, EXTERNAL:
Wing span	11.77 m (38 ft 7 in)
Length overall	14.70 m (48 ft 2¾ in)
Height	5.52 m (18 ft 1½ in)

AREA:
Wings, gross	52.0 m² (560 sq ft)

WEIGHTS (approx):
Weight empty	10,000 kg (22,050 lb)
Fuel	4,535 kg (10,000 lb)
Max T-O weight, clean	14,515 kg (32,000 lb)

PERFORMANCE:
Max speed at height	Mach 2.0+

EUROFIGHTER (EFA)

Details of this military aircraft programme, in which British Aerospace is participating with companies from West Germany, Italy and Spain, can be found in the International section.

BAe NIMROD

BAe's involvement with major Nimrod developments ended in 1986, when the final conversion from MR. Mk 1 to MR. Mk 2 was re-delivered to the RAF and the AEW. Mk 3 airborne early warning variant was abandoned because of radar problems. Two prototype and 46 production MR. Mk 1 maritime reconnaissance variants were built, of which 35 were upgraded to MR. Mk 2 and returned to the RAF from August 1979 onwards. A further 11 were converted to AEW. Mk 3 configuration and have been held in RAF storage pending a decision on their future. Three elint/sigint Nimrod R. Mk 1s (lacking an MAD tailboom) were built under a separate contract. The Nimrod was last described fully in the 1987-88 (Mks 1/2) and 1986-87 (Mk 3) editions of *Jane's*.

BAe (BAC/VICKERS) VC10 K. Mk 2/Mk 3 TANKERS

In addition to operating 13 of its original 14 VC10 C. Mk 1 transports, delivered in 1966-68 to No. 10 Squadron, the RAF has received tanker variants converted from former airline aircraft in the form of five VC10 K. Mk 2s (from July 1983) and four Super VC10 K. Mk 3s (from February 1985) for No. 101 Squadron. Modification work was undertaken by BAe at Filton, the final aircraft flying on 9 August 1985, and involved installing an internal Flight Refuelling Mk 17B hose-and-drum unit, plus wing-mounted FR Mk 32/2800 HDUs. The basic VC10 and Super VC10 were last described fully in the 1969-70 *Jane's* under the British Aircraft Corporation entry, and specific tanker modifications in the 1987-88 edition.

Fourteen British Airways Super VC10s were bought by the RAF in 1981, plus a Gulf Air VC10 in 1982. After instructional disposals and scrapping, six Super VC10s remained in storage in 1988 as possible candidates for a simplified tanker conversion with only the two underwing pods.

BAe HOTOL

HOTOL (horizontal take-off and landing) is the name of a space transport study undertaken by the British Aerospace divisions at Warton (Military Aircraft Division), Stevenage (Space and Communications Division) and Filton (Civil Aircraft Division) in conjunction with Rolls-Royce. The initial objective was a reusable unmanned launch vehicle able to carry satellites into orbit for one fifth the cost of current procedures. Later versions were expected to carry personnel into orbit to service space stations or other objects in low Earth orbits.

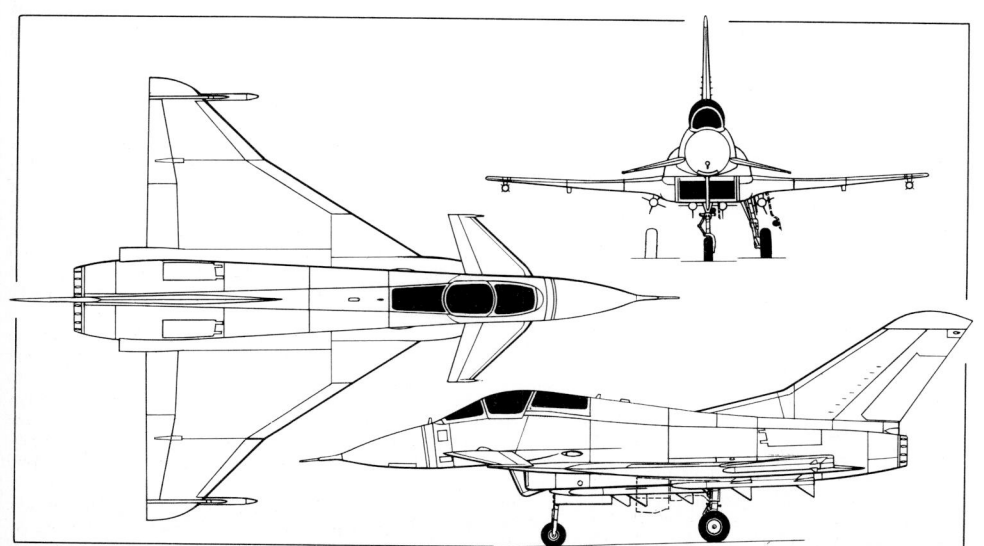

Three-view drawing of BAe EAP demonstrator *(Pilot Press)*

In February 1986 the British National Space Centre of the Department of Trade announced that it had allocated £375,000 to initiate a two-year proof of concept study costing £3 million. The initial funds covered the first six months of the study, in 1987; an equal amount was made available by industry. From October 1987, the study was maintained by additional BAe funds, but the British government announced in July 1988 that it would provide no further funding and the future of the programme is uncertain.

HOTOL would take off and land like a conventional aircraft. Novel features include a laser guided trolley for take-off, which would be left behind in the interests of weight saving. Landing would be on a relatively lightweight gear carried on board. This arrangement was adopted because the take-off weight would be about five times the landing weight. The key to the HOTOL concept is a revolutionary hybrid power plant under study by Rolls-Royce. Known as the RB545 Swallow, this would act as an air-breathing turbofan in the atmosphere, and as an oxygen/hydrogen rocket in space. Speed at transition from air-breathing to rocket power would be Mach 5 at 26,000 m (85,000 ft). Initial rig tests of critical components of the engine were conducted in 1986.

Detail design is at an early stage, but BAe states that re-entry heat protection would be by a metal skin and not by tiles of the kind used on the US Space Shuttle. Titanium would be used on the upper surfaces.

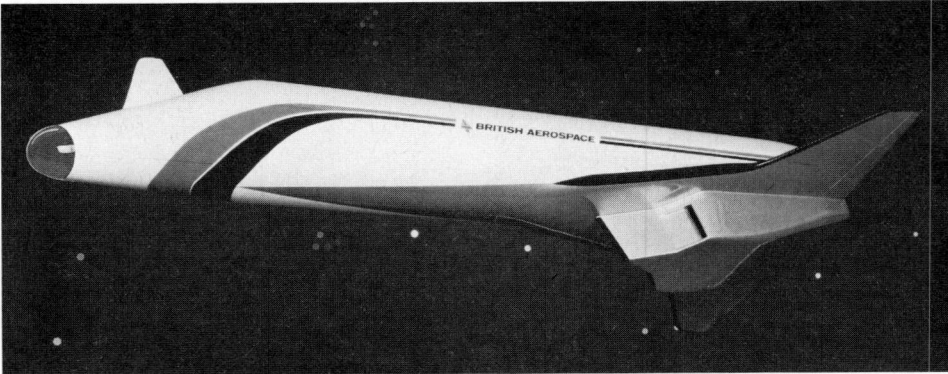

Model of latest configuration of HOTOL aerospacecraft

DIMENSIONS (provisional):
Wing span	28.34 m (93 ft 0 in)
Length overall	62.97 m (206 ft 7¼ in)
Height overall	12.83 m (42 ft 1⅛ in)

WEIGHTS (provisional):
T-O weight	250,000 kg (551,155 lb)
Landing weight	47,500 kg (104,719 lb)

PERFORMANCE (provisional):
Payload into 300 km (162 mile) equatorial Earth orbit	8,000 kg (17,635 lb)
T-O speed	278 knots (515 km/h; 320 mph)
Landing speed	150 knots (278 km/h; 173 mph)
Landing run: dry runway	1,145 m (3,750 ft)
wet runway	1,500 m (4,925 ft)

BROOKLANDS
BROOKLANDS AIRCRAFT LIMITED
(Subsidiary of Brooklands Aerospace Group PLC)

Old Sarum Airfield, Salisbury, Wiltshire SP4 6BJ
Telephone: 0722 21812
Telex: 47106 AERODS
Fax: 0722 337100
CHAIRMAN: Alan Curtis
MARKETING DIRECTOR: W. L. Pender

The original company responsible for the Optica programme, Edgley Aircraft Ltd, was formed in 1974 to design, build and market a specialised observation aircraft that would combine the all-round field of view of a helicopter with the lower operating costs of a fixed-wing aircraft. Fuel consumption of the Optica is claimed to be 16-24% of that for a comparable light turbine helicopter, and operating costs (fixed and direct for 500 hours per year) 31%.

Production of the Optica started in 1983 in the company's 6,505 m² (70,000 sq ft) premises at Old Sarum Airfield. The first production aircraft (c/n 003, G-BLFC) was rolled out and first flew on 4 August 1984. CAA type certification was granted on 8 February 1985, for day VFR flying and was extended to night and IFR clearance in time for the delivery of the first customer's aircraft in April 1985.

The company encountered financial difficulties, and was purchased from the receiver by Mr A. Haikney of Aero-Docks Ltd in December 1985. A new company, Optica Industries Ltd, re-started production in January 1986. Its plan to produce 46 aircraft in 1987 was disrupted by a severe fire on 16 January 1987, which destroyed the aircraft hangar and most of the completed aircraft inside.

Following the fire, on 14 April 1987, the company was renamed Brooklands Aircraft Ltd. The aircraft was renamed Optica Scout and will be referred to as the Scout in the UK market. By February 1988, excluding a prototype, a demonstrator, nine destroyed before delivery and a static test airframe, four Opticas had been delivered to customers. Brooklands' initial production target is one Optica Scout per month.

BROOKLANDS OPTICA SCOUT Mk II

First flown on 14 December 1979, the Optica is a three-seat observation aircraft, designed particularly for pipeline and powerline inspection; forestry and coastal patrol; police duties; frontier patrol; aerial photography; film, TV and press reporting; and touring. The cabin configuration is designed to give the best possible all-round view. Power plant is a ducted propulsor unit, offering quietness, both within the cabin and from the ground. A low wing loading, pre-set inboard flaps and a low stalling speed facilitate continuous en-route flight at low speeds. Generous flap area provides good field performance from both hard and soft strips. Stability increases at low speeds.

TYPE: Three-seat slow flying observation aircraft; stressed to BCAR Section K (non-aerobatic category) and FAR Pt 23 (Normal category).

WINGS: Cantilever mid-wing monoplane. Wing section NASA GA(W)-1; thickness/chord ratio 17%. Dihedral 3° on outer panels. Incidence 0°. Constant chord single-spar non-swept wings of L72 duralumin stressed skin construction. Wingtips (also fin/tailplane fillets, nosewheel mudguard and some power plant fairings) of glassfibre. Fowler trailing-edge flaps (29 per cent of total wing chord) inboard and outboard of tailbooms. Electrically actuated outboard flaps can be set at angles up to 50° for landing; inboard flaps set permanently at 10°, giving the effect of a slotted wing, for continuous low

Brooklands Optica Scout three-seat slow flying observation aircraft (*Air Portraits*)

speed flying. Bottom hinged, mass balanced slotted ailerons outboard of outer flaps, operated by pushrods. No spoilers, airbrakes or tabs.

CABIN: 'Insect eye' shaped structure, built of aluminium alloy with ICI Perspex windows, optionally tinted. Outward visibility approximately 270° in vertical plane and 340° in horizontal plane. Cabin attached to fan shroud and rest of airframe by six stators of steel tube and aluminium alloy shear web construction. Steel tube and aluminium alloy nose beam supports cabin floor. Horizontal window frame member just above floor level, together with nosewheel box, is designed to withstand 9g impact. Tinted windows optional. Two movable 9 kg (20 lb) ballast weights may be positioned on the nose beam. Two lamps are also mounted in the nose beam, one as a landing lamp, the other as a taxi/standby landing lamp.

TAIL UNIT: Twin-tailboom configuration, basically of aluminium alloy stressed skin tubular construction. Limited GRP content in non-load-bearing areas. Tailboom pick-up points at extremities of wing centre-section. Angular, inward canted fins and balanced rudders. Fixed incidence tailplane, with elevator, bridging space between tops of fins. Inset trim tab occupies port half of elevator trailing-edge; no rudder tabs. Two movable 9 kg (20 lb) ballast weights may be positioned, one in each fin.

LANDING GEAR: Non-retractable tricycle type, with steerable nosewheel offset to port. Mainwheel legs embody rubber in compression shock absorption. Nosewheel shock absorption by bungee rubber in tension. Single wheel on

each unit, tyre sizes 6.00-6 (main) and 5.00-5 (nose). Hydraulic disc brakes on mainwheels.

POWER PLANT: Ducted propulsor unit, with engine and fan forming a power pod separate from the main shroud. Pod is attached to fan shroud with four Lord rubber mountings, and supported by four stators of steel channel and aluminium alloy shear web construction, with steel tube engine bearers. Five-blade Hydulignum fixed-pitch fan, driven by a 194 kW (260 hp) Textron Lycoming IO-540-V4A5D flat-six engine, mounted in a duct downstream of the fan. Fuel tank of 128 litres (33.8 US gallons; 28 Imp gallons) capacity in each wing leading-edge, immediately outboard of tailbooms and forward of wing spar. Tanks are of full wing section, but are designed not to be stressed by wing bending and torsion. Total usable fuel capacity 250 litres (66 US gallons; 55 Imp gallons). Refuelling point in upper surface of each wing. Oil capacity 7.6 litres (2.0 US gallons; 1.7 Imp gallons).

ACCOMMODATION: Cabin designed to accommodate up to three persons side by side on fixed seats, with either single- or two-pilot operation (left hand and centre seats). Dual controls standard. Baggage space aft of seats. Single elliptical door on each side, hinged at front and opening forward. Can be flown with doors removed. Cabin heated, by hot air from engine, and ventilated. A Janitrol combustion heater is offered as an extra.

SYSTEMS: Hydraulics for mainwheel brakes only. Electrical system (24V) includes engine driven alternator and storage battery for engine starting and actuation of flaps.

AVIONICS AND EQUIPMENT: Standard nav/com avionics by King (Silver Crown). Alternative avionics could be provided. Special equipment which has been tested successfully includes Barr & Stroud IR18 Mk II and an air-to-ground video relay. Other equipment such as FLIR, GEC Avionics TICM II, searchlights and loudspeakers is being assessed.

DIMENSIONS, EXTERNAL:

Wing span	12.00 m (39 ft 4 in)
Wing chord: basic, constant	1.32 m (4 ft 4 in)
over 10° fixed flaps	1.45 m (4 ft 9 in)
Wing aspect ratio	9.1
Length overall	8.15 m (26 ft 9 in)
Height over fan shroud (excl aerial)	1.98 m (6 ft 6 in)
Diameter of fan shroud	1.68 m (5 ft 6 in)
Diameter of fan	1.22 m (4 ft 0 in)
Shroud ground clearance	0.25 m (10 in)
Height over tailplane	2.31 m (7 ft 7 in)
Tailplane span:	
c/l of tailbooms	3.40 m (11 ft 2 in)
intersection fin chord	2.60 m (8 ft 6½ in)
Wheel track	3.40 m (11 ft 2 in)
Wheelbase	2.73 m (9 ft 0 in)
Doors (each): Long axis	1.35 m (4 ft 5 in)
Short axis	0.96 m (3 ft 1¾ in)
Height to sill	0.51 m (1 ft 8 in)

DIMENSIONS, INTERNAL:

Cabin: Length	2.44 m (8 ft 0 in)
Max width (to door Perspex)	1.68 m (5 ft 6 in)
Max height	1.35 m (4 ft 5 in)
Floor area	0.72 m² (7.75 sq ft)

AREAS:

Wings, gross	15.84 m² (170.5 sq ft)
Ailerons (total)	1.55 m² (16.68 sq ft)
Trailing-edge flaps:	
inboard (total)	0.61 m² (6.57 sq ft)
outboard (total)	1.59 m² (17.12 sq ft)

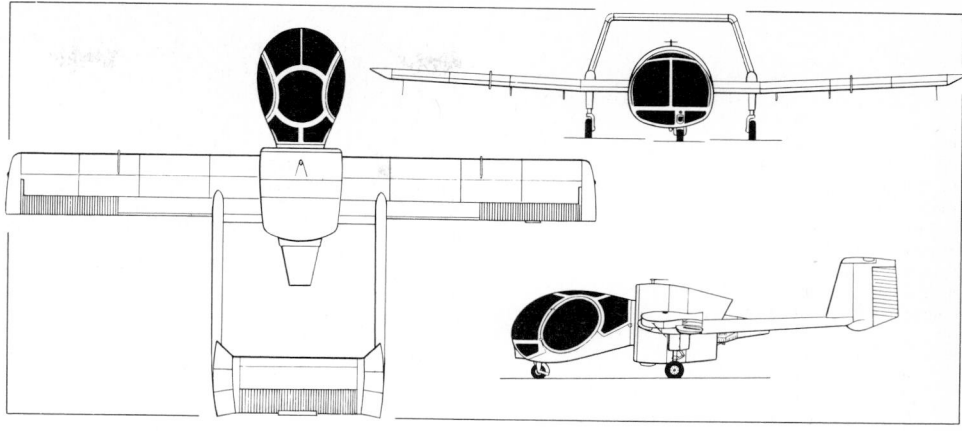

Brooklands Optica Scout (Textron Lycoming IO-540 engine) *(Pilot Press)*

Fins (total)	1.98 m² (21.31 sq ft)
Rudders (total)	1.10 m² (11.84 sq ft)
Tailplane	1.62 m² (17.44 sq ft)
Elevator, incl tab	1.26 m² (13.56 sq ft)

WEIGHTS AND LOADINGS:

Weight empty	948 kg (2,090 lb)
Max cabin load	231 kg (510 lb)
Max T-O weight	1,315 kg (2,900 lb)
Max wing loading	83.0 kg/m² (17.0 lb/sq ft)
Max power loading	6.78 kg/kW (11.2 lb/hp)

PERFORMANCE (at max T-O weight, forward limit CG):

Never-exceed speed	140 knots (259 km/h; 161 mph)
Max level speed	115 knots (213 km/h; 132 mph)
Loiter speed (40% power)	70 knots (130 km/h; 81 mph)
Cruising speed:	
(50% power)	86 knots (159 km/h; 99 mph)
(70% power)	103 knots (191 km/h; 119 mph)
Stalling speed: outboard flaps up	58 knots (108 km/h; 67 mph)
Max rate of climb at S/L	247 m (810 ft)/min
Service ceiling	4,275 m (14,000 ft)
T-O run	330 m (1,082 ft)
Landing run	278 m (912 ft)
Range with max fuel (45 min reserves):	
at 70 knots (130 km/h; 81 mph)	570 nm (1,056 km; 656 miles)
at 110 knots (204 km/h; 127 mph)	370 nm (685 km; 426 miles)
Endurance (45 min reserves):	
at 70 knots (130 km/h; 81 mph)	8 h
at 110 knots (204 km/h; 127 mph)	2 h 45 min
g limits	+3.8/−1.5

CMC

CHICHESTER-MILES CONSULTANTS LTD

West House, The Old Rectory, Ayot St Lawrence, Welwyn, Hertfordshire AL6 9BT
Telephone: 0438 820341
CHAIRMAN: I. Chichester-Miles

CMC LEOPARD

Mr Ian Chichester-Miles, formerly Chief Research Engineer of British Aerospace Aircraft Division at Hatfield, Hertfordshire, established Chichester-Miles Consultants to develop a high performance light business jet. Design of the four-seat Leopard started in January 1981 and was sufficiently advanced for a mockup to be completed in early 1982. Detail design and construction of a prototype by Designability Ltd of Dilton Marsh, Wiltshire, began in July 1982, under contract to CMC. First flight of this aircraft was scheduled for the first half of 1988. It has lower-powered engines, and lacks the full pressurisation/air-conditioning system, avionics and instrumentation of the production aircraft.

TYPE: Four-seat light business aircraft.

WINGS: Cantilever mid-wing monoplane. ARA designed wing section and 3D profiles combining laminar flow and supercritical wing technology. Thickness/chord ratio 14% at root, 11% at tip. Sweepback at quarter-chord 25°. Two-spar structure, primarily of GRP, with some carbonfibre reinforcement. Full span electrically actuated trailing-edge plain flaps of carbonfibre, with deflections of ±45° for high drag landing and air-braking/lift dumping. No ailerons or spoilers. Liquid de-icing and decontamination system in leading-edge.

FUSELAGE: Built in three sections: unpressurised nose section accommodating avionics and nosewheel gear when retracted, pressurised cabin section, and unpressurised rear section providing a baggage bay, with fuel tanks below and equipment bays to rear. Basic monocoque structure, primarily of GRP with some carbonfibre reinforcement; fore and aft cabin bulkheads, engine and tailplane axle frames moulded in. Pressure cabin section divided approximately along aircraft horizontal datum, with upper section formed by electrically actuated upward opening canopy hinged at windscreen leading-edge. Multiple latches around canopy lower edge. Bonded-in acrylic side windows carry pressurisation tension. Nose opens for access to avionics.

TAIL UNIT: All-moving fin and tailplane of all-composites construction. Fin sternpost projects to bottom of rear fuselage. Low-set tailplane in two independent sections, each mounted on a steel axle projecting from side of rear fuselage. Tailplane sections are operated collectively for control in pitch and differentially for roll control. Fin and tailplane sections each have a carbonfibre geared anti-servo tab, adjustable for trim. Anti-icing as for wings.

LANDING GEAR: Electrically retractable tricycle type, main units retracting inward into wingroot wells, nosewheels forward. Well closure doors linked mechanically to landing gear units. Gravity extension assisted by bias springs and aerodynamic drag. Long stroke shock absorber in each unit, using synthetic elastomers in compression. Main units, each with single Cleveland wheel, size 500 × 5, have tyres size 11 × 4, pressure 4.82 bars (70 lb/sq in) on prototype, 7.24 bars (105 lb/sq in) on production aircraft. Twin-wheel nose unit has wheels size 400 × 3 and tyres size 8.5 × 2.75 in on prototype; tyre pressure 2.75 bars (40 lb/sq in). Tyre pressure 3.8 bars (55 lb/sq in) on production aircraft. Hydraulic disc brakes. Parking brake.

POWER PLANT: Prototype has two Noel Penny Turbines NPT 301-3 turbojets each of nominal 1.42 kN (319 lb st) rating. Production aircraft will have two low-bypass Noel Penny Turbines NPT 754 turbofans, each of 3.34 kN (750 lb st). Each engine in nacelle, mounted on composite crossbeam located elastically in rear fuselage. Nacelles of composite construction, with stainless steel firewalls and liquid de-icing system for leading-edges. Fuel tanks in fuselage, below baggage bay. Prototype has total fuel capacity of 455 litres (120 US gallons; 100 Imp gallons). Production aircraft will have maximum capacity of 591 litres (156 US gallons; 130 Imp gallons). Refuelling point on upper surface of fuselage, near base of fin.

ACCOMMODATION: Cabin seats four, in two pairs, on semi-reclining (35°) seats beneath upward opening jettisonable canopy. Options include dual controls, and accommodation for pilot, stretcher and attendant in medevac role. Unpressurised baggage bay aft of cabin, capacity 54 kg (120 lb), with external door in upper surface of fuselage.

SYSTEMS (production aircraft): Air-conditioning and pressurisation (max differential 0.55 bars: 8 lb/sq in) by engine bleed air, with simple Normalair-Garrett air cycle cold air/dehumidifier unit. Electrical system powered by dual engine driven 3kVA starter/generators. Hydraulic system for brakes only.

AVIONICS AND EQUIPMENT (production aircraft): Full nav/com and weather radar systems. Avionics, mounted in nose bay, supply data to three CRTs in pilot's instrument panel and one below: they comprise EADI, EHSI, engine management display, and systems management display. CRT displays can be transferred in the failure mode. Reduced scale electromechanical standby flight instruments. All avionics systems fully integrated with digital autopilot.

DIMENSIONS, EXTERNAL:

Wing span	7.16 m (23 ft 6 in)
Wing chord: at root	1.14 m (3 ft 9 in)
at tip	0.36 m (1 ft 2 in)
Wing aspect ratio	8.78
Length overall	7.52 m (24 ft 8 in)
Height overall	2.06 m (6 ft 9 in)
Height to canopy sill	0.76 m (2 ft 6 in)
Tailplane span	3.91 m (12 ft 10 in)
Wheel track	3.45 m (11 ft 4 in)
Wheelbase	3.20 m (10 ft 6 in)

DIMENSIONS, INTERNAL:

Cabin: Length	2.74 m (9 ft 0 in)
Max width	1.14 m (3 ft 9 in)
Max height	0.94 m (3 ft 1 in)
Baggage bay volume	0.40 m³ (14 cu ft)

AREAS:

Wings, gross	5.85 m² (62.9 sq ft)
Trailing-edge flaps	1.24 m² (13.3 sq ft)
Fin	0.86 m² (9.3 sq ft)
Tailplane (incl tabs)	2.14 m² (23.0 sq ft)

Prototype of CMC Leopard business jet *(Brian M. Service)*

WEIGHTS AND LOADINGS (A: prototype, B: production aircraft, estimated):

Weight empty, equipped: B	862 kg (1,900 lb)
Max fuel weight: A	367 kg (810 lb)
B	476 kg (1,050 lb)
Max T-O weight: A	1,156 kg (2,550 lb)
B	1,701 kg (3,750 lb)
Max zero-fuel weight: A	1,043 kg (2,300 lb)
B	1,224 kg (2,700 lb)
Max landing weight: A	1,156 kg (2,880 lb)
B	1,497 kg (3,300 lb)
Max wing loading: A	197.7 kg/m² (40.5 lb/sq ft)
B	291.0 kg/m² (59.6 lb/sq ft)

PERFORMANCE (production aircraft, estimated, ISA):

Never-exceed speed	Mach 0.81
	(300 knots; 556 km/h; 345 mph) EAS
Max level speed at 9,450 m (31,000 ft)	
	469 knots (869 km/h; 540 mph)
Max and econ cruising speed at 13,100 m (43,000 ft)	
	434 knots (804 km/h; 500 mph)
Stalling speed, full flap, at AUW of 1,406 kg (3,100 lb)	
	82 knots (152 km/h; 95 mph)
Max rate of climb at S/L	1,370 m (4,500 ft)/min
Rate of climb at S/L, one engine out	
	365 m (1,200 ft)/min
Service ceiling	12,955 m (42,500 ft)
Service ceiling, one engine out	6,400 m (21,000 ft)
T-O to 15 m (50 ft)	727 m (2,385 ft)
T-O balanced field length	838 m (2,750 ft)
Landing from 15 m (50 ft) at AUW of 1,406 kg (3,100 lb)	
	747 m (2,450 ft)
Landing factored field length	823 m (2,700 ft)
Range with max fuel and max payload, with reserves	
	1,500 nm (2,775 km; 1,725 miles)

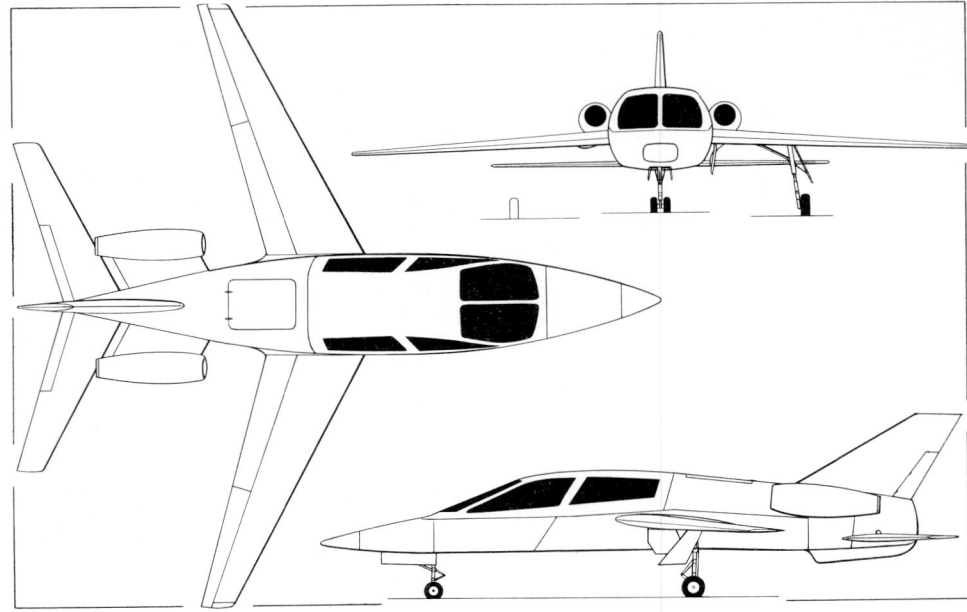

CMC Leopard (two Noel Penny Turbines NPT 301-3 turbojets) (*Pilot Press*)

CRANFIELD
CRANFIELD INSTITUTE OF TECHNOLOGY, COLLEGE OF AERONAUTICS

Cranfield, Bedfordshire MK43 0AL
Telephone: 0234 750111
Telex: 825072
Fax: 0234 751181
ACTING HEAD OF COLLEGE AND PROFESSOR OF AIRCRAFT DESIGN, DIRECTOR OF PROJECTS: Prof D. Howe
CHIEF DESIGNER: J. H. Webb
HEAD OF FLIGHT SYSTEMS AND MEASUREMENT LABORATORIES: D. A. Williams

The College of Aeronautics is a fully CAA and MoD(PE) approved design and manufacturing organisation based on the Cranfield Institute of Technology airfield. It undertakes major conversions and installations for MoD(PE) and commercial organisations. These have included various special flight control, avionics and FLIR installations in Comets, Varsities, Canberras, Hunters and BAC One-Elevens. Recent work has involved the design, manufacture and installation of modifications to an RAE Buccaneer, including the installation of pitch and roll controls in the rear cockpit, plus installation of major avionics in the bomb bay, in addition to the VAAC Harrier and ASTRA Hawk, last described fully in the 1987-88 *Jane's*. It designed and manufactured the Cranfield A1 aerobatic aircraft and A2 Machan RPV, also described in earlier editions of *Jane's*.

ASTRA HAWK

The BAe Hawk T. Mk 1 (XX341) conversion, known as the ASTRA (Advanced System Training Aircraft), provides the Empire Test Pilots School (ETPS) with an advanced variable stability aircraft to replace an earlier Cranfield-modified Beagle Basset. The aircraft's first flight after modification, but using only the normal control system, was made on 21 August 1986. Trials in full ASTRA configuration, with the variable stability system operational, began on 29 September 1987. After initial delivery to the A&AEE at Boscombe Down in May 1988, XX341 was due to be handed back to the ETPS in the last quarter of 1988.

CRANFIELD/OPERATION ABILITY MODIFIED ORION

Mr Philip Scott, who is 85% paralysed, has formed a company known as Operation Ability Ltd (The Meadows,

Mr Philip Scott with partially complete G-802 Orion modified for flight by an 85% disabled pilot

Firgrove Road, Whitehill, Bordon, Hampshire GU35 9DY, *telephone* 04203 5062). Its first objective is a programme to enable Mr Scott, who has lost the use of his legs, body, hands and much of his arms, to gain a Private Pilot's Licence, and Mr Scott is the first tetraplegic to have passed a CAA medical examination accepting him as 'fit to learn'.

A special design, the Cranfield A3, was prepared to meet the requirement, but the high cost has led to an alternative approach which involves changes to the fuselage of a G-802

Orion powered by a Turbomeca Marboré turbojet. By May 1988, the aircraft was substantially complete at Cranfield and design was under way of modifications to permit entry and exit by a disabled person, and operation of the controls. Sponsors include Racal Avionics, which has provided on long-term loan a fully automatic navigation system with moving map display. A description of the standard Orion can be found under the Aérodis heading in the French part of the Sport Aircraft section.

CRANFIELD AERONAUTICAL SERVICES LIMITED

No. 2 Hangar, Cranfield Airfield, Wharley End, Cranfield, Bedfordshire MK43 0AL
Telephone: 0234 752746
Fax: 0234 751181
DIRECTORS:
Prof D. Howe
M. J. R. Sheehan
Prof J. L. Stollery
SECRETARY: B. Benson

Cranfield Aeronautical Services is fully CAA and MoD(PE) approved for the design and manufacture of aircraft and major modifications. Recent projects include the water bomber conversion of a BAe 748 turboprop airliner (see 1987-88 *Jane's*) and range-extension modifications for the BAC One-Eleven.

BAC ONE-ELEVEN AUXILIARY FUEL SYSTEM

Cranfield Aeronautical Services has designed, and is manufacturing and marketing, an auxiliary fuel system for

BAC One-Eleven transports. The first two installations, in Series 475 aircraft, each provide an additional 6,814 litres (1,800 US gallons; 1,498 Imp gallons) of fuel in nine cells. However, the modular design of the system allows the tankage to be increased or decreased to meet specific range/weight/volumetric constraints and requirements for particular executive, corporate and paramilitary customers up to a maximum of 9,615 litres (2,540 US gallons; 2,115 Imp gallons) for a 13-cell installation in a One-Eleven 500.

The first modified aircraft was returned to its operator (McAlpine Aviation) on 15 March 1988, following CAA certification.

EVERETT

R. J. EVERETT ENGINEERING LTD

Abbey Oaks, Sproughton, Nr Ipswich, Suffolk
Telephone: 0473 47685

EVERETT AUTOGYRO

The Everett autogyro was designed with knowledge gained from the Bensen and Campbell Cricket single-seat light autogyros (see 1975-76 *Jane's*). Detail design was by R. J. Everett Engineering Ltd, which was granted CAA Manufacturers Approval on 8 May 1985. The autogyro is marketed in ready for flight form, with alternative 1,600 cc or 1,830 cc converted Volkswagen motorcar engines. First flight of an Everett autogyro was made on 15 February 1984. An initial batch of 25 is under construction, 16 of which had been sold by the Spring of 1987.

DIMENSIONS, EXTERNAL:

Rotor diameter	6.63 m (21 ft 9 in)
Length overall	3.43 m (11 ft 3 in)
Height overall	2.08 m (6 ft 10 in)
Wheel track	1.59 m (5 ft 2½ in)

WEIGHTS:

Weight empty	139 kg (307 lb)
Max T-O weight	272 kg (600 lb)

PERFORMANCE:

Never-exceed speed	69 knots (129 km/h; 80 mph)
Max cruising speed	65 knots (120 km/h; 75 mph)
Normal cruising speed	56 knots (104 km/h; 65 mph)
Max rate of climb at S/L	182 m (600 ft)/min
T-O run: with spin-up	164 m (538 ft)
without spin-up	256 m (840 ft)
Landing run	2.5 m (8 ft)
Range with max fuel	130 nm (240 km; 150 miles)
Endurance with max fuel	approx 2 h 30 min

Everett single-seat light autogyro (*Brian M. Service*)

ISLAND AIRCRAFT — *see ARV*

MARSHALL

MARSHALL OF CAMBRIDGE (ENGINEERING) LTD (Aircraft Division)

Airport Works, Cambridge CB5 8RX
Telephone: 0223 61133
Telex: 81208
Fax: 0223 321032
CHAIRMAN: Sir Arthur Marshall, OBE
ENGINEERING DIRECTOR/CHIEF DESIGNER:
R. E. Ward
SALES MANAGER: G. McA. Bacon
PUBLIC RELATIONS MANAGER: C. Buisseret

The Aircraft Division of this company (known as Marshalls Flying School Ltd until 1962) has specialised for many years in the modification, overhaul and repair of aircraft, including the design and installation of interior furnishing for executive transports and of avionics fits up to and including the complete outfitting of aircraft for calibration and electronic countermeasures roles.

In 1966, Marshall was appointed the designated centre for Royal Air Force Hercules transport aircraft, and in 1973 the company completed the conversion of an RAF Hercules C. Mk 1 to W. Mk 2 configuration, as detailed in the 1979-80 and earlier editions of *Jane's*. It has since undertaken the conversion of Hercules into flight refuelling tanker/receivers, and the lengthening of RAF Hercules C. Mk 1 transports to C. Mk 3 standard. The last of 29 C. Mk 3 conversions undertaken by Marshall was completed on 25 November 1985, as described in the 1987-88 and earlier editions of *Jane's*. Marshall now has a major contract to convert ex-airline TriStars into flight refuelling tankers and freighters for the RAF.

First Lockheed Hercules C. Mk 3P with probe for in-flight refuelling

Lockheed TriStar K. Mk 1, equipped by Marshall as a flight refuelling tanker (*S. G. Richards*)

HERCULES C. Mk 1K TANKER and HERCULES C. Mk 1P/3P RECEIVER AIRCRAFT

Six Royal Air Force Lockheed Hercules C. Mk 1 aircraft have been converted by Marshall into flight refuelling tanker/receivers by fitting a Mk 17 hose drum unit (HDU) on the cargo compartment ramp, a drogue deployment box on the outside of the cargo bay door, four long-range fuel tanks in the cabin, and an in-flight refuelling probe over the flight deck. Modified in this way, each aircraft retains the availability of a pressurised cargo compartment for normal flight, but depressurises when operating with the drogue deployed. The first converted aircraft, designated Hercules **C. Mk 1K**, first flew on 8 June 1982 and became operational with No. 1312 Flight from Ascension Island in early August 1982. At least three further Mk 1/1Ks have been further modified by Marshall with a pod under each wingtip, presumably for elint/sigint duties.

Sixteen RAF Hercules C. Mk 1 aircraft have each been fitted with a probe to provide an in-flight refuelling capability, and are now designated **C. Mk 1P**. During the 1982 Falklands campaign, one of them remained in the air for 28 h on an operational mission, creating a record for duration of flight in a Hercules. It is intended that all C. Mk 1 and C. Mk 3 Hercules will be equipped with probes, and the first **C. Mk 3P** (XV214) was returned to RAF Lyneham in February 1986, after conversion.

In 1987, RAF Hercules began receiving IR jamming equipment and chaff/flare dispensers on each side of the rear fuselage, and a contract was placed with General Instrument for AN/ALR-66 radar warning receivers.

MARSHALL (LOCKHEED) TRISTAR TANKER CONVERSION

To meet a growing Royal Air Force requirement for flight refuelling tanker support, Marshall of Cambridge is converting to this role six Lockheed L-1011-500 TriStar transport aircraft purchased from British Airways in 1982 and three more purchased from Pan Am in 1984. Work started in 1983 and the converted aircraft have been given the following RAF designations:

TriStar K. Mk 1. Two interim (ZD950 and 953) and two full (ZD951 and 949) conversions to tanker/passenger standard, each with twin Flight Refuelling Mk 17T in-flight refuelling hose drum units and a total of seven fuel tanks in the fore and aft baggage compartments, to provide an additional 45,360 kg (100,000 lb) of fuel, giving a total aircraft fuel capacity of 136,080 kg (300,000 lb). The hose

drum units deliver this fuel at a rate of 1,814 kg (4,000 lb)/min at 3.45 bars (50 lb/sq in). A flight refuelling probe is installed above the forward fuselage to provide a receiver capability. There is also a crew rest area for use by the non-operating crew on long sorties. Total fuel management during refuelling and defuelling is controlled from a panel at the engineer's station. Closed circuit TV enables the crew to monitor all in-flight refuelling operations. The first K. Mk 1 (ZD950) flew for the first time on 9 July 1985. Its max T-O weight is increased to 244,940 kg (540,000 lb) and it was in process of gaining CA Release to Service early in 1988. ZD953 was the first to re-join the RAF after conversion, on 24 March 1986, followed by ZD951 and 949 later the same year.

TriStar KC. Mk 1. Two aircraft (ZD948 and 952) being converted to tanker/freighter role beginning in 1985. In addition to embodiment of the fuel system modifications, this requires the installation of a 2.64 m × 3.56 m (104 in × 140 in) cargo door on the port side, forward of the wing leading-edge, together with a cargo handling system. The passenger floor is strengthened to provide for high density loadings. In these aircraft all items carried on the cabin floor will be mounted on pallets. Thus, passengers can be carried when seat equipped pallets are fitted. Following re-delivery of the initial two aircraft, interim K. Mk 1s ZD950 and 953 will be converted with freight doors to this standard.

TriStar K. Mk 2. Three ex-Pan Am aircraft (ZE704-706), for planned conversion to the tanker/passenger role by the early 1990s. Fuel capacity 4,535 kg (10,000 lb) less than that of K. Mk 1. Two (ZE704 and 705) operated initially for trooping flights in airline standard accommodation.

All nine RAF TriStars are assigned to No. 216 Squadron, at RAF Brize Norton. In addition to the current internal hose drum units in the tankers, a Flight Refuelling Mk 32 refuelling pod will be fitted later under each wing; these will be capable of delivering fuel at a rate of 1,134 kg (2,500 lb)/min at 3.45 bars (50 lb/sq in) simultaneously from each pod. General Instrument AN/ALR-66 radar warning receivers will be fitted to RAF TriStars.

MARSHALL (LOCKHEED) TRISTAR MODIFICATION

Marshall is undertaking a variety of modification packages for several TriStar operators, including the Sunset III work for British Airways, which involves internal re-design.

NAC
THE NORMAN AEROPLANE COMPANY LTD

Cardiff (Wales) Airport, Barry, South Glamorgan CF6 9AY, Wales
Telephone: 0446 711884
Telex: 497245 NORAC G; 497504 NORAC G
Fax: 0446 711490
MANAGING DIRECTOR: N. D. Norman, CBE, CEng, FRAeS
COMMERCIAL DIRECTOR: Mrs B. E. Norman
CHIEF ENGINEER: W. J. Morris
REGIONAL SALES MANAGER: N. Tyler

Mr N. D. Norman founded this company, as NDN Aircraft Ltd, in 1976. The company name was changed to The Norman Aeroplane Company with effect from 22 July 1985, simultaneously with a transfer of its manufacturing centre to Wales.

Aircraft for which The Norman Aeroplane Company is responsible are described in this entry. Production is taking place in a purpose-built factory at Cardiff (Wales) International Airport.

NAC FIRECRACKER

The development history of the Firecracker was last described under the Hunting Firecracker entry in the 1984-85 *Jane's*. Responsibility for the aircraft has reverted to The Norman Aeroplane Company, which will build Firecrackers to order.

The prototype of the turbine-engined Firecracker (G-SFTR) flew for the first time on 1 September 1983 and was certificated on 23 March 1984. It is one of two aircraft of this type which were acquired subsequently by Specialist Flying Training Ltd for use in its training operations; the other is G-SFTS. In 1988, NAC was discussing a number of potential orders with representatives of undisclosed countries.

The following details apply to the aircraft in its certificated civil form, except where indicated. Military Firecrackers can be offered with a PT6A-25D engine, rated at 559 kW (750 shp), Stencel Ranger zero/zero rocket escape system, extra fuel (435 kg; 960 lb max) and air-conditioning. The fully certificated piston engined version (described in 1983-84 *Jane's*) is also available.

TYPE: Two-seat turboprop powered training aircraft.
WINGS: Cantilever low-wing monoplane. Wing section NACA 23012, modified on centre-section, where forward extension of leading-edge reduces thickness/chord ratio at wingroot. Extended chord (dog-tooth) on leading-edge of outer wing panels of civil registered aircraft. Dihedral 5° on outer wing panels only. Incidence 3°. Leading-edge of inner wing panels swept back approximately 20°. Light alloy three-spar structure, with Frise ailerons and electrically operated single-slotted trailing-edge flaps. Trim tab in starboard aileron; balance tab in port aileron. All controls manually operated. No de-icing system.
FUSELAGE: Semi-monocoque stressed skin structure of light alloy. Hydraulically operated light alloy door type airbrake in fuselage undersurface, at wing trailing-edge.
TAIL UNIT: Cantilever stressed skin structure of light alloy. Fixed incidence tailplane. Trim tab in starboard half of elevator and in rudder. No de-icing system.
LANDING GEAR: Hydraulically retractable tricycle type with single wheel on each unit. Steerable nosewheel retracts rearward, main units inward. Tyres remain partially exposed when retracted, to reduce damage in wheels-up landing. Oleo-pneumatic shock absorber in each unit. Cleveland type 551-751 mainwheels with size 6.00-6 Goodyear tyres. Cleveland type 551-753 nosewheel, with size 5.00-5 Goodyear tyre. Cleveland Model 30-83A hydraulically operated disc brakes. Parking brake. Emergency extension of main units by free fall; nose unit is extended by CO_2 pressure from an emergency bottle.
POWER PLANT: One 533 kW (715 ehp) Pratt & Whitney Canada PT6A-25A turboprop, flat rated at 410 kW (550 shp) at S/L, and driving a Hartzell type HC-B3TN-3/T10173-17 three-blade constant-speed fully-feathering and reversible-pitch metal propeller with spinner. Goodrich electric propeller de-icing optional. Two integral fuel tanks in each wing and a fuselage collector tank, with a combined capacity of 405 litres (107 US gallons; 89 Imp gallons). Two non-jettisonable auxiliary fuel tanks, each of 145 litres (38.4 US gallons; 32 Imp gallons), can be carried on underwing hardpoints. Overwing refuelling points for main fuel system. Oil capacity 13 litres (3.5 US gallons; 2.9 Imp gallons). Engine air intakes have a Centrisep particle separator for air cleaning/ice protection.
ACCOMMODATION: Two seats in tandem beneath sideways opening (to starboard) transparent canopy. Stencel crew

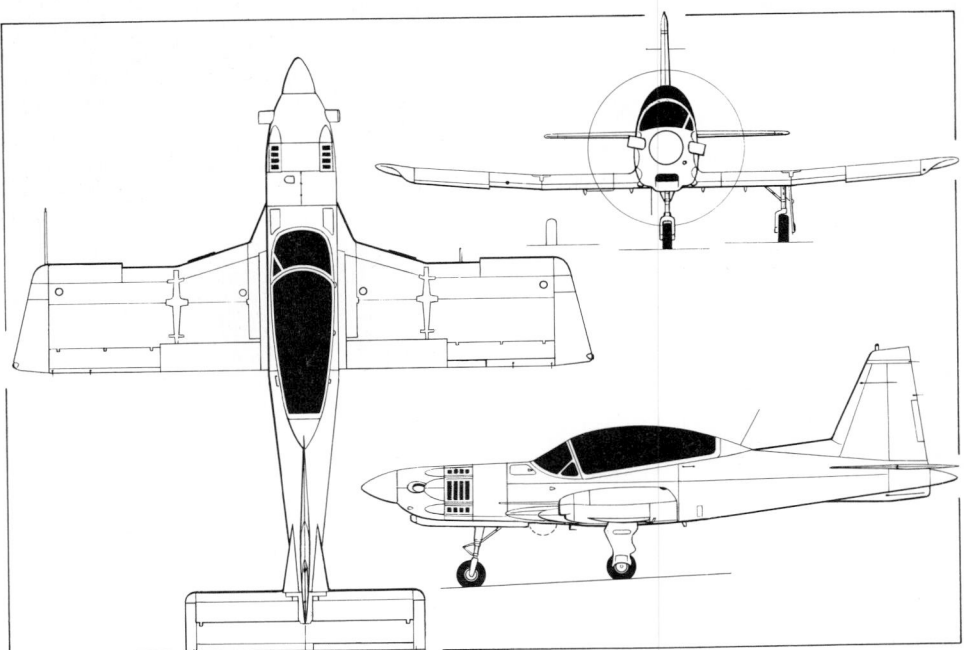

Three-view drawing *(Pilot Press)* **and photograph of the NAC Firecracker tandem-seat trainer**

ejection system available optionally. Canopy can be jettisoned in emergency. Rear seat is raised 10 cm (4 in) above level of forward seat for improved view. Baggage space (0.25 m³; 9 cu ft) aft of rear seat. Accommodation heated and ventilated.
SYSTEMS: Hydraulic system, pressure 103.5 bars (1,500 lb/sq in), supplied by electro-hydraulic pump with hand operated emergency pump. Gas bottle for emergency nosewheel extension. Electrical system powered by a Prestolite engine driven 28V 70A alternator. 12V 35Ah battery for aerobatics. Air-conditioning and oxygen systems optional.
AVIONICS: Options include dual VHF nav/com, DME and glideslope receivers, Becker ADF 2079 ADF, ATC 2000 transponder, AL3B audio control centre and intercom.
ARMAMENT: Four underwing hardpoints, each of 181 kg (400 lb) capacity, for the carriage of two auxiliary fuel tanks and/or Portsmouth Aviation FN 7.62 mm or FFV Unipod 0.50 in gun pods; rocket launchers including Aerea AL 18-50, AL 8-70 and AL 6-80, Brandt, LAU 32, Matra F2, SNIA and SURA-D; SAMP EU 70 and EU 32 GP bombs, SAMP EU 13 fragmentation bombs; photo reconnaissance pods; and SAMAR, SATER and EMER. PACK survival kits. An SP.800 HUD can be installed in the cockpit to provide the pupil pilot with information relating to weapons aiming and vital aircraft systems failure warnings.

DIMENSIONS, EXTERNAL:
Wing span	7.92 m (26 ft 0 in)
Wing chord: at root	1.83 m (6 ft 0 in)
at tip	1.45 m (4 ft 9 in)
Wing aspect ratio	5.28
Length overall	8.33 m (27 ft 4 in)
Height overall	3.25 m (10 ft 8 in)
Tailplane span	3.35 m (11 ft 0 in)
Wheel track	3.05 m (10 ft 0 in)
Wheelbase	2.10 m (6 ft 10½ in)
Propeller diameter	2.13 m (7 ft 0 in)

AREAS:
Wings, gross	11.89 m² (128.0 sq ft)
Ailerons (total, incl tabs)	1.20 m² (12.89 sq ft)
Trailing-edge flaps (total)	1.23 m² (13.20 sq ft)
Fin	0.48 m² (5.13 sq ft)
Rudder, incl tab	0.66 m² (7.14 sq ft)
Tailplane	1.56 m² (16.77 sq ft)
Elevator, incl tab	1.27 m² (13.66 sq ft)
Dive brake	0.26 m² (2.75 sq ft)

WEIGHTS (A: civil version, B: military version):
Basic weight empty, equipped:	A	1,117 kg (2,462 lb)
	B	1,210 kg (2,667 lb)
Typical customer options:	A	41 kg (90 lb)
Max T-O and landing weight:	A	1,633 kg (3,600 lb)
	B	1,832 kg (4,040 lb)
* Military overload T-O weight		1,927 kg (4,250 lb)

* *from smooth hard surface*

PERFORMANCE (civil version at max T-O weight, except where indicated):
Never-exceed speed	288 knots (533 km/h; 331 mph) EAS
Max level speed at 4,575 m (15,000 ft)	198 knots (367 km/h; 228 mph)
Econ cruising speed at 6,100 m (20,000 ft)	180 knots (333 km/h; 207 mph)
Stalling speed, flaps down and engine idling	60 knots (111 km/h; 69 mph) EAS
Max rate of climb at S/L	628 m (2,060 ft)/min
Service ceiling	8,260 m (27,100 ft)
T-O run	347 m (1,140 ft)
T-O to 15 m (50 ft)	500 m (1,640 ft)

Landing from 15 m (50 ft) at AUW of 1,451 kg (3,200 lb)
   with reverse thrust   677 m (2,220 ft)
Range with max fuel, incl external auxiliary tanks, no
   reserves   1,100 nm (2,038 km; 1,266 miles)
Range with max standard fuel, no reserves
                625 nm (1,158 km; 720 miles)
g limits at normal max T-O weight   +6/−3
PERFORMANCE (military version, estimated at max T-O
   weight, ISA):
   Max level speed at S/L
              223 knots (413 km/h; 257 mph)
   Time to 4,575 m (15,000 ft)   6 min 15 s
   T-O to 15 m (50 ft)   457 m (1,500 ft)
   g limits   +6.7/−3.5

NAC 6 FIELDMASTER

The NAC 6 Fieldmaster was designed by Mr Desmond Norman, with financial support from the UK National Research Development Corporation, specifically for agricultural, firefighting and oil pollution control work. Representing an entirely new approach to the design of agricultural aircraft, it has a titanium chemical hopper which is an integral part of the fuselage structure, its outer surface being contoured to serve as the skin of that fuselage section. The power plant is mounted on the front of this hopper, the aft fuselage to its rear, and the wings are attached directly to each side of the hopper's base. The cockpit, in the rear fuselage, is protected by a strong rollover structure, and is large enough to accommodate a second seat in tandem. Removable dual controls are available, to simplify flight training and checkout procedures. The wing is fitted with wide span auxiliary aerofoil trailing-edge flaps, embodying a liquid spray dispersal system that discharges directly into the downwash of the flaps, and so ensures that the spray droplets achieve the best possible crop penetration.

For the firefighting role the Fieldmaster can be fitted with a scoop gear enabling it to refill its water tank in flight. A retractable boom, extending rearward along the underside of the fuselage, can be lowered in flight to an angle of about 45°. A scoop at the rear end of the boom penetrates the surface when the aircraft's wheels are about 3 m (10 ft) above the water, and the dynamic pressure generated by the scoop's passage through the water refills the tank in less than one minute. Operation of a dump lever unlatches a 101.5 × 48.25 cm (40 × 19 in) door in the bottom of the tank to release the water load on to a fire zone, the door being closed electro-hydraulically after dumping.

The prototype Fieldmaster (G-NRDC) made its first flight at Sandown, Isle of Wight, on 17 December 1981, and by March 1986 had flown 300 hours during flight testing, demonstrations and in-service spraying trials by an agricultural operator. The first production Fieldmaster (G-NACL) flew on 29 March 1987, and certification was received on 27 April.

In July 1987, the first two production Fieldmasters began a season of fire patrol flights and water bombing sorties in the Maritime Alps under contract to France Aviation. Turn-round time between firefighting sorties averaged 3 min. These two aircraft are included in five purchased by Croplease Ltd of Shannon, Ireland.

Under a contract signed in December 1987, NAC accepted the first three of an initial 200 sets of main airframe parts for the Fieldmaster produced by the Yugoslav aircraft manufacturer UTVA in May 1988. Assisted by Prva Petoletka-Trstenik (landing gear) and Soko (machined airframe parts), UTVA will supply all components except the hopper and engine frame, up to a maximum of 500 units

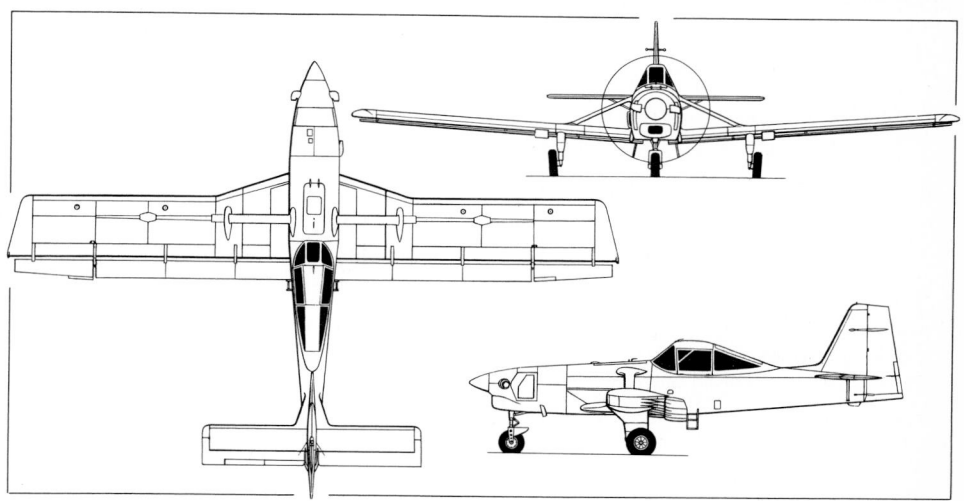

Photograph and three-view drawing *(Pilot Press)* **of NAC 6 Fieldmaster agricultural aircraft prototype (Pratt & Whitney Canada PT6A-34AG turboprop)**

over ten years. Planned output by NAC is three aircraft in 1988 and 12 in 1989.

Prospects of up to 100 sales in Yugoslavia have prompted consideration of an alternative power plant, in the form of a Walter turboprop manufactured in Czechoslovakia.

TYPE: Two-seat large capacity agricultural aircraft.

WINGS: Low-wing monoplane, with an overwing streamline section bracing strut each side. Wing section NACA 23012, modified on inner panels, where forward extension of leading-edge reduces thickness/chord ratio to 8.6% at wingroot. Dihedral 4° 15′. Incidence 4° 30′. Conventional all-metal structure with full corrosion proofing. Electrically actuated wide span auxiliary aerofoil trailing-edge flaps, which incorporate plumbing for 24 standard spray nozzles on each wing. Micronair spray system (total 12 nozzles) optional. The ailerons are also of auxiliary aerofoil type. Servo tab on starboard aileron, linked mechanically to rudder pedals, ensuring some bank with rudder movement.

FUSELAGE: Forward fuselage comprises structural titanium hopper with capacity of 2,032 kg (4,480 lb) dry, or 2,366 litres (625 US gallons; 520 Imp gallons) of liquid chemicals, and incorporating large access door, vent system, inspection windows, and light. Firefighting modifications include additional 53 litre (14 US gallon; 11.6 Imp gallon) tank for Moussant fire-retardant, which is mixed with water before release. Rear fuselage, attached to the rear of this hopper, is of semi-monocoque light alloy construction, fully corrosion proofed, and with easy access for cleaning and maintenance.

TAIL UNIT: Braced conventional structure of light alloy. Fixed incidence tailplane. Trim tab in port elevator. Servo tab on rudder controlled by stick movement, so that tab is moved automatically with bank.

LANDING GEAR: Non-retractable tricycle type, with single wheel on each unit. Nosewheel has alternative steerable or castoring facility. Main units of levered suspension type. Nosewheel tyre size 7.00-8, pressure 3.45 bars (50 lb/sq in); mainwheels have tubed tyres, diameter 736 mm (29 in), pressure 3.79 bars (55 lb/sq in). Cleveland hydraulic disc brakes. Landing gear incorporates wire cutters.

POWER PLANT: One 559 kW (750 shp) Pratt & Whitney Canada PT6A-34AG turboprop, driving a Hartzell type HC-B3TN-3/T10282+4 three-blade fully-feathering reversible-pitch metal propeller with spinner. Four integral fuel tanks, two per wing. Main tanks, each of 757 litres (200 US gallons; 166.5 Imp gallons), inboard; ferry tanks, each of 734 litres (194 US gallons; 161.5 Imp gallons), outboard. Total fuel capacity 1,490 litres (394 US gallons; 328 Imp gallons). Oil capacity 13 litres (3.5 US gallons; 2.9 Imp gallons). Engine air intake has a Centrisep filtration system.

ACCOMMODATION: Standard accommodation for pilot only, on fully adjustable seat in an enclosed cockpit, with rollover protective structure. Rear trainee/passenger seat optional. Dual controls optional, those for pupil easily removable. Crew safety helmets with headsets optional. Baggage space in fuselage. Sideways hinged door on each side. Birdproof armoured glass windscreen, two-speed windscreen wiper and windscreen wash system optional. Accommodation ventilated; air-conditioning and heating system optional. Wirecutters forward of windscreen, and cable deflecting wire from top of windscreen to tip of fin.

SYSTEMS: Electrical system includes 24V 200A starter/generator. Hydraulic system for brakes only. Central warning system standard.

AVIONICS AND EQUIPMENT: Intercom standard. Avionics, and IFR instrument package, to customer requirements. Standard equipment includes an external power socket.

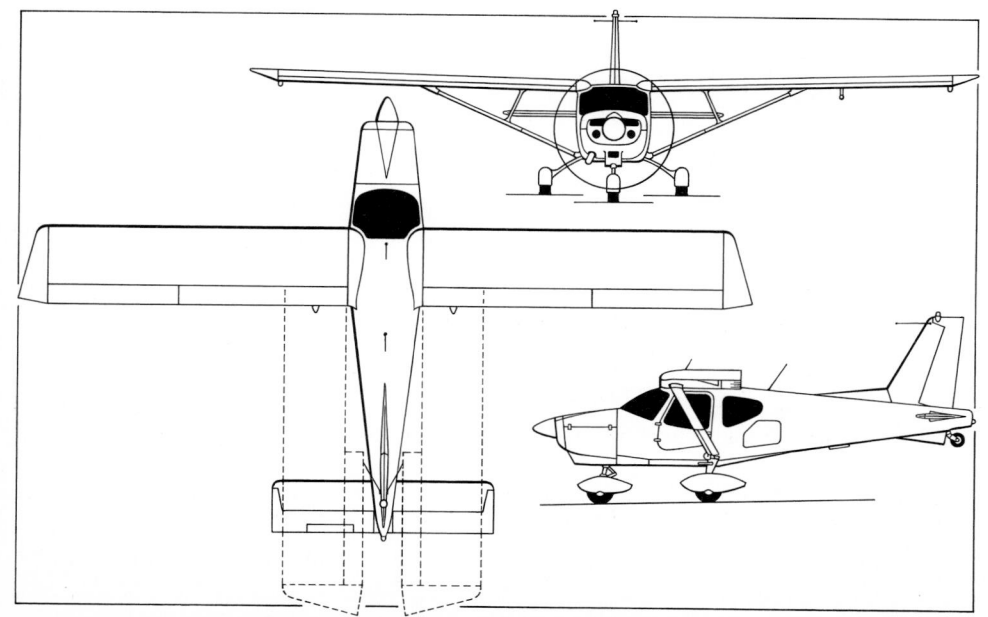

NAC1 Freelance four-seat utility aircraft *(Jane's/Mike Keep)*

Optional equipment includes airframe and engine hour meter; instrument lighting, navigation lights, fin and wingtip strobe lights; two forward looking retractable work lights, each 765,000 candlepower; automatic flagman installation; firefighting dump door and water scoop (see introductory copy); Transland gatebox, high volume spreader, quick disconnect flange kit, and side loading system; and Micronair installation, with flowmeter and rpm indicator.

DIMENSIONS, EXTERNAL:

Wing span	16.23 m (53 ft 3 in)
Wing chord (excl flaps): at root	2.01 m (6 ft 7¼ in)
at tip	1.45 m (4 ft 9 in)
Wing aspect ratio	7.96
Length overall	11.02 m (36 ft 2 in)
Height overall	4.12 m (13 ft 6 in)
Wheel track	5.28 m (17 ft 4 in)
Wheelbase	3.35 m (11 ft 0 in)
Propeller diameter	2.69 m (8 ft 10 in)

DIMENSION, INTERNAL:

Hopper volume	2.36 m³ (83 cu ft)

AREA:

Wings, gross	33.25 m² (358.0 sq ft)

WEIGHTS AND LOADINGS:

Standard empty weight:	2,266 kg (4,995 lb)
Max T-O and landing weight:	
BCAR Public Transport Category	3,855 kg (8,500 lb)
UK CAA AN 90	4,535 kg (10,000 lb)
Max zero-fuel weight	3,855 kg (8,500 lb)
Max wing loading (AN 90)	136.37 kg/m² (27.93 lb/sq ft)
Max power loading (AN 90)	8.11 kg/kW (13.33 lb/shp)

PERFORMANCE ('clean', with main landing gear fairings installed, at max Public Transport Category T-O weight, S/L, ISA, except where indicated):

Never-exceed speed	172 knots (318 km/h; 198 mph)
Max level speed, clean:	
at S/L	143 knots (265 km/h; 165 mph)
at 1,830 m (6,000 ft)	147 knots (272 km/h; 169 mph)
Design manoeuvring speed	
	126 knots (233 km/h; 145 mph)
Stalling speed: flaps up	70 knots (129 km/h; 81 mph)
flaps down (30°)	60 knots (111 km/h; 69 mph)
Max rate of climb at S/L	293 m (960 ft)/min
Service ceiling	5,547 m (18,200 ft)
T-O run	419 m (1,375 ft)
T-O to 15 m (50 ft)	625 m (2,050 ft)
Landing from 15 m (50 ft)	472 m (1,550 ft)

Landing run at typical landing weight of 2,720 kg (6,000 lb), with propeller reversal 152 m (500 ft)
Range at 3,050 m (10,000 ft) with two crew, 454 kg (1,000 lb) of equipment and max fuel, no reserves:
1,000 nm (1,853 km; 1,150 miles)

g limits	+3.4/−1.7

NAC1 FREELANCE

The prototype Freelance (G-NACI) made its first flight on 29 September 1984. Production aircraft will have a wider fuselage, a larger glazed area and certain other features to maximise passenger comfort. The initial production aircraft (G-NACA) flew early in 1988, and NAC anticipates appointing a subcontractor to provide most components for the Cardiff assembly line from 1989 onwards. It was planned to produce about eight Freelances in 1988.

The Freelance is intended to be suitable for a wide range of specialist tasks, including air ambulance, glider and banner towing, agricultural spraying, photography and parachutist duties, with interchangeable wheel, ski and float landing gear.

Fitment is under consideration of a 175 kW (235 hp) engine to satisfy the requirements of a potential military customer in the Far East.

TYPE: Four-seat multi-purpose utility aircraft.

Prototype NAC1 Freelance multi-purpose utility aircraft with wings folded *(Brian M. Service)*

WINGS: Strut braced high-wing monoplane. Wing section NACA 23012 (modified). Dihedral 30′ from roots. Incidence 3°. No sweepback. Constant chord conventional two-spar all-metal structure of Alclad light alloy, including trailing-edge flaps and ailerons, braced on each side by single strut from fuselage floor line. No tabs. Wing folding system enables wings to be swung back, permitting aircraft to be stored within a 4 × 9 m (13 ft 1 in × 29 ft 6 in) space.

FUSELAGE: Conventional semi-monocoque structure of basically rectangular section, with frames, stringers and Alclad light alloy sheet covering. Composites engine cowling.

TAIL UNIT: Cantilever all-metal structure, with sweptback vertical surfaces and non-swept rectangular horizontal surfaces. Small dorsal fin. Trim tab in port elevator.

LANDING GEAR: Non-retractable tricycle gear standard. All three wheels same size; tyre size 600 × 6, pressure 2.07 bars (30 lb/sq in). Wheel/ski and float gear, and balloon tyres, available optionally.

POWER PLANT: One 134 kW (180 hp) Textron Lycoming O-360-A4M flat-four engine, driving a Sensenich two-blade fixed-pitch (optionally constant-speed) metal propeller with spinner. Textron Lycoming engines of 157 kW (210 hp) (turbocharged) and 175 kW (235 hp) to be available optionally. Fuel tank in each wing, combined capacity 280 litres (74.5 US gallons; 62 Imp gallons) usable. Refuelling point above each wing.

ACCOMMODATION: Individual seats for pilot and three passengers in fully enclosed cabin. Forward opening door on each side. Baggage space behind rear seats, with loading door on port side of fuselage. Rear (sliding) door optional, for paradropping. Cabin can be configured for one specially designed full-length stretcher, plus medical attendant, in addition to pilot.

SYSTEMS: Hydraulic system, pressure 34.5 bars (500 lb/sq in), for mainwheel brakes. DC electrical system includes 28V 60A alternator and 25Ah battery. Exhaust muff heater with punka louvres for cabin ventilation.

AVIONICS: Normal instrumentation for VFR and IFR flying. General Aviation Class 1 radio equipment optional.

EQUIPMENT: Wide variety of equipment options, according to role. These can include towing gear for sailplane (up to 907 kg; 2,000 lb AUW) or banners; passengers' ski carrying bin in rear fuselage; a 378.5 litre (100 US gallon; 83.3 Imp gallon) detachable belly spraytank, plus boom and nozzles or Micronair atomisers; outward opening cabin windows for aerial photography; rear (sliding) door for paradropping; ambulance kit (see 'Accommodation' paragraph); and underwing hardpoints.

DIMENSIONS, EXTERNAL:

Wing span	12.25 m (40 ft 2½ in)
Wing chord, constant	1.32 m (4 ft 4 in)
Wing aspect ratio	9.51
Width, wings folded	3.66 m (12 ft 0 in)
Length overall	7.42 m (24 ft 4 in)
Height overall	3.00 m (9 ft 10 in)
Tailplane span	3.66 m (12 ft 0 in)
Wheel track	2.26 m (7 ft 5 in)
Wheelbase	1.75 m (5 ft 9 in)
Propeller diameter	1.93 m (6 ft 4 in)
Passenger door (port): Height	0.91 m (3 ft 0 in)
Width	0.86 m (2 ft 10 in)
Height to sill	0.76 m (2 ft 6 in)

DIMENSIONS, INTERNAL:

Cabin: Length	2.69 m (8 ft 10 in)
Max width	1.04 m (3 ft 5 in)
Max height	1.22 m (4 ft 0 in)

AREAS:

Wings, gross	15.79 m² (170.0 sq ft)
Ailerons (total)	1.38 m² (14.9 sq ft)
Trailing-edge flaps (total)	1.86 m² (20.0 sq ft)
Fin	0.72 m² (7.74 sq ft)
Rudder	0.62 m² (6.63 sq ft)
Tailplane	2.01 m² (21.6 sq ft)
Elevators (total)	1.24 m² (13.4 sq ft)

WEIGHTS AND LOADINGS:

Basic weight empty, equipped	709 kg (1,564 lb)
Max T-O and landing weight	1,247 kg (2,750 lb)
Max wing loading	78.97 kg/m² (16.18 lb/sq ft)
Max power loading	9.31 kg/kW (15.28 lb/hp)

PERFORMANCE (at max T-O weight):

Max level speed at S/L	
	124 knots (230 km/h; 143 mph)
Cruising speed at S/L (75% power)	
	119 knots (220 km/h; 137 mph)
Stalling speed, power off:	
flaps up	57 knots (105 km/h; 65 mph)
flaps down	52 knots (97 km/h; 60 mph)
Max rate of climb at S/L	186 m (611 ft)/min
Service ceiling	4,235 m (13,900 ft)
T-O run	298 m (976 ft)
T-O to 15 m (50 ft)	606 m (1,988 ft)
Landing from 15 m (50 ft)	431 m (1,415 ft)
Landing run	170 m (557 ft)

Max range at 75% power at 2,440 m (8,000 ft), with allowances for start, taxi, T-O, climb and 45 min reserves 808 nm (1,496 km; 930 miles)
Max range at 3,050 m (10,000 ft), allowances as above
1,056 nm (1,955 km; 1,215 miles)

NASH

NASH AIRCRAFT LTD (a subsidiary of Kinetrol Ltd)

Trading Estate, Farnham, Surrey GU9 9NU
Telephone: 0252 723688
Telex: 858567
DIRECTORS:
A. R. B. Nash (Managing)
Roy G. Procter
R. C. Nash

Mr Alan Nash acquired a controlling interest in Procter Aircraft Associates Ltd in early 1978, as a result of which the company was renamed Nash Aircraft Ltd in 1980. Its principal current activity is the development and manufacture of the Petrel two-seat light aircraft.

NASH PETREL

The company prototype of the Petrel (G-AXSF) made its first flight on 8 November 1980. In initial glider towing trials, it towed Vega, Mini-Nimbus and Nimbus sailplanes to a height of 610 m (2,000 ft) in under 4 min. During 1982 the original Textron Lycoming O-320-D2A engine was

replaced by a 134 kW (180 hp) Textron Lycoming O-360-A3A, to optimise aircraft performance in the glider towing and pilot training roles. During 1983 a new high tailplane was designed and fitted, to improve stability and spin recovery. In 1984 upswept tips were fitted to the wings to improve handling. Early in 1985 cuffs were fitted to the wing leading-edge, extending from 50 per cent span to the tips.

A pre-production batch of five Petrels is under construction. These will have either an O-320 or O-360 engine according to individual customer requirements.

TYPE: Two-seat light aircraft.

WINGS: Cantilever low-wing monoplane. Wing section NACA 3415. Dihedral 5° on outer panels. No sweepback or washout. All-metal constant chord structure, built in three sections: centre-section, integral with fuselage, to which outer panels are each attached with three bolts. Single main spar at 30 per cent chord and lightweight auxiliary spar at 66 per cent chord. Multiple ribs, with no spanwise stiffeners. All-metal NACA slotted flaps and Frise ailerons on outer panels. Flaps are operated manually by pushrod and torque tube; ailerons are operated by pushrods.

FUSELAGE: All-metal structure. Four longeron basic structure, with flat sides and bottom and single-curvature top decking. Integral wing centre-section forms seat and main landing gear attachment structure.

TAIL UNIT: Cantilever all-metal structure. Fixed incidence tailplane. Manually operated tab in starboard elevator. Tab on rudder. Control surfaces mass balanced. Rudder operated by cables; elevators by pushrods.

LANDING GEAR: Non-retractable tricycle type. Nose unit consists of a telescopic strut with elastomeric shock absorption, carrying a Goodyear 5.00-6 wheel, and is steerable from the rudder pedals. Main gear is of cantilever steel leaf spring type, with Goodyear 6.00-6 wheels and hydraulic disc brakes. Tyre pressure (all) 1.72 bars (25 lb/sq in).

POWER PLANT: One 134 kW (180 hp) Textron Lycoming O-360-A3A flat-four engine, driving a Sensenich two-blade fixed-pitch metal propeller with spinner. Provision for alternative engines of 88-134 kW (118-180 hp). Removable fuel tanks in wing centre-section leading-edges, capacity 104.5 litres (27.6 US gallons; 23 Imp gallons).

ACCOMMODATION: Two persons side by side, on seats with individually adjustable backs. One-piece rearward sliding bubble canopy. Dual controls standard. Baggage space aft of seats.

EQUIPMENT: Starter, generator and basic instrumentation. Radio, navigation and other equipment to customer's requirements.

DIMENSIONS, EXTERNAL:

Wing span	9.04 m (29 ft 8 in)
Wing chord, constant	1.37 m (4 ft 6 in)
Wing aspect ratio	6.3
Length overall	6.22 m (20 ft 5 in)
Height overall	2.23 m (7 ft 4 in)
Tailplane span	3.35 m (11 ft 0 in)
Wheel track	2.24 m (7 ft 4 in)
Wheelbase	1.52 m (5 ft 0 in)

AREA:

Wings, gross	13.00 m² (140.0 sq ft)

WEIGHTS:

Weight empty	544 kg (1,200 lb)
Max T-O weight	794 kg (1,750 lb)

PERFORMANCE (at max T-O weight):

Max level speed	115 knots (213 km/h; 132 mph)
Cruising speed	90 knots (167 km/h; 104 mph)
Stalling speed: flaps up	46 knots (86 km/h; 53 mph)
flaps down	40 knots (74 km/h; 46 mph)
Max rate of climb at S/L	350 m (1,150 ft)/min

Company owned prototype of the Nash Petrel two-seat light aircraft

---

OPTICA AVIATION — *see Brooklands Aircraft Co Ltd*

PILATUS BRITTEN-NORMAN
PILATUS BRITTEN-NORMAN LTD
(Subsidiary of Oerlikon-Bührle Holding Ltd)

The Airport, Bembridge, Isle of Wight PO35 5PR
Telephone: 0983 872511
Telex: 86277 PBNBEM G
MANAGING DIRECTOR: Dr E. Haefliger
TECHNICAL DIRECTOR: R. Wilson
PUBLIC RELATIONS: Mrs Alice Day

In 1979 Pilatus Aircraft Ltd of Switzerland acquired all assets of Britten-Norman (Bembridge) Ltd, including the facilities on the Isle of Wight and the former Fairey SA Islander/Trislander production hardware at Gosselies in Belgium.

The previous history of this company can be found in the 1978-79 and earlier editions of *Jane's*. It produces the Islander transport aircraft in a variety of forms; the Islander is manufactured in Romania by IAv Bucuresti (which see), and more than 400 had been delivered to Pilatus Britten-Norman from that source by mid-1988. In addition to the Bembridge and Romanian production lines, Philippine Aerospace Development Corporation had an Islander production line in Manila, for the production of 115 aircraft under licence in four phases during the period 1974-1980. Only 55 aircraft were built, but assembly of BN-2Bs is being continued in the Philippines by PADC (which see). A licence to manufacture the three-engined Trislander in the USA is held by International Aviation Corporation (see 1987-88 *Jane's*). The last Trislander produced by Pilatus Britten-Norman was delivered to the Botswana Defence Force in September 1984.

PILATUS BRITTEN-NORMAN BN-2B ISLANDER

Detail design of the Islander began in April 1964 and construction of the prototype (G-ATCT) was started in September of the same year. It flew for the first time on 13 June 1965, powered by two 157 kW (210 hp) Rolls-Royce Continental IO-360-B engines and with wings of 13.72 m (45 ft) span. Subsequently, the prototype was re-engined with more powerful Textron Lycoming O-540 engines, with which it flew for the first time on 17 December 1965. The wing span was also increased by 1.22 m (4 ft) to bring the prototype to initial production standard.

The production prototype BN-2 Islander (G-ATWU) flew for the first time on 20 August 1966. The Islander received its domestic C of A on 10 August 1967 and an FAA Type Certificate on 19 December 1967.

Deliveries of Islanders began in August 1967, and various models, including military Defenders, have been supplied to operators in approx 120 countries. By June 1988 deliveries totalled 1,100, including 17 complete aircraft and two kits for PADC of the Philippines delivered in 1987.

Initial production Islanders were designated **BN-2**. Those built as standard from 1 June 1969 had the designation **BN-2A**, as described in the 1977-78 *Jane's*. The current standard piston engined model, from 1978, is the **BN-2B** Islander, which has a higher max landing weight and improved interior design. It is available with a choice of two piston engine power plants and either standard fuel tanks or standard tanks plus optional tanks in wingtips. Features, compared with the BN-2A (which is still available to order), include a range of passenger seats and covers, more robust door locks, improved door seals and stainless steel sills, redesigned fresh air system to improve ventilation in hot and humid climates, smaller diameter propellers to

Pilatus Britten-Norman BN-2B-26 Islander operated by South East Air *(Geoffrey P. Jones)*

decrease cabin noise, and redesigned flight deck and instrument panel. The two basic versions are designated **BN-2B-26** (with O-540 engines) and **BN-2B-20** (with IO-540s); BN-2B-27 and BN-2B-21 versions are no longer available, but new improved tip tanks are available as options to the basic BN-2B-26 and BN-2B-20 aircraft. The **BN-2T Turbine Islander**, powered by two Allison 250-B17C turboprops, and the military **Defender** and **Maritime Defender**, are described separately.

A series of modification kits is available as standard or as an option for new production aircraft, and can also be supplied to operators in the field for retrospective fitting to existing aircraft. An extended nose, incorporating 0.62 m³ (22 cu ft) of additional baggage space, was introduced as an optional feature in 1972.

A Rajay turbocharging installation was developed in the United States by Jonas Aircraft, the New York based distributors for Pilatus Britten-Norman aircraft. The Rajay installation is a bolt-on unit, which can be fitted on to standard 194 kW (260 hp) engines.

The following description applies to the standard piston engined versions of the BN-2B:

TYPE: Twin-engined feederline transport.

WINGS: Cantilever high-wing monoplane. NACA 23012 constant wing section. No dihedral. Incidence 2°. No sweepback. Conventional riveted two-spar torsion box structure in one piece, using L72 aluminium-clad aluminium alloys. Flared-up wingtips of Britten-Norman design. Integral fuel tanks in wingtips optional. Slotted ailerons and single-slotted flaps of metal construction. Flaps operated electrically, ailerons by pushrods and cables. Ground adjustable tab on starboard aileron. BTR-Goodrich pneumatic de-icing boots optional.

FUSELAGE: Conventional riveted four-longeron semi-monocoque structure of pressed frames and stringers and metal skin, using L72 aluminium clad aluminium alloys.

TAIL UNIT: Cantilever two-spar structure, with pressed ribs and metal skin, using L72 aluminium-clad aluminium alloys. Fixed incidence tailplane and mass balanced elevator. Rudder and elevator are actuated by pushrods and cables. Trim tabs in rudder and elevator. Pneumatic de-icing of tailplane and fin optional.

LANDING GEAR: Non-retractable tricycle type, with twin wheels on each main unit and single steerable nosewheel. Cantilever main legs mounted aft of rear spar. All three legs fitted with oleo-pneumatic shock absorbers. All five wheels and tyres size 16 × 7-7, supplied by Goodyear. Tyre pressure: main 2.41 bars (35 lb/sq in); nose 2.00 bars (29 lb/sq in). Foot operated aircooled Cleveland hydraulic brakes on main units. Parking brake. Wheel/ski gear available optionally.

POWER PLANT: Two Textron Lycoming flat-six engines, each driving a Hartzell HC-C2YK-2B or -2C two-blade constant-speed feathering metal propeller. Propeller synchronisers optional. Standard power plant is the 194 kW (260 hp) O-540-E4C5, but the 224 kW (300 hp) IO-540-K1B5 can be fitted at customer's option. Optional Rajay turbocharging installation on 194 kW (260 hp) engines, to improve high altitude performance. Integral fuel tank between spars in each wing, outboard of engine. Total fuel capacity (standard) 518 litres (137 US gallons; 114 Imp gallons). With optional fuel tanks in wingtips, total capacity is increased to 855 litres (226 US gallons; 188 Imp gallons). Additional pylon mounted underwing auxiliary tanks, each of 227 litres (60 US gallons; 50 Imp gallons) capacity, available optionally. Refuelling point in upper surface of wing above each internal tank. Total oil capacity 22.75 litres (6 US gallons; 5 Imp gallons).

ACCOMMODATION: Up to 10 persons, including pilot, on side by side front seats and four bench seats. No aisle. Seat backs fold forward. Access to all seats via three forward opening doors, forward of wing and at rear of cabin on port side and forward of wing on starboard side. Baggage compartment at rear of cabin, with port side loading door in standard versions. Exit in emergency by removing door windows. Special executive layouts available. Can be operated as freighter, carrying more than a ton of cargo; in this configuration the passenger seats can be stored in the rear baggage bay. In ambulance role, up to three stretchers and two attendants can be accommodated. Other layouts possible, including photographic and geophysical survey, parachutist transport or trainer (with accommodation for up to eight parachutists and a

Pilatus Britten-Norman BN-2T Turbine Islander with Micronair underwing spray system

dispatcher), firefighting, public health spraying and crop-spraying.

SYSTEMS: Southwind cabin heater standard. 45,000 BTU Stewart Warner combustion unit, with circulating fan, provides hot air for distribution at floor level outlets and at windscreen demisting slots. Fresh air, boosted by propeller slipstream, is ducted to each seating position for on-ground ventilation. Electrical DC power, for instruments, lighting and radio, from two engine driven 24V 50A self-rectifying alternators and a controller to main busbar and circuit breaker assembly. Emergency busbar is supplied by a 24V 17Ah heavy duty lead-acid battery in the event of a twin alternator failure. Ground power receptacle provided. Optional electric de-icing of propellers and windscreen, and pneumatic de-icing of wing and tail unit leading-edges. Intercom system, including second headset, and passenger address system are standard. Oxygen system available optionally for all versions.

AVIONICS AND EQUIPMENT: Standard items include blind-flying instrumentation, autopilot, dual flying controls and brake system, and a wide range of VHF and HF communications and navigation equipment.

DIMENSIONS, EXTERNAL:

Wing span	14.94 m (49 ft 0 in)
Wing chord (constant)	2.03 m (6 ft 8 in)
Wing aspect ratio	7.4
Length overall	10.86 m (35 ft 7¾ in)
Fuselage: Max width	1.21 m (3 ft 11½ in)
Max depth	1.46 m (4 ft 9¾ in)
Height overall	4.18 m (13 ft 8¾ in)
Tailplane span	4.67 m (15 ft 4 in)
Wheel track (c/l of shock absorbers)	
	3.61 m (11 ft 10 in)
Wheelbase	3.99 m (13 ft 1¼ in)
Propeller diameter	1.98 m (6 ft 6 in)
Cabin door (front, port):	
Height	1.10 m (3 ft 7½ in)
Width: top	0.64 m (2 ft 1¼ in)
Height to sill	0.59 m (1 ft 11¼ in)
Cabin door (front, starboard):	
Height	1.10 m (3 ft 7½ in)
Max width	0.86 m (2 ft 10 in)
Height to sill	0.57 m (1 ft 10½ in)
Cabin door (rear, port): Height	1.09 m (3 ft 7 in)
Width: top	0.635 m (2 ft 1 in)
bottom	1.19 m (3 ft 11 in)
Height to sill	0.52 m (1 ft 8½ in)
Baggage door (rear, port): Height	0.69 m (2 ft 3 in)

DIMENSIONS, INTERNAL:

Passenger cabin, aft of pilot's seat:

Length	3.05 m (10 ft 0 in)
Max width	1.09 m (3 ft 7 in)
Max height	1.27 m (4 ft 2 in)
Floor area	2.97 m² (32 sq ft)
Volume	3.68 m³ (130 cu ft)

Baggage space aft of passenger cabin

1.39 m³ (49 cu ft)

Freight capacity:

aft of pilot's seat, incl rear cabin baggage space
4.70 m³ (166 cu ft)

with four bench seats folded into rear cabin baggage space
3.68 m³ (130 cu ft)

AREAS:

Wings, gross	30.19 m² (325.0 sq ft)
Ailerons (total)	2.38 m² (25.6 sq ft)
Flaps (total)	3.62 m² (39.0 sq ft)
Fin	3.41 m² (36.64 sq ft)
Rudder, incl tab	1.60 m² (17.2 sq ft)
Tailplane	6.78 m² (73.0 sq ft)
Elevator, incl tabs	3.08 m² (33.16 sq ft)

WEIGHTS AND LOADINGS (A: 194 kW; 260 hp engines, B: 224 kW; 300 hp engines):

Weight empty, equipped (without avionics):

A   1,866 kg (4,114 lb)

B		1,925 kg (4,244 lb)
Max payload: A		929 kg (2,048 lb)
B		870 kg (1,918 lb)
Max fuel weight: standard: A, B		354 kg (780 lb)
with optional tanks in wingtips: A, B	585 kg (1,290 lb)	
Max T-O and landing weight: A, B		2,993 kg (6,600 lb)

Max zero-fuel weight (BCAR):

A, B		2,855 kg (6,300 lb)
Max wing loading: A, B	99.1 kg/m² (20.3 lb/sq ft)	

Max floor loading, without cargo panels:

A, B		586 kg/m² (120 lb/sq ft)
Max power loading: A		7.71 kg/kW (12.7 lb/hp)
B		6.68 kg/kW (11.0 lb/hp)

PERFORMANCE (at max T-O weight. A and B as above):

Never-exceed speed:

A, B   183 knots (339 km/h; 211 mph) IAS

Max level speed at S/L:

A	148 knots (274 km/h; 170 mph)
B	151 knots (280 km/h; 173 mph)

Max cruising speed (75% power) at 2,135 m (7,000 ft):

A	139 knots (257 km/h; 160 mph)
B	142 knots (264 km/h; 164 mph)

Cruising speed (67% power) at 2,750 m (9,000 ft):

A	134 knots (248 km/h; 154 mph)
B	137 knots (254 km/h; 158 mph)

Cruising speed (59% power) at 3,660 m (12,000 ft):

A	130 knots (241 km/h; 150 mph)
B	132 knots (245 km/h; 152 mph)

Stalling speed:

flaps up: A, B	50 knots (92 km/h; 57 mph) IAS
flaps down: A, B	40 knots (74 km/h; 46 mph) IAS

Max rate of climb at S/L: A	262 m (860 ft)/min
B	344 m (1,130 ft)/min

Rate of climb at S/L, one engine out:

A	44 m (145 ft)/min
B	61 m (200 ft)/min

Absolute ceiling: A	4,145 m (13,600 ft)
B	6,005 m (19,700 ft)

Service ceiling: A	3,445 m (11,300 ft)
B	5,240 m (17,200 ft)

Service ceiling, one engine out: A	1,525 m (5,000 ft)
B	1,980 m (6,500 ft)

Min ground turning radius   9.45 m (31 ft 0 in)

T-O run at S/L, zero wind, hard runway:

A	278 m (913 ft)
B	264 m (866 ft)

T-O run at 1,525 m (5,000 ft): A   396 m (1,299 ft)

B   372 m (1,221 ft)

T-O to 15 m (50 ft) at S/L, zero wind, hard runway:

A	371 m (1,218 ft)
B	352 m (1,155 ft)

T-O to 15 m (50 ft) at 1,525 m (5,000 ft):

A	528 m (1,732 ft)
B	496 m (1,628 ft)

Landing from 15 m (50 ft) at S/L, zero wind, hard runway: A, B   299 m (980 ft)

Landing from 15 m (50 ft) at 1,525 m (5,000 ft):

A, B   357 m (1,170 ft)

Landing run at 1,525 m (5,000 ft): A, B   171 m (560 ft)

Landing run at S/L, zero wind, hard runway:

A, B   140 m (460 ft)

Range at 75% power at 2,135 m (7,000 ft):

A, standard fuel   622 nm (1,153 km; 717 miles)

A, with optional tanks

1,023 nm (1,896 km; 1,178 miles)

B, standard fuel   555 nm (1,028 km; 639 miles)

B, with optional tanks 920 nm (1,704 km; 1,059 miles)

Range at 67% power at 2,750 m (9,000 ft):

A, standard fuel   713 nm (1,322 km; 822 miles)

A, with optional tanks

1,159 nm (2,147 km; 1,334 miles)

B, standard fuel   577 nm (1,070 km; 665 miles)

B, with optional tanks 975 nm (1,807 km; 1,123 miles)

Range at 59% power at 3,660 m (12,000 ft):

A, standard fuel   755 nm (1,400 km; 870 miles)

A, with optional tanks

1,216 nm (2,253 km; 1,400 miles)

B, standard fuel   613 nm (1,136 km; 706 miles)

B, with optional tanks

1,061 nm (1,965 km; 1,221 miles)

PILATUS BRITTEN-NORMAN DEFENDER

The Defender is a variant of the civil Islander which can be adapted for a wide variety of government and military roles such as search and rescue, internal security, long-range patrol, forward air control, troop transport, logistic support and casualty evacuation. It is available with the same choices of wing configuration as the current civil versions and can be equipped with a wide range of sophisticated avionics, including nose mounted weather radar, providing the aircraft with a marine search capability. For an electronic warfare role, equipment can range from a simple radar warning receiver to a comprehensive passive electronics intelligence gathering system, ESM, and ECM coupled to the ESM to provide radar jamming or defensive chaff/IR flare dispensing. Other optional equipment includes four NATO standard underwing pylons for a variety of external stores, the inboard pair each carrying up to 317.5 kg (700 lb) and the outboard pair up to 204 kg (450 lb).

Typical underwing loads include twin 7.62 mm machine-guns in pod packs, 250 lb or 500 lb GP bombs, Matra rocket packs, SURA rocket clusters, wire guided missiles, 5 in reconnaissance flares, anti-personnel grenades, smoke bombs, marker bombs and 227 litre (60 US gallon; 50 Imp gallon) drop tanks.

Internal capacity for passengers, stretcher cases or cargo is the same as that of the civil Islander.

Britten-Norman Defenders/Islanders have been delivered to the Abu Dhabi Defence Force, Belgian Army, Belize Defence Force, Botswana Defence Force, British Army Parachute Association, Ciskei Defence Force, Ghana Air Force, Guyana Defence Force, Haitian Air Corps, Indonesian Army, Jamaica Defence Force, Malagasy Air Force, Presidential Flight of the Mexican Air Force, Royal Hong Kong Auxiliary Air Force, Panamanian Air Force, Somali Aeronautical Corps, Sultan of Oman's Air Force, Suriname Air Force, Mauritania Islamic Defence Force, the Seychelles Ministry of Agriculture and Fisheries, the Malawi Army Air Wing, Venezuelan Army Air Regiment, Zaïre Air Force, Zimbabwe Air Force and the Rwanda Air Force. Those operated by Ciskei, Haiti, Indonesia, Iraq, Somalia, Venezuela, Zaïre, Zimbabwe, Israel and Qatar are military Islanders, and are not equipped to carry offensive weapons; those which serve with the Cyprus National Guard, Indian Navy and Philippine Navy are Maritime Islanders.

The description given for the BN-2B Islander applies also to the Defender, except as follows:

POWER PLANT: Two 224 kW (300 hp) Textron Lycoming IO-540-K1B5 flat-six engines standard.

AVIONICS: Typical installation comprises 720 channel VHF nav/com transceivers with VOR/LOC and VOR/ILS, ADF, marker beacon receiver, transponder, HF com transceiver, weather radar and full autopilot. Optional equipment includes RWR, ESM and ECM.

PILATUS BRITTEN-NORMAN MARITIME DEFENDER

Generally similar to the Defender, the Maritime Defender differs by having a modified nose with a larger (Bendix RDR-1400) search radar, capable of detecting a 100 m² (1,076 sq ft) target in sea state 4-5 at a range of 36 nm (67 km; 41.5 miles). Scanning 60° on each side of the flight path, the radar provides a search width of 60 nm (111 km; 69 miles) at optimum altitude. The interior layout provides for pilot and co-pilot, a radar operator at a mid-cabin position on the starboard side, and two observers in the rear of the cabin, one aft of the radar operator, and one adjacent to a window on the port side.

Intended for coastal patrol, fishery and oil rig protection duties, as well as search and rescue support, the Maritime Defender is suitable for all-weather operation, by day or night, and carries the equipment necessary to fulfil such roles. This can include compass/HSI, horizon gyro (radar stabilisation), autopilot, ground mapping and weather radar, VLF/Omega, radio altimeter, dual VHF com, dual VHF nav/ILS, VHF marine band com, ADF, transponder, DME, encoding altimeter and SSB HF com. Specialised equipment includes a searchlight installation and hand held camera; the four underwing pylons can be used to carry a loudspeaker pod, flares, parachute dinghy packs and a variety of weapons.

The description of the Defender applies also to the Maritime Defender, except that overall length is increased to 11.07 m (36 ft 3¾ in).

PILATUS BRITTEN-NORMAN BN-2T TURBINE ISLANDER and DEFENDER

On 2 August 1980 the prototype (G-BPBN) was flown of the BN-2T Turbine Islander, powered by two Allison 250-B17C turboprops. These enable the BN-2T to use available low cost jet fuel instead of scarce and costly Avgas, and offer a particularly low operating noise level.

British CAA certification of the Turbine Islander was received at the end of May 1981; FAR Pt 23 US type approval was granted on 15 July 1982. Full icing clearance to FAR Pt 25 was granted on 23 July 1984. The first production aircraft was delivered during December 1981. The company announced in January 1983 the receipt of an order for four BN-2T Turbine Islanders for service with Transportes e Trabalhos Aereos, the domestic airline of Mozambique. Nineteen aircraft had been delivered by early 1988. Deliveries include one to RAF Weston-on-the-Green, incorporating an in-flight sliding parachute door, and three to the Malawi Police. Two BN-2Ts were delivered in mid-1988 to the Netherlands Police, equipped with a very comprehensive Collins avionics fit, plus Bendix RDR 1400C radar and blister windows.

The Turbine Islander is available for the same range of applications as the piston engined Islander, including a military **Turbine Defender**. Five such aircraft were ordered for the UK Army Air Corps in early 1988, as replacements for DHC-2 Beavers used for surveillance, notably in Northern Ireland. Deliveries were due to begin in late 1988.

The description of the BN-2B Islander applies also to the BN-2T, except as follows:

TYPE: Twin-turboprop feederline transport.

FUSELAGE: Generally as for BN-2B.

POWER PLANT: Two 298 kW (400 shp) Allison 250-B17C turboprops, flat rated at 238.5 kW (320 shp), and each driving a Hartzell three-blade constant-speed fully-feathering metal propeller. Fuel capacity 814 litres (215 US gallons; 179 Imp gallons). Pylon mounted underwing tanks, each of 227 litres (60 US gallons; 50 Imp gallons) capacity, are available optionally for special purposes. Total oil capacity 5.7 litres (1.5 US gallons; 1.25 Imp gallons).

ACCOMMODATION: Generally as for BN-2B. In ambulance role can accommodate, in addition to the pilot, a single stretcher, one medical attendant, and five seated occupants; or two stretchers, one attendant, and three passengers; or three stretchers, two attendants, and one passenger. Other possible layouts include photographic and geophysical survey; parachutist transport or trainer (with accommodation for up to eight parachutists and a dispatcher); and pest control or other agricultural spraying. Maritime Turbine Islander/Defender versions available for fishery protection, coastguard patrol, pollution survey, search and rescue, and similar applications. Offered as an option is an in-flight sliding parachute door.

AVIONICS AND EQUIPMENT: Standard avionics and equipment generally similar to BN-2B. Other equipment, according to mission, includes fixed tail 'sting' or towed 'bird'

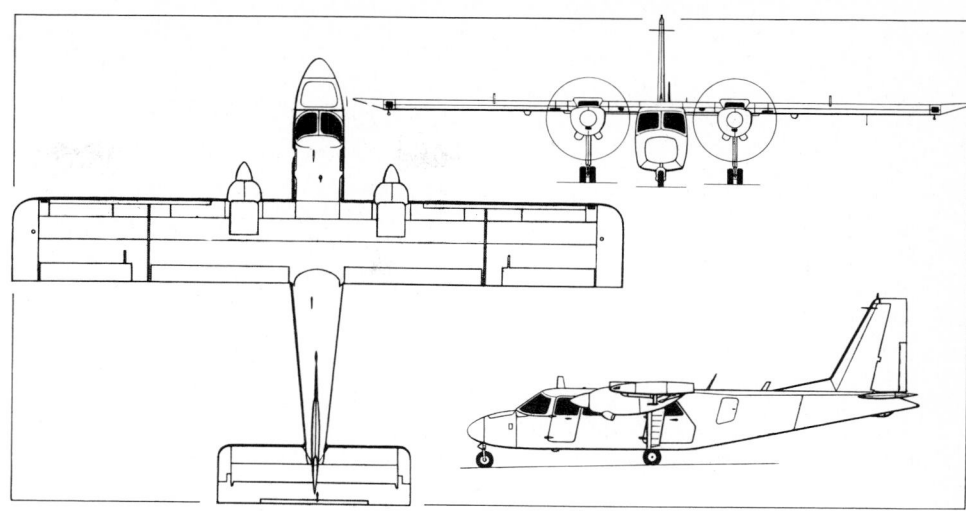

Pilatus Britten-Norman BN-2T Turbine Islander *(Pilot Press)*

magnetometer, spectrometer, or electromagnetic detection/analysis equipment (geophysical survey); one or two cameras, navigation sights, and appropriate avionics (photographic survey); 188.7 litre (50 US gallon; 41.5 Imp gallon) Micronair underwing spraypods complete with pump and rotary atomiser (pest control/agricultural spraying versions); radar, VLF/Omega nav system, radar altimeter, marine band and VHF transceivers, dinghies, survival equipment, and special crew accommodation (maritime versions).

DIMENSIONS, EXTERNAL:
As for BN-2B, except
Length overall: standard nose   10.87 m (35 ft 7¾ in)
     weather radar nose   11.07 m (36 ft 3¾ in)
Propeller diameter   2.03 m (6 ft 8 in)

WEIGHTS:
Weight empty, equipped (incl pilot)   1,914 kg (4,220 lb)
Payload with max fuel   608 kg (1,340 lb)
Max T-O weight   3,175 kg (7,000 lb)
Max landing weight   3,084 kg (6,800 lb)
Max zero-fuel weight   2,994 kg (6,600 lb)

PERFORMANCE (standard aircraft and Turbine Defender, at max T-O weight, ISA, except where indicated):

Max cruising speed at 3,050 m (10,000 ft)
     170 knots (315 km/h; 196 mph)
Max cruising speed at S/L
     154 knots (285 km/h; 177 mph)
Cruising speed, 72% power at 3,050 m (10,000 ft)
     150 knots (278 km/h; 173 mph)
Cruising speed, 72% power at 1,525 m (5,000 ft)
     142 knots (263 km/h; 164 mph)
Stalling speed, power off:
   flaps up   52 knots (97 km/h; 60 mph) IAS
   flaps down   45 knots (84 km/h; 52 mph) IAS
Max rate of climb at S/L   320 m (1,050 ft)/min
Rate of climb at S/L, one engine out
     66 m (215 ft)/min
Service ceiling   over 7,620 m (25,000 ft)
Absolute ceiling, one engine out   3,080 m (10,100 ft)
T-O run   255 m (837 ft)
T-O to 15 m (50 ft)   381 m (1,250 ft)
Landing from 15 m (50 ft)   340 m (1,115 ft)
Landing run   228 m (747 ft)
Range (IFR) with max fuel, reserves for 45 min hold plus 10%   590 nm (1,093 km; 679 miles)
Range (VFR) with max fuel, no reserves
     728 nm (1,349 km; 838 miles)

Pilatus Britten-Norman ASTOR Defender with original Ferranti surveillance radar in nose

PILATUS BRITTEN-NORMAN ASTOR DEFENDER

ASTOR (Airborne STand-Off Radar) is the current acronym for a British Ministry of Defence programme which is seeking to fulfil a requirement for an airborne surveillance radar to provide an overall picture of a battle area. It is intended to operate in conjunction with a battlefield reconnaissance RPV called Phoenix, which would be sent in to obtain a closer look at any area or target shown by the ASTOR aircraft to be deserving of more detailed examination.

Two platforms are being evaluated for ASTOR, the high-level option being represented by a BAC/English Electric Canberra. The more versatile Defender could be selected for production systems if it proves able to acquire sufficient data from medium heights. Radar trials have included GEC equipment in the Canberra and Ferranti equipment in the Defender, and a modified Thorn EMI Searchwater has been flying in the Canberra testbed since 1982. Up to 12 ASTOR platforms are required.

Pilatus Britten-Norman began work on an ASTOR (then CASTOR) Turbine Defender testbed (G-DLRA, c/n 2140) on 5 March 1984, and the converted aircraft made its first flight on 12 May, with the undernose radome containing ballast only. Flight trials with a version of the Thorn EMI Skymaster radar were due to begin in the Autumn of 1988. This installation significantly alters the Defender's nose shape, but is considered the best location to provide optimum lookdown capability for the scanner. To provide ground clearance for the radar in this position, the nosewheel leg is lengthened by 30.5 cm (12 in) and a Trislander main landing gear fitted. Despite the ungainly appearance, flight tests demonstrated adequate performance and virtually unaltered handling characteristics.

The ASTOR radar will be a lightweight all-weather multi-mode I-band data acquisition system, designed to meet UK General and Air Staff Requirement 3956, and to provide primary intelligence information in the immediate battle zone and beyond, while operating well within friendly territory. It will have full 360° scan, and will offer a wide area of coverage against moving and fixed targets. The associated transmitter, receiver and processing equipment will be housed in the fuselage of the Islander, which will be flown and operated by a two-man crew. Data acquired will be processed and transmitted automatically, via an airborne link, to one or more ground stations.

The description of the standard BN-2T Turbine Islander applies also to the ASTOR Defender, except as follows:

Pilatus Britten-Norman ASV Maritime Defender with Sea Skua missiles and Seaspray radar

TYPE: Twin-turboprop experimental battlefield surveillance aircraft.

FUSELAGE: Modified nose, as described in introductory paragraphs.

LANDING GEAR: Modified BN-2A Mk III Trislander main landing gear. Longer nosewheel leg to provide adequate ground clearance for radome. Main landing gear tyre size 6.50 × 8, pressure 2.4 bars (35 lb/sq in).

SYSTEMS AND AVIONICS: Multi-mode radar installed in nose, as described in introductory paragraphs. Other systems and avionics generally as described for Islander/Turbine Islander.

DIMENSIONS, EXTERNAL:
Wing span	14.94 m (49 ft 0 in)
Wing aspect ratio	7.4
Length overall	approx 11.89 m (39 ft 0 in)
Propeller diameter	2.03 m (6 ft 8 in)

WEIGHT:
Design max T-O weight	3,630 kg (8,000 lb)

PILATUS BRITTEN-NORMAN AEW, AEW/MR and ASW/ASV MARITIME DEFENDERS

To meet the need for a lightweight high performance AEW system, Pilatus Britten-Norman and Thorn EMI Electronics have collaborated on a private venture basis to install the Thorn EMI Skymaster multi-mode radar into the Pilatus Britten-Norman Defender airframe (G-TEMI), and so create the **AEW Defender**. As the illustration shows, the nose radome of the AEW Defender is deeper, more bulbous and less angular than that of the original ASTOR aircraft, to house the Skymaster radar. In an AEW role this long-range radar, using pulse-Doppler processing, can acquire and track automatically large numbers of targets flying at all altitudes against a land or sea background. For maritime reconnaissance (MR) the operator selects a non-coherent, frequency agile mode of operation, optimising the radar for the detection of small surface targets in high sea states out to the radar horizon.

The Defender's STOL performance enables it to be operated from forward unprepared strips, and in the air the aircraft's low radar cross section aids survivability. The **AEW/MR Defender** is fitted with a second console to increase operational flexibility and target handling capacity. An air-to-air and air-to-ground data link, ESM, IFF and navigation equipments may be fully integrated with the radar display and control system.

Future developments will include a border surveillance role, with the radar optimised for the detection of moving targets at long range. A synthetic aperture mode would provide high resolution mapping video, which could be linked to provide ground commanders with an all-weather real-time display showing enemy dispositions and movements.

A further variant, the **ASW/ASV Maritime Defender**, made its first appearance at the Hanover Air Show in May 1984. This aircraft may be equipped to varying standards, to the customer's specification. Equipment can include a 360° radar, FLIR, sonobuoys, acoustic processing

Pilatus Britten-Norman AEW Defender with nose-mounted Thorn EMI Skymaster radar

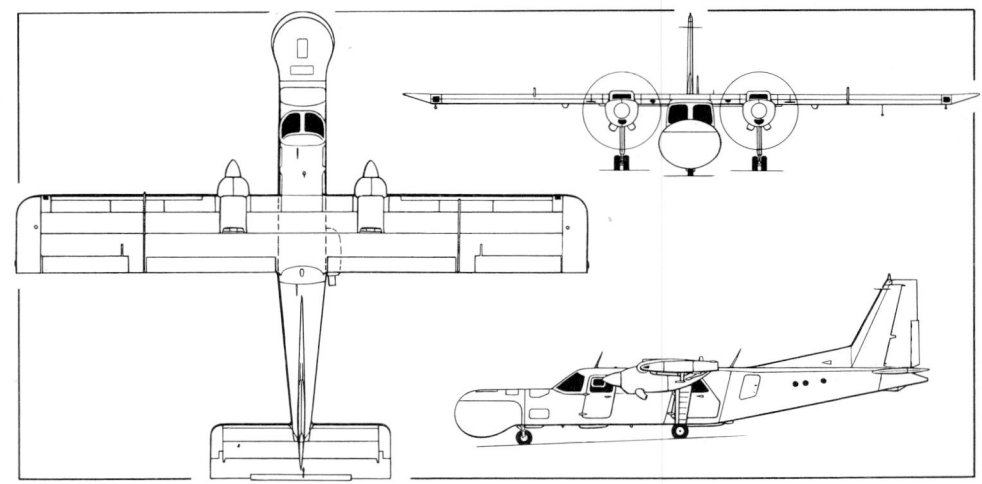

Pilatus Britten-Norman AEW Defender, a Turbine Islander development with Skymaster maritime surveillance radar *(Pilot Press)*

equipment, and a magnetic anomaly detector. Four underwing hardpoints can be used to carry two Sting Ray lightweight torpedoes, four Sea Skua missiles, depth charges, ECM and ESM pods, survival packs, rockets, gun pods or other stores. A crew of three is normal, with room for a trainee.

The UK Ministry of Defence purchased Pilatus Britten-Norman's former Turbine Defender demonstrator (G-OPBN) in 1986, for use by the Royal Navy's Directorate-General of Underwater Weapons torpedo trials unit as ZF573.

The 1988 **Elint Defender** is mentioned in the Addenda.

SHORTS
SHORT BROTHERS PLC

PO Box 241, Airport Road, Belfast BT3 9DZ, Northern Ireland
Telephone: 0232 458444
Telex: 74688
OTHER FACTORIES: Newtownards, Castlereagh, Belfast (3)
LONDON OFFICE: Glen House, Stag Place, Victoria, London SW1E 5AG
Telephone: (01) 828 9838
CHAIRMAN: Rodney Lund
MANAGING DIRECTOR: R. W. R. McNulty, BA, BComm, CA
DIRECTOR, AIRCRAFT ENGINEERING: M. Wilson
MARKETING DIRECTOR: A. F. C. Roberts, OBE
PUBLIC RELATIONS MANAGER: Miss M. O'Neill

Short Brothers were first established, as aeronauts, in 1898, and in 1901 they began the manufacture of balloons at Hove, Sussex. Works were later established in London, first at premises off the Tottenham Court Road and, in 1906, at Battersea. In March 1909 Shorts opened the United Kingdom's first purpose built aircraft factory at Shellbeach, Isle of Sheppey. (The Short No. 1 had been ordered by F. T. McClean in January 1909.) The contract placed with Shorts by the Wright brothers in March 1909, for six Flyers, was the first aircraft series production contract to be placed in the UK. The main aircraft works moved to Eastchurch in 1909-10, and to Rochester in 1913-14.

In June 1936 Short Brothers, in collaboration with Harland & Wolff Ltd, formed a new company known as Short & Harland Ltd to build aircraft in Belfast, and in 1947 activities were concentrated in Belfast under the name Short Bros & Harland Ltd. The name Short Brothers Ltd was re-adopted on 1 June 1977.

The British government now owns, directly or indirectly, 100% of the issued shareholding. In 1985 the company received the Queen's Award to Industry for the 15th time. It had 7,200 employees in December 1987.

The company's current products include the 30-seat Shorts 330 and 36-seat Shorts 360 commuter airliners, in use throughout the world for passenger, freight, military and miscellaneous operations. The earlier Skyvan STOL light transport remains available to order.

Important collaborative agreements between Shorts and Embraer of Brazil were announced in May 1984. As a first step, Shorts is marketing and manufacturing under licence a new version of the EMB-312 Tucano turboprop basic trainer, which was selected in March 1985 as the replacement for the Royal Air Force's Jet Provosts. The Shorts Tucano is being manufactured in the company's Shorlac (Shorts Light Aircraft Company) facility at the former Royal Naval Air Station Sydenham, Belfast.

Shorts retains responsibility for major overhaul and refurbishment of RAF Canberra PR. Mk 9s built under licence in the 1950s.

A proportion of the composite components for the Tucano, Canberra and some other military contracts is manufactured by Short Brothers (Dunmurry) Limited, a wholly-owned subsidiary formed in 1985.

Internationally, Shorts is collaborating as a risk sharing partner with Fokker in development and production of the Fokker 100, with responsibility for the wings. Shorts also holds contracts to produce landing gear doors for the Boeing 747, inboard trailing-edge flap assemblies for the Boeing 757, and rudder assemblies for the Boeing 737-300.

Shorts is also quality approved subcontractor to many major US and UK aerospace companies. Conversely, production of the wings for the Shorts 330/360 is undertaken jointly by CATIC of China and Fokker of the Netherlands.

During 1967, Shorts began the design and manufacture of pods for Rolls-Royce jet engines. It is currently podding RB211 engines for the Boeing 747, 757 and 767, and had produced pods for more than 1,200 RB211s by January 1988. Those produced for the 757 from mid-1983 utilise carbonfibre for the outer skin barrel of the nose cowl, offering a 25 per cent weight saving compared with aluminium alloy. The company also produces pods for the Textron Lycoming ALF 502 turbofans of the British Aerospace 146, and was responsible for the design and manufacture of the first flight test pod for the PW2037 turbofan chosen to power some Boeing 757s.

In September 1984 Shorts and Rohr Industries of the USA joined forces to offer a nacelle system for the advanced V2500 turbofan being developed by International Aero Engines AG for 150-seat jetliners; and in January 1985 it was announced that the Shorts/Rohr team had been selected to produce the pods for V2500 engines selected for the Airbus Industrie A320. Assembly of the pods began in 1987.

In September 1986 Shorts and the de Havilland Division of Boeing Canada signed an agreement under which the companies were to study jointly the requirements for a new-generation transport aircraft for regional airline and corporate use. It was anticipated that the resultant NRA 90 25-seat twin-turboprop aircraft would be ready to enter service in 1991; but in 1987 the programme was suspended for at least 12 months. Details of the NRA 90-A and 90-B designs will be found in the International section of the addenda to the 1987-88 edition of *Jane's*.

In addition to its activities in the field of piloted aircraft, Shorts is engaged in development and production of missiles and supersonic target drones, and production to UK Ministry of Defence contract of the Skeet target drone.

The company's Flying Services Division operates maintenance units and airfields for various civil and military organisations, and flies and maintains aircraft and target drones for the Ministry of Defence. Short Brothers Air Services Limited, a subsidiary company, operates targets for the Ministry of Defence and provides a service for overseas countries.

SHORTS 330

The Shorts 330 is a 30-passenger twin-turboprop transport aircraft derived from the smaller Skyvan STOL utility transport, and retaining many of the latter type's well proven characteristics, including the large cabin cross-section. The first prototype (G-BSBH) flew for the first time on 22 August 1974. Eight days earlier, the first order for the

Shorts 330 regional airliner in the livery of Olympic Airways

330 was placed by Command Airways of Poughkeepsie, New York, for three aircraft. CAA certification to full Transport Category requirements was granted on 18 February 1976; this was followed on 18 June 1976 by US FAR Pt 25 and Pt 36 approval, and subsequently by approvals from the Canadian Dept of Transport, the West German LBA and the Australian Dept of Transport. The 330 conforms with CAB Pt 298 (US) and meets the noise requirements of FAR Pt 36 by a substantial margin. Initial deliveries began in June 1976; first to enter service, on 24 August 1976, was a Time Air 330.

By the beginning of 1988 orders and options for all variants of the 330 (including 330-UTT and Sherpa) totalled 169 aircraft.

The first 26 Shorts 330s are powered by 875 kW (1,173 shp) PT6A-45A engines; the next 40 have PT6A-45B engines. Subsequent aircraft have more powerful PT6A-45R engines and a number of items as standard which were available only as options on the original version.

Three versions of the 330 are available:

330-200. Standard passenger version, as described in detail.

330-UTT. Military utility tactical transport version. Described separately.

Sherpa. Freighter version of 330-200, from which it differs mainly in having a ramp type full width rear loading door. In service with US Air Force under designation C-23A. Described separately.

In addition, the US Army leases six ex-airline 330s, including four modified to military standards by Field Aircraft Services of Calgary, Alberta, for operation in the Kwajalein area of the Pacific.

The following description applies to the standard 330-200 passenger version:

TYPE: Twin-turboprop transport aircraft.

WINGS: Braced high-wing monoplane, of all-metal safe-life construction, built in three sections. Wing sections NACA 63A series (modified). Thickness/chord ratio 18% at root, 14% on outer panels. Dihedral 3° on outer panels. Centre-section, integral with top of centre-fuselage, has taper on leading- and trailing-edges, and is a two-spar single-cell box structure of light alloy with conventional skin and stringers. The strut braced outer panels, which are pin jointed to the centre-section, are reinforced Skyvan constant chord units, built of light alloy, and each consists of a two-cell box having wing skins made up of a smooth outer skin bonded to a corrugated inner skin. All-metal single-slotted ailerons. Geared trim tabs in ailerons. All-metal single-slotted flaps, each in three sections. Primary control surfaces are

rod actuated. Optional Goodrich pneumatic boot de-icing of leading-edges.

FUSELAGE: Light alloy structure, built in two main portions: nose (including flight deck, nosewheel bay and forward baggage compartment); and the centre (including main wing spar attachment frames and lower transverse beams which carry the main landing gear and associated fairings) and rear portion (including aft baggage compartment and tail unit attachment frames). The nose and rear underfuselage are of conventional skin/stringer design. The remainder is composed of a smooth outer skin bonded to a corrugated inner skin and stabilised by frames.

TAIL UNIT: Cantilever all-metal two-spar structure with twin fins and rudders, basically similar to that of the Skyvan. Fixed incidence tailplane, with reinforced leading-edge. Full span elevator, aerodynamically balanced by set-back hinges. Rudders each have an unshielded horn aerodynamic balance. Primary control surfaces are rod actuated. Geared trim tabs in elevator and starboard rudder (port rudder, trim only). Optional Goodrich pneumatic boot de-icing of leading-edges.

LANDING GEAR: Menasco retractable tricycle type, with single wheel on each unit. Main units carried on short sponsons, into which the wheels retract hydraulically. Oleo-pneumatic shock absorbers. Nosewheel is steerable. Mainwheel tyre size 34 × 10.75-16; nosewheel tyre size 9-6. Normal tyre pressures: main units 5.45 bars (79 lb/sq in), nose unit 3.79 bars (55 lb/sq in).

POWER PLANT: Two 893 kW (1,198 shp) Pratt & Whitney Canada PT6A-45R turboprops, each driving a Hartzell five-blade constant-speed fully-feathering metal low-speed propeller. Fuel tanks in wing centre-section/fuselage fairing; total usable capacity increased from original 2,182 litres (576 US gallons; 480 Imp gallons) to 2,546 litres (672.5 US gallons; 560 Imp gallons) in January 1985. Normal cross-feed provisions to allow for pump failure. Single pressure refuelling point in starboard landing gear fairing, backed by three gravity refuelling points in fuselage spine.

ACCOMMODATION: Crew of two on flight deck, plus cabin attendant. Dual controls standard. Standard seating for 30 passengers, in ten rows of three at 76 cm (30 in) pitch, with wide aisle. Seat rails fitted to facilitate changes in configuration. Galley, toilet and cabin attendant's seat at rear. Large overhead baggage lockers. Entire accommodation soundproofed and air-conditioned. Baggage compartments in nose (1.27 m³; 45 cu ft) and to rear of cabin (2.83 m³; 100 cu ft), each with external access and capable of holding a combined total of 500 kg (1,100 lb)

of baggage. Passenger door is at rear of cabin on port side. Passenger version has two emergency exits on the starboard side, two on the port side (including passenger door) and one in the flight deck roof. Mixed traffic version has full access to these emergency exits. For mixed passenger/freight operation a partition divides the cabin into a rear passenger area (typically for 18 persons) and a forward cargo compartment, the latter being loaded through a large port side door, capable of admitting ATA 'D' type containers. In all-cargo configuration the cabin can accommodate up to seven 'D' type containers, with ample space around them for additional freight. Cabin floor is flat throughout its length, and is designed to support loadings of 181 kg (400 lb) per foot run at 610.3 kg/m² (125 lb/sq ft). Locally reinforced areas of higher strength are also provided. Seat rails can be used as cargo lashing points. Freight loading is facilitated by the low-level cabin floor.

SYSTEMS: Hamilton Standard air-conditioning system, using engine bleed air. Hydraulic system of 207 bars (3,000 lb/sq in), supplied by engine driven pumps, operates landing gear, nosewheel steering, flaps and brakes (at half pressure) and includes emergency accumulators. Air/oil reservoir pressurised to 1.72 bars (25 lb/sq in) at 20°C. Main electrical system, for general services, is 28V DC and is of the split busbar type with cross-coupling for essential services. Lucas 28V 250A DC starter/generator for engine starting and aircraft services, with separate 1.5kW 200V AC output for windscreen anti-icing and demisting. Special AC sources of 115V and 26V available at 400Hz for certain instruments, avionics and fuel booster pumps. Anti-icing standard for engine intake ducts, inlet lips and propellers. Optional de-icing of wing and tailplane leading-edges.

AVIONICS AND EQUIPMENT: Passenger safety equipment standard. Wide range of radio and navigation equipment available to customer's requirements. Typical standard avionics comprise duplicated VHF communications and navigation systems, two glideslope/marker beacon receivers, two ILS repeaters, two radio magnetic indicators, one ADF, one transponder, one DME, PA system and weather radar. Flight data recorder and voice recorder available as standard options.

DIMENSIONS, EXTERNAL:

Wing span	22.76 m (74 ft 8 in)
Wing chord (standard mean)	1.85 m (6 ft 0.7 in)
Length overall	17.69 m (58 ft 0½ in)
Height overall	4.95 m (16 ft 3 in)
Tailplane span	5.68 m (18 ft 7¾ in)
Wheel track	4.24 m (13 ft 10⅞ in)
Wheelbase	6.15 m (20 ft 2 in)
Propeller diameter	2.82 m (9 ft 3 in)
Propeller ground clearance	1.83 m (6 ft 0 in)
Cabin floor: Height above ground	0.94 m (3 ft 1 in)
Passenger door (port, rear):	
Height	1.57 m (5 ft 2 in)
Width	0.71 m (2 ft 4 in)
Height to sill	0.94 m (3 ft 1 in)
Cargo door (port, forward):	
Height	1.68 m (5 ft 6 in)
Width	1.42 m (4 ft 8 in)
Height to sill	0.94 m (3 ft 1 in)

DIMENSIONS, INTERNAL:

Cabin: Max length, incl toilet	9.47 m (31 ft 1 in)
Max width	1.93 m (6 ft 4 in)
Max height	1.93 m (6 ft 4 in)
Floor area	18.77 m² (202 sq ft)
Volume (all-cargo)	34.83 m³ (1,230 cu ft)
Baggage compartments volume (total usable)	
	4.11 m³ (145 cu ft)
Cabin overhead lockers (total)	1.13 m³ (40 cu ft)

AREAS:

Wings, gross	42.1 m² (453.0 sq ft)
Ailerons (total, aft of hinges)	2.55 m² (27.5 sq ft)

Shorts 330 twin-turboprop commuter and utility transport, with added side view (bottom) of Sherpa
(Pilot Press)

Trailing-edge flaps (total) 7.74 m^2 (83.3 sq ft)
Fins (total) 8.65 m^2 (93.1 sq ft)
Rudders (total, aft of hinges) 2.24 m^2 (24.1 sq ft)
Tailplane 7.77 m^2 (83.6 sq ft)
Elevator (total, aft of hinges) 2.55 m^2 (27.4 sq ft)

WEIGHTS AND LOADINGS:
Weight empty, equipped (incl crew of three):
330-200 for 30 passengers 6,680 kg (14,727 lb)
Fuel 2,032 kg (4,480 lb)
Max payload for normal max T-O weight:
30 passengers and baggage 2,653 kg (5,850 lb)
cargo 3,400 kg (7,500 lb)
Max T-O weight 10,387 kg (22,900 lb)
Max landing weight 10,251 kg (22,600 lb)
Max wing loading 246.8 kg/m^2 (50.55 lb/sq ft)
Max power loading 5.81 kg/kW (9.56 lb/shp)

PERFORMANCE (at max T-O weight, ISA at S/L, except where indicated):
Max cruising speed at 3,050 m (10,000 ft), AUW of 9,525 kg (21,000 lb) 190 knots (352 km/h; 218 mph)
Econ cruising speed at 3,050 m (10,000 ft), AUW of 9,525 kg (21,000 lb) 160 knots (296 km/h; 184 mph)
Stalling speed, flaps and landing gear up
90 knots (167 km/h; 104 mph) EAS
Stalling speed at max landing weight, flaps and landing gear down 73 knots (136 km/h; 85 mph) EAS
Max rate of climb at S/L 360 m (1,180 ft)/min
Service ceiling, one engine out, AUW of 9,072 kg (20,000 lb) 3,500 m (11,500 ft)
T-O distance (FAR Pt 25 and BCAR Gp A):
ISA 1,042 m (3,420 ft)
ISA + 15°C 1,295 m (4,250 ft)
Landing distance, AUW of 9,072 kg (20,000 lb):
BCAR 1,143 m (3,750 ft)
FAR 1,030 m (3,380 ft)
Runway LCN at max T-O weight 10.7
Range with max passenger payload, cruising at 3,050 m (10,000 ft), no reserves 473 nm (876 km; 544 miles)
Range with max fuel, cruising at 3,050 m (10,000 ft), no reserves:
passenger version, 1,966 kg (4,335 lb) payload
915 nm (1,695 km; 1,053 miles)
cargo version, 2,306 kg (5,085 lb) payload
758 nm (1,403 km; 872 miles)

OPERATIONAL NOISE LEVELS (FAR Pt 36):
Take-off 88.9 EPNdB
Sideline 84.7 EPNdB
Approach 92.9 EPNdB

SHORTS 330-UTT

Shorts stated on 7 September 1982 that production had begun of this military utility tactical transport version of the Model 330. The Royal Thai Army took delivery of two (one in June 1984 and one in March 1985). The Royal Thai Border Police took two (in October 1984 and April 1985) and now operate also one of the Army UTTs.

The basic airframe and power plant remain unchanged, but max payload is increased to 3,630 kg (8,000 lb) and max operational necessity T-O weight to 11,158 kg (24,600 lb). Other changes include a strengthened cabin floor and reconfigured avionics panel. Cabin accommodation can be provided for up to 33 troops, 30 paratroops plus a jumpmaster (exit via inward opening rear door each side), or 15 stretchers plus four seated personnel.

PERFORMANCE:
Cruising speed at 3,050 m (10,000 ft), AUW of 9,979 kg (22,000 lb):
high-speed cruise, max continuous power
201 knots (372 km/h; 231 mph)
long-range cruise 160 knots (296 km/h; 184 mph)
Max rate of climb at S/L at normal max T-O weight of 10,387 kg (22,900 lb):
two engines 381 m (1,250 ft)/min
one engine 89 m (290 ft)/min
STOL T-O run at S/L, 15° flap 415 m (1,360 ft)
STOL T-O to 15 m (50 ft), 15° flap 644 m (2,110 ft)
STOL landing from 15 m (50 ft) at AUW of 9,525 kg (21,000 lb), flaps down, propeller reversal
488 m (1,600 ft)
STOL landing run, conditions as above 235 m (770 ft)
Range with 30 fully armed assault troops
600 nm (1,112 km; 691 miles)

SHORTS SHERPA

US Air Force designation: C-23A

The Sherpa is a freighter version of the Shorts 330-200. It retains many features of the all-passenger version, to allow utility passenger transport operations to be undertaken. The forward freight door and wide-body hold of the 330-200 are unchanged, but the Sherpa's design incorporates a full width rear cargo door, which permits through loading.

The hydraulically actuated rear ramp/door, which is operated from inside or outside the aircraft, can be lowered to a variety of positions to simplify loading from a wide range of ground equipment. The forward baggage compartment of the Shorts 330-200 is retained and this, being lockable, is suitable for high value cargo. Standard airline containers can be accommodated in the main cabin, up to the size of the LD3, making the Sherpa particularly suited for the operation of short-haul cargo feeder services.

Shorts Sherpa, with rear ramp/door, for CVG Edelca of Venezuela

Typical loads can include two LD3 containers and nine passengers; four LD3 or seven CO8 containers; two half ton vehicles in the class of the Land-Rover, using load spreaders; and a wide range of bulky cargo. The cabin is suitable for the installation of specialist role equipment and, for example, lends itself readily to onboard sorting of letters and small packages. Roller conveyor systems, including pallet locks which pick up on the aircraft's standard seat rails, are available optionally (standard on the C-23A).

The prototype of the Sherpa was flown for the first time on 23 December 1982. In March 1984 the US Air Force ordered 18 Sherpas for use by the 10th Military Airlift Squadron of Military Airlift Command in the EDSA (European Distribution System Aircraft) role. The fleet is based at Zweibrücken in West Germany, for the transport of high priority spares between more than 20 peacetime US Air Force bases in Europe. The initial contract included ten years' logistic support and servicing. In addition, the US Air Force took options on a further 48 aircraft, which were extended in November 1986 for a further four years.

The first Sherpa, designated C-23A in the EDSA role, made its first flight on 6 August 1984; with the second aircraft, it was delivered in November 1984. The remaining 16 C-23As were delivered by 6 December 1985. A civil Sherpa has been delivered to Venezuela to support hydro-electric power development schemes.

TYPE: Twin-turboprop freight/utility aircraft.

AIRFRAME AND POWER PLANT: As described for Shorts 330-200 except for constant width rear fuselage with hydraulically actuated rear loading ramp/door.

ACCOMMODATION: Crew of two on flight deck, plus flight mechanic. Dual controls standard. Flight deck air-conditioned. Main cabin air-conditioning optional. Baggage compartment in nose (1.27 m^3; 45 cu ft) with external access. Passenger door at rear of cabin on port side. Cargo door at front of cabin on port side. Hydraulically actuated full width rear loading ramp/door. In an all-cargo configuration the cabin can accommodate up to seven CO8 or four LD3 containers. Cabin floor is flat throughout its length and is designed to support 181 kg (400 lb) per foot run at 610.3 kg/m^2 (125 lb/sq ft). The locally reinforced centre cabin area is able to carry 272 kg (600 lb) per foot run at 732.4 kg/m^2 (150 lb/sq ft). A further 272 kg (600 lb) total load can be stowed on the ramp/door. Seat rails can be used as cargo lashing points. Freight loading is facilitated by the low-level cabin floor.

AVIONICS AND EQUIPMENT: Avionics on the C-23As for the US Air Force include single UHF and HF radios, dual VHF-AM/FM, two flight directors, dual VOR/ILS, a Litton LTN-96 ring laser gyro inertial navigation system, Tacan, dual ADF, flight data recorder, cockpit voice recorder, IFF transponder, GPWS, radar altimeter, and a Collins RNS-300 colour weather radar with terrain mapping.

DIMENSIONS, EXTERNAL: As for 330-200 plus:
Rear loading door: Height 1.98 m (6 ft 6 in)
Width 1.98 m (6 ft 6 in)

DIMENSIONS, INTERNAL:
Cabin: Max length 9.09 m (29 ft 10 in)
Max width 1.98 m (6 ft 6 in)
Max height 1.98 m (6 ft 6 in)
Volume (all-cargo) 35.68 m^3 (1,260 cu ft)
Baggage compartment (nose) 1.27 m^3 (45 cu ft)

WEIGHTS AND LOADINGS: As for 330-200, except:
Max payload 3,175 kg (7,000 lb)

PERFORMANCE (at max T-O weight, ISA, except where indicated):
Max cruising speed at AUW of 9,525 kg (21,000 lb) at 3,050 m (10,000 ft) 190 knots (352 km/h; 218 mph)
Econ cruising speed at AUW of 9,525 kg (21,000 lb) at 3,050 m (10,000 ft)
157 knots (291 km/h; 181 mph)
Max rate of climb at S/L 360 m (1,180 ft)/min
Service ceiling, one engine out, AUW of 9,072 kg (20,000 lb) 3,930 m (12,900 ft)
T-O distance (FAR Pt 25 and BCAR Gp A):
ISA 1,042 m (3,420 ft)
ISA + 15°C 1,295 m (4,250 ft)
Landing distance at max landing weight:
BCAR: normal field 1,225 m (4,020 ft)
short field 960 m (3,150 ft)
FAR 1,113 m (3,650 ft)
Range with max fuel, reserves for 45 min hold and 43 nm (80 km; 50 mile) diversion:
with 3,175 kg (7,000 lb) payload
195 nm (362 km; 225 miles)
with 2,268 kg (5,000 lb) payload
669 nm (1,239 km; 770 miles)

SHORTS 360-300

On 10 July 1980, Shorts released first details of the Model 360 'stretched' development of the Model 330, seating six more passengers in a lengthened fuselage and having strengthened outer wing panels and bracing struts, and a new tail unit, as well as more powerful and more fuel-efficient engines.

Designed specifically for short haul airline operation, over typical commuter average stage lengths of about 120 nm (222 km; 138 miles), the Shorts 360 retains the basic configuration of the Model 330, the major external differences being the lengthened fuselage (a 0.91 m; 3 ft plug is inserted forward of the wings) and the introduction of a sweptback single fin and rudder instead of the latter's twin assembly. Power plant is a higher rated version of the proven PT6A turboprop.

Pressurisation was considered unnecessary in view of the short stage lengths over which the aircraft would operate, and this enables the Shorts 360 to retain the same 'walkabout' headroom, square section wide-bodied interior, seating comfort, air-conditioning and other amenities as its predecessor. The new rear fuselage/tail configuration is designed to reduce drag, improve fuel efficiency, and provide even greater baggage capacity. Considerable emphasis is placed on the 360's ability to provide more than 0.20 m^3 (7 cu ft) of baggage space for each of its 36 passengers.

The prototype (G-ROOM) made its first flight on 1 June 1981, some six months ahead of schedule, powered initially by PT6A-45 engines. The PT6A-65R power plant which had been selected for production aircraft was installed subsequently, and CAA certification was obtained on 3 September 1982. FAA certification, to FAR Pt 25 and Pt 36, followed in early November 1982. The first production 360 made its first flight on 19 August 1982, and entered commercial service with Suburban Airlines of Pennsylvania on 1 December 1982.

From November 1985, manufacture turned to the Shorts 360 Advanced, which was powered by two 1,062 kW (1,424 shp) PT6A-65AR turboprops. This has been superseded by the current variant, the **Shorts 360-300**.

Several enhancements are featured by the Series 300, including six-blade propellers with synchrophasing, new cambered wing lift struts, and engine nacelles with low-drag exhaust stubs. New lightweight seats offer improved passenger comfort and reduced maintenance. The improved power plant provides an increase in maximum cruising speed and substantially improved weight/altitude/temperature limits, giving better 'hot and high' performance and an improved en-route climb performance, and permitting an increased maximum take-off weight.

Optional extras include a Category II autopilot, reclining seats, a wet sink facility in the galley, a supplementary ground air-conditioning system and protective liners for freight operations.

The first two Shorts 360-300 airliners, accepted by Philippine Airlines on 18 March 1987, represented part of an order for four being supplied under operating leases from the Shannon based GPA Jetprop company. In October 1987, Capital Airlines of the UK began operations with the first Shorts 360-300 to be certificated for the carriage of 39 passengers.

By 9 May 1988 orders and options for all versions of the

Shorts 360-300 commuter transport (39-seat modification) for Capital Airlines of Leeds/Bradford

Shorts 360 totalled 150, of which 138 had been delivered.

TYPE: Twin-turboprop commuter transport.

WINGS: Generally as for Shorts 330-200.

FUSELAGE: As Shorts 330-200, but lengthened by insertion of 0.91 m (3 ft) plug forward of wings. Rear fuselage modified to cater for redesigned tail unit.

TAIL UNIT: Cantilever all-metal two-spar structure, with single sweptback fin and rudder and constant chord non-swept tailplane. Trim tabs in each elevator. Heavy-duty floor panels for freight handling in Series 300.

LANDING GEAR: Similar to Shorts 330-200, but of Dowty Rotol design with Dunlop tyres. Mainwheel tyres size 37 × 11.75-16, pressure 5.38 bars (78 lb/sq in). Maxaret anti-skid units standard.

POWER PLANT: Two 1,062 kW (1,424 shp) Pratt & Whitney Canada PT6A-67R turboprops, each driving a Hartzell advanced technology six-blade constant-speed fully-feathering propeller with spinner. New engine nacelles with low-drag exhaust stubs on Series 300. Fuel capacity 2,182 litres (576 US gallons; 480 Imp gallons).

ACCOMMODATION: Crew of two on flight deck, plus cabin attendant. Dual controls standard. Main cabin accommodation similar to Shorts 330-200, but seating 36 passengers in 12 rows of three (optionally, 39 passengers). Standard ground and in-flight air conditioning. Large overhead baggage lockers. Baggage compartments in nose and to rear of cabin, each with external access, giving equivalent of almost 0.17 m³ (6 cu ft) of baggage space per passenger (0.20 m³; 7.2 cu ft per passenger if locker space is included). Self-contained passenger stairs.

SYSTEMS: Generally as for Shorts 330-200 except for electrical system, which has Lear Siegler 28V 300A DC starter/generators and three 400VA single-phase static inverters for AC power. Full de-icing and anti-icing systems standard.

AVIONICS: From Collins Pro Line II range, including dual FDS-65 flight director systems, dual VHF-21A com, dual VIR-32 VHF nav, dual DME-42, dual TDR-90 transponders, dual RMI-36, ADF-60A, dual MCS-65 magnetic compasses, and WXR-220 colour weather radar, plus Sundstrand Mk II GPWS, Honeywell YG7500 radar altimeter, Fairchild A100A voice recorder and Plessey PV1584G data recorder. Options include Collins HF-230 HF com, APS-65 Cat II autopilot and second ADF.

DIMENSIONS, EXTERNAL: As for Shorts 330-200 except:

Wing span	22.80 m (74 ft 9½ in)
Length overall	21.58 m (70 ft 9⅝ in)
Height overall	7.27 m (23 ft 10¼ in)
Tailplane span	7.19 m (23 ft 7 in)
Wheelbase	7.06 m (23 ft 2 in)
Propeller diameter	2.74 m (9 ft 0 in)
Propeller ground clearance	1.78 m (5 ft 10 in)
Rear door sill height	0.98 m (3 ft 2¼ in)

DIMENSIONS, INTERNAL:

Cabin: Length	11.02 m (36 ft 2 in)
Max width	1.93 m (6 ft 4 in)
Max height	1.93 m (6 ft 4 in)
Passenger compartment volume	41.06 m³ (1,450 cu ft)
Baggage compartment volume:	
forward	1.27 m³ (45 cu ft)
rear	4.81 m³ (170 cu ft)
lockers	1.47 m³ (52 cu ft)

AREAS: As for Shorts 330-200 except:

Wing area	42.18 m² (454 sq ft)
Vertical tail surfaces (total)	8.49 m² (91.4 sq ft)
Horizontal tail surfaces (total)	9.85 m² (106.0 sq ft)

WEIGHTS:

Typical operating weight empty	7,870 kg (17,350 lb)
Max payload:	
36 passengers and baggage	3,184 kg (7,020 lb)
cargo	3,765 kg (8,300 lb)

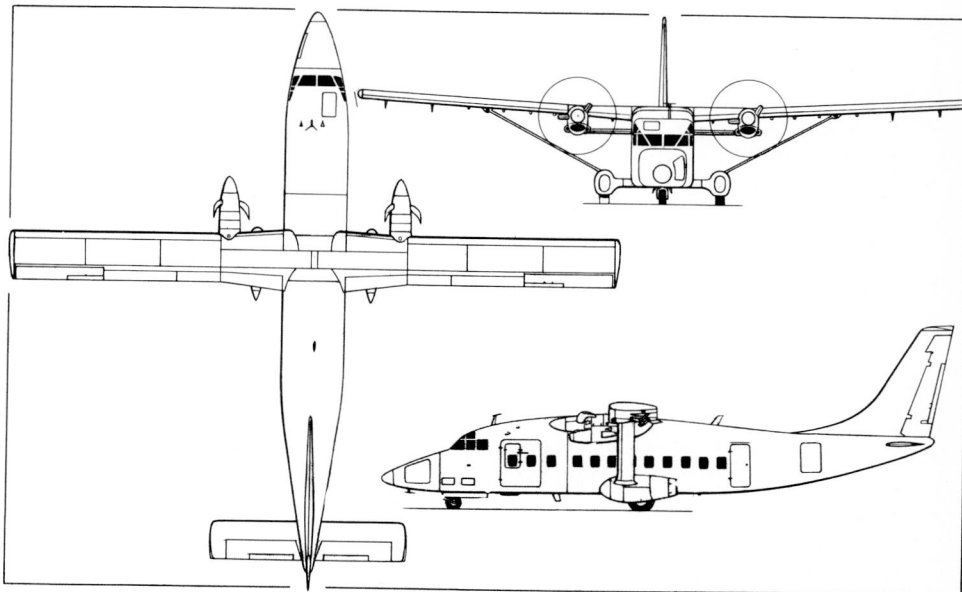

Shorts 360-300 commuter transport (two P&WC PT6A-67R turboprop engines) *(Pilot Press)*

Max fuel load	1,741 kg (3,840 lb)
Max T-O weight	12,292 kg (27,100 lb)
Max ramp weight	12,337 kg (27,200 lb)
Max landing weight	12,020 kg (26,500 lb)

PERFORMANCE (to FAR Pt 25: at max T-O weight except where indicated):

Cruising speed at 3,050 m (10,000 ft) and 11,340 kg (25,000 lb) aircraft weight

	216 knots (400 km/h; 249 mph)
Max rate of climb at S/L: ISA	290 m (952 ft)/min
ISA +15°C	282 m (925 ft)/min
Single-engine ceiling	2,667 m (8,750 ft)
Balanced T-O field length: ISA	1,305 m (4,280 ft)
ISA +15°C	1,402 m (4,600 ft)

Landing distance at max landing weight:

ISA	1,220 m (4,000 ft)
Runway LCN	14.1

Range at 3,050 m (10,000 ft), cruising at 216 knots (400 km/h; 249 mph), 50 nm (93 km; 57 mile) diversion, 45 min hold, 54 kg (119 lb) fuel allowance, 36 passengers with baggage at 86 kg (190 lb) each:

402 nm (745 km; 463 miles)

Range as above at 182 knots (337 km/h; 210 mph) with 31 passengers with baggage

636 nm (1,178 km; 732 miles)

SHORTS 360-300F

Capitalising on the 360's low noise levels (well within FAR Pt 36 and ICAO Annex 16), Shorts is promoting an all-freight adaptation of the 360-300 directed towards the overnight parcels market. The 360-300F is windowless apart from normal cockpit glazing and two transparencies in the forward freight door. Payload is up to 4,536 kg (10,000 lb), and with the optional addition of a second freight door in place of the rear passenger door, five LD3 containers may be accommodated. An optional integrated handling system is available in the form of a roller conveyor with pallet locks; directional transfer mat; side guidance rails; and a forward cargo restraint barrier.

Details as Shorts 360-300 except:

DIMENSIONS, INTERNAL:

Cabin: Width at floor level	1.88 m (6 ft 2 in)
Height	1.98 m (6 ft 6 in)

WEIGHT:

Max payload: cargo	4,536 kg (10,000 lb)

SHORTS SC.7 SKYVAN Srs 3M

Design of the SC.7 Skyvan was started as a private venture in 1959, and the first prototype (G-ASCN) flew for the first time on 17 January 1963, with Continental GTSIO-520 piston engines. It was re-engined with 388 kW (520 shp) Astazou II turboprops and first flew in its new form on 2 October 1963. The change to Garrett TPE331 turboprops was made on the Skyvan Series 3 in 1967.

Orders for all versions of the Skyvan totalled 150. The most recent delivery was of an aircraft to the Sharjah Amiri Guard Air Wing in February 1986, although further Skyvans are available to order. A full description of the civil Skyvan Series 3 and military Series 3M can be found in the 1986-87 *Jane's*. The Series 3M-200 differs in being cleared for non-civil operation at a higher max T-O weight. An abbreviated entry follows:

TYPE: STOL utility light transport.

POWER PLANT: Two 533 kW (715 shp) Garrett TPE331-2-201A turboprops, each driving a Hartzell HC-B3TN-5/T10282H three-blade variable-pitch propeller. Fuel in four tanks in pairs on top of fuselage between wingroots, each pair consisting of one tank of 182 litres (48 US gallons; 40 Imp gallons) capacity and one of 484 litres (128 US gallons; 106.5 Imp gallons) capacity. Total fuel capacity of 1,332 litres (352 US gallons; 293 Imp gallons). Provision for increase in total fuel capacity to 1,773 litres (468 US gallons; 390 Imp gallons) by installing four specially designed tanks in spaces between fuselage frames on each side, beneath main fuel tank. Oil capacity 7.73 litres (2.04 US gallons; 1.7 Imp gallons).

ACCOMMODATION: Crew of one, with provision for two. Srs 3M can accommodate 22 equipped troops; 16 paratroops and a dispatcher; 12 stretcher cases and two medical attendants; or 2,358 kg (5,200 lb) of freight. Full-width rear loading door can be opened in flight to permit the parachuting of loads up to 1.37 m (4 ft 6 in) in height. Cabin unpressurised.

EQUIPMENT: Port side blister window for an air dispatcher; two anchor cables for parachute static lines; a guard rail beneath the tail to prevent control surface fouling by the static lines; inward facing paratroop seats with safety nets; parachute signal light; mounts for NATO stretchers; and roller conveyors for easy loading and paradropping of pallet mounted supplies.

DIMENSIONS, EXTERNAL:
Wing span	19.79 m (64 ft 11 in)
Wing chord (constant)	1.78 m (5 ft 10 in)
Wing aspect ratio	11.0
Length overall: without radome	12.21 m (40 ft 1 in)
with radome	12.60 m (41 ft 4 in)
Height overall	4.60 m (15 ft 1 in)
Tailplane span	5.28 m (17 ft 4 in)
Wheel track	4.21 m (13 ft 10 in)
Wheelbase	4.52 m (14 ft 10 in)
Propeller diameter	2.59 m (8 ft 6 in)
Propeller ground clearance	1.52 m (5 ft 0 in)
Crew and passenger doors (fwd, port and stbd):	
Height	1.52 m (5 ft 0 in)
Width	0.51 m (1 ft 8 in)
Height to sill	1.14 m (3 ft 9 in)
Rear loading door: Height	1.78 m (5 ft 10 in)
Width	1.98 m (6 ft 6 in)
Height to sill	0.74 m (2 ft 5 in)

DIMENSIONS, INTERNAL:
Cabin, excl flight deck: Length	5.67 m (18 ft 7 in)
Max width	1.98 m (6 ft 6 in)
Max height	1.98 m (6 ft 6 in)
Floor area	11.15 m² (120 sq ft)
Volume	22.09 m³ (780 cu ft)

WEIGHTS AND LOADINGS (with 1,332 litres; 352 US gallons; 293 Imp gallons of fuel):
Basic operating weight: 3M	3,356 kg (7,400 lb)
3M-200, equipped	3,768 kg (8,307 lb)
Typical operating weight as freighter	3,456 kg (7,620 lb)
Typical operating weight:	
with troops	3,778 kg (8,330 lb)
3M-200 paratroop transport	3,943 kg (8,692 lb)
Max payload for normal T-O weight	2,358 kg (5,200 lb)
Max payload for overload T-O weight	2,721 kg (6,000 lb)
Max fuel weights: standard tanks	1,052 kg (2,320 lb)
with additional tanks	1,415 kg (3,120 lb)
Max T-O weight: normal	6,214 kg (13,700 lb)
3M, overload	6,577 kg (14,500 lb)
3M-200	6,804 kg (15,000 lb)
Max landing weight: 3M	6,123 kg (13,500 lb)
3M-200	6,577 kg (14,500 lb)
Max wing loading: 3M	179.1 kg/m² (36.7 lb/sq ft)
3M-200	196.3 kg/m² (40.2 lb/sq ft)
Max power loading: 3M	6.17 kg/kW (9.58 lb/shp)
3M-200	6.38 kg/kW (10.49 lb/shp)

PERFORMANCE (at max T-O weight, except where noted, with 1,332 litres; 352 US gallons; 293 Imp gallons of fuel):
Never-exceed speed	217 knots (402 km/h; 250 mph) EAS
Max cruising speed at 3,050 m (10,000 ft):	
3M at max continuous power	175 knots (324 km/h; 202 mph)
3M-200 at max continuous power at AUW of 6,577 kg (14,500 lb)	174 knots (322 km/h; 200 mph)
3M at cruise power	168 knots (311 km/h; 193 mph)
3M-200 at cruise power at AUW of 6,577 kg (14,500 lb)	166 knots (308 km/h; 191 mph)
Econ cruising speed at 3,050 m (10,000 ft):	
3M	150 knots (278 km/h; 173 mph)
3M-200 at AUW of 6,577 kg (14,500 lb)	150 knots (278 km/h; 173 mph)
Stalling speed, flaps down	62 knots (115 km/h; 71 mph) EAS
Max rate of climb at S/L	466 m (1,530 ft)/min
Service ceiling (30.5 m; 100 ft/min climb)	6,705 m (22,000 ft)
Service ceiling, one engine out (15 m; 50 ft/min climb)	2,895 m (9,500 ft)
Min ground turning radius	3.76 m (12 ft 4 in)

Runway LCN at AUW of 5,670 kg (12,500 lb):
standard tyres	3.5
low pressure tyres	3.0
T-O run, STOL, unfactored: 3M	238 m (780 ft)
3M-200	290 m (950 ft)
T-O to 15 m (50 ft), STOL, unfactored:	
3M	384 m (1,260 ft)
3M-200	488 m (1,600 ft)
Landing from 15 m (50 ft), at max landing weight:	
3M (STOL, unfactored)	425 m (1,395 ft)
3M-200 (STOL, unfactored)	457 m (1,500 ft)
Landing run, at max landing weight:	
3M (STOL, unfactored)	212 m (695 ft)
Range at long-range cruising speed, 45 min reserves	580 nm (1,075 km; 670 miles)

Range at long-range cruising speed, 45 min reserves:
3M (typical freighter) with 2,268 kg (5,000 lb) payload,

Shorts Skyvan operated by the Amiri Guard of Sharjah

ISA	208 nm (386 km; 240 miles)
3M-200 with 1,815 kg (4,000 lb) payload, ISA + 10°C	540 nm (1,000 km; 621 miles)

SHORTS FJX

In March 1988, Shorts released details of its projected FJX (Fan-Jet Experimental) 44-seat twin-turbofan regional airliner, and began seeking a risk-sharing manufacturing partner prior to launching full scale development, with the target of 1993-94 service entry. The FJX is intended to break into a sector of the market currently dominated by turboprop aircraft and will employ a pair of small turbofans in the 24.91 kN (5,600 lb st) class.

DIMENSIONS, EXTERNAL:
Wing span	22.49 m (73 ft 9⅝ in)
Length overall	24.96 m (81 ft 10¾ in)
Height overall	7.89 m (25 ft 10¾ in)

WEIGHTS:
Basic operating weight, empty	11,428 kg (25,195 lb)
Max T-O weight	18,325 kg (40,400 lb)

PERFORMANCE (estimated):
Max cruising speed	428 knots (793 km/h; 493 mph)
Range at long-range cruising speed, with reserves	973 nm (1,803 km; 1,120 miles)

SHORTS S312 TUCANO
RAF designation: Tucano T. Mk 1

Under the terms of a co-operation agreement between Shorts and Embraer of Brazil, announced in May 1984, Shorts undertook to develop from the basic EMB-312 Tucano (see Embraer entry in Brazilian section) a new version of the turboprop trainer that would meet or exceed all requirements of the UK Ministry of Defence Air Staff Target 412 for a Jet Provost replacement.

The UK Government announced on 21 March 1985 that the Shorts Tucano had been selected for this role. The decision ended a competition that had lasted two years. The decisive consideration, according to the UK Secretary of State for Defence, was the "cost factor", the Shorts offer being the least expensive "by a clear margin". Initially, 130 Tucanos are being built for the Royal Air Force.

To exceed Air Staff Target 412, the Shorts Tucano embodies significant modifications compared with the basic EMB-312. These include a changed power plant to improve speed, particularly at low altitude, and provide an increased rate of climb; a ventral airbrake to control speed during descent; structural strengthening for increased manoeuvre loads and fatigue life; a new cockpit layout to meet RAF requirements; and wide use of UK equipment. For export sales purposes, the design incorporates four wing strong points to provide armament training and light attack capability. The Shorts Tucano has a safe design fatigue life of 12,000 hours.

The first flight of a Tucano with a Garrett engine (PP-ZTC), as chosen for the RAF version, took place in Brazil on 14 February 1986. After completing 14.35 hours of test flying there, it was airfreighted to the UK, reassembled in Belfast, and made its first flight with a British test flight serial (G-14-007, later G-BTUC) on 11 April 1986. During that flight it demonstrated its ability to fly at a sea level speed of 268 knots (496 km/h; 308 mph), as required by the RAF. The first Shorts-built production Tucano T. Mk 1 (ZF135) flew for the first time on 30 December 1986, although the formal rollout ceremony did not take place until 20 January 1987. It was delivered to the Aeroplane & Armament Experimental Establishment at Boscombe Down on 26 June 1987, followed on 1 October 1987 by ZF136, both being engaged on provisional type certification trials. Deliveries to the RAF began with ZF138 on 16 June 1988.

Following delivery of up to six Tucanos to the Central Flying School at Scampton, student training on the aircraft was due to begin at No. 7 Flying Training School, Church Fenton, late in 1988. Subsequent operators will be No. 1 FTS at Linton-on-Ouse and the RAF College, Cranwell. The baseline Tucano course will be 146 h 30 min (1 h less than the current Jet Provost syllabus), for students who have received prior piston-engined training of 63 hours on Chipmunks. They will then progress to Hawks for advanced training and weapons instruction; or Jetstreams for multi-engined training. Estimates indicate that the Tucano will have direct operating costs only 49% of those of the Jet

Artist's impression of the projected Shorts FJX regional airliner

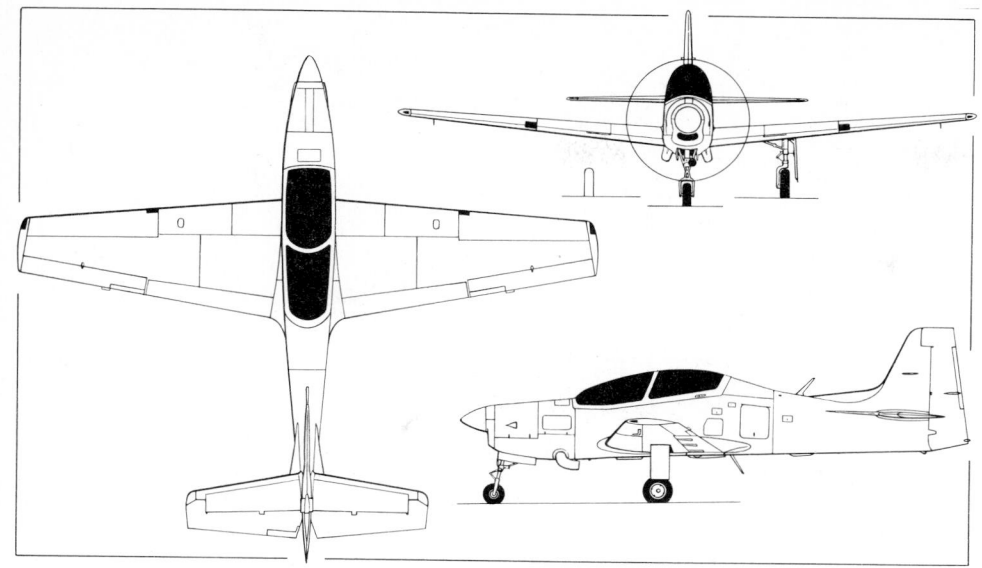

Shorts S312 Tucano basic trainer (Garrett TPE331-12B turboprop) *(Pilot Press)*

The first production Shorts S312 Tucano, under test from Belfast

climates. Single hydraulic system, pressure 207 bars (3,000 lb/sq in), for landing gear extension and retraction, and airbrake. Accumulator to lower landing gear in emergency. DC electrical power provided by a 28V 200A starter/generator and two 24Ah alkaline batteries. Static inverter for 115V and 26V AC power at 400Hz. Normalair-Garrett oxygen system supplied from a single bottle, capacity 2,250 litres (80 cu ft). Emergency oxygen bottle, capacity 70 litres (2.5 cu ft), mounted on each ejection seat. Engine air intake de-iced by engine bleed air; propeller, pitot head, static vents, and stall warning system de-iced electrically. Optional windscreen anti-icing.

AVIONICS AND EQUIPMENT: Standard avionics include VHF/UHF/audio by Marconi, Plessey and Dowty; gyromagnetic compass, VOR/ILS/marker beacon receiver, GEC Avionics AD2780 Tacan, and Narco transponder.

ARMAMENT: Optional provision on export variant for up to 454 kg (1,000 lb) of weapons distributed on four underwing pylons. Details as for Embraer Tucano.

DIMENSIONS, EXTERNAL:

Wing span	11.28 m (37 ft 0 in)
Propeller diameter	2.39 m (7 ft 10 in)
Propeller ground clearance	0.32 m (12.6 in)

AREAS:

Wings, gross	19.33 m² (208.08 sq ft)
Fin, excl dorsal fin	2.08 m² (22.40 sq ft)
Rudder, incl tab	1.46 m² (15.70 sq ft)
Tailplane, incl fillets	4.57 m² (49.20 sq ft)

WEIGHTS AND LOADINGS (A, aerobatic configuration; B, full weapons configuration):

Basic weight empty: A	2,017 kg (4,447 lb)
Max internal fuel: A, B	555 kg (1,223 lb)
Max ramp weight: A	2,720 kg (5,997 lb)
B	3,295 kg (7,264 lb)
Max T-O weight: A	2,700 kg (5,952 lb)
B	3,275 kg (7,220 lb)
Max landing weight: A	2,700 kg (5,952 lb)
B	2,900 kg (6,393 lb)
Max zero-fuel weight: A	2,028 kg (4,471 lb)
Max wing loading: A	139.7 kg/m² (28.61 lb/sq ft)
Max power loading: A	3.29 kg/kW (5.41 lb/shp)

PERFORMANCE (at max T-O weight of 2,700 kg; 5,952 lb, except where indicated):

Never-exceed speed	280 knots (518 km/h; 322 mph) EAS
Max level and cruising speed at 3,050-4,575 m (10,000-15,000 ft)	274 knots (507 km/h; 315 mph)
Econ cruising speed at 6,100 m (20,000 ft)	220 knots (407 km/h; 253 mph)
Stalling speed, power off:	
flaps and landing gear down	69 knots (128 km/h; 80 mph) EAS
flaps and landing gear up	75 knots (139 km/h; 87 mph) EAS
Max rate of climb at S/L	1,070 m (3,510 ft)/min
Service ceiling	10,365 m (34,000 ft)
T-O run	329 m (1,080 ft)
T-O to 15 m (50 ft)	524 m (1,720 ft)
Landing from 15 m (50 ft) at 2,600 kg (5,732 lb)	573 m (1,880 ft)
Landing run	302 m (990 ft)
Radius of action with 454 kg (1,000 lb) of weapons at T-O weight of 3,275 kg (7,220 lb)	430 nm (797 km; 495 miles)
Range at 7,620 m (25,000 ft) with max fuel, 30 min reserves	900 nm (1,665 km; 1,035 miles)
Endurance at econ cruising speed at 7,620 m (25,000 ft), 30 min reserves	5 h 12 min
g limits:	+7/–3.6 aerobatic
	+4.4/–2.2 full weapons

Provost. Shorts will be responsible for logistic supplies at RAF stations operating the Tucano.

Early in 1988, Kenya was reportedly interested in obtaining between ten and 20 Tucanos from Shorts.

The main description of the Tucano can be found under the Embraer heading in the Brazilian section. The Shorts Tucano T. Mk 1 for the RAF differs in the following respects:

WINGS: Incidence 1° 13′. Aluminium alloy two-spar torsion box structure of 7075-T73511 and 7075-T76 and 2024-T3 sheet. Leading-edge strengthened for bird strike protection. Electrically actuated trim tab in, and small ground adjustable tab on, each aileron.

FUSELAGE: Hydraulically actuated ventral airbrake.

LANDING GEAR: Nosewheel unit supplied by Fairey Hydraulics. Dunlop wheels and tyres, size 22 × 6.75-10 on

mainwheels, 5.00-5 on nosewheel. Dunlop hydraulic single-disc brakes on mainwheels.

POWER PLANT: One 820 kW (1,100 shp) Garrett TPE331-12B turboprop, driving a Hartzell four-blade constant-speed fully-feathering reversible-pitch propeller with spinner. Two integral fuel tanks in each wing, total capacity 724 litres (191 US gallons; 159 Imp gallons). Gravity refuelling point in each wing upper surface. Provision for two external tanks with total capacity of 660 litres (174 US gallons; 145 Imp gallons). Oil capacity 4.25 litres (1.13 US gallons; 0.94 Imp gallon).

ACCOMMODATION: Instructor and pupil in tandem, on Martin-Baker Mk 8LCP lightweight ejection seats.

SYSTEMS: Cockpit air-conditioning by engine bleed air plus recirculated cockpit air through a regenerative turbofan system. Alternative freon system available for hot

---

SLINGSBY
SLINGSBY AVIATION LIMITED

Ings Lane, Kirkbymoorside, North Yorkshire YO6 6EZ
Telephone: 0751 32474
Telex: 57597 SLINAV G
Fax: 0751 31173
CHIEF EXECUTIVE:
James S. Tucker, BSc (Eng), CEng, MRAeS
CHIEF DESIGNER: B. Mellers
EXPORT SALES MANAGER AND PRESS CONTACT:
J. Dignan
HOME SALES MANAGER AND PRESS CONTACT:
Roger C. Bull, BSc (Eng)

Slingsby was initially recognised primarily as a manufacturer of sailplanes. This aspect of the company's activities has ended and Slingsby is concentrating on development and production of the T67 two-seat aerobatic trainer aircraft. The company specialises in the application of modern composite materials, and also manufactures hovercraft and other marine products. Slingsby is responsible for manufacture of the gondola, propulsion ducts, flying control surfaces, nosecone and battens of the Airship Industries Skyship 600 airships, and also for the installation of electrics and avionics. MoD work includes major overhaul of Venture powered gliders and re-covering and painting of 36 Chipmunks. In early 1988 its covered

works area was approx 9,290 m² (100,000 sq ft) and it had a workforce of 210.

SLINGSBY T67

The original T67A was a licence built version of the Fournier RF6B light aircraft. Production by Fournier, in France, was limited to 45 RF6B-100s and a single RF6B-120, which flew for the first time on 14 August 1980 and received FAR Pt 23 certification on 7 November 1980. Slingsby built ten T67As (similar to the RF6B-120), of which the first (G-BIOW) flew for the first time on 15 May 1981. This model, which was described in the 1982-83 *Jane's*, has been superseded by new versions, built primarily of GRP instead of wood, including the military T67M Firefly (described separately). To speed the T67M programme, a T67A (G-BJNG) was modified to Firefly 160 standard by installation of a 119 kW (160 hp) engine and constant-speed propeller for tests that included spinning trials at extreme CG limits.

Current versions for civil use are as follows:

T67B. Basic version, of GRP construction, as described in detail. Powered by an 86.5 kW (116 hp) Textron Lycoming O-235-N2A flat-four engine driving a two-blade fixed-pitch propeller with spinner.

T67C. As T67B, but with 119 kW (160 hp) Textron Lycoming engine, metal fixed-pitch propeller, 24V 70A engine driven alternator and 24V 12Ah battery.

T67D. As T67C, but with constant-speed propeller and increased fuel. Certification programme proceeding in Spring 1988.

By February 1988 a total of 55 civil and military T67s had been delivered, with a further 15 in production. Subsequent deliveries included two T67Cs to the Oxford Air Training School, these being converted from T67Bs. The military versions are described separately.

The following details apply to the T67B:

TYPE: Two-seat aerobatic, training and sporting aircraft.

WINGS: Cantilever low-wing monoplane. Wing section NACA 23015 at root, NACA 23013 at tip. Dihedral 3° 30′. Incidence 3°. Wings, Frise ailerons and manually operated plain trailing-edge flaps all of GRP construction.

FUSELAGE: Oval section structure of GRP.

TAIL UNIT: Cantilever structure of GRP. Fixed incidence tailplane. Trim tab in port elevator. Spin strakes forward of tailplane roots.

LANDING GEAR: Non-retractable tricycle type. Oleo-pneumatic shock absorber in each unit. Steerable nosewheel. Mainwheel tyres size 6.00-6, pressure 1.4 bars (20 lb/sq in). Nosewheel tyre size 5.00-5, pressure 2.5 bars (37 lb/sq in). Hydraulic disc brakes. Parking brake. GRP mainwheel fairings optional.

POWER PLANT: One flat-four engine as described in model listings. Fuselage fuel tank, immediately aft of firewall, capacity 114 litres (30 US gallons; 25 Imp gallons). Refuelling point on fuselage upper surface, forward of windscreen. Oil capacity 4 litres (1.06 US gallons; 0.88 Imp gallon). Oil system permits short periods of inverted flight.

ACCOMMODATION: Two seats side by side under one-piece transparent canopy, which swings upward and rearward for access to cockpit. Optional canopy has fixed windscreen, and upward hinged and rearward opening rear section. Dual controls standard. Adjustable rudder pedals. Cockpit heated and ventilated. Baggage space aft of seats.

SYSTEMS: Hydraulic system for brakes only. Vacuum system for blind-flying instrumentation. Electrical power supplied by 12V 60A engine driven alternator and 12V 25Ah battery.

AVIONICS AND EQUIPMENT: Standard equipment includes artificial horizon and directional gyro, with vacuum system and vacuum gauge, electric turn co-ordinator, rate of climb indicator, recording tachometer, stall warning system, clock, outside air temperature gauge, accelerometer; cabin fire extinguisher, heated pitot; instrument, landing, navigation and strobe lights; tiedown rings and towbar. Optional avionics, available to customer requirements, include equipment by Becker, King and Narco, up to full IFR standard.

DIMENSIONS, EXTERNAL:

Wing span	10.59 m (34 ft 9 in)
Wing chord: at root	1.53 m (5 ft 0¼ in)
at tip	0.83 m (2 ft 8¾ in)
Wing aspect ratio	8.88
Length overall	7.32 m (24 ft 0¼ in)
Height overall	2.51 m (8 ft 3 in)
Tailplane span	3.40 m (11 ft 1¾ in)
Wheel track	2.44 m (8 ft 0 in)
Wheelbase	1.50 m (4 ft 11 in)
Propeller diameter	1.83 m (6 ft 0 in)

DIMENSIONS, INTERNAL:

Cabin: Length	2.05 m (6 ft 8¾ in)
Max width	1.08 m (3 ft 6½ in)
Max height	1.08 m (3 ft 6½ in)

AREAS:

Wings, gross	12.63 m² (136.0 sq ft)
Ailerons (total)	1.24 m² (13.35 sq ft)
Trailing-edge flaps (total)	1.74 m² (18.73 sq ft)
Fin	0.80 m² (8.61 sq ft)
Rudder	0.81 m² (8.72 sq ft)
Tailplane	1.65 m² (17.76 sq ft)
Elevators (incl tab)	0.99 m² (10.66 sq ft)

WEIGHTS AND LOADINGS:

Weight empty (basic): T67B	610 kg (1,345 lb)
T67C	630 kg (1,390 lb)
T67D	635 kg (1,400 lb)
Max fuel: T67B, T67C	82 kg (181 lb)
T67D	114 kg (252 lb)
Max baggage: T67B	18 kg (40 lb)
T67C, T67D	30 kg (66 lb)
Max T-O and landing weight: T67B	862 kg (1,900 lb)
T67C, T67D	907 kg (2,000 lb)
Max wing loading: T67B	68.21 kg/m² (13.97 lb/sq ft)
T67C, T67D	71.82 kg/m² (14.71 lb/sq ft)
Max power loading: T67B	9.97 kg/kW (16.38 lb/hp)
T67C, T67D	7.62 kg/kW (12.50 lb/hp)

PERFORMANCE (at max T-O weight):

Never-exceed speed:	
T67B	165 knots (305 km/h; 190 mph)
T67C, T67D	180 knots (333 km/h; 207 mph)
Max level speed at S/L:	
T67B	115 knots (213 km/h; 132 mph)
T67C	135 knots (250 km/h; 155 mph)
T67D	138 knots (256 km/h; 159 mph)
Max cruising speed (75% power) at 2,440 m (8,000 ft):	
T67B	110 knots (204 km/h; 126 mph)
T67C	125 knots (231 km/h; 144 mph)
T67D	128 knots (237 km/h; 147 mph)
Stalling speed, power off, flaps up:	
T67B	55 knots (102 km/h; 64 mph)
Stalling speed, power off, flaps down:	
T67B	46 knots (85 km/h; 53 mph)
T67C, T67D	49 knots (91 km/h; 57 mph)
Max rate of climb at S/L: T67B	201 m (660 ft)/min
T67C	320 m (1,050 ft)/min
T67D	335 m (1,100 ft)/min
Service ceiling: T67B	3,660 m (12,000 ft)
T-O run: T67B	223 m (733 ft)
T67C	201 m (660 ft)
T67D	190 m (623 ft)
T-O to 15 m (50 ft): T67B	537 m (1,760 ft)
T67C	442 m (1,450 ft)
T67D	402 m (1,319 ft)
Landing from 15 m (50 ft): T67B	521 m (1,710 ft)
T67C, T67D	533 m (1,750 ft)
Landing run: T67B	213 m (700 ft)
T67C, T67D	232 m (760 ft)
Range with max fuel (65% power at 2,440 m; 8,000 ft), allowances for T-O and climb, 45 min reserves at 45% power: T67B	451 nm (835 km; 519 miles)
T67C	360 nm (666 km; 414 miles)
T67D	565 nm (1,046 km; 650 miles)
g limits	+6/−3

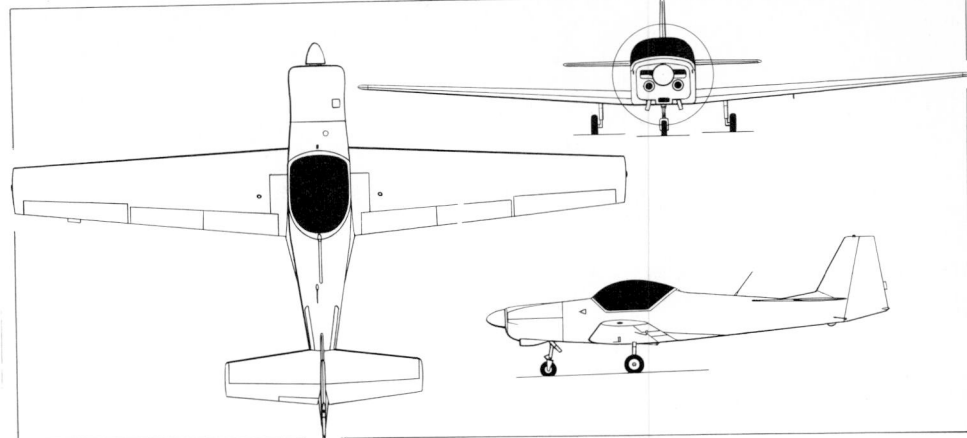

Slingsby T67M Firefly 160 (Textron Lycoming AEIO-320-D1B engine) with original canopy *(Pilot Press)*

SLINGSBY T67M FIREFLY 160

This military basic trainer version of the T67 is based on the T67B of GRP construction. The description of the T67B applies also to the T67M, except as detailed below. A first flight of this version (G-BKAM), known as the Firefly 160, was made on 5 December 1982, and CAA certification was achieved in September 1983.

TYPE: Two-seat military basic trainer.

WINGS, FUSELAGE, TAIL UNIT AND LANDING GEAR: Generally as for T67B.

POWER PLANT: One 119 kW (160 hp) Textron Lycoming AEIO-320-D1B flat-four engine, driving a Hoffmann HO-V72 two-blade constant-speed wooden propeller with spinner. Fuel and oil systems suitable for inverted flight. Fuel tanks in leading-edge of wings, capacity 162 litres (42.6 US gallons; 35.5 Imp gallons). Refuelling point in upper wing surface. Oil capacity 7.7 litres (2.0 US gallons; 1.7 Imp gallons).

ACCOMMODATION AND SYSTEMS: As for T67B, except that current aircraft have new canopy with fixed windscreen and upward hinged and rearward opening rear section. Inertia reel lockable shoulder harness standard, and air-conditioning optional.

AVIONICS AND EQUIPMENT: Avionics to customer requirements. Blind-flying instrumentation standard.

DIMENSIONS AND AREAS: As for T67B

WEIGHTS AND LOADINGS:

Weight empty, equipped	649 kg (1,430 lb)
Max fuel weight	114 kg (252 lb)
Max T-O, aerobatic and landing weight	907 kg (2,000 lb)
Max wing loading	71.82 kg/m² (14.71 lb/sq ft)
Max power loading	7.62 kg/kW (12.5 lb/hp)

PERFORMANCE (at max T-O weight):

Never-exceed speed	180 knots (333 km/h; 207 mph)
Max level speed at S/L	138 knots (256 km/h; 159 mph)
Max cruising speed, 75% power at 2,440 m (8,000 ft)	128 knots (237 km/h; 147 mph)
Stalling speed, power off, flaps down	49 knots (91 km/h; 57 mph)
Max rate of climb at S/L	335 m (1,100 ft)/min
Service ceiling	4,575 m (15,000 ft)
T-O run	190 m (623 ft)
T-O to 15 m (50 ft)	402 m (1,319 ft)
Landing from 15 m (50 ft)	533 m (1,750 ft)
Landing run	232 m (760 ft)
Range with max fuel at 75% power, allowances for T-O, climb and 45 min reserves at 45% power	529 nm (980 km; 608 miles)
g limits at 884 kg (1,950 lb) AUW	+6/−3

SLINGSBY T67M200 FIREFLY

A development of the T67M, this version has a 149 kW (200 hp) Textron Lycoming AEIO-360-A1E engine, driving a Hoffmann HO-V123 three-blade variable-pitch propeller. The description and dimensions of the T67M apply also to the T67M200; weight and performance data are given below. This version flew for the first time on 16 May 1985. First customer was the Turkish Aviation Institute at Ankara, to which five aircraft were delivered in 1985, followed by five more in 1988. Dutch operator King Air

Slingsby T67M Firefly 200 two-seat military basic trainer of the Royal Hong Kong Auxiliary Air Force

Slingsby T67M200 Firefly operated by King Air of Seppe, Netherlands

flies four T67Ms as screening trainers for prospective pilots of the RNethAF.

WEIGHTS AND LOADINGS:

Weight empty	685 kg (1,510 lb)
Max fuel	114 kg (252 lb)
Max baggage	30 kg (66 lb)
Max T-O and landing weight	975 kg (2,150 lb)
Max wing loading	77.20 kg/m² (15.81 lb/sq ft)
Max power loading	6.54 kg/kW (10.75 lb/hp)

PERFORMANCE:

Never-exceed speed	180 knots (333 km/h; 207 mph)
Max level speed at S/L	140 knots (259 km/h; 161 mph)
Max cruising speed (75% power, at 2,440 m; 8,000 ft)	133 knots (246 km/h; 153 mph)
Stalling speed, power off, flaps down	51 knots (95 km/h; 59 mph)
Max rate of climb at S/L	350 m (1,150 ft)/min
T-O run	168 m (550 ft)

T-O to 15 m (50 ft)	345 m (1,130 ft)
Landing from 15 m (50 ft)	549 m (1,800 ft)
Landing run	247 m (810 ft)
Range with max fuel (65% power at 2,440 m; 8,000 ft), allowances for T-O and climb, 45 min reserves at 45% power	500 nm (926 km; 575 miles)
g limits	+6/−3

TRAGO MILLS

TRAGO MILLS LTD (Aircraft Division)

Treswithick Farm, Cardinham, Bodmin, Cornwall PL30 4BU

Telephone: 020 882 485

CHIEF DESIGNER: Sydney A. Holloway

TEST PILOT AND PRESS CONTACT:

Air Vice-Marshal Geoffrey Cairns

Trago Mills has built the prototype of Mr Sydney Holloway's SAH-1 two-seat light aircraft. The company is CAA approved for light aircraft design, development, manufacture and testing, and has retained as design consultant Mr Frank H. Robertson, who has held engineering and senior design appointments with Vought Corporation in the USA, and with Miles, Saunders-Roe and Shorts in the UK.

TRAGO MILLS SAH-1

Design of the SAH-1 started in October 1977, and construction of a prototype began in January 1978. Both design and construction are to full CAA and FAR Pt 23 standards. The first flight of the prototype (G-SAHI) was made on 23 August 1983 and a full Certificate of Airworthiness, Public Transport Category, was obtained on 12 December 1985.

Early in 1988, negotiations were underway with the Hungarian Ministry of Agriculture and Fishing Air Service for Hungarian investment to permit full-scale production to be launched. Levels of industrial involvement up to the manufacture of 'green' aircraft in Hungary have been considered. Pending a decision, Trago Mills was proceeding at reduced tempo on an initial batch of five SAH-1s.

In addition to the basic SAH-1, with O-235 engine, a more powerful version is expected to be made available, with a 119 kW (160 hp) Textron Lycoming AEIO-320-DB flat-four engine driving a constant-speed propeller. Estimated weights and performance for this model are included in the following specification of the basic version:

TYPE: Two-seat fully aerobatic light aircraft.

WINGS: Cantilever low-wing monoplane. Wing section NACA 2413.6 (constant). Dihedral 5° from roots. Incidence 3° at root, 1° at tip. Tapered, non-swept aluminium alloy wings, with L65 spar booms and L72 sheet skins, stabilised with PVC foam. Trailing-edge single-slotted flaps and slotted ailerons of similar construction.

FUSELAGE: Aluminium alloy stressed skin structure, with radiused corners, incorporating centre-section spars.

TAIL UNIT: Aluminium alloy cantilever structure, stabilised with PVC foam. Constant chord tailplane, attached to fuselage, with horn balanced elevators; full span trim tab in starboard elevator. Sweptback fin and horn balanced rudder. Ventral fin.

LANDING GEAR: Non-retractable tricycle type, with single wheel on each unit. Oleo-pneumatic shock absorber in nosewheel leg; spring steel main legs. Cleveland mainwheels and tyres size 6.00-6, pressure 1.24 bars (18.0 lb/sq in). Nosewheel and tyre size 5.00-5, pressure 1.03 bars (15 lb/sq in). Cleveland hydraulic brakes.

POWER PLANT: One 88 kW (118 hp) Textron Lycoming O-235-L2A flat-four engine, driving a two-blade fixed-pitch propeller with spinner. Integral fuel tank in each wing leading-edge, total capacity 114 litres (30 US gallons; 25 Imp gallons). Refuelling point in upper surface of each wing. Oil capacity 5.7 litres (1.5 US gallons; 1.25 Imp gallons).

ACCOMMODATION: Two seats side by side under rearward sliding bubble canopy. Baggage space aft of seats. Cockpit heated and ventilated.

SYSTEM: 60A engine driven alternator.

AVIONICS AND EQUIPMENT: Blind-flying instrumentation standard. Radio to customer's specification.

DIMENSIONS, EXTERNAL:

Wing span	9.36 m (30 ft 8.4 in)
Wing chord: at root	1.515 m (4 ft 11⅔ in)
at tip	0.81 m (2 ft 8 in)
Wing aspect ratio	7.5
Length overall	6.58 m (21 ft 7¼ in)

Height overall	2.38 m (7 ft 9.6 in)
Tailplane span	2.74 m (9 ft 0 in)
Wheel track	2.40 m (7 ft 10½ in)
Wheelbase	1.46 m (4 ft 9.6 in)
Propeller diameter	1.68 m (5 ft 6 in)
Propeller ground clearance	0.30 m (12 in)

DIMENSIONS, INTERNAL:

Cockpit: Length	1.52 m (5 ft 0 in)
Max width	1.21 m (3 ft 11½ in)
Baggage space	0.4 m³ (14.0 cu ft)

AREAS:

Wings, gross	11.15 m² (120.0 sq ft)
Ailerons (total)	0.89 m² (9.6 sq ft)
Trailing-edge flaps (total)	1.30 m² (14.0 sq ft)
Fin	0.96 m² (10.3 sq ft)
Rudder	0.63 m² (6.8 sq ft)
Tailplane	1.11 m² (12.0 sq ft)
Elevators, incl tab	0.93 m² (10.0 sq ft)

WEIGHTS AND LOADINGS (A, O-235 engine; B, AEIO-320 engine):

Weight empty, equipped: A	460 kg (1,014 lb)
B	571 kg (1,259 lb)
Max fuel load: A	85 kg (188 lb)
Max T-O weight: A	748 kg (1,649 lb)
B	870 kg (1,919 lb)
Max wing loading: A	67.06 kg/m² (13.74 lb/sq ft)
B	78.04 kg/m² (15.99 lb/sq ft)
Max power loading: A	8.50 kg/kW (13.97 lb/hp)
B	7.31 kg/kW (11.99 lb/hp)

PERFORMANCE (at max T-O weight, B estimated):

Never-exceed speed:	
A	202 knots (374 km/h; 232 mph) EAS
B	232 knots (430 km/h; 267 mph) EAS
Max level speed at S/L:	
A	121 knots (224 km/h; 139 mph)
B	140 knots (259 km/h; 161 mph)
Max cruising speed, 75% power at S/L:	
A	110 knots (204 km/h; 127 mph)
B	126 knots (233 km/h; 145 mph)
Econ cruising speed, 50% power at S/L:	
A	93 knots (172 km/h; 107 mph)
B	110 knots (204 km/h; 127 mph)
Stalling speed:	
flaps up: A	54 knots (100 km/h; 63 mph) EAS
B	57 knots (106 km/h; 66 mph) EAS
flaps down: A	47 knots (88 km/h; 55 mph) EAS
B	51 knots (95 km/h; 59 mph) EAS
Max rate of climb at S/L: A	279 m (915 ft)/min
B	393 m (1,290 ft)/min
Service ceiling: A	5,000 m (16,400 ft)
B	6,645 m (21,800 ft)
T-O run: A	247 m (812 ft)
B	223 m (730 ft)
T-O to 15 m (50 ft): A	374 m (1,228 ft)
B	315 m (1,033 ft)
Landing from 15 m (50 ft): A	290 m (953 ft)
B	315 m (1,033 ft)

Range with max fuel, 13.6 litres (3 Imp gallons) reserves:
A at 78 knots (145 km/h; 90 mph) at 1,525 m (5,000 ft) — 620 nm (1,149 km; 714 miles)
B at 95 knots (175 km/h; 109 mph) at 3,050 m (10,000 ft) — 490 nm (907 km; 564 miles)

Trago Mills SAH-1 side by side two-seat light aircraft

UAT

UNITED AEROSPACE TECHNOLOGIES LTD

Unit 11, Haxter Close, Belliver, Plymouth, Devon

Telephone: 0303 77222

SALES CONTACT: Transavia Ltd, Luton International Airport, Bedfordshire LU2 9NF

Telephone: 0582 415600

Telex: 826945 TRANSA G

DIRECTORS:

Group Captain S. A. Edwards, OBE

T. Luscombe

United Aerospace Technologies owns the rights of T. Luscombe designs and has the consultancy of T. Luscombe and G. Miles.

UAT also jointly owns Semiduct High Lift Technology with the Custer Channel Wing Corporation, USA, as used on the P.20 V/STOL Airlifter (Joint Services) project.

Current Luscombe initiated aircraft are the Ranger, Super Ranger and Twin Ranger, of which details follow:

UAT RANGER

The Ranger owes much to development work on tandem-wing aircraft performed by Luscombe over a fourteen-year period and in particular to the Rattler ultralight aircraft. Constructed almost entirely of Kevlar and GRP, with some carbonfibre, it combines strength with light weight, and is corrosion-proof. In addition, the sound deadening properties of the Nomex fuselage help to ensure crew comfort during very long flights. This was considered important in an aircraft intended to cover the entire spectrum from long distance cruising to military utility duties with STOL ability and low radar signature. The power plant is fully cowled with Kevlar panels and, if required, the engine heat and exhaust can be mixed with cold air and released above the wing to minimise IR emissions.

In addition to stores carried on two standard NATO 14 in underwing attachments, the Ranger can carry a variety of stores and equipment in a unique conformal pod attached beneath the floor of the cockpit on further NATO 14 in attachments. As well as making the pod quickly removable, and jettisonable, this feature enables the aircraft to carry stores under the fuselage when the conformal pod is not fitted. Versatility will be increased further in due course by the availability of retractable flotation equipment, permitting operation from land, water, ice or snow without major sacrifice of performance. The flotation gear will also provide platforms for stretcher carrying when the aircraft is used for military, police, maritime or search and rescue casevac duties.

TYPE: Two-seat tandem-wing general purpose aircraft.

WINGS: High-wing monoplane, with single streamline-section bracing strut each side. Centre-section and two main panels of composite construction, with moderate sweepback. No dihedral. Ailerons operate in conjunction with spoiler in upper surface of each wing. Split flap extends from each wingroot to inboard edge of aileron. Sweptback fin and rudder, of composite construction, mounted at each wingtip.

FOREPLANES: Cantilever all-moving surfaces of composite construction, mounted on each side of fuselage nose. No dihedral or sweep.

FUSELAGE: Short pod of Nomex sandwich construction, with removable and jettisonable conformal pod contoured to bottom lines. Pod can be airdropped by parachute or released during slow flight at minimum height above surface. Compartment for avionics or equipment in nose, which can have optically flat 45° window at front.

LANDING GEAR: Non-retractable tricycle type, with single wheel on each unit. Steerable nosewheel.

POWER PLANT: One 145 kW (195 hp) Continental O-360 flat-six engine, driving a three-blade Hartzell constant-speed pusher propeller.

ACCOMMODATION: Pilot and passenger side by side in enclosed, heated and ventilated cabin.

OPERATIONAL EQUIPMENT: Provision for carrying laser target marker, IR or TV sensor in nose. Two hardpoints under each wing for standard NATO 14 in attachments, able to carry a maximum of 181 kg (400 lb) of rockets, bombs, armament or equipment pods, surveillance equipment, spraygear or other loads under each wing. Underfuselage conformal pod can house twin machine-guns and magazines; inflatable liferaft and survival equipment for sea rescue missions; tent, rations and survival equipment for overland SAR; medical supplies; additional fuel or spraying equipment. Instead of pod, aircraft can carry 227 kg (500 lb) of bombs, mines or other stores under the fuselage.

DIMENSIONS, EXTERNAL:
Wing span	8.89 m (29 ft 2 in)
Foreplane span	3.71 m (12 ft 2 in)
Length overall	5.79 m (19 ft 0 in)
Height overall	2.95 m (9 ft 8 in)

AREAS:
Wings, gross	9.01 m² (97.0 sq ft)
Foreplanes, gross	1.67 m² (18.0 sq ft)

WEIGHTS:
Weight empty	544 kg (1,200 lb)
Max T-O weight	1,088 kg (2,400 lb)

PERFORMANCE (estimated):
Max speed	156 knots (290 km/h; 180 mph)
Cruising speed	122 knots (225 km/h; 140 mph)
Loiter speed	43 knots (80 km/h; 50 mph)
Range:	
standard fuel	1,042 nm (1,931 km; 1,200 miles)
with auxiliary tanks	3,126 nm (5,793 km; 3,600 miles)
Endurance with standard fuel	11 hours

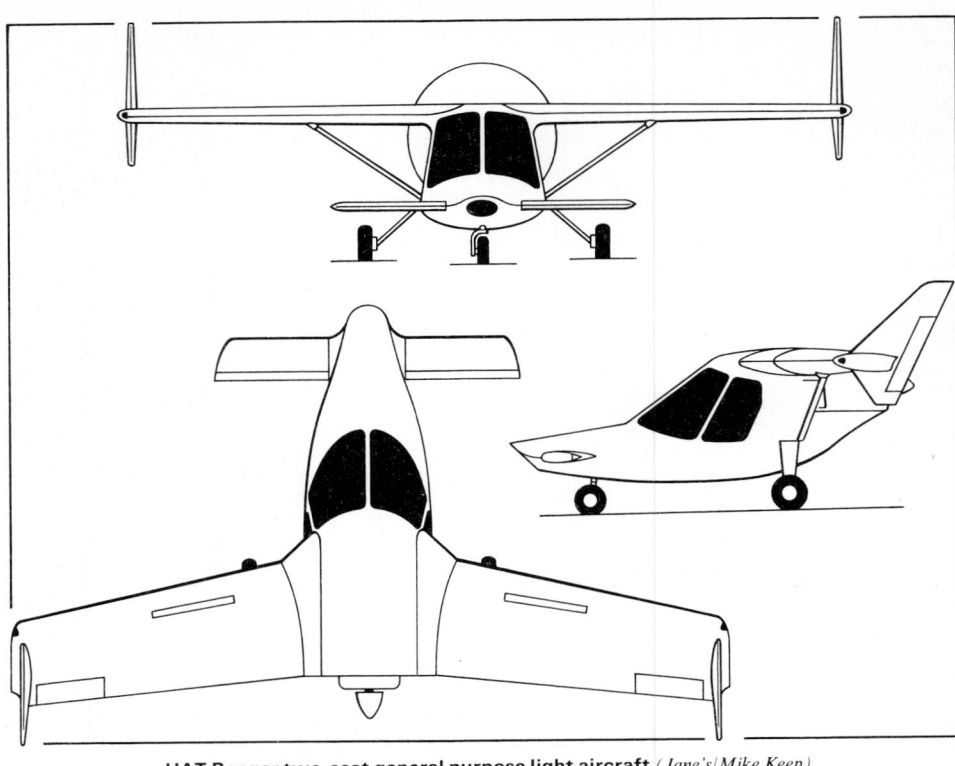

UAT Ranger two-seat general purpose light aircraft *(Jane's/Mike Keep)*

UAT SUPER RANGER

Using 85 per cent of the components of the Ranger, the Super Ranger is a 'stretched' variant with the fuselage lengthened to accommodate two additional seats. The extra space at the rear enables a retractable landing gear to be fitted.

The principal market for the Super Ranger is seen as 'long distance, comfortable cruising, with excellent economy'.

The description and details of the Ranger apply also to the Super Ranger, except as follows:

TYPE: Four-seat lightweight tandem-wing aircraft.

WINGS: As for Ranger, but of slightly increased span.

FOREPLANES: As for Ranger, but of increased span.

FUSELAGE: As for Ranger, but with a 0.51 m (1 ft 8 in) plug inserted between rear of pilot/co-pilot seats and the rear stressed bulkhead. A glazed emergency escape panel is installed in the roof above the rear seats.

LANDING GEAR: Retractable tricycle type, with single wheel on each unit. Electro-hydraulic actuation.

POWER PLANT: One 142 kW (190 hp) Teledyne Continental IOL-300 liquid-cooled flat-six engine.

ACCOMMODATION: Pilot and passenger side by side, and two side by side passenger seats in enclosed, heated and air-conditioned cabin.

AVIONICS: Provision for comprehensive avionics, to customer's requirements.

DIMENSIONS, EXTERNAL (provisional):
Wing span	9.14 m (30 ft 0 in)
Length overall	6.30 m (20 ft 8 in)
Height overall	2.84 m (9 ft 4 in)

WEIGHTS (estimated):
Weight empty	726 kg (1,600 lb)
Max fuel load (normal)	159 kg (350 lb)
Max T-O weight	1,292 kg (2,850 lb)

PERFORMANCE (estimated):
Max range at econ cruising speed	
	1,736 nm (3,218 km; 2,000 miles)
Endurance	8 h

UAT TWIN RANGER

The Twin Ranger is a twin-engined development of the Ranger with accommodation for six people. To provide adequate directional control, the wingtip fins and rudders are replaced by a single swept conventional fin and rudder on the rear fuselage. Many parts of the Twin Ranger are common with those of the Ranger and Super Ranger.

The description of the Ranger applies also to the Twin Ranger, except as follows:

TYPE: Six-seat lightweight tandem-wing aircraft.

WINGS: Outer wings as for the Ranger, except for winglet instead of fin and rudder on each wingtip.

FOREPLANES: As for Ranger, but of increased area.

FUSELAGE: Of Nomex sandwich construction. Front fuselage common with Ranger. Centre-section entirely new to accommodate the twin-engine power plant.

TAIL UNIT: Sweptback fin and horn balanced rudder at rear of fuselage pod.

LANDING GEAR: Retractable tricycle type. Twin wheels on nose unit, single wheel on each main unit. Electro-hydraulic actuation. Main units retract inward into fuselage.

POWER PLANT: Two 142 kW (190 hp) Teledyne Continental IOL-300 liquid-cooled flat-six engines, mounted on trailing-edge of centre-section. Fuel tanks in wingroots, total capacity 682 litres (180 US gallons; 150 Imp gallons).

ACCOMMODATION: Enclosed cabin seats six people, including the pilot. Passenger seats quickly detachable to provide usable payload volume of 4.2 m³ (148 cu ft), without severe restraints on loading due to CG considerations. Cabin soundproofed and air-conditioned.

DIMENSIONS, EXTERNAL (provisional):
Wing span	11.23 m (36 ft 10 in)
Length overall	8.08 m (26 ft 6 in)
Height overall	3.35 m (11 ft 0 in)

WEIGHTS (estimated):
Weight empty	862 kg (1,900 lb)
Max T-O weight	1,932 kg (4,260 lb)

PERFORMANCE (estimated):
Range, with reserves	
	2,952 nm (5,471 km; 3,400 miles)
Max endurance	over 14 h

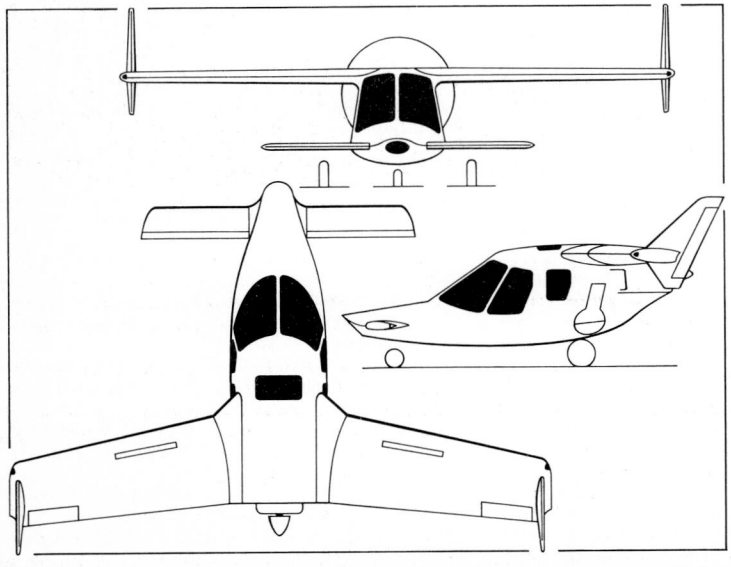

Provisional drawing of UAT Super Ranger four-seat general purpose light aircraft *(Jane's/Mike Keep)*

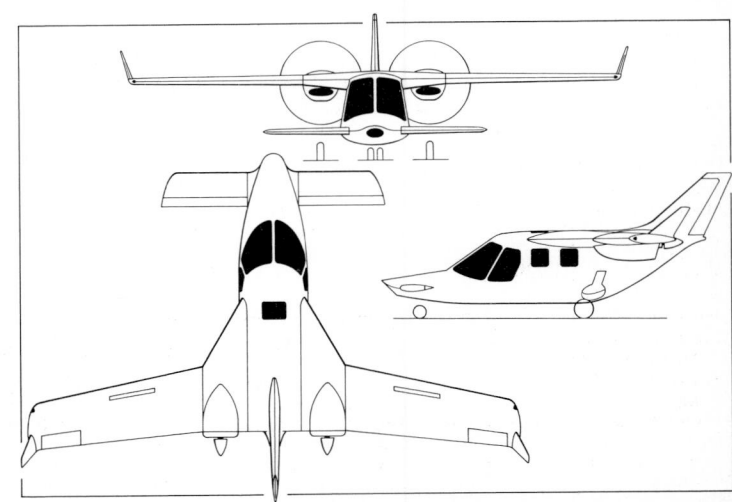

Provisional drawing of UAT Twin Ranger six-seat general purpose light aircraft *(Jane's/Mike Keep)*

WALLIS
WALLIS AUTOGYROS LTD

Reymerston Hall, Norfolk NR9 4QY
Telephone: 0362 850418
MANAGING DIRECTOR:
Wg Cdr K. H. Wallis, CEng, FRAeS, FRSA, RAF (Retd)

The first Wallis single-seat ultralight autogyro introduced many patented features, including a rotor head with offset gimbal system to provide hands and feet off stability and to eliminate pitch-up and 'tuck-under' hazards; a high speed flexible rotor spin-up shaft with positive disengagement during flight; an automatic system of controlling rotor drive on take-off which allows power to be applied until the last moment; centrifugal stops to control rotor blade teetering; and a novel safe starting arrangement.

Many other Wallis autogyros have since been completed. Wallis Autogyros does not engage in production for public sale; it builds these aircraft only for operation within the company. However, three Wallis autogyros (two WA-116s and a WA-117) have been evaluated by RARDE, Christchurch, in the role of airfield battle damage reconnaissance.

WALLIS WA-116 and WA-116-T

The WA-116 represents the original Wallis design, of which the prototype (G-ARRT) flew for the first time on 2 August 1961, powered by a 54 kW (72 hp) modified McCulloch 4318 piston engine. Four more WA-116s were built by Beagle and five by Wg Cdr Wallis, as described in the 1973-74 *Jane's*. The last of these was later dismantled for construction of the two-seat G-AXAS, a WA-116-T.

WA-116/Mc. The prototype (G-ARRT) is re-engined with a 67 kW (90 hp) McCulloch. This aircraft, and the 'James Bond' WA-116/Mc (G-ARZB), continue to perform well. The latter has appeared in more than 500 displays, as far afield as Australia and the USA.

WA-116/F. Designation applied following the refitting of G-ASDY in 1971 with a 44 kW (60 hp) Franklin 2A-120-A engine. It is currently fitted with a Franklin 2A-120-B engine, driving a specially designed two-blade propeller, and has carried out specialised aerial photographic work, as detailed in earlier editions of *Jane's*.

A particularly successful WA-116/F is G-ATHM which currently holds nine world rotorcraft records. This aircraft underwent more extensive conversion than its predecessors, mainly to increase fuel capacity and pilot comfort to fit it for special long range flights. It has a 50 litre (13.2 US gallon; 11 Imp gallon) internal fuel tank, and began test flying, for range, in April 1974. Fitted also with a 36 litre (9.6 US gallon; 8 Imp gallon) jettisonable long range ventral tank, it set up on 13 July 1974 new Class E3 and E3a world records, for nonstop distance in a closed circuit, of 361.91 nm (670.26 km; 416.48 miles). Additionally, this flight set new 100 km (Class E3a only) and 500 km (Class E3 and E3a) closed circuit speed records of 70.51 knots (130.67 km/h; 81.19 mph) and 68.07 knots (126.14 km/h; 78.38 mph) respectively. A 91 litre (24 US gallon; 20 Imp gallon) ventral tank was next fitted, and on 28 September 1975, with this tank containing some 70 litres (18.5 US gallons; 15.5 Imp gallons), Wg Cdr Wallis made a nonstop flight from Lydd, Kent, to Wick, Caithness. This flight set Class E3 and E3a records for nonstop distance in a straight line of 472.092 nm (874.315 km; 543.274 miles). The ventral tank was not jettisoned after being emptied, and G-ATHM landed with sufficient fuel remaining for a further 65 nm (121 km; 75 miles). Its time of 6 h 25 min is a record for duration in both Class E3 and Class E3a. On 14 October 1984 **WA-116/F/S** G-BLIK set new Class E3 and E3a speed records over 15 km of 102.365 knots (189.58 km/h; 117.80 mph). On 17 April 1985 it set new Class E3 and E3a world speed records over 100 km of 102.81 knots (190.41 km/h; 118.31 mph); and on 18 September 1986 new speed records over 3 km of 104.5 knots (193.6 km/h; 120.3 mph). The suffix S denotes 'Special' because of the numerous cleaning up refinements embodied. Thus, WA-116s hold all the major autogyro world records for speed, range and endurance. Future plans for this aircraft include a further attempt on the non-stop distance record.

WA-116-T/Mc. The McCulloch engined WA-116-T/ Mc, G-AXAS, is a tandem two-seat autogyro which flew for the first time on 3 April 1969. Recent activities include work utilising the slow flight and short take-off and landing capability, and also electrostatically charged spraying tests, employing a spray system that can be lowered beneath the lowest part of the aircraft in flight.

WEIGHTS (WA-116/F):

Weight empty	143 kg (316 lb)
Max T-O weight	317.5 kg (700 lb)

PERFORMANCE (WA-116/F):

Max level speed	not fully explored
Cruising speed without long-range tank	
	87 knots (161 km/h; 100 mph)
Max rate of climb at S/L	305 m (1,000 ft)/min
Max range with long-range tank (estimated)	
	651 nm (1,207 km; 750 miles)

WALLIS WA-116/X

In 1985 Wg Cdr Wallis began the development of a new autogyro for a particular reconnaissance role. The requirement calls for a day and night all-weather capability, together with very low vibration levels.

As part of the development programme a series of flight tests is being conducted with current and new technology engines. Current engines tested include a special version of the 59.6 kW (80 hp) Limbach L 2000, a 37 kW (50 hp) Fuji 440 cc two-cylinder aircooled two-stroke, and the 47.7 kW (64 hp) Rotax 520 Bombardier geared two-cylinder liquid cooled two-stroke engine. Modified engines include the Rootes Imp and a two-cylinder engine made from components of the Rolls-Royce Continental O-240. New technology engines in the programme include a special version of the Norton Motors P62 twin-rotor Wankel type and a supercharged or turbocharged 1,360 cc automobile engine. The radiator for the Rotax and Norton engines is in the nose of the cockpit nacelle, providing some cockpit heating in inclement weather conditions.

Airframes being used for these flight tests are a basic WA-116 (G-AVDG), with appropriate modifications, and a new one (G-BMJX) provisionally designated WA-116/X, the suffix X indicating the unknown quantity pending selection of a suitable engine.

The WA-116/X programme is expected to lead to the next generation of Wallis autogyros, emphasis being placed on easy adaptation to new technology engines as they become available. Future aircraft will be equipped for night flying and the carriage of a range of sensors, and will be easily adaptable for military, police and similar roles.

WALLIS WA-117/R-R

Details of the WA-117, which combines the WA-116 airframe with a fully certificated engine, the 74 kW (100 hp) Rolls-Royce Continental O-200-B, can be found in the 1986-87 *Jane's*.

Wallis WA-116/F/S which holds Class E3 and E3a speed records, showing fixed foreplane surfaces

Wallis WA-117/R-R equipped for airfield damage assessment research *(RAE Farnborough)*

Wallis WA-201 twin-engined research autogyro

The WA-117/R-R has been engaged during the past year in important operations, under Ministry of Defence contracts, to demonstrate the effectiveness of Wallis autogyros for all-weather day and night damage reconnaissance of military airfields. It is shown in an accompanying illustration equipped with a British Aerospace miniature infra-red linescan and real-time ground link, and a 70 mm camera.

WALLIS WA-120/R-R

The WA-120 (G-AYVO) was last described in the 1987-88 *Jane's*.

WALLIS WA-121

The WA-121 is the smallest and lightest Wallis autogyro to date. Three versions were projected: a high-speed **WA-121/Mc** with a Wallis-McCulloch engine of about 74 kW (100 hp); a cross-country **WA-121/F** with a 44.5 kW (60 hp) Franklin 2A-120-B engine; and a high-altitude **WA-121/M Meteorite 2** with a supercharged 89 kW

(120 hp) Meteor Alfa 1 radial two-stroke engine and transistorised ignition. There are currently no plans to proceed with construction of the two last-mentioned variants.

The prototype WA-121/Mc (G-BAHH) has a high-mounted tailplane and an open cockpit, and made its first flight on 28 December 1972. It employs a number of improvements in control system design, resulting in greater stability at speed, better head resistance and greater pilot comfort. It set new Class E3 and E3a height records on 20 July 1982, when Wg Cdr Wallis flew it to a height of 5,643.7 m (18,516 ft) at Boscombe Down. Special features in the rotor head suspension, incorporated originally in the WA-117 prototype G-AVJV, are incorporated also in the WA-120 and WA-121. Now fitted with an improved oxygen system, and a wider track main landing gear to standardise it with other autogyros in the Wallis range, the WA-121 is intended to undertake experimental flying using rotor blades designed for high speeds and may make an attempt to better its height record.

WALLIS WA-122/R-R

A two-seat trainer development of the similar WA-116-T (G-BGGW) first flew on 16 July 1980 as the WA-122/R-R. Further details appeared in the 1987-88 and previous editions of *Jane's*.

WALLIS WA-201

The WA-201 is a research vehicle designed to prove the concept of a twin-engined version of the Wallis type of light autogyro. The aircraft is powered by two 47.7 kW (64 hp) Rotax 532 Bombardier geared two-cylinder liquid cooled two-stroke engines, mounted entirely separately in tandem so that the front engine drives a pusher propeller and the rear engine a tractor propeller. The two propellers are counter rotating and have no offset thrust. The power available is sufficient for take-off and flight using only one engine. The two engines give an exceptional lift-to-empty weight ratio and rate of climb, making the WA-201 potentially an effective aircraft for post-attack airfield damage assessment.

WESTLAND
WESTLAND PLC

Yeovil, Somerset BA20 2YB
Telephone: 0935 75222
Telex: 46277 WHLYEO G
LONDON OFFICE: 4 Carlton Gardens, Pall Mall, SW1
Telephone: (01) 839 4061
GROUP CHIEF EXECUTIVE: H. P. Stewart, LLB, FCA
HEAD OF PUBLIC RELATIONS: Ian Woodward

Westland Aircraft Ltd (now Westland plc) was formed in July 1935, to take over the aircraft branch of Petters Ltd, known previously as the Westland Aircraft Works, which had been engaged in aircraft design and construction since 1915. It entered the helicopter industry in 1947 by acquiring a licence to build the US Sikorsky S-51, which it produced as the Westland Dragonfly. This technical association with Sikorsky Division of United Technologies has continued since the decision was taken to concentrate on the design, development and construction of helicopters.

In 1959, Westland acquired Saunders-Roe Ltd. In 1960 it

acquired the Helicopter Division of Bristol Aircraft Ltd and Fairey Aviation Ltd, and has been subsequently the only major helicopter design and manufacturing organisation in the United Kingdom.

In April 1983 the Aerospace Division of British Hovercraft Corporation was combined with the Westland Helicopters Industrial Division to form the Aerospace Division of Westland plc. In October 1985 three additional divisions were created: Helicopter Division, Helicopter Customer Support Division and Technologies Division. Early in 1987 the Helicopter Division and the Customer Support Division were amalgamated to create a new Helicopter Division with responsibility for both manufacturing and product support. The various Divisions subsequently became consolidated into limited liability companies, as Westland Helicopters Ltd, Westland Aerospace Ltd and Westland Technologies Ltd.

A shareholders' meeting in February 1986 approved a financial reconstruction package under which United Technologies (USA) and Fiat (Italy) acquired a minority holding in Westland plc.

Programmes on which Westland Aerospace is engaged include the production of centre wings for the Shorts 330 and 360 transport aircraft, composite engine cowlings for the Boeing of Canada DHC-8 Dash 8, missile and satellite structures, fuel pods and transmission components for Boeing CH-47 Chinook helicopters, and gears and gearboxes for other aerospace companies. Its latest products include composite structures for McDonnell Douglas, Boeing and Airbus aircraft.

The collaboration between Westland and Agusta of Italy, already well established with the EH 101 programme (see International section), has been extended to include design, manufacture and marketing across the joint product range.

A joint Westland/Agusta management company, EHI Limited, has been set up in London to support the EH 101 civil and military helicopter. EHI Inc is a subsidiary of EHI in the USA. It also has a Canadian subsidiary in Ottawa, known as EHI Canada.

Westland Group activities in the USA, Central America and the Caribbean are represented by Westland Inc, a wholly owned subsidiary.

WESTLAND HELICOPTERS LIMITED

Yeovil, Somerset BA20 2YB
Telephone: 0935 75222
Telex: 46277 WHLYEO G
Fax: 0935 704201
MANAGING DIRECTOR: J. Varde
ENGINEERING DIRECTOR: R. I. Case
MARKETING DIRECTOR: M. I. Leese
HEAD OF PUBLIC RELATIONS: Ian Woodward

Helicopters in current production at Yeovil are the Sea King and Lynx, manufacture of the Westland 30 having been completed. In addition, Westland Helicopters and Agusta of Italy are collaborating through a joint company named EH Industries Ltd to develop and produce the EH 101 naval, commercial and utility helicopter (see International section).

Composite main rotor blades, based on carbonfibre and glassfibre materials, are in production at Yeovil as direct replacements for metal blades on S-61, SH-3 and Westland Sea King helicopters.

Advanced design composite main rotor blades have been successfully test flown on the Lynx, Lynx-3, Westland TT300 and EH 101.

WESTLAND SEA KING

The Westland Sea King development programme stemmed from a licence agreement for the S-61 helicopter concluded originally with Sikorsky in 1959. This permitted Westland to utilise the basic airframe and rotor system of the Sikorsky SH-3 now described under Agusta in the Italian section. Considerable changes were made in the power plant and in specialised equipment, initially to meet a Royal Navy requirement for an advanced anti-submarine helicopter with prolonged endurance. The Sea King can also undertake secondary roles, such as search and rescue, tactical troop transport, casualty evacuation, cargo carrying and long-range self-ferry. A land based general purpose version, the Commando, is described separately.

Current versions of the Sea King are as follows:

Sea King AEW. Mk 2A. Version developed in mid-1982 to provide Royal Navy with airborne early warning capability. By 1987, ten (plus an aerodynamic prototype) had been converted, of which only eight are operational at any one time. Described and illustrated in 1986-87 edition.

Sea King HAR. Mk 3. Uprated version for SAR duties with the Royal Air Force. Provision for flight crew of two pilots, air electronics/winch operator and loadmaster/winchman; up to six stretchers, or two stretchers and 11 seated survivors, or 19 persons. Nav system includes Decca TANS F computer, accepting inputs from Mk 19 Decca nav receiver and Type 71 Doppler. MEL radar. First HAR. Mk 3 flew on 6 September 1977; deliveries of 16 completed in 1979. Three more ordered in 1983 were delivered in 1985. Operated by No. 202 Squadron at Finningley (HQ) and

detachments at Boulmer, Brawdy, Manston, Lossiemouth and Leconfield; plus No. 78 Squadron on Falkland Islands. Latter's aircraft fitted with radar warning receivers and chaff/flare dispensers.

Sea King HC. Mk 4. Utility version of Commando Mk 2 (which see) for Royal Navy.

Sea King HAS. Mk 5. Updated ASW and SAR version for the Royal Navy. Thirty new-build aircraft ordered in three batches (17, 8 and 5), of which the first two (ZA126/127) were handed over officially on 2 October 1980. Delivery of the first batch was completed in October 1982; delivery of the next eight began in September 1984, and the final five were delivered between January and July 1986. The Fleet Air Arm's workshops had brought all surviving older Sea Kings up to recent standards by early 1987. Of 56 HAS. Mk 1s, 47 were converted to HAS. Mk 2A (including 35 subsequently to HAS. Mk 5 and 11 to AEW. Mk 2A) and one directly to HAS. Mk 5. All except one of the 21 new-build HAS. Mk 2s also became Mk 5s.

The nav/attack system of the Sea King HAS. Mk 5 utilises Tans G coupled to Decca 71 Doppler and MEL Sea Searcher radar. Also fitted are Racal MIR-2 ESM, passive sonobuoy dropping equipment, and associated GEC Avionics LAPADS acoustic processing and display equipment. The increased size of the rotating antenna necessitated the Mk 5's larger dorsal radome.

Using this new equipment, the Sea King can pinpoint the position of an enemy submarine at far greater range than has been possible in the past, and attack it with torpedoes. In addition to monitoring signals from its own sonobuoys, the Sea King can handle information from buoys dropped by RAF Nimrod aircraft in a joint search. It can remain on station, up to 87 nm (160 km; 100 miles) from its parent ship, for long periods.

The Sea King HAS. Mk 5 carries a crew of four, with the dunking sonar operator also monitoring the LAPADS equipment at an additional crew station. To make room for the extra equipment, the cabin has been enlarged by moving the rear bulkhead nearly 1.83 m (6 ft 0 in) further into the tail.

The sonar system in the Royal Navy's fleet of HAS. Mk 5 Sea Kings is being updated under a contract awarded to the Maritime Aircraft Systems Division of GEC Avionics in 1987. Previously fitted with two separate 'stand-alone' systems (Plessey 195 dipping sonar and GEC Avionics AQS-902C sonobuoy processing), the HAS. Mk 5 will be retrofitted with a new and enhanced combined system known as AQS-902G-DS. This will replace the analog computing element of the Plessey 195 with a digital processor, and present integrated information from both the free sonobuoys and the dipping sonar on a single CRT display. The contract provides for 31 new AQS-902G-DS

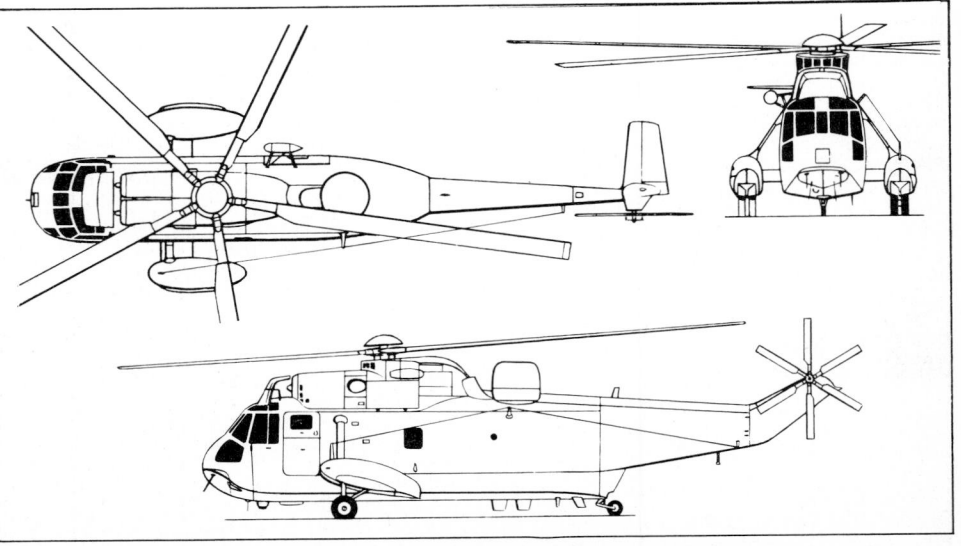

Westland Sea King HAS. Mk 5 anti-submarine helicopter *(Pilot Press)*

systems, plus the modification of 112 AQS-902C systems to the upgraded standard.

Max T-O weight of the Sea King HAS. Mk 5 is 9,525 kg (21,000 lb).

Sea King HAS. Mk 6. Updated ASW and SAR version for the Royal Navy. Four new-build aircraft ordered October 1987 and 25 HAS. Mk 5s being retrofitted to this standard from 1987 onwards. The first Mk 6 (a conversion of Mk 5 XZ581) first flew at Yeovil on 15 December 1987. Equipment changes include modifications to the Plessey sonar to increase 'dunking' depth; installation of CRT displays for AQS-902 sonar systems; upgrading of ESM to 'Orange Crop II' standard; and fitment of additional communications equipment. Performance remains the same as for Sea King HAS. Mk 5.

Sea King Mk 42. ASW version for Indian Navy. Original order for six, which are in service with No. 330 Squadron. Delivery of a further six was completed in 1974, and these are in service with Nos. 330 and 336 Squadrons. Follow-on order announced in June 1977 for three uprated aircraft, designated **Mk 42A**, with hauldown capability for small ship operation, which were delivered in March 1980.

Advanced Sea King. Version with 1,092 kW (1,465 shp) Rolls-Royce Gnome H.1400-1T engines, uprated main gearbox with emergency lubrication and strengthened main lift frames. Other changes include composite main and tail rotor blades, and improved search radar. Maximum AUW increased to 9,752 kg (21,500 lb) to give an improved payload/range performance. Through life costs reduced.

Sea King Mk 42B. ASW version of the Advanced Sea King of which 12 were ordered for the Indian Navy in July 1983, followed by eight more. Features include GEC Avionics AQS-902 sonobuoy processor and tactical processing system; MEL Super Searcher radar; integrated Alcatel HS-12 dipping sonar; Chelton 700 sonics homing; Marconi Hermes ESM; and ability to carry British Aerospace Sea Eagle long-range anti-ship missiles. First aircraft (IN513) flown 17 May 1985; none delivered by early 1988.

Sea King Mk 42C. Utility transport version of the Advanced Sea King of which six have been ordered for the Indian Navy. Navigation systems similar to HAR. Mk 3, except that the MEL radar is replaced by Bendix RDR 1400C, nose mounted; the ADF and IFF are produced by HAL. First aircraft (IN555) flew on 25 September 1986; handed over 5 February 1987.

Sea King Mk 42D. Proposed equivalent of AEW. Mk 2 for Indian Navy. No purchases known.

Other versions, for which orders have been completed, were described in the 1983-84 *Jane's* and included the Sea King HAS. Mk 1 (Royal Navy), Sea King HAS. Mk 2 (Royal Navy), Sea King Mk 4X (Royal Aerospace Establishment), Sea King Mk 41 (Federal German Navy), Sea King Mk 43 (Norwegian Air Force - for which an extra aircraft is on order), Sea King Mk 45 (Pakistan Navy), Sea King Mk 47 (Egyptian Navy), Sea King Mk 48 (Belgian Air Force) and Sea King Mk 50 (Royal Australian Navy).

A total of more than 330 Sea Kings and Commandos had been ordered by January 1988, of which 286 had been delivered.

The following details apply to current production Advanced Sea Kings:

AIRFRAME: Generally similar to Agusta-Sikorsky ASH-3H (see Italian section), but with main and tail rotor blades of composite materials. Stabiliser on starboard side of tail pylon is unbraced. New five-blade tail rotor to give increased capability in side wind.

POWER PLANT: Two 1,238 kW (1,660 shp) (max contingency rating) Rolls-Royce Gnome H.1400-1T turboshafts, mounted side by side above cabin. Transmission rating 2,200 kW (2,950 shp). Fuel in six underfloor bag tanks, total capacity 3,714 litres (981 US gallons; 817 Imp gallons). Internal auxiliary tank, capacity 863 litres (228

Prototype Westland Sea King HAS. Mk 6 (XZ581) prior to first flight *(Paul Jackson)*

US gallons; 190 Imp gallons) may be fitted for long range ferry purposes. Pressure refuelling point on starboard side, two gravity points on port side. Flat plate debris guard for engine air intakes. Optional Centrisep air cleaner unit.

ACCOMMODATION: Crew of four in ASW role; accommodation for up to 22 survivors in SAR role; and up to 28 troops in utility role. Two-section airstair door at front on port side, cargo door at rear on starboard side. Entire accommodation heated and ventilated. Cockpit doors and windows, and two windows each side of cabin, can be jettisoned in an emergency.

SYSTEMS: Three main hydraulic systems. Primary and auxiliary systems operate main rotor control. System pressure 103.5 bars (1,500 lb/sq in); flow rate 22.7 litres/min at 87.9 bars (6 US gallons; 5 Imp gallons/min at 1,275 lb/sq in). Unpressurised reservoir. Utility system for main landing gear, sonar and rescue winches, blade folding and rotor brake. System pressure 207 bars (3,000 lb/sq in); flow rate 41 litres/min at 186.2 bars (10.8 US gallons; 9 Imp gallons/min at 2,700 lb/sq in). Unpressurised reservoir. Electrical system includes two 20kVA 200V three-phase 400Hz engine driven generators, a 26V single-phase AC supply fed from the aircraft's 22Ah nickel-cadmium battery through an inverter, and DC power provided as a secondary system from two 200A transformer-rectifier units.

OPERATIONAL EQUIPMENT (ASW models): As equipped for this role, the Sea King is a fully integrated all-weather hunter/killer weapon system, capable of operating independently of surface vessels, and the following equipment and weapons can be fitted to achieve this task: Plessey Type 195, Bendix AN/AQS-13B or Alcatel HS-12 dipping sonar, GEC Avionics Doppler navigation system, MEL Super Searcher radar in dorsal radome, transponder beneath rear fuselage, Honeywell AN/APN-171 radar altimeter, Sperry GM7B Gyrosyn compass system, Louis Newmark Mk 31 automatic flight control system, two No. 4 marine markers, four No. 2 Mk 2 smoke floats, Ultra Electronics mini-sonobuoys, up to four Mk 46 or Sting Ray homing torpedoes, or four Mk 11 depth charges or one Clevite simulator. Observer/navigator has tactical display on which sonar contacts are integrated with search radar and navigational information. Radio equipment comprises Collins ARC-182 UHF/VHF and homer, Ultra D 403M standby UHF, Collins 718U-5 HF radio, Racal B693 intercom,

Telebrief system and IFF provisions. CAE Electronics internal MAD ordered for RN Sea Kings in 1987. For secondary role a mounting is provided on the aft frame of the starboard door for a general purpose machine-gun. The Mk 31 AFCS provides radio altitude displays for both pilots; artificial horizon displays; three axis stabilisation in pilot controlled manoeuvres; attitude hold, heading hold and height hold in cruising flight; controlled transition manoeuvres to and from the hover; automatic height control and plan position control in the hover; and an auxiliary trim facility.

OPERATIONAL EQUIPMENT (non-ASW models): A wide range of radio and navigation equipment may be installed, including VHF/UHF communications, VHF/UHF homing, radio compass, Doppler navigation system, radio altimeter, VOR/ILS, radar and transponder, of Collins, Plessey, Honeywell and GEC Avionics manufacture. A Sperry compass system and a Louis Newmark automatic flight control system are also installed. Sea Kings equipped for search and rescue have in addition a Breeze BL 10300 variable speed hydraulic rescue hoist of 272 kg (600 lb) capacity mounted above the starboard side cargo door. Automatic main rotor blade folding and spreading is standard; for shipboard operation the tail pylon can also be folded. With search radar fitted, a total of 18 survivors and medical staff can be carried; this total can be increased to 22 if the search radar is omitted. In the casualty evacuation role, the Sea King can accommodate up to 9 stretchers and two medical attendants, or intermediate combinations of seats and stretchers; a typical layout might provide for 15 seats and six stretchers. In the troop transport role, the Sea King can accommodate 28 troops. As a cargo transport, the aircraft has an internal capacity of 3,628 kg (8,000 lb) and the same max external load capacity when a low response sling is fitted.

DIMENSIONS, EXTERNAL:

Main rotor diameter	18.90 m (62 ft 0 in)
Tail rotor diameter	3.16 m (10 ft 4 in)
Length overall (rotors turning)	22.15 m (72 ft 8 in)
Length of fuselage	17.02 m (55 ft 10 in)
Length overall:	
main rotor folded	17.42 m (57 ft 2 in)
rotors and tail folded	14.40 m (47 ft 3 in)
Height overall: rotors turning	5.13 m (16 ft 10 in)
rotors spread and stationary	4.85 m (15 ft 11 in)
Height to top of rotor head	4.72 m (15 ft 6 in)
Width overall (rotors folded):	
with flotation bags	4.98 m (16 ft 4 in)
without flotation bags	4.77 m (15 ft 8 in)
Wheel track (c/l of shock absorbers)	3.96 m (13 ft 0 in)
Cabin door (port): Height	1.68 m (5 ft 6 in)
Width	0.91 m (3 ft 0 in)
Cargo door (stbd): Height	1.52 m (5 ft 0 in)
Width	1.73 m (5 ft 8 in)
Height to sill	1.14 m (3 ft 9 in)

DIMENSIONS, INTERNAL:

Cabin: Length: ASW	5.87 m (19 ft 3 in)
SAR	7.59 m (24 ft 11 in)
Max width	1.98 m (6 ft 6 in)
Max height	1.92 m (6 ft 3½ in)
Floor area (incl area occupied by radar, sonar etc):	
ASW	12.08 m² (130 sq ft)
SAR	13.94 m² (150 sq ft)

AREAS:

Main rotor disc	280.6 m² (3,020.3 sq ft)
Tail rotor disc	7.8 m² (83.9 sq ft)

WEIGHTS AND LOADINGS (A: anti-submarine, B: anti-surface vessel, C: airborne early warning, D: SAR, E: troop transport, F: external cargo):

Basic weight (depending on version)		approx 5,530 kg (12,194 lb)
Weight equipped (typical):	A	6,236 kg (13,749 lb)
	B	6,454 kg (14,229 lb)
	C	6,929 kg (15,275 lb)

Indian Sea King Mk 42B destined for INS *Vikrant* *(Paul Jackson)*

D	6,280 kg (13,844 lb)
E	5,438 kg (11,990 lb)
F	5,424 kg (11,958 lb)
Max T-O weight	9,752 kg (21,500 lb)
Max disc loading	34.75 kg/m² (7.12 lb/sq ft)
Max power loading	4.44 kg/kW (7.29 lb/shp)

PERFORMANCE (at max T-O weight, ISA):

Never-exceed speed (British practice) at S/L	
	122 knots (226 km/h; 140 mph)
Cruising speed at S/L	110 knots (204 km/h; 126 mph)
Max rate of climb at S/L	619 m (2,030 ft)/min
Max vertical rate of climb at S/L	246 m (808 ft)/min
Service ceiling, one engine out	1,220 m (4,000 ft)
Max contingency ceiling (1 hour rating)	
	1,067 m (3,500 ft)
Hovering ceiling: IGE	1,982 m (6,500 ft)
OGE	1,433 m (4,700 ft)
Range with max standard fuel, at 1,830 m (6,000 ft)	
	800 nm (1,482 km; 921 miles)
Ferry range with max standard and auxiliary fuel, at 1,830 m (6,000 ft)	940 nm (1,742 km; 1,082 miles)

PERFORMANCE (at typical mid-mission weight):

Never-exceed speed (British practice) at S/L	
	146 knots (272 km/h; 169 mph)
Cruising speed at S/L	132 knots (245 km/h; 152 mph)

WESTLAND COMMANDO

First flown on 12 September 1973, the Commando is a tactical helicopter based on the Sea King.

The payload/range performance and endurance capabilities of the Sea King have been optimised in the design of the Commando, which is intended to operate with maximum efficiency in the primary roles of tactical troop transport, logistic support and cargo transport, and casualty evacuation. In addition, the Commando can operate effectively in the secondary roles of air-to-surface strike and SAR.

The following versions have been announced:

Commando Mk 1. Designation of first five Commandos, ordered on behalf of the Egyptian Air Force by the Saudi Arabian government. Minimally modified version; essentially a standard Sea King Mk 41 aircraft, able to transport up to 21 troops. First two delivered to Egypt in January/February 1974.

Commando Mk 2. Major production version, to which detailed description applies. Flew for first time (G-17-12) on 16 January 1975. Saudi Arabian order included 17 Mk 2s and two VIP Mk 2Bs for the Egyptian Air Force. Four Mk 2s (three Mk 2As and one VIP Mk 2C) delivered to Qatar Emiri Air Force. The Egyptian Air Force also received in 1979-80 four Commando **Mk 2Es** equipped with Elettronica IHS-6 ECM/ESM for an electronic warfare role.

Commando Mk 3. Eight ordered by Qatar. First flown (QA30) 14 June 1982; deliveries between December 1982 and January 1984. Provision for armament, including Exocet anti-ship missiles and ATMs. Based on Advanced Sea King.

Sea King HC. Mk 4. Utility version of Commando Mk 2 for Royal Navy. Has folding main rotor blades and folding tail pylon of Sea King, but retains non-retractable wheeled landing gear of Commando. Designed to carry up to 28 fully equipped troops, or 2,720 kg (6,000 lb) of cargo, and to operate in Arctic and tropical conditions. Max slung load 3,628 kg (8,000 lb). Equipped for parachuting and abseiling. Revised avionics, including Decca TANS with chart display and Decca 71 Doppler navigation system. One cabin mounted 7.62 mm machine-gun. For service with Nos. 707, 771, 845 and 846 (Naval Air Commando) Squadrons. First flight (by ZA290) 26 September 1979. Seventeen ordered initially, of which the first was handed over to the Royal Navy in November 1979. This figure of 17

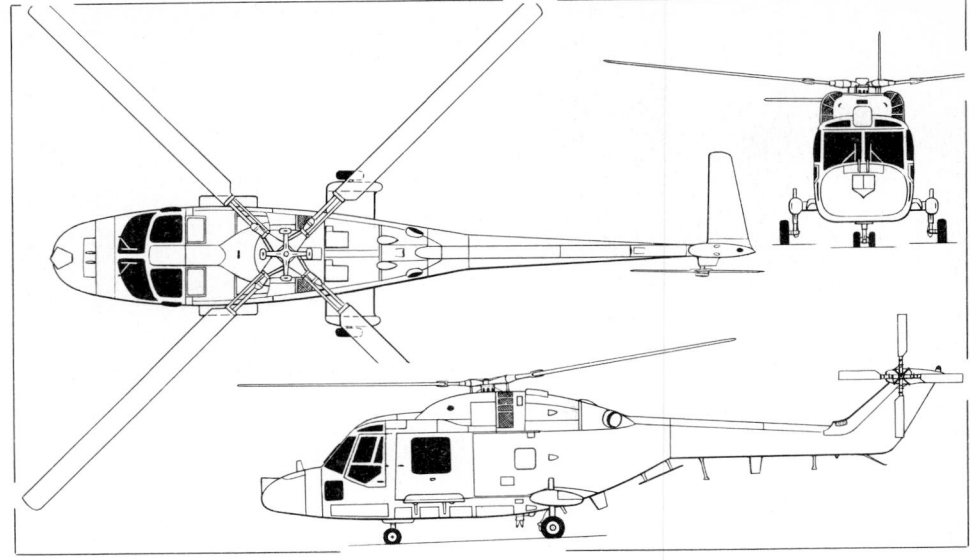

Westland Lynx HAS. Mk 2 anti-submarine helicopter for the Royal Navy (*Pilot Press*)

includes two Sea King Mk 4X for supply to RAE Farnborough. In 1982, following the Falkland Islands campaign, it was announced that a further eight had been ordered for the Royal Navy. Four more were ordered in 1984 and delivered in 1985, and ten more in 1985, of which the last was delivered in April 1987. The 28th HC.Mk 4 (ZF115) was the first production Sea King to fly from the start with composites main rotor blades, on 14 November 1985, although others had been retrofitted. One ordered in 1987 for February 1989 delivery to Empire Test Pilots School, and three in October 1987 for naval duties.

The following data apply to current production aircraft:

TYPE: Twin-turboshaft tactical military helicopter.

ROTOR SYSTEM: Five-blade main and tail rotors, of composite construction. Main rotor blades, of NACA 0012 section, attached to hub by multiple bolted joint. Rotor brake fitted. Automatic folding of main rotor blades available as an option.

ROTOR DRIVE: Twin input four-stage reduction main gearbox, with single bevel intermediate and tail gearboxes. Main rotor/engine rpm ratio 93.43; tail rotor/engine rpm ratio: 15.26.

FUSELAGE: Light alloy stressed skin structure, unpressurised. Sea King sponsons replaced by stub wings.

TAIL UNIT: Similar to Advanced Sea King, with starboard side stabiliser at top of fixed tail rotor pylon. Folding tail pylon available as an option.

LANDING GEAR: Non-retractable tailwheel type, with twin-wheel main units. Oleo-pneumatic shock absorbers. Mainwheel tyres size 6.50-10, tailwheel tyre size 6.00-6.

POWER PLANT: As for current versions of Advanced Sea King.

ACCOMMODATION: Crew of two on flight deck. Seats along cabin sides, and single jump seat, for up to 28 troops. Two-piece airstair door at front on port side, cargo door at rear on starboard side. Entire accommodation heated and ventilated. Cockpit doors and windows, and two windows each side of main cabin, are jettisonable in an emergency.

SYSTEMS: Primary and secondary hydraulic systems for flight controls. No pneumatic system. Electrical system includes two 20kVA alternators.

AVIONICS AND EQUIPMENT: Wide range of radio, radar and navigation equipment available to customer's requirements. Cargo sling and rescue hoist optional.

ARMAMENT: Wide range of guns, missiles, etc may be carried, to customer's requirements.

DIMENSIONS, EXTERNAL:

Main rotor diameter	18.90 m (62 ft 0 in)
Tail rotor diameter	3.16 m (10 ft 4 in)
Distance between rotor centres	11.10 m (36 ft 5 in)
Main rotor blade chord	0.46 m (1 ft 6¼ in)
Length overall (rotors turning)	22.15 m (72 ft 8 in)
Length of fuselage	17.02 m (55 ft 10 in)
Height overall (rotors turning)	5.13 m (16 ft 10 in)
Height to top of rotor head	4.72 m (15 ft 6 in)
Wheel track (c/l of shock absorbers)	3.96 m (13 ft 0 in)
Wheelbase	7.21 m (23 ft 8 in)
Passenger door (fwd, port):	
Height	1.68 m (5 ft 6 in)
Width	0.91 m (3 ft 0 in)
Cargo door (rear, stbd): Height	1.52 m (5 ft 0 in)
Width	1.73 m (5 ft 8 in)

DIMENSIONS, INTERNAL: As Advanced Sea King (SAR version)

AREAS: As for Advanced Sea King, plus:

Main rotor blades (each)	4.14 m² (44.54 sq ft)
Tail rotor blades (each)	0.23 m² (2.46 sq ft)
Tailplane	1.80 m² (19.40 sq ft)

WEIGHTS:

Operating weight empty (troop transport, 2 crew, typical)	5,620 kg (12,390 lb)
Max T-O weight	9,752 kg (21,500 lb)

PERFORMANCE (at max T-O weight): As given for Advanced Sea King, plus:

Range with max payload (28 troops), reserves for 30 min standoff	214 nm (396 km; 246 miles)

WESTLAND LYNX and SUPER LYNX

The Lynx is one of three types of aircraft (Puma, Gazelle and Lynx) covered by the Anglo-French helicopter agreement first proposed in February 1967 and confirmed on 2 April 1968. Westland has design leadership in the Lynx, which fulfils general purpose and naval roles.

The first of 13 Lynx prototypes (XW835) flew for the first time on 21 March 1971 and was followed by XW837, the third prototype (second Lynx to fly), on 28 September 1971. Details of subsequent development aircraft can be found in the 1975-76 *Jane's*. Production versions are as follows:

Lynx AH. Mk 1. General purpose and utility version for British Army. Total of 113 built. Described in 1986-87 and earlier editions of *Jane's*.

Lynx HAS. Mk 2. Version for Royal Navy, for advanced shipborne anti-submarine and other duties. Gem 2 engines. Ferranti Seaspray search and tracking radar in modified nose. Capable of operation on anti-submarine classification and strike, air to surface vessel search and strike, search and rescue, reconnaissance, troop transport, fire support, communication and fleet liaison, and vertical replenishment duties. Total of 60 delivered, plus 26 to French Navy, designated **HAS. Mk 2(FN)**. First production aircraft (XZ227) flown on 20 February 1976. First operational RN unit, No. 702 Squadron, formed on completion of Navy intensive flight trials in December 1977. Able to carry Sea Skua anti-ship missiles. In late 1985, the Royal Navy workshops at Yeovilton began converting HAS Mk 2s to Mk 3 standard (see below). By early 1988, the majority of the 55 active RN first-series Lynx had been thus modified.

Lynx HAS. Mk 3. Royal Navy aircraft with uprated power plant, comprising two 835 kW (1,120 shp) Rolls-Royce Gem 41-1 turboshaft engines. Delivery of original series of 20, plus three Falklands War replacements, began

Westland Sea King HC. Mk 4 logistic support version of the Commando for the Royal Navy (*RNAS Yeovilton*)

Lynx Mk 1/5 ZD285 with experimental GECAv nose turret for helmet-mounted low-light video display trials *(Paul Jackson)*

in March 1982 and was completed in April 1985. One was built for the Empire Test Pilots School, but stored in a semi-complete condition in 1987. Seven more were ordered in July 1985 and delivered from November 1987 onwards. Lynx operations centred on Portland, where 815 and 829 Squadrons provide detachments of one or two helicopters to RN warships, and 702 Squadron is training unit.

Lynx Mk 4. Second batch of 14 aircraft ordered for French Navy in May 1980 with Gem 41-1 engines and uprated transmission to permit an increase in AUW to 4,763 kg (10,500 lb). Deliveries began on 28 April 1982 and were completed in September 1983. All supplied 'green' for equipment installation by Aérospatiale and subsidiaries.

Lynx AH. Mk 5. Uprated aircraft for British Army. Similar to AH. Mk 1 but with Gem 41-1 turboshaft engines, three-pinion main gearbox and 4,535 kg (10,000 lb) AUW. Two trials aircraft built initially for RAE Bedford: AH. Mk 1/5 (ZD285), first flown 21 November 1984, with uprated three-pinion gearbox, naval Lynx sonar well and Gem 2 engines; Mk 5X (ZD559), first flown 11 February 1985, with Gem 41-1s, uprated transmission and max T-O weight of 4,535 kg (10,000 lb). Nine AH. Mk 5s ordered. Initial example (ZE375) flew on 23 February 1985 and was used for engine trials. Remainder transferred to AH. Mk 7 contract, although ZE376 flew initially as Mk 5 on 23 April 1986.

In 1987, ZD285 completed a two-year modification programme and was transferred to RAE Farnborough with a swivelling nose turret by GEC Avionics containing an image-intensifying camera and equipment (English Electric Valve Ltd/Instrument Technology Ltd). Images are fed to a pair of 25 mm video tubes in the pilot's Ferranti/GEC helmet-mounted display for trials of an operational night flying system which includes overlaid flight parameter symbology (Arcom Control Systems Ltd). Following flight trials down to 3 m (10 ft) in starlight conditions, ZD285 will be fitted with a Smiths airborne mission management system 'glass cockpit' for control of navigation, communications, threat warning and weapons systems.

Lynx AH. Mk 7. Uprated aircraft to meet GSR 3947 requirement for the British Army. As Mk 5 but with improved systems, reversed-direction (clockwise when seen from port side) tail rotor with composite blades, and 4,876 kg (10,750 lb) AUW. The more powerful tail rotor reduces noise and improves the ability to hover for extended periods at high weights, important during anti-tank operations. Eight transferred from AH. Mk 5 contract, plus five more ordered in 1985. First AH. Mk 7 (ZE376) flew for first time on 7 November 1985.

In May 1985, it was announced that Westland, with Racal Avionics as subcontractor, is developing a central tactical system (CTS) for the Lynx. This will ease the crew's workload by centrally processing all sensor data and presenting mission information on a multi-function electronic display. First flight of the CTS took place in 1987.

Lynx HAS. Mk 8. Current development proposed for the RN, having passive identification system, increased max T-O weight to 5,125 kg (11,300 lb), improved tail rotor control, BERP composite main rotor blades and a central tactical system. As first stage of Mk 8 update, two Lynx HAS. Mk 3s modified from 1987 with GECAv Sea Owl thermal imager in place of nose-mounted radar. MEL Super Searcher or Ferranti Sea Spray Mk 3 was intended for installation in under fuselage radome, but MoD cancelled 360° radar requirement in early 1988. Instead, Sea Spray radar to be retained alongside Sea Owl, and MIR-2 ESM system to be updated. Racal RAMS 4000 mission management system in prospect.

Lynx AH. Mk 9. Variant of Mk 7 with tricycle (wheel) landing gear in place of skids, and other modifications. Sixteen ordered in 1987 (plus eight conversions from Mk 1) to support newly formed 24 Airmobile Brigade, British Army. No armament.

Lynx Mk 88. ASW version for use on board frigates of the Federal German Navy. Generally similar to HAS. Mk 2 but with Gem 41-2 engines, non-folding tail and Bendix AN/AQS-18 sonar. Original batch of 12 delivered. Two more ordered in 1984 for 1986 delivery. Another five ordered in February 1986 for delivery in 1988.

Lynx Mk 90. Improved version of Royal Danish Navy Mk 80, having Racal MIR-2 'Orange Crop' ESM and tactical data system (to which standard earlier Lynx being updated). First flown (S-249) 15 April 1987 as conversion of embargoed Argentine Mk 87 and ex-demonstrator G-BKBL. Delivered 22 May 1987. Second airframe (S-256) was 90% complete Mk 87 finished by Danish military workshop. Surviving Argentine Mk 23 purchased in 1987 for modification by Westland (as S-035).

Other versions, for which orders have been completed (described in the 1983-84 *Jane's*), comprise Lynx Mk 2 (FN) (14 French Navy), Mk 21 (nine Brazilian Navy), Mk 23 (two Argentine Navy), Mk 25 (six Netherlands Navy UH-14A), Mk 27 (ten Netherlands Navy SH-14B), Mk 28 (three Qatar Police), Mk 80 (eight Danish Navy), Mk 81 (eight Netherlands Navy SH-14C), Mk 86 (six Norwegian Air Force/Coast Guard) and Mk 89 (three Nigerian Navy). Versions not built were: Mk 6 (Royal Marines), Mk 22 (Egyptian Army), Mk 24 (Iraqi Army), Mk 26 (Iraqi Army - armed), Mk 82 (Egyptian utility export), Mk 83 (Saudi Army), Mk 84 (Qatar Army), Mk 85 (United Arab Emirates Army) and Mk 87 (Argentine Navy - embargoed).

Well over 300 Lynx are in service. Production is shared in the ratio of 70 per cent by Westland to 30 per cent by Aérospatiale.

Under development is a new export version of the Navy Lynx known as **Super Lynx**, with extended range and payload and all-weather day/night capability, using advanced dipping sonar and 360° radar. Powered by 835 kW (1,120 shp) Rolls-Royce Gem 42-1 engines, it will be fitted with a new high-efficiency tail rotor and Westland's new advanced technology swept-tip composites main rotor blades. Weapons will include Penguin and Sea Skua missiles and Sting Ray torpedoes.

On 11 August 1986, the Lynx demonstrator G-LYNX set the current world's absolute speed record for helicopters by averaging 216.45 knots (400.87 km/h; 249.09 mph) over a 15/25 km course. The Lynx was modified for the attempt, with BERP III main rotor blades, Westland 30 type tail surfaces and other performance enhancements (see 1986-87 *Jane's*).

The following description applies to both the military general purpose and naval versions with the Gem 2 power plant, except where indicated:

TYPE: Twin-engined multi purpose helicopter.

ROTOR SYSTEM: Single four-blade semi-rigid main rotor and four-blade tail rotor. Each blade is attached to the main rotor hub by titanium root attachment plates and a flexible arm. The rotor hub and inboard portions of the flexible arms are built as a complete unit, in the form of a titanium monobloc forging. Tail rotor blades have a light alloy spar, stainless steel leading-edge sheath, and rear section similar to that of main rotor blades. Main rotor blades of both versions can be folded.

ROTOR DRIVE: Drives are taken from the front of the engines into the main gearbox, which is mounted above the cabin forward of the engines. This gearbox interconnects the two engines, with speed reduction in two stages. In flight, the accessory gears, which are all at the front of the main gearbox, are driven by one of the two through shafts from the first stage reduction gears. For system checking on the ground without the rotor turning, the accessories can be driven by the port engine. Freewheel units are mounted in each engine gearbox shaft, and also within the accessory drive chain of gears. Rotor head controls are actuated by three identical tandem servo jacks, trunnion mounted from the main rotor gearbox and powered by two independent hydraulic systems. Control system incorporates a simple stability augmentation system. Provision is made for in-flight blade tracking. Each engine embodies an independent control system which provides full authority rotor speed governing, pilot control being limited to selection of the desired rotor speed range. In the event of an engine failure, this system will restore power up to single engine maximum contingency rating. On the naval versions, the main rotor can provide negative thrust to increase stability on deck after touchdown. Tail rotor drive is taken from the main ring gear. A hydraulically operated rotor brake is mounted on the main gearbox.

FUSELAGE AND TAIL UNIT: Conventional semi-monocoque pod and boom structure, mainly of light alloy. Glassfibre components used for access panels, doors and fairings. Single large window in each of the main cabin sliding doors. Provision for internally mounted defensive armament, and for universal flange mountings on each side of the exterior to carry weapons or other stores. Tailboom is a light alloy monocoque structure bearing the sweptback vertical fin/tail rotor pylon, which has a half tailplane near the tip on the starboard side. Tail pylon leading- and trailing-edges, and bullet fairing over tail rotor gearbox, are of glassfibre. Tail pylon of naval version can be folded and spread manually, to reduce overall length for stowage.

LANDING GEAR (general purpose military version): Non-retractable tubular skid type. Provision for a pair of adjustable ground handling wheels on each skid. Flotation gear optional.

LANDING GEAR (naval versions): Non-retractable oleo-pneumatic tricycle type. Single-wheel main units, carried on sponsons, are fixed at 27° toe-out for deck landing, and can be manually turned into line and locked fore and aft for movement of aircraft into and out of ship's hangar. Twin-wheel nose unit can be steered hydraulically through 90° by the pilot to facilitate independent take-off into wind. Sprag brakes (wheel locks) fitted to each wheel prevent rotation on landing or inadvertent deck roll. These locks are disengaged hydraulically and will re-engage automatically in the event of hydraulic failure. Flotation gear, and hydraulically actuated harpoon deck lock securing system, optional.

POWER PLANT: Two Rolls-Royce Gem 2 turboshafts, each with max contingency rating of 671 kW (900 shp) in Lynx AH. 1, HAS. 2 and early export variants. Later versions have Gem 41-1 or 41-2 engines, each with max contingency rating of 835 kW (1,120 shp), or Gem 42-1 engines, each with max contingency rating of 846 kW (1,135 shp). Engines of British and French Lynx in service being converted to Mk 42 standard during regular overhauls from 1987 onwards. Engine oil tank capacity 6.8 litres (1.8 US gallons; 1.5 Imp gallons). Main rotor gearbox oil capacity 18 litres (4.8 US gallons; 4 Imp gallons).

ACCOMMODATION: Pilot and co-pilot or observer on side by side seats. Dual controls optional. Individual forward hinged cockpit door and large rearward sliding cabin door on each side; all four doors jettisonable. Cockpit accessible from cabin area. Maximum high density layout (general purpose version) for one pilot and 10 armed troops or paratroops, on lightweight bench seats in soundproofed cabin. Alternative VIP layouts for four to seven passengers, with additional cabin soundproofing. Seats can be removed quickly to permit the carriage of up to 907 kg (2,000 lb) of freight internally. Tiedown rings are provided. In the casualty evacuation role, with a crew of two, the Lynx can accommodate three standard stretchers and a medical attendant. Both basic versions have secondary capability for search and rescue (up to nine survivors) and other roles.

SYSTEMS: Two independent hydraulic systems, pressure 141 bars (2,050 lb/sq in). A third hydraulic system is provided in the naval version when sonar equipment, MAD or a hydraulic winch system is installed. No pneumatic system. 28V DC electrical power supplied by two 6kW engine driven starter/generators and an alternator. External power sockets. 24V 23Ah (optionally 40Ah) nickel-cadmium battery fitted for essential services and emergency engine starting. 200V three-phase AC power available at 400Hz from two 15kVA transmission driven alternators. Graviner Triple FD engine fire detection system; two separate fire suppression systems fitted. Optional cabin heating and ventilation system. Optional supplementary cockpit heating system. Electric anti-icing and demisting of windscreen, and electrically operated windscreen wipers, standard; windscreen washing system optional.

Prototype Westland Lynx AH. Mk 7 for British Army

AVIONICS AND FLIGHT EQUIPMENT: All versions equipped as standard with navigation, cabin and cockpit lights; adjustable landing light under nose; anti-collision beacon; first aid kit(s); and hand fire extinguishers for cabin. Avionics common to all roles (general purpose and naval versions) include GEC Avionics duplex three-axis automatic stabilisation equipment; Sperry GM9 Gyrosyn compass system; Decca tactical air navigation system (TANS); Decca 71 Doppler, E2C standby compass; and S.G. Brown intercom system. Optional role equipment for both versions includes GEC Avionics automatic flight control system (AFCS); Collins VOR/ILS; DME; Collins ARN-118 Tacan; I-band transponder (naval version only); Plessey PTR 446, Collins APX-72, Siemens STR 700/375 or Italtel APX-77 IFF; and vortex sand filter for engine air intakes. Additional units are fitted in naval version, when sonar is fitted, to provide automatic transition to hover and automatic Doppler hold in hover.

ARMAMENT AND OPERATIONAL EQUIPMENT: For armed escort, anti-tank or air-to-surface strike missions, general purpose version can be equipped with one 20 mm cannon mounted in the cabin; or two 20 mm cannon mounted externally so as to permit the carriage also of anti-tank missiles or a pintle-mounted 7.62 mm machine-gun inside the cabin; or a side mounted 25 mm Oerlikon cannon. External pylon can be fitted on each side of cabin for a variety of stores, including two Minigun or other self-contained gun pods; two rocket pods; or up to eight Aérospatiale/MBB Hot, Rockwell Hellfire, Hughes TOW, or similar air-to-surface missiles. An additional six or eight missiles can be carried in cabin, for rearming in forward areas, and a stabilised sight is fitted for target detection and missile direction. British Army Lynx aircraft equipped with TOW missiles have roof mounted Hughes sight manufactured under licence by British Aerospace. The TOW roof sight is being upgraded to have a night vision capability in the far infra-red waveband to increase operational versatility in low-light night conditions or poor daylight visibility. The Lynx can transport anti-tank teams of three gunners with missiles and launchers. Sanders AN/ALQ-144 infra-red jammer installed beneath tailboom of some British Army Lynx from 1987. Requirement issued for radar warning receiver. For search and rescue role, with three crew, both versions can have a waterproof floor and a 272 kg (600 lb) capacity 'clip-on' hoist on starboard side of cabin. Optional equipment, according to role, can include lightweight sighting system with alternative target magnification, vertical and/or oblique cameras, flares for night operation, low light level TV, infra-red linescan, searchlight, and specialised communications equipment. Naval version can carry out a number of these roles, but has specialised equipment for its primary duties. For ASW role, this includes two Mk 44, Mk 46 or Sting Ray homing torpedoes, one each on an external pylon on each side of fuselage, and six marine markers; or two Mk 11 depth charges. Detection of submarines is by means of dipping sonars or magnetic anomaly detector. The dipping sonars are operated by a hydraulically powered winch and cable hover mode facilities within the AFCS. CAE Electronics internal MAD ordered for RN Lynx in 1987. Tracor M-130 chaff/flare dispensers and Whittaker Microwave Systems AN/ALQ-167(V) D-J band anti-anti-ship missile jamming pods installed on RN Lynx patrolling Arabian Gulf, 1987. Ferranti Seaspray lightweight search and tracking radar, for detecting small surface targets in low visibility/high sea conditions. Armament includes four BAe Sea Skua semi-active homing missiles for attacking light surface craft; alternatively, four AS.12 or similar wire guided missiles can be employed in conjunction with AF 530 or APX-334 lightweight stabilised optical sighting system.

DIMENSIONS, EXTERNAL (A: general purpose version; N: naval version):

Main rotor diameter (A, N)	12.80 m (42 ft 0 in)
Tail rotor diameter (A, N)	2.21 m (7 ft 3 in)
Length overall:	
A, N both rotors turning	15.163 m (49 ft 9 in)
N, main rotor blades and tail folded	10.618 m (34 ft 10 in)
Width overall, main rotor blades folded:	
A	2.94 m (9 ft 7¾ in)
N	3.75 m (12 ft 3¾ in)
Height overall, both rotors stopped:	
A	3.504 m (11 ft 6 in)
N	3.48 m (11 ft 5 in)
Height overall, main rotor blades and tail folded:	
N	3.20 m (10 ft 6 in)
Skid track: A	2.032 m (6 ft 8 in)
Wheel track: N	2.778 m (9 ft 1.4 in)
Wheelbase: N	2.94 m (9 ft 7¾ in)

DIMENSIONS, INTERNAL:

Cabin, from back of pilots' seats:	
Min length	2.057 m (6 ft 9 in)
Max width	1.778 m (5 ft 10 in)
Max height	1.422 m (4 ft 8 in)
Floor area	3.72 m² (40.04 sq ft)
Volume	5.21 m³ (184 cu ft)

AREAS:

Main rotor disc	128.7 m² (1,385.4 sq ft)
Tail rotor disc	3.84 m² (41.28 sq ft)

Westland Super Lynx, advanced version of Navy Lynx *(Pilot Press)*

Westland Lynx HAS. Mk 3 carrying Sea Skua missiles and ALQ-167 'Yellow Veil' jamming pod
(HMS Heron)

WEIGHTS (A: general purpose version, N: naval version):

Manufacturer's empty weight: A	2,578 kg (5,683 lb)
N	2,740 kg (6,040 lb)
Manufacturer's basic weight: A	2,658 kg (5,860 lb)
N	3,030 kg (6,680 lb)
Operating weight empty, equipped:	
A, troop transport (pilot and 10 troops)	2,787 kg (6,144 lb)
A, anti-tank strike (incl weapon pylons, firing equipment and sight)	3,072 kg (6,772 lb)
A, search and rescue (crew of three)	2,963 kg (6,532 lb)
N, anti-submarine strike	3,343 kg (7,370 lb)
N, reconnaissance (crew of two)	3,277 kg (7,224 lb)
N, anti-submarine classification and strike	3,472 kg (7,654 lb)
N, air to surface vessel search and strike (crew of two and four Sea Skuas)	3,414 kg (7,526 lb)
N, search and rescue (crew of three)	3,416 kg (7,531 lb)
N, dunking sonar search and strike	3,650 kg (8,047 lb)
Max T-O weight: A	4,535 kg (10,000 lb)
N	4,763 kg (10,500 lb)

PERFORMANCE (at normal max T-O weight at S/L, ISA, except where indicated. A: general purpose version; N: naval version):

Max continuous cruising speed:	
A	140 knots (259 km/h; 161 mph)
N	125 knots (232 km/h; 144 mph)
A (ISA + 20°C)	130 knots (241 km/h; 150 mph)
N (ISA + 20°C)	114 knots (211 km/h; 131 mph)
Speed for max endurance:	
A, N (ISA and ISA + 20°C)	70 knots (130 km/h; 81 mph)

Max forward rate of climb: A	756 m (2,480 ft)/min
N	661 m (2,170 ft)/min
A (ISA + 20°C)	536 m (1,760 ft)/min
N (ISA + 20°C)	469 m (1,540 ft)/min
Max vertical rate of climb:	
A	472 m (1,550 ft)/min
N	351 m (1,150 ft)/min
A (ISA + 20°C)	390 m (1,280 ft)/min
N (ISA + 20°C)	244 m (800 ft)/min
Hovering ceiling OGE: A	3,230 m (10,600 ft)
N	2,575 m (8,450 ft)

Typical range, with reserves:
A, troop transport   292 nm (540 km; 336 miles)
Radius of action, out and back at max sustained speed, allowances for T-O and landing, 30 min loiter in search area, 3 min hover for each survivor, and 10% fuel reserves at end of mission:
N, search and rescue (crew of 3 and 2 survivors)
115 nm (212 km; 132 miles)
N, search and rescue (crew of 3 and 7 survivors)
96 nm (178 km; 111 miles)

Time on station at 50 nm (93 km; 58 miles) radius, out and back at max sustained speed, with 2 torpedoes, smoke floats and marine markers, allowances for T-O and landing and 10% fuel reserves at end of mission:
N, anti-submarine classification and strike, loiter speed on station   2 h 0 min
N, anti-submarine strike, loiter on station
2 h 29 min
N, dunking sonar search and strike, 50% loiter speed and 50% hover on station   1 h 5 min

Time on station at 50 nm (93 km; 58 miles) radius, out and back at max sustained speed, with crew of 2 and 4 Sea Skuas, allowances and reserves as above:

N, air to surface vessel strike, en-route radar search
and loiter speed on station 1 h 36 min
Max range: A 340 nm (630 km; 392 miles)
N 320 nm (593 km; 368 miles)
Max endurance: A 2 h 57 min
N (ISA + 20°C) 2 h 50 min
Max ferry range with auxiliary cabin tanks:
A 724 nm (1,342 km; 834 miles)
N 565 nm (1,046 km; 650 miles)

WESTLAND LYNX-3
The Lynx-3 dedicated anti-tank helicopter flew for the
first time in 1984. One prototype (ZE477) was built, but the
programme has now been abandoned. Full details of the
Lynx-3 last appeared in the 1987-88 edition.

WESTLAND 30 (TT30 and TT300)
Production of the Westland 30 ended in January 1988
with completion of the 38th airframe, including 21 delivered
to Pawan Hans (formerly the Helicopter Corporation of
India), prototypes and demonstrators. Westland remains
prepared to re-open the production line in the event of an
economical order being received, but readers are meanwhile
referred to the 1987-88 and earlier editions of *Jane's* for a
full history and technical description.

WESTLAND/SIKORSKY WS 70
Following agreement of full partnership with United
Technologies, Westland received US State Department
approval to produce a version of the Sikorsky Black Hawk
helicopter designated WS 70. The Westland board set aside
£3 million for a demonstrator (ZG468), which was
assembled from a Sikorsky kit to US Army S-70A
battlefield transport standards. Powered by two General
Electric T700 turboshaft engines, it flew for the first time on
1 April 1987 and is used for training and market support
activities. First order, for 80 WS 70s, was reportedly placed
by Saudi Arabia in July 1988.
The details given for the S-60A Black Hawk in the US
section apply to the Westland WS 70 except as follows:

POWER PLANT: Two 1,126 kW (1,510 shp) General Electric
T700-GE-701A turboshafts.
AVIONICS AND EQUIPMENT: Communications equipment
includes Racal B693 com, GEC AD3400 V/UHF AM
and FM, Collins HF 9000, Chelton Series 7 VHF/FM
homing, plus customer specified equipment. Navigation
equipment includes AN/ASN-43 compass, Racal Decca
91 Doppler, Racal RNS 252 navigation system, Bendix
DMS 44 DME, Cossor 2720 IFF, plus customer specified
equipment.

WEIGHTS:
Weight empty 4,915 kg (10,835 lb)
Mission T-O weight 7,632 kg (16,825 lb)
Max alternative T-O weight 9,979 kg (22,000 lb)

EH 101
Details of this programme, in which Westland is in
partnership with Agusta of Italy, can be found in the
International section.

Prototype of the Westland/Sikorsky WS 70 (two General Electric T700 turboshaft engines)

UNITED STATES OF AMERICA

AAI
AMERICAN AVIATION INDUSTRIES
16700 Roscoe Boulevard, Van Nuys, California 91406
Telephone: (818) 786 1921
Telex: 662903 ACI USA
CHIEF EXECUTIVE OFFICER: Geoff Miller
VICE-PRESIDENT, MARKETING: Don Sterling
Aviation Consultants Inc formed American Aviation
Industries to re-engine Lockheed JetStar business jets with
new turbofans. The modified aircraft is known as the
FanStar. AAI also planned re-engining programmes for
other business jet and commuter aircraft, including the
Fairchild Swearingen Metro II.

AAI FANSTAR
The FanStar conversion involves the removal of the four
14.68 kN (3,300 lb st) Pratt & Whitney JT12 turbojets or the
four 16.46 kN (3,700 lb st) Garrett TFE731-3 turbofans
from Lockheed JetStar I and II aircraft respectively, and
replacing them with two General Electric CF34-3A high
bypass turbofans, each rated at 40.70 kN (9,150 lb st) with
automatic power reserve (APR), 38.48 kN (8,650 lb)
without APR, installed in new translating sleeve, short-cowl
nacelles with cascade type thrust reversers. Fuel capacity is
10,069 litres (2,660 US gallons; 2,215 Imp gallons) in four
integral wing tanks and two non-removable external tanks.
Other changes include replacement of the aircraft's DC
electrical system by an AC system with power rectified into
DC, with static inverters to supply regulated AC where
needed. The inverters are of the dual split-bus type, with no
load shedding, and permit operation of all AC components
in the event of engine failure. A dual fuel pump system is
installed if not already fitted, and a new high-flow
high-pressure Sundstrand Turbomach APU is supplied.
Structural changes include the addition of a 0.61 m (2 ft 0
in) extension and 1.22 m (4 ft 0 in) high NASA (Whitcomb)
winglet to each wingtip, and a 0.76 m (2 ft 6 in) extension to
the rudder below the tailplane for improved yaw control,
connected to a rudder bias system for enhanced directional
control in engine-out situations. A Collins APS-85 digital
autopilot with solid state heading and reference systems
replaces all existing gyros and autopilot components. A full
EFIS display and long-range navigation equipment are
available.
AAI claims a reduction in direct operating costs of 34 per
cent over the unconverted JetStar, with a 10-year extension
of service life. A further advantage is compliance with FAR
Part 36 noise regulations. The proof of concept prototype, a
JetStar Dash 8 (N380AA), was delivered in May 1985 to
General Electric's Mojave Flight Test Center in California,
and made its first flight, with lower rated CF34-1A engines,
on 5 September 1986. FAA approval, by Supplemental
Type Certificate, was anticipated in July 1987, with

Prototype American Aviation Industries FanStar conversion of Lockheed JetStar business jet

simultaneous start of production conversions. By January
1987 AAI had received orders for 17 FanStar conversions,
since when no further information has been received.
DIMENSIONS, EXTERNAL:
Wing span 18.79 m (61 ft 8 in)
Wing chord: at root 4.16 m (13 ft 7¾ in)
at tip 1.14 m (3 ft 9 in)
Wing aspect ratio 6.0
Length overall 18.41 m (60 ft 5 in)
Height overall 6.22 m (20 ft 5 in)
Tailplane span 7.54 m (24 ft 9 in)
Wheel track 3.75 m (12 ft 3½ in)
Wheelbase 6.68 m (20 ft 7 in)
DIMENSIONS, INTERNAL:
Cabin: Length 8.60 m (28 ft 2½ in)
Max width 1.89 m (6 ft 2½ in)
Max height 1.85 m (6 ft 1 in)
Floor area 15.33 m² (165 sq ft)
Volume 29.31 m³ (1,035 cu ft)
AREAS:
Wings, gross 52.72 m² (567.5 sq ft)
Ailerons (total) 4.53 m² (48.8 sq ft)
Trailing-edge flaps (total) 5.81 m² (62.6 sq ft)
Leading-edge slats (total) 3.16 m² (34.0 sq ft)
Winglets (total) 2.28 m² (24.5 sq ft)
Speed-brake 0.85 m² (9.2 sq ft)
Fin 8.73 m² (94.0 sq ft)
Rudder 1.50 m² (16.2 sq ft)
Tailplane 10.94 m² (117.8 sq ft)
Elevators (total) 2.90 m² (31.2 sq ft)
WEIGHTS AND LOADINGS:
Weight empty 10,511 kg (23,174 lb)

Max fuel weight 8,266 kg (18,224 lb)
Max T-O weight 20,185 kg (44,500 lb)
Max ramp weight 20,298 kg (44,750 lb)
Max zero-fuel weight 12,474 kg (27,500 lb)
Max landing weight 16,329 kg (36,000 lb)
Max wing loading 382.9 kg/m² (78.4 lb/sq ft)
Max power loading 249.4 kg/kN (2.44 lb/lb st)
PERFORMANCE (estimated at max T-O weight except where
indicated):
Never-exceed speed Mach 0.87
Max level speed at 7,010 m (23,000 ft)
479 knots (888 km/h; 551 mph)
Max cruising speed at 13,100 m (43,000 ft)
459 knots (851 km/h 528 mph)
Econ cruising speed at 12,500 m (41,000 ft)
418 knots (775 km/h; 481 mph)
Stalling speed, T-O flap setting
123 knots (228 km/h; 142 mph)
Max rate of climb at S/L 1,225 m (4,020 ft)/min
Rate of climb at S/L, one engine out
366 m (1,200 ft)/min
Service ceiling 13,105 m (43,000 ft)
Service ceiling, one engine out 6,400 m (21,000 ft)
T-O run 980 m (3,216 ft)
T-O to 15 m (50 ft) 1,707 m (5,600 ft)
Landing run 1,067 m (3,500 ft)
Range with max fuel 3,550 nm (6,579 km; 4,088 miles)

OPERATIONAL NOISE LEVELS (estimated):
T-O 79.4 EPNdB
Approach 89.4 EPNdB
Sideline 84.9 EPNdB

ACA

ACA INDUSTRIES INC

28603 Trailriders Drive, Rancho Palos Verdes, California 90274
Telephone: (213) 539 7121
PRESIDENT: Dr Julian Wolkovitch

In 1974 Englishman Dr Julian Wolkovitch flew a proof-of-concept glider featuring his patented joined wing configuration which comprises two sets of wings arranged to form diamond shapes in plan and front views. The configuration was adopted subsequently for the Summit Trident T-3 microlight aircraft (see Sport Aircraft section of 1987-88 *Jane's*).

The Defense Advanced Research Projects Agency (DARPA), NASA and the US Navy have supported research into the joined wing concept for application to aircraft and missiles. Claimed benefits of the configuration, drawn from wind tunnel tests and structural analyses, include lighter weight, greater stiffness, less induced drag, lower wave drag, higher trimmed maximum lift coefficient and inbuilt direct lift and sideforce capabilities.

Studies by its Ames Research Center having shown that a joined wing weighs some 40 per cent less than aerodynamically equivalent conventional wing and tail surfaces, NASA awarded ACA a contract to design a manned research aircraft. ACA is studying applications for joined wings, which may include transport and general aviation aircraft, fighters, VTOL aircraft, agricultural aircraft and RPVs, and is providing consultancy services to Rockwell International and other manufacturers working on joined wing aircraft projects.

ACA JW-1, JW-2 and JW-3

In March 1986 ACA Industries began work on redesigning the Ames/NASA AD-1 oblique wing research aircraft (described in the 1981-82 *Jane's*) as a joined wing technology demonstrator. It proposes to use the fuselage, engines and landing gear of the AD-1 mated to a new joined wing which will have removable tip panels, enabling the aircraft to be progressively modified to configurations with the wing joint located at 60 per cent, 80 per cent and 100 per cent of span. Initially the aircraft will be configured with the joint at 60 per cent span, and designated **JW-1**. The tip panels will subsequently be removed in two phases to create the **JW-2** (joint at 80 per cent span) and **JW-3** (joint at 100 per cent span). NASA wind tunnel tests of ⅙ scale models of the JW-1, JW-2 and JW-3 were completed during 1987. Detail design work was in progress in early 1988, with a first flight in JW-1 configuration scheduled for 1990.

TYPE: Single-seat research aircraft.

WINGS: Front and rear wings in joined wing configuration. Two-spar fail-safe structure of composite materials. Wing section specially designed by NASA. Thickness/chord ratio 11.3% on front wing, 12.1% on rear wing. Dihedral 5° on front wing. Anhedral 20° on rear wing. Sweepback 30° 28' on front wing. Sweepforward at quarter-chord 31° 50' on rear wing. In JW-1 configuration front wing has six trailing-edge control surfaces, rear wing four trailing-edge control surfaces, which can operate in a variety of combinations to provide pitch, roll and direct lift control.

FUSELAGE: Fail-safe structure of composite construction. Single airbrake on each side of fuselage.

TAIL UNIT: Single vertical fin with rudder. Streamlined 'bullet' fairing at junction with rear wing.

LANDING GEAR: Non-retractable tricycle type.

POWER PLANT: Two Ames Industrial Corporation TRS 18-046 turbojets, each rated at 0.978 kN (220 lb st), mounted in pods aft of front wing/fuselage junction.

ACCOMMODATION: Pilot only, in enclosed cockpit with canopy. Cockpit is not pressurised.

DIMENSIONS, EXTERNAL (A: JW-1, B: JW-2, C: JW-3):

Wing span, front: A	12.19 m (40 ft 0 in)
B	9.84 m (32 ft 3½ in)
C	7.31 m (24 ft 0 in)
rear, all	7.31 m (24 ft 0 in)
Wing chord: at root: all	1.19 m (3 ft 11 in)
at tip: A	0.48 m (1 ft 6¾ in)
B	0.61 m (2 ft 0 in)
C	0.76 m (2 ft 6 in)
Wing aspect ratio, front: A	11.18
B	8.07
C	5.21

AREAS:

Wings, gross: A	13.29 m² (143.1 sq ft)
B	12.01 m² (129.3 sq ft)
C	10.27 m² (110.6 sq ft)
Front wing: A	10.17 m² (109.5 sq ft)
B	8.89 m² (95.7 sq ft)
C	7.15 m² (77.0 sq ft)
Rear wing: all	3.12 m² (33.6 sq ft)

WEIGHT AND LOADINGS:

Max T-O weight	973 kg (2,145 lb)
Max wing loading: A	73.21 kg/m² (14.99 lb/sq ft)
B	81.01 kg/m² (16.59 lb/sq ft)
C	94.74 kg/m² (19.39 lb/sq ft)

PERFORMANCE (estimated):

Max level speed at 2,135 m (7,000 ft):

A	276 knots (511 km/h; 318 mph)
B	283 knots (524 km/h; 326 mph)
C	291 knots (539 km/h; 335 mph)

Max rate of climb at S/L, ISA:

A, B, C	518 m (1,700 ft)/min

Rate of climb at S/L, ISA, one engine out:

A, B	152 m (500 ft)/min
C	91 m (300 ft)/min

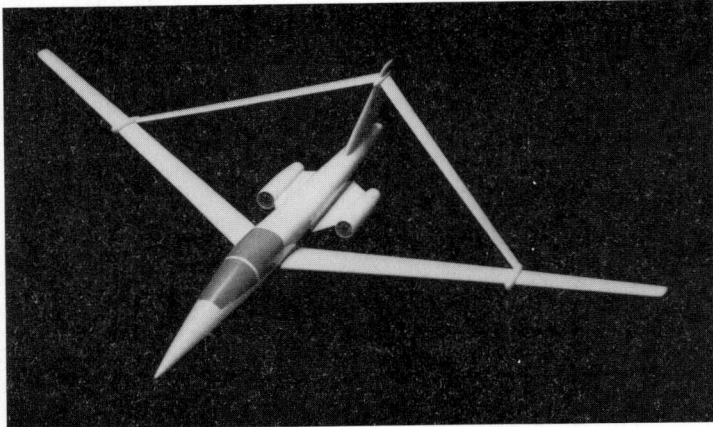
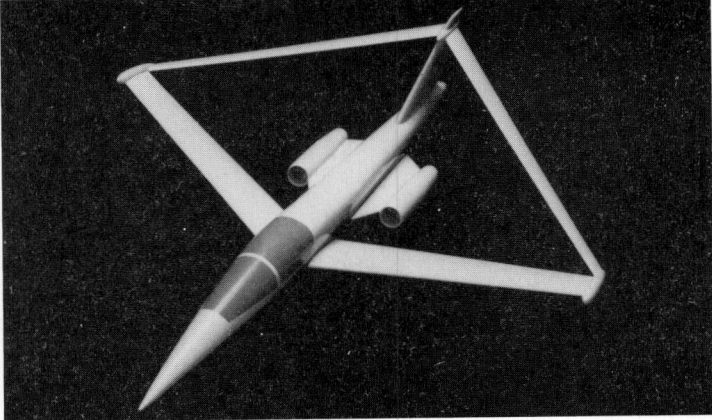

Models of the ACA JW-1 (left) and JW-3 long- and short-span versions of NASA's joined wing research aircraft

ADVANCED AIRCRAFT

ADVANCED AIRCRAFT CORPORATION

2016 Palomar Airport Road, Carlsbad, California 92008
Telephone: (619) 438 1964
Telex: 249075 (ATSD UR)
PRESIDENT: Neil F. Martin
GENERAL MANAGER: Leland L. Dimon III

This company was formed on 1 July 1983. It has acquired the production facilities of the former Riley Aircraft Manufacturing Inc (see 1983-84 *Jane's*). The following conversions of Cessna aircraft were available in 1987, since when no further information has been received.

ADVANCED AIRCRAFT TURBINE P-210

The basic Cessna Model 210 Centurion, and the variations for the Pressurised Centurion, have been described fully under the Cessna entry in previous editions of *Jane's*. The Advanced Aircraft Turbine P-210 (previously known as the Spirit 750) is a turboprop conversion of the Pressurised Centurion, developed by Riley Aircraft Manufacturing. The Riley prototype, powered by a Pratt & Whitney Canada PT6A-112 turboprop flat rated at 373 kW (500 shp), made its first flight on 30 June 1982. Development was delayed subsequently during financial reorganisation of the Riley company, and manufacturing and marketing rights for the modification were acquired by Advanced Aircraft Corporation in 1983. Flight testing resumed in March 1984, but the prototype was lost on 18 May during spinning trials with a radar pod on the starboard wing. A second prototype began flying in November 1984, and an FAA Supplemental Type Certificate was granted during 1985.

The current Turbine P-210 is powered by a 559 kW (750 shp) PT6A-135 turboprop, flat rated at 335.5 kW (450 shp) and driving a Hartzell three-blade constant-speed fully-feathering and reversible-pitch Q-tip propeller with spinner. The conversion includes modified control surfaces, the addition of a ventral fin, installation of a glassfibre aerodynamic cowling with inertial separator and electric induction air lip de-icing, electric propeller de-icing, a Lear Siegler 28V 200A starter/generator, a 28V 50A standby generator, Gill 639T heavy duty battery, fuel computer, a new engine instrument panel, a 24V electrical system to meet FAA requirements, Flint wingtip fuel tanks with a combined capacity of 62.5 litres (16.5 US gallons; 13.7 Imp gallons), and 3M Stormscope radar.

DIMENSIONS, EXTERNAL: As for Cessna Centurion, except:

Length overall	9.17 m (30 ft 1 in)
Propeller diameter	1.98 m (6 ft 6 in)

WEIGHTS AND LOADINGS:

Weight empty	1,199 kg (2,621 lb)
Max ramp weight	1,822 kg (4,016 lb)
Max T-O weight	1,814 kg (4,000 lb)
Max landing weight	1,723 kg (3,800 lb)
Max wing loading	102.53 kg/m² (21.0 lb/sq ft)
Max power loading	5.41 kg/kW (8.88 lb/shp)

PERFORMANCE (at max T-O weight except where indicated):

Max cruising speed at 7,010 m (23,000 ft)	253 knots (470 km/h; 292 mph)
Econ cruising speed	213 knots (394 km/h; 245 mph)

Stalling speed:

flaps up	67 knots (125 km/h; 78 mph) IAS
30% flap	63 knots (117 km/h; 73 mph) IAS
flaps down	58 knots (108 km/h; 67 mph) IAS
Max rate of climb at S/L	549 m (1,800 ft)/min

Advanced Aircraft Turbine P-210 turboprop conversion of Cessna Pressurised Centurion, before addition of ventral fin

A WORLD OF OPPORTUNITIES WAITING TO BE SHARED

At McDonnell Douglas, we've established an enviable heritage of sharing with international partners the benefits of our company's capabilities and talents in aviation, space and information systems.

Global financiers count on our fast and accurate Tymnet® information systems. European manufacturers trust us for cad/cam. Great Britain shares with us the advanced development of the vertical takeoff fighter, the Harrier II, as well as the T45 training system. We join with Korea in the manufacture of helicopters. Canada, China, Italy and Sweden know us for the MD airliners they help us develop and build. In Australia, Canada and Spain we work jointly on F/A-18 Hornets.

International ventures such as these have introduced new technologies and expanded others, helping McDonnell Douglas keep its promises to create human opportunities, foster economic growth and bring new commerce to our international business partners. For more than 65 years, we've given customers products that promised performance —and delivered.

MCDONNELL DOUGLAS
Giving the nations of the world their money's worth.

INFORMATION SYSTEMS   HEALTH CARE   HELICOPTERS   MILITARY AND COMMERCIAL AIRCRAFT   SPACE AND MISSILE SYSTEMS

IT'S GOT OUR NAME WRITTEN ALL OVER IT.

We're the leading edge in wings. And the last word in communications.

We're a proven direction in avionics. And the propulsion systems that get you there.

We're the air you breathe. And the muscle to stop a 200-ton jumbo.

We can hit Mach 3+. Or a target the size of this page.

We're hypersonic. We're undersea. We're armored and armor-piercing.

We can give you sight in the dark. Or electricity on the moon.

We can project an electronic map. And fly you to it by wire.

We're military. And civilian.

We're commercial aviation. And general aviation.

We're Allied-Signal Aerospace.

A more aerodynamic aerospace company.

Allied-Signal Aerospace Company

Service ceiling   above 7,010 m (23,000 ft)
T-O to 15 m (50 ft) at AUW of 1,542 kg (3,400 lb)
                                      334 m (1,095 ft)
Landing from 15 m (50 ft) at AUW of 1,542 kg (3,400 lb)
                                      394 m (1,291 ft)
Range with max fuel, ISA, max cruise power at 7,010 m
(23,000 ft), allowances for start, taxi, take-off, climb
and descent, 45 min reserves
                            1,008 nm (1,868 km; 1,160 miles)

ADVANCED AIRCRAFT REGENT 1500

Known formerly as the Riley Turbine Eagle 421, this
modification unites the Cessna 421C Golden Eagle airframe
with Pratt & Whitney Canada PT6A turboprops, mounted
in new low-drag nacelles. Each engine has more than double
the power output of the one it replaces, yet weighs some 40
per cent less. The Riley prototype flew for the first time in
late November 1979, at Palomar Airport, and the
certification programme was completed during 1980.

A description of the Cessna 421C Golden Eagle appeared
under the Cessna entry in the 1985-86 edition; it applies also
to the Regent 1500 (421CP), except as follows:

POWER PLANT: Two Pratt & Whitney Canada PT6A-135
  turboprops, each flat rated at 559 kW (750 shp), and
  driving Hartzell three-blade constant-speed autofeathering reversible-pitch propellers with Q-tips and spinners.
  Standard fuel as for Cessna 421C, but auxiliary tanks in
  rear of nacelles with combined capacity of 568 litres (150
  US gallons; 125 Imp gallons). Optionally, the rear
  nacelles can be replaced by new all-glassfibre fuel tanks
  which increase standard fuel capacity by a total of 605
  litres (160 US gallons; 133 Imp gallons). Advanced
  aerodynamic cowlings incorporate inertial separators.
  Electric de-icing of propellers and air intakes.
SYSTEMS: Generally as for Cessna 421C, except bleed air unit
  for pressurisation system; electrical system with 200A
  starter/generators and heavy duty battery; engine fire
  detection system; and pneumatic leading-edge de-icing
  boots for wings and tail unit.

Advanced Aircraft Regent 1500, with Pratt & Whitney Canada PT6A-135 turboprops

WEIGHTS:
Weight empty	2,404 kg (5,300 lb)
Max T-O weight	3,447 kg (7,600 lb)
Max zero-fuel weight	2,993 kg (6,600 lb)
Max landing weight	3,266 kg (7,200 lb)

PERFORMANCE (at max T-O weight except where indicated):
Max cruising speed, at max cruise power, AUW of 3,220
  kg (7,100 lb):
    at 8,230 m (27,000 ft)   315 knots (584 km/h; 363 mph)
    at 6,705 m (22,000 ft)   278 knots (515 km/h; 320 mph)
    at 4,875 m (16,000 ft)   251 knots (465 km/h; 289 mph)
Max rate of climb at S/L:
    at max T-O weight   945 m (3,100 ft)/min
    at 3,175 kg (7,000 lb) AUW   1,310 m (4,300 ft)/min
Service ceiling   9,145 m (30,000 ft)
Service ceiling, one engine out, at 3,175 kg (7,000 lb)
  AUW   7,620 m (25,000 ft)
T-O run   462 m (1,517 ft)
T-O to 15 m (50 ft)   694 m (2,277 ft)

Landing from 15 m (50 ft) with propeller reversal
                                      606 m (1,988 ft)
Landing run with propeller reversal   324 m (1,064 ft)
Range with max fuel, ISA, allowances for start, taxi,
take-off, climb and descent, 45 min reserves:
  max cruise power:
    at 4,875 m (16,000 ft)
                            832 nm (1,542 km; 958 miles)
    at 6,705 m (22,000 ft)
                            987 nm (1,829 km; 1,136 miles)
    at 8,230 m (27,000 ft)
                          1,169 nm (2,166 km; 1,346 miles)
  max range power:
    at 5,485 m (18,000 ft)
                            908 nm (1,682 km; 1,045 miles)
    at 6,705 m (22,000 ft)
                          1,112 nm (2,060 km; 1,280 miles)
    at 8,230 m (27,000 ft)
                          1,276 nm (2,364 km; 1,469 miles)

AERODYNE
AERODYNE SYSTEMS ENGINEERING LTD
PRESIDENT: James J. Solano

Aerodyne Systems' ML74 Wasp and M79 Hornet light
helicopters were described and illustrated in the 1987-88
and earlier editions of *Jane's*. No recent information has
been received from the company, which is no longer at its
former address and is assumed to have ceased trading.

AERO MOD
AERO MOD GENERAL
Chelan Municipal Airport, Washington 98816
Telephone: (509) 682 5150

No information has been received on Aero Mod
General's products since the Summer of 1985. All known
details of its Ag-Cat and Ayres Thrush conversions can be
found in the 1987-88 *Jane's*.

AERO UNION
AERO UNION CORPORATION
Municipal Airport, 100 Lockheed Avenue, Chico,
California 95926
Telephone: (916) 896 3000
Telex: 171359 AEROUNION CICO
Fax: (916) 893 8585
PRESIDENT: Dale P. Newton
VICE-PRESIDENT, MARKETING: Richard E. Foy

This company was established in 1959 as an aerial
firefighting operation, using converted war surplus aircraft
for aerial retardant delivery. It developed tank systems for
such aircraft as the Boeing B-17, Douglas DC-4, DC-6 and
DC-7, Fairchild C-119 and Grumman S-2. A description of
its Douglas DC-3 aerial spraying system can be found in
the 1984-85 *Jane's*. In 1980 the company received CAB
certification as an all-cargo air service carrier using DC-4,
Carvair and Guppy aircraft. Aero Union also manufactures
a variety of equipment, including aircraft fuel tanks,
airstairs, retardant delivery and aerial spraying systems,
and dorsal fin assemblies.

AERO UNION MODULAR AIRBORNE FIRE FIGHTING SYSTEM (MAFFS)

Designed for cargo aircraft such as the Lockheed C-130
which use the USAF 463L pallet system, the Aero Union
MAFFS comprises five retardant tank modules with a total
capacity of 11,356 litres (3,000 US gallons; 2,498 Imp
gallons), a control module, and a dispensing module with
two retractable nozzles providing a retardant swath 13-61 m
(43-200 ft) wide, and 180-610 m (590-2,000 ft) long,
depending on aircraft altitude and speed. The MAFFS,
which has an installed weight, empty, of 2,177 kg (4,800 lb),
is powered by compressed air stored in reservoirs at each
tank module. The control module is battery powered. An
installation time of less than one hour is claimed for the
C-130 if the MAFFS is assembled on a loader outside the
aircraft, with a typical turnaround time of 15 minutes for

replenishing the system in operational use. The MAFFS can
be operated at altitudes of 30-150 m (98-492 ft) and at
speeds of 130-140 knots (241-259 km/h; 150-161 mph).

AERO UNION C-130 AUXILIARY FUEL SYSTEM

Aero Union has developed an auxiliary fuel system for
the Lockheed C-130 which can be used for in-flight
refuelling, extra fuel capacity, or fuel transportation. The
system consists of a 6.1 m (20 ft) platform on which two
cylindrical tanks are mounted by means of a pair of cradles.
The plumbing is in compliance with MIL-F-17874 and
offers a flow rate of 1,136 litres (300 US gallons; 250 Imp
gallons)/minute. The unit interfaces with the Lockheed air
refuelling manifold, and a passage is provided for crew
access fore and aft of the tank installation. Tank capacity
(total) 13,627 litres (3,600 US gallons; 2,998 Imp gallons);
length 5.26 m (17 ft 3 in); width 3.0 m (9 ft 10¼ in); height,
excluding plumbing, 1.68 m (5 ft 6 in); weight empty approx
1,542 kg (3,400 lb).

AERO UNION HELIBORNE AERIAL FIRE FIGHTING SYSTEM (HAFFS)

The Heliborne Aerial Fire Fighting System is a
second generation development of MAFFS, designed for
installation in large helicopters such as the Boeing
CH-47/Model 234 series. It has a capacity of 7,571 litres
(2,000 US gallons; 1,665 Imp gallons). Extinguishing agent
is dispersed through a remotely operated, variable pattern
foam cannon capable of delivering up to 2,271 litres (600 US
gallons; 500 Imp gallons)/min at a standoff distance of more
than 61 m (200 ft). All or part of the payload may also be
dropped directly on a fire in under 10 s. The HAFFS will
saturate a half-acre area at a density of 40.3 litres/m² (0.99
US gallon; 0.82 Imp gallon/sq ft). Empty weight of the
installation is 1,749 kg (3,857 lb). A smaller system, capacity
2,650-3,785 litres (700-1,000 US gallons; 583-833 Imp
gallons), is being developed for Boeing CH-46/Kawasaki
KV107 helicopters. Aero Union is also evaluating
derivative designs for such helicopters as the Aérospatiale
AS 332, EHI EH 101, Mil Mi-8 and Sikorsky UH-60.

Lockheed C-130B of the North Carolina Air National Guard equipped with Aero Union MAFFS
(Mike Jerram)

AERO UNION (GRUMMAN) HU-16B ALBATROSS TANKER CONVERSION

Aero Union has developed a firefighting conversion of

the standard HU-16B Albatross amphibian that enables the aircraft to carry 3,785 litres (1,000 US gallons; 833 Imp gallons) of water or retardant in two side by side tanks in the fuselage. The tanks can be filled from two retractable probes which extend into the water while the aircraft is planing on the step, or on land by a single filling point in the fuselage side. The retardant tanks can be emptied individually or simultaneously, and refilled from a body of water within 10 s at a speed of 70 knots (130 km/h; 81 mph).

WEIGHTS:

Weight empty	9,956 kg (21,950 lb)
Max T-O weight	15,036 kg (33,150 lb)

PERFORMANCE:

Max level speed	220 knots (408 km/h; 253 mph)
Cruising speed	162 knots (300 km/h; 186 mph)

AIRMASTER

AIRMASTER INC

850 West Perimeter Road, Renton, Washington 98055
Telephone: (206) 255 1422
Telex: 185195 AMAST UT
PRESIDENT: Lawrence Matanski
VICE-PRESIDENT, MARKETING: Harold W. Mallet

Airmaster Inc was formed in 1980 to develop and manufacture the Avalon turboprop amphibian. The Avalon 680 proof of concept prototype (described in the 1986-87 edition) was flown for the first time in 1983, and in 1987 Airmaster was putting its main effort into the much refined Avalon Twin Star 1000 and A-1200 Guardian with a more conventional flying-boat hull.

AIRMASTER AVALON TWIN STAR 1000

The Twin Star 1000 is intended to be the basic model in Airmaster's family of modern turboprop amphibians. It has a conventional flying-boat hull, with twin turboprops mounted in pusher configuration above the wings, instead of the single-engined twin-boom configuration of the Avalon 680. Construction of a prototype was started in February 1985, but no recent news of subsequent progress has been received.

TYPE: Twin-turboprop multi-purpose amphibian.
WINGS: Cantilever high-wing monoplane of constant chord. NACA 23015 (modified) wing section. Dihedral 2°. Incidence 4°. Aluminium alloy fail-safe structure, with Frise ailerons and Fowler single-slotted trailing-edge flaps over full span except for wingtips. Electric aileron trim. Pneumatic leading-edge de-icing boots optional.
FUSELAGE: Conventional flying-boat hull of high length-to-beam ratio, with single step. Aluminium alloy (2024-T3) semi-monocoque structure, with 14 watertight compartments. Stabilising floats carried on cantilever aerofoil shape sponsons mid-mounted on hull beneath wings. Hull drains and manifold bilge pumping.
TAIL UNIT: Conventional cantilever structure of aluminium alloy, with unswept tailplane mounted on sweptback vertical surfaces, well above top of hull. Horn balanced rudder and elevators, each with electric trim. Large dorsal fin. Optional pneumatic de-icing boots on leading-edge of fin and tailplane.
LANDING GEAR: Hydraulically retractable tricycle type, with emergency manual backup. Nosewheel retracts forward, enabling tyre to serve as fender for nose. Main units retract rearward into stabilising floats. Oleo-pneumatic shock absorbers. Single wheel on each unit. Mainwheel tyres size 7.00-6; nosewheel tyre size 6.00-6. Cleveland brakes.
POWER PLANT: Two 373 kW (500 shp) Pratt & Whitney Canada PT6A-11 turboprops, each driving a Hartzell three-blade constant-speed fully-feathering and reversible-pitch metal pusher propeller, with spinner. Main fuel tank in fuselage between sponsons, capacity 568 litres (150 US gallons; 125 Imp gallons), with refuelling point above sponson. Auxiliary tank, capacity 189 litres (50 US gallons; 41.6 Imp gallons), in each wing, with flush refuelling point in wing upper surface. Total fuel capacity 1,060 litres (280 US gallons; 233 Imp gallons). Oil capacity (total) 11.4 litres (3 US gallons; 2.5 Imp gallons). Engine air intakes each have heated lip for anti-icing. Propellers anti-iced automatically by hot engine exhaust.
ACCOMMODATION: Pilot and six passengers in 2-2-3 forward facing seats in enclosed cabin, with forward hinged door on each side. Airstairs for land operation. Heating and ventilation standard. Baggage space behind rear seats. Optional alcohol de-icing system and wipers for windscreen.
SYSTEMS: Optional freon air-conditioning and pressurisation system, with max pressure differential of 0.24 bars (3.5 lb/sq in). Single electro-hydraulic system, with emergency hand pump. Pneumatic system pressure 82 bars (1,200 lb/sq in). 24V electrical system. Standby oxygen system optional.
AVIONICS AND EQUIPMENT: Blind-flying instrumentation standard. Avionics, autopilot, weather radar, stormscope and fuel management computer optional.

DIMENSIONS, EXTERNAL:

Wing span	13.41 m (44 ft 0 in)
Wing aspect ratio	7.3
Length overall	11.13 m (36 ft 6 in)
Fuselage width	1.42 m (4 ft 8 in)
Height overall	4.42 m (14 ft 6 in)
Tailplane span	4.67 m (15 ft 3½ in)
Wheel track	3.51 m (11 ft 6 in)
Wheelbase	4.63 m (15 ft 2½ in)
Propeller diameter (each)	2.54 m (8 ft 4 in)
Propeller ground clearance	1.46 m (4 ft 9½ in)
Distance between propeller centres	3.60 m (11 ft 9½ in)
Passenger doors:	
Height: port	1.22 m (4 ft 0 in)
stbd	0.89 m (2 ft 11 in)
Width: port	0.84 m (2 ft 9 in)
stbd	0.81 m (2 ft 8 in)

DIMENSIONS, INTERNAL:

Cabin: Length	3.05 m (10 ft 0 in)
Max width	1.27 m (4 ft 2 in)
Max height	1.57 m (5 ft 2 in)

AREAS:

Wings, gross	24.53 m² (264.0 sq ft)
Ailerons (total)	2.16 m² (23.3 sq ft)
Trailing-edge flaps (total)	4.74 m² (51.0 sq ft)
Fin	2.38 m² (25.6 sq ft)
Rudder	1.58 m² (17.0 sq ft)
Tailplane	3.81 m² (41.0 sq ft)
Elevators	2.55 m² (27.5 sq ft)

WEIGHTS AND LOADINGS:

Weight empty	1,769 kg (3,900 lb)
Max T-O weight	2,948 kg (6,500 lb)
Max landing weight	2,812 kg (6,200 lb)
Max wing loading	120.18 kg/m² (24.62 lb/sq ft)
Max power loading	3.95 kg/kW (6.50 lb/shp)

PERFORMANCE (estimated at max T-O weight):

Never-exceed speed	217 knots (402 km/h; 250 mph)
Max level speed and max cruising speed at 3,660 m (12,000 ft)	207 knots (383 km/h; 238 mph)
Econ cruising speed	180 knots (333 km/h; 207 mph)
Stalling speed, flaps down	58 knots (108 km/h; 67 mph)
Max rate of climb at S/L	731 m (2,400 ft)/min
Service ceiling	7,925 m (26,000 ft)
Service ceiling, one engine out	3,810 m (12,500 ft)
T-O run: on land	256 m (840 ft)
on water	336 m (1,100 ft)
Landing run: on land	183 m (600 ft)
on water	198 m (650 ft)
Range with max fuel:	
at cruise power	695 nm (1,287 km; 800 miles)
at econ cruise power	869 nm (1,609 km; 1,000 miles)

AIRMASTER A-1200 GUARDIAN

The Airmaster A-1200 Guardian is basically similar to the Twin Star 1000, except for the installation of military or maritime patrol equipment and/or armament. It can be upgraded with two 507 kW (680 shp) PT6A-27 or 559 kW (750 shp) PT6A-34 turboprops to improve its STOL performance. Total fuel capacity can be increased to 1,514 litres (400 US gallons; 333 Imp gallons) to extend the patrol range to 1,216 nm (2,253 km; 1,400 miles) with standard PT6A-11 engines. JATO rockets can be attached on each side of the rear fuselage for emergency short take-off in rough water.

Operational equipment can include radar mounted in the nose of the port engine nacelle and a high intensity searchlight in the nose of the starboard nacelle. Six hardpoints under the wings can carry lightweight rocket launchers, grenade launchers, 7.62 mm machine-gun pods, or air-to-air missiles on standard NATO pylons. A Gatling type machine-gun can be pod mounted above the port stabilising float. Mini-torpedoes can be carried outboard of the stabilising floats.

DIMENSIONS, WEIGHTS AND PERFORMANCE:
Generally as for Twin Star 1000

Artist's impressions of the Airmaster Twin Star 1000 (left) and A-1200 Guardian amphibians

AIR TRACTOR

AIR TRACTOR INC

PO Box 485, Municipal Airport, Olney, Texas 76374
Telephone: (817) 564 5616
Telex: 910 890 4792
PRESIDENT: Leland Snow

The Air Tractor series of agricultural aircraft embodies more than 30 years' experience by their designer, Mr Leland Snow, who designed, developed, certificated and put into production the earlier Snow S-2 series of agricultural aircraft. The latter, which later became the Rockwell S-2R Thrush, have been described in previous editions of *Jane's*.

Eight versions of the Air Tractor series were available in 1988: the Models AT-301, AT-301B, AT-401 and AT-501 with Pratt & Whitney radial engine; and the AT-400, AT-400A, AT-502 and AT-503 with various types of Pratt & Whitney Canada PT6A turboprop.

AIR TRACTOR MODEL AT-301/301B AIR TRACTOR

The first prototype/pre-production Model **AT-301** Air Tractor flew for the first time in September 1973, and received FAA certification under FAR Pt 23 in November of that year. At that time the aircraft was also flight tested to meet FAR Pt 8 requirements. The Model **AT-301B**, introduced in 1987 to replace the AT-301A (see 1986-87 *Jane's*), is identical to the AT-301 except for the installation of a larger hopper, with a 0.97 m (3 ft 2 in) wide gatebox for high application rates of dry chemicals.

By 1 January 1988 a total of 710 AT-301/301Bs had been ordered, of which 679 had been completed, and production was continuing at a rate of four aircraft per month.

TYPE: Single-seat agricultural aircraft.
WINGS: Cantilever low-wing monoplane. Wing section NACA 4415. Dihedral 3° 30′. Incidence 2°. No sweepback. Conventional two-spar structure of 2024-T3 light alloy. Ailerons of light alloy construction, interconnected with trailing-edge flaps to droop 10° at maximum flap deflection of 30°. Electrically operated Fowler trailing-edge flaps of light alloy construction. No trim tabs. Wing ribs and skins zinc chromated before assembly. Wingroots and skin overlaps sealed against chemical entry.
FUSELAGE: Welded structure of 4130N steel tube, oven stress relieved and oiled internally. Quickly detachable skins of 2024-T3 light alloy, with Camloc fasteners. Rear fuselage lightly pressurised to prevent chemical ingress.
TAIL UNIT: Light alloy structure, with cantilever fin and strut braced tailplane. Fabric covered rudder and elevators. Trim tab in each elevator.
LANDING GEAR: Non-retractable tailwheel type. Cantilever spring steel main gear; flat spring suspension for

castoring and lockable tailwheel. Cleveland mainwheels with tyres size 8.50-10 (8-ply), pressure 2.83 bars (41 lb/sq in). Tailwheel tyre size 12.50-4, pressure 2.42 bars (35 lb/sq in). Cleveland type 30-89 hydraulic disc brakes.

POWER PLANT: One 447 kW (600 hp) Pratt & Whitney R-1340 aircooled radial engine, driving a Hamilton Standard 12D40/6101A-12 two-blade constant-speed metal propeller without spinner, or a Pacific Propeller 22D40 constant-speed Hydromatic propeller. Fuel in two integral wing tanks with combined capacity of 477 litres (126 US gallons; 105 Imp gallons). Refuelling points on upper surface of wings at root. Oil capacity 30.3 litres (8 US gallons; 6.7 Imp gallons).

ACCOMMODATION: Single seat in enclosed cabin which is sealed to prevent chemical ingress. Downward hinged window/door on each side. Baggage compartment in bottom of fuselage, aft of cabin, with door on port side. Cabin ventilation by 0.10 m (4 in) diameter airscoop.

SYSTEMS: Agricultural dispersal system comprises a 1,211 litre (320 US gallon; 266 Imp gallon) glassfibre hopper, mounted in the forward fuselage for the AT-301; 1,325 litre (350 US gallon; 291 Imp gallon) hopper for the AT-301B; Transland gatebox; Transland valve and strainer; 5 cm (2 in) Agrinautics pump; 5 cm (2 in) stainless steel plumbing; and up to 69 nozzles in spraybars mounted below and just aft of wing trailing-edges. 24V electrical system, supplied by 60A engine driven alternator.

AVIONICS AND EQUIPMENT: Optional avionics include Narco Com 811 radio, King KX 155 nav/com, King KR 87 ADF, Narco AT-150 transponder and Narco ELT-10 emergency locator transmitter. Optional equipment includes 600W retractable landing light in port wingtip; night flying package of strobe/navigation, instrument, post and dome lights; night working lights; directional and attitude gyro instrument package; glassfibre engine cowling ring; Hydromatic propeller; Cleveland 29-11 wheels and high-flotation tyres; external power socket; and ferry fuel system. Alternative agricultural equipment includes Transland high volume and extra high volume spreader systems, and six- or eight-unit Micronair installations, and windscreen washer.

DIMENSIONS, EXTERNAL:
Wing span	13.75 m (45 ft 1¼ in)
Wing chord, constant	1.83 m (6 ft 0 in)
Wing aspect ratio	7.5
Length overall	8.23 m (27 ft 0 in)
Height overall	2.59 m (8 ft 6 in)
Propeller diameter	2.77 m (9 ft 1 in)

AREAS:
Wings, gross	25.08 m² (270 sq ft)
Ailerons (total)	3.55 m² (38.2 sq ft)
Trailing-edge flaps (total)	3.34 m² (36.0 sq ft)
Fin	0.90 m² (9.7 sq ft)
Rudder	1.30 m² (14.0 sq ft)
Tailplane	2.42 m² (26.0 sq ft)
Elevators (incl tabs)	2.36 m² (25.4 sq ft)

WEIGHTS AND LOADINGS (A: AT-301; B: AT-301B):
Weight empty, spray equipped: A	1,723 kg (3,800 lb)
B	1,746 kg (3,850 lb)
Certificated gross weight (FAR 23):	
A, B	2,268 kg (5,000 lb)
Typical operating weight (CAM 8):	
A	3,356 kg (7,400 lb)
B	3,492 kg (7,700 lb)
Max wing loading: A	133.8 kg/m² (27.4 lb/sq ft)
B	139.1 kg/m² (28.5 lb/sq ft)
Max power loading: A	7.51 kg/kW (12.33 lb/hp)
B	7.81 kg/kW (12.83 lb/hp)

Air Tractor Model AT-301 Air Tractor (Pratt & Whitney R-1340 engine)

Air Tractor Model AT-400 Turbo Air Tractor (P&WC PT6A-15AG turboprop)

PERFORMANCE (at max T-O weight except where indicated):
Max level speed at S/L:	
A	146 knots (270 km/h; 168 mph)
B	142 knots (264 km/h; 164 mph)
Max level speed at S/L with dispersal equipment:	
A	139 knots (257 km/h; 160 mph)
B	135 knots (251 km/h; 156 mph)
Cruising speed at 1,825 m (6,000 ft), spraypump removed	
for ferrying: A	135 knots (249 km/h; 155 mph)
B	132 knots (245 km/h; 152 mph)
Typical working speed:	
A, B	104-121 knots (193-225 km/h; 120-140 mph)
Stalling speed at 2,268 kg (5,000 lb) AUW:	
flaps up: A, B	64 knots (118 km/h; 73 mph)
flaps down: A, B	53 knots (98 km/h; 61 mph)
Stalling speed as usually landed:	
A, B	49 knots (90 km/h; 56 mph)
Max rate of climb at S/L, dispersal equipment installed,	
AUW of 2,268 kg (5,000 lb): A	488 m (1,600 ft)/min
B	457 m (1,500 ft)/min
T-O run at AUW of 2,268 kg (5,000 lb):	
A, B	244 m (800 ft)
T-O run at AUW of 3,175 kg (7,000 lb):	
A, B	396 m (1,300 ft)
Landing run at normal landing weight: A	91 m (300 ft)

Range with max fuel, no allowances:
A	469 nm (869 km; 540 miles)

AIR TRACTOR MODEL AT-400 and 400A TURBO AIR TRACTOR

These versions of the Air Tractor incorporate a 1,514 litre (400 US gallon; 333 Imp gallon) hopper and 0.97 m (3 ft 2 in) wide gatebox. The **AT-400** is powered by a 507 kW (680 shp) Pratt & Whitney Canada PT6A-15AG, -27 or -28 turboprop, the **AT-400A** by a customer-furnished used 410 kW (550 shp) PT6A-20, in each case driving a Hartzell three-blade constant-speed reversible-pitch propeller. All models have steel alloy wing lower spar caps for indefinite fatigue life, and a reinforced leading-edge to prevent bird strike damage; size 29-11 high-flotation tyres and wheels as standard; and a 250A starter/generator and two 24V 21Ah batteries. Fuel capacity is 477 litres (126 US gallons; 105 Imp gallons). Optional equipment includes Transland extra high volume dispersal system.

A total of 85 AT-400s had been delivered by 1 January 1988.

WEIGHTS AND LOADINGS:
Weight empty, spray equipped	1,610 kg (3,550 lb)
Certificated gross weight (FAR 23)	2,721 kg (6,000 lb)
Typical operating weight (CAM 8)	3,538 kg (7,800 lb)
Max wing loading	141.1 kg/m² (28.9 lb/sq ft)
Max power loading	6.98 kg/kW (11.47 lb/shp)

PERFORMANCE (at max T-O weight except where indicated):
Max level speed at S/L, 'clean'	174 knots (322 km/h; 200 mph)
Max level speed at S/L with dispersal equipment	160 knots (298 km/h; 185 mph)
Cruising speed, 55% power at 2,440 m (8,000 ft), spraypump removed for ferrying	143 knots (265 km/h; 165 mph)
Typical working speed	113-126 knots (209-233 km/h; 130-145 mph)
Stalling speed at 2,721 kg (6,000 lb) AUW:	
flaps up	66 knots (122 km/h; 76 mph)
flaps down	58 knots (106 km/h; 66 mph)
Stalling speed as usually landed	48 knots (89 km/h; 55 mph)
Max rate of climb at S/L, dispersal equipment installed, AUW of 2,721 kg (6,000 lb)	457 m (1,500 ft)/min
T-O run at AUW of 2,721 kg (6,000 lb)	305 m (1,000 ft)
Landing run as usually landed	152 m (500 ft)

AIR TRACTOR MODEL AT-401 AIR TRACTOR

This version of the Air Tractor was developed during 1986 and is based on the Pratt & Whitney R-1340 powered Model AT-301, but with an increased wing span and a larger capacity hopper. Ten AT-401s were delivered during 1987 to customers in Brazil, Kenya and the United States. Differences from the AT-301 are as follows:

Air Tractor Model AT-401 (Pratt & Whitney R-1340 radial engine)

WINGS: As for AT-301 but with 1.22 m (4 ft 0 in) increase in span, alloy steel lower spar cap and bonded doubler on inside of wing leading-edge for increased impact damage resistance. Glassfibre wingroot fairings.

TAIL UNIT: As for AT-301 but with metal skinned elevators and rudder, sealed against chemical ingress.

LANDING GEAR: Heavy duty landing gear spring, Cleveland four-piston brakes and thicker brake discs.

POWER PLANT: As for AT-301 but three-blade Hydromatic propeller of 2.59 m (8 ft 6 in) diameter optional.

ACCOMMODATION: Redesigned 'line of sight' instrument panel with improved instrument access via swing-down lower panel.

SYSTEM: 1,514 litre (400 US gallon; 333 Imp gallon) hopper standard.

DIMENSIONS, EXTERNAL: As for AT-301 except:

Wing span	14.97 m (49 ft 1¼ in)
Wing aspect ratio	8.2

AREAS: As for AT-301 except:

Wings, gross	27.31 m² (294.0 sq ft)
Trailing-edge flaps (total)	3.75 m² (40.4 sq ft)

WEIGHTS:

Weight empty, spray equipped	1,851 kg (4,080 lb)
Certificated max T-O weight	2,721 kg (6,000 lb)
Typical operating weight	3,565 kg (7,860 lb)

PERFORMANCE:

Max level speed at S/L, with spray equipment
136 knots (252 km/h; 157 mph)
Cruising speed at 1,830 m (6,000 ft), spraypump removed
for ferrying 130 knots (241 km/h; 150 mph)
Typical working speed
104-121 knots (193-225 km/h; 120-140 mph)
Stalling speed as usually landed
47 knots (87 km/h; 54 mph)

AIR TRACTOR MODEL AT-501

The original Model AT-500, which was described briefly in the 1985-86 *Jane's*, was a market research prototype for a new series of larger Air Tractors, and resulted in the production AT-501 variant which was certificated on 23 June 1987 with subsequent delivery of two aircraft. The AT-501 is powered by a 447 kW (600 hp) Pratt & Whitney R-1340-S3H1G radial engine, driving a three-blade Hydromatic propeller, but may be converted to turboprop AT-502 configuration in the field, since the two models are identical aft of the engine firewall. Fuel capacity is 477 litres (126 US gallons; 105 Imp gallons); hopper capacity 1,900 litres (502 US gallons; 418 Imp gallons).

DIMENSIONS, EXTERNAL:

Wing span	15.24 m (50 ft 0 in)
Wing chord, constant	1.83 m (6 ft 0 in)
Length overall	9.05 m (29 ft 8½ in)
Height overall	2.99 m (9 ft 9½ in)
Wheel track	3.11 m (10 ft 2½ in)
Propeller diameter	3.30 m (10 ft 10 in)

AREA:

Wings, gross	27.87 m² (300.0 sq ft)

WEIGHTS:

Weight empty	2,086 kg (4,600 lb)
Design gross weight	3,629 kg (8,000 lb)
Normal operating weight	4,173 kg (9,200 lb)

PERFORMANCE:

Max level speed, with spray equipment
139 knots (257 km/h; 160 mph)
Cruising speed 121 knots (225 km/h; 140 mph)
Working speed
104-121 knots (193-225 km/h; 120-140 mph)
Stalling speed at normal landing weight
49 knots (91 km/h; 56 mph)

AIR TRACTOR MODEL AT-502

Increased usage of low-density nitrogen based fertilisers such as urea in various parts of the world prompted development of the Air Tractor AT-502, which has a larger chemical hopper than the AT-400, increased wing span, and safety glass centre windscreen with wiper. The AT-502 is designed for installation of a variety of Pratt & Whitney Canada PT6A turboprops. FAA type certification was granted on 23 June 1987, and three Model AT-502s were delivered in the latter half of that year. Differences from the AT-400 are as follows:

WINGS: As for AT-400 but with 1.52 m (5 ft 0 in) increase in span, alloy steel lower spar cap and bonded doubler on inside of wing leading-edge for increased resistance to impact damage, and glassfibre wingroot fairings.

FUSELAGE: Length increased by 0.56 m (1 ft 10 in), width increased by 0.25 m (10 in), and larger diameter tubular frame members used to cater for increased max T-O weight.

Air Tractor Model AT-502 (P&WC PT6A turboprop engine)

TAIL UNIT: As AT-400 but with metal skinned elevators and rudder, sealed against chemical ingress.

LANDING GEAR: As for AT-503.

POWER PLANT: One 507 kW (680 shp) Pratt & Whitney Canada PT6A-15AG, PT6A-27, PT6A-28, PT6A-34 or PT6A-34AG turboprop.

ACCOMMODATION: As for AT-400, but with new quick-detachable instrument panel and removable fuselage skin panels for ease of maintenance.

SYSTEMS: Agricultural dispersal system comprising 1,900 litre (502 US gallon; 418 Imp gallon) glassfibre hopper, Transland gatebox, Agrinautics pump, 5 cm (2 in) stainless steel plumbing and up to 81 nozzles on underwing spraybars.

AVIONICS AND EQUIPMENT: As for AT-301.

DIMENSIONS, EXTERNAL:

Wing span	15.24 m (50 ft 0 in)
Wing chord, constant	1.83 m (6 ft 0 in)
Wing aspect ratio	8.3
Length overall	9.91 m (32 ft 6 in)
Height overall	2.99 m (9 ft 9½ in)
Wheel track	3.11 m (10 ft 2½ in)
Wheelbase	6.64 m (21 ft 9½ in)
Propeller diameter	2.69 m (8 ft 10 in)

AREAS:

Wings, gross	27.87 m² (300.0 sq ft)
Ailerons (total)	3.53 m² (38.0 sq ft)
Trailing edge-flaps (total)	3.75 m² (40.4 sq ft)
Fin	0.90 m² (9.7 sq ft)
Rudder	1.30 m² (14.0 sq ft)
Tailplane	2.41 m² (26.0 sq ft)
Elevators (total, incl tab)	2.44 m² (26.3 sq ft)

WEIGHTS AND LOADINGS:

Weight empty, equipped	1,887 kg (4,160 lb)
Max T-O weight (CAM 8)	3,856 kg (8,500 lb)
Max landing weight	3,629 kg (8,000 lb)
Max wing loading	138.36 kg/m² (28.33 lb/sq ft)
Max power loading	7.61 kg/kW (12.5 lb/shp)

PERFORMANCE (at max T-O weight, with spray equipment installed)

Max level speed at S/L 148 knots (274 km/h; 170 mph)
Max cruising speed at 2,440 m (8,000 ft)
141 knots (261 km/h; 162 mph)
Stalling speed, power off, flaps down, max landing weight
60 knots (111 km/h; 69 mph)
Stalling speed as usually landed
46 knots (85 km/h; 53 mph)
Max rate of climb at S/L 213 m (700 ft)/min
T-O run 366 m (1,200 ft)
Range with max fuel 435 nm (805 km; 500 miles)

AIR TRACTOR MODEL AT-503

Design of the **AT-503** began in September 1985 in response to a US State Department requirement for aerial application aircraft suitable for eradication of narcotics crops. The AT-503 is larger than previous Air Tractor models and is the company's first two-seat design. It is intended for special purpose operations such as fire-bombing, forest spraying in mountainous terrain and high-volume seeding or fertiliser applications, in addition to anti-drug enforcement operations. The prototype made its first flight on 25 April 1986, flown by its designer, Mr Leland Snow. An FAA Type Certificate for the AT-503 was granted on 2 October 1986.

The description which follows applies to the Air Tractor AT-503:

TYPE: Two-seat agricultural aircraft.

WINGS: As for AT-400 except increased wing and flap spans and heavier gauge skins.

FUSELAGE: As for AT-400 except length increased by 0.56 m (1 ft 10 in), width by 0.25 m (10 in), and larger diameter tubular members employed for increased MTOW.

TAIL UNIT: As for AT-301, but metal skinned. Elevator trim tabs actuated electrically.

LANDING GEAR: Non-retractable tailwheel type. Cantilever spring steel main units; flat spring suspension for castoring and lockable tailwheel. Cleveland mainwheels with Goodyear high flotation tyres, size 29-11, pressure 2.96 bars (43 lb/sq in). Cleveland disc brakes.

POWER PLANT: One Pratt & Whitney Canada PT6A-45R turboprop, flat rated at 820 kW (1,100 shp), driving a Hartzell five-blade feathering and reversible-pitch constant-speed metal propeller. Frakes Aviation 'Jet Thrust' exhaust outlets. Fuel in two integral tanks and two self-sealing bladder tanks in wings, total usable capacity 984 litres (260 US gallons; 216.5 Imp gallons). Self-sealing tanks are of FTL No. 1 type, resistant to 0.50 in rounds.

ACCOMMODATION: Two seats in tandem in enclosed cabin, which is sealed to prevent chemical ingress and protected with overturn structure. Four downward hinged doors, two on each side, with 25.4 mm (1 in) square chromoly tube frames. Rear seat position windows are bulged to provide downward and forward view for observer/instructor. Windscreen is constructed of bullet-proof laminated acrylic/polycarbonate. Windscreen washer/wiper system optional. Separate ram airscoops for ventilation of each cockpit.

SYSTEM: Integral chemical hopper, capacity 1,900 litres (502 US gallons; 418 Imp gallons).

DIMENSIONS, EXTERNAL:

Wing span	14.63 m (48 ft 0 in)
Wing chord, constant	1.83 m (6 ft 0 in)
Wing aspect ratio	8.0
Length overall	10.21 m (33 ft 6 in)
Height overall	2.99 m (9 ft 9½ in)
Wheel track	3.11 m (10 ft 2½ in)
Wheelbase	6.64 m (21 ft 9½ in)
Propeller diameter	2.82 m (9 ft 3 in)

AREAS:

Wings, gross	26.76 m² (288.0 sq ft)
Ailerons (total)	3.53 m² (38.0 sq ft)
Trailing-edge flaps (total)	3.40 m² (36.6 sq ft)
Fin	0.90 m² (9.70 sq ft)
Rudder	1.30 m² (14.0 sq ft)
Tailplane	2.41 m² (26.0 sq ft)
Elevators (total, incl tab)	2.44 m² (26.3 sq ft)

WEIGHTS AND LOADINGS:

Weight empty, equipped	2,109 kg (4,650 lb)
Payload	2,644 kg (5,830 lb)
Max T-O weight (CAM 8)	4,754 kg (10,480 lb)
Max landing weight	3,629 kg (8,000 lb)
Max wing loading	177.65 kg/m² (36.39 lb/sq ft)
Max power loading	5.80 kg/kW (9.53 lb/shp)

PERFORMANCE (at max T-O weight):

Max level speed at S/L 191 knots (340 km/h; 220 mph)
Max cruising speed at 2,440 m (8,000 ft)
182 knots (338 km/h; 210 mph)
Ferry speed 156 knots (290 km/h; 180 mph)
Stalling speed, power off, flaps down, at max landing
weight 60 knots (111 km/h; 69 mph)
Max rate of climb, no hopper load
1,067 m (3,500 ft)/min
Service ceiling 10,975 m (36,000 ft)
T-O run 85 m (280 ft)
Range with max fuel 695 nm (1,287 km; 800 miles)
g limit +3.8

ALLISON

ALLISON GAS TURBINE DIVISION GMC

PO Box 420-SC U13A, Indianapolis, Indiana 46206-0420
Telephone: (317) 230 3158
Telex: 276411
Fax: (317) 230 5100
PUBLIC RELATIONS OFFICER: Anthony A. Perona

ALLISON TURBINE BONANZA

Allison, in conjunction with Soloy Conversions Ltd (which see), has obtained FAA certification of a turboprop conversion of the Beechcraft Model A36 Bonanza, known as the Allison Turbine Bonanza. The conversion involves replacement of the Bonanza's standard 212.5 kW (285 hp) Continental IO-520-BB piston engine with an Allison 250-B17C Turbine Pac rated at 313 kW (420 shp) and driving a three-blade metal feathering and reversing Hartzell propeller.

During the course of conversion two additional support spars are added to the bottom of the aircraft's fuselage for added strength and the lighter Allison engine is installed 0.53 m (1 ft 9 in) further forward than the Continental

power plant, to maintain the aircraft's centre of gravity position. A new engine mount and cowlings are provided. The resulting space behind the engine installation is available for baggage stowage. Other standard modifications include new engine and propeller controls, new fuel lines with a Shadin fuel flow monitor, Osborne wingtip tanks, each of 75.7 litres (20 US gallons; 16.6 Imp gallons) capacity, bringing total usable fuel capacity to 424 litres (112 US gallons; 93 Imp gallons) and incorporating a small sweptback outward canted winglet on the upper surface, a 24V electrical system with Gill lead-acid battery and 150A starter/generator, dual actuators for the elevator trim tabs, audible VNE overspeed warning, Casey cabin heating system, nosecowl mounted landing light, and Goodrich propeller de-icing system. Optional equipment includes an oxygen system, air-conditioning and alternative instrument air supply. The conversion is available for Model A36 and A36TC Bonanzas, but not the F33. Allison had received orders for 15 Turbine Bonanzas, of which 13 had been completed, by March 1988.

DIMENSIONS, EXTERNAL:

Wing span, between tips of winglets	10.20 m (33 ft 5½ in)
Length overall	8.89 m (29 ft 2 in)
Height overall	2.62 m (8 ft 7 in)
Tailplane span	3.71 m (12 ft 2 in)
Wheel track	2.92 m (9 ft 7 in)
Propeller diameter	2.29 m (7 ft 6 in)
Propeller ground clearance	0.18 m (7¼ in)

WEIGHTS:

Weight empty	1,089 kg (2,400 lb)
Max T-O weight	1,739 kg (3,833 lb)
Max landing weight	1,656 kg (3,650 lb)

PERFORMANCE:

Max level speed	210 knots (389 km/h; 242 mph)
Cruising speed:	
at 4,570 m (15,000 ft)	200 knots (371 km/h; 230 mph)
at 6,100 m (20,000 ft)	195 knots (361 km/h; 224 mph)
Stalling speed, flight idle power:	
flaps up	65 knots (120 km/h; 75 mph)
flaps down	57 knots (106 km/h; 66 mph)
Max rate of climb at S/L, at max T-O weight	579 m (1,900 ft)/min
Service ceiling	above 7,620 m (25,000 ft)
T-O run, 15° flap	177 m (580 ft)
T-O to 15 m (50 ft), 15° flap	244 m (800 ft)
Landing from 15 m (50 ft), 30° flap	160 m (525 ft)
Landing run, 30° flap	99 m (325 ft)
Range, with max fuel, allowances for start, taxi, T-O, climb and 45 min reserves at max cruising power:	
at 3,050 m (10,000 ft)	820 nm (1,520 km; 944 miles)
at 4,570 m (15,000 ft)	985 nm (1,825 km; 1,134 miles)
at 6,100 m (20,000 ft)	1,065 nm (1,974 km; 1,226 miles)

Allison Turbine Bonanza conversion of the Beechcraft Model A36 Bonanza

Prototype Allison Turbine Mentor turboprop conversion of the Beechcraft T-34 trainer

ALLISON TURBINE MENTOR

Allison has developed a turboprop conversion of the Beechcraft T-34 Mentor (Model 45) two-seat military trainer which involves replacement of the 152.9 kW (225 hp) and 212.5 kW (285 hp) Continental piston engines originally installed with a 313 kW (420 shp) Allison 250B-17D turboprop, employing a similar engine mount to that developed for the Allison Turbine Bonanza. Part of the space gained by the more forward location of the turboprop is used for an electrical bay and baggage compartment. Other modifications include strengthening of the wing to withstand a maximum load of 6g, and additional fuel tanks which increase standard capacity from 189 litres (50 US gallons; 41.6 Imp gallons) to 303 litres (80 US gallons; 66.6 Imp gallons). Wingtip tanks, each of 76 litres (20 US gallons; 16.6 Imp gallons) capacity, are optional. The Allison conversion can be carried out on Model T-34A and T-34B Mentors. Alternative versions of the Allison 250 power plant with 261 kW (350 shp) or 372.8 kW (500 shp) ratings will be available on production aircraft. The prototype Turbine Mentor (N4CN) made its public debut at the Paris Air Show in June 1987 and was demonstrated subsequently to a number of potential military operators. Orders from several countries were anticipated by the Autumn of 1988.

DIMENSIONS, EXTERNAL AND INTERNAL:

Wing span	10.00 m (32 ft 9⅞ in)
Wing chord: at root	2.13 m (7 ft 0 in)
at tip	1.07 m (3 ft 6 in)
Wing aspect ratio	6.1
Length overall	8.56 m (28 ft 1 in)
Height overall	2.92 m (9 ft 7 in)
Tailplane span	3.71 m (12 ft 2⅛ in)
Wheel track	2.92 m (9 ft 7 in)
Propeller diameter	2.29 m (7 ft 6 in)
Propeller ground clearance	0.31 m (1 ft 0¼ in)
Baggage door, rear:	
Height	0.48 m (1 ft 7⅛ in)
Max width	0.54 m (1 ft 9⅛ in)
Baggage door, forward:	
Height	0.35 m (1 ft 2 in)
Width	0.30 m (1 ft 0 in)
Baggage capacity, total	0.30 m³ (10.5 cu ft)

AREAS:

Wings, gross	16.50 m² (177.6 sq ft)
Ailerons (total)	1.07 m² (11.5 sq ft)
Flaps (total)	1.98 m² (21.3 sq ft)
Fin, incl dorsal fin	1.06 m² (11.46 sq ft)
Rudder, incl tab	0.62 m² (6.63 sq ft)

Tailplane	2.07 m² (22.25 sq ft)
Elevators (total, incl tabs)	1.39 m² (15.0 sq ft)

WEIGHTS:

Weight empty	916 kg (2,020 lb)
Max T-O weight	1,542 kg (3,400 lb)

PERFORMANCE:

Never-exceed speed	219 knots (406 km/h; 252 mph)
Max cruising speed at 3,050 m (10,000 ft)	210 knots (389 km/h; 242 mph)
Max rate of climb at S/L	640 m (2,100 ft)/min
Service ceiling	7,620 m (25,000 ft)
T-O run	137 m (450 ft)
T-O to 15 m (50 ft)	213 m (700 ft)
Landing run	107 m (350 ft)
Landing from 15 m (50 ft)	229 m (750 ft)
Range	1,080 nm (2,001 km; 1,244 miles)
g limits	+6/−3

ALLISON TURBO FLAGSHIP ATF 580S

Allison has decided not to certificate this 'stretched' Convairliner conversion (see 1987-88 *Jane's*), nor to market it. Future status of this aircraft was not known at the time of going to press.

ARCTIC

ARCTIC AIRCRAFT COMPANY

PO Box 6-141, Anchorage, Alaska 99502
Telephone: (907) 243 1580
PRESIDENT: William A. Diehl

The S1B2 Arctic Tern is an updated and much improved version of the Interstate S1A, first flown in 1940. Built to CAR.04a (aerobatic) standard, it was certificated for operation on optional Edo floats on 20 January 1981. No information has been received concerning numbers built since that time.

ARCTIC AIRCRAFT INTERSTATE S1B2 ARCTIC TERN

TYPE: Two-seat sporting and general utility aircraft.
AIRFRAME: See 1987-88 *Jane's*.
POWER PLANT: One 112 kW (150 hp) Textron Lycoming O-320 flat-four engine, driving a McCauley two-blade fixed-pitch metal propeller. One fuel tank in each wing, total capacity 151 litres (40 US gallons; 33.3 Imp gallons). Underbelly auxiliary fuel tank optional.
ACCOMMODATION: Two seats in tandem; rear seat removable to provide additional space for cargo. Cabin door on starboard side, beneath wing. Cabin step. Baggage space in rear fuselage, with external door on starboard side, capacity 45 kg (100 lb). Tinted windows and cabin skylight optional. Safety belts and fittings standard. Dual controls standard. Cabin soundproofed, heated and ventilated. Windscreen de-icing by hot air.

Arctic Aircraft Interstate S1B2 Arctic Tern (*Neil A. Macdougall*)

SYSTEM: Electrical system includes 55A engine driven alternator, 12V DC storage battery and engine starter.

AVIONICS AND EQUIPMENT: A range of radios and equipment is available (see 1987-88 edition for details).

DIMENSIONS, EXTERNAL:

Wing span	11.18 m (36 ft 8 in)
Wing chord (constant)	1.57 m (5 ft 2 in)

Length overall: landplane	7.01 m (23 ft 0 in)
seaplane	7.32 m (24 ft 0 in)
Height overall	2.13 m (7 ft 0 in)
Tailplane span	3.35 m (11 ft 0 in)

DIMENSIONS, INTERNAL:

Cabin: Max width	0.66 m (2 ft 2 in)
Volume	1.38 m³ (48.7 cu ft)
Baggage compartment volume	0.84 m³ (29.63 cu ft)

AREA:

Wings, gross	17.30 m² (186.2 sq ft)

WEIGHTS AND LOADINGS (A: landplane; B: seaplane with Edo 2000 floats):

Weight empty: A	487 kg (1,073 lb)
B	521.5 kg (1,150 lb)
Max T-O weight: A	862 kg (1,900 lb)
B	965 kg (2,127 lb)
Max wing loading: A	49.8 kg/m² (10.2 lb/sq ft)
B	55.7 kg/m² (11.4 lb/sq ft)
Max power loading: A	7.7 kg/kW (12.67 lb/hp)
B	8.62 kg/kW (14.18 lb/hp)

PERFORMANCE:

Never-exceed speed: A	152 knots (282 km/h; 175 mph)

Max cruising speed at S/L, 75% power:

A	102 knots (188 km/h; 117 mph)
B	91 knots (169 km/h; 105 mph)

Cruising speed, 65% power at optimum altitude:

A	96 knots (178 km/h; 111 mph)

Stalling speed, flaps down:

A, B	30 knots (55 km/h; 34 mph)

Max rate of climb at S/L, at max T-O weight:

A	389 m (1,275 ft)/min
B	305 m (1,000 ft)/min

Service ceiling: A, B	5,790 m (19,000 ft)
T-O run at max T-O weight: A	99 m (325 ft)

T-O to 15 m (50 ft) at max T-O weight:

A	152 m (500 ft)
Landing from 15 m (50 ft): A	137 m (450 ft)

Range with max fuel, 45 min reserves:

A, 75% power	479 nm (888 km; 552 miles)
A, 65% power	566 nm (1,049 km; 652 miles)

Range with max fuel, no reserves:

B	499 nm (925 km; 575 miles)

AROCET
AROCET INC

18702 58th Avenue Northeast, Arlington, Washington 98223.
Telephone: (206) 435 6606

AROCET AT-9 TACTICAL TRAINER

Arocet Inc, in co-operation with Stoddart-Hamilton Aircraft Inc, is developing this turboprop version of the Glasair III all-composite homebuilt aircraft described in the Sport Aircraft section of this edition. The aircraft is powered by a 313 kW (420 shp) Allison 250-B17D turboprop and will be marketed as a low cost, high performance fully aerobatic military trainer adaptable to combat roles such as ground support, patrol, air defence, and search and rescue. Subject to successful flight testing, the AT-9 may also be made available in homebuilt kit or FAA certificated form if there is sufficient market interest. The prototype Arocet AT-9 made its first flight on 24 July 1988.

TYPE: Two-seat turboprop powered training aircraft.
WINGS: Cantilever low-wing monoplane. Wing section LS(1)-0413 series. All-composite structure with glassfibre single-piece main spar, ribs and rear spar. Electrically operated flaps of composite construction. Composite ailerons with integral trim system.
FUSELAGE: Composite sandwich monocoque moulded in two half-shells.
TAIL UNIT: Conventional cantilever tail unit of composite construction, as for wings. Fixed sweptback fin, integral with moulded fuselage. Elevators and rudder manually operated.

LANDING GEAR: Hydraulically retractable tricycle type; nosewheel retracts rearward, mainwheels inward into wingroots. Oleo-pneumatic shock absorber in each unit.
POWER PLANT: One 313 kW (420 shp) Allison 250-B17D turboprop, driving a three-blade McCauley constant-speed reversing metal propeller. Fuel contained in integral glassfibre tanks in wings, max capacity 333 litres (88 US gallons; 73 Imp gallons). Wing surfaces treated with Thorstrand aluminised coating to protect fuel system from lightning strikes.
ACCOMMODATION: Crew of two side by side in enclosed cabin with zero/zero pilot extraction system and dual controls. Control system response can be adjusted to varying degrees of sensitivity.
AVIONICS AND EQUIPMENT: Full IFR avionics with gunsight and armament management equipment. All antennae integral with airframe structure to reduce drag and installation weight.
ARMAMENT: Two hardpoints, each with max load of 125 kg (275 lb), beneath wings outboard of main landing gear can carry a variety of stores including 7- or 19-tube rocket launchers, practice bomb racks, machine-gun pods, cartridge launchers and rescue pods.

DIMENSIONS, EXTERNAL:

Wing span	7.10 m (23 ft 3½ in)
Length overall	6.64 m (21 ft 9½ in)
Height overall	2.21 m (7 ft 3 in)
Propeller diameter	2.03 m (6 ft 8 in)

DIMENSIONS, INTERNAL:
Cabin:

Max width	1.07 m (3 ft 6¼ in)

AREA:

Wings, gross	7.54 m² (81.2 sq ft)

WEIGHTS AND LOADINGS:

Weight empty	680 kg (1,500 lb)
Max fuel weight	261 kg (576 lb)
Max T-O weight	1,225 kg (2,700 lb)
Max wing loading	162.46 kg/m² (33.25 lb/sq ft)
Max power loading	3.91 kg/kW (6.43 lb/shp)

PERFORMANCE (estimated, at max T-O weight unless otherwise indicated):

Never-exceed speed	350 knots (649 km/h; 403 mph)
Max level speed: at S/L	300 knots (556 km/h; 345 mph)
at 3,050 m (10,000 ft)	331 knots (613 km/h; 381 mph)

Cruising speed at 7,620 m (25,000 ft)

	318 knots (589 km/h; 366 mph)
Stalling speed	61 knots (113 km/h; 70 mph)

Max rate of climb at S/L, at T-O weight of 1,089 kg

(2,400 lb)	1,013 m (3,325 ft)/min
Service ceiling	11,280 m (37,000 ft)
Max operating altitude	7,620 m (25,000 ft)
T-O run	160 m (525 ft)
T-O to 15 m (50 ft)	267 m (875 ft)

Landing from 15 m (50 ft) with propeller reversal

	206 m (675 ft)
Landing run with propeller reversal	110 m (360 ft)

Range with max fuel: at cruising speed of 236 knots (437 km/h; 272 mph) at 4,575 m (15,000 ft), 30 min fuel

reserves	1,378 nm (2,554 km; 1,587 miles)

at cruising speed of 318 knots (589 km/h; 366 mph) at 7,620 m (25,000 ft), reserves as above

	1,200 nm (2,224 km; 1,382 miles)
g limits	+6.9/-4

AVTEK
AVTEK CORPORATION

4680 Calle Carga, Camarillo, California 93010
Telephone: (805) 482 2700
Telex: 183218 AVTEK UD
Fax: (805) 987 0068
PRESIDENT: Robert F. Adickes
SENIOR VICE-PRESIDENT, ENGINEERING: Niels Andersen
DIRECTOR OF MARKETING: Robert D. Honeycutt

Avtek Corporation was established in 1982 to design, develop and certificate the Avtek Model 400A all-composite twin-turboprop six/nine-seat business aircraft of canard configuration. The aircraft was designed initially by the late Al W. Mooney, founder of Mooney Aircraft Corporation, and later refined by Niels Andersen, Ford Johnston and Irvin Culver. NASA provided computer analysis of the aerodynamic configuration, and wind tunnel testing. The company benefits also from research by Dow Chemical Company and Dr Leo Windecker, designer of the Windecker Eagle which was the first all-composite aircraft to gain FAA certification. Dow Chemical Company has licensed its basic patents developed during the Eagle programme to Avtek Corporation.

E. I. duPont de Nemours, Dow Chemical Company, Air Rotor GmbH of West Germany, Nomura Securities of Japan, the Pennsylvania state government and Valmet Corporation of Finland are investors in Avtek Corporation. Funding from the Commonwealth of Pennsylvania will contribute towards the building of a 3,716 m² (40,000 sq ft) facility near Lock Haven for subassembly work on the production Avtek 400A. Meanwhile, Avtek Corporation is seeking a site larger than its present location to undertake final assembly and flight testing.

AVTEK MODEL 400A

Design of the Avtek 400A was initiated in March 1981, and construction of the first prototype started on 1 January 1982. This proof of concept (POC) aircraft (N400AV) flew for the first time on 17 September 1984.

Major changes made in the Spring of 1985 included a fuselage 'stretch' of 0.20 m (8 in) forward and 0.76 m (2 ft 6 in) aft of the forward pressure bulkhead; an increase in cabin width; a new wing incorporating additional fuel capacity in large wingroot leading-edge extensions; a new foreplane of greater span and reduced chord; relocated main landing gear legs; and specially developed Pratt & Whitney PT6A-3 turboprops, mounted closer to the wing.

On 20 March 1985 Valmet Corporation of Finland purchased an option to build an 'Explorer' derivative of the Avtek 400A for special missions such as maritime surveillance, liaison, coastal patrol, aerial survey, search and reconnaissance, and ESM, tailored to individual customer requirements. DuPont has an option to build the first 100 production airframes, which are constructed primarily from its proprietary polyaramid materials. The Avtek 400A structure is all-composite, comprising 72% DuPont Kevlar and Nomex, 16% graphite/carbonfibre, and smaller quantities of R-glass, S-glass, aluminium and nickel fibres.

Avtek Corporation is reported to have received deposit payments for 81 Avtek 400As, and plans to achieve FAA certification in late 1989, beginning customer deliveries in early 1990.

A description of the proof of concept prototype can be found in the 1985-86 *Jane's*. This aircraft was retrofitted and flown with PT6A-135M engines (PT6A-35s with counter-rotating gearboxes from the PT6A-66) and four-blade propellers, but it is not otherwise planned to modify it to production configuration. The following details apply to the pre-production second prototype, which was expected to fly in 1988:

TYPE: Six/nine-seat business aircraft.
WINGS: Cantilever low-wing monoplane, with large wingroot leading-edge extensions. Wing section Avtek 12. Anhedral 2° 30′ from roots. Sweepback 50° inboard of nacelles, 15° 30′ outboard. All-composites fail-safe structure. Mass balanced two-section ailerons of composite construction, inner sections functioning as pitch trim stabilisers. All control surfaces operated through bellcranks and rigid pushrods. No trim tabs. No trailing-edge flaps. Pneumatic de-icing boots on leading-edges.
FOREPLANE: Cantilever structure of composite materials, located on upper fuselage above forward end of cabin. Dihedral 1°. Conventional elevators, mass balanced and operated through bellcranks and pushrods. No trim tabs. Electric or engine bleed air de-icing of leading-edges.
FUSELAGE: All-composites fail-safe monocoque structure. Cabin and cabin baggage compartment pressurised.
TAIL UNIT: Conventional sweptback vertical fin and rudder, of all-composites construction. Rudder mass balanced and operated through bellcranks and pushrods. No trim tab. Pneumatic de-icing of fin leading-edge. Two large triangular ventral fins under tailcone, each at 45° anhedral angle.
LANDING GEAR: Hydraulically retractable tricycle type, main units retracting inward and nosewheel forward. Emergency extension system. Oleo-pneumatic shock absorber in each unit. Single wheel on each unit, mainwheels size 6.00-6 with Goodyear tyres size 17.5-6.25

× 7.5, pressure 7.0 bars (102 lb/sq in). Steerable nosewheel unit with wheel size 5.00-5 and Goodyear tyre size 14.2-5.5 × 6.5, pressure 5.0 bars (73 lb/sq in). Cleveland hydraulic disc brakes.
POWER PLANT: Two Pratt & Whitney Canada PT6A-3L/R turboprops, derived from the PT6A-135 and flat rated at 507 kW (680 shp), one mounted within nacelle above each wing. Hartzell four-blade constant-speed fully-feathering reversible-pitch pusher propellers (metal blades on prototype, Kevlar on production version). Propellers are opposite rotating, with automatic synchrophasing, full Beta control reversing and autofeathering. In-flight start capability. Integral fuel tank in each wingroot leading-edge. Total fuel capacity 1,003 litres (265 US gallons; 221 Imp gallons), of which 18.9 litres (5 US gallons; 4.2 Imp gallons) are unusable. Refuelling point in upper surface of each wing. Dual anti-icing inlets for each engine.
ACCOMMODATION: Pilot and five to nine passengers according to interior layout. Optional configurations include eight-passenger Pullman or Salon; eight-passenger Lounge; six-passenger Conference; Ambulance with stretcher, medical equipment and seats for three ambulatory patients or medical attendants; and Cargo with seats for pilot and one passenger. Two-section door on port side of cabin, with step incorporated in lower half. Emergency exit on starboard side opposite cabin door. Baggage compartment at rear of cabin with internal access. Unpressurised baggage compartment in nose with external door on port side. Accommodation is pressurised, air-conditioned, heated and ventilated.
SYSTEMS: AiResearch bleed air pressurisation system with max differential of 0.52 bars (7.6 lb/sq in), and air cycle air-conditioning system. Electrically driven hydraulic pump provides pressure of 138 bars (2,000 lb/sq in) for landing gear actuation. Electrical system includes dual 28V 300A engine driven generators, dual 29Ah storage batteries and external power socket. Oxygen system of 1.39 m³ (49 cu ft) capacity, pressure 128 bars (1,850 lb/sq in), provides constant flow for passengers and demand flow for pilot. Anti-icing of windscreen by electrical system, of propellers by engine efflux; alcohol anti-icing of wing and fin leading-edges optional; electrically heated pitot. Engine fire extinguishing system optional.
AVIONICS AND EQUIPMENT: Wide range of optional avionics by Bendix, Collins and Sperry, including EFIS and EICAS, and colour radar by RCA. Full IFR instrumentation optional.

DIMENSIONS, EXTERNAL:

Wing span	10.67 m (35 ft 0 in)
Foreplane span	6.92 m (22 ft 8½ in)

Length overall	11.99 m (39 ft 4 in)	Max width	1.40 m (4 ft 7¼ in)
Length of fuselage	10.41 m (34 ft 2 in)	Max height	1.37 m (4 ft 6 in)
Height overall	3.47 m (11 ft 4¾ in)	AREAS:	
Propeller diameter	1.93 m (6 ft 4 in)	Wings, gross	13.40 m² (144.2 sq ft)
Passenger door (port): Height	1.17 m (3 ft 10 in)	Foreplane, gross	4.52 m² (48.7 sq ft)
Width	0.76 m (2 ft 6 in)	WEIGHTS:	
Height to sill	0.76 m (2 ft 6 in)	Weight empty, equipped	1,714 kg (3,779 lb)
Baggage door (port, nose): Height	0.51 m (1 ft 8 in)	Max ramp weight	2,976 kg (6,560 lb)
Width	0.56 m (1 ft 10 in)	Max T-O and landing weight	2,948 kg (6,500 lb)
Height to sill	0.79 m (2 ft 7 in)	PERFORMANCE (estimated):	
Emergency exit (stbd): Height	0.51 m (1 ft 8 in)	Max level speed at S/L	255 knots (473 km/h; 294 mph)
Width	0.67 m (2 ft 2½ in)	Max cruising speed	
DIMENSIONS, INTERNAL:		at 3,050 m (10,000 ft)	297 knots (550 km/h; 342 mph)
Cabin: Length	3.14 m (10 ft 3½ in)	at 6,700 m (22,000 ft)	364 knots (675 km/h; 419 mph)

at 12,500 m (41,000 ft)	338 knots (626 km/h; 389 mph)
Stalling speed	83 knots (154 km/h; 96 mph)
Max rate of climb at S/L	1,411 m (4,630 ft)/min
Max rate of climb at S/L, one engine out	
	578 m (1,897 ft)/min
Service ceiling	12,950 m (42,500 ft)
Service ceiling, one engine out	10,060 m (33,000 ft)
T-O to 15 m (50 ft)	463 m (1,520 ft)
Landing from 15 m (50 ft)	390 m (1,280 ft)
Range with max fuel:	
no reserves	2,276 nm (4,218 km; 2,621 miles)
NBAA IFR reserves	1,922 nm (3,562 km; 2,213 miles)

AYRES

AYRES CORPORATION

PO Box 3090, Albany, Georgia 31708-5201
Telephone: (912) 883 1440
Telex: 547629 AYRESPORT ABN
Fax: (912) 439 9790
SALES MANAGERS: Marvin H. Wilson (Domestic)
Bill Brodbeck (International)

AYRES THRUSH S2R-600

Ayres Corporation purchased the manufacturing and world marketing rights of the Rockwell Thrush Commander-600 and -800 from Rockwell International's General Aviation Division in late November 1977, and now offers the following versions of this large agricultural aircraft:

Thrush S2R-600. Basic version with Pratt & Whitney R-1340 Wasp aircooled radial engine. Previously known as S2R-R1340. Available with one or two seats.

Bull Thrush S2R-R1820. As Thrush S2R-600, but with a Wright R-1820 engine. Described separately.

Turbo-Thrush S2R. As Thrush S2R-600, but with a Pratt & Whitney Canada PT6A-11, -15, -34 or -65AG turboprop. Described separately.

By early 1988 a total of 1,651 piston engined Thrushes had been delivered.

The Thrush S2R-600 has a corrosion-proof, polyurethane finish, and is certificated to both CAR 3 Normal category and CAM 8 Restricted category requirements.

The following details refer to the basic single-seat Thrush S2R-600, but apply also to the Bull Thrush, except as described in the separate entry for the latter aircraft.

TYPE: Single-seat (optionally two-seat) agricultural aircraft.

WINGS: Cantilever low-wing monoplane. Dihedral 3° 30'. Two-spar structure of light alloy throughout, except for main spar caps of 4130 chrome molybdenum steel. Leading-edge formed by heavy main spar and the nose skin. Light alloy plain ailerons. Electrically operated flaps. Wingroots sealed against chemical entry. Wing extensions, adding 2.79 m² (30 sq ft) of effective lifting surface, are standard on S2R-600, optional on Turbo-Thrush.

FUSELAGE: Welded chrome molybdenum steel tube structure covered with quickly removable light alloy panels. Underfuselage skin of stainless steel.

TAIL UNIT: All-metal aluminium alloy structure with cantilever fin and strut braced tailplane. Trim tab in each elevator. Deflector cable from cockpit to fin tip.

LANDING GEAR: Non-retractable tailwheel type. Main units have rubber in compression shock absorption and 29 × 11.00-10 wheels with 10-ply tyres. Hydraulically operated disc brakes. Parking brakes. Wire cutters on main gear. Steerable, locking tailwheel, size 12.5 × 4.5 in.

POWER PLANT: One 447 kW (600 hp) Pratt & Whitney R-1340 Wasp nine-cylinder aircooled radial engine, driving a Hamilton Standard type 12D40/EAC AG-100-2 two-blade constant-speed metal propeller, is standard. Fuel contained in wing tanks with combined capacity of 401 litres (106 US gallons; 88.3 Imp gallons).

ACCOMMODATION: Single adjustable mesh seat in 'safety pod' sealed cockpit enclosure is standard, with steel tube overturn structure. Dual tandem seating optional, with forward or rear facing second seat. Dual controls optional with forward facing rear seat, for pilot training. Adjustable rudder pedals. Downward hinged door on each side. Tempered safety glass windscreen. Cockpit wire cutter. Dual inertia reel safety harness with optional second seat. Baggage compartment standard on single-seat aircraft. Windscreen wiper and washer.

SYSTEM: Electrical system powered by a 24V 50A alternator. Lightweight 24V 35Ah battery.

AVIONICS: To customer's requirements.

EQUIPMENT: Transland glassfibre hopper forward of cockpit with capacity of 1.50 m³ (53 cu ft) can hold 1,514 litres (400 US gallons; 333 Imp gallons) of liquid or 1,487 kg (3,280 lb) of dry chemical. Hopper has a 0.33 m² (3.56 sq ft) lid, openable by two handles, and cockpit viewing window. Standard equipment includes Universal spray system with external 50 mm (2 in) stainless steel plumbing, 50 mm pump with wooden fan, Transland gate, 50 mm valve, quick-disconnect pump mount and strainer. Streamlined spraybooms with outlets for 68 nozzles. Micro-adjust valve control (spray) and calibrator (dry). A 63 mm (2.5 in) side loading system is installed on

Ayres Thrush S2R-600 (600 hp Pratt & Whitney R-1340 Wasp engine)

Ayres Turbo-Thrush NEDS dedicated narcotics eradication aircraft

the port side. Stainless steel rudder cables. Navigation lights, instrument lights and two strobe lights. Optional equipment includes a rear cockpit to accommodate aft facing crew member, or forward facing seat for passenger, or flying instructor if optional dual controls installed; space can be used alternatively for cargo. Other optional items are a Transland high-volume spreader, agitator installation; ten-unit AU5000 Micronair installation in lieu of standard booms and nozzles; Transland gatebox with stiffener casting; quick-disconnect flange and kit; night working lights including landing light and wingtip turn lights; cockpit fire extinguisher; and water bomber configuration.

DIMENSIONS, EXTERNAL:
Wing span	14.48 m (47 ft 6 in)
Length overall (tail up)	8.95 m (29 ft 4½ in)
Height overall	2.79 m (9 ft 2 in)
Tailplane span	5.18 m (17 ft 0 in)
Wheel track	2.72 m (8 ft 11 in)
Propeller diameter	2.74 m (9 ft 0 in)

AREA:
Wings, gross	33.13 m² (356.6 sq ft)

WEIGHTS AND LOADINGS:
Weight empty, equipped	1,678 kg (3,700 lb)
Max T-O weight: CAR 3	2,721 kg (6,000 lb)
CAM 8	3,130 kg (6,900 lb)
Max wing loading	103.0 kg/m² (21.1 lb/sq ft)
Max power loading	6.99 kg/kW (11.5 lb/hp)

PERFORMANCE (with spray equipment installed and at CAR 3 max T-O weight, except where indicated):
Max level speed	122 knots (225 km/h; 140 mph)
Max cruising speed, 70% power	
	108 knots (200 km/h; 124 mph)
Working speed, 70% power	
	91-100 knots (169-185 km/h; 105-115 mph)
Stalling speed: flaps up	58 knots (108 km/h; 67 mph)
flaps down	55 knots (101 km/h; 63 mph)
Stalling speed at normal landing weight:	
flaps up	47 knots (87 km/h; 54 mph)
flaps down	45 knots (84 km/h; 52 mph)
Max rate of climb at S/L	317 m (1,040 ft)/min

Service ceiling	4,575 m (15,000 ft)
T-O run	215 m (705 ft)
Landing run	139 m (455 ft)
Ferry range with max fuel at 70% power	
	350 nm (648 km; 403 miles)

AYRES BULL THRUSH S2R-R1820/510

Claimed by Ayres to be the most powerful production agricultural aircraft in the world, the Bull Thrush is generally similar to the Thrush S2R-600 except for smaller wings and the installation of a Wright R-1820 engine and a chemical hopper of increased capacity. The description of the Thrush S2R-600 applies also to the Bull Thrush, except as follows:

POWER PLANT: One 895 kW (1,200 hp) Wright R-1820 Cyclone nine-cylinder aircooled radial engine, driving a Hamilton Standard three-blade constant-speed metal propeller. Fuel system as for Thrush, but total usable fuel capacity 863 litres (228 US gallons; 190 Imp gallons).

AVIONICS AND EQUIPMENT: Generally as for Thrush, except that the chemical hopper is of 1.93 m³ (68.2 cu ft) or 1,930 litres (510 US gallons; 425 Imp gallons) capacity.

DIMENSIONS, EXTERNAL: As for Thrush, except:
Wing span	13.54 m (44 ft 5 in)
Length overall	9.60 m (31 ft 6 in)
Height overall	2.92 m (9 ft 7 in)
Wheel track	2.74 m (9 ft 0 in)

AREA:
Wings, gross	30.34 m² (326.6 sq ft)

WEIGHTS:
Weight empty, equipped	2,263 kg (4,990 lb)
Typical operating weight (CAM 8)	4,536 kg (10,000 lb)

PERFORMANCE (with spray equipment, at CAM 8 max T-O weight, except where indicated):
Max level speed	138 knots (256 km/h; 159 mph)
Cruising speed, 50% power	
	135 knots (249 km/h; 155 mph)
Working speed, 30-50% power	
	87-130 knots (161-241 km/h; 100-150 mph)
Stalling speed: flaps up	61 knots (113 km/h; 70 mph)
flaps down	58 knots (107 km/h; 66 mph)

Stalling speed at normal landing weight:
flaps up	52 knots (95 km/h; 59 mph)
flaps down	50 knots (92 km/h; 57 mph)
Max rate of climb at S/L	620 m (2,033 ft)/min
Service ceiling	8,535 m (28,000 ft)
T-O run	168 m (550 ft)
Landing run at normal landing weight	290 m (950 ft)
Ferry range at 40% power	
	582 nm (1,078 km; 670 miles)

AYRES TURBO-THRUSH S2R and TERR-MAR TURBO SEA THRUSH

Five versions of the turbine engined Turbo-Thrush S2R are currently available:

Turbo-Thrush S2R-T11: Version with a 373 kW (500 shp) Pratt & Whitney Canada PT6A-11AG turboprop and available only with the standard 1,514 litre (400 US gallon; 333 Imp gallon) chemical hopper.

Turbo-Thrush S2R-T15: Version with a 507 kW (680 shp) Pratt & Whitney Canada PT6A-15AG turboprop, available with a 1,514 litre (400 US gallon; 333 Imp gallon) or, optionally, 1,930 litre (510 US gallon; 425 Imp gallon) chemical hopper.

Turbo-Thrush S2R-T34: This version has a 559 kW (750 shp) Pratt & Whitney Canada PT6A-34AG turboprop and is available with standard and optional chemical hoppers as above.

Turbo-Thrush S2R-T65/400 NEDS: Ayres has developed a special version of the Turbo-Thrush, known as the Narcotics Eradication Delivery System (NEDS), for the US State Department, to which nine aircraft were delivered during 1983-85. This aircraft is powered by a 1,026 kW (1,376 shp) Pratt & Whitney Canada PT6A-65AG turboprop driving a five-blade propeller of 2.82 m (9 ft 3 in) diameter and features a two-seat armoured cockpit, armour protection around the engine compartment and a 75.7 litre (20 US gallon; 16.7 Imp gallon) self-sealing auxiliary fuel tank mounted in a bulletproof structure in addition to standard Turbo-Thrush wing fuel tanks. The aircraft are operated by the State Department's International Narcotics Matters Bureau and have been used on 'Operation Roundup' drug eradication missions in such countries as Burma, Colombia and Thailand against poppy crops, in Mexico against marijuana and poppies, and in Belize and Guatemala against marijuana. A chemical herbicide known as 'Roundup' is carried in a 1,514 litre (400 US gallon; 333 Imp gallon) tank and is sprayed on the plants to make them overfertilise, grow rapidly, then wilt and die. Delivery rate, at a working speed of 104-113 knots (193-209 km/h; 120-130 mph), is some 265 litres (70 US gallons; 60 Imp gallons) per acre, a typical marijuana field being about 0.3 ha (0.7 acre). In Belize, Turbo-Thrush NEDS have operated under escort from an armed Pilatus Britten-Norman Defender which could provide fire support in an emergency, such as forced landing. The Turbo-Thrush NEDS is usually operated by two crew in case of injury from groundfire, and is equipped with King VLF Omega 660, ADF, VOR, HF and VHF avionics.

Terr-Mar Turbo Sea Thrush. Terr-Mar Aviation Corporation of Vancouver, Canada, holds FAA type approval for a water bombing version of the Turbo-Thrush mounted on twin Wipline amphibious floats. A Terr-Mar probe enables the 1,930 litre (510 US gallon; 425 Imp gallon) hopper to be filled 'on the step' in 15 s. A gravity activated drop door beneath the hopper is closed by airflow.

With the exception of the Turbo-Thrush NEDS, in each case the turboprop drives a Hartzell three-blade constant-speed fully-feathering and reversible-pitch metal propeller with spinner. To compensate for the small size and light weight of the turboprop, it is mounted well forward of the firewall, in a slender cowling. Current installations have cowlings which comprise individual panels to improve access. Standard and optional equipment is generally as detailed for the basic Thrush. Total usable fuel capacity is 863 litres (228 US gallons; 190 Imp gallons).

Advantages claimed for this conversion include greatly improved take-off and climb performance; improved short landing capability; a 454 kg (1,000 lb) increase in payload due to reduced power plant weight; ability to operate on

Ayres Bull Thrush S2R-R1820 (1,200 hp Wright R-1820 engine)

Terr-Mar Aviation Corporation Turbo Sea Thrush conversion of the Ayres Turbo-Thrush agricultural aircraft

aviation turbine fuel, or diesel fuel; a TBO of 3,500 h; quieter operation; and the ability to feather the propeller during fuelling and loading operations without shutting down the engine, because of the free-turbine configuration.

By early 1988 a total of 280 Turbo-Thrushes had been delivered.

DIMENSIONS, EXTERNAL, AND AREA: As for Bull Thrush S2R-R1820 except:
Length overall	10.06 m (33 ft 0 in)
Height overall	2.79 m (9 ft 2 in)

WEIGHTS AND LOADINGS (A: standard hopper; B: optional 1,930 litre; 510 US gallon; 425 Imp gallon hopper):
Weight empty: A	1,633 kg (3,600 lb)
B	1,769 kg (3,900 lb)
Max T-O weight (CAR 3): A, B	2,721 kg (6,000 lb)
Typical operating weight (CAM 8):	
A	3,719 kg (8,200 lb)
B	3,856 kg (8,500 lb)
Max wing loading	127.1 kg/m² (26.0 lb/sq ft)
Max power loading	7.6 kg/kW (14.17 lb/shp)

PERFORMANCE (A and B with PT6A-34AG power plant, at max T-O weight except where indicated):
Max level speed with spray equipment	
	138 knots (256 km/h; 159 mph)
Cruising speed, 50% power	
	130 knots (241 km/h; 150 mph)
Working speed, 30-50% power	
	82-130 knots (153-241 km/h; 95-150 mph)
Stalling speed: flaps up	61 knots (113 km/h; 70 mph)
flaps down	57 knots (106 km/h; 66 mph)
Stalling speed at normal landing weight:	
flaps up	51 knots (95 km/h; 59 mph)
flaps down	50 knots (92 km/h; 57 mph)
Max rate of climb at S/L	530 m (1,740 ft)/min
Service ceiling	7,620 m (25,000 ft)
T-O run	183 m (600 ft)
Landing run	152 m (500 ft)
Landing run with propeller reversal	91 m (300 ft)
Ferry range at 40% power	
	664 nm (1,231 km; 765 miles)

BALDWIN
BALDWIN AIRCRAFT INTERNATIONAL
CHIEF EXECUTIVE OFFICER: Gary Baldwin

BALDWIN ASP-XJ

In May 1988 Baldwin Aircraft International's ASP-XJ (Armed Surveillance and Patrol - Experimental Jet) two-seat all-composite jet surveillance and patrol aircraft was displayed at the Air/Space America 88 air show held at San Diego, California, reportedly following successful flight trials. As can be seen from the accompanying photograph, the ASP-XJ is of tail-less delta configuration similar in appearance to a Dassault Mirage III. The entire airframe is manufactured from composites, primarily Kevlar, with some boron, Nomex, graphite and S and E glass materials. The aircraft is said to be suitable for such

Prototype Baldwin Aircraft International ASP-XJ all-composite light jet military aircraft

roles as pilot training, military patrol and surveillance, or commercial use.

First details of Baldwin Aircraft's project were revealed in the Autumn of 1984 when the prototype of a light ground attack fighter was said to be nearing completion. At that time the subsonic ASP-XJ was to have been powered by a General Electric CJ610-8A turbojet rated at 13.12 kN (2,950 lb st). Other data included a wing span of 4.20 m (13 ft 9½ in) and a max T-O weight of 2,041 kg (4,500 lb). A single-seat supersonic version known as ASP-XJS was to be powered by a General Electric J85-GE-21 engine rated at 22.24 kN (5,000 lb st) with afterburning, with max T-O weight of 3,266 kg (7,200 lb). Both variants were then said to feature fly by wire control systems and were to be equipped with four underwing stores hardpoints for the carriage of weapons or external fuel tanks. No further details have been received.

BEECHCRAFT
BEECH AIRCRAFT CORPORATION
(Subsidiary of Raytheon Company)
9709 East Central, Wichita, Kansas 67201-0085
Telephone: (316) 681 7111
Telex: 203603
BRANCH DIVISION: Salina, Kansas
CHAIRMAN EMERITUS, AND CHAIRMAN OF BEECH AIRCRAFT FOUNDATION: Mrs Olive Ann (Walter H.) Beech
CHAIRMAN: Thomas L. Phillips
PRESIDENT AND CHIEF EXECUTIVE OFFICER: Max E. Bleck
EXECUTIVE VICE-PRESIDENT:
  Charles W. Dieker (Marketing)
VICE-PRESIDENTS:
  C. Don Cary (Product Marketing)
  Robert D. Dickerson (Engineering)
  George D. Rodgers (Sales and Marketing Services)
  Elbert L. Rutan
DIRECTOR OF CORPORATE COMMUNICATIONS:
  Drew Steketee

Beech Aircraft Corporation was founded jointly in 1932 by Mrs Olive Ann Beech and the late Walter H. Beech, pioneer designer and builder of light aeroplanes in the USA. On 8 February 1980 it became a wholly owned subsidiary of Raytheon. It continues to operate as a separate entity, and is currently engaged in the production of civil and military aircraft, missile targets, and aircraft and missile components.

Deliveries by Beech in 1987 were made up of 90 King Airs, 26 Barons, 165 Bonanzas, 4 Duchesses, 15 Model 1900 Airliners and 14 Beechjets. By 1 January 1988 Beech had delivered 5,250 pressurised aircraft since introducing the King Air 90 in 1964. Total production of Beech aeroplanes reached 48,463 by the beginning of 1988.

A wholly owned subsidiary, Beech Aerospace Services Inc (BASI), of Jackson, Mississippi, is currently responsible for worldwide logistic support of Army/Air Force/Navy C-12s, and Beech MQM-107 targets, in more than 74 locations in 37 countries.

Beech Aircraft had 8,500 employees worldwide at the end of 1987 and occupies 315,127 m² (3,392,000 sq ft) of plant area at its two major facilities in Wichita and Salina, Kansas.

The Salina division supplies all wings, non-metallic interior components, ventral fins, nosecones and tailcones used in Wichita production, and is responsible for manufacture and final assembly of the T-34C trainer. Work performed in Wichita includes manufacture under subcontract of composites winglets and landing gear doors for the McDonnell Douglas C-17 military transport aircraft.

Wholly owned subsidiaries of the parent company include Scaled Composites (which see), acquired in June 1985 to serve as an advanced development arm for the company; Beech Acceptance Corporation Inc, engaged in business aircraft retail finance and leasing; Beechcraft AG, in Zurich, Switzerland, which supports in Europe the sales, liaison and other activities of the parent company; Travel Air Insurance Company Ltd, a Bermuda-based company organised to provide aircraft liability insurance; Beech Holdings Inc, which provides marketing support to the parent company; Beech International Sales Corporation, Wichita, through which all Beech export sales are made;

Beech Aerospace Services Inc, which provides worldwide support of Beech military aircraft, missile targets and related products; and the following sales outlets which are wholly owned subsidiaries of Beech Holdings Inc: Beechcraft East Inc, Farmingdale, New York, and Bedford, Massachusetts; Hangar One Inc, Atlanta, Hartsfield, DeKalb-Peachtree, and Fulton County, Georgia; Birmingham, Alabama; and Opa Locka, Orlando and Tampa, Florida; United Beechcraft Inc, Wichita, Kansas; Beechcraft West, Ontario, Hayward, Van Nuys, and Fresno, California; Indiana Beechcraft Inc, Indianapolis, Indiana, where Beech's Commuter Spares Parts Supply operation is based; and Hartzog Aviation, Rockford, Illinois.

BEECHCRAFT T-34C
US Navy designation: T-34C
The original piston engined Beechcraft Model 45 was built as the T-34A Mentor for the USAF (450) and as the similar T-34B for the US Navy (423). Design of the upgraded T-34C, with a PT6A-25 turboprop and updated avionics, began in March 1973, and the first of two YT-34C prototypes flew on 21 September that year. Under successive US Navy contracts, Beech delivered 334 new-production T-34Cs between November 1977 and April 1984. Six T-34Cs have been transferred to the US Army's Airborne Special Operations Test Board at Fort Bragg, North Carolina, where they serve as chase and photographic aircraft. In May 1987 the US Navy ordered a further 19 T-34Cs for delivery between June 1989 and April 1990. By mid-1987 the US Navy's T-34C fleet had logged nearly one million flight hours and had established the lowest accident rate for aircraft in the service's current inventory. An export civil version, known as the **Turbine Mentor 34C**, is in service at the Algerian national pilot training school, which received six in 1979. A limited number of Turbine Mentor 34Cs was offered to private commercial operators in the Autumn of 1987, but no orders had been received up to the end of that year.

A **T-34C-1** armament systems trainer version is also available and, in addition to its basic role, is capable of carrying out forward air control (FAC) and tactical strike training missions. Deliveries of T-34C-1s were made to Argentina (Navy 15), Ecuador (Air Force 20, Navy 3),

Beechcraft T-34C-1 in service with the Navy of Peru

Gabon (Presidential Guard 4), Indonesia (Air Force 25), Morocco (Air Force 12), Peru (Navy 7), Taiwan (40) and Uruguay (Navy 3).

TYPE: Two-seat turbine powered primary training and light strike training aircraft.

WINGS: Cantilever low-wing monoplane. Wing section NACA 23016.5 (modified) at root, NACA 23012 at tip. Dihedral 7°. Incidence 4° at root, 1° at tip. No sweepback. Conventional box beam structure of light alloy. Ailerons of light alloy construction. Single-slotted trailing-edge flaps of light alloy. Manually operated trim tab in port aileron. Servo tabs in both ailerons.

FUSELAGE: Semi-monocoque light alloy structure.

TAIL UNIT: Cantilever structure of light alloy. Fixed incidence tailplane. Manually operated trim tabs in elevators and rudder. Twin ventral fins under rear fuselage.

LANDING GEAR: Electrically retractable tricycle type. Main units retract inward, nosewheel aft. Beech oleo-pneumatic shock absorbers. Single wheel on each unit. Mainwheels size 7.00-8, pressure 6.20 bars (90.0 lb/sq in). Nosewheel and tyre size 5.00-5, pressure 4.83 bars (70.0 lb/sq in). Goodyear multiple-disc hydraulic brakes.

POWER PLANT: One 533 kW (715 shp) Pratt & Whitney Canada PT6A-25 turboprop, torque limited to 298 kW (400 shp), driving a Hartzell three-blade constant-speed fully-feathering metal propeller with spinner. Version of same engine derated to 410 kW (550 shp) is available optionally. Two bladder fuel cells in each wing, in inboard leading-edge and aft of main spar outboard of landing gear; total usable capacity 492 litres (130 US gallons; 108 Imp gallons). Oil capacity 15 litres (4 US gallons; 3.33 Imp gallons).

ACCOMMODATION: Instructor and pupil in tandem beneath rearward sliding cockpit canopy. Cockpit ventilated, heated by engine bleed air and air-conditioned. Dual controls standard. All armament controls in forward cockpit of T-34C-1.

SYSTEMS: Hydraulic system for brakes only. Pneumatic system for emergency opening of cockpit canopy. Diluter demand gaseous oxygen system, pressure 103.5 bars (1,500 lb/sq in). Electrical power supplied by 250A starter/generator. Freon air-conditioner for cockpit cooling.

AVIONICS AND EQUIPMENT: Standard avionics can include UHF or VHF com, VOR or Tacan nav, DME, transponder, angle of attack indicator, ADF, marker beacon receiver, compass and intercom system. R/Nav, Loran, HF and specialised tactical systems available to customer's requirements. US Navy T-34C has ARC-159V UHF com, VIR-30A VOR/Omni, dual 255Y-1 ICS/audio, TCN-40 Tacan and PN-101 remote compass, all by Collins; two TDR-950 transponders and a CIR-11-2 emergency locator transmitter. Blind-flying instrumentation standard. Electrically heated pitot.

ARMAMENT (T-34C-1): CA-513 fixed-reticle reflector gunsight. Four underwing hardpoints are provided for the carriage of stores. The inboard stations are rated at 272 kg (600 lb) each, the outboard stations at 136 kg (300 lb) each, with a maximum load of 272 kg (600 lb) each side and 544 kg (1,200 lb) total. Weapons which can be carried on MA-4 racks include AF/B37K-1 bomb containers with practice bombs or flares, LAU-32 or LAU-59 rocket pods, Mk 81 bombs, SUU-11 Minigun pods, BLU-10/B incendiary bombs, AGM-22A wire guided anti-tank missiles and TA8X towed target equipment.

DIMENSIONS, EXTERNAL:

Wing span	10.16 m (33 ft 3⅞ in)
Wing chord: at root	2.55 m (8 ft 4½ in)
at tip	1.05 m (3 ft 5¼ in)
Wing aspect ratio	6.2

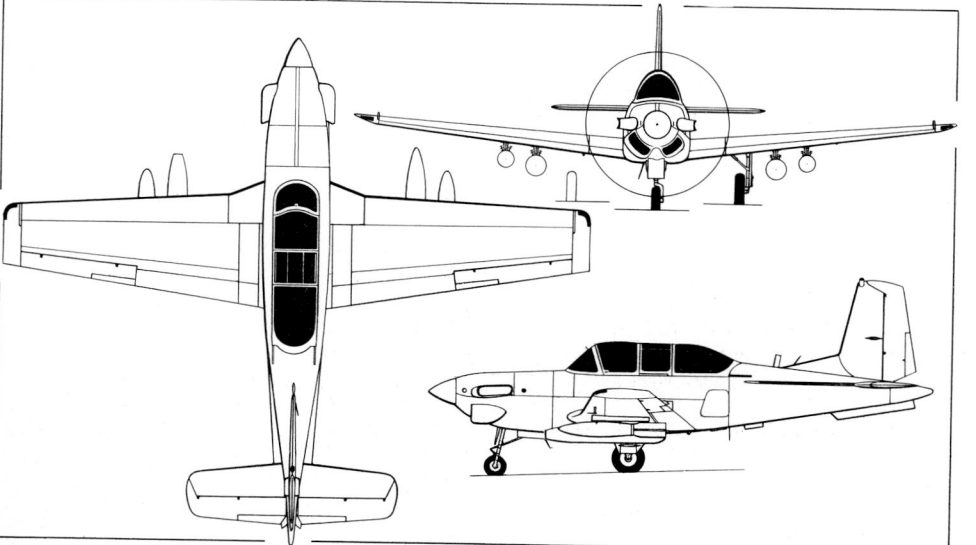
Beechcraft T-34C-1 turboprop powered training/light attack aircraft *(Pilot Press)*

Length overall	8.75 m (28 ft 8½ in)
Height overall	2.92 m (9 ft 7 in)
Tailplane span	3.71 m (12 ft 2⅛ in)
Wheel track	2.95 m (9 ft 8 in)
Wheelbase	2.41 m (7 ft 11 in)
Propeller diameter	2.29 m (7 ft 6 in)
Propeller ground clearance	0.29 m (11¼ in)

DIMENSIONS, INTERNAL:

Cabin: Length	2.74 m (9 ft 0 in)
Max width	0.86 m (2 ft 10 in)
Max height	1.22 m (4 ft 0 in)

AREAS:

Wings, gross	16.69 m² (179.6 sq ft)
Ailerons (total)	1.06 m² (11.4 sq ft)
Trailing-edge flaps (total)	1.98 m² (21.3 sq ft)
Fin	1.20 m² (12.9 sq ft)
Rudder, incl tab	0.64 m² (6.9 sq ft)
Tailplane	3.46 m² (37.2 sq ft)
Elevators, incl tabs	1.26 m² (13.6 sq ft)

WEIGHTS AND LOADING:

Weight empty: T-34C	1,342 kg (2,960 lb)
T-34C-1	1,356 kg (2,990 lb)
Max T-O and landing weight:	
T-34C	1,950 kg (4,300 lb)
T-34C-1, strike role	2,494 kg (5,500 lb)
Max ramp weight: T-34C	1,962 kg (4,325 lb)
Max wing loading: T-34C	108.3 kg/m² (22.2 lb/sq ft)

PERFORMANCE (T-34C, at T-O weight of 1,910 kg; 4,210 lb, except where indicated):

Never-exceed speed	280 knots (518 km/h; 322 mph)
Max cruising speed at 5,180 m (17,000 ft)	
	214 knots (396 km/h; 246 mph)
Stalling speed, flaps down, power off, at typical landing weight of 1,588 kg (3,501 lb)	
	53 knots (98 km/h; 61 mph)
Max rate of climb at S/L	451 m (1,480 ft)/min
Service ceiling	over 9,145 m (30,000 ft)
T-O run	352 m (1,155 ft)
T-O to 15 m (50 ft)	586 m (1,920 ft)
Landing from 15 m (50 ft)	547 m (1,795 ft)
Landing run	226 m (740 ft)
Range with max fuel:	
at 181 knots (335 km/h; 208 mph) at 305 m (1,000 ft)	
	427 nm (790 km; 491 miles)
at 202 knots (374 km/h; 232 mph) at 3,050 m (10,000 ft)	
	523 nm (968 km; 601 miles)
at 180 knots (333 km/h; 207 mph) at 6,100 m (20,000 ft)	
	708 nm (1,311 km; 814 miles)
g limits	+6/−3

PERFORMANCE (T-34C-1 with 410 kW; 550 shp engine, estimated. A with two stores at AUW of 2,222 kg; 4,900 lb. B with four stores at AUW of 2,494 kg; 5,500 lb, except where indicated):

Max level speed at 5,500 m (18,000 ft):	
A	209 knots (387 km/h; 241 mph)
B	206 knots (382 km/h; 237 mph)
Stalling speed, flaps down, idle power:	
A	65 knots (120 km/h; 75 mph) CAS
B	69 knots (128 km/h; 80 mph) CAS
Max rate of climb at S/L: A	540 m (1,771 ft)/min
B	436 m (1,431 ft)/min
Typical combat radius:	
FAC mission at AUW of 2,429 kg (5,355 lb), with four stores and optional max fuel, incl 2.6 h loiter over target and 20 min +5% reserves	
	100 nm (185 km; 115 miles)
Strike mission at AUW of 2,473 kg (5,452 lb), with four stores and optional max fuel, incl 20 min +5% reserves	
	300 nm (555 km; 345 miles)

BEECHCRAFT BONANZA MODEL F33A/C

The **F33A** version of the Bonanza is a four/five-seat single-engined executive aircraft, similar in general configuration to the Bonanza Model V35B, but distinguished by a conventional tail unit with sweptback vertical surfaces. The prototype flew for the first time on 14 September 1959, and the production models were known as Debonairs until 1967. The 1985 model introduced as standard equipment a large cargo door, three-blade propeller, super soundproofing, and the avionics and equipment listed in the appropriate paragraph, representing full IFR standard.

The Mexican Air Force received 21 aerobatic **F33C**s in 1986 and three other F33Cs, built to special order, were delivered to civilian customers in late 1986/early 1987. Earlier F33C recipients included the Imperial Iranian Air Force (16), Mexican Navy (5), Netherlands Government Flying School (16), and Spanish Air Force/Air Ministry (74). This model remains available to special order. The large cargo door, air-conditioning and fifth seat are not available for the Bonanza F33C.

A total of 2,655 Model 33s had been built by 1 January 1988. The company expected to build 100 F33As during 1988.

TYPE: Four/five-seat light cabin monoplane.
WINGS: Cantilever low-wing monoplane. Wing section Beech modified NACA 23016.5 at root, modified NACA 23012 at tip. Dihedral 6°. Incidence 4° at root, 1° at tip. Sweepback 0° at quarter-chord. Each wing is a two-spar semi-monocoque box-beam of conventional aluminium alloy construction. Symmetrical section ailerons and

Beechcraft Model F33A Bonanza four/five-seat cabin monoplane

single-slotted three-position flaps of aluminium alloy construction. Ground adjustable trim tab in each aileron.
FUSELAGE: Conventional aluminium alloy semi-monocoque structure. Hat section longerons and channel type keels extend forward from cabin section, making the support structure for the engine and nosewheel an integral part of the fuselage.
TAIL UNIT: Conventional cantilever all-metal stressed-skin structure, primarily of aluminium alloy but with beaded magnesium skin on elevators. Large trim tab in each elevator. Fixed tab in rudder.
LANDING GEAR: Electrically retractable tricycle type, with steerable nosewheel. Mainwheels retract inward into wings, nosewheel rearward. Beech oleo-pneumatic shock absorbers in all units. Cleveland mainwheels, size 6.00-6, and tyres, size 7.00-6, pressure 2.28-2.76 bars (33-40 lb/sq in). Cleveland nosewheel and tyre, size 5.00-5, pressure 2.76 bars (40 lb/sq in). Cleveland ring-disc hydraulic brakes. Parking brake. 'Magic Hand' landing gear system optional.
POWER PLANT: One 212.5 kW (285 hp) Continental IO-520-BB flat-six engine, driving a McCauley three-blade constant-speed metal propeller with spinner. Propeller de-icing optional. Manually adjustable engine cowl flaps. Two standard fuel tanks in wing leading-edges, with total usable capacity of 280 litres (74 US gallons; 61.6 Imp gallons). Refuelling points above tanks. Oil capacity 11.5 litres (3 US gallons; 2.5 Imp gallons).
ACCOMMODATION: Enclosed cabin with four individual seats in pairs as standard, plus optional forward facing fifth seat (F33A only). Baggage compartment and hat shelf aft of seats. Passenger door and baggage compartment door on starboard side. Heater standard. Large cargo door, on starboard side of fuselage, standard on F33A. F33C has removable seat cushions, to accommodate parachutes, and a quick-release passenger door.
SYSTEMS: Optional 12,000 BTU refrigeration type air-conditioning system comprises evaporator located beneath pilot's seat, condenser on lower fuselage and engine mounted compressor. Air outlets on centre console, with two-speed blower. Electrical system supplied by 28V 60A alternator, 24V 15.5Ah battery; a 100A alternator is available as an option, as is a standby generator. Hydraulic system for brakes only. Pneumatic system for instrument gyros and refrigeration type air-conditioning system optional. Oxygen system optional.
AVIONICS AND EQUIPMENT: Standard avionics include King KX 165-05 720-channel com transceiver, 200-channel nav/glideslope receiver/converter with KI 206 VOR/ILS indicator, King KY 165-04 720-channel com transceiver, 200-channel nav receiver/converter with KI 202 VOR/LOC indicator, KR 87 ADF with 227-00 indicator, KN 63 DME with KDI 572 indicator, DME hold and nav 1/nav 2 switching, KT 76A transponder, KMA 24-03 audio control/marker beacon receiver, microphone, headset, cabin speaker and static wicks. A wide range of optional avionics is available, including Loran C. King and S-Tec autopilots, Sperry WeatherScout radar and 3M/Ryan Stormscope are optional. Standard equipment includes electric clock, exhaust gas temperature gauge, outside air temperature gauge, rate of climb indicator, sensitive altimeter, turn co-ordinator, 3 in horizon and directional gyros, four fore and aft adjustable and reclining seats, armrests, headrests, single diagonal strap shoulder harness with inertia reel for all occupants, pilot's storm window, sun visors, ultraviolet-proof windscreen and windows, large cargo door, emergency locator transmitter, stall warning device, alternate static source, heated pitot, rotating beacon, three light strobe system, carpeted floor, coat hooks, glove compartment, in-flight

storage pockets, approach plate holder, utility shelf, cabin dome light, reading lights, instrument post lights, control wheel map light, electroluminescent sub-panel lighting, landing light, taxi light, full-flow oil filter, three-colour polyurethane exterior paint, external power socket and towbar. Optional equipment includes control wheel clock, dual controls, co-pilot's wheel brakes, fifth seat, super soundproofing, control wheel map lights, entrance door courtesy light, internally lit instruments and fresh air vent blower. Also available is a Beech designed 'Magic Hand' landing gear safety system. Designed to eliminate the possibility of wheels-up landing or inadvertent retraction of the landing gear on the ground, it lowers the gear automatically on approach when the engine manifold pressure falls below approximately 508 mm (20 in) and airspeed has been reduced to 104 knots (193 km/h; 120 mph). On take-off, it keeps the gear down until the aircraft is airborne and has accelerated to 78 knots (145 km/h; 90 mph) IAS. The system can be switched off by the pilot at will. F33C has accelerometer, second boost pump with indicator light, non-baffled fuel cells, heavy-gauge rudder cables and reinforced fuselage, wings and tail surfaces as standard.

DIMENSIONS, EXTERNAL:

Wing span	10.21 m (33 ft 6 in)
Wing chord: at root	2.13 m (7 ft 0 in)
at tip	1.07 m (3 ft 6 in)
Wing aspect ratio	6.2
Length overall	8.13 m (26 ft 8 in)
Height overall	2.51 m (8 ft 3 in)
Tailplane span	3.71 m (12 ft 2 in)
Wheel track	2.92 m (9 ft 7 in)
Wheelbase	2.13 m (7 ft 0 in)
Propeller diameter	2.03 m (6 ft 8 in)
Passenger door: Height	0.91 m (3 ft 0 in)
Width	0.94 m (3 ft 1 in)
Cargo door (F33A): Height	0.57 m (1 ft 10½ in)
Width	0.96 m (3 ft 2 in)
Baggage compartment door:	
Height	0.57 m (1 ft 10½ in)
Width	0.47 m (1 ft 6½ in)

DIMENSIONS, INTERNAL:

Cabin, aft of firewall: Length	3.07 m (10 ft 1 in)
Max width	1.07 m (3 ft 6 in)
Max height	1.27 m (4 ft 2 in)
Volume	3.31 m³ (117 cu ft)
Baggage space	0.99 m³ (35 cu ft)

AREAS:

Wings, gross	16.80 m² (181 sq ft)
Ailerons (total)	1.06 m² (11.4 sq ft)
Trailing-edge flaps (total)	1.98 m² (21.3 sq ft)
Fin	0.93 m² (10.0 sq ft)
Rudder, incl tab	0.52 m² (5.6 sq ft)
Tailplane	1.75 m² (18.82 sq ft)
Elevators, incl tabs	1.67 m² (18.0 sq ft)

WEIGHTS AND LOADINGS:

Weight empty	1,015 kg (2,237 lb)
Max T-O and landing weight	1,542 kg (3,400 lb)
Max T-O weight, F33C in Aerobatic category	
	1,270 kg (2,800 lb)
Max ramp weight	1,548 kg (3,412 lb)
Max wing loading	91.8 kg/m² (18.8 lb/sq ft)
Max power loading	7.26 kg/kW (11.93 lb/hp)

PERFORMANCE (at max T-O weight, except cruising speeds at mid-cruise weight):

Max level speed at S/L	182 knots (338 km/h; 209 mph)
Cruising speed:	
75% power at 1,830 m (6,000 ft)	
	172 knots (319 km/h; 198 mph)

66% power at 3,050 m (10,000 ft)
   168 knots (311 km/h; 193 mph)
55% power at 3,660 m (12,000 ft)
   157 knots (291 km/h; 181 mph)
45% power at 2,440 m (8,000 ft)
   136 knots (253 km/h; 157 mph)

Stalling speed, power off:

flaps up	64 knots (118 km/h; 74 mph) IAS
30° flap	51 knots (94 km/h; 59 mph) IAS
Max rate of climb at S/L	353 m (1,157 ft)/min
Service ceiling	5,443 m (17,858 ft)
T-O run	305 m (1,000 ft)
T-O to 15 m (50 ft)	530 m (1,740 ft)
Landing from 15 m (50 ft)	396 m (1,300 ft)
Landing run	232 m (760 ft)

Range with max usable fuel, allowances for engine start, taxi, T-O, climb and 45 min reserves at 45% power:

75% power at 1,830 m (6,000 ft)
   715 nm (1,325 km; 823 miles)
66% power at 3,050 m (10,000 ft)
   777 nm (1,440 km; 894 miles)
55% power at 3,660 m (12,000 ft)
   838 nm (1,553 km; 964 miles)
45% power at 2,440 m (8,000 ft)
   889 nm (1,648 km; 1,023 miles)

BEECHCRAFT BONANZA MODEL A36

The current version of the A36, introduced on 3 October 1983, succeeded the earlier 212.5 kW (285 hp) Continental IO-520-BB powered model. It is a full six-seat utility aircraft developed from the Bonanza Model V35B, but has a conventional tail unit with sweptback vertical surfaces, similar to that of the Bonanza F33 series. In addition, the A36 has large double doors on the starboard side aft of the wing root, to facilitate loading and unloading of bulky cargo when used in a utility role. The cabin volume is increased by 0.54 m³ (18.9 cu ft) compared with the F33, due to a fuselage extension of 0.25 m (10 in), and an increase of 0.28 m³ (10 cu ft) in the baggage compartment volume.

Like all Bonanzas, the Model A36 is licensed in the FAA Utility category at full gross weight, with no limitation of performance. The current model has as standard a Continental IO-550-B engine, redesigned instrument panels with 40% more space for instruments and avionics, dual controls, throttle control power levers, exhaust gas temperature gauge, automatically-dimming landing gear and annunciator lights for night operation, a three-blade propeller and a standby vacuum system. Landing gear and flap controls have been repositioned to conform to GAMA recommendations. Optional extras include instrument post lights, internally-lit instruments, courtesy lights for entrance door and rear step, co-pilot's vertically adjusting seat, refrigeration type air-conditioning system and all other items mentioned under the Model F33A Bonanza entry, except for the large cargo door.

A total of 2,840 Model 36 Bonanzas had been delivered by 1 January 1988. In April 1985 Saudia (Saudi Arabian Airlines) received four Model A36 Bonanzas for pilot training. The Finnair Training Centre at Pori, Finland, took delivery of three Model A36 Bonanzas during 1987.

TYPE: Four/six-seat utility light cabin monoplane.

WINGS: As for Model F33A.

FUSELAGE: As F33A but lengthened by 0.25 m (10 in).

TAIL UNIT: As for Model F33A.

LANDING GEAR: As for Model F33A, but without 'Magic Hand' system option.

POWER PLANT: One 224 kW (300 hp) Continental IO-550-B flat-six engine, driving a McCauley three-blade constant-speed propeller. The engine is equipped with an altitude-compensating fuel pump which automatically leans and enriches the fuel/air mixture during climb and descent respectively. Fuel capacity as for Model F33A.

ACCOMMODATION: Enclosed cabin seating four to six persons on individual seats. Pilot's seat is vertically adjustable. Dual controls standard. Two rear removable seats and two folding seats permit rapid conversion to utility configuration. Optional club seating with rear facing third and fourth seats, executive writing desk, refreshment cabinet, headrests for third and fourth seats, reading lights and fresh air outlets for fifth and sixth seats. Double doors of bonded aluminium honeycomb construction on starboard side facilitate loading of cargo. As an air ambulance, one stretcher can be accommodated with ample room for a medical attendant and/or other passengers. Extra windows provide improved view for passengers. Stowage for 181 kg (400 lb) of baggage.

SYSTEMS: Electrical system as for F33A. Hydraulic system for brakes only. Pneumatic system for instrument gyros, and refrigeration type air-conditioning system, optional.

AVIONICS AND EQUIPMENT: Standard avionics include King KX 155 720-channel nav/com, with KI 208 VOR/LOC Omni converter/indicator, but a wide range of optional avionics is available. An optional ground communication switch permits use of one com radio without turning on the battery master switch. Optional equipment is as detailed for the F33A Bonanza, except as noted.

DIMENSIONS, EXTERNAL AND AREAS: As for F33A except:

Length overall	8.38 m (27 ft 6 in)
Height overall	2.62 m (8 ft 7 in)
Wheelbase	2.39 m (7 ft 10¼ in)

Beechcraft Model A36 Bonanza of the Finnair Training Centre

Rear passenger/cargo door: Height	1.02 m (3 ft 4 in)
Width	1.14 m (3 ft 9 in)

DIMENSIONS, INTERNAL:

Cabin, aft of firewall: Length, incl extended baggage compartment	3.84 m (12 ft 7 in)
Max width	1.07 m (3 ft 6 in)
Max height	1.27 m (4 ft 2 in)
Volume	3.85 m³ (135.9 cu ft)

WEIGHTS AND LOADINGS:

Weight empty, standard	1,028 kg (2,266 lb)
Max T-O weight	1,655 kg (3,650 lb)
Max ramp weight	1,661 kg (3,663 lb)
Max wing loading	98.6 kg/m² (20.2 lb/sq ft)
Max power loading	7.40 kg/kW (12.2 lb/hp)

PERFORMANCE (max speed at minimum weight; cruising speeds at mid-cruise weight):

Max level speed   184 knots (340 km/h; 212 mph)

Max cruising speed:

2,500 rpm at 1,830 m (6,000 ft)
   176 knots (326 km/h; 202 mph)
2,300 rpm at 2,440 m (8,000 ft)
   167 knots (309 km/h; 192 mph)
2,100 rpm at 1,830 m (6,000 ft)
   160 knots (296 km/h; 184 mph)
2,100 rpm at 3,050 m (10,000 ft)
   153 knots (283 km/h; 176 mph)

Stalling speed, power off:

flaps up	68 knots (126 km/h; 78 mph) IAS
30° flap	59 knots (109 km/h; 68 mph) IAS
Max rate of climb at S/L	368 m (1,210 ft)/min
Service ceiling	3,638 m (18,500 ft)
T-O run: 0° flap	360 m (1,182 ft)
12° flap	296 m (971 ft)
T-O to 15 m (50 ft): 0° flap	640 m (2,100 ft)
12° flap	583 m (1,913 ft)
Landing from 15 m (50 ft)	442 m (1,450 ft)
Landing run	280 m (920 ft)

Range with max usable fuel, with allowances for engine start, taxi, T-O, climb and 45 min reserves at economy cruise power:

2,500 rpm at 3,660 m (12,000 ft)
   875 nm (1,621 km; 1,008 miles)
2,300 rpm at 3,660 m (12,000 ft)
   903 nm (1,672 km; 1,039 miles)
2,100 rpm at 1,830 m (6,000 ft)
   914 nm (1,692 km; 1,052 miles)

BEECHCRAFT TURBO BONANZA MODEL B36TC

Beech introduced a turbocharged version of the A36 Bonanza in 1979, following FAA certification on 7 December 1978, and 271 of the initial A36TC version were delivered. In 1982 Beech introduced the improved B36TC, with a wing of greater span and increased capacity, and 471 of this model had been delivered by 1 January 1988. The B36TC is generally similar to the A36, except as follows:

WINGS: Wing section NACA 23010.5 at tip. Incidence 0° at tip.

POWER PLANT: One 223.7 kW (300 hp) Continental TSIO-520-UB turbocharged flat-six engine, driving a three-blade constant-speed metal propeller with spinner. Fixed engine cowl flaps. Two fuel tanks in each wing leading-edge, with total usable capacity of 386 litres (102 US gallons; 85 Imp gallons). Refuelling points above tanks. Oil capacity 11.5 litres (3 US gallons; 2.5 Imp gallons).

ACCOMMODATION AND SYSTEMS: Air-conditioning optional.

AVIONICS AND EQUIPMENT: As for Model A36, except that exhaust gas temperature gauge is not available. Turbine inlet temperature gauge is standard.

DIMENSIONS, EXTERNAL: As for Model A36, except:

Wing span	11.53 m (37 ft 10 in)
Wing chord at tip	0.91 m (3 ft 0 in)
Wing aspect ratio	7.6
Propeller diameter	1.98 m (6 ft 6 in)

DIMENSIONS, INTERNAL: As for Model A36

AREA:

Wings, gross	17.47 m² (188.1 sq ft)

WEIGHTS AND LOADINGS:

Weight empty, standard	1,093 kg (2,410 lb)
Max T-O and landing weight	1,746 kg (3,850 lb)
Max ramp weight	1,753 kg (3,866 lb)
Max wing loading	100.1 kg/m² (20.5 lb/sq ft)
Max power loading	7.81 kg/kW (12.8 lb/hp)

PERFORMANCE (at max T-O weight, except speeds are at mid-cruise weight):

Max level speed at 6,700 m (22,000 ft)
   213 knots (394 km/h; 245 mph)

Cruising speed at 7,620 m (25,000 ft):

79% power	200 knots (370 km/h; 230 mph)
75% power	195 knots (361 km/h; 224 mph)
69% power	188 knots (348 km/h; 216 mph)
56% power	173 knots (320 km/h; 199 mph)

Stalling speed, power off:

flaps up	65 knots (120 km/h; 75 mph) IAS
30° flap	57 knots (106 km/h; 66 mph) IAS
Max rate of climb at S/L	319 m (1,049 ft)/min
Service ceiling	over 7,620 m (25,000 ft)
T-O run, 15° flap	311 m (1,020 ft)
T-O to 15 m (50 ft), 15° flap	649 m (2,130 ft)
Landing run	298 m (976 ft)

Range with max fuel, allowances for engine start, taxi, T-O, cruise climb, descent, and 45 min reserves at 50% power:

79% power at 7,620 m (25,000 ft)
   956 nm (1,770 km; 1,100 miles)
75% power at 7,620 m (25,000 ft)
   984 nm (1,822 km; 1,132 miles)
69% power at 7,620 m (25,000 ft)
   1,022 nm (1,892 km; 1,176 miles)
56% power at 6,100 m (20,000 ft)
   1,092 nm (2,022 km; 1,256 miles)

BEECHCRAFT BARON MODEL 58

Beech introduced this new version of the Baron in late 1969. Developed from the Baron D55, it differed by having the forward cabin section extended by 0.254 m (10 in), allowing the windscreen, passenger door, instrument panel and front seats to be moved forward and so provide a more spacious cabin. This change was made without affecting the wing main spar location, but the wheelbase was extended by moving the nosewheel forward, to improve ground handling. New features included double passenger/cargo doors on the starboard side, extended propeller hubs, redesigned engine nacelles to improve cooling, and a fourth window on each side. The Model 58 was licensed by the FAA in the Normal category on 19 November 1969.

Beech had delivered 2,168 of this Baron series (including Baron 58Ps and 58TCs) by 1 January 1988. Deliveries include four for the Indonesian Civil Flying Academy, Java, and three for the Centre Multi-National Formation Aviation Civile of M'Vengue, Gabon.

TYPE: Four/six-seat cabin monoplane.

WINGS: Cantilever low-wing monoplane. Wing section NACA 23016-5 at root, NACA 23010-t at tip. Dihedral 6°. Incidence 4° at root, 0° at tip. No sweepback. Each wing is a two-spar semi-monocoque box beam of conventional aluminium alloy construction, with beaded skins. Electrically operated single-slotted light alloy trailing-edge flaps, with beaded skins. Manually operated trim tab in port aileron. Pneumatic rubber de-icing boots optional.

FUSELAGE: Semi-monocoque aluminium alloy structure. Hat section longerons and channel type keels extend forward from the cabin section, making the support structure for the forward nose section and nosewheel gear an integral part of the fuselage.

TAIL UNIT: Cantilever all-metal structure. Elevators have smooth magnesium alloy skins. Manually operated trim tab in each elevator and in rudder. Pneumatic rubber de-icing boots optional.

LANDING GEAR: Electrically retractable tricycle type. Main units retract inward into wings, nosewheel aft. Beech oleo-pneumatic shock absorbers in all units. Steerable nosewheel with shimmy damper. Cleveland wheels, with mainwheel tyres size 6.50-8, pressure 3.59-3.96 bars (52-56 lb/sq in). Nosewheel tyre size 5.00-5, pressure 3.79-4.14 bars (55-60 lb/sq in). Cleveland ring-disc hydraulic brakes. Heavy duty brakes optional. Parking brake.

POWER PLANT: Two 224 kW (300 hp) Continental IO-550-C flat-six engines, each driving a McCauley three-blade constant-speed fully feathering metal propeller with spinner. The standard fuel system has a usable capacity of 514 litres (136 US gallons; 113 Imp gallons), with optional usable capacity of 628 litres (166 US gallons; 138 Imp gallons). Optional 'wet wingtip' installation also available, increasing usable capacity to 734 litres (194 US gallons; 161.5 Imp gallons).

ACCOMMODATION: Standard model has four individual seats in pairs in enclosed cabin, with door on starboard side. Single diagonal strap shoulder harness with inertia reel standard on all seats. Vertically adjusting pilot's seat is standard. Vertically adjusting co-pilot's seat, folding fifth and sixth seats, or club seating comprising folding fifth and sixth seats and aft facing third and fourth seats, are optional. Executive writing desk available as option with club seating. Baggage compartment in nose, capacity 136 kg (300 lb). Double passenger/cargo doors on starboard side of cabin provide access to space for 181 kg (400 lb) of baggage or cargo behind the third and fourth seats. Pilot's storm window. Openable windows adjacent to the third and fourth seats are used for ground ventilation and as emergency exits. Cabin heated and ventilated. Windscreen defrosting standard.

SYSTEMS: Cabin heated by Janitrol 50,000 BTU heater, which serves also for windscreen defrosting. Oxygen system of 1.41 m³ (49.8 cu ft) or 1.87 m³ (66 cu ft) capacity optional. Electrical system includes two 28V 60A engine driven alternators with alternator failure lights and two 12V 25Ah batteries. Two 100A alternators optional. Hydraulic system for brakes only. Pneumatic pressure system for air driven instruments, and optional wing and tail unit de-icing system. Oxygen system optional. Cabin air-conditioning and windscreen electric anti-icing systems optional.

AVIONICS AND EQUIPMENT: Standard avionics include King KX 155-09 720-channel com transceiver with audio amplifier, 200-channel nav receiver with KI 208 VOR/LOC converter/indicator, KR 87 ADF with KI 227-00 indicator, King combined loop/sense antenna, microphone, headset, cabin speaker, nav and com antennae. Bendix, King and Sperry weather radars optional. Optional avionics by Collins, King and S-Tec. Standard equipment includes dual controls, blind-flying instruments, control wheel clock, outside air temperature gauge, sensitive altimeter, turn co-ordinator, pilot's storm window, sun visors, ultraviolet-proof windscreen and cabin windows, armrests, adjustable rudder pedals (retractable on starboard side), emergency locator transmitter, heated pitot head, instrument panel floodlights, map light, lighted trim tab position indicator, step and entrance door courtesy lights, reading lights, navigation and position lights, steerable taxi light, dual landing lights, cabin carpeting and soundproofing, headrests, heated fuel vents, cabin dome light, door ajar warning light, nose baggage compartment light, heated fuel and stall warning vanes, external polyurethane paint finish, EGT and CHT gauges, synchroscope, engine winterisation kit, towbar and external power socket. Options include a true airspeed indicator, engine and flight hour recorders, instantaneous vertical speed indicator, alternate static source, internally illuminated instruments, rotating beacon, strobe lights, electric windscreen anti-icing, wing ice detection light, static wicks, cabin club seating, executive writing desk, refreshment cabinet, cabin fire extinguisher, ventilation blower, super soundproofing, and approach plate holder.

DIMENSIONS, EXTERNAL:

Wing span	11.53 m (37 ft 10 in)
Wing chord: at root	2.13 m (7 ft 0 in)
at tip	0.90 m (2 ft 11.6 in)
Wing aspect ratio	7.2
Length overall	9.09 m (29 ft 10 in)
Height overall	2.97 m (9 ft 9 in)
Tailplane span	4.85 m (15 ft 11 in)
Wheel track	2.92 m (9 ft 7 in)
Wheelbase	2.72 m (8 ft 11 in)
Propeller diameter	1.96 m (6 ft 5 in)
Rear passenger/cargo doors:	
Max height	1.02 m (3 ft 4 in)
Width	1.14 m (3 ft 9 in)
Baggage door (fwd): Height	0.56 m (1 ft 10 in)
Width	0.64 m (2 ft 1 in)

DIMENSIONS, INTERNAL:

Cabin, incl rear baggage area:	
Length	3.84 m (12 ft 7 in)
Max width	1.07 m (3 ft 6 in)
Max height	1.27 m (4 ft 2 in)
Floor area	3.72 m² (40 sq ft)
Volume	3.85 m³ (135.9 cu ft)
Baggage compartment: fwd	0.49 m³ (17.2 cu ft)

AREAS:

Wings, gross	18.51 m² (199.2 sq ft)
Ailerons (total)	1.06 m² (11.40 sq ft)
Trailing-edge flaps (total)	1.98 m² (21.30 sq ft)
Fin	1.46 m² (15.67 sq ft)
Rudder, incl tab	0.81 m² (8.75 sq ft)
Tailplane	4.95 m² (53.30 sq ft)
Elevators, incl tabs	1.84 m² (19.80 sq ft)

WEIGHTS AND LOADINGS:

Weight empty	1,579 kg (3,481 lb)
Max T-O weight	2,495 kg (5,500 lb)
Max landing weight	2,449 kg (5,400 lb)
Max ramp weight	2,506 kg (5,524 lb)
Max wing loading	143.4 kg/m² (27.6 lb/sq ft)
Max power loading	5.60 kg/kW (9.2 lb/hp)

PERFORMANCE (at max T-O weight, except cruising speeds at average cruise weight):

Max level speed at S/L	208 knots (386 km/h; 239 mph)
Max cruising speed, 2,500 rpm at 1,525 m (5,000 ft)	203 knots (376 km/h; 234 mph)
Cruising speed, 2,500 rpm at 3,050 m (10,000 ft)	198 knots (367 km/h; 228 mph)
Econ cruising speed, 2,100 rpm at 3,660 m (12,000 ft)	163 knots (302 km/h; 188 mph)

Stalling speed, power off:

flaps up	84 knots (156 km/h; 97 mph) IAS
flaps down	75 knots (139 km/h; 86 mph) IAS
Max rate of climb at S/L	529 m (1,735 ft)/min
Rate of climb at S/L, one engine out	119 m (390 ft)/min
Service ceiling	6,306 m (20,688 ft)
Service ceiling, one engine out	2,220 m (7,284 ft)
T-O run	427 m (1,400 ft)
T-O to 15 m (50 ft)	701 m (2,300 ft)
Landing from 15 m (50 ft)	747 m (2,450 ft)
Landing run	434 m (1,425 ft)

Range with 734 litres (194 US gallons; 161.5 Imp gallons) usable fuel, with allowances for engine start, taxi, T-O, climb and 45 min reserves at econ cruise power:

max cruising speed (power/altitude settings as above)	1,150 nm (2,130 km; 1,324 miles)
cruising speed (power/altitude settings as above)	1,411 nm (2,615 km; 1,625 miles)
econ cruising speed (power/altitude settings as above)	1,575 nm (2,919 km; 1,814 miles)

Beechcraft Baron Model 58 four/six-seat cabin monoplane

BEECHCRAFT BARON MODEL 58P

Production of the pressurised Model 58P Baron has ceased. A total of 492 of this model was delivered. A description and photograph may be found in the 1987-88 and earlier editions of *Jane's*.

BEECHCRAFT KING AIR MODEL C90A

The King Air C90A is a pressurised six/ten-seat twin-turboprop business aircraft which superseded the Models 90, A90, B90, C90 and C90-1 King Air. In April 1987 Beech announced structural changes which result in a 204 kg (450 lb) increase in max T-O weight, permitting two more passengers and additional baggage to be carried. Deliveries of the higher gross weight Model C90A began in the fourth quarter of 1987.

A total of 1,159 commercial and 226 military King Air 90/A90/B90/C90/C90-1/C90As had been delivered by 1 January 1988.

TYPE: Six/ten-seat twin-turboprop business aircraft.

WINGS: Cantilever low-wing monoplane. Wing section NACA 23014.1 (modified) at root, NACA 23016.22 (modified) at outer end of centre-section, NACA 23012 at tip. Dihedral 7°. Incidence 4° 48' at root, 0° at tip. No sweepback at quarter-chord. Two-spar aluminium alloy structure. All-metal ailerons of magnesium, with adjustable trim tab on port aileron. Single-slotted aluminium alloy flaps. Automatic pneumatic de-icing boots on leading-edges are standard.

FUSELAGE: Aluminium alloy semi-monocoque structure.

TAIL UNIT: Cantilever all-metal structure with sweptback vertical surfaces. Fixed incidence tailplane, with 7° dihedral. Trim tabs in rudder and each elevator. Automatic pneumatic de-icing boots on leading-edges of fin and tailplane are standard.

LANDING GEAR: Hydraulically retractable tricycle type. Nosewheel retracts rearward, mainwheels forward into engine nacelles. Mainwheels protrude slightly beneath nacelles when retracted, for safety in a wheels-up emergency landing. Fully castoring steerable nosewheel with shimmy damper. Beech oleo-pneumatic shock absorbers. Goodrich mainwheels with tyres size 8.50-10, pressure 3.79 bars (55 lb/sq in). Goodrich nosewheel with tyre size 6.50-10, pressure 3.59 bars (52 lb/sq in). Goodrich heat-sink and aircooled multi-disc hydraulic brakes. Parking brakes.

POWER PLANT: Two 410 kW (550 shp) Pratt & Whitney Canada PT6A-21 turboprops, each driving a Hartzell three-blade constant-speed fully-feathering propeller with spinner. Propeller electrothermal anti-icing, auto ignition system, environmental fuel drain collection system, and magnetic chip detector, standard. Automatic propeller feathering, and propeller synchrophaser, optional. Fuel in two tanks in engine nacelles, each with usable capacity of 231 litres (61 US gallons; 50.8 Imp gallons), and auxiliary bladder tanks in outer wings, each with capacity of 496 litres (131 US gallons; 109 Imp gallons). Total usable fuel capacity 1,454 litres (384 US gallons; 320 Imp gallons). Refuelling points in top of each engine nacelle and in wing leading-edge outboard of each nacelle. Oil capacity 13.2 litres (3.5 US gallons; 2.9 Imp gallons) per engine. Engine anti-icing system standard. Engine fire detection and extinguishing system optional.

ACCOMMODATION: Two seats side by side in cockpit with dual controls standard. Normally, four reclining seats in main cabin, in pairs facing each other fore and aft. Standard furnishings include cabin forward partition, with fore and aft partition curtain and coat rack, hinged nose baggage compartment door, seat belts and inertia reel shoulder harness for all seats. Optional arrangements seat up to eight persons, some with two- or three-place couch, lateral tracking chairs, and refreshment cabinets. Baggage racks at rear of cabin on starboard side, with optional toilet on port side. Door on port side aft of wing, with built-in airstairs. Emergency exit on starboard side of cabin. Entire accommodation pressurised and air-conditioned. Electrically heated windscreen, windscreen defroster and windscreen wipers standard.

SYSTEMS: Pressurisation by dual engine bleed air system with pressure differential of 0.34 bars (5.0 lb/sq in). Cabin heated by 45,000 BTU dual engine bleed air system and auxiliary electrical heating system. Hydraulic system for landing gear actuation. Electrical system includes two 28V 250A starter/generators, 24V 45Ah aircooled nickel-cadmium battery with failure detector. Complete de-icing and anti-icing equipment. Oxygen system, 0.62 m^3 (22 cu ft), 1.39 m^3 (49 cu ft) or 1.81 m^3 (64 cu ft) capacity, optional. Vacuum system for flight instruments.

AVIONICS AND EQUIPMENT: Standard Collins Pro Line avionics package comprises APS-65 autopilot/flight director; dual Collins VHF-251 VHF transceivers; dual Collins VIR-351 Omni nav receivers; Collins AMR-350 audio system; Collins ADF-650A ADF; dual Collins marker beacon receiver integral with AMR-350, plus marker lights; dual Collins GLS-350 glideslope receivers; Collins DME-451, with Nav 1/Nav 2 switching and DME hold; dual transponders; Collins PN-101 compass system (pilot); Standard Electric gyro horizon (pilot); CF gyro horizon and directional gyro (co-pilot); radio altimeter; dual Flite-Tronics PC-125 125VA inverters with failure light; avionics transient protection; dual flight instrumentation; sectional instrument panel; white lighting; radio accessories, static wicks and Beech metal radio panel; microphone key button in pilot and co-pilot control wheels; dual microphones, headsets and cockpit speakers; and avionics master switch. Optional avionics include a wide range of equipment by Bendix, Collins, King, Edo-Aire Mitchell, RCA and Sperry. Standard equipment includes dual blind-flying instrumentation with sensitive altimeters, standby magnetic compass, outside air temperature gauge, LCD digital clock/chronometer, vacuum gauge, de-icing pressure gauge, cabin rate of climb indicator, cabin altitude and pressure differential indicators, dual load meters, voltage meter with bus selector switch, propeller de-ice meter, pilot and co-pilot four-way adjustable seats with shoulder harness, map pockets, control locks, storm windows, tracked sun visors, automatic fuel heater system, emergency locator transmitter, heated pitots, heated stall warning transmitter, stall warning device, cabin windows with adjustable polarised shades, carpeted floor, internal corrosion proofing, 'No smoking—Fasten seat belt' sign, fresh air outlets, dual map lights, primary and secondary instrument light systems, indirect cabin lighting, two overhead cabin spotlights, entrance door light, adjustable reading lights, aft compartment lights, dual landing lights, taxi light, position lights, dual rotating beacons, wing ice lights, heated fuel vents, external power socket, static wicks, and external urethane paint. Optional equipment includes flight hour recorder, instantaneous vertical speed indicator, cockpit and cabin fire extinguishers, a range of cabin seats, cabinets, storage drawers and toilets, entrance door step lights, tail floodlights, strobe lights, and wingtip recognition lights.

DIMENSIONS, EXTERNAL:

Wing span	15.32 m (50 ft 3 in)
Wing chord: at root	2.15 m (7 ft 0½ in)
at tip	1.07 m (3 ft 6 in)
Wing aspect ratio	8.6
Length overall	10.82 m (35 ft 6 in)
Height overall	4.34 m (14 ft 3 in)
Tailplane span	5.26 m (17 ft 3 in)
Wheel track	3.89 m (12 ft 9 in)
Wheelbase	3.73 m (12 ft 3 in)
Propeller diameter	2.36 m (7 ft 9 in)
Propeller ground clearance	0.305 m (1 ft 0 in)
Passenger door: Height	1.30 m (4 ft 3½ in)
Width	0.69 m (2 ft 3 in)
Height to sill	1.22 m (4 ft 0 in)

Beechcraft King Air C90A business aircraft with 'pitot' cowlings

DIMENSIONS, INTERNAL:

Total pressurised length	5.43 m (17 ft 10 in)
Cabin: Length	3.86 m (12 ft 8 in)
Max width	1.37 m (4 ft 6 in)
Max height	1.45 m (4 ft 9 in)
Floor area	6.50 m^2 (70 sq ft)
Volume	8.88 m^3 (313.6 cu ft)
Baggage compartment, rear	1.51 m^3 (53.5 cu ft)

AREAS:

Wings, gross	27.31 m^2 (293.94 sq ft)
Ailerons (total)	1.29 m^2 (13.90 sq ft)
Trailing-edge flaps (total)	2.72 m^2 (29.30 sq ft)
Fin	2.20 m^2 (23.67 sq ft)
Rudder, incl tab	1.30 m^2 (14.00 sq ft)
Tailplane	4.39 m^2 (47.25 sq ft)
Elevators, incl tabs	1.66 m^2 (17.87 sq ft)

WEIGHTS AND LOADINGS:

Weight empty	2,985 kg (6,580 lb)
Max T-O weight	4,581 kg (10,100 lb)
Max ramp weight	4,608 kg (10,160 lb)
Max landing weight	4,354 kg (9,600 lb)
Max wing loading	167.7 kg/m^2 (34.4 lb/sq ft)
Max power loading	5.59 kg/kW (9.2 lb/shp)

PERFORMANCE (at max T-O weight except where indicated):

Max cruising speed at AUW of 3,855 kg (8,500 lb):

at 3,660 m (12,000 ft)	242 knots (448 km/h; 278 mph)
at 4,880 m (16,000 ft)	247 knots (457 km/h; 284 mph)
at 6,400 m (21,000 ft)	243 knots (450 km/h; 280 mph)

Stalling speed, power off:

wheels and flaps up	88 knots (163 km/h; 101 mph) IAS
wheels and flaps down	78 knots (144 km/h; 90 mph) IAS
Max rate of climb at S/L	610 m (2,003 ft)/min
Rate of climb at S/L, one engine out	169 m (554 ft)/min
Service ceiling	8,809 m (28,900 ft)
Service ceiling, one engine out	4,346 m (14,260 ft)
Min ground turning radius	10.82 m (35 ft 6 in)
T-O run	574 m (1,885 ft)
T-O to 15 m (50 ft)	785 m (2,577 ft)
Accelerate/stop distance	1,232 m (4,042 ft)
Landing from 15 m (50 ft) at max landing weight, with propeller reversal	633 m (2,078 ft)
Landing run at max landing weight, with propeller reversal	316 m (1,036 ft)

Range with max fuel at max cruising speed, incl allowance for starting, taxi, take-off, climb, descent and 45 min reserves at max range power, ISA, at:

6,400 m (21,000 ft)	1,075 nm (1,992 km; 1,238 miles)
4,875 m (16,000 ft)	933 nm (1,729 km; 1,074 miles)
3,660 m (12,000 ft)	866 nm (1,605 km; 997 miles)

Max range at econ cruising power, allowances as above, at:

6,400 m (21,000 ft)	1,277 nm (2,366 km; 1,470 miles)
4,875 m (16,000 ft)	1,155 nm (2,140 km; 1,330 miles)
3,660 m (12,000 ft)	1,054 nm (1,953 km; 1,214 miles)

BEECHCRAFT KING AIR MODEL F90-1

Production of the King Air Model F90-1 has now ceased. A total of 231 F90s and F90-1s was delivered. A full description and photograph may be found in the 1987-88 and earlier editions of *Jane's*.

BEECHCRAFT SUPER KING AIR B200

Design of the Super King Air 200 began in October 1970. The first prototype (c/n BB1) flew for the first time on 27 October 1972. FAA certification under FAR Part 23 was awarded on 14 December 1973, the aircraft satisfying also the icing requirements of FAR Part 25.

In February 1977 Beech delivered to the French Institut Géographique National two specially modified Super King Airs. These have twin Wild RC-10 Superaviogon camera installations and Doppler navigation systems, and were the first Super King Airs to be equipped with optional wingtip fuel tanks, which increase the total usable fuel capacity from 2,059 litres (544 US gallons) to 2,460 litres (650 US gallons) to provide a max endurance of 10.3 h. Designated **Model 200T**, they are fitted with high-flotation main landing gear, and are operated under a special French airworthiness certificate which allows max T-O and landing weights of 6,350 kg (14,000 lb) and 6,123 kg (13,500 lb) respectively. They can be operated with or without the wingtip tanks, for high-altitude photography and weather observation.

Beech announced on 25 April 1977 a specially equipped **Maritime Patrol** version of the Super King Air, which is described separately.

A Super King Air supplied to the Egyptian government in 1978 is used to conduct water, uranium and other natural resources exploration in the Sinai and Egyptian deserts. This aircraft is equipped with remote sensing equipment, specialised avionics, and sophisticated cameras. In June 1978, Beech delivered to the government of Taiwan a Super King Air equipped to check ground based navigation systems; and Malaysia uses two Super King Airs for airways calibration and flight inspection. A second special mission aircraft was delivered to Taiwan's Ministry of the Interior in May 1979. Two Super King Airs were delivered to the Royal Hong Kong Auxiliary Air Force in 1986 and 1987.

The **Super King Air B200**, introduced in March 1981, is generally similar to the Super King Air 200, except for the installation of Pratt & Whitney Canada PT6A-42 turboprops, which provide better cruise and altitude performance than the PT6A-41s in the original Super King Air 200. In addition, max zero-fuel weight is increased by 272 kg (600 lb) and cabin pressure differential is increased from 0.41 bars (6.0 lb/sq in) to 0.44 bars (6.5 lb/sq in). Design of the B200 began in March 1980, the prototype being a modified Super King Air 200 (c/n BB343). Manufacture of production aircraft began in May 1980, and FAA certification was granted on 13 February 1981. Five versions are available:

Super King Air B200. Basic version.

Super King Air B200C. As Super King Air B200, but with a 1.32 × 1.32 m (4 ft 4 in × 4 ft 4 in) cargo door.

Super King Air B200T. Generally similar to Maritime Patrol 200T, with standard provision to carry removable wingtip tanks to increase maximum fuel capacity by 401 litres (106 US gallons; 88.25 Imp gallons), to a total of 2,460 litres (650 US gallons; 541 Imp gallons). Span without tip-tanks 16.92 m (55 ft 6 in).

Super King Air B200CT. Version with both cargo door and wingtip tank provisions as standard.

Super King Air 300. Described separately.

By 1 January 1988 Beech had delivered 1,420 Super King Air 200 series aircraft to commercial and private operators and 282 military versions (described separately) to the US armed forces and foreign customers.

The following description applies to the B200:

TYPE: Twin-turboprop passenger, cargo or executive light transport.

WINGS: Cantilever low-wing monoplane, with constant chord centre-section and tapered outer panels. Leading-edges extended forward just outboard of engine nacelles. Wing section NACA 23018.5 (modified) at root, NACA 23011.3 at tip. Dihedral 6°. Incidence 3° 48′ at root, −1° 7′ at tip. No sweepback at quarter-chord. Two-spar light alloy structure. Conventional ailerons of light alloy construction, with trim tab in port aileron. Single-slotted trailing-edge flaps of light alloy construction. Pneumatic de-icing boots standard.

FUSELAGE: Light alloy semi-monocoque structure of safe-life design.

TAIL UNIT: Conventional cantilever T tail structure of light alloy with swept vertical and horizontal surfaces. Dorsal fin, and shallow ventral fin. Fixed incidence tailplane. Trim tab in each elevator. Anti-servo tab in rudder. Pneumatic de-icing boots standard, on leading-edge of tailplane only.

LANDING GEAR: Hydraulically retractable tricycle type, with twin wheels on each main unit. Single wheel on steerable nose unit, with shimmy damper. Main units retract forward, nosewheel rearward. Beech oleo-pneumatic shock absorbers. Goodrich mainwheels and tyres size 18 × 5.5, pressure 7.25 bars (105 lb/sq in). Oversize and/or 10-ply mainwheel tyres optional. Goodrich nosewheel size 6.50 × 10, with tyre size 22 × 6.75-10, pressure 3.93 bars (57 lb/sq in). Goodrich hydraulic multiple-disc brakes. Parking brake.

POWER PLANT: Two 634 kW (850 shp) Pratt & Whitney Canada PT6A-42 turboprops, each driving a Hartzell three-blade constant-speed fully-feathering reversible-pitch metal propeller with spinner. Bladder fuel tanks in each wing, with main system capacity of 1,461 litres (386 US gallons; 321.5 Imp gallons) and auxiliary system capacity of 598 litres (158 US gallons; 131.5 Imp gallons). Total usable fuel capacity 2,059 litres (544 US gallons; 453 Imp gallons). Two refuelling points in upper surface of each wing. Wingtip tanks optional, providing an additional 401 litres (106 US gallons; 88.25 Imp gallons) and raising maximum usable capacity to 2,460 litres (650 US gallons; 541 Imp gallons). Oil capacity 29.5 litres (7.8 US gallons; 6.5 Imp gallons). Anti-icing of engine air intakes by hot air from engine exhaust is standard. Electrothermal anti-icing for propellers standard; automatic feathering and synchrophaser optional.

ACCOMMODATION: Pilot only, or crew of two side by side, on flight deck, with full dual controls and instruments as standard. Six cabin seats standard, each equipped with seat belts and inertia reel shoulder harness; alternative layouts for a maximum of 13 passengers in cabin and 14th beside pilot. Partition with sliding door between cabin and flight deck, and partition at rear of cabin. Door at rear of cabin on port side, with integral airstair. Large cargo door optional. Inward opening emergency exit on starboard side over wing. Lavatory and stowage for up to 249 kg (550 lb) baggage in aft fuselage. Maintenance access door in rear fuselage; radio compartment access doors in nose. Standard equipment includes reading lights and fresh air outlets for all passengers, triple cabin windows with polarised glare control, fully carpeted floor, 'No smoking'—'Fasten seat belt' sign, cabin coat rack, fluorescent cabin lighting, aisle and door courtesy lights. Electrically heated windscreens, hot air windscreen defroster, dual storm windows, sun visors, map pockets and windscreen wipers. Cabin is air-conditioned and pressurised, with radiant heat panels to warm cabin before engine starting.

SYSTEMS: Cabin pressurisation by engine bleed air, with a maximum differential of 0.44 bars (6.5 lb/sq in). Cabin air-conditioner of 34,000 BTU capacity. Auxiliary cabin heating by radiant panels standard. Oxygen system for flight deck, and 0.62 m³ (22 cu ft) oxygen system for cabin, with automatic drop-down face masks; standard system of 1.39 m³ (49 cu ft); 1.81 m³ (64 cu ft) or 2.15 m³ (76 cu ft) optional. Dual vacuum system for instruments. Hydraulic system for landing gear retraction and extension, pressurised to 171-191 bars (2,475-2,775 lb/sq in). Separate hydraulic system for brakes. Pneumatic system for wing and tailplane de-icing. Electrical system has two 250A 28V starter/generators and a 24V 45Ah aircooled nickel-cadmium battery with failure detector. AC power provided by dual 250VA inverters. Engine fire detection system standard; engine fire extinguishing system optional.

AVIONICS AND EQUIPMENT: Standard Collins Pro Line avionics include dual Collins VHF-20A VHF transceivers; Collins VIR-30AGM automatic Omni No. 1 with 331A-3G indicator; Collins VIR-30AG automatic Omni No. 2 with IND31C indicator; dual Omni range filters; Collins dual DB system Model 415 with dual Model 210 voice activated interphone, ADF voice/range filters and dual audio switches; Collins ADF-60A ADF, less indicator; dual Collins marker beacon receivers, integral with VIR-30 No. 1; dual Collins glideslopes, integral with VIR-30 No. 1 and No. 2; Sperry Primus 200 colour weather radar, Sperry C-14-A compass system, with servo amplifier (pilot); Collins RMI-30, with Nav 1/ADF on single needle, Nav 2/ADF on double needle; Collins TDR-90 transponder; dual Collins DME-40 with Nav 1/Nav 2 switching and DME hold; dual Flite-Tronics PC-250 250VA inverters with failure light; sectional instrument panel; dual flight instrumentation; Standard Electric gyro horizon (pilot); CF gyro horizon (co-pilot); Beech edge-lit radio panel, radio accessories, microphone key button in pilot's and co-pilot's control wheels, static wicks, and white lighting; dual microphones, headsets and cockpit speakers; cabin paging system; avionics master switch; and avionics overvoltage protection. A

wide range of optional avionics by Bendix, Collins, King, RCA, Sperry and SunAir is available to customer's requirements, including a Collins EFIS with three colour CRT displays replacing the HSI, ADI and conventional radar screen; and Collins FMS-90, flight management system, combining FMS-90 VLF/Omega, VOR/DME and R/Nav navigation functions. Also available is a two-CRT Sperry EFIS, and Sperry SPZ 4000 autopilot/flight control system with digital computer. Standard equipment is generally as listed for King Air C90A, plus dual max allowable airspeed indicators, control wheel mounted chronographs, toilet, fluorescent cabin lighting instead of indirect lighting, aisle courtesy light, transistor controlled blue/white cockpit lighting, passenger door light, rudder boost system, and yaw damper system. Optional equipment includes a flight hour recorder, instantaneous vertical speed indicator, cockpit and cabin fire extinguishers, a range of cabin chairs, cabinets and table, flushing toilet, aft cabin air-conditioning installation, passenger door step lights, wingtip recognition lights, strobe lights, and fin illumination lights.

DIMENSIONS, EXTERNAL:	
Wing span	16.61 m (54 ft 6 in)
Wing chord: at root	2.18 m (7 ft 1¾ in)
at tip	0.90 m (2 ft 11⅝ in)
Wing aspect ratio	9.8
Length overall	13.34 m (43 ft 9 in)
Height overall	4.57 m (15 ft 0 in)
Tailplane span	5.61 m (18 ft 5 in)
Wheel track	5.23 m (17 ft 2 in)
Wheelbase	4.56 m (14 ft 11½ in)
Propeller diameter	2.50 m (8 ft 2½ in)
Propeller ground clearance	0.37 m (1 ft 2½ in)
Distance between propeller centres	5.23 m (17 ft 2 in)
Passenger door: Height	1.31 m (4 ft 3½ in)
Width	0.68 m (2 ft 2¾ in)
Height to sill	1.17 m (3 ft 10 in)
Cargo door (optional): Height	1.32 m (4 ft 4 in)
Width	1.24 m (4 ft 1 in)
Nose avionics service doors (port and stbd):	
Max height	0.57 m (1 ft 10½ in)
Width	0.63 m (2 ft 1 in)
Height to sill	1.37 m (4 ft 6 in)
Emergency exit (stbd): Height	0.66 m (2 ft 2 in)
Width	0.50 m (1 ft 7¾ in)
DIMENSIONS, INTERNAL:	
Cabin (from forward to rear pressure bulkhead):	
Length	6.71 m (22 ft 0 in)
Max width	1.37 m (4 ft 6 in)
Max height	1.45 m (4 ft 9 in)
Floor area	7.80 m² (84 sq ft)
Volume	11.10 m³ (392 cu ft)
Baggage hold, rear of cabin:	
Volume	1.51 m³ (53.5 cu ft)
AREAS:	
Wings, gross	28.15 m² (303.0 sq ft)
Ailerons (total)	1.67 m² (18.0 sq ft)
Trailing-edge flaps (total)	4.17 m² (44.9 sq ft)
Fin	3.46 m² (37.2 sq ft)
Rudder, incl tab	1.40 m² (15.1 sq ft)
Tailplane	4.52 m² (48.7 sq ft)
Elevators, incl tabs	1.79 m² (19.3 sq ft)
WEIGHTS AND LOADINGS:	
Weight empty	3,656 kg (8,060 lb)
Max fuel	1,653 kg (3,645 lb)
Max T-O and landing weight	5,670 kg (12,500 lb)

Max ramp weight	5,710 kg (12,590 lb)
Max zero-fuel weight	4,990 kg (11,000 lb)
Max wing loading	201.6 kg/m² (41.3 lb/sq ft)
Max power loading	4.47 kg/kW (7.35 lb/shp)

PERFORMANCE (at max T-O weight ISA, except where indicated):

Never-exceed speed	259 knots (480 km/h; 298 mph) IAS
Max operating Mach No.	0.52
Max level speed at 7,620 m (25,000 ft), average cruise weight	294 knots (545 km/h; 339 mph)
Max cruising speed at 7,620 m (25,000 ft), average cruise weight	289 knots (536 km/h; 333 mph)
Econ cruising speed at 7,620 m (25,000 ft), average cruise weight, normal cruise power	282 knots (523 km/h; 325 mph)
Stalling speed:	
flaps up	99 knots (183 km/h; 114 mph) IAS
flaps down	75 knots (139 km/h; 86 mph) IAS
Max rate of climb at S/L	747 m (2,450 ft)/min
Rate of climb at S/L, one engine out	226 m (740 ft)/min
Service ceiling	over 10,670 m (35,000 ft)
Service ceiling, one engine out	6,675 m (21,900 ft)
T-O run, 40% flap	566 m (1,856 ft)
T-O to 15 m (50 ft), 40% flap	786 m (2,579 ft)
Landing from 15 m (50 ft):	
without propeller reversal	867 m (2,845 ft)
with propeller reversal	632 m (2,074 ft)
Landing run	536 m (1,760 ft)

Range with max fuel, allowances for start, taxi, climb, descent, and 45 min reserves at max range power, ISA:

max cruise power at:
5,485 m (18,000 ft)
1,190 nm (2,205 km; 1,370 miles)
8,230 m (27,000 ft)
1,550 nm (2,872 km; 1,785 miles)
9,450 m (31,000 ft)
1,750 nm (3,243 km; 2,015 miles)
10,670 m (35,000 ft)
1,965 nm (3,641 km; 2,263 miles)
econ cruise power at:
5,485 m (18,000 ft)
1,517 nm (2,811 km; 1,747 miles)
8,230 m (27,000 ft)
1,860 nm (3,447 km; 2,142 miles)
9,450 m (31,000 ft)
1,974 nm (3,658 km; 2,273 miles)

BEECHCRAFT MARITIME PATROL B200T

Beech announced on 9 April 1979 that it had begun to flight test a maritime patrol version of its Super King Air 200 twin-turboprop light transport, for FAA certification as the Maritime Patrol 200T.

In production form, the current B200T can be equipped for missions such as surface and subsurface monitoring of exclusive economic zones, detecting pollution, inspecting offshore installations, and conducting search and rescue flights. Special missions for which it could also be used include aerial photography, environmental and ecological research, airways and ground based navigation equipment checks, target towing, and ambulance duties.

Modifications to the standard Super King Air to adapt it to Maritime Patrol B200T configuration include fitting new outboard wing assemblies, with mountings for a 200.5 litre (53 US gallon; 44 Imp gallon) removable fuel tank at each wingtip; strengthened landing gear to cater for higher

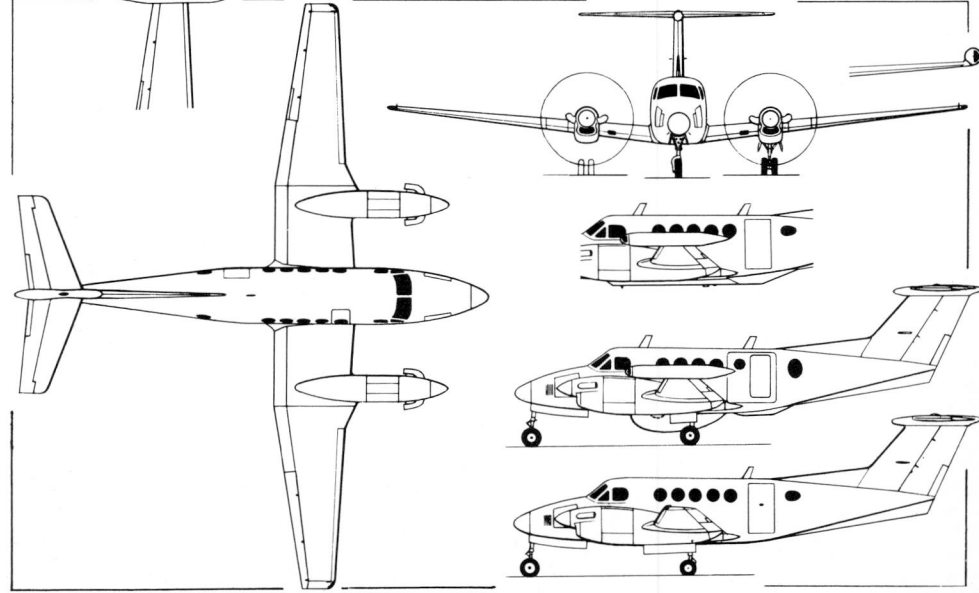

Beechcraft Super King Air B200 twin-turboprop transport, with additional side view of Maritime Patrol 200T (centre right); scrap views of wingtip tanks and centre-fuselage of photo survey aircraft for IGN *(Pilot Press)*

Beechcraft Super King Air B200 eight/fifteen-seat pressurised transport

take-off and landing weights; two bubble observation windows in the rear of the cabin for visual search and photography; a hatch for dropping survival equipment; and a search radar with 360° scan in a radome beneath the fuselage. Advanced navigation equipment is available; standard avionics include VLF/Omega which provides ground stabilisation and is coupled with the autopilot. This permits a search pattern to be programmed before take-off or en route. An integrated systems approach is utilised, with controls and displays located on the cabin operator's console.

Deliveries include 16 Maritime Patrol 200Ts to Japan's Maritime Safety Agency, two for the Algerian Ministry of Defence, three to Peru and one to the Uruguayan Navy.

The description of the Super King Air B200 applies also to the B200T, except as follows:

TYPE: Maritime patrol or multi-mission aircraft.

WINGS: As for Super King Air B200, except for new outboard wing panels redesigned to permit mounting of removable wingtip tanks. Optional wingtip ESM antennae.

LANDING GEAR: Strengthened to cater for higher operating weights.

POWER PLANT: As for Super King Air B200, including removable wingtip tanks which increase maximum usable fuel capacity by 401 litres (106 US gallons; 88.25 Imp gallons), to a total of 2,460 litres (650 US gallons; 541 Imp gallons).

AVIONICS AND EQUIPMENT: Standard items as detailed in introductory description. Optional avionics include ESM integrated with INS, VHF-FM com, HF and VHF com, Northrop Seehawk FLIR, LLLTV, sonobuoys and processor, OTPI, multispectral scanner, tactical navigation computer, and two alternative search radar systems, both with 360° scan and weather avoidance capability and integrated with INS.

DIMENSIONS, EXTERNAL: As for Super King Air B200, except:
Wing span over tip tanks 17.25 m (56 ft 7 in)
Wing aspect ratio 10.5
DIMENSIONS, INTERNAL: As for Super King Air B200, except:
Cabin: Length (excl flight deck) 5.08 m (16 ft 8 in)
WEIGHTS (A: Normal category; B: Restricted category):
Weight empty: A, B 3,744 kg (8,255 lb)
Max T-O weight: A 5,670 kg (12,500 lb)
B 6,350 kg (14,000 lb)
Max landing weight: A 5,670 kg (12,500 lb)
B 6,123 kg (13,500 lb)
PERFORMANCE (at max T-O weight except where indicated):
Max cruising speed, AUW of 4,990 kg (11,000 lb) at 4,265 m (14,000 ft) 265 knots (491 km/h; 305 mph)
Typical patrol speed 140 knots (259 km/h; 161 mph)
Range with max fuel, patrolling at 227 knots (420 km/h; 261 mph) at 825 m (2,700 ft), 45 min reserves 1,790 nm (3,317 km; 2,061 miles)
Typical endurance at 140 knots (259 km/h; 161 mph), at 610 m (2,000 ft), 45 min reserves 6 h 36 min
Max time on station, with wingtip fuel tanks 9 h 0 min

BEECHCRAFT SUPER KING AIR 200/B200 (MILITARY VERSIONS)
US military designation: C-12

The first three production Super King Airs were acquired by the US Army in 1974 as **RU-21Js**, as noted in previous editions of *Jane's*. In August 1974, Beech received an initial contract to build and support 34 modified military versions of the Super King Air designated C-12A. Worldwide deployment of the C-12s began in July 1975. They are described as "standard off-the-shelf Super King Air types, modified slightly to meet military flight requirements and to orient the control systems for two-pilot operation which is standard military practice". Accommodation is provided for eight passengers, plus two pilots, with easy conversion to cargo and other missions. The large baggage area has provisions for storing survival gear.

Orders for the C-12 series totalled 308 by 1 January 1988, of which 282 had been delivered. The following versions have been announced:

C-12A. Initial Model A200 for US Army (60) and US Air Force (30), with two 559 kW (750 shp) Pratt & Whitney Canada PT6A-38 turboprops and Hartzell three-blade constant-speed fully-feathering reversible-pitch propellers. Wing span 16.61 m (54 ft 6 in); auxiliary tanks. Weights, loadings and performance given in 1980-81 *Jane's*. Army aircraft later refitted with PT6A-41 engines are redesignated C-12C; USAF C-12As refitted with PT6A-42s are redesignated C-12E. Total of 91 delivered, including one for Foreign Military Sales. Entered service July 1975.

UC-12B. US Navy/Marine Corps version (Model A200C), with 634 kW (850 shp) PT6A-41 turboprops, cargo door and high-flotation landing gear. Total of 66 (49 Navy, 17 Marine Corps) delivered by 31 May 1982.

C-12C. As C-12A, for US Army (14), but built from outset with PT6A-41 engines. Deliveries completed.

C-12D (Model A200CT). As C-12C, for US Army, but with cargo door, high flotation landing gear and provisions for tip tanks. Wing span (over tip tanks) 16.92 m (55 ft 6 in). Total of 50 delivered (including 13 modified to RC-12Ds, which see, six for USAF and five for Foreign Military Sales).

RC-12D Improved Guardrail V (Model A200CT). Special mission US Army version, acquired to supplement earlier unpressurised RU-21H Guardrail V aircraft for battlefield duties in Europe and South Korea. The RC-12D serves as the aerial platform for the AN/USD-9 Improved Guardrail remotely controlled communications intercept and direction finding system, with direct reporting to tactical commanders at corps level and below. It is configured with an aircraft survivability equipment (ASE) suite, a Carousel IV-E inertial platform and Tacan set, and mission equipment including a radio data link, AN/ARW-83(V)5 airborne relay facility, associated antennae above and below the wings, and ECM in wingtip pods which increase overall span to 17.63 m (57 ft 10 in). Other system components are an AN/TSQ-105(V)4 integrated processing facility, AN/ARM-63(V)4 AGE flightline van, and AN/TSC-87 tactical commander's terminal. Thirteen RC-12Ds are included in total given for C-12D, with deliveries from Summer 1983. Prime system contractor is ESL Inc, with Beech as mission equipment integrator. Max T-O weight 6,441 kg (14,200 lb).

C-12E. Designation of upgraded C-12A for US Air Force, when refitted with PT6A-42 engines.

C-12F. Operational support aircraft (OSA), generally similar to Model B200C, with PT6A-42 engines and hydraulically retractable landing gear. Forty purchased for US Air Force following initial five-year lease contract. First C-12F delivered in May 1984. Alternative payloads include eight passengers, more than 1,043 kg (2,300 lb) of cargo, or two litter patients with attendants. Cargo door standard. Produced also for US Army (12 delivered in 1986/1987) which ordered five more in May 1986.

UC-12F. US Navy equivalent of C-12F with PT6A-42 engines and hydraulically retractable landing gear. Deliveries of 12 began in 1986.

RC-12H Guardrail Common Sensor. Special Mission US Army version, with max T-O weight of 6,804 kg (15,000 lb). Six delivered in 1985.

C-12J. Variant of Beechcraft 1900C (which see), not Super King Air.

RC-12K Guardrail Common Sensor. Electronics special missions aircraft. Nine ordered by US Army in October 1985 to be converted from C-12D, for delivery from Spring 1988. PT6A-67 turboprops, large cargo door and oversized landing gear standard. Max T-O weight 7,257 kg (16,000 lb).

UC-12M. US Navy equivalent of C-12F. Deliveries of 12 began in 1987.

Retouched photograph of US Army RC-12D in Improved Guardrail V configuration

Beechcraft C-12F operational support aircraft of USAF Military Airlift Command

BEECHCRAFT SUPER KING AIR 300

The Super King Air 300 is an improved version of the Model B200 with two 783 kW (1,050 shp) Pratt & Whitney Canada PT6A-60A engines, increased maximum take-off and landing weights to FAA SFAR 41C standards, redesigned 'pitot cowl' engine air inlets of 451 cm² (70 sq in) area compared with 567 cm² (88 sq in) on the B200, aerodynamically faired exhausts, a 12.7 cm (5 in) forward extension of the inboard wing leading-edges, 13.2 cm (5.2 in) forward extension of the propeller line, hydraulically actuated landing gear and numerous interior and equipment changes.

Design began in August 1980. A modified Model 200 testbed began flight trials in October 1981; a production prototype made its first flight in September 1983 and was awarded FAA type certification on 24 January 1984. Customer deliveries of the Model 300 began in the Spring of 1984 and totalled 135 by 1 January 1988.

In the Summer of 1986 the US Federal Aviation Administration ordered 19 Super King Air 300s for airways calibration duties. These aircraft, deliveries of which started on 4 April 1988, are equipped with an onboard automatic flight inspection system (AFIS), with accommodation for a flight inspection technician, observer, passenger/observer and a flight crew of two. They are based at Atlanta, Georgia; Atlantic City, New Jersey; Battle Creek, Michigan; Oklahoma City, Oklahoma; and Sacramento, California.

The following description applies to those features of the Model 300 which differ from the Super King Air 200 series:

WINGS: Inboard leading-edges extended forward and fitted with strakes.

LANDING GEAR: Hydraulically retractable tricycle type. Goodrich mainwheels and tyres size 19 × 6.75-8, pressure 6.20 bars (90 lb/sq in) at max T-O weight. Goodrich nosewheel and tyre size 22 × 6.75-10, pressure 3.79-4.13 bars (55-60 lb/sq in). Beech brake de-icing optional.

POWER PLANT: Two 783 kW (1,050 shp) Pratt & Whitney Canada PT6A-60A turboprops, each driving a Hartzell four-blade constant-speed fully-feathering reversible-pitch metal propeller with spinner. Bladder cells and integral tanks in each wing, with total capacity of 1,438 litres (380 US gallons; 316.5 Imp gallons); auxiliary tanks inboard of engine nacelles, capacity 601 litres (159 US gallons; 132.5 Imp gallons). Total fuel capacity 2,039 litres (539 US gallons; 449 Imp gallons). No provision for wingtip tanks. Oil capacity 30.2 litres (8 US gallons; 6.66 Imp gallons).

ACCOMMODATION: As for Model B200, except for additional emergency exit on port side of cabin, opposite starboard emergency exit and of the same dimensions. Pilot and co-pilot storm windows standard. Cabin features single-piece upper sidewall panels, indirect overhead lighting system with rheostat controls, stereo system with graphic equaliser and overhead speakers, larger executive tables incorporating magnetic game boards, seats with inflatable lumbar support adjustment, fore-and-aft, reclining and lateral tracking movement as standard. Crew seats have 2½° or 5° tilt positions. Emergency exit lighting standard. Electric heating on ground standard. Optional radiant heat panels of B200 not available.

SYSTEMS: As for Model B200, except for automatic bleed air type heating and 22,000 BTU cooling system with high capacity ventilation system; 2.18 m³ (77 cu ft) oxygen system standard; hydraulic landing gear retraction and extension system; two 300A 28V starter/generators with triple bus electrical distribution system.

AVIONICS AND EQUIPMENT: Collins Pro Line avionics including dual Collins VHF-22A transceivers; dual Collins VIR-32 VOR/LOC/glideslope/marker beacon receivers, with dual 331A-3G indicators and CTL-32 controllers; dual DB system Model 415, with dual DB system Model 210 voice-activated interphone; Collins ADF-60A; dual Collins marker beacon receivers (included in VIR-32s), with marker lights; dual Collins glideslopes (included in VIR-32s); Sperry Primus 200 colour weather radar; Sperry C-14A compass system or Collins MCS-65 compass system; dual Collins RMI-30s with Nav 1/ADF on single needle, Nav 2/ADF on double needle; Collins TDR-90 transponder; IDC encoding altimeter; Collins DME-42; dual 250VA Flite-Tronics PC-250 inverters with failure light. Sectional instrument panel. Dual flight instrumentation with 5 in instruments standard, internally lit. Pilot's Standard Electric gyro horizon; co-pilot's 3 in CF gyro horizon. Custom edge-lit radio panel, microphone key button in pilot's and co-pilot's control wheels, static wicks, white lighting. Dual microphones, headsets and cockpit speakers. External interphone with jack plug in nosewheel bay, cabin paging and avionics master switch. Dual level electrically heated, safety plate glass windscreens, hot-air windscreen defroster; fail safe (dual pane) cockpit side windows; dual adjustable sun visors; map pocket; oxygen outlets and overhead-mounted diluter demand masks with microphones; pedestal mounted oxygen controls; dual cockpit speakers; fire extinguisher; two-speed bleed air system; POH storage container. Standard cabin equipment includes: fail safe (dual pane) cabin windows with polarised sun shades; six fully adjustable cabin chairs, each with shoulder harness, lap belt and retractable inboard armrest; forward partition with

Beechcraft Super King Air 300 of the US Federal Aviation Administration

sliding doors; aft partition with sliding doors; private lavatory; aft compartment retractable coat rods; airstair door with folding steps; airstair door courtesy light; emergency exit lights; wing ice lights; two landing lights; nosewheel taxi light; flush position lights; dual white rotating beacons; dual map lights; adjustable reading light for each cabin seat; indirect cabin lighting; two cockpit overhead floodlights; entrance door area illumination light; blue white cockpit lighting; cabin door inspection lights; aft compartment lights; primary and secondary instrument lighting systems.

DIMENSIONS, EXTERNAL: As for Model B200 except:

Length overall	13.36 m (43 ft 10 in)
Height overall	4.37 m (14 ft 4 in)
Propeller diameter	2.67 m (8 ft 9 in)
Propeller ground clearance	0.25 m (10 in)

DIMENSIONS, INTERNAL: As for Model B200 except:
Emergency exit doors (each side of cabin, above wing):

Height	0.66 m (2 ft 2 in)
Width	0.95 m (1 ft 7¾ in)

WEIGHTS AND LOADINGS:

Weight empty	3,851 kg (8,490 lb)
Max baggage weight	249 kg (550 lb)
Max T-O and landing weight	6,350 kg (14,000 lb)
Max ramp weight	6,396 kg (14,100 lb)
Max zero-fuel weight	5,216 kg (11,500 lb)
Max wing loading	225.6 kg/m² (46.2 lb/sq ft)
Max power loading	4.05 kg/kW (6.7 lb/shp)

PERFORMANCE (at max T-O weight, ISA):
Never-exceed speed

	259 knots (480 km/h; 298 mph) IAS
Max operating Mach No.	0.58
Max level speed	317 knots (587 km/h; 365 mph)
Max cruising speed	315 knots (583 km/h; 363 mph)
Econ cruising speed	307 knots (568 km/h; 353 mph)

Stalling speed:

flaps up	100 knots (185 km/h; 115 mph) IAS
flaps down	81 knots (150 km/h; 93 mph) IAS
Max rate of climb at S/L	867 m (2,844 ft)/min

Rate of climb at S/L, one engine out

	264 m (867 ft)/min
Max certificated ceiling	10,670 m (35,000 ft)
Service ceiling, one engine out	6,970 m (22,875 ft)
T-O run, 40% flap	411 m (1,350 ft)
T-O to 15 m (50 ft), 40% flap	607 m (1,992 ft)
Accelerate/stop distance, 40% flap	1,122 m (3,682 ft)
Landing from 15 m (50 ft)	886 m (2,907 ft)

Landing run, without propeller reversal

	514 m (1,686 ft)

Range with max fuel, allowances for start, taxi, T-O, climb, descent and 45 min reserves at max range power:
max cruise power at:

5,485 m (18,000 ft)	
	1,055 nm (1,955 km; 1,215 miles)
7,315 m (24,000 ft)	
	1,240 nm (2,298 km; 1,428 miles)
8,535 m (28,000 ft)	
	1,400 nm (2,594 km; 1,612 miles)
10,670 m (35,000 ft)	
	1,748 nm (3,235 km; 2,010 miles)

max range power at:

5,485 m (18,000 ft)	
	1,429 nm (2,647 km; 1,645 miles)
8,535 m (28,000 ft)	
	1,795 nm (3,326 km; 2,067 miles)
10,670 m (35,000 ft)	
	1,959 nm (3,630 km; 2,256 miles)

BEECHCRAFT C99 AIRLINER

Production of the Beechcraft C99 Airliner has ceased. A total of 239 aircraft in the Beechcraft 99 series was delivered, of which 75 were Model C99s delivered in 1981-86. A description and photograph may be found in the 1987-88 and earlier editions of *Jane's*.

BEECHCRAFT 1300 COMMUTER

In January 1988 Beech announced development of this regional airliner variant of the Super King Air B200, designed for operations on long routes with light passenger loads. The Model 1300 provides accommodation for 13 passengers with individual air, light and oxygen outlets at every seat, and is equipped with dual overwing emergency exits. The adoption of panel mounted avionics as standard has enabled a baggage compartment to be provided in the aircraft's nose, capacity 0.37 m³ (13 cu ft). Three-blade propellers with autofeathering, hydraulically actuated landing gear, airframe anti- and de-icing systems, air-conditioning, cabin paging system, front-mounted post lit instruments interchangeable with those of the Beech 99 Airliner, and radiant heat cabin warming, are standard. A belly cargo pod, capacity 1.25 m³ (44 cu ft), engine fire extinguishing system, and landing gear and brake de-icing systems, are optional. Dual outward-canted ventral fins are installed for increased stability at low airspeeds and high angles of attack. Typical empty weight is approx 3,573 kg (7,877 lb), and the Model 1300 will cruise at 265 knots (491 km/h; 305 mph). Max operating altitude will be 7,620 m (25,000 ft).

Launch customer for the Beechcraft 1300 Commuter is Mesa Airlines of Farmington, New Mexico, which ordered five for delivery beginning in late 1988, with options on three additional aircraft. In June 1988 flight testing was well advanced, with certification expected within a few weeks.

Prototype Beechcraft 1300 Commuter airliner, with wool tufting for airflow distribution tests

BEECHCRAFT 1900C AIRLINER and 1900 EXEC-LINER
US military designation: C-12J

Beech began design of the basic 1900 commuter airliner during 1979, and the first flight of the performance prototype (UA-1) was made on 3 September 1982, followed by the systems prototype (UA-2) on 30 November 1982. The third prototype (UA-3) was used for function and reliability testing, equipment certification, and demonstration; it is now in operational service. FAA certification under SFAR Pt 41C, obtained on 22 November 1983, included single pilot approval under FAR 135 Appendix A.

The Beech 1900 is offered in two variants: **Model 1900C Airliner** with cargo door, the first of which was delivered in February 1984; and **1900 Exec-Liner**, which is the corporate version. By the Summer of 1988 a total of 100 Model 1900C Airliners were in service with 11 US and two European regional operators. Recent orders include ten aircraft, with ten options, for Texas Air Corporation, to be operated by its Continental Express subsidiary, of which deliveries began in December 1987, and five for Conquest Airlines Corporation of Beaumont, Texas, delivery of which was completed in May 1988. The first delivery of an Exec-Liner (N34GT) was made to General Telephone Company of Illinois in the Summer of 1985.

In March 1986 the United States Air Force ordered six Model 1900Cs for delivery commencing September 1987. These aircraft, designated **C-12J**, serve as Air National Guard mission support aircraft, and replaced Convair C-131s.

Six Model 1900Cs have been ordered by the Egyptian Air Force for delivery in 1988. Four of these are configured for electronic surveillance missions, and two as maritime patrol aircraft. For this latter role the aircraft are equipped with Litton search radar, Motorola sideways looking airborne multi-mode radar (SLAMMR) and Singer S-3075 ESM systems. Deliveries of 12 Model 1900Cs for the Taiwan Air Force began in January 1988.

From aircraft c/n UC-1 onwards, all Beechcraft 1900 series aircraft (including those for the US Air Force and Egyptian Air Force) are equipped with a 'wet wing' providing a maximum fuel capacity of 2,593 litres (685 US gallons; 570 Imp gallons).

The description which follows applies to the commercial Model 1900C and 1900 Exec-Liner:

TYPE: Twin-turboprop commuter/cargo airliner and executive transport.

WINGS: Cantilever low-wing monoplane. Wing section NACA 23000. Thickness/chord ratio 18% at root, 12% at tip. Dihedral 6°. Incidence 3° 29′ at root, –1° 4′ at tip. No sweepback at quarter-chord. Semi-monocoque fail-safe structure of aluminium alloy, riveted and bonded, with a continuous main spar. Single-slotted trailing-edge flaps, in two sections on each wing, of aluminium alloy construction; symmetrical ailerons of similar construction. Trim tab at inboard end of port aileron. Pneumatic de-icing boots on wing leading-edges.

FUSELAGE: Semi-monocoque fail-safe pressurised structure of aluminium alloy, mainly of bonded construction but including some riveting. Small horizontal vortex generator on each side of wing leading-edge.

TAIL UNIT: Aluminium alloy structure comprising a cantilever T tail with sweptback vertical and horizontal surfaces. Small fin (tail-let) beneath each side of tailplane, near tip; and auxiliary fixed horizontal tail surface (stabilon) on each side of rear fuselage. Trim tabs in elevators and rudder. Pneumatic de-icing boots on leading-edges of tailplane and stabilons.

LANDING GEAR: Hydraulically retractable tricycle type. Main units retract forward and nose unit rearward. Beech oleo-pneumatic shock absorber in each unit. Twin Goodyear wheels on each main unit, size 6.50 × 10, with Goodyear tyres size 22 × 6.75-10, pressure 6.07 bars (88 lb/sq in); Goodrich steerable nosewheel size 6.5 × 8, with Goodrich tyre size 19.5 × 6.75-8, pressure 6.07 bars (88 lb/sq in). Multiple-disc hydraulic brakes. Beech/Hydro-Aire anti-skid units and power steering optional.

POWER PLANT: Two Pratt & Whitney Canada PT6A-65B turboprops, each flat rated at 820 kW (1,100 shp) and driving a Hartzell four-blade constant-speed fully-feathering reversible-pitch composite propeller with spinner. 'Wet wing' fuel storage, with a total capacity of 2,593 litres (685 US gallons; 570 Imp gallons), of which 2,536 litres (670 US gallons; 558 Imp gallons) are usable. Refuelling point in each wing leading-edge, inboard of engine nacelle. Oil capacity (total) 27.2 litres (7.2 US gallons; 6 Imp gallons).

ACCOMMODATION: Crew of one (FAR Pt 91) or two (FAR Pt 135) on flight deck, with standard accommodation in cabin of commuter version for 19 passengers, in single seats on each side of centre aisle. Forward and rear carry-on baggage lockers, underseat baggage stowage, rear baggage compartment and nose baggage compartment. Forward and rear doors, incorporating airstairs, on port side. Upward hinged cargo door instead of rear passenger door on Model 1900C. Two emergency exits over wing on starboard side, plus one on port side (1900C only). Accommodation is air-conditioned, heated, ventilated and pressurised. Exec-Liner has 12/18-passenger cabin with forward and rear compartments, combination lavatory/passenger seat and two beverage bars at cabin compartment division. Club seating optional. Customised interiors to customer choice.

SYSTEMS: Bleed air cabin heating and pressurisation, max differential 0.33 bars (4.8 lb/sq in). Air cycle and vapour cycle air-conditioning. Hydraulic system, pressure 207 bars (3,000 lb/sq in) for landing gear actuation. Electrical system includes two 300A engine starter/generators and one 22Ah nickel-cadmium battery. Constant flow oxygen system of 4.33 m³ (153 cu ft) capacity standard.

AVIONICS: Duplicated King com/nav, glideslope receiver, transponder, audio, ADF, DME, marker beacon receiver and Bendix RDR-160 weather radar. Sperry EFIS, and Collins autopilot and Pro Line II equipment, optional.

DIMENSIONS, EXTERNAL:

Wing span	16.61 m (54 ft 6 in)
Wing chord: at root	2.18 m (7 ft 1¾ in)
at tip	0.91 m (2 ft 11¾ in)
Wing aspect ratio	9.8
Length overall	17.63 m (57 ft 10 in)
Height overall	4.55 m (14 ft 11 in)
Tailplane span	5.64 m (18 ft 6 in)
Wheel track	5.23 m (17 ft 2 in)
Wheelbase	7.26 m (23 ft 10 in)
Propeller diameter	2.78 m (9 ft 1½ in)
Propeller ground clearance	0.36 m (1 ft 2 in)
Distance between propeller centres	5.23 m (17 ft 2 in)
Passenger doors (fwd and rear, port, each):	
Height	1.32 m (4 ft 4 in)
Width	0.69 m (2 ft 3 in)
Height to sill: fwd	1.28 m (4 ft 2½ in)
rear	1.15 m (3 ft 9¼ in)
Cargo door (rear, port): Height	1.32 m (4 ft 4 in)
Width	1.32 m (4 ft 4 in)
Height to sill	1.15 m (3 ft 9¼ in)
Baggage door (nose, port):	
Max height	0.56 m (1 ft 10 in)
Width	0.66 m (2 ft 2 in)
Height to sill	1.45 m (4 ft 9 in)
Emergency exits (two stbd; plus one port on 1900C only; all overwing): Height	0.70 m (2 ft 3½ in)
Width	0.51 m (1 ft 8 in)

DIMENSIONS, INTERNAL:

Cabin, incl flight deck and rear baggage compartment:	
Length	12.02 m (39 ft 5½ in)
Max width	1.37 m (4 ft 6 in)
Max height	1.45 m (4 ft 9 in)
Floor area	15.28 m² (164.5 sq ft)
Pressurised volume	20.00 m³ (706 cu ft)
Baggage space:	
Cabin:	
1900C, fwd: standard	0.42 m³ (15.0 cu ft)
optional	1.19 m³ (41.9 cu ft)
rear (both)	4.36 m³ (154.0 cu ft)
Nose compartment	0.38 m³ (13.5 cu ft)

AREAS:

Wings, gross	28.15 m² (303.0 sq ft)
Ailerons (total)	1.67 m² (18.0 sq ft)
Trailing-edge flaps (total)	4.17 m² (44.9 sq ft)
Fin	3.42 m² (36.85 sq ft)
Rudder (incl tab)	1.106 m² (11.9 sq ft)
Tail-lets (total)	0.305 m² (3.28 sq ft)
Tailplane	4.52 m² (48.7 sq ft)
Elevator (incl tab)	1.79 m² (19.3 sq ft)
Stabilons (total, exposed)	1.44 m² (15.46 sq ft)

WEIGHTS AND LOADINGS:

Weight empty (typical)	4,128 kg (9,100 lb)
Max fuel (usable)	2,027 kg (4,470 lb)
Max baggage	866 kg (1,910 lb)

Beechcraft Model 1900C twin-turboprop commuter airliner

Max T-O weight	7,530 kg (16,600 lb)
Max ramp weight	7,580 kg (16,710 lb)
Max landing weight	7,302 kg (16,100 lb)
Max zero-fuel weight	6,350 kg (14,000 lb)
Max wing loading	267.5 kg/m² (54.8 lb/sq ft)
Max power loading	4.59 kg/kW (7.55 lb/shp)

PERFORMANCE (at max T-O weight except where indicated):
Max cruising speed (provisional) at AUW of 6,350 kg (14,000 lb):

at 2,440 m (8,000 ft)	267 knots (495 km/h; 307 mph)
at 4,875 m (16,000 ft)	267 knots (495 km/h; 307 mph)
at 7,620 m (25,000 ft)	254 knots (471 km/h; 292 mph)

T-O speed, 20° flap
    105 knots (194 km/h; 121 mph) CAS
Approach speed at max landing weight
    113 knots (209 km/h; 130 mph) CAS
Stalling speed at max T-O weight:
    wheels and flaps up
        101 knots (187 km/h; 116 mph) CAS
    wheels down and 20° flap
        95 knots (176 km/h; 109 mph) CAS
Stalling speed at max landing weight, wheels and flaps down   87 knots (161 km/h; 100 mph) CAS
Max rate of climb at S/L   710 m (2,330 ft)/min
Rate of climb at S/L, one engine out
        149 m (490 ft)/min
Service ceiling   exceeds certificated ceiling
        of 7,620 m (25,000 ft)
Service ceiling, one engine out   3,960 m (13,000 ft)
T-O run, 20° flap   671 m (2,200 ft)
T-O to 15 m (50 ft), 20° flap   991 m (3,250 ft)
Landing from 15 m (50 ft) at max landing weight
        774 m (2,540 ft)
Landing run at max landing weight   466 m (1,530 ft)
Accelerate/stop distance, 20° flap   1,158 m (3,800 ft)
Range with 15 passengers, at high speed cruise power, with allowances for starting, taxi, T-O, climb and descent (provisional):
    with NBAA VFR reserves
        1,286 nm (2,383 km; 1,481 miles)

BEECHCRAFT MODEL 2000 STARSHIP 1

The first flight took place on 29 August 1983 of an 85 per cent scale proof of concept prototype of this new Beechcraft turboprop powered corporate aircraft. It was built by Mr 'Burt' Rutan's Scaled Composites Inc (which see, now a Beech subsidiary), and provided data for the full size Starship 1. By early 1986 the scale version had completed over 500 flight hours with its initial power plant of 559 kW (750 shp) PT6A-135A engines. It was first flown with Pratt & Whitney Canada PT6A-67 engines on 29 August 1985.

Six pre-production Starship 1s were built, three for flight testing and one each for static, damage tolerance and pressure cycle testing. Bell Aerospace was contracted to manufacture the CFRP foreplanes for these aircraft. The first full scale prototype (N2000S) made its first flight from Wichita on 15 February 1986, followed by a 'commemorative first flight' on 24 February. This aircraft was powered initially by PT6A-65A-4 engines pending delivery of the production standard PT6A-67 power plants. A second prototype (N3042S), fitted with the Collins advanced integrated avionics system specified for production Starships, joined the flight test programme on 14 June 1986, and was followed on 5 January 1987 by the third prototype (N3234S; c/n NC-3), which had a furnished cabin and performed function and reliability testing.

By June 1988 the three Starship prototypes had completed more than 1,650 flights totalling more than 2,000 hours. In June 1987 NC-3/N3234S was flown to France, where it made its first public appearance outside the USA at the Paris Air Show. Basic certification for two-crew operation was granted by the FAA on 14 June 1988, with

Beechcraft C-12J of the United States Air National Guard

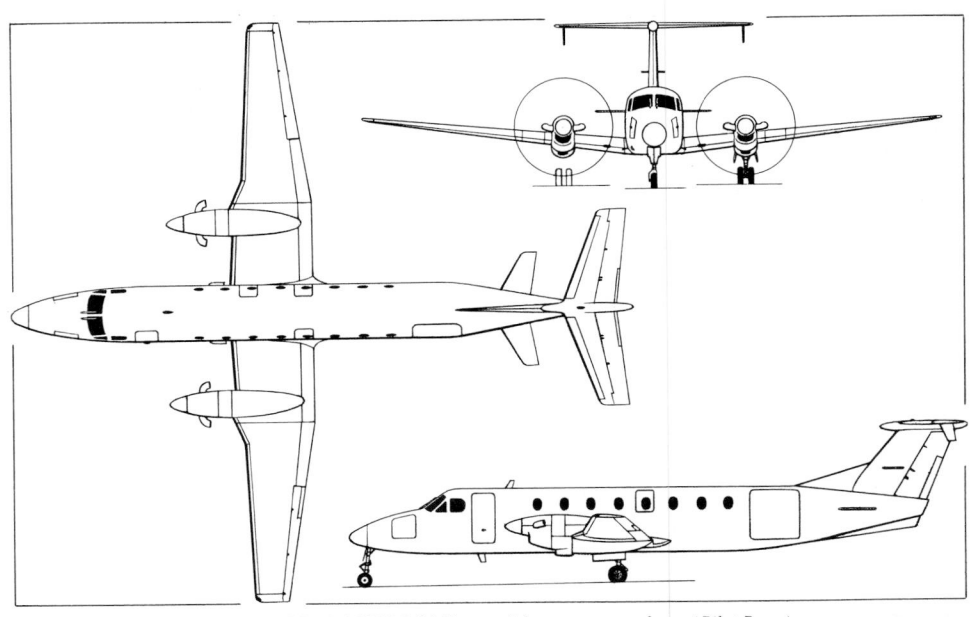

Beechcraft Model 1900C Airliner with rear cargo door *(Pilot Press)*

certification of the autopilot system and for flight into known icing conditions anticipated before the end of the year. A demonstrator aircraft, c/n NC-4, is expected to fly in the Spring of 1989, followed by the first customer aircraft by mid-year. In June 1988 Beech held orders for more than 50 Starships from customers in Canada, Europe, the United Kingdom and United States.

The description applies to the full size Starship 1:

TYPE: Eight/eleven-seat business aircraft.

WINGS: Cantilever mid/low-wing monoplane. Specially developed wing section. Dihedral 1° 18′ 36″. Incidence 2° at root. Sweepback 24° 24′ at quarter-chord. Continuous tip to tip structure of honeycomb and graphite/epoxy monocoque, semi-monocoque and honeycomb sandwich, with titanium used in high stress areas such as landing gear mountings and wing/tipsail junctions. Wingtip stabilisers (which the company terms tipsails) of composite construction, incorporating rudders and trim tabs. Elevons and Fowler flaps of composite construction. Electric trim tab in each rudder.

FUSELAGE: Circular section fuselage of fail-safe construction, using similar materials to wings, produced by manual lay-up method. A ventral fin has a movable surface for yaw trim/damping.

FOREPLANES: Low-set, electrically operated variable geometry foreplanes, of similar construction to wings, each with vortex generators and an elevator. Foreplane sweep is electronically interconnected with the flaps to counter pitch moment changes, over sweep range 4° forward to 30° back. Trim tabs on elevators.

LANDING GEAR: Retractable tricycle type, hydraulically operated with emergency backup. Main units retract inward, nose unit forward. Beech oleo-pneumatic shock absorbers. Twin Goodyear mainwheels with tyres size 19.5 × 6.75-10, pressure 5.38 bars (78 lb/sq in). Single Goodrich nosewheel with tyre size 19.5 × 6.75-8, pressure 5.38 bars (78 lb/sq in). Goodyear multi-disc brakes with carbon heat sink.

POWER PLANT: Two Pratt & Whitney Canada PT6A-67 turboprops, each flat rated at 895 kW (1,200 shp) and driving a Hartzell five-blade fully-feathering and reversible-pitch composite pusher propeller with spinner. Fuel, total capacity 1,923 litres (508 US gallons; 423 Imp gallons), contained in integral wing tanks with flush refuelling point in upper surface of each wing.

ACCOMMODATION: To be certificated for single pilot operation, but provision for two crew on three-way adjustable seats on flight deck, separated from cabin by bulkhead with door. Standard 'double club' seating for eight in swivelling, reclining, lateral tracking, and fore and aft adjustable seats. Individual stereo headset,

Third prototype Beechcraft Starship 1 photographed during its first flight on 5 January 1987

ashtray/drink holder, indirect cabin lighting, reading light and fresh air vent by each seat. Sidewall console houses folding work tables and storage for cabin accessories. Forward toilet compartment opposite cabin entrance door, with hot/cold water and mirror; pull-out flushing toilet; privacy doors to cockpit and cabin enclose the forward baggage compartment, which has hang-up storage. Rear baggage compartment, accessible in flight via mirrored door in rear cabin bulkhead. Hi-fi speakers in one-piece cabin headliner. Cabin trim panels secured to isolation mounts to enhance acoustics and eliminate vibration. 'No smoking' and 'Fasten seat belt' signs. Cabin is bleed air heated, with electric augmentation, vapour cycle air-conditioned and blower ventilated.

SYSTEMS: Pressurisation system with max differential of 0.58 bars (8.5 lb/sq in) to provide a cabin altitude of 2,440 m (8,000 ft) at 12,495 m (41,000 ft). Freon vapour cycle cooling system. Engine bleed air provides pressurisation, heating and ventilation. 28V DC three-bus electrical system supplied by single aircooled 34Ah battery and starter/generator mounted on each engine and connected in parallel. Oxygen cylinder capacity 2.18 m³ (77 cu ft) rated at 124 bars (1,800 lb/sq in), mounted in nose, provides passenger oxygen supply automatically via drop-down masks until cabin altitude reaches 4,115 m (13,500 ft). Quick-donning masks for crew. De-icing and anti-icing systems for windscreen, engine air inlets, fuel vents, pitot static probes and stall warning sensor.

AVIONICS AND EQUIPMENT: Collins integrated avionics package comprising 12 colour and two monochrome CRT displays in 'all glass' cockpit. Pilot and co-pilot have duplicated instrument panels, each with two 15.2 × 17.8 cm (6 × 7 in) EFIS displays for primary flight and navigation functions and two 10.2 × 10.2 cm (4 × 4 in) airspeed indicator and altitude/vertical speed indicator CRTs. Monochrome sensor display units (SDUs) provide heading bearings, DME and ILS functions and latitude/longitude information from a VLF/Omega long-range navigation system, and can be used as a primary navigation display in the event of EFIS failure. Dual control/display units (CDUs) control EFIS, weather radar, navigation radios and flight management functions. Engine indication caution and advisory system (EICAS) provides nearly 100 specific pieces of information in analog or digital form on a 15.2 × 17.8 cm (6 × 7 in) colour CRT display, with a priority message system to override extraneous information. Dual multi-function displays (MFDs) provide weather radar images from Collins TWR-850 turbulence weather radar system, maps, checklists and diagnostic and maintenance data, and serve as backup to EICAS. Two radio tuning units provide gas discharge tube alphanumerics for displaying navigation and transponder frequencies and codes, and can be used for display of engine parameters if EICAS fails. Dual flight management system (FMS) keyboards control all navigation frequencies, selected from onboard microdisc storage which is updated every 28 days. Dual clocks, altitude awareness panels, a course heading panel, reversionary switching panels and standby electromagnetic airspeed indicator, gyro horizon and altimeter are provided. Information from sensors and data acquisition units located throughout the aircraft is available to all instruments through an ARINC 429 digital databus system. Teledyne stall warning system. Stick pusher limits max attainable angle of attack.

DIMENSIONS, EXTERNAL:
Wing span (reference)	16.60 m (54 ft 4¾ in)
Winglet height, each	2.45 m (8 ft 0½ in)
Foreplane span: sweptforward	7.58 m (24 ft 10½ in)
sweptback	6.37 m (20 ft 11 in)
Length overall	14.05 m (46 ft 1 in)
Fuselage: Length	13.67 m (44 ft 10 in)
Diameter (constant section)	1.78 m (5 ft 10 in)
Height overall	3.68 m (12 ft 11 in)
Wheel track	5.13 m (16 ft 10 in)
Wheelbase	6.86 m (22 ft 6 in)
Propeller diameter	2.54 m (8 ft 4 in)
Propeller ground clearance	0.89 m (2 ft 11 in)
Distance between propeller centres	3.07 m (10 ft 1 in)
Passenger door: Height	1.88 m (4 ft 8 in)
Width	0.71 m (2 ft 4 in)
Emergency exit: Height	0.56 m (1 ft 10 in)
Width	0.66 m (2 ft 2 in)

DIMENSIONS, INTERNAL:
Cabin, excl flight deck: Length	5.08 m (16 ft 8 in)
Max width	1.68 m (5 ft 6 in)
Max height	1.66 m (5 ft 5½ in)
Floor area	5.94 m² (64 sq ft)
Volume (between pressure bulkheads)	
	14.24 m³ (503 cu ft)
Baggage holds: forward	0.56 m³ (20 cu ft)
rear	0.99 m³ (35 cu ft)

AREAS:
Wings, gross	26.09 m² (280.9 sq ft)
Elevons (total)	1.59 m² (17.1 sq ft)
Trailing-edge flaps (total)	4.78 m² (51.5 sq ft)
Ventral fin	1.25 m² (13.5 sq ft)
Foreplane (forward position)	5.67 m² (61.0 sq ft)
Elevators (total)	1.01 m² (10.9 sq ft)
Winglets (total)	4.92 m² (53.0 sq ft)
Rudders (total, incl tabs)	1.04 m² (11.2 sq ft)

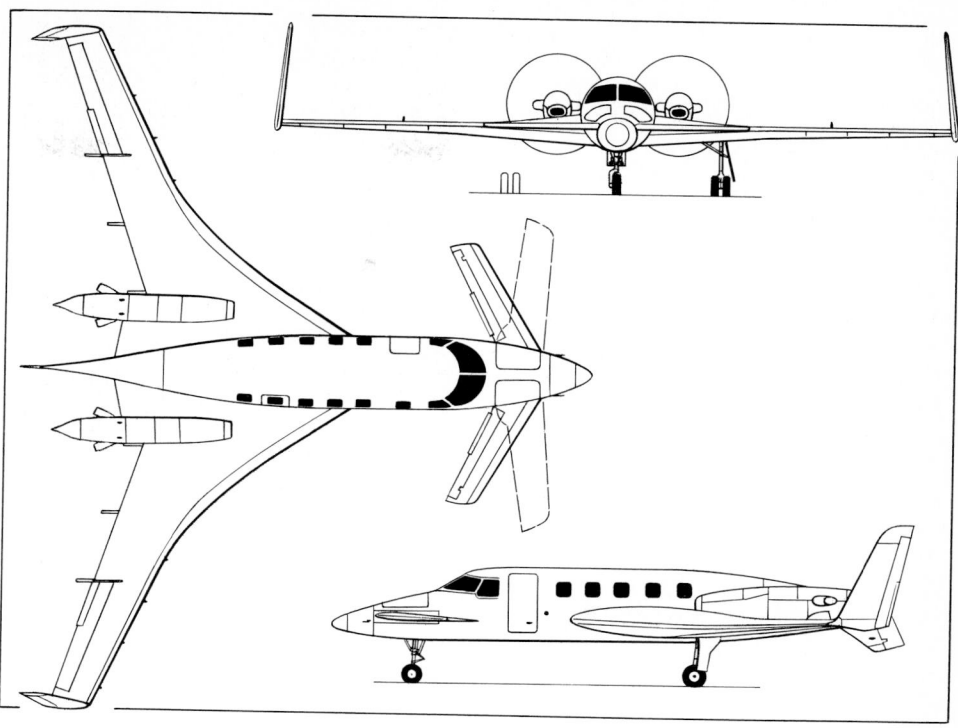

Beechcraft Starship 1 eight/eleven-seat business aircraft *(Pilot Press)*

WEIGHTS AND LOADINGS:
Basic weight empty	4,044 kg (8,916 lb)
Max payload	1,308 kg (2,884 lb)
Max fuel weight	1,732 kg (3,819 lb)
Max T-O weight	6,350 kg (14,000 lb)
Max zero-fuel weight	5,352 kg (11,800 lb)
Max landing weight	6,033 kg (13,300 lb)
Max wing loading	243.4 kg/m² (49.84 lb/sq ft)
Max power loading	3.55 kg/kW (5.83 lb/shp)

PERFORMANCE (estimated at AUW of 5,670 kg; 12,500 lb):
Never-exceed speed	Mach 0.76
Max level speed and max cruising speed at 7,620 m	
(25,000 ft)	352 knots (652 km/h; 405 mph)
Max cruising speed at 10,670 m (35,000 ft)	
	338 knots (626 km/h; 389 mph)
Econ cruising speed	270 knots (500 km/h; 311 mph)
Stalling speed, power off:	
flaps up	99 knots (183 km/h; 114 mph)
flaps down	84 knots (156 km/h; 97 mph)
Max rate of climb at S/L	1,030 m (3,380 ft)/min
Rate of climb at S/L, one engine out	
	314 m (1,030 ft)/min
Max operating altitude	12,495 m (41,000 ft)
Service ceiling, one engine out	7,040 m (23,100 ft)
T-O run	392 m (1,285 ft)
T-O to 15 m (50 ft), flaps up	628 m (2,060 ft)
Landing from 15 m (50 ft)	963 m (3,160 ft)
Landing run	658 m (2,160 ft)

Range with max fuel, four passengers, 45 min reserves:
at max cruise power 1,992 nm (3,691 km; 2,294 miles)
at econ cruise power 2,176 nm (4,032 km; 2,506 miles)

BEECHCRAFT MODEL 400 BEECHJET

In December 1985 Beech Aircraft Corporation acquired from Mitsubishi Heavy Industries and Mitsubishi Aircraft International the Diamond II business jet programme. The aircraft is now known as the Beechjet, for which Beech has

worldwide marketing rights outside Japan. Mitsubishi Aircraft International (see 1986-87 *Jane's*) ceased all general aviation operations outside of Japan on 31 March 1986, but initially supplied assemblies and subassemblies for final assembly by Beech. In January 1988 Beech announced that all Beechjet manufacturing was being transferred to its facilities at Salina and Wichita, with total transfer scheduled for completion in June 1989.

Beech, through its dealer network, is providing support for existing Mitsubishi aircraft delivered prior to its acquisition of the Diamond II/Beechjet, including the MU-2 turboprop series and the Diamond I and IA business jets. Details of the development of the Mitsubishi Diamond series can be found under the MAI entry in the 1985-86 edition of *Jane's*.

Beech has introduced as standard on the Beechjet an extended range fuel tank, capacity 363 litres (96 US gallons; 80 Imp gallons), and a tailcone baggage compartment, both of which were optional on the Diamond II. Other improvements introduced by Beech include optional Bendix/King and Honeywell EFIS and new interior styling and furnishings.

The first Beech assembled aircraft was rolled out on 19 May 1986, and deliveries began in the following month. By 1 January 1988 a total of 25 Beechjets had been delivered.

Beech has teamed with McDonnell Douglas and FlightSafety International to offer the Beechjet for the USAF's Tanker-Transport-Bomber Training System (TTBTS) requirement.

TYPE: Twin-turbofan business aircraft.

WINGS: Cantilever low-wing monoplane. Mitsubishi computer-designed wing sections: thickness/chord ratio 13.2% at root, 11.3% at tip. Dihedral from roots. Incidence 3° at root. Washout 6° 30′. Sweepback 20° at quarter-chord. Wings are of machine milled aluminium alloy, built in two panels. Each has two primary box beam spars, forming an integral fuel tank. Narrow chord

Beechcraft Model 400 Beechjet twin-turbofan business aircraft

Fowler type flaps over most of trailing-edges, actuated hydraulically and having double-slotted inboard and single-slotted outboard segments. Immediately forward of flaps are long span narrow chord spoilers, for roll control; these also serve as airbrakes, and can be used as lift dumpers to assist braking on touchdown. Outboard of each outer trailing-edge flap is a small, short span aileron for roll trim. Leading-edges anti-iced by hot air.

FUSELAGE: Pressurised, fail-safe fatigue resistant semi-monocoque structure, of oval cross-section with flattened cabin floor. Construction is mainly of aluminium alloy, using multiple load paths, bonded doublers and small skin panels in the principal load-bearing members. Built in three main portions: forward (including flight deck), centre and rear.

TAIL UNIT: Cantilever T tail, with sweepback on all surfaces; construction generally similar to that of wings. Curved dorsal fin, plus small underfin. A small horizontal strake is fitted on each side of rear fuselage, abreast of main fin, to assist airflow control. Trim tab in base of rudder. Small yaw damping control surface above rudder. Variable incidence tailplane, with elevators.

LANDING GEAR: Sumitomo retractable tricycle type, with single wheel and oleo-pneumatic shock absorber on each unit. Hydraulic actuation, controlled electrically. Emergency free-fall extension. Nosewheel, which is steerable by rudder pedals, retracts forward; mainwheels retract inward into fuselage. Goodyear wheels, with Goodrich tyres, on all units. Goodyear brakes.

POWER PLANT: Two Pratt & Whitney Canada JT15D-5 turbofans, each rated at 12.9 kN (2,900 lb st) for take-off. Rohr thrust reversers optional. Total usable fuel capacity 3,134 litres (828 US gallons; 689 Imp gallons). One refuelling point in top of each wing, and one in rear fuselage for fuselage tank only, which can also be filled by transferring fuel from wing tanks using electric boost pump. Oil capacity 7.7 litres (2 US gallons; 1.7 Imp gallons).

ACCOMMODATION: Crew of two on flight deck. Standard layout seats eight passengers in pressurised cabin, with four tracking, reclining seats in facing pairs, each with integral headrest and armrest, and a three-place couch with reclining backrest. Nine-seat interior optional. Side facing seat incorporating flushing toilet on starboard side at front. Baggage compartment at rear, capacity 204 kg (450 lb). Additional baggage space in tailcone area.

SYSTEMS: Pressurisation system, with normal differential of 0.62 bars (9.0 lb/sq in). Backup pressurisation system, using engine bleed air, for use in emergency. Hydraulic system, pressure 103.5 bars (1,500 lb/sq in), for actuation of flaps, landing gear and other services. Each variable volume output engine driven pump has a maximum flow rate of 14.76 litres (3.9 US gallons; 3.25 Imp gallons)/min, and one pump can actuate all hydraulic systems. Reservoirs, capacity 4.16 litres (1.1 US gallons; 0.9 Imp gallon), pressurised by filtered engine bleed air at 1.03 bars (15 lb/sq in). All systems are, wherever possible, of modular conception: for example, entire hydraulic installation can be removed as a single unit. Stick shaker as backup stall warning device.

AVIONICS: Standard avionics include Sperry SPZ-900 integrated flight control system with pilot's AD-650A ADI and HSI with vertical gyro and gyro compass, AAR 3137 RMI, dual VHF-22A transceivers, dual VIR-32A VOR/ILS receivers, TDR-90 transponders, Collins ADF-60A, DME-42 and ALT-55B radio altimeter, Sperry Primus 300SL weather radar, and dual Gables G-6686 audio system. Optional avionics include Bendix/King EFS-10 three-tube EFIS with dual channel, fail-safe KFC400 digital flight control system; KNS660 FMS with vertical navigation (VNAV); Series III CNI package; and RDS 86 digital colour weather radar: or Honeywell (Sperry) EFIS with Primus 650 weather radar and FMZ-600 FMS coupled to the standard SPZ-900 IFCS; second ADF-60A, second DME-42, Foster LNS-616A

Artist's impression of the Beechcraft cabin class twin, a prototype of which flew in July 1988

area navigation system with Loran C update, Global GNS-500A VLF/Omega navigation system, Sperry EDZ-601 flight director, Primus 400SL or Primus 800 weather radar, Sperry SPI-501 co-pilot's flight director, King KHF 950 HF transceiver, and Wulfsburg Flitefone VI.

DIMENSIONS, EXTERNAL:
Wing span	13.25 m (43 ft 6 in)
Wing aspect ratio	7.5
Length overall	14.75 m (48 ft 5 in)
Fuselage: Length	13.15 m (43 ft 2 in)
Max width	1.68 m (5 ft 6 in)
Max depth	1.85 m (6 ft 1 in)
Height overall	4.19 m (13 ft 9 in)
Tailplane span	5.00 m (16 ft 5 in)
Wheel track	2.84 m (9 ft 4 in)
Wheelbase	5.86 m (19 ft 3 in)
Crew/passenger door: Height	1.27 m (4 ft 2 in)
Width	0.71 m (2 ft 4 in)

DIMENSIONS, INTERNAL:
Cabin:	
Max length, incl flight deck	6.37 m (20 ft 11 in)
Length, excl flight deck	4.76 m (15 ft 7 in)
Max width	1.50 m (4 ft 11 in)
Max height	1.45 m (4 ft 9 in)
Volume: incl flight deck	11.33 m³ (400 cu ft)
excl flight deck	8.64 m³ (305 cu ft)
Baggage compartment volume	0.93 m³ (33 cu ft)

AREAS:
Wings, net	22.43 m² (241.4 sq ft)
Trailing-edge flaps (total)	5.22 m² (56.4 sq ft)
Spoilers (total)	0.57 m² (6.2 sq ft)
Fin, incl dorsal fin	5.91 m² (63.6 sq ft)
Rudder, incl yaw damper	1.12 m² (12.1 sq ft)
Tailplane	5.25 m² (56.5 sq ft)
Elevators, incl tab	1.56 m² (16.8 sq ft)

WEIGHTS AND LOADINGS:
Basic operating weight, incl crew, avionics and interior fittings	4,588 kg (10,115 lb)
Max fuel weight	2,224 kg (4,904 lb)
Max T-O weight	7,157 kg (15,780 lb)
Max ramp weight	7,189 kg (15,850 lb)
Max zero-fuel weight	5,656 kg (12,470 lb)
Max landing weight	6,450 kg (14,220 lb)
Max wing loading	319.1 kg/m² (65.37 lb/sq ft)
Max power loading	277.4 kg/kN (2.72 lb/lb st)

PERFORMANCE (at max T-O weight except where indicated):

Never-exceed speed	Mach 0.785
Max level speed at 8,840 m (29,000 ft)	
	461 knots (854 km/h; 531 mph)
Typical cruising speed at 11,890 m (39,000 ft)	
	447 knots (828 km/h; 515 mph)
Long-range cruising speed at 12,500 m (41,000 ft)	
	388 knots (719 km/h; 447 mph)
Stalling speed, flaps down, idling power	
	87 knots (161 km/h; 100 mph) IAS
Max operating altitude	12,500 m (41,000 ft)
FAA (FAR 25) T-O to 10.7 m (35 ft) at S/L, ISA	
	1,204 m (3,950 ft)
FAA landing distance from 15 m (50 ft) at S/L, ISA, max landing weight	862 m (2,830 ft)
Range with four passengers, max fuel, ISA, zero wind, with allowance for climb and descent, long-range cruise power:	
NBAA VFR reserves	
	1,930 nm (3,575 km; 2,222 miles)

BEECH RESEARCH & DEVELOPMENT PROJECTS

Beech has announced brief details of research and development projects being undertaken by Burt Rutan and the Beech-owned subsidiary Scaled Composites Inc (see entry in this section), including a medium-sized cabin class pressurised twin-engined design which draws on technology developed for the Starship 1. It features composites construction and has a three-surface configuration with foreplane, swept wings, a T tail with rearward swept fin and forward swept tailplane, and a ventral fin. The airframe has been designed to be readily adaptable to rotary, turboprop or turbofan power plants. A six/eight-seat turbofan version, powered by Williams FJ44 turbofans of 8.00 kN (1,800 lb) thrust, will have a max T-O weight of 4,309 kg (9,500 lb) and a max cruising speed of Mach 0.77 at 10,668 m (35,000 ft). Wing span is 14.63 m (48 ft 0 in), length overall 11.89 m (39 ft 0 in). A proof of concept prototype completed at Scaled's Mojave, California, facility made its first flight on 12 July 1988.

The all-composite five-seat single-piston-engined aircraft, based on Rutan Design No 81, which was illustrated in the 1987-88 Jane's, was test flown during 1987 and the evaluation programme has ended. No further development will be undertaken by Beech, which was to begin marketing studies in 1988 for a new six-seat single-engined aircraft to replace the Beechcraft Bonanza.

BEECHCRAFT ADVANCED TECHNOLOGY TACTICAL TRANSPORT

Under a $2.5 million Defense Advanced Research Projects Agency (DARPA) contract, Beech subsidiary Scaled Composites Inc (which see) has designed, built and test flown a scale proof of concept (POC) version of an Advanced Technology Tactical Transport (AT³) intended to fill the void in military airlift capability between the Lockheed C-130 and large helicopters.

The AT³ proof of concept prototype (N133SC), designed by Scaled's President Mr Burt Rutan, made a public 'commemorative' first flight from Mojave Airport, California, on 20 January 1988, although it had flown for the first time on 29 December 1987. The aircraft is 62 per cent scale size, with an airframe of composite glassfibre/foam and carbonfibre construction. To fulfil design goals of STOL performance and advanced aerodynamics the aircraft features a 'trimaran' configuration with tandem high aspect ratio wings connected by long engine nacelles each housing a 522 kW (700 shp) Pratt & Whitney Canada PT6A-135 turboprop and the main units of the retractable tricycle-type landing gear. The forward wing has dihedral, the rear one anhedral. Eight fast-acting, electrically actuated flaps are extended (but not lowered) for the start of take-off roll, then lowered rapidly (full deflection takes about 1.5 s) to increase lift as rotation speed is reached, enhancing STOL

Beech/Scaled Composites Inc 62 per cent scale Advanced Technology Tactical Transport proof of concept prototype

capability. All fuel is contained in wings and engine nacelles, leaving the fuselage free for cargo. A flight-openable rear loading door is incorporated for airdropping of supplies or paratroops. The conventional cruciform tail surfaces have a sweptback fin and two-segment rudder.

The DARPA contract provides for some 40 flights by the POC scale demonstrator. Lockheed-Georgia has joined Beech in the project, which may lead to full scale development of an AT³ intended to carry a payload of 14 troops and 2,268 kg (5,000 lb) of cargo at 326 knots (604

km/h; 375 mph) over a low-altitude unrefuelled range of 2,400 nm (4,448 km; 2,764 miles), while operating from unimproved airstrips 305 m (1,000 ft) long. Maximum gross weight of the full size AT³ would be in the 22,680 kg (50,000 lb) class.

BELL

BELL HELICOPTER TEXTRON INC
(Subsidiary of Textron Inc)

PO Box 482, Fort Worth, Texas 76101
Telephone: (817) 280 2011
Telex: 75 8229 and 75 8313

SENIOR VICE-PRESIDENT, CORPORATE RELATIONS:
 Dwayne K. Jose
SENIOR VICE-PRESIDENT, COMMERCIAL BUSINESS, AND GENERAL
 MANAGER, CUSTOMER SUPPORT AND SERVICE DIVISION:
 Gainor J. Lindsey
SENIOR VICE-PRESIDENT, RESEARCH & ENGINEERING:
 Robert R. Lynn
SENIOR VICE-PRESIDENT, GOVERNMENT BUSINESS:
 Charles R. Rudning
VICE-PRESIDENT, COMMERCIAL MARKETING:
 James A. Hamilton
VICE-PRESIDENT, INTERNATIONAL MARKETING:
 Philip S. Prince
VICE-PRESIDENT, DEVELOPMENT ENGINEERING:
 Stanley Martin
VICE-PRESIDENT, MILITARY BUSINESS DEVELOPMENT:
 Ray Swindell
DIRECTOR, PUBLIC AFFAIRS: Carl L. Harris

From 1970-81 Bell Helicopter Textron was an unincorporated division of Textron Inc. Since 3 January 1982 it has been a wholly owned subsidiary of Textron Inc.

In early 1988 a total of 8,344 people were employed in the USA by Bell, which, with its licensees, has manufactured more than 30,000 helicopters. Of these, more than 9,000 were delivered for commercial use.

In October 1983 Bell Helicopter Canada (see entry in Canadian section) was formed under a contract with the Canadian government to establish a manufacturing plant at Mirabel, near Montreal, Quebec. To make more space available at Fort Worth for the V-22 Osprey programme, Bell completed the transfer of its Model 206B JetRanger and Model 206L LongRanger production lines to Mirabel in January 1987. The lines for the Models 212 and 412 are being transferred in mid-1988 and early 1989 respectively.

Available details of the range of military and commercial helicopters in current production or under development by Bell Helicopter Textron are published in this entry and under the Bell heading in the Canadian section. Several models are also built under licence by Agusta in Italy and Fuji in Japan (which see). Korea Bell Helicopter Company (KBHC, which see) will co-produce helicopters in the Republic of Korea with Bell Helicopter Textron.

Bell Helicopter de Venezuela CA, a joint venture with Maquinarias Mendoza CA and Aerotecnica SA, was established in early 1984, in Caracas, to provide marketing and support services in Venezuela. Bell Helicopter Asia (Pte) Ltd is a wholly owned Singapore-based company providing marketing and support for the Southeast Asia region.

BELL MODEL 205
US military designations: UH-1D/H/V, EH-1H and HH-1H Iroquois
Canadian military designation: CH-118 Iroquois

Although basically similar to the earlier Model 204 (see *1971-72 Jane's*), the Model 205 introduced a longer fuselage, increased cabin space to accommodate a much larger number of passengers, and other changes. Details of the full range of military variants have been recorded in

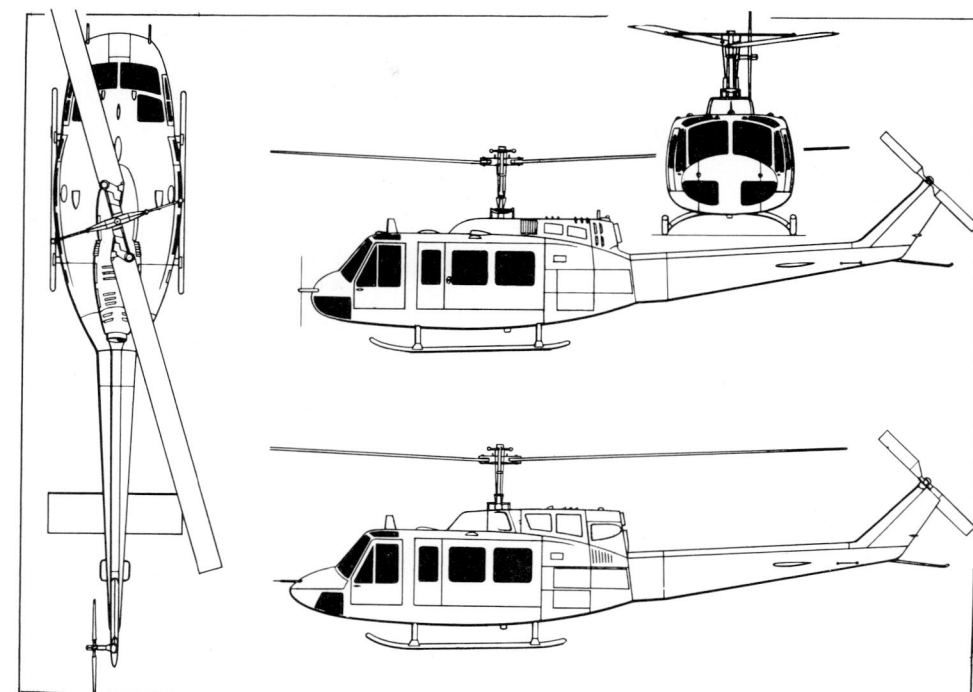

Bell UH-1H Iroquois, with additional side view (bottom) of UH-1N, described in Canadian section *(Pilot Press)*

previous editions of *Jane's*. The final production version is the **UH-1H**. Deliveries of this version to the US Army began in September 1967 and totalled 3,573. Production of the UH-1H continued subsequently to satisfy export orders, which totalled 1,317 by Spring 1985. It ended temporarily in December 1980, but was restarted in order to build 55 for Turkey. Deliveries of these were due to be completed in 1987. The Model 205 was also manufactured by Agusta in Italy, and (as the HU-1H) is still produced by Fuji in Japan. Twelve of the Japan Ground Self-Defence Force helicopters are each being equipped to carry and lay about 100 mines, with plans to equip 40 more. In addition, under a licensing agreement, 118 UH-1Hs were produced for the Nationalist Chinese Army, with much of the manufacturing and assembly carried out by AIDC (which see).

Up to FY 1980, a total of $47 million was provided to modify UH-1Hs to **EH-1H** electronic countermeasures configuration, with the Quick Fix I airborne communications interception, emitter locating and jamming system, including an AN/APR-39V2 radar warning receiver, XM130 chaff/flare dispenser and AN/ALQ-144 infra-red jammer. The FY 1981 budget added $5.1 million to convert initial Quick Fix IA systems in the EH-1H to Phase IB configuration, plus survivability equipment to protect the aircraft against known and postulated threats, including hot metal/plume suppression. By April 1981, three of the EH-1Hs had been delivered, with seven more to follow. However, the Quick Fix mission has been taken over by the much larger Sikorsky EH-60A version of the Black Hawk utility transport helicopter (which see).

About 220 UH-1Hs have been converted by US Army Electronics Command to **UH-1V** medevac configuration. Avionics and equipment in this version include a radio altimeter, AEL AN/ARN-124 DME, glideslope and rescue hoist.

The US Army plans to retain at least 2,700 improved UH-1Hs in service beyond the year 2000 to perform such operations as resupply, troop transport, command and control, electronic warfare, medical evacuation and minefield emplacement. To make such a plan realistic, a product improvement programme for the Army's UH-1H fleet introduced improved or new avionics and equipment including an AN/ALQ-144 infra-red jammer, AN/APN-209 radar altimeter, AN/APR-39 radar warning receiver, AN/ARC-164 UHF/AM radio, AN/ARN-124 DME, XM130 chaff/flare dispenser, NOE communications (FM/ HF), communications security, infra-red suppressor (hot metal and plume), altimeter lighting (5V), crashworthy auxiliary fuel system, closed circuit refuelling, fuel tank vent, improved main input driveshaft, and main rotor mast plug. In addition, it is planned to introduce, as a minimum, new composite main rotor blades; improved stabiliser bar, tail rotor hub and servo cylinders; a split engine deck, and improved oil filtration; a night vision compatible cockpit; built-in Vibrex connections; an improved AN/ASN-43 gyro magnetic compass; and Doppler navigation.

A US Army Request for Proposal for composite main rotor blades for the UH-1H was issued on 16 November 1981. The Army's schedule called for a qualified blade to be ready for production after 32 months. Procurement of 6,000 blades is anticipated in 1985-89, at a cost of $20,000 or less per blade in FY 1981 dollars. Bell tendered a joint proposal with Boeing, and this team was awarded a $19 million development contract during 1982 by the US Army Aviation Research and Development Command. Bell designed the composite blade for the UH-1H, but both companies fabricated test blades and supported laboratory and flight testing to ensure compliance with Army requirements. The composite rotor blades provide a 6 per cent improvement in the UH-1H's hovering capability and a 5-8 per cent reduction in fuel flow in forward flight. Bell provided manufacturing tools and fixtures and transferred specific manufacturing knowledge to Boeing, so that both companies are equally capable and qualified to manufacture production blades, for which contracts are expected to exceed $100 million. The first flight of the composite rotor blades on a UH-1H took place in early 1985. Production deliveries were scheduled to begin in mid-1988.

The following details apply to the military UH-1H in its current form:

TYPE: Single-rotor general purpose helicopter.

ROTOR SYSTEM: Two-blade semi-rigid main rotor. Interchangeable blades, built up of extruded aluminium spars and laminates, now being replaced by new composite blades, with unidirectional glassfibre roving spar, afterbody of glassfibre skin over a Nomex honeycomb core, unidirectional glassfibre roving trailing-edge, and a

Bell Model 205 Iroquois helicopter of the Turkish Army

polyurethane leading-edge abrasion strip. A stainless steel sheath under this strip on the outboard portion of the blade reinforces the inertia weight attachment and enhances tree cutting capability. Stabilising bar above and at right angles to main rotor blades. Underslung feathering axis head. Two-blade all-metal tail rotor of honeycomb construction. Blades do not fold.

ROTOR DRIVE: Shaft drive to both main and tail rotors. Transmission rating 820 kW (1,100 shp). Main rotor rpm 294-324.

FUSELAGE: Conventional all-metal semi-monocoque structure.

TAIL SURFACE: Small synchronised elevator on rear fuselage is connected to the cyclic control to increase allowable CG travel.

LANDING GEAR: Tubular skid type. Lock-on ground handling wheels and inflated nylon float bags available.

POWER PLANT: One 1,044 kW (1,400 shp) Textron Lycoming T53-L-13 turboshaft, mounted aft of the transmission on top of the fuselage and enclosed in cowlings. Five interconnected rubber fuel cells, total capacity 844 litres (223 US gallons; 186 Imp gallons), of which 799 litres (211 US gallons; 176 Imp gallons) are usable. Overload fuel capacity of 1,935 litres (511 US gallons; 425 Imp gallons) usable, obtained by installation of kit comprising two 568 litre (150 US gallon; 125 Imp gallon) internal auxiliary fuel tanks interconnected with the basic fuel system.

ACCOMMODATION: Pilot and 11-14 troops, or six litters and a medical attendant, or 1,759 kg (3,880 lb) of freight. Crew doors open forward and are jettisonable. Two doors on each side of cargo compartment; front door is hinged to open forward and is removable, rear door slides aft. Forced air ventilation system.

AVIONICS AND EQUIPMENT: FM, UHF, VHF radio sets, IFF transponder, Gyromatic compass system, direction finder set, VOR receiver and intercom standard. Optional nav/com systems. Standard equipment includes bleed air heater and defroster, comprehensive range of engine and flight instruments, power plant fire detection system, 30V 300A DC starter/generator, navigation, landing and anti-collision lights, controllable searchlight, hydraulically boosted controls. Optional equipment includes external cargo hook, auxiliary fuel tanks, rescue hoist, 150,000 BTU muff heater.

DIMENSIONS, EXTERNAL:
Main rotor diameter	14.63 m (48 ft 0 in)
Tail rotor diameter	2.59 m (8 ft 6 in)
Main rotor blade chord	0.53 m (1 ft 9 in)
Tail rotor blade chord	0.213 m (8.4 in)
Length:	
overall (main rotor fore and aft)	17.62 m (57 ft 9⅝ in)
fuselage	12.77 m (41 ft 10¾ in)
Height:	
overall, tail rotor turning (excl fin tip antenna)	4.41 m (14 ft 5½ in)
to top of main rotor head	3.60 m (11 ft 9¾ in)
Stabiliser span	2.84 m (9 ft 4 in)
Width over skids	2.91 m (9 ft 6½ in)

DIMENSIONS, INTERNAL:
Cabin: Max width	2.34 m (7 ft 8 in)
Max height	1.25 m (4 ft 1¼ in)
Volume (excl flight deck)	approx 6.23 m³ (220 cu ft)

AREAS:
Main rotor disc	168.11 m² (1,809.56 sq ft)
Tail rotor disc	5.27 m² (56.7 sq ft)

WEIGHTS AND LOADINGS:
Weight empty, equipped	2,363 kg (5,210 lb)
Basic operating weight (troop carrier mission)	2,520 kg (5,557 lb)
Mission weight	4,100 kg (9,039 lb)
Max T-O and landing weight	4,309 kg (9,500 lb)
Max zero-fuel weight	3,660 kg (8,070 lb)
Max disc loading	25.6 kg/m² (5.25 lb/sq ft)
Max power loading	4.13 kg/kW (8.63 lb/shp)

PERFORMANCE (at max T-O weight):
Never-exceed speed	110 knots (204 km/h; 127 mph)
Max level and cruising speed	110 knots (204 km/h; 127 mph)
Econ cruising speed at 1,735 m (5,700 ft)	110 knots (204 km/h; 127 mph)
Max rate of climb at S/L	488 m (1,600 ft)/min
Service ceiling	3,840 m (12,600 ft)
Hovering ceiling: IGE	4,145 m (13,600 ft)
OGE	1,220 m (4,000 ft)
Range with max fuel, no allowances, no reserves, at S/L	276 nm (511 km; 318 miles)

BELL MODELS 206B JETRANGER III and 206L-3 LONGRANGER III

By January 1988, Bell and its licensees had manufactured well over 7,000 helicopters of the Model 206 series, more than 4,600 of them for commercial customers. Production of the JetRanger and LongRanger is now undertaken at Bell Helicopter Canada's plant at Mirabel, near Montreal. A description and illustrations of these helicopters may be found in the Canadian section of this edition.

BELL SEARANGER
US Navy designation: TH-57

Production of SeaRanger training versions of the

JetRanger has ceased. Details of the TH-57A, TH-57B and TH-57C may be found in the 1987-88 and earlier editions of *Jane's*.

BELL KIOWA
US Army designation: OH-58A, B and C
Canadian military designation: CH-136

Details of the OH-58A, B and C Kiowa series of light observation helicopters may be found in the 1987-88 and earlier editions of *Jane's*.

BELL MODEL 406 (AHIP)
US Army designations: OH-58D and AH-58D Warrior

The US Army announced on 21 September 1981 that Bell's Model 406 proposal had been selected as winner of its Army Helicopter Improvement Program (AHIP) competition to develop a near-term scout helicopter. Its configuration includes an MDAC/Northrop mast mounted sight and a Honeywell Sperry cockpit control and display subsystem. The US Army planned to modify at least 578 existing OH-58A Kiowa helicopters in 1985-91, under the designation OH-58D. Of these 171 had been funded by FY 1988, in five lots (16, 44, 39, 36 and 36), with a further 36 included in the FY 1989 budget request. Deliveries totalled 87 by early February 1988, and included 15 of an armed version known as the **AH-58D Warrior**.

The first of five prototype OH-58Ds made its first flight on 6 October 1983. Two were delivered in December 1985, and 64 were in the US Army inventory by the beginning of July 1987. The first shipment to units in Europe began on 11 June 1987, when 12 OH-58Ds were loaded on board a single C-5A Galaxy, complete with all needed support and maintenance equipment.

TYPE: Two-seat scout helicopter.

ROTOR SYSTEM: Four-blade soft-in-plane main rotor. Blade section BHTI M406183. Glassfibre composite blades, with hollow spar, and afterbody skins supported by Nomex honeycomb core. Main rotor head has glassfibre yoke and elastomeric bearings. Each blade attached to head by two side by side pins. Main rotor blades fold and have a bendable tab at 60 per cent radius. No rotor brake. Two-blade non-lubricated tail rotor on port side of tailboom; blades of glassfibre composite with nickel coated abrasion strip.

ROTOR DRIVE: Steel spiral bevel and planetary gear transmissions in aluminium and magnesium cast housings. Transmission rating 454 kW (609 shp) maximum, 339 kW (455 shp) continuous. Main gearbox beneath main rotor, tail rotor gearbox at tail rotor. Main rotor/engine rpm ratio 0.065668:1. Tail rotor/engine rpm ratio 0.39584:1.

FUSELAGE: Stressed aluminium semi-monocoque fail-safe structure incorporating skins, longerons, two upper longitudinal roof beams and a lower curved honeycomb sandwich underfuselage panel. Tapered stressed aluminium semi-monocoque tailboom, composed of bulkheads and skins.

TAIL UNIT: Fixed stabiliser of aluminium monocoque construction with inverted aerofoil section on starboard side of tailboom. Fixed vertical fin in sweptback upper and ventral sections.

LANDING GEAR: Light alloy tubular skids bolted to extruded cross-tubes.

Bell OH-58D (AHIP) with mast mounted sight

POWER PLANT: One Allison 250-C30R turboshaft, with an intermediate power rating of 485 kW (650 shp) at S/L ISA. One self-sealing crash resistant fuel cell, capacity 399 litres (105.4 US gallons; 87.8 Imp gallons) located aft of the cabin area. Refuelling point on starboard side of fuselage. Oil capacity 5.7 litres (1.5 US gallons; 1.2 Imp gallons).

ACCOMMODATION: Pilot and co-pilot/observer seated side by side. Door on each side of fuselage. Accommodation is heated and ventilated.

SYSTEMS: Single hydraulic system, pressure 69 bars (1,000 lb/sq in) for main and tail rotor controls and SCAS system. Maximum flow rate 11.36 litres (3 US gallons; 2.5 Imp gallons)/min. Open-type reservoir. Primary electrical power provided by 10kVA 400Hz three-phase 120/208V AC alternator with 200A 28V DC transformer/rectifier unit for secondary DC power. Backup power provided by 500VA 400Hz single-phase 115V AC solid state inverter and 200A 28V DC starter/generator.

AVIONICS AND EQUIPMENT: Multi-function displays for vertical and horizontal situation indication, mast mounted sight day/night viewing and communications control, with selection via control column handgrip switches. Five com transceivers, data link and secure voice equipment. Doppler, strapdown INS. Equipped for day/night VFR. Mast mounted sight houses 12x magnification TV camera, auto-focusing IR thermal imaging sensor and laser rangefinder/designator, with automatic target tracking and in-flight automatic boresighting. Night vision goggles; AHRS; and airborne target handoff subsystem (ATHS).

ARMAMENT (optional): Four Stinger air-to-air or Hellfire air-to-surface missiles, or two rocket pods, or two 0.50 in machine-gun pods, mounted on outriggers on cabin sides.

DIMENSIONS, EXTERNAL:
Main rotor diameter	10.67 m (35 ft 0 in)
Main rotor blade chord	0.24 m (9½ in)
Tail rotor diameter	1.65 m (5 ft 5 in)
Length: overall, rotors turning	12.85 m (42 ft 2 in)
fuselage, excl rotors	10.31 m (33 ft 10 in)
Width, rotors folded	1.97 m (6 ft 5½ in)
Height: to top of rotor head	2.59 m (8 ft 6 in)
overall	3.90 m (12 ft 9½ in)
Skid track	1.88 m (6 ft 2 in)
Cabin doors (port and stbd, each):	
Height	1.04 m (3 ft 5 in)
Width	0.91 m (3 ft 0 in)
Height to sill	0.66 m (2 ft 2 in)

AREAS:
Main rotor blades (each)	1.30 m² (13.95 sq ft)
Tail rotor blades (each)	0.13 m² (1.43 sq ft)
Main rotor disc	89.37 m² (962.0 sq ft)
Tail rotor disc	2.14 m² (23.04 sq ft)
Fin	0.85 m² (9.1 sq ft)
Stabiliser (stbd)	0.90 m² (9.74 sq ft)

WEIGHTS AND LOADINGS:
Weight empty	1,281 kg (2,825 lb)
Max fuel weight	321 kg (707 lb)
Max T-O and landing weight	2,041 kg (4,500 lb)
Max zero-fuel weight	1,711 kg (3,773 lb)
Max disc loading	22.95 kg/m² (4.7 lb/sq ft)
Max power loading	6.27 kg/kW (10.3 lb/shp)

PERFORMANCE (at max T-O weight, 'clean'):

Never-exceed speed	130 knots (241 km/h; 149 mph)
Max level speed at 1,220 m (4,000 ft)	
	128 knots (237 km/h; 147 mph)
Max cruising speed at 610 m (2,000 ft)	
	120 knots (222 km/h; 138 mph)
Econ cruising speed at 1,220 m (4,000 ft)	
	110 knots (204 km/h; 127 mph)
Max rate of climb: at S/L, ISA	469 m (1,540 ft)/min
at 1,220 m (4,000 ft), 35°C (95°F)	
	over 152 m (500 ft)/min
Vertical rate of climb: at S/L, ISA	232 m (760 ft)/min
at 1,220 m (4,000 ft), 35°C (95°F)	
	over 152 m (500 ft)/min
Service ceiling	over 3,660 m (12,000 ft)
Hovering ceiling: IGE, ISA	over 3,660 m (12,000 ft)
OGE, ISA	3,415 m (11,200 ft)
OGE, 35°C (95°F)	1,735 m (5,700 ft)
Range with max fuel, no reserves	
	300 nm (556 km; 345 miles)
Endurance	2 h 30 min

BELL MODEL 406 CS

The Model 406 CS (for Combat Scout) is a lighter and simplified variant of the AHIP OH-58D, equipped with a quick-change weapons system. First flown in June 1984, this multi-mission helicopter omits the MMS, specialised avionics and integrated multiplex cockpit of the AHIP 406, but incorporates many OH-58D features including AHIP dynamics and drive train, mated to a damage-resistant, 10,000 hour fail-safe four-blade rigid rotor of composites construction and a high-thrust composites tail rotor. Power plant is a 485 kW (650 shp) Allison 250-C30L turboshaft; transmission rating is 380 kW (510 shp) continuous. Armament can comprise two GIAT 20 mm M621 gun pods, each with 180 rds, four TOW 2 anti-tank missiles, or a mix of Stinger air-to-air missiles, 70 mm rockets and 7.62 mm or 0.50 in machine-guns.

In 1987 a Combat Scout successfully completed simulated air-to-air combat trials at NAS Patuxent River, Maryland, armed with a Lucas Aerospace gun turret and laser designator.

Saudi Arabia has announced its intention to purchase 15 Combat Scouts.

WEIGHTS:

Weight empty	1,028 kg (2,266 lb)
Max T-O weight	2,041 kg (4,500 lb)

PERFORMANCE (at max T-O weight):

Max level speed	124 knots (230 km/h; 143 mph)
Max cruising speed	120 knots (222 km/h; 138 mph)
Hovering ceiling: IGE	6,035 m (19,800 ft)
OGE	5,210 m (17,100 ft)
Range with max fuel	217 nm (402 km; 250 miles)
Endurance	2 h 30 min

BELL MODEL 209 HUEYCOBRA, SEACOBRA and SUPERCOBRA

US Army designations: AH-1G, AH-1Q and AH-1R
US Navy/Marine Corps designations: AH-1J, AH-1T and AH-1W

Bell initiated the Model 209 in March 1965 as a company funded development of the UH-1B/C Iroquois intended specifically for armed helicopter missions. The prototype made its first flight on 7 September 1965, and the US Army's intention to order the aircraft was announced on 11 March 1966, the initial model being the AH-1G HueyCobra. Total orders to date for all versions of the HueyCobra/SeaCobra exceed 1,800.

The following versions have been built:

AH-1G HueyCobra. Original version for US Army (1,075); described in 1987-88 and earlier editions of *Jane's*. Production included 38 for USMC, six for Israel, eight for Spain, and some conversions to TH-1G dual control trainer and JAH-1G armament testbed.

AH-1J SeaCobra. Initial twin-turboshaft version for US Marine Corps (69) and Imperial Iranian Army Aviation (202). Production completed; last described in 1987-88 *Jane's*.

AH-1Q HueyCobra. Interim (converted AH-1G) anti-armour version for US Army; production completed. Details in 1982-83 and earlier *Jane's*.

AH-1S HueyCobra. Advanced and modernised TOW-capable version for US Army; described separately. In production.

AH-1T Improved SeaCobra. Improved version of twin-engined AH-1J for US Marine Corps, described in 1987-88 and earlier editions of *Jane's*. Total of 57 built; production completed, but March 1988 contract provides for 21 to be upgraded to AH-1W configuration by May 1990.

AH-1W SuperCobra. Most recent production version, originating from 1980 flight test by Bell of a USMC AH-1T powered by two General Electric T700-GE-700 turboshafts with a combined output in excess of 2,386 kW (3,200 shp). Improvements, proposed subsequently for retrofit to existing AH-1Ts, included installation of General Electric T700-GE-401 turboshafts with a combined output of 2,423 kW (3,250 shp); a new combining gearbox; and a number of detail improvements. The T700-GE-401 has intermediate and contingency ratings of 1,260 kW (1,690 shp) and 1,285 kW (1,723 shp) respectively. The fuel system is designed to

Bell Model 406CS Combat Scout, armed with GIAT 20 mm M621 gun pods

survive 23 mm shell damage. A T700-GE-401 testbed helicopter, then designated AH-1T+, made its first flight on 16 November 1983 and in early 1984 Congressional approval was given for the procurement of 44 production AH-1W SuperCobras, 22 each in FYs 1985 and 1986. The first AH-1W was delivered on 27 March 1986 for a seven-month test programme with Naval Air Systems Command. A second AH-1W began a three-month electromagnetic interference test programme in the Spring of 1986. Deliveries of all 44 AH-1Ws had been completed by early 1988. Two aircraft have been equipped with an interim FLIR capability. The USMC also plans to update its fleet of approximately 40 AH-1Ts to AH-1W standard, with the first modification funded for delivery in 1989.

The first AH-1T uprated to AH-1W standard for the USMC is being fitted with a larger main rotor based on Bell's Model 680 bearingless research rotor. First flight was scheduled for 1988.

Missions assigned to the AH-1W include anti-armour, troop carrying helicopter escort, multiple weapon fire support, armed reconnaissance, and search and target acquisition. A night targeting system, known as the Cobra laser night attack system (CLNAS), is under development by Israel Aircraft Industries for USMC AH-1Ws and Israeli operated AH-1S HueyCobras. The description below refers to the AH-1W SuperCobra:

TYPE: Twin-engined close support and attack helicopter.

ROTOR SYSTEM AND DRIVE: Two-blade main rotor system, similar to that of Bell Model 214, with strengthened main rotor head incorporating Lord Kinematics Lastoflex elastomeric and Teflon faced bearings. Main rotor blades, section Wortmann FX69-H-098, have aluminium spar with steel leading-edge and aluminium faced honeycomb material aft of spar. Single tab on each main rotor blade. Tail rotor also similar to that of Model 214,

with increased diameter and blade chord, constructed from aluminium honeycomb with stainless steel skin and leading-edge. Main rotor brake standard. Main rotor/engine rpm ratio: 1 : 64.354. Tail rotor/engine rpm ratio 1 : 13.708.

WINGS: Small mid-mounted stub-wings, to carry armament and offload rotor in flight, of conventional all-metal construction. Section NACA 0024-0030. Dihedral 0°. Incidence 14°. Sweepback at quarter-chord 14° 42'.

FUSELAGE: Conventional all-metal semi-monocoque fail-safe structure, with low silhouette and narrow profile.

TAIL UNIT: Sweptback vertical fin/tail rotor pylon. Elevator, of inverted aerofoil section and conventional construction, mid-mounted on tailboom forward of fin.

LANDING GEAR: Non-retractable tubular skid type. Ground handling wheels optional.

POWER PLANT: Two General Electric T700-GE-401 turboshafts, each rated at 1,260 kW (1,690 shp). Fuel contained in two interconnected self-sealing rubber fuel cells in fuselage, with protection from damage by 0.50 in ballistic ammunition, total capacity 1,153 litres (304.5 US gallons; 253.5 Imp gallons). Gravity refuelling point in forward fuselage, pressure refuelling point in aft fuselage. Provision for carriage of two or four external fuel tanks each of 291 litres (77 US gallons; 64 Imp gallons) capacity; or two 378 litre (100 US gallon; 83 Imp gallon) tanks; or two 100 and two 77 US gallon tanks; on underwing stores stations. Oil capacity 19 litres (5 US gallons; 4.2 Imp gallons).

ACCOMMODATION: Crew of two in tandem, with co-pilot/gunner in front seat and pilot at rear. Cockpit is heated, ventilated and air-conditioned. Dual controls, night vision capabilty and armour protection standard. Forward crew door on port side and rear crew door on starboard side, both upward opening.

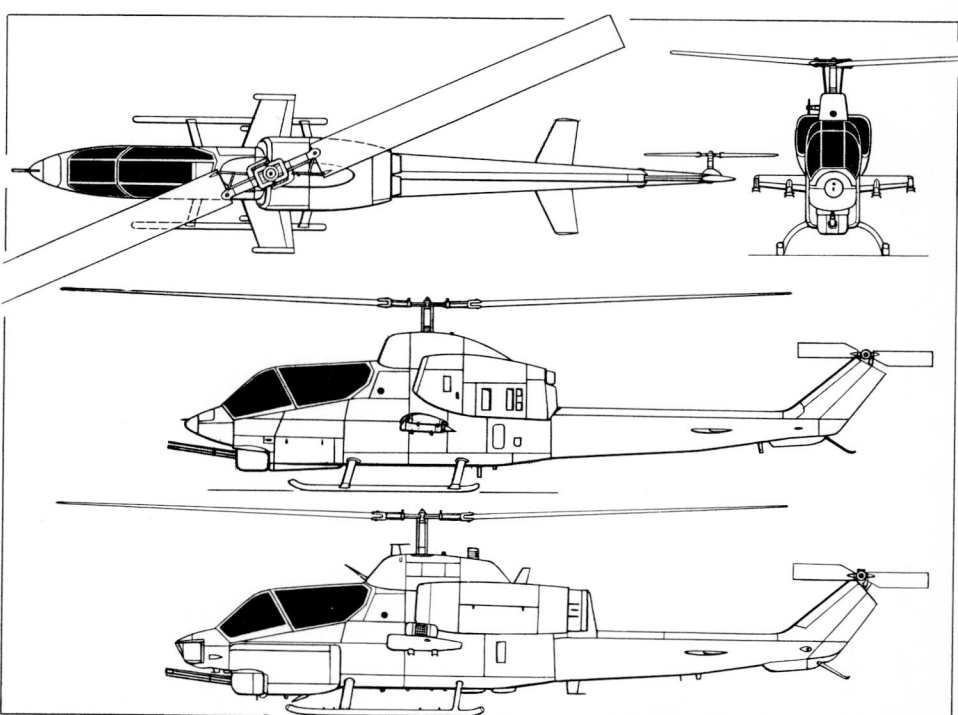

Bell AH-1T Improved SeaCobra, with added side view (bottom) of AH-1W SuperCobra *(Pilot Press)*

SYSTEMS: Three independent hydraulic systems, pressure 207 bars (3,000 lb/sq in), for flight controls and other services. Electrical system comprises two 28V 400A DC generators, two 24V 34.5Ah batteries and five inverters: main 115V AC, 1kVA, single-phase at 400Hz, standby 115V AC, 750VA, three-phase at 400Hz. AiResearch environmental control unit.

AVIONICS: AN/ASN-75B compass set, AN/ARN-89B ADF, AN/APX-100(V) transponder, AN/ARN-118 Tacan, AN/APN-154(V) radar beacon set, AN/ARC-182(V), AN/APN-194 radar altimeter, AN/APR-39(V) radar signal detecting set, AN/APR-44(V) radar warning system, KY-58 TSEC secure voice set and AN/ALQ-144(V) countermeasures set.

ARMAMENT: Electrically operated General Electric under-nose turret housing an M197 three-barrel 20 mm gun. A 750-rd ammunition container is located in the fuselage directly aft of the turret; firing rate is 750 rds/min, but a 16-round burst limiter is incorporated in the firing switch. Gun can be tracked 110° to each side, 18° upward, and 50° downward, but barrel length of 1.52 m (5 ft) makes it imperative that the M197 is centralised before wing stores are fired. Underwing attachments for up to four LAU-61A (19 tube), LAU-68A, LAU-68A/A, LAU-68B/A or LAU-69A (seven-tube) 2.75 in Zuni rocket launcher pods; two CBU-55B fuel-air explosive weapons; four SUU-44/A flare dispensers; two M118 grenade dispensers; Mk 45 parachute flares; or two GPU-2A or SUU-11A/A Minigun pods. Provision for carriage of up to eight TOW missiles in two two-round clusters, eight AGM-114 Hellfire missiles, or one AIM-9L Sidewinder missile, on each outboard underwing stores station. Canadian Marconi TOW/Hellfire control system. AN/ALE-39 chaff system with one MX-7721 dispenser mounted on each stub wing.

DIMENSIONS, EXTERNAL:

Main rotor diameter	14.63 m (48 ft 0 in)
Main rotor blade chord	0.84 m (2 ft 9 in)
Tail rotor diameter	2.97 m (9 ft 9 in)
Tail rotor blade chord	0.305 m (1 ft 0 in)
Distance between rotor centres	8.89 m (29 ft 2 in)
Wing span	3.23 m (10 ft 7 in)
Wing aspect ratio	3.74
Length overall, rotors turning	17.68 m (58 ft 0 in)
Length of fuselage	13.87 m (45 ft 6 in)
Width overall	3.28 m (10 ft 9 in)
Height to top of rotor head	4.11 m (13 ft 6 in)
Height overall	4.32 m (14 ft 2 in)
Elevator span	2.11 m (6 ft 11 in)
Width over skids	2.13 m (7 ft 0 in)

AREAS:

Main rotor blades (each)	6.13 m² (66.0 sq ft)
Tail rotor blades (each)	0.45 m² (4.835 sq ft)
Main rotor disc	168.11 m² (1,809.56 sq ft)
Tail rotor disc	6.94 m² (74.70 sq ft)
Vertical fin	2.01 m² (21.70 sq ft)
Horizontal tail surfaces	1.41 m² (15.20 sq ft)

WEIGHTS:

Weight empty	4,627 kg (10,200 lb)
Mission fuel load	946 kg (2,086 lb)
Max useful load (fuel and disposable ordnance)	2,065 kg (4,552 lb)
Max T-O and landing weight	6,690 kg (14,750 lb)

PERFORMANCE (at max T-O weight, ISA):

Never-exceed speed	190 knots (352 km/h; 219 mph)
Max level speed at S/L	152 knots (282 km/h; 175 mph)
Max cruising speed	150 knots (278 km/h; 173 mph)
Rate of climb at S/L, one engine out	244 m (800 ft)/min
Service ceiling	more than 4,270 m (14,000 ft)
Service ceiling, one engine out	more than 3,660 m (12,000 ft)
Hovering ceiling: IGE	4,495 m (14,750 ft)
OGE	914 m (3,000 ft)
Range at S/L with standard fuel, no reserves	343 nm (635 km; 395 miles)

BELL MODEL 209 HUEYCOBRA (MODERNISED VERSIONS)
US Army designations: AH-1E, AH-1F, AH-1P, AH-1S and TH-1S

The AH-1S was introduced as an advanced version of the single-engined HueyCobra for the US Army, with TOW missile capability, upgraded power plant, gearbox, transmission and many other improvements. The first of a succession of US Army contracts was placed in 1975, involving both the conversion of earlier AH-1G Cobras and a three-stage production programme of new-build aircraft with varying degrees of upgrading. The modernisation programme gave rise to the following new US Army designations:

AH-1S. Applies to 337 AH-1Gs (including 92 previously converted to AH-1Q) when retrofitted with the TOW missile system, a 1,342 kW (1,800 shp) Textron Lycoming T53-L-703 turboshaft, and the rotor system dynamics of the AH-1P. (Bell designation is Mod AH-1S.) Some aircraft also fitted with equipment specified for AH-1E and AH-1F, including an M197 gun, ALQ-144 infra-red jammer, APR-39 radar warning receiver, AAS-32 laser rangefinder and tracker, hot metal and plume infra-red suppressor. Ten converted by Northrop to **TH-1S** 'Night Stalker' configuration, to give US Army pilots experience in

Bell AH-1W SuperCobra armed with Hellfire missiles

operation of the Martin Marietta FLIR-based night vision system and Honeywell integrated helmet and display sighting system (IHADSS) fitted to AH-64 Apache helicopters.

AH-1P. First batch of new-production TOW Cobras (Bell designation: Production AH-1S), of which 100 delivered to US Army in 1977-78. Flat-plate canopy, improved nap-of-the-earth (NOE) instrument panel layout, continental United States (CONUS) navigation equipment, radar altimeter, improved communication radios, uprated engine and transmission, push/pull anti-torque controls, and (from the 67th aircraft onwards) Kaman developed composite rotor blades.

AH-1E (Bell designation: Up-gun AH-1S). Next 98 new-build aircraft, with improvements detailed for AH-1P plus ECAS (enhanced Cobra armament system) changes which included a universal 20/30 mm gun turret, improved wing stores management system for the 2.75 in rockets, automatic compensation for off-axis gun firing, and a 10kVA alternator to provide the necessary additional electric power. Delivered in 1978-79.

AH-1F. Fully upgraded TOW version (Bell designation: Modernised AH-1S), and final new-production model. Total of 99 built for US Army (deliveries completed in 1981); Army National Guard has acquired 50. To the improvements already mentioned for the AH-1P and AH-1E are added a new fire control subsystem (comprising a laser rangefinder and tracker, ballistics computer, low-airspeed sensor, and pilot's head-up display), air data system, Doppler navigation system, IFF transponder, infra-red jammer, hot metal and plume infra-red suppressor, closed circuit refuelling, new secure voice communications, and new composite rotor blades developed by Kaman.

The last AH-1 production buy for the US Army was completed in 1986, but modification programmes are continuing. Those funded up to mid-1988 include C-Nite, ATAS (air-to-air Stinger), C-Flex (Cobra fleet life extension), engine air filter, redesigned swashplate, M-43 nuclear/biological/chemical mask, AN/AVR-2 laser warning, and improved SCAS (stability control augmentation system) roll modifications. **C-Nite** provides the capability of detecting, acquiring and engaging targets during reduced visibility and at night. **ATAS** will provide a mid-range defensive and offensive air-to-air capability. The **C-Flex** programme adds several service life extension modifications, of which the Night Fix lighting, AH-1G to S upgrade, and K-Flex driveshaft efforts have been completed. Remaining C-Flex efforts are rotor improve-

ments, improved TOW test set, and radio upgrade. These and other improvements significantly enhance the safety of the aircraft and crew, as well as providing reliability and maintainability that will extend the life and increase the operational readiness of the Cobra fleet.

Forty-six AH-1S, of a planned total of 73, have been ordered by the Japan Ground Self-Defence Force for delivery between 1985 and 1989. These are assembled under licence in Japan, with Fuji as prime contractor and sub-licence from Mitsui. Other deliveries of the AH-1S have included 24 for Jordan and 20 for Pakistan. The supply of ten to Israel, four for Royal Thai Army Aviation, and 42 for the South Korean government has been authorised. Overseas operators of Bell AH-1s have shown interest in retrofitting the C-Nite sighting system.

The major differences between the modernised versions and earlier single-engined HueyCobras may be summarised as follows:

TYPE: Anti-armour attack helicopter.

ROTOR SYSTEM AND DRIVE: Upgraded gearbox and transmission, the latter rated at 962 kW (1,290 shp) for take-off, 845 kW (1,134 shp) continuous. From 67th AH-1P onward, main rotor blades of composite construction are fitted, developed by Kaman Aerospace Corporation and equipped with tungsten carbide bearing sleeves. The outer 15 per cent of these blades, which are tolerant of damage by weapons of up to 23 mm calibre, is tapered in both chord and thickness.

FUSELAGE: Tailboom strengthened to increase survivability against weapons of up to 23 mm calibre. Entire airframe has an infra-red-suppressant paint finish.

POWER PLANT: One 1,342 kW (1,800 shp) Textron Lycoming T53-L-703 turboshaft. Closed circuit refuelling on AH-1F. Fuel capacity 980 litres (259 US gallons; 216 Imp gallons).

ACCOMMODATION: Flat-plate canopy has seven planes of viewing surfaces, designed to minimise glint and reduce possibility of visual detection during nap-of-the-earth (NOE) flying; it also provides increased headroom for pilot. Improved instrument layout and lighting, compatible with use of night vision goggles. Improved, independently operating window/door ballistic jettison system to facilitate crew escape in emergency.

SYSTEMS: 10kVA 400Hz AC alternator with emergency bus added to electrical system. Hydraulic system pressure 103.5 bars (1,500 lb/sq in), maximum flow rate 22.7 litres (6 US gallons; 5 Imp gallons)/min. Open reservoir. Battery driven Abex standby pump, for use in event of main hydraulic system failure, can be used for collective

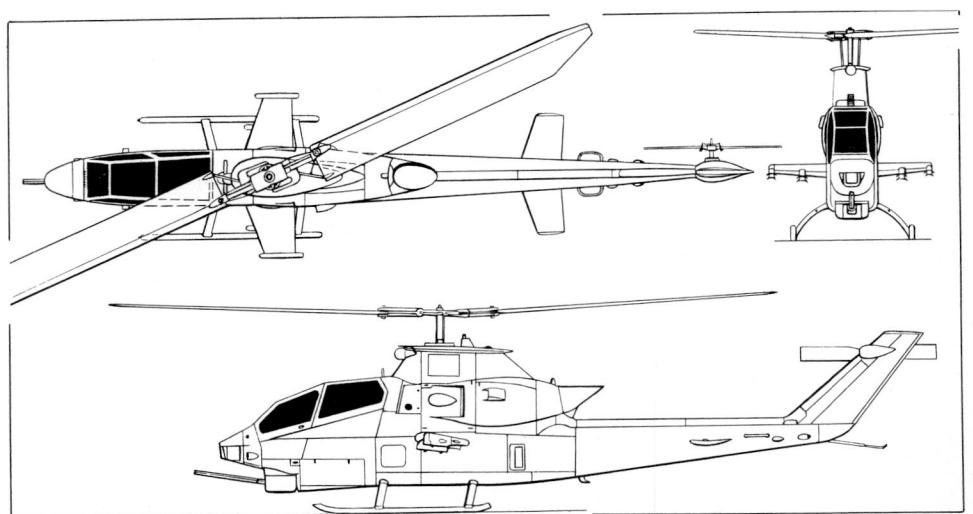

Bell AH-1S HueyCobra (Textron Lycoming T53-L-703 turboshaft) *(Pilot Press)*

pitch control and for boresighting turret and TOW missile system. Improved environmental control and fire detection systems.

AVIONICS AND EQUIPMENT: Standard lightweight avionics equipment (SLAE) in AH-1S includes AN/ARC-114 FM, AN/ARC-164 UHF/AM voice com, and E-Systems (Memcor Division) AN/ARC-115 VHF/AM voice com (compatible with KY-58 single-channel secure voice system). Other avionics include AN/ASN-128 Doppler nav system in AH-1F; APR-39 radar warning receiver; ALQ-144 infra-red jammer; HSI; VSI; radar altimeter; push/pull anti-torque controls for tail rotor; co-pilot's standby magnetic compass. C-Flex upgrade includes introduction of Magnavox AN/ARC-164(V) UHF/AM, Collins AN/ARC-186 VHF/AM-FM, ITT AN/ARC-201 (SINCGARS) VHF/FM, and LaBarge AN/ARN-89B D/F.

ARMAMENT AND OPERATIONAL EQUIPMENT: M65 system with eight Hughes TOW missiles, disposed as two two-round clusters on each of the outboard underwing stations. The inboard wing stations remain available for other stores. Beginning with the first AH-1E, the M28 (7.62/40 mm) turret in earlier HueyCobras was replaced by a new electrically powered General Electric universal turret, designed to accommodate either a 20 mm or a 30 mm weapon and to improve standoff capability. The 20 mm M197 three-barrel cannon (with 750 rds) is mounted in this turret. Rate of fire is 730 rds/min. Turret position is controlled by the pilot or co-pilot/gunner through helmet sights, or by the co-pilot using the M65 TOW missile system's telescopic sight unit. Field of fire is up to 110° to each side of aircraft, 20.5° upward and 50° downward. Also from the first AH-1E, the helicopter is equipped with a Baldwin Electronics M138 wing stores management subsystem, providing the means to select and fire, singly or in groups, any one of five types of external 2.75 in rocket store. These are mounted in launchers each containing from 7 to 19 tubes, and are additional to the TOW missile capability.

In addition to these installations the first AH-1F introduced a fire control subsystem which includes a Kaiser head-up display for the pilot, Teledyne Systems digital fire control computer for the turreted weapon and underwing rockets, omnidirectional airspeed system to improve cannon and rocket accuracy, Hughes laser rangefinder (accurate over 10,000 m; 32,800 ft), and a Rockwell AN/AAS-32 automatic airborne laser tracker. Other operational equipment includes a Hughes LAAT stabilised sight (see 1987-88 *Jane's*), a GEC Avionics M-143 air data subsystem, Bendix AN/APX-100 solid-state IFF transponder, Sanders AN/ALQ-144 infra-red jammer (above engine), suppressor for infra-red signature from engine hot metal and exhaust plume, and AN/APR-39 radar warning receiver.

DIMENSIONS, EXTERNAL:

Main rotor diameter	13.41 m (44 ft 0 in)
Main rotor blade chord (from 67th AH-1P onward)	
	0.76 m (2 ft 6 in)
Tail rotor diameter	2.59 m (8 ft 6 in)
Tail rotor blade chord	0.305 m (1 ft 0 in)
Wing span	3.28 m (10 ft 9 in)
Length overall, rotors turning	16.18 m (53 ft 1 in)
Width of fuselage	0.99 m (3 ft 3 in)
Height to top of rotor head	4.09 m (13 ft 5 in)
Width over TOW pods	3.56 m (11 ft 8 in)
Elevator span	2.11 m (6 ft 11 in)
Width over skids	2.13 m (7 ft 0 in)

AREAS:

Main rotor disc	141.26 m² (1,520.23 sq ft)
Tail rotor disc	5.27 m² (56.75 sq ft)

WEIGHTS (AH-1S):

Operating weight empty	2,993 kg (6,598 lb)
Mission weight	4,524 kg (9,975 lb)
Max T-O and landing weight	4,535 kg (10,000 lb)

PERFORMANCE (AH-1S at max T-O weight, ISA):

Never-exceed speed (TOW configuration)	
	170 knots (315 km/h; 195 mph)
Max level speed (TOW configuration)	
	123 knots (227 km/h; 141 mph)
Max rate of climb at S/L, normal rated power	
	494 m (1,620 ft)/min
Service ceiling, normal rated power	3,720 m (12,200 ft)
Hovering ceiling IGE	3,720 m (12,200 ft)
Range at S/L with max fuel, 8% reserves	
	274 nm (507 km; 315 miles)

BELL MODELS 212 and 412

The production lines for these two helicopters are being transferred to Bell's Canadian facility (in mid-1988 and January 1989 respectively), and their descriptions can therefore now be found in the Canadian section.

BELL MODEL 214ST SUPERTRANSPORT

The Model 214ST was developed originally for major production and service in Iran. It was expected to serve primarily as a military transport helicopter; but Bell has since developed the 214ST also as a commercial transport with multi-mission capability. Originally, the suffix ST indicated Stretched Twin: it now indicates SuperTransport.

The prototype 214ST flew for the first time in February 1977, and construction of three pre-production examples

Bell AH-1F HueyCobra of the US Army

began in 1978. The decision to manufacture an initial series of 100 production 214STs was announced in November 1979. FAA and CAA certification for two-pilot IFR operation was obtained in 1982, and deliveries started soon afterwards. The Model 214ST has been certificated under transport category airworthiness requirements in Canada, Japan, the United Kingdom and United States. The CAA has approved it for flight into icing conditions with added icing kit.

Initial contracts included three for British Caledonian Helicopters for offshore support in the North Sea. To enhance the helicopter's value for such missions, on which it is now operated worldwide, the FAA approved a new configuration with seats for a crew of two and 18 (instead of the original 16) passengers in Spring 1982. Other orders include four for the People's Republic of China, and one for the North Slope Borough Search and Rescue team based at Barrow, Alaska, equipped for emergency medical service and SAR duties.

Military transport models have been sold to Brunei (one), Iraq (20), Peru (11), Thailand (nine) and Venezuela (four).

By early 1988 a total of 78 214STs had been delivered.

TYPE: Twin-turboshaft commercial transport helicopter.

ROTOR SYSTEM: Two-blade advanced technology main rotor. Each blade has a unidirectionally laid glassfibre spar, with a ±45°-wound torque casing of glassfibre cloth. The trailing-edge is also of unidirectional glassfibre, and the space between spar and trailing-edge is filled by a Nomex honeycomb core. The entire blade is then bonded together by glassfibre wrapping, with the leading-edge protected by a titanium abrasion strip and the tip by a replaceable stainless steel cap. Two-blade tail rotor; interchangeable blades, each with a stainless steel leading-edge spar and covering, aluminium honeycomb core and glassfibre trailing-edge strip. Main rotor head incorporates elastomeric bearings. Second-generation Noda-Matic nodal suspension system. Nodal beam requires no lubrication. Main rotor brake standard.

ROTOR DRIVE: Main transmission has a maximum rating of 1,752 kW (2,350 shp), maximum continuous rating of 1,454 kW (1,950 shp), and single-engine rating of 1,286 kW (1,725 shp). Combining, intermediate and tail rotor gearboxes, each with one-hour run-dry capability.

FUSELAGE: Conventional all-metal semi-monocoque structure, incorporating rollover protection ring.

Bell Model 214ST SuperTransport helicopter in offshore service

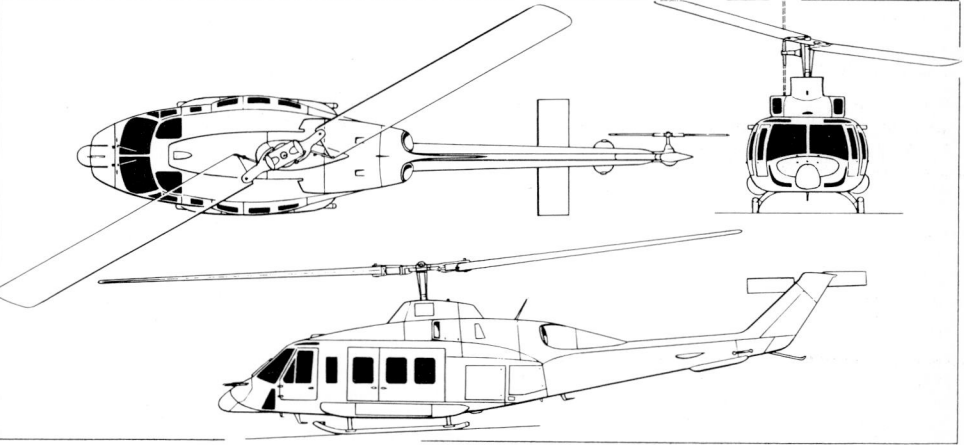

Bell Model 214ST SuperTransport (two General Electric CT7-2A turboshafts) *(Pilot Press)*

TAIL SURFACE: Electronically controlled elevator, which minimises trim changes with alterations of power and CG, and improves longitudinal stability.

LANDING GEAR: Energy absorbing non-retractable tubular skid type or tricycle type wheeled landing gear standard.

POWER PLANT: Two 1,212 kW (1,625 shp) General Electric CT7-2A turboshafts, connected to a combining gearbox. In the event of an engine failure, the remaining engine is capable of developing 1,286 kW (1,725 shp) to provide continued flight capability. Standard fuel capacity 1,647 litres (435 US gallons; 362 Imp gallons), contained in seven interconnected rupture resistant cells, arranged to provide two independent fuel systems as required by FAR Pt 29. Single-point refuelling. Auxiliary fuel system optional, consisting of two tanks in rear of cabin, each of 329 litres (87 US gallons; 72 Imp gallons) capacity; 95 litre (25 US gallon; 21 Imp gallon) underseat auxiliary fuel tanks also available. Engine anti-icing and inlet screens standard.

ACCOMMODATION: Standard seating for pilot, co-pilot and up to 18 passengers. Dual controls standard. Crew seats adjustable. Passenger seats in three rows across cabin plus a two-place bench seat on each side of rotor mast. Standard configuration offers utility or deluxe interiors with contemporary or energy attenuating seats. Jettisonable crew door each side. Large cabin door on each side for passengers or easy loading of cargo. Glass windscreens, with standard anti-icing system. Two emergency exits on each side. Baggage space aft of cabin, capacity 1.84 m³ (65 cu ft). Passenger seating removable to provide 9.23 m³ (326 cu ft) of cargo capacity. Cabin heated and ventilated.

SYSTEMS: Dual engine driven hydraulic pumps for fully redundant hydraulic power for flight control system; pressure 207 bars (3,000 lb/sq in), maximum flow rate 25.4 litres (6.7 US gallons; 5.6 Imp gallons)/min for primary control system; 19 litres (5 US gallons; 4.2 Imp gallons)/min for utility system. Closed bootstrap pressurised reservoirs. Third system operates oil cooler blower for transmission and combiner gearbox. Redundant electrical system with dual engine driven generators. Stability and control augmentation system (SCAS). Main rotor blade in-flight tracking system. Attitude/altitude retention system (AARS). Computer controlled fly by wire automatic elevator trim system.

AVIONICS AND EQUIPMENT: Standard avionics include dual com, dual nav, R/Nav, ADF, transponder, DME, air data computer, and standby attitude indicator to provide IFR capability. Avionics options include radar, nav coupling, and VLF nav system. Optional equipment includes anti-icing kit, emergency flotation gear, external cargo suspension system, internal rescue hoist, and two pneumatically ejected 10- or 12-person liferafts inside engine cowl fairing forward of rotor mast.

DIMENSIONS, EXTERNAL:

Main rotor diameter	15.85 m (52 ft 0 in)
Tail rotor diameter	2.95 m (9 ft 8 in)
Main rotor blade chord	0.84 m (2 ft 9 in)
Tail rotor blade chord	0.36 m (1 ft 2 in)
Length: overall, rotors turning	18.95 m (62 ft 2¼ in)
fuselage	15.02 m (49 ft 3½ in)
Height overall	4.84 m (15 ft 10½ in)
Skid track	2.64 m (8 ft 8 in)
Wheel track	2.83 m (9 ft 3½ in)

DIMENSIONS, INTERNAL:

Cabin: Length, instrument panel to centre rear bulkhead	3.42 m (11 ft 2¾ in)
Max length	4.13 m (13 ft 6¾ in)
Max width	2.41 m (7 ft 11 in)
Volume	8.95 m³ (316 cu ft)

AREAS:

Main rotor disc	197.30 m² (2,123.7 sq ft)
Tail rotor disc	6.82 m² (73.39 sq ft)

WEIGHT:

Max T-O weight: internal or external load	7,938 kg (17,500 lb)

PERFORMANCE (at max T-O weight except where indicated):

Normal cruising speed at S/L, at average cruise weight	140 knots (259 km/h; 161 mph)
Max cruising speed at 1,220 m (4,000 ft)	138 knots (256 km/h; 159 mph)
Max rate of climb at S/L, ISA	543 m (1,780 ft)/min
Service ceiling, one engine out, ISA	1,460 m (4,800 ft)
Hovering ceiling IGE	1,950 m (6,400 ft)
Range at 1,220 m (4,000 ft) with max standard fuel, no reserves	463 nm (858 km; 533 miles)
Range, ISA, VFR, standard fuel, no reserves	439 nm (813 km; 505 miles)
Ferry range with auxiliary fuel, pilot only, no payload, no reserves	over 550 nm (1,019 km; 633 miles)

BELL MODEL 222

The first of five prototypes of the Model 222, described as the first commercial light twin-engined helicopter to be built in the USA, flew for the first time on 13 August 1976. FAA certification for a Model 222 in pre-production configuration was received on 16 August 1979. The production 222 received approval for VFR operation on 20 December, and the first delivery, to Petroleum Helicopters Inc, was made on 16 January 1980. FAA certification

Bell Model 222UT Utility Twin helicopter

for single-pilot IFR operations in Category I weather conditions was granted on 15 May 1980. A Model 222 delivered to Omniflight Helicopters on 18 January 1981 was the 25,000th Bell helicopter built. Another is serving as a flying testbed for Bell's Model 680 rotor system (described separately).

Current production aircraft are available in the following configurations:

Basic 222B. Basic model, as described. On 29 July 1982 the 222B became the first transport category helicopter to be certificated by the FAA for single-pilot IFR flight without stability augmentation.

222B Executive. Fully equipped for both single and dual pilot IFR flight. Sperry coupled automatic flight control system to provide stability augmentation and automatic hold for attitude, altitude, heading and airspeed, plus VOR/LOC course and glideslope hold during approach. Collins ProLine avionics include dual VHF com, dual VOR nav with glideslope, ADF, marker beacon receiver, transponder, DME and area navigation. Luxury accommodation for five or six passengers, with automatic temperature control, fluorescent and reading lights, window curtains and ceiling speakers. Optional stereo system and refreshment cabinet.

222UT (Utility Twin). Utility version of the Model 222, incorporating the improvements and power plant detailed for the Model 222B. Retractable tricycle landing gear replaced by tubular skid gear with lock-on ground handling wheels. Fuselage mounted flotation system optional. Standard seating for a pilot and six or seven passengers. Optional layout for a pilot and eight passengers. VFR and single-pilot IFR certification received in Spring 1983; customer deliveries began in September 1983. Customers include Lloyd Helicopters of Australia, which has six intended primarily for offshore oil support, the New York City Police Department, and the Port Authority of New York and New Jersey. This model is used widely for air ambulance duties.

By January 1988 a total of 167 Model 222s had been delivered.

The following details refer to the basic Model 222B, except where indicated:

TYPE: Twin-turbine light commercial helicopter.

ROTOR SYSTEM: Two-blade main rotor. Blade section Wortmann 090. Thickness/chord ratio 8%. Each blade comprises a stainless steel spar with bonded glassfibre safety straps to retard crack propagation and offer secondary load path; replaceable stainless steel leading-edge; and afterbody of Nomex honeycomb covered with glassfibre skin. Each blade is attached to the rotor head by two chordwise bolts. Small trim tab on each blade. Completely dry titanium main rotor hub has conical elastomeric bearings. Two-blade tail rotor of stainless

steel construction, with preconing, underslung feathering axis and skewed flapping axis. Rotor blades do not fold. A rotor brake is standard.

ROTOR DRIVE: Rotors shaft driven through gearbox with two spiral bevel reductions and one planetary reduction. Transmission rating (two engines) 690 kW (925 shp). Single-engine rating 548 kW (735 shp). Main rotor/engine rpm ratio 1:27.4; tail rotor/engine rpm ratio 1:5.08.

SPONSONS: Short span cantilever sponson set low on each side of fuselage, serving as main landing gear housings, fuel tanks and work platforms. Section NACA 0035. Dihedral 3° 12′. Incidence 5°. Sweepback at quarter-chord 3° 30′. All-metal structure of light alloy sheet and honeycomb. No movable surfaces.

FUSELAGE: Semi-monocoque structure of light alloy, with limited use of light alloy honeycomb panels. Fail-safe structure in critical areas. One-piece nosecone tilts forward and down for access to avionics and equipment bay.

TAIL UNIT: Cantilever structure of light alloy. Fixed vertical fin in sweptback upper and lower sections. Tailplane, with slotted leading-edge and endplate fins, mounted midway along rear fuselage. Small skid below ventral fin for protection in tail-down landing.

LANDING GEAR: Hydraulically retractable tricycle type. All units retract forward, mainwheels into sponsons. Free-fall extension in emergency. Oleo-pneumatic shock absorbers, with scissored yoke. Self-centring nosewheel, swivelling through 360°. Single wheel and tyre on each unit. Mainwheel tyres size 6.00-6, pressure 5.18 bars (75 lb/sq in). Nosewheel tyre size 5.00-5, pressure 4.14 bars (60 lb/sq in). Hydraulic disc brakes. New type water-activated emergency 'pop-out' floats optional. Model 222UT has skid type landing gear and lock-on ground handling wheels, with fuselage mounted flotation system optional.

POWER PLANT: Two Textron Lycoming LTS 101-750C-1 turboshafts, each rated at 510 kW (684 shp) for take-off, mounted in a streamline housing above the cabin and aft of the rotor pylon. Bell focused pylon with nodalisation. Fuel contained in five crash resistant internal bladders, in fuselage and sponsons, with total capacity of 710 litres (187.5 US gallons; 156.1 Imp gallons) in Model 222B. Model 222UT has max fuel capacity of 931 litres (246 US gallons; 204.8 Imp gallons). Rear seat fuel tank, capacity 246 litres (65 US gallons; 54.1 Imp gallons), and parcel shelf fuel tank, capacity 181 litres (48 US gallons; 40 Imp gallons), optional on both models. Single-point refuelling on starboard side of fuselage. Oil capacity 6.5 litres (1.7 US gallons; 1.43 Imp gallons) per engine.

ACCOMMODATION: Pilot and seven passengers in standard 2-3-3 layout; alternatively pilot, co-pilot and six passengers. Two additional passengers can be accommodated in

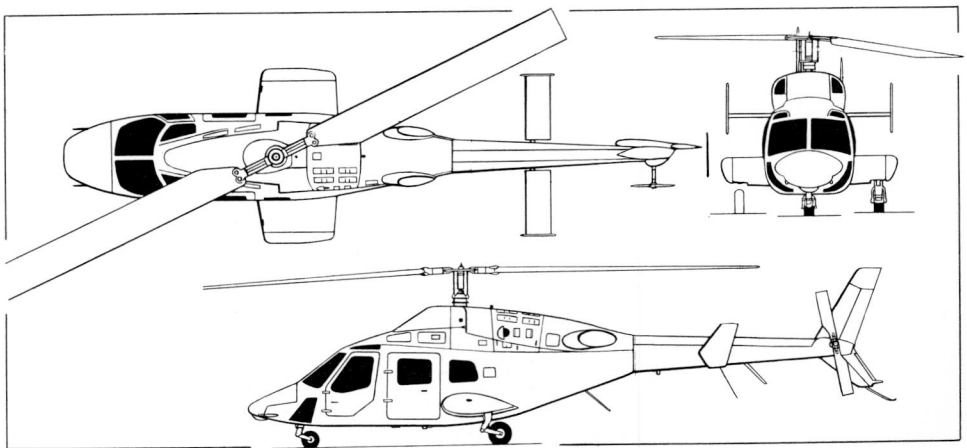

Bell Model 222B twin-turbine light commercial helicopter (*Pilot Press*)

a high-density 2-2-3-3 arrangement. Energy attenuating seats, all with shoulder harness in Model 222B. Crew door at forward end of cabin on each side; cabin door on each side immediately forward of wing. Space for 1.05 m³ (37 cu ft) of baggage aft of cabin, with external door on starboard side. Ventilation standard; air-conditioning and heating optional.

SYSTEMS: Dual hydraulic systems, pressure 103.5 bars (1,500 lb/sq in). Maximum flow rate 15.1 litres (4 US gallons; 3.3 Imp gallons)/min. Open reservoir. Electrical system of Model 222B supplied by dual 150A DC generators, dual 250VA AC inverters, and 17Ah nickel-cadmium storage battery. Dual inverters deleted in Model 222UT, and 17Ah battery replaced by one of 34Ah capacity.

AVIONICS AND EQUIPMENT: Standard avionics in 222B comprise VHF transceiver and intercom system. Collins Pro Line and King Gold Crown Series III avionics optional. Sperry SPZ-7000 digital automatic flight control system approved for single-pilot IFR operation in 222UT. Other avionics, blind-flying instrumentation and equipment, including Sperry Helipilot system, Bendix RDR-1400 weather radar and 1,270 kg (2,800 lb) capacity cargo hook kit, to customer's requirements.

DIMENSIONS, EXTERNAL:

Main rotor diameter	12.80 m (42 ft 0 in)
Tail rotor diameter	2.10 m (6 ft 10½ in)
Main rotor blade chord	0.66 m (2 ft 2 in)
Tail rotor blade chord	0.254 m (10 in)
Sponson chord: at root	1.55 m (5 ft 1 in)
at tip	1.49 m (4 ft 10¾ in)
Length: overall, rotors turning	15.36 m (50 ft 4¾ in)
fuselage	12.85 m (42 ft 2 in)
Width overall	3.46 m (11 ft 4 in)
Height overall	3.51 m (11 ft 6 in)
Wheel track: 222B	2.77 m (9 ft 1 in)
Wheelbase: 222B	3.70 m (12 ft 1¾ in)
Passenger doors (each): Height	1.30 m (4 ft 3 in)
Width	0.99 m (3 ft 3 in)
Height to sill	0.46 m (1 ft 6 in)
Baggage door (stbd, rear): Height	0.62 m (2 ft 0½ in)
Width	0.89 m (2 ft 11 in)
Height to sill	1.14 m (3 ft 9 in)

DIMENSIONS, INTERNAL:

Cabin (passenger area): Length	2.01 m (6 ft 7 in)
Max width	1.41 m (4 ft 7½ in)
Max height	1.30 m (4 ft 3 in)
Volume, incl crew area	5.52 m³ (195 cu ft)
Baggage hold	1.05 m³ (37 cu ft)
Hatbox (aft of cabin seats)	0.14 m³ (5 cu ft)

AREAS:

Main rotor blades (each)	4.23 m² (45.50 sq ft)
Tail rotor blades (each)	0.23 m² (2.45 sq ft)
Main rotor disc	128.7 m² (1,385.4 sq ft)
Tail rotor disc	3.46 m² (37.2 sq ft)
Vertical tail surfaces (total)	1.44 m² (15.5 sq ft)
Horizontal tail surfaces (total)	1.37 m² (14.8 sq ft)

WEIGHTS AND LOADING (A: 222B; B: 222UT):

Weight empty: A	2,223 kg (4,900 lb)
B	2,210 kg (4,874 lb)
Max T-O and landing weight:	
internal payload	3,742 kg (8,250 lb)
external payload	1,270 kg (2,800 lb)
Max disc loading:	
internal payload	29.1 kg/m² (5.95 lb/sq ft)

PERFORMANCE (at max T-O weight, ISA. A: 222B; B: 222UT):

Never-exceed speed:	
at S/L: A, B	150 knots (278 km/h; 172 mph)
at 1,220 m (4,000 ft):	
A, B	156 knots (289 km/h; 179 mph)
Econ cruising speed, S/L to 1,220 m (4,000 ft):	
A	140 knots (259 km/h; 161 mph)
B	133 knots (246 km/h; 153 mph)
Max rate of climb at S/L: A, B	512 m (1,680 ft)/min
Service ceiling: A, B	4,815 m (15,800 ft)
Service ceiling, one engine out:	
A, B	2,285 m (7,500 ft)
Hovering ceiling: IGE: A, B	2,165 m (7,100 ft)
OGE: A, B	1,950 m (6,400 ft)

Bell XV-15 tilt-rotor research aircraft making its first flight with advanced technology rotor blades in November 1987

Range with max fuel at 1,220 m (4,000 ft), 20 min		
reserves: A	287 nm (532 km; 330 miles)	
B	373 nm (691 km; 429 miles)	
Range with max fuel at S/L, 20 min reserves:		
A	255 nm (472 km; 294 miles)	
B	330 nm (610 km; 380 miles)	

BELL MODEL D292 (ACAP)

Under the US Army's Advanced Composite Airframe Program (ACAP), Bell was one of two manufacturers awarded a contract to design and develop a prototype advanced composite-airframe helicopter. Phase I engineering design and design support testing was completed by the end of 1982. Phase II, the construction and testing of three airframes, began in October 1982. The first was a tool-proofing article (TPA) used for repairability demonstrations and ballistics testing. The second became the D292 flight test vehicle (FTV) after systems installation and made its initial hover flight on 30 August 1985. It was used for shake testing, controls proof loading and EMC testing, in addition to 15 hours of ground running and 50 hours of flight testing which was completed in October 1985.

A five-phase militarisation test and evaluation programme (MT & E) began in 1985 and was due to be completed in 1988, following evaluation of landing gear crashworthiness, lightning protection system, internal acoustics, additional repairability demonstrations, and static test article (STA) drop tests at rates of impact up to 15.2 m (50 ft)/s (12.8 m; 42 ft/s vertical and 2.5 m; 27 ft/s horizontal).

The purpose of the ACAP programme was to achieve the Army's goal of reducing weight and cost, and improving military helicopter characteristics, by demonstrating the application of advanced composite materials. Goals included a weight reduction of 22 per cent in airframe structure, a 17 per cent saving in cost, survivability in a vertical crash, and reduced radar signature. Bell and Sikorsky each also designed a duplicate aircraft in current conventional metal construction for baseline comparison against the composite-construction aircraft.

A description of the Model D292's structure may be found in the 1987-88 edition of *Jane's*.

BELL MODEL 301
US Army designation: XV-15

Bell Helicopter has been working on tilt-rotor technology since the late 1940s, proving the concept feasible with its XV-3 prototype, described in the 1962-63 *Jane's*. Since that time development of tilt-rotor systems has progressed

steadily, leading initially to the Model 301 which Bell proposed to meet a 1973 NASA/US Army requirement. The two research aircraft have the Army designation XV-15; US Navy funding was provided in 1979 and 1980. First flights were made on 3 May 1977 and 23 April 1979; first complete in-flight transition to aeroplane mode was made by the second aircraft (N703NA) on 24 July 1979. The two XV-15s are now being used in a research programme to explore the limits of the operational flight envelope and assess its application to military and civil transport needs.

Details of the early stages of this programme can be found in the 1980-81 and previous editions of *Jane's*. Test achievements by the end of 1982 were summarised in the 1984-85 edition, and 1983-84 progress in the 1985-86 *Jane's*. New advanced technology rotor blades, built of carbonfibre, glassfibre and Nomex, and developed by Boeing Helicopters as part of the V-22 Osprey programme, were first flown on the second XV-15 on 13 November 1987. Some 30 hours of flight testing were planned for 1988.

The XV-15 structure, tilt-rotor and control systems were described in detail in the 1983-84 *Jane's*. An abbreviated description follows:

TYPE: Tilt-rotor research aircraft.

ROTOR SYSTEM: Two three-blade rotors, spring restrained, stiff in plane and gimballed, with composite blades of high-twist semi-tapered design attached to titanium head by tension/torsion straps and roller pitch bearings. Elastomeric flapping restraints to increase helicopter mode control power and damping. Blades do not fold. No rotor brake.

ROTOR DRIVE: Each rotor is driven by individual engine via reduction gear, engine coupling, rotor planetary gear and shaft centrebox. Interconnected driveshafts and redundant tilting mechanisms permit single-engine operation and fail-operative tilt capability.

POWER PLANT: Two 1,156 kW (1,550 shp) Textron Lycoming LTC1K-4K turboshafts, each with a two minute contingency rating of 1,343 kW (1,800 shp), wingtip mounted with tilt mechanism operated by SPECO interconnected double ballscrew actuators. Two fuel tanks in each wing, total capacity 867 litres (229 US gallons; 190.7 Imp gallons).

ACCOMMODATION: Pilot and co-pilot on Rockwell-Columbus LW-3B ejection seats, side by side on flight deck, with access to cabin. Currently in austere test configuration for research equipment; cabin could accommodate nine personnel.

DIMENSIONS, EXTERNAL:

Rotor diameter (each)	7.62 m (25 ft 0 in)
Wing span over engine nacelles	10.72 m (35 ft 2 in)
Width overall, rotors turning	17.42 m (57 ft 2 in)
Length: fuselage	12.50 m (41 ft 0 in)
overall	12.83 m (42 ft 1 in)
Height: over tail fins	3.86 m (12 ft 8 in)
overall, nacelles vertical	4.67 m (15 ft 4 in)
Tail unit span (incl fins)	3.91 m (12 ft 10 in)
Wheel track, c/l of shock absorbers	2.64 m (8 ft 8 in)
Wheelbase	4.80 m (15 ft 9 in)

DIMENSIONS, INTERNAL:

Cabin (excl flight deck): Length	4.53 m (14 ft 10½ in)
Max width	1.52 m (5 ft 0 in)
Max height	1.52 m (5 ft 0 in)
Floor area	5.40 m² (58.1 sq ft)
Volume	8.50 m³ (300 cu ft)

AREAS:

Rotor discs (each)	45.60 m² (490.9 sq ft)
Wings, gross	15.70 m² (169.0 sq ft)

WEIGHTS AND LOADING:

Weight empty	4,341 kg (9,570 lb)
Max payload (STOL)	1,542 kg (3,400 lb)
Max fuel weight	676 kg (1,490 lb)
Design T-O weight (VTO)	5,897 kg (13,000 lb)

Bell Model D292 ACAP prototype

Max T-O weight (STO)	6,804 kg (15,000 lb)
Max disc loading	74.2 kg/m² (15.2 lb/sq ft)

PERFORMANCE (at design T-O weight):

Never-exceed speed	364 knots (674 km/h; 419 mph)
Max level speed at 5,180 m (17,000 ft)	
	332 knots (615 km/h; 382 mph)
Max cruising speed at 4,970 m (16,300 ft)	
	303 knots (561 km/h; 349 mph)
Econ cruising speed at 6,100 m (20,000 ft)	
	200 knots (371 km/h; 230 mph)
Max rate of climb at S/L	960 m (3,150 ft)/min
Service ceiling	8,840 m (29,000 ft)
Service ceiling, one engine out	4,570 m (15,000 ft)
Hovering ceiling: IGE	3,200 m (10,500 ft)
OGE	2,635 m (8,650 ft)
Range with max fuel	445 nm (824 km; 512 miles)

BELL/BOEING V-22 OSPREY

This joint programme is described under a separate Bell/Boeing main heading.

BELL MODEL 680 ROTOR

On 27 May 1982 Bell began test flying its new Model 680 composite bearingless rotor system, which promises significant improvements in performance, noise levels and ride quality. By May 1985, after more than 375 hours of flight testing in four-blade form on a Model 222, indications were that all basic goals had been achieved. The Model 680 system, intended for application to future rather than present Bell designs, consists of a one-piece glassfibre yoke with inboard flapping flexures and outboard feathering elements. Elastomeric shear pads for lead-lag damping and elastomeric shear restraints to control feathering motion are incorporated between the yoke and the cuff assemblies. All major components are of composite construction, with at least 50 per cent fewer parts and a weight reduction of 15 per cent. (See entry for Bell AH-1W SuperCobra.)

On 10 November 1987 the Bell 222 Model 680 test vehicle made its first flight with adaptive engine control, a digital control system developed jointly by Bell and Lucas Aerospace Limited which is intended to improve aircraft performance by providing the engine control with the ability to 'adapt' its characteristics in flight.

BELL ARTI and LHX

In 1982 the US Army invited manufacturers to submit design concepts for its Light Helicopter Experimental (LHX) programme, now representing a requirement for some 2,100 helicopters in three variants: armed reconnaissance, light attack and air to air combat, all using the same dynamic systems. Bell began a contracted study which included derivative variants of the UH-1 and AH-1, as well as new designs for helicopters and high-performance (tilt-rotor) craft. The US Army subsequently announced that a conventional helicopter was wanted for the LHX requirement. Accordingly, Bell and its partner, McDonnell Douglas Helicopter Company, are concentrating on a single main rotor design incorporating an advanced bearingless main rotor system, composite materials adapted from the ACAP programme, a ring-fin tail rotor, and twin 895 kW (1,200 shp) T800 turboshafts. In accordance with US Army specifications it will be designed to fire Hellfire and Stinger missiles and other advanced weapons.

A major supporting contract for the LHX was the Advanced Rotorcraft Technology Integration (ARTI) effort for which Bell, in partnership with Sperry Flight Systems, Honeywell Inc and Texas Instruments, conducted 'hands-off' flight tests of the digital fly by wire AFCS using the experimental YAH-1S four-blade Model 249 HueyCobra as the testbed aircraft. The ARTI programme has been completed.

Bell artist's impression of possible LHX contender

BELL/BOEING
BELL HELICOPTER TEXTRON and BOEING HELICOPTERS
PROGRAMME MANAGER: Brig Gen Harry W. Blot, USMC

BELL/BOEING V-22 OSPREY

Bell Helicopter Textron and Boeing Helicopters are teamed in a joint programme to meet the US Defense Department's Joint Services Advanced Vertical Lift Aircraft (formerly JVX) requirement. This was initiated as an Army-led programme in FY 1982, but was transferred in January 1983 to the US Navy as executive service, the Army subsequently withdrawing from the programme. The selected aircraft, based on the technology of Bell's Model 301/XV-15 tilt-rotor research aircraft, was named V-22 Osprey in January 1985. Bell is responsible for the wings, nacelles, rotor and transmission systems, and engine integration; Boeing's contribution is the fuselage, tail unit, landing gear, fairings, and avionics integration.

A 24-month preliminary design contract was awarded by Naval Air Systems Command on 26 April 1983, and in January 1984 Bell began a simulated V-22 flight test programme using data from wind tunnel tests and analyses. Formal evaluation by military pilots, using NASA/Ames simulation, began in the following March. Boeing built a two-thirds scale rotor/wing model to prove hover performance predictions, and a fuselage mockup, and testing of critical structural components was co-ordinated by both partners.

A seven-year FSED phase started in FY 1986 with the award on 2 May of a first instalment contract covering the manufacture of six flying prototypes (Nos. 1, 3 and 6 by Bell, Nos. 2, 4 and 5 by Boeing), plus three non-flying airframes for static, ground and fatigue testing. Rollout of the first flying prototype (BuAer number 163911) took place at Bell's Flight Research Center at Arlington, Texas, on 23 May 1988, and it was scheduled to make its first flight from this location in late 1988.

The Osprey is conceived as a joint service multi-mission aircraft, production deliveries of which are planned to begin in late 1991/early 1992 to the US Marine Corps, 1993 to the US Air Force, and 1995 to the US Navy. Production is planned in the following versions:

MV-22A. First and major production variant, for US Marine Corps, which has a requirement for 552 as amphibious troop assault and support transports to replace CH-46 Sea Knight and CH-53 Sea Stallion helicopters. Flight crew of three. Required to carry 24 combat-equipped Marines or equivalent cargo at a speed of 250 knots (463 km/h; 288 mph) over an operational radius of 200 nm (370 km; 230 miles), with the ability to hover midway through the mission at 915 m (3,000 ft) at an ambient air temperature of 33°C (91.4°F).

HV-22A. Combat search and rescue, special warfare and fleet logistics support variant for US Navy (requirement for 50), to replace HH-3 helicopters. Normal crew of five. In CSAR roles the Osprey would be required to operate at 250 knots (463 km/h; 288 mph) over a 460 nm (852 km; 530 mile) radius and hover mid-mission for 15 min at 915 m (3,000 ft) OGE, with accommodation for four survivors.

CV-22A. Long-range special operations variant for US Air Force, which has a requirement for 55 (originally 80)

Two views of the first prototype of the Bell/Boeing V-22 Osprey *(Jay Miller/Aerofax)*

such aircraft, each able to carry 12 special forces troops or up to 1,306 kg (2,880 lb) of internal cargo over a 520 nm (964 km; 599 mile) mission radius at 250 knots (463 km/h; 288 mph), with capability to hover OGE at 1,220 m (4,000 ft) at 35°C (95°F).

The following variant is also under consideration:

SV-22A. The US Navy has expressed an interest in up to 300 V-22s for anti-submarine warfare duties, to replace the fixed-wing S-3 Viking. Features would include AN/APS-137 radar, dipping sonar, sonobuoy racks, external fuel tanks, FLIR, and anti-shipping and self-defence missiles. Development go-ahead has been deferred to allow USN to study sensor requirements and to examine alternative option of re-opening the S-3 production line.

The US Army, although not involved in the development phase, originally had plans to procure 231 aircraft in the Marine Corps configuration for multi-mission transport duties, but has since withdrawn its requirement, although maintaining a presence in the V-22 programme office.

Additional requirements specified by one or more of the services for the V-22 include an unrefuelled ferry range of 2,100 nm (3,892 km; 2,418 miles) for self-deployability; in-flight refuelling capability; ability to carry outsize external loads of up to 4,536 kg (10,000 lb); all-weather low-altitude capability; self-protection; and low maintenance. To meet the Navy/Marine Corps requirement for operation from US Navy amphibious assault ships, the wing and rotor system must 'fold' in 90 seconds.

Procurement plans currently anticipate a production go-ahead in FY 1989, with funding of 12 pre-production aircraft in FY 1990 and the first 45 full production Ospreys in FY 1991, followed by a further 61 in FY 1992.

TYPE: Twin-turboshaft multi-mission tilt-rotor aircraft.

AIRFRAME (general): Approx 59 per cent of aircraft is constructed of advanced composties, of which principal ones are Hercules IM-6 graphite/epoxy for wings and Hercules AS4 for fuselage and tail unit. Metal in the V-22's structure accounts for only about 454 kg (1,000 lb) of aircraft empty weight. Safe emergency flotation is provided by fuselage sponsons, with engine nacelles serving as pontoons for additional stability on water.

ROTOR SYSTEM: Two Bell counter-rotating three-blade propeller/rotors, with graphite/glassfibre, tapered, statically and aerodynamically balanced blades of high-twist design, elastomeric spherical bearings, and glassfibre spinners. Three Bendix swashplate actuators in each rotor head, each actuator being triple redundant electrically and dual redundant hydraulically. Rotor braking standard. Litton Poly-Scientific folding and de-icing systems for rotor blades. Stage 1 of shipboard stowage sequence begins with aircraft in helicopter mode (nacelles vertical), rotors then being braked with one blade positioned inboard and parallel to wing leading-edge. Remaining blades are sequenced automatically to fold inward alongside first blade; nacelles are then tilted to horizontal position prior to unlocking and rotating the wing.

ROTOR DRIVE: Each rotor is driven by individual engine via engine coupling and one prop/rotor gearbox in each nacelle. Prop/rotor gearboxes are interconnected by gearboxes and driveshafts to permit single-engine operation. Main transmission rated at 3,408 kW (4,570 shp) for normal operation and 4,415 kW (5,920 shp) with one engine inoperative.

WINGS: Cantilever high-wing monoplane, with constant chord and slight forward sweep. Main wing built by Bell, with control surfaces and fixed trailing-edge by Lockheed-Georgia. Construction is mainly of composites, with one-piece moulded two-spar torsion box, moulded graphite/epoxy ribs, bonded stringers, and continuous one-piece upper and lower moulded skin panels. Trailing-edge of fixed portion is of graphite. Three-segment detachable leading-edge on each side, of aluminium alloy with Nomex honeycomb core. Two-segment single-slotted graphite flaperon, with titanium fittings, on each trailing-edge, operated by FBW signalling of Moog hydraulic actuators. No tabs. Pneumatic boot de-icing of leading-edges. Second stage of shipboard stowage sequence, after rotor blade folding and tilting of nacelles to horizontal position, involves unlocking wing and rotating it clockwise through 90° on a 2.31 m (7 ft 7 in) diameter stainless steel carousel, to lie fore and aft along top of fuselage with port nacelle at front. Wing locking/unlocking and rotation is performed hydraulically via Lucas Aerospace actuators. A Litton wire-twist capsule maintains integrity of electrical connections passing through carousel during rotation sequence.

FUSELAGE: Semi-monocoque structure, built by Boeing Helicopters, of rectangular cross-section and comprising frames, longerons and skins of composites and aluminium alloy construction. Large overwing fairings, housing wing rotation carousel and some equipment bays. Sponson on each side of lower centre-fuselage to house main landing gear, fuel and environmental control unit.

TAIL UNIT: Cantilever structure, manufactured by Grumman, comprising horizontal surfaces mounted on top of rear fuselage with twin sweptback endplate fins and rudders. Entire structure built of Hercules AS4 graphite/epoxy laminates except for hinges, fittings and fasteners.

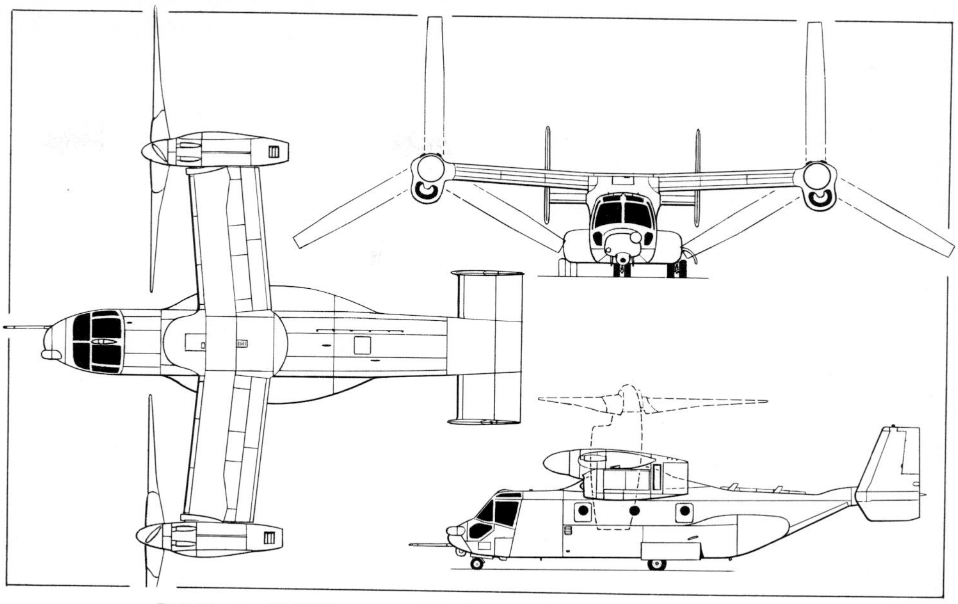

Bell/Boeing V-22 Osprey multi-mission tilt-rotor aircraft *(Pilot Press)*

Three hydraulic actuators (by Moog) on elevator and one (by Dowty Boulton Paul) on each rudder, all signalled electrically by FBW system. No elevator or rudder tabs. Pneumatic boot de-icing of fin and tailplane leading-edges.

LANDING GEAR: Dowty hydraulically actuated retractable tricycle type, with twin wheels and oleo-pneumatic shock absorbers on each unit, Menasco Canada steerable nose unit. Dowty Canada two-stage shock absorption in main gear is designed for landing impacts of up to 3.66 m (12 ft)/s normal, 4.48 m (14.7 ft)/s maximum, and has been drop tested to 7.32 m (24 ft)/s. All units retract rearward, main gear into sponsons on lower sides of centre-fuselage. Manual and nitrogen pressurised standby systems for emergency extension. Parker Bertea wheels and multi-disc hydraulic carbon brakes.

POWER PLANT: Two Allison T406-AD-400 (501-M80C) turboshafts, each with T-O and intermediate rating of 4,586 kW (6,150 shp) and max continuous rating of 4,392 kW (5,890 shp), installed in Bell built tilting nacelles at wingtips. Each nacelle has GFRP cowling panels and pylon support structures, and a Garrett infra-red emission suppressor at the rear. Air particle separator and Lucas inlet/spinner ice protection system for each engine. Lucas Aerospace full authority digital engine control (Fadec) for each engine, with analog electronic backup control. Pratt & Whitney has been named as second production source for engines, starting with production lot 5. Internal fuel (JP-5) in up to 13 crash resistant, self-sealing (nitrogen pressurised) cells: one 1,431 kg (3,155 lb) forward cell in each sponson, a 925 kg (2,040 lb) cell in rear of starboard sponson, four 227 kg (500 lb) auxiliary cells in each wing leading-edge, and a 306 kg (675 lb) engine feed cell outboard of the auxiliary tanks in each wing. (Not all versions have all tanks.) Pressure refuelling point in starboard wing leading-edge; gravity point in upper surface of each wing. Simmonds fuel management system. Provision for a further 7,235 kg (15,950 lb) of fuel to be carried in two additional tanks in main cabin for self-deployment mission. In-flight refuelling probe in lower starboard side of forward fuselage.

ACCOMMODATION: Normal crew complement of pilot (in starboard seat), co-pilot and crew chief in USMC variant. Flight deck has overhead and knee-level side transparencies in addition to large windscreen and main side windows, plus an overhead rearview mirror. Main window frame is of titanium. Main cabin has composites floor panels, and can accommodate up to 24 combat-equipped troops, on inward facing crashworthy fold away seats, plus two gunners; up to 12 litters plus medical attendants; or an equivalent cargo load with energy absorbing tiedowns. Main cabin door at front on starboard side, top portion of which opens upward and inward, lower portion (with built-in steps) downward and outward. Full width rear loading ramp/door in underside of rear fuselage, operated by Parker Bertea hydraulic actuators. Emergency exit windows on port side; escape hatch in fuselage roof aft of wing.

SYSTEMS: Environmental control system, utilising engine bleed air; control unit in rear of port main landing gear sponson. Three hydraulic systems (two independent main systems and one standby), all at operating pressure of 345 bars (5,000 lb/sq in), with Parker Bertea reservoirs. Electrical power supplied by two 40kVA constant frequency AC generators, two 50/80kVA variable frequency DC generators (one driven by APU), rectifiers, and a 15Ah battery. General Electric Aerospace triple redundant digital fly by wire flight control system, incorporating triple primary FCS (PFCS) and triple automatic FCS (AFCS) processors, and dual flight control computers (FCC) each linked to a MIL-STD-1553B databus; two PFCSs and one AFCS are fail-operational. FBW system signals hydraulic actuation of flaperons, elevator and rudders, controls aircraft transition between helicopter and aeroplane modes, and can be programmed for automatic management of airspeed, nacelle tilting and angle of attack. FCCs provide interfaces for swashplate, conversion actuator, flaperon, elevator, rudder and pylon primary actuators, flight deck central drive, force feel, and nosewheel steering. Dual 1750A processors for PFCS and single 1750A for AFCS incorporated in each FCC. Non-redundant standby analogue computer provides control of aircraft, including Fadec and pylon actuation, in the event of FBW system failure. Sundstrand Turbomach 261 kW (350 shp) APU, in rear portion of wing centre-section, provides power for mid-wing gearbox which, in turn, drives two electrical generators and an air compressor. Anti-icing of windscreens and engine air intakes; de-icing of rotor blades and spinners. Clifton Precision combined oxygen (OBOGS) and nitrogen (OBIGGS) generating systems for cabin and fuel tank pressurisation respectively. Systron Donner pneumatic fire protection systems for engines, APU and wing dry bays.

AVIONICS AND EQUIPMENT: VHF/AM-FM, HF/SSB and (USAF only) UHF secure voice com; Tacan, VOR/ILS, AHRS, radar altimeter and digital map displays; IFF; Honeywell AN/AAR-47 missile warning system; radar/infra-red warning system; J.E.T. ADI-350W standby attitude indicator; Aydin Vector data acquisition and storage system. Major tactical sensors are a Hughes Aircraft AN/AAQ-16 FLIR detector in undernose fairing and (USAF and USN only) a Texas Instruments AN/APQ-174 terrain following multifunction radar in offset (to port) nose 'thimble', with two Allied Signal IP-1555 full colour multifunction displays. Two Control Data AN/AYK-14 mission computers, with Boeing/IBM software. Pilots' night vision system and Honeywell integrated helmet display system. Chaff/flare dispensers. Provision for rescue hoist over forward (starboard) cabin door.

DIMENSIONS, EXTERNAL:

Rotor diameter, each	11.58 m (38 ft 0 in)
Wing span, excl nacelles	14.02 m (46 ft 0 in)
Wing chord, constant	2.54 m (8 ft 4 in)
Distance between rotor centres	14.19 m (46 ft 6¾ in)
Width overall, rotors turning	25.78 m (84 ft 6.8 in)
Length: fuselage	17.47 m (57 ft 4 in)
overall, wings stowed/blades folded	19.09 m (62 ft 7.6 in)
Height: over tail fins	5.38 m (17 ft 7.8 in)
wings stowed/blades folded	5.51 m (18 ft 1 in)
overall, nacelles vertical (= rotor ground clearance)	6.35 m (20 ft 10 in)
Nacelle ground clearance, nacelles vertical	1.58 m (5 ft 2½ in)
Tail span, over fins	5.61 m (18 ft 5 in)
Wheel track (c/l of outer mainwheels)	4.62 m (15 ft 2 in)
Dorsal escape hatch: Length	1.02 m (3 ft 4 in)
Width	0.74 m (2 ft 5 in)

DIMENSIONS, INTERNAL:

Cabin: Length	7.37 m (24 ft 2 in)
Max width	1.80 m (5 ft 11 in)
Max height	1.83 m (6 ft 0 in)
Usable volume	24.3 m^3 (858 cu ft)

AREA:

Rotor discs, each	105.4 m^2 (1,134 sq ft)

WEIGHTS AND LOADING:

Weight empty, equipped	approx 13,993 kg (30,850 lb)
Max fuel weight: standard	6,215 kg (13,700 lb)
with self-ferry cabin tanks	13,450 kg (29,650 lb)
Max internal payload (cargo)	9,072 kg (20,000 lb)
Cargo hook capacity: single	4,536 kg (10,000 lb)
two hooks (combined weight)	6,804 kg (15,000 lb)
Normal mission T-O weight: VTO	21,545 kg (47,500 lb)
STO	24,947 kg (55,000 lb)
Max STO weight for self-ferry	27,442 kg (60,500 lb)
Max cabin floor loading (cargo)	1,464 kg/m² (300 lb/sq ft)

PERFORMANCE (estimated):
Max cruising speed:
at S/L, helicopter mode
100 knots (185 km/h; 115 mph)
at S/L, aeroplane mode
275 knots (509 km/h; 316 mph)
at optimum altitude, aeroplane mode
300 knots (556 km/h; 345 mph)
Max forward speed with max slung load
200 knots (370 km/h; 230 mph)
Service ceiling   7,925 m (26,000 ft)
T-O run at normal mission STO weight
less than 152 m (500 ft)

Range:
VTO at 21,146 kg (46,619 lb) gross weight, incl 5,443 kg
(12,000 lb) payload
1,200 nm (2,224 km; 1,382 miles)
STO at 24,947 kg (55,000 lb) gross weight, incl 9,072 kg
(20,000 lb) payload
1,800 nm (3,336 km; 2,073 miles)
STO at 27,442 kg (60,500 lb) self-ferry gross weight, no
payload   2,100 nm (3,892 km; 2,418 miles)

BELLANCA
BELLANCA INC
PO Box 964, Alexandria, Minnesota 56308
Telephone: (612) 762 1501
CHAIRMAN: Marge Mitchell
PRESIDENT: Donald Jensen
SECRETARY/TREASURER: Gerald E. Sather

Viking Aviation acquired in 1982 the assets of the former Bellanca Aircraft Corporation (see 1981-82 and earlier editions of *Jane's*), which went into liquidation in 1981. The purchase agreement included rights to the Bellanca name,

and on 7 May 1982 Viking Aviation Inc was renamed Bellanca Inc.

The company's initial activity was limited to provision of product support for the Bellanca Viking series of four-seat light business aircraft (of which 1,598 had been built by January 1979) and various 14 Series models; replacement parts for the Viking are being manufactured under FAA-PMA approval. Bellanca Inc holds the type certificates and production inventory for Models 14-19, 14-19-2, 14-19-3, 14-19-3A, 17-30, 17-31, 17-31TC, 17-30A, 17-31A and 17-31ATC. Production of the Bellanca Viking was

resumed in 1984. Two aircraft were completed in 1986-87; 1988 production was expected to increase to some eight aircraft. Details and an illustration of the Viking can be found in the 1986-87 *Jane's*.

In 1984 Bellanca Inc also acquired the FAA type certificate and production jigs for the Eagle Aircraft Eagle agricultural biplane (see 1983-84 *Jane's*). Bellanca provides support for existing Eagles, but has no immediate plans to resume production.

BOEING
THE BOEING COMPANY
PO Box 3707, Seattle, Washington 98124
Telephone: (206) 655 2121
Telex: 329430
Fax: (206) 655 1171
ESTABLISHED: July 1916

CHAIRMAN AND CHIEF EXECUTIVE OFFICER:
Frank A. Shrontz
VICE-CHAIRMAN: Malcolm T. Stamper
EXECUTIVE VICE-PRESIDENT & CHIEF FINANCIAL OFFICER:
Harold W. Haynes
Operating components of The Boeing Company include:
Boeing Aerospace
See next entry

Boeing Commercial Airplanes
See pages 352
Boeing Helicopters
See pages 364
Boeing Military Airplanes
See pages 368

BOEING AEROSPACE
PO Box 3999, Seattle, Washington 98124
PRESIDENT: M. K. Miller
Telephone: (206) 773 2121
Telex: 32 9430

Boeing Aerospace has its headquarters at the division's space centre at Kent, Washington, some 12 miles south of Seattle. It consists of four major divisions: Information Systems, Space Systems, Ballistic Systems, and Defense Systems. Subsidiary companies are: Boeing Agri-Industrial Company; Boeing Technical Operations; Boeing Technical and Management Services, and Boeing Petroleum Services. Major programmes and activities concern airborne warning and control, the E-6 Tacamo aircraft, the Inertial Upper Stage, Minuteman ICBM, Peacekeeper ICBM ground support system, air-launched cruise missile, ASW standoff weapon, and Roland and Avenger air defence systems. Responsible for much of Boeing's military and space effort, it has a labour force of approximately 17,000.

BOEING E-3 SENTRY
USAF designation: E-3
RAF designation: Sentry AEW. Mk 1
The E-3 Sentry AWACS (Airborne Warning And Control System) is effectively a mobile, flexible, survivable and jamming-resistant high capacity radar station, command, control and communications centre, installed within a Boeing 707 airframe. It offers the potential of long-range high- or low-level surveillance of all air vehicles, manned or unmanned, and provides detection, tracking and identification capability within its surveillance capacity during all weathers and above all kinds of terrain. The radar system of later production aircraft also incorporates a maritime surveillance mode. Each of these aircraft is able to support a variety of tactical and/or air defence missions with no change in configuration. Its data storage and processing capability can provide real-time assessment of enemy action, and of the status and position of friendly resources.

In US Air Force service, the E-3 has a dual use: as a command and control centre to support quick-reaction deployment and tactical operations by Tactical Air Command units; and as a survivable early warning airborne command and control centre for identification, surveillance and tracking of airborne enemy forces, and for the command and control of NORAD (North American Air Defense) forces over the continental USA. The E-3 provides comprehensive surveillance out to a range of more than 200 nm (370 km; 230 miles) from the aircraft for low-flying targets, and still further for targets at higher altitudes.

Design of the E-3A is based on the airframe of the Model 707-320B commercial jet transport, but with a strengthened fuselage and powered by Pratt & Whitney TF33 turbofans. Two aircraft, with the prototype designation EC-137D, were modified initially for comparative trials with two prototype downward looking radars, of which that produced by Westinghouse was eventually selected. The full scale development test programme, completed at the end of 1976, involved three aircraft completely equipped with mission avionics, and a fourth aircraft equipped for airworthiness testing. Thirty-five E-3s (including upgraded

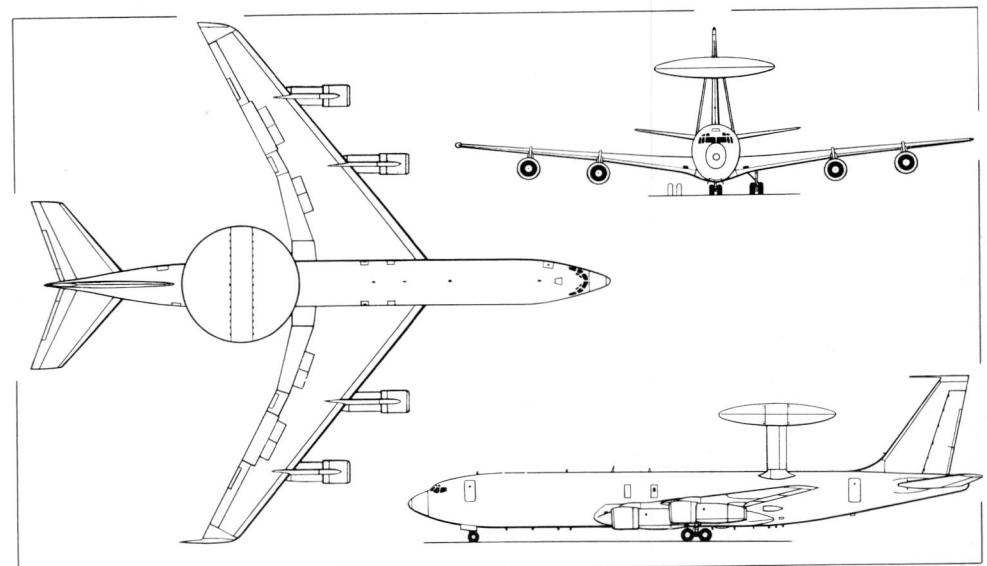

Three-view drawing *(Pilot Press)* **and photograph** *(S. G. Richards)* **of NATO Boeing E-3A Sentry AWACS aircraft**

prototypes) were delivered subsequently to the USAF, the last of them in June 1984. A further 18 were built for NATO.

These USAF and NATO AWACS have been developed and produced to four differing standards, as follows:

Core E-3A. Initial form of the first 24 production Sentries delivered to USAF. Equipment as detailed in 1987-88 *Jane's*.

E-3B. Under the USAF Block 20 modification programme, the two EC-137Ds and 22 USAF core-configured E-3As (aircraft Nos. 4 to 9 and 11 to 26) are being updated to E-3B standard by the installation of ECM-resistant voice communications; one more HF (making three in all) and five more UHF radios (making 12); a new and faster IBM CC-2 computer with much expanded memory and greatly increased processing speed compared with the original CC-1; five additional SDCs (making 14); and an austere maritime surveillance capability which Westinghouse developed for incorporation in the basic radar system. The E-3B also has provisions for Have Quick anti-jamming improvements to UHF radios, self defence, and a radio teletypewriter. First E-3B was re-delivered to USAF, after modification, on 18 July 1984. Remaining 23 are being modified by USAF at Tinker AFB, using Boeing kits.

US/NATO Standard E-3A. Original standard for USAF aircraft Nos. 27 to 35, of which delivery began in December 1981, and of the updated aircraft No. 3. Radar modified to embody full maritime surveillance capability; CC-2 computer; additional HF radios; ECM-resistant voice communications; radio teletypewriter; provisions for self defence and ECM. The 18 NATO aircraft are to this standard and retain E-3A designation.

E-3C. Under USAF Block 25 modification programme, begun in 1984, upgrading of the 10 USAF Standard E-3As to E-3C configuration is adding five more SDCs, five more UHF radios, and provisions for Have Quick anti-jamming improvements.

The USAF Electronic Systems Division has proposed a $425 million MSIP for the E-3, phased over five years, to give the radar greater 'detectability', add passive sensors, and make other improvements. Eventually, all USAF and NATO E-3s will be equipped with the Joint Tactical Information Distribution System (JTIDS) for anti-jam communications.

As a first step, in May 1987, Boeing was awarded a $241.5 million USAF contract for E-3 improvements that include full-scale development and integration into US and NATO E-3s of an ESM system to detect signals emitted by both hostile and friendly targets. Additional enhancements to be made to US E-3s, under what is known as the Block 30/35 programme, include a radar sensitivity improvement programme (RSIP), upgrading of JTIDS to TADIL-J (tactical digital information link-J) capability; CC-2 computer memory upgrade, using VLSI (very large scale integration) and bubble memory electronics technologies; and ability to employ the GPS (Global Positioning System). IOC for the Block 30/35 improvements is scheduled for 1993.

The first production core-configured E-3A Sentry was delivered on 24 March 1977 to Tactical Air Command's 552nd Airborne Warning and Control Wing (later Division), based at Tinker AFB, Oklahoma. E-3As achieved initial operational status in April 1978, and have since completed deployments to Iceland, West Germany, Saudi Arabia, Sudan, the Mediterranean area, South West Asia and the Pacific. E-3 aircraft are also employed in support of the US drug enforcement programme.

E-3As began to assume a role in US continental air defence on 1 January 1979, when NORAD personnel started to augment E-3A flight crews from TAC on all operational NORAD missions from Tinker AFB. The operating component was redesignated 552nd AWAC Wing in April 1985; it consists of several subordinate units. At Tinker, these include the 963rd and 964th AWAC Squadrons, the 966th AWAC Training Squadron, the 552nd Aircraft Generation Squadron (systems support), the 552nd Component Repair Squadron, and the 8th Tactical Deployment Control Squadron (flying EC-135/WC-135 aircraft). Overseas units of the 28th Air Division include the 960th, 961st and 962nd AWAC Squadrons. Based respectively at NAS Keflavik, Iceland, Kadena AB, Okinawa, Japan and Elmendorf AFB, Alaska, they provide command and control capability to CINCLANT (through the Commander, Iceland Defence Force) and CINCPAC.

Much of the avionics for NATO E-3As were produced in West Germany, with Dornier as systems integrator. NATO funded a third HF radio, to cover the maritime environment; a new data analysis and programming group; underwing hardpoints for self defence system stores; and a radio teletype to link the AWACS with the Organisation's maritime forces and commands. The first NATO production E-3A flew for the first time at Renton on 18 December 1980, was delivered to Dornier on 19 March 1981, and was handed over to NATO on 22 January 1982. The final aircraft was delivered on 25 April 1985.

The NATO AWACS aircraft's main operating base is at Geilenkirchen in West Germany. Initial forward operating bases were at Oerland, Norway, and Konya, Turkey. Additional forward operating bases became operational during 1985 at Preveza, Greece and Trapani, Italy.

The sale of five E-3 AWACS aircraft to the Royal Saudi Air Force was approved during October 1981, under a programme known as Peace Sentinel. Also included in the sale were six E-3 derivative tanker aircraft, designated **KE-3A**, and in 1984 the Saudi government exercised an option to increase the number of KE-3As to eight. In the same year, agreement was reached to equip the RSAF aircraft with 97.9 kN (22,000 lb st) CFM56-2A-2 engines, fitted with Hispano-Suiza thrust reversers. The first Saudi E-3 was handed over on 30 June 1986, and deliveries of all 13 aircraft were completed by 24 September 1987. These aircraft are not expected to be equipped with JTIDS, the latest-standard ECCM or Have Quick provisions.

On 18 December 1986 the British Government announced its intention to order six E-3 AWACS aircraft for the Royal Air Force, and exercised an option on a seventh in October 1987. RAF E-3s will be designated **Sentry AEW. Mk 1.** They will be powered by CFM56 engines and will be delivered to the UK for installation, integration and flight testing of avionics systems by British contractors. Boeing offered 130 per cent offset to British companies on the RAF E-3 procurement. In 1987 France ordered four similar aircraft, all for 1991 delivery. An option is held on two further aircraft. A similar industrial offset programme to that negotiated with the UK has been offered to France.

The following details apply specifically to the USAF E-3A except where indicated:

TYPE: Airborne early warning and command post aircraft.

AIRFRAME: As described in 1987-88 and earlier *Jane's*.

POWER PLANT: Four Pratt & Whitney TF33-PW-100/100A turbofans, each rated at 93.4 kN (21,000 lb st), mounted in pods beneath the wings. Fuel contained in integral wing tanks. Provision for in-flight refuelling, with receptacle for boom over flight deck.

ACCOMMODATION: Basic operational crew of 20 includes a flight crew complement of four plus 16 AWACS specialists, though this latter number can vary for tactical and defence missions. Aft of flight deck, from front to rear of fuselage, are communications, data processing and other equipment bays; multi-purpose consoles; communications, navigation and identification equipment; and crew rest area, galley and parachute storage rack.

SYSTEMS: A liquid cooling system provides protection for the radar transmitter. An air cycle pack system, a draw-through system, and two closed loop ram-cooled environmental control systems ensure a suitable environment for crew and avionics equipment. Electrical power generation has a 600kVA capability. Distribution centre for mission equipment power and remote avionics in lower forward cargo compartment. Rear cargo compartment houses radar transmitter and an APU. External sockets allow intake of power when aircraft is on ground. Two separate and independent hydraulic systems power essential flight and mission equipment, but either system can satisfy requirements of both equipment groups in an emergency.

AVIONICS AND EQUIPMENT: Elliptical cross-section rotodome of 9.14 m (30 ft) diameter and 1.83 m (6 ft) max depth, mounted 3.35 m (11 ft) above fuselage, comprises four essential elements: a turntable, strut mounted above rear fuselage, supporting rotary joint assembly to which are attached sliprings for electrical and waveguide continuity between rotodome and fuselage; structural centre section of aluminium skin and stiffener supporting the Westinghouse AN/APY-1 surveillance radar and IFF/TADIL C antennae, radomes, auxiliary equipment for radar operation and environmental control of the rotodome interior; liquid cooling of the radar antennae; and two radomes of multi-layer glassfibre sandwich material, one for surveillance radar and one for IFF/TADIL C array. For surveillance operations rotodome is hydraulically driven at 6 rpm, but during non-operational flights it is rotated at only ¼ rpm, to keep bearings lubricated. Radar operates in S band and can function as both a pulse and/or a pulse-Doppler radar for detection of aircraft targets. A similar pulse radar mode with additional pulse compression and sea clutter adaptive processing is used to detect maritime/ship traffic. Radar is operable in six modes: PDNES (pulse-Doppler non-elevation scan), when range is paramount to elevation data; PDES (pulse-Doppler elevation scan), providing elevation data with some loss of range; BTH (beyond the horizon), giving long-range detection with no elevation data; Maritime, for detection of surface vessels in various sea states; Interleaved, combining available modes for all-altitude longer-range aircraft detection, or for both aircraft and ship detection; and Passive, which tracks enemy ECM sources without transmission-induced vulnerability. Radar antennae, spanning about 7.32 m (24 ft), and 1.52 m (5 ft) deep, scan mechanically in azimuth, and electronically from ground level up into the stratosphere. Heart of the data processing capability of the first 24 aircraft in their original core E-3A form is an IBM 4 Pi CC-1 high-speed computer (see 1987-88 *Jane's* for details). From 25th aircraft, the new and improved IBM CC-2 computer was installed from the start, with a main storage capacity of 665,360 words. Data display and control are provided by Hazeltine high resolution colour situation display consoles (SDC) and auxiliary display units (ADU). The E-3B carries 14 SDCs and two ADUs. Navigation/guidance relies upon two Delco AN/ASN-119 Carousel IV inertial navigation platforms, a Northrop AN/ARN-120 Omega set which continuously updates the inertial platforms, and a Teledyne Ryan AN/APN-213 Doppler velocity sensor to provide airspeed and drift information. Communications equipment provides HF, VHF and UHF channels through which information can be transmitted or received in clear or secure mode, in voice or digital form. A weather radar is carried in the nose. Identification is based on an Eaton (AIL) AN/APX-103 interrogator set which is the first airborne IFF interrogator to offer complete AIMS Mk X SIF air traffic control and Mk XII military identification friend or foe (IFF) in a single integrated system. Simultaneous Mk X and Mk XII multi-target and multi-mode operations allow the operator to obtain instantaneously the range, azimuth and elevation, code identification, and IFF status, of all targets within radar range. NATO E-3As carry, and USAF aircraft have provisions for, a radio teletype. All aircraft from c/n 25 have an inboard underwing hardpoint on each side. There is no immediate requirement for either USAF or NATO AWACS to carry weapons; but on NATO E-3As these hardpoints can be used to mount additional podded items of ECM equipment.

DIMENSIONS, EXTERNAL:

Wing span	44.42 m (145 ft 9 in)
Length overall	46.61 m (152 ft 11 in)
Height overall	12.73 m (41 ft 9 in)

WEIGHT:

Max T-O weight	147,417 kg (325,000 lb)

PERFORMANCE:

Max level speed	460 knots (853 km/h; 530 mph)
Service ceiling	over 8,850 m (29,000 ft)
Endurance on station, 870 nm (1,610 km; 1,000 miles) from base	6 h
Max unrefuelled endurance	more than 11 h

BOEING TACAMO

US Navy designation: E-6A

On 29 April 1983, Boeing Aerospace received a contract to develop a survivable airborne communications system to provide an on-station/all-ocean link between the US National Command Authorities and the US Navy's Trident ballistic nuclear submarine (SSBN) fleet. Designated E-6A, the new aircraft will augment and partially replace the EC-130Q version of the Lockheed Hercules used currently for this mission, known as Tacamo (TAke Charge And Move Out), and is fitted with the EC-130Q's existing AVLF avionics.

The airframe of the E-6A is almost identical with that of the E-3 Sentry, and is assembled on the same production line. The prototype (BuAer number 62782) made its first short flight from Renton to Boeing Field, Seattle, on 19 February 1987. After installation of the aircraft's avionics, full flight testing began on 1 June 1987. Three production E-6As were ordered in FY 1987, deliveries of which are due to begin in Spring 1989, and long-lead funding to begin production of a further seven aircraft was approved for FY 1989. The USN requirement is for 16 E-6As.

In 1988 it was announced that USAF planned to purchase 21 similar aircraft, designated E-8A, to carry the J-STARS (Joint Surveillance Target Attack Radar System), with Grumman's Melbourne Systems Division acting as the system's integrator. Further details of the E-8A programme are given under the Boeing Military Airplanes heading.

The following details apply to the E-6A prototype:

TYPE: Long endurance communications relay aircraft, to carry the US Navy's airborne very low frequency (AVLF) communications systems.

AIRFRAME: Retains more than 75 per cent commonality with that of the E-3A, main differences being deletion of the dorsal radome and its support structure, the addition of wingtip ESM/Satcom pods and HF antenna fairings, and increased corrosion protection. Also retained is the nuclear/EMP (electromagnetic pulse) 'hardening' of the E-3A airframe. Additions include incorporation of the large forward freight door of the commercial Boeing 707-320C. Landing gear is identical to that of the E-3A.

POWER PLANT: Four 97.9 kN (22,000 lb st) CFM International F108-CF-100 (CFM56-2A-2) turbofans in individual underwing pods, as on E/KE-3As for Saudi Arabia. Fuel contained in integral tanks in wings, with single-point refuelling. In-flight refuelling via boom receptacle above flight deck.

ACCOMMODATION: Basic militarised interior sidewalls, ceilings and lighting are same as in E-3A. Interior divided into three main functional areas: forward of wings (flight deck and crew rest area), overwing (six-man mission crew), and aft of wings (equipment). Forward crew area, 50 per cent common with that of E-3A, accommodates a four-man flight crew on flight deck. Compartment immediately aft of this contains food storage, galley, dining area, toilets, and an eight-bunk rest area for spare crew carried on extended or remote deployment missions. Crew enter by ladder and hatch in floor of this compartment. Then follows the C³ overwing compartment with central and other consoles, their operators, and an airborne control officer (ACO). Through this is reached, to the rear, the compartment containing the R/T racks, transmitters, trailing wire antennae and their winches, parachutes, equipment spares, and a baggage

Boeing E-6A Tacamo prototype during its first flight on 19 February 1987, before fitting of wingtip pods and other avionics

storage area. There is a bale-out door at rear of this compartment on the starboard side.

SYSTEMS: Some 75 per cent of the E-6A's systems are the same as those in the E-3A. Among those retained are the liquid cooling system for the transmitters, the 'draw-through' cooling system for other avionics, the 600 kVA electrical power generation system, the APU, the liquid oxygen system, and MIL specification hydraulic oil.

AVIONICS AND OPERATIONAL EQUIPMENT: Three Collins AN/ARC-182 VHF/UHF com transceivers, all with secure voice capability; two Collins AN/ARC-190 HF com (one transceiver, one receive only); and Hughes Aircraft AIC-29 crew intercom with secure voice capability. External aerials for Satcom UHF reception in each wingtip pod; fairings beneath each pod house antennae for standard HF reception. Navigation by triplex Litton LTN-90 ring laser gyro-based inertial reference system integrated with a Litton LTN-211 VLF/Omega system and duplex Smiths Industries SFM 102 digital/analog flight management computer system (FMCS). Bendix APS-133 colour weather radar, in nosecone, with capability for short range terrain mapping, tanker beacon homing, and waypoint display. Honeywell APN-222 high/low-range (0-15,240 m; 0-50,000 ft) radio altimeter, and Collins low-range (0-762 m; 0-2,500 ft) radio altimeter, with ILS and GPWS. General Instruments ALR-66(V)4 electronic support measures (ESM), in starboard wingtip pod, provide information on threat detection, identification, bearing and approximate range. In overwing compartment, overseen by ACO, are two banks of three consoles and a new communications central console, which incorporate ERCS (emergency rocket communications system) receivers, Satcom cryptographic equipment, new teletypes, tape recorders, and other C³ equipment, all hardened against electromagnetic interference. In each operational area the E-6A links 'upward' with the airborne command posts and the Presidential E-4, to satellites, and to the ERCS; and 'downward' to VLF ground stations and the SSBN fleet. The main VLF antenna is a 7,925 m (26,000 ft) long trailing wire aerial (LTWA), with a 41 kg (90 lb) drogue at the end, which is winched out from the middle part of the rear cabin compartment through an opening in the cabin floor. The LTWA, with its drogue, weighs about 495 kg (1,090 lb) and creates some 907 kg (2,000 lb) of drag when fully deployed. Acting as a dipole is a much shorter (1,220 m; 4,000 ft) trailing wire (STWA), winched out from beneath the rear fuselage just forward of the tailplane. At patrol altitude, with the LTWA deployed, the aircraft enters a tight orbit and the drogue stalls, causing the wire to be almost vertical (70 per cent verticality is required for effective sub-sea communications) and the aircraft/wire combination acts like a lasso being whirled above the head, only in reverse: i.e., the path of the drogue is that of the hand holding the rope, while the orbit of the aircraft is the lasso. Signals transmitted through the trailing wire antennae use 200 kW of power, and can be received by submerged SSBNs via a towed buoyant wire antenna. Mean time

between failures of complete mission avionics is approx 20 h, but the E-6 is able to carry spares, and a spare crew, to permit extended missions of up to 72 h with in-flight refuelling, and/or deployment to remote bases.

ARMAMENT: None.

DIMENSIONS, EXTERNAL:

Wing span	45.16 m (148 ft 2 in)
Length overall	46.61 m (152 ft 11 in)
Height overall	12.93 m (42 ft 5 in)
Wheel track	6.73 m (22 ft 1 in)
Wheelbase	17.98 m (59 ft 0 in)
Forward cargo door: Height	2.34 m (7 ft 8 in)
Width	3.40 m (11 ft 2 in)
Height to sill	3.20 m (10 ft 6 in)

AREA:

Wings, gross	283.4 m² (3,050.0 sq ft)

WEIGHTS:

Operating weight empty	78,378 kg (172,795 lb)
Max fuel	70,305 kg (155,000 lb)
Max T-O weight	155,128 kg (342,000 lb)

PERFORMANCE (S/L, ISA, estimated):

Dash speed	530 knots (981 km/h; 610 mph)
Cruising speed at 12,200 m (40,000 ft)	455 knots (842 km/h; 523 mph)
Patrol altitude	7,620-9,150 m (25,000-30,000 ft)
Ceiling	12,800 m (42,000 ft)
Critical field length	2,042 m (6,700 ft)
Max effort T-O run	1,646 m (5,400 ft)
Max effort T-O run with fuel for 2,500 nm (4,630 km; 2,875 miles)	732 m (2,400 ft)
Landing run at max landing weight	793 m (2,600 ft)
Mission range, unrefuelled	6,350 nm (11,760 km; 7,307 miles)
Endurance: unrefuelled	15 h 24 min
on-station, 1,000 nm (1,850 km; 1,150 miles) from T-O	10 h 30 min
with one refuelling	28.9 h
with multiple refuelling	72 h

BOEING 767 AOA

In July 1984, Boeing Aerospace received a contract from the US Army Strategic Defence Command to develop an

Boeing's Airborne Optical Adjunct conversion of the prototype 767, produced as an element of the SDI programme

aircraft capable of detecting missile warheads as they re-enter the atmosphere. The aircraft modified under this 67-month programme is the original prototype of the Boeing 767 commercial transport (N767BA), now known as the Airborne Optical Adjunct (AOA). Identified by a large equipment housing above its cabin, and two ventral fins, it flew for the first time in its new form on 21 August 1987.

After initial qualification of the aerodynamic shape, equipment for the AOA task will be supplied by Boeing's two principal subcontractors. Hughes Aircraft Company was to deliver the infra-red sensors during 1988, for evaluation in flight in 1989. The AOA's computers are being provided by the Space and Strategic Avionics Division of Honeywell.

Eventual testing of the complete AOA system, as an element of the SDI programme, will be conducted over the Pacific, with the aircraft flying at normal airline cruising heights. It will carry a crew of 10 to 15 personnel on four to six hour missions. The targets for its sensors will be inert ICBM warheads.

BOEING (LOCKHEED) P-3C UPDATE IV

After competitive bidding against Lockheed, Boeing Aerospace was selected by the US Navy to develop ASW mission avionics for the P-3C Orion Update IV programme. The contract includes development and installation of acoustic and non-acoustic sensors, communications equipment, distributed processing, databus architecture and programmable colour displays and controls. Equipment suppliers named by October 1987 were Texas Instruments for the AN/APS-137 radar and General Instruments for the AN/ALR-66(U)5 ESM.

A trial installation is being made in a P-3C delivered to Boeing in August 1987, with redelivery to the Naval Air Test Center at Patuxent River NAS scheduled for Summer 1990. Present plans envisage retrofit of the Update IV avionics in 80 existing P-3C Update II Orions, and installation as standard equipment in the 125 new Long-Range Air ASW-Capable Aircraft (**LRAACA**, formerly P-3D and P-3G) required by the US Navy to follow completion of Orion production.

BOEING COMMERCIAL AIRPLANES

PO Box 3707, Seattle, Washington 98124

Telephone: (206) 237 2121

Telex: 0650 329430 BOEING Co C

Fax: (206) 237 1706

PRESIDENT: Dean D. Thornton

EXECUTIVE VICE-PRESIDENTS:
R. R. Albrecht (Chairman, Boeing Canada, and Sales, Marketing, Contracts, Financial Controls and Customer Relations)
Philip M. Condit (Engineering, Manufacturing, Product Development and Customer Services)

VICE-PRESIDENT, ENGINEERING: Ben A. Cosgrove

VICE-PRESIDENT, SALES: J. C. Longridge

Boeing Commercial Airplanes, with headquarters at the company's Renton, Washington, facility just south of Seattle, was reorganised in 1983 into three divisions. Renton Division is responsible for manufacture of 707, 727, 737 and 757 series aircraft; the Everett Division handles the 747 and 767 programmes; and the Fabrication Division serves the other operating groups with its massive NC machine capability. A Materiel Division was created in 1984 to consolidate activities of purchasing, quality control and vendor supplies.

Including military derivatives, 9 Model 707s, 161 Model 737s, 23 Model 747s, 40 Model 757s and 37 Model 767s were delivered in 1987. A further 79 Model 737s, 14 Model 747s, 25 Model 757s and 33 Model 767s were delivered during the first six months of 1988. Schedules then called for the delivery of 86 Model 737s, 16 Model 747s, 23 Model 757s and 19 Model 767s during the remainder of 1988. Cumulative total of announced orders was 6,488 aircraft on 30 June 1988, of which 5,482 had been delivered.

BOEING MODEL 707
USAF designations: VC-137, E-6A and E-8A

The prototype for the Boeing Model 707, designated Model 367-80, made its first flight on 15 July 1954, and a developed version was ordered in large numbers as a flight refuelling tanker/transport for the US Air Force under the designation KC-135 (Boeing Model 717). Commercial developments of the prototype, with the basic designations of Boeing 707 and 720, were manufactured in many versions. Details can be found in the 1980-81 and earlier editions of *Jane's*. The last commercially configured example, a 707-320C for the Moroccan government, was delivered in March 1982.

Manufacture has continued solely to provide airframes for the military AWACS and other defence programmes, details of which can be found in other Boeing sections of this entry. Orders for all commercial and military models totalled 999 by 26 May 1988. At 30 June 1988, military 707s still to be delivered comprised 12 E-3s (one for USAF, four

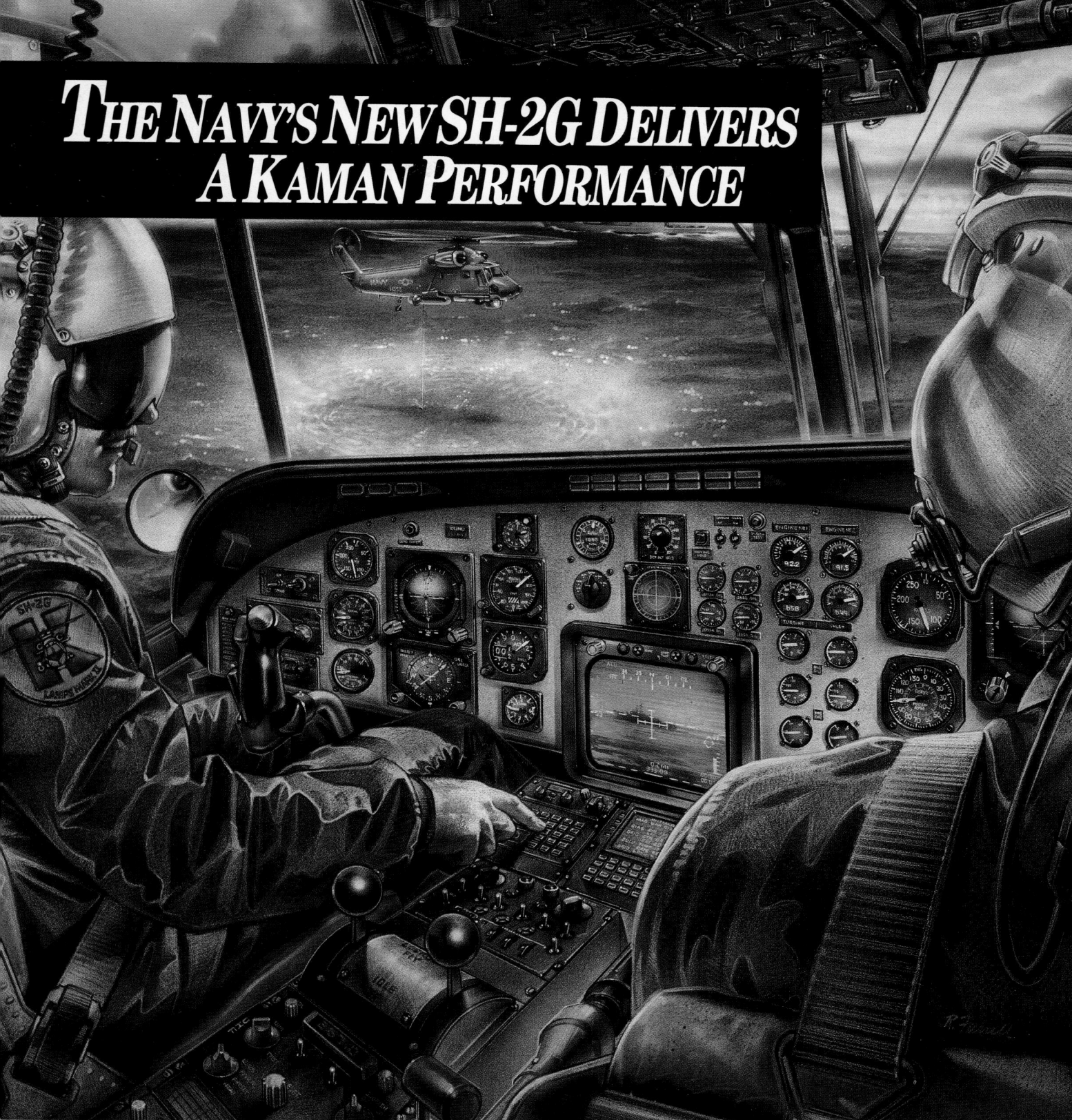

THE NAVY'S NEW SH-2G DELIVERS A KAMAN PERFORMANCE

Kaman. The name says command. An appropriate thought for the Navy's new ASW attack helicopter. The Kaman SH-2G.

Already in production, the SH-2G builds upon the proven record of the SH-2F. The Navy's most recent evolution of the unbeatable Kaman design.

But we've upgraded it with two powerhouse T700 engines. New avionics. And high-performance dynamics.

Now there's even an on-board acoustic processor for totally autonomous missions against submarines. Plus superb sonobuoy and sonar capabilities.

When the situation gets hot, the SH-2G lets you add critical components. Like dipping sonar. An array of missiles and special weapons. And more advanced ESM.

All of which help counter increasingly sophisticated threats at sea. And on land.

That's what it takes to deliver performance. Now. And well into the 21st century.

Fly farther. Fight harder. Let us put you in Kaman today!

For more information, write or call: Kaman Aerospace Corporation, P.O. Box 2, Bloomfield, CT 06002, (203) 243-7551.

KAMAN
A KAMAN PERFORMANCE

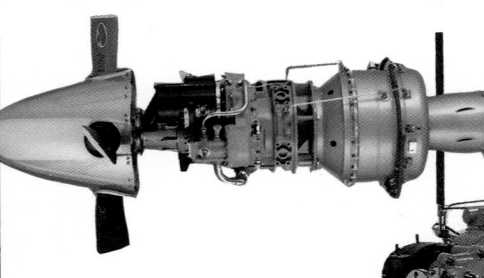

for France, seven for the UK) and six E-6As. Boeing Military Airplanes is offering tanker/transport conversions of ex-airline 707s, as described under its entry.

BOEING MODEL 737-200

USAF designation: T-43A

The original Model 737 was designed to utilise many components and assemblies already in production for the Boeing 727. Design began on 11 May 1964, and the first Model 737 flew on 9 April 1967. Deliveries began before the end of 1967, following FAA certification on 15 December. Details of the early production versions of the Model 737, and of subsequent design development, can be found in the 1974-75 *Jane's*.

The Boeing 737 was the third commercial transport to reach a sales total of one thousand, and in June 1987 became the world's best selling commercial airliner when orders for all models surpassed the previous record total of 1,831 sales set by the Boeing 727. They passed the 2,000 mark on 3 March 1988. By 30 June 1988 Boeing 737 orders totalled 2,137, of which 1,563 had been delivered. These totals include 19 Model 737-200s modified as T-43A navigation trainers for the US Air Force (see 1975-76 *Jane's*) and three maritime reconnaissance 737-200 Surveillers for Indonesia. By 30 June 1988 the worldwide fleet of Boeing 737s had carried an estimated 1.94 billion passengers, recorded 29.7 million revenue hours and covered a combined distance of more than 11.6 billion miles.

Production of the Model 737-200 was scheduled to end in August 1988. It was built in the following versions:

Advanced 737-200. Standard model, with max ramp weight of 52,615 kg (116,000 lb) and max T-O weight of 52,390 kg (115,500 lb). JT8D-15A engines (each 68.9 kN; 15,500 lb st) standard; JT8D-17A (71.2 kN; 16,000 lb st) optional; basic fuel capacity of 19,532 litres (5,160 US gallons; 4,296 Imp gallons). Accommodation for 120 passengers and baggage, with 81 cm (32 in) pitch seating, or up to 130 passengers in 76 cm (30 in) pitch seating with no reduction in cabin facilities. Use of graphite composite in place of former aluminium honeycomb in later production aircraft reduced the weight of the rudder, elevators and ailerons. Coupled with further use of composites in a new advanced technology interior, this resulted in a total weight reduction of more than 454 kg (1,000 lb).

Advanced 737-200C/QC. Standard convertible passenger/cargo model with strengthened fuselage and floor, and a large two-position upper deck cargo door with effective opening of 2.15 m × 3.40 m (7 ft 0½ in × 11 ft 2 in). The quick change (QC) feature allows more rapid conversion by using palletised passenger seating and other special interior furnishings. Typical mixed interior configuration provides accommodation for three cargo pallets and 65 passengers with 81 cm (32 in) pitch seating. Total of 104 ordered and delivered by 30 June 1988.

Corporate version. Same as standard Advanced 737-200, except interiors are adapted to special business and executive luxury requirements. Additional fuel capacity offered by installation of fuel cells in lower cargo compartments. With max fuel this model can carry a 1,134 kg (2,500 lb) payload up to 4,000 nm (7,412 km; 4,606 miles).

Advanced 737-200 High Gross Weight Structure. Higher gross weight models of the Advanced 737-200/200C, for longer-range use, in two versions. One has a maximum ramp weight of 56,700 kg (125,000 lb) and a maximum T-O weight of 56,472 kg (124,500 lb) with JT8D-15A or JT8D-17A engines, and a fuel capacity of either 21,009 litres (5,550 US gallons; 4,621 Imp gallons) or 22,598 litres (5,970 US gallons; 4,971 Imp gallons). The additional capacity for increased range capability is provided by a 1,476 litre (390 US gallon; 325 Imp gallon) or a 3,066 litre (810 US gallon; 674 Imp gallon) fuel tank installed in the aft lower cargo compartment. The second version, with a maximum ramp weight of 58,332 kg (128,600 lb), maximum T-O weight of 58,105 kg (128,100 lb), design landing weight of 48,534 kg (107,000 lb), and maximum zero-fuel weight of 43,091 kg (95,000 lb), has approximately 650 nm (1,204 km; 748 miles) greater range capability than the standard Advanced 737-200. Sectors of 2,300 nm (4,262 km; 2,648 miles) can be served with a 130-passenger payload and typical fuel reserves. Aircraft is identical to the Advanced 737-200 except for the auxiliary fuel tank, new wheels, tyres and brakes.

All 737-200 versions meet FAR Pt 36 and ICAO Annex 16 in respect of noise characteristics.

In January 1987 the Boeing 737-200 with JT8D-9/9A/15/15A/17/17A engines received FAA approval for extended range operations, permitting flights over water or undeveloped land areas by these twin-engined commercial airliners without their being subject to restrictions requiring such aircraft to remain within one hour's flying time of a suitable airport at single-engine cruising speeds. Operators must, however, apply for regulatory permission to operate extended range services with the aircraft.

An FAA certificated kit is available which enables the Model 737 to operate from unpaved or gravel runways. The kit includes a vortex dissipator for each engine, consisting of a short hollow boom that protrudes from under each engine's forward edge. The boom is capped by a plug with downward facing orifices. Pressurised engine bleed air forced through these orifices destroys any ground level vortex and prevents small pieces of gravel being ingested by the engines. Other items include a gravel deflection 'ski' on the nosewheel, deflectors between the main landing gear wheels, protective shields over hydraulic tubing and speed brake cable on the main gear strut, glassfibre reinforcement of lower inboard flap surfaces, application of Teflon-base paint to fuselage and wing undersurfaces and provision of more robust DME, ATC and VHF antennae.

Boeing 737-200 short-range transport (Pratt & Whitney JT8D-17A turbofans) in the insignia of Ethiopian Airlines

British Airways Advanced 737s, known as 'Super 737s', are equipped with advanced flight deck avionics, including a Sperry SP-177 digital automatic flight control system. Lufthansa ordered 38 Advanced 737s with similar equipment. Category IIIA certification of these AFCS versions was granted on 2 December 1981.

Surveiller. Specially equipped maritime surveillance 737-200 for Indonesian Air Force (three built), fitted also with 14 first class and 88 tourist class seats so that they can be used for government transport purposes. Details in 1987-88 and earlier editions of *Jane's*.

The description which follows applies to the commercial versions of the 737-200:

TYPE: Twin-turbofan short-range transport.

WINGS: Cantilever low-wing monoplane. Special Boeing wing sections. Average thickness/chord ratio 12.89%. Dihedral 6°. Incidence 1° at root. Sweepback at quarter-chord 25°. Aluminium alloy dual-path fail-safe two-spar structure. Ailerons of graphite composite construction. Triple-slotted trailing-edge flaps of aluminium, with trailing-edges of aluminium honeycomb. Aluminium alloy Krueger flaps on leading-edge, inboard of nacelles. Three leading-edge slats of aluminium alloy with aluminium honeycomb trailing-edge on each wing from engine to wingtip. Two aluminium honeycomb flight spoilers on each outer wing serve both as airbrakes in the air and for lateral control, in association with ailerons. Two aluminium honeycomb ground spoilers on each wing, one outboard and one inboard of engine, are used only during landing. Ailerons are hydraulically powered by two hydraulic systems with manual reversion. Trailing-edge flaps are hydraulically powered, with electrical backup. Leading-edge slats and Krueger flaps are symmetrically powered by one hydraulic system normally, and by a second hydraulic system for alternate extension. Flight spoilers are symmetrically powered by the two main individual hydraulic systems. Engine bleed air for anti-icing supplied to engine nose cowls and all wing leading-edge slats.

FUSELAGE: Aluminium alloy semi-monocoque fail-safe structure.

TAIL UNIT: Cantilever aluminium alloy multi-spar structure, with graphite composite control surfaces. Variable incidence tailplane. Elevator has dual hydraulic power, with manual reversion. Rudder is powered by a dual actuator from two main hydraulic systems, with a standby hydraulic actuator and system. Tailplane trim has dual electric drive motors, with manual backup. Elevator control tabs for manual reversion are locked out during hydraulic actuation.

LANDING GEAR: Hydraulically retractable tricycle type, with free-fall emergency extension. Nosewheels retract forward, main units inward. No main-gear doors: wheels form wheel well seal. Twin wheels on each main and nose unit. Boeing oleo-pneumatic shock absorbers. Mainwheels and tyres size 40 × 14-16 (low pressure 40 × 18-17 tyres, or C40 × 14-21/H40 × 14.5-19 tyres with heavy duty wheel brakes, are available optionally). Nosewheels and tyres size 24 × 7.7 (low pressure 24.5 × 8.5 tyres available optionally). Bendix or Goodrich multi-disc brakes. Hydro-Aire Mk III anti-skid units and automatic brakes standard.

POWER PLANT: Two Pratt & Whitney JT8D turbofans (details under individual model listings), in underwing pods. High performance target type thrust reversers, with full sound attenuation quiet nacelles. All models have standard fuel capacity of up to 19,532 litres (5,160 US gallons; 4,296 Imp gallons), with integral fuel cells in wing centre-section as well as two integral wing tanks. Long-range version has auxiliary fuel tank in rear lower cargo compartment, giving max fuel capacity of 22,598 litres (5,970 US gallons; 4,971 Imp gallons). Single-point pressure refuelling through leading-edge of starboard wing. Fuelling rate 1,135 litres (300 US gallons; 250 Imp gallons)/min. Auxiliary overwing fuelling points. Total oil capacity 41.5 litres (11 US gallons; 9.1 Imp gallons).

ACCOMMODATION: Crew of two side by side on flight deck. Details of passenger accommodation given under individual model descriptions. Passenger versions are equipped with forward airstair; a rear airstair is optional. Convertible passenger/cargo versions have the rear airstair as standard and forward airstair optional. One plug type door at each corner of cabin, with passenger doors on port side and service doors on starboard side. Overwing emergency exit on each side. Basic passenger cabin has one lavatory and one galley at each end. Large-volume hand baggage overhead bins. Provision for a wide variety of interior arrangements. Freight holds forward and aft of wing, under floor.

SYSTEMS: Air-conditioning and pressurisation system utilises engine bleed air. Max differential 0.52 bars (7.5 lb/sq in). Two functionally independent hydraulic systems with a third standby system, using fire resistant hydraulic fluid, for flying controls, flaps, slats, landing gear, nosewheel steering and brakes; pressure 207 bars (3,000 lb/sq in). No pneumatic system. Electrical supply provided by engine driven generators. Garrett APU for air supply and electrical power in flight and on the ground, as well as engine starting.

AVIONICS AND EQUIPMENT: Equipment to satisfy FAA Category II low weather minimum criteria is standard, as well as a Lear Siegler performance data computer system. Autopilot, specially designed for ILS localiser and glideslope control, with control wheel steering. Optional equipment will permit Category IIIA capability. Very low frequency (VLF-Omega) navigation systems, and a range of flight management systems with various levels of automation, including autothrottle and automatic flight control, are available as options.

DIMENSIONS, EXTERNAL:

Wing span	28.35 m (93 ft 0 in)
Wing chord: at root	4.71 m (15 ft 5.6 in)
at tip	1.60 m (5 ft 3 in)
Wing aspect ratio	8.8
Length overall	30.53 m (100 ft 2 in)
Length of fuselage	29.54 m (96 ft 11 in)
Height overall	11.28 m (37 ft 0 in)
Tailplane span	10.97 m (36 ft 0 in)
Wheel track	5.23 m (17 ft 2 in)
Wheelbase	11.38 m (37 ft 4 in)
Main passenger door (port, fwd):	
Height	1.83 m (6 ft 0 in)
Width	0.86 m (2 ft 10 in)
Height to sill	2.62 m (8 ft 7 in)
Passenger door (port, rear): Height	1.83 m (6 ft 0 in)
Width	0.76 m (2 ft 6 in)
Width with airstair	0.86 m (2 ft 10 in)
Height to sill	2.74 m (9 ft 0 in)
Emergency exits (overwing, port and stbd, each):	
Height	0.97 m (3 ft 2 in)
Width	0.51 m (1 ft 8 in)
Galley service door (stbd, fwd):	
Height	1.65 m (5 ft 5 in)
Width	0.76 m (2 ft 6 in)
Height to sill	2.62 m (8 ft 7 in)
Service door (stbd, rear): Height	1.65 m (5 ft 5 in)
Width	0.76 m (2 ft 6 in)
Height to sill	2.74 m (9 ft 0 in)
Freight hold door (stbd, fwd): Height	1.22 m (4 ft 0 in)
Width	1.30 m (4 ft 3 in)
Height to sill	1.30 m (4 ft 3 in)
Freight hold door (stbd, rear): Height	1.22 m (4 ft 0 in)
Width	1.22 m (4 ft 0 in)
Height to sill	1.55 m (5 ft 1 in)

DIMENSIONS, INTERNAL:
Cabin, incl galley and toilet: Length   20.88 m (68 ft 6 in)
  Max width   3.53 m (11 ft 7 in)
  Max height   2.13 m (7 ft 0 in)
  Floor area   63.8 m² (687 sq ft)
  Volume   131.28 m³ (4,636 cu ft)
  Freight hold (fwd) volume   10.48 m³ (370 cu ft)
  Freight hold (rear) volume   14.30 m³ (505 cu ft)
AREAS:
Wings, gross   102.00 m² (1,098.0 sq ft)
Ailerons (total)   2.49 m² (26.8 sq ft)
Trailing-edge flaps (total)   16.87 m² (181.6 sq ft)
Slats (total)   6.52 m² (70.2 sq ft)
Ground spoilers (total)   3.68 m² (39.6 sq ft)
Flight spoilers (total)   2.64 m² (28.4 sq ft)
Fin   20.81 m² (224.0 sq ft)
Rudder   5.22 m² (56.2 sq ft)
Tailplane   28.99 m² (312.0 sq ft)
Elevators, incl tabs (total)   6.55 m² (70.5 sq ft)
WEIGHTS AND LOADINGS (standard aircraft at brake release
weight of 52,390 kg; 115,500 lb except where indicated):
Operating weight empty (JT8D-17A engines):
  200   27,445 kg (60,507 lb)
  200C all-passenger   28,828 kg (63,555 lb)
  200C all-cargo   27,231 kg (60,034 lb)
  200QC all-passenger   30,141 kg (66,450 lb)
  200QC all-cargo   27,500 kg (60,629 lb)
Max payload: 200   15,645 kg (34,493 lb)
  200C all-passenger   14,263 kg (31,445 lb)
  200C all-cargo   15,860 kg (34,966 lb)
  200QC all-passenger   12,950 kg (28,550 lb)
  200QC all-cargo   15,590 kg (34,371 lb)
Max T-O weight (all-models):
  basic   52,390 kg (115,500 lb)
  optional   53,070 kg (117,000 lb)
        or 56,472 kg (124,500 lb)
        or 58,105 kg (128,100 lb)
Max ramp weight (all models):
  basic   52,615 kg (116,000 lb)
  optional   53,295 kg (117,500 lb)
        or 56,700 kg (125,000 lb)
        or 58,332 kg (128,600 lb)
Max zero-fuel weight (all models):
  basic   43,091 kg (95,000 lb)
  optional for 200C   44,906 kg (99,000 lb)
Max landing weight (all models):
  basic   46,720 kg (103,000 lb)
  optional   47,627 kg (105,000 lb)
        or 48,534 kg (107,000 lb)
Wing loading (all models):
  basic   575.5 kg/m² (117.9 lb/sq ft)
  max optional   638.2 kg/m² (130.7 lb/sq ft)
Power loading (JT8D-17A engines, all models):
  basic   368 kg/kN (3.61 lb/lb st)
  max optional   408 kg/kN (4.00 lb/lb st)
WEIGHTS AND LOADINGS (at brake release weight of 56,472
kg; 124,500 lb):
  Operating weight empty   27,574 kg (60,790 lb)
  Max payload   15,517 kg (34,210 lb)
  Max T-O weight   56,472 kg (124,500 lb)
  Max ramp weight   56,700 kg (125,000 lb)
  Max zero-fuel weight   43,091 kg (95,000 lb)
  Max landing weight   48,534 kg (107,000 lb)
  Max wing loading   620.24 kg/m² (127.04 lb/sq ft)
  Max power loading (JT8D-17A engines)
            397 kg/kN (3.9 lb/lb st)
PERFORMANCE (ISA, with JT8D-17A engines):
Max operating speed, all models
    Mach 0.84 (350 knots; 648 km/h; 402 mph EAS)
Max cruising speed, at an average cruise weight of 45,359
kg (100,000 lb) at 10,060 m (33,000 ft)
        462 knots (856 km/h; 532 mph)
Econ cruising speed at 10,060 m (33,000 ft)   Mach 0.73
Stalling speed, flaps down, at 46,720 kg (103,000 lb)
  landing weight   102 knots (189 km/h; 117 mph)

Runway LCN (at max ramp weight of 52,615 kg; 116,000
lb, optimum tyre pressure and 20 in flexible pavement):
  40 × 14-16 tyres   53
  C40 × 14-21 tyres   53
  C40 × 18-17 tyres   38
FAR T-O distance to 10.7 m (35 ft), 737-200 at 49,435 kg
(109,000 lb) AUW and 28.9°C (84°F):
  JT8D-9A engines   2,027 m (6,650 ft)
  JT8D-17A engines   1,615 m (5,300 ft)
FAR landing distance from 15 m (50 ft), 737-200 at
landing weight of 46,720 kg (103,000 lb)
                 1,372 m (4,500 ft)
Min ground turning radius   17.58 m (57 ft 8 in)
Range, JT8D-17A engines, FAR domestic reserves,
cruising at 10,060 m (33,000 ft), at 52,615 kg (116,000
lb) ramp weight with 115 passengers and 19,533 litres
(5,160 US gallons; 4,296 Imp gallons) fuel
          1,855 nm (3,437 km; 2,136 miles)
Range, conditions as above, except 58,332 kg (128,600 lb)
ramp weight and 22,599 litres (5,970 US gallons; 4,971
Imp gallons) fuel
          2,530 nm (4,688 km; 2,913 miles)
Range, conditions as above, with 130 passengers
          2,255 nm (4,179 km; 2,596 miles)
OPERATIONAL NOISE LEVELS (JT8D-9 engines and nacelle
acoustic treatment, FAR Pt 36):
T-O at 52,390 kg (115,500 lb) brake release weight
                     95.3 EPNdB
Sideline at 52,390 kg (115,500 lb) brake release
weight   100.6 EPNdB
Approach at 46,720 kg (103,000 lb) max landing
weight   101.1 EPNdB

BOEING MODEL 737-300

Work on the 737-300 was started in early 1980.
Lengthening of the fuselage, to accommodate additional
passengers and underfloor freight, and the installation of
new-generation turbofan engines, offer much reduced fuel
consumption per seat-mile and lower noise levels compared
with the earlier model. It has the same approval for
extended range overwater operations as the 737-200 (which
see).

Following production go-ahead in March 1981, work
began in mid-1982 and the prototype 737-300 made its first
flight on 24 February 1984. A second aircraft joined the
flight test programme on 2 March. Certification was
granted on 14 November 1984, with the first delivery (to US
Air) on 28 November. The first revenue service with a
737-300 was flown by Southwest Airlines on 7 December
1984.

Orders for the 737-300 totalled 790 by 11 August 1988;
425 of these had been delivered by 5 July.

The executive version of the 737-300 is equipped typically
for about 20 passengers, with conference room, bedroom,
bathroom and full dining facilities. Three had been sold by
mid-1988, including one to the Royal Thai Air Force.

The description of the 737-200 applies also to the
737-300, except as follows:

WINGS: Generally similar to the 737-200 except: modified
aerofoil section for leading-edge slats outboard of engine
nacelles; revised trailing-edge flap sections and flap track
fairings aft of engines; additional spoilers outboard; wing
structure strengthened; and each wingtip extended by
0.28 m (11 in).

FUSELAGE: As for 737-200, but lengthened by a total of
2.64 m (8 ft 8 in), by insertion of a 1.12 m (3 ft 8 in) plug
forward of the wing, and a 1.52 m (5 ft 0 in) plug aft of the
wing carry-through structure. In addition to providing
increased passenger capacity, this 'stretch' gives a lower
freight hold volume which by 5.47 m³ (193 cu ft) than that
of the standard 737-200.

TAIL UNIT: As for 737-200, except dorsal fin area and
tailplane span increased. Some fins manufactured by the
Xian Aircraft Co in the People's Republic of China.

Composite material rudders manufactured by Short
Brothers (UK).

LANDING GEAR: Generally as for 737-200, but nose unit
repositioned and modified to ensure adequate ground
clearance for larger engine nacelles. Twin nosewheels
have tyres size 27 × 7.75. Main units have heavy duty
wheels, H40 × 14.5-19 heavy duty tyres, and Bendix
or Goodrich heavy duty wheel brakes as standard.
Mainwheel tyre pressure 13.45-14.00 bars (195-203 lb/sq
in). Nosewheel tyre pressure 11-45-11.85 bars (166-172
lb/sq in).

POWER PLANT: Two 88.97 kN (20,000 lb st) CFM
International CFM56-3B-1 or B-2 turbofans, pylon
mounted one on each wing. Nacelles are forward of
wings, and higher than those of 737-200; each is fitted
with an aerodynamic fence. Standard fuel capacity up to
20,104 litres (5,311 US gallons; 4,422 Imp gallons), with
integral fuel cells in wing centre-section and integral wing
tanks. Optional fuel capacities of 21,580 litres (5,701 US
gallons; 4,747 Imp gallons) and 23,170 litres (6,121
US gallons; 5,097 Imp gallons). Single-point pressure
refuelling through leading-edge of starboard wing.

ACCOMMODATION: Crew of two side by side on flight deck
(unchanged from 737-200). Alternative cabin layouts seat
from 128 to 149 passengers. Typical arrangements offer 8
first class seats four-abreast at 96.5 cm (38 in) pitch and
120 tourist class seats six-abreast at 81 cm (32 in) in mixed
class; and 141 or 149 all-tourist class at seat pitches of 81
cm (32 in) or 76 cm (30 in) respectively. One plug type
door at each corner of cabin, with passenger doors on
port side and service doors on starboard side. Airstair for
forward cabin door optional. Overwing emergency exit
on each side. One or two galleys and one lavatory
forward, and one or two galleys and lavatories aft,
depending on configuration. New lightweight interior,
using advanced crushed core materials, providing total
overhead baggage capacity of 6.80 m³ (240 cu ft),
equivalent to 0.048 m³ (1.7 cu ft) per passenger.
Underfloor freight holds, forward and aft of wing, with
access doors on starboard side.

SYSTEMS: Generally as for 737-200. AiResearch bleed air
control system for air-conditioning and thermal anti-icing
systems; Garrett GTCP 85-129(C) APU.

AVIONICS AND EQUIPMENT: Equipped to FAA Category II
low weather minimum criteria as standard. Flight
management computer system (FMCS), with performance and navigation functions, includes FAA Category II
SP-300 digital autopilot with optional Category IIIA
capability, inertial reference system (IRS) with laser
gyros in lieu of gimbal type, 12.7 cm (5 in) electro-
mechanical flight displays, 10 cm (4 in) electrical air data
displays, dual digital air data computers, and full-range
digital autothrottle. Other items include dual nav/com,
VHF nav, colour digital radar, and digital autobrake.
Optional equipment includes VLF/Omega nav system
and dual INS. An EFIS installation received FAA
certification on 24 July 1986. Also FAA approved is
Boeing's windshear detection and guidance system.

DIMENSIONS, EXTERNAL:
Wing span   28.88 m (94 ft 9 in)
Wing chord at root   4.71 m (15 ft 5.6 in)
Length overall   33.40 m (109 ft 7 in)
Height overall   11.13 m (36 ft 6 in)
Tailplane span   12.70 m (41 ft 8 in)
Wheel track   5.23 m (17 ft 2 in)
Wheelbase   12.45 m (40 ft 10 in)
Passenger, service and freight hold door
  sizes   as for 737-200
DIMENSIONS, INTERNAL:
Cabin, incl galley and toilet:
  Length   23.52 m (77 ft 2 in)
  Max width   3.45 m (11 ft 4 in)
  Max height   2.13 m (7 ft 0 in)
  Freight hold (fwd) volume   12.03 m³ (425 cu ft)
  Freight hold (rear) volume   18.21 m³ (643 cu ft)

Boeing 737-300 short-range transport of Norway Airlines

AREAS: As for 737-200 except:

Wings, gross	105.4 m² (1,135.0 sq ft)
Slats (total)	7.23 m² (77.8 sq ft)
Ground spoilers (total)	5.00 m² (53.8 sq ft)
Fin	23.13 m² (249.0 sq ft)
Tailplane	31.31 m² (337.0 sq ft)

WEIGHTS:

Operating weight empty	31,479 kg (69,400 lb)
Max payload: standard	16,148 kg (35,600 lb)
optional	16,828 kg (37,100 lb)
Max T-O weight: standard	56,472 kg (124,500 lb)
optional	62,822 kg (138,500 lb)
Max ramp weight: standard	56,700 kg (125,000 lb)
optional	63,049 kg (139,000 lb)
Max zero-fuel weight: standard	47,625 kg (105,000 lb)
optional	48,307 kg (106,500 lb)
Max landing weight	51,710 kg (114,000 lb)

PERFORMANCE: (A: at brake release weight of 56,472 kg; 124,500 lb. B: at optional BRW of 62,822 kg; 138,500 lb):

T-O field length, S/L, at 29°C (84°F):

A	2,027 m (6,650 ft)
B	2,749 m (9,020 ft)

Wet landing field length, 40° flap, at max landing weight:

A, B	1,603 m (5,260 ft)

Still air range with 141 passengers, T-O at S/L:

A	1,615 nm (2,993 km; 1,860 miles)
B	2,590 nm (4,800 km; 2,982 miles)

BOEING MODEL 737-400

Details of this new variant were announced in June 1986. The Model 737-400 offers all the new technology of the 737-300, but has a fuselage lengthened by 3.05 m (10 ft 0 in) by means of two 'plugs', one of 1.83 m (6 ft 0 in) forward of the wing and one of 1.22 m (4 ft 0 in) aft. The aircraft is powered by either two CFM International CFM56-3B-2 turbofans, each rated at 97.86 kN (22,000 lb st), or two CFM56-3C turbofans, each rated at 104.5 kN (23,500 lb st). The outer wings and landing gear are strengthened to permit a maximum landing weight of 54,885-56,245 kg (121,000-124,000 lb). A tail bumper is standard. In typical mixed-class configuration the 737-400 seats 146 passengers and up to 170 passengers in inclusive-tour charter configuration; lower cargo hold volume is 38.93 m³ (1,375 cu ft).

Firm orders for the 737-400 totalled 125 by 28 July 1988.

The first 737-400 (N73700) was rolled out on 26 January 1988 and made it first flight on 19 February, followed by the second aircraft on 25 March. A third 737-400 joined the test programme in June, and certification was expected in September 1988.

The general specification of the 737-300 applies also to the 737-400 except as follows:

DIMENSIONS, EXTERNAL:

Length overall	36.45 m (119 ft 7 in)

DIMENSIONS, INTERNAL:

Cabin, incl galley and toilet:

Length	27.18 m (89 ft 2 in)

WEIGHTS:

Operating weight empty: standard	32,976 kg (72,700 lb)
optional	33,430 kg (73,700 lb)
Max payload: standard	18,280 kg (40,300 lb)
optional	19, 640 kg (43,300 lb)
Max T-O weight: standard	62,822 kg (138,500 lb)
optional	68,039 kg (150,000 lb)
Max ramp weight: standard	63,049 kg (139,000 lb)
optional	68,265 kg (150,500 lb)
Max zero-fuel weight: standard	51,256 kg (113,000 lb)
optional	53,070 kg (117,000 lb)
Max landing weight: standard	54,885 kg (121,000 lb)
optional	56,245 kg (124,000 lb)

PERFORMANCE (estimated. A: at T-O weight of 62,822 kg; 138,500 lb. B: at optional T-O weight of 68,039 kg; 150,000 lb):

T-O field length, S/L, at 30°C: A   2,316 m (7,600 ft)

B, with optional CFM56-3C engines
2,499 m (8,200 ft)

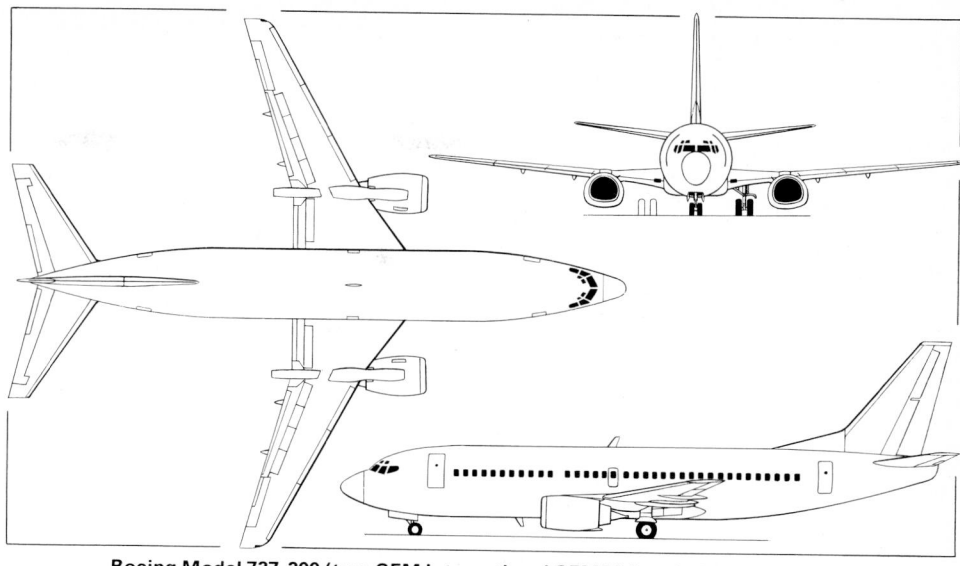

Boeing Model 737-300 (two CFM International CFM56-3 turbofans) *(Pilot Press)*

Wet landing field length, 40° flap:

A at 54,885 kg (121,000 lb) landing weight
1,722 m (5,650 ft)
B at 56,245 kg (124,000 lb) landing weight
1,850 m (6,070 ft)

Still air range with 146 passengers, T-O at S/L:

A	2,160 nm (4,003 km; 2,487 miles)
B	2,500 nm (4,633 km; 2,879 miles)

BOEING MODEL 737-500

Known initially as the 737-1000 during early design studies, this variant was announced on 20 May 1987 and combines the advanced technology of the 737-300 and -400 with a fuselage shortened to give an overall length of 31.0 m (101 ft 9 in), providing accommodation for 108-132 passengers and lower hold volume of 23.3 m³ (823 cu ft).

The aircraft will be powered by two CFM International CFM56-3B-1 turbofans, each rated at 88.97 kN (20,000 lb st) or derated to 82.29 kN (18,500 lb st) according to customer preference, and will be available with a choice of max T-O weights from 52,390 to 60,554 kg (115,500-133,500 lb). When equipped with auxiliary fuel tanks and the more powerful engines, a 737-500 with mixed class accommodation for 108 passengers will have a maximum range of 2,996 nm (5,552 km; 3,450 miles).

Major launch customers for the 737-500 are Braathens SAFE of Norway, which ordered 25 aircraft, and Southwest Airlines, 20 with options on a further 20. Firm orders totalled 133 by 25 August 1988. The first 737-500 is scheduled for rollout in May 1989, first flight in June 1989, with first customer deliveries following in March 1990. The 737-500 will replace the 737-200 in the Boeing range.

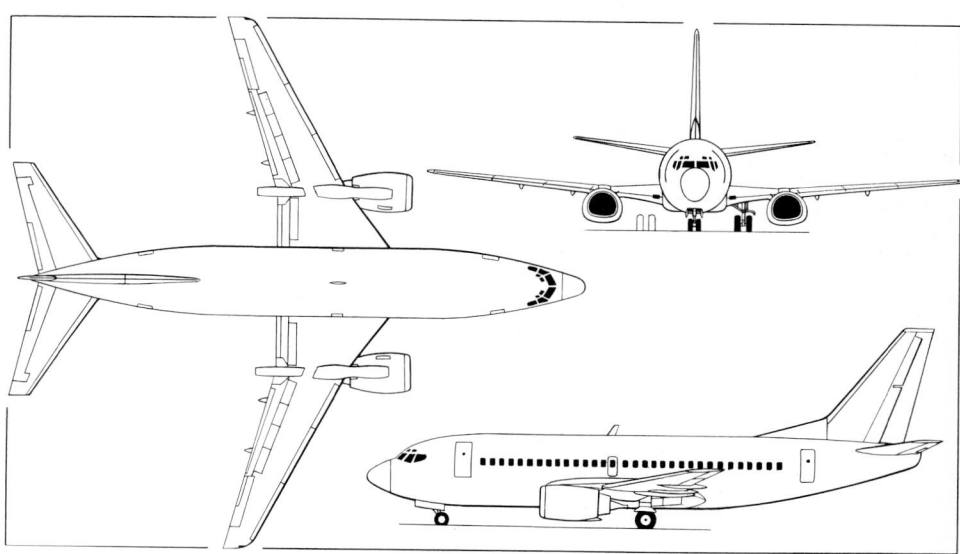

Boeing 737-500 short/medium-range transport *(Pilot Press)*

The first Boeing 737-400 taking off for the first time on 19 February 1988

BOEING MODEL 747

First details of this wide-body commercial transport were announced on 13 April 1966, simultaneously with the news that Pan American had ordered 25 Boeing 747s, including spares. Programme go-ahead followed on 25 July 1966.

The first 747 (designated RA001) flew for the first time on 9 February 1969. FAA certification of the basic 747 was granted on 30 December 1969. The first 747 to be delivered was received by Pan American on 12 December 1969, and entered commercial service on the airline's New York/London route on 22 January 1970.

Orders for all versions of the 747, including military E-4s, totalled 868 by 30 June 1988, by which date 700 of these had been delivered. The total 747 fleet operating in July 1988 carried more than 7 million passengers each month, and had flown more than 23 million hours in revenue service.

Versions of the Boeing 747 are as follows:

747-100. The original 747-100 was introduced into commercial service in January 1970, and 167 were sold. (Two of these have since been converted to -200B Combis and are included in the total given for that version.) The -100B incorporates strengthened wing, fuselage and landing gear structure. Initial order, with 213.5 kN (48,000 lb st) JT9D-7F engines, was placed by Iran Air in 1978, and this aircraft was delivered on 5 July 1979. Subsequent versions, with max taxi weights of 323,411 kg (713,000 lb), 334,751 kg (738,000 lb), and 341,555 kg (753,000 lb), allow for the installation of a variety of optional engines in addition to the basic 206.8 kN (46,500 lb st) General Electric CF6-45A2, including the 233.5 kN (52,500 lb st) CF6-50E2, and 236.25 kN (53,110 lb st) Rolls-Royce RB211-524D4. Nine ordered and delivered by mid-1988.

747SP. Lighter weight, shorter bodied derivative of the 747-100B. Described separately.

747-100SR. This short-range version of the 747-100B embodies structural changes required for high take-off and landing cycles. It is available at max taxi weights up to 273,515 kg (603,000 lb) with the same engines as the 747-100B. The first 747-100SR flew on 4 September 1973 and was delivered on 26 September 1973. Total of 29 ordered and delivered by mid-1988.

747-200B. Passenger version, with same accommodation as 747-100B. First flown on 11 October 1970 and certificated on 23 December 1970; deliveries began on 15 January 1971. Available at taxi weights up to 379,200 kg (836,000 lb). Standard engines include 243.5 kN (54,750 lb st) JT9D-7R4G2; 233.5 kN (52,500 lb st) CF6-50E2 and 236.25 kN (53,110 lb st) RB211-524D4. Optional engines include 252.2 kN (56,700 lb st) CF6-80C2B1 and 236.25 kN (53,110 lb st) RB211-524D4-B. Total of 233 ordered and 223 delivered by 30 June 1988. Selected by US Air Force for Presidential transport to replace VC-137 aircraft (further details in Boeing Military Airplanes entry, under 'Air Force One' heading).

747-200C Convertible. Version of 747-200 which can be converted from all-passenger to all-cargo, or five combinations of both. The first 747-200C flew on 23 March 1973, was certificated on 17 April, and was delivered to World Airways on 27 April 1973. Max T-O weight of 377,840 kg (833,000 lb) with Pratt & Whitney JT9D-7R4G2, Rolls-Royce RB211-524D4, General Electric CF6-50E2 or CF6-80C2 engines. Thirteen ordered, 12 delivered, by mid-1988.

747-200F Freighter. Version of the 747-200 capable of delivering 90,720 kg (200,000 lb) of palletised cargo over a range of 4,480 nm (8,300 km; 5,159 miles). Described separately.

747-200M. Combi version of the basic 747-200B, incorporating a cargo door in the port side of the fuselage, aft of the wing. This permits main deck layouts for passengers only, or for passengers and up to 12 main deck pallets/containers, with passenger and cargo areas separated by removable bulkhead. The first modification to Combi configuration was carried out on a Sabena 747-100, and redelivery was made in February 1974. The first production Combi was delivered to Air Canada in March 1975. Total of 77 ordered and delivered by mid-1988.

747-300. Version with extended upper deck to increase passenger accommodation. Described separately.

747-300M. Combi version of 747-300; described separately.

747-300SR. Short-range version of 747-300. Described separately.

747-400 and 400M. Advanced and Combi versions of 747-300; described separately.

E-4. Advanced Airborne Command Post version of 747, developed for US Air Force. Four built. Described under Boeing Aerospace heading in 1986-87 *Jane's*.

747 modification programmes. A major modification to enhance capability is available to operators of 747-100 and -200B aircraft. Performed at Boeing facilities, it includes installation of a side cargo door. The side cargo door modification enables an operator to convert 747-100 or -200B passenger aircraft into a version with main deck cargo capability. Variations include an all-cargo Special Freighter, a 6- or 12-pallet Combi, and an all-passenger or all-cargo Convertible. Like the Combi, the Convertible configuration can also be operated in a mixed passenger/cargo mode. The major elements of the side door modification include installation of a 3.05 m (10 ft 0 in) high by 3.40 m (11 ft 2 in) wide side cargo door, strengthened main deck floor, a fully powered or manual cargo handling system, and an option to increase certificated design weights of the aircraft. By early 1985 four side-cargo Combi models, and 24 all-freighter models had been delivered to nine airlines. Boeing Military Airplanes (which see) is modifying 19 Pan American 747s into the passenger/convertible configuration to support the US Air Force's CRAF (Civil Reserve Air Fleet) enhancement programme. The first converted aircraft was redelivered to Pan American on 31 May 1985. These aircraft are known by the military designation **C-19A**.

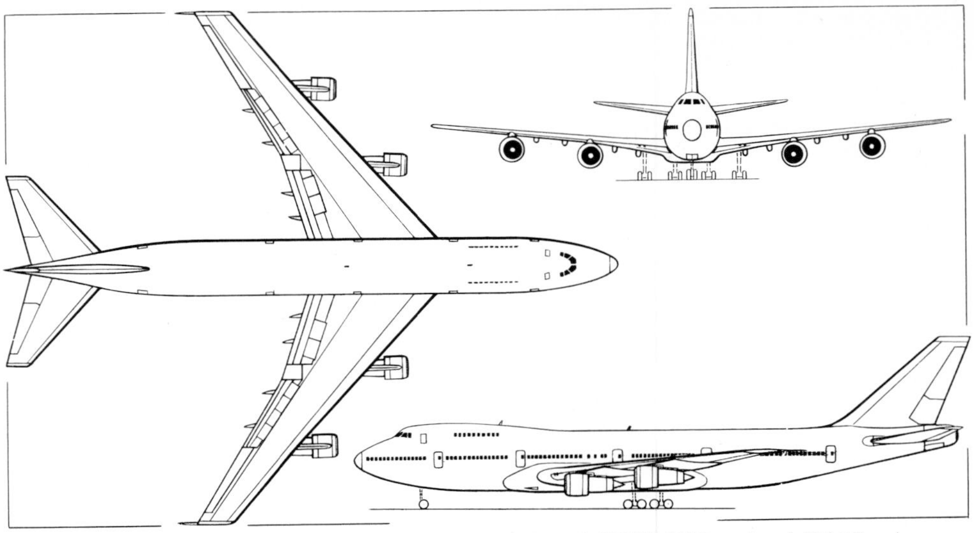

Boeing 747-200B four-turbofan heavy transport aircraft (P&W JT9D engines) *(Pilot Press)*

The 747 can be fitted, or retrofitted, with a performance management system (PMS) developed by Boeing and Delco. The PMS computer memory is programmed with airline economic factors and the performance characteristics of the individual aircraft/engine combination, and receives continuous inputs of altitude, airspeed, air temperature, fuel flow, wind velocity and other data during flight. Using these data, coupled with existing autopilot, autothrottle and inertial navigation systems, the PMS calculates, displays and controls automatically the optimum or desired airspeed, engine power setting, attitude and flight path of the aircraft for minimum fuel burn and/or minimum operating cost. The first complete system was delivered for airline service in June 1982. Results of in-service airline evaluations show trip fuel burn reductions in excess of one per cent. Fifteen airlines had ordered a total of 162 Delco/Boeing 747 PMS units by early 1987.

The following details apply specifically to the basic Model 747-100/200B passenger airliner:

TYPE: Four-turbofan heavy commercial transport.

WINGS: Cantilever low-wing monoplane. Special Boeing wing sections. Thickness/chord ratio 13.44% inboard, 7.8% at mid-span, 8% outboard. Dihedral 7°. Incidence 2°. Sweepback 37° 30′ at quarter-chord. Aluminium alloy dual-path fail-safe structure. Low-speed outboard ailerons; high-speed inboard ailerons. Triple-slotted trailing-edge flaps. Six aluminium honeycomb spoilers on each wing, comprising four flight spoilers outboard and two ground spoilers inboard. Ten variable camber leading-edge flaps outboard and three-section Krueger flaps inboard on each wing leading-edge. All controls fully powered.

FUSELAGE: Conventional semi-monocoque structure, consisting of aluminium alloy skin, longitudinal stiffeners and circumferential frames. Structure is of fail-safe design, utilising riveting, bolting and structural bonding.

TAIL UNIT: Cantilever aluminium alloy dual-path fail-safe structure. Variable incidence tailplane. No trim tabs. All controls fully powered.

LANDING GEAR: Hydraulically retractable tricycle type. Twin-wheel nose unit retracts forward. Main gear comprises four four-wheel bogies: two, mounted side by side under fuselage at wing trailing-edge, retract forward; two, mounted under wings, retract inward. Cleveland Pneumatic oleo-pneumatic shock absorbers. All 18 wheels and tubeless tyres of Model 747-100B are size 46 × 16 Type VII. Tyre pressure: mainwheels 14.49 bars (210 lb/sq in), nosewheels 13.11 bars (190 lb/sq in). Mainwheels and tyres size 49 × 17 on 747-200B model, pressure 14.15 bars (205 lb/sq in). The high gross weight aircraft has 49 × 19 tyres at a pressure of 13.46 bars (195 lb/sq in). Disc brakes on all mainwheels, with individually controlled anti-skid units.

POWER PLANT: Four Pratt & Whitney, General Electric or Rolls-Royce turbofans, as detailed in model listings, in pods pylon-mounted on wing leading-edges. Fuel in seven integral tanks. Capacity of centre wing tank varies according to version: 747-100B: 49,966 litres (13,200 US gallons; 10,991 Imp gallons); 747-200: 64,973 litres (17,164 US gallons; 14,292 Imp gallons). Remaining tanks common to all versions: two inboard main tanks, each 47,492 litres (12,546 US gallons; 10,447 Imp gallons); two outboard main tanks, each 16,966 litres (4,482 US gallons; 3,732 Imp gallons); two inboard reserve tanks, each 2,021 litres (534 US gallons; 445 Imp gallons). Outboard mains are reduced by 1,234 litres (326 US gallons; 271 Imp gallons) when CF6-50E2 or CF6-80C2 engines are installed. 747-200 also available with two outboard reserve tanks, each 2,983 litres (788 US gallons; 656 Imp gallons). Fuselage tank, capacity 6,511 litres (1,720 US gallons; 1,432 Imp gallons) optional. Total capacity, including manifolds, 747-100B: 183,380 litres (48,445 US gallons; 40,339 Imp gallons); 747-200: 204,355 litres (53,985 US gallons; 44,952 Imp gallons). Refuelling point on each wing between inboard and outboard engines. Total usable oil capacity 19 litres (5 US gallons; 4.2 Imp gallons).

ACCOMMODATION: Normal operating crew of three, on flight deck above level of main deck. Observer station and provision for second observer station are provided. Crew rest area available as option at rear of upper deck. Basic accommodation for 452 passengers, made up of 32 first class and 420 economy class, which includes a 32-passenger upper deck (extended on 747-300, which see). Alternative layouts accommodate 447 economy class passengers in nine-abreast seating or 516 ten-abreast, with 32 passengers on upper deck. All versions have two aisles. Five passenger doors on each side, of which two forward of wing on each side are normally used. Freight holds under floor, forward and aft of wing, with doors on starboard side. One door on forward hold, two on rear hold. Aircraft is designed for fully mechanical loading of baggage and freight. An optional side cargo door is available for passenger, convertible and freighter versions of the Model 747. Installed aft of door 4 on the port side of the fuselage, it allows the carriage of main deck cargo on passenger versions. Addition of this door to the freighter allows loads up to 3.05 m (10 ft) in height to be accommodated aft of the flight deck, and also makes possible simultaneous nose and side cargo handling.

SYSTEMS: Air cycle air-conditioning system. Pressure differential 0.61 bars (8.9 lb/sq in). Four independent hydraulic systems, pressure 207 bars (3,000 lb/sq in), maximum capacity 265 litres (70 US gallons; 58 Imp gallons)/min at 196.5 bars (2,850 lb/sq in), each with one engine driven and one pneumatically driven pump. The latter pumps supplement or substitute for engine driven pumps. Reservoir in each system, pressurised by engine bleed air via a pressure regulation module. Reservoir relief valve pressure is nominal 4.48 bars (65 lb/sq in). A small AC powered electric pump is installed to charge the brake accumulator during towing of the aircraft. Electrical supply from four aircooled 60kVA generators mounted one on each engine. Two 60kVA generators (supplemental cooling allows 90kVA each) mounted on APU for ground operation and to supply primary electrical power when engine mounted generators are not operating. Three-phase 400Hz constant frequency AC generators, 115/200V output. 28V DC power obtained from transformer-rectifier units. 24V 36Ah nickel-cadmium battery for selected ground functions and as in-flight backup. Gas turbine APU for pneumatic and electrical supplies.

AVIONICS AND EQUIPMENT: Standard avionics include three ARINC 566 VHF communications systems, two ARINC 533A HF communications systems, one ARINC 531 Selcal, three ARINC 547 VOR/ILS navigation systems, two ARINC 570 ADF, marker beacon receiver, two ARINC 568 DME, two ARINC 572 ATC, three ARINC 552 low-range radio altimeters, two ARINC 564 weather radar units, three ARINC 561 inertial navigation systems, two heading reference systems, ARINC 412 interphone, ARINC 560 passenger address system, multiple passenger service and entertainment system, ARINC 573 flight recorder, ARINC 557 cockpit voice recorder, integrated electronic flight control system with autothrottle and rollout guidance to provide automatic stabilisation, path control and pilot assist functions for Category II and III landing conditions, two ARINC 565 central air data systems, stall warning system, central instrument warning system, ground proximity warning system, attitude and navigation instrumentation, and standby attitude indication.

DIMENSIONS, EXTERNAL:
Wing span 59.64 m (195 ft 8 in)
Wing chord: at root 16.56 m (54 ft 4 in)
at tip 4.06 m (13 ft 4 in)
Wing aspect ratio 7.0
Length overall 70.66 m (231 ft 10 in)
Length of fuselage 68.63 m (225 ft 2 in)
Height overall 19.33 m (63 ft 5 in)
Tailplane span 22.17 m (72 ft 9 in)
Wheel track 11.00 m (36 ft 1 in)
Wheelbase 25.60 m (84 ft 0 in)
Passenger doors (ten, each): Height 1.93 m (6 ft 4 in)
Width 1.07 m (3 ft 6 in)
Height to sill approx 4.88 m (16 ft 0 in)
Baggage door (front hold): Height 1.68 m (5 ft 6 in)
Width 2.64 m (8 ft 8 in)
Height to sill approx 2.64 m (8 ft 8 in)
Baggage door (forward door, rear hold):
Height 1.68 m (5 ft 6 in)
Width 2.64 m (8 ft 8 in)
Height to sill approx 2.69 m (8 ft 10 in)
Bulk loading door (rear door on rear hold):
Height 1.19 m (3 ft 11 in)
Width 1.12 m (3 ft 8 in)
Height to sill approx 2.90 m (9 ft 6 in)
Optional cargo door (port): Height 3.05 m (10 ft 0 in)
Width 3.40 m (11 ft 2 in)

DIMENSIONS, INTERNAL:
Cabin, incl toilets and galleys:
Length 57.00 m (187 ft 0 in)
Max width 6.13 m (20 ft 1½ in)
Max height 2.54 m (8 ft 4 in)
Floor area, passenger deck 327.9 m² (3,529 sq ft)
Volume, passenger deck 789 m³ (27,860 cu ft)
Baggage hold (fwd, containerised) volume 78.4 m³ (2,768 cu ft)
Baggage hold (rear, containerised) volume 68.6 m³ (2,422 cu ft)
Bulk volume 28.3 m³ (1,000 cu ft)

AREAS:
Wings, reference area 511 m² (5,500 sq ft)
Ailerons (total) 20.6 m² (222 sq ft)
Trailing-edge flaps (total) 78.7 m² (847 sq ft)
Leading-edge flaps (total) 48.1 m² (518 sq ft)
Spoilers (total) 30.8 m² (331 sq ft)
Fin 77.1 m² (830 sq ft)
Rudder 22.9 m² (247 sq ft)
Tailplane 136.6 m² (1,470 sq ft)
Elevators 32.5 m² (350 sq ft)

WEIGHTS (letters are used to denote engine installations as follows: A: JT9D-7R4G2; B: CF6-45A2; C: CF6-50E2; D: CF6-80C2; and E: RB211-524D4):
Operating weight empty (approx) for max available gross weights:
747-100SR (550 pass): B 162,431 kg (358,100 lb)
747-100B (366 pass): B 169,417 kg (373,500 lb)
E 171,866 kg (378,900 lb)
747-200B (366 pass): A 169,961 kg (374,700 lb)
C 171,548 kg (378,200 lb)
D 172,728 kg (380,800 lb)
E 173,998 kg (383,600 lb)
747-200M (257 pass and 7 pallets):
A 171,821 kg (378,800 lb)
C 173,408 kg (382,300 lb)
D 174,587 kg (384,900 lb)
E 175,858 kg (387,700 lb)
747-200C (366 pass): A 175,313 kg (386,500 lb)
C 176,901 kg (390,000 lb)
D 178,080 kg (392,600 lb)
E 179,350 kg (395,400 lb)
747-200C (28 pallets): A 163,973 kg (361,500 lb)
C 165,561 kg (365,000 lb)
D 166,740 kg (367,600 lb)
E 168,010 kg (370,400 lb)
Max fuel weight:
747-100B, 747-100SR:
B, C 147,181 kg (324,480 lb)
E 148,324 kg (327,000 lb)
747-200B, 747-200M, 747-200C:
A, E 165,289 kg (364,400 lb)
C, D 164,141 kg (361,870 lb)
Max structural payload:
747-100SR (550 pass): B 76,385 kg (168,400 lb)
747-100B (366 pass): B, C 69,399 kg (153,000 lb)
E 66,950 kg (147,600 lb)
747-200B (366 pass): A 68,855 kg (151,800 lb)
C 67,268 kg (148,300 lb)
D 66,088 kg (145,700 lb)
E 64,818 kg (142,900 lb)
747-200M (257 pass and 7 pallets):
A 75,387 kg (166,200 lb)
C 73,799 kg (162,700 lb)
D 72,620 kg (160,100 lb)
E 71,350 kg (157,300 lb)
747-200C (366 pass): A 92,306 kg (203,500 lb)
C 90,718 kg (200,000 lb)
D 89,539 kg (197,400 lb)
E 88,269 kg (194,600 lb)
747-200C (28 pallets): A 103,646 kg (228,500 lb)
C 102,058 kg (225,000 lb)
D 100,879 kg (222,400 lb)
E 99,609 kg (219,600 lb)
Max T-O weight:
747-100SR: B 235,870 kg (520,000 lb)
or 272,155 kg (600,000 lb)
747-100B: B, E 322,050 kg (710,000 lb)
or 333,390 kg (735,000 lb)
or 340,195 kg (750,000 lb)
747-200B, -200M, -200C:
A, C, D, E 351,534 kg (775,000 lb)
or 356,070 kg (785,000 lb)
or 362,875 kg (800,000 lb)
or 371,945 kg (820,000 lb)
or 377,840 kg (833,000 lb)
Max ramp weight:
747-100B: B, C, E 341,555 kg (753,000 lb)
747-200B, -200M, -200C:
A, C, D, E 379,200 kg (836,000 lb)
Max zero-fuel weight:
747-100SR: B 238,815 kg (526,500 lb)
747-100B: B, E 238,815 kg (526,500 lb)
747-200B: A, C, D, E 238,815 kg (526,500 lb)
747-200M: A, C, D, E 247,205 kg (545,000 lb)
747-200C: A, C, D, E 267,620 kg (590,000 lb)
Max landing weight:
747-100SR: B 229,065 kg (505,000 lb)
or 238,135 kg (525,000 lb)
747-100B: B, E 255,825 kg (564,000 lb)
747-200B: A, C, D, E 255,825 kg (564,000 lb)
or 265,350 kg (585,000 lb)
or 285,765 kg (630,000 lb)
747-200M: A, C, D, E 285,765 kg (630,000 lb)
747-200C: A, C, D, E 285,765 kg (630,000 lb)

PERFORMANCE (747-100B at max T-O weight of 340,195 kg; 750,000 lb, 747-200B at max T-O weight of 377,840 kg; 833,000 lb, except where indicated. Engines as designated under 'Weights'):
Max level speed at 9,150 m (30,000 ft):
747-100B at AUW of 272,160 kg (600,000 lb):
B 525 knots (973 km/h; 604 mph)
747-200B at AUW of 317,515 kg (700,000 lb):
A 527 knots (977 km/h; 607 mph)
C 523 knots (968 km/h; 602 mph)
D 530 knots (981 km/h; 610 mph)
E 522 knots (967 km/h; 601 mph)
Cruise ceiling, all versions 13,715 m (45,000 ft)
Min ground turning radius 22.86 m (75 ft 0 in)
Runway LCN (W: 334,750 kg; 738,000 lb, X: 341,555 kg; 753,000 lb, Y: 366,500 kg; 808,000 lb, Z: 379,200 kg; 836,000 lb max taxi weight on h = 0.51 m; 20 in flexible pavement): W 81
X 83
Y 86
Z 88
Runway LCN (weights as above, on 11.02 m; 40 in rigid pavement): W 87
X 89
Y 93
Z 95
FAR T-O distance to 10.7 m (35 ft) at S/L, ISA:
747-100B: B 3,050 m (10,000 ft)
747-200B: A 3,170 m (10,400 ft)
C 3,292 m (10,800 ft)
D 3,079 m (10,100 ft)
E 3,155 m (10,350 ft)
FAR landing field length:
747-100B, -200B at 255,825 kg (564,000 lb) 1,881 m (6,170 ft)
747-200B at 265,350 kg (585,000 lb) 1,942 m (6,370 ft)
747-200B at 285,765 kg (630,000 lb) 2,112 m (6,930 ft)
Range, long-range cruise, typical international reserves of 5% trip fuel, 200 nm (371 km; 230 mile) alternate, 30 min hold at 457 m (1,500 ft):
747-100B with 366 passengers and baggage:
B 5,500 nm (10,193 km; 6,333 miles)
747-200B with 366 passengers and baggage:
A 6,550 nm (12,138 km; 7,542 miles)
C 6,350 nm (11,760 km; 7,307 miles)
D 6,900 nm (12,778 km; 7,940 miles)
E 6,600 nm (12,223 km; 7,595 miles)
Ferry range, long-range cruise, reserves as above:
747-100B: B 7,300 nm (13,520 km; 8,400 miles)
747-200B: A 7,450 nm (13,797 km; 8,573 miles)
C 7,200 nm (13,334 km; 8,285 miles)
D 7,900 nm (14,630 km; 9,091 miles)
E 7,500 nm (13,890 km; 8,631 miles)

OPERATIONAL NOISE LEVELS (As per FAR Pt 36, A: RB211-524C2 engines at brake release weight (BRW) of 340,195 kg; 750,000 lb and landing weight of 265,350 kg; 585,000 lb, B: JT9D-7R4G2 at BRW of 377,840 kg; 833,000 lb and landing weight of 285,765 kg; 630,000 lb):
T-O: A 104 EPNdB
B 106 EPNdB
Approach: A 107 EPNdB
B 107 EPNdB
Sideline: A 97 EPNdB
B 99 EPNdB

BOEING MODEL 747-200F FREIGHTER

The 747-200F Freighter is a version of the standard Model 747-200, capable of delivering 90,720 kg (200,000 lb) of containerised or palletised main deck cargo over a range of more than 4,500 nm (8,340 km; 5,180 miles). The first 747-200F flew for the first time on 30 November 1971. It was certificated on 7 March 1972 and delivered to Lufthansa two days later. A total of 66 had been ordered by 30 June 1988, of which 60 had been delivered.

To ensure maximum utilisation, the 747-200F has a special loading system that enables two men to handle and stow the maximum load of up to 112,400 kg (247,800 lb) in 30 min. This system was fully described in the 1977-78 *Jane's*.

The 747-200F can carry up to 29 containers measuring 3.05 × 2.44 × 2.44 m (10 ft long, 8 ft high and 8 ft wide), plus 30 lower-lobe containers, each of 4.90 m³ (173 cu ft) capacity, and 22.65 m³ (800 cu ft) of bulk cargo. The main deck can accommodate ANSI/ISO containers of up to 12.2 m (40 ft) in length, and many combinations of pallets and igloos. The lower hold can accommodate combinations of IATA-A1 or -A2, and ATA LD-1 or -3 half-width containers, full-width or main-deck baggage containers, and many combinations of pallets and igloos.

The nose loading door, which is hinged just below the flight deck to allow it to swing forward and upward, gives clear access to the main deck to facilitate the handling of long or large loads. A side cargo door is available as an option, allowing simultaneous nose and side loading. The side cargo door will accept palletised loads up to 3.05 m (10 ft 0 in) in height.

The description of the Model 747-200B applies also to the Model 747-200F except as follows:

TYPE: Four-turbofan heavy commercial freighter.

FUSELAGE: As for Model 747-200B, except for nose cargo loading door, which is hinged at the top and opens forward and upward. No windows in freight hold.

ACCOMMODATION: Normal operating crew of three on flight deck. Nose cargo loading door, hinged at top. Lower lobe cargo doors, on starboard side, one forward and one aft of wing. Bulk compartment cargo door, on starboard side, aft of lower lobe cargo door. Two doors for crew on port side of aircraft. Aircraft is designed for fully mechanical loading of freight.

DIMENSIONS, EXTERNAL: As for Model 747-200B except:
Crew doors (two, each): Height 1.93 m (6 ft 4 in)
Width 1.07 m (3 ft 6 in)
Height to sill approx 4.88 m (16 ft 0 in)
Nose cargo loading door: Height 2.49 m (8 ft 2 in)
Width at top (min) 2.67 m (8 ft 9 in)
Max width 3.81 m (12 ft 6 in)
Height to sill approx 4.90 m (16 ft 1 in)

DIMENSIONS, INTERNAL:
Main cargo deck: Height 2.54 m (8 ft 4 in)
Max width at floor level 5.92 m (19 ft 5 in)
Lower lobe: Width at floor level 3.18 m (10 ft 5 in)
Total cargo volume 687.0 m³ (24,260 cu ft)

AREAS: As for Model 747-200B

WEIGHTS (letters are used to denote engine installations as follows: A: JT9D-7R4G2; B: CF6-50E2; C: CF6-80C2; and D: RB211-524D4):
Operating weight empty (approx) for max available gross weights: A 155,219 kg (342,200 lb)
B 156,807 kg (345,700 lb)
C 157,986 kg (348,300 lb)
D 159,256 kg (351,100 lb)
Max fuel weights as for 747-200B
Max payload (29 pallets): A 112,400 kg (247,800 lb)
B 110,812 kg (244,300 lb)
C 109,633 kg (241,700 lb)
D 108,363 kg (238,900 lb)
Max T-O weight: A, B, C, D 351,535 kg (775,000 lb)
or 356,070 kg (785,000 lb)
or 362,875 kg (800,000 lb)
or 371,945 kg (820,000 lb)
or 377,840 kg (833,000 lb)
Max ramp weight: A, B, C, D 379,200 kg (836,000 lb)
Max zero-fuel weight:
A, B, C, D 267,620 kg (590,000 lb)
Max landing weight:
A, B, C, D 285,765 kg (630,000 lb)

PERFORMANCE (at max T-O weight of 377,840 kg; 833,000 lb, except where indicated. Engines as designated under 'Weights'):
Max level speed at AUW of 317,515 kg (700,000 lb), at 9,150 m (30,000 ft):
A 527 knots (977 km/h; 607 mph)
B 523 knots (968 km/h; 602 mph)
C 530 knots (981 km/h; 610 mph)
D 522 knots (967 km/h; 601 mph)
Cruise ceiling 13,715 m (45,000 ft)
Min ground turning radius 22.86 m (75 ft 0 in)
FAR T-O distance to 10.7 m (35 ft) at S/L, ISA:
A 3,170 m (10,400 ft)
B 3,292 m (10,800 ft)

Boeing 747-200F Freighter of Nippon Cargo Airlines

C	3,079 m (10,100 ft)
D	3,155 m (10,350 ft)

FAR landing field length:

at AUW of 255,825 kg (564,000 lb)	1,881 m (6,170 ft)
at AUW of 265,350 kg (585,000 lb)	1,942 m (6,370 ft)
at AUW of 285,765 kg (630,000 lb)	2,112 m (6,930 ft)

Range, long-range step cruise, typical international reserves of 5% trip fuel, 200 nm (371 km; 230 mile) alternate, 30 min hold at 457 m (1,500 ft), with 90,720 kg (200,000 lb) payload:

A	4,700 nm (8,704 km; 5,408 miles)
B	4,550 nm (8,426 km; 5,236 miles)
C	4,900 nm (9,075 km; 5,639 miles)
D	4,650 nm (8,612 km; 5,351 miles)

Ferry range, long-range step cruise, reserves as above:

A	7,900 nm (14,630 km; 9,091 miles)
B	7,650 nm (14,168 km; 8,803 miles)
C	8,300 nm (15,371 km; 9,551 miles)
D	7,950 nm (14,723 km; 9,148 miles)

BOEING MODEL 747SP

A lower-weight longer-range version of the basic Model 747, the 747SP (special performance), was introduced for use on lower-density routes. Retaining a 90 per cent commonality of components with the standard Model 747, the major change is a reduction in overall length of 14.35 m (47 ft 1 in). It made its first flight on 4 July 1975, and FAA certification was received on 4 February 1976. First delivery was made on 5 March that year. By 30 June 1988, a total of 44 had been ordered and delivered.

The description of the basic Model 747-100B/-200B applies also to the 747SP, except for the following details:

WINGS: As Model 747, except that trailing-edge flaps are of single-slotted variable pivot type, and wing structural materials are of reduced gauge. Large flap track fairings replaced by small link fairings. New wing/body fairings and leading-edge fillets.

FUSELAGE: As Model 747, except length reduced.

TAIL UNIT: Similar to 747, but tailplane span increased by 3.05 m (10 ft). Two-segment elevators. Height of fin increased by 1.52 m (5 ft 0 in). Double-hinged rudder.

LANDING GEAR: As Model 747, except structural weight reduced. Mainwheel tyres size 46 × 16, pressure 12.63 bars (183 lb/sq in). Nosewheel tyres size 49 × 17, pressure 13.8 bars (200 lb/sq in). Higher gross weight aircraft use 747-100 wheels and brakes. Modified 747-100 steel brakes by Bendix.

POWER PLANT: Four General Electric CF6-45A2 or CF6-50E2F turbofans, each of 206.8 kN (46,500 lb st); four Pratt & Whitney JT9D-7A turbofans, each of 205.7 kN (46,250 lb st); four Rolls-Royce RB211-524B2 turbofans, each of 222.8 kN (50,100 lb st), RB211-524C2 engines each of 229.5 kN (51,600 lb st), or RB211-524D4 engines each of 236.25 kN (53,110 lb st). Fuel system and oil capacity as for Model 747-100B, but with an additional 5,966 litres (1,576 US gallons; 1,312 Imp gallons) reserve fuel, providing a total capacity of 190,625 litres (50,359 US gallons; 41,932 Imp gallons).

ACCOMMODATION: Normal operating crew of three on flight deck above level of main deck. Observer station and provision for second observer station are provided. Crew rest area, as described for Model 747-400, is optional. Accommodation for 299 passengers on main deck, with 28 first class seats in forward area and ten-abreast seating throughout the major part of the main cabin. Seating for 32 passengers on upper deck, giving total capacity of 331 passengers. Max high-density accommodation for 440 passengers. Four doors on each side, two forward and

two aft of the wing. Crew door on starboard side giving access to upper deck. Freight holds under floor, forward and aft of wing box, each with one door on starboard side.

SYSTEMS, AVIONICS AND EQUIPMENT: As for Model 747.

DIMENSIONS, EXTERNAL: As for 747-100B/200B except:

Length overall	56.31 m (184 ft 9 in)
Height overall	19.94 m (65 ft 5 in)
Tailplane span	25.22 m (82 ft 9 in)
Wheelbase	20.52 m (67 ft 4 in)

DIMENSIONS, INTERNAL:

Cabin, incl toilets and galleys:

Length	42.27 m (138 ft 8 in)
Max width	6.13 m (20 ft 1½ in)
Max height	2.54 m (8 ft 4 in)
Floor area, passenger deck	253.2 m² (2,725 sq ft)
Volume, passenger deck	613.34 m³ (21,660 cu ft)
Baggage hold volume (fwd)	48.99 m³ (1,730 cu ft)
Baggage hold volume (rear, containerised)	48.99 m³ (1,730 cu ft)
Bulk compartment volume (rear)	11.33 m³ (400 cu ft)

AREAS: As for 747-100B/200B except:

Ailerons (total)	20.37 m² (219.3 sq ft)
Trailing-edge flaps (total)	78.78 m² (848 sq ft)
Fin	82.22 m² (885 sq ft)
Tailplane	142.51 m² (1,534 sq ft)

WEIGHTS: (RB211-524D4 engines):

Operating weight empty (approx, with 276 passengers):

	151,454 kg (333,900 lb)
Max fuel weight	149,361 kg (329,285 lb)
Max payload	34,518 kg (76,100 lb)
	or 41,322 kg (91,100 lb)
Max T-O weight (dry engines)	285,765 kg (630,000 lb)
	or 299,370 kg (660,000 lb)
	or 303,905 kg (670,000 lb)
	or 312,980 kg (690,000 lb)
	or 315,700 kg (696,000 lb)
	or 317,515 kg (700,000 lb)
Max ramp weight	284,485 kg (636,000 lb)
	or 302,090 kg (666,000 lb)
	or 306,630 kg (676,000 lb)
	or 315,700 kg (696,000 lb)
	or 318,875 kg (703,000 lb)
Max zero-fuel weight	185,975 kg (410,000 lb)
	or 192,775 kg (425,000 lb)
Max landing weight	204,115 kg (450,000 lb)
	or 210,920 kg (465,000 lb)

PERFORMANCE (with RB211-524D4 engines, at T-O weight of 317,515 kg; 700,000 lb, except where indicated):

Never-exceed speed	Mach 0.92
Max level speed, AUW of 226,795 kg (500,000 lb) at 9,150 m (30,000 ft)	538 knots (996 km/h; 619 mph)
Service ceiling	13,745 m (45,100 ft)
Min ground turning radius over outer wingtip	22.25 m (73 ft 0 in)

Runway LCN (Y: 302,090 kg; 666,000 lb, Z: 317,515 kg; 700,000 lb taxi weight on h = 0.51 m; 20 in flexible pavement): Y   70

Z   75

Runway LCN (weights as above, on l = 1.02 m; 40 in rigid pavement): Y   76

Z   80

FAR T-O distance to 10.7 m (35 ft) at S/L, ISA   2,347 m (7,700 ft)

FAR landing field length:

at AUW of 204,115 kg (450,000 lb)	1,594 m (5,230 ft)
at AUW of 210,920 kg (465,000 lb)	1,646 m (5,400 ft)

Range, long-range step cruise, typical international reserves, with 276 passengers and baggage   6,650 nm (12,324 km; 7,658 miles)

Ferry range, long-range step cruise, typical international reserves   8,000 nm (14,826 km; 9,212 miles)

BOEING MODEL 747-300

On 12 June 1980, Boeing announced an option for the Model 747 which incorporates structural changes to the aircraft's upper deck area to increase passenger carrying capacity and provide an optional crew rest area, as described for the Model 747-400. The upper forward fuselage is extended aft by 7.11 m (23 ft 4 in) to increase upper deck accommodation from 32 to a maximum of 69 passengers in all-economy class configuration. Seating is six abreast, with a single aisle, and panniers between the outer seats and cabin wall are provided for hand baggage. Alternative configurations include 26 first class sleeper seats on the extended upper deck. In addition, seven additional seats can be accommodated on the main deck as a result of deleting the standard circular stairway. It is replaced by a new straight stairway at the rear of the upper deck area. Two new doors 1.83 m (6 ft 0 in) high and 1.07 m (3 ft 6 in) wide replace the existing 1.22 × 0.61 m (4 ft 0 in × 2 ft 0 in) upper deck exits. Other structural changes include the provision of a new emergency exit and additional windows. The extended upper deck option was made available initially on existing aircraft of the 747-100 and -200 series, which then became known as **747-300s**; maximum take-off weights are unchanged, but operating weight empty is increased by about 4,220 kg (9,310 lb). Most efficient high speed cruise is increased from Mach 0.84 to Mach 0.85 by the revised upper contours. Flight testing with JT9D-7R4G2 engines began on 5 October 1982, followed on 10 December by the first 747-300 with CF6-50E2 engines, and FAA certification of the -300 was announced by Boeing on 7 March 1983. Initial deliveries were to Swissair and UTA, with whom the aircraft entered service on 28 March and 1 April 1983 respectively. Orders for new 747-300s totalled 80, including four short-range **747-300SRs** (for Japan Air Lines) and 20 **747-300M** Combis, by 30 June 1988. At that date 75, including the four-300SRs and 17 of the -300Ms, had been delivered.

On 19 July 1987, a 747-300 powered by General Electric CF6-80C2 turbofans took off from Glasgow, Montana, at a weight of 395,085 kg (871,000 lb). This was claimed to be the greatest weight at which a civil airliner had become airborne, but was exceeded by the prototype 747-400 on 27 June 1988 when that aircraft, powered by PW4000 engines, took off from Moses Lake, Washington, at a gross weight of 404,808 kg (892,450 lb).

The detailed specification for the Boeing 747-100B/200B applies also to the 747-300 except as follows:

WEIGHTS (A: JT9D-7R4G2; B: CF6-50E2; C: CF6-80C2 and D: RB211-524D4):

Operating weight empty (approx) for max available gross weights:

747-300 (400 pass):	A	174,134 kg (383,900 lb)
	B	175,721 kg (387,400 lb)
	C	176,901 kg (390,000 lb)
	D	178,171 kg (392,800 lb)
747-300M (289 pass and 7 pallets):		
	A	175,585 kg (387,100 lb)
	B	177,173 kg (390,600 lb)
	C	178,352 kg (393,200 lb)
	D	179,622 kg (396,000 lb)
Max fuel weights		as for 747-200B

Max payload:

747-300 (400 pass):	A	68,538 kg (151,100 lb)
	B	66,950 kg (147,600 lb)

Boeing 747-300 of Saudia, Saudi Arabian Airlines, with extended upper deck

C	65,771 kg (145,000 lb)
D	64,501 kg (142,200 lb)

747-300M (289 pass and 7 pallets):

A	80,694 kg (177,900 lb)
B	79,106 kg (174,400 lb)
C	77,927 kg (171,800 lb)
D	76,657 kg (169,000 lb)

Max T-O weight:

747-300, -300M: A, B, C, D	351,535 kg (775,000 lb)
	or 356,070 kg (785,000 lb)
	or 362,875 kg (800,000 lb)
	or 371,945 kg (820,000 lb)
	or 377,840 kg (833,000 lb)

Max ramp weight:

747-300, -300M: A, B, C, D	379,200 kg (836,000 lb)

Max zero-fuel weight:

747-300: A, B, C, D	242,670 kg (535,000 lb)
747-300M: A, B, C, D	256,280 kg (565,000 lb)

Max landing weight:

747-300: A, B, C, D	260,360 kg (574,000 lb)
	or 265,350 kg (585,000 lb)
	or 285,765 kg (630,000 lb)
747-300M: A, B, C, D	285,765 kg (630,000 lb)

PERFORMANCE (at max T-O weight of 377,840 kg; 833,000 lb, except where indicated. Engines as designated under 'Weights'):

Max level speed at AUW of 317,515 kg (700,000 lb) at 9,150 m (30,000 ft):

A	530 knots (982 km/h; 610 mph)
B	529 knots (979 km/h; 608 mph)
C	538 knots (996 km/h; 619 mph)
D	526 knots (974 km/h; 605 mph)

FAR T-O distance to 10.7 m (35 ft) at S/L, ISA:

A	3,170 m (10,400 ft)
B	3,292 m (10,800 ft)
C	3,079 m (10,100 ft)
D	3,155 m (10,350 ft)

FAR landing field length:

at AUW of 255,825 kg (564,000 lb)	1,881 m (6,170 ft)
at AUW of 265,350 kg (585,000 lb)	1,942 m (6,370 ft)
at AUW of 285,765 kg (630,000 lb)	2,112 m (6,930 ft)

Range, long-range cruise, typical international reserves of 5% trip fuel, 200 nm (371 km; 230 mile) alternate, 30 min hold at 457 m (1,500ft), with 400 passengers and baggage:

A	6,300 nm (11,675 km; 7,254 miles)
B	6,100 nm (11,297 km; 7,020 miles)
C	6,700 nm (12,408 km; 7,710 miles)
D	6,250 nm (11,575 km; 7,192 miles)

Ferry range, long-range cruise, reserves as above:

A	7,250 nm (13,436 km; 8,348 miles)
B	7,000 nm (12,964 km; 8,055 miles)
C	7,750 nm (14,353 km; 8,918 miles)
D	7,300 nm (13,520 km; 8,400 miles)

BOEING MODEL 747-400

Boeing announced in May 1985 development of the Model 747-400, an advanced long-range version of the 747-300. Improvements include 258.0 kN (58,000 lb st) class CF6-80C2, PW4256 or RB211-524G engines, a modern two-crew digital flight deck, more flexible interior configurations, increased range and better fuel economy.

The 747-400 shares the extended upper deck fuselage of the 747-300. A 1.83 m (6 ft 0 in) extension has been added to each wingtip, with a 1.83 m (6 ft 0 in) winglet, canted outboard at an angle of 22° and sweptback 60°, the combined tip extension and winglet installation offering a claimed increase in range of some three per cent. By employing advanced aluminium alloys developed for the Models 757 and 767 in the 747-400's wing structure, Boeing engineers have achieved a weight saving of 2,721 kg (6,000 lb). Substitution of carbon brakes for steel brakes, and new 0.56 m (1 ft 10 in) wide wheels with low-profile tyres, has provided a further weight saving of 816 kg (1,800 lb) in the aircraft's landing gear. New engine nacelles and support pylons have been designed, offering commonality with those of the Boeing 767. The 747-400's flight deck is

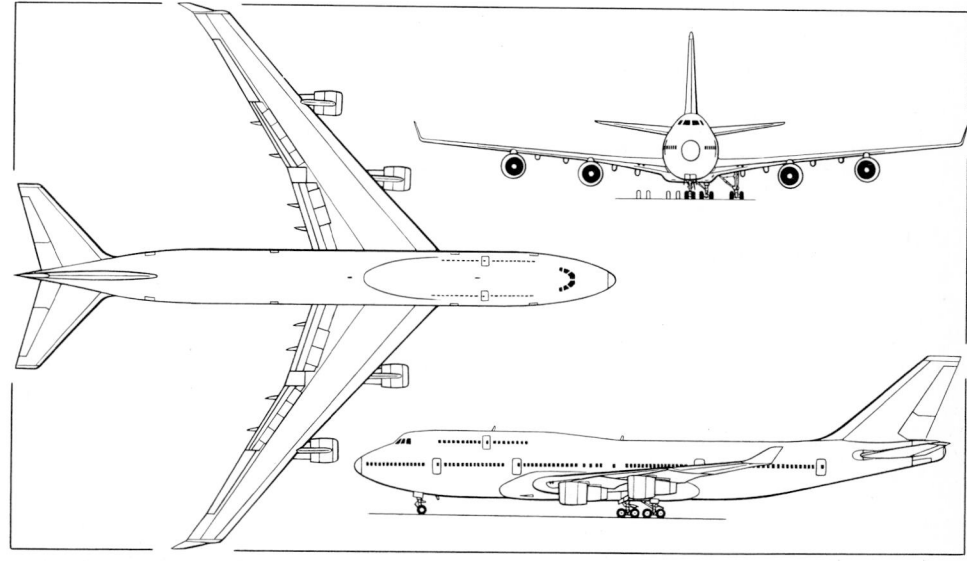

Boeing 747-400 advanced long-range version of the 747-300 (General Electric CF6-80C2 engines)
(Pilot Press)

Small winglets are a distinctive feature of the Boeing 747-400, first flown on 29 April 1988

configured for two-crew operation with digital avionics, sharing many common features with the 757/767 and resulting in a 60 per cent reduction in the number of instruments and gauges on the 747 flight deck. The final flight deck configuration may include a head-down display of fuel status on the engine indicating and crew alerting (EICAS) CRT displays rather than on overhead panels.

Improvements to the cabin area of the 747-400 include increased overhead storage facilities, alternative galley and toilet positions, a wireless cabin entertainment system in which audio and visual signals are picked up from floor mounted transmitters, and greater flexibility in interior design to permit airlines to react quickly to changes in market requirements which demand different mixes of first, business and economy class seating. An overhead crew rest area located above the main deck in the aft section of the passenger cabin is optional, with accommodation for four bunks and four seats; or eight bunks and two seats; or two bunks, two seats and five sleeper seats. A Combi cargo/passenger variant is designated **747-400M**.

A new feature of the 747-400 is provision for the carriage of 12,492 litres (3,300 US gallons; 2,748 Imp gallons) of fuel in the horizontal tail surfaces, in tanks located between the front and rear spars. No provision is made for transferring this fuel as a means of adjusting longitudinal trim or maintaining aft centre of gravity. As a result of the increased fuel capacity, greater fuel economy of new generation engines and structural weight savings, the 747-400 will offer a 1,000 nm (1,853 km; 1,151 mile) increase in range over the 747-300. Maximum range, with a payload of 412 passengers in three-class accommodation, will be 7,300 nm (13,528 km; 8,406 miles). Depending on the engines selected, the 747-400 is expected to burn 9-12 per cent less fuel than a 747-300 and to offer fuel burned per passenger seat reductions of up to 24 per cent over a 747-200. A Pratt & Whitney Canada APU is installed in the tailcone.

Design go-ahead for the 747-400 was granted in July 1985. Construction of the first aircraft (N401PW) began in mid-1986 with rollout occuring on 26 January 1988, and first flight on 29 April 1988. FAA certification and first customer deliveries were anticipated in the last quarter of that year. In October 1985 Northwest Orient Airlines became the launch customer for the 747-400 with an order for 10 aircraft, powered by PW4000 series engines. The Northwest Orient aircraft will be configured for 450 passengers. Delivery will take place during 1988-1990. Total 747-400 firm orders, including Combis, had reached 146 by 30 June 1988. Other customers include: Air France (16 with CF6 engines); Air New Zealand (1 with RB211s); British Airways (17 with RB211s); Cathay Pacific (2 with RB211s); CAAC of China (3 Combis); China Airlines (5 with PW4000s); International Lease Finance (4); Japan Air Lines (20 with CF6s); Japanese Government (2); KLM (8, incl 4 Combis with CF6s); Korean Air (9, with PW4000s); Lufthansa (10 with CF6s, 3 of them Combis); MAS (2 Combis with CF6s); Qantas (4 with RB211s); Singapore Airlines (14 with PW4000s); Thai Airways International (2); United Air Lines (15 with PW4000s); and UTA (2 with CF6s).

DIMENSIONS, EXTERNAL: As for 747-100/200, except:
Wing span   64.92 m (213 ft 0 in)

WEIGHTS (letters are used to denote engine installations as follows: A: PW4256; B: CF6-80C2; C: RB211-524D4D):
Operating weight empty (approx) for max available gross weights: A   177,354 kg (391,000 lb)
    B   177,218 kg (390,700 lb)
    C   178,661 kg (393,880 lb)
Max fuel weights: A, C   175,392 kg (386,674 lb)
    B   174,553 kg (384,824 lb)
Max payload:
    A   65,317 kg (144,000 lb)
    B   65,453 kg (144,300 lb)
    C   64,011 kg (141,120 lb)
Max T-O weight   362,875 kg (800,000 lb)
                         or 385,555 kg (850,000 lb)
                         or 394,625 kg (870,000 lb)
Max ramp weight   364,235 kg (803,000 lb)
                         or 386,915 kg (853,000 lb)
                         or 395,986 kg (873,000 lb)
Max zero-fuel weight   242,670 kg (535,000 lb)
Max landing weight   260,360 kg (574,000 lb)
                         or 285,765 kg (630,000 lb)

PERFORMANCE (estimated, at T-O weight of 394,625 kg (870,000 lb) except where indicated. Engines as designated under 'Weights'):
Max level speed at 9,150 m (30,000 ft):
    A   529 knots (979 km/h; 608 mph)
    B   532 knots (985 km/h; 612 mph)
    C   527 knots (976 km/h; 606 mph)
FAR T-O distance to 10.7 m (35 ft) at S/L, ISA:
    A   3,383 m (11,100 ft)
    B   3,353 m (11,000 ft)
    C   3,323 m (10,900 ft)
FAR landing field length at max landing weight of 285,765 kg (630,000 lb): A, B, C   2,134 m (7,000 ft)
Range, long-range cruising speed, 412 passengers and baggage, typical international reserves:
    A, B, C   7,300 nm (13,528 km; 8,406 miles)
Ferry range, typical international reserves:
    A, B, C   8,400 nm (15,569 km; 9,673 miles)

BOEING MODEL 757

In the early months of 1978, Boeing announced a proposal to develop a new family of advanced technology commercial aircraft, to which it gave the Model designations 757, 767 and 777. The short/medium-range 757 was intended to differ considerably from the other two, being based on the Boeing 727 fuselage. Improved performance would come from two new high bypass engines, and an advanced technology wing with less sweepback than that of the Model 727.

On 31 August 1978 Eastern Air Lines and British Airways announced their intention to purchase 21 and 19 Model 757s respectively, the former taking an option on an additional 24, and the latter on 18. Following the signature in early 1979 of formal contracts by both of these airlines, Boeing announced on 23 March 1979 that the company had initiated full production of the Model 757. The first 757 (N757A) made its first flight on 19 February 1982. This, and the next four aircraft off the production line, were used in the certification programme, which resulted in type certification by the FAA on 21 December 1982 and the UK CAA on 14 January 1983. Deliveries to Eastern Air Lines and British Airways began on 22 December 1982 and 25 January 1983, with respective revenue services starting on 1 January and 9 February 1983. Aircraft for these two airlines are designated **Model 757-200** and were powered initially by 166.4 kN (37,400 lb st) Rolls-Royce 535C turbofans. This was the first time that Boeing had launched a new airliner with a non-American engine. The first PW2037 engined 757 made its first flight on 14 March 1984; it was certificated in October and deliveries to Delta began on 5 November 1984. The first 757 with uprated Rolls-Royce 535E4 engines was delivered to Eastern on 10 October 1984. With the 535C engines, the 757-200 provides 53 per cent more seat miles per unit of fuel than earlier medium-range aircraft. With 535E4 and PW2037 engines the advantage is 76 per cent. A corporate/executive transport version and an extended range variant are available. The first example of the extended range model was delivered to Royal Brunei Airlines in May 1986.

Boeing announced in January 1986 a dedicated freighter version of the 757-200 designated Model **757-200PF** (Package Freighter). This aircraft features a large side cargo door in the forward fuselage, a single crew door and a windowless interior which will accept up to 15 standard 2.24 × 3.18 m (88 × 125 in) cargo pallets on the main deck. United Parcel Service has ordered 20 Model 757-200PFs powered by PW2040 engines. The first 757-200PF was type certificated on 3 September 1987 and delivered to UPS the same day. Seven had been delivered by 30 June 1988.

In February 1986 Boeing announced the **Model 757-200M** Combi, which, unlike the 757-200PF, retains all passenger windows and doors but has a mixed cargo/passenger configuration with an upward opening 3.40 × 2.18 m (134 × 86 in) cargo door on the port side of

the forward fuselage. The 757-200M can carry up to three 2.24 m × 2.74 m (88 × 108 in) cargo containers and 150 passengers. Royal Nepal Airlines is launch customer for the Combi, with an order for a single aircraft which flew for the first time on 15 July 1988 and was scheduled for delivery in September.

In January 1987 the Boeing 757 with Rolls-Royce 535E4 engines received FAA approval for extended range operation over water or undeveloped land areas. Boeing's windshear detection and guidance system also received FAA approval for commercial operation on 757s in the following month.

On 8 April 1988 a Boeing 757-200 on delivery to Air Europe set a distance record for the type, flying the 4,988 nm (9,244 km; 5,744 miles) from Seattle to Palma de Mallorca in 10 h 21 min. By 30 June 1988 firm orders totalled 358, of which 181 had been delivered.

The Model 757 retains the same fuselage cross-section as the 707/727/737 family. The original design provided for a T tail configuration, but as a result of wind tunnel testing it was decided to mount the tailplane on the fuselage.

TYPE: Twin-turbofan short/medium-range transport aircraft.

WINGS: Cantilever low-wing monoplane. Special Boeing wing sections. Dihedral 5°. Incidence 3° 12′. Sweepback at quarter-chord 25°. All aluminium alloy two-spar fail-safe wing box structure, manufactured by Boeing, with wing in-spar ribs by Hawker de Havilland of Australia. Centre-section continuous through fuselage. All-speed fully-powered ailerons outboard of double-slotted inboard and outboard trailing-edge flaps. Inboard flaps manufactured by Shorts of Northern Ireland; outboard flaps by CASA of Spain. High-lift full span leading-edge slats, in five sections on each wing, manufactured by Boeing Renton; Boeing Helicopters fixed leading-edges. Five flight spoilers and one ground spoiler on wing upper surface forward of trailing-edge flaps, manufactured by Grumman. Lateral control provided by ailerons, plus flight spoilers operated differentially. Spoilers operated collectively as speed brakes. Extensive use of honeycomb, and graphite composites and laminates, in construction of ailerons, flaps and spoilers. Thermal anti-icing of wing leading-edges. Wing/fuselage fairings and flap track fairings, of graphite/Kevlar, manufactured by Heath Tecna; wingtips by Schweizer.

FUSELAGE: All-metal semi-monocoque fail-safe structure, its cross-section based on two circular arcs of different radii, the larger above, and faired into a smooth contoured oval. Flight deck manufactured by Boeing Military Airplanes at Wichita; main cabin sections by Boeing Renton; extreme rear fuselage by LTV.

TAIL UNIT: Tailplane consists of full span torque boxes of conventional light alloy construction, and is attached at pivot points and to an actuator. The fin comprises a

First Boeing 757-200PF package freighter for United Parcel Service

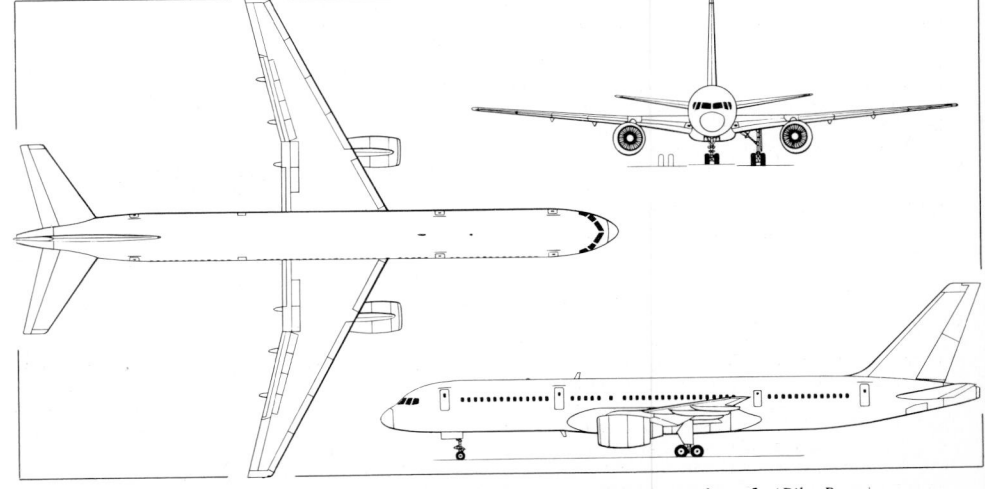

Boeing 757-200 twin-turbofan short/medium-range transport aircraft *(Pilot Press)*

Boeing 757-200 (Rolls-Royce 535E4 turbofans) in the insignia of Royal Brunei Airlines

three-spar dual-cell light alloy torque box attached to the fuselage. Elevators and rudder have graphite/epoxy honeycomb skins, supported by honeycomb and laminated spar and rib assemblies. Fin and tailplane manufactured by LTV; rudder and elevators of graphite by Boeing.

LANDING GEAR: Retractable tricycle type, with main and nose units manufactured by Menasco. Each main unit comprises a four-wheel bogie, fitted with Dunlop wheels, carbon brakes and tyres. Twin-wheel nose unit, also with Dunlop tyres. All landing gear doors of graphite/Kevlar.

POWER PLANT: Two 166.4 kN (37,400 lb st) Rolls-Royce 535C; 170 kN (38,200 lb st) Pratt & Whitney PW2037; 178.4 kN (40,100 lb st) Rolls-Royce 535E4; or 185.5 kN (41,700 lb st) Pratt & Whitney PW2040 turbofans, mounted in underwing pods. Engine support struts supplied by Rohr Industries. Fuel capacity 42,597 litres (11,253 US gallons; 9,370 Imp gallons).

ACCOMMODATION: Crew of two on flight deck, with provision for an observer. Five to seven cabin attendants. Nine standard interior arrangements for 178 (16 first class/162 tourist), 186 (16 first class/170 tourist), 202 (12 first class/190 tourist), 208 (12 first class/196 tourist) mixed class passengers, or 214, 220, 223, 224 or 239 all-tourist passengers. First class seats are four-abreast, at 96.5 cm (38 in) pitch; tourist seat pitch is 81 or 86 cm (32 or 34 in), basically six-abreast, in mixed class arrangements. Large overhead bins of Kevlar provide approximately 0.054 m³ (1.9 cu ft) of stowage per passenger. Choice of two cabin door configurations, with either three passenger doors and two overwing emergency exits on each side (used with 186, 208, 220 and 224 seat interiors); or four doors on each side (used with 178, 202, 214, 223 and 239 seat interiors). All versions have a galley at the front on the starboard side and another at the rear (two on 178 and 186 passenger versions and three on the 239 version plus one amidships); a toilet at the front on the port side and three more at the rear (186, 202, 208, 220, 224 passengers or two at the rear 239) or amidships (178, 214, 223 passengers). Coat closet at front of first class cabins and 214/220 passenger interiors. Baggage/cargo hold doors on starboard side.

SYSTEMS: AiResearch environmental control system; General Electric engine thrust management system; Sperry-Vickers engine driven hydraulic pumps; four Abex electric hydraulic pumps. Hydraulic system maximum flow rate 140 litres (37 US gallons; 30.8 Imp gallons)/min at T-O power on engine driven pumps; 25.4-34.8 litres (6.7-9.2 US gallons; 5.6-7.7 Imp gallons)/min on electric motor pumps; 42.8 litres (11.3 US gallons; 9.4 Imp gallons)/min on ram air turbine. Independent reservoirs, pressurised by air from pneumatic system, maximum pressure 207 bars (3,000 lb/sq in) on primary pumps. Sundstrand electrical power generating system and ram air turbine; and Garrett GTCP331-200 APU.

AVIONICS: Collins FCS-700 autopilot flight director system (AFDS), EFIS-700 electronic flight instrument system, engine indication and crew alerting system (EICAS), RMI-743 radio distance magnetic indicator (RDMI) and optional radio magnetic indicator (RMI). Avionics also include a Honeywell inertial reference system (IRS). In this IRS, conventional mechanical gyroscopes are replaced by laser gyroscopes, and utilisation, in both the Models 757 and 767, represents their first commercial application. The IRS provides position, velocity and attitude information to flight deck displays, and the flight management computer system (FMCS) and digital air data computer (DADC) supplied by Sperry Flight Systems. The FMCS provides automatic en-route and terminal navigation capability, and also computes and commands both lateral and vertical flight profiles for optimum fuel efficiency, maximised by electronic linkage

of the FMCS with automatic flight control and thrust management systems. Boeing windshear detection and guidance system is optional. Aircraft for British Airways and Monarch Airlines have Bendix ARINC 700 series avionics, including colour weather radar and seven digital com, nav and identification systems.

DIMENSIONS, EXTERNAL:

Wing span	38.05 m (124 ft 10 in)
Wing chord: at root	8.20 m (26 ft 11 in)
at tip	1.73 m (5 ft 8 in)
Wing aspect ratio	7.8
Length overall	47.32 m (155 ft 3 in)
Length of fuselage	46.96 m (154 ft 10 in)
Height overall	13.56 m (44 ft 6 in)
Tailplane span	15.21 m (49 ft 11 in)
Wheel track	7.32 m (24 ft 0 in)
Wheelbase	18.29 m (60 ft 0 in)
Passenger doors (two, fwd, port):	
Height	1.83 m (6 ft 0 in)
Width	0.84 m (2 ft 9 in)
Passenger door (rear, port): Height	1.83 m (6 ft 0 in)
Width	0.76 m (2 ft 6 in)
Service door (fwd, stbd): Height	1.65 m (5 ft 5 in)
Width	0.76 m (2 ft 6 in)
Service door (stbd, opposite second passenger door):	
Height	1.83 m (6 ft 0 in)
Width	0.84 m (2 ft 9 in)
Service door (rear, stbd): Height	1.83 m (6 ft 0 in)
Width	0.76 m (2 ft 6 in)
Emergency exits (four, overwing):	
Height	0.97 m (3 ft 2 in)
Width	0.51 m (1 ft 8 in)
Emergency exits, optional (two, aft of wings):	
Height	1.32 m (4 ft 4 in)
Width	0.61 m (2 ft 0 in)

DIMENSIONS, INTERNAL:

Cabin (aft of flight deck to rear pressure bulkhead):	
Length	36.09 m (118 ft 5 in)
Max width	3.53 m (11 ft 7 in)
Max height	2.13 m (7 ft 0 in)
Floor area	116.04 m² (1,249 sq ft)
Passenger area volume	230.50 m³ (8,140 cu ft)
Underfloor cargo volume (bulk loading):	
fwd	19.82 m³ (700 cu ft)
rear	30.87 m³ (1,090 cu ft)

AREAS:

Wings, gross	185.25 m² (1,994 sq ft)
Ailerons (total)	4.46 m² (48.0 sq ft)
Trailing-edge flaps (total)	30.38 m² (327 sq ft)
Leading-edge slats (total)	18.39 m² (198 sq ft)
Flight spoilers (total)	10.96 m² (118 sq ft)
Ground spoilers (total)	12.82 m² (138 sq ft)
Fin	34.37 m² (370 sq ft)
Rudder	11.61 m² (125 sq ft)
Tailplane	50.35 m² (542 sq ft)
Elevators (total)	12.54 m² (135 sq ft)

WEIGHTS AND LOADINGS (with 186 passengers. A: 535E4 engines; B: PW2037s; C: PW2040s):

Operating weight empty: A	57,180 kg (126,060 lb)
B, C	57,039 kg (125,750 lb)
Max basic T-O weight: A, B, C	99,790 kg (220,000 lb)
Max T-O weight (medium range):	
A, B, C	104,325 kg (230,000 lb)
Max T-O weight (long range):	
A, B, C	113,395 kg (250,000 lb)
Max landing weight: A, B, C	89,810 kg (198,000 lb)
757-200PF	95,255 kg (210,000 lb)
Max zero-fuel weight: A, B, C	83,460 kg (184,000 lb)
757-200PF	90,720 kg (200,000 lb)
Max wing loading:	
A, B, C at max basic T-O weight	538.5 kg/m² (110.3 lb/sq ft)

A, B, C at long range max T-O weight	587.8 kg/m² (120.4 lb/sq ft)
Max power loading:	
at max basic T-O weight:	
A	279.68 kg/kN (2.74 lb/lb st)
B	293.5 kg/kN (2.88 lb/lb st)
C	268.97 kg/kN (2.64 lb/lb st)
at long range max T-O weight:	
A	317.81 kg/kN (3.12 lb/lb st)
B	333.51 kg/kN (3.27 lb/lb st)
C	305.1 kg/kN (3.00 lb/lb st)

PERFORMANCE (nominal, with 186 passengers, US mixed class operations; at max basic T-O weight, except where indicated, and with engines as above):

Max operating speed: A, B, C	Mach 0.86
Cruising speed: A, B, C	Mach 0.80
Approach speed at S/L, flaps down, max landing weight:	
A, B, C	132 knots (245 km/h; 152 mph) EAS
Initial cruising height: A	11,878 m (38,970 ft)
B, C	11,674 m (38,300 ft)
Min ground turning radius: over wingtip	29.87 m (98 ft)
nose gear	21.64 m (71 ft)

Runway LCN at ramp weight of 100,244 kg (221,000 lb), optimum tyre pressure and subgrade C flexible pavement: H40 × 14.5-19.0 tyres 36

T-O field length (S/L, 29°C):	
at max basic T-O weight: A	1,646 m (5,400 ft)
B	1,791 m (5,875 ft)
C	1,637 m (5,370 ft)
at long range max T-O weight: A	2,134 m (7,000 ft)
B	2,792 m (9,160 ft)
C	2,118 m (6,950 ft)
Landing field length at max landing weight:	
A	1,411 m (4,630 ft)
B, C	1,460 m (4,790 ft)
Range with 186 passengers:	
at max basic T-O weight:	
A	2,820 nm (5,226 km; 3,247 miles)
B, C	2,980 nm (5,522 km; 3,431 miles)
at long range max T-O weight:	
A	3,820 nm (7,079 km; 4,399 miles)
B, C	4,000 nm (7,408 km; 4,603 miles)
757-200PF, max long range T-O weight, 22,680 kg (50,000 lb) payload:	
A	3,700 nm (6,857 km; 4,261 miles)
B, C	3,885 nm (7,200 km; 4,474 miles)

OPERATIONAL NOISE LEVELS (FAR Pt 36 Stage 3):

T-O, at max basic T-O weight, cutback power:	
A	82.2 EPNdB
B	86.2 EPNdB
C (estimated)	84.7 EPNdB
Approach at max landing weight, 30° flaps:	
A	95.0 EPNdB
B, C	97.7 EPNdB
Sideline: A	93.3 EPNdB
B	94.0 EPNdB
C (estimated)	94.6 EPNdB

BOEING MODEL 767

On 14 July 1978, Boeing announced its intention to launch full scale development of the twin-turbofan Model 767, following receipt of an order for 30 from United Air Lines. Construction of the first Model 767 began on 6 July 1979, with a fuselage 1.17 m (3 ft 10 in) wider than that of the Model 757, permitting a two-aisle seating layout. A 220-passenger version known as the **767-200** was selected as the basic model. The first Model 767 (N767BA) made its first flight on 26 September 1981, powered by Pratt & Whitney JT9D turbofans. The fifth aircraft, the first powered by General Electric CF6-80A engines, flew for the first time on 19 February 1982.

Boeing 767-200ER of Air Mauritius photographed during its record-setting delivery flight in April 1988

FAA certification of the initial JT9D-7R4D version was received on 30 July 1982, and on 30 September 1982 for the CF6-80A version. Delivery of the first 767, to United Air Lines, was made on 19 August 1982, this airline operating its initial revenue service on 8 September. The first CF6-engined 767 was delivered to Delta on 25 October and entered service on 15 December 1982.

As well as the basic model, an optional medium-range version of the 767-200 with reduced fuel capacity, and an optional higher gross weight version, certificated in June 1983, are available. In addition, an extended-range **767-200ER** (first flown on 6 March 1984), with still higher gross weight and increased fuel capacity, is in production. The basic extended-range version, with gross weight increased to 156,490 kg (345,000 lb) and increased fuel capacity due to wing centre-section tanks, was first delivered, to Ethiopian Airlines on 23 May 1984. Versions with optional gross weights of 159,210 kg (351,000 lb), 172,365 kg (380,000 lb) and 175,540 kg (387,000 lb) and with additional fuel capacity are also available.

In February 1983 Boeing announced the addition to the line of a 269-seat **767-300**, with the same max T-O weight as the basic 767-200ER, strengthened main and nose landing gear, and additional metal thickness in certain areas of the fuselage and wing lower surface. The fuselage is extended by a 3.07 m (10 ft 1 in) plug forward of the wing, and a 3.35 m (11 ft) plug aft of the wing. Flight deck, cabin cross-section and systems are as for the other 767 models; power plant options are as for the 767-200ER. The first order for the 767-300 was received on 29 September 1983. The first 767-300 flew for the first time on 30 January 1986, powered by JT9D-7R4D engines, and was certificated on 22 September 1986, at which time the version with CF6-80A2s was also certificated. Deliveries (to JAL) began on 25 September 1986. In August 1987 British Airways ordered 11 767-300s, with options on a further 15, all with Rolls-Royce RB211-524H engines, for delivery between November 1989 and February 1992.

In January 1985 Boeing began development of an extended range, higher gross weight version of the 767-300, designated **767-300ER**. This version, with optional gross weights of 172,365 kg (380,000 lb), 175,540 kg (387,000 lb) or 181,439 kg (400,000 lb), and further enlarged wing

centre-section fuel tanks, is powered by advanced General Electric CF6-80C2, Pratt & Whitney PW4000 series or Rolls-Royce RB211-524H engines. Structural changes have been incorporated to accommodate the increased fuel capacity and higher gross weight. Launch customer for the 767-300ER was American Airlines, which ordered 15 for delivery commencing in February 1988. Certification of the 767-300ER was obtained in late 1987.

In January 1987 the 767-200 with JT9D-7R4 and CF6-80A or A2 engines received FAA approval for extended range operation over water or undeveloped land areas. By February, the FAA had also approved the installation on 767-200s and -300s of Boeing's windshear detection and guidance system.

On 17 April 1988 a Boeing 767-200ER established a distance record for a twin-jet commercial airliner, flying from Halifax, Nova Scotia, to Plaisance Airport, Mauritius, in the Indian Ocean, a distance of 7,579 nm (14,044 km; 8,727 miles). The aircraft, which was on its delivery flight to Air Mauritius, completed the journey in 16 h 27 min.

By 30 June 1988 orders for the Model 767-200/200ER/ 300/300ER totalled 295 (119, 74, 51 and 51 respectively); of these, 226 (114, 65, 34 and 13) had been delivered. Details of the modification of the original prototype as an element of the SDI programme can be found in the 767 AOA entry, under Boeing Aerospace.

Boeing awarded Model 767 manufacturing subcontracts to Grumman Aerospace Corporation (wing centre-section, an adjacent lower fuselage section, and fuselage bulkheads); to LTV (horizontal tail); and to Canadair Ltd (rear fuselage). In other major work-sharing programmes, Aeritalia of Italy and member companies of the Japanese aerospace industry participate as follows:

Aeritalia: Wing control surfaces, flaps and leading-edge slats; wingtips; elevators; fin, rudder; and nose radome.

Fuji: Wing fairings and main landing gear doors.

Kawasaki: Centre-fuselage body panels, exit hatches and wing in-spar ribs.

Mitsubishi: Rear-fuselage body panels, stringers, passenger and cargo doors, and dorsal fin.

The following details apply to the basic Model 767-200, except where indicated:

TYPE: Twin-turbofan medium-range commercial transport.

WINGS: Cantilever low-wing monoplane. Special Boeing wing sections. Thickness/chord ratio 15.1% at root, 10.3% at tip. Dihedral 6°. Incidence 4° 15′. Sweepback 31° 30′ at quarter-chord. Fail-safe structure of aluminium alloy. Plain inboard (all-speed) and outboard (low-speed) ailerons with extensive use of graphite hybrid composites. Single-slotted linkage-supported aluminium outboard trailing-edge flaps; double-slotted inboard flaps. Conventional inboard and outboard spoilers of graphite composite construction are provided for roll control, to act as airbrakes, and for lift dumping. Track mounted leading-edge slats of light alloy construction. Roll trim through spring feel system. All control surfaces are powered hydraulically. Anti-icing of outboard wing leading-edges.

FUSELAGE: Conventional semi-monocoque structure of aluminium alloy, consisting of skin, longitudinal stringers and circumferential frames. Structure is of fail-safe design, and is pressurised except for tailcone aft of passenger cabin, landing gear wheel wells and air cycle machine wells.

TAIL UNIT: Cantilever fail-safe structure of aluminium alloy and aluminium honeycomb. Variable incidence tailplane. Elevators of single hinge type with redundant parallel actuators. No trim tabs. All controls are powered hydraulically. Yaw trim through spring feel system. No anti-icing.

LANDING GEAR: Hydraulically retractable tricycle type. Menasco twin-wheel nose unit retracts forward. Cleveland Pneumatic main gear, comprising two four-wheel bogies which retract inward. Oleo-pneumatic shock absorbers. Bendix wheels and brakes. Mainwheel tyres size 45 × 17-20, pressure 12.6 bars (183 lb/sq in). Nosewheel tyres size 37 × 14-15, pressure 10.0 bars (145 lb/sq in). Steel disc brakes on all mainwheels. Electronically controlled anti-skid units.

POWER PLANT: Two high bypass turbofans in pods pylon-mounted on the wing leading-edges. Alternative engines available for all models of the Boeing 767 are the General Electric CF6-80A and Pratt & Whitney JT9D-7R4D, both rated at 213.5 kN (48,000 lb st), and the CF6-80A2 and JT9D-7R4E and JT9D-7R4E4, rated at 222.4 kN (50,000 lb st). Additionally, the 767-200,

First Boeing 767-300ER extended range version of the 767-300

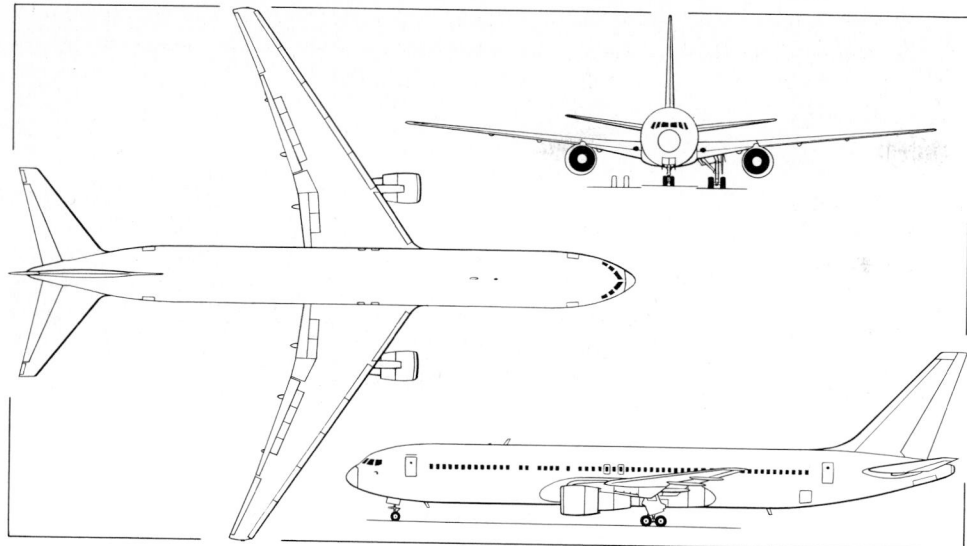

Boeing 767-300 wide-bodied medium-range commercial transport aircraft *(Pilot Press)*

767-200ER and 767-300 are available with the Pratt & Whitney PW4050 rated at 222.4 kN (50,000 lb st); PW4052 rated at 231.3 kN (52,000 lb st) and the General Electric CF6-80C2B2 rated at 233.5 kN (52,500 lb st). The General Electric CF6-80C2B4, rated at 257.5 kN (57,900 lb st), is available on the 767-200ER, 767-300 and 767-300ER. The Pratt & Whitney PW4056, rated at 252.4 kN (56,750 lb st), PW4060 and General Electric CF6-80C2B6, both rated at 266.9 kN (60,000 lb st), are available only on extended range versions. The Rolls-Royce RB211-524G, rated at 269.6 kN (60,600 lb st), will be available on 767s entering service from early 1990. Fuel in one integral tank in each wing, and in a centre tank, with total capacity of 63,216 litres (16,700 US gallons; 13,905 Imp gallons) in 200/300; 767-200ER has additional 14,195 litres (3,750 US gallons; 3,122 Imp gallons) in a second centre-section tank, raising total capacity to 77,412 litres (20,450 US gallons; 17,028 Imp gallons). The 767-300ER has a further expanded wing centre-section tank (optional on the -200ER), bringing total capacity to 91,039 litres (24,050 US gallons; 20,026 Imp gallons). Refuelling point in port outer wing. Anti-icing of engine air inlets.

ACCOMMODATION: Normal operating crew of two on flight deck, with third position optional. Basic accommodation in -200 models for 216 passengers, made up of 18 first class passengers forward in six-abreast seating at 96.5 cm (38 in) pitch, and 198 tourist class in mainly seven-abreast seating at 87 cm (34 in) pitch. Type A inward opening plug doors are provided at both the front and rear of the cabin on each side of the fuselage, with a Type III emergency exit over the wing on each side. A total of five toilets is installed, two centrally in the main cabin, two aft in the main cabin, and one forward in the first class section. Galleys are situated at forward and aft ends of the cabin. Alternative single class layouts provide for 230 tourist passengers, seated seven-abreast at 86 cm (34 in) pitch; 242 passengers seated seven-abreast at 81 cm (32 in) pitch; or 255 passengers mainly seven-abreast (two-three-two) at 76 cm (30 in) pitch, or eight-abreast (two-four-two) at 81 cm (32 in) pitch. Max seating capacity in -200 models (requiring additional overwing emergency exit) for 290 passengers, mainly eight-abreast, at 76 cm (30 in) pitch, or in -300 for 290 passengers seven-abreast. Underfloor cargo holds of -200 versions can accommodate, typically, up to 22 LD2 or 11 LD1 containers. The 767-300 underfloor cargo holds can accommodate 30 LD2 or 15 LD1 containers. Forward and rear cargo doors of equal size are standard on the 767-200 and 767-300, but a larger (1.75 by 3.40 m; 5 ft 9 in by 11 ft 2 in) forward cargo door is standard on the 767-200ER and 767-300ER and optional on 767-200 and 767-300, to permit loading of Type 2 pallets, three such pallets being accommodated in the -200/200ER and four in the -300/300ER. Bulk cargo door at rear on port side. Overhead stowage for carry-on baggage. Cabin is air-conditioned, cargo holds heated.

SYSTEMS: AiResearch dual air cycle air-conditioning system. Pressure differential 0.59 bars (8.6 lb/sq in). Electrical supply from two alternating 90 kVA three-phase 400 Hz constant frequency AC generators, 115/200V output. 90 kVA generator mounted on APU for ground operation or for emergency use. Three hydraulic systems at 207 bars (3,000 lb/sq in), for flight control and utility functions, supplied from engine driven pumps and a Garrett bleed air powered hydraulic pump or APU. Maximum generating capacity of port and starboard systems is 163 litres (43 US gallons; 35.8 Imp gallons)/min; centre system 185.5 litres (49 US gallons; 40.8 Imp gallons), at 196.5 bars (2,850 lb/sq in). Reservoirs pressurised by engine bleed air via a pressure regulation module. Reservoir relief valve pressure is nominally 4.48 bars

(65 lb/sq in). An additional hydraulic motor driven generator, to provide essential functions for extended range operations, is standard on the 767-200ER and 767-300ER and optional on the 767-200 and 767-300. Nitrogen chlorate oxygen generators in passenger cabin, plus gaseous oxygen for flight crew. Anti-icing for air data sensors and windscreen. APU in tailcone to provide ground and in-flight electrical power and pressurisation.

AVIONICS AND EQUIPMENT: Standard avionics include ARINC 700 Series equipment (Bendix VOR/marker beacon receiver, ILS receiver, radio altimeter, transponder, DME, ADF and RDR-4A colour weather radar in aircraft for All Nippon, Britannia and Transbrasil). Collins caution annunciator, dual digital flight management systems, and triple digital flight control computers, including FCS-700 flight control system, EFIS-700 electronic flight instrument system and RMI-743 radio distance magnetic indicator. Honeywell IRS, and Sperry Flight Systems FMCS and DADC, as described in Boeing Model 757 entry. Options include Boeing's windshear detection and guidance system.

DIMENSIONS, EXTERNAL:

Wing span	47.57 m (156 ft 1 in)
Wing chord: at root	8.57 m (28 ft 1¼ in)
at tip	2.29 m (7 ft 6 in)
Wing aspect ratio	7.9
Length overall: 200/200ER	48.51 m (159 ft 2 in)
300/300ER	54.94 m (180 ft 3 in)
Length of fuselage: 200/200ER	47.24 m (155 ft 0 in)
300/300ER	53.67 m (176 ft 1 in)
Fuselage: Max width	5.03 m (16 ft 6 in)
Height overall	15.85 m (52 ft 0 in)
Tailplane span	18.62 m (61 ft 1 in)
Wheel track	9.30 m (30 ft 6 in)
Wheelbase: 200/200ER	19.69 m (64 ft 7 in)
300/300ER	22.76 m (74 ft 8 in)

Passenger doors (two, fwd and rear, port):
Height	1.88 m (6 ft 2 in)
Width	1.07 m (3 ft 6 in)

Galley service door (two, fwd and rear, stbd):
Height	1.83 m (6 ft 0 in)
Width	1.07 m (3 ft 6 in)

Emergency exits (two, each): Height 0.97 m (3 ft 2 in)
Width 0.51 m (1 ft 8 in)

Cargo doors (two, fwd and rear, stbd):
Height	1.75 m (5 ft 9 in)
Width	1.78 m (5 ft 10 in)

Optional cargo door (fwd, port):
Height	1.75 m (5 ft 9 in)
Width	3.40 m (11 ft 2 in)

DIMENSIONS, INTERNAL:
Cabin, excl flight deck:
Length: 200/200ER	33.93 m (111 ft 4 in)
300/300ER	40.36 m (132 ft 5 in)
Max width	4.72 m (15 ft 6 in)
Max height	2.87 m (9 ft 5 in)
Floor area: 200/200ER	154.9 m² (1,667 sq ft)
300/300ER	184.0 m² (1,981 sq ft)
Volume: 200/200ER	428.2 m³ (15,121 cu ft)
300/300ER	483.9 m³ (17,088 cu ft)
Volume, flight deck	13.5 m³ (478 cu ft)

Baggage holds (containerised), volume:
200/200ER	74.8 m³ (2,640 cu ft)
300/300ER	101.9 m³ (3,600 cu ft)

Bulk cargo hold volume:
all models	12.2 m³ (430 cu ft)

Combined baggage hold/bulk cargo hold volume:
200/200ER	87.0 m³ (3,070 cu ft)
300/300ER	114.1 m³ (4,030 cu ft)

Total cargo hold volume:
200/200ER	111.3 m³ (3,930 cu ft)
300/300ER	147.0 m³ (5,190 cu ft)

AREAS:
Wings, gross	283.3 m² (3,050 sq ft)
Ailerons (total)	11.58 m² (124.6 sq ft)
Trailing-edge flaps (total)	36.88 m² (397.0 sq ft)
Leading-edge slats (total)	28.30 m² (304.6 sq ft)
Spoilers (total)	15.83 m² (170.4 sq ft)
Fin	30.19 m² (325.0 sq ft)
Rudder	15.95 m² (171.7 sq ft)
Tailplane	59.88 m² (644.5 sq ft)
Elevators (total)	17.81 m² (191.7 sq ft)

WEIGHTS (A: 767-200 basic/JT9D-7R4D engines; B: 767-200 basic/CF6-80A; C: medium-range version/JT9D-7R4D; D: medium-range version/CF6-80A; E: 767-200ER/PW4050; F: 767-200ER/CF6-80C2B2; G: 767-200ER/PW4056; H: 767-200ER/CF6-80C2B4; J: 767-300/PW4050; K: 767-300/CF6-80C2B2; L: 767-300 higher gross weight version/PW4050; M: 767-300 higher gross weight version/CF6-80C2B2; N: 767-300ER/PW4056; P: 767-300ER/CF6-80C2B4; Q: 767-300ER/PW4060):

Manufacturer's weight empty:
A, C	74,752 kg (164,800 lb)
B, D	74,344 kg (163,900 lb)
E	76,339 kg (168,300 lb)
F	76,249 kg (168,100 lb)
G	76,566 kg (168,800 lb)
H	76,476 kg (168,600 lb)
J, L	79,560 kg (175,400 lb)
K, M	79,379 kg (175,000 lb)
N	80,785 kg (178,100 lb)
P	80,603 kg (177,700 lb)
Q	81,374 kg (179,400 lb)

Operating weight empty: A, C 80,921 kg (178,400 lb)
B, D	80,512 kg (177,500 lb)
E	83,552 kg (184,200 lb)
F	83,461 kg (184,000 lb)
G	83,778 kg (184,700 lb)
H	83,688 kg (184,500 lb)
J, L	87,135 kg (192,100 lb)
K, M	86,953 kg (191,700 lb)
N	89,312 kg (196,900 lb)
P	89,131 kg (196,500 lb)
Q	89,902 kg (198,200 lb)

Max payload (767-200, 216 passengers; 767-200ER, 174 passengers; 767-300, 261 passengers; 767-300ER, 210 passengers): A, B, C, D 19,595 kg (43,200 lb)
E, F, G, H	16,574 kg (36,540 lb)
J, K, L, M	23,677 kg (52,200 lb)
N, P, Q	20,003 kg (44,100 lb)

Max fuel weight:
A, B, C, D, J, K, L, M	51,131 kg (112,725 lb)
E, F	62,613 kg (138,038 lb)
G, H, N, P, Q	73,635 kg (162,338 lb)

Max T-O weight: A, B 136,078 kg (300,000 lb)
C, D	142,881 kg (315,000 lb)
E, F, J, K	156,489 kg (345,000 lb)
G, H, N, P	175,540 kg (387,000 lb)
L, M	159,211 kg (351,000 lb)
Q	181,437 kg (400,000 lb)

Max ramp weight: A, B 136,985 kg (302,000 lb)
C, D	143,789 kg (317,000 lb)
E, F, J, K	157,396 kg (347,000 lb)
G, H, N, P	175,994 kg (388,000 lb)
L, M	159,664 kg (352,000 lb)
Q	181,890 kg (401,000 lb)

Max zero-fuel weight: A, B 112,491 kg (248,000 lb)
C, D	113,398 kg (250,000 lb)
E, F	114,757 kg (253,000 lb)
G, H	117,934 kg (260,000 lb)
J, K, L, M, N, P	126,098 kg (278,000 lb)
Q	130,634 kg (288,000 lb)

Max landing weight: A, B 122,470 kg (270,000 lb)
C, D	123,377 kg (272,000 lb)
E, F	126,098 kg (278,000 lb)
G, H	129,273 kg (285,000 lb)
J, K, L, M, N, P	136,078 kg (300,000 lb)
Q	145,149 kg (320,000 lb)

PERFORMANCE (at max T-O weight except where indicated):
Normal cruising speed, all versions Mach 0.80
Approach speed at max landing weight:
A, B, C, D	136 knots (252 km/h; 157 mph)
E	138 knots (256 km/h; 159 mph)
F, G, H	140 knots (259 km/h; 161 mph)
J, K, L, M, N, P	141 knots (261 km/h; 162 mph)
Q	145 knots (269 km/h; 167 mph)

Initial cruise altitude: A 11,950 m (39,200 ft)
B	12,100 m (39,700 ft)
C	11,650 m (38,200 ft)
D	11,800 m (38,700 ft)
E	11,215 m (36,800 ft)
F	11,460 m (37,600 ft)
G	10,925 m (35,850 ft)
H	10,850 m (35,600 ft)
J, M	11,250 m (36,900 ft)
K	11,340 m (37,200 ft)
L	11,125 m (36,500 ft)
N, P	10,600 m (34,800 ft)
Q	10,400 m (34,100 ft)

Service ceiling, one engine out: A, C 6,525 m (21,400 ft)
B, D	6,430 m (21,100 ft)
E	6,850 m (22,500 ft)

F	7,200 m (23,600 ft)
G	7,250 m (23,800 ft)
H	7,375 m (24,200 ft)
J, L	6,035 m (19,800 ft)
K, M	6,150 m (20,200 ft)
N, P	6,615 m (21,700 ft)
Q	6,550 m (21,500 ft)
T-O field length: A, B	1,798 m (5,900 ft)
C	1,951 m (6,400 ft)
D	1,981 m (6,500 ft)
E	2,347 m (7,700 ft)
F	2,316 m (7,600 ft)
G, H	2,774 m (9,100 ft)
J	2,560 m (8,400 ft)
K	2,469 m (8,100 ft)
L, M	2,652 m (8,700 ft)
N	2,926 m (9,600 ft)
P	2,956 m (9,700 ft)
Q	2,774 m (9,100 ft)
Design range: A	3,160 nm (5,856 km; 3,639 miles)
B	3,220 nm (5,967 km; 3,708 miles)
C	3,795 nm (7,033 km; 4,370 miles)
D	3,850 nm (7,135 km; 4,433 miles)
E	5,365 nm (9,942 km; 6,178 miles)
F	5,410 nm (10,026 km; 6,230 miles)
G	6,770 nm (12,546 km; 7,796 miles)
H	6,805 nm (12,611 km; 7,836 miles)
J	4,000 nm (7,413 km; 4,606 miles)
K	4,020 nm (7,450 km; 4,629 miles)
L	4,230 nm (7,839 km; 4,871 miles)
M	4,260 nm (7,895 km; 4,905 miles)
N	5,740 nm (10,637 km; 6,610 miles)
P	5,760 nm (10,674 km; 6,633 miles)
Q	6,060 nm (11,230 km; 6,978 miles)

OPERATIONAL NOISE LEVELS (FAR Pt 36, Stage 3):

T-O at max basic T-O weight: B	87.1 EPNdB
H	90.4 EPNdB
Approach at max landing weight: B	101.6 EPNdB
H	101.7 EPNdB
Sideline: B	95.4 EPNdB
H	96.6 EPNdB

Model of proposed Boeing Model 7J7 (*Jay Miller/Aerofax*)

BOEING MODEL 7J7

In March 1986 The Boeing Company and the Japanese companies of Mitsubishi Heavy Industries, Kawasaki Heavy Industries, Fuji Heavy Industries and the Japan Aircraft Development Corporation signed a memorandum of understanding for the design, development and production of an advanced technology airliner known as the Model 7J7. The Japanese companies will have a 25 per cent equity share in the programme and will participate on a full partnership basis. Hawker de Havilland Ltd of Australia, Saab-Scania of Sweden and Shorts of Belfast have also signed understandings with Boeing to participate as programme associates.

The 7J7 will be an entirely new design using very high bypass engines driving propfans, an advanced wing design, new structural materials, advanced avionics and digital communications equipment and fly by wire and fly by light technologies. Boeing has selected the General Electric UDF power plant for the 7J7. The general configuration of the aircraft can be seen in the accompanying illustration.

Boeing predicts a 45 per cent increase in fuel efficiency and a ten per cent reduction in direct operating costs for the aircraft when compared with the latest turbofan airliners which will be available at the end of the decade.

In February 1987, under a contract from Boeing, Calspan Corporation began flight testing key elements of the 7J7's advanced digital fly by wire flight control system on the NC-131H Total In-Flight Simulator (TIFS) aircraft that it maintains, modifies and operates on behalf of the USAF Flight Dynamics Laboratory (see 1980-81 and earlier editions of *Jane's*). Equipment evaluated included both sidestick and centre column controllers.

In December 1987 Boeing announced that it was delaying 7J7 programme timing "until a more defined requirement of airplane and engine size can be obtained from key customers". Company workforce assigned to the programme was reduced from 900 to 300, and 1993/94 is now regarded as the earliest likely date for entry into service.

BOEING HELICOPTERS

Boeing Center, PO Box 16858, Philadelphia, Pennsylvania 19142
Telephone: (215) 591 2121
Telex: 510 669 2217 BOEMORA MOR
PRESIDENT: Donald R. Chesnut
VICE-PRESIDENT, RESEARCH AND ENGINEERING:
John Diamond
DIRECTOR, INTERNATIONAL SALES AND MARKETING:
John F. Hayden
DIRECTOR, COMMUNICATIONS: Robert Torgerson

Boeing Helicopters, established in 1960 as Boeing Vertol Company, has produced and delivered more than 2,500 tandem-rotor helicopters to the US military services, as well as to many foreign nations. Its primary production programme involves modernisation of early model CH-47 Chinooks to CH-47D configuration for the US Army. Production of H-46 Sea Knight SR&M improvement kits for the US Navy and Marine Corps is also continuing.

Boeing Helicopters is teamed with Bell Helicopter Textron to develop and produce the V-22 Osprey, as described under the Bell/Boeing entry in this section. On 3 June 1985 Boeing Helicopters signed a memorandum of understanding with Sikorsky Aircraft to enter a joint design to meet the US Army's LHX light helicopter requirement, with Boeing Military Airplanes responsible for the avionics integration. The Boeing Helicopters/Sikorsky contender will have a gross weight of approx 3,629 kg (8,000 lb). With Sikorsky, Boeing Helicopters has also begun manufacture of replacement rotor blades for the US Army's UH-60 Black Hawk. The blades are of graphite reinforced glassfibre with a Nomex honeycomb core.

Boeing Helicopters also produces the fixed portions of the wing leading-edges of the Model 737, 747, 757 and 767 commercial transports, and metal leading-edge slats for the 757.

In early 1987 an 11,055 m² (119,000 sq ft) development facility and a 17,466 m² (188,000 sq ft) office/computer centre were added to Boeing Helicopters' Philadelphia headquarters.

Employment within Boeing Helicopters stood at 6,600 at the beginning of 1988.

BOEING HELICOPTERS MODEL 107
USN and USMC designations: CH-46/UH-46 Sea Knight

A total of 624 CH/UH-46 Sea Knights was delivered to the US Marine Corps and US Navy in the 1964-1971 period. With a view to modernising the Marine Corps' fleet of CH-46s, two were modified by Boeing Helicopters in 1975, and the US Marine Corps subsequently updated 273 CH-46s to **CH-46E** configuration, with 1,394 kW (1,870 shp) General Electric T58-GE-16 turboshafts and other modifications (see 1985-86 and earlier editions of *Jane's*).

In April 1975 Boeing Helicopters received a contract from Naval Air Systems Command to initiate the development of glassfibre main rotor blades for the H-46

Boeing Helicopters updated CH-46E for the US Marine Corps with SR&M improvements

fleet. Following testing in 1977-78, the first production order was issued by the US Navy in December 1977; follow-on orders maintained deliveries of glassfibre blades up to the end of 1986. During 1981 Boeing Helicopters received contracts to provide 96 glassfibre rotor blades for Canadian Armed Forces CH-113/113A helicopters, 33 blades for Columbia Helicopters Inc and 103 blades for Swedish HKP-4s. All were delivered in 1983-86.

In December 1980 the Naval Air Systems Command awarded Boeing Helicopters the first of a series of contracts for a multi-year US Navy/Marine Corps helicopter improvement programme. Known as the safety, reliability and maintainability (SR&M) programme, this is aimed at reducing the operating costs of HH-46A, CH-46D and CH-46E helicopters beyond the end of this century. Improvements involve an aircraft retrofit kit to update the hydraulic flight control system, electrical system, rotor drive system, airframe and landing gear, manufactured by Boeing Helicopters for installation by the Navy. During the eight-year programme, 357 modification kits are being supplied. A prototype SR&M modified CH-46E flew for the first time on 23 November 1983. The production phase began during the first quarter of 1984, with delivery to the Navy of the first production kit in July 1985. Service

deliveries of CH-46Es with SR&M improvements began in December 1985 from MCAS Cherry Point, North Carolina. Production of kits is due to be completed in January 1989.

Development testing of rapid-inflating emergency flotation bags for CH-46Es was completed during 1985. When deflated, the bags are stowed in fuselage side panels measuring approximately 1.78 m × 0.81 m (5 ft 10 in × 2 ft 8 in). All US Navy and US Marine Corps CH-46Es are to be fitted with provisions for the equipment, beginning in late 1988.

Under a US Navy contract received in September 1987, Boeing Helicopters is developing kits to increase the fuel capacity of US Marine Corps H-46Es. A production programme involving 169 shipsets is under consideration, to start in late 1989.

BOEING HELICOPTERS MODELS 114 and 414
US Army designation: CH-47 Chinook
Canadian Armed Forces designation: CH-147
Royal Air Force designation: Chinook HC. Mk 1B
Spanish Army designation: HT.17

Development of the CH-47 Chinook began in 1956, to meet a US Army requirement for an all-weather medium transport helicopter. The first of five YCH-47As made its initial hovering flight on 21 September 1961. Details of the initial production **CH-47A** (354 for US Army and **CH-47B** (108 for US Army) can be found in the 1974-75 edition of *Jane's*. Transmissions of some existing US Army As and Bs were later uprated to CH-47C standard.

Current domestic and export versions are as follows:

CH-47C. Increased performance from a combination of strengthened transmissions, two 2,796 kW (3,750 shp) T55-L-11A engines and increased integral fuel capacity. First flight 14 October 1967; deliveries of 270 to US Army began in Spring 1968. Total of 182 US Army CH-47Cs undergoing retrofit with glassfibre rotor blades.

A crashworthy fuel system and an integral spar inspection system (ISIS) were introduced from 1973, incorporation of the crashworthy fuel system on US Army CH-47Cs being accomplished by retrofit kits. Chinooks delivered to Australia also have this system, which provides a total fuel capacity of 3,944 litres (1,042 US gallons; 867.6 Imp gallons). Nine CH-47Cs, designated **CH-147**, were delivered to Canada from September 1974. Details of these can be found in the 1985-86 and earlier editions. There is a full description of the CH-47C in the 1980-81 edition. Nine of the Spanish Army's Chinooks are CH-47Cs.

CH-47D. Under a 1976 US Army contract Boeing Helicopters modified three earlier model CH-47s (one A, one B and a C) as D standard prototypes, the first one being flown on 11 May 1979. In October 1980 the initial CH-47D 'production' modernisation contract was awarded by the US Army, and the first 'production' example made its initial flight as a CH-47D on 26 February 1982. It was handed over to the US Army on 20 May 1982, as the first of a planned total of 472 aircraft which are being remanufactured to this much-modified and modernised standard, extending the service life of the Army's Chinook fleet into the next century. Initial operational capability for the CH-47D was achieved on 28 February 1984, with the aircraft first equipping the 101st Airborne Division. A total of 328 CH-47Ds had been funded by mid-1988, of which 240 are covered by a multi-year procurement contract. Deliveries totalled more than 210 at that time, and are scheduled to continue until November 1993, at a current rate of four per month. All deliveries to active Army units in the continental USA have been completed; units based in Europe are being equipped from the current production line, starting in November 1987. Boeing has proposed completion of the final 144 aircraft to CH-47E standard (which see).

The CH-47D remanufacturing programme involves stripping the Chinooks down to their basic airframes before refitting them with improved components and systems to bring them up to the new standard. Any necessary body or other repairs and modifications are done at the same time.

Thirteen major improvements are involved in the conversion. Textron Lycoming T55-L-712 turboshafts replace the lower-rated T55-L-7C or -11 engines of earlier models. Rotor transmission rating is increased, with integral lubrication and cooling, and composite rotor blades are fitted. The flight deck is reconfigured to reduce pilot workload. Other changes include redundant and improved electrical systems, modular hydraulic systems, an advanced flight control system, improved avionics, aircraft survivability equipment, and night vision goggle compatibility. A Solar T62-T-2B APU runs the accessory gear drive, thereby operating all hydraulic and electrical systems, and a single-point pressure refuelling system and triple cargo

Boeing Helicopters CH-47D Chinook of the US Army

hooks are installed. Some 10-15 per cent (by weight) of the CH-47D airframe is of composite construction. The basic airframe structure, landing gear and seats are the only major components not replaced or rebuilt. Some 300 subcontractors are engaged in the conversion programme.

At a max gross weight of 22,680 kg (50,000 lb) in US Army service the CH-47D has more than double the useful load capability of the CH-47A (10,334 kg; 22,783 lb compared with 4,990 kg; 11,000 lb). Its versatility covers a variety of combat and support missions, including troop movement, artillery emplacement, and battlefield resupply. It is the prime mover for the Army's M198 towed 155 mm howitzer; this artillery piece, plus 32 rounds of ammunition and an 11-man gun crew, represents a combined internal/external load of approx 9,980 kg (22,000 lb). The CH-47D is the only Army helicopter capable of lifting, using the centre underfuselage hook, the 11,225 kg (24,750 lb) D5 caterpillar bulldozer. It is able to airlift Army Milvans (supply containers) at speeds of up to 138 knots (256 km/h; 159 mph), and carry (using all three hooks) up to seven 1,893 litre (500 US gallon; 416 Imp gallon), 1,587 kg (3,500 lb) rubber fuel blivets in a single mission. According to the US Army, the CH-47D offers more than 100 per cent increase in performance over the A model Chinook when operated in a standard European climate, and a 68 per cent increase in 'hot and high' conditions.

Following successful in-flight refuelling trials conducted by the US Army Aviation Engineering Flight Activity unit based at Edwards AFB, California, using a US Air Force HC-130 tanker aircraft, some CH-47Ds are being equipped with an in-flight refuelling system comprising a single-piece graphite boom with aluminium fuel tube mounted on the lower starboard side of the helicopter. The boom measures 8.93 m (29 ft 3½ in) overall. Refuelling has been accomplished at speeds up to 120 knots (222 km/h; 138 mph), at night and in moderate turbulence, at a refuelling rate of 568 litres (150 US gallons; 125 Imp gallons)/min, permitting the CH-47D to be refuelled completely in six minutes.

CH-47E. Proposed 'Advanced Chinook' for US Army, based on updated CH-47D airframe with four-blade

rotor system with de-icing equipment, Textron Lycoming T55-L-714 engines, 'glass' cockpit with CRT displays, additional fuel capacity, and enhanced self-defence capability. Initial proposal is for 144 CH-47Es with deliveries commencing in November 1990.

MH-47E. On 2 December 1987 Boeing Helicopters received an $81.8 million contract to develop an MH-47E variant of the Chinook for the US Army's Special Operations Forces. The MH-47E will be based on a modified CH-47D airframe with 2,983 kW (4,000 shp) Textron Lycoming T55-L-714 engines featuring full authority digital electronic control (FADEC); fuel capacity as for the Model 234LR commercial Chinook, with in-flight refuelling capability; an IBM integrated avionics subsystem to upgrade and extend the helicopter's communications, navigation and survivability capability; multifunction displays; FLIR; a multi-mode radar similar to that being developed for the V-22 Osprey; inertial cargo handling system and additional troop seats; Breeze rescue hoist; provision for two door-mounted 0.50 in machine-guns; rotor brake; and onboard oxygen generating system. The MH-47E will perform clandestine deep penetration missions under adverse weather conditions, by day or night, and over all types of terrain. US Army procurement is for an initial batch of 16 MH-47Es, with options for an additonal 34.

Chinook HC. Mk 1. Version for Royal Air Force, originally ordered in 1978. First example (ZA670) made its initial flight on 23 March 1980. First 33 were similar to Canadian CH-147, with Textron Lycoming T55-L-11E turboshafts, but with provision for glassfibre/carbonfibre rotor blades and three external cargo hooks (capacity 12,700 kg; 28,000 lb on centre hook, or 9,072 kg; 20,000 lb total on forward and rear hooks); accommodation for up to 44 troops or 24 standard NATO stretchers; and other airframe and equipment changes as detailed in the 1985-86 and earlier *Jane's*. Entered service with Nos. 18 and 7 Squadrons in 1981 and 1982 respectively. The first 14 RAF Chinooks were retrofitted with glassfibre rotor blades and a single-point pressure fuelling system by the Royal Navy's Aircraft Yard at Fleetlands, Gosport, Hants. Radar warning receivers were added in another retrofit pro-

CH-47D CHINOOK WEIGHTS AND PERFORMANCE

	Condition 1	Condition 2	Condition 3	Condition 4
Take-off condition				
Altitude	1,220 m (4,000 ft)	Sea level	1,220 m (4,000 ft)	Sea level
Temperature	35°C (95°F)	15°C (59°F)	35°C (95°F)	15°C (59°F)
Empty weight	10,500 kg (23,149 lb)	10,500 kg (23,149 lb)	10,423 kg (22,980 lb)	10,265 kg (22,630 lb)
T-O weight	19,178 kg (42,280 lb)	22,679 kg (50,000 lb)	19,657 kg (43,336 lb)	22,679 kg (50,000 lb)
Payload: external	7,081 kg (15,612 lb)	10,455 kg (23,049 lb)	—	—
internal	—	—	6,423 kg (14,160 lb)	—
Max level speed, S/L, ISA,				
max continuous power, no external load	161 knots (298 km/h; 185 mph)	161 knots (298 km/h; 185 mph)	154 knots (285 km/h; 177 mph)	
Average cruising speed	120 knots (222 km/h; 138 mph)	132 knots (245 km/h; 152 mph)	134 knots (248 km/h; 154 mph)	138 knots (256 km/h; 159 mph)
Max rate of climb, S/L,				
ISA, intermediate rated power	669 m (2,195 ft)/min	464 m (1,522 ft)/min	640 m (2,100 ft)/min	464 m (1,522 ft)/min
Hovering ceiling OGE, ISA, max power	3,130 m (10,270 ft)	1,524 m (5,000 ft)	2,972 m (9,750 ft)	1,524 m (5,000 ft)
Mission radius	30 nm (55.5 km; 34.5 miles)	30 nm (55.5 km; 34.5 miles)	100 nm (185 km; 115 miles)	
Ferry range	—	—	—	1,111 nm (2,059 km; 1,279 miles)

Condition 1
T-O weight is gross weight for 61 m (200 ft)/min vertical rate of climb to hover OGE at 1,220 m/35°C (4,000 ft/95°F). External payload is carried outbound only. Fuel reserve is 30 min cruise fuel. Max speed shown is at T-O weight less external payload.

Condition 2
T-O gross weight is max structural T-O weight for which vertical climb capability at S/L, ISA is 271 m (890 ft)/min. Otherwise same as Condition 1.

Condition 3
T-O weight is gross weight for hover OGE at 1,220 m/35°C (4,000 ft/95°F). Radius is with inbound payload 50 per cent of outbound internal payload. Fuel reserve is 30 min cruise fuel. Max speed shown is at T-O weight.

Condition 4
T-O weight is max structural T-O weight. Max ferry range (internal and external auxiliary fuel). Optimum cruise climb to 2,440 m (8,000 ft) and complete cruise at 2,440 m (8,000 ft). Fuel reserve is 10 per cent of initial fuel.

gramme. Eight more HC. Mk 1s (beginning ZD574), with uprated T55-L-712 engines as in the CH-47D, were delivered in 1984-86. All RAF Chinooks now have T55-L-712 engines and glassfibre rotor blades, and are designated **HC. Mk 1B.** The Secure Radio Division of Marconi Defence Systems has been awarded a £2 million contract to develop a secure speech system for the RAF's Chinook force.

Model 234. Commercial version, described separately.

Model 414. International military version of CH-47C, described in 1985-86 *Jane's*. Now superseded by CH-47D International Chinook (which see). Eight delivered to Spanish Army Aviation's 5th Helicopter Transport Battalion (Bheltra-V) at Colmenar Viejo, Madrid; last six of these have nose mounted Bendix RDR-1400 weather radar.

CH-47D International Chinook. Model 414-100, starting with aircraft for the Japanese programme which began in Spring 1984 when the Japan Defence Agency approved the purchase of two for the JGSDF and one for the JASDF. The first production International CH-47D (N7425H) made its first flight in January 1986, and, with the second, was shipped to Kawasaki Heavy Industries of Japan in April 1986 for avionics and interior installation prior to a co-production arrangement in which Kawasaki is manufacturing 21 CH-47Ds using some Boeing Helicopters supplied components and some locally produced assemblies. Deliveries of the two Boeing Helicopters assembled Chinooks to the JGSDF and JASDF were made in November and December 1986 respectively. Further details of the Japanese (**CH-47J**) programme are given under the entry for Kawasaki.

Total US Army procurement of CH-47A/B/C models was 732. Other military customers for US built Chinooks include Argentina (5), Australia (12), Canada (9), Japan (7), Spain (18), Taiwan (undisclosed), Thailand (4, ex-US Army), and the UK (41). Orders for Agusta/EM built CH-47Cs have been received from Egypt (15), Greece (10), Iran (68), Italy (28), Libya (20) and Morocco (9), with 11 more now in service with the Pennsylvania Army NG.

The following data apply generally to the CH-47D and International CH-47D, except where a specific version is indicated:

TYPE: Twin-engined medium transport helicopter.

ROTOR SYSTEM: Two three-blade rotors in tandem, rotating in opposite directions and driven through interconnecting shafts which enable both rotors to be driven by either engine. Rotor blades, of glassfibre, have Boeing Helicopters VR7 and VR8 aerofoil sections, cambered leading-edge, D shaped glassfibre spar, and a fairing assembly consisting of Nomex honeycomb core with crossply glassfibre laminates for skin. Blades can survive hits by 22 mm API and HEI munitions and still provide a 'fly home' capability. All blades can be folded manually. Rotor heads fully articulated with pitch, flapping and drag hinges. All bearings submerged completely in oil. Provisions for optional rotor brake.

ROTOR DRIVE: Power transmitted from each engine through individual overrunning clutches, into the combiner transmission, thereby providing a single power output to the interconnecting shafts. Rotor/engine rpm ratio 1 : 67. Combined transmission rating 5,593 kW (7,500 shp) and single-engine transmission emergency rating of 3,430 kW (4,600 shp) in CH-47D and International CH-47D at 225 rpm.

FUSELAGE: Semi-monocoque mainly metal structure comprising flight deck, cabin, rear fuselage, and pylon sections. The cabin is of constant cross-section, with the lower half sealed during manufacture to form a watertight compartment that provides water landing capability. Rear of fuselage contains cargo ramp and door.

LANDING GEAR: Non-retractable quadricycle type, with twin wheels on each forward unit and single wheels on each rear unit. Oleo-pneumatic shock absorbers in all units. Rear units fully castoring and steerable; power steering installed on starboard rear unit. All wheels are size 24 × 7.7-VII, with tyres size 8.50-10-III, pressure 4.62 bars (67 lb/sq in). Two single-disc hydraulic brakes. Provision for fitting detachable wheel-skis.

POWER PLANT: Two Textron Lycoming T55-L-712 turboshafts, pod-mounted on sides of the rear pylon, and each with a standard power rating of 2,796 kW (3,750 shp) and emergency rating of 3,356 kW (4,500 shp). Textron Lycoming T55-L-712 SSB engine has standard power rating of 3,264 kW (4,378 shp) and emergency rating of 3,451 kW (4,628 shp). Self-sealing pressure refuelled crashworthy fuel tanks in external fairings on sides of fuselage. Total fuel capacity 3,899 litres (1,030 US gallons; 858 Imp gallons). Oil capacity 14 litres (3.7 US gallons; 3.1 Imp gallons).

ACCOMMODATION: Two pilots on flight deck, with dual controls. Jump seat for crew chief or combat commander. Jettisonable door on each side of flight deck. Depending on seating arrangement, 33 to 55 troops can be accommodated in main cabin, or 24 litters plus two attendants, or vehicles and freight. Rear loading ramp can be left completely or partially open, or can be removed to permit transport of extra-long cargo and in-flight parachute or free-drop delivery of cargo and equipment. Main cabin door, at front on starboard side, comprises upper hinged section which can be opened in

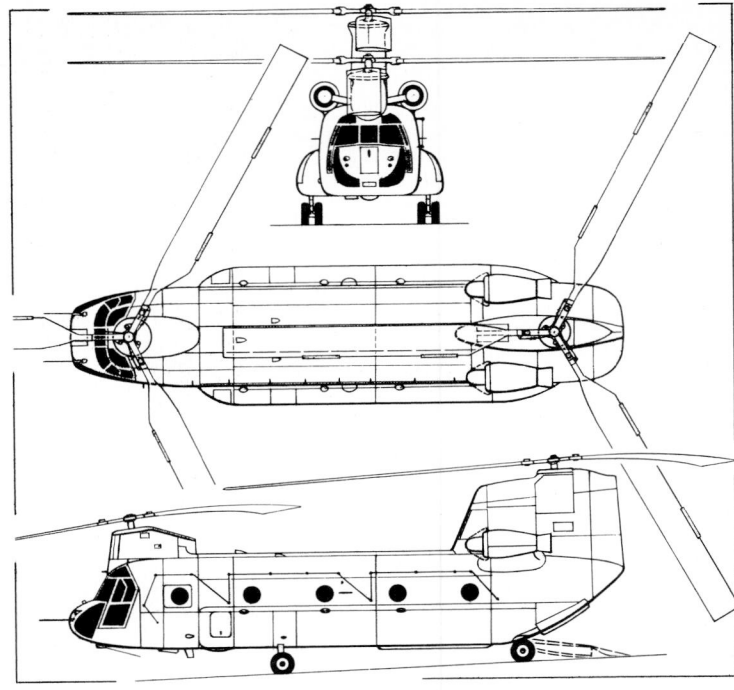

Boeing Helicopters CH-47D military helicopter. Broken lines show rear loading ramp lowered *(Pilot Press)*

Artist's impression of Boeing Helicopters MH-47E helicopter for the US Army's Special Operations Forces

flight, and lower section with integral steps. Lower section is jettisonable. Triple external cargo hook system, as on Model 234, with centre hook rated to carry max load of 11,790 kg (26,000 lb) and the forward and rear hooks 7,710 kg (17,000 lb) each. Provisions are installed for a power-down ramp and water dam to permit ramp operation on water; for forward and aft cargo hooks, ferry fuel tanks, external rescue hoist, and windscreen washers.

SYSTEMS: Cabin heated by 200,000 BTU heater/blower. Hydraulic system provides pressure of 207 bars (3,000 lb/sq in) for flying controls. Max flow rate 53.0 litres (14 US gallons; 11.65 Imp gallons) per minute. Spherical hydraulic reservoir, volume 5,326 cm³ (325 cu in), pressurised to 1.72 bars (25 lb/sq in). Utility hydraulic system, pressure 231 bars (3,350 lb/sq in), max flow rate 51.5 litres (13.6 US gallons; 11.3 Imp gallons) per minute. Piston type reservoir, volume 7,014 cm³ (428 cu in), of which 5,326 cm³ (325 cu in) are usable, pressurised to 3.86 bars (56 lb/sq in). Electrical system includes two 40kVA aircooled alternators driven by transmission drive system. Solar T62-T-2B APU runs accessory gear drive, thereby operating all hydraulic and electrical systems.

AVIONICS AND EQUIPMENT (International CH-47D: US Army CH-47D assumed to be generally similar. Avionics for RAF HC. Mk 1 listed in 1985-86 and earlier editions): Standard avionics include ARC-102 HF com radio, Collins ARC-186 UHF/AM-FM, Magnavox ARC-164 UHF/AM com; C-6533 intercom; Bendix APX-100 IFF; APN-209 radar altimeter; ARN-89B ADF; ARN-123 VOR/glideslope/marker beacon receiver; and ASN-43 gyromagnetic compass. Flight instruments are standard

for IFR, and include an AQU-6A horizontal situation indicator. AFCS maintains helicopter stability, eliminating the need for constant small correction inputs by the pilot to maintain desired attitude. The AFCS is a redundant system using two identical control units and two sets of stabilisation actuators. Standard equipment includes a hydraulically powered winch for rescue and cargo handling, rearview mirror, plus integral work stands and step for maintenance. Provisions for static lines, and maintenance davits for removal of major components.

DIMENSIONS, EXTERNAL:
Rotor diameter (each)	18.29 m (60 ft 0 in)
Rotor blade chord (each)	0.81 m (2 ft 8 in)
Distance between rotor centres	11.94 m (39 ft 2 in)
Length overall, rotors turning	30.18 m (99 ft 0 in)
Length of fuselage	15.54 m (51 ft 0 in)
Width, rotors folded	3.78 m (12 ft 5 in)
Height to top of rear rotor head	5.68 m (18 ft 7.8 in)
Wheel track (c/l of shock absorbers)	3.20 m (10 ft 6 in)
Wheelbase	6.86 m (22 ft 6 in)
Passenger door (fwd, stbd): Height	1.68 m (5 ft 6 in)
Width	0.91 m (3 ft 0 in)
Height to sill	1.09 m (3 ft 7 in)
Rear loading ramp entrance: Height	1.98 m (6 ft 6 in)
Width	2.31 m (7 ft 7 in)
Height to sill	0.79 m (2 ft 7 in)

DIMENSIONS, INTERNAL:
Cabin, excl flight deck: Length	9.19 m (30 ft 2 in)
Width (mean)	2.29 m (7 ft 6 in)
Width at floor	2.51 m (8 ft 3 in)
Height	1.98 m (6 ft 6 in)

Floor area	21.0 m² (226 sq ft)
Usable volume	41.7 m³ (1,474 cu ft)

AREAS:

Rotor blades (each)	7.43 m² (80.0 sq ft)
Rotor discs (total)	525.3 m² (5,655 sq ft)

WEIGHTS (International CH-47D):

Internal payload over 100 nm (185 km; 115 mile) radius at 1,220 m (4,000 ft), 35°C day, hovering OGE at T-O, 20 min reserves 7,136 kg (15,733 lb)

External payload over 100 nm (185 km; 115 mile) radius at 1,220 m (4,000 ft), 35°C day, hovering OGE at T-O, 20 min reserves 6,908 kg (15,229 lb)

Internal payload over 100 nm (185 km; 115 mile) radius at 1,525 m (5,000 ft), ISA, hovering OGE at T-O, 20 min reserves 10,287 kg (22,679 lb)

External payload over 100 nm (185 km; 115 mile) radius at 1,525 nm (5,000 ft), ISA, hovering OGE at T-O, 20 min reserves 10,118 kg (22,307 lb)

Design gross weight	14,968 kg (33,000 lb)
Alternative gross weight	20,865 kg (46,000 lb)
Max T-O weight	24,494 kg (54,000 lb)

PERFORMANCE (International CH-47D, at max continuous power, ISA, at gross weights of A: 22,680 kg; 50,000 lb, B: 20,865 kg; 46,000 lb, C: 14,968 kg; 33,000 lb):

Max level speed at S/L:

A	149 knots (276 km/h; 171 mph)
B	154 knots (285 km/h; 177 mph)
C	163 knots (302 km/h; 188 mph)

Service ceiling, max continuous power:

A	2,775 m (9,100 ft)
B	3,690 m (12,100 ft)
C	6,735 m (22,100 ft)

Hovering ceiling OGE, T-O power:

A	1,860 m (6,100 ft)
B	2,710 m (8,900 ft)
C	5,395 m (17,700 ft)

Boeing Helicopters 234 which made a demonstration tour in the People's Republic of China in 1987

BOEING HELICOPTERS MODEL 234 COMMERCIAL CHINOOK

This development of the military CH-47 Chinook is produced as a commercial passenger transport, cargo carrier, and for specialised tasks such as servicing offshore oil and natural gas rigs, remote resources exploration and extraction, logging, and construction work. The airframe is based on that of the latest military Chinook, but includes features such as wide chord glassfibre rotor blades; redesigned fuselage side fairings; a lengthened nose to accommodate the weather radar antenna; and repositioning further forward of the front landing gear units.

Initial order was placed by British Airways Helicopters, which ordered three Model 234 LRs in 1978 (later increased to six), primarily for North Sea oil rig support operations. First flight was made on 19 August 1980. FAA and UK CAA certification was received on 19 and 26 June 1981 respectively. The first 234 LR went into service with BAH (now British International Helicopters) on 1 July 1981, and all six had been delivered by 1 June 1982. FAA and CAA certification of a 234 LR 'combi' was received in the Summer of 1982.

Three basic versions of the Model 234 are offered:

Long-range model (234 LR). Identified by continuous fuselage-side fairings, approximately twice as large as those of the military Chinook and containing large fuel tanks. Equipped to airline standards as a passenger, passenger/freight 'combi', or all-cargo transport. Six built for BAH/BIH and three for Helicopter A/S of Norway in 1981-85; no other orders known.

Extended-range model (234 ER). Version of 234 LR with two internal auxiliary fuel tanks and fewer seats. Typical configuration has 17 seats for passengers and fuel for up to 875 nm (1,621 km; 1,008 miles). Can also be configured for 32 passengers and a single internal fuel tank where maximum range is not required. FAA certification granted in May 1983 for operation with internal and external loads at the max T-O weights listed. Leased to Arco Alaska (two in 1983) and ERA Helicopters (one in 1985); no other customers known.

Utility model (234 UT). Fuselage side fuel tanks replaced by two drum shaped internal tanks, mounted longitudinally side by side at front of cabin. Fuselage-side fairings removed, leaving only an individual blister around each landing gear mounting. Received supplemental type certification from FAA in October 1981 at a max gross weight of 23,133 kg (51,000 lb) for external cargo lift operations. The FAA approval included also the carriage of 24 passengers, external loads of up to 12,700 kg (28,000 lb) on the aircraft's single cargo hook, and external cargo lift missions at altitudes of up to 3,660 m (12,000 ft) under max gross weight conditions. No orders known.

Multi-purpose long-range model (234 MLR). Similar to 234 LR but with airline standard interior replaced by utility interior. Three delivered to a Far East government operator in 1985.

Conversion from one configuration of the Model 234 to another is estimated to take eight hours, and requires four persons to handle the fuel tanks of the utility model and the ramp baggage bins of the passenger carrying helicopter.

TYPE: Twin-turbine commercial transport helicopter.

ROTOR SYSTEM: Similar to that of International CH-47D. Wide chord glassfibre blades, with VR7 section over inboard 85 per cent of span, and VR8 section on outer 15 per cent of span; thickness/chord ratio 12% and 8% respectively. Overall blade twist 12°. An aluminium screen inserted in the skin provides lightning protection, discharging strikes via the titanium leading-edge. Outboard 25 per cent of leading-edge capped with replaceable nickel section. Blade balancing by tracking weights in tips. Two blades of each rotor can be folded manually. Heads fully articulated, with pitch, flapping and drag hinges. All bearings submerged completely in oil. Blades embody electric de-icing blankets, permitting addition of a de-icing kit if required. Rotor rpm 225.

ROTOR DRIVE: As described for CH-47D. Auxiliary transmission lubrication system enables flight to be completed after total loss of oil in primary system. Transmission rated at 5,033 kW (6,750 shp) at 225 rotor rpm, and 3,430 kW (4,600 shp) for single-engine operation.

FUSELAGE: All-metal semi-monocoque structure of basically square section. Loading ramp forms undersurface of upswept rear fuselage. External fuel pods of long-range model made of advanced composites, including glassfibre, graphite/epoxy and Nomex nylon honeycomb.

These fairing pods provide flotation capability adequate to meet British airworthiness requirements applicable to a sea state seven (9.15 m; 30 ft waves. Wave length-to-height ratio 15) without added flotation gear.

LANDING GEAR: As described for CH-47D, but with tyre pressures of 8.55 bars (124 lb/sq in) on forward gear, 7.20 bars (104.4 lb/sq in) on rear gear.

POWER PLANT: Two Textron Lycoming AL 5512 turboshafts, pod-mounted on sides of rear rotor pylon. Each engine has max T-O rating of 3,039 kW (4,075 shp), max continuous rating of 2,218.5 kW (2,975 shp), and 30 min contingency rating of 3,247 kW (4,355 shp). Long-range model has two fuel tanks, one in each fuselage side fairing, with total capacity of 7,949 litres (2,100 US gallons; 1,749 Imp gallons). Utility model has two drum-shape internal tanks, with total capacity of 3,702 litres (978 US gallons; 814 Imp gallons). Extended-range model has both fuselage side and internal drum tanks. Single-point pressure refuelling.

ACCOMMODATION: Two pilots side by side on flight deck, with dual controls. Passenger cabin of long-range model seats up to 44 persons four-abreast, with centre aisle. Each seat has overhead bin and underseat stowage for carry-on baggage; larger items are stowed over the rear ramp in the main baggage compartment. Galley, with cabin attendant's seat, and toilet, are standard, between flight deck and cabin. Basic FAA/CAA approved 'combi' versions offer 8-32 passenger seats, with cargo at rear of cabin, loaded via rear ramp; or 22-32 passenger seats, with cargo stowed on only one side of cabin's centre aisle. All passenger facilities can be removed, and heavy duty floor installed, for freight-only service. Passenger door at front of cabin on starboard side. Crew door on each side of flight deck. Cabin floor supported by dynamically tuned fittings to reduce vibration. Hydraulically powered cargo ramp can be stopped at any intermediate position to match the level of the loading vehicle being used. Single central cargo hook is standard on utility model for carrying external loads of up to 12,700 kg (28,000 lb). Optional dual tandem hooks for precision operations and for load stability in high-speed flight; or three tandem hooks for delivering multiple loads.

SYSTEMS: Heating and ventilation systems maintain comfortable flight deck/cabin temperature in ambient temperatures down to –32°C. Duplicated flying control, hydraulic and electrical systems, as described for CH-47D/Model 414. Solar T62T-2B APU, rated at 71 kW (95 shp), drives auxiliary gearbox on rear transmission to start engines and provide power for two flying control system hydraulic pumps and two alternators. All critical systems heated to inhibit ice build-up.

AVIONICS AND EQUIPMENT: Duplicated full blind-flying instrumentation, weather radar, and dual four-axis automatic flight control system with built-in test equipment, provide all-weather capability. Optional equipment includes passenger interior furnishings for the utility model, 'combi' interior, downward-shining cargo load light, rescue hoist of 272 kg (600 lb) capacity, glassfibre wheel-skis, an ice detector probe, and ditching equipment that includes two liferafts, each with an overload capacity of 36 persons. Standard items include integral work platforms, and a maintenance panel that allows 26 separate checks to be made from a single ground-level position.

DIMENSIONS, EXTERNAL: As CH-47D except:

Length of fuselage	15.87 m (52 ft 1 in)
Width over fuselage side fairings	4.78 m (15 ft 8 in)

Wheel track:

fwd landing gear	3.20 m (10 ft 6 in)
rear landing gear	3.40 m (11 ft 2 in)
Wheelbase	7.87 m (25 ft 9.9 in)

DIMENSIONS, INTERNAL:

Passenger cabin	as for CH-47D

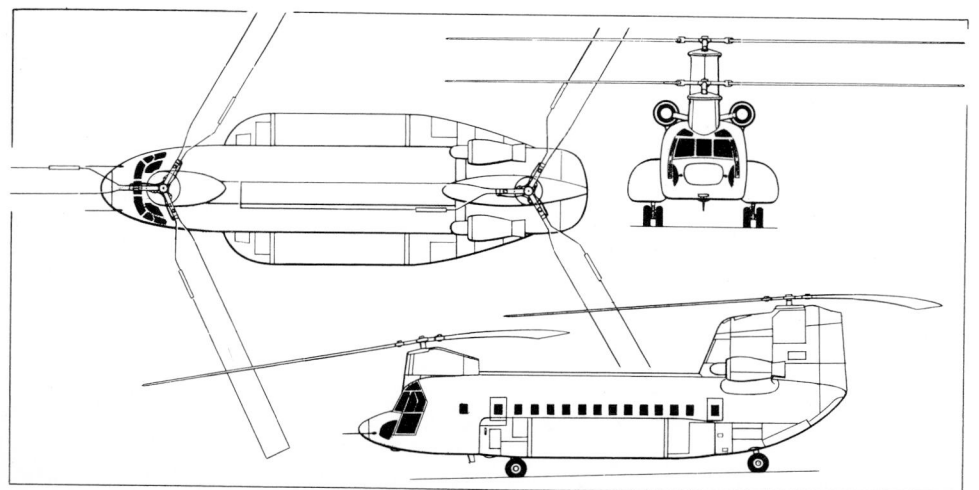

Boeing Helicopters Model 234 LR long-range Commercial Chinook *(Pilot Press)*

Baggage compartment volume	4.42 m³ (156 cu ft)
Utility model, cargo hold volume	41.03 m³ (1,449 cu ft)

WEIGHTS:
Manufacturer's weight empty:

LR	11,748 kg (25,900 lb)
ER	12,020 kg (26,500 lb)
MLR	11,113 kg (24,500 lb)
UT	9,797 kg (21,600 lb)
Operating weight empty: LR	12,292 kg (27,100 lb)
ER	12,406 kg (27,350 lb)
MLR	11,317 kg (24,950 lb)
UT	10,002 kg (22,050 lb)
Fuel load: LR, MLR	6,391 kg (14,091 lb)
ER	9,368 kg (20,653 lb)
UT	2,976 kg (6,562 lb)
Max payload: LR, MLR, internal	9,072 kg (20,000 lb)
ER, UT, internal	8,731 kg (19,250 lb)
ER, MLR, UT, external	12,700 kg (28,000 lb)

Max T-O weight:

ER, LR, MLR, internal load	22,000 kg (48,500 lb)
UT, internal load	19,051 kg (42,000 lb)
ER, LR, MLR, UT, external load	23,133 kg (51,000 lb)

PERFORMANCE:
Never-exceed speed:

ER, LR, MLR	150 knots (278 km/h; 173 mph)
UT	140 knots (259 km/h; 161 mph)

Max cruising speed at 610 m (2,000 ft):

ER, LR, MLR, internal load, at 22,000 kg (48,500 lb) AUW	145 knots (269 km/h; 167 mph)
UT, internal load, at 19,051 kg (42,000 lb) AUW	140 knots (259 km/h; 161 mph)

Cruising speed for optimum range, with load at 610 m (2,000 ft):

ER, LR, MLR, UT, internal load, at all gross weights	135 knots (250 km/h; 155 mph)

Max rate of climb at S/L at max T-O weight:

ER, LR, MLR, internal load	360 m (1,180 ft)/min
UT, internal load	457 m (1,500 ft)/min

Operational ceiling:

ER, LR, MLR, UT	4,570 m (15,000 ft)

Hovering ceiling IGE:

ER, LR, MLR, internal load	2,590 m (8,500 ft)
UT, internal load	4,085 m (13,400 ft)

Hovering ceiling OGE:

ER, LR, MLR, internal load	820 m (2,700 ft)
UT, internal load	3,505 m (11,500 ft)

Range with 45 min IFR reserves:

LR, 44 passengers	530 nm (982 km; 610 miles)
ER, 17 passengers	830 nm (1,538 km; 956 miles)
LR, MLR, with max fuel	620 nm (1,149 km; 714 miles)
ER with max fuel	1,035 nm (1,918 km; 1,192 miles)
UT with max internal load	229 nm (424 km; 264 miles)
UT with max external load	145 nm (269 km; 167 miles)

Max endurance:

LR, MLR, internal load	5 h 18 min
ER, internal load	8 h 25 min
UT, external load	2 h 18 min

BOEING HELICOPTERS MODEL 360

Boeing Helicopters has designed and built as a private venture the prototype of a twin-turboshaft twin-rotor cargo helicopter known as the Model 360. Similar in size to the CH-46/UH-46 Sea Knight, it makes extensive use of composites materials in the fuselage, rotor hubs, upper

Boeing Helicopters Model 360 advanced technology demonstrator

controls and drive system components. An advanced flight control and flight management system is installed. The prototype (N360BV) made its first flight on 10 June 1987 and had accumulated about 50 hours' flying by the beginning of 1988.

TYPE: Twin-turbine medium-size cargo/utility helicopter.

ROTOR SYSTEM: Two four-blade rotors in tandem, turning in opposite directions and linked through interconnecting shafts to enable both rotors to be driven by either engine. All-composites rotor blades of new VR12 and VR15 aerofoil section, which improve hovering efficiency and high speed performance. Rotor head is constructed almost entirely of glassfibre and graphite composites, with elastomeric bearings. Automatic blade-folding motors and linkages are integrated with the lead-lag damping system. Many transmission and control system components made of carbonfibre or glassfibre, including rotor shafts and rotor swashplates.

FUSELAGE: Basic structure of graphite fuselage frames and longerons, covered by preformed panels of Kevlar diagonal-weave skins with Nomex honeycomb core; graphite reinforcement is provided at the panel edges and for all cut-outs. Panels attached to structure by combination of cold bonding and metallic fasteners. The floor is formed as a separate assembly incorporating the fuel tanks and cargo handling roller system, and is suspended on sprung counterweights to isolate it from vibration; the entire flight deck is mounted similarly. The rear of the fuselage, containing the one-piece cargo ramp and door, is of new drag-reducing design.

LANDING GEAR: Retractable tricycle type with twin wheels on each unit. Main landing gear retraction beams are of carbonfibre composites.

POWER PLANT: Two Textron Lycoming AL5512 turboshafts, mounted one in each side of the rear fuselage, each with a standard power rating of 3,132 kW (4,200 shp). Fuel in one 901 litre (238 US gallon; 198 Imp gallon) self-sealing

tank at rear and two 1,109 litre (293 US gallon; 244 Imp gallon) tanks forward, giving total capacity of 3,119 litres (824 US gallons; 686 Imp gallons).

SYSTEMS: Hydraulic and electrical system components are modular in nature, and grouped to allow systems and structure to be integrated during construction.

AVIONICS AND EQUIPMENT: Full nav/com equipment. Doppler radar and optional remote map reader. Honeywell digital automatic flight control system forms part of Bendix integrated flight control and flight management system incorporating six CRT displays with multi-function keyboards, and computer controlled EADI and EHSI displays for pilot and co-pilot, linked to a heading and attitude reference system via a multiplex databus.

DIMENSIONS, EXTERNAL:

Length of fuselage	15.54 m (51 ft 0 in)
Height overall	5.91 m (19 ft 4¾ in)
Wheel track	3.96 m (13 ft 0 in)

DIMENSIONS, INTERNAL:

Cabin: Max width	3.99 m (13 ft 1 in)
Max height	3.43 m (11 ft 3 in)

WEIGHT (estimated):

Design T-O weight	13,834 kg (30,500 lb)

PERFORMANCE (estimated):

Normal cruising speed	200 knots (370 km/h; 230 mph)

BELL/BOEING V-22 OSPREY

Boeing Helicopters is teamed with Bell Helicopter Textron to develop the V-22 Osprey tilt-rotor aircraft to meet the US government's Joint Services Vertical Lift Aircraft requirement. A full description of the aircraft appears under the Bell/Boeing entry in this section. Boeing Helicopters is responsible for the V-22 fuselage, and is developing the advanced technology graphite/glassfibre rotor blades for this aircraft. A smaller diameter (7.62 m; 25 ft) rotor with composites blades is currently being test flown on the Bell XV-15 research aircraft.

BOEING MILITARY AIRPLANES

PO Box 7730, Wichita, Kansas 67277-7730
Telephone: (316) 687 2020
Telex: 910 741 6900 BOEWICA WIC
PRESIDENT: R. L. Dryden
EXECUTIVE VICE-PRESIDENT: Charles F. Tiffany
PUBLIC RELATIONS: Allen Hobbs

Boeing Military Airplanes, the formation of which was announced on 23 October 1979, is responsible for all work on the B-52 Stratofortress bomber and KC-135 jet tanker-transport series, and the offensive avionics system of the Rockwell B-1B strategic bomber. It manufactures parts and assemblies for the Boeing series of commercial transports, including the nose section and nacelles of the 757 and 767, and pylons for the 747 and 767. It also undertakes conversion of Boeing aircraft from passenger to freight carrying and other configurations, installs new interiors and embodies structural modifications. Boeing Military Airplanes is avionics integrator for the Bell/Boeing V-22 Osprey programme (see Bell/Boeing entry) and Boeing/Sikorsky's development work for the LHX helicopter competition, and has been awarded an R & D contract for the US National Aerospace Plane trans-atmospheric aircraft. It was responsible for installing the mission-adaptive wing on NASA's AFTI F-111 research aircraft, and is currently teamed with General Dynamics and Lockheed Burbank in development work for the USAF's advanced tactical fighter (ATF) programme (which see, under USAF heading).

The Wichita facility occupies an area of 376.5 ha (930 acres), including 810,950 m² (8,729,000 sq ft) of covered space. Boeing Military Airplanes also has facilities in Huntsville, Alabama, at Edwards AFB, California, and

a major design and development centre in Seattle, Washington. At the beginning of 1987, the company had a total Kansas workforce of 21,000 persons.

In May 1985 the company was selected to design, develop and produce replacement wings for the US Navy's fleet of Grumman A-6 Intruder attack aircraft. The new wing is made primarily of graphite/epoxy composites. Control surfaces are of aluminium alloy. Titanium is used in high-stress areas, such as the wing fold fittings. Design improvements include split fuel tanks, so that supply can be maintained if one is damaged in combat; enhanced lightning and fire protection; and easier repair and maintenance. Contracts for 179 new wings had been placed by March 1988, with options for a total of 341. Boeing is to install the wings initially on 11 A-6Es, together with upgrade kits to improve bulkhead structure and other systems unique to the new wing. For newly built A-6Es, the wings are being installed by Grumman. First deliveries of production replacement wings to Grumman were made in May 1988.

A NASA contract to modify a Boeing 747-100 as a second carrier aircraft for Space Shuttle Orbiter vehicles was received in early 1988. In another current programme, two of the four USAF C-22Bs (ex-airline 727-100s) are being modified to carry an additional 4,164 litres (1,100 US gallons; 916 Imp gallons) of fuel and having their landing gear rated for an increased max landing weight of 77,112 kg (170,000 lb) for use by the Air National Guard on operational support airlift missions.

BOEING B-52 STRATOFORTRESS

The early development history of the B-52 has been recorded in previous editions of *Jane's*, and a structural

description can be found in the 1964-65 edition. The two versions in squadron service in 1988 are the **B-52G** and **B-52H**, of which a combined total of 263 remain operational (167 Gs and 96 Hs), serving with the 2nd, 7th, 42nd, 97th, 379th, 410th and 416th Bomb Wings of the Eighth Air Force; and the 5th, 43rd, 92nd, 93rd and 320th Bomb Wings of the Fifteenth Air Force.

Full scale development of B-52 carrier aircraft equipment for AGM-86 air-launched cruise missiles, began in early 1978, and the current programme calls for 98 B-52Gs and 96 B-52Hs each to be modified to carry 12 AGM-86s externally (six on each inboard underwing pylon), in addition to an internal load of SRAMs or other weapons.

SAC's 416th Bomb Wing at Griffiss AFB, NY, became the first unit to attain operational capability with the AGM-86 in December 1982. It was followed by the 379th Wing at Wurtsmith AFB, Michigan. Other stations equipped with ALCM-equipped B-52s include Blytheville AFB, Arkansas; Fairchild AFB, Washington; and Barksdale AFB, Louisiana. All 98 B-52Gs, and about 12 B-52Hs, had been equipped for external cruise missile carriage by early 1988. Completion of this phase of the programme is scheduled for FY 1990.

The B-52Hs are being further modified to carry eight more ALCMs, SRAMs, advanced cruise missiles or free-fall nuclear weapons on an internal common strategic rotary launcher (CSRL). This programme was initiated in 1982, and the first CSRL began flight testing in September 1985. A total of 104 CSRLs is to be produced, of which 54 had been ordered by January 1988. Boeing Military Airplanes is building 96 B-52H modification kits and providing depot and base activation support. The production programme is managed by Oklahoma City Air Logistics Center at Tinker

Boeing B-52G Stratofortress, armed with AGM-86B air-launched cruise missiles

AFB, and modification and installation is being performed at Kelly AFB, Texas. The first fully modified aircraft was scheduled to be delivered to Carswell AFB, Texas, in April 1988, permitting the first B-52Hs to be put on full alert with both internal and external ALCMs by September 1989. The system should be fully operational at all SAC B-52H bases by August 1993, including Fairchild AFB, Washington; K. I. Sawyer AFB, Michigan; and Minot AFB, North Dakota.

Cruise missile carrying B-52Gs have a distinctive fairing (known as a 'strakelet') at the leading-edge of each wingroot to give them a recognisable appearance in accordance with provisions of the unratified SALT II agreement. B-52Hs do not need 'strakelets', as all carry cruise missiles and are already recognisably different from other versions of the Stratofortress.

The 69 B-52Gs not modified for use as cruise missile carriers have been adapted for a long-range conventional force projection role. Thirty of them have also each been equipped to carry eight Harpoon anti-shipping missiles externally in a maritime support role. Two squadrons of Harpoon-equipped B-52Gs are now operational. All 69 aircraft are being fitted with an integrated conventional stores management system (ICSMS) permitting them to carry either nuclear weapons or conventional weapons as required, by rearranging data stored in the weapons systems computer by means of a pre-programmed removable software cassette. IOC for ICSMS-equipped B-52Gs was planned for 1988. Future plans call for an increase in the number of B-52G/Hs assigned to the dual-role mission.

The following details apply to the B-52G and B-52H:

POWER PLANT (B-52G): Eight 61.2 kN (13,750 lb st) J57-P-43WB turbojets. Fuel capacity 174,130 litres (46,000 US gallons; 38,303 Imp gallons) internally, plus two 2,650 litre (700 US gallon; 583 Imp gallon) underwing drop tanks.

POWER PLANT (B-52H): Eight 75.6 kN (17,000 lb st) Pratt & Whitney TF33-P-3 turbofans. Fuel capacity as for B-52G.

ACCOMMODATION (B-52G/H): Crew of six (pilot and co-pilot, side by side on flight deck, navigator, radar navigator, ECM operator and gunner).

AVIONICS AND OPERATIONAL EQUIPMENT: All currently operational B-52Gs and Hs have an AN/ASQ-151 Electro-optical Viewing System (EVS) to improve low level penetration capability. The EVS sensors are housed in two steerable, side by side chin turrets. The starboard turret houses a Hughes Aircraft AAQ-6 forward-looking infra-red (FLIR) scanner, while the port turret contains a Westinghouse AVQ-22 low light level TV camera. Phase VI avionics include Motorola ALQ-122 SNOE (Smart Noise Operation Equipment) and Northrop AN/ALQ-155(V) advanced ECM; an AFSATCOM kit which permits worldwide communication via satellite; a Dalmo Victor ALR-46 digital radar warning receiver; Westinghouse ALQ-153 pulse-Doppler tail warning radar; and improved versions of the ITT Avionics ALQ-117 ECM system for the B-52G and ALQ-172 ECM system for the B-52H. Boeing OAS (offensive avionics system), introduced from 1980, is a digital solid state system, and includes Tercom (terrain comparison) guidance, a Teledyne Ryan Doppler radar, Honeywell AN/ASN-131 gimballed electrostatic airborne inertial navigation system (GEANS), IBM/Raytheon ASQ-38 analog bombing/navigation system with IBM digital processing, Lear Siegler attitude heading and reference system, Honeywell radar altimeter, Sperry controls and displays, and Norden Systems modernised strategic radar. Under Phase II of the programme, scheduled for completion by FY 1989, all 167 B-52Gs and 96 Hs are being equipped with OAS.

ARMAMENT (B-52G): Four 0.50 in machine-guns in tail turret, remotely operated by AGS-15 fire control system, remote radar control, or closed circuit TV. Twelve

CSRL installed in weapons bay of a B-52H

AGM-86 air-launched cruise missiles, or up to 20 Boeing AGM-69 SRAM short-range attack missiles (eight on rotary launcher in internal weapons bay, and six under each wing, plus nuclear free-fall bombs) on 98 aircraft. Other 69 aircraft equipped to carry conventional bombs and/or (on 30 aircraft) Harpoon air-to-surface missiles, as described in earlier paragraphs.

ARMAMENT (B-52H): Single 20 mm Vulcan multi-barrel cannon in tail turret instead of four machine-guns. All aircraft being equipped to carry 12 AGM-69 cruise missiles externally and eight internally on CSRL.

DIMENSIONS, EXTERNAL:
Wing span	56.39 m (185 ft 0 in)
Wing area, gross	371.6 m² (4,000 sq ft)
Length overall	49.05 m (160 ft 10.9 in)
Height overall	12.40 m (40 ft 8 in)
Wheel track (c/l of shock struts)	2.51 m (8 ft 3 in)
Wheelbase	15.48 m (50 ft 3 in)

DIMENSION, INTERNAL:
Weapons bay volume	29.53 m³ (1,043 cu ft)

WEIGHT:
Max T-O weight	more than 221,350 kg (488,000 lb)

PERFORMANCE:
Max level speed at high altitude
        Mach 0.90 (516 knots; 957 km/h; 595 mph)
Cruising speed at high altitude
        Mach 0.77 (442 knots; 819 km/h; 509 mph)
Penetration speed at low altitude   Mach 0.53 to 0.55
    (352-365 knots; 652-676 km/h; 405-420 mph)
Service ceiling   16,765 m (55,000 ft)

T-O run: G   3,050 m (10,000 ft)
        H   2,900 m (9,500 ft)
Range with max fuel, without in-flight refuelling:
    G   more than 6,513 nm (12,070 km; 7,500 miles)
    H   more than 8,685 nm (16,093 km; 10,000 miles)

BOEING KC-135 STRATOTANKER

Of the 732 **KC-135A** tanker-transports built by Boeing for the US Air Force, to support Strategic Air Command aircraft and those of other US Air Force commands, the US Navy and Marine Corps, and other nations, 594 remained operational in early 1988. Many of these have been modified to later standards.

Since 1975 Boeing at Wichita has been engaged in a programme to extend the flying life of each KC-135 by 27,000 hours, by replacing sections of the lower wing skins. This is to enable the aircraft to remain fully operational well past the year 2020, and justified a programme to retrofit modern technology engines, to improve fuel economy and reduce noise. Selection of the 97.9 kN (22,000 lb st) CFM International CFM56-2B-1 turbofan (military designation F108-CF-100) for evaluation on a KC-135A testbed aircraft was announced in early 1980, and the USAF plans to acquire 375 modification kits by FY 1992.

The re-engined aircraft, the first of which (61-0293) made its first flight on 4 August 1982, have the new USAF designation **KC-135R**. Electrical, hydraulic, performance and fuel management, and flight control systems are also undergoing modification, the main landing gear is being strengthened, and dual APUs are being installed for quick engine starting. The first nine KC-135R 'production' conversions for the USAF were funded in the FY 1982 budget, and 256 modification kits had been funded by 20 April 1988. A total of 110 aircraft had been redelivered by Boeing Military Airplanes to the USAF by that date, and KC-135Rs were in service at McConnell AFB, Kansas, Castle AFB, California, Robins AFB, Georgia, Altus AFB, Oklahoma, and Ellsworth AFB, South Dakota. Eleven similar **C-135FR** conversions have been completed for the French Air Force; the first of these was returned to service officially on 26 August 1985, and the 11th aircraft was redelivered on 13 April 1988.

Compared with the standard turbojet KC-135A, Boeing estimated that the KC-135R would be able to offload 65 per cent more fuel over a 1,500 nm (2,775 km; 1,725 mile) radius at average T-O gross weight, and 150 per cent more at 2,500 nm (4,630 km; 2,875 mile) radius. Increased thrust enables it to take off to 762 m (2,500 ft) before a KC-135A could leave the ground. Its noise footprint is 98 per cent smaller in terms of a 90 EPNdB landing/take-off contour. Max take-off weight of the KC-135R is 146,285 kg (322,500 lb), compared with 136,800 kg (301,600 lb) for the KC-135A. Max fuel load is 92,210 kg (203,288 lb) compared with the KC-135A's 86,047 kg (189,702 lb).

Air Force Systems Division is reported to have received funding for trials of Flight Refuelling Ltd Mk 32B hose-reel refuelling pods on a KC-135R, with a view to supplementing the aircraft's standard boom refuelling system.

To satisfy the near-term critical requirements for replacing the turbojets of Air National Guard and Air Force Reserve KC-135s with turbofans, the US Air Force acquired many retired commercial Boeing 707-100B/720B/320B/320C airliners, together with spare JT3D-3B turbofans. The airliners were flown to the Military Aircraft Storage and Disposition Center, Tucson, Arizona, to be stripped of their engines, pylons, tailplanes and other components intended for overhaul/refurbishment and transfer to the Air Force's KC-135 aircraft.

The initial US Air Force programme for the replacement of turbojets by JT3D turbofans involved 18 special-purpose -135 aircraft, comprising three C-135Es, one KC-135E, two NKC-135Es, five EC-135Hs, two EC-135Ks, two EC-135Ns, two EC-135Ps, and one RC-135T. These were redelivered to the USAF in 1981 and continue in service for airborne command post and other special communications missions. Three more have since been re-engined.

Follow-on contracts covered the retrofit of five special purpose -135s, and the entire fleet of 134 Air National Guard and Air Force Reserve KC-135 aircraft, with JT3D engines. Simultaneously with this modification, five-rotor

Boeing KC-135R of the US Air Force, re-engined with CFM56-2B-1 turbofans *(Mike Jerram)*

wheel brakes and a Mark II/III anti-skid system were installed. The first re-engined **KC-135E** for the ANG (57-1496) was delivered to Phoenix, Arizona, on 26 July 1982; the last KC-135E was delivered in January 1988. Further details of this programme were given in the 1987-88 and earlier editions of *Jane's*.

BOEING EC-18B ARIA

Aeronautical Systems Division of the US Air Force procured eight former American Airlines Boeing 707-323C transport aircraft under the designation C-18A, of which four have been modified to replace EC-135N Advanced Range Instrumentation Aircraft (ARIA) operated by its 4950th Test Wing. Like the ARIA EC-135Ns, each of the 707s is converted to house the world's largest airborne steerable antenna (diameter 2.13 m; 7 ft) in a bulbous nose, a probe antenna on each wingtip, and a totally new cockpit configuration, with navigation station, a new flight director, modified electrical system and improved environmental control system. Designated EC-18B after conversion, the aircraft carry a crew of 16 to 24 on an average ARIA mission and have a greater payload capability than the EC-135Ns they replace, making them better able to support the expanding ARIA mission. This includes support of unmanned space launches, cruise missile and SDI tests, Army and Navy ballistic missile tests, and the Space Transportation System (Shuttle) programme.

The first EC-18B made its first flight after conversion on 27 February 1985 and entered operational service in January 1986. All four were expected to be fully operational by 1988, together with three remaining EC-135s. A future modification will incorporate the sonobuoy missile impact location system (SMILS) currently installed on some US Navy P-3 Orion aircraft.

BOEING EC-18C and E-8A (J-STARS)

On 27 September 1985, Grumman Corporation received a $657 million contract for full scale development of the USAF/US Army Joint Surveillance Target Attack Radar System (J-STARS). Boeing has modified two C-18A (former American Airlines Boeing 707-323C transport aircraft) airframes as testbeds for the airborne equipment. Grumman is responsible for subsystems installation, integration and flight testing of the equipment, which includes a Norden multi-mode side looking radar antenna in a canoe shape radome some 9.1 m (30 ft) long, under the front fuselage of each aircraft. The radar will operate in synthetic aperture radar (SAR) mode to detect and locate stationary objects such as parked tanks, and will alternate between SAR and Doppler to locate slow moving targets. The J-STARS system will then direct attack on the targets, via the Joint Tactical Information Distribution System (JTIDS).

The first aircraft to be modified arrived at Boeing Military Airplanes' Wichita facility in January 1986 and was delivered to Grumman's Melbourne Systems Division on 31 July 1987. A second Boeing 707-323C arrived at Wichita for modification in June 1986, for delivery to Grumman in Autumn 1988. Each is expected to carry a crew of 17 US Army and USAF specialists to man the radar processing and communications consoles in the cabin.

The first of two completed testbed aircraft, redesigned **EC-18C**, was due to fly for the first time in full J-STARS configuration in late 1988. The demonstration programme is scheduled for completion by 1991, when a decision will be taken on whether to proceed to production of up to 21 operational **E-8As** and ground stations to receive data from the aircraft.

BOEING EC-18D

This designation applies to the two remaining USAF C-18As, which it is proposed to modify as cruise missile mission control platforms. Announcement of the EC-18D choice of contractor was expected in mid-1988.

BOEING 707 TANKER/TRANSPORT
Royal Saudi Air Force designation: KE-3A

In 1982 BMA initiated a programme to demonstrate the use of the commercial Model 707-320 Intercontinental airframe modified as an aerial refuelling tanker. A former TWA 707-320C was converted as a demonstration aircraft, making its first flight in this form in early 1983. This aircraft is equipped with three hose and drogue refuelling points, one on the fuselage centreline and one at each wingtip, the latter being housed in pods similar to those used on earlier tanker modifications of the Model 707 for such operators as the Canadian Armed Forces and the Royal Moroccan Air Force. The centreline station is a new modification. When not required for the tanker role the aircraft can be converted easily into an all-passenger, all-cargo, or combination passenger/cargo transport, and with special interiors for VIP or aeromedical transport. Seats, cargo handling equipment, as well as most executive interior partitions and furnishings, are mounted on permanently installed tracks with quick disconnect fittings.

A variety of refuelling system options is available, including a probe or receptacle in the nose, Beech or Sargent-Fletcher wingtip pods deploying a hose and drogue, a Sargent-Fletcher rear fuselage centreline hose and drogue installation, or a Boeing centreline boom refuelling installation of the type developed for the USAF's KC-135

Boeing EC-18B ARIA of USAF's 4950th Test Wing

Boeing Model 707 tanker/transport demonstrator with its three hose and drogue refuelling systems deployed

tanker/transports. These can be combined to customer requirements, enabling the Boeing 707 tanker/transport to be equipped in a configuration that is compatible with any type of Western fighter. Increased fuel capacity can be provided by the installation of an optional 19,040 litre (5,030 US gallon; 4,188 Imp gallon) tank in the rear lower cargo hold. With this, the 707-320's standard 90,299 litre (23,855 US gallon; 19,863 Imp gallon) wing fuel tanks, and triple refuelling points, the tanker can rendezvous with fighters 1,000 nm (1,853 km; 1,151 miles) from its base and transfer 55,878 kg (123,190 lb) of fuel.

In addition to installation of the refuelling pods or boom, basic modifications include a refuelling control panel at the flight engineer's station; improved hydraulic system and fuel pumps; strengthening of the outer wing; new wingtips, military avionics and a TV scanner; and either a boom operator's or pod observer's station. Military avionics include dual UHF with DF, Tacan, IFF, weather radar, rendezvous radar, and dual INS. The quick-change capability of the interior makes the 707 tanker/transport easily adaptable for a range of military roles including coastal patrol, electronic countermeasures, maritime missions, and tactical command and control (C²). By the installation of wing hardpoints or dispensing bays, it could also be used as a platform for the deployment of sonobuoys or other ASW sensors, mines and bombs, air-to-air or standoff missiles, and chaff or flares.

Twenty-five 707 tanker/transports were in, or scheduled for, service in four countries by 1987. These are in various hose-drogue, boom, or combined boom/hose-drogue configurations. Depending on the configuration selected by the customer, Boeing can deliver 707 tanker/transports within 12 to 18 months from order, and can provide all required support to allow effective utilisation of the multi-role capabilities of these aircraft. Customers include the Brazilian Air Force (four tanker-only aircraft converted from former VARIG Boeing 707s) and Spanish Air Force (two, each with a VIP interior for about 66 passengers), the first of which was delivered in the Spring of 1988.

The eight tankers delivered to the Royal Saudi Air Force, simultaneously with five E-3A Sentry AWACS aircraft, are designated **KE-3A**. They differ from standard 707 tankers in having CFM56 turbofan engines, with Hispano-Suiza thrust reversers, to provide commonality with the RSAF's E-3As.

A description of the Model 707-320C can be found in the 1980-81 and earlier editions of *Jane's*.

BOEING VC-25A 'AIR FORCE ONE'

The US Air Force has selected two Boeing 747-200Bs to provide airlift for the President of the United States. They will replace the current Boeing VC-137Cs (707-320Cs) which entered the presidential fleet on 12 October 1962 and 4 August 1972, and will be designated VC-25A. The main airframes were built in Everett, Washington, and flown to Boeing Military Airplanes for configuration as 'Air Force One', the radio call sign used by the 89th Military Airlift Wing at Andrews AFB for an aircraft carrying the President. Deliveries to the USAF are scheduled for November 1988 and May 1989.

Powered by four 252.4 kN (56,750 lb st) General Electric F103-GE-102 (CF6-80C2B1) turbofans, the VC-25As have a fuel capacity of 202,940 litres (53,611 US gallons; 44,640 Imp gallons), providing an unrefuelled range in excess of 6,000 nm (11,120 km; 6,910 miles). Self-sufficiency will be enhanced by utilising self-contained airstairs in the lower lobe and the addition of a second Garrett GTCP331-200 APU in the tail.

The new aircraft will have a Bendix Aerospace EFIS-10 electronic flight instrument system and complete onboard state-of-the-art communications equipment, including secure voice terminals and cryptographic equipment for writing and deciphering classified messages. E-Systems will provide the mission communication system kits, which Boeing will install along with normal aircraft communications equipment. Litton will supply the aircraft's ring laser gyro inertial navigation systems. Each VC-25A will

NASA's AFTI F-111/MAW testbed aircraft, modified by Boeing Military Airplanes

accommodate 80 passengers and 23 crew, including ground crew required to travel with the aircraft.

Extensively modified to meet presidential requirements, the 371.6 m² (4,000 sq ft) of interior floor space of each 'Air Force One' will include an executive suite with presidential office, stateroom and lavatory; two galleys, each capable of providing food for 50 persons; an emergency treatment medical facility; and work and rest areas for the presidential staff, news media representatives and USAF crew.

WEIGHTS:

Long-range mission T-O weight	364,552 kg (803,700 lb)
Max zero-fuel weight	238,816 kg (526,500 lb)
Design mission zero-fuel weight	202,302 kg (446,000 lb)
Max landing weight	285,763 kg (630,000 lb)

BOEING 747 CRAF PROGRAMME
US Air Force designation: C-19A

Under the CRAF (Civil Reserve Air Fleet) programme, Boeing Military Airplanes is modifying 19 Boeing 747s of Pan American World Airways to supplement military transport forces by providing airlift of bulk and oversize cargo during emergencies. The main deck floor of each aircraft is being strengthened, and a cargo handling system and side cargo door installed. Empty weight of the aircraft is increased by 5,900 kg (13,000 lb), for which the airline receives compensation during commercial operations.

The first modified 747 (N655PA) was returned to Pan American on 31 May 1985 and continues to operate in all-passenger configuration. The programme was scheduled for completion by June 1988.

BOEING/USAF/NASA MISSION ADAPTIVE WING

Under a 1979 USAF contract, Boeing Military Airplanes modified the wings of NASA's General Dynamics F-111A (63-9778) to Mission Adaptive Wing (MAW) configuration. Instead of utilising flaps, slats, ailerons or spoilers, this concept alters wing camber to satisfy a variety of flight conditions and yet maintain a smooth, uninterrupted upper surface. Mechanisms built inside the MAW act upon flexible single-segment leading- and three-segment trailing-edge surfaces to change wing camber during flight. The smooth, flexible surface of this unique wing is made of glassfibre, and its contours are altered by internal link driven by power hinges. The leading-edge has a range of movement from 1° up to 20° down; the trailing-edge can be varied from 1° up to 18° down, and can also twist spanwise. The resulting variations in curvature produce extremely efficient airflow over and under the wing. In addition to demonstrating the performance improvements of smooth variable camber wings, the programme is intended to check and validate the deformable portion of the glassfibre structure, and to evaluate the agility and increased buffet-free envelope of the aircraft with the MAW as part of the USAF/NASA continuing AFTI (advanced fighter technology integration) programme.

The MAW offers six control modes: roll, manoeuvre camber, cruise camber, manoeuvre load, gust alleviation and manoeuvre enhancement. Six mission modes are expected to provide tighter manoeuvring radii for evasive action and survivability; increased fatigue life; improved handling; greater weapons platform stability; and a more comfortable ride with reduced crew fatigue.

The first flight of the AFTI F-111 MAW took place from Edwards AFB, California, on 18 October 1985 and was followed by a second flight on 22 November. Wing sweep was fixed at 26° for these flights. The flight test programme is divided into two year-long phases which will cover performance improvements of the MAW over the standard F-111 wing; determination of optimum camber for all phases of flight; verification of wing loadings at specific flight conditions; determination of MAW handling characteristics; and confirmation of anticipated improvements in the buffet envelope. Phase 1, successfully completed during 1986, consisted of 26 flights and was conducted with the MAW controlled in manual mode. Further development in Phase 2, which began on 6 August 1987, is testing the wing in five modes (cruise camber, manoeuvre camber,

Artist's impression of the proposed Boeing 757 long-range ASW aircraft (LRAACA)

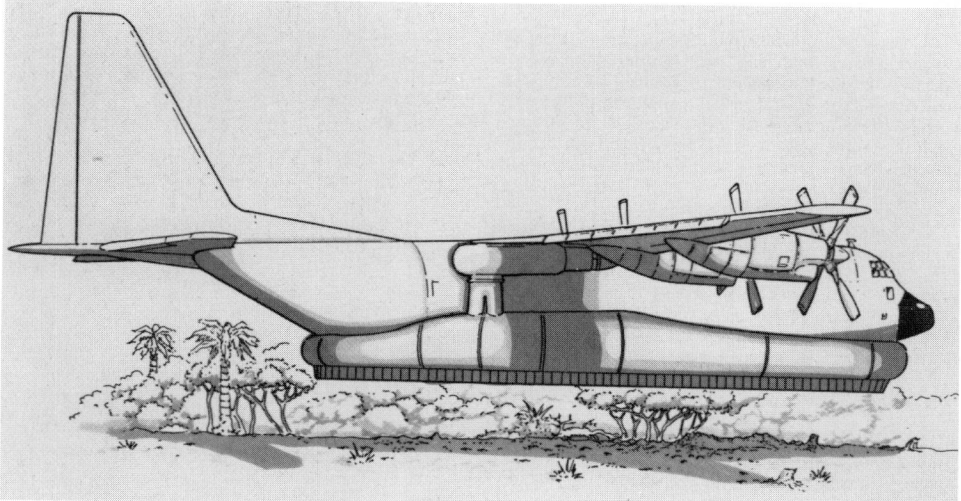

Artist's impression of the Boeing Military Airplanes cargo aircraft ground mobility system (CAGMS)

manoeuvre load, gust alleviation and manoeuvre enhancement) under automatic control, intended eventually to prove the wing's capability to configure itself automatically to suit prevailing flight conditions and requirements. This second phase was due for completion in July 1988.

BOEING 757 LRAACA

Boeing Military Airplanes has proposed an anti-submarine warfare variant of the Model 757-200 airliner to meet the US Navy's Long Range Air ASW Capability Aircraft (LRAACA) requirement. Modifications would include deletion of cabin windows and passenger doors, a modified lower fuselage area incorporating forward and aft weapons bays, six sonobuoy launching tubes, three additional fuel tanks, an extended nose to accommodate search radar, an MAD tail 'sting', and wing modifications to improve weight capability and to incorporate provision for weapons hardpoints and wingtip antennae. An Update IV avionics suite would be installed, and Boeing has chosen the 192.7 kN (43,310 lb st) Pratt & Whitney F117-PW-100 (PW2043) turbofan as power plant, this engine having a larger gearbox than standard commercial Model 757 engines, permitting more electrical power to be generated for onboard equipment. A crew of ten is specified.

Following the issue of RFPs on 23 September 1987, bids for the LRAACA contract were submitted by Boeing, Lockheed (with a modernised P-3) and McDonnell Douglas (for an MD-87 variant with UHB engines). Contractor selection was expected in Autumn 1988, leading to a prototype first flight in mid-1990 and initial production deliveries in early 1991. The US Navy requirement is for up to 125 of the selected aircraft.

BOEING CARGO AIRCRAFT GROUND MOBILITY SYSTEM

Under contract from the US Air Force, Boeing Military Airplanes, in conjunction with Textron Marine Systems, is developing an air cushion Cargo Aircraft Ground Mobility System (CAGMS) which would enable USAF Lockheed C-130 transport aircraft to operate from bomb-damaged airfields or other rough surfaces. The CAGMS, the general configuration of which is illustrated in an accompanying artist's impression, would be used for landing and would enable a C-130 to touch down on soft, unstable terrain and to clear obstacles up to 0.46 m (1 ft 6 in) high. After touchdown the aircraft's conventional landing gear would be lowered to enhance slow-speed stability and manoeuvrability when parking. The CAGMS is a strap-on unit which could be attached to a C-130 when required, and quickly removed for normal airfield operations.

BRANSON
BRANSON AIRCRAFT CORPORATION

3790 Wheeling Street, Denver, Colorado 80239
Telephone: (303) 371 9112
Telex: 45-4577 BRANSON DVR
Fax: (303) 371 1813
PRESIDENT: Carl F. Branson
EXECUTIVE VICE-PRESIDENT: Roger P. Kirwan

Founded in 1966, Branson Aircraft Corporation provides engineering and custom manufacturing services for aircraft manufacturers and owners. The company has developed a series of auxiliary fuel tanks for business aircraft such as the Beechcraft Beechjet, Canadair Challenger, Cessna Citation, Learjet family and Mitsubishi Diamond, and has also designed conformal supplementary fuel tanks for installation in the cargo bays of commercial jet airliners. Other activities include the design, manufacture and installation of special mission equipment such as that required for medical transport, weather research and aerial photography.

CITATION EXTENDED RANGE FUEL SYSTEM

Branson holds an FAA FAR Pt 25 supplemental type certificate for its 454 litre (120 US gallon; 100 Imp gallon) auxiliary fuel tank installation in the Cessna Model 500 Citation, Citation I, II and S/II business jets. The tank installation and associated structural work weighs 36 kg (80 lb) empty and permits a 295 kg (650 lb) increase in the aircraft's maximum gross weight, enabling Citation I operators to carry an additional three passengers, plus 27 kg (60 lb) of baggage, and provides an extended maximum range of 1,654 nm (3,065 km; 1,905 miles). The first of these installations, which takes six weeks to complete, was made in January 1985.

DIAMOND I LONG-RANGE TANK

Branson has developed a 363 litre (96 US gallon; 80 Imp gallon) long-range fuel tank for the Mitsubishi Diamond I and IA and Beechcraft Model 400 Beechjet. In the latter aircraft the tank is standard equipment. The tank mounts in

the aircraft's fuselage against the rear pressure bulkhead. Also available for the Diamond is a transfer system for filling the aircraft's fuselage fuel tank from the port wing tank, eliminating the need for manual filling of the fuselage tank. A Branson tailcone baggage compartment, capacity 0.93 m³ (33 cu ft), maximum load 204 kg (450 lb), is also available for retrofit to Diamond IA aircraft. Branson has also received FAA approval for a gross weight increase kit for the Diamond IA which increases max T-O weight to 7,031 kg (15,500 lb).

LEARJET 55 LONG-RANGE TANKS

Branson has developed long-range auxiliary fuel tanks for the Learjet Model 55 business jet which provide an additional 378.5 litres (100 US gallons; 83.5 Imp gallons) or 757 litres (200 US gallons; 167 Imp gallons) of fuel. The installation takes approximately four weeks for the 378 litre tank, and five weeks for the 757 litre tank, which extends the aircraft's range by 400 nm (741 km; 461 miles)

CITATION EXTENDED WIDTH CARGO DOOR

Branson has developed a cabin door modification for Cessna Citation I, II and S/II business jets which provides a 0.91 m (3 ft 0 in) wide door permitting the loading of full size medical stretchers, palletised cargo, research equipment, large aerial cameras and other outsize items. The extended width cargo door installation weighs 28.6 kg (63 lb), does not interfere with existing cabin seating or furnishings, and meets FAA FAR Pt 25 requirements. The installation takes six weeks to complete. Ten Citations had been modified by February 1988, including a dedicated critical care medical transport aircraft for the University of Alabama.

CITATION AIR AMBULANCE EQUIPMENT

Branson has developed a medical equipment installation package for the Cessna Citation I, II and S/II which includes installation of the extended width cabin door, single or dual stretchers, medical oxygen supply, compressed air, vacuum and electrical outlets. The first such installation has been completed on a Citation II operated by Air Express of Oslo, Norway.

BROMON
BROMON AIRCRAFT CORPORATION

4085 Nevso Drive, Las Vegas, Nevada 89103
Telephone: (702) 362 7121
Telex: 510 1002000 BROMON
PRESIDENT: James H. Brown
SENIOR VICE-PRESIDENT: Joseph A. Mico-Monaco
DIRECTOR OF ENGINEERING: Dale Ruhmel

BROMON BR2000

In June 1987 Bromon Aircraft Corporation announced that it was developing the BR2000 twin-turboprop aircraft, which it believes will meet commercial and military requirements for a rugged STOL transport fulfilling such roles as commuter airliner, overnight package carrying, tactical troop transport, LAPES delivery, helicopter refuelling, gunship, medevac, border patrol, drug enforcement, coastal patrol, disaster relief, forestry patrol, surveillance and scientific mission work.

Key features of the concept, which was inspired by the four-engined Ahrens 404 transport (last described in the 1981-82 edition of *Jane's*), are simplicity, systems redundancy, accessibility and ease of maintenance combined with reliability, low acquisition and operating costs and quiet operation. The BR2000 has been designed to meet FAR Pt 25 certification requirements.

In commercial roles the BR2000 will accommodate up to 46 passengers in two-abreast seating with 76 cm (30 in) seat pitch. A quick-change interior enables the aircraft to be adapted to combined passenger/cargo or all-cargo configurations, with accommodation for three 'A' series freight containers or six LD3 containers. For military applications the BR2000 can accommodate up to 36 combat-equipped ground troops, or 30 paratroopers, or 36 casualty litters. As an assault aircraft it can operate into unimproved or soft landing surfaces with a CBR of 4, at a maximum descent rate of 213 m (700 ft)/min, and can accommodate up to three 1,361 kg (3,000 lb) 463L military pallets or two Army High Mobility Multipurpose Wheeled Vehicles (Hummers) or a single Hummer and M119 howitzer, or two F100 or F110 turbofans on standard A3000 trailers. The aircraft is also suitable for special missions operations and, it is claimed, can be reconfigured from special missions to cargo role in under 35 minutes and from cargo to troop transport role in under one hour by a team of four groundcrew.

Design of the BR2000 began in 1985. Detail design continued in 1987, with factory tooling and construction of the first of five prototypes beginning in 1988 in anticipation of the first flight in Spring 1989. FAA certification and first customer deliveries are expected in 1990. The BR2000 is being built at the former Ramey AFB at Aquadilla, Puerto Rico. By the end of the second year of production Bromon predicts a production rate of two aircraft per month. In July 1988, announcement of an order for approximately 15 aircraft by the Philippine Air Force was said to be imminent.

TYPE: Twin-turboprop utility aircraft.
WINGS: Cantilever high-wing monoplane of all-metal construction. Centre-section of constant chord, with tapered outer panels. All-metal ailerons extending to wingtips, with trim tabs. All-metal trailing-edge flaps, each in two sections, electrically actuated. Primary control surfaces are cable and pulley actuated.
FUSELAGE: All-metal structure of square cross-section.
TAIL UNIT: Cantilever all-metal structure with single fin and rudder. Fin is sweptback. Large dorsal fin. Trim tabs in elevators and rudder. Electric trim standard.
LANDING GEAR: Retractable tricycle type with twin wheels on each unit. Main units housed in streamlined sponsons on fuselage sides. Retraction and extension of landing gear is hydraulically actuated, with free-fall emergency backup system. When retracted all wheels remain slightly proud of fuselage lower surface. Nose unit steerable. Anti-skid brakes standard, with nitrogen actuated emergency braking system. Tyre pressures (military soft-field configuration): main units 3.58 bars (52 lb/sq in); nose unit 3.86 bars (56 lb/sq in).
POWER PLANT: Two 1,394 kW (1,870 shp) General Electric CT7-9B turboprops, each driving a four-blade feathering and reversing Hamilton Standard propeller with spinner. Integral wet wing fuel tanks, maximum capacity 4,732 litres (1,250 US gallons; 1,041 Imp gallons). Overwing and single-point refuelling standard. Self-sealing fuel tanks optional.
ACCOMMODATION: Crew of two on flight deck. Dual controls standard. Cabin is unpressurised. Standard seating for 46 passengers in 23 rows of two at 76 cm (30 in) seat pitch, with wide aisle. Seat rails are installed to facilitate changes of configuration. Toilet at front of cabin on starboard side. Cold refreshment centre at rear. Baggage compartment at rear of cabin. Large overhead baggage lockers. Three passenger doors, one to rear of flight deck on port side and one on each side aft of main landing gear. Paradropping capability from side doors or rear loading ramp/door. Single emergency exit window on each side beneath wing. Electrically actuated full width rear loading ramp/door with integral cargo winch.
SYSTEMS: Hydraulic system for landing gear and brake operation. Electrical system includes DC starter/generator on each engine, and AC inverter.
AVIONICS: Integrated flight system comprising dual VHF nav/com, ADI/EHSI, flight directors and transponders, ADF, AHRS, DME, radio altimeter, colour weather radar, autopilot, cockpit voice and flight data recorders. Programmable text facility, Omega/VLF, long range navigation systems, inertial navigation systems and HF com equipment optional.

DIMENSIONS, EXTERNAL:
Wing span	24.59 m (80 ft 8 in)
Length overall	23.49 m (77 ft 1 in)
Height overall	8.53 m (28 ft 0 in)
Rear cargo door: Height	2.41 m (7 ft 11 in)
Width	2.39 m (7 ft 10 in)
Fuselage ground clearance	0.84 m (2 ft 9 in)

DIMENSIONS, INTERNAL:
Cabin: Max length excl flight deck	10.51 m (34 ft 6 in)
Max width	2.49 m (8 ft 2 in)
Max height	2.41 m (7 ft 11 in)
Volume	63.15 m³ (2,230.0 cu ft)
Baggage compartment volume	9.51 m³ (336.0 cu ft)

WEIGHTS:
Weight empty	7,051 kg (15,545 lb)
Max fuel weight	3,799 kg (8,375 lb)
Max T-O weight	13,494 kg (29,750 lb)
Max ramp weight	13,608 kg (30,000 lb)

PERFORMANCE (estimated):
Max cruising speed	224 knots (415 km/h; 258 mph)
Normal cruising speed	210 knots (389 km/h; 242 mph)
Min single-engine control speed (V_{MC})	61 knots (113 km/h; 70 mph)
Stalling speed, flaps down	68 knots (126 km/h; 78 mph)
Max rate of climb at S/L	674 m (2,210 ft)/min
Service ceiling	7,620 m (25,000 ft)
STOL T-O to 15 m (50 ft), conditions as above	510 m (1,675 ft)
FAA balanced field length	less than 915 m (3,000 ft)
Landing from 15 m (50 ft)	350 m (1,150 ft)
Min ground turning radius	7.62 m (25 ft 0 in)
Range with 2,656 kg (5,855 lb) payload, 45 min reserves	2,000 nm (3,706 km; 2,303 miles)
Range with 5,443 kg (12,000 lb) payload, 45 min reserves	300 nm (556 km; 345 miles)
Range, military transport with 36 troops and equipment	1,000 nm (1,853 km; 1,151 miles)
Ferry range, 45 min reserves	2,500 nm (4,633 km; 2,879 miles)
On-station endurance, special missions configuration with 1,134 kg (2,500 lb) mission payload	11 h 30 min

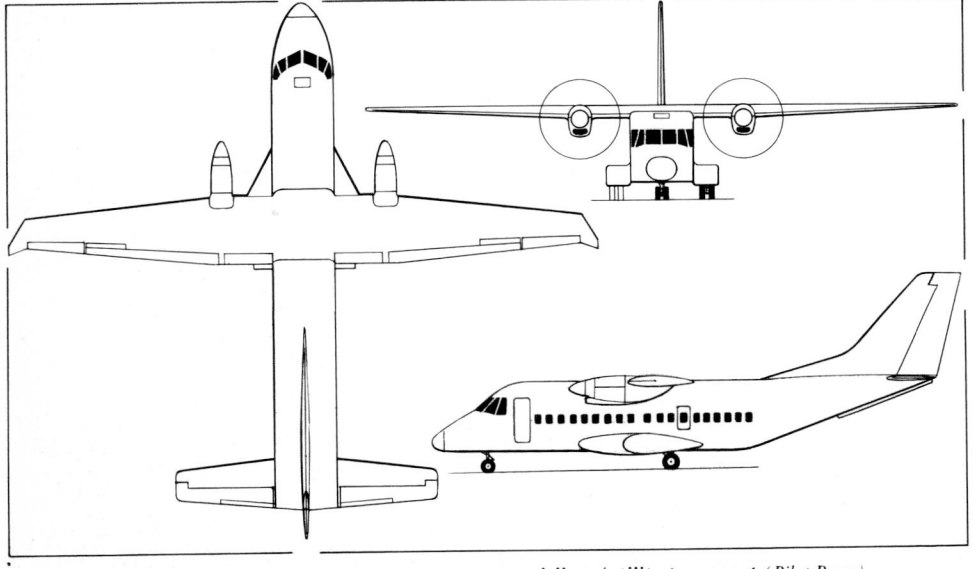

Bromon BR2000 twin-turboprop commuter airliner/utility transport (*Pilot Press*)

BUSH
BUSH CONVERSIONS INC

Box 431, Udall, Kansas 67146
Telephone: (316) 782 3851
VICE-PRESIDENT: Barbara Williams

BOLEN 'TAILDRAGGER' CONVERSIONS

Bush Conversions Inc is offering the 'Taildragger' conversions which the former Ralph Bolen Inc designed as a tailwheel landing gear conversion for application to Cessna 150/152, 172/Skyhawk, R172K and 175 aircraft. Flight testing has indicated an average 8.5-10.5 knots (16-19.5 km/h; 10-12 mph) increase in speed resulting from removal of the nosewheel unit; but this change in landing gear configuration is intended also to improve performance from short fields and rough surfaces, to permit a tighter turn radius on narrow strips, and to simplify operation on floats or skis when this is desirable.

The conversion is carried out by the addition of two bulkheads in the front fuselage and a new main landing gear attachment box, just forward of the existing box, to which new cantilever main-gear legs are installed in the case of Cessna Models 172 and 175. Cessna 150 series F, G, H, J and K, and Cessna 152s, retain their existing main-gear legs, but these are removed from their original mounting and attached to the new forward box. Earlier versions require new legs of the design fitted to Cessna 150s of the above series, so that the now-standard wheel with 15 × 6.00-6 tyre and wheel brakes can be installed. The remainder of the conversion covers the removal of the nose gear, and the installation of a new tailwheel unit that includes a Scott 3200 wheel. This unit is attached by stress plates and stringers, so that the tailwheel assembly becomes an integral part of the fuselage structure. No skin removal is required for the conversion.

The 'Taildragger' modification of the landing gear system

has been so designed that on completion there is no shift in the CG position. The STC for most of the Cessna Model 150/152 series, and for the Model 172, R172K and 175, covers operation on Fluidyne snow skis. No weight penalty results from conversion of Model 150/152 aircraft; the longer and stronger main-gear units introduced on the Models 172/175, and accompanying structure, increase weight by 13.6 kg (30 lb).

Bolen 'Taildragger' conversion of a Cessna Model 150 (*Mike Jerram*)

CALIFORNIA HELICOPTER

CALIFORNIA HELICOPTER INTERNATIONAL INC

2935 Golf Course Drive, Ventura, California 93003
Telephone: (805) 644 5800
Telex: 6831165 CHI UW
Fax: (805) 644 5132
PRESIDENT: Gary A. Podolny
EXECUTIVE VICE-PRESIDENT: Harry R. Smith

CALIFORNIA HELICOPTER (SIKORSKY) S-58T

On 22 December 1981, California Helicopter acquired from Sikorsky the rights to the S-58T helicopter, a twin-turbine (Pratt & Whitney Canada PT6T-6) conversion of the piston engined Sikorsky S-58. Details of the conversion can be found under the Sikorsky entry in the 1978-79 and earlier editions of *Jane's*; that company had delivered approximately 146 converted aircraft and/or conversion kits when negotiations with California Helicopter were finalised in 1981. These covered rights to manufacture turbine conversion kits and spare parts, and support of the worldwide fleet of S-58/S-58T aircraft.

California Helicopter is currently manufacturing conversion kits and offers remanufactured H-34 helicopter airframes for use with the kits, together with a component exchange programme.

The S-58T is operated commercially on a variety of services ranging from passenger transport to heavy lift external cargo. The FAA and British Civil Aviation Authority have approved the aircraft for IFR operation.

New York Airways uses two S-58Ts with 14-passenger configuration on its shuttle operation from Manhattan to the New York metropolitan airports. Others are operated throughout the world.

The Indonesian Air Force has converted and delivered to

California Helicopter conversion of Sikorsky S-58 to twin-turbine S-58T configuration

its own units a total of 12 S-58Ts, with the purchase of four more planned. The Royal Thai Air Force has acquired 18 S-58Ts. Two additional S-58Ts have been acquired by the Thai Ministry of Agriculture as VIP transports, and California Helicopter received a number of enquiries from agencies of the Thai government for S-58Ts to be used in applications that include cargo and troop transport, search and rescue, and multi-role operation.

WEIGHTS AND LOADINGS:
Weight empty	3,437 kg (7,577 lb)
Max T-O and landing weight	5,896 kg (13,000 lb)
Max disc loading	25.8 kg/m² (5.29 lb/sq ft)
Max power loading	4.72 kg/kW (7.76 lb/shp)

PERFORMANCE (at max T-O weight. A: PT6T-3; B: PT6T-6):
Max level speed at S/L:
A, B	120 knots (222 km/h; 138 mph)

Cruising speed:
A, B	110 knots (204 km/h; 127 mph)
Hovering ceiling OGE: A	1,433 m (4,700 ft)
B	1,980 m (6,500 ft)
Single-engine absolute ceiling: A	640 m (2,100 ft)
B	1,280 m (4,200 ft)

Range with 1,071 litres (283 US gallons; 236 Imp gallons) usable fuel, including 20 min reserves at cruising speed:
A	260 nm (481 km; 299 miles)
B	242 nm (447 km; 278 miles)

CAVENAUGH

CAVENAUGH AVIATION INC

Route 22, Box 965, Conroe, Texas 77303
Telephone: (409) 539 5900
Telex: 821734 CAVENAVIA
PRESIDENT: Dudley N. Cavenaugh.
DIRECTOR OF MARKETING: William H. Reynolds

CAVENAUGH CARGOLINER

Cavenaugh Aviation commenced design work on this cargo conversion of the Mitsubishi MU-2 pressurised twin-turboprop business transport in mid-1984, and began construction of a prototype modification a year later, subsequently obtaining FAA certification. The Cargoliner is based on the long fuselage MU-2G, MU-2J, MU-2L, MU-2N and Marquise models of the aircraft, last described under the MAI heading in the US section of the 1985-86 *Jane's*.

The conversion involves substitution of a crew door, hinged at its forward edge and with integral step, for the flight deck window on the port or starboard side of the fuselage; installation of a bulkhead, stressed to 9g, between flight deck and cabin area and containing a door for access to the cargo area; the addition of a smooth plastic liner in the former cabin area, and cargo nets which divide the area into three compartments, each accessible from the front or rear of the aircraft. A one-piece upward opening cargo door, 1.17 m (3 ft 10 in) high × 1.32 m (4 ft 4 in) wide, is optional and replaces the MU-2's standard door on the port side of the fuselage. The MU-2's pressurisation system is

Cavenaugh Cargoliner conversion of the Mitsubishi MU-2, with optional rear cargo door

not affected by the conversion. By March 1987 Cavenaugh Aviation had completed 11 Cargoliners, including the prototype.

DIMENSIONS, EXTERNAL:
Crew door: Height		0.61 m (2 ft 0 in)
Width: at top edge		0.41 m (1 ft 4 in)
at bottom edge		0.84 m (2 ft 9 in)

DIMENSIONS, INTERNAL:
Cargo hold: Length	4.9 m (16 ft 1 in)
Max height: at forward bulkhead	1.29 m (4 ft 3 in)
at rear bulkhead	1.17 m (3 ft 10 in)
Volume	7.64 m³ (270.0 cu ft)

CESSNA

CESSNA AIRCRAFT COMPANY (Subsidiary of General Dynamics Corporation)

PO Box 1521, Wichita, Kansas 67201
Telephone: (316) 685 9111
Telex: 417 400

CHAIRMAN AND CHIEF EXECUTIVE OFFICER:
Russell W. Meyer Jr
VICE-PRESIDENT: Roy H. Norris (Citation Marketing)
DIRECTOR OF PUBLIC RELATIONS: H. Dean Humphrey
Cessna Aircraft Company was founded by the late Clyde V. Cessna, a pioneer in US aviation in 1911, and was

incorporated on 7 September 1927. Its former Pawnee and Wallace aircraft divisions in Wichita were consolidated as production facilities within the company's Aircraft Division in mid-1984. In 1985 General Dynamics Corporation acquired the company as a wholly owned subsidiary.
Subsidiary companies owned by Cessna are the

McCauley Accessory Division of Dayton, Ohio; Fluid Power Division of Hutchinson, Kansas; Cessna Fluid Power Ltd of Glenrothes, Fife, Scotland; and Cessna Finance Corporation in Wichita. It has a 49 per cent interest in Reims Aviation of France.

By 31 December 1987, the company had produced a total of 177,008 aircraft. During 1987, its sales totalled 187 aircraft, including units delivered by Reims Aviation of France (which see). Total employment within the company stood at 5,000 on 1 January 1988.

The company's announced range of production aircraft for 1988 consisted of five types: the Caravan I and II, and three models of the Citation business jet. Restoration of piston engined models to the production line is not anticipated before mid-1989.

CESSNA MODEL 152

A total of 7,500 standard Model 152s and Model 152 Aerobats had been built by 31 December 1986, including 640 built by Reims Aviation in France. Manufacture of the Aerobat has ended. Production of the standard Model 152 has been suspended. Descriptions of both can be found in the 1984-85 *Jane's*.

CESSNA SKYHAWK

The Skyhawk is certificated for operation as a floatplane, and can be fitted with skis. A version designated F 172 is produced in France by Reims Aviation.

A total of 35,773 commercial aircraft in the Model 172/Skyhawk series had been built by 31 December 1987, including 2,144 F 172s built in France. In addition, 864 were built during 1966-1983 as T-41A, T-41B, T-41C and T-41D Mescalero military basic trainers.

Production of the Skyhawk has been suspended. A description can be found in the 1985-86 *Jane's*.

CESSNA CUTLASS RG

The Cutlass RG combined the airframe of the Model 172 Skyhawk with the retractable landing gear developed for the Skylane RG.

A total of 1,159 Cutlass RGs had been sold by 31 December 1987. Production has been suspended. A description can be found in the 1985-86 *Jane's*.

CESSNA SKYLANE

A total of 19,812 Model 182/Skylanes of various models had been built by 31 December 1987, including 169 F 182s built by Reims Aviation. Production of the Model 182/Skylane has been suspended. A description appeared in the 1985-86 edition.

CESSNA SKYLANE RG and TURBO SKYLANE RG

Production of these retractable landing gear versions of the Skylane has been suspended.

By 31 December 1987 a total of 2,102 Skylane RGs had been built, including 73 assembled by Reims Aviation in France as Reims 182 Skylane RGs. A description can be found in the 1985-86 *Jane's*.

CESSNA MODEL 185 SKYWAGON

A total of 4,356 Model 185 Skywagons, including 497 military U-17A/B/Cs, had been built by 31 December 1987.

Skywagon production has been suspended. A full description and illustration can be found in the 1985-86 *Jane's*.

CESSNA AG TRUCK and AG HUSKY

Production of both of these agricultural aircraft was suspended in 1985. By 31 December 1987, sales of the Ag Truck totalled 1,949, and 386 examples of the Ag Husky had been delivered. Abbreviated descriptions of both models can be found in the 1985-86 *Jane's*, with a full description of the Ag Truck in the 1984-85 edition.

CESSNA STATIONAIR 6 and TURBO STATIONAIR 6
US Air Force designation: U-26A (Turbo Stationair)

Cessna first renamed the former U206 Skywagon and TU206 Turbo Skywagon as the Stationair and Turbo Stationair respectively. In 1978 a further name change to Stationair 6 and Turbo Stationair 6 highlighted the six-seat capacity of these cargo/utility aircraft. Production of the U206G and TU206G models has been suspended. Full descriptions of both can be found in the 1985-86 *Jane's*.

A total of 7,652 Model 206 Skywagons and Stationairs had been built by 31 December 1987, including 643 de luxe Super Skylanes of similar basic design.

CESSNA MODEL 208 CARAVAN I/U-27A

First flown on 9 December 1982, the engineering prototype of the Caravan I (N208LP) bore little resemblance to any previous Cessna design. The aircraft was claimed by the company to be the first all-new single-engined turboprop general aviation aircraft, and was intended to supplement or replace the thousands of de Havilland Canada Beavers and Otters, and Cessna 180s, 185s and 206s, operated throughout the world in a variety of utility roles.

The Caravan I's basic ability to fly fast with a heavy load, to get into and out of unprepared airstrips, and to offer

Turboprop powered Cessna Model 208 Caravan I amphibian of Royal Canadian Mounted Police

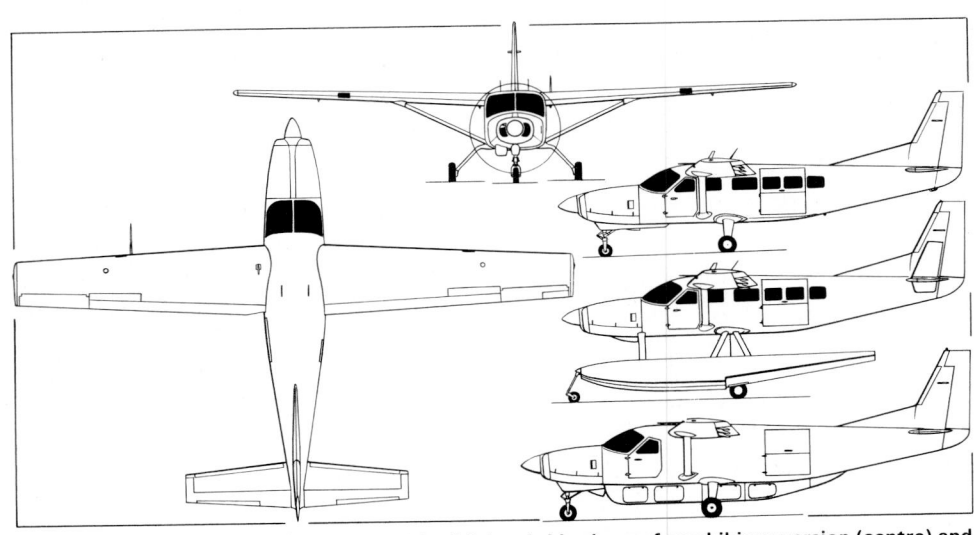

Cessna Model 208 Caravan I landplane, with additional side views of amphibious version (centre) and 'stretched' Model 208B (bottom) *(Pilot Press)*

economy and reliability with minimum maintenance, can be extended by the addition of weather radar, air-conditioning and oxygen systems. Other packages of optional equipment enable it to perform aerial firefighting, photographic, agricultural spraying, ambulance/hearse, border patrol, parachuting and supply dropping, surveillance, and a variety of government utility duties, on wheels, floats and skis.

The first production Caravan I was rolled out in August 1984. FAA certification was obtained on 23 October, in landplane configuration, with full production beginning in 1985. FAA certification of an amphibian version was obtained in March 1986. The first production amphibian was delivered to the Royal Canadian Mounted Police for use in remote areas of the Province of Quebec. One Caravan I is in service with the Brazilian Air Force, one with the Liberian Army, and ten were ordered in mid-1986 by the Royal Thai Army.

In December 1983 Federal Express Corporation of Memphis, Tennessee, placed an initial order for 30 **Model 208A** Caravan Is, and subsequently ordered nine more of this model, which differs from the standard aircraft in having a King avionics installation, no cabin windows or starboard side rear door, more freight tiedowns, an

additional cargo net, an underfuselage cargo pannier constructed from composites materials, a 15.2 cm (6 in) vertical extension to the fin/rudder, realigned exhaust outlet to keep exhaust gases clear of the pannier, and a max T-O weight of 3,629 kg (8,000 lb).

On 3 March 1986 the prototype (N9767F) of a 'stretched' version of the Caravan I made its first flight. This aircraft, known as the **Model 208B** and developed at the request of Federal Express Corporation, has a 1,587 kg (3,500 lb) payload and 12.7 m³ (450 cu ft) of cargo space, including belly cargo pod. Certification was achieved in October 1986. One hundred and sixty of the total of 199 Caravan Is on order for Federal Express will be 'stretched' versions, which have a 1.22 m (4 ft 0 in) increase in fuselage length achieved by plug inserts fore and aft of the wing centre-section. The first Model 208B was delivered to Federal Express Corporation on 31 October 1986, and a total of 98 Caravan Is of both models had been delivered by 20 January 1988. At that time the carrier's Caravan Is had logged a total flight time of 80,000 hours with a 99.7 per cent despatch reliability rate. Deliveries to Federal Express, which operates the aircraft in Canada, France, Hawaii and the United States, continued in 1988 at the rate of four per month.

Cessna Model 208B Caravan I operated by Union Flights of Sacramento, California, on behalf of Federal Express *(John Wegg)*

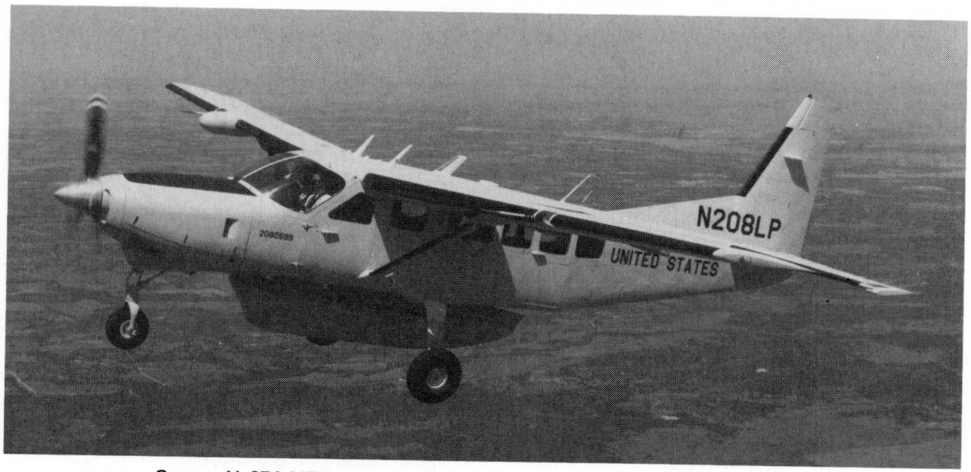

Cessna U-27A LIRA reconnaissance aircraft with underbelly recce pod

The all-freight versions of the Model 208A and Model 208B developed for Federal Express are known as the **Cargomaster** and **Super Cargomaster** respectively.

The Caravan I is the first single-engined aircraft to achieve FAA certification for Category II ILS operations. Federal Express will equip 104 of its aircraft for Cat II operations.

In the Spring of 1985 Cessna released details of a military derivative of the Caravan I with the factory designation **U-27A**. This is similar to the civilian model, but with increased ramp, T-O and landing weights, and is intended for troop transport, medevac, cargo, surveillance, VIP and forward air control roles. A demonstrator (N9514F, c/n 208-0079) was exhibited at the US Army Aviation Association of America convention in April 1986, and began a tour of US Army installations immediately afterwards. It was evaluated for possible lease or purchase for air ambulance duties and/or use as an airborne control station for RPVs. The U-27A has the 2.83 m³ (84 cu ft) cargo pannier of the Model 208A, and can be fitted with six underwing stations for a variety of stores, including drop tanks.

During 1987 Cessna began demonstrations to US and foreign military operators of a low intensity reconnaissance aircraft (LIRA) variant of the U-27A. This aircraft (N208LP, c/n 208-0699) is equipped with a General Dynamics reconnaissance pod derived from that being evaluated on the F-16 Recce. The pod, mounted on an underbelly centreline station, can house a variety of sensors, including high resolution optical cameras and IR linescan. A Sperry data link provides real-time transmission through ground stations to battlefield commanders or other aircraft within a radius of 174 nm (322 km; 200 miles).

By 31 December 1987 Cessna had delivered a total of 193 Caravan Is.

The name Caravan II applies to the unrelated twin turboprop business and utility transport developed jointly by Cessna and Reims Aviation of France, and described under the latter company's entry. The following description applies to Cessna's single-engined Model 208 Caravan I:

TYPE: Single-engined turboprop utility aircraft.

WINGS: Braced high-wing monoplane, with constant chord inner panels and tapered outer panels. Wing section NACA 23017.424 at root, NACA 23012 at tip. Dihedral 3° from roots. Incidence 2° 37′ at root, –0° 36′ at tip. Fail-safe two-spar structure. Single streamline section bracing strut each side. Electrically actuated wide span single-slotted flaps occupy more than 70 per cent of wing trailing-edge, and extend to 30° setting for low landing speeds. Ailerons operate in conjunction with slot-lip spoilers for positive roll control. Aileron trim standard.

FUSELAGE: Conventional semi-monocoque structure.

TAIL UNIT: Cantilever structure, with long dorsal fin. All control surfaces horn balanced. Large trim tab in starboard elevator. Rudder trim standard. Floatplane versions have an auxiliary fin mounted on the leading-edge of the tailplane on each side.

LANDING GEAR: Non-retractable tricycle type, with single wheel on each unit. Tubular spring cantilever main units; oil-damped spring nosewheel unit. Mainwheel tyres size 6.50-10; nosewheel 6.50-8. Oversize tyres, mainwheels 8.50-10, nosewheel 22 × 8.00-8, optional. Hydraulically actuated single-disc brake on each mainwheel. Certificated in floatplane and amphibian versions, with floats by Wipline, and with ski landing gear.

POWER PLANT: One Pratt & Whitney Canada PT6A-114 turboprop, flat rated at 447 kW (600 shp) to 3,800 m (12,500 ft), and driving a Hartzell three-blade constant-speed reversible-pitch and feathering composites propeller type HC-B3MN3/M10083 with spinner. Integral fuel tanks in wings, total capacity 1,268 litres (335 US gallons; 279 Imp gallons), of which 1,257 litres (332 US gallons; 276.5 Imp gallons) are usable.

ACCOMMODATION: Pilot and up to nine passengers or 1,360 kg (3,000 lb) of cargo. Maximum seating capacity with FAR Pt 23 waiver is 14. Cabin has a flat floor with Brownline cargo track attachments for a combination of two- and three-abreast seating, with an aisle between the seats. Forward hinged door for pilot, with direct vision window, on each side of forward fuselage. Airstair door for passengers at rear of cabin on starboard side. Cabin is heated and ventilated. Optional air-conditioning. Two-section horizontally split cargo door at rear of cabin on port side, flush with floor at bottom and with square corners. Upper portion hinges upward, lower portion forward 180°. In a cargo role cabin will accommodate typically two D-size cargo containers or up to ten 208 litre (55 US gallon; 45.8 Imp gallon) drums.

SYSTEMS: Electrical system is powered by 28V 200A starter/generator and 24V 45Ah lead-acid battery (24V 40Ah nickel-cadmium battery optional). Standby electrical system, with 95A alternator, optional. Hydraulic system for brakes only. Oxygen system, capacity 3.31 m³ (116.95 cu ft), optional. Vacuum system standard. Cabin air-conditioning system optional on c/n 208-00030 onwards. De-icing system, comprising electric propeller de-icing boots, pneumatic wing, wing strut and tail surface boots, electric heated windscreen panel, heated pitot/static probe, ice detector light and standby electrical system, all optional.

AVIONICS AND EQUIPMENT: Standard avionics include Sperry Series 300 nav/com, ADF, 400 transponder and audio console/intercom. Optional avionics include Sperry Series 400, with autopilot and area navigation system, King Silver Crown Basic and IFR avionics packages and Bendix RDS-82 colour weather radar, pod mounted on starboard wing leading-edge. Standard equipment includes sensitive altimeter, electric clock, magnetic compass, attitude and directional gyros, true airspeed indicator, turn and bank indicator, vertical speed indicator, ammeter/voltmeter, fuel flow indicator, ITT indicator, oil pressure and temperature indicator, windscreen defrost, ground service plug receptacle, variable intensity instrument post lighting, map light, overhead courtesy lights (3) and overhead floodlights (pilot and co-pilot), approach plate holder, cargo tiedowns, internal corrosion proofing, vinyl floor covering, emergency locator beacon, partial plumbing for oxygen system, adjustable fore/aft/vertical/reclining pilot's seat with seatbelt and dual inertia reel shoulder restraints, tinted windows, control surface bonding straps, heated pitot and stall warning systems, retractable crew steps (port side), tiedowns and towbar. Optional equipment includes co-pilot's and passenger seats, stowable, folding utility seats, digital clock, fuel totaliser, turn co-ordinator, flight hour recorder, fire extinguisher, dual controls, co-pilot flight instruments, floatplane kit (on c/n 208-00030 onwards), hoisting rings (for floatplane), inboard fuel filling provisions (included in floatplane kit), ice detection light, courtesy lights on wing leading-edge, passenger reading lights, omniflash beacon, rudder gust lock, retractable crew step for starboard side, oversized tyres, electric trim system, oil quick drain valve and fan driven ventilation system.

DIMENSIONS, EXTERNAL (Model 208):
Wing span 15.88 m (52 ft 1 in)
Wing chord: at root 1.98 m (6 ft 6 in)
  at tip 1.22 m (4 ft 0 in)
Wing aspect ratio 9.6
Length overall: landplane 11.46 m (37 ft 7 in)
Height overall: landplane 4.32 m (14 ft 2 in)
  amphibian (on land) 5.33 m (17 ft 6 in)
Tailplane span 6.25 m (20 ft 6 in)
Wheel track: landplane 3.56 m (11 ft 8 in)
  amphibian 3.25 m (10 ft 8 in)
Wheelbase: landplane 3.54 m (11 ft 7½ in)
  amphibian 4.44 m (14 ft 7 in)
Propeller diameter 2.54 m (8 ft 4 in)
Airstair door: Height 1.27 m (4 ft 2 in)
  Width 0.61 m (2 ft 0 in)
Cargo door: Height 1.27 m (4 ft 2 in)
  Width 1.24 m (4 ft 1 in)

DIMENSIONS, INTERNAL (Model 208):
Cabin: Length, excl baggage area 4.57 m (15 ft 0 in)
  Max width 1.57 m (5 ft 2 in)
  Max height 1.30 m (4 ft 3 in)
  Volume 9.67 m³ (341.4 cu ft)

AREAS:
Wings, gross 25.96 m² (279.4 sq ft)
Vertical tail surfaces (incl dorsal fin) 3.57 m² (38.41 sq ft)
Horizontal tail surfaces 6.51 m² (70.04 sq ft)

WEIGHTS AND LOADINGS (Civil Model 208. L: landplane, F: floatplane, A: amphibian):
Weight empty: L 1,724 kg (3,800 lb)
  F 2,020 kg (4,454 lb)
  A 2,177 kg (4,799 lb)
Max baggage (all) 147 kg (325 lb)
Max fuel (all) 1,009 kg (2,224 lb)
Max ramp weight: L 3,327 kg (7,335 lb)
  F, A 3,463 kg (7,635 lb)
Max T-O and landing weight, and max zero-fuel weight:
  L 3,311 kg (7,300 lb)
  F, A 3,447 kg (7,600 lb)
Max wing loading: L 127.4 kg/m² (26.1 lb/sq ft)
  F, A 132.8 kg/m² (27.2 lb/sq ft)
Max power loading: L 7.41 kg/kW (12.2 lb/shp)
  F, A 7.71 kg/kW (12.7 lb/shp)

WEIGHTS (U-27A: L, F and A as above):
Weight empty, standard: L 1,769 kg (3,900 lb)
  F 2,020 kg (4,454 lb)
  A 2,177 kg (4,799 lb)
Max ramp weight: L 3,645 kg (8,035 lb)
  F, A 3,463 kg (7,635 lb)
Max T-O weight: L 3,629 kg (8,000 lb)
  F, A 3,447 kg (7,600 lb)
Max landing weight: L 3,538 kg (7,800 lb)
  F, A 3,311 kg (7,300 lb)

PERFORMANCE (Civil Model 208. L: landplane, F: floatplane, A: amphibian):
Max operating speed (all) 175 knots (325 km/h; 202 mph) IAS
Max cruising speed at 3,050 m (10,000 ft):
  L 184 knots (341 km/h; 212 mph)
  F 159 knots (295 km/h; 183 mph)
  A 153 knots (283 km/h; 176 mph)
Stalling speed, power off:
  L, flaps up 73 knots (135 km/h; 84 mph) CAS
  L, flaps down 60 knots (111 km/h; 69 mph) CAS
  F, A, landing configuration 58 knots (107 km/h; 67 mph) CAS
Max rate of climb at S/L: L 370 m (1,215 ft)/min
  F 306 m (1,004 ft)/min
  A 290 m (952 ft)/min
Service ceiling: L 8,410 m (27,600 ft)
  F 7,285 m (23,900 ft)
  A 7,010 m (23,000 ft)
Max operating altitude (all) 9,145 m (30,000 ft)
T-O run: L 296 m (970 ft)
T-O run, water: F 468 m (1,535 ft)
  A 469 m (1,540 ft)
T-O to 15 m (50 ft): L 507 m (1,665 ft)
T-O to 15 m (50 ft), water: F 843 m (2,765 ft)
  A 859 m (2,820 ft)
Landing from 15 m (50 ft): L 472 m (1,550 ft)
Landing run: L 197 m (645 ft)
Range with max fuel, at max cruise power, allowances for start, taxi and reserves stated:
  L at 3,050 m (10,000 ft, 45 min) 970 nm (1,797 km; 1,117 miles)
  L at 6,100 m (20,000 ft, 45 min) 1,275 nm (2,362 km; 1,468 miles)
  F at 3,050 m (10,000 ft), 30 min 898 nm (1,664 km; 1,034 miles)
  A at 3,050 m (10,000 ft), 30 min 868 nm (1,608 km; 999 miles)
Range with max fuel at max range power, allowances as above:
  L at 3,050 m (10,000 ft) 1,115 nm (2,066 km; 1,284 miles)
  L at 6,100 m (20,000 ft) 1,370 nm (2,539 km; 1,578 miles)
g limits +3.8/–1.52

PERFORMANCE (U-27A: L, F and A as above):
Max cruising speed at 3,050 m (10,000 ft):
  L 182 knots (337 km/h; 209 mph)
  F 158 knots (293 km/h; 182 mph)
  A 153 knots (283 km/h; 176 mph)
Stalling speed in landing configuration:
  L, F, A 61 knots (113 km/h; 71 mph)
Max rate of climb at S/L: L 314 m (1,030 ft)/min
  F 288 m (944 ft)/min
  A 271 m (889 ft)/min
Service ceiling: L 7,410 m (24,300 ft)
  F 7,285 m (23,900 ft)
  A 7,010 m (23,000 ft)
T-O run at S/L: L 365 m (1,195 ft)
T-O run at S/L, water: F 575 m (1,886 ft)
  A 588 m (1,927 ft)
T-O to 15 m (50 ft) at S/L: L 662 m (2,170 ft)
T-O to 15 m (50 ft) at S/L, water: F 989 m (3,243 ft)
  A 1,019 m (3,341 ft)
Landing from 15 m (50 ft) at S/L, without propeller reversal: L 496 m (1,625 ft)

Landing run at S/L, without propeller reversal:
L 218 m (715 ft)
Range at 3,050 m (10,000 ft) at max cruise power, allowances for T-O climb, cruise, descent, and 45 min reserves: L 950 nm (1,760 km; 1,094 miles)
F 898 nm (1,664 km; 1,034 miles)
A 868 nm (1,608 km; 1,000 miles)

CESSNA CENTURION, TURBO CENTURION and PRESSURISED CENTURION

A total of 8,453 Model 210/Centurions, plus an additional 51 Pressurised Centurions, had been delivered by 31 December 1987. Production of all models of the Centurion has been suspended. Full descriptions can be found in the 1985-86 *Jane's*.

CESSNA MODEL T303 CRUSADER

Production of this six-seat, turbocharged twin-engined aircraft has been suspended. A total of 297 T303 Crusaders had been delivered by 31 December 1987. The aircraft was fully described and illustrated in the 1985-86 *Jane's*.

CESSNA MODEL 402C

Production of the Model 402C Utiliner and Model 402C Businessliner has been suspended. A total of 1,540 Model 402s had been delivered by 31 December 1987. Full descriptions and illustrations can be found in the 1985-86 *Jane's*.

REIMS-CESSNA MODEL F 406/CARAVAN II

Details of this joint programme for a twin-turboprop business/utility transport can be found under the Reims Aviation entry in the French section.

CESSNA MODEL 414A CHANCELLOR

Production of the pressurised Model 414A Chancellor has been suspended. By 31 December 1987 Cessna had delivered 1,067 Model 414/Chancellors. A full description of the Model 414A appeared in the 1985-86 *Jane's*.

CESSNA MODEL 421 GOLDEN EAGLE

The prototype of this six/eight-seat pressurised twin-engined business aircraft flew for the first time on 14 October 1965. FAA type approval was received on 1 May 1967 and deliveries began in the same month.

Two developed versions were produced subsequently as the 421B Golden Eagle and 421B Executive Commuter, remaining in production until replaced by the Model 421C Golden Eagle in 1976.

A total of 1,909 Model 421s had been delivered by 31 December 1987. Production was suspended in 1985. A full description and illustration can be found in the 1985-86 *Jane's*.

CESSNA MODEL 425 CONQUEST I

Known as the Corsair until late 1982, the Conquest I is a twin-turboprop business aircraft based on the airframe of the Model 421 Golden Eagle. FAA certification was gained by mid-1980. Initial deliveries of production aircraft were made in November 1980, and 132 Corsairs were delivered. A total of 232 Corsairs and Conquest Is had been delivered by 31 December 1987. Production of the Conquest I has been suspended. A full description and illustrations can be found in the 1986-87 *Jane's*.

CESSNA MODEL 441 CONQUEST II

Production of the twin-turboprop Conquest II has been suspended. A total of 360 had been delivered by 31 December 1987. A full description and illustrations of the Conquest II, together with brief details of the Pratt & Whitney Canada PT6A-engined **Model 435**, may be found in the 1986-87 *Jane's*.

CESSNA MODEL 550 CITATION II

Announced on 14 September 1976, the Citation II introduced a fuselage lengthened by 1.14 m (3 ft 9 in) compared with the Citation I, an increased span high aspect ratio wing, increased fuel and baggage capacity, and Pratt & Whitney Canada JT15D-4 turbofan engines. The prototype (N550CC) flew for the first time on 31 January 1977, and certification to FAR Pt 25 Transport Category requirements was received in late March 1978 for two-pilot operation. The Model 551 Citation II/SP was subsequently introduced for single-pilot operation, with up to 10 passengers, at a max T-O weight of 5,670 kg (12,500 lb), conforming to FAR Pt 23 requirements.

Production of the Citation II was phased out during 1984 in favour of the improved Citation S/II (which see), at which time 503 Citation IIs had been delivered. At the National Business Aircraft Association convention at New Orleans in September 1985, Cessna announced that it would resume production of the Citation II. By 31 December 1987 a total of 14 new production Citation IIs had been delivered. The following description applies to the current production Model 550 (c/n 0550 and later) unless otherwise indicated:

TYPE: Eight/twelve-seat twin-turbofan executive transport.

WINGS: Cantilever low-wing monoplane without sweepback. Wing section at c/l NACA 23014 (modified), at wing station 247.95 NACA 23012. Incidence 2° 30′ at c/l, -0° 30′ at wing station 247.95. Dihedral 4°. All-metal fail-safe structure with two primary spars, an auxiliary spar, three fuselage attachment points, and conventional ribs and stringers. Manually operated ailerons, with manual trim on port aileron. Electrically operated single-slotted trailing-edge flaps. Hydraulically operated aerodynamic speed brakes. Wing leading-edge forward of each engine is electrically anti-iced. Pneumatic de-icing boots on outer leading-edges.

FUSELAGE: All-metal pressurised structure of circular section. Fail-safe design, providing multiple load paths.

TAIL UNIT: Cantilever all-metal structure. Horizontal surfaces have dihedral of 9°. Large dorsal fin and smaller ventral fin. Manually operated control surfaces. Electric elevator trim with manual override; manual rudder trim.

LANDING GEAR: Hydraulically retractable tricycle type with single wheel on each unit. Main units retract inward into the wing, nose gear forward into fuselage nose. Free-fall and pneumatic emergency extension systems. Goodyear mainwheels with tyres size 22.0 × 8-10, 10-ply rating, pressure 6.90 bars (100 lb/sq in). Steerable nosewheel with Goodyear wheel and tyre size 18.0 × 4.4, 10-ply rating, pressure 8.27 bars (120 lb/sq in). Goodyear hydraulic brakes. Parking brake and pneumatic emergency brake system. Anti-skid system optional.

POWER PLANT: Two Pratt & Whitney Canada JT15D-4 turbofans, each rated at 11.12 kN (2,500 lb st) for take-off, mounted in pod on each side of rear fuselage. Integral fuel tanks in wings, with usable capacity of 2,808 litres (742 US gallons; 618 Imp gallons).

ACCOMMODATION: Crew of two on separate flight deck, on fully adjustable seats, with seat belts and inertia reel shoulder harness, and sun visors. Fully carpeted main cabin equipped with seats for six to ten passengers, with toilet in six/eight-seat versions. Main baggage area at rear of cabin. Second baggage area in nose. Total baggage capacity 522 kg (1,150 lb). Cabin is pressurised, heated and air-conditioned. Individual reading lights and air inlets for each passenger. Dropout constant-flow oxygen system for emergency use. Plug type door with integral airstair at front on port side and one emergency exit on starboard side. Doors on each side of nose baggage compartment. Tinted windows, each with curtains. Pilot's storm window, birdproof windscreen with de-fog system, anti-icing, standby alcohol anti-icing and bleed air rain removal system.

SYSTEMS: Pressurisation system supplied with engine bleed air, max pressure differential 0.61 bars (8.8 lb/sq in), maintaining a sea level cabin altitude to 6,720 m (22,040 ft), or a 2,440 m (8,000 ft) cabin altitude to 12,495 m (41,000 ft). Hydraulic system, pressure 103.5 bars (1,500 lb/sq in), with two pumps to operate landing gear and speed brakes. Separate hydraulic system for wheel brakes. Electrical system supplied by two 28V 400A DC starter/generators, with two 350VA inverters and 24V 40Ah nickel-cadmium battery. Oxygen system of 0.62 m^3 (22 cu ft) capacity includes two crew demand masks and five dropout constant flow masks for passengers. High capacity oxygen system optional. Engine fire detection and extinguishing systems.

DIMENSIONS, EXTERNAL:
Wing span 15.76 m (51 ft 8½ in)
Wing aspect ratio 8.3
Length overall 14.39 m (47 ft 2½ in)
Height overall 4.57 m (15 ft 0 in)
Wheel track 5.36 m (17 ft 7 in)
Wheelbase 5.55 m (18 ft 2½ in)

DIMENSIONS, INTERNAL:
Cabin:
Length, front to rear bulkhead 6.37 m (20 ft 10¾ in)
Max height 1.46 m (4 ft 9½ in)
Baggage capacity 1.84 m^3 (65.0 cu ft)

AREAS:
Wings, gross 30.00 m^2 (322.9 sq ft)
Horizontal tail surfaces (total, incl tab) 6.56 m^2 (70.6 sq ft)
Vertical tail surfaces (total) 4.73 m^2 (50.9 sq ft)

WEIGHTS:
Weight empty, equipped 3,351 kg (7,388 lb)
Max fuel weight 2,272 kg (5,009 lb)
Max T-O weight 6,033 kg (13,300 lb)
Max ramp weight 6,123 kg (13,500 lb)
Max zero-fuel weight: standard 4,309 kg (9,500 lb)
optional 4,990 kg (11,000 lb)
Max landing weight 5,760 kg (12,700 lb)

PERFORMANCE (at max T-O weight, ISA, except where indicated):
Max operating speed:
S/L to 4,265 m (14,000 ft) 262 knots (486 km/h; 302 mph) IAS
4,265 m (14,000 ft) to 8,530 m (28,000 ft) 277 knots (513 km/h; 319 mph) IAS
8,530 m (28,000 ft) and above Mach 0.705
Cruising speed at average cruise weight of 4,990 kg (11,000 lb) at 7,620 m (25,000 ft) 385 knots (713 km/h; 443 mph)
Stalling speed, clean, at max T-O weight 94 knots (174 km/h; 108 mph) CAS
Stalling speed at max landing weight 82 knots (152 km/h; 95 mph) CAS
Max rate of climb at S/L 1,027 m (3,370 ft)/min
Rate of climb at S/L, one engine out 322 m (1,055 ft)/min
Max certificated altitude 13,105 m (43,000 ft)
Service ceiling, one engine out 7,680 m (25,200 ft)
T-O to 15 m (50 ft) 727 m (2,385 ft)
T-O balanced field length (FAR Pt 25) 912 m (2,990 ft)
FAR Pt 25 landing runway length at max landing weight 692 m (2,270 ft)
Range with max fuel, crew of two and six passengers, allowances for T-O, climb, cruise at 13,105 m (43,000 ft), descent, and 45 min reserves 1,662 nm (3,080 km; 1,914 miles)

OPERATIONAL NOISE LEVELS (FAR Pt 36):
T-O 80.1 EPNdB
Approach 90.5 EPNdB
Sideline 86.7 EPNdB

CESSNA MODEL S550 CITATION S/II

US Navy designation: T-47A

Cessna announced on 4 October 1983 first details of the Citation S/II, an eight/ten-seat version of the Citation II. The improvements were introduced on the production line from aircraft c/n 506, delivered in the late Summer of 1984. They include a new wing aerofoil section, utilising Citation III supercritical technology, to reduce high-speed drag while retaining the Citation II's slow-speed handling and short-field capability; a modified wing/fuselage fairing to improve localised airflow; an extended wing inboard leading-edge, increasing wing area/lift and providing greater fuel capacity; modified engine pylon contours to reduce drag; sealed aileron/speed brake gaps, and faired flap coves, to reduce drag and improve lift; hydraulically actuated Fowler flaps of graphite composite construction, in two panels on each wing, which extend further inboard to provide additional lift/drag; ailerons of graphite composite construction with geared trim tabs to improve roll access response; a TKS glycol anti-icing system for the wing leading-edges; and a new -4B version of the Citation II's Pratt & Whitney Canada JT15D turbofans, which provides greater thrust at high altitudes. Tail unit anti-icing systems are no longer required.

Internal refinements include an increase in tailcone baggage volume to 0.79 m^3 (28.0 cu ft); a headroom increase of 12.7 cm (5 in) in the totally private toilet area; soft-touch

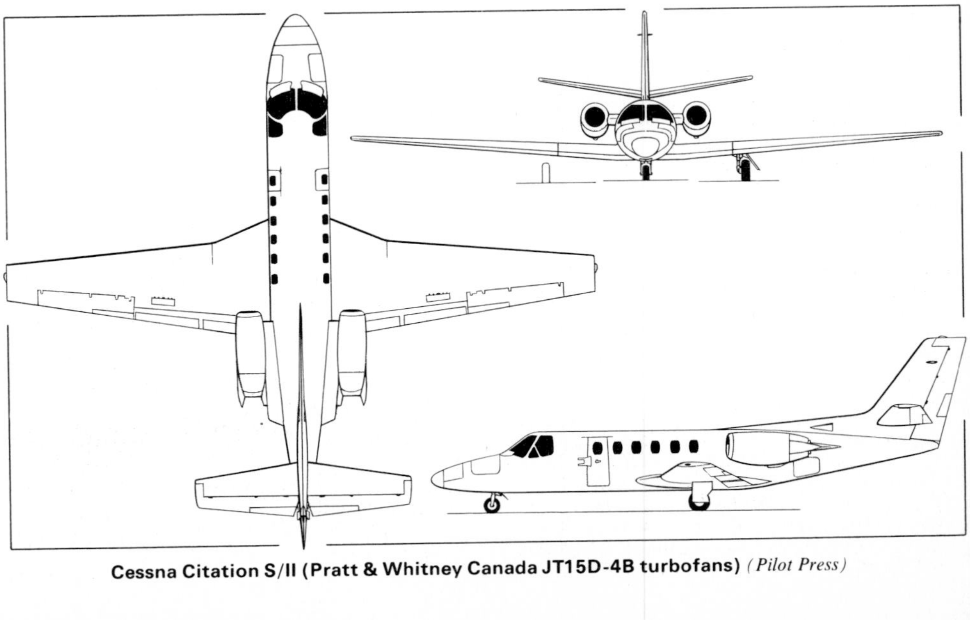

Cessna Citation S/II (Pratt & Whitney Canada JT15D-4B turbofans) *(Pilot Press)*

Cessna Citation S/II executive jet

headliners that reduce sound levels; Citation III style seats with shoulder harness, lateral tracking for more head and elbow room, and built-in life jacket storage; and redesigned sidewall air ducts which improve cabin insulation and heating and also provide a better than ten per cent increase in aisle width. Options include a vanity unit for the toilet, refreshment centres of composite construction, a wide door for use in cargo, air ambulance and other special applications, and Sperry EFIS. In April 1987 Cessna introduced high capacity brakes as standard. These units, available also for retrofit to earlier Model S550s, reduce landing distance at max landing weight by some 13 per cent.

The first production configuration Citation S/II made its first flight on 14 February 1984; FAA certification, with exemption for single-pilot operation, was granted in July 1984. A total of 139 Citation S/IIs had been delivered by 31 December 1987.

In late 1985 Cessna delivered its first Citation S/II ambulance aircraft to the Province of Manitoba, Canada. The aircraft can accommodate single or double stretchers, up to four medical attendants and large quantities of medical oxygen. Five specially-equipped Citation S/IIs have also been delivered to the Chinese government for use by the Airborne Remote Sensing Centre of the Chinese Academy of Sciences. They are operated by the Flight Test Research Institute in Xian.

Since 1985 the US Navy has operated 15 Citation S/IIs, known as the **Model 552** and designated **T-47A**, instead of the T-39Ds used previously to train personnel in use of air-to-air, air-to-surface, intercept and other radar equipment. These aircraft are part of a five-year programme, plus a three-year option, covering provision of the aircraft, simulators, maintenance and pilot services. The T-47As differ from standard Citation S/IIs in having JT15D-5 turbofans, a shorter wing span, to increase rate of climb and make possible a speed of Mach 0.733 at 12,200 m (40,000 ft), and an Emerson nose mounted APQ-159 radar. The crew normally comprises a civilian pilot, Navy instructor and three students. The first T-47A made its first flight on 15 February 1984 and received FAA certification on 21 November 1984. By June 1987 the T-47A fleet had logged nearly 35,000 flight hours and achieved a mission completion rate in excess of 95 per cent.

In January 1988 Cessna delivered its 1,500th Citation, a Model S/II for Executive Jet Aviation of Columbus, Ohio. At that time the worldwide Citation fleet, operating in 53 countries, had completed more than four million flight hours.

The following description applies to the current production Model S550 (c/n 0115 and later), except where indicated:

TYPE: Eight/ten-seat twin-turbofan executive transport.

WINGS: Cantilever low-wing monoplane without sweepback. Incidence 2° 30′ at c/l, –0° 30′ at wing station 247.95. Dihedral 4°. All-metal fail-safe structure with two primary spars, an auxiliary spar, three fuselage attachment points, and conventional ribs and stringers. Manually operated ailerons, of graphite composite construction, each with geared trim tab. Hydraulically operated trailing-edge Fowler flaps of graphite composite construction. Hydraulically operated aerodynamic speed brakes. Glycol anti-icing of leading-edges.

FUSELAGE: All-metal pressurised structure of circular section. Fail-safe design, providing multiple load paths.

TAIL UNIT: Cantilever all-metal structure. Horizontal surfaces have dihedral of 9°. Dorsal fin. Manually operated control surfaces. Electric elevator trim with manual override; manual rudder trim.

LANDING GEAR: Hydraulically retractable tricycle type with single wheel on each unit. Main units retract inward into the wing, nose gear forward into fuselage nose. Free-fall and pneumatic emergency extension systems. Goodyear mainwheels with tyres size 22.0 × 8-10, 12-ply rating, pressure 8.27 bars (120 lb/sq in). Steerable nosewheel with Goodyear wheel and tyre size 18.0 × 4.4, 10-ply rating, pressure 8.27 bars (120 lb/sq in). High capacity brakes manufactured by Aircraft Wheel and Brake

Division of Parker Hannifin Corporation. Parking brake and pneumatic emergency brake system. Anti-skid system optional.

POWER PLANT: Two Pratt & Whitney Canada JT15D-4B turbofans, each rated at 11.12 kN (2,500 lb st) for take-off, mounted in a pod each side of rear fuselage. Integral fuel tanks in wings, with combined usable capacity of 3,263 litres (862 US gallons; 718 Imp gallons).

ACCOMMODATION: Crew of two on separate flight deck, on fully adjustable seats, with seat belts and inertia reel shoulder harness, and sun visors. Seating for six to eight passengers in main cabin. Standard interior configuration provides for six passenger seats, two forward and four aft facing, each with headrest, seat belt and diagonal inertia reel harness; flushing toilet aft; tracked refreshment centre; forward cabin divider with privacy curtain, aft cabin divider with sliding doors. Passenger service units containing an oxygen mask, air vent and reading light for each passenger. Three separate baggage areas, one in nose section, externally accessible, one in aft cabin area, and one in tailcone area, with a combined capacity of up to 658 kg (1,450 lb).

SYSTEMS: Pressurisation system supplied with engine bleed air, max pressure differential 0.61 bars (8.8 lb/sq in), maintaining a sea level cabin altitude to 6,962 m (22,842 ft), or a 2,440 m (8,000 ft) cabin altitude to 13,105 m (43,000 ft). Hydraulic system, pressure 103.5 bars (1,500 lb/sq in), with two pumps to operate landing gear and speed brakes. Pressurised reservoir. Separate hydraulic system for wheel brakes. Electrical system supplied by two 28V 300A engine driven DC starter/generators, with two 350VA inverters and 24V 40Ah nickel-cadmium battery. Oxygen system of 0.62 m³ (22 cu ft) capacity includes two crew demand masks and five dropout constant flow masks for passengers. High capacity oxygen system optional. Engine fire detection and extinguishing systems.

AVIONICS AND EQUIPMENT: Standard avionics package comprises Sperry SPZ-500 integrated flight director/autopilot system, with single-cue command bars, Sperry C-14D compass system, Sperry RD-450 (starboard) HSI, dual Collins VHF-22A com transceivers, dual Collins VIR-32 nav receivers with VOR/LOC, glideslope and marker beacon receivers, dual Collins RMI-30, Collins DME-42 with 339F-12 indicator, TDR-90 transponder, Collins ADF-60, and Sperry Primus 300SL colour weather radar. Optional advanced avionics and instrumentation are available according to customer choice, and include Bendix Series III integrated EFIS, nav/com and radar systems.

DIMENSIONS, EXTERNAL:

Wing span over lights: S/II	15.90 m (52 ft 2½ in)
T-47A	14.18 m (46 ft 6 in)
Wing chord (mean): S/II	2.06 m (6 ft 9 in)
Wing aspect ratio: S/II	7.8
Length overall: S/II	14.39 m (47 ft 2½ in)
T-47A	14.60 m (47 ft 10¾ in)
Height overall: S/II	4.57 m (15 ft 0 in)
T-47A	4.51 m (14 ft 9¾ in)
Wheel track	5.36 m (17 ft 7 in)
Wheelbase	5.55 m (18 ft 2½ in)
Tailplane span: S/II	5.79 m (19 ft 0 in)
Cabin door (S/II, optional): Height	1.14 m (3 ft 9 in)
Width	0.89 m (2 ft 11 in)

DIMENSIONS, INTERNAL (S/II):

Cabin:	
Length, front to rear bulkhead	6.37 m (20 ft 10¾ in)
Max height	1.45 m (4 ft 9½ in)
Max width	1.49 m (4 ft 10¾ in)
Baggage capacity (total)	2.27 m³ (80.0 cu ft)

AREAS (S/II):

Wings, gross	31.83 m² (342.6 sq ft)
Horizontal tail surfaces (total)	6.48 m² (69.8 sq ft)
Vertical tail surfaces (total)	4.73 m² (50.9 sq ft)

WEIGHTS AND LOADINGS:

Weight empty, equipped: S/II	3,655 kg (8,059 lb)
T-47A	4,098 kg (9,035 lb)
Max baggage weight (S/II): internal	272 kg (600 lb)
external	385 kg (850 lb)
Max ramp weight: S/II	6,940 kg (15,300 lb)
Max fuel weight: S/II	2,640 kg (5,820 lb)
Max T-O weight: S/II	6,849 kg (15,100 lb)
T-47A	6,804 kg (15,000 lb)
Max landing weight: S/II	6,350 kg (14,400 lb)
Max zero-fuel weight: S/II	4,990 kg (11,200 lb)
Max wing loading S/II	215.17 kg/m² (44.07 lb/sq ft)
Max power loading S/II	1.42 kg/kN (3.02 lb/lb st)

PERFORMANCE (S/II at max T-O weight, except where indicated):

Max operating speed:	
S/L to 2,440 m (8,000 ft)	
	261 knots (483 km/h; 300 mph) IAS
2,440 m (8,000 ft) to 8,935 m (29,315 ft)	
	276 knots (511 km/h; 318 mph)
above 8,935 m (29,315 ft)	Mach 0.721
Cruising speed at mid-cruise weight of 5,443 kg	
(12,000 lb) at 10,670 m (35,000 ft)	
	403 knots (746 km/h; 463 mph)
Stalling speed, clean, at max T-O weight	
	94 knots (174 km/h; 108 mph) CAS
Stalling speed at max landing weight	
	82 knots (152 km/h; 94 mph) CAS
Max rate of climb at S/L	926 m (3,040 ft)/min
Rate of climb at S/L, one engine out	
	262 m (860 ft)/min
Max operating altitude	13,105 m (43,000 ft)
Service ceiling, one engine out	7,315 m (24,000 ft)
T-O balanced field length (FAR Pt 25)	
	987 m (3,240 ft)
FAR 25 landing runway length at max landing weight	
(high capacity brakes)	805 m (2,640 ft)
Range with four passengers, two crew and baggage, zero wind, IFR reserves	1,739 nm (3,223 km; 2,002 miles)
Range with max fuel	1,998 nm (3,701 km; 2,300 miles)

OPERATIONAL NOISE LEVELS (FAR Pt 36):

T-O	78.0 EPNdB
Approach	91.0 EPNdB
Sideline	90.4 EPNdB

CESSNA MODEL 560 CITATION V

Cessna announced development of the Model 560 Citation V at the 1987 National Business Aircraft Association convention in New Orleans, following the first flight of the engineering prototype (N560CC) during August. The Citation V is a development of the Citation S/II, powered by two 12.89 kN (2,900 lb st) Pratt & Whitney Canada JT15D-5A turbofans and with a fuselage lengthened by nearly 0.6 m (2 ft) to provide increased passenger space and a fully enclosed private toilet/vanity area in its eight-seat cabin. Apart from its longer fuselage, the principal external change is the addition of a seventh cabin window on each side. Two baggage compartments, outside the main passenger cabin area, with a total volume

Cessna T-47A, a US Navy training version of the Citation S/II

Prototype Cessna Model 560 Citation V business jet

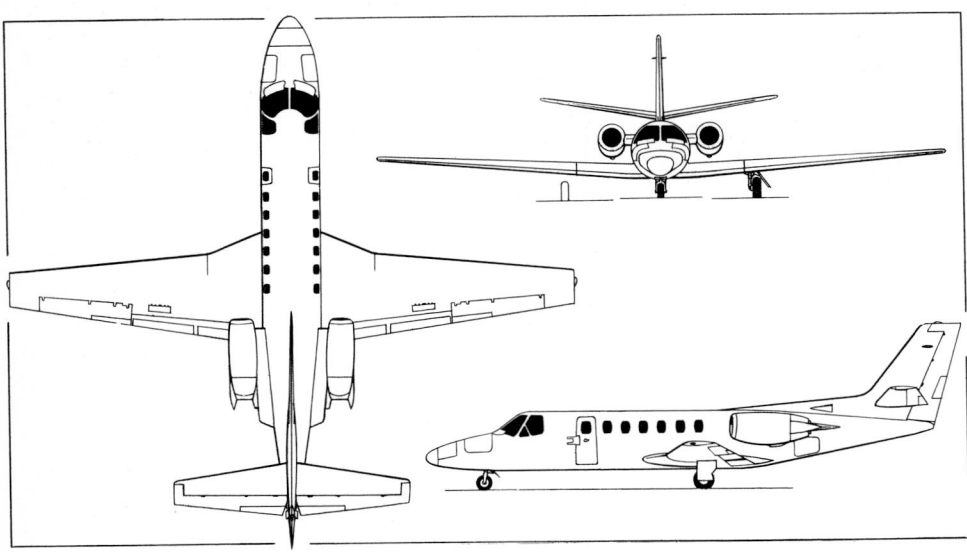

Cessna Model 560 Citation V (two Pratt & Whitney Canada JT15D-5A turbofans) *(Pilot Press)*

of 1.16 m³ (41 cu ft), can accommodate up to 385 kg (850 lb) of baggage.

The Citation V features a new anti-ice/de-ice system, comprising inboard wing cuff leading-edges heated by engine bleed air and 'silver' low profile de-icer boots on the leading-edges of the outer wing panels and tailplane. Standard equipment includes Category II avionics, comprising an integrated Sperry autopilot and flight guidance system, EFIS in the pilot's panel, a Global GNS-X navigation management system, advanced weather radar, dual transponders, encoding and radio altimeters; thrust reversers; engine synchronisers; a 1.8 m³ (64 cu ft) oxygen system; recognition lights; and an in-flight telephone.

By November 1987 the prototype Citation V had completed more than 100 flight hours. This aircraft is being used for low speed aerodynamic certification and primary systems development. A second pre-production prototype, which joined the test programme in early 1988, is being used for high speed aerodynamic and systems certification. FAA certification of the Citation V was scheduled for November 1988, with first customer deliveries anticipated in February 1989.

The following data are provisional:

DIMENSIONS, EXTERNAL: As for Citation S/II except:
Length overall	14.90 m (48 ft 10¾ in)
Tailplane span	6.55 m (21 ft 6 in)
Wheelbase	6.06 m (19 ft 10¾ in)

DIMENSIONS, INTERNAL As for Citation S/II except:
Length, front to rear bulkhead	6.89 m (22 ft 7¼ in)

AREAS: As for Citation S/II except:
Horizontal tail surfaces (total)	7.88 m² (84.8 sq ft)

WEIGHTS:
Weight empty, equipped	4,004 kg (8,828 lb)
Max fuel weight	2,640 kg (5,820 lb)
Max T-O weight	7,212 kg (15,900 lb)
Max ramp weight	7,303 kg (16,100 lb)
Max landing weight	6,895 kg (15,200 lb)
Max zero-fuel weight	5,080 kg (11,200 lb)

PERFORMANCE:
Max operating speed:
at 2,440 m (8,000 ft) to 8,810 m (28,900 ft)	
	292 knots (541 km/h; 336 mph) IAS
above 8,810 m (28,900 ft)	Mach 0.755
Cruising speed at 10,060 m (33,000 ft)	
	427 knots (791 km/h; 492 mph)
Stalling speed, 'clean', at max T-O weight	
	87 knots (161 km/h; 100 mph)
Max rate of climb at S/L	1,112 m (3,650 ft)/min

Rate of climb at S/L, one engine out
	360 m (1,180 ft)/min
Max operating altitude	13,715 m (45,000 ft)
Service ceiling, one engine out	9,480 m (31,100 ft)
T-O balanced field length (FAR 25)	963 m (3,160 ft)
FAR 25 landing field length, S/L, ISA, at max landing weight	890 m (2,920 ft)

Range with six passengers, two crew, zero wind, at high-speed cruise speed with allowances for T-O, climb, cruise, descent and VFR reserves
1,920 nm (3,558 km; 2,211 miles)

CESSNA MODEL 650 CITATION III

The Citation III represented Cessna's entry into the high-speed medium-size business jet market. First flight of the first prototype (N650CC) was made on 30 May 1979. The second prototype flew for the first time on 2 May 1980,

and FAA certification under FAR Pt 25 Transport Category requirements was gained on 30 April 1982. Flight test experience allowed the maximum operating speed to be increased to Mach 0.83. A maximum speed of Mach 0.90 was demonstrated successfully in a dive.

The first production Citation III was delivered to the Citation Marketing Division in December 1982. It was used as a demonstrator, together with the second and third production aircraft, prior to the start of delivery to customers in Spring 1983. By 31 December 1987 Citation III deliveries totalled 143 aircraft. The Citation III was certificated by the United Kingdom Civil Aviation Authority in April 1988. Within Europe, it is also certificated in Austria, Denmark, France, West Germany, Italy, Spain, Sweden and Switzerland.

TYPE: Twin-turbofan eight/eleven-seat long-range executive transport.

WINGS: Cantilever low-wing monoplane. NASA-developed supercritical section. Dihedral 3°. Sweepback at quarter-chord 25°. Conventional two-spar fail-safe structure of light alloy, utilising bonded and riveted construction and built in three sections. Electrically actuated trailing-edge flaps, in three sections on each wing, are of Kevlar and graphite composite construction. Four hydraulically actuated spoilers on the upper surface of each wing, immediately forward of the flaps. The two centre spoilers on each wing can be operated as airbrakes in flight. All eight spoilers can be used for emergency descent, and for lift dumping after touchdown. Hydraulically powered ailerons, with manual reversion, are complemented by the outboard spoiler panel on each wing, which provides additional roll authority after approx 3° of aileron deflection. Stall strips and a stall fence are mounted at approx semi-span of each outer wing panel. Anti-icing of wing leading-edges by engine bleed air.

FUSELAGE: Conventional semi-monocoque light alloy structure of circular cross-section. Fail-safe in pressurised area.

TAIL UNIT: Cantilever T tail structure of light alloy, with swept horizontal and vertical surfaces. Variable incidence tailplane has 3° anhedral. Electric anti-icing of tailplane leading-edges. Fin leading-edge is not anti-iced. Rudder incorporates a boost system to minimise yaw in asymmetric thrust conditions.

LANDING GEAR: Hydraulically retractable tricycle type. Main units retract inward into the undersurface of the wing centre-section, nosewheel forward and upward into the nose. Main units of trailing link type, each with twin wheels; nose unit has a single wheel. Oleo-pneumatic shock absorber in each unit. Hydraulically powered nosewheel steering, with an accumulator to provide steering after a loss of normal hydraulic power. Emergency landing gear extension by manual release and free-fall to locked position; pneumatic blowdown system for backup. Mainwheel tyres size 22.0 × 5.75, 10-ply rating, pressure 10.20 bars (148 lb/sq in). Nosewheel tyre size 18.0 × 4.4, 10-ply rating, pressure 8.62 bars (125 lb/sq in). Fully modulated hydraulically powered anti-skid brake system. In the event of hydraulic system failure, an electrically driven standby pump provides pressure for the brakes. Emergency pneumatic brake system. Parking brake.

POWER PLANT: Two Garrett TFE731-3B-100S turbofans, each rated at 16.24 kN (3,650 lb st) for take-off, mounted in pod on each side of rear fuselage. Hydraulically operated Rohr target type thrust reversers standard. Two independent fuel systems, with integral tanks in each wing; usable capacity 4,183 litres (1,105 US gallons; 920 Imp gallons). Additional fuel cell behind rear fuselage bulkhead. Single-point pressure refuelling on starboard side of fuselage, to rear of wing trailing-edge. Gravity

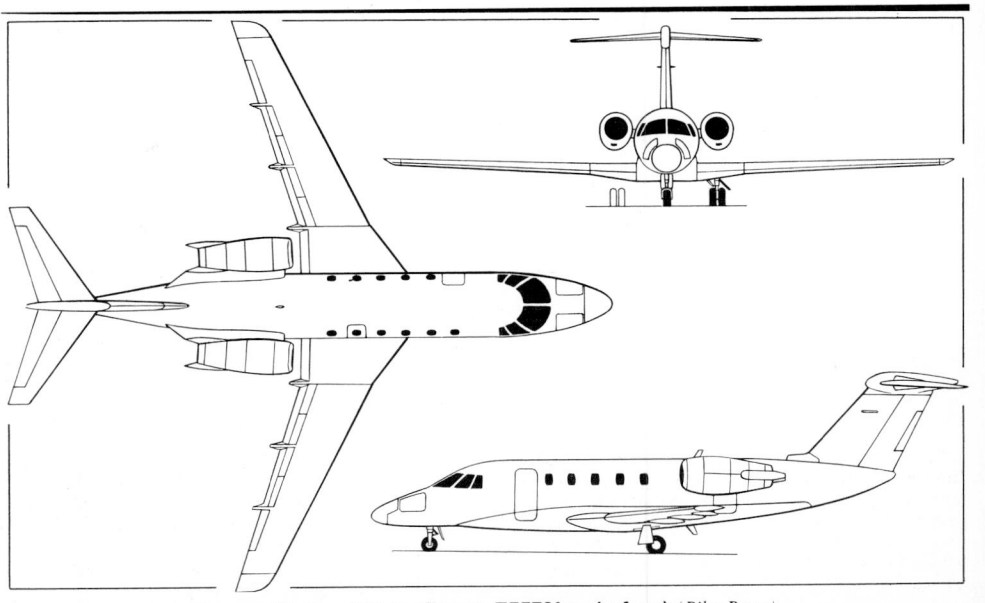

Cessna Citation III (two Garrett TFE731 turbofans) *(Pilot Press)*

Cessna Citation III eight/eleven-seat executive transport

refuelling point on upper surface of each wing. A boost pump in the port wing fills the fuselage tank when pressure refuelling is not available. Engine intake anti-icing system.

ACCOMMODATION: Crew of two on separate flight deck, and up to nine passengers. Standard interior has six individual seats, with toilet at rear of cabin. The fuselage nose incorporates a radome, high resolution radar, avionics bay and a storage compartment for crew baggage. Electrically heated baggage compartment in rear fuselage with external door on port side. Airstair door forward of wing on port side. Overwing emergency escape hatch on starboard side. Cabin is pressurised, heated and air-conditioned. Windscreen anti-icing by engine bleed air, with alcohol spray backup for port side of the windscreen. Windscreen defogging by warm air, and rain removal by engine bleed air and a mechanically actuated airflow deflector.

SYSTEMS: Environmental control system, with separate control of flight deck and cabin conditions. Direct engine bleed pressurisation system, with nominal pressure differential of 0.67 bars (9.7 lb/sq in), provides 2,440 m (8,000 ft) cabin environment to max certificated altitude and can maintain a sea level cabin environment to approx 7,620 m (25,000 ft). Electrical system includes two 28V 400A DC starter/generators, two 200/115V 5kW three-phase engine driven alternators, two 115V 400Hz solid state static inverters, two 24V 22Ah nickel-cadmium batteries and an external power socket in the tailcone. Hydraulic system of 207 bars (3,000 lb/sq in) powered by two engine driven pressure compensated pumps for operation of spoilers, brakes, landing gear, nosewheel steering and thrust reversers. Hydraulic reservoir with integral reserve and an electrically driven hydraulic pump to provide emergency power. Oxygen system of 1.39 m³ (49 cu ft) capacity with automatic dropout constant-flow oxygen mask for each passenger and a quick-donning pressure demand mask for each crew member. Engine fire detection and extinguishing system.

AVIONICS AND EQUIPMENT: Standard avionics include a Sperry SPZ-650 integrated flight director/autopilot system with AD650A ADI, RD650A HSI and C-14D compass system; Sperry GH-14 ADI and RD450 HSI with C-14D compass system for co-pilot; AA-300 radio altimeter; dual Collins VHF-22A 720-channel transceivers, dual VIR-32 nav receivers which include VOR, localiser, glideslope and marker beacon receivers,

dual RMI-30, DME-42 DME, TDR-90 transponder; Sperry Primus 300SL colour weather radar; Collins ADF-60 ADF; JET standby attitude gyro; Teledyne angle of attack system; air data computer; dual Avtech audio amplifiers; and Telex microphones, headsets and speakers. A wide range of optional avionics is available including Bendix Series III integrated EFIS, nav/com and radar system. Standard equipment includes dual altimeters, Mach/airspeed indicators, angle of attack indicator, digital clock, instantaneous rate of climb indicators, outside air temperature gauge, crew seats with vertical, fore, aft and recline adjustments, seat belts, shoulder harnesses and inertia reels, six individual passenger seats, three each forward and aft facing with vertical, fore and aft adjustment, lateral tracking and recline adjustments, seat belts and shoulder harnesses, sun visors, flight deck divider with curtain, openable storm windows, electroluminescent and edge-lit instrument panels, stall warning system, cockpit and cabin fire extinguishers, indirect cabin lighting, cabin aisle lights, door courtesy lights, 'Fasten seat belt—No smoking' signs, refreshment centre, cup holders, ashtrays, executive table, aft cabin divider with curtain, emergency exit signs, internal corrosion proofing, emergency battery pack, emergency portable cabin oxygen, navigation and recognition lights, dual landing and taxi lights, dual anti-collision strobe lights, red flashing beacon, dual wing ice lights, lightning protection, static discharge wicks and tiedown provisions.

DIMENSIONS, EXTERNAL:	
Wing span	16.31 m (53 ft 6 in)
Wing mean aerodynamic chord	2.08 m (6 ft 9¾ in)
Wing aspect ratio	8.9
Length overall	16.90 m (55 ft 5½ in)
Height overall	5.12 m (16 ft 9½ in)
Tailplane span	5.60 m (18 ft 4½ in)
Wheel track	2.84 m (9 ft 4 in)
Wheelbase	6.50 m (21 ft 4 in)
Cabin door: Width	0.61 m (2 ft 0 in)
Height	1.37 m (4 ft 6 in)

DIMENSIONS, INTERNAL:	
Cabin:	
Length, front to rear bulkhead	7.01 m (23 ft 0 in)
Length, aft of cockpit divider	5.66 m (18 ft 7 in)
Max width	1.73 m (5 ft 8 in)
Max height	1.78 m (5 ft 10 in)

Baggage capacity (aft)	1.88 m³ (66.4 cu ft)
Crew baggage compartment (nose)	0.17 m³ (6.0 cu ft)
AREAS:	
Wings, gross	29.00 m² (312.0 sq ft)
Horizontal tail surfaces (total)	6.26 m² (67.4 sq ft)
Vertical tail surfaces (total)	6.04 m² (65.0 sq ft)
WEIGHTS:	
Weight empty, standard	5,357 kg (11,811 lb)
Max fuel weight	3,349 kg (7,384 lb)
Max T-O weight	9,979 kg (22,000 lb)
Max ramp weight	10,070 kg (22,200 lb)
Max landing weight	9,072 kg (20,000 lb)
Max zero-fuel weight	6,940 kg (15,300 lb)

PERFORMANCE (at max T-O weight, ISA, except where indicated):

Max operating speed:	
S/L to 2,440 m (8,000 ft)	305 knots (565 km/h; 351 mph) IAS
at 11,132 m (36,524 ft)	278 knots (515 km/h; 320 mph) IAS
above 11,132 m (36,524 ft)	Mach 0.851

Max cruising speed at 10,670 m (35,000 ft) and 7,257 kg (16,000 lb) cruise weight
472 knots (874 km/h; 543 mph)

Stalling speed, 'clean', at max T-O weight
125 knots (232 km/h; 144 mph) CAS

Stalling speed, flaps and wheels down, at max landing weight
97 knots (515 km/h; 112 mph) CAS

Max rate of climb at S/L	1,127 m (3,700 ft)/min
Rate of climb at S/L, one engine out	245 m (805 ft)/min
Time to 13,100 m (43,000 ft)	33 min
Certificated ceiling	15,545 m (51,000 ft)
Ceiling, one engine out	7,165 m (23,500 ft)
FAR 25 T-O field length at S/L	1,579 m (5,180 ft)
FAR 25 landing field length at max landing weight	884 m (2,900 ft)

Range, zero wind, with allowances for T-O, climb, descent and 45 min reserves:
2 crew, 4 passengers
2,346 nm (4,348 km; 2,701 miles)

g limits	+3.2/–1

OPERATIONAL NOISE LEVELS (FAR Pt 36):

T-O	74.0 EPNdB
Approach	85.0 EPNdB
Sideline	81.0 EPNdB

CHADWICK
CHADWICK HELICOPTERS INC
PO Box 6179, Aloha, Oregon 97007-6179

Chadwick Helicopters Inc is a subsidiary of Chadwick Incorporated, which was founded in 1964 and manufactures a number of helicopter accessories including auxiliary fuel systems, electronic underslung load indicators, external cargo racks, firefighting and aerial applications equipment, a high-pressure wash system for aerial cleaning of insulators on high tension power transmission lines, and computerised weighing devices for aircraft.

CHADWICK C-122S
Chadwick began designing a single-seat ultralight helicopter in 1983. The development programme included building and flight testing a 'flying platform' to test and confirm dynamic components. The prototype Model C-122S was completed during 1985 and made its public debut at the 38th Helicopter Association International convention at Anaheim, California, in January 1986. The C-122S is intended for commercial and sporting applications including farming, forestry control, traffic watch, training and news gathering, and for paramilitary missions such as border and coastal patrol, drug enforce-

ment, observation, armed reconnaissance, radio relay, command and control, target acquisition and artillery control, limited photo reconnaissance and pilot training.

To meet specialised requirements Chadwick Helicopters is also developing a two-seat trainer version of the helicopter designated **C-122T**, an agricultural model **C-122AG**, a 'police interceptor' variant to be known as the **C-122PI**, a **C-122R** RPV version, and the **C-122W** weapons platform. A helicopter training platform (HTP) has also been developed which enables a C-122S to be attached to a scissor arm so that a pupil pilot may gain experience of handling the helicopter in tethered flight. The scissor arm is raised by the C-122S's rotor power and permits vertical and tilting movement, the tilt feature being lockable for the early stages of pilot training.

The C-122S has been designed to meet FAA FAR Pt 103 certification requirements for ultralight aircraft. Work on finalising production design and flight testing was proceeding in early 1987, since when no further information has been received.

TYPE: Single-seat ultralight helicopter.

ROTOR SYSTEM: Four-blade fully articulated main rotor with offset flapping hinges. Blades are of metal construction with two extruded aluminium spars, one forming the forward portion of the aerofoil section, with the flush riveted aluminium skinning forming the rear section. Leading-edge coated with abrasion resistant polymer material. Blades feature ogee tip design claimed to increase efficiency and reduce noise. One fixed trim tab on each main rotor blade. Blades fold after removal of a single locking pin per blade. Two-blade teetering tail rotor of flush riveted and bonded aluminium alloy.

ROTOR DRIVE: Vertically mounted idler shaft driven by cog belt from engine, with final stage reduction pulley driving main rotor hub via a second cog belt. Overrunning clutch disengages automatically for autorotation and engine shutdown. Rotor hub supported on non-rotating rotor mast. All controls and oscillating components are mounted on sealed, life-lubricated bearings. Tail rotor driven by V belt.

FUSELAGE: Monocoque structure of glassfibre/polyester composite formed around truss bulkhead supporting engine, main rotor mast, idler shaft assembly, control mixer, pilot's seat and landing gear. Attachments for cargo hook, agricultural equipment, navigation lights, landing light, anti-collision light and armament optional.

TAIL UNIT: Single boom supports tail rotor, rotor ring guard, stub horizontal stabiliser and sweptback ventral fin.

LANDING GEAR: Fixed aluminium alloy tube skids with shock absorber units. Replaceable skid shoes. Ground handling wheels, float gear, and tundra pads optional.

POWER PLANT: One 47 kW (63 hp) Rotax 503 two-cylinder aircooled two-stroke engine, mounted vertically at rear of cockpit area. Power plant has tuned venturi-type carburettors and tuned exhausts, and is controlled by microprocessor and linear stepper motor to provide constant rotor rpm. Auto rewind rope starting system. Single fuel tank in lower fuselage area below and to rear of pilot's seat, total capacity 18.9 litres (5 US gallons; 4.2 Imp gallons).

ACCOMMODATION: Single seat for pilot integral with cabin floor and primary bulkhead. Seat belts standard; provision for inertia reel harness. One-piece windscreen. Transparent cabin doors optional. Centrally mounted instrument panel incorporates flight and engine instruments and warning and caution lights. Conventional cyclic and collective pitch controls, and tail rotor control pedals.

SYSTEM: Electrical system, powered by 12V generator. Nickel-cadmium batteries for microprocessor are charged by engine's electrical generating system.

AVIONICS AND EQUIPMENT: Standard equipment includes airspeed indicator, altimeter, engine and main rotor

Prototype of the Chadwick C-122S single-seat ultralight helicopter

tachometers, engine power limit, low fuel warning and generator charging lights, pitot tube cover and main rotor tiedowns. Optional equipment includes lighting kit, electric starting system, battery and voltage regulator, cabin doors, cabin heating, rotor brake, engine compartment doors, tinted windscreen, fire extinguisher, first aid kit, engine running time meter, utility floats incorporating baggage compartment, cargo hook, auxiliary fuel system, agricultural spray system, inertia reel harnesses, emergency locator transmitter, VHF antennae, tundra pads, outside air temperature gauge, custom paint scheme, compact tool kit, ignition lock, ground handling wheels, quick blade folding kit, blade stowage rack, and armour protection for pilot and engine compartments. (Some optional equipment is not permissible under FAA FAR Pt 103 certification regulations for ultralight aircraft.)

DIMENSIONS, EXTERNAL:

Main rotor diameter	5.64 m (18 ft 6 in)
Tail rotor diameter	0.90 m (2 ft 11½ in)
Main rotor blade chord	0.23 m (9 in)
Tail rotor blade chord	0.13 m (5 in)
Distance between rotor centres	3.53 m (11 ft 7 in)
Length overall: rotors turning	6.86 m (22 ft 6 in)
main rotor folded	5.79 m (19 ft 0 in)
Fuselage: Max width	0.79 m (2 ft 7 in)
Height overall	2.19 m (7 ft 2¼ in)
Skid track	1.22 m (4 ft 0 in)

AREAS:

Main rotor blades (total)	2.27 m² (24.42 sq ft)
Tail rotor blades (total)	0.08 m² (0.87 sq ft)
Main rotor disc	24.97 m² (268.8 sq ft)
Tail rotor disc	0.64 m² (6.87 sq ft)
Horizontal stabiliser	0.15 m² (1.6 sq ft)
Ventral fin	0.31 m² (3.3 sq ft)

WEIGHTS AND LOADINGS:

Weight empty	115 kg (253 lb)
Max T-O weight (normal)	227 kg (500 lb)
Max design weight	317 kg (700 lb)
Max disc loading	12.69 kg/m² (2.6 lb/sq ft)
Max power loading	6.74 kg/kW (11.11 lb/hp)

PERFORMANCE (at max T-O weight of 227 kg; 500 lb):

Never-exceed speed	100 knots (185 km/h; 115 mph)
Max cruising speed:	
at S/L	82 knots (151 km/h; 94 mph)*
at 1,220 m (4,000 ft)	80 knots (148 km/h; 92 mph)*
at 2,440 m (8,000 ft)	76 knots (142 km/h; 88 mph)*
Econ cruising speed at S/L	
	64 knots (119 km/h; 74 mph)*
Vertical rate of climb at S/L	288 m (945 ft)/min
Rate of climb at S/L, T-O power:	
ISA	357 m (1,170 ft)/min
ISA + 20°C	317 m (1,040 ft)/min
Service ceiling	4,110 m (13,480 ft)
Hovering ceiling IGE: ISA	3,860 m (12,670 ft)
Hovering ceiling OGE: ISA	2,875 m (9,440 ft)
ISA + 20°C	2,470 m (8,100 ft)
Range, 2 min warmup, no reserves:	
at S/L	104 nm (193 km; 120 miles)
at 1,220 m (4,000 ft)	91 nm (169 km; 105 miles)

*To meet FAR Pt 103 requirements, speed is limited by electronic microprocessor to 55 knots (101 km/h; 63 mph)

CHRISTEN
CHRISTEN INDUSTRIES INC

Aircraft Manufacturing Division
PO Box 547, Afton, Wyoming 83110
Telephone: (307) 886 3151
Fax: (307) 886 9674
PRESIDENT AND GENERAL MANAGER: E. H. Andersen Jr

In November 1983 Christen Industries, whose Eagle biplanes are described in the Sport Aircraft section, acquired the former Pitts Aerobatics company, together with manufacturing and marketing rights to the Pitts Special series of aerobatic biplanes designed by Mr Curtis Pitts. The former Pitts Aerobatics facility at Afton, Wyoming, has been retained as the corporate headquarters of Christen Industries, where manufacture, assembly and testing of the aircraft take place. In early 1988 Christen Industries had a workforce of 70 people.

CHRISTEN A-1 HUSKY

Work began in November 1985 on the design of a new utility aircraft designated A-1 Husky, which Christen Industries believes is suitable for a range of duties such as bush flying, border patrol, fish and wildlife protection and pipeline inspection. Although it is externally similar in appearance to the Piper Super Cub, the Husky is an entirely new design created with computer-aided design (CAD) techniques. The prototype (N6070H) began flight testing in 1986, and received FAA certification in 1987. By 15 January 1988 a total of 35 Huskys had been delivered. Certification of the Husky for float operation was expected in the Spring of 1988. The US Border Patrol service has ordered 12 Huskys to replace its fleet of Piper Super Cubs.

TYPE: Two-seat light cabin monoplane.

WINGS: Braced high-wing monoplane, with steel tube V bracing struts each side. Wing section modified Clark Y USA 35B. Aluminium spars and ribs, aluminium sheet leading-edge, with Dacron covering overall. Drooped

Plane Booster wingtips. Slotted flaps and symmetrical section ailerons of light alloy construction with metal skin, each with 'spade' type aerodynamic counterbalance. No tabs.

FUSELAGE: Welded full-depth truss structure of 4130 chrome molybdenum steel tubing, metal skinned to rear of cabin area, the remainder Dacron covered.

TAIL UNIT: Wire and strut braced structure of welded steel tubes and channels, covered with Dacron. Internal bungee trim system exerts trim forces on elevator control rods.

LANDING GEAR: Non-retractable tailwheel type. Two faired side Vs and half-axles hinged to bottom of fuselage, with internal (under front seat) bungee cord shock absorption. Cleveland mainwheels, tyres size 8.00-6. Oversize 'tundra' tyres optional. Cleveland mainwheel brakes. Steerable leaf-spring tailwheel. Skis and floats optional.

POWER PLANT: One 134 kW (180 hp) Textron Lycoming O-360-C1G flat-four engine, driving a Hartzell two-blade constant-speed metal propeller with spinner. Fuel contained in two metal tanks, one in each wing, total capacity 208 litres (55 US gallons; 45.75 Imp gallons), of

Christen A-1 Husky two-seat light cabin monoplane (*J. M. G. Gradidge*)

which 189 litres (50 US gallons; 41.6 Imp gallons) are usable. Fuel filler point in upper surface of each wing, near root.

ACCOMMODATION: Enclosed cabin seating two in tandem, with dual controls. Downward-hinged door on starboard side, with upward-hinged window above. Skylight window in roof.

SYSTEM: Electrical system includes lights and 60A alternator.

DIMENSIONS, EXTERNAL:

Wing span	10.73 m (35 ft 2½ in)
Length overall	6.88 m (22 ft 7 in)
Height overall	2.01 m (6 ft 7 in)
Propeller diameter	1.93 m (6 ft 4 in)

AREAS:

Wings, gross	16.72 m² (180.0 sq ft)
Ailerons (total)	1.43 m² (15.4 sq ft)
Trailing-edge flaps (total)	2.09 m² (22.5 sq ft)
Fin	0.43 m² (4.66 sq ft)
Rudder	0.62 m² (6.76 sq ft)
Tailplane	1.48 m² (15.9 sq ft)
Elevators, incl tabs	1.31 m² (14.1 sq ft)

WEIGHTS AND LOADINGS:

Weight empty	540 kg (1,190 lb)
Max T-O weight	816 kg (1,800 lb)
Max baggage weight	22.7 kg (50 lb)
Max wing loading	48.8 kg/m² (10.0 lb/sq ft)
Max power loading	7.45 kg/kW (10.0 lb/hp)

PERFORMANCE:

Never-exceed speed   132 knots (245 km/h; 152 mph)
Cruising speed, 75% power at 1,220 m (4,000 ft)
                          122 knots (226 km/h; 140 mph)
Cruising speed, 55% power
                          115 knots (212 km/h; 132 mph)

Stalling speed, flaps up	48 knots (80 km/h; 49 mph)
Stalling speed, flaps down	37 knots (68 km/h; 42 mph)
Max rate of climb at S/L	457 m (1,500 ft)/min
Service ceiling	6,100 m (20,000 ft)
T-O run	46 m (150 ft)
T-O to 15 m (50 ft)	229 m (750 ft)
Landing from 15 m (50 ft)	427 m (1,400 ft)
Landing run, full flap	107 m (350 ft)

PITTS SPECIAL S-1 SERIES

The original single-seat Pitts Special was designed in 1943-44. Construction of a prototype began in 1944 and it flew in September of that year.

The current production version of the S-1 is the **S-1T**, described below. Details of the earlier S-1S factory built aircraft may be found in the 1987-88 and earlier editions of *Jane's*. Christen Industries no longer markets kits or plans for Pitts designs.

PITTS S-1T SPECIAL

Production of this advanced version of the S-1 series began in early 1981, and it is available as a factory built aircraft to special order only. Generally similar to other versions of the S-1, it has symmetrical ailerons and wing sections, and the wings have been moved forward 11.5 cm (4½ in) to compensate for the installation of a more powerful engine. FAA type certification was gained in the Autumn of 1982.

TYPE: Single-seat sporting biplane.

WINGS: Braced biplane type, with single faired interplane strut each side and N type cabane struts. Dual streamline flying and landing wires. Wing section M6. Thickness/chord ratio 12%. Dihedral 0° on upper wing, 3° on lower wings. Incidence 1° 30′ on upper wing, 0° on lower wings. Sweepback at quarter-chord 6° 40′ on upper wing only. Wooden structure, with fabric covering. Frise ailerons on both upper and lower wings, of similar construction to wings. No flaps or tabs.

FUSELAGE: Welded steel tube structure with wooden stringers, with aluminium top decking and side panels, remainder fabric covered.

TAIL UNIT: Wire braced steel tube structure, fabric covered. Fixed incidence tailplane. Trim tab in each elevator.

LANDING GEAR: Non-retractable tailwheel type. Rubber cord shock absorption. Cleveland mainwheels with 6-ply tyres, size 5.00-5, pressure 2.07 bars (30 lb/sq in). Cleveland hydraulic disc brakes. Steerable tailwheel. Glassfibre fairing on mainwheels.

POWER PLANT: One 149 kW (200 hp) Textron Lycoming AEIO-360-A1E flat-four engine, driving a Hartzell two- or three-blade constant-speed propeller with spinner. Fuel tank aft of firewall, capacity 75 litres (20 US gallons; 16.6 Imp gallons). Refuelling point on upper surface of fuselage, forward of windscreen. Oil capacity 7.5 litres (2 US gallons; 1.7 Imp gallons). Inverted fuel and oil systems standard.

ACCOMMODATION: Single seat. Sliding cockpit canopy standard.

DIMENSIONS, EXTERNAL:

Wing span, upper	5.28 m (17 ft 4 in)
Wing chord (constant, both)	0.91 m (3 ft 0 in)

Wing aspect ratio	5.8
Length overall	4.72 m (15 ft 6 in)
Height overall	1.91 m (6 ft 3 in)
Tailplane span	1.98 m (6 ft 6 in)
Propeller diameter	1.93 m (6 ft 4 in)

AREA:

Wings, gross	9.15 m² (98.5 sq ft)

WEIGHTS AND LOADINGS:

Weight empty	376 kg (830 lb)
Max T-O weight	521 kg (1,150 lb)
Max wing loading	57.05 kg/m² (11.68 lb/sq ft)
Max power loading	3.50 kg/kW (5.75 lb/hp)

PERFORMANCE (at max T-O weight):

Never-exceed speed	176 knots (326 km/h; 203 mph)
Max level speed at S/L	161 knots (298 km/h; 185 mph)
Max cruising speed at S/L	
	152 knots (282 km/h; 175 mph)
Stalling speed	56 knots (103 km/h; 64 mph)
Max rate of climb at S/L	853 m (2,800 ft)/min

Range with max fuel, 55% power, 30 min reserves
                          268 nm (497 km; 309 miles)

g limits	+9/-4.5

PITTS MODEL S-2B

This two-seater differs from the earlier S-2A (described in the 1987-88 and earlier editions of *Jane's*) in having a 194 kW (260 hp) Textron Lycoming AEIO-540-D4A5 flat-six engine, and is intended to be capable of unlimited aerobatics carrying two persons. The heavier power plant necessitated moving the wings and landing gear forward about 15 cm (6 in), and made possible more room in the front cockpit.

The prototype S-2B was completed during September 1982. Its capability was demonstrated shortly afterwards when Clint McHenry, carrying a passenger, took first place in the Advanced Category at the US Nationals held at Sherman, Texas.

The S-2B was awarded FAA type certification in the Spring of 1983, in the Aerobatic category, under FAR Pt 23. Christen expected to manufacture 26 Pitts S-2Bs in 1988.

TYPE: Two-seat aerobatic biplane.

WINGS: Braced biplane type, with single faired interplane strut each side and N type cabane struts. Wing section NACA 6400 series on upper wing, 00 series on lower wings. Two-spar spruce structure with fabric covering. Ailerons on both upper and lower wings, with aerodynamic 'spade' balances on lower ailerons. No flaps or tabs.

FUSELAGE: Welded 4130 steel tube structure with wooden stringers, covered with Dacron except for aluminium top decking and side panels.

TAIL UNIT: Wire braced 4130 steel tube structure. Fixed surfaces metal covered, control surfaces fabric covered. Trim tab in each elevator.

LANDING GEAR: Non-retractable tailwheel type. Rubber cord shock absorption. Steerable tailwheel. Streamlined fairings on mainwheels.

POWER PLANT: One 194 kW (260 hp) Textron Lycoming AEIO-540-D4A5 flat-six engine, driving a McCauley Type 1A/200 two-blade constant-speed metal propeller with spinner. Fuel tank in fuselage, immediately aft of firewall, capacity 110 litres (29 US gallons; 24 Imp

gallons). Refuelling point on fuselage upper surface forward of windscreen. Oil capacity 11.35 litres (3 US gallons; 2.5 Imp gallons). Inverted fuel and oil systems standard.

ACCOMMODATION: Two seats in tandem cockpits, with dual controls. Sideways opening one-piece canopy covers both cockpits. Space for 9.1 kg (20 lb) baggage aft of rear seat when flown in non-aerobatic category.

SYSTEM: Electrical system powered by 12V 40A alternator and non-spill 12V battery.

DIMENSIONS, EXTERNAL:

Wing span: upper	6.10 m (20 ft 0 in)
lower	5.79 m (19 ft 0 in)
Wing chord (constant, both)	1.02 m (3 ft 4 in)
Length overall	5.71 m (18 ft 9 in)
Height overall	2.02 m (6 ft 7½ in)

AREA:

Wings, gross	11.6 m² (125.0 sq ft)

WEIGHTS AND LOADINGS:

Weight empty	521 kg (1,150 lb)
Max T-O weight	737 kg (1,625 lb)
Max wing loading	63.55 kg/m² (13.0 lb/sq ft)
Max power loading	3.80 kg/kW (6.25 lb/hp)

PERFORMANCE (at max T-O weight):

Never-exceed speed	182 knots (338 km/h; 210 mph)
Max cruising speed	152 knots (282 km/h; 175 mph)
Stalling speed	52 knots (97 km/h; 60 mph)
Max rate of climb at S/L	823 m (2,700 ft)/min
Service ceiling	6,400 m (21,000 ft)

Range with max fuel, 55% power, 30 min reserves
                          277 nm (513 km; 319 miles)

PITTS MODEL S-2S

Production of this single-seat version of the S-2A began in late 1978. It has a forward fuselage shortened by 0.36 m (14 in) to accommodate a 194 kW (260 hp) Textron Lycoming AEIO-540-D4A5 flat-six engine, driving a McCauley Type 1A/200 two-blade fixed-pitch metal propeller with spinner. It also differs from the S-2A by having a maximum fuel capacity of 132.5 litres (35 US gallons; 29.1 Imp gallons) and an oil capacity of 11.4 litres (3 US gallons; 2.5 Imp gallons). The first flight of the prototype was made on 9 December 1977; full type certification was gained in June 1981. The Model S-2S is available to special order only.

DIMENSIONS, EXTERNAL: As for Model S-2B except:

Length overall	5.28 m (17 ft 4 in)
Height overall	2.02 m (6 ft 7½ in)

WEIGHTS AND LOADINGS:

Weight empty	499 kg (1,100 lb)
Max T-O weight	680 kg (1,500 lb)
Max wing loading	58.6 kg/m² (12.0 lb/sq ft)
Max power loading	3.51 kg/kW (5.77 lb/hp)

PERFORMANCE (at max T-O weight):

Never-exceed speed	176 knots (326 km/h; 203 mph)
Max level speed at S/L	162 knots (301 km/h; 187 mph)
Max cruising speed at S/L	
	152 knots (282 km/h; 175 mph)
Stalling speed	51 knots (94 km/h; 58 mph)
Max rate of climb at S/L	853 m (2,800 ft)/min
g limits	+9/-4.5

Christen Pitts two-seat Model S-2B, capable of unlimited aerobatics with both seats occupied

CLASSIC
CLASSIC AIRCRAFT CORPORATION

Capital City Airport, Lansing, Michigan 48906

Telephone: (517) 321 7500

Telex: 229 430

PRESIDENT: Richard S. Kettles

ENGINEERING MANAGER: Donald P. Zurfluh

SALES MANAGER: Donald C. Kettles

CLASSIC WACO CLASSIC F-5

In March 1984 Classic Aircraft Corporation began construction of a prototype Waco Classic F-5 biplane, based on the original Waco YMF-5 and built under the same FAA type certificate. The prototype (N1935B) made its first flight on 20 November 1985. Although externally similar to the earlier Waco YMF-5, the Waco Classic F-5 incorporates modern constructional techniques, tolerances and materials.

No news has been received from the company since 1986, during which year it expected the aircraft to receive FAA certification. A full description appeared in the 1987-88 *Jane's*; the following is a shortened version:

TYPE: Three-seat sporting biplane.

AIRFRAME: See 1987-88 *Jane's*.

POWER PLANT: One 182.7 kW (245 hp) Jacobs R-755-B2 aircooled radial engine (remanufactured), driving a two-blade fixed-pitch wooden propeller. Constant-speed propeller optional. Engine enclosed with streamline aluminium 'bump' cowling. Fuel contained in two aluminium tanks in upper wing centre-section, total capacity 182 litres (48 US gallons; 40 Imp gallons). Refuelling point for each tank in upper wing surface. Auxiliary tanks, capacity 45 litres (12 US gallons; 10 Imp gallons) each, optional in either or both inboard upper wing panels. Standard oil capacity 15 litres (4 US gallons; 3.33 Imp gallons); with auxiliary fuel tanks 19 litres (5 US gallons; 4.2 Imp gallons).

ACCOMMODATION: Three seats in tandem open cockpits, two side by side in front position, single seat at rear. Dual controls, seat belts with shoulder harness, and pilot's adjustable seat, standard. Front baggage compartment, capacity 11.3 kg (25 lb); rear baggage compartment, volume 0.2 m³ (7.5 cu ft), capacity 34 kg (75 lb).

SYSTEMS, AVIONICS AND EQUIPMENT: See 1987-88 *Jane's*.

DIMENSIONS, EXTERNAL:

Wing span: upper	9.14 m (30 ft 0 in)
lower	8.18 m (26 ft 10 in)
Length overall	7.10 m (23 ft 3⅝ in)
Height overall	2.57 m (8 ft 5⅜ in)
Wheelbase	1.95 m (6 ft 5 in)
Propeller diameter	2.44 m (8 ft 0 in)

AREA:

Wings, gross	21.69 m² (233.5 sq ft)

WEIGHTS AND LOADINGS:

Basic weight empty	816 kg (1,800 lb)

Prototype Classic Waco Classic F-5 re-creation of the Waco YMF-5 three-seat biplane

Max T-O and landing weight	1,134 kg (2,500 lb)
Max wing loading	52.26 kg/m² (10.71 lb/sq ft)
Max power loading	6.21 kg/kW (10.20 lb/hp)
PERFORMANCE (at max T-O weight except where indicated):	
Never-exceed speed	186 knots (344 km/h; 214 mph)
Max level speed at S/L	117 knots (217 km/h; 135 mph)
Max cruising speed at S/L	
	104 knots (193 km/h; 120 mph)

Econ cruising speed at 2,440 m (8,000 ft)	
	95 knots (177 km/h; 110 mph)
Stalling speed, power off	48 knots (88 km/h; 55 mph)
Max rate of climb at S/L	396 m (1,300 ft)/min
T-O run	61 m (200 ft)
Range, standard fuel, 30 min reserves	
	286 nm (531 km; 330 miles)

COLEMILL

COLEMILL ENTERPRISES INC

PO Box 60627, Cornelia Fort Air Park, Nashville, Tennessee 37206
Telephone: (615) 226 4256
Telex: 555 197
PRESIDENT: Ernest Colbert

Colemill specialises in performance improvement conversions of light single- and twin-engined aircraft.

COLEMILL PANTHER NAVAJO

Colemill's conversion of the Navajo or Navajo C/R involves a power plant change, redesigned nacelles, additional continuous running fuel pumps, a digital fuel totaliser, heavy duty brakes, and wingtip mounted landing lights. Conversion normally takes 10-14 days. Colemill has also developed 'Zip-Tip' winglets for Panther Navajo and Chieftain conversions. The winglets improve stability in the lower-speed flight zone, down to stalling speed, and provide cruising speed increases of 4-9 knots (8-16 km/h; 5-10 mph) at altitudes between 3,960 and 7,620 m (13,000 and 25,000 ft), at engine power settings between 45% and 65% of maximum power. This increase is, therefore, able to match the cruising speed of the standard Panther Navajo (without winglets) at power settings which offer greater fuel economy.

Following the award of a Supplemental Type Certificate in Summer 1982, operators of Panther conversions of Navajo and Chieftain aircraft can specify winglets from new or as retrofit modifications, replacing the normal extended wingtips of the conversion. They increase wing span to 13.16 m (43 ft 2 in) and wing area by 0.56 m² (6 sq ft).

The basic description of the Navajo, which can be found

Colemill Panther Navajo with winglets *(Austin J. Brown)*

under the Piper entry in the 1982-83 *Jane's*, applies also to the Panther Navajo, except as follows:

WINGS: New wingtips with marked undercamber, which increase wing span and area; or alternative choice of winglets, as described in opening paragraph.

LANDING GEAR: Cleveland four-spot heavy duty disc brakes.

POWER PLANT: Two 261 kW (350 hp) Textron Lycoming TIO-540-J2BD turbocharged engines, each driving a Hartzell four-blade constant-speed fully-feathering metal propeller with 'Q' tips. Pressurised magnetos, Woodward

propeller governors, synchrophasers and unfeathering accumulators standard. Fuel system as for basic Navajo, except for the addition of continuous running electrically operated fuel pumps.

EQUIPMENT: Generally as for standard Navajo, but existing fuel flow gauges are replaced by a Shadin Digiflow fuel management computer giving digital readout of fuel remaining/fuel consumed. Supplemental wingtip landing lights can be operated independently of the standard nosewheel mounted landing light, prior to lowering of landing gear.

DIMENSION, EXTERNAL:

Wing span	13.00 m (42 ft 8 in)

LOADING:

Max power loading	5.65 kg/kW (9.3 lb/hp)

PERFORMANCE (at max T-O weight):

Max level speed	269 knots (498 km/h; 309 mph)
Max cruising speed, 75% power at optimum altitude	
	248 knots (459 km/h; 285 mph)
Cruising speed, 65% power:	
at 7,315 m (24,000 ft)	
	235 knots (435 km/h; 270 mph)
at 3,660 m (12,000 ft)	
	206 knots (381 km/h; 237 mph)
Max rate of climb at S/L	610 m (2,000 ft)/min
Rate of climb at S/L, one engine out	
	122 m (400 ft)/min
Short-field T-O run	229 m (750 ft)
T-O to 15 m (50 ft)	458 m (1,500 ft)
Landing from 15 m (50 ft)	427 m (1,400 ft)

COLEMILL PANTHER II

Colemill's Panther II conversion is based on the Piper Chieftain and includes the installation of new 261 kW (350

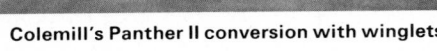

Colemill's Panther II conversion with winglets

hp) Textron Lycoming TIO-540-J2BD and LTIO-540-J2BD turbocharged engines, each driving a Hartzell four-blade constant-speed fully-feathering metal propeller with 'Q' tips. A digital fuel management computer, Woodward propeller governors and synchrophaser, and Cleveland four-spot heavy duty brakes, are also standard. 'Zip-Tip' winglets are optional.

COLEMILL EXECUTIVE 600

The Executive 600 is a Cessna 310, of Model F to Q series, or Cessna 320 (up to and including Model 320C), re-engined by Colemill with two 224 kW (300 hp) Continental IO-520-E flat-six engines, each driving a McCauley three-blade propeller. Dimensions are unchanged; empty weight is increased by about 14 kg (30 lb); other data are as follows:

WEIGHTS:
Max T-O weight: 310		2,358 kg (5,200 lb)
320		2,404 kg (5,300 lb)

PERFORMANCE (at max T-O weight):
Max cruising speed (75% power):
310   205 knots (379 km/h; 236 mph)
320   202 knots (374 km/h; 232 mph)
Cruising speed (65% power):
310   195 knots (361 km/h; 224 mph)
320   192 knots (355 km/h; 221 mph)
Stalling speed, wheels and flaps down:
310, 320   64 knots (119 km/h; 74 mph)
Max rate of climb at S/L: 310   762 m (2,500 ft)/min
320   777 m (2,550 ft)/min
Service ceiling: 310, 320   5,940 m (19,500 ft)
T-O to 15 m (50 ft): 310, 320   518 m (1,700 ft)
Landing from 15 m (50 ft): 310, 320   unchanged
Range with max fuel, 45 min reserves:
310   1,050 nm (1,944 km; 1,208 miles)
320   1,060 nm (1,963 km; 1,220 miles)

COLEMILL PRESIDENT 600

The President 600 is a Beechcraft B55 Baron re-engined by Colemill with two 224 kW (300 hp) Continental IO-520-E flat-six engines, each driving a three-blade propeller. Some 250 President 600 conversions have been delivered. Dimensions are unchanged; empty weight is increased by about 14 kg (30 lb); other data are as follows:

WEIGHT:
Max T-O weight   2,313 kg (5,100 lb)
PERFORMANCE (at max T-O weight):
Max cruising speed (75% power)
      203 knots (376 km/h; 233 mph)
Cruising speed (65% power)
      193 knots (357 km/h; 222 mph)
Stalling speed, wheels and flaps down
      66 knots (123 km/h; 76 mph)
Max rate of climb at S/L   823 m (2,700 ft)/min
Service ceiling   5,940 m (19,500 ft)
T-O to 15 m (50 ft)   497 m (1,631 ft)
Landing from 15 m (50 ft)   unchanged
Range with max fuel, 45 min reserves
      1,050 nm (1,944 km; 1,208 miles)

COLEMILL FOXSTAR BARON

The Foxstar is a Beechcraft Baron Model 55 or 58 re-engined with two 224 kW (300 hp) Teledyne Continental IO-550C engines with heavy duty crankcases, each driving a Hartzell Sabre Blade four-blade Q-tip propeller. Other modifications include the installation of Woodward propeller governors and synchrophase system, Shadin Digiflow fuel computer, 'Zip-Tip' winglets, and 60A alternators. The Foxstar conversion is FAA STC approved for all Model C55, D55, E55 and Model 58 Barons, and offers improvements in rate of climb, cruising speed, engine-out performance, and cabin noise and vibration levels.

WEIGHT:
Max T-O weight   2,449 kg (5,400 lb)
PERFORMANCE (at max T-O weight):
Max cruising speed, 75% power
      205 knots (380 km/h; 236 mph)
Cruising speed, 65% power
      200 knots (371 km/h; 230 mph)
Stalling speed, landing gear and flaps down
      74 knots (137 km/h; 85 mph)
Max rate of climb at S/L   561 m (1,840 ft)/min
Service ceiling   6,400 m (21,000 ft)
T-O to 15 m (50 ft)   610 m (2,000 ft)
Landing from 15 m (50 ft)   734 m (2,410 ft)
Range with max fuel, 45 min reserves
      1,131 nm (2,096 km; 1,302 miles)

COLEMILL STARFIRE BONANZA

The Starfire is a Beechcraft Bonanza re-engined with a 224 kW (300 hp) Teledyne Continental IO-550B engine, driving a Hartzell Sabre Blade four-blade Q-tip propeller. Other modifications include the installation of a Woodward propeller governor, Shadin Digiflow fuel computer/totaliser, 'Zip-Tip' winglets, and a 60A alternator. The Starfire conversion has received FAA STC approval for all Beechcraft Model C33A, E33A, F33A, S35, V35A, V35B and A36 Bonanzas. The conversion offers improvements in rate of climb, cruising speed and cabin noise and vibration levels.

PERFORMANCE:
Cruising speed   176 knots (326 km/h; 203 mph)
Max rate of climb at S/L   369 m (1,210 ft)/min
T-O run   296 m (971 ft)
T-O to 15 m (50 ft)   583 m (1,912 ft)

COMMANDER

COMMANDER AIRCRAFT COMPANY

Washington, DC
Telephone: (202) 457 9060
PRESIDENT: Randy Greene
VICE-PRESIDENT, ENGINEERING: Dave Ellis

In the Summer of 1988 Commander Aircraft Company acquired from Gulfstream Aerospace Corporation the manufacturing, marketing and product support rights for the Rockwell Commander 112 and 114 series of single-engined light aircraft, last described in the 1978-79 edition of *Jane's*. Initially the company plans to provide

spares and product support services for existing aircraft, but expects to begin deliveries of new Commander 112s and 114s during 1989.

COMTRAN

COMTRAN LTD

8507 Broadway, San Antonio, Texas 78217
Telephone: (512) 821 6301
Telex: 767438 COMTRAN UD
Fax: (512) 822 7766
PROGRAMME DIRECTOR: John T. Jennings

COMTRAN SUPER Q

Comtran Ltd has developed a modification and upgrading programme for Boeing 707 jet airliners known as the Comtran Super Q. The extensive refurbishment includes installation of Comtran Q-707 engine nacelle hush kits which enable the aircraft to meet FAR 36 Stage II and ICAO Annex 16, Chapter 2 noise requirements. The hush kit uses Rohr Industries' DynaRohr surface liner material within a modified engine nacelle on which the engine inlet and fan exit ducts are lengthened, and results in a claimed reduction in the 100 EPNdB footprint area from 5.6 nm (10.5 km; 6.5 miles) for a standard Boeing 707 to 2.8 nm (5.1 km; 3.2 miles) for the Super Q. Hush kit installation does not interfere with existing engine systems such as anti-icing and thrust reversers.

The Super Q also features a new passenger cabin with wide-body styling incorporating new technology lightweight passenger seats, overhead storage bins, a new cabin entertainment system with video monitors and individual seat mounted controls, new cabin soundproofing, new cabin headliner with 'wash' lighting, headliner and aisle illuminated emergency escape lighting systems, overhauled galleys and lavatories fore and aft, new liferafts, lifejackets and emergency exit chutes, and new floor and side panel liners in the baggage compartments. The cabin provides accommodation for up to 186 passengers in four-class configuration. Optional interior arrangements provide for standard first and tourist class, high-density single class, combined passenger/cargo and all-cargo configurations. Use of fireblocking materials in all seats,

Artist's impression of Comtran Super Q conversion of the Boeing 707 in Combi configuration

and non-toxic polycarbonate composite materials for overhead panels and seat trim, plus supplementary emergency floor lighting, enables the Super Q to meet ICAO, FAA and European S-2000 fire, safety and toxicity standards.

The Super Q's flight deck features upgraded Collins avionics including FD109Y flight directors, long range navigation systems, colour weather radar, a new cockpit audio system, and new wiring and switching as required.

The prototype Super Q conversion (N730Q) was displayed at the Paris Air Show in June 1987.

For a typical mission carrying a full complement of passengers and crew, and 65,975 kg (145,450 lb) of fuel including 9,072 kg (20,000 lb reserves), at a max brake release weight of 150,955 kg (332,800 lb), cruising at Mach 0.8 at 10,670 m (35,000 ft), the Super Q has an estimated range of 4,365 nm (8,089 km; 5,026 miles).

DAEDALUS

DAEDALUS RESEARCH INC

Route 4, PO Box 327A1, Petersburg, Virginia 23803
Telephone: (804) 732 4696

PRESIDENT: Edward H. Allen
CHIEF OPERATING OFFICER: Edward S. Weil
Development of the **Daedalus GTP-350 Gemini** turboprop multi-mission aircraft, described and illustrated

in the 1987-88 *Jane's*, has been slowed down to allow Daedalus staff to concentrate on a smaller (227 kg; 500 lb gross weight) unmanned craft of similar appearance for a US Defense Department customer.

DEE HOWARD

THE DEE HOWARD COMPANY

International Airport, PO Box 17300, San Antonio, Texas 78217
Telephone: (512) 828 1341

Telex: 767380
PRESIDENT AND CHIEF EXECUTIVE OFFICER: Dee Howard
A 40% holding in The Dee Howard Company, with option on a further 20%, was acquired by Aeritalia (see Italian section) in the Spring of 1988.

DEE HOWARD XR LEARJET

The Dee Howard Company has developed an overall performance improvement system suitable for retrofit on all Model 24 and 25 Learjets having General Electric CJ610-6 or -8A turbojets. The improvements incorporated in the XR

Learjet include a new centre-section glove which reduces drag, improves spanwise lift, and accommodates an additional 245 kg (540 lb) of fuel; a new engine pylon/nacelle configuration that eliminates adverse flow pressure characteristics and channel flow Mach problems, and also improves engine bay cooling; two small span flow limiters, boundary layer energisers and stall turbulators at the junction of the inboard and outboard leading-edge on each wing, to produce stall buffet and improve overall stall performance; a new leading-edge profile to optimise cruise drag and low-speed stall characteristics; improved ailerons, trailing-edge flaps, outer wing panels, and new tip tank fin cuffs to improve cruise performance; a new engine exhaust nozzle that improves specific fuel consumption; and installation of a Teledyne angle of attack system, or retention of the Conrac angle of attack system if the modified aircraft has the Century III wing.

Conversion of a suitable Model 24 or 25 to XR Learjet configuration provides an extra 400 nm (741 km; 460 miles) of range at a constant cruising speed of Mach 0.78, plus an increase of 680 kg (1,500 lb) in maximum take-off weight, and increased payload.

DEE HOWARD BAC 1-11

In February 1986 The Dee Howard Company signed agreements with Rolls-Royce and British Aerospace which will lead to certification of the 67.17 kN (15,100 lb st) Rolls-Royce Tay 650 turbofan in BAC One-Eleven Series 400, 475 and 500 aircraft. All prototype modification and flight test work is undertaken at the company's San Antonio facility. The first converted aircraft was rolled out in May 1988 and began engine runs in June, with the first flight anticipated in early 1989 and FAA certification about a year later. Replacement of the One-Eleven's Spey 511

engines with the Tay power plant is expected to provide corporate configured 400 series aircraft with an NBAA IFR range of 3,100 nm (5,745 km; 3,570 miles) and to offer a reduction in balanced field length requirements of as much as 30 per cent under 'hot and high' conditions. The modification includes new engine nacelles and Dee Howard-developed thrust reversers, and will enable the aircraft to meet FAR Pt 36 Stage 3 noise requirements. At the time of its agreement with the engine and airframe manufacturers, the company held one order for the conversion, which is available to corporate and airline operators of the BAC One-Eleven. Dee Howard foresees a potential market for up to 170 conversions. After completion of the first three aircraft, the conversion is expected to take between 42 and 90 days. Installation kits will be made available to airlines capable of undertaking the work themselves.

ECTOR
ECTOR AIRCRAFT COMPANY INC
414 East Hillmont Road, Odessa, Texas 79765
Telephone: (915) 362 1841
PRESIDENT: Timothy H. Parker

ECTOR MOUNTAINEER

For a number of years the Ector Aircraft Company has produced civil versions of the Cessna L-19 Bird Dog (last described in the 1964-65 *Jane's*). Generally similar to the original L-19, Ector's aircraft are rebuilt completely from new off the shelf or serviceable components. The entire airframe is corrosion proofed with zinc chromate before assembly; mounting brackets for floats are built into the basic airframe; and all four side windows can be opened in flight. The rear seat is removable to permit the carriage of cargo.

Production of the more powerful Super Mountaineer model has ceased. A description may be found in the 1985-86 *Jane's*. By 1 January 1987 a total of 42 Mountaineers had been produced for service with various organisations as glider tugs, for patrol and general purpose duties, and for use as sporting aircraft.

TYPE: Two-seat (optional three-seat) cabin monoplane.
AIRFRAME: As described in 1987-88 and earlier *Jane's*.
POWER PLANT: One 159 kW (213 hp) Teledyne Continental O-470-11 flat-four engine, driving a two-blade fixed-pitch metal propeller. One fuel tank in each wingroot, total capacity 151 litres (40 US gallons; 33.3 Imp gallons). Refuelling points on wing upper surface. Oil capacity 9.4 litres (2.5 US gallons; 2.1 Imp gallons).
ACCOMMODATION: Normally two seats in tandem in enclosed cabin with 360° field of view. Door on starboard side. All four cabin side windows can be opened fully. Six skylights in roof. Space for baggage behind rear seat. With rear seat removed, 0.85 m³ (30 cu ft) of space is available for freight. Optional conversion to provide three seats. Cabin heated and ventilated.

Ector Mountaineer, a civil version of the Cessna L-19 Bird Dog

AVIONICS AND EQUIPMENT: Radio equipment available to customer's requirements. Navigation and landing lights, heated pitot, stall warning indicator, Hobbs hour meter and Whelen three-light strobe system standard. External power socket and wing racks optional.

DIMENSIONS, EXTERNAL:
Wing span	10.97 m (36 ft 0 in)
Length overall	7.86 m (25 ft 9½ in)
Height overall	2.29 m (7 ft 6 in)
Propeller diameter	2.29 m (7 ft 6 in)
Door: Height	0.64 m (2 ft 1 in)
Width	0.81 m (2 ft 8 in)
Height to sill	1.12 m (3 ft 8 in)

WEIGHTS:
Weight empty, equipped	658 kg (1,450 lb)
Max T-O weight	1,043 kg (2,300 lb)

PERFORMANCE (at max T-O weight):
Max level speed at S/L	87 knots (161 km/h; 100 mph) IAS
Max rate of climb at S/L	366 m (1,200 ft)/min
Service ceiling	6,980 m (22,900 ft)
T-O run	122 m (400 ft)
Landing run	98 m (320 ft)
Range with max fuel, no reserves	651 nm (1,207 km; 750 miles)

ELECTROSPACE SYSTEMS
ELECTROSPACE SYSTEMS INC
(subsidiary of The Chrysler Corporation)
PO Box 831359, 1301 East Collins Boulevard, Richardson, Texas 75083-1359
Telephone: (214) 783 2000
Telex: 163590 ESI UT
Fax: (214) 470 2466
PRESIDENT: James R. Lightner
VICE-PRESIDENT, MARKETING: Donald E. Heitzman

ELECTROSPACE SYSTEMS (MCDONNELL DOUGLAS) EC-24A

Under a US Navy contract awarded in August 1984, Electrospace Systems Inc has converted a McDonnell Douglas DC-8-54 airliner for fleet electronic warfare

support group (FEWSG) missions, under the designation EC-24A. Airframe modifications to the aircraft (BuAer 163050) were performed by the company's Aircraft Modification Center at Waco, Texas; following systems installation and integration by Electrospace Systems, the aircraft was delivered to the US Navy in August 1987. The EC-24A is based at Tulsa, Oklahoma.

The EC-24A carries ECM, ESM and C³CM systems and high-power broad-band jamming equipment. Visible changes to the DC-8 airframe include the addition of two ventral canoe-shaped radome fairings and a high frequency probe antenna at each wingtip. The equipment installed by Electrospace Systems for FEWSG missions includes: dual AN/ALT-40 radar jamming systems with steerable antennae; dual AN/ASQ-191 communications transceiver/jamming systems; dual AN/ALE-43 chaff dispensers capable of producing chaff in almost any dipole length within the A-J radar bands; dual AN/ALR-75 ESM receiver

systems with pulse analysers to give onboard signal identification capability; six AN/ARC-159 UHF transceivers; dual AN/ARC-186 VHF transceivers; four AN/ARC-190 HF transceivers; dual OE-320 DF systems; dual HP-9826 computer systems; KY-58 secure communications system; and supportive electrical generators and cooling equipment. Systems operator positions are provided in the aircraft's cabin.

A typical mission crew for the EC-24A comprises pilot, co-pilot, flight engineer, and seven systems operators, one of whom is the mission commander. In addition, the aircraft has capacity for up to 1,361 kg (3,000 lb) of cargo and seats for 20 maintenance personnel or additional crew members, enabling it to self-deploy to any part of the world. Unrefuelled range is approximately 4,800 nm (8,895 km; 5,527 miles) and endurance 11 h. The additional drag of the FEWSG mission radomes and antennae reduces overall performance of the DC-8-54 by six per cent.

Electrospace Systems EC-24A conversion of a McDonnell Douglas DC-8-54 for fleet electronic warfare support group missions

ENSTROM

THE ENSTROM HELICOPTER CORPORATION

PO Box 277, Twin County Airport, Menominee, Michigan 49858

Telephone: (906) 863 9971
Telex: 261912
Fax: (906) 863 6821

CHAIRMAN: Dean Kamen
PRESIDENT: Robert M. Tuttle
VICE-PRESIDENT, SALES AND SERVICE: Richard E. Loynachan

The history of Enstrom, since the company was founded in 1959, has been outlined in previous editions of *Jane's*. Ownership passed to Bravo Investments BV of the Netherlands in January 1980. In September 1984 Enstrom was acquired by a group of American investors headed by Mr Dean Kamen and Mr Robert Tuttle.

A total of more than 830 Enstrom helicopters had been built by 1 January 1988.

ENSTROM MODELS F-28 and 280

Details of the basic Model F-28A and the Model 280 Shark can be found in the 1978-79 *Jane's*. They were replaced by turbocharged versions of both models, under the designations F28C and 280C respectively. These received FAA certification on 8 December 1975 and were last described in the 1984-85 *Jane's*. Production of these models ceased in November 1981. They were succeeded by the Models F28F, 280F Shark (described in 1985-86 *Jane's* and now out of production), and the Model 280FX. Currently available versions are as follows:

F28F Falcon. Basic version, which received FAA certification in January 1981. Recent developments, applicable to all Enstrom models, include a redesigned main rotor gearbox with heavy wall main rotor shaft and a lightweight exhaust muffler system which offers reductions in noise levels of 40 per cent in the hover and 30 per cent when flying at an altitude of 152 m (500 ft). The new main rotor gearbox is fitted as standard on current production helicopters and may be retrofitted to earlier 'F' series Enstroms. The muffler assembly is available as an option on new helicopters, and may also be retrofitted to Models F28F, 280F and 280FX.

An Enstrom wet or dry dispersal agricultural kit is available for fitment to the F28F. It comprises two side-mounted hoppers with large quick-fill openings, and spraybooms with a normal span of 9.04 m (29 ft 8 in), but extendable to 11.07 m (36 ft 4 in). A manually operated clutch provides positive control of the centrifugal pump, which has a liquid capacity of 227 litres (60 US gallons; 50 Imp gallons)/min. Dry discharge rate is variable from 0 to 272 kg (600 lb)/min. Weight of the entire quickly removable dispersal system is 48 kg (105 lb). Hopper capacity is 303 litres (80 US gallons; 67 Imp gallons) of liquid or 0.5 m³ (17.4 cu ft) of dry chemicals.

F28F-P Sentinel. Dedicated police patrol version of the F28F, developed for the Pasadena Police Department in California, which took delivery of its first F28F-P in October 1986. The F28F-P may be fitted with a Locator IIA, Locator IIB, Spectrolab SX-5 or Carter searchlight, and specialised police radio packages. Specifications and performance are identical to those of the standard F28F Falcon.

Model 280FX. Modified version of the Model 280F Shark, which began flight testing in December 1983 and received FAA certification under CAR Pt 6 on 14 January 1985. The Model 280FX features completely faired landing gear, a redesigned air inlet system, redesigned horizontal and vertical tail surfaces incorporating endplate fins on the horizontal stabiliser, covered tail rotor shaft, and a tail rotor guard. New seats including lumbar support and energy-absorbing foam have been installed. Main and tail rotor gearboxes contain chip detectors. Range can be increased to 339 nm (627 km; 390 miles) by installing an internal auxiliary tank. Claimed to remain stable if flown 'feet-off' at 87 knots (161 km/h; 100 mph).

TYPE: Three-seat light helicopter.

ROTOR SYSTEM: Fully articulated metal three-blade main rotor. Blades are of bonded light alloy construction, each attached to hub by retention pin and drag link. Blade section NACA 0013.5. Two-blade teetering tail rotor, with blades of bonded light alloy construction. Tail rotor on port side. Blades do not fold.

ROTOR DRIVE: Poly V-belt drive system. Right angle drive reduction gearbox. Main rotor/engine rpm ratio 1 : 8.678; tail rotor/engine rpm ratio 1 : 1.213.

FUSELAGE: Glassfibre and light alloy cab structure, with welded steel tube centre-section. Semi-monocoque aluminium tailcone structure.

TAIL UNIT: Horizontal stabiliser forward of tail rotor, with endplate fins.

LANDING GEAR: Skids carried on Enstrom oleo-pneumatic shock absorbers. Air Cruiser inflatable floats available optionally.

POWER PLANT: One 168 kW (225 hp) Textron Lycoming HIO-360-F1AD flat-four engine with Rotomaster 3BT5EE10J2 turbocharger. Two fuel tanks, each of 79.5 litres (21 US gallons; 17.5 Imp gallons). Total standard fuel capacity 159 litres (42 US gallons; 35 Imp gallons) of which 151 litres (40 US gallons; 33.3 Imp gallons) are

Enstrom F28F-P Sentinel police patrol helicopter

usable. Auxiliary tank, capacity 49 litres (13 US gallons; 10.8 Imp gallons), can be installed in the baggage compartment. Oil capacity 9.5 litres (2.5 US gallons; 2.1 Imp gallons).

ACCOMMODATION: Pilot and two passengers, side by side on bench seat; centre place removable. Fully transparent removable door on each side of cabin. Baggage space aft of engine compartment, capacity 49 kg (108 lb), with external access door. Cabin heated and ventilated.

SYSTEM: Electrical power provided by 12V 70A engine driven alternator; 24V 70A system optional.

AVIONICS AND EQUIPMENT: Standard equipment includes airspeed indicator, sensitive altimeter, Hamilton vertical card compass (optional on 280FX), outside air temperature gauge, turn-and-bank indicator, rotor/engine tachometer, low rotor rpm warning light, manifold pressure/fuel flow gauge, fuel pressure warning lights, gearbox and oil temperature gauges, cylinder head temperature gauge, fuel quantity gauge, Alcor exhaust gas temperature gauge (F28F) or Insight graphic engine monitor (280FX), overboost, low fuel pressure and clutch disengagement warning lights. Also standard are ground handling wheels with handle, kick-in service steps, floor carpeting, lap belts for all seats, shoulder harnesses for two seats, instrument lighting with dimmer control, position light on each horizontal stabiliser tip, anti-collision strobe light, landing lights, adjustable nose light, soundproofing, main and tail rotor covers and blade tiedowns. Additionally, the Model 280FX has as standard an annunciator warning panel, baggage compartment, sliding vent windows and custom seating, and an avionics package comprising King KY 197 com with intercom, KT 76A transponder, II Morrow Model 611 Loran C and Bose headsets. Optional equipment includes dual controls, electric clutch actuator, cabin heater, fire extinguisher, first aid kit, custom interior and custom paint scheme, floor switch, external power receptacle, starter warning light, third shoulder harness, auxiliary fuel tank, baggage compartment and sliding vent windows (both standard on 280FX), corrosion protection, eight-day clock, three-place intercom, floats, cargo hook, hardpoints for agricultural equipment or night sign, and wet or wet/dry agricultural dispersal systems. Optional instrumentation includes R. C. Allen attitude gyro and turn co-ordinator, directional gyro, instantaneous vertical speed indicator, EC-200 entertainment centre with stereo headsets and a variety of avionics fits from AR Nav, II Morrow, King, Narco and Northstar.

DIMENSIONS, EXTERNAL:
Main rotor diameter	9.75 m (32 ft 0 in)
Tail rotor diameter	1.42 m (4 ft 8 in)
Distance between rotor centres	5.56 m (18 ft 3 in)
Main rotor blade chord	0.24 m (9½ in)
Tail rotor blade chord	0.11 m (4½ in)
Length overall, rotors stationary	8.94 m (29 ft 4 in)
Height to top of rotor head	2.79 m (9 ft 2 in)
Skid track	2.24 m (7 ft 4 in)
Cabin doors (each): Height	1.04 m (3 ft 5 in)
Width	0.84 m (2 ft 9 in)
Height to sill	0.64 m (2 ft 1 in)
Baggage door: Height	0.55 m (1 ft 9½ in)
Width	0.39 m (1 ft 3½ in)
Height to sill	0.86 m (2 ft 10 in)

DIMENSIONS, INTERNAL (A: F28F; B: 280FX):
Cabin: Max width: A	1.55 m (5 ft 1 in)
B	1.50 m (4 ft 11 in)
Baggage compartment volume	0.18 m³ (6.3 cu ft)

AREAS:
Main rotor disc	74.69 m² (804.0 sq ft)
Tail rotor disc	1.66 m² (17.88 sq ft)

WEIGHTS AND LOADINGS (A: F28F Normal category; B: 280FX):
Weight empty, equipped: A	703 kg (1,550 lb)
B	712 kg (1,570 lb)
Max T-O weight: A, B	1,179 kg (2,600 lb)
Max disc loading: A, B	15.77 kg/m² (3.23 lb/sq ft)
Max power loading: A, B	7.02 kg/kW (11.55 lb/hp)

PERFORMANCE (both versions at AUW of 1,066 kg; 2,350 lb except where indicated):

Max level speed, S/L to 915 m (3,000 ft):
A	97 knots (180 km/h; 112 mph) IAS
B	102 knots (188 km/h; 117 mph) IAS
Max cruising speed: A	97 knots (180 km/h; 112 mph)
B	102 knots (188 km/h; 117 mph)
Econ cruising speed: A	83 knots (154 km/h; 96 mph)
B	96 knots (177 km/h; 110 mph)
Max rate of climb at S/L	442 m (1,450 ft)/min
Certificated operating ceiling	3,660 m (12,000 ft)
Hovering ceiling: IGE	4,025 m (13,200 ft)

IGE at AUW of 1,179 kg (2,600 lb)
2,345 m (7,700 ft)
OGE at AUW of 1,066 kg (2,350 lb) 2,650 m (8,700 ft)

Max range, standard fuel, no reserves:
A	228 nm (423 km; 263 miles)
B	260 nm (483 km; 300 miles)
Max endurance	3 h 30 min

Enstrom Model 280FX three-seat light helicopter

EXCALIBUR
EXCALIBUR AVIATION COMPANY
8337 Mission Road, San Antonio, Texas 78214
Telephone: (512) 927 6201
PRESIDENT: Michael M. Davis

Excalibur Aviation continues to produce its improved versions of the Beechcraft Queen Air. These modified aircraft, named Queenaire 800 and Queenaire 8800, continue to be completed at the rate of one per month, notably for operators in South America. In addition to this continuing programme, Excalibur Aviation is currently modifying military U-8F (Beech Queen Air 65) aircraft for the US National Guard Bureau, Washington, DC. The conversions provide improved reliability, speed and range, together with reduced operating costs.

By early 1988 Excalibur Aviation had completed a total of 166 Queenaire conversions, including 51 for the US Army. Some 45 Beech Model 50 Twin-Bonanzas have also been modified by the company.

EXCALIBUR QUEENAIRE 800 and 8800
The Excalibur modification of Queen Air 65s and 80s includes installation of two 298 kW (400 hp) Textron Lycoming IO-720-A1B eight-cylinder engines, each driving a Hartzell three-blade constant-speed and fully-feathering metal propeller with spinner; new engine mountings; new exhaust system; new low drag engine nacelles; new (or zero-time overhauled and certificated) accessories; and Excalibur fully enclosed wheel well doors. Modifications of the Beechcraft Queen Air 65, A65 and 80 of all serial numbers are designated Queenaire 800; similar modifications to the Queen Air A80 and B80 of all serial numbers have the designation Queenaire 8800.

WEIGHTS (A: Queenaire 800; B: Queenaire 8800):

Weight empty, equipped (average):
A	2,449 kg (5,400 lb)
B	2,631 kg (5,800 lb)
Max T-O weight: A	3,628 kg (8,000 lb)
B	3,991 kg (8,800 lb)
Max landing weight: A	3,447 kg (7,600 lb)
B	3,792 kg (8,360 lb)

An Excalibur Queenaire 800 conversion of a Beech U-8F for the Missouri Army National Guard

PERFORMANCE (at max T-O weight):

Cruising speed, 75% power:
A, B at 2,530 m (8,300 ft)
201 knots (372 km/h; 231 mph)
Cruising speed, 65% power:
A, B at 3,050 m (10,000 ft)
195 knots (362 km/h; 225 mph)
Cruising speed, 45% power at 3,050 m (10,000 ft):
A, B 172 knots (319 km/h; 198 mph)
Stalling speed, gear and flaps up:
A 80 knots (148 km/h; 92 mph)
B 86 knots (160 km/h; 99 mph)
Stalling speed, gear and flaps down:
A 68 knots (126 km/h; 78 mph)
B 70 knots (129 km/h; 80 mph)
Max rate of climb at S/L: A 468 m (1,535 ft)/min
B 454 m (1,490 ft)/min

Rate of climb at S/L, one engine out:
A 110 m (360 ft)/min
B 76 m (250 ft)/min
Service ceiling: A 6,005 m (19,700 ft)
B 5,700 m (18,700 ft)
Service ceiling, one engine out:
A 3,595 m (11,800 ft)
B 3,110 m (10,200 ft)
T-O to 15 m (50 ft): A 520 m (1,706 ft)
B 625 m (2,050 ft)
Landing from 15 m (50 ft): A 663 m (2,176 ft)
B 747 m (2,450 ft)
Range with max fuel at 3,050 m (10,000 ft), with 113.5 litres (30 US gallons; 20.8 Imp gallons) reserves:
A 1,322 nm (2,451 km; 1,523 miles)
B 1,547 nm (2,867 km; 1,782 miles)

FAIRCHILD

Fairchild Industries Inc closed down or sold its military and commercial aircraft manufacturing divisions in late 1987. Details of the **Fairchild Republic Company**'s A-10A Thunderbolt II and T-46A Next Generation Trainer aircraft may be found in the 1987-88 and earlier editions of *Jane's*.

FAIRCHILD AIRCRAFT
FAIRCHILD AIRCRAFT CORPORATION
PO Box 790490, San Antonio, Texas 78279-0490
Telephone: (512) 824 9421
Telex: 767-315
PRESIDENT: Thomas J. Smith
EXECUTIVE VICE-PRESIDENT, OPERATIONS: David P. Bartles
VICE-PRESIDENT, INTERNATIONAL SALES: A. Bruce Chuber
VICE-PRESIDENT, ENGINEERING: Rawland Scott
DIRECTOR, PUBLIC RELATIONS: Brian Loflin

In December 1987 Fairchild Industries completed the sale of Metro Aviation, which owned 97% of the stock of Fairchild Aircraft Corporation, to GMF Investments Inc. The company continues to manufacture the Merlin series of twin-turboprop pressurised executive aircraft and the Metro airliner. Fairchild delivered a total of 15 Metro/Merlin series aircraft during 1987. In April 1988 North American Ventures of East Hartford, Connecticut, announced that it had reached agreement to purchase Metro Aviation from GMF Investments.

FAIRCHILD MODEL SA227-AC METRO III and EXPEDITER I
Swedish Air Force designation: Tp88
US military designation: C-26A

The **Metro III** is a 19/20-passenger all-weather pressurised, air-conditioned airliner, certificated under the FAA's Special Federal Air Regulations 41 and 41B, which provide for compliance with ICAO Annex 8 specifications for operation at a gross weight in excess of 5,670 kg (12,500 lb). The standard Metro III is certificated for operation at a max T-O weight of 6,577 kg (14,500 lb), providing a useful load increase of 672 kg (1,482 lb) compared with the Metro II which it superseded. The optional high gross weight version of the Metro III has a max T-O weight of 7,257 kg (16,000 lb). British CAA certification was expected in June 1988, following modifications that include a new dual-redundant stall avoidance system, dual continuous alcohol/water injection system, externally operable escape hatches, and a modified aileron aerofoil section. Britavia of the UK assisted Fairchild in carrying out the modifications.

The changes from the Metro II include a 3.05 m (10 ft 0 in) increase in wing span; more powerful engines, each driving a slow-turning four-blade propeller; new main landing gear doors, to improve take-off and landing performance and provide better access for maintenance; new streamline nacelle cowlings, with quick-action latches, and hinged at the rear to improve engine access; improved handling characteristics; and new fire prevention and containment features, with all inflammable fluid pipework isolated physically from all electric current-carrying components and wiring. The Metro III is certificated for flight into known icing conditions, and has lightning strike protection which the company claims is equal to that in the latest generation of commercial jet transports.

One Metro III was delivered to the Swedish Air Force for use as a VIP transport, and is known in Swedish service as the **Tp88**. In March 1988 Fairchild Aircraft Corporation received an order for six Metro IIIs, with an option for seven more aircraft, for the US Air National Guard under the designation **C-26A**. The aircraft, which will serve in the ANGOSTA (Air National Guard Operational Support Transport Aircraft) role, will be delivered between March and August 1989. They will have a quick-change interior, enabling passenger seats to be replaced by a medevac or all-cargo carrying configuration.

An all-cargo version, known as the **Expediter I**, is available, with cabin air-conditioning ducts repositioned to increase cargo space, reinforced cabin floor, cargo nets and guards, and a reduced empty weight which permits a max cargo payload of more than 2,268 kg (5,000 lb). First operator of the Expediter was SAT-AIR, on behalf of United Parcel Service. In April 1985 the first of ten Expediter Is was delivered to the US small package carrier DHL Worldwide Courier Express. This version has structurally reinforced landing gear and main spar to permit an increase in max T-O weight to 7,257 kg (16,000 lb).

TYPE: Twin-turboprop 19/20-passenger commuter airliner.

WINGS: Cantilever low-wing monoplane. Wing section NACA 65_2A215 at root, NACA 64_2A415 at tip. Dihedral 5°. Incidence 1° at root, −2° 30′ at tip. Sweepback at quarter-chord 0° 54′. All-metal two-spar fail-safe structure of aluminium alloy, constructed in one piece. The main spar beams have laminated caps and these, in the centre-section, have titanium laminations. Hydraulically operated double-slotted trailing-edge flaps. Manually controlled trim tab in each aileron. Goodrich pneumatic de-icing boots on wing leading-edges, with automatic bleed air cycling system.

FUSELAGE: All-metal cylindrical semi-monocoque fail-safe structure of 2024 aluminium alloy, flush riveted throughout. All but the nose section is pressurised. Glassfibre honeycomb nosecap can accommodate a 0.46 m (18 in) weather radar antenna.

TAIL UNIT: Cantilever all-metal structure with sweptback surfaces and dorsal fin. Small ventral fin. Electrically adjustable variable incidence tailplane. Manually controlled rudder trim. Goodrich pneumatic de-icing boots on tailplane leading-edges, with automatic bleed air cycling system.

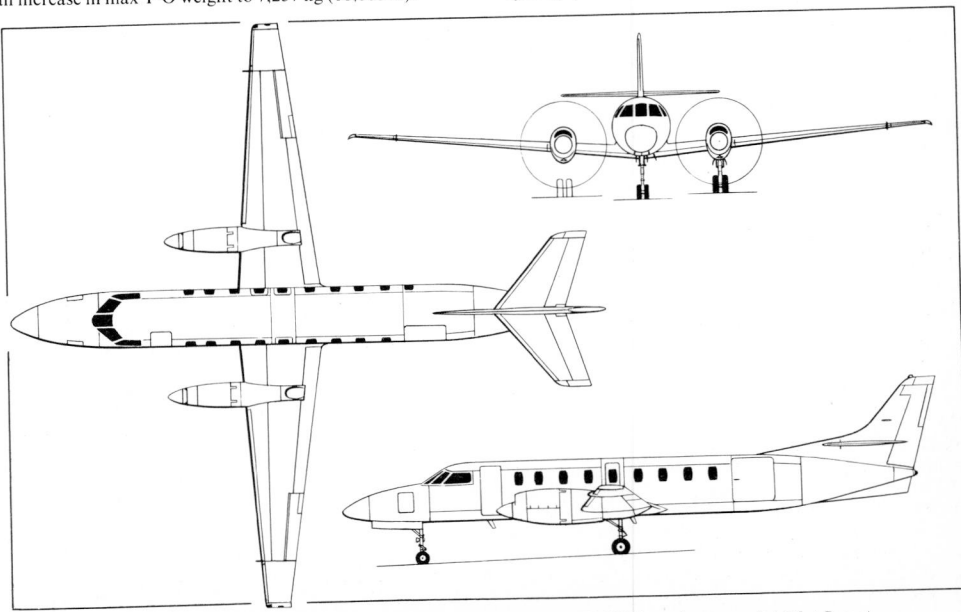

Fairchild Metro III commuter airliner (two Garrett TPE331 turboprops) *(Pilot Press)*

Fairchild Expediter I twin-turboprop cargo aircraft of DHL Worldwide Courier Express

LANDING GEAR: Retractable tricycle type with twin wheels on each unit. Hydraulic retraction, with dual actuators on each unit. All wheels retract forward, main gear into engine nacelles, nosewheels into fuselage. Ozone Aircraft Systems oleo-pneumatic shock absorber struts. Nosewheel steerable. Free-fall emergency extension system, with backup of hand operated hydraulic pump. Goodrich mainwheels with low-pressure tubeless tyres, size 18 × 5.50, type VII. Jay-Em nosewheels and Goodyear low-pressure tubeless tyres, size 16 × 4.40, type VII. Tyre pressures: nosewheel (T-O weight 6,577 kg/14,500 lb): 3.79 bars (55 lb/sq in); (T-O weight 7,257 kg/16,000 lb): 4.76 bars (69 lb/sq in). Mainwheels (T-O weight 6,577 kg/14,500 lb): 5.60 bars (87 lb/sq in); (T-O weight 7,257 kg/16,000 lb): 7.10 bars (103 lb/sq in). Goodrich self-adjusting hydraulically operated disc brakes and anti-skid system.

POWER PLANT: Two 745.5 kW (1,000 shp) dry/820 kW (1,100 shp) wet Garrett TPE331-11U-612G turboprops with continuous alcohol/water injection system, each driving a Dowty Rotol four-blade constant-speed fully-feathering reversible-pitch metal propeller with spinner. Automatic propeller synchrophasing, and full Beta control reversing, standard. In-flight windmill start capability. Integral fuel tank in each wing, each with a usable capacity of 1,226 litres (324 US gallons; 270 Imp gallons). Total usable fuel capacity 2,452 litres (648 US gallons; 540 Imp gallons). Refuelling point on each outer wing panel. Automatic fuel heating. Oil capacity 15.1 litres (4 US gallons; 3.3 Imp gallons). Engine inlet de-icing by bleed air. Electric oil cooler inlet anti-icing. Electric propeller de-icing. Flush mounted fuel vents. Single-point rapid defuelling provisions. Negative torque sensing, single red line/autostart, automatic engine temperature limiting, and engine fire extinguishing systems.

ACCOMMODATION: Crew of two on flight deck, each with four-way adjustable seat with folding armrests and shoulder harness, separated from passenger/cargo area by partial bulkhead on port side and armrest height curtain on starboard side. Dual controls standard. Bulkhead between cabin and flight deck optional. Standard accommodation for 19-20 passengers seated two abreast, on each side of centre aisle. 'No smoking' and 'Fasten seat belt' signs. High-back, tracking, quickly-removable passenger seats standard. Interior convertible to all-cargo or mixed passenger/cargo configuration with movable bulkhead between passenger and cargo sections. Snap-in carpeting. Self-stowing aisle filler. Tiedown fittings for cargo at 0.76 m (30 in) spacing. Integral-step passenger door on port side of fuselage, immediately aft of flight deck. Large cargo loading door on port side of fuselage at rear of cabin, hinged at top. Three window emergency exits, one on the port, two on the starboard side. Forward baggage/avionics compartment in nose, capacity 363 kg (800 lb). Pressurised rear cargo compartment, capacity 385 kg (850 lb). Cabin air-conditioned and pressurised. Electric windscreen de-icing. Two-speed windscreen wipers.

SYSTEMS: AiResearch automatic cabin pressure control system: max differential 0.48 bars (7.0 lb/sq in), providing a sea level cabin altitude to 5,120 m (16,800 ft). Engine bleed air heating, dual air cycle cooling system, with automatic temperature control. Air blower system for on-ground ventilation. Independent hydraulic system for brakes. Dual engine driven hydraulic pumps, using fire resistant MIL-H-83282 hydraulic fluid, provide 138 bars (2,000 lb/sq in) to operate flaps, landing gear actuators

and nosewheel steering. Hydraulic system flow rates 30.3 litres (8 US gallons; 6.7 Imp gallons)/min at idle power, both engines; 46.7 litres (12.34 US gallons; 10.27 Imp gallons)/min at T-O and climb power. Air/oil reservoir, pressure 2.27 bars (33 lb/sq in). Electrical system supplied by two 300A 28V DC starter/generators. Fail-safe system with overload and overvoltage protection. Redundant circuits for essential systems. Two 350VA solid state inverters supply 115V and 26V AC. Two SAFT 24V 23Ah nickel-cadmium batteries for main services. Engine fire detection system and fire extinguishing system standard. Wing overheat detection system. Oxygen system of 1.39 m³ (49 cu ft) capacity with flush outlets at each seat; system with capacity of 5.04 m³ (178 cu ft) optional. Stall avoidance system comprising angle indicator, visual and aural warning.

AVIONICS AND EQUIPMENT: Two flight deck and four cabin speakers standard; provisions for installation of remotely mounted or panel mounted avionics, customer furnished weather radar and autopilot. Standard equipment includes pilot and co-pilot foot warmers; edge lit consoles, pedestal and switch panels; integrally lit instruments; annunciator panel with 48 indicators; internally operated control locks, individual reading lights and air vents for each passenger; heated pitot; heated static sources; baggage compartment, cargo compartment, entrance, map and instrument panel, ice inspection, retractable landing, navigation, rotating beacon and taxi lights; automatic engine start cycle; external power socket; and static wicks.

DIMENSIONS, EXTERNAL:

Wing span	17.37 m (57 ft 0 in)
Wing mean aerodynamic chord	1.84 m (6 ft 0.33 in)
Wing aspect ratio	10.5
Length overall	18.09 m (59 ft 4¼ in)
Height overall	5.08 m (16 ft 8 in)
Tailplane span	4.86 m (15 ft 11½ in)
Wheel track	4.57 m (15 ft 0 in)
Wheelbase	5.83 m (19 ft 1½ in)
Propeller diameter	2.69 m (8 ft 10 in)
Passenger door (fwd): Height	1.35 m (4 ft 5 in)
Width	0.64 m (2 ft 1 in)
Cargo door (rear): Height	1.30 m (4 ft 3¼ in)
Width	1.35 m (4 ft 5 in)
Height to sill	1.30 m (4 ft 3¼ in)
Forward baggage doors (two, each):	
Height	0.64 m (2 ft 1 in)
Width	0.46 m (1 ft 6 in)
Emergency exits (three, each):	
Height	0.71 m (2 ft 4 in)
Width	0.51 m (1 ft 8 in)

DIMENSIONS, INTERNAL:
Cabin, excl flight deck and rear cargo compartment:

Length	7.75 m (25 ft 5 in)
Max width	1.57 m (5 ft 2 in)
Max height (aisle)	1.45 m (4 ft 9 in)
Floor area	13.01 m² (140 sq ft)
Volume	13.88 m³ (490 cu ft)
Rear cargo compartment (pressurised):	
Length	2.34 m (7 ft 8 in)
Max width	1.57 m (5 ft 2 in)
Max height	1.32 m (4 ft 4 in)
Volume	4.06 m³ (143.5 cu ft)
Nose cargo compartment (unpressurised):	
Length	1.75 m (5 ft 9 in)
Volume	1.13 m³ (40 cu ft)

AREAS:

Wings, gross	28.71 m² (309.0 sq ft)
Ailerons (total)	1.31 m² (14.12 sq ft)
Trailing-edge flaps (total)	3.78 m² (40.66 sq ft)
Fin, incl dorsal fin	3.40 m² (36.62 sq ft)
Rudder, incl tab	1.80 m² (19.38 sq ft)
Tailplane	5.08 m² (54.70 sq ft)
Elevators	1.98 m² (21.27 sq ft)

WEIGHTS AND LOADINGS:

*Operating weight empty:	
Commuter	4,164 kg (9,180 lb)
Expediter	3,960 kg (8,730 lb)
Max fuel weight	1,969 kg (4,342 lb)
Max T-O weight: standard	6,577 kg (14,500 lb)
optional	7,257 kg (16,000 lb)
Max ramp weight: standard	6,622 kg (14,600 lb)
optional	7,303 kg (16,100 lb)
Max zero-fuel weight	6,305 kg (13,900 lb)
Max landing weight: standard	6,350 kg (14,000 lb)
optional	7,031 kg (15,500 lb)
Max wing loading	252.8 kg/m² (51.78 lb/sq ft)
Max power loading	4.42 kg/kW (7.27 lb/shp)

increased by 38 kg (84 lb) for aircraft with optional T-O weight of 7,257 kg (16,000 lb)

PERFORMANCE (at max T-O weight of 6,577 kg; 14,500 lb, ISA, except where indicated):

Design diving speed
311 knots (576 km/h; 358 mph) CAS
Max operating speed
248 knots (459 km/h; 285 mph) CAS
Max operating Mach No.   0.52
Max cruising speed at mid-cruise weight of 5,670 kg (12,500 lb):
at 4,575 m (15,000 ft)
278 knots (515 km/h; 320 mph)
at 6,100 m (20,000 ft)
273 knots (506 km/h; 314 mph)
at 7,620 m (25,000 ft)
263 knots (487 km/h; 303 mph)
Min single-engine control speed (V_{MC})
87 knots (161 km/h; 100 mph) IAS
Stalling speed:
flaps and wheels up
98 knots (182 km/h; 113 mph) IAS
flaps and wheels down
87 knots (161 km/h; 100 mph) IAS
Max rate of climb at S/L   722 m (2,370 ft)/min
Rate of climb at S/L, one engine out 210 m (690 ft)/min
Service ceiling   8,380 m (27,500 ft)
Service ceiling, one engine out   4,330 m (14,200 ft)
T-O to 15 m (50 ft), dry power   991 m (3,250 ft)
Landing from 15 m (50 ft)   747 m (2,450 ft)
Range with max standard fuel, two crew, 19 passengers and baggage, 45 min reserves:
at max T-O weight of 6,577 kg (14,500 lb)
575 nm (1,065 km; 662 miles)
at max T-O weight of 7,257 kg (16,000 lb)
1,150 nm (2,131 km; 1,324 miles)

FAIRCHILD SPECIAL MISSION AIRCRAFT

Fairchild offers a variety of aircraft, designed specifically for special mission applications, some 35 examples of which have been delivered. Variations based on the Metro III include models for maritime patrol, anti-submarine warfare, flight navigation systems inspection, photo reconnaissance, electronic intelligence, airborne early warning and airborne critical care missions. The maritime patrol variant has a 360° scan Litton AN/APS-504(V) or (V)5, or AIL AN/APS-128D, radar in an underbelly blister fairing, an Omega nav system linked to hand held cameras, and two bulged observation windows, staggered one on each side of the rear fuselage. The ASW version carries sonobuoys and a sonobuoy signal processor, an OTP indicator, and MAD tailboom. Optional equipment for both versions includes a searchlight, IR linescanner, low light level TV, FLIR, side-looking TV, Doppler radar, droppable liferafts and survival kits, and two 288 litre (76 US gallon; 63 Imp gallon) underwing auxiliary fuel tanks. At a max T-O weight of 7,257 kg (16,000 lb), and with underwing tanks, the surveillance versions can complete a 10 hour mission over a radius of 1,050 nm (1,946 km; 1,209 miles) from base, at a height of 7,620 m (25,000 ft) with 45 min fuel reserves.

In 1982 the Swedish Defence Materiel Administration (FMV) contracted Fairchild Aircraft Corporation to begin studies for an airborne early warning variant of the Metro III incorporating an active array radar housed in a dorsal antenna. Initial wind tunnel testing was conducted in LTV's Dallas facility during 1983, and in early 1986 the FMV ordered a Metro III to test the Ericsson PS-890 static, electronically scanned E/F band radar, which scans one side at a time in a 120° arc. The aircraft was first flown in October 1986 with a mockup antenna, and completed 116 hours of aerodynamic and handling tests with Fairchild before it was delivered to Sweden in early October 1987 for installation and integration of mission electronics and data link by Ericsson Radio and other subcontractors. First flight with an operating radar is anticipated in late 1989 or early 1990.

The radar will be carried in a 9.14 m (30 ft) long housing of composite construction which is mounted on pylons on top of the fuselage. A ram air cooling intake is incorporated in the forward end of the housing, and an exhaust outlet at the rear. The antenna is inclined at an incidence of –2°, permitting the Metro III to be flown at the high angle of attack/low airspeeds dictated by the FMV's requirement for long endurance while maintaining the antenna in a horizontal position. Sweptback vertical auxiliary fins or 'tail-lets' have been added to the upper and lower surfaces of the tailplane, and a larger ventral fin installed to enhance directional stability. 60kVA of electrical power for the radar is provided by a Turbomach T-62T APU, installed in an E-Systems pod carried on a centreline stores station beneath the wing centre-section. Other modifications include the installation of a periscope sight in the flight deck roof, and a larger emergency exit on the port side of the cabin. No decision has been announced on the choice of data link that will connect the radar with Sweden's STRIL 60/90 air defence system. Provisional performance data include loiter speeds of 135-146 knots (250-270 km/h; 155-168 mph) with flaps at 50%, 164-175 knots (305-325 km/h; 189-202 mph) with flaps at 25%, and an endurance of 4-6 h in a patrol area 100 nm (185 km; 115 miles) away from base. Sweden has a requirement for 10-15 such surveillance aircraft.

FAIRCHILD MERLIN 300 (SA227 TT/41)

This aircraft series originated with the Merlin III, which received FAA certification on 27 July 1970, and was described in the 1974-75 *Jane's*. The later Merlin IIIA was described in the 1977-78 edition, the Merlin IIIB in the 1980-81 edition, and the Merlin IIIC in the 1983-84 edition.

Production of the Merlin IIIC ended in late 1982. It was superseded by a modified version, known then as the Fairchild 300, of which development began in April 1983.

Deliveries of the Merlin 300 began in the Winter of 1984-85, and totalled 10 by late 1987. The power plant is unchanged, the emphasis being primarily on aerodynamic and control system improvements for increased performance and enhanced handling, notably in roll. External changes include the introduction of 0.76 m (2 ft 6 in) winglets and reshaped ailerons. Internally, the control system utilises larger cables and pulleys, requiring much reduced travel of the yoke for roll control.

TYPE: Eight/ten-passenger twin-turboprop executive transport.

WINGS: Generally as for Metro III, but without the increase in wing span, and with winglets and reshaped ailerons.

FUSELAGE: All-metal cylindrical semi-monocoque fail-safe structure of 2024 aluminium alloy, flush riveted throughout. Glassfibre honeycomb nosecap will accommodate a 0.46 m (18 in) weather radar antenna.

TAIL UNIT: As for Metro III.

LANDING GEAR: As for Metro III, except for new power braking and anti-skid systems.

POWER PLANT: Two 671 kW (900 shp) Garrett TPE331-10U-513G turboprops, each driving a Dowty Rotol R.321 four-blade fully-feathering and reversible-pitch metal propeller with synchrophaser. Continuous alcohol/water injection system optional. Fuel system, engine inlet de-icing, and other power plant systems generally as for Metro III.

ACCOMMODATION: Crew of two on flight deck, each on four-way adjustable seat with shoulder harness; dual controls standard. Bulkhead with sliding door divides flight deck from cabin. Accommodation for eight to ten passengers with seats disposed on each side of a central aisle. Rapid relocation of seats and couches is made possible by continuous tracks recessed into floor,

Fairchild Merlin 300 twin-turboprop business aircraft

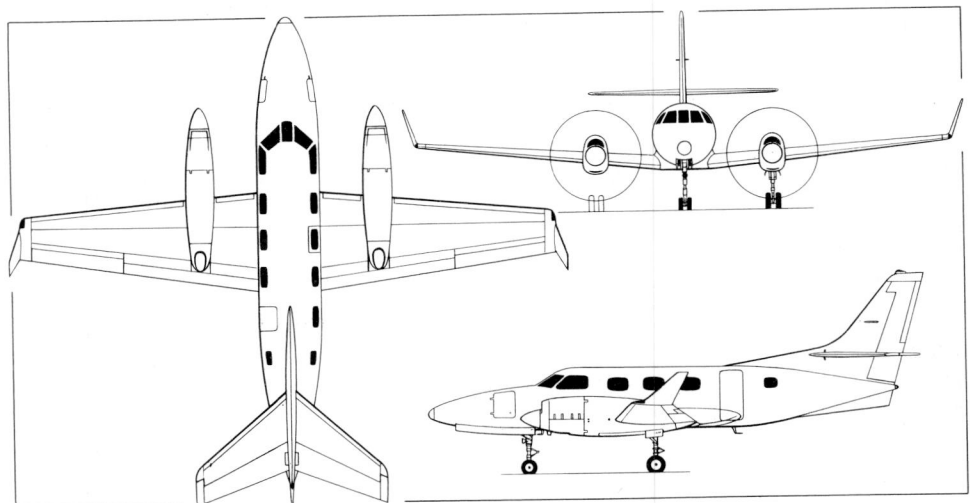

Fairchild Merlin 300 eight/ten-passenger executive transport aircraft (*Pilot Press*)

permitting layout to be varied according to mission. Passenger door at rear of cabin on port side, with integral airstair. Emergency exit on starboard side of cabin. Sliding door at rear end of cabin to separate it from the entrance vestibule. Baggage space in vestibule to accommodate 136 kg (300 lb); baggage and avionics in unpressurised nose compartment, capacity 272 kg (600 lb). Accommodation pressurised, air-conditioned and ventilated. Electrically heated windscreen. Two-speed windscreen wipers.

SYSTEMS: Generally as for Metro III, except that oxygen system has a capacity of 0.62 m³ (22 cu ft).

AVIONICS AND EQUIPMENT: Optional avionics, and standard and optional equipment, are generally as for Metro III, with the addition of a Collins EHSI-74 electronic horizontal situation indicator.

DIMENSIONS, EXTERNAL:

Wing span	16.60 m (47 ft 10¾ in)
Wing mean aerodynamic chord	1.94 m (6 ft 4½ in)
Wing aspect ratio	7.7
Length overall	12.85 m (42 ft 2 in)
Height overall	5.13 m (16 ft 10 in)
Tailplane span	4.86 m (15 ft 11½ in)
Wheel track	4.57 m (15 ft 0 in)
Wheelbase	3.23 m (10 ft 7 in)
Propeller diameter	2.69 m (8 ft 10 in)
Passenger door (port, rear): Height	1.35 m (4 ft 5 in)
Width	0.64 m (2 ft 1 in)

DIMENSIONS, INTERNAL:

Cabin, excl flight deck and rear compartment:	
Length	3.23 m (10 ft 7 in)
Max width	1.57 m (5 ft 2 in)
Max height	1.45 m (4 ft 9 in)
Volume	9.09 m³ (321 cu ft)
Rear baggage compartment volume (pressurised)	2.12 m³ (75.0 cu ft)
Nose baggage/avionics compartment volume (unpressurised)	1.27 m³ (45.0 cu ft)

AREAS: As for Metro III, except:

Wings, gross	25.78 m² (277.50 sq ft)

WEIGHTS AND LOADINGS:

Weight empty, equipped	3,833 kg (8,450 lb)
Max fuel weight	1,969 kg (4,342 lb)
Max T-O and landing weight	6,001 kg (13,230 lb)
Max ramp weight	6,046 kg (13,330 lb)
Max zero-fuel weight	5,670 kg (12,500 lb)
Max wing loading	232.8 kg/m² (47.68 lb/sq ft)
Max power loading	4.47 kg/kW (7.35 lb/shp)

PERFORMANCE (at max T-O weight, ISA, except where indicated):

Never-exceed speed	265 knots (490 km/h; 305 mph) CAS
Max operating Mach No.	0.63

Max cruising speed, at mid-cruise weight of 5,670 kg (12,500 lb):

at 3,050 m (10,000 ft)	296 knots (548 km/h; 340 mph)
at 6,100 m (20,000 ft)	300 knots (555 km/h; 345 mph)
at 7,620 m (25,000 ft)	289 knots (535 km/h; 332 mph)
at 9,150 m (30,000 ft)	283 knots (524 km/h; 325 mph)

Min single-engine control speed (VMC)	109 knots (202 km/h; 125 mph) IAS

Stalling speed:

flaps and wheels up	104 knots (193 km/h; 120 mph)
flaps and wheels down	91 knots (169 km/h; 105 mph)
Max rate of climb at S/L	792 m (2,600 ft)/min
Rate of climb at S/L, one engine out	228 m (750 ft)/min
Service ceiling	9,450 m (31,000 ft)
Service ceiling, one engine out	4,815 m (15,800 ft)
T-O to 15 m (50 ft)	890 m (2,920 ft)
Landing from 15 m (50 ft)	855 m (2,805 ft)

Range with max fuel, allowances for start, T-O, climb and descent plus 45 min reserves:

at long-range cruise power at 8,535 m (28,000 ft)
2,312 nm (4,284 km; 2,662 miles)

at max cruise power at 4,575 m (15,000 ft)
1,795 nm (3,326 km; 2,067 miles)

FAIRCHILD MERLIN IV C (SA227-AT)

The Merlin IV C is a corporate version of the Metro III commuter airliner, differing primarily in its internal configuration. It has reclining passenger seats, couches, and a more luxurious standard of interior furniture, decor and lighting. The refreshment and entertainment centre includes a large buffet cabinet with beverage and food storage and preparation facilities, television and stereo equipment. At the rear of the cabin, separated by a bulkhead and hinged door, are a toilet and baggage compartment.

The Merlin IV C is certificated under the SFAR Pt 41B and ICAO Annex 8 specifications, and has a max T-O and landing weight of 6,577 kg (14,500 lb) or, optionally, 7,257 kg (16,000 lb). Its large cabin volume, and the availability of movable bulkheads and interchangeable cabin furnishings, makes it easily convertible to meet a company's airlift requirements in virtually any arrangement of passengers and/or cargo.

The description and specification of the Metro III apply also to the Merlin IV C, except as follows:

TYPE: Eleven/fourteen-passenger corporate transport.

AVIONICS AND EQUIPMENT: In late 1986 the Merlin IV C was certificated for a King/Bendix KFC 400 flight control system with KNS660 flight management system integrated with the Bendix EFIS-10 five-tube electronic flight instrument system comprising two ADIs, two HSIs and a multi-function display.

WEIGHTS AND LOADINGS: As Metro III, except:
Weight empty, equipped   4,318 kg (9,520 lb)

PERFORMANCE (at max T-O weight, ISA, except where indicated):
Max cruising speed, at mid-cruise weight of 5,670 kg (12,500 lb):
  at 3,050-4,575 m (10,000-15,000 ft)
                        283 knots (524 km/h; 326 mph)
  at 6,100 m (20,000 ft) 281 knots (521 km/h; 323 mph)
  at 7,620 m (25,000 ft) 273 knots (506 km/h; 314 mph)
Max rate of climb at S/L   750 m (2,460 ft)/min
Rate of climb at S/L, one engine out 207 m (680 ft)/min
Range with max standard fuel, max cruise power at 7,925 m (26,000 ft), 45 min reserves:
  eight occupants   1,653 nm (3,063 km; 1,903 miles)
  thirteen occupants   974 nm (1,805 km; 1,121 miles)
Ferry range, conditions and allowances as above, but with two flight crew only
                    2,117 nm (3,923 km; 2,438 miles)

FAIRCHILD METRO V and MERLIN V

Fairchild Aircraft was developing the Metro V in 1988 in place of previously announced models known as Metro IV, Metro VI and Merlin 400SP. In corporate form, the Metro V will be known as the Merlin V.

The Metro V is powered by two 834 kW (1,119 shp) Garrett TPE331-12-612G turboprops, with McCauley propellers, and will meet new FAA FAR Pt 23 CC

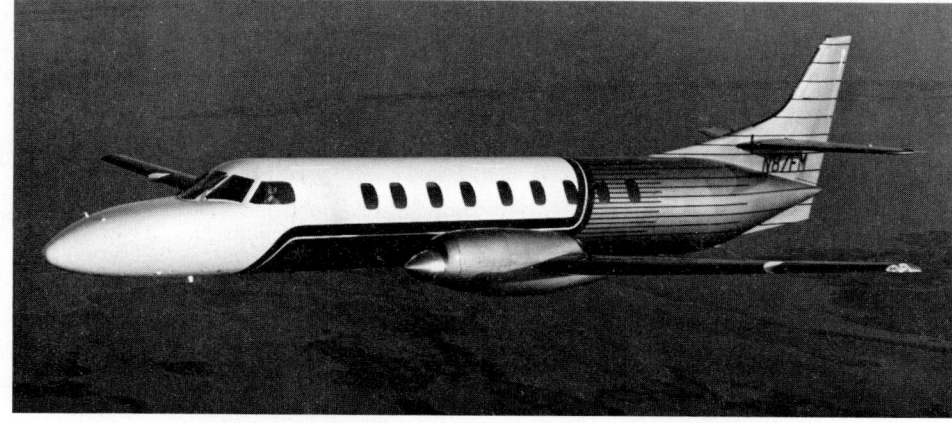

Fairchild Merlin IV C twin-turboprop corporate transport

commuter airliner certification requirements. Features of the new design include a new wing of increased area, with semi-Fowler flaps over 90 per cent of its span; a T tail configuration; improved ailerons and rudder; improved electrical and safety systems; a stand-up cabin for 19 passengers; and a redesigned flight deck.

First flight of the prototype Metro V is scheduled for February 1990, with initial customer deliveries in January 1991.

The following data apply to the Metro V:
DIMENSIONS, EXTERNAL:
Wing span   17.37 m (57 ft 0 in)
Length overall   18.41 m (60 ft 5 in)
Height overall   5.09 m (16 ft 8½ in)
Propeller diameter   2.69 m (8 ft 10 in)
DIMENSIONS, INTERNAL:
Cabin: Max width   1.63 m (5 ft 4 in)

Max height   1.73 m (5 ft 8 in)
Volume   17.56 m³ (620 cu ft)
WEIGHTS:
Weight empty, equipped   4,450 kg (9,810 lb)
Max fuel weight (2,460 litres; 650 US gallons; 541 Imp gallons)   1,968 kg (4,340 lb)
Max payload   2,127 kg (4,690 lb)
Max T-O weight   7,484 kg (16,500 lb)
PERFORMANCE (estimated):
Max cruising speed   280 knots (519 km/h; 322 mph)
Max rate of climb at S/L   731 m (2,400 ft)/min
Rate of climb at S/L, one engine out
                             207 m (680 ft)/min
T-O to 15 m (50 ft)   1,091 m (3,580 ft)
Landing from 15 m (50 ft)   686 m (2,250 ft)
Range with 19 passengers, IFR reserves
                    900 nm (1,668 km; 1,036 miles)

FRAKES
FRAKES AVIATION INC
Route 3, PO Box 229-B, Cleburne Airport, Cleburne, Texas 76031
Telephone: (817) 645 9136
Telex: 75-8390 FRAKES CLEB
PRESIDENT: J. Fred Frakes
VICE-PRESIDENT: Joseph Frakes

FRAKES KING AIR CONVERSION
This company has developed an engine nacelle and inlet system modification for the Beech Model 90 King Air series of turboprop business aircraft. Frakes claims that the modification, which is available on all Model 90-F90 King Airs, offers lower drag, increased ram air recovery, enhanced take-off, climb and altitude performance, and a 13-26 knot (24-48 km/h; 15-30 mph) increase in cruising speed, depending on model.

FRAKES TURBO-ALBATROSS
No news of this proposed turboprop conversion of the Grumman HU-16 Albatross (see 1987-88 *Jane's*) has been received since early 1986.

GARRETT
GARRETT GENERAL AVIATION SERVICES DIVISION
(Division of Allied Signal Aerospace Company)
Los Angeles International Airport, 6201 West Imperial Highway, Los Angeles, California 90045
Telephone: (213) 568 3700
Telex: 181827 A/B AIRE AVI LSA
VICE-PRESIDENT, MARKETING & SALES: Richard A. Graser
Garrett General Aviation Services Division offers a Garrett TFE731 engine retrofit programme for the Dassault-Breguet Mystère-Falcon 20.

GARRETT 731 HAWKER
This Garrett TFE731-3 turbofan conversion programme for the British Aerospace HS 125 Series 400 business jet has been completed. Sixty-seven aircraft were converted. A description and photograph may be found in the 1987-88 *Jane's*.

GARRETT FALCON 20 RE-ENGINING PROGRAMME
In May 1987 Garrett General Aviation Services announced plans to offer an engine retrofit to operators of Dassault-Breguet Mystère-Falcon 20 business jets. The modification, developed in conjunction with the French manufacturer, involves replacing the Falcon 20's General Electric CF700 power plant with Garrett TFE731-5AR turbofans. Under the terms of the joint venture Dassault-Breguet will complete engineering studies leading to FAA certification, and will supply Falcon 900 engine nacelles to Garrett, which will be responsible for providing retrofit kits and for marketing activities.

The TFE731 retrofit is expected to increase the range of the Falcon 20 by 50 per cent. Estimated range of the 'C' model is extended to 1,920 nm (3,555 km; 2,209 miles), that of the 'D' and 'E' models to 2,100 nm (3,889 km; 2,416

Model of the Garrett TFE731 turbofan powered Falcon 20 business jet

miles), and that of the 'F' model to 2,130 nm (3,949 km; 2,450 miles). In each case, a payload of eight passengers is assumed, operating at a speed of Mach 0.72, with NBAA IFR fuel reserves.

In November 1987 a Falcon 20F was delivered to Istres, France, for calibration flights by Dassault-Breguet, to establish baseline performance figures for the unconverted aircraft, prior to installation of new pylons for the TFE731

engines. This aircraft, which was scheduled to make its first flight with TFE731 engines in September 1988, is being used for certification of the Garrett retrofit, and will also serve as development and certification testbed for Dee Howard TR-5020 thrust reversers on the re-engined Falcons. Work was expected to begin on the first customer engine retrofit in December 1988. In mid-1988 Garrett General Aviation Services held orders for 23 Falcon 20 retrofits.

GATES LEARJET — *See Learjet Corporation*

GENERAL DYNAMICS
GENERAL DYNAMICS CORPORATION
Pierre Laclede Center, St Louis, Missouri 63105
Telephone: (314) 889 8200
Telex: 6841036
Fax: (314) 889 8839
CHAIRMAN AND CHIEF EXECUTIVE OFFICER: Stanley C. Pace
PRESIDENT AND CHIEF OPERATING OFFICER:
Herbert F. Rogers
Convair Division:
PO Box 85357, San Diego, California 92138
Telephone: (619) 573 8000
CORPORATE VICE-PRESIDENT AND GENERAL MANAGER:
John E. McSweeny
VICE-PRESIDENT, RESEARCH AND ENGINEERING:
J. William Vega
Fort Worth Division:
PO Box 748, Fort Worth, Texas 76101
Telephone: (817) 777 2000
CORPORATE VICE-PRESIDENT AND GENERAL MANAGER:
Charles A. Anderson
VICE-PRESIDENT, F-16 ENGINEERING: W. D. Buntin
VICE-PRESIDENT, RESEARCH AND ENGINEERING:
E. M. Petrushka
VICE-PRESIDENT, INTERNATIONAL MARKETING:
Dain M. Hancock
VICE-PRESIDENT, MARKETING: D. J. Wheaton

General Dynamics conducts its US aerospace activities at six divisions: Convair Division, with operations at San Diego, California; Fort Worth Division, with operations at Fort Worth, Texas; Pomona Division, with headquarters at Pomona, California; Electronics Division, with headquarters in San Diego; Valley Systems Division, with headquarters at Rancho Cucamonga, California; and Space Systems Division, with headquarters in San Diego. Convair Division is responsible for the design, development and production of offensive missile systems and aircraft structures. Fort Worth Division is engaged in the design, development and production of military aircraft and avionics. Pomona Division is engaged in the development and production of tactical missile and gun systems. Electronics Division is involved in new technology to support the development and production of advanced electronics systems. Valley Systems Division produces Stinger and RAM missiles, and is developing terminally guided submunitions.

Fort Worth is currently responsible for production of the F-16 Fighting Falcon multi-role fighter; spares, support and modification/update for the F-111 fighter-bomber; and various ground based radar systems. Convair Division produces a major portion of the fuselage for the McDonnell Douglas KC-10A Extender tanker/cargo aircraft. It retains detailed tooling for high usage spares for the Convair-Liner 240/340/440 series of piston-engined transports, and continues to manufacture components for these types.

On 3 March 1985 General Dynamics acquired the Cessna Aircraft Company of Wichita, Kansas (see separate entry in this section).

GENERAL DYNAMICS/MCDONNELL DOUGLAS A-12
In December 1987 General Dynamics, in equal partnership with McDonnell Douglas, was selected to develop the US Navy's Advanced Tactical Aircraft (ATA), now designated A-12, which will replace the Grumman A-6 in the 1990s. The A-12, which is expected to fly in 1992, will be powered by an uprated version of the General Electric F404 engine, and will employ 'stealth' technology. Total US Navy requirement is for some 450 aircraft. Further details of the A-12 programme are given under a separate General Dynamics/McDonnell Douglas heading.

GENERAL DYNAMICS F-16 FIGHTING FALCON
The F-16 had its origin in the US Air Force's Lightweight Fighter (LWF) prototype programme, in 1972. The history of this programme and a description of the YF-16 prototypes can be found in the 1978-79 and 1977-78 editions of *Jane's* respectively.

The first of two YF-16 prototypes (72-01567) made its official first flight on 2 February 1974 and was followed by the second YF-16 (72-01568) on 9 May 1974. On 13 January 1975 the Secretary of the US Air Force announced that the F-16 had been selected for full scale engineering development. The original YF-16 requirement for an air superiority day fighter was expanded, to give equal emphasis to the air-to-surface role, including provision of radar and all-weather navigation capabilities. The manufacture of eight pre-production aircraft, comprising six single-seat **F-16As** and two two-seat **F-16Bs**, began in July 1975. The first full scale development F-16A made its first flight on 8 December 1976, and the first F-16B on 8 August 1977.

Initially, the US Air Force planned to procure a total of 650 F-16s. This was increased first to 1,388 aircraft, including 204 two-seaters, to replace McDonnell Douglas F-4s in the active force and to modernise the Air Force Reserve and Air National Guard, and subsequently to a planned total of 2,729, of which 1,859 had been contracted and 1,247 delivered by 1 January 1988. In addition, 15 other

General Dynamics F-16C Fighting Falcon of the Israeli Air Force

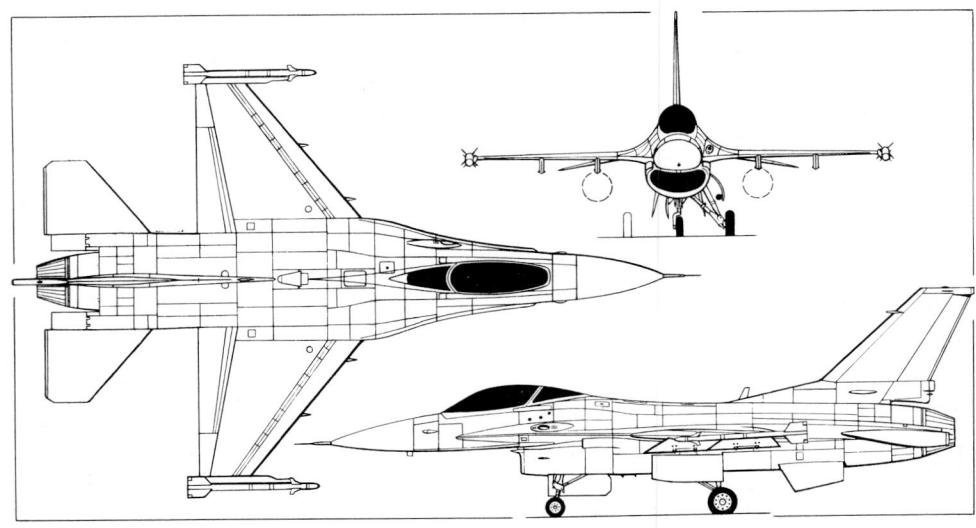

Three-view drawing of General Dynamics F-16C Fighting Falcon *(Pilot Press)*

air forces have ordered a total of 1,158 F-16s (for details see 1986-87 *Jane's*). Production at Fort Worth for the USAF continues at the rate of 180 a year for FY 1986-89, with a contract option to increase this to 216 a year. By December 1987 deliveries to all customers from Fort Worth totalled 1,569, with a further 410 delivered from European assembly lines in Belgium and the Netherlands, and air forces of 16 nations had announced plans to acquire a total of 4,062 F-16s.

Current operational, experimental and planned or proposed versions of the F-16 are as follows:

A-16. Proposed close air support (CAS) version for US Air Force Tactical Air Command. If adopted, would be based on modified aircraft from current procurement.

In January 1988 the USAF selected General Dynamics Fort Worth as one of six contractors to provide options on a successor for the Fairchild Republic A-10A.

F-16A. First production version, for air-to-air and air-to-surface roles. Production for USAF completed in March 1985, but still available to other customers. Pratt & Whitney F100-PW-200 turbofan, rated at approx 106.0 kN (23,830 lb st) with afterburning. Westinghouse APG-66 pulse-Doppler range and angle track radar. First aircraft (78-0001) flew for the first time on 7 August 1978. Entered service with USAF's 388th Tactical Fighter Wing at Hill AFB, Utah, on 6 January 1979, and achieved combat-ready status in October 1980, in which year the name **Fighting Falcon** was adopted. Standard equipment in TAC, USAFE, PACAF, ANG and AFRES, and with the Thunderbirds air demonstration squadron. Operated also by the air forces of Belgium, Denmark, Egypt, Israel, the Netherlands, Norway, Pakistan and Venezuela; ordered by Indonesia (8, with F100-PW-220 engines, plus 4 F-16Bs), Singapore (4, plus 4 F-16Bs, with potential force of 20) and Thailand (14, plus 4 F-16Bs). Extension of fin root fairing houses Loral Rapport ECM equipment in Belgian and Israeli F-16As and F-16Bs, a braking parachute in aircraft for Norway and Venezuela. F-16s of the Pakistan Air Force carry Thomson-CSF Atlis laser target designation pods. The first aircraft for Singapore, an F-16B and the 2,000th production Fighting Falcon, was handed over at Fort Worth on 10 February 1988. Singapore's eight F-16s will remain in the USA, at Luke AFB, Arizona, for crew training until 1989-90. Deliveries to Thailand began in May 1988, and those to Indonesia are to start in 1989. Further details of service history may be found in the 1986-87 and earlier editions of *Jane's*.

USAF and NATO operators are co-operating in an operational capabilities upgrade (OCU) programme to enable F-16A/Bs to utilise next-generation air-to-air and

air-to-surface weapons systems. Changes will be made to existing radar systems and software, and the aircraft's fire control and stores management computers will be improved. A data transfer unit and combined altitude radar altimeter will be installed.

F-16(ADF). In October 1986 the USAF awarded General Dynamics a contract to modify a total of 270 F-16As and Bs as air defence fighters (ADF) to replace F-4s and F-106s in eleven Air National Guard continental air defence squadrons. The aircraft's APG-66 radar will be upgraded with AMRAAM data link, improved ECCM and improved capability against cruise missiles. It will also be equipped with HF radio, IFF interrogator, ID light, a crash survivable flight data recorder and provisions for the Global Positioning System. The contract calls for addition of a drag chute and 2,271 litre (600 US gallon; 500 Imp gallon) external fuel tanks; requirements for these are under review. The aircraft will be modified to launch AIM-7 Sparrow missiles, two of which can be carried on underwing launchers. Alternatively, it will carry up to six AIM-120 AMRAAM or AIM-9 Sidewinder missiles, or combinations of all three air-to-air weapons. The F-16(ADF) will retain the M61 20 mm gun. First flight, by an ADF modified F-16B, was expected to take place in March 1988. Programme completion is scheduled for FY 1992.

F-16B. Two-seat variant of F-16A with two cockpits in tandem, each fully systems-operational. Service use as for F-16A. Length unchanged.

F-16C/D. Single-seat (F-16C) and two-seat (F-16D) versions embodying results of USAF Multinational Staged Improvement Programme (MSIP) implemented in February 1980. MSIP expands the aircraft's growth capability to incorporate systems for ground attack and beyond-visual-range intercept missions by day and night, and in all weather conditions. Stage I of the programme, introduced on Block 15 F-16A and F-16B aircraft delivered from November 1981, included wiring and structural provisions for emerging systems. Stage II, applicable to Block 25 production deliveries of F-16C and F-16D aircraft from July 1984, incorporates core avionics, cockpit and other airframe changes. Stage III, scheduled to begin during 1987, involves selected installation of advanced systems as these become available.

The only external feature distinguishing the F-16C from the F-16A is a slightly expanded forward tail fin root fairing to house ASPJ (airborne self-protection jamming) when it becomes available. Internal changes include a Westinghouse APG-68 multi-mode radar offering increased range, sharper resolution, expanded operating modes and advanced ECCM by comparison with the APG-66; an

General Dynamics F-16D 'Wild Weasel' for the Israeli Air Force *(Doyle Guerry, via Aerofax)*

advanced cockpit with improved pilot/vehicle interface, including up-front controls, two multi-function displays, radar altimeter, GEC Avionics wide-angle holographic HUD (being delivered from Spring 1988), FLIR video and Fairchild mission data transfer equipment; avionics growth capability through increases in both the speed and memory of core computers and solid state cartridge system for loading mission data; increased capacity electrical power and cooling systems; structural changes for increased max T-O weight and gross weight manoeuvring limits; and MIL-STD-1760 weapons interface to provide compatibility with advanced 'smart' weapons such as AMRAAM and AGM-65D Maverick imaging infra-red missiles.

At Block 30 (July 1986 deliveries) a common engine bay was incorporated which facilitated installation of either the Pratt & Whitney F100-PW-220 or the General Electric F110-GE-100 engine developed under the USAF's Alternate Fighter Engines programme. Other changes included computer memory expansion and seal-bonded fuselage fuel tanks. First USAF wing to receive F-16C/Ds with F110 engines was the 86th TFW at Ramstein AB, West Germany. At Block 30B (from Spring 1987) a software change provides full level IV multi-target compatibility with AMRAAM. Further additions in 1987 included a voice message unit, Shrike anti-radiation missiles, crash survivable flight data recorder, and a modular common inlet duct which provides more air and full available thrust from the F110 engine at lower airspeeds. One Block 30 F-16D has been diverted to Calspan Corporation as the NF-16D (which see).

At Block 40 (December 1988 delivery) planned upgrades include a digital flight control system, automatic terrain following, diffractive optics HUD, expanded core computers, advanced IFF, increased max T-O weight, a Martin Marietta LANTIRN pod set (low altitude navigation and targeting infra-red for night) and GPS. Block 70 (mid-1991 delivery) is being planned to incorporate full HARM/Shrike missile capability, radar and cockpit improvements, an on-board oxygen generating system (OBOGS), reliability and maintainability improvements, ASPJ, advanced threat warning (ALR-74 or ALR-56M), ALE-47 advanced chaff/flares, and increased performance F100-PW-229 and F110-GE-IPE engines.

The first F-16C for the US Air Force (83-118) was delivered on 19 July 1984; the first F-16D was delivered in September 1984; first operational unit to equip with these models was the 33rd TFS at Shaw AFB, South Carolina. F-16Cs and F-16Ds have been ordered also by Bahrain (12 F-16C/Ds with F110-GE-100 engines), Egypt (34 F-16Cs and 6 F-16Ds, the first of which, with an F100-PW-220 engine, was handed over at Fort Worth on 15 August 1986), Greece (40, with F110-GE-100 engines, deliveries commencing 1988, with potential force of 60); Israel (60 F-16Cs and 15 F-16Ds with F110-GE-100s, deliveries of which were scheduled for completion by the end of 1987, with potential for a further 30 aircraft); South Korea (30 F-16Cs and 6 F-16Ds with F100-PW-220 engines, the first delivered in March 1986, with a potential force totalling 156); and Turkey (136 F-16Cs and 24 F-16Ds with F110-GE-100 engines; last of eight built at Fort Worth was delivered in late January 1988, remaining 152 being built by TAI in Turkey, the first of which, an F-16C, was flown on 11 October 1987).

F-16Cs and F-16Ds of USAF's 52nd TFW at Spangdahlem AB, West Germany, are operated alongside F-4G Phantoms on 'Wild Weasel' defence suppression missions. An accompanying illustration shows an F-16D modified for similar duties with the Israeli Air Force. The special operational equipment is housed in a large rectangular-section dorsal spine, extending from the canopy to beyond the jet nozzle.

F-16N. Selected in January 1985 as US Navy supersonic adversary aircraft (SAA). Contract for 26 aircraft with deliveries commencing Spring 1987 and scheduled for completion in May 1988. The airframe is derived from that of Block 30 F-16Cs with minor structural modifications involving the substitution of titanium for aluminium in lower wing fittings and cold working the lower wing skin holes to meet the increased frequency of *g* loading in

adversary roles. The F-16N configuration includes the General Electric F110-GE-100 engine, substitution of the APG-66 radar for the APG-68, and deletion of the M61 gun. The F-16N normally carries only wingtip launchers for practice AIM-9 missiles and ACMI AIS pods, but is capable of carrying the full complement of F-16 fuel tanks and other external stores. Four aircraft are two-seat versions, similar to the F-16D and designated **TF-16N**. F-16Ns and TF-16Ns serve with the fighter weapons school (eight) and VF-126 squadron (six) at NAS Miramar, California; and with VF-45 (twelve) at NAS Key West, Florida.

F-16 Agile Falcon and SX-3. Agile Falcon is proposed successor to F-16C/D with composites wings of same planform but with area increased to 34.84 m² (375.0 sq ft) and lighter in weight, with refined aerodynamics. Updated avionics and a developed General Electric F110 improved performance engine (IPE) rated at 129.0 kN (29,000 lb st) with afterburning. Offered initially to European NATO operators of F-16A/B, and suggested as replacement for abandoned Israeli Lavi.

On 19 October 1987 the Japan Defence Agency announced that it had selected a developed version of the F-16 for its FS-X fighter requirement. The aircraft, now designated **SX-3**, will be developed jointly by Japan and the United States. It will retain the larger wing surfaces of the Agile Falcon, with an extended fuselage to provide increased fuel capacity, additional mission avionics in a longer nose radome, forward canard surfaces, and leading-edge flaps of radar absorbent materials. Avionics will include an active phased-array radar developed by Mitsubishi Electronics, and provision will be made for underwing carriage of four Mitsubishi Type 80 anti-shipping missiles. Initial requirement for the SX-3, which will be manufactured in Japan, is for 130 aircraft, with a potential requirement for 170. The SX-3 will begin flight testing in 1993 and enter JASDF service in 1997, progressively replacing Mitsubishi F-1s.

F-16 Recce. A reconnaissance capability is being designed for the F-16, using pod mounted sensors and requiring only minor changes to any existing F-16 model. Compatibility has been flight demonstrated with four existing European built sensor pods, including that used on the Tornado. F-16s have been operational as tactical reconnaissance aircraft with the Royal Netherlands Air Force, as F-16A(R)s since 1983.

An extensive flight test programme conducted in 1986 verified the suitability of a new General Dynamics designed underbelly reconnaissance pod built especially for the F-16, and the feasibility and effectiveness of near-real-time reconnaissance capability. The semi-conformal pod, installed on an F-16B (75-0752), housed advanced electro-

optical and infra-red sensors for day/night operation, at all speeds and altitudes, and with stand-off capability. The three multi-position sensors served the function of seven cameras in current fixed-mount arrangements. The system provided real-time cockpit viewing and sensor positioning, imagery review/manipulation/frame selection, and digital data link of selected frames to distant ground stations. Ground station operators were able to analyse, annotate and disseminate this imagery and their reports electronically only minutes after the images were taken, compared with the hours required to process film-based systems. In addition to electro-optical equipment, a Texas Instruments RS-710 infra-red linescanner, extendable data link antenna and a Control Data Corporation imagery management system, the pod can also carry wide-angle and long-range Chicago Aerial KS-153 cameras. The pod is 4.40 m (14 ft 5 in) long, weighs 454-567 kg (1,000-1,250 lb), and has a design load factor of 9*g*. Development status of the F-16 Recce is uncertain, but highly probable by the early 1990s.

AFTI/F-16. Modified F-16A testbed aircraft for Air Force Systems Command's Advanced Fighter Technology Integration (AFTI) programme; first flown on 10 July 1982. Digital flight control system and twin fuselage-mounted ventral foreplanes, permitting 'decoupled' or six degrees of freedom flight modes and also providing integrated manoeuvring capability for making flat (unbanked) turns without sideslip and manoeuvre enhancement/gust alleviation. Detailed account of programme in 1986-87 *Jane's*, and of the automated manoeuvre and attack system (AMAS) programme (completed April 1987) in 1987-88 edition. Test programme in 1988 (beginning on 10 February) was aimed at improving communications between aircraft and ground troops during close air support missions. Aircraft modifications include a two-way digital data link with forward air controllers, refinement of terrain management and display system and its Sandia software, and improvements to FLIR/laser tracker and pilot's helmet sight. The CAS test flights will also continue work begun in the AMAS programme to provide a ground collision avoidance system. Future plans call for upgrades of AFTI/F-16's radar and other sensors to enhance aircraft's all terrain capability.

NF-16D. F-16D Block 30 modified as variable stability in-flight simulator test aircraft (VISTA) for Calspan Corporation, replacing earlier NT-33A variable stability testbed. VISTA features include vertical surface direct-force generators above and below wings, variable-stability flight control system and fully programmable cockpit controls and displays. The NF-16D, which was expected to be delivered to Calspan during 1988, will be used for research into flying qualities, displays and flight control, and for test pilot training.

Development of the F-16 is continuing. Initial operational testing of LANTIRN began in mid-January 1986 on an F-16 from McChord AFB, Washington. Delivery of 700 navigation pods began in March 1987.

Flight testing of an infra-red system known as Falcon Eye FLIR was scheduled to begin in 1987. This utilises a head-mounted display and head-steered FLIR sensor forward of the F-16's windscreen. Claimed advantages are night vision without need for an external pod and off-boresight field of vision correlated to the pilot's head position.

Other research and development subjects being investigated for the F-16 include artificial intelligence, modular avionics architecture, VHSIC, various weapons, sensors and cockpit displays, secure/anti-jam communications and data links, advanced navigation systems, chemical and electromagnetic pulse hardening, signature reduction and vulnerability reduction. The F-16 is a candidate for a defence suppression role in the USAF's Follow-On Weasel programme. A Falcon Century programme has been instituted to monitor and evaluate developments and to

F-16 Recce test aircraft equipped with General Dynamics reconnaissance pod

maintain a master plan for F-16 developments into the next century.

The following description applies to the F-16C and F-16D:

TYPE: Single-seat day/night multi-role fighter (F-16C) and two-seat fighter/trainer (F-16D).

WINGS: Cantilever mid-wing monoplane, of blended wing/body design and cropped delta planform. The blended wing/body concept is achieved by flaring the wing/body intersection, thus not only providing lift from the body at high angles of attack but also giving less wetted area and increased internal fuel volume. In addition, thickening of the wingroot gives a more rigid structure, with a weight saving of some 113 kg (250 lb). Basic wing is of NACA 64A-204 section, with 40° sweepback on leading-edges. Structure is mainly of aluminium alloy, with 11 spars, 5 ribs and single upper and lower skins, and is attached to fuselage by machined aluminium fittings. Leading-edge manoeuvring flaps are programmed automatically as a function of Mach number and angle of attack. The increased wing camber maintains effective lift coefficients at high angles of attack. These flaps are one-piece bonded aluminium honeycomb sandwich structures and are driven by rotary actuators. The trailing-edges carry large flaperons (flaps/ailerons), which are interchangeable left with right and are actuated by integrated servo-actuators. The maximum rate of flaperon movement is 52°/s.

FUSELAGE: Semi-monocoque all-metal structure of frames and longerons, built in three main modules: forward (to just aft of cockpit), centre and aft. Nose radome built by Brunswick Corporation. Highly swept vortex control strakes along the fuselage forebody increase lift and improve directional stability at high angles of attack.

TAIL UNIT: Cantilever structure with sweptback surfaces. Fin is multi-spar multi-rib aluminium structure with graphite epoxy skins, aluminium tip and dorsal fin. Optional extension of rear root fairing to house brake-chute (standard in F-16Cs for Turkey and F-16As for Norway) or Rapport III ECM. Interchangeable all-moving tailplane halves, constructed of graphite epoxy composite laminate skins mechanically attached to a corrugated aluminium substructure. Each tailplane half has an aluminium pivot shaft, and a removable full depth bonded honeycomb leading-edge. Ventral fins have bonded aluminium honeycomb core with aluminium skins. Split speed-brake inboard of rear portion of each horizontal tail surface to each side of nozzle, each deflecting 60° from the closed position.

LANDING GEAR: Menasco hydraulically retractable type, nose unit retracting rearward and main units forward into fuselage. Nosewheel is located aft of intake, to reduce the risk of foreign objects being thrown into the engine during ground operation, and rotates 90° during retraction to lie horizontally under engine air intake duct. Oleo-pneumatic struts in all units. Goodyear mainwheels and brakes; Goodrich mainwheel tyres, size 25.5 × 8-14, pressure 14.48-15.17 bars (210-220 lb/sq in) at T-O weights less than 11,340 kg (25,000 lb). Steerable nosewheel with Goodrich tyre, size 18 × 5.5-8, pressure 14.82-15.51 bars (215-225 lb/sq in) at T-O weights less than 11,340 kg (25,000 lb). All but two main unit components interchangeable. Brake by wire system on main gear, with Goodyear anti-skid units. Runway arrester hook under rear fuselage. Landing/taxying light on each main landing gear leg.

POWER PLANT: One General Electric F110-GE-100, rated at 122.8 kN (27,600 lb st) with afterburning, or one Pratt & Whitney F100-PW-220 turbofan, rated at 104.3 kN (23,450 lb st) with afterburning, as alternative standard engines, mounted in rear fuselage. Fixed geometry intake, with boundary layer splitter plate, beneath fuselage. Standard fuel contained in wing and five seal-bonded fuselage cells which function as two tanks; see under 'Weights' for quantities. In-flight refuelling receptacle in top of centre-fuselage, aft of cockpit. Auxiliary fuel can be carried in drop tanks on underwing and underfuselage hardpoints.

ACCOMMODATION: Pilot only in F-16C in air-conditioned cockpit. McDonnell Douglas ACES II zero/zero ejection seat. Tinted bubble canopy made of polycarbonate advanced plastics material. The windscreen and forward canopy are an integral unit without a forward bow frame, and are separated from the aft canopy by a simple support structure which serves also as the breakpoint where the forward section pivots upward and aft to give access to the cockpit. A redundant safety lock feature prevents canopy loss. Windscreen/canopy design provides 360° all-round view, 195° fore and aft, 40° down over the side, and 15° down over the nose. To enable the pilot to sustain high g forces, and for pilot comfort, the seat is inclined 30° aft and the heel line is raised. In normal operation the canopy is pivoted upward and aft by electrical power; the pilot is also able to unlatch the canopy manually and open it with a backup handcrank. Emergency jettison is provided by explosive unlatching devices and two rockets. A limited displacement, force sensing control stick is provided on the right hand console, with a suitable armrest, to provide precise control inputs during combat manoeuvres. The F-16D has two cockpits in tandem, equipped with all controls, displays, instruments, avionics and life support systems required to perform both training and combat missions.

The layout of the F-16D second station is essentially the same as that of the F-16C, and is fully systems-operational. A single-enclosure polycarbonate transparency, made in two pieces and spliced aft of the forward seat with a metal bow frame and lateral support member, provides outstanding view from both cockpits.

SYSTEMS: Regenerative 12kW environmental control system, with digital electronic control, uses engine bleed air for pressurisation and cooling of crew station and avionics compartments. Two separate and independent hydraulic systems supply power for operation of the primary flight control surfaces and the utility functions. System pressure (each) 207 bars (3,000 lb/sq in), rated at 161 litres (42.5 US gallons; 35.4 Imp gallons)/min. Bootstrap type reservoirs, rated at 5.79 bars (84 lb/sq in). Electrical system powered by engine driven Westinghouse 60kVA main generator and 10kVA standby generator (including ground annunciator panel for total electrical system fault reporting), with Sundstrand constant speed drive and powered by a Sundstrand accessory drive gearbox. Four dedicated, sealed cell batteries provide transient electrical power protection for the fly by wire flight control system. Application of the control configured vehicle (CCV) principle of relaxed static stability produces a significant reduction in trim drag, especially at high load factors and supersonic speeds. The aircraft centre of gravity is allowed to move aft, reducing both the tail drag and the change in drag on the wing due to changes in lift required to balance the download on the tail. Relaxed static stability imposes a requirement for a highly reliable, full-time-operating, stability augmentation system, including reliable electronic, electrical and hydraulic provisions. The signal paths in this quad-redundant system are used to control the aircraft, replacing the usual mechanical linkages. Pilot commands are processed by a four-channel Lear Siegler flight control computer which generates the electrical signals for the servo actuators. An onboard Sundstrand/Solar jet fuel starter is provided for engine self-start capability. Simmonds fuel measuring system. Garrett emergency power unit automatically drives a 5kVA emergency generator and emergency pump to provide uninterrupted electrical and hydraulic power for control in the event of the engine or primary power systems becoming inoperative.

AVIONICS AND EQUIPMENT: Westinghouse APG-68 pulse-Doppler range and angle track radar, with planar array in nose. Radar provides air-to-air modes for range-while-search, uplook search, velocity search, air combat, track-while-scan (ten targets), raid cluster resolution, single target track and (later) high PRF track to provide target illumination for AIM-7 missiles; and air-to-surface modes for ground mapping, Doppler beam sharpening, ground moving target, sea target, fixed target track, target freeze after pop-up, beacon for nav fix and offset weapon delivery with ground FAC, and air-to-ground ranging. Forward avionics bay, immediately forward of cockpit, contains radar, air data equipment, inertial navigation system, flight control computer, and combined altitude radar altimeter (CARA). Rear avionics bay contains ILS, Tacan and IFF, with space for future equipment. A Dalmo Victor AN/ALR-69 radar warning system is installed. Communications equipment includes Magnavox AN/ARC-164 UHF 'Have Quick' transceiver; provisions for a Magnavox KY-58 secure voice system; Collins AN/ARC-186 VHF AM/FM transceiver; government furnished AN/AIC-18/25 intercom; and Novatronics interference blanker. Sperry Flight Systems central air data computer. Litton LN-39 standard inertial navigation system; Collins AN/ARN-108 ILS; Collins AN/ARN-118 Tacan; Teledyne Electronics AN/APX-101 IFF transponder with a government furnished IFF control; government furnished National Security Agency KIT-1A/TSEC cryptographic equipment; Lear Siegler stick force sensors; GEC Avionics wide-angle holographic electronic head-up display with raster video capability and integrated keyboard; horizontal situation indicator; Teledyne Avionics angle of attack transmitter; Gull Airborne angle of attack indicator; Clifton Precision attitude director indicator; General Dynamics advanced stores management computer; Delco fire control computer; Sperry multi-function display set; data entry/cockpit interface by Litton-Canada and General Dynamics, Fort Worth; and cockpit/TV set. Cockpit and core avionics integrated on two MIL-STD-1553B multiplex buses. Optional equipment includes VIR-130 VOR/ILS and ARC-190 HF radio. Essential structure and wiring provisions are built into the airframe to allow for easy incorporation of future avionics systems under development for the F-16 by the US Air Force. Israeli Air Force F-16s have been extensively modified with Israeli designed and manufactured equipment, as well as optional US equipment, to tailor them to the IAF defence role.

ARMAMENT: General Electric M61A1 20 mm multi-barrel cannon in the port side wing/body fairing, equipped with a General Electric ammunition handling system and a 'snapshoot' gunsight (part of the head-up display system) and 515 rounds of ammunition. There is a mounting for an air-to-air missile at each wingtip, one underfuselage centreline hardpoint, and six underwing hardpoints for additional stores. For manoeuvring flight at 5.5g the underfuselage station is stressed for a load of up to 1,000

kg (2,200 lb), the two inboard underwing stations for 2,041 kg (4,500 lb) each, the two centre underwing stations for 1,587 kg (3,500 lb) each, the two outboard underwing stations for 318 kg (700 lb) each, and the two wingtip stations for 193 kg (425 lb) each. For manoeuvring flight at 9g the underfuselage station is stressed for a load of up to 544 kg (1,200 lb), the two inboard underwing stations for 1,134 kg (2,500 lb) each, the two centre underwing stations for 907 kg (2,000 lb) each, the two outboard underwing stations for 204 kg (450 lb) each, and the two wingtip stations for 193 kg (425 lb) each. There are mounting provisions on each side of the inlet shoulder for the specific carriage of sensor pods (electro-optical, FLIR, etc); each of these stations is stressed for 408 kg (900 lb) at 5.5g, and 250 kg (550 lb) at 9g. Typical stores loads can include two wingtip mounted AIM-9J/L Sidewinders, with up to four more on the outer underwing stations; Sargent-Fletcher 1,400 litre (370 US gallon; 308 Imp gallon) or 2,271 litre (600 US gallon; 500 Imp gallon) drop tanks on the inboard underwing stations; a 1,136 litre (300 US gallon; 250 Imp gallon) drop tank on the underfuselage station; a Martin Marietta Pave Penny laser spot tracker pod along the starboard side of the nacelle; and single or cluster bombs, air-to-surface missiles, or flare pods, on the four inner underwing stations. Stores can be launched from Aircraft Hydro-Forming MAU-12C/A bomb ejector racks, Hughes LAU-88 launchers, or Orgen triple or multiple ejector racks. Westinghouse AN/ALQ-119 and AN/ALQ-131 ECM (jammer) pods can be carried on the centreline and two underwing stations. Provision for future internal installation of Westinghouse/ITT AN/ALQ-165 airborne self-protection jammer (ASPJ) instead of ECM pods. ALE-40 internal chaff/flare dispensers. Current capabilities include air-to-air combat with gun and Sidewinder missiles; and air-to-ground attack with gun, rockets, conventional bombs, special weapons, laser guided and electro-optical weapons. Specific structure, wiring provisions, and system architecture, are built in to ensure acceptance of future sensor and weapon systems, including electro-optical and FLIR pods, and advanced beyond-visual-range missiles. Weapons already launched successfully from F-16s, in addition to Sidewinders and AMRAAM, include radar guided Sparrow and Sky Flash air-to-air missiles, AGM-65A/B/D Maverick air-to-surface missiles and Penguin Mk 3 anti-ship missile. Also, the GPU-5/A 30 mm gun pod has been fired successfully from the F-16 fuselage station. F-16s of the Norwegian Air Force carry Penguin anti-shipping missiles. F-16s can be equipped with a variety of reconnaissance pods (eg, Orpheus on RNethAF aircraft) and the Thomson-CSF Atlis laser designator pod, as carried by those of Pakistan Air Force.

DIMENSIONS, EXTERNAL (F-16C, D):

Wing span over missile launchers	9.45 m (31 ft 0 in)
Wing span over missiles	10.00 m (32 ft 9¾ in)
Wing aspect ratio	3.0
Length overall	15.03 m (49 ft 4 in)
Height overall	5.09 m (16 ft 8½ in)
Tailplane span	5.58 m (18 ft 3¾ in)
Wheel track	2.36 m (7 ft 9 in)
Wheelbase	4.00 m (13 ft 1½ in)

AREAS (F-16C, D):

Wings, gross	27.87 m² (300.0 sq ft)
Flaperons (total)	5.82 m² (62.64 sq ft)
Leading-edge flaps (total)	6.82 m² (73.42 sq ft)
Vertical tail surfaces (total)	5.09 m² (54.75 sq ft)
Rudder	1.08 m² (11.65 sq ft)
Horizontal tail surfaces (total)	5.92 m² (63.70 sq ft)

WEIGHTS AND LOADINGS:

Weight empty:	
F-16C: F100-PW-220	8,316 kg (18,335 lb)
F-110-GE-100	8,663 kg (19,100 lb)
Max internal fuel: F-16C	3,162 kg (6,972 lb)
F-16D	2,624 kg (5,785 lb)
Max external fuel (both)	3,066 kg (6,760 lb)
Max external load (both)	5,443 kg (12,000 lb)
Typical combat weight:	
F-16C	9,790 kg (21,585 lb)
Max T-O weight:	
air-to-air, no external tanks:	
F-16C	11,372 kg (25,071 lb)
F-16D	11,114 kg (24,502 lb)
with external load:	
F-16C	19,187 kg (42,300 lb)
F-16D	17,010 kg (37,500 lb)
Wing loading:	
at 11,839 kg (26,100 lb) AUW	425 kg/m² (87.0 lb/sq ft)
at 17,010 kg (37,500 lb) AUW	610 kg/m² (125.0 lb/sq ft)
Thrust/weight ratio ('clean')	1.1 to 1

PERFORMANCE:

Max level speed at 12,200 m (40,000 ft)	above Mach 2.0
Service ceiling	more than 15,240 m (50,000 ft)
Radius of action	more than 500 nm (925 km; 575 miles)
Ferry range, with drop tanks	more than 2,100 nm (3,890 km; 2,415 miles)
Max symmetrical design g limit with full internal fuel	+9

GENERAL DYNAMICS/ MCDONNELL DOUGLAS

PRINCIPAL PROGRAMME OFFICE: General Dynamics Corporation, Fort Worth Division, PO Box 748, Fort Worth, Texas 76101
Telephone: (817) 777 2000

GENERAL DYNAMICS/MCDONNELL DOUGLAS ATA
US Navy designation: A-12

On 23 December 1987 the US Navy announced that it had selected General Dynamics and McDonnell Douglas to develop its A-12 carrier-based Advanced Tactical Aircraft

(ATA). A fixed-price contract valued at $4.379 billion has been awarded for the development programme. Few details have yet been released for the aircraft, which will be powered by two General Electric F404 derivative turbofans, operated by a two-man crew, and feature integrated avionics and electronic warfare systems. A two-year demonstration/validation programme was expected to be initiated in late FY 1988, with the first flight of a prototype A-12 planned for the mid-1990s and service entry at the end of that decade. Announced subcontractors on the ATA programme include Westinghouse (combined function FLIR), Norden Systems and Texas Instruments (multifunction radar), Harris (multifunction antenna system), General Electric Aircraft Electronics Division (missile warning

system), Garrett (air data computer), Bendix (main landing gear, wheels and carbon brakes), Litton (inertial navigation system), Garrett Auxiliary Power Division (airframe-mounted accessory drive gearbox system), Litton Industries Amecom Division (electronic surveillance measures system), Martin Marietta (navigational FLIR), and Sundstrand Turbomach Division (auxiliary power unit). The US Navy has a requirement for up to 450 ATAs to replace Grumman A-6 Intruders in the all-weather attack role. After completion of the FSED programme, General Dynamics and McDonnell Douglas will compete annually for production contracts.

GREAT LAKES
GREAT LAKES AIRCRAFT COMPANY INC

Production of the Great Lakes Sport Trainer was revived in 1974 in Wichita, Kansas, and in 1978 moved to Eastman,

Georgia, where manufacture was suspended in 1982. In 1984, under new ownership, Great Lakes Aircraft Company Inc was re-established in Claremont, New Hampshire. The manufacturing facility was to be expanded by April 1986 to

a total of 4,273 m² (46,000 sq ft), with plans to produce up to two aircraft a month, but no news has been received since that time. A description and illustration of the Model 2T-1A-2 can be found in the 1987-88 *Jane's*.

GRUMMAN
GRUMMAN CORPORATION

1111 Stewart Avenue, Bethpage, New York 11714-3580
Telephone: (516) 575 0574
Telex: 961430
CHAIRMAN, PRESIDENT AND CHIEF EXECUTIVE OFFICER:
John O'Brien
VICE-CHAIRMAN, TECHNOLOGY: Renso L. Caporali
VICE-PRESIDENT, MARKETING: David L. Walsh
VICE-PRESIDENT, PUBLIC AFFAIRS: Weyman B. Jones

Grumman Aircraft Engineering Corporation was incorporated on 6 December 1929. Important changes in its corporate structure were announced in 1969, resulting in the formation of Grumman Corporation as a small holding company, with Grumman Aerospace Corporation, Grumman Allied Industries Inc and Grumman Data Systems Corporation. In February 1985 Grumman Corporation announced the creation of ten operating divisions, each matched to a specific market: Aerostructures; Aircraft Systems; Allied (Vehicles and Marine); Data Systems; Electronics Systems; International; Melbourne Systems;

Space Systems; St Augustine; and Technical Services. Melbourne Systems Division is prime contractor and responsible for avionics installation in the E-8A Joint STARS (modified Boeing 707) aircraft, of which further details are given under the entry for Boeing Military Airplanes. A Corporate Services Division provides legal, purchasing, contracts and other common services to all the operating divisions. A Space Station Program Support division was formed during 1987.
Employment within the corporation totalled 33,700 at 31 December 1987.

GRUMMAN AIRCRAFT SYSTEMS DIVISION

PRESIDENT: Peter B. Oram
Current aircraft products of this division include versions of the A-6 Intruder, C-2A Greyhound, EA-6B Prowler, E-2C Hawkeye and F-14 Tomcat for the US Navy. It has also designed and built two examples of a small forward swept wing (FSW) technology demonstrator designated X-29A, under contract from the US Defense Advanced Research Projects Agency. A contract to manufacture 270 shipsets of engine nacelles and thrust reversers for the Tay turbofans of Gulfstream IV and Fokker 100 transport aircraft was received in February 1984. An initial contract covering design and manufacture of complete tail sections of the Bell/Boeing V-22 Osprey advanced vertical lift aircraft (see Bell/Boeing entry) was received in August 1984. In April 1987 Grumman announced that it had been awarded an initial $28 million contract for the manufacture of two sets of composite structure ailerons, elevators and rudders for the McDonnell Douglas C-17A tactical airlifter.

A contract was awarded in January 1987 by the Government of Pakistan to study the technical feasibility of integrating US engines and avionics into Chinese manufactured F-7 fighter aircraft for the Pakistan Air Force. On 5 August 1987 the US Air Force awarded Grumman contracts totalling $245 million for the development, installation and flight testing of avionics upgrades for

Chinese Shenyang J-8 II fighter aircraft. Further details of these programmes are given under the CAC and SAC headings in the Chinese section.
Aircraft delivered during 1987 comprised eight F-14s, nine E-2Cs, nine EA-6Bs, seven A-6Es and eight C-2As.

GRUMMAN HAWKEYE
US Navy designations: E-2B, E-2C and TE-2C

The E-2 Hawkeye was developed as a carrier borne early warning aircraft, but is suitable also for land based operations. The first of three prototypes flew for the first time on 21 October 1960; these were followed by 56 E-2As, all operational examples of which had been updated to E-2B standard by the end of 1971. Details of these versions have appeared in earlier editions of *Jane's*.

The first of two E-2C prototypes flew on 20 January 1971. Production began in mid-1971 and the first flight of a production aircraft was made on 23 September 1972. Orders from the US Navy for this version now cover 144 aircraft; 121 of these had been delivered by the beginning of 1988, and it is planned for production to continue at the rate of six per year until the early 1990s. Four E-2Cs were supplied to Israel in 1981; Japan accepted four each in 1982 and 1984, and plans to buy five more: three in FY 1989 and two in FY 1990. Egypt has accepted five aircraft, the last three of which were delivered in October 1987. The government of Singapore has taken delivery of four aircraft.

The US Coast Guard and US Customs Service each have two aircraft for use in anti-narcotics smuggling operations. These four aircraft were taken from the US Navy inventory, and replaced by increasing FY 1988 procurement from six aircraft to ten. Six E-2Cs were funded in FY 1989.

The E-2C entered service, with airborne early warning squadron VAW-123 at NAS Norfolk, Va, in November 1973, and went to sea on board USS *Saratoga* in late 1974. Sixteen other squadrons, including two naval reserve squadrons, have since received E-2C aircraft, and two TE-2C training aircraft are also in service.

The Hawkeye can maintain patrol on naval task force defence perimeters in all weathers, at an operating height of about 9,150 m (30,000 ft), and can detect and assess any threat from approaching enemy aircraft over ranges approaching 260 nm (480 km; 300 miles). An AN/APS-139 radar system superseded the earlier AN/APS-125 and AN/APS-138 in new production E-2Cs in 1988. A retrofit programme is in progress for all previously delivered aircraft. The system includes a new total radiation aperture control antenna (TRAC-A) to reduce sidelobes and offset increased jamming threats. The radar is capable of detecting airborne targets anywhere in a three million cubic mile surveillance envelope while simultaneously monitoring maritime traffic. Long-range detection, automatic target track initiation and high-speed processing combine to enable each E-2C to track, automatically and simul-

Grumman E-2C Hawkeye early warning and control aircraft of the Japan Air Self-Defence Force *(Katsumi Hinata)*

taneously, more than 2,000 targets and to control more than 40 airborne intercepts. A Randtron Systems AN/APA-171 antenna system is housed in a 7.32 m (24 ft) diameter saucer-shaped rotodome, mounted above the rear fuselage of the aircraft, which revolves in flight at 6 rpm. The Yagi type radar arrays within the rotodome are interfaced to the onboard avionic systems, providing radar sum and difference signals plus IFF.

The AN/APS-139 search radar can detect targets as small as a cruise missile at ranges in excess of 145 nm (268 km; 167 miles). It also monitors movement of enemy ships and land vehicles. The AN/ALR-73 passive detection system (PDS) alerts operators to the presence of electronic emitters at distances up to twice the detection range of the radar system, thus expanding significantly the surveillance capability of the E-2C. Functions of these and other key elements of the E-2C's avionics systems were described more fully in the 1979-80 *Jane's*.

In 1986, the US Navy began evaluation of an E-2C with new Grumman/General Electric APS-145 radar system, able to track more targets, at greater ranges, decrease the effects of jamming, and offer sharper overland detection. The APS-145 is expected to go into production aircraft towards the end of 1991. Work continues on further improvements to the E-2C's radar detection and processing capabilities, and on a wing strengthening programme.

E-2Cs are used to monitor air traffic in the Florida skies surrounding Cape Canaveral during Space Shuttle launches and to direct US Coast Guard and US Customs fixed-wing and helicopter crews in many successful interceptions of drug smuggling aircraft. They are also used to direct Israeli fighters engaged in combat missions in the Middle East.

The following details apply to the E-2C Hawkeye:

TYPE: Airborne early warning aircraft.

WINGS: Cantilever high-wing monoplane of all-metal construction. Incidence 4° at root, 1° at tip. Centre-section is a structural box consisting of three beams, ribs and machined skins. Hinged leading-edge is non-structural and provides access to flying and engine controls. The outer panels fold rearward about skewed-axis hinge fittings mounted on the rear beams, to stow parallel with the rear fuselage on each side. Folding is done through a double acting hydraulic cylinder. Trailing-edges of outer panels and part of centre-section consist of long span ailerons and hydraulically actuated Fowler flaps. When flaps are lowered, ailerons are drooped automatically. All control surfaces are power operated and incorporate devices to produce artificial feel forces. Automatic flight control system (AFCS) can be assigned sole control of the system hydraulic actuators, or AFCS signals can be superimposed on the pilot's mechanical inputs for stability augmentation. Pneumatically inflated rubber de-icing boots on leading-edges.

FUSELAGE: Conventional all-metal semi-monocoque structure.

TAIL UNIT: Cantilever structure, with four fins and three double-hinged rudders. Tailplane dihedral 11°. Portions of tail unit made of glassfibre to reduce radar reflection. Power control and artificial feel systems as for ailerons. Pneumatically inflated rubber de-icing boots on all leading-edges.

LANDING GEAR: Hydraulically retractable tricycle type. Pneumatic emergency extension. Steerable nosewheel unit retracts rearward. Mainwheels retract forward, and rotate to lie flat in bottom of nacelles. Twin wheels on nose unit only. Oleo-pneumatic shock absorbers. Mainwheel tyres size 36 × 11 Type VII 24-ply, pressure 17.9 bars (260 lb/sq in) on ship, 14.5 bars (210 lb/sq in) ashore. Hydraulic brakes. Hydraulically operated retractable tailskid. A-frame arrester hook under tail.

POWER PLANT: Two 3,661 kW (4,910 ehp) Allison T56-A-425 turboprops, driving Hamilton Standard type 54460-1 four-blade fully-feathering reversible-pitch constant-speed propellers. These have foam filled blades which have a steel spar and glassfibre shell. Spinners and blades incorporate electric anti-icing. Production E-2Cs delivered from 1988 onwards have T56-A-427 engines

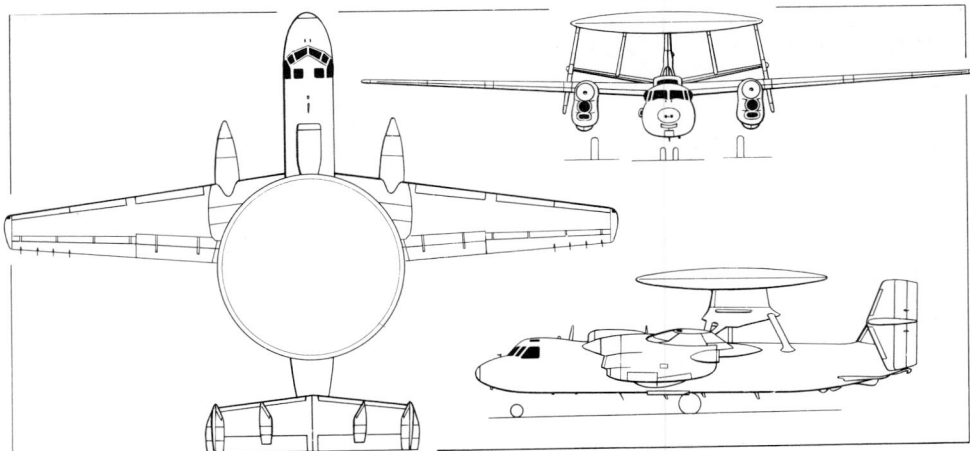

Grumman E-2C Hawkeye twin-turboprop airborne early warning aircraft (*Pilot Press*)

which provide a two per cent power increase and lower fuel consumption.

ACCOMMODATION: Normal crew of five on flight deck and in ATDS compartment in main cabin, consisting of pilot, co-pilot, combat information centre officer, air control officer and radar operator. Downward hinged door, with built-in steps, on port side of centre-fuselage.

AVIONICS: Randtron AN/APA-171 rotodome (radar and IFF antennae), General Electric AN/APS-139 advanced radar processing system (ARPS) with overland/overwater detection capability (with APS-145 scheduled for introduction in 1991 and eventual retrofit in all E-2Cs), RT-988/A IFF interrogator with Hazeltine OL-76/AP IFF detector processor, Litton AN/ALR-73 passive detection system, Hazeltine AN/APA-172 control indicator group, Litton OL-77/ASQ computer programmer (L-304), ARC-158 UHF data link, ARQ-34 HF data link, ASM-440 in-flight performance monitor, Collins ARC-51A UHF com, AIC-14A intercom, Litton AN/ASN-92 (LN-15C) CAINS carrier aircraft inertial navigation system, GEC Avionics standard central air data computer, APN-153 (V) Doppler, ASN-50 heading and attitude reference system, ARN-52 (V) Tacan, Collins ARA-50 UHF ADF, ASW-25B ACLS and Honeywell APN-171 (V) radar altimeter.

DIMENSIONS, EXTERNAL:
Wing span	24.56 m (80 ft 7 in)
Wing chord: at root	3.96 m (13 ft 0 in)
at tip	1.32 m (4 ft 4 in)
Wing aspect ratio	9.3
Width, wings folded	8.94 m (29 ft 4 in)
Length overall	17.54 m (57 ft 6¾ in)
Height overall	5.58 m (18 ft 3¾ in)
Diameter of rotodome	7.32 m (24 ft 0 in)
Tailplane span	7.99 m (26 ft 2½ in)
Wheel track	5.93 m (19 ft 5¾ in)
Wheelbase	7.06 m (23 ft 2 in)
Propeller diameter	4.11 m (13 ft 6 in)

AREAS:
Wings, gross	65.03 m² (700.0 sq ft)
Ailerons (total)	5.76 m² (62.0 sq ft)
Trailing-edge flaps (total)	11.03 m² (118.75 sq ft)
Fin, incl rudder and tab:	
outboard (total)	10.25 m² (110.36 sq ft)
inboard (total)	4.76 m² (51.26 sq ft)
Tailplane	11.62 m² (125.07 sq ft)
Elevators (total)	3.72 m² (40.06 sq ft)

WEIGHTS:
Weight empty	17,265 kg (38,063 lb)
Max fuel (internal, usable)	5,624 kg (12,400 lb)
Max T-O weight	23,556 kg (51,933 lb)

PERFORMANCE (at max T-O weight):
Max level speed	323 knots (598 km/h; 372 mph)
Max cruising speed	311 knots (576 km/h; 358 mph)
Cruising speed (ferry)	268 knots (496 km/h; 308 mph)
Approach speed	103 knots (191 km/h; 119 mph)
Stalling speed (landing configuration)	
	74 knots (138 km/h; 86 mph)
Service ceiling	9,390 m (30,800 ft)
Min T-O run	610 m (2,000 ft)
T-O to 15 m (50 ft)	793 m (2,600 ft)
Min landing run	439 m (1,440 ft)
Ferry range	1,394 nm (2,583 km; 1,605 miles)
Time on station, 175 nm (320 km; 200 miles) from base	
	3-4 h
Endurance with max fuel	6 h 6 min

GRUMMAN C-2A GREYHOUND

Production of a second series of C-2A carrier on-board delivery (COD) aircraft for the US Navy was authorised in February 1982, and 39 were funded under a multi-year contract signed in early 1983, in annual batches of 8, 6, 8, 8 and 9. The first new-production C-2A, which made its first flight on 4 February 1985, was retained by Grumman for carrier suitability and flight dynamic tests; the second was used to check avionics integration and electromagnetic compatibility in a test programme completed in September 1985. Deliveries to the US Navy began in May 1985 and are scheduled for completion in late 1989. Six new procurement C-2As are with VR-24 squadron serving the Mediterranean Fleet from Sigonella, Sicily. A second squadron, VRC-50, became operational in 1986 at Cubi Point in the Philippines. VRC-30 at North Island, California, VRC-40 at Norfolk, Virginia, and replacement air groups VAW-120 and VAW-110 have also received new C-2As.

The last of the original C-2A Greyhounds, of which 19 were delivered during the 1960s, were retired from service during 1987. Newly manufactured Greyhounds have uprated engines and avionics, improved anti-corrosion protection, and increased passenger comfort. They also introduced a new APU to reduce the need for ground support equipment and provide self-sufficiency for operation at remote locations.

The description which follows is applicable to the current production C-2A based on the E-2C version of the Hawkeye:

TYPE: Twin-turboprop carrier on-board delivery (COD) transport.

FUSELAGE: Cargo door, with integral ramp, forms undersurface of rear fuselage, which is more upswept than that of E-2C.

TAIL UNIT: Basically as for E-2C, but without tailplane dihedral.

LANDING GEAR: Basically as for E-2C, but with stronger nose gear (adapted from that of A-6A Intruder) to cater for higher AUW. Each nosewheel fitted with 20 × 5.5 Type VII 12-ply tyre. Mainwheel tyre pressure 13.8 bars (200 lb/sq in) on ship, 11.4 bars (165 lb/sq in) ashore.

POWER PLANT: Two 3,661 kW (4,910 ehp) Allison T56-A-425 turboprops, each driving a Hamilton Standard Type 54460-1 four-blade fully-feathering reversible-pitch constant-speed propeller with spinner. Two fuel tanks, total capacity 6,905 litres (1,824 US gallons; 1,519 Imp gallons), occupy entire wing centre-section between the beams and the centreline and wing-fold ribs. Fuelling point on inboard side of starboard nacelle. For long-range ferrying, fuel tanks can be supplemented by six 920 litre (243 US gallon; 202 Imp gallon) tanks in main cabin. Oil capacity (usable) 23.5 litres (6.2 US gallons; 5.2 Imp gallons). Available, but not specified for US Navy C-2As, is the capability for mounting a flight refuelling probe above the front fuselage.

ACCOMMODATION: Pilot and co-pilot side by side on flight deck, with dual controls. Third crew member is loadmaster. Lavatory and baggage space aft of flight deck. High-strength cargo compartment floor (1,465 kg/m²; 300 lb/sq ft) incorporates flush tracks for attaching tiedown fittings. Cargo door has integral ramp with detachable treadways. Provision for remotely controlled cargo handling winch. Alternative payloads include 28 passengers or 12 litters and attendants. Door

Grumman C-2A Greyhound carrier on-board delivery (COD) transport of second production series

at front of cabin on port side. Although not required for US Navy C-2As, compartment can be adapted to accept Military Airlift Command 463L material handling and support system, with choice of either three 2.74 × 2.24 m (108 × 88 in) master pallets or five 2.24 × 1.37 m (88 × 54 in) modular pallets.

SYSTEMS: Air-conditioning system max pressure differential 0.45 bars (6.5 lb/sq in). Two independent hydraulic systems, pressure 207 bars (3,000 lb/sq in). Flight system has two pumps, each rated at 28.4 litres (7.5 US gallons; 6.2 Imp gallons) per min, with an air/oil separated reservoir, capacity 5 litres (1.31 US gallons; 1.09 Imp gallons). The combined system has two pumps, each rated at 94.6 litres (25 US gallons; 21 Imp gallons) per min, with an air/oil separated reservoir, capacity 12.6 litres (3.34 US gallons; 2.78 Imp gallons). Both systems supply control actuators. One system is also responsible for actuating wing fold system, cargo door, steering damper, arrester hook, brakes, landing gear, windscreen wipers, flaps and auxiliary generator. Liquid oxygen breathing system, with two 10 litre (2.6 US gallon; 2.2 Imp gallon) converters, plus portable unit for cargo or personnel attendant. Primary electrical system supplied by two independent 115/200V 400Hz three-phase engine driven generators, each rated at 60kVA. 28V DC secondary subsystem supplied by two independent transformer-rectifiers. Gas turbine APU drives a 10kVA generator through an auxiliary hydraulic pump for ground operation, and also allows ground starting of the turboprop engines without external equipment. In flight, the 10kVA generator functions as an emergency generator.

AVIONICS: HF, VHF, UHF com; Omega, Doppler radar, AHRS, dual VOR, UHF ADF, LF ADF and weather radar. GEC Avionics standard central air data computer.

DIMENSIONS, EXTERNAL: As for E-2C except:

Length overall	17.32 m (56 ft 10 in)
Height overall	4.84 m (15 ft 10½ in)

DIMENSIONS, INTERNAL:

Cabin: Volume	54.4 m³ (1,920 cu ft)
Cargo compartment: Length	8.38 m (27 ft 6 in)
Max width	2.24 m (7 ft 4 in)
Max height	1.65 m (5 ft 5 in)

AREAS: As for E-2C

WEIGHTS:

Weight empty	16,486 kg (36,346 lb)
Internal fuel weight	5,625 kg (12,400 lb)
Max payload: carrier operation	4,536 kg (10,000 lb)
land operation	6,804 kg (15,000 lb)
Max T-O weight	26,081 kg (57,500 lb)

PERFORMANCE (at max T-O weight):

Max level speed	310 knots (574 km/h; 357 mph)
Max cruising speed	260 knots (482 km/h; 299 mph)
Max rate of climb at S/L	796 m (2,610 ft)/min
Service ceiling, ferry mission	10,210 m (33,500 ft)
Min T-O run	665 m (2,180 ft)
T-O to 15 m (50 ft)	932 m (3,060 ft)
Landing from 15 m (50 ft)	691 m (2,266 ft)
Min landing run	435 m (1,428 ft)
Range with 4,536 kg (10,000 lb) freight	
	over 1,040 nm (1,930 km; 1,200 miles)
Max range, ferry mission	
	1,560 nm (2,891 km; 1,796 miles)

GRUMMAN A-6E INTRUDER
US Navy designations: A-6E, EA-6A and KA-6D

The basic A-6A (originally A2F-1) Intruder was conceived as a carrier-borne low-level attack bomber equipped specifically to deliver nuclear or conventional weapons on targets completely obscured by weather or darkness. Of more than 660 A-6s built, in successive versions, approximately 350 currently equip operational US Navy and Marine Corps squadrons, and three readiness training squadrons.

The A-6A, A-6B and A-6C early models, last described in the 1978-79 *Jane's*, are no longer operational, most available examples having been converted to A-6E/TRAM or EA-6A configuration or into KA-6D tankers (78 converted from A-6A and seven from A-6E, details in 1980-81 *Jane's*). The latest **KA-6D** configuration deletes all weapon systems capability and includes provision for the carriage of five 1,514 litre (400 US gallon; 333 Imp gallon) drop tanks.

The following versions of the A-6 are still in production:

EA-6B Prowler. Advanced electronics development of the EA-6A, described separately.

A-6E Intruder. First produced as an advanced conversion of the A-6A (240 converted) with multi-mode radar and an IBM computer similar to that first tested in the EA-6B. First flight of an A-6E was made on 10 November 1970. First squadron deployment was made in September 1972, and the A-6E was approved officially for service use in December 1972. Procurement of new airframes totalled 195 up to and including FY 1987, of which approx 176 had been delivered by the end of 1987. Current Intruders are to **A-6E/TRAM** (target recognition and attack multisensor) standard, first flown in October 1974. Delivery of fully provisioned TRAM aircraft began on 14 December 1978, and the first carrier deployment was completed successfully in May 1980. All older A-6Es were due to be converted to

Grumman KA-6D in-flight refuelling tanker aircraft (*Katsumi Hinata*)

TRAM standard by 1988. A-6E/TRAM training is carried out using Grumman TC-4C (modified Gulfstream I) aircraft, eight of which are in US Navy/US Marine Corps service.

Fifty A-6Es were equipped to carry McDonnell Douglas Harpoon anti-shipping missiles (four per aircraft). Harpoon-capable A-6Es began to be deployed during 1981, and all subsequent new production and converted aircraft are equipped to carry this missile.

A-6F Intruder II and A-6G. See separate entry.

Boeing Military Airplanes has a contract to develop and manufacture new graphite/epoxy wings for the A-6, to overcome fatigue problems believed to result from operation at heavier weights and higher load factors than were envisaged when the original A-6 was designed. Flight trials, starting in 1987, are expected to lead to production of the new wings for all existing and future A-6s, and to provide an 8,800-hour service life. The initial contract covers manufacture of 120 sets of wings, with options for a total of 336. Up to 102 existing A-6s will be re-winged by Boeing, beginning in early 1988.

The following description applies to the A-6E:

TYPE: Two-seat carrier-based bomber for all-weather close air support, interdiction and deep strike missions.

WINGS: Cantilever mid-wing monoplane, with 25° sweepback at quarter-chord. All-metal structure. Hydraulically operated almost full span leading-edge slats and trailing-edge single-slotted, tracked, Fowler type flaps, with inset spoilers (flaperons) of same span as flaps forward of trailing-edge flaps for roll control. Trailing-edge of each wingtip, outboard of flap, splits to form speed-brakes which project above and below wing when extended. Two short fences above each wing. Outer panels fold upward and inward.

FUSELAGE: Conventional all-metal semi-monocoque structure. Bottom is recessed between engines to carry semi-exposed store.

TAIL UNIT: Cantilever all-metal structure. All-moving tailplane, without separate elevators. Electronic antenna in rear part of fin, immediately above rudder.

LANDING GEAR: Hydraulically retractable tricycle type. Twin-wheel nose unit retracts rearward. Single-wheel main units retract forward and inward into air intake fairings. A-frame arrester hook under rear fuselage.

POWER PLANT: Two 41.4 kN (9,300 lb st) Pratt & Whitney J52-P-8B turbojets. Max internal fuel capacity 8,873 litres (2,344 US gallons; 1,952 Imp gallons). Provision for up to five external fuel tanks under wing and centreline stations, each of 1,135 litres (300 US gallons; 250 Imp gallons) or 1,514 litres (400 US gallons; 333 Imp gallons) capacity. Removable flight refuelling probe projects upward immediately forward of windscreen.

Grumman A-6E/TRAM Intruder of VA-55 'War Horses' Squadron landing on USS *Coral Sea* (*Brian Service*)

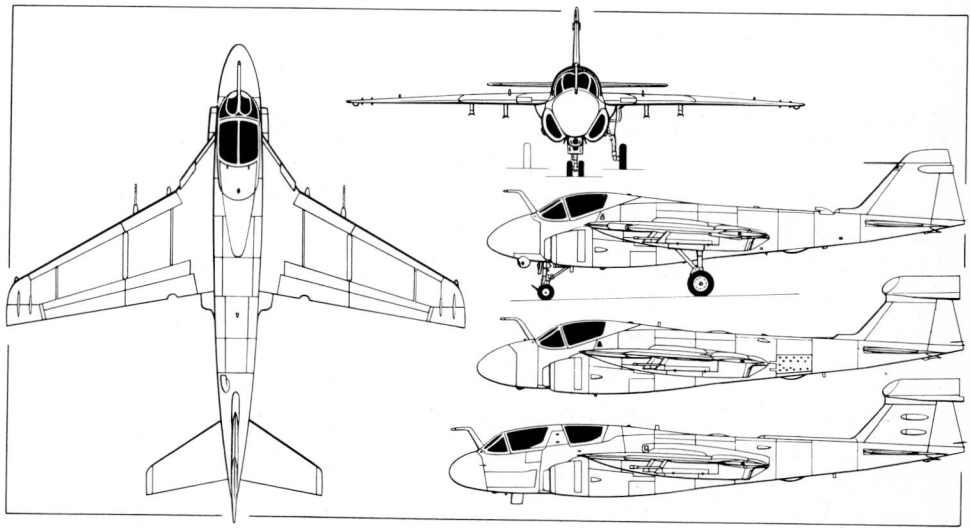

Grumman A-6E/TRAM, with additional side views of EA-6A (centre) and EA-6B (bottom) (*Pilot Press*)

ACCOMMODATION: Crew of two on Martin-Baker GRU7 ejection seats, which can be reclined to reduce fatigue during low-level operations. Bombardier/navigator slightly behind and below pilot to starboard. Hydraulically operated rearward sliding canopy.

SYSTEMS: AiResearch environmental control system for cockpit and avionics bay. Dual hydraulic systems for operation of flight controls, leading-edge and trailing-edge flaps, wingtip speed-brakes, landing gear brakes and cockpit canopy, each rated at 119.4 litres (31.5 US gallons; 26.2 Imp gallons) per min, with air/oil separated reservoir, pressurised at 2.76 bars (40 lb/sq in). One electrically driven hydraulic pump provides restricted flight capability by supplying the tailplane and rudder actuators only, each rated at 11.4 litres (3 US gallons; 2.5 Imp gallons) per min, with internally pressurised reservoir, pressurised at 1.08 bars (15.7 lb/sq in). Electrical system powered by two Garrett constant speed drive units that combine engine starting and electric power generation, each delivering 30kVA. A Garrett ram air turbine, mounted so that it can be projected into the airstream above the port wing root, provides in-flight emergency electric power for essential equipment.

AVIONICS AND EQUIPMENT: Single Norden AN/APQ-148 simultaneous multi-mode nav/attack radar, replaces two earlier radar systems in A-6A. IBM and Fairchild nav/attack computer system and interfacing data converter. Conrac Corporation armament control unit. RCA video tape recorder for post-strike assessment of attacks. Litton AN/ALR-67 radar warning receiver. Norden radar provides simultaneous ground mapping; identification, tracking, and rangefinding of fixed or moving targets; and terrain clearance or terrain following manoeuvres. During 1981-83, it was updated by an improved AMTI (airborne moving target indication) to enhance its ability to detect moving targets. Cockpit displays for pilot and bombardier/navigator; terrain data presented on vertical display indicator ahead of pilot. IBM AN/ASQ-133 solid state digital computer is coupled to A-6E's radar, inertial and Doppler navigational equipment, communications and AFCS. As mission data is measured in flight by onboard aerodynamic and electronic sensors, computer compares data with programmed information, computes differences, and provides corrective data to alter parameters of mission. Fairchild signal data converter accepts analog input data from up to 60 sensors, converting data to a digital output that is fed into nav/attack system computer. Conrac armament control unit (ACU) provides all inputs and outputs necessary to select and release weapons. Master arming switch has a 'practice' position that allows ACU to be cycled up to point of firing command. Kaiser AN/AVA-1 multi-mode display serves as a primary flight aid for navigation, approach, landing and weapons delivery. Basic vertical display indicator (VDI) is a 0.20 m (8 in) CRT which shows a synthetic landscape, sky and electronically generated command flight path that move to simulate the motion of these features as they would be seen by pilot through windscreen. Symbols are superimposed to augment basic attitude data, and for attack a second set of superimposed information provides a target symbol, steering symbol, and release and pull-up markers. A solid state radar data scan converter can provide on the same display an apparent real-world perspective of terrain, ten shades of grey defining terrain elevation at ten different segmented contour intervals up to 8.7 nm (16 km; 10 miles) ahead of aircraft. This makes it possible for pilot to fly in either terrain following or terrain avoidance mode at low altitude. Flight path and attack symbols can be superimposed over terrain elevation data on VDI, enabling pilot to attack while avoiding or following terrain in target area. Kaiser micromesh filter prevents 'washout' of data displayed on VDI in sunlight. Naval pilots use VDI as a primary flight instrument, for precise steering in navigation, weapons cues, progress, and status information during attack. For carrier landing, unit is used as a flight director and, linked to the APQ-148 radar, presents steering information, allowing pilot to select descent angle for final approach. Aircraft fitted with TRAM package have, in addition, an undernose precision-stabilised turret, with a sensor package containing both infra-red and laser equipment; INS updated with Litton AN/ASN-92 CAINS; new communications-navigation-identification (CNI) equipment including AN/ARC-159 UHF, AN/ARN-84 Tacan and AN/APX-72 IFF transponder; and automatic carrier landing capability. Sensor package is integrated with multi-mode radar, providing capability to detect, identify and attack a wide range of targets (as well as view the terrain) under adverse weather conditions, and with improved accuracy, using either conventional or laser guided weapons. Bombardier/navigator operates TRAM system by first acquiring target on his radar screen. He then switches to FLIR (forward looking infra-red) system, using an optical zoom to enlarge target's image. After identifying and selecting his targets, bombardier uses a laser designator to mark target with a laser spot, on which his own laser guided weapons, or those from another aircraft, will home. Using TRAM's laser spot detector, A-6E can also acquire a target being illuminated from another aircraft, or designated by a forward air controller on the ground. GEC Sensors Ltd FLIR system, for night attack navigation, under development in 1988.

ARMAMENT: Five weapon attachment points, each with a 1,633 kg (3,600 lb) capacity (max external stores load 8,165 kg; 18,000 lb). Typical weapon loads are twenty-eight 500 lb bombs in clusters of six, or three 2,000 lb general purpose bombs plus two 1,135 litre (300 US gallon; 250 Imp gallon) drop tanks. AIM-9 Sidewinder missiles can be carried for air-to-air use. Harpoon missile capability added to weapons complement of A-6E/TRAM. The HARM missile has been test flown on the A-6E. Flight and firing tests have been carried out with the AGM-123A Skipper II, also on an A-6E.

DIMENSIONS, EXTERNAL:

Wing span	16.15 m (53 ft 0 in)
Wing mean aerodynamic chord	3.32 m (10 ft 10¾ in)
Width, wings folded	7.72 m (25 ft 4 in)
Length overall	16.69 m (54 ft 9 in)
Height overall	4.93 m (16 ft 2 in)
Tailplane span	6.21 m (20 ft 4½ in)
Wheel track	3.32 m (10 ft 10½ in)
Wheelbase	5.24 m (17 ft 2¼ in)

AREAS:

Wings, gross	49.1 m^2 (528.9 sq ft)
Flaperons (total)	3.81 m^2 (41.0 sq ft)
Trailing-edge flaps (total)	9.66 m^2 (104.0 sq ft)
Leading-edge slats (total)	4.63 m^2 (49.8 sq ft)
Fin	5.85 m^2 (62.93 sq ft)
Rudder	1.52 m^2 (16.32 sq ft)
Tailplane	10.87 m^2 (117.0 sq ft)

WEIGHTS AND LOADING:

Weight empty	12,132 kg (26,746 lb)
Fuel load: internal	7,230 kg (15,939 lb)
external (five tanks)	4,558 kg (10,050 lb)
Max external load	8,165 kg (18,000 lb)
Max T-O weight: catapult	26,580 kg (58,600 lb)
field	27,397 kg (60,400 lb)
Max zero-stores weight	20,166 kg (44,460 lb)
Max landing weight: carrier	16,329 kg (36,000 lb)
field	20,411 kg (45,000 lb)
Max wing loading	557. kg/m^2 (114.2 lb/sq ft)

PERFORMANCE (no stores, except where stated):

Never-exceed speed	700 knots (1,297 km/h; 806 mph)
Max level speed at S/L	560 knots (1,037 km/h; 644 mph)
Cruising speed at optimum altitude	412 knots (763 km/h; 474 mph)
Approach speed	110 knots (204 km/h; 127 mph)
Stalling speed: flaps up	142 knots (264 km/h; 164 mph)
flaps down	98 knots (182 km/h; 113 mph)
Max rate of climb at S/L	2,323 m (7,620 ft)/min
Rate of climb at S/L, one engine out	646 m (2,120 ft)/min
Service ceiling	12,925 m (42,400 ft)
Service ceiling, one engine out	6,400 m (21,000 ft)
Min T-O run	1,185 m (3,890 ft)
T-O to 15 m (50 ft)	1,390 m (4,560 ft)
Landing from 15 m (50 ft)	774 m (2,540 ft)
Min landing run	521 m (1,710 ft)
Range with max military load	878 nm (1,627 km; 1,011 miles)
Ferry range with max external fuel: tanks retained	2,380 nm (4,410 km; 2,740 miles)
tanks jettisoned when empty	2,818 nm (5,222 km; 3,245 miles)

GRUMMAN A-6F INTRUDER II and A-6G

Under a contract awarded in June 1984, Grumman initiated a major update programme for the Intruder, known originally as the A-6E Upgrade. Norden Systems was chosen to develop a new Ku band APQ-173 multi-mode radar to replace the A-6E's AN/APQ-148. The new radar features increased range for target recognition, acquisition and tracking with standoff weapon capability; inverse synthetic aperture radar capability for long-range ship classification; an air-to-air mode for use with AIM-9L/M Sidewinder or AIM-120 AMRAAM air-to-air self defence missiles, for which an additional stores station is provided on each outer wing panel; and improved reliability and maintainability. To accommodate the increased information available from the radar, the A-6F would have five multi-function display units in a redesigned cockpit. The pilot would have vertical and horizontal situation displays; the bombardier/navigator would have forward looking infra-red (FLIR), radar and weapons management displays. The MFDs, two AYK-14 tactical computers, ASW-27 two-way data link and signal data recording and maintenance aid system and Kaiser Electronics HUD, which replaces the A-6E's optical sight, would be common with those of the F-14D Tomcat.

Other additions and improvements to be incorporated in the A-6F included an ALR-67 radar warning system; Collins ARC-182 VHF/UHF airborne radio communication system; ARN-118 Tacan; Litton ASN-130 inertial navigation system; ALQ-165 airborne self-protection jammer; replacement of the APN-153 Doppler radar with a Collins global positioning system; improved tactical software; standard common air data computer; FLIR autotracker for automatic target lock-on and tracking; improved bomb racks; two 40kVA generators; windscreen rain removal system; and extension of the databus for weapons pylons to accommodate Maverick, Harpoon and HARM missiles.

General Electric was selected to provide a 48.0 kN (10,800 lb st) non-afterburning version of its F404 turbofan, designated F404-GE-400D, for the A-6F, which also has a Garrett APU, aircraft mounted accessory drive on each engine, revised fuel system with self-sealing armoured fuel lines, fire detecting stations throughout the airframe, and void-filling foam between the outer shell of the airframe and the fuel tanks. Total internal fuel load, in three fuselage and four wing tanks, is 7,228 kg (15,936 lb).

Design work on the A-6F began in July 1984, and construction of a prototype was started during 1985. The programme called for five development prototypes, the first of which (162183) first flew on 25 August 1987 and the second on 23 November 1987. Funding for the A-6F programme was withdrawn by Congress in FY 1989 US defence budget cuts, and a number of alternatives was being considered, including the upgrading of a total of 167 A-6Es to **A-6G** configuration. The A-6G would include all of the planned digital avionics upgrades of the A-6F, but would be powered by J52-P-408/409 turbofans, obviating the need for major airframe redesign. The existing A-6F prototypes have been placed in storage pending an A-6G decision.

GRUMMAN EA-6B PROWLER

The EA-6B is an advanced electronics development of the EA-6A for which Grumman received a prototype design and development contract in the Autumn of 1966. Except for a 1.37 m (4 ft 6 in) longer nose section and large fin pod, the external configuration of this version is the same as that of the basic A-6.

The longer nose section provides accommodation for a total crew of four, the two additional crewmen being necessary to operate the more advanced ECM equipment. This comprises high-powered electronic jammers and modern computer-directed receivers, which provided the US Navy with its first aircraft designed and built specifically for tactical electronic warfare. The prototype EA-6B flew for the first time on 25 May 1968.

Deliveries of the first 12 production aircraft began in January 1971, and a total of 149 EA-6Bs had been ordered up to and including FY 1988, of which 127 had been delivered. It is planned to increase the Prowler force by ordering nine aircraft per year from FYs 1989 to 1992 inclusive.

ICAP (increased capability) versions of the EA-6B, with substantially increased jamming efficiency, are now standard. The first 21 production EA-6Bs were modified by Grumman to ICAP-1 configuration, and new-built aircraft up to 1983 were also to this standard. Modifications included an expanded onboard tactical jamming system with eight frequency bands, reduced response time, and a new multi-format display. In addition, an automatic carrier landing system (ACLS) to permit carrier recovery in zero-zero weather, a new defensive electronic countermeasures system (DECM) and new communications-navigation-identification (CNI) equipment are installed.

The prototype of a more advanced ICAP-2 version, with further improved jamming capability, made its first flight on 24 June 1980, and aircraft delivered since early 1984 have been to this higher standard. Each of the five pods carried under the EA-6B's wings and fuselage originally generated signals within a single frequency band. An ICAP-2 exciter in each pod generates signals in any one of seven frequency bands, and each pod can jam in two different bands simultaneously. ICAP-2 attained IOC in 1984 on new aircraft; some early EA-6Bs are being updated to ICAP-2 standard.

To follow this, an ADVCAP (advanced capability) programme was initiated in 1983, when Litton Industries' Amecom Division, with Texas Instruments and ITT as subcontractors, received a contract to develop a new receiver/processor group for the EA-6B's tactical jamming system. The ADVCAP EA-6B will carry HARM anti-radar missiles or drop tanks on two inboard underwing stations, with an additional outboard station under each wing for ECM pods. The fin pod will be larger than on earlier EA-6Bs, and it will have an antenna group beneath the rear fuselage. Deliveries of production EA-6Bs to ADVCAP standard was expected to begin in 1989, with retrofit of up to 100 ICAP-2 Prowlers starting in 1991.

Twelve US Navy squadrons (VAQ-129, 130, 131, 132, 133, 134, 135, 136, 137, 138, 139 and 140) were equipped with the Prowler by 1987. The first detachment of US Marine Corps Prowler squadron VMAQ-2 began training on the EA-6B in September 1977 at NAS Whidbey Island, Washington, and the detachment deployed in late 1978. Two additional detachments have since completed training, and at least one is deployed at all times. Deployment with reserve units is scheduled to begin in FY 1989.

As part of the US Navy's vehicle improvement programme (VIP) for the EA-6B, Grumman was modifying one aircraft in 1988 as a VIP testbed for airframe changes aimed at improving stall and manoeuvring limitations. Narrow triangular glove strakes are being added immediately forward of the wingroot; the tail fin is being extended

Grumman EA-6B Prowler ICAP-2 tactical jamming aircraft

0.46 m (1 ft 6 in) above the fin pod; wingtip speed brakes are modified to operate also as ailerons, deflecting with the flaperons for roll control; droop of the inboard and outboard leading-edge slats is increased; and the rear undersurface of the wings, including the trailing-edge flaps, is reconstructed. The VIP testbed aircraft, which is also refitted with more powerful (53.4 kN; 12,000 lb st) J52-P-409 turbojets, is due to make its first flight in late 1989.

The description of the standard A-6E Intruder applies also to the EA-6B, except as follows:

TYPE: Four-seat carrier- or land-based advanced ECM aircraft.

WINGS: As for A-6E, but reinforced to cater for increased gross weight, fatigue life and 5.5g load factor.

FUSELAGE: As for A-6E, but reinforcement of underfuselage structure in areas of arrester hook and landing gear attachments, and lengthened by 1.37 m (4 ft 6 in).

TAIL UNIT: As for A-6E, except for provision of a large fin-tip pod to house ECM equipment.

LANDING GEAR: As for A-6E, except for reinforcement of attachments, A-frame arrester hook, and upgrading of structure to cater for increased gross weight.

POWER PLANT: Two Pratt & Whitney J52-P-408 turbojets, each rated at 49.8 kN (11,200 lb st).

ACCOMMODATION: Crew of four under two separate upward opening canopies. Martin-Baker GRUEA 7 ejection seats for flight crew. The two additional crewmen are ECM Officers to operate the ALQ-99 equipment from the rear cockpit. Either ECMO can independently detect, assign, adjust and monitor the jammers. The ECMO in the starboard front seat is responsible for communications, navigation, defensive ECM and chaff dispensing.

SYSTEMS: Generally as for A-6E.

AVIONICS: AN/ALQ-99F tactical jamming system, in five integrally powered pods, with a total of 10 jamming transmitters. Each pod covers one of seven frequency bands. Sensitive surveillance receivers in the fin-tip pod for long-range detection of radars; emitter information is fed to a central digital computer (AYK-14 in ICAP-2 aircraft) that processes the signals for display and recording. Detection, identification, direction-finding and jammer-set-on sequence can be performed automatically or with manual assistance from crew. PRB Associates AN/TSQ-142 tactical mission support system. Teledyne Systems AN/ASN-123 navigation system with digital display group.

ARMAMENT: Originally unarmed, but currently being equipped to carry Texas Instruments AGM-88A HARM anti-radar missiles underwing (due for introduction in August 1988). Four underwing hardpoints on ICAP-2 aircraft, six on ADVCAP EA-6B.

DIMENSIONS, EXTERNAL: As for A-6E, except:
Width, wings folded	7.87 m (25 ft 10 in)
Length overall	18.24 m (59 ft 10 in)
Height overall	4.95 m (16 ft 3 in)
Wheelbase	5.23 m (17 ft 2 in)

WEIGHTS AND LOADING:
Weight empty	14,588 kg (32,162 lb)
Internal fuel load	6,995 kg (15,422 lb)
Max external fuel load	4,547 kg (10,025 lb)
T-O weight from carrier in standoff jamming configuration (5 ECM pods)	24,703 kg (54,461 lb)
T-O weight from field in ferry range configuration (max internal and external fuel)	27,492 kg (60,610 lb)
Max T-O weight, catapult or field	29,483 kg (65,000 lb)
Max zero-fuel weight	17,708 kg (39,039 lb)
Max landing weight, carrier or field	20,638 kg (45,500 lb)
Max wing loading	600.5 kg/m² (123 lb/sq ft)

PERFORMANCE (A: no stores; B: 5 ECM pods):
Never-exceed speed		710 knots (1,315 km/h; 817 mph)
Max level speed at S/L:		
	A	566 knots (1,048 km/h; 651 mph)
	B	530 knots (982 km/h; 610 mph)
Cruising speed at optimum altitude:		
	A, B	418 knots (774 km/h; 481 mph)

Stalling speed, flaps up, max power:		
	A	124 knots (230 km/h; 143 mph)
Stalling speed, flaps down, max power:		
	A	84 knots (156 km/h; 97 mph)
Max rate of climb at S/L:	A	3,932 m (12,900 ft)/min
	B	3,057 m (10,030 ft)/min
Rate of climb at S/L, one engine out:		
	A	1,189 m (3,900 ft)/min
Service ceiling:	A	12,550 m (41,200 ft)
	B	11,580 m (38,000 ft)
Service ceiling, one engine out:	A	8,930 m (29,300 ft)
T-O run:	B	814 m (2,670 ft)
T-O to 15 m (50 ft):	A	869 m (2,850 ft)
	B	1,065 m (3,495 ft)
Landing from 15 m (50 ft):	A	823 m (2,700 ft)
Landing run:	A	579 m (1,900 ft)
	B	655 m (2,150 ft)
Range with max external load, 5% reserves plus 20 min at S/L:	B	955 nm (1,769 km; 1,099 miles)
Ferry range with max external fuel:		
tanks retained		1,756 nm (3,254 km; 2,022 miles)
tanks jettisoned when empty		
		2,085 nm (3,861 km; 2,399 miles)

GRUMMAN TOMCAT
US Navy designation: F-14

The Tomcat was declared winner of the US Navy's VFX carrier-based fighter competition on 15 January 1969, and the first of 12 development aircraft made its initial flight on 21 December 1970. Originally, the planned programme was intended to provide 497 Navy Tomcats, including the 12 development aircraft, but this total is now to be increased considerably, extending production into the 1990s. By the end of 1987 the US Navy was scheduled to have 28 Tomcat squadrons, including four reserve and two training squadrons, operating from 12 aircraft carriers and the Naval Air Stations at Miramar, California, Oceana, Virginia, and Dallas, Texas.

Production versions are as follows:

F-14A. Initial version, deployed from October 1972, initially with USN squadrons VF-1 and VF-2. Total of 557, including the 12 R & D aircraft, delivered to US Navy by

April 1987, when production of this version ended. Early aircraft powered by TF30-P-412A turbofans, but those delivered from FY 1983 (final 102 aircraft) have improved TF30-P-414As of the same rating. Thirty-two are being upgraded to F-14A(Plus) standard, with F110 engines. In addition, 79 F-14As were delivered to Iran in 1976-78; those retained the Phoenix weapon system but had slightly different ECM equipment from US Navy Tomcats.

F-14A(Plus). Interim updated version, now in production pending introduction of F-14D. Development began in July 1984, when Grumman was awarded a $984 million fixed price contract for an F-14A update programme which provided for development of the F-14A(Plus) 'Super Tomcat' with F110-GE-400 engines but otherwise mostly unchanged, and for the F-14D with F110-GE-400s, digital avionics and a new radar. Grumman is prime contractor for the engine and avionics upgrades, with General Electric and Hughes Aircraft as subcontractors. The F110-GE-400 is rated at 62.3 kN (14,000 lb st) dry and 102.75 kN (23,100 lb st) with max afterburning, and offers 82 per cent parts commonality with the F110-GE-100 engine for the USAF's F-15s and F-16s. A 1.27 m (4 ft 2 in) plug is inserted in the afterburner section to match the engine to F-14A inlet position and airframe contours, and only secondary structure requires modification to accept the new engine. Operational improvements conferred by the new engine include unrestricted throttle movement throughout the aircraft's flight envelope and fewer compressor stalls.

Grumman's full scale development programme involves five aircraft, including the F-14B prototype (157986) which first flew with definitive F110-GE-400 engines on 29 September 1986 as part of the F-14A(Plus) programme. Three, the first of which was flown on 24 November 1987, will be used for avionics and radar development, in conjunction with a TA-3B Skywarrior aircraft. One will be completed to full F-14D standard and will join that programme after serving on the F-14A(Plus) development programme. The development schedule includes some 36 months of flight testing. Production of the F-14A(Plus) followed completion of the F-14A programme, with the first of 38 aircraft flown for the first time on 14 November 1987 and delivered to VF-101 at NAS Oceana, Virginia, on 11 April 1988. IOC with two US Navy fleet squadrons is anticipated in early 1989, and completion of F-14A(Plus) deliveries by May 1990. In addition, 32 F-14As will be upgraded to F-14A(Plus) standard, with F110 engines.

F-14D. The F-14D upgrade modifies some 60 per cent of the F-14A's analog avionics, providing new weapons management, navigation, displays and control functions, with digital bus integration of the Litton ALR-67 threat warning and recognition system, Westinghouse/ITT ALQ-165 airborne self protection jammer (ASPJ), joint tactical information distribution system (JTIDS), infra-red search and track sensor (IRST) and television camera set (TCS), with emphasis on hardware and software commonality with F/A-18 and latest A-6 programmes. The new Hughes radar, designated APG-71, is based on the AN/AWG-9 radar, with improved ECCM capability and incorporating monopulse angle tracking, digital scan control, target identification and raid assessment. The APG-71 features non-co-operative target identification and is able to counter sophisticated ECM by means of a low-sidelobe antenna and sidelobe blanking guard channel, frequency agility, and a new high-speed digital signal processor based on elements of the USAF's multi-stage improvement programme (MSIP) of the F-15's APG-70 radar. Provision is also made for integration of the

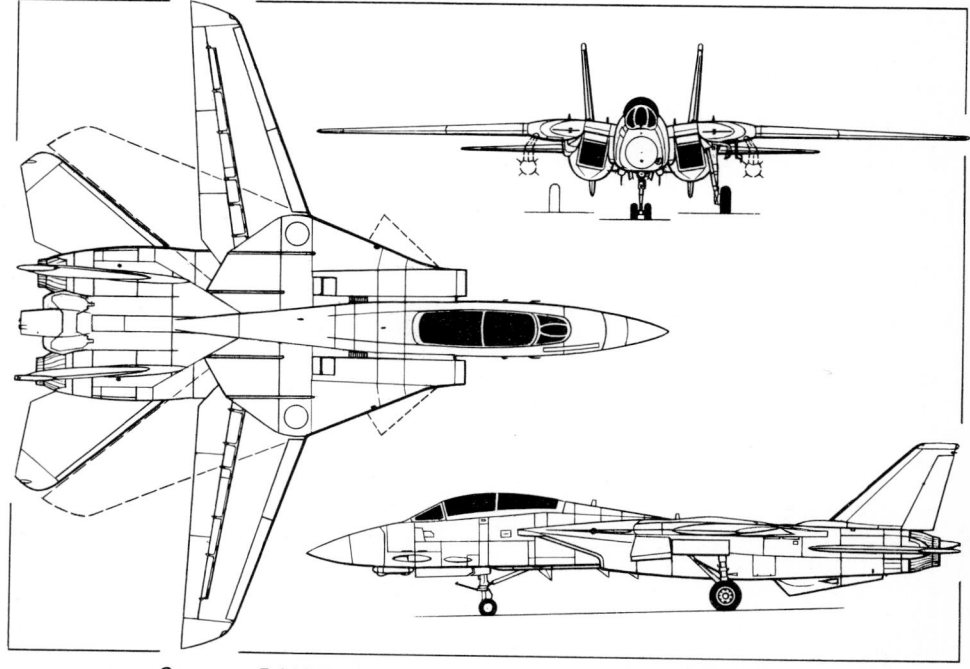

Grumman F-14A Tomcat carrier based multi-role fighter (*Pilot Press*)

AMRAAM missile. The F-14D is equipped with Martin-Baker Navy aircrew common ejection seats (NACES).

A total of 127 new-production F-14Ds is planned, of which the first seven were funded in FY 1988 and a further 12 in FY 1989. Deliveries are due to begin in March 1990. In addition, approximately 400 F-14A and F-14A(Plus) aircraft are to be remanufactured to F-14D standard, beginning in FY 1990.

The F110-GE-400 powered F-14A(Plus) and F-14D are expected to show significant performance benefits resulting from the engine's 43 per cent increase in afterburning and 37 per cent increase in military (non-afterburning) thrust over the Pratt & Whitney TF30-P-414A engine. Specific excess energy is increased by 20 per cent, afterburning specific fuel consumption is reduced by 30 per cent, and deck launch intercept radius and combat air patrol time on station are expected to be increased by 62 and 34 per cent respectively, as a result of lower fuel burns and the F110 engined Tomcat's ability to be launched without use of afterburner. Time to 10,670 m (35,000 ft) is expected to be reduced by 61 per cent, and acceleration time by 43 per cent.

The following description applies to the current operational F-14A:

TYPE: Two-seat carrier based multi-role fighter.

WINGS: Variable geometry mid-wing monoplane, with 20° of leading-edge sweep in the fully forward position and 68° when fully swept. Oversweep position of 75° for carrier stowage. Wing position is programmed automatically for optimum performance throughout the flight regime, but manual override is provided. A short movable wing outer panel, needing only a comparatively light pivot structure, results from the wide fuselage and fixed centre-section 'glove', with pivot points 2.72 m (8 ft 11 in) from the centreline of the airframe. The inboard wing sections, adjacent to the fuselage, arc upward slightly to minimise cross-sectional area and wave drag, and consist basically of a one-piece electron beam-welded assembly, 6.70 m (22 ft) in span, made from Ti-6Al-4V titanium alloy. Small canard surfaces, known as glove vanes, swing out from the leading-edge of the fixed portion of the wing, to a maximum of 15° in relation to the leading-edge, as Mach number is increased. Spoilers on upper surfaces of wing. Stabilisation in pitch, provided by the canard surfaces, leaves the differential tailplane free to perform its primary control function. Trailing-edge flaps extend over almost entire span. Leading-edge slats.

FUSELAGE: All-metal semi-monocoque structure, with machined frames, main longerons of titanium, and light alloy stressed skin. The centre-fuselage section is a simple, fuel-carrying box structure; forward fuselage section comprises cockpit and upward hinged nose giving access to radar. The aft section has a tapered aerofoil shape to minimise drag, with a fuel dump pipe projecting from the rear. Speed brakes located on the upper and lower surfaces, between the bases of the vertical tail fins. Rear fuselage and vertical tail surfaces manufactured by Fairchild Republic.

TAIL UNIT: Twin vertical fins, mounted at the rear of each engine nacelle. Fins and rudders of light alloy honeycomb sandwich. Outward canted ventral fin under each nacelle. The all-flying multi-spar horizontal surfaces have skins of boron epoxy composite material and honeycomb trailing-edges.

LANDING GEAR: Retractable tricycle type. Twin-wheel nose unit and single-wheel main units retract forward, main units inward into bottom of engine air intake trunks. Original beryllium brakes were replaced with Goodyear lightweight carbon brakes from Spring 1981. Arrester hook under rear fuselage, housed in small ventral fairing. Nose-tow catapult attachment on nose unit.

ENGINE INTAKES: Straight two-dimensional external compression inlets. A double-hinged ramp extends down from the top of each intake, and these are programmed to provide the correct airflow to the engines automatically under all flight conditions. Each intake is canted slightly away from the fuselage, from which it is separated by some 0.25 m (10 in) to allow sufficient clearance for the turbulent fuselage boundary layer to pass between fuselage and intake without causing turbulence within the intake. Engine inlet ducts and aft nacelle structures are manufactured by Rohr Corporation. The inlet duct, constructed largely of aluminium alloy honeycomb, is about 4.27 m (14 ft) long; the aft nacelle structure, of bonded aluminium alloy honeycomb and conventional aluminium alloy sheet, is about 4.88 m (16 ft) in length.

POWER PLANT: Early aircraft have two Pratt & Whitney TF30-P-412A turbofans of 93 kN (20,900 lb st) with afterburning, mounted in ducts which open to provide 180° access for ease of maintenance. F-14As delivered from 1984-87 have TF30-P-414As of the same rating. Garrett ATS200-50 air turbine starter. Integral fuel tanks in outer wings, each with capacity of 1,117 litres (295 US gallons; 246 Imp gallons); between engines in rear fuselage, with capacity of 2,453 litres (648 US gallons; 539 Imp gallons); and forward of wing carry-through structure, capacity 2,616 litres (691 US gallons; 575 Imp gallons); plus two feeder tanks with combined capacity of 1,726 litres (456 US gallons; 380 Imp gallons). Total internal fuel capacity 9,029 litres (2,385 US gallons; 1,986 Imp gallons). An external auxiliary fuel tank can be carried beneath each intake trunk, each containing 1,011 litres (267 US gallons; 222 Imp gallons). Retractable flight refuelling probe on starboard side of fuselage near front cockpit.

Grumman F-14A Tomcat of US Navy Squadron VF-31 from USS *Forrestal (Alex Hay Porteous)*

ACCOMMODATION: Pilot and naval flight officer seated in tandem on Martin-Baker GRU7A rocket assisted zero/zero ejection seats, under a one-piece bubble canopy, hinged at the rear and offering all-round view.

AVIONICS: Hughes AN/AWG-9 weapons control system, with ability to detect airborne targets at ranges of more than 65-170 nm (120-315 km; 75-195 miles) according to their size, and ability to track 24 enemy targets and attack six of them simultaneously at varied altitudes and distances. Fairchild AN/AWG-15F fire control set; CP-1066/A central air data computer; CP-1050/A computer signal data converter; AN/ASW-27B digital data link; AN/APX-76(V) IFF interrogator; AN/APX-72 IFF transponder; AN/ASA-79 multiple display indicator group; Kaiser Aerospace AN/AVG-12 vertical and head-up display system. AN/ARC-51 and AN/ARC-159 UHF com; AN/ARR-69 UHF auxiliary receiver; KY-28 cryptographic system; LS-460/B intercom; AN/ASN-92(V) INS; A/A24G39 AHRS; AN/APN-154 beacon augmentor; AN/APN-194(V) radar altimeter; ARA-63A receiver-decoder; AN/ARN-84 micro Tacan; AN/ARA-50 UHF ADF; AN/APR-27/50 radar receiver; AN/APR-25/45 radar warning set. TV optical unit in undernose pod.

ARMAMENT AND OPERATIONAL EQUIPMENT: One General Electric M61A-1 Vulcan 20 mm gun mounted in the port side of forward fuselage, with 675 rounds of ammunition. Four Sparrow air-to-air missiles mounted partially submerged in the underfuselage, or four Phoenix missiles carried on special pallets which attach to the bottom of the fuselage. Two wing pylons, one under each fixed wing section, can carry four Sidewinder missiles or two additional Sparrow or Phoenix missiles with two Sidewinders. Various combinations of missiles and bombs. ECM equipment includes Goodyear AN/ALE-29 and AN/ALE-39 chaff and flare dispensers, with integral jammers. Since 1979, Northrop Corporation has been manufacturing television camera sets (TCSs) for installation on F-14As. The TCS is a closed-circuit TV system, offering both wide-angle (acquisition) and telescopic (identification) fields of view. Mounted beneath the nose of the F-14A, the TCS automatically searches for, acquires and locks on to distant targets, displaying them on monitors for the pilot and flight officer. By allowing early identification of targets, the system permits crews to make combat decisions earlier than was possible previously. Small undernose pod for Sanders AN/ALQ-100/126 deception jamming system, relocated under camera package of aircraft with Northrop TCS. During 1980-81, a total of 49 F-14As were allocated to carry TARPS (tactical air reconnaissance pod system), containing a KS-87B frame camera, KA-99 low altitude panoramic camera, and AN/AAD-5 infra-red reconnaissance equipment, on underbelly attachment.

DIMENSIONS, EXTERNAL:

Wing span: unswept	19.54 m (64 ft 1½ in)
swept	11.65 m (38 ft 2½ in)
overswept	10.15 m (33 ft 3½ in)
Wing aspect ratio	7.28
Length overall	19.10 m (62 ft 8 in)
Height overall	4.88 m (16 ft 0 in)
Tailplane span	9.97 m (32 ft 8½ in)
Distance between fin tips	3.25 m (10 ft 8 in)
Wheel track	5.00 m (16 ft 5 in)
Wheelbase	7.02 m (23 ft 0½ in)

AREAS:

Wings, gross	52.49 m^2 (565.0 sq ft)
Leading-edge slats (total)	4.29 m^2 (46.2 sq ft)
Trailing-edge flaps (total)	9.87 m^2 (106.3 sq ft)
Spoilers (total)	1.97 m^2 (21.2 sq ft)
Horizontal tail surfaces (total)	13.01 m^2 (140.0 sq ft)
Fins (total)	7.90 m^2 (85.0 sq ft)
Rudders (total)	3.06 m^2 (33.0 sq ft)

WEIGHTS (P-414A engines):

Weight empty	18,191 kg (40,104 lb)
Fuel (usable): internal	7,348 kg (16,200 lb)
external	1,724 kg (3,800 lb)
Max external weapon load	6,577 kg (14,500 lb)
T-O weight, 'clean'	26,632 kg (58,715 lb)
T-O weight with 4 Sparrow	27,086 kg (59,714 lb)
T-O weight with 6 Phoenix	32,098 kg (70,764 lb)
Max T-O weight	33,724 kg (74,349 lb)
Design landing weight	23,510 kg (51,830 lb)

PERFORMANCE:

Max level speed: at height	Mach 2.34 (1,342 knots; 2,485 km/h; 1,544 mph)
at low level	Mach 1.2 (792 knots; 1,468 km/h; 912 mph)
Max cruising speed	400-550 knots (741-1,019 km/h; 460-633 mph)
*Carrier approach speed	134 knots (248 km/h; 154 mph)
*Stalling speed	115 knots (213 km/h; 132 mph)
Max rate of climb at S/L	over 9,140 m (30,000 ft)/min
Service ceiling	above 15,240 m (50,000 ft)
Min T-O distance	427 m (1,400 ft)
Min landing distance	884 m (2,900 ft)
Max range with external fuel	approx 1,735 nm (3,220 km; 2,000 miles)

**carrier landing design gross weight*

GRUMMAN OV-1/RV-1 MOHAWK

Although production of the OV-1 Mohawk surveillance aircraft ended in the early 1970s, those still in US Army service have undergone a succession of conversion and modernisation programmes. The most recent of these to be completed, in FY 1987, was the conversion of 78 OV-1Bs (SLAR reconnaissance) and OV-1Cs (infra-red and photographic reconnaissance) to **OV-1D** (interchangeable SLAR/IR) configuration, to augment 37 aircraft built from the outset as OV-1Ds. Of these 115 aircraft, about 95 remained in service in 1988. Specific mission avionics and equipment installed in the OV-1D include AN/AAS-24 infra-red detection system, AN/ALQ-147A(V)1 infra-red jammer, AN/APN-171 radar altimeter, AN/APR-39(V)2 or AN/APR-44 radar warning receiver, AN/APS-94F side looking airborne radar, AN/APX-72 IFF transponder, AN/ARN-103 Tacan, AN/ASN-86 inertial navigation system, AN/AYA-10 signal processor, and a KS-113A photographic survey system with KA-60C and KA-76 cameras.

In an earlier programme known as Quick Look II, completed in 1983, a total of 28 other OV-1Bs were converted as **RV-1D** electronic warfare aircraft equipped with AN/ALQ-133 jamming ECM, AN/USQ-61 digital data set, AN/USM-393 simulation set, AN/ALM-153/154 test sets, and an AN/MSA-34 antenna group.

Various updates and improvements are being made to US Army OV-1Ds to enable them to continue operating effectively into the late 1990s. Funding for current updates, initiated in FY 1986, covers wing and fuselage strengthening of 18 aircraft to increase fatigue life from 7,000 to 12,000 hours, conducting of fatigue testing and monitoring, and the fitting of one aircraft with new com/nav equipment and cockpit display systems. The com/nav 'prototype' was due to be delivered to the Army for evaluation during 1988, and Grumman anticipates orders to modify at least 58 more OV-1Ds to this standard. Airframe strengthening of 20 more OV/RV-1s was approved in the FY 1987 budget, making 38 aircraft scheduled for this treatment, and actual conversion of the first ten of these was also beginning in 1988.

The US Army has flight tested in recent years an OV-1D fitted with more powerful engines, and Grumman has tested improved stall warning and electrical power/anti-icing systems for the Mohawk.

GRUMMAN (GENERAL DYNAMICS) RAVEN

US Air Force designation: EF-111A

The programme to convert 42 General Dynamics F-111As into EF-111A electronic warfare aircraft has been described in the 1986-87 and previous editions of *Jane's*.

Grumman X-29A FSW (forward swept wing) technology demonstrator

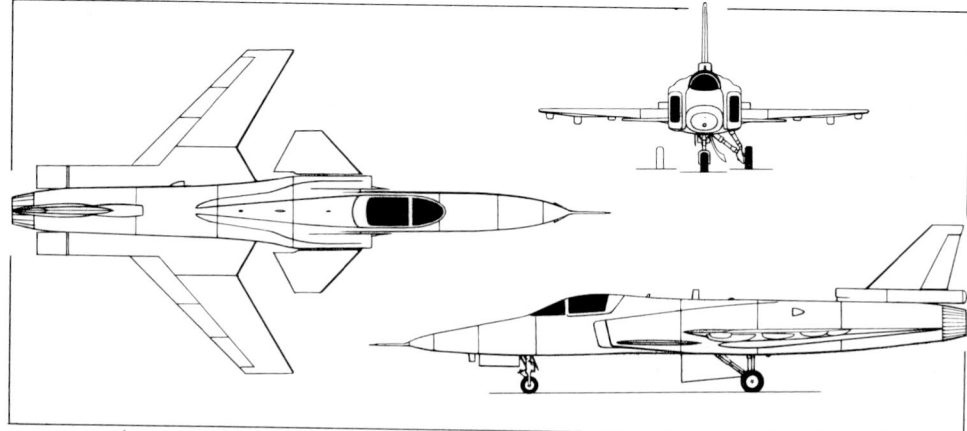

Grumman X-29A FSW demonstrator (General Electric F404-GE-400 turbofan) *(Pilot Press)*

The contract to upgrade the EF-111A's AN/ALQ-99 tactical jamming system, mentioned briefly in the 1987-88 *Jane's*, was terminated on 20 May 1988 due to delays and cost overruns. Alternative upgrade programmes were then being considered, including an improved radar warning system and the use of ECM pods and/or expendable decoys.

In January 1987 the US Air Force awarded Grumman a contract for an EF-111A avionics modernisation programme (AMP). The upgrade will include improved cockpit control-display functions, enhanced terrain-following and navigation radars, installation of a ring laser gyro inertial navigation system and global positioning system (GPS), and the addition of two digital computers using two dual-redundant multiplex buses to provide digital interfacing. An FSD trials aircraft was scheduled to fly in January 1989, with delivery of production modernisation kits following a year later.

GRUMMAN MODEL 712 FORWARD SWEPT WING DEMONSTRATOR
US Air Force designation: X-29A

Grumman has been exploring for some time the benefits offered by a forward swept wing (FSW) design, and conducted a series of wind tunnel test programmes that were funded by the Defense Advanced Research Projects Agency. Monitored by the US Air Force, these programmes verified the aerodynamic benefits of such a design. As a result, Grumman was awarded an $80 million contract in 1981 to build two single-seat FSW demonstrator aircraft that would be designated X-29A. Construction of the airframes began in January 1982, and on 14 December 1984 the first X-29A made its initial flight from NASA's Ames-Dryden Flight Research Center at Edwards AFB, California. On 12 March 1985 the aircraft was delivered to USAF Aeronautical Systems Division, which handed it over to NASA, and it made its first flight with a NASA pilot in command on 2 April. By the end of first phase testing in December 1986 the X-29A had made 104 flights, totalling 92.6 flight hours, and had attained a maximum speed of Mach 1.46, a maximum loading of 5.7g and a maximum 21° angle of attack. Before the second phase began in June 1987, a calibrated engine with two thrust measuring systems for performance data was installed, together with a NASA noseboom calibrated for air data measurements and upgraded instrumentation. Performance and asymmetric load testing has been completed, the 200th flight was made on 8 June 1988, and the second phase of the programme was scheduled to be completed that Summer.

Funding has been allocated for preparation of the No. 2 aircraft for high angle of attack testing by the US Air Force. Work on design modifications and installation of flight test instrumentation and an anti-spin parachute began in the Summer of 1987. The aircraft was due to be delivered in October 1988 and is expected to fly for the first time in March 1989. The test programme will include some 45-60 flights. These will expand the X-29A's angle of attack envelope to 40° initially, and later to a maximum of 70°. NASA anticipates a flying rate of two flights per week when both X-29As are operational.

Grumman's FSW design offers the promise of a new generation of tactical aircraft that will be smaller, lighter in weight, less costly, but more efficient than contemporary fighters. The aerodynamic advantages of forward wing sweep include improved manoeuvrability, with virtually spin-proof characteristics, better low-speed handling, and reduced stalling speeds. In addition, such aircraft have the advantage of lower drag across the entire operational envelope, particularly at speeds approaching Mach 1, which will permit the use of a less powerful engine.

With an FSW aircraft of conventional (ie metal) construction, when aerodynamic stresses flex the wing in flight, this increases the angle of attack (and hence the lift) of the outer wing sections. This, in turn, increases the air loads and causes further deformation of the wings; higher speeds raise these forces until they eventually exceed the strength of the wing structure. The advent of advanced composite materials, exceptionally strong and light in weight, has made possible an FSW tailored to eliminate twisting when the wing bends. The single-seat X-29As have a thin supercritical wing of metal/composite construction, with a variable camber trailing-edge that changes the shape of the wing to match flight conditions. A close-coupled foreplane reduces supersonic trim drag. The aircraft is designed to be highly (35 per cent) unstable longitudinally. A standard Northrop F-5A forward fuselage and nose landing gear, and many off-the-shelf components such as F-16 main landing gear and control surface actuators, were utilised to reduce costs. Sufficient flexibility is being built into the programme to allow for the flight testing of other advanced concepts relating to cockpits, multi-axis thrust vectoring exhaust nozzles, weapons carriage, and techniques to reduce further the take-off and landing speed of FSW aircraft.

TYPE: FSW demonstrator aircraft.

WINGS: Cantilever low/mid-wing monoplane. Supercritical wing section. Thickness/chord ratio at root 6.2%, at tip 4.9%. No dihedral. Incidence –6° at WS 20 to +0.8° at WS 163.22. Forward sweep at quarter-chord 33° 44'. Safe-life construction, with substructure of aluminium alloy and titanium, and graphite epoxy composite skins. Full span dual hinged camber-changing trailing-edge flaperons, with two National Water Lift integrated servo actuators in each wing. A wing strake extends aft from the trailing-edge at each wing root, each strake with a trailing-edge flap which has its own Moog integrated servo actuator to augment foreplanes for pitch control. No wing de-icing system.

FOREPLANES: All-moving (30° up, 60° down) canard surfaces of conventional aluminium alloy construction, one on each side of the centre-fuselage, outboard of engine inlet ducts. Operated by National Water Lift servo actuators for primary pitch control. No anti-icing system.

FUSELAGE: Semi-monocoque fail-safe structure of aluminium alloy, incorporating pressurised cockpit section.

TAIL UNIT: Sweptback fin and rudder only, of aluminium alloy construction. Rudder operated by National Water Lift integrated servo actuator. No anti-icing system.

LANDING GEAR: Hydraulically retractable tricycle type, all three units retracting forward. Menasco oleo-pneumatic shock absorber in each unit. Goodrich wheels and tyres. Nosewheel tyre size 18 × 6-8, pressure 10.35 bars (150 lb/sq in); mainwheel tyres each 24 × 5.5, pressure 17.25 bars (250 lb/sq in). Goodrich hydraulic carbon disc brakes, aircooled; Goodyear anti-skid units.

POWER PLANT: One General Electric F404-GE-400 afterburning turbofan in the 71.2 kN (16,000 lb st) class. Two bladder fuel cells within the fuselage, and integral tank in each wing strake, giving total capacity of 1,804 kg (3,978 lb) of JP5 fuel. No flight refuelling capability.

ACCOMMODATION: Pilot only, on Martin-Baker GRQ7A ejection seat, beneath upward opening canopy hinged at rear. Accommodation air-conditioned and pressurised.

SYSTEMS: AiResearch bootstrap air cycle air-conditioning and pressurisation system, providing cockpit pressure differential of 0.34 bars (5 lb/sq in). Dual engine driven Abex hydraulic pumps for two independent systems, each 207 bars (3,000 lb/sq in) for operation of flight control actuators, landing gear and utility systems. Electrical system includes Westinghouse 40kVA engine driven generator and Lear Siegler 5kVA emergency generator, 500VA converter, two transformer-rectifiers, 20Ah storage battery, and external power socket. Liquid oxygen system with converter. Garrett emergency power unit, operated by engine bleed air and/or hydrazine fuel, to drive the Lear Siegler emergency generator and a Vickers hydraulic pump of 83 litres (22 US gallons; 18.3 Imp gallons)/min output. Systron-Donner engine fire detection and extinguishing system.

AVIONICS: Include Litton LR-80 attitude and heading reference system and other navigation equipment, Magnavox AN/ARC-164 UHF com, and Teledyne RT-1063B/APX-101V IFF/SIF. Honeywell triple redundant digital fly by wire flight control system.

DIMENSIONS, EXTERNAL:

Wing span	8.29 m (27 ft 2½ in)
Wing chord: at root	2.96 m (9 ft 8½ in)
at tip	1.19 m (3 ft 11 in)

Retouched photograph showing engine configuration of Grumman S-2T Turbo Tracker with Garrett TPE331-1-5AW turboprops

Wing aspect ratio	3.9
Foreplane span	4.15 m (13 ft 7½ in)
Length overall, incl nose probe	16.44 m (53 ft 11¼ in)
Length of fuselage	14.66 m (48 ft 1 in)
Height overall	4.36 m (14 ft 3½ in)
Wheel track	2.30 m (7 ft 6½ in)
Wheelbase	5.48 m (17 ft 11¾ in)
AREAS (exposed):	
Wings	17.54 m² (188.84 sq ft)
Foreplanes (total)	3.34 m² (35.96 sq ft)
Vertical tail surfaces (total)	3.02 m² (32.51 sq ft)
WEIGHTS:	
Weight empty	6,260 kg (13,800 lb)
Max fuel weight	1,804 kg (3,978 lb)
Max T-O weight	8,074 kg (17,800 lb)

PERFORMANCE:
No details received, but max level speed approx Mach 1.6

GRUMMAN S-2T TURBO TRACKER

Grumman has received a $260 million US Navy foreign military sales contract for a turboprop modification of its S-2 Tracker anti-submarine warfare aircraft which involves replacing the S-2's 1,141 kW (1,530 hp) Curtiss-Wright R-1820-82 piston engines with 1,227 kW (1,645 shp) Garrett TPE331-1-5AW turboprops driving four-blade Dowty Rotol advanced technology propellers. The Turbo Tracker will have a 270 knot (500 km/h; 311 mph) maximum speed at 1,525 m (5,000 ft), a 500 kg (1,102 lb) increase in payload, and improvements in cruising speed, T-O and landing distances, single-engine rate of climb and engine TBO.

Prototype installation, in two S-2G aircraft, is being carried out by Tracor Aviation, with first flight of the prototype expected in July 1988. Included in the modification programme is a new avionics and ASW package which comprises a GEC Avionics MAPADS 902F acoustic processor, ASQ-504(V) magnetic anomaly detector, AN/APS-509 radar, ARR-84 acoustic receivers and an ASN-150 tactical navigation system coupled with the 72R inertial navigation system and Collins avionics. Thirty-two S-2Ts, including a pre-production aircraft due to fly in late 1988, are to be supplied to Taiwan under a US Navy FMS contract. Grumman will convert two of these, and supply conversion kits for local modification of the remainder. Other potential customers include Argentina, Brazil, Peru, South Korea, Thailand and Turkey.

GULFSTREAM AEROSPACE

GULFSTREAM AEROSPACE CORPORATION
(Subsidiary of Chrysler Corporation)

PO Box 2206, Savannah International Airport, Savannah, Georgia 31402-2206
Telephone: (912) 964 3000
Telex: 546470 GULF AERO
Fax: (912) 964 3775
CHAIRMAN AND CHIEF EXECUTIVE OFFICER:
  Allen E. Paulson
PRESIDENT, US OPERATIONS: Albert H. Glenn
SENIOR VICE-PRESIDENT, ENGINEERING:
  Charles N. Coppi
SENIOR VICE-PRESIDENT, MARKETING:
  Robert H. Cooper
VICE-PRESIDENT, INTERNATIONAL SALES:
  Joseph E. Anckner
VICE-PRESIDENT, DOMESTIC MARKETING AND ADMINISTRATION:
  Herbert B. Franck
CORPORATE COMMUNICATIONS DIRECTOR:
  Alvin F. Balaban

On 16 August 1985 the Chrysler Corporation acquired Gulfstream Aerospace Corporation, which is currently producing the Gulfstream IV business aircraft. Gulfstream had 4,500 personnel in 1988.

In March 1986 Gulfstream acquired a 9,290 m² (100,000 sq ft) aircraft completion facility at Long Beach International Airport, California, which had been operated formerly by AiResearch Aviation. This facility has expanded the company's ability to outfit and complete Gulfstream IVs for customer delivery, and includes a product support centre.

GULFSTREAM AEROSPACE GULFSTREAM III
US military designation: C-20

Production of the Gulfstream III business jet was completed in 1986 after a total of 202 aircraft had been built. An abbreviated description may be found in the 1987-88 edition; full descriptions and photographs of the Gulfstream III and its SRA-1 surveillance and reconnaissance variant appeared in the 1986-87 and earlier editions of *Jane's*.

GULFSTREAM AEROSPACE G1159C GULFSTREAM IV
US Navy designation: EC-20F

Design of this advanced version of the Gulfstream III was initiated in March 1983, and construction of four production prototypes (one for static testing) began in 1985. Rollout of the first aircraft (N404GA) occurred on 11 September 1985, with a first flight following on 19 September. The second prototype flew on 11 June 1986, followed by the third in August 1986. FAA certification was granted on 22 April 1987, following 1,412 hours of flight

testing. By June 1987 Gulfstream Aerospace held orders for more than 100 Gulfstream IVs, of which 26 had been delivered by the end of that year. A further 60 were expected to be delivered by the end of 1988.

The US Department of Defense has ordered three Gulfstream IVs, under the designation **EC-20F**, to replace Douglas ERA-3 Skywarriors used by the US Navy in the tactical ECM training role. One was to be delivered in 1988 and the other two in 1989.

On 12 June 1987 the third production Gulfstream IV (N440GA), with company Chairman Mr Allen Paulson in command, flew from le Bourget Airport, Paris, on an attempt to set a westbound around-the-world record. Routing via fuel stops at Edmonton, Alberta; Midway Island; Kota Kinabalu, Malaysia; and Dubai, UAE, the aircraft returned to Paris on 14 June after covering a total distance of 19,887.9 nm (36,832.44 km; 22,886.6 miles) in 45 h 25 min 10 s at an average speed of 437.86 knots (810.93 km/h; 503.89 mph). Gulfstream achieved a total of 22 world records with this flight.

On 26/27 February 1988 a Gulfstream IV (N400GA) captained by Mr Paulson flew from Houston, Texas, on an attempt to set an eastbound around-the-world record. The aircraft, named *Pursuit of Perfection*, routed via fuel stops at Shannon, Ireland; Dubai, UAE; Taipei, Taiwan; and Maui, Hawaii, returning to Houston after covering a total distance of 20,028.68 nm (37,093.1 km; 23,048.6 miles) in 36 h 8 min 34 s, at an average speed of 554.15 knots (1,026.29 km/h; 637.71 mph). Gulfstream was awarded eleven records for the flight which broke an around-the-world record set 30 days previously by a United Airlines Boeing 747SP. The Gulfstream IV was equipped with an additional fuel tank in its cabin, capacity 3,629 kg (8,000 lb), for the flight, for which its T-O weight was 34,782 kg (76,681 lb). This tank installation is available as an option for civil and SRA-4 versions of the Gulfstream IV.

Generally similar to the Gulfstream III, the Gulfstream IV differs primarily in having a structurally redesigned wing, incorporating 30 per cent fewer parts and offering a weight saving of 395 kg (870 lb) with provision for 453 kg (1,000 lb) more internal fuel capacity; a tailplane of increased span; a fuselage lengthened by 1.37 m (4 ft 6 in); a sixth window on each side of the cabin; rudder, ailerons and spoilers made of carbonfibre; Rolls-Royce RB183-03 Tay Mk 610-8 turbofans; and a flight deck incorporating advanced CRT displays and digital avionics.

TYPE: Twin-turbofan executive transport.

WINGS: Cantilever low-wing monoplane of light alloy construction, with carbonfibre ailerons and spoilers; manufactured by Textron Aerostructures. Advanced sonic rooftop wing section. Thickness/chord ratio of 10% at wing station 50 and 8.6% at wing station 414. Dihedral 3°. Incidence 3° 30' at root, −2° at tip. Sweepback at quarter-chord 27° 40'. NASA (Whitcomb) aluminium honeycomb winglets. Plain ailerons of aluminium alloy, hydraulically powered with manual reversion.

Single-slotted Fowler trailing-edge flaps. Three spoilers on upper surface of each wing at 12 per cent chord, immediately forward of trailing-edge flaps, operated differentially to complement ailerons for roll control and collectively to serve as airbrakes. Trim tab in port aileron. Four vortilons and a single 'tripper' strip under leading-edge of each wing to enhance low speed stall characteristics. Anti-icing of leading-edges by engine bleed air.

FUSELAGE: Conventional semi-monocoque fail-safe pressurised structure of light alloy, with carbonfibre in cabin floor and flight deck areas.

TAIL UNIT: Cantilever T tail of light alloy, except for rudder and some tailplane components of carbonfibre. Swept horizontal and vertical surfaces. Trim tab in rudder and each elevator. Hydraulically powered controls with manual reversion.

LANDING GEAR: Retractable tricycle type with twin wheels on each unit. Main units retract inward, steerable nose unit forward. Mainwheel tyres size 34 × 9.25-16, pressure 12.07 bars (175 lb/sq in). Nosewheel tyres size 21 × 7.25-10, pressure 7.9 bars (115 lb/sq in). Goodyear aircooled carbon brakes, with Goodyear fully modulating anti-skid units. Goodyear digital electronic brake-by-wire system. Dowty electronic steer-by-wire system.

POWER PLANT: Two Rolls-Royce Tay Mk 611-8 turbofans, each flat rated at 61.6 kN (13,850 lb st) to ISA +15°C. Target type thrust reversers. Fuel in two integral wing tanks, with total capacity of 16,542 litres (4,370 US gallons; 3,639 Imp gallons). Single pressure fuelling point in leading-edge of starboard wing.

ACCOMMODATION: Crew of two or three. Standard seating for 14 to 19 passengers in pressurised and air-conditioned cabin. Galley, toilet and large baggage compartment, capacity 907 kg (2,000 lb), at rear of cabin. Integral airstair door at front of cabin on port side. Baggage compartment door on port side. Electrically heated wraparound windscreen. Six cabin windows, including one overwing emergency exit, on each side.

SYSTEMS: Cabin pressurisation system max differential 0.65 hbars (9.45 lb/sq in). Air-conditioning system. Two independent hydraulic systems, each 207 bars (3,000 lb/sq in). Maximum flow rate 83.3 litres (22 US gallons; 18.3 Imp gallons)/min. Two bootstrap type hydraulic reservoirs, pressurised to 4.14 bars (60 lb/sq in). Garrett GTCP36-100 APU in tail compartment, flight rated to 9,150 m (30,000 ft). Electrical system includes two 36kVA alternators with two solid state 30kVA converters to provide 23kVA 115/200V 400Hz AC power and 250A of regulated 28V DC power; two 24V 40Ah nickel-cadmium storage batteries and external power socket.

AVIONICS AND EQUIPMENT: Standard items include a Sperry SPZ-8000 digital automatic flight control system, Sperry FMZ-800 flight management system and six 20.3 cm × 20.3 cm (8 in × 8 in) colour CRT displays, two each for primary flight instruments, navigation and engine instrument and crew alerting systems (EICAS); dual fail-operational flight guidance systems including auto throttles; dual air data systems; dual flight management systems with vertical and lateral navigation and performance management; and digital colour radar. System integration is accomplished through a Sperry avionics standard communications bus (ASCB). Other factory-installed avionics include dual VHF/HF com; dual VOR/LOC/GS and markers; dual DME; dual ADF; dual radio altimeters; dual transponders; dual cockpit audio; dual flight guidance and performance computers; dual laser INS; dual ILS receivers with Cat III capability; attitude/heading reference system; and cockpit voice recorder. The system is designed to provide growth potential for interface with MLS, GPS and VLF Omega in future developments.

DIMENSIONS, EXTERNAL:

Wing span over winglets	23.72 m (77 ft 10 in)
Wing chord:	
at root (fuselage centreline)	5.94 m (19 ft 5⅞ in)
at tip	1.85 m (6 ft 0¾ in)
Wing aspect ratio	6.0
Length overall	26.92 m (88 ft 4 in)
Fuselage length	24.03 m (78 ft 10 in)
Fuselage: Max diameter	2.39 m (7 ft 10 in)
Height overall	7.57 m (24 ft 10 in)

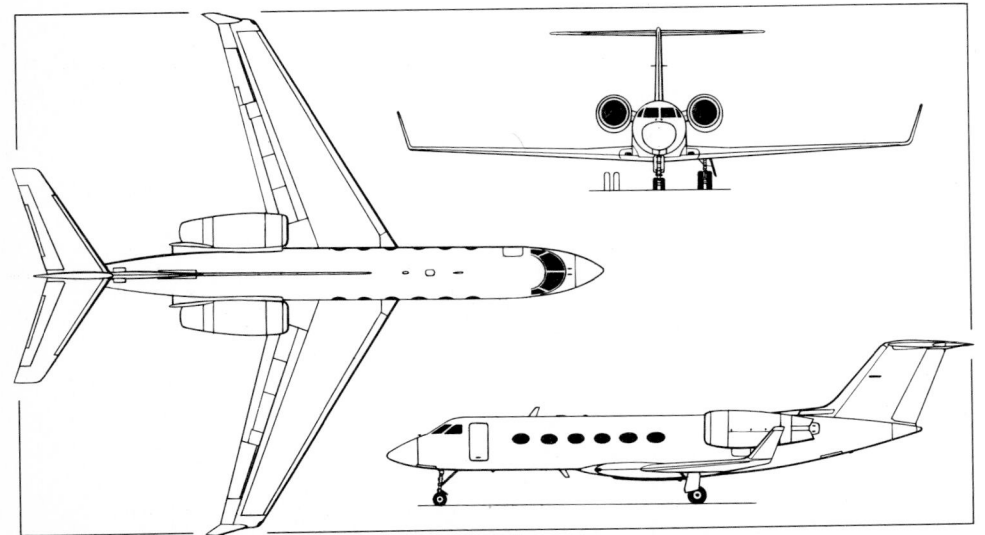

Gulfstream Aerospace Gulfstream IV twin-turbofan executive transport (*Pilot Press*)

Gulfstream IV *Pursuit of Perfection* **which set an eastbound around-the-world speed record in February 1988**

Tailplane span	9.75 m (32 ft 0 in)
Wheel track	4.17 m (13 ft 8 in)
Wheelbase	11.61 m (38 ft 1¼ in)
Passenger door (fwd, port): Height	1.57 m (5 ft 2 in)
Width	0.91 m (3 ft 0 in)
Baggage door (rear): Height	0.72 m (2 ft 4½ in)
Width	0.91 m (2 ft 11¾ in)

DIMENSIONS, INTERNAL:
Cabin:

Length, incl galley, toilet and baggage compartment

	13.74 m (45 ft 1 in)
Max width	2.24 m (7 ft 4 in)
Max height	1.85 m (6 ft 1 in)
Floor area	22.9 m² (247 sq ft)
Volume	47.62 m³ (1,682 cu ft)
Cabin volume	42.84 m³ (1,513 cu ft)
Passenger area volume	30.50 m³ (1,077 cu ft)
Flight deck volume	3.51 m³ (124 cu ft)
Rear baggage compartment volume	4.78 m³ (169 cu ft)

AREAS:

Wings, gross	88.29 m² (950.39 sq ft)
Ailerons (total, incl tab)	2.68 m² (28.86 sq ft)
Trailing-edge flaps (total)	11.97 m² (128.84 sq ft)
Spoilers (total)	7.46 m² (80.27 sq ft)
Winglets (total)	2.38 m² (25.60 sq ft)
Fin	10.92 m² (117.53 sq ft)
Rudder, incl tab	4.16 m² (44.75 sq ft)
Horizontal tail surfaces (total)	18.77 m² (202.0 sq ft)
Elevators (total, incl tabs)	5.22 m² (56.22 sq ft)

WEIGHTS AND LOADINGS:

Manufacturer's weight empty	16,102 kg (35,500 lb)
Typical operating weight empty	19,278 kg (42,500 lb)
Max payload	1,814 kg (4,000 lb)
Max usable fuel	13,381 kg (29,500 lb)
Max T-O weight	33,203 kg (73,200 lb)
Max ramp weight	33,384 kg (73,600 lb)
Max zero-fuel weight	21,092 kg (46,500 lb)
Max landing weight	26,535 kg (58,500 lb)
Max wing loading	375.9 kg/m² (77.02 lb/sq ft)
Max power loading	269.6 kg/kN (2.64 lb/lb st)

PERFORMANCE (at max T-O weight, ISA, except where indicated):
Max operating speed

340 knots (629 km/h; 391 mph) CAS
or Mach 0.88

Max cruising speed at 9,450 m (31,000 ft)

509 knots (943 km/h; 586 mph)

Normal cruising speed at 13,715 m (45,000 ft)

Mach 0.80 (459 knots; 850 km/h; 528 mph)

Stalling speed at max landing weight:
wheels and flaps up 122 knots (227 km/h; 141 mph)
wheels and flaps down

108 knots (200 km/h; 124 mph)

Approach speed at max landing weight

140 knots (259 km/h; 161 mph)

Max rate of climb at S/L	1,220 m (4,002 ft)/min

Rate of climb at S/L, one engine out

337 m (1,105 ft)/min

Max operating altitude	13,715 m (45,000 ft)
Runway LCN	35

FAA balanced T-O field length at S/L

	1,600 m (5,250 ft)
Landing from 15 m (50 ft)	1,026 m (3,366 ft)

Range with max payload, normal cruising speed and NBAA IFR reserves

3,694 nm (6,845 km; 4,254 miles)

Range with max fuel, eight passengers, at Mach 0.80 and with NBAA IFR reserves

4,220 nm (7,820 km; 4,859 miles)

OPERATIONAL NOISE LEVELS (FAR Pt 36):

T-O	76.8 EPNdB
Approach	91.0 EPNdB
Sideline	87.3 EPNdB

GULFSTREAM SRA-4

Gulfstream Aerospace has extended the special missions concept of the Gulfstream IV under the designation **SRA-4**. The aircraft is available with integrated systems and equipment for surveillance/reconnaissance, maritime patrol, anti-submarine warfare, medical evacuation, priority cargo and administrative transport roles, with cabin interiors configured to permit rapid changes of role. An upward opening cargo door 1.6 m (5 ft 3 in) high and 2.1 m (6 ft 11 in) wide can be installed in the starboard forward fuselage area, aft of the flight deck, to facilitate loading and unloading of bulky cargo, mission equipment or stretchers.

In typical maritime patrol configuration the SRA-4 is equipped with a nose mounted high definition surface search radar, forward looking infra-red detection system, electronic support measures, flare/marker launch tubes, radar/IRDS, nav/com and ESM consoles, positions for up to eight observers/console operators, stowage and deployment facilities for survival equipment, and a crew rest area. With a crew of six, and a mission payload of 2,811 kg (6,198 lb), including 272 kg (600 lb) of expendable stores, the SRA-4 could operate over a 600 nm (1,112 km; 690 mile) radius of action, cruising to the patrol area at 12,500 m (41,000 ft) at 454 knots (841 km/h; 523 mph), and remain on station for six hours, manoeuvring at 61 m (200 ft) for up to 33 per cent of that time, and searching at 3,050 m (10,000 ft) for the remainder, returning to base at 13,715 m (45,000 ft).

In electronic surveillance/reconnaissance roles the SRA-4 can be equipped with a variety of sensors, including side-looking synthetic aperture radar in a belly-mounted pod beneath the forward fuselage section, long range oblique photographic camera (LOROP), ESM, VHF/UHF/HF communications for C³ functions, chaff dispensers, infra-red countermeasures housed in the tailcone, SAR equipment and accommodation for mission specialists for each sensor. A typical electronic surveillance mission profile with six crew and a total mission payload of 2,373 kg (5,231 lb) would permit 10.5 hours on station at loiter altitudes between 10,670 and 15,550 m (35,000-51,000 ft).

For anti-submarine warfare applications the SRA-4 can be equipped with a nose-mounted high definition maritime surveillance radar offering periscope/snorkel detection capability, FLIR, sonobuoy launchers and acoustic processor, a tailcone-mounted magnetic anomaly detector (MAD) boom, ESM, torpedo stowage in a weapons bay beneath the forward fuselage, and provision for carriage and launch of one anti-shipping missile on each underwing stores hardpoint. With a mission payload of 2,503 kg (5,518 lb), including six crew, an ASW SRA-4 could operate over a 1,000 nm (1,853 km; 1,151 mile) radius of action with 4.3 hours on station in hi-lo loitering and manoeuvring. In an anti-shipping role the SRA-4 could fly 1,350 nm (2,502 km; 1,554 miles) at high altitude, descend to 61 m (200 ft) for a 350 knot (649 km/h; 403 mph)/100 nm (185 km; 115 miles) attack run and launch a standoff weapon at 50 nm (93 km; 57 miles) range from target before climbing to 13,715 m (45,000 ft) for return to base.

In a medical evacuation role the SRA-4's cabin can accommodate up to 15 litter patients plus medical attendants; while for priority cargo transport, in addition to the cargo door, the aircraft can be equipped with a floor-mounted cargo roller system for rapid loading.

The Indian government is reported to have ordered two reconnaissance-configured SRA-4s for delivery during 1988.

GULFSTREAM AEROSPACE TECHNOLOGIES (Oklahoma Operations)

Wiley Post Airport, Box 22500, Oklahoma City, Oklahoma 73123
Telephone: (405) 789 5000
Telex: 747193
PRESIDENT: Robert N. Buckley
VICE-PRESIDENT, MARKETING: Clifford M. Shirley

Gulfstream Aerospace's 46,452 m² (500,000 sq ft) Oklahoma facility, used formerly for the production of the Gulfstream Commander Jetprop series of turboprop business aircraft, now provides manufacturing and engineering services for government agencies, aerospace equipment manufacturers and defence contractors. The Commander 112 and 114 single-engined range was sold by Gulfstream Aerospace in 1988 to Commander Aircraft Company of Washington, DC.

Under a major agreement announced on 2 May 1988 Gulfstream Aerospace Technologies has been authorised by McDonnell Douglas to manufacture spare parts for all out-of-production Douglas transport aircraft from the DC-3 up to and including the DC-10.

Employment at Oklahoma City totalled 825 in Spring 1988.

HAMILTON
HAMILTON AEROSPACE
San Antonio, Texas

HAMILTON H-1
Hamilton Aerospace is developing a turbofan powered military trainer and close support tactical aircraft based on the airframe of the all-composite two-seat Hamilton HX-321 homebuilt aircraft described in the Sport Aircraft section of this edition. The Hamilton H-1 is powered by one Garrett TFE731-5 turbofan rated at 20.02 kN (4,500 lb st), but will also be offered with a 373 kW (500 shp) Allison 250-C20 turboprop according to customer preference. A prototype was expected to fly during the Summer of 1988.

HAWK
HAWK INTERNATIONAL
57430 Aviation Drive, Yucca Valley, California 92284
Telephone: (619) 365 1831
PRESIDENT: Ernest Hawk

Hawk International specialises in equipment for oil and water well drilling and fencing. As a result of difficulties in transporting its products, the company's President initiated in July 1977 the design of a freight carrying aircraft that might overcome both the slowness of road transport and the high cost and loading/unloading difficulties of conventional aircraft. He named his project GafHawk 125, signifying general aviation freighter.

HAWK GAFHAWK 125

Features considered of prime importance in design of the GafHawk included STOL capability for operation into and from small unprepared strips, a turboprop power plant for economic operation, a square-section fuselage for maximum utilisation of internal capacity, undertail loading of bulk cargo at truckbed height, and a single engine for economy, ease of certification and single-pilot operation.

A small scale flying testbed known as the MiniHawk, which consisted of an extensively rebuilt Piper Tri-Pacer light aircraft, made its first flight in 1978 and was described and illustrated in the 1980-81 *Jane's*.

The GafHawk 125 prototype (N101GH) was flown for the first time on 19 August 1982, powered by an 893 kW (1,198 shp) Pratt & Whitney Canada PT6A-45R turboprop. Negotiations were continuing in 1988 for the establishment of an offshore production facility, at which time Hawk International held firm orders for 20 GafHawk 125s, with options on a further 93 pending certification.

The GafHawk is intended to be certificated initially at a gross weight of 5,670 kg (12,500 lb) under FAR Pt 23, although it would be capable of operating at a max T-O weight of 6,577 kg (14,500 lb). Larger and smaller developed versions of the GafHawk 125 are under consideration. Certification of the prototype had not been obtained by early 1988.

TYPE: Single-engined all-metal turboprop freighter.
AIRFRAME: As described in 1987-88 *Jane's*.
POWER PLANT: One Pratt & Whitney Canada PT6A-65B/R turboprop, with a max continuous rating of 875 kW (1,173 shp), driving a Hartzell five-blade reversible-pitch constant-speed metal propeller with spinner. Fuel tank, made of transparent glassfibre and with a capacity of 1,363 litres (360 US gallons; 300 Imp gallons), mounted above forward fuselage, directly over the wing, and providing gravity feed to engine. Refuelling point on upper surface of tank. Two aluminium fuel tanks, with a combined capacity of 3,785 litres (1,000 US gallons; 833 Imp gallons), can be installed in the main cargo hold for long ferry flights. Electrically heated de-icing boots for propeller and engine air intake.
ACCOMMODATION: Pilot and co-pilot on flight deck. Dual controls and full blind-flying instrumentation for both pilots standard. Door to flight deck on each side of fuselage; communicating door between flight deck and cargo hold in forward bulkhead. Cabin door on each side, aft of wing. Electrically actuated upward/inward-opening

Prototype Hawk GafHawk 125 single-engined turboprop freighter

main cargo door, in undersurface of upswept rear fuselage, can be opened in flight. Heavy duty corrugated light alloy floor in cargo hold, with cargo tiedowns along walls at each fuselage gusset frame, and tailgate for loading. Main cabin volume augmented by usable space under flight deck, accommodating pipes and timber up to 6.1 m (20 ft) in length with rear loading door closed. Accommodation heated and ventilated.
SYSTEMS, AVIONICS AND EQUIPMENT: As detailed in 1987-88 *Jane's*.
DIMENSIONS, EXTERNAL:

Wing span	21.79 m (71 ft 6 in)
Wing chord (constant)	2.08 m (6 ft 10 in)
Wing aspect ratio	10.4
Length overall	14.30 m (46 ft 11 in)
Height overall	5.49 m (18 ft 0 in)
Tailplane span	7.01 m (23 ft 0 in)
Wheel track (c/l outer tyres)	3.38 m (11 ft 1 in)
Wheelbase	4.39 m (14 ft 5 in)
Propeller diameter	2.74 m (9 ft 0 in)
Rear ramp/door: Height	1.93 m (6 ft 4 in)
Width	1.96 m (6 ft 5 in)

DIMENSIONS, INTERNAL:

Cabin: Length at floor level, excl flight deck	
	4.72 m (15 ft 6 in)
Max width	2.03 m (6 ft 8 in)
Max height	2.13 m (7 ft 0 in)
Volume	20.22 m³ (714.0 cu ft)

AREA:

Wings, gross	45.8 m² (493.0 sq ft)

WEIGHTS AND LOADINGS (estimated):

Weight empty	3,085 kg (6,800 lb)
Max design T-O weight	6,577 kg (14,500 lb)
Max wing loading	143.6 kg/m² (29.4 lb/sq ft)
Max power loading	7.52 kg/kW (12.36 lb/shp)

PERFORMANCE (prototype, at max design T-O weight):

Max cruising speed at 3,050 m (10,000 ft)	
	120 knots (222 km/h; 138 mph)
Econ cruising speed (55% power) at 3,050 m (10,000 ft)	
	110 knots (204 km/h; 127 mph)
Stalling speed, flaps down, power on	
	47 knots (87 km/h; 54 mph)
Max rate of climb at S/L	280 m (920 ft)/min
Service ceiling	5,485 m (18,000 ft)
T-O run	287 m (940 ft)
T-O to 15 m (50 ft)	506 m (1,660 ft)
Landing from 15 m (50 ft)	436 m (1,430 ft)
Landing run	201 m (660 ft)
Range with max fuel	716 nm (1,326 km; 824 miles)

HAYES

HAYES INTERNATIONAL CORPORATION (Dothan Division)

PO Box 929, Dothan-Houston County Airport, Dothan, Alabama 36302-0929
Telephone: (205) 983 4571
Telex: 782123
VICE-PRESIDENT AND GENERAL MANAGER:
Donald E. Blish

HAYES (BAe) 146-200 CARGO CONVERSION

Hayes International's Dothan Division was appointed by British Aerospace to undertake the prototype conversion of a BAe 146 Series 200 (see UK section) to all-cargo configuration. Hayes designed, manufactured and installed a port-side upward opening door (3.30 m; 10 ft 10 in wide by 1.98 m; 6 ft 6 in deep) in the rear fuselage, forward of the rear passenger door; undertook the necessary structural strengthening; and installed interior furnishings and cargo handling equipment.

After such conversion, a BAe 146 is operable in either all-cargo or passenger/cargo combi configuration. It is marketed by BAe, but Hayes was responsible for obtaining the FAA supplemental type certificate and is undertaking production conversions.

HAYES (LOCKHEED) L-1011F TRISTAR

Under contract to Aircraft Sales Company, Hayes converted an ex-Eastern Air Lines Lockheed L-1011-1 passenger airliner to all-cargo configuration, as the L-1011F. In addition to installing a 2.84 m by 4.32 m (9 ft 4 in × 14 ft 2 in) cargo door in the port side of the cabin, forward of the wing, the conversion required a 9g bulkhead aft of the flight deck, replacement of the cabin windows by blanking plates, and installation of tracks and roller conveyors on the upper and lower decks. Max payload is 54,430 kg (120,000 lb). FAA type approval was received after the L-1011F's first flight, on 7 May 1987. Further conversions can be made to order.

HELIO

HELIO AIRCRAFT LTD

This company is no longer at its former Pittsburg, Kansas, address, and is presumed to have ceased trading. Brief descriptions and illustrations of the Helio Courier 700 and 800 STOL aircraft and Model 21A Rat'ler agricultural aircraft may be found in the 1987-88 and earlier editions of *Jane's*.

HILLER — *see Rogerson*

HUGHES — *see McDonnell Douglas*

HYNES

This company was formed on 1 January 1975 (initially as Brantly-Hynes Helicopter Inc). Its President, Mr M. K. Hynes, acquired ownership of the type certificates for the Brantly B-2, B-2A, B-2B and Model 305, reinstating production of the B-2B and 305 as the Hynes H-2 and H-5 respectively.

In Spring 1987 the company's assets were put up for sale, and plans have since been made for these two helicopters to be produced in India by Naras Aviation. Their descriptions can therefore be found under that company's heading.

IAC

INTERNATIONAL AEROMARINE CORPORATION

1011 S Sanford Avenue, Sanford, Florida 32771
Telephone: (305) 323 4360
PRESIDENT: Joseph W. Gurnow
VICE-PRESIDENT, ENGINEERING: David B. Thurston

International Aeromarine Corporation, which is partly owned by Thurston Aeromarine Corporation, was formed to develop and gain certification of the TA16 Seafire, the latest in a series of light amphibians designed by Mr David B. Thurston.

IAC TA16 SEAFIRE

Following design and development of the TA16 Trojan amphibian, of which 50 are under construction by Canadian and US homebuilders, Mr Thurston decided to market a production version. This has been named Seafire to distinguish it from the homebuilt version. The Seafire prototype (N16SA), completed in March 1982, was structurally designed and statically tested to the requirements of FAR Pt 23, Amendment 24. It flew for the first time on 10 December 1982 and IAC expected to complete its certification by the end of 1987. By mid-1987 the company held orders for ten Seafires, since when no further information has been received.
TYPE: Four-seat light amphibian.

WINGS: Cantilever shoulder-wing monoplane. Wing section NACA 64₂A215. Dihedral 3°. Incidence 4°. Constant chord wings with no sweepback. All-metal structure. All-metal ailerons of Thurston design, each with ground adjustable trim tab. Single-slotted all-metal trailing-edge flaps. Small fixed stabilising float beneath each wing at approximately two-thirds span.
HULL: All-metal hull of planing type with single step. Retractable water rudder.
TAIL UNIT: Cantilever all-metal T tail. Bungee trim system for elevators.
LANDING GEAR: Hydraulically retractable tricycle type. Main units retract inward; steerable nosewheel retracts forward to close opening in hull, which needs no

closure doors. IAC oleo-pneumatic shock absorbers. Parker-Hannifin aluminium alloy wheels, all three size 6.00-6, with tyre size 17.5 × 6.30, 6-ply rating. Tyre pressures: mainwheels 2.76 bars (40 lb/sq in), nosewheel 2.07 bars (30 lb/sq in). Parker-Hannifin dual-pad disc brakes. Parking brake. Wheel landing gear designed to meet Canadian DoT snow-ski load conditions.

POWER PLANT: One 186 kW (250 hp) Textron Lycoming O-540-A4D5 flat-six engine, pylon mounted and braced from the upper surface of the hull directly over the wing, driving a Hartzell two-blade constant-speed metal tractor propeller with spinner. Fuel tank in leading-edge of each wing, with combined capacity of 340 litres (90 US gallons; 75 Imp gallons). Refuelling point on upper surface of each wing. Oil capacity 11.5 litres (3 US gallons; 2.5 Imp gallons). Engine air intake incorporates filter and automatic inlet door which opens if main duct becomes blocked by ice or debris.

ACCOMMODATION: Pilot and three passengers in pairs in enclosed cabin, with two-section rearward sliding canopy. Forward section slides aft over rear canopy, and both may then be rotated to either side of hull, or removed, to facilitate loading/unloading of bulky items. All glass tinted. Adjustable seats with belts and shoulder harness. Dual controls and toe brakes. Cabin carpeted. Space for baggage or freight at rear of cabin. Accommodation is heated and ventilated.

SYSTEMS: Electrical system powered by 24V 70A engine driven alternator; 24V 37Ah battery. Electrically driven hydraulic pump provides system pressure of 69 bars (1,000 lb/sq in) for actuation of landing gear. Oxygen system optional.

AVIONICS AND EQUIPMENT: Standard Narco avionics include Nav 122 with localiser, glideslope and marker beacon receiver; Nav 121, ADF 141, CP-135, dual Com 120 and AT-150 transponder. Optional nav/com systems to customer's requirements. Blind-flying instrumentation and emergency locator transmitter standard. Dual IFR instrumentation optional. Standard equipment includes instrument panel, cabin interior, landing and taxi lights; Whelen nav/strobe lights; external power socket; control locks; baggage tiedown straps.

Prototype IAC TA16 Seafire four-seat amphibian *(Howard Levy)*

DIMENSIONS, EXTERNAL:

Wing span	11.28 m (37 ft 0 in)
Wing chord, constant	1.52 m (5 ft 0 in)
Wing aspect ratio	7.5
Length overall	8.28 m (27 ft 2 in)
Length of hull	7.42 m (24 ft 4 in)
Height overall	3.28 m (10 ft 9 in)
Tailplane span	3.05 m (10 ft 0 in)
Wheel track	4.01 m (13 ft 2 in)
Wheelbase	3.28 m (10 ft 9 in)
Propeller diameter	2.03 m (6 ft 8 in)

DIMENSIONS, INTERNAL:

Cabin: Length	2.13 m (7 ft 0 in)
Max width	1.01 m (3 ft 4 in)
Max height	1.22 m (4 ft 0 in)
Floor area	1.86 m² (20.0 sq ft)
Volume	2.26 m³ (80.0 cu ft)

AREAS:

Wings, gross	17.00 m² (183.0 sq ft)
Ailerons (total)	1.11 m² (12.0 sq ft)
Trailing-edge flaps (total)	2.51 m² (27.0 sq ft)
Fin	2.34 m² (25.2 sq ft)
Dorsal fin	0.12 m² (1.30 sq ft)
Rudder	0.67 m² (7.2 sq ft)
Tailplane	1.95 m² (21.0 sq ft)
Elevators	1.45 m² (15.6 sq ft)

WEIGHTS AND LOADINGS:

Weight empty, equipped	885 kg (1,950 lb)
Max fuel weight	245 kg (540 lb)
Max T-O and landing weight	1,451 kg (3,200 lb)
Max wing loading	85.44 kg/m² (17.5 lb/sq ft)
Max power loading	7.80 kg/kW (12.8 lb/hp)

PERFORMANCE (at max T-O weight):

Never-exceed speed	160 knots (298 km/h; 185 mph) IAS
Max level speed at 2,135 m (7,000 ft)	152 knots (281 km/h; 175 mph) IAS
Max cruising speed, 75% power at 2,135 m (7,000 ft)	139 knots (257 km/h; 160 mph)
Econ cruising speed, 67% power at 2,135 m (7,000 ft)	135 knots (249 km/h; 155 mph)
Stalling speed, engine idling:	
flaps up	63 knots (117 km/h; 73 mph)
flaps down	52 knots (97 km/h; 60 mph)
Max rate of climb at S/L	323 m (1,060 ft)/min
Service ceiling	5,485 m (18,000 ft)
T-O run: land	198 m (650 ft)
water	259 m (850 ft)
T-O to 15 m (50 ft): land	305 m (1,000 ft)
water	366 m (1,200 ft)
Landing from 15 m (50 ft):	
land or water	366 m (1,200 ft)
Range with max fuel	868 nm (1,609 km; 1,000 miles)

JETCRAFT

JETCRAFT USA

3801 Highway 146, Las Vegas, Nevada 89124
Telephone: (702) 361 6409
PRESIDENT AND CHAIRMAN: John E. Morgan
CHIEF ENGINEER: Floyd Snow

JetCraft USA has announced plans to develop a family of business jets, using airframe parts based on those of the de Havilland Vampire T. Mk 11 jet trainer, but of new manufacture. A British company, Strato Jet UK Ltd, is supplying all components for the aircraft, which will be assembled in a 9,290 m² (100,000 sq ft) factory in Las Vegas.

JETCRAFT EXECUTIVE MARK I

Initial model in the JetCraft range is a six/seven-passenger business jet called Executive Mark I. Certification is anticipated in July 1989 under FAR Pt 23. It has a new metal fuselage, with a conventional enclosed pressurised cabin forward of the wing main spar, and new fins and rudders mated to the Vampire's wings and tailbooms. The power plant is a General Electric CF700-2D2 turbofan, rated at 20.02 kN (4,500 lb st) at T-O. Standard fuel capacity is 1,745 litres (461 US gallons; 384 Imp gallons), of which 1,703 litres (450 US gallons; 375 Imp gallons) are usable. Total fuel capacity with external fuel tanks is 2,653 litres (701 US gallons; 584 Imp gallons).

DIMENSIONS, EXTERNAL:

Wing span	11.58 m (38 ft 0 in)
Length overall	12.50 m (41 ft 0 in)
Height overall	2.59 m (8 ft 6 in)

AREAS:

Wings, gross	19.32 m² (208.0 sq ft)
Horizontal tail surfaces (total)	5.20 m² (56.0 sq ft)

WEIGHTS (estimated):

Weight empty	2,449 kg (5,400 lb)
Max T-O and landing weight with external fuel	5,624 kg (12,400 lb)

Prototype JetCraft Executive Mark I

PERFORMANCE (estimated):

Max operating speed	486 knots (901 km/h; 560 mph) IAS *or* Mach 0.82
Max cruising speed	470 knots (870 km/h; 541 mph)
Stalling speed:	
landing gear and flaps up	80 knots (148 km/h; 92 mph)
landing gear and flaps down	75 knots (138 km/h; 86 mph)
Max rate of climb at S/L	1,890 m (6,200 ft)/min
T-O run at S/L, ISA	366 m (1,200 ft)
Max certificated operating ceiling	12,500 m (41,000 ft)
Range with external fuel	3,220 nm (5,967 km; 3,708 miles)

JETCRAFT MARK II JET CRUISER

This six-passenger executive aircraft is generally similar to the Executive Mark I, but is projected with either a Pratt & Whitney Canada PT6A-65AR or Garrett TPE331-14 turboprop in a 'pusher' installation in the same location as the Mark I's turbofan. Estimated range is 3,300 nm (6,115 km; 3,800 miles), with a max cruising speed of 373 knots (692 km/h; 430 mph).

JETCRAFT MARK III EXECUTIVE COMMUTER

Generally similar in configuration to the Mark I and Mark II aircraft, the Mark III is offered as a ten-seater, with larger cabin (53 cm; 21 in longer and 20 cm; 8 in wider) and a side by side pair of 11.12 kN (2,500 lb st) Pratt & Whitney Canada JT15D-4 turbofans. Estimated range is 1,823 nm (3,379 km; 2,100 miles), with a max cruising speed of 460 knots (853 km/h; 530 mph).

KAMAN

KAMAN AEROSPACE CORPORATION
(a subsidiary of Kaman Corporation)

Old Windsor Road, PO Box No. 2, Bloomfield, Connecticut 06002
Telephone: (203) 242 4461
Telex: 710 425 3411
PRESIDENT AND CHIEF EXECUTIVE OFFICER:
Walter R. Kozlow

VICE-PRESIDENT, ENGINEERING:
Dr Roger A. Massey
DIRECTOR, PUBLIC RELATIONS:
Kenneth J. Nasshan

The original Kaman Aircraft Corporation was founded in 1945 by Mr Charles H. Kaman, who is now President and Chairman of the Board of Kaman Corporation. Its initial programme was to develop and test a novel servo-flap control system for helicopter rotors, and the current production H-2 Seasprite naval helicopter continues to utilise this system.

Current research and development programmes under the sponsorship of the US Army, Air Force, Navy and NASA include the advanced design of helicopter rotor systems, blades and rotor control concepts, component fatigue life determination, and structural dynamic analysis and testing.

Kaman Aerospace is a major subcontractor in many aircraft and space programmes. This work includes design, tooling and fabrication of components in metal, metal honeycomb, bonded and composite construction, using techniques such as filament winding and braiding. Military and commercial aircraft programmes in which Kaman participates include the Grumman A-6 and F-14, Rockwell B-1B, Lockheed C-5B, Bell/Boeing V-22, Boeing 767, Sikorsky UH-60 and NASA Space Shuttle Orbiter. Kaman also supplies acoustic engine ducts and spare parts for various aircraft types to the US military, and thrust reversers for CF6 engines to General Electric Company.

Kaman designed, and since mid-1977 has been producing, all-composite rotor blades for Bell AH-1 HueyCobras in service with the US Army and other countries. Improved performance, life and operational features have been demonstrated. Kaman is also a supplier of helicopters reconfigured as remotely piloted target drones for US Army weapons testing and training.

Through its diversified technologies operations, of which Kaman Aerospace is a part, Kaman Corporation provides scientific services and systems development primarily for the US armed services and government agencies; advanced technology products for military and commercial applications; helicopters, helicopter modifications and spare parts for the US Navy; and aerospace subcontracting for defence and commercial prime contractors.

KAMAN SEASPRITE
US Navy designations: HH-2 and SH-2

The prototype Seasprite flew for the first time on 2 July 1959, and many versions (described in previous editions of *Jane's*) were produced subsequently for the US Navy. Production of the SH-2F version was restarted in 1981.

From 1967, all single-engined UH-2A/B Seasprites were converted progressively to UH-2C twin-engined configuration, with 932 kW (1,250 shp) General Electric T58-GE-8B turboshafts in place of the former T58. They later underwent further modification, under the US Navy's Mk I LAMPS (Light Airborne Multi-Purpose System) programme, to provide helicopters for ASW (anti-submarine warfare), ASST (anti-ship surveillance and targeting), SAR (search and rescue), and utility operations. All but two of the US Navy's SH-2s were subsequently upgraded to SH-2F standard, with increased strength landing gear, T58-GE-8F engines and improved rotor system.

Operational deployment of HSL LAMPS Mk I squadrons began on 7 December 1971. By February 1988 more than 580,000 flight hours had been accumulated by LAMPS Mk I detachments deployed on successive long cruises on the following ship classes: FFG-7, DD-963, DDG-993, CG-47, FFG-1, FF-1052, FF-1040, CG-26, CGN-35, CGN-38 and BB-61. US Coast Guard WMEC and WHEC cutters are also being made capable of operating with the SH-2. In addition to the eight active Navy LAMPS Mk I HSL squadrons, formation of three Naval Air Reserve HSL squadrons began in 1984, and 24 SH-2Fs have been transferred to Reserve units as new production aircraft were delivered. Active and Reserve LAMPS Mk I SH-2s are scheduled to remain operational at least to the year 2010.

The following versions were in service in February 1987:

HH-2D. One aircraft, without LAMPS modifications, assigned to oceanography work.

NHH-2D. One aircraft assigned to special test programmes.

SH-2F. Mk I LAMPS version, of which 88 were delivered initially between May 1973 and 1982, plus 16 earlier SH-2Ds uprated to SH-2F configuration; first unit became operational with squadron HSL-33, deployed in the Pacific, on 11 September 1973. Seventy-nine of original 88 remained in US Navy service in February 1988. Further 54 new production SH-2Fs ordered in FYs 1982-86 (18, 18, 6, 6, and 6), of which 48 had been delivered by February 1988. Further six, ordered in FY 1987, will instead be completed to T700 powered SH-2G configuration (see next paragraph). For description and illustrations of SH-2F, see 1987-88 *Jane's*. US Navy plans to retrofit SH-2F fleet to SH-2G standard, and June 1987 contract included funds to intiate such retrofit on 42 aircraft. Additional funding has been made available for conversion of two existing SH-2Fs as pre-production YSH-2Gs.

SH-2G. Improved **Super Seasprite**, of which six ordered in FY 1987. To keep pace with the increasing threat, the US Navy initiated an SH-2F upgrade programme with FY 1987 production, under this designation. The primary airframe changes include the installation of new fuel efficient T700-GE-401 engines to replace the T58-GE-8F engines, and incorporation of newly developed composite main rotor blades. The avionics improvements include a MIL-STD-1553B digital databus, onboard acoustic processor (yet to be selected), multi-function raster display, TACNAV data transfer, and 99-channel sonobuoys. Evaluation of a YSH-2G prototype fitted with T700 engines was completed in 1985. US Navy tests have proved the SH-2 suitable for dipping sonar operations, air-to-surface missile firing, forward looking infra-red sensors and equipment with various guns, rockets and countermeasures. Export models of the SH-2 are offered with this equipment.

The following description refers to the SH-2G Super Seasprite:

Kaman YSH-2G Super Seasprite prototype (two General Electric T700-GE-401 engines)

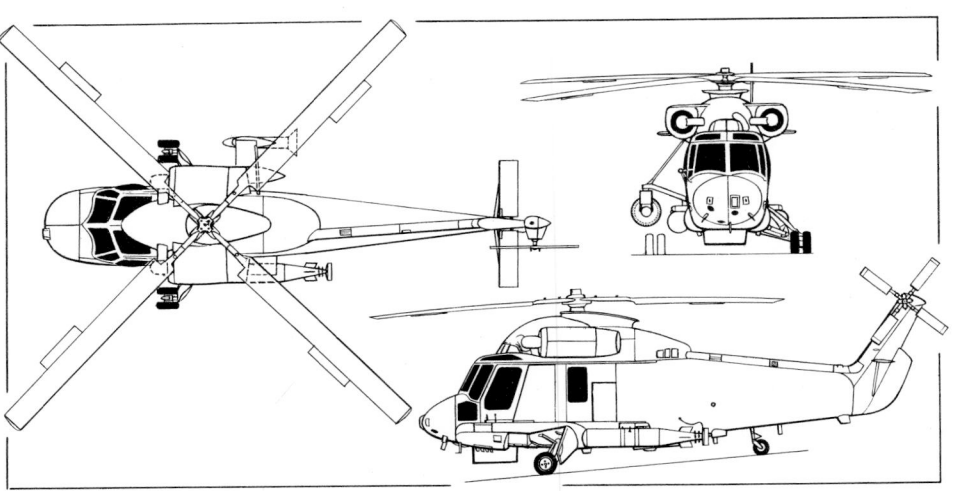

Kaman SH-2G Super Seasprite LAMPS Mk I helicopter *(Pilot Press)*

TYPE: Naval anti-submarine warfare and anti-ship surveillance and targeting helicopter, with secondary capability for search and rescue, observation and utility missions.

ROTOR SYSTEM: Four-blade main rotor utilising titanium hub and composite rotor blades, with composite servo-flap controls. Four-blade tail rotor. All eight blades folded manually. Main rotor rpm 298.

FUSELAGE AND TAIL UNIT: All-metal semi-monocoque structure, with flotation hull housing main fuel tanks. Nose split on centreline, to fold rearward on each side to reduce stowage space required. Fixed horizontal stabiliser on tail rotor pylon.

LANDING GEAR: Tailwheel type, with forward retracting twin mainwheels and non-retractable tailwheel. Liquid spring shock absorbers in main-gear legs; oleo-pneumatic shock absorber in tailwheel unit, which is fully castoring for taxying but locked fore and aft for T-O and landing. Mainwheels have 8-ply tubeless tyres size 17.5 × 6.25-11, pressure 17.25 bars (250 lb/sq in); tailwheel 10-ply tube-type tyre size 5.00-5, pressure 11.04 bars (160 lb/sq in).

POWER PLANT: Two 1,285 kW (1,723 shp) General Electric T700-GE-401 turboshafts, one on each side of rotor pylon structure. Basic fuel capacity of 1,802 litres (476 US gallons; 396 Imp gallons), including up to two external auxiliary tanks with a combined capacity of 757 litres (200 US gallons; 166.5 Imp gallons). Ship-to-air helicopter in-flight refuelling (HIFR).

ACCOMMODATION: Crew of three, consisting of pilot, co-pilot/tactical co-ordinator, and sensor operator. One passenger or litter patient with LAMPS equipment installed; four passengers or two litters with sonobuoy launcher removed. Provision for transportation of internal or external cargo.

AVIONICS, ARMAMENT AND OPERATIONAL EQUIPMENT: LAMPS Mk I mission equipment includes Canadian Marconi LN-66HP surveillance radar; General Instruments AN/ALR-66A(V)1 radar warning/ESM; Teledyne Systems AN/ASN-150 tactical management system; dual Collins AN/ARC-159(V)1 UHF radios; Texas Instruments AN/ASQ-81(V)2 magnetic anomaly detector; Computing Devices AN/UYS-503 acoustic processor; Rospatch AN/ARR-84 sonobuoy receiver; Tele-Dynamics AN/AKT-22(V)7 sonobuoy data link; 15 DIFAR and

DICASS sonobuoys; AN/ALE-39 chaff dispensers; AN/ASQ-188 torpedo presetter; one or two Mk 46 or Mk 50 torpedoes; eight Mk 25 marine smoke markers; cargo hook for external loads, capacity 1,814 kg (4,000 lb); and folding rescue hoist, capacity 272 kg (600 lb).

DIMENSIONS, EXTERNAL:

Main rotor diameter	13.51 m (44 ft 4 in)
Main rotor blade chord	0.59 m (1 ft 11 in)
Tail rotor diameter	2.46 m (8 ft 1 in)
Tail rotor blade chord	0.236 m (9.3 in)
Length of fuselage, excl tail rotor	12.19 m (40 ft 0 in)
Length overall (rotors turning)	16.08 m (52 ft 9 in)
Length overall, nose and blades folded	11.68 m (38 ft 4 in)
Height overall (rotors turning)	4.58 m (15 ft 0½ in)
Height (blades folded)	4.14 m (13 ft 7 in)
Width overall, incl MAD	3.74 m (12 ft 3 in)
Stabiliser span	2.97 m (9 ft 9 in)
Wheel track (outer wheels)	3.30 m (10 ft 10 in)
Wheelbase	5.13 m (16 ft 10 in)
Tail rotor ground clearance	2.12 m (6 ft 11½ in)

AREAS:

Main rotor blades (each)	3.96 m² (42.63 sq ft)
Tail rotor blades (each)	0.295 m² (3.175 sq ft)
Main rotor disc	143.41 m² (1,543.66 sq ft)
Tail rotor disc	4.77 m² (51.32 sq ft)

WEIGHTS:

Weight empty	3,483 kg (7,680 lb)
Max T-O weight	6,123 kg (13,500 lb)

PERFORMANCE (at max T-O weight, ISA):

Max level speed at S/L	130 knots (241 km/h; 150 mph)
Normal cruising speed	120 knots (222 km/h; 138 mph)
Max rate of climb at S/L	472 m (1,550 ft)/min
Service ceiling	5,090 m (16,700 ft)
Service ceiling one engine out	2,985 m (9,800 ft)
Hovering ceiling: IGE	4,390 m (14,400 ft)
OGE	3,320 m (10,900 ft)
Max range, 20 min reserves	440 nm (815 km; 506 miles)

Time on station (20 min reserves):

ASW at 35 nm (65 km; 40 miles) from base, 1 torpedo	2 h 10 min
ASW as above, 2 torpedoes	1 h 30 min
Max endurance, 20 min reserves	4 h 35 min

KING'S

THE KING'S ENGINEERING FELLOWSHIP

Municipal Airport, Orange City, Iowa 51041
Telephone: (712) 737 4444
PRESIDENT: Carl A. Mortenson

The Angel, developed for and by The King's Engineering Fellowship through donations, was designed by Mr Carl Mortenson, who designed and built an earlier light twin named Evangel for similar missionary work in the 1960s (see 1974-75 and earlier editions of *Jane's*). Eight Evangels were built, of which seven were still serving with missionaries in Alaska, Colombia, Micronesia and Peru in 1988.

KING'S MODEL 44 ANGEL

The King's Angel is a twin-engined light transport intended specifically for missionary aviation duties. Design goals included low manufacturing costs, STOL capability, suitability for rough and soft field operation, sturdiness, easy maintenance and repair in the field, and the ability to accommodate bulky cargo. The design phase has involved more than 16,000 manhours of work on over 1,000 drawings, and the prototype (N44KE) was built on production tooling. It flew for the first time in January 1984, and had logged over 550 flying hours by January 1988. During the test programme, the engines were raised above the wing on pylons for a period, and outboard 'trimmerons' were added for improved single-engine control (roll control being normally by means of spoilers). Later, the engines were replaced immediately on top of the wings, in longer nacelles, to increase cruising speed by an estimated 13 knots (24 km/h; 15 mph).

Recent changes incorporated as a result of flight testing include increased span on the horizontal tail surfaces to improve pitch trim with power changes. Final performance testing was expected to be completed in March 1988, after which destructive testing will begin once funding is obtained. No firm production date has been set because of funding uncertainties, but mid-1989 is seen as the earliest target, after which the Angel could be manufactured at a rate of one every two to three months, for missionary and other uses.

TYPE: Twin-engined light utility transport.
WINGS: Cantilever low-mid wing monoplane. Wing section modified NACA 23018-23010 with modified leading-edge; thickness/chord ratio of 18% at root, 10% at tip. All-metal riveted structure, with built-up aluminium alloy capstrip spars and 19 die formed ribs each side. Near full span hydraulically actuated Fowler flaps, with 37° max deflection. Multiple small-plate spoilers, forward of flaps, for roll control, supplemented by outboard 'trimmeron' between flap and wingtip on each trailing-edge.

FUSELAGE: Conventional aluminium alloy riveted semi-monocoque structure.
TAIL UNIT: Cantilever aluminium alloy riveted structure, with sweptback vertical surfaces and long dorsal fin.
LANDING GEAR: Retractable tricycle type. Electro-hydraulic retraction, mainwheels inward into wingroots, nosewheel rearward. Emergency extension by handpump or gravity. Tyre size: mainwheels 8.50-10, nosewheel 8.50-6. Cleveland brakes.
POWER PLANT: Two 224 kW (300 hp) Textron Lycoming IO-540-M flat-six engines, mounted on top of the inboard wings and each driving a Hartzell three-blade constant-speed feathering pusher propeller. Total usable fuel capacity 855 litres (226 US gallons; 188 Imp gallons). Oil capacity 22.7 litres (6 US gallons; 5 Imp gallons).
ACCOMMODATION: Enclosed cabin seating up to eight persons, including pilot. Five seats can be removed for carrying cargo, including four 208 litre (55 US gallon; 46 Imp gallon) drums. Rearmost bench seat is fixed. Four large windows and one smaller circular window on each side of cabin. Horizontally divided 'clamshell' door on port side at front of cabin; emergency exit on starboard side. Heating and window air vents standard. Compartment for 90 kg (200 lb) of baggage at rear of fuselage, with door on port side.
SYSTEMS: Hydraulic system, with electric pump, for landing gear and flap actuation. Electrical system includes 12V battery in fuselage nose.

Prototype King's Angel light twin for missionary aviation duties *(Howard Levy)*

AVIONICS AND EQUIPMENT: Blind-flying instrumentation standard. King avionics, including twin com/nav transceivers, glideslope, and dual ADF. Weather radar, Loran-C and HF com optional.

DIMENSIONS, EXTERNAL:
Wing span	12.19 m (40 ft 0 in)
Wing chord at root	2.29 m (7 ft 6 in)
Length overall	10.13 m (33 ft 3 in)
Height overall	3.51 m (11 ft 6 in)
Wheel track	3.96 m (13 ft 0 in)
Wheelbase	4.57 m (15 ft 0 in)

WEIGHTS:
Weight empty	1,701 kg (3,750 lb)
Max T-O weight	2,631 kg (5,800 lb)

PERFORMANCE:
Cruising speed, 65% power at 3,050 m (10,000 ft)	
	174 knots (322 km/h; 200 mph)
Landing speed	57 knots (105 km/h; 65 mph)
Service ceiling	5,790 m (19,000 ft)
Service ceiling, one engine out	2,135 m (7,000 ft)
T-O run	183 m (600 ft)
T-O to 15 m (50 ft)	366 m (1,200 ft)
Landing from 15 m (50 ft)	335 m (1,100 ft)
Landing run	183 m (600 ft)
Range with max fuel, with reserves	
	1,390 nm (2,575 km; 1,600 miles)
Endurance: with 8 occupants	4 h
with max fuel and 4 occupants	8 h

LAKE

LAKE AIRCRAFT INC

606 Dyer Boulevard, Kissimmee Airport, Kissimmee, Florida 32741
Telephone: (305) 847 9000
Telex: 52-3258 Lake Air Kiss
PRESIDENT: Armand E. Rivard
EXECUTIVE VICE-PRESIDENT: Gordon Collins
VICE-PRESIDENT, INTERNATIONAL: Haig Hagopian

LAKE LA4-200 AMPHIBIAN

The original C-1 Skimmer prototype flew for the first time in May 1948. From it were developed the improved C-2 Skimmer IV and the Lake LA-4, LA-4A, LA-4P, LA-4S and LA-4T, as described in previous editions of *Jane's*. By early 1988 more than 1,200 Lake amphibians had been delivered. The further improved LA4-200 received FAA certification in 1970, and is now manufactured in two versions, as follows:

LA4-200 EP. Standard version, as described in detail, which introduced a 13 cm (5 in) longer propeller shaft to increase efficiency and reduce cabin noise; a Textron Lycoming IO-360-A1B6 engine, dynamically balanced for smoother operation; an aerodynamically improved engine nacelle, which reduces drag and noise; wing trailing-edge fillets at intersection of wingroot and fuselage, to improve low-speed stability and protect the propeller from water

spray erosion; hull hydro boosters for improved on-water operation; reinforced floats and hull station 97 bulkhead; improved canopy; new instrument panel glareshield; new fresh air vents; additional corrosion proofing; and a new polyurethane paint finish.

LA4-200 EPR. Identical to above, but with reversible-pitch constant-speed propeller, which allows the aircraft to taxi in reverse during such on-water operations as docking or mooring.

Lake delivered nine LA4-200 EPs in 1987.
TYPE: Single-engined four-seat amphibian.
WINGS: Cantilever shoulder-wing monoplane with tapered wing panels attached directly to sides of hull. Wing section NACA 4415 at root, NACA 4409 at tip. Dihedral 5° 30'. Incidence 3° 15'. Structure consists of duralumin leading- and trailing-edge torsion boxes separated by a single duralumin main spar. All-metal ailerons and hydraulically operated slotted flaps over 80 per cent of span. Ground adjustable trim tabs on ailerons. Wing balancer floats are light alloy monocoque structures.
HULL: Single-step all-metal structure, with double-sealed boat hull. Alodined and zinc chromated inside and out against corrosion, with polyurethane paint exterior finish.
TAIL UNIT: Cantilever all-metal structure. Outboard elevator section separate from inboard section and actuated hydraulically for trimming. Retractable water rudder in base of aerodynamic rudder.

LANDING GEAR: Hydraulically retractable tricycle type. Consolidated oleo-pneumatic shock absorbers in main gear, which retracts inward into wings. Nosewheel, with long-stroke oleo, retracts forward. Gerdes mainwheels with Goodyear tyres, size 6.00-6, pressure 2.41 bars (35 lb/sq in). Gerdes nosewheel with Goodyear tyre size 5.00-5, pressure 1.38 bars (20 lb/sq in). Gerdes disc brakes. Parking brake. Nosewheel is free to swivel 30° each side.
POWER PLANT: One 149 kW (200 hp) Textron Lycoming IO-360-A1B6 flat-four engine, mounted on pylon above hull and driving a Hartzell two-blade constant-speed metal pusher propeller. Rajay turbocharger, reversible-pitch and Q-tip propeller, optional. Standard usable fuel capacity 204 litres (54 US gallons; 45 Imp gallons); optional usable fuel capacity of 340 litres (90 US gallons; 75 Imp gallons). Oil capacity 7.5 litres (2 US gallons; 1.7 Imp gallons).
ACCOMMODATION: Enclosed cabin seating pilot and three passengers. Front and rear seats removable. Front seats have inertia reel shoulder harness as standard. Dual controls standard; dual brakes for co-pilot optional. Entry through two forward-hinged windscreen sections. Upward hinged gull wing cargo door standard. Baggage compartment, capacity 90.5 kg (200 lb), aft of cabin. Dual windscreen defroster system.
SYSTEMS: Vacuum system for flight instruments. Hydraulic system, pressure 86.2 bars (1,250 lb/sq in), for flaps, horizontal trim and landing gear actuation; handpump provided for emergency operation. Engine driven 12V 60A alternator and 12V 30Ah battery. Janitrol 30,000 BTU heater optional.
AVIONICS AND EQUIPMENT: Basic avionics installation includes com and nav antennae, cabin speaker, microphone and circuit breakers. An extensive range of avionics by Collins, King and Narco, and autopilots by Brittain and Edo-Aire Mitchell, are available to customers' requirements. Standard equipment includes full blind-flying instrumentation, electric clock, manifold pressure gauge, outside air temperature gauge, recording tachometer, fuel pressure and quantity indicators, oil pressure and temperature indicators, cylinder head temperature gauge, ammeter, stall warning device, control locks, carpeted floor, four fresh air vents, tinted glass for all windows, dual windscreen defrosters, inertia

Two Lake LA4-200 amphibians emerging from the water

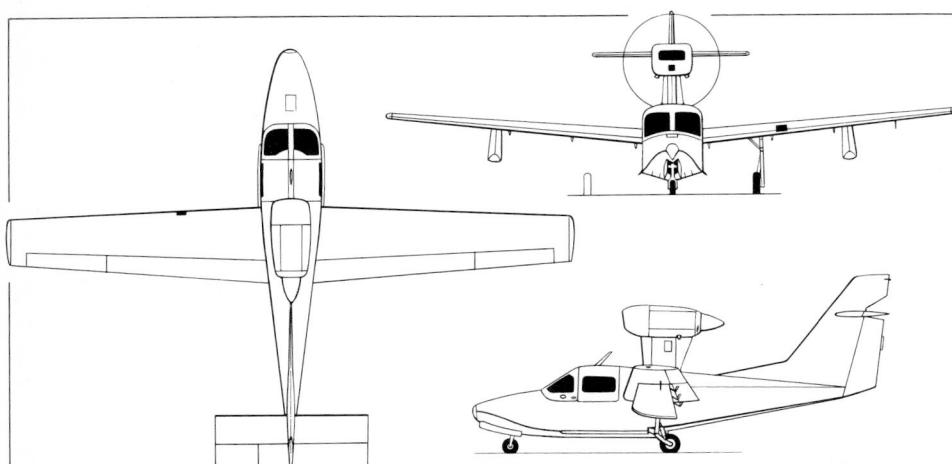

Lake LA-250 Renegade, showing cargo door location

Lake Renegade six-seat amphibian *(Pilot Press)*

reel shoulder harness on front seats, shoulder restraint on rear seats, map pocket on front seats, baggage tiedown straps, landing and taxi lights, navigation lights, strobe light, heated pitot, fuselage nose bumper, paddle, cleat, line, full flow oil filter, quick fuel drains, and inboard and outboard tiedown rings. Optional equipment includes hour meter, true airspeed indicator, shoulder harness for rear seats, alternate static source, manual/automatic bilge pump, cabin fire extinguisher, and external metallic paint finish.

DIMENSIONS, EXTERNAL:

Wing span	11.58 m (38 ft 0 in)
Wing chord, mean	1.35 m (4 ft 5.1 in)
Wing aspect ratio	8.7
Length overall	7.59 m (24 ft 11 in)
Height overall	2.84 m (9 ft 4 in)
Tailplane span	3.05 m (10 ft 0 in)
Wheel track	3.40 m (11 ft 2 in)
Wheelbase	2.69 m (8 ft 10 in)
Propeller diameter	1.88 m (6 ft 2 in)

DIMENSIONS, INTERNAL:

Cabin: Length	1.57 m (5 ft 2 in)
Max width	1.05 m (3 ft 5½ in)
Max height	1.32 m (3 ft 11½ in)
Floor area	approx 1.53 m² (16.5 sq ft)
Volume	approx 1.70 m³ (60.0 cu ft)
Baggage hold	0.24 m³ (8.5 cu ft)

AREAS:

Wings, gross	15.79 m² (170.0 sq ft)
Ailerons (total)	1.16 m² (12.5 sq ft)
Trailing-edge flaps (total)	2.28 m² (24.5 sq ft)
Fin	1.25 m² (13.5 sq ft)
Rudder	0.79 m² (8.5 sq ft)
Tailplane	1.45 m² (15.6 sq ft)
Elevators	0.78 m² (8.4 sq ft)

WEIGHTS AND LOADINGS:

Weight empty, equipped	753 kg (1,660 lb)
Max T-O and landing weight	1,220 kg (2,690 lb)
Max wing loading	74.2 kg/m² (15.2 lb/sq ft)
Max power loading	8.19 kg/kW (13.45 lb/hp)

PERFORMANCE (at max T-O weight. A: EP/EPR; B: EP/EPR with turbocharger):

Max level speed at S/L:

A   134 knots (248 km/h; 154 mph) IAS

Max cruising speed: 75% power at 2,440 m (8,000 ft):

A   130 knots (241 km/h; 150 mph)

75% power at 6,100 m (20,000 ft):

B   143 knots (265 km/h; 164 mph)

Stalling speed:

A, B, flaps and landing gear up

53 knots (98 km/h; 61 mph)

A, B, flaps and landing gear down

39 knots (73 km/h; 45 mph)

Max rate of climb at S/L: A	299 m (980 ft)/min

Rate of climb at 2,440 m (8,000 ft):

B	244 m (800 ft)/min
Service ceiling: A	3,810 m (12,500 ft)
Max operating altitude: B	6,100 m (20,000 ft)

T-O run: on land: A	183 m (600 ft)
on water: A	335 m (1,100 ft)
Landing run on land: A	145 m (475 ft)
Alighting run on water: A	183 m (600 ft)

Range with max fuel, at normal cruising speed, with

reserves: A   564 nm (1,046 km; 650 miles)

Max range with max fuel, with reserves:

A   716 nm (1,327 km; 825 miles)

Endurance (75% power):

A at 2,440 m (8,000 ft)	5 h 36 min
B at 6,100 m (20,000 ft)	5 h 12 min

LAKE LA-250 RENEGADE and TURBO RENEGADE

The **Renegade** is basically a development of the LA4-200 with lengthened fuselage, providing six-seat accommodation, and has a more powerful engine, together with tail surfaces of greater area. It was designed for STOL capability and is able to make high-speed step turns on water. FAA certification was received in August 1983. It is available also in turbocharged form as the **Turbo Renegade**. Lake delivered 14 Renegades in 1987.

The description of the LA4-200 applies also to the LA-250, except as follows:

TYPE: Single-engined six-seat amphibian.

HULL: Generally as for LA4-200, but lengthened by 1.05 m (3 ft 5 in). Deeper V hull bottom and added hull strakes for improved water handling.

TAIL UNIT: Cantilever all-metal structure, with swept fin and rudder and dorsal fillet. High-set tailplane. Outboard portion of elevator on port side is actuated hydraulically and independently as large trim tab. Fin is notched at tailplane position to permit elevator movement. Small retractable water rudder in base of rudder.

LANDING GEAR: As for LA4-200, except wheelbase increased by 0.43 m (1 ft 5 in), and oleo extension increased to provide greater ground clearance.

POWER PLANT: One 186 kW (250 hp) Textron Lycoming IO-540-C4B5 flat-six engine in Renegade, driving a Hartzell three-blade constant-speed Q-tip metal pusher

propeller. Turbocharged TIO-540 engine in Turbo Renegade. Standard usable fuel capacity 204 litres (54 US gallons; 45 Imp gallons); optional usable capacity of 340 litres (90 US gallons; 75 Imp gallons).

ACCOMMODATION: As for LA4-200, but lengthened cabin provides seating for a pilot and five passengers, with increased baggage capacity. Gull wing cargo door standard.

DIMENSIONS, EXTERNAL:

Wing span	11.68 m (38 ft 4 in)
Length overall	8.64 m (28 ft 4 in)
Height overall	3.05 m (10 ft 0 in)
Wheelbase	3.13 m (10 ft 3 in)
Propeller diameter	1.93 m (6 ft 4 in)

DIMENSION, INTERNAL:

Cabin: Length	2.03 m (6 ft 8 in)

WEIGHTS AND LOADINGS:

Weight empty, equipped	839 kg (1,850 lb)
Max T-O and landing weight	1,383 kg (3,050 lb)
Max wing loading	87.6 kg/m² (17.94 lb/sq ft)
Max power loading	7.42 kg/kW (12.2 lb/hp)

PERFORMANCE (at max T-O weight, S/L, ISA):

Never-exceed speed	148 knots (274 km/h; 170 mph)

Max level speed at 1,980 m (6,500 ft)

139 knots (258 km/h; 160 mph)

Max cruising speed, 75% power at 1,980 m (6,500 ft)

132 knots (245 km/h; 152 mph)

Stalling speed, power off:

landing gear and flaps up

53 knots (99 km/h; 61 mph) IAS

landing gear and flaps down

48 knots (89 km/h; 56 mph) IAS

Max rate of climb at S/L	274 m (900 ft)/min
Service ceiling	4,480 m (14,700 ft)
T-O run: on land	268 m (880 ft)
on water	381 m (1,250 ft)

Range with max fuel, 30 min reserves

900 nm (1,668 km; 1,036 miles)

LAKE SEAWOLF

The Seawolf, introduced in early 1985, is a military/maritime surveillance variant of the LA-250 Renegade, with an Alkan 6091 rack under each wing to carry a variety of external stores including bombs of up to 200 lb size, rocket launchers, cartridge launchers and machine-gun pods. The weapons boresight position is constant and repeatable even after store removal and re-installation. In addition, the Seawolf can carry and release wing mounted rescue pods designed for use at sea or over land, with contents suitable for desert, Arctic and sea survival. Sea search and rescue pods are equipped with a liferaft, rations, homing and signalling devices; while desert pods have tent, rations, water, and other necessary equipment for survival and rescue.

A variety of radar systems is available, with the antenna mounted at the forward face of the engine pod, between the cooling inlets. The systems offer colour weather detection, a range of 240 nm (445 km; 276 miles), and three search modes: Search 1, employing sea clutter rejection circuitry to assist in detecting small boats down to a minimum range of 275 m (900 ft); Search 2, designed for precision surface mapping where high target resolution is important; and Search 3, which offers normal surface mapping for such tasks as the detection and tracking of oil slicks.

Interface units are available to provide a moving map display, waypoint designation, checklists, beacon navigation and multiple indicators. Provision has also been made for the installation of Loran or Omega navigation equipment.

Lake Aircraft claims that the Seawolf can fulfil a variety of paramilitary roles, including patrol and reconnaissance, search and rescue, special missions, liaison and logistics support, anti-smuggling duties, fish and wildlife protection, pollution control, law enforcement, and medevac duties. In medevac configuration the cabin can accommodate two litter patients and an attendant, as well as emergency medical equipment, once the passenger seats have been removed.

The prototype Seawolf (N1401G), which made its public debut at the 1985 Paris Air Show, retained the standard 12V electrical system of the civil Renegade; production versions will have a 28V system.

Typical mission profiles for the Seawolf are:

Lake Seawolf maritime patrol amphibian with underwing SAR pods

Maritime patrol, with standard fuel and two gun pods; pilot only; take-off weight 1,485 kg (3,274 lb), 70 min fuel reserves; radius of action 100 nm (185 km; 115 miles); outbound leg flown at 120 knots (222 km/h; 138 mph) at 1,830 m (6,000 ft), with 6 h 30 min on station at 450 m (1,500 ft), returning to base at 120 knots at 2,440 m (8,000 ft).

Single strike mission, with standard fuel, and bombs or rockets; pilot only; take-off weight 1,517 kg (3,344 lb), 70 min fuel reserves; flying outbound to target 400 nm (740 km; 460 miles) from base at 120 knots at 6,000 ft, with ten min over target, returning to base at 125 knots (231 km/h; 144 mph) at 3,050 m (10,000 ft).

Multiple strike mission, with standard fuel and rockets; two crew; take-off weight 1,565 kg (3,450 lb), 1 h 50 min fuel reserves; flying to initial target 200 nm (370 km; 230 miles) distant at 6,000 ft, ten min over target, continuing to second target 150 nm (278 km; 172 miles) beyond, ten min over target, returning to base at 10,000 ft.

Search and rescue mission, with external fuel and two SAR packs; pilot only; take-off weight 1,568 kg (3,457 lb), 1 h 50 min fuel reserves; to search locality 250 nm (463 km; 287 miles) from base at 6,000 ft, time on station 8 hours, returning to base at 120 knots at 10,000 ft.

Photo reconnaissance mission, with standard fuel and two reconnaissance pods; two crew; take-off weight 1,430 kg (3,152 lb), 1 h 30 min fuel reserves; flying at 120 knots to three locations at 50 nm (93 km; 57 mile) intervals from base, one hour loiter over each at 1,500 ft, returning 150 nm to base at 120 knots at 6,000 ft.

Ferry flight, with external fuel; two crew; take-off weight 1,563 kg (3,445 lb), 1 h 50 min fuel reserves; range 1,500 nm (2,775 km; 1,726 miles) at 120 knots; endurance 12 h 30 min.

The description of the Renegade applies also to the Seawolf, except as follows:

TYPE: Single-engined multi-role amphibian.

HULL: Interior LPS preservative spray optional.

POWER PLANT: Standard fuel capacity 333 litres (88 US gallons; 73.3 Imp gallons); optional capacity, with external tanks, 568 litres (150 US gallons; 125 Imp gallons).

ACCOMMODATION: Enclosed cabin capable of seating up to six persons. All seats except pilot's removable, with a variety of optional internal configurations according to mission. Entry through two forward-hinged windscreen sections. Upward hinged gull wing cargo door standard.

ARMAMENT: Standard Alkan 6091 stores mounts on underwing hardpoints, one inboard and one outboard of each wing balancer float, can accommodate a variety of stores, including external fuel tanks, parachute flares, SAR pods, ECM pods, gun pods, reconnaissance pods, rocket launchers, photo-reconnaissance pods, cartridge throwers, flare dispensers, hazardous material containers, practice and general purpose bombs. Inboard stores points can each carry up to 100 kg (220 lb), outboard points can each carry up to 35 kg (77 lb).

DIMENSIONS AND AREAS: As for Renegade

WEIGHTS:

Weight empty	998 kg (2,200 lb)
*Max ramp and T-O weight	1,565 kg (3,450 lb)
Max landing weight, on land	1,383 kg (3,050 lb)

PERFORMANCE:

As for Renegade, except:

Cruising speed, 55% power	110 knots (204 km/h; 127 mph)
Landing distance, land and water	230 m (755 ft)
Range with standard fuel at 120 knots (222 km/h; 138 mph), with 38 litres (10 US gallons; 8.3 Imp gallons) fuel reserves	876 nm (1,622 km; 1,008 miles)
Range with external tanks at 120 knots (222 km/h; 138 mph), with 38 litres (10 US gallons; 8.3 Imp gallons) fuel reserves	1,500 nm (2,780 km; 1,727 miles)
Endurance: with standard fuel	8 h 30 min
with external tanks	14 h 30 min

**181 kg (400 lb) must be underwing stores*

LEARJET

LEARJET CORPORATION

Mid-Continent Airport, PO Box 7707, Wichita, Kansas 67277

Telephone: (316) 946 2000

Telex: 417441

CHAIRMAN: Robert J. Edgreen

PRESIDENT AND CHIEF EXECUTIVE OFFICER: Beverly N. Lancaster

EXECUTIVE VICE-PRESIDENT: William A. Boettger

VICE-PRESIDENT RESALE MARKETING: Michael I. Berger

VICE-PRESIDENT ENGINEERING: William W. Greer

VICE-PRESIDENT MARKETING: Frank E. de Monchaux

DIRECTOR, CORPORATE PUBLIC RELATIONS: John V. Alexander

Founded in 1960 by the late William P. Lear Sr, this company was known originally as the Swiss American Aviation Corporation, which was formed to manufacture a high-speed twin-jet executive aircraft known as the Learjet 23 (formerly SAAC-23). In 1962 all company activities were relocated at Wichita, Kansas, and shortly afterwards the company became known as Lear Jet Corporation. In 1967 Mr Lear's interests (approx 60%) were acquired by The Gates Rubber Company of Denver, Colorado, and in January 1970 the company name was changed to Gates Learjet Corporation. In early September 1987, Integrated Acquisition Inc acquired a 64.8% interest in Gates Learjet, and renamed the company Learjet Corporation. In January 1988 the company announced that it would close its plant at Tucson, Arizona, and concentrate all Learjet manufacturing operations in Wichita, where total employment was expected to exceed 1,540 by the Summer of 1988.

Improved 'Century III' models of the Learjet 24, 25 and 35/36, incorporating a cambered wing and other changes to reduce stall and approach speeds and balanced field length, were introduced in late 1975. Further details of these improvements can be found in the 1981-82 *Jane's*.

Since 1 July 1979, all newly delivered Learjets have also embodied a 'Softflite' handling package to improve stall characteristics. Available for retrofit on earlier aircraft, this comprises a full chord shallow fence on each wing, small devices on the inboard leading-edge, and two rows of boundary layer energisers forward of each aileron, to energise the airflow and delay the onset of compressibility. Vortex generators are removed; the stick shaker/pusher is retained but unlikely to be required. A Softflite I performance kit was developed subsequently, and is FAA certificated for all early model Learjet 20 series aircraft with the so-called straight-wing or standard wing configuration, including the original Model 23. The modification incorporates a unique treatment of the wing leading-edge in place of conventional stall strips, and includes the full chord wing fences and boundary layer energisers that form part of the original Softflite package. Designed to improve low-speed performance and handling qualities, the Softflite I modification greatly enhances the aerodynamic stall characteristics of those early 20 series aircraft not equipped with Century III and original Softflite systems improvements.

Advanced models, with wings of increased span fitted with supercritical winglets, were announced in 1977. Designated Learjet 28/29 and Learjet 55, these subsequently joined the earlier models in production; manufacture of the Learjet 28/29 ended in 1982. Models 35, 36 and 55 continue in production, and were joined in 1987 by a new Model 31, combining the Learjet 35/36 fuselage and power plant with a wing similar to that of the earlier 28/29.

LEARJET 35A and 36A

US Air Force designation: C-21A

A prototype turbofan powered Learjet (known originally as the Model 26) made its first flight with Garrett TFE731-2 engines on 4 January 1973. The production 35 and 36, announced in May 1973, are almost identical, differing in fuel capacity and accommodation. FAA certification was awarded in July 1974, and customer deliveries began later that year. French and UK certification were gained during 1979.

Century III improvements, the 'Softflite' handling package (see introductory notes) and engine synchronisers are standard for both models; a higher max T-O weight of 8,300 kg (18,300 lb), originally an option, is now standard on the current 35A/36A. Improvements introduced in the Autumn of 1983 include the T/R-4000 thrust reverser system developed in co-operation with The Dee Howard Company (which see). The T/R-4000 has a hydraulic accumulator permitting operation even if the aircraft hydraulic system fails, single-engine deployment capability, quick removal hot section, a locking arrangement preventing deployment at high thrust settings, reverse thrust availability within two seconds after touchdown, throttle retard system, and lower engine (N_1) speed at equivalent reverser thrust. The T/R-4000 is optional on new Learjet 35A/36As, and is available for retrofit to all Century III 30-series Learjets.

A new 'special class' interior for the Model 35A was introduced in Autumn 1985, offering increased leg and headroom. Four passengers can be accommodated in club seating on Erda seats which recline and have an electrically actuated inboard, fore and aft tracking facility. A centre console between the rear pair of seats contains stereo headsets and an in-flight telephone. Solid doors fore and aft of the lavatory area, electronic control of the adjustable washbasin cabinet, and 0.61 m (2 ft 0 in) wide fold-out conference/dining tables, are also featured in the new cabin configuration.

One of 80 Learjet C-21As sold to US Air Force for operational support missions *(Jay Miller/Aerofax)*

During 1984-85 the USAF received, originally on lease, 80 Model 35As, designated **C-21A**, for the Operational Support Aircraft (OSA) programme, to replace CT-39 Sabreliners in the Military Airlift Command inventory on high-priority and time-sensitive cargo delivery, passenger airlift and other operational support missions, including medical evacuation. In September 1986 USAF exercised its option to purchase the 80 C-21As for $180 million. They are based throughout the USA and in Japan and the Federal Republic of Germany. In the Summer of 1987 the Air National Guard acquired four C-21As to replace T-39s based at Andrews AFB, Maryland.

By early 1988 a total of 690 Learjet Model 35As and 36As had been delivered.

TYPE: Twin-turbofan light executive transport.

WINGS: Cantilever low-wing monoplane. Wing section NACA 64A 109 with modified leading-edge. Dihedral 2° 30′. Incidence 1°. Sweepback 13° at quarter-chord. All-metal eight-spar structure with milled alloy skins. Manually operated, aerodynamically balanced all-metal ailerons. The Softflite handling package consists of two rows of boundary layer energisers forward of each aileron, full-chord fences, and stall strips on the wing leading-edges. Hydraulically acutated all-metal single-slotted flaps. Hydraulically actuated all-metal spoilers ahead of flaps. Electrically operated trim tab in port aileron. Balance tab in each aileron. Anti-icing by engine bleed air ducted into leading-edges.

FUSELAGE: All-metal flush riveted semi-monocoque fail-safe structure.

TAIL UNIT: Cantilever all-metal sweptback structure, with electrically actuated variable incidence T tailplane and small ventral fin. Conventional manually operated control surfaces. Electrically operated trim tab in rudder. Electrically heated de-icing of tailplane leading-edges.

LANDING GEAR: Retractable tricycle type, with twin wheels on each main unit and single steerable nosewheel. Hydraulic actuation, with backup pneumatic extension. Oleo-pneumatic shock absorbers. Goodyear multiple-disc hydraulic brakes. Pneumatic emergency braking system. Parking brakes. Fully modulated anti-skid system.

POWER PLANT: Two Garrett TFE731-2-2B turbofans, each rated at 15.6 kN (3,500 lb st), pod-mounted on sides of rear fuselage. Fuel in integral wing and wingtip tanks and a fuselage tank, with a combined usable capacity (Learjet 35A) of 3,524 litres (931 US gallons; 775 Imp gallons). Learjet 36A has a larger fuselage tank, giving a combined usable total of 4,201 litres (1,110 US gallons; 924 Imp gallons). Refuelling point on upper surface of each wingtip tank. Fuel jettison system. Engine nacelle leading-edges anti-iced by engine bleed air.

ACCOMMODATION: Crew of two on flight deck, with dual controls. Up to eight passengers in Learjet 35A; one on inward facing bench seat on starboard side at front, then two pairs of swivel seats which face fore and aft for take-off and landing, with centre aisle, and three on forward facing couch at rear of cabin. Alternative 'mid-cabin' arrangement, available optionally, places a refreshment area in the middle of the cabin, accessible from fore and aft club seating areas, each for four passengers. Learjet 36A can accommodate up to six passengers, one pair of swivel seats being removed. Toilet and stowage space under front inward facing seat which can be screened from remainder of cabin. Refreshment cabinet opposite this seat, aft of passenger door. Baggage compartment with capacity of 226 kg (500 lb) aft of cabin.

Two-piece clamshell door at forward end of cabin on port side, with integral steps built into lower half. Emergency exit on starboard side of cabin. Birdproof windscreens.

SYSTEMS: Environmental control system comprises cabin pressurisation, ventilation, heating and cooling. Heating and pressurisation by engine bleed air, with a max pressure differential of 0.65 bars (9.4 lb/sq in), maintaining a cabin altitude of 1,980 m (6,500 ft) to an actual altitude of 13,715 m (45,000 ft). Freon R12 vapour cycle cooling system supplemented by a ram-air heat exchanger. Flight control system includes dual yaw dampers, dual stick pushers, dual stick shakers and Mach trim. Anti-icing system includes distribution of engine bleed air for wing, tailplane and engine nacelle leading-edges and windscreen; electrical heating of pitot heads, stall warning vanes and static ports; and alcohol spray on windscreen and nose radome. Hydraulic system supplied by two engine driven pumps, each pump capable of maintaining alone the full system pressure of 103.5 bars (1,500 lb/sq in), for operation of landing gear, brakes, flaps and spoilers. Hydraulic system maximum flow rate 15 litres (4 US gallons; 3.33 Imp gallons) per min. Cylindrical reservoir pressurised to 1.38 bars (20 lb/sq in). Electrically driven hydraulic pump for emergency operation of all hydraulic services. Pneumatic system of 124 to 207 bars (1,800 to 3,000 lb/sq in) pressure for emergency extension of landing gear and operation of brakes. Electrical system powered by two 30V 400A brushless generators, two 1kVA solid state inverters to provide AC power, and two 24V 37Ah lead-acid batteries. Oxygen system for emergency use, with crew demand masks and drop-out masks for each passenger.

AVIONICS: Standard avionics include dual Collins FIS-84/EHSI-74 flight directors, one integrated with J.E.T. FC-530 FCS and dual yaw dampers; dual Collins VHF-22A com transceivers; dual VIR-32 nav receivers; ADF-60; dual DME-42 with IND-42C indicators; dual Allen 3137 RMIs; dual Collins TDR-90 transponders; Collins ALT-55B radio altimeter with DRI-55 indicator; Universal UNS-1A long range nav system; King KHF-950 HF; Fredrickson Jetcal-5 selcal; Wulfsberg Flitefone VI; Sperry Primus 450 colour weather radar; dual J.E.T. VG-206D vertical gyros; dual J.E.T. DN-104B directional gyros; J.E.T. PS-835D and AI-804 emergency battery and attitude gyro; IDC electric encoding altimeter with altitude alerter and IDC air data unit (pilot's side); IDC barometric altimeter (co-pilot); dual Teledyne IVSIs; dual marker beacon indicators; dual Avtech audio systems; IDC SAT/TAT/TAS indicator; Rosemount temperature probe; eight-day wind-up clock (pilot's side); Davtron 877 clock (co-pilot); nacelle heat annunciator; N_1 reminder; avionics master switch; chip detector and flap pre-select.

EQUIPMENT: Standard equipment includes thrust reversers, dual angle of attack indicators, engine synchronisation meter, cabin differential pressure gauge, cabin rate of climb indicator, interstage and turbine temperature gauges, turbine and fan speed gauges, wing temperature indicator, alternate static source, depressurisation warning, engine fire warning lights, Mach warning system, dual stall warning system, fire axe, cabin fire extinguisher, cabin stereo system, flotation jackets for crew and passengers, sound-proofing; baggage compartment, courtesy, instrument panel, flood, map, and reading lights; dual anti-collision, landing, navigation, recognition, strobe, and taxi lights, wing ice detection light; dual engine fire extinguishing systems with 'systems armed' and fire warning lights, engine synchronisation system, control lock, external power socket, and lightning protection system.

DIMENSIONS, EXTERNAL:
Wing span over tip tanks	12.04 m (39 ft 6 in)
Wing chord: at root	2.74 m (9 ft 0 in)
at tip	1.55 m (5 ft 1 in)
Wing aspect ratio	5.7
Length overall	14.83 m (48 ft 8 in)
Height overall	3.73 m (12 ft 3 in)
Tailplane span	4.47 m (14 ft 8 in)
Wheel track	2.51 m (8 ft 3 in)
Wheelbase	6.15 m (20 ft 2 in)
Passenger door:	
Standard: Height	1.57 m (5 ft 2 in)
Width	0.61 m (2 ft 0 in)
Optional: Height	1.57 m (5 ft 2 in)
Width	0.91 m (3 ft 0 in)
Emergency exit: Height	0.71 m (2 ft 4 in)
Width	0.48 m (1 ft 7 in)

DIMENSIONS, INTERNAL (A: Learjet 35A; B: Learjet 36A):
Cabin: Length, incl flight deck: A	6.63 m (21 ft 9 in)
B	5.77 m (18 ft 11 in)
Max width	1.50 m (4 ft 11 in)
Max height	1.32 m (4 ft 4 in)
Volume, incl flight deck: A	9.12 m³ (322.0 cu ft)
B	7.25 m³ (256.0 cu ft)
Baggage compartment: A	1.13 m³ (40.0 cu ft)
B	0.76 m³ (27.0 cu ft)

AREA:
Wings, gross	23.53 m² (253.3 sq ft)

WEIGHTS AND LOADINGS (Learjet 35A and 36A):
Weight empty, equipped	4,462 kg (9,838 lb)
Max payload	1,361 kg (3,000 lb)

Max T-O weight	8,300 kg (18,300 lb)
Max ramp weight	8,391 kg (18,500 lb)
Max landing weight	6,940 kg (15,300 lb)
Max wing loading	347.1 kg/m² (71.1 lb/sq ft)
Max power loading	261.7 kg/kN (2.57 lb/lb st)

PERFORMANCE (Learjet 35A and 36A, at max T-O weight, except where indicated):
Never-exceed speed	Mach 0.83
Max level speed at 7,620 m (25,000 ft)	
	471 knots (872 km/h; 542 mph)
Max cruising speed, mid-cruise weight, at 12,500 m (41,000 ft)	460 knots (852 km/h; 529 mph)
Econ cruising speed, mid-cruise weight, at 13,700 m (45,000 ft)	418 knots (774 km/h; 481 mph)
Stalling speed, wheels and flaps down, engines idling	
	96 knots (178 km/h; 111 mph) IAS
Max rate of climb at S/L	1,322 m (4,339 ft)/min
Rate of climb at S/L, one engine out	
	389 m (1,276 ft)/min
Service ceiling	13,715 m (45,000 ft)
Service ceiling, one engine out	7,165 m (23,500 ft)
T-O balanced field length, FAR Pt 25:	
at 7,711 kg (17,000 lb)	1,287 m (4,224 ft)
at 8,300 kg (18,300 lb)	1,515 m (4,972 ft)
Landing distance, FAR Pt 25, at max landing weight	
	937 m (3,075 ft)
Range with 4 passengers, max fuel and 45 min reserves:	
Learjet 35A	2,232 nm (4,136 km; 2,570 miles)
Learjet 36A	2,635 nm (4,916 km; 3,055 miles)

OPERATIONAL NOISE LEVELS (FAR Pt 36):
T-O	83.9 EPNdB
Approach	91.4 EPNdB
Sideline	87.8 EPNdB

LEARJET 35A/36A SPECIAL MISSIONS VERSIONS

In addition to the commercial Model 35A/36A, Learjet offers specialised aircraft for a wide range of civilian and paramilitary applications such as aerial survey, aeronautical research, airways calibration, anti-submarine warfare, atmospheric research, border patrol, ECM/ESM, geophysical survey, maritime patrol, pilot training, radar surveillance, reconnaissance, search and rescue, and weather modification. Special mission Learjets are operating in 20 countries, including Argentina, Australia, Bolivia, Brazil, Chile, the People's Republic of China, Finland, West Germany, Japan, Mexico, Peru, Saudi Arabia, Sweden, Switzerland, Thailand and Yugoslavia. Most special missions modifications are applicable to the Models 35A and 36A, according to customer requirements.

Versions announced to date are:

EC-35A. Electronic warfare version for EW training simulation or use as a standoff ECM/ESM platform.

PC-35A. Maritime patrol version. A prototype (N80SM) based on a modified Learjet 35A and then known as the Sea Patrol Learjet, was exhibited at the 1979 Paris Air Show. Equipment available includes 360° sea surveillance digital radar housed in underbelly radome; high resolution television; forward looking infra-red (FLIR); infra-red linescanner (IRLS); electronic support measures (ESM); magnetic anomaly detector; integrated tactical displays; VLF Omega and other long range navigation systems; a hardpoint under each wing with an Alkan 165B ejector for the carriage and ejection of external stores weighing up to

453 kg (1,000 lb); drop hatch for rescue gear; multi-track digital recorders; direction finding (homing) systems; ASW sonobuoy drop and detection equipment, and data annotated hand-held cameras.

RC-35A. Reconnaissance version. Standard installations include long range oblique photographic (LOROP) cameras, side looking synthetic aperture radar, and pod-mounted surveillance camera systems carried as external stores. Three RC-35As, each equipped with geological survey equipment, including Goodyear SLAR in an underbelly pack, were delivered to the People's Republic of China in 1985, to supplement two similarly equipped **RC-36As** delivered in 1984.

UC-35A. Utility version with configurations to suit such applications as aerial survey, airways calibration, cargo/passenger transport, medevac, target towing and weather modification. In September 1984 Learjet announced certification of the Marquardt MTR-101 aerial target launch and recovery tow reel for use aboard Learjet aircraft. The Hayes Universal Tow Target System is also approved. Three Learjet 35As have been delivered to the Finnish Air Force, equipped for a variety of missions, including aerial mapping, air ambulance, air pollution control, oblique photography, rescue and sea patrol, in addition to their primary role of target towing for the Air Force's BAe Hawk combat trainers.

U-36A. Extensively modified version of Learjet 36A for Japan's Maritime Self Defence Force (JMSDF). Two delivered, one each in November 1985 and late 1986, for target towing, anti-ship sea skimming missile simulation and ECM duties. To meet the Japan Defence Agency's mission profile for the aircraft, Learjet, in association with Shin Meiwa, introduced longer and increased diameter wingtip tanks to accommodate the HWQ-1T missile seeker simulator, ALQ-6 jammer and camera equipment; an underbelly fairing for long range ocean surveillance radar; an ALE-43 chaff dispenser; an ARS-1-L high speed tow sleeve with scoring; a new two-piece windscreen with electric demisting system for increased speed during low level missions; expanded underwing stores capability; and increases in max T-O and landing weights to accommodate mission equipment. Further deliveries of U-36As to the JMSDF are anticipated into the 1990s.

PERFORMANCE (PC-35A):
Operating speed:	
at 11,275-12,500 m (37,000-41,000 ft)	
	415 knots (769 km/h; 478 mph)
at 4,575-7,620 m (15,000-25,000 ft)	
	319 knots (590 km/h; 367 mph)
S/L to 610 m (2,000 ft)	
	250 knots (463 km/h; 288 mph)
Rate of climb at S/L	1,380 m (4,525 ft)/min
Range:	
at high altitude	2,249 nm (4,168 km; 2,590 miles)
at medium altitude	1,617 nm (2,996 km; 1,862 miles)
at low altitude	1,060 nm (1,964 km; 1,220 miles)

LEARJET 31

Learjet introduced the Learjet Model 31 at the National Business Aircraft Association Covention at New Orleans in late September 1987. This aircraft combines the fuselage, eight-passenger cabin and 15.6 kN (3,500 lb st) Garrett TFE731-2-2B turbofans of the Learjet 35A and 36A with a longer span wing with winglets, similar to that employed on

Special missions Learjet Model 35A with drop hatch, LOROP camera windows, air turbine target reeling packs, surveillance radar and ESM system

the earlier turbojet Learjet Model 28/29 'Longhorns'. A new feature introduced on the Learjet 31 is a pair of outward-canted ventral strakes which Learjet calls Delta-Fins. Installed on each side of the lower rear fuselage, the aluminium and composite fins have a 65° leading-edge sweepback that produces vortex lift at high angles of attack, to enhance directional stability at all airspeeds. They are most effective at low speed and high angles of attack, where they produce lift in undisturbed airflow and exert a nose-down pitching moment as the aircraft approaches the stall. As a result, the Learjet 31 is not required to have a stick pusher system, although a stick shaker is installed as a precaution, and the aircraft exhibits such improved yaw and Dutch roll characteristics that only a single yaw damper is required and is not a vital operational item for flight dispatch.

The prototype Learjet 31, modified from a Learjet 35A airframe, first flew on 11 May 1987 and was used for aerodynamic testing. The first production aircraft (N311DF) served as systems testbed. By April 1988 the two aircraft had completed 390 hours of flight testing. FAA certification was expected in July 1988, with first customer deliveries in August. A total of eight Learjet 31s was expected to be manufactured during 1988, with an increase in production rate anticipated in 1989.

The following data are provisional:

POWER PLANT: As for Learjet 35A/36A. Fuel capacities 2,320 litres (613 US gallons; 510 Imp gallons) standard, 2,597 litres (686 US gallons; 571 Imp gallons) optional.

AVIONICS: Standard Collins avionics package comprises dual VHF-22A com with CTL-22 controls, dual VIR-32 nav receivers with CTL-32 controls, pilot's ADI-70/HSI-70 and co-pilot's AIM-510-24HG/HSI-70 flight instruments integrated with J.E.T. FC-530 autopilot, ADF-60 with CTL-62 control, DME-42 with IND-42A indicator, TDR-90 with CTL-92 control, dual Allen 3137 RMIs, dual marker beacon receivers, dual DB audio systems, Bendix RDS-81 four-colour weather radar, dual J.E.T. DN-104B compass systems, J.E.T. VG-206D vertical gyro, I.D.C. electric encoding altimeter with altitude alert and I.D.C. air data unit, co-pilot's I.D.C. barometric altimeter, dual Teledyne IVSIs, dual Davtron 877 digital clocks, dual I.D.C. Mach/IAS indicators, J.E.T. PS-835D/AI-804 emergency battery and attitude gyro, avionics master switch, and single J.E.T. yaw damper.

EQUIPMENT: Gravity flow fuel system, fuel filler screens, throttle-mounted landing gear warning mute and go-around switches, nacelle heat annunciator, dual Gill-Teledyne G-6381E high capacity lead-acid batteries, recognition light, wing ice light, emergency press override switches, transponder ident switch in pilot's control wheel, engine synchroniser and syncroscope, flap preselect, crew lifejackets, cockpit dome lights, cockpit speakers, crew oxygen masks and fire extingusiher are standard. Cabin furnishings include a three-seat divan, four individual tracking and reclining seats, side facing seat with toilet, two folding tables, refreshment cabinet with ice chest, baggage compartment, coffee warmer, water dispenser, cup and miscellaneous storage, coat rod, forward privacy curtain, overhead panels with reading lights, indirect lighting, air vents and oxygen masks, and passenger lifejackets.

Data as for Learjet 35A except:

DIMENSIONS, EXTERNAL:
Wing span	13.36 m (43 ft 10 in)
Length overall	14.83 m (48 ft 8 in)
Height overall	3.73 m (12 ft 3 in)

DIMENSION, INTERNAL:
Cabin: Length, excl flight deck	5.21 m (17 ft 1 in)

AREA:
Wings, gross	24.57 m² (264.5 sq ft)

WEIGHTS:
Weight empty: standard	4,471 kg (9,857 lb)
optional	4,489 kg (9,896 lb)
Basic operating weight	4,652 kg (10,257 lb)
Payload with max fuel	627 kg (1,383 lb)
Max fuel weight: standard	2,000 kg (4,410 lb)
optional	2,249 kg (4,958 lb)
Max T-O weight: standard	7,031 kg (15,500 lb)
optional	7,258 kg (16,000 lb)
Max ramp weight: standard	7,144 kg (15,750 lb)
optional	7,371 kg (16,250 lb)
Max landing weight: standard and optional	
	6,940 kg (15,300 lb)
Max zero-fuel weight: standard and optional	
	5,715 kg (12,600 lb)

PERFORMANCE (at max standard T-O weight, S/L, ISA, except where indicated):
Never-exceed speed	
	300 knots (555 km/h; 345 mph) IAS
Max operating speed	Mach 0.78
Cruising speed (typical)	
	400-447 knots (741-828 km/h; 461-515 mph)
Stalling speed at typical landing weight	
	84 knots (156 km/h; 97 mph) CAS
Max rate of climb at S/L	1,670 m (5,480 ft)/min
Rate of climb at S/L, one engine out	
	576 m (1,890 ft)/min
Max certificated ceiling	15,545 m (51,000 ft)
T-O balanced field length, FAR Pt 25	
	899 m (2,950 ft)

Learjet 31 eight-passenger twin-turbofan business aircraft

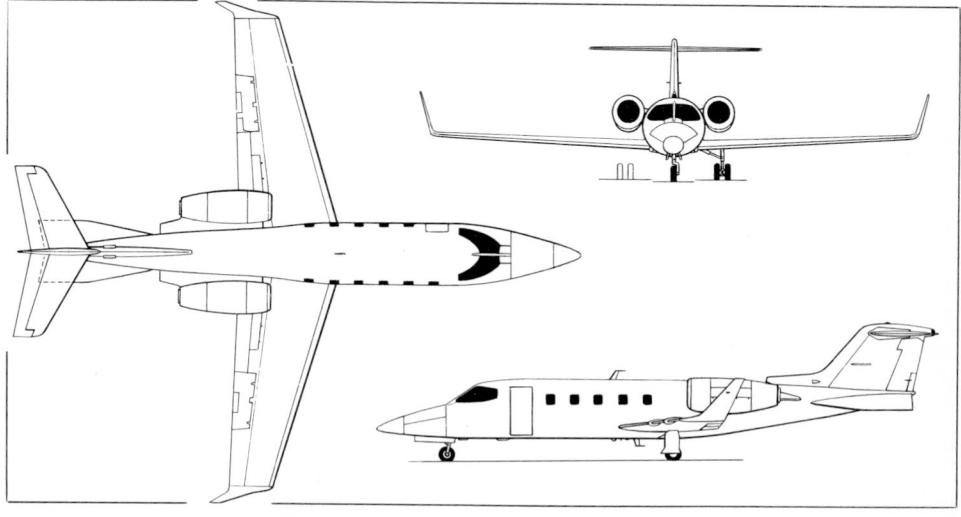

Three-view drawing of Learjet 31 *(Pilot Press)*

Landing distance at max landing weight
884 m (2,900 ft)
Range at econ cruising speed with four passengers, 45 min reserves:
standard fuel	1,630 nm (3,021 km; 1,877 miles)
extended range fuel	1,850 nm (3,428 km; 2,130 miles)

LEARJET 55C

The first of two Learjet 55 prototypes (N551GL) flew for the first time on 19 April 1979; the second (N552GL) flew on 15 November 1979, and the first production example on 11 August 1980. Certification under FAR Pt 25 was received on 18 March 1981. The initial customer delivery was made on 30 April 1981, and 133 Model 55s had been delivered by the end of 1987.

FAA certification was received in July 1983 of a Phase 1 performance improvement package for Model 55s, which included replacement of the original leading-edge stall strips with new strips each containing five small inverted triangular wedges approx 1.5 mm (¹/₁₆ in) thick, plus installation of seven individually mounted triangles at a location on the leading-edge forward of the ailerons; installation of automatic ground spoilers; and the addition of automatic performance reserve (APR) to the TFE731-3A-2B turbofans, automatically provides an additional 0.80 kN (180 lb) of thrust from one engine if thrust from the other engine drops by five per cent or more. Phase 1 improvements are incorporated in all Learjet 55s manufactured since 1 July 1983, and are available as a retrofit package for earlier production aircraft. A Garrett energy management system (GEMS) is available optionally as an extension of APR.

A further performance improvement package, Phase 1A, was introduced on the production line in the Spring of 1984. This features high-energy brakes with 13 per cent greater capacity and up to 50 per cent increased life claimed; new wheels; longer axles, and modified landing gear doors, fairings and actuators. The doors and fairings are manufactured from graphite/epoxy and Kevlar/epoxy, respectively. Phase 1A, certificated in February 1984, is available as a retrofit to earlier Model 55s, with Phase 1 as a prerequisite. The package offers substantial increases in the Learjet 55's high-altitude, hot-day performance. Other improvements introduced from c/n 55-107 included an optional 9,752 kg (21,500 lb) max T-O weight and 8,165 kg (18,000 lb) max landing weight.

In September 1986 Learjet announced the Learjet Model 55B which featured an all-digital flight deck, increased max T-O weight as standard, aerodynamic refinements to the wing, and interior changes, which provide better take-off performance, increased range and greater mission flexibility than those of earlier Learjet 55s. Details of the Model 55B can be found in the 1987-88 *Jane's*. The current model, announced at the 1987 NBAA Convention in New Orleans,

is the **Learjet Model 55C** which is similar to the Model 55B but incorporates ventral Delta-Fins, each 2.88 m (9 ft 3 in) long, which improve balanced field length performance and confer aerodynamic and handling benefits, particularly at low airspeed and high angles of attack. They also obviate the need for a stick pusher system and permit installation of a single yaw damper. New low-drag engine pylons have also been introduced on the 55C.

Three versions were available in 1988:

Learjet 55C. Basic version, as described in detail.

Learjet 55C/ER. Extended range version, with an additional fuel tank of 163 kg (359 lb) capacity in the tailcone baggage compartment. This tank is available for retrofit on standard 55s already delivered.

Learjet 55C/LR. Long-range version; as 55C/ER, plus an additional fuel tank of 298 kg (658 lb) capacity between the standard fuselage tank and rear cabin baggage compartment. Typical seating for seven passengers and two crew. Retrofit of existing 55s to this standard to be available.

The Learjet 55B is certificated in and operating from Australia, Austria, Brazil, Canada, France, West Germany, Saudi Arabia, Spain, Switzerland, the United States and Venezuela. Certification of the 55C was expected in August 1988.

TYPE: Twin-turbofan light executive transport.

WINGS: Cantilever low-wing monoplane. Sweepback 13° at quarter-chord. All-metal multi-spar structure with cavity milled wing skins. Wing upper surface skin tapers in thickness from wing root to wingtip to save weight. The design incorporates an advanced cambered leading-edge, the 'Softflite' handling package (see introductory notes to company entry), boundary layer energisers and supercritical winglets. Manually operated ailerons. Electrically operated trim tab in port aileron. Hydraulically operated all-metal single-slotted trailing-edge flaps. Hydraulically operated all-metal spoilers mounted on wing upper surface just forward of flaps. Anti-icing by engine bleed air ducted into leading-edges.

FUSELAGE: All-metal flush riveted semi-monocoque fail-safe structure.

TAIL UNIT: Cantilever all-metal sweptback structure, with electrically actuated variable incidence T tailplane. Twin ventral 'Delta-Fins' on lower rear fuselage, canted outward. Electrically heated de-icing of tailplane leading-edge.

LANDING GEAR: Hydraulically retractable tricycle type, with twin wheels on each main unit and single steerable nosewheel. Mainwheel tyres size 17.5 × 5.75-8, 12 ply, pressure 12.4 bars (180 lb/sq in); nosewheel tyre size 18.0 × 4.4, 10 ply, pressure 7.24 bars (105 lb/sq in). High pressure pneumatic system for emergency extension. Oleo-pneumatic shock absorbers. Chined nosewheel tyre. Mainwheel doors are of composites construction.

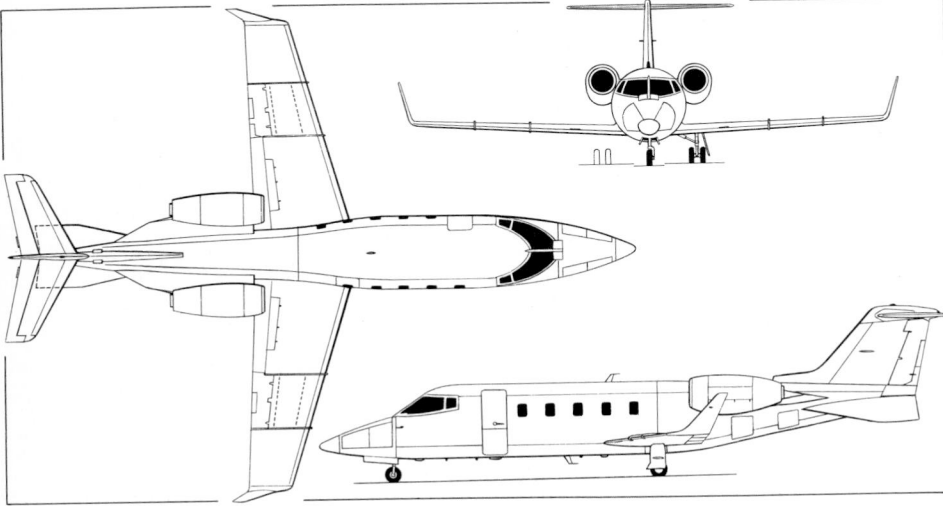

Three-view drawing (*Pilot Press*) **and photograph of the Learjet 55C executive transport**

High energy hydraulic braking system, with pneumatic backup. Fully modulated anti-skid units.

POWER PLANT: Two Garrett TFE731-3A-2B turbofans, each rated at 16.46 kN (3,700 lb st), plus 0.80 kN (180 lb st) automatic power reserve, pod-mounted on sides of fuselage aft of wing. Thrust reversers standard. Fuel in integral wing tanks and a fuselage bladder tank, with a combined capacity of 3,789 litres (1,001 US gallons; 833 Imp gallons) in standard Model 55B. Additional fuel capacity of extended-range versions detailed in model listings. Single-point refuelling. Engine nacelle leading-edges and fan hubs anti-iced by engine bleed air.

ACCOMMODATION: Crew of two on flight deck, with dual controls. IPECO fully adjustable crew seats. Seating for four to eight passengers in a choice of six interior layouts. Two folding tables. Carpeted floor. Galley refreshment cabinet. Toilet. Baggage space at rear of cabin, and in fuselage nose and tailcone of basic Model 55C. Tailcone baggage space reduced on long range versions, but 55C/LR has baggage area at front of cabin. Two-piece clamshell door at forward end of cabin on port side, with integral steps built into the lower section. Emergency exit/baggage door on starboard side of cabin.

SYSTEMS: Environmental control system comprises cabin pressurisation, ventilation, heating and cooling. Heating and pressurisation are provided by engine bleed air, with a maximum pressure differential of 0.65 bars (9.4 lb/sq in), maintaining a cabin altitude of 2,440 m (8,000 ft) to 15,545 m (51,000 ft). Freon vapour-cycle cooling system, supplemented by a ram air system. Anti-icing system includes distribution of engine bleed air to wing leading-edges, engine nacelle leading-edges and fan hubs, and pilot and co-pilot windscreens; electric anti-icing of tailplane leading-edge, pitot heads, stall warning vanes and static ports; and alcohol anti-icing of windscreens. Hydraulic system supplied by two engine driven variable-volume constant-pressure pumps, one on each engine, each capable of maintaining alone the full system pressure of 103.5 bars (1,500 lb/sq in) for operation of landing gear, brakes, flaps and spoilers. Hydraulic system maximum flow rate 15 litres (4 US gallons; 3.33 Imp gallons) per min. Cylindrical reservoir pressurised to 1.38 bars (20 lb/sq in). Electrically driven hydraulic pump for emergency operation of all hydraulic services. Pneumatic system of 124 to 207 bars (1,800 to 3,000 lb/sq in) pressure for emergency extension of landing gear and operation of brakes. Electrical system powered by two 28V 400A engine driven brushless generators, either of which is capable of maintaining adequate DC power to operate all

electrical services; two 1kVA solid state inverters to provide AC power; and two 24V 37Ah lead-acid batteries. Oxygen system of 1.08 m³ (38 cu ft) capacity, with crew demand masks; dropout mask for each passenger, which is presented automatically if cabin altitude exceeds 4,265 m (14,000 ft). Sundstrand Turbomach APU optional (not on 55C/ER or 55C/LR).

AVIONICS: From aircraft c/n 134 onwards standard avionics include a Collins five-tube EFIS-85L-12 electronic flight instrumentation system with dual AHS-85 AHRS; Collins APS-85 digital autopilot with glareshield controller and dual flight data computers; dual ADC-82 air data systems; dual VHF-22A nav/coms with CTL-22 controls; dual VIR-32 nav receivers with CTL-32 controls; dual DME-42 with IND-42C indicators; ADF-60 with CTL-62 control; dual RMI-30; dual TDR-90 transponders with CTL-92 controls; ALT-55B radio altimeter, Collins WXR-350 Sensor weather radar, Universal UNS-1A long-range nav system; King KHF-950 HF; Frederickson Jetcal-5 secal; Collins flight profile advisory system; and Wulfsberg Flitefone VI. Other standard flight deck equipment includes dual Collins encoding altimeters; MSI-80 Mach/airspeed indicators; VSI-80 instantaneous vertical speed indicators; Collins altitude pre-selector/alerter; TAS/SAT/TAT temperature indicator; IDC two-inch standby Mach/IAS indicator and altimeter; J.E.T. PS-835D and AI-804 emergency battery and attitude gyro; dual marker beacon systems; dual Avtech audio systems; dual Davtron 877 clocks; yaw damper; dual stall warning indicators; engine synchroniser and synchroscope; annunciator panels; avionics master switch; N$_1$ reminder, chip detector and flap preselect.

EQUIPMENT: Standard equipment includes sun visors; map lights; life jackets; fire extinguisher; writing tables; dome lights; oxygen masks; manual storage compartments, and dividing panel between flight deck and cabin. Cabin equipment includes two folding tables; four individual seats with tracking, swivel, recline and sideways motions; three-seat forward facing divan with storage and tracking and recline motions, single side facing seat, galley refreshment cabinet with decanters, bottle cooler, ice chest, oven, tray carrier, hot and cold liquid containers and storage area; forward coat closet; stereo and tape storage; magazine rack; convenience panel with reading lights, air vents, cabin speakers and oxygen masks; lighting control panel; opaque and tinted window shades; indirect lighting; aisle lighting; entrance step light; flushing toilet with vanity mirror and light; baggage

compartment light; passenger life jackets; auxiliary cabin heater; fire extinguisher and axe; nose and tail baggage compartment lights; wing ice light and maintenance interphone jack plug sockets.

DIMENSIONS, EXTERNAL:	
Wing span	13.34 m (43 ft 9 in)
Wing chord: at root	2.74 m (9 ft 0 in)
at tip	1.07 m (3 ft 6 in)
Wing aspect ratio	6.7
Length overall	16.79 m (55 ft 1 in)
Length of fuselage	15.93 m (52 ft 3 in)
Height overall	4.47 m (14 ft 8 in)
Tailplane span	4.47 m (14 ft 8 in)
Wheel track	2.51 m (8 ft 3 in)
Wheelbase	7.01 m (23 ft 0 in)
Cabin door: Height	1.70 m (5 ft 7 in)
Width	0.61 m (2 ft 0 in)

DIMENSIONS, INTERNAL:	
Cabin: Length between pressure bulkheads:	
55C, 55C/ER	6.71 m (22 ft 0 in)
55C/LR	6.30 m (20 ft 8 in)
Length, cockpit/cabin divider to rear pressure bulkhead: 55C, 55C/ER	5.08 m (16 ft 8 in)
55C/LR	4.67 m (15 ft 4 in)
Max width	1.80 m (5 ft 11 in)
Max height	1.74 m (5 ft 8½ in)
Volume, incl flight deck:	
55C, 55C/ER	13.37 m³ (472 cu ft)
55C/LR	12.88 m³ (455 cu ft)
Baggage capacity: 55C rear cabin	0.93 m³ (33.0 cu ft)
nose	0.17 m³ (6.0 cu ft)
tail	0.52 m³ (18.5 cu ft)
55C/ER, total	1.36 m³ (48.0 cu ft)
55C/LR, total	1.81 m³ (64.0 cu ft)

AREAS:	
Wings, gross	24.57 m² (264.5 sq ft)
Ailerons (total)	1.09 m² (11.70 sq ft)
Trailing-edge flaps (total)	3.42 m² (36.85 sq ft)
Winglets (total)	1.11 m² (12.00 sq ft)
Spoilers (total)	0.65 m² (7.05 sq ft)
Fin	4.67 m² (50.29 sq ft)
Rudder	0.99 m² (10.65 sq ft)
Tailplane	5.02 m² (54.00 sq ft)
Elevators (total)	1.31 m² (14.13 sq ft)

WEIGHTS AND LOADINGS:	
Weight empty: 55C	5,725 kg (12,622 lb)
55C/ER	5,754 kg (12,686 lb)
55C/LR	5,813 kg (12,816 lb)
Max fuel weight: 55C	3,035 kg (6,690 lb)
55C/ER	3,197 kg (7,049 lb)
55C/LR	3,496 kg (7,707 lb)
Max T-O weight: 55C	9,525 kg (21,000 lb)
55C/ER & LR	9,752 kg (21,500 lb)
Max zero-fuel weight:	
all versions	6,804 kg (15,000 lb)
Max landing weight:	
all versions	8,165 kg (18,000 lb)
Max wing loading:	
55C	387.6 kg/m² (79.4 lb/sq ft)
55C/ER & LR	396.9 kg/m² (81.3 lb/sq ft)
Max power loading:	
55C	289.3 kg/kN (2.84 lb/lb st)
55C/ER & LR	296.2 kg/kN (2.90 lb/lb st)

PERFORMANCE (at max T-O weight except where indicated):

Never-exceed speed:	
below 2,440 m (8,000 ft)	300 knots (555 km/h; 345 mph) IAS
2,440 m (8,000 ft) to 11,275 m (37,000 ft)	350 knots (648 km/h; 403 mph) IAS
11,275 m (37,000 ft) to 13,715 m (45,000 ft)	Mach 0.81 to Mach 0.79
above 13,715 m (45,000 ft)	Mach 0.79
Max level speed at 9,150 m (30,000 ft)	477 knots (884 km/h; 549 mph)
Max cruising speed at 12,500 m (41,000 ft)	455 knots (843 km/h; 524 mph)
Econ cruising speed at 14,325 m (47,000 ft)	419 knots (776 km/h; 482 mph)
Max rate of climb at S/L: 55C	1,273 m (4,176 ft)/min
55C/ER & LR	1,237 m (4,059 ft)/min
Max rate of climb at S/L, one engine out:	
55C	378 m (1,240 ft)/min
55C/ER & LR	305 m (1,000 ft)/min
Max certificated ceiling	15,545 m (51,000 ft)
T-O balanced field length, FAR Pt 25:	
55C	1,494 m (4,900 ft)
55C/ER & LR	1,570 m (5,150 ft)
Landing distance, FAR Pt 91 at max landing weight	945 m (3,100 ft)
Range with crew of two, four passengers, allowances for taxi, T-O, climb, cruise at long-range power, descent and 45 min reserves:	
55C	2,250 nm (4,170 km; 2,591 miles)
55C/ER	2,370 nm (4,392 km; 2,729 miles)
55C/LR	2,540 nm (4,707 km; 2,925 miles)

LOCKHEED
LOCKHEED CORPORATION

4500 Park Granada Boulevard, Calabasas, California 91399-0610

Telephone: (818) 712 2000
CHAIRMAN, PRESIDENT AND CHIEF EXECUTIVE OFFICER:
Daniel M. Tellep
VICE-CHAIRMEN:
Robert A. Fuhrman
Vincent N. Marafino

The early history of this company was outlined briefly in previous editions of *Jane's*. In September 1977 the former Lockheed Aircraft Corporation was renamed Lockheed Corporation, to reflect the company's diversified activities. These include the design and production of aircraft, electronics, satellites, space systems, missiles, ocean systems, information systems, and systems for strategic defence and for command, control, communications and intelligence.

In 1988, Lockheed Corporation's total facilities covered more than 2,322,575 m² (25,000,000 sq ft), and it had approximately 98,000 employees in 25 US states and on worldwide company assignments. On 3 September 1987, it announced that its aircraft design, development, manufacturing and modification programmes, undertaken previously by Lockheed-California Company, Lockheed-Georgia Company and Lockheed Aircraft Service Company, were being integrated under three divisions of a new Lockheed Aeronautical Systems Company (LASC), with headquarters in Burbank, California. Details of the new organisation follow:

LOCKHEED AERONAUTICAL SYSTEMS COMPANY (LASC)

2555 North Hollywood Way (PO Box 551), Burbank, California 91520

Telephone: (818) 847 6121

DIVISIONAL HEADQUARTERS: Burbank, California; Marietta, Georgia; Ontario, California

PRESIDENT: John C. Brizendine
EXECUTIVE VICE-PRESIDENTS:
Harold T. Bowling (General Manager Ontario Division)
Kenneth W. Cannestra (General Manager Georgia Division)
E. Lloyd Graham (General Manager Headquarters Operations)
R. Richard Heppe (General Manager ATF Programmes)

Ben R. Rich (General Manager Advanced Development Projects)
Lockheed Aeronautical Systems Company employs 43,000 people at facilities in California, Georgia, Mississippi, Pennsylvania, South Carolina, Texas and West Virginia.

LASC BURBANK DIVISION

2555 North Hollywood Way (PO Box 551), Burbank, California 91520
Telephone: (818) 847 6121
Telex: 67208

This division of LASC is responsible for production of the P-3 Orion land based anti-submarine warfare aircraft, special aircraft modifications programmes, and components for the TR-1 high-altitude reconnaissance aircraft and Lockheed-Georgia's C-5B. It is engaged in several important research and development programmes, of which few details are yet available. One of them, covered in part by a $4.7 million USAF contract received in Spring 1986, is a four-year four-phase programme involving integrated vehicle and propulsion system concepts applicable to future supersonic cruise aircraft. Another, current in 1988, is for a supersonic advanced STOVL fighter with a hybrid fan vectored thrust engine and gross weight of about 19,050 kg (42,000 lb), being developed under a conceptual design contract from NASA.

LOCKHEED 'RF-19' and XST

In the so-called 'Skunk Works' at Burbank, this division has built, under a DARPA-funded contract from the USAF's Flight Dynamics Laboratory, many examples of a single-seat fighter/reconnaissance aircraft, of which primary features are low radar, infra-red and optical signatures.

A proof of concept/demonstrator aircraft, known as **XST** (Experimental Stealth Technology), is believed to have made its first flight in 1977. The XST was reportedly a very small aircraft, powered by two 11.12-12.46 kN (2,500-2,800 lb st) General Electric CJ610 turbojet engines. Between five and seven XSTs are believed to have been built, and two at least are thought to have crashed.

An operational derivative made its first flight during 1982 and was designed to offer minimal radar, infra-red, acoustic and visual signatures. General configuration is of blended wing/fuselage design, with foreplanes on blended fuselage chines. Two canted fins, one on each side of the engine exhaust outlets, assist IR shielding. A special paint finish also reduces both IR and radar signatures. There are no electromagnetic emissions from the aircraft during its mission.

The aircraft is said to be powered by two General Electric F404-GE-400 turbofans, each rated at 48.0 kN (10,800 lb st) without afterburner. Its size is believed to be similar to that of the F/A-18 Hornet, with folding wings to permit air transportation by C-5 Galaxy. It is said to make little or no exhaust noise, even at close range. US Air Force designation is rumoured to be RF-19, although AR-2 and AR-19 have also been suggested but no official confirmation received. The official acronym for its assignment has been reported as CSIRS (covert survivable in-weather reconnaissance-strike). In early 1986 reports were received

that the 'RF-19' was in series production and that up to 40 aircraft were operational, examples of which had been deployed outside the United States to bases which included one in the United Kingdom. The operating unit for the aircraft is believed to be the 4450th Tactical Test Group, based at Nellis AFB, Nevada. On 11 July 1986 a USAF pilot attached to this unit was killed in the crash of an unidentified aircraft near Bakersfield, California. The crash site was declared a national security area while wreckage was recovered. Another crash said to have involved a 'USAF Stealth fighter' occurred on 14 October 1987 in a restricted area near Nellis AFB.

The following data are estimated and highly provisional:
DIMENSIONS, EXTERNAL:

Wing span	9.65 m (31 ft 8 in)
Width, wings folded	5.0 m (16 ft 5 in)
Length overall	18.0 m (59 ft 0 in)
Height overall	4.0 m (13 ft 1½ in)

WEIGHTS:

Weight empty	10,000 kg (22,050 lb)
Max T-O weight	15,000 kg (33,070 lb)

PERFORMANCE:
Max cruising speed at S/L
560 knots (1,038 km/h; 645 mph)
Combat radius 300-400 nm (556-741 km; 345-460 miles)

LOCKHEED YF-22A (ATF)

For available details of the US Air Force's Advanced Tactical Fighter (ATF) programme, see the US Air Force Systems Command entry in this section. Lockheed is contracted to build two YF-22A prototypes, in partnership with General Dynamics (Fort Worth Division) and Boeing Military Airplanes. General Dynamics will build the centre fuselage and tail unit, Boeing the wings and rear fuselage. Subcontractors so far announced include Curtiss-Wright (leading-edge flap drive), GEC Astronics (digital flight control computers), GEC Avionics (head-up display), General Electric with Martin Marietta (infra-red search/track system), Harris (databus interface modules), Hughes Radar Systems (common integrated processors), Menasco (landing gear), National Water Lift and Parker Hannifin (flight control actuators), Sterer (nosewheel steering), Sundstrand Turbomach (APU), Texas Instruments (central mission processing computer), and Westinghouse/Texas Instruments (active array radar).

First flight of the YF-22A is scheduled for late 1989/early 1990.

LOCKHEED ER-2, U-2R and TR-1

The configuration of the TR-1 is basically that of a powered sailplane, which explains its unusual 'bicycle' landing gear, combined with underwing balancer units which provide stability during take-off and are then jettisoned. Range can, when necessary, be extended by

shutting off the engine and gliding. After touchdown, the aircraft comes to rest on one of the down-turned wingtips, which serve as skids.

There are three versions of the TR-1 series, as follows:
TR-1A. Single-seat tactical reconnaissance version, described by the Department of Defense as being "equipped with a variety of electronic sensors to provide continuously available, day or night, high-altitude all-weather standoff surveillance of the battle area in direct support of the US and Allied ground and air forces during peace, crises, and war situations". The TR-1A has the same basic airframe as the U-2R (1983-84 *Jane's*), with a J75-P-13B engine, but with the significant addition of an advanced synthetic aperture radar system (ASARS) in the form of a UPD-X side-looking airborne radar (SLAR) and modern electronic countermeasures (ECM). The TR-1A is intended primarily for use in Europe, where its SLAR provides the capability to 'see' approximately 30 nm (55 km; 35 miles) into hostile territory without the need to overfly an actual or potential battle area. A TR-1A variant reported in 1984 has a satellite data link antenna mounted above its fuselage (see illustration in 1986-87 *Jane's*). The first TR-1A (80-1066) flew for the first time on 1 August 1981. Deliveries began in September 1981, initially to Beale AFB, California. Total of 26 TR-1As funded by FY 1987. Two additional U-2Rs, fitted with 'superpods', have been ordered for 1989 delivery.

TR-1B. Two-seat training version of TR-1A. Second cockpit in tandem, above and behind standard cockpit. Two built; both delivered to Beale AFB in 1983.

ER-2. Basically similar to TR-1A but modified for use by NASA as an Earth resources research aircraft. One aircraft, delivered to Ames Research Center in June 1981. Described under NASA entry in 1982-83 *Jane's*. A second ER-2 has been ordered, for 1989 delivery.

Fourteen TR-1s are being stationed at RAF Alconbury, Cambridgeshire, England with the USAF's 95th Reconnaissance Squadron, 17th Tactical Reconnaissance Wing. A detachment of this aircraft has been housed at RAF Wethersfield. Although operating in Europe, they remain under the jurisdiction of Strategic Air Command, and not USAFE. The first of these TR-1s was flown to Alconbury during February 1983, and all 14 were scheduled for delivery by early 1987. The TR-1 programme is scheduled for completion in 1989.

The following details apply to the TR-1A except where indicated:
TYPE: High-altitude reconnaissance and research aircraft.
AIRFRAME: As described in 1987-88 *Jane's*.
POWER PLANT: One 75.6 kN (17,000 lb st) Pratt & Whitney J75-P-13B turbojet. All fuel in inboard and outboard main tanks filling each wing except for tip, each with overwing gravity refuelling point. Normal internal fuel capacity approx 4,448 litres (1,175 US gallons; 978 Imp gallons).

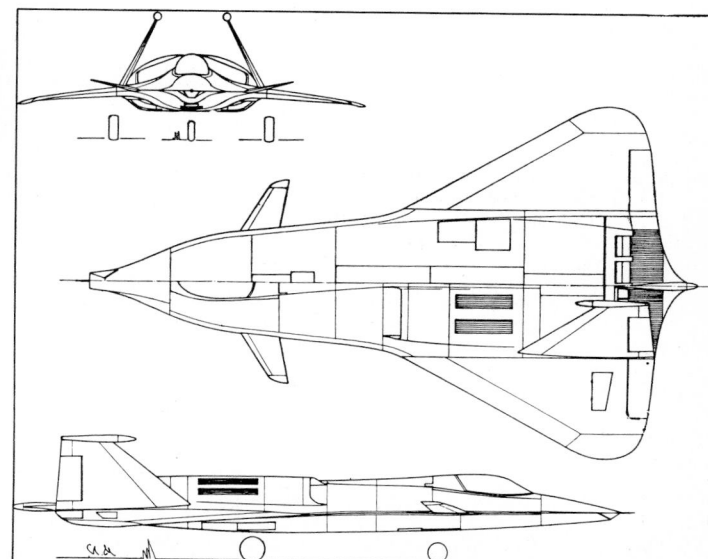

These conjectural drawings of the Lockheed RF-19, by Hideo Maki, are reproduced by courtesy of *AiReview*, **Tokyo**

ACCOMMODATION: Pilot only, on ejection seat. Side-hinged transparent canopy, protected internally against ultra-violet radiation. Accommodation is air-conditioned and pressurised. Rearview periscope on most aircraft (positions vary), to check that contrails are not being produced in flight. Food warmer, with spaceflight type tubes of food. Second (instructor's) cockpit above and behind standard cockpit in TR-1B.

AVIONICS AND EQUIPMENT: Typical standard avionics include HF, UHF and VHF com, INS, Tacan, ILS, autopilot, ADF, air data computer, compass, and (for night flying) astro-compass. Equipment includes one vertical and two lateral cameras for training flights, or side-looking airborne radar and T-35 tracking camera for operational missions. Main avionics and equipment compartments are in detachable modular nose section, in a 'Q' bay aft of

the cockpit (replaced by second cockpit in TR-1B), and in two large pods mounted underwing at approx one-third span. Each pod is approx 8.23 m (27 ft) long; has a volume of about 2.55 m³ (90 cu ft), and weighs about 544 kg (1,200 lb) complete with sensors and/or equipment. There is a smaller 'E' bay between the 'Q' bay and mainwheel bay; additional small areas in the bottom of the rear fuselage and in the tailcone can also be used to house mission equipment.

DIMENSIONS, EXTERNAL:
Wing span	31.39 m (103 ft 0 in)
Wing aspect ratio	approx 10.6
Length overall	19.20 m (63 ft 0 in)
Height overall	4.88 m (16 ft 0 in)

AREA:
Wings, gross	approx 92.9 m² (1,000 sq ft)

WEIGHTS:
Weight empty, excl power plant and equipment pods	under 4,535 kg (10,000 lb)
Max T-O weight	18,144 kg (40,000 lb)

PERFORMANCE:
Max cruising speed at normal operational height of 21,650 m (70,000 ft)	more than 373 knots (692 km/h; 430 mph)
Operational ceiling	27,430 m (90,000 ft)
Min ground turning radius	68.6 m (225 ft)
Max range	more than 2,605 nm (4,830 km; 3,000 miles)
Max endurance	12 h
g limit	+2.5

Close-up photograph of Lockheed TR-1A shows clearly the shape of the starboard sensor pod

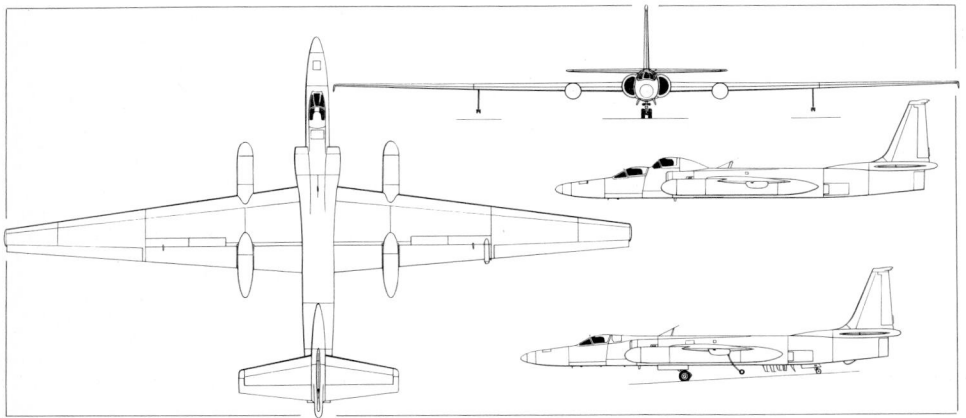

Lockheed TR-1A high-altitude reconnaissance and research aircraft, with additional side elevation (centre) of TR-1B *(Pilot Press)*

LOCKHEED MODEL 185/285 ORION
US Navy designation: P-3
CAF designation: CP-140 Aurora

In 1958 Lockheed won a US Navy competition for an 'off-the-shelf' ASW aircraft with a developed version of its Electra four-turboprop commercial transport. An aerodynamic prototype flew for the first time on 19 August 1958. A second aircraft, designated YP-3A (formerly YP3V-1), with full avionics, flew on 25 November 1959.

Details of the P-3A initial production version (157 built) and WP-3A can be found in the 1978-79 *Jane's*. The P-3B (144 built) and EP-3B were last described in the 1983-84 edition. Other versions, including special conversions, are as follows:

P-3B (Portugal). In late 1985 the Portuguese Air Force ordered six P-3Bs. These aircraft, formerly operated by the Royal Australian Air Force, will receive major systems updates to improve their ASW effectiveness and are destined for service with Esquadron 601. Following completion of a prototype by Lockheed in 1988, the remaining aircraft will be modified by Oficinas Gerais de Material Aeronáutico (OGMA) in Portugal (which see).

P-3C. Advanced version with the A-NEW system of sensors and control equipment, built around a Univac digital computer that integrates all ASW information and permits retrieval, display and transmission of tactical data in order to eliminate routine log keeping functions. First flight was made on 18 September 1968 and the P-3C entered service in 1969. A total of 279 P-3Cs had been delivered to the US Navy by 1 April 1986. Nine aircraft were funded in FY 1986 and nine in FY 1987.

The prototype Update III P-3C Orion photographed during test and evaluation by the US Navy

Aircraft delivered from January 1975 were to **P-3C Update I** standard, with new avionics and electronics software developed to enhance their effectiveness. Equipment includes a magnetic drum that gives a sevenfold increase in computer memory capacity, a new versatile computer language, Omega navigation system, improved acoustic processing sensitivity, a tactical display for two of the sensor stations, and an improved magnetic tape transport. **Update II**, initiated in 1976, added an infra-red detection system (IRDS) and a sonobuoy reference system (SRS). The Harpoon missile and control system were incorporated into production aircraft from August 1977. Ten Update II P-3Cs were delivered to the Royal Australian

Air Force in 1978-79 for service with No. 10 Squadron, followed by ten more in 1984-86. The Royal Netherlands Navy received 13 Update II P-3Cs, between 1981 and 1984, one of which was being used in 1987 for operational trials of a Phillips USfa thermal imaging system. Japan has ordered 78 of a planned 100, of which four were assembled and the remainder are being licence built in Japan by Kawasaki (which see), following delivery of three US built aircraft during 1981. Kawasaki had delivered 40 of the remaining 71 by 31 March 1988.

Update III, of which production deliveries began in May 1984, involves mainly ASW avionics, including a new IBM Proteus acoustic processor to analyse signals picked up

from the sea, a new sonobuoy receiver which replaces DIFAR (directional acoustic frequency analysis and recording), an improved APU, and environmental controls to cater for increased heat from the avionics and to improve crew comfort further. The first delivery of P-3C Update IIIs to a US Navy reserve patrol squadron was scheduled for FY 1988. Four have been ordered by the Royal Norwegian Air Force for delivery in 1989 and three by the Pakistan Navy for 1991 delivery.

In addition to new production Update III aircraft, Lockheed has developed a retrofit kit, which was installed on a P-3C of VP-31 in early 1987. Installation of 18 more kits was scheduled to begin in June 1987, with the possibility of retrofitting a total of 113 Update II P-3Cs eventually.

Update IV, now being developed for introduction in the early 1990s, will have improved processing capabilities, Texas Instruments AN/APS-137(V) radar, and a new family of acoustic sensors designed to counter the 'quieting' trend of the Soviet submarine force. Aerodynamic trials by Lockheed of a P-3C equipped with an Eaton AIL Division AN/ALR-77 tactical electronic support measures (ESM) system were expected to be followed by technical and operational evaluation at the Naval Air Test Center, Patuxent River, Maryland. The AN/ALR-77 system comprises four wingtip quadrants providing 360° coverage with 36 interferometer antennae, each sub-band being covered by a triplet of antennae. Overall FSED contractor for Update IV is Boeing Aerospace; up to 80 Update II P-3Cs are expected to receive Update IV modification.

EP-3C. Elint version of P-3C being developed by Kawasaki for JMSDF. First example funded in 1987, for delivery in March 1991. Eight more expected to be funded for operation by mid-1990s.

EP-3E. Ten P-3As and two EP-3Bs were converted to EP-3E configuration to replace Lockheed EC-121s in service with VQ-1 and VQ-2 squadrons. Identified by large canoe shape radars on upper and lower surfaces of fuselage and ventral radome forward of wing. EP-3E avionics suites are believed to comprise GTE-Sylvania AN/ALR-60 communications, interception and analysis sytem; Raytheon AN/ALQ-76 noise jamming pod; Loral AN/ALQ-78 automatic ESM system; Magnavox AN/ALQ-108 IFF jammer; Sanders AN/ALR-132 infra-red jammer; ARGO Systems AN/ALR-52 instantaneous frequency measuring equipment; Texas Instruments AN/APS-115 frequency agile search radar; Hughes AN/AAR-37 infra-red detector; Loral AN/ASA-66 tactical display; Cardion AN/ASA-69 scan converter; and Sperry Univac AN/ASQ-114 computer.

P-3F. Six aircraft, similar to mid-1970s US Navy P-3Cs, for Imperial Iranian Air Force. Used initially for long-range surface surveillance and subsequently also for ASW missions. Delivery completed in January 1975.

P-3G. Proposed new variant, powered by a version of the Allison 501-M80C turboshaft adopted for the Bell/Boeing V-22A Osprey tilt-rotor aircraft. This programme now represents LASC's entry for the US Navy's LRAACA (long range air ASW combat aircraft) competition, which is expected to lead to a contract for 125 aircraft for 1990-94 procurement.

CP-140 Aurora. Version for Canadian Armed Forces (18 built). Described in detail in 1981-82 *Jane's*.

P-3 Sentinel. Airborne early warning and control (AEW&C) variant. Prototype (N91LC), converted from ex-Royal Australian Air Force P-3B, made first flight on 14 June 1984, fitted with a 7.32 m (24 ft) diameter Randtron APA-171 rotodome above rear fuselage but without radar. For military AEW&C operations the Sentinel would be equipped with General Electric AN/APS-139 radar (as on Grumman E-2C Hawkeye); a C³ system to receive, process and transmit tactical information through HF, UHF, VHF and Satcom channels; AR-187 satellite communications system and Collins EFIS-86B five-tube colour CRT electronic flight instrument system. Testing of an installed APS-138 was scheduled to begin in the Summer or Autumn of 1988.

In May 1987 the US Customs Service became launch customer for the P-3 Sentinel, with an order for one aircraft and options on three more. The first Sentinel for US Customs is based on the company demonstrator airframe equipped with General Electric AN/APS-125 radar, with which it was flown for the first time on 8 April 1988. Delivery was due to be made in the following June. The aircraft, named *Blue Sentinel*, will be used for anti-drug smuggling operations in the Caribbean and Gulf of Mexico.

Possible military customers for the P-3 Sentinel include Australia, which has a requirement for four AEW aircraft, Canada, Japan and the US Navy. The General Electric AN/APS-145 radar will be available for the aircraft from late 1989.

By August 1988 Lockheed had delivered more than 620 P-3s of all versions.

In June 1987 Lockheed and MBB of West Germany signed a teaming agreement to propose the P-3 for the Federal Republic of Germany's planned maritime patrol aircraft (MPA) programme, for which there is a requirement for up to 18 aircraft.

The following data refer to the P-3C, but are generally applicable to other versions, except for the details noted:
TYPE: Four-turboprop ASW aircraft.
WINGS: Cantilever low-wing monoplane. Wing section NACA 0014 (modified) at root, NACA 0012 (modified) at tip. Dihedral 6°. Incidence 3° at root, 0° 30′ at tip.

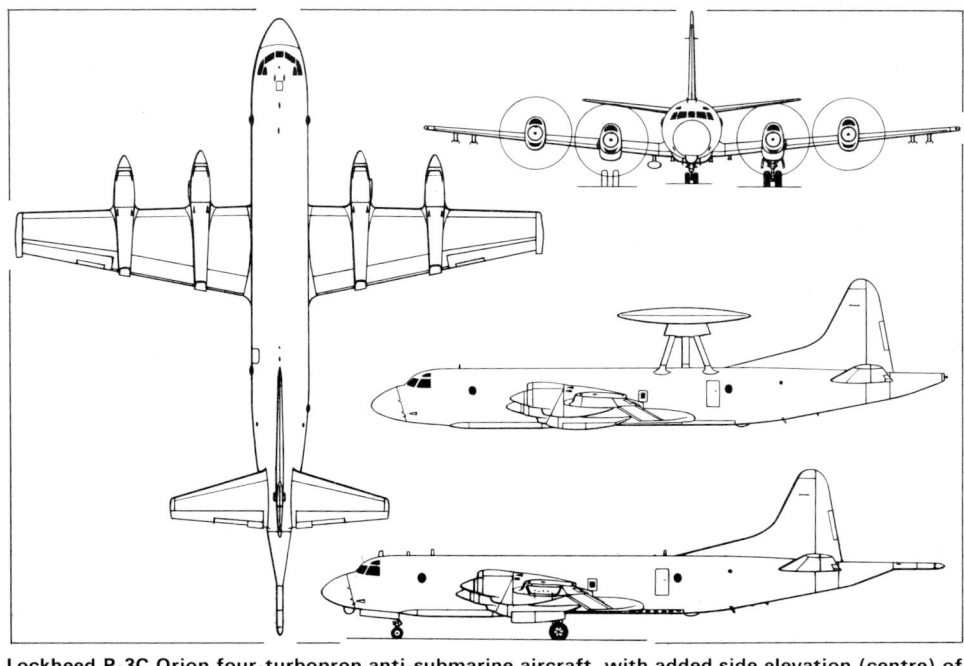

Lockheed P-3C Orion four-turboprop anti-submarine aircraft, with added side elevation (centre) of Sentinel version (*Pilot Press*)

Lockheed EP-3E of US Navy squadron VQ-1 landing at Atsugi, Japan, in May 1985 (*Katsumi Hinata*)

Aerodynamic prototype of P-3 Sentinel airborne early warning and control version of the Orion

Fail-safe box beam structure of extruded integrally stiffened aluminium alloy. Lockheed-Fowler trailing-edge flaps. Hydraulically boosted aluminium ailerons. Anti-icing by engine bleed air ducted into leading-edges.

FUSELAGE: Conventional aluminium alloy semi-monocoque fail-safe structure.

TAIL UNIT: Cantilever aluminium alloy structure with dihedral tailplane and dorsal fin. Fixed incidence tailplane. Hydraulically boosted rudder and elevators. Leading-edges of fin and tailplane have electric anti-icing system.

LANDING GEAR: Hydraulically retractable tricycle type, with twin wheels on each unit. All units retract forward, mainwheels into inner engine nacelles. Oleo-pneumatic shock absorbers. Mainwheels have size 40-14 type VII 26-ply tubeless tyres, pressures 7.58-12.41 bars (110-180 lb/sq in) at 36,287 kg (80,000 lb) T-O weight; 12.41 bars (180 lb/sq in) at 57,606 kg (127,000 lb) T-O weight; 13.10 bars (190 lb/sq in) at 61,235 kg (135,000 lb) max normal T-O weight. Nosewheels have size 28-7.7 type VII tubeless tyres, pressure 10.34 bars (150 lb/sq in). Hydraulic brakes. No anti-skid units.

POWER PLANT: Four 3,661 kW (4,910 ehp) Allison T56-A-14 turboprops, each driving a Hamilton Standard 54H60 four-blade constant-speed propeller. Fuel in one tank in fuselage and four wing integral tanks, with total usable capacity of 34,826 litres (9,200 US gallons; 7,660 Imp gallons). Four overwing gravity fuelling points and central pressure refuelling point. Oil capacity (min usable) 111 litres (29.4 US gallons; 24.5 Imp gallons) in four tanks. Electrically de-iced propeller spinners.

ACCOMMODATION: Normal ten-man crew. Flight deck has wide-vision windows, and circular windows for observers are provided fore and aft in the main cabin, each bulged to give 180° view. Main cabin is fitted out as a five-man tactical compartment containing advanced electronic, magnetic and sonic detection equipment, an all-electric galley and large crew rest area.

SYSTEMS: Air-conditioning and pressurisation system supplied by two engine driven compressors. Pressure differential 0.37 bars (5.4 lb/sq in). Hydraulic system, pressure 207 bars (3,000 lb/sq in), for flaps, control surface boosters, landing gear actuation, brakes and bomb bay doors. Three hydraulic pumps, each rated at 30.3 litres (8.0 US gallons; 6.7 Imp gallons)/min at 0-2,200 lb/sq in, 22.7 litres (6.0 US gallons; 5.0 Imp gallons)/min at 2,975 lb/sq in. Class one non-separated air/oil reservoir, Type B pressurised. Electrical system utilises three 60kVA generators for 120/208V 400Hz AC supply. 24V DC supply. Integral APU with 60kVA generator for ground air-conditioning, electrical supply and engine starting.

AVIONICS AND EQUIPMENT: The ASQ-114 general purpose digital computer is the heart of the P-3C system. Together with the AYA-8 data processing equipment and computer controlled display systems, it permits rapid analysis and utilisation of electronic, magnetic and sonic data. Nav/com system comprises two LTN-72 inertial navigation systems; AN/APN-227 Doppler; ARN-81 Loran A and C; AN/ARN-118 Tacan; two VIR-31A VOR/LOC/GS/MB receivers; ARN-83 LF-ADF; ARA-50 UHF direction finder; AJN-15 flight director indicator for tactical directions; HSI for long-range flight directions; glideslope indicator; on-top position indicator; two ARC-161 HF transceivers; two ARC-143 UHF transceivers; ARC-101 VHF receiver/transmitter; AGC-6 teletype and high-speed printer; HF and UHF secure communication units; ACQ-5 data link communication set and AIC-22 interphone set; APX-72 IFF transponder and APX-76 SIF interrogator. Electronic computer controlled display equipment includes ASA-70 tactical display; ASA-66 pilot's display; ASA-70 radar display and two auxiliary readout (computer stored data) displays. ASW equipment includes two ARR-72 sonar receivers; two AQA-7 DIFAR (directional acoustic frequency analysis and recording) sonobuoy indicator sets; hyperbolic fix unit; acoustic source signal generator; time code generator and AQH-4(V) sonar tape recorder; ASQ-81 magnetic anomaly detector; ASA-64 submarine anomaly detector; ASA-65 magnetic compensator; ALQ-78 electronic countermeasures set; APS-115 radar set (360° coverage); ASA-69 radar scan converter; KA-74 forward computer assisted camera; KB-18A automatic strike assessment camera with horizon-to-horizon coverage; RO-308 bathythermograph recorder. Additional equipment includes APN-194 radar altimeter; two APQ-107 radar altimeter warning systems; A/A24G-9 true airspeed computer and ASW-31 automatic flight control system. P-3Cs delivered from 1975 have the avionics/electronics package updated by addition of an extra 393K memory drum and fourth logic unit, Omega navigation, new magnetic tape transport, and an ASA-66 tactical display for the sonar operators. To accommodate the new systems a new operational software computer programme was written in CMS-2 language. GEC Avionics AQS-901 acoustic signal processing and display system in RAAF P-3Cs. AN/ALR-77 passive radar detection system (ESM), to be housed in wingtip pods, is under development for Update IV P-3C by Eaton Corpn (AIL Division), and will also provide targeting data for the aircraft's Harpoon missiles. Wing span increased by

some 0.81 m (2 ft 8 in) to accommodate ESM antennae and receivers. Update IV FSED contract awarded to Boeing Aerospace in Spring 1987, for completion in 1992. Subcontractors include Magnavox (acoustic system), Resdel (sonobuoy receiver), General Instrument (ESM), Honeywell (AN/AQH-4[V]2 data recorders) and M/A Com (satellite communications).

ARMAMENT: Bomb bay, 2.03 m wide, 0.88 m deep and 3.91 m long (80 in × 34.5 in × 154 in), forward of wing, can accommodate a 2,000 lb Mk 25/39/55/56 mine, three 1,000 lb Mk 36/52 mines, three Mk 57 depth bombs, eight Mk 54 depth bombs, eight Mk 43/44/46 torpedoes or a combination of two Mk 101 nuclear depth bombs and four Mk 43/44/46 torpedoes. Ten underwing pylons for stores: two under centre-section each side can carry torpedoes or 2,000 lb mines; three under outer wing each side can carry respectively (inboard to outboard) a torpedo or 2,000 lb mine (or searchlight on starboard wing), a torpedo or 1,000 lb mine or rockets singly or in pods; a torpedo or 500 lb mine or rockets singly or in pods. Torpedoes can be carried underwing only for ferrying; mines can be carried and released. Search stores, such as sonobuoys and sound signals, are launched from inside cabin area in the P-3A/B. In the P-3C sonobuoys are loaded and launched externally and internally. Max total weapon load includes six 2,000 lb mines under wings and a 3,290 kg (7,252 lb) internal load made up of two Mk 101 depth bombs, four Mk 44 torpedoes, pyrotechnic pistol and 12 signals, 87 sonobuoys, 100 Mk 50 underwater sound signals (P-3A/B), 18 Mk 3A marine markers (P-3A/B), 42 Mk 7 marine markers, two B.T. buoys, and two Mk 5 parachute flares. Sonobuoys are ejected from P-3C aircraft with explosive cartridge actuating devices (CAD), eliminating the need for a pneumatic system. Australian P-3Cs use Barra sonobuoys.

DIMENSIONS, EXTERNAL:
Wing span	30.37 m (99 ft 8 in)
Wing chord: at root	5.77 m (18 ft 11 in)
at tip	2.31 m (7 ft 7 in)
Wing aspect ratio	7.5
Length overall	35.61 m (116 ft 10 in)
Height overall	10.27 m (33 ft 8½ in)
Fuselage diameter	3.45 m (11 ft 4 in)
Tailplane span	13.06 m (42 ft 10 in)
Wheel track (c/l shock absorbers)	9.50 m (31 ft 2 in)
Wheelbase	9.07 m (29 ft 9 in)
Propeller diameter	4.11 m (13 ft 6 in)
Cabin door: Height	1.83 m (6 ft 0 in)
Width	0.69 m (2 ft 3 in)

DIMENSIONS, INTERNAL:
Cabin, excl flight deck and electrical load centre:
Length	21.06 m (69 ft 1 in)
Max width	3.30 m (10 ft 10 in)
Max height	2.29 m (7 ft 6 in)
Floor area	61.13 m² (658.0 sq ft)
Volume	120.6 m³ (4,260 cu ft)

AREAS:
Wings, gross	120.77 m² (1,300.0 sq ft)
Ailerons (total)	8.36 m² (90.0 sq ft)
Trailing-edge flaps (total)	19.32 m² (208.0 sq ft)
Fin, incl dorsal fin	10.78 m² (116.0 sq ft)
Rudder, incl tab	5.57 m² (60.0 sq ft)
Tailplane	22.39 m² (241.0 sq ft)
Elevators, incl tabs	7.53 m² (81.0 sq ft)

WEIGHTS (P-3B/C):
Weight empty	27,890 kg (61,491 lb)
Max fuel weight	28,350 kg (62,500 lb)
Max expendable load	9,071 kg (20,000 lb)

Max normal T-O weight	61,235 kg (135,000 lb)
Max permissible weight	64,410 kg (142,000 lb)
Design zero-fuel weight	35,017 kg (77,200 lb)
Max landing weight	47,119 kg (103,880 lb)

PERFORMANCE (P-3B/C, at max T-O weight, except where indicated otherwise):
Max level speed at 4,575 m (15,000 ft) at AUW of 47,625 kg (105,000 lb)
411 knots (761 km/h; 473 mph)
Econ cruising speed at 7,620 m (25,000 ft) at AUW of 49,895 kg (110,000 lb)
328 knots (608 km/h; 378 mph)
Patrol speed at 457 m (1,500 ft) at AUW of 49,895 kg (110,000 lb)
206 knots (381 km/h; 237 mph)
Stalling speed: flaps up 133 knots (248 km/h; 154 mph)
flaps down 112 knots (208 km/h; 129 mph)
Max rate of climb at 457 m (1,500 ft)
594 m (1,950 ft)/min
Service ceiling 8,625 m (28,300 ft)
Service ceiling, one engine out 5,790 m (19,000 ft)
T-O run 1,290 m (4,240 ft)
T-O to 15 m (50 ft) 1,673 m (5,490 ft)
Landing from 15 m (50 ft) at design landing weight
845 m (2,770 ft)
Mission radius (3 h on station at 457 m; 1,500 ft)
1,346 nm (2,494 km; 1,550 miles)
Max mission radius (no time on station) at 61,235 kg (135,000 lb)
2,070 nm (3,835 km; 2,383 miles)

LOCKHEED VIKING
US Navy designation: S-3

Production of 187 **S-3As** (see 1978-79 *Jane's*) for the US Navy ended in mid-1978. All tooling was then placed in storage at Burbank pending a US Navy decision on further orders, and in early 1980 demonstrator versions of the **US-3A** (COD) and **KS-3A** (tanker) were evaluated by the Navy. In 1982 three of the earlier production S-3As were modified to US-3A configuration. The sole KS-3A was also converted to US-3A configuration in late 1983.

As an alternative to the KS-3A dedicated tanker configuration, tests of an S-3A with a 'buddy' refuelling pack under its port wing were conducted in 1984. This technique, which transfers fuel from the tanker's standard internal tanks, and an external tank under the starboard wing, without affecting its multi-mission capability, may be adopted for operational use.

Lockheed announced on 18 August 1981 the receipt of a full scale engineering development contract, from the US Naval Air Systems Command, for an improved avionics system for S-3A Vikings currently in service with the US Navy. With initial funding of $14.5 million, it followed a contract awarded by the Navy in 1980, under which Lockheed developed the specifications for an S-3A weapons system improvement programme (WSIP).

Aircraft modified under the WSIP are redesignated **S-3B**. Improvements include increased acoustic processing capacity, expanded electronic support measure capability, better radar processing, a new sonobuoy telemetry receiver system, and provisions for the Harpoon missile. It is anticipated that a total of 160 S-3As will be retrofitted under the programme. Two FSED (full scale engineering development) S-3As were modified initially, the first of which (159742) began flight testing on 13 September 1984; the flight test schedule was completed in August 1985, with redelivery to the US Navy in October. Following a three-month technical evaluation by the Naval Air Test Center at Patuxent River NAS, Maryland, the two S-3Bs undertook a six-month operational evaluation.

Lockheed S-3B Viking with Harpoon missiles, and updated avionics and weapon systems

Two prototype kits to convert S-3As to S-3B production standard were delivered in 1987, and on 28 April 1986 the US Navy contracted Lockheed to supply a first production series of 22 modification kits, together with spares, support equipment and integrated logistics support, at the rate of two per month. Modification of S-3As to S-3B standard is undertaken at Cecil Field NAS, Florida, where the first modified S-3B was delivered to squadron VS-27 on 17 December 1987. To equip a projected 15-carrier fleet, Lockheed has also submitted proposals for follow-on production of 82 or 103 new S-3Bs.

In March 1988 Lockheed Aeronautical Systems Company was awarded a $66 million US Navy contract for prototype development of an electronic reconnaissance variant of the S-3A, designated **ES-3A**. The ES-3A will replace EA-3B Skywarriors, giving the US Navy a carrier-based sigint aircraft capable of performing over-the-horizon electronic surveillance of potentially hostile forces. Lockheed took delivery of an S-3A from NAS Cecil Field, Florida, on 1 March 1988 and will remove its ASW equipment and install government-furnished electronic equipment which is expected to include a sensor suite based on that used in the Lockheed EP-3E. The ES-3A development programme, which is scheduled to last four years, began in the Summer of 1988 with the modification of a flying qualities test airframe to examine the aerodynamic effects of adding some 60 new aerials to the S-3A's fuselage. First flight of the ES-3A prototype is anticipated for August 1989. The ES-3A will be operated by a four-man crew and is expected to equip two new US Navy squadrons, VQ-5 and VQ-6, based respectively at NAS Agana and NAS Rota in support of the Pacific and Atlantic/Mediterranean fleets.

The ES-3A contract provides an option for the production of kits and modification of a further 15 aircraft. Sanders Associates of Nashua, New Hampshire, is providing cockpit display screens; Lockheed missiles and Space Company's Austin, Texas, division will provide wiring and electronics racks; and electronics installation will be undertaken by LASC at its Greenville, South Carolina, Aeromod Center after airframe modifications at Burbank.

AVIONICS, ARMAMENT AND OPERATIONAL EQUIPMENT (S-3B): AYS-1 Proteus acoustic signal processor; modified Sanders AN/OL-320/AYS data processing memory group integrated with IBM AN/UYS-1; updated Sperry Univac AYK-10A(V) air data computer, interfaced with Harpoon air-to-surface missile and other new systems; improved electronic support measures (ESM); Hazeltine AN/ARR-78 sonobuoy receiver system; Precision Echo AN/AQH-7 analog tape recorder, Cubic AN/ARS-2 sonobuoy reference system; Texas Instruments AN/APS-137(V)1 radar, incorporating inverse synthetic aperture radar (ISAR) techniques; modified Goodyear AN/ALE-39 chaff/flare dispensing system; IBM AN/ALR-76 ESM; and provision for carrying McDonnell Douglas Harpoon standoff air-to-surface missiles, and for future advanced navigation and communications systems including Global Positioning System and Joint Tactical Information Distribution System.

LOCKHEED L-1011 (MODEL 385) TRISTAR
Details of the early history of the L-1011 TriStar, of which 250 were built, can be found in the 1983-84 and

previous editions of *Jane's*.

Lockheed has delivered modification kits to Delta Air Lines for uprating six of its TriStars to **L-1011-250** extended range configuration. The kits increase total fuel capacity of each aircraft from 71,668 kg (158,000 lb) to 96,905 kg (213,640 lb), to provide a 2,000 nm increase in range to 5,085 nm (9,415 km; 5,850 miles) with 280 passengers and baggage. Key structural sections of the wings, fuselage and landing gear are strengthened to cater for an 18 per cent increase in max T-O weight to 231,330 kg (510,000 lb). The original engines are replaced by higher thrust Rolls-Royce RB211-524B4 turbofans under separately negotiated arrangements.

The Dash 250 modification is available for approximately 150 other TriStars (from c/n 1052 onwards) produced after design changes were implemented to improve the CG envelope. The L-1011-500 version already incorporates the Dash 250 elements.

Under a similar contract from First Chicago Leasing Corporation, Lockheed is supplying kits to uprate four early production TriStars to a new **L-1011-150** extended range configuration. This modification, which is applicable also to about 50 L-1011-1 models, increases range from 2,800 nm (5,185 km; 3,220 miles) to 3,600 nm (6,665 km; 4,140 miles) and max T-O weight from 195,045 kg (430,000 lb) to 213,190 kg (470,000 lb).

Details of the L-1011 tanker/freighter conversion for the Royal Air Force can be found under the Marshall of Cambridge entry in the UK section of this edition. The **L-1011F** all-cargo conversion is described briefly under the Hayes International Corporation entry in this section.

LASC GEORGIA DIVISION
86 South Cobb Drive, Marietta, Georgia 30063
Telephone: (404) 424 4411
Telex: 542642 LOCKHEED MARA
GENERAL MANAGER: Kenneth W. Cannestra
EXECUTIVE VICE-PRESIDENT: H. Bard Allison
PUBLIC INFORMATION: Joseph E. Dabney

The main building occupied by this division at Marietta is one of the world's largest aircraft production plants under a single roof. Aircraft in current production on its assembly lines are the C-5B Galaxy heavy logistics transport, the C-130 Hercules turboprop transport and its commercial counterpart, the L-100. A major modification programme on USAF C-5A Galaxy transports was completed in 1987.

Lockheed had approximately 20,000 employees in Marietta at the beginning of 1988, and had delivered 2,826 aircraft from Georgia Division by that time.

LOCKHEED MODEL 382 HERCULES
US Air Force designations: C-130, AC-130, DC-130, EC-130, HC-130, JC-130, LC-130, MC-130, RC-130 and WC-130
US Navy designations: C-130, DC-130, EC-130 and LC-130
US Marine Corps designation: KC-130
US Coast Guard designation: HC-130
Canadian Armed Forces designation: CC-130
RAF designations: Hercules C. Mk 1, W. Mk 2 and C. Mk 3
Export designations: C-130H, C-130H-30, KC-130H and C-130H-MP

The C-130 was designed to a specification issued by the US Air Force Tactical Air Command in 1951. Lockheed was awarded its first production contract for the C-130A in September 1952, and 461 C-130As and C-130Bs were manufactured. Details of these basic versions and of many

Lockheed C-130H Hercules of No. 401 Squadron, 1st Transport Wing, Japan Air Self Defence Force
(Katsumi Hinata)

variants for special duties can be found in previous editions of *Jane's*. Later military versions of the C-130 are as follows:

C-130H. Similar to earlier Hercules models except for updated avionics, improved wing and more powerful engines: T56-A-15 turboprops rated at 3,661 kW (4,910 ehp) for take-off, but limited to 3,362 kW (4,508 ehp). Deliveries to USAF began in April 1975. In service with many other air forces. In early 1988 total orders for the C-130H and derivatives stood at 337 aircraft for the USAF,

US Navy and US Coast Guard and 468 for international customers.

C-130H-MP. Maritime patrol, search and rescue version, based on C-130H. Max T-O weight 70,310 kg (155,000 lb). Max payload 18,630 kg (41,074 lb). Four 3,362 kW (4,508 ehp) T56-A-15 engines. Standard and optional equipment includes sea search radar, scanner seats with observation windows, computerised INS/Omega navigation system, crew rest and lavatory/galley slide-in

Lockheed C-130H-30 of the Indonesian Air Force

module, flare launcher, loudspeaker system, rescue kit airdrop platform, side looking airborne radar, passive microwave imager, low light TV, infra-red scanner, camera with data annotation, and ramp equipment pallet which includes a station for an observer. Search time at an altitude of 1,525 m (5,000 ft) is 2 h 30 min at a radius of 1,800 nm (3,333 km; 2,070 miles); 16 h 50 min at radius of 200 nm (370 km; 230 miles). One each delivered to the Indonesian Air Force and US Coast Guard, and three to the Royal Malaysian Air Force.

C-130H-30. 'Stretched' version, with structural changes similar to those of RAF Hercules C.Mk 3 (see C-130K paragraph). Seven delivered to the Algerian Air Force, one to the Cameroun Air Force, one to the Dubai Air Wing, three to the French Air Force, seven to the Indonesian Air Force, three to the Nigerian Air Force, one to Saudi Arabia, one to the Spanish Air Force, one to the Royal Thai Air Force, and four to an unnamed air force in the Far East. Two of the Nigerian aircraft are convertible into 90-passenger transports, by inserting 15-seat pallets into the cargo hold. Conversion takes less than one hour.

AC-130H 'Spectre'. Gunship version with side-firing weapons including various combinations of 105 mm howitzer, 40 mm cannon, two 20 mm Vulcan cannon and two 7.62 mm Miniguns. Equipped with sensors and target acquisition systems including forward looking infra-red and low light level TV, and in-flight refuelling capability. In service with the 23rd Air Force's 1st Special Operations Wing. Improvement programme announced in Spring 1987 and known as SOFI (Special Operations/Forces Improvements) will include new fire control computers, navigation equipment and sensors, scheduled for completion in FY 1992.

EC-130H 'Compass Call'. Operated by 41st Electronic Combat Squadron (a geographically separated unit of the 28th Air Division, Tinker AFB, Oklahoma) at Davis-Monthan AFB, Arizona and the 66th Electronic Combat Wing at Sembach, West Germany. Works with ground mobile C³CM systems to jam enemy command control and communications systems.

HC-130H. Extended range version for Aerospace Rescue and Recovery Service of the US Air Force for aerial recovery of personnel or equipment and other duties; total of 43 delivered, of which the first one flew on 8 December 1964. Update programme announced in Spring 1987 includes Self Contained Navigation System (SCNS), night vision goggles lighting and new communications and navigation equipment for 31 HC-130Hs, 21 of which will also be equipped for in-flight refuelling. The US Coast Guard subsequently ordered 27, and a further two aircraft ordered in the Spring of 1987. Details in 1979-80 *Jane's*. Four modified as **JC-130H** with added equipment for aerial recovery of re-entering space capsules. One modified to **DC-130H** for drone control duties.

KC-130H. Probe-drogue tanker version, very similar to the KC-130R. Exported to Argentina (2), Brazil (2), Israel (2), Morocco (2), Saudi Arabia (8), Spain (5) and Singapore (1).

LC-130H. Similar to LC-130R (which see). Four acquired by US Air Force Air Reserve Forces.

MC-130H. Combat Talon II version of C-130H, modified by USAF for special tactical missions including day/night infiltration and exfiltration, resupply of Special Operations ground forces, psychological warfare missions, aerial reconnaissance, and airdropping and surface-to-air retrieval of personnel. Crew of 9-11. Deeper nose radome, carrying Fulton STAR retrieval yoke of type fitted to HC-130H. Other equipment includes Emerson Electric AN/APQ-170 terrain following radar, precision ground mapping, inertial navigation system, automatic computed air release point, high-speed low-level aerial delivery and container release systems, ground acquisition receiver/interrogator, Texas Instruments AN/AAQ-15 infra-red detection system, secure voice UHF/VHF/FM radios, retractable FLIR pod, angle of attack probe and ALQ-8

Lockheed EC-130H 'Compass Call' electronic warfare aircraft, identified by fuselage side blisters and undertail antennae

First MC-130H Combat Talon II special operations aircraft for the USAF

ECM pod under port wing, plus in-flight refuelling capability. IBM Federal Systems Division is prime contractor for systems integration, with E-Systems as subcontractor for avionics installation and modification. Eighteen funded during FY 1983-87, with expected USAF MC-130H inventory of 24 aircraft by 1991. The first MC-130H began flight tests with E-Systems at Greenville, Texas, in the Spring of 1988, preceding a formal flight test programme scheduled to begin at Edwards AFB, California, in June. MC-130Hs will supplement earlier MC-130Es with MAC's 23rd Air Force, 1st Special Operations Wing at Hulburt Field, Florida.

C-130K. This is basically a C-130H, modified to meet requirements of the Royal Air Force. Much of the avionics and instrumentation is of UK manufacture. Sixty-six delivered as **Hercules C. Mk 1**, of which the first flew on 19 October 1966. One modified by Marshall of Cambridge (Engineering) Ltd in the UK for use by the RAF Meteorological Research Flight, under the designation **Hercules W. Mk 2**. Thirty of the others have been lengthened by 4.57 m (15 ft 0 in) (2.54 m; 8 ft 4 in plug forward of wing, 2.03 m; 6 ft 8 in aft of wing), equivalent to commercial L-100-30 standard. This increases payload capacity to seven cargo pallets instead of five, or two Land-Rovers and four trailers (instead of 3 + 2), or 128 troops instead of 92, or 92 fully equipped paratroops instead of 64, or 97 stretcher patients instead of 74. The first aircraft was modified at Marietta in 1979; the remaining 29 were lengthened by Marshall of Cambridge (see UK section). After modification, these aircraft are redesignated **Hercules C. Mk 3**.

HC-130N. Search and rescue version of the C-130H for recovery of aircrew and retrieval of space capsules after re-entry, using advanced direction finding equipment. Fifteen delivered to US Air Force.

HC-130P. Version of the C-130H, modified to have capability of refuelling helicopters in flight and for mid-air retrieval of parachute-borne payloads. Twenty built for USAF Aerospace Rescue and Recovery Service. Details in 1979-80 *Jane's*.

EC-130Q. Similar to earlier EC-130G, but with improved equipment and crew accommodation, for US Navy command communications (Tacamo) duties. Described as "the only airborne, survivable, communications link with submarine forces, providing HF and VLF SIMOP (simultaneous operations) capability in a collocated environment". Eighteen built.

KC-130R. Probe-drogue tanker version of C-130H: 14 for US Marine Corps. Changes from earlier KC-130F (1975-76 *Jane's*) include engines of 3,362 kW (4,508 ehp), increased T-O and landing weights, pylon mounted fuel tanks to provide additional 10,296 litres (2,720 US gallons; 2,265 Imp gallons) of fuel, and removable 13,627 litre (3,600 US gallon; 2,997 Imp gallon) fuel tank in cargo compartment. All fuel can be used by tanker for extended range. Single-point fuelling of installed and removable tanks via normal filler in wheel well. Operating weight empty 36,279 kg (79,981 lb). Max T-O weight 75,433 kg (166,301 lb). Able to offload up to 23,587 kg (52,000 lb) of fuel, equivalent to 30,283 litres (8,000 US gallons; 6,661 Imp gallons), at mission radius of 1,000 nm (1,850 km; 1,150 miles).

LC-130R. Basically a C-130H with wheel-ski gear for US Navy Squadron VXE-6. Six converted, for service in the Antarctic. Details in 1979-80 *Jane's*.

KC-130T. Tanker for US Marine Corps (Reserve). Similar to KC-130R but with updated avionics, including 'state of the art' INS, Omega and Tacan, a new autopilot and flight director, and solid state search radar. KC-130Ts delivered in late 1984 featured Bendix AN/APS-133 colour radar, flush mounted antennae and orthopaedically designed crew seats. Able to refuel helicopters as well as fighters. Delivery of 10 to Marine Aerial Refueler Transport Squadron 234 (VMGR-234) of Marine Air Control Group 48 at NAS Glenview, Illinois, began on 23 October 1983. Four additional KC-130Ts on order.

AC-130U 'Spectre'. New gunship version of C-130H. Prototype to be modified by Rockwell International from a C-130H, for first flight in early 1990. Total of 12 planned, to replace 10 AC-130As. To be fitted with a 105 mm howitzer, single 25 mm and 40 mm cannon, Hughes AN/APG-70 digital fire control radar, Texas Instruments FLIR, Ball Aerospace LLL TV, HUD, new EW suite, combined INS/GPS nav, triple 1553B databuses, baron/Kevlar armour protection, in-flight refuelling, and bad-weather attack radar.

Commercial versions of the Hercules are described separately.

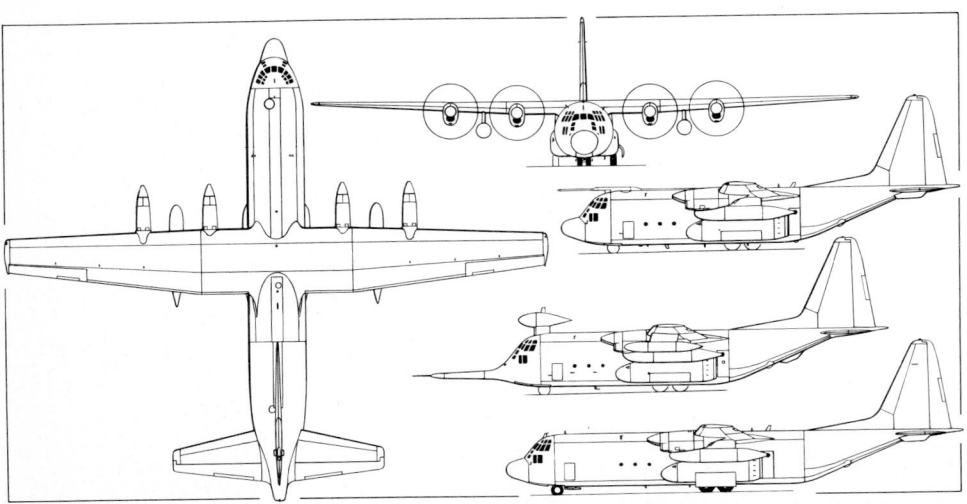

Lockheed C-130H-30 'stretched' Hercules (RAF C. Mk 3) with upper side view of C-130K (RAF C. Mk 1) and centre side view of W. Mk 2 *(Pilot Press)*

The C-130 is able to deliver single loads of up to 11,340 kg (25,000 lb) by the ground proximity extraction method. This involves making a flypast 1.2-1.5 m (4-5 ft) above the ground with the rear loading ramp open. The aircraft trails a hook which is attached by cable to the palletised cargo. The hook engages a steel cable on the ground and the cargo is extracted from the aircraft and brought to a stop on the ground in about 30 m (100 ft) by an energy absorption system manufactured by All American Engineering of Wilmington, Delaware. An alternative extraction technique known as LAPES (low altitude parachute extraction system) involves deploying a 6.70 m (22 ft) ribbon parachute to drag the pallet from the cabin. Loads of up to 22,680 kg (50,000 lb) have been delivered by this method.

By January 1988 firm orders for all versions of the Hercules exceeded 1,830 for 60 nations. The 1,800th aircraft was delivered on 2 December 1986, with production continuing at the rate of approx three a month.

The following details refer specifically to the international C-130H, except where indicated otherwise:

TYPE: Medium/long-range combat transport.

WINGS: Cantilever high-wing monoplane. Wing section NACA 64A318 at root, NACA 64A412 at tip. Dihedral 2° 30′. Incidence 3° at root, 0° at tip. Sweepback at quarter-chord 0°. All-metal two-spar stressed skin structure, with integrally stiffened tapered machined skin panels up to 14.63 m (48 ft 0 in) long. Conventional aluminium alloy ailerons have tandem-piston hydraulic boost, operated by either of two independent hydraulic systems. Lockheed-Fowler aluminium alloy trailing-edge flaps. Trim tab in each aileron. Leading-edges anti-iced by engine bleed air.

FUSELAGE: Semi-monocoque structure of aluminium and magnesium alloys.

TAIL UNIT: Cantilever all-metal stressed skin structure. Fixed incidence tailplane, with Kevlar afterbody strake on undersurface at each side, close to fuselage. Trim tab in each elevator and rudder. Elevator tabs use AC electrical power as primary source and DC as emergency source. Control surfaces have tandem-piston hydraulic boost. Hot air anti-icing of tailplane leading-edge, by engine bleed air.

LANDING GEAR: Hydraulically retractable tricycle type. Each main unit has two wheels in tandem, retracting into fairings built on to the sides of the fuselage. Nose unit has twin wheels and is steerable through 60° each side of centre. Oleo shock absorbers. Mainwheel tyres size 56 × 20-20, pressure 6.62 bars (96 lb/sq in). Nosewheel tyres size 39 × 13-16, pressure 4.14 bars (60 lb/sq in). Goodyear aircooled multiple disc hydraulic brakes with anti-skid units. Retractable combination wheel-skis available.

POWER PLANT: Four 3,362 kW (4,508 ehp) Allison T56-A-15 turboprops, each driving a Hamilton Standard type 54H60 four-blade constant-speed fully-feathering reversible-pitch propeller. Fuel in six integral tanks in wings, with total capacity of 26,344 litres (6,960 US gallons; 5,795 Imp gallons) and two optional underwing pylon tanks, each with capacity of 5,146 litres (1,360 US gallons; 1,132 Imp gallons). Total fuel capacity 36,636 litres (9,680 US gallons; 8,060 Imp gallons). Single pressure refuelling point in starboard wheel well. Overwing gravity fuelling. Oil capacity 182 litres (48 US gallons; 40 Imp gallons).

ACCOMMODATION: Crew of four on flight deck, comprising pilot, co-pilot, navigator and systems manager (fully performance qualified flight engineer on USAF aircraft). Provision for fifth man to supervise loading. Sleeping quarters for relief crew, and galley. Flight deck and main cabin pressurised and air-conditioned. Standard complements for C-130H are as follows: troops (max) 92, paratroops (max) 64, litters 74 and 2 attendants. Corresponding figures for C-130H-30 are 128 troops, 92 paratroops, and 97 litters. As a cargo carrier, loads can include heavy equipment such as a 12,080 kg (26,640 lb) type F.6 refuelling trailer or a 155 mm howitzer and its high-speed tractor, or up to five 463L pallets of freight (seven in C-130H-30). Hydraulically operated main loading door and ramp at rear of cabin. Paratroop door on each side aft of landing gear fairing. Two emergency exit doors standard; two additional doors optional on C-130H-30.

SYSTEMS: Air-conditioning and pressurisation system max pressure differential 0.52 bars (7.5 lb/sq in). Three independent hydraulic systems, utility and booster systems operating at a pressure of 207 bars (3,000 lb/sq in), rated at 65.1 litres (17.2 US gallons; 14.3 Imp gallons)/min for utility and booster systems, 30.3 litres (8.0 US gallons; 6.7 Imp gallons)/min for auxiliary system. Reservoirs are unpressurised. Auxiliary system has handpump for emergencies. Electrical system supplied by four 40kVA AC alternators, plus one 40kVA auxiliary alternator driven by APU in port main landing gear fairing. Four transformer-rectifiers for DC power. Current production aircraft incorporate systems and component design changes for increased reliability. There are differences between the installed components for US government and export versions.

AVIONICS: Dual 628T-2A HF com, dual 618M-3A VHF com, AN/ARC-164 UHF com, AN/AIC-13 PA system, AN/AIC-18 intercom, dual 621A-6A ATC transponders, DF-301E UHF nav, dual 51RV-4B VHF nav, CMA 771 Omega nav, LTN-72 INS, dual DF-206 ADF, 51Z-4 marker beacon receiver, dual 860E-5 DME, AL-101 radio altimeter, RDR-1F weather radar, dual C-12 compass systems, Mk II GPWS, AP-105V autopilot, and dual FD-109 flight directors.

DIMENSIONS, EXTERNAL:

Wing span	40.41 m (132 ft 7 in)
Wing chord: at root	4.88 m (16 ft 0 in)
mean	4.16 m (13 ft 8½ in)
Wing aspect ratio	10.1
Length overall:	
all except HC-130H and C-130H-30	29.79 m (97 ft 9 in)
C-130H-30	34.37 m (112 ft 9 in)
Height overall	11.66 m (38 ft 3 in)
Tailplane span	16.05 m (52 ft 8 in)
Wheel track	4.35 m (14 ft 3 in)
Wheelbase	9.77 m (32 ft 0¾ in)
Propeller diameter	4.11 m (13 ft 6 in)
Main cargo door (rear of cabin):	
Height	2.77 m (9 ft 1 in)
Width	3.05 m (10 ft 0 in)
Height to sill	1.03 m (3 ft 5 in)
Paratroop doors (each): Height	1.83 m (6 ft 0 in)
Width	0.91 m (3 ft 0 in)
Height to sill	1.03 m (3 ft 5 in)
Emergency exits (each): Height	1.22 m (4 ft 0 in)
Width	0.71 m (2 ft 4 in)

DIMENSIONS, INTERNAL:

Cabin, excl flight deck:	
Length without ramp:	
C-130H	12.22 m (40 ft 1¼ in)
C-130H-30	16.79 m (55 ft 1¼ in)
Length with ramp: C-130H	15.73 m (51 ft 8½ in)
C-130H-30	20.33 m (66 ft 8½ in)
Max width	3.12 m (10 ft 3 in)
Max height	2.81 m (9 ft 2¾ in)
Floor area, excl ramp: C-130H	39.5 m^2 (425.0 sq ft)
Volume, incl ramp: C-130H	127.4 m^3 (4,500.0 cu ft)
C-130H-30	165.5 m^3 (5,845.0 cu ft)

AREAS:

Wings, gross	162.12 m^2 (1,745.0 sq ft)
Ailerons (total)	10.22 m^2 (110.0 sq ft)
Trailing-edge flaps (total)	31.77 m^2 (342.0 sq ft)
Fin	20.90 m^2 (225.0 sq ft)
Rudder, incl tab	6.97 m^2 (75.0 sq ft)
Tailplane	35.40 m^2 (381.0 sq ft)
Elevators, incl tabs	14.40 m^2 (155.0 sq ft)

WEIGHTS AND LOADINGS:

Operating weight empty:	
C-130H	34,686 kg (76,469 lb)
C-130H-30	36,397 kg (80,242 lb)
Max fuel weight: internal	20,520 kg (45,240 lb)
external	8,020 kg (17,680 lb)
Max payload: C-130H	19,356 kg (42,673 lb)
C-130H-30	17,645 kg (38,900 lb)
Max normal T-O weight	70,310 kg (155,000 lb)
Max overload T-O weight	79,380 kg (175,000 lb)
Max normal landing weight	70,310 kg (155,000 lb)
Max overload landing weight	79,380 kg (175,000 lb)
Max zero-fuel weight, 2.5*g*	54,040 kg (119,142 lb)
Max wing loading	434.5 kg/m^2 (89 lb/sq ft)
Max power loading	5.23 kg/kW (8.6 lb/ehp)

PERFORMANCE (C-130H at max T-O weight, unless indicated otherwise):

Max cruising speed	325 knots (602 km/h; 374 mph)
Econ cruising speed	300 knots (556 km/h; 345 mph)
Stalling speed	100 knots (185 km/h; 115 mph)
Max rate of climb at S/L	579 m (1,900 ft)/min
Service ceiling at 58,970 kg (130,000 lb) AUW	10,060 m (33,000 ft)
Service ceiling, one engine out, at 58,970 kg (130,000 lb) AUW	8,075 m (26,500 ft)
Min ground turning radius	19.2 m (63 ft)
Runway LCN at 70,310 kg (155,000 lb) AUW:	
asphalt	37
concrete	42
T-O run	1,091 m (3,580 ft)
T-O to 15 m (50 ft)	1,573 m (5,160 ft)
Landing from 15 m (50 ft) at 45,360 kg (100,000 lb) AUW	731 m (2,400 ft)
Landing from 15 m (50 ft) at 58,967 kg (130,000 lb) AUW	838 m (2,750 ft)
Landing run at 58,967 kg (130,000 lb) AUW	518 m (1,700 ft)
Range with max payload, with 5% reserves and allowance for 30 min at S/L	2,046 nm (3,791 km; 2,356 miles)
Range with max fuel, incl external tanks, 7,081 kg (15,611 lb) payload, reserves of 5% initial fuel plus 30 min at S/L	4,250 nm (7,876 km; 4,894 miles)

LOCKHEED L-100 SERIES COMMERCIAL HERCULES

Details of initial versions of the commercial Hercules have appeared in previous editions of *Jane's*; current models are as follows:

L-100-20 (Model 382E). Certificated on 4 October 1968, this 'stretched' version of the Hercules has a 2.54 m (100 in) fuselage extension. A 1.52 m (60 in) fuselage plug is inserted aft of the forward crew door and a 1.02 m (40 in) plug aft of the rear personnel doors. Allison 501-D22A engines. Military operators/owners in January 1988 were the Gabon Air Force (1), Peruvian Air Force (5) and Philippine Air Force (3).

L-100-30 (Model 382G). Generally similar to the L-100-20, but with the fuselage extended a further 2.03 m (80 in). Early models did not have aft personnel doors which are now standard. Saturn Airways (now Transamerica Airlines) was the first operator of this model, in December 1970. Military operators/owners in 1988 included the air forces of Dubai (1), Ecuador (1), Gabon (3), Indonesia (1), Kuwait (4), Pakistan (1), Peru (5) and the Philippines (4).

In 1988 efforts to obtain an FAA supplemental type certificate with ditching provision to enable the civil L-100-30 to carry up to 100 passengers were awaiting a launch customer. All C-130 and L-100 aircraft delivered since April 1984 have two 0.61 × 1.22 m (24 × 48 in) emergency exits, one on each side of the aircraft, as standard equipment. Together with the current rear personnel doors, these provide the necessary exits for up to 79 passengers. An optional additional exit on each side of the fuselage will provide exits for 100 passengers. Various passenger, galley and toilet configurations are available, with a supplemental oxygen system for passengers.

Lockheed has developed an airborne hospital version of the L-100-30, designated **L-100-30HS**. Five of this variant have been delivered to Saudi Arabia after modification by Ontario division, with operating theatres and intensive care, advanced anaesthesia and X-ray facilities. Electrical generators and air conditioners contained in underwing pods enable the aircraft to function as remote emergency hospitals for up to 72 hours without external support. Described under Ontario division entry.

A total of 109 commercial Hercules (all versions) had been ordered by January 1988. Details given for the C-130H apply also to the L-100-20 and L-100-30, except as follows:

TYPE: Medium/long-range transport.

LANDING GEAR: As for C-130H, except mainwheel tyre pressure 3.24-7.38 bars (47-107 lb/sq in) and nosewheel tyre pressure 4.14 bars (60 lb/sq in).

POWER PLANT: Four 3,362 kW (4,508 ehp) Allison 501-D22A turboprops.

DIMENSIONS, EXTERNAL:

Length overall: L-100-20	32.33 m (106 ft 1 in)
L-100-30	34.37 m (112 ft 9 in)
Wheelbase: L-100-20	11.30 m (37 ft 1 in)
L-100-30	12.32 m (40 ft 5 in)

Lockheed L-100-30 'Super Hercules' of China Air Cargo

Crew door (integral steps): Height	1.14 m (3 ft 9 in)
Width	0.76 m (2 ft 6 in)
Height to sill	1.04 m (3 ft 5 in)

DIMENSIONS, INTERNAL:

Cabin, excl flight deck:	
Length: L-100-20	15.04 m (49 ft 4 in)
L-100-30: excl ramp	17.07 m (56 ft 0 in)
incl ramp	19.93 m (65 ft 4¾ in)
Max height	2.74 m (9 ft 0 in)
Floor area, excl ramp: L-100-20	46.36 m² (499.0 sq ft)
L-100-30	52.30 m² (563.0 sq ft)
Floor area, ramp	9.57 m² (103.0 sq ft)
Volume, incl ramp: L-100-20	150.28 m³ (5,307 cu ft)
L-100-30	171.5 m³ (6,057 cu ft)

WEIGHTS AND LOADINGS:

Operating weight empty:	
L-100-20	34,781 kg (76,680 lb)
L-100-30	35,260 kg (77,736 lb)
Max payload: L-100-20	23,637 kg (52,110 lb)
L-100-30	23,158 kg (51,054 lb)
Max ramp weight	70,670 kg (155,800 lb)
Max T-O weight	70,308 kg (155,000 lb)
Max landing weight	61,235 kg (135,000 lb)
Max zero-fuel weight	58,420 kg (128,790 lb)
Max fuel weight	29,380 kg (64,772 lb)
Max wing loading	433.5 kg/m² (88.8 lb/sq ft)
Max power loading	5.23 kg/kW (8.6 lb/ehp)

PERFORMANCE (at max T-O weight except where indicated):

Max cruising speed at 6,100 m (20,000 ft) at 54,430 kg (120,000 lb) AUW	308 knots (571 km/h; 355 mph)
Landing speed	124 knots (230 km/h; 143 mph)
Max rate of climb at S/L	518 m (1,700 ft)/min
Min ground turning radius: L-100-20	26.8 m (88 ft)
L-100-30	27.5 m (90 ft)
Runway LCN: asphalt	37
concrete	42
FAR T-O field length	1,905 m (6,250 ft)
FAR landing field length, at max landing weight	1,478 m (4,850 ft)
Range:	
with max payload, 45 min reserves	1,334 nm (2,472 km; 1,536 miles)
with zero payload	4,830 nm (8,951 km; 5,562 miles)

OPERATIONAL NOISE LEVELS (FAR Pt 36, Stage 2):

T-O	98.4 EPNdB
Approach	99.1 EPNdB
Sideline	93.9 EPNdB

LOCKHEED HTTB

This high technology testbed (HTTB) conversion of a commercial model L-100-20 Hercules, developed to provide a platform for evaluating new technologies in an airborne environment, first flew on 19 June 1984. It is being used to conduct STOL flight research, in the development of avionics subsystems, and to develop high lift systems, advanced flight controls, cockpit displays, navigation, guidance and enroute survivability systems for future tactical airlift aircraft. Externally apparent features include the addition of a long dorsal fin, similar extensions known as 'horsals' (horizontal dorsals) forward of each tailplane root, and an electrically isolated sensor boom of composite materials forward of each wingtip.

During the first of several planned modification programmes, the HTTB was fitted with a 1,000-channel data gathering, analysis and display system known as LADS (Lockheed airborne data system), enabling engineers to run tests and evaluate data in real time aboard the aircraft. In addition to LADS, the HTTB carries in its cargo compartment a 10 m (33 ft) long mobile data centre van equipped with telemetry links to analyse data on the ground at remote test sites. Early test flights also verified a new electronics mission pod known as SAMSON (Special Avionics Mission Strap-On Now). This uses a Hercules external wing fuel tank, containing its own generator, to house an easily attachable special avionics package, providing special mission capability without physical

modification of the airframe. Lockheed believes that the SAMSON facility will offer worldwide C-130 operators a viable low-cost electronics mission capability.

The HTTB set new FAI Class N time-to-height records on 5 March 1985. Taking off at a gross weight of 44,724 kg (98,600 lb), using only 427 m (1,400 ft) of runway, the aircraft climbed to 3,000 m in 3 min 59.4 s; to 6,000 m in 9 min 19.75 s; and to 9,000 m in 18 min 33.72 s.

Planned modifications to the HTTB which were scheduled for completion by April 1988 include the installation of fully-powered flight controls, fast-acting double-slotted trailing-edge flaps, drooped high camber fixed wing leading-edges, fly by wire composite construction spoilers for direct lift control and enhanced roll control, extended-chord ailerons and rudder with servo tab, and a new landing gear which will permit sink rates up to 3.05 m (10.0 ft)/s at a landing weight of 58,967 kg (130,000 lb). Wind tunnel testing indicated that the external modifications could offer an increase in lift of up to 95 per cent. Target STOL performance includes a landing from 15 m (50 ft) in 457 m (1,500 ft) at a landing weight of 63,500 kg (140,000 lb). Landing speed is expected to be about 80 knots (148 km/h; 92 mph).

The HTTB was modified during 1987 to incorporate a number of systems improvements, including a triplex digital flight control system (DFCS) developed jointly by LASC Georgia division and Sperry Aerospace and Marine Group. The DFCS drives five independent electromechanical actuator systems (EMAS), some of which function as series servos in the pitch, roll and yaw stability augmentation systems. The remaining EMAS units drive rudder and elevator servotabs which aerodynamically balance the surfaces and provide backup fly by wire control in case hydraulic power should be lost. An onboard command guidance system with laser rangefinder, FLIR and a computer-generated head-up display guides the pilot through the final approach and landing phases of flight to touchdown without the normal level-off and flare, thus reducing landing distance. Flight testing of this autonomous landing guidance system was expected to begin in April 1988. In the last quarter of 1988 Lockheed-Georgia was expected to install 3,915 kW (5,250 shp) Allison T-56 Series IV engines in the HTTB to improve take-off performance. In each phase of the HTTB modification programme Georgia division is running a pilot participation programme in which pilot and flight engineer crews from selected industry and service organisations fly the aircraft, providing

feedback which will be used in establishing future advanced tactical transport requirements. In addition to industry research programmes, the HTTB is being offered to university faculties and graduate students who will have opportunities to place experiments aboard the aircraft and to take part in the flight testing of their equipment. Lockheed will also test a 14 × 2 m (4.27 × 0.6 ft) phased array radar antenna installed on the starboard fuselage side of the HTTB. The installation, which was expected to be completed in the Spring of 1988, is a private venture aimed at the US Air Force's Air Defence Initiative.

LOCKHEED ARTB

Due for completion in mid-1988, the ARTB (advanced radar testbed) is a modified Lockheed C-141 StarLifter four-turbofan transport aircraft for use by USAF's 4950th Test Wing to evaluate the response of modern airborne radars to jamming and other ECCM. The aircraft was modified by Georgia division, with Hughes and Westinghouse as subcontractors, and can accommodate a number of different radar antennae in interchangeable nose radomes. The programme, which is expected to improve the anti-jamming capabilities of current airborne radars, is scheduled to run until April 1990.

LOCKHEED GALAXY
USAF designation: C-5

Full structural and specification details of the original C-5A can be found in the 1975-76 *Jane's*. An abbreviated entry appeared in the 1978-79 edition.

In early 1978 Lockheed received a USAF contract to manufacture two new sets of wings for the **C-5A**, of a design intended to increase service life to 30,000 h. Apart from the moving surfaces, these wings are of virtually new design, using 7175-T73511 aluminium alloy for greater strength and increased resistance to corrosion, and were built under subcontract by Avco Aerostructures Textron. The first re-winged Galaxy was redelivered to the USAF in early 1981, and the remaining 76 in operational service were fitted with the new wings in a modification programme which was completed in July 1987. Under a $10 million 1986 contract from the USAF, Georgia division is modifying a number of C-5As to enable them to carry oversized Space Shuttle cargo that is currently beyond existing airlift capability. This contract is due for completion in September 1989.

The 433rd MAW at Kelly AFB, Texas, became the first AFRES unit to receive the C-5A when the first of eight aircraft was delivered in December 1984. The Air National Guard's 105th MAG, based at Stewart Airport, Newburgh, New York, received its first C-5As in July 1985. A total of 44 C-5As is scheduled to be transferred to AFRES and ANG units.

In the Summer of 1982, Congress approved a Lockheed proposal to manufacture a C-5N (N : new) version of the Galaxy, to meet an urgent US Air Force requirement for additional heavy airlift capacity. Funding was approved for a total of 50 of these transports under the service designation **C-5B**.

The aircraft internal arrangements and external aero-dynamic configuration are the same as those of the C-5A, but the new version includes all of the changes, improvements and modifications incorporated in its predecessor during its years of service with the US Air Force.

The first C-5B was rolled out on 12 July, and made its first flight from Dobbins AFB on 10 September 1985. First delivery to the USAF was made on 8 January 1986, and 21 had been delivered by 1 January 1988. Four of these were in service with the 443rd Military Airlift Wing (the MAC training centre) at Altus AFB, Oklahoma. The two operational C-5B units, each due to receive 23 aircraft, are the 60th MAW at Travis AFB, California, and the 436th

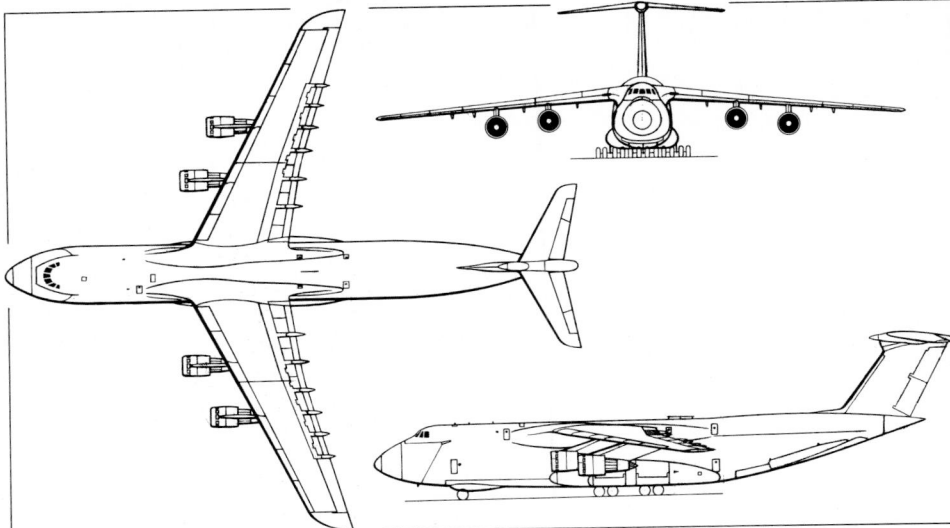

Lockheed C-5B Galaxy heavy logistics transport aircraft (*Pilot Press*)

Lockheed's all-black high technology testbed (HTTB) Hercules, a converted L-100-20

Lockheed C-5B Galaxy heavy logistics transport aircraft of the USAF

MAW at Dover AFB, Delaware. Final delivery is scheduled for February 1989. Production was continuing at the rate of two aircraft per month in early 1988.

The following description applies to the C-5B:

TYPE: Heavy logistics transport aircraft.

WINGS: Cantilever high-wing monoplane. Wing section NACA 0012 (mod) at 20 per cent span, NACA 0011 (mod) at 43.7 per cent and 70 per cent span. Anhedral 5° 30′ at quarter-chord. Incidence 3° 30′ at root. Sweepback at quarter-chord 25°. Conventional fail-safe box structure of built-up spars and machined aluminium alloy extruded skin panels. Statically balanced aluminium alloy ailerons. Modified Fowler aluminium alloy trailing-edge flaps. Simple hinged aluminium alloy spoilers forward of flaps. No trim tabs. Sealed inboard slats and slotted outboard slats on leading-edges. Ailerons and spoilers operated by hydraulic servo actuators. Trailing-edge flaps and leading-edge slats actuated by ball screwjack and torque tube system. Major wing assemblies are built by Avco Aerostructures Textron and joined by Lockheed. Leading-edge slats and slat tracks, leading-edge ribs, and ailerons, are built under subcontract by Canadair Ltd.

FUSELAGE: Conventional semi-monocoque fail-safe structure of 7049-T73, 7050-T736, 7075-T73 and 7475 aluminium alloys.

TAIL UNIT: Cantilever all-metal T tail. All surfaces swept; anhedral on tailplane. All components are single-cell box structures with integrally stiffened aluminium alloy skin panels. Variable incidence tailplane. Elevators in four sections; rudder in two sections. No trim tabs. Rudder and elevators operated through hydraulic servo actuators. Tailplane actuated through hydraulically powered screwjack. No anti-icing equipment.

LANDING GEAR: Retractable tricycle type. Nose unit retracted rearward by hydraulically driven ballscrews. Main units rotated through 90° and retracted inward via hydraulically driven gearbox. Single nose shock absorber and four main gear shock absorbers are of Bendix oleo-pneumatic dual-chamber type. Four wheels on nose unit. Four main units (two in tandem on each side) each comprise a 'triangular footprint' six-wheel bogie made up of a pair of wheels forward of the shock absorber and two pairs aft. All 28 tyres size 49 × 17-20 type VII 26-ply. Tyre pressures: nosewheels 9.45 bars (137 lb/sq in), mainwheels 7.65 bars (111 lb/sq in) with in-flight deflation capability. Goodrich wheels, tyres and carbon disc brakes. Hydro-Aire fully modulating anti-skid units. Ground manoeuvrability enhanced by castoring rear main units.

POWER PLANT: Four General Electric TF39-GE-1C turbofans, each rated at 191.2 kN (43,000 lb st). Twelve integral fuel tanks in wings, between front and rear spars, comprising two outboard main tanks (each 13,874 litres; 3,665 US gallons; 3,052 Imp gallons), two inboard main tanks (each 14,755 litres; 3,898 US gallons; 3,246 Imp gallons), two outboard auxiliary tanks (each 18,034 litres; 4,764 US gallons; 3,967 Imp gallons), two inboard auxiliary tanks (each 18,401 litres; 4,861 US gallons; 4,078 Imp gallons); two outboard extended range tanks (each 15,865 litres; 4,191 US gallons; 3,490 Imp gallons), and two inboard extended range tanks (each 15,883 litres; 4,196 US gallons; 3,494 Imp gallons). Total capacity 193,624 litres (51,150 US gallons; 42,591 Imp gallons). Two refuelling points each side, in forward part of main landing gear pods. Flight refuelling capability, via inlet in upper forward fuselage, over flight engineer's station (compatible with KC-135 and KC-10 tankers). Oil capacity 138 litres (36.4 US gallons; 30.3 Imp gallons).

ACCOMMODATION: Standard crew of five, consisting of pilot, co-pilot, flight engineer and two loadmasters, with rest area for 15 people (relief crew, couriers, etc) at front of upper deck. Basic version has seats for 75 troops on rear part of upper deck, aft of wing box. Provision for carrying 270 troops on lower deck, but aircraft will be employed primarily as freighter. Typical loads include two M1 Abrams tanks or sixteen ¾ ton lorries; or one M1 and two Bradley armoured fighting vehicles; or six AH-64A Apache attack helicopters; or 10 Pershing misiles with tow and launch vehicles; or 36 standard 463L load pallets. 'Visor' type upward hinged nose, and loading ramp, permit straight-in loading into front of hold, under flight deck. Rear straight-in loading via ramp which forms undersurface of rear fuselage. Side panels of rear fuselage, by ramp, hinge outward to improve access on ground but do not need to open for airdrop operations in view of width of ramp. Ramp and associated side panels built under subcontract by Canadair Ltd. Provision for aerial delivery system (ADS) kits for paratroops or cargo. Two passenger doors, one each on port and starboard sides at rear end of lower deck. One crew door on port side at forward end of lower deck. Five evacuation slides and four 25-person liferafts, all supplied by Garrett Air Cruisers. Entire accommodation pressurised and air-conditioned.

SYSTEMS: Electronically controlled air-conditioning and pressurisation systems: pressure differential 0.57 bars (8.2 lb/sq in). Four separate hydraulic systems, pressure 207 bars (3,000 lb/sq in) each, supply flying control and utility systems, with power supplied by two identical variable volume, constant pressure pumps on each engine, each rated at 227 litres (60 US gallons; 50 Imp gallons)/min. Each system contains an unpressurised hydraulic reservoir. Electrical system includes four 60/80 kVA AC engine driven generators. Two APUs provide auxiliary pneumatic and electrical power. Ground hydraulic power is supplied by two air turbine motors.

AVIONICS AND EQUIPMENT: Communications and navigation equipment to military requirements. Bendix colour weather radar. Three Delco inertial navigation units with triple-mix capabilities. Special equipment includes updated electronic malfunction detection, analysis and recoding subsystem (MADAR II) which scans and analyses more than 800 test points.

DIMENSIONS, EXTERNAL:
Wing span	67.88 m (222 ft 8½ in)
Wing chord: at root	13.85 m (45 ft 5¼ in)
at tip	4.67 m (15 ft 4 in)
Wing aspect ratio	7.75
Length overall	75.54 m (247 ft 10 in)
Length of fuselage	70.29 m (230 ft 7¼ in)
Height overall	19.85 m (65 ft 1½ in)
Tailplane span	20.94 m (68 ft 8½ in)
Wheel track (between outer wheels)	11.42 m (37 ft 5½ in)
Wheelbase (c/l main gear to c/l nose gear)	22.22 m (72 ft 11 in)
Crew door (lower deck): Height	1.80 m (5 ft 11 in)
Width	1.02 m (3 ft 4 in)
Height to sill	3.94 m (12 ft 11 in)
Passenger door (lower deck): Height	1.83 m (6 ft 0 in)
Width	0.91 m (3 ft 0 in)
Height to sill	3.56 m (11 ft 8 in)
Aft loading opening (ramp lowered):	
Max height	3.93 m (12 ft 10¾ in)
Max width	5.79 m (19 ft 0 in)
Aft straight-in loading:	
Max height	2.90 m (9 ft 6 in)
Max width	5.79 m (19 ft 0 in)
Forward loading opening (ramp lowered or straight-in):	
Max height	4.11 m (13 ft 6 in)
Max width	5.79 m (19 ft 0 in)

Height to floor (kneeled): forward	1.34 m (4 ft 4¾ in)
rear	1.45 m (4 ft 9 in)

DIMENSIONS, INTERNAL:
Cabins, excl flight deck:
Length:	
upper deck, forward	11.99 m (39 ft 4 in)
upper deck, rear	18.20 m (59 ft 8½ in)
lower deck, without ramps	36.91 m (121 ft 1 in)
lower deck, with ramps	44.09 m (144 ft 8 in)
Max width:	
upper deck, forward	4.20 m (13 ft 9½ in)
upper deck, rear	3.96 m (13 ft 0 in)
lower deck	5.79 m (19 ft 0 in)
Max height:	
upper deck	2.29 m (7 ft 6 in)
lower deck	4.09 m (13 ft 5 in)
Floor area:	
upper deck, forward	50.17 m² (540.0 sq ft)
upper deck, rear	72.10 m² (776.1 sq ft)
lower deck, without ramp	213.76 m² (2,300.9 sq ft)
Volume:	
upper deck, forward	56.91 m³ (2,010 cu ft)
upper deck, rear	170.46 m³ (6,020 cu ft)
lower deck	985.29 m³ (34,795 cu ft)

AREAS:
Wings, gross	576.0 m² (6,200 sq ft)
Ailerons (total)	23.49 m² (252.8 sq ft)
Trailing-edge flaps (total)	92.13 m² (991.7 sq ft)
Leading-edge slats (total)	60.25 m² (648.5 sq ft)
Spoilers (total)	40.01 m² (430.7 sq ft)
Fin	89.29 m² (961.1 sq ft)
Rudder	21.06 m² (226.7 sq ft)
Tailplane	89.73 m² (965.8 sq ft)
Elevators	24.03 m² (258.7 sq ft)

WEIGHTS AND LOADINGS (for 2.25g):
Operating weight empty, equipped	169,643 kg (374,000 lb)
Max payload	118,387 kg (261,000 lb)
Max fuel weight	150,815 kg (332,500 lb)
Max T-O weight	379,657 kg (837,000 lb)
Max zero-fuel weight	288,030 kg (635,000 lb)
*Max landing weight	288,415 kg (635,850 lb)
Max wing loading	659 kg/m² (135.48 lb/sq ft)
Max power loading	496.4 kg/kN (4.88 lb/lb st)

*at 2.7 m (9 ft)/s descent rate

PERFORMANCE (estimated at max T-O weight, except where indicated):
Never-exceed speed	402 knots (745 km/h; 463 mph) CAS or Mach 0.875
Max level speed at 7,620 m (25,000 ft)	496 knots (919 km/h; 571 mph)
Max cruising speed at 7,620 m (25,000 ft)	480-490 knots (888-908 km/h; 552-564 mph)
Econ cruising speed at 7,620 m (25,000 ft)	450 knots (833 km/h; 518 mph)
Stalling speed at max landing weight, 40° flap, power off	104 knots (193 km/h; 120 mph)
Max rate of climb at S/L	525 m (1,725 ft)/min
Service ceiling at AUW of 278,960 kg (615,000 lb)	10,895 m (35,750 ft)
Min ground turning radius	45.11 m (148 ft 0 in)
Runway LCN: asphalt	69
concrete	44
T-O run at S/L, ISA	2,530 m (8,300 ft)
T-O to 15 m (50 ft) at S/L, ISA	2,987 m (9,800 ft)
Landing from 15 m (50 ft), max landing weight at S/L, ISA	1,164 m (3,820 ft)
Landing run, max landing weight at S/L, ISA	725 m (2,380 ft)

Range with max payload, ISA, fuel reserves 5% of initial
fuel plus 30 min loiter at S/L
          2,982 nm (5,526 km; 3,434 miles)
Range with max fuel, ISA, reserves as above
          5,618 nm (10,411 km; 6,469 miles)

LOCKHEED GEORGIA/NASA PROPFAN

LASC's Georgia division was contracted by NASA to
flight test an advanced propeller (propfan) system. The
Propfan Test Assessment (PTA) contract covered design,
modification and airborne tests of the propfan at speeds up
to Mach 0.8 and altitudes up to 10,670 m (35,000 ft).
Lockheed designed a new nacelle to house an Allison
570-M78 industrial turboshaft which drives the propfan
system. The propfan features eight thin profile blades of
2.74 m (9 ft 0 in) diameter with highly swept tips. The nacelle
and propfan assembly are mounted on the port wing of a
Lockheed owned Gulfstream II business jet (c/n 118,
N650PF/NASA 650) which made its first flight on 6 March
1987 at Savannah, Georgia, and was delivered to Lockheed
seven days later. First flight with the full propfan
installation was made on 29 April 1987. In addition to
substantial redesign of the Gulfstream II's wings, the
aircraft has a balance boom installed on the starboard
wingtip and carries an instrument-ation and data recording
system drawing information from some 598 onboard
sensors. The PTA flight test programme is expected to last
150 hours and several stages had been completed by the end
of 1987. It was due to continue in March 1988 to assess
cabin noise levels, after delivery to Georgia of a special
3.05 m (10 ft) long acoustically treated cabin compartment
manufactured for the aircraft by Burbank division.

Lockheed/NASA Gulfstream II experimental Propfan Test Assessment aircraft

The PTA programme is managed by NASA's Lewis
Research Center in Cleveland, Ohio. Lockheed's partners in
the programme are Allison Gas Turbine (power plant);
Gulfstream Aerospace (modification and support of

testbed aircraft); Hamilton Standard (propfan system);
LASC Burbank division (acoustics); and Rohr Industries
(propulsion drive system and nacelles).

LASC ONTARIO DIVISION

PO Box 33, Ontario International Airport, Ontario,
   California 91761-0033
Telephone: (714) 395 2411
GENERAL MANAGER: Harold T. Bowling
VICE-PRESIDENT, ENGINEERING: George L. Morgan
VICE-PRESIDENT, NEW BUSINESS DEVELOPMENT:
   Paul S. Norton
DIRECTOR, PUBLIC RELATIONS: John R. Dailey

This division of the Lockheed Aeronautical Systems
Company is claimed to be the world's largest aircraft
maintenance and modification unit, with some 3,350
employees. It has designed and installed major modifications, including cargo conversions and specialised
interiors, for such aircraft as the Boeing KC-135 and 707;
Douglas DC-8; and Lockheed C-130, C-141, L-188 Electra,
L-1011 and P-3. Lockheed Aeromod Center in Greenville,
South Carolina, provides aircraft maintenance and modification services to military and commercial customers.

LOCKHEED C-130 CONVERSIONS

LASC Ontario division specialises in engineering design
and modification of aircraft for electronic warfare,
command, control and communications, and other high
technology systems, including Sigint. During 1981 it
completed the modification of a C-130H to airborne
emergency hospital configuration for the Royal Saudi Air
Force (illustration in 1982-83 *Jane's*). Patients enter via a
ramp at the rear of the aircraft, into a reception area; this is
followed by three compartments comprising an examination room, operating theatre and intensive care unit.
Non-standard underwing pods house APUs which draw

fuel from the aircraft's wing tanks when the main engines
are shut down. Each APU is able to provide essential
ground power for up to 72 hours, including the operation
of medical equipment, environmental systems such as
air-conditioning and heating, lighting, and communications. The aircraft is equipped with HF and UHF
communications systems.

By the Spring of 1986, Saudi Arabia had a total of ten
modified C-130 type aircraft employed in its nationwide
rapid-response aeromedical service. The three latest aircraft
are L-100-30HS stretched 'hospital ships'. The fleet includes
aircraft which carry onboard four-wheel drive ambulances,
a 52-patient air evacuation aircraft with onboard surgical
capability, and an aircraft which can provide opthalmology,
ear, nose and throat and dental examination and treatment.
Three Saudi Arabian C-130 medical aircraft took part in the
evacuation and emergency treatment of casualties from the
hijacking and subsequent crash of a Boeing 737 near Arar
on 25 December 1986.

In late 1985 Ontario division was awarded a US Air
Force contract to update the Special Operations Forces'
AC-130H gunships with new navigation and fire control
systems. The company is also engaged in developing other
Special Mission C-130s for the US Air Force, and in
gunship modifications of C-130s for export customers.

LOCKHEED P-3A CONVERSIONS

A P-3A Orion was modified by Ontario division in 1984
for use by the US Customs Service, to interdict ships and
aircraft smuggling illegal drugs into the USA. The original
Texas Instruments nose radar was replaced by a Hughes
APG-63 radar and infra-red detection system, for all-

weather day/night operations. Three more P-3As were
subsequently modified for the US Customs Service by
Lockheed Aeromod Center Inc at Greenville, South
Carolina, using kits produced at Ontario. In addition to the
APG-63 radar, all of these aircraft have new inertial
navigation systems and multi-frequency communications
radios compatible with US Customs and Coast Guard
ground stations, as well as civilian law enforcement
agencies. Ontario division was also responsible for modifying the prototype P-3 (AEW&C) Sentinel to carry its
rotodome above the rear fuselage.

Since 1985 Ontario division has been awarded contracts
by the US Navy for the design and conversion of VP special
mission P-3s, and in 1986 was contracted to convert two
P-3Cs to EP-3E configuration, with options for a further 10
aircraft. Six of these options have been taken up and are due
for completion in 1989.

LOCKHEED L-1011 CONVERSIONS

Ontario division completed two special L-1011-500
conversions in 1986 for foreign governments. The modifications included interiors suitable for heads of state,
worldwide airborne communications systems and EW
self-protection systems.

Previously, in a programme completed in 1981, this
division modified the first nine L-1011-500 TriStars to
incorporate an active flight control system. Under another
programme, completed in 1982, six L-1011-500 aircraft
were equipped with a digital autopilot system. Modification
of L-1011-500 aircraft to meet individual airline specifications was continuing in 1987.

LTV

LTV AIRCRAFT PRODUCTS GROUP
(A unit of The LTV Corporation)

9314 West Jefferson, PO Box 655907, Dallas, Texas
   75265-5907
Telephone: (214) 266 2011
PRESIDENT: Billie M. Smith
SENIOR VICE-PRESIDENT:
   Robert J. Patton (Business Development Operations)
DIRECTOR, PUBLIC RELATIONS AND ADVERTISING:
   Lynn J. Farris
Aircraft Modernization and Support Division
PRESIDENT: Larry J. Cherry
Commercial Aircraft Division
PRESIDENT: John J. Ryan
VICE-PRESIDENT AND GENERAL MANAGER: S. C. Laden
Military Aircraft Division
PRESIDENT: Gordon L. Williams
VICE-PRESIDENT, ENGINEERING: Robert W. Stoner

The former Chance Vought Aircraft Inc, founded in 1917
and a leading producer of aircraft for the US Navy
throughout its history, became the Chance Vought
Corporation on 31 December 1960. On 31 August 1961,
it merged with Ling-Temco Electronics Inc, to form
Ling-Temco-Vought Inc (now The LTV Corporation). On
29 September 1986, LTV reorganised its aerospace/defence
operations into two groups: LTV Aircraft Products Group,
which consists of the above-mentioned three divisions
based in Dallas, Texas: and LTV Missiles and Electronics

Group, which consists of AM General Division, South
Bend, Indiana; Sierra Research Division of Buffalo, New
York; and Missiles Division of Grand Prairie, Texas.

Current aerospace products include McDonnell Douglas
DC-10 and KC-10 tailplanes and elevators, Boeing 747 tail
assemblies, complete tailplane assemblies for the Boeing
Model 767, complete tail units for the Boeing 757, and two
prototype YA-7F attack aircraft. In 1986 the company
was selected by McDonnell Douglas Corporation to
manufacture engine nacelles and tail unit sections for the
C-17A transport. A teaming agreement with Aérospatiale
Helicopter Corporation and LHTEC, to pursue US
government military applications of a T800 engined version
of the SA 365 Dauphin helicopter, was announced in May
1988.

In October 1985 LTV's Sierra Research Division was
awarded a $34 million US Air Force contract for airborne
platform/telemetry relay systems to be installed on two
DHC-8 Dash 8 aircraft for operation as part of the Gulf
Range Instrumentation System based at Tyndall AFB,
Florida. The installation includes a large electronically
steerable phased-array antenna mounted on the lower
starboard fuselage side of the aircraft, an eight-channel
UHF voice communication relay system, and an AN/APS-
128D pulse compression radar for sea surveillance. Both
aircraft were modified and delivered by the Summer of
1988. (See also Boeing Canada entry.) In the Spring of 1988
Sierra Research Division was awarded a contract to
undertake systems installation in six British Aerospace
125-800 business jets for the US Air Force's flight
inspection (C-FIN) role, under the USAF designation
C-29A.

LTV CORSAIR II
US military designation: A-7

An initial contract to develop and build three A-7As was
awarded by the US Navy on 19 March 1964; first flight was
made on 27 September 1965. Several versions of the A-7
were developed subsequently as Corsair IIs, for the US
Navy, the US Air Force, the Hellenic Air Force and the
Portuguese Air Force. Details of the A-7A, A-7B, A-7C,
A-7D and A-7E can be found in the 1983-84, 1979-80 and
earlier editions of *Jane's*.

Orders for all versions totalled 1,545 new-build aircraft
when production ended in 1983. The most recent versions of
the Corsair II are:

TA-7C. Designation of 60 A-7Bs and A-7Cs converted
into tandem two-seat trainers, with operational capability;
first example flew on 8 December 1976. Described in
previous editions of *Jane's*. Re-delivery began on 22
January 1985 of 49 aircraft upgraded with Allison TF41
engines, new Stencel ejection seats, automatic manoeuvring
flaps and an engine monitoring system. Delivery of these
was completed in August 1987. Six other aircraft are fitted
with electronic warfare equipment and are designated
EA-7L.

A-7H. Land based version of A-7E, retaining the folding
wings but without in-flight refuelling capability. First A-7H
flew for the first time on 6 May 1975. Total of 60 delivered
to two squadrons of the Hellenic Air Force.

TA-7H. Two-seat version for the Hellenic Air Force,
with an Allison TF41-A-400 engine. Configuration similar
to TA-7C, but no in-flight refuelling capability. Five
delivered between July and October 1980.

A-7K. Two-seat version of the US Air Force's A-7D,

with fuselage lengthened by 0.86 m (2 ft 10 in), and powered by 64.5 kN (14,500 lb st) Allison TF41-A-1 engine. Total of 31 delivered to US Air National Guard. Basically trainers, these aircraft retain combat capability.

A-7P. Designation of modernised A-7As for Esquadra 302 (Grupo 52) of Portuguese Air Force at Mantijo, with TF30-P-408 engines and the latest A-7D and A-7E-standard navigation and weapons delivery avionics. Initial flight 20 July 1981. Deliveries of initial 20 completed September 1982. A further 30, including six **TA-7P** two-seaters, were ordered in 1983; deliveries of these were completed in October 1984. These aircraft can carry a Northrop AN/ALQ-171(V) ECM pod to defeat surface and airborne radar controlled terminal threat systems.

A full structural description can be found in the 1983-84 and previous editions of *Jane's*; a shorter description of the A-7E appeared in the 1985-86 edition.

LTV CORSAIR UPDATE PROGRAMMES

Current activity is centred on a series of update programmes for the Corsair II. A total of 80 Air National Guard A-7Ds and A-7Ks is being equipped with low-altitude night attack (LANA) capability under contracts awarded by the Air Force's Oklahoma City Air Logistics Center. The first LANA equipped aircraft, an A-7K (81-0076) of the 162nd TFTS, Arizona ANG, made its first flight from Dallas on 2 October 1986. Deliveries, to the 150th TFG of the New Mexico ANG at Kirtland AFB, began in the Summer of 1987. LTV is retrofitting 72 A-7Ds and eight two-seat A-7Ks with forward looking infra-red (FLIR) and automatic terrain following (ATF) capability, together with a new GEC Avionics wide angle HUD derived from that fitted to the F-16C/D, to provide around-the-clock, under-the-weather capability. LTV is also manufacturing 40 FLIR pods incorporating a Texas Instruments AN/AAR-49 IR seeker.

Future plans, as yet unfunded, include AIM-9L Sidewinder air-to-air missile capability, and a birdproof windscreen.

On 7 May 1987, LTV received a contract from USAF Aeronautical Systems Division to upgrade two A-7D Corsair IIs to supersonic **A-7 Plus** (formerly Strikefighter) configuration, for prototype evaluation in 1989-90 as a potential improvement to the Air Force's air-to-ground support task, including close air support/battlefield air interdiction (CAS/BAI). These prototypes, which are being modified under the designation **YA-7F**, will feature a common engine bay enabling Pratt & Whitney F100-PW-220 or General Electric F100-GE-100 afterburning turbofans to be installed, but will be test flown with the Pratt & Whitney engine. Other modifications include a lengthened fuselage with additional fuel and avionics capacity; airframe mounted accessory drive unit for self-contained ground operation; a new technology trailing-edge flap system and lift dump/spoiler system to permit shorter landing run on unimproved or battle damaged runways; extended vertical tail surfaces; wingroot strakes; anhedral tailplane; improved avionics, including a GEC HUD and air data computer; improved environmental control system; and a molecular sieve oxygen generating system (MSOGS). If the YA-7F is selected for production, up to 337 existing ANG Corsair IIs will be modified to the A-7 Plus standard. First flight was expected in Autumn 1988.

Other developments under evaluation, but not incorporated in the YA-7F prototypes, include hands-on throttle and stick (HOTAS); a data link for improved close air support; advanced tactical hand-off system (ATHS); improved radar warning system; ground proximity warning system and improved landing gear warning system. LTV stated that the A-7 Plus will offer 16 per cent greater speed (Mach 1.12 with afterburner), 45 per cent decrease in T-O

Artist's impression of the A-7 Plus supersonic conversion of A-7D/K aircraft

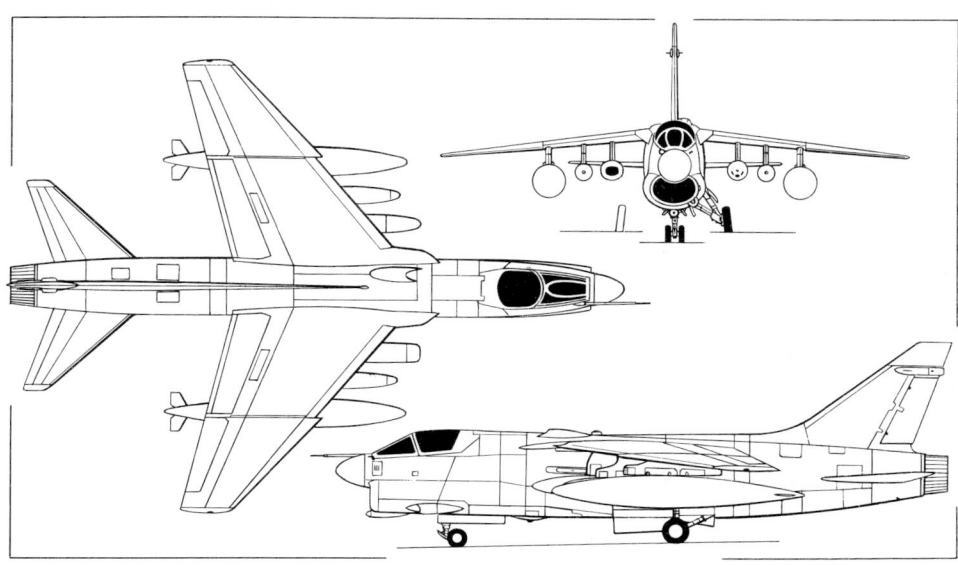

Provisional three-view of LTV YA-7F prototype for A-7 Plus *(Pilot Press)*

roll and 30 per cent decrease in landing roll over existing A-7s and will provide greater agility and survivability while operating with minimal support in forward battle areas.

ARMAMENT (A-7 Plus): One internally mounted Mk 61 20 mm Gatling gun, with 1,000 rounds of ammunition. Six underwing and two fuselage weapon stations, capable of carrying all USAF, USN, and assorted NATO munitions (max external load more than 7,711 kg; 17,000 lb). Weapon carriers include MAU-12, MER-10N, and TER-9A bomb racks; LAU-3 and LAU-681 wing mounted rocket launchers; AERO-38 fuselage mounted missile launchers; and pods containing 20 or 30 mm guns,

ECM, chaff, or auxiliary fuel. Provision also to carry 'buddy' air-to-air refuelling pods.

WEIGHTS (A-7 Plus):
Weight empty	9,555 kg (21,066 lb)
Max T-O weight	20,865 kg (46,000 lb)

TYPICAL MISSION PERFORMANCE (A-7 Plus with F100-PW-220 at T-O weight of 17,078 kg; 37,651 lb, with six Mk 82 bombs and 1,000 rds of 20 mm ammunition):
Max level speed at S/L	642 knots (1,190 km/h; 737 mph)
Time to 9,150 m (30,000 ft)	1.6 min
T-O run	640 m (2,100 ft)

MACHEN
MACHEN INC
South 3608 Davison Boulevard, Spokane, Washington 99204

Telephone: (509) 838 5326

EXECUTIVE VICE-PRESIDENT, MARKETING: James Christy

Machen's current products in 1987 were the Superstar 650 and 680. The Turbo 350 Bonanza and Laser Jet programmes, described in the 1985-86 *Jane's*, are no longer active.

MACHEN SUPERSTAR 650

Under the name Superstar 650, Machen Inc has developed a conversion of the Piper (Ted Smith) Aerostar 600, 601, 601P and 602P which provides new turbochargers, controllers, fuel pumps, fuel injection servos, and improved pressurisation components, as well as uprating each of the Textron Lycoming TIO-540-S1A5 engines to 242 kW (325 hp). Performance improvements include a better twin- and single-engine rate of climb, a higher single-engine service ceiling, and reduced take-off distance and noise levels. By February 1986 a total of 65 Superstar 650 conversions had been completed; no later total has been received.

Machen also markets and installs an FAA approved aerodynamic modification kit (SB 73-1) for the standard Aerostar 600 series and Superstar 650, which restores the unrestricted use of flaps and the original centre of gravity

Machen Superstar 650 conversion of the Piper Aerostar 601P

limits, following limitations imposed on the 600 series by the FAA in 1983. The kit comprises aileron and rudder hinge gap seals, a strake on the forward fuselage, leading-edge stall strips, and vortex generators on the lower wing surface and on the fin.

Machen announced in early 1987 that it had developed

a compact turbo-intercooling system for turbocharged models of the Aerostar series. The system offers improvements in hot day take-off, cruise climb and single-engine climb performance.

The Aerostar 600 was described fully under the Piper entry in the 1982-83 *Jane's*, the 601 and 601P in the 1981-82

Jane's, and the 602P in the 1984-85 edition. The descriptions of these aircraft apply also to the Superstar 650, except as noted in this entry.

PERFORMANCE: As for appropriate Aerostar model except:
Cruising speed, average cruise weight at 7,620 m (25,000 ft): 75% power   240 knots (445 km/h; 276 mph)
65% power   226 knots (419 km/h; 260 mph)
Min single-engine control speed (VMC)
79 knots (146 km/h; 91 mph)
Max rate of climb at S/L   596 m (1,955 ft)/min
Rate of climb at S/L, one engine out   123 m (402 ft)/min
Service ceiling, one engine out   4,575 m (15,000 ft)
T-O to 15 m (50 ft)   604 m (1,980 ft)

MACHEN SUPERSTAR 680

Machen Inc began producing in 1980 a further conversion of the Piper (Ted Smith) Aerostar 601P, known as the Superstar 680, to provide improved performance. The major element of this modification is the addition of induction air intercoolers to the Superstar 650 model. Four-blade Hartzell propellers are optional.

The description of the Aerostar 601P under the Piper entry in the 1981-82 *Jane's* applies also to the Machen Superstar 680 modification, except as noted. Changed full-conversion weight and performance figures include:

WEIGHTS:
Weight empty, equipped   1,863 kg (4,106 lb)
Max ramp weight   2,812 kg (6,200 lb)
Max T-O weight   2,812 kg (6,200 lb)
Max landing weight   2,721 kg (6,000 lb)

PERFORMANCE (at max T-O weight except where indicated):
Max cruising speed at 7,620 m (25,000 ft)
265 knots (491 km/h; 305 mph)
Cruising speed, average cruise weight at 7,620 m (25,000 ft):
75% power   250 knots (463 km/h; 288 mph)
65% power   242 knots (448 km/h; 279 mph)
55% power   232 knots (430 km/h; 267 mph)
Min single-engine control speed (VMC)
79 knots (146 km/h; 91 mph)
Max rate of climb at S/L   596 m (1,955 ft)/min
Rate of climb at S/L, one engine out   122 m (402 ft)/min
Service ceiling   7,620 m (25,000 ft)
Service ceiling, one engine out   7,010 m (23,000 ft)
T-O to 15 m (50 ft)   603 m (1,980 ft)
Range, standard fuel, 45 min reserves
1,137 nm (2,107 km; 1,309 miles)
Range, auxiliary fuel   1,441 nm (2,670 km; 1,659 miles)

MARSH
MARSH AVIATION COMPANY

5060 East Falcon Drive, Mesa, Arizona 85205
Telephone: (602) 832 3770
Telex: 165 028
Fax: (602) 985 2840
PRESIDENT: Floyd D. Stilwell

MARSH S2R-T TURBO THRUSH

Marsh Aviation converted the piston engined Rockwell Thrush Commander to turbine power by installing a Garrett TPE331-1-101 turboprop. Derated to 447 kW (600 shp) for this conversion, the engine drives a Hartzell constant-speed fully-feathering and reversible-pitch propeller, and the full 580 kW (778 shp) output of the TPE331 is available in an emergency. Single cycle air-conditioning and cockpit heating are provided by engine bleed air, which also operates the agricultural spraypump. The empty weight of the Turbo Thrush is 227 kg (500 lb) less than that of the standard Thrush Commander, providing increased payload capability and improved speed and performance. For agricultural operators working in remote areas, the TPE331 installation has the advantage that ordinary automotive diesel fuel can be used if jet fuel is not available.

Standard fuel capacity of the Turbo Thrush is 401 litres (106 US gallons; 88.3 Imp gallons). Standard hopper capacity is 1.50 m³ (53 cu ft) or 1,514 litres (400 US gallons; 333 Imp gallons). A larger hopper is available optionally, capacity 1.89 m³ (66.8 cu ft) or 1,892.5 litres (500 US gallons; 416 Imp gallons).

Following more than 600 h of flight by two prototypes, an FAA Supplemental Type Certificate was issued and the first production conversion was handed over in September 1976. Turbo Thrush deliveries totalled 75 by February 1985, the majority for operators in Africa, Europe, Mexico, the Middle East and the USA. No further examples have been notified since that time.

Details of the Rockwell Thrush Commander can be found in the 1977-78 *Jane's*, and weight and performance data for the Turbo Thrush in the 1987-88 edition.

MARSH G-164 C-T TURBO CAT

Marsh Aviation developed this turbine engine conversion for the Grumman/Gulfstream Aerospace/Schweizer G-164 Super Ag-Cat C by replacing the original piston engine with a 580 kW (778 shp) Garrett TPE331-1-101 turboprop, derated to 447 kW (600 shp).

Certification was gained in 1980, and six Turbo Cats (one A, four Bs and a C) had been completed by 1981. No more have been built since, although the aircraft remains available. Details of the Schweizer Super Ag-Cat C can be found in the 1981-82 *Jane's*, and of the Turbo Cat in the 1984-85 edition.

MARSH/BEECHCRAFT T-34 TURBO MENTOR

A description of Marsh Aviation's prototype turboprop conversion of the Beechcraft T-34A/B Mentor two-seat primary trainer appeared in the 1983-84 *Jane's*. No news of this programme has been received since 1986.

MARSH/GRUMMAN TURBO S-2 CONVERSION

Marsh Aviation has developed a turbine engine conversion for the Grumman S-2 Tracker anti-submarine aircraft. Modifications include extensive aerodynamic changes to the fuselage and engine nacelles, to reduce drag, and replacement of the S-2's original Wright R-1820 piston engines with Garrett TPE331-14 turboprops, each driving a Hartzell five-blade reversible-pitch propeller of 2.92 m (9 ft 7 in) diameter. The aim was to increase cruising speed by 60 knots (111 km/h; 69 mph) by comparison with the standard S-2, with a 50 per cent reduction in fuel consumption at high speed. Other performance improvements were expected to include a 25 per cent reduction in take-off and landing runs, and an increase of about 230 m (750 ft)/min in single-engine rate of climb at max T-O weight.

For its first flight, on 21 November 1986, the TPE331-14 turboprops of the first Marsh Turbo S-2 conversion (N426DF) were each flat rated at 932 kW (1,250 shp),

Marsh Turbo Thrush conversion of the Rockwell International Thrush Commander

Prototype Marsh Turbo S-2 conversion of the S-2 Tracker

instead of their max rating of 1,227 kW (1,645 shp). In this form, during subsequent early testing, it demonstrated true airspeeds in excess of 287 knots (531 km/h; 330 mph) and initial climb rates of up to 1,225 m (4,020 ft)/min. This aircraft has computerised engine controls to reduce pilot workload and enhance reliability.

A military version of the Turbo S-2 is available with integrated mission equipment for maritime patrol and anti-submarine warfare roles, including search radar, FLIR, MAD, sonobuoy launchers, pictorial navigation avionics with automatic search and attack modes, six underwing stores positions and a torpedo bay. In late 1987 the Argentine Navy was reported to be considering Marsh Turbo S-2 conversion of its fleet of Grumman S-2As and S-2Es.

Following certification, the Turbo S-2 was to be evaluated in the firefighting role by the California Forestry Department. Marsh Aviation foresees a market for between 60 and 80 conversions worldwide.

WEIGHTS:
Weight empty   6,278 kg (13,840 lb)
Max fuel weight   1,624 kg (3,580 lb)
Max T-O weight   11,793 kg (26,000 lb)
Max landing weight   11,113 kg (24,500 lb)
PERFORMANCE:
Cruising speed at 3,050 m (10,000 ft)
230 knots (426 km/h; 265 mph)
Cruising speed at 7,925 m (26,000 ft)
270 knots (500 km/h; 311 mph)
Retardant drop speed   130 knots (241 km/h; 150 mph)
Max rate of climb at S/L   884 m (2,900 ft)/min
Max range at cruising speed of 210 knots (389 km/h; 241 mph) at 7,620 m (25,000 ft), no reserves
1,468 nm (2,720 km; 1,690 miles)

MAULE

MAULE AIR INC

Lake Maule, Route 5, Moultrie, Georgia 31768
Telephone: (912) 985 2045
Telex: 804613 MAULE MOUL
PRESIDENT: Belford D. Maule
SALES MANAGER: Dan Spader

This company succeeded Maule Aircraft Corporation, which was formed to manufacture the M-4 four-seat light aircraft, production of which ended in 1975. The former company transferred to Moultrie, Georgia, in September 1968, and Maule Air Inc was formed in 1984 to continue production of the uprated M-5 Lunar Rocket and M-7 Super Rocket. The Lunar Rocket has since been discontinued, but the following versions of the Super Rocket and Star Rocket, and the turboprop Star Craft, are currently available:

MAULE STAR ROCKET and SUPER ROCKET

Models of the Star Rocket and Super Rocket available in 1988 were as follows:

M-6 Super Rocket. Generally similar to the earlier M-5-235C (1983-84 *Jane's*), but differs by having a revised wing of increased span, with changes to the ailerons and trailing-edge flaps. FAA certification awarded on 25 June 1981. Available as M-6-235 with a 175 kW (235 hp) Textron Lycoming O-540-J1A5D or IO-540-W1A5D engine, and with wheel landing gear or amphibious floats.

MX-7 Star Rocket. Certificated on 9 November 1984, the Star Rocket combines the shorter span wing of the former M-5 series with the glassfibre wingtips, increased fuel capacity, ailerons and five-position flaps of the M-7, and the fuselage of the M-6. It is available as the **MX-7-180** with 134 kW (180 hp) Textron Lycoming O-360-C1F, or as the **MX-7-235** with 175 kW (235 hp) Textron Lycoming O-540-J1A5D or IO-540-W1A5D engine, and with optional tricycle gear in addition to other landing gear options.

M-7-235 Super Rocket. This 1984 development of the earlier four-seat M-6-235 is a five-seater with a three-place rear bench. Wing span and weights are increased. Power plant is a 175 kW (235 hp) Textron Lycoming O-540-J1A5D or fuel injected IO-540-W1A5D flat-six engine. It is available as a landplane or on Edo 797-2500 amphibious floats or Edo 2440B standard floats.

Production of all versions totals more than 1,200, of which 54 were sold in 1987.

TYPE: Four-seat or five-seat STOL light aircraft.
WINGS: Braced high-wing monoplane. Streamline section V bracing strut each side. USA 35B (modified) wing section. Dihedral 1°. Incidence 0° 30′. All-metal two-spar structure with metal covering and glassfibre tips. All-metal ailerons and flaps. Ailerons linked with rudder tab, so that aircraft can be controlled in flight by using only the control wheel in the cockpit. Flaps have maximum deflection of 48°, with negative setting of −7° for enhanced cruise performance. Cambered wingtips standard.
FUSELAGE: Welded 4130 steel tube structure. Covered with glassfibre, except for metal doors and aluminium skin around cabin.
TAIL UNIT: Braced steel tube structure with glassfibre covering. Trim tab in port elevator. Servo tab in rudder linked to aileron movement. Starboard rudder trim via spring to starboard rudder pedal. Underfin on floatplane and amphibious versions.
LANDING GEAR: Non-retractable tailwheel type. Maule oleo-pneumatic shock absorbers in main units. Maule steerable tailwheel. Cleveland mainwheels with Goodyear or McCreary tyres size 17 × 6.00-6, pressure 1.79 bars (26 lb/sq in). Tailwheel tyre size 8 × 3.50-4, pressure 1.03-1.38 bars (15-20 lb/sq in). Cleveland hydraulic disc brakes. Parking brake. Oversize tyres, size 20 × 8.50-6 (pressure 1.24 bars; 18 lb/sq in), and fairings aft of mainwheels optional. Tricycle gear optional on MX-7. Provisions for fitting optional Edo Model 248B2440 floats or Edo Model 797-2500 amphibious floats, Pee

Maule M-7-235 Super Rocket five-seat STOL aircraft (*Air Portraits*)

Kay Model 2300 or Aqua Model 2400 floats, or Federal Model C2200H or C3000H or Fli-Lite 3000 Mk IIIA skis.
POWER PLANT: One flat-four or flat-six engine, driving a Hartzell two-blade constant-speed propeller, as detailed in model listings. (Three-blade McCauley propeller standard on Trigear MX-7, optional on other models.) Two fuel tanks in wings with total usable capacity of 151 litres (40 US gallons; 33 Imp gallons). Optional auxiliary fuel tanks in outer wings, to provide total capacities of 254 litres (67 US gallons; 56 Imp gallons) in M-6, 265 litres (70 US gallons; 58 Imp gallons) in M-7, and 269 litres (71 US gallons; 59 Imp gallons) in MX-7. Refuelling points on wing upper surface. Oil capacity 7.5 litres (2 US gallons; 1.7 Imp gallons) on all models except Super Rocket with O-540-J1A5D engine which has 9.5 litres (2.5 US gallons; 2.1 Imp gallons).
ACCOMMODATION: Pilot and three passengers in Star Rocket, four in Super Rockets, on two front bucket seats and rear bench seat, or optional quickly removed rear sling seat. One door on port side of fuselage, hinged at front edge and opening forward. Three doors on starboard side of fuselage, the forward and centre doors hinged at the front edge, the rear baggage door hinged at the rear edge. The centre and rear doors can be opened together to provide an opening 1.30 m (4 ft 3 in) wide to facilitate loading of bulky cargo. Accommodation heated and ventilated. Windscreen defroster standard. Tinted windscreen optional.
SYSTEMS: Hydraulic system for brakes only. Electrical system powered by 60A engine driven alternator. 28V electrical system optional.
AVIONICS AND EQUIPMENT: A wide range of Collins Micro Line, Bendix King, Genave and Narco communication and navigation equipment is available to customer's requirements. Standard equipment includes cylinder head temperature gauge, clock, stall warning device, instrument and cabin dome lights, cabin steps, cargo tiedown rings, navigation lights and port landing lights. Optional equipment includes blind-flying instrumentation, autopilot, wing levelling system, turn co-ordinator, rate of climb indicator, exhaust gas temperature gauge, angle of attack indicator, encoding altimeter, economy mixture control and Sorensen agricultural spraygear.
DIMENSIONS, EXTERNAL:

Wing span: M-6	10.03 m (32 ft 11 in)
M-7	10.26 m (33 ft 8 in)
MX-7	9.40 m (30 ft 10 in)
Wing chord, constant: all	1.60 m (5 ft 3 in)
Wing aspect ratio: M-6	6.5
M-7	6.4
MX-7	6.0
Length overall: all	7.19 m (23 ft 7¼ in)

Height overall: all (landplane)	1.93 m (6 ft 4 in)
all (amphibian)	3.05 m (10 ft 0 in)
Tailplane span: all	3.28 m (10 ft 9 in)
Wheel track: all	1.83 m (6 ft 0 in)
Wheelbase: all	4.82 m (15 ft 10 in)
Propeller diameter:	
M-6, MX-7	1.98 m (6 ft 6 in)
M-7	2.06 m (6 ft 9 in)
Cabin doors: all (fwd, each):	
Height	0.84 m (2 ft 9 in)
Width	0.76 m (2 ft 6 in)
Height to sill	0.94 m (3 ft 1 in)
Cabin door: all (centre, stbd):	
Height	0.75 m (2 ft 5½ in)
Width	0.69 m (2 ft 3 in)
Height to sill	0.76 m (2 ft 6 in)
Baggage door: all (rear, stbd):	
Height	0.58 m (1 ft 11 in)
Width	0.56 m (1 ft 10 in)
Height to sill	0.61 m (2 ft 0 in)

AREAS:

Wings, gross: M-6	15.38 m² (165.6 sq ft)
M-7	16.44 m² (177.0 sq ft)
MX-7	14.67 m² (157.9 sq ft)
Ailerons (total): MX-7	1.19 m² (12.8 sq ft)
M-6, M-7	1.07 m² (11.56 sq ft)
Trailing-edge flaps (total): MX-7	1.75 m² (18.8 sq ft)
M-6, M-7	2.32 m² (25.0 sq ft)
Fin: all	1.22 m² (13.14 sq ft)
Rudder, incl tab: all	0.54 m² (5.83 sq ft)
Tailplane: all	1.32 m² (14.2 sq ft)
Elevators, incl tab: all	1.58 m² (17.0 sq ft)

WEIGHTS AND LOADINGS (L: landplane, F: floatplane, A: amphibian):

Weight empty:	
M-6 (L), M-7 (L)	681 kg (1,500 lb)
M-6 (F), M-7 (F), MX-7-235 (F)	794 kg (1,750 lb)
M-6 (A), M-7 (A), MX-7-235 (A)	907 kg (2,000 lb)
MX-7-180 (L)	613 kg (1,350 lb)
MX-7-235 (L)	669 kg (1,475 lb)
Max baggage (all)	45 kg (100 lb)
Max cargo (all)	317 kg (700 lb)
Max T-O and landing weight:	
all models (L)	1,134 kg (2,500 lb)
all models (F, A)	1,247 kg (2,750 lb)
Max wing loading:	
M-6 (L)	73.69 kg/m² (15.10 lb/sq ft)
M-6 (F, A)	81.06 kg/m² (16.61 lb/sq ft)
M-7 (L)	68.91 kg/m² (14.12 lb/sq ft)
M-7 (F, A)	75.83 kg/m² (15.54 lb/sq ft)
MX-7 (L)	77.25 kg/m² (15.83 lb/sq ft)
MX-7 (F, A)	85.01 kg/m² (17.42 lb/sq ft)
Max power loading:	
M-6 (L), M-7 (L), MX-7-235 (L)	
	6.48 kg/kW (10.64 lb/hp)
M-6 (F, A), M-7 (F, A), MX-7-235 (F, A)	
	7.12 kg/kW (11.70 lb/hp)
MX-7-180 (L)	8.45 kg/kW (13.89 lb/hp)

PERFORMANCE (at max T-O weight, ISA: L, F and A are for 'Weights'):

Max level speed at S/L:	
M-6/O-540 (L), M-7/O-540 (L), MX-7-235/O-540 (L)	
	144 knots (267 km/h; 166 mph)
M-6/IO-540 (L), M-7/IO-540 (L), MX-7-235/IO-540 (L)	
	147 knots (273 km/h; 170 mph)
M-6 (F, A)	126 knots (233 km/h; 145 mph)
M-7 (F, A), MX-7-235 (F, A)	
	130 knots (241 km/h; 150 mph)
MX-7-180 (L)	134 knots (248 km/h; 154 mph)
Max cruising speed (75% power) at optimum altitude:	
M-6 (L), M-7 (L), MX-7-235 (L)	
	139 knots (257 km/h; 160 mph)
M-6 (F, A)	121 knots (224 km/h; 139 mph)
M-7 (F, A), MX-7-235 (F, A)	
	125 knots (232 km/h; 144 mph)

Turboprop powered Maule M-7 Star Craft with Edo 797-2500 amphibious landing gear (*Howard Levy*)

MX-7-180 (L) 126 knots (233 km/h; 145 mph)
Stalling speed, flaps down, power off:
M-6 (L), M-7 (L) 31 knots (57 km/h; 35 mph)
M-6 (F, A) 49 knots (91 km/h; 56 mph)
M-7 (F, A), MX-7-235 (F, A)
47 knots (87 km/h; 54 mph)
MX-7 (L) 35 knots (65 km/h; 40 mph)
Max rate of climb at S/L:
M-6 (L), MX-7-235 (L) 579 m (1,900 ft)/min
M-6 (F, A), MX-7-235 (F, A) 381 m (1,250 ft)/min
M-7 (L) 610 m (2,000 ft)/min
M-7 (F, A) 411 m (1,350 ft)/min
MX-7-180 (L) 366 m (1,200 ft)/min
Service ceiling:
M-6 (L), M-7 (L), MX-7-235 (L) 6,100 m (20,000 ft)
M-6 (F, A), M-7 (F, A), MX-7-235 (F, A)
5,180 m (17,000 ft)
MX-7-180 (L) 4,575 m (15,000 ft)
T-O run on land:
M-6 (L), M-7 (L), MX-7-235/IO-540 (L),
MX-7-235 (A) 38 m (125 ft)
M-6 (A), M-7 (A) 69 m (225 ft)
MX-7-180 (L) 61 m (200 ft)
MX-7-235/O-540 (L) 46 m (150 ft)
T-O run on water:
M-6 (F, A), M-7 (F, A) 305 m (1,000 ft)
MX-7-235 (F, A) 335 m (1,100 ft)
T-O to 15 m (50 ft) on land:
M-6 (L), M-7 (L), MX-7 (L) 183 m (600 ft)
M-6 (A), M-7 (A), MX-7-235 (A) 152 m (500 ft)
T-O to 15 m (50 ft) on water:
M-6 (F, A), M-7 (F, A) 381 m (1,250 ft)
MX-7-235 (F, A) 412 m (1,350 ft)
Landing from 15 m (50 ft) on land:
M-6 (L), M-7 (L), MX-7 (L) 152 m (500 ft)
M-6 (A), M-7 (A), MX-7-235 (A) 305 m (1,000 ft)
Landing from 15 m (50 ft) on water:
M-6 (F, A), M-7 (F, A), MX-7-235 (F, A)
305 m (1,000 ft)
Landing run on land and water:
M-6 (A), M-7 (A), MX-7-235 (A) 244 m (800 ft)
Range with standard fuel, 45 min reserves:
M-6/O-540 (L), M-7/O-540 (L), MX-7-235/O-540 (L)
425 nm (788 km; 490 miles)

M-6/IO-540 (L), M-7/IO-540 (L),
MX-7-235/IO-540 (L) 460 nm (853 km; 530 miles)
M-6/O-540 (F, A) 265 nm (491 km; 305 miles)
M-6/IO-540 (F, A) 299 nm (555 km; 345 miles)
M-7/O-540 (F, A), MX-7-235/O-540 (F, A)
286 nm (531 km; 330 miles)
M-7/IO-540 (F, A), MX-7-235/IO-540 (F, A)
321 nm (595 km; 370 miles)
MX-7-180 (L) 560 nm (1,038 km; 645 miles)
Range with optional auxiliary fuel, 45 min reserves:
M-6/O-540 (L), M-7/O-540 (L), MX-7-235/O-540 (L)
747 nm (1,384 km; 860 miles)
M-6/IO-540 (L), M-7/IO-540 (L),
MX-7-235/IO-540 (L) 807 nm (1,496 km; 930 miles)
M-6/O-540 (F, A) 586 nm (1,086 km; 675 miles)
M-6/IO-540 (F, A) 647 nm (1,199 km; 745 miles)
M-7/O-540 (F, A), MX-7-235/O-540 (F, A)
608 nm (1,126 km; 700 miles)
M-7/IO-540 (F, A), MX-7-235/IO-540 (F, A)
669 nm (1,239 km; 770 miles)
MX-7-180 (L) 977 nm (1,810 km; 1,125 miles)

MAULE M-7 and MX-7 STAR CRAFT

Maule has built and flown prototypes of turboprop versions of both the **MX-7-420** (N5666K) and **M-7-420** (N5671K), powered in each case by an Allison 250-B17C engine. Named Star Craft, the turboprop models have airframes generally identical to those of the piston engined MX-7 and longer span M-7, with the same option of wheel, float or Edo 797-2500 amphibious landing gear. Certification of both models was expected in mid-1988.
POWER PLANT: One 313 kW (420 shp) Allison 250-B17C turboprop, driving a Hartzell HC-B3TF-7/T10173F-21R three-blade metal propeller with autofeathering, reverse pitch and Beta control. Intake anti-icing. Fuel capacity (usable) is 265 litres (70 US gallons; 58 Imp gallons) standard, increasable to 378 litres (100 US gallons; 83 Imp gallons) with optional outer-wing tanks.
SYSTEMS: 28V DC electrical system standard, with 150A starter/generator, solid state regulators and 24V 19Ah battery.

DIMENSIONS, EXTERNAL: As for piston engined M-7/MX-7 except:
Length overall (landplane) 7.32 m (24 ft 0 in)
WEIGHTS AND LOADINGS:
Weight empty:
M-7-420: landplane 853 kg (1,880 lb)
floatplane 771 kg (1,700 lb)
amphibian 884 kg (1,950 lb)
MX-7-420: landplane 626 kg (1,380 lb)
Max T-O weight:
M-7-420 (all landing gears) 1,247 kg (2,750 lb)
MX-7-420 (landplane) 1,134 kg (2,500 lb)
Max wing loading:
M-7-420 75.83 kg/m² (15.54 lb/sq ft)
MX-7-420 77.25 kg/m² (15.83 lb/sq ft)
Max power loading:
M-7-420 3.99 kg/kW (6.55 lb/shp)
MX-7-420 3.62 kg/kW (5.95 lb/shp)
PERFORMANCE (at max T-O weight. A: M-7-420 floatplane, B: M-7-420 amphibian, C: MX-7-420 landplane):
Max level speed at S/L:
A, B 149 knots (277 km/h; 172 mph)
Max cruising speed (75% power):
A, B, at 1,370 m (4,500 ft)
143 knots (265 km/h; 165 mph)
C at 4,575 m (15,000 ft)
170 knots (315 km/h; 196 mph)
Stalling speed: A, B 47 knots (87 km/h; 54 mph)
Max rate of climb at S/L:
A, B 677 m (2,222 ft)/min
C 1,432 m (4,700 ft)/min
Service ceiling: A, B 7,620 m (25,000 ft)
C 6,100 m (20,000 ft)
T-O run: A, B (water) 229 m (750 ft)
B (land) 54 m (175 ft)
C 92 m (300 ft)
T-O to 15 m (50 ft): A, B (water) 259 m (850 ft)
B (land) 107 m (350 ft)
Landing from 15 m (50 ft):
A, B (land and water) 305 m (1,000 ft)
Landing run:
A, B (land and water) 244 m (800 ft)
Range: A, B, standard fuel 456 nm (845 km; 525 miles)

MBB

MBB HELICOPTER CORPORATION
(Subsidiary of Messerschmitt-Bölkow-Blohm GmbH)
900 Airport Road, PO Box 2349, West Chester, Pennsylvania 19380
Telephone: (215) 431 4150
Telex: 173102
PRESIDENT AND CHIEF EXECUTIVE OFFICER: David O. Smith
SENIOR VICE-PRESIDENT, MARKETING: Andreas Aastad
MANAGER, COMMUNICATIONS: Lynda Kate

Messerschmitt-Bölkow-Blohm of West Germany (which see) established this subsidiary company in the USA, in early 1979, to take over marketing and product support of the company's family of twin-turbine helicopters in the United States, Central America and Mexico.
In 1983 the company opened the MBB North American Service Center, a 3,252 m² (35,000 sq ft) building housing spares, mechanic and pilot training, and helicopter assembly and modification facilities, and a 2,787 m² (30,000 sq ft) administration building. An additional 3,716 m² (40,000 sq ft) completion centre was opened in the Spring of 1988. The MBB complex is located on a 17 hectare (42 acre)

site adjacent to the Brandywine Airport, West Chester, Pennsylvania.
MBB Helicopter Corporation is responsible for marketing, sales and technical support of the entire range of MBB helicopters, which includes the BO 105CBS, BO 105LS and BK 117, described in the German, Canadian and International sections respectively. In 1988 it introduced a modified offshore version of the BK 117, with six seats instead of nine, provision for carrying liferafts, and an optional rear cargo compartment.

MCDONNELL DOUGLAS

MCDONNELL DOUGLAS CORPORATION
Box 516, St Louis, Missouri 63166
Telephone: (314) 232 0232
Telex: 44-857
Corporate Office
CHAIRMAN AND CHIEF EXECUTIVE OFFICER:
John F. McDonnell
PRESIDENT: Gerald A. Johnston
VICE-CHAIRMAN, GOVERNMENT BUSINESS:
Robert C. Little

DIRECTOR, PUBLIC RELATIONS: John L. Cooke
McDonnell Douglas Corporation was formed on 28 April 1967, by the merger of the former Douglas Aircraft Company Inc and the McDonnell company. It encompasses both of the original companies and their subsidiaries, and the former Hughes Helicopters Inc, which became a subsidiary in 1984.
At the beginning of July 1988 McDonnell Douglas employed 117,980 people worldwide. Total office, engineering, laboratory and manufacturing floor area was 3.8 million m² (41 million sq ft).

Major operating components of McDonnell Douglas Corporation Aerospace Group are as follows:
McDonnell Aircraft Company
Follows this entry
Douglas Aircraft Company
Follows McDonnell Aircraft Co entry
McDonnell Douglas Helicopter Company
Follows Douglas Aircraft Co entry
McDonnell Douglas Astronautics Company

MCDONNELL AIRCRAFT COMPANY
(A Division of McDonnell Douglas Corporation)
Box 516, St Louis, Missouri 63166
Telephone: (314) 232 0232
PRESIDENT: William S. Ross
EXECUTIVE VICE-PRESIDENTS:
Irving L. Burrows
John D. Wolf
VICE-PRESIDENT, INTERNATIONAL MARKETING:
James P. Caldwell
VICE-PRESIDENT, MARKETING: Thomas M. Gunn
VICE-PRESIDENT, ENGINEERING: Herman W. Hamm
VICE-PRESIDENT, ENGINEERING TECHNOLOGY:
Leonard F. Impellizzeri
VICE-PRESIDENT, GENERAL MANAGER NEW AIRCRAFT
PRODUCTS: James M. Sinnett
VICE-PRESIDENT, AIRCRAFT ENGINEERING:
Donald D. Snyder
DIRECTOR OF COMMUNICATIONS: Timothy J. Beecher

Development and production at St Louis continues to be concentrated on versions of the F-15 Eagle air superiority fighter, AV-8B Harrier II and F/A-18 Hornet naval strike fighter.

MCDONNELL DOUGLAS F-4 PHANTOM II

To reduce injuries to aircrew of F-4s, and loss of aircraft, due to bird strikes during low-level missions, McDonnell Douglas and Goodyear Aerospace have developed an improved, one-piece, bird-resistant windscreen. The first two F-4Es fitted retrospectively with the new windscreen successfully completed a one year test and evaluation programme with the Missouri Air National Guard in 1986. Made from two layers of polycarbonate between three layers of acrylic plastics, the 2.3 cm (0.92 in) thick windscreen is designed to withstand impact by a 1.8 kg (4 lb) bird at an aircraft speed of 500 knots (925 km/h; 575 mph). Elimination of the former windscreen frame also improves the pilot's field of view.
Under a contract announced in October 1986, McDonnell Douglas is equipping US Air Force F-4G 'Wild Weasels' with updated equipment to detect and locate hostile radar transmitters. The contract involves production under subcontract, by Honeywell Sperry, of the CP-1674/APR-47 Weasel attack signal processor, a major component of the F-4G's AN/APR-47 radar receiving set.

MCDONNELL DOUGLAS/BAe AV-8B HARRIER II

Details of the AV-8B Harrier II can be found in the International section.

MCDONNELL DOUGLAS F-15 EAGLE

Against competing designs from Fairchild and North American Rockwell, the USAF selected the McDonnell Douglas F-15 in December 1969 to meet its requirement for a new air superiority fighter. The resulting contract called for 20 aircraft for development testing, these to comprise 18 single-seat **F-15As** and two TF-15A two-seat trainers. First flight of the F-15A was made on 27 July 1972, and the first flight of a two-seat TF-15A trainer (redesignated subsequently **F-15B**) on 7 July 1973. An F-15B (the 21st Eagle built) was the first Eagle delivered to the US Air Force, on 14 November 1974. Production of the F-15A and B totalled 361 and 58 respectively. These early variants were described in previous editions of *Jane's*.
The F-15A and B were followed from June 1979 by the **F-15C** (single-seat) and **F-15D** (two-seat), which are able to carry two McDonnell low-drag conformal fuel tanks (CFT) developed specially for the F-15. Made in 'handed' pairs, these attach to the sides of the engine air intake trunks, are designed to the same load factors as the basic aircraft, and can be removed in 15 minutes. CFTs could be configured to accommodate avionics such as reconnaissance sensors, radar detection and jamming equipment, a laser designator, low light level TV system, and reconnaissance cameras, in addition to fuel. All external stores stations remain available with the CFTs in use, and a

McDonnell Douglas F-15C Eagles of the USAF's 57th FIS escorting a Tu-95 'Bear-D'

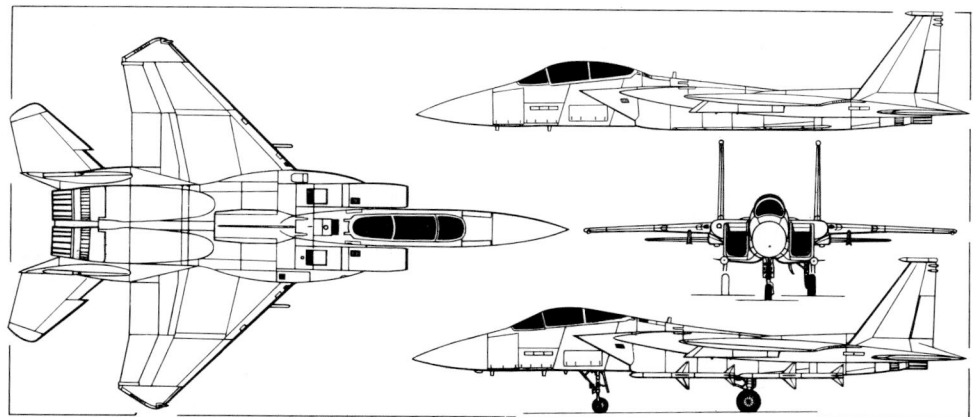

McDonnell Douglas F-15C Eagle single-seat air superiority fighter, with additional side view (top) of two-seat F-15B *(Pilot Press)*

Conformal reconnaissance pod under development as a private venture for two-seat F-15s

new weapon attachment system can extend the operating radius with large external loads by up to 40 per cent. Known as tangential carriage, it involves the installation of rows of stub pylons on the lower corner and bottom of each CFT. Up to twelve 1,000 lb class or four 2,000 lb class weapons can be carried on these pylons. AIM-7F Sparrow missiles can also be attached directly to the CFTs.

The first F-15C (78-468) flew for the first time on 26 February 1979, and the first F-15D on 19 June of that year. In aircraft built since 1980 the radar can operate in a high-resolution raid assessment mode able to identify clustered targets individually. F-15Cs and F-15Ds delivered prior to availability of the programmable signal processor and expanded computer which provide this capability will be retrofitted to bring them up to standard. An overload warning system is installed in current F-15C/D aircraft which permits the pilot to manoeuvre safely to 9g throughout most of the flight envelope at flight design gross weights. It too is being retrofitted to all F-15s delivered earlier.

An initial multi-staged improvement programme (MSIP), first funded in 1983, covers the introduction of a Hughes APG-70 radar with memory increase to 1,000K and trebled processing speed; upgrading the aircraft's central computer to store four times as much data and process it three times as quickly; and replacing the original armament control system panel by a single multi-purpose Sperry colour video screen. Linked to a computer, the armament control system is programmable, allowing for the addition of advanced versions of the AIM-7 and AIM-9 and AMRAAM. Other MSIP improvements include a tactical electronic system consisting of a Northrop enhanced ALQ-135 internal countermeasures system, Loral ALR-56C radar warning receiver, Tracor ALE-45 chaff/flare dispenser, and Magnavox electronic warfare warning system. Flight testing of the new system began in December 1984. The first production F-15C built under MSIP was unveiled at McDonnell Douglas' St Louis plant on 20 June 1985.

By March 1988 nearly 1,100 Eagles had been delivered, including 850 to the USAF. Active USAF units included the 57th FWW at Nellis AFB, Nevada, the 405th TTW at Luke AFB, Arizona, the 1st TFW at Langley AFB, Virginia, the 36th TFW at Bitburg AB, West Germany, the 49th TFW at Holloman AFB, New Mexico, the 33rd TFW at Eglin AFB, Florida, the 18th TFW at Kadena AB, Okinawa, and the 32nd TFS at Soesterberg in the Netherlands. The 48th FIS

at Langley AFB, Virginia, was the first US air defence squadron to receive the Eagle. The 21st TFW at Elmendorf AFB, Alaskan Air Command, in support of air defence, became operational with F-15s during 1982; other Fighter Interceptor Squadrons now include the 318th at McChord AFB, Washington, the 5th at Minot, North Dakota, and the 57th at Keflavik, Iceland.

Equipment of Air National Guard units with F-15As and F-15Bs began on 29 June 1985 with the 122nd TFS, at New Orleans, Louisiana, and these models now equip the 116th TFW at Dobbins AFB, Georgia; the 159th TFG at New Orleans, Louisiana; the 199th TFS, 154th Composite Group, Hawaii ANG, at Hickam AFB; and the 102nd Fighter Interceptor Wing at Otis ANG Base, Massachusetts.

The F-15 has also been selected by the US Air Force for assignment to the Rapid Deployment Force Central Command. To ensure optimum effectiveness for the aircraft allocated to this mission, the US Air Force has procured 322 sets of conformal fuel tanks.

Exports include 51 Eagles for Israel (22 As, two Bs and 26 Cs in service) and 60 for Saudi Arabia (45 Cs and 15 Ds). The JASDF plans to purchase a total of 187 **F-15Js** and **F-15DJs**, of which 173 are being licence built in Japan, with Mitsubishi as the prime contractor. The first of the 14 US built aircraft was handed over on 15 July 1980, and the first two were flown to Japan in March 1981.

McDonnell Douglas has developed an air-to-ground attack version of the Eagle, known as the **F-15E** dual role fighter; this is described separately. Also described separately is an advanced **F-15S/MTD** (STOL/Manoeuvring Technology Demonstrator) version of the Eagle which McDonnell Douglas is developing and will flight test for the US Air Force.

McDonnell Douglas has proposed a version of the F-15 Eagle for the USAF's Follow-on Wild Weasel defence suppression aircraft requirement to replace F-4G Wild Weasels in the USAF inventory. As a private venture the company developed a conformal reconnaissance pod designed to be carried on the centreline stores station of two-seat F-15s. The pod, which was flight tested in the Summer of 1987, could transmit imagery to ground stations via a data link, providing near real-time reconnaissance.

Excluding the 20 development aircraft, USAF procurement of the F-15A/B/C/D/E is expected to total 1,266 by the mid-1990s. Up to FY 1988, a total of 470 F-15Cs and Ds

had been funded for the USAF. Production for the USAF then switched to the F-15E. Early F-15s had Pratt & Whitney F100-PW-100 turbofans, but the F100-PW-220 has been standard since 1985.

The following description applies to the current standard F-15C:

TYPE: Single-seat twin-turbofan air superiority fighter, with secondary attack role.

WINGS: Cantilever shoulder-wing monoplane. Wing uses NACA 64A aerofoil section with varying thickness/chord ratios, ranging from 6.6% at the root to 3% at the tip. Leading-edges modified with conical camber. Anhedral 1°. Incidence 0°. Sweepback at quarter-chord 38° 42'. Fail-safe structure, comprising a torque box with integrally stiffened machined skins and conventionally machined ribs, of light alloy and titanium. Leading- and trailing-edges are of conventional light alloy rib/skin construction, and wingtips of aluminium honeycomb. Plain ailerons and plain trailing-edge flaps of aluminium honeycomb. No spoilers or trim tabs. Powered controls, hydraulically operated by National Water Lift actuators. No anti-icing system.

FUSELAGE: All-metal semi-monocoque structure. Speedbrake on upper centre-fuselage, constructed of graphite/epoxy, aluminium honeycomb and titanium.

TAIL UNIT: Cantilever structure with twin fins and rudders. All-moving horizontal tail surfaces outboard of fins, with extended chord on outer leading-edges. Ronson Hydraulic Units rudder servo actuators; National Water Lift actuators for horizontal surfaces. Moog boost and pitch compensator for control stick.

LANDING GEAR: Hydraulically retractable tricycle type, with single wheel on each unit. All units retract forward. Cleveland nose and main units, each incorporating an oleo-pneumatic shock absorber. Nosewheel and tyre by Goodyear, size 22 × 6.6-10, pressure 17.93 bars (260 lb/sq in). Mainwheels by Bendix, with Goodyear tyres size 34.5 × 9.75-18, pressure 23.44 bars (340 lb/sq in). Bendix carbon heat-sink brakes. Hydro-Aire wheel braking skid control system.

POWER PLANT: Two Pratt & Whitney F100-PW-220 turbofans, each rated at 104.3 kN (23,450 lb st) with afterburning for take-off. Internal fuel in eight Goodyear fuselage tanks, total capacity 7,836 litres (2,070 US gallons; 1,724 Imp gallons). Simmonds fuel gauge system. Optional conformal fuel tanks attached to side of engine air intakes, beneath wing, each containing 2,839 litres (750 US gallons; 624 Imp gallons). Provision for up to three additional 2,309 litre (610 US gallon; 508 Imp gallon) external fuel tanks. Max total internal and external fuel capacity 20,441 litres (5,400 US gallons; 4,496 Imp gallons).

ENGINE INTAKES: Straight two-dimensional external compression inlets, on each side of the fuselage. Air inlet controllers by Hamilton Standard. Air inlet actuators by National Water Lift.

ACCOMMODATION: Pilot only, on McDonnell Douglas ACES II ejection seat. Stretched acrylic canopy and windscreen. Windscreen anti-icing valve by Dynasciences Corporation.

SYSTEMS: AiResearch air-conditioning system. Three independent hydraulic systems (each 207 bars; 3,000 lb/sq in) powered by Abex engine driven pumps; modular hydraulic packages by Hydraulic Research and Manufacturing Company. Lear Siegler generating system for electrical power, with Sundstrand 40/50kVA generator constant speed drive units and Electro Development Corpn transformer-rectifiers. The oxygen system includes a Simmonds liquid oxygen indicator. Garrett APU for engine starting, and for the provision of electrical or hydraulic power on the ground independently of the main engines.

AVIONICS AND EQUIPMENT: General Electric automatic analog flight control system standard. Hughes Aircraft APG-63 X-band pulse-Doppler radar (being upgraded to APG-70 by MSIP modification), equipped since 1980 with a Hughes Aircraft programmable signal processor provides long-range detection and tracking of small high-speed targets operating at all altitudes down to treetop level, and feeds accurate tracking information to the IBM CP-1075 96K (24K on early F-15C/Ds) central computer to ensure effective launch of the aircraft's missiles or the firing of its internal gun. For close-in dogfights, the radar acquires the target automatically and the steering/weapon system information is displayed on a McDonnell Douglas Electronics AN/AVQ-20 head-up display. A Teledyne Electronics AN/APX-101 IFF transponder informs ground stations and other suitably equipped aircraft that the F-15 is friendly. It also supplies data on the F-15's range, azimuth, altitude and identification to air traffic controllers. A Hazeltine AN/APX-76 IFF interrogator informs the pilot if an aircraft seen visually or on radar is friendly. A Litton reply evaluator for the IFF system operates with the AN/APX-76. A Sperry vertical situation display set, using a cathode ray tube to present radar, electro-optical identification and attitude director indicator formats to the pilot, permits inputs received from the aircraft's sensors and the central computer to be visible to the pilot under any light conditions. Sperry also developed the AN/ASK-6 air data computer and AN/ASN-108 AHRS for the F-15, the latter also serving as a backup to the Litton AN/ASN-109 INS which provides the basic navigation data and is the aircraft's primary attitude reference. In addition to giving the aircraft's position at all times, the INS provides pitch, roll, heading, acceleration and speed information. Other specialised equipment for flight control, navigation and communications includes a Collins AN/ARN-118 Tacan; Collins HSI to present aircraft navigation information on a symbolic pictorial display; Collins ADF and AN/ARN-112 ILS receivers; Magnavox AN/ARC-164 UHF transceiver and UHF auxiliary transceiver. The communications sets have cryptographic capability. Dorne and Margolin glideslope localiser antenna, and Teledyne Avionics angle of attack sensors. Northrop (Defense Systems Division) Enhanced AN/ALQ-135(V) internal countermeasures set provides automatic jamming of enemy radar signals; Loral AN/ALR-56C radar warning receiver; Magnavox AN/ALQ-128 electronic warfare warning set; and Tracor AN/ALE-45 chaff dispenser. Bendix tachometer, fuel and oil indicators; Plessey feel trim actuators.

ARMAMENT: Provision for carriage and launch of a variety of air-to-air weapons over short and medium ranges, including four AIM-9L/M Sidewinders, four AIM-7F/M Sparrows or eight AMRAAM, and a 20 mm M61A1 six-barrel gun with 940 rounds of ammunition. General Electric lead-computing gyro. A Dynamic Controls Corporation armament control system keeps the pilot informed of weapons status and provides for their management. Three air-to-surface weapon stations (five if configured with conformal fuel tanks) allow for the carriage of up to 10,705 kg (23,600 lb) of bombs, rockets or additional ECM equipment. AN/AWG-20 armament control system.

DIMENSIONS, EXTERNAL:

Wing span	13.05 m (42 ft 9¾ in)
Length overall	19.43 m (63 ft 9 in)
Height overall	5.63 m (18 ft 5½ in)
Tailplane span	8.61 m (28 ft 3 in)
Wheel track	2.75 m (9 ft 0¼ in)
Wheelbase	5.42 m (17 ft 9½ in)

AREAS:

Wings, gross	56.5 m² (608.0 sq ft)
Ailerons (total)	2.46 m² (26.48 sq ft)
Flaps (total)	3.33 m² (35.84 sq ft)
Fins (total)	9.78 m² (105.28 sq ft)
Rudders (total)	1.85 m² (19.94 sq ft)
Tailplanes (total)	10.34 m² (111.36 sq ft)

First full scale development McDonnell Douglas F-15E Eagle dual role fighter

WEIGHTS:

Weight empty, equipped (no fuel, ammunition, pylons or external stores)	12,973 kg (28,600 lb)
Max fuel load: internal	6,103 kg (13,455 lb)
CFTs (2, total)	4,422.5 kg (9,750 lb)
auxiliary tanks (3, total)	5,395.5 kg (11,895 lb)
max internal and external	15,921 kg (35,100 lb)
T-O weight (interceptor, full internal fuel and 4 Sparrows)	20,244 kg (44,630 lb)
T-O weight (incl three 2,309 litre; 610 US gallon; 508 Imp gallon drop tanks)	26,521 kg (58,470 lb)
Max T-O weight: with CFTs	30,845 kg (68,000 lb)

PERFORMANCE:

Max level speed	more than Mach 2.5 (800 knots; 1,482 km/h; 921 mph CAS)
Approach speed	125 knots (232 km/h; 144 mph) CAS
T-O run (interceptor)	274 m (900 ft)
Landing run (interceptor), without braking parachute	1,067 m (3,500 ft)
Service ceiling	18,300 m (60,000 ft)
Ferry range: with external tanks, without CFTs	more than 2,500 nm (4,631 km; 2,878 miles)
with CFTs	3,100 nm (5,745 km; 3,570 miles)
Max endurance: with in-flight refuelling	15 h 0 min
unrefuelled, with CFTs	5 h 15 min
Design g limits	+9/-3

MCDONNELL DOUGLAS F-15E EAGLE

The F-15E is a two-seat dual role version of the Eagle capable of performing long-range, deep interdiction, high ordnance payload air-to-ground missions by day or night, and in adverse weather, while retaining its proven air-to-air capabilities. An industry funded prototype, known initially as the Strike Eagle, was modified from a two-seat F-15B (71-291). The rear cockpit was upgraded with four multi-purpose CRT displays for radar, weapon selection, and monitoring of enemy tracking systems. Production F-15Es also have front cockpit modifications that include redesigned 'up front' controls, a wide field of view HUD, and three colour CRTs providing multi-purpose displays for improved navigation, weapons delivery and systems operation, including moving map displays, weapons options, precision radar mapping, and terrain following.

For tactical target missions at night and in all-weather conditions, the F-15E has advanced radar and infra-red systems. A new high resolution synthetic aperture Hughes APG-70 radar, wide-field forward looking infra-red (FLIR) and Martin Marietta AN/AAQ-14 LANTIRN navigation and targeting pods will ensure target detection/identification and improve the accuracy of weapons delivery. Successful integration of these systems was demonstrated during 1982 in flight tests at Edwards AFB, California, and Eglin AFB, Florida, resulting in accurate 'blind' weapons delivery. Integrated internal countermeasures equipment is fitted.

Some 60 per cent of the F-15's structure was redesigned to create the F-15E, the airframe of which is expected to have a fatigue life of 16,000 flying hours. To accommodate the new avionics, internal fuel capacity has been reduced slightly, to 7,643 litres (2,019 US gallons; 1,681 Imp gallons), by reducing the capacity of one fuselage tank, but for increased payload/range capability the F-15E can utilise standard F-15 conformal fuel tanks with a full complement of bombs carried on integral, tangential weapon racks. The conformal tanks add 5,678 litres (1,500 US gallons; 1,249 Imp gallons) of fuel for increased range, and can be used in conjunction with up to three 2,309 litre (610 US gallon; 508 Imp gallon) external fuel tanks. In addition to carrying a variety of guided and unguided bombs and other air-to-ground weapons, the F-15E retains its air superiority performance and weapons (AIM-7 Sparrow, AIM-9 Sidewinder and AIM-120 AMRAAM missiles).

A digital, triple redundant Lear Siegler Astronautics flight control system is installed in the F-15E, permitting coupled automatic terrain following, and a Honeywell ring laser gyro INS provides quick reaction alignment and improved navigational accuracy. A new engine bay developed by McDonnell Douglas enables the F-15E to be powered by either General Electric F110 or Pratt & Whitney F100 engines. The engine bay structure consists of large titanium sections manufactured with superplastic forming and diffusion bonding processes, and will permit future installation of growth versions of these engines, providing a total of up to 266.9 kN (60,000 lb st) in the aircraft's two-engine installation. An F-15 powered by Pratt & Whitney's improved F100-PW-220 engine was delivered to the 33rd TFW at Eglin AFB, Florida, in August 1986 for in-service evaluation. The F-15E incorporates digital electronic engine control, engine trimming and monitoring systems. Other improvements include foam filled fuel tanks for greater survivability, higher rated generators, and an improved environmental control system.

Product improvements for the F-15E were flight tested on four Eagles, including an F-15C, an F-15D and the prototype Strike Eagle, between November 1982 and April 1983. During these tests, an F-15 took off for the first time at a gross weight of 34,019 kg (75,000 lb), ie 3,175 kg (7,000 lb) more than the standard max T-O weight of the F-15C with conformal fuel tanks. On this occasion, the aircraft was equipped with two CFTs, three other external tanks, and eight 500 lb Mk 82 bombs. In the overall programme 16 different stores loads configurations were tested, including the carriage of 2,000 lb Mk 84 bombs and BDU-38 and CBU-58 weapons, delivered by both visual and radar means.

Go-ahead for the dual role Eagle programme was announced by the USAF on 24 February 1984, and the first of three full scale development F-15Es (86-183) made its first flight on 11 December 1986. First night flight of an F-15E took place on 1 July 1987. The first production F-15E was scheduled for delivery to the USAF's 405th Tactical Training Wing at Luke AFB, Arizona, in Spring 1988. In FYs 1986-88 the USAF funded 92 F-15Es (8, 42 and 42 respectively); a further 36 were included in the FY 1989 budget request. The US Air Force plans to procure 392 dual role Eagles. IOC is expected in Autumn 1989.

The following description refers to the F-15E where it differs from the F-15C:

TYPE: Two-seat dual role attack/air superiority fighter.

FUSELAGE: Upper rear fuselage, rear fuselage keel structure, main landing gear doors and some rear fuselage fairings incorporate superplastic-formed/diffusion bonded (SPF/DB) titanium structure, providing additional engine bay volume to permit compatibility with alternative engines.

LANDING GEAR: Bendix wheels and Michelin AIR X radial tyres on all units. Nosewheel tyre size 22 × 7.75-9, mainwheel tyres size 36 × 11-18; tyre pressure 21.03 bars (305 lb/sq in) on all units. Bendix five-rotor carbon disc brakes.

ACCOMMODATION: Two crew, pilot and weapon systems officer, in tandem on McDonnell Douglas ACES II ejection seats. Single-piece, upward-hinged canopy.

ARMAMENT: 20 mm M61A1 six-barrel gun in starboard wing root, with 512 rds. General Electric lead computing gyro. Provision on underwing (one per wing) and centreline pylons for air-to-air and air-to-ground weapons and external fuel tanks. Wing pylons use standard rail and ejection launchers for AIM-9 Sidewinder and AIM-120 AMRAAM air-to-air missiles; AIM-7 Sparrow and

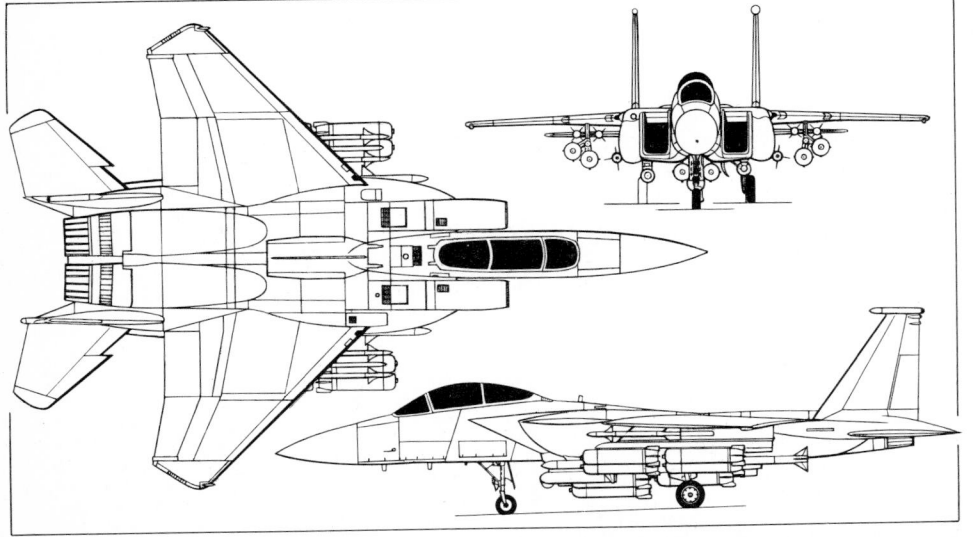

McDonnell Douglas F-15E Eagle equipped for high ordnance payload air-to-ground mission *(Pilot Press)*

Artist's impression of the advanced technology S/MTD version of the F-15 Eagle

AIM-120 AMRAAM can be carried on launchers on centreline station or on tangential stores carriers on conformal fuel tanks (maximum total load four each AIM-7 or AIM-9, up to eight AIM-120). Single or triple rail launchers for AGM-65 Maverick air-to-ground missiles can be fitted to wing stations only. Tangential carriage on CFTs provides for up to six bomb racks on each tank, with provision for triple ejector racks on wing and centreline stations. The F-15E can carry a wide variety and quantity of guided and unguided air-to-ground weapons, including Mk 20 Rockeye (26), Mk 82 (26), Mk 83 (15), Mk 84 (seven), BSU-49 (26), BSU-50 (seven), GBU-8 (five), GBU-10 (seven), GBU-12 (15), GBU-15 (two), GBU-22 (15), GBU-24 (five), CBU-52 (25), CBU-58 (25), CBU-71 (25), CBU-87 (25), CBU-89 (25), CBU-90 (25), CBU-92 (25), CBU-93 (25) bombs; LAU-3A rockets (nine), SUU-20 training weapons (five), A/A-37 U-33 tow target (one), B-57 and B-61 series nuclear weapons (five), and AGM-65 Maverick (six). An AXQ-14 data link pod is used in conjunction with the GBU-15; LANTIRN pod illumination is used to designate targets for the GBU-12, -22 and -24 laser guided bombs. AN/AWG-27 armament control system.

WEIGHTS:

Basic operating weight empty	14,379 kg (31,700 lb)
Max weapon load	10,659 kg (23,500 lb)
Max fuel weight: internal	5,952 kg (13,123 lb)
external (2 CFTs and 3 610 USG drop tanks)	
	9,818 kg (21,645 lb)
Max T-O weight	36,741 kg (81,000 lb)
Max zero-fuel weight	28,440 kg (62,700 lb)
Max landing weight:	
unrestricted	20,094 kg (44,300 lb)
at reduced sink rates	36,741 kg (81,000 lb)

MCDONNELL DOUGLAS F-15S/MTD

In October 1984 McDonnell Douglas was awarded a $117.8 million cost-sharing contract to develop and flight test for the US Air Force Wright Aeronautical Laboratories an advanced technology version of the F-15 with short take-off and landing (STOL) and new manoeuvring capabilities, designated F-15S/MTD (STOL/Manoeuvring Technology Demonstrator). The programme will investigate four specific technologies: two-dimensional (2-D) thrust vectoring/reversing jet nozzles; integrated flight/propulsion control; rough/soft field STOL landing gear; and advanced pilot/vehicle interfaces.

McDonnell Douglas has modified its No. 1 F-15B flight test aircraft for the programme. Controllable foreplanes, adapted from the tailplanes of the F/A-18A Hornet, were installed above the F-15B's engine air intake trunks, forward of the wings. Mounted at a dihedral angle of 20°, the foreplanes operate symmetrically or asymmetrically to provide pitch and roll moments, and are used as stability maintaining surfaces rather than for primary flight control. They permit the F-15B's maximum allowable load factor to be increased from 7.33g to 9g without additional structural strengthening. Rectangular, two-dimensional vectoring nozzles manufactured from carbonfibre are installed at the rear of the aircraft's F100 engines, replacing the F-15B's standard afterburner ducts. The nozzles vector engine thrust by up to 20° upward or downward from the longitudinal axis to enhance take-off performance and flight manoeuvring. Thrust reverser vanes in the nozzles are flight-deployable for rapid deceleration in addition to their short-landing-roll function.

A digital fly by wire system integrates with the flight control system all functions of foreplanes, flaperons, horizontal tail surfaces and vectoring nozzles to provide high precision control of the aircraft's flight path for landing approach. Structurally reinforced landing gear permits 3.66 m (12 ft)/s landing impact loads. The F-15S/MTD employs F-15E avionics and cockpit displays. All flight control surfaces on the F-15S/MTD are actuated hydraulically, and McDonnell Douglas is using the requirements of this aircraft to design a new 552 bar (8,000 lb/sq in) hydraulic power system for future fighters.

The F-15S/MTD incorporates new aluminium-lithium alloy skins, 5 per cent stronger and 9 per cent lighter than the conventional aluminium parts they replace.

Performance parameters specified for the F-15S/MTD include take-off and landing runs of 457 m (1,500 ft) on a 15 m (50 ft) wide, hard, wet, rough surface runway, at night and in adverse weather, with fuel, gun, ammunition and a 2,721 kg (6,000 lb) external payload. McDonnell Douglas is aiming for take-off and landing runs of 305 m (1,000 ft) and 381 m (1,250 ft) respectively. A 6 to 7 per cent increase in manoeuvring performance over the standard F-15 is anticipated, with a 4,536 kg (10,000 lb) increase in payload when operating from a 457 m (1,500 ft) runway, a 27 per cent reduction in take-off run, 13 per cent improvement in cruise range, 24 per cent better roll rate and up to 100 per cent improvement in pitch rate.

The F-15S/MTD was scheduled to make its first flight in July 1988. The initial test programme will include some 150 hours of flight testing. Major subcontractors in the programme are Pratt & Whitney, General Electric's Flight Control Division, and the National Water Lift Division of Pneumo Corporation.

MCDONNELL DOUGLAS F/A-18A HORNET

Canadian AF designations: CF-18A/B
Spanish Air Force designations: C.15 and CE.15

In the Spring of 1974 the US Department of Defense accepted a proposal from the US Navy to study a low-cost lightweight multi-mission fighter, then identified as the VFAX. In August of that year Congress terminated the VFAX concept, directing instead that the Navy should investigate versions of the General Dynamics YF-16 and Northrop YF-17 lightweight fighter prototypes then under evaluation for the USAF. McDonnell Douglas, deciding that the YF-17 could be redesigned to meet the Navy's requirements, teamed with Northrop to propose a derivative, for which it would serve as prime contractor. Identified

as the Navy Air Combat Fighter (NACF), this was named Hornet when selected for development. Two single-seat versions were proposed originally, the F-18A for fighter duties and the A-18 for attack missions. Except for a small amount of operational equipment and missile armament, the two proved so similar that a single configuration, the F/A-18, was able eventually to undertake both missions. Under a 1985 agreement, McDonnell Douglas became prime contractor for all existing and future versions of the aircraft, with Northrop as principal subcontractor.

The first Hornet (160775) made its first flight on 18 November 1978; the second flew on 12 March 1979, and all 11 development aircraft were flying by March 1980, including two F/A-18B two-seat combat-capable trainers.

F/A-18A. Initial single-seat production version, ordered as escort fighter/interdictor replacing F-4, armed with fuselage mounted Sparrows; and as attack aircraft replacing A-7, with FLIR and a laser tracker replacing the Sparrow missiles. Total of 410 (including two-seat F/A-18Bs) built for USN/USMC under FY 1979-1985 contracts. Deliveries began in May 1980 and were completed in 1987. Production for export customers (see later paragraphs) is continuing until 1990. The first development squadron (VFA-125) was formed at NAS Lemoore, California, in November 1980, and the Hornet officially entered operational service on 7 January 1983, with Marine Fighter/Attack Squadron 314 at MCAS El Toro, California. On 1 February 1985 the first Atlantic Fleet F/A-18A operational squadrons began forming at Cecil Field NAS, Florida, after training at NAS Lemoore, California. Also in February, two F/A-18A squadrons, VFA-113 'Stingers' and VFA-25 'Fist of the Fleet' embarked in the aircraft carrier USS *Constellation* for the aircraft's first extended deployment at sea.

F/A-18B. Tandem two-seat version of F/A-18A for training, with combat capability, formerly known as TF/A-18A. Fuel capacity reduced by under 6 per cent.

F/A-18C and F/A-18D. Single- and two-seat aircraft purchased from FY 1986 onwards: total of 324 (243 Cs and 81 Ds) funded by FY 1989. Similar to F/A-18A/B, but with provision for carriage of up to six AMRAAM weapons, two fuselage mounted and two on each outboard wing stores station; up to four imaging infra-red Maverick missiles, one on each wing station; provisions for AN/ALQ-165 airborne self-protection jammer (ASPJ), permitting interchangeability with AN/ALQ-126B; provisions for reconnaissance equipment; upgraded stores management set with 128K memory, Intel 8086 processor, upgraded armament multiplex bus to meet MIL-STD 1553B and MIL-STD 1760 weapons interface capability; flight incident recorder and monitoring set (FIRAMS) which incorporates an integrated fuel/engine indicator, data storage set for recording maintenance and flight incidents data, a signal data processor interfacing with the fuel system to provide overall system control, enhanced built-in-test capability and automatic adjustment of aircraft centre of gravity as fuel is consumed in flight; a maintenance status panel enabling avionics faults to be isolated at circuit card level; and new XN-6 mission computer with higher processing speed and double the memory of the F/A-18A/B's XN-5.

The first production F/A-18C flew on 3 September 1987 and was delivered to NATC Patuxent River on 21 September. All F/A-18Cs and Ds delivered from October 1989 will have all-weather night attack capability, including provision for pilot's night vision goggles, a Hughes Aircraft AN/AAR-50 FLIR thermal imaging navigation set (TINS) which presents TV-like images on a raster head-up display, multi-function colour displays and a Honeywell colour digital moving map system. The F/A-18D will also incorporate a fully mission capable rear cockpit featuring independent display selection. An F/A-18D equipped as the night attack prototype made its first flight on 6 May 1988. In the night attack role the control column and throttles are removed from the F/A-18D's rear cockpit and replaced by two stationary hand controllers with which a naval flight officer can operate the aircraft's weapon systems and three colour CRT display screens. After initial flight testing by the manufacturer, the night attack prototype was scheduled

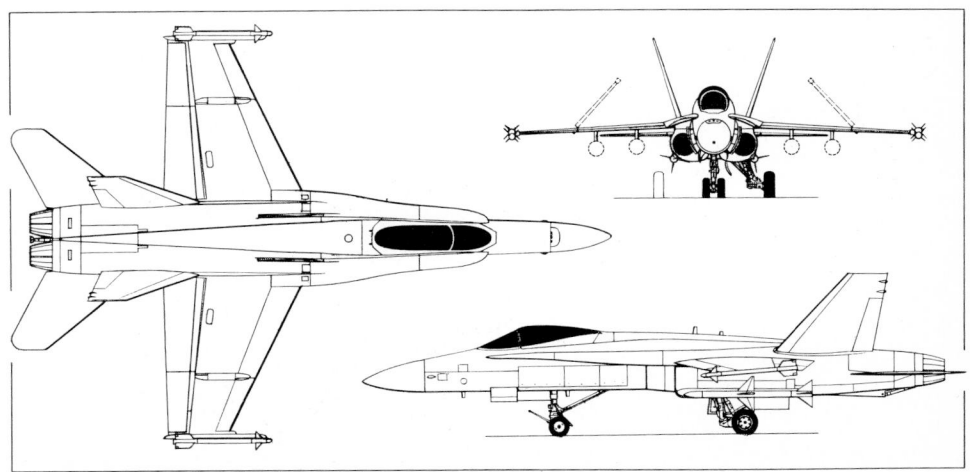

McDonnell Douglas F/A-18A Hornet (two General Electric F404-GE-400 turbofans) *(Pilot Press)*

F/A-18D prototype of the McDonnell Douglas night attack Hornet

to undergo a seven-month test and evaluation programme at the Naval Weapons Center, NAS China Lake, California.

F/A-18(RC). The US Navy began evaluation of a simple reconnaissance conversion of the standard F/A-18A in the Autumn of 1982. This involved removal of the gun from the aircraft's nose, and its replacement by a twin-sensor package with two windows in a slightly bulged underfairing. Flight testing of the first F/A-18 fitted with reconnaissance equipment began on 15 August 1984. A reconnaissance version of the F/A-18D is now being developed for the US Marine Corps as the F/A-18(RC), incorporating the Advanced Tactical Airborne Reconnaissance System (ATARS) that is being developed separately. An all-weather reconnaissance pod for carriage on the centreline stores station, under development by Loral, houses a version of the UPD-4 SLAR high resolution synthetic aperture side-looking radar to supplement the F/A-18's nose mounted optical and infra-red sensors. Imagery is transmitted in real time via a datalink but could be displayed in the rear cockpit of the F/A-18(RC), with growth potential within the pod for installation of an electro-optical camera. The pod, datalink and digital processing equipment has been successfully tested on a US Marine Corps RF-4B. It will be possible to convert the F/A-18(RC) overnight to the fighter/attack configuration within the operational squadron.

CF-18A. Version for Canadian Armed Forces, which plan to purchase 138, including 24 **CF-18B** two-seaters. Selection announced on 10 April 1980. First example made its initial flight on 29 July 1982. Deliveries began with CAF901 and CAF902 on 25 October 1982 and are scheduled to continue at the rate of two per month until 1989. By January 1988 a total of 120 CF-18s had been delivered. First CAF unit was No. 410 Squadron, based at CFB Cold Lake, Alberta, followed by No. 425 at Bagotville, Quebec, and Nos. 439, 409 and 421 Squadrons of No. 1 Canadian Air Group at Sollingen, West Germany. CF-18s are replacing CF-101s, CF-104s and CF-5s. By comparison with US Navy version, CF-18 has different ILS, added spotlight on port side of fuselage for night identification of other aircraft in flight, and provision for carrying LAU-5003 rocket pods.

AF-18A and ATF-18A. Versions for the Royal Australian Air Force. The intention to procure 75 Hornets was announced on 20 October 1981. Two two-seat ATF-18As, manufactured by McDonnell Douglas, were delivered to the RAAF on 17 May 1985. The first ATF-18A assembled by Aerospace Technologies of Australia (ASTA, which see) made its first flight on 26 February 1985 and was handed over to the RAAF's No. 2 operational conversion unit on 4 May. The first Australian manufactured aircraft (ATF-18A A21-104) made its first flight on 3 June 1985. The RAAF's Hornets (57 single-seat AF-18As and 18 two-seat ATF-18As) are replacing Dassault Mirage III-Os. Three operational squadrons are being formed, with deliveries scheduled for completion in 1990. The first squadron, No. 3 based at Williamtown, took delivery of its first AF-18As (A21-8 and A21-9) in Autumn 1986. Re-equipment of No. 77 Squadron began in July 1987.

EF-18A and B. Versions for Spanish Air Force, which ordered 72 in May 1983, with an option for 12 more. First aircraft rolled out 22 November 1985. Thirty-three delivered by January 1988; deliveries due for completion in July 1990. In Spanish Air Force service, aircraft are designated **C.15** (single-seat) and **CE.15** (two-seat).

A total of 1,168 Hornets, including the 11 development aircraft, is planned for the US Navy and Marine Corps. More than 150 of those built will be two-seat trainers. A total of 675 Hornets had been delivered to all customers by 16 May 1988. Northrop builds the centre and rear fuselage sections, which are delivered totally assembled to McDonnell Douglas at St Louis, where final assembly and testing are centred. As part of the EF-18 industrial co-operation programme, CASA of Madrid manufactures horizontal tail surfaces, flaps, leading-edge extensions, speed brakes, rudders and rear side panels for all F/A-18s.

By January 1988 a total of 17 US Navy and 8 US Marine Corps squadrons were equipped with F/A-18s, which had completed 450,000 flight hours. They first saw combat action in April 1986, when aircraft from VFA-131, VFA-132, VMFA-314 and VMFA-323, operating from USS *Coral Sea*, attacked targets in Libya.

In February 1986 the F/A-18A was selected to replace the US Navy Blue Angels Flight Demonstration Squadron's A-4F Skyhawks and made its public debut with the team at MCAS Yuma, Arizona, on 25 April 1987. Eight early production aircraft, not suitable for shipboard operation and including a single F/A-18B, have been fitted with smoke-generating systems and special seat harnesses.

The following information applies to the single-seat US Navy F/A-18C, but is generally applicable to all versions:

TYPE: Single-seat naval multi-mission fighter.

WINGS: Cantilever mid-wing monoplane. Anhedral 3°. Sweepback 20° at quarter-chord. Multi-spar structure primarily of light alloy, with graphite/epoxy inter-spar skin panels and trailing-edge flaps. Boundary layer control achieved by wing root slots. Full span leading-edge manoeuvring flaps have a maximum extension angle of 30°. Single-slotted trailing-edge flaps, actuated by Bertea hydraulic cylinders, deploy to a maximum of 45°. Ailerons, with Hydraulic Research actuators, can be drooped to 45°, providing the advantages of full span flaps for low approach speeds. Leading- and trailing-edge flaps are computer programmed to deflect for optimum lift and drag in both manoeuvring and cruise conditions, and ailerons and flaps are also deflected differentially for roll. Light alloy wingroot leading-edge extensions (LEX) permit flight at angles of attack exceeding 60°. Wings fold upward through 100°, by means of AiResearch mechanical drive, at the inboard end of each aileron.

FUSELAGE: Semi-monocoque basic structure, primarily of light alloy, with graphite/epoxy used for access doors/panels. Titanium firewall between engines. Airbrake in upper surface of fuselage between tail fins. Pressurised cockpit section of fail-safe construction.

TAIL UNIT: Cantilever structure with swept vertical and horizontal surfaces, made primarily of graphite/epoxy over light alloy honeycomb core. Twin 20° outward-canted fins and rudders, mounted forward of all-moving horizontal surfaces (stabilators), which have 2° anhedral and are actuated collectively and differentially by National Water Lift servo-cylinder hydraulic units for pitch and roll control.

LANDING GEAR: Retractable tricycle type, with twin-wheel nose and single-wheel main units. Nose unit retracts forward, mainwheels rearward, turning 90° to stow horizontally inside the lower surface of the engine air ducts. Bendix wheels and brakes. Nosewheel tyres size 22 × 6.6-10, 20 ply, pressure 24.13 bars (350 lb/sq in) for carrier operations, 10.34 bars (150 lb/sq in) for land operations. Mainwheel tyres size 30 × 11.5-14.5, 24 ply, pressure 24.13 bars (350 lb/sq in) for carrier operations, 13.79 bars (200 lb/sq in) for land operations. Ozone nosewheel steering unit. Nose unit towbar for catapult launch. Arrester hook, for carrier landings, under rear fuselage.

POWER PLANT: Two General Electric F404-GE-400 low bypass turbofans, each producing approx 71.2 kN (16,000 lb thrust) with afterburning. Self-sealing fuel tanks and fuel lines; foam in wing tanks and fuselage voids. Internal fuel capacity approx 6.435 litres (1,700 US gallons; 1,415 Imp gallons). Provision for up to three 1,250 litre (330 US gallon; 275 Imp gallon) external tanks. Flight refuelling probe retracts into upper starboard side of nose. Simmonds fuel gauging system. Fixed ramp air intakes.

ACCOMMODATION: Pilot only, on Martin-Baker SJU-5/6 ejection seat, in pressurised, heated and air-conditioned cockpit. Upward opening canopy, with separate windscreen.

SYSTEMS: Two completely separate hydraulic systems, each at 207 bars (3,000 lb/sq in). Max flow rate 212 litres (56 US gallons; 46.6 Imp gallons)/min. Bootstrap type

McDonnell Douglas F/A-18A Hornet carrying two Harpoon air-to-surface missiles

reservoir, pressure 5.86 bars (85 lb/sq in). Quadruplex digital fly by wire flight control system, with direct electrical backup to all surfaces, and direct mechanical backup to stabilators. AiResearch air-conditioning system. General Electric electrical power system. Garrett APU for engine starting and ground pneumatic, electric and hydraulic power. Oxygen system. Fire detection and extinguishing systems.

AVIONICS AND EQUIPMENT: Include an automatic carrier landing system (ACLS) for all-weather carrier operations; a Hughes Aircraft AN/APG-65 multi-mode digital air-to-air and air-to-ground tracking radar, with air-to-air modes which include velocity search (VS), range while search (RWS), track while scan (TWS), which can track ten targets and display eight to the pilot, and raid assessment mode (RAM). Ford AN/AAS-38 attack FLIR; Honeywell digital moving map display; Smiths Industries multi-purpose colour cockpit display; Collins AN/ARN-118 Tacan; AN/ARC-182 UHF/VHF com and DF-301E UHF/DF; Magnavox AN/ALR-50 and Litton AN/ALR-67 radar warning receivers; Ferranti Type 117 laser designator; Goodyear AN/ALE-39 chaff dispenser; Sanders AN/ALQ-126B ECM; Harris AN/ASW-25 radio data link; Eaton AN/ARA-63 receiver/decoder; Ferranti FID 2035 horizontal situation display; Bendix HSI; J.E.T. ID-1791/A flight director indicator; ITT/Westinghouse AN/ALQ-165 airborne self-protection jammer (ASPJ); General Electric quadruple-redundant fly by wire flight control system; two Control Data AN/AYK-14 digital computers; Litton AN/ASN-130A inertial navigation system; two Kaiser multi-function CRTs, central Ferranti/Bendix CRT and Kaiser AN/AVQ-28 head-up display; Conrac communications system control; Normalair-Garrett digital data recorder for Bendix maintenance recording system; flight incident recording and monitoring system (FIRAMS); Smiths standby altimeter; and Kearflex standby airspeed indicator, standby vertical speed indicator, and cockpit pressure altimeter.

ARMAMENT: Nine external weapon stations, comprising two wingtip stations for AIM-9 Sidewinder air-to-air missiles; two outboard wing stations for an assortment of air-to-air or air-to-ground weapons, including AIM-7 Sparrows, AIM-9 Sidewinders, AIM-120 AMRAAMs, AGM-84 Harpoons and AGM-65 Maverick missiles; two inboard wing stations for external fuel tanks or air-to-ground weapons; two nacelle fuselage stations for Sparrows or Martin Marietta AN/ASQ-173 laser spot tracker/strike camera (LST/SCAM) and Ford AN/AAS-38 FLIR pods; and a centreline fuselage station for external fuel or weapons. Air-to-ground weapons include GBU-10 and -12 laser guided bombs, Mk 82 and Mk 84 general purpose bombs, and CBU-59 cluster bombs. An M61 20 mm six-barrel gun, with 570 rounds, is mounted in the nose and has a McDonnell Douglas director gunsight, with a conventional sight as backup.

DIMENSIONS, EXTERNAL:

Wing span	11.43 m (37 ft 6 in)
Wing span over missiles	12.31 m (40 ft 4¾ in)
Wing chord: at root	4.04 m (13 ft 3 in)
at tip	1.68 m (5 ft 6 in)
Wing aspect ratio	3.5
Width, wings folded	8.38 m (27 ft 6 in)
Length overall	17.07 m (56 ft 0 in)
Height overall	4.66 m (15 ft 3½ in)
Tailplane span	6.58 m (21 ft 7¼ in)
Distance between fin tips	3.60 m (11 ft 9½ in)
Wheel track	3.11 m (10 ft 2½ in)
Wheelbase	5.42 m (17 ft 9½ in)

AREAS:

Wings, gross	37.16 m² (400.0 sq ft)
Ailerons, total	2.27 m² (24.4 sq ft)
Leading-edge flaps, total	4.50 m² (48.4 sq ft)
Trailing-edge flaps, total	5.75 m² (61.9 sq ft)
Fins, total	9.68 m² (104.2 sq ft)
Rudders, total	1.45 m² (15.6 sq ft)
Tailplanes, total	8.18 m² (88.1 sq ft)

WEIGHTS:

Weight empty	10,455 kg (23,050 lb)
Max fuel weight: internal	4,926 kg (10,860 lb)
external	3,053 kg (6,732 lb)
Max external stores load	7,710 kg (17,000 lb)
Fighter mission T-O weight	16,651 kg (36,710 lb)
Attack mission T-O weight	22,328 kg (49,224 lb)

PERFORMANCE:

Max level speed	more than Mach 1.8
Max speed, intermediate power	more than Mach 1.0
Approach speed	134 knots (248 km/h; 154 mph)
Acceleration from 460 knots (850 km/h; 530 mph) to 920 knots (1,705 km/h; 1,060 mph) at 10,670 m (35,000 ft)	under 2 min
Combat ceiling	approx 15,240 m (50,000 ft)
T-O run	less than 427 m (1,400 ft)
Combat radius, fighter mission	more than 400 nm (740 km; 460 miles)
Combat radius, attack mission	575 nm (1,065 km; 662 miles)
Ferry range, unrefuelled	more than 2,000 nm (3,706 km; 2,303 miles)

MCDONNELL DOUGLAS HORNET 2000

As part of a study commissioned by the US Department of Defense in 1987, McDonnell Douglas is examining five potential configurations for an upgraded F/A-18 Hornet known as the Hornet 2000, for the development of which international partners are being sought. Configuration 1 features an enhanced performance engine; integrated communications, navigation and identification avionics (ICNIA) performing all communications, navigation and IFF functions; an optional active array antenna for the APG-65 radar; and weapons system improvements, including replacement of existing cockpit displays, front control panel and HUD control panel by flat plate displays. In Configuration 2 the Hornet 2000 would also feature missile detection, laser warning and C³ receiver systems; a 50 per cent increase in wing stiffness to raise weapons carriage speeds; engines such as the projected General Electric Growth 2 F404, each delivering 88.97 kN (20,000 lb thrust); and a dorsal fuel tank increasing internal fuel capacity by 1,225 kg (2,700 lb). Configuration 3 would feature a new wing with 25 per cent greater area than that of the F/A-18; a dorsal tank containing an additional 1,678 kg (3,700 lb) of fuel; and enlarged horizontal tail surfaces. In Configuration 3A the larger wing and tail surfaces would be complemented by vertical surfaces of increased area, but an additional 1,225 kg (2,700 lb) of fuel would be carried in a 0.70 m (2 ft 3½ in) fuselage 'plug' tank rather than the dorsal tank. Configuration 4 features an entirely new wing of cranked-arrow planform, with forward canard surfaces; a 1,450 kg (3,197 lb) capacity fuselage fuel tank plug; and the power plant, avionics and defensive systems improvements previously described.

NORTHROP/MCDONNELL DOUGLAS YF-23A (ATF)

McDonnell Douglas and Northrop signed a teaming agreement covering their individual proposals for the US Air Force's Advanced Tactical Fighter. Northrop's design was one of two selected by the USAF on 31 October 1986. Northrop is prime contractor for all phases of the programme and McDonnell Douglas is principal subcontractor. For further details of the ATF programme see the USAF entry.

GENERAL DYNAMICS/MCDONNELL DOUGLAS A-12

See separate entry under GD/MCDD heading in this section.

DOUGLAS AIRCRAFT COMPANY (Division of McDonnell Douglas Corporation)

HEADQUARTERS: 3855 Lakewood Boulevard, Long Beach, California 90846
Telephone: (213) 593 5511
PRESIDENT: James E. Worsham
SENIOR VICE-PRESIDENT, COMMERCIAL PRODUCTS:
  William T. Gross
SENIOR VICE-PRESIDENT, GOVERNMENT PRODUCTS:
  Thomas M. Ryan Jr
VICE-PRESIDENTS, COMMERCIAL MARKETING:
  Glenn L. Hickerson (International)
  Russell Ray (The Americas)
VICE-PRESIDENT, ENGINEERING: Dale Warren
DIRECTOR, MEDIA RELATIONS: Donald N. Hanson

Douglas Aircraft Company operates plants at Long Beach and Torrance, California, Macon, Georgia, and Salt Lake City, Utah. The DC (Douglas Commercial) series of designations which had identified the company's civil designs since the DC-1 of 1933 was superseded in 1983 by a system using the McDonnell Douglas initials MD. First to bear an MD designation was the Super 80 series of DC-9 derivatives, now known as the MD-80. Existing DC-8, DC-9 and DC-10 designations remain unchanged.

MCDONNELL DOUGLAS MD-80 SERIES

Known previously as the Super 80, the MD-80 Series was developed from the DC-9 specifically to meet the needs of operators on short/medium-range routes who require an aircraft of increased capacity. Compared with the DC-9 Series 50, the wings are increased in span by the insertion of root plugs and by a 0.61 m (2 ft 0 in) extension on each tip, and the fuselage is extended by plugs forward and aft of the wing. The cabin has 'wide look' decor, with large enclosed overhead baggage compartments, acoustic ceiling and soft fluorescent lighting. Standard fuel capacity is increased as a result of the larger wing. Systems improvements include a new digital electronics integrated flight guidance and control system; a 'dial a flap' system to permit more accurate selection of flap angle for optimum take-off and landing performance; flow-through cooling of the aircraft's avionics compartment; a larger capacity APU; a new recirculating system for ventilation air; and an advanced digital fuel quantity gauging system.

A performance management system (PMS) similar to that certificated for the DC-10 (which see) became standard on all MD-80s delivered from April 1983. Other improvements include aerodynamic refinements; increased use of composites, such as a Kevlar wing/fuselage fillet that became standard during 1983; and cockpit and avionics changes, including advanced attitude and heading reference systems. A Honeywell Sperry EFIS system is offered as an optional replacement for electro-mechanical primary flight instrument displays, together with flat plate LED displays and flight management systems. Honeywell Sperry has also developed a windshear detection and guidance system for the MD-80 series, for scheduled certification in the last quarter of 1988. The windshear detection and guidance system will be standard equipment on all new MD-80 series aircraft, and will be available for retrofit to aircraft already in service.

The first aircraft in the Super 80/MD-80 series made its initial flight on 18 October 1979; second and third prototypes (N1002G and N1002W) flew on 6 December 1979 and 29 February 1980 respectively. FAA certification was granted on 26 August 1980, and on 12 September the first production aircraft was delivered to Swissair, which had placed an order for 15 in October 1977.

Available models are as follows:

MD-81. Basic version, powered by two Pratt & Whitney JT8D-209 turbofans. Emergency thrust reserve becomes available automatically in an engine-out situation. Entered service, with Swissair, on 5 October 1980.

MD-82. Announced on 16 April 1979, with Pratt & Whitney JT8D-217 turbofans. Regarded as being particularly suitable for operation from 'hot and high' airports. The higher thrust available makes possible an increased payload and range when operating from standard airports. First flown on 8 January 1981, and certificated on 30 July 1981 at a max T-O weight of 66,680 kg (147,000 lb), it entered commercial service in August 1981. Otherwise generally similar to MD-81, with same fuel capacity and max landing weight. A second version, with JT8D-217A engines and higher max T-O weight, was certificated in mid-1982, and became available from Autumn 1982. On 12

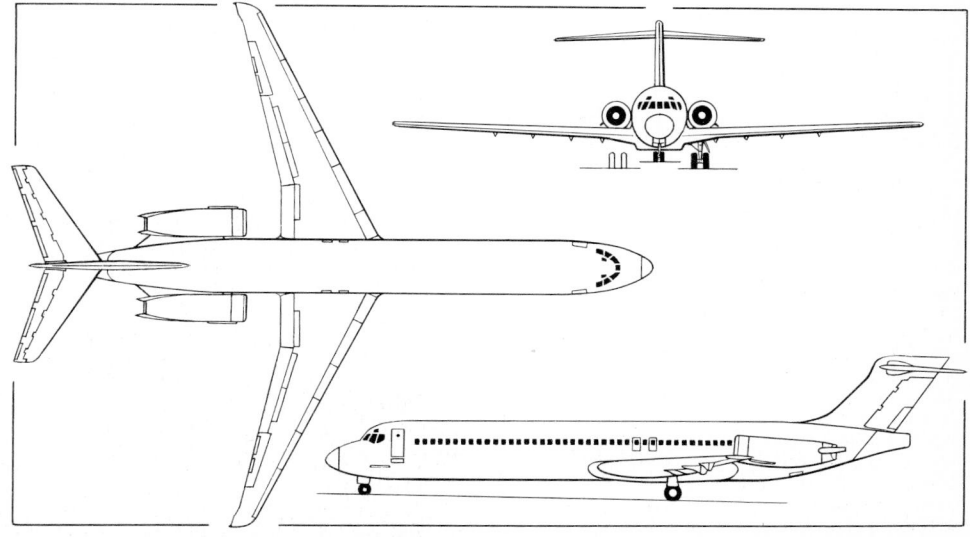

McDonnell Douglas MD-87, a short-fuselage variant of the MD-80 series of twin-turbofan transports
(Pilot Press)

First McDonnell Douglas MD-87 for Swiss carrier CTA *(Anton Wettstein)*

April 1985 agreement was reached with the government of the People's Republic of China for the sale of 26 MD-82s, of which 25 are being partially assembled in the United States and shipped to China for final completion by the Shanghai Aviation Industrial Corporation (SAIC). The sole US assembled aircraft arrived in China on 30 September 1985. First subassemblies were delivered to SAIC in January 1986; the first SAIC assembled MD-82 flew for the first time on 2 July 1987 and entered service with CAAC on 4 August, followed by delivery of the second aircraft on 18 December 1987. The FAA certificate was extended to Chinese built MD-82s on 9 November 1987. Four had been completed by SAIC by June 1988, with two more due by year-end, seven in 1989 and eight in 1990. The original Chinese option for 15 additional MD-82s has been allowed to lapse.

MD-83. This longer-range version of the MD-80, powered by Pratt & Whitney JT8D-219 engines, was announced on 31 January 1983. These engines offer a 2 per cent improvement in fuel consumption by comparison with -217A turbofans; greater fuel capacity is provided by the introduction of two extra fuel tanks in the cargo compartment.

The MD-83 flew for the first time on 17 December 1984. FAA certification was received in 1985, with service entry with launch customers Alaska Airlines and Finnair taking place in early 1986. On 14 November 1985 Finnair's first MD-83 made the longest nonstop flight ever recorded by an MD-80 variant, flying from Montreal to Helsinki, a distance of 3,404 nm (6,308 km; 3,920 miles) in 7 h 26 min. On 9 September 1987 an MD-83 of the Swedish charter carrier Transwede flew the MD-80 series' first transatlantic revenue service, flying from Stockholm to Fort Lauderdale, Florida, a distance of 4,533 nm (8,401 km; 5,220 miles), routing via stops at Oslo, Norway, and Gander, Newfoundland.

MD-87. Announced on 3 January 1985, the MD-87 is a short-fuselage variant of the MD-80, with accommodation for 130 single class passengers or 109 passengers in mixed class configuration. Standard power plant is two Pratt & Whitney JT8D-217C engines, offering a 2 per cent improvement in fuel consumption over -217A engines. The JT8D-219 or other engines in the JT8D-200 series may be fitted in the MD-87. Standard fuel capacity can be increased by optional auxiliary tanks in the cargo compartment. The MD-87 incorporates McDonnell Douglas' MD-80 series cruise performance improvement package, which includes a fillet fairing between fuselage and engine pylons, a fairing on the APU, improved sealing on the horizontal tail surfaces, low drag flap hinge fairings, and an extended low

drag tailcone. The MD-87 was also the first of the MD-80 series to have as standard an electronic flight instrument system, AHRS and head-up display.

Assembly of the first MD-87 began in April 1986, followed by the first flight on 4 December. Certification was received on 21 October 1987, permitting deliveries to begin to launch customers Finnair and Austrian Airlines. Other orders include four for Toa Domestic Airlines, ten for SAS, and eight, with options on 28 more, for Midway Airlines (with JT8D-219 engines). Compagnie de Transport Aerier (CTA) of Switzerland has ordered four MD-87s, the first of which was delivered on 30 March 1988, and Iberia of Spain has ordered 17, for delivery commencing in Autumn 1989. A total of 57 MD-87s had been ordered by 1 April 1988, including one executive version.

MD-88. Announced on 23 January 1986, the MD-88 is powered by Pratt & Whitney JT8D-219 engines and features EFIS cockpit displays, a flight management system, an onboard windshear detection system and increased use of composites materials in the airframe. A new interior design provides accommodation for 142 passengers (14 first class and 128 coach class) in five-abreast seating, with wider aisle and redesigned overhead storage bins. First flight was made on 15 August 1987, and FAA certification was granted on 9 December. The first of 53 MD-88s ordered by launch customer Delta Air Lines, which has 57 more on option, entered service on 5 January 1988. Other customers include Wandair of Canada, which has ordered eight MD-88s, with options on a further eight, for delivery between June 1989 and June 1991.

MD-80 Executive Jets. McDonnell Douglas offers corporate and executive variants of the MD-83 and MD-87. In typical corporate configurations seating 20 passengers the MD-83 offers a maximum range of 4,100 nm (7,598 km; 4,721 miles), while the MD-87 has a maximum range of 4,500 nm (8,339 km; 5,182 miles), each being equipped with auxiliary fuel tanks. In March 1987 McDonnell Douglas announced the sale of the first MD-87 executive jet to the Aladdin Hotel and Casino in Las Vegas, Nevada. The aircraft was delivered in 'green' configuration for final outfitting and installation of auxiliary fuel tanks providing an additional capacity of 13,627 litres (3,600 US gallons; 2,998 Imp gallons).

By 1 July 1988 orders and options for the MD-80 series totalled 1,111, of which 502 had been delivered.

The following description applies specifically to the MD-81, and generally also to the other models, except where indicated:

TYPE: Twin-turbofan short/medium-range airliner.

WINGS: Cantilever low-wing monoplane. Mean thickness/chord ratio 11.0%. Dihedral 3°. Incidence 1° 15'. Sweepback at quarter-chord 24° 30'. All-metal construction, with two spars and spanwise stringers riveted to skin. Glassfibre trailing-edges on wings, ailerons and flaps. Manually controlled aileron on each wing. Wing mounted speed brakes. Full span leading-edge slats. Hydraulically actuated double-slotted trailing-edge flaps over 67 per cent of semi-span. Single boundary layer fence (vortillon) under each wing. Three spoilers per wing; two outboard segments act as flight and ground spoilers, inboard segment is ground spoiler only. Detachable wingtips. Thermal anti-icing of leading-edges.

FUSELAGE: All-metal semi-monocoque fail-safe structure of heat treated light alloy. Majority of cabin floor constructed of balsa or Nomex core composite. Engine pylons built by Calcor, fuselage panels by Aeritalia.

TAIL UNIT: Cantilever all-metal structure with electrically actuated variable incidence T tailplane. Manually controlled elevators with control tabs. Hydraulically controlled rudder with manual override. Glassfibre trailing-edges on control surfaces.

LANDING GEAR: Retractable tricycle type of Cleveland Pneumatic manufacture, with steerable nosewheels. Hydraulic retraction, nose unit forward, main units inward. Twin Goodyear wheels and tyres on each unit. Mainwheel tyres size 44.5 × 16.5-20, pressure 11.38 bars (165 lb/sq in). Nosewheel tyres size 26 × 6.6-14, pressure 10.34 bars (150 lb/sq in). Goodyear disc brakes. Hydro-Aire Mk IIIA anti-skid units. Douglas ram air brake cooling.

POWER PLANT: Two Pratt & Whitney JT8D-209 turbofans in MD-81, pod mounted one each side of rear fuselage, and each rated at 82.3 kN (18,500 lb st), with emergency thrust reserve of 3.34 kN (750 lb st). MD-82 has JT8D-217s, each rated at 89 kN (20,000 lb st), with emergency thrust reserve of 3.78 kN (850 lb st), or -217As of similar rating. MD-83 has JT8D-219 engines of 93.4 kN (21,000 lb st). MD-87 has JT8D-217C engines of 89 kN (20,000 lb st), with an emergency thrust reserve of 3.78 kN (850 lb st). MD-88 has 93.4 kN (21,000 lb st) JT8D-219 turbofans. Standard fuel capacity in MD-81/82/87/88 is 21,876 litres (5,779 US gallons; 4,812 Imp gallons); increased in MD-83 (and, optionally, MD-87) to 26,260 litres (6,939 US gallons; 5,778 Imp gallons) by two 2,195 litre (580 US gallon; 483 Imp gallon) auxiliary tanks in cargo compartment. Pressure refuelling point in

First McDonnell Douglas MD-88 taking off on its first flight, in the markings of Delta Air Lines

starboard wing leading-edge. Overwing gravity refuelling points.

ACCOMMODATION: Crew of two and observer on flight deck, plus cabin attendants. Seating arrangements are optional to meet specific airline requirements. Maximum optional seating capacity is for 172 passengers (139 in MD-87). Fully pressurised and air-conditioned. One toilet forward on port side, two at rear of cabin. Provisions for galley at both forward and rear ends of cabin. Passenger door at front of cabin on port side, with built-in electrically operated airstairs, and rear hydraulically operated ventral stairway, are standard. Servicing and emergency exit doors at starboard forward end and port rear end of cabin. Three cargo doors for underfloor holds on starboard side. Overwing emergency exits, two each side.

SYSTEMS: AiResearch dual air cycle air-conditioning and pressurisation system utilising engine bleed air, max differential 0.54 bars (7.77 lb/sq in). Two separate 207 bar (3,000 lb/sq in) hydraulic systems for operation of spoilers, flaps, slats, rudder, landing gear, nosewheel steering, brakes, rotated thrust reversers and ventral stairway. Maximum flow rate 30.3 litres (8 US gallons; 6.7 Imp gallons)/min. Airless bootstrap type reservoirs, output pressure 2.07 bars (30 lb/sq in). Pneumatic system, for air-conditioning/pressurisation, engine starting and ice protection, utilises 8th or 13th stage engine bleed air and/or APU. Electrical system includes three 40kVA 120/208V three-phase 400Hz alternators, two engine driven, one driven by APU. Oxygen system of diluter demand type for crew on flight deck; continuous flow chemical canister type with automatic mask presentation for cabin passengers. Anti-icing of wing and engine inlets, and de-icing of tailplane, by engine bleed air. Electric de-icing of windscreen. APU provides pneumatic and electrical power on ground, and electrical power in flight.

AVIONICS AND EQUIPMENT: All-digital avionics, including dual Honeywell Sperry integrated flight systems; Honeywell Sperry Cat IIIA autoland; autopilot and stability augmentation system; performance management system; speed command with digital full-time autothrottles; thrust rating indicator system; dual Honeywell air data systems; automatic reserve thrust; ADF system; and colour weather radar display. Sundstrand head-up display optional.

DIMENSIONS, EXTERNAL (all versions, except as indicated):
Wing span	32.87 m (107 ft 10 in)
Wing chord: at root	7.05 m (23 ft 1½ in)
at tip	1.10 m (3 ft 7½ in)
Wing aspect ratio	9.62
Length overall: except MD-87	45.06 m (147 ft 10 in)
MD-87	39.75 m (130 ft 5 in)
Length of fuselage:	
except MD-87	41.30 m (135 ft 6 in)
MD-87	36.30 m (119 ft 1 in)
Height overall: except MD-87	9.04 m (29 ft 8 in)
MD-87	9.30 m (30 ft 6 in)
Tailplane span	12.24 m (40 ft 2 in)
Wheel track	5.08 m (16 ft 8 in)
Wheelbase: except MD-87	22.07 m (72 ft 5 in)
MD-87	19.18 m (62 ft 11 in)
Passenger door (port, fwd):	
Height	1.83 m (6 ft 0 in)
Width	0.86 m (2 ft 10 in)
Height to sill	2.24 m (7 ft 4 in)
Servicing door (stbd, fwd): Height	1.22 m (4 ft 0 in)
Width	0.69 m (2 ft 3 in)
Height to sill	2.24 m (7 ft 4 in)
Servicing door (port, rear): Height	1.52 m (5 ft 0 in)
Width	0.69 m (2 ft 3 in)
Height to sill	2.67 m (8 ft 9 in)
Freight and baggage hold doors:	
Height	1.27 m (4 ft 2 in)
Width	1.35 m (4 ft 5 in)
Height to sill: fwd	1.17 m (3 ft 10 in)
centre	1.30 m (4 ft 3 in)
rear	1.52 m (5 ft 0 in)
Rear cargo door (MD-87): Height	1.27 m (4 ft 2 in)
Width	0.91 m (3 ft 0 in)
Emergency exits (overwing, port and stbd):	
Height	0.91 m (3 ft 0 in)
Width	0.51 m (1 ft 8 in)

DIMENSIONS, INTERNAL:
Cabin, excl flight deck, incl toilets:
Length	30.78 m (101 ft 0 in)
Max width	3.07 m (10 ft 1 in)
Max height	2.06 m (6 ft 9 in)
Floor area	89.65 m² (965 sq ft)
Volume	191.9 m³ (6,778 cu ft)
Freight holds (underfloor, MD-81/82):	
fwd	13.14 m³ (464 cu ft)
centre	9.80 m³ (346 cu ft)
rear	12.54 m³ (443 cu ft)
Freight holds (underfloor, MD-83):	
total	29.1 m³ (1,028 cu ft)

AREAS:
Wings, gross	118 m² (1,270 sq ft)
Ailerons (total)	3.53 m² (38.0 sq ft)
Fin, excl dorsal fin	9.51 m² (102.4 sq ft)
Rudder	6.07 m² (65.3 sq ft)
Tailplane	29.17 m² (314.0 sq ft)

WEIGHTS AND LOADINGS (A: MD-81, B: MD-82, C: MD-83, D: MD-87, E: MD-88):
Operating weight empty: A		35,571 kg (78,421 lb)
B		35,629 kg (78,549 lb)
C		36,543 kg (80,563 lb)
D standard fuel		33,183 kg (73,157 lb)
D optional fuel		33,851 kg (74,629 lb)
Fuel load:		
A, B, D standard		17,748 kg (39,128 lb)
C, D optional		21,273 kg (46,900 lb)
Max payload (weight limited): A		17,952 kg (39,579 lb)
B		19,709 kg (43,451 lb)
C		18,795 kg (41,437 lb)
D standard		17,619 kg (38,843 lb)
D optional		16,951 kg (37,371 lb)
Max T-O weight: A (-217 engines), D standard		
		63,503 kg (140,000 lb)
A (-217A engines), B, D optional, E standard		
		67,812 kg (149,500 lb)
C, E optional		72,575 kg (160,000 lb)
Max zero-fuel weight: A		53,524 kg (118,000 lb)
B, C		55,338 kg (122,000 lb)
D		50,802 kg (112,000 lb)
Max landing weight:		
A, D standard		58,060 kg (128,000 lb)
B, D optional		58,967 kg (130,000 lb)
C		63,276 kg (139,500 lb)
Max wing loading:		
A, D standard		534.6 kg/m² (109.5 lb/sq ft)
B, D optional, E standard		574.7 kg/m² (117.7 lb/sq ft)
C, E optional		615.0 kg/m² (126.0 lb/sq ft)
Max power loading: A		385.8 kg/kN (3.78 lb/lb st)
B, D optional		381.0 kg/kN (3.74 lb/lb st)
C, E optional		388.5 kg/kN (3.81 lb/lb st)
D standard		356.8 kg/kN (3.50 lb/lb st)
E standard		363.3 kg/kN (3.56 lb/lb st)

PERFORMANCE (at max T-O weight except where indicated):
Max level speed (all)		500 knots (925 km/h; 575 mph)
Max cruising speed (all)		Mach 0.80
Normal cruising speed (all)		Mach 0.76
FAA T-O field length: A		2,210 m (7,250 ft)
B		2,271 m (7,450 ft)
C		2,553 m (8,375 ft)
D		1,859 m (6,100 ft)
FAA landing field length, at max landing weight:		
A		1,478 m (4,850 ft)
B		1,500 m (4,920 ft)
C		2,585 m (5,200 ft)
D		1,430 m (4,690 ft)
Range with max fuel:		
D standard		2,980 nm (5,522 km; 3,431 miles)
D optional		3,650 nm (6,764 km; 4,203 miles)

Range (A, B, C with 155 passengers, domestic reserves; D with 130 passengers, domestic reserves):
A		1,563 nm (2,896 km; 1,800 miles)
B		2,049 nm (3,798 km; 2,360 miles)
C		2,501 nm (4,635 km; 2,880 miles)
D standard		2,372 nm (4,395 km; 2,731 miles)
D optional		2,829 nm (5,243 km; 3,260 miles)

OPERATIONAL NOISE LEVELS (FAR Pt 36):
T-O: A, B, C		90.4 EPNdB
D estimated		88.7 EPNdB
Sideline: A, B, C		94.6 EPNdB
D estimated		92.8 EPNdB
Approach: A, B, C		93.3 EPNdB
D estimated		93.3 EPNdB

MCDONNELL DOUGLAS UHB MD-90 PROGRAMME

McDonnell Douglas, Aeritalia of Italy, Saab-Scania of Sweden and Shanghai Aviation Industrial Corporation of China are co-operating on the development of ultra high bypass (UHB) engine technology as the basis for a range of derivative and new short-to-medium-range airliners. The General Electric Company and the Allison Gas Turbine Division of General Motors are developing demonstrator UHB engines which began flight testing in the port nacelle of a modified MD-80 at Edwards AFB, California, on 18 May 1987. For initial testing the General Electric GE36 UDF engine was equipped with two eight-blade fans of nearly 3.66 m (12 ft 0 in) diameter. An improved engine with a ten-blade fan in front and an eight-blade fan at the rear began flight trials on 15 August 1987. The flight test programme included customer demonstration flights for which the aircraft was outfitted with an 18-passenger standard mixed class airline interior in the aft fuselage section. The programme was completed on 25 March 1988 after the aircraft had logged 165 hours in 93 flights, reaching a maximum altitude of 11,280 m (37,000 ft) and a maximum speed of Mach 0.865. The UDF engine was then removed for inspection by General Electric engineers.

Design studies indicate that on an average length short-haul flight an MD-80 size airliner with UHB propulsion could burn some 25 to 35 per cent less fuel than an advanced turbofan aircraft, and as much as 50 per cent less than current turbofan airliners. The **MD-91** is planned as an MD-80 derivative seating 114 passengers. Projected max T-O weight is 46,266 kg (102,000 lb), with a 1,500 nm (2,779 km; 1,727 mile) range at a cruising speed of Mach 0.78. Certification and first deliveries could be achieved by Autumn 1992. An **MD-92** version could seat up to 165 passengers.

The **MD-9XX** is a projected propfan airliner of entirely new design in the 160 to 180 passenger class. In addition to UHB engines, the aircraft would feature laminar and turbulent boundary layer control, very high aspect ratio supercritical wings, flight-critical active stability augmentation, all-electric secondary power systems, digital control systems, fly by wire and fly by light technologies, and cockpit sidestick controllers. Certification could be achieved by the end of the 1990s.

McDonnell Douglas also proposes a UHB retrofit programme for the MD-80 series. Timing of such a programme would depend on development of the MD-91. The company predicts that an **MD-80 Retrofit** would offer a 41 per cent reduction in fuel burn over a 500 nm (926 km; 575 mile) flight at Mach 0.78 with 142 passengers against an MD-82 flying the same route. Estimated operating weight empty is 38,562 kg (85,015 lb), and max T-O weight 62,142 kg (137,000 lb).

MCDONNELL DOUGLAS P-9D

McDonnell Douglas is studying an ultra high bypass (UHB) powered aircraft for the US Navy's Long Range Air-ASW Capable Aircraft (LRAACA) requirement. Known by the company designation P-9D, the twin-engined aircraft would be similar in size to the MD-87, with a wing span of 32.86 m (107 ft 9½ in), length overall of 40.29 m (132 ft 2½ in) and max T-O weight of 74,843 kg (165,000 lb). The 111.2 kN (25,000 lb st) General Electric G36 UDF and Pratt & Whitney/Allison 578 power plants are under consideration for the aircraft, which would feature a modern 'all glass' two-crew cockpit with CRT displays and

Artist's impression of McDonnell Douglas P-9D UHB anti-submarine warfare aircraft

McDonnell Douglas MD-80 UHB demonstrator

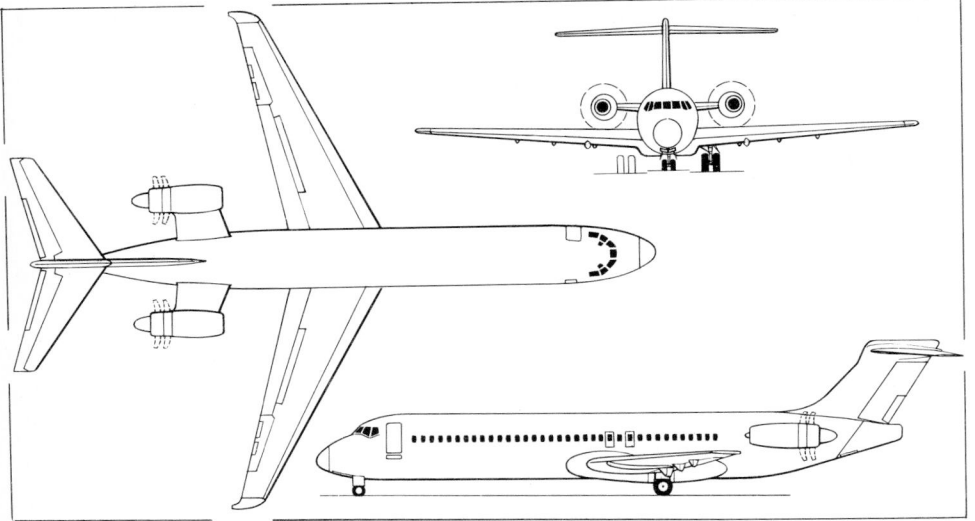

McDonnell Douglas MD-91, one of a proposed new range of UHB powered airliners *(Pilot Press)*

digital avionics. Two internal weapons bays forward of the wing would enable it to carry Harpoon anti-ship missiles, bombs, mines or torpedoes, in addition to underwing stores carried on six weapons pylons. A full range of detection equipment and sensors would be carried, including search radar, magnetic anomaly detector and acoustic receivers. The P-9D would be able to launch 40 sonobuoys from externally loaded chutes, and a further 125 from crew loaded chutes. Projected performance includes a maximum speed of 430 knots (797 km/h; 495 mph), and up to 4 hours loiter time on station over a target area nearly 2,000 nm (3,706 km; 2,303 miles) from base.

MCDONNELL DOUGLAS DC-10

The DC-10 was developed as an all-purpose commercial transport able to operate economically over ranges from 260 nm to 5,730 nm (480 to 10,620 km; 300 to 6,600 miles), according to Series, and able to carry 270 mixed class passengers, or a maximum of 380 passengers in an all-economy configuration.

There have been five basic civil production versions, as follows:

Series 10. Initial version at 185,970 kg (410,000 lb) max T-O weight for use on domestic services, powered by three General Electric CF6-6D or -6D1 turbofans, each rated at 178 kN (40,000 lb st) or 182.4 kN (41,000 lb st) respectively. First flight 29 August 1970. Type certificated by FAA on 29 July 1971. First scheduled passenger flight 5 August 1971, by American Airlines. Subsequent version at 206,385 kg (455,000 lb) max T-O weight, and with added centre-wing fuel. Details in 1987-88 and earlier *Jane's*.

Series 15. Basically as Series 10, but with max T-O weight of 206,385 kg (455,000 lb), and 207 kN (46,500 lb st) General Electric CF6-50C2F engines. First flight 8 January 1981. Certificated on 12 June 1981. Seven built. Details in 1987-88 and earlier *Jane's*.

Series 30. Extended range version for intercontinental operations, powered by three General Electric CF6-50A or -50C turbofans, each rated at 218 kN (49,000 lb st) or 227 kN (51,000 lb st) respectively. Initial deliveries at 251,745 kg (555,000 lb) max T-O weight. Later versions have CF6-50C1 or C2 engines rated at 233.5 kN (52,500 lb st), or C2B engines rated at 236 kN (53,000 lb st) and max T-O weight of up to 263,085 kg (580,000 lb). Increased fuel capacity. Wing span increased by 3.05 m (10 ft 0 in). Landing gear supplemented by additional dual-wheel bogie

unit, mounted on the fuselage centreline between the four-wheel bogie main units. First flight 21 June 1972. FAA certification granted 21 November 1972, simultaneously with first deliveries of production aircraft to KLM and Swissair. Convertible and cargo versions, designated **Series 30CF** and **30F**, are described separately.

Series 30ER. Developed version of Series 30, with range extended still further by installing auxiliary fuel tank in rear of cargo compartment. More powerful (240.2 kN; 54,000 lb st) CF6-50C2B engines. First order (for two) placed by Swissair in July 1980, plus kits to convert two of its existing DC-10s to Srs 30ER configuration. Other customers include Thai Airways International and Toa Domestic Airlines of Japan.

Series 40. Extended range version for intercontinental operations, powered by three Pratt & Whitney turbofan engines. Twenty-two early models, built for Northwest Orient Airlines, had JT9D-20 turbofans, each rated at 220 kN (49,400 lb st) with water injection. First flight 28 February 1972; FAA certification received 20 October 1972. Last flight, built for Japan Air Lines, equipped with JT9D-59A turbofans, each rated at 236 kN (53,000 lb st). First flight of a Series 40 with this latter power plant was on 25 July 1975.

In early 1983, FAA certification was received for a Delco Electronics performance management system (PMS), for installation on the DC-10, which is able to provide fuel savings of 1-3 per cent. The PMS is coupled through the autopilot and autothrottle systems to control automatically the aircraft's pitch and thrust to obtain maximum fuel efficiency during climb, cruise and descent. First PMS-equipped DC-10 to enter service, in March 1983, was a JAL Series 40.

By 1 April 1988, McDonnell Douglas had received firm orders for 386 commercial DC-10s, of which 378 had been delivered. Production was due to be phased out by the end of that year, as manufacture of the MD-11 gets under way.

The following description applies to the Series 30, 30ER and 40:

TYPE: Three-turbofan commercial transport.

WINGS: Cantilever low-wing monoplane of all-metal fail-safe construction. Several different Douglas wing sections. Thickness/chord ratio varies from slightly more than 12.2% at root to less than 8.4% at tip. Dihedral 5° 14.4' inboard, 3° 1.8' outboard. Incidence positive at wingroot, negative at tip. Sweepback at quarter-chord 35°. All-metal inboard and outboard ailerons, the former

used conventionally, the latter only when the leading-edge slats are extended. Double-slotted all-metal trailing-edge flaps mounted on external hinges, with an inboard and outboard flap panel on each wing. Five all-metal spoiler panels on each wing, at the rear edge of the fixed wing structure, forward of the flaps. All spoilers operate in unison as lateral control, speed brake and ground spoilers. Full span three-position all-metal leading-edge slats. Ailerons are powered by Bertea hydraulic actuators, spoilers by Parker-Hannifin hydraulic actuators. Each aileron is powered by either of two hydraulic systems; each spoiler is powered by a single system. All leading-edge slat segments outboard of the engines are anti-iced with engine bleed air.

FUSELAGE: Aluminium alloy semi-monocoque fail-safe structure of circular cross-section. Except for auxiliary areas the entire fuselage is pressurised.

TAIL UNIT: Cantilever all-metal structure standard. Variable incidence tailplane, actuated by Vickers hydraulic motors. Longitudinal and directional controls are fully powered and comprise inboard and outboard elevators, each segment powered by a Bertea tandem actuator; upper and lower rudder each powered by a Bertea actuator. Rudder standby power supplied by two Abex transfer motor pumps. Twelve DC-10s in current service have upper rudder segments made of graphite epoxy.

LANDING GEAR: Hydraulically retractable tricycle type, with gravity free-fall for emergency extension. Twin-wheel steerable nose unit retracts forward; Menasco main units inward into fuselage. Main gear comprises two four-wheel bogies, with an additional dual-wheel main unit mounted on the fuselage centreline between the bogie units and retracting forward. Oleo-pneumatic shock absorbers in all units. Goodyear nosewheels and tyres size 40 × 15.5-16, pressure 12.41 bars (180 lb/sq in). Main units and centreline unit have Goodyear wheels and tyres size 52 × 20.5-23. The former have a pressure of 11.38 bars (165 lb/sq in), the latter 9.65 bars (140 lb/sq in). Goodyear disc brakes and anti-skid system, with individual wheel control.

POWER PLANT: Three turbofans (details under Series descriptions), two of which are mounted on underwing pylons, the third above the rear fuselage at the base of the fin. All engines are fitted with thrust reversers for ground operation. Engine air inlets have load carrying acoustically treated panels for noise attenuation, and each engine fan case and fan exhaust is similarly treated. Four integral wing fuel tanks and an auxiliary tank in the wing centre-section with a connected structural compartment fitted with a bladder cell, giving total capacity of approximately 138,165 litres (36,500 US gallons; 30,392 Imp gallons). Four standard pressure refuelling adapters, two in each wing outboard of the engine pylons. Lower cargo hold can be used to carry an optional long-range tank of either 5,807 litres (1,534 US gallons; 1,277 Imp gallons) or 12,556 litres (3,317 US gallons; 2,762 Imp gallons). Oil capacity, Series 30: 34.1 litres (9 usable US gallons; 7.5 Imp gallons); Series 40: 56.8 litres (15 usable US gallons; 12.5 Imp gallons).

ACCOMMODATION: Crew of three (pilot, first officer, flight engineer), with seating for two observers, plus cabin attendants. Standard seating for 255 or 270 in mixed class versions, with a maximum of 380 passengers in an economy class arrangement. Two aisles run the length of the cabin, which is separated into sections by cloakroom dividers. In the first class section, with three pairs of reclining seats abreast, the aisles are 0.78 m (2 ft 7 in) wide. In the coach class section, four pairs of seats, with a table between the centre pairs, also have two aisles, these being 0.51 m (1 ft 8 in) wide. One pair of seats is exchanged for a three-seat unit in the nine-abreast high-density layout. Up to nine lavatories located throughout the passenger cabin. Cloakrooms of standard and elevating type distributed throughout the cabin. Overhead stowage modules, fully enclosed and providing

McDonnell Douglas DC-10 Series 30 in the insignia of Swissair, under charter to Air Afrique

stowage for passengers' personal effects, are located on the sidewalls and extend the full length of the cabin. Optional centreline overhead baggage racks available. Eight passenger doors, four on each side, open by sliding inward and upward into the above-ceiling area. Containerised or bulk cargo compartments located immediately forward and aft of the wing, with outward opening doors on the starboard side. A bulk cargo compartment is located in the lower rear section of the fuselage, with its door on the port side. Entire accommodation is fully air-conditioned, with five separate control zones for the below-floor galley configuration. Optional main cabin galley to replace the lower galley, and in this configuration there are four separate control zones for the air-conditioning. The lower deck galley is provided with five to eight high-temperature ovens, and with refrigerators, storage space for linen, china and other accessories. Serving carts are taken to cabin level by two electric elevators, to a buffet service centre, from where stewardesses serve passengers. To permit quick turnround at terminals, without interference to passenger movement in the main cabin, the kitchen is provisioned through the cargo doors at ground level.

SYSTEMS: Three parallel continuously operating and completely separate hydraulic systems supply the fully powered flight controls and wheel brakes. Normally, one of the systems supplies power for landing gear actuation. Two reversible motor pumps, each sized to deliver power from one of the other two systems for standby operation of landing gear, can also power any other hydraulically operated unit. Each hydraulic system is powered by two identical engine driven pumps, capable of delivering a total of 265 litres (70 US gallons; 58.3 Imp gallons)/min at 207 bars (3,000 lb/sq in) at take-off. All three hydraulic systems are applied to each primary control axis in a manner which ensures maximum control effectiveness in the event of single or dual hydraulic system failures. A Garrett TSCP-700-4 APU provides ground electrical and pneumatic power, including main engine starting, and auxiliary electrical power in flight.

AVIONICS AND EQUIPMENT: A dual fail-operative landing system is installed to meet Category IIIA weather minima. Triple inertial navigation system meeting ARINC 561 requirements on Srs 30 and 40, with optional dual area navigation system capability.

DIMENSIONS, EXTERNAL:
Wing span 50.40 m (165 ft 4½ in)
Wing chord: at root 10.71 m (35 ft 1¾ in)
at tip 2.73 m (8 ft 11½ in)
Wing aspect ratio 7.5
Length overall 55.50 m (182 ft 1 in)
Length of fuselage 51.97 m (170 ft 6 in)
Height overall 17.70 m (58 ft 1 in)
Tailplane span 21.69 m (71 ft 2 in)
Wheel track 10.67 m (35 ft 0 in)
Wheelbase: Series 30 22.05 m (72 ft 4 in)
Series 40 22.07 m (72 ft 5 in)

DIMENSIONS, INTERNAL:
Cabin: Length, from rear bulkhead of flight deck to rear cabin bulkhead approx 41.45 m (136 ft 0 in)
Max width 5.72 m (18 ft 9 in)
Height (basic) 2.41 m (7 ft 11 in)
Series 30, 40 in lower-galley configuration:
Forward baggage and/or freight hold (forward of wing):
containerised volume 27.2 m³ (960 cu ft)
bulk volume 37.9 m³ (1,339 cu ft)
Centre baggage and/or freight hold (aft of wing):
containerised volume 36.2 m³ (1,280 cu ft)
bulk volume 43.9 m³ (1,552 cu ft)
Rear hold:
bulk volume 22.8 m³ (805 cu ft)
Series 30, 40 in upper-galley configuration:
Forward baggage and/or freight hold (forward of wing):
containerised volume 72.5 m³ (2,560 cu ft)
bulk volume 86.2 m³ (3,045 cu ft)
Centre baggage and/or freight hold (aft of wing):
containerised volume 45.3 m³ (1,600 cu ft)
bulk volume 54.8 m³ (1,935 cu ft)
Rear hold:
bulk volume 14.4 m³ (510 cu ft)

AREAS:
Wings, gross 367.7 m² (3,958 sq ft)
Ailerons: inboard (total) 7.68 m² (82.7 sq ft)
outboard (total) 9.76 m² (105.1 sq ft)
Trailing-edge flaps (total) 62.1 m² (668.2 sq ft)
Leading-edge slats (total) 43.84 m² (471.9 sq ft)
Spoilers (total) 12.73 m² (137.0 sq ft)
Fin 45.92 m² (494.29 sq ft)
Rudders (total) 10.29 m² (110.71 sq ft)
Tailplane 96.6 m² (1,040.2 sq ft)
Elevators (total) 27.7 m² (298.1 sq ft)

WEIGHTS AND LOADINGS:
Basic weight empty: Series 30 121,198 kg (267,197 lb)
Series 40 122,951 kg (271,062 lb)
Max payload: Series 30 48,330 kg (106,550 lb)
Series 40 46,243 kg (101,950 lb)
Max fuel weight:
standard 111,387 kg (245,566 lb)
small auxiliary tank installed 116,049 kg (255,844 lb)
large auxiliary tank installed 121,467 kg (267,790 lb)
Max T-O weight:
Series 30 259,450-263,085 kg (572,000-580,000 lb)
Series 40 (-20 engines) 251,745 kg (555,000 lb)
Series 40 (-59A engines) 259,450 kg (572,000 lb)
Max ramp weight:
Series 30 260,815 kg (575,000 lb)
Series 40 (-20 engines) 253,105 kg (558,000 lb)
Series 40 (-59A engines) 260,815 kg (575,000 lb)
Max zero-fuel weight:
Series 30, 40 166,922 kg (368,000 lb)
Max landing weight:
Series 30, 40 182,798 kg (403,000 lb)
Max wing loading:
Series 30 705.6 kg/m² (144.5 lb/sq ft)
Series 40 (-20 engines) 684.6 kg/m² (140.2 lb/sq ft)
Series 40 (-59A engines) 705.6 kg/m² (144.5 lb/sq ft)

PERFORMANCE (at max T-O weight except where indicated):
Never-exceed speed Mach 0.95
Max level speed at 7,620 m (25,000 ft) Mach 0.88 (530 knots; 982 km/h; 610 mph)
Max cruising speed at 9,145 m (30,000 ft):
Series 30 490 knots (908 km/h; 564 mph)
Series 40 (-20 engines) 489 knots (906 km/h; 563 mph)
Series 40 (-59A engines) 498 knots (922 km/h; 573 mph)
Normal cruising speed, all versions Mach 0.82
T-O speed (V_2):
Series 30 (-50C engines) 189 knots (351 km/h; 218 mph)
Series 40 (-20 engines) 187 knots (346 km/h; 215 mph)
Series 40 (-59A engines) 178 knots (330 km/h; 205 mph)
Landing speed (with full load of passengers and baggage):
Series 30, 40 138 knots (256 km/h; 159 mph)
Max rate of climb at S/L:
Series 30 884 m (2,900 ft)/min
Series 40 (-20 engines) 829 m (2,720 ft)/min
Series 40 (-59A engines) 762 m (2,500 ft)/min
Service ceiling:
Series 30 at 249,475 kg (550,000 lb) AUW 10,180 m (33,400 ft)
Series 40 (-20 engines) at 242,670 kg (535,000 lb) AUW 9,660 m (31,700 ft)
Series 40 (-59A engines) 9,965 m (32,700 ft)
En-route climb altitude, one engine out:
Series 30 at 251,744 kg (555,000 lb) AUW 4,360 m (14,300 ft)
Series 40 (-20 engines) at 247,205 kg (545,000 lb) AUW 3,565 m (11,700 ft)
Series 40 (-59A engines) at 254,010 kg (560,000 lb) AUW 5,135 m (16,850 ft)
FAA T-O field length:
Series 30 (-50C2 engines) 3,170 m (10,400 ft)
Series 40 (-59A engines) 3,135 m (10,280 ft)
FAA landing field length:
Series 30, 40 1,630 m (5,350 ft)
Range with max fuel, no payload:
Series 30 6,504 nm (12,055 km; 7,490 miles)
Series 40 6,305 nm (11,685 km; 7,260 miles)
Range with max payload at max zero-fuel weight:
Series 30 4,000 nm (7,413 km; 4,606 miles)
Series 40 (-20 engines) 3,500 nm (6,485 km; 4,030 miles)
Series 40 (-59A engines) 4,050 nm (7,505 km; 4,663 miles)

MCDONNELL DOUGLAS DC-10 SERIES 30CF and 30F

The **Series 30CF** is a convertible freighter version of the McDonnell Douglas DC-10 transport. Generally similar to the basic DC-10 Series 30 and 40, it is designed for easy conversion to either passenger or cargo configuration. Its payload can consist of 380 passengers and baggage or 64,860 kg (143,000 lb) of cargo over full intercontinental range; or up to 70,626 kg (155,700 lb) of cargo on domestic transcontinental routes.

The first Series 30CF was powered by three General Electric CF6-50A turbofans. It flew for the first time on 28 February 1973 and initial deliveries were made that year to Trans International Airlines and Overseas National Airways. In 1977, Overseas National Airways took delivery of two of the later DC-10 Srs 30CFs, powered by General Electric CF6-50C1 engines rated at 233.5 kN (52,500 lb st). More than 30 Series 30CFs were ordered, and this version also formed the basis for the USAF's **KC-10 Extender** tanker/transport described in a later entry.

In the passenger configuration, interior layout of the Series 30CF is generally similar to that of the DC-10, but the CF was designed to permit overnight conversion to an all-cargo configuration. This entails removal of seats, overhead baggage racks, forward food service centre, cloakrooms and carpeting from the main cabin, and installation of freight loading tracks and rollers, a cargo tiedown system and restraint nets. Coffee service fixtures and lavatories in the rear cabin may also be removed but are retained normally for regular cargo flights.

For cargo loading, two-channel network of roller conveyors, adjustable guide rails and pallet restraint fittings is installed in the seat tracks in the cabin floor by use of simple stud and locking pin devices. A 2.59 m high × 3.56 m wide (8 ft 6 in × 11 ft 8 in) cargo door in the side of the fuselage swings upward and allows easy loading of bulky freight.

A total of 30 standard 2.24 × 2.74 m (7 ft 4 in × 9 ft) cargo pallets, or 22 larger pallets measuring 2.24 × 3.18 m (7 ft 4 in × 10 ft 5 in) or 2.44 × 3.05 m (8 × 10 ft), can be accommodated in the main cabin. The Series 30CF with upstairs galleys also has 132.2 m³ (4,670 cu ft) of cargo space in the two lower cargo compartments for bulk freight, or for 26 half-size containers, or for five full-size pallets and 16 half-size containers.

The **Series 30F** is an all-freighter version of the DC-10. Generally similar to the Series 30CF, it does not incorporate those features which permit conversion to passenger configuration. Its payload capability is 80,282 kg (176,992 lb) of cargo over intercontinental range. The Series 30F is powered by CF6-50C2 engines. Nine DC-10 Series 30Fs were ordered by Federal Express. The first was delivered on 24 January 1986, and the last was due in 1988.

The main deck cargo compartment can accommodate 23 standard 2.24 × 3.18 m (7 ft 4 in × 10 ft 5 in) cargo pallets, or 51 1.57 × 2.24 m (5 ft 2 in × 7 ft 4 in) demi containers, or 30 pallets measuring 2.24 × 2.74 m (7 ft 4 in × 9 ft). Below-deck forward and centre cargo compartments can accommodate a further 117.8 m³ (4,160 cu ft) of bulk freight using 13 full-width containers, or 116.3 m³ (4,108 cu ft) using 26 half-width containers. The rear below-deck compartment provides a further 14.4 m³ (510 cu ft) of cargo volume.

Weight and performance figures are generally similar to those of the DC-10 Series 30 except as follows:

WEIGHTS:
Weight empty: CF 108,385 kg (238,948 lb)
F 106,505 kg (234,800 lb)
Max T-O weight: CF 267,620 kg (590,000 lb)
F 263,085 kg (580,000 lb)
Max landing weight: CF 190,962 kg (421,000 lb)
F 197,765 kg (436,000 lb)

PERFORMANCE:
Landing speed at max landing weight:
CF 149 knots (275 km/h; 171 mph)
F 152 knots (282 km/h; 175 mph)
FAA T-O field length at max T-O weight:
CF 3,170 m (10,400 ft)
F 3,292 m (10,800 ft)
FAA landing field length at max landing weight:
CF 1,868 m (6,130 ft)
F 1,926 m (6,320 ft)
Max range with max cargo:
CF 3,581 nm (6,637 km; 4,124 miles)
F 3,281 nm (6,080 km; 3,778 miles)

MCDONNELL DOUGLAS EXTENDER

US Air Force designation: KC-10A

The US Air Force announced on 19 December 1977 that, following evaluation of the Boeing 747 and McDonnell Douglas DC-10 to meet its requirement for an advanced tanker/cargo aircraft (ATCA), the DC-10 was selected to fulfil this role. Subsequently, the aircraft was designated KC-10A and named Extender.

On 20 November 1978, the Air Force authorised McDonnell Douglas to begin production of two KC-10As. Four more were ordered in November 1979, six in February 1981 and four in January 1982. Then, in December 1982, the Air Force entered into a multi-year contract with McDonnell Douglas for the purchase of 44 more KC-10s during the fiscal years 1983 to 1987, bringing the total to 60, the 59th of which was delivered in 1988. The last aircraft will be delivered in 1989, after 'prototype' conversion to add a hose-and-drogue capability (see later paragraph).

The first KC-10A (serial number 79-0433) made its first flight on 12 July 1980. The first to enter service (serial number 79-0434) was delivered on 17 March 1981 to Barksdale AFB, Louisiana, and the Extender is now in service with the US Air Force's 9th Air Refueling Squadron at March AFB, California, 32nd ARS at Barksdale AFB, and the 344th ARS and 911th ARS at Seymour Johnson AFB, North Carolina. The Air Force Reserve's 77th ARS (Associate) at Seymour Johnson, the 78th ARS (Associate) at Barksdale and the 79th ARS (Associate) at March share the aircraft with the active duty squadrons at their respective bases. By mid-1988 USAF KC-10As had completed their 14th consecutive six-month period in which they achieved a launch reliability of 99 per cent.

The modifications necessary to convert the DC-10-30CF to KC-10A configuration include the installation of fuel cells in the lower fuselage compartment; provision of a boom operator station, an aerial refuelling boom, a refuelling receptacle, an improved cargo handling system, and some military avionics systems. Various seating layouts are available in the forward area to permit the transport of a fighter squadron's essential support personnel. Seven bladder fuel cells are installed in the lower fuselage

KC-10A Extender military tanker/transport, in latest low visibility camouflage scheme, refuelling a Lockheed SR-71

compartments, three forward and four aft of the wing, mounted within framework that restrains and supports the cells. These are interconnected with the aircraft's basic fuel system, comprising 108,062 kg (238,236 lb). All can be used for extended range, or fuel from the lower deck cells and the aircraft's basic fuel system can be used for in-flight refuelling. The KC-10A is able to deliver 90,718 kg (200,000 lb) of fuel to a receiver 1,910 nm (3,540 km; 2,200 miles) from its home base, and return to base. In February 1985 a KC-10A made a nonstop, unrefuelled flight from Riyadh, Saudi Arabia, to March AFB, covering the 7,800 nm (14,455 km; 8,982 miles) in 17.8 hours and consuming 139,253 kg (307,000 lb) of fuel.

In June 1987 McDonnell Douglas was awarded a US Air Force contract to modify the KC-10A to three-point tanker configuration by fitting two Flight Refuelling Ltd Mk 32B underwing hose/drogue refuelling pods. Modification work will include additional wiring to the flight engineer's and refuelling operator's stations, a closed circuit television camera and monitor for the refuelling operator and piping and structural work in the aircraft's wings. The initial contract is for development of the removable pod system in the 60th KC-10A on order for the US Air Force. All other aircraft in the inventory will subsequently be modified to accept the pods, of which 39 more will be purchased. The pods will increase the KC-10A's fuel offload capability and offer system redundancy in over-water deployments of US Navy and US Marine Corps aircraft which use the hose and drogue method of in-flight refuelling.

The aerial refuelling operator's station, with access from the upper main deck, is sited in the lower rear fuselage and can accommodate the boom operator, an instructor and an observer, although only the boom operator is needed for a refuelling mission. The station has a rear window and a periscope observation system to give a wide field of view, and is pressurised and air-conditioned. The advanced aerial refuelling boom provides greater capability than the type installed in the KC-135; in particular, it has a greater transfer flow rate, being rated at 5,678 litres (1,500 US gallons; 1,249 Imp gallons)/min. The boom operator 'flies' it by means of a digital fly by wire control system supplied by Sperry Flight Systems. A hose/reel unit for probe and drogue refuelling is also installed, so that the KC-10A can service US Navy, US Marine Corps and NATO aircraft, as well as older types of fighter still serving with Reserve and ANG units.

The provision of a refuelling receptacle, above the flight deck of the KC-10A, allows greater flexibility on long-range cargo or refuelling operations, extending the range beyond the nominal 6,000 nm (11,112 km; 6,905 miles) with a 45,400 kg (100,000 lb) payload. The improved cargo handling system, by comparison with the basic DC-10-30CF, includes an increased floor area covered by omni-directional rollers, power rollers, and a portable winch to move cargo fore and aft.

Changes to the avionics are concerned chiefly with the deletion of equipment intended specifically for commercial operations, and the addition of UHF and secure com systems, Tacan, IFF, beacon transponder and a radar beacon mode. In addition to its tanker/transport role, the KC-10A can also act as a pathfinder for the aircraft it is refuelling, by providing supplementary navigation and communications services during long-range deployments.

The description of the DC-10 Series 30CF applies to the KC-10A, except as follows:

TYPE: Military flight refuelling/cargo aircraft.

WINGS, FUSELAGE, TAIL UNIT: As for DC-10-30, except for omission of most upper deck cabin windows and Srs 30CF lower deck cargo doors.

LANDING GEAR: As for DC-10-30, except nosewheel tyre pressure increased to 13.10 bars (190 lb/sq in); pressure in tyres on main units and centreline unit increased to 13.79 bars (200 lb/sq in) and 10.69 bars (155 lb/sq in) respectively.

POWER PLANT: Three 233.53 kN (52,500 lb st) General Electric CF6-50C2 turbofans. Basic aircraft fuel system comprises three integral main wing fuel tanks, and an integral auxiliary tank in the wing centre-section with a connected structural compartment fitted with a bladder cell, giving a total capacity of approximately 132,331 litres (34,958 US gallons; 29,108 Imp gallons). Details of transfer fuel loads given in introductory copy and under 'Avionics and Equipment'. Oil capacity 34.1 litres (9 US gallons; 7.5 Imp gallons).

ACCOMMODATION: Three crew on flight deck. Various seating arrangements for a limited number of essential support personnel at forward end of main cabin. Aerial refuelling station, with accommodation and large observation windows for boom operator, instructor and a student observer at aft end of lower fuselage compartment. Five passenger doors on main deck. A 2.59 × 3.56 m (8 ft 6 in × 11 ft 8 in) cargo door on the port side of the fuselage permits loading of standard USAF 463L pallets, bulk cargo or wheeled vehicles. Maximum capacity for 25 pallets with access from both sides of the compartment, or 27 pallets with a single aisle on the starboard side.

SYSTEMS: As for DC-10-30.

AVIONICS AND EQUIPMENT: Include some additional military avionics, comprising navigation, communication, Tacan, IFF transponder, and modified commercial weather radar. Seven Goodyear Aerospace rubberised fabric fuel cells mounted in the lower fuselage compartments, with combined capacity of 53,446 kg (117,829 lb) fuel, equivalent to approx 68,610 litres (18,125 US gallons; 15,092 Imp gallons), which are interconnected into the aircraft's basic fuel system. Flight refuelling boom mounted under rear fuselage, plus hose/reel unit for probe and drogue refuelling (24.4 m; 80 ft long hose and 66 cm; 26 in diameter drogue). Director lights to guide receiver. Flight refuelling receptacle mounted on fuselage upper surface above flight deck.

DIMENSIONS, EXTERNAL: As for DC-10-30 except:
Length overall	55.35 m (181 ft 7 in)
Height overall	17.70 m (58 ft 1 in)
Wheel track	10.57 m (34 ft 8 in)

AREAS: As for DC-10-30

WEIGHTS AND LOADING:
Operating weight empty:	
tanker	109,328 kg (241,027 lb)
cargo	110,945 kg (244,591 lb)
Fuel at T-O: tanker	158,291 kg (348,973 lb)
Design fuel capacity	161,508 kg (356,065 lb)
Max cargo payload	76,843 kg (169,409 lb)
Design max T-O weight	267,620 kg (590,000 lb)
Max wing loading	727.8 kg/m² (149.06 lb/sq ft)

PERFORMANCE:
Critical field length	3,124 m (10,250 ft)
Max range with max cargo	
	3,797 nm (7,032 km; 4,370 miles)
Max ferry range, unrefuelled	
	9,993 nm (18,507 km; 11,500 miles)

MCDONNELL DOUGLAS MD-11

First details of the MD-11, an advanced medium/long-range successor to the DC-10, were revealed at the 1985 Paris Air Show; development began in July 1985, with prototype construction commencing in March 1987. Derived from the DC-10, the aircraft features a longer fuselage than the DC-10 Series 30, aerodynamic improvements including upper and lower, outward inclined winglets, an advanced horizontal tail design with cambered aerofoil, reduced sweepback and integral 'trim tank' with a fuel capacity of 7,571 litres (2,000 US gallons; 1,665 Imp gallons), extended tailcone, an advanced two-crew all-digital flight deck, and restyled passenger interior. Power plants are either three General Electric CF6-80C2D1F, or three Pratt & Whitney PW4360 turbofans, providing a 27 per cent improvement in range over the DC-10 Series 30, with increased passenger capacity and a 31 per cent forecast reduction in seat/mile costs. The Rolls-Royce RB211-524L will become an option in 1993.

The use of composite materials is a key feature of the MD-11 design. More than 20 airframe components, including virtually all control surfaces on the wings and horizontal tail, engine inlets and cowls, and wing/fuselage fillets, are manufactured from composite materials such as carbonfibre, glassfibre and Kevlar. Aluminium-lithium fuselage floor beams will be introduced from the 14th production aircraft.

Four variants of the MD-11 were offered initially. The standard **MD-11** provides two-class accommodation for 323 passengers, with a maximum range of 7,008 nm (12,987 km; 8,070 miles). The extended-range **MD-11ER** has a fuselage 5.79 m (19 ft 0 in) shorter than the MD-11 and offers accommodation for 277 passengers, with a maximum range of 7,877 nm (14,597 km; 9,070 miles). The **MD-11 Combi** is a mixed passenger/cargo aircraft capable of carrying 4-10 cargo pallets and 168-240 two-class passengers, depending on configuration, at maximum ranges between 5,210 nm (9,656 km; 6,000 miles) and 6,947 nm (12,875 km; 8,000 miles). The **MD-11F** is an all-freight variant.

In the Spring of 1988 McDonnell Douglas announced plans to launch an **MD-11 Super Stretch** version which will have a fuselage some 5.49 m (18 ft 0 in) longer than that of the standard MD-11, offering standard seating for 370 passengers or, for airlines not requiring additional underfloor cargo space, an optional lower deck cabin that could accommodate 40 business class, 60 coach class or 90 economy class passengers, bringing total capacity to 450. The lower-deck cabin will be nearly 21.34 m (70 ft 0 in) long, with a maximum height of 1.98 m (6 ft 6 in) and four-abreast seating with a single aisle. Maximum range of the MD-11

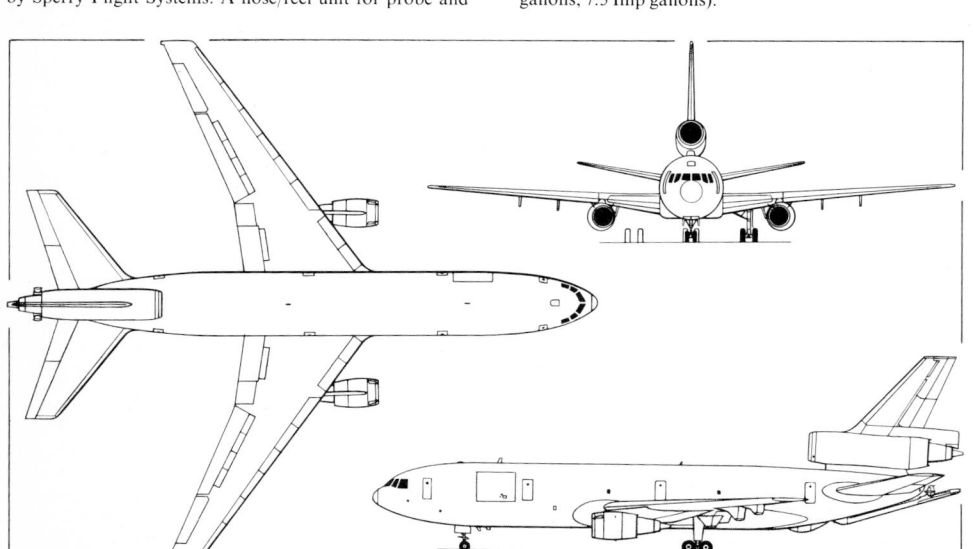

McDonnell Douglas KC-10A Extender advanced tanker/cargo aircraft for the US Air Force (*Pilot Press*)

Super Stretch will be about 4,460 nm (8,265 km; 5,136 miles).

Production of the MD-11 range is expected to reach the rate of one per week by 1991.

On 3 December 1986 the (then) British Caledonian Airways became launch customer for the MD-11 with an order for nine aircraft. This was followed on 8 December by an order from Mitsui & Company Limited of Japan for five MD-11s, and on 17 December by an order for 12 from Scandinavian Airlines System. McDonnell Douglas officially launched the MD-11 programme on 30 December 1986. By 1 July 1988 a total of 38 firm orders and 70 options/reservations had been received from customers including Alitalia (6 MD-11 Combis, with 4 options), Dragonair, Federal Express Corporation, Finnair (2 orders, 2 options), Guinness Peat Aviation, JAT (2 orders, 3 options); Korean Air (8 orders and options), Mitsui (5 for lease with CF6 engines), SAS (12), Swissair (12 orders, 6 options, with PW4360 engines), Thai Airways International (4 orders, 4 options with CF6 engines), Varig, and ZAS Airline of Egypt (1 Combi ordered, 1 option).

Assembly of the first MD-11 began on 9 March 1988. The first flight is scheduled for March 1989, followed by FAA certification a year later and airline service entry in April 1990. Suppliers for the MD-11 programme include Aeritalia (vertical stabiliser, rudder, fuselage panels and winglets), AP Precision Hydraulics (centreline and nose landing gear), Bendix Brake and Strut (mainwheels and carbon brakes), CASA (horizontal tail surfaces), Convair Division of General Dynamics (fuselage sections), Embraer (outboard flap sections), Fischer GmbH (composite flap hinge fairings), Pneumo Abex Corporation (main landing gear), Rohr Industries (engine pylons), Honeywell Sperry Flight Systems (advanced flight deck) and Westland Aerospace (flap vanes).

TYPE: Three-turbofan commercial transport.

WINGS: Cantilever low-wing monoplane of all-metal fail-safe construction, comprising two-spar structural box and chordwise ribs and bulkheads, and skins with spanwise stiffeners. Aerofoil section is a Douglas design. Dihedral 6°. Incidence 5° 51' at wing/fuselage intersection. Sweepback at quarter-chord 35°. Winglet extending above and below each wingtip. Upper winglet is of metal construction with ribs, spars and stiffened aluminium alloy skin, with carbonfibre trailing-edge; lower winglet is of carbonfibre construction. Inboard ailerons have metal structure with composites skin; outboard ailerons entirely of composite materials. Double-slotted trailing-edge flaps mounted on external hinges, with composite-skinned metal (inboard) and all-composites (outer flap) panel on each wing. Five all-metal spoiler panels on each wing, at rear edge of fixed wing structure, forward of flaps. Spoilers are of aluminium alloy honeycomb construction with aluminium alloy skinning. Full-span two-position all-metal leading-edge slats, eight segments per wing. Ailerons are powered by National Water Lift hydraulic actuators. All leading-edge outer slat segments are anti-iced with engine bleed air.

FUSELAGE: Aluminium alloy semi-monocoque fail-safe structure of circular cross-section. Passenger and cargo areas are pressurised.

TAIL UNIT: Electro-hydraulically actuated variable incidence tailplane has metal spars and ribs, aluminium alloy skinning, and carbonfibre trailing-edge. Slotted elevators of carbonfibre construction. Elevators powered by Parker Hannifin and Teijin Seiki actuators. Leading-edge of tailplane is anti-iced with bleed air from No. 2 engine.

LANDING GEAR: Hydraulically retractable tricycle type, with additional twin-wheel main unit mounted on the fuselage centreline. Nosewheel and centreline units retract forward, main units inward into fuselage. Twin-wheel steerable nose unit. Main gear comprises two four-wheel bogies. Oleo-pneumatic shock absorbers in all units.

Loral nosewheels and Goodyear tyres size 40 × 15.5-16, pressure 13.44 bars (195 lb/sq in). Main and centreline units have Bendix wheels and Goodyear tyres size 54 × 21-24, pressure 13.79 bars (200 lb/sq in). Bendix carbon brakes with air convection cooling; Loral anti-skid system.

POWER PLANT: Three Pratt & Whitney PW4360 turbofans, each rated at 266.9 kN (60,000 lb st), or three General Electric CF6-80C2D1F turbofans, each rated at 273.57 kN (61,500 lb st), or three Rolls-Royce RB211-524L turbofans, each rated at 289-311 kN (65,000-70,000 lb st), two of which are mounted on underwing pylons, the third above the rear fuselage at the base of the fin. Rear engine inlet duct and fan cowl doors, and nose cowl outer barrels on wing-mounted engines, are of composites construction. Inner surfaces of engine nacelles are acoustically treated. Refuelling point in leading-edge of each wing.

ACCOMMODATION: Crew of two. Standard mixed class seating for 323 (MD-11), 214 (Combi) or 277 (MD-11ER). Crew door and three passenger doors each side, all eight of which open sliding inward and upward. Two freight holds below cabin, forward and aft of wing, and one bulk cargo compartment in rear fuselage. Forward freight hold is heated and ventilated; rear freight hold heated only. MD-11 Combi has a cargo door in centre compartment on port side of fuselage for loading of pallets, a main deck cargo door on port rear side of cabin, and two additional emergency exit doors, one on each side of passenger cabin immediately forward of the main deck cargo door.

SYSTEMS: Air-conditioning system comprises three AiResearch air bearing air cycle units with two automatic digital pressure controllers and electro-manual backup. Cabin max pressure differential 0.59 bars (8.6 lb/sq in). Three independent hydraulic systems for operation of flight controls and braking, with motor/pump interconnects to allow one system to power another. Electrical system comprises three 400Hz, 100/120kVA integrated drive generators, one per engine; one 90kVA generator in APU; 50Ah battery; four transformer-rectifiers to convert AC power to DC; and 25kVA drop-out air driven emergency generator. Pneumatic system, max controlled pressure 0.27-0.41 bars (4-6 lb/sq in) at 230°C, supplies air-conditioning, anti-icing for wing (outer slats) and tailplane leading-edges, galley vent jet pump, and cargo compartment floor heating. Plumbed gaseous oxygen system for crew, using EROS equipment; chemical oxygen generators with automatically deploying masks for passengers. Portable oxygen cylinders for attendants and first aid. Engine bleed air anti-icing for wing and tailplane leading-edges and engine cowlings. De-icing for windscreens, angle-of-attack sensors, TAT probe and static port plate. Garrett TSCP700-4E APU.

AVIONICS: Avionics integrator Honeywell responsible for flight guidance/flight deck system consisting of 44 line-replaceable units. These include aircraft system controllers (ASC) that perform flight engineering control and monitoring functions, providing automated hydraulic, electrical, environmental and fuel systems; a central fault display system (CFDS); an electronic instrument system (EIS) using six 20 × 20 cm (8 × 8 in) colour CRTs; a flight management system (FMS); an automatic flight system (AFS) featuring Cat IIIB autoland, windshear detection and guidance computer with escape capability and full-time longitudinal stability augmentation; a laser inertial reference system (IRS); and a digital air data computer (DADC).

The following data apply to the standard MD-11, except where indicated:

DIMENSIONS, EXTERNAL:

Wing span	51.66 m (169 ft 6 in)
Wing chord: at root	10.71 m (35 ft 1¾ in)
at tip	2.73 m (8 ft 11½ in)
Wing aspect ratio	7.5
Length overall: standard	61.21 m (200 ft 10 in)
MD-11ER	55.55 m (182 ft 3 in)
Fuselage length: standard	58.65 m (192 ft 5 in)
MD-11ER	52.86 m (173 ft 5 in)
Max fuselage diameter	6.02 m (19 ft 9 in)
Height overall	17.60 m (57 ft 9 in)
Tailplane span	18.03 m (59 ft 2 in)
Wheel track	10.57 m (34 ft 8 in)
Wheelbase: standard	24.61 m (80 ft 9 in)
MD-11ER	22.07 m (72 ft 5 in)
Crew doors (two, each): Height	1.93 m (6 ft 4 in)
Width	0.81 m (2 ft 8 in)
Passenger doors (six, each): Height	1.93 m (6 ft 4 in)
Width	1.07 m (3 ft 6 in)
* Forward cargo door: Height	1.68 m (5 ft 6 in)
Width	2.64 m (8 ft 8 in)
Centre cargo door (standard): Height	1.68 m (5 ft 6 in)
Width	1.78 m (5 ft 10 in)
Bulk cargo door: Height	0.91 m (3 ft 0 in)
Width	0.76 m (2 ft 6 in)
Combi main deck cargo door (port, rear):	
Height	2.59 m (8 ft 6 in)
Width	4.06 m (13 ft 4 in)
Combi emergency exits (two, each):	
Height	1.52 m (5 ft 0 in)
Width	0.71 m (2 ft 4 in)

* Centre cargo door of Combi also this size

DIMENSIONS, INTERNAL:

Cabin:	
Length, flight deck door to rear bulkhead	
	46.51 m (152 ft 7¼ in)
Max width	5.71 m (18 ft 9 in)
Max height	2.41 m (7 ft 11 in)
Floor area, incl galleys and toilets	
	244.7 m² (2,634.0 sq ft)
Volume, incl galleys and toilets	
	599.3 m³ (21,165 cu ft)
Baggage holds, volume:	
forward	80.5 m³ (2,844 cu ft)
centre	62.6 m³ (2,212 cu ft)
rear	14.4 m³ (510 cu ft)

AREAS:

Wings, gross	338.9 m² (3,648 sq ft)
Winglets, each	3.71 m² (40.0 sq ft)
Vertical tail surfaces, total	56.2 m² (605.0 sq ft)
Horizontal tail surfaces, total	85.5 m² (920.0 sq ft)

WEIGHTS:

Weight empty	100,153 kg (220,800 lb)
Max payload	55,656 kg (122,700 lb)
Max fuel weight	117,480 kg (259,000 lb)
Max T-O weight	273,289 kg (602,500 lb)
Max zero-fuel weight	181,437 kg (400,000 lb)
Max landing weight	195,044 kg (430,000 lb)

PERFORMANCE (estimated: A: MD-11, B: MD-11ER, C: MD-11F, D: MD-11 Combi):

Never-exceed speed: all	Mach 0.95
Max level speed at 8,230 m (27,000 ft): all	
	Mach 0.87 (519 knots; 962 km/h; 597 mph)
Max cruising speed at 9,150 m (30,000 ft):	
A, C, D	503 knots (932 km/h; 579 mph)
B	502 knots (930 km/h; 578 mph)
Econ cruising speed at 10,670 m (35,000 ft): all	
	473 knots (876 km/h; 544 mph)
Stalling speed, power on:	
10° flap:	
A, C, D	148 knots (274 km/h; 171 mph)
B	149 knots (276 km/h; 172 mph)
25° flap:	
A, C, D	142 knots (263 km/h; 164 mph)
B	144 knots (267 km/h; 166 mph)
Max rate of climb at S/L: A, C, D	844 m (2,770 ft)/min
B	850 m (2,790 ft)/min
Rate of climb at S/L, one engine out:	
A, C, D	414 m (1,360 ft)/min
B	401 m (1,380 ft)/min
Service ceiling: A, C, D	9,935 m (32,600 ft)
B	9,845 m (32,300 ft)
Service ceiling, one engine out:	
A, C, D	6,310 m (20,700 ft)
B	6,400 m (21,000 ft)
T-O run: A, C, D	2,207 m (7,240 ft)
B	2,109 m (6,920 ft)
T-O to 10.7 m (35 ft): A, C, D	2,926 m (9,600 ft)
B	2,807 m (9,210 ft)
Landing from 15 m (50 ft) at max landing weight:	
A	1,966 m (6,450 ft)
B	1,917 m (6,290 ft)
C	2,130 m (6,990 ft)
D	2,079 m (6,820 ft)
Runway LCN, rigid pavement, taxi weight of 276,010 kg (608,500 lb)	105
Runway ACN, conditions as above	65
Range with max payload, at max zero-fuel weight:	
A	5,002 nm (9,270 km; 5,760 miles)
B	5,700 nm (10,563 km; 6,564 miles)
C	3,542 nm (6,564 km; 4,079 miles)
D	4,024 nm (7,457 km; 4,634 miles)

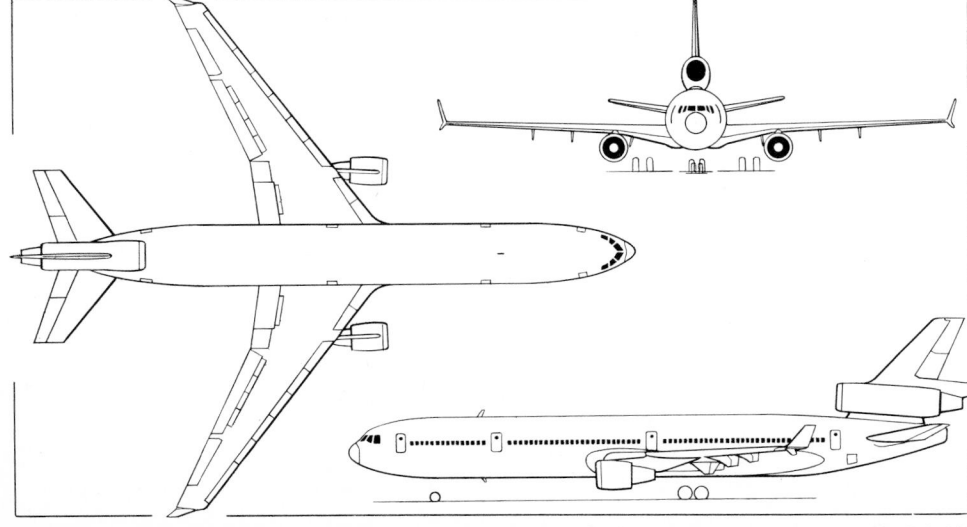

McDonnell Douglas MD-11, designed as an advanced higher-capacity successor to the DC-10
(Pilot Press)

McDONNELL DOUGLAS C-17A

The US Air Force announced on 29 August 1981 that McDonnell Douglas had been selected as prime contractor to develop the new C-17A long-range cargo aircraft, following evaluation of three designs entered for its C-X competition.

The C-17A will be a long-range, heavy lift air-refuellable cargo transport, intended primarily to provide inter-theatre airlift of outsize loads, including tanks and infantry fighting vehicles, directly into airfields in potential conflict areas. Design requirements therefore include outstanding STOL performance.

In January 1982 the Air Force stated that it did not plan full scale development and production of the C-17A at that time. However, on 26 July 1982 McDonnell Douglas received a contract for a 'modestly paced' research and development programme, to include such C-17A technologies as would also benefit other airlift programmes, and preserving the option to proceed to full scale engineering development of the C-17A if eventually deemed appropriate. A full scale development contract, covering the construction of one flying prototype and two structural test aircraft was awarded on 31 December 1985.

Construction of the first C-17A began in 1987, with the first flight scheduled for August 1990 and the FSD phase continuing until July 1992. The first two production C-17As, ordered on 20 January 1988, are due to fly in late 1990 and early 1991. The first four production aircraft and the prototype will be used in the test programme. The USAF plans to acquire 210 aircraft by the year 2000, at a unit cost of $178 million. The 437th MAW at Charleston AFB, South Carolina, has been designated as the first C-17A unit, and is due to achieve IOC in 1992.

Major subassemblies are produced at Salt Lake City, Utah, and Macon, Georgia. Subcontractors in the C-17A programme include Beech Aircraft Corporation (composite winglets); Delco Electronics Corporation (mission computer and electronic display system); Grumman Aerostructures (composite ailerons, rudder and elevators); GEC Avionics (advanced head-up displays); Lockheed Burbank (wing spars, stringers, ribs, bulkheads, leading-edge slats and main wing assembly); Honeywell Inc (support equipment); Vought Aero Products (vertical and horizontal stabilisers, engine nacelles and thrust reversers); Murdock Engineering Company (engine pylons); Reynolds Metals Company (wing skins); Plessey (fuel pumps); and Honeywell Sperry (electronic flight control system and air data computers). McDonnell Douglas Helicopter Co will manufacture the tailcone, wing/fuselage fillets, wing trailing-edge panels, main landing gear fairings and flap hinge fairings, all of composites materials.

The C-17A, making use of technology developed for the company's earlier YC-15 advanced medium STOL transport prototypes (see 1979-80 *Jane's*), will be able to airlift outsize combat equipment which at present can be carried only by the Lockheed C-5 Galaxy, and offer a short field performance currently provided only by the C-130 Hercules. It will be able to operate from runways only 915 m (3,000 ft) long and 18.3 m (60 ft) wide; on the ground, it will be able to execute a 180° turn in only 27.4 m (90 ft); and a fully loaded aircraft, using thrust reversal, will be able to reverse up a 1 in 50 gradient.

TYPE: Long-range heavy lift cargo transport.

AIRFRAME: General survivability features include ample provisions for crew and troop shielding; redundant load paths, to minimise the effects of battle damage; facility for critical line-replaceable units (LRUs) to be replaced in flight, and for all LRUs to be replaced without removing other equipment.

WINGS: Cantilever high-wing monoplane, of supercritical section with 25° sweepback. NASA type 2.90 m (9.5 ft) tall winglet of composites construction at each tip, also of supercritical section. Full span leading-edge slats. Externally blown flap system, developed from that used on McDonnell Douglas YC-15, to reduce final approach and landing speeds by directing engine efflux over single-hinged, double-slotted Fowler trailing-edge flaps to provide extra lift. Flaps extend over approx two-thirds of each trailing-edge. Four-segment spoilers/lift dumpers forward of flaps on each wing. Ailerons are of composites construction.

FUSELAGE: Conventional semi-monocoque fail-safe structure, upswept at rear. Rear-loading ramp/door in underside of rear fuselage. Twin strakes under extreme rear of fuselage.

TAIL UNIT: Cantilever T tail. Sweptback fin, with small dorsal fillet; inset rudder, in upper and lower segments. Sweptback tailplane, with two inboard and two outboard elevators.

LANDING GEAR: Hydraulically retractable tricycle type, with free-fall emergency extension. Twin-wheel Menasco nose unit and six-wheel main units, designed for sink rate of 5.03 m (16.5 ft)/s and suitable for operation from paved runways or unpaved strips. Cleveland mainwheel units, each consisting of two legs in tandem with three wheels on each leg, retract into fairings on lower fuselage sides; Menasco nose unit is forward retracting.

POWER PLANT: Four 164.6 kN (37,000 lb st) Pratt & Whitney F117-PW-100 turbofans, pylon-mounted in individual underwing pods and each fitted with a directed-flow thrust reverser deployable both in flight and on the ground. Provision for in-flight refuelling.

ACCOMMODATION: Normal flight crew of pilot and co-pilot, side by side on flight deck, plus a loadmaster. Provision for additional crew members if required for special missions. Access to flight deck via downward opening airstair door on port side of lower forward fuselage. Bunks for crew immediately aft of flight deck area; crew comfort station at forward end of cargo hold. Main cargo hold able to accommodate Army wheeled vehicles, including five-ton expandable vans in two side by side rows, or Jeeps in triple rows, or up to three AH-64A Apache attack helicopters, with straight-in loading via hydraulically actuated rear loading ramp which forms underside of rear fuselage when retracted. Alternatively, aircraft can be equipped as a troop transport, with rows of stowable tip-up seats along each side wall and a row of seats which can be erected along the centreline, or with litters for medical evacuation mission. Airdrop capability includes single platforms of up to 27,215 kg (60,000 lb), or up to 102 paratroops. The C-17A will be the only aircraft able to airdrop outsize firepower such as the US Army's new infantry fighting vehicle (three of which comprise one deployment load); it will also be able to carry the M1 main battle tank in combination with other vehicles. The cargo handling system includes rails for airdrops and rails/rollers for normal cargo handling. Each row of rails/rollers can be converted quickly by a single loadmaster from one configuration to the other. Cargo tiedown rings, each with an 11,340 kg (25,000 lb) load restraint capability, are installed throughout the cargo area floor. Three quick-erecting litter stanchions, each supporting four litters, permanently installed. Main access to cargo hold is via rear loading ramp, which is itself capable of supporting 18,145 kg (40,000 lb) of cargo. Undersurface of rear fuselage aft of ramp is formed by door which moves upward inside fuselage to facilitate loading and unloading. Paratroop door at rear on each side, and two overwater emergency exits overhead, aft of the paratroop doors, and two overhead forward of the wing box.

SYSTEMS: Include AiResearch electronically controlled bleed air system; fully redundant flight control and hydraulic systems; independent fuel feed systems; electrical system; Garrett GTCP331 APU (in starboard landing gear pod), operable in flight, provides power for environmental control system, engine starting, and on-ground electronics requirements; onboard inert gas generating system (OBIGGS); explosion protection system, pressurised by engine bleed air at 3.1 bars (45 lb/sq in) to produce NEA 4 gas and governed by a Gull Inc system controller; and fire suppression system. All phases of cargo operation and configuration change capable of being handled by one loadmaster.

AVIONICS AND EQUIPMENT: Honeywell Sperry electronic flight control system, and dual air data computers, with advanced digital avionics and four full-colour multi-function displays (MFDs), two GEC Avionics full flight regime head-up displays, plus integrated mission and communications keyboards (MCKs) and displays (MCDs). Primary flight data presented on HUD and a selectable mode for the MFD. Horizontal navigation situation computer-generated flight plan and weather radar overlay selectable on MFD. Station keeping (SKE), engine and flight control configuration data available on MFDs. All frequency tuning for nav/com accomplished from glareshield control panel. MCD has frequency and channel pre-storage facility and provides for flight plan entry manually or by pre-programmed cassette, permitting insertion of in-flight planning changes without disturbing ongoing navigation. All MCD information for flight and navigation monitoring is presented on the HUD and MFDs. Teledyne Controls warning and caution system. Master warning caution annunciator provides automatic monitoring of all main systems and provides visual alerts on glareshields, aural and voice alerts on intercom. Cargo hold equipment includes integral rails and roller conveyors, in floor (incl ramp); sidewall rails; tiedown rings of 11,340 kg (25,000 lb) rating, spaced at 61 cm (24 in) intervals; cargo winch and retrieval winch; and Oxford type tow/release for cargo platforms. Other equipment suppliers include Bendix (AN/APS-133(V) weather/mapping radar), Delco Electronics (mission computer and electronic control system), Hamilton Standard (aircraft and propulsion data management computer), Honeywell (automatic test equipment, and support equipment data acquisition and control system), LTV (Sierra Research Division) (station keeping equipment), and Telephonic Corporation (radio management system). Development of defensive electronic systems was authorised in 1988.

DIMENSIONS, EXTERNAL:

Wing span	50.29 m (165 ft 0 in)
Length overall	53.39 m (175 ft 2 in)
Height overall	17.68 m (58 ft 0 in)

DIMENSIONS, INTERNAL:

Cargo compartment:

Length, incl 5.99 m (19 ft 8 in) rear loading ramp	
	26.82 m (88 ft 0 in)
Max width	5.49 m (18 ft 0 in)
Height under wing	3.76 m (12 ft 4 in)
Max height	4.11 m (13 ft 6 in)
Volume	592 m³ (20,900 cu ft)

AREAS:

Wings, gross	353 m² (3,800 sq ft)
Ailerons, total	11.83 m² (127.34 sq ft)

WEIGHTS:

Operating weight empty	120,200 kg (265,000 lb)
Typical payload:	
inter-theatre logistics mission (2.5g load factor)	
	58,605 kg (129,200 lb)
heavy logistics mission (2.25g load factor)	
	71,895 kg (158,500 lb)
Max payload (2.25g load factor)	
	78,110 kg (172,200 lb)
Max T-O weight	263,083 kg (580,000 lb)

PERFORMANCE (estimated):

Normal cruising speed at high altitude	Mach 0.77
Max cruising speed at low altitude	
	350 knots (648 km/h; 403 mph) CAS
Airdrop speed at S/L	
	115-250 knots (213-463 km/h; 132-288 mph) CAS
Airdrop speed at 7,620 m (25,000 ft)	
	130-250 knots (241-463 km/h; 150-288 mph) CAS
Approach speed with max payload	
	115 knots (213 km/h; 132 mph) CAS
Min ground turning radius:	
three-point turn	25 m (82 ft)
180° turn	34.74 m (114 ft)
wingtip/tailplane clearance	72.24 m (237 ft)
Runway LCN (paved surface)	better than 40
T-O field length with 75,750 kg (167,000 lb) payload	
	2,320 m (7,600 ft)
Landing field length with 75,750 kg (167,000 lb) payload, using thrust reversal	915 m (3,000 ft)
Radius, T-O with 39,055 kg (86,100 lb) payload in 975 m (3,200 ft), land in 760 m (2,500 ft), T-O with similar payload in 885 m (2,900 ft) and land in 730 m (2,400 ft), all at load factor of 3g, no in-flight refuelling	
	500 nm (925 km; 575 miles)
Radius, T-O with 63,865 kg (140,800 lb) payload in 2,320 m (7,600 ft) at load factor of 2.25g, land in 915 m	

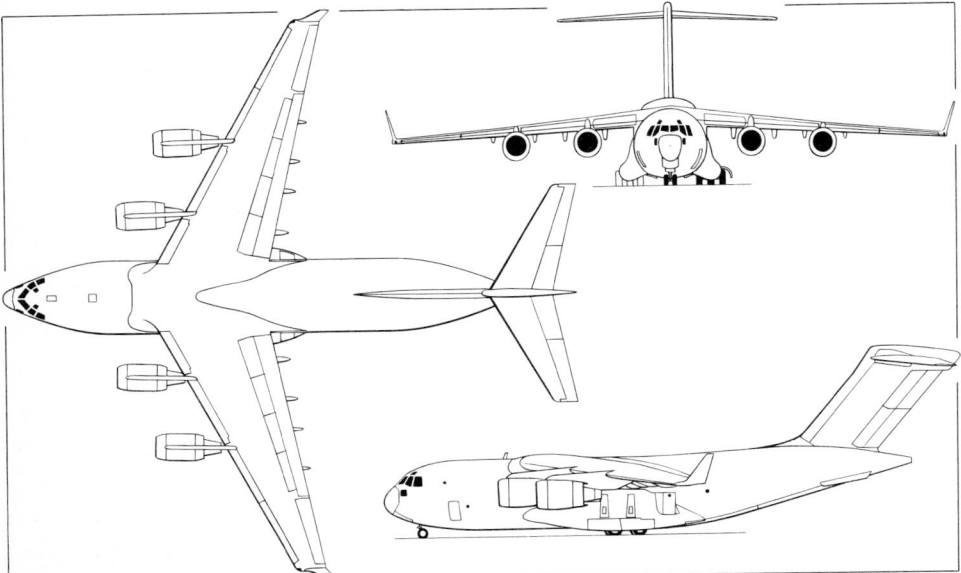

McDonnell Douglas C-17A long-range heavy lift cargo transport (*Pilot Press*)

(3,000 ft), T-O with zero payload (load factor of 3*g*) in 730 m (2,400 ft) and land in 610 m (2,000 ft), no in-flight refuelling 1,900 nm (3,520 km; 2,190 miles)
Range with payloads indicated, with no in-flight refuelling:
75,750 kg (167,000 lb), T-O in 2,320 m (7,600 ft), land in 915 m (3,000 ft), load factor of 2.25*g*
2,400 nm (4,445 km; 2,765 miles)
71,895 kg (158,500 lb), T-O in 2,320 m (7,600 ft), land in 885 m (2,900 ft), load factor of 2.25*g*
2,700 nm (5,000 km; 3,110 miles)
58,605 kg (129,200 lb), T-O in 1,830 m (6,000 ft), land in 795 m (2,600 ft), load factor of 2.5*g*
2,800 nm (5,190 km; 3,225 miles)
self-ferry (zero payload), T-O in 1,100 m (3,600 ft), land in 610 m (2,000 ft), load factor of 2.5*g*
5,000 nm (9,265 km; 5,755 miles)

MCDONNELL DOUGLAS/BAe T45TS

US Navy designation: T-45 Goshawk

Details of the T-45 can be found under the McDonnell Douglas/BAe entry in the International section.

MCDONNELL DOUGLAS HELICOPTER COMPANY (Subsidiary of McDonnell Douglas Corporation)

5000 East McDowell Road, Mesa, Arizona 85205-9797
Telephone: (602) 891 3000
Telex: 3719337 MD HC C MESA
Fax: (602) 891 5599
OTHER WORKS: Culver City, California 90230
Telephone: (213) 305 5000
Telex: 182436 HU HELI C CULV
CHAIRMAN: Robert C. Little
PRESIDENT AND CHIEF EXECUTIVE OFFICER:
William P. Brown
EXECUTIVE VICE-PRESIDENTS:
Allen C. Haggerty (Engineering and Operations)
Norman B. Hirsh (Programme Management)
VICE-PRESIDENT, RESEARCH AND ENGINEERING:
Dean C. Borgman
VICE-PRESIDENT, MARKETING: VeLoy J. Varner
DIRECTOR, PUBLIC AFFAIRS: Robert W. Mack

On 6 January 1984, Hughes Helicopters Inc became a subsidiary of the McDonnell Douglas Corporation; on 27 August 1985 the company name was changed to McDonnell Douglas Helicopter Company. More than 4,000 of nearly 7,000 helicopters produced are in operation by civil and military operators in nearly 100 countries worldwide, and a series of advanced models is being developed. Research activities include work on composites rotor blades, hubs and tailbooms, metal insulation and IR suppression systems, the US Army's LHX programme, and Chain Gun ordnance systems for air and ground applications.

Mesa, Arizona, the site of the company's main production and flight test facility, comprises a 52,955 m² (570,000 sq ft) Apache assembly, flight test and delivery centre, to which was added a further 123,980 m² (1,334,500 sq ft) complex of office, engineering and other buildings completed in 1986. In mid-1986 Mesa became the new official headquarters of the company, with a workforce due to total 5,000 by the end of 1987 and 7,000 by 1990. The MD 500/530 line was transferred to Mesa from California in the Winter of 1986-87. The combined production rate of MD 500/530s and Apaches is about 16 per month.

In 1986 MDHC sold its Model 300 helicopter line to Schweizer Aircraft Corporation of Elmira, New York (which see), which had been producing the helicopter under a licensing agreement since 1983. Licensees building McDonnell Douglas helicopters in 1988 were RACA in Argentina (500D and 500E civil variants); Kawasaki in Japan (500D civil and military variants);Korean Air in the Republic of Korea (500D and 500E civil and military, excluding TOW variants, and fuselages for all MD 500s sold worldwide); and BredaNardi in Italy (300C, 500D, 500E and 530F civil variants).

McDonnell Douglas MD 500E executive helicopter

MCDONNELL DOUGLAS MD 500/520/530 (CIVIL VERSIONS)

The MD 500, which entered full scale production in November 1968, originated as a civil development of the OH-6A Cayuse military helicopter last described in the 1977-78 *Jane's*. From it have since been developed several military export versions; these are listed separately. Including the OH-6A, more than 4,000 helicopters of the MD 500/530 series had been built by early 1988.

Civil versions of the MD 500 are as follows:

MD 500. Initial basic production version, with Allison 250-C18A turboshaft.

MD 500C. Similar to MD 500, but with Allison 250-C20 engine and improved 'hot and high' performance. Licence manufacture was also undertaken by RACA (Argentina) and Kawasaki (Japan). US production ended in 1978.

MD 500D. Announced in February 1975, the 500D is similar in size and general appearance to the MD 500C. It differs in having a derated Allison 250-C20B engine; a five-blade main rotor; and a T tail, which gives greater flight stability in both high and low speed regimes, as well as better handling characteristics in abnormal manoeuvres. First flight of the prototype took place in August 1974, and the first flight of a production aircraft was made on 9 October 1975. Now replaced on US production line by MD 500E. Licence manufacture continues by RACA (Argentina), BredaNardi (Italy), Kawasaki (Japan) and Korean Air (South Korea). US production ended in 1983.

MD 500E. Longer and more streamlined nose, providing increased legroom for front seat occupants. Replaced MD 500D in 1982 as basic US production version. It retains the 500D's Allison 250-C20B engine. Rear seat passengers have 12 per cent more headroom, additional legroom and, as a result of lowering the bulkhead between front and rear seats, a 50 per cent improvement in forward view. First flown (N5294A) on 28 January 1982, the MD 500E incorporates improvements that include a new auxiliary fuel tank, better soundproofing around the transmission and cooling fan, longer main rotor blade abrasion strips, new endplate fins, new 'T' grouping of flight instruments, and an improved heating system. A four-blade tail rotor, a fore-and-aft litter kit, and an air-conditioning system are optional. Deliveries began in December 1982, following FAA certification in the preceding month. By early 1988 more than 225 had been delivered, including specially equipped models for law enforcement delivered to Police Departments in Atlanta, Oklahoma City, Puerto Rico, St Louis, Tampa, Washington DC, and to 25 law enforcement agencies in the State of California, including 10 for the Los Angeles County Sheriff's Department. Typically, law enforcement MD 500Es are each equipped with a 30 million candlepower SX-16 Nightsun searchlight, siren, emergency services communications systems and a rescue net. A four-blade 'Quiet Knight' tail rotor has also been developed to reduce the helicopter's noise level from the ground. Eight MD 500Es have been delivered to the US Army Aviation Systems Command at St Louis.

In June 1987 the Italian Air Force selected the MD 500E for its future helicopter pilot training requirements. BredaNardi SpA, MDHC's Italian licensee, is responsible for the prototype conversion, which includes provision for IFR operation. Up to 50 MD 500Es are required by the Italian Air Force.

The original MD 500E prototype was retrofitted with an Allison 250-C20R turboshaft in support of the certification of this engine for use in the MD 520L. It first flew in this form on 8 December 1986, and completed the planned 15 hours of engineering flight tests on 21 August 1987.

MD 520L. Developed version of MD 500E scheduled for certification in December 1988. New features include an Allison 250-C20R turboshaft rated at 317 kW (425 shp) for T-O and 280 kW (375 shp) max continuous; larger five-blade main rotor; four-blade 'quiet' tail rotor; extended tail boom; new tail rotor gearbox which reduces tail rotor speed and noise; enhanced lifting capability; and increased high altitude operating capability.

MD 520N. Modified MD 500 with NOTAR tailboom. Described separately.

MD 530F Lifter. Derived from the MD 500D, this version is intended for operation at high altitudes or high temperatures. It has the fuselage configuration of the 500E and a derated Allison 250-C30 turboshaft engine which fits into the same engine compartment as the 250-C20B. FAA approval to increase the T-O rating from 280 kW (375 shp) to 317 kW (425 shp) was granted on 11 July 1985. To provide additional lift capability, the main rotor has a 0.3 m (1 ft) increase in diameter, and diameter of the tail rotor is increased by 5 cm (2 in). A cargo hook kit is available, capable of lifting an external load of up to 907 kg (2,000 lb). First flight was made on 22 October 1982; FAA certification was granted on 29 July 1983 and the first customer aircraft was delivered to Rogers Helicopters Inc on 20 January 1984. Deliveries include 26 for Iraq, for use in training, transportation and agricultural roles.

MD 530K. Developed version of MD 530F, with improvements as listed for MD 520L, but powered by an Allison 250-C30 turboshaft. Certification expected in June 1989.

McDonnell Douglas Helicopter Company delivered 69 completed MD 500/530s and assembly kits during 1987, and expected to deliver 80 in 1988.

The following details apply to the current MD 500E and 530F, except where indicated:

TYPE: Turbine powered civil light helicopter.

ROTOR SYSTEM: Five-blade fully articulated main rotor, with blades attached to laminated strap retention system by means of quick-disconnect pins for folding. Each blade consists of an extruded aluminium spar hot-bonded to one-piece wraparound aluminium skin. Trim tab outboard on each blade. Main rotor blades can be folded. Two-blade tail rotor, each blade comprising a swaged steel tube spar and metal skin covering. Four-blade 'quiet' tail rotor, and main rotor brake, optional.

ROTOR DRIVE: Three sets of bevel gears, three driveshafts and one overrunning clutch. Main rotor/engine rpm ratio 1 : 12.594. Tail rotor/engine rpm ratio 1 : 1.956.

FUSELAGE: Aluminium semi-monocoque structure of pod and boom type. Clamshell doors at rear of pod give access to engine and accessories.

TAIL UNIT: T tail with horizontal stabiliser at tip of narrow chord sweptback fin; small auxiliary fin at tip of tailplane on each side; narrow chord sweptback ventral fin with integral tailskid to protect tail rotor in tail-down attitude near ground.

LANDING GEAR: Tubular skids carried on McDonnell Douglas oleo-pneumatic shock absorbers. Utility floats, snow skis and emergency inflatable floats optional.

POWER PLANT: MD 500E is powered by a 313 kW (420 shp) Allison 250-C20B turboshaft, which is derated to 280 kW (375 shp) for T-O and has a max continuous rating of 261 kW (350 shp). Allison 250-C20R, rated at 317 kW (425 shp) for T-O and 280 kW (375 shp) max continuous, optional for 500E and 530F, standard for 520L. MD 530F has a 485 kW (650 shp) Allison 250-C30 turboshaft, derated to 317 kW (425 shp) for take-off and 261 kW (350 shp) max continuous. Two interconnected bladder fuel tanks with combined usable capacity of 240 litres (63.4 US gallons; 52.8 Imp gallons). Self-sealing fuel tank optional. Refuelling point on starboard side of fuselage. Auxiliary fuel system, with 79.5 litre (21 US gallon; 17.5 Imp gallon) internal tank, available optionally. Oil capacity 5.7 litres (1.5 US gallons; 1.2 Imp gallons).

ACCOMMODATION: Forward bench seat for pilot and two passengers, with two or four passengers, or two litter patients and one medical attendant, in rear portion of cabin. Low-back front seats and individual rear seats, with fabric or leather upholstery, optional. Baggage space, capacity 0.31 m³ (11 cu ft), under and behind rear seat in five-seat form. Clear space for 1.19 m³ (42 cu ft) of cargo or baggage with only three front seats in place. Two doors on each side. Interior soundproofing optional.

SYSTEMS: Aero Engineering Corporation air-conditioning system or Fargo pod mounted air-conditioner optional. Electrical system in 500D includes a 150A engine driven generator and a nickel-cadmium battery.

AVIONICS AND EQUIPMENT (500E): Optional avionics include dual King KY 195 com, KX 175 nav/com, KR 85 ADF, and KT 76 transponder; dual Collins VHF-251 com, VHF-251/351 nav/com, IND-350 nav indicator, ADF-650 ADF, and TDR-950 transponder; intercom system, headsets, microphones; and public address system. Standard equipment includes outside air temperature gauge, 8-day clock, engine hour meter, five sets inertia reel shoulder harness, cargo tiedown fittings, fire extinguisher, first aid kit, passenger steps, ground handling wheels, external power socket, landing light, skid-tip position light, anti-collision strobe lights, navigation lights, cockpit utility light, aft cabin light, and instrument lights. Optional equipment includes shatterproof glass, heating/demisting system, radios and intercom, attitude and directional gyros, rate of climb indicator, nylon mesh seats, dual controls, cargo hook, cargo racks, underfuselage cargo pod, heated pitot tube, extended landing gear, blade storage rack, litter kit, emergency inflatable floats and inflated utility floats. FAA supplemental certification has been received for installing a 30 million candlepower Spectrolab SX-16 Nightsun searchlight.

DIMENSIONS, EXTERNAL:
Main rotor diameter: 500E	8.03 m (26 ft 4 in)
520L	8.66 m (28 ft 4¾ in)
530F	8.33 m (27 ft 4 in)
Main rotor blade chord	0.171 m (6¾ in)
Tail rotor diameter: 500E	1.40 m (4 ft 7 in)
520L, 530F	1.45 m (4 ft 9 in)
Distance between rotor centres:	
500E	4.67 m (15 ft 4 in)
530F	4.88 m (16 ft 0 in)
Length overall, rotors turning:	
500E	9.40 m (30 ft 10 in)
530F	9.78 m (32 ft 1 in)
Length of fuselage	7.29 m (23 ft 11 in)
Height to top of rotor head (standard skids)	
500E	2.49 m (8 ft 2 in)
530F	2.44 m (8 ft 0 in)
Tailplane span	1.65 m (5 ft 5 in)
Skid track (standard)	1.96 m (6 ft 5 in)
Cabin doors (each): Height	1.13 m (3 ft 8½ in)
Max width	0.76 m (2 ft 6 in)
Height to sill: 500E	0.79 m (2 ft 7 in)
530F	0.76 m (2 ft 6 in)
Cargo compartment doors (each):	
Height	1.12 m (3 ft 8¼ in)
Width	0.88 m (2 ft 10½ in)
Height to sill: 500E	0.71 m (2 ft 4 in)
530F	0.66 m (2 ft 2 in)

DIMENSIONS, INTERNAL:
Cabin: Length	2.44 m (8 ft 0 in)
Max width	1.31 m (4 ft 3½ in)
Max height	1.52 m (5 ft 0 in)

AREAS:
Main rotor blades (each): 500E	0.690 m² (7.43 sq ft)
530F	0.71 m² (7.69 sq ft)
Tail rotor blades (each): 500E	0.095 m² (1.02 sq ft)
530F	0.098 m² (1.05 sq ft)
Main rotor disc: 500E	50.89 m² (547.81 sq ft)
520L	58.83 m² (633.28 sq ft)
530F	54.58 m² (587.50 sq ft)
Tail rotor disc: 500E	1.53 m² (16.50 sq ft)
520L, 530F	1.65 m² (17.72 sq ft)
Fin	0.56 m² (6.05 sq ft)
Horizontal stabiliser	0.76 m² (8.18 sq ft)

WEIGHTS AND LOADINGS:
Weight empty: 500E	654 kg (1,441 lb)
530F	709 kg (1,564 lb)
Max normal T-O weight: 500E	1,361 kg (3,000 lb)
530F	1,406 kg (3,100 lb)
Max overload T-O weight:	
500E, 530F	1,610 kg (3,550 lb)
Max gross weight, external load:	
530F	1,701 kg (3,750 lb)
Max normal disc loading:	
500E	26.76 kg/m² (5.48 lb/sq ft)
530F	25.78 kg/m² (5.28 lb/sq ft)
Max normal power loading:	
500E	4.35 kg/kW (7.14 lb/shp)
530F	2.90 kg/kW (4.77 lb/shp)

PERFORMANCE (A: 500E, B: 530F, at max normal T-O weight):
Never-exceed speed at S/L:	
A, B	152 knots (282 km/h; 175 mph)
Max cruising speed at S/L:	
A	139 knots (258 km/h; 160 mph)
Max cruising speed at 1,525 m (5,000 ft):	
A	134 knots (248 km/h; 154 mph)
B	135 knots (250 km/h; 155 mph)
Max cruising speed from S/L to 1,525 m (5,000 ft):	
B	135 knots (250 km/h; 155 mph)
Econ cruising speed at S/L:	
A	129 knots (238 km/h; 148 mph)
B	130 knots (241 km/h; 150 mph)
Econ cruising speed at 1,525 m (5,000 ft):	
A	119 knots (220 km/h; 137 mph)
B	123 knots (229 km/h; 142 mph)
Max rate of climb at S/L: A	572 m (1,875 ft)/min
B	640 m (2,100 ft)/min
Vertical rate of climb at S/L: A	277 m (910 ft)/min
B	427 m (1,400 ft)/min
Service ceiling: A, B	4,875 m (16,000 ft)
Hovering ceiling IGE: ISA: A	2,590 m (8,500 ft)
B	4,328 m (14,200 ft)
ISA + 20°C: A	1,830 m (6,000 ft)
B	3,660 m (12,000 ft)

Hovering ceiling OGE: ISA: A	1,860 m (6,100 ft)
B	3,660 m (12,000 ft)
ISA + 20°C: A	945 m (3,100 ft)
B	2,985 m (9,800 ft)
Range, 2 min warm-up, standard fuel, no reserves:	
A at S/L	255 nm (473 km; 294 miles)
B at S/L	212 nm (395 km; 245 miles)
A at 1,525 m (5,000 ft)	278 nm (515 km; 320 miles)
B at 1,525 m (5,000 ft)	239 nm (443 km; 275 miles)

MCDONNELL DOUGLAS MODEL 500/530 DEFENDER

US Army designation: MH-6A

Details of the 500MD Scout Defender, 500MD/TOW Defender, 500MD/ASW Defender, and 500MD Defender II variants of the MD 500 may be found in the 1987-88 and earlier editions of *Jane's*.

Military versions of the MD 500/530 available in 1988 were as follows:

500MG Defender. As 530MG, but with 313 kW (420 shp) Allison 250-C20B turboshaft and MD 500E rotor system. In July 1985 a **Paramilitary MG Defender** version was introduced which is intended as a low cost helicopter suitable for use by police, border patrol, rescue, narcotics control and internal security authorities. It is offered in both 500E and 530F configurations. In February 1986 McDonnell Douglas Helicopter completed delivery of six 500MG Defenders to the Colombian Air Force, which also received two commercial MD 500Es to serve as trainers.

530MG Defender. Based on airframe and power plant of the commercial MD 530F Lifter. Development began in late 1982, and demonstrator (N530MG) flew for first time on 4 May 1984. Integrated crew station provides a compact multi-function display which enhances cockpit field of view and enables hands-on control of the helicopter at all times, with all weapons delivery, communications management, and flight control conducted via the collective and cyclic sticks. A 79.5 litre (21 US gallon; 17.5 Imp gallon) internal auxiliary fuel tank is optional.

The 530MG Defender is designed primarily for point attack and anti-armour missions, but is equally suitable for

scout, day and night surveillance, utility, cargo lift, and light attack duties. A programme is under way to develop an over-the-horizon capability for naval applications.

Equipment includes Racal Avionics RAMS 3000 integrated control and display system for all-weather and NOE flight, designed to operate with a MIL-STD-1553B interface and comprising a processor interface unit (PIU), a control display unit (CDU), and a data transfer device (DTD) linked by a dual 1553B databus. A multi-function display incorporates a high resolution monochrome CRT with alpha-numeric and symbolic data overlay capability. The CDU incorporates a monochrome CRT with line keys and keyboard and can be used to conduct all normal flight planning, navigational, frequency selection, and subsystem management functions by use of dedicated keys on the CDU keyboard. Data are transferred to the DTD from a ground loader unit via an RS-232C serial data link which is placed in a cockpit receptacle for update transfer to the data base of the PIU. Other equipment includes Astronautics Corpn autopilot; Decca Doppler navigation system integrated with Racal Doppler velocity sensor; Ferranti FIN 1110 AHRS; twin Collins VHF/UHF AM/FM radios; King HF radio, ADF/VOR, radar altimeter and transponder; Telephonics intercom; and SFENA attitude indicator. Optional avionics include Hughes Aircraft TOW mast mounted sight system, FLIR, radar warning receiver, IFF, GPWS and laser rangefinder.

Standard 14 in NATO racks are provided for external stores. Weapons qualified or tested by 1987 included TOW 2 anti-armour missiles, FN pods containing two 7.62 mm or one 0.50 in machine-gun, and 2.75 in rockets in 7-tube or 12-tube launchers. Additional weapons are planned to include four General Dynamics Stinger air-to-air missiles and a 7.62 mm McDonnell Douglas Chain Gun automatic machine-gun. Chaff and infra-red decoy flares can be carried, with automatic chaff ejection on threat detection facility. Both cyclic sticks have triggers for gun or rocket firing; the co-pilot/gunner's visual image display has two handgrips for TOW/FLIR operation.

Nightfox. Introduced in January 1986 as low cost helicopter for night surveillance and military operations. Equipment includes a FLIR Systems Inc Series 2000

McDonnell Douglas 530MG Defender with TOW missile launchers and nose mounted Hughes M65 sight

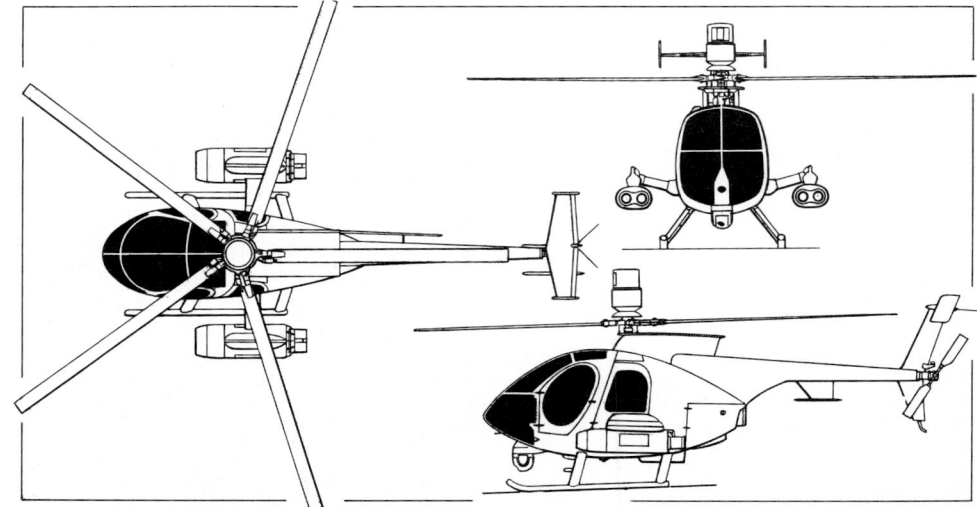

McDonnell Douglas 530MG Defender, with TOW missiles and mast mounted sight *(Pilot Press)*

McDonnell Douglas 530MG Nightfox helicopter with FLIR thermal imaging system and EX-34 Chain Gun installation

thermal imager and night vision goggles, with weapons as for 530MG. Available in both 500MG and 530MG configurations. Four MD 500MG Nightfoxes reportedly delivered to Colombian Air Force.

MH-6A. Version in limited service with the US Army Special Operations Aviation Group. Aircraft of this type, flying from the frigate USS *Jarrett*, took part in the action against the Iranian Navy minelayer *Iran Ajr* in the Persian Gulf in September 1987. The MH-6A is an MD 530MG Defender equipped with FLIR, used in conjunction with pilot's night vision goggles. Armament is said to include machine-guns and rockets.

DIMENSIONS, EXTERNAL (A: 500MD/TOW, B: 530MG):
As for 500E/530F except:

Length of fuselage: A	7.62 m (25 ft 0 in)
B	7.29 m (23 ft 11 in)
Height to top of rotor head: A	2.64 m (8 ft 8 in)
B	2.62 m (8 ft 7 in)
B with MMS	3.41 m (11 ft 2½ in)
Height over tail (endplate fins):	
A, B	2.71 m (8 ft 10¾ in)
Width over skids: A	1.95 m (6 ft 4¾ in)
B	1.96 m (6 ft 5 in)
Width over TOW pods: A	3.23 m (10 ft 7¼ in)
Tailskid ground clearance: A	0.67 m (2 ft 2½ in)
B	0.41 m (1 ft 4 in)

WEIGHTS:

Weight empty, equipped: A	896 kg (1,976 lb)
Max T-O weight: A	1,361 kg (3,000 lb)
B, normal	1,406 kg (3,100 lb)
B, max overload	1,610 kg (3,550 lb)

PERFORMANCE (at max normal T-O weight, ISA, except where indicated):

Never-exceed speed at S/L:	
A	130 knots (241 km/h; 150 mph)
Max cruising speed at S/L:	
A, B	119 knots (221 km/h; 137 mph)
Max cruising speed at 1,525 m (5,000 ft):	
A	115 knots (213 km/h; 132 mph)
B	122 knots (226 km/h; 140 mph)
Max rate of climb at S/L: A, ISA	503 m (1,650 ft)/min
B, up to ISA + 20°C	631 m (2,070 ft)/min
Vertical rate of climb at S/L:	
B, ISA	606 m (1,990 ft)/min
B, ISA + 20°C	558 m (1,830 ft)/min
Service ceiling: A	4,205 m (13,800 ft)
B	over 4,880 m (16,000 ft)
Hovering ceiling IGE: A, ISA	2,315 m (7,600 ft)
B, ISA	5,060 m (16,600 ft)
A, ISA + 20°C	1,525 m (5,000 ft)
B, ISA + 20°C	4,270 m (14,000 ft)
A, 35°C	1,100 m (3,600 ft)
B, 35°C	2,680 m (8,800 ft)
Hovering ceiling OGE: A, ISA	1,770 m (5,800 ft)
B, ISA	4,300 m (14,100 ft)
A, ISA + 20°C	915 m (3,000 ft)
B, ISA + 20°C	3,475 m (11,400 ft)
A, 35°C	640 m (2,100 ft)
B, 35°C	2,135 m (7,000 ft)
Range with standard fuel, 2 min warmup, no reserves:	
A at S/L	210 nm (389 km; 242 miles)
B at S/L	180 nm (333 km; 207 miles)
A at 1,525 m (5,000 ft)	231 nm (428 km; 266 miles)
B at 1,525 m (5,000 ft)	203 nm (376 km; 233 miles)
Endurance with standard fuel, 2 min warmup, no reserves: A at S/L	2 h 34 min
B at S/L	2 h 6 min
A at 1,525 m (5,000 ft)	2 h 47 min
B at 1,525 m (5,000 ft)	2 h 18 min

MCDONNELL DOUGLAS MD 520N NOTAR HELICOPTER

Under a $2.2 million 24-month contract from the US Army Applied Technology Laboratory and the Defense Advanced Research Projects Agency, an Army OH-6A helicopter (12917) was modified to serve as the prototype of the no-tail-rotor (NOTAR) helicopter, and was flown for the first time in this form on 17 December 1981. Details of the programme can be found in the 1982-83 *Jane's*. During 1985 the NOTAR prototype was extensively modified, with a new forward fuselage similar in profile to that of the MD 500E, a 313 kW (420 shp) Allison 250-C20B turboshaft, a new fan with composite blades of smaller diameter and greater chord than the original metal bladed fan, and a second air circulation slot on the tailboom. Flight testing of the helicopter resumed on 12 March 1986 and was completed in June. At the Helicopter Association International convention held at Anaheim, California, in February 1988, McDonnell Douglas Helicopter Company announced development of a prototype NOTAR version of the MD 500 designated MD 520N, for which detailed design work began in May 1988. Modifications to the MD 500 include an increased diameter rotor, new tailboom of composites construction, an advanced NOTAR circulation fan and new tail surface design. The MD 520N will be powered by an Allison 250-C20R turboshaft. First flight is scheduled for May 1989, with certification anticipated at the end of that year. Two structural test airframes will also be constructed.

Advantages claimed for the NOTAR concept include reduced operating costs, significant reduction in pilot workload, increased safety for pilot and ground personnel, and enhanced flight characteristics, particularly in sideways and rearward flight.

MCDONNELL DOUGLAS MDX

At the Helicopter Association International convention at Anaheim, California, in February 1988, McDonnell Douglas announced development of a new twin-engined commercial helicopter designated MDX. The MDX will seat ten in utility configuration and eight in an executive transport role. Gross weight will be in the 2,268 kg (5,000 lb) class. Proposed features include the NOTAR system, an integrated 'glass' cockpit combining most flight instruments on a single CRT display screen, grease-lubricated main rotor transmission, and Flexbeam main rotor blades of composites construction. Programme go-ahead was expected at the end of 1988.

MCDONNELL DOUGLAS APACHE
US Army designation: AH-64A

The Hughes (now McDonnell Douglas Helicopter Company) Model 77 was designed to meet the US Army's requirement for an advanced attack helicopter (AAH) capable of undertaking a full day/night/adverse weather anti-armour mission, and of fighting, surviving and 'living with' troops in a front-line environment. Two YAH-64 flight test prototypes made their initial flights on 30 September and 22 November 1975 respectively. Details of the prototype and full scale engineering development programmes can be found in the 1984-85 and earlier editions of *Jane's*. Selection of the AH-64 for the US Army was announced in December 1976, and it was given the name Apache in late 1981.

Teledyne Ryan is responsible for building the AH-64 fuselage, wings, engine nacelles, avionics bays, canopy and tail unit. The production programme began with a Lot 1 production contract for 11 Apaches, the first of which was delivered on 26 January 1984. On 7 December 1987 the 300th production Apache was delivered, at which time production was at the rate of 10 per month, and the total delivered had risen to 357 by 10 June 1988. Thirty-four US Army and National Guard battalions are scheduled to equip with Apaches, of which seven had received the AH-64 by mid-1988.

Self-deployment capability was demonstrated on 4 April 1985, when the 14th production Apache, with four 871 litre (230 US gallon; 191 Imp gallon) external fuel tanks, made a 1,020 nm (1,891 km; 1,175 mile) nonstop flight from Mesa to Santa Barbara, landing with 30 minutes' fuel remaining. Such ferry range permits deployment from the USA to Europe via a northern Atlantic route, with stops at Goose Bay, Frobisher Bay, Søndrestrøm, Reykjavik and Prestwick. If the required deployment is farther than ferry range, the Apache can be carried in C-141B StarLifter and C-5 Galaxy transports (two and six Apaches respectively). Loading trials have also been conducted with a mockup of the McDonnell Douglas C-17A, which could accommodate up to three Apaches.

Initial operational capability was achieved in July 1986 by the 6th Cavalry Regiment's 3rd Squadron. In 1987 the North Carolina Army National Guard's 1st Attack Helicopter Battalion, 130th Aviation, received the first of 18 Apaches, becoming the first Guard or Reserve unit to operate the type. These NCARNG Apaches are based at Raleigh-Durham Airport. Three more NG battalions of Apaches are funded for equipping in 1989-90.

In September 1987 the first US Army AH-64A unit to be based overseas deployed to West Germany. The 2nd Squadron, 6th Cavalry Brigade (Air Combat), is assigned to the VII Corps Aviation Brigade at Illesheim, with 18 Apaches. With helicopters from the 1st Squadron, 6th Cavalry Brigade, from Fort Hood, Texas, the Apaches took part in Exercise 'Reforger '87', flying more than 680 hours, mostly at night, in support of a NATO 'certain strike' operation in West Germany.

In October 1987 McDonnell Douglas Helicopter Company began a $10 million, 11 month programme to integrate General Dynamics Stinger air-to-air missiles with the Apache. The helicopter will be able to carry up to four Stingers, mounted in pairs on the outboard weapons pylon on each stub wing. Successful test firing of two AIM-9 Sidewinder air-to-air missiles was carried out in late November 1987 at the US Army's White Sands, New Mexico, ranges as part of a programme to explore the

McDonnell Douglas NOTAR testbed, modified from an OH-6A

Apache's air-to-air combat capability. The firings were made in the hover, and in forward flight at a speed of 80 knots (148 km/h; 92 mph). The Apache also conducted laser ranging and tracking tests, using Bell UH-1 helicopters and LTV A-7 attack aircraft as aerial targets.

McDonnell Douglas has received funding for its proposal to equip Apaches with an Airborne Target Handover System (ATHS). Developed by Honeywell's Sperry Defense Systems Division, the ATHS enables the Apache to transmit or receive target acquisition information using other aircraft or ground stations. The information is automatically transmitted by coded signal without voice communications. Ten prototype units have been evaluated on US Army AH-64As at Fort Rucker, Alabama. Deliveries of ATHS units will be made between 1990 and 1993.

McDonnell Douglas Helicopter Company has received contracts from the US Army Aviation Applied Directorate to develop an advanced composite main rotor hub and fibre-reinforced thermoplastic secondary structures for the AH-64A, and to develop artificial intelligence applications for fault isolation and diagnosis of the helicopter's systems. A production AH-64A has been allocated for a five-year vibration analysis study funded by NASA's Langley Research Center.

In April 1987 MDHC announced preliminary details of a proposed **Advanced Apache**, based on studies for an advanced development for the US Army which had been under way for 18 months. This helicopter has also been proposed for the West German Army's PAH-2 anti-tank helicopter requirement, and would include advanced avionics and fly by wire flight controls, a new Honeywell ring laser INS, a data transfer system permitting cassette loading of mission data, ATHS, 1,491 kW (2,000 shp) T700 engines with digital control, improved cockpit fields of view, provision for air-to-air Stinger missiles slaved to the gunner's helmet for off-axis aiming, rearward looking TV with a fin mounted video camera, and a gun with longer barrel, active recoil and digital turret control. The Advanced Apache would have 75 per cent commonality with the AH-64A. Initial funding for it was included in the FY 1989 budget amendment proposals.

Meanwhile, MDHC is working with the US Army to define details of a multi-stage improvement programme (MSIP) which will include upgrading of the Apache's weapon, sensor and fire control systems, digital databus and crew displays. Improvements will include an airborne adverse weather weapons system (AAWWS) to provide a 'fire and forget' capability for the Hellfire missiles, plus some of the changes being explored for the Advanced Apache. Initial MSIP funds were provided in the FY 1988 budget, allowing work to begin in mid-1988 for a scheduled delivery date of 1993. Army and company funds are also being used to develop various air-to-air missile installations for the helicopter, and to enhance the M230 Chain Gun for the air-to-air role. Stinger, Sidewinder and Mistral missiles have been integrated with the AH-64A's weapons system, with the first Stinger test firing due in Autumn 1988. On 25 April 1988 a Sidearm missile fired from an Apache at the US Naval Weapons Center hit an armoured vehicle containing an RF emitter.

TYPE: Twin-engined attack helicopter.

ROTOR SYSTEM: Four-blade fully articulated main rotor and four-blade tail rotor; all blades manufactured by Tool Research and Engineering Corpn (Composite Structures Division). Main rotor blades are of high-camber aerofoil section and broad chord, with sweptback tips, and can be folded or removed for air transportation. Each blade has five stainless steel spars lined with structural glassfibre tubes, a laminated stainless steel skin and a composite rear section, bonded together. Blades are attached to hub by a laminated strap retention system, and are fitted with elastomeric lead/lag dampers and offset flapping hinges. Tail rotor comprises two pairs of blades, mounted on port side of pylon/fin support structure at optimum quiet setting of approx 55°/125° to each other. AEG-

McDonnell Douglas AH-64A Apache twin-turboshaft attack helicopter

Telefunken blade de-icing system. Main rotor driveshaft rotates within a fixed, hollow outer shaft, permitting removal of main transmission without dismantling main rotor system. This results in improved drive system reliability, as flight loads are transmitted to airframe via static mast instead of through main transmission. Entire system is capable of flight in negative *g* conditions.

ROTOR DRIVE: Litton (Precision Gear Division) main transmission and engine nose gearbox; transmission to tail rotor via Aircraft Gear Corpn grease-lubricated intermediate and tail rotor gearboxes, with Bendix driveshafts and couplings. Garrett cooling fan for tail rotor gearbox. Main transmission designed to operate for one hour after loss of oil; gearboxes can tolerate ballistic damage and continue to operate for up to one hour without failure. Selected dynamic components constructed of 7049 aluminium and electro-slag remelt (ESR) steel; critical parts of transmission (eg, bearings) have ESR collars for protection against hits by 12.7 mm ammunition. Rotor/engine rpm ratios approx 1 : 72.4 for main rotor, approx 1 : 14.9 for tail rotor.

WINGS: Cantilever mid-mounted wings of low aspect ratio, located aft of the cockpit. Wings are removable, and attach to sides of fuselage for transport and storage. Two hardpoints beneath each wing for the carriage of mixed ordnance or ferry tanks.

FUSELAGE: Conventional semi-monocoque aluminium structure. Designed to survive hits by 12.7 mm and 23 mm ammunition.

TAIL UNIT: Bolted pylon structure, with tail rotor mounted on port side. Low-mounted all-moving tailplane, with Simmonds actuators and Hamilton Standard control electronics.

Close-up of the Apache's nose mounted TADS/ PNVS installation *(Brian M. Service)*

LANDING GEAR: Menasco trailing arm type, with single mainwheels and fully castoring, self-centring and lockable tailwheel. Mainwheel tyres size 8.50-10, tailwheel tyre size 5.00-4. Hydraulic brakes on main units. Main gear is non-retractable, but legs fold rearward to reduce overall height for storage and transportation. Energy absorbing main and tail gears are designed for normal descent rates of up to 3.05 m (10 ft)/s and heavy landings at up to 12.8 m (42 ft)/s. Take-offs and landings can be made at structural design gross weight on terrain slopes of up to 12° (head-on) and 10° (side-on).

POWER PLANT: Two 1,265 kW (1,696 shp) General Electric T700-GE-701 turboshafts, derated for normal operations to provide reserve power for combat emergencies, and with automatic one engine out rating of 1,285 kW (1,723 shp). Engines mounted one on each side of fuselage, above wings, with key components armour-protected. Upper cowlings let down to serve as maintenance platforms. Two crash resistant fuel cells in fuselage, combined capacity 1,422 litres (376 US gallons; 313 Imp gallons).

ACCOMMODATION: Crew of two in tandem: co-pilot/gunner in front, pilot behind on 48 cm (19 in) elevated seat. Crew seats, by Simula Inc, are of lightweight Kevlar. Teledyne Ryan canopy, with PPG transparencies and transparent acrylic blast barrier between cockpits, is designed to provide optimum field of view. Crew stations are protected by Ceradyne Inc lightweight boron armour shields in cockpit floor and sides, and between cockpits, offering protection against 23 mm high explosive and armour piercing rounds. Sierracin electric heating of windscreen. Seats and structure designed to give crew a 95 per cent chance of surviving ground impacts of up to 12.8 m (42 ft)/s.

SYSTEMS: AiResearch totally integrated pneumatic system includes a shaft driven compressor, air turbine starters, pneumatic valves, temperature control unit and environmental control unit. Parker Bertea dual hydraulic systems, operating at 207 bars (3,000 lb/sq in), with actuators ballistically tolerant to 12.7 mm direct hits. Redundant flight control system for both rotors. In the event of a dual hydraulic system failure, the system adjusts to Sperry Flight Systems secondary fly by wire control. Bendix electrical power system, with two 35kVA fully redundant engine driven AC generators, two 300A transformer-rectifiers, and URDC standby DC battery. Garrett GTP 36-55(H) 93 kW (125 shp) APU for engine starting and maintenance checking.

AVIONICS AND EQUIPMENT: Main avionics bays are adjacent to co-pilot/gunner's position, in large fairings on sides of fuselage. Communications equipment includes AN/ ARC-164 UHF, AN/ARC-186 UHF/VHF, Tempest C-10414 intercom, KY-28/58/TSEC crypto secure voice, and C-8157 secure voice control. Singer-Kearfott AN/ ASN-128 lightweight Doppler navigation system, with Litton LR-80 (AN/ASN-143) strapdown attitude and heading reference system (AHRS). Doppler system, with AHRS, permits nap-of-the-earth navigation and provides for storing target locations. Avionics fit includes an AN/ARN-89B ADF and an AN/APX-100 IFF transponder with KIT-1A secure encoding. Sperry Flight Systems digital automatic stabilisation equipment (DASE). Aircraft survivability equipment (ASE) consists of an Aerospace Avionics AN/APR-39 passive radar warning receiver, an AN/AVR-2 laser warning receiver, a Sanders AN/ALQ-144 infra-red jammer, chaff dispensers, and an AN/ALQ-136 radar jammer. Other avionics include Astronautics Corpn HSI, an AN/APU-209 radar altimeter video display unit, and remote magnetic indicator, and Pacer Systems omnidirectional air data system. A Sperry Flight Systems all-raster symbology generator processes TV data from IR and other sensors, superimposes symbology, and distributes the combination to CRT and helmet mounted displays in the aircraft. 'Black Hole' IR suppression system protects aircraft from heat-seeking missiles: this eliminates an engine bay cooling fan, by operating from engine exhaust gas through ejector nozzles to lower the gas plume and metal temperatures. BITE fault detection/location system.

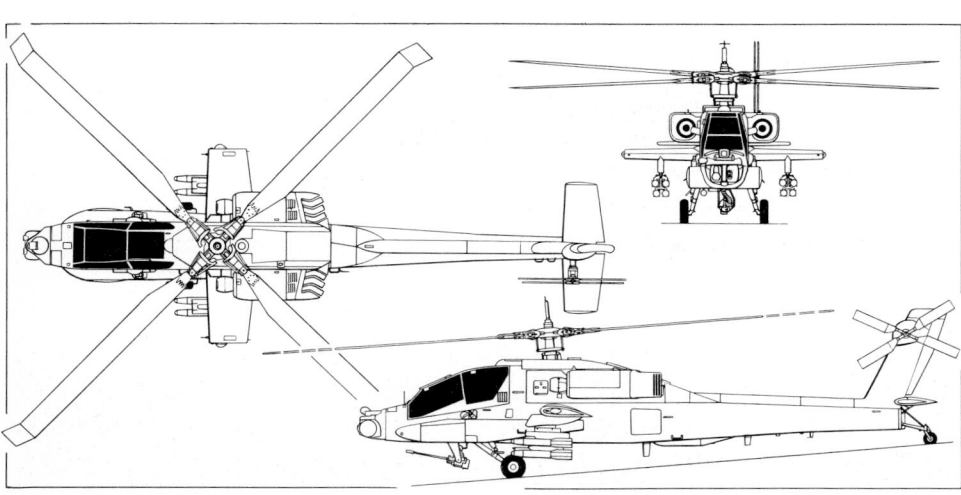

McDonnell Douglas AH-64A Apache tandem two-seat advanced attack helicopter *(Pilot Press)*

Sidewinder air-to-air missile and Hellfire anti-tank missiles on an AH-64A *(Ivo Sturzenegger)*

ARMAMENT AND OPERATIONAL EQUIPMENT: Armament consists of a McDonnell Douglas M230 Chain Gun 30 mm automatic cannon, located between the mainwheel legs in an underfuselage mounting with Lear Siegler electronic controls. Normal rate of fire is 625 rds/min of Honeywell TP (target practice), HE or HEDP (high explosive dual purpose) ammunition, which is interoperable with NATO Aden/DEFA 30 mm ammunition. Max ammunition load is 1,200 rds. Gun mounting is designed to collapse into fuselage between pilots in the event of a crash landing. Four underwing hardpoints, with Aircraft Hydro-Forming pylons and ejector units, on which can be carried up to sixteen Rockwell Hellfire anti-tank missiles; or up to seventy-six 2.75 in FFAR (folding fin aerial rockets) in their launchers; or a combination of Hellfires and FFAR. Hellfire remote electronics by Rockwell; Bendix aerial rocket control system; multiplex (MUX) system units by Sperry Flight Systems. Co-pilot/gunner (CPG) has primary responsibility for firing gun and missiles, but pilot can override his controls to fire gun or launch missiles. Martin Marietta Orlando Aerospace target acquisition and designation sight and AN/AAQ-11 pilot's night vision sensor (TADS/PNVS) comprises two independently functioning systems mounted on the nose. The TADS consists of a rotating turret (±120° in azimuth, +30/–60° in elevation) that houses the sensor subsystems, an optical relay tube in the CPG's cockpit, three electronic units in the avionics bay, and cockpit-mounted controls and displays. It is used principally for target search, detection and laser designation, with the CPG as primary operator (though it can also provide backup night vision to the pilot in the event of a PNVS failure. Once acquired by the TADS, targets can be tracked manually or automatically for autonomous attack with gun, rockets or Hellfire missiles. The TADS daylight sensor consists of a TV camera with narrow (0.9°) and wide angle (4.0°) fields of view; direct view optics (4° narrow and 18° wide angle); a laser spot tracker; and an International Laser Systems laser range finder/designator. The night sensor, in the starboard half of the turret, incorporates a FLIR sight with narrow, medium and wide angle (3.1, 10.1 and 50.0°) fields of view. The PNVS consists of a FLIR sensor (30° × 40° field of view) in a rotating turret (±90° in azimuth, +20/–45° in elevation) mounted above the TADS; an electronics unit in the avionics bay; and the pilot's display and controls. It provides the pilot with thermal imaging that permits nap-of-the-earth flight to, from and within the battle area at night or in adverse daytime weather, at altitudes low enough to avoid detection by the enemy. PNVS imagery is displayed on a single monocle in front of one of the pilot's eyes; flight information such as airspeed, altitude and heading is superimposed on this imagery to simplify the piloting task. The monocle is a part of the Honeywell Avionics integrated helmet and display sighting system (IHADSS) worn by both crew members.

DIMENSIONS, EXTERNAL:

Main rotor diameter	14.63 m (48 ft 0 in)
Main rotor blade chord	0.53 m (1 ft 9 in)
Tail rotor diameter	2.79 m (9 ft 2 in)
Length overall: tail rotor turning	14.68 m (48 ft 2 in)
both rotors turning	17.76 m (58 ft 3⅛ in)
Wing span	5.23 m (17 ft 2 in)
Height: over tail fin	3.52 m (11 ft 6½ in)
over tail rotor	4.30 m (14 ft 1¼ in)
to top of rotor head	3.84 m (12 ft 7 in)
overall (top of air data sensor)	4.66 m (15 ft 3½ in)
Distance between c/l of pylons:	
inboard pair	3.20 m (10 ft 6 in)
outboard pair	4.72 m (15 ft 6 in)
Tailplane span	3.40 m (11 ft 2 in)
Wheel track	2.03 m (6 ft 8 in)
Wheelbase	10.59 m (34 ft 9 in)

AREAS:

Main rotor disc	168.11 m² (1,809.5 sq ft)
Tail rotor disc	6.13 m² (66.0 sq ft)

WEIGHTS:

Weight empty	4,881 kg (10,760 lb)
Max internal fuel weight	1,157 kg (2,550 lb)
Max external stores weight	771 kg (1,700 lb)
Structural design gross weight	6,650 kg (14,660 lb)
Primary mission gross weight	6,552 kg (14,445 lb)
Max T-O weight	9,525 kg (21,000 lb)

GENERAL PERFORMANCE (at 6,552 kg; 14,445 lb AUW, ISA except where indicated):

Never-exceed speed	197 knots (365 km/h; 227 mph)
Max level and max cruising speed	
	160 knots (296 km/h; 184 mph)
Max vertical rate of climb at S/L	762 m (2,500 ft)/min
Service ceiling	6,400 m (21,000 ft)
Service ceiling, one engine out	3,290 m (10,800 ft)
Hovering ceiling: IGE	4,570 m (15,000 ft)
OGE	3,505 m (11,500 ft)
Max range, internal fuel	260 nm (482 km; 300 miles)
Ferry range, max internal and external fuel, still air	
	918 nm (1,701 km; 1,057 miles)
Endurance at 1,220 m (4,000 ft) at 35°C	1 h 50 min
Max endurance, internal fuel	3 h 9 min
g limits at low altitude and airspeeds up to 164 knots	
(304 km/h; 189 mph)	+3.5/–0.5

WEIGHTS FOR TYPICAL MISSION PERFORMANCE (A: anti-armour at 1,220 m/4,000 ft and 35°C, 4 Hellfire and 320 rds of 30 mm ammunition; B: as A, but with 1,200 rds; C: as A, but with 6 Hellfire and 540 rds; D: anti-armour at 610 m/2,000 ft and 21°C, 8 Hellfire and 1,200 rds; E: air cover at 1,220 m/4,000 ft and 35°C, 4 Hellfire and 1,200 rds; F: as E but at 610 m/2,000 ft and 21°C, 4 Hellfire, 19 rockets, 1,200 rds; G: escort at 1,220 m/4,000 ft and 35°C, 19 rockets and 1,200 rds; H: escort at 610 m/2,000 ft and 21°C, 38 rockets and 1,200 rds):

Mission fuel: A	727 kg (1,602 lb)
G	741 kg (1,633 lb)
E	745 kg (1,643 lb)
C	902 kg (1,989 lb)
B	1,029 kg (2,269 lb)

D	1,063 kg (2,344 lb)
H	1,077 kg (2,374 lb)
F	1,086 kg (2,394 lb)
Mission gross weight: A	6,552 kg (14,445 lb)
E	6,874 kg (15,154 lb)
G	6,932 kg (15,282 lb)
B, C	7,158 kg (15,780 lb)
D	7,728 kg (17,038 lb)
F	7,813 kg (17,225 lb)
H	7,867 kg (17,343 lb)

TYPICAL MISSION PERFORMANCE (A-H as above):

Cruising speed at intermediate rated power:

C	147 knots (272 km/h; 169 mph)
D	148 knots (274 km/h; 170 mph)
F	150 knots (278 km/h; 173 mph)
B	151 knots (280 km/h; 174 mph)
E, H	153 knots (283 km/h; 176 mph)
A	154 knots (285 km/h; 177 mph)
G	155 knots (287 km/h; 178 mph)

Max vertical rate of climb at intermediate rated power:

B, C	137 m (450 ft)/min
H	238 m (780 ft)/min
F, G	262 m (860 ft)/min
E	293 m (960 ft)/min
D	301 m (990 ft)/min
A	448 m (1,470 ft)/min

Mission endurance: A, E, G	1 h 50 min
C	1 h 17 min
D, F, H	2 h 30 min
B	2 h 40 min

MCDONNELL DOUGLAS SEA-GOING APACHE

Under a company initiated programme, McDonnell Douglas is evaluating the concept of a sea-going Apache for attack, surveillance and air-to-air combat missions, operating in outer air battle regions from small warships. The sea-going Apache would have high capacity retractable landing gear, a folding main rotor and tail section, APG-65 search and track radar and provision for Sidewinder, AMRAAM and Sparrow air-to-air missiles and Penguin and Harpoon anti-shipping missiles. Integration of existing naval mission electronics, avionics and weapons would simplify and reduce the cost of logistical support.

At the Naval Helicopter Association meeting held in San Diego, California, in March 1988, McDonnell Douglas revealed details of the latest design concept for a sea-going Apache. Forward avionics bays have been moved to the underside of the fuselage, enabling a larger cockpit canopy to be installed, and fuel capacity has been increased to 3,229 litres (853 US gallons; 710 Imp gallons). Other proposed features of the helicopter are infra-red search and track capability, targeting radar, extendable in-flight refuelling probe, and a recovery, assist, securing and traversing (RAST) system. With a maximum width (rotors folded) of 11 ft 0 in (3.35 m), the sea-going Apache could be carried on board ships of frigate, destroyer or cruiser classes. On a typical surveillance mission, operating at a max T-O weight of 8,618 kg (19,000 lb) and armed with two AIM-9s, the sea-going Apache could operate over a radius of 200 nm (370 km; 230 miles) from its ship, remaining on station for 4 h and returning to the ship with 30 min fuel reserves.

MCDONNELL DOUGLAS/BELL LHX

Details of revised requirements for the US Army's LHX programme, for which McDonnell Douglas Helicopter Company and Bell Helicopter Textron are teamed, may be found under the US Army entry in this section.

Artist's impression of McDonnell Douglas Sea-Going Apache concept

MELEX

MELEX USA INC

1221 Front Street, Raleigh, North Carolina 27609
Telephone: (919) 828 7645
Telex: 825868 MELEX UF
Fax: (919) 834 7290
VICE-PRESIDENT: George Lundy

This company, a subsidiary of Pezetel (PZL) of Poland (which see), is responsible for sales and operational support of PZL Mielec M-18 and M-18A Dromader agricultural aircraft operating in the western hemisphere.

T45 TURBINE DROMADER

Turbines Inc of Terre Haute, Indiana, in co-operation with Melex USA Inc, has developed a turboprop conversion of the M-18, based on the 895 kW (1,200 shp) Pratt & Whitney Canada PT6A-45AG engine (derated to 735 kW; 986 shp) driving a five-blade propeller and known as the T45 Turbine Dromader. The prototype (N2856G) flew for the first time on 17 August 1985, and a supplemental type certificate was obtained on 25 April 1986. An annual conversion rate of three to four aircraft is anticipated for the US market alone.

The conversion, which reduces the Dromader's empty weight by about 363 kg (800 lb), provides an increase in normal operating speed of some 20 knots (37 km/h; 23 mph) and a 10 per cent decrease in take-off distance at max T-O weight. Standard fuel capacity has been increased to 719 litres (190 US gallons; 158 Imp gallons). Improvements have also been made to the hydraulic and electrical systems. Provision has been made for carrying a second occupant in

Prototype T45 Turbine Dromader conversion with Pratt & Whitney Canada PT6A-45AG engine

a rearward facing seat, and a dual control version is also available for pilot training.

MELEX DROMADER WATER BOMBER

Melex USA is also developing a firefighting version of the

Dromader which would be able to replenish its tanks by collecting water via scoops while taxiing. In early 1988 the company was investigating the use of hydro-skis for stabilising the aircraft on water as a possible alternative to conventional float landing gear.

MERLYN

MERLYN PRODUCTS INC

West 7510 Hall Avenue, Spokane, Washington 99204
Telephone: (509) 838 1141
PRESIDENT: Suzanne Evans

This company is developing a pressurisation system for

the Beech Model 36 Bonanza series of piston engined light aircraft, described under the Beechcraft entry in this section. The modification will include the installation of a Dukes Inc pressurisation system to provide a 0.29 bar (4.25 lb/sq in) cabin pressure differential. Extensive structural changes to the Bonanza's fuselage are anticipated. Turbocharged models of the Bonanza 36 will also have intercoolers

installed as part of the modification, the first example of which was expected to be completed in the Summer of 1988.

Other products developed by Merlyn include intercooler kits for the Beech Bonanza and Duke, and an intercooler and propeller modification for the Piper Aerostar series known as the **Samurai 350**.

MID-CONTINENT

MID-CONTINENT AIRCRAFT CORPORATION

Drawer L, Hayti, Missouri 63851
Telephone: (314) 359 0500
Telex: 447183
CHAIRMAN: Richard Reade
PRESIDENT: Ken Mauk

MID-CONTINENT KING CAT

Mid-Continent Aircraft Corporation, an operator and distributor of Schweizer (Grumman) Ag-Cats, has obtained an FAA supplemental type certificate for an aircraft known as the King Cat. This is an Ag-Cat re-engined with an 895 kW (1,200 hp) Wright R-1820-202A radial engine, driving a three-blade metal propeller. The engineering work for the STC was carried out by Serv-Aero Engineering Inc. The King Cat has since been certificated in Canada.

Based on the airframe of the Super Ag-Cat C, which has a hopper accommodating 1,893 litres (500 US gallons; 416 Imp gallons) of spray or 1,814 kg (4,000 lb) of dry chemicals, the King Cat offers improved high-altitude/ high-temperature performance. It is available as a conversion of a Super Ag-Cat C, or a kit is obtainable for installation by the customer or his maintenance organisation. Options which are available include upper wing installation height increase of 20.3 cm (8 in), Serv-O ailerons, increased fuel capacity of 431.5 litres (114 US gallons; 95 Imp gallons), Collins cockpit air-conditioning and a 1,893 litre (500 US gallon; 416 Imp gallon) water bombing system for fire control.

By 1 January 1988 Mid-Continent had completed 23 King Cat conversions. Examples are in service in the United States, Canada and South Africa.

Mid-Continent King Cat, a Wright engined conversion of a Super Ag-Cat C

WEIGHTS AND LOADINGS:

Weight empty: basic		2,184 kg (4,816 lb)
spray equipped		2,257 kg (4,976 lb)
dust equipped		2,225 kg (4,906 lb)
Max T-O weight: FAR 23		2,857 kg (6,300 lb)
CAM 8		3,855 kg (8,500 lb)
Max wing loading:		
FAR 23	78.5 kg/m² (16.07 lb/sq ft)	
CAM 8	105.9 kg/m² (21.68 lb/sq ft)	
Max power loading:		
FAR 23	3.19 kg/kW (5.25 lb/hp)	
CAM 8	4.31 kg/kW (7.08 lb/hp)	

PERFORMANCE:

Ferry speed	117 knots (217 km/h; 135 mph)
Typical working speed	87-113 knots (161-209 km/h; 100-130 mph)
Stalling speed, power off, at AUW of 2,857 kg (6,300 lb)	60 knots (111 km/h; 69 mph) CAS
T-O run with 907 kg (2,000 lb) hopper load	293 m (960 ft)
T-O to 15 m (50 ft) with 907 kg (2,000 lb) hopper load	427 m (1,400 ft)
Landing from 15 m (50 ft) at weight of 2,257 kg (4,976 lb)	363 m (1,190 ft)
Landing run at weight of 2,257 kg (4,976 lb)	179 m (588 ft)

THE MOD SQUAD

THE MOD SQUAD INC

11 Robin Lane, Fenton, Missouri 63026
Telephone: (800) 825 9445

MOD SQUAD THUNDERBIRD 211

This company has developed a modification programme for Mooney M20-series light aircraft which it claims updates the aircraft to the appearance and performance

standards of current Mooney models. The modification is typically based on a 1966-68 Mooney M20E or M20F and involves dismantling and inspection of the airframe, followed by rebuilding with a Mooney 201-style engine cowling, windscreen, instrument panel, propeller spinner, landing gear doors and aerodynamic fairings. A zero-timed, tuned and balanced 149 kW (200 hp) Textron Lycoming engine prepared by High Performance Aircraft of Mena, Arkansas, is installed. Interior modifications include new

soundproofing, thicker cabin windows, new seats with inflatable lumbar support for the pilot, and a reconditioned IFR panel of Narco avionics. Consumable items such as brake pads and hoses are replaced, and the aircraft is finished in a custom exterior paint scheme. Claimed performance for the Thunderbird 211 includes a cruising speed at 75% power of 169-178 knots (314-330 km/h; 195-205 mph), and a 91 m (300 ft)/min improvement in max climb rate over the unmodified aircraft.

MOLLER

MOLLER INTERNATIONAL

1222 Research Park Drive, Davis, California 95616
Telephone: (916) 756 5069
PRESIDENT: Paul S. Moller

MARKETING DIRECTOR: Jack G. Allison

Since 1960 Moller International has undertaken research and development projects in aerodynamics, noise suppression and vehicle design, leading to the construction and testing of a number of experimental VTOL aircraft which

are said to combine the best features of helicopters, fixed-wing aircraft and cars. Prototypes known originally as the Discojet and later designated **Model XM-4** and **Model 200X Aerobot** were of 'flying saucer' configuration with two-piece glassfibre airframes. Accommodation was provided for two occupants in a centrally mounted cockpit, around which were mounted eight 37.3 kW (50 hp) Wankel rotary ducted fans which provided lift for hovering flight and thrust for forward flight.

A developed production version known as the **Merlin 300 Aerobot** will seat three occupants, and is illustrated in the accompanying photograph of a production mockup. Work on the prototype slowed down in 1987 due to increased interest in unmanned versions, but a limited number of Merlin 300s are expected to be available as experimental civilian aircraft in 1990, with FAA certification to follow. The Merlin 300 will be powered by six rotary engines driving two-rotor ducted fans. Four redundant computers provide stability in pitch and roll axes. Vertical and yaw axes are artificially stabilised with manual override. A ballistic parachute recovery system is installed. The Merlin 300 will be offered in kit form for home assembly and operation in the FAA Experimental category, or in production form in the proposed Primary Aircraft certification category.

Projected variants include a tandem two-seat **Merlin 150** with power plants totalling 447.5 kW (600 hp), giving a cruising speed of 287 knots (532 km/h; 330 mph); and the four-seat **Merlin 400** which is similar to the Merlin 300 but with increased power, totalling 894.8 kW (1,200 hp), and a cruising speed of 293 knots (544 km/h; 338 mph).

MERLIN 300 AEROBOT
(all data provisional)

POWER PLANT: Six 119.3 kW (160 hp) liquid-cooled rotary engines driving two-rotor ducted fans. Maximum fuel capacity 189 litres (50 US gallons; 42 Imp gallons).

DIMENSIONS, EXTERNAL:

Length overall	5.79 m (19 ft 0 in)
Width overall	2.44 m (8 ft 0 in)
Height overall	1.83 m (6 ft 0 in)

WEIGHTS:

Max payload	295 kg (650 lb)
Max T-O weight	850 kg (1,875 lb)

PERFORMANCE:

Max level speed	350 knots (649 km/h; 403 mph)
Cruising speed at 55% power	
	280 knots (518 km/h; 322 mph)
Rate of climb at 75% power	1,280 m (4,200 ft)/min
Hovering ceiling	2,896 m (9,500 ft)
Service ceiling	5,791 m (19,000 ft)
Max range	738 nm (1,368 km; 850 miles)

Engineering prototype of the Moller Merlin 300 Aerobot ducted fan VTOL craft

MOONEY

MOONEY AIRCRAFT CORPORATION

PO Box 72, Kerrville, Texas 78029-0072
Telephone: (512) 896 6000
Telex: Easylink 62913770 OESL UD
CHAIRMAN AND PRESIDENT: Alexandre Couvelaire
GENERAL MANAGER: Robert A. Kromer
DIRECTOR OF MARKETING: Brant D. Dahlfors
DIRECTOR OF ENGINEERING: Rocky G. Peters

The original Mooney Aircraft Inc was formed in June 1948, in Wichita, Kansas, from where the single-seat Model M-18 Mooney Mite was produced until 1952. Its subsequent history and name changes were detailed in the 1987-88 and earlier *Jane's*.

In 1985 M Alexandre Couvelaire, President of the Paris based Euralair/Avialair jet charter and fixed base operator, and M Michel Seydoux, President of MSC, jointly acquired 70 per cent of Mooney Aircraft, and Lake Aircraft (which see) acquired the remaining 30 per cent.

In June 1987 Mooney and Aérospatiale of France announced joint development of the TBM 700 pressurised turboprop light aircraft, details of which can be found under TBM International in the International section of this edition. Mooney delivered a total of 143 aircraft during 1987.

Mooney 201 'Lean Machine' four-seat light aircraft (200 hp Textron Lycoming IO-360-A3B6D)

MOONEY 201 (M20J)

The original Mooney 201 first flew in June 1976 and received FAA certification in September 1976. The 1988 model, known as the Mooney 201 Lean Machine, dispenses with all equipment that is not essential while retaining full IFR capability, including an autopilot. Mooney expected to deliver 30-35 Model 201s during 1988.

TYPE: Four-seat cabin monoplane.

WINGS: Cantilever low-wing monoplane. Wing section NACA 63$_2$-215 at root, NACA 64$_1$-412 at tip. Dihedral 5° 30'. Incidence 2° 30' at root, 1° at tip. Sweepforward 2° 29'. Light alloy structure with flush riveted stretch formed wraparound skins. Full span main spar; rear spar terminates at mid-span of flaps. Sealed-gap differentially operated light alloy ailerons. Electrically operated single-slotted light alloy flaps over 70 per cent of trailing-edge. Vacuum operated, electrically controlled speedbrake optional, in upper surface of each wing at quarter span/two-thirds chord. No tabs.

FUSELAGE: Composite all-metal structure. Cabin section is of welded 4130 chrome molybdenum steel tube with light alloy covering. Rear section is of semi-monocoque construction, with light alloy bulkheads and skin and extruded light alloy stringers.

TAIL UNIT: Cantilever light alloy structure, with variable incidence tailplane. All surfaces covered with wrap-around metal skin.

LANDING GEAR: Electrically retractable levered suspension tricycle type with airspeed safety switch bypass. Nosewheel retracts rearward, main units inward into wings. Rubber disc shock absorbers in main units. Cleveland mainwheels, size 6.00-6, and steerable nosewheel, size 5.00-5. Tyre pressure: mainwheels 2.07 bars (30 lb/sq in), nosewheel 3.38 bars (49 lb/sq in). Cleveland hydraulic single-disc brakes on mainwheels. Parking brake.

POWER PLANT: One 149 kW (200 hp) Textron Lycoming IO-360-A3B6D flat-four engine, driving a McCauley B2D34C214/90DHB-16 two-blade constant-speed metal propeller. Q-tip propeller and propeller anti-icing optional. Two integral fuel tanks in wings, with combined usable capacity of 242 litres (64 US gallons; 53.3 Imp gallons). Refuelling points in wing upper surface. Oil capacity 7.5 litres (2 US gallons; 1.7 Imp gallons).

ACCOMMODATION: Cabin accommodates four persons in pairs on individual seats with reclining back and armrests. Fully adjustable seats with lumbar support and luxury fabric optional. Dual controls standard. Overhead ventilation system. Cabin heating and cooling system, with adjustable outlets and illuminated control. One-piece wraparound windscreen. Tinted Plexiglas windows. Starboard front seat and rear seats removable for freight stowage. Rear seats fold forward for carrying cargo.

Single door on starboard side. Compartment for 59 kg (130 lb) baggage behind cabin, with access from cabin or through door on starboard side. Windscreen defrosting system standard.

SYSTEMS: Hydraulic system for brakes only. Electrical system includes 60A alternator, 12V 35Ah battery, voltage regulator and warning lights, together with protective circuit breakers. Standby generator and vacuum system optional. Oxygen system optional.

AVIONICS AND EQUIPMENT: Standard King KSP 88001 avionics package includes KMA 24 audio panel, KX 155 nav/com with glideslope, KI 209 VOR/LOC/GS indicator, KX 155 nav/com, KI 208 VOR/LOC indicator, KR 86 ADF, KT 76A transponder, KAP 100 autopilot and emergency locator transmitter. Options include King KN 64 DME, and KAP 150 or Century 2000 single- or two-axis autopilot systems. Standard equipment includes airspeed indicator, sensitive altimeter, vertical speed indicator, turn co-ordinator, magnetic compass, ammeter, oil pressure gauge, oil temperature gauge, fuel pressure gauge, manifold pressure gauge, tachometer, two electric fuel quantity gauges, outside air temperature gauge, CHT and EGT gauges, alternate static source, instrument panel annunciator lights, rheostat controlled glareshield post lights, navigation lights, landing/taxi light, cabin lighting, three high intensity strobe lights, seat belts and shoulder harnesses for all seats, assist straps and baggage straps, hatrack, multiple cabin fresh air vents, cargo tiedowns, wing jackpoints and external tiedowns, towbar, fuel tank quick drains and fuel sampler cup, epoxy and zinc chromate anti-corrosion treatment, and overall external urethane enamel paint finish. Optional equipment includes export altimeter with millibar subscale, second altimeter, auxiliary power plug, co-pilot's toe brakes, rudder pedal extension kit, deluxe control wheels, seat headrests, halon fire extinguisher, rotating beacon, vertically adjustable seats, static wicks, sun visors and collapsible towbar.

DIMENSIONS, EXTERNAL:

Wing span	11.00 m (36 ft 1 in)
Wing chord, mean	1.50 m (4 ft 11¼ in)
Wing aspect ratio	7.45
Length overall	7.52 m (24 ft 8 in)
Height overall	2.54 m (8 ft 4 in)
Tailplane span	3.58 m (11 ft 9 in)
Wheel track	2.79 m (9 ft 2 in)
Wheelbase	1.82 m (5 ft 11½ in)
Propeller diameter	1.88 m (6 ft 2 in)
Propeller ground clearance	0.24 m (9½ in)

DIMENSIONS, INTERNAL:

Cabin: Length	2.90 m (9 ft 6 in)
Max width	1.10 m (3 ft 7½ in)
Max height	1.13 m (3 ft 8½ in)
Baggage door: Width	0.53 m (1 ft 9 in)
Height	0.43 m (1 ft 5 in)
Baggage compartment	0.38 m³ (13.5 cu ft)

AREAS:

Wings, gross	16.24 m² (174.8 sq ft)
Ailerons (total)	1.06 m² (11.4 sq ft)
Trailing-edge flaps (total)	1.66 m² (17.9 sq ft)
Fin	0.73 m² (7.92 sq ft)
Rudder	0.58 m² (6.23 sq ft)
Tailplane	1.99 m² (21.45 sq ft)
Elevators	1.11 m² (12.05 sq ft)

WEIGHTS AND LOADINGS:

Weight empty	758 kg (1,671 lb)
Max T-O and landing weight	1,243 kg (2,740 lb)
Max wing loading	76.5 kg/m² (15.67 lb/sq ft)
Max power loading	8.34 kg/kW (13.7 lb/hp)

PERFORMANCE (at max T-O weight):

Never-exceed speed	196 knots (364 km/h; 226 mph)
Max level speed at S/L	175 knots (325 km/h; 202 mph)

Max cruising speed, 75% power at 2,470 m (8,100 ft)
169 knots (314 km/h; 195 mph)
Econ cruising speed, 55% power at 2,470 m (8,100 ft)
152 knots (282 km/h; 175 mph)
Stalling speed:
flaps up 63 knots (117 km/h; 73 mph) IAS
wheels and flaps down
53 knots (98 km/h; 61 mph) CAS

Max rate of climb at S/L	314 m (1,030 ft)/min
Service ceiling	5,730 m (18,800 ft)
T-O to 15 m (50 ft)	463 m (1,517 ft)
Landing from 15 m (50 ft)	491 m (1,610 ft)
Landing run	235 m (770 ft)

Range, 55% power, no reserves
1,059 nm (1,962 km; 1,219 miles)
Range, 75% power, no reserves
951 nm (1,762 km; 1,095 miles)

MOONEY 205 (M20J)

Introduced in mid-1986, the Mooney 205 is developed from the Mooney 201, but embodies aerodynamic refinements to improve performance, notably in terms of max cruising speed and rate of climb. New landing gear doors fully enclose the main legs and wheels when retracted. The engine cooling flaps have been enlarged and are controlled electrically. A new 28V electrical system gives increased power for cold-weather engine starting and optional avionics. Three new preselected flap positions permit initial extension to 15° at a speed of 132 knots (244 km/h; 152 mph) instead of the former 115 knots (213 km/h; 132 mph). New wingtips incorporate faired navigation and strobe lights. Trailing-edge position lights are standard.

The Mooney 205 has a Textron Lycoming IO-360-A3B6D engine, like the 201, but can be distinguished externally by its rounded cabin windows and changed paint scheme. FAA certification was granted on 9 June 1986. Mooney was scheduled to deliver 25 Model 205s during 1988.

AVIONICS AND EQUIPMENT: Choice of optional IFR avionics packages from Narco and King. Other avionics options include Century 2000 and King KAP 100, KAP 150 or KFC 150 autopilots, Foster, II Morrow and Northstar Loran C systems, 3M WX-10A, WX-8 or WX-11 Stormscope weather avoidance systems, S-Tec yaw damper, King KT 96 radio telephone and EC 200 AM/FM stero cassette entertainment centre. Standard equipment generally as for Mooney 201, plus sun visors. Special Edition interior option on Model 205SE includes vertically adjustable front seats with adjustable lumbar support; fabric seats with leather trim, 'comfort cushions', folding centre arm and adjustable headrests; Graystone finish instrument panel and control wheels; exclusive exterior paint scheme with metallic trim colours and Special Edition insignia, and chrome-plated towbar. Equipment options generally as for Mooney 201 plus

Mooney 205, showing revised cabin window outlines

leather seats with fabric inserts or all-leather seats, access step, true airspeed indicator, Davtron digital clock, quartz analog clock, rear window curtains, encoding altimeter, Terra blind encoder, four-probe EGT gauge, instantaneous vertical speed indicator, oxygen system capacities 2.16 or 3.22 m³ (77 or 115 cu ft), propeller de-icing system, polished propeller and spinner, Hartzell Q-tip propeller, high intensity wingtip recognition lights, speed brake kit, standby vacuum system, and windscreen defroster blower.

DIMENSIONS AND AREAS:
As for Mooney 201
WEIGHT:

Max T-O weight	1,243 kg (2,740 lb)

PERFORMANCE (at max T-O weight):
Max level speed 178 knots (330 km/h; 205 mph)
Max cruising speed, 75% power at 2,440 m (8,000 ft)
171 knots (317 km/h; 197 mph)
Stalling speed:
wheels and flaps up
61 knots (113 km/h; 70 mph) IAS
wheels and flaps down
54 knots (100 km/h; 62 mph) IAS

Max rate of climb at S/L	323 m (1,060 ft)/min
Service ceiling	5,670 m (18,600 ft)
Endurance at max cruising speed	5 h 2 min

MOONEY 252TSE (M20K)

Mooney introduced the Model 252TSE (Turbo Special Edition) in late 1985 as a replacement for the Turbo Mooney 231, described in the 1985-86 *Jane's*. A total of 889 Model 231s was manufactured. Externally similar to the Model 231, the Mooney 252TSE differs in having a 156.6 kW (210 hp) Continental TSIO-360-MB-1 engine with Garrett TE04 turbocharger with automatic wastegate operation, an intercooler, electric cowl flap, NACA duct for induction air, a 28V electrical system and new landing gear doors which fully enclose the main legs and wheels when retracted. Principal external difference is the rounded cabin window design. Mooney expected to deliver some 40 Model 252s during 1988.

TYPE: Four-seat cabin monoplane.

WINGS: Cantilever low-wing monoplane. Wing section NACA 63₂-215 at root, NACA 64₁-412 at tip. Dihedral 5° 30'. Incidence 2° 30' at root, 1° at tip. No sweepback, except on wingroot leading-edges. Conventional tapered all-metal two-spar structure of light alloy. Horn balanced plain ailerons and electrically actuated trailing-edge flaps of light alloy construction. No tabs.

FUSELAGE AND TAIL UNIT: As for 201.

LANDING GEAR: Electrically retractable tricycle type. Steerable nosewheel retracts rearward, main units inward into wings. All wheels faired by doors when retracted. Shock absorption of nosewheel and mainwheel units by Lord rubber discs. Cleveland wheels, with mainwheel tyres size 6.00-6 (6-ply), pressure 2.90 bars (42 lb/sq in). Nosewheel tyre size 5.00-5 (6-ply), pressure 3.38 bars (49 lb/sq in). Cleveland hydraulic brakes. Parking brake.

POWER PLANT: One 156.5 kW (210 hp) Continental TSIO-360-MB-1 flat-six turbocharged engine, driving a McCauley 2A34C216/90DHB-16E constant-speed metal propeller. Q-tip propeller optional. Goodrich propeller de-icing optional. Two integral fuel tanks in inner wings, with combined capacity of 297.5 litres (78.6 US gallons; 65.4 Imp gallons), of which 286 litres (75.6 US gallons; 63 Imp gallons) are usable. Refuelling points in upper surface of the inboard section of each wing. Oil capacity 7.5 litres (2 US gallons; 1.7 Imp gallons).

ACCOMMODATION: Cabin accommodates four persons in pairs on individual seats. Front seats fully adjustable, with lumbar support. Rear seats fold flat for carriage of bulky items of cargo. Dual controls standard. Forward hinged door on starboard side. Baggage space aft of rear seat, accessible from cabin and via baggage door on starboard side. Accommodation heated and ventilated.

SYSTEMS: Hydraulic system for brakes only. 28V DC electrical system powered by a 70A engine driven alternator. Dual 70A alternators optional. 28V 20Ah battery. Electric standby vacuum system standard. Oxygen system standard.

AVIONICS AND EQUIPMENT: Avionics options as for Mooney 205. Standard and optional equipment generally as for Mooney 205 except that standby vacuum system, push/pull vernier primary engine controls, turbine inlet

Mooney 252TSE (210 hp turbocharged Continental TSIO-360-MB-1)

temperature gauge, pressurised magnetos and air/oil separator are standard, and dual alternators, six-probe EGT gauge, oil cooler winterisation kit and air-conditioning system are optional.

DIMENSIONS, EXTERNAL AND INTERNAL:
As Mooney 201, except:

Length overall	7.75 m (25 ft 5 in)
Cabin door (stbd, over wing):	
Height	1.13 m (3 ft 8½ in)
Width	0.74 m (2 ft 5 in)
Baggage door (stbd, aft): Height	0.52 m (1 ft 8½ in)
Width	0.43 m (1 ft 5 in)
Height to sill	1.17 m (3 ft 10 in)

AREAS:

Fin	0.72 m² (7.80 sq ft)
Rudder	0.58 m² (6.25 sq ft)
Tailplane	1.99 m² (21.42 sq ft)
Elevators	1.21 m² (13.0 sq ft)

WEIGHTS AND LOADINGS:

Weight empty	816 kg (1,800 lb)
Max baggage	54 kg (120 lb)
Max ramp, T-O and landing weight	1,315 kg (2,900 lb)
Max wing loading	80.97 kg/m² (16.6 lb/sq ft)
Max power loading	8.4 kg/kW (13.8 lb/hp)

PERFORMANCE (at max T-O weight):

Max level speed	219 knots (406 km/h; 252 mph)
Max cruising speed, 78.6% power at 8,535 m (28,000 ft)	202 knots (374 km/h; 233 mph)
Econ cruising speed, 55% power at 7,010 m (23,000 ft)	178 knots (330 km/h; 205 mph)
Stalling speed:	
landing gear and flaps up	61 knots (113 km/h; 71 mph)
landing gear and flaps down	59 knots (110 km/h; 68 mph)
Max rate of climb at S/L	329 m (1,080 ft)/min
Certificated ceiling	8,535 m (28,000 ft)
T-O to 15 m (50 ft)	655 m (2,150 ft)
Endurance at max cruising speed	5 h 48 min

MOONEY PFM (M20L)

Design started in April 1986 of the Mooney M20L, the engineering prototype of which (N20PM) made its first flight in May 1987. Known as the Mooney PFM, the aircraft is powered by a Porsche PFM 3200-3 power plant. The airframe is generally similar to that of the Mooney 252TSE, but with an increase in fuselage length aft of the cabin area. The first production standard Mooney PFM (N10MP) made its first flight in October 1987 and was officially rolled out at the company's Kerville headquarters on 12 November. FAA certification was received in May 1988, when first customer deliveries bagan. Mooney was scheduled to manufacture 65-68 PFMs during 1988, with production expected to reach a rate of 5.5 aircraft per month by the end of the year. Orders for 40 had been received by the Spring of 1988, of which 10 had been completed.

The description for the Mooney 201 and 252TSE applies also to the PFM except as follows:

FUSELAGE: Generally as for Mooney 201, 205 and 252TSE, but with cabin tubular structure extended aft of rear seats by 0.305 m (1 ft 0 in) and nosewheel mounting point moved forward by 0.20 m (8 in).

LANDING GEAR: As for previously described models, except that the inner pair of main landing gear doors is deleted and mainwheels are unfaired when retracted.

POWER PLANT: One 162 kW (217 hp) Porsche PFM 3200-N03 flat-six aircooled engine attached to three-point overhead tubular mount structure and driving a two-blade constant-speed composite construction Hartzell BHC-J2YF-1BF/B7421 propeller via 0.442:1 reduction gearing. Engine has Bosch K-Jetronic fuel injection with automatic mixture control, dual solid-state Magneti Marelli electronic ignition systems, and single lever power control. Two integral fuel tanks in inboard wing leading-edges, with combined capacity of 252 litres (66.5 US gallons; 55.4 Imp gallons) of which 229 litres (60.5 US gallons; 50.4 Imp gallons) are usable. Oil capacity 12.8 litres (3.375 US gallons; 2.8 Imp gallons).

ACCOMMODATION: Porsche AG-styled interior standard.

SYSTEMS: Dual 28V DC electrical systems including 70A alternators, dual 24V 22Ah batteries and dual bus systems. Scott oxygen system and propeller de-icing system optional.

AVIONICS AND EQUIPMENT: Standard and optional avionics as for Mooney 252TSE. Standard equipment includes true airspeed indicator, sensitive altimeter, magnetic compass, vertical speed indicator, turn co-ordinator, electric directional gyro, Terra blind encoder, electric pictorial artificial horizon, dual alternator output loadmeter/voltmeter, digital engine monitoring gauges, oil pressure gauge, fuel pressure gauge, oil temperature gauge, tachometer, fuel flow indicator, OAT and CHT gauges, electric clock/flight hour recorder, alternate static source, internally lit instruments, glareshield panel dimmer control, auxiliary power receptacle point, vertically adjustable seats and custom designed exterior paint finish. Optional equipment generally as for Mooney 252TSE except Special Edition interior and polished propeller are not available and dual alternators, access step, recognition lights and seat headrests are standard.

The data for the Mooney 252TSE apply also to the Mooney PFM except as follows:

DIMENSIONS, EXTERNAL:

Length overall	15.44 m (26 ft 11 in)
Wheel track	2.76 m (9 ft 0¾ in)
Wheelbase	2.02 m (6 ft 7½ in)
Propeller ground clearance	0.28 m (11 in)
Passenger door: Height	0.89 m (2 ft 11 in)
Width	0.74 m (2 ft 5 in)
Baggage door: Height	0.52 m (1 ft 8½ in)
Width	0.43 m (1 ft 5 in)
Height to sill	1.19 m (3 ft 10 in)

DIMENSIONS, INTERNAL:

Cabin: Length	3.20 m (10 ft 6 in)
Floor area	3.53 m² (38.0 sq ft)
Volume	3.88 m³ (137 cu ft)
Baggage compartment volume	0.64 m³ (22.6 cu ft)

AREA:

Wings, gross	16.23 m² (174.7 sq ft)

WEIGHTS AND LOADINGS:

Weight empty	922 kg (2,033 lb)
Max T-O and landing weight	1,315 kg (2,900 lb)
Max wing loading	81.0 kg/m² (16.6 lb/sq ft)
Max power loading	8.13 kg/kW (13.36 lb/hp)

PERFORMANCE (at max T-O weight):

Never-exceed speed	195 knots (361 km/h; 224 mph)
Max level speed at S/L	171 knots (317 km/h; 197 mph)
Max cruising speed at S/L	168 knots (311 km/h; 193 mph)
Cruising speed at 2,745 m (9,000 ft):	
75% power	160 knots (296 km/h; 184 mph)
65% power	152 knots (282 km/h; 175 mph)
55% power	145 knots (269 km/h; 170 mph)
Stalling speed, power off:	
clean	63 knots (117 km/h; 72 mph) CAS
wheels and flaps down	57 knots (106 km/h; 66 mph) CAS
Max rate of climb at S/L	317 m (1,040 ft)/min
Service ceiling	5,883 m (19,300 ft)
T-O run	396 m (1,300 ft)
T-O to 15 m (50 ft)	792 m (2,600 ft)
Landing from 15 m (50 ft)	579 m (1,900 ft)
Landing run	244 m (800 ft)
Range, 45 min reserves:	
with max fuel	970 nm (1,798 km; 1,117 miles)
with max payload	500 nm (927 km; 576 miles)

MORRISEY

MORRISEY AIRCRAFT COMPANY
PO Box 6247, Kingman, Arizona 86402
Telephone: (602) 757 1240

MORRISEY MODEL 2000C

Mr Bill Morrisey, who originally designed the Morrisey Nifty light aircraft from which was derived the more powerful Varga Kachina (described in the 1984-85 *Jane's*), has re-acquired the rights to the design, which is now being marketed as the Morrisey Model 2000C. Also available are the Morrisey Bravo OM-1 and Padre, which were described in the Sport Aircraft section of the 1987-88 *Jane's*.

The Model 2000C is similar in general configuration to the earlier Nifty illustrated, with welded steel tube fuselage, metal skinned to aft of the cockpit section and fabric covered using the Stits process on the rear fuselage. Cockpit side panels are removable for maintenance. The wings and tail surfaces are of all-metal aluminium alloy construction with glassfibre wingtips. The cockpit seats two in tandem and is fully enclosed by a three-piece canopy, with access via a hinged centre section opening sideways to starboard. Streamlined rear decking is optional. The standard landing gear is of the non-retractable tricycle type, but a tailwheel version may be offered according to demand. Initial production aircraft will be powered by a 74.6 kW (100 hp) piston engine, driving a fixed-pitch two-blade propeller, but more powerful engines will be offered in the future. Buyers may also supply Morrisey Aircraft Company with their own engines and propellers to reduce purchase cost. The

Morrisey Nifty two-seat light aircraft, now in production as the Morrisey Model 2000C

Morrisey Model 2000C has received FAA type approval in Normal and Utility categories.

DIMENSIONS, EXTERNAL:

Wing span	9.14 m (30 ft 0 in)
Length overall	6.10 m (20 ft 0 in)

WEIGHT:

Max T-O weight	703 kg (1,550 lb)

PERFORMANCE:

Max level speed	more than 108 knots (201 km/h; 125 mph)

MTC

MOSHIER TECHNOLOGIES CORPORATION
599-A Fairchild Drive, Mountain View, California 94043
Telephone: (415) 968 6550
PRESIDENT AND CHIEF EXECUTIVE OFFICER:
Michael W. Moshier

Moshier Technologies Corporation (MTC) was formed in early 1986 to develop small, practical VTOL aircraft. The results of an earlier feasibility study indicated that such an aircraft could be built successfully using many existing off-the-shelf components and technologies.

Design goals established by MTC included a mechanically simple propulsion system, with no moving parts except for those of an advanced turbine engine; a compact airframe, built of composites, with small ground footprint; low acoustic and infra-red signatures; reliability and ease of operation; and multi-fuel capability. A family of such aircraft, collectively known as Aurora, will each incorporate the same generic fluidic propulsion system. A variant known as the Aurora Model 400-M is being developed for military roles such as personnel transport, reconnaissance, surveillance, rescue, VIP/courier, scout/attack (SCAT) and offensive/defensive duties. Also under development is a family of VTOL RPVs, for military and commercial applications.

Two- and four-seat commercial derivatives of the aircraft are planned in the long term. MTC foresees these aircraft serving in the business aviation and paramilitary roles such as VIP transport, charter, courier, ambulance/medevac, surveillance, law enforcement, and forest, border and customs patrol duties.

A generic version of the aircraft's fluidic propulsion system has been tested successfully at NASA's Ames facility. In early 1987 MTC began construction of a one-fifth scale model of the Aurora 400-C which began preliminary flight tests in November 1987. After successful testing of low-speed scale models has been completed MTC will seek joint-venture partners to continue full scale prototype development.

MTC AURORA 400-C

The following data should be regarded as provisional:
TYPE: Four-seat VTOL utility aircraft.
AIRFRAME: Semi-monocoque glassfibre and carbonfibre laminated structure over skeletal metal frame.
WINGS: Cantilever main wings at rear of airframe, with sweepback and slight anhedral. Outward-canted winglet

at each tip. Cantilever all-moving canard surfaces, forward swept and with slight anhedral.

LANDING GEAR: 'Three point' type with two retractable legs and one fixed skid. No wheels.

POWER PLANT: One turbofan of unspecified type rated at 8.01 kN (1,800 lb st). Fluidic amplification propulsion system, nominal ratio 1.6:1, nominal entrainment ratio 17:1, with no moving parts, claimed low dynamic pressure and exhaust temperature, and substantial noise attenuation. Fuel capacity 416 litres (110 US gallons; 92 Imp gallons).

ACCOMMODATION: Four seats in unpressurised enclosed cabin with upward opening 'gull wing' doors.

SYSTEMS: Fly by wire and fly by light three-axis control system, with multiple level redundancy.

DIMENSIONS, EXTERNAL:
Wing span	7.62 m (25 ft 0 in)
Length overall	4.27 m (14 ft 0 in)
Height (without skids)	1.52 m (5 ft 0 in)

AREA:
Wings, gross	7.62 m² (82.0 sq ft)

WEIGHTS AND LOADING:
Weight empty	497 kg (1,095 lb)
Max T-O weight	964 kg (2,125 lb)
Max wing loading	126.5 kg/m² (25.9 lb/sq ft)

PERFORMANCE (estimated, S/L, ISA):
Max level speed	460 knots (853 km/h; 530 mph)
Cruising speed at 610 m (2,000 ft), 33% power	208 knots (386 km/h; 240 mph)
Hover ceiling	2,743 m (9,000 ft)

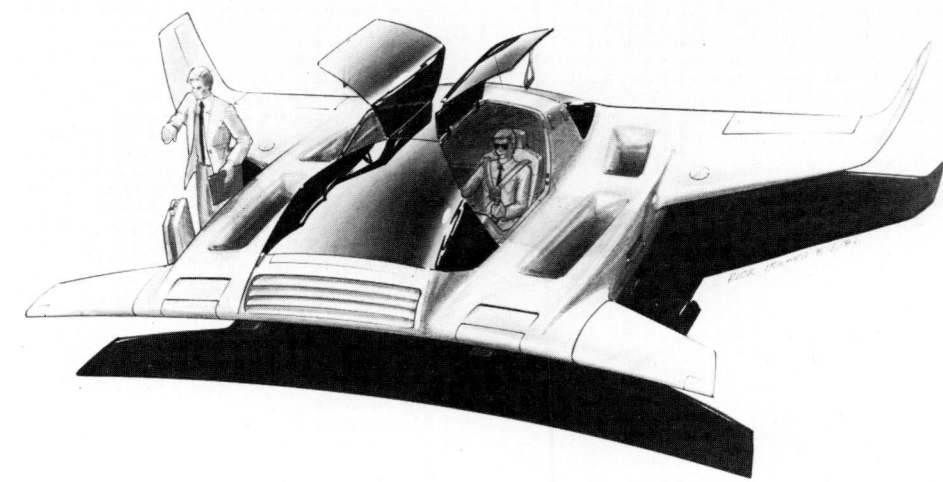

Artist's impression of Moshier Technologies Corporation Aurora Model 400-C VTOL aircraft

Range, standard flight profile of 3% engine operation in ground idle, 5% in VTOL/hover/translation, 92% in cruising flight   more than 347 nm (644 km; 400 miles)

Ferry range	more than 868 nm (1,609 km; 1,000 miles)
Endurance	more than 2 h

MU-2

MU-2 MODIFICATIONS INC

Box 7331, Dallas, Texas 75209
Telephone: (214) 358 3528
Fax: (214) 350 9261
PRESIDENT: Steve Gage
MARKETING: Barron Thomas Aviation Inc, Love Field, Dallas, Texas 75209

MU-2 EXPRESS CONVERSIONS

MU-2 Modifications Inc has developed and certificated cargo and medevac conversions of the long fuselage variants of the Mitsubishi MU-2 twin-turboprop business aircraft. Work commenced on the first conversion in April 1985, and FAA certification by supplemental type certificate was obtained in September and October of that year for the company's crew and cargo door modifications respectively.

The **MU-2 Express** conversion involves installation of a crew door in place of the cockpit window on the port side of the flight deck, hinged at its forward edge; a rear cargo door measuring 1.22 m (4 ft 0 in) high by 1.35 m (4 ft 5 in) wide in place of the aircraft's standard cabin door on the fuselage port side; and cargo nets in the cabin area. The rear cargo door can be a one-piece unit hinged at the top, or a twin door, vertically divided, hinged at front and rear, with a window in the forward door portion. It is available for use in either pressurised or unpressurised form. The MU-2 Express provides a total of 7.64 m³ (270.0 cu ft) of cargo space.

The **MU-2 Medi-Vac Express** is a dedicated emerg-

MU-2 Modifications Inc MU-2 Express twin-turboprop cargo aircraft

ency medical services aircraft which incorporates the crew door and a pressurised rear cargo door and provides accommodation for three stretcher patients, three medical attendants and associated life-support equipment. Other variants offered include a commuter aircraft with accommodation for ten passengers, a Combi passenger/cargo aircraft, and an Executive/Cargo quick-change aircraft.

An optional weight reduction programme carried out concurrently with the other modifications increases the aircraft's useful load to 1,678 kg (3,700 lb). By early 1988 MU-2 Modifications had delivered 29 MU-2 Express/ Medi-Vac Express conversions to customers in Italy, Spain and the United States.

NASA

NATIONAL AERONAUTICS AND SPACE ADMINISTRATION (Office of Aeronautics and Space Technology)

600 Independence Avenue SW, Washington, DC 20546
Telephone: (202) 453 1000
Telex: 89530 NASA WSH
Fax: (202) 426 4256
ACTING ASSOCIATE ADMINISTRATOR:
Dr William F. Ballhaus Jr
DIRECTOR OF AERONAUTICS: Cecil C. Rosen
DIRECTOR OF NASP OFFICE: Duncan E. McIver

NASA has several research programmes involving the use of specially developed, specially equipped or modified aircraft. Details of some of these follow:

NATIONAL AERO-SPACE PLANE
US Air Force designation: X-30

In his State of the Union address on 4 February 1986, President Reagan announced plans for an "aerospace plane" that "could shrink travel times between Washington, DC, and Tokyo . . . to less than two hours".

NASA and the US Department of Defense then initiated plans for a joint National Aero-Space Plane (NASP) research programme which could lead to a new generation of economic, reusable aerospace vehicles for the 21st century. The programme brings together hypersonic research programmes undertaken separately by DoD and NASA over a number of years, and follows an initial research phase of concept studies for a Transatmospheric Vehicle (TAV) conducted by aerospace manufacturers during 1984-85 under the direction of Air Force Systems Command's Aeronautical Systems and Space Divisions.

Rockwell International artist's impression of the X-30 National Aero-Space Plane

The Aero-Space Plane concept is based on an air-breathing hydrogen-fuelled aircraft, which would probably embody hybrid power plants combining rockets for take-off with supersonic combustion ramjets (scramjets), and be capable of horizontal take-off and landing. As a space vehicle it would be able to make single-stage entry into space and achieve orbital speeds up to Mach 25. As an aeroplane it would cruise in the upper atmosphere at sustained hypersonic velocities of Mach 5 to Mach 15 (5,250 to 15,750 km/h; 3,000 to 10,000 mph) at altitudes

around 32,000 m (105,000 ft).

Research already conducted in the areas of hypersonic propulsion, advanced materials and structures, fluid dynamics, supersonic combustion ramjet theory, development of lightweight, high strength, high temperature structural materials, and the availability of supercomputers for engine and airframe design integration, suggests that the first versions of such aircraft could be operational by the year 2000.

Aero-Space Planes, in various configurations, are expected to have both military and commercial applications. They could serve as low-cost satellite and orbital payload launch vehicles, long range air defence interceptors, and space platforms for laser and rocket systems of the kind proposed for the Strategic Defense Initiative (SDI) programme. NASP 'airliners', operating within the atmosphere at speeds up to Mach 15, would reduce dramatically the transit time on intercontinental routes, while operating from existing airport sites.

The US Air Force has been assigned overall responsibility for the NASP research programme, with NASA responsible for overall technology maturation and commercial applications. The current technology development phase of the NASP programme involves five major contractors for propulsion and airframe development. The propulsion contracts were awarded to Rocketdyne and Pratt & Whitney; General Dynamics, McDonnell Douglas and Rockwell International received the airframe contracts. Each contractor is pursuing a particular prime technology, although a mixture of them will almost certainly be needed in the eventual selected configuration. GD is taking the lead in studying carbon structures, while McDonnell Douglas studies silicone carbide fibre reinforced titanium and Rockwell pursues titanium aluminide honeycomb.

In the third phase of the programme an experimental subscale aircraft, designated X-30, will be used to develop, prove, and demonstrate Aero-Space Plane technologies throughout the flight envelope for hypersonic cruise and acceleration to low Earth orbit. Final selection of contractors for prototype manufacture is expected in late 1990, with a first flight of the X-30 anticipated in the mid-1990s.

NASA HIDEC F-15

The Highly Integrated Digital Electronic Control (HIDEC) programme is being used to evaluate performance gains provided by the integration of propulsion and flight control systems, and is being conducted jointly by NASA, the US Air Force and industry.

A McDonnell Douglas F-15 Eagle (NASA 287) has been modified with a digital flight control system, advanced digitally controlled Pratt & Whitney PW1128 engines, and integrating hardware connecting the two systems. Initial testing began on 25 June 1986 and demonstrated significant improvement in aircraft performance and fuel economy. Additional testing was continuing in 1987.

NASA PROPFAN TEST ASSESSMENT PROGRAMME

Details of the NASA Propfan Test Assessment Programme (PTA) may be found under the LASC Georgia division entry in this section.

NASA MISSION ADAPTIVE WING RESEARCH

A description of the joint Boeing/US Air Force/NASA Mission Adaptive Wing (MAW) programme, using a modified General Dynamics AFTI F-111A testbed aircraft, appears in the Boeing Military Airplanes entry.

NASA WINGTIP VORTEX TURBINE RESEARCH

Flight testing at NASA Langley of wingtip mounted vortex turbines installed on a modified Piper PA-28R Arrow III (N519NA/NASA 519) have shown the feasibility of reducing induced drag by recovering the energy of

NASA's Highly Integrated Digital Electronic Control McDonnell Douglas F-15 Eagle

wingtip vortices. The aircraft was illustrated in the 1987-88 *Jane's*.

Sundstrand Aviation Mechanical supplied turbines for which NASA designed tapered and cambered blades. One turbine is attached to each wingtip of the Arrow, recovering without drag penalty 2.2 kW (3 hp) out of 10.4 kW (14 hp) needed to offset total induced drag on the aircraft. NASA believes that on an aircraft such as a Boeing 747 wingtip vortex turbines could offer power recovery of the order of 298 kW (400 hp).

NASA ATOPS

NASA has selected Honeywell's Air Transport Systems Division to supply an air data/inertial reference system (ADIRS), similar to that developed for the Airbus A320, to provide data for the aft research cockpit of its Boeing 737-100 Advanced Transport Systems Research Vehicle (see 1986-87 *Jane's*). The ADIRS was due for delivery in May 1988 and will be used in NASA's ATOPS (advanced transport operating system) programme.

NASA/US NAVY F-8 OBLIQUE-WING DEMONSTRATOR

In late 1984 NASA and the US Navy signed an agreement to flight test an oblique wing variable-sweep demonstrator aircraft, based on NASA's LTV F-8 Crusader digital fly by wire research aircraft. The oblique wing concept was first tested on NASA's AD-1 subsonic experimental aircraft in 1979. The NASA/Navy programme will extend flight testing to transonic and supersonic speeds. On 13 November 1985 NASA awarded a contract for preliminary design of the oblique wing to Rockwell International's North American Aircraft Operations Division, and a wing of 16.86 m (55 ft 4 in) span and 27.87 m² (300 sq ft) area at 0° sweep has been proposed, with a thickness/chord ratio of 14% (constant). A follow-on contract covers construction and ground testing of the oblique wing demonstrator, with an initial one year, 40-flight test programme expected to begin in 1989.

The oblique wing F-8 is expected to be capable of speeds up to at least Mach 1.4 with a maximum wing sweep of 60-65°. The first year's flight test programme will be aimed at expanding the flight envelope of the oblique wing configuration, demonstrating its transonic and supersonic capabilities, with some emphasis on high altitude cruise and

manoeuvring capabilities, and at adapting the modular software of the F-8's digital flight computers to accommodate the characteristics of the oblique wing. Potential applications for future US Navy aircraft include the use of oblique wings on carrier based aircraft, on which the straight-wing configuration could be used for take-off, landing and loiter, and the oblique position for high speed interception of hostile targets.

NASA HIGH-ALPHA RESEARCH F/A-18

NASA's Ames-Dryden Research Center is conducting a high angle of attack technology programme to research flight control concepts which employ various combinations of aerodynamics and thrust vector control at subsonic and high alpha flight conditions. NASA has contracted McDonnell Douglas Corporation to modify its F/A-18 Hornet high-alpha research aircraft with a thrust vector control system for pitch and yaw axes. Work began on modifying the F/A-18 in June 1987.

NASA STOVL and ASTOVL PROGRAMMES

NASA has awarded a two-stage contract to Lockheed Aeronautical Systems Company for a supersonic STOVL (short take-off/vertical landing) fighter. Under the first stage, Lockheed's Burbank division developed a conceptual design for such a fighter that could fly after the year 2001, powered by a hybrid fan vectored thrust (HFVT) turbine engine based on "a proprietary Rolls-Royce design". The study, aimed at identifying technologies that would make STOVL aircraft operationally cost-effective, is now in its second stage, in which Lockheed will assemble a scale model of the design to assess its hovering capabilities.

Under a separate programme, NASA's Ames Research Center was due to conduct wind tunnel testing in 1988 of a joint design by General Dynamics and Boeing Canada's de Havilland division for an advanced STOVL (ASTOVL) fighter featuring ejector-lift short take-off and vertical landing. Designated E-7, the GD/Boeing concept features large delta wings of NASA-Ames design, with 12 ejector intakes in each wingroot just aft of the leading-edge. The non-flying E-7 test model is powered by a Rolls-Royce Spey turbofan initially, though plans are to refit it with a General Electric F110 later.

NORTHROP
NORTHROP CORPORATION

1840 Century Park East, Los Angeles, California 90067-2199
Telephone: (213) 553 6262
Telex: 192893 NORTHROP 1
Fax: (213) 201 3023, 553 2076, or 552 3104
CHAIRMAN AND CHIEF EXECUTIVE OFFICER:
　Thomas V. Jones
PRESIDENT AND CHIEF OPERATING OFFICER: Kent Kresa
SENIOR VICE-PRESIDENT, PUBLIC AFFAIRS:
　Les Daly
VICE-PRESIDENT, PUBLIC INFORMATION: A. W. Cantafio

This company was formed in 1939 by John K. Northrop and others to undertake the design and manufacture of military aircraft. Although continuing its activities in the

design, development and production of aircraft, missiles and target drone systems, Northrop broadened its scope of operation to include electronics, space technology, communications, support services and commercial products. To reflect this changing character of its business, the company changed its name from Northrop Aircraft Inc to Northrop Corporation in 1959. Since 1986, its operations have been handled by the Aircraft and B-2 (formerly Advanced Systems) Divisions, an Electronics Systems Group, and a subsidiary known as Northrop Worldwide Aircraft Services Inc.

The Aircraft Division is responsible for the design and manufacture of fighter aircraft, the manufacture of commercial aircraft major assemblies, and the work of Northrop Ventura in RPVs and targets. B-2 Division manages a number of aerospace programmes and is prime contractor to the USAF for research and development of

the B-2 advanced technology bomber. Northrop Worldwide Aircraft Services Inc, of Lawton, Oklahoma, provides technical and support services. Electronics Systems Group comprises an Electronics Division; Electro-Mechanical Division, which handles advanced missile programmes, electro-optical systems for target identification and target designation; Defense Systems Division, designer and manufacturer of electronic countermeasures systems, including the internal countermeasures set (ICS) for the US Air Force's F-15 Eagle; and Precision Products Division; and a subsidiary, Northrop Services Inc, which provides technical support to NASA at Johnson Space Center in Houston, Texas, the Environmental Protection Agency, the National Institute of Health and the National Cancer Institute.

Northrop had over 45,000 employees in early 1988.

AIRCRAFT DIVISION

One Northrop Avenue, Hawthorne, California 90250
Telephone: (213) 332 1000
Telex: 181861 NORTHR A HWTH
VICE-PRESIDENT AND AIRCRAFT DIVISION GENERAL MANAGER:
　Joseph T. Gallagher
VICE-PRESIDENT, ADVANCED DESIGN: Delbert H. Jacobs
VICE-PRESIDENT, ENGINEERING: Thomas R. Rooney
VICE-PRESIDENT, INFORMATION RESOURCES: Robert W. Slusser

Northrop Ventura
1515 Rancho Conejo Boulevard, Newbury Park, California 91320
Telephone: (805) 373 2000
Telex: 683 9403 NOCVNP

Current production at Northrop's Aircraft Division, which has about 14,000 employees, is centred on the F/A-18 Hornet multi-mission fighter (see McDonnell Douglas entry), and major Boeing 747 subcontract work, which includes manufacture of the main fuselage section, the extra-large side loading cargo door, passenger doors and upper deck.

Northrop is principal subcontractor for the Hornet, with design and production responsibility for the centre and rear fuselage and the twin vertical tails, including internal

systems such as fuel, the environmental control system and auxiliary power system. The 600th shipset of these components was delivered in May 1987.

Northrop is prime contractor for research and development of the US Air Force's B-2 advanced technology bomber (ATB). It is also one of the two selected prime contractors in the USAF's advanced tactical fighter (ATF) programme, with McDonnell Douglas Corporation as principal subcontractor; and is engaged in research projects involving advanced simulators and composite materials.

Northrop Ventura became a unit of the Aircraft Division in 1987.

NORTHROP TIGER II
USAF designations: F-5E and F-5F

Although series production of the Northrop F-5 series ended in early 1987 with the delivery of two F-5Es to the Air Force of Bahrain, Northrop assembled four F-5Es and three F-5Fs from major spares components during 1987 and delivered the aircraft to the Singapore Air Force. Two more F-5Es were due to follow in December 1988 and a further three in April 1989.

Details of the F-5E, F-5F and RF-5E TigerEye may be found in the 1986-87 and earlier editions of *Jane's*.

NORTHROP YF-23A (ATF)
For available details of the US Air Force's Advanced Tactical Fighter (ATF) programme, see the US Air Force Systems Command entry in this section. Northrop is contracted to build two YF-23A prototypes, in partnership with McDonnell Douglas as principal subcontractor. Other

YF-23A subcontractors include a Hamilton Standard/General Electric team (flight control computer) and ATT/TRW (central digital processor).

B-2 DIVISION
8900 East Washington Boulevard, Pico Rivera, California 90660-3737
Telephone: (213) 942 3000
VICE-PRESIDENT AND GENERAL MANAGER: John Patierno
VICE-PRESIDENT, DEPUTY GENERAL MANAGER AND B-2
  PROGRAMME MANAGER: Ed Smith

NORTHROP B-2
The B-2 advanced technology bomber (ATB) is being developed to meet a USAF requirement, first outlined publicly in late 1981, for a highly survivable strategic penetration bomber to complement and eventually replace the Rockwell B-1B. Popularly known as the 'stealth bomber' due to its adoption of low-observables (LO) technology, it has been developed by Northrop, with assistance from Boeing Aerospace and LTV's Vought Aero Products Division, under an October 1981 contract from the USAF's Aeronautical Systems Division. General Electric has been selected to furnish the aircraft's four F101-GE-102 turbofans, and six development aircraft have reportedly been funded. The USAF has a declared requirement for 132 B-2s, of which 120 would be nuclear-capable, and is seeking initial operational capability in the early 1990s. It awarded Northrop a $2 billion contract on 19 November 1987 to initiate B-2 production.

The ATB programme is so highly classified that it came as a surprise when, on 20 April 1988, USAF issued an artist's impression showing the aircraft's general appearance. As expected, this revealed that the B-2 has a flying-wing configuration, and USAF's Chief of Staff, Gen Larry D. Welch, subsequently told reporters: "Everything you see in that representation, if it's there, is right". For security reasons, however, the drawing omits much detail that might disclose finer details of the design, and there has been speculation that the inlet geometry, for example, may be changed on later prototypes. The wing appears to have about 35° sweepback on the leading-edges, and a zig-zag trailing-edge that presumably is a compromise between the conflicting requirements of 'stealth' and aerodynamics. Construction almost certainly relies extensively upon

Artist's impression of Northrop B-2 advanced technology bomber

graphite/epoxy (carbonfibre) and other composite materials, much of it possibly of a honeycomb nature to absorb radar emissions. In the absence of a vertical tail unit, movable control surfaces are likely to consist of inboard flaps and outboard elevons on the trailing-edge.

Initial information shows that the aircraft is smaller than previously expected, with a gross weight in the order of 108,860-122,470 kg (240,000-270,000 lb) rather that the previously suggested figures in the 158,760-170,100 kg (350,000-375,000 lb) range. The engines, with streamline overwing intake ducts and underwing trailing-edge nozzles, are non-afterburning and are mounted in pairs, each side of the central 'fuselage' bulge housing the two- or three-man crew and the main weapons bay. Internal weapons load, confirmed by USAF officials as being smaller than that of the B-1B, will normally consist of about 16 medium-range cruise missiles or an equivalent weight of B-83 nuclear bombs, a total weight in the region of 34,000 kg (75,000 lb). Performance, which is high subsonic, is expected to include an unrefuelled range of up to 6,500 nm (12,000 km; 7,500

miles) and the ability to operate at altitudes ranging from a few hundred feet to above 15,240 m (50,000 ft).

First flight of a B-2 prototype, previously due to take place in late 1987, was said in the following April to be scheduled for the Autumn of 1988, taking off from the assembly facility (USAF Plant 42) at Palmdale, California, and flying to the nearby Air Force Flight Test Center at Edwards AFB. Meanwhile, some of the flight control and other avionics intended for the B-2 were reportedly being flown at Edwards in an unidentified testbed aircraft in the Spring of 1988. The B-2's initial operating base will be Whiteman AFB, Missouri, where 34 B-2 hangars and additional support facilities are currently under construction. Two other bases will be designated later. Oklahoma City Air Logistics Center has been selected as the primary depot facility for the B-2.

DIMENSIONS (approx):

Wing span	52.43 m (172 ft)
Length overall	21.03 m (69 ft)
Height overall	5.18 m (17 ft)

OMAC
OMAC INC
PO Box 3530, 1 Rockwell Avenue, Albany, Georgia 31708
Telephone: (912) 436 2425
Fax: (912) 436 2488
CHIEF EXECUTIVE OFFICER: Charles V. Mihaylo
NATIONAL SALES MANAGER: David J. Rooney

OMAC was founded in Reno, Nevada, to develop and market a low cost high performance and economical six/eight-seat turboprop powered business aircraft of canard configuration, known as the Laser 300 (originally OMAC I).

On 30 January 1985 OMAC began operations at a 19,138 m² (206,000 sq ft) headquarters at Albany Municipal Airport, Georgia.

OMAC LASER 300
The OMAC 1 prototype flew for the first time on 11 December 1981, but was slightly damaged in a ground accident in the Spring of 1982. In June of that year modifications were made to the original configuration, as detailed in earlier editions of *Jane's*. This aircraft had completed 249 flights by the Summer of 1987, when it was retired from the test programme and displayed in the Museum of Flight at Boeing Field, Seattle, Washington.

A second prototype (N81PH) flew for the first time on 19 February 1983, becoming an experimental testbed for further modification and design changes. Among these was replacement of the original Textron Lycoming LTP 101-700A-1A turboprop with a similarly rated Garrett TPE331-9 in 1984, and the addition of larger wingtip fins. Following research in the wind tunnels at NASA's Langley facility, the Laser 300 production design was 'frozen' in April 1985 with further changes which included reconfigured over-cabin strake fuel tanks, modified nose contours, enlarged circular cabin cross-section, forward and rear baggage compartments, and adoption of a P&WC PT6A-135A power plant. The first production Laser 300 (N301L) was rolled out in early June 1988, and made its first flight on 29 July. FAA certification and first customer deliveries are anticipated in early 1989.

The following description applies to the Laser 300 production version:

TYPE: Lightweight all-metal business aircraft of fail-safe, fatigue resistant design.

WINGS: Cantilever high-wing monoplane, with constant chord and 20° sweepback at quarter-chord. Wing section Hicks modified NACA 63-A215 (Mod B) at root, 63-A212 (Mod B) at tip, with drooped outboard leading-edge. Dihedral 1° 30'. Conventional two-spar structure of aluminium alloy. Electro-mechanically operated trailing-edge flaps, of single-slotted Fowler type. Coventional cable actuated ailerons. Tip fins fitted at wingtips extend above and below wing. Each lower segment incorporates cable operated rudder. Electrically actuated bungee roll and yaw trim system.

FUSELAGE: Conventional aluminium alloy semi-monocoque pressurised structure. Dorsal and ventral fins.

FOREPLANE: Cantilever monoplane of constant chord and NASA LS(1)0417 modified section. Conventional

two-spar light alloy structure. Full span elevator each side. Electro-mechanically actuated bungee trim tab in port elevator.

LANDING GEAR: Hydraulically retractable tricycle type. Free-castoring nosewheel retracts forward. Hydraulic shock absorption. Main units have tubular spring steel legs and retract rearward and inward on a skewed axis. Nosewheel tyre size 6.00-6. Mainwheels have heavy duty tyres size 17.5 × 5.75. Hydraulic brakes. Rear 'tail bumper' comprising rearward retracting urethane roller protects propeller from damage in the event of over-rotation.

POWER PLANT: One Pratt & Whitney Canada PT6A-135A turboprop, flat rated at 559 kW (750 shp) and driving a McCauley three-blade feathering and reversing metal

Retouched photograph of first prototype OMAC Laser 300

pusher propeller. Fuel in integral strake tanks along top of cabin, and in inboard wing tanks and wing centre-section tank, with combined capacity of 1,136 litres (300 US gallons; 250 Imp gallons).

ACCOMMODATION: Standard seating for two pilots and five passengers. Two seats for pilot and co-pilot/passenger, two single seats and a three-seat divan, all forward facing. Seats track mounted to permit easy conversion for passenger/cargo use. Club seating arrangement with executive work tables, or two forward facing seats with a three-seat bench on starboard side, are optional, as are other layouts seating up to 10 persons including crew. Baggage compartments forward or aft of cabin seats, with space at front or rear for toilet. Airstair door at front on port side. Emergency exit at rear on starboard side. Unpressurised baggage compartments in nose and tailcone.

SYSTEMS: Pressurisation system with max cabin differential of 0.38 bars (5.5 lb/sq in). Hydraulic system with dual electrically powered pumps for operation of landing gear. TKS anti-icing system on windscreen, canard and wing. Freon air-conditioning optional.

AVIONICS AND EQUIPMENT: King Silver Crown avionics will be offered as standard factory fit. Emergency oxygen and external power socket standard.

DIMENSIONS, EXTERNAL (all data provisional):

Wing span	12.65 m (41 ft 6 in)
Foreplane span	7.16 m (23 ft 6 in)
Length overall	9.02 m (29 ft 7 in)
Height overall	3.00 m (9 ft 10 in)
Propeller diameter	2.69 m (8 ft 10 in)

DIMENSIONS, INTERNAL:

Cabin: Length, excl flight deck	3.18 m (10 ft 5¼ in)
Max height	1.52 m (5 ft 0 in)
Max width	1.53 m (5 ft 0½ in)
Volume	6.94 m³ (245.0 cu ft)
Baggage compartment volume (total)	2.18 m³ (77.0 cu ft)

AREAS:

Wings, gross	24.15 m² (260.0 sq ft)
Foreplane	6.13 m² (66.0 sq ft)

WEIGHTS:

Weight empty	2,313 kg (5,100 lb)
Max fuel weight	1,474 kg (3,250 lb)
Max baggage	236 kg (520 lb)
Max T-O and landing weight	3,787 kg (8,350 lb)

PERFORMANCE (estimated at max T-O weight):

Max cruising speed at 7,620 m (25,000 ft)	253 knots (468 km/h; 291 mph)
Econ cruising speed	200 knots (370 km/h; 230 mph)
Stalling speed	61 knots (113 km/h; 71 mph)
Max rate of climb at S/L	613 m (2,010 ft)/min
Certification ceiling	7,620 m (25,000 ft)
Service ceiling	9,150 m (30,000 ft)
T-O to 15 m (50 ft)	610 m (2,000 ft)
Landing from 15 m (50 ft)	701 m (2,300 ft)
Range:	
with max payload	1,398 nm (2,591 km; 1,610 miles)
with max fuel	2,095 nm (3,882 km; 2,412 miles)

ORLANDO
ORLANDO HELICOPTER AIRWAYS INC
2774 Carrier Avenue, Sanford, Florida 32771
Telephone: (305) 323 1756
Telex: 52 9450
PRESIDENT: Fred P. Clark
VICE-PRESIDENT OF SALES: Troy E. Simmons

Orlando Helicopter Airways Inc was founded at Sanford, Florida, in 1964, since when the company has been engaged in the remanufacture, sale and operation of Sikorsky helicopters. The company has large stocks of parts and components for Sikorsky S-52, S-55/H-19 and S-58/H-34 helicopters and owns the FAA type certificates for all models of the H-19 series and the H-34. Rotorparts Inc, an affiliate company, claims the world's largest stocks of Sikorsky S-55 parts, and supplies components for S-55, S-58, S-61 and S-62 helicopters to many overseas governments. Total sales of Sikorsky helicopters remanufactured by Orlando Helicopter Airways exceed 100. Future plans include conversions of later models such as the S-61, S-62 and S-64 series as they are declared surplus by military forces; turbine engine conversions of piston engined helicopters; and experimentation with alternative fuels such as gasoline/alcohol and propane gas in helicopters for agricultural operation.

On 27 October 1985 an agreement was signed with the Guangzhou Machinery Tool Company for the production of Orlando OHA-S-55 Bearcat helicopters in the People's Republic of China. A new company, Guangzhou Orlando Helicopters (which see), will initially assemble US manufactured parts, leading to production of components in China. The 20-year joint venture includes the establishment and operation of helicopter passenger services in China, and will also offer rotor blade overhaul and repair facilities for Far East operators. Future plans include the assembly of larger helicopter types in China. Orlando Helicopter Airways and Bates Associates of Hong Kong have also formed Orlando Helicopter Far East Ltd to handle export marketing of helicopters manufactured in China.

ORLANDO/SIKORSKY S-52
Orlando Helicopter Airways offers a four-seat civilian conversion of the S-52 which includes dual controls, night lighting, VHF transceiver and FAA certification. In 1983 the company, in conjunction with Kaylor Energy Products Inc of Menlo Park, California, converted an S-52 to electric power. The proof-of-concept machine has been extensively modified for the installation of four electric motors linked by a common shaft to the main transmission. A battery pack of twelve 72V lead-acid batteries is mounted forward of the motors and provides approximately ten minutes' power from a full charge. The power produced by the electric motors is in the order of 183 kW (245 hp). Ground trials began in late 1983. The next phases of the test programme will include use of silver zinc batteries to extend flight time to 30 minutes, and replacement of batteries with an 'instantly rechargeable' lithium hydroxide power system. In the final test phase the four electric motors will be replaced with a single motor. Orlando Helicopter Airways points out a number of advantages to electric powered helicopters, including low noise levels, lack of exhaust emissions, no infra-red signature from the motor, and simplicity of the power system.

A four-seat turbine engined conversion of the S-52, powered by a 313 kW (420 shp) Allison 250-C20B turboshaft engine, is known as the Orlando **OHA-S-52T Clipper.**

ORLANDO/SIKORSKY S-55/H-19
Several remanufactured models of Sikorsky S-55/H-19 series helicopters are offered by Orlando Helicopter Airways:

Vistaplane. Passenger/air ambulance version seating eight passengers in standard version or 11 passengers in high density configuration. For ambulance work up to six litters and two attendants can be accommodated. Cabin floor viewing window optional.

Orlando Helicopter Airways OHA-S-55 Bearcat agricultural helicopter

Heli-Camper. VIP model with sleeping facilities for four passengers in fully carpeted and soundproofed cabin; hot and cold water; refrigerator; two-burner stove; shower and wash basin; toilet; air-conditioning. Other standard features include colour television and AM/FM stereo radio and tape deck, roll-up awning, tinted windows, bar and storage cabinets, dual flight controls, full night lighting and dual landing lights, interphone communication system, King 360-channel VHF transceiver and VOR, King transponder, and emergency locator transmitter. Options include an electro-mechanical cargo sling, hydraulic hoist, amphibious floats, rotating spot light, and King KT-96 radio telephone. The Heli-Camper has a stripped and remanufactured airframe, new instruments, new or overhauled dynamic components including main and tail rotor blades, and an overhauled 596 kW (800 hp) Wright Cyclone R-1300-3D piston engine. Fuel capacity 715 litres (189 US gallons; 157.5 Imp gallons); max T-O weight 3,266 kg (7,200 lb); cruising speed 78 knots (145 km/h 90 mph); range 304 nm (563 km; 350 miles).

OHA-S-55 Nite-Writer. Aerial advertising model incorporating a 12.2 × 2.4 m (40 × 8 ft) Sky Sign Inc computerised electronic billboard, mounted at 40° to the side of the helicopter's fuselage. Continuously running messages, graphics and logos can be displayed on the sign, with a claimed night legibility range of up to 1.7 nm (3.2 km; 2 miles).

OHA-S-55 Bearcat. Designed for Orlando-developed combination spray and dry dispensing systems for quick conversion from liquid chemicals to dry fertilisers or seeds. Glassfibre chemical tank, capacity 946 litres (250 US gallons; 208 Imp gallons) standard. System also allows dry material to be carried internally rather than in underslung bucket. Also adaptable for firefighting. Orlando Helicopter Airways has obtained FAA approval for S-55 operators using Pratt & Whitney R-1340 engines under FAR Parts 91 (Standard), 137 (Agricultural) and 133 (External Load) to use automobile fuel in their helicopters, and all Orlando-modified S-55s with R-1340 engines include this approval. The OHA-S-55 is equipped with a 'super quiet' engine muffler system. Kysor cockpit air-conditioning system optional.

Heavy Lift. External load model for logging, construction and firefighting operations, with 1,361 kg (3,000 lb) useful load.

As noted in the Chinese section of this edition, an **OHA-S-55T Challenger** version, with a 522 kW (700 shp) Textron Lycoming LTS 101-700A-3 turboshaft engine, is, together with the standard OHA-S-55, the subject of a co-production agreement with the People's Republic of China, where it will be known as the **Panda.** A proposed **OHA-S-55T Phoenix** variant will feature Pratt & Whitney Canada PT6 single- or twin-turbine engines mounted on the transmission deck, and a new streamlined nose section.

Hind Look-alike. Under US Army Missile Command contract, Orlando is modifying 15 H-19/S-55s into simulated representations of the Soviet Mil Mi-24 'Hind-E' combat helicopter for use by troops in battlefield training and recognition, and as pilotless targets. Modification

Orlando Helicopter Airways S-58T Orlando Airliner

involves fitting a larger, reshaped nose, a new tailboom, stub wings, weapon pylons, 'operational' blisters, and a new five-blade main rotor. The new nose was designed by 3D Industries of Madison Heights, Michigan, which is supplying moulds and canopies for the aircraft. The drone flight control package will be provided by Honeywell. Deliveries were scheduled for completion by November 1988.

ORLANDO/SIKORSKY S-58/H-34

Five remanufactured models of Sikorsky S-58/H-34 series helicopters are offered. The **Agricultural** and **Heavy Lift** versions have a 1,137 kW (1,525 hp) Wright Cyclone R-1820-84 piston engine and are similarly equipped to equivalent versions of the Orlando S-55/H-19.

Heli-Camper. Similarly equipped to S-55 Heli-Camper, but with additional standard features: 8.73 m² (94 sq ft) living area with sculptured carpeting, entertainment centre, separate bar, sleeping accommodation for six passengers, full-size four-burner stove and 0.11 m³ (3.9 cu ft) refrigerator, 3,500W generator, super soundproofing, tinted glass and wraparound windscreen. 1,137 kW (1,525 hp) Wright Cyclone R-1820-84 radial piston engine. Fuel capacity 992 litres (262 US gallons; 218 Imp gallons); max T-O weight 5,670 kg (12,500 lb); cruising speed 96 knots (177 km/h; 110 mph); range 304 nm (563 km; 350 miles).

Orlando Airliner. High density version of the Sikorsky S-58T twin-turbine helicopter (see California Helicopters entry in this section). Standard equipment includes dual flight controls; toe brakes; hydraulic rotor brake; two independent servo control systems; cabin, cockpit, instrument, position, night and landing lights; rotating beacon; 24V battery, 1,071 litre (283 US gallon; 235.6 Imp gallon) fuel system; 2,268 kg (5,000 lb) capacity cargo sling; new paintwork; an extended passenger cabin; 18 additional cabin windows (for a total of 22); 18 airline-standard seats (15 forward facing and three rearward facing, standard or lightweight); Flightex soundproofing; tinted cabin windows; and ram air scoop for cabin cooling. Options available for the Orlando Airliner include a 272 kg (600 lb) capacity rescue hoist; pop-out emergency floats; 568 litre (150 US gallon; 125 Imp gallon) capacity external auxiliary

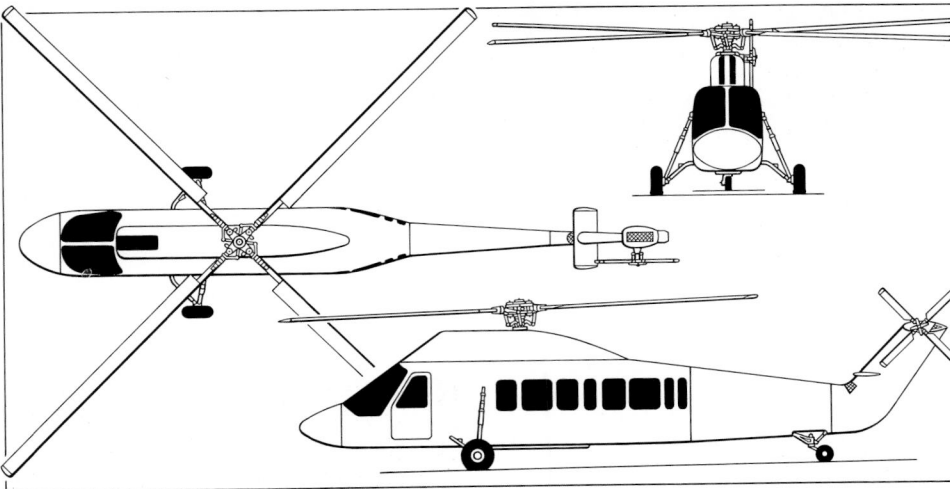
Orlando Helicopter Airways OHA-S-58T Viking twin-turbine conversion of Sikorsky S-58 *(Jane's/Mike Keep)*

fuel tank; stereo system; toilet; air-conditioning; one-piece windscreen; and customer choice of avionics. By early 1984, the latest data for which a total has been received, Orlando Helicopter Airways had delivered ten Orlando Airliners, including two for New York Helicopter Airways. The Orlando Airliner has a useful load of over 2,268 kg (5,000 lb), maximum speed at S/L of 120 knots (222 km/h; 138 mph), hovering ceiling OGE of 2,440 m (8,000 ft), and range, with auxiliary fuel and 20 min reserves, of 373 nm (692 km; 430 miles).

Flying Armoured Personnel Carrier. Military version of S-58T with extended passenger cabin and 18 opening cabin windows. The entire lower fuselage below the line of the cabin windows is protected with Kevlar soft armour plating. Fuel system similarly armoured, and

incorporates self-sealing tanks. Pilot and co-pilot side windows are made from Lexan bullet resistant material, with 6.35 mm (¼ in) 'boiler plate' wing panels for added crew protection, and soft Kevlar armour around and under seats and in engine compartment. Two additional doors, each 0.56 m × 1.17 m (22 in × 46 in) on port side of fuselage, supplementing main cabin sliding door on starboard side. Provision for mounting heavy weapons at door and window stations, and for carrying external stores.

A new version of the Orlando S-58 is under development, designated **OHA-S-58T Viking.** It will be powered by twin Pratt & Whitney Canada PT6 turbine engines mounted on the transmission deck and will have a redesigned streamlined nose.

PHALANX
PHALANX ORGANIZATION INC

PHALANX MP-18 DRAGON

In the Spring of 1986 a full-size 'plug' had been completed for the twin-turbofan multi-role MP-18, from which

moulds were to be created for the aircraft's Kevlar/Nomex composite airframe components. Work was progressing on the construction of five prototypes for demonstrating the Dragon's various configurations. A first flight was then tentatively scheduled for early 1988, but in 1987 it was reported that Phalanx's assets had been sold to a company

known as American Aerospace Inc, and no subsequent news of the venture has been received. A description and illustration of the MP-18 can be found in the 1987-88 *Jane's*.

PIA
PITTSBURGH INSTITUTE OF AERONAUTICS

Box 10897, Pittsburgh, Pennsylvania 15236
Telephone: (412) 462 9011
PRESIDENT: Ivan D. Livi

PIA MODIFIED GRUMMAN OV-1A MOHAWK

To enhance the versatility of its Mohawk aircraft, used for testing engines and avionics, electrical and hydraulic systems, this aviation technician school has installed two Westinghouse J34 turbojets in underwing pods. The turbojets occupy the outer wing stations used formerly for external fuel tanks, and supplement the aircraft's normal Textron Lycoming T53 turboprops. The new mountings are designed to facilitate engine changes, and the Mohawk can be operated with either the turbojets or turboprops in use.

Pittsburgh Institute of Aeronautics' Grumman OV-1A Mohawk with Westinghouse J34 turbojet engines in underwing pods *(Frank Bria)*

PIASECKI
PIASECKI AIRCRAFT CORPORATION

2nd Street West, Essington, Pennsylvania 19029
Telephone: (215) 521 5700
PRESIDENT: Frank N. Piasecki
VICE-PRESIDENT, ENGINEERING: Donald N. Myers
INDUSTRIAL ENGINEER: Kenneth R. Meenen

The Piasecki Aircraft Corporation was formed in 1955 by Mr Frank Piasecki, who was formerly Chairman of the Board and President of the Piasecki Helicopter Corporation (now Boeing Helicopters). The company has a wholly owned subsidiary, Piasecki Aircraft of Canada Ltd, in Ottawa, Ontario. Latest proposals for the company's Heli-Stat hybrid VTOL vehicle are given in the Lighter than Air section of this edition.

PIASECKI 16H-3 PATHFINDER

On 29 March 1988 Piasecki Aircraft Corporation announced plans for the development of a high-speed compound helicopter known as the Model 16H-3 Pathfinder, the general configuration of which can be seen in the accompanying artist's impression. The Pathfinder is

Artist's impression of Piasecki 16H-3 Pathfinder 15-seat compound helicopter

intended to compete with fixed-wing corporate and commuter aircraft, carrying up to 15 passengers at cruising speeds in excess of 174 knots (322 km/h; 200 mph). It will be powered by two 761 kW (1,020 shp) Pratt & Whitney Canada PT6B-36 turboshafts, and will employ an advanced version of Piasecki's 'ring tail' vertical thrust ducted propeller (VTDP) design which is being developed under contract from the US Army for prototype installation, and testing in NASA-Langley's wind tunnel. The VTDP concept has been successfully demonstrated on the prototype Piasecki 16H-1A compound helicopter which has achieved a maximum speed of 170 knots (362 km/h; 225 mph).

Piasecki is seeking domestic and overseas manufacturing and marketing partners for the Pathfinder project. The following data are provisional:

DIMENSIONS, EXTERNAL:
Rotor diameter	13.48 m (44 ft 2¾ in)
Wing span	6.10 m (20 ft 0 in)
Length overall, rotor turning	14.81 m (48 ft 7¼ in)
Fuselage length	13.04 m (42 ft 9½ in)
Height overall	3.75 m (12 ft 3½ in)
Wheel track	2.44 m (8 ft 0 in)
Wheelbase	7.22 m (23 ft 8½ in)

WEIGHTS:
Weight empty	2,701 kg (5,955 lb)
Max T-O weight:	
vertical T-O	4,717 kg (10,400 lb)
short T-O	4,853 kg (10,700 lb)

PERFORMANCE (estimated, at max T-O weight, ISA at S/L):
Max cruising speed at 1,525 m (5,000 ft):	
VTO	184 knots (341 km/h; 212 mph)
STO	177 knots (328 km/h; 204 mph)
Max rate of climb at S/L:	
at VTO max T-O weight	704 m (2,310 ft)/min
at STO max T-O weight	574 m (1,885 ft)/min
Max rate of climb at 915 m (3,000 ft), one engine out:	
at VTO max T-O weight	55 m (180 ft)/min
at STO max T-O weight	46 m (150 ft)/min
Max range, no reserves	417 nm (772 km; 480 miles)

PIPER

PIPER AIRCRAFT CORPORATION

2926 Piper Drive, PO Box 1328, Vero Beach, Florida 32960
Telephone: (305) 567 4361
Telex: 441426

SENIOR VICE-PRESIDENT, ADVANCED ENGINEERING:
LeRoy LoPresti

VICE-PRESIDENT, MARKETING AND SALES:
C. Raymond Johnson

DIRECTOR OF MARKETING: J. Earle Boyter

Effective 1 March 1984, Piper Aircraft became a subsidiary of Lear Siegler Inc. The manufacturing and R&D facilities at Lock Haven, Pennsylvania, and sheet metal plant at Piper, Pennsylvania, were closed during the second half of 1984. The last of 76,992 aircraft to be manufactured at Lock Haven, a Piper Mojave, left the plant in August 1984, and phasing out of the Lakeland, Florida, facility was completed by October 1985. All Piper manufacturing activities are now concentrated at Vero Beach, where a new 12,077 m² (130,000 sq ft) plant was completed in October 1986, to accommodate production of the Cheyenne IIIA and 400 turboprop aircraft which had formerly been built at Lakeland.

On 12 May 1987 Piper was acquired by Mr. M. Stuart Millar, a California businessman. In December 1987 a subsidiary company, LoPresti Piper Advanced Engineering Group, was established under the direction of Mr LeRoy LoPresti to explore and develop aerodynamic improvements to selected Piper aircraft models, including some out-of-production types.

Piper has agreements with Chincul SA (which see) for the manufacture of a broad range of Piper products in Argentina; with Embraer (which see) for the development, production and marketing of Piper aircraft in Brazil; and with PZL Mielec (which see) of Poland, which produces a modified version of the Piper Seneca II light twin-engined aircraft, known as the M-20 Mewa, in that country.

PIPER (PA-18-150) SUPER CUB

Intention to resume production of the popular Super Cub, in both flyaway and kit form, was announced by Piper in the Spring of 1988. Power plant will be a 112 kW (150 hp) Textron Lycoming O-320-A2D flat-four, which will be mandatory for homebuilt examples; usable fuel capacity is 135.5 litres (35.8 US gallons; 29.8 Imp gallons).

The Super Cub was last described under the WTA heading in the 1986-87 *Jane's*.

PIPER (PA-28-161) WARRIOR II

Design of the Warrior began in June 1972, an important feature being replacement of the earlier constant chord wings of the Cherokee series by a longer span wing with tapered outer panels. As a result of its introduction the Warrior, which at that time had essentially the same 112 kW (150 hp) engine as the discontinued Cherokee Cruiser, was certificated at a maximum T-O weight 79 kg (175 lb) greater. First flight of a prototype was made on 17 October 1972, and FAA certification of the original Model PA-28-151 was granted on 9 August 1973.

The current PA-28-161 Warrior II version, first flown on 27 August 1976, has a 119 kW (160 hp) engine which operates on 100 octane low-lead fuel. The current version offers a basic optional equipment package, **Executive**, comprising: blind-flying instrumentation with 3 in gyros; clock; outside air temperature gauge; exhaust gas temperature gauge; rate of climb and true airspeed indicators; instrument panel white backlighting; overhead red spotlight; cabin dome, avionics dimming, navigation, landing and taxi lights; rotating beacon; assist strap at door; aircraft step; engine primer system; engine driven and electric vacuum pump with vacuum gauge; quick oil drain; wheel fairings; towbar; pilot's vertically adjustable seat, sun visors, alternate static source, heated pitot, emergency locator transmitter, strobe lights, external power socket, and 35Ah battery.

In addition, four optional avionics groups are available for factory installation in the Warrior II.

A total of 2,935 Warriors had been sold by 1 January 1988. Recent sales include 12 for the Royal Jordanian Air Academy and 19 for British Aerospace Flying College at Prestwick Airport, Scotland. These aircraft are used for

Piper Warrior II ab initio trainers at the British Aerospace Flying College, Prestwick

training commercial and military pilot cadets, commencing in January 1988 with trainees sponsored by British Airways.

TYPE: Four-seat cabin monoplane.

WINGS: Cantilever low-wing monoplane. Wing section NACA 65₂-415 on inboard panels; outboard leading-edge incorporates modification No. 5 of NACA TN 2228. Dihedral 7°. Incidence 2° at root, -1° at tip. Sweepback at quarter-chord 5°. Light alloy single-spar structure with glassfibre wingtips. Plain ailerons of light alloy construction. Four-position manually actuated trailing-edge flaps of light alloy with ribbed skins.

FUSELAGE: Light alloy semi-monocoque structure with glassfibre nose cowl and tailcone.

TAIL UNIT: Cantilever structure of light alloy, except for glassfibre tips on fin and tailplane. Fin and rudder have ribbed light alloy skins. One-piece all-moving tailplane, with combined anti-servo and trim tab. Rudder trimmable, but no trim tab in rudder.

LANDING GEAR: Non-retractable tricycle type. Steerable nosewheel. Piper oleo-pneumatic shock absorbers; single wheel on each unit. Cleveland wheels with 4-ply tyres size 6.00-6 on main units, pressure 1.65 bars (24 lb/sq in). Cleveland nosewheel and 4-ply tyre size 5.00-5, pressure 1.65 bars (24 lb/sq in). Cleveland disc brakes. Parking brake. Glassfibre wheel fairings optional.

POWER PLANT: One 119 kW (160 hp) Textron Lycoming O-320-D3G flat-four engine, driving a Sensenich two-blade fixed-pitch metal propeller type 74DM6-0-60 with spinner. Fuel in two wing tanks, with total capacity of 189 litres (50 US gallons; 41.6 Imp gallons), of which 181.5 litres (48 US gallons; 40 Imp gallons) are usable. Refuelling point on upper surface of each wing. Oil capacity 7.5 litres (2 US gallons; 1.7 Imp gallons).

ACCOMMODATION: Four persons in pairs in enclosed cabin. Individual adjustable front seats with seat belts and shoulder harnesses; bench type rear seat with seat belts. Dual controls and brakes standard. Large door on starboard side. Baggage compartment at rear of cabin, with volume of 0.68 m³ (24 cu ft) and capacity of 91 kg (200 lb). External baggage door on starboard side. Heating, ventilation and windscreen defrosting standard.

SYSTEMS: Hydraulic system for brakes only. Electrical system powered by 14V 60A engine driven alternator. 12V 25Ah battery standard, 12V 35Ah battery optional (standard with Executive equipment package). Dual vacuum system for optional blind-flying instrumentation is available, complete with vacuum gauge, regulator, filter, and annunciator light. Piper Aire air-conditioning system optional.

AVIONICS AND EQUIPMENT: Nav/coms, ADF, autopilot, glideslope and marker beacon receivers, and transponders, by Century Flight Systems, Collins, King and Narco are available in five optional groups, together with an extensive range of other optional avionics. Standard equipment includes recording tachometer, sensitive altimeter, inertial reel shoulder harnesses for all seats, armrests, map pockets, pilot's storm window, stall

warning device, carpeted floor, soundproofing, automatic emergency locator transmitter, provisions for air-conditioning, full flow oil filter, tiedown rings and fuel tank quick drains. Optional equipment, in addition to that listed under Executive package, includes encoding altimeter, digital clock, approach plate holder, engine hour recorder, pilot and co-pilot's vertically adjustable seats, pilot and co-pilot headrests, cabin fire extinguisher, improved soundproofing, cup holders, floor and/or overhead ventilation with booster fan, stainless steel control cables, tinted windows, carburettor ice detection system, lockable fuel tank caps, external power receptacle, zinc chromate paint for aluminium parts and polyurethane paint for exterior finish.

DIMENSIONS, EXTERNAL:
Wing span	10.67 m (35 ft 0 in)
Wing chord: at root	1.60 m (5 ft 3 in)
at tip	1.07 m (3 ft 6¼ in)
Wing aspect ratio	7.2
Length overall	7.25 m (23 ft 9½ in)
Height overall	2.22 m (7 ft 3½ in)
Tailplane span	3.96 m (12 ft 11¾ in)
Wheel track	3.05 m (10 ft 0 in)
Wheelbase	2.03 m (6 ft 8 in)
Propeller diameter	1.88 m (6 ft 2 in)
Propeller ground clearance	0.21 m (8¼ in)
Cabin door: Height	0.89 m (2 ft 11 in)
Width	0.91 m (3 ft 0 in)
Baggage door: Height	0.51 m (1 ft 8 in)
Max width	0.56 m (1 ft 10 in)
Height to sill	0.71 m (2 ft 4 in)

DIMENSIONS, INTERNAL:
Cabin: Length (instrument panel to rear bulkhead)	2.46 m (8 ft 1 in)
Max width	1.05 m (3 ft 5½ in)
Max height	1.24 m (4 ft 1 in)
Floor area	2.28 m² (24.5 sq ft)
Volume (incl baggage area)	3.00 m³ (106.0 cu ft)

AREAS:
Wings, gross	15.8 m² (170.0 sq ft)
Ailerons (total)	1.23 m² (13.2 sq ft)
Trailing-edge flaps (total)	1.36 m² (14.6 sq ft)
Fin	0.69 m² (7.4 sq ft)
Rudder	0.38 m² (4.1 sq ft)
Tailplane, incl tab	2.46 m² (26.5 sq ft)

WEIGHTS AND LOADINGS:
Weight empty, standard	613 kg (1,352 lb)
Max T-O and landing weight	1,106 kg (2,440 lb)
Max ramp weight	1,110 kg (2,447 lb)
Max wing loading	70.06 kg/m² (14.35 lb/sq ft)
Max power loading	9.33 kg/kW (15.25 lb/hp)

PERFORMANCE (at max T-O weight):
Never-exceed speed	153 knots (282 km/h; 176 mph)
*Max level speed at S/L	127 knots (235 km/h; 146 mph)
*Best power cruising speed:	
75% power at 2,745 m (9,000 ft)	
	126 knots (233 km/h; 145 mph)

65% power at 3,810 m (12,500 ft)
        118 knots (219 km/h; 136 mph)
55% power at 3,810 m (12,500 ft)
        107 knots (198 km/h; 123 mph)
*Best econ cruising speed:
  75% power at 2,745 m (9,000 ft)
        122 knots (225 km/h; 140 mph)
  65% power at 3,810 m (12,500 ft)
        116 knots (215 km/h; 134 mph)
  55% power at 3,810 m (12,500 ft)
        105 knots (195 km/h; 121 mph)
Stalling speed:
  flaps up   56 knots (104 km/h; 65 mph) CAS
  flaps down   50 knots (93 km/h; 58 mph) CAS
Max rate of climb at S/L   196 m (644 ft)/min
Service ceiling   3,355 m (11,000 ft)
T-O run   320 m (1,050 ft)
T-O to 15 m (50 ft)   503 m (1,650 ft)
Landing from 15 m (50 ft) 354 m (1,160 ft)
Landing run   191 m (625 ft)
*Range with max fuel with allowances for taxi, T-O, climb
  and descent, and 45 min reserves at max range power:
  at best power settings:
    75% power at 2,745 m (9,000 ft)
          525 nm (972 km; 604 miles)
    65% power at 3,810 m (12,500 ft)
          553 nm (1,025 km; 637 miles)
    55% power at 3,810 m (12,500 ft)
          565 nm (1,047 km; 651 miles)
  at best econ power settings:
    75% power at 2,745 m (9,000 ft)
          590 nm (1,092 km; 679 miles)
    65% power at 3,810 m (12,500 ft)
          633 nm (1,173 km; 729 miles)
    55% power at 3,810 m (12,500 ft)
          640 nm (1,186 km; 737 miles)
*With optional wheel fairings

PIPER (PA-28-161) CADET

The Cadet, announced under this new name in April 1988, is a variant of the Warrior II with instrumentation optimised for VFR or IFR training. Other changes include deletion of the rear baggage compartment and third cabin window each side. By mid-1988 Piper had received orders for more than 100 Cadets, including 50 for the FlightSafety Academy division of FlightSafety International at Vero Beach, Florida, which has an option on 50 more. Deliveries of the Cadet were due to begin in September 1988.

PIPER (PA-28-181) ARCHER II

On 9 October 1972 Piper introduced the Cherokee Challenger as successor to the Cherokee 180. In 1974 this was superseded by the Cherokee Archer, with the same basic airframe and power plant, but with many additional equipment and avionics options. In 1976 this aircraft was redesignated PA-28-181 Cherokee Archer II, and in 1978 introduced the tapered wings of the Warrior II.

The Archer II can be fitted with the generally similar optional Executive equipment package, as well as the five optional avionics packages, which are available for the Warrior II. The 1986 model of the Archer II introduced as standard equipment a basic lighting package comprising instrument panel white backlighting, overhead red lighting, cabin dome and radio lights, landing, taxi, navigation and wingtip strobe lights, entrance step, automatic emergency locator transmitter and wheel fairings. The **Executive** package (as for the Warrior II, with deletion of towbar and engine primer system; adding 52.2 kg (115.1 lb) to aircraft basic weight.

A total of 9,797 Cherokee 180s and PA-28-181 Archer IIs had been sold by 1 January 1988. Recent sales include a second batch of four for primary flying training of future flight crew of Saudi Arabian Airlines.

TYPE: Four-seat cabin monoplane.

WINGS: Cantilever low-wing monoplane. Wing section NACA 65$_2$-415 on inboard panels; outboard leading-edge has modification No. 5 of NACA TN 2228. Dihedral 7°. Incidence 2° at root, –1° at tip. Sweepback at quarter-chord 5°. Light alloy single-spar structure with glassfibre wingtips. Plain ailerons of light alloy construction. Light alloy trailing-edge flaps with ribbed skins.

FUSELAGE: Aluminium alloy semi-monocoque structure. Glassfibre engine cowling.

TAIL UNIT: Cantilever structure of aluminium alloy, except for glassfibre tips on fin and tailplane. Fin and rudder have corrugated metal skin. One-piece all-moving horizontal surface with combined anti-servo and trim tab. Trim tab in rudder.

LANDING GEAR: Non-retractable tricycle type. Steerable nosewheel. Piper oleo-pneumatic shock absorbers. Cleveland wheels and Schenuit tyres, size 6.00-6, 4-ply rating, on all three wheels. Mainwheel tyre pressure 1.65 bars (24 lb/sq in), nosewheel 1.24 bars (18 lb/sq in). Cleveland high capacity disc brakes. Parking brake. Wheel speed fairings optional.

POWER PLANT: One 134 kW (180 hp) Textron Lycoming O-360-A4M flat-four engine, driving a Sensenich two-blade fixed-pitch metal propeller with spinner. Fuel in two tanks in wing leading-edges, with total capacity of 189 litres (50 US gallons; 41.6 Imp gallons), of which

Piper Archer II, which has the tapered wings introduced on the Warrior

181.5 litres (48 US gallons; 40 Imp gallons) are usable. Oil capacity 7.5 litres (2 US gallons; 1.7 Imp gallons).

ACCOMMODATION: Four persons in pairs in enclosed cabin. Individual adjustable front seats, with dual controls; individual rear seats. Large door on starboard side. Baggage compartment at rear of cabin, with volume of 0.74 m³ (26 cu ft) and capacity of 90 kg (200 lb); door on starboard side. Hatshelf. Rear seats removable to provide 1.25 m³ (44 cu ft) cargo space. Accommodation heated and ventilated. Windscreen defrosting.

SYSTEMS: Optional Piper Aire air-conditioning system. Electrical system includes 14V 60A alternator and 12V 25Ah battery. 35Ah battery optional (standard with Executive equipment package). Hydraulic system for brakes only. Vacuum system optional.

AVIONICS AND EQUIPMENT: As for Warrior II, except that sun visors and towbar are standard. An exhaust gas temperature gauge is optional for the Executive version.

DIMENSIONS, EXTERNAL AND INTERNAL:
As for Warrior II, except:
Tailplane span	3.92 m (12 ft 10½ in)
Wheelbase	2.00 m (6 ft 7 in)
Propeller diameter	1.93 m (6 ft 4 in)

AREAS: As for Warrior II

WEIGHTS AND LOADINGS:
Weight empty, equipped (standard)	657 kg (1,449 lb)
Max T-O and landing weight	1,156 kg (2,550 lb)
Max ramp weight	1,160 kg (2,558 lb)
Max wing loading	73.2 kg/m² (15.0 lb/sq ft)
Max power loading	8.63 kg/kW (14.17 lb/hp)

PERFORMANCE (at max T-O weight):
Never-exceed speed
          148 knots (275 km/h; 171 mph) CAS
*Max level speed at S/L   129 knots (239 km/h; 148 mph)
*Best power cruising speed:
  75% power at 2,440 m (8,000 ft)
        129 knots (239 km/h; 148 mph)
  65% power at 3,660 m (12,000 ft)
        125 knots (231 km/h; 144 mph)
  55% power at 3,810 m (12,500 ft)
        111 knots (206 km/h; 128 mph)
*Best econ cruising speed:
  75% power at 2,440 m (8,000 ft)
        126 knots (233 km/h; 145 mph)
  65% power at 3,660 m (12,000 ft)
        122 knots (225 km/h; 140 mph)

55% power at 3,810 m (12,500 ft)
        107 knots (198 km/h; 123 mph)
Stalling speed:
  flaps up   59 knots (109 km/h; 68 mph) CAS
  flaps down   53 knots (98 km/h; 61 mph) CAS
Max rate of climb at S/L   224 m (735 ft)/min
Service ceiling   4,160 m (13,650 ft)
Absolute ceiling   4,800 m (15,750 ft)
T-O run   265 m (870 ft)
T-O to 15 m (50 ft)   506 m (1,660 ft)
Landing from 15 m (50 ft) 424 m (1,390 ft)
Landing run   282 m (925 ft)
*Range with max fuel, allowances for taxi, T-O, climb and descent, and 45 min reserves at max range power:
  at best power settings:
    75% power at 2,440 m (8,000 ft)
          520 nm (963 km; 599 miles)
    65% power at 3,660 m (12,000 ft)
          565 nm (1,047 km; 650 miles)
    55% power at 3,810 m (12,500 ft)
          580 nm (1,075 km; 668 miles)
  at best econ power settings:
    75% power at 2,440 m (8,000 ft)
          600 nm (1,112 km; 691 miles)
    65% power at 3,660 m (12,000 ft)
          645 nm (1,196 km; 743 miles)
    55% power at 3,810 m (12,500 ft)
          670 nm (1,242 km; 772 miles)
*With optional wheel fairings

PIPER (PA-28RT-201T) TURBO ARROW IV

The Piper Arrow derived from the Cherokee Arrow II, which was generally similar to the Cherokee Archer II but had a retractable landing gear, more powerful engine, and the untapered wings of the 1975 PA-28-180 Archer. In 1977, Piper updated this model by fitting long span tapered wings identical with those of the Archer II, but with increased fuel capacity, giving improved performance. The 1978 version of this aircraft was named Arrow III, the prototype of which flew for the first time on 16 September 1975, followed by the first production aircraft on 7 January 1977. Piper designation was PA-28R-201. The Turbo Arrow III differed by having a turbocharged engine, mounted in a streamline cowling, and the first production example of this version flew on 1 December 1976.

Piper Turbo Arrow IV retractable gear four-seat cabin monoplane with T tail

In 1979 Piper introduced an improved model with an all-moving T tailplane, but production of the Arrow IV with normally aspirated Textron Lycoming IO-360-C1C6 engine ended in 1982. The Turbo Arrow IV embodies the improvements detailed for the Archer II. A total of 909 Turbo Arrow IVs had been sold by 1 January 1988.

The 1986 Turbo Arrow IV introduced as standard an engine driven vacuum pump system; standby electric vacuum pump; advanced instrument panel including gyro horizon, directional gyro, turn rate indicator, rate of climb indicator, outside air temperature gauge and electric clock; heated pitot head; automatic emergency locator beacon; wingtip strobe lights; and a basic lighting package comprising instrument panel white backlighting and red overhead lighting, cabin dome light, navigation, taxi and landing lights and avionics dimming.

An optional **Executive** package comprises deluxe interior with four headrests and window curtains; tinted windscreen and side windows; overhead vent system and vent fan; true airspeed indicator; alternate static source; pilot's and co-pilot's vertically adjustable seats; crew cup holders; 'Quietized' cabin soundproofing; external power receptacle; cigarette lighter; 35Ah battery; and wingtip recognition lights, adding 27.3 kg (60.2 lb) to aircraft basic weight. Other optional equipment includes a three-blade propeller; polished spinner (with three-blade propeller only); cold weather starting kit; engine hour recorder; digital clock; control wheel approach plate holder; lockable fuel caps; and zinc chromate protective finish.

In addition to the above equipment, six avionics packages are available optionally for the Turbo Arrow IV.

The description of the Archer II applies also to the Turbo Arrow IV, except for the following details:

TAIL UNIT: Cantilever T tail of light alloy construction. All-moving tailplane with trim tab. Rudder trim.

LANDING GEAR: Tricycle type, retracted hydraulically with an electrically operated pump supplying the hydraulic pressure. In addition to the usual 'gear up' warning horn and red light, an automatic extension system drops the landing gear automatically if power is reduced and airspeed drops below 91 knots (169 km/h; 105 mph). The sensing system consists of a small probe mounted on the port side of the fuselage. Being located in the propeller slipstream, it can differentiate between a climb with power on and an approach to land with power reduced. A free-fall emergency extension system is also fitted. An 'anti-retraction' system guards against premature retraction of the landing gear below an airspeed of 74 knots (137 km/h; 85 mph) at take-off, or accidental retraction on the ground. There is also a manual override lever by which the pilot can hold the landing gear retracted as airspeed falls below 91 knots (169 km/h; 105 mph). Main units retract inward into wings, nose unit rearward. All units fitted with oleo-pneumatic shock absorbers. Mainwheels and tyres size 6.00-6, 6-ply rating, pressure 2.07 bars (30 lb/sq in). Nosewheel and tyre size 5.00-5, 4-ply rating, pressure 1.86 bars (27 lb/sq in). High capacity dual hydraulic disc brakes and parking brake.

POWER PLANT: One 149 kW (200 hp) Continental TSIO-360-FB flat-six turbocharged engine, driving a Hartzell two-blade constant-speed metal propeller with spinner. A three-blade propeller is optional, but essential if optional built-in oxygen system is installed. Fuel tanks in wing leading-edges with total capacity of 291 litres (77 US gallons; 64 Imp gallons), of which 273 litres (72 US gallons; 60 Imp gallons) are usable. Oil capacity 7.5 litres (2 US gallons; 1.7 Imp gallons).

SYSTEMS: Generally as for Archer II and Warrior II, plus electro-hydraulic system for landing gear actuation. An oxygen system of 1.37 m³ (48.3 cu ft) capacity is available optionally.

AVIONICS AND EQUIPMENT: Optional avionics and standard equipment generally as detailed for Warrior II, plus cylinder head temperature gauge, exhaust gas temperature gauge, 65A electric generator, dual range electric auxiliary fuel pump as standard equipment. Optional equipment as listed in Executive paragraph and for Archer II and Warrior II, plus cold weather start kit.

DIMENSIONS, EXTERNAL:
Wing span 10.80 m (35 ft 5 in)
Wing chord: at root 1.60 m (5 ft 3 in)
at tip 1.07 m (3 ft 6¼ in)
Length overall 8.33 m (27 ft 3¾ in)
Height overall 2.52 m (8 ft 3¼ in)
Tailplane span 3.30 m (10 ft 10 in)
Wheel track 3.19 m (10 ft 5½ in)
Wheelbase 2.39 m (7 ft 10¼ in)
Propeller diameter 1.93 m (6 ft 4 in)
Cabin door (stbd): Width 0.91 m (3 ft 0 in)
Height 0.89 m (2 ft 11 in)
Baggage door (stbd): Width 0.56 m (1 ft 10 in)
Height 0.51 m (1 ft 8 in)

DIMENSIONS, INTERNAL:
Cabin:
Length, panel to rear bulkhead 2.46 m (8 ft 1 in)
Max width 1.05 m (3 ft 5½ in)
Max height 1.24 m (4 ft 1 in)
Volume (incl baggage area) 3.00 m³ (106.0 cu ft)

AREA:
Wings, gross 15.79 m² (170.0 sq ft)

WEIGHTS AND LOADINGS:
Weight empty 786 kg (1,732 lb)
Max T-O weight 1,315 kg (2,900 lb)
Max ramp weight 1,321 kg (2,912 lb)
Max wing loading 83.29 kg/m² (17.06 lb/sq ft)
Max power loading 8.83 kg/kW (14.5 lb/hp)

PERFORMANCE (at max T-O weight):
Never-exceed speed 186 knots (344 km/h; 214 mph) CAS
Max level speed at 4,265 m (14,000 ft) 178 knots (330 km/h; 205 mph)
Best power cruising speed at optimum altitude:
75% power 172 knots (319 km/h; 198 mph)
65% power 167 knots (309 km/h; 192 mph)
55% power 157 knots (291 km/h; 181 mph)
Best econ cruising speed at optimum altitude:
75% power 168 knots (311 km/h; 193 mph)
65% power 164 knots (304 km/h; 189 mph)
55% power 153 knots (284 km/h; 176 mph)
Stalling speed:
flaps up 63 knots (117 km/h; 72 mph) CAS
flaps down 58 knots (108 km/h; 67 mph) CAS
Max rate of climb at S/L 287 m (940 ft)/min
Max approved operating altitude 6,100 m (20,000 ft)
T-O run 338 m (1,110 ft)
T-O to 15 m (50 ft) 494 m (1,620 ft)
Landing from 15 m (50 ft) 475 m (1,560 ft)
Landing run 197 m (645 ft)
Range with max fuel, allowances for taxi, T-O, climb and descent, and 45 min reserves at max range power:
at best power settings:
75% power 695 nm (1,287 km; 800 miles)
65% power 725 nm (1,343 km; 835 miles)
55% power 775 nm (1,435 km; 892 miles)
at best econ power settings:
75% power 790 nm (1,465 km; 910 miles)
65% power 830 nm (1,539 km; 956 miles)
55% power 900 nm (1,667 km; 1,036 miles)

PIPER (PA-28-236) DAKOTA

Piper introduced in 1978 an addition to the Warrior, Archer, Arrow line known as the PA-28-236 Dakota, which differs primarily by having a 175 kW (235 hp) Textron Lycoming engine to provide increased performance, and increased capacity fuel tanks to cater for this power plant.

The 1986 version of the Dakota introduced the same standard items as listed for the Turbo Arrow IV, plus high performance wheel fairings. An **Executive** package as detailed for the Arrow IV is also available, and adds 26.9 kg (59.3 lb) to aircraft basic weight. A range of Collins, King and Narco avionics packages is also available optionally.

Licence assembly of the Dakota was undertaken by the Chilean aircraft industry (ENAER, which see); a total of 27 was completed. Ten Dakotas were delivered to Argentina's Instituto Nacionale de Aviació Civil (INAC) in 1987 for airline pilot training. The aircraft carry Argentine Air Force markings. Piper sales of the PA-28-236 Dakota totalled 726 at 1 January 1988.

The description of the Archer II applies also to the Dakota, except as follows:

POWER PLANT: One 175 kW (235 hp) Textron Lycoming O-540-J3A5D flat-six engine, driving a Hartzell two-blade constant-speed metal propeller with spinner. Two integral fuel tanks in each wing, with a total capacity of 291.5 litres (77 US gallons; 64 Imp gallons), of which 272.5 litres (72 US gallons; 60 Imp gallons) are usable. Refuelling points on upper surface of each wing. Oil capacity 11.5 litres (3 US gallons; 2.5 Imp gallons).

AVIONICS AND EQUIPMENT: As for the Turbo Arrow IV, six optional factory installed avionics packages are available, as well as a wide range of other avionics equipment to customer's requirements. Optional equipment includes items provided in the Executive package, plus engine hour recorder, digital clock, carburettor ice detector, approach plate holder, cabin fire extinguisher, rotating beacon, external power receptacle, polished propeller spinner, Piper Aire air-conditioning, stainless steel control cables, lockable fuel tank caps, heavy duty tyres and brakes, and zinc chromate treatment of aluminium parts.

DIMENSIONS, EXTERNAL AND INTERNAL: As for Archer II except:
Length overall 7.54 m (24 ft 8¾ in)
Height overall 2.18 m (7 ft 2 in)
Wheelbase 1.98 m (6 ft 6 in)

WEIGHTS AND LOADINGS:
Weight empty 758 kg (1,672 lb)
Max T-O weight 1,361 kg (3,000 lb)
Max ramp weight 1,366 kg (3,011 lb)
Max wing loading 85.93 kg/m² (17.6 lb/sq ft)
Max power loading 7.78 kg/kW (12.8 lb/hp)

PERFORMANCE (at max T-O weight):
Max level speed at S/L 148 knots (274 km/h; 170 mph)
Best power cruising speed at optimum altitude:
75% power 144 knots (267 km/h; 166 mph)
65% power 139 knots (257 km/h; 160 mph)
55% power 130 knots (241 km/h; 150 mph)
Best econ cruising speed at optimum altitude:
75% power 139 knots (258 km/h; 160 mph)
65% power 134 knots (248 km/h; 154 mph)
55% power 126 knots (234 km/h; 145 mph)
Stalling speed:
flaps up 63 knots (117 km/h; 73 mph) CAS
flaps down 56 knots (104 km/h; 65 mph) CAS
Max rate of climb at S/L 338 m (1,110 ft)/min
Service ceiling 5,335 m (17,500 ft)
Absolute ceiling 5,945 m (19,500 ft)
T-O run 270 m (886 ft)
T-O to 15 m (50 ft) 371 m (1,216 ft)
Landing from 15 m (50 ft):
standard brakes 526 m (1,725 ft)
heavy duty brakes 466 m (1,530 ft)
Landing run: standard brakes 252 m (825 ft)
heavy duty brakes 195 m (640 ft)
Range with max fuel, allowances for taxi, T-O, climb, cruise, descent, and 45 min reserves at max range power:
at best power settings at optimum altitude:
75% power 650 nm (1,205 km; 748 miles)
65% power 710 nm (1,315 km; 817 miles)
55% power 750 nm (1,390 km; 863 miles)
at best econ power settings at optimum altitude:
75% power 720 nm (1,334 km; 829 miles)
65% power 770 nm (1,427 km; 886 miles)
55% power 810 nm (1,501 km; 933 miles)

PIPER (PA-32-301) SARATOGA

On 17 December 1979, Piper announced that it had begun production of a new family of six-seat single-engined aircraft known as Saratogas, to replace the PA-32 SIX 300 and T tail Lance series (all described in 1979-80 *Jane's*). All Saratogas have a common airframe, with a conventional low-mounted tailplane and a semi-tapered wing of longer span than the wing of the aircraft they supersede.

Three versions of the Saratoga are available:

PA-32-301 Saratoga. Basic version, as described in detail.

PA-32R-301 Saratoga SP. Retractable landing gear version of the Saratoga, described separately.

PA-32R-301T Turbo Saratoga SP. Turbocharged version of the Saratoga SP, described separately.

These aircraft are available with nine optional factory installed avionics packages.

The 1986 versions of the Saratoga introduced as standard equipment blind-flying instrumentation with 3 in attitude and directional gyros; electric clock; outside air temperature

Piper Dakota, a four-seat aircraft with non-retractable landing gear

gauge; pictorial turn rate, rate of climb and airspeed indicators; basic lighting package which comprises avionics dimming, instrument panel white backlighting and overhead red lighting; waterfall switch panel light; cabin dome, map and reading lights; landing/taxi and navigation lights; rotating beacon; wing strobe lights; entrance step; wheel fairings; engine driven and electric standby vacuum systems with vacuum gauge, regulator, filter and warning lights; 35Ah battery; and automatic emergency locator beacon.

An optional **Executive** package includes a deluxe lounge interior with club seating, headrests for all seats, window curtains, refreshment console and fold-down armrests for fifth and sixth seats; tinted windscreen and side windows; pilot's and co-pilot's vertically adjustable seats; ventilation fan; wingtip recognition lights; 'Quietized' cabin soundproofing; true airspeed indicator; cigarette lighter; 35Ah battery; external power receptacle with weather-tight cap; crew cupholders; courtesy light package comprising automatic forward compartment light, cabin entrance door light and rear cabin entrance door light; heavy duty brakes and tyres on main landing gear; and heavy duty tyre on 6 in nosewheel. The package adds 33.1 kg (73.1 lb) to basic aircraft weight.

At 1 January 1988, sales of Saratoga models totalled 370.

TYPE: Six-seat cabin monoplane.

WINGS: Cantilever low-wing monoplane. Light alloy single-spar structure with glassfibre wingtips. Plain ailerons of light alloy construction. Electrically operated trailing-edge flaps of light alloy construction with ribbed skins.

FUSELAGE: Conventional semi-monocoque structure of light alloy. Glassfibre engine cowling.

TAIL UNIT: Cantilever structure of light alloy, except for glassfibre tips on fin and tailplane. Fin and rudder have ribbed metal skins. One-piece all-moving horizontal surface with combined anti-servo and trim tab. Trimmable rudder.

LANDING GEAR: Non-retractable tricycle type. Steerable nosewheel. Piper oleo-pneumatic shock absorbers. Single wheel on each unit. Mainwheel tyres size 6.00-6, 8-ply rating, pressure 3.79 bars (55 lb/sq in). Nosewheel tyre size 5.00-5, 6-ply rating, pressure 2.41 bars (35 lb/sq in). Nosewheel tyre size 6.00-6 optional. High capacity disc brakes. Parking brake. Wheel fairings optional. Heavy duty brakes and tyres optional.

POWER PLANT: One 224 kW (300 hp) Textron Lycoming IO-540-K1G5 flat-six engine, driving a Hartzell two-blade constant-speed metal propeller with spinner. Three-blade propeller optional. Polished spinner optional (three-blade propeller only). Two fuel tanks in each wing with combined capacity of 405 litres (107 US gallons; 89 Imp gallons), of which 386 litres (102 US gallons; 85 Imp gallons) are usable. Refuelling points on wing upper surface. Oil capacity 11.5 litres (3 US gallons; 2.5 Imp gallons).

ACCOMMODATION: Enclosed cabin, seating six people in pairs. Dual controls and toe brakes standard. Two forward hinged doors, one on starboard side forward, overwing; one on port side at rear end of cabin. Space for 45 kg (100 lb) baggage at rear of cabin, with external baggage/utility door on port side. Additional baggage space, capacity 45 kg (100 lb), between engine fireproof bulkhead and instrument panel, with external door on starboard side. Pilot's storm window. Sun visors. Accommodation heated and ventilated. Windscreen defroster standard.

SYSTEMS: Piper Aire air-conditioning, vacuum and oxygen systems optional, including a built-in oxygen system of 1.81 m³ (64.0 cu ft) capacity. Hydraulic system for brakes only. Electrical system includes a 14V 60A engine driven alternator, and 12V 25Ah battery. 35Ah battery optional (standard with Executive package).

AVIONICS AND EQUIPMENT: A wide range of avionics is available to customer's requirements, including weather radar with internal wing mounted antenna. Standard equipment includes recording tachometer, sensitive altimeter, dual cylinder head temperature and exhaust gas temperature gauges, fore and aft adjustable pilot and co-pilot seats with shoulder and safety belts, armrests, map pockets, glove compartment, soundproofing, stall warning device, provisions for emergency locator transmitter, alternator failure and low oil pressure warning lights, full flow oil filter, fuel quick drains, oil quick drain, jack pads, stowable towbar, and tiedown rings. Optional equipment includes items detailed in Executive package, plus digital clock; encoding altimeter; engine hour recorder; cabin fire extinguisher; stainless steel control cables; and zinc chromate treatment of aluminium parts.

DIMENSIONS, EXTERNAL:
Wing span	11.02 m (36 ft 2 in)
Length overall: Saratoga	8.44 m (27 ft 8½ in)
Turbo Saratoga	8.59 m (28 ft 2 in)
Height overall	2.49 m (8 ft 2 in)
Tailplane span	3.94 m (12 ft 11 in)
Wheel track	3.23 m (10 ft 7 in)
Wheelbase	2.36 m (7 ft 9 in)
Cabin door (fwd, stbd): Height	0.89 m (2 ft 11 in)
Width	0.91 m (3 ft 0 in)
Cabin door (rear, port): Height	0.72 m (2 ft 4½ in)
Width	0.71 m (2 ft 4 in)
Baggage door (fwd): Height	0.41 m (1 ft 4 in)
Width	0.56 m (1 ft 10 in)

Piper PA-32-301 Saratoga six-seat cabin monoplane

Baggage/utility door (rear): Height	0.52 m (1 ft 8½ in)
Width	0.66 m (2 ft 2 in)

DIMENSIONS, INTERNAL:
Cabin: Length (instrument panel to rear bulkhead)	3.15 m (10 ft 4¼ in)
Max width	1.24 m (4 ft 1 in)
Max height	1.07 m (3 ft 6 in)
Volume (incl rear baggage area)	5.53 m³ (195.3 cu ft)
Baggage compartment volume:	
forward	0.20 m³ (7.0 cu ft)
rear	0.49 m³ (17.3 cu ft)

AREA:
Wings, gross	16.56 m² (178.3 sq ft)

WEIGHTS AND LOADINGS:
Weight empty	906 kg (1,998 lb)
Max T-O weight	1,633 kg (3,600 lb)
Max ramp weight	1,640 kg (3,615 lb)
Max wing loading	98.6 kg/m² (20.2 lb/sq ft)
Max power loading	7.30 kg/kW (12.0 lb/hp)

PERFORMANCE (at max T-O weight):
Max level speed at optimum altitude	152 knots (282 km/h; 175 mph)
Best power cruising speed at optimum altitude:	
at 75% power	150 knots (278 km/h; 173 mph)
at 65% power	146 knots (270 km/h; 168 mph)
at 55% power	136 knots (252 km/h; 156 mph)
Best econ cruising speed at optimum altitude:	
at 75% power	148 knots (274 km/h; 170 mph)
at 65% power	144 knots (267 km/h; 166 mph)
at 55% power	133 knots (246 km/h; 153 mph)
Stalling speed:	
flaps up	66 knots (122 km/h; 76 mph) CAS
flaps down	60 knots (111 km/h; 69 mph) CAS
Max rate of climb at S/L	302 m (990 ft)/min
Service ceiling	4,875 m (16,000 ft)
T-O run: 2-blade propeller	361 m (1,183 ft)
3-blade propeller	309 m (1,013 ft)
T-O to 15 m (50 ft): 2-blade propeller	536 m (1,759 ft)
3-blade propeller	479 m (1,573 ft)
Landing from 15 m (50 ft):	
standard brakes	491 m (1,612 ft)

heavy duty brakes	466 m (1,530 ft)
Landing run: standard brakes	223 m (732 ft)
heavy duty brakes	198 m (650 ft)

Range with max fuel, allowances for taxi, T-O, climb, descent, and 45 min reserves at max range power:
best power settings at optimum altitude:
75% power	745 nm (1,381 km; 858 miles)
65% power	805 nm (1,492 km; 927 miles)
55% power	849 nm (1,573 km; 978 miles)

best econ power settings at optimum altitude:
75% power	823 nm (1,525 km; 948 miles)
65% power	911 nm (1,688 km; 1,049 miles)
55% power	960 nm (1,778 km; 1,105 miles)

PIPER (PA-32R-301) SARATOGA SP

This is a retractable landing gear model of the Saratoga, of which two versions were introduced in 1980:

PA-32R-301 Saratoga SP. Basic version, similar to the PA-32-301 Saratoga but with retractable landing gear and new options as described.

PA-32R-301T Turbo Saratoga SP. As Saratoga SP, but power plant comprises one 224 kW (300 hp) Textron Lycoming TIO-540-S1AD flat-six turbocharged engine, driving a Hartzell two-blade constant-speed metal propeller. (Three-blade propeller optional.) Additional standard equipment for Turbo Saratoga SP includes cylinder head and exhaust gas temperature gauges, engine overboost warning light and manually controlled cowl flaps. Options available for this version include electric propeller and windscreen de-icing, pneumatic wing and tail surface de-icing, and a built-in oxygen system.

Both models are available with nine optional factory installed avionics packages, including a King flight director. The 1986 versions of the Saratoga SP and Turbo Saratoga SP introduced as standard those items listed for the Saratoga, with the exception of wheel fairings and rotating beacon.

An optional **Executive** package, similar to that listed for the Saratoga, is available for both models, and adds 33.1 kg (73.1 lb) to basic aircraft weight.

Piper PA-32R-301T Turbo Saratoga SP

At 1 January 1988 sales of the Saratoga SP and Turbo Saratoga SP totalled 392 and 385 respectively.

The description of the Saratoga applies also to the retractable landing gear versions, except as follows:

WINGS AND TAIL UNIT: Pneumatic de-icing system for wing and tail unit leading-edges is available optionally for the Turbo Saratoga SP.

LANDING GEAR: Hydraulically retractable tricycle type with single wheel on each unit. Main units retract inward, nosewheel aft. Integrated automatic system which extends the landing gear at 102 knots (189 km/h; 117 mph), unless overridden by pilot. Emergency free-fall extension system. Piper oleo-pneumatic shock absorbers. Steerable nosewheel. Mainwheels and tyres size 6.00-6, 8-ply rating, pressure 2.62 bars (38 lb/sq in). Nosewheel and tyre size 5.00-5, 6-ply rating, pressure 2.41 bars (35 lb/sq in). High capacity hydraulic disc brakes. Parking brake. Heavy duty tyres and brakes optional.

POWER PLANT: As for Saratoga except as detailed for Turbo Saratoga SP. Propeller de-icing optional for Turbo Saratoga SP.

ACCOMMODATION: As for Saratoga, but inertia reel safety harnesses standard for all forward facing seats, and pilot's electrically heated windscreen plate optional for Turbo Saratoga SP.

SYSTEMS: As for Saratoga, but electrically driven hydraulic pump for landing gear actuation; built-in oxygen system of 1.81 m³ (64 cu ft) capacity and 95A alternator available optionally for Turbo Saratoga SP.

AVIONICS AND EQUIPMENT: Generally as listed for Saratoga, with amendments as noted in this entry, plus optional wing ice inspection light for Turbo Saratoga SP.

DIMENSIONS, EXTERNAL: As for Saratoga, except:

Length overall: Saratoga SP	8.45 m (27 ft 8½ in)
Turbo Saratoga SP	8.69 m (28 ft 6 in)
Height overall	2.59 m (8 ft 6 in)
Wheel track	3.39 m (11 ft 1½ in)
Wheelbase	2.43 m (7 ft 11½ in)

WEIGHTS AND LOADINGS (A: Saratoga SP; B: Turbo Saratoga SP): As for Saratoga, except:

Weight empty: A	926 kg (2,041 lb)
B	961 kg (2,119 lb)

PERFORMANCE (at max T-O weight. A: Saratoga SP/two-blade propeller; B: Turbo Saratoga SP/two-blade propeller; C: Saratoga SP/three-blade propeller; D: Turbo Saratoga SP/three-blade propeller):

Max level speed at optimum altitude:

A	164 knots (304 km/h; 189 mph)
B	191 knots (354 km/h; 220 mph)
D	195 knots (361 km/h; 225 mph)

Best power cruising speed at optimum altitude:

at 75% power: A	159 knots (295 km/h; 183 mph)
	B	177 knots (328 km/h; 204 mph)
at 65% power: A	153 knots (283 km/h; 176 mph)
	B	166 knots (307 km/h; 191 mph)
at 55% power: A	144 knots (267 km/h; 166 mph)
	B	152 knots (282 km/h; 175 mph)

Best econ cruising speed at optimum altitude:

at 75% power: A	157 knots (291 km/h; 181 mph)
	B	171 knots (317 km/h; 197 mph)
at 65% power: A	151 knots (280 km/h; 174 mph)
	B	160 knots (296 km/h; 184 mph)
at 55% power: A	141 knots (261 km/h; 162 mph)
	B	145 knots (269 km/h; 167 mph)

Stalling speed, flaps up:

A	65 knots (121 km/h; 75 mph) CAS
B	63 knots (118 km/h; 73 mph) CAS

Stalling speed, flaps down:

A	59 knots (110 km/h; 68 mph) CAS
B	60 knots (111 km/h; 69 mph) CAS

Max rate of climb at S/L: A 308 m (1,010 ft)/min
B 341 m (1,120 ft)/min

Service ceiling: A	5,090 m (16,700 ft)
*B	6,100 m (20,000 ft)
Absolute ceiling: A	5,595 m (18,350 ft)
*B	6,100 m (20,000 ft)

T-O run, and T-O to 15 m (50 ft):
as for Saratoga and Turbo Saratoga
Landing from 15 m (50 ft), and landing run:
as for Saratoga and Turbo Saratoga
Range with max fuel, allowances for taxi, T-O, climb, descent, and 45 min reserves at max range power:

Best power settings at optimum altitude:

75% power: A	784 nm (1,453 km; 903 miles)
	B	730 nm (1,353 km; 840 miles)
65% power: A	828 nm (1,533 km; 953 miles)
	B	790 nm (1,465 km; 910 miles)
55% power: A	869 nm (1,611 km; 1,001 miles)
	B	843 nm (1,562 km; 971 miles)

Best econ power settings at optimum altitude:

75% power: A	865 nm (1,603 km; 996 miles)
	B	844 nm (1,564 km; 972 miles)
65% power: A	937 nm (1,736 km; 1,079 miles)
	B	920 nm (1,704 km; 1,059 miles)
55% power: A	983 nm (1,822 km; 1,132 miles)
	B	950 nm (1,760 km; 1,094 miles)

*Max certificated altitude

PIPER (PA-42-720) CHEYENNE IIIA

Announced on 26 September 1977, the **Cheyenne III** differed from the I and II by having increased wing span, a

Piper Cheyenne IIIA six/eleven-seat turboprop business aircraft

lengthened fuselage, a T tail and more powerful PT6A-41 engines. The production prototype flew for the first time on 18 May 1979; FAA certification was gained in early 1980, and 89 had been delivered before the Cheyenne III was superseded by the **Cheyenne IIIA**.

Piper received FAA certification for the Cheyenne IIIA in March 1983. It differs principally in having PT6A-61 turboprop engines, and offers performance improvements which include increased max cruising speed and higher certificated ceiling. Other features include improvements to the interior layout, air-conditioning and electrical systems. Forty-eight had been delivered by 1 January 1988.

A Cheyenne IIIA, equipped with special sensors, was delivered to the US Drug Enforcement Administration on 15 February 1984 for use on a variety of surveillance and identification missions by day and night, and in March 1985 an order for a further eight Cheyenne IIIA Customs High Endurance Tracker (CHET) aircraft was announced by Piper. These aircraft, equipped with infra-red sensors and long-range radars, were delivered at one month intervals commencing in late September 1985. The US Customs Service has options on a further eight Cheyenne IIIAs.

In December 1984 Lufthansa German Airlines ordered three Cheyenne IIIAs, with an option (since taken up) on a fourth, for delivery commencing in the Spring of 1987. The aircraft, which are equipped with Collins EFIS on flight decks configured to resemble those of Lufthansa's Airbus A310 jet transports, are used for pilot training by Lufthansa and the Swiss airline Swissair. Three Cheyenne IIIAs were ordered by the Italian carrier Alitalia in the Autumn of 1986 for advanced pilot training.

The Cheyenne IIIA is available with Standard and Executive interior options, and a Co-pilot Flight Group which adds 8.7 kg (19.2 lb) to the aircraft's basic empty weight, comprising airspeed and rate of climb indicator, altimeter, electric turn rate indicator, attitude and directional gyros, clock, heated pitot, static system with alternate source, co-pilot's toe brakes, and windscreen wiper.

A full IFR avionics package, including autopilot/flight director and weather radar, plus full icing protection, is standard equipment on the current Cheyenne IIIA, to which the following description applies:

TYPE: Six/eleven-seat corporate and commuter airline transport.

WINGS: Cantilever low-wing monoplane. Wing section NACA 63₂A415, modified, at root, NACA 63₁A212 at tip. Dihedral 5°. Incidence 1° 30'. No sweepback. Three-spar safe-life structure of light alloy. Ailerons and trailing-edge flaps as for Cheyenne IA. Goodrich pneumatic de-icing boots for wing leading-edges are standard.

FUSELAGE: Conventional semi-monocoque safe-life structure of light alloy.

TAIL UNIT: Cantilever T tail of light alloy construction, with sweptback vertical surfaces. Fixed incidence tailplane. Elevators and rudder of light alloy. Servo tab in rudder; anti-servo tab in elevator. Goodrich de-icing equipment standard for leading-edges of tailplane and fin.

LANDING GEAR: Hydraulically retractable tricycle type with single wheel on each unit. Main units retract inward, nosewheel aft. Pneumatic blow-down system for emergency landing gear extension, with manually operated hydraulic system as backup. Piper oleo-pneumatic shock absorbers. Cleveland mainwheels with tyres size 6.50-10 12-ply Type III, pressure 6.90 bars (100 lb/sq in).

Cleveland steerable nosewheel with tyre size 17.5 × 6.25, 10-ply rating Type III, pressure 4.83 bars (70 lb/sq in). Goodrich hydraulically operated disc brakes. Parking brake.

POWER PLANT: Two Pratt & Whitney Canada PT6A-61 turboprops, each flat rated at 537 kW (720 shp) and driving a Hartzell three-blade constant-speed feathering and reversible-pitch metal propeller with Q-tips. Automatic propeller feathering system and synchrophaser optional. Each wing has four interconnected fuel cells and a tip tank, with a combined total capacity of 2,158 litres (570 US gallons; 474.5 Imp gallons), of which 2,120 litres (560 US gallons; 466 Imp gallons) are usable. NACA type anti-icing and non-siphoning fuel vents incorporating flame arresters. Refuelling points on upper surface of each tip tank and engine nacelle. Oil capacity 24.6 litres (6.5 US gallons; 5.4 Imp gallons). Electric intake anti-icing and propeller de-icing.

ACCOMMODATION: Pilot and co-pilot on four-way adjustable seats with armrests, headrests, shoulder safety belts with inertia reels, and stowage for oxygen mask beneath seats. To be certificated for single pilot operation. Dual controls standard. Pilot's storm window. Cabin seats up to nine passengers, but standard interior includes six reclining and adjustable passenger seats with armrests, headrests, and magazine storage on seat back. Four optional executive interiors available, plus a wide range of options for cabin furnishing. Door with built-in airstair on port side, with seven locking pins and inflatable pressurisation seal. Emergency exit window on starboard side. Baggage compartments in nose and rear of cabin, each with capacity of 136 kg (300 lb), and in each engine nacelle, with a capacity of 45 kg (100 lb), giving a maximum total baggage capacity of 363 kg (800 lb). Accommodation is pressurised, heated and air-conditioned. Pilot's windscreen heated; provisions for heating co-pilot windscreen. Pilot and co-pilot windscreen wipers standard.

SYSTEMS: AiResearch pressurisation system with max differential of 0.43 bars (6.3 lb/sq in), maintaining a cabin altitude of 3,050 m (10,000 ft) to a height of 10,060 m (33,000 ft). Environmental control system, combining the functions of heater, air-conditioner and dehumidifier. Hydraulic system supplied by dual engine driven pumps. Pneumatic system and vacuum system supplied by engine bleed air. Electrical system includes two 28V 250A engine driven generators and 24V 43Ah storage battery. Oxygen system of 0.62 m³ (22 cu ft) capacity with ten outlets. Pneumatic wing and tailplane de-icing boots, electric anti-icing of engine air intakes, heated pitots, electric propeller de-icing, and windscreen heating.

AVIONICS AND EQUIPMENT: Generally as for Cheyenne IA (1986-87 *Jane's*), including King 300 and Collins AP-106 autopilot/flight directors. Extensive standard installed equipment includes 'No smoking-Fasten seat belt' sign; carpeted floor; tinted cabin windows; pull-down window shades; curtain between flight deck and cabin; oxygen system with individual masks in storage compartments; indirect fluorescent lighting, individual reading lights, and courtesy lights. Optional equipment includes cabin chimes; stereo system; cabin instrument cluster giving digital readouts of altitude, outside air temperature, time, and true airspeed; cabin fire extinguisher; emergency locator transmitter; and engine fire extinguishing systems.

DIMENSIONS, EXTERNAL:

Wing span over tip tanks	14.53 m (47 ft 8 in)
Wing chord: at root	3.12 m (10 ft 3 in)
at tip	0.97 m (3 ft 2 in)
Wing aspect ratio	7.8
Length overall	13.23 m (43 ft 4¾ in)
Height overall	4.50 m (14 ft 9 in)
Tailplane span	6.65 m (21 ft 10 in)
Wheel track	5.72 m (18 ft 9 in)
Wheelbase	3.23 m (10 ft 7¼ in)
Propeller diameter	2.41 m (7 ft 11 in)
Distance between propeller centres	5.38 m (17 ft 8 in)
Passenger door: Height	1.16 m (3 ft 10 in)
Width	0.73 m (2 ft 5 in)
Nose baggage doors:	
Fwd: height	0.30 m (1 ft 0 in)
width	0.61 m (2 ft 0 in)
Rear: height	0.51 m (1 ft 8 in)
width	0.66 m (2 ft 2 in)
Utility door (aft): Height	0.76 m (2 ft 6 in)
Width	0.47 m (1 ft 6½ in)

DIMENSIONS, INTERNAL:

Cabin (incl flight deck and rear baggage area):	
Length	6.99 m (22 ft 11 in)
Max width	1.30 m (4 ft 3 in)
Max height	1.32 m (4 ft 4 in)
Volume	approx 9.91 m³ (350.0 cu ft)
Nose baggage compartment	0.46 m³ (16.25 cu ft)
Rear baggage compartment	0.88 m³ (31.0 cu ft)
Nacelle baggage locker (two, each)	0.16 m³ (5.6 cu ft)

AREAS:

Wings, gross	27.22 m² (293.0 sq ft)
Ailerons (total)	1.25 m² (13.5 sq ft)
Trailing-edge flaps (total)	3.98 m² (42.8 sq ft)
Fin	2.17 m² (23.36 sq ft)
Rudder, incl tab	1.88 m² (20.2 sq ft)
Tailplane	3.48 m² (37.5 sq ft)
Elevators, incl tab	2.26 m² (24.3 sq ft)

WEIGHTS AND LOADINGS:

Basic weight empty	3,101 kg (6,837 lb)
Max T-O weight	5,080 kg (11,200 lb)
Max ramp weight	5,119 kg (11,285 lb)
Max zero-fuel weight	4,241 kg (9,350 lb)
Max landing weight	4,685 kg (10,330 lb)
Max wing loading	186.6 kg/m² (38.22 lb/sq ft)
Max power loading	4.73 kg/kW (7.78 lb/shp)

PERFORMANCE (at max T-O weight except where indicated):

Max level speed at average cruise weight of 4,218 kg (9,300 lb)	314 knots (582 km/h; 362 mph)
Cruising speed at max cruise power, at average cruise weight of 4,127 kg (9,100 lb):	
at 6,700 m (22,000 ft)	305 knots (565 km/h; 351 mph)
at 7,620 m (25,000 ft)	302 knots (560 km/h; 348 mph)
at 9,150 m (30,000 ft)	293 knots (543 km/h; 337 mph)
at 10,670 m (35,000 ft)	282 knots (523 km/h; 325 mph)
Minimum single-engine control speed (V_{MC})	91 knots (169 km/h; 105 mph)
Stalling speed, engine idling:	
flaps and gear up	102 knots (189 km/h; 118 mph) IAS
flaps and gear down	89 knots (165 km/h; 103 mph) IAS
Rotation speed	95 knots (176 km/h; 110 mph) IAS
Approach speed	111 knots (206 km/h; 128 mph) IAS
Max rate of climb at S/L	725 m (2,380 ft)/min
Rate of climb at S/L, one engine out	191 m (625 ft)/min
Service ceiling	10,925 m (35,840 ft)
Service ceiling, one engine out	7,070 m (23,200 ft)
T-O run	447 m (1,465 ft)
T-O to 15 m (50 ft)	695 m (2,280 ft)
Landing from 15 m (50 ft)	928 m (3,043 ft)
Landing from 15 m (50 ft) with propeller reversal	788 m (2,586 ft)
Landing run	583 m (1,914 ft)
Landing run with propeller reversal	444 m (1,457 ft)
Accelerate/stop distance	1,025 m (3,363 ft)
Range with max fuel, allowances for taxi, T-O, climb, descent, 45 min reserves at max range power:	
max cruising power at:	
6,700 m (22,000 ft)	1,372 nm (2,542 km; 1,580 miles)
7,620 m (25,000 ft)	1,510 nm (2,798 km; 1,739 miles)
9,460 m (31,000 ft)	1,840 nm (3,409 km; 2,118 miles)
10,670 m (35,000 ft)	2,055 nm (3,808 km; 2,366 miles)
max range power at:	
6,700 m (22,000 ft)	1,803 nm (3,341 km; 2,076 miles)
7,620 m (25,000 ft)	1,945 nm (3,604 km; 2,240 miles)
9,460 m (31,000 ft)	2,170 nm (4,021 km; 2,499 miles)
10,670 m (35,000 ft)	2,270 nm (4,207 km; 2,614 miles)

Piper Cheyenne 400, powered by Garrett TPE331-14A/14B turboprops

PIPER (PA-42-1000) CHEYENNE 400

Announced in September 1982, this eight-seat business aircraft (known initially as the Cheyenne IV and later as the Cheyenne 400 LS) combines the basic airframe structure, components and systems of the Cheyenne IIIA with a new power plant, updated electrical system and other changes to ensure optimum performance and economy of operation. The prototype Cheyenne 400 (N400PT) flew for the first time on 23 February 1983, followed by a second prototype on 23 June. FAA certification was obtained on 13 July 1984, and deliveries began with an aircraft handed over to the Garrett Turbine Engine Company on 26 July. At 1 January 1988 a total of 33 Cheyenne 400s had been delivered.

The '400' in the designation marks the claim that this is the only corporate turboprop aircraft capable of achieving 400 mph.

TYPE: Twin-turboprop eight-seat light business transport.

WINGS: Cantilever low-wing monoplane, basically similar to those of Cheyenne IIIA, adapted for new power plant and flush riveted throughout. Area inboard of each wheel well strengthened and modified to accept new main landing gear. Outer panels modified to incorporate integral fuel tanks and to carry wingtip tanks to supplement fuel capacity and provide endplate aerodynamic benefits.

FUSELAGE: Basically as for Cheyenne IIIA, but strengthened to cater for increased pressurisation and to embody new multi-ply stretched acrylic cabin windows. Flush riveted throughout.

TAIL UNIT: As for Cheyenne IIIA, with minor modifications to cater for higher speeds. Flush riveted throughout.

LANDING GEAR: Hydraulically retractable tricycle type, with single wheel on each unit. Main units retract inward into wings, nosewheel rearward. Redesigned by comparison with Cheyenne IIIA, for improved ground attitude and increased landing weight. Mainwheels and tyres size

6.50-10, 12-ply rating, pressure 7.58 bars (110 lb/sq in). Steerable nosewheel, size 6.00-6, with 17.5 × 6.25-6 tyre, 10-ply rating, pressure 5.52 bars (80 lb/sq in). Hydraulically actuated dual disc brakes, with multiple brake pads, on each mainwheel.

POWER PLANT: Two 1,226.5 kW (1,645 shp) Garrett TPE331-14A/14B counter-rotating turboprops, each flat rated at 746 kW (1,000 shp) and driving a Dowty Rotol ARA-D constant-speed reversible-pitch advanced technology propeller with four carbonfibre/epoxy blades. Blade design and construction incorporates protection from both erosion and lightning strike. The installation of each engine includes new mountings, a new nacelle enclosing the exhaust system, new inlet incorporating bleed air anti-icing, and an exhaust system which discharges the efflux over the wing. Propeller synchrophaser standard. Fuel system as for Cheyenne IIIA. The engines have automatic negative torque control, automatic start sequencing, and use a micro-computer system to record in-flight performance data for engine trend monitoring.

ACCOMMODATION: Crew of two side by side on separate flight deck. Standard cabin has two rearward facing seats at front. Flat floor and table between these seats and two pairs of forward facing seats, with dropped aisle between each pair. Toilet, with solid divider and door, and walk-in baggage area, capacity 136 kg (300 lb), at rear of cabin. Alternative cabin layouts available. Airstair door at rear of cabin on port side. Optional cargo door immediately aft of this, to provide unobstructed wide opening. Double glazed windows. Emergency exit over wing on starboard side. Nose baggage compartment, capacity 136 kg (300 lb), large enough to accommodate skis and golf bags, with two doors on port side.

SYSTEMS: Environmental control system utilises engine bleed air from both engines for heating, cooling and

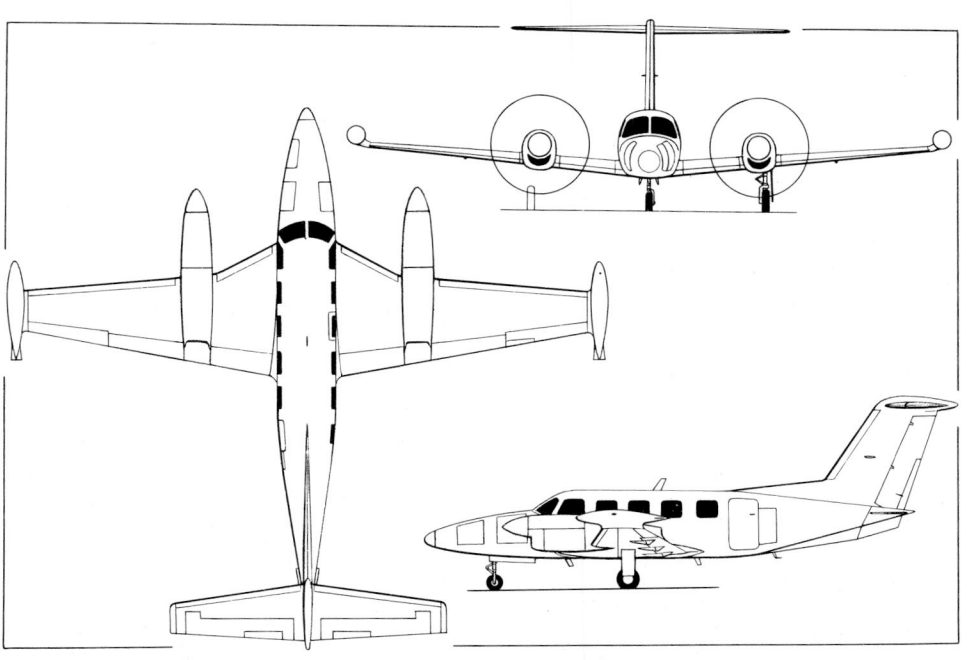

Piper Cheyenne 400 twin-turboprop eight-seat business transport *(Pilot Press)*

pressurisation. Max pressure differential 0.51 bars (7.5 lb/sq in). Independent emergency bleed air pressurisation system. Completely new electrical system includes two engine driven generators and two batteries. Automatic dropout oxygen masks.

AVIONICS AND EQUIPMENT: A full IFR avionics package, including autopilot/flight director and weather radar, plus full icing protection, is standard equipment. Complete optional system by Collins includes pilot's electronic ADI and electric HSI; multi-function display for radar and nav as well as system functions; co-pilot's mechanical ADI and electronic HSI; digital air data system, FCS 65 flight control system with latest technology digital autopilot; and a complete line of com, nav, radar and long range nav systems. Similar system by Bendix is in form of a five-tube electronic display comprising pilot and co-pilot electronic ADI and electronic HSI; multi-function radar display; electronic engine instrument and crew alerting options; digital air data system; digital autopilot flight control system; and complete line of com, short and long range nav and radar systems.

DIMENSIONS, EXTERNAL: As for Cheyenne IIIA, except:

Height overall	5.00 m (16 ft 5 in)
Propeller diameter	2.69 m (8 ft 10 in)

DIMENSIONS, INTERNAL: As for Cheyenne IIIA, except:

Cabin: Max height	1.42 m (4 ft 8 in)
Baggage compartment volume:	
nose	0.48 m³ (17.0 cu ft)
rear	0.88 m³ (31.0 cu ft)

AREAS: As for Cheyenne IIIA, except:

Fin	2.68 m² (28.81 sq ft)
Rudder, incl tab	1.60 m² (17.25 sq ft)
Elevators, incl tabs	2.26 m² (24.30 sq ft)

WEIGHTS:

Weight empty, standard	3,431 kg (7,565 lb)
Max usable fuel	1,732 kg (3,819 lb)
Max T-O weight	5,466 kg (12,050 lb)
Max ramp weight	5,504 kg (12,135 lb)
Max landing weight	5,035 kg (11,100 lb)
Max zero-fuel weight	4,536 kg (10,000 lb)

PERFORMANCE (at max T-O weight except where indicated):

Max operating speed
Mach 0.62 (246 knots; 455 km/h; 283 mph EAS)

Cruising speed at max cruise power at AUW of 4,536 kg (10,000 lb):
at 7,315 m (24,000 ft) 351 knots (650 km/h; 404 mph)
at 8,850 m (29,000 ft) 346 knots (641 km/h; 398 mph)
at 10,670 m (35,000 ft) 334 knots (620 km/h; 385 mph)
at 12,500 m (41,000 ft) 294 knots (544 km/h; 338 mph)

Minimum single-engine control speed (VMC) 99 knots (183 km/h; 114 mph)

Stalling speed, engines idling:
flaps and landing gear up 93 knots (172 km/h; 107 mph) IAS
flaps and landing gear down 84 knots (156 km/h; 97 mph) IAS

Max rate of climb at S/L	988 m (3,242 ft)/min
Rate of climb at S/L, one engine out	304 m (997 ft)/min
Service ceiling	above 12,500 m (41,000 ft)
Service ceiling, one engine out	8,745 m (28,700 ft)
T-O to 15 m (50 ft)	709 m (2,325 ft)
Landing from 15 m (50 ft) at max landing weight:	
without reverse thrust	706 m (2,317 ft)
with reverse thrust	621 m (2,038 ft)
Accelerate/stop distance	969 m (3,180 ft)

Range at max cruise power at 10,670 m (35,000 ft), with allowances for start, taxi, T-O, climb, descent and 45 min reserves at max range power:
with 8 passengers 1,243 nm (2,304 km; 1,432 miles)
with 2 passengers 1,821 nm (3,375 km; 2,097 miles)

Max range, at max range power at 12,500 m (41,000 ft), allowances as above:
with 8 passengers 1,431 nm (2,652 km; 1,648 miles)
with 2 passengers 2,176 nm (4,033 km; 2,506 miles)

PIPER (PA-34-220T) SENECA III

On 23 September 1971, Piper announced a twin-engined light aircraft which had the company designation PA-34 and, following Piper tradition, the Indian name Seneca. Built at Piper's Vero Beach, Florida, factory, the aircraft was redesignated Seneca II from 1975. On 15 February 1981 Piper introduced the improved PA-34-220T Seneca III, with more powerful engines.

The Seneca III has counter-rotating (C/R) engine and propeller installations. The retractable landing gear is operated by an electro-hydraulic system and includes an emergency extension system which allows the wheels to free fall into the down and locked position. A dual-vane stall warning system provides warning by horn well in advance of the stall in either clean or gear/flaps-down configuration.

The 1985 Seneca III versions introduced as standard an instrument package which includes blind-flying instrumentation with 3 in attitude and directional gyros, electric clock, outside air temperature gauge, pictorial turn rate indicator, rate of climb indicator, airspeed indicator, and dual engine driven pneumatic pumps; a lighting package which includes

Piper Seneca III, powered by two Continental TSIO-360-KB turbocharged counter-rotating engines

instrument panel white lighting and overhead red lighting, avionics dimming, cabin dome, map, reading, landing, navigation, taxi, and wing strobe lights; heated pitot; and automatic emergency locator beacon.

Optional equipment groups available for the Seneca III are as follows:

Executive. Comprising deluxe lounge interior with headrests for all seats, window curtains, assist strap, club seating, refreshment console and fold-down armrest; tinted windscreen and side windows; pilot's and co-pilot's vertically adjustable seats; ventilation fan; wingtip recognition lights; 'Quietized' cabin soundproofing; true airspeed indicator; external power receptacle; crew cup holders; courtesy lighting package including forward baggage compartment light, cabin entrance door light and rear cabin entrance door light; heavy duty brakes and tyres for main landing gear and heavy duty tyre on six inch nosewheel; and towbar, adding 33.1 kg (73.1 lb) to basic aircraft weight.

De-icing Group. Comprising pneumatic de-icing boots for wing and tail unit leadng-edges, electric propeller de-icing, luminous outside air temperature gauge, ice inspection light, electric windscreen de-icing plate for pilot, heated pitot head and two heated lift detectors; adding 22.6 kg (49.9 lb) to basic empty weight.

It was announced on 3 January 1977 that Piper had signed an agreement with Pezetel, the Polish foreign trade organisation, enabling PZL Mielec (which see) to assemble, manufacture and distribute the Seneca in Eastern Europe. These aircraft (several hundred are involved in the agreement) are powered by 164 kW (220 hp) PZL-F engines and are named **M-20 Mewa** (Gull). In June 1987 Pezetel awarded Western world marketing rights for the M-20 to the British company Aircraft International.

At 1 January 1988 a total of 4,365 Senecas had been delivered: 918 Seneca Is, 2,602 Seneca IIs and 845 Seneca IIIs. Recent sales include six Seneca IIIs for the Royal Jordanian Air Academy and six for the BAe Flying College.

TYPE: Six-seat twin-engined light aircraft.

WINGS: Cantilever low-wing monoplane. Dihedral 7°. Single-spar wings, Frise ailerons, and wide span electrically operated slotted flaps, of light alloy construction. Glassfibre wingtips. Pneumatic de-icing boots for leading-edges optional.

FUSELAGE: Light alloy semi-monocoque structure.

TAIL UNIT: Cantilever structure of light alloy. One-piece all-moving horizontal surface with combined anti-balance and trim tab. Anti-servo tab in rudder. Pneumatic de-icing boots for fin and tailplane leading-edges optional.

LANDING GEAR: Hydraulically retractable tricycle type. Main units retract inward, nose unit forward. Oleo-pneumatic shock absorbers. Steerable nosewheel. Emergency free-fall extension system. Mainwheels and tyres size 6.00-6, 8-ply rating, pressure 3.79 bars (55 lb/sq in); nosewheel and tyre size 6.00-6, 6-ply rating, pressure 2.76 bars (40 lb/sq in). Nosewheel safety mirror. High capacity disc brakes. Parking brake. Heavy duty tyres and brakes optional.

POWER PLANT: One 164 kW (220 hp) Continental TSIO-360-KB and one 164 kW (220 hp) Continental LTSIO-360-KB flat-six turbocharged counter-rotating engines, each driving a Hartzell two-blade constant-speed fully-feathering metal propeller with spinner. Three-blade propellers, propeller de-icing, automatic unfeathering and propeller synchrophasers optional. Fuel in two tanks in wings, with a total capacity of 371 litres (98 US gallons; 81.6 Imp gallons) of which 352 litres (93 US gallons; 77.4 Imp gallons) are usable. Optional 57 litre (15 US gallon; 12.5 Imp gallon) auxiliary tank in each wing to provide a max capacity of 485 litres (128 US gallons; 106.6 Imp gallons) of which 466 litres (123 US gallons; 102.4 Imp gallons) are usable. Oil capacity 7.5 litres (2 US gallons; 1.7 Imp gallons). Glassfibre engine cowlings.

ACCOMMODATION: Enclosed cabin, seating six people in pairs on individual seats with 0.25 m (10 in) centre aisle. Dual controls standard. Pilot's storm window. Two forward hinged doors, one on starboard side at front, the other on port side at rear. Large optional door adjacent to rear cabin door provides an extra-wide opening for loading bulky items. Passenger seats removable easily to provide different seating/baggage/cargo combinations. Space for 45 kg (100 lb) baggage at rear of cabin, and for 45 kg (100 lb) in nose compartment with external door on port side. Cabin heated and ventilated. Windscreen defrosters standard. Electrically de-iced windscreen for pilot, and ice inspection light, optional.

SYSTEMS: Electro-hydraulic system for landing gear actuation. Electrical system powered by two 14V 65A alternators. 12V 35Ah battery. Oxygen system with six outlets, or built-in oxygen system of 1.81 m³ (64 cu ft), optional. Dual engine driven pneumatic pumps for flight instruments optional. Piper Aire air-conditioning system of 14,500 BTU capacity optional. Janitrol 45,000 BTU combustion heater standard.

AVIONICS AND EQUIPMENT: Four optional factory installed packages of avionics are available, these including nav/coms, ADF, autopilot, DME, glideslope and marker beacon receivers, and transponder, by Collins, King and Piper. Options include alternative to or duplication of the above equipment, plus autopilot/flight director systems, encoding altimeter, HF transceiver, R/Nav, radio altimeter, and weather radar, by manufacturers which include the above, plus 3M, Bendix, King, Narco, SunAir and United. Standard equipment includes dual cylinder head and exhaust gas temperature gauges, dual manifold pressure gauges, dual electric tachometers, sensitive altimeter and alternate static source. Pilot's and co-pilot's seats are fore and aft adjustable and reclining, and have inertia reel shoulder and safety belts and armrests; pilot's storm window, sun visors, stall warning device, provisions for emergency locator transmitter, carpeted floor, soundproofing, fuel tank quick drains, jack pads, and tiedown rings. Items in operational groups are available optionally, plus co-pilot's blind-flying instrumentation, encoding altimeter, digital clock, cabin heater, hour recorder, cabin fire extinguisher, vertically adjustable seats for pilot and co-pilot, inertia reel shoulder belt systems for crew and passenger seats, headrests, window curtains, tables, refreshment console, tinted windows, ventilation fan, stainless steel control cables, in-flight recognition lights, towbar, and zinc chromate finish for aluminium parts.

DIMENSIONS, EXTERNAL:

Wing span	11.85 m (38 ft 10¾ in)
Wing chord, constant	1.60 m (5 ft 3 in)
Length overall	8.72 m (28 ft 7½ in)
Height overall	3.02 m (9 ft 10¾ in)
Tailplane span	4.14 m (13 ft 6¾ in)
Wheel track	3.38 m (11 ft 1¼ in)
Wheelbase	2.13 m (7 ft 0 in)
Propeller diameter	1.93 m (6 ft 4 in)
Distance between propeller centres	3.80 m (12 ft 5½ in)
Cabin door (stbd, fwd): Height	0.89 m (2 ft 11 in)
Width	0.91 m (3 ft 0 in)
Cabin door (port, rear): Height	0.72 m (2 ft 4½ in)
Width	0.71 m (2 ft 4 in)
Baggage door (stbd, rear): Height	0.52 m (1 ft 8½ in)
Width	0.66 m (2 ft 2 in)
Baggage door (port, fwd): Height	0.53 m (1 ft 9 in)
Width	0.61 m (2 ft 0 in)

DIMENSIONS, INTERNAL:

Cabin (incl flight deck): Length	3.17 m (10 ft 5 in)
Max width	1.24 m (4 ft 1 in)
Max height	1.07 m (3 ft 6 in)
Volume	5.53 m³ (195.3 cu ft)

Forward baggage compartment 0.43 m³ (15.3 cu ft)
Rear baggage compartment 0.49 m³ (17.3 cu ft)

AREAS:
Wings, gross 19.39 m² (208.7 sq ft)
Ailerons, incl tab (total) 1.17 m² (12.60 sq ft)
Trailing-edge flaps (total) 1.94 m² (20.84 sq ft)
Fin 1.14 m² (12.32 sq ft)
Rudder, incl tab 0.71 m² (7.62 sq ft)
Horizontal tail surfaces (total) 3.60 m² (38.74 sq ft)

WEIGHTS AND LOADINGS:
Weight empty, standard 1,310 kg (2,888 lb)
Max usable fuel weight: standard 253 kg (558 lb)
optional 385 kg (738 lb)
Max T-O weight 2,154 kg (4,750 lb)
Max ramp weight 2,165 kg (4,773 lb)
Max zero-fuel weight 2,027 kg (4,470 lb)
Max landing weight 2,047 kg (4,513 lb)
Max wing loading 111.1 kg/m² (22.76 lb/sq ft)
Max power loading 6.57 kg/kW (10.8 lb/hp)

PERFORMANCE (at max T-O weight except where indicated):
Max level speed at optimum altitude, mid cruise weight
196 knots (363 km/h; 226 mph)
Cruising speed at optimum altitude, mid cruise weight:
75% power 193 knots (357 km/h; 222 mph)
65% power 191 knots (354 km/h; 220 mph)
55% power 180 knots (333 km/h; 207 mph)
45% power 168 knots (311 km/h; 193 mph)
Cruising speed at 3,050 m (10,000 ft), mid cruise weight:
75% power 179 knots (332 km/h; 206 mph)
65% power 175 knots (324 km/h; 202 mph)
55% power 159 knots (295 km/h; 183 mph)
45% power 143 knots (265 km/h; 165 mph)
Minimum single-engine control speed (VMC)
65 knots (120 km/h; 75 mph)
Stalling speed: flaps and landing gear up
66 knots (122 km/h; 76 mph) CAS
flaps and landing gear down
62 knots (115 km/h; 72 mph) CAS
Max rate of climb at S/L 427 m (1,400 ft)/min
Rate of climb at S/L, one engine out 73 m (240 ft)/min
Max certificated ceiling 7,620 m (25,000 ft)
Service ceiling, one engine out 3,750 m (12,300 ft)
T-O run 280 m (920 ft)
T-O to 15 m (50 ft) 369 m (1,210 ft)
Landing from 15 m (50 ft):
standard brakes 658 m (2,160 ft)
heavy duty brakes 603 m (1,978 ft)
Landing run: standard brakes 427 m (1,400 ft)
heavy duty brakes 371 m (1,218 ft)
Accelerate/stop distance:
standard brakes 732 m (2,400 ft)
heavy duty brakes 636 m (2,088 ft)
Range with standard fuel, allowances for taxi, T-O, climb, descent, and 45 min reserves at max range power:
at optimum altitude:
75% power 463 nm (858 km; 533 miles)
65% power 550 nm (1,018 km; 633 miles)
55% power 630 nm (1,166 km; 725 miles)
45% power 670 nm (1,240 km; 771 miles)
at 3,050 m (10,000 ft):
75% power 450 nm (833 km; 517 miles)
65% power 535 nm (990 km; 615 miles)
55% power 610 nm (1,129 km; 702 miles)
45% power 632 nm (1,170 km; 727 miles)
Range with max optional fuel, allowances as above:
at optimum altitude:
75% power 665 nm (1,232 km; 765 miles)
65% power 785 nm (1,454 km; 904 miles)
55% power 920 nm (1,705 km; 1,059 miles)
45% power 990 nm (1,834 km; 1,140 miles)
at 3,050 m (10,000 ft):
75% power 640 nm (1,186 km; 737 miles)
65% power 758 nm (1,405 km; 873 miles)
55% power 860 nm (1,593 km; 990 miles)
45% power 903 nm (1,673 km; 1,040 miles)

PIPER (PA-46-310P) MALIBU

PA-46-310P Malibu, claimed by Piper to be the first cabin class, pressurised, piston powered single-engined aircraft

Piper announced on 20 November 1982 a new six-seat cabin monoplane, the PA-46-310P Malibu, which the company claims to be the world's first cabin class, pressurised, piston powered single-engined aircraft. The almost circular section fuselage of the Malibu has practically no taper over the length of the cabin, providing each passenger with an equal level of comfort. The engineering and pre-production prototypes had completed more than 400 and almost 60 flight hours respectively at the time of the company's announcement, and during this period these aircraft met or exceeded all design performance goals. FAA certification was received in September 1983. Production deliveries began in November 1983, and by 1 January 1988 a total of 361 aircraft had been delivered.

An optional **Executive** group equipment package comprises executive writing table; forward refreshment centre; cabin stereo system; true airspeed indicator; polished propeller spinner; external power receptacle; lockable fuel caps; and vinyl floor runner, and adds 20.4 kg (45.0 lb) to basic aircraft weight.

At the Paris Air Show in June 1987 Piper's new owner confirmed that derivative models of the Malibu, including a turboprop version (described separately) and a twin-engined variant, were under examination for possible future development.

TYPE: Six-seat all-metal cabin monoplane.

WINGS: Cantilever low-wing monoplane of high aspect ratio. Dihedral 4°. Conventional ailerons and hydraulically actuated trailing-edge flaps. Pneumatic de-icing boots on leading-edges optional.

FUSELAGE: Semi-monocoque structure, primarily of light alloy, with fail-safe construction in the pressurised area.

TAIL UNIT: Conventional tail unit, with swept vertical surfaces and an extended dorsal fin blended into the upper surface of the rear fuselage. Horn balanced control surfaces. Trim tab in elevator. Pneumatic de-icing boots on leading-edges optional.

LANDING GEAR: Hydraulically retractable tricycle type with single wheel on each unit; main units retract inward into wing roots, nosewheel rearward, rotating 90° to lie flat under baggage compartment. Oleo-pneumatic shock absorber in each unit. Hydraulic brakes on mainwheels. Parking brake.

POWER PLANT: One 231 kW (310 hp) Continental TSIO-520-BE flat-six turbocharged engine, driving a Hartzell two-blade constant-speed propeller with spinner. Fuel system capacity 462 litres (122 US gallons; 101.6 Imp gallons), of which 454 litres (120 US gallons; 100 Imp gallons) are usable. Oil capacity 7.5 litres (2 US gallons; 1.7 Imp gallons).

ACCOMMODATION: Pilot and five passengers in pressurised, heated and ventilated cabin. Centre and rear contoured reclining seats in facing pairs. Foldaway writing table. Airstair door immediately to rear of wing trailing-edge on port side. Overwing emergency exit on starboard side. Unpressurised baggage compartment in nose, and pressurised space at rear of cabin, each with capacity of 45 kg (100 lb). Heated windscreen optional.

SYSTEMS: Pressurisation system with max differential of 0.38 bars (5.5 lb/sq in), to provide a cabin altitude of 2,440 m (8,000 ft) to a height of 7,620 m (25,000 ft). Hydraulic system pressure 107 bars (1,550 lb/sq in). One engine driven vacuum pump standard; second pump optional. Standard electrical system has one 60A alternator; second 60A alternator optional. 24V 15Ah battery. Full icing protection is optional, with pneumatic de-icing boots on wing and tail surfaces, electrically heated propeller, pilot's electrically heated anti-ice windscreen plate, wing ice inspection light, heated pitot head, heated lift detector, and dual alternators and vacuum pumps. Approval for flight into known icing conditions was obtained in July 1984.

AVIONICS AND EQUIPMENT: Standard King avionics comprise dual nav/coms; VOR/LOC and glideslope; HSI; ADF; DME; transponder; automatic flight control system and automatic emergency locator beacon. Options include alternatives to or duplication of the above equipment, plus R/Nav; yaw damper; RMI; Texas Instruments and Foster Loran systems; Sperry WeatherScout I colour weather radar; 3M Stormscope; SunAir ASB-100A HF transceiver; and Wulfsberg Flitefone. Standard equipment includes airspeed indicator; magnetic compass; Piper pictorial turn rate indicator; rate of climb indicator; altimeter; eight-day clock; 3 in artificial horizon; electric 3 in pictorial navigation indicator; luminous outside air temperature gauge; heated pitot; ammeter; annunciator panel; electric tachometer; fuel quantity gauge; manifold pressure/fuel flow gauge; oil temperature gauge; oil pressure gauge; cylinder head temperature gauge; turbine inlet temperature gauge; engine hour meter; alternate static source; dual control wheels with elevator trim switch on pilot's wheel; and pilot's and co-pilot's toe brakes. Pilot's and co-pilot's seats are vertically and fore/aft adjusting and have inertia reel shoulder harnesses and safety belts; armrests for all six seats; ashtrays; map holders; pilot's storm window; emergency exit; sun visors; passenger club seating with inertia reel shoulder harnesses and seatbelts on forward facing seats; window curtains; cigar lighter; super soundproofing; fuel tank quick drains; fuel sampler; jack pads and towbar standard. Optional equipment includes ground clearance energy saver system supplying battery power to one com and audio system; panel-mounted digital clock; co-pilot's flight instruments; oxygen system; relief tube; hand held fire extinguisher; stainless steel control cables; and Irish weave or all-leather seats.

DIMENSIONS, EXTERNAL:
Wing span 13.11 m (43 ft 0 in)
Length overall 8.66 m (28 ft 4¾ in)
Height overall 3.44 m (11 ft 3½ in)
Tailplane span 4.42 m (14 ft 6 in)
Wheel track 3.75 m (12 ft 3½ in)
Wheelbase 2.44 m (8 ft 0 in)
Propeller diameter 2.03 m (6 ft 8 in)
Passenger door (port, rear):
Height 1.17 m (3 ft 10 in)
Width 0.61 m (2 ft 0 in)
Baggage door (port, nose):
Height 0.58 m (1 ft 11 in)
Width 0.48 m (1 ft 7 in)

DIMENSIONS, INTERNAL:
Cabin: Length, instrument panel to rear pressure bulkhead 3.76 m (12 ft 4 in)
Max width 1.26 m (4 ft 1½ in)
Max height 1.19 m (3 ft 11 in)
Baggage compartment volume:
nose 0.40 m³ (14.0 cu ft)
rear cabin 0.57 m³ (20.0 cu ft)

AREA:
Wings, gross 16.26 m² (175.0 sq ft)

WEIGHTS AND LOADINGS:
Weight empty, standard 1,068 kg (2,354 lb)
Max usable fuel weight 326 kg (720 lb)
Max T-O weight 1,860 kg (4,100 lb)
Max ramp weight 1,868 kg (4,118 lb)
Max wing loading 114.25 kg/m² (23.4 lb/sq ft)
Max power loading 8.05 kg/kW (13.23 lb/hp)

PERFORMANCE (at max T-O weight, S/L, ISA, except where indicated):
Max level speed at mid cruise weight
234 knots (434 km/h; 269 mph)
Cruising speed at mid cruise weight at optimum altitude:
75% power 215 knots (398 km/h; 248 mph)
65% power 205 knots (380 km/h; 236 mph)
55% power 196 knots (363 km/h; 226 mph)
Stalling speed:
flaps up 68 knots (126 km/h; 79 mph) CAS
flaps down 58 knots (108 km/h; 67 mph) CAS
Max rate of climb at S/L 348 m (1,143 ft)/min
Service ceiling 7,620 m (25,000 ft)
T-O run 439 m (1,440 ft)
T-O to 15 m (50 ft) 617 m (2,025 ft)
Landing from 15 m (50 ft) 463 m (1,520 ft)
Landing run 195 m (640 ft)
Range with max fuel at optimum altitude with allowances for taxi, T-O, climb and descent, and 45 min reserves at max range power:
75% power 1,330 nm (2,464 km; 1,531 miles)
65% power 1,420 nm (2,631 km; 1,635 miles)
55% power 1,555 nm (2,881 km; 1,790 miles)

PIPER TURBINE MALIBU

In October 1987 Piper announced plans to develop a turbine engined version of the Malibu, to be powered by a 298 kW (400 shp) flat rated Pratt & Whitney Canada PT6A-11 turboprop. A prototype was expected to fly in early 1988, with first customer deliveries anticipated in late 1989. The following data are provisional:

DIMENSIONS, EXTERNAL: As for Malibu except:
Length overall 9.78 m (32 ft 1¼ in)
Height overall 3.60 m (11 ft 9½ in)

WEIGHT:

Max T-O weight	1,996 kg (4,400 lb)

PERFORMANCE (estimated, at max T-O weight):

Never-exceed speed 222 knots (411 km/h; 256 mph) CAS	
Max level speed 200 knots (371 km/h; 230 mph) CAS	
Max cruising speed at 7,620 m (25,000 ft)	
	240 knots (445 km/h; 276 mph)
Max rate of climb at S/L	
	more than 457 m (1,500 ft)/min
Service ceiling	7,620 m (25,000 ft)
Range at max cruising speed, 45 min reserves	
	1,000 nm (1,853 km; 1,151 miles)

PIPER DYNA-CAM ENGINE PROJECT

In June 1987 Piper began flight testing a 156.6 kW (210 hp) liquid-cooled Dyna-Cam engine in an experimental Piper Arrow III. The engine, known originally as the Hermann Cam-Drive, was first developed in 1940. It consists of two cylinder blocks, twelve cylinders and six double-ended pistons. It was certificated by the Federal Aviation Administration in 1957 and briefly test flown in a Piper Comanche in 1961. Claimed advantages of the Dyna-Cam engine are smooth running, high torque at low rpm, long engine life and very low frontal area. The Piper flight test programme was expected to last about nine months.

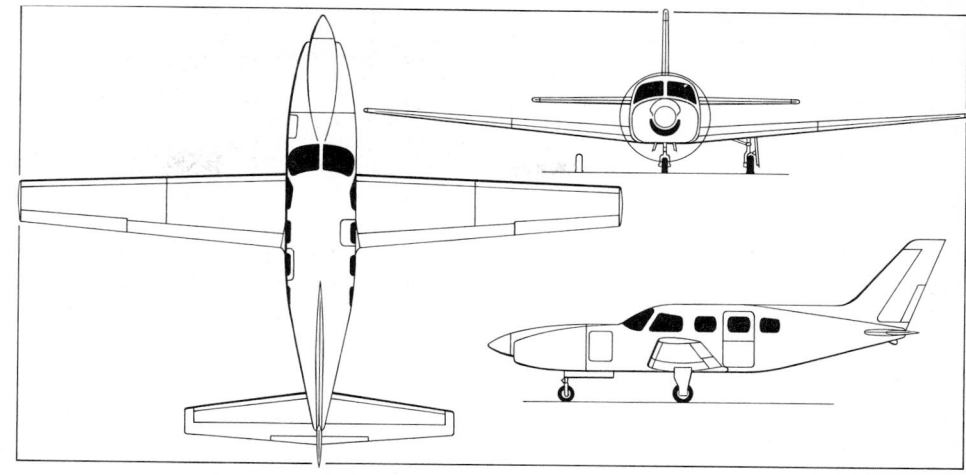

Piper Turbine Malibu (P&WC PT6A-11 turboprop), due for certification in 1989 *(Jane's/Mike Keep)*

PORSCHE
PORSCHE AVIATION PRODUCTS INC

Galesburg Municipal Airport, RR2, Box 118A, Galesburg, Illinois 61401
Telephone: (309) 342 0800
Fax: (309) 342 1078
PRESIDENT: Donald R. Krull
VICE-PRESIDENT, SALES AND PRODUCT SUPPORT:
Pat Millard

Porsche Aviation Products Inc was founded in mid-1986 as a subsidiary of Porsche AG of the Federal Republic of Germany and is responsible for sales, marketing and product support services for the Porsche PFM 3200 power plant (described in the Engines section of this edition) in North and South America.

The company is supplying engines to Mooney Aircraft Corporation for its Mooney PFM aircraft (which see), and will market refurbished Cessna Model 172 Skyhawk and Model 182 Skylane aircraft which will be re-engined with Porsche power plants and equipped with new avionics, updated cabin interiors and custom external paint schemes. Initially, both Porsche-Cessna models will be sold with a 161.8 kW (217 hp) naturally aspirated Porsche PFM 3200 engine. The Cessna 182 will also be offered with a 178.9 kW (240 hp) turbocharged and intercooled variant of the power plant. FAA certification of the Porsche-Cessna 172 was expected during the first quarter of 1988, with customer deliveries scheduled to begin shortly thereafter. All aircraft powered by Porsche PFM engines feature 'single lever' power control with automatic mixture and propeller control, dual electrical systems and dual electronic ignition.

Cessna Model 182 Skylane re-engined with 161.8 kW (217 hp) Porsche PFM 3200 power plant

RAISBECK
RAISBECK ENGINEERING INC

7675 Perimeter Road South, Boeing Field International, Seattle, Washington 98108
Telephone: (206) 763 2000
CHIEF EXECUTIVE OFFICER: James D. Raisbeck
VICE-PRESIDENT, MARKETING: John McCarthy

Raisbeck Engineering Inc continues the work of its founder and Chief Executive Officer, James D. Raisbeck, of developing, certificating, and marketing to the general aviation community advanced technology systems aimed at increasing aircraft performance, productivity and safety. Products available in early 1988 are described below.

RAISBECK MARK VI SYSTEM

In April 1982, Raisbeck Engineering formed a joint venture with Morrison-Knudsen's Western Aircraft Maintenance Inc of Boise, Idaho, to develop its Mark VI System for the Beechcraft Super King Air 200 series. The partnership with Western Aircraft Maintenance Inc was terminated in December 1985, but the Mark VI System is fully certificated and continues to be marketed by Raisbeck.

Improvements embodied by the Mark VI System include new inboard wing leading-edges of composite material which increase speed and intercooler efficiency through advanced aerodynamics; Goodrich flush wing de-icing boots made practicable by recessing the new inboard leading-edges; flap and aileron seals; extended rear underwing fairings of composite material on engine nacelles to reduce drag; wheel doors which enclose completely the oversize tyres on those Super King Air 200s fitted with high flotation landing gear; low drag windscreen wipers; a flexible stainless steel coupling between exhaust stack and inlet; flush automatic nose vane door which increases air-conditioning efficiency when open and reduces drag by closing when not needed; vanes which direct inlet air up to the compressor with full supercharging effect; and twin ventral strakes under the rear fuselage, instead of the single standard ventral fin, to improve airflow and increase stability and speed.

Beechcraft Super King Air 200 embodying Raisbeck Mark VI System

Altitude	T-O weight	Ambient conditions	Torque increase	True airspeed increase
5,485 m (18,000 ft)	4,990 kg (11,000 lb)	ISA	29.45 kg-m (213 ft-lb)	27 knots (50 km/h; 31 mph)
9,450 m (31,000 ft)	4,990 kg (11,000 lb)	ISA	16.73 kg-m (121 ft-lb)	31 knots (57 km/h; 36 mph)

Typical Raisbeck Mark VI incremental performance gains

Altitude	T-O weight	Ambient conditions	Ice doors stowed	Ice doors deployed
S/L to 9,450 m (31,000 ft)	5,443 kg (12,000 lb)	ISA	8 minutes less	22 minutes less

Typical Raisbeck Mark VI reductions in time to climb

The Raisbeck Mark VI system received British CAA certification in the Spring of 1986. It is available as a series of individually certificated kits for easy local installation.

HARTZELL/RAISBECK QUIET TURBOFAN PROPELLER SYSTEM

In February 1985 Raisbeck certificated a four-blade propeller conversion for the Super King Air 200, known as the Raisbeck Quiet Prop, which it claims results in considerably reduced flight deck and cabin noise, shorter take-off and landing runs and a rate of climb of 1,102 m (3,616 ft)/min instead of 898 m (2,945 ft)/min for the Mark VI equipped Super King Air with the usual three-blade propellers. The conversion utilises new advanced technology lightweight 2.39 m (7 ft 10 in) diameter 'turbofan' propellers developed by Hartzell, and includes new timers, slip rings and a Goodrich hot propeller de-icing system. First flight of the propeller took place on a Mark VI-equipped Beechcraft Super King Air B200 on 25 June 1984. By March 1987 more than 100 Quiet Prop systems had been delivered, and production was running at 8-10 per month.

By 7 August 1986 Raisbeck had received FAA certification of a Quiet Prop installation for the de Havilland Canada DHC-6-300 Twin Otter, and began deliveries of a further system for Beechcraft King Air 90 series aircraft in the Autumn of that year.

RAISBECK SHORT-FIELD ENHANCEMENT SYSTEM

In June 1987 Raisbeck announced FAA certification and first production deliveries of its Short-Field Enhancement System for Super King Air 200/B200 aircraft. The modification comprises new composite construction inboard wing leading-edges, intercooler ducting, wing-to-fuselage fairings and flush mounted Goodrich de-icing boots.

When combined with the Hartzell/Raisbeck Quiet Turbofan propeller system, the modification provides a

Raisbeck Short-Field Enhancement System modification for Beech Model 200 series Super King Airs

claimed 18 knot (33 km/h; 21 mph) reduction in flaps-up V_2 take-off speed; 35 per cent reduction in FAA T-O distance; 50 per cent reduction in FAA accelerate-go T-O distance; increased engine-out climb rate; reduced FAA-approved reference and approach speeds; and a 56 per cent reduction in stopping distance using maximum reverse thrust.

PERFORMANCE (at AUW of 5,670 kg; 12,500 lb, S/L, ISA):

T-O speed (V_2)	103 knots (191 km/h; 119 mph)
Approach speed	97 knots (180 km/h; 112 mph)
T-O to 15 m (50 ft)	686 m (2,250 ft)
Accelerate-go distance	1,061 m (3,480 ft)
Accelerate-stop distance	987 m (3,240 ft)

RAISBECK MARK VII SYSTEM

Raisbeck's Mark VII System for all versions of the Beechcraft King Air 90 has been broken down into a series of 12 kits which are being certificated individually. The first kit, comprising fully enclosed main landing gear speed doors, was certificated in June 1983; production deliveries began immediately afterwards. Their effect is to decrease time to climb by 14 per cent and add 6 knots (11 km/h; 7 mph) to the cruising speed of the aircraft at 7,315 m (24,000 ft).

The second kit, certificated in September 1983, introduced new area ruled wing lockers, aft of the engine nacelles. These have a combined volume of 0.45 m³ (16 cu ft), with a capacity of 317 kg (700 lb), and will accommodate outsize items such as six pairs of 2.2 m (7 ft 2½ in) skis, while at the same time decreasing drag and increasing cruising speed. They can be installed on Beechcraft King Air, Super King Air and Model 99 aircraft. Deliveries began in April 1986.

The remaining ten kits will include rear fuselage ventral strakes, increased efficiency intakes, advanced technology four-blade propellers for the King Air 90 series, and a TKS full span ice protection system, replacing the current de-icing boots and associated with wing leading-edge aerodynamic improvements.

RAISBECK RAM AIR RECOVERY SYSTEM

Raisbeck Engineering Inc has developed a Ram Air Recovery System (RARS) for Beechcraft Super King Air 200 aircraft which provides improvements in cruising speeds and rates of climb. RARS comprises the installation of a more complete sealing of the engine nacelle air inlet section, a new fixed turning vane, the addition of a 'Coanda effect' curved surface on the rear portion of the movable inertial separator vane, and a new highly porous ice shedder screen. Deliveries of RARS equipped aircraft began on 15 June 1986. The system is approved by Pratt & Whitney Canada, which manufactures the Super King Air 200's engines, and has received FAA certification.

RAM

RAM AIRCRAFT CORPORATION

Waco-Madison Cooper Airport, PO Box 5219, Waco, Texas 76708-0219
Telephone: (817) 752 8381
Telex: 910 894 5248
Fax: (817) 752 3307

PRESIDENT:
Jack M. Riley Jr (Engineering)
INTERNATIONAL SALES: Mike McMains
SALES MANAGER: David Seesing
PRESS RELATIONS, MARKETING AND ADVERTISING:
Chuck Morrow

RAM Aircraft Corporation specialises in the modification of selected single- and twin-engined general aviation aircraft to provide increased performance and efficiency. This is achieved by the installation of engines of greater horsepower, driving propellers of advanced design. All of the resulting modifications have been FAA approved by the award of a supplemental type certificate (STC). Export STC modification kits are available, and these can include either new engines or RAM-remanufactured 100 per cent balanced versions of the Continental TSIO-520 engine in N, NB, VB, A, E, EB, B, BB, C, F, H, M, P and R models and GTSIO-520-L and N. RAM's Cessna 310, 320, 340 and 414A conversions are now identified as Series I (310 hp) and Series III (325 hp) when Teledyne Continental camshafts are fitted, and Series II and Series IV respectively with RAM economy camshaft developed by Crane Cams Inc of Daytona Beach, Florida, which affords easier starting and smoother idling, with claimed reductions in cruising power fuel consumption of 3-5 per cent. The company offers also an aircraft refurbishing service at its Waco works, including repainting and airframe maintenance.

Any performance figures not listed in this entry may be considered to be the same as specified by the aircraft's manufacturer.

RAM/CESSNA 172

RAM modifications of the Cessna 172, models D-N, involves the installation of a 119 kW (160 hp) Textron Lycoming O-320-D2G flat-four engine or a RAM-remanufactured Textron Lycoming O-320-E2D with power output increased from 112 kW (150 hp) to 119 kW (160 hp).

RAM/PIPER PA-28-140/PA-28-151

RAM modification of these two Piper models involves the installation of a 119 kW (160 hp) Textron Lycoming O-320-D3G flat-four engine.

RAM/CESSNA T206/210

RAM modification of these two Cessna models covers replacement of the 212 kW (285 hp) Continental TSIO-520-C/H flat-six engine in early production aircraft by a 231 kW (310 hp) TSIO-520-M/R. This RAM-remanufactured engine provides performance generally the same as that of later model Cessna production aircraft powered by a 231 kW (310 hp) engine. A Hartzell Q-tip propeller or wide chord McCauley propeller can be included in the modification.

RAM/CESSNA T310

In this modification the 212 kW (285 hp) Continental TSIO-520-B flat-six engines can be replaced by 224 kW (300 hp) TSIO-520-E, or 242 kW (325 hp) TSIO-520-NBR RAM-remanufactured engines. With 242 kW (325 hp) engines the modified aircraft is known as RAM 310 Series IV. Either separately or in conjunction with this modification, RAM can install aerial mapping/photo reconnaissance dual camera ports, the STC approved installation being suitable for cameras as large as the Wild RC10 and Zeiss RMKA 15/23.

PERFORMANCE (A: 224 kW; 300 hp, B: 242 kW; 325 hp engines, at max T-O weight of 2,572 kg; 5,670 lb):

Cruising speed, 75% power at 5,485 m (18,000 ft):	
A	213 knots (394 km/h; 245 mph)
B	235 knots (434 km/h; 270 mph)
Max rate of climb at S/L: A	640 m (2,100 ft)/min
B	915 m (3,000 ft)/min
Rate of climb at S/L, one engine out:	
A	137 m (450 ft)/min
B	183 m (600 ft)/min

RAM/CESSNA 340/340A

RAM's modification of the Cessna 340/340A replaces 212 kW (285 hp) Continental TSIO-520-K engines by RAM-remanufactured 231 kW (310 hp) TSIO-520-Ns or 242 kW (325 hp) TSIO-520-NBRs. In 231 kW (310 hp) form the modified aircraft is known as the RAM 340 Series II, and in 242 kW (325 hp) form as the 340 Series IV. Hartzell Q-tip propellers are part of the modification package. With the 231 kW (310 hp) engines, useful load and max T-O weight of the Cessna 340 and 340A are increased by 68 kg (150 lb), and with the 242 kW (325 hp) engines, by 136 kg (300 lb).

PERFORMANCE (A: 231 kW; 310 hp engines with Q-tip propellers. B: 242 kW; 325 hp engines, at max T-O weight of 2,853 kg; 6,290 lb):

Cruising speed, 75% power at 6,100 m (20,000 ft):	
A, B	225 knots (417 km/h; 259 mph)
Max rate of climb at S/L: A	564 m (1,850 ft)/min
B	655 m (2,150 ft)/min
Rate of climb at S/L, one engine out:	
A	105 m (345 ft)/min
B	114 m (375 ft)/min
Time to 5,485 m (18,000 ft): A	20 min
B	17 min
Acceleration to 87 knots (161 km/h; 100 mph): A	20 s
B	16 s

RAM/CESSNA 401/402A/402B/402C

In this modification RAM installs remanufactured 224 kW (300 hp) Continental TSIO-520-E or 242 kW (325 hp) TSIO-520-VB engines in Cessna 401 and 402A-C aircraft. Standard equipment includes replacement of engine accessories with new or overhauled equipment, Slick 6220 pressurised magnetos, a red silicone rubber baffle seal kit, Alcor 46158 exhaust gas temperature gauge and combustion analyser. Options include an electronic fuel flow management system, Woodward propeller synchrophaser, RAM super soundproofing, Cleveland heavy duty brakes, polished and balanced propellers and three-colour polyurethane external paint finish.

RAM/CESSNA 414/414A

In this modification RAM replaces the 231 kW (310 hp) Continental TSIO-520-J engines installed in Cessna 414s built between 1970 and 1976 by 231 kW (310 hp) TSIO-520-Ns or 242 kW (325 hp) TSIO-520-NBRs, when they are known respectively as the RAM 414 Series II and IV. The installation includes the same standard and optional items as for the Cessna 340A and 402C. The Hartzell Q-tip propellers are available only for modifications with the 242 kW (325 hp) engines, with which they are standard.

PERFORMANCE (A: 231 kW; 310 hp. B: 242 kW; 325 hp engines, at max T-O weight of 2,953 kg; 6,510 lb):

Cruising speed, 75% power at 6,100 m (20,000 ft):	
A	210 knots (389 km/h; 241 mph)
B	215 knots (398 km/h; 247 mph)
Max rate of climb at S/L: A	533 m (1,750 ft)/min
B	610 m (2,000 ft)/min
Rate of climb at S/L, one engine out:	
A	88 m (290 ft)/min
B	104 m (340 ft)/min
Time to 5,485 m (18,000 ft): A	20 min
B	18 min
Acceleration to 87 knots (161 km/h; 100 mph): A	22 s
B	19 s

RAM/CESSNA 414AW

RAM's modification of the Cessna 414A replaces the standard 231 kW (310 hp) Continental TSIO-520-J engines by remanufactured TSIO-520-N/NBs of the same horsepower (Series II) or (in the 414AW Series IV) by 242 kW (325 hp) TSIO-520-NBRs, with Hartzell Q-tip propellers. FAA approval of this aircraft, which is fitted with 0.89 m (2 ft 11 in) high winglets at each wingtip, was received on 1 March 1983, and subsequently by the civil aviation authorities in Australia. The RAM/Cessna 414AW operates at a gross weight increase of 153 kg (337 lb), providing a 136 kg (300 lb) net increase in useful load.

PERFORMANCE (at max T-O weight: A with 231 kW; 310 hp engines, B with 242 kW; 325 hp engines):

Cruising speed, 75% power at 6,100 m (20,000 ft):	
75% power:	
A	210 knots (389 km/h; 242 mph)
B	215 knots (398 km/h; 247 mph)
55% power:	
A	188 knots (348 km/h; 216 mph)
B	195 knots (361 km/h; 224 mph)
Max rate of climb at S/L:	
A	494 m (1,620 ft)/min
B	533 m (1,750 ft)/min
Rate of climb at S/L, one engine out:	
A	91 m (300 ft)/min
B	98 m (320 ft)/min
Time to 5,485 m (18,000 ft):	
A	22 min
B	18 min
Acceleration to 87 knots (161 km/h; 100 mph):	
A	23 s
B	22 s

RAM/CESSNA 421C and 421CW

RAM's modification of the Cessna 421B and 421C Golden Eagle series includes RAM or TCM factory remanufactured GTSIO-520-L/N engines, propellers and accessories. The RAM engine conversion provides a 50 kg (110 lb) increase in useful load for the Cessna 421C. RAM replaces the standard engine cooling baffles, exhaust risers, slip joints and magnetos with a 'RAM Reliability Package' which includes new red silicone rubber/glassfibre cooling baffle seal material, remanufactured exhaust system and slip joints, and Bendix S6RN-1250 pressurised magnetos. Also included are a Hoskins computerised fuel management system and Alcor direct reading exhaust gas temperature system. In November 1984 RAM received FAA approval for the installation of 0.89 m (2 ft 11 in) winglets to Cessna 421C aircraft up to factory serial number 0799. The first converted aircraft, known as the **RAM/Cessna 421CW**, was delivered in October 1984, and 20 conversions had been completed by February 1988. Australian certification of the RAM/Cessna 421CW was obtained in 1987.

The winglet installation for the Cessna 421C involves removal of the standard 0.46 m (1 ft 6 in) wingtip and replacement with a wing extension and winglet assembly each of which measures 0.93 m (3 ft 0½ in) to the base of the winglet. This adds a total of 0.94 m (3 ft 1 in) to the standard Cessna 421C's wing span. The RAM winglet is constructed from bidirectional carbon graphite cloth impregnated with epoxy resins, with an outer layer which includes interwoven aluminium cloth for electrical conductivity and lighting protection. Existing landing lights, position lights and wingtip strobe lights are installed in the new wingtip/winglet assembly. The RAM/Cessna 421CW Supplemental Type Certificate includes certification for flight into known icing conditions. With winglets installed the RAM/Cessna 421CW has a 23 kg (50 lb) increase in useful load over the standard Cessna 421C. RAM claims a 25 per cent increase in max rate of climb for the winglet equipped aircraft.

A description of the Cessna 421C can be found in the 1985-86 *Jane's*.

DIMENSIONS, EXTERNAL (421CW): As for Cessna 421C except:

Basic wing span	13.47 m (44 ft 2½ in)
Span, winglet tip to winglet tip	13.83 m (45 ft 4½ in)
Wing aspect ratio (basic)	8.64
Effective wing aspect ratio, including winglets	9.74
Winglet cant angle	10°
Winglet toe-out angle	2°

AREA (421CW):

Wings, gross (basic)	21.0 m² (226.0 sq ft)

First production RAM conversion of a Cessna 421C with winglets, known as RAM/Cessna 421CW

WEIGHTS AND LOADINGS (421CW):

Max T-O weight	3,429 kg (7,560 lb)
Max zero-fuel weight	2,963 kg (6,533 lb)
Max wing loading	163.3 kg/m² (33.45 lb/sq ft)
Max power loading	6.12 kg/kW (10.06 lb/hp)

PERFORMANCE (421CW):

Cruising speed at 75% power at 6,100 m (20,000 ft)
228 knots (422 km/h; 262 mph)
Cruising speed at 65% power at 6,100 m (20,000 ft)
223 knots (413 km/h; 257 mph)
Max rate of climb, one engine out at 1,525 m (5,000 ft),
ISA   91 m (300 ft)/min
Time to 7,315 m (24,000 ft)   24 min

RAM/BEECH BARON 58

This modification installs 231 kW (310 hp) Continental TSIO-520-L/LB or 242 kW (325 hp) TSIO-520-WB engines in Beech Baron Models 58P and 58TC. Standard items include Alcor exhaust gas temperature gauge and combus-

tion analyser, Airborne dry vacuum pumps, Woodward Type II synchrophase system with Woodward propeller governors, red silicone rubber baffle seals, Teflon fuel and oil hoses, Cleveland brakes and wheels, RAM super soundproofing, polished and balanced propellers, and optional three-colour polyurethane external paint finish. A Hoskins electronic fuel flow system is optional.

PERFORMANCE (Baron 58P. A: 231 kW; 310 hp, B: 242 kW; 325 hp):

Cruising speed, 75% power at 6,100 m (20,000 ft):

A	202 knots (374 km/h; 233 mph)
B	210 knots (389 km/h; 242 mph)

Max rate of climb at S/L: A   449 m (1,475 ft)/min
B   457 m (1,500 ft)/min

Rate of climb at S/L, one engine out:

A	62 m (204 ft)/min
B	82 m (270 ft)/min

RANKIN

RANKIN AIRCRAFT

Rankin Airport, Route 3, Maryville, Missouri 64468
Telephone: (816) 582 3791
PRESIDENT: Joe Rankin

RANKIN COLLEGIATE

Mr Joe Rankin acquired the type certificate and manufacturing drawings for the former Porterfield CP-65 Collegiate two-seat light aeroplane, more than 400 of which were manufactured prior to the Second World War. A

number of modifications were made to update the design, which is now known as the Rankin Collegiate.

No sales had been reported up to the time of going to press. A description and illustration of the Collegiate can be found in the 1987-88 *Jane's*.

RILEY

RILEY INTERNATIONAL CORPORATION

2206 Palomar Airport Road, Suite B-2, Carlsbad, California 92008
Telephone: (619) 438 9089
Telex: 140414
PRESIDENT: Jack M. Riley

This company was formed by Mr Jack Riley to continue marketing his well-known conversions of commercially produced light aircraft. Those currently available are described in this entry. Details of the Riley Rocket 340, Riley Turbine 404, Riley Rocket Power 414 and Riley-Modified Corsair may be found in the 1983-84 *Jane's*. The former Riley Turbine P-210 conversion is now listed under the Advanced Aircraft Corporation entry in this section. The former Riley Turbine Eagle 421 appears as the Regent 1500 in the same entry.

RILEY P-210 ROCKET

In 1983 Riley announced development of the P-210 Rocket conversion of the Cessna Model 210 Pressurised Centurion. This conversion involves the installation of a Riley intercooler system for the standard 231 kW (310 hp) turbocharged Continental TSIO-520-AF engine. Riley claims that the induction air intercooler with flush NACA duct in the cowling reduces induction air temperatures by up to 45 per cent, greatly improving engine efficiency. Other modifications include additional soundproofing and electro-pneumatic door seals, double-skinned cabin windows, new wheels, tyres, brakes and battery, dual alternators, metal instrument panel, dual vacuum pumps, Flint wingtip fuel tanks which increase the P-210's fuel capacity to 462 litres (122 US gallons; 102 Imp gallons), Bendix/King Silver Crown avionics with Bendix/King KFC 200 or Cessna 400 autopilot, Loran C, and new exterior paint. The Riley P-210 Rocket received an FAA supplemental type certificate in late 1984. The Riley induction air intercooler modification has also received FAA approval for the Cessna Turbo Centurion.

PERFORMANCE:

Cruising speed:
at 5,485 m (18,000 ft)   210 knots (389 km/h; 242 mph)
at 7,000 m (23,000 ft)   217 knots (402 km/h; 250 mph)
Max rate of climb at S/L   305 m (1,000 ft)/min

Time to 7,000 m (23,000 ft)   23 min
Service ceiling   7,000 m (23,000 ft)

RILEY SUPER 310

The Super 310 (formal designation R310 Super) represents a similar conversion to that of the Super 340, the existing power plants in the Cessna 310/320 being replaced by 231 kW (310 hp) Continental TSIO-520-Ns with intercoolers. The conversion is FAA approved for the Cessna 310I to 310R, 320B to 320F and T310P to T310R. Installation of the complete kit requires 12 working days.

A description of the Cessna Model 310 appears under the Cessna entry in the 1981-82 *Jane's*. It applies also to the Riley Super 310, except as follows:

POWER PLANT: As described for Riley Super 340, except installed engines are TSIO-520-Ns instead of TSIO-520-Js.

WEIGHTS AND LOADINGS: As for the appropriate Cessna 310/320 model except as follows:

Weight empty	increased by 10 kg (22 lb)
Max payload	reduced by 10 kg (22 lb)
Max power loading	5.11 kg/kW (8.4 lb/hp)

PERFORMANCE (at max T-O weight):

Max cruising speed, 75% power:
at 7,315 m (24,000 ft)   261 knots (483 km/h; 300 mph)
at 5,485 m (18,000 ft)   243 knots (451 km/h; 280 mph)
at 4,265 m (14,000 ft)   234 knots (435 km/h; 270 mph)
Max rate of climb at S/L   792 m (2,600 ft)/min
Rate of climb at S/L, one engine out
158 m (520 ft)/min
Service ceiling   10,670 m (35,000 ft)
Service ceiling, one engine out   7,620 m (25,000 ft)
T-O to 15 m (50 ft)   503 m (1,650 ft)
Landing from 15 m (50 ft)   546 m (1,790 ft)
Range with max fuel, max cruising speed at 7,315 m (24,000 ft), 30 min reserves
1,042 nm (1,931 km; 1,200 miles)
Range with max fuel, econ cruising speed at optimum altitude, 30 min reserves
1,737 nm (3,218 km; 2,000 miles)

RILEY SUPER 340

The Riley Super 340 (formal designation R340 Super) differs from the standard Cessna 340 primarily through

replacement of the latter's TSIO-520-K engines by TSIO-520-Js. The most important change associated with this new engine installation is the addition of an intercooler which allows a higher power output and also improves specific fuel consumption, critical altitude, engine life and reliability.

The prototype Super 340 received FAA certification in June 1974. The standard Cessna 340A for 1976 was updated in a manner similar to that of the Riley Super 340. Consequently, only Cessna 340 aircraft constructed from 1972 until the last of the 1975 models were completed are suitable for this conversion, which is completed by Riley engineers in five working days.

A description of the Cessna Model 340A appears under the Cessna entry in the 1984-85 *Jane's*. It applies also to the Riley Super 340, except as follows:

POWER PLANT: Two 231 kW (310 hp) Continental TSIO-520-J flat-six turbocharged and intercooled engines, each driving a McCauley three-blade propeller. Engine installation upgraded from Cessna 340 to Cessna 414 configuration. Fuel system as for Cessna 340. Optional aft nacelle fuel tanks, each of 75.7 litres (20 US gallons; 16.6 Imp gallons), provide max optional fuel capacity of 920 litres (243 US gallons; 202 Imp gallons) when used in conjunction with the Cessna optional 768 litre (203 US gallon; 169 Imp gallon) system.

WEIGHTS AND LOADINGS:

Weight empty	1,754 kg (3,868 lb)
Max payload	904 kg (1,993 lb)
Max T-O weight	2,710 kg (5,975 lb)
Max wing loading	158.6 kg/m² (32.47 lb/sq ft)
Max power loading	5.87 kg/kW (9.64 lb/hp)

PERFORMANCE (at max T-O weight):

Max level speed at 7,315 m (24,000 ft)
252 knots (467 km/h; 290 mph)
Max cruising speed, 75% power:
at 7,315 m (24,000 ft)
234 knots (435 km/h; 270 mph)
at 5,485 m (18,000 ft)
226 knots (418 km/h; 260 mph)
at 4,265 m (14,000 ft)
217 knots (402 km/h; 250 mph)
Econ cruising speed at 7,315 m (24,000 ft)
208 knots (386 km/h; 240 mph)
Max rate of climb at S/L   549 m (1,800 ft)/min

Cruise rate of climb at max cruising power
305 m (1,000 ft)/min
Rate of climb at S/L, one engine out
107 m (350 ft)/min
Service ceiling   9,755 m (32,000 ft)
Service ceiling, one engine out   4,875 m (16,000 ft)
T-O run   457 m (1,500 ft)
T-O to 15 m (50 ft)   594 m (1,950 ft)
Landing from 15 m (50 ft)   561 m (1,840 ft)
Landing run   233 m (765 ft)
Range with max fuel, max cruising speed at 7,315 m
(24,000 ft), 30 min reserves
1,042 nm (1,931 km; 1,200 miles)
Range with max fuel, econ cruising speed at 7,315 m
(24,000 ft), 30 min reserves
1,737 nm (3,218 km; 2,000 miles)

RILEY TURBINE ROCKET 421

This Riley conversion of the pressurised Cessna 421

involves installation of Textron Lycoming LTP 101-700 turboprops, each rated normally at 522 ekW (700 ehp), but flat rated in this application at approximately 70 per cent of normal T-O power. Both the Cessna Model 421B and 421C are suitable for this conversion, under the formal designations of R421BL and R421CL respectively. First flight of a Turbine Rocket 421 was made on 10 January 1978, followed by the first production conversion on 4 June 1978. The R421BL was certificated in June 1981.

The description of the Cessna 421C Golden Eagle which appeared under the Cessna entry in the 1985-86 *Jane's* applies also to the Riley Turbine Rocket 421, except that the landing gear is equipped with Cleveland 199-76 heavy duty brakes; each engine drives a Hartzell propeller with Q-tips and Beta propeller reversal; and optional wing fuel tanks are available to add 363 litres (96 US gallons; 80 Imp gallons) to the max total capacity.

WEIGHT AND LOADINGS:
Max T-O weight   3,470 kg (7,650 lb)

Max wing loading   173.7 kg/m² (35.58 lb/sq ft)
Max power loading   4.75 kg/kW (7.81 lb/ehp)
PERFORMANCE (at T-O weight of 3,453 kg; 7,612 lb, ISA):
Max cruising speed at 8,230 m (27,000 ft)
270 knots (500 km/h; 311 mph)
Max rate of climb at S/L   1,067 m (3,500 ft)/min
Rate of climb at S/L, one engine out
224 m (735 ft)/min
Service ceiling   over 9,145 m (30,000 ft)
Service ceiling, one engine out   6,400 m (21,000 ft)
Min landing field length   686 m (2,250 ft)
Landing run with propeller reversal   152 m (500 ft)
Range with max fuel, IFR reserves
1,300 nm (2,407 km; 1,496 miles)

ROBINSON

ROBINSON HELICOPTER COMPANY INC

24747 Crenshaw Boulevard, Torrance, California 90505
Telephone: (213) 539 0508
Telex: 18-2554
Fax: (213) 539 5198
PRESIDENT: Franklin D. Robinson
VICE-PRESIDENT, MARKETING: Barbara K. Robinson

Robinson Helicopter Company was formed to design and manufacture the R22 as a lightweight helicopter competitive in price with current two/four-seat fixed-wing light aircraft. Design began in June 1973, the first prototype flew for the first time on 28 August 1975, and the second was completed in early 1977. FAA certification was granted on 16 March 1979, and deliveries of production R22s began in October 1979. United Kingdom CAA certification was gained in June 1981.

FAA certification of the improved R22 Alpha was received in October 1983, permitting a 31.75 kg (70 lb) increase in gross weight, to allow development of the R22 for police work and for IFR training. The further improved R22 Beta model was announced on 5 August 1985.

By February 1988 a total of 760 R22s (all models) had been delivered. Robinson delivered 127 during 1987, including 20 to Australia and 16 each to Japan and the United Kingdom. In January 1988 five R22 IFR trainers were delivered to Bristow Helicopters at Redhill Aerodrome, England, for use by the company's commercial helicopter pilot school. Two others are operated by the Indira Gandhi Memorial Flying Academy in India.

Three standard R22s operated by Ranger Helicopters set five Class E1a records in Canada on 11-12 May 1982. A speed of 95 knots (176 km/h; 109 mph) was achieved over both 3 km and 25 km courses. Average speed over a 100 km course was 92.233 knots (170.817 km/h; 106.140 mph). Distance records were set by flights of 142.340 nm (263.615 km; 163.802 miles) over a straight course, and 140.655 nm (260.494 km; 161.863 miles) in a closed circuit.

ROBINSON MODEL R22 BETA, MARINER and POLICE

Current standard version of the Robinson helicopter, from c/n 501 onwards, is the **R22 Beta**. It has been available also with floats and ground handling wheels, as the **R22 Mariner**, since 1985. Mariners are operating as tuna-spotters in Mexico (2) and Venezuela (4). A law enforcement variant, the **R22 Police**, is also available, with specialist equipment as detailed below.

A load carrying hook kit, complete with electric release switches for both pilots and mechanical emergency release, is available from Classic Helicopter Corporation, 6505 Perimeter Road, Boeing Field, Seattle, Washington 98108. Applicable to any R22 with a factory installed hardpoint, the kit is certificated for a max load of 181 kg (400 lb) and imposes a never-exceed speed of 75 knots (139 km/h; 86 mph) when in use. The installation weighs 2.3 kg (5 lb) and can be installed in approx six hours. It is expected to be used primarily for sling training.

TYPE: Two-seat lightweight helicopter.
ROTOR SYSTEM: Two-blade semi-articulated main rotor, with a tri-hinged underslung rotor head to reduce blade flexing, rotor vibration and control force feedback and an elastic teeter hinge stop to prevent blade/boom contact when starting or stopping the rotor in high winds. Main rotor blade section NACA 63-015 (modified). Rigid in plane, and free to flap, these blades are of bonded all-metal construction, with a stainless steel spar and leading-edge, light alloy skin and light alloy honeycomb core. One fixed trim tab on main rotor blades. The two-blade tail rotor, mounted on the port side, is of light alloy bonded construction. Rotor brake standard.
ROTOR DRIVE: V belt drive with sprag type overrunning clutch. The main and tail gearboxes each utilise spiral bevel gears. Maintenance-free flexible couplings of proprietary manufacture are used in both the main and tail rotor drive systems. Main rotor/engine rpm ratio 1:5. Tail rotor/engine rpm ratio 1.28:1.

The Robinson R22 Police helicopter of the Oklahoma State Highway Patrol

Float equipped Robinson R22 Mariner

FUSELAGE: Welded steel tube and light alloy primary structure for cabin, rotor pylon and engine mounting, with full monocoque tailcone. Cabin skins of light alloy and glassfibre.
TAIL UNIT: Cruciform light alloy structure with fixed horizontal stabiliser and vertical fin. Small spring skid (small float on Mariner version) beneath lower half of fin to give protection in a tail-down landing.
LANDING GEAR: Welded steel tube and light alloy skid landing gear, with energy absorbing crosstubes. Twin float/skid gear on Mariner.
POWER PLANT: One 119 kW (160 hp) Textron Lycoming O-320-B2C flat-four engine (derated to 97.5 kW; 131 hp for T-O), mounted in the lower rear section of the main fuselage, and partially exposed to improve cooling and

simplify maintenance. Light alloy main fuel tank in upper rear section of the fuselage on port side, usable capacity 72.5 litres (19.2 US gallons; 16 Imp gallons). Optional auxiliary fuel tank, capacity 39.75 litres (10.5 US gallons; 8.7 Imp gallons), available from 1985 on new R22 Alphas and Betas only. Oil capacity 5.7 litres (1.5 US gallons; 1.25 Imp gallons).
ACCOMMODATION: Two seats side by side in enclosed cabin, with inertia reel shoulder harness. Cyclic control stick mounted between seats, with dual grips on yoke so that aircraft can be flown from either seat. Conventional dual collective and throttle controls mounted at the port side of each seat. Cyclic control pivots to either side to simplify entry and exit and to permit resting control hand on knee while flying, for more relaxed piloting position.

Curved two-panel windscreen. Removable door, with window, on each side. Police version has observation doors with bubble windows, which are also available as options on other models. Baggage space beneath each seat. Cabin heated and ventilated.

SYSTEM: Electrical system, powered by 12V DC alternator, includes navigation, panel and map lights, dual landing lights, anti-collision light and battery. Second battery optional.

AVIONICS AND EQUIPMENT: A King KY 197 com transceiver is standard; optional avionics include a KN 53 nav receiver, Morrow Apollo I Loran-C, KT 76A transponder and KR 87 ADF. Standard equipment includes rate of climb indicator, sensitive altimeter, quartz clock, hour meter, low rotor rpm warning horn, temperature and chip warning lights for main gearbox and chip warning light for tail gearbox, high-capacity oil cooler, rotor brake, windscreen cover, rotor blade tiedowns, soundproofing, fire extinguisher, and ground handling wheels. Optional equipment includes Hamilton vertical compass, AIM 305-1AL artificial horizon, AIM-205-1AL directional gyro, remote altitude encoder, cabin heater/demister, engine primer, removable port side controls and windscreen covers.

Police version standard equipment as above plus: dual com control panel, Wulfsberg Flitefone 40 VHF or UHF radio, removable port side controls, 70A alternator and fire extinguisher. Police version optional equipment: searchlight with dual lamps, PA speaker and siren, second Wulfsberg Flitefone 40 VHF or UHF radio and King KT 76A transponder.

IFR trainer standard avionics and equipment: AIM 500 DVF artificial horizon, King KEA 129 encoding altimeter, Astronautics DC turn co-ordinator, King KCS 55A HSI, King KR 87 ADF, King KX 165 nav/com digital display radio, King KT 76A transponder, King KR 22 marker beacon receiver, and Astro Tech LC-2 digital clock. Standard equipment is the same as for basic Alpha. IFR trainer optional avionics: second Narco Nav 121 VOR, or King KN 63 DME.

DIMENSIONS, EXTERNAL:

Main rotor diameter	7.67 m (25 ft 2 in)
Tail rotor diameter	1.07 m (3 ft 6 in)
Main rotor blade chord	0.18 m (7.2 in)
Distance between rotor centres	4.39 m (14 ft 5 in)
Length overall (rotors turning)	8.76 m (28 ft 9 in)
Length of fuselage	6.30 m (20 ft 8 in)
Fuselage: Max width	1.12 m (3 ft 8 in)
Height overall	2.67 m (8 ft 9 in)
Skid track	1.93 m (6 ft 4 in)

DIMENSION, INTERNAL:

Cabin: Max width	1.12 m (3 ft 8 in)

AREAS:

Main rotor blades (each)	0.70 m² (7.55 sq ft)
Tail rotor blades (each)	0.037 m² (0.40 sq ft)
Main rotor disc	46.21 m² (497.4 sq ft)
Tail rotor disc	0.89 m² (9.63 sq ft)
Fin	0.21 m² (2.28 sq ft)
Stabiliser	0.14 m² (1.53 sq ft)

WEIGHTS AND LOADINGS:

Weight empty (without auxiliary fuel tank)	
	374 kg (824 lb)
Fuel weight: standard	52 kg (115 lb)
auxiliary	28.6 kg (63 lb)

Max T-O and landing weight	621 kg (1,370 lb)
Max zero-fuel weight	569 kg (1,255 lb)
Max disc loading	13.43 kg/m² (2.75 lb/sq ft)
Max power loading	5.22 kg/kW (8.56 lb/hp)

PERFORMANCE (at max T-O weight):

Never-exceed speed	102 knots (190 km/h; 118 mph)
Max level speed	97 knots (180 km/h; 112 mph)
Cruising speed, 75% power at 2,440 m (8,000 ft)	
	96 knots (177 km/h; 110 mph)
Econ cruising speed	82 knots (153 km/h; 95 mph)
Max rate of climb at S/L	366 m (1,200 ft)/min
Rate of climb at 1,525 m (5,000 ft)	
	323 m (1,060 ft)/min
Service ceiling	4,265 m (14,000 ft)
Hovering ceiling IGE	2,125 m (6,970 ft)
Range with auxiliary fuel and max payload, no reserves	
	319 nm (592 km; 368 miles)
Endurance at 65% power, auxiliary fuel, no reserves	
	3 h 20 min

ROBINSON R44

In the Summer of 1986 Robinson Helicopter Company announced that it was developing a four-seat version of its R22 helicopter, to be designated R44. The R44 will be powered by a piston engine, for which the 194 kW (260 hp) Textron Lycoming O-540, 212.5 kW (285 hp) Teledyne Continental IO-520 and 158 kW (212 hp) Porsche PFM 3200 are under consideration. The helicopter is expected to be similar to the R22, but with no parts commonality, and is not likely to become available until the early 1990s.

ROCKWELL INTERNATIONAL

ROCKWELL INTERNATIONAL CORPORATION

600 Grant Street, Pittsburgh, Pennsylvania 15219

Telephone: (412) 565 2000

Telex: 866213

CHAIRMAN AND CHIEF EXECUTIVE OFFICER:
Robert Anderson

PRESIDENT AND CHIEF OPERATING OFFICER:
Donald R. Beall

SENIOR VICE-PRESIDENT, RESEARCH AND ENGINEERING:
Robert L. Cattoi

VICE-PRESIDENT, AND PRESIDENT AEROSPACE OPERATIONS:
Sam F. Iacobellis

DIRECTOR OF MEDIA RELATIONS: William D. Mellon

North American Aviation Inc, incorporated in Delaware in 1928 and a manufacturer of aircraft of various kinds from 1934, and Rockwell-Standard Corporation of Pittsburgh, Pennsylvania, a manufacturer of automotive components and builder of the Aero Commander line of civilian aircraft, merged on 22 September 1967 to form North American Rockwell Corporation.

This adopted its present name in 1973, to reflect its expanding international business. The corporation applies advanced technology to a wide range of products in its four major businesses: **Aerospace**, which is engaged in the research, development and manufacture of military aircraft, manned and unmanned space systems and rocket engines, advanced space-based surveillance systems and high energy laser and other directed energy programmes; **Automotive**; **Electronics**, engaged in research, development, manufacture and marketing of a broad range of defence and commercial electronics systems and products for precision guidance and control, tactical weapons command, control, communications and intelligence, precision navigation, avionics, telecommunications and semiconductor applications; and **General Industries**.

NORTH AMERICAN AIRCRAFT

100 North Sepulveda Boulevard, El Segundo, California 90245

Telephone: (213) 647 1000

PRESIDENT: John J. Pierro

Palmdale Facility:
2825 East Avenue P, Palmdale, California 93550
Telephone: (805) 273 6000

VICE-PRESIDENT AND GENERAL MANAGER: C. W. Bright

Columbus Facility (planned closure during 1989):
4300 East Fifth Avenue, Columbus, Ohio 43216
Telephone: (614) 239 3344

VICE-PRESIDENT AND GENERAL MANAGER: A. H. Smith

Tulsa Facility:
2000 North Memorial Drive, Tulsa, Oklahoma 74158
Telephone: (918) 835 3111

VICE-PRESIDENT AND GENERAL MANAGER:
William P. Swiech

In addition to the programmes of which details follow, Rockwell's North American Aircraft unit is one of the three airframe contractors selected for current work on the US National Aero-Space Plane (see NASA entry in this section). It is also teamed with British Aerospace in offering a modified BAe 125 aircraft as a candidate for the US Air Force's Tanker Transport Training System (TTTS) programme.

ROCKWELL INTERNATIONAL B-1B

The early history of the B-1 bomber has been recorded in previous editions of *Jane's*. The decision to order 100 derivative B-1Bs for the US Air Force was announced by President Reagan in October 1981, and the first production B-1B flew for the first time on 18 October 1984. The remaining 99 were ordered under the FY 1983-1986 defence budgets (7, 10, 34 and 48 respectively). Initial delivery, of the second production aircraft (first flown 4 May 1985), to the 96th Bomb Wing at Dyess AFB, Texas, took place on 7 July 1985. This base achieved IOC in September 1986 and had received all 29 of its aircraft by the end of the year. Deliveries continued throughout 1987 and early 1988 at a rate of approximately four per month to the 28th Bomb Wing at Ellsworth AFB, South Dakota (35 aircraft), the 319th Bomb Wing at Grand Forks AFB, North Dakota (17), and the 384th Bomb Wing at McConnell AFB, Kansas (17). Each base also deploys supporting tankers. The 100th and final B-1B was rolled out on 20 January 1988, at which time the Air Force had accepted 80 aircraft. Deliveries were completed on 30 April 1988. Three B-1Bs are allocated for test and development flying.

Operational B-1Bs are able to carry, in three weapons bays, varying combinations of nuclear air-to-ground

Rockwell International B-1B strategic bomber in flight with wings fully spread

missiles, conventional or nuclear free-fall bombs, and auxiliary fuel. Using electronic jamming equipment, infra-red countermeasures, radar location and warning systems, other advanced avionics and 'low observable' technology to defeat hostile defensive systems, the B-1B will be able to penetrate present and predicted sophisticated enemy defences well into the 1990s and to operate within less heavily defended areas into the next century. It will also be suitable for deployment in a variety of roles now flown by the Boeing B-52, including anti-submarine patrol or maritime surveillance at long ranges, and aerial minelaying.

The first launch of an AGM-69 short range attack missile (SRAM) from a B-1B was made successfully on 16 January 1987, while the bomber was flying at Mach 0.9 at a height of 150 m (500 ft). First live launch of an AGM-86B ALCM, with an instrument package replacing the warhead, was made on 24 November 1987.

Outwardly the B-1B is generally similar to the B-1 prototype No. 4, but has major airframe improvements that include a strengthened landing gear; a movable bulkhead in the forward weapons bay to allow for the carriage of a wide range of different sized weapons; optional weapons bay fuel tanks to give extended range; and external stores stations beneath the fuselage to accommodate additional fuel or weapons. The variable engine inlets of the original B-1 are replaced by fixed inlets, with new engine nacelles and simplified overwing fairings. These modifications are designed to provide optimum performance for the high-subsonic low altitude penetration role.

The B-1B has, through the application of 'low observable' technology, a radar signature only one per cent that of a B-52. Offensive avionics include advanced forward-looking and terrain following radar, an extremely accurate inertial navigation system, a link to the Air Force Satellite Communications (AFSATCOM) system, a new computer-driven avionics system, and a strategic Doppler radar altimeter. The defensive avionics are built around the AN/ALQ-161 ECM system, with extended frequency coverage, and include tail warning radar and expendable decoys such as chaff and flares. Development of the full potential of this system will not be achieved for several more years.

The structure of the B-1B is hardened to withstand nuclear blast and overpressure. More than 60 per cent of the structure and equipment was subcontracted, with some 3,000 subcontractors and suppliers being involved in the programme in addition to AIL/Eaton (defensive avionics), Boeing (offensive avionics) and General Electric (power plant). Principal subcontractors were listed in the 1987-88 and earlier editions of *Jane's*.

During the Summer of 1987, a series of international speed and distance with payload records was set by the B-1B. On 4 July, a 2,000 km closed circuit was covered at a speed of 582.18 knots (1,078.2 km/h; 669.96 mph) with a payload of 30,000 kg (66,140 lb). On 17 September a similar payload was carried around a 5,000 km circuit at 569.225 knots (1,054.206 km/h; 655.05 mph).

TYPE: Long-range multi-role strategic bomber.

WINGS: Cantilever low-wing fail-safe blended wing/body structure, with variable geometry on outer panels. Wing carry-through structure, sealed as an integral fuel tank, is mainly of diffusion bonded 6AL-4V titanium. Wing pivot mechanism is of same material, with a pin made from a single 6AL-4V forging on each side, in spherical steel bearings, above and below which are integrally stiffened double cover plates of machined titanium. Wing sweep is actuated by screwjacks, driven by four hydraulic motors; it can be powered by any two of aircraft's four hydraulic systems, asymmetric movement being prevented by a torque shaft between the two screwjacks. Sweep actuators are covered by a leading-edge 'knuckle' fairing which prevents a gap from opening when outer panels are swept back. Aft of the wing pivot on each side are overwing fairings which blend the wing trailing-edges and engine nacelles. Each of outer wing panels, which have 15° of leading-edge sweep when fully forward and 67° 30′ when fully swept, is a conventional two-spar aluminium alloy torsion box structure, with machined spars, ribs, and one-piece integrally stiffened top and bottom skin panels. Wingtips, wing/body fairings, and some outer wing skin panels, are of GRP. Full span seven-segment leading-edge slats on each outer panel can be drooped 20° for take-off and landing. Six-segment single-slotted trailing-edge flaps on each outer panel, with maximum downward deflection of 40°. No ailerons: lateral control is provided by four-segment airbrake/spoilers on each outer wing, forward of outer four flap segments, with max upward deflection of 70°. All control surfaces operated electro-hydraulically by rods, cables, pulleys and bellcrank levers, except for two outboard spoilers on each wing which are controlled by a fly by wire system.

FUSELAGE: Conventional area ruled fail-safe stressed-skin structure of closely spaced frames and longerons, built mainly of 2025 and 7075 aluminium alloys. Built in five main sections comprising forward, forward intermediate, wing carry-through, rear intermediate and rear fuselage, last two of these being manufactured by LTV (Vought Aero Products Division). Titanium used for engine bays and firewalls, tail support structure, rear fuselage skins and other high load or high heat areas. Dorsal spine of steel/boron filled titanium sandwich construction. Nose radome of polyimide quartz; dielectric panels of GRP. Small sweptback movable vane of composite material, with 30° anhedral, on each side of nose, actuated by structural mode control system (SMCS) accelerometers in fuselage. These sense lateral and vertical motion of forward fuselage in turbulent conditions and compensate for it by relaying electrical signals to move vanes, providing both yaw and pitch damping.

TAIL UNIT: Cantilever fail-safe structure with sweepback on all surfaces. Fin is a conventional titanium and aluminium alloy torsion box structure, secured to rear fuselage by a double shear attachment, bolts on tailplane spindle, a vertical shear pin in tailplane spindle fitting, and a shear-bolt joint on front beam of box. Aluminium alloy rudder is in three sections, all of which have 25° of travel each side. Two-section all-moving tailplane is operated collectively for control in pitch (between 10° up and 25° down) and differentially (± 20°) for roll, the two halves moving independently on the steel spindle. Rudder and tailplane actuated hydraulically, with fly by wire

Rockwell International B-1B fitted with clamshell hardpoints for Advanced Cruise Missiles (ACMs)

backup system for use in the event of a mechanical system failure.

LANDING GEAR: Hydraulically retractable tricycle type. Each main unit, which retracts inward and rearward, has two pairs of wheels in tandem. Steerable nose unit has twin wheels and retracts forward. Oleo-pneumatic shock absorber in each unit. Goodyear wheels and carbon brakes, with anti-skid system. Goodrich tyres. Mainwheel diameter 60 cm (23½ in), tyre size 46 × 16-325, 30-ply rating, pressure 15.2-19.0 bars (220-275 lb/sq in). Nosewheel diameter 41 cm (16 in), tyre size 35 × 11.5-16, 22-ply rating, pressure 14.5 bars (210 lb/sq in).

POWER PLANT: Four General Electric F101-GE-102 augmented turbofans, each rated at 136.9 kN (30,780 lb st), mounted in pairs beneath fixed centre-section of wing, close to CG, to provide optimum stability in low-altitude turbulence conditions. Fixed geometry inlets. Integral fuel tanks in fuselage and outer wings; provision for auxiliary fuel tanks to be carried in two forward weapons bays and beneath fuselage. Fuel capacity increased considerably over that of original B-1. Simmonds Precision fuel management system maintains CG trim automatically as fuel is consumed. Receptacle in upper nose section, forward of windscreen, for in-flight refuelling; aircraft is compatible with KC-10 and KC-135 tankers.

ACCOMMODATION: Four-man operational crew comprising pilot, co-pilot and two systems operators (defensive and offensive) on Weber ACES II ejection seats in a pressurised crew compartment. Pilots have control sticks rather than conventional bomber/transport yokes. Radiation glareshield standard. Crew access via downward opening door and electrically retractable ladder under fuselage, aft of nosewheel unit.

SYSTEMS: All systems and subsystems are either fail-operative or fail-safe, to ensure that no single system failure prevents accomplishment of primary mission, and

that no second failure in same system prevents a safe return to base. Hamilton Standard air-conditioning and pressurisation systems. Four independent hydraulic systems, each 276 bars (4,000 lb/sq in) pressure, for actuation of wing sweep, control surfaces, landing gear and weapons bay doors. Hydraulic system maximum flow rate 238.5 litres (63 US gallons; 52.4 Imp gallons)/min each. Gas/oil reservoirs, pressurised to approx 11.03 bars (160 lb/sq in). No pneumatic system. Main electrical system has three 115kVA integrated engine driven constant-speed generators, supplying 230/400V three-phase AC power at 400Hz through four main buses. Harris Corporation self testing electrical multiplex system (EMUX), using mini-computers, controls major subsystems: it collects and conditions signals at remote terminals and transmits them from point to point over a common databus and also supervises all signal data, using a centralised controller/processor. Requiring only two two-wire cables for its operations, EMUX is designed to control such functions as electrical power distribution to subsystems and avionics equipment, engine instruments, environmental control system, fuel system, landing gear, lights and weapons system operations. Two Garrett APUs, installed between pairs of turbofans, provide self-start capability for operation from advance airfields and drive an emergency generator to power the essential bus. Quadruplex automatic flight control system (AFCS) controls flight path, roll attitude, altitude, airspeed, autothrottle and terrain following. Flight director panel has heading hold, navigation and automatic approach modes. Central air data computer; gyro stabilisation system; stability control augmentation system; and structural mode control subsystem (SMCS). Engine fire extinguishing system.

AVIONICS: Standard GFE (government furnished equipment) includes communications, IFF, ILS, intercom, some navigation equipment, Honeywell ASN-131 SPN/GEANS radar altimeter (similar to that in B-52) and altimeter indicator, rescue beacon and transponder. Boeing Military Airplanes is responsible for the offensive avionics system (OAS). This includes a Singer Kearfott high accuracy inertial navigation system (developed from that used in the F-16); a Teledyne Ryan AN/APN-218 Doppler velocity sensor, comprising a single antenna/receiver/transmitter unit; Westinghouse AN/APQ-164 multi-mode offensive radar system (ORS), derived from the AN/APG-66 in the F-16, which includes a low-observable phased-array antenna to provide low altitude terrain following and precise navigational functions; IBM avionics control units (ACUs), including two for terrain following based on those used in B-52 plus a mass storage device (MSD), using AP-101C computers initially (1750As later) to provide programme instructions for navigation, weapons delivery, bomb damage assessment, defensive system computation, and central integrated test; Sperry Flight Systems offensive display sets, similar to those in B-52, comprising three multi-function displays (two at offensive systems operator's station and one for defensive systems operator), an electronics display unit, and a video recorder similar to that used in B-52; Sanders Associates electronic CRT display units, modified from those developed for original B-1, to allow defensive systems operator to analyse threat situations and assign appropriate countermeasures; and Sundstrand data transfer units (similar to those in B-52) to gather and store mission and flight data.

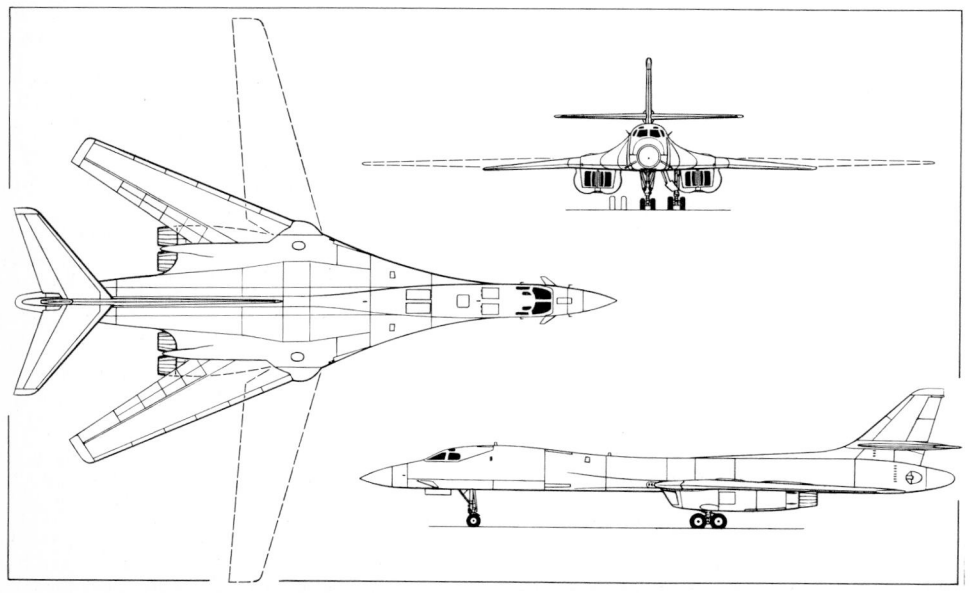

Rockwell International B-1B long-range multi-role strategic bomber *(Pilot Press)*

The defensive avionics system, which is the responsibility of Eaton Corporation's AIL Division, is based on that company's AN/ALQ-161 system, which comprises an AN/ALQ-161A radio frequency surveillance/ECM system (RFS/ECMS), tail warning function (TWF), AN/ASQ-184 defensive management system and an expendable countermeasures system, totalling 108 separate elements. Developed to support the original B-1 over a broad spectrum of missions, including deep solo penetration of hostile airspace, the system subsequently received additions to extend both the frequency coverage and repertoire of electronic jamming techniques of the original design. The current AN/ALQ-161 system, which will enable the B-1B to penetrate present and predicted enemy defences well into the 1990s, is controlled by a network of digital computers which can be reprogrammed easily; in addition, all electronic systems boxes 'plug in' to a dedicated databus network, enabling system to be upgraded continuously to adapt to future threats until well into the next century. To protect the B-1B, the system must counter a very dense environment of signals from increasingly sophisticated hostile radar networks. A single AN/ALQ-161 system contains and controls a large number of Northrop (Defense Systems Divsion) jamming transmitters and Raytheon phased-array antennae. In addition to jamming hardware, a sophisticated control system, managed by a network of special digital computers, is employed. This network can control the jamming chains so rapidly that each can jam signals from many radars simultaneously. The numerous jamming chains are deployed around periphery of B-1B to jam signals in any frequency band coming from any direction. Integrated with jamming control subsystem is an equally sophisticated network of separate receiving antennae, receivers and processors which act as 'ears' of system. By means of these new signals can be picked up, identified and jammed, with optimised jamming techniques, in a fraction of a second. One of the advantages of having the receiving function completely integrated with the jamming function, is that it allows receiving system to detect new signals and continue to monitor old signals while jamming in same frequency band. A special subsystem allows this to be accomplished by monitoring output of jamming transmitters and adjusting receivers continuously. All main systems computers on B-1B, including AN/ALQ-161's main computer, are identical, and communicate over a MIL-STD-1553B databus. Via this, the AN/ALQ-161 communicates with controls and displays used by defensive systems operator. It also uses this bus to send status reports to a central integrated test system (CITS), which records all in-flight failures and battle damage for later diagnosis and repair. Within the AN/ALQ-161 itself is a local status monitoring network called SEAT (status evaluation and test), which reports to CITS and allows system automatically to route electronic signals around failed components and maintain full jamming response against highest priority threat signals. Exclusive of cabling, displays and controls, the current AN/ALQ-161 system weighs approx 2,360 kg (5,200 lb) and consumes about 120 kW of power in 'all-out' jamming mode. Other defensive equipment includes expendable decoys such as chaff and flares.

ARMAMENT: Three internal weapons bays, comprising 9.53 m (31 ft 3 in) double bay forward of wing carry-through structure and a single 4.57 m (15 ft) long bay aft, with hydraulically actuated doors. Forward bay incorporates a movable bulkhead permitting accommodation of a wide variety of weapons, of various sizes, and mixed loads. Internal capacity in a nuclear role for up to eight AGM-86B air-launched cruise missiles (ALCMs), twenty-four AGM-69 short range attack missiles (SRAMs), twelve B-28 or twenty-four B-61 or B-83 free fall nuclear bombs; or, in a non-nuclear role, for up to eighty-four 500 lb Mk 82 bombs or 500 lb Mk 36 mines. Six external stores stations beneath fuselage, on which can be carried an additional twelve ALCMs.
The forward and aft bays can be combined to carry eight ALCMs on a common strategic rotary launcher.

DIMENSIONS, EXTERNAL:

Wing span: fully spread	41.67 m (136 ft 8½ in)
fully swept	23.84 m (78 ft 2½ in)
Length overall	44.81 m (147 ft 0 in)
Height overall	10.36 m (34 ft 0 in)
Tailplane span	13.67 m (44 ft 10 in)
Wheel track (c/l of shock absorbers)	4.42 m (14 ft 6 in)
Wheelbase	17.53 m (57 ft 6 in)

AREA:

Wings, gross	approx 181.2 m² (1,950 sq ft)

WEIGHTS AND LOADING:

Weight empty, equipped	87,090 kg (192,000 lb)
Max weapons load:	
internal	34,019 kg (75,000 lb)
external	26,762 kg (59,000 lb)
Max fuel load	88,450 kg (195,000 lb)
Typical conventional weapon load	29,030 kg (64,000 lb)
Max T-O weight	216,365 kg (477,000 lb)
Max wing loading	approx 1,194 kg/m² (244.6 lb/sq ft)

PERFORMANCE (design):

Max level speed	approx Mach 1.25
Low-level penetration speed at approx 61 m (200 ft)	more than 521 knots (965 km/h; 600 mph)
Max unrefuelled range	approx 6,475 nm (12,000 km; 7,455 miles)

ROCKWELL (LOCKHEED) AC-130U 'SPECTRE'

It was announced on 6 July 1987 that the USAF had awarded a $155,233,489 contract to Rockwell's North American Aircraft Operations to cover research and development of this new gunship version of the Lockheed Hercules. Request for the first six AC-130Us was included in the FY 1989 budget proposals. This will lead to rollout of the first AC-130U at Palmdale in 1990, followed by ten months of flight testing at the Air Force Flight Test Center, Edwards AFB, California. This aircraft, and eleven additional AC-130Us, will then enter service with the Special Operations Forces at Hurlburt Field, Florida, between late 1991 and the end of 1992.

All twelve gunship airframes will be new C-130Hs built by Lockheed's Georgia division. Conversion to gunship configuration began in 1988, and includes installation of a highly accurate suite of 105 mm, 40 mm and 25 mm guns which can be slaved to FLIR, low light level TV or strike radar, permitting night and/or adverse weather operations against ground targets. The AC-130U will utilise the highly-banked circular (pylon) turn technique first practised with 'Puff the Magic Dragon' C-47 gunships in Southeast Asia in the mid-1960s, and will combine intense firepower with the latest methods of target location and increased loitering capability. The modified APG-70 fire control radar will be supplied by Hughes Aircraft Company. ECM will enhance survivability in a low-to-medium threat environment.

Apart from its primary role of precision fire suppression, the in-flight refuellable AC-130U will be capable of performing other special operations roles, including escort, surveillance, search, rescue and armed reconnaissance/interdiction.

Full details of the basic C-130H can be found in the LASC Georgia entry in this section.

NORTH AMERICAN SPACE OPERATIONS

2230 East Imperial Highway, El Segundo, California 90245
Telephone: (213) 647 5000
PRESIDENT: George W. Jeffs

Satellite Systems Division

2600 Westminster Boulevard, Seal Beach, California 90740-7644
Telephone: (213) 594 3311
PRESIDENT: Glynn S. Lunney

Rocketdyne Division

6633 Canoga Avenue, Canoga Park, California 91304
Telephone: (818) 710 6300
PRESIDENT: Richard Schwartz

Space Transportation Systems Division

12214 Lakewood Boulevard, Downey, California 90241
Telephone: (213) 922 2111
PRESIDENT: Rocco A. Petrone

The Space Transportation Systems Division is responsible for Rockwell International Corporation's engineering design and development, fabrication and assembly, and test and evaluation of both manned and unmanned space systems.

Under contract to NASA, the Rockwell group designed, built and tested the four Shuttle spacecraft (Orbiters) named *Columbia, Challenger, Discovery* and *Atlantis.*

Rockwell's space group, with its major facilities in Downey and Palmdale, California, has contractual support units based in NASA Centers at the Johnson Space Center, Texas, the Kennedy Space Center, Florida, the Marshall Space Flight Center, Alabama, and the National Space Technology Laboratories, Mississippi.

Shuttle Operations Company

600 Gemini Avenue, Houston, Texas 77058
Telephone: (713) 282 3000
PRESIDENT: Robert G. Minor

Rockwell's Shuttle Operations Company performs mission support operations for Johnson Space Center under a contract which consolidated work previously performed by 16 different contractors. Its tasks include project management, maintenance and operations of Mission Control Center-Houston, Shuttle Mission Simulator, Shuttle Avionics Integration Laboratory, Software Production Facility and the Central Computing Facility; sustaining engineering, flight preparation production, and direct mission operations, testing and support for Space Shuttle operations at the Johnson Space Center. The Rockwell team includes Bendix Field Engineering Corporation, System Development Corporation, Omniplan Corporation, RMS Technologies Incorporated, and System Management American Corporation.

Space Station Systems Division

12214 Lakewood Boulevard, Downey, California 90241
Telephone: (213) 922 2111
PRESIDENT: Seymour Z. Rubenstein

Rockwell's Space Station Systems Division was awarded a $27 million contract by NASA on 15 April 1985 for definition and preliminary design of elements of a permanently manned Space Station to be operational in low-Earth orbit by the mid-1990s. Following the completion of the 21-month contract in 1987 NASA plans to enter into the final design and development of the Space Station, including definition and preliminary design of the structural framework; interface between the Space Station and the Space Shuttle; mechanisms such as the Remote Manipulator Systems; attitude control, thermal control; communications; tracking; data management systems; plans for equipping a module with sleeping quarters, wardroom and galley; and plans for extravehicular activity (EVA).

SPACE TRANSPORTATION SYSTEM

The NASA Space Shuttle was the world's first reusable space transportation system, and will be the keystone of America's space programme for the remainder of this century.

The Shuttle system includes the Rockwell International Shuttle spacecraft (see next entry), an external propellant tank and two solid propellant rocket boosters. Other prime contractors are Martin Marietta for the external tank, and Thiokol for the boosters. In operation, the Shuttle is launched vertically, with all engines firing. At an altitude of about 43 km (27 miles), the booster stages separate and descend into the sea by parachute, for recovery. The Shuttle spacecraft continues under its own power, and jettisons its large external propellant tank just before attaining orbit.

In space, the Shuttle spacecraft manoeuvres by means of the two orbit manoeuvring engines. The reaction control engines are used for minor course corrections and adjustments of altitude. Its main tasks are to place satellites into orbit, retrieve satellites from orbit, and repair and service satellites in orbit. It can also be used to put propulsive stages and satellites into precise low Earth orbit, for subsequent transfer to synchronous orbit or to an 'escape' mission into space. It can be used for short duration scientific and applications missions, as an orbiting research laboratory or reconnaissance vehicle, for space rescue, as a tanker for space refuelling, and for support of orbiting space stations.

On some flights a pressurised Spacelab, developed by ten European countries under the leadership of the European Space Agency, is carried in the payload bay. Spacelab is the means by which man-associated experiments can be performed in the payload bay. It includes a pressurised enclosure housing support equipment (to make it habitable) as well as the experimental equipment. When sensors require direct exposure to the space environment, a pallet is used in association with the pressurised enclosure. On other types of mission, a pallet may be used alone, with control of the instruments being exercised from the Shuttle spacecraft cabin or even from the ground. The Spacelabs are designed around a basic seven-day mission.

On conclusion of its mission, the Shuttle spacecraft flies back into the atmosphere towards its land base, protected by a form of heat shielding which is designed to survive 100 missions, unlike ablative heatshields. Once through the re-entry phase, the Shuttle spacecraft is able to glide up to 950 nm (1,760 km; 1,100 miles) to its base, steered by aerodynamic controls.

Special equipment developed for use on the Space Shuttle includes a new type of spacesuit and a rescue system known as a Personal Rescue Enclosure. This consists of a 0.86 m 34 in) diameter ball which contains its own short term simplified life support and communication systems. The ball has three layers (urethane, Kevlar and an outside thermal protective layer) and a small viewing port of tough Lexan.

Essential details of missions flown in 1981-85 can be found in previous editions of *Jane's*.

Details of the boosters and the external tank used with the spacecraft in its original form are as follows:

BOOSTERS (STS-8 and subsequent missions): Two Thiokol solid propellant rocket boosters (each 14,679 kN; 3,300,000 lb st for lift-off) are attached one on each side of the external propellant tank. Current steel skinned boosters each weigh 586,051 kg (1,292,000 lb) at launch. In 1986 the steel skinned boosters will be replaced by boosters with filament wound casings, each weighing 571,082 kg (1,259,000 lb) at launch. The booster cases are designed for 20 re-uses.

EXTERNAL PROPELLANT TANK: Contains the main propellants for the Orbiter. It is of aluminium alloy semi-monocoque construction, with a 25 mm (1 in) thick foam external insulation. In the forward end of the tank is a 559 m³ (19,786 cu ft) tank holding 617,774 kg (1,361,936 lb) of liquid oxygen; in the rear end is a 1,514 m³ (53,518 cu ft) tank holding 103,257 kg (227,641 lb) of liquid hydrogen. Total propellant weight 721,031 kg (1,589,577 lb). Between propellant tanks is an unpressurised intertank which houses instrumentation and electrical components. Current missions use a lightweight tank weighing 750,980 kg (1,655,600 lb) when filled.

Basic dimensions and weights of the complete Space Transportation System are as follows:

DIMENSIONS, EXTERNAL:

Length overall	56.14 m (184 ft 2.4 in)
Length of external tank	47.00 m (154 ft 2.4 in)
Length of boosters	45.46 m (149 ft 2.0 in)
Height overall	23.35 m (76 ft 7.2 in)

WEIGHTS:

Shuttle system complete (typical)	2,042,576 kg (4,503,033 lb)
Shuttle spacecraft (empty)	67,876 kg (149,642 lb)
External tank (full)	750,980 kg (1,655,600 lb)
Boosters (2), each	586,051 kg (1,292,000 lb)

THRUST:

Total, at lift-off	34,360 kN (7,725,000 lb)
Shuttle main engines (3), each	1,668 kN (375,000 lb)
Boosters (2), each	14,678 kN (3,300,000 lb)

PERFORMANCE:

Payload:

in 185 km (115 mile) orbit, due east	29,485 kg (65,000 lb)
in 500 km (310 mile) orbit, 55° inclination	11,340 kg (25,000 lb)
in 185 km (115 mile) polar orbit	14,515 kg (32,000 lb)

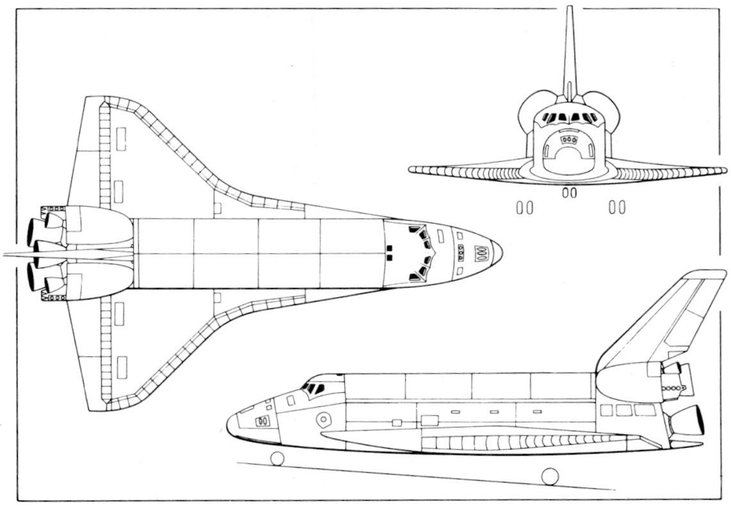

NASA/Rockwell International Shuttle spacecraft *(Michael A. Badrocke)*

ROCKWELL INTERNATIONAL SHUTTLE SPACECRAFT

The Shuttle spacecraft, primary component of NASA's Space Transportation System, lifts off from Earth like a rocket, operates in orbit as a spacecraft, and returns to land in a manner similar to that of a conventional aeroplane.

Shuttle spacecraft *Columbia* (OV-102) made the first successful, 36-orbit, test flight in April 1981, manned by astronauts John Young (commander) and Capt Robert Crippen (pilot), and has since completed six more successful orbital missions. After STS-5, the Orbiter was modified at Kennedy Space Center, to enable it to carry Spacelab and to accommodate a six-man crew to fly the spacecraft and conduct experiments. After STS-9, *Columbia* returned to Rockwell's Palmdale facility for major modifications, including the installation of operational systems, and returned to service in early 1986.

Challenger (OV-099), the second Earth orbital flight spacecraft, made its first flight on 4 April 1983. It became the first operational spacecraft, with all onboard systems qualified to operate for a minimum of 100 missions without major overhaul. *Challenger* was destroyed in a post-launch explosion during mission 51L on 28 January 1986. *Discovery* (OV-103) made its first flight on 30 August 1984. *Atlantis* (OV-104) was launched for the first time on 3 October 1985, on military mission 51J. *Discovery* and *Atlantis* are approximately 453 kg (1,000 lb) lighter than *Challenger* was, due primarily to replacement of the majority of the low-temperature insulation tiles used on earlier Orbiters by thermal protection blankets. In August 1986 President Reagan ordered a new Shuttle spacecraft to replace *Challenger*. The programme was expected to resume in 1988.

The following description refers to the spacecraft in its original form:

TYPE: Reusable space transportation vehicle.

WINGS: Cantilever low-wing monoplane, of ogival planform. Wing section NACA 0010 (modified). Sweepback 81° on inner leading-edges, 45° on outer leading-edges. Dihedral 3° 30′ on trailing-edges. The main wing assembly, for which Grumman is responsible, is primarily a conventional aluminium alloy structure made up of a corrugated spar web, truss ribs, and riveted skin/stringer and honeycomb skins. Wing has a very blunt leading-edge and is more than 1.52 m (5 ft) thick at the thickest point. Two-segment hydraulically actuated elevons on each trailing-edge, for pitch and roll control, are of aluminium honeycomb construction with a titanium rubbing strip on each of their leading-edges. Hinged panels on the wing upper surface, of titanium and Inconel sandwich, are used to seal the wing/elevon gap; these are the only areas of the wing not covered by the thermal protection system.

FUSELAGE: Conventional semi-monocoque aluminium alloy structure, built in three main portions. Forward fuselage contains the crew module, three forward electronics bays, forward reaction control system and nosewheel unit. The mid fuselage portion is an 18.28 m (60 ft) long section of primary load carrying structure, built by General Dynamics (Convair), and includes the wing carry-through structure. Upper half of the mid fuselage consists of structural payload bay doors, hinged along the side and meeting at the top centreline. These doors are of graphite epoxy bonded honeycomb sandwich construction, with a Nomex core. The forward 9.14 m (30 ft) of each door incorporates Vought radiator panels that are deployed in orbit. Fixed radiator panels are attached to the remaining inner surface on the front of each aft door. The rear of the aft doors can be fitted with fixed radiator panels if required by a specific mission. The rear fuselage interfaces with the removable orbital manoeuvring system (OMS)/reaction control system (RCS) pods, the wing rear spar, the vertical tail assembly, the body flap, the external tank rear supports, the main propulsion system, the launch umbilical panel, the three rear electronics bays, and other discrete system equipment. A bulkhead heatshield at the rear of the vehicle protects the main engine systems. A large body flap at the rear fuselage protects the main engine nozzles during re-entry, and is actuated hydraulically to serve also as a trimming surface.

TAIL UNIT: Vertical surfaces only, built by Fairchild Republic, of wedge section with 45° sweepback on fin leading-edge. Fin is a conventional aluminium alloy structure. The rudder/speed brake assembly has an aluminium honeycomb skin and is divided into upper and lower sections. Each of these is also split longitudinally and actuated individually to serve as both rudder and speed brake, operated by a Sundstrand hydraulic rotary actuator. The Inconel honeycomb seal over these is the only part of the vertical tail not covered by the thermal protection system. Mission requirements call for a locked rudder/speed brake during boost, orbit and re-entry. The speed brake control is provided from approx Mach 10 to Mach 5; from Mach 5 to landing the rudder and speed brake controls are combined as required. Primary system control is automatic, with manual override.

THERMAL PROTECTION SYSTEM: The thermal protection system (TPS) consists of materials applied externally to maintain the airframe outer skins within an acceptable temperature limit of 176°C (350°F) during re-entry. The TPS materials are designed to perform a minimum of 100 missions, in which temperatures will range from −156°C (−250°F) in space to re-entry temperatures of nearly 1,648°C (3,000°F) on the wing leading-edge and fuselage nose. Coated Nomex felt reusable surface insulation (FRSI) is used where temperatures are less than 371°C (700°F), on the upper portion of the payload bay doors, mid and rear fuselage sides, upper wing, and part of the orbital manoeuvring system (OMS) pods. On OV-102 *Columbia*, low-temperature reusable surface insulation (LRSI) tiles are used where temperatures go below 648°C (1,200°F) and above 371°C (700°F) nominal. These areas are the lower portion of payload bay doors; forward fuselage; parts of the mid and rear fuselage; upper wing; vertical tail and a portion of the OMS pods. These tiles have a white surface coating, which provides better thermal characteristics in orbit. On OV-099 *Challenger*, some of the LRSI tiles on the OMS pods were replaced with a composite blanket, advanced, flexible, reusable surface insulation (AFRSI), a quilted fabric blanket that is easier to produce, more durable, easier to install and lighter. On *Discovery* and *Atlantis*, AFRSI replaces the majority of the LRSI tiles. High-temperature reusable surface insulation (HRSI) tiles are used where temperatures are below 1,260°C (2,300°F) and above 648°C (1,200°F). The areas are the forward fuselage, lower mid fuselage, lower wing, selected areas of the vertical tail, a portion of the OMS pods, and around the forward fuselage windows. The HRSI has two different densities: one weighs 4 kg/m³ (9 lb/cu ft) and is used in all areas except around the nose and main landing gear doors, nose cap interface, wing leading-edge, reinforced carbon-carbon/HRSI interface, external tank umbilical doors, vent doors, and fin leading-edge. These areas use HRSI tiles with a density of 9.9 kg/m³ (22 lb/cu ft) and have a black surface coating for entry emittance. When the higher density HRSI tiles have been expended, fibrous refractory insulation (FRCI) tiles will be used instead. The FRCI-12 tiles have a density of 5.4 kg/m³ (12 lb/cu ft), and improved strength, durability and resistance to cracking.

LANDING GEAR: Retractable tricycle type, with twin wheels and Menasco oleo-pneumatic shock absorbers on each unit. Hydraulic release, with a pyrotechnic backup for deployment in flight. Landing gear cannot be retracted in flight, after release. Nose unit is retracted forward into fuselage and main units forward into wings before launch. Nose unit is steerable; main units are fitted with Goodrich brakes and Hydro-Aire anti-skid units. All units have Goodrich wheels and tyres. Landing gear is designed to facilitate safe landing at speeds of up to 225 knots (415 km/h; 258 mph). The main gear tyres are rated at 20,410 kg (45,000 lb) and the brakes at 240 × 10⁶ ft-lb.

MAIN PROPULSION: Three Rocketdyne SSME (Space Shuttle Main Engines) high-pressure liquid oxygen/liquid hydrogen engines, each rated at 1,668 kN (375,000 lb st) at sea level and 2,091 kN (470,000 lb thrust) in vacuum at 100 per cent; 1,752 kN (393,800 lb) at sea level and 2,174 kN (488,800 lb) vacuum at 104 per cent; 1,856 kN (417,300 lb) at sea level and 2,283 kN (513,250 lb) vacuum at 109 per cent. The engines can be throttled over a range of 65 to 109 per cent of their rated power level. Each engine is designed for 7½ h of operation, with 55 starts.

ORBIT MANOEUVRING ENGINES: Two Aerojet Liquid Rocket Company (ALRC) bipropellant liquid rocket engines, running on monomethylhydrazine (MMH) and nitrogen tetroxide (N_2O_4), are used for the Orbiter's orbit manoeuvring subsystem (OMS). These engines are housed in pods, one on each side of the Orbiter's rear fuselage. The OMS engines, for which a usable total of 10,830 kg (23,876 lb) of propellant is carried, are used to position the spacecraft in orbit; each develops 26.7 kN (6,000 lb thrust) in space.

REACTION CONTROL ENGINES: The reaction control subsystem (RCS) utilises 38 Marquardt R-40A bipropellant liquid rocket engines (each 3.88 kN; 872 lb vacuum thrust) and six Marquardt R-1E-3 bipropellant liquid rocket vernier thrusters (each 0.11 kN; 25 lb vacuum thrust). Fourteen of the R-40A engines are on the nose and 24 on the aft end, 12 in each OMS/RCS pod; there are two of the R-1E verniers on the nose and two in each aft pod. Propellants are the same as for the OMS engines; 1,096 kg (2,418 lb) is carried in the RCS tanks, and there is provision for crossfeed between the aft OMS and aft RCS tanks.

CREW COMPARTMENT: Self-contained crew module has a fuselage side hatch for access, a hatch into the airlock from the mid section, and a hatch from the airlock into the payload bay. It is divided into three levels, the upper (flight deck) level having side by side seating for two flight crewmen with dual controls. Behind them are seats for one or two mission specialists. On the middle deck provisions are made for three more seats, bunks and a galley, dependent upon particular flight requirements, hygiene section, airlock, three electronics bays, and payload bay access. For rescue missions, seats for three more persons can be fitted in place of the bunks. The lower deck contains environmental control equipment and crew equipment storage.

PAYLOAD BAY: In centre of fuselage, 18.29 m (60 ft) long and 4.57 m (15 ft) in diameter. Retractable manipulator arm on left hand side if required for a particular flight (with provision for a second one on the right), for deploying and retrieving payloads. Complete closed circuit TV system by RCA Astro-Electronics includes a colour camera in the crew compartment and several black and white and or colour cameras in the cargo bay and on the manipulator arm. These facilitate payload handling and provide TV coverage for engineers and the general public on Earth.

SYSTEMS: Environmental control and life support system, made up of four subsystems: atmosphere revitalisation subsystem (ARS), to control atmospheric environment for occupants and thermal environment for electronics; food, water and waste subsystem (FWW), to provide hygiene, and other life support functions; active thermal control subsystem (ATCS), to maintain subsystems and components within specified temperature limits and to provide, via payload door radiator panels, active heat rejection to protect payloads; and an airlock support subsystem. Three redundant hydraulic systems, each of 207 bars (3,000 lb/sq in), supply actuators for the elevons, body flap, rudder/speed brake, and power to actuate main engine thrust vector controls, landing gear, brakes and steering. Electrical power subsystem (EPS) consists, functionally, of a fuel cell power plant (FCP) subsystem, and a power reactant storage and distribution (PRSD) subsystem. There are three FCPs, each providing power at 27.5V to 32.5V DC over a power range of 2-12kW and each connected to one of the three main DC buses; these supply the primary in-flight electrical power used by the Shuttle, generated through the chemical combination and conversion of cryogenic oxygen and hydrogen. In the PRSD subsystem, the cryogenic oxygen and hydrogen tanks are defined as a tank set. The tank sets installed are dependent upon specific flight requirements; up to five sets can be accommodated. Westinghouse remote power control system and master timing unit. Honeywell four channel fly by wire electrical flight control subsystem for operation of all control surfaces and main engine controls. APU subsystem consists of three Sundstrand independent APUs (each 100.7 kW; 135 shp), deriving their energy from the decomposition of hydrazine (N_2H_4).

AVIONICS AND EQUIPMENT: Fully fail-operational/fail-safe guidance, navigation and control system, including three Singer-Kearfott KT-70/SKN-2600 type inertial measuring units; triplex Ku-band microwave scan beam landing system, by the AIL Division of Eaton Corpn; head-up displays (HUD); three Northrop rate gyro assemblies; three Hoffman L-band Tacan; three Bendix accelerometer assemblies; two Honeywell C-band radar altimeters; four AiResearch air data transducers; three Lear Siegler attitude director indicators; two Collins horizontal situation indicators; two Sperry alpha/Mach indicators two Bendix altitude/vertical velocity indicators; two Bendix surface position indicators; two Sperry barometric altimeters; and two Sperry ATC transponders. Communications and tracking equipment includes one (optionally two) Ku-band rendezvous radar/satellite com on starboard side of cargo bay; two Ball star trackers; two 100W Watkins-Johnson S-band TWT amplifiers; two P-band UHF for EVA/ATC com; Conrac S-band FM for Orbiter/ground and Orbiter/payload com; and Ku-band radio for Orbiter/ground com and Ku band for rendezvous. Central data processing is by means of five IBM Advanced System/4 Pi Model AP-101 digital computers and two mass memory units. Four of the computers are interconnected to process guidance, navigation and control inputs and to relay commands to FBW flight control systems; the fifth is provided for independent backup and systems management.

DIMENSIONS, EXTERNAL:
Wing span 23.79 m (78 ft 0.68 in)
Wing aspect ratio 2.265
Wing mean aerodynamic chord 12.06 m (39 ft 6.81 in)
Length 37.19 m (122 ft 0.2 in)
Height 17.25 m (56 ft 7 in)

DIMENSIONS, INTERNAL:
Payload bay: Length 18.29 m (60 ft 0 in)
Diameter 4.57 m (15 ft 0 in)
Crew module: Volume 74.33 m^3 (2,625 cu ft)

AREAS:
Wings, gross 249.91 m^2 (2,690 sq ft)
Elevons (total) 38.38 m^2 (413.14 sq ft)
Rudder/speed brake 9.09 m^2 (97.84 sq ft)
Vertical tail surfaces (total) 38.39 m^2 (413.25 sq ft)
Body flap 12.61 m^2 (135.75 sq ft)

WEIGHTS:
Weight dry: *Columbia* 70,606 kg (155,661 lb)
Design landing weight with payload 14,515 kg (32,000 lb) 96,162 kg (212,000 lb)

PERFORMANCE:
Orbital speed
approx 15,285 knots (28,325 km/h; 17,600 mph)
Nominal touchdown speed (unpowered)
180 knots (334 km/h; 208 mph) EAS

ROGERSON

ROGERSON HILLER CORPORATION
(Subsidiary of Rogerson Aircraft Corporation)

William R. Fairchild International Airport, Port Angeles, Washington 98362
PRESIDENT: Gerald J. Tobias
VICE-PRESIDENT, INTERNATIONAL MARKETING:
Victor Milner Jr,
2201 Alton Avenue, Irvine, California 92714
Telephone: (714) 660 0666
Telex: (910) 595 2843

This company was formed in January 1973, as Hiller Aviation Inc, to acquire from Fairchild Industries the design rights, production tooling and spares of the Hiller 12E series of light helicopters. Initially, it provided product support for helicopters of this type in worldwide service, before restarting production of piston engined and turbine powered versions in three-seat and four-seat configurations. The five-seat FH-1100 was added following purchase from Fairchild in 1980.

In April 1984, Hiller Aviation became a wholly owned subsidiary of Rogerson Aircraft Corporation, which manufactures aircraft control system parts, fuel tanks, composite materials and components for the aerospace industry. It was renamed Hiller Helicopters, resuming deliveries of the UH-12E and redesignated RH-1100 in July 1984, and has since been renamed Rogerson Hiller Corporation.

In November 1985 Rogerson Hiller occupied a new 13,006 m^2 (140,000 sq ft) manufacturing facility at William R. Fairchild International Airport, Port Angeles, Washington. In September 1985 the company acquired L.O.M. Corporation, manufacturer of helicopter rotor blades, and renamed the latter company Aerobond. Production of rotor blades is undertaken at the Port Angeles factory.

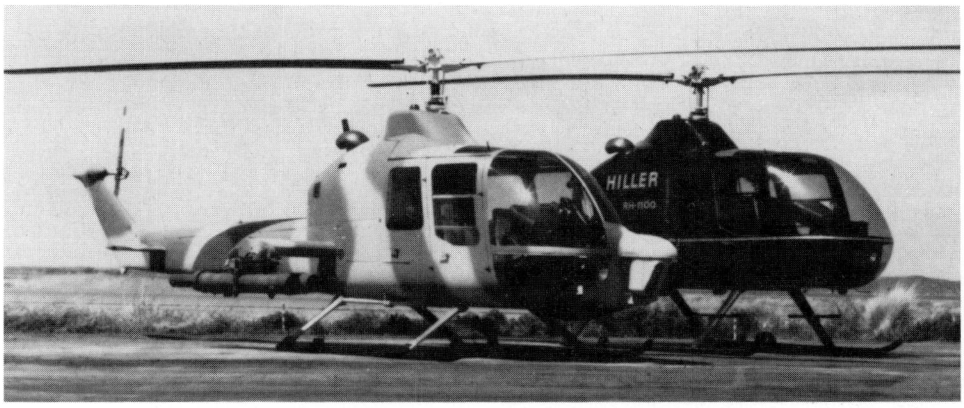

Prototype RH-1100M Hornet with civilian RH-1100 in background

HILLER RH-1100

The original FH-1100 was a refined development of the OH-5A designed for the US Army's LOH (Light Observation Helicopter) competition. A total of 246 FH-1100s had been built when production ended in 1974.

The current, improved, RH-1100 has a more powerful engine and main rotor blades of 76 mm (3 in) greater chord, together with a larger diameter tail rotor and a new drive coupling between the engine and the main rotor transmission, to allow operation at a higher gross weight and increased maximum speed. Production aircraft will incorporate composite materials in their structure in place of some aluminium components.

The prototype of a multi-mission military variant of the helicopter, designated **RH-1100M Hornet**, made its debut at the 1985 Paris Air Show. The RH-1100M can carry interchangeable weapons systems including two 2.75 in folding fin rocket pods, 7.62 mm machine-guns, 0.50 calibre machine-guns and four TOW missiles. The RH-1100M has provision for an autopilot, forward looking infra-red anti-missile warning systems, air-to-air missile system capability, and chin or roof mounted sight. Hiller believes the RH-1100M's primary markets would be in South America, Africa and parts of Asia.

By early 1988 the company had delivered single examples of the FH-1100 to Sri Lanka, Taiwan and Venezuela, and expects to make first customer deliveries of the new RH-1100 in March 1989.

The following description applies to the standard civil RH-1100, except where indicated:

TYPE: Five-seat utility helicopter.

ROTOR SYSTEM: Two-blade semi-rigid main rotor of all-metal construction. Blade section NACA 63_2015. Each blade attached to rotor head by single main retention bolt and drag link. Droop stops standard. The main rotor blades each have a rolled stainless steel leading-edge spar bonded to an aluminium trailing section with a honeycomb core. Two-blade tail rotor of stainless steel and honeycomb construction. Main rotor blades fold. Rotor brake optional. Electrically controlled trim system.

ROTOR DRIVE: Mechanical drive through single-stage bevel and two-stage planetary main transmission, with intermediate and tail rotor gearboxes. Main rotor/engine rpm ratio 1:16.30. Tail rotor/engine rpm ratio 1:2.47.

FUSELAGE: Aluminium alloy semi-monocoque structure of pod and boom type.

TAIL UNIT: Vertical fin, and fixed horizontal surface, both of aluminium alloy and honeycomb construction. Tubular guard to protect rotor in tail-down landing.

LANDING GEAR: Skid type with torsion tube suspension, with choice of standard or extended support struts. Extended struts necessary with optional inflatable float installation. Ground handling wheels standard.

POWER PLANT: One 313 kW (420 shp) Allison 250-C20B turboshaft, derated to 204 kW (274 shp). Single bladder fuel tank in bottom of centre-fuselage with usable capacity of 259 litres (68.5 US gallons; 57 Imp gallons). Refuelling point on starboard side of rear fuselage. Oil capacity 2.6 litres (0.7 US gallons; 0.6 Imp gallons).

ACCOMMODATION: Pilot and co-pilot side by side with three passengers to rear, or pilot and four passengers. Four forward hinged doors, two on each side of cabin, with removable centre door post for cargo loading. Dual internal stretcher kit optional. Baggage compartment to rear of cabin, capacity 0.30 m^3 (10.5 cu ft). Accommodation ventilated. Cabin heater and windscreen defroster optional.

SYSTEMS: Hydraulic system for cyclic and collective pitch controls. Electrical system includes a 28V 60A DC starter/generator and nickel-cadmium battery.

AVIONICS: A range of nav/com systems is available to customer's requirements.

EQUIPMENT: Standard equipment includes clock, engine hour meter, outside air temperature gauge, fuel filter warning system, night lighting system including two rotating beacons, edge-lit instrument panel, seatbelts, shoulder harness on front seats, sliding rear windows, tinted windows, hardpoint for optional external cargo hook, external power socket, and choice of exterior paint scheme and interior trim. Optional equipment includes stability augmentation system, dual controls, rear seat shoulder harness, cabin fire extinguisher, first aid kit, strobe lights, engine auto relight, reverse scoop intake, heated pitot, loudspeaker/siren, quick-release cargo hook, cargo racks, ambulance kit, dual litter kit, searchlight and Simplex agricultural spraygear.

DIMENSIONS, EXTERNAL:
Main rotor diameter 10.80 m (35 ft 5 in)
Tail rotor diameter 1.83 m (6 ft 0 in)
Distance between rotor centres 6.29 m (20 ft 7½ in)
Main rotor blade chord 0.33 m (13 in)
Length overall, rotors turning 12.57 m (41 ft 3 in)
Length of fuselage 9.08 m (29 ft 9½ in)
Width, rotors folded 1.32 m (4 ft 4 in)
Height overall 2.83 m (9 ft 3½ in)
Skid track 2.20 m (7 ft 2¾ in)

AREAS:
Main rotor disc 91.0 m^2 (979.0 sq ft)
Tail rotor disc 2.63 m^2 (28.3 sq ft)

WEIGHTS (A: RH-1100, B: RH-1100M):
Weight empty: A 687 kg (1,515 lb)
B (TOW) 1,048 kg (2,310 lb)
B (Scout) 726 kg (1,600 lb)
Max payload: A 462 kg (1,020 lb)
Max standard fuel weight: A, B 200.5 kg (442 lb)
Max T-O weight: A 1,292 kg (2,850 lb)
B 1,406 kg (3,100 lb)

PERFORMANCE (at max T-O weight, A and B as above):
Max level speed at S/L:
A, B 110 knots (204 km/h; 127 mph)
Max cruising speed at 1,525 m (5,000 ft):
A 110 knots (204 km/h; 127 mph)
Econ cruising speed: A 106 knots (196 km/h; 122 mph)
Max rate of climb at S/L 488 m (1,600 ft)/min
Vertical rate of climb at S/L: A 244 m (800 ft)/min
Service ceiling: A 5,275 m (17,300 ft)
Hovering ceiling: IGE: A 5,180 m (17,000 ft)
OGE: A 3,660 m (12,000 ft)
Range at 1,525 m (5,000 ft) with max fuel, no reserves:
A 340 nm (629 km; 391 miles)
B (Scout) 534 nm (990 km; 615 miles)
Max endurance at 1,525 m (5,000 ft), no reserves:
A 3 h 24 min
B 5 h 0 min

HILLER UH-12E HAULER

Rogerson Hiller has resumed delivery of the basic model UH-12E light helicopter. Customers include the government of India, to which deliveries of Haulers equipped for agricultural work began in May 1986.

TYPE: Three-seat utility helicopter.

ROTOR SYSTEM: Two-blade main rotor mounted universally on driveshaft, with small servo rotor; the latter is connected directly to the pilot's cyclic control stick, through a universally mounted transfer bearing and simple linkage. Movement of the control stick introduces positive or negative pitch changes to the servo rotor paddles. The resulting aerodynamic forces tilt the rotor head and produce cyclic pitch changes to the rotor blades. Main rotor blades are of bonded stainless steel, with aluminium honeycomb core, and wedge tips. Thickness/chord ratio 12%. Blades are interchangeable individually and are bolted to forks which are retained at the rotor head by tension-torsion bars. Blades do not fold. Rotor brake optional. Two-blade tail rotor of light alloy construction, mounted on port side of tailboom.

ROTOR DRIVE: Mechanical drive through two-stage planetary main transmission. Bevel gear drive to auxiliaries. Tail rotor gearbox (and fan gearbox on piston engined versions). Separate transmission oil system. Main rotor/engine rpm ratio 1 : 8.66. Tail rotor/engine rpm ratio 1 : 1.44.

FUSELAGE: Light alloy fully stressed semi-monocoque platform structure supporting the non-stressed cabin enclosure, engine mounting and landing gear. Tailboom of beaded light alloy sheet with no internal stiffeners.

TAIL UNIT: Horizontal stabiliser on starboard side of tailboom of three-seat versions, with steel tube spar, light alloy ribs and skin. Incidence ground-adjustable. Inverted V stabilising surfaces forward of tail rotor on four-seat versions.

LANDING GEAR: Wide track light alloy tube skids carried on spring steel cross members. Optional extended legs. Ground handling wheels standard. Optional 'zip-on' pontoons can be attached above the skids to permit water or land operations, but require extended landing gear.

POWER PLANT: One 253.5 kW (340 hp) Textron Lycoming VO-540-C2A flat-six engine, installed vertically and derated to 227.5 kW (305 hp). Engine muffler optional. Single bladder fuel cell, capacity 174 litres (46 US gallons; 38 Imp gallons), mounted in lower portion of rear fuselage, beneath engine. Two optional auxiliary fuel tanks, mounted in fuselage on each side of engine; capacity 76 litres (20 US gallons; 16.6 Imp gallons) each. Oil capacity 12.5 litres (3.3 US gallons; 2.7 Imp gallons).

ACCOMMODATION: Three persons side by side on bench seat. Seat belts for all occupants; provision for shoulder harness. Dual controls optional. Forward-hinged door on each side, with sliding window. Baggage compartment immediately aft of engine. Heater/defroster optional.

SYSTEM: Electrical system includes a 72A alternator, nickel-cadmium battery, and battery temperature monitor.

AVIONICS AND EQUIPMENT: A range of optional avionics is available. Standard equipment includes engine hour meter, edge-lit instrument panel, outside air temperature gauge, eight-day clock, electrically controlled trim system, tinted glazing, cargo hook hardpoint, external power socket, and polyurethane paint finish. Optional equipment includes Mason cyclic control grip, fire extinguisher, first aid kit, night lighting equipment including two rotating beacons, strobe lights, 454 kg (1,000 lb) capacity quick-release cargo hook, twin heavy duty cargo racks, agricultural spray equipment, loudspeaker/siren, searchlight, and tropical doors. Agricultural equipment includes Simplex Model 3300 system with 9.75 m (32 ft) folding spraybooms and two glassfibre tanks, with total capacity of 416 litres (110 US gallons; 91 Imp gallons) or 530 litres (140 US gallons; 166 Imp

New production Hiller UH-12E with Simplex cropspraying system

gallons), designed for quick change to dry system; or Simplex Model 4500 system with single tank, capacity 530 litres (140 US gallons; 116 Imp gallons) and folding booms.

DIMENSIONS, EXTERNAL:
Main rotor diameter	10.80 m (35 ft 5 in)
Main rotor blade chord (constant)	0.33 m (1 ft 1 in)
Servo rotor diameter	3.05 m (10 ft 0 in)
Tail rotor diameter	1.68 m (5 ft 6 in)
Distance between rotor centres	6.17 m (20 ft 3 in)
Length overall, rotors turning	12.41 m (40 ft 8½ in)
Length of fuselage	8.69 m (28 ft 6 in)
Height to top of rotor head	3.08 m (10 ft 1¼ in)
Skid track	2.29 m (7 ft 6 in)
Cabin doors (standard, each):	
Height	1.13 m (3 ft 8½ in)
Max width	0.81 m (2 ft 8 in)
Height to sill	0.58 m (1 ft 11 in)

DIMENSIONS, INTERNAL:
Cabin: Length	1.52 m (5 ft 0 in)
Max width	1.50 m (4 ft 11 in)
Max height	1.35 m (4 ft 5 in)
Floor area	1.16 m² (12.5 sq ft)

AREAS:
Tail rotor blades (each)	0.094 m² (1.01 sq ft)
Main rotor disc	91.97 m² (990.0 sq ft)
Tail rotor disc	2.57 m² (27.7 sq ft)

WEIGHTS AND LOADINGS:
Weight empty	798 kg (1,759 lb)
Max T-O weight	1,406 kg (3,100 lb)
Max disc loading	15.28 kg/m² (3.13 lb/sq ft)
Max power loading	6.18 kg/kW (10.16 lb/hp)

PERFORMANCE (at max T-O weight, except where indicated):
Never-exceed and max level speed	83 knots (154 km/h; 96 mph)
Cruising speed	78 knots (145 km/h; 90 mph)
Max rate of climb at S/L	393 m (1,290 ft)/min
Vertical rate of climb at S/L	225 m (740 ft)/min
Service ceiling:	
at AUW of 1,270 kg (2,800 lb)	4,570 m (15,000 ft)
at max T-O weight	2,255 m (7,400 ft)
Hovering ceiling IGE:	
at AUW of 1,270 kg (2,800 lb)	3,170 m (10,400 ft)
at max T-O weight	2,315 m (7,600 ft)
Hovering ceiling OGE:	
at AUW of 1,270 kg (2,800 lb)	2,070 m (6,800 ft)
at max T-O weight	1,155 m (3,800 ft)
Range, 30 min reserves:	
standard fuel	150 nm (278 km; 173 miles)
auxiliary fuel	316 nm (585 km; 364 miles)
Endurance with auxiliary fuel, 30 min reserves	4 h 1 min

R/STOL — *see Sierra Industries Inc*

SABRELINER
SABRELINER CORPORATION

6161 Aviation Drive, St Louis, Missouri 63134
Telephone: (314) 731 2260
Telex: 44-7227
OTHER WORKS: Perryville Municipal Airport, Missouri
CHAIRMAN AND CHIEF EXECUTIVE OFFICER:
F. Holmes Lamoreux
VICE-PRESIDENT, GOVERNMENT OPERATIONS:
Reuben D. Best
VICE-PRESIDENT, COMMERCIAL MARKETING:
Karl R. Childs
VICE-PRESIDENT, ENGINEERING:
Bob D. Hanks

Sabreliner Corporation was formed in July 1983 as a subsidiary of the New York merchant banking company Wolsey & Co, following the latter's purchase of the Sabreliner Division of Rockwell International Corporation.

The main activities of Sabreliner Corporation are to provide product support for Sabreliner models currently in service, a total of about 600 aircraft, and refurbishment and upgrading of Lockheed T-33 and AT-33 aircraft for resale, primarily to operators in Central and South America. Deliveries have included two Sabreliner Model 40R executive transports, 13 AT-33s and six T-33s to the Ecuadorian Air Force, with five more AT-33s on order. The company also offers a modification programme for Sabreliner Model 40 and Model 60 aircraft which involves the installation of extended life Pratt & Whitney JT12 engines, Collins EFIS displays, interior and exterior

refurbishing and zero-timed engines. In early 1985 Sabreliner Corporation was awarded a logistics support contract for US Navy Grumman TC-4C aircraft based at Whidbey Island, Washington; Oceana, Virginia; and Cherry Point, North Carolina. In September 1987 it was awarded a five-year contract for worldwide support of US Navy and US Marine Corps CT-39 Sabreliner aircraft. It is also making structural repairs and modifications to ten USAF Sabreliners (two T-39As and eight T-39Bs), the first of which was re-delivered in the Spring of 1988.

SABRELINER MODEL 85
Development of this proposed new model of the Sabreliner business jet has been temporarily suspended. A description, specification and artist's impression may be found in the 1987-88 *Jane's*.

SADLER
SADLER AIRCRAFT COMPANY

8225 East Montebello, Scottsdale, Arizona 85253
Telephone: (602) 994 4631
Telex: 285776 VAMP UR
Fax: (602) 481 0574
PRESIDENT: William G. Sadler
MARKETING DIRECTOR: F. Brent Stewart

SADLER A-22
Sadler Aircraft Company (formerly American Microflight Inc), whose Vampire ultralight aircraft is described in the Sport Aircraft section of this edition, has developed a low cost ground support aircraft, provisionally designated A-22, for attack and defence roles and also for such applications as border control, drug enforcement, counterinsurgency and interdiction.

Sadler A-22 single-seat lightweight ground attack aircraft

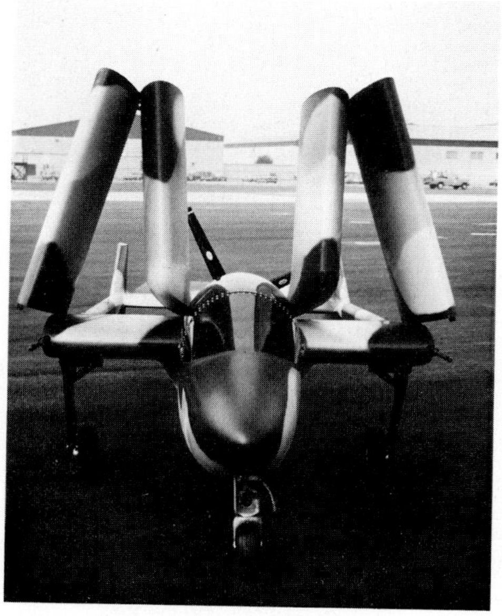

Sadler A-22 with wings folded

The A-22 is externally similar to the Vampire, but has a watercooled 224 kW (300 hp) modified Chevrolet V-6 engine with heavy duty reduction drive, strengthened airframe, increased fuel capacity, retractable landing gear, and bullet resistant fuselage pod and cockpit canopy providing protection for the pilot, engine and fuel system. Provision is made for the installation of a single 7.62 mm Hughes Chain Gun in the leading-edge of each inboard wing section, with ammunition storage to the rear, and for the carriage of stores, including 2.75 in rocket launching pods and bombs, on a total of four underwing hardpoints. Development of the A-22 began during 1985. Rollout of a prototype was made in July 1987, with customer demonstrations due to begin in June 1988 after flight testing had been completed. A two-seat dual control trainer version of the A-22 is expected to become available in early 1989.

Sadler Aircraft Company has also flight tested a smaller low cost RPV version of the Vampire under contract for a customer.

TYPE: Single-seat lightweight ground attack aircraft.

WINGS: Cantilever shoulder-wing monoplane of constant chord. NACA 66-A218 laminar flow wing section. Single aluminium alloy main spar, stamped ribs and flush riveted skin of aluminium alloy sheet. Aluminium alloy ailerons and four-position trailing-edge flaps. Outer wings fold upward in two hinged sections for transportation and storage.

FUSELAGE: Bullet resistant Kevlar fuselage pod and twin aluminium alloy tailbooms.

TAIL UNIT: Twin fins and rudders, interconnecting tailplane and elevator of similar construction to wings.

LANDING GEAR: Retractable tricycle type, with trailing link suspension. Fully swivelling nosewheel with steering through differential braking of main wheels.

POWER PLANT: One 224 kW (300 hp) watercooled Chevrolet V-6 all-aluminium fuel injected engine, modified for aircraft use, with heavy duty reduction drive to a four-blade composites pusher propeller. Standard fuel capacity 75.7 litres (20 US gallons; 16.6 Imp gallons). Turbocharged version available for high altitude operations.

ACCOMMODATION: Pilot only, in enclosed cockpit, with tinted bullet resistant Lexan canopy.

DIMENSIONS, EXTERNAL:

Wing span	6.70 m (22 ft 0 in)
Wing chord (constant)	1.27 m (4 ft 2 in)
Wing aspect ratio	5.28
Length overall	4.98 m (16 ft 4 in)
Height overall	1.14 m (3 ft 9 in)
Height, wings folded	2.13 m (7 ft 0 in)
Width, wings folded	2.29 m (7 ft 6 in)
Propeller diameter	1.37 m (4 ft 6 in)

AREA:

Wings, gross	8.51 m² (91.6 sq ft)

WEIGHTS:

Weight empty	340 kg (750 lb)
Max ordnance load	454 kg (1,000 lb)
Max T-O weight	907 kg (2,000 lb)

PERFORMANCE (estimated, at AUW of 680 kg; 1,500 lb, at S/L):

Never-exceed speed	251 knots (466 km/h; 290 mph)
Max level speed	195 knots (362 km/h; 225 mph)
Stalling speed, flaps down	53 knots (97 km/h; 60 mph)
Max rate of climb	1,067 m (3,500 ft)/min
Service ceiling	5,485 m (18,000 ft)
T-O and landing run	91 m (300 ft)

SCALED

SCALED COMPOSITES INC (Subsidiary of Beech Aircraft Corporation)

Hangar 78, Mojave Airport, Mojave, California 93501
Telephone: (805) 824 4541
Fax: (805) 824 4174

PRESIDENT: Elbert L. (Burt) Rutan

VICE-PRESIDENT AND GENERAL MANAGER: Herbert A. Iversen

Scaled Composites Inc was acquired by Beech Aircraft Corporation in June 1985, for operation as a wholly owned subsidiary. It had been established by Mr 'Burt' Rutan, who continues as President of SCALED in addition to serving as a Vice-President of Beech, to provide an independent research and development organisation that could hire its services to individuals or companies requiring assistance with advanced aeronautical concepts. Aircraft to which it contributed were the NASA AD-1 oblique-wing research aircraft, for which detail design was carried out by Mr Rutan (see 1981-82 *Jane's*); the Fairchild/Ames 62% scale NGT, for which Mr Rutan completed the detail scaling from Fairchild's NGT lofting drawings (see 1982-83 *Jane's*); the M115-6.85 SCAT 1 85% scale demonstrator of the Beech Model 2000 Starship 1 (see Beech Aircraft Corporation in this section); a prototype of the Aviation Composites Mercury canard microlight (see Sport Aircraft section in 1987-88 *Jane's*); the Model 120-9E proof-of-concept Predator 480 agricultural aircraft, (described under the ATAC entry in the 1985-86 *Jane's*); the full scale demonstrator of California Microwave Inc's CM-44 manned RPV (described and illustrated under that company's heading in the RPVs and Targets section of the 1987-88 *Jane's*); the 62% scale Beech/DARPA AT³, (described under Beech Aircraft Corporation's entry in this edition); and the short-run production of the Teledyne Ryan Aeronautical Scarab Mach 0.8 ground launched reconnaissance RPV.

SCALED's 2,787 m² (30,000 sq ft) facility at Mojave Airport, which is literally next door to Rutan Aircraft Factory, is well equipped for the construction of one or two prototypes of a particular design concept, and facilities include a large hangar, instrumentation and flight test departments, a short run production shop, plus a small machine shop. Future programmes are expected to involve commercial and military projects of a proprietary nature. In early 1986 a new 1,858 m² (20,000 sq ft) composites fabrication facility was added to the existing plant.

POND RACER PR-01

SCALED is building for Mr Robert J. Pond of Minnesota a twin-engined all-composites racing aircraft designed by Mr Burt Rutan. The aircraft is of twin-boom configuration, similar to the Lockheed P-38 Lightning, with tapered forward swept wings featuring aeroelastic tailoring. A cockpit nacelle mounted between the booms is supported by the rear surface of the wing centre-section and the tailplane. The tail unit is of three-fin configuration, with a central fin integral with the fuselage pod, while each tailboom has a sweptback, outward canted 'butterfly' fin and a small dorsal finlet. The area of the 'butterfly' fins will be progressively reduced during flight testing to optimum size. A retractable tailwheel type landing gear is fitted. The airframe is of carbonfibre/foam construction. Power plant comprises two 746 kW (1,000 hp) Electromotive/Nissan VG-30 liquid-cooled, turbocharged and intercooled V-6 automobile piston engines mounted ahead of the wing leading-edge, each driving a specially developed four-blade advanced technology propeller via reduction gearing. Fuel is contained in six integral tanks, three in each nacelle boom. Wing span is 7.62 m (25 ft 0 in); max T-O weight is expected to be about 1,361 kg (3,000 lb).

The Pond Racer has been designed to compete in Unlimited class air racing and is expected to be capable of maximum speeds of up to 521 knots (966 km/h; 600 mph). Following rollout in April 1989, it is scheduled to begin flight testing in June. Test pilot for the aircraft is Dick Rutan, brother of the designer and pilot of the round-the-world Voyager aircraft. The Pond Racer is expected to make its racing debut at the National Championship Air Races at Reno, Nevada, in September 1989. Mr Pond has also announced his intention to use the aircraft for attempts to set new speed records for piston-engined aircraft in all categories.

SCHAFER

SCHAFER AIRCRAFT MODIFICATIONS INC

Route 10, Box 301, Madison Cooper Airport, Waco, Texas 76708
Telephone: (817) 753 1551
Telex: 795902 SCHAFER CFTO
Fax: (817) 753 8416

PRESIDENT: Earl Schafer

EXECUTIVE VICE-PRESIDENT AND DIRECTOR OF MARKETING: R. B. Stevens

Mr Earl Schafer established this company during 1977. Initially, work was concentrated on the design and manufacture of auxiliary fuel tanks and the embodiment of modifications in Cessna business aircraft of the 300 and 400 series. Since 1979 the company has developed aircraft modification programmes of its own concept, of which details follow:

SCHAFER COMANCHERO

The Comanchero is a conversion of the Piper Pressurised Navajo with 559 kW (750 shp) Pratt & Whitney Canada PT6A-135 turboprops, flat rated at 462 kW (620 shp), replacing the standard 317 kW (425 hp) Textron Lycoming TIGO-541-E1A piston engines. This increases the useful load by 345 kg (760 lb) and offers a considerably longer max range. Max fuel capacity is increased to 1,363 litres (360 US gallons; 300 Imp gallons). The company received an FAA STC for the Comanchero in January 1981. A dual camera port installation for high altitude aerial photography is available optionally.

SECA, a subsidiary of Aérospatiale of France, has been appointed sole modification and service centre for Schafer Comanchero modifications for Europe, the Middle East and Africa.

WEIGHTS AND LOADINGS:

Weight empty	2,177 kg (4,800 lb)
Max baggage weight	218 kg (480 lb)
Max T-O weight	3,538 kg (7,800 lb)
Max wing loading	176.9 kg/km² (36.24 lb/sq ft)
Max power loading	4.07 kg/kW (6.7 lb/shp)

PERFORMANCE: As for Pressurised Navajo except:

Max cruising speed at 6,100 m (20,000 ft)	282 knots (522 km/h; 325 mph)
Max rate of climb at S/L	1,067 m (3,500 ft)/min
Rate of climb at S/L, one engine out	250 m (820 ft)/min
Service ceiling	more than 11,280 m (37,000 ft)
Service ceiling, one engine out	6,860 m (22,500 ft)
T-O to 15 m (50 ft)	533 m (1,750 ft)
Landing from 15 m (50 ft)	564 m (1,850 ft)
Max range at 8,840 m (29,000 ft), 45 min reserves	1,530 nm (2,835 km; 1,761 miles)

SCHAFER COMANCHERO 500

The Comanchero 500 is a conversion of the Piper Chieftain which, basically, replaces the standard piston engines with turboprops of greater power. Design originated in mid-1980, and the prototype began flight testing in late August 1981.

Conversion of the Chieftain to **Comanchero 500B** standard involves replacement of its 261 kW (350 hp) Textron Lycoming TIO-540-J2BD piston engines by two 533 ekW (715 ehp) Pratt & Whitney Canada PT6A-27 turboprops, each flat rated at 431 ekW (578 ehp). Optionally, customers can select **Comanchero 500A** standard, with lower cost 410 kW (550 shp) PT6A-20s installed, if they do not require the hot day/high altitude performance offered by the flat rated PT6A-27s. In addition to turboprop engines, the conversion adds a 132 litre (35 US gallon; 29 Imp gallon) supplementary fuel tank in each engine nacelle, increases max T-O weight, and includes as standard an inspection of the airframe and replacement, if necessary, of such items as control surface and system bearings and bushings, landing gear bushings, and hydraulic components. Options include special interiors, avionics to customers' requirements, a detachable underfuselage cargo pod with capacity of 0.44 m³ (15.5 cu ft), and 341 litre (90 US gallon; 75 Imp gallon) supplementary nacelle tanks in lieu of the standard installation. By early 1987 a total of 25 Comanchero 500 conversions had been completed.

In early 1984 Schafer contracted with Embraer of Brazil for the licence manufacture of 50 Comanchero 500Bs in Brazil, where the aircraft is known as the Neiva NE-821 Carajá and has 410 kW (550 shp) derated PT6A-34 engines. Two modification kits were supplied by Schafer; the remainder are being manufactured locally by Neiva Indústria Aeronáutica SA, under whose entry further details of the Carajá can be found.

WEIGHT:

Max T-O weight	3,629 kg (8,000 lb)

PERFORMANCE (A, Comanchero 500A; B, Comanchero 500B):

Max cruising speed: A, B at 3,660 m (12,000 ft)	240 knots (445 km/h; 276 mph)
Max rate of climb at S/L: A	853 m (2,800 ft)/min
B	732 m (2,400 ft)/min
Rate of climb at S/L, one engine out: A, B	259 m (850 ft)/min
Service ceiling: A	8,840 m (29,000 ft)
Service ceiling, one engine out: A, B	4,725 m (15,500 ft)
T-O to 15 m (50 ft): A	759 m (2,490 ft)
Landing from 15 m (50 ft): A	724 m (2,375 ft)

Range with pilot and ten passengers, 13.6 kg (30 lb) baggage allowance per passenger, and 45 min reserves, with standard fuel: A, B   500 nm (926 km; 575 miles)
Range with pilot and 181 kg (400 lb) payload:
B   1,300 nm (2,410 km; 1,500 miles)

SCHAFER COMANCHERO 750

Schafer gained an STC during May 1981 for this re-engined version of the Piper Cheyenne II. This modification involves replacement of the standard 462 ekW (620 ehp) Pratt & Whitney Canada PT6A-28 turboprops by PT6A-135s flat rated at 559 kW (750 shp). A dual camera port installation for high altitude aerial photography is available optionally.

PERFORMANCE:
Max cruising speed at 7,620 m (25,000 ft)
        278 knots (515 km/h; 320 mph)
Max rate of climb at S/L   869 m (2,850 ft)/min
Rate of climb at S/L, one engine out   198 m (650 ft)/min
Max range, econ cruising power at 8,840 m (29,000 ft)
        1,630 nm (3,020 km; 1,877 miles)

SCHAFER DOUGLAS DC-3-65TP

Schafer, in conjunction with Aero Modifications International of Fort Worth, Texas, has developed a turboprop conversion for the Douglas DC-3 which involves replacing the aircraft's piston engines with two Pratt & Whitney Canada PT6A-65AR turboprops. The conversion also includes a fuselage 'stretch' forward of the wingroot to maintain the aircraft's centre of gravity envelope. The hydraulic system is modified and fuel capacity increased.

Design work on the modification, which is known as the Schafer DC-3-65TP, began in January 1985. The prototype (N70BF) made its first flight on 1 August 1986. Work began on the first production conversion in September 1986. By early 1987 Schafer had received orders for three DC-3-65TPs.

FUSELAGE: As for standard DC-3 but with 1.02 m (3 ft 4 in) plug forward of wingroot. Plug section can incorporate one additional cabin window on each side if required for passenger operation.

TAIL UNIT: As for DC-3 but with minor changes to horizontal tail surfaces for improved stability.

POWER PLANT: Two 1,062 kW (1,424 shp) Pratt & Whitney Canada PT6A-65AR turboprops, each flat rated at 917 kW (1,230 shp) and driving a Hartzell five-blade feathering and reversing propeller with de-icing. Engines have inertial separators and hot lip intake de-icing. One additional fuel tank, usable capacity 447 litres (118 US gallons; 98.25 Imp gallons), in each engine nacelle. One forward auxiliary fuel tank, usable capacity 765 litres (202 US gallons; 168 Imp gallons), and one rear auxiliary fuel tank, usable capacity 753 litres (199 US gallons; 166 Imp gallons), in each inboard wing, giving total usable fuel capacity of 3,930 litres (1,038 US gallons; 864 Imp gallons). Oil capacity 9.5 litres (2.5 US gallons; 2.1 Imp gallons).

SYSTEMS: Two engine driven 250A starter/generators. Redesigned electrical system with dual batteries providing simultaneous engine start capability.

DIMENSIONS, EXTERNAL: As for standard DC-3, except:
Length overall   20.34 m (66 ft 9 in)
Propeller diameter   2.79 m (9 ft 2 in)
Baggage door: Height   1.42 m (4 ft 8 in)
        Width   2.13 m (7 ft 0 in)
DIMENSIONS, INTERNAL:
Cabin: Length   12.50 m (41 ft 0 in)
        Max width   2.18 m (7 ft 2 in)
        Max height   1.95 m (6 ft 5 in)
        Floor area   26.72 m² (287.6 sq ft)
        Volume   48.85 m³ (1,725 cu ft)

Schafer Comanchero 500 conversion of Piper Chieftain

Schafer Douglas DC-3-65TP conversion with Pratt & Whitney Canada PT6A-65AR turboprops

WEIGHTS AND LOADINGS:
Basic operating weight   7,167 kg (15,800 lb)
Max fuel weight   3,154 kg (6,954 lb)
Max T-O and landing weight   12,202 kg (26,900 lb)
Max zero-fuel weight   11,793 kg (26,000 lb)
Max wing loading   132.8 kg/m² (27.2 lb/sq ft)
Max power loading   6.65 kg/kW (10.9 lb/shp)
PERFORMANCE:
Never-exceed speed
        187 knots (346 km/h; 215 mph) IAS
Max level speed at 3,050 m (10,000 ft)
        217 knots (402 km/h; 250 mph)
Max cruising speed at 3,050 m (10,000 ft)
        196 knots (363 km/h; 226 mph)
Econ cruising speed at 3,050 m (10,000 ft)
        185 knots (343 km/h; 213 mph)

Stalling speed, flight idle power
        52 knots (96 km/h; 60 mph) IAS
Max rate of climb at S/L   610 m (2,000 ft)/min
Rate of climb at S/L, one engine out   137 m (450 ft)/min
Service ceiling   7,620 m (25,000 ft)
Service ceiling, one engine out   3,685 m (12,100 ft)
T-O run   1,051 m (3,450 ft)
T-O to 15 m (50 ft)   1,122 m (3,680 ft)
Landing from 15 m (50 ft)   670 m (2,200 ft)
Range: with max fuel and 2,268 kg (5,000 lb) payload
        1,300 nm (2,409 km; 1,497 miles)
with 4,536 kg (10,000 lb) payload
        100 nm (185 km; 115 miles)

SCHWEIZER
SCHWEIZER AIRCRAFT CORPORATION

PO Box 147, Elmira, New York 14902
Telephone: (607) 739 3821
Telex: 932459 SCHWEIZER BIGF
Fax: (607) 796 2488
PRESIDENT: Paul Hardy Schweizer
VICE-PRESIDENT:
Leslie E. Schweizer (Chief Engineer)
SALES MANAGER, AG-CAT: T. C. Kosier
HELICOPTER MARKETING DIRECTOR: Larry A. Brooks
MARKETING COORDINATOR: Barbara Tweedt

Schweizer Aircraft Corporation was established in 1939 to design and manufacture sailplanes. Its current sailplane products are described in the appropriate section of this edition.

From mid-1957 until 1979 Schweizer also produced the Grumman (later Gulfstream American) Ag-Cat agricultural aircraft under subcontract. In January 1981 it purchased all rights to the Ag-Cat design, and deliveries of Schweizer Super-B Ag-Cats began in October 1981, since supplemented by a new turboprop version. All marketing and support for the Ag-Cat is undertaken from the Elmira facility.

It was announced on 13 July 1983 that Schweizer was to take over, under licence, sole US manufacture of the Hughes Model 300 series light helicopter, which had been in production by Hughes Helicopters since the late 1950s.

Schweizer also became responsible for providing product support for Model 300s already in service, including the TH-55A military training version. Production tooling was shipped to Schweizer during the Summer of 1983, and the first Elmira built Model 300C was completed in June 1984. On 21 November 1986 Schweizer purchased all US manufacturing rights to the Model 300C from McDonnell Douglas Helicopter Corporation.

Schweizer is well known also as an aircraft subcontractor and is engaged currently in work for Beech, Bell Helicopter, Boeing, Sikorsky and other companies. It is engaged in contractual design and prototyping, and in projects to develop heavy lift vehicles, aerial applicators for pheromones, centrifuges, and spatial disorientation trainers.

SCHWEIZER SA 2-37A

The SA 2-37A is a modified version of Schweizer's SGM 2-37 motor glider (see Sailplanes section), developed primarily for use as a special purpose aircraft for law enforcement, border surveillance and other selected military applications. The wings are of slightly greater span, with modified leading-edges to improve stalling characteristics; and the SA 2-37A has a much more powerful engine, fitted with mufflers (long exhaust on each side of cowling) and driving a three-blade 'quiet' propeller. The aircraft is certificated under FAR Pt 23 for day and night VFR and IFR operations, and has a very low acoustic signature.

Requiring only approximately 38.8 kW (52 hp) from the 175 kW (235 hp) IO-540 engine to maintain altitude in the quiet mission mode, it is said to be inaudible when flying at 'quiet mode' speed at 610-915 m (2,000-3,000 ft) above the ground.

Standard fuel capacity is more than trebled compared with the motor glider, and can be increased further by use of an optional auxiliary tank. Behind the new bulged cockpit canopy is a 1.84 m³ (65 cu ft) payload bay designed to accept various sensor pallets such as low light level TV, infra-red imaging systems, standard cameras, or other payloads specified by customers. The pallet can be removed quickly for replacement or maintenance, and a removable underfuselage skin and rear hatch doors provide access to the entire rear section of the aircraft. Other power plants and larger payload versions of the SA 2-37A are possible, both for specific surveillance applications and for such alternative roles as basic and advanced training, mission operator training, glider and banner towing and priority cargo delivery.

First flight of the SA 2-37A prototype (N9237A, a modified SGM 2-37) was made in 1986, and two similar aircraft are believed to have been built subsequently for an unspecified US government agency. The prototype is fitted with an underfuselage Hughes Aircraft Corporation AN/AAQ-16 thermal imaging system.

TYPE: Two-seat special missions aircraft.

AIRFRAME: Generally similar to that of SGM 2-37 motor glider (which see), with wings extended in span and having Wortmann root and tip sections of FX-61-163 and FX-60-126 (modified) respectively. Leading-edges have chord extended by cuffs on portions of outer panels to improve stall characteristics. Fuselage slightly longer, and modified in forward areas to accommodate change of engine and enlarged canopy. Centre-section, outer wing panels and horizontal tail surface removable for storage and transportation. Speed fairings and hydraulic parking brakes on mainwheels.

POWER PLANT: One 175 kW (235 hp) Textron Lycoming IO-540-W3A5D flat-six engine, driving a McCauley three-blade constant-speed propeller with spinner. Standard fuel capacity of 196.8 litres (52 US gallons; 43.3 Imp gallons), increasable optionally to 253.6 litres (67 US gallons; 55.8 Imp gallons).

ACCOMMODATION: Seats for two persons side by side under two-piece upward opening canopy, hinged on centreline. Dual controls, seat belts and inertia reel harnesses standard. Compartment aft of seats enlarged to accommodate pallet containing up to 340 kg (750 lb) of sensors or other equipment.

SYSTEMS: 28V DC electrical system standard, with 100A alternator. A 300A generator and 110/120V 400Hz AC inverter are optional. Other options include air-conditioning and 1.81 m³ (64 cu ft) Scott oxygen system.

AVIONICS AND EQUIPMENT: Litton inertial navigation system. Standard King avionics comprise dual KX 155 nav/com (one with VOR/ILS, one with VOR indicator) and single KG 258 artificial horizon, KEA 129 encoding altimeter, KR 87 ADF with indicator, KT 76 transponder, KR 21 marker beacon receiver, and KMA 24H audio control panel. Flight and engine instrumentation includes compass, ASI, rate of climb indicator, altimeter, fuel pressure and quantity gauges, oil temperature and pressure gauges, tachometer and voltmeter. Other standard equipment includes directional gyro, turn and bank indicator, exhaust gas and cylinder head temperature gauges, vacuum system, two David Clark headsets, digital clock, dual engine mufflers with resonator quiet kit, navigation/strobe/landing lights, interior post lights, flood/map light, and static wicks. Optional avionics and equipment include King KNS 80 R/Nav, KCS 55A compass system, KFC 150 autopilot (requiring KCS 55A slave compass), and KRA 10A radar altimeter; Loran system; Storm Scope WX-11; Shadin fuel flow system; 56.8 litre (15 US gallon; 12.5 Imp gallon) auxiliary fuel tank; 10 in tailwheel; armour seat protection; tinted glass; and lighting compatible with night vision goggles.

DIMENSIONS, EXTERNAL:
Wing span	18.745 m (61 ft 6 in)
Wing aspect ratio	19.0
Fuselage length	8.46 m (27 ft 9 in)
Height overall (tail down)	2.36 m (7 ft 9 in)
Tailplane span	3.24 m (10 ft 7½ in)
Wheel track	2.79 m (9 ft 2 in)
Wheelbase	5.99 m (19 ft 8 in)
Propeller diameter	2.18 m (7 ft 2 in)
Propeller ground clearance (tail up)	0.55 m (1 ft 9.7 in)

AREAS:
Wings, gross	18.52 m² (199.4 sq ft)
Ailerons (total)	1.01 m² (10.90 sq ft)
Airbrakes (total)	0.82 m² (8.79 sq ft)
Vertical tail surfaces (total)	1.62 m² (17.43 sq ft)
Horizontal tail surfaces (total)	2.13 m² (22.95 sq ft)

WEIGHTS AND LOADINGS:
Weight empty	918 kg (2,025 lb)
Max mission payload	340 kg (750 lb)
Max T-O weight	1,587 kg (3,500 lb)
Max wing loading	85.65 kg/m² (17.55 lb/sq ft)
Max power loading	9.06 kg/kW (14.89 lb/hp)

Prototype of the Schweizer SA 2-37A two-seat surveillance aircraft

PERFORMANCE (at max T-O weight):
Max permissible diving speed	176 knots (326 km/h; 202 mph) CAS

Cruising speed at 1,525 m (5,000 ft):
75% power	138 knots (256 km/h; 159 mph)
65% power	129 knots (239 km/h; 148 mph)
Approach speed	117 knots (217 km/h; 135 mph) CAS

Quiet mode speed
70-80 knots (130-148 km/h; 80-92 mph)
Optimum climbing speed
77 knots (142 km/h; 88 mph) CAS

Stalling speed:
airbrakes open	71 knots (132 km/h; 82 mph)
airbrakes closed	67 knots (124 km/h; 77 mph)
Max rate of climb at S/L	292 m (960 ft)/min
Service ceiling	5,490 m (18,000 ft)

T-O run (S/L, ISA): hard surface 387 m (1,270 ft)
grass 533 m (1,750 ft)
T-O to 15 m (50 ft) (S/L, ISA):
hard surface 612 m (2,010 ft)
grass 759 m (2,490 ft)
Landing from 15 m (50 ft) (S/L, ISA):
hard surface 680 m (2,230 ft)
grass 732 m (2,400 ft)
Best glide ratio 20
g limits +6.6/−3.3

SCHWEIZER AG-CAT SUPER-B and AG-CAT TURBINE

The prototype of the original (Grumman designed) Ag-Cat agricultural biplane flew for the first time on 27 May 1957. First deliveries were made in 1959 and 2,455 Ag-Cats (1,730 G-164A, 659 G-164B, 44 G-164C and 22 G-164D) were built by Schweizer under subcontract. Schweizer resumed production in October 1981 with two versions of an improved G-164B known as the Ag-Cat Super-B. It has also developed the turboprop powered Ag-Cat Super-B Turbine. Recent deliveries included three G-164Bs to SMA Agriculture in Sudan. Details of current models are as follows:

Ag-Cat Super-B/600 (G-164B). This is the basic Schweizer Ag-Cat, with a 447.5 kW (600 hp) Pratt & Whitney R-1340 nine-cylinder radial aircooled engine, driving a Pacific Propeller Type 12D40/AG100 two-blade constant-speed metal propeller. Improvements incorporated in the Super-B include a hopper with 40 per cent greater capacity (1.51 m³; 53.5 cu ft) than that of earlier models, a 0.97 m (3 ft 2 in) wide stainless steel gatebox and bottom loader valve as standard equipment, plus numerous equipment and airframe improvements. The upper wing is raised 20 cm (8 in) to improve the pilot's view, and increase load carrying capability, operating speed and climb performance.

Ag-Cat 450B (G-164B). This alternative version of the Super-B is generally similar to the basic model, but is powered instead by a 335.5 kW (450 hp) Pratt & Whitney R-985 nine-cylinder radial aircooled engine. Usable fuel capacity is 242 litres (64 US gallons; 53.3 Imp gallons). The 450B has a 1.23 m³ (43.5 cu ft) hopper, capacity 1,230 litres (325 US gallons; 271 Imp gallons). It is available only to special order.

Ag-Cat Super-B Turbine (G-164B). Generally similar to the basic Ag-Cat Super-B, but powered by a Pratt & Whitney Canada PT6A turboprop. Alternative power plants available for this version are the 373 kW (500 shp) PT6A-11AG, 507 kW (680 shp) PT6A-15AG, and 559 kW (750 shp) PT6A-34AG.

The following description applies generally to all three production models, except where indicated:

TYPE: Single-seat agricultural biplane.

WINGS: Single-bay staggered biplane. NACA 4412 (modified) wing section. Dihedral 3°. Incidence 6°. Aluminium alloy (6061-T6) two-spar structure with 6061-T6 skins on entire top surface, around leading-edge and back to front spar on undersurface. Remainder of undersurface fabric covered. Each D leading-edge is made of five separate sections to facilitate replacement if damaged. Glassfibre wingtips. N type interplane struts. Light alloy ailerons on all four wings, with ground adjustable tab on lower port aileron. No flaps.

FUSELAGE: Welded 4130 chrome-molybdenum steel tube structure, covered with duralumin sheet. Removable side panels.

TAIL UNIT: Welded 4130 chrome-molybdenum steel tube structure, covered with fabric and wire braced. Cable deflector wire from tip of fin to top of cockpit canopy. Controllable trim tab in port elevator. Ground adjustable tabs on rudder and starboard elevator.

LANDING GEAR: Non-retractable tailwheel type. Cantilever spring steel legs. Cleveland wheels with tyres size 8.50-10 8-ply, pressure 2.42 bars (35 lb/sq in). Steerable tailwheel with tyre size 12.4-4.5, pressure 3.45 bars (50 lb/sq in). Cleveland heavy duty aircooled hydraulic disc brakes. Parking brake.

POWER PLANT: One Pratt & Whitney nine-cylinder aircooled radial engine with Pacific Propeller constant-speed propeller, or Pratt & Whitney Canada PT6A turboprop, as detailed in model listings. Fuel tanks in upper wing with combined usable capacity of 302 litres (80 US gallons; 66.6 Imp gallons). Single-point refuelling on upper surface of upper wing centre-section. Oil capacity 32.2 litres (8.5 US gallons; 7.1 Imp gallons).

ACCOMMODATION: Single seat in enclosed cockpit. Reinforced fairing aft of canopy for turnover protection. Canopy side panels open outward and down, canopy top upward and to starboard, to provide access. Baggage compartment. Cockpit pressurised against dust ingress

Schweizer Ag-Cat Super-B/600 agricultural aircraft

and ventilated by ram air. Safety padded instrument panel. Air-conditioning by J.B. Systems optional.

SYSTEMS: Hydraulic system for brakes only. Optional electrical system with 24V alternator, navigation lights and/or strobe lights, external power socket, and electric engine starter.

EQUIPMENT: Radio optional. Standard equipment includes control column lock, instrument glareshield, seat belt and shoulder harness, tinted windscreen, stall warning light, refuelling steps and assist handles, tiedown rings, and urethane paint external yellow finish.

AGRICULTURAL EQUIPMENT: Forward of cockpit, over CG, is a 1.51 m³ (53.5 cu ft) glassfibre hopper, capacity 1,514 litres (400 US gallons; 333 Imp gallons), for agricultural chemicals (dry or liquid) with distributor beneath fuselage. Low-volume, ULV or high-volume spray system, with leading- or trailing-edge booms. Emergency dump system for hopper load; can be used also for water bomber operations.

DIMENSIONS, EXTERNAL (A: Super-B/600, B: Super-B Turbine, C: 450B):

Wing span	12.93 m (42 ft 5 in)
Wing chord (constant)	1.47 m (4 ft 10 in)
Wing aspect ratio: upper wing	8.7
biplane, effective mean	5.5
Length overall: A	7.44 m (24 ft 5 in)
B	8.38 m (27 ft 6 in)
C	7.54 m (24 ft 9 in)
Height overall: A, C	3.51 m (11 ft 6 in)
B	3.68 m (12 ft 1 in)
Tailplane span	3.96 m (13 ft 0 in)
Wheel track	2.44 m (8 ft 0 in)
Wheelbase	5.59 m (18 ft 4 in)
Propeller diameter (max)	2.74 m (9 ft 0 in)
Propeller ground clearance	0.27 m (10.8 in)

AREAS:

Wings, gross	36.42 m² (392.0 sq ft)
Ailerons (total)	2.93 m² (31.5 sq ft)
Fin	1.67 m² (17.97 sq ft)
Rudder	1.12 m² (12.0 sq ft)
Tailplane	2.12 m² (22.8 sq ft)
Elevators	2.06 m² (22.2 sq ft)

WEIGHTS AND LOADINGS:
Weight empty equipped, spray and duster versions:

A	1,656 kg (3,650 lb)
B	1,429 kg (3,150 lb)
C	1,508 kg (3,325 lb)
Certificated AUW	2,358 kg (5,200 lb)
Max T-O weight (CAM.8)	3,184 kg (7,020 lb)
Max wing loading	87.42 kg/m² (17.91 lb/sq ft)
Max power loading: A	7.12 kg/kW (11.71 lb/hp)
B	5.70-8.54 kg/kW (9.36-14.04 lb/shp)
C	9.49 kg/kW (15.6 lb/hp)

PERFORMANCE (A: Super-B/600, B: Super-B Turbine with PT6A-15AG engine, C: 450B):

Working speed: A, C	100 knots (185 km/h; 115 mph)
B	113 knots (209 km/h; 130 mph)

T-O to 15 m (50 ft) at 2,358 kg (5,200 lb) certificated

AUW: A	320 m (1,050 ft)
B	274 m (900 ft)
C	396 m (1,300 ft)
Design g loadings, all versions	+4.2/-1

SCHWEIZER MODEL 300C

The early history of this helicopter can be found under the Hughes Helicopters entry in previous editions of *Jane's*, and a detailed description of the basic Model 300 in the 1976-77 edition. Hughes built more than 2,800 of all versions, including the TH-55A Osage for the US Army, before transferring production to Schweizer in July 1983. In November 1986, Schweizer purchased the Model 300 programme in its entirety.

The current Model 300C is a developed version, with improvements to allow a 45 per cent increase in payload. The prototype made its first flight in August 1969, followed by the first Hughes production model in December 1969. FAA certification was received in May 1970. The first production Schweizer Model 300C flew in June 1984 and was delivered on 29 June. In late 1985 the US Army awarded Schweizer a $4.9 million contract for the supply of 30 Model 300Cs and spare parts. In March 1986 Schweizer began delivery of 24 TH-300C training versions to the Royal Thai Army, which ordered a further 24 TH-300Cs for delivery during 1988. The 100th Schweizer built Model 300C was delivered in January 1987. Schweizer expected to manufacture 68 Model 300Cs in 1988. The Model 300C is manufactured also in Italy, by BredaNardi (which see).

The specially equipped 300C available for police patrol has safety mesh seats with inertia reel shoulder harness, ballistic glassfibre armour beneath each seat, a high power public address/siren system, a high intensity controllable searchlight system, an integrated communications system based on the King KY 195 VHF transceiver, a heavy duty 28V 100A electrical system, cabin heater, night lights with strobe beacons, cabin utility light, external power socket, fire extinguisher, first aid kit and mapcase.

TYPE: Three-seat light utility helicopter.

ROTOR SYSTEM: Fully articulated metal three-blade main rotor. Fully interchangeable blades of bonded construction, with constant section extruded aluminium spar, wraparound skin and a trailing-edge section. Blade

Schweizer Model 300C helicopter

section NACA 0015. Tracking tabs on blades at three-quarters radius. Elastomeric dampers. Electric cyclic trim. Two-blade teetering tail rotor, each blade comprising a steel tube spar with glassfibre skin. Limited blade folding. No rotor brake.

ROTOR DRIVE: Combination V-belt/pulley and reduction gear drive system. Main rotor and tail rotor gearbox have spiral bevel right-angle drive. Main rotor/engine rpm ratio 1 : 6.8. Tail rotor/engine rpm ratio 1.97 : 1.03.

FUSELAGE: Welded steel tube centre structure, with light alloy, stainless steel and Plexiglas cabin and one-piece light alloy tube tailboom.

TAIL UNIT: Horizontal and vertical fixed stabilising surfaces, made of light alloy ribs and skins.

LANDING GEAR: Skids carried on oleo-pneumatic shock absorbers. Replaceable skid shoes. Two ground handling wheels with 0.25 m (10 in) balloon tyres, pressure 4.14-5.17 bars (60-75 lb/sq in). Available optionally on floats made of polyurethane coated nylon fabric, 4.70 m (15 ft 5 in) long and with a total installed weight of 27.2 kg (60 lb).

POWER PLANT: One 168 kW (225 hp) Textron Lycoming HIO-360-D1A flat-four engine, derated to 142 kW (190 hp), mounted horizontally aft of seats. Two aluminium fuel tanks, total capacity 185.5 litres (49 US gallons; 40.8 Imp gallons) mounted externally aft of cockpit. Crash resistant fuel tank optional. Oil capacity 9.5 litres (2.5 US gallons; 2.1 Imp gallons).

ACCOMMODATION: Three persons side by side on sculptured and cushioned bench seat, with shoulder harness, in Plexiglas enclosed cabin. Carpet and tinted canopy standard. Forward hinged, removable door on each side. Dual controls optional. Baggage capacity 45 kg (100 lb). Exhaust muff heating and ventilation kits available.

SYSTEMS: Standard electrical system includes 24V 70A alternator, 24V battery, starter and external power socket.

AVIONICS AND EQUIPMENT: Optional avionics include Collins VHF-253 or King KY 196 com transceiver and headsets, and ADF650A or KR 86 ADFs, TDR 950 or KT 76A transponders. Standard equipment includes mapcase, first aid kit, fire extinguisher, engine hour meter, and main rotor blade tiedown kit. Optional equipment

includes amphibious floats, litter kits, cargo racks with combined capacity of 91 kg (200 lb), external load sling of 408 kg (900 lb) capacity, Simplex Model 5200 agricultural spray or dry powder dispersal kits, Sky Night law enforcement package; instrument training package; throttle governor; start-up overspeed control unit, night flying kit, dual controls, all-weather cover, heavy duty skid plates, single or dual exhaust mufflers, door lock, dual oil coolers, and tinted glass for cabin windows.

DIMENSIONS, EXTERNAL:

Main rotor diameter	8.18 m (26 ft 10 in)
Main rotor blade chord	0.171 m (6¾ in)
Tail rotor diameter	1.30 m (4 ft 3 in)
Distance between rotor centres	4.66 m (15 ft 3½ in)
Length overall, max over rotors	9.40 m (30 ft 10 in)
Height over rotor head	2.66 m (8 ft 8⅝ in)
Width, rotor partially folded	2.44 m (8 ft 0 in)
Height to top of cabin	2.19 m (7 ft 2 in)
Cabin width	1.30 m (4 ft 3 in)
Skid track	1.99 m (6 ft 6½ in)
Length of skids	2.51 m (8 ft 3 in)
Passenger doors (each): Height	1.09 m (3 ft 7 in)
Width	0.97 m (3 ft 2 in)
Height to sill	0.91 m (3 ft 0 in)

AREAS:

Main rotor blades (each)	0.70 m² (7.55 sq ft)
Tail rotor blades (each)	0.08 m² (0.86 sq ft)
Main rotor disc	52.5 m² (565.5 sq ft)
Tail rotor disc	1.32 m² (14.2 sq ft)
Fin	0.23 m² (2.5 sq ft)
Horizontal stabiliser	0.246 m² (2.65 sq ft)

WEIGHTS AND LOADING:

Weight empty	474 kg (1,046 lb)
Max T-O weight: Normal category	930 kg (2,050 lb)
external load	975 kg (2,150 lb)
Max disc loading	17.67 kg/m² (3.62 lb/sq ft)

PERFORMANCE (at max Normal T-O weight, ISA):
Never-exceed speed at S/L

	91 knots (169 km/h; 105 mph)
Max cruising speed	82 knots (153 km/h; 95 mph)
Speed for max range, at 1,220 m (4,000 ft)	
	67 knots (124 km/h; 77 mph)
Max rate of climb at S/L	229 m (750 ft)/min
Service ceiling	3,110 m (10,200 ft)

Schweizer Model 330 Sky Knight (Allison 225-C10A turboshaft)

Hovering ceiling: IGE	1,800 m (5,900 ft)
OGE	840 m (2,750 ft)
Range at 1,220 m (4,000 ft), 2 min warm-up, max fuel, no reserves	194 nm (360 km; 224 miles)
Max endurance at S/L	3 h 24 min

SCHWEIZER MODEL 330 SKY KNIGHT

At the 1987 Airborne Law Enforcement Association convention in Sacramento, California, Schweizer Aircraft displayed a mockup of a three/four-seat turbine engined development of the Model 300C helicopter designated Model 330 Sky Knight. The helicopter, a prototype of which (N330TT) made its first flight in public on 14 June 1988, is powered by a 261 kW (350 shp) Allison 225-C10A turboshaft (derated to 149 kW; 200 shp) and uses most systems, controls, rotors and dynamic components of the piston engined aircraft. Main rotor speed is 471 rpm. The integrated avionics are supplied by Honeywell.

A new forward fuselage provides an increase in cabin length of some 0.61 m (2 ft 0 in) and an increase in width of 0.43 m (1 ft 5 in) and incorporates an aerodynamically improved transparency. The centre passenger seat has been raised and moved rearward in the training version, enabling it to be used by a second, observing, student. Flight controls can be provided at all three seat positions. A new pedestal mounted instrument console incorporates an IFR flight panel with dual multi-function CRT displays. Max fuel capacity is 227 litres (60 US gallons; 50 Imp gallons). Streamlined fairings have been added to the rear fuselage and tailboom.

Schweizer was to make a production decision on the Sky Knight in August 1988, following initial flight testing and market surveys. It expects to market the helicopter for a variety of duties, including scout/observation, aerial photography, law enforcement, light utility, agricultural spraying and VIP transportation.

Schweizer is teamed with Flight Safety International, Allison and Honeywell as a contender for the US Army's SCAT (single contractor aviator training) programme.

DIMENSIONS, EXTERNAL:

Main rotor diameter	8.18 m (26 ft 10 in)
Tail rotor diameter	1.30 m (4 ft 3 in)
Length overall, max over rotors	9.40 m (30 ft 10 in)
Height overall	2.64 m (8 ft 8 in)
Skid track	1.98 m (6 ft 6 in)

DIMENSIONS, INTERNAL:

Cabin: Width at seat	1.72 m (5 ft 7½ in)
Height at seat	1.35 m (4 ft 5¼ in)

WEIGHTS:

Weight empty	476 kg (1,050 lb)
Max T-O weight: Normal category	930 kg (2,050 lb)
external load	975 kg (2,150 lb)

PERFORMANCE (at Normal T-O weight):

Max cruising speed	100 knots (185 km/h; 115 mph)
Normal cruising speed	91 knots (169 km/h; 105 mph)
Hovering ceiling: IGE	5,485 m (18,000 ft)
OGE	4,265 m (14,000 ft)
Max range at 1,220 m (4,000 ft), no reserves	252 nm (466 km; 290 miles)
Max endurance, no reserves	3 h 30 min

SEAPLANES INC — *see Turbotech*

SEGUIN

SEGUIN AVIATION INC

2075 Highway 46, Seguin, Texas 78155
Telephone: (512) 379 3278
GENERAL MANAGER: Paul Holman

SEGUIN GERONIMO

Seguin Aviation has named this modification of the Piper PA-23-150 and PA-23-160 Apache twin-engined light aircraft after the famous leader of the Chiracahua Apache tribe of North American Indians. The Geronimo modification package, individual elements of which may be ordered separately, includes replacement of the Apache's original 112 kW (150 hp) Textron Lycoming O-320 or 119 kW (160 hp) O-320-B engines with two new 134 kW (180 hp) Textron Lycoming O-360-A1D power plants, each driving a Hartzell HC-C2YK-2RB-7666A2 two-blade metal constant-speed and feathering propeller; new streamlined glassfibre engine cowlings with new air induction and oil cooling systems; extended glassfibre nosecone which increases fuselage length by 0.79 m (2 ft 7 in) and incorporates a nose baggage compartment; fully enclosed wheel well doors for nose and main landing gears; new Hoerner type wingtips which reduce wing span by 0.56 m (1 ft 10 in); new square tipped fin and rudder with extended dorsal fin and strobe light; new tailcone; one-piece bubble or slanted windscreen with tinted glass; engine nacelle and wingroot fairings; gap seals for the trailing-edge flaps; and external power receptacle.

Internal modifications include a new shock mounted instrument panel with dual instrument post lighting, dual Radair EGT gauges; dual 'ram's horn' control wheels; custom furnishings with new headliner, seat upholstery, side panels and carpet; tinted sun visors; two 50A alternators; 35Ah battery, and Southwind 20,000 BTU cabin heater. The Geronimo is also finished in a new three-colour polyurethane external paint scheme.

Other Seguin modifications available to owners of PA-23s and to customers for Geronimo conversions include a gross weight increase to 1,814 kg (4,000 lb), Hartzell Q tip propellers, Hoerner contoured wingtip fuel tanks which increase total fuel capacity by 182 litres (48 US gallons; 40

Seguin Geronimo conversion of the Piper PA-23 Apache *(Jon King Keisling)*

Imp gallons), sixth seat with kick-out emergency window, third cabin window on each side, cargo door, inflatable door seal, rear baggage compartment, inner panes for all windows, three density soundproofing kit, and a dual brake modification. Wingtip tanks, sixth seat, door seals, rear baggage compartment, instrument panel improvements and soundproofing modifications are also approved for Piper PA-23/27 Apache 235 and Aztec 250 aircraft. Some 300 Seguin Geronimo conversions have been completed.

The following data refer to the Geronimo with complete modification package as described:

PERFORMANCE (at T-O weight of 1,724 kg; 3,800 lb):

Never-exceed speed	197 knots (365 km/h; 227 mph) IAS
Max level speed	174 knots (322 km/h; 200 mph)
Cruising speed:	
75% power at 1,220 m (4,000 ft)	165-170 knots (306-315 km/h; 190-196 mph)
65% power at 1,830 m (6,000 ft)	160-165 knots (296-306 km/h; 184-190 mph)
Minimum single-engine control speed (V$_{MC}$), feathered propeller	56 knots (105 km/h; 65 mph)
Stalling speed, power off, flaps and landing gear down	47 knots (87 km/h; 54 mph) IAS
Max rate of climb at S/L	610 m (2,000 ft)/min
Rate of climb at S/L, one engine out	229 m (750 ft)/min
Service ceiling	7,010 m (23,000 ft)
Service ceiling, one engine out	3,660 m (12,000 ft)
T-O and landing run	122 m (400 ft)
T-O to 15 m (50 ft)	198 m (650 ft)
Landing from 15 m (50 ft)	206 m (675 ft)
Range with max standard fuel, no reserves:	
75% power	907 nm (1,680 km; 1,043 miles)
65% power	972 nm (1,800 km; 1,118 miles)

SIERRA

SIERRA INDUSTRIES INC

Garner Municipal Airport, PO Box 5184, Uvalde, Texas 78802-5184
Telephone: (512) 278 4381
Telex: 9102402612
Fax: (512) 278 7649
PRESIDENT: Mark Huffstutler

On 24 September 1986 Sierra Industries Inc acquired the assets of the former R/STOL Systems Inc, including some 100 supplemental type certificates for STOL and performance modifications to 40 aircraft types, as detailed in this entry.

Sierra Industries holds an FAA Supplemental Type Certificate covering the installation of RCA WeatherScout I radar inside the leading-edge of the starboard wing of a number of aircraft including the Cessna 182, 206F, T206F, TU206G, U206G and 210 series. The truncated 13 × 30 cm (5 × 12 in) antenna is housed inside a leading-edge cutaway, with the receiver/transmitter built integrally at the back of the antenna. The wing structure is reinforced around the cutaway. A reinforced epoxy/glassfibre radome encloses the opening. Total system weight is 10.5 kg (23.1 lb). WeatherScout I is basically a weather radar, but provides limited ground mapping capability.

SIERRA INDUSTRIES CESSNA AUXILIARY FUEL SYSTEMS

Sierra Industries has developed an auxiliary fuel system for Cessna Model 180, 182, 185, 206 and 207 aircraft which increases the total fuel capacity of the aircraft by 204 litres (54 US gallons; 45 Imp gallons). The modification involves the installation of three vulcanised rubber fuel bladders in each wing panel outboard of the aircraft's standard wing fuel tank. Installation is accomplished in approximately 50 man hours, and is FAA certificated to FAR Pt 23 requirements.

SIERRA INDUSTRIES CESSNA 210 LANDING GEAR DOOR MODIFICATION

Sierra Industries has developed an FAA approved modification kit for Cessna Model 210, T210 and P210 Centurions manufactured between 1970 and 1978 (c/ns 21059200-21062954 inclusive), which enables the main landing gear doors to be removed. The conversion involves the substitution of prefabricated metal fairings to close gaps left by the door removal. Claimed advantages of the modification are an 8.6 kg (19 lb) increase in useful load, reduced maintenance, reduced landing gear retraction and extension times, elimination of possible door-fouling problems and enhanced appearance comparable to that of 1979 and later model Centurions.

SIERRA/BEECH, SIERRA/CESSNA and SIERRA/PIPER SAFETY and PERFORMANCE CONVERSIONS

Continuous improvement has been made on Sierra's line of Hi-Lift systems for Beech, Cessna and Piper single-engined and smaller twin-engined aircraft. The Sierra modification, first applied to a Cessna 182, comprises full span wing leading-edge and trailing-edge high-lift systems which greatly reduce the take-off and landing distances normally required by such aircraft.

The existing ailerons are used as an integral part of the full span trailing-edge flap system. When the conventional inboard flaps are lowered for take-off or landing, the ailerons droop with them, virtually doubling the wing lift at low speeds. The ailerons retain their differential operation for roll control when drooped.

In addition, the wing is fitted with a full span distributed-camber leading-edge to provide an optimum spanwise lift distribution for maximum cruise efficiency. The cambered leading-edge also reduces the aerofoil leading-edge pressure peak at high angles of attack, to impart maximum resistance to stall and to provide highly responsive manoeuvrability at low airspeeds. Some types of Cessna single-engined aircraft built since 1972 include this leading-edge as a standard production feature.

The full span flap system, in combination with conical

cambered wingtips, dorsal and ventral fins, belly mounted vortex generators, and flap/elevator automatic trim system, is applied to various models to offer increased performance.

To improve controllability at low speeds, stall fences are provided between flaps and ailerons, and to complete the Hi-Lift modification the aileron gap is sealed with a strip of aluminium sheet or rubberised canvas These modifications permit safe STOL landings and take-offs by even novice pilots, and cruising speed and range are increased by 2-4 per cent.

Maximum gross weight increases have accompanied the certification of modifications of twin-engined aircraft such as the Cessna Super Skymaster and Piper Twin Comanche. This is due primarily to their increased climb performance and slower take-off and landing speeds.

Development of a Hi-Lift system for the Cessna 400 series of twin-engined business aircraft entailed complete redesign of the wings from the rear spar aft to allow installation of 100 per cent Fowler flaps and flap actuated drooping ailerons. This system, in combination with an automatic pitch trim system and double hinged rudder, led to FAA certificated decreases in take-off and landing field lengths of approximately 40 per cent.

In 1974, the FAA certificated the Sierra equipped Piper Seneca I, with wing upper surface spoilers for roll control, full span slotted flaps, cambered wingtips and an anti-servo rudder tab. These modifications allow shorter take-off and landing distances; minimum control speed is reduced by 16 per cent, the best rate of climb speed is lowered by 19 per cent, single-engine service ceiling is raised by 213 m (700 ft) and roll response is increased greatly at all speeds and configurations. A similar modification of the Seneca II was certificated during 1976.

More recent activities have entailed fitting full span trailing-edge flaps and spoilers for roll control on a Piper Cherokee SIX; and developing a high differential aileron droop Hi-Lift system for high performance single-engined aircraft, such as the Cessna Model P210 Pressurised Centurion. In this application a new and improved control mechanism droops both ailerons symmetrically to 15° when the trailing-edge flaps are extended to 20° for take-off. For roll control the ailerons travel up and down in high ratio differential: thus, with the control wheel fully to starboard, the starboard aileron moves up 42° to act as a spoiler (27° up from its normal faired position); at the same time the port aileron is deflected downward an additional 12° to a total of 27°. Ailerons are also drooped symmetrically by 15° when the trailing-edge flaps are extended to 30° for approach and landing.

Benefits from this advanced Hi-Lift system include a greatly reduced adverse yaw tendency in turns, and a high roll rate for more precise control when flaps are down and speed low. Control wheel forces are significantly less than with unmodified aircraft, due to a tailoring of aerodynamic forces on the up-moving aileron and a crossover cable which minimises friction in the control runs

Four stall strips, two on each wing, retain the desirable stall characteristics common to all Sierra Hi-Lift systems. For aircraft fitted with wing leading-edge de-icing boots, rubber strips are cemented to the rubber boots; when these are not fitted, aluminium stall strips are riveted to the wing leading-edge. A strip 130 mm (5 in) long, close to the wing root, initiates an early warning signal that the aircraft is approaching the stall. A longer strip, mounted further outboard and lower than the first, initiates the stall of the inboard and centre wing sections, while the outboard section and the wingtip are still unaffected by stall conditions. When the aircraft stalls it noses forward and down, under the complete control of ailerons which remain unstalled and effective for roll control.

The Sierra integrated high-lift and safety systems have been designed for easy field maintenance. They are designed to be applicable to almost the entire range of Cessna and Piper aircraft, and the Beechcraft Bonanza.

Full details of the basic Beech, Cessna and Piper airframes are given under the appropriate company headings in this and earlier editions of *Jane's*, and apply also to the Sierra versions, except for the added Hi-Lift systems as described. Weights and performance details of the Cessna and Piper range of Hi-Lift modifications are given in the accompanying tables. The conversions can be fitted as a retrospective modification to any of the models listed, irrespective of year.

Data for the modified Bonanzas are as follows:

WEIGHTS:
Weight empty, equipped:	
V35B	987 kg (2,176 lb)
A36	1,009 kg (2,225 lb)
Max T-O weight: V35B	1,542 kg (3,400 lb)
A36	1,633 kg (3,600 lb)

PERFORMANCE:
Max level speed:	
V35B	181 knots (335 km/h; 208 mph)
A36	177 knots (327 km/h; 204 mph)
Max cruising speed:	
V35B	176 knots (325 km/h; 202 mph)
A36	169 knots (313 km/h; 194 mph)
Stalling speed, wheels and flaps down:	
V35B	53 knots (98 km/h; 61 mph)
A36	54 knots (100 km/h; 62 mph)
Max rate of climb at S/L:	
V35B	343 m (1,125 ft)/min
A36	309 m (1,015 ft)/min
Service ceiling: V35B	5,445 m (17,858 ft)
A36	4,875 m (16,000 ft)
T-O run: V35B*	239 m (785 ft)
A36	276 m (904 ft)
T-O to 15 m (50 ft): V35B*	420 m (1,377 ft)
A36	485 m (1,590 ft)
Landing from 15 m (50 ft):	
V35B*	279 m (914 ft)
A36	305 m (1,000 ft)
Landing run: V35B*	146 m (478 ft)
A36	168 m (550 ft)
Max range, with optional long-range tanks:	
V35B	875 nm (1,620 km; 1,007 miles)
A36	833 nm (1,543 km; 958 miles)

*Normal operation

Beechcraft A36 Bonanza as certificated with Sierra Hi-Lift system, including full span flaps

Sierra/Cessna T210, showing clearly the high differential aileron droop Hi-Lift system

Sierra/Cessna Century V Eagle, a Citation 500 conversion with advanced wing aerofoil section and JT15D-4 turbofans

Sierra Industries conversion of the Piper Seneca II features full span trailing-edge flaps, with wing upper surface spoilers for roll control

SIERRA/CESSNA EAGLE, EAGLE SP, LONGWING and CENTURY V EAGLE

The Sierra **Eagle** (formerly Astec Eagle and R/STOL Eagle) conversion entails modifications to the wing contours of the Cessna Citation 500 and Citation I twin-turbofan executive transport aircraft.

Changes to the basic Citation 500 wing include use of an advanced technology aerofoil section of increased thickness and length over the inboard portion of the wing; wingtip extensions of 0.51 m (1 ft 8 in); and the addition of cove seals to the trailing-edge flaps. The thickened wing and the wingtip extensions contain an additional 392 kg (865 lb) of fuel, accounting for about 75 per cent of the approximate 600 nm (1,112 km; 691 mile) increase in range over the basic Citation 500. The remainder of the increase is due to improved aerodynamic efficiency of the Eagle wing.

The Sierra **Eagle SP** conversion introduces identical modifications to the Citation 501, which is certificated under FAR Pt 23 and approved for single-pilot operation.

The **Longwing** conversion was introduced in 1983 and uses the Eagle wingtip extensions on Citation 500 aircraft, but does not include the wingroot modifications. The conversion increases fuel capacity (by approximately 54 kg; 120 lb on aircraft c/n 001-213) and provides a 10 per cent increase in range. Rate of climb is also improved, and approach speeds reduced.

The **Century V Eagle** designation applies to the Sierra Eagle with its JT15D-1 or -1A power plant replaced by more powerful JT15D-4 engines, each of 11.12 kN (2,500 lb st). The production rate for Eagle conversions has been set at eight per year.

The description of the Citation I under Cessna's entry in this section applies also to the Eagle, except as follows:

WINGS: Thickness/chord ratio of inboard portions increased from 14% to 19%, and supercritical technology incorporated to improve wing/fuselage airflow. Span increased by comparison with Citation 500, by addition of wingtip extensions.

POWER PLANT: As for Citation 500, except increased fuel capacity provided in the thicker wing centre-section and wingtip extensions.

DIMENSIONS, EXTERNAL:

Wing span	14.35 m (47 ft 0½ in)
Wing chord: at root	2.95 m (9 ft 8⅛ in)
at tip	0.93 m (3 ft 0½ in)
Wing aspect ratio	7.92
Length overall	13.26 m (43 ft 6 in)
Height overall	4.36 m (14 ft 3¾ in)
Wheel track	3.84 m (12 ft 7⅛ in)
Wheelbase	4.78 m (15 ft 8¼ in)

WEIGHTS (A: JT15D-1, B: JT15D-1A, C: JT15D-4 power plant):

Weight empty: A, B	2,971 kg (6,550 lb)
C	3,016 kg (6,650 lb)
Max fuel weight: A, B, C	2,045 kg (4,510 lb)
Max T-O weight: A, B, C	5,670 kg (12,500 lb)
Max zero-fuel weight: A, B, C	4,309 kg (9,500 lb)
Max landing weight: A, B, C	5,148 kg (11,350 lb)

PERFORMANCE (at max T-O weight except where indicated):

Max cruising speed, AUW of 4,309 kg (9,500 lb), at 10,670 m (35,000 ft):

A	341 knots (631 km/h; 392 mph)
B	357 knots (661 km/h; 411 mph)
C	386 knots (715 km/h; 444 mph)

Cruising speed, AUW of 4,309 kg (9,500 lb), at 12,500 m (41,000 ft):

A	317 knots (587 km/h; 365 mph)
B	336 knots (623 km/h; 387 mph)
C	375 knots (695 km/h; 432 mph)

Stalling speed at max landing weight:

A, B, C	78 knots (145 km/h; 90 mph)

Max certificated altitude: A   10,670 m (35,000 ft)

B	12,500 m (41,000 ft)
C	13,105 m (43,000 ft)

Balanced T-O field length: A, B   907 m (2,975 ft)

C	762 m (2,500 ft)

FAA landing field length at max landing weight:

A, B, C	722 m (2,370 ft)

Max range, with 227 kg (500 lb) fuel reserves:

A	1,800 nm (3,336 km; 2,073 miles)
C	1,900 nm (3,521 km; 2,188 miles)

SIERRA VERSIONS OF CESSNA MODELS

	Weight empty equipped	Weight gross	Max level speed	Max cruising speed	Stalling speed, wheels and flaps down	Max rate of climb at S/L	Single-engine rate of climb at S/L	Service ceiling	T-O run	T-O to 15 m (50 ft)	Landing from 15 m (50 ft)	Landing run	Max range**	Min control speed
	kg (lb)	kg (lb)	knots (km/h; mph)	knots (km/h; mph)	knots (km/h; mph)	m (ft)/ min	m (ft)/ min	m (ft)	m (ft)	m (ft)	m (ft)	m (ft)	nm (km; miles)	knots (km/h; mph)
Model 150 and Commuter	449 (990)	725 (1,600)	110 (204; 127)	105 (195; 121)	26 (48.3; 30)	213 (700)		3,930 (12,900)	A 129 (422) B 161 (527)	A 248 (815) B 273 (895)	A 193 (632) B 230 (755)	A 90 (295) B 106 (348)	790 (1,464; 910)	
Model 172 and Skyhawk	572 (1,263)	1,043 (2,300)	126 (233; 145)	118 (219; 136)	28 (51.5; 32)	206 (675)		4,150 (13,600)	A 140 (460) B 175 (575)	A 274 (900) B 302 (990)	A 223 (730) B 267 (875)	A 92 (302) B 109 (356)	738 (1,367; 850)	
Model 172 and Skyhawk floatplane*	646 (1,425)	1,007 (2,220)	97 (180; 112)	94 (174; 108)	28 (51.5; 32)	191 (625)		3,765 (12,350)	A 256 (840) B 320 (1,050)	A 405 (1,330) B 451 (1,480)	A 267 (875) B 296 (970)	A 145 (475) B 171 (560)	477 (885; 550)	
Model 180 Skywagon	707 (1,560)	1,270 (2,800)	152 (282; 175)	144 (267; 166)	32.2 (60; 37)	364 (1,195)		6,215 (20,400)	A 110 (360) B 137 (450)	A 216 (710) B 239 (785)	A 207 (680) B 254 (835)	A 88 (290) B 104 (342)	1,098 (2,035; 1,265)	
Model 180 Skywagon floatplane	850 (1,875)	1,338 (2,950)	142 (264; 164)	133 (246; 153)	32.2 (60; 37)	332 (1,090)		5,425 (17,800)	A 245 (805) B 307 (1,006)	A 369 (1,210) B 402 (1,320)	A 254 (832) B 308 (1,010)	A 145 (475) B 171 (560)	1,063 (1,971; 1,225)	
Model 182 and Skylane	725 (1,599)	1,338 (2,950)	150 (278; 173)	143 (266; 165)	33 (62; 38)	288 (945)		5,610 (18,400)	A 131 (430) B 164 (537)	A 248 (815) B 270 (885)	A 237 (777) B 280 (920)	A 99 (325) B 117 (384)	1,050 (1,947; 1,210)	
Model 182 RG	800 (1,764)	1,412 (3,112)	187 (347; 215)	173 (321; 199)	42 (80; 48)	317 (1,040)		6,100 (20,000)	A 133 (435)	A 248 (815)	A 237 (777)	A 119 (389)	1,030 (1,909; 1,186)	
Model 185 Skywagon	721 (1,590)	1,519 (3,350)	159 (295; 183)	149 (277; 172)	34 (63; 39)	320 (1,050)		5,440 (17,850)	A 114 (375) B 143 (469)	A 233 (763) B 265 (870)	A 230 (755) B 271 (890)	A 95 (310) B 111 (365)	972 (1,802; 1,120)	
Model 185 Skywagon floatplane	866 (1,910)	1,505 (3,320)	149 (277; 172)	140 (259; 161)	34 (63; 39)	311 (1,020)		5,210 (17,100)	A 182 (596) B 227 (745)	A 332 (1,090) B 364 (1,195)	A 265 (870) B 326 (1,070)	A 146 (480) B 173 (566)	903 (1,673; 1,040)	
Model 188 Ag Wagon 230	836 (1,844)	1,723 (3,800)	124 (230; 143)	116 (214; 133)	38.5 (71; 44)	245 (805)		4,330 (14,200)	A 207 (680) B 259 (850)	A 338 (1,110) B 431 (1,420)	A 186 (610) B 256 (840)	A 94 (308) B 111 (363)	303 (563; 350)	
Model A188 Ag Wagon 300†	843 (1,859)	1,814 (4,000)	135 (251; 156)	127 (235; 146)	40 (74; 46)	302 (990)		4,905 (16,100)	A 183 (600) B 229 (750)	A 293 (960) B 381 (1,250)	A 186 (610) B 256 (840)	A 94 (308) B 111 (363)	390 (724; 450)	
Model 206 Stationair 6†	785 (1,732)	1,633 (3,600)	155 (288; 179)	148 (274; 170)	36 (66; 41)	296 (970)		4,695 (15,400)	A 147 (482) B 184 (603)	A 302 (990) B 352 (1,155)	A 226 (740) B 270 (885)	A 92 (301) B 108 (355)	916 (1,697; 1,055)	
Model 206 Stationair 6 floatplane	943 (2,080)	1,587 (3,500)	144 (267; 166)	136 (253; 157)	36 (66; 41)	276 (905)		4,450 (14,600)	A 248 (815) B 311 (1,019)	A 454 (1,490) B 486 (1,595)	A 280 (917) B 343 (1,125)	A 148 (485) B 174 (572)	833 (1,544; 960)	

A, B, *, **, †, see notes at end of Cessna table.

CESSNA MODELS—continued

	Weight empty equipped	Weight gross	Max level speed	Max cruising speed	Stalling speed, wheels and flaps down	Max rate of climb at S/L	Single-engine rate of climb at S/L	Service ceiling	T-O run	T-O to 15 m (50 ft)	Landing from 15 m (50 ft)	Landing run	Max range**	Min control speed
	kg (lb)	kg (lb)	knots (km/h; mph)	knots (km/h; mph)	knots (km/h; mph)	m (ft)/ min	m (ft)/ min	m (ft)	m (ft)	m (ft)	m (ft)	m (ft)	nm (km; miles)	knots (km/h; mph)
Model T206 Turbo Stationair 6	831 (1,832)	1,633 (3,600)	178 (330; 205)	163 (303; 188)	36 (66; 41)	322 (1,055)		8,260 (27,100)	A 148 (485) B 185 (606)	A 303 (995) B 358 (1,175)	A 226 (740) B 270 (885)	A 92 (301) B 108 (355)	963 (1,786; 1,110)	
Model T206 Turbo Stationair 6 floatplane	979 (2,160)	1,633 (3,600)	164 (304; 189)	148 (274; 170)	36 (66; 41)	311 (1,020)		7,650 (25,100)	A 241 (790) B 301 (987)	A 442 (1,450) B 475 (1,560)	A 283 (928) B 344 (1,130)	A 151 (495) B 178 (584)	911 (1,690; 1,050)	
Model 207 Skywagon and Stationair 7	862 (1,902)	1,723 (3,800)	150 (278; 173)	142 (264; 164)	38.5 (71; 44)	262 (860)		4,205 (13,800)	A 155 (510) B 194 (637)	A 332 (1,090) B 390 (1,280)	A 244 (800) B 298 (975)	A 97 (318) B 114 (375)	829 (1,536; 955)	
Model T207 Turbo Skywagon and Turbo Stationair 7	908 (2,002)	1,723 (3,800)	168 (312; 194)	156 (290; 180)	38.5 (71; 44)	277 (910)		7,650 (25,100)	A 155 (510) B 194 (637)	A 332 (1,090) B 390 (1,280)	A 244 (800) B 298 (975)	A 97 (318) B 114 (375)	812 (1,504; 935)	
Model 210 Centurion II	953 (2,102)	1,723 (3,800)	178 (330; 205)	167 (309; 192)	38.5 (71; 44)	274 (900)		4,905 (16,100)	A 155 (510) B 194 (637)	A 326 (1,070) B 376 (1,232)	A 239 (783) B 293 (960)	A 93 (305) B 110 (360)	1,137 (2,108; 1,310)	
Model T210 Turbo Centurion II	998 (2,202)	1,723 (3,800)	204 (378; 235)	192 (356; 221)	38.5 (71; 44)	293 (960)		9,020 (29,600)	A 160 (525) B 200 (656)	A 328 (1,075) B 401 (1,318)	A 239 (783) B 293 (960)	A 93 (305) B 110 (360)	1,133 (2,100; 1,305)	
Model P210 Pressurised Turbo Centurion II	1,008 (2,222)	1,723 (3,800)	204 (378; 235)	192 (356; 221)	49 (91; 57)	293 (960)		9,020 (29,600)	200 (656)	401 (1,318)	293 (960)	110 (360)	1,133 (2,100; 1,305)	
Model P210 Pressurised Centurion	1,064 (2,345)	1,822 (4,016)	206 (381; 237)	††	55 (102; 63)	283 (930)		7,010 (23,000)	366 (1,200)	607 (1,990)	271 (890)	424 (1,390)	925 (1,714; 1,065)	
Model 310R	1,701 (3,750)	2,495 (5,500)	237 (439; 273)	223 (414; 257)	64 (119; 74)	518 (1,700)	119 (390)	8,350 (27,400)	B 290 (950)	B 448 (1,470)	B 355 (1,165)	B 219 (720)	1,242 (2,301; 1,430)	69 (129; 80) CAS
Model 337 Super Skymaster	1,196 (2,638)	2,100 (4,630)	177 (328; 204)	168 (312; 194)	39 (72.5; 45)	369 (1,210)	99 (325)	6,125 (20,100)	A 130 (428) B 163 (535)	A 265 (870) B 322 (1,055)	A 273 (895) B 323 (1,060)	A 105 (343) B 123 (405)	†† ††	
Model T337 Turbo Super Skymaster	1,289 (2,843)	2,131 (4,700)	204 (378; 235)	200 (370; 230)	40 (74; 46)	353 (1,160)	93 (305)	9,265 (30,400)	A 136 (445) B 169 (556)	A 280 (920) B 332 (1,088)	A 273 (895) B 323 (1,060)	A 107 (352) B 126 (415)	†† ††	
Model T337 Pressurised Super Skymaster	1,315 (2,900)	2,132 (4,700)	217 (402; 250)	208 (385; 239)	40 (74; 46)	353 (1,160)	126 (415)	6,100 (20,000)	A 126 (413) B 157 (516)	A 280 (920) B 332 (1,088)	A 273 (895) B 323 (1,060)	A 107 (352) B 126 (415)	†† ††	
Model 340	1,878 (4,140)	2,717 (5,990)	242 (447; 278)	228 (421; 262)	61 (114; 71)	503 (1,650)	96 (315)	9,085 (29,800)					1,372 (2,542; 1,580)	75 (140; 87) CAS
Model 401/402	1,673 (3,690)	2,858 (6,300)	226 (420; 261)	208 (386; 240)	65.5 (121; 75)	491 (1,610)	69 (225)	7,980 (26,180)	A 240 (786) B 300 (983)	A 378 (1,240) B 472 (1,550)	A 354 (1,160) B 442 (1,450)	A 155 (510) B 183 (600)	†† ††	72 (134; 83) 72 (134; 83)
Model 402C	1,849 (4,076)	3,107 (6,850)	††	††	65 (121; 75)	442 (1,450)	91 (300)	9,145 (30,000)	329 (1,080)	533 (1,750)	427 (1,400)	259 (850)	1,220 (2,261; 1,405)	74 (137; 85)
Model 414	1,872 (4,126)	2,880 (6,350)	††	††	67 (124; 77)	457 (1,500)	61 (200)	7,925 (26,000)	A 278 (912) B 347 (1,140)	A 381 (1,250) B 465 (1,525)	A 340 (1,115) B 425 (1,395)	A 183 (600) B 276 (905)	†† ††	72 (134; 83) 72 (134; 83)
Model 414A	1,975 (4,354)	3,062 (6,750)	††	††	65 (121; 75)	480 (1,575)	88 (290)	9,145 (30,000)	329 (1,080)	533 (1,750)	405 (1,330)	238 (780)	1,300 (2,409; 1,497)	73 (135; 84)
Model 421A	1,932 (4,260)	3,102 (6,840)	240 (444; 276)	224 (414; 258)	69 (128; 79)	512 (1,680)	88 (290)	8,230 (27,000)	A 307 (1,008) B 384 (1,260)	A 443 (1,452) B 553 (1,815)	A 419 (1,375) B 524 (1,720)	A 208 (683) B 245 (804)	1,488 (2,756; 1,713) ††	83 (153; 95) 83 (153; 95)
Model 421B	2,011 (4,435)	3,379 (7,450)	245 (454; 282)	230 (426; 265)	71 (132; 82)	564 (1,850)	93 (305)	9,450 (31,000)	A 313 (1,028) B 365 (1,196)	A 428 (1,403) B 535 (1,754)	A 427 (1,400) B 534 (1,752)	A 134 (440) B 158 (517)	1,490 (2,762; 1,716) ††	78 (145; 90) 78 (145; 90)
Model 421C	2,173 (4,790)	3,379 (7,450)	256 (475; 295)	240 (444; 276)	71 (132; 82)	591 (1,940)	107 (350)	9,200 (30,200)	B 396 (1,300)	B 558 (1,830)	B 518 (1,700)	B 317 (1,040)	1,487 (2,755; 1,712)*	77 (143; 89) CAS

A: STOL operation.   B: normal operation.   *Available also with engines of increased horsepower.
**With optional long-range tanks fitted, if available.
†Leading-edge already installed by Cessna on current models.   ††No change from standard aircraft.

SIERRA VERSIONS OF PIPER MODELS

	Weight empty equipped	Weight gross	Max level speed	Max cruising speed	Stalling speed, wheels and flaps down	Max rate of climb at S/L	Single-engine rate of climb at S/L	Service ceiling	T-O run	T-O to 15 m (50 ft)	Landing from 15 m (50 ft)	Landing run	Max range**	Min control speed
	kg (lb)	kg (lb)	knots (km/h; mph)	knots (km/h; mph)	knots (km/h; mph)	m (ft)/ min	m (ft)/ min	m (ft)	m (ft)	m (ft)	m (ft)	m (ft)	nm (km; miles)	knots (km/h; mph)
PA-28-140 Cherokee	558 (1,232)	975 (2,150)	126 (223; 145)	120 (222; 138)	29 (53.2; 33)	206 (675)		4,480 (14,700)	A 171 (560) B 189 (620)	A 354 (1,160) B 404 (1,325)	A 192 (630) B 221 (725)	A 94 (310) B 110 (360)	†† ††	
PA-28-160 Cherokee	576 (1,270)	997 (2,200)	128 (237; 147)	121 (224; 139)	31 (56.5; 35)	216 (710)		4,970 (16,300)	A 152 (500) B 177 (580)	A 341 (1,120) B 390 (1,280)	A 204 (670) B 226 (740)	A 104 (340) B 114 (375)	†† ††	
PA-28-180 Cherokee	638 (1,406)	1,111 (2,450)	129 (238; 148)	122 (227; 141)	36 (66; 41)	221 (725)		4,313 (14,510)	A 165 (540) B 186 (610)	A 351 (1,150) B 399 (1,310)	A 238 (780) B 262 (860)	A 131 (430) B 146 (480)	596 (1,104; 686) ††	
PA-28R-180 Cherokee Arrow II	611 (1,349)	1,134 (2,500)	149 (275; 171)	142 (262; 163)	35 (64.5; 40)	270 (885)		4,695 (15,400)	A 171 (560) B 195 (640)	A 347 (1,140) B 396 (1,300)	A 259 (850) B 299 (980)	A 145 (475) B 168 (550)	911 (1,690; 1,050)	
PA-28R-200 Cherokee Arrow II	693 (1,528)	1,202 (2,650)	152 (282; 175)	143 (266; 165)	37 (69; 43)	274 (900)		4,570 (15,000)	A 175 (575) B 198 (650)	A 344 (1,130) B 393 (1,290)	A 283 (930) B 319 (1,045)	A 168 (550) B 187 (615)	782 (1,448; 900)	
PA-28-235 Cherokee 235	712 (1,570)	1,361 (3,000)	140 (259; 161)	132 (245; 152)	39 (72; 45)	244 (800)		3,660 (12,000)	A 168 (550) B 191 (625)	A 265 (870) B 302 (990)	A 274 (900) B 312 (1,025)	A 149 (490) B 171 (560)	926 (1,716; 1,066)	
PA-32-260 Cherokee SIX	783 (1,726)	1,542 (3,400)	144 (267; 166)	137 (254; 158)	38 (71; 44)	259 (850)		4,420 (14,500)	A 180 (590) B 238 (780)	A 317 (1,040) B 341 (1,120)	A 247 (810) B 267 (875)	A 155 (510) B 171 (560)	964 (1,786; 1,110)	
PA-32-300 Cherokee SIX	825 (1,819)	1,542 (3,400)	151 (280; 174)	146 (270; 168)	38 (71; 44)	320 (1,050)		4,955 (16,250)	A 171 (560) B 226 (740)	A 299 (980) B 320 (1,050)	A 247 (810) B 267 (875)	A 158 (520) B 168 (550)	921 (1,706; 1,060)	
PA-24-180 Comanche	694 (1,530)	1,157 (2,550)	149 (277; 172)	143 (266; 165)	35 (64; 40)	293 (960)		5,850 (19,200)	A 183 (600) B 302 (990)	A 324 (1,065) B 475 (1,560)	A 262 (860) B 326 (1,070)	A 128 (420) B 149 (490)	868 (1,609; 1,000)	
PA-24-250 Comanche	776 (1,710)	1,315 (2,900)	168 (311; 193)	161 (298; 185)	35.5 (66; 41)	427 (1,400)		6,310 (20,700)	A 187 (615) B 290 (950)	A 296 (970) B 389 (1,275)	A 256 (840) B 347 (1,140)	A 140 (460) B 213 (700)	1,537 (2,848; 1,770)	
PA-24-260 Comanche	812 (1,792)	1,451 (3,200)	174 (322; 200)	164 (304; 189)	36 (66; 41)	410 (1,345)		6,355 (20,850)	A 200 (655) B 302 (990)	A 338 (1,110) B 401 (1,315)	A 268 (880) B 360 (1,180)	A 152 (500) B 226 (740)	1,137 (2,108; 1,310)	
PA-24-260 Turbo Comanche	821 (1,810)	1,451 (3,200)	213 (394; 245)	201 (372; 231)	36 (66; 41)	410 (1,345)		7,620 (25,000)	A 200 (655) B 302 (990)	A 338 (1,110) B 401 (1,315)	A 268 (880) B 360 (1,180)	A 152 (500) B 226 (740)	1,306 (2,422; 1,505)	
PA-24-400 Comanche	966 (2,130)	1,633 (3,600)	196 (364; 226)	189 (351; 218)	39 (72; 45)	506 (1,660)		6,155 (20,200)	A 126 (415) B 168 (550)	A 233 (765) B 271 (890)	A 303 (995) B 379 (1,245)	A 184 (605) B 216 (710)	1,568 (2,905; 1,805)	
PA-30 Twin Comanche*	1,022 (2,253)	1,724 (3,800)	158 (293; 182)	153 (283; 176)	45 (84; 52)	427 (1,400)	79 (260)	6,100 (20,000)	B 206 (675)	B 341 (1,120)	B 355 (1,165)	B 186 (610)	1,481 (2,744; 1,705)	69 (129; 80)
PA-30 Turbo Twin Comanche*	1,088 (2,399)	1,724 (3,800)	213 (394; 245)	197 (365; 227)	45 (84; 52)	427 (1,400)	69 (225)	7,620 (25,000)	B 206 (675)	B 341 (1,120)	B 355 (1,165)	B 186 (610)	1,528 (2,832; 1,760)	69 (129; 80)
PA-39 Twin Comanche C/R*	1,022 (2,253)	1,724 (3,800)	181 (336; 209)	174 (322; 200)	45 (84; 52)	445 (1,460)	79 (260)	6,100 (20,000)	B 206 (675)	B 320 (1,050)	B 355 (1,165)	B 186 (610)	1,468 (2,720; 1,690)	65 (121; 75)
PA-39 Turbo Twin Comanche C/R*	1,088 (2,399)	1,724 (3,800)	212 (393; 244)	197 (365; 227)	45 (84; 52)	427 (1,400)	69 (225)	7,620 (25,000)	B 158 (520)	B 323 (1,060)	B 355 (1,165)	B 189 (620)	1,515 (2,808; 1,745)	65 (121; 75)
PA-23-235 Aztec	1,241 (2,735)	2,177 (4,800)	182 (338; 210)	175 (325; 202)	40 (74; 46)	465 (1,525)	62 (205)	5,515 (18,100)	B 210 (690)	B 331 (1,085)	B 381 (1,250)	B 195 (640)	1,090 (2,020; 1,255)	54 (98; 62)
PA-E23-250 Aztec	1,339 (2,953)	2,266 (4,995)	197 (365; 227)	191 (354; 220)	41 (76; 47)	509 (1,670)	99 (325)	6,615 (21,700)	B 190 (625)	B 315 (1,035)	B 395 (1,295)	B 203 (665)	1,112 (2,060; 1,80)	56 (103; 64)
PA-23-250 Aztec	1,326 (2,925)	2,359 (5,200)	188 (348; 216)	179 (332; 206)	45.5 (84; 52)	491 (1,610)	85 (280)	6,035 (19,800)	B 195 (640)	B 323 (1,060)	B 395 (1,295)	B 203 (665)	916 (1,697; 1,055)	56 (105; 65)
PA-23-250 Turbo Aztec	1,397 (3,080)	2,359 (5,200)	222 (412; 256)	182 (388; 210)	43 (79; 49)	372 (1,220)	64 (210)	9,145 (30,000)	B 195 (640)	B 323 (1,060)	B 395 (1,295)	B 203 (665)	1,050 (1,947; 1,210)	56 (105; 65)
PA-34 Seneca I	1,160 (2,557)	1,905 (4,200)	170 (315; 196)	162 (300; 187)	58 (106; 66)	414 (1,360)	57 (190)	5,730 (18,800)	B 195 (640)	B 320 (1,050)	B 381 (1,250)	B 196 (645)	743 (1,378; 856)	57 (106; 65)
PA-34 Seneca II	1,280 (2,823)	2,073 (4,570)	195 (361; 225)	190 (352; 219)	66 (122; 76)	421 (1,380)	67 (220)	7,620 (25,000)	B 198 (650)	B 332 (1,090)	B 573 (1,880)	B 213 (700)	882 (1,633; 1,015)†	57 (106; 65)

A: STOL operation.   B: normal operation.   *Available also with engines of increased horsepower.
**With optional long-range tanks fitted, if available.
†1,192 (2,207; 1,371) with optional long-range tanks.   ††No change from standard aircraft.

SIKORSKY

SIKORSKY AIRCRAFT, DIVISION OF UNITED TECHNOLOGIES CORPORATION

6900 North Main Street, Stratford, Connecticut 06601-1381
Telephone: (203) 386 4000
Telex: 96 4372
OTHER WORKS: Fort Rucker, Alabama; Tallassee, Alabama; Troy, Alabama; South Avenue, Bridgeport, Connecticut; Shelton, Connecticut; Sikorsky Memorial Airport, Stratford, Connecticut; and Development Flight Test Center, West Palm Beach, Florida
PRESIDENT: Eugene Buckley
SENIOR VICE-PRESIDENTS:
  Robert C. Harris (Business Integration and Planning)
  Ray D. Leoni (Engineering and Operations)
VICE-PRESIDENT, INTERNATIONAL MARKETING:
  John A. Kerns
VICE-PRESIDENT, RESEARCH AND ENGINEERING:
  Kenneth C. Mard
VICE-PRESIDENT, AVIONICS SYSTEMS INTEGRATION:
  William E. McClure
VICE-PRESIDENT, COMMERCIAL MARKETING:
  Mackie D. Mott
VICE-PRESIDENT, GOVERNMENT BUSINESS DEVELOPMENT:
  Gary F. Rast
DIRECTOR OF COMMUNICATIONS: Robert Stangarone
MANAGER OF PUBLIC RELATIONS: Martin H. Moore

Founded on 5 March 1923 by the late Igor I. Sikorsky as the Sikorsky Aero Engineering Corporation, this company has been a division of United Technologies since 1929. It became involved in helicopter production in the 1940s, since which time it has produced more than 6,000 rotating-wing aircraft.

Sikorsky's company headquarters and main plant are at Stratford, Connecticut, with a secondary facility nearby at Bridgeport. Development flight test, commercial service and training centres are at West Palm Beach, Florida, where UTC subsidiary Pratt & Whitney has its military engine operation. Employment at all Sikorsky facilities totalled about 16,000 in 1988, making the company the largest helicopter manufacturer outside the Soviet Union. Current production is centred on the UH-60A Black Hawk and its derivatives, the CH-53E Super Stallion heavy lift helicopter and its derivatives, and the S-76 series.

On 3 June 1985 Sikorsky signed a memorandum of understanding with Boeing Helicopters to bid jointly for development of the US Army's LHX helicopter.

Sikorsky licensees include Westland of Great Britain, Agusta of Italy, Aérospatiale of France, MBB in West Germany, Mitsubishi of Japan, and Pratt & Whitney Canada Ltd. In the Summer of 1983 Sikorsky and Brazilian manufacturer Embraer signed an agreement for the transfer of technology involved in the design and manufacture of components made from composites materials. In June 1984 Sikorsky and Construcciones Aeronauticas SA (CASA) signed a memorandum of understanding to establish a long term helicopter industrial co-operation programme in Spain. CASA builds tail rotor pylon, tailcone and stabiliser components for the H-60 and S-70 helicopters, and has responsibility for final assembly and test flying of Sikorsky helicopters supplied to Spain, which ordered six S-70Bs for delivery in 1987-88. The first CASA manufactured S-70 components were delivered to Sikorsky in early January 1986.

On 12 February 1986 shareholders of Westland PLC (see United Kingdom section) approved a joint Sikorsky/Fiat plan involving financial and technical support and minor equity participation in the British company. Under the terms of the agreement Westland is licensed to manufacture the S-70 series of helicopters.

In February 1988 Sikorsky announced plans to establish an S-76 production line in South Korea within five years. A new company, Daewoo-Sikorsky Aerospace Ltd (DSA), has been established, with a production facility at Chang-Won in which civil and military variants of the S-76 will be manufactured.

SIKORSKY S-61/SH-3 SEA KING

Manufacture of the S-61 series by Sikorsky has ended, but various military and commercial models remain in production by Agusta in Italy, Mitsubishi in Japan, and Westland in the UK, under whose entries they are described or listed.

As a follow-on to an earlier US Navy programme that upgraded 119 SH-3s to SH-3H configuration, Agusta has a contract for one prototype and 11 production Service Life Extension Programme (SLEP) kits to convert US Navy SH-3Ds to SH-3H standard. A further 14 kits will be produced by Sikorsky. During the upgrade, each aircraft will also be fitted with new sonobuoy launcher, acoustic signal receiver, MAD, data link, UHF radio, AHRS, sonar and flight refuelling system.

SIKORSKY H-53E

US Navy designations: CH-53E Super Stallion and MH-53E Sea Dragon

The **CH-53E Super Stallion** is a major development of the US Marine Corps' CH-53D Stallion twin-engined heavy duty transport helicopter, last described in the 1978-79 *Jane's*. The longer fuselage of the CH-53E, its different rotor system, three engines, uprated transmission

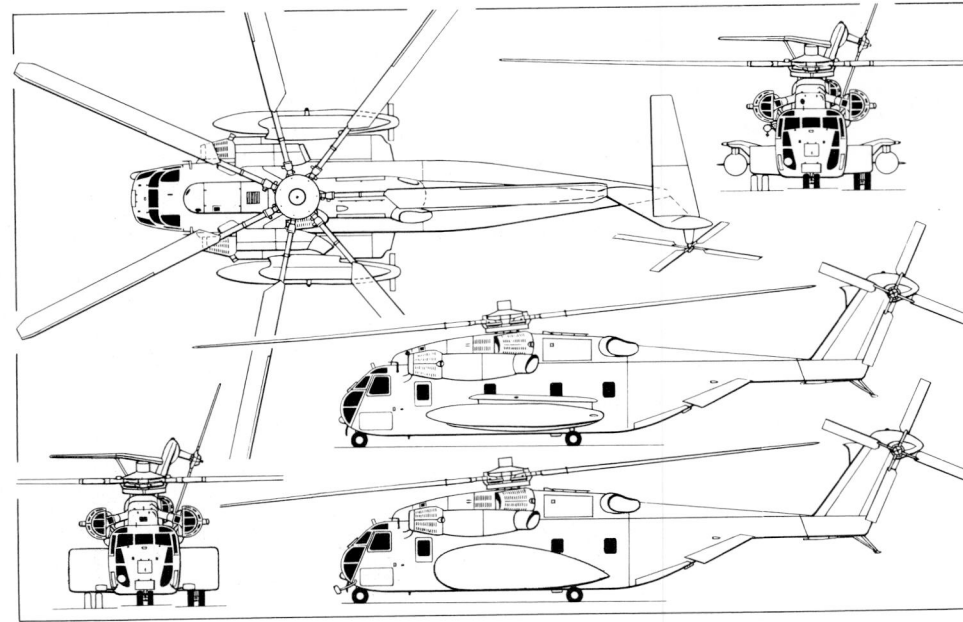

Sikorsky CH-53E Super Stallion, with lower side view and lower front view of MH-53E Sea Dragon (*Pilot Press*). **See page 487 for details of S-80 export versions**

Sikorsky CH-53E Super Stallion heavy-lift helicopter of the US Marine Corps with flight refuelling nose-probe retracted

and doubled lift capability make it the largest and most powerful helicopter yet put into production outside the Soviet Union.

Sikorsky received initial US Navy funding in 1973 to proceed with Phase I of the CH-53E development programme, and the first of two YCH-53E prototypes flew for the first time on 1 March 1974. The first production prototype flew on 8 December 1975, and the second in March 1976. Fourteen production CH-53Es (first flight 13 December 1980) were ordered in 1978, and deliveries to the US Marine Corps began on 16 June 1981. A total of 107 had been funded up to and including FY 1988, of which Sikorsky had delivered 93 to the US Marine Corps and Navy. A further seven CH-53Es were included in the FY 1989 budget request. Total requirement is for 125 production CH-53Es.

The US Marine Corps operates the CH-53E in an amphibious assault role. Although capable of carrying up to 55 fully armed troops, its primary role is the transport of

heavy equipment and armament, and retrieval of disabled aircraft. The US Navy uses it for vertical onboard delivery (VOD), transport duties, and removal of damaged aircraft from aircraft carriers. Operational use, in the Mediterranean area, began in Summer 1983.

Planned improvements for the CH-53E include all-composites tail rotor blades, uprated General Electric T64-416 power plants, Omega navigation system, ground proximity warning system, flight crew night vision system, and improvements to the internal cargo handling system. Missile alerting system, chaff/flare decoy ejectors, a nitrogen fuel inerting system and the ability to refill the hydraulic system from the cargo hold will also be incorporated. The modified CH-53Es may also be equipped with air-to-air missiles for self defence. Initial firing trials with an AIM-9 Sidewinder missile have been conducted at the Naval Air Test Center, NAS Patuxent River, Maryland.

In June 1986 Sikorsky began full scale development of a helicopter night vision system (HNVS) for the CH-53E, in

First Sikorsky MH-53E Sea Dragon airborne mine countermeasures helicopter delivered to US Navy

co-operation with Northrop's Electro-Mechanical Division. The HNVS comprises a Martin Marietta pilot night vision system, Honeywell integrated helmet and display sighting system and equipment developed by Northrop for the Bell AH-1S surrogate trainer programme. The HNVS will permit low-level night operations in adverse weather. Ground testing of an HNVS equipped CH-53E was scheduled to begin in August 1988, with flight testing following two months later and a US Navy operational evaluation programme commencing in August 1989.

The **MH-53E Sea Dragon** is an airborne mine countermeasures (AMCM) version of the Super Stallion able to tow through the water mechanical, acoustic and magnetic hydrofoil sweeping gear. Its early history was described in the 1982-83 *Jane's*. The MH-53E has enlarged sponsons to carry nearly 3,785 litres (1,000 US gallons; 833 Imp gallons) more fuel; improved hydraulic and electrical systems; and minefield, navigational and AFC systems, including automatic tow couplers and automatic approach to/depart from hover features to enhance its AMCM capabilities. The first pre-production MH-53E made its initial flight on 1 September 1983. Deliveries to the US Navy began on 26 June 1986 and the MH-53E entered operational service with HM-12 on 1 April 1987. Another MH-53E delivered to HM-12 (now the AMCM training unit) in Spring 1987 was the 100th H-53E. The combined fleet of CH-53Es and MH-53Es had by then logged more than 90,000 flying hours. Current operational units are HM-14 (Atlantic Fleet) and HM-15 (Pacific Fleet).

Twenty-four production MH-53Es were funded in FY 1985-88 (2, 10, 4 and 8 respectively), with a further seven requested in FY 1989. Production of the CH-53E was halted for a period between October 1986 and July 1988, to concentrate entirely on the MH-53E, of which more may be ordered during FY 1990. Japan plans to acquire up to 12 helicopters similar to the MH-53E (see S-80 entry).

The following details refer to the CH-53E, but are generally applicable also to the MH-53E, except for the changes listed in the previous paragraphs:

TYPE: Triple-turbine heavy duty multi-purpose helicopter.

ROTOR SYSTEM AND TRANSMISSION: Fully articulated seven-blade main rotor. Blade twist 14°. Each blade has a titanium spar, Nomex honeycomb core and glassfibre epoxy composite skin. Sikorsky blade inspection method (BIM) embodied, utilising pressurised spar. Titanium and steel main rotor head. Hydraulic power folding system for main rotor blades. Four-blade aluminium tail rotor mounted on pylon canted 20° to port. Main gearbox is mounted in blister above main cabin and is rated at 10,067 kW (13,500 shp) for T-O. Rotor brake standard.

FUSELAGE: Watertight semi-monocoque primary structure of light alloy, steel and titanium. Separate cockpit section of glassfibre/epoxy composite. Extensive use of Kevlar for rotor/transmission blister and engine cowlings. Tail rotor pylon folds hydraulically to starboard side. Fuselage stressed to withstand crash force of 20g vertically and 10g laterally.

TAIL SURFACE: Strut braced stabiliser of gull-wing type on starboard side of inclined tail rotor pylon. Stabiliser and pylon made of Kevlar.

LANDING GEAR: Retractable tricycle type, with twin wheels on each unit. Main units retract into rear of sponsons on each side of fuselage. Fully castoring nosewheels.

POWER PLANT: Three General Electric T64-GE-416 turbo-shafts, each with a max rating of 3,266 kW (4,380 shp) for 10 min, intermediate rating of 3,091 kW (4,145 shp) for 30 min and max continuous power rating of 2,756 kW (3,696 shp). Self-sealing bladder fuel cell in forward part of each sponson, each with capacity of 1,192 litres (315 US gallons; 262 Imp gallons). Additional two-cell unit, with capacity of 1,465 litres (387 US gallons; 322 Imp gallons) brings total standard internal capacity to 3,849 litres (1,017 US gallons; 847 Imp gallons). (Total internal capacity of MH-53E is 12,113 litres; 3,200 US gallons; 2,664 Imp gallons.) Optional drop tank outboard of each sponson of CH-53E, total capacity 4,921 litres (1,300 US gallons; 1,082 Imp gallons). (MH-53E can carry seven internal range extension tanks, total capacity 7,949 litres; 2,100 US gallons; 1,748 Imp gallons.) Forward extendable probe for in-flight refuelling. Alternatively, aircraft can refuel by hoisting hose from surface vessel while hovering.

ACCOMMODATION: Crew of three. Main cabin will accommodate up to 55 troops on folding canvas seats along walls and in centre of cabin. Door on forward starboard side of main cabin. Hydraulically operated rear loading ramp. Typical freight loads include seven standard 102 × 122 cm (3 ft 4 in × 4 ft) pallets. Single-point central hook for slung cargo, capacity 16,330 kg (36,000 lb).

SYSTEMS: Hydraulic system, with four pumps, for collective, cyclic pitch, roll, yaw and feel augmentation flight control servo mechanisms; engine starters; landing gear actuation; cargo winches; loading ramp; and blade and tail pylon folding. System pressure 207 bars (3,000 lb/sq in), except for engine starter system which is rated at 276 bars (4,000 lb/sq in). (Separate hydraulic system in MH-53E to power AMCM equipment.) Electrical system includes three 115V 400Hz 40-60kVA AC alternators, and two 28V 200A transformer-rectifiers for DC power. Solar APU.

AVIONICS AND EQUIPMENT: Hamilton Standard automatic flight control system, using two digital onboard computers and a four-axis autopilot. Equipment in MH-53E includes Westinghouse AN/AQS-14 towed sonar, AN/AQS-17 mine neutralisation device, AN/ALQ-141 electronic sweep, and Edo AN/ALQ-166 towed hydrofoil sled for detonating magnetic mines.

DIMENSIONS, EXTERNAL (CH-53E and MH-53E):

Main rotor diameter	24.08 m (79 ft 0 in)
Main rotor blade chord	0.76 m (2 ft 6 in)
Tail rotor diameter	6.10 m (20 ft 0 in)
Length overall, rotors turning	30.19 m (99 ft 0½ in)
Length, rotor and tail pylon folded	18.44 m (60 ft 6 in)
Length of fuselage	22.35 m (73 ft 4 in)
Width of fuselage	2.69 m (8 ft 10 in)
Width, rotor and tail pylon folded:	
CH-53E	8.66 m (28 ft 5 in)
MH-53E	8.41 m (27 ft 7 in)
Height to top of main rotor head	5.32 m (17 ft 5½ in)
Height overall, tail rotor turning	8.97 m (29 ft 5 in)
Height, rotor and tail pylon folded	5.66 m (18 ft 7 in)
Wheel track (c/l of shock struts)	3.96 m (13 ft 0 in)
Wheelbase	8.31 m (27 ft 3 in)

DIMENSIONS, INTERNAL (CH-53E and MH-53E):

Cabin:

Length (rear ramp/door hinge to fwd bulkhead)	
	9.14 m (30 ft 0 in)
Max width	2.29 m (7 ft 6 in)
Max height	1.98 m (6 ft 6 in)

AREAS (CH-53E and MH-53E):

Main rotor disc	455.38 m² (4,901.7 sq ft)
Tail rotor disc	29.19 m² (314.2 sq ft)

WEIGHTS:

Weight empty: CH-53E	15,072 kg (33,228 lb)
MH-53E	16,482 kg (36,336 lb)
Internal payload (100 nm; 185 km; 115 miles radius):	
CH-53E	13,607 kg (30,000 lb)
External payload (50 nm; 92.5 km; 57.5 miles radius):	
CH-53E	14,515 kg (32,000 lb)
Max external payload: CH-53E	16,330 kg (36,000 lb)
Useful load, influence sweep mission:	
MH-53E	11,793 kg (26,000 lb)
Max T-O weight (CH-53E and MH-53E):	
internal payload	31,640 kg (69,750 lb)
external payload	33,340 kg (73,500 lb)

Sikorsky HH-53H Pave Low III, to which the new MH-53J will be generally similar

PERFORMANCE (CH-53E and MH-53E, ISA, at T-O weight
of 25,400 kg; 56,000 lb):
Max level speed at S/L   170 knots (315 km/h; 196 mph)
Cruising speed at S/L   150 knots (278 km/h; 173 mph)
Max rate of climb at S/L, 11,340 kg (25,000 lb) payload
                                762 m (2,500 ft)/min
Service ceiling at max continuous power
                                5,640 m (18,500 ft)
Hovering ceiling at max power:
  IGE   3,520 m (11,550 ft)
  OGE   2,895 m (9,500 ft)
Self-ferry range, unrefuelled, at optimum cruise condition
for best range:
  CH-53E   1,120 nm (2,075 km; 1,290 miles)

SIKORSKY MH-53J

As one element of a programme to upgrade the combat
rescue and recovery fleet of the USAF Special Operations
Forces, Sikorsky is converting all 31 remaining twin-
turboshaft HH-53B/C Super Jolly Green Giant helicopters
to a new **MH-53J** Pave Low Enhanced configuration.
They will be generally similar to the eleven MH-53H Pave
Low III helicopters converted earlier by Sikorsky, of which
one is shown in an accompanying illustration. For night and
adverse weather operation, these aircraft have an inertial
navigation system, stabilised FLIR, Doppler navigation
equipment, a computer projected map display, and radar
from an A-7D Corsair II in an offset thimble radome on the
nose. The first was delivered in Summer 1987.

SIKORSKY S-70A

**US Army designations: UH-60A Black Hawk,
EH-60A and MH-60K**
**US Air Force designation: UH-60A, MH-60G Pave
Hawk**
US Marine Corps designation: VH-60A

A detailed account of the development and early history
of the S-70/UH-60A can be found in the 1982-83 and earlier
editions of *Jane's*. The helicopter was designed to meet the
US Army's Utility Tactical Transport Aircraft System
(UTTAS) requirement for an aircraft capable of carrying all
the elements of an 11-man infantry squad, to replace the
UH-1 Iroquois. The first of three Sikorsky YUH-60A
prototypes flew for the first time on 17 October 1974. After
fly-off evaluation against prototypes of a Boeing Vertol
competitor, the Sikorsky design was declared the winner on
23 December 1976.

The initial, and major, production version is:

UH-60A Black Hawk. Assault transport version for
the US Army. First production example flown in October
1978. Designed primarily to carry 11 fully equipped troops
plus a crew of three. Large cabin enables it also to be used
without modification for medical evacuation, reconnaissance, command and control purposes or troop resupply.
For external lift missions its cargo hook has a capacity of up
to 3,630 kg (8,000 lb). Design is compact, so that the
helicopter itself can be airlifted over long ranges. One can be
carried in a C-130 Hercules, two in a C-141 StarLifter and
six in a C-5 Galaxy, using Sikorsky developed air
transportability kits. In January 1988 Sikorsky was
awarded a third multi-year contract for 252 UH-60As,
bringing the total contracted to 1,107. The US Army
anticipates a total procurement of 2,251 aircraft. By
February 1988, Black Hawk deliveries exceeded 900. By
that time US Army Black Hawks had logged more than
650,000 flight hours.

The UH-60A is deployed with the 101st Airborne
Division (Air Assault) at Fort Campbell, Kentucky; 82nd
Airborne Division at Fort Bragg, North Carolina; Ninth
Infantry Division at Fort Lewis, Washington; 24th Infantry
Division at Fort Stewart, Georgia; with US Army forces in
Hawaii, Korea, Panama and West Germany; and with
Army National Guard aviation units in Alaska, Arizona,
Kentucky, North Carolina, Ohio, Oklahoma and Virginia.
Eight medical evacuation kits for installation in Black
Hawks were delivered to the US Army in 1981, two of the
kits equipping aircraft delivered to the 326th Medical
Battalion, Fort Campbell, Kentucky. This Battalion will
eventually have 12 medevac equipped aircraft which, in
addition to being used for training in military medevac
missions, will also be available to provide medical
evacuation assistance to civil authorities in parts of Indiana,
Illinois, Kentucky and Tennessee.

A hover infra-red suppressor subsystem (HIRSS), which
cools the engine exhaust so that it no longer presents a target
for heat-seeking missiles, is installed on current production
aircraft and will be retrofitted to earlier UH-60s. The system
does not require the helicopter to be in forward motion for
effectiveness, as earlier IR suppressing systems did. By June
1987 Sikorsky had completed missile qualification for the
Hellfire anti-armour missile which had been launched from
UH-60As in forward, rearward and sideways flight, in the
hover at night, and with the pilot wearing night vision
goggles. Test firings had also been completed to evaluate the
Airborne Target Handover System (ATHS) which allows
for digital burst communications between a designating
aircraft and the firing aircraft. US Army development
testing of ATHS was scheduled to begin in July 1987.
Exterior and interior lighting systems compatible with night
vision goggles have been incorporated on production
UH-60As from November 1985 and have been retrofitted to
earlier production aircraft. Testing of a Honeywell Volcano

Sikorsky UH-60A Black Hawk with underslung load of field gun and ammunition

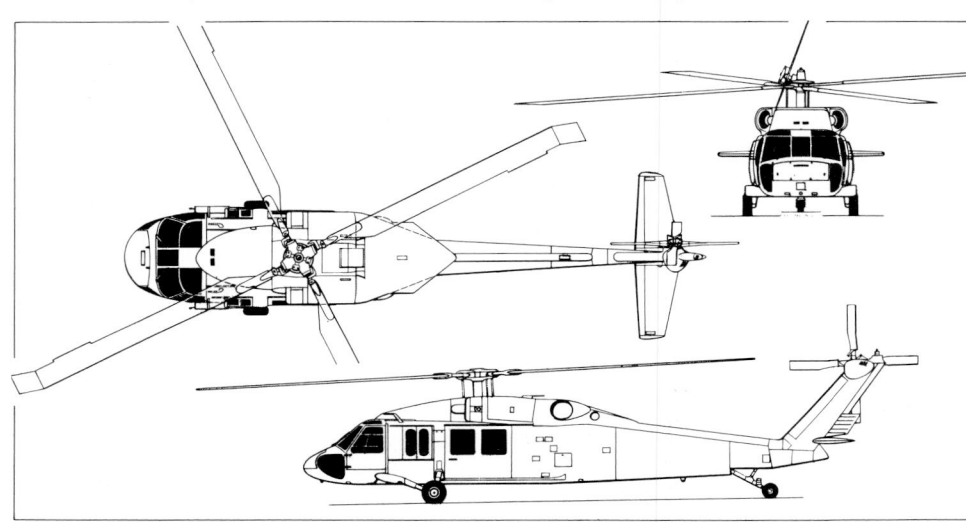

Sikorsky UH-60A Black Hawk combat assault helicopter *(Pilot Press)*

multiple delivery mine system was completed in early 1987,
and US Army development testing of the system began in
July 1987. Volcano dispenses up to 960 Gator anti-tank and
anti-personnel mines from externally mounted expendable
canisters on each side of the fuselage.

A usage monitor, which measures certain rotor loadings,
is being installed on 30 UH-60As to enable the US Army
and Sikorsky to determine optimum replacement times for
dynamic components. During 1987 a wire strike protection
system and an accident data recorder system were being
tested on the UH-60A. Data recorders were to be
incorporated on UH-60As and EH-60As during the course
of the year.

The basic design of the UH-60A has proved suitable for a
number of derivatives, as follows:

EH-60A. In October 1980, Sikorsky received a US Army
contract to prepare a YEH-60A prototype for the
installation of 816 kg (1,800 lb) of Quick Fix IIB electronic
countermeasures equipment designed to intercept, locate,
monitor and jam enemy battlefield communications. Prime
contractor for the AN/ALQ-151 ECM kit was Electronic
Systems Laboratories, a subsidiary of TRW. The equipment
includes four dipole antennae mounted beneath the fuselage
together with a deployable whip antenna, and a data bank
in the cabin. A hover infra-red suppressor subsystem
(HIRSS) is standard. The YEH-60A flew for the first time
on 24 September 1981. In October 1984 Tracor Aerospace
Group was awarded a $51 million contract for the
conversion of an initial quantity of 40 UH-60As to EH-60A
ECM/ESM configuration. Tracor produces, integrates and

installs the ECM/ESM systems, and flight tests the
converted helicopters. The first production EH-60A was
delivered on 28 July 1987, as an element of the US Army's
special electronics mission aircraft (SEMA) programme.
Sixty-six had been funded by FY 1987. The programme was
terminated in 1988.

VH-60A. Nine aircraft for US Marine Corps (first flight
6 October 1987), to replace Bell VH-1Ns of the Executive
Flight Detachment of Marine Helicopter Squadron One
(HMX-1) at Quantico, Virginia.

MH-60G Pave Hawk. Designation for 20 aircraft,
delivered originally as UH-60As, which began to enter
service with USAF's 55th Aerospace Rescue and Recovery
Squadron at Eglin AFB, Florida, in 1982-83 as an interim
remedy for a shortfall in rescue helicopters. The USAF
has contracted Sikorsky Support Services Inc of Troy,
Alabama, to modify these to MH-60G Pave Hawks to
incorporate an aerial refuelling probe, 443 litre (117 US
gallon; 97.5 Imp gallon) internal auxiliary fuel tank and a
fuel management panel. All will be fitted eventually with
Doppler/INS, an electronic map display, Tacan, RDR-14
lightweight weather/ground mapping radar, secure HF and
Satcom, 0.50 in machine-guns and Pave Low III FLIR, as
installed in the MH-53H/J. The Pave Hawk programme
replaces that for the HH-60A Night Hawk (see 1987-88
Jane's), which did not receive DoD funding.

MH-60K. In January 1988 Sikorsky received a contract
from the US Army to build and test fly a prototype
MH-60K special operations aircraft (SOA) based on the
Black Hawk. Due to fly in early 1990, the helicopter will

feature an extended range fuel system, air-to-air refuelling capability, integrated avionics system with modernised CRT displays, Hughes AN/AAQ-16 FLIR, Texas Instruments AN/APQ-168 terrain following radar, and uprated engines and gearbox. Armament will include two 0.50 in machine-guns and provision for Stinger air-to-air missiles. An initial procurement of 22 MH-60Ks is anticipated by the US Army, with options for a further 38.

UH-60B. Proposed new variant of UH-60A for US Army, under development. Major design improvements proposed include an advanced composites main rotor system, with blades of increased area having a Boeing aerofoil section inboard, Sikorsky swept-taper tips, carbonfibre reinforced spars, and a glassfibre-skinned Nomex core; improved durability gearbox; strengthened flight controls; advanced cockpit with CRT displays and integrated avionics; improved forward view from cockpit; wire strike protection; self defence systems including General Dynamics ATAS missiles; enhanced safety systems; and General Electric T700-GE-701C uprated engines. Predicted max T-O weight is 10,750 kg (23,700 lb). If adopted, deliveries of US Army UH-60Bs could begin by July 1991.

SH-60B Seahawk. US Navy ASW/ASST helicopter, described separately.

SH-60F Ocean Hawk. US Navy 'CV-Helo' version to replace SH-3H Sea King. See Seahawk entry.

HH-60H. Combat search and rescue/special warfare helicopter for US Navy. See Seahawk entry.

HH-60J. Medium range rescue helicopter for US Coast Guard. See Seahawk entry.

S-70A. Tactical utility version of UH-60A, in production for the export market. Two **S-70A-5s** have been delivered to the air force of the Philippines. The Royal Australian Air Force has ordered 39 **S-70A-9s**, to replace Bell UH-1s, with deliveries commencing in October 1987 and continuing at the rate of two per month until late 1990. These have General Electric T700-GE-701A-1 turboshafts, a modified SH-60B flight control system, external rescue hoist, main rotor brake, folding tail pylon, special communications and navigation equipment and ESSS. No. 9 Squadron, based at Townsville, Queensland, was the first RAAF unit to receive the S-70A-9. The first aircraft, completed by Sikorsky at Stratford, flew on 11 September 1987 and was delivered on 22 February 1988. Assembly and testing of the remaining 38 aircraft are being performed in Australia by Hawker de Havilland. The Black Hawks will be transferred to the Royal Australian Army in early 1989, although the RAAF will still be responsible for their maintenance. In July 1988 five Black Hawks were delivered to the Colombian Air Force for anti-narcotics operations. In March 1988 Israel announced that it had selected the S-70A to replace Israeli Air Force Bell 212 helicopters, and on 25 May the US Army awarded Sikorsky an FMS contract for 12 "UH-60 aircraft modified to **Desert Hawk** configuration". A total Israeli requirement for some 40 S-70As is anticipated.

S-70C. Commercial version, described separately.

WS-70. UK designation for S-70A assembled by Westland Helicopters from Sikorsky supplied kits. Described under Westland entry in UK section.

The following description applies to the standard UH-60A, except where indicated:

TYPE: Twin-turbine combat assault squad transport.

ROTOR SYSTEM: Four-blade main rotor. Sikorsky SC-1095 blade section, with thickness/chord ratio of 9.5%. Middle section has leading-edge droop and trailing-edge tab to overcome vortex impingement from preceding blade in cruising flight. Blade twist 18°. Blade tips sweptback 20°. Each blade consists of a hollow oval titanium spar, Nomex honeycomb core, graphite trailing-edge and root, covered with glassfibre/epoxy, with glassfibre leading-edge counterweight, titanium leading-edge sheath and Kevlar tip. Blades are tolerant to 23 mm gunfire damage, and are pressurised and equipped with gauges providing fail-safe confirmation of blade structural integrity. Electrically heated de-icing mat in leading-edge of each blade of both main and tail rotors. Forged titanium one-piece rotor head with elastomeric bearings which require no lubrication, reducing rotor head maintenance by 60 per cent. Bifilar self-tuning vibration absorber on rotor head. Manual blade folding. Canting of tail rotor (20° to port) increases vertical lift and allows greater CG travel. 'Cross beam' four-blade tail rotor of composite materials, eliminating all rotor head bearings.

ROTOR DRIVE: Conventional transmission system with both turbines driving through freewheeling units to main gearbox. This is of modular construction to simplify maintenance. Transmission can operate for 30 min following total oil loss. Intermediate and tail rotor gearboxes oil lubricated. Main rotor shaft can be lowered for storage or air transport.

FUSELAGE: Conventional semi-monocoque light alloy structure, designed to retain 85 per cent of its passenger and flight deck space in a vertical crash at 11.5 m (38 ft)/s, a lateral crash at 9.1 m (30 ft)/s and a longitudinal crash at 12.2 m (40 ft)/s. It can also withstand a combined force of 20*g* forward and 10*g* downward. Composite materials including glassfibre and Kevlar are used for the cockpit doors, canopy, fairings and engine cowlings. Glassfibre/Nomex floors.

Sikorsky YEH-60A communications jamming version of the Black Hawk, with whip antenna retracted under rear fuselage

TAIL UNIT: Pylon structure with port-canted tail rotor mounted on starboard side. Tail pylon design permits normal forward flight and roll-on landing if tail rotor is destroyed. Large variable incidence tailplane has a control system which senses airspeed, collective lever position, pitch attitude rate and lateral acceleration. Tailplane is set at about +34° incidence in the hover, and -6° for autorotation. Tailplane moved by dual electric actuators, with manual backup. Tailboom folds (to starboard) immediately forward of tail pylon for transport and storage.

LANDING GEAR: Non-retractable tailwheel type with single wheel on each unit. Energy absorbing main gear with a tailwheel which gives protection for the tail rotor in taxying over rough terrain or during a high-flare landing. Axle assembly and main gear oleo shock absorbers by General Mechatronics. Mainwheel tyres size 26 × 10.00-11, pressure 8.96-9.65 bars (130-140 lb/sq in); tailwheel tyre size 15 × 6.00-6, pressure 6.21-6.55 bars (90-95 lb/sq in).

POWER PLANT: Two 1,151 kW (1,560 shp) General Electric T700-GE-700 turboshafts; combined transmission rating 2,109 kW (2,828 shp). (T700-GE-701A engines with max T-O rating of 1,285 kW; 1,723 shp optional in export models.) Two crashworthy, bulletproof fuel cells, with combined usable capacity of 1,361 litres (360 US gallons; 299.5 Imp gallons), aft of cabin. Single-point pressure refuelling; or gravity refuelling via point on each tank. Auxiliary fuel can be carried internally in one of several optional arrangements, or externally by the ESSS system.

ACCOMMODATION: Two-man flight deck, with pilot and co-pilot on armour protected seats. A third crew member is stationed in the cabin at the gunner's position. Forward hinged jettisonable door on each side for access to flight deck area. Main cabin open to cockpit to provide good communication with flight crew and forward view for squad commander. Accommodation for 11 fully equipped troops, or 14 in high density configuration. Eight troop seats can be removed and replaced by four litters for medevac missions, or to make room for internal cargo. An optional layout is available to accommodate a maximum of six litter patients. Cabin heated and ventilated. External cargo hook, having a 3,630 kg (8,000 lb) lift capability, enables UH-60A to transport a 105 mm howitzer, its crew of five and 50 rounds of ammunition. Rescue hoist of 272 kg (600 lb) capacity optional. Large rearward sliding door on each side of fuselage for rapid entry and exit. Electric windscreen de-icing. (Executive configured interiors for 7-12 passengers are available for the S-70A.)

SYSTEMS: Solar 67 kW (90 hp) T-62T-40-1 APU; Garrett engine start system. An optional winterisation kit provides a second hydraulic accumulator installed in parallel with the APU hydraulic start accumulator, maintaining engine start capability at low ambient temperatures; Bendix 30/40kVA and 20/30kVA electrical power generators; 17Ah nickel-cadmium battery. Engine fire extinguishing system. Rotor blade de-icing system standard on US Army aircraft, optional for export versions.

AVIONICS: Com equipment comprises E-Systems AN/ARC-186 VHF-FM, GTE Sylvania AN/ARC-115 VHF-AM, Magnavox AN/ARC-164 UHF-AM, Collins AN/ARC-186(V) VHF-AM/FM, Bendix AN/APX-100 IFF transponder, Magnavox TSEC/KT-28 voice security set, and intercom. Nav equipment comprises Emerson AN/ARN-89 ADF, Bendix AN/ARN-123(V)1 VOR/marker beacon/glideslope receiver, Sperry AN/ASN-43 gyro compass, Singer Kearfott AN/ASN-128 Doppler, and Honeywell AN/APN-209(V)2 radar altimeter. E-Systems Melpar/Memcor AN/APR-39(V)1 radar warning receiver and Sanders AN/ALQ-144 infra-red countermeasures set. Hamilton Standard AFCS with digital three-axis autopilot.

ARMAMENT AND OPERATIONAL EQUIPMENT: New production UH-60As from c/n 431 onward incorporate hardpoints for an external stores support system (ESSS). This consists of a combination of fixed provisions built into the airframe and four removable external pylons from which fuel tanks and a variety of weapons can be suspended. Able to carry more than 2,268 kg (5,000 lb) on each side of the helicopter, the ESSS can accommodate two 870 litre (230 US gallon; 191.5 Imp gallon) fuel tanks outboard, and two 1,703 litre (450 US gallon; 375 Imp gallon) tanks inboard. This allows the UH-60A to self deploy 1,200 nm (2,220 km; 1,380 miles) without refuelling. The ESSS also enables the Black Hawk to carry Hellfire anti-armour missiles, gun or M56 mine dispensing pods, ECM packs, rockets and motorcycles. Up to 16 Hellfires can be carried externally on the ESSS, with another 16 in the cabin to provide the capability to land and reload. Infra-red jamming flares and Tracor XM130 chaff dispenser.

DIMENSIONS, EXTERNAL:
Main rotor diameter 16.36 m (53 ft 8 in)
Main rotor blade chord 0.53 m (1 ft 8¾ in)
Tail rotor diameter 3.35 m (11 ft 0 in)
Length overall, rotors turning 19.76 m (64 ft 10 in)
Length, rotors and tail pylon folded 12.60 m (41 ft 4 in)
Length of fuselage:
UH-60A/MH-60G, excl flight refuelling probe 15.26 m (50 ft 0¾ in)
MH-60G, incl retracted refuelling probe 17.38 m (57 ft 0¼ in)
Fuselage: Max width: UH-60A 2.36 m (7 ft 9 in)
MH-60G with auxiliary tanks 5.46 m (17 ft 11 in)
Max depth 1.75 m (5 ft 9 in)
Height: overall, tail rotor turning 5.13 m (16 ft 10 in)
to top of rotor head 3.76 m (12 ft 4 in)
in air transportable configuration 2.67 m (8 ft 9 in)
Tailplane span 4.38 m (14 ft 4½ in)
Wheel track 2.705 m (8 ft 10½ in)
Wheelbase 8.83 m (28 ft 11¾ in)
Tail rotor ground clearance 1.98 m (6 ft 6 in)
Cabin doors (each): Height 1.37 m (4 ft 6 in)
Width 1.75 m (5 ft 9 in)

DIMENSION, INTERNAL:
Cabin: Volume 11.61 m³ (410.0 cu ft)

AREAS:
Main rotor blades (each) 4.34 m² (46.70 sq ft)
Tail rotor blades (each) 0.41 m² (4.45 sq ft)
Main rotor disc 210.05 m² (2,261 sq ft)
Tail rotor disc 8.83 m² (95.0 sq ft)
Tailplane 4.18 m² (45.0 sq ft)
Vertical stabiliser 3.00 m² (32.3 sq ft)

WEIGHTS:
Weight empty: UH-60A 5,118 kg (11,284 lb)
Mission T-O weight: UH-60A 7,708 kg (16,994 lb)
Max alternative T-O weight:
UH-60A, S-70A 9,979 kg (22,000 lb)

PERFORMANCE (UH-60A at mission T-O weight, except where indicated):
Max level speed at S/L 160 knots (296 km/h; 184 mph)
Max level speed at max T-O weight 158 knots (293 km/h; 182 mph)
Max cruising speed at 1,220 m (4,000 ft) and 35°C (95°F) 145 knots (268 km/h; 167 mph)
Single-engine cruising speed at 1,220 m (4,000 ft), and 35°C (95°F) 105 knots (195 km/h; 121 mph)
Vertical rate of climb at S/L over 137 m (450 ft)/min
Service ceiling 5,790 m (19,000 ft)
Hovering ceiling IGE at 35°C 2,895 m (9,500 ft)
Hovering ceiling OGE: ISA 3,170 m (10,400 ft)
at 35°C 1,705 m (5,600 ft)
Range with max internal fuel at max T-O weight, 30 min reserves 324 nm (600 km; 373 miles)
Range with external fuel tanks on ESSS pylons:
with two 870 litre (230 US gallon; 191.5 Imp gallon) tanks 880 nm (1,630 km; 1,012 miles)
with two 870 litre (230 US gallon; 191.5 Imp gallon) and two 1,703 litre (450 US gallon; 375 Imp gallon) tanks 1,200 nm (2,220 km; 1,380 miles)
Endurance: UH-60A 2 h 18 min
MH-60G with max fuel 4 h 51 min

SIKORSKY S-70B

US Navy designations: SH-60B Seahawk, SH-60F Ocean Hawk, and HH-60H

US Coast Guard designation: HH-60J

The US Navy's LAMPS (light airborne multi-purpose system) programme was initiated in 1970, when the Kaman SH-2D Seasprite won the contract for the LAMPS Mk I aircraft. In 1974, IBM Federal Systems Division was selected as prime contractor for LAMPS Mk III, the proposed Mk II having been cancelled. Fly-off tests of competitive airframes from Boeing and Sikorsky were conducted in 1977, each manufacturer submitting a developed version of the aircraft it had built for the US Army's UTTAS competition. Sikorsky was selected to supply the LAMPS Mk III airframe, and General Electric to supply a navalised version of the T700 engine.

A key factor in selection of the Sikorsky S-70B was its promise of reduced development costs, due to the high degree of commonality with the Army's UH-60A Black Hawk. The designation **SH-60B** and name **Seahawk** were allocated to the Navy model, which embodies changes to integrate the mission equipment and to provide shipboard compatibility. These changes include the addition of chin mounted pods for ESM equipment, pylons for two torpedoes or auxiliary fuel tanks, and a pylon for MAD equipment on the starboard side; installation of more powerful navalised engines; addition of a sensor operator's station and port side launcher for 25 sonobuoys in the cabin; increased fuel capacity; a rescue hoist; automatic main rotor folding system; main rotor brake; folding tail rotor pylon; modified, shorter-wheelbase landing gear; a DAF Indal RAST (recovery assist, secure and traversing) device to haul down the helicopter in rough seas on to a small deck, and to stow it in the ship's hangar; a sliding cabin door; hover in-flight refuelling system; and buoyancy features. The pilot's and co-pilot's seats are not armoured.

The first of five SH-60B prototypes (BuAer number 161169) flew on 12 December 1979, and details of subsequent development and operational testing can be found in the 1982-83 *Jane's*. Production of a first batch of 18 SH-60Bs was authorised in FY 1982, followed by 27 more in FY 1983. Total planned requirement by the US Navy is 204 aircraft. The first production Seahawk flew on 11 February 1983, and deliveries to the Navy continue at the rate of two per month, with a total of 85 delivered by June 1987. First USN squadron was HSL-41, at NAS North Island, San Diego, California. Operational deployment began in 1984 and by the Summer of 1987 six US Navy squadrons were operational (HSLs -41, -43 and -45 at NAS North Island, and -40, -42 and -44 at NAS Mayport, Florida), with four SH-60B detachments operating with the Atlantic Fleet and three with the Pacific Fleet. Mission capability of 97 per cent has been recorded by the USN's SH-60B fleet.

US Navy SH-60Bs will be deployed on a total of 95 'Oliver Hazard Perry' class frigates, 'Spruance' class and Aegis equipped destroyers, and 'Ticonderoga' class guided missile cruisers. They will provide all-weather capability for detection, classification, localisation and interdiction of surface vessels and submarines. Compared with the LAMPS Mk I, range, loiter time and endurance are increased significantly. ASW listening time is increased by 57 min, ASST (anti-ship surveillance and targeting) loiter time by 45 min. The helicopter interfaces with its mother ship via a data link, but can also operate independently. Secondary missions include search and rescue (SAR), vertical replenishment (vertrep), medical evacuation (medevac), fleet support and communications relay.

Under a US Navy contract with Sikorsky and Rolls-Royce Turbomeca, an SH-60B began initial flight tests on 3 April 1987 re-engined with 1,566 kW (2,100 shp) RTM 322 turboshafts. A US Navy flight evaluation involving some 60 hours of flight testing was scheduled to follow at Sikorsky's West Palm Beach facility and at the Naval Air Test Center, NAS Patuxent River. No use of RTM 322s in US Navy H-60 series helicopters is currently contemplated.

Japan has selected the SH-60B to replace the SH-3A/Bs of the JMSDF. Two Sikorsky built Seahawk airframes, designated **XSH-60J**, were delivered to Mitsubishi at Nagoya for installation of Japanese electronics and mission equipment under a $27 million contract from the Japan Defence Agency's Technical Research and Development Institute. The first of these helicopters flew on 31 August 1987, and was followed by the second in early October, beginning a two-year testing programme. The SH-60J Seahawk will be built by Mitsubishi (which see), and is scheduled to enter service with the JMSDF in the early 1990s, with replacement of SH-3s completed by the middle of the decade.

On 9 October 1984 the Royal Australian Navy confirmed an initial order for eight Seahawks for its full-spectrum ASW requirement, and ordered a further eight in May 1986. These Seahawks, designated **S-70B-2** RAWS (role adaptable weapon system), will operate from the RAN's 'Adelaide' (FFG-7) class guided missile frigates. The first RAN Seahawk (N7265H) flew from Sikorsky's West Palm Beach facility on 4 December 1987. Fourteen of the S-70B-2 RAWS will be assembled in Australia by Hawker de Havilland. The RAN helicopters will be equipped with MEL Super Searcher radar and Collins advanced integrated avionics including cockpit controls and displays, navigation receivers and communications transceivers, an airborne target off-hand data link, and a tactical data system (TDS). The Spanish Navy took delivery of six S-70Bs in December 1988, for operation from its frigates.

On 6 March 1985 Sikorsky received a $50.9 million contract for full scale development and production options for a 'CV-Helo' version of the Seahawk designated **SH-60F Ocean Hawk** and known officially as the CV Inner Zone ASW helicopter. Intended as a replacement for

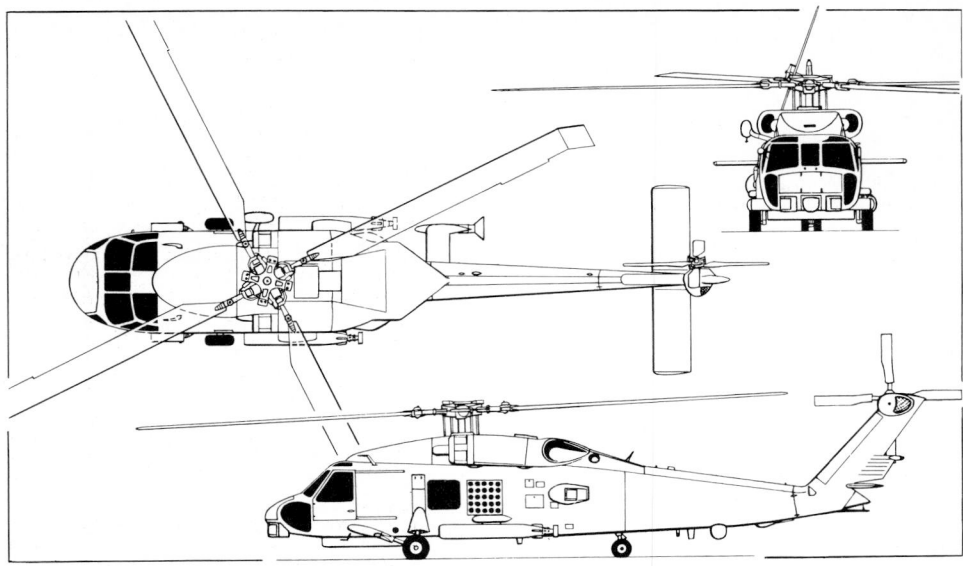

Sikorsky SH-60B Seahawk twin-turbine ASW/ASST helicopter *(Pilot Press)*

Sikorsky SH-60B Seahawk LAMPS Mk III helicopter with parent ship USS *Crommelin* **(FFG 37)**

the SH-3H Sea King, this helicopter will operate from aircraft carriers to protect the inner zone of a carrier battle group from submarine attack, with a mission endurance of four hours. The SH-60F differs from the SH-60B in having all LAMPS Mk III avionics, sensors and pneumatic sonobuoy launcher equipment removed, together with the cargo hook, RAST system main probe, and tail probe and control panel, although installation provisions will be retained. An integrated ASW mission avionics suite is installed, comprising a MIL-STD-1553B tactical data management system with dual Teledyne Systems AN/ASN-150 tactical navigation computers, a redundant digital databus, a tactical data link to other aircraft, a communications control system, and multi-function keypads and display units for each of the four crew members. Seahawk prototype 161170 was modified as the SH-60F test aircraft.

Additional equipment in the SH-60F includes an Allied Signal (Bendix Oceanics) AN/AQS-13F dipping sonar system, internal/external auxiliary fuel system and an additional weapons station on an extended pylon on the port side of the fuselage. Armament includes two Mk 50 acoustic homing torpedoes. Modifications include rearrangement of the cabin interior, removal of external sensor fairings, and improvements to the automatic flight control system to permit increased rates of deceleration on automatic approaches, in addition to automatic coupled sonar cable angle hover or coupled Doppler hover. Provision is made for a chaff/sonobuoy launcher system, an attitude/heading reference system and global positioning system, with future growth potential for a fatigue monitoring system, surface search radar, FLIR, night vision equipment, passive ESM, MAD, air-to-surface missile capability, a sonobuoy data link, and an increase in max T-O weight to 10,659 kg (23,500 lb). Secondary missions will include SAR and standby during launch and recovery of the carriers' fixed-wing aircraft to provide a rescue service in case of ditching. The US Navy requirement is for 175 SH-60Fs. The initial contract provides production options for 76 helicopters in five lots. In January 1986 Sikorsky received a contract for seven SH-60Fs, the first of which flew on 19 March 1987. Together with a second SH-60F, it was used for Navy operational evaluation. Five more will be delivered between May and September 1989. A Lot 3 batch of 18 full-rate production aircraft was ordered in Spring 1988, with deliveries scheduled to begin in October 1989.

In September 1986, the US Navy awarded Sikorsky a

contract for an initial production increment of five combat search and rescue/special warfare support (HCS) helicopters for the Navy, designated **HH-60H**, and two medium range recovery (MRR) helicopters for the Coast Guard, designated **HH-60J**. These orders have since been increased to nine HH-60Hs and five HH-60Js. The HH-60H/J 'Rescue Hawks' are close derivatives of the SH-60F, with the same T700-401C engines as those installed in current production SH-60B/Fs. It is expected that 18 will eventually serve with the Navy and 35 with the Coast Guard, with deliveries commencing in 1989 and 1990 respectively. Initial US Navy deliveries will be to HCS-4 and HCS-5 squadrons. The Japan Air Self-Defence Force was seeking funding for three HH-60J SAR helicopters in FY 1988 budget requests.

The following description applies to the SH-60B:

TYPE: Twin-turbine ASW/ASST (anti-ship surveillance and targeting) helicopter.

ROTOR SYSTEM: As for UH-60A, except that main rotor blades can be folded by electrical power, and a rotor brake is provided.

AIRFRAME: Identical to UH-60A in construction. Wheelbase is shortened by 46.6 per cent, with twin wheels on tail unit, tyre size 17.5 × 6.00-6. Multiple disc brakes on mainwheels. Landing gear structure is less complex since the SH-60B's vertical impact requirement is 71.5 per cent below that of the UH-60A.

POWER PLANT: Two 1,260 kW (1,690 shp) General Electric T700-GE-401 turboshafts in early aircraft; 1,417 kW (1,900 shp) T700-401C turboshafts introduced in 1988. Internal fuel capacity 2,233 litres (590 US gallons; 491 Imp gallons). Hovering in-flight refuelling capability. Two auxiliary fuel tanks on fuselage pylons optional.

ACCOMMODATION: Pilot and airborne tactical officer/backup pilot in cockpit, sensor operator in specially equipped station in cabin. Dual controls standard. Sliding door with jettisonable window on starboard side. Accommodation is heated, ventilated and air-conditioned.

SYSTEMS: Generally as for UH-60A.

AVIONICS AND EQUIPMENT: Com equipment comprises Collins AN/ARC-159(V)2 UHF and AN/ARC-174(V)2 HF, Hazeltine AN/APX-76A(V) and Bendix AN/APX-100(V)1 IFF transponders, TSEC/KY-75 voice security set, TSEC/KG-45(E-1) com security, Telephonics OK-374/ASC com system control group and Sierra Research AN/ARQ-44 data link and telemetry. Nav equipment comprises Collins AN/ARN-118(V) Tacan, Honeywell AN/APN-194(V) radar altimeter, Teledyne Ryan AN/APN-217 Doppler, and Collins AN/ARA-50 UHF DF. Mission equipment includes Sikorsky sonobuoy launcher, Edmac AN/ARR-75 and R-1651/ARA sonobuoy receiving sets, Texas Instruments AN/ASQ-81(V)2 MAD, Raymond MU-670/ASQ magnetic tape memory unit, Astronautics IO-2177/ASQ altitude indicator, Fairchild AN/ASQ-164 control indicator set and AN/ASQ-165 armament control indicator set, Texas Instruments AN/APS-124 search radar (under front fuselage), IBM AN/UYS-1(V)2 Proteus acoustic processor and CV-3252/A converter display, Control Data AN/AYK-14 (XN-1A) digital computer, and Raytheon AN/ALQ-142 ESM (in chin mounted pods). External cargo hook and rescue hoist standard.

ARMAMENT: Includes two Mk 46 torpedoes and provision for Norwegian Penguin Mk 2 Mod 7 anti-shipping missiles (being qualified for 1989 introduction).

DIMENSIONS, EXTERNAL: As UH-60A except:

Length overall (rotors and tail pylon folded)	12.47 m (40 ft 11 in)
Width (rotors folded)	3.26 m (10 ft 8½ in)
Height: to top of rotor head	3.63 m (11 ft 11 in)
overall, tail rotor turning	5.18 m (17 ft 0 in)
overall, pylon folded	4.04 m (13 ft 3¼ in)
Wheel track	2.79 m (9 ft 2 in)
Wheelbase	4.83 m (15 ft 10 in)

AREAS: As UH-60A

WEIGHTS (A, ASW mission; B, ASST mission; C, Utility role):

Weight empty: A	6,191 kg (13,648 lb)
Mission gross weight: A	9,182 kg (20,244 lb)
B	8,334 kg (18,373 lb)
Max gross weight: C	9,926 kg (21,884 lb)

PERFORMANCE:

Dash speed at 1,525 m (5,000 ft), tropical day	126 knots (234 km/h; 145 mph)
Vertical rate of climb at S/L, 32.2°C (90°F)	213 m (700 ft)/min
Vertical rate of climb at S/L, 32.2°C (90°F), one engine out	137 m (450 ft)/min

SIKORSKY S-70C

The S-70C is a commercial variant of the H-60 helicopter series which can be configured for a range of utility missions including heavy construction, external lift, maritime and environmental survey, mineral exploration, forestry and conservation. It uses the H-60 airframe, dynamics and systems, but is powered by two General Electric CT7-2C or -2D engines. Options available include a de-icing kit for main and tail rotors, 3,630 kg (8,000 lb) capacity external cargo hook, cabin mounted rescue hoist, aeromedical evacuation kit, and a winterisation kit. The S-70C is certificated under FAR Pt 21.25. Delivery of 24 with undernose radar to the People's Republic of China was completed in December 1985. Fourteen have been ordered by the Chinese Nationalist Air Force, Taiwan. Other export sales include two to Brunei, three to Jordan, two to the Philippines and one each to Rolls-Royce and Westland PLC in the United Kingdom.

An S-70C (G-RRTM) is being used by Rolls-Royce in the UK as a flying testbed for the Rolls-Royce Turbomeca RTM 322 turboshaft engine.

The Sikorsky S-70C is generally similar to the UH-60A, except as follows:

TYPE: Twin-turbine utility helicopter.

POWER PLANT: Two 1,212 kW (1,625 shp) General Electric CT7-2C or 1,285 kW (1,723 shp) CT7-2D turboshafts. Combined transmission rating (continuous) 2,334 kW (3,130 shp). Maximum fuel capacity 1,370 litres (362 US gallons; 301 Imp gallons).

ACCOMMODATION: Flight deck crew of two, with provision for 12 passengers in standard cabin configuration and up to 19 passengers in high density layout. Forward hinged door on each side of flight deck for access to cockpit area. Large rearward sliding door on each side of main cabin.

DIMENSIONS, INTERNAL:

Cabin: Length	3.84 m (12 ft 7 in)
Max width	2.34 m (7 ft 8 in)
Max height	1.37 m (4 ft 6 in)
Floor area	8.18 m² (88.0 sq ft)
Volume	10.96 m³ (387.0 cu ft)
Baggage compartment volume	0.52 m³ (18.5 cu ft)

WEIGHTS:

Weight empty	4,607 kg (10,158 lb)
Max external load	3,630 kg (8,000 lb)
Max T-O weight	9,185 kg (20,250 lb)

PERFORMANCE (ISA, at max T-O weight):

Never-exceed speed	195 knots (361 km/h; 224 mph)
Max level speed at S/L	157 knots (290 km/h; 180 mph)
Cruising speed at S/L	145 knots (268 km/h; 167 mph)
Max rate of climb at S/L	615 m (2,020 ft)/min
Service ceiling	4,360 m (14,300 ft)
Service ceiling, one engine out	1,095 m (3,600 ft)
Hovering ceiling OGE	1,204 m (3,950 ft)

Range at 135 knots (250 km/h; 155 mph) at 915 m (3,000 ft) with max standard fuel, 30 min reserves
255 nm (473 km; 294 miles)

Range, max fuel, no reserves
297 nm (550 km; 342 miles)

Sikorsky SH-60F Ocean Hawk CV-Helo lowering its sonar during US Navy operational evaluation

Artist's impression of the Sikorsky HH-60H combat search and rescue/special warfare support helicopter

Sikorsky S-70C commercial derivative of the UH-60 series

SIKORSKY S-76 MARK II

The 12-passenger twin-turbine commercial S-76 was announced on 19 January 1975 as the first stage of a programme intended to give the company a bigger share of the civil aircraft market. Construction of four prototypes began in May 1976, and the first flight was made, by the No. 2 aircraft (N762SA), on 13 March 1977. FAR Pt 29 certification was received in November 1978 and deliveries began in early 1979.

The S-76 benefits from work carried out on the dynamic system of the UH-60A Black Hawk. The main rotor, for example, is a scaled-down version of that developed for the UH-60A. The helicopter conforms with FAR Pt 29 Category A IFR. Offshore oil support, corporate executive transport, medical care and general utility operations are its primary markets.

All aircraft delivered since 1 March 1982 have been designated **S-76 Mark II** and embody more than 40 standard improvements, including a new cabin ventilation system to provide ample fresh air with no performance penalty; refinements in the major dynamic components; and an increased number of fuselage access panels, these latter features being intended to improve reliability and simplify maintenance. Kits incorporating the Mark II refinements are available to update earlier S-76 aircraft to this standard, most of them without charge.

On 18 February 1982, Sikorsky announced the availability of three quick-change medical kits to convert any S-76 to an ambulance configuration. These include an air medical evacuation system (AMES) kit for operators placing primary emphasis on air ambulance operations, providing maximum intensive care for two patients treated by two attendants; a quick-change single-stretcher kit for use where intensive care transport may be needed quickly on a standby basis; and a kit for the installation of three stretchers, when the S-76 is to be used more specifically as a civil defence or SAR type ambulance. In late 1986 Sikorsky announced a new Emergency Medical Service configuration which includes built-in redundant systems for medical gases, suction and electrical power.

The special Allison turboshaft fitted in the Mark II, designated Allison 250-C30S (for Sikorsky), has a 5 per cent higher take-off rating of 485 kW (650 shp). Allison is developing a new version of this engine, designated 250-C34, to provide a further 10 per cent increase in power. A digital computerised fuel control system is being developed by Hamilton Standard to complement this power plant. When equipped with the 250-C34 the S-76 Mark II will be certificated at a maximum T-O weight of 4,989 kg (11,000 lb) and have an uprated transmission to handle the increased power.

Between 4-9 February 1982 a production S-76 Mark II, without special modification, was used to establish 12 records in FAI classes E1d and E1e. Details of these have been given in the 1987-88 and previous editions of *Jane's*.

In 1987 an S-76A (F-WZSA) was fitted with 522 kW (700 shp) Turbomeca Arriel 1S turboshafts for test flying leading to FAA certification in April 1988, since when the Turbomeca power plant has been available as a retrofit option on the helicopter.

In the Spring of 1985 Sikorsky began testing an experimental higher harmonic control (HHC) system in an S-76 which has demonstrated a vibration reduction of up to 90 per cent over the standard S-76. In the HHC system, one rod in each of the three channels of the main rotor mechanical control system is replaced with an HHC actuator which drives the corresponding main hydraulic servo mechanism to produce a vibration-cancelling motion of the rotor blades. In a production system the actuators would probably be built into the main servos. The benefits of higher harmonic control include improved crew and passenger comfort, better systems reliability, improved

fatigue life, greater stability for weapons aiming and firing, and a potential reduction in weight compared to current generation 'passive' vibration absorbers. Sikorsky has also been developing a composite rotor head and all-composite main rotor blades with graphite-glassfibre spars for the S-76, together with an ice protection kit weighing 68 kg (150 lb), of which 45 kg (100 lb) is removable during the Summer months.

The following versions of the S-76 had been announced by early 1988:

S-76. Original general purpose all-weather transport, generally as described below for the S-76 Mark II, and covering aircraft delivered prior to 1 March 1982.

S-76 Mark II. Current production version from 1 March 1982, as described in detail.

S-76B. With Pratt & Whitney Canada PT6B-36 power plant; described separately.

S-76 Utility. More basic version of the S-76 Mark II,

for a variety of roles. Sliding doors on each side of the cabin, dual controls, and a cabin floor designed for cargo loadings of up to 976 kg/m² (200 lb/sq ft), are standard. Optional features include non-retractable landing gear with low pressure tyres, to increase rough terrain ground clearance, crash resistant fuel tanks, a similar auxiliary tank of 416 litres (110 US gallons; 91.5 Imp gallons) capacity for installation in the baggage compartment, armoured crew seats, removable troop seats, cargo hook, rescue hoist, engine air particle separators and provisions for stretcher installation. The Philippine Air Force received 17 military S-76 Utility helicopters, of which 12 are **AUH-76s** configured for COIN, troop/logistic support and medevac duties. Two others are configured for SAR, one with a 12-passenger utility cabin, and two with an 8-passenger cabin.

H-76 Eagle. Military development of the S-76B; described separately.

H-76N. Naval development of the H-76, described separately.

The following description and specification details apply to the standard S-76 Mark II, with Allison engines, except where indicated:

TYPE: Twin-turbine general purpose all-weather helicopter.

ROTOR SYSTEM: Four-blade main rotor, with Sikorsky SC-1095 blade section. Each blade consists of a hollow oval titanium spar, titanium and nickel leading-edge abrasion strips, and glassfibre composite outer covering over Nomex honeycomb core. Blades have swept tips of Kevlar (30° on leading-edges, 10° on trailing-edges). Fully articulated aluminium rotor head, with elastomeric bearings which need no lubrication. Hydraulic lead-lag dampers and bifilar vibration absorbers on rotor head. Cross-beam four-blade tail rotor of composite materials. Rotor brake optional.

ROTOR DRIVE: Conventional transmission system, with both turbines driving through freewheeling units to main gearbox. Intermediate and tail rotor gearboxes are oil lubricated. Max continuous rating of main transmission 969 kW (1,300 shp).

FUSELAGE: Composite structure, comprising glassfibre nose, light alloy honeycomb cabin, semi-monocoque light alloy tailcone and Kevlar doors and fairings.

TAIL UNIT: Pylon structure with tail rotor on port side. All-moving tailplane, which serves also to protect passengers or ground crew from contact with tail rotor.

LANDING GEAR: Hydraulically retractable tricycle type, with

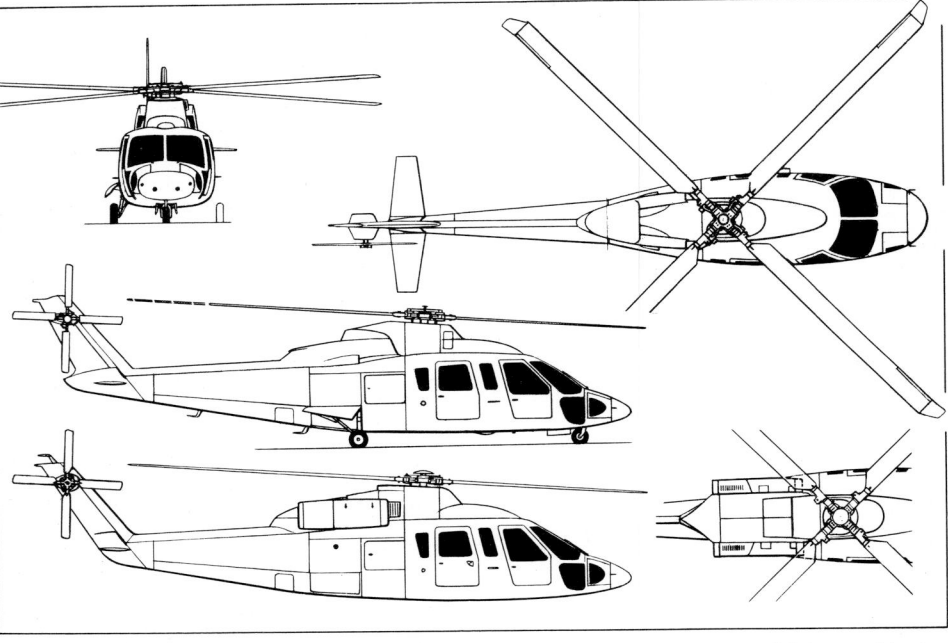

Sikorsky S-76 Mark II eight/twelve-passenger commercial transport helicopter, with lower side view and scrap detail of S-76B *(Pilot Press)*

Sikorsky S-76 Mark II general purpose helicopter in service with the Royal Jordanian Air Force
(Ivo Sturzenegger)

single wheel on each unit. Nosewheel retracts rearward, main units inward into rear fuselage; all three units are enclosed by wheel doors when retracted. Mainwheel tyres size 14.5 × 5.5-6, pressure 11.38 bars (165 lb/sq in); nosewheel tyre size 13 × 5.00-4, pressure 9.31 bars (135 lb/sq in). Hydraulic brakes; hydraulic mainwheel parking brake. Non-retractable tricycle gear, with low pressure tyres, optional on Utility version.

POWER PLANT: Two 485 kW (650 shp) Allison 250-C30S turboshafts, with max continuous rating of 415 kW (557 shp), mounted above the cabin aft of the main rotor shaft. Two 522 kW (700 shp) Turbomeca Arriel 1S turboshafts optional for retrofit. Standard fuel system has a capacity of 1,064 litres (281 US gallons; 234 Imp gallons). Extended range fuel tanks, capacity 401 litres (106 US gallons; 88 Imp gallons), optional.

ACCOMMODATION: Pilot and co-pilot plus a maximum of 12 passengers. In this configuration passengers are seated on three four-abreast rows of seats, floor mounted at a pitch of 79 cm (31 in). A number of executive layouts are available, including a four-passenger 'office in the sky' configuration. Executive versions have luxurious interior trim, full carpeting, special soundproofing, radio telephone, and co-ordinated furniture. Dual controls optional. Two large doors on each side of fuselage, hinged at their forward edges; sliding doors are available optionally. Baggage hold aft of cabin, with external access door on each side of the fuselage. Cabin heated and ventilated. Windscreen demisting and dual windscreen wipers. Windscreen heating and external cargo hook optional.

SYSTEMS: Hydraulic system at pressure of 207 bars (3,000 lb/sq in) supplied by two pumps driven from main gearbox. Hydraulic system maximum flow rate 15.9 litres (4.2 US gallons; 3.5 Imp gallons) per minute. Bootstrap reservoir. Pump head pressure 3.45 bars (50 lb/sq in). In VFR configuration, electrical system comprises two 200A DC starter/generators and a 24V 17Ah nickel-cadmium battery. In IFR configuration, system comprises gearbox driven 7.5kVA generator, and a 115V 600VA 400Hz static inverter for AC power. 34Ah battery optional. Engine fire detection and extinguishing system.

AVIONICS AND EQUIPMENT: Wide range of optional avionics available, according to configuration, including Honeywell SPZS-7000 single-pilot digital AFCS with EFIS, Hamilton Standard AFCS, VHF nav receivers, transponder, compass system, weather radar, flight director system, radar altimeter, ADF, DME, VLF nav system, and ELT and sonic transmitters. Standard equipment includes provisions for dual controls; cabin fire extinguishers; cockpit, cabin, instrument, navigation and anti-collision lights; landing light; external power socket; first aid kit; and utility soundproofing. Collins VHF-20 com transceiver and intercom system standard. Optional equipment includes air-conditioning, cargo hook, rescue hoist, emergency flotation gear, engine air particle separators, full IFR instrumentation and litter installation.

DIMENSIONS, EXTERNAL (A: Mark II, B: Mark II Utility):
Main rotor diameter	13.41 m (44 ft 0 in)
Main rotor blade chord	0.39 m (1 ft 3½ in)
Tail rotor diameter	2.44 m (8 ft 0 in)
Tail rotor blade chord	0.16 m (6½ in)
Length overall, rotors turning	16.00 m (52 ft 6 in)
Fuselage: Length	13.22 m (43 ft 4½ in)
Max width	2.13 m (7 ft 0 in)
Max depth	1.83 m (6 ft 0 in)
Height overall, tail rotor turning:	
A	4.41 m (14 ft 5¾ in)
B	4.52 m (14 ft 9¾ in)
Tailplane span: A	3.05 m (10 ft 0 in)
B	3.15 m (10 ft 4 in)
Wheel track: A	2.44 m (8 ft 0 in)
B	2.54 m (8 ft 4 in)
Wheelbase	5.00 m (16 ft 5 in)
Tail rotor ground clearance	1.97 m (6 ft 5¾ in)

DIMENSIONS, INTERNAL:
Cabin: Length	2.46 m (8 ft 1 in)
Max width	1.93 m (6 ft 4 in)
Max height	1.35 m (4 ft 5 in)
Floor area	4.18 m² (45.0 sq ft)
Volume	5.78 m³ (204.0 cu ft)
Baggage compartment volume	1.08 m³ (38.0 cu ft)

AREAS:
Main rotor disc	141.21 m² (1,520 sq ft)
Tail rotor disc	4.67 m² (50.27 sq ft)
Tailplane	2.00 m² (21.5 sq ft)

WEIGHTS AND LOADINGS:
Weight empty, standard equipment	2,540 kg (5,600 lb)
Max fuel weight: standard	861 kg (1,898 lb)
auxiliary	325 kg (716 lb)
Max payload	2,132 kg (4,700 lb)
Max external load	1,497 kg (3,300 lb)
Max T-O weight	4,672 kg (10,300 lb)
Max disc loading	33.07 kg/m² (6.77 lb/sq ft)
Max power loading	4.82 kg/kW (7.92 lb/shp)

PERFORMANCE (A: at gross weight of 4,536 kg; 10,000 lb, B: at gross weight of 3,810 kg; 8,400 lb):
Never-exceed speed	155 knots (286 km/h; 178 mph)
Max cruising speed: A	145 knots (269 km/h; 167 mph)
B	155 knots (286 km/h; 178 mph)

Sikorsky S-76B with 716 kW (960 shp) Pratt & Whitney Canada PT6B-36 turboshafts

Cruising speed for max range:
A	125 knots (232 km/h; 144 mph)
Max rate of climb at S/L	411 m (1,350 ft)/min
Service ceiling: A	4,575 m (15,000 ft)
Service ceiling, one engine out: A	1,890 m (6,200 ft)
B	3,445 m (11,300 ft)
Hovering ceiling IGE: A	1,890 m (6,200 ft)
B	3,415 m (11,200 ft)
Range with 12 passengers, standard fuel, 30 min reserves	404 nm (748 km; 465 miles)
Range with 8 passengers, auxiliary fuel and offshore equipment	600 nm (1,112 km; 691 miles)

SIKORSKY S-76B

The Sikorsky S-76B is a version of the S-76 Mark II with Pratt & Whitney Canada PT6B-36 turboshafts. Development installation began in October 1983, when a ground test airframe was modified for a 200 hour ground test programme which ended on 7 April 1984. A second PT6B-36 powered S-76B (N3123U) began flight testing on 22 June 1984, and was joined by the ground test machine in February 1985. FAA Cat A certification was granted in early 1987. The PT6B-36 engines provide the S-76B with a 48 per cent increase in take-off power, resulting in a 51 per cent increase in useful load under hot and high conditions. Maximum take-off weight is increased by 499 kg (1,100 lb), and the main transmission rating is increased to 1,118 kW (1,500 shp). Other modifications include a 15 per cent reduction in tail rotor pylon area, and reconfigured engine exhaust fairings.

By June 1987 Sikorsky had delivered 31 S-76Bs to customers in Japan, the Netherlands, South Korea, the USA and West Germany. Flight testing for UK certification began on 2 July 1987. By 1 January 1988 the S-76B fleet had logged more than 9,000 flight hours.

The description of the S-76 Mark II applies also to the S-76B, except as follows:

POWER PLANT: Two 716 kW (960 shp) Pratt & Whitney Canada PT6B-36 turboshafts, maximum continuous power rating 649 kW (870 shp). Standard fuel capacity 1,064 litres (281 US gallons; 234 Imp gallons); auxiliary tank capacity 208 litres (55 US gallons; 46 Imp gallons).

WEIGHTS AND LOADINGS:
Weight empty	2,970 kg (6,548 lb)
Max T-O weight	5,171 kg (11,400 lb)
Max external load	1,497 kg (3,300 lb)
Max disc loading	36.62 kg/m² (7.50 lb/sq ft)
Max power loading	3.61 kg/kW (5.94 lb/shp)

PERFORMANCE (ISA, at max T-O weight):
Never-exceed speed	155 knots (287 km/h; 178 mph)
Max cruising speed	145 knots (269 km/h; 167 mph)
Econ cruising speed	131 knots (243 km/h; 151 mph)
Max rate of climb at S/L	457 m (1,500 ft)/min

Rate of climb at S/L, one engine out	160 m (525 ft)/min
Service ceiling	4,572 m (15,000 ft)
Service ceiling, one engine out	2,377 m (7,800 ft)
Hovering ceiling OGE	1,646 m (5,400 ft)
Range at 130 knots (241 km; 150 mph) at 915 m (3,000 ft), standard fuel with 30 min reserves	312 nm (578 km; 359 miles)

SIKORSKY H-76 EAGLE

The H-76 Eagle is a military development of the S-76B. The prototype (N3124G), which made its first flight in February 1985, incorporated the optional armoured crew seats, sliding cabin doors and heavy duty floor of that version, and introduced a wide range of optional items that include weapon pylons, an optical sight mounted above the instrument panel, self-sealing high strength fuel tanks, and provisions for door mounted weapons. The main transmission is upgraded, as are the intermediate and tail rotor gearboxes. The main rotor hub and shaft are strengthened, chord of the horizontal tail surface increased, dual spars employed in the vertical fin, and tail rotor blade chord increased. Fuselage skin thickness is increased to withstand the blast of weapons launch. The H-76 can be equipped for troop transport/logistic support, as a gunship, and for roles including airborne assault, air observation post, combat SAR, evacuation, ambulance, and conventional SAR.

The Eagle can be equipped with either a mast mounted (MMS) or roof mounted sight (RMS). Further planned developments include a version with air-to-air missiles, of which the helicopter could carry up to 16, although a more likely weapons load would be eight AAMs and two cannon pods; head-up display; laser rangefinder; integrated armament management system; self-protection systems including a radar warning receiver, infra-red jammer and chaff/flare dispensers; high-clearance landing gear; and a Honeywell SPZ-7000 automatic flight control system.

In early 1987 the H-76 prototype successfully completed weapons firing tests on a four-station pitch-compensated armament pylon (PCAP) at Mojave, California. The PCAP, which has a faired leading-edge, permits a speed increase of 3-4 knots over previously installed pylons and was tested with a GIAT M261 20 mm cannon pod, 7.62 mm and 12.7 mm machine-gun pods, the VS-MD-H mine dispenser and 70 mm rockets. The pod is one of several integrated improvements to the H-76's weapons systems, which include operation of the integrated armament management system (IAMS) from the collective pitch lever as well as from the panel, and provision of system-ready signals and a sideslip trim ball on the head-up display.

Sikorsky and Daewoo Industries of South Korea have formed Daewoo-Sikorsky Aerospace Ltd and are proposing the H-76 Eagle for the Republic of Korea's medium

Sikorsky H-76 Eagle military utility helicopter (Pratt & Whitney Canada PT6B-36 turboshafts)

helicopter requirement. If successful, a production rate of 24 per year is anticipated to meet the ROK's 150-175 aircraft requirement.

The description of the S-76 Mark II applies also to the H-76, except as follows:

TYPE: Twin-turbine armed utility helicopter.

ROTOR SYSTEM, ROTOR DRIVE, FUSELAGE, TAIL UNIT and LANDING GEAR: Generally as for UH-60A. Strobex rotor blade tracker optional.

POWER PLANT: As for S-76B, except fuel is contained in two high strength, optionally self-sealing, tanks located below the rear cabin, with a total capacity of 993 litres (262.4 US gallons; 218.4 Imp gallons). Gravity refuelling point on each side of fuselage. Engine ice protection by bleed air anti-icing system. Engine fire detection and extinguishing systems. Engine air particle separator optional.

ACCOMMODATION: Pilot and co-pilot, plus varying troop/passenger loads according to role. Armoured pilot seats optional. Ten fully armed troops can be transported, or seven troops when configured as an airborne assault vehicle with multi-purpose pylon system (MPPS) and one 7.62 mm door gun installed. For evacuation use the cabin can be equipped with 12 seats or, in emergency, all seats can be removed and 16 persons can be airlifted sitting on the cabin floor. For SAR use the cabin will accommodate three patients on litters, or six persons lying prone on the floor and on the rear cabin raised deck. The standard medevac layout provides for three litters and a bench seat for two medical attendants.

SYSTEMS: Generally as for S-76B, except electrical system has a 17 or optional 34Ah battery.

AVIONICS AND EQUIPMENT: Typical avionics include VHF-20A VHF transceiver, AN/ARC-186 VHF-AM/FM com, 719A UHF com, ADF-60A ADF, DF-301E UHF DF, VIR-30A VOR with ILS, glideslope and marker beacon receivers, DME-40 DME, TDR-90 transponder and dual RMI-36 RMI, all by Collins, course deviation indicators, ELT, Andrea A301-61A intercom, cabin speaker system and loudhailer. Typical equipment includes dual controls and instrumentation, stability augmentation system, dual 5 in VGIs, Allen RCA-26 standby self-contained attitude indicator, Collins ALT-50A radio altimeter, soundproofing, 'Fasten seat belt—No smoking' signs, first aid kit, two cabin fire extinguishers, external power socket, provisions for optional emergency flotation system, and provisions for installation of cargo hook with certificated capacity of 1,497 kg (3,300 lb), rescue hoist of 272 kg (600 lb) capacity. Standard lighting includes cockpit, cabin and instrument lights, navigation lights, anti-collision strobe light, and a battery operated self-contained cabin emergency light.

ARMAMENT: One 7.62 mm machine-gun can be pintle mounted in each doorway and fired with or without the MPPS system installed. Pintles incorporate field of fire limiters and will accept Fabrique National or Maramount M60D machine-guns. The MPPS can be installed on the cabin floor, providing the capability to carry and deploy pods containing single or twin 7.62 mm machine-guns, 0.50 in machine-guns, 2.75 in and 5 in rocket pods, Mk 66 2.75 in rockets, Oerlikon 68 mm rockets, Hellfire, TOW, Sea Skua and Stinger missiles, and Mk 46 torpedoes. Targeting equipment can include FLIR, Saab-Scania reticle sight, TOW roof sight or TOW mast mounted sight and laser rangefinder.

DIMENSIONS, EXTERNAL AND INTERNAL, AND AREAS:
Generally as for S-76B

WEIGHTS:

Weight empty	2,545 kg (5,610 lb)
Weight empty, equipped (typical)	3,030 kg (6,680 lb)
Max fuel weight	792 kg (1,745 lb)
Max T-O weight	5,171 kg (11,400 lb)

PERFORMANCE:
Similar to S-76B, but range highly variable according to loading and mission

SIKORSKY H-76N

In February 1984 Sikorsky announced development of an H-76N naval version of the H-76, designed for anti-ship

Sikorsky Helicopter Advanced Demonstrator of Operator Workload (SHADOW), based on an S-76

Sikorsky S-72X1 X-Wing rotor systems research aircraft pictured during its first flight on 2 December 1987

surveillance and targeting, anti-submarine warfare, surface attack, search and rescue, and utility missions, operating from frigate sized ships. Over-the-horizon targeting (OTHT) and anti-ship (ASV) variants will be available with Ferranti Seaspray 3 and MEL Super Searcher radars in mounted pods. The ASV H-76N will be armed with two BAe Sea Skua air-to-surface missiles. The anti-submarine warfare version will have a dipping sonar, processing suite and two Gould Mk 46 or Marconi Sting Ray torpedoes. Other developments planned for the H-76N include a dual digital AFCS-coupled hover capability, target information data link, a tactical navigation system, hover in-flight refuelling system, roof- or mast-mounted FLIR system, ECM pod, chaff/flare dispensers on the tailboom, strengthened landing gear providing greater ground/deck clearance, folding main rotor blades, and provision for deck securing.

The H-76N will be offered with a choice of Allison 250-C34S or Pratt & Whitney Canada PT6B-36 engines. Provisional specifications include an estimated empty weight (all versions) of 2,812 kg (6,200 lb) and max T-O weights of 4,473 kg (9,861 lb) for the OTHT variant, 4,968 kg (10,953 lb) for the ASV version and 4,754 kg (10,481 lb) for an H-76N equipped with a 136 kg (300 lb) ECM pod for secondary role jamming. Total fuel capacity for all proposed variants is 999 litres (264 US gallons; 210 Imp gallons).

SIKORSKY S-76 SHADOW

In 1985 Sikorsky modified an S-76 helicopter to have a new single-pilot cockpit attached to the forward fuselage, to test advanced automated cockpit concepts for the US Army's Advanced Rotorcraft Technology Integration (ARTI) programme. Known as the Sikorsky Helicopter Advanced Demonstrator of Operator Workload

(SHADOW), it features large window areas which can be partially or totally covered during testing to evaluate cockpit visibility impact on pilot workload and effectiveness. The SHADOW made its first flight on 24 June 1985, with the single-pilot cockpit unmanned. After an initial 15-hour flight test programme it was fitted with advanced equipment, including fly by wire sidearm control stick, voice interactive system, remote map reader, FLIR, and a programmable symbol generator feeding a head-up display, a visually coupled helmet mounted display, and dual CRT displays with touch-sensitive screens. Standard flight deck controls are retained in the main cabin, to permit a safety pilot to monitor testing. Flight trials of the fully instrumented evaluation cockpit began in the Spring of 1986. Further flight trials were due to begin in the Spring of 1988.

Sikorsky's partners in the SHADOW programme include Bendix, Kaiser, Litton, Northrop, Pacer Systems, Rockwell Collins, Singer Kearfott and United Technologies Hamilton Standard division.

SIKORSKY S-72X1 X-WING PROJECT

Early in 1984 Sikorsky was awarded a contract valued at $77 million to modify one of NASA's two S-72 Rotor Systems Research Aircraft (RSRA: see 1979-80 *Jane's*) into a concept demonstrator for the NASA/Defense Advanced Research Projects Agency (DARPA) X-Wing rotor programme.

As a first step, an S-72 began a 13-flight test programme at NASA's Ames-Dryden Flight Research Facility on 8 May 1984 to prove the aircraft's suitability for flight in a fixed-wing mode. With its main rotor removed and long span wings installed, it expanded its proven performance envelope to 262 knots (485 km/h; 301 mph) and an altitude of 3,050 m (10,000 ft).

Sikorsky designed the X-Wing to replace the conventional rotor on the other S-72 (N741NA/NASA 741), which was rolled out on 19 August 1986 and subsequently moved to NASA's Ames-Dryden Flight Research Facility at Edwards Air Force Base, California, where, after a 16-second pre-planned lift-off during high-speed taxi tests on 13 November 1987, it made a 38-minute first flight (without the X-Wing) on 2 December 1987. After three further flights, however, the original contract funding expired and Sikorsky suspended all work on the X-Wing programme pending resolution of how further development should be funded. Sikorsky has said that it could not continue to fund the programme unaided.

For the initial phase of flight testing the aircraft's variable incidence fixed wing was to have been used to establish baseline weight, centre of gravity and performance data. During 1988 two of the four X-Wing blades were to have been installed for the second phase of testing, leading to the third phase with all four blades installed. The X-Wing would enable the aircraft to operate in the rotating-wing mode for take-off and hover, and then convert to fixed-wing

Artist's impression of Sikorsky H-76N naval helicopter with MEL Super Searcher radar and torpedoes

flight for speeds up to 250 knots (463 km/h; 288 mph). Initial test flights would be conducted with the X-Wing locked in the stationary position.

A full description of the S-72X1 can be found in the 1987-88 *Jane's*.

SIKORSKY S-80

The S-80 is an export version of the USN/USMC CH-53E heavy duty helicopter. It is available in two forms:

the **S-80E** is the basic heavy transport helicopter equivalent to the CH-53E; the **S-80M** is the export form of the airborne mine countermeasures MH-53E.

In its simplest configuration, the S-80E has a single-point cargo hook and operates in VFR conditions. Customers can enhance its capability with a variety of optional extras, including troop seats, cabin soundproofing, an internal cargo winch, external hoist of 272 kg (600 lb) capacity, two-point external cargo attachment, automatic blade and

tail folding, two 2,460.5 litre (650 US gallon; 541 Imp gallon) drop tanks, ground to air and/or in-flight refuelling capability, engine air particle separators, and a wide range of com/nav equipment.

Japan has authorised funding for six S-80Ms, four in FY 1986 and two in FY 1987. Six more are planned, four in FY 1989 and two in FY 1990. Deliveries were expected to begin in 1988.

SKYTRADER

SKYTRADER CORPORATION

Richards-Gebaur Airport, 15900 Kensington, Kansas City, Missouri 64147
Telephone: (816) 322 2811
Telex: 755964 SKYTRADER UD
Fax: (816) 322 2934
PRESIDENT, CHAIRMAN AND CHIEF EXECUTIVE OFFICER:
John J. Dupont
EXECUTIVE VICE-PRESIDENT, MARKETING: James F. Hudson
EXECUTIVE VICE-PRESIDENT, ENGINEERING AND GOVERNMENT PROGRAMMES: Ronald P. Barrett

SKYTRADER ST1700 CONESTOGA/ST1700 MD EVADER

A prototype Skytrader 800 was built by Dominion Aircraft Corporation Ltd, a Canadian company with facilities at Renton, Washington. Much of the design work was undertaken by former Boeing Company employees. This aircraft (N800ST) made its first flight on 21 April 1975, and was last described in the 1979-80 edition of *Jane's*. It was powered by two 298 kW (400 hp) Textron Lycoming IO-720-B1A piston engines.

Dominion Aircraft ceased trading in 1979, and the project lay dormant until 1983 when Mr John J. Dupont acquired it and formed Skytrader Aircraft (renamed Skytrader Corporation in 1984). In October 1984 first details were announced of the planned **Skytrader ST1700 Conestoga** which, although based on the earlier Skytrader 800 design, differs in having a T tail, extended and drooped nose ahead of the flight deck for improved lift and field of view, cambered wing and tailplane tips incorporating aerodynamic twist, strengthened main landing gear legs with twin wheels, and overhead cockpit 'eyebrow' windows. The ST1700's cabin is 46 cm (18 in) longer and 10 cm (4 in) wider than that of the Skytrader 800, permitting a variety of quick-change internal configurations.

At the 1985 convention of the Army Aviation Association of America in St Louis, the **Skytrader ST1700 MD** (military derivative) **Evader** was revealed, and development of this version is now expected to precede production of the commercial ST1700. The Evader has a considerably greater max T-O weight and payload. It will be suitable for a wide variety of military missions, including tactical transport, with accommodation for up to 26 combat-equipped troops, casualty evacuation, cargo carrying and airdropping. A ½463L cargo roller system enables full LAPES, CARP, HARP and HALO airdrop techniques to be employed. There will be four hardpoints under the wings for stores, including external fuel tanks and gun pods, and pylons on the fuselage sides for two Sidewinder self-defence air-to-air missiles. Operations into landing strips 152 m (500 ft) long will be practicable, and a bolt-on fuselage float attaching to the main landing gear structure will permit operation off water. To permit night and 'stealth' missions the ST1700 MD's flight deck will be compatible with night vision goggles. Provision is made for in-flight refuelling capability. No choice of power plant for the ST1700 MD had been announced by April 1988.

TYPE: Twin-turboprop all-metal STOL commuter airliner and cargo aircraft.

WINGS: High-wing monoplane, with single bracing strut on each side. Constant chord wings, with electrically operated leading-edge slats. Aerofoil section NACA 230-13M. Full span ailerons and flaps on trailing-edge. Trim tab in each aileron. Cambered wingtips.

FUSELAGE: Conventional structure with rectangular cabin section and upswept rear end. Flight deck has large single window on each side forward of crew door and extending from floor height to below instrument panel mounting. Square cabin windows, eight on port side, seven on starboard.

TAIL UNIT: Cantilever T tail, with horizontal surfaces of constant chord. Dorsal fin. Trim tab in rudder.

LANDING GEAR: Non-retractable type. Twin wheels on nose and main legs, with oversize, low pressure tyres.

ACCOMMODATION: Crew of two at front of cabin. 'Quick-change' cabin interior provides various internal arrangements including 18-passenger layout with 76 cm (30 in) pitch seating and 41 cm (16 in) aisle width, or all-freight. Access to flight deck via forward hinged door on each side, and to main cabin by airstair door on port side aft of wing. Hydraulically operated rear loading ramp/door, openable in flight for airdropping; double doors on starboard side at rear for oversized items or direct fork-lift loading. Cargo compartment can accept up to six D-type containers, each 1.02 × 1.02 × 1.02 m (40 × 40 × 40 in), or palletised or other cargo. Nose baggage

Prototype Skytrader SCOUT-STOL utility transport with nose-mounted FLIR turret

compartment, capacity 136 kg (300 lb), accessible via upward opening door on port side.

AVIONICS: King Silver Crown system, including KNS81 R/Nav, Bendix RDS-81 digital four-colour weather radar and King GC381A radar graphics unit, standard.

DIMENSIONS, EXTERNAL:
Wing span	17.98 m (59 ft 0 in)
Wing chord (constant)	2.03 m (6 ft 8 in)
Length overall	15.85 m (52 ft 0 in)
Height overall	6.10 m (20 ft 0 in)
Fuselage: Max width	1.68 m (5 ft 6 in)
Tailplane span	7.11 m (23 ft 4 in)
Fuselage ground clearance	0.71 m (2 ft 4 in)
Wheel track (c/l of shock struts)	4.27 m (14 ft 0 in)
Rear cargo loading door: Length	2.44 m (8 ft 0 in)
Height from ground to top of cargo compartment	
	2.44 m (8 ft 0 in)
Double doors (stbd): Height	1.37 m (4 ft 6 in)
Width	1.39 m (4 ft 7 in)
Height to sill	0.91 m (3 ft 0 in)

DIMENSIONS, INTERNAL:
Cabin:
Length, excl flight deck and space above ramp/door	
	7.11 m (23 ft 4 in)
Max width	1.37 m (4 ft 6 in)
Max height	1.65 m (5 ft 5 in)
Cargo volume, incl nose baggage compartment	
	17.98 m³ (635.0 cu ft)
Nose baggage compartment	0.69 m³ (24.5 cu ft)

WEIGHTS AND LOADING:
Weight empty: transport	3,810 kg (8,400 lb)
cargo	3,651 kg (8,050 lb)
Max T-O weight	7,710 kg (17,000 lb)
Max power loading	10.89 kg/kW (8.95 lb/shp)

ESTIMATED PERFORMANCE: Details not yet available

SKYTRADER SCOUT-STOL

On 16 May 1986 Skytrader Corporation rolled out its SCOUT-STOL short take-off and landing aircraft, based on the airframe of the earlier Skytrader 800 prototype. This aircraft was powered by two 298 kW (400 hp) Textron Lycoming IO-720-B1A piston engines; but in October 1987 Skytrader Corporation announced an agreement with Teledyne Continental Motors for installation of two 373 kW (500 shp) TP-500 turboprops in the prototype SCOUT-STOL for engine flight testing. Installation of the turboprop power plant was undertaken by Soloy Conversions Ltd. During 1988 the SCOUT-STOL was scheduled for demonstrations to the US Military Special Operations Command.

The SCOUT-STOL is intended as a multi-role utility/combat aircraft and has a cabin volume of 9.49 m³ (335 cu ft), accommodating up to 16 people, with a flight-openable rear loading ramp/paratroop dropping door. Flight Systems

Inc has been commissioned to develop a weapons system for the military gunship role, permitting the carriage of 2.75 in Hydra rockets, Stinger and Hellfire missiles and BEI 0.50 in calibre machine-gun pods. The McDonnell Douglas Helicopter ABP-30 Viper 30 mm modular sideways- and forward-firing demountable gun can be installed for deep reconnaissance missions. The SCOUT-STOL is also capable of carrying the McDonnell Douglas Battlefield Surveillance System (AMMS) module. Other optional equipment for military versions of the SCOUT-STOL includes FLIR Systems Inc forward looking infra-red in a steerable pod mounted beneath the aircraft's nose; SLAR; computerised onboard data processing; a steerable high intensity searchlight; underwing hardpoints for the carriage of sonobuoys, flares, long-range fuel tanks, navigational equipment or surveillance system pods; reconnaissance, mapping and long-range optical (LOROP) high-resolution cameras; LLLTV with videotape recording; and medevac equipment. Avionics include a King Radio KNS 660 multi-function navigation management system integrated to a King KFS 325 autopilot/flight director; King KHF 950 HF; multi-spectral scan fully integrated all-weather deep reconnaissance surveillance modules; Bendix/King all-weather utility avionics systems; portable MLS system; and Rockwell Collins MIL-STD-1553 navigation and GPWS avionics.

A launch order for five SCOUT-STOLS, configured for ocean surveillance missions, was received in January 1988 from Northstar Maritime Corporation of the Marshall Islands, which also holds an option on a further 10 aircraft. They will be used to patrol and protect fishing rights in the Pacific Basin. Mission equipment will include FLIR, Northstar Avionics Loran-C, a King Radio navigation system, and 35 mm cameras in the cockpit for documentation of surveillance and detection data. Delivery is scheduled to begin during 1989.

POWER PLANT: Two 373 kW (500 shp) Teledyne Continental TP-500 turboprops. Standard fuel contained in bladder tanks in wings, max capacity 908 litres (240 US gallons; 200 Imp gallons). Two optional long-range fuel tanks, each of 314 litres (83 US gallons; 69 Imp gallons), can be mounted on underwing stores pylons.

SYSTEMS: Electrical system includes two 250A DC starter/generators. Janitrol hot-air engine fuel fed anti-icing system optional. Air-conditioning system and auxiliary onboard GPU optional.

DIMENSIONS, EXTERNAL:
Wing span	16.76 m (55 ft 0 in)
Wing aspect ratio	7.9
Length overall	12.80 m (42 ft 0 in)
Height overall	5.79 m (19 ft 0 in)

DIMENSIONS, INTERNAL:
Cargo bay: Length	4.57 m (15 ft 0 in)
Max width (constant section)	1.37 m (4 ft 6 in)

Max height	1.68 m (5 ft 6 in)
Total cargo volume, incl nose bay	11.2 m³ (396.0 cu ft)
Cargo bay volume, constant section	
	10.50 m³ (371.0 cu ft)
Nose bay volume	0.57 m³ (20.0 cu ft)

AREA:

Wings, gross	35.77 m² (385.0 sq ft)

WEIGHTS AND LOADINGS:

Weight empty	3,175 kg (7,000 lb)
Fuel: standard	653 kg (1,440 lb)
with optional tanks	1,105 kg (2,436 lb)
Max T-O weight	4,536 kg (10,000 lb)
Max wing loading	126.8 kg/m² (25.97 lb/sq ft)
Max power loading	6.08 kg/kW (10.0 lb/shp)

PERFORMANCE (estimated at max T-O weight, ISA, S/L):

Max level speed at S/L	174 knots (322 km/h; 200 mph)
Cruising speed:	
75% power at 3,050 m (10,000 ft)	
	161 knots (298 km/h; 185 mph)
55% power at 760 m (2,500 ft)	
	130 knots (241 km/h; 150 mph)
Min control speed, one engine out	
	61 knots (113 km/h; 70 mph)
Stalling speed, slats and flaps extended	
	52 knots (97 km/h; 60 mph)
Max rate of climb at S/L	549 m (1,800 ft)/min
Rate of climb at S/L, one engine out	79 m (260 ft)/min
Service ceiling	7,315 m (24,000 ft)
Service ceiling, one engine out	3,355 m (11,000 ft)
T-O run	207 m (680 ft)
T-O to 15 m (50 ft)	305 m (1,000 ft)
Landing from 15 m (50 ft)	290 m (950 ft)
Range at 75% power:	
standard fuel	386 nm (714 km; 444 miles)
Range at 55% power:	
standard fuel	482 nm (893 km; 555 miles)
optional fuel	782 nm (1,448 km; 900 miles)

SKYTRADER 1400 COMMUTERLINER and SCOUT-A

The Skytrader 1400 Commuterliner is a projected 19-passenger version of the SCOUT-STOL, from which it differs primarily in having a fuselage some 1.83 m (6 ft 0 in) longer and two 533 kW (715 shp) Garrett TPE331-5 turboprops driving four-blade Hartzell Quiet Props. STOL capability is retained. All-weather avionics are standard. The cabin is quickly convertible for small package utility transport operations, with rear ramp loading and offloading, and a container system compatible with road delivery vans. Halon fire suppression systems for the cockpit, cabin, wings and engines contribute to safety standards that surpass the requirements of FAR Pt 121. Seat pitch is 73.6 cm (29 in). A military utility paratroop version of the Skytrader 1400 is designated **SCOUT-A**.

Standard fuel capacity is 908 litres (240 US gallons; 200 Imp gallons), increasable optionally to 1,287 litres (340 US gallons; 283 Imp gallons).

Model of the 19-passenger Skytrader 1400 Commuterliner

In December 1987 Skytrader Corporation announced the sale of five Skytrader 1400 Commuterliners to Marshalls Pacific Airline Ltd of Majuro, Republic of the Marshall Islands. This was followed in January 1988 by an order for four aircraft for Lang Aire Inc of Las Vegas, Nevada. Skytrader expects to manufacture nine aircraft during 1989, with customer deliveries scheduled to begin in the last quarter of that year. All subassemblies will be manufactured by Gulfstream Aerospace Technologies at Bethany, Oklahoma, with final assembly taking place at Skytrader's Kansas City facility. Customer completion work and after-sales support will be performed by AAR Oklahoma Inc of Oklahoma City.

DIMENSIONS, EXTERNAL:

Wing span	16.76 m (55 ft 0 in)
Wing aspect ratio	7.85
Length overall	14.94 m (49 ft 0 in)
Height overall	5.79 m (19 ft 0 in)

DIMENSIONS, INTERNAL:

Passenger/cargo cabin: Length	6.40 m (21 ft 0 in)
Max width	1.37 m (4 ft 6 in)
Max height	1.67 m (5 ft 6 in)
Volume	14.72 m³ (520.0 cu ft)
Total cargo volume, incl nose bay and tailcone	
	15.71 m³ (555.0 cu ft)

AREA:

Wings, gross	35.77 m² (385.0 sq ft)

WEIGHTS AND LOADINGS:

Weight empty	3,175 kg (7,000 lb)
Fuel: standard	653 kg (1,440 lb)
optional	925 kg (2,040 lb)
Max T-O weight	5,896 kg (13,000 lb)
Max wing loading	164.8 kg/m² (33.77 lb/sq ft)
Max power loading	5.53 kg/kW (9.09 lb/shp)

PERFORMANCE (estimated at max T-O weight, ISA):

Max level speed at S/L	191 knots (354 km/h; 220 mph)
Cruising speed:	
at 3,050 m (10,000 ft)	173 knots (322 km/h; 200 mph)
at 760 m (2,500 ft)	156 knots (290 km/h; 180 mph)
Stalling speed, flaps and slats extended	
	52 knots (97 km/h; 60 mph)
Min fully manoeuvrable speed, flaps and slats extended	
	50 knots (92 km/h; 57 mph)
Min single-engine control speed	
	52 knots (97 km/h; 60 mph)
Max rate of climb at S/L	640 m (2,100 ft)/min
Rate of climb at S/L, one engine out	177 m (580 ft)/min
Service ceiling	8,535 m (28,000 ft)
Service ceiling, one engine out	3,810 m (12,500 ft)
T-O run	250 m (821 ft)
T-O to 15 m (50 ft)	466 m (1,529 ft)
Landing from 15 m (50 ft)	281 m (920 ft)
Landing from 15 m (50 ft), with reverse pitch	
	165 m (540 ft)
Range:	
with max standard fuel	417 nm (772 km; 480 miles)
with optional fuel	591 nm (1,094 km; 680 miles)

SMITH
MIKE SMITH AERO INC

PO Box 430, Highway 160, Johnson City, Kansas 67855
Telephone: (316) 492 6840
PRESIDENT: Michael D. Smith

SMITH TRI-TAIL BONANZA

Three of these conventional-tail conversions for the Beech V-tail Bonanza light aircraft were completed. Details and a photograph may be found in the 1987-88 *Jane's*.

SMITH BONANZA 400

Mike Smith Aero has developed a conversion of the Beechcraft Model A36 Bonanza in which the aircraft's standard 224 kW (300 hp) Teledyne Continental IO-550-B engine is replaced with a 298 kW (400 hp) Textron Lycoming IO-720 eight-cylinder power plant. The Bonanza 400 is also equipped with wingtip fuel tanks, each with a capacity of 76 litres (20 US gallons; 16.7 Imp gallons), bringing total usable fuel capacity to 431 litres (114 US gallons; 95 Imp gallons). A prototype (N1LX) was flown for the first time on 9 July 1985. In early 1988 customer interest was being sought prior to taking a decision on seeking FAA certification under a Supplemental Type Certificate. Provisional data include:

WEIGHT:

Weight empty	1,074 kg (2,367 lb)

PERFORMANCE:

Cruising speed at 3,050 m (10,000 ft)	
	203 knots (376 km/h; 234 mph)
Max rate of climb at S/L	
	in excess of 610 m (2,000 ft)/min.

SOLOY
SOLOY CONVERSIONS LTD

450 Pat Kennedy Way SW, Olympia, Washington 98502
Telephone: (206) 754 7000
Telex: 510 785 0241
PRESIDENT: Joe I. Soloy
SALES MANAGER: J. T. Koester
MARKETING GROUP MANAGER: R. K. Furtick

Soloy Conversions has long been known for its turbine engine conversions of Bell 47G and Hiller UH-12E series helicopters. It is now devoting its major effort to expanding production of the Bell 47G conversion, and to work on its Turbine Pac specialised turboprop conversion scheme, development of which is being shared by the Allison Gas Turbine Division of General Motors Corporation (which see, in this section). The Turbine Pac can be produced in 16 configurations, ranging from 313 to an eventual 548 kW (420-735 shp).

SOLOY TURBINE PAC CONVERSIONS

The Turbine Pac is a specialised turboprop conversion unit that can be used to update and improve the performance of a variety of fixed-wing aircraft. In its current form it is built around a 313 kW (420 shp) Allison 250-C20S, a 373 kW (500 shp) Allison 250-C28C, or a 485 kW (650 shp) Allison 250-C30 turboshaft, with a separate shaft driven 1,800 rpm reduction gearbox to provide the propeller drive. This gearbox is rated at more than 522 kW (700 shp) to allow for future growth versions of the engine.

Military version of Cessna Model 206 with Soloy Turbine Pac power plant and high flotation landing gear

Flight testing of the Turbine Pac began on 23 November 1981, using a Cessna Model 185 (N5010Y) and an Allison 250-C20 engine. Details of the subsequent development programme can be found in the 1987-88 and earlier editions of *Jane's*. Three models (Cessna 206, Cessna 207 and Beechcraft A36 Bonanza) are STC approved and in production. The Soloy Turbine Pac Cessna 185 and Allison/Soloy Beechcraft T-34 are available to government agencies and others able to use non-certificated aircraft; a Cessna Model 185/U-17 with Soloy Turbine Pac power plant has been evaluated by the Royal Thai Army. Soloy Turbine Pac Cessnas have been delivered to the US Drug Enforcement Administration and the Government of Costa Rica. Several Allison turboprop A36 Bonanzas have been sold for private and business use; this conversion is described under the Allison heading. Under development is an adaptation of the more powerful Allison Series IV turboshaft for single- and twin-engined aircraft. Soloy has also completed the installation of a 485 kW (650 shp) Allison 250-C30M in an Aérospatiale Astar 350D helicopter, certification of which was granted in early 1986. A prototype installation of the 313 kW (420 shp) Allison 250-B17 in the Chilean ENAER Aucán prototype (1987–88 *Jane's*) made its first flight on 12 February 1986, prior to returning to Chile for evaluation. In early 1988 a subsidiary company, Soloy Dual Pac Inc, was developing a new Dual Pac system, which combines the power section of two 373 kW (500 shp) Teledyne Continental TP-500 turboprops with a Soloy gearbox, each engine providing independent drive to a single Hartzell propeller through a separate reduction system. Soloy believes the Dual Pac, which can operate on a single power section for fuel economy during extended flight, will provide power redundancy for 'single-engined' aircraft operating under FAR Pt 135 IFR passenger carrying requirements, and improve the safety of twin-engined aircraft in the event of engine failure. A prototype installation in a cabin class general aviation aircraft was expected to fly during 1988.

Soloy Turbine Pac installation in a Cessna 207 on PK amphibious floats

SOLOY CESSNA 206 TURBINE PAC

The Soloy Turbine Pac conversion for the Cessna 206 received FAA certification on 22 May 1984 and is in production, with converted aircraft delivered to customers in Australia, Bolivia, Switzerland and the United States. The aircraft is approved for operation on Wipline and PK floats, and EDO 3500 amphibious floats. A military version of this aircraft, intended primarily for liaison and observation missions, is equipped with 'super flotation' landing gear with oversize low pressure tyres for operation off unprepared terrain, and an extended range fuel system in the wings.

POWER PLANT: One 313 kW (420 shp) Soloy Model 763 Turbine Pac/Allison 250-C20S turboprop, driving a Hartzell three-blade constant-speed fully-feathering propeller. Fuel capacity 230-348 litres (61-92 US gallons; 51-77 Imp gallons), depending on airframe model. Extended range fuel tanks, total usable capacity 189 litres (50 US gallons; 42 Imp gallons), optional on military model. Oil capacity 7.1 litres (1.9 US gallons; 1.6 Imp gallons).

WEIGHTS:
Weight empty	866 kg (1,910 lb)
Max T-O weight	1,633 kg (3,600 lb)

PERFORMANCE (at max T-O weight):
Never-exceed speed
148 knots (274 km/h; 170 mph) IAS
Max level speed and max cruising speed at 3,050 m (10,000 ft)   163 knots (302 km/h; 188 mph)
Econ cruising speed at 6,100 m (20,000 ft)
142 knots (263 km/h; 164 mph)
Stalling speed:
flaps up, power off
58 knots (107 km/h; 67 mph) CAS
flaps down, power off
52 knots (96 km/h; 60 mph) CAS
Max rate of climb at S/L   594 m (1,950 ft)/min
Service ceiling   6,100 m (20,000 ft)
T-O run   174 m (570 ft)
T-O to 15 m (50 ft)   324 m (1,063 ft)

Soloy Turbine Pac conversion of a Cessna Model 185 Skywagon in military configuration

Landing from 15 m (50 ft)   334 m (1,094 ft)
Landing run   168 m (553 ft)
Range with 333 litres (88 US gallons; 73 Imp gallons) usable fuel, max range power at 6,100 m (20,000 ft)
882 nm (1,635 km; 1,016 miles)

SOLOY CESSNA 207 TURBINE PAC

Prototype installation of a 313 kW (420 shp) Soloy Turbine Pac/Allison 250-C20S turboprop in a Cessna Model 207 (N21190) was flown for the first time on 14 January 1984. A second Cessna 207 joined the test programme in Spring 1985, and certification was achieved in early 1986.

WEIGHTS:
Weight empty	893 kg (1,969 lb)
Max T-O weight	1,814 kg (4,000 lb)

PERFORMANCE:
Max level speed:
at 1,525 m (5,000 ft)   157 knots (291 km/h; 181 mph)
at 3,050 m (10,000 ft)   164 knots (304 km/h; 189 mph)
Stalling speed:
flaps up, power off
59 knots (109 km/h; 68 mph) CAS
flaps down, power off
53 knots (98 km/h; 61 mph) CAS
Max rate of climb at S/L   500 m (1,640 ft)/min
Service ceiling   7,620 m (25,000 ft)
T-O run   224 m (736 ft)
Range with 303 litres (80 US gallons; 67 Imp gallons) usable fuel, max range power at 3,050 m (10,000 ft)
558 nm (1,034 km; 642 miles)

SUMMIT

SUMMIT AVIATION INC

Summit Airport, Middletown, Delaware 19709
Telephone: (302) 834 5400
Telex: 83-5499
CHIEF EXECUTIVE OFFICER: Caroline DuPont
PRESIDENT: Patrick J. Foley

SUMMIT SENTRY O2-337

Summit Aviation developed this version of the Cessna Model T337 for a wide range of military missions. These include forward air control, helicopter escort, light air-to-ground attack, convoy protection, maritime patrol, six-seat personnel carrier, light cargo transport, aerial photography, psychological warfare and airborne dis-

charge. Special configurations are available for VIP transport, medevac and high-altitude missions. In all configurations day or night capability can be provided.

Summit's modifications begin with the purchase of a Model T337, which was described under the Cessna entry in the 1980-81 *Jane's*. Power plant comprises two 168 kW (225 hp) Continental TSIO-360 turbocharged flat-six engines. For orders of fewer than 20 aircraft, Summit rebuilds Cessna T337 airframes to zero-time status. For larger orders the Cessna factory was originally expected to supply new airframes, as required, for Summit to outfit according to customer specification.

With four standard NATO MALL-4A pylons mounted beneath the wings, each able to carry a max load of 159 kg (350 lb), the Summit Sentry can carry weapons which include SUU-11A/A 7.62 mm gun pods; FFV UNI 12.7

mm gun pods; LAU-32A/A, 32B/A, 59A, 68A and 68B/A rocket launchers; CBU-14, SUU/14/A containers and bombs, LUU-1B, 5B, and Mod 6 Mk 3 markers; Mk 24 flares; ADSID; and a combined search radar and speaker system.

Summit supplied six Sentry O2-337s to the Royal Thai Navy air arm in 1980 and a further four in 1983. Other reported operators include the air forces of Haiti, Honduras, Nicaragua and Senegal. According to the *Washington Post* newspaper, at least three were supplied to the Nicaraguan contras, via the CIA, under Operation Elephant Herd in 1984.

Available specifications and performance details are as follows:

WEIGHTS:
Weight empty, approx	1,433 kg (3,160 lb)
Max T-O weight	2,359 kg (5,200 lb)
Max landing weight	2,200 kg (4,850 lb)

PERFORMANCE (at max T-O weight):
Max level speed: at S/L   163 knots (302 km/h; 188 mph)
at 3,050 m (10,000 ft)   179 knots (332 km/h; 206 mph)
Max cruising speed:
at S/L   150 knots (278 km/h; 173 mph)
at 1,525 m (5,000 ft)   155 knots (287 km/h; 178 mph)
at 3,050 m (10,000 ft)   165 knots (306 km/h; 190 mph)
Max rate of climb at S/L   335 m (1,100 ft)/min
Service ceiling   8,690 m (28,500 ft)
T-O run   164 m (538 ft)
Landing run   137 m (449 ft)
Range at 75% power with 560 litres (148 US gallons; 123 Imp gallons) usable fuel
955 nm (1,770 km; 1,100 miles)
Max range, long-range cruise power, fuel as above
1,175 nm (2,177 km; 1,353 miles)

Summit O2-337s for the Royal Thai Navy air arm awaiting delivery

SUPER 580
SUPER 580 AIRCRAFT COMPANY
2192 Palomar Airport Road, Carlsbad, California 92008
Telephone: (619) 438 3600
Telex: 140414
Fax: (619) 753 1531
PRESIDENT: Ted Vallas
VICE-PRESIDENT, SALES: James Coleman

This company, a division of Flight Trails Inc, has the licence for a turboprop conversion and remanufacturing programme for the Convair 340/440/580 series of passenger/cargo transports, known as the Super 580, from the Allison Gas Turbine Division of General Motors Corporation.

SUPER 580 AIRCRAFT SUPER 580

The Super 580 conversion employs two Allison 501-D22G turboprops, each flat rated at 2,983 kW (4,000 shp), and driving a Hamilton Standard 54H60-77 four-blade, constant-speed feathering and reversing propeller, replacing the Pratt & Whitney R-2800 radial piston engines of the Convair 340/440 or the earlier Allison 501-D13 turboprops of the Convair 580. Compared with the Convair 580, of which some 170 were converted by Convair, the Super 580 is claimed to offer a 2.5 per cent improvement in specific fuel consumption, improved engine-out performance, greater reliability, a 13 per cent increase in range, a 40 per cent increase in hot-day payload capability, cruising speeds up to 325 knots (602 km/h; 374 mph), and a 40 per cent reduction in operating costs.

The Allison 501-D22G engine conversion has been designed as a quick-change nacelle/engine module, manufactured by subcontractor Jay Dee Aircraft Supply Co of Santa Monica, California. Standard fuel capacity is 6,738 litres (1,780 US gallons; 1,482 Imp gallons), with 7,790 litres (2,058 US gallons; 1,714 Imp gallons) or 11,008 litres (2,908 US gallons; 2,421 Imp gallons) available optionally. A Garrett 95.90 APU is installed in the starboard engine nacelle, and a new fire extinguisher system is standard. A tail-mounted APU is optional.

The Super 580 remanufacturing programme includes a redesigned flight deck with a King Gold Crown Series 3 avionics package and two Sperry Flight Systems flight directors. A Rockwell Collins flight director system, incorporating an EFIS display and two digital flight directors, is optional. All electrical wiring is replaced, but the aircraft's existing DC electrical system is retained. An AC system may be introduced at a later date, either as standard equipment or as an option. The Super 580's passenger cabin, pressurised at 0.29 bars (4.16 lb/sq in), is configured for 50 passengers in airline seats with 0.91 m (36 in) pitch, and features upgraded soundproofing, lavatory and galley facilities, 0.12 m³ (4.4 cu ft) capacity overhead baggage bins, indirect fluorescent lighting and individual reading lights and air vents.

Three cabin baggage compartments are provided: a 1.44 m³ (50.9 cu ft) forward compartment with a capacity of 227 kg (500 lb); a 5.64 m³ (199.2 cu ft) aft compartment, capacity 816 kg (1,800 lb); and a stowage area for carry-on baggage and garment bags. A 2.20 m³ (77.8 cu ft) belly compartment can accommodate 453 kg (1,000 lb) of cargo.

Piston engined Convair 340/440 aircraft undergoing remanufacture as Super 580s also require modifications to their tail surfaces. A 0.30 m (1 ft 0 in) fin extension and a larger rudder with an additional 1.11 m² (12.0 sq ft) of surface area are added, fin/rudder attachment points strengthened, and horizontal tail surfaces increased in span

Super 580 turboprop conversion of a Convairliner

by 0.51 m (1 ft 8 in) at each tip, with an additional 1.58 m² (17.0 sq ft) of elevator added. An anti-skid braking system is available optionally.

The first Super 580 conversion was performed by Hamilton Aviation, Tucson, Arizona. First flown after conversion on 21 March 1984, it was configured for quick-change corporate/commuter operations and delivered to The Way International of New Knoxville, Ohio, in June 1984 after receiving FAA approval to CAR 4b by means of a Supplemental Type Certificate. Like Hamilton Aviation's conversion, the first Super 580 Aircraft Company modification, which made its first flight on 20 November 1984, was based on a Convair 580 airframe. The third Super 580, of which conversion began in the Spring of 1985, was the first to be based on a piston engined Convair 440. Air Resorts Airlines, which is also a division of Flight Trails Inc, planned to convert three of its Convair 440s to Super 580s during 1988, and will eventually convert all 11 of its aircraft.

The Super 580 Aircraft Company has joined with Westinghouse Electric Corporation in a proposal put before the US Treasury Department for an anti-drug surveillance version of the Super 580. This aircraft, known as the **Super 580 Falcon**, would be equipped with a Westinghouse AN/APG-66S radar mounted on the underside of the fuselage. Super 580 Aircraft has proposed an initial retrofit of 12 Convair 440s for use by the US Drug Enforcement Agency or US Customs Service to patrol southern border areas of the United States. An extension of the programme to 50 aircraft is envisaged. Aerodynamic engineering for the Super 580 Falcon would be performed by General Dynamics' Convair Division. The first conversion could be ready for flight testing in 20 months after go-ahead, with production aircraft available 24 months after contract award. The aircraft would have a cruising speed of 325 knots (602 km/h; 374 mph) and a range of 2,800 nm (5,189 km; 3,224 miles). A typical mission could involve a 200 nm (371 km; 230 mile) positioning leg, a 12 h 30 min loiter and return to base with IFR fuel reserves.

The following data apply to the standard transport version:

DIMENSIONS, EXTERNAL:

Wing span	32.08 m (105 ft 3 in)

Length overall	24.84 m (81 ft 6 in)
Height overall	8.89 m (29 ft 2 in)

DIMENSIONS, INTERNAL:

Cabin: Length	15.75 m (51 ft 8 in)
Max height	1.98 m (6 ft 6 in)
Max width	2.69 m (8 ft 10 in)

WEIGHTS:

Basic operating weight	14,742 kg (32,500 lb)
Max fuel weight	5,421 kg (11,951 lb)
Max ramp and max T-O weight	26,383 kg (58,165 lb)
Max landing weight:	
without anti-skid	23,587 kg (52,000 lb)
with anti-skid	24,040 kg (53,000 lb)
Max zero-fuel weight	22,680 kg (50,000 lb)

PERFORMANCE:

Never-exceed speed	349 knots (647 km/h; 402 mph)
Max cruising speed:	
at S/L	280 knots (519 km/h; 322 mph)
at 3,050 m (10,000 ft)	
	310 knots (574 km/h; 357 mph)
Stalling speed	
	75-93 knots (139-173 km/h; 86-107 mph)
Max rate of climb at S/L	872 m (2,860 ft)/min
Rate of climb at S/L, one engine out	
	258 m (848 ft)/min
Service ceiling	7,620 m (25,000 ft)
Service ceiling, one engine out	6,860 m (22,500 ft)
Range with 18 passengers	
	1,920 nm (3,558 km; 2,211 miles)
Max range, FAR domestic reserves	
	2,000 nm (3,706 km; 2,303 miles)

SUPER 580 AIRCRAFT SUPER 580 ST

In 1984 the Convair Division of General Dynamics Corporation, under subcontract to Allison Division of General Motors, conducted feasibility studies for a 'stretch' of existing Convair 340/440, CV-580 and CV-640 airframes to permit increased payloads of up to 78 passengers or 9,525 kg (21,000 lb) of cargo, typically in nine LD3 containers or on up to seven 2.2 × 2.7 m (88 × 108 in) pallets. Super 580 Aircraft has applied for FAA Supplemental Type Certification for the conversion, to be known as the Super 580 ST (Stretch). Tooling design for the conversion has been completed by San Diego Aircraft Engineering, and a prototype was expected to fly in late 1988. Super 580 Aircraft estimates that some 270 Convair airframes are potential candidates for Super 580 ST conversion.

DIMENSIONS (preliminary):

Length overall	29.18 m (95 ft 9 in)
Cabin: Volume	87.7 m³ (3,096 cu ft)
Floor area	48.1 m² (518.0 sq ft)

WEIGHTS (provisional):

Weight empty: passenger	16,951 kg (37,370 lb)
cargo	14,968 kg (33,000 lb)
Baggage: standard	201 kg (444 lb)
optional	228 kg (502 lb)
Max T-O weight	28,576 kg (63,000 lb)
Max landing weight	26,308 kg (58,000 lb)
Max zero-fuel weight	24,948 kg (55,000 lb)

Artist's impression of the Super 580 ST, based on the Convair CV-580 airframe

SWEARINGEN
SWEARINGEN ENGINEERING AND TECHNOLOGY INC
Suite A, 1234 99th Street, San Antonio, Texas 78214
Telephone: (512) 921 1208 and 0198
PRESIDENT: E. J. Swearingen
VICE-PRESIDENT, ENGINEERING: C. H. Green
VICE-PRESIDENT, MARKETING: O. L. Anderson

Well known as the designer of the Merlin and Metro twin-turboprop executive transports, Mr 'Ed' J. Swearingen initiated a modification programme to enhance the performance and operating economy of Beechcraft King Air 90 models.

Swearingen Aircraft (formerly Jetcrafters) also manufactures PT6A engine nacelles for Dornier GmbH for the Dornier 128-6, and prototype JT15D nacelles for Pratt & Whitney Canada.

SWEARINGEN TAURUS MODIFICATION

Any model of the Beechcraft King Air 90 series (except the T tail F90) can be improved by incorporation of the Swearingen Taurus modification. This involves replacing the existing engines with Pratt & Whitney Canada PT6A-135 turboprops, each flat rated at 522 kW (700 shp); modification of the existing engine nacelles to reduce their height and cross-sectional area; provision of new cowls,

engine air inlets, inertial water/ice separators, a new low-profile exhaust system to reduce drag and increase thrust, new oil cooler airflow control system, and a new integral nacelle fuel tank with full lightning strike protection; removal of the existing engine driven cabin supercharger and provision of a new flow control system to provide dual bleed air pressurisation; and the supply of new engine torque indicators.

After embodiment of the Taurus modification, the King Air 90, A90, B90, C90 and E90 are redesignated respectively Taurus 90, A90, B90, C90 and E90. By early 1985 Swearingen had completed 12 Taurus modifications.

Brief details of performance improvements follow:

PERFORMANCE (A: Taurus 90, B: A90, C: B90, D: C90, and E: E90):

Max cruising speed at optimum altitude:
A, B, C, D, E	278 knots (515 km/h; 320 mph)

Stalling speed, flaps down:
A, B, C, D, E	69 knots (127 km/h; 79 mph)

Max rate of climb at S/L: A ... 913 m (2,995 ft)/min
B	884 m (2,900 ft)/min
C, D	852 m (2,795 ft)/min
E	814 m (2,670 ft)/min

Service ceiling: A, B, C, D, E ... 11,430 m (37,500 ft)

T-O to 15 m (50 ft): A, B ... 625 m (2,050 ft)
C	533 m (1,750 ft)
D	689 m (2,261 ft)
E	617 m (2,024 ft)

Landing from 15 m (50 ft): A, B ... 716 m (2,350 ft)
C, D	613 m (2,010 ft)
E	643 m (2,110 ft)

SWEARINGEN SA-30 FANJET

On 30 October 1986 Swearingen announced its intention to design and build an advanced technology light twin-jet aircraft known as the SA-30 Fanjet. By June 1988 all wind tunnel testing had been completed, and construction of the prototype was well under way. First flight was then scheduled for early 1989.

TYPE: Twin-turbofan executive transport.

WINGS: Cantilever low-wing monoplane, of all-metal fail-safe construction. Sweptback, tapered planform, and advanced technology computer-designed section. Main wing box forms integral fuel tanks. Double-slotted Fowler trailing-edge flaps and leading-edge slats for low landing speeds. Lateral control by combination of ailerons and spoilers (latter in five segments on each wing, forward of flaps); spoilers serve also as airbrakes/lift dumpers. Flaps and slats are mechanically synchronised, and positioned by electrically operated screwjacks; spoilers are actuated electro-hydraulically; ailerons are actuated mechanically, and have electrically actuated trim tabs. Leading-edges are de-iced with a TKS system.

FUSELAGE: Pressurised all-metal (aluminium alloy) semi-monocoque structure of basically circular section, with chemically milled skins.

TAIL UNIT: Cantilever all-metal T tail, with sweepback on all surfaces. All-moving tailplane is positioned by electrically actuated pitch trim actuators. Rudder is mechanically actuated, and fitted with an electrically actuated trim tab. TKS de-icing of tailplane leading-edges.

LANDING GEAR: Retractable tricycle type, with twin wheels and oleo-pneumatic shock absorber on each unit. Hydraulic actuation, main units retracting inward and rearward into fuselage. Hydraulically steerable nose unit retracts forward.

POWER PLANT: Two 8.01 kN (1,800 lb st) Williams International FJ44 turbofans, pod-mounted on pylons on sides of rear fuselage. Inlets de-iced by engine bleed air. Fuel in three integral tanks, one in each wing and one in rear fuselage, with combined capacity of 1,893 litres (500 US gallons; 416 Imp gallons). Single-point refuelling of all three tanks.

ACCOMMODATION: Pilot and one passenger (or co-pilot) on flight deck. Main cabin, separated by a bulkhead, is fitted as standard with four chairs in facing pairs, each with adjustable reclining backs and retractable armrests, plus two foldaway tables and an optional refreshment centre at front, with toilet, washbasin and storage cabinets at rear. Other layouts, and additional seating, available optionally. Airstair passenger door at front on port side. Baggage compartment aft of main cabin, with external access via port-side door aft of wing. Two-piece wraparound windscreen, birdproof and electrically heated.

SYSTEMS: Cabin pressurised to 0.69 bars (10.0 lb/sq in), and heated, by engine bleed air; and cooled by a freon-cycle system. Hydraulic system for actuation of spoilers, landing gear extension/retraction and nosewheel steering. Electrical DC power supplied by two 300A engine driven starter/generators, with all necessary AC provided by static inverters. Redundant frequency-wild alternators provide power for windscreen heating.

AVIONICS: Collins Pro Line II avionics standard, including com, nav, marker beacon receivers, glideslopes, audios, DMEs, transponders, RMIs and inverters (all dual), plus ADF, compass, colour weather radar and autopilot/flight director.

DIMENSIONS, EXTERNAL:
Wing span	11.07 m (36 ft 4 in)
Wing aspect ratio	8.0
Length overall	12.77 m (41 ft 10¾ in)
Height overall	3.94 m (12 ft 11 in)

DIMENSIONS, INTERNAL:
Cabin: Length:	
between pressure bulkheads	4.89 m (16 ft 0½ in)
passenger section	3.41 m (11 ft 2½ in)
Max width	1.43 m (4 ft 8½ in)
Max height	1.31 m (4 ft 3½ in)
Volume	8.38 m³ (296.0 cu ft)

AREA:
Wings, gross	15.33 m² (165.0 sq ft)

WEIGHTS:
Weight empty, equipped	2,358 kg (5,200 lb)
Fuel weight	1,519 kg (3,350 lb)
Max ramp weight	4,218 kg (9,300 lb)
Max T-O weight	4,196 kg (9,250 lb)
Max landing weight	4,082 kg (9,000 lb)

PERFORMANCE (estimated, at max T-O weight except where indicated):
Max operating speed	Mach 0.82 (470 knots; 871 km/h; 541 mph)
Max cruising speed	450 knots (834 km/h; 518 mph)
Long-range cruising speed	413 knots (765 km/h; 475 mph)
Stalling speed at max landing weight	80 knots (149 km/h; 93 mph)
Max rate of climb at S/L	1,228 m (4,030 ft)/min
Max operating altitude	12,500 m (41,000 ft)
FAA T-O balanced field length	997 m (3,270 ft)
FAA landing distance	733 m (2,405 ft)

Range at Mach 0.72 (413 knots; 765 km/h; 475 mph):
NBAA VFR reserves	2,170 nm (4,021 km; 2,499 miles)
NBAA IFR reserves	1,830 nm (3,391 km; 2,107 miles)

Swearingen Taurus modification of a Beechcraft King Air Model 90

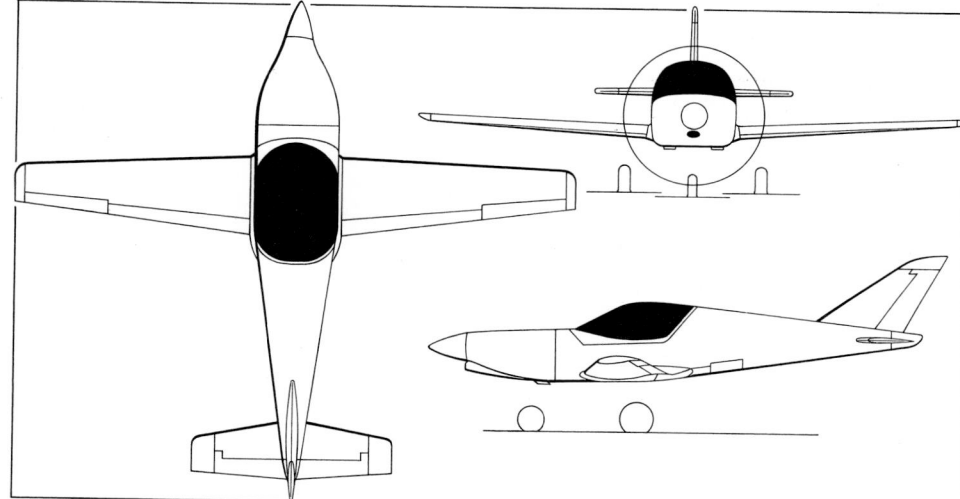

Jaffe/Swearingen SA-32T side by side two-seat turboprop powered trainer (Jane's/Mike Keep)

Artist's impression of the Swearingen SA-30 Fanjet executive transport

JAFFE/SWEARINGEN SA-32T

Swearingen is in the process of designing a two-seat turboprop powered training aircraft, designated SA-32T, powered by an Allison 250-B17D engine. A prototype was under construction in mid-1988, with first flight scheduled for March 1989. General appearance is shown in the accompanying three-view drawing. Except for the power plant and canopy design, the airframe appears to be almost identical with that of Mr Swearingen's SX300 two-seat light aircraft, described and illustrated in the Sport Aircraft section of the 1987-88 Jane's. (See Jaffe in Addenda.)

TYPE: Two-seat training aircraft.

WINGS: Cantilever low-wing monoplane, of tapered planform and mainly metal construction, including ailerons and hydraulically actuated trailing-edge flaps. Wingtips and wing/fuselage fairings of composite materials. Ailerons have electric trim.

FUSELAGE: Conventional all-metal stressed skin primary structure. Tailcone and engine cowling panels of composites construction.

TAIL UNIT: Metal structure, comprising sweptback fin and rudder, non-swept tailplane and elevators. Fin and tailplane tips are of composite materials. Electrically operated trim tab in elevator.

LANDING GEAR: Hydraulically retractable tricycle type, with single wheel and oleo-pneumatic shock absorber on each unit. Manual hydraulic pump for emergency extension, and gas-spring powered secondary emergency extension. Steerable nose unit, with shimmy damper. Mainwheel tyres size 6.00-6, nosewheel tyre size 5.00-5 (all three 6-ply). Hydraulic disc brakes and parking brake.

POWER PLANT: One 313 kW (420 shp) Allison 250-B17D turboprop, driving a three-blade constant-speed propeller with spinner. Inlet anti-iced by engine bleed air. Fuel in two integral wing tanks (each 128.5 litres; 34 US gallons; 28 Imp gallons usable) and a 72 litre (19 US gallon; 16 Imp gallon) fuselage header tank, giving total usable capacity of 329 litres (87 US gallons; 72 Imp gallons).

ACCOMMODATION: Side by side seats for instructor and pupil, with full-shoulder inertia reel safety harness for each occupant. Dual controls standard. Hydraulically actu-

ated 'omnivision' canopy, with windscreen demisting. Baggage space aft of seats (no external access). Accommodation heated (by engine bleed air) and ventilated.

SYSTEMS: Hydraulic system for actuation of flaps, landing gear and mainwheel brakes. Electrical system (28V DC), with lead-acid battery and 70A alternator, provides power for engine start, aileron and elevator trim, hydraulic pumps, navigation, strobe, landing and cockpit lights.

DIMENSION, INTERNAL:
Wing span	7.43 m (24 ft 4½ in)
Wing aspect ratio	8.3
Length overall	6.86 m (22 ft 6 in)
Height overall	2.37 m (7 ft 9¼ in)

DIMENSIONS INTERNAL:
Cockpit: Max width	1.04 m (3 ft 5 in)

AREA:
Wings, gross reference	6.64 m² (71.5 sq ft)

WEIGHTS:
Average weight empty, equipped	707 kg (1,560 lb)

Fuel weight (usable)	264 kg (583 lb)
Baggage (max)	32 kg (70 lb)
Max T-O and landing weight	1,179 kg (2,600 lb)

PERFORMANCE (estimated, at max T-O weight except where indicated):
Max level speed at S/L	288 knots (534 km/h; 332 mph)
Normal cruising speed at 6,100 m (20,000 ft)	274 knots (508 km/h; 315 mph)
Stalling speed at 1,134 kg (2,500 lb) AUW:	
gear and flaps up	86 knots (160 km/h; 100 mph)
gear and flaps down	73 knots (136 km/h; 85 mph)
Max rate of climb at S/L at 1,134 kg (2,500 lb) AUW	1,128 m (3,700 ft)/min
Service ceiling	more than 7,620 m (25,000 ft)
T-O run	427 m (1,400 ft)
T-O to 15 m (50 ft)	518 m (1,700 ft)
Landing from 15 m (50 ft)	701 m (2,300 ft)
Landing run	335 m (1,100 ft)
Max range at normal cruising speed, no reserves	960 nm (1,779 km; 1,105 miles)

TAP
THOMPSON AERO PRODUCTS
PO Box 3280, 4 Jackpine, Sunriver, Oregon 97707
Telephone: (503) 593 1484
PROPRIETOR: W. D. Thompson

This company manufactures and installs auxiliary spoilers and dive brakes for Cessna Model 177 and 177RG Cardinal and Model 210, T210 and P210 Centurion light aircraft. The dive brakes (total area 0.088 m²; 0.947 sq ft) and spoilers (total area 0.28 m²; 3.02 sq ft) are of external hinged plate type and mixed aluminium alloy/graphite/Kevlar/glassfibre construction. Spoilers are mounted above the aircraft's wing inboard of the mid-span position, dive brakes below the wing in the same position, and are operated by a pneumatic system drawing suction from the aircraft's intake manifold or vacuum pump. The spoiler and dive brake systems can be mounted independently or in

combination. A position indicating system with alerting light and auxiliary vacuum system are optional (the latter mandatory on turbocharged aircraft). Installation of the complete systems takes some 120 man hours.

Claimed advantages of the systems are faster approach speeds to short runways, enhanced crosswind handling, improved deceleration with lift dumping providing reductions in landing run of up to 35 per cent, improved stall/spin recovery, rapid descents at cruise power avoiding engine shock cooling, and precise speed control in rapid descents and steep approaches. The curved spoiler plate is claimed to reduce T-O run by 15-20 per cent in conditions of sluggish acceleration, such as when operating from soft fields or from high elevation airports at max T-O weight, and to reduce stalling speed in take-off configuration by 1.7 nm (3 km/h; 2 mph).

Thompson Aero Products auxiliary spoiler shown in the deployed position

TAYLORCRAFT
TAYLORCRAFT AVIATION CORPORATION
PO Box 947, 820 East Bald Eagle Street, Lock Haven, Pennsylvania 17745
PRESIDENT: George A. Ruckle

Taylorcraft Aviation Corporation, which was re-formed on 1 April 1968 primarily to provide product support, also put into production a two-seat trainer/sporting aircraft designated Model F-19 Sportsman 100, based on the well known Taylorcraft Model B of Second World War origin.

In early 1980, the Model F-19 (see 1979-80 *Jane's*) was taken out of production, and the company certificated a higher powered verson designated F-21. This was supplemented by a new Model F-21A for 1983, but the latter model was replaced by the F-21B during 1985.

On 9 July 1985 the company was acquired by a group of former Piper Aircraft Company employees, and the production facility was moved to the Piper Memorial Airport at Lock Haven, Pennsylvania. The first production aircraft from the new assembly line was rolled out on 9 January 1986. In early 1986 Taylorcraft acquired manufacturing rights for Edo floats.

No information has been received from the company since it filed for protection under Chapter 11 of the US bankruptcy laws in late 1986, but it was reported in Spring 1988 to be continuing with certification flight testing of the F-22.

TAYLORCRAFT F-21B
In Spring 1985 Taylorcraft built a prototype of the Model F-21B, and production was reportedly at the rate of one per week in March 1986. The F-21B is similar to the F-21 (1987-88 *Jane's*) but with some modifications to the structure, to permit an increased max T-O weight, and a new fuel system.

Production has reportedly been suspended, but the F-21B has received Australian certification, giving rise to hopes that it may be resumed in the near future.

TYPE: Two-seat trainer/sporting aircraft.

WINGS: Braced high-wing monoplane with V bracing struts each side. Wing section NACA 23012. Dihedral 1°. Composite structure with aluminium I beam spars, stamped metal ribs and Dacron covering. Plain wide-span ailerons of similar construction. No trim tabs.

FUSELAGE: Welded structure of 4130 steel tube with aluminium skinned underside and Dacron covering elsewhere.

TAIL UNIT: Wire braced welded steel tube structure with Dacron covering. Trim tab in port elevator.

LANDING GEAR: Non-retractable tailwheel type. Two side Vs and half-axles. Mainwheels fitted with 6.00-6 4-ply tyres; swivelling tailwheel has 8 in pneumatic tyre as standard. Scott 8 in tailwheel or Maule P8B-1-2 tundra tailwheel optional. Dual hydraulic toe brakes standard. Floats and Aero M1500 or M2000 skis optional.

POWER PLANT: One 88 kW (118 hp) Textron Lycoming O-235-L2C flat-four engine, driving a Sensenich 72CK-O-50 two-blade fixed-pitch metal propeller with spinner. One fuel tank in each wing, with combined capacity of 159 litres (42 US gallons; 35 Imp gallons). Oil capacity 5.7 litres (1.5 US gallons; 1.2 Imp gallons).

ACCOMMODATION: Two seats, with shoulder harness, side by side in enclosed cabin. Dual controls standard. Metal door with sliding window each side. Standard equipment includes door locks and window latches, carpeted floor and cargo tiedown straps. Baggage compartment aft of seats, standard capacity 91 kg (200 lb), with extension tube 1.22 m (4 ft) long by 15 cm (6 in) diameter for fishing equipment, and side windows. Accommodation heated and ventilated.

SYSTEM: Electrical system powered by 12V 60A engine driven alternator, with 12V storage battery. Wiring provisions for navigation lights. Engine driven vacuum pump when optional blind-flying instrumentation installed.

AVIONICS AND EQUIPMENT: Optional avionics to customer requirements. Standard equipment includes large instrument panel with radio rack in centre, wiring for landing light in port wing, skylight windows, and tiedown rings. Optional equipment includes full blind-flying instrumentation; attitude and directional gyros, electric clock, vacuum system, Whelen wingtip strobe lights and fin strobe light, streamline wheel fairings, Stewart Warner oil cooler installation, and choice of internal and external colour schemes.

DIMENSIONS, EXTERNAL:
Wing span	10.97 m (36 ft 0 in)
Wing chord (constant)	1.60 m (5 ft 3 in)
Length overall	6.74 m (22 ft 1¼ in)

Height overall	1.98 m (6 ft 6 in)
Tailplane span	3.05 m (10 ft 0 in)
Wheel track	1.83 m (6 ft 0 in)
Propeller diameter	1.83 m (6 ft 0 in)

AREAS:
Wings, gross	17.07 m² (183.71 sq ft)
Ailerons (total)	1.86 m² (20.0 sq ft)
Fin	0.34 m² (3.7 sq ft)
Rudder	0.59 m² (6.3 sq ft)
Tailplane	1.21 m² (13.0 sq ft)
Elevators, incl tab	0.99 m² (10.66 sq ft)

WEIGHTS AND LOADINGS:
Weight empty	465 kg (1,025 lb)
Max T-O weight	794 kg (1,750 lb)
Max wing loading	46.48 kg/m² (9.52 lb/sq ft)
Max power loading	9.02 kg/kW (14.83 lb/hp)

PERFORMANCE (at max T-O weight except where indicated):
Never-exceed speed	128 knots (237 km/h; 147 mph)
Max level speed	108 knots (201 km/h; 125 mph)
Stalling speed, power off	42 knots (78 km/h; 48 mph)
Max rate of climb at S/L	229 m (750 ft)/min
T-O run	107 m (350 ft)
T-O to, and landing from, 15 m (50 ft)	130 m (425 ft)
Landing run	152 m (500 ft)
Range, 75% power with 30 min reserves	636 nm (1,178 km; 732 miles)

g limits:
Normal category, max T-O weight	+3.8/−1.52
Utility category at 626 kg (1,380 lb) AUW	+4.4/−1.76

TAYLORCRAFT F-22 PHOENIX
The Model F-22 made its public debut in prototype form (N44191) at the 1985 EAA Convention at Oshkosh. A development of the Model F-21B, it differs principally in

Prototype Taylorcraft F-22 Phoenix with tricycle landing gear (*J.M.G. Gradidge*)

having a tricycle landing gear, and manually operated wing flaps which reduce the stalling speed, power off, by 4 knots (8 km/h; 5 mph). Description is as for the Model F-21B except that adjustable bucket seats with storage compartments, and swing-out door windows, are standard, and the tubular structure in the cabin area has been redesigned to facilitate entry and exit. A 91 × 173 cm (36 × 68 in) or 91 × 91 cm (36 × 36 in) skylight window is optional. The aircraft will be certificated in the Normal and Utility categories, and will be offered with a choice of tailwheel, tricycle, ski or float landing gear.

Certification test flying was reported to be continuing in the Spring of 1988.

WEIGHTS:
Weight empty	494 kg (1,090 lb)
Baggage capacity	91 kg (200 lb)

PERFORMANCE (estimated):
Stalling speed, power off, flaps down	38 knots (70 km/h; 43 mph)
T-O run, flaps down	91 m (300 ft)
T-O to, and landing from, 15 m (50 ft)	115 m (375 ft)

TELEDYNE RYAN

TELEDYNE RYAN AERONAUTICAL

2701 Harbor Drive, PO Box 80311, San Diego, California 92138-9012
Telephone: (619) 291 7311
Telex: 910 335 1180 TDYRYN SDG
PRESIDENT: Hudson B. Drake
VICE-PRESIDENT, ENGINEERING: Gene Dotson
PUBLIC RELATIONS: Jack G. Broward

For many years the major production items of Teledyne Ryan Aeronautical have been the Firebee series of jet powered targets and special purpose vehicles (pre-programmed and remotely piloted) for various types of reconnaissance mission. The most recent of these is the Model 410.

TELEDYNE RYAN MODEL 410

The Model 410 was designed for use on exceptionally long-range or long-endurance reconnaissance/surveillance (manned or unmanned), and related unmanned missions such as electronic countermeasures. A prototype (N53578) was completed in the Autumn of 1987 and made its first (manned) flight on 27 May 1988. An initial test programme, comprising seven flights and 36 take-offs and landings, has been completed.

Ability to stay aloft with a 45.4 kg (100 lb) payload for 80 hours, and to use unimproved airstrips or short stretches of roadway, are features of the design. Maximum equipment load, in unmanned form, is 454 kg (1,000 lb), allowing the use of standard sized rather than specially miniaturised sensors. The Model 410's exceptionally long endurance permits either great range or extended loiter capability, or combinations of the two, conferring considerable potential for cost-effective military reconnaissance as well as civilian surveillance of coastlines, borders or other sensitive areas. As initially configured, with a 2:1 turbocharger ratio, it can fly at an altitude of more than 9,150 m (30,000 ft); with optional higher ratio turbocharging this ceiling can be increased to 13,725 m (45,000 ft). In unmanned form, the Model 410 can be equipped to fly autonomous (pre-programmed) missions beyond the range of ground controllers, or can be flown as an RPV with a direct data link, carrying frame or video cameras. Also claimed are all-weather and day/night operation.

According to early TRA announcements, a larger (11.28 m; 37 ft 0 in span, 1,088 kg; 2,400 lb gross weight) version, with greater endurance, is also envisaged. The following description applies to the initial version:

Teledyne Ryan Model 410 on manned flight test

AIRFRAME: Cantilever high-wing monoplane, of pod-and-twin-boom configuration, fitted with wing trailing-edge flaps and conventional three-axis control surfaces (ailerons, elevator and rudders). Main structure is built using glassfibre/epoxy skins with an infill of high-density structural foam plastics. Wings have graphite/epoxy spars and can be detached for transportation and storage. Tricycle landing gear has non-retractable mainwheels mounted on cantilever self-sprung legs of graphite/epoxy; nosewheel can be fully retracted rearward to avoid interference with forward looking sensors. For manned flight test phase, prototype is fitted with a single-seat cockpit under a sideways opening 'teardrop' canopy.

POWER PLANT: One 119 kW (160 hp) Textron Lycoming TIO-320-C1B flat-four turbocharged engine, mounted in rear of fuselage pod and driving a three-blade pusher propeller with spinner. All fuel is carried in tanks in wings.

AVIONICS AND EQUIPMENT: Flight control system can store multiple mission programmes, and can be re-programmed in flight or controlled from a base station when aircraft is within range. Data link range can be supplemented by relaying data via land, sea or air vehicles, including other Model 410s. Satellite link can be provided for real-time data transmission, and onboard data recording is standard. Ground control centre permits a two-person crew to monitor eight Model 410s and their sensors via a two-way long-range data link.

DIMENSIONS:
Wing span	9.55 m (31 ft 4 in)
Width, wings removed	2.44 m (8 ft 0 in)
Length overall	6.60 m (21 ft 8 in)
Propeller diameter	1.60 m (5 ft 3 in)
Payload compartment volume	0.68 m³ (24.0 cu ft)

WEIGHT:
Max payload	454 kg (1,000 lb)

PERFORMANCE:
Max level speed	190 knots (352 km/h; 219 mph)
Typical operating speed range	85-140 knots (157-259 km/h; 98-161 mph)
Service ceiling:	
2:1 turbocharger ratio	over 9,150 m (30,000 ft)
optional higher ratio	13,725 m (45,000 ft)
T-O and landing run	229 m (750 ft)
Max endurance at 100 knots (185 km/h; 115 mph):	
with 45.4 kg (100 lb) payload	80 h
with max payload	24 h

THORP

THORP 211 AIRCRAFT COMPANY INC

Old Man's Airport, Pedricktown, New Jersey 08067
Telephone: (609) 299 3634
OWNERS: Tom Kurtz and Earl McGuire
VICE-PRESIDENT, MARKETING AND SALES: Donald H. Smith

THORP T211

This two-seat light aircraft, designed by Mr John Thorp, originated as the T-11 Sky Scooter, which flew for the first time in 1946 with a 48.5 kW (65 hp) engine and was last described in the 1950-51 *Jane's*. Several versions were developed, but plans to market them in kit form did not materialise. Adams Industries subsequently put the type into limited production as the Thorp T211, with a more powerful engine, for business, recreational and training purposes.

In 1985, Mr Tom Kurtz, Mr Harry Gehrke and Mr Earl McGuire purchased all rights in the aircraft from Adams Industries, together with tooling and components. Under the new company name, the T211 is again on the market, offered initially in kit form. In January 1987 plans for production of FAA-certificated aircraft were in progress, but no date for the start of production deliveries had been set and no subsequent news has been received.

TYPE: Two-seat cabin monoplane.

WINGS: Cantilever low-wing monoplane. All-metal structure with ribbed skins. Wide span manually operated three-position trailing-edge flaps, and plain ailerons, both with ribbed skins. No trim tabs.

FUSELAGE: All-metal semi-monocoque structure of light alloy.

TAIL UNIT: Cantilever structure of light alloy; elevators, all-moving tailplane and rudder have ribbed skins. Ground adjustable tab on rudder.

LANDING GEAR: Non-retractable tricycle type, with single wheel on each unit. Oleo-pneumatic shock absorber in each unit. All three wheels size 500 × 4. Handbrake and parking brake.

POWER PLANT: One 74.5 kW (100 hp) Continental O-200-A flat-four engine, driving a McCauley two-blade fixed-pitch metal propeller with spinner. Fuel cell aft of cabin, capacity 91 litres (24 US gallons; 20 Imp gallons), of which 87 litres (23 US gallons; 19.2 Imp gallons) are usable. Oil capacity 5.7 litres (1.5 US gallons; 1.25 Imp gallons).

ACCOMMODATION: Two seats side by side beneath rearward sliding transparent canopy. Baggage compartment behind seats, capacity 36 kg (80 lb).

SYSTEM: Electrical system supplied by 12V 20A generator and 12V 25Ah storage battery.

AVIONICS AND EQUIPMENT: Optional avionics package by Collins includes VHF-251 com, VIR-351 nav, IND-350 VOR/LOC receiver/indicator, TDR-950 transponder, noise cancelling microphone and emergency locator transmitter.

DIMENSIONS, EXTERNAL:
Wing span	7.62 m (25 ft 0 in)
Length overall	5.49 m (18 ft 0 in)
Height overall	2.44 m (8 ft 0 in)
Propeller diameter	1.70 m (5 ft 7 in)

AREA:
Wings, gross	9.75 m² (105.0 sq ft)

WEIGHTS AND LOADINGS:
Weight empty	332 kg (733 lb)
Max T-O and landing weight	576 kg (1,270 lb)
Max wing loading	59.1 kg/m² (12.1 lb/sq ft)
Max power loading	7.73 kg/kW (12.7 lb/hp)

PERFORMANCE (at max T-O weight):
Max level speed at S/L	137 knots (254 km/h; 158 mph)
Cruising speed (75% power)	104 knots (193 km/h; 120 mph)
Stalling speed, flaps down	34 knots (63 km/h; 39 mph)
Max rate of climb at S/L	290 m (950 ft)/min
Service ceiling	5,790 m (19,000 ft)
T-O run	91 m (300 ft)
Landing run	61 m (200 ft)
Range at 55% power, with max fuel and reserves	417 nm (772 km; 480 miles)

Thorp T211, offered initially in kit form by Thorp 211 Aircraft Inc (*Geoffrey P. Jones*)

TURBOTECH

TURBOTECH INC

Pearson Air Park, 1115 E 5th Street, PO Box 61586,
Vancouver, Washington 98666
Telephone: (206) 694 6287
PRESIDENT: L. W. Soukup

Turbotech Inc (formerly Seaplanes Inc) carries out
STOL and/or performance improvements to a variety of
lightplanes manufactured by Beech, Cessna, Gulfstream
American, Maule, Piper, Stinson and Waco. Performance
increases result largely from replacing the original power
plant by an engine of increased power. The company has
also designed a STOL kit for installation on Cessna 170B,
172, 175, 180, 182, 185, 206 and 210 aircraft. This includes a
stall fence, leading-edge cuff and aileron gap seals, which
improve take-off and landing performance by approx 7 per
cent.

Power plant replacements include removal of the existing
engine from Cessna 170, 172 and 175, and Stinson 108
aircraft, and the installation of a 164 kW (220 hp) Franklin
flat-six engine and constant-speed propeller. The 186 kW
(250 hp) turbocharged Franklin, also with constant-speed
propeller, can be installed in the Cessna 172, 175, Stinson
108 and Waco Vela. This power plant is used also for
installation in the Maule M-5 Lunar Rocket in lieu of a 157
kW (210 hp) Continental or 164 kW (220 hp) Franklin
engine. The 172 kW (230 hp) Continental O-470 is also
available for the Stinson 108.

The 224 kW (300 hp) Textron Lycoming IO-540-K is
used for one installation in the Cessna 185, but Turbotech
obtained Supplemental Type Certificates during 1982 for
two additional engine modifications on this aircraft. These
cover the installation of a 261 kW (350 hp) Textron

Turbotech Inc conversion of Cessna 185F with 261 kW (350 hp) Textron Lycoming TIO-540-J2BD turbocharged engine

Lycoming TIO-540-J2BD, and the introduction of a
Garrett turbocharger for the 224 kW (300 hp) Continental
IO-520-D of the standard Cessna 185. These conversions
give the aircraft full performance to a service ceiling of 7,620
m (25,000 ft) and 7,315 m (24,000 ft) respectively. The
Cessna 206 has also been approved with the 261 kW
(350 hp) Textron Lycoming TIO-540-J2BD turbocharged
engine. A gross weight increase of 93 kg (205 lb) with
installation of tip tanks was approved in July 1983.

Recent developments include the installation of a
turbocharger on a 224 kW (300 hp) Continental IO-520-D
for the Cessna 180, and an add-on turbocharger modification on the Gulfstream American AA-5B Tiger powered
by a 134 kW (180 hp) Textron Lycoming O-360-A4K
flat-four engine. The **Turbo Tiger** modification includes a

high strength stainless exhaust system, retractable cowl
flaps, additional oil cooler, Electronics International
induction temperature gauge, high pressure fuel pump, and
a combined manifold/fuel pressure gauge. The conversion
adds 13.6 kg (30 lb) to the aircraft's empty weight.
Performance, at max T-O weight, includes a max level speed
at 1,070 m (3,500 ft) of 129 knots (240 km/h; 149 mph) IAS;
max level speed at 3,050 m (10,000 ft) of 118 knots (219
km/h; 136 mph) IAS; max level speed at 7,620 m (25,000 ft)
of 92 knots (170 km/h; 106 mph) IAS; max rate of climb at
S/L of 274 m (900 ft)/min; and service ceiling of 7,620 m
(25,000 ft).

Performance figures for all other Turbotech conversions
that had been certificated by early 1987 are given in the
accompanying table.

		Max level speed knots (km/h; mph)	Max cruising speed at 2,135 m (7,000 ft) knots (km/h; mph)	Max rate of climb at S/L m (ft)/min	Service ceiling m (ft)	T-O run m (ft)	Range nm (km; miles)
Cessna 170A/B	A	148 (274; 170)	137 (254; 158)	457 (1,500)	5,485 (18,000)	91 (300)	434 (804; 500)
	F	126 (233; 145)	116 (216; 134)	366 (1,200)	4,265 (14,000)	152 (500)	478 (885; 550)
	G	139 (257; 160)	126 (233; 145)	396 (1,300)	4,875 (16,000)	122 (400)	478 (885; 550)
Cessna 172 land	A	145 (269; 167)	135.5 (251; 156)	427 (1,400)	5,485 (18,000)	91 (300)	521 (966; 600)
Cessna 172 float	A**	126 (233; 145)	118 (217; 135)	335 (1,100)	4,875 (16,000)	320 (1,050)	412 (764; 475)
Cessna 172 land turbo	B	148 (274; 170)*	148 (274; 170)	549 (1,800)	7,620 (25,000)*	84 (275)	521 (966; 600)
Cessna 172 float turbo	B**	135 (249; 155)	135 (249; 155)	457 (1,500)	6,100 (20,000)*	381 (1,250)	412 (764; 475)
Cessna 175	A	145 (269; 167)	135.5 (251; 156)	427 (1,400)	5,485 (18,000)	91 (300)	521 (966; 600)
Cessna 175 turbo	B	148 (274; 170)*	148 (274; 170)	549 (1,800)	7,620 (25,000)	84 (275)	521 (966; 600)
Cessna 180 turbo	J	154 (285; 177)*	165 (306; 190)	366 (1,200)	7,315 (24,000)	244 (800)	651 (1,207; 750)
Cessna 185 land	C	158 (293; 182)	151 (280; 174)	351 (1,150)	5,790 (19,000)	244 (800)	695 (1,287; 800)
Cessna 185 float	C	144 (267; 166)	136 (253; 157)§	326 (1,070)	5,180 (17,000)	411 (1,350)	608 (1,126; 700)
Cessna 185 turbo	I	174 (322; 200)	169 (314; 195)§	610 (2,000)	7,620 (25,000)	229 (750)	651 (1,207; 750)
Cessna 185 turbo	J	154 (285; 177)*	165 (306; 190)§§	366 (1,200)	7,315 (24,000)	244 (800)	651 (1,207; 750)
Cessna 206 turbo	I	169 (314; 195)	165 (306; 190)	533 (1,750)	8,230 (27,000)	255 (835)	805 (1,492; 927)
Stinson 108-2/-3	A	139 (257; 160)	131 (243; 151)	488 (1,600)	5,485 (18,000)	91 (300)	521 (966; 600)φ
Stinson 108-2/-3 turbo	B	139 (257; 160)*	139 (257; 160)	579 (1,900)	7,620 (25,000)*	84 (275)	521 (966; 600)φ
Stinson 108-2/-3	D	139 (257; 160)*	126 (233; 145)	488 (1,600)	5,640 (18,500)	84 (275)	521 (966; 600)φ
Stinson 108-2/-3	H	122 (225; 140)	113 (209; 130)	335 (1,100)	4,875 (16,000)	137 (450)	521 (966; 600)φ
Beech Bonanza A35-C35 turbo	B	181 (336; 209)	181 (336; 209)	518 (1,700)	6,400 (21,000)*	256 (840)	868 (1,609; 1,000)†
Maule M-4 turbo	B	152 (282; 175)	142 (264; 164)	549 (1,800)	7,620 (25,000)*	84 (275)	564 (1,046; 650)
Maule M-5 turbo	E	149 (277; 172)	156 (290; 180)	411 (1,350)	7,620 (25,000)*	91 (300)	695 (1,287; 800)
Waco Vela turbo	B	169 (314; 195)	161 (298; 185)	442 (1,450)	6,100 (20,000)*	258 (845)	912 (1,690; 1,050)

A 164 kW (220 hp) Franklin 6A-350
B 186 kW (250 hp) Franklin 6AS-350 turbocharged
C 224 kW (300 hp) Textron Lycoming IO-540-K
D 172 kW (230 hp) Continental O-470-K/L/R
E 175 kW (235 hp) Textron Lycoming O-540-J1A5D turbocharged
F 123 kW (165 hp) Franklin 6A4-165-B3
G 134 kW (180 hp) Franklin 6A-335-B
H 134 kW (180 hp) Textron Lycoming O-360

I 261 kW (350 hp) Textron Lycoming TIO-540-J2BD turbocharged
J 224 kW (300 hp) Continental IO-520-D turbocharged
* max certificated speed/altitude
** gross weight increased to 1,134 kg (2,499 lb)
φ Stinson 108-2 range 434 nm (804 km; 500 miles)
§ 187 knots (346 km/h; 215 mph) at 6,700 m (22,000 ft)
§§ 178 knots (330 km/h; 205 mph) at 6,700 m (22,000 ft)
† with tip tanks

UNIVAIR

UNIVAIR AIRCRAFT CORPORATION

2500 Himalaya Road, Aurora, Colorado 80011
Telephone: (303) 364 7661
Telex: 317327
Fax: (303) 344 3254
PRESIDENT: Stephen E. Dyer
MARKETING MANAGER: Michael D. Sellers

Univair Aircraft Corporation, founded in 1946, is a
company specialising in the manufacture of components for

light aircraft. It holds 19 type certificates and 36
supplemental type certificates, drawings, production tooling and rights to manufacture many post-war 'classic' US
light aircraft, including the Ercoupe, Alon, Forney and
Mooney M-10 Cadet series; and the Stinson 108 series. The
company also manufactures spares under FAA parts
manufacture approvals (PMAs) for older designs produced
originally by such companies as Aeronca, Cessna,
Luscombe, Navion, Piper and Taylorcraft, and has
acquired Piper Aircraft Corporation's inventory of spare

parts for out of production Piper aircraft, including the J-3
Cub, J-4 Cub Coupé, J-5 Cub Cruiser, PA-11 Cub Special,
PA-12 Super Cruiser, PA-14 Family Cruiser, PA-15 Vagabond, PA-16 Clipper, PA-20 Pacer and PA-22
Tri-Pacer, Caribbean and Colt series.

A description and photograph of the Univair Stinson 108
with Textron Lycoming IO-360-A1A engine conversion
may be found in the 1987-88 and earlier editions of *Jane's*.

USAF

UNITED STATES AIR FORCE SYSTEMS COMMAND

Aeronautical Systems Division, Wright-Patterson AFB,
Dayton, Ohio 45433-6503
Telephone: (513) 255 3334
PUBLIC AFFAIRS OFFICER: Capt Jamie S. Scearse
ATF PROGRAMME DIRECTOR: Colonel James A. Fain Jr

USAF ADVANCED TACTICAL FIGHTER (ATF)
US Air Force designations: YF-22A and YF-23A

The Advanced Tactical Fighter (ATF) programme is

intended to meet a United States Air Force requirement for
a new air superiority fighter to replace the McDonnell
Douglas F-15 Eagle in the mid-1990s. The ATF programme
also includes development of an advanced technology
engine for the aircraft. Concept definition study contracts
were awarded in September 1983 to Boeing, General
Dynamics, Grumman, Lockheed, McDonnell Douglas,
Northrop and Rockwell. These companies submitted their
prototype design proposals to the USAF on 28 July 1986.

On 31 October 1986 the USAF announced the selection
of Lockheed-Burbank and Northrop to begin the demon-
stration/validation phase of the ATF programme. Under
respective designations **YF-22A** and **YF-23A**, each

contractor is building two flying prototypes and a ground
based avionics testbed for demonstration and validation
purposes, leading to selection of the successful ATF
contender in mid-1991 when the full scale development
phase will begin. The prototypes are expected to fly in early
1990, and the FSD ATF in the third quarter of FY 1993.
Engines for the ATF will be developed from ground
demonstrator power plants which began testing in 1987.
Pratt & Whitney's PW5000-derived prototype engine is
designated YF119 and General Electric's YF120. Each of
the prototype aircraft will be required to fly with GE and
P&W engines.

Design goals for the ATF include greatly improved

reliability and maintainability, with high sortie generation rates, increased survivability achieved through 'first-look, first-kill' opportunities using low observable 'stealth' techniques and passive sensors. Compared to current front-line fighters the ATF will have significantly reduced T-O and landing distances, increased supersonic cruise and manoeuvrability performance and greatly increased combat radius on internal fuel.

Airframe design will draw on the most recent advances in flight control, including the use of fibre optics and digital flight control for stability and handling, and widespread use of composite materials. Technologies being evaluated include low-observable 'stealth' techniques, conformal sensors and hydraulically actuated weapons racks. The

ATF is being designed to carry existing and planned air-to-air weapons including AMRAAM, AIM-9 Sidewinder and ASRAAM, and will be equipped with an internal gun. Power plant technologies under evaluation include integrated flight/propulsion controls, STOL capability and two-dimensional convergent/divergent engine nozzles. Flat panel CRT displays, extra-wide field of view HUDs, pilot's articulating seats for enhanced g load tolerance, and advanced display processing, are among technologies which may be incorporated in the ATF's advanced cockpit concept.

The USAF has a requirement for up to 750 ATFs, with IOC anticipated in the mid-1990s. The US Navy is also evaluating the ATF as a possible replacement for the

Grumman F-14 Tomcat as a fleet air defence interceptor at the end of this century. Up to 619 'navalised' ATFs could be required.

C-27

The USAF's C-27 requirement is for a twin-turboprop STOL transport, with a rear-loading ramp/door, for the intra-theatre airlift of troops and cargo (payload capacity 4,536 kg; 10,000 lb) using short and/or impaired runways. Initial plans were to order ten C-27s in FY 1988 and 1989, with option for a further eight to be funded in FY 1990, but deletion of funds for the first five from the 1988 budget has resulted in the programme being deferred for re-definition of the requirement. Likely candidates are the Bromon BR-2000, Boeing Canada Dash 8, Aeritalia G222 and Airtech CN-235.

TTTS

The TTTS (Tanker/Transport Training System) requirement is for an off-the-shelf multi-engined turbofan powered business aircraft to provide advanced pilot training for USAF large multi-engined aircraft, and replaced the CTA (Companion Trainer Aircraft) that was cancelled in 1982. The USAF has a requirement for 211 of the aircraft eventually selected, although procurement funding is not expected to be sought before at least FY 1990. Aircraft for which proposals have been submitted include the BAe 125 Series 800, Beechcraft Beechjet, Cessna Citation S/II, Dassault-Breguet Falcon, IAI Astra and Learjet 31. An RFP (request for proposals) was expected to be issued in the Summer of 1988, followed by selection of the winning type in mid-1989.

STRATEGIC RECONNAISSANCE AIRCRAFT

According to early 1988 press reports, US Defense Department officials have confirmed that a new long-range reconnaissance aircraft is being developed to replace the USAF's now-ageing SR-71, of which comparatively few remain in service. The only details given were that the new aircraft is being designed for speeds of up to 3,300 knots (6,100 km/h; 3,800 mph) and altitudes of above 30,500 m (100,000 ft), will have in-flight refuelling capability, and will employ the latest low-observables 'stealth' design techniques and materials. It is generally believed that Lockheed's Burbank division is the prime contractor.

Artist's impression of a possible configuration for the USAF's Advanced Tactical Fighter

VALSAN
VALSAN PARTNERS
1 Horatio Street, Jackson Square, New York, NY 10014
Telephone: (212) 807 6622
Telex: 825379 VALSAN UF
Fax: (212) 242 6405
PRESIDENT: Robert E. Wagenfeld
VICE-PRESIDENT, MARKETING: Walter H. Johnson

VALSAN 'QUIET 727'
Valsan has developed a programme for re-engining the

Boeing 727-200 to enable the aircraft to meet the more stringent noise regulations of FAR Pt 36 Stage 3 and ICAO Annex 16 Chapter 3. Conversion of a Sterling Airways 727-200 'prototype' (OY-SAS) began in late 1987 and was completed in June 1988, with first flight following on 12 July and award of a Supplemental Type Certificate anticipated in September 1988. The modification, carried out by Lockheed, involves acoustic treatment of the centre engine, and removal of its thrust reverser, and replacement of the outer pair of engines with two Pratt & Whitney JT8D-217C turbofans. In mid-1988 Valsan reported 85 orders and

options for this modification, which also incorporates a flight deck reconfigured for a flight crew of two instead of three.

Flight testing of a 727 with added winglets was expected to begin in September 1988 and achieve certification by January 1989. Other future modifications being considered include 'stretched' cargo and passenger versions of the 727-200, with plugs of 2.54 m (8 ft 4 in) forward of the wing and 2.03 m (6 ft 8 in) aft; and a two-person 'glass cockpit' with EICAS (electronic engine instrument and crew alerting system) and dual computers and CRT displays.

VAT
VERTICAL AVIATION TECHNOLOGY
1430 Elm Avenue, Winter Park, Florida 32789
PROPRIETORS:
Bradford Clark
Ron Mander
CONSULTANT ENGINEER: Ralph Alex

VAT S-52-3
Vertical Aviation Technology was formed to develop and market improved and updated versions of the Sikorsky S-52 four-seat helicopter, which will be offered in kit form. A prototype (N9329R), fitted with a reconfigured glassfibre nosecone, new windscreen, restyled vertical tail surfaces and electric trim system, is being tested for compliance with FAA Supplemental Type Certificate requirements. The standard S-52 is powered by a 183 kW (245 hp) Franklin O-425-1 piston engine, but Vertical Aviation is considering supplying a 201 kW (270 hp) watercooled Javelin V-6 power plant or 373 kW (500 shp) Allison 250-C18 or -C20 turboshaft with its conversion kits, which will have all dynamic components pre-assembled. Assembly time for the helicopter is estimated at 1,000 man hours.

Prototype Vertical Aviation Technology S-52-3 conversion of Sikorsky S-52 helicopter *(Howard Levy)*

DIMENSIONS, EXTERNAL:

Main rotor diameter	10.06 m (33 ft 0 in)
Main rotor blade chord	0.26 m (10¼ in)
Tail rotor diameter	1.62 m (5 ft 4 in)
Length overall	8.38 m (27 ft 6 in)
Height overall	2.64 m (8 ft 8 in)

WEIGHTS:

Weight empty	816 kg (1,800 lb)
Max T-O weight	1,225 kg (2,700 lb)

PERFORMANCE:

Never-exceed speed	95 knots (176 km/h; 109 mph)
Cruising speed	85 knots (157 km/h; 98 mph)
Max rate of climb at S/L	320 m (1,050 ft)/min

VERILITE
VERILITE AIRCRAFT COMPANY INC
(a subsidiary of De Vore Aviation Corporation)
6104B Kircher Boulevard NE, Albuquerque, New Mexico 87109
Telephone: (505) 345 8713
Telex: 660436
PRESIDENT: Gilbert De Vore

Founded in 1954, De Vore Aviation specialised initially in consultancy and contract engineering services for aircraft manufacturers. In 1969 it acquired manufacturing rights to the PK range of seaplane and amphibian floats, and was appointed exclusive supplier of Aerojet General aircraft standby rocket engines (formerly known as JATO). In 1970 De Vore developed its Tel-Tail aircraft vertical tail floodlighting system, and in 1976 began development of a single-box airport visual approach aid, the pulsed light

approach slope indicator (PLASI) which has been FAA approved for fixed- and rotating-wing aircraft. In October 1983 De Vore formed Verilite Aircraft Company Inc and announced its entry into light aircraft manufacturing.

VERILITE MODEL 100 SUNBIRD
The design goal for the Sunbird 'Affordable Airplane', initially named Sundancer in a public naming contest, was

to produce a light aeroplane to sell for under $20,000 in 1983 values. Initial funding was not available until the late Spring of 1985, at which time detail design was started.

Taxying trials took place at Albuquerque in February 1987, in the course of which the aircraft was accidentally damaged. After rebuilding and the incorporation of some small improvements a so-called 'second prototype' (N100VL) flew successfully on 5 October 1987. NASA Langley co-operated in the tunnel testing of the partially drooped leading-edge which gives the Sunbird 'unspinnable' flying characteristics. Flight testing is taking place at Roswell, New Mexico. In October 1987 Verilite held orders for 32 Sunbirds.

TYPE: Two-seat single-engined light aircraft.

WINGS: Strut braced high-wing monoplane. Wing section NACA 64₁212 Mod B inboard, with extended drooped leading-edge from 57% semi-span outboard. Dihedral 2°. Incidence 2° at root, 0° at tip. No sweepback. Single bracing strut on each side. Structure of foam core sandwich with pre-preg glassfibre faces. Plain flaps and ailerons of same construction as wings. Ailerons have internal spring trim.

FUSELAGE: Aluminium keel and bulkheads, with skins of pre-preg glassfibre/foam core sandwich.

TAIL UNIT: Cantilever structure of pre-preg glassfibre/foam core sandwich. Elevators and rudder have internal spring trim system.

LANDING GEAR: Non-retractable tricycle type. Bungee suspension on nosewheel leg; aluminium spring struts on main units. Tyre size (all) 5.00-5; pressure 2.14 bars (31.0 lb/sq in). Brakes on mainwheels.

POWER PLANT: One 52.2 kW (70 hp) Emdair CF-092B two-cylinder four-stroke engine, driving a two-blade fixed-pitch pusher propeller. Single fuel tank in centre-section, capacity 49 litres (13 US gallons; 10.8 Imp gallons).

ACCOMMODATION: Two seats, side by side, in fully enclosed cabin. Canopy slides forward for access. Baggage area behind seats, capacity 22.7 kg (50 lb). Ram air ventilation.

SYSTEMS: Generator/battery electrical system for engine starting, minimum avionics and navigation lights.

AVIONICS: Nav/com optional. VOR standard.

DIMENSIONS, EXTERNAL:

Wing span   9.75 m (32 ft 0 in)

Verilite Model 100 Sunbird prototype

Wing chord: at root	1.25 m (4 ft 1¼ in)	Ailerons (total)	1.03 m² (11.10 sq ft)
at tip	1.28 m (4 ft 2¼ in)	Trailing-edge flaps (total)	1.97 m² (21.20 sq ft)
Wing aspect ratio	7.6	Fin	0.80 m² (8.60 sq ft)
Length overall	7.21 m (23 ft 7¾ in)	Rudder	0.59 m² (6.30 sq ft)
Height overall	2.54 m (8 ft 4 in)	Tailplane	1.58 m² (17.00 sq ft)
Tailplane span	3.28 m (10 ft 9 in)	Elevators	1.12 m² (12.10 sq ft)
Wheel track	2.08 m (6 ft 10 in)	WEIGHTS:	
Wheelbase	2.44 m (8 ft 0 in)	Weight empty	345 kg (760 lb)
Propeller diameter	1.73 m (5 ft 8 in)	Max T-O weight	567 kg (1,250 lb)
Passenger door: Height	0.86 m (2 ft 10 in)	PERFORMANCE:	
Width	1.11 m (3 ft 8 in)	Never-exceed speed at S/L	
Height to sill	0.63 m (2 ft 1 in)		132 knots (245 km/h; 152 mph)
DIMENSIONS, INTERNAL:		Max level speed at S/L	111 knots (206 km/h; 128 mph)
Cabin: Length	1.73 m (5 ft 8 in)	Max cruising speed (75% power) at S/L	
Max width	1.01 m (3 ft 4 in)		100 knots (185 km/h; 115 mph)
Max height	1.14 m (3 ft 9 in)	Stalling speed: flaps up	40 knots (74 km/h; 46 mph)
Floor area	1.58 m² (17.0 sq ft)	flaps down	37 knots (68 km/h; 43 mph)
Volume	approx 1.42 m³ (50.0 cu ft)	Max rate of climb at S/L	204 m (670 ft)/min
AREAS:		Range with max fuel and max payload	
Wings, gross	12.58 m² (135.4 sq ft)		400 nm (741 km; 461 miles)

WIPAIRE

WIPAIRE INC

South End Doane Trail, Inver Grove Heights, Minnesota 55075
Telephone: (612) 451 1205
Telex: 297051
PRESIDENT: Robert Wiplinger

WIPAIRE SUPER BEAVER

This company, well known for its range of Wipline floats and amphibious floats for light and utility aircraft, has developed a modification for the de Havilland Canada DHC-2 Beaver. Known as the Wipaire Super Beaver, the conversion is based on surplus US Army and USAF L-20 Beaver airframes, which are completely dismantled, stripped and inspected using dye penetrant tests on all structural attachment points. All nuts, bolts and rod ends are replaced with new items, and old control cables with stainless steel cables. Roof windows are faired over, additional side windows (two per side) added aft of the cabin doors, and a rear cargo hatch installed. The rear cabin area is extended by 0.71 m (2 ft 4 in), and a 0.58 m × 0.35 m (23 in × 14 in) baggage hatch installed. To adjust the aircraft's centre of gravity the battery is moved forward from this area. Heavy soundproofing, tinted windows and articulating Cessna seats are installed in the cabin. All engine accessories for the 335.5 kW (450 hp) Pratt & Whitney R-985 power plant are replaced, and the engine extensively overhauled. A Hartzell three-blade constant-speed metal propeller with spinner replaces the standard two-blade Hamilton Standard unit. Wipaire Model 6000 amphibious floats are available optionally.

The first Super Beaver was delivered to an Alaskan customer in April 1983 and 24 had been completed by Summer 1987. The company anticipates sales of at least six aircraft per year.

Wipaire Inc Super Beaver on amphibious floats

WREN

WREN AIRCRAFT INC

Municipal Airport, Route 2, Box 351, Buckeye, Arizona 85326
Telephone: (602) 386 6204
PRESIDENT: Todd Peterson

Production of the Wren 460 by the original Wren Aircraft Corporation, then based at Fort Worth, Texas, came to an end in 1969. Production was resumed by a newly formed Wren Aircraft Inc in February 1982.

WREN 460P

The Wren 460P is a four-seat STOL light aircraft based on the airframe of a Cessna 182. The original prototype flew for the first time in 1963, and FAA certification was received in June 1964. Subsequent versions benefited from improvements made annually by Cessna in the Model 182.

Upgrading to Wren 460P configuration makes no changes to the power or gross weight of the basic Cessna 182 airframe. Four Wren devices provide the aircraft with its slow flying and STOL capabilities, as follows:

1. Full span double-slotted Fowler flaps are installed. The outer panel of the new flaps, on each wing, operates as both an aileron and a flap in the flaps-extended position. Wing lift coefficient increases from 1.5 to 2.6 as the flaps deflect to their maximum 30° position. A button control on the pilot's control wheel enables the flaps to be retracted instantly on touchdown, for faster braking, without the pilot needing to remove his hands from the wheel or throttle.

2. The basic NACA 2412 wing section nose radius of 2.6 cm (1.01 in) is increased to 3.8 cm (1.50 in) by the use of a sheet metal glove. This postpones wing stalling from the normal 16° angle of attack to 20° and provides a lift coefficient increment of 0.4 independent of flap deflection. The stalling characteristics are extremely docile, with no trace of lateral roll-off.

3. A set of small articulated horizontal control surfaces, known as the ULS (ultra low speed) nose control system, is mounted on the nose of the aircraft, immediately aft of the propeller. These control surfaces, each comprising a stabiliser, elevator and tab, are connected permanently to the conventional elevator control system and work in conjunction with this system. They act in the propeller slipstream to augment pitch control in slow-speed flight.

The ULS controls serve to reduce the balancing tail download required to trim out the nose-down pitching moment when the flaps are extended, and this provides an increase in the aircraft's total lift.

4. A set of five feathering drag plates, known as 'Wren's Teeth', is added to each wing upper surface. These drag plates operate on a harmonic linkage with the ailerons and deflect outward through 60° when the aileron is deflected up. This further decreases lift on the downgoing wing and, more importantly, increases drag on the downgoing wing so that the normal adverse aileron yaw is overcome and the aircraft yaws into rather than away from its turn. Positive and immediate roll response to control deflection is achieved down to an indicated airspeed of 31 knots (56 km/h; 35 mph) in ground effect.

The Wren 460 is unusual in its ability to utilise fully its slow flying capability. At 39-52 knots (72-97 km/h; 45-60 mph) only 30 per cent power is required and the aircraft can maintain level flight, in level attitude, with no engine heating or cooling problems. At these speeds, it is even more manoeuvrable than at high cruising speeds.

TYPE: Four-seat STOL light aircraft.

WINGS: Braced high-wing monoplane with single streamline section bracing strut each side. Wing section NACA 2412 (modified) with constant radius leading-edge cuff (fixed droop). Dihedral 1° 44'. Incidence 0° 55' at root, −3° 8' at tip. All-metal structure. Flaps, ailerons and drag plates described in introductory copy.

FUSELAGE, LANDING GEAR: As for standard Cessna 182, except that larger wheels and tyres are fitted. Mainwheels and tyres size 8.00-6, pressure 1.72 bars (25 lb/sq in). Nosewheel and tyre size 6.00-6, pressure 1.45 bars (21 lb/sq in) standard. Nosewheel tyre size 8.00-6 optional, for use on extra rough or extra soft landing areas. Float and ski installations optional.

TAIL UNIT: As for Cessna 182, but with electrically actuated automatic trim system, which adjusts tailplane incidence as flaps are raised and lowered, giving reduced landing and take-off runs.

POWER PLANT: One 172 kW (230 hp) Continental O-470-R flat-six engine, driving a McCauley two-blade constant-speed metal propeller. Hartzell reversible-pitch propeller optional. Standard fuel capacity 303 litres (80 US gallons; 66.6 Imp gallons). Oil capacity 11.4 litres (3 US gallons; 2.5 Imp gallons).

ACCOMMODATION: Four seats in pairs in enclosed cabin, with

Wren 460P four-seat STOL light aircraft (*Neil A. Macdougall*)

provision for additional seat for a child. Dual controls optional. Forward hinged door on each side. Three seats removable for freight carrying. Space aft of seats for 54 kg (120 lb) baggage.

SYSTEMS: Air-conditioning system optional. Hydraulic system for brakes. Oxygen system optional. 12V electrical system.

DIMENSIONS, EXTERNAL:

Wing span	10.92 m (35 ft 10 in)
Length overall	8.33 m (27 ft 4 in)
Height overall	2.74 m (9 ft 0 in)
Tailplane span	3.55 m (11 ft 8 in)
ULS surfaces span	2.29 m (7 ft 6 in)
Wheel track	2.74 m (9 ft 0 in)
Wheelbase	1.69 m (5 ft 6½ in)
Propeller diameter: standard	2.08 m (6 ft 10 in)
optional	2.24 m (7 ft 4 in)

DIMENSIONS, INTERNAL:

Cabin: Length	2.74 m (9 ft 0 in)
Max width	1.09 m (3 ft 7 in)
Max height	1.27 m (4 ft 2 in)

AREAS:

Wings, gross	16.30 m² (175.4 sq ft)
Ailerons (total)	1.50 m² (16.1 sq ft)
Trailing-edge flaps, including ailerons (total)	4.25 m² (45.7 sq ft)
Drag plates (total)	0.29 m² (3.1 sq ft)
Fin, incl dorsal fin	1.08 m² (11.6 sq ft)
Rudder	0.65 m² (7.0 sq ft)

Tailplane	1.90 m² (20.4 sq ft)
Elevators	1.46 m² (15.7 sq ft)
ULS surfaces	0.65 m² (7.0 sq ft)

WEIGHTS AND LOADINGS:

Weight empty, equipped	770 kg (1,697 lb)
Max fuel weight	254 kg (560 lb)
Max T-O and landing weight:	
Normal	1,270 kg (2,800 lb)
Restricted category	1,655 kg (3,650 lb)
Max wing loading:	
Normal	77.9 kg/m² (15.96 lb/sq ft)
Max power loading:	
Normal	7.41 kg/kW (12.17 lb/hp)

PERFORMANCE (at max T-O weight):

Max cruising speed at 2,440 m (8,000 ft)	139 knots (257 km/h; 160 mph)
Econ cruising speed at 1,830 m (6,000 ft)	122 knots (225 km/h; 140 mph)
Stalling speed, flaps down, power off	26 knots (47 km/h; 29 mph)
Max rate of climb at S/L	329 m (1,080 ft)/min
Service ceiling	5,850 m (19,200 ft)
T-O and landing run	82 m (270 ft)
T-O to and landing from 15 m (50 ft)	171 m (560 ft)
Landing from 15 m (50 ft), reversible pitch propeller	138 m (454 ft)
Landing run, reversible pitch propeller	62 m (205 ft)
Range with max fuel and max payload	851 nm (1,577 km; 980 miles)

WTA
WTA INC

Lubbock International Airport, Route 3, Box 48A, Lubbock, Texas 79401
Telephone: (806) 765 7242
Telex: 744439
VICE-PRESIDENT: Larry T. Neal

WTA Inc acquired from Piper Aircraft Corporation marketing rights to the PA-18-150 Super Cub and the PA-36 Brave agricultural aircraft, and renamed the latter as the New Brave in versions with 279 kW (375 hp) and 298 kW (400 hp) engines. The PA-18-150 has now been restored to production by Piper (which see); deliveries by WTA totalled 250.

WTA (PIPER) PA-36 NEW BRAVE

Piper Aircraft Corporation first gave details of the original PA-36 Brave agricultural aircraft on 9 October 1972. With the acquisition of marketing rights for this aircraft, WTA decided to concentrate on versions with 279 and 298 kW (375 and 400 hp) engines and renamed them New Braves.

The basic configuration seats the pilot well aft. The long nose is designed to collapse progressively in an emergency. The fuselage is graded in strength to provide high energy absorption and progressive collapse. A sturdy overturn pylon is an integral part of the fuselage structure. The laminated wing spars provide structural redundancy.

The pilot's capsule keeps him well clear of main structural members. The floor is 0.30 m (1 ft 0 in) above the lower longerons, and cockpit width allows for substantial deformation of the fuselage without hazard to the pilot. The seat is articulated to allow the pilot's position to change with fuselage deformation. The cockpit capsule is sealed to

prevent the ingress of toxic chemicals; and all protrusions, knobs and levers which might cause injury are eliminated. The instrument panel is equipped with a large energy absorbing crash roll.

The cockpit capsule is ventilated via an airscoop in the top of the canopy, which filters the incoming air before discharge through two adjustable diffusers. A heating system is standard, and the inflow of ventilating and/or heated air has the effect of pressurising the cockpit, further discouraging any inflow of toxic fumes or chemicals.

The fuel tanks, located in the wing roots, are filled with reticulated polyurethane foam to serve both as a fire suppressant and as a constant baffle to reduce fuel surge. Fire resistant fuel pipes are wire-reinforced at potential rupture points.

High, medium or low volume spray systems are available, the first dispensing chemicals at a rate equivalent to 168 litres/hectare (18 US gallons/acre; 15 Imp gallons/acre), with a 24.4 m (80 ft) swath width. Location of the spraybooms just aft of the wing trailing-edges reduces drag and allows the pilot to make visual checks of their operation.

All parts of the New Brave's airframe are treated to prevent corrosion damage, with extensive use of polyurethane coating, selection of stainless steel for cables and other moving components in vulnerable areas, and internal oiling of lower truss sections. The design eliminates dust traps and inaccessible areas, and fuselage covering is spaced away from the frame to permit thorough hosing down. To facilitate washing, inspection and maintenance, the side panels are attached by quick release fasteners.

Two versions of the New Brave are available:

New Brave 375. Equipped with one 279 kW (375 hp) Textron Lycoming IO-720-D1C flat-eight engine, driving a Hartzell three-blade constant-speed metal propeller with spinner.

New Brave 400. Latest model, with a 298 kW (400 hp) version of the Textron Lycoming IO-720-D1C engine.

By early 1987 a total of 150 New Braves had been delivered. The following description applies to both versions:

TYPE: Single-seat agricultural aircraft.

WINGS: Cantilever low-wing monoplane. Wing section NACA 63₃-618. Dihedral 6°. Incidence 2° 30' at root, 0° 30' at tip. Conventional two-spar metal structure. Light alloy laminated spars with two-bolt main spar attachment to fuselage structure. Light alloy covering, detachable leading-edges and glassfibre wingtips. Conventional ailerons and trailing-edge flaps. Landing lights in wing leading-edges.

FUSELAGE: Welded chrome-molybdenum steel tube structure. Metal underskin and removable side panels. Glassfibre engine cowling.

TAIL UNIT: Cantilever all-metal structure. Tailplane has glassfibre tips. Tab on rudder and in each elevator. Cable from top of cockpit structure to tip of fin to deflect cables.

LANDING GEAR: Non-retractable tailwheel type. Interchangeable cantilever spring steel main-gear struts, with wire cutters on leading-edges. Cleveland mainwheels type 40-101 with tyres size 8.50-10, 6-ply rating, pressure 1.93-2.21 bars (28-32 lb/sq in). Scott steerable tailwheel type 3450-21 with tyre of 0.25 m (10 in) diameter, pressure 2.41-3.10 bars (35-45 lb/sq in). Cleveland type 30-67B hydraulic brakes. Parking brake.

POWER PLANT: One engine as detailed in model listings. One fuel tank in each wingroot. Total fuel capacity for both versions 337 litres (89 US gallons; 74 Imp gallons), of which 325.5 litres (86 US gallons; 71.5 Imp gallons) are usable. Refuelling point in upper surface of each wing. Fuel tanks filled with reticulated polyurethane safety foam (Safom). Oil capacity 16 litres (4.25 US gallons; 3.5 Imp gallons).

ACCOMMODATION: Pilot only, on adjustable seat in an isolated cockpit capsule with steel tube overturn structure. Seat, equipped with double shoulder harness and inertia reel, is attached to overturn structure. Wire cutter mounted in centre of windscreen. Combined window and door on each side, hinged at bottom. Entrance steps optional.

SYSTEMS: Electrical system supplied by 28V 70A alternator with two 12V 25Ah batteries in series. 35Ah capacity batteries optional. Hydraulic system for brakes only.

AVIONICS: Optional factory installed avionics available, as well as a range of transponders.

EQUIPMENT: Hopper/tank of 1.08 m³ (38 cu ft) capacity, for 1,041 litres (275 US gallons; 229 Imp gallons) of liquid chemical. Maximum capacity for dry chemicals 998 kg (2,200 lb). Venturi type dry material spreaders of stainless steel available, including a basic design capable of

New Brave agricultural aircraft, for which WTA has exclusive marketing rights

application rates of 5.6 to 224 kg/hectare (5 to 200 lb/acre). Spray system comprises an easily removable wind driven spraypump and 38 mm (1½ in) diameter spraybooms equipped with 60 nozzles. Belt driven hydraulic spray system with stainless steel dropped booms optional. Other optional equipment includes 8-day clock; sensitive altimeter; turn co-ordinator; emergency locator transmitter; night working light package which includes two 600W cockpit adjustable/retractable working lights, two 450W ground adjustable turning lights, hopper light, and related switching; landing and taxi lights; navigation, instrument panel, rotating beacon, and anti-collision lights; cockpit fire extinguisher; and heater.

DIMENSIONS, EXTERNAL:

Wing span	11.82 m (38 ft 9½ in)
Wing chord: at root	2.03 m (6 ft 8 in)
at tip	1.75 m (5 ft 9 in)
Wing aspect ratio	6.7
Length overall	8.38 m (27 ft 6 in)
Height overall	2.29 m (7 ft 6 in)
Tailplane span	4.01 m (13 ft 1¾ in)
Wheel track	2.65 m (8 ft 8¾ in)
Wheelbase	5.91 m (19 ft 4¾ in)
Propeller diameter	2.18 m (7 ft 2 in)
Propeller ground clearance	0.23 m (9 in)
Cockpit doors: Height	0.76 m (2 ft 6 in)
Width	0.71 m (2 ft 4 in)
Height to sill	1.57 m (5 ft 2 in)
Hopper loading door: Length	1.27 m (4 ft 2 in)
Width	0.48 m (1 ft 7 in)

DIMENSIONS, INTERNAL:

Cockpit: Max width	0.97 m (3 ft 2 in)
Max height	1.32 m (4 ft 4 in)

AREAS:

Wings, gross	20.96 m² (225.65 sq ft)
Ailerons (total)	2.01 m² (21.6 sq ft)
Trailing-edge flaps (total)	2.32 m² (25.0 sq ft)
Fin	0.95 m² (10.2 sq ft)
Rudder	0.90 m² (9.7 sq ft)
Tailplane	2.11 m² (22.67 sq ft)
Elevators (incl tabs)	1.92 m² (20.66 sq ft)

WEIGHTS AND LOADINGS (A: Normal category, B: Restricted category):

Weight empty:	
no dispersal equipment	1,118 kg (2,465 lb)
sprayer	1,154 kg (2,544 lb)
duster	1,152 kg (2,540 lb)
Max T-O weight: A	1,769 kg (3,900 lb)
B	2,177 kg (4,800 lb)
Max landing weight: A, B	1,769 kg (3,900 lb)
Max wing loading: A	84.4 kg/m² (17.3 lb/sq ft)
B	103.9 kg/m² (21.3 lb/sq ft)
Max power loading, New Brave 375:	
A	6.33 kg/kW (10.4 lb/hp)
B	7.79 kg/kW (12.8 lb/hp)
Max power loading, New Brave 400:	
A	5.94 kg/kW (9.75 lb/hp)
B	7.31 kg/kW (12.0 lb/hp)

PERFORMANCE (New Brave 375 at Normal category max T-O weight, no dispersal equipment installed):

Max level speed at optimum altitude	139 knots (257 km/h; 160 mph)
Cruising speed, best power mixture:	
75% power at 1,705 m (5,600 ft)	129 knots (240 km/h; 149 mph)
65% power at 2,895 m (9,500 ft)	126 knots (233 km/h; 145 mph)
55% power at 4,265 m (14,000 ft)	119 knots (220 km/h; 137 mph)
Cruising speed, best econ mixture:	
75% power at 1,705 m (5,600 ft)	128 knots (236 km/h; 147 mph)
65% power at 2,895 m (9,500 ft)	124 knots (230 km/h; 143 mph)
55% power at 4,265 m (14,000 ft)	117 knots (217 km/h; 135 mph)
Stalling speed:	
flaps up	63 knots (116 km/h; 72 mph) CAS
flaps down	58 knots (106 km/h; 66 mph) CAS
Max rate of climb at S/L	320 m (1,051 ft)/min
T-O run	218 m (715 ft)
T-O to 15 m (50 ft)	368 m (1,208 ft)
Landing from 15 m (50 ft)	564 m (1,850 ft)

Landing run	226 m (740 ft)

Range with max fuel, best econ mixture, with allowances for start, taxi, T-O, climb, descent, and 45 min reserves:

75% power at 1,705 m (5,600 ft)	465 nm (861 km; 535 miles)
65% power at 2,895 m (9,500 ft)	495 nm (917 km; 570 miles)
55% power at 4,265 m (14,000 ft)	525 nm (974 km; 605 miles)

PERFORMANCE (New Brave 375 at Restricted category max T-O weight, except where indicated. A: sprayer, B: duster):

Max level speed at optimum altitude:	
A	123 knots (229 km/h; 142 mph)
B	119 knots (220 km/h; 137 mph)
Cruising speed, best power mixture at AUW of 1,542 kg (3,400 lb): A	118 knots (219 km/h; 136 mph)
B	113 knots (209 km/h; 130 mph)
Max rate of climb at S/L: A	168 m (550 ft)/min
B	116 m (380 ft)/min
Max rate of climb at S/L at AUW of 1,769 kg (3,900 lb):	
A	280 m (920 ft)/min
B	201 m (660 ft)/min
T-O run: A	442 m (1,450 ft)
B	533 m (1,750 ft)
T-O run at AUW of 1,769 kg (3,900 lb):	
A	274 m (900 ft)
B	351 m (1,150 ft)
T-O to 15 m (50 ft): A	701 m (2,300 ft)
B	762 m (2,500 ft)
T-O to 15 m (50 ft) at AUW of 1,769 kg (3,900 lb):	
A	457 m (1,500 ft)
B	533 m (1,750 ft)
Landing from 15 m (50 ft) at max landing weight:	
A, B	439 m (1,440 ft)
Landing run at max landing weight:	
A, B	140 m (460 ft)

Range with max fuel, best power mixture, with allowances for start, taxi, T-O, climb, cruise, descent and 45 min reserves at 45% power:

A	392 nm (727 km; 452 miles)
B	372 nm (689 km; 428 miles)

YUGOSLAVIA

SOKO
SOUR VAZDUHOPLOVNA INDUSTRIJA SOKO

88 000 Mostar
Telephone: (088) 22-121, 33-831, 35-244, 35-541, 37-943, 55-120
Telex: 46-180 YU SOKOMO
PRESIDENT: Dipl Ing Milenko Pjescić
VICE-PRESIDENT, RESEARCH AND DEVELOPMENT:
    Dipl Ing M. Zadro
DIRECTOR, COMMERCIAL: Dipl Oec N. Milović
DIRECTOR, ENGINEERING, AIRCRAFT DIVISION:
    Dipl Ing Šefik Karabeg

Founded in 1951, this company manufactures aircraft of its own design and is participating, with Romania, in developing and producing the Orao/IAR-93 strike aircraft described under the SOKO/CNIAR heading in the International section.

SOKO also continues to build under licence the Aérospatiale SA 342L Gazelle helicopter, on behalf of the Yugoslav government.

SOKO G-4 SUPER GALEB (SEAGULL)

This light strike and training aircraft was designed to replace the earlier G2-A Galeb and Lockheed T-33 in basic and advanced training units of the Yugoslav Air Force. The first of two Super Galeb prototypes flew for the first time on 17 July 1978. The second was flown on 18 December 1979, followed by the first of several pre-production aircraft on 17 December 1980. The production Super Galeb, for which the Yugoslav Air Force placed a substantial order, differs from the pre-production aircraft model in having an all-moving tailplane with considerable anhedral, instead of the original conventional horizontal tail surfaces with elevators and no anhedral. A substantial proportion of the quantity ordered initially had been delivered by early 1987.

TYPE: Two-seat basic trainer and light strike aircraft.

WINGS: Cantilever low-wing monoplane. No dihedral. Sweepback at quarter-chord 22°; leading-edge sweep increased near the wing roots. One-piece two-spar all-metal structure, with integrally machined skin panels inboard and chemically milled skin towards wingtips. Shallow boundary layer fence on upper surface of each wing, forward of inboard end of aileron. Wings attached to fuselage at six points. Entire trailing-edge made up of conventional all-metal sealed ailerons and flaps. Ailerons actuated by hydraulic servo jacks, with artificial feel, flaps by electrically controlled hydraulic actuators. No slats or tabs.

FUSELAGE: All-metal semi-monocoque structure, with air intake trunk blended into each side. Rear portion, complete with tail surfaces, detachable for access to

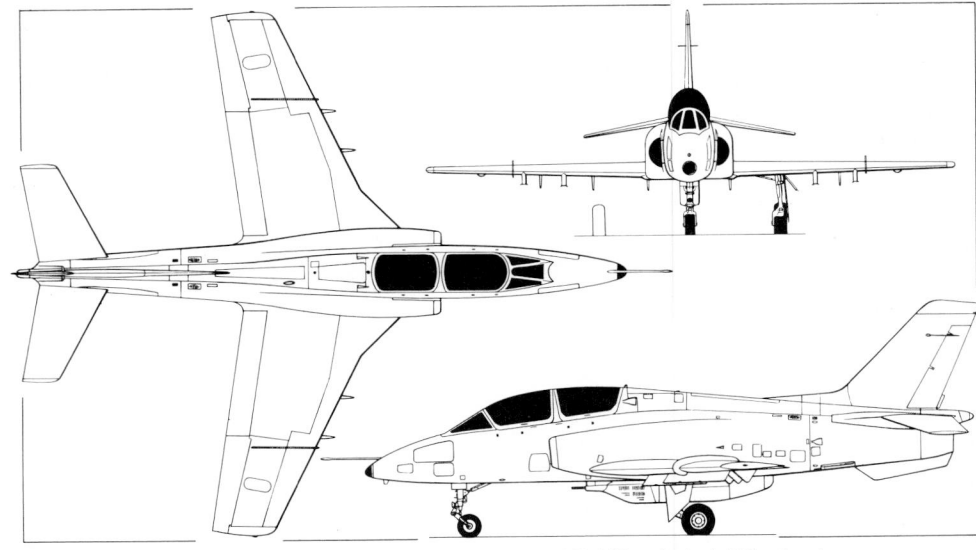

SOKO G-4 Super Galeb (Rolls-Royce Viper Mk 632 turbojet) *(Pilot Press)*

SOKO G-4 Super Galeb jet training and light attack aircraft

engine. Door type airbrake under rear fuselage. Landing light in nose, forward of large equipment bay.

TAIL UNIT: Conventional cantilever all-metal structure, with all surfaces sweptback. All-moving horizontal surfaces have 10° anhedral, and are actuated by hydraulic servo jacks, with artificial feel. Mechanically actuated rudder.

Dorsal fin. Ground adjustable tab on rudder. Two ventral strakes under jetpipe.

LANDING GEAR: Hydraulically retractable tricycle type, with single wheel on each unit. Nosewheel retracts forward, main units inward into wings. Oleo-pneumatic shock absorber in each leg. Hydraulically steerable nose unit optional (not on current aircraft). Trailing link main units. Mainwheels fitted with Dunlop tyres size 615 × 225-10, pressure 4.4 bars (64 lb/sq in), and hydraulic brakes. Nosewheel has Dunlop tyre size 6.50-5.5 TC, pressure 3.0 bars (43.5 lb/sq in). Brake parachute container at base of rudder. Provision for attaching two assisted take-off rockets under centre-fuselage.

POWER PLANT: One Rolls-Royce Viper Mk 632 turbojet, rated at 17.8 kN (4,000 lb st). Fuel in three flexible bag tanks in centre-fuselage and an integral tank between the spars of each inner wing. Total internal fuel capacity 1,720 litres (454.4 US gallons; 378.5 Imp gallons). Provision for two underwing auxiliary tanks, on inboard pylons, total capacity 625 litres (165.1 US gallons; 137.5 Imp gallons). Max fuel capacity 2,345 litres (619.5 US gallons; 516 Imp gallons). Gravity refuelling system standard.

ACCOMMODATION: Crew of two in tandem on Martin-Baker zero/zero Mk J10 ejection seats (zero height/90 knot Mk J8 optional but not on current aircraft), with ejection through the individual sideways hinged (to starboard) canopy over each seat. Rear seat raised by 25 cm (10 in) to give occupant forward view over front seat occupant. Cockpit pressurised and air-conditioned.

SYSTEMS: Engine compressor bleed air used for pressurisation, air-conditioning, anti-g suit and windscreen anti-icing systems, and to pressurise fuel tanks. Dual hydraulic system, pressure 210 bars (3,045 lb/sq in), for flying control servos, flap and airbrake actuators, landing gear retraction and extension, and wheel brakes. Hydraulic system flow rate 45 litres (12 US gallons; 10 Imp gallons)/min for main system, 16 litres (4.2 US gallons; 3.5 Imp gallons)/min for flight control system. Electrical system supplied by 9kW 28V DC generator, with nickel-cadmium battery for ground/emergency power and self contained engine starting. Two static inverters, total output 600VA, provide 115V 400Hz AC power. Gaseous oxygen system adequate for two crew for 2 h 30 min.

AVIONICS AND EQUIPMENT: Dual controls and full blind-flying instrumentation in each cockpit. Standard nav/com equipment comprises EAS type ER4.671D or RC E163 Kondor VHF com radio, GEC Avionics AD 370B or Iskra VARK-1 radio compass, Collins VIR-30 VOR/ILS, Iskra 75R4 VOR marker beacon receiver, Collins DME 40 and TRT AHV-6 radio altimeter. Optional UHF and V/UHF com, gyro platform and other equipment to customer's specification.

ARMAMENT AND OPERATIONAL EQUIPMENT: Removable ventral gun pod containing 23 mm GSh-23L twin-barrel rapid fire cannon with 200 rds. Two attachments under each wing, with capacity of 500 kg (1,102 lb) inboard and 350 kg (772 lb) outboard. Total weapon load capability, with centreline gun pod, 1,950 kg (4,300 lb). In addition to standard high explosive bombs and napalm pods, typical Yugoslav stores include S-8-16 cluster bombs, each with eight 16 kg fragmentation munitions; KPT-150 expendable containers, each with up to 40 anti-personnel or 54 anti-tank bomblets; L-57-16MD pods, each with sixteen 57 mm rockets; L-128-04 pods, each with four 128 mm rockets; adaptors for twin 5 in HVAR rockets, single 57 mm VRZ-57 training rockets; SN-3-050 triple carriers for 50 kg bombs; SN-3-100 triple carriers for 100 kg bombs; KM-3 pods each containing a single 12.7 mm (0.50 in) gun; SAM Z-80 towed target system; and auxiliary fuel tanks on the inboard attachments. Ferranti D282 gyro gunsight standard. Other types of fire control system optional. A photo reconnaissance/infra-red line-scan pod and night illumination system have been under development for several years, but an off-the-shelf system may be selected for economic reasons.

DIMENSIONS, EXTERNAL:

Wing span	9.88 m (32 ft 5 in)
Wing aspect ratio	5.0
Length overall	11.86 m (38 ft 11 in)
Height overall	4.28 m (14 ft 0½ in)
Tailplane span	3.97 m (13 ft 0¼ in)
Wheel track	3.49 m (11 ft 5½ in)
Wheelbase	4.15 m (13 ft 7½ in)

AREAS:

Wings, gross	19.5 m² (209.9 sq ft)
Ailerons (total)	1.358 m² (14.62 sq ft)
Trailing-edge flaps (total)	3.340 m² (35.95 sq ft)
Airbrake	0.438 m² (4.71 sq ft)
Fin	3.130 m² (33.69 sq ft)
Rudder	0.689 m² (7.42 sq ft)
Horizontal tail surfaces	4.669 m² (50.26 sq ft)

WEIGHTS:

Weight empty, equipped	3,250 kg (7,165 lb)
T-O weight, training mission	4,760 kg (10,495 lb)
T-O weight, normal combat mission, with 1,350 kg (2,975 lb) of weapons	6,110 kg (13,470 lb)
Max T-O weight, combat overload	6,330 kg (13,955 lb)

PERFORMANCE (at AUW of 4,760 kg; 10,495 lb, except where indicated):

Never-exceed speed	Mach 0.866
Max level speed at 6,000 m (19,680 ft)	491 knots (910 km/h; 565 mph)
Landing speed	89 knots (165 km/h; 103 mph)
Max rate of climb at S/L:	
AUW as above	1,800 m (5,905 ft)/min
with 50% internal fuel (AUW of 3,890 kg; 8,575 lb)	2,330 m (7,645 ft)/min
Time to 8,000 m (26,240 ft)	6 min
Absolute ceiling	15,000 m (49,200 ft)
T-O run	532 m (1,745 ft)
T-O to 15 m (50 ft)	850 m (2,790 ft)
Landing from 15 m (50 ft) at landing weight of 3,800 kg (8,375 lb)	750 m (2,460 ft)
Landing run at above landing weight	550 m (1,805 ft)

Combat radius, with gun pack and full internal fuel, 10% reserves:

with four BL755 cluster bombs:	
lo-lo-lo	208 nm (386 km; 240 miles)
hi-lo-hi	260 nm (483 km; 300 miles)
with two BL755 and two aux fuel tanks:	
lo-lo-lo	321 nm (595 km; 370 miles)
hi-lo-hi	438 nm (812 km; 504 miles)
Range at 11,000 m (36,000 ft), with two aux fuel tanks, 10% reserves	1,420 nm (2,630 km; 1,635 miles)
Endurance at 11,000 m (36,000 ft), with two aux fuel tanks	4 h 20 min
g limits	+8/-4.2

NOVI AVION

Known as the Novi Avion at this stage, a multi-role fighter to replace the MiG-21 in the Yugoslav Air Force has been under development for several years. No details are available, but it can be assumed that the development programme is directed by the Vazduhoplovno Tehnicki Institut in Zarkovo, near Belgrade, which was responsible for the Yugoslav input to the international J-22 Orao attack aircraft programme. Production will almost certainly be undertaken by Soko.

It is understood that discussions concerning collaborative airframe development have taken place with various European and US manufacturers, and that engine proposals from Rolls-Royce, General Electric and Pratt & Whitney are being studied.

UTVA

UTVA—SOUR METALNE INDUSTRIJE, RO FABRIKA AVIONA

Jabucki Put BB, 26 000 Pancevo
Telephone: (013) 512584
Telex: 13250 FA UTVA YU
GENERAL MANAGER: Dipl Ing Soso Milan
MANAGER OF AIRCRAFT DEVELOPMENT:
Dipl Ing Stamatov Petar
CHIEF DESIGNER: Dipl Ing Dimić Dragoslav

UTVA-75A21

The UTVA-75A21 is a side by side two-seat training, glider towing and utility lightplane, which was projected, designed and built in partnership by UTVA-Pancevo, Prva Petoletka-Trstenik, Vazduhoplovno Tehnicki Institut and Institut Masinskog Fakulteta of Belgrade. Design was started in 1974, to the requirements of FAR Pt 23 (Utility category). Construction of two prototypes was undertaken in 1975; the first of these flew for the first time on 19 May 1976 and the second on 18 December 1976. Series production began immediately and is continuing. More than 100 UTVA-75A21s have been delivered to civilian flying clubs, others to the Yugoslav Air Force.

TYPE: Two-seat light aircraft.

WINGS: Cantilever low-wing monoplane, with short span centre-section and two constant chord outer panels. Wing section NACA 65₂415. Dihedral 0° on centre-section, 6° on outer panels. Conventional all-metal two-spar structure. Ailerons and flaps, with fluted skin, along entire trailing-edge of outer panels, except for tips. Flettner trim tab on each aileron.

FUSELAGE: Conventional all-metal semi-monocoque structure.

TAIL UNIT: Cantilever all-metal structure, with sweptback vertical surfaces. Fluted skin on fin, rudder and elevator. Rudder and elevator horn balanced. Controllable tab on elevator; ground adjustable tab on rudder.

LANDING GEAR: Non-retractable tricycle type, with single wheel on each unit, and small tail bumper. Prva Petoletka-Trstenik oleo-pneumatic shock absorbers. Dunlop tyres, size 6.00-6 on mainwheels, 5.00-5 on nosewheel. Prva Petoletka-Trstenik hydraulic brakes.

POWER PLANT: One 134 kW (180 hp) Textron Lycoming IO-360-B1F flat-four engine, driving a Hartzell HC-C2YK-1BF/F7666A two-blade variable-pitch metal propeller. Two integral fuel tanks in wings, total capacity 160 litres (42.3 US gallons; 35 Imp gallons). Provision for carrying two 100 litre (26.4 US gallon; 22 Imp gallon) drop tanks under wings, raising max total capacity to 360 litres (95.1 US gallons; 79 Imp gallons). Oil capacity 10 litres (2.6 US gallons; 2.2 Imp gallons).

ACCOMMODATION: Two seats side by side in enclosed cabin, with large upward opening jettisonable canopy door over each seat, hinged on centreline. Dual stick type controls standard. Cabin heated and ventilated.

SYSTEMS: Dual hydraulic systems for brakes. 14V DC electrical system, with 35Ah battery, navigation lights, rotating beacon and landing lights as standard equipment.

AVIONICS AND EQUIPMENT: King KY 195B radio optional. Standard equipment includes radio compass.

ARMAMENT AND MILITARY EQUIPMENT: Two fittings for light weapon loads underwing on military UTVA-75s. Each can carry a bomb, 100 kg (220 lb) cargo container, two-round rocket launcher or machine-gun pod.

DIMENSIONS, EXTERNAL:

Wing span	9.73 m (31 ft 11 in)
Wing chord (constant)	1.55 m (5 ft 1 in)
Wing aspect ratio	6.5

UTVA-75A21 two-seat trainer with underwing pylons for light weapon loads

Length overall	7.11 m (23 ft 4 in)
Height overall	3.15 m (10 ft 4 in)
Tailplane span	3.80 m (12 ft 5½ in)
Wheel track	2.58 m (8 ft 5½ in)
Wheelbase	1.99 m (6 ft 6¼ in)
Propeller diameter	1.93 m (6 ft 4 in)
Propeller ground clearance	0.295 m (11¾ in)

AREAS:

Wings, gross	14.63 m² (157.5 sq ft)
Ailerons (total)	1.38 m² (14.85 sq ft)
Flaps (total)	1.61 m² (17.33 sq ft)
Horizontal tail surfaces (total)	3.34 m² (35.95 sq ft)

WEIGHTS:

Weight empty, equipped	685 kg (1,510 lb)
Max crew/military load/baggage	210 kg (463 lb)
Max fuel: standard	103 kg (227 lb)
with drop tanks	256 kg (564 lb)
Max T-O weight	960 kg (2,116 lb)

PERFORMANCE (at max T-O weight):

Max level speed	116 knots (215 km/h; 133 mph)

Max cruising speed	100 knots (185 km/h; 115 mph)
Econ cruising speed	89 knots (165 km/h; 102 mph)
Stalling speed, engine idling:	
flaps up	52 knots (95 km/h; 59 mph)
25° flap	45 knots (82 km/h; 51 mph)
Max rate of climb at S/L	270 m (885 ft)/min
Service ceiling	4,000 m (13,125 ft)
T-O run	125 m (410 ft)
T-O to 15 m (50 ft)	250 m (820 ft)
Landing from 15 m (50 ft)	340 m (1,115 ft)
Landing run	100 m (328 ft)
Range with max standard fuel	
	432 nm (800 km; 497 miles)
Range with drop tanks, no reserves	
	1,080 nm (2,000 km; 1,242 miles)
g limits	+6/−3

UTVA-75A41

The UTVA-75A41 is a four-seat version of the UTVA-75A21 for training, glider towing and utility operations. Design and construction were started in 1984 in partnership by UTVA-Pancevo, Prva Petoletka-Trstenik, Vazduhoplovno Tehnicki Institut and Institut Masinskog Fakulteta of Belgrade, to the requirements of FAR Pt 23 (Normal category). The prototype UTVA-75A41 flew for the first time in 1986. Series production began immediately afterwards, in parallel with continued manufacture of the two-seat UTVA-75A21. Deliveries were expected to begin in 1987.

TYPE: Four-seat light utility and training aircraft.

WINGS, FUSELAGE, TAIL UNIT, LANDING GEAR, POWER PLANT AND SYSTEMS: As for UTVA-75A21.

ACCOMMODATION: Four seats in pairs in enclosed cabin, with large upward opening jettisonable canopy door over each fore and aft pair of seats, hinged on centreline. Dual stick type controls standard. Cabin heated and ventilated.

AVIONICS AND EQUIPMENT: King equipment standard, including dual KY 197 720-channel VHF com transceivers; KR 87 digitally tuned ADF with integral electronic flight timer and pushbutton elapsed timer; panel mounted R/Nav system comprising a KNS 81 200-channel nav, 40-channel glideslope indicator and 9-waypoint digital R/Nav computer, combined with a KI 525A pictorial nav indicator; KI 229 RMI; KN 53 200-channel VHF nav with integral 40-channel glideslope indicator and KI 525A indicator; KN 62A 200-channel DME with digital distance, ground speed and time-to-station; KT 79 all solid state digital transponder featuring cross-check readout of encoded altitude and automatic VFR code selection; and KMA 24 audio control console with integral marker beacon receiver.

ARMAMENT: None.

DIMENSIONS, EXTERNAL, and AREAS:
As for UTVA-75A21

WEIGHTS:

Weight empty, equipped	700 kg (1,544 lb)
Max payload	310 kg (683 lb)
Max fuel: standard	103 kg (227 lb)
with drop tanks	256 kg (564 lb)
Max T-O weight	1,163 kg (2,564 lb)

PERFORMANCE (at max T-O weight):

Max level speed	113 knots (210 km/h; 130 mph)
Max cruising speed	97 knots (180 km/h; 112 mph)
Econ cruising speed	86 knots (160 km/h; 99 mph)
Stalling speed, engine idling:	
flaps up	57 knots (105 km/h; 65 mph)
25° flap	49 knots (90 km/h; 56 mph)
Max rate of climb at S/L	264 m (866 ft)/min
Service ceiling	4,000 m (13,125 ft)
T-O run	200 m (656 ft)
T-O to 15 m (50 ft)	400 m (1,312 ft)
Landing from 15 m (50 ft)	340 m (1,115 ft)
Landing run	180 m (590 ft)
Range with max standard fuel	
	432 nm (800 km; 497 miles)
Range with drop tanks, no reserves	
	1,080 nm (2,000 km; 1,242 miles)
g limits	+3.8/−2.2

UTVA-75A11

The UTVA-75A11 is an agricultural aircraft with an airframe almost identical to that of the UTVA-75A21 except for changes associated with the installation of a chemical hopper forward of a high-set single-seat cabin in the centre-fuselage. The landing gear is upgraded to cope with operations at a higher gross weight, from grass surfaces; and a more powerful engine is fitted.

Design of the UTVA-75A11 was started on 20 December 1986. Construction of the prototype began on 15 June 1987 and the first flight was scheduled for May 1988.

Differences by comparison with the UTVA-75A21 are as follows:

TYPE: Single-seat agricultural aircraft.

FUSELAGE: Basically as for UTVA-75A21, but greater use of composites, particularly for pilot's cabin. Chemical hopper, capacity 870 litres (230 US gallons; 191 Imp gallons), forward of cabin.

LANDING GEAR: Tyres size 7.00-8 on mainwheels, 6.00-6 on nosewheel.

POWER PLANT: One 224 kW (300 hp) Textron Lycoming IO-540-L1A5D flat-six engine, driving a Hartzell HC-

C2YK-1BF/F8475D-4 propeller. Two fuel tanks in wings, with total capacity of 160 litres (42.3 US gallons; 35 Imp gallons). Provision for two 150 litre (39.6 US gallon; 33 Imp gallon) underwing tanks.

ACCOMMODATION: Pilot only, in high-set cabin. Downward hinged canopy/door on each side.

SYSTEMS: Electrical system is 24V 60A DC, with a 19Ah nickel-cadmium battery.

AVIONICS AND EQUIPMENT: Prototype has Rudičajavec VHF radio, blind-flying instrumentation, navigation and landing lights, and rotating beacon.

DIMENSIONS, EXTERNAL:
As for UTVA-75A21 except:

Length overall	7.21 m (23 ft 8 in)
Propeller diameter	2.03 m (6 ft 8 in)
Propeller ground clearance	0.47 m (1 ft 6 in)

WEIGHTS:

Weight empty	847 kg (1,868 lb)
Max payload	780 kg (1,720 lb)
Max fuel, internal	103 kg (227 lb)
Max T-O weight	1,730 kg (3,814 lb)
Max landing weight	1,400 kg (3,086 lb)

PERFORMANCE (at max T-O weight, estimated):

Never-exceed speed	173 knots (320 km/h; 199 mph)
Max level speed	121 knots (225 km/h; 140 mph)
Max cruising speed	102 knots (190 km/h; 118 mph)
Econ cruising speed	89 knots (165 km/h; 102 mph)
Stalling speed: flaps down	62 knots (115 km/h; 72 mph)
flaps up	67 knots (124 km/h; 77 mph)
Max rate of climb at S/L	240 m (787 ft)/min
Service ceiling	5,000 m (16,400 ft)
T-O run	340 m (1,115 ft)
T-O to 15 m (50 ft)	630 m (2,067 ft)
Landing from 15 m (50 ft)	540 m (1,772 ft)
Landing run	250 m (820 ft)
Range with max internal fuel	162 nm (300 km; 186 miles)
Range with underwing tanks	442 nm (820 km; 510 miles)

UTVA LASTA (SWALLOW)

First shown publicly in model form at the 1985 Paris Air Show, the Lasta was designed by the Vazduhoplovno Tehnicki Institut at Zarkovo, near Belgrade, as a primary trainer to the requirements of FAR Pt 23. Although similar in configuration and purpose to the French Epsilon, and with the same power plant, it is a larger and heavier aircraft. Pupil pilots are intended to progress from the Lasta directly to the SOKO G-4 Super Galeb jet basic trainer, and the cockpits of the two aircraft are fundamentally similar. The Lasta is intended to be suitable for basic, aerobatic, navigation, instrument and night flying training, for basic training in gunnery, rocket firing and bombing, for formation flying and combat manoeuvres.

Manufacture of the Lasta is being undertaken by Fabrika Aviona UTVA at Pancevo. The first of two prototypes flew for the first time in 1985. Tooling was being prepared at that time for a pre-series of ten production Lastas.

TYPE: Tandem two-seat primary trainer and light attack aircraft.

WINGS: Cantilever low-wing monoplane of conventional light alloy two-spar stressed-skin construction. Dihedral from roots. Ailerons and flaps over full span. Trim tab in inboard trailing-edge of each aileron.

FUSELAGE: Conventional light alloy semi-monocoque structure.

TAIL UNIT: Cantilever light alloy stressed-skin structure. Fixed incidence tailplane. Horn balanced rudder. Long dorsal fin and shallow ventral fin. Trim tab in rudder and starboard elevator.

LANDING GEAR: Hydraulically retractable tricycle type of Prva Petoletka-Trstenik design and manufacture, with single wheel on each unit. Nosewheel retracts rearward, main units inward. Oleo-pneumatic shock absorbers. Nosewheel steerable to 30° each way, via rudder pedals. Dunlop tyres: size 6.00-6 (8PR), pressure 3.8 bars (55

Model of UTVA-75A11 single-seat agricultural aircraft

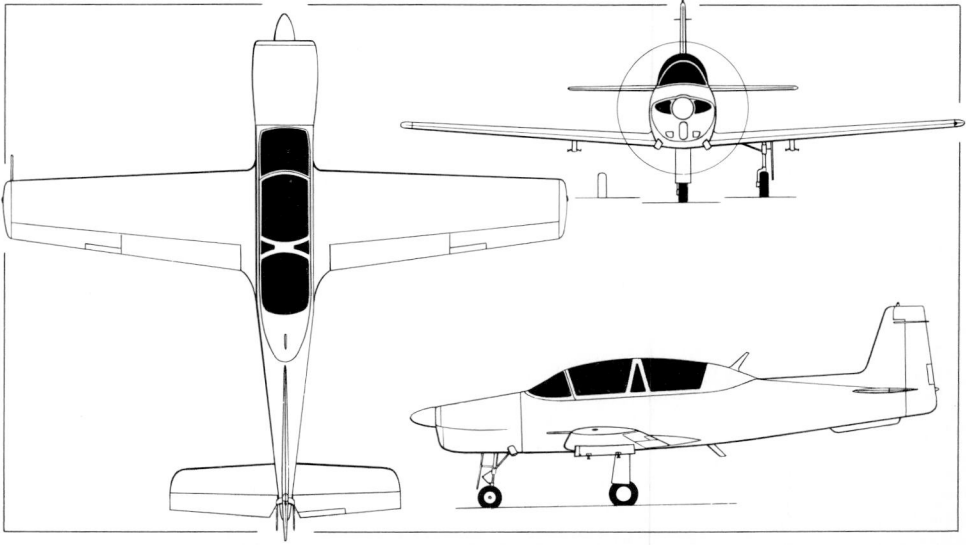

UTVA Lasta (Textron Lycoming AEIO-540-L1B5D engine) *(Pilot Press)*

lb/sq in), on mainwheels; size 5.00-5 (8PR), pressure 4.2 bars (61 lb/sq in), on nosewheel. Hydraulic disc brakes.

POWER PLANT: One 224 kW (300 hp) Textron Lycoming AEIO-540-Z1B5D flat-six engine, driving a Hoffmann HO-V-123K-V three-blade constant-speed propeller with spinner. Integral fuel tanks in wings.

ACCOMMODATION: Two seats in tandem, with rear seat raised 76 mm (3 in). Separate canopy over each seat, sideways hinged to starboard.

SYSTEMS: Hydraulic, electrical and oxygen systems standard. Full night lighting.

AVIONICS: Standard equipment will include VHF, VOR, ILS and DME.

ARMAMENT: Two underwing hardpoints for bombs, rocket packs and pods containing twin machine-guns, with total external load of up to 400 kg (882 lb).

DIMENSIONS, EXTERNAL:
Wing span	8.34 m (27 ft 4½ in)
Wing aspect ratio	6.3
Length overall	8.04 m (26 ft 4½ in)
Height overall	4.45 m (14 ft 7¼ in)

AREA:
Wings, gross	11.0 m² (118.4 sq ft)

WEIGHTS:
Weight empty, equipped	1,060 kg (2,337 lb)
Max T-O weight	1,630 kg (3,593 lb)

Prototype UTVA Lasta primary trainer and light attack aircraft

PERFORMANCE (estimated, at max T-O weight):
Never-exceed speed	302 knots (560 km/h; 348 mph)	Max rate of climb at S/L	540 m (1,770 ft)/min
Max level speed at S/L	186 knots (345 km/h; 214 mph)	T-O run	320 m (1,050 ft)
		Landing run	310 m (1,017 ft)

SPORT AIRCRAFT
(incorporating Homebuilt, Microlight and Racing aircraft)

AUSTRALIA

BLUE MAX
BLUE MAX ULTRALIGHT
PO Box 42, Nagambie, Victoria 3608
Telephone: (058) 561622
OWNER: Werner Bekker

BLUE MAX ULTRALIGHT BLUE MAX
This single-seat microlight is available in ready to fly form. The engine can be switched off and restarted in flight for periods of gliding.
TYPE: Single-seat microlight.

AIRFRAME: Mainframe and boom constructed of aluminium alloy, with optional glassfibre cockpit pod. Ceconite covered wings, with glassfibre ribs, leading-edges and tips. Ceconite covered tail unit. Three-axis control. Non-retractable tailwheel landing gear.
POWER PLANT: One 33.6 kW (45 hp) Rotax 447. Optionally, a 21 kW (28 hp) König 570. Fuel capacity 41 litres (10.8 US gallons; 9 Imp gallons).
DIMENSIONS, EXTERNAL: Not quoted
WEIGHTS:

Weight empty	115 kg (254 lb)
Max pilot weight	95 kg (210 lb)
Max T-O weight	239 kg (527 lb)

PERFORMANCE (A: König 570, B: Rotax 447 engine):
Max level and cruising speed:

A	54 knots (100 km/h; 62 mph)
B	59 knots (109 km/h; 68 mph)
Max rate of climb at S/L: A	122 m (400 ft)/min
B	427 m (1,400 ft)/min
Service ceiling: A	1,220-1,525 m (4,000-5,000 ft)
T-O run: A	91 m (300 ft)
Landing run: A	76 m (250 ft)
Range with max fuel: A	250 nm (463 km; 287 miles)
Endurance: A	2 h 45 min
B	2 h

CORBY
JOHN C. CORBY
34 Coronet Court, North Rocks, Sydney, NSW 2151

CORBY CJ-1 STARLET
Details of the first Starlet can be found in the 1974-75 *Jane's*. More than 20 have been completed from plans, with approximately 50 more under construction in Australia, New Zealand and the USA.
TYPE: Single-seat homebuilt.
AIRFRAME: All-wooden construction, except for fabric covering on wings from main spar aft, and on rudder and elevators. Wing section NACA 43012A. Non-retractable tailwheel landing gear.
POWER PLANT: Any suitable engine of up to 56 kW (75 hp) and 72 kg (160 lb) weight. Fuel capacity 36-43 litres (9.6-11.4 US gallons; 8-9.5 Imp gallons).
DIMENSIONS, EXTERNAL:

Wing span	5.64 m (18 ft 6 in)
Length overall	4.50 m (14 ft 9 in)
Height overall	1.47 m (4 ft 10 in)
Propeller diameter	1.37 m (4 ft 6 in)

AREA:

Wings, gross	6.36 m² (68.5 sq ft)

WEIGHTS:

Weight empty	183-212 kg (405-467 lb)
Max T-O weight	322 kg (710 lb)

PERFORMANCE (with 56 kW; 75 hp VW engine at max T-O weight):

Max level speed	145 knots (269 km/h; 167 mph)
Max cruising speed	125 knots (232 km/h; 144 mph)
Stalling speed, power off	42 knots (79 km/h; 49 mph)
Typical rate of climb at S/L	320 m (1,050 ft)/min
Range with max fuel	231 nm (428 km; 266 miles)
g limits	±4.5

EASTWOOD
EASTWOOD AIRCRAFT PTY LTD
Stevens Road, PO Box 564, Currency Creek, South Australia 5214
Telephone: (085) 554011
MANAGER: Geoff Eastwood

EASTWOOD TYRO Mk II
The prototype Tyro first flew in December 1981. The current Tyro II is available ready built, or in plans and kit forms (with or without engine) for amateur construction. At least five ready-built Tyro IIs have been delivered. The Tyro's strong construction and bungee rubber suspension allow it to operate off very short grass airstrips and it is said to be ideally suited to rural work. Assembly for flight takes 10 minutes.

TYPE: Single-seat microlight; conforms to ANO 95-10.
AIRFRAME: Strut-braced wings, with NACA 4418 section. Light alloy mainframe, with Dacron covered wings and tail surfaces. Three-axis control. Non-retractable tailwheel landing gear.
POWER PLANT: One 20 kW (27 hp) Rotax 277 standard; 32 kW (43 hp) Rotax 447 optional. Fuel capacity 20 litres (5.3 US gallons; 4.4 Imp gallons).
DIMENSIONS, EXTERNAL:

Wing span	8.90 m (29 ft 2 in)
Length overall	5.33 m (17 ft 6 in)
Propeller diameter (Rotax 277 engine)	1.63 m (5 ft 4 in)

AREA:

Wings, gross	10.50 m² (113.0 sq ft)

WEIGHTS:

Weight empty	113 kg (250 lb)
Pilot weight range	54.4-91 kg (120-200 lb)
Max T-O weight	218 kg (482 lb)

PERFORMANCE (Rotax 277 engine):

Max level speed at S/L	69 knots (129 km/h; 80 mph)
Max cruising speed at S/L	56 knots (105 km/h; 65 mph)
Stalling speed, power off	20 knots (37 km/h; 23 mph)
Max rate of climb at S/L	259 m (850 ft)/min
T-O run	61 m (200 ft)
Landing run	92 m (300 ft)
Range	130 nm (241 km; 150 miles)
Endurance	2 h 30 min
g limits:	+4/-2 design
	+6/-3 ultimate

HUGHES
HOWARD HUGHES ENGINEERING PTY LTD
PO Box 89, 11 Smith Drive, Ballina, NSW 2478
Telephone: (066) 86 3148

HUGHES LIGHTWING R55
The prototype LightWing first flew in June 1986, and by February 1988 twenty-nine LightWings conforming to ANO 101-28 requirements had been built. Approval is being sought to sell kits under homebuilt or ANO 101-55 regulations, in non-retractable tailwheel and twin-float configurations. Four kits had been completed by February 1988. Construction of a prototype four-seater under ANO 101-31 is planned.
TYPE: Two-seat microlight, ARV and homebuilt.
AIRFRAME: Strut braced wings of 6061-T6 aluminium alloy construction, and welded steel tube fuselage and tail unit, all fabric covered. Glassfibre engine cowling. Three-axis control. Non-retractable tailwheel or twin float landing gear.
POWER PLANT: One 47 kW (63 hp) Rotax 532. The 71 kW (95 hp) Norton rotary is a planned engine option when available. Fuel capacity 35 litres (9.2 US gallons; 7.7 Imp gallons).
DIMENSIONS, EXTERNAL:

Wing span	9.70 m (31 ft 10 in)
Length overall	5.80 m (19 ft 0½ in)
Height overall	1.90 m (6 ft 2¾ in)
Propeller diameter	1.68 m (5 ft 6 in)

AREA:

Wings, gross	14.55 m² (156.61 sq ft)

WEIGHTS:

Weight empty	207 kg (456 lb)
Max pilot weight	100 kg (220 lb)
Max T-O weight	450 kg (992 lb)

PERFORMANCE:
Max level speed at 915 m (3,000 ft)

	80 knots (148 km/h; 92 mph)
Econ cruising speed	60 knots (111 km/h; 69 mph)
Stalling speed	32 knots (60 km/h; 37 mph)
Max rate of climb at S/L	366 m (1,200 ft)/min
Service ceiling (ANO 101-55)	915 m (3,000 ft)
T-O run	31 m (100 ft)
Landing run	92 m (300 ft)
Range	150 nm (278 km; 172 miles)
g limits	+6/-3

HUGHES LIGHTWING AEROPOWER 28
The new Aeropower 28 is almost identical to the R55, again intended to be available in ready assembled and kit forms and produced under ANO 101-28 and 101-55 regulations, but with no microlight version. The prototype A28 first flew in March 1988 and production was expected to begin in June of the same year. Airframe details are similar to those for the R55.
TYPE: Two-seat homebuilt.
POWER PLANT: One 58.2 kW (78 hp) Norton. Fuel capacity 40 litres (10.5 US gallons; 8.8 Imp gallons).
DIMENSIONS, EXTERNAL:

Wing span	8.70 m (27 ft 10½ in)
Length overall	5.70 m (18 ft 8½ in)
Height overall	1.90 m (6 ft 2¾ in)
Propeller diameter	1.57 m (5 ft 2 in)

WEIGHTS:

Weight empty	250 kg (551 lb)
Max pilot weight	90 kg (198 lb)
Max T-O weight	450 kg (992 lb)

PERFORMANCE:

Max level speed	95 knots (176 km/h; 109 mph)
Max and econ cruising speed	
	87 knots (161 km/h; 100 mph)
Stalling speed	36 knots (67 km/h; 42 mph)
Service ceiling	3,050 m (10,000 ft)
T-O run	61 m (200 ft)
Landing run	92 m (300 ft)
Range	300 nm (556 km; 345 miles)
Endurance	3 h 30 min
g limits	+6/-3

KIMBERLEY
GARETH J. KIMBERLEY
255 Woniora Road, Blakehurst, NSW 2221
Telephone: Sydney (02) 546 4143

KIMBERLEY SKY-RIDER
Design of the Sky-Rider started in early 1977 and the first flight was achieved on 5 November 1978. Plans are available to amateur constructors, and 185 sets had been sold in 17 countries (mainly Australia and the USA) by February 1988. Six are known to have flown.
TYPE: Single-seat microlight; conforms to ANO 95-10 and FAR Pt 103.
AIRFRAME: Wire braced monoplane. Structure of tubular aluminium alloy, with Dacron covering on wings, flaps, ailerons and tail surfaces. Three-axis control; flaps also fitted. Non-retractable tailwheel landing gear. Floats and skis optional, as is ballistic recovery parachute.

POWER PLANT: Typically, one 13.5 kW (18 hp) 250 cc Fuji Robin. Fuel capacity 6.8 litres (1.8 US gallons; 1.5 Imp gallons). Optional engines include Rotax, Cuyuna 430 and KFM types.
DIMENSIONS, EXTERNAL:

Wing span	9.86 m (32 ft 4 in)
Length overall	5.94 m (19 ft 6 in)
Height overall	2.39 m (7 ft 10 in)
Propeller diameter	1.37 m (4 ft 6 in)

Blue Max single-seat microlight (Rotax 447 engine)

Eastwood Tyro Mk II single-seat microlight

Corby Starlet built by Mr Laurie Wincen and Mr John Atkinson of Cairns, Australia (56 kW; 76 hp Revmaster 2,100 cc engine)

Kimberley Sky-Rider single-seat microlight

Hughes LightWing R55 in twin-float configuration

Laser Aerobatics Akro Model Z homebuilt aircraft *(Austin J. Brown)*

AREA:			
Wings, gross	13.38 m² (144.0 sq ft)		
WEIGHTS (with 250 cc Fuji Robin engine):			
Weight empty	95 kg (210 lb)		
Max pilot weight	91 kg (200 lb)		
Max T-O weight	181.5 kg (400 lb)		
PERFORMANCE (with 250 cc Fuji Robin engine):			
Max level speed	43 knots (80 km/h; 50 mph)		
Max cruising speed	39 knots (72 km/h; 45 mph)		

Econ cruising speed	35 knots (64 km/h; 40 mph)
Stalling speed:	
flaps up	22 knots (41 km/h; 25 mph)
flaps down, engine idling	18 knots (32 km/h; 20 mph)
Stalling speed IGE	16 knots (29 km/h; 18 mph)
Max rate of climb at S/L	91 m (300 ft)/min
Max permitted flying height (in Australia)	
	152 m (500 ft)
T-O run	75 m (246 ft)

Landing run	50 m (164 ft)
Range with max fuel	35 nm (64 km; 40 miles)
Endurance with max fuel	1 h
g limits	+2/nil normal
	+4.5/–1.5 ultimate
	(not stressed for aerobatics)

LABAHAN
ROBERT LABAHAN
6 Victoria Street, Seville, Victoria 3139
Telephone: (059) 64 4730

The Hitchiker is available in ready assembled form only.

LABAHAN HITCHIKER
TYPE: Single-seat microlight; conforms to ANO 95-10.
AIRFRAME: Strut braced monoplane. Aluminium alloy tubular fuselage structure and fabric covered wooden wings. Three-axis control. Cockpit pod optional. Non-retractable tailwheel landing gear.
POWER PLANT: One 20 kW (27 hp) Rotax 277. Fuel capacity 27 litres (7.1 US gallons; 6 Imp gallons).

DIMENSIONS, EXTERNAL:
Wing span	8.05 m (26 ft 5 in)
Length overall	4.80 m (15 ft 9 in)
Propeller diameter	1.27 m (4 ft 2 in)

WEIGHTS:
Weight empty	100 kg (220 lb)
Max T-O weight	204 kg (450 lb)

PERFORMANCE:
Max level speed	61 knots (113 km/h; 70 mph)
Econ cruising speed	55 knots (102 km/h; 63 mph)
Stalling speed	26 knots (48 km/h; 30 mph)
T-O run	46 m (150 ft)
Landing run	61 m (200 ft)
Range	156 nm (290 km; 180 miles)

LASER
LASER AEROBATICS
Lot 60-61, Mount Dandenong Tourist Road, Olinda, Victoria 3788
Telephone: (03) 7511745
CHIEF ENGINEER: David J. Pilkington, BE, MSc

LASER AEROBATICS AKRO MODEL Z
The Laser Aerobatics Akro Model Z has its ancestry in the American Stephens Akro. However, apart from a general similarity of configuration, the style of wing attachment, the aileron layout and similar main landing gear legs, the two aircraft are different designs.

Plans for the Akro Model Z are available, and three examples are known to have flown in Australia and one in the UK. Others were being built in Australia (three), continental Europe and the USA in 1987. Mr Pilkington believes that construction should be undertaken only by experienced builders.

TYPE: Single-seat aerobatic and sporting homebuilt monoplane.
AIRFRAME: All wooden wings, with NACA 21012 section, modified at root. Wide span ailerons, with steel tube spar and wooden ribs, fabric covered. Welded steel tube fuselage, covered with aluminium sheet forward of cockpit and fabric aft. Braced welded steel tube tail unit, fabric covered. Each elevator fitted with trim/balance tab. Non-retractable tailwheel landing gear.

POWER PLANT: One 149 kW (200 hp) Textron Lycoming IO-360. Fuel capacity 77 litres (20 US gallons; 17 Imp gallons).

DIMENSIONS, EXTERNAL:
Wing span	7.42 m (24 ft 4 in)
Length overall	6.20 m (20 ft 4 in)
Propeller diameter	1.93 m (6 ft 4 in)

AREA:
Wings, gross	9.10 m² (98.0 sq ft)

WEIGHTS:
Weight empty	438 kg (965 lb)
Max T-O weight: aerobatic	553 kg (1,220 lb)
normal	589 kg (1,298 lb)

Skywise Ultraflight Sadler Vampire single-seat microlight

Prototype Percy Maya single-seat microlight

Prototype Ligeti Stratos single-seat pusher microlight (König 430 cc engine)
(Howard Levy)

PERFORMANCE (constant-speed propeller):				
Max level speed at S/L	160 knots (296 km/h; 184 mph)	Max rate of climb at S/L	762 m (2,500 ft)/min	Range with max fuel, no reserves
Stalling speed	56 knots (104 km/h; 65 mph) CAS	T-O to 15 m (50 ft)	305 m (1,000 ft)	300 nm (556 km; 345 miles)
		Landing from 15 m (50 ft)	457 m (1,500 ft)	

LIGETI

LIGETI AERO-NAUTICAL PTY LTD
Essendon Airport, Building 44, PO Box 362, North Balwyn, Victoria 3104
Telephone: (03) 374 2077

LIGETI STRATOS
The Stratos was conceived to combine the efficiency of a canard, the large wing area and small span of a tandem wing configuration, and the strength of an externally braced biplane. The prototype first flew on 25 April 1985. However, following the death of Mr Ligeti the future of the programme is not known.

Because of the small size of the Stratos, it can be transported fully assembled on a trailer behind a car, and kept in an average family garage, eliminating assembly and dismantling. Its aerodynamically clean configuration makes it suitable for soaring.

TYPE: Single-seat microlight; conforms to ANO 95-10.
AIRFRAME: Joined-wing aircraft, with Wortmann 67 series wing sections. All-composites structure of Kevlar and glassfibre skins over shaped rigid foam, with carbonfibre spars. Three-axis control. Non-retractable landing gear.
POWER PLANT: Prototype has one 21 kW (28 hp) König SD 570. Optional engines up to 37.3 kW (50 hp). Standard fuel capacity 22 litres (5.8 US gallons; 4.8 Imp gallons).
DIMENSIONS, EXTERNAL (prototype):

Wing span	5.36 m (17 ft 7 in)
Foreplane span	5.18 m (17 ft 0 in)
Length overall	2.49 m (8 ft 2 in)
Height overall	0.99 m (3 ft 3 in)
Fan diameter	0.65 m (2 ft 1½ in)

AREA (prototype):

Wings, gross	7.53 m² (81.0 sq ft)

WEIGHTS (prototype):

Weight empty	78 kg (172 lb)

Pilot weight range	55-83 kg (121-183 lb)
Max T-O weight	188 kg (414 lb)

PERFORMANCE (prototype):

Max level speed	108 knots (200 km/h; 124 mph)
Max cruising speed	97 knots (180 km/h; 112 mph)
Econ cruising speed	86 knots (160 km/h; 99 mph)
Stalling speed: power on	32 knots (58 km/h; 36 mph)
power off	33 knots (61 km/h; 38 mph)
Max rate of climb at S/L	205 m (670 ft)/min
Service ceiling	4,500 m (14,760 ft)
T-O run	110 m (360 ft)
Landing run	85 m (278 ft)
Range with max standard fuel	388 nm (720 km; 447 miles)
Endurance with max standard fuel	5 h 15min
g limits	+9/-6

PERCY

GRAHAM J. PERCY
PO Box 135, 50 Baxter-Tooradin Road, Pearcedale, Victoria 3912
Telephone: (059) 78 6490

PERCY MAYA
The prototype Maya first flew in January 1985. Plans are available to amateur constructors, and although the aircraft was designed to suit a König engine, other two-stroke engines can be fitted as long as power plant weight (including reduction gear, mounts, exhaust, cowling and propeller) does not exceed 27.2 kg (60 lb). Accommodation

with the standard cockpit canopy suits pilots up to 1.83 m (6 ft) tall.
TYPE: Single-seat microlight; conforms to ANO 95-10.
AIRFRAME: All-wooden structure, covered with Stits Poly-Fiber. Detachable wings use NACA 4412.5 (mod) section. Three-axis control. Non-retractable tailwheel landing gear.
POWER PLANT: One 21 kW (28 hp) König SD 570. Alternative engines can be fitted (see introduction). Fuel capacity 14.8 litres (3.9 US gallons; 3.25 Imp gallons).
DIMENSIONS, EXTERNAL:

Wing span	8.48 m (27 ft 10 in)
Length overall	5.33 m (17 ft 6 in)

Height overall	1.65 m (5 ft 5 in)
Propeller diameter	1.30 m (4 ft 3 in)

AREA:

Wings, gross	10.28 m² (110.7 sq ft)

WEIGHTS (prototype):

Weight empty	112.5 kg (248 lb)
Max pilot/baggage weight	91 kg (200 lb)
Max T-O weight	217 kg (480 lb)

PERFORMANCE (design, with König engine):

Max rough-air and cruising speed	55 knots (101 km/h; 63 mph)
Stalling speed	32 knots (60 km/h; 37 mph)
Max rate of climb at S/L	152 m (500 ft)/min

SKYTEK

SKYTEK AUSTRALIA PTY LTD
Willetton, Western Australia
DESIGNER: Graham Swannell

SKYTEK MAVERICK
This new aerobatic and cross-country homebuilt first flew as a prototype on 24 December 1987. Plans and kits are to be made available.(See Addenda for illustration.)
TYPE: Single-seat homebuilt.
AIRFRAME: Constructed mainly of glassfibre, epoxy resins,

carbonfibre and foam, with fuselage built as self-jigging sandwich structure. Non-retractable tailwheel landing gear.
POWER PLANT: One 74.5 kW (100 hp) Ellison conversion of a Continental O-200 in prototype. Options include an 85.75 kW (115 hp) engine for unlimited aerobatics. Christen inverted fuel and oil system allows 3 min inverted flight. Fuel capacity 111 litres (29 US gallons; 24.5 Imp gallons).
DIMENSIONS, EXTERNAL:

Length overall	2.80 m (9 ft 2 in)
Height overall	1.80 m (5 ft 11 in)

WEIGHT:

Weight empty	300 kg (661 lb)
Max T-O weight	476 kg (1,050 lb)

PERFORMANCE:

Cruising speed at 3,050 m (10,000 ft)	150 knots (278 km/h; 173 mph)
Stalling speed	51 knots (95 km/h; 59 mph)
Max rate of climb at S/L	366 m (1,200 ft)/min
Endurance with 45 min reserves	4 h 30 min
g limits, design: at 408 kg (900 lb) AUW	+6/-3
at max T-O weight	+4.4/-2.2

SKYWISE

SKYWISE ULTRAFLIGHT PTE LTD
PO Box 226, Hornsby, NSW 2077
Telephone: (02) 476 4788
Telex: AA 176672
MANAGING DIRECTOR: Douglas W. Kewley

SKYWISE ULTRAFLIGHT SADLER VAMPIRE
Manufacture of this refined version of the US Sadler Vampire microlight is undertaken under licence in Australia by Skywise Ultraflight. Two versions are available, as follows:

SV-1. With KFM 107ER engine.
SV-2. With Rotax 447 engine.
TYPE: Single-seat microlight; conforms to ANO 95-25.
AIRFRAME: Wings, using NACA 63₃-A218 aerofoil section, are constructed of 2024-T3 Alclad aluminium alloy. Kevlar/glassfibre fuselage pod. Tail unit of similar

construction to wings. Remainder of airframe of 6061-T6 aluminium alloy, including flush riveted wing and tailplane skins. Three-axis control. Non-retractable tricycle landing gear.

POWER PLANT: One 22.4 kW (30 hp) KFM 107ER MAXI or 30.6 kW (41 hp) Rotax 447. Fuel capacity 16 litres (4.2 US gallons; 3.5 Imp gallons) in SV-1, 21 litres (5.5 US gallons; 4.6 Imp gallons) in SV-2. Optional second tank of similar capacity. Inverted flight fuel system available optionally.

DIMENSIONS, EXTERNAL (A: SV-1, B: SV-2):

Wing span: A	6.75 m (22 ft 1¾ in)
B	7.00 m (22 ft 11½ in)
Length overall: A, B	5.14 m (16 ft 10½ in)
Height overall: A	1.19 m (3 ft 11 in)
B	1.20 m (3 ft 11¼ in)
Propeller diameter: A, B	1.32 m (4 ft 4 in)

AREAS (A and B as above):

Wings, gross: A	8.55 m² (92.03 sq ft)
B	8.65 m² (93.11 sq ft)

WEIGHTS (A and B as above):

Weight empty: A	155 kg (342 lb)
B	166.5 kg (367 lb)
Max pilot weight: A, B	90 kg (198 lb)
Max T-O weight: A	265 kg (584 lb)

PERFORMANCE (A and B as above):

Max level speed: A	83 knots (154 km/h; 96 mph) IAS
B	88 knots (163 km/h; 101 mph) IAS
Cruising speed: A	70 knots (130 km/h; 81 mph) IAS
B	75 knots (139 km/h; 86 mph) IAS
Stalling speed: A, B	35 knots (65 km/h; 41 mph) IAS
Max rate of climb at S/L: A	152 m (500 ft)/min
B	305 m (1,000 ft)/min
T-O run: A	100 m (328 ft)
B	80 m (263 ft)

SMITH
ALLAN C. SMITH DEVELOPMENTS PTY LTD
16 Loyalty Road, North Rocks, NSW 2151
Telephone: 630 0211

SMITH FSRW-1
Development of this two-seat homebuilt amphibian is believed to be continuing, although no news has been received for this edition. Full details and an illustration can be found in the 1987-88 *Jane's.*

SV
SV AIRCRAFT PTY LTD
PO Box 85, Nagambie, Victoria 3608
Telephone: (057) 942711
DIRECTOR: Glenn Lyon

SV 11B FARMATE
The Farmate is sold in ready to fly form.
TYPE: Single-seat microlight.
AIRFRAME: Aluminium alloy structure, with glassfibre skin overall, double surfaced over 19 per cent of wings. Three-axis control. Non-retractable tailwheel landing gear.
POWER PLANT: One 20 kW (27 hp) Rotax 277. Fuel capacity 25 litres (6.6 US gallons; 5.5 Imp gallons).

DIMENSIONS, EXTERNAL:

Wing span	8.00 m (26 ft 3 in)
Length overall	5.30 m (17 ft 4¾ in)
Height overall	1.30 m (4 ft 3¼ in)
Propeller diameter	1.22 m (4 ft 0 in)

AREA:

Wings, gross	8.0 m² (86.1 sq ft)

WEIGHTS:

Weight empty	150 kg (331 lb)
Pilot weight range	75-95 kg (165-209 lb)
Max T-O weight	265 kg (584 lb)

PERFORMANCE:

Max level and max cruising speed	80 knots (148 km/h; 92 mph)
Econ cruising speed	60 knots (111 km/h; 69 mph)
Stalling speed: power on	30 knots (56 km/h; 35 mph)
power off	32 knots (60 km/h; 37 mph)
Max rate of climb at S/L	152 m (500 ft)/min
Service ceiling	3,050 m (10,000 ft)
T-O run	122 m (400 ft)
Landing run	183 m (600 ft)
Range with max fuel	180 nm (333 km; 207 miles)
Endurance with max fuel	3 h
g limits	+6/-4

SV 14
A single prototype of this two-seat microlight had been completed by mid-1985. No more recent news has been received. Full details and an illustration can be found in the 1987-88 *Jane's.*

THRUSTER
THRUSTER AIRCRAFT (AUSTRALIA) PTY LTD
458 The Boulevarde, Kirrawee, NSW 2232
Telephone: (02) 542 1990
Telex: AA 73953
Fax: (02) 542 3004
GENERAL MANAGER: Ken Asplin

THRUSTER TST
The 1988 dual-control Thruster TST incorporates a number of new features, while retaining the unique wing design which allows each wing to 'rack' and fold inside the double surface skins for ease of transportation and rapid rigging. Sales of the ready-to-fly Thruster totalled 476 by March 1988.

The European licenced manufacturer is Thruster Aircraft (UK) Ltd, Unit 3B, Highfield Road Industrial Estate, Camelford, Cornwall PL32 9RA, England (*Telephone:* 0840 213322).
TYPE: Two-seat microlight; conforms to ANO 95-25, BCAR Section S and CASO 19.
AIRFRAME: Mainframe constructed of anodised aluminium alloy. Dacron covered wings and tail unit. Three-axis control. Non-retractable tailwheel landing gear. Optional floats, skis and agricultural spray equipment.
POWER PLANT: One 43.25 kW (58 hp) Rotax 503. Fuel capacity 40 litres (10.6 US gallons; 8.8 Imp gallons).

DIMENSIONS, EXTERNAL:

Wing span	9.60 m (31 ft 6 in)
Length overall	5.50 m (18 ft 0 in)
Height overall	1.90 m (6 ft 2¾ in)
Propeller diameter	1.63 m (5 ft 4 in)

AREA:

Wings, gross	15.00 m² (161.5 sq ft)

WEIGHTS:

Weight empty	150 kg (330 lb)
Pilot weight range	55-180 kg (121-397 lb)
Max T-O weight	370 kg (816 lb)

PERFORMANCE:

Max level speed	68 knots (126 km/h; 78 mph)
Max cruising speed	65 knots (120 km/h; 75 mph)
Econ cruising speed	52 knots (96 km/h; 60 mph)
Stalling speed: power off, flaps up, at 330 kg (727 lb) AUW	31 knots (58 km/h; 36 mph)
Max rate of climb at S/L	250 m (820 ft)/min
T-O run	45 m (147 ft)
Landing run	50 m (164 ft)
Range with max fuel	156 nm (289 km; 179 miles)
Endurance, 50% power	3 h
g limits	+7/-4

WAACO
WEST AUSTRALIAN AIRCRAFT COMPANY
15 Lynwood Avenue, Ringwood East, Victoria 3135
Telephone: (03) 879 4747

WAACO STAGGERBIPE Mk 1
The Waaco Staggerbipe is a single-seat, single-engined air recreational vehicle with negative-stagger biplane wings, first flown in November 1985. It was planned to make kits available, but no recent news has been received. Full details and an illustration can be found in the 1987-88 *Jane's.*

WHEELER
RON WHEELER AIRCRAFT (SALES) PTY LTD
152 Bellevue Parade, Carlton, NSW 2218
Telephone: (02) 546 2501

WHEELER SCOUT MK III
First flown in May 1974, the Scout 'minimum aircraft' can be quickly dismantled and carried on the roof rack of a motorcar. It has been in production since August 1976, and worldwide sales in Mk I, Mk II and current Mk III forms have totalled several hundred aircraft. The Scout is available as a ready assembled aircraft only.

The Scout Mk III, to which the data apply, was introduced in 1982 and features three-axis control, and a 13.4 kW (18 hp) Fuji Robin EC 25 engine in **Mk IIIRN** form and a 26 kW (35 hp) Rotax 377 engine in **Mk IIIRX** form. Fuel capacity is 17 litres (4.5 US gallons; 3.7 Imp gallons).
TYPE: Single-seat microlight; conforms to ANO 95-10.
AIRFRAME: Mainframe of wire braced aluminium alloy extrusions, with Dacron covered wings and tail surfaces. No ailerons or wing warping. Tail surfaces are all-moving, operated by the control column and rudder pedals for three-axis control. Non-retractable tailwheel landing gear.

DIMENSIONS, EXTERNAL:

Wing span (nominal)	8.69 m (28 ft 6 in)
Length overall	5.20 m (17 ft 0¾ in)
Height overall	1.57 m (5 ft 2 in)
Propeller diameter: IIIRN	1.22 m (4 ft 0 in)
IIIRX	1.37 m (4 ft 6 in)

AREA:

Wings, gross	13.56 m² (146.0 sq ft)

WEIGHTS:

Weight empty, equipped: IIIRN	68 kg (150 lb)
IIIRX	82 kg (181 lb)
Max pilot weight	79 kg (175 lb)
Max T-O weight	141 kg (310 lb)

PERFORMANCE:

Max level speed	57 knots (105 km/h; 65 mph)
Cruising speed	42-44 knots (78-82 km/h; 48-51 mph)
Stalling speed	18 knots (32 km/h; 20 mph)
Max rate of climb at S/L	168 m (550 ft)/min
T-O run	30-40 m (98-131 ft)
Landing run	20-25 m (66-82 ft)
Range	48 nm (90 km; 56 miles)
Endurance	1 h 20 min

WINTON
SCOTT WINTON
Mr Scott Winton is the designer of a single-seat microlight aircraft known as the Sapphire. The sole manufacturer and supplier in Australia is:
J. and P. Heard, North Creek Road, Ballina, NSW 2478

WINTON SAPPHIRE
The Sapphire is in production in two forms:
Sapphire 10. Basic version, conforming to ANO 95-10. Powered by 26 kW (35 hp) Rotax 377. Available as an airframe kit; as an advanced kit complete with engine, propeller and control systems; or in ready to fly form.
Sapphire LSA. Lightweight sport aircraft, with reduced wing area, and 30 kW (40 hp) Rotax 447. Available only in ready to fly form, conforming to ANO 95-25.
TYPE: Single-seat microlight.
AIRFRAME: Wings of GRP/foam sandwich, with fabric covering on Sapphire 10, GRP skin on Sapphire LSA. Ailerons all GRP construction. GRP semi-monocoque fuselage pod and tailboom. Tail fin of GRP. All-moving horizontal surfaces and rudder of GRP and aluminium alloy tubing with fabric covering. Non-retractable tailwheel landing gear.

POWER PLANT: One Rotax engine (see model listings). Sapphire 10 fuel capacity 22 litres (5.8 US gallons; 4.8 Imp gallons); Sapphire LSA 40 litres (10.6 US gallons; 8.8 Imp gallons).

DIMENSIONS, EXTERNAL:

Wing span	8.84 m (29 ft 0 in)
Length overall	4.93 m (16 ft 2 in)
Height overall	1.27 m (4 ft 2 in)
Propeller diameter	1.31 m (4 ft 3½ in)

AREAS (A: Sapphire 10, B: Sapphire LSA):

Wings, gross: A	10.03 m² (108.0 sq ft)
B	9.13 m² (98.3 sq ft)

SV 11B Farmate single-seat microlight

Single-seat prototype of the Airtech Canada Skylark

Thruster TST two-seat microlight

Birdman Enterprises Chinook 2-S with float landing gear

WEIGHTS:						
Weight empty: A	104 kg (230 lb)	Cruising speed (50% power):		T-O run: A	50 m (164 ft)	
B	141 kg (310 lb)	A	62 knots (115 km/h; 71 mph)	B	60 m (197 ft)	
Max T-O weight: A	227 kg (500 lb)	B	65 knots (120 km/h; 75 mph)	Landing run: A	90 m (295 ft)	
B	250 kg (552 lb)	Stalling speed: A	32 knots (60 km/h; 37 mph)	B	100 m (328 ft)	
		B	35 knots (65 km/h; 41 mph)	g limits	+8/-4	
PERFORMANCE:		Max rate of climb at S/L: A	396 m (1,300 ft)/min			
Max level speed: A, B	80 knots (148 km/h; 92 mph)	B	335 m (1,100 ft)/min			

BELGIUM

SCWAL
SCWAL SA
Avenue De Fré 267/20, B-1180 Brussels
Telephone: (32 2) 375 38 93
Telex: 65892 GRYF B
MANAGING DIRECTOR: Charles Rifon
   SCWAL, with offices in Brussels and a small manufacturing plant at Baileux, was established in 1979. In addition to producing its own SCWAL 101 light aircraft, it began manufacture and sale in September 1987 of an improved version of the American Aircraft Falcon, under licence from Sonaca.

SCWAL 101
   The SCWAL 101 is intended to be a fully certificated aircraft fitting between microlights and conventional light

aeroplanes. Design goals were easy maintenance, road transportability, and the ability to use non-aviation fuel. Applications include civil and military training, surveillance and crop dusting in addition to sport flying. A twin-engined version may follow. The first flight was achieved on 26 April 1984.
TYPE: Side by side two-seat monoplane; conforms to FAR Pt 23 normal category.
AIRFRAME: Bolted aluminium/steel tubular mainframe. All aluminium wing and tail surfaces. Wortmann wing section. Three-axis control, including flaperons. Optional enclosed Perspex transparent cockpit pod with two doors. Non-retractable tricycle landing gear.
POWER PLANT: One 52.2 kW (70 hp) BMW converted motorcycle engine. Fuel capacity 60 litres (16 US gallons; 13.2 Imp gallons).

DIMENSIONS, EXTERNAL:	
Wing span	11.00 m (36 ft 1 in)
Length overall	5.50 m (18 ft 0½ in)
AREA:	
Wings, gross	13.75 m² (148.0 sq ft)
WEIGHTS:	
Weight empty	300 kg (661 lb)
Max T-O weight	520 kg (1,146 lb)
PERFORMANCE:	
Max level speed	75 knots (140 km/h; 87 mph)
Stalling speed: flaps up	38 knots (70 km/h; 44 mph)
flaps down	33 knots (60 km/h; 38 mph)
Max rate of climb at S/L	162 m (530 ft)/min
T-O run	125 m (410 ft)
Endurance	8 h
g limits	+5.7/-2.85 ultimate

CANADA

AIRTECH
AIRTECH CANADA
PO Box 415, Peterborough Municipal Airport, Peterborough, Ontario K9J 6Z3
Telephone: (705) 743 9483
Telex: 06 962912
Fax: (705) 749 0841
PRESIDENT: John O'Dwyer

AIRTECH CANADA SKYLARK
   The Skylark prototype was first flown on 12 October 1984. It is available in kit (100-200 hours construction time) and ready assembled forms; ten had been built by February 1988.
   A side by side two-seat version has been designed as the

Skylark II, and a special derivative of this for carrying heavy loads at high altitudes is under consideration.
   The following data refer to the single-seat Skylark:
TYPE: Single-seat microlight aircraft; conforms to FAR Part 23.
AIRFRAME: Constructed of aluminium alloy sheet, extrusions and angles (including stamped ribs), with glassfibre cockpit fairing. Wings and tail surfaces Ceconite 7600 fabric covered. NASA wing section. Three-axis control. Non-retractable tricycle landing gear. Floats and skis optional.
POWER PLANT: One 21 kW (28 hp) König. Fuel capacity 19 litres (5 US gallons; 4.2 Imp gallons).
DIMENSIONS, EXTERNAL:
   Wing span   10.97 m (36 ft 0 in)

Length overall	5.49 m (18 ft 0 in)
Propeller diameter	1.83 m (6 ft 0 in)
AREA:	
Wings, gross	16.54 m² (178.0 sq ft)
WEIGHTS:	
Weight empty	129 kg (284 lb)
Max T-O weight	244 kg (539 lb)
PERFORMANCE:	
Max level speed	51 knots (95 km/h; 59 mph)
Normal cruising speed	43 knots (80 km/h; 50 mph)
Max rate of climb at S/L	186 m (610 ft)/min
T-O run	18 m (60 ft)
Landing run	under 18 m (60 ft)
Design g limits	+5/-2.5

BIRDMAN
BIRDMAN ENTERPRISES 1986 LTD
Box 609, 702 12th Avenue, Nisku, Alberta T0C 2G0
Telephone: (403) 955 7878
Telex: 037 2459
GENERAL MANAGER: Barry Metcalfe

BIRDMAN CHINOOK 1-S
   First flown on 12 December 1982, the Chinook 1-S is offered in kit form (40-100 hours to assemble). Several hundred have been produced in two versions with differing engines. The Chinook does not spin.
TYPE: Single-seat microlight; conforms to FAI and FAR Pt 103 requirements.

AIRFRAME: Mainframe of aluminium alloy tube and sheet, with steel tube bracing struts and non-retractable tailwheel landing gear. Dacron covered wings and tail surfaces. Three-axis control, plus flaps. Marsden UA80/1 (modified) wing section. Wings detachable. Optional spray equipment, floats and skis.

POWER PLANT: One 20 kW (27 hp) Rotax 277 or 26.8 kW (36 hp) Rotax 377 engine. Standard fuel capacity 19 litres (5 US gallons; 4.2 Imp gallons). Optional 9.5 or 15 litre (2.5 or 4 US gallon; 2-3.3 Imp gallon) tank in each wing.

DIMENSIONS, EXTERNAL (with 277 engine):

Wing span	10.67 m (35 ft 0 in)
Length overall	5.34 m (17 ft 6 in)
Height overall	1.68 m (5 ft 6 in)
Propeller diameter	1.37 m (4 ft 6 in)

AREA:

Wings, gross	13.01 m² (140.0 sq ft)

WEIGHTS (277 engine):

Weight empty	113 kg (250 lb)

Pilot weight range: A	50-113 kg (110-250 lb)
Max T-O weight	283 kg (625 lb)

PERFORMANCE (at max T-O weight, 277 engine):

Max level speed at S/L	52 knots (97 km/h; 60 mph)
Econ cruising speed	43 knots (80 km/h; 50 mph)
Stalling speed:	
power on	22 knots (41 km/h; 25 mph) IAS
power off	25 knots (45 km/h; 28 mph) IAS
Max rate of climb at S/L	213 m (700 ft)/min
Service ceiling	4,575 m (15,000 ft)
T-O run	31-62 m (100-200 ft)
Landing run	31-62 m (100-200 ft)
Range at cruising speed, 65% power	
	130-173 nm (241-321 km; 150-200 miles)

Endurance with standard fuel	4 h 24 min
g limits	+6/−3

BIRDMAN CHINOOK 2-S

First flown on 15 October 1983, the Chinook 2-S is a tandem two-seat version of the single-seat Chinook for flight training, sport flying, cropspraying, photography and light transport use. Structurally similar to the single-seater, the Chinook 2-S has a greater wing span (11.28 m; 37 ft 0 in), a 12.7 cm (5 in) longer cabin with more side glazing, external fuel tanks as standard, a 30 kW (40 hp) Rotax 447 or 35 kW (47 hp) Rotax 503 engine, and strengthened structure. Dual controls are standard and a door is provided for each occupant. Float and ski landing gear remain options.

CANAERO DYNAMICS
CANAERO DYNAMICS AIRCRAFT INC

RR 2, Kettleby, Ontario L0G 1J0
Telephone: (416) 833 1250
GENERAL MANAGER: Lorry R. Smith

CANAERO DYNAMICS TOUCAN SERIES II

The Toucan resembles an ARV version of the Cessna Skymaster, with an engine mounted in the nose and another at the rear of the fuselage pod. It has full single engine flight capability.

The prototype flew for the first time in September 1983 and the first production aircraft in January 1986. The Toucan is available in kit and ready assembled forms, and by February 1988 fifteen had been built.

TYPE: Two-seat ARV, suited to recreational flying, pilot training, agricultural spraying, surveillance and aerial photography.

AIRFRAME: Strut braced rigid wing of aluminium alloy, with UV resistant skins and glassfibre wingtips. Three-axis control, plus flaps. Semi-monocoque fuselage of welded 4130 chrome-molybdenum steel, with twin tailbooms. Non-retractable tricycle landing gear. Floats optional. Recovery parachute standard.

POWER PLANT: Two 30.5 kW (41 hp) Rotax 447 engines in 'push and pull' configuration. Fuel capacity 68 litres (18 US gallons; 15 Imp gallons). Optional 23 litre (6 US gallon; 5 Imp gallon) auxiliary tank.

DIMENSIONS, EXTERNAL:

Wing span	11.74 m (38 ft 6 in)
Length overall	6.10 m (20 ft 0 in)
Height overall	2.85 m (9 ft 4 in)
Propeller diameter	1.52 m (5 ft 0 in)

AREA:

Wings, gross	17.34 m² (186.6 sq ft)

WEIGHTS:

Weight empty	218 kg (480 lb)
Crew weight range	45.5-136 kg (100-300 lb)
Max T-O weight	476 kg (1,050 lb)

PERFORMANCE (at max T-O weight):

Max level speed at 610 m (2,000 ft)	
	68 knots (126 km/h; 78 mph)
Econ cruising speed at 610 m (2,000 ft)	
	52 knots (97 km/h; 60 mph)
Stalling speed, flaps up, engine idling	
	26 knots (49 km/h; 30 mph)
Max rate of climb at S/L	244 m (800 ft)/min
Service ceiling	3,050 m (10,000 ft)
T-O run	46 m (150 ft)
Landing run	31 m (100 ft)
Range with max payload	173 nm (321 km; 200 miles)
Endurance	4 h 30 min
g limits	+6/−3

CIRCA
CIRCA REPRODUCTIONS

8027 Argyll Road, Edmonton, Alberta T6C 4A9
Telephone: (403) 469 2692
DESIGNER/PROPRIETOR: Graham R. Lee

Circa Reproductions markets plans of ⅞th scale reproductions of First World War fighters.

CIRCA REPRODUCTIONS NIEUPORT 11

The prototype Nieuport 11 reproduction first flew on 25 July 1984. Plans, including drawings for a wooden replica Lewis gun, are available, and by January 1988 a total of 375 sets had been sold. About 105 aircraft are reportedly under active construction. A prefabricated engine cowling and fuel tank are available from the designer. Estimated building time is 600 working hours.

The Nieuport 11 is capable of meeting both Canadian and US ultralight regulations, though the company prefers that it be built as an Experimental category aircraft with a weight that makes it a homebuilt. If he wishes the homebuilder can complete the aircraft as a Nieuport 16, 17, 24, 24*bis* or 27, the 17 onwards having a greater wing area of about 11.6 m² (125 sq ft), or as a German Siemens-Schuckert D.I.

TYPE: Single-seat replica microlight or homebuilt; conforms as microlight to FAR Pt 103 and Canadian regulations.

AIRFRAME: Tubular 6061-T6 aluminium alloy structure, with 2024-T3 duralumin gussets and covered with Ceconite and aluminium sheet. Three-axis control. Non-retractable tailskid or tailwheel landing gear. Skis optional.

POWER PLANT: One 22.4 kW (30 hp) Cuyuna ULII-02. Optional engines of up to 30 kW (40 hp). Fuel capacity 48 litres (12.7 US gallons; 10.5 Imp gallons) or 19 litre (5 US gallon; 4.2 Imp gallon) tank, according to regulation requirements.

DIMENSIONS, EXTERNAL:

Wing span	6.55 m (21 ft 6 in)
Length overall	4.98 m (16 ft 4 in)
Height overall	2.29 m (7 ft 6 in)
Propeller diameter	1.83 m (6 ft 0 in)

AREA:

Wings, gross	10.59 m² (114.0 sq ft)

WEIGHTS:

Weight empty	115 kg (254 lb)
Max pilot weight	88.5 kg (195 lb)
Max T-O weight	249 kg (550 lb)

PERFORMANCE (at 211 kg; 465 lb AUW):

Max level speed with 18.6 kW (25 hp) engine	
	67 knots (124 km/h; 77 mph) IAS
Econ cruising speed	43 knots (80 km/h; 50 mph)
Stalling speed	23 knots (42 km/h; 26 mph) IAS
Max rate of climb at S/L	137 m (450 ft)/min
T-O run	76 m (250 ft)
Landing run	61 m (200 ft)
Range with max fuel	
	more than 173 nm (322 km; 200 miles)
Endurance with max fuel	4 h 45 min
g limits	+5.5/−3.5

CIRCA REPRODUCTIONS NIEUPORT 12

Plans of this ⅞th scale reproduction of the two-seat Nieuport 12C-2 will eventually be made available.

TYPE: Two-seat replica homebuilt aircraft; conforms to US and Canadian Experimental regulations.

AIRFRAME: Braced sesquiplane, with UA-81 University of Alberta wing section. Wooden or sheet aluminium upper wing spars and oval tube lower spar. Remainder of airframe constructed of 6061-T6 aluminium alloy tubing, with aluminium gussets and fabric covering. Three-axis control. Non-retractable tailskid landing gear. Optional tailwheel.

POWER PLANT: One 38.8 kW (52 hp) Rotax 503 or, optionally, a Continental C65 or C85 of up to 63.4 kW (85 hp). Fuel capacity 45.5 litres (12 US gallons; 10 Imp gallons).

DIMENSIONS, EXTERNAL:

Wing span: upper	8.08 m (26 ft 6 in)
lower	6.93 m (22 ft 9 in)
Length overall	6.55 m (21 ft 6 in)
Height overall	2.29 m (7 ft 6 in)
Propeller diameter (prototype)	1.83 m (6 ft 0 in)

AREA:

Wings, gross	17.62 m² (189.7 sq ft)

WEIGHTS (prototype):

Weight empty	186 kg (410 lb)
Max T-O weight	454 kg (1,000 lb)

PERFORMANCE (prototype, estimated):

Max level speed	65 knots (121 km/h; 75 mph)
Max rate of climb at S/L	137 m (450 ft)/min
T-O run	122 m (400 ft)
Landing run	61 m (200 ft)
g limits	+5/−3

CIRCA REPRODUCTIONS SOPWITH TRIPLANE

A prototype of the ⅞th scale Sopwith Triplane has not yet been completed. Plans to allow amateur construction will become available in due course.

TYPE: Single-seat replica microlight; conforms to Canadian microlight regulations and Experimental aircraft category.

AIRFRAME: Structural materials, control and landing gear (with ski gear option) as for Nieuport 11 replica.

POWER PLANT: Prototype has one 30 kW (40 hp) Volkswagen modified motorcar engine. Max fuel capacity estimated at 45.5 litres (12 US gallons; 10 Imp gallons).

DIMENSIONS, EXTERNAL:

Wing span	7.06 m (23 ft 2 in)
Length overall	5.03 m (16 ft 6 in)
Height overall	2.82 m (9 ft 3 in)
Propeller diameter	1.83-2.01 m (6 ft 0 in-6 ft 7 in)

AREA:

Wings, gross	18.30 m² (197.0 sq ft)

WEIGHT:

Weight empty	147 kg (325 lb)

ELMWOOD
ELMWOOD AVIATION

RR 4 Elmwood Drive, Belleville, Ontario K8N 4Z4
Telephone: (613) 967 1853
DESIGNER/PROPRIETOR: Ronald B. Mason

ELMWOOD CA-05 CHRISTAVIA Mk I

The prototype Christavia Mk I (C-GENC) first flew on 3 October 1981. Elmwood Aviation is offering plans, and considers the aircraft suitable for the type of flying carried out by professional organisations like Mission Aviation Fellowship. By early 1988, more than 300 Christavia Mk Is were under construction; about 40 had flown. Those under construction include several for the mission field.

TYPE: Tandem two-seat homebuilt.

AIRFRAME: Braced two-spar wing structure of Sitka spruce, with truss ribs and Dacron covering. Aluminium can be used alternatively to fabricate spars and ribs. Computer designed wing section. Frise ailerons of wooden construction with Dacron covering. Fuselage of welded 4130 and

1025 steel tube, Dacron covered. Wire-braced tail unit of steel tube, with mild steel plate ribs, Dacron covered. Non-retractable tailwheel landing gear. Optional floats or skis.

POWER PLANT: Prototype has a 48.5 kW (65 hp) Continental A65. Engines of 37.25 to 112 kW (50 to 150 hp) can be fitted. Main fuel tank, capacity 57 litres (15 US gallons; 12.5 Imp gallons), in fuselage aft of firewall; auxiliary tank, capacity 23 litres (6 US gallons; 5 Imp gallons), in each wing.

DIMENSIONS, EXTERNAL:

Wing span	9.91 m (32 ft 6 in)
Length overall	6.30 m (20 ft 8 in)
Height overall	2.13 m (7 ft 0 in)
Propeller diameter	1.83 m (6 ft 0 in)

AREA:

Wings, gross	13.59 m² (146.25 sq ft)

WEIGHTS (48.5 kW; 65 hp engine, 15 US gallons fuel):

Weight empty	338 kg (745 lb)
Max T-O weight	590 kg (1,300 lb)

PERFORMANCE (at max T-O weight, engine and fuel as above):

Max level speed at S/L	104 knots (193 km/h; 120 mph)
Cruising speed at 610 m (2,000 ft), 45% power	
	74 knots (137 km/h; 85 mph)
Stalling speed: power off	37 knots (68 km/h; 42 mph)
power on	31 knots (57 km/h; 35 mph)
Rate of climb at S/L	259 m (850 ft)/min
Service ceiling	3,960 m (13,000 ft)
T-O run	107 m (350 ft)
Landing from 15 m (50 ft)	198 m (650 ft)
Range with standard fuel, 45% power	
	382 nm (708 km; 440 miles)
g limits	+4.5/−2.8

ELMWOOD CH-8 CHRISTAVIA Mk 4

This four-seat development of the Christavia Mk I first flew on 3 January 1986. Plans and an information kit are available, and in early 1988 about 50 were under construction.

TYPE: Four-seat homebuilt cabin monoplane.

AIRFRAME: Similar to Christavia Mk I.

Canaero Dynamics Toucan 'push and pull' twin-engined ARV

Circa Reproductions Nieuport 12 replica *(Howard Levy)*

Circa Reproductions Nieuport 11 Experimental category scale replica, built by Mr Richard Starks of Parkville, Missouri (1,700 cc Volkswagen engine)

Magal Holdings Cuby II two-seat microlight

Elmwood Aviation CH-8 Christavia Mk 4 four-seat homebuilt

POWER PLANT: One 112 kW (150 hp) Textron Lycoming O-320 or converted motorcar engine. Fuel capacity 136.4 litres (36 US gallons; 30 Imp gallons).

DIMENSIONS, EXTERNAL:
Wing span 10.67 m (35 ft 0 in)
Length overall 7.01 m (23 ft 0 in)
Height overall 1.98 m (6 ft 6 in)
Propeller diameter 1.78 m (5 ft 10 in)
AREA:
Wings, gross 16.26 m² (175.0 sq ft)

WEIGHTS (112 kW; 150 hp engine):
Weight empty 522 kg (1,150 lb)
Max T-O weight 1,043 kg (2,300 lb)
PERFORMANCE:
Max level speed at 610 m (2,000 ft) 111 knots (206 km/h; 128 mph)
Econ cruising speed, 65% power 102 knots (188 km/h; 117 mph)
Stalling speed: flaps up 35 knots (65 km/h; 40 mph)
12° flap 31 knots (57 km/h; 35 mph)

Max rate of climb at S/L 244 m (800 ft)/min
Service ceiling 5,485 m (18,000 ft)
T-O run 91 m (300 ft)
Landing run 152 m (500 ft)
Range with max fuel 548 nm (1,017 km; 632 miles)

MACAIR
MACAIR INDUSTRIES INC
PO Box 11, Rosemont, Ontario L0N 1R0
Telephone: (705) 435 9224

MACAIR MERLIN
The Merlin is a new cabin microlight, available in kit (about 150 working hours) and ready assembled forms. (See Addenda for illustration.)
TYPE: Side by side two-seat microlight.
AIRFRAME: Strut braced wings with aluminium D-cell and reinforced foam ribs, Ceconite 103 covered. Welded 4130 steel tube fuselage and tail unit, Falconar fabric covered. Glassfibre engine cowling. Non-retractable tailwheel landing gear. Three-axis control.
POWER PLANT: One 37.3 kW (50 hp) Rotax 503.
DIMENSIONS, EXTERNAL:
Wing span 9.75 m (32 ft 0 in)
Length overall 6.10 m (20 ft 0 in)
Height overall 1.68 m (5 ft 6 in)
AREA:
Wings, gross 14.03 m² (151.0 sq ft)

WEIGHT:
Max T-O weight 190.5 kg (420 lb)
PERFORMANCE (two crew):
Cruising speed 56 knots (105 km/h; 65 mph)
Stalling speed 34 knots (63 km/h; 39 mph)
Max rate of climb at S/L 168 m (550 ft)/min
Service ceiling 3,660 m (12,000 ft)
T-O run 92 m (300 ft)
g limits +6/–3

MAGAL
MAGAL HOLDINGS LTD
19 Pensville Road South East, Calgary, Alberta T2A 4K3
Telephone: (403) 248 9386
REPRESENTATIVES: Hal Arthur and Brian Stephens
This organisation offers through dealerships two two-seat strut braced cabin microlights of generally similar appearance, designed in Piper Cub style but with modern features. The wings can be removed for transportation.

MAGAL CUBY I
Version with fully enclosed accommodation and a Rotax engine in the 20-37.3 kW (27-50 hp) range. Fuel capacity 36.4 litres (9.6 US gallons; 8 Imp gallons). Three-axis control. Non-retractable tailwheel landing gear standard; floats and possibly skis are optional.
DIMENSIONS, EXTERNAL:
Wing span 9.75 m (32 ft 0 in)
Length overall 5.94 m (19 ft 6 in)
Height overall 1.76 m (5 ft 9½ in)
AREA:
Wings, gross 13.00 m² (140.0 sq ft)
WEIGHTS:
Weight empty 122 kg (270 lb)
Max baggage weight 13.6 kg (30 lb)
Max T-O weight 363 kg (800 lb)
PERFORMANCE (Rotax 447 engine):
Cruising speed 61 knots (113 km/h; 70 mph)
Stalling speed 25 knots (45 km/h; 28 mph)
Max rate of climb at S/L 213 m (700 ft)/min
T-O and landing run (land) 46 m (150 ft)
g limits +5/–1

MAGAL CUBY II
The larger Cuby II appears to differ from the Cuby I mainly in having accommodation suited to pilots up to 1.98 m (6 ft 6 in) tall and 136 kg (300 lb) weight, no cabin side doors are fitted, the wings have ailerons and flaps over the full span, and engines of 31.3-47.7 kW (42-64 hp) can be selected. Fuel capacity is 45.5 litres (12 US gallons; 10 Imp gallons).
DIMENSIONS, EXTERNAL:
Wing span 10.21 m (33 ft 6 in)
Length overall 6.25 m (20 ft 6 in)
Height overall 1.76 m (5 ft 9½ in)
AREA:
Wings, gross 14.86 m² (160.0 sq ft)
WEIGHTS:
Weight empty 163 kg (360 lb)
Max baggage weight 13.6 kg (30 lb)
Max T-O weight 453 kg (1,000 lb)
PERFORMANCE (Rotax 503 engine):
Cruising speed 61 knots (113 km/h; 70 mph)
Stalling speed 26 knots (49 km/h; 30 mph)
Max rate of climb at S/L 213 m (700 ft)/min
T-O and landing run (land) 61 m (200 ft)
g limits +4/–1

McASCO — *see MacFam in US section*

MURPHY
MURPHY AVIATION LTD
8880 Young Road South, Chilliwack, British Columbia
V2P 4P5
Telephone: (604) 792 5855
Fax: (604) 792 6496
PRESIDENT: Darryl Murphy

MURPHY RENEGADE II
The prototype Renegade II first flew in May 1985. Ready assembled aircraft, plans and kits are available, the latter in four standards ranging from a partial parts kit to a 300-400 working hour quick build kit with all parts pre-manufactured plus assembled fuselage, wings and engine mounting. By February 1988 six ready assembled aircraft had been completed, with 25 sets of plans and 30 kits delivered. Two plans-built and 20 kit-built Renegade IIs were then flying.
TYPE: Two-seat dual-control ARV and homebuilt biplane; also conforms to microlight regulations in Canada and some European countries.
AIRFRAME: Strut and wire braced biplane of fabric covered all-metal construction. NACA 23012 wing section. Frise ailerons on lower only or all four wings. Optional extended wings with rounded tips. Non-retractable tailwheel landing gear. Optional floats, skis, agricultural spraygear and parachute.

POWER PLANT: One 35.8 kW (48 hp) Rotax 503 standard; 39.5 kW (53 hp) twin-carburettor Rotax 503 optional. Alternative engines include Rotax 532 and Continental O65, O75 and O85. Fuel in two 29.5 litre (7.8 US gallon; 6.5 Imp gallon) tanks.

DIMENSIONS, EXTERNAL:
Wing span: upper	6.48 m (21 ft 3 in)
lower	6.05 m (19 ft 10 in)
Length overall	5.61 m (18 ft 5 in)
Height overall	2.08 m (6 ft 10 in)
Propeller diameter	1.73 m (5 ft 8 in)

AREA:
Wings, gross	14.29 or 15.61 m² (153.8 or 168.0 sq ft)

WEIGHTS:
Weight empty	163-181 kg (360-400 lb)
Max T-O weight	408 kg (900 lb)

PERFORMANCE (Rotax 503 engine and 2 crew, unless stated otherwise):
Max level speed at 305 m (1,000 ft)	74 knots (136 km/h; 85 mph)
Econ cruising speed	61 knots (113 km/h; 70 mph)
Stalling speed, power off	29 knots (53 km/h; 33 mph)
Max rate of climb at S/L	213 m (700 ft)/min
Service ceiling	3,660 m (12,000 ft)
T-O and landing run	61 m (200 ft)
Range with max payload	195 nm (362 km; 225 miles)

Endurance	4 h 30 min
g limits (pilot only)	+10/-6 ultimate

MURPHY RENEGADE SPIRIT
Added to the range of Renegade kits available in July 1987, the Renegade Spirit has the 47.7 kW (64 hp) Rotax 532 as its standard power plant, in a radial type cowling, and introduces a number of other internal and external refinements. Continental O65, O75, and O85 engines can be fitted.
The prototype Renegade Spirit (C-IJLW) first flew on 6 May 1987. By February 1988, 45 kits and 12 sets of plans had been delivered; 18 kit-built and one plans-built aircraft were flying.
DIMENSIONS, EXTERNAL AND WEIGHTS: As for Renegade II
PERFORMANCE (two crew):
Max level speed	87 knots (161 km/h; 100 mph)
Econ cruising speed	65 knots (120 km/h; 75 mph)
Stalling speed, power off	29 knots (53 km/h; 33 mph)
Max rate of climb at S/L	335 m (1,100 ft)/min
Service ceiling	3,660 m (12,000 ft)
T-O run	53 m (175 ft)
Landing run	61 m (200 ft)
Range with max payload	195 nm (362 km; 225 miles)
Endurance	4 h 30 min
g limits (pilot only)	+10/-6 ultimate

REPLICA PLANS
REPLICA PLANS
14752 90th Avenue, Surrey, British Columbia V3R 1A4
Telephone: 589 9386

REPLICA PLANS S.E.5A REPLICA
The S.E.5A replica was designed to be an easy to build and inexpensive 85 per cent scale representation of the famous First World War fighter. The first prototype flew initially in 1970, and by early 1988 approximately 45-50 others had been built from the 380 sets of plans sold.
TYPE: Single-seat homebuilt sporting biplane.

AIRFRAME: Braced biplane wings of Clark CYH section, with spruce struts. Fabric covered wooden wings, except for glassfibre or aluminium leading-edges. Ply skinned fuselage box structure, with fabric covered turtledeck and aluminium forward top decking. Tail unit structure generally similar to that of wings. Non-retractable tailwheel landing gear.
POWER PLANT: Various engines can be installed. Performance figures quoted are for aircraft with 63.5 kW (85 hp) Continental C85-12. Fuel capacity 72 litres (19 US gallons; 15.8 Imp gallons).
DIMENSIONS, EXTERNAL:
Wing span	7.11 m (23 ft 4 in)
Length overall	5.54 m (18 ft 2 in)
Height overall	2.34 m (7 ft 8 in)
Propeller diameter	1.83 m (6 ft 0 in)

AREA:
Wings, gross	13.56 m² (146.0 sq ft)

WEIGHTS:
Weight empty	358 kg (790 lb)
Max T-O weight	499 kg (1,100 lb)

PERFORMANCE:
Max level speed at S/L	78 knots (145 km/h; 90 mph)
Max cruising speed	74 knots (137 km/h; 85 mph)
Stalling speed	31 knots (57 km/h; 35 mph)
Max rate of climb at S/L	183 m (600 ft)/min

SEAWIND
SEAWIND INTERNATIONAL INC
PO Box 878, Haliburton, Ontario K0M 1S0
Telephone: (705) 457 1438
PRESIDENT: Leonard R. Creelman

SEAWIND INTERNATIONAL SEAWIND 2000
The production prototype Seawind (C-GFNL) flew for the first time on 23 August 1982. An illustration can be found in the 1987-88 *Jane's*. The Seawind 2000 is the much refind version of which kits are available, each containing pre-moulded components that are supplied as complete subassemblies where possible. Assembly takes about 1,000 working hours.
TYPE: Four-seat dual-control homebuilt amphibian; exceeds FAR Pt 23 minimum performance requirements.

AIRFRAME: Wing section NLF(1)-0215F. Built-up GRP wing spar and PVC foam ribs, covered with GRP skins. Ailerons, plain flaps, wingtip floats and single-step flying-boat hull all of GRP/PVC foam construction. GRP tail unit. Hydraulically retractable tricycle landing gear.
POWER PLANT: One 149 kW (200 hp) Textron Lycoming IO-360-C1C. Two integral fuel cells in wings; total capacity 302 litres (80 US gallons; 66.6 Imp gallons).

DIMENSIONS, EXTERNAL:
Wing span	10.67 m (35 ft 0 in)
Length overall	8.23 m (27 ft 0 in)
Height overall	2.90 m (9 ft 6 in)
Propeller diameter	1.93 m (6 ft 4 in)

AREA:
Wings, gross	14.59 m² (157.0 sq ft)

WEIGHTS:
Weight empty	771 kg (1,700 lb)
Max T-O weight: from water	1,270 kg (2,800 lb)
from land	1,360 kg (3,000 lb)

PERFORMANCE:
Max level speed at S/L	161 knots (298 km/h; 185 mph)
Econ cruising speed	143 knots (266 km/h; 165 mph)
Stalling speed: flaps up	52 knots (97 km/h; 60 mph)
flaps and landing gear down	48 knots (89 km/h; 55 mph)
Max rate of climb at S/L	366 m (1,200 ft)/min
Service ceiling	5,180 m (17,000 ft)
T-O run: land	198 m (650 ft)
water	396 m (1,300 ft)
Landing run	366 m (1,200 ft)
Range with max standard fuel	1,042 nm (1,931 km; 1,200 miles)

SEVILLE
SEVILLE AIRCRAFT INC
751 Main Street E, No 1, Milton, Ontario L9T 3Z3
Telephone: (416) 878 1901
PRESIDENT: Sandy Sinclair

SEVILLE TWO PLACE
This aircraft is available in kit form or ready to fly.
TYPE: Tandem two-seat lightweight training aircraft.
AIRFRAME: Strut braced wings, with aluminium alloy D-spar, foam ribs and fabric covering. Welded steel tube fuselage with glassfibre nose and Mylar covering. Aluminium alloy tail unit. Three-axis control. Non-retractable tricycle landing gear.
POWER PLANT: One 29.4 kW (39.4 hp) Rotax 447. Fuel capacity 19 litres (5 US gallons; 4.2 Imp gallons).

DIMENSIONS, EXTERNAL:
Wing span	11.43 m (37 ft 6 in)
Length overall	6.25 m (20 ft 6 in)
Height overall	2.59 m (8 ft 6 in)
Propeller diameter	1.63 m (5 ft 4 in)

AREA:
Wings, gross	16.72 m² (180.0 sq ft)

WEIGHTS:
Weight empty	173 kg (380 lb)
Max T-O weight	385 kg (850 lb)

PERFORMANCE (two crew):
Cruising speed	52 knots (97 km/h; 60 mph)
Stalling speed	23 knots (42 km/h; 26 mph)
Max rate of climb at S/L	198 m (650 ft)/min
g limits	+6/-3

SPECTRUM
SPECTRUM AIRCRAFT INC
No. 3-9531 192nd Street, Surrey, British Columbia V3T 4W2
Telephone: (604) 888 2055
SALES AND MARKETING MANAGER: Allan K. Hunkin

SPECTRUM BEAVER RX-28
Marketed in kit and ready-assembled forms, the Beaver RX-28 microlight was designed for rough-field operation.
TYPE: Single-seat microlight aircraft; conforms to FAR Pt 103 and Canadian regulations.
AIRFRAME: Aluminium alloy structure, with Dacron covered wings and tail unit. Mylar reinforced leading-edges. Three-axis control. Glassfibre cockpit fairing. Non-retractable tricycle landing gear. Options include fully enclosed cockpit fairing, floats, skis and recovery parachute.
POWER PLANT: One 20 kW (27 hp) Rotax 277; 26 kW (35 hp) Rotax optional. Fuel capacity 19 litres (5 US gallons; 4.2 Imp gallons) standard.

DIMENSIONS, EXTERNAL:
Wing span	9.45 m (31 ft 0 in)
Length overall	5.38 m (17 ft 8 in)
Height overall	1.73 m (5 ft 8 in)
Propeller diameter	1.52 m (5 ft 0 in)

AREA:
Wings, gross	13.75 m² (148.0 sq ft)

WEIGHTS:
Weight empty	115 kg (253 lb)
Pilot weight range	59-109 kg (130-240 lb)
Max T-O weight	252 kg (556 lb)

PERFORMANCE (with 79 kg; 175 lb pilot):
Max level speed	50 knots (93 km/h; 58 mph)
Econ cruising speed	35 knots (64 km/h; 40 mph)
Stalling speed	21 knots (39 km/h; 24 mph)
Max rate of climb at S/L	213 m (700 ft)/min
Service ceiling	3,660 m (12,000 ft)
T-O run	28 m (90 ft)
Landing run	34 m (110 ft)
Range with max fuel	87 nm (161 km; 100 miles)
Endurance	2 h 5 min
g limits	+7.5/-3 ultimate

SPECTRUM BEAVER RX-35 and RX-35 FLOATER
Believed to be available in kit and ready assembled forms, the **RX-35** is the standard tricycle landing gear model, while the **Floater** has amphibious landing gear and a

Seawind 2000 amphibian on exhibition at EXPO 86, showing latest form of engine cowling and canopy

Murphy Renegade II two-seat homebuilt biplane (Neil A. Macdougall)

Murphy Renegade Spirit, with radial cowling (Howard Levy)

Seville Two Place lightweight training aircraft

Replica Plans S.E.5A, built by Mr Ismall Cruz of Kirkland, Washington, and finished in colours and markings of 25th Pursuit Squadron, American Expeditionary Force (Peter M. Bowers)

Spectrum Beaver RX-35 (Geoffrey P. Jones)

Spectrum Beaver RX-550 Floater with float landing gear

---

choice of engines. Both are structurally similar to the RX-28. Details, where they differ from the RX-28, are as follows:

TYPE: Single-seat microlight; conforms to Canadian regulations.

POWER PLANT: One 26 kW (35 hp) Rotax 377. Floater has option of 33.5 kW (45 hp) Rotax 447. Fuel capacity 19 litres (5 US gallons; 4.2 Imp gallons) standard; optional auxiliary tank, capacity 38 litres (10 US gallons; 8.4 Imp gallons).

DIMENSIONS, EXTERNAL:

Wing span	9.45 m (31 ft 0 in)
Length overall	5.38 m (17 ft 8 in)
Height overall: RX-35	1.73 m (5 ft 8 in)
Floater	1.85 m (6 ft 1 in)
Propeller diameter	1.63 m (5 ft 4 in)

AREA:

Wings, gross	13.75 m² (148.0 sq ft)

WEIGHTS (A: RX-35, B: Floater):

Weight empty: A	121.5 kg (268 lb)
B	149 kg (328 lb)

Pilot weight range: A	59-118 kg (130-260 lb)
B	59-102 kg (130-225 lb)
Max T-O weight: A	244 kg (539 lb)
B	265 kg (585 lb)

PERFORMANCE (A: RX-35, B: Floater):

Max level speed: A	56 knots (103 km/h; 64 mph)
B	52 knots (97 km/h; 60 mph)
Econ cruising speed:	
A, B	36 knots (68 km/h; 42 mph)
Stalling speed:	
A, power on	22 knots (41 km/h; 25 mph)
B, power on	26 knots (47 km/h; 29 mph)
A, power off	25 knots (45 km/h; 28 mph)
B, power off	22 knots (41 km/h; 25 mph)
Max rate of climb at S/L: A	335 m (1,100 ft)/min
B	119 m (390 ft)/min
Service ceiling: A	3,960 m (13,000 ft)
B	3,660 m (12,000 ft)
T-O run: A	18 m (60 ft)
B	46 m (150 ft)

Landing run: A	35 m (115 ft)
B	31 m (100 ft)
Range with max standard fuel:	
A	78 nm (145 km; 90 miles)
B	69 nm (128 km; 80 miles)
Endurance	2 h
g limits: A	+7.3/-2.9
B	+6.75/-3

SPECTRUM BEAVER RX-550 SERIES

The Beaver RX-550 is a tandem-seat training version of the RX-28, suited also to many commercial and military/para-military applications. The airframe is structurally similar to that of the single-seat model, but larger and with full dual controls.

The three models of RX-550 differ as follows:

RX-550. Standard version with 33.5 kW (45 hp) Rotax 447 engine.

RX-550 Floater. Rotax 503 engine of 35.8 kW (48 hp). Heavier empty and max T-O weights and higher performance.

RX-550SP. Similar to Floater but with max payload of 227 kg (500 lb) and useful load of 204 kg (450 lb) for commercial applications. New 34 litre (9 US gallon; 7.5 Imp gallon) seat tank standard to allow 4 h endurance and range of 182 nm (338 km; 210 miles). Heavier suspension using Spectrum's shock absorber landing gear system. Options include agricultural spraygear, and various types of cargo and baggage compartments. Can be flown as a two-seater or with the cargo/baggage compartments in place of the rear seat.

THOR
THOR AIR
457 Fenmar Drive, Weston, Ontario M9L 2R6
Telephone: (416) 745 4657
Telex: 065-27383
GENERAL MANAGER: Guenter Weber

THOR AIR THOR T-1
Three versions have been offered: the single-seat **T-1** (to which the following description applies) and **T-1A**, with 31.3 kW (42 hp) Rotax 447 engine, and the two-seat **T-2**, with 35 kW (47 hp) Rotax 503. A large number of kits have been sold, and a 'military version' of the T-2 has been under development.
TYPE: Single-seat microlight.
AIRFRAME: Strut braced, of aluminium tube and Dacron. Non-retractable tailwheel landing gear. Optional cockpit enclosure, floats and skis.
POWER PLANT: One 20 kW (27 hp) Rotax 277. Fuel capacity 19 litres (5 US gallons; 4.2 Imp gallons).

DIMENSIONS, EXTERNAL:
Wing span	9.83 m (32 ft 3 in)
Length overall	4.19 m (13 ft 9 in)
Height overall	2.36 m (7 ft 9 in)
Propeller diameter	1.27 m (4 ft 2 in)

AREA:
Wings, gross	15.51 m² (167.0 sq ft)

WEIGHTS:
Weight empty	108 kg (238 lb)
Max T-O weight	227 kg (500 lb)

PERFORMANCE:
Max level speed	55 knots (101 km/h; 65 mph)
Max cruising speed	48 knots (89 km/h; 55 mph)
Stalling speed	19 knots (36 km/h; 22 mph)
Max rate of climb at S/L	213 m (700 ft)/min
Service ceiling	3,050 m (10,000 ft)
g limits	+6/−4

THOR AIR JUNO
The Juno is basically an update of the Thor T-1, available in kit and ready assembled forms.
TYPE: Side by side two-seat microlight; conforms to FAR Pt 103 and Canadian Transport regulations.
AIRFRAME: Strut braced, with aluminium alloy mainframe and Dacron covering on fuselage sides, wings and tail unit. Three-axis control. Non-retractable tailwheel landing gear. Options include cockpit enclosure, skis, floats, ballistic parachute and instrument pack.
POWER PLANT: One 20 kW (27 hp) Rotax 277; optional 31.3 kW (42 hp) Rotax 447. Fuel tank capacity 20 litres (5.3 US gallons; 4.4 Imp gallons).

DIMENSIONS, EXTERNAL:
Wing span	9.86 m (32 ft 4 in)
Length overall	4.45 m (14 ft 7 in)
Height overall	1.93 m (6 ft 4 in)
Propeller diameter	1.52 m (5 ft 0 in)

AREA:
Wings, gross	15.51 m² (167.0 sq ft)

WEIGHTS:
Weight empty	129 kg (284 lb)
Pilot weight range	45.5-113 kg (100-250 lb)
Max T-O weight	256 kg (564 lb)

PERFORMANCE:
Max level speed	52 knots (97 km/h; 60 mph)
Econ cruising speed	35 knots (64 km/h; 40 mph)
Stalling speed: power on	18 knots (33 km/h; 20 mph)
power off	19 knots (36 km/h; 22 mph)
Max rate of climb at S/L	213 m (700 ft)/min
Service ceiling	3,050 m (10,000 ft)
T-O run	23 m (75 ft)
Landing run	15 m (50 ft)
Range with max fuel	130 nm (241 km; 150 miles)
Endurance	3 h
g limits	+6/−3

ULTIMATE
ULTIMATE AIRCRAFT CORP
Guelph Airpark, Guelph, Ontario N1H 6H8
Telephone: (519) 836 8622
PRESIDENT: Gordon Price

ULTIMATE AIRCRAFT 10 DASH 100/300
Ultimate Aircraft is offering sets of plans, kits and ready assembled examples of three closely related single-seat biplanes of the 10 Dash series. The basic model is the **10 Dash 100**, designed to be an affordable sporting biplane with a 74.5 or 134 kW (100 or 180 hp) engine. Power plants between these ratings can be installed at the customer's option. A typical power plant is a 74.5 kW (100 hp) Continental O-200. The prototype 10 Dash 100 flew for the first time on 6 October 1985.

The **10 Dash 200** was designed as a modern competition aerobatic aircraft, utilising a 134-149 kW (180-200 hp) engine with Ellison throttle body injector and a constant-speed Hoffmann or MT composites propeller. The final model in the range is the **10 Dash 300**, a state of the art competition aircraft, with longer-span wings, incorporating full-span symmetrical ailerons; a longer fuselage; and a 224 kW (300 hp) or 261 kW (350 hp) Textron Lycoming engine, driving a three-blade Hoffmann propeller.
TYPE: Single-seat homebuilt sporting and aerobatic biplane.
AIRFRAME: Braced biplane, with Ceconite covered wooden wings. Near symmetrical wing section. Upper and lower full-span ailerons of aluminium alloy. 'Macro flap' control (5° aileron droop with 30° 'up' elevator). Welded steel tube fuselage structure, aluminium alloy and Ceconite covered. Aluminium alloy turtledeck. Glassfibre nose cowlings. Braced steel tube tail unit, Ceconite covered. Non-retractable tailwheel landing gear.
POWER PLANT: See introduction. 10-100 has fuel capacity of 83 litres (22 US gallons; 18.3 Imp gallons). Optional 57 litre (15 US gallon; 12.5 Imp gallon) strap-on centre-section tank. Inverted fuel system.

DIMENSIONS, EXTERNAL:
Wing span: 10-100, 10-200	4.83 m (15 ft 10 in)
10-300	5.95 m (19 ft 6 in)
Length overall: 10-100	5.33 m (17 ft 6 in)
10-200	5.49 m (18 ft 0 in)
10-300	6.40 m (21 ft 0 in)
Height overall: 10-100, 10-200	1.68 m (5 ft 6 in)

AREAS:
Wings, gross: 10-100, 10-200	8.92 m² (96.0 sq ft)
10-300	11.15 m² (120.0 sq ft)

WEIGHTS:
Weight empty: 10-100	358 kg (790 lb)
10-200	420 kg (925 lb)
10-300	522 kg (1,150 lb)
Max T-O weight: 10-100, 10-200	612 kg (1,350 lb)
10-300	748 kg (1,650 lb)

PERFORMANCE:
Max level speed:	
10-100	165 knots (306 km/h; 190 mph)
10-200	191 knots (354 km/h; 220 mph)
10-300	217 knots (402 km/h; 250 mph)
Cruising speed, 75% power:	
10-100	122 knots (225 km/h; 140 mph)
10-200	148 knots (273 km/h; 170 mph)
10-300	165 knots (305 km/h; 190 mph)
Stalling speed:	
10-100: power off	46 knots (86 km/h; 53 mph)
power on	44 knots (81 km/h; 50 mph)
Max rate of climb at S/L: 10-100	350 m (1,150 ft)/min
10-300	915 m (3,000 ft)/min
T-O run: 10-100	180 m (590 ft)
Landing run: 10-100	155 m (510 ft)
Range: 10-100	564 nm (1,046 km; 650 miles)
10-200	434 nm (804 km; 500 miles)
10-300	520-781 nm (965-1,448 km; 600-900 miles)
Rate of roll: 10-200	360°/sec
g limits: all	+7/−5 operating

ULTIMATE AIRCRAFT 20 DASH 300
The Ultimate Aircraft 20 Dash 300 is identical to the 10 Dash 300 except for having two seats in tandem under a one-piece bubble canopy. It offers the same choice of Textron Lycoming engines and other options, and is available in two forms: the **20 Dash 300T** is a two-seat aerobatic training aircraft; the **20 Dash 300E** is the exhibition model.
As for 10-300
WEIGHTS:
Weight empty	545 kg (1,200 lb)
Max T-O weight	907 kg (2,000 lb)

PERFORMANCE:
Max level speed	217 knots (402 km/h; 250 mph)
Cruising speed, 75% power	165 knots (305 km/h; 190 mph)
Range	434-608 nm (804-1,126 km; 500-700 miles)

ULTIMATE AIRCRAFT (PITTS) SPECIAL
The standard Pitts S-1 and S-2 Specials are described in detail under the Christen heading in the main US Aircraft section of this edition. Basic feature of the Ultimate versions of these aircraft is the use of new wings with larger control surfaces and significantly increased strength of construction. These make it possible to roll at 360°/s at normal flying speeds and 240°/s at low speeds, and to perform five vertical rolls on take-off. The wings are jig built to fit any Pitts Special without modification. Other features include low-profile glassfibre engine cowlings and Plexiglas cockpit canopy, and the option to build the fuselage up to 21 cm (8½ in) longer to increase comfort.
POWER PLANT: Conformal auxiliary fuel tanks, filled with Explosafe explosion-proof metal foil, strapped above centre-section of top wing. Capacity 34 or 57 litres (9 or 15 US gallons; 7.5 or 12.5 Imp gallons) for S-1; 68 litres (18 US gallons; 15 Imp gallons) for S-2.

DIMENSION, EXTERNAL (S-1):
Wing span (upper and lower)	4.77 m (15 ft 8 in)

ULTRAFLIGHT
ULTRAFLIGHT SALES LTD
PO Box 370, Port Colborne, Ontario L3K 1B7
Telephone: (416) 735 8352
Telex: 061-5497
GENERAL MANAGER: Mrs Linda M. Kramer

ULTRAFLIGHT LAZAIR
The Lazair first flew in November 1978. It is available in kit form for amateur construction or ready assembled. Sales were well in excess of 1,000 by January 1988.

The Lazair is offered in three versions: **Series III** is the standard aircraft and is also available in **Series IIIEC** (enclosed cockpit) form with an enclosure of glassfibre reinforced plastic and a Lexan windscreen; **SS Surveillance Special** with two 17 kW (23 hp) KFM 107E engines, increased wing area, radios, lights, public address equipment for police duties and electric starting, also available in EC form; and the **Elite**, which is similar to the SS but, being intended for the recreational microlight pilot who requires a high performance aircraft, is powered by two 15 kW (20 hp) JPX PUL 425 engines. An EC version is available.

The Lazair SS is too heavy to be operated in the USA under microlight regulations, the SS/EC cannot be operated in the USA or Canada under microlight regulations, and the Elite EC is also too heavy for the US microlight regulations.
The following data apply to the Lazair Series III, unless stated otherwise:
TYPE: Single-seat microlight.
AIRFRAME: Tedlar-covered all-aluminium alloy structure, except for foam plastics ribs. Three-axis control by ailerons and 'ruddervators'. Non-retractable tailwheel landing gear. Options are cockpit fairing, floats and skis.
POWER PLANT: Two 7 kW (9.5 hp) 185 cc Rotax engines. Fuel capacity 19 litres (5 US gallons; 4.2 Imp gallons).

DIMENSIONS, EXTERNAL:
Wing span	11.07 m (36 ft 4 in)
Length overall: standard	4.27 m (14 ft 0 in)
EC versions	4.88 m (16 ft 0 in)
Height overall	1.93 m (6 ft 4 in)
Propeller diameter	0.71 m (2 ft 4 in)

AREA:
Wings, gross	13.19 m² (142.0 sq ft)

WEIGHTS:
Weight empty	100 kg (220 lb)
Max pilot weight	113.5 kg (250 lb)
Max T-O weight	208 kg (460 lb)

PERFORMANCE (Series III, with 77 kg; 170 lb pilot):
Max level speed	53 knots (98 km/h; 61 mph)
Max cruising speed	35 knots (64 km/h; 40 mph)
Stalling speed	21 knots (39 km/h; 24 mph)
Max rate of climb at S/L	114 m (375 ft)/min
T-O run	37 m (120 ft)
Range with max fuel	more than 139 nm (257 km; 160 miles)
Endurance with max fuel	4 h
g limits	+4/−1.3

ULTRAFLIGHT LAZAIR II
First flown on 10 November 1981, the Lazair II is a side by side two-seat version of the Lazair, intended primarily for training, with dual controls. KFM 107E engines of 17 kW (23 hp) each, with electric starting, are available as an option, with which the aircraft is known as the **Lazair II EL**.
The following data apply to the Lazair II, unless stated otherwise:
TYPE: Two-seat, dual-control microlight.
POWER PLANT: Two 15 kW (20 hp) JPX PUL 425 engines. Fuel tank capacity 19 litres (5 US gallons; 4.2 Imp gallons).

Thor Air Juno two-seat microlight

Ultimate Aircraft upgraded Pitts S-1 Special *(J.M.G. Gradidge)*

Ultimate Aircraft 10 Dash 100 *(J.M.G. Gradidge)*

Two-seat Lazair II with twin nosewheels *(Peter M. Bowers)*

DIMENSIONS, EXTERNAL:		WEIGHTS:		Max rate of climb at S/L	110 m (360 ft)/min
Wing span	11.58 m (38 ft 0 in)	Weight empty	130 kg (287 lb)	T-O run	91 m (300 ft)
Length overall	4.27 m (14 ft 0 in)	Max T-O weight	329 kg (725 lb)	g limits	+4/–2
Height overall	1.93 m (6 ft 4 in)	PERFORMANCE (77 kg; 170 lb pilot):			
Propeller diameter	0.86 m (2 ft 10 in)	Max level speed	47 knots (88 km/h; 55 mph)		
AREA:		Cruising speed	35 knots (64 km/h; 40 mph)		
Wings, gross	14.03 m² (151.0 sq ft)	Stalling speed	22 knots (41 km/h; 25 mph)		

ULTRAVIA

ULTRAVIA AERO INC

609 Iberville, Repentigny (Montreal), Quebec J6A 6Y7
Telephone: (514) 585 6132
Telex: 05 268897
Fax: 849 6720
VICE-PRESIDENT: Mrs Lorraine Chauvin

ULTRAVIA LE PELICAN and LONGNOSE PELICAN

Le Pelican flew for the first time in May 1982 and was put on the market in plan, kit and parts forms for amateur construction, or ready to fly. More powerful models, the Super Pelican and LongNose Pelican, were introduced thereafter. The LongNose Pelican is structurally identical to Le Pelican. The following description is applicable to Le Pelican, unless otherwise specified.

TYPE: Single-seat microlight, designed to FAR Pt 23 standards; conforms to FAR Pt 103 and TCAR Section 101.
AIRFRAME: Built of aircraft grade aluminium alloy, with D-cell wing leading-edge, composite foam/aluminium wing ribs, one-piece glassfibre engine cowling, and Dacron covering. Three-axis control. Non-retractable tailwheel landing gear. Optional floats, skis and cabin doors.
POWER PLANT: Original Le Pelican has one 15.7 kW (21 hp) Briggs and Stratton 42CL. LongNose has one 20 kW (27 hp) Rotax 277. Removable (portable) fuel tank, capacity 19 litres (5 US gallons; 4.2 Imp gallons).

DIMENSIONS, EXTERNAL:
Wing span 10.67 m (35 ft 0 in)
Length overall 4.57 m (15 ft 0 in)
Height overall 1.98 m (6 ft 6 in)
Propeller diameter 1.22 m (4 ft 0 in)
AREA:
Wings, gross 12.63 m² (136.0 sq ft)
WEIGHTS:
Weight empty 113 kg (250 lb)

Pilot weight range 45-113 kg (100-250 lb)
Max T-O weight 238 kg (525 lb)
PERFORMANCE (with 79 kg; 175 lb pilot):
Max level speed 56 knots (105 km/h; 65 mph)
Econ cruising speed 43 knots (80 km/h; 50 mph)
Stalling speed:
  power on 21 knots (39 km/h; 24 mph)
  power off 24 knots (45 km/h; 27.5 mph)
Max rate of climb at S/L 152 m (500 ft)/min
Service ceiling 4,575 m (15,000 ft)
T-O and landing run (typical) 30 m (100 ft)
Range with max fuel 217 nm (402 km; 250 miles)
Endurance with max fuel 5 h
g limits +4/–2 normal
 +6/–3 ultimate

ULTRAVIA SUPER PELICAN

The Super Pelican is externally and structurally identical to the original Le Pelican and the LongNose Pelican. Specifications, where different from LongNose Pelican, are as follows:
POWER PLANT: One 26 kW (35 hp) Global.
DIMENSIONS, EXTERNAL:
Propeller diameter 1.47 m (4 ft 10 in)
PERFORMANCE (with 79 kg; 175 lb pilot):
Max level speed 65 knots (121 km/h; 75 mph)
Econ cruising speed 56 knots (105 km/h; 65 mph)
Max rate of climb at S/L 290 m (950 ft)/min
T-O run (typical) 15 m (50 ft)
Endurance with max fuel 4 h

ULTRAVIA PELICAN CLUB

The Pelican Club first flew as a prototype in 1984. Three versions are available as the GS, S and UL, with varying wing spans/areas and engine choices. Kits are available and by March 1988 65 had been delivered, of which 60 had then been assembled. Ten ready built aircraft had also been completed in addition to the prototypes.

The following details refer to the S version with a Rotax 532, unless stated otherwise.
TYPE: Two-seat dual-control homebuilt aircraft.
AIRFRAME: Strut braced wings of aluminium alloy, with glassfibre/foam sandwich ribs, Dacron covered. Wing section NACA 6315. Vacuum moulded monocoque fuselage of glassfibre/epoxy/Clark foam construction. Non-retractable tailwheel landing gear standard. Optional tricycle gear, floats and skis.
POWER PLANT: One 38.8 kW (52 hp) Rotax 503 or 47.7 kW (64 hp) Rotax 532. GS has options of 48.5 kW (65 hp) Continental A65 or HAPI engine of up to 61 kW (82 hp). Fuel capacity 38 litres (10 US gallons; 8.3 Imp gallons). Two auxiliary fuel tanks optional, each of 23 litres (6 US gallons; 5 Imp gallons) capacity.
DIMENSIONS, EXTERNAL:
Wing span: UL 10.67 m (35 ft 0 in)
  S 10.21 m (33 ft 6 in)
  GS 9.35 m (30 ft 8 in)
Length overall 5.94 m (19 ft 6 in)
Height overall 2.54 m (8 ft 4 in)
Propeller diameter 1.73 m (5 ft 8 in)
AREAS:
Wings, gross: UL 14.86 m² (160.0 sq ft)
  S 13.47 m² (145.0 sq ft)
  GS 12.54 m² (135.0 sq ft)
WEIGHTS (Pelican Club S):
Weight empty 227 kg (500 lb)
Baggage capacity 22.7 kg (50 lb)
Max T-O weight 431 kg (950 lb)
PERFORMANCE (Pelican Club S):
Max level speed 104 knots (193 km/h; 120 mph)
Econ cruising speed 82 knots (153 km/h; 95 mph)
Stalling speed:
  flaps down 26 knots (49 km/h; 30 mph)
  flaps up 31 knots (57 km/h; 35 mph)
Max rate of climb at S/L 267 m (875 ft)/min
Service ceiling 5,180 m (17,000 ft)
T-O run 46 m (150 ft)
g limits +6/–3 ultimate

WESTERN

WESTERN AIRCRAFT SUPPLIES

623 Markerville Road NE, Calgary, Alberta T2E 5X1
Telephone: (403) 276 3087
DIRECTOR: Jean J. Peters

WESTERN PGK-1 HIRONDELLE

The prototype Hirondelle first flew on 27 June 1976. Plans and wood kits are available, as well as some preformed components.
TYPE: Side by side two-seat, dual-control homebuilt aircraft.
AIRFRAME: Wing section NACA 23012. All wooden structure, with Dacron covering on wings and rear fuselage. Glassfibre cabin top. Non-retractable tailwheel landing gear.
POWER PLANT: One 86 kW (115 hp) Textron Lycoming O-235-C1B. Two fuel tanks, each 54.5 litres (14.4 US gallons; 12 Imp gallons) capacity.
DIMENSIONS, EXTERNAL:
Wing span 7.92 m (26 ft 0 in)

Length overall 6.27 m (20 ft 7 in)
Height overall 2.29 m (7 ft 6 in)
Propeller diameter 1.68 m (5 ft 6 in)

AREA:
Wings, gross 10.96 m² (118.0 sq ft)

WEIGHTS:
Weight empty, equipped 428 kg (944 lb)
Max T-O weight 669 kg (1,475 lb)

PERFORMANCE (at max T-O weight):
Max level speed 123 knots (228 km/h; 142 mph)
Max cruising speed 117 knots (217 km/h; 135 mph)
Stalling speed 53 knots (97 km/h; 60 mph)
Max rate of climb at S/L over 305 m (1,000 ft)/min
Service ceiling 3,840 m (12,600 ft)
T-O run approx 228 m (750 ft)
Endurance, with 45 min reserves 3 h 36 min

ZENAIR

ZENAIR LTD

Huronia Airport, Midland, Ontario L4R 4K8
Telephone: (705) 526 2871
PRESIDENT AND DESIGNER: Christophe Heintz

Zenair began by marketing the Zénith two-seat homebuilt aircraft, and by early 1988 more than 400 Zéniths of all versions were flying. Its Zipper microlight series has recently been withdrawn.

ZENAIR MONO Z-CH 100

The single-seat Mono Z-CH 100 is of generally similar construction to the two-seat Zénith, but is smaller and less powerful. The prototype (C-GNYM) made its first flight on 8 May 1975.

Construction drawings and manual, materials, parts and complete kits are available, and at least 130 sets had been sold by early 1988. Building time is estimated at under 600 working hours.

TYPE: Single-seat homebuilt aircraft.

AIRFRAME: All-metal semi-monocoque construction. Wing section GAW-1 (modified). Non-retractable tricycle or, optionally, tailwheel landing gear.

POWER PLANT: One 41 kW (55 hp) 1,700 cc converted Volkswagen engine in prototype. Engines from 33.5 kW (45 hp) 1,600 cc Volkswagen to 74.5 kW (100 hp) Continental O-200 optional. Fuel capacity 55 litres (14.4 US gallons; 12 Imp gallons).

DIMENSIONS, EXTERNAL:
Wing span 6.71 m (22 ft 0 in)
Length overall 5.94 m (19 ft 6 in)
Height overall 1.98 m (6 ft 6 in)
Propeller diameter 1.47 m (4 ft 10 in)

AREA:
Wings, gross 8.50 m² (91.5 sq ft)

WEIGHTS (48.5 kW; 65 hp engine):
Weight empty 286 kg (630 lb)
Baggage capacity 11.3 kg (25 lb)
Max T-O weight 435 kg (960 lb)

PERFORMANCE (engine as above):
Max level speed 109 knots (200 km/h; 125 mph)
Cruising speed (75% power) 95 knots (177 km/h; 110 mph)
Stalling speed 42 knots (77 km/h; 48 mph)
Max rate of climb at S/L 250 m (820 ft)/min
Service ceiling over 3,660 m (12,000 ft)
T-O and landing run 168 m (550 ft)
Range with max fuel 350 nm (645 km; 400 miles)
g limits ±9 ultimate

ZENAIR ACRO-ZÉNITH CH 150

Developed from the Mono Z-CH 100, the CH 150 is intended for aerobatic training and competition flying. The prototype first flew on 19 May 1980. Kits, complete except for engine, are available to amateur constructors. All of the more critical parts, such as wing spars and ribs, are premanufactured.

TYPE: Single-seat homebuilt aircraft.

AIRFRAME: All-metal semi-monocoque construction. Wing section NACA 0015. Non-retractable tailwheel landing gear. Skis optional.

POWER PLANT: One 112 kW (150 hp) Textron Lycoming O-320 standard. Engines of 74.5-134 kW (100-180 hp) can be fitted. Fuel capacity 55 litres (14.4 US gallons; 12 Imp gallons). Can be increased to 136 litres (36 US gallons; 30 Imp gallons) by use of ferry tank. Fuel and oil systems equipped for inverted flight.

DIMENSIONS, EXTERNAL:
Wing span 6.15 m (20 ft 2 in)
Length overall 6.17 m (20 ft 3 in)
Height overall 1.52 m (5 ft 0 in)
Propeller diameter 1.78 m (5 ft 10 in)

AREA:
Wings, gross 7.83 m² (84.3 sq ft)

WEIGHTS (112 kW; 150 hp O-320 engine. Wooden propeller and ferry tank fitted. No electrics):
Weight empty 331 kg (730 lb)
Typical aerobatic T-O weight 440 kg (970 lb)
Baggage capacity 20 kg (44 lb)
Max T-O weight 522 kg (1,150 lb)

PERFORMANCE (conditions as above):
Max level speed at S/L 156 knots (290 km/h; 180 mph)
Econ cruising speed at 915 m (3,000 ft) 126 knots (233 km/h; 145 mph)
Stalling speed 48 knots (89 km/h; 55 mph)
Max rate of climb at S/L 670 m (2,200 ft)/min
Service ceiling over 4,875 m (16,000 ft)
T-O run 213 m (700 ft)
Landing run 183 m (600 ft)
Range with standard fuel 260 nm (483 km; 300 miles)
Range at 55% power, with ferry fuel 660 nm (1,223 km; 760 miles)
Endurance 2 h
g limits ±12 ultimate

ZENAIR SUPER ACRO-ZÉNITH CH 180

The first Super Acro-Zénith CH 180 (C-GZEN) was an unlimited aerobatic aircraft, powered by a 171.5 kW (230 hp) Textron Lycoming IO-360 engine. It differed from the Acro-Zénith CH 150 in several respects, apart from engine, the most obvious external changes being a revised tail unit and wings without dihedral. The front fuel tank capacity is 45.5 litres (12 US gallons; 10 Imp gallons) and the rear, with header, 77 litres (20.4 US gallons; 17 Imp gallons). Construction time is 800 working hours. Engines of up to 149 kW (200 hp) can be fitted.

DIMENSIONS, EXTERNAL:
Wing span 6.15 m (20 ft 2 in)
Length overall 6.17 m (20 ft 3 in)
Height overall 1.65 m (5 ft 5 in)

AREA:
Wings, gross 7.90 m² (85.0 sq ft)

WEIGHTS:
Weight empty 363 kg (800 lb)
Max T-O weight 521 kg (1,150 lb)

PERFORMANCE (149 kW; 200 hp engine):
Cruising speed (75% power) 165 knots (305 km/h; 190 mph)
Stalling speed 42 knots (77 km/h; 48 mph)
Max rate of climb at S/L 915 m (3,000 ft)/min
Max rate of roll 270°/s
Range with max fuel, 55% power (123 litres; 27 Imp gallons of fuel) 565 nm (1,046 km; 650 miles)
g limits: ±8 normal
±12 ultimate

ZENAIR ZÉNITH-CH 200

The prototype Zénith-CH 200 flew for the first time on 22 March 1970. Sets of plans and a constructional manual are available to amateur builders, together with materials, parts and complete kits. By early 1988 many hundreds of kits and sets of plans for the CH 200 and generally similar CH 250 (which see) had been sold to customers in 44 countries; at least 120 kits have been assembled and 28 aircraft built from plans.

The following description applies to the standard Zénith-CH 200:

TYPE: Side by side two-seat, dual-control homebuilt aircraft.

AIRFRAME: All-metal semi-monocoque construction, except for glassfibre engine cowling and fairings. NACA 64A515 (modified) wing section. Plans show rudder only, with no fin. Conventional fin and rudder can be fitted if desired. Non-retractable tricycle or, optionally, tailwheel landing gear. Floats and skis optional.

POWER PLANT: Design suitable for engines from 63.5 kW (85 hp) to 119 kW (160 hp). Fuel capacity 90 litres (24 US gallons; 20 Imp gallons). Optional fuel tanks in wing leading-edges, total capacity 72.5 litres (19.2 US gallons; 16 Imp gallons).

DIMENSIONS, EXTERNAL:
Wing span 7.00 m (22 ft 11¾ in)
Length overall 6.25 m (20 ft 6 in)
Height overall 2.11 m (6 ft 11 in)
Propeller diameter 1.83 m (6 ft 0 in)

AREA:
Wings, gross 9.80 m² (105.9 sq ft)

WEIGHTS (93 kW; 125 hp engine):
Weight empty 422 kg (930 lb)
Baggage capacity 35 kg (77 lb)
Max T-O weight 680 kg (1,500 lb)

PERFORMANCE (at max T-O weight. 93 kW; 125 hp engine):
Max level speed at S/L 131 knots (243 km/h; 151 mph)
Cruising speed (75% power) at S/L 122 knots (227 km/h; 141 mph)
Stalling speed, flaps down 47 knots (87 km/h; 54 mph)
Max rate of climb at S/L 335 m (1,100 ft)/min
T-O and landing run 244 m (800 ft)
Range with max fuel 391 nm (724 km; 450 miles)
g limit +9 ultimate

ZENAIR ZÉNITH-CH 250

The Zénith-CH 250 is a de luxe version of the Zénith-CH 200 with two 65 litre (16.8 US gallon; 14 Imp gallon) fuel tanks in the wings and a 0.71 m³ (25 cu ft) baggage area. A forward sliding canopy and rear windows similar to those of the Tri-Z CH 300 are fitted. Recommended engines are in the 86-119 kW (115-160 hp) range. A tailwheel or float landing gear can be fitted as alternatives to the standard tricycle type.

WEIGHTS (112 kW; 150 hp engine):
Weight empty 449 kg (990 lb)
Max T-O weight 730 kg (1,610 lb)

PERFORMANCE (engine as above):
Max level speed 144 knots (267 km/h; 166 mph)
Cruising speed (75% power) 130 knots (241 km/h; 150 mph)
Stalling speed 45 knots (84 km/h; 52 mph)
Max rate of climb at S/L 518 m (1,700 ft)/min
T-O and landing run 198 m (650 ft)
Range with standard fuel 469 nm (869 km; 540 miles)

ZENAIR TRI-Z CH 300

The three-seat Tri-Z CH 300 is a 'stretched' version of the two-seat CH 200, with an enlarged cabin to provide room for a rear bench seat able to carry a third adult, two children or 95 kg (210 lb) of baggage. Electrically actuated slotted flaps are fitted. Recommended power is in the 93-134 kW (125-180 hp) range. Fuel is carried in two 65 litre (16.8 US gallon; 14 Imp gallon) wing tanks. Extra fuel can be carried in further wing tanks. The prototype made its first flight on 9 July 1977.

Sets of plans and a constructional manual are available to amateur builders, as are materials, prefabricated component parts and complete kits. Construction from kits takes 1,000 working hours on average.

DIMENSIONS, EXTERNAL:
Wing span 8.10 m (26 ft 6¾ in)
Length overall 6.85 m (22 ft 5¾ in)
Height overall 2.08 m (6 ft 10 in)

AREA:
Wings, gross 12.00 m² (129.2 sq ft)

WEIGHTS (93 kW; 125 hp engine):
Weight empty 476 kg (1,050 lb)
Max T-O weight 816 kg (1,800 lb)

PERFORMANCE (engine as above):
Max level speed 130 knots (241 km/h; 150 mph)
Econ cruising speed 109 knots (201 km/h; 125 mph)
Stalling speed, flaps down 45 knots (82 km/h; 51 mph)
Max rate of climb at S/L 244 m (800 ft)/min
Range (75% power) 521 nm (965 km; 600 miles)
g limits ±5.7 ultimate

ZENAIR ZODIAC CH 600

The first flight of the CH 60 was achieved in June 1984. Plans and a kit of component parts (45 per cent premanufactured) for the improved CH 600 are available to amateur builders. Construction from a kit takes about 400 working hours. It is suited to the first time builder.

TYPE: Side by side two-seat, dual-control homebuilt aircraft.

AIRFRAME: All-metal construction. No fixed fin. Wing section NACA 65018. Non-retractable tricycle or tailwheel landing gear. Skis and floats optional.

POWER PLANT: One 48.5 kW (65 hp) JPX modified 1,875 cc Volkswagen, 47.7 kW (64 hp) Rotax 532, 48.5-74.5 kW (65-100 hp) Continental, 37.3 kW (50 hp) VW without electric starting or 52 kW (70 hp) VW engine. Fuel capacity 60 litres (16 US gallons; 13.3 Imp gallons).

DIMENSIONS, EXTERNAL:
Wing span 8.20 m (26 ft 10¾ in)
Length overall 5.65 m (18 ft 6½ in)
Height overall 1.90 m (6 ft 2¾ in)
Propeller diameter 1.52 m (5 ft 0 in)

AREA:
Wings, gross 12.1 m² (130.2 sq ft)

WEIGHTS:
Weight empty, equipped 268 kg (590 lb)
Max T-O weight 476 kg (1,050 lb)

PERFORMANCE (at max T-O weight):
Max level speed at S/L 100 knots (185 km/h; 115 mph)
Econ cruising speed 87 knots (161 km/h; 100 mph)
Stalling speed 39 knots (71 km/h; 44 mph)
Max rate of climb at S/L 219 m (720 ft)/min
Service ceiling 3,050 m (10,000 ft)
T-O run 183 m (600 ft)
Landing run 200 m (656 ft)
Range with max fuel, 75% power 364 nm (676 km; 420 miles)
Endurance 4 h
g limits ±6.9

ZENAIR STOL CH 701

The prototype of this Experimental category aircraft was flown for the first time in Summer 1986. The CH 701 is a strut braced high-wing cabin monoplane, capable of being completed with a tricycle or tailwheel landing gear, and with floats, amphibious and ski gears as options. Power is provided by a 37.3 kW (50 hp) Rotax 503 engine in the prototype, but a 47.7 kW (64 hp) Rotax 532, 44.7-52 kW (60-70 hp) VW, or 48.5-67 kW (65-90 hp) Continental engine are optional alternatives. To achieve STOL performance, full span leading-edge flaps are fitted to the near constant chord wings. An agricultural version is available with a Micro AG spraying/dusting system.

DIMENSIONS, EXTERNAL:
Wing span 8.23 m (27 ft 0 in)
Length overall 5.49 m (18 ft 0 in)
Propeller diameter 1.73 m (5 ft 8 in)

Ultravia Pelican Club GS with optional tricycle landing gear

Zenair Zénith-CH 200 with float landing gear

Ultravia LongNose Pelican

Zenair Zénith-CH 250 homebuilt (*Geoffrey P. Jones*)

Prototype Western PGK-1 Hirondelle two-seat light aircraft

Zenair Zodiac CH 600 with a tricycle landing gear

Zenair Mono Z-CH 100 with optional tailwheel landing gear (*Neil A. Macdougall*)

Super Acro-Zénith CH 180 unlimited aerobatic aircraft (*Neil A. Macdougall*)

Prototype Zenair STOL CH 701

AREA:
Wings, gross   11.33 m² (122.0 sq ft)
WEIGHTS:
Weight empty   195 kg (430 lb)
Max T-O weight   399 kg (880 lb)
PERFORMANCE (48.5 kW; 65 hp engine, at max T-O weight):
Max level speed at S/L   74 knots (137 km/h; 85 mph)
Normal cruising speed   65 knots (121 km/h; 75 mph)
Max rate of climb at S/L   366 m (1,200 ft)/min
T-O run   37 m (120 ft)
Landing run   28 m (90 ft)
g limits   ±6

ZENAIR ZÉNITH CH 2000

Fitting into the Zenair range as a side by side two-seat and smaller span derivative of the Tri-Z CH 300, the Zénith CH 2000 is intended to conform to Canadian Recreational category regulations, but is aimed at the primary training market. The first flight was scheduled for Summer 1988.

AIRFRAME: All-metal construction. Wing section LS (1) 0417 (mod). Non-retractable tricycle landing gear, with optional floats and skis.

POWER PLANT: One 74.5 kW (100 hp) Continental O-200. Fuel capacity 100 litres (26.4 US gallons; 22 Imp gallons)

standard, 200 litres (52.8 US gallons; 44 Imp gallons) optional.
DIMENSIONS, EXTERNAL:
Wing span   7.60 m (24 ft 11¼ in)
Length overall   6.85 m (22 ft 5¾ in)
Height overall   2.30 m (7 ft 6½ in)
Propeller diameter   1.83 m (6 ft 0 in)
AREA:
Wings, gross   11.00 m² (118.4 sq ft)
WEIGHTS (A: aerobatic category, B: standard):
Max payload: A   180 kg (396 lb)
B, with baggage   230 kg (507 lb)

Max T-O weight: A	630 kg (1,389 lb)	Stalling speed	42 knots (78 km/h; 49 mph)	Range with max standard and optional fuel:		
B	680 kg (1,499 lb)	Max rate of climb at S/L	259 m (850 ft)/min	B	928 nm (1,720 km; 1,068 miles)	

PERFORMANCE (estimated):
Max level speed 124 knots (230 km/h; 143 mph)
Econ cruising speed 103 knots (190 km/h; 118 mph)

Service ceiling more than 3,660 m (12,000 ft)
T-O run 213 m (700 ft)
Landing run 183 m (600 ft)

Range with max payload and standard fuel:
B 464 nm (860 km; 534 miles)

CHINA
(PEOPLE'S REPUBLIC)

BIAA
BEIJING INSTITUTE OF AERONAUTICS & ASTRONAUTICS
37 Xue yuan Road, Beijing 100083
Telephone: 201 7251
Telex: 22036 BIAAT CN
VICE-PRESIDENT: Shen Shituan

In addition to microlights, which are available in both ready assembled and kit forms, the Beijing Institute of Aeronautics & Astronautics has built the Mifeng-6 (Bee-6) hot-air airship (see Lighter-than-Air section).

BIAA MIFENG-2 (BEE-2)
The **Mifeng-1**, described and illustrated in the 1982-83 *Jane's*, was a single-seat microlight aircraft with a Rogallo type wing. The prototype **Mifeng-2**, like the Mifeng-1, was first flown in radio-controlled form (in 1982) before piloted tests began. It utilised the same fuselage, landing gear and 11.2 kW (15 hp) power plant as the Mifeng-1, but had new single-surface rectangular planform semi-rigid wings, with dihedral, conventional tail surfaces and two-axis control (rudder and elevators).

The following details refer to the current production version, with 19.4 kW (26 hp) engine and three-axis control (ailerons, elevators and rudder).

DIMENSIONS, EXTERNAL:
Wing span 10.00 m (32 ft 9¾ in)
Length overall 5.05 m (16 ft 7 in)
Height overall 2.70 m (8 ft 10¼ in)
AREA:
Wings, gross 15.40 m² (165.8 sq ft)
WEIGHTS:
Weight empty 100 kg (220 lb)
Max T-O weight 220 kg (485 lb)
PERFORMANCE:
Max level speed 40 knots (75 km/h; 47 mph)
Stalling speed 22 knots (40 km/h; 25 mph)
T-O run 32 m (105 ft)
Landing run 45 m (148 ft)
Range 97 nm (180 km; 112 miles)

BIAA MIFENG-3 (BEE-3)
The two-seat Mifeng-3 sesquiplane was developed from the Mifeng-2. The prototype made its first flight on 21 August 1983, and this aircraft is now in production for agricultural operations, touring, flight training, forest protection and aerial photography. The main differences compared with the Mifeng-2 are a lengthened fuselage pod, additional short-span lower wings with N interplane struts, and a more powerful engine.

Mifeng-3s are flying in China, New Zealand, the USA and elsewhere.
TYPE: Tandem two-seat utility and touring microlight; conforms to BCAR Section S-CAP 482.

AIRFRAME: Steel tube fuselage pod, and aluminium alloy wing and tail unit structures, fabric covered. Three-axis control. Non-retractable tricycle landing gear.

POWER PLANT: One 31.3 kW (42 hp) Rotax 447. Fuel capacity 25 litres (6.6 US gallons; 5.5 Imp gallons).

DIMENSIONS, EXTERNAL:
Wing span 10.00 m (32 ft 9¾ in)
Length overall 6.14 m (20 ft 1¾ in)
Height overall 2.72 m (8 ft 11 in)
Propeller diameter 1.57 m (5 ft 2 in)
AREA:
Upper wing, gross 15.40 m² (168.0 sq ft)
WEIGHTS:
Weight empty 150 kg (331 lb)
Max T-O weight 330 kg (727 lb)
PERFORMANCE:
Max level speed 51 knots (95 km/h; 59 mph)
Cruising speed 35 knots (65 km/h; 40 mph)
Stalling speed 23 knots (42 km/h; 26 mph)
Rate of climb at S/L 132 m (433 ft)/min
Service ceiling 3,400 m (11,150 ft)
T-O run 54 m (177 ft)
Landing run 70 m (230 ft)
Max range 88 nm (163 km; 101 miles)
g limit +4

BIAA MIFENG-4 and 4A (BEE-4 and 4A)
The Mifeng-4 is a refinement of the Mifeng-3, utilising the same fuselage and engine. It is said to have improved controllability and performance, and is more suited to field work due to the reduced rigging time for the wings. Unlike the Mifeng-3, it has double-surface covering on the wings, and the lower wings are enlarged.

The Mifeng-4 has been used as a flying platform by TV stations and the Chinese Ministry of Nuclear Industry. It also established a Chinese national distance record for microlights, at more than 1,000 km.

A version of the Mifeng-4 with shorter-span wings and higher performance is known as the **Mifeng-4A**.

DIMENSIONS, EXTERNAL (Mifeng-4):
Wing span 10.44 m (34 ft 3 in)
Length overall 6.14 m (20 ft 1¾ in)
Height overall 2.38 m (7 ft 9¾ in)
Propeller diameter 1.73 m (5 ft 8 in)
WEIGHTS (Mifeng-4):
Weight empty 180 kg (397 lb)
Max T-O weight 380 kg (838 lb)
PERFORMANCE (Mifeng-4):
Max level speed 51 knots (95 km/h; 59 mph)
Cruising speed 35-38 knots (65-70 km/h; 40-43 mph)
Stalling speed 26 knots (48 km/h; 30 mph)
Max rate of climb at S/L 132 m (435 ft)/min
Service ceiling 3,200 m (10,500 ft)
T-O run 60 m (197 ft)
Range 86 nm (159 km; 99 miles)

BIAA MIFENG-5 (BEE-5)
In the Spring of 1985, BIAA co-operated with another factory to design a light multi-purpose aircraft suited to operations from grass. The first of two flight test prototypes flew in September 1985.

Compared with earlier Mifeng aeroplanes, the Mifeng-5 is larger, with tandem accommodation for three persons, or a 140 kg (309 lb) payload in addition to the pilot. It is three-axis control.

NAI
NANJING AERONAUTICAL INSTITUTE
29 Yudaojei Street, Nanjing, Jiangsu Province
Telephone: 46131 2152
Telex: 34155 NAINJ CN
PRESIDENT: Prof Yu Chenye

NAI AD-100 TRAVELLER
Brief details and an illustration of the all-composites AD-100 Traveller canard microlight can be found in the 1987-88 *Jane's*.

SHIJIAZHUANG
SHIJIAZHUANG AIRCRAFT PLANT
Shijiazhuang, Hebei Province

SHIJIAZHUANG QINGTING 5 series (DRAGONFLY 5)
First flown in late 1983, the **Qingting 5** single-seat microlight is powered by a 22.4 kW (30 hp) piston engine and carries 9 kg (19.8 lb) of fuel.

The side by side two-seat **Qingting 5A** is generally similar to the Qingting 5, with unchanged power plant; the tandem two-seat **Qingting 5B**, built in 1985, uses a 33.6 kW (45 hp) engine and is fitted with cockpit and side fairings.
TYPE: Single- and two-seat microlight.
DIMENSIONS, EXTERNAL (A: Qingting 5, B: Qingting 5A, C: Qingting 5B):
Wing span: A, B 10.55 m (34 ft 7½ in)
C 10.62 m (34 ft 10 in)
Length overall: A, B 5.36 m (17 ft 7 in)
C 5.77 m (18 ft 11¼ in)
Height overall: A, B 2.84 m (9 ft 3¾ in)
C 2.86 m (9 ft 4½ in)
Propeller diameter: A 1.32 m (4 ft 4 in)

AREAS (A, B and C as above):
Wings, gross: A, B, C 15.10 m² (162.5 sq ft)
WEIGHTS (A, B and C as above):
Weight empty: A 123 kg (271 lb)
B 135 kg (298 lb)
C 157 kg (346 lb)
Max T-O weight: A 241 kg (531 lb)
B 294 kg (648 lb)
C 320 kg (705 lb)
PERFORMANCE (A, B and C as above):
Max level speed: A 47 knots (88 km/h; 54 mph)
B 41 knots (77 km/h; 47 mph)
C 58 knots (107 km/h; 66 mph)
Normal cruising speed:
A 24-40 knots (45-75 km/h; 28-47 mph)
B 27-38 knots (50-70 km/h; 31-43 mph)
C 35 knots (65 km/h; 40 mph)
Max rate of climb at S/L: A 204 m (670 ft)/min
B 84 m (275 ft)/min
C 171 m (560 ft)/min
T-O run (grass): A 27 m (89 ft)
B 51 m (167 ft)
C 53 m (174 ft)
Landing run: A 33 m (108 ft)
B 23 m (76 ft)
C 65 m (213 ft)

Range: A 56 nm (104 km; 64 miles)
B 46.5 nm (86 km; 53 miles)
C 63 nm (117 km; 72 miles)

SHIJIAZHUANG QINGTING 6 (DRAGONFLY 6)
The Qingting 6 is a three-axis control single-seat homebuilt of more refined design than the Qingting 5 series of microlights. The structure is said to be all-metal. Power is provided by a 59.7 kW (80 hp) Revmaster engine.

DIMENSIONS, EXTERNAL:
Wing span 9.802 m (32 ft 2 in)
Length overall 6.676 m (21 ft 10¾ in)
Height overall 1.74 m (5 ft 8½ in)
AREA:
Wings, gross 11.52 m² (124.0 sq ft)
WEIGHTS:
Weight empty 253 kg (558 lb)
Max T-O weight 500 kg (1,102 lb)
PERFORMANCE:
Max level speed 70 knots (130 km/h; 81 mph)
Normal cruising speed 49 knots (90 km/h; 56 mph)
Max rate of climb at S/L 128 m (420 ft)/min
Service ceiling 3,500 m (11,480 ft)
T-O run 107 m (351 ft)
Landing run 87 m (285 ft)
Range 72 nm (134 km; 83 miles)

FINLAND

TERVAMÄKI
JUKKA TERVAMÄKI
Harmaapaadentie 12A, 00930 Helsinki 93

TERVAMÄKI JT-5
The prototype JT-5 autogyro flew for the first time on 7 January 1973. It was later sold, together with production

rights, tools and moulds, to Sig Vittorio Magni of Italy. In 1979 plans, component parts, materials and complete kits of the Magni-Tervamäki MT-5 were made available to

BIAA Mifeng-2 single-seat microlight in production form

BIAA Mifeng-5 three-seat multi-purpose light aircraft

BIAA Mifeng-4A, a development of the Mifeng-3

Shijiazhuang Qingting 5B with cockpit fairing

Shijiazhuang Qingting 6 homebuilt aircraft

Tervamäki JT-5 completed by Veikko and Matti Silvennoinen of Jyväskylä, Finland

amateur constructors by VPM SnC (via per Besnate 10, 21040 Jerago, Italy).

The following details apply to the standard JT-5:

TYPE: Single-seat homebuilt autogyro.

ROTOR SYSTEM: Two-blade semi-rigid rotor of glassfibre reinforced epoxy resin, with polyurethane plastics foam core. NACA 8-H-12 blade section. Rotor mast of steel tubing. Rotor head is compact offset-gimbal type with centrifugal teeter stops and rotor brake. Normal rotor rpm is 400, maximum 600. Rotor spin-up of 300 rpm can be achieved.

AIRFRAME: Basic structure of welded 4130 steel tubing with a glassfibre/RFB honeycomb sandwich cockpit. All internal cockpit structures of glassfibre reinforced epoxy resin. One-piece aluminium engine cowling. Central fin and rudder of glassfibre reinforced epoxy resin, with rigid

PVC foam ribs and Courtauld carbonfibre stiffeners. Horizontal tail and auxiliary endplate fins of glassfibre sandwich with honeycomb core. Non-retractable tricycle landing gear. Small tailwheel beneath fin.

POWER PLANT: One 56 kW (75 hp) 1.7 litre Volkswagen engine, converted for autogyro use by Limbach Motorenbau. Fuel capacity 50 litres (13.2 US gallons; 11 Imp gallons).

DIMENSIONS, EXTERNAL:

Rotor diameter	7.00 m (22 ft 11½ in)
Length of fuselage	3.50 m (11 ft 5¾ in)
Height overall	2.00 m (6 ft 6¾ in)
Propeller diameter	1.20 m (3 ft 11¼ in)

AREAS:

Rotor blades (each)	0.63 m² (6.78 sq ft)
Rotor disc	38.50 m² (414.4 sq ft)

WEIGHTS:

Weight empty, equipped	167 kg (368 lb)
Max T-O weight	290 kg (639 lb)

PERFORMANCE (at max T-O weight):

Max level speed at S/L	92 knots (170 km/h; 106 mph)
Econ cruising speed	70 knots (130 km/h; 81 mph)
Min level speed	19 knots (35 km/h; 22 mph)
Max rate of climb at S/L	180 m (590 ft)/min
Service ceiling	4,000 m (13,125 ft)
T-O run	70 m (230 ft)
Landing run	5 m (16 ft)
Range with max fuel, no reserves	
	189 nm (350 km; 217 miles)

FRANCE

AERMAS
AUTOMOBILES MARTINI SA
ZI, 58470 Magny-Cours
Telephone: 86 58 14 25

This company, well known for its Formula 3 racing cars, has developed an ultralight aircraft which was exhibited at the 1987 Paris Air Show.

AERMAS 386
TYPE: Side by side two-seat, dual-control microlight; conforms to FAR Pt 23 Normal category.

AIRFRAME: Light alloy two-spar wings with glassfibre leading-edge and fabric covering. Steel tube centre-frame, supporting wings, Kevlar reinforced glassfibre honeycomb sandwich cockpit pod, and light alloy boom carrying fabric covered light alloy tail unit. Three-axis control. Non-retractable tricycle landing gear.

POWER PLANT: One 38 kW (51 hp) Rotax 462.

DIMENSIONS, EXTERNAL:

Wing span	11.16 m (36 ft 7½ in)
Length overall	7.20 m (23 ft 7½ in)

AREA:

Wings, gross	17.5 m² (188.4 sq ft)

WEIGHTS:

Weight empty	174 kg (384 lb)
Max T-O weight	390 kg (860 lb)

PERFORMANCE:

Cruising speed	65 knots (120 km/h; 75 mph)
Max level speed in rough air	
	57 knots (105 km/h; 65 mph)
Stalling speed, pilot only	25 knots (45 km/h; 28 mph)
Max rate of climb at S/L, pilot only	270 m (885 ft)/min
g limits	+5.7/−2.8

AÈRODIS

AÈRODIS SARL

Notaire, Allee de la Ronce, 10340 Les Riceys
Telephone: 25 29 30 34
Telex: 830 607F
EXECUTIVE Alain Carsenti

GRINVALDS G-802 ORION

The original version of the Orion was the G-801, the prototype of which flew for the first time on 2 June 1981. A prototype of the developed G-802 first flew on 4 November 1983. Plans and kits of this version are marketed. Aerodis America Inc is no longer associated with the Orion.

The following description applies to the standard kit version of the G-802.

TYPE: Four-seat, dual-control homebuilt aircraft.
AIRFRAME: Wing and tail unit structures of glassfibre reinforced locally with Kevlar and carbonfibre. Wing section NACA 43015 at root, NACA 43012 at tip. Composites fuselage of glassfibre/epoxy resin, Kevlar and graphite reinforced. Retractable tricycle landing gear.
POWER PLANT: One 134 kW (180 hp) Textron Lycoming IO-360 in first Orion, driving a 'tail-pusher' propeller. Suited to engines of 112-149 kW (150-200 hp). Two fuel tanks, total capacity 220 litres (58 US gallons; 48.4 Imp gallons). Long range tanks available when flown with pilot and one passenger only, capacity 400 litres (106 US gallons; 88 Imp gallons), or 490 litres (129 US gallons; 108 Imp gallons) with pilot only.

DIMENSIONS, EXTERNAL:
Wing span	9.00 m (29 ft 6½ in)
Length overall	6.85 m (22 ft 5½ in)
Height overall	2.50 m (8 ft 2½ in)
Propeller diameter	1.50 m (4 ft 11 in)

AREA:
Wings, gross	11.22 m² (120.8 sq ft)

WEIGHTS (134 kW; 180 hp engine):
Weight empty, equipped	610 kg (1,345 lb)
Baggage capacity	30 kg (66 lb)
Max T-O weight	1,050 kg (2,315 lb)

PERFORMANCE (134 kW; 180 hp engine):
Max level speed at 2,440 m (8,000 ft)	178 knots (330 km/h; 205 mph)
Econ cruising speed at 2,440 m (8,000 ft)	135 knots (250 km/h; 155 mph)
Stalling speed: flaps up	54 knots (100 km/h; 63 mph)
20° flap	49 knots (90 km/h; 56 mph)
Max rate of climb at S/L	270 m (885 ft)/min
Service ceiling	4,500 m (14,775 ft)
T-O to 15 m (50 ft)	600 m (1,970 ft)
Landing run	200 m (655 ft)
Range at cruising speed, standard fuel	809 nm (1,500 km; 932 miles)
Max range with long range fuel tanks (65% power)	1,618 nm (3,000 km; 1,864 miles)

AÈRONAUTIC 2000

AÈRONAUTIC 2000

52 rue Galande, 75005 Paris
In 1987 Zenith-Aviation, which in 1983 had acquired from Aéronautic 2000 a full licence to build, market and support the latter's Baroudeur microlight, sold back its rights to Aéronautic 2000.

AÈRONAUTIC 2000 BAROUDEUR

The Baroudeur first flew in September 1981 and was subsequently developed in both single- and two-seat versions, of which only the two-seater remains current. The prototype two-seat Baroudeur flew for the first time in 1982. A military anti-tank version capable of carrying two or four rocket launchers was evaluated by the French Army in 1983, and by Indian pilots in 1984 as a military trainer and flying club aircraft. Details of rocket firing trials can be found in the 1987-88 *Jane's*.

The following details apply to the current two-seat version of the Baroudeur, in recreational and training form, unless stated otherwise.

TYPE: Side by side two-seat, dual-control microlight.
AIRFRAME: Duralumin mainframe. Double surface fabric covered wings and control surfaces. Wing section TK7315. Three-axis control. Non-retractable tricycle landing gear. Options include cockpit enclosure, floats, skis, recovery parachute and agricultural spraygear.
POWER PLANT: One 38 kW (51 hp) Rotax 462 or 37.3 kW (50 hp) Fuji Robin. Standard fuel capacity 20 litres (5.3 US gallons; 4.4 Imp gallons); 40 litre (10.6 US gallon; 8.8 Imp gallon) tank optional.
ARMAMENT: Four or six launchers for 89 mm Luchaire rockets can be carried underwing on military version.

DIMENSIONS, EXTERNAL:
Wing span	10.90 m (35 ft 9¼ in)
Length overall	5.60 m (18 ft 4½ in)
Height overall	2.40 m (7 ft 10½ in)
Propeller diameter	1.60 m (5 ft 3 in)

AREA:
Wings, gross	17.00 m² (182.99 sq ft)

WEIGHTS:
Weight empty	175 kg (385 lb)
Max T-O weight	385 kg (849 lb)

PERFORMANCE (at max T-O weight):
Max level speed at S/L	54 knots (100 km/h; 62 mph)
Econ cruising speed	38 knots (70 km/h; 43 mph)
Stalling speed	25 knots (45 km/h; 28 mph)
Max rate of climb at S/L	180 m (590 ft)/min
Service ceiling	3,000 m (9,840 ft)
T-O run	50 m (164 ft)
Landing run	40 m (132 ft)
Range: standard fuel	54 nm (100 km; 62 miles)
40 litre tank	151 nm (280 km; 174 miles)
Endurance: standard fuel	2 h
40 litre tank	3 h

AIR CREATION

AIR CREATION SARL

Z I Lavilledieu, 07170 Villeneuve-de-Berg
Telephone: 75 94 24 10
Telex: 345790F
Fax: 75 93 50 87
EXPORT MANAGER: Jean-Luc Tilloy

Air Creation offers three trike units, namely the single-seat Racer, 1 + 1 Safari G-T and two-seat Safari G-T BI, all except the Racer having a choice of various Air Creation wings to form microlights. The Safari G-T BI also has a choice of three Rotax engines. Crop-dusting and banner-towing versions of the Safari G-T are available. The following details refer to the Safari G-T BI and the Racer in completed microlight forms.

AIR CREATION SAFARI G-T BI

First flown in October 1982, a total of 415 ready-assembled microlights using Safari trikes had been sold by April 1988.

TYPE: Two-seat microlight.
AIRFRAME: Aluminium alloy trike unit. 40% double surface Plus 20, or 80% double-surface Quartz 18, or 90% double surface Quartz 16SX flexwings, with aluminium alloy frames, Mylar leading-edges and fabric surfaces (Trilam used on upper surface of Quartz). Optional composites cockpit fairing. Weight shift control. Tricycle landing gear; optional skis. (Safari G-T has a choice of 50% double surface Plus 17 or 90% double surface Quartz 16 flexwings.)
POWER PLANT: One 38.8 kW (52 hp) Rotax 462, or 31.3 kW (42 hp) Rotax 447, or 34 kW (45.6 hp) Rotax 503 engine. Fuel capacity 22 litres (5.8 US gallons; 4.8 Imp gallons) standard. Optional 20 litre (5.3 US gallon; 4.4 Imp gallon) auxiliary tank. (Safari G-T has Rotax 447.)

DIMENSIONS, EXTERNAL:
Wing span	10.00 m (32 ft 9¾ in)
Propeller diameter	1.50 m (4 ft 11 in)

AREA (Quartz 18):
Wings, gross	15.50 m² (166.84 sq ft)

WEIGHTS (Quartz 18 flexwing):
Weight empty	142 kg (313 lb)
Pilot weight range	40-120 kg (88-264 lb)
Max T-O weight	230 kg (507 lb)

PERFORMANCE (Quartz 18 flexwing and Rotax 462 engine):
Max level speed	59 knots (110 km/h; 68 mph)
Econ cruising speed	42 knots (78 km/h; 48 mph)
Stalling speed	22 knots (40 km/h; 25 mph)
Max rate of climb at S/L	210 m (690 ft)/min
Service ceiling	7,000 m (22,965 ft)
T-O run	50 m (164 ft)
Landing run	55 m (180 ft)
Range with max standard fuel	135 nm (250 km; 155 miles)
Endurance	2 h 30 min
g limits	+6/−3

AIR CREATION RACER

First flown in December 1986, the Racer uses only the Air Creation 12 SX flexwing which has 100% double surface covering. Trike construction is similar to that of the Safaris and power is provided by a 31.3 kW (42 hp) Rotax 447 engine, with similar fuel capacity.

DIMENSION, EXTERNAL:
Propeller diameter	1.45 m (4 ft 9 in)

WEIGHTS: As for Safari except:
Weight empty	110 kg (242 lb)

PERFORMANCE:
Max level speed	70 knots (130 km/h; 81 mph)
Econ cruising speed	46 knots (85 km/h; 53 mph)
Stalling speed	20 knots (37 km/h; 23 mph)
Max rate of climb at S/L	420 m (1,380 ft)/min
T-O run	40 m (131 ft)
Landing run	45 m (148 ft)
Range with standard fuel	135 nm (250 km; 155 miles)
Endurance	3 h 30 min
g limits	+6/−3

A.I.R'S SA

AIR INTERNATIONAL SERVICE

26 rue des Roses, 75018 Paris
Telephone: 48 03 36 34
The Maestro and Allegro are offered in ready assembled form, with a wide range of options.

A.I.R'S MAESTRO

TYPE: Two-seat microlight.
AIRFRAME: Constructed from AU4G 2217 aluminium alloy tubing, with fabric covered rigid wing and tail unit. Wing section NACA 4412. Three-axis control. Non-retractable tricycle landing gear. Skis, floats and cockpit fairing optional.
POWER PLANT: One 34 kW (45.6 hp) Rotax 503. Optional 38 kW (51 hp) Rotax or 47 kW (63 hp) Rotax 532; latter is standard on the agricultural version.

DIMENSIONS, EXTERNAL:
Wing span	10.50 m (34 ft 5½ in)
Length overall	5.50 m (18 ft 0½ in)
Height overall	2.55 m (8 ft 4½ in)

AREA:
Wings, gross	17.0 m² (183.0 sq ft)

WEIGHTS:
Weight empty	167 kg (368 lb)
Max T-O weight	380 kg (838 lb)

PERFORMANCE:
Max level speed	59 knots (110 km/h; 68 mph)
Cruising speed	49 knots (90 km/h; 56 mph)
Stalling speed	22 knots (40 km/h; 25 mph)
Max rate of climb at S/L	180 m (590 ft)/min
T-O run	40 m (131 ft)
Landing run	50 m (164 ft)
Endurance with standard fuel	1 h 30 min
g limits	+6/−4

A.I.R'S ALLEGRO

The three-axis single-seat Allegro was derived from the Maestro and is of similar construction and layout. A large cockpit fairing semi-encloses the seat.

POWER PLANT: One 26 kW (34.9 hp) Rotax 377 or 38 kW (51 hp) Rotax.

DIMENSIONS, EXTERNAL:
Wing span	9.00 m (29 ft 6¼ in)
Length overall	5.50 m (18 ft 0½ in)
Height overall	2.55 m (8 ft 4½ in)

AREA:
Wings, gross	13.50 m² (145.3 sq ft)

WEIGHTS:
Weight empty	125 kg (276 lb)
Max T-O weight	300 kg (661 lb)

PERFORMANCE:
Max level speed	75 knots (140 km/h; 87 mph)
Cruising speed	59 knots (110 km/h; 68 mph)
Stalling speed	22 knots (40 km/h; 25 mph)
Max rate of climb at S/L	300 m (985 ft)/min
T-O run	30 m (98 ft)
Landing run	50 m (164 ft)
Endurance	1 h 45 min
g limits	+8/−4

ASL

CLUB D'AVIONS SUPERS LÉGERS DU CHER

45 rue Guilbeau, 18000 Bourbes

ASL 18

The prototype ASL 18 first flew on 12 August 1986.
TYPE: Two-seat dual-control microlight.
AIRFRAME: Strut braced biplane of wood construction, with light alloy cabane and interplane struts. Dacron covering on wings and tail control surfaces, and glassfibre nose fairing. Lower wings pivoted for roll control. Wing section NACA 23009. Non-retractable tricycle landing gear.

Aermas 386 side by side two-seat ultralight

Air Creation Racer single-seat trike fitted with the 12 SX flexwing

The first Grinvalds G-802 Orion all-plastics homebuilt aircraft

A.I.R'S Maestro two-seat microlight *(Wolfgang Wagner)*

Aéronautic 2000 Baroudeur exhibited at 1987 Paris Air Show, with fully enclosed cockpit, new engine cowlings and spinner *(Brian M. Service)*

ASL 18 two-seat ultralight biplane *(Geoffrey P. Jones)*

POWER PLANT: One 1,600 cc converted Volkswagen motorcar engine.

DIMENSIONS, EXTERNAL:

Wing span, both	7.86 m (25 ft 9½ in)
Length overall	6.24 m (20 ft 5¾ in)
Propeller diameter	1.30 m (4 ft 3¼ in)

AREA:

Wings, gross	17.56 m² (189.0 sq ft)

WEIGHTS:

Weight empty	175 kg (386 lb)
Max T-O weight	365 kg (805 lb)

PERFORMANCE (estimated):

Max level speed	67 knots (125 km/h; 78 mph)
Stalling speed	25 knots (45 km/h; 28 mph)
Max rate of climb at S/L	144 m (472 ft)/min
g limits	+7/−3

AVIASUD

AVIASUD ENGINEERING SA

Zone Industrielle la Palud, 83600 Fréjus
Telephone: (33) 94 53 94 00
Telex: 461 172F AVIASUD
GENERAL MANAGER: François Goethals

In addition to marketing the Sirocco and Mistral, Aviasud distributes the Marco J-5 (see Hewa-Technics).

AVIASUD SIROCCO

The first flight of the Sirocco was achieved in July 1982. By early 1988 at least 160 had been built.

TYPE: Single-seat microlight aircraft; conforms to FAR Pt 103.

AIRFRAME: Mostly aluminium wing structure, with glass-fibre front D spar, 6005A-T6 aluminium rear spar and ribs, and double surface Dacron covering. MacCready TK 7315 (modified) aerofoil section. Fuselage boom of Kevlar reinforced glassfibre; fuselage pod of moulded glassfibre and polyester, with epoxy resin. Three-axis control. Integral tail fin stiffened with Klegecell PVC foam ribs. Non-retractable tricycle landing gear. Floats and skis optional.

POWER PLANT: One 26 kW (35 hp) Rotax 377, 17 kW (23 hp) König 430RD, 22.4 kW (30 hp) KFM 107ER or 19.4 kW (26 hp) JPX PUL 425. Fuel capacity 20 litres (5.3 US gallons; 4.4 Imp gallons) standard, 40 litres (10.6 US gallons; 8.8 Imp gallons) optional.

DIMENSIONS, EXTERNAL:

Wing span	10.12 m (33 ft 2½ in)
Length overall	5.85 m (19 ft 2¼ in)
Height overall	2.80 m (9 ft 2¼ in)
Propeller diameter (Rotax engine)	1.45 m (4 ft 9 in)

AREA:

Wings, gross	13.80 m² (148.5 sq ft)

WEIGHTS:

Weight empty	114-130 kg (251-286 lb)
Pilot weight range	55-120 kg (121-264 lb)
Baggage capacity	30 kg (66 lb)
Max T-O weight	250 kg (551 lb)

PERFORMANCE:

Max level speed	62 knots (115 km/h; 71 mph)
Econ cruising speed	43 knots (80 km/h; 50 mph)
Stalling speed, engine idling	21 knots (40 km/h; 25 mph)
Max rate of climb at S/L	300 m (985 ft)/min
Service ceiling	6,500 m (21,325 ft)
T-O run	35 m (115 ft)
Landing run	30-50 m (98-164 ft)
Range with standard fuel	162 nm (300 km; 186 miles)
Range with max fuel	270 nm (500 km; 310 miles)
Endurance with max standard fuel	4 h
g limits	+6.7/−3.6

AVIASUD MISTRAL

The Mistral is designed for recreational flying but is also suited to professional activities normally performed by high-cost conventional aeroplanes and helicopters, such as pilot training, aerial photography, TV and surveillance, banner towing, and cropspraying. It is sold in ready to fly form.

TYPE: Side by side two-seat microlight and ARV aircraft; designed to FAR Pt 23.

AIRFRAME: Braced biplane, with NACA 23012 wing section. Duralumin wing spars and wooden ribs, double surface covered; tail unit similarly constructed. Glassfibre/carbonfibre/epoxy and polyester semi-monocoque fuselage. Three-axis control. Non-retractable tricycle landing gear, with optional floats and skis.

POWER PLANT: One 47 kW (63 hp) Rotax 532. Fuel capacity 68 litres (18 US gallons; 15 Imp gallons).

DIMENSIONS, EXTERNAL:

Wing span	9.40 m (30 ft 10 in)
Length overall	5.90 m (19 ft 4 in)
Height overall	2.20 m (7 ft 2½ in)
Propeller diameter	1.70 m (5 ft 7 in)

AREA:

Wings, gross	17.90 m² (192.7 sq ft)

WEIGHTS:

Weight empty	174 kg (383 lb)

Baggage capacity	20 kg (44 lb)
Max T-O weight	400 kg (882 lb)

PERFORMANCE (at max T-O weight):

Max level speed at S/L	81 knots (150 km/h; 93 mph)
Econ cruising speed	54 knots (100 km/h; 62 mph)
Stalling speed:	
power on	30 knots (55 km/h; 34.5 mph)
power off	33 knots (60 km/h; 38 mph)
Max rate of climb at S/L	240 m (785 ft)/min
Service ceiling	4,000 m (13,125 ft)
T-O and landing run	80 m (262 ft)
Range	270 nm (500 km; 310 miles)
Endurance	8 h

AVIASUD MISTRAL 503

Also in production is this new version of the Mistral, which offers improved economy. A superlight version, with an empty weight of 149.9 kg (330 lb), has been developed for the Federal German market.

POWER PLANT: One 37.3 kW (50 hp) Rotax 503. Fuel capacity 33 litres (8.7 US gallons; 7.3 Imp gallons).

PERFORMANCE (two crew of 75 kg; 165 lb each, full fuel):

Max level speed	70 knots (130 km/h; 81 mph)

g limits	+4/–2 design
	+6/–3 ultimate

Max cruising speed	49 knots (90 km/h; 56 mph)
Stalling speed: power on	30 knots (55 km/h; 34 mph)
power off	32 knots (58 km/h; 36 mph)
Max rate of climb at S/L	180 m (590 ft)/min
Service ceiling	3,000 m (9,850 ft)
T-O run	100 m (330 ft)
Landing run	80 m (262 ft)
Range	162 nm (300 km; 186 miles)
Endurance	4 h
g limits	+4/–2 limit
	+6/–3 ultimate

BROC
BERNARD BROC ENTERPRISE
Route de Freycenet, Borne, 43350 St Paulien
Telephone: 71 00 43 21
PROPRIETOR: Bernard Broc

BROC PAPILLON

A single prototype has been built of this tandem-wing microlight, which first flew in 1985. It is unclear whether it is intended for future marketing to amateur builders.

TYPE: Single-seat microlight.

AIRFRAME: Aluminium alloy wings and glassfibre fuselage pod. Three-axis control. Non-retractable tricycle landing gear. Floats optional.

POWER PLANT: Two small radial engines. Fuel capacity 47 litres (12.4 US gallons; 10.3 Imp gallons).

DIMENSIONS, EXTERNAL:

Length overall	2.90 m (9 ft 6¼ in)
Height overall	1.50 m (4 ft 11 in)
Propeller diameter (each)	1.05 m (3 ft 5½ in)

WEIGHTS:

Weight empty	170 kg (375 lb)
Max T-O weight	320 kg (705 lb)

PERFORMANCE:

Max cruising speed	65 knots (120 km/h; 75 mph)
Econ cruising speed	54 knots (100 km/h; 62 mph)
Max rate of climb at S/L	240 m (785 ft)/min
Service ceiling	4,000 m (13,125 ft)
T-O run	70 m (230 ft)
Landing run	60 m (197 ft)
Range	323 nm (600 km; 372 miles)
Endurance	5 h 30 min
g limits	+6/–3

CENTRAIR
SA CENTRAIR
Aérodrome Le Blanc, BP 44, 36300 Le Blanc
Telephone: (54) 37 07 96
Telex: 750 272 F

CENTRAIR PARAFAN

Development of this parawing microlight was started in November 1984. Many Parafans have been delivered, some to the armed forces of France and foreign countries. This aircraft offers pendulum stability in flight, and can be landed safely power-off. The maximum acceptable wind speed on the ground for take-off is a steady 12 knots (22 km/h; 14 mph), without major gusting.

TYPE: Single-seat parawing microlight.

AIRFRAME: Welded AG3 aluminium alloy trike unit, suspended under an eleven-cell NASA type ram air sports parachute wing (manufactured by PF and Aérazur) by two clusters of steering cables. Two-axis control. Non-retractable tricycle landing gear.

POWER PLANT: One 29.4 kW (39.4 hp) Rotax 447. Fuel capacity 20 litres (5.3 US gallons; 4.4 Imp gallons).

DIMENSIONS, EXTERNAL:

Parawing span	10.10 m (33 ft 1¾ in)
Trike: length	2.40 m (7 ft 10½ in)
width	1.70 m (5 ft 7 in)
height	1.70 m (5 ft 7 in)

AREA:

Parawing, gross	31.40 m² (338.0 sq ft)

WEIGHTS:

Weight empty	105 kg (231 lb)
Max payload	100 kg (220 lb)

PERFORMANCE:

Cruising speed	22-24 knots (40-45 km/h; 25-28 mph)
Max rate of climb	90-120 m (295-395 ft)/min
Theoretical ceiling	3,500 m (11,480 ft)
T-O run (no wind):	
with ground assistance	20-40 m (66-131 ft)
without ground assistance	30-50 m (98-164 ft)
Landing run (no wind)	0-20 m (0-66 ft)

CENTRAIR PARAFAN II

This is a two-seat version of the Parafan, powered by a 34 kW (45.6 hp) Rotax 503 or 38 kW (51 hp) Rotax 462 engine. Fuel capacity remains the same.

DIMENSIONS, EXTERNAL:

Parawing span	10.00 m (32 ft 9¾ in)
Trike: length	2.70 m (8 ft 10¼ in)
width	1.70 m (5 ft 7 in)
height	1.80 m (5 ft 11 in)

AREA:

Parawing, gross	44.0 m² (473.6 sq ft)

WEIGHTS:

Weight empty	140 kg (309 lb)
Max payload	200 kg (441 lb)

PERFORMANCE:

Cruising speed	27-31 knots (50-58 km/h; 31-36 mph)
Max rate of climb	90-240 m (295-785 ft)/min
Theoretical ceiling	3,500 m (11,480 ft)
T-O run (no wind):	
with ground assistance	20-40 m (66-131 ft)
without ground assistance	30-50 m (98-164 ft)

CHASLE
YVES CHASLE
8 Lotissement-Concorde, Odos, 65310 Laloubére

CHASLE YC-100/101/110/111 HIRONDELLE (SWALLOW)

The YC-100 prototype first flew on 1 May 1985. Plans are available in four versions, as follows:

YC-100. With wings of 3.20.16Y section, derived from the Aérospatiale V.16F aerofoil. Powered by a 16.4 kW (22 hp) JPX PUL 425/503 or 18 kW (24 hp) König SC 430 engine. Prototype has König SC 430. Second aircraft, built in Brazil, has JPX.

YC-101. Generally similar to YC-100, but with increased wing span. Recommended power plants are JPX PUL 865, 21 kW (28 hp) König SD 570 and 22.4 kW (30 hp) KFM 107ER.

YC-110. Generally similar to YC-100, but with wings of NACA 23015 section and with two-section auxiliary

aerofoil ailerons of the type fitted to many wartime Junkers aircraft, of almost full span. Recommended power plants as for YC-100, plus 21 kW (28 hp) König SD 570.

YC-111. Generally similar to YC-110, but with increased wing span. Recommended power plants are König SD 570, KFM 107ER, JPX PUL 865, 26 kW (34.9 hp) Rotax 377 or 29.4 kW (39.4 hp) Rotax 447.

TYPE: Single-seat microlight.

AIRFRAME: Strut braced, of fabric covered wooden construction, except for Styrofoam wing ribs. Non-retractable tricycle landing gear. Three-axis control.

POWER PLANT: As described under model listings. Fuel capacity 24 litres (6.3 US gallons; 5.3 Imp gallons).

DIMENSIONS, EXTERNAL (A: YC-100, B: YC-101, C: YC-110, D: YC-111):

Wing span: A	8.30 m (27 ft 2¾ in)
B, D	9.35 m (30 ft 8¼ in)
C	8.25 m (27 ft 0¾ in)

Length overall: all models	5.43 m (17 ft 9¾ in)
Height overall: all models	1.71 m (5 ft 7½ in)

AREAS:

Wings, gross: A	11.25 m² (121.1 sq ft)
B	12.85 m² (138.3 sq ft)
C	12.55 m² (135.1 sq ft)
D	13.50 m² (145.3 sq ft)

WEIGHTS:

Weight empty: A	110 kg (243 lb)
C	118 kg (260 lb)
Max T-O weight: A	210 kg (463 lb)
C	218 kg (480 lb)

PERFORMANCE:

Max level speed: A	70 knots (130 km/h; 80 mph)
Cruising speed: A, C	54 knots (100 km/h; 62 mph)
Stalling speed: A, C	25 knots (45 km/h; 28 mph)
T-O run: A, on grass	under 100 m (330 ft)
Landing run: A, on grass	25-30 m (82-100 ft)

COLOMBAN
MICHEL COLOMBAN
37*bis* rue Lakanal, 92500 Rueil-Malmaison
Telephone: 47 51 88 76

In addition to marketing plans and a manual for building the Cricri light aircraft, M Michel Colomban is completing the prototype of a new side by side two-seater. It is similar in construction to the Cricri, lightweight, and capable of being dismantled in three minutes for transport on a trailer. No details are yet available except that it is intended to be economical to operate, while offering good performance and aerobatic capability.

COLOMBAN MC 15 CRICRI

The MC 10 Cricri prototype was first flown on 19 July 1973. Early amateur-built Cricris were designated MC 12 and used Valmet SM 160J engines. The current model is the JPX powered MC 15. The Cricri is said to handle like a single-engined aircraft. This results from the fact that the two small engines are mounted close together, and from the carefully conceived shape of the cockpit canopy which

deflects the propeller slipstream over the tail surfaces in such a way that the failure of one engine produces no dangerous handling problems. Plans are available in the French and English languages, with European standard metric dimensions; 458 sets had been sold by early 1988 to amateur builders in France and neighbouring countries, and between 50 and 60 aircraft were then flying.

TYPE: Single-seat light homebuilt aircraft.

AIRFRAME: Entire basic structure is of light alloy, except for Klégécel ribs in wings and tail unit, and Klégécel stringers in fuselage. Laminar-flow aerofoil derived from a Wortmann section. Full span auxiliary aerofoil wing flaps operate collectively as high-lift devices and differentially as ailerons. Non-retractable tricycle landing gear.

POWER PLANT: Two JPX PUL 212 engines, each rated at 11 kW (15 hp). Fuel capacity 23 litres (6 US gallons; 5 Imp gallons).

DIMENSIONS, EXTERNAL:

Wing span	4.90 m (16 ft 0¾ in)
Length overall	3.91 m (12 ft 10 in)
Height overall	1.20 m (3 ft 11¼ in)
Propeller diameter	0.695 m (2 ft 3½ in)

AREA:

Wings, gross	3.10 m² (33.4 sq ft)

WEIGHTS:

Weight empty	80 kg (176 lb)
Max T-O and landing weight	170 kg (375 lb)

PERFORMANCE (MC 15 at max T-O weight):

Max speed measured in dive	159 knots (295 km/h; 183 mph)
Max cruising speed (75% power)	108 knots (200 km/h; 124 mph)
Stalling speed:	
flaps down	39 knots (72 km/h; 45 mph)
flaps up	50 knots (93 km/h; 58 mph)
Max rate of climb at S/L	390 m (1,280 ft)/min
Service ceiling	5,000 m (16,400 ft)
T-O run	100 m (330 ft)
Landing run	150 m (495 ft)
Range with max fuel	215 nm (400 km; 248 miles)
g limits	+9/–4.5 ultimate

Aviasud Mistral microlight/ARV *(Geoffrey P. Jones)*

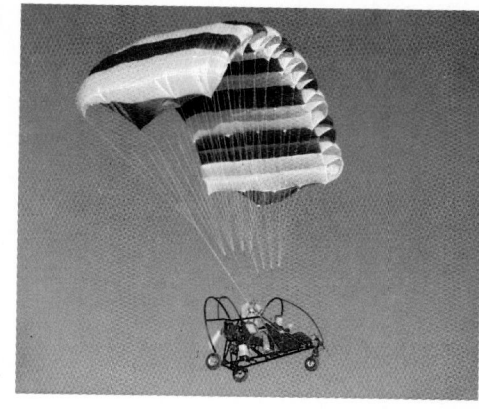

Centrair Parafan II two-seat parawing microlight

Prototype Chasle YC-100 Hirondelle microlight monoplane

Aviasud Sirocco single-seat microlight aircraft

Colomban MC 15 in inverted flight

Bernard Broc Papillon microlight

Coupé-Aviation JC-01 two-seat lightplane

COUPÉ-AVIATION
JACQUES COUPÉ
La Trute, Azay-sur-Cher, 37270 Montlouis sur Loire
Telephone: (47) 50 41 84

COUPÉ-AVIATION JC-01
The prototype JC-01 was flown for the first time on 16 March 1976. Plans are available to amateur constructors, together with plans of the more powerful JC-2.
TYPE: Two-seat, dual-control homebuilt sporting aircraft.
AIRFRAME: All-wood structure, with fabric covered wings, rear fuselage, and flying control surfaces. Non-retractable tailwheel landing gear.
POWER PLANT: One 48.5 kW (65 hp) Continental A65-8F. Fuel capacity 60 litres (15.9 US gallons; 13 Imp gallons).
DIMENSIONS, EXTERNAL:
Wing span   8.35 m (27 ft 4¾ in)
Length overall   6.40 m (21 ft 0 in)
AREA:
Wings, gross   11.69 m² (125.83 sq ft)
WEIGHTS:
Weight empty   330 kg (728 lb)
Max T-O weight   580 kg (1,279 lb)

PERFORMANCE (as originally flown, at max T-O weight):
Max level speed   108 knots (200 km/h; 124 mph)
Econ cruising speed   76 knots (140 km/h; 87 mph)
T-O speed   27 knots (50 km/h; 31 mph)
Stalling speed   25 knots (45 km/h; 28 mph)
T-O run   90 m (295 ft)

COUPÉ-AVIATION JC-2
The JC-2 is generally similar to the JC-01 but has a more powerful engine and tricycle landing gear. The prototype first flew in May 1981. At least six JC-2s are under construction by amateurs or have flown, with 74.5 kW (100 hp) engines. It was intended to market the JC-2 also in kit form.
TYPE: Side by side two-seat homebuilt aircraft.
AIRFRAME: All-wood structure, with Dacron covered wings, ailerons, flaps, rear fuselage, elevators and rudder. Wing section NACA 23012. Non-retractable tricycle landing gear.
POWER PLANT: One 67 kW (90 hp) Continental engine in prototype. Fuel capacity 90 litres (23.8 US gallons; 19.75 Imp gallons).

DIMENSIONS, EXTERNAL:
Wing span   8.35 m (27 ft 4¾ in)
Length overall   6.40 m (21 ft 0 in)
AREA:
Wings, gross   11.70 m² (126.0 sq ft)
WEIGHTS:
Weight empty   500 kg (1,103 lb)
Baggage capacity   20 kg (44 lb)
Max T-O weight   750 kg (1,653 lb)
PERFORMANCE (with 67 kW; 90 hp engine):
Max level speed   108 knots (200 km/h; 124 mph)
Econ cruising speed   86 knots (160 km/h; 99 mph)
Stalling speed: flaps up   27 knots (50 km/h; 31 mph)
flaps down   24 knots (45 km/h; 28 mph)

COUPÉ-AVIATION JC-3
The JC-3 differs from the JC-01 primarily in having a sweptback fin and a 51 kW (68 hp) Volkswagen 1,700 cc converted motorcar engine. Two examples were under construction by amateurs in 1985, but no recent news has been received.

CROSES

EMILIEN CROSES

63 route de Davayé (Aérodrome), 71000 Charnay les Macon
Telephone: (85) 38 07 31

CROSES EAC-3 POUPLUME

The Pouplume single-seat tandem-wing biplane has a fixed rear wing and a pivoted forward wing which dispenses with the need for ailerons and elevators. Construction is of wood, with fabric covered wings, and a non-retractable tailwheel landing gear. The prototype has a 7.8 kW (10.5 hp) Moto 232 cc motorcycle engine; fuel capacity is 10 litres (2.6 US gallons; 2.2 Imp gallons).

The EAC-3-01 Pouplume flew for the first time in June 1961. It was followed, in 1967, by a second prototype (EAC-3-02) with a 20 cm (8 in) longer fuselage. Plans are available.

A version known as the **Pouplume Sport** differs in having a 1,500 cc Volkswagen engine and reduced span of 6.40 m (21 ft 0 in).

The following data apply to the standard Moto-powered Pouplume:

DIMENSIONS, EXTERNAL:

Wing span: forward wing	7.80 m (25 ft 7 in)
rear wing	7.00 m (23 ft 0 in)
Length overall	4.70 m (15 ft 3 in)
Height overall	1.80 m (5 ft 11 in)

AREA:

Wings, gross	16.02 m² (172.2 sq ft)

WEIGHTS:

Weight empty	110-140 kg (243-310 lb)
Max T-O weight	220-260 kg (485-573 lb)

PERFORMANCE (A: 7.8 kW; 10.5 hp engine, B: 13.4 kW; 18 hp engine):

Max level speed: A	38 knots (70 km/h; 43 mph)
B	65 knots (120 km/h; 75 mph)
Econ cruising speed: A	27 knots (50 km/h; 31 mph)
B	38 knots (70 km/h; 43 mph)
T-O run: A	60 m (200 ft)
B	40 m (131 ft)
Landing run: A	24 m (80 ft)

CROSES EC-6 CRIQUET (LOCUST)

The Criquet is a side by side two-seater, using the same tandem-wing formula as the Pouplume. The EC-6-01 prototype flew for the first time on 6 July 1965.

TYPE: Side by side two-seat tandem-wing homebuilt aircraft.
AIRFRAME: Wings have wooden structure, with plywood leading-edge, overall fabric covering and some components of glassfibre. NACA 23012 (modified) wing section. Wooden fuselage, covered with plywood. Glass-fibre engine cowling. Plywood covered spruce fin and rudder. Non-retractable tailwheel landing gear.
POWER PLANT: One 67 kW (90 hp) Continental engine. Fuel capacity originally 60 litres (15.9 US gallons; 13 Imp gallons); planned to be increased to 90 litres (23.8 US gallons; 19.75 Imp gallons).

DIMENSIONS, EXTERNAL:

Wing span: forward wing	7.80 m (25 ft 7 in)
rear wing	7.00 m (22 ft 11½ in)
Length overall	4.65 m (15 ft 3 in)

AREA:

Wings, gross	16.02 m² (172.2 sq ft)

WEIGHTS:

Weight empty	290 kg (639 lb)
Max T-O weight	550 kg (1,213 lb)

PERFORMANCE (officially certificated, at max T-O weight):

Max level speed at S/L	115 knots (213 km/h; 132 mph)
Econ cruising speed	86 knots (160 km/h; 99 mph)
Will not stall	
Time to 2,000 m (6,560 ft)	6 min 14 s

CROSES EC-8 TOURISME

This three-seat touring aircraft is generally similar to the standard wooden Criquet but can have an 'all-terrain' landing gear comprising two tandem pairs of mainwheels.

DISTRI

DISTRI SNAP SARL

86 avenue de Saint-Ouen, 75018 Paris
Telephone: (1) 42 28 40 42
MANAGER: Yves Chemarin

DISTRI SNAP AIRCROSS

The Aircross is a tandem two-seat microlight of typical aluminium alloy tubular trike and flexwing type, powered by a 29.4 kW (39.4 hp) Rotax 447 engine. Two flexwings are offered, the 18.5 m² (199.13 sq ft) Appolo CX and the 18.00 m² (193.75 sq ft) Midi 18. The following performance figures are with the Appolo CX flexwing, which has a span of 10.5 m (34 ft 5½ in).

PERFORMANCE:

Max level speed	49 knots (90 km/h; 56 mph)
Max cruising speed	40 knots (75 km/h; 47 mph)
Stalling speed	22 knots (40 km/h; 25 mph)
Max rate of climb	180 m (590 ft)/min

DISTRI SNAP EPSILON

The Epsilon is another tandem two-seat microlight, offered with three engine options and a choice of two flexwings of similar span and area. The standard **Epsilon's** wing is single surface, with Mylar reinforced leading-edges and offering +6/–3 g limits. The **Epsilon Plus** has a wing with 70% double surface, its leading-edges made rigid by high density foam; g limits are +6/–3. Options for the Epsilon include floats or skis to replace the standard tricycle landing gear. Either model can carry agricultural gear, survey equipment, a stretcher or other specialised equipment, except when powered by the C-16 engine.

The following details refer to the Epsilon with a C-22 engine.

POWER PLANT: One 35.8 kW (48 hp) C-16, 47 kW (63 hp) C-18 or 58 kW (78 hp) C-22 engine. Fuel capacity 27 litres (7 US gallons; 6 Imp gallons).
EQUIPMENT: Installation of agricultural spraygear takes 4 min. The polyester hopper has a capacity of 110 litres (29 US gallons; 24 Imp gallons). The low volume system dispenses 15-25 litres/hectare (1.6-2.7 US gallons; 1.3-2.2 Imp gallons/acre). Ultra low volume system dispenses 3-15 litres/hectare (0.3-1.6 US gallons; 0.25-1.3 Imp gallons/acre).

DIMENSION, EXTERNAL:

Wing span	11.00 m (36 ft 1 in)

WEIGHTS:

Weight empty	175 kg (386 lb)
Max T-O weight	410 kg (904 lb)

PERFORMANCE (Epsilon Plus, C-22 engine):

Max level speed	46 knots (85 km/h; 53 mph)
Stalling speed	27 knots (50 km/h; 31 mph)
Max rate of climb at S/L	300 m (985 ft)/min
Service ceiling	4,000 m (13,125 ft)
T-O run	80 m (262 ft)
Endurance	2-3 h

GATARD

AVIONS A. GATARD

Villa la Devallée, 17130 Montendre s/Royan
Telephone: (46) 49 42 76

GATARD STATOPLAN AG 02Sp POUSSIN (CHICK)

The Poussin is the most popular of a series of designs by M Albert Gatard, all with a special control system that involves use of a variable incidence 'lifting' tailplane of large area. Instead of altering the wing angle of attack to increase lift, the pilot lowers full-span slotted aileron/flaps and adjusts the tailplane to maintain pitching equilibrium. In consequence, the aircraft climb with the fuselage datum at no more than 4° to the horizontal, which preserves a good forward view and low body drag.

Early Poussins built by amateur constructors are of the original **AG 02** model, as described in detail. The **AG 02Sp** shown on current plans has more rounded wingtips, inset ailerons, an improved landing gear which increases cruising speed by approx 5 per cent, and an increased max T-O weight of 305 kg (672 lb).

TYPE: Single-seat homebuilt monoplane.
AIRFRAME: Wooden structure, plywood covered. NACA 23012 wing section. Aileron/flaps linked with variable incidence 'lifting' tailplane of NACA 2309 section, and with underfuselage airbrake which operates automatically when aileron/flaps are lowered at large angles, as for landing. Non-retractable tailwheel landing gear.
POWER PLANT: One 18 kW (24 hp) modified Volkswagen engine. Provision for alternative engine of up to 30 kW (40 hp) weighing between 50 and 60 kg (110-132 lb). Fuel capacity 30 litres (7.9 US gallons; 6.6 Imp gallons).

DIMENSIONS, EXTERNAL:

Wing span	6.40 m (21 ft 0 in)
Length overall	4.53 m (14 ft 10½ in)
Height overall	1.50 m (4 ft 11 in)

AREA:

Wings, gross	6.15 m² (66.2 sq ft)

WEIGHTS:

Weight empty	170 kg (375 lb)
Max T-O weight	280 kg (617 lb)

PERFORMANCE (at max T-O weight):

Max cruising speed	77 knots (144 km/h; 89 mph)
Max speed for aerobatics	69 knots (130 km/h; 80 mph)
Stalling speed	35 knots (65 km/h; 41 mph)
Max rate of climb at S/L	132 m (435 ft)/min
T-O run	190 m (625 ft)
Landing run	200 m (655 ft)

GUERPONT

GUERPONT BIPLUM

The Biplum flew for the first time in 1985, by which time 14 other amateur builders had acquired plans.
TYPE: Single-seat ultralight biplane.
AIRFRAME: Mostly of bonded wooden construction, with Dacron covered wings and rear fuselage. Entire lower wings pivot to function as ailerons. Wing section NACA 23009. Non-retractable tailwheel landing gear.
POWER PLANT: One 16.4 kW (22 hp) König SC 430. JPX 425 engine optional. Fuel capacity 23 litres (6 US gallons; 5 Imp gallons).

DIMENSIONS, EXTERNAL:

Wing span	6.50 m (21 ft 4 in)
Length overall	5.10 m (16 ft 8¾ in)

AREA:

Wings, gross	12.7 m² (136.7 sq ft)

WEIGHTS:

Weight empty	95 kg (210 lb)
Max T-O weight	190 kg (419 lb)

PERFORMANCE:

Max level speed at S/L	58 knots (107 km/h; 66 mph)
Max cruising speed (75% power)	50 knots (92 km/h; 57 mph)
Max rate of climb at S/L	120 m (394 ft)/min
Theoretical ceiling	4,600 m (15,100 ft)

HYDROPLUM

HYDROPLUM SARL

Fior di Linu, Pietranera, 20200 Bastia, Corsica
Telephone: (95) 31 67 67
M Claude Tisserand designed two amphibians: the single-seat Hydroplum monoplane and two-seat Hydroplum II sesquiplane. Both are said to conform to microlight (ULM) and Experimental regulations. Plans are available, plus kits for the two-seater, which can also be purchased in ready to fly form.

TISSERAND HYDROPLUM

The Hydroplum first flew in September 1983.
TYPE: Single-seat amphibian.
AIRFRAME: Plywood construction. Wing section NACA 2415. Three-axis control with water rudder attached to heel of single-step hull. Retractable taildragger landing gear.
POWER PLANT: One 30 kW (40 hp) 440 cc Hirth. Fuel capacity 40 litres (10.6 US gallons; 8.8 Imp gallons).

DIMENSIONS, EXTERNAL:

Wing span	9.25 m (30 ft 4¼ in)
Length overall	5.90 m (19 ft 4¼ in)
Height overall	1.40 m (4 ft 7 in)
Propeller diameter	1.40 m (4 ft 7 in)

AREA:

Wings, gross	13.00 m² (139.93 sq ft)

WEIGHTS:

Weight empty	145 kg (319 lb)
Pilot weight range	60-90 kg (133-198 lb)
Max T-O weight	260 kg (573 lb)

PERFORMANCE (at max T-O weight):

Max level speed	59 knots (110 km/h; 68 mph)
Econ cruising speed	43 knots (80 km/h; 50 mph)
Stalling speed	30 knots (55 km/h; 34 mph)
Max rate of climb at S/L	300 m (985 ft)/min
T-O run: on land	80 m (262 ft)
on water	100 m (328 ft)
Landing run: on land	80 m (262 ft)
on water	50 m (164 ft)
Range with max standard fuel	145 nm (270 km; 167 miles)

TISSERAND HYDROPLUM II/PETREL

The Hydroplum II is a two-seat sesquiplane development of the Hydroplum which flew for the first time on 1 November 1986. Kits, requiring about 500 working hours to assemble, and ready to fly aircraft (known by the name **Petrel**) are available from Société Morbihannaise d'Aéro Navigation (SMAN) of Anse de Mané Braz, Saint-Philibert,

Croses EAC-3 Pouplume light aircraft (Moto engine)

Hydroplum amphibian, designed by M Claude Tisserand

Croses EC-6 Criquet (*M.J. Hooks*)

Gatard AG 02 Poussin No. 19, built by M P. Buatois of Dijon (*M.J. Hooks*)

Distri Snap Epsilon with agricultural equipment during trials in Ethiopia

Guerpont Biplum single-seat ultralight biplane (*M.J. Hooks*)

Tisserand Hydroplum II amphibian

Jodel D.92, a modified version of the Bébé (*Geoffrey P. Jones*)

56470 La Trinité-sur-Mer, France; tel 97 55 00 26.

TYPE: Side by side two-seat amphibian.

AIRFRAME: Wings have tubular main spar, glassfibre/epoxy leading-edge and glassfibre/foam/epoxy ribs, with Dacron covering. Wing section NACA 2412. Three-axis control. Moulded monocoque single step hull of glassfibre/epoxy, with Kevlar reinforcement; carbonfibre/epoxy tailboom with water rudder at heel. Boom supports tail unit of wood with fabric covering on fin and control surfaces. Retractable tricycle landing gear. Optional fully enclosed cockpit.

POWER PLANT: One 47.7 kW (64 hp) Rotax 532. Four-stroke engine of same power can be installed for operation in homebuilt category. Fuel capacity 50 litres (13.2 US gallons; 11 Imp gallons).

DIMENSIONS, EXTERNAL:
Wing span: upper	8.90 m (29 ft 2½ in)
Length overall	5.90 m (19 ft 4¼ in)
Height overall	1.80 m (5 ft 11 in)
Propeller diameter	1.60 m (5 ft 3 in)

AREA:
Wings, gross	16.50 m² (177.6 sq ft)

WEIGHTS:
Weight empty, equipped	185 kg (408 lb)
Max T-O weight	360 kg (793 lb)

PERFORMANCE (at max T-O weight):
Max level speed	81 knots (150 km/h; 93 mph)
Econ cruising speed	54 knots (100 km/h; 62 mph)
Stalling speed	30 knots (55 km/h; 34 mph)
Max rate of climb at S/L	300 m (985 ft)/min
T-O run: on land	50 m (164 ft)
on water	100 m (328 ft)
Landing run: on land, without brakes	100 m (328 ft)
on water	50 m (164 ft)

JODEL
AVIONS JODEL SA

HEAD OFFICE: 37 Route de Seurre, 21200 Beaune
DESIGN OFFICE: 21-Darois
PRESIDENT-DIRECTOR GENERAL: Jean Delemontez

Jodel designs have been built both commercially and by amateurs, and more than 5,000 aircraft of Jodel type have flown throughout the world.

JODEL D.9 BÉBÉ SERIES

The prototype Bébé flew for the first time in January 1948. Construction can take as little as 500 working hours.

TYPE: Single-seat homebuilt aircraft.

AIRFRAME: All-wood construction, except for fabric covering on the wings, rudder and elevators. Non-retractable tailwheel or tailskid landing gear.

POWER PLANT: One modified Volkswagen engine is standard, but other engines of 18.6 to 48.5 kW (25 to 65 hp) may be fitted. Fuel capacity 25 litres (6.6 US gallons; 5.5 Imp gallons).

DIMENSIONS, EXTERNAL:
Wing span	7.00 m (22 ft 11 in)
Length overall	5.45 m (17 ft 10½ in)

AREA:
Wings, gross	9.0 m² (96.8 sq ft)

WEIGHTS:
Weight empty 190 kg (420 lb)
Max T-O weight 320 kg (705 lb)
PERFORMANCE (30 kW; 40 hp engine, at max T-O weight):
Max level speed at S/L 87 knots (160 km/h; 100 mph)
Cruising speed 74 knots (137 km/h; 85 mph)
Stalling speed 35 knots (65 km/h; 40 mph)
Max rate of climb at S/L 180 m (590 ft)/min
T-O run 110 m (360 ft)
Landing run 100 m (330 ft)
Range with max fuel 217 nm (400 km; 250 miles)

JODEL D.11 and D.119

The original D.11, with 33.6 kW (45 hp) Salmson engine, was the basic model in the series of Jodel two-seaters for amateur and commercial production. The version for amateur construction with 67 kW (90 hp) Continental engine is designated D.119.

The wing is of wood, covered with Dacron, the fuselage and tail unit of wood covered with glassfibre. The following details refer to a D.11 which spans 8.23 m (27 ft 0 in), has an empty weight of 340 kg (750 lb) and loaded weight of 562 kg (1,240 lb), and is powered by a 48.5 kW (65 hp) Continental A65-8 flat-four engine:

PERFORMANCE:
Max level speed at S/L 93 knots (173 km/h; 108 mph)
Cruising speed 86 knots (161 km/h; 100 mph)
Max rate of climb at S/L 152 m (500 ft)/min
Service ceiling 4,875 m (16,000 ft)
T-O run 152 m (500 ft)
Landing run 244 m (800 ft)
Range with max fuel 260 nm (482 km; 300 miles)

JODEL D.112 CLUB and D.113

The D.112 is a two-seat dual-control version of the D.9. Except for increased overall dimensions, a wider fuselage and enclosed side by side cockpit, the D.112 conforms in layout and structure to the D.9, but is fitted normally with a 48.5 kW (65 hp) Continental flat-four engine. Fuel capacity is 60 litres (15.9 US gallons; 13 Imp gallons).

The version built in Sweden as the D.113 differs from the D.112 in several minor respects.

DIMENSIONS, EXTERNAL:
Wing span 8.20 m (26 ft 10 in)
Length overall 6.36 m (20 ft 10 in)
AREA:
Wings, gross 12.72 m² (136.9 sq ft)
WEIGHTS:
Weight empty 270 kg (600 lb)
Max T-O weight 520 kg (1,145 lb)
PERFORMANCE (at max T-O weight):
Max level speed at S/L 102 knots (190 km/h; 118 mph)
Econ cruising speed 81 knots (150 km/h; 93 mph)
Stalling speed 38 knots (70 km/h; 43 mph)
Max rate of climb at S/L 193 m (632 ft)/min
T-O run 137 m (450 ft)
Landing run 120 m (395 ft)
Range with max fuel 323 nm (600 km; 373 miles)

JODEL D.18

The 1981-82 *Jane's* contained details of the Delemontez-Cauchy DC-1. No plans of this are available, but M Delemontez is marketing plans of a slightly modified version, known as the Jodel D.18, with a different wing section, revised ailerons, all-moving tailplane and other changes. It has a typical Jodel light wooden airframe, with coarse dihedral on the tapered outer wing panels. Installation of a 43 kW (58 hp) 1,600 cc Volkswagen engine, instead of the usual Continental, has resulted in a more streamlined cowling and improved performance. Fuel capacity is 65 litres (17 US gallons; 14.3 Imp gallons).

The prototype D.18 was flown for the first time on 21 May 1984.

DIMENSIONS, EXTERNAL:
Wing span 7.50 m (24 ft 7¼ in)
Length overall 5.70 m (18 ft 8½ in)
AREA:
Wings, gross 9.83 m² (105.8 sq ft)
WEIGHTS:
Weight empty 230-250 kg (507-551 lb)
Max T-O weight 460 kg (1,014 lb)
PERFORMANCE:
Max level speed 135 knots (250 km/h; 155 mph)
Cruising speed 92 knots (170 km/h; 105 mph)
Stalling speed 39 knots (72 km/h; 45 mph)
Max rate of climb at S/L 180 m (590 ft)/min
T-O to 15 m (50 ft) 260 m (853 ft)
Landing from 15 m (50 ft) 450 m (1,477 ft)
Endurance 5 h

JODEL D.19

This is the designation of D.18s constructed with tricycle landing gear. Examples are under construction in France.

JURCA

MARCEL JURCA

2 rue des Champs Philippe, 92250 La Garenne-Colombes
Telephone: 1459 40138

M Marcel Jurca is the designer of a series of high-performance light aircraft of which plans have been supplied to other constructors on a purely amateur basis. More recently, he has produced plans for representations of Second World War fighters, usually to two-thirds or three-quarters of the original size. The latest and final aircraft in this series is the M.J.70, a full-size representation of the P-51D Mustang that was expected to be available by the end of 1988.

For builders in North America, Australia and New Zealand, Jurca plans are available from Mr Ken Heit, 1733 Kansas, Flint, Michigan 48506, USA (telephone 313 232 5395). Mr Simon Richards, a Briton living in France and builder of the M.J.100 prototype, supplies plans to UK builders (Ecorsaint, 21150 Les Laumes, France), while Claus Colling Ltd (Priel 5A, 8051 Gammelsdorf, Federal Republic of Germany) manufactures all metal components, landing gears and flight controls for the Jurca representations of Second World War fighters.

JURCA M.J.2 and M.J.22 TEMPÊTE

The prototype **M.J.2** Tempête was flown for the first time on 27 June 1956. At least 45 Tempêtes are now flying.

The type of engine fitted to a particular aircraft is indicated by a suffix letter in its designation. Suffix letters are A for the 48.5 kW (65 hp) Continental A65, B for the 56 kW (75 hp) Continental A75, C for the 63.5 kW (85 hp) Continental C85, D for the 67 kW (90 hp) Continental C90-8/C90-14F, E for the 74.5 kW (100 hp) Continental O-200-A, F for the 78.5 kW (105 hp) Potez 4 E-20, G for the 86 kW (115 hp) Potez 4 E-30, H for the 78.5-86 kW (105-115 hp) Textron Lycoming O-235, I for the 93 kW (125 hp) Textron Lycoming O-290-G, K for the 101-104 kW (135-140 hp) Textron Lycoming O-290-D2, N for the 112 kW (150 hp) Textron Lycoming or Continental, P for the 119 kW (160 hp) Textron Lycoming or Continental, and R for the 134 kW (180 hp) Textron Lycoming or Continental. The standard version is the M.J.2A. The M.J.2D cruises at 105 knots (195 km/h; 121 mph) and climbs to 1,000 m (3,280 ft) in 3 minutes. It can also perform aerobatics without loss of height.

A version known as the **M.J.22** has a 112 kW (150 hp) engine and strengthened airframe.

The Tempête is basically a single-seat aircraft, but the 112 and 134 kW (150 and 180 hp) versions have provision for carrying behind the pilot on cross-country flights a second person weighing not more than 55 kg (121 lb). This is not permitted by the DGAC in France. The suffix 'A' is added to the aircraft designation in two-seat configuration.

The following details apply generally to all basic single-seat M.J.2 models:

TYPE: Single-seat homebuilt aircraft.

AIRFRAME: All-wood construction, except for fabric covering on the wings, ailerons, elevators and rudder. NACA 23012 wing section. Non-retractable tailwheel (or tailskid) landing gear.

POWER PLANT: See introduction. Fuel capacity 60 litres (15.9 US gallons; 13.2 Imp gallons).

DIMENSIONS, EXTERNAL:
Wing span 6.00 m (19 ft 8 in)
Length overall 5.855 m (19 ft 2½ in)
Height overall 2.40 m (7 ft 10 in)
AREA:
Wings, gross 7.98 m² (85.9 sq ft)
WEIGHTS (48.5 kW; 65 hp engine):
Weight empty 90 kg (639 lb)
Max T-O weight 430 kg (950 lb)
PERFORMANCE (48.5 kW; 65 hp engine):
Max level speed 104 knots (193 km/h; 120 mph)
Cruising speed 89 knots (165 km/h; 102 mph)
Max rate of climb at S/L 170 m (555 ft)/min
Service ceiling 3,500 m (11,500 ft)
T-O run 250 m (820 ft)
Endurance 3 h 20 min

JURCA M.J.5 SIROCCO

The M.J.5 Sirocco is a tandem two-seat development of the M.J.2 Tempête. It is fully aerobatic when flown as a two-seater. The prototype M.J.5 flew for the first time on 3 August 1962, powered by a 78.5 kW (105 hp) Potez 4 E-20 engine. A factory built model was awarded subsequently a certificate of airworthiness in the Utility category.

The version of the Sirocco for amateur construction is generally similar to the factory built version, with non-retractable or retractable landing gear, including optional retractable tailwheel. The type of engine fitted to a particular aircraft is indicated by a suffix letter in its designation. Suffix letters are A for the 67 kW (90 hp) Continental C90-8 or -14F, B for the 74.5 kW (100 hp) Continental O-200-A, C for the 78.5 kW (105 hp) Potez 4 E-20, D for the 86 kW (115 hp) Potez 4 E-30, E for the 78.5 kW (105 hp) Hirth, F for the 93 kW (125 hp) Textron Lycoming, G for the 100.5 kW (135 hp) Regnier, H for the 119.5 kW (160 hp) Textron Lycoming, K for the 134 kW (180 hp) Textron Lycoming and L for the 149 kW (200 hp) Textron Lycoming. Addition of the numeral 1 indicates a non-retractable landing gear; the numeral 2 indicates a retractable main landing gear; 2A indicates that the tailwheel also retracts.

One aircraft has a 119 kW (160 hp) PRV modified motorcar engine and P-51 Mustang type underbelly airscoop.

The details which follow refer to a Sirocco with an 86 kW (115 hp) Textron Lycoming O-235-C2B engine and 1.85 m (6 ft 0¾ in) diameter propeller, and a modified rudder of reduced height and greater chord:

DIMENSIONS, EXTERNAL:
Wing span 7.00 m (23 ft 0 in)
Length overall 6.15 m (20 ft 2 in)
Height overall, tail up 2.60 m (8 ft 6¼ in)
(standard Sirocco 2.80 m; 9 ft 2¼ in)
AREA:
Wings, gross 10.00 m² (107.64 sq ft)
WEIGHTS:
Weight empty 430 kg (947 lb)
Max T-O weight 680 kg (1,499 lb)
PERFORMANCE (at max T-O weight):
Max level speed 127 knots (235 km/h; 146 mph)
Cruising speed 116 knots (215 km/h; 134 mph)
Stalling speed 44 knots (80 km/h; 50 mph)
Time to 1,000 m (3,280 ft) 4 min
Service ceiling 5,000 m (16,400 ft)
T-O run 250 m (820 ft)
Landing run 200 m (655 ft)
Endurance 4 h 20 min

JURCA M.J.5 SIROCCO (SPORT WING)

A special version of the Sirocco, with 86 kW (115 hp) engine and increased span, has been developed for the New Zealand and Australian market. The wing of this aircraft, known as a 'Sport' wing, embodies one additional rib and inter-rib bay each side. The modification is available in the English language set of Sirocco plans.

JURCA M.J.51 SPEROCCO

The tandem two-seat Sperocco (the name being a contraction of 'Special Sirocco') is intended for high performance aerobatic and competition flying and incorporates features of the M.J.5 and M.J.7. The fuselage is of completely new design, with a basically triangular cross-section, but is of similar construction to that of the M.J.5. Landing gear is of the M.J.5 type and is fully retractable.

Any horizontally opposed engine of 112-179 kW (150-240 hp) may be installed. Fuel is contained in two wing tanks, each of 55 litres (14.5 US gallons; 12 Imp gallons) capacity, and one fuselage tank of 45 or 100 litres (11.9 or 26.4 US gallons; 10 or 22 Imp gallons) capacity.

The first M.J.51, powered by a 149 kW (200 hp) Textron Lycoming AIO-360 engine, is being constructed by M Serge Brillant at Melun.

DIMENSIONS, EXTERNAL:
Wing span 7.623 m (25 ft 0 in)
Length overall 7.24 m (23 ft 9 in)
AREA:
Wings, gross 11.00 m² (118.4 sq ft)
WEIGHT:
Max T-O weight 730 kg (1,653 lb)
PERFORMANCE (estimated, with 112 kW; 150 hp Textron Lycoming engine):
Max level speed 149 knots (275 km/h; 171 mph)
Max cruising speed (75% power) 135 knots (250 km/h; 155 mph)
Stalling speed 49 knots (90 km/h; 56 mph)
Time to 1,000 m (3,280 ft) 1 min 30 s

JURCA M.J.52 ZÉPHYR

The all-wooden M.J.52 Zéphyr is a very light two-seat monoplane, based on the M.J.5 Sirocco but using a converted Volkswagen motorcar engine or Continental engine in the 30-48.5 kW (40-65 hp) range. It can have a non-retractable or retractable landing gear.

Plans of the M.J.52 have been available since Spring 1985, and a prototype is under construction. It has been designed to conform to FAR Pt 23 Utility category requirements, yet to be simple to construct in a garage or similar building and inexpensive in terms of materials and working hours.

DIMENSIONS, EXTERNAL:
Wing span 9.06 m (29 ft 8¾ in)
Length overall 6.28 m (20 ft 7¼ in)
AREA:
Wings, gross 13.50 m² (145.3 sq ft)
WEIGHTS:
Weight empty 333 kg (734 lb)
Max T-O weight 517 kg (1,140 lb)
PERFORMANCE (37.3 kW; 50 hp engine):
Max level speed 59 knots (110 km/h; 68 mph)
Stalling speed 22 knots (40 km/h; 25 mph)
Endurance 5 h
g limits +8/−4 ultimate

JURCA M.J.7 and M.J.77 GNATSUM

The Gnatsum is a precise scale replica, for amateur construction, of the North American P-51 Mustang

Jodel D.18 with Volkswagen engine *(Geoffrey P. Jones)*

Jodel D.112 Club two-seat homebuilt aircraft *(Geoffrey P. Jones)*

Jurca M.J.5L2 Sirocco (149 kW; 200 hp Textron Lycoming engine) built by M Jean Y. Guillou

Jurca M.J.2D Tempête built by Mr Al Painton of Painton, Missouri, USA

Jurca M.J.7 Gnatsum built by M Jacques Danton of Nangis, France (Potez 4 D-32 engine)

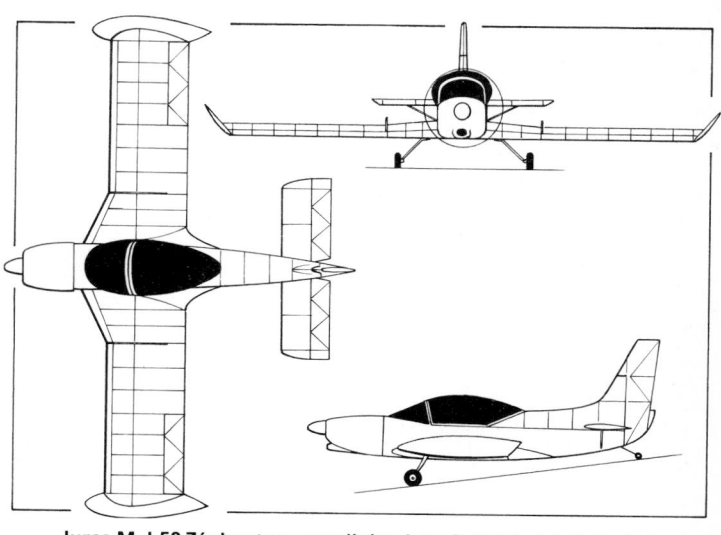

Jurca M.J.52 Zéphyr two-seat light aircraft *(Michael A. Badrocke)*

Jurca M.J.8 1-Nine-OH built by Mr Ronald Kitchen of Carson City, Nevada

Jurca M.J.10 Spit built by Mr Don McMurtrie of Bartlesville, Oklahoma

---

single-seat fighter of the Second World War. Its name 'Gnatsum' is 'Mustang' reversed. Drawings for two versions are available as follows:

M.J.7. To two-thirds scale. Suitable engines include 149 kW (200 hp) Ranger and 134 kW (180 hp) Textron Lycoming O-360. Prototype first flew on 31 July 1969. Plastics fuselage shells for the M.J.7 are available from Boeve Brothers of Holland, Michigan, USA.

M.J.77. To three-quarters scale. Seven examples are under construction, or flying, in France, all using the 194 kW (260 hp) Potez 4 D-32 engine. Others are being built in the USA and West Germany.

Jurca plans provide for alternative plywood covered semi-monocoque fuselage construction, a wooden box structure covered with two plastics shells, a structure of metal tubing covered with two plastics shells or aluminium sheet, or the tubular structure covered with polyurethane foam and glassfibre. Manually retractable landing gear is standard. The M.J.77 being built by Herr Claus Colling of

West Germany has a 298 kW (400 hp) Chevrolet engine and uses plastics shells fabricated by Rattray in the USA over a metal tubing fuselage.

DIMENSIONS, EXTERNAL (all-wood M.J.77 with 4 D-32 engine):

Wing span	8.50 m (27 ft 10½ in)
Length overall	7.40 m (24 ft 3¼ in)

AREA (M.J.77 as above):

Wings, gross	13.40 m² (144.2 sq ft)

WEIGHTS (M.J.77 as above):

Weight empty	1,035 kg (2,281 lb)
Max T-O weight	1,300 kg (2,866 lb)

PERFORMANCE (M.J.77 as above, with two 80 kg; 176 lb occupants):

Max level speed	167 knots (310 km/h; 193 mph)
Cruising speed at 2,400 rpm	151 knots (280 km/h; 174 mph)
Stalling speed:	
clean	54 knots (100 km/h; 62 mph)

landing configuration	46 knots (85 km/h; 53 mph)
Max rate of climb at S/L	366 m (1,200 ft)/min
T-O run	300 m (985 ft)

JURCA M.J.70

Full-size representation of the P-51D Mustang. No details available.

JURCA M.J.8 and M.J.80 1-NINE-OH

The **M.J.8** is a single-seat sporting aircraft which was designed by M Jurca by scaling down to three-quarters of the original dimensions the airframe of the Focke-Wulf Fw 190A fighter. The **M.J.80** is similar but is designed to full scale. The prototype M.J.8, which flew for the first time on 30 March 1975, now has a 231 kW (310 hp) Textron Lycoming engine, and the design is suitable for the alternative use of any horizontally opposed or radial engine in the 119-231 kW (160-310 hp) range. The M.J.80 can be fitted with engines of 186-373 kW (250-500 hp), including the Pratt & Whitney R-1340. The landing gear of both models is retractable.

DIMENSIONS, EXTERNAL (M.J.8):

Wing span	7.87 m (25 ft 10 in)
Length overall	6.63 m (21 ft 9 in)

AREA:

Wings, gross	10.20 m² (109.8 sq ft)

WEIGHTS (M.J.8 with 119.5 kW; 160 hp engine):

Weight empty	400 kg (880 lb)
Max T-O weight	626 kg (1,380 lb)

PERFORMANCE (M.J.8, estimated, with 119.5 kW; 160 hp engine):

Max level speed at S/L	139 knots (257 km/h; 160 mph)
Max cruising speed	124 knots (230 km/h; 143 mph)
Stalling speed	49 knots (90 km/h; 56 mph)
Max rate of climb at S/L	503 m (1,650 ft)/min

JURCA M.J.9 ONE-OH-NINE

Three-quarter scale representation of the Messerschmitt Bf 109 fighter of the Second World War. The prototype is under construction.

JURCA M.J.90

This is a full-size representation of a Bf 109G, to which it is dimensionally the same. Its method of construction is similar to that of the M.J.9. Plans are available.

JURCA M.J.10 SPIT

The M.J.10 is a single-seat, three-quarter scale representation of the Supermarine Spitfire that can also be completed as a two-seater. It is suitable for any horizontally opposed or inline engine of 119-231 kW (160-310 hp), although slight variations from the Spitfire's contours are

necessary in the former case. Construction is normally of wood, except for glassfibre engine cowling and fabric covering on the control surfaces, but the standard plans also detail a tubular fuselage. The landing gear is manually retractable.

The basic plans adopted the Spitfire Mk IX as the standard M.J.10, but alternative detail plans represent both Merlin and Griffon engined models, including the Mks VC and XIV, and show clipped, standard or extended span wings.

The first M.J.10 flew in 1982.

DIMENSIONS, EXTERNAL:

Wing span:

standard	8.40 m (27 ft 6¾ in)
clipped	7.46 m (24 ft 5½ in)
Length overall	7.125 m (23 ft 4½ in)

AREA:

Wings, gross	12.60 m² (135.6 sq ft)

WEIGHTS (119.5 kW; 160 hp engine):

Weight empty	658 kg (1,450 lb)
Max T-O weight	907 kg (2,000 lb)

PERFORMANCE (estimated, with 119.5 kW; 160 hp engine):

Max level speed at S/L	139 knots (257 km/h; 160 mph)
Cruising speed	124 knots (230 km/h; 143 mph)
Stalling speed	49 knots (90 km/h; 56 mph)
Max rate of climb at S/L	503 m (1,650 ft)/min
T-O run	200 m (660 ft)

JURCA M.J.100

Plans are available for a full-size representation of the Supermarine Spitfire, known as the M.J.100. It can be built with an all-wood airframe, or with a metal tube fuselage, in standard or reinforced form according to the engine fitted,

and provision can be made for a passenger. With the metal fuselage structure, either aluminium alloy or foam and glassfibre skins are used. The tailwheel landing gear is retractable. The power plant will normally be a low cost engine in the 224-298 kW (300-400 hp) range. Engines of up to 447 kW (600 hp), or others weighing up to 600 kg (1,322 lb) with cowling and propeller, can be fitted. It is estimated that an experienced builder could complete an M.J.100 in approximately 1,800 working hours, and an inexperienced builder in 3,000 hours or less. A prototype, powered by a 298 kW (400 hp) geared and turbocharged Jaguar motorcar engine, was expected to fly in 1988.

DIMENSIONS, EXTERNAL: As for original Spitfire of selected mark.

WEIGHTS (373 kW; 500 hp engine):

Standard weight empty	about 952.5 kg (2,100 lb)
Max T-O weight	1,361 kg (3,000 lb)

PERFORMANCE (engine as above, estimated):

Max level speed	250 knots (463 km/h; 288 mph)

Stalling speed:

flaps down	50 knots (93 km/h; 58 mph)
flaps up	55 knots (102 km/h; 64 mph)
Max rate of climb at S/L	915 m (3,000 ft)/min

JURCA M.J.12 PEE-40

The M.J.12 is a three-quarter scale representation of the Curtiss P-40 single-seat fighter of the Second World War. It spans 8.524 m (27 ft 11½ in) and has an overall length (tail up) of 7.62 m (25 ft 0 in). All-wood or metal tube fuselage construction, with moulded glassfibre fuselage shells. Wings and tail unit are plywood covered. Provision can be made for a passenger.

LASCAUD
ETS D. LASCAUD

41 rue de Crussol, 07500 Granges-Lès-Valence

Telephone: (75) 44 47 02

LASCAUD BIFLY

This is a revised version of the Belgian Butterfly, designed by Mr R. Mossoux (see 1984-85 *Jane's*). Two standards of kits are offered, with and without an engine, plus ready to fly aircraft. Construction takes 150-160 hours.

TYPE: Single-seat microlight aircraft.

AIRFRAME: Tandem wings, each with 2024-T3 aluminium alloy spars and PVC foam ribs, Dacron covered. NACA 23012 wing section. Fuselage of welded AG5 rectangular

section tube and AU4G sheet. Rudder-only tail unit of similar construction to wings. Composites nose fairing with small windscreen optional. Two-axis control. Non-retractable tailwheel landing gear.

POWER PLANT: One 15 kW (20 hp) J-C-V 274 cc engine. Fuel capacity 12 litres (3.2 US gallons; 2.6 Imp gallons).

DIMENSIONS, EXTERNAL:

Wing span: front

front	6.19 m (20 ft 3¾ in)
rear	4.36 m (14 ft 3¾ in)
Length overall	3.25 m (10 ft 8 in)
Height overall	1.48 m (4 ft 10¼ in)
Propeller diameter	1.20 m (3 ft 11¼ in)

AREA:

Wings, gross	11.68 m² (125.7 sq ft)

WEIGHTS:

Weight empty	65 kg (143 lb)
Max T-O weight	160 kg (353 lb)

PERFORMANCE:

Max level speed	59 knots (110 km/h; 68 mph)
Cruising speed	38 knots (70 km/h; 43 mph)
Stalling speed	16.5 knots (30 km/h; 19 mph)
Max rate of climb at S/L	120 m (395 ft)/min
Service ceiling	3,050 m (10,000 ft)
T-O run	30-40 m (98-131 ft)
Landing run	5-20 m (17-65 ft)
Range at cruising speed	89 nm (165 km; 102 miles)
g limits	±6 ultimate

LEDERLIN
FRANÇOIS LEDERLIN

2 rue Charles Peguy, 38000 Grenoble

This aircraft was derived from the Mignet HM-380, but retains little of the original except for the wing section. First flight was made on 14 September 1965.

Plans of the 380-L, annotated in English and with both English and metric measurements, are available to amateur constructors.

LEDERLIN 380-L

TYPE: Side by side two-seat homebuilt aircraft.

AIRFRAME: Tandem-wing biplane. Wing section 3.40-13. Wooden wings, with plywood leading-edge and overall fabric covering. Variable incidence front wing. No

ailerons or flaps. Welded steel tube fuselage, covered with light alloy to front of cabin and with fabric on rear fuselage, over wooden formers. Wooden tail unit with fabric covering. Non-retractable tailwheel landing gear.

POWER PLANT: One 67 kW (90 hp) Continental C90-14F. Fuel capacity 85 litres (22.5 US gallons; 18.75 Imp gallons).

DIMENSIONS, EXTERNAL:

Wing span: forward

forward	7.92 m (26 ft 0 in)
rear	6.00 m (19 ft 8¼ in)
Length overall	4.77 m (15 ft 7¾ in)
Height overall	2.08 m (6 ft 10 in)
Propeller diameter	1.83 m (6 ft 0 in)

AREAS:

Wings, gross: forward	9.92 m² (106.8 sq ft)
rear	7.43 m² (80.0 sq ft)

WEIGHTS:

Weight empty	360 kg (794 lb)
Max T-O weight	600 kg (1,323 lb)

PERFORMANCE (at max T-O weight):

Max level speed at 305 m (1,000 ft)

	109 knots (201 km/h; 125 mph)

Econ cruising speed at 610 m (2,000 ft)

	87 knots (161 km/h; 100 mph)
Stalling speed, power off	26 knots (49 km/h; 30 mph)
Max rate of climb at S/L	275 m (900 ft)/min
Service ceiling	over 3,660 m (12,000 ft)
T-O run	122 m (400 ft)
Landing run	153 m (500 ft)

Range at econ cruising speed

	477 nm (885 km; 550 miles)

LENDEPERGT
PATRICK LENDEPERGT

112 rue de la Jarry, 94300 Vincennes

Telephone: (1) 43 65 61 95

LENDEPERGT LP-01 SIBYLLE

The prototype of this amphibian was first flown in July 1984. It is available in kit form, and possibly ready assembled, and by February 1988 thirty had been ordered. In addition to sport flying, it can be adapted for surveillance (with nose mounted EAS ATAL TV system), stretcher carrying and other uses.

TYPE: Four-seat amphibious homebuilt aircraft.

AIRFRAME: All-composites, of pre-moulded carbonfibre, Kevlar and epoxy. Laminar flow wings. Single-step hull. Retractable tricycle landing gear, with water rudder.

POWER PLANT: One 119 kW (160 hp) Textron Lycoming O-320-D2F. Alternative Textron Lycoming engine of up to 156.6 kW (210 hp), Mazda, or Allison Model 250 turboprop. Fuel capacity 290 litres (76.6 US gallons; 63.8 Imp gallons) standard; optional 80 litre (21 US gallon; 17.6 Imp gallon) auxiliary tank.

DIMENSIONS, EXTERNAL:

Wing span	9.40 m (30 ft 10 in)
Length overall	6.60 m (21 ft 8 in)
Height overall	2.50 m (8 ft 2½ in)
Propeller diameter	1.62 m (5 ft 3¾ in)

AREA:

Wings, gross	12.40 m² (133.5 sq ft)

WEIGHTS:

Weight empty	600 kg (1,323 lb)
Max T-O weight	1,300 kg (2,866 lb)

PERFORMANCE:

Max level speed	151 knots (280 km/h; 174 mph)
Econ cruising speed	130 knots (240 km/h; 149 mph)

Stalling speed:

flaps up	49 knots (90 km/h; 56 mph)
flaps down	41 knots (75 km/h; 47 mph)
Max rate of climb at S/L	120 m (363 ft)/min
Service ceiling	5,000 m (16,400 ft)

T-O run:

from land	600 m (1,970 ft)
from water	750 m (2,460 ft)
Landing run, on land	150 m (492 ft)
Range with max fuel	1,080 nm (2,000 km; 1,240 miles)
Endurance	8 h
g limits	+4/−3

LUCAS
EMILE LUCAS

Corbonod, 01420 Seyssel

Telephone: (50) 59 27 54

LUCAS L5

The prototype L5 was first flown on 13 August 1976. Plans are available to amateur builders, and more than 35 L5s are known to be flying or under construction, in three basic versions, as follows:

L5. Two/three-seat model, similar to prototype.

L5 200. Airframe generally similar to L5, but three seats standard. Suitable power plants include 70 kW (94 hp) Rolls-Royce Continental O-200-E and Textron Lycoming O-320. Fuel capacity 123 litres (32.5 US gallons; 27 Imp gallons). Accommodation for three persons and no baggage, or two persons and 65 kg (143 lb) baggage.

L5 360. As basic L5, but with four seats in pairs. Prototype has 134 kW (180 hp) Textron Lycoming O-360. One fuel tank in fuselage, capacity 80 litres (21.1 US gallons;

17.6 Imp gallons) and two in wings, each 50 litres (13.2 US gallons; 11 Imp gallons). Space for 30 kg (66 lb) of baggage when carrying three persons.

The following details apply to the basic L5 but the airframe description is generally applicable to all versions:

TYPE: Two/three-seat homebuilt monoplane.

AIRFRAME: All-metal airframe of light alloy. Wing section NACA 23015(mod). Non-retractable tricycle or retractable tailwheel landing gear.

POWER PLANT: Prototype had one 85.75 kW (115 hp)

Lascaud Bifly single-seat tandem-wing microlight *(Geoffrey P. Jones)*

Lederlin 380-L two-seat light aircraft (Continental C90-14F engine)
(Peter J. Bish)

Lendepergt LP-01 Sibylle amphibian

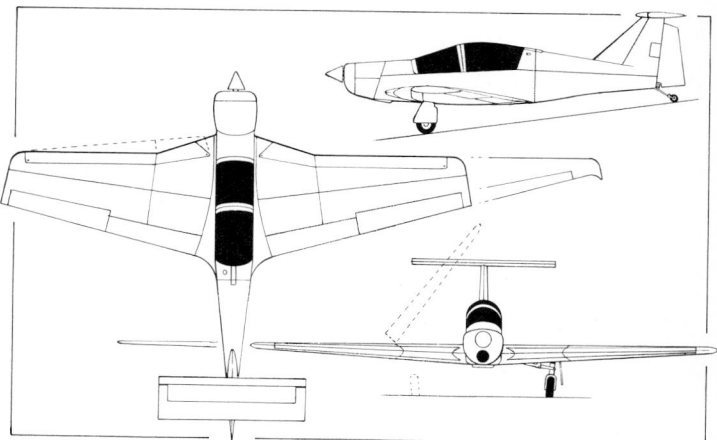

Lucas L5 with retractable tailwheel landing gear *(Geoffrey P. Jones)*

Lucas L6-7 sport aircraft, with extended-wing motor glider version shown in
scrap view *(Michael A. Badrocke)*

Avions Mignet HM-1000 Balerit two-seat microlight, fitted with optional
cockpit fairing

Textron Lycoming O-235. Basic L5s built to plans can
have an engine of between 93 and 134 kW (125-180 hp).
Fuel capacity 75 or 115 litres (19.8 or 30.4 US gallons;
16.5 or 25.3 Imp gallons) in L5; see model listings for
other versions.

DIMENSIONS, EXTERNAL:

Wing span	9.20 m (30 ft 2¼ in)
Length overall	6.30 m (20 ft 8 in)
Height overall	2.10 m (6 ft 10¾ in)
Propeller diameter	1.70 m (5 ft 7 in)

AREA:

Wings, gross	11.90 m² (128.1 sq ft)

WEIGHTS (prototype):

Weight empty, equipped	505 kg (1,113 lb)
Max T-O weight	746 kg (1,644 lb)

PERFORMANCE (prototype):

Max level speed:

with retractable landing gear

	146 knots (270 km/h; 168 mph)
with fixed gear	127 knots (235 km/h; 146 mph)

Econ cruising speed:

with retractable landing gear

	116 knots (215 km/h; 134 mph)
with fixed gear	97 knots (180 km/h; 112 mph)
Max rate of climb at S/L	300 m (985 ft)/min
T-O to 15 m (50 ft)	280 m (920 ft)
Landing from 15 m (50 ft)	380 m (1,245 ft)
Range with max fuel	539 nm (1,000 km; 621 miles)

LUCAS L6-7

Design of this tandem two-seat light aircraft was started
in 1981, and the prototype was expected to fly during 1987.
By adding wingtip extensions, it can be flown as a motor
glider (see Sailplanes section). It is expected to be marketed
in the form of plans and kits.

TYPE: Two-seat homebuilt aircraft.

AIRFRAME: All-metal airframe of aluminium alloy. Wing
section NACA 65_3618. Retractable tailwheel or tricycle
landing gear.

POWER PLANT: One 62 kW (83 hp) Limbach. Optionally one
112 kW (150 hp) Textron Lycoming O-320 for aerobatic
training. Fuel capacity 50 litres (13.2 US gallons; 11 Imp
gallons).

DIMENSIONS, EXTERNAL (Sport aircraft):

Wing span	9.50 m (31 ft 2 in)
Length overall	7.00 m (22 ft 11½ in)
Height overall	1.85 m (6 ft 1 in)
Propeller diameter	1.61 m (5 ft 3½ in)

AREA (Sport aircraft):

Wings, gross	13.0 m² (140.0 sq ft)

WEIGHTS (Sport aircraft, Limbach engine):

Weight empty	350 kg (772 lb)
Max T-O weight	530 kg (1,168 lb)

PERFORMANCE (Sport aircraft, Limbach engine, estimated):

Max cruising speed	205 knots (380 km/h; 236 mph)
Econ cruising speed	180 knots (333 km/h; 207 mph)
T-O run	200 m (657 ft)
Landing run	160 m (525 ft)

MIGNET
SOCIÉTÉ D'EXPLOITATION DES AÉRONEFS HENRI MIGNET

Logis des Pierrières, Saint-Romain de Benêt, 17600 Saujon
Telephone: (46) 02 26 00

DIRECTOR: Alain Mignet

In addition to producing the Balerit, this company is
developing a new two-seat microlight with a front mounted
engine, a fuselage with a composites fairing and windscreen,
a Dacron covered metal wing, and tricycle landing gear.

AVIONS MIGNET HM-1000 BALERIT

The Balerit represents a microlight adaptation of the
well-known Mignet Pou du Ciel (Flying Flea) tandem-wing
configuration, in which the aircraft is controlled by means
of the pivoted forward wing and a rudder, with no
conventional roll control surfaces. Like all Mignet designs,

it cannot stall or spin. The prototype flew for the first time
on 9 April 1984.

TYPE: Side by side two-seat, dual-control microlight aircraft.

AIRFRAME: Tandem-wing biplane, primarily of light alloy
construction, but with carbonfibre rudder. Each wing
built in three sections that can be folded and stacked
for transportation. Two-axis control. Non-retractable
tricycle landing gear. Optional floats, skis, glassfibre
cockpit fairing, and front wing extensions to increase
total area to 19.30 m² (207.7 sq ft).

POWER PLANT: One 34.3 kW (46 hp) Rotax 503. Fuel
capacity 24 litres (6.3 US gallons; 5.3 Imp gallons).
Optional 38 kW (51 hp) Rotax 503.2V or 47 kW (63 hp)
Rotax 532 engine.

DIMENSIONS, EXTERNAL:

Wing span: front, standard

	7.30 m (23 ft 11½ in)
rear	5.50 m (18 ft 0½ in)

Length overall	5.00 m (16 ft 5 in)
Height overall	1.88 m (6 ft 2 in)
Propeller diameter	1.48 m (4 ft 10¼ in)

AREA (standard front wing):

Wings, gross (total)	17.55 m² (189.0 sq ft)

WEIGHTS:

Weight empty	175 kg (386 lb)
Max T-O weight	374 kg (824 lb)

PERFORMANCE (Rotax 503, at max T-O weight, with
standard front wing):

Max level speed	57 knots (105 km/h; 65 mph)
Cruising speed	46 knots (85 km/h; 53 mph)
Min flying speed	27 knots (50 km/h; 31 mph)
Max rate of climb at S/L	180 m (590 ft)/min
T-O run	45 m (148 ft)
Landing run	25 m (82 ft)
g limits	+7/−3

NICOLLIER
AVIONS H. NICOLLIER
13 rue de Verdun, 25000 Besançon
Telephone: (81) 53 57 01

NICOLLIER HN 433 MENESTREL
The prototype of this single-seat aircraft flew for the first time on 25 November 1962. Wing spars and kits of materials are available from the Siravia company, of Pons. Moulded canopies, cowlings and wheel fairings, together with plans, are available from Avions H. Nicollier.
TYPE: Single-seat homebuilt aircraft.
AIRFRAME: All-wood structure, with some plywood covering and Dacron overall. Non-retractable tailwheel landing gear.
POWER PLANT: One 22 kW (30 hp) converted Volkswagen 1,300 cc motorcar engine in prototype. Recommended are Rectimo-VW engines of 22-37.3 kW (30-50 hp).
DIMENSIONS, EXTERNAL:

Wing span	7.00 m (22 ft 11½ in)
Length overall	5.30 m (17 ft 4½ in)
Height overall	1.48 m (4 ft 10¼ in)

AREA:

Wings, gross	8.20 m² (88.26 sq ft)

WEIGHTS:

Weight empty	201 kg (443 lb)
Max T-O weight	330 kg (727 lb)

PERFORMANCE (with 1,500 cc engine, at max T-O weight):

Max level speed at S/L	108 knots (200 km/h; 124 mph)
Max cruising speed	97 knots (180 km/h; 112 mph)
Stalling speed:	
engine idling	26 knots (48 km/h; 30 mph)
power on	22 knots (40 km/h; 25 mph)
Max rate of climb at S/L	258 m (845 ft)/min
T-O run	100 m (328 ft)
Max range	278 nm (515 km; 320 miles)
g limits	+4.4/-2.2

NICOLLIER HN 434 SUPER-MENESTREL
A completely redesigned version of the Menestrel has been developed as the HN 434 Super-Menestrel, plans of which are available to amateur constructors. A 1,500 cc or 1,600 cc Volkswagen modified motorcar engine gives improved performance, and fuel capacity is increased. Pilot comfort is improved. The Super-Menestrel is also simpler to construct.

NICOLLIER HN 600 WEEK-END
The HN 600 Week-end is a single-seat light aircraft, designed for economical construction and operation by amateurs. The structure is simple, of wood and fabric, with some components of Klégécel foam. Plans became available in 1981. A number of major components, such as the wing spar, ribs, cowlings and canopy, were to be made available in completed form from the Siravia company of Pons. Recommended power plant is a converted Volkswagen 1,500 cc motorcar engine of 22-37 kW (30-50 hp).
DIMENSIONS, EXTERNAL:

Wing span	7.00 m (22 ft 11½ in)
Length overall	5.25 m (17 ft 2¾ in)

AREA:

Wings, gross	8.20 m² (88.26 sq ft)

WEIGHTS:

Weight empty	185 kg (408 lb)
Max T-O weight	310 kg (683 lb)

PERFORMANCE (estimated, at max T-O weight):

Max level speed	108 knots (200 km/h; 124 mph)
Max cruising speed	92 knots (170 km/h; 106 mph)
Stalling speed	33 knots (60 km/h; 38 mph)
Max rate of climb at S/L	210 m (688 ft)/min
Range with max fuel at 86 knots (160 km/h; 99 mph)	
	345 nm (640 km; 397 miles)

NOIN
ETS NOIN AÉRONAUTIQUES
RN 85, Châteauvieux, 05130 Tallard
Telephone: (92) 54 15 04
This company markets in plans, kit and ready to fly forms a single-seat self-launching motor-glider known as Sirius. The prototype first flew in 1985 and by March 1988 three kits and ten sets of plans had been sold.

NOIN SIRIUS
TYPE: Single-seat microlight motor-glider.
AIRFRAME: All-composites, of Styrofoam, glassfibre and epoxy. Göttingen 549 wing section. Three-axis control. Two non-retractable wheels in tandem form landing gear, with skids at bottom of tailfin and at wingtips.
POWER PLANT: One 15.4 kW (20 hp) JPX 425. Fuel capacity 11 litres (2.9 US gallons; 2.4 Imp gallons).
DIMENSIONS, EXTERNAL:

Wing span	12.00 m (39 ft 4½ in)
Length overall	5.90 m (19 ft 4¼ in)
Propeller diameter	0.98 m (3 ft 2½ in)

AREA:

Wings, gross	13.24 m² (142.5 sq ft)

WEIGHTS:

Weight empty	135 kg (298 lb)
Pilot weight (max)	90 kg (198 lb)
Max T-O weight	240 kg (529 lb)

PERFORMANCE, POWERED:

Max level speed	48 knots (90 km/h; 56 mph)
Econ cruising speed	40 knots (75 km/h; 47 mph)
Stalling speed	27 knots (50 km/h; 31 mph)
Max rate of climb at S/L	102 m (335 ft)/min
T-O run	100-120 m (328-394 ft)
Landing run	60-100 m (197-328 ft)
Endurance with max fuel	1 h 40 min

PERFORMANCE, UNPOWERED:

Best glide ratio at 40 knots (75 km/h; 47 mph)	20
Min rate of sink	0.85 m (2.8 ft)/s
g limits	+4.4/-2.2 normal
	+6.6/-2.2 ultimate

PIEL
AVIONS CLAUDE PIEL
Le Mas de Darnetz, 19300 Egletons
Telephone: (16 55) 93 09 79
PROPRIETOR: Mme Claude Piel
The authorised distributor for plans of Piel designs available to amateur constructors is:
D. Trivisonno, 10426 Parc Georges Blvd, Montreal, Quebec H1H 4Y3, Canada.

PIEL EMERAUDE and SUPER EMERAUDE
More than 425 sets of plans of the Emeraude and Super Emeraude have been sold, and several versions have been factory-built. Current versions are as follows:
C.P.301. With 67 kW (90 hp) Continental C90-12F engine.
C.P.304. With 63.4 kW (85 hp) Continental C85-12F engine and wing flaps.
C.P.305. With 86 kW (115 hp) Textron Lycoming engine.
C.P.308. With 56 kW (75 hp) Continental engine.
C.P.320. With Super Emeraude wings, a 74.5-85.75 kW (100-115 hp) Continental engine and alternative tailwheel or tricycle landing gear.
C.P.320A. As C.P.320, but with sweptback fin.
C.P.321. As C.P.320, with 78.5 kW (105 hp) Potez engine.
C.P.323A. With 112 kW (150 hp) Textron Lycoming engine and sweptback fin. **C.P.323AB** has tricycle landing gear.
C.P.324 Emeraude Club. With 56 kW (75 hp) JPX 2100 engine.
TYPE: Side by side two-seat, dual-control homebuilt.
AIRFRAME: All-wood airframe, fabric covered except for wooden skins on tailplane. NACA 23012 wing section. Non-retractable tailwheel landing gear. Some aircraft have non-standard retractable gear.
POWER PLANT: Engine as in model listings. Fuel capacity 80 litres (21.1 US gallons; 17.6 Imp gallons). Provision for auxiliary tank, capacity 40 litres (10.6 US gallons; 8.8 Imp gallons).
DIMENSIONS, EXTERNAL:

Wing span	8.04 m (26 ft 4½ in)
Length overall: C.P.301	6.30 m (20 ft 8 in)
C.P.320	6.45 m (21 ft 2 in)
Height overall: C.P.301	1.85 m (6 ft 0¾ in)
C.P.320	1.90 m (6 ft 2¾ in)
Propeller diameter: C.P.301	1.80 m (5 ft 11 in)
C.P.320	1.78 m (5 ft 10 in)

AREA:

Wings, gross	10.85 m² (116.7 sq ft)

WEIGHTS:

Weight empty: C.P.301	380 kg (838 lb)
C.P.320	410 kg (903 lb)
Max T-O weight: C.P.301	650 kg (1,433 lb)
C.P.320	700 kg (1,543 lb)

PERFORMANCE (at max T-O weight):

Max level speed:	
C.P.301	110 knots (205 km/h; 127 mph)
C.P.320	124 knots (230 km/h; 143 mph)
Econ cruising speed (65% power) at 1,200 m (3,940 ft):	
C.P.301	101 knots (187 km/h; 116 mph)
C.P.320	110 knots (205 km/h; 127 mph)
Stalling speed, flaps up:	
C.P.301	51 knots (92 km/h; 58 mph)
C.P.320	53 knots (97 km/h; 61 mph)
Stalling speed, flaps down:	
C.P.301	46 knots (85 km/h; 53 mph)
C.P.320	49 knots (90 km/h; 56 mph)
Max rate of climb at S/L: C.P.301	168 m (551 ft)/min
C.P.320	240 m (787 ft)/min
Service ceiling: C.P.301	4,000 m (13,125 ft)
C.P.320	4,300 m (14,100 ft)
T-O run: C.P.301	250 m (820 ft)
C.P.320	230 m (755 ft)
Landing run: C.P.301	250 m (820 ft)
C.P.320	260 m (853 ft)
Range at econ cruising speed:	
C.P.301, C.P.320	538 nm (1,000 km; 620 miles)

PIEL C.P.1320
Designed to combine the general characteristics of the Super Emeraude with the Super Diamant's three-seat cabin and fuel tanks in the wings, the C.P.1320 can be fitted with engines of 112 kW (150 hp) to 149 kW (200 hp). More than 40 sets of plans sold in France; others by Mr Trivisonno.
TYPE: Three-seat homebuilt.
AIRFRAME: Wooden construction. NACA 23012 wing section. Retractable tailwheel landing gear.
POWER PLANT: Prototype has one 119 kW (160 hp) Textron Lycoming engine. Fuel capacity 140 litres (37 US gallons; 30.8 Imp gallons).
DIMENSIONS, EXTERNAL:

Wing span	7.90 m (25 ft 11 in)
Length overall	6.60 m (21 ft 8 in)
Height overall	1.80 m (5 ft 11 in)
Propeller diameter	1.80 m (5 ft 11 in)

AREA:

Wings, gross	11.10 m² (119.48 sq ft)

WEIGHTS:

Weight empty	470 kg (1,036 lb)
Max T-O weight	800 kg (1,764 lb)

PERFORMANCE:

Max level speed	162 knots (300 km/h; 186 mph)
Econ cruising speed (65% power)	
	132 knots (245 km/h; 152 mph)
Stalling speed: flaps up	54 knots (100 km/h; 62 mph)
flaps down	52 knots (95 km/h; 59 mph)
Max rate of climb at S/L	600 m (1,968 ft)/min
Service ceiling	5,000 m (16,400 ft)
T-O run	200 m (657 ft)
Landing run	300 m (984 ft)

Range with max fuel (65% power)	
	593 nm (1,100 km; 683 miles)
g limits: normal	+5/-2.5
aerobatic (two occupants, max T-O weight 720 kg; 1,585 lb)	+6/-3

PIEL SUPER DIAMANT
The Super Diamant is essentially a three/four-seat version of the Emeraude, of which more than 50 sets of plans have been sold. Current versions are as follows:
C.P.604. Prototype flown in Summer of 1964, with a 108 kW (145 hp) Continental engine. Current version has swept vertical tail surfaces.
C.P.605. Much-modified four-seat ('2+2') version, with 112 kW (150 hp) Textron Lycoming O-320-E2A engine. Fully certificated for commercial production, as well as for amateur construction. Details in 1973-74 *Jane's*.
C.P.605B. Version of C.P.605 with retractable tricycle landing gear.
TYPE: Three/four-seat homebuilt.
AIRFRAME: All-wood airframe, fabric covered except for fixed tail surfaces which are plywood covered. Wing section NACA 23012. C.P.604 has non-retractable tailwheel landing gear. C.P.605B has retractable tricycle landing gear.
POWER PLANT: One flat-four engine (typically 119 kW; 160 hp Textron Lycoming IO-320-B1A or O-360-D1C). Fuel capacity 85 litres (22.5 US gallons; 18.7 Imp gallons). Provision for additional tankage to give total capacity of 160 litres (42.3 US gallons; 35 Imp gallons).
DIMENSIONS, EXTERNAL (C.P.605B):

Wing span	9.20 m (30 ft 2¼ in)
Length overall	7.00 m (22 ft 11¾ in)
Height overall	2.00 m (6 ft 6¾ in)
Propeller diameter	1.80 m (5 ft 11 in)

AREA:

Wings, gross	13.30 m² (143.2 sq ft)

WEIGHTS (C.P.605B):

Weight empty	520 kg (1,146 lb)
Max T-O weight	850 kg (1,873 lb)

PERFORMANCE (C.P.605B, at max T-O weight):

Max level speed	141 knots (260 km/h; 162 mph)
Econ cruising speed (65% power) at 1,200 m (3,940 ft)	
	124 knots (230 km/h; 143 mph)
Stalling speed: flaps up	49 knots (90 km/h; 56 mph)
flaps down	45 knots (82 km/h; 51 mph)
Max rate of climb at S/L	330 m (1,082 ft)/min
Service ceiling	5,000 m (16,400 ft)
T-O run	160 m (525 ft)
Landing run	270 m (886 ft)
Range at econ cruising speed	
	620 nm (1,150 km; 714 miles)

PIEL C.P.70, C.P.750 and C.P.751 BERYL
The **C.P.70 Beryl** combines the wing of the C.P.30 Emeraude, virtually unchanged, with a fuselage containing

Nicollier HN 433 Menestrel (Austin J. Brown)

Piel C.P. 1320 built by M A.Kieger (Geoffrey P. Jones)

Piel Emeraude constructed by Mr Ted Hendrickson of Snohomish, Washington (John Wegg)

Nicollier HN 600 Week-end (Volkswagen 1,500 cc motorcar engine) (Michael A. Badrocke)

Piel C.P.750 Beryl built by Mr Scott Christiansen of Salt Lake City, Utah (John Wegg)

Noin Sirius self-launching microlight glider (J.M.G. Gradidge)

Piel C.P.80 (c/n 3) single-seat racing aircraft (Air Photo Supply)

---

two seats in tandem, and non-retractable tricycle landing gear. It is powered by a 48.5 kW (65 hp) Continental C65-8F engine. Plans of this version are not available from Mr Trivisonno of Canada.

Intended for aerobatic flying, the **C.P.750 Beryl** is also similar in general appearance to the Emeraude but has a longer, steel tube fuselage seating two persons in tandem, slightly reduced span, and other changes. The C.P.750 has been built principally by amateur constructors in Canada.

A further variant, the **C.P.751**, introduced several new design features and has a 134 kW (180 hp) Textron Lycoming O-360-A engine. Several are under construction or flying in Canada and the USA.

The following details refer to the C.P.750 Beryl.

TYPE: Two-seat homebuilt aerobatic monoplane.

AIRFRAME: All-wood wings, with fabric covering. Wing section NACA 23012. Fabric covered welded steel tube fuselage. Wooden tail unit; fixed surfaces plywood covered, control surfaces fabric covered. Non-retractable tailwheel landing gear.

POWER PLANT: One 112 kW (150 hp) Textron Lycoming O-320-E2A. Fuel capacity 70 litres (18.5 US gallons; 15.4 Imp gallons), with provision for two auxiliary tanks to give total capacity of 140 litres (37 US gallons; 30.75 Imp gallons).

DIMENSIONS, EXTERNAL (C.P.750):

Wing span	8.04 m (26 ft 4½ in)
Length overall	6.90 m (22 ft 7¾ in)
Height overall	2.10 m (6 ft 10¾ in)
Propeller diameter	1.80 m (5 ft 11 in)

AREA (C.P.750):

Wings, gross	11.00 m² (118.4 sq ft)

WEIGHTS:

Weight empty	480 kg (1,058 lb)
Max T-O weight	760 kg (1,675 lb)

PERFORMANCE (C.P.750, at max T-O weight):

Max level speed	151 knots (280 km/h; 174 mph)
Econ cruising speed (65% power) at 1,200 m (3,940 ft)	135 knots (250 km/h; 155 mph)
Stalling speed: flaps up	54 knots (100 km/h; 63 mph)
flaps down	52 knots (95 km/h; 59 mph)
Max rate of climb at S/L	390 m (1,280 ft)/min
Service ceiling	5,200 m (17,060 ft)
T-O run	190 m (623 ft)
Landing run	280 m (919 ft)
Range at econ cruising speed	593 nm (1,100 km; 683 miles)

PIEL C.P.80

The C.P.80 was designed as a single-seat racing aircraft for amateur construction. Twelve C.P.80s are known to be flying.

TYPE: Single-seat homebuilt racing aircraft.

AIRFRAME: All-wood, except for polyester plastics wingtips and engine cowling. Wing section NACA 23012. Non-retractable tailwheel landing gear.

POWER PLANT: One 67 kW (90 hp) Continental C90-8F. Provision for other engines, including 48.5 kW (65 hp) Continental. Fuel capacity 40 litres (10.6 US gallons; 8.8 Imp gallons).

DIMENSIONS, EXTERNAL:

Wing span	6.00 m (19 ft 8¼ in)
Length overall	5.30 m (17 ft 4¾ in)
Height overall	1.70 m (5 ft 7 in)
Propeller diameter	1.52 m (5 ft 0 in)

AREA:

Wings, gross	6.20 m² (66.7 sq ft)

WEIGHTS (67 kW; 90 hp engine):

Weight empty	260 kg (573 lb)
Max T-O weight	380 kg (837 lb)

PERFORMANCE (estimated, with 67 kW; 90 hp engine, at max T-O weight):

Max level speed	167 knots (310 km/h; 193 mph)
Econ cruising speed (65% power) at 1,200 m (3,940 ft)	130 knots (240 km/h; 149 mph)
Stalling speed	52 knots (95 km/h; 59 mph)
Max rate of climb at S/L	720 m (2,360 ft)/min
Service ceiling	6,000 m (19,685 ft)
T-O and landing run	200 m (656 ft)
Range at econ cruising speed	243 nm (450 km; 280 miles)
g limits	+8/−6

PIEL C.P.90 PINOCCHIO

The C.P.90 Pinocchio is essentially a smaller, single-seat development of the Emeraude, intended for aerobatic and general sporting flying.

AIRFRAME: All-wood, fabric covered. Wing section NACA 23012. Non-retractable tailwheel landing gear.

POWER PLANT: One 74.5 kW (100 hp) Continental O-200. Fuel capacity 60 litres (15.9 US gallons; 13.2 Imp gallons).
DIMENSIONS, EXTERNAL:

Wing span	7.20 m (23 ft 7½ in)
Length overall	6.00 m (19 ft 8¼ in)
Height overall	1.80 m (5 ft 11 in)
Propeller diameter	1.80 m (5 ft 11 in)

AREA:

Wings, gross	9.65 m² (103.9 sq ft)

WEIGHTS:

Weight empty	335 kg (738 lb)
Max T-O weight	500 kg (1,102 lb)

PERFORMANCE (estimated, at max T-O weight):

Max level speed	141 knots (260 km/h; 162 mph)
Econ cruising speed (65% power) at 1,200 m (3,940 ft)	
	124 knots (230 km/h; 143 mph)

Stalling speed	41 knots (75 km/h; 47 mph)
Max rate of climb at S/L	480 m (1,575 ft)/min
Service ceiling	6,000 m (19,685 ft)
T-O run	180 m (590 ft)
Landing run	160 m (525 ft)
Range at econ cruising speed	
	296 nm (550 km; 341 miles)

PIEL C.P.150 ONYX

The Onyx was the last aircraft designed by the late M Claude Piel, and plans are currently available only from Mme Piel, in France. Construction of at least 110 Onyx is known to have been undertaken, and several have flown.
TYPE: Single-seat tandem-wing microlight.
AIRFRAME: All-wood construction standard, except for Klégécel ribs in wings, fins and rudders, which are all Tergal fabric covered. Forward wing is pivoted for variable incidence. Rear wings have tip mounted fins and rudders and inset ailerons. Elevator in centre-section of forward wing. Non-retractable tricycle landing gear. Alternative glassfibre fuselage being utilised by some builders.
POWER PLANT: One 8.8 kW (12 hp) Solo.
DIMENSIONS, EXTERNAL:

Wing span	7.30 m (23 ft 11½ in)
Length overall	3.53 m (11 ft 7 in)

AREAS:

Wings, gross: rear wing	9.10 m² (97.95 sq ft)
front wing	3.70 m² (39.83 sq ft)

WEIGHTS:

Weight empty	70 kg (154 lb)
Max T-O weight	180 kg (397 lb)

PERFORMANCE: No details received

POTTIER
JEAN POTTIER
4 rue de Poissy, 78130 les Mureaux
Telephone: 099 13-85
Details of the Pottier P.80S, P.100TS, P.110TS and P.105TS can be found in the 1987-88 *Jane's.* Plans are available for the following types:

POTTIER P.50 BOUVREUIL (BULLFINCH)
TYPE: Single-seat homebuilt racing aircraft.
AIRFRAME: All-wood, except for plastics engine cowling and mainwheel fairings. Wing section NACA 23015 at root, NACA 23012 at tip. Alternative retractable (P.50R) or non-retractable (P.50) tailwheel landing gear.
POWER PLANT: One 67 kW (90 hp) Continental C90 standard. Other engines of 48.5 to 86 kW (65-115 hp) are optional. Fuel capacity 60 litres (15.9 US gallons; 13 Imp gallons) for racing, 100 litres (26.4 US gallons; 22 Imp gallons) for touring. Provision for carrying auxiliary fuel tank under each wing.
DIMENSIONS, EXTERNAL:

Wing span	6.20 m (20 ft 4 in)
Length overall	5.65 m (18 ft 6½ in)

AREA:

Wings, gross	7.50 m² (80.7 sq ft)

WEIGHTS:

Weight empty	270 kg (595 lb)
Max T-O weight	400 kg (882 lb)

PERFORMANCE (with non-retractable landing gear):

Max level speed	167 knots (310 km/h; 192 mph)
Max cruising speed (75% power)	
	151 knots (280 km/h; 174 mph)
Stalling speed	44 knots (80 km/h; 50 mph)
g limits	±10

POTTIER P.70S
TYPE: Single-seat homebuilt sporting aircraft.
AIRFRAME: All-metal, of 2024 alloy. Wing section NACA 4415. Non-retractable tricycle landing gear.
POWER PLANT: One 30-44.7 kW (40-60 hp) Volkswagen converted motorcar engine. Fuel capacity 40 litres (10.6 US gallons; 8.75 Imp gallons).

DIMENSIONS, EXTERNAL:

Wing span	5.85 m (19 ft 2¼ in)
Length overall	5.15 m (16 ft 10¾ in)
Height overall	1.60 m (5 ft 3 in)
Propeller diameter	1.30 m (4 ft 3¼ in)

AREA:

Wings, gross	7.20 m² (77.5 sq ft)

WEIGHTS:

Weight empty, equipped	215 kg (474 lb)
Max T-O and landing weight	325 kg (716 lb)

PERFORMANCE (A: standard P.70S with 30 kW; 40 hp engine, B: 44.7 kW; 60 hp engine, at max T-O weight except where indicated):

Max level speed at S/L:	
A	97 knots (180 km/h; 112 mph)
B	116 knots (215 km/h; 133 mph)
Econ cruising speed at S/L:	
A	65 knots (120 km/h; 75 mph)
Stalling speed, flaps down:	
A, B	38 knots (70 km/h; 44 mph)
Max rate of climb at S/L: A	150 m (490 ft)/min
B	330 m (1,080 ft)/min
Service ceiling: A	4,500 m (14,775 ft)
T-O run: A	350 m (1,150 ft)
B	200 m (657 ft)
Range: A, B	215 nm (400 km; 248 miles)
g limit: A, B	+9 ultimate

POTTIER P.170S
The P.170S is a tandem two-seat version of the P.70S. It is of all-metal construction and has a retractable tricycle landing gear. Engine is a 37.3-52 kW (50-70 hp) Volkswagen. Plans are available to amateur constructors.
TYPE: Two-seat sporting homebuilt.
DIMENSIONS, EXTERNAL:

Wing span	5.95 m (19 ft 6¼ in)
Length overall	5.70 m (18 ft 8½ in)
Height overall	1.65 m (5 ft 5 in)

AREA:

Wings, gross	7.40 m² (79.65 sq ft)

WEIGHTS:

Weight empty	230 kg (507 lb)
Max T-O weight	445 kg (981 lb)

PERFORMANCE (A: 37.3 kW; 50 hp engine, B: 52 kW; 70 hp engine):

Max level speed: A	95 knots (175 km/h; 109 mph)
B	108 knots (200 km/h; 124 mph)
Max cruising speed: A	84 knots (155 km/h; 96 mph)
B	102 knots (190 km/h; 118 mph)
Stalling speed: A, B	41 knots (75 km/h; 47 mph)
Max rate of climb at S/L: A	150 m (490 ft)/min
B	300 m (980 ft)/min
T-O run: A	380 m (1,250 ft)
B	220 m (722 ft)
Landing from 15 m (50 ft): A, B	350 m (1,150 ft)
Range with standard 50 litres (11 Imp gallons) of fuel, 45 min reserves: A, B	215 nm (400 km; 248 miles)
g limit: A, B	+6.6 ultimate

POTTIER P.180S
The P.180S is a side by side two-seat sporting aircraft, of all-metal construction and with a non-retractable tricycle landing gear. Power plant is a 41-67 kW (55-90 hp) Volkswagen. Plans are available to amateur constructors.
TYPE: Two-seat sporting aircraft.
DIMENSIONS, EXTERNAL:

Wing span	6.50 m (21 ft 4 in)
Length overall	5.35 m (17 ft 6½ in)
Height overall	1.70 m (5 ft 7 in)

AREA:

Wings, gross	7.80 m² (83.96 sq ft)

WEIGHTS:

Weight empty	240 kg (529 lb)
Max T-O weight	470 kg (1,036 lb)

PERFORMANCE (estimated, 41 kW; 55 hp engine):

Max level speed	97 knots (180 km/h; 112 mph)
Max cruising speed	89 knots (165 km/h; 102 mph)
Stalling speed	41 knots (75 km/h; 47 mph)
Max rate of climb at S/L	168 m (550 ft)/min
T-O run	330 m (1,080 ft)
Landing from 15 m (50 ft)	350 m (1,150 ft)
Range	270 nm (500 km; 310 miles)
g limit	+5.7 ultimate

SOYER/BARRITAULT
CLAUDE SOYER and JEAN BARRITAULT
Claude Soyer: BP 19, 49160 Longue-Jumelles
Jean Barritault: 10 rue G. Clémenceau, 49150 Baugé

SOYER/BARRITAULT SB1 ANTARÈS
The SB1 Antarès first flew on 24 May 1984. Plans available to amateur builders show an airframe of more simple design, a three-seat cabin with two side by side front seats and a rear bench, a non-retractable tricycle landing gear, and 89.5 kW (120 hp) engine. The following description applies to the prototype:

TYPE: Tandem two-seat touring homebuilt.
AIRFRAME: Mostly all-wooden, with Dacron covering overall. Alternate wood and Klégécel wing nose ribs. Large polyester fairings over wing/fuselage junctions. Wing section NACA 4417. Retractable tricycle landing gear.
POWER PLANT: One 119 kW (160 hp) Textron Lycoming O-320-D2A. Fuel capacity 300 litres (79.25 US gallons; 66 Imp gallons).
DIMENSIONS, EXTERNAL:

Wing span	9.88 m (32 ft 5 in)
Length overall	7.20 m (23 ft 7½ in)
Height overall	1.90 m (6 ft 3 in)

AREA:

Wings, gross	12.20 m² (131.3 sq ft)

WEIGHTS:

Weight empty	642 kg (1,415 lb)
Max T-O weight	1,012 kg (2,231 lb)

PERFORMANCE:

Cruising speed	135 knots (250 km/h; 155 mph)
Range with max fuel, 45 min reserves	
	1,215 nm (2,250 km; 1,398 miles)

STERN
RENÉ STERN
10 rue du Château, 57730 Folschviller

STERN ST 80 BALADE
The ST 80 flew for the first time on 17 July 1983. Plans are available to amateur builders, together with kits containing major component parts.
TYPE: Single-seat homebuilt.
AIRFRAME: All-wood with fabric covering, except for fuselage which has wooden skins. Wing section NACA 43015 at root, NACA 43012 at tip. Non-retractable tricycle type.
POWER PLANT: One 45 kW (60 hp) Limbach 1,700 cc in prototype. Alternative Volkswagen modified motorcar engine in 1,600 cc to 2,000 cc range. Fuel capacity 32 litres (8.5 US gallons; 7 Imp gallons).
DIMENSIONS, EXTERNAL:

Wing span	6.40 m (21 ft 0 in)
Length overall	4.90 m (16 ft 0¾ in)
Propeller diameter	1.40 m (4 ft 7 in)

AREA:

Wings, gross	7.0 m² (75.35 sq ft)

WEIGHTS:

Weight empty	230 kg (507 lb)
Max T-O weight	340 kg (750 lb)

PERFORMANCE:

Max level speed	
	97-108 knots (180-200 km/h; 112-124 mph)
Max cruising speed	86 knots (160 km/h; 99 mph)
Stalling speed	44 knots (80 km/h; 50 mph)
Max rate of climb at S/L	240 m (785 ft)/min

TISSERAND — *see Hydroplum*

ZENITH-AVIATION — *see Aéronautic 2000*

The SB1 Antarès designed and built in Baugé, France, by M Claude Soyer and M Jean Barritault

Pottier P.70S with standard tricycle landing gear *(M.J. Hooks)*

Almost complete Piel C.P.90 Pinocchio II constructed by M Pradurous

Pottier P.180S *(M.J. Hooks)*

Piel C.P.150 Onyx with non-standard glassfibre fuselage *(Geoffrey P. Jones)*

Pottier P.50 Bouvreuil (60 kW; 80 hp Limbach LB 2000 EB1 engine) built by Mr Anton Seger of Basle, Switzerland *(Wolfgang Wagner)*

Stern ST 80 single-seat homebuilt aircraft with wings folded *(M.J. Hooks)*

GERMANY
(FEDERAL REPUBLIC)

AKAFLIEG MÜNCHEN
**FLUGTECHNISCHE FORSCHUNGSGRUPPE
an der TECHNISCHEN UNIVERSITÄT
MÜNCHEN**

Arcisstrasse 21, Postfach 202420, 8000 Munich 2

Telephone: 089 28 61 11

DIRECTOR: Wolfgang Fischer

AKAFLIEG MÜNCHEN Mü 30 SCHLACRO
The Mü 30 is a tandem two-seat aerobatic monoplane suitable also for glider towing, hence its name Schlacro (schlepp = towing, acro = aerobatic). The first flight was scheduled for the end of 1987, but no news has been received.

The one-piece symmetrical single-spar wing is of carbonfibre and Kevlar composites sandwich construction. Wing section is Mü 17/40/22/15P. The fabric covered steel tube fuselage and carbonfibre/Kevlar composites tail unit were designed to optimise aerobatics. Control surfaces have a carbonfibre structure, fabric covered. Power plant is a 156 kW (210 hp) Porsche PFM 3200, and fuel capacity is 148 litres (39 US gallons; 32.5 Imp gallons). A non-retractable tailwheel landing gear is fitted.

DIMENSIONS, EXTERNAL:
Wing span	8.70 m (28 ft 6½ in)
Length overall (flying attitude)	7.30 m (23 ft 11½ in)

Height overall	2.20 m (7 ft 2½ in)
Propeller diameter	2.00 m (6 ft 6¾ in)

AREA:

Wings, gross	11.80 m² (127.0 sq ft)

WEIGHTS (estimated):

Weight empty	565 kg (1,245 lb)
T-O weight for glider towing	700 kg (1,543 lb)
Max T-O weight	850 kg (1,874 lb)

PERFORMANCE (estimated, at max T-O weight except where indicated):

Max level speed	162 knots (300 km/h; 186 mph)
Cruising speed, 75% power	146 knots (270 km/h; 168 mph)
Max rate of climb at S/L	560 m (1,840 ft)/min
T-O to 15 m (50 ft)	270 m (886 ft)
Landing from 15 m (50 ft)	310 m (1,017 ft)

g limits: at max T-O weight	±8
at 700 kg (1,543 lb) aerobatic weight	±10

BINDER

BINDER AVIATIK GmbH

Flugplatz Donaueschingen-Villingen, 7710 Donaueschingen
Telephone: 0771 3078/9
Telex: 7 92 889 AVIAT D
MANAGER: Heinz Westphal

BINDER BA83 MISTRAL II

The Mistral was designed and developed for Binder Aviatik GmbH by Ikarusflug Bodensee; the first of three prototypes flew on 30 September 1983. It is being manufactured in co-operation between the two companies.
TYPE: Single-seat microlight, conforming to West German national standards.

AIRFRAME: Mainframe of aluminium alloy tubing. Wings have aluminium spars and glassfibre reinforced leading-edges, Dacron covered. Wing section Mü-14%. Dacron covered tail unit. Three-axis control. Non-retractable tricycle landing gear.
POWER PLANT: One 21 kW (28 hp) König SD 570. Fuel capacity 20 litres (5.3 US gallons; 4.4 Imp gallons).

DIMENSIONS, EXTERNAL:

Wing span	9.40 m (30 ft 10 in)
Length overall	5.88 m (19 ft 3½ in)
Height overall	2.60 m (8 ft 6¼ in)
Propeller diameter	1.37 m (4 ft 6 in)

AREA:

Wings, gross	13.90 m² (149.6 sq ft)

WEIGHTS:

Weight empty	114 kg (251 lb)
Pilot weight range	70-117 kg (154-258 lb)
Max T-O weight	231 kg (509 lb)

PERFORMANCE:

Max level and max cruising speed	46 knots (85 km/h; 53 mph)
Econ cruising speed	32 knots (60 km/h; 37 mph)
Stalling speed:	
power on	24.5 knots (45 km/h; 28 mph)
power off	25 knots (46 km/h; 29 mph)
Max rate of climb at S/L	90 m (295 ft)/min
T-O run	70 m (230 ft)
Landing run	50 m (164 ft)
Range with max fuel	102 nm (190 km; 118 miles)
Endurance with max fuel	2 h 12 min
g limits	+6/-3

BOROWSKI — *see Technoflug*

COZY — *see Co Z Development Corporation in US section*

DALLACH

DALLACH FLUGZEUGE GmbH

Stauferstrasse 20, 7076 Wissgoldingen
Telephone: (071 62) 23497

DALLACH SUNRISE II

This aircraft is available in ready to fly or kit form.
TYPE: Single/two-seat microlight; optional dual controls.
AIRFRAME: Wings have GFRP sandwich leading-edge torsion box, carbonfibre spar booms, ribs of GFRP/foam and Dacron covering. Welded steel tube fuselage, with GFRP sandwich decking and overall Dacron covering. Wire braced tail unit of Dacron covered GFRP sandwich. Non-retractable tailwheel landing gear. Skis optional.
POWER PLANT: One 30 kW (40 hp) KKHD engine, based on Citroën Visa.

DIMENSIONS, EXTERNAL:

Wing span	13.10 m (42 ft 11¾ in)
Length overall	5.30 m (17 ft 4¾ in)

AREA:

Wings, gross	15.4 m² (165.75 sq ft)

WEIGHTS:

Weight empty	approx 150 kg (330 lb)
Max T-O weight	340 kg (750 lb)

PERFORMANCE (at max T-O weight, except where indicated):

Max level speed	65 knots (120 km/h; 75 mph)
Cruising speed (50% power)	43 knots (80 km/h; 50 mph)
Stalling speed:	
max T-O weight	24 knots (45 km/h; 28 mph)
pilot only	22 knots (40 km/h; 25 mph)
Max rate of climb at S/L:	
max T-O weight	114 m (374 ft)/min
pilot only	174 m (570 ft)/min
T-O run: max T-O weight	100 m (328 ft)
pilot only	70 m (230 ft)
Range with max fuel (50% power)	143 nm (266 km; 165 miles)

HEWA-TECHNICS

HEWA-TECHNICS

AIRCRAFT DIVISION: Dorfstrasse 77, 8939 Markt Wald
Telephone: 08262 1868
Telex: 539625 HEWAT D
GENERAL MANAGER: Heinz Wagenseil

The original J-5 composites light aircraft was designed in Poland by Mr Jaroslaw Janowski. An aircraft branch of the Marko-Elektronic Company was established in that country to offer for export kits of component parts to construct the J-5. Hewa-Technics of West Germany markets the aircraft in kit and ready-assembled forms, under the name of Marco J-5. The kit is claimed to take approximately 600 working hours to assemble.

HEWA-TECHNICS MARCO J-5

TYPE: Single-seat homebuilt.
AIRFRAME: Built entirely of glassfibre and epoxy, except for the flaperons which are glassfibre and duralumin. Wortmann FX 67-K170/17 wing section. Three-axis control. Landing gear comprises retractable mainwheel, non-retractable tailwheel and wingtip balancers. Polish-assembled example illustrated has new non-retractable conventional tailwheel gear.
POWER PLANT: One 22.4 kW (30 hp) KFM 107ER. Fuel capacity 25 litres (6.6 US gallons; 5.5 Imp gallons).

DIMENSIONS, EXTERNAL:

Wing span	8.10 m (26 ft 7 in)
Length overall	4.70 m (15 ft 5 in)
Height overall	1.40 m (4 ft 7¼ in)
Propeller diameter	1.15 m (3 ft 9¼ in)

AREA:

Wings, gross	6.50 m² (70.0 sq ft)

WEIGHTS:

Weight empty	140 kg (309 lb)
Pilot weight range	60-95 kg (132-209 lb)
Max T-O weight	260 kg (575 lb)

PERFORMANCE:

Max level speed	113 knots (210 km/h; 130 mph)
Econ cruising speed	81 knots (150 km/h; 93 mph)
Stalling speed	42 knots (78 km/h; 49 mph)
Max rate of climb at S/L	150 m (490 ft)/min
Service ceiling	5,000 m (16,400 ft)
T-O run	200 m (656 ft)
Landing run	150 m (490 ft)
Range with max fuel	378 nm (700 km; 435 miles)
g limits	+4/-3

HFL

HFL-FLUGZEUGBAU GmbH

Hohenhorststrasse 1b, 2120 Lüneburg
Telephone: (04131) 5 60 68
Telex: 2182181 ARTO D
TECHNICAL MANAGER: Dipl Ing Konrad Herz
Developed from the HFL-UL convertible monoplane/biplane, the original Stratos first flew in 1985. The current 'production' Stratos II is certificated as a microlight aircraft by the Deutsche Aeroklub, but has the characteristics of a motor glider.

HFL STRATOS II

TYPE: Single-seat microlight motor glider.

AIRFRAME: Aluminium alloy tubing fuselage frame; carbon-Kevlar tubes supporting tail surfaces. Carbonfibre/GFRP wing structure, of Wortmann FX-63-137 section. Polyester fabric covering. Three-axis control. Non-retractable tricycle landing gear.
POWER PLANT: One 17.9 kW (24 hp) König SC 430. Fuel capacity 32 litres (8.5 US gallons; 7 Imp gallons).

DIMENSIONS, EXTERNAL:

Wing span	13.60 m (44 ft 7½ in)
Length overall	6.60 m (21 ft 8 in)
Height overall	2.00 m (6 ft 6¾ in)
Propeller diameter	1.96 m (6 ft 5 in)

AREA:

Wings, gross	15.00 m² (161.5 sq ft)

WEIGHTS:

Weight empty	150 kg (331 lb)
Pilot weight range	60-100 kg (132-220 lb)
Max T-O weight	280 kg (617 lb)

PERFORMANCE:

Max level speed	70 knots (130 km/h; 81 mph)
Max cruising speed	62 knots (115 km/h; 71 mph)
Stalling speed	24 knots (43 km/h; 27 mph)
Max rate of climb at S/L	150 m (490 ft)/min
T-O run	80 m (263 ft)
Landing run	40 m (132 ft)
Range	216 nm (400 km; 248 miles)
Min rate of sink (power off)	48 m (157 ft)/min

IKARUS

IKARUS DEUTSCHLAND COMCO GmbH

Tannenweg 20, 7031 Aidlingen
Telephone: (0 70 34) 4081/83

IKARUS-COMCO SHERPA I

The Sherpa I was designed in Switzerland by Hans Gigax and made its first flight in May 1982. Production has been licensed to Ikarus-Comco in West Germany. Orders for several hundred Sherpa Is have been received.
TYPE: Single-seat microlight.
AIRFRAME: Aluminium tube framework. Wire-braced fabric covered wings. Non-retractable tricycle landing gear. Three-axis control.
POWER PLANT: One 16.4 kW (22 hp) Hirth 263R. Fuel capacity 26 litres (6.9 US gallons; 5.7 Imp gallons).

DIMENSIONS, EXTERNAL:

Wing span	10.50 m (34 ft 5½ in)
Length overall	4.95 m (16 ft 3 in)
Height overall	2.82 m (9 ft 3 in)
Propeller diameter	1.40 m (4 ft 7 in)

AREA:

Wings, gross	15.70 m² (169.0 sq ft)

WEIGHTS:

Weight empty	100 kg (220 lb)
Max T-O weight	215 kg (474 lb)

PERFORMANCE:

Max level speed	48 knots (90 km/h; 56 mph)
Max cruising speed	43 knots (80 km/h; 50 mph)
Stalling speed	22 knots (40 km/h; 25 mph)
Max rate of climb at S/L	91 m (300 ft)/min
T-O run	60 m (197 ft)
Landing run	40 m (131 ft)
Range with max fuel	81 nm (150 km; 93 miles)
g limits	+6/-3 ultimate

IKARUS-COMCO SHERPA II

The Sherpa II is a more powerful two-seat version of the Sherpa I which entered production in the Summer of 1983. Description as for Sherpa I except as follows:
POWER PLANT: One 31.3 kW (42 hp) Hirth 276R.

Model of the Akaflieg München Mü 30 Schlacro aerobatic and glider towing aircraft

Binder BA83 Mistral II with cockpit fairing

Dallach Sunrise II single/two-seat microlight aircraft

Ikarus-Comco Sherpa II

HFL Stratos II microlight motor glider

Polish-assembled Marco J-5 with new non-retractable tailwheel landing gear (Martin Fricke)

Ikarus-Comco Fox-C22 two-seat microlight

WEIGHTS:
Weight empty	115 kg (253 lb)
Max T-O weight	300 kg (661 lb)

PERFORMANCE:
Max level speed	43 knots (80 km/h; 50 mph)
Max cruising speed	38 knots (70 km/h; 43 mph)
Stalling speed	23 knots (42 km/h; 26 mph)
Max rate of climb at S/L	122 m (400 ft)/min
T-O run	45 m (148 ft)
Landing run	35 m (115 ft)

IKARUS-COMCO FOX-D

This Gigax-designed microlight is a single-seater, which first flew in December 1982. It has an aluminium alloy frame with partially enclosed cockpit pod. Three-axis control. Tricycle landing gear, or optional floats.

POWER PLANT: One 16.4 kW (22 hp) Hirth 383 cc. Fuel capacity 13 litres (3.4 US gallons; 2.8 Imp gallons). Provision for auxiliary tank.

DIMENSIONS, EXTERNAL:
Wing span	10.00 m (32 ft 9¾ in)
Length overall	4.75 m (15 ft 7 in)
Height overall	2.65 m (8 ft 8¼ in)
Propeller diameter	1.60 m (5 ft 3 in)

AREA:
Wings, gross	13.20 m² (142.0 sq ft)

WEIGHTS:
Weight empty	100 kg (221 lb)
Max T-O weight	215 kg (474 lb)

PERFORMANCE:
Max cruising speed	40 knots (75 km/h; 47 mph)
Stalling speed	23 knots (42 km/h; 26 mph)

Max rate of climb at S/L	120 m (395 ft)/min
T-O and landing run on grass	30-40 m (98-131 ft)
Range with max fuel	
	approx 108 nm (200 km; 124 miles)
g limits	+6/−3 ultimate

IKARUS-COMCO FOX-C22

The Fox-C22 is basically a side by side two-seat derivative of the Fox-D, of greater dimensions and higher power. Dual controls are standard.

POWER PLANT: One 28.3 kW (38 hp) Rotax 462. Fuel capacity 20 litres (5.3 US gallons; 4.4 Imp gallons).

DIMENSIONS, EXTERNAL:
Wing span	10.40 m (34 ft 1½ in)
Length overall	6.25 m (20 ft 6 in)
Height overall	2.20 m (7 ft 2½ in)

AREA:		Max T-O weight	330 kg (728 lb)
Wings, gross	15.20 m² (163.6 sq ft)	PERFORMANCE:	
WEIGHTS:		Max cruising speed	43 knots (80 km/h; 50 mph)
Weight empty	148 kg (326 lb)	Stalling speed	25 knots (45 km/h; 28 mph)

Max rate of climb at S/L: pilot only 240 m (785 ft)/min
two persons 168 m (550 ft)/min
T-O and landing run on grass 50-60 m (164-197 ft)
Range about 135 nm (250 km; 155 miles)

KONSUPROD

KONSUPROD GmbH & CO KG

Gwinnerstrasse 13, 6000 Frankfurt am Main
Telephone: (069) 41 60 29
Telex: 4 17 362 KONS D

KONSUPROD ULM-1B MOSKITO

The Moskito microlight is available as a kit of pre-moulded component parts or ready assembled. The prototype first flew on 9 August 1986. By early 1988 15 ready assembled aircraft had been built.
TYPE: Single-seat microlight.
AIRFRAME: Wings and tail unit constructed of GFRP and PVC foam, cotton fabric covered. Wing section

Wortmann FX-63-137. Fuselage of carbonfibre/Kevlar/ glassfibre. Three-axis control. Non-retractable tricycle landing gear.
POWER PLANT: One 17 kW (23 hp) König SC 430. Fuel capacity 20 litres (5.3 US gallons; 4.4 Imp gallons)

DIMENSIONS, EXTERNAL:
Wing span 10.40 m (34 ft 1½ in)
Length overall 5.85 m (19 ft 2¼ in)
Height overall 1.80 m (5 ft 11 in)
Propeller diameter 1.30 m (4 ft 3¼ in)
AREA:
Wings, gross 12.90 m² (138.9 sq ft)
WEIGHTS:
Weight empty 123 kg (271 lb)

Pilot weight range 55-95 kg (122-209 lb)
Max T-O weight 235 kg (518 lb)
PERFORMANCE:
Max level and cruising speed
54 knots (100 km/h; 62 mph)
Econ cruising speed
38-43 knots (70-80 km/h; 43-50 mph)
Stalling speed 25 knots (45 km/h; 28 mph)
Max rate of climb at S/L 72 m (236 ft)/min
Service ceiling 4,000 m (13,125 ft)
T-O to 15 m (50 ft) 280 m (920 ft)
Landing from 15 m (50 ft) 350 m (1,150 ft)
Range with max fuel 140 nm (260 km; 161 miles)
Endurance 4 h 15 min
g limits +4/−2

LEICHTFLUGZEUG

LEICHTFLUGZEUG GmbH & CO KG

Leopoldweg 3, 5982 Neuenrade
Telephone: (0 23 92) 63 09

LEICHTFLUGZEUG SKY WALKER II

TYPE: Tandem two-seat, dual control microlight.
AIRFRAME: Tubular metal mainframe and fabric covered flying and control surfaces. Three-axis control. Non-

retractable tricycle landing gear, with optional floats or wheel-skis.
POWER PLANT: One 26.8 kW (36 hp) Göbler Hirth 2702. (Sky Walker II-300 has 38.8 kW; 52 hp Göbler Hirth 2703.)
DIMENSIONS, EXTERNAL:
Wing span 10.15 m (33 ft 3½ in)
Length overall 5.70 m (18 ft 8½ in)
Height overall 1.95 m (6 ft 4¾ in)
AREA:
Wings, gross 15.20 m² (163.6 sq ft)

WEIGHTS:
Weight empty 150 kg (331 lb)
Max T-O weight 350 kg (772 lb)
PERFORMANCE (Sky Walker II):
Max level speed 54 knots (100 km/h; 62 mph)
Cruising speed 43 knots (80 km/h; 50 mph)
Max rate of climb at S/L 78 m (256 ft)/min
T-O run 20-80 m (66-262 ft)
g limits +6/−4

TECHNOFLUG

TECHNOFLUG LEICHTFLUGZEUGBAU GmbH

Industriestrasse 6, 7230 Schramberg-2
Telephone: (07422) 8423
DESIGNER: Dipl Ing B. Karrais

TECHNOFLUG PICCOLO

The Piccolo is a modified and slightly larger version of the Neukom AN-20B, which first flew in prototype form in May 1986. It is now available in ready-assembled form; 35 had been ordered and eleven delivered by April 1988.
TYPE: Single-seat microlight motor glider; conforms to JAR 22.

AIRFRAME: Wings have a single GFRP composites spar and sandwich skins, and carry upper surface spoilers. Wing section Wortmann FX 63-137. Monocoque fuselage and tail unit of GFRP construction. Three-axis control. Non-retractable tricycle landing gear.
POWER PLANT: One 17 kW (23 hp) Solo 2350B. Fuel capacity 22 litres (5.8 US gallons; 4.8 Imp gallons).
DIMENSIONS, EXTERNAL:
Wing span 13.30 m (43 ft 7½ in)
Length overall 6.65 m (21 ft 9¾ in)
Height overall 1.02 m (3 ft 4¼ in)
Propeller diameter 1.18 m (3 ft 10½ in)
AREA:
Wings, gross 10.60 m² (114.1 sq ft)
WEIGHTS:
Weight empty 170 kg (375 lb)

Baggage weight 10 kg (22 lb)
Pilot weight range 65-110 kg (144-242 lb)
Max T-O weight 285 kg (628 lb)
PERFORMANCE (at max T-O weight):
Max level speed 74 knots (138 km/h; 86 mph)
Econ cruising speed 65 knots (120 km/h; 75 mph)
Stalling speed 30 knots (54 km/h; 34 mph)
Max rate of climb at S/L 126 m (413 ft)/min
Service ceiling 3,500 m (11,500 ft)
T-O to 15 m (50 ft) 258 m (846 ft)
Landing run 50 m (164 ft)
Range with max fuel 248 nm (460 km; 285 miles)
Endurance 4 h
g limits +5.3/−2.6

ULTRALEICHT

ULTRALEICHT-FLUGGERÄTEBAU GmbH

Twist 9, 4455 Wietmarschen
Telephone: 059 36 64 80
Telex: 98617

ULTRALEICHT WILDENTE

TYPE: Single-seat microlight.
AIRFRAME: Wings have light alloy basic structure, with metal covered leading-edge, some structure of PVC hard foam and glassfibre. Steel tube fuselage, with fabric covering on tailboom. Three-axis control. Non-retractable tricycle landing gear. Optional wheel-skis.
POWER PLANT: One 16.4 kW (22 hp) Göbler-Hirth F 263. Fuel capacity 20 litres (5.3 US gallons; 4.4 Imp gallons).
DIMENSIONS, EXTERNAL:
Wing span 10.50 m (34 ft 5½ in)
Length overall 6.10 m (20 ft 0 in)
Height overall 2.75 m (9 ft 0¼ in)
Propeller diameter 1.35 m (4 ft 5¼ in)

AREA:
Wings, gross 15.4 m² (165.75 sq ft)
WEIGHTS:
Weight empty 145 kg (320 lb)
Max T-O weight 240 kg (529 lb)
PERFORMANCE:
Max level speed 54 knots (100 km/h; 62 mph)
Min flying speed 27 knots (50 km/h; 31 mph)
Stalling speed at AUW of 220 kg (485 lb)
25 knots (45 km/h; 28 mph)
Max rate of climb at S/L at max T-O weight
108 m (354 ft)/min
T-O run 50-70 m (164-230 ft)
Landing run 40-50 m (131-164 ft)
Range 140 nm (260 km; 162 miles)
g limits +4/−2

ULTRALEICHT WILDENTE 2

This tandem two-seat version of the Wildente has an open steel tube tailboom extending from the bottom of its

fuselage structure, and a 28 kW (38 hp) Göbler-Hirth F27 02R engine.
DIMENSIONS, EXTERNAL:
Wing span 11.00 m (36 ft 1 in)
Length overall 7.10 m (23 ft 3½ in)
Height overall 2.50 m (8 ft 2½ in)
Propeller diameter 1.62 m (5 ft 3¾ in)
AREA:
Wings, gross 16.50 m² (177.6 sq ft)
WEIGHTS:
Weight empty 150 kg (331 lb)
Max T-O weight 350 kg (772 lb)
PERFORMANCE:
Stalling speed at max T-O weight
27 knots (50 km/h; 31 mph)
Max rate of climb at S/L 102 m (335 ft)/min
T-O run 90-100 m (295-328 ft)
Landing run 90 m (295 ft)
g limits +4/−2

VOGT

HELMUT VOGT

Mörikestrasse 20, 7982 Baienfurt
Telephone: 0751 46840

VOGT LO-120

The LO-120 flew for the first time on 10 May 1984. Kits of the major component parts are available to amateur builders. Assembly takes about 400 working hours.
TYPE: Tandem two-seat, dual-control microlight trainer and homebuilt aircraft.
AIRFRAME: Single surface wood and GFRP composite wings of Göttingen G-625 section. Wooden fuselage. Three-axis control. Non-retractable tricycle landing gear.

POWER PLANT: One 27 kW (36 hp) Rotax 377. Fuel capacity 32 litres (8.5 US gallons; 7 Imp gallons). Optional engines are 21 kW (28 hp) Hirth or 16.4 kW (22 hp) Lloyd LS 400.
DIMENSIONS, EXTERNAL:
Wing span 12.00 m (39 ft 4½ in)
Length overall 7.00 m (22 ft 11½ in)
Height overall 1.75 m (5 ft 9 in)
Propeller diameter 1.60 m (5 ft 3 in)
AREA:
Wings, gross 18.00 m² (193.75 sq ft)
WEIGHTS:
Weight empty 150 kg (331 lb)
Pilot weight range 60-130 kg (132-286 lb)
Max T-O weight 340 kg (749 lb)

PERFORMANCE (Lloyd engine):
Max level speed 53 knots (98 km/h; 61 mph)
Econ cruising speed 38 knots (70 km/h; 43 mph)
Stalling speed 26 knots (48 km/h; 30 mph)
Max rate of climb at S/L 108 m (355 ft)/min
Service ceiling 4,000 m (13,125 ft)
T-O run 60 m (197 ft)
Landing run 150 m (492 ft)
Range with max standard fuel
215 nm (400 km; 248 miles)

VULCAN

VULCAN UL-AVIATION

Kiefernweg 13, 8011 Zorneding bei München
Telephone: (08106) 29148

VULCAN UL-AVIATION ALBATROS

TYPE: Side by side two-seat microlight.
AIRFRAME: Structure of light alloy tube, with fabric covered wings and tail unit, and glassfibre nose fairing. Three-axis control. Non-retractable tricycle landing gear. Optional floats.

POWER PLANT: One 28.3 kW (38 hp) Rotax 462 standard (47 kW; 63 hp Rotax 532 in export floatplanes). Fuel capacity 40 litres (10.6 US gallons; 8.8 Imp gallons).

DIMENSIONS, EXTERNAL:
Wing span 9.60 m (31 ft 6 in)

Konsuprod Moskito single-seat microlight

Leichtflugzeug Sky Walker two-seat microlight *(Wolfgang Wagner)*

Technoflug Piccolo in production form

Vulcan UL-Aviation Albatros

Vogt LO-120 tandem two-seat microlight trainer and homebuilt aircraft

Two-seat Ultraleicht Wildente 2 microlight *(Wolfgang Wagner)*

SciCraft Gambit two-seat homebuilt canard light aircraft *(G. Feinblatt/Media)*

Length overall	6.00 m (19 ft 8¼ in)	WEIGHTS:		Cruising speed	43 knots (80 km/h; 50 mph)
Height overall	3.07 m (10 ft 1 in)	Weight empty	150 kg (331 lb)	Stalling speed	21 knots (38 km/h; 24 mph)
		Max T-O weight	358 kg (789 lb)	Max rate of climb at S/L	150 m (490 ft)/min
AREA:		PERFORMANCE:		T-O run	30-50 m (98-164 ft)
Wings, gross	17.7 m² (190.5 sq ft)	Max level speed	62 knots (115 km/h; 71 mph)	Range	162 nm (300 km; 186 miles)

ISRAEL

SCICRAFT

**SCICRAFT LTD
(subsidiary of Cyclone Aviation Products Ltd)**

D N Misgav 20100
Telephone: (04) 962214
Telex: 46384 CYCLV
Fax: (04) 962220
PRESIDENT: Baruch Levanon
VICE-PRESIDENT: E. Jonathan Glinert

SCICRAFT GAMBIT

The Gambit, of which three models are available in kit form, is aimed mainly at private recreational pilots and training markets, though amphibious, agricultural and military applications are planned. Construction takes less than 400 working hours.

TYPE: Side by side two-seat homebuilt.

AIRFRAME: Wings have aluminium alloy leading-edges, composites cambered tips and winglets, and optional Tedlar or Ceconite skins. Composites ailerons on wings.

Composites foreplane of glassfibre/graphite/foam core sandwich. Elevators on foreplane. Rudder on each winglet, deflecting outward only. Composites fuselage of Kevlar/graphite/foam core sandwich. Non-retractable tricycle landing gear. Dual controls optional.

POWER PLANT: Available as **Gambit 600** with 47 kW (63 hp) Rotax 532, **Gambit 700** with 56 kW (75 hp) Hewland, or **Gambit 900** with 67 kW (90 hp) Norton rotary engine. Fuel capacity 60 litres (16 US gallons; 13.2 Imp gallons) standard; optional 30 litre (8 US gallon; 6.6 Imp gallon) auxiliary tank.

DIMENSIONS, EXTERNAL:		Weight empty: A		277 kg (610 lb)		B		100 knots (185 km/h; 115 mph)
Wing span	10.01 m (32 ft 10 in)	B:		299 kg (660 lb)		Min flying speed: A		39 knots (73 km/h; 45 mph)
Foreplane span	3.86 m (12 ft 8 in)	Max baggage: A		16 kg (35 lb)		B		42 knots (78 km/h; 48 mph)
Length overall	5.13 m (16 ft 10 in)	B		25 kg (55 lb)		Max rate of climb at S/L: A		183 m (600 ft)/min
Height overall	2.44 m (8 ft 0 in)	Max T-O weight: A		476 kg (1,050 lb)		B		259 m (850 ft)/min
Propeller diameter	1.52 m (5 ft 0 in)	B		506 kg (1,115 lb)		Range with standard fuel:		
AREAS:		PERFORMANCE (A and B as above):				A		217 nm (402 km; 250 miles)
Wings, gross	13.65 m² (147.0 sq ft)	Max level speed: A		87 knots (161 km/h; 100 mph)		B		347 nm (643 km; 400 miles)
Foreplanes, gross	1.77 m² (19.1 sq ft)	B		113 knots (209 km/h; 130 mph)		g limits: A		+7/−2.8
WEIGHTS (A: Gambit 600, B: Gambit 900):		Max cruising speed: A		78 knots (145 km/h; 90 mph)		B		+6.6/−2.64

ITALY

AEROSERVICE
AEROSERVICE ITALIANA SRL
Frazione Masio 103, Valle Masio, 10046 Poirino (To)
Telephone: (011) 945 18 04/945 24 66
Telex: 215069
Fax: (11) 945 11 31
GENERAL MANAGER: Claudio Gabriele
MARKETING MANAGER: Ing Diego Carnevale

AEROSERVICE ITALIANA EAGLE XL
A description of the original US built Eagle can be found under the American Aerolights heading in the 1983-84 *Jane's*. The XL is essentially a full three-axis version, with roll control spoilers added and a Rotax engine as standard.
TYPE: Single-seat microlight; conforms to FAR Pt 103.
AIRFRAME: Mainframe is of aluminium alloy, carbonfibre and Kevlar, with Dacron covering. Three-axis control by spoilers, foreplane elevator and wingtip rudders. Non-retractable tricycle landing gear. Optional floats and skis.
POWER PLANT: One 26 kW (35 hp) Rotax 377 or 29.4 kW (39.4 hp) Rotax 447. Fuel capacity 15 litres (4 US gallons; 3.3 Imp gallons).

DIMENSIONS, EXTERNAL:	
Wing span	10.67 m (35 ft 0 in)
Foreplane span	2.74 m (9 ft 0 in)
Length overall	4.57 m (15 ft 0 in)
Height overall	2.93 m (9 ft 7¼ in)
Propeller diameter	1.37 m (4 ft 6 in)
AREA:	
Wings/foreplane, gross	16.44 m² (177.0 sq ft)
WEIGHTS:	
Weight empty	102 kg (225 lb)
Pilot weight range	54.5-109 kg (120-240 lb)
Max T-O weight	231 kg (510 lb)
PERFORMANCE (with 68 kg; 150 lb pilot; Rotax 377):	
Max level speed	43 knots (80 km/h; 50 mph)
Econ cruising speed	32 knots (60 km/h; 37 mph)
Min flying speed	21 knots (39 km/h; 24 mph)
Max rate of climb at S/L	229 m (750 ft)/min
Service ceiling	5,335 m (17,500 ft)
T-O and landing run	38 m (125 ft)
Range with max fuel	78 nm (145 km; 90 miles)
Endurance with max fuel	2 h 30 min
g limits	+8/−2.5

AEROSERVICE ITALIANA COUNTRY EAGLE XL
The Country Eagle is an agricultural spraying aircraft, derived directly from the Eagle XL. The strong airframe and higher powered engine (38.8 kW; 52 hp Rotax 462 or 44.7 kW; 60 hp Arrow GT-500) allow safe transportation of 80 litres (21 US gallons; 17.6 Imp gallons) of chemicals. Spraying density can vary between 10 and 30 litres (2.6 and 7.9 US gallons; 2.2 and 6.6 Imp gallons) per hectare, with low density and high anti-drift mixtures. It is said to be particularly suited to spraying herbicides, insecticides and fungicides.
Known details where they vary from the Eagle XL are as follows:

AREA:	
Wings/foreplane, gross	16.98 m² (182.8 sq ft)
WEIGHTS:	
Weight empty	145 kg (320 lb)
Max T-O weight	335 kg (738 lb)
PERFORMANCE:	
Max level speed	46 knots (85 km/h; 53 mph)
Spraying speed	27-32 knots (50-60 km/h; 31-37 mph)
T-O run (rough field)	50 m (164 ft)
Endurance	1 h 30 min

AEROSERVICE ITALIANA EAGLE 2 PLC
This two-seat version of the Eagle XL has a more powerful 34.3 kW (46 hp) Rotax 503 engine, and does not conform to FAR Pt 103. The few known dimensional, weight and performance differences compared with the single-seater are as follows:

AREA:	
Wings/foreplane, gross	16.98 m² (182.8 sq ft)
WEIGHT:	
Weight empty	137 kg (302 lb)
PERFORMANCE:	
Max level speed	49 knots (90 km/h; 56 mph)
Cruising speed	35 knots (65 km/h; 40 mph)
Min flying speed	25 knots (46 km/h; 29 mph)
T-O run	70 m (230 ft)
Endurance	1 h 30 min

AEROSERVICE ITALIANA F2-FOXCAT
The F2-Foxcat is an all-composites version of the American Aircraft Falcon single-seat microlight. It can be

fitted with engines of 18.6-22.4 kW (25-30 hp), with an Arrow GT-254 as standard. The airframe is built of Kevlar/carbonfibre/glassfibre and epoxy resin composites and honeycomb. The wing/foreplane covering is Tedlar. Fuel capacity is 20 litres (5.3 US gallons; 4.4 Imp gallons).

DIMENSIONS, EXTERNAL:	
Wing span	10.97 m (36 ft 0 in)
Length overall	4.33 m (14 ft 2½ in)
Height overall	1.71 m (5 ft 7¼ in)
AREA:	
Wings, gross	16.26 m² (175.0 sq ft)
WEIGHTS:	
Weight empty	115 kg (253 lb)
Max T-O weight	240 kg (529 lb)
PERFORMANCE:	
Max level speed	65 knots (120 km/h; 75 mph)
Econ cruising speed	49 knots (90 km/h; 56 mph)
Min flying speed	21 knots (39 km/h; 25 mph)
Max rate of climb at S/L	244 m (800 ft)/min
Service ceiling	over 4,500 m (14,760 ft)
T-O run	50 m (164 ft)
Range with max fuel	over 162 nm (300 km; 186 miles)

AEROSERVICE ITALIANA F2-FOXCAT 2 PLC
This is a two-seat derivative of the single-seat Foxcat, powered by a 48.5 kW (65 hp) Arrow GT-500 two-stroke flat-twin engine or, optionally, the 34 kW (45.6 hp) Rotax 503.

DIMENSIONS, EXTERNAL:	
Wing span	10.97 m (36 ft 0 in)
Length overall	5.63 m (18 ft 5¾ in)
Height overall	1.78 m (5 ft 10 in)
AREA:	
Wings, gross	16.26 m² (175.0 sq ft)
WEIGHTS:	
Weight empty	150 kg (331 lb)
Max T-O weight	400 kg (882 lb)
PERFORMANCE:	
Max level speed	86 knots (160 km/h; 99 mph)
Econ cruising speed	65 knots (120 km/h; 75 mph)
Min flying speed	27 knots (49 km/h; 31 mph)
Max rate of climb at S/L	213 m (700 ft)/min
Service ceiling	4,500 m (14,765 ft)
T-O run	100 m (328 ft)
Range with max fuel	over 270 nm (500 km; 310 miles)

ALIFERRARI
ALIFERRARI
Zona Industriale 24, 45026 Lendinara (RO)
Telephone: (0425) 62018
This leading Italian manufacturer of trikes built in 1986 the prototype of a two-seat microlight named Cormorano.

ALIFERRARI CORMORANO
TYPE: Two-seat microlight.
AIRFRAME: Welded steel tube airframe. Flying surfaces Dacron covered. Non-retractable tricycle landing gear.

POWER PLANT: One 47 kW (63 hp) Rotax 532. Fuel capacity 20 litres (5.25 US gallons; 4.4 Imp gallons).

DIMENSIONS, EXTERNAL:	
Wing span	10.20 m (33 ft 5½ in)
Length overall	6.00 m (19 ft 8¼ in)
Height overall	2.50 m (8 ft 2½ in)
AREA:	
Wings, gross	18.00 m² (193.75 sq ft)
WEIGHTS:	
Weight empty	165 kg (364 lb)
Max T-O weight	365 kg (805 lb)

PERFORMANCE:	
Max level speed	59 knots (110 km/h; 68 mph)
Cruising speed	48 knots (90 km/h; 56 mph)
Stalling speed	23 knots (42 km/h; 26 mph)
Max rate of climb at S/L	240 m (787 ft)/min
T-O run	35 m (115 ft)
Landing run	40 m (132 ft)
g limits	+4.5/−2.5

AUI
AVIAZIONE ULTRALEGGERA ITALIANA
Via Sempione 9, 28040 Marano Ticino (NO)
Telephone: (0321) 97565/6
Telex: 616332 RIERO I
PRESIDENT: Gabriele Concato
ENGINEERING: Emilio Garatti
MARKETING: Claudio Garatti
AUI was formed to design and manufacture the first all-Italian microlight production aircraft, the T7 Leone, which flew for the first time on 15 August 1984.

AUI T7 LEONE
TYPE: Single-seat microlight.
AIRFRAME: Wire-braced wings and tail unit of aluminium

alloy tubing with Dacron covering. Welded chrome molybdenum steel tube fuselage, with one-piece light alloy tubular tailboom. Non-retractable tailwheel landing gear.
POWER PLANT: One 22.4 kW (30 hp) KFM 107ER.

DIMENSIONS, EXTERNAL:	
Wing span	9.40 m (30 ft 10 in)
Length overall	6.40 m (21 ft 0 in)
Height overall	2.80 m (9 ft 2¼ in)
AREA:	
Wings, gross	13.50 m² (145.3 sq ft)
WEIGHTS:	
Weight empty	115 kg (254 lb)
Max T-O weight	230 kg (507 lb)

PERFORMANCE:	
Max level speed	65 knots (120 km/h; 74 mph)
Cruising speed	51 knots (95 km/h; 59 mph)
Stalling speed	24 knots (43 km/h; 27 mph)
Max rate of climb at S/L	180 m (590 ft)/min
Service ceiling	3,050 m (10,000 ft)
T-O and landing run	35 m (115 ft)
Endurance with max fuel	4 h

AUI T8 LEONE
The T8 Leone is a side by side two-seat derivative of the T7, with a Rotax 503 or 532 engine. Dimensions and performance are generally similar to those of the T7.

CUP
CENTRO ULTRALEGGERI PARTENOPEO
Via S. Maria del Pianto 42, 80143 Naples
Telephone: (81) 759 00 45
DIRECTOR: Fabrizio Pisani
DESIGNERS: Franco Curcio and Franco Nuzzo

CUP F-3
First flown on 25 April 1986, the F-3 will be offered to experienced pilots in kit and ready assembled forms.
TYPE: Single-seat microlight.
AIRFRAME: All-metal construction, except for Dacron covering on wings and tailplane, and glassfibre winglet

type wingtips, fairing aft of cockpit and nosecone. Wing section NACA 2415. Three-axis control. Non-retractable tricycle landing gear. Optional floats and skis.
POWER PLANT: One 18.6 kW (25 hp) KFM 107ER. Fuel capacity 19 litres (5 US gallons; 4.2 Imp gallons).

Aeroservice Italiana Eagle XL single-seat microlight *(Avio Data)*

AUI T7 Leone single-seat microlight *(Avio Data)*

Aeroservice Italiana F2-Foxcat 2 PLC

CUP F-3 single-seat microlight

Aliferrari Cormorano prototype two-seat microlight *(Avio Data)*

Dedalus Poppy single-seat cabin monoplane *(Avio Data)*

DIMENSIONS, EXTERNAL:	
Wing span	9.55 m (31 ft 4 in)
Length overall	5.06 m (16 ft 7¼ in)
Height overall	1.70 m (5 ft 7 in)
Propeller diameter	1.00 m (3 ft 3½ in)
AREA:	
Wings, gross	13.30 m² (143.2 sq ft)
WEIGHTS:	
Weight empty	115 kg (254 lb)
Pilot weight range	60-91 kg (133-200 lb)
Max T-O weight	220 kg (485 lb)
PERFORMANCE:	
Max level speed	55 knots (102 km/h; 63 mph)
Cruising speed	47 knots (87 km/h; 54 mph)
Stalling speed	24 knots (44 km/h; 28 mph)
Max rate of climb at S/L	180 m (590 ft)/min

Service ceiling	2,400 m (7,875 ft)
T-O run	50 m (164 ft)
Endurance	3 h
g limits:	+4.4/−2.2
	+6.6/−3.3 ultimate

CUP BF-3

This side by side two-seat version of the F-3 was expected to fly for the first time in August 1988, with production beginning the following December. Kits and ready assembled aircraft will be offered.

TYPE: Two-seat microlight; conforms to FAR Pt 103.

AIRFRAME: Similar construction to F-3 and similar landing gear options.

POWER PLANT: One 28 kW (37.5 hp) Rotax 462. Fuel capacity 19 litres (5 US gallons; 4.2 Imp gallons).

DIMENSIONS, EXTERNAL:	
Wing span	10.40 m (34 ft 1½ in)
Length overall	5.45 m (17 ft 10½ in)
Height overall	1.90 m (6 ft 2¾ in)
Propeller diameter	1.35 m (4 ft 5¼ in)
AREA:	
Wings, gross	14.56 m² (156.7 sq ft)
WEIGHTS:	
Weight empty	150 kg (331 lb)
Crew weight range	57-150 kg (126-331 lb)
Max T-O weight	330 kg (727 lb)
PERFORMANCE: To be evaluated	
Design g limits	+4/-3.8

DEDALUS
DEDALUS Srl

Viale Campania 29, 20133 Milan
Telephone: (02) 71 63 41
GENERAL MANAGER: Marco Baggi

DEDALUS POPPY

The prototype Poppy flew for the first time in May 1984. Kits are available, requiring about 300 working hours to assemble. Many completed aircraft are flying.

TYPE: Single-seat homebuilt.

AIRFRAME: Airframe is geodetic structure of Sitka spruce, with Dacron fabric covering, although aluminium alloy bracing struts are used and the engine cowling can be of glassfibre. Wing section Rhode St Genese 34. Non-retractable tailwheel landing gear.

POWER PLANT: One 18.6 kW (25 hp) KFM 107E. Fuel capacity 20 litres (5.3 US gallons; 4.4 Imp gallons).

DIMENSIONS, EXTERNAL:	
Wing span	10.60 m (34 ft 9¼ in)
Length overall	5.90 m (19 ft 4¼ in)
Height overall	1.90 m (6 ft 2¾ in)
Propeller diameter	1.40 m (4 ft 7 in)
AREA:	
Wings, gross	15.00 m² (161.5 sq ft)

WEIGHTS:	
Weight empty	114 kg (252 lb)
Max T-O weight	210 kg (463 lb)
PERFORMANCE:	
Max level speed	54 knots (100 km/h; 62 mph)
Econ cruising speed	43 knots (80 km/h; 50 mph)
Stalling speed	22 knots (40 km/h; 25 mph)
Max rate of climb at S/L	183 m (600 ft)/min
Service ceiling	3,050 m (10,000 ft)
T-O to 15 m (50 ft)	50 m (164 ft)
Landing from 15 m (50 ft)	100 m (328 ft)
Range with max fuel	108 nm (200 km; 124 miles)

HOBBYSTICA
HOBBYSTICA AVIO

Via Migliara 52/5, 04014 Pontinia (Latina)
Telephone: (0773) 85 01 22
DIRECTOR: Roberto Ragogna

HOBBYSTICA AVIO A-2-S BARRACUDA

First flown in 1983, the Barracuda is available in ready assembled form.

TYPE: Single-seat microlight.

AIRFRAME: Wings constructed of aluminium alloy, steel tubing and wood, Dacron covered, with conical cambered glassfibre tips. Wing section NACA 4412. Aluminium alloy and steel tube fuselage structure, and light alloy tail unit. Three-axis control. Non-retractable tricycle landing gear.

POWER PLANT: One 30 kW (40 hp) 521 cc Hirth. Fuel capacity 20 litres (5.3 US gallons; 4.4 Imp gallons).

DIMENSIONS, EXTERNAL:
Wing span	8.20 m (26 ft 10¾ in)
Length overall	6.02 m (19 ft 9 in)
Height overall	2.30 m (7 ft 6½ in)
Propeller diameter	1.45 m (4 ft 9 in)

AREA:
Wings, gross	10.50 m² (113.0 sq ft)

WEIGHTS:
Weight empty	130 kg (287 lb)
Max T-O weight	240 kg (529 lb)

PERFORMANCE:
Max level speed	73 knots (135 km/h; 84 mph)
Econ cruising speed	46 knots (85 km/h; 53 mph)
Stalling speed, flaps down	22 knots (40 km/h; 25 mph)
Max rate of climb at S/L	180 m (590 ft)/min

Service ceiling	4,000 m (9,850 ft)
T-O run	60-65 m (197-213 ft)
Landing run	50-60 m (164-197 ft)
Range with max fuel	188 nm (350 km; 217 miles)
Endurance	2 h
g limits	+6/-3

HOBBYSTICA AVIO A-2-2 BARRACUDA

This is a tandem two-seat version of the A-2-S Barracuda, differing in the following details:
TYPE: Tandem two-seat, dual-control microlight.
AIRFRAME: Wing section NACA 4416.
POWER PLANT: One 48.5 kW (65 hp) Arrow engine, with 20 litres (5.3 US gallons; 4.4 Imp gallons) of fuel.

DIMENSIONS, EXTERNAL:
Wing span	10.05 m (32 ft 11¾ in)
Propeller diameter	1.70 m (5 ft 7 in)

AREA:
Wings, gross	16.98 m² (182.8 sq ft)

WEIGHTS:
Weight empty	165 kg (364 lb)
Max T-O weight	400 kg (882 lb)

PERFORMANCE:
Max level speed	70 knots (130 km/h; 81 mph)
Stalling speed at AUW of 350 kg (770 lb)	26 knots (48 km/h; 30 mph)
g limits at AUW of 350 kg (770 lb)	+4.4/-1.75

IANNOTTA
DOTT ING ORLANDO IANNOTTA

Via Nicolardi 254, 80131 Naples
Telephone: (081) 741 9324

IANNOTTA I-66L SAN FRANCESCO

Plans to build the San Francesco are available.
TYPE: Two-seat, dual-control homebuilt motor glider.
AIRFRAME: All wood wings, with plywood leading-edges and fabric covering overall. Wing section NACA 23012. Fabric covered steel tube fuselage structure, with wooden formers. Wire braced tail unit of welded steel tube, fabric covered. Non-retractable tailwheel landing gear.
POWER PLANT: One 51 kW (68 hp) Limbach SL 1700E. Fuel capacity 70 litres (18.5 US gallons; 15.4 Imp gallons).

DIMENSIONS, EXTERNAL:
Wing span	9.34 m (30 ft 7¾ in)
Length overall	6.60 m (21 ft 8 in)
Propeller diameter	1.45 m (4 ft 9 in)

AREA:
Wings, gross	13.61 m² (146.5 sq ft)

WEIGHTS:
Weight empty	268 kg (591 lb)
Max T-O weight	462 kg (1,018 lb)

PERFORMANCE, POWERED:
Max level speed	81 knots (150 km/h; 93 mph)
Cruising speed at S/L	70 knots (130 km/h; 81 mph)
Landing speed	35 knots (65 km/h; 41 mph)
Max rate of climb at S/L	210 m (690 ft)/min
Service ceiling	3,800 m (12,470 ft)
Range with max fuel	378 nm (700 km; 435 miles)

PERFORMANCE, UNPOWERED:
Best glide ratio at 50 knots (93 km/h; 58 mph)	14
Min rate of sink at 48 knots (88 km/h; 55 mph)	84 m (275 ft)/min

IANNOTTA 940 ZEFIRO

First flown on 25 April 1986. Plans are available to amateur constructors.
TYPE: Single-seat microlight; conforms to FAR Pt 103.
AIRFRAME: Wire braced all-wood structure, with fabric covered wings and tail surfaces. Wing section Göttingen 532 modified. Monowheel landing gear.

POWER PLANT: One 22.4 kW (30 hp) KFM 107ER Maxi. Fuel capacity 19 litres (5 US gallons; 4.2 Imp gallons).

DIMENSIONS, EXTERNAL:
Wing span	11.22 m (36 ft 9¾ in)
Length overall	6.20 m (20 ft 4 in)
Height overall	2.27 m (7 ft 5½ in)
Propeller diameter	1.05 m (3 ft 5¼ in)

AREA:
Wings, gross	16.20 m² (174.4 sq ft)

WEIGHTS:
Weight empty	115 kg (253 lb)
Pilot weight range	50-100 kg (110-220 lb)
Max T-O weight	225 kg (496 lb)

PERFORMANCE:
Max level speed	54 knots (100 km/h; 62 mph)
Econ cruising speed	32 knots (60 km/h; 37 mph)
Stalling speed	20 knots (37 km/h; 23 mph)
T-O to 15 m (50 ft)	250 m (820 ft)
Landing from 15 m (50 ft)	100 m (328 ft)
g limits	+4.4/-2.0

NIKE
NIKE AERONAUTICA SRL

Via Ferrarese 10, 40013 Castelmaggiore, Bologna
Telephone: (051) 765105
SALES MANAGER: Fabbri Giampiero

NIKE AERONAUTICA ITALZAIR

The Italzair is an Italian derivative of the Canadian Ultraflight Lazair microlight, the first example of which was built and flown in 1983. Production of a much improved version was expected to begin in mid-1987, but no news has been received.
TYPE: Single-seat microlight.

AIRFRAME: Aluminium alloy structure, except for composites wing ribs and Dacron covering. Three-axis control. Non-retractable tailwheel landing gear. Optional floats.
POWER PLANT: Two 7 kW (9.5 hp) 185 cc Rotax. Fuel capacity 25 litres (6.6 US gallons; 5.5 Imp gallons).

DIMENSIONS, EXTERNAL:
Wing span	11.07 m (36 ft 4 in)
Length overall	4.30 m (14 ft 1¼ in)
Height overall	1.93 m (6 ft 4 in)
Propeller diameter	0.90 m (2 ft 11½ in)

AREA:
Wings, gross	13.19 m² (142.0 sq ft)

WEIGHTS:
Weight empty	110 kg (243 lb)
Pilot weight range	60-90 kg (133-198 lb)
Max T-O weight	200 kg (441 lb)

PERFORMANCE:
Max level speed	54 knots (100 km/h; 62 mph)
Econ cruising speed	38 knots (70 km/h; 43 mph)
Stalling speed, power off	19 knots (34 km/h; 21 mph)
Max rate of climb at S/L	180 m (590 ft)/min
T-O run	50 m (164 ft)
Landing run	60 m (197 ft)
Range with max fuel	129 nm (240 km; 149 miles)
g limits	+4/-2

POLARIS
POLARIS MOTOR SRL

Via Flaminia 208, 06021 Costacciaro (PG)
Telephone: (075) 917 0492
Telex: 564006 POLARE I
MANAGING DIRECTOR: Doi Malingri
Polaris has two main centres of activity, namely hang gliders (see Hang Glider section) and microlights using these flexwings.

POLARIS AIR-DINGHY

The Polaris Air-Dinghy can be operated as a normal aerofoil boat or, with a hang glider flexwing, as a microlight water-based aircraft. More than 700 have been built.
TYPE: Single-seat boat or microlight.
AIRFRAME: Fuselage pod, two floats and connecting structure of GRP and Kevlar. Standard hang glider flexwing. Control by weight shift.
POWER PLANT: One 47.7 kW (64 hp) Arrow GT500. Fuel capacity 20 litres (5.3 US gallons; 4.4 Imp gallons).

DIMENSIONS, EXTERNAL (aircraft):
Length overall	3.93 m (12 ft 10¾ in)
Height overall	3.47 m (11 ft 4¾ in)

WEIGHTS (aircraft):
Weight empty	105 kg (232 lb)
Max T-O weight	280 kg (617 lb)

PERFORMANCE (aircraft):
Max level speed	43 knots (80 km/h; 50 mph)
Cruising speed	32 knots (60 km/h; 37 mph)
Stalling speed	16 knots (30 km/h; 19 mph)

T-O and landing run	30 m (99 ft)
Endurance	4 h

POLARIS AIR-DINGHY 1+1

This is identical to the Air-Dinghy but for higher weights and with provision for a passenger. Take-off and landing requires an experienced pilot if crew weight exceeds 140 kg (309 lb). Differences compared with the single-seat Air-Dinghy are as follows:

WEIGHTS:
Weight empty	125 kg (275 lb)
Max crew weight	180 kg (396 lb)
Max T-O weight	310 kg (683 lb)

PERFORMANCE:
Max level speed	38 knots (70 km/h; 43 mph)
Stalling speed	25 knots (45 km/h; 28 mph)

POLARIS CROSS-COUNTRY

The Cross-Country is a single- or tandem two-seat (1 + 1) land operated microlight, based on a 7215-61 light alloy tube trike and a Polaris flexwing hang glider with weight shift control. Power is provided by a 35.8 kW (48 hp) Rotax 503 engine.

WEIGHTS (excl wings):
Weight empty	64 kg (141 lb)
Max T-O weight	234 kg (516 lb)

POLARIS DYNAMIC TRICK

The Dynamic Trick is a convertible tandem two-seat microlight landplane/flying-boat/boat. In its conventional form it is a stainless steel trike fitted with a Polaris Gryps flexwing and powered by a Rotax engine. By removing the wheels and shock absorbers, and attaching a Dynamic EV 37 inflatable boat, the aircraft becomes a microlight flying-boat able to operate from water. When detached, the EV 37 can be used as a boat carrying four persons at 32 knots (60 km/h; 37 mph). The prototype was first flown in February 1987 and production of kits began in the following month.
TYPE: Two-seat microlight, flying-boat or boat.
POWER PLANT: One 35.8 kW (48 hp) Rotax 503. Fuel capacity 20 litres (5.3 US gallons; 4.4 Imp gallons).

DIMENSION:
Wing span	10.60 m (34 ft 9½ in)

AREA:
Wings, gross	19.00 m² (205.0 sq ft)

WEIGHTS (flying-boat):
Weight empty	130 kg (286 lb)
Crew weight range	60-180 kg (133-397 lb)
Max T-O weight	273 kg (602 lb)

PERFORMANCE (flying-boat):
Max level speed	43 knots (80 km/h; 50 mph)
Cruising speed	32-38 knots (60-70 km/h; 37-43 mph)
Stalling speed	19 knots (34 km/h; 21 mph)
T-O and landing run	30-50 m (99-164 ft)
Range	108 nm (200 km; 124 miles)
Endurance	3 h

T.E.D.A.
TECNOLOGIA EUROPEA DIVISIONE AERONAUTICA SRL

Via Canova 8, 20145 Milan

Telephone: (02) 3491841

Telex: 314003 MEC FIN I

Fax: 342026

T.E.D.A. LUCKY and RANGER

TYPES: Single-seat (Lucky) and tandem two-seat (Ranger) microlights.

AIRFRAME: Strut braced aluminium alloy wings with fabric covering. All-glassfibre pod and boom fuselage, reinforced with Derakane resin. Non-retractable tailwheel landing gear.
POWER PLANT: Lucky: One 22.4 kW (30 hp) IAME KFM 107. Ranger: One 35.8 kW (48 hp) Rotax 503. One 18 litre (4.75 US gallon; 4 Imp gallon) fuel tank in Lucky; two tanks in Ranger, each of 10 litres (2.6 US gallons; 2.2 Imp gallons) capacity.

DIMENSIONS, EXTERNAL (A: Lucky, B: Ranger):
Wing span: A	10.11 m (33 ft 2 in)
B	10.40 m (34 ft 1 in)
Length overall: A	5.83 m (19 ft 1½ in)
B	6.24 m (20 ft 5¾ in)
Height overall: A	2.20 m (7 ft 2½ in)
B	2.10 m (6 ft 10½ in)

T.E.D.A. Lucky single-seat microlight *(Avio Data)*

Prototype Nike Aeronautica Italzair single-seat microlight

Iannotta 940 Zefiro microlight (foreground) and I-66L San Francesco homebuilt

Polaris Dynamic Trick with EV 37 Dynamic inflatable boat hull

Polaris Cross-Country microlight

Polaris Air-Dinghy 1 + 1

Hobbystica Avio A-2-2 Barracuda two-seat microlight

Propeller diameter: A	1.30 m (4 ft 3¼ in)	Payload: A	110 kg (242 lb)	Stalling speed: A	22 knots (41 km/h; 25 mph)
B	1.50 m (4 ft 11 in)	B	160 kg (353 lb)	B	25 knots (45 km/h; 28 mph)
AREAS:		Max T-O weight: A	241 kg (531 lb)	Max rate of climb at S/L: A, B	275 m (900 ft)/min
Wings, gross: A	13.75 m² (148.0 sq ft)	B	330 kg (727 lb)	T-O run: A	35 m (115 ft)
B	17.20 m² (185.0 sq ft)			B	40 m (131 ft)
WEIGHTS:		PERFORMANCE:		Landing run, with brakes: A	20 m (66 ft)
Weight empty: A	114 kg (251 lb)	Max level speed: A, B	54 knots (100 km/h; 62 mph)	B	30 m (98 ft)
B	150 kg (330 lb)	Cruising speed: A	46 knots (85 km/h; 53 mph)	g limits: A	+4/−2
		B	51 knots (95 km/h; 59 mph)	B	+3.8/−1.9

LUXEMBOURG

WOLFF
ATELIERS PAUL WOLFF
1 Rue des Romains, L-8284 Kehlen
Telephone: Luxembourg 309954

WOLFF FLASH-3
The Flash-3 was exhibited at the 1985 RSA meeting at Brienne in France, before it had made its first flight. It is offered in the form of a series of component kits, with an estimated construction time of 650 to 750 hours.

TYPE: Three-seat homebuilt aircraft.

AIRFRAME: Entire airframe constructed of vinylester and resin composites, partially strengthened with carbonfibre. Wing section NACA 43012₅ at root, 43010 at tip. Retractable tricycle landing gear.

POWER PLANT: One 112 kW (150 hp) Textron Lycoming O-320. Other engines of up to 194 kW (260 hp) can be fitted. Fuel capacity: standard tank 261 litres (69 US gallons; 57.4 Imp gallons); long range tank 541 litres (143 US gallons; 119 Imp gallons); long range tank with tip tanks 641 litres (169.3 US gallons; 141 Imp gallons).

DIMENSIONS, EXTERNAL:
Wing span, over tip tanks	8.53 m (27 ft 11¾ in)
Length overall	7.93 m (26 ft 0¼ in)
Height overall	2.11 m (6 ft 11 in)
Propeller diameter	1.93 m (6 ft 4 in)

AREA:
Wings, gross	10.00 m² (107.64 sq ft)

WEIGHTS:
Weight empty   508 kg (1,120 lb)
Baggage capacity   120 kg (264 lb)
Max T-O weight: without tip tanks   996 kg (2,196 lb)
   with tip tanks   1,066 kg (2,350 lb)
PERFORMANCE (at max T-O weight):
Max level speed at S/L   197 knots (365 km/h; 227 mph)

Econ cruising speed at 3,050 m (10,000 ft)
   180 knots (334 km/h; 207 mph)
Stalling speed, flaps down   44 knots (81 km/h; 50 mph)
Max rate of climb at S/L   366 m (1,200 ft)/min
Service ceiling   5,430 m (17,820 ft)
T-O run   230 m (755 ft)
Landing run   210 m (689 ft)

Range with standard fuel, two occupants and baggage
   1,776 nm (3,291 km; 2,045 miles)

POLAND

JANOWSKI
JAROSLAW JANOWSKI
ul Nowomiejska 2 m 29, 91-061 Lodz

JANOWSKI J-2 POLONEZ
The prototype Polonez flew for the first time on 22 August 1977. The following description applies to this aircraft in its current form:
TYPE: Single-seat homebuilt microlight.

AIRFRAME: All-wood construction, except for fabric covering on wings, ailerons, tailplane and rudder. Wing section NACA 23012. Non-retractable tailwheel landing gear.
POWER PLANT: One 22.5 kW (30 hp) Trabant motorcar engine. Aircraft may be fitted with any other suitable engine of 18.5-30 kW (25-40 hp).
DIMENSIONS, EXTERNAL:
Wing span   7.00 m (23 ft 0 in)
Length overall   4.84 m (15 ft 10½ in)
Height overall   1.35 m (4 ft 5¼ in)
Propeller diameter   1.06 m (3 ft 6 in)

AREA:
Wings, gross   7.00 m² (75.35 sq ft)
WEIGHTS:
Weight empty   105 kg (231 lb)
Normal T-O weight   235 kg (518 lb)
PERFORMANCE:
Max level speed   86 knots (160 km/h; 99 mph)
Cruising speed   65 knots (120 km/h; 75 mph)
Stalling speed   33 knots (60 km/h; 38 mph)
Max rate of climb at S/L   180 m (590 ft)/min
Endurance   3 h

MARGANSKI
EDWARD MARGANSKI
ul Poprzeczna 21, 43-300 Bielsko-Biala

MARGANSKI DK-3 KASIA
This very small twin-engined homebuilt aircraft flew for the first time on 29 October 1984. It was designed to be suited to fast cross-country flights of up to 1,000 km range and for operation from prepared airfields. A single-engined version has also been designed, using an engine in the 30-44.5 kW (40-60 hp) range. The following details refer to the twin-engined DK-3:

TYPE: Single-seat homebuilt; conforms to FAR Pt 23.
AIRFRAME: GFRP structure. Wing section Wortmann FX-67-170K. Non-retractable tricycle landing gear.
POWER PLANT: Two 18.6 kW (25 hp) KFM 107Es. Fuel capacity 60 litres (15.9 US gallons; 13 Imp gallons).
DIMENSIONS, EXTERNAL:
Wing span   7.10 m (23 ft 3½ in)
Length overall   5.45 m (17 ft 10½ in)
Height overall   1.80 m (5 ft 11 in)
Propeller diameter   0.87 m (2 ft 10¼ in)
AREA:
Wings, gross   3.50 m² (37.67 sq ft)

WEIGHTS:
Weight empty, equipped   180 kg (397 lb)
Max T-O weight   310 kg (683 lb)
PERFORMANCE:
Max level speed   140 knots (260 km/h; 162 mph)
Max cruising speed   113 knots (210 km/h; 130 mph)
Stalling speed   57 knots (105 km/h; 66 mph)
T-O run   350 m (1,148 ft)
Landing run   250 m (820 ft)
Max range   540 nm (1,000 km; 621 miles)
g limits   +4.5/-1.8

ORLIŃSKI
ROMAN ORLIŃSKI
ul Lesna 4, 82-200 Malbork

ORLIŃSKI RO-7 ORLIK (EAGLET)
The prototype Orlik was flown for the first time on 22 February 1987. Plans are available to amateur builders. Some wing and fuselage components will be available in glassfibre from 1989.
TYPE: Single-seat homebuilt.
AIRFRAME: Wing section NACA 23012. Wings of mostly

wood construction, with plywood D-section leading-edge and fabric covering aft of spar. Welded steel tube forward fuselage; wooden semi-monocoque rear fuselage. Non-retractable tailwheel landing gear.
POWER PLANT: One 48.5 kW (65 hp) Walter Mikron III. Fuel capacity 30 litres (7.9 US gallons; 6.6 Imp gallons).
DIMENSIONS, EXTERNAL:
Wing span   7.60 m (24 ft 11¼ in)
Length overall   5.50 m (18 ft 0½ in)
Height overall   1.95 m (6 ft 4¾ in)
Propeller diameter   1.45 m (4 ft 9 in)

AREA:
Wings, gross   8.75 m² (94.18 sq ft)
WEIGHTS:
Weight empty   220 kg (485 lb)
Max T-O weight   320 kg (705 lb)
PERFORMANCE:
Max level speed at S/L   81 knots (150 km/h; 93 mph)
Econ cruising speed at S/L   49 knots (90 km/h; 56 mph)
Stalling speed   39 knots (71 km/h; 45 mph)
Max rate of climb at S/L   300 m (985 ft)/min
T-O run   100 m (328 ft)

SOUTH AFRICA

MFS
MICROLIGHT FLIGHT SYSTEMS PTY LTD
53 Old Main Road, Hillcrest, 3610 Natal
Telephone: (031) 75 3920
MANAGING DIRECTOR: John Young

MFS SHADOW
This aircraft is known as the Shadow Trainer in the USA.
TYPE: Two-seat microlight; conforms to South African Department of Civil Aviation certification requirements.
AIRFRAME: Main structure of aluminium alloy tubing, with

fabric covered wings and tail unit. Three-axis control. Non-retractable tricycle landing gear.
POWER PLANT: One 39.5 kW (53 hp) Rotax 503. Fuel capacity 20 litres (5.3 US gallons; 4.4 Imp gallons).
DIMENSIONS, EXTERNAL:
Wing span   9.75 m (32 ft 0 in)
Length overall   5.69 m (18 ft 8 in)
Height overall   3.07 m (10 ft 1 in)
Propeller diameter   1.35 m (4 ft 5 in)
AREA:
Wings, gross   14.86 m² (160.0 sq ft)

WEIGHTS:
Weight empty   146 kg (321 lb)
Max T-O weight   317 kg (700 lb)
PERFORMANCE:
Cruising speed (79% power) 39 knots (72 km/h; 45 mph)
Stalling speed   23 knots (42 km/h; 26 mph)
Max rate of climb at S/L   198 m (650 ft)/min
Service ceiling   3,660 m (12,000 ft)
T-O run   30.5 m (100 ft)
Landing run   25 m (80 ft)

SWEDEN

ANDREASSON
BJÖRN ANDREASSON
Collins Väg 22B, 23600 Höllviksnäs
In addition to the aircraft described here, Mr Andreasson's BA-12 Slandan and BA-14 are detailed under the MFI heading in this section.

ANDREASSON BA-4B
Plans to build the BA-4B are available.
TYPE: Single-seat fully aerobatic homebuilt biplane.
AIRFRAME: Braced biplane. Alternative all-metal wings, or all-wood wing structure, covered with heavy plywood skin. Ailerons, of simplified sheet metal construction, on lower wings only. Provision for detachable plastics wingtips. Sheet metal fuselage and tail unit. Turtledeck either sheet metal or reinforced plastics. Non-retractable tailwheel landing gear.
POWER PLANT: Prototype has 74.5 kW (100 hp) Rolls-Royce Continental O-200-A. Provision for other engines, including Volkswagen conversions. Standard fuel capacity 50 litres (13.2 US gallons; 11 Imp gallons). Provision for external 'bullet' tank of 50 litres (13.2 US gallons; 11 Imp gallons) capacity under fuselage.

DIMENSIONS, EXTERNAL:
Wing span: upper   5.34 m (17 ft 7 in)
   lower   5.14 m (16 ft 11 in)
Length overall   4.60 m (15 ft 0 in)
AREA:
Wings, gross   8.30 m² (89.3 sq ft)
WEIGHT:
Max T-O weight   375 kg (827 lb)
PERFORMANCE (prototype, at max T-O weight):
Max level speed   122 knots (225 km/h; 140 mph)
Max cruising speed   104 knots (193 km/h; 120 mph)
Min flying speed   35 knots (64 km/h; 40 mph)
Max rate of climb at S/L   610 m (2,000 ft)/min
T-O and landing run   less than 100 m (330 ft)
Range with standard fuel   152 nm (280 km; 175 miles)

ANDREASSON MFI-9 HB
The prototype BA-7 made its first flight on 10 October 1958. It entered production, and was followed by the MFI-9 version which also went into production.
Plans for the MFI-9 HB, a redrawn version of the MFI-9 for amateur builders, are currently available and the description and data refer to this version. Kits of

component parts were also made available from the Cana Aircraft Company in Singapore.
TYPE: Side by side two-seat, dual control homebuilt; conforms to FAR Pt 23 in Utility category.
AIRFRAME: All-metal construction, except for glassfibre reinforced plastics wingtips. Wing section NACA 23009, modified to have leading-edge droop. Non-retractable tricycle landing gear. Optional floats or skis.
POWER PLANT: One 74.5 kW (100 hp) Continental O-200-A. Other engines of similar weight and power rating can be used. Fuel capacity 80 litres (21 US gallons; 17.6 Imp gallons).
DIMENSIONS, EXTERNAL:
Wing span   7.43 m (24 ft 4½ in)
Length overall   5.85 m (19 ft 2¼ in)
Height overall   2.00 m (6 ft 6¾ in)
AREA:
Wings, gross   8.70 m² (93.65 sq ft)
WEIGHTS:
Weight empty   340 kg (750 lb)
Baggage capacity   20 kg (44 lb)
Max T-O weight   575 kg (1,267 lb)
PERFORMANCE:
Max level speed   130 knots (240 km/h; 149 mph)

Andreasson BA-4B single-seat fully aerobatic homebuilt biplane
(Geoffrey P. Jones)

MFS Shadow two-seat microlight

Wolff Flash-3 three-seat homebuilt aircraft

Janowski J-2 Polonez built by Mr Josef Leniec (Andrzej Glass)

Marganski DK-3 Kasia twin-engined single-seat light aircraft (A. Proszalek)

MFI-9B built in Sweden by Malmö

Orliński RO-7 single-seat homebuilt aircraft (Tomasz Szulc)

Ekström Humlan (67 kW; 90 hp McCulloch 4318 engine) built by Mr Tommy Nilsson of Björklinge, Sweden

Econ cruising speed at S/L		Max rate of climb at S/L	270 m (885 ft)/min	Landing run	130 m (427 ft)
	113 knots (210 km/h; 130 mph)	Service ceiling	4,500 m (14,775 ft)	Range with max payload	431 nm (800 km; 497 miles)
Stalling speed, power off	44 knots (80 km/h; 50 mph)	T-O run, grass	150 m (492 ft)		

EKSTRÖM
STAFFAN W. EKSTRÖM
Jupitervägen 43, 181 6 Lidingö
Telephone: (08) 766 34 48

EKSTRÖM HUMLAN

The Humlan prototype flew for the first time in June 1973. At least 11 Humlans have been completed and flown in Sweden.

TYPE: Single-seat homebuilt autogyro.

ROTOR SYSTEM: Two-blade semi-rigid rotor. Ztan Zee aluminium blades. Blade section NACA 8H-12.

AIRFRAME: Chassis of 6061-T6 square-section aluminium tube, on which is mounted a pod type nacelle. Fin, rudder and fixed tailplane built of aluminium sheet. Non-retractable tricycle landing gear. Optional glassfibre floats or skis.

POWER PLANT: One 67 kW (90 hp) McCulloch AF 100-X3 standard. Alternative engines include 1,700 cc Limbach and 1,834 cc converted Volkswagen motorcar engine. Fuel capacity 32 litres (8.45 US gallons; 7 Imp gallons).

DIMENSIONS, EXTERNAL (wheel landing gear):	
Rotor diameter	6.80 m (22 ft 3¾ in)
Length overall	3.42 m (11 ft 2¾ in)
Height overall	1.98 m (6 ft 6 in)
Propeller diameter	1.20 m (3 ft 11¼ in)

WEIGHTS (wheel landing gear):	
Weight empty	145 kg (320 lb)
Max T-O weight	295 kg (650 lb)

PERFORMANCE (wheel landing gear):	
Max cruising speed	81 knots (150 km/h; 93 mph)
Econ cruising speed	65 knots (120 km/h; 74 mph)
Max rate of climb at S/L	300 m (984 ft)/min
T-O run	60 m (197 ft)
Landing run, zero wind	5 m (16 ft)
Max range, no reserves	97 nm (180 km; 112 miles)

MFI
MALMÖ FORSKNINGS & INNOVATIONS AB
(Malmö Research & Development Ltd)
Smedstorpsgatan, S-212 28 Malmö
Telephone: (040) 18 07 05
Telex: 12442 FOTEX S
TECHNICAL MANAGER: Bjorn Andreasson

ANDREASSON BA-12 SLANDAN (DRAGONFLY)
The single-seat BA-12 Slandan (Dragonfly) was Mr Andreasson's first microlight design, of which a prototype flew in 1984. The Slandan is being handled by MFI and is at present being produced, in kit form and as a completed aircraft, by the Royal Swedish Aero Club. MFI had itself completed the first five aircraft as demonstrators.

The Slandan is of all-composites construction, using glassfibre, Kevlar and carbonfibre/Derakane. The wings have a low-speed aerofoil section developed in Sweden. Alternative 21 kW (28 hp) König or 26 kW (35 hp) Rotax

447 engines can be fitted. Fuel capacity is 19 litres (5 US gallons; 4.2 Imp gallons).

DIMENSIONS, EXTERNAL:	
Wing span	10.00 m (32 ft 9¾ in)
Length overall	5.00 m (16 ft 4¾ in)
Height overall	2.00 m (6 ft 6¾ in)

WEIGHTS:	
Weight empty	135 kg (298 lb)
Fuel	20 kg (44 lb)
Max T-O weight	250 kg (551 lb)

PERFORMANCE:	
Max cruising speed	54 knots (100 km/h; 62 mph)
Stalling speed	22 knots (40 km/h; 25 mph)
Max rate of climb at S/L	245 m (805 ft)/min
T-O run	50 m (164 ft)
Range, with König engine	108 nm (200 km; 124 miles)

ANDREASSON BA-14
This aircraft combines features of Mr Andreasson's earlier conventional side by side two-seat light aircraft and the BA-12, notably in adopting the latter's composites

construction and Vee 'butterfly' tail unit. The prototype was built by MFI but the second aircraft (and presumably subsequent examples) are to be produced by the Royal Swedish Aero Club.

The BA-14 is a strut braced aircraft with forward-swept high-lift wings carrying ailerons and flaps. The tail unit has horn-balanced elevators, while a small ventral fin supports a tail bumper skid. A non-retractable tricycle landing gear is standard, and accommodation is probably similar to that in the MFI-9. Engine options are a Textron Lycoming O-235 or Rotax 532, to be joined by the Rotax 912 after its development has been completed.

DIMENSION, EXTERNAL:	
Wing span	11.4 m (37 ft 4¾ in)

WEIGHT:	
Max T-O weight	450 kg (992 lb)

PERFORMANCE (with Rotax 532, estimated):	
Cruising speed	86 knots (159 km/h; 99 mph)
Stalling speed	33 knots (61 km/h; 38 mph)
T-O and landing run	75 m (246 ft)
Endurance at 75% power	4 h

SWITZERLAND

BRÄNDLI
MAX BRÄNDLI
Höheweg 2, CH-2553 Safnern
Telephone: (032) 55 18 23

BRÄNDLI BX-2 CHERRY
The prototype Cherry made its first flight on 24 April 1982. Plans (written in German) are available, and 88 sets had been sold by January 1988. The canopy and main spar are available in prefabricated form.

TYPE: Two-seat homebuilt.
AIRFRAME: Wings and tail unit have wood spars and Styrofoam skins covered with glassfibre. Wing section NACA 747A15. Ailerons and flaps of foam and glassfibre construction. Wood fuselage structure, plywood and glassfibre covered. Retractable tricycle landing gear.

POWER PLANT: One 48.5 kW (65 hp) Continental A65. Alternative engines include Limbach L 2000 or L 2400, JPX, HAPI, Continental C75 or C90. Fuel capacity 72 litres (19 US gallons; 15.8 Imp gallons).

DIMENSIONS, EXTERNAL:	
Wing span	7.00 m (22 ft 11½ in)
Length overall	5.23 m (17 ft 2 in)
Height overall	2.02 m (6 ft 7½ in)
Propeller diameter	1.60 m (5 ft 3 in)

AREA:	
Wings, gross	8.50 m² (91.5 sq ft)

WEIGHTS:	
Weight empty, equipped	310 kg (683 lb)
Max payload	190 kg (419 lb)
Max baggage	40 kg (88 lb)
Max T-O and landing weight	550 kg (1,212 lb)

PERFORMANCE (with A65 engine, at max T-O weight, except where indicated):	
Max level speed at 915 m (3,000 ft)	121 knots (225 km/h; 140 mph)
Max cruising speed at 915 m (3,000 ft)	113 knots (210 km/h; 130 mph)
Stalling speed, flaps down, engine idling, at AUW of 510 kg (1,125 lb)	45 knots (84 km/h; 52 mph)
Max rate of climb at S/L	180 m (590 ft)/min
Service ceiling	4,200 m (13,775 ft)
T-O run	280 m (918 ft)
Landing run	150 m (492 ft)
Range with max fuel	539 nm (1,000 km; 621 miles)
Endurance	5 h 5 min
g limits	+3.8/-1.9

BRÜGGER
MAX BRÜGGER
CH 1724 Zénauva
Telephone: (037) 33 29 20

BRÜGGER MB-2 COLIBRI 2
The prototype Colibri 2 flew for the first time on 1 May 1970. Plans are available, and about 250 Colibri 2s are under construction or flying in Europe.

TYPE: Single-seat homebuilt.
AIRFRAME: All-wood construction, except for fabric covering on wings and ailerons. No fixed fin. Wing section NACA 23012. Non-retractable tailwheel landing gear.

POWER PLANT: One 30 kW (40 hp) 1,600 cc Volkswagen engine (Brügger modification). Fuel capacity 33 litres (8.7 US gallons; 7.25 Imp gallons).

DIMENSIONS, EXTERNAL:	
Wing span	6.00 m (19 ft 8¼ in)
Length overall	4.80 m (15 ft 9 in)
Height overall	1.60 m (5 ft 3 in)
Propeller diameter	1.38 m (4 ft 6⅓ in)

AREA:	
Wings, gross	8.20 m² (88.25 sq ft)

WEIGHTS:	
Weight empty	215 kg (474 lb)
Max T-O and landing weight	330 kg (727 lb)

PERFORMANCE (at max T-O weight):	
Max speed at 1,000 m (3,280 ft)	97 knots (180 km/h; 111 mph)
Econ cruising speed (70% power) at 1,000 m (3,280 ft)	86 knots (160 km/h; 99 mph)
Stalling speed	33 knots (60 km/h; 38 mph)
Max rate of climb at S/L	180 m (590 ft)/min
Service ceiling	4,500 m (14,760 ft)
T-O and landing run	200 m (656 ft)
Range with max fuel	270 nm (500 km; 310 miles)

SWISS AEROLIGHT
CP 444, Pt Lancy 1, 1213 Geneva
Telephone: (022) 93 37 22
DIRECTOR: Dominique Loup

SWISS AEROLIGHT FUN FLY
The Fun Fly first flew as a prototype on 15 September 1983. It is available in plans, kit, individual component part and ready assembled forms. Many have flown.

TYPE: Side by side two-seat microlight.
AIRFRAME: Wood and aluminium alloy wings, with polystyrene ribs, Dacron covered. Ailerons and tail surfaces of aluminium alloy and wood, Dacron covered. Fuselage of light alloy tubing. Optional cockpit fairing.

Three-axis control. Non-retractable tricycle landing gear. Optional floats or skis. Space for carrying baggage or equipment such as tents, skis, a folding bicycle or windsurfing board.

POWER PLANT: One 39.5 kW (53 hp) Rotax 503. Provision for alternative power plants weighing not more than 70 kg (154 lb). Fuel capacity 48 litres (12.7 US gallons; 10.5 Imp gallons). Provision for two further tanks of same capacity.

DIMENSIONS, EXTERNAL:	
Wing span	11.20 m (36 ft 9 in)
Length overall	5.50 m (18 ft 0½ in)
Height overall	2.20 m (7 ft 2½ in)
Propeller diameter	1.55 m (5 ft 1 in)

AREA:	
Wings, gross	17.50 m² (188.4 sq ft)

WEIGHTS:	
Weight empty	175 kg (386 lb)
Max T-O weight	375 kg (826 lb)

PERFORMANCE:	
Max level speed	65 knots (120 km/h; 74 mph)
Econ cruising speed	43 knots (80 km/h; 50 mph)
Stalling speed	30 knots (55 km/h; 35 mph)
Max rate of climb at S/L	305 m (1,000 ft)/min
T-O and landing run	50 m (164 ft)
Service ceiling	4,500 m (14,775 ft)
Range	215 nm (400 km; 248 miles)
g limits	+9.5/-4.5 ultimate

UNION OF SOVIET SOCIALIST REPUBLICS

ANTONOV

ANTONOV SLAVUTITCH M-1
This powered version of the Slavutitch-UT (see Hang Gliders subsection) made its first flight on 1 August 1982. It uses a trike fitted with a 17.2 kW (23 hp) Neptun engine.

Fuel capacity is approx 10 litres (2.6 US gallons; 2.2 Imp gallons).

DIMENSIONS, EXTERNAL:	
Wing span	8.80 m (28 ft 10½ in)
Length overall	4.40 m (14 ft 5¼ in)
Height overall	3.40 m (11 ft 2 in)

Propeller diameter	0.91 m (3 ft 0 in)

AREA:	
Wings, gross	17.40 m² (187.3 sq ft)

WEIGHTS:	
Weight empty	74.5 kg (164 lb)

Brändli BX-2 Cherry two-seat homebuilt aircraft

Brügger MB-2 Colibri 2 built by Nadal Patrick *(Geoffrey P. Jones)*

Swiss Aerolight Fun Fly two-seat microlight

Andreasson (MFI) BA-12 Slandan microlight

LAK (Oshkinis) BROK-1M Garnis single-seat microlight

Max pilot weight	87.5 kg (193 lb)	Max cruising speed	30 knots (55 km/h; 34 mph)	Service ceiling	500 m (1,640 ft)
Max T-O weight	170 kg (375 lb)	Stalling speed	22 knots (40 km/h; 25 mph)	Range	16 nm (30 km; 18.5 miles)
PERFORMANCE:					
Max level speed	35 knots (65 km/h; 40 mph)	Max rate of climb at S/L	360 m (1,181 ft)/min		

LAK

LITOVSKAYA AVIATSIONNAYA KONSTRUKTSIYA (Lithuanian Aircraft Construction)

Prenaisk, Litovsk (Lithuania)
OFFICERS: see Sailplanes section

LAK BROK-1M GARNIS

The single-seat BROK-1M is a modified and powered microlight version of the Oshkinis BRO-23KR Garnis primary training glider (see Sailplanes section). It uses an 18.4 kW (25 hp) Zuzycie engine, and can be operated on a central skid or tricycle landing gear.

DIMENSIONS, EXTERNAL:
Wing span	8.2 m (26 ft 11 in)
Length overall	5.1 m (17 ft 1½ in)

AREA:
Wings, gross	10.4 m² (111.9 sq ft)

WEIGHTS:
Weight empty	115 kg (253 lb)
Max T-O weight	195 kg (430 lb)

PERFORMANCE:
Never-exceed speed	59 knots (110 km/h; 68 mph)
Max level speed	40-46 knots (75-85 km/h; 47-53 mph)
Stalling speed	27 knots (50 km/h; 31 mph)
T-O run	30-50 m (98-164 ft)

UNITED KINGDOM

AEROTECH

AEROTECH INTERNATIONAL LTD

Unit 2, Buckingham Road Industrial Estate, Brackley, Northants
Telephone: (0280) 700289

Telex: 946240 CWEASY G
CHIEF EXECUTIVE: M. J. McBride

The Sorcerer microlight, designed by Mr Michael W. J. Whittaker, is currently manufactured under licence by Aerotech International, which is offering the MW5B version in ready-assembled form. A few MW5 Sorcerers are also under construction from plans offered by Mr Whittaker.

The MW5B Sorcerer first flew on 7 March 1986. Full details can be found under the Whittaker heading.

AMF

AMF MICROFLIGHT LTD

Membury Airfield, Lambourn, Berkshire RG16 7TJ
Telephone: (0488) 72224
Telex: 848507 MIFLI
MANAGING DIRECTOR: A. M. Fleming

AMF MICROFLIGHT CHEVVRON 2-32

The Chevvron was first flown in 1983. By March 1988, five production aircraft had been ordered and built.
TYPE: Side by side two-seat microlight/trainer; conforms to BCAR Section S.

AIRFRAME: Airframe of glassfibre/carbonfibre/Kevlar and foam construction. Wortmann wing section. Three-axis control. Non-retractable tricycle landing gear.
POWER PLANT: One 24 kW (32 hp) König SD 570. Fuel capacity 27 or 54 litres (7.2 or 14.4 US gallons; 6 or 12 Imp gallons).

DIMENSIONS, EXTERNAL:
Wing span	13.41 m (44 ft 0 in)
Length overall	6.86 m (22 ft 6 in)
Height overall	1.91 m (6 ft 3 in)
Propeller diameter	1.52 m (5 ft 0 in)

AREA:
Wings, gross	16.35 m² (176.0 sq ft)

WEIGHTS:
Weight empty	150 kg (331 lb)
Pilot weight range	50-180 kg (110-396 lb)
Max T-O weight	370 kg (815 lb)

PERFORMANCE:
Max level and cruising speed	65 knots (120 km/h; 75 mph)
Econ cruising speed	45 knots (83 km/h; 52 mph)
Stalling speed: power off	29 knots (54 km/h; 34 mph)
power on	27 knots (50 km/h; 31 mph)
Max rate of climb at S/L	178 m (585 ft)/min
Service ceiling	3,050 m (10,000 ft)
T-O run	91 m (300 ft)
Landing run	137 m (450 ft)
Range with standard fuel	347 nm (643 km; 400 miles)
g limits	+4/−2

AVIATION COMPOSITES

AVIATION COMPOSITES
22 Hambridge Road, Newbury, Berkshire
Telephone: 0635 38022

AVIATION COMPOSITES MERCURY

This side by side two-seat all-composites light aircraft was designed by Burt Rutan, originally for Lotus Cars Ltd. Pre-production examples were built by Aviation

Composites of the UK, the first of which flew for the first time in April 1987, in Florida.

The Mercury is a sweptwing canard with three-axis control and a tricycle landing gear with retractable nosewheel. Power plant is a 30 kW (40 hp) Norton rotary engine. The airframe structure is of glassfibre/foam/graphite/epoxy.

DIMENSIONS, EXTERNAL:

Wing span	9.75 m (32 ft 0 in)
Length overall	5.54 m (18 ft 2 in)

AREA:

Wings, gross	14.03 m² (151.0 sq ft)

PERFORMANCE (estimated):

Cruising speed	87 knots (161 km/h; 100 mph)
Max rate of climb at S/L	186 m (610 ft)/min
Range	290 nm (537 km; 334 miles)

CFM

COOK FLYING MACHINES
(trading as CFM Metal-Fax Ltd)
Unit 2D, Eastlands Industrial Estate, Leiston, Suffolk IP16 4LL
Telephone: 0728 832353/833076
Telex: 8950511 ONEONE G 38201001
Fax: 0728 832 498
MANAGING DIRECTOR: David G. Cook

CFM SHADOW

The Shadow first flew as a prototype in 1983. By January 1988 a total of 80 fully assembled aircraft and kits had been produced. Type approval to BCAR CAP 482 Section S was gained in May 1985. A dual control version received CAA certification in January 1986.

ULV cropspraying trials have demonstrated the suitability of the Shadow in this role. A multi-function surveillance fit for photography, video recording, and closed-circuit TV microwave transmission to a command vehicle/station is also available.

TYPE: Tandem two-seat microlight; conforms to FAI and UK CAA requirements.

AIRFRAME: Wings constructed of aluminium alloy and wood, with foam/glassfibre ribs, plywood covering on forward section and polyester fabric aft. Fuselage pod of Fibrelam; aluminium tube tailboom. Three-axis control. Non-retractable tricycle landing gear. Overseas options include floats, agricultural spraygear and other specialised equipment.

POWER PLANT: One 30 kW (40 hp) 437 cc Rotax 447. Standard fuel capacity 23 litres (6 US gallons; 5 Imp gallons). Overseas options include a 43 litre (11.4 US gallon; 9.5 Imp gallon) auxiliary fuel tank.

DIMENSIONS, EXTERNAL:

Wing span	10.03 m (32 ft 11 in)
Length overall	6.40 m (21 ft 0 in)
Height overall	1.73 m (5 ft 8 in)
Propeller diameter	1.30 m (4 ft 3 in)

AREA:

Wings, gross	15.0 m² (162.0 sq ft)

WEIGHTS:

Weight empty	150 kg (331 lb)
Pilot weight range	55-90 kg (121-198 lb)
Max passenger/payload weight	90 kg (198 lb)
Max T-O weight	348 kg (767 lb)

PERFORMANCE (at max T-O weight):

Max level speed	82 knots (153 km/h; 95 mph)
Econ cruising speed	56 knots (105 km/h; 65 mph)
Min flying speed	33 knots (62 km/h; 38 mph)
Max rate of climb at S/L	213 m (700 ft)/min
Service ceiling (without oxygen)	3,050 m (10,000 ft)
T-O run from metalled surface	90 m (295 ft)
Landing run, with braking	75 m (246 ft)
Range, with reserves	113 nm (209 km; 130 miles)
Endurance, with reserves: standard fuel	1 h 45 min
optional fuel	8 h
g limits	+6/−3 static, ultimate

FULTON

FULTON AIRCRAFT LTD
Fulton House, Wood Wharf Business Park, Prestons Road, London Docklands, London E14 9SF
Telephone: (01) 538 0751
Telex: 887951 FULCOL G
Fax: (01) 538 4743
CHAIRMAN: A. Fulton

FULTON FA-1

Development of the FA-1 took place in Canada, where the prototype first flew in August 1985. A production prototype was built in the UK.

TYPE: Side by side two-seat, dual-control microlight trainer; conforms to FAI/CAA requirements, and to CAP 482 Section S.

AIRFRAME: Constructed of rigid composite materials (glassfibre, epoxy and PVC foam plastics). Three-axis control. Non-retractable tricycle landing gear.

POWER PLANT: One 38.7 kW (52 hp) Rotax 503 2V. Fuel capacity 36.5 litres (9.6 US gallons; 8 Imp gallons).

DIMENSIONS, EXTERNAL:

Wing span	9.375 m (30 ft 9 in)
Length overall	6.08 m (19 ft 11 in)
Height overall	2.29 m (7 ft 6 in)
Propeller diameter	1.65 m (5 ft 5 in)

AREA:

Wings, gross	15.0 m² (161.5 sq ft)

WEIGHTS (open cockpit version):

Weight empty	148 kg (326 lb)
Crew weight range	50-180 kg (110-396 lb)
Max T-O weight	360 kg (794 lb)

PERFORMANCE (at max T-O weight):

Max level speed	70 knots (129 km/h; 80 mph)
Max cruising speed	65 knots (120 km/h; 75 mph)
Stalling speed	25 knots (46 km/h; 29 mph)
Max rate of climb at S/L	225 m (740 ft)/min
Endurance with max fuel, with reserves	2 h
g limits	+6/−3

ISAACS

JOHN O. ISAACS
23 Linden Grove, Chandler's Ford, Hampshire SO5 1LE
Telephone: 0703 260885

ISAACS FURY II

The prototype Fury flew for the first time on 30 August 1963. In 1966-67 Mr Isaacs modified this prototype to Mk II standard, by restressing the airframe and installing a larger engine.

Many plans have been supplied to amateur constructors throughout the world, and 18 Furies were known to have flown by January 1988.

TYPE: Single-seat 7/10th scale fighter representation.

AIRFRAME: Braced biplane of wooden construction, with fabric covered wings, upper wing ailerons and tail unit, and plywood covered fuselage. Wing section RAF 28. Non-retractable tailskid landing gear.

POWER PLANT (prototype): One 93 kW (125 hp) Textron Lycoming O-290. Fuel capacity 45.5 litres (12 US gallons; 10 Imp gallons) or 54.5 litres (14.4 US gallons; 12 Imp gallons).

DIMENSIONS, EXTERNAL:

Wing span: upper	6.40 m (21 ft 0 in)
lower	5.54 m (18 ft 2 in)
Length overall	5.87 m (19 ft 3 in)
Height over tail (flying attitude)	2.16 m (7 ft 1 in)

AREA:

Wings, gross	11.50 m² (123.8 sq ft)

WEIGHTS (prototype):

Weight empty	322 kg (710 lb)
Max permissible T-O weight	450 kg (1,000 lb)

PERFORMANCE (prototype with uncowled engine):

Max level speed	100 knots (185 km/h; 115 mph)
Stalling speed	33 knots (61 km/h; 38 mph)
Max rate of climb at S/L	488 m (1,600 ft)/min
g limit	+9

ISAACS SPITFIRE

The prototype of Isaacs' 6/10th-scale Spitfire first flew on 5 May 1975. Plans are available to homebuilders, and 18 sets had been sold by January 1988.

TYPE: Single-seat homebuilt fighter representation.

AIRFRAME: All-wood construction, except for fabric covered ailerons. Wing section NACA 2200 series. Non-retractable tailwheel landing gear.

POWER PLANT: One 74.5 kW (100 hp) Continental O-200. Fuel capacity 45.5 litres (12 US gallons; 10 Imp gallons).

DIMENSIONS, EXTERNAL:

Wing span	6.75 m (22 ft 1½ in)
Length overall	5.88 m (19 ft 3 in)
Height overall	1.73 m (5 ft 8 in)

AREA:

Wings, gross	8.08 m² (87.0 sq ft)

WEIGHTS:

Weight empty	366 kg (805 lb)
Max T-O weight	499 kg (1,100 lb)

PERFORMANCE (at max T-O weight):

Max level speed	130 knots (240 km/h; 150 mph)
Cruising speed	116 knots (215 km/h; 134 mph)
Stalling speed, 'clean'	45-47 knots (84-87 km/h; 52-54 mph)
Stalling speed, with optional fuselage airbrake extended	41 knots (76 km/h; 47 mph)
Max rate of climb at S/L	336 m (1,100 ft)/min
g limits	+9/−4.5 factored

MAINAIR

MAINAIR SPORTS LTD
Unit 2, Alma Industrial Estate, Regent Street, Rochdale, Lancashire OL12 0HQ
Telephone: 0706 55134
Telex: 635091 ALBION G attn MAINAIR
DIRECTORS: John A. Hudson and Peter W. Hudson

Mainair's sales consist mostly of complete microlights, comprising trikes and flexwings of its own manufacture. It is also developing the Skybike, a ground mobile aircraft combining a flexwing microlight and a motorcycle.

MAINAIR GEMINI FLASH 2 ALPHA

Details of several long distance flights made by Gemini Flash microlights can be found in the 1987-88 *Jane's*. The current model is the Gemini Flash 2 Alpha, with a sealed nosewheel unit, increased fuel capacity and higher powered engine options compared with previous models. The CS Flash single-seat agricultural aircraft mentioned in the 1987-88 *Jane's* has been superseded by a Rotax 532-engined version of the Gemini Flash 2 Alpha.

TYPE: Two-seat flexwing microlight; conforms to FAI/CAA requirements, and meets BCAR Section S requirements for dual control microlights.

AIRFRAME: Trike unit of anodised aluminium alloy. Glassfibre cockpit pod. Flash extremely taut flexible wing, with 76% double surface Dacron covering, and small fin. Non-retractable tricycle landing gear. Optional skis. Agricultural version might use 50 litre (13.2 US gallon; 11 Imp gallon) chemical tank and twin spraybooms.

POWER PLANT: One 34 kW (45.6 hp) Rotax 503, 38 kW (51 hp) Rotax 462, or 47 kW (63 hp) Rotax 532, the latter for cropspraying version. Fuel capacity 45.5 litres (12 US gallons; 10 Imp gallons).

DIMENSIONS, EXTERNAL:

Wing span	10.6 m (34 ft 9½ in)
Length overall	3.46 m (11 ft 4¼ in)
Height overall	3.83 m (12 ft 6¾ in)
Propeller diameter	1.575 m (5 ft 2 in)

AREA:

Wings, gross	15.57 m² (167.6 sq ft)

WEIGHTS:

Weight empty	148 kg (326 lb)
Total crew weight range	70-180 kg (154-397 lb)
Max T-O weight	344 kg (758 lb)

PERFORMANCE:

Cruising speed	43 knots (80 km/h; 50 mph)
Econ cruising speed	42 knots (78 km/h; 48 mph)
Stalling speed: power on	25 knots (47 km/h; 29 mph)
power off	24 knots (45 km/h; 28 mph)
Max rate of climb at S/L: solo	300 m (985 ft)/min
dual	150 m (492 ft)/min
Service ceiling	3,050 m (10,000 ft)
T-O to 15 m (50 ft)	180 m (591 ft)
Landing from 15 m (50 ft)	150 m (492 ft)
Range with standard fuel	69 nm (128 km; 80 miles)
Endurance	3 h 30 min
g limits	+6/−4 ultimate

MAINAIR SCORCHER

Suited to the pilot wishing for high performance or competition, the Scorcher is Mainair's highest powered single-seat microlight.

The general description of the airframe of the Gemini Flash 2 Alpha applies also to the Scorcher, except that the Scorcher wing is 83% double surface.

TYPE: Single-seat microlight.

AMF Microflight Chevvron 2-32 two-seat microlight

Aviation Composites Mercury all-composites light aircraft *(Peter R. March)*

Fulton Aircraft FA-1 two-seat microlight trainer

Mainair Gemini Flash 2

Whittaker MW5B Sorcerer manufactured by Aerotech

CFM Shadow two-seat microlight

Isaacs Fury II single-seat homebuilt biplane *(R. Kunert)*

Prototype Isaacs Spitfire single-seat light sporting aircraft *(Geoffrey P. Jones)*

POWER PLANT: One 34 kW (45.6 hp) Rotax 503. Fuel capacity 24 litres (6.3 US gallons; 5.2 Imp gallons) standard; optional 20 litre (5.3 US gallon; 4.4 Imp gallon) auxiliary tank.

DIMENSIONS, EXTERNAL:
Wing span 9.20 m (30 ft 2 in)
Length overall 2.88 m (9 ft 5½ in)

Height overall 3.60 m (11 ft 10 in)
Propeller diameter 1.575 m (5 ft 2 in)
AREA:
Wings, gross 12.6 m² (135.6 sq ft)
WEIGHTS:
Weight empty 134 kg (295 lb)
Max pilot weight 90 kg (198 lb)

Max T-O weight 262 kg (577 lb)
PERFORMANCE:
Never-exceed speed 78 knots (145 km/h; 90 mph)
Cruising speed 43 knots (80 km/h; 50 mph)
Stalling speed 26 knots (49 km/h; 30 mph)
Max rate of climb at S/L 228 m (750 ft)/min
g limits +6/–4 ultimate

MEDWAY
MEDWAY MICROLIGHTS
Burrows Lane, Middle Stoke, Rochester, Kent
Telephone: (0634) 270780
MANAGING DIRECTOR: Chris Draper

MEDWAY MICROLIGHTS HYBRED 440R
Mated to a Raven wing, the Hybred 440R trike flew for

the first time in 1986. Ready assembled microlights are offered.
TYPE: Tandem two-seat flexwing microlight.
AIRFRAME: Trike unit comprises an aluminium alloy structure, attached to the double surface Raven wing, with weight-shift control. Non-retractable tricycle landing gear. Optional floats and skis.
POWER PLANT: One 29.4 kW (39.4 hp) Rotax 447. Fuel capacity 20.5 litres (5.4 US gallons; 4.5 Imp gallons).

DIMENSIONS, EXTERNAL:
Wing span 10.97 m (36 ft 0 in)
Propeller diameter 1.57 m (5 ft 2 in)
WEIGHTS:
Weight empty 149 kg (328 lb)
Crew weight range 75-180 kg (166-397 lb)
Max T-O weight 343 kg (756 lb)
PERFORMANCE:
Max level speed 74 knots (137 km/h; 85 mph)

Econ cruising speed	56 knots (105 km/h; 65 mph)
Stalling speed	35 knots (65 km/h; 41 mph)
Max rate of climb at S/L	183 m (600 ft)/min
Service ceiling	3,050 m (10,000 ft)
T-O run	220 m (722 ft)
Landing run	245 m (804 ft)
Range	130 nm (241 km; 150 miles)

MEDWAY MICROLIGHTS HALF PINT

The first flight of a prototype Half Pint trike unit fitted with an Aerial Arts 130SX flexwing took place in 1984. Currently fitted with either a Medway Microlights Hawk or Gnat wing, it is available only for export until CAA approval has been gained.

TYPE: Single-seat trike unit with Hawk or Gnat flexwing.

AIRFRAME: Aluminium framed flexwing, with double surface covering. Aluminium alloy trike unit. Non-retractable tricycle landing gear.

POWER PLANT: One 20 kW (27 hp) Rotax 277, 16.4 kW (22 hp) JPX PUL 425 or JPX PUL 500, or Fuji Robin 250 or 330 engine.

WEIGHT:	
Weight empty	70 kg (154 lb)
PERFORMANCE:	
Econ cruising speed	19 knots (35 km/h; 22 mph)

MICROFLIGHT

MICROFLIGHT AIRCRAFT LTD
Hangar 6, Shobdon Airfield, Herefordshire HR6 9NR
Telephone: (056 881) 606/8864
DIRECTORS:
John Hollings (Managing)
David Corbett

MICROFLIGHT SPECTRUM

Developed from Mr Michael Campbell-Jones' Ladybird, the Spectrum is available in ready assembled form.

TYPE: Two-seat microlight; conforms to FAI/CAA requirements.

AIRFRAME: Aluminium alloy airframe, with double surfaced glassfibre and carbonfibre composite wing, and fuselage pod of similar composites construction. Wing section NACA 4412 modified. Three-axis control. Non-retractable tricycle landing gear. Optional recovery parachute and floats.

POWER PLANT: One 30 kW (40 hp) Rotax 447. Fuel capacity 36.4 litres (9.6 US gallons; 8 Imp gallons).

DIMENSIONS, EXTERNAL:	
Wing span	12.00 m (39 ft 4½ in)
Length overall	5.89 m (19 ft 4 in)
Height overall	2.69 m (8 ft 10 in)
Propeller diameter	1.57 m (5 ft 2 in)
AREA:	
Wings, gross	15.0 m² (161.5 sq ft)
WEIGHTS:	
Weight empty	150 kg (330 lb)
Pilot weight range	50-180 kg (110-396 lb)
Max T-O weight	356 kg (785 lb)
PERFORMANCE:	
Max level speed	61 knots (113 km/h; 70 mph)
Econ cruising speed	48 knots (89 km/h; 55 mph)
Stalling speed, power on	25 knots (47 km/h; 29 mph)
Max rate of climb at S/L	244 m (800 ft)/min
Service ceiling	3,660 m (12,000 ft)
T-O run	65 m (213 ft)
Landing run	50 m (164 ft)
Range	173 nm (322 km; 200 miles)
g limits	+ 6/-4

NIPPER

NIPPER KITS AND COMPONENTS LTD
Foxley, Blackness Lane, Keston, Kent BR2 6HL
Telephone: (0689) 58351
CHAIRMAN: D. P. L. Antill

NIPPER Mk IIIb

This light aircraft was developed and manufactured originally by Avions Fairey in Belgium. Plans, kits of component parts and an advisory service are available, and in early 1988 five Nippers were known to be under construction. Many others have been flown.

TYPE: Single-seat aerobatic homebuilt.

AIRFRAME: Wooden wing, aileron, tailplane and elevator structures, and welded steel tube fuselage and rudder structures, all fabric covered except for glassfibre underfuselage fairing and wood skins on tailplane and elevators. No fin. Modified NACA 43012A wing section. Non-retractable tricycle landing gear.

POWER PLANT: One 41 kW (55 hp) Rollason Ardem XI. Alternatively, Nipper recommends the 48.5 kW (65 hp) Barry Smith aerobatic engine of 1,834 cc, with fuel and oil systems for inverted flight. Fuel capacity 34 litres (9 US gallons; 7.5 Imp gallons). Provision for two 16.5 litre (4.3 US gallon; 3.6 Imp gallon) wingtip fuel tanks.

DIMENSIONS, EXTERNAL:	
Wing span: without tip tanks	6.00 m (19 ft 8 in)
with tip tanks	6.25 m (20 ft 6 in)
Length overall	4.56 m (15 ft 0 in)
Height overall	1.91 m (6 ft 3 in)
AREA:	
Wings, gross	7.50 m² (80.70 sq ft)
WEIGHTS (Ardem engine):	
Weight empty	210 kg (465 lb)
Max T-O weight: Aerobatic	310 kg (685 lb)
Normal	340 kg (750 lb)

PERFORMANCE (Ardem engine at max T-O weight, unless stated otherwise):
Max level speed at S/L:	
without tip tanks	93 knots (173 km/h; 107 mph)
Barry Smith engine	113 knots (209 km/h; 130 mph)
Econ cruising speed at S/L	78 knots (145 km/h; 90 mph)
Stalling speed, power off	33 knots (61 km/h; 38 mph)
Max rate of climb at S/L:	198 m (650 ft)/min
Barry Smith engine	305 m (1,000 ft)/min
Service ceiling	3,660 m (12,000 ft)
T-O run	85 m (280 ft)
Landing run	110 m (360 ft)
Range with tip tanks	390 nm (720 km; 450 miles)
g limits	+ 6/-3

NOBLE HARDMAN

NOBLE HARDMAN AVIATION LTD
Elvicta Estate, Crickhowell, Powys NP8 1DF, Wales
Telephone: (0873) 811570
Telex: 437269
MANAGING DIRECTOR: D. L. Hardman

NOBLE HARDMAN AVIATION SNOWBIRD Mk IV

The prototype Snowbird flew for the first time on 2 September 1984. The current version is the Mk IV, to which the details apply:

TYPE: Side by side two-seat microlight trainer; conforms to FAI and French Veritas requirements, and to BCAR Section S.

AIRFRAME: Dacron covered aluminium alloy structure, wings using superplastic Supral 150. Three-axis control. Non-retractable tricycle landing gear. Computerised instrument panel standard.

POWER PLANT: One 44.7 kW (60 hp) Rotax 532. Fuel capacity 30 litres (7.9 US gallons; 6.6 Imp gallons).

DIMENSIONS, EXTERNAL:	
Wing span	9.45 m (31 ft 0 in)
Length overall	6.10 m (20 ft 0 in)
Height overall	2.13 m (7 ft 0 in)
AREA:	
Wings, gross	15.14 m² (163.0 sq ft)
WEIGHTS:	
Weight empty	181 kg (398 lb)
Max T-O weight	384 kg (847 lb)
PERFORMANCE:	
Econ cruising speed	55 knots (102 km/h; 63 mph)
Stalling speed	33 knots (61 km/h; 38 mph)
Max rate of climb at S/L	213 m (700 ft)/min
T-O run	70 m (230 ft)
Landing from 15 m (50 ft)	198 m (650 ft)
Range	104 nm (193 km; 120 miles)
g limits	+ 4/-2

PEGASUS

PEGASUS TRANSPORT SYSTEMS LTD
56 George Lane, Marlborough, Wiltshire SN8 4BY
Telephone: 0672 53504
DIRECTORS: S. M. G. Rose and Graham Slater

The CAA approved manufacturing subsidiary of Pegasus Transport Systems Ltd is Solar Wings Ltd (see Hang Gliders subsection).

PEGASUS XL

The Pegasus XL flew for the first time in Autumn 1984. By early 1988 approximately 400 were flying worldwide. The **XL-SE** (special edition) is an XL offered with registration, registration letters, a Permit to Fly and an ASI inclusive in the price.

TYPE: Two-seat flexwing microlight; conforms to FAI/CAA definitions and built to BCAR Section S standards.

AIRFRAME: Aluminium alloy trike unit, joined to Pegasus flexible wing with 55 per cent double-surface covering. Weight-shift control. Non-retractable tricycle landing gear. Options include recovery parachute.

POWER PLANT: One 30 kW (40 hp) Rotax 447 or 38 kW (51 hp) Rotax 462. Fuel capacity 24 litres (6.3 US gallons; 5.2 Imp gallons) standard or 45 litres (11.9 US gallons; 10 Imp gallons) optional.

DIMENSIONS, EXTERNAL:	
Wing span	10.36 m (34 ft 0 in)
Height of trike	2.54 m (8 ft 4 in)
Propeller diameter	1.52 m (5 ft 0 in)
AREA:	
Wings, gross	17.65 m² (190.0 sq ft)
WEIGHTS:	
Weight empty	145 kg (320 lb)
Max suspended load	301 kg (663 lb)
Total crew weight range	55-190 kg (121-419 lb)
Max T-O weight	350 kg (771 lb)

PERFORMANCE (Rotax 447):
Cruising speed	45 knots (83 km/h; 52 mph)
Stalling speed	24 knots (45 km/h; 28 mph)
Max rate of climb at S/L: solo	320 m (1,050 ft)/min
dual	168 m (550 ft)/min
g limits	+ 6/-4 tested at max AUW
	+ 4/-2 recommended

PEGASUS Q

This two-seat sports microlight has a speed range of 22-65 knots (40-121 km/h; 25-75 mph) and its high speed cruise with light pitch inputs makes long journeys less tiring. The lightweight airframe and short span wing offer a saving of 8.6 kg (19 lb) weight compared with the XL's wing. The eliptical tip design gives an efficient transverse airflow for good slow speed flying characteristics. Power is supplied by the same engine options as for the Pegasus XL, with a 24.4 or 47 litre (6.45 or 12.4 US gallon; 5.4 or 10.33 Imp gallon) fuel tank.

DIMENSION, EXTERNAL:	
Wing span	10.36 m (34 ft 0 in)
AREA:	
Wings, gross	15.27 m² (164.4 sq ft)
WEIGHT:	
Wing	43 kg (95 lb)

PERFORMANCE (approx):
Cruising speed	43 knots (80 km/h; 50 mph)
Stalling speed	22 knots (41 km/h; 25 mph)
Max rate of climb at S/L: solo	320 m (1,050 ft)/min
dual	168 m (550 ft)/min

PFA

THE POPULAR FLYING ASSOCIATION
Terminal Building, Shoreham Airport, Shoreham-by-Sea, West Sussex BN4 5FF
Telephone: 0273 461616
Fax: 0273 463390
VICE-CHAIRMAN AND CHIEF EXECUTIVE: F. I. V. Walker

The PFA markets plans of the three aircraft described, plus the Isaacs Fury, Evans VP-1 and VP-2, and Pazmany PL-4 detailed under their designers' names in this section.

CURRIE WOT

The Wot was designed by Mr J. R. Currie in 1937. The following details refer to aircraft built to standard plans, as obtainable from the PFA. An average of seven sets of plans is sold each year.

TYPE: Single-seat fully aerobatic homebuilt biplane.

AIRFRAME: Wings and tail unit have wood structure with fabric covering. Wing section Clark Y. Plywood box fuselage with fabric covering overall. Non-retractable tailskid landing gear; some built with tailwheels.

POWER PLANT: One Volkswagen 1,600 cc modified motorcar engine, or other engine of up to 74.5 kW (100 hp), including 48.5 kW (65 hp) Walter Mikron III or 67 kW (90 hp) Continental C90. Fuel capacity 54.5 litres (14.4 US gallons; 12 Imp gallons).

DIMENSIONS, EXTERNAL:	
Wing span (both)	6.73 m (22 ft 1 in)
Length overall	5.58 m (18 ft 3½ in)
Height overall	2.06 m (6 ft 9 in)

Currie Wot built by Mr Don Lord *(PFA)*

Microflight Aircraft Spectrum two-seat microlight

Nipper Mk IIIb single-seat light aircraft *(Tim Griffith)*

Luton L.A.4a Minor light monoplane

Noble Hardman Aviation Snowbird Mk IV trainer

Druine D31 Turbulent

Pegasus XL microlight aircraft

AREA:
Wings, gross	13.0 m² (140.0 sq ft)

WEIGHTS:
Weight empty	250 kg (550 lb)
Max T-O weight	408 kg (900 lb)

PERFORMANCE (at max T-O weight):
Max level speed at 610 m (2,000 ft)
83 knots (153 km/h; 95 mph)
Econ cruising speed at 610 m (2,000 ft)
69 knots (129 km/h; 80 mph)
Stalling speed 35 knots (65 km/h; 40 mph)
Max rate of climb at S/L 183 m (600 ft)/min
Range with max fuel 208 nm (385 km; 240 miles)

DRUINE D31 TURBULENT

The following data apply to the D31 Turbulent as factory-built in the UK for many years by Rollason Aircraft and Engines Ltd. The fitting of optional wheel fairings and a sliding canopy increases speed by about 7 knots (13 km/h; 8 mph).

Plans for the Turbulent are available to amateur constructors, from the PFA, and an average of four or five sets is sold each year.

TYPE: Single-seat homebuilt.

AIRFRAME: Wings and tail control surfaces have wood structure with fabric covering. Wing section NACA 23012. Plywood covered wooden fuselage and fixed tail surfaces. Non-retractable tailwheel landing gear, with optional tailskid and skis.

POWER PLANT: One 33.5 kW (45 hp) Rollason Ardem 4CO2 Mk IV or 41 kW (55 hp) Ardem Mk V. Fuel capacity 39 litres (10.2 US gallons; 8.5 Imp gallons).

DIMENSIONS, EXTERNAL:
Wing span	6.58 m (21 ft 7 in)
Length overall	5.33 m (17 ft 6 in)
Height overall	1.52 m (5 ft 0 in)

AREA:
Wings, gross	7.20 m² (77.5 sq ft)

WEIGHTS:
Weight empty	179 kg (395 lb)
Baggage capacity	11.5 kg (25 lb)
Max T-O weight	281 kg (620 lb)

PERFORMANCE (with 33.5 kW; 45 hp engine, at max T-O weight):
Max level speed 95 knots (176 km/h; 109 mph)
Econ cruising speed 76 knots (141 km/h; 87 mph)
Stalling speed 39 knots (71 km/h; 44 mph)
Max rate of climb at S/L 137 m (450 ft)/min
Service ceiling 2,740 m (9,000 ft)
T-O run from grass 95 m (310 ft)
Landing run on grass 52 m (170 ft)
Range with max fuel, normal allowances
217 nm (400 km; 250 miles)

LUTON L.A.4a MINOR

The first Luton Minor flew in 1936. In 1960, the design was modernised and restressed completely to the latest British Airworthiness Requirements, allowing for a power increase to 41 kW (55 hp) and a maximum flying weight of 340 kg (750 lb).

Minors are under construction in many parts of the world, and a considerable number of amateur built examples have been completed and flown.

The following description applies to the aircraft in the form previously marketed by Phoenix, except where indicated.

TYPE: Single-seat homebuilt.

AIRFRAME: All-wood structure, except for steel tube lift and cabane struts, and fabric covering on most of wings, ailerons, fuselage top decking aft of cockpit and tail unit. Coupé cockpit enclosure optional. Wing section RAF 48. Non-retractable tailwheel landing gear.

POWER PLANT: One 1,600 cc Volkswagen modified motorcar engine is usually installed. Fuel capacity 29.5 litres (7.8 US gallons; 6.5 Imp gallons). Provision for additional tanks in wings.

DIMENSIONS, EXTERNAL:
Wing span	7.62 m (25 ft 0 in)
Length overall	6.32 m (20 ft 9 in)
Height overall	2.29 m (7 ft 6 in)

AREA:		
Wings, gross		11.6 m² (125.0 sq ft)

WEIGHTS:
Weight empty	177 kg (390 lb)
Max T-O weight	340 kg (750 lb)

PERFORMANCE (Volkswagen 1,600 cc engine, at normal T-O weight):

Max level speed at 457 m (1,500 ft)	
	65 knots (120 km/h; 75 mph)
Normal cruising speed	60 knots (111 km/h; 69 mph)
Stalling speed	25 knots (45 km/h; 28 mph)
Max rate of climb at S/L	107 m (350 ft)/min
T-O run	92 m (300 ft)
Landing run	36.5 m (120 ft)

Range:		
with standard fuel		155 nm (290 km; 180 miles)
with auxiliary tanks		340 nm (645 km; 400 miles)

ROMAIN
J. ROMAIN & SONS
111 Burnham Green Road, Burnham Green, Welwyn, Hertfordshire
Telephone: (043879) 525

ROMAIN COBRA MK 1
The Cobra Mk 1 is to be made available in ready assembled and kit forms. The prototype flew for the first time on 28 October 1986.
TYPE: Single-seat microlight; conforms to BCAR Section S-CAP 482.
AIRFRAME: Strut and wire braced biplane, with Ceconite covered aluminium alloy airframe, except for area of fuselage forward of cockpit which is metal skinned. Three-axis control. Non-retractable tricycle landing gear.
POWER PLANT: One 22.4 kW (30 hp) IAME KFM. Fuel capacity 20.5 litres (5.4 US gallons; 4.5 Imp gallons).

DIMENSIONS, EXTERNAL:
Wing span	5.69 m (18 ft 8 in)
Length overall	4.42 m (14 ft 6 in)
Height overall	1.68 m (5 ft 6 in)
Propeller diameter	1.57 m (5 ft 2 in)

WEIGHTS:
Weight empty	69.5 kg (153 lb)
Pilot weight range	55-90 kg (122-198 lb)
Max T-O weight	180 kg (397 lb)

PERFORMANCE:
Max level speed at 305 m (1,000 ft)	
	78 knots (145 km/h; 90 mph)
Econ cruising speed at 457 m (1,500 ft)	
	52 knots (97 km/h; 60 mph)
Stalling speed, power off	20 knots (36 km/h; 22 mph)
Max rate of climb at S/L	305 m (1,000 ft)/min
T-O run	31 m (100 ft)
Landing run	25 m (80 ft)
Range with max fuel	87 nm (161 km; 100 miles)
Endurance	2 h
g limits	+6/−4

SOUTHDOWN
SOUTHDOWN AEROSTRUCTURE LTD
Lasham Airfield, Alton, Hampshire GU34 5SR
Telephone: 025 683 359

DIRECTOR: M. K. Fripp
The Pipistrelle 2C is temporarily out of production. Full details and an illustration can be found in the 1987-88 *Jane's*.

TAYLOR
T. TAYLOR
79 Springwater Road, Eastwood, Essex SS9 5BW
Telephone: (0702) 521484

TAYLOR J.T.1 MONOPLANE
The prototype J.T.1 Monoplane first flew on 4 July 1959. Plans are available and by February 1988 about 800 sets had been sold. Approximately 110 plans-built Monoplanes have flown. Wood kits are available in Canada and the USA.
TYPE: Single-seat fully aerobatic homebuilt.
AIRFRAME: All-wood structure, with fabric covering part of wings, elevators and rudder, the remainder plywood covered. Wing section RAF 48. Non-retractable tailwheel landing gear standard.
POWER PLANT: One 30 kW (40 hp) Volkswagen 1,500 cc modified motorcar engine. Other engines fitted by constructors include a 30 kW (40 hp) Aeronca E 113, 48.5 kW (65 hp) Continental A65, 48.5 kW (65 hp) Textron Lycoming, and a 53.7 kW (72 hp) McCulloch. Aircraft with the 48.5 kW (65 hp) engines have a 10 cm (4 in) longer nose and 25 cm (10 in) longer rear fuselage to maintain the correct CG position. Fuel capacity 32 litres (8.4 US gallons; 7 Imp gallons).

DIMENSIONS, EXTERNAL:
Wing span	6.40 m (21 ft 0 in)
Length overall	4.57 m (15 ft 0 in)
Height over tail	1.47 m (4 ft 10 in)
Propeller diameter	1.14 m (3 ft 9 in)

AREA:
Wings, gross	7.06 m² (76.0 sq ft)

WEIGHTS:
Weight empty	195 kg (430 lb)
Baggage capacity	4.5 kg (10 lb)
Max T-O weight	299 kg (660 lb)

PERFORMANCE:
Max level speed at S/L	100 knots (185 km/h; 115 mph)
Econ cruising speed	87 knots (161 km/h; 100 mph)
Stalling speed, power off flaps up	
	35 knots (65 km/h; 40 mph)
flaps down	31 knots (57 km/h; 35 mph)
Max rate of climb at S/L	305 m (1,000 ft)/min
Service ceiling	4,115 m (13,500 ft)
T-O to 15 m (50 ft)	107 m (350 ft)
Landing from 15 m (50 ft)	229 m (750 ft)
Range	252 nm (466 km; 290 miles)
Endurance	3 h
g limits	±6

TAYLOR J.T.2 TITCH
The prototype Titch first flew on 4 January 1967. Plans are available and by February 1988 about 500 sets had been sold. Thirty-two plans-built aircraft have flown. Wood kits are available in Canada and the USA.
TYPE: Single-seat homebuilt.
AIRFRAME: All-wood structure. Wings plywood and fabric covered. Fuselage and fixed tail surfaces plywood covered, except for aluminium cockpit side panels. Rudder and elevators fabric covered. Taylor modified NACA 23012 wing section. Non-retractable tailwheel landing gear.
POWER PLANT: One 63.5 kW (85 hp) Continental C85. Plans-built Titches fitted with engines ranging from 33.6 kW (45 hp) Volkswagen 1,600 cc modified motorcar engine to 78.3 kW (105 hp) Textron Lycoming O-235. Fuel capacity 45.5 litres (12 US gallons; 10 Imp gallons). (1,834 cc VW engined version has 32 litre; 8.4 US gallon; 7 Imp gallon fuel tank.)

DIMENSIONS, EXTERNAL:
Wing span	5.72 m (18 ft 9 in)
Length overall	5.05 m (16 ft 7 in)
Height overall	1.42 m (4 ft 8 in)
Propeller diameter	1.52 m (5 ft 0 in)

AREA:
Wings, gross	6.60 m² (71.0 sq ft)

WEIGHTS (Continental C85 engine):
Weight empty	229 kg (505 lb)
Baggage capacity	4.5 kg (10 lb)
Max T-O weight	345 kg (760 lb)

PERFORMANCE (engine as above):
Max level speed	174 knots (322 km/h; 200 mph)
Max and Econ cruising speed	
	135 knots (250 km/h; 155 mph)
Stalling speed, power off:	
flaps up	51 knots (94 km/h; 58 mph)
flaps down	44 knots (81 km/h; 50 mph)
Service ceiling	5,485 m (18,000 ft)
Max rate of climb at S/L	488 m (1,600 ft)/min
T-O to 15 m (50 ft)	107 m (350 ft)
Landing from 15 m (50 ft)	274 m (900 ft)
Range	330 nm (611 km; 380 miles)
g limits	±6

WESTWIND
WESTWIND CORPORATION LTD
29 Hillcrest Avenue, Edgware, Middlesex HA8 8NZ
Telephone: (01) 958 8539
DIRECTOR: Joe Sudwarts

WESTWIND PHOENIX SG-1
Production of this 'working' microlight has ended, but Westwind is prepared to build it to special order. Full details can be found in the 1987-88 *Jane's*.

WHITTAKER
MICHAEL W. J. WHITTAKER
Dawlish Cottage, Pincots Lane, Wickwar, Wotton-under-Edge, Gloucestershire GL12 8NY
Telephone: (045 424) 598
Mr Michael Whittaker's MW5 Sorcerer is currently being manufactured under licence as an assembled aircraft by Aerotech International, in MW5B form. Plans for the MW5 are available directly from Mr Whittaker.

WHITTAKER/AEROTECH MW5 SORCERER
The following details refer to the MW5B version, as built under licence by Aerotech International.
TYPE: Single-seat microlight; conforms to FAI/CAA requirements.
AIRFRAME: Wing has aluminium alloy spar tubes and drag struts, plywood ribs, and fabric covering. NACA 4412 wing section. Fuselage mainframe of tubular aluminium alloy. Nose fairing with windscreen. Three-axis control. Non-retractable tricycle landing gear. Optional floats and skis.
POWER PLANT: One 37.3 kW (50 hp) Fuji Robin EC44 PM02, or Rotax 377 or 447. Fuel capacity 31 litres (8.2 US gallons; 6.8 Imp gallons).

DIMENSIONS, EXTERNAL:
Wing span	9.16 m (30 ft 0½ in)
Length overall	4.80 m (15 ft 9 in)
Height overall	2.17 m (7 ft 1½ in)
Propeller diameter	1.57 m (5 ft 2 in)

AREA:
Wings, gross	14.16 m² (152.4 sq ft)

WEIGHTS (60 hp engine):
Weight empty	140 kg (308 lb)
Pilot weight range	55-100 kg (122-220 lb)
Max T-O weight	260 kg (573 lb)

PERFORMANCE (60 hp engine, at max T-O weight):
Max level speed	65 knots (120 km/h; 75 mph)
Econ cruising speed	50 knots (92 km/h; 57 mph)
Stalling speed	31 knots (58 km/h; 36 mph)
Max rate of climb at S/L	183 m (600 ft)/min
T-O run	50 m (164 ft)
Landing from 15 m (50 ft)	170 m (558 ft)
Range	150 nm (278 km; 172 miles)
Endurance with max fuel	2 h 50 min
g limits	+4/−2

WHITTAKER MW6 MERLIN
This two-seat version of the MW5 first flew in May 1986. Plans are available.
TYPE: Tandem two-seat homebuilt and microlight aircraft.
AIRFRAME: Wing has aluminium alloy spar, wooden ribs, and is double surface fabric covered. NACA 4412 wing section. Fuselage mainframe of aluminium alloy tubes, bolted together. Three-axis control. Non-retractable tricycle landing gear.
POWER PLANT: One 37.3 kW (50 hp) Fuji Robin EC44PM 432 cc, or Rotax 503 or 532. Fuel capacity 18 litres (4.8 US gallons; 4 Imp gallons).

DIMENSIONS, EXTERNAL:
Wing span	9.75 m (32 ft 0 in)
Length overall	5.33 m (17 ft 6 in)
Height overall	2.59 m (8 ft 6 in)
Propeller diameter	1.57 m (5 ft 2 in)

AREA:
Wings, gross	14.86 m² (160.0 sq ft)

WEIGHTS:
Weight empty	150 kg (330 lb)
Crew weight range	46-181 kg (100-400 lb)
Max T-O weight	340 kg (750 lb)

Romain Cobra Mk 1 microlight biplane

Whittaker MW6 Merlin two-seat aircraft *(Edwin A. Shackleton)*

Taylor J.T.1 Monoplane fitted with bubble canopy and owned by Mr D. Hunter

Baby Ace Model D with optional wheel spats and headrest fairing

Taylor J.T.2 Titch owned by Mr Roy Newton

Acro Sport I built by M Georges Coussement and M Alfred Haeck of Belgium

PERFORMANCE:					
Max level speed	55 knots (102 km/h; 63 mph)	Max rate of climb at S/L: solo	290 m (950 ft)/min	Landing run	91 m (300 ft)
Econ cruising speed	45 knots (83 km/h; 52 mph)	dual	152 m (500 ft)/min	Range with max standard fuel	78 nm (144 km; 90 miles)
Stalling speed, power off	28 knots (52 km/h; 33 mph)	Service ceiling	3,050 m (10,000 ft)		
		T-O run	61 m (200 ft)		

UNITED STATES OF AMERICA

ACE

ACE AIRCRAFT COMPANY
05-134th Street, Chesapeake, West Virginia 25315
Telephone: (304) 949 3098
OWNER: Denny Meadows
The Ace Aircraft Company offers plans, material kits and some pre-welded components for the Baby Ace Model D and Jr Ace Model E (see also Acro-Sport Corben Jr Ace).

BABY ACE MODEL D
The prototype of the redesigned Baby Ace Model D flew for the first time on 15 November 1956. About 350 have since been built by amateurs.
TYPE: Single-seat homebuilt.
AIRFRAME: Wing section Clark Y (modified). Wooden wings and ailerons, and welded steel tube fuselage and tail unit, all fabric covered. Non-retractable tailwheel landing gear. Optional floats.
POWER PLANT: One Continental A65, A85, C65 or C85 engine of 48.5 or 63.5 kW (65 or 85 hp). Fuel capacity 63.6 litres (16.8 US gallons; 14 Imp gallons).
DIMENSIONS, EXTERNAL:
Wing span   8.05 m (26 ft 5 in)

Length overall   5.40 m (17 ft 8¾ in)
Height overall   2.02 m (6 ft 7¾ in)
AREA:
Wings, gross   10.43 m² (112.3 sq ft)
WEIGHTS (landplane, unless stated otherwise):
Weight empty, equipped   261 kg (575 lb)
Baggage capacity   4.5 kg (10 lb)
Max T-O weight: 48.5 kW (65 hp)   431 kg (950 lb)
   63.5 kW (85 hp) landplane or seaplane
     522 kg (1,150 lb)
PERFORMANCE (48.5 kW; 65 hp landplane, at max T-O weight):
Max level speed at S/L   96 knots (177 km/h; 110 mph)
Max cruising speed
     87-91 knots (161-169 km/h; 100-105 mph)
Stalling speed   30 knots (54.7 km/h; 34 mph)
Max rate of climb at S/L   365 m (1,200 ft)/min
Service ceiling   4,875 m (16,000 ft)
T-O and landing run   76 m (250 ft)
Range with max fuel   304 nm (560 km; 350 miles)

JUNIOR ACE MODEL E
The Junior Ace Model E differs from the Baby Ace

Model D in being a side by side two-seater. It is powered usually by a 63.5 kW (85 hp) Continental C85, and the details refer to a typical aircraft with this power plant that also has a cockpit 7.5 cm (3 in) wider and 10 cm (4 in) deeper than that of the standard Model E, a full electrical system and increased fuel capacity of 85 litres (22.5 US gallons; 18.75 Imp gallons).

DIMENSIONS, EXTERNAL:
Wing span   7.92 m (26 ft 0 in)
Length overall   5.50 m (18 ft 0 in)
Height overall   2.00 m (6 ft 7 in)
WEIGHTS:
Weight empty   367 kg (809 lb)
Max T-O weight   606 kg (1,335 lb)
PERFORMANCE:
Max level speed at S/L   113 knots (209 km/h; 130 mph)
Cruising speed   91 knots (169 km/h; 105 mph)
Landing speed   57 knots (105 km/h; 65 mph)
Service ceiling   3,050 m (10,000 ft)
T-O run   122 m (400 ft)
Landing run   183 m (600 ft)
Range with max fuel   304 nm (560 km; 350 miles)

ACRO SPORT

ACRO SPORT INC
PO Box 462, Hales Corners, Wisconsin 53130
Telephone: (414) 529 2609

PRESIDENT: LaFonda Jean Kinnaman
The Acro Sport I, Super Acro Sport, Acro Sport II and Pober Pixie were all designed by Mr Paul H. Poberezny, President of the entirely separate Experimental Aircraft Association.

ACRO SPORT I
The Acro Sport I was designed specifically for construction by school students as a pupils' project. First flight of the prototype (N1AC) was made on 11 January 1972. Plans and construction manuals are available to homebuilders, and

about 1,250 sets had been sold by early 1988. More than sixty Acro Sport Is were then flying.

The following details apply to the prototype:

TYPE: Single-seat aerobatic homebuilt biplane.

AIRFRAME: Wooden wings and ailerons (on all four wings), fabric covered. Wing section Munk M-6. Glassfibre wingtips. Fuselage of welded steel tube, with wooden stringers, fabric covered. Glassfibre nose cowl and light alloy engine cowlings. Welded steel tube tail unit, with fabric covering. Non-retractable tailwheel landing gear, modified from Piper J-3 components.

POWER PLANT: Prototype has 134 kW (180 hp) Textron Lycoming engine. Basic power plant is a 74.5 kW (100 hp) Continental O-200. Fuel capacity 104 litres (20 US gallons; 16.7 Imp gallons).

DIMENSIONS, EXTERNAL: *

Wing span: upper	5.97 m (19 ft 7 in)
lower	5.82 m (19 ft 1 in)
Length overall	5.33 m (17 ft 6 in)
Height overall	1.83 m (6 ft 0 in)
Propeller diameter	1.93 m (6 ft 4 in)

AREA:

Wings, gross	10.73 m² (115.5 sq ft)

WEIGHTS:

Weight empty, equipped	335 kg (739 lb)
Baggage capacity	16 kg (35 lb)
Max T-O and landing weight	534 kg (1,178 lb)

PERFORMANCE (at max T-O weight):

Max level speed	132 knots (245 km/h; 152 mph)
Econ cruising speed	91 knots (169 km/h; 105 mph)
Stalling speed	44 knots (81 km/h; 50 mph)
Max rate of climb at S/L	518 m (1,700 ft)/min
T-O run	46 m (150 ft)
Landing run	244 m (800 ft)
Range with max fuel	304 nm (563 km; 350 miles)

SUPER ACRO SPORT

The Super Acro Sport prototype first flew on 21 March 1973. The aircraft is intended for unlimited International Class aerobatic competition at world championship level.

The differences by comparison with the standard Acro Sport I are covered in a supplement to the basic plans available from Acro Sport Inc. The description of the Acro Sport I applies also to the Super Acro Sport, except as follows:

TYPE: Single-seat advanced homebuilt aerobatic biplane.

AIRFRAME: As for Acro Sport I, except wing section NACA 23012.

POWER PLANT: Prototype has 149 kW (200 hp) Textron Lycoming IO-360-A2A.

DIMENSIONS, EXTERNAL: As for Acro Sport I, except:

Length overall	5.30 m (17 ft 4½ in)

WEIGHTS:

Weight empty	401 kg (884 lb)
Max T-O weight	612 kg (1,350 lb)

PERFORMANCE (at max T-O weight):

Max level speed at S/L	135 knots (251 km/h; 156 mph)
Max cruising speed	117 knots (217 km/h; 135 mph)
Stalling speed	44 knots (81 km/h; 50 mph)
Max rate of climb at S/L	549 m (1,800 ft)/min
Service ceiling	4,575 m (15,000 ft)
T-O run	38 m (125 ft)
Landing run	244 m (800 ft)
Range with max fuel	260 nm (482 km; 300 miles)

ACRO SPORT II

The Acro Sport II is a two-seat aerobatic biplane derived

from the Acro Sport I, for the pilot with only a low number of flying hours to his credit. The first flight was achieved on 9 July 1978. Plans are available to homebuilders and approximately 1,050 sets had been sold by early 1988. More than 40 Acro Sport IIs were flying at that time.

TYPE: Tandem two-seat homebuilt aerobatic biplane.

AIRFRAME: As for Acro Sport I.

POWER PLANT: Prototype has 134 kW (180 hp) Textron Lycoming O-360-A4B. Can be powered by engines of 74.5-149 kW (100-200 hp). Fuel capacity 98.4 litres (26 US gallons; 21.6 Imp gallons).

DIMENSIONS, EXTERNAL:

Wing span: upper	6.60 m (21 ft 8 in)
lower	6.32 m (20 ft 9 in)
Length overall	5.75 m (18 ft 10¼ in)
Height overall	2.03 m (6 ft 7¾ in)

AREA:

Wings, gross	14.12 m² (152.0 sq ft)

WEIGHTS:

Weight empty	397 kg (875 lb)
Baggage capacity	13.6 kg (30 lb)
Max T-O weight	689 kg (1,520 lb)

PERFORMANCE (prototype):

Max cruising speed	107 knots (198 km/h; 123 mph)
Stalling speed	46 knots (86 km/h; 53 mph)
Max rate of climb at S/L	457 m (1,500 ft)/min
T-O run	91 m (300 ft)
g limits	+6.5/-4.5

POBER P-9 PIXIE

The prototype Pixie made its first flight in July 1974, with a Volkswagen engine. Some Pixies currently flying use the 48.5 kW (65 hp) Continental engine.

Plans are available to amateur constructors, and approximately 950 sets had been sold by early 1988.

TYPE: Single-seat sporting homebuilt.

AIRFRAME: Wooden wing structure, plywood and fabric covered. Clark Y wing section. Welded fuselage of 4130 chrome molybdenum steel tubing with wood formers and fabric covering. Tail unit of welded 4130 chrome molybdenum steel tubing, fabric covered. Non-retractable tailwheel landing gear standard.

POWER PLANT: One 44.5 kW (60 hp) Limbach SL 1700 EA. Equally suited to other Volkswagen and 48.5 kW (65 hp) engines. Fuel capacity 46.6 litres (12.3 US gallons; 10.2 Imp gallons).

DIMENSIONS, EXTERNAL:

Wing span	9.09 m (29 ft 10 in)
Length overall	5.26 m (17 ft 3 in)
Height overall	1.88 m (6 ft 2 in)
Propeller diameter	1.35 m (4 ft 5 in)

AREA:

Wings, gross	12.47 m² (134.25 sq ft)

WEIGHTS:

Weight empty	246 kg (543 lb)
Baggage capacity	9 kg (20 lb)
Max T-O weight	408 kg (900 lb)

PERFORMANCE (at max T-O weight):

Max level speed at S/L	89 knots (166 km/h; 103 mph)
Max cruising speed	72 knots (134 km/h; 83 mph)
Stalling speed	26 knots (49 km/h; 30 mph)
Max rate of climb at S/L	213 m (700 ft)/min
Service ceiling	3,810 m (12,500 ft)
T-O and landing run	91 m (300 ft)
Range with max fuel	251 nm (466 km; 290 miles)

COUGAR MODEL 1

This aircraft was designed by Mr Robert E. Nesmith, to encourage aviation among teenage boys. More than 100 Cougars have been built from plans.

TYPE: Side by side two-seat homebuilt.

AIRFRAME: All-wood wings, using modified NACA 4900-series section. Ailerons of 4130 steel tubing with aluminium trailing-edges. Welded steel tube fuselage and tail unit, with fabric covering. Glassfibre nose cowling and light alloy engine cowlings. Non-retractable tailwheel landing gear.

POWER PLANT: Suitable engines range from 48.5 to 93.2 kW (65-125 hp), including the Continental C65, C85 and O-200; and Textron Lycoming O-235 and O-290. Fuel capacity 11.4 kg (25 lb).

DIMENSIONS, EXTERNAL:

Wing span	6.25 m (20 ft 6 in)
Length overall	5.77 m (18 ft 11 in)
Height overall	1.68 m (5 ft 6 in)
Propeller diameter	1.63 m (5 ft 4 in)

AREA:

Wings, gross	7.62 m² (82.0 sq ft)

WEIGHTS:

Weight empty: standard	283 kg (624 lb)
with folding wings	312 kg (689 lb)
Max T-O weight	567 kg (1,250 lb)

PERFORMANCE (at max T-O weight):

Max level speed	152 knots (281 km/h; 175 mph)
Econ cruising speed	104 knots (193 km/h; 120 mph)
Stalling speed	46 knots (86 km/h; 53 mph)
Max rate of climb at S/L	396 m (1,300 ft)/min
T-O run	152 m (500 ft)
Landing run	183 m (600 ft)
Range with max fuel	521 nm (965 km; 600 miles)

CORBEN Jr ACE

The Corben Jr Ace was designed by Mr O. G. Corben in the 1920s. The following details apply to the plans marketed by Acro Sport (see also Ace Aircraft Company):

TYPE: Side by side two-seat homebuilt.

AIRFRAME: Wooden wings and ailerons, fabric covered. Wing section Clark Y. Fuselage structure of welded steel tube and wooden stringers, fabric covered. Light alloy engine cowling. Fabric covered steel tube tail unit. Non-retractable tailwheel landing gear.

POWER PLANT: One 33.6 kW (45 hp) Szekely, Aeromarine AR-350, Continental C65 or similar engine. Fuel capacity 38 litres (10 US gallons; 8.3 Imp gallons).

DIMENSIONS, EXTERNAL:

Wing span	10.35 m (33 ft 11½ in)
Length overall	5.73 m (18 ft 9½ in)
Height overall	2.29 m (7 ft 6 in)
Propeller diameter	1.93 m (6 ft 4 in)

AREA:

Wings, gross	15.61 m² (168.0 sq ft)

WEIGHTS:

Weight empty	255 kg (563 lb)
Max T-O weight	442 kg (975 lb)

PERFORMANCE (at max T-O weight):

Max level speed at S/L	74 knots (137 km/h; 85 mph)
Econ cruising speed	61 knots (113 km/h; 70 mph)
Stalling speed	31 knots (57 km/h; 35 mph)
Max rate of climb at S/L	152 m (500 ft)/min
Service ceiling	over 3,960 m (13,000 ft)
T-O and landing run	46 m (150 ft)
Range with max fuel	173 nm (322 km; 200 miles)

ADVANCED AVIATION
ADVANCED AVIATION INC

323 North Ivey Lane, PO Box 16716, Orlando, Florida 32861

Telephone: (305) 298 2920

MARKETING MANAGER: Angel Matos

The Advanced Aviation range of aircraft now includes the Sierra sailplane (see Sailplanes section).

ADVANCED AVIATION COBRA

The prototype of the single-seat Cobra flew for the first time in 1982. The current standard model is thought to be the **B377 Cobra B**, which qualifies under both microlight and Experimental regulations. The basically similar **B447 Cobra VIP** has disc brakes and a cushioned seat as standard, and is powered by the higher rated Rotax 447 engine, putting it in the Experimental category. The Rotax 532LC-engined **B532 AG Cobra** is equipped for cropspraying. Many hundreds of Cobra kits have been sold.

The following details refer to the Cobra B, unless stated otherwise.

TYPE: Single-seat microlight; conforms to FAR Pt 103. Cobra VIP and AG Cobra conform to FAA Experimental category as homebuilt aircraft.

AIRFRAME: Aluminium alloy structure throughout, with double surface wing covering. Three-axis control. Options include nose cowling and recovery parachute. Non-retractable tricycle landing gear. Floats and skis optional.

POWER PLANT: One 26 kW (35 hp) Rotax 377. Cobra VIP has 30 kW (40 hp) Rotax 447. AG Cobra uses a 48.5 kW (65 hp) Rotax 532LC which is also optional for Cobra VIP.

All models have 19 litre (5 US gallon; 4.2 Imp gallon) fuel capacity.

DIMENSIONS, EXTERNAL:

Wing span	10.57 m (34 ft 8 in)
Length overall	5.46 m (17 ft 10¾ in)
Height overall	2.51 m (8 ft 3 in)
Propeller diameter	1.52 m (5 ft 0 in)

AREA:

Wings, gross	13.56 m² (146.0 sq ft)

WEIGHTS (Cobra B):

Weight empty	114 kg (252 lb)
Pilot weight range	50-102 kg (110-225 lb)
Max T-O weight	238 kg (525 lb)

PERFORMANCE (Cobra B):

Max level speed	55 knots (101 km/h; 63 mph)
Econ cruising speed	39 knots (72 km/h; 45 mph)
Stalling speed	21 knots (39 km/h; 24 mph)
Max rate of climb at S/L	229 m (750 ft)/min
Service ceiling	4,575 m (15,000 ft)
T-O run	30 m (100 ft)
Landing run	46 m (150 ft)
Range	78 nm (145 km; 90 miles)
Endurance	2 h

ADVANCED AVIATION B532 KING COBRA B

This two-seat Experimental version of the Cobra is powered normally by a 48.5 kW (65 hp) Rotax 532, with optional engines of 32 kW (43 hp), 34.3 kW (46 hp) and 37.3 kW (50 hp). It flew for the first time in 1983 and is similar in construction to the single-seat Cobras.

WEIGHTS:

Weight empty	147 kg (325 lb)
Crew weight range	50-190 kg (110-420 lb)
Max T-O weight	351 kg (775 lb)

PERFORMANCE:

Max level speed	59 knots (109 km/h; 68 mph)
Econ cruising speed	43 knots (80 km/h; 50 mph)
Stalling speed	27 knots (50 km/h; 31 mph)
Max rate of climb at S/L	198 m (650 ft)/min
Service ceiling	3,660 m (12,000 ft)
T-O and landing run	76 m (250 ft)
Range	65 nm (120 km; 75 miles)
Endurance	1 h 30 min

ADVANCED AVIATION (HIGHCRAFT) BUCCANEER

The Buccaneer was made available by Advanced Aviation as a bolt-together kit primarily for amphibious flying-boat use although it can be built as a landplane for later upgrade to amphibian. Construction time was quoted as 50 hours.

The following details refer to the **Model XA/350** amphibian.

TYPE: Single-seat amphibious microlight aircraft; conforms to FAR Pt 103.

AIRFRAME: Aluminium alloy wings and tail unit, double surface Dacron covered; glassfibre two-step hull and stabilising floats. Three-axis control. Retractable tailwheel landing gear. Options include skis and recovery parachute.

POWER PLANT: One 26 kW (35 hp) Rotax 377. Fuel capacity 17 litres (4.5 US gallons; 3.75 Imp gallons). Optional 20

Acro Sport II built by Mr Steve Blake of McHenry, Illinois, USA, and fitted with an Airplane Factory two-place canopy

Corben Jr Ace built by Mr Wilton Weser of DesPlaines, Illinois

Acro Sport Pober P-9 Pixie built by Mr G. Haegeman of Gosselies, Belgium, the first to be completed in Europe, in 1983 (*M. J. Hooks*)

Advanced Aviation Cobra Carrera single-seat landplane (*Howard Levy*)

Cougar Model 1 (Textron Lycoming O-290 engine) (*John Wegg*)

Two-seat Advanced Aviation King Cobra (*Brian M. Service*)

kW (27 hp) Rotax 277 in **Model XA/280** or 30 kW (40 hp) Rotax 447 in **Model XA/430**.

DIMENSIONS, EXTERNAL (all models):

Wing span	10.21 m (33 ft 6 in)
Length overall: landplane	5.33 m (17 ft 6 in)
amphibian	5.84 m (19 ft 2 in)
Height overall	2.26 m (7 ft 4¾ in)
Propeller diameter	1.52 m (5 ft 0 in)

AREA (all models):

Wings, gross	15.05 m² (162.0 sq ft)

WEIGHTS (XA/350):

Weight empty	144 kg (318 lb)
Pilot weight range	50-113 kg (110-250 lb)
Max T-O weight	272 kg (600 lb)

PERFORMANCE (XA/350 with 77 kg; 170 lb pilot):

Max level speed at S/L	55 knots (101 km/h; 63 mph)
Econ cruising speed at S/L	39 knots (72 km/h; 45 mph)
Stalling speed at S/L	21 knots (39 km/h; 24 mph)
Max rate of climb at S/L	229 m (750 ft)/min
Service ceiling	3,960 m (13,000 ft)
T-O run: on land	38 m (125 ft)
on water	49 m (160 ft)
Landing from 15 m (50 ft): on land	137 m (450 ft)
Range	87 nm (161 km; 100 miles)
Endurance	2 h 15 min
g limits	+5/−3.5

ADVANCED AVIATION COBRA CARRERA

This is a single-seat land-based-only derivative of the Buccaneer with a non-retractable landing gear and elongated nose. It is offered with four engine options, the models with a 20 kW (27 hp) Rotax 277, a 26 kW (35 hp) Rotax 377 and 30 kW (40 hp) Rotax 447 meeting FAR Pt 103-7 microlight requirements or coming under Experimental regulations, and the 34 kW (45.6 hp) Rotax 503 model being classified as an Experimental category type only. All have a fuel capacity of 19 litres (5 US gallons; 4.2 Imp gallons). Construction time is 50 h.

The following details refer to the Rotax 377-engined model:

DIMENSIONS, EXTERNAL:

Wing span	8.43 m (27 ft 8 in)
Length overall	6.22 m (20 ft 5 in)
Height overall	1.68 m (5 ft 6 in)
Propeller diameter	1.52 m (5 ft 0 in)

AREA:

Wings, gross	12.45 m² (134.0 sq ft)

WEIGHTS:

Weight empty	120 kg (265 lb)
Max pilot weight	113 kg (250 lb)
Max T-O weight	249 kg (550 lb)

PERFORMANCE (77 kg; 170 lb pilot):

Max level speed	55 knots (101 km/h; 63 mph)
Cruising speed	48 knots (89 km/h; 55 mph)
Stalling speed	22 knots (41 km/h; 25 mph)
Max rate of climb at S/L	305 m (1,000 ft)/min
Service ceiling	4,265 m (14,000 ft)
T-O and landing run	46 m (150 ft)
g limits	+6/−3

ADVANCED AVIATION XA/650 BUCCANEER II

This side by side two-seat derivative of the Buccaneer amphibian flew for the first time on 14 March 1986. The landing gear is retracted via a cockpit lever instead of manually. Power plant is a 48.5 kW (65 hp) Rotax 532. Fuel capacity is 45 litres (12 US gallons; 10 Imp gallons). Kits are available.

DIMENSIONS, EXTERNAL:

Wing span	10.21 m (33 ft 6 in)
Length overall	6.65 m (21 ft 9½ in)
Height overall	2.13 m (7 ft 0 in)
Propeller diameter	1.73 m (5 ft 8 in)

AREA:

Wings, gross	15.89 m² (171.0 sq ft)

WEIGHTS:

Weight empty	236 kg (520 lb)
Max crew weight	195 kg (430 lb)
Max T-O weight	465 kg (1,025 lb)

PERFORMANCE (preliminary, crew weight 154 kg; 340 lb):

Max level speed at S/L	65 knots (120 km/h; 75 mph)
Econ cruising speed at S/L	50 knots (92 km/h; 57 mph)
Stalling speed: power off	29 knots (53 km/h; 33 mph)
Max rate of climb at S/L	167 m (550 ft)/min
T-O run: on land or water	77 m (250 ft)

ADVANCED AVIATION BUCCANEER SX

This new single-seat amphibian is reportedly to supersede the earlier model. Available in the same bolt-together aluminium tube, Dacron covering and glassfibre hull kit form, it utilises the airframe of the Carrera but with the addition of a hull and wing floats, and has a cockpit lever to retract the landing gear. Power plant options are a 30 kW (40 hp) Rotax 447, 34 kW (45.6 hp) Rotax 503, or 48.5 kW (65 hp) Rotax 532. Fuel capacity is 19 litres (5 US gallons; 4.2 Imp gallons) in the microlight category, or 49.2 litres (13 US gallons; 10.8 Imp gallons) in the Experimental category. Construction takes about 60 working hours.

DIMENSIONS, EXTERNAL:
Wing span	8.43 m (27 ft 8 in)
Length overall	6.22 m (20 ft 5 in)
Height overall	1.68 m (5 ft 6 in)

WEIGHTS:
Weight empty	144 kg (318 lb)
Max T-O weight	272 kg (600 lb)

PERFORMANCE (Rotax 447 engine):
Max level speed	69 knots (129 km/h; 80 mph)
Cruising speed	52 knots (97 km/h; 60 mph)
Stalling speed	25 knots (45 km/h; 28 mph)
Max rate of climb at S/L	275 m (900 ft)/min
T-O run: from land	38 m (125 ft)
from water	46 m (150 ft)

AEROCAR
AEROCAR INC

PO Box 1171, Longview, Washington 98632
Telephone: (206) 423 8260
PRESIDENT AND GENERAL MANAGER: Moulton B. Taylor

In February 1948 Aerocar Inc began developing a flying automobile designed by Mr M. B. Taylor. The prototype *Aerocar*, with a Textron Lycoming O-290 engine, was completed in October 1949. Design and theoretical work continue on the concept, now in its CRX fourth generation form.

Fully active Aerocar programmes are detailed in this entry; separate entries for Brown and Holcomb cover other aircraft

AEROCAR SOOPER-COOT MODEL A

The prototype Sooper-Coot flew for the first time in February 1971. Its 'float-wing' configuration permits rough-water operation and, since the close proximity of the wings to the water forms a 'pressure wedge', unusually low take-off and landing speeds are possible without recourse to flaps or other lift enhancing devices.

The structure is basically of wood, but the tailboom and tail unit can be of steel tube and fabric, wood monocoque or all-metal construction. Wing section is NACA 4415. The fabric covered ailerons are of metal construction. A manually retractable tricycle landing gear is standard, but an alternative powered retraction system is shown on the plans.

Recommended power plant for the Sooper-Coot is a Franklin of either 134 or 164 kW (180 or 220 hp). However, many builders are fitting a 157 kW (210 hp) Continental IO-360. To minimise expenditure, others are fitting Textron Lycoming O-320 and O-320-B engines of 119 kW (160 hp). Maximum fuel capacity is 189 litres (50 US gallons; 41.6 Imp gallons).

Certain component parts (including the glassfibre engine cowls, glassfibre hull shell, foredeck, instrument panel, tail fairings, engine cooling fan blades and spring steel main landing gear legs), and plans, are available to amateur constructors. Many hundreds of Sooper-Coots are under construction, and more than 130 are known to be flying.

DIMENSIONS, EXTERNAL:
Wing span	10.97 m (36 ft 0 in)
Length overall	6.10 to 6.71 m (20 ft 0 in to 22 ft 0 in)
Height overall	2.44 m (8 ft 0 in)

AREA:
Wings, gross	16.72 m² (180.0 sq ft)

WEIGHTS:
Weight empty	499 kg (1,100 lb)
Max T-O weight	884 kg (1,950 lb)

PERFORMANCE (134 kW; 180 hp engine, at max T-O weight):
Max cruising speed	113 knots (209 km/h; 130 mph)
Econ cruising speed at 50% power	
	95 knots (177 km/h; 110 mph)
Max rate of climb at S/L	381 m (1,250 ft)/min
T-O run (land)	61 m (200 ft)

AEROCAR MINI-IMP

The Mini-Imp is a single-seat version of the Aerocar Imp, to which it is generally similar (see 'Brown' entry in this section). The basic structure is all metal. Plans are available, together with parts kits. More than 250 amateur-built Mini-Imps are being constructed, and a number are flying. Average time taken for construction is 1,500 working hours.

The description of the Imp applies also to the Mini-Imp, except as follows:

TYPE: Single-seat sporting homebuilt.

POWER PLANT: Recommended engine is a 47 kW (63 hp) Rotax 532. Alternative engines in the 44.5-74.5 kW (60-100 hp) range may be installed. Fuel capacity 45.4 litres (12 US gallons; 10 Imp gallons), plus tip tanks, each of 34 litres (9 US gallons; 7.5 Imp gallons) capacity.

DIMENSIONS, EXTERNAL:
Wing span	7.77 m (25 ft 6 in)
Length overall	4.88 m (16 ft 0 in)
Height over fuselage	1.24 m (4 ft 1 in)
Propeller diameter	1.45 m (4 ft 9 in)

WEIGHTS:
Weight empty	236 kg (520 lb)
Max T-O weight	362 kg (800 lb)

PERFORMANCE (51 kW; 68 hp Limbach 1,900 cc engine, except where indicated):

Max cruising speed at S/L
	130 knots (241 km/h; 150 mph)

Max cruising speed (Revmaster engine, estimated)
	over 173 knots (322 km/h; 200 mph)
Stalling speed	44 knots (81 km/h; 50 mph)
Max rate of climb at S/L	366 m (1,200 ft)/min
T-O run	183 m (600 ft)
Range	over 434 nm (804 km; 500 miles)
g limits	±9

AEROCAR MICRO-IMP

The Micro-Imp is of similar configuration to the Mini-Imp, but is constructed primarily of glassfibre reinforced paper known as TPG (Taylor Paper Glass). The prototype made its first flight in the Summer of 1981. Drawings to allow amateur constructors to build the Micro-Imp are almost complete, but the programme was still delayed in early 1988, pending the availability of a suitable engine.

TYPE: Single-seat sporting homebuilt.

AIRFRAME: Structure made almost entirely of TPG. This comprises paper core covered with glassfibre in a matrix of polyester resin, covered overall with ripstop Dacron. Metal inlays built into TPG to accommodate compressive loadings. Wing section NASA GA(PC)-1. Full-span constant chord 'flaperons' of similar construction to wings. Non-structural and removable fuselage nosecone of moulded glassfibre. Retractable tricycle landing gear.

POWER PLANT: One 47 kW (63 hp) Rotax 532 currently recommended. Fuel capacity 26.5 litres (7 US gallons; 5.8 Imp gallons).

DIMENSIONS, EXTERNAL:
Wing span	8.23 m (27 ft 0 in)
Length overall	4.57 m (15 ft 0 in)
Height overall	1.22 m (4 ft 0 in)
Propeller diameter	1.07 m (3 ft 6 in)

WEIGHTS:
Weight empty	113 kg (250 lb)
Max T-O weight	238 kg (525 lb)

PERFORMANCE (estimated):
Max level speed	104 knots (193 km/h; 120 mph)
Econ cruising speed	87 knots (161 km/h; 100 mph)
Stalling speed	42 knots (78 km/h; 48 mph)
Max rate of climb at S/L	152 m (500 ft)/min
Service ceiling	3,050 m (10,000 ft)
T-O run	152 m (500 ft)
Landing run	122 m (400 ft)

TAYLOR BULLET 2100

Following the success of the TPG method of construction for the Micro-Imp, Aerocar designed a two-seat counterpart also utilising TPG. It is known as the Taylor Bullet 2100, because of its similarity in configuration to the Gallaudet Bullet of 1912. The prototype began its taxying tests in February 1985.

Plans to allow amateur construction of the Bullet 2100 are not yet available, but will be offered eventually, together with some difficult to fabricate component parts such as the landing gear, driveshaft unit, welded components, wheels and brakes.

TYPE: Side by side two-seat homebuilt.

AIRFRAME: Wing section GA(PC)-1. Warren truss type wing structure using laminated paper ribs and basic spar webs (TPG), with some use of aluminium and wood. Wing leading-edges covered with moulded glassfibre skins. Overall Dacron wing covering. Warren truss full span 'flaperons'. Y tail surfaces, with TPG spars and ribs (with aluminium inlays on spars) and glassfibre skins, covered overall with Dacron, as are tailboom and main fuselage. Non-retractable tailwheel landing gear.

POWER PLANT: One 52.2 kW (70 hp) Revmaster 2100D. Design suited to other engines, including 74.5 kW (100 hp) Revmaster, Continental O-200 or Textron Lycoming O-235. Fuel capacity of 83 litres (22 US gallons; 18.3 Imp gallons).

DIMENSIONS, EXTERNAL:
Wing span	10.36 m (34 ft 0 in)
Length overall	5.72 m (18 ft 9 in)
Height overall	1.83 m (6 ft 0 in)
Propeller diameter	1.42 m (4 ft 8 in)

AREA:
Wings, gross	12.63 m² (136.0 sq ft)

WEIGHTS:
Weight empty	453 kg (1,000 lb)
Max baggage	35 kg (78 lb)
Max T-O weight	748 kg (1,650 lb)

PERFORMANCE (estimated at max T-O weight):
Max level speed at S/L	130 knots (241 km/h; 150 mph)
Max cruising speed	122 knots (225 km/h; 140 mph)
Stalling speed	42 knots (78 km/h; 48 mph)
Max rate of climb at S/L	213 m (700 ft)/min
T-O run	152 m (500 ft)
Landing run (with reverse pitch)	152 m (500 ft)
Range with max fuel	434 nm (805 km; 500 miles)
g limits	+4 normal
	+6 ultimate

AERO COMPOSITE
AERO COMPOSITE TECHNOLOGY INC

Rt 3, Box 107B, Somerset, Pennsylvania 15501
Telephone: (814) 445 8608
OWNERS: William D. Forrest and Tom Wright

AERO COMPOSITE SEA HAWKER

Under the original owners, Aero Gare, design of the Sea Hawker began in 1981 and a prototype flew for the first time in July 1982. The present owners purchased the Sea Hawker from Aero Composites Inc in July 1987. They are marketing kits comprising 22 pre-moulded components and all raw materials, with cadmium plating on all welded or machined parts. By March 1988, a total of 234 kits had been sold, together with 331 sets of plans only. Thirty-two Sea Hawkers had then flown. Average construction time is between 1,400 and 1,600 working hours.

The Sea Hawker's amphibious rough-field landing gear permits landings on water, asphalt, grass, snow, mud, and rough fields. The glassfibre covered rubbing strips on the hull allow a safe gear-up emergency landing on hard surfaces.

TYPE: Side by side two-seat homebuilt amphibious biplane.

AIRFRAME: NASA wing section. Composite wings of glassfibre and carbonfibre. Full-span slotted ailerons on lower wings deflect with slotted flaps on upper wings for take-off and landing. Single-step hull of Kevlar, glassfibre and carbonfibre, with integral fin. Retractable tricycle landing gear. Water rudder under fin.

POWER PLANT: One 112 kW (150 hp) Textron Lycoming O-320 recommended. Two fuel tanks, each with 132.5 litre (35 US gallon; 29 Imp gallon) capacity.

DIMENSIONS, EXTERNAL:
Wing span	7.32 m (24 ft 0 in)
Length overall	6.55 m (21 ft 6 in)
Height overall	2.29 m (7 ft 6 in)
Propeller diameter	1.63 m (5 ft 4 in)

AREA:
Wings, gross	10.96 m² (118.0 sq ft)

WEIGHTS (112 kW; 150 hp engine):
Weight empty	386 kg (850 lb)
Max T-O weight	726 kg (1,600 lb)

PERFORMANCE (112 kW; 150 hp engine):

Max level and cruising speed at S/L
	129 knots (238 km/h; 148 mph)
Econ cruising speed	120 knots (222 km/h; 138 mph)
Stalling speed, flaps down	37 knots (68 km/h; 42 mph)
Max rate of climb at S/L	335 m (1,100 ft)/min
Service ceiling	5,475 m (18,000 ft)
T-O run: from land	153 m (500 ft)
from water	305 m (1,000 ft)
Landing run: on land	213 m (700 ft)
on water	183 m (600 ft)
Range with max fuel, 45 min reserves	
	1,042 nm (1,931 km; 1,200 miles)
g limits	+5/-3

AERO DESIGNS
AERO DESIGNS INC

635 Blakeley, San Antonio, Texas 78209
Telephone: (512) 650 3398

AERO DESIGNS PULSAR

Aero Designs is marketing the Pulsar in kit form, including engine. It is basically a side by side two-seat version of the Star-Lite, designed also by Mr Mark Brown. Construction takes about 400 working hours.

AIRFRAME: Construction similar to Star-Lite. Wing section MSI-0313. Non-retractable tricycle landing gear.

POWER PLANT: One 47.7 kW (64 hp) Rotax 532. Fuel capacity 60 litres (16 US gallons; 13.3 Imp gallons).

Aerocar Mini-Imp single-seat sporting monoplane

Aerocar Sooper-Coot Model A amphibian

Aero Composite Sea Hawker amphibious biplane *(Debby LeGare)*

Aero Dynamics Sparrow Hawk Mk II two-seat light aircraft

Buccaneer II two-seat homebuilt amphibian, marketed by Advanced Aviation *(Howard Levy)*

Advanced Aviation Buccaneer SX (Rotax 447 engine) *(Howard Levy)*

Aero Designs Pulsar homebuilt prototype *(Howard Levy)*

DIMENSIONS, EXTERNAL:		WEIGHTS:		Service ceiling	4,570 m (15,000 ft)
Wing span	7.62 m (25 ft 0 in)	Weight empty	195 kg (430 lb)	T-O and landing run	91 m (300 ft)
Length overall	5.94 m (19 ft 6 in)	Max T-O weight	394 kg (870 lb)	Range	347 nm (644 km; 400 miles)
Height overall	1.92 m (6 ft 3½ in)	PERFORMANCE:		g limits	+6/-4
Propeller diameter	1.42 m (4 ft 8 in)	Cruising speed	113 knots (209 km/h; 130 mph)		
AREA:		Stalling speed	37 knots (68 km/h; 42 mph)		
Wings, gross	7.43 m² (80.0 sq ft)	Max rate of climb at S/L	366 m (1,200 ft)/min		

AERO DYNAMICS
AERO DYNAMICS LTD
19131 59th Drive NE, Arlington Airport, Arlington, Washington 98223
Telephone: (206) 435 8558

AERO DYNAMICS SPARROW HAWK Mk II
Four separate kits are available to construct the Sparrow Hawk Mk II.
TYPE: Side by side two-seat homebuilt.
AIRFRAME: All-metal wings, ailerons and tailplane. All-composites fuselage and rudders of Kevlar/foam sandwich construction. Twin tailbooms of Kevlar, with carbonfibre reinforcement. Non-retractable tricycle landing gear.

POWER PLANT: One 47 kW (63 hp) Rotax 532. Optional two- or four-stroke engine of between 44.7 and 74.5 kW (60-100 hp). Fuel capacity 53 litres (14 US gallons; 11.7 Imp gallons) standard; optionally 60 litres (16 US gallons; 13.3 Imp gallons).

DIMENSIONS, EXTERNAL:	
Wing span	10.49 m (34 ft 5 in)
Length overall	5.44 m (17 ft 10 in)
Height overall	2.11 m (6 ft 11 in)
AREA:	
Wings, gross	13.29 m² (143.0 sq ft)
WEIGHTS:	
Weight empty	318 kg (700 lb)
Max T-O weight	635 kg (1,400 lb)

PERFORMANCE:
*Max level speed
  91-113 knots (169-209 km/h; 105-130 mph)
*Cruising speed
  82-104 knots (153-193 km/h; 95-120 mph)
Stalling speed   32 knots (58 km/h; 36 mph)
Max rate of climb at S/L: dual   229 m (750 ft)/min
  solo   335 m (1,100 ft)/min
Service ceiling   6,100 m (20,000 ft)
T-O run   76 m (250 ft)
Landing run   91 m (300 ft)
Range   312-608 nm (579-1,125 km; 360-700 miles)
g limits   +6/-4
*Depending on power plant options

AEROLITES

AEROLITES INC

Route 1, Box 187, Welsh, Louisiana 70591
Telephone: (318) 734 3865
Telex: 6503079915 (via WUI)
PRESIDENT: Daniel J. Roché

In October 1986 the manufacturing rights to the Bearcat homebuilt aircraft were purchased from Litecraft by AeroLites Inc. A side by side two-seat version is currently under development.

AEROLITES BEARCAT

First shown publicly in 1984, the Bearcat bears a close external resemblance to the Piper Cub. Kits are available. Estimated building time is 60-90 working hours.

TYPE: Single-seat homebuilt.

AIRFRAME: Constructed of 4130 chrome molybdenum steel tube and covered with Dacron (double surface on wings), polyester and glassfibre. Non-retractable tailwheel landing gear. Optional floats, skis, full cockpit enclosure and ballistic parachute.

POWER PLANT: One 31.3 kW (42 hp) Rotax 447; 38.8 kW (52 hp) Rotax 503 available optionally. Fuel capacity 19 litres (5 US gallons; 4.2 Imp gallons).

DIMENSIONS, EXTERNAL:
Wing span	9.14 m (30 ft 0 in)
Length overall	5.33 m (17 ft 6 in)
Height overall	1.96 m (6 ft 5 in)
Propeller diameter	1.73 m (5 ft 8 in)

AREA:
Wings, gross	13.93 m² (150.0 sq ft)

WEIGHTS:
Weight empty	125 kg (275 lb)
Max pilot weight	113 kg (250 lb)
Max T-O weight	317 kg (700 lb)

PERFORMANCE (at max T-O weight):
Max level speed	65 knots (121 km/h; 75 mph)
Max cruising speed	52 knots (97 km/h; 60 mph)
Stalling speed: power on	23 knots (42 km/h; 26 mph)
power off	24 knots (44 km/h; 27 mph)
Max rate of climb at S/L	366 m (1,200 ft)/min
T-O and landing run	46 m (150 ft)
Landing from 15 m (50 ft)	137 m (450 ft)
Range with max fuel	104 nm (193 km; 120 miles)
Endurance	2 h
g limits	+6/-4

AEROLITES AG BEARCAT

The Ag Bearcat was created jointly by AeroLites and Louisiana AgriLites. Only slight modification was required to the airframe to accept the Spray Miser Ag system. The standard engine is a 47 kW (63 hp) Rotax 532; fuel capacity is 38 litres (10 US gallons; 8.3 Imp gallons). Full span trailing-edge ailerons help to improve pilot control. Standard equipment includes a 12V high volume electric pump capable of flow rates of over 30.3 litres (8 US gallons; 6.7 Imp gallons)/min at 1.38 bars (20 lb/sq in), a 91 litre (24 US gallon; 20 Imp gallon) glassfibre underbelly chemical tank with emergency dump, and welded aluminium 'wet' booms. Options include a ballistic parachute, high flotation tyres and Mylar coated fabric.

DIMENSIONS, EXTERNAL:
Wing span	9.25 m (30 ft 4 in)
Length overall	5.33 m (17 ft 6 in)
Height overall	1.96 m (6 ft 5 in)
Propeller diameter	1.73 m (5 ft 8 in)

AREA:
Wings, gross	14.77 m² (159.0 sq ft)

WEIGHTS:
Weight empty	193 kg (425 lb)
Max T-O weight	431 kg (950 lb)

PERFORMANCE (ISA, S/L with 88 kg; 195 lb pilot, except where indicated):
Max level speed	78 knots (145 km/h; 90 mph)
Cruising and spraying speed	61 knots (113 km/h; 70 mph)
Stalling speed, power on	31 knots (57 km/h; 35 mph)
Max rate of climb at S/L	427 m (1,400 ft)/min
Service ceiling	6,400 m (21,000 ft)
T-O run at max T-O weight	107 m (350 ft)
Landing run	46 m (150 ft)
Range with max fuel	121 nm (225 km; 140 miles)
Endurance with max fuel	2 h
g limits	+6/-4

AERO MIRAGE

AERO MIRAGE INC

3009 NE 20th Way, Gainesville, Florida 32609
Telephone: (904) 377 4146

AERO MIRAGE TC-2

The prototype of this high performance commuter homebuilt first flew on 16 May 1983 and the TC-2 is now available in kit form to amateur builders.

The following details refer to the prototype, unless stated otherwise:

TYPE: Side by side two-seat homebuilt.

AIRFRAME: Wing and tailplane spars of glassfibre reinforced plastics with foam core webs. Remainder of airframe constructed of Kevlar, Klégécel, S glass and vinylester resin. Wing section NACA 64415. Retractable tricycle landing gear.

POWER PLANT: One 74.5 kW (100 hp) Continental O-200-A. Other engines recommended as suitable up to 74.5 kW (100 hp), though both a Textron Lycoming O-235 and O-290 are being fitted to Mirages. Standard fuel capacity 95 litres (25 US gallons; 20.8 Imp gallons); capacity with auxiliary tanks 144 litres (38 US gallons; 31.6 Imp gallons).

DIMENSIONS, EXTERNAL:
Wing span	6.40 m (21 ft 0 in)
Length overall	5.05 m (16 ft 7 in)
Height overall	1.78 m (5 ft 10 in)
Propeller diameter	1.57 m (5 ft 2 in)

AREA:
Wings, gross	5.95 m² (64.0 sq ft)

WEIGHTS (with 48.5 kW; 65 hp engine):
Weight empty	238 kg (525 lb)
Baggage capacity	18 kg (40 lb)
Max T-O weight	431 kg (950 lb)

PERFORMANCE (engine as above, unless stated otherwise):
Max level speed at S/L	157 knots (291 km/h; 181 mph)
Cruising speed, 75% power, at S/L	142 knots (264 km/h; 164 mph)
Stalling speed, prototype:	
flaps down	50 knots (92 km/h; 57 mph)
flaps up	55 knots (102 km/h; 63 mph)
Landing run	137 m (450 ft)

AEROSPORT

AEROSPORT LTD

Box 278, Holly Springs, North Carolina 27540
Telephone: (919) 552 6375
PRESIDENT: E. B. Trent

AEROSPORT SCAMP A

The prototype Scamp flew for the first time on 21 August 1973. The Scamp A can be used for limited aerobatics; and emphasis has been placed on simple construction techniques to make it an easy project for the homebuilder.

Plans and parts are available to amateur constructors. A total of at least 905 sets of plans had been sold by 1988. More than 40 have flown, and some examples of an agricultural version, known as Scamp B, were assembled in South America (see under Colombia in main Aircraft section of the 1984-85 *Jane's*).

TYPE: Single-seat homebuilt biplane.

AIRFRAME: All-metal construction, with light alloy semi-monocoque fuselage. Wing section NACA 23012. Non-retractable tricycle landing gear.

POWER PLANT: Prototype has 44.5 kW (60 hp) 1,834 cc Volkswagen modified motorcar engine. Design suitable for Volkswagen engines of up to 2,100 cc, though Aerosport recommends 1,834 cc as optimum. Fuel capacity 30.5 litres (8 US gallons; 6.66 Imp gallons).

DIMENSIONS, EXTERNAL:
Wing span	5.33 m (17 ft 6 in)
Length overall	4.27 m (14 ft 0 in)
Height overall	1.69 m (5 ft 6½ in)
Propeller diameter	1.42 m (4 ft 8 in)

AREA:
Wings, gross	9.75 m² (105.0 sq ft)

WEIGHTS:
Weight empty	236-249 kg (520-550 lb)
Max T-O weight	348-362 kg (768-798 lb)

PERFORMANCE (1,834 cc engine):
Max level speed	91 knots (169 km/h; 105 mph)
Cruising speed	78 knots (145 km/h; 90 mph)
Stalling speed	39 knots (73 km/h; 45 mph)
Service ceiling (estimated)	3,660 m (12,000 ft)
T-O and landing run	122 m (400 ft)
Range at cruising speed	108 nm (201 km; 125 miles)
g limits	+6/-3

AIR COMMAND

AIR COMMAND MANUFACTURING INC

Liberty Landing Airport, Route 3, Box 197A, Liberty, Missouri 64068
Telephone: (816) 781 9313
Fax: (816) 781 9366
PRESIDENT: Dennis Fetters

AIR COMMAND 447 COMMANDER

The 447 Commander is marketed as a ready assembled aircraft or as a kit that can be assembled quickly, using just six hand tools. Approximately 200 single-seat Commanders have been sold.

TYPE: Single-seat microlight gyroplane; conforms to FAR Pt 103.

AIRFRAME: Aluminium alloy structure. Rotor has two McCutchen SkyWheel laminar flow blades, of carbonfibre and glassfibre composite construction with aluminium alloy leading-edge spar. Non-retractable tricycle landing gear. Options include Wunderlich rotor spin-up, rotor brake, floats and skis.

POWER PLANT: One 30 kW (40 hp) Rotax 447. Seat fuel tank, capacity 19 litres (5 US gallons; 4.2 Imp gallons). One 34 litre (9 US gallon; 7.5 Imp gallon) auxiliary tank optional.

DIMENSIONS, EXTERNAL:
Rotor diameter	7.01 m (23 ft 0 in)
Length overall	3.25 m (10 ft 8 in)
Height overall	2.13 m (7 ft 0 in)
Propeller diameter	1.50 m (4 ft 11 in)

AREA:
Rotor disc	38.6 m² (415.5 sq ft)

WEIGHTS:
Weight empty	114 kg (252 lb)
Pilot weight range	55-136 kg (120-300 lb)
Max T-O weight	388 kg (856 lb)

PERFORMANCE (Rotax 447 engine):
Max level and cruising speed	55 knots (101 km/h; 63 mph)
Econ cruising speed	39 knots (72 km/h; 45 mph)
Min flying speed	7-9 knots (13-16 km/h; 8-10 mph)
Max rate of climb at S/L	244 m (800 ft)/min
Service ceiling	4,575 m (15,000 ft)
T-O run: with pre-rotation	18 m (60 ft)
without pre-rotation	152 m (500 ft)
Range with standard fuel	87 nm (161 km; 100 miles)
Endurance	2 h
g limit	+9

AIR COMMAND 503 COMMANDER

This gyroplane uses the same airframe as the 447 Commander, but has a 38.8 kW (52 hp) Rotax 503 engine as standard. It conforms to FAR Pt 103.

AIR COMMAND 532 COMMANDER ELITE

The 532 Commander Elite became available in kit form in Spring 1985. It has the same airframe as the 447 Commander, but uses the 47.7 kW (64 hp) Rotax 532 engine as standard, with a five-blade propeller. It conforms to FAA Experimental homebuilt requirements, and as such the kit is less than 50 per cent completed. Options include a partial enclosure.

WEIGHTS:
Weight empty	125 kg (275 lb)
Max T-O weight	215 kg (475 lb)

PERFORMANCE:
Max cruising speed	87 knots (161 km/h; 100 mph)
Econ cruising speed	65 knots (121 km/h; 75 mph)
Max rate of climb at S/L	366 m (1,200 ft)/min
Service ceiling	4,570 m (15,000 ft)
T-O run, with pre-rotation	18 m (60 ft)
Landing run	0-3 m (0-10 ft)
Range with standard fuel	78 nm (145 km; 90 miles)
Range with auxiliary fuel	173 nm (322 km; 200 miles)
g limit	+9

AIR COMMAND 532 COMMANDER ELITE TWO-SEATER

By means of a simple bolt-on conversion kit, a standard 532 Commander Elite can be modified into a side by side two-seater under homebuilt regulations. Fitting a second control stick makes it suitable for training purposes. A rotor of 7.01 m (23 ft) or 7.62 m (25 ft) diameter can be employed.

WEIGHTS:
Weight empty	141 kg (310 lb)
Max T-O weight	340 kg (750 lb)

PERFORMANCE (two persons):
Max level speed	65 knots (121 km/h; 75 mph)
Cruising speed, 75% power	39 knots (72 km/h; 45 mph)
Max rate of climb at S/L	152 m (500 ft)/min
T-O run: with pre-rotation	46 m (150 ft)
without pre-rotation	214 m (700 ft)
Landing run	0-1.5 m (0-5 ft)

AeroLites Ag Bearcat agricultural homebuilt aircraft

Aero Mirage TC-2 all-composites lightplane

Aerosport Scamp A biplane built by Mr Jack Stafford of Greenville, South Carolina

Air Command 532 Commander Elite with optional partial enclosure and wheel fairings

Aircraft Designs (Hollmann) Bumble Bee microlight gyroplane

Aircraft Designs (Hollmann) HA-2M Sportster two-seat gyroplane
(J. M. G. Gradidge)

AIRCRAFT DESIGNS
AIRCRAFT DESIGNS INC
11082 Bel Aire Court, Cupertino, California 95014
Telephone: (408) 255 8688
PRESIDENT: Martin Hollmann

HOLLMANN HA-2M SPORTSTER
The Sportster prototype first flew in October 1974. Plans, materials and component parts are available, and by early 1988 more than 77 Sportsters were under construction or flying.

TYPE: Side by side two-seat homebuilt gyroplane.

ROTOR SYSTEM: Two-blade rotor of NACA 8-H-12 section. Metal blades, each made up of a leading-edge extrusion, aluminium formed ribs and Alclad skin, riveted and bonded together. Pre-rotator and rotor brake standard.

AIRFRAME: All aluminium alloy construction, except for glassfibre fairings and tail unit tips. Non-retractable tricycle landing gear.

POWER PLANT: One 97 kW (130 hp) Franklin Sport 4B on prototype. Most aircraft powered by a 112 kW (150 hp)

Textron Lycoming O-320. Fuel capacity 45.4 litres (12 US gallons; 10 Imp gallons).

DIMENSIONS, EXTERNAL:
Rotor diameter	8.53 m (28 ft 0 in)
Length overall	3.66 m (12 ft 0 in)
Height to top of rotor head	2.34 m (7 ft 8 in)
Propeller diameter	1.68 m (5 ft 6 in)

WEIGHTS (112 kW: 150 hp engine, unless stated otherwise):
Weight empty, equipped (prototype)	281 kg (620 lb)
Max T-O weight	500 kg (1,100 lb)

PERFORMANCE (112 kW; 150 hp engine, unless stated otherwise):
Max cruising speed at S/L (prototype)	65 knots (121 km/h; 75 mph)
Econ cruising speed at S/L (prototype)	52 knots (97 km/h; 60 mph)
Stalling speed (prototype)	25 knots (45 km/h; 28 mph)
Max rate of climb at S/L	274 m (900 ft)/min
Service ceiling	2,440 m (8,000 ft)
T-O run	107 m (350 ft)
Landing run	0-6 m (0-20 ft)
Range: with max fuel	78 nm (145 km; 90 miles)
with max payload	61 nm (112 km; 70 miles)

HOLLMANN BUMBLE BEE
The Bumble Bee first flew in prototype form in January 1984 and is now available in bolt together kit form or can be built from plans, using prefabricated component parts. By February 1988 at least nine Bumble Bees had been sold.

TYPE: Single-seat microlight gyroplane; conforms to FAR Pt 103.

AIRFRAME: Fuselage structure of square aluminium alloy tubing, with glassfibre/foam sandwich cruciform tail surfaces. Two-blade rotor of NACA 8-H-12 section, with aluminium alloy leading-edges and glassfibre/foam/epoxy trailing-edges. Rotor pre-spin available. Non-retractable tricycle landing gear.

POWER PLANT: One 30 kW (40 hp) Rotax 447. Fuel capacity 19 litres (5 US gallons; 4.2 Imp gallons).

DIMENSIONS, EXTERNAL:
Rotor diameter	7.01 m (23 ft 0 in)
Length overall	3.35 m (11 ft 0 in)
Height overall	2.29 m (7 ft 6 in)
Propeller diameter	1.52 m (5 ft 0 in)

AREA:
Rotor disc	38.55 m² (415.0 sq ft)

WEIGHTS:	
Weight empty	102 kg (225 lb)
Pilot weight range	68-113 kg (150-250 lb)
Max T-O weight	227 kg (500 lb)
PERFORMANCE:	
Max level speed	56 knots (103 km/h; 64 mph)

Econ cruising speed	35 knots (64 km/h; 40 mph)
Min flying speed	4.5 knots (8 km/h; 5 mph)
Max rate of climb at S/L	366 m (1,200 ft)/min
Service ceiling	3,660 m (12,000 ft)
T-O run, without rotor pre-spin	76 m (250 ft)
with rotor pre-spin	30 m (100 ft)

Range with max fuel	56 nm (105 km; 65 miles)
Endurance	1 h
g limits	+3.5/−1

AIRCRAFT DEVELOPMENT

AIRCRAFT DEVELOPMENT INC

1326, N. Westlink Boulevard, Wichita, Kansas 67212
Telephone: (316) 722 7736
PRESIDENT: Richard Jimenez

AIRCRAFT DEVELOPMENT EZ-1

The prototype EZ-1 made its first flight on 31 July 1983.
TYPE: Single-seat microlight; conforms to FAR Pt 103 requirements.
AIRFRAME: Aluminium alloy fuselage structure. Wing and tail surface spars made from foam/glassfibre/graphite sandwich with aluminium skinning using self-adhesive 'Scotch-A-Frame' bonding technique over 85 per cent of the structure. Three-axis control, plus wing flaps. Non-retractable tricycle landing gear.
POWER PLANT: One 15 kW (20 hp) Zenoah G25B-1. Fuel capacity 16.3 litres (4.3 US gallons; 3.6 Imp gallons).

DIMENSIONS, EXTERNAL:	
Wing span	9.45 m (31 ft 0 in)
Length overall	5.33 m (17 ft 6 in)
Height overall	1.98 m (6 ft 6 in)
Propeller diameter	1.27 m (4 ft 2 in)
AREA:	
Wings, gross	11.98 m² (129.0 sq ft)
WEIGHTS:	
Weight empty	106 kg (234 lb)
Pilot weight range	45-102 kg (100-225 lb)

Max T-O weight	229 kg (505 lb)

PERFORMANCE (at max T-O weight, 20 hp engine):

Max level speed	43 knots (80 km/h; 50 mph)
Econ cruising speed	36 knots (67 km/h; 42 mph)
Stalling speed	23 knots (42 km/h; 26 mph)
Max rate of climb at S/L	106 m (348 ft)/min
Service ceiling	2,285 m (7,500 ft)
T-O run	91 m (300 ft)
Landing run	61 m (200 ft)
Range with max fuel	67 nm (124 km; 77 miles)
Endurance with max fuel	1 h 43 min
g limits:	+6/−3 ultimate

AIRPLANE FACTORY

THE AIRPLANE FACTORY INC

PO Box 24035, Dayton, Ohio 45424
Telephone: (513) 849 6533
PRESIDENT: W. Douglas Hoy

DAS ULTRALIGHTERFIGHTER

This aircraft is supplied in prefabricated kit form.
TYPE: Single-seat microlight Fokker E.III replica; conforms to FAR Pt 103.
AIRFRAME: Structure of aluminium alloy and chromoly steel, Dacron covered. Three-axis control. Non-retractable taildragger landing gear. Parachute recovery system, floats and replica machine-gun optional.

POWER PLANT: One 20 kW (27 hp) Rotax 277. Fuel capacity 16.7 litres (4.4 US gallons; 3.7 Imp gallons).

DIMENSIONS, EXTERNAL:	
Wing span	10.97 m (36 ft 0 in)
Length overall	6.25 m (20 ft 6 in)
Height overall	2.29 m (7 ft 6 in)
Propeller diameter	1.63 m (5 ft 4 in)
AREA:	
Wings, gross	13.66 m² (147.0 sq ft)
WEIGHTS:	
Weight empty	112 kg (247 lb)
Max pilot weight	102 kg (225 lb)
Max T-O weight	229 kg (505 lb)

PERFORMANCE (with 77 kg; 170 lb pilot):

Max level and max cruising speed	55 knots (101 km/h; 63 mph)
Stalling speed:	
power on	20 knots (37 km/h; 23 mph)
power off	22 knots (40 km/h; 25 mph)
Max rate of climb at S/L	183 m (600 ft)/min
Service ceiling	2,750 m (9,000 ft)
T-O run	30 m (100 ft)
Landing run	46 m (150 ft)
Range with max fuel	130 nm (241 km; 150 miles)
Endurance with max fuel	4 h
g limits	+6/−3

ALDERFER

ALDERFER GYROCHOPPER AIRCRAFT CORPORATION

4278 Shafor Road, Hamilton, Ohio 45011
Telephone: (513) 844 2857
GENERAL MANAGER: Edward Alderfer

ALDERFER GYROCHOPPER II

The prototype Gyrochopper II made its first flight in June 1984. Mr Alderfer will construct further examples, one at a time, for sale to experienced autogyro pilots, once he has logged 500 flying hours on the prototype.
TYPE: Single-seat homebuilt autogyro.
ROTOR SYSTEM: Two-blade teetering rotor of composites construction.
AIRFRAME: Inverted T airframe basic structure of square section aluminium alloy tubing. Non-retractable tricycle landing gear.
POWER PLANT: One 67 kW (90 hp) Volkswagen 2,180 cc modified motorcar engine. Fuel capacity 30 litres (8 US gallons; 6.66 Imp gallons).

DIMENSIONS, EXTERNAL:	
Rotor diameter	7.31 m (24 ft 0 in)
Length overall	4.57 m (15 ft 0 in)
Height overall	2.13 m (7 ft 0 in)
Propeller diameter	1.32 m (4 ft 4 in)
WEIGHTS:	
Weight empty	204 kg (450 lb)
Pilot weight range	68-102 kg (150-225 lb)
Max T-O weight	317 kg (700 lb)
PERFORMANCE:	
Max level speed	74 knots (137 km/h; 85 mph)
Econ cruising speed	52 knots (97 km/h; 60 mph)
Max rate of climb at S/L	244 m (800 ft)/min
Service ceiling	4,575 m (15,000 ft)
T-O run	244 m (800 ft)
Landing run	0-9 m (0-30 ft)
Range: with max fuel	104 nm (193 km; 120 miles)
with max payload	87 nm (161 km; 100 miles)
Endurance	2 h 30 min

ALDERFER GYROCHOPPER III

The follow-on Gyrochopper III first flew as a prototype in August 1986. Further examples may be built later for experienced pilots.
TYPE: Tandem two-seat homebuilt autogyro.

ROTOR SYSTEM: Two-blade teetering rotor of composites construction.
AIRFRAME: Square-section aluminium alloy tubular structure. Non-retractable tricycle landing gear.

POWER PLANT: One 47 kW (63 hp) Rotax 532. Fuel capacity 45.4 litres (12 US gallons; 10 Imp gallons).

DIMENSIONS, EXTERNAL:	
Rotor diameter	7.62 m (25 ft 0 in)
Length overall	4.57 m (15 ft 0 in)
Height overall	2.44 m (8 ft 0 in)
Propeller diameter	1.73 m (5 ft 8 in)
WEIGHTS:	
Weight empty	161 kg (355 lb)
Baggage capacity	23 kg (50 lb)
Max T-O weight	385 kg (850 lb)

PERFORMANCE: As for Gyrochopper II, except:

Max rate of climb at S/L	305 m (1,000 ft)/min
T-O run	152 m (500 ft)
Range: with max fuel	130 nm (241 km; 150 miles)
with max payload	104 nm (193 km; 120 miles)
Endurance	1 h 45 min

AMERICAN AIR

AMERICAN AIR TECHNOLOGY

The address given in the 1987-88 *Jane's* is no longer current. Details of the company's Solo and Dual aircraft, and an illustration, can be found in that edition.

AMERICAN AIRCRAFT

AMERICAN AIRCRAFT INC

EXECUTIVE OFFICES: 650 Sacramento Street, San Francisco, California 94111
Telephone: (415) 989 0141
Telex: 9103502332
MARKETING AND SALES: PO Box 9346, Albuquerque, New Mexico 87119
Versions of these aircraft are produced in Belgium by SCWAL SA and in Italy by Ultrasport.

AMERICAN AIRCRAFT FALCON

The prototype Falcon was flown at the 1982 EAA Fly-in at Oshkosh, Wisconsin. Release of ready to fly production aircraft began in the Spring of 1983, and several hundred are in service.
TYPE: Single-seat microlight; conforms to FAR Pt 103.
AIRFRAME: Foreplane constructed of aluminium alloy, carbonfibre, glassfibre, Kevlar and foam plastics. Swept-back main wings, with foam ribs and double surface Tedlar covering. Low-drag Kevlar/graphite/epoxy fuselage pod. Three-axis control. Non-retractable tricycle landing gear. Options include ballistic parachute and full cockpit canopy.
POWER PLANT: One 20 kW (27 hp) Rotax 277. Fuel capacity 19 litres (5 US gallons; 4.2 Imp gallons).

DIMENSIONS, EXTERNAL:	
Wing span	10.97 m (36 ft 0 in)
Foreplane span	3.71 m (12 ft 2 in)
Length overall	4.34 m (14 ft 3 in)
Height overall	1.70 m (5 ft 7 in)
Propeller diameter	1.37 m (4 ft 6 in)
AREA:	
Wings and foreplane, gross	16.75 m² (180.3 sq ft)
WEIGHTS:	
Weight empty	113 kg (250 lb)
Pilot weight range	50-95 kg (110-210 lb)
Max T-O weight	240 kg (530 lb)

PERFORMANCE (with 77 kg; 170 lb pilot):

Max level speed	55 knots (101 km/h; 63 mph)
Cruising speed	52 knots (97 km/h; 60 mph)
Stalling speed	24 knots (44 km/h; 27 mph)
Max rate of climb at S/L	198 m (650 ft)/min
Service ceiling	4,570 m (15,000 ft)
T-O run	61 m (200 ft)
Landing run	76 m (250 ft)
Range with max fuel	105 nm (194 km; 121 miles)
Endurance with max fuel	2 h 48 min
g limits	+5.8/−2.9

AMERICAN AIRCRAFT FALCON XP

This is basically a tandem two-seat version of the Falcon, conforming to Experimental regulations and powered by a 38 kW (51 hp) Rotax 503 engine. Full details can be found in the 1987-88 *Jane's*.

AMERICAN AIR JET

AMERICAN AIR JET INC

710 Sunnywood Place, Woodland Park, Colorado 80863
Telephone: (719) 633 5588
REGISTERED AGENT: Stephen L. Willman
American Air Jet Inc was founded in 1987 with the purchased assets of the former Eagle Helicopter Corporation.

AMERICAN AIR JET AMERICAN

Expected to be first flown in May 1988, this rotor-tip, cold air, pressure-jet helicopter is being offered initially in kit form (with deliveries from late 1988), to be followed by ready assembled examples for export. FAA certification of production aircraft will be sought if US demand proves sufficient.
TYPE: Tandem or side by side two-seat homebuilt helicopter.
ROTOR SYSTEM: Single rotor with two hollow glassfibre blades, controlled by mechanical swashplate system. No tail rotor.

Aircraft Development EZ-1 single-seat microlight

The Airplane Factory Das Ultralighterfighter

Alderfer Gyrochopper III two-seat autogyro

Alderfer Gyrochopper II single-seat autogyro

American Aircraft Falcon single-seat microlight aircraft

BAC Freedom 28 single-seat microlight aircraft

Prototype American Air Jet American pressure-jet helicopter *(Howard Levy)*

AIRFRAME: Aluminium alloy structure, with glassfibre nosecone and steel tube engine mounting. Twin skid landing gear, with optional ground handling wheels and floats. Directional control by twin rudders.

POWER PLANT: Prototype has 209 kW (280 hp) Mazda 13-B rotary engine, driving a centrifugal compressor to provide compressed air to thrust-jets at trailing-edge of blade tips. 'Production' engine is 268.5 kW (360 hp) rotary, with alternative turbine engine of similar rating.

Standard fuel capacity 182 litres (48 US gallons; 40 Imp gallons).

DIMENSIONS, EXTERNAL:
Rotor diameter	10.97 m (36 ft 0 in)
Fuselage length	5.49 m (18 ft 0 in)
Height overall	2.44 m (8 ft 0 in)

WEIGHTS:
Weight empty	340 kg (750 lb)
Max T-O weight	726 kg (1,600 lb)

PERFORMANCE (estimated, with 268.5 kW; 360 hp engine):
Max level speed	122 knots (225 km/h; 140 mph)
Cruising speed	87 knots (161 km/h; 100 mph)
Service ceiling	3,660 m (12,000 ft)
Hovering ceiling: IGE	2,135 m (7,000 ft)
OGE	1,220 m (4,000 ft)
Range at optimum speed	260 nm (483 km; 300 miles)
Endurance at 61 knots (113 km/h; 70 mph)	4 h

BAC
BRUTSCHE AIRCRAFT CORPORATION
1800 West 1887 South, Woods Cross, Utah 84087
Telephone: (801) 295 5222
PRESIDENT AND DESIGNER: Neal H. Brutsche

BAC FREEDOM 28
The Freedom 28 was expected to become available in kit form, taking an average of 200-300 working hours to assemble.

TYPE: Single-seat microlight.

AIRFRAME: Airframe of pop riveted Alclad aluminium alloy, except for Ceconite covering on wings aft of main spar and elevators. Eppler 591 wing section. Full span flaperons. Non-retractable tailwheel landing gear. Optional floats and cabin side windows.

POWER PLANT: One 20 kW (27 hp) Rotax 277. Fuel capacity 19 litres (5 US gallons; 4.2 Imp gallons).

DIMENSIONS, EXTERNAL:
Wing span	8.48 m (27 ft 10 in)
Length overall	5.31 m (17 ft 5 in)
Height overall	1.78 m (5 ft 10 in)
Propeller diameter	1.52 m (5 ft 0 in)

AREA:
Wings, gross	10.13 m² (109.0 sq ft)

WEIGHTS:
Weight empty	115 kg (254 lb)
Max baggage	18 kg (40 lb)
Max T-O weight	227 kg (500 lb)

PERFORMANCE (at max T-O weight):
Max cruising speed	55 knots (102 km/h; 63 mph)
Cruising speed (75% power)	53 knots (98 km/h; 61 mph)
Stalling speed, flaperons down	21 knots (39 km/h; 24 mph)

Max rate of climb at S/L	160 m (525 ft)/min
Service ceiling	3,050 m (10,000 ft)
T-O run	69 m (225 ft)
Landing run	61 m (200 ft)
Endurance	2 h-3 h 30 min

FREEDOM 48

Expected homebuilt version of the Freedom 28, with a heavier wing and more powerful Rotax 503 engine.

BARNETT

BARNETT ROTORCRAFT
4307 Olivehurst Avenue, Olivehurst, California 95961
Telephone: (916) 742 7416
PRESIDENT: K. Jerrie Barnett

Plans, materials and kits of parts were made available to construct the J 3M and J 4B gyroplanes. However, although the J 3M remained available for purchase in early 1988, it is being phased out. Details of this model can be found in the *1976-77 Jane's.*

BARNETT J 4B and J 4B-2

The single-seat J 4B first flew in prototype form on 15 July 1968. For those wishing to construct a two-seat J 4B-2, a set of J 4B plans has to be purchased along with a set of modification plans which details the necessary changes to produce the two-seat configuration. The aluminium rotor blades, hand laid-up nacelle and engine cooling cowls are available ready fabricated.
TYPE: Single-seat (J 4B) and two-seat (J 4B-2) autogyros.
ROTOR SYSTEM: Two-blade autorotating rotor, of bonded aluminium alloy.

AIRFRAME: All-metal structure of welded 4130 chrome-molybdenum steel tubing, with fabric covered tail surfaces. Glassfibre fuselage nacelle. Non-retractable tricycle landing gear.
POWER PLANT: One 48.5-74.5 kW (65-100 hp) Continental engine, of A65 through to O-200 type, or Mazda or other converted motorcar engine. Fuel capacity 56 litres (15 US gallons; 12.5 Imp gallons).
DIMENSIONS, EXTERNAL (A: J 4B, B: J 4B-2):
Rotor diameter: A		7.01 m (23 ft 0 in)
B		7.72 m (25 ft 4 in)
Length overall, without rotor: A		3.76 m (12 ft 4 in)
B		4.17 m (13 ft 8 in)
Height overall: A		2.34 m (7 ft 8 in)
B		2.46 m (8 ft 1 in)

AREAS:
Rotor disc: A	38.70 m² (416.59 sq ft)
B	46.95 m² (505.39 sq ft)

WEIGHTS (A and B as above):
Baggage capacity: A	13.6 kg (30 lb)
B	9 kg (20 lb)

Normal T-O weight: A, no battery	333 kg (734.5 lb)
B	456 kg (1,005.5 lb)
Max T-O weight: A	363 kg (800 lb)
B	492 kg (1,085 lb)

PERFORMANCE (A and B as above):
Max level speed: A	109 knots (201 km/h; 125 mph)
B	97 knots (180 km/h; 112 mph)
Cruising speed (75% power):	
A	91 knots (169 km/h; 105 mph)
B	81 knots (150 km/h; 93 mph)
Max rate of climb at S/L: A	457 m (1,500 ft)/min
B	152 m (500 ft)/min
Service ceiling: A	3,660 m (12,000 ft)
B	2,440 m (8,000 ft)
T-O run: A	107 m (350 ft)
B	183 m (600 ft)
Landing run: A	0-6 m (0-20 ft)
B	8 m (25 ft)

BARRACUDA

W. B. BUETHE ENTERPRISES INC
PO Box 486, Cathedral City, California 92234
Telephone: (619) 324 9454
PRESIDENT: Dr William B. Buethe

BARRACUDA

The prototype Barracuda flew for the first time on 29 June 1975. Plans and kits are available, and about 25 Barracudas are believed to be flying.
TYPE: Side by side two-seat, dual-control sporting homebuilt.
AIRFRAME: Plywood covered all-wood construction, except for glassfibre used in ailerons and for tailplane tips. Wing section NACA 64₂415. Retractable tricycle landing gear.
POWER PLANT: One 186 kW (250 hp) Textron Lycoming IO-540-C4B5 or other engine of 112-224 kW (150-300 hp). Fuel capacity 166.5 litres (44 US gallons; 36.6 Imp gallons). Provision for two 23 litre (6 US gallon; 5 Imp gallon) auxiliary tanks in outboard wing panels.
DIMENSIONS, EXTERNAL:
Wing span	7.54 m (24 ft 9 in)
Length overall	6.55 m (21 ft 6 in)
Propeller diameter	2.18 m (7 ft 2 in)

AREA:
Wings, gross	11.15 m² (120.0 sq ft)

WEIGHTS:
Weight empty	712 kg (1,570 lb)
Baggage capacity	27 kg (60 lb)
Max T-O weight	1,043 kg (2,300 lb)

PERFORMANCE:
Max level speed at 2,135 m (7,000 ft)	181 knots (335 km/h; 208 mph)
Cruising speed (62% power) at 2,450 m (8,050 ft)	162 knots (300 km/h; 187 mph)
Stalling speed: 'clean'	56 knots (103 km/h; 64 mph)
wheels and flaps down	54 knots (100 km/h; 62 mph)
Max rate of climb at S/L	762 m (2,500 ft)/min
Range at max T-O weight, 65% power, with auxiliary tank, 30 min reserves	800 nm (1,480 km; 920 miles)

BOAC

BARNEY OLDFIELD AIRCRAFT COMPANY
PO Box 228, Needham, Massachusetts 02192

OLDFIELD 'BABY' LAKES

Plans and material kits are available for this scaled-down version of the Great Lakes Sport Trainer. More than 930 sets of plans have been sold and about 100 aircraft are flying.
TYPE: Single-seat homebuilt sporting biplane.
AIRFRAME: Wooden wings, fabric covered. Wing section modified M6, tapering to USA 27 46 cm (18 in) from tips. Ailerons on lower wings only. Welded steel tube fuselage and tail unit, fabric covered. Non-retractable tailwheel landing gear.
POWER PLANT: One 63.4 kW (85 hp) Continental. Provision for alternative engines of between 37.25 and 74.5 kW (50 and 100 hp). Fuel capacity 45 litres (12 US gallons; 10 Imp gallons).
DIMENSIONS, EXTERNAL:
Wing span: upper	5.08 m (16 ft 8 in)
Length overall	4.19 m (13 ft 9 in)
Height overall	1.37 m (4 ft 6 in)

AREA:
Wings, gross	7.99 m² (86.0 sq ft)

WEIGHTS (59.5 kW; 80 hp Continental A80 engine):
Weight empty	215 kg (475 lb)
Max T-O weight	385 kg (850 lb)

PERFORMANCE (A80 engine, at max T-O weight):
Max level speed at S/L	117 knots (217 km/h; 135 mph)
Cruising speed at S/L	102 knots (190 km/h; 118 mph)
Stalling speed	44 knots (81 km/h; 50 mph)
Max rate of climb at S/L	610 m (2,000 ft)/min
Service ceiling	5,200 m (17,000 ft)
T-O run	91 m (300 ft)
Landing run (no brakes)	122 m (400 ft)
Max range	217 nm (400 km; 250 miles)
g limits	±9

OLDFIELD 'SUPER BABY' LAKES

The prototype 'Super Baby' Lakes flew for the first time in 1976. It was developed as a more powerful and modified variant of the 'Baby' Lakes. Plans are available.
POWER PLANT: One Textron Lycoming engine in 80.5-93 kW (108-125 hp) range. Header tank fitted.
DIMENSIONS, EXTERNAL:
As for 'Baby' Lakes, except:
Length overall	4.34 m (14 ft 3 in)

WEIGHTS:
Weight empty	218 kg (480 lb)

Max T-O weight	385 kg (850 lb)

PERFORMANCE:
Max level speed	135 knots (249 km/h; 155 mph) IAS
Cruising speed (75% power)	117 knots (217 km/h; 135 mph) IAS
Stalling speed	48 knots (89 km/h; 55 mph) IAS
Max rate of climb at S/L	915 m (3,000 ft)/min
T-O run	69 m (225 ft)
Landing run	130 m (425 ft)
Max range, with wing tanks	260 nm (483 km; 300 miles)

OLDFIELD 'BUDDY BABY' LAKES

The two-seat 'Buddy Baby' utilises standard 'Baby' wings and tail unit. To prevent a significant increase in wing loading, a 41 cm (16 in) upper wing centre-section has been introduced, together with short stub-wings built integrally with the fuselage to increase the lower span by a similar amount.

The fuselage has been widened and stretched to permit seating positions for two average-sized (77 kg; 170 lb) people in a configuration much like that of a 'buddy seat' on a motorcycle. Dual throttle and rudder pedals are provided, with a single dual-position joystick. The aircraft is flown solo from the rear seat and dual from the front position. Plans were to be made available.

BOUNSALL

BOUNSALL AIRCRAFT
PO Box 506, Mesquite, Nevada 89024
Telephone: (702) 346 5722

Details and an illustration of the Prospector and Super Prospector bush monoplanes can be found in the 1987-88 *Jane's*. No recent news has been received from Bounsall Aircraft.

BOWERS

PETER M. BOWERS
10458 16th Avenue South, Seattle, Washington 98168
Telephone: (206) 242 2582

BOWERS FLY BABY 1-A

The prototype Fly Baby monoplane was produced to compete in an Experimental Aircraft Association design contest, organised to encourage the development of a simple, low-cost, easy-to-fly aeroplane that could be built by inexperienced amateurs for recreational flying. It flew for the first time on 27 July 1960. Plans are available and 4,230 sets had been sold by mid-1988. Construction of well over 700 Fly Babys is known to have been undertaken, of which about 400 have flown.

Several individual amateur builders amended the plans during 1973 to allow for construction of two-seat versions of the Fly Baby. Although Mr Bowers does not recommend this conversion, he has made some additions to the plans to cater for it.

The following description applies to the original single-seat Fly Baby 1-A:
TYPE: Single-seat homebuilt.
AIRFRAME: All-wood construction, except for Dacron covering on wings and tail unit. Wing section NACA 4412. Non-retractable tailwheel landing gear. Examples have flown with floats and skis. Cockpit canopy optional.
POWER PLANT: One 63.5 kW (85 hp) Continental C85. Suited to modified Volkswagen engines of over 1,800 cc. Fuel capacity 60.5 litres (16 US gallons; 13.3 Imp gallons).
DIMENSIONS, EXTERNAL:
Wing span	8.53 m (28 ft 0 in)
Length overall	5.64 m (18 ft 6 in)
Height, wings folded	1.98 m (6 ft 6 in)

WEIGHTS:
Weight empty	274 kg (605 lb)
Max T-O weight	419 kg (924 lb)

PERFORMANCE (at max T-O weight):
Max level speed at S/L	over 104 knots (193 km/h; 120 mph)

Bowers Fly Baby 1-A (Continental A65 engine) built by Mr Eugene Fisher of Seattle, Washington *(Peter M. Bowers)*

Barnett Rotorcraft J 4B-2 with enclosed cockpit *(J. M. G. Gradidge)*

Barracuda two-seat sporting monoplane, built by Dr W. B. Buethe

Modified Bowers Fly Baby 1-B built by Mr Itz Kowitz *(Howard Levy)*

Oldfield (BOAC) 'Baby' Lakes (Continental A65 engine) *(Peter M. Bowers)*

BX-200 cross-country homebuilt, designed by Mr Uriel Bristol *(Howard Levy)*

Cruising speed	
	91-96 knots (169-177 km/h; 105-110 mph)
Landing speed	39 knots (73 km/h; 45 mph)
Max rate of climb at S/L	335 m (1,100 ft)/min
T-O and landing run	76 m (250 ft)
Range with max fuel	277 nm (515 km; 320 miles)

BOWERS FLY BABY 1-B

During 1968 Mr Bowers designed and built a set of interchangeable biplane wings for the original prototype Fly Baby and with these fitted it flew for the first time on 27 March 1969. Fifteen more biplanes, designated Fly Baby 1-B, have been completed and flown. The biplane wings have the same aerofoil section and incidence as those of the monoplane version, but incorporate aluminium alloy wingtip bows. Ailerons are fitted to the lower wings only. Changeover from monoplane to biplane configuration can be accomplished by two people in approximately one hour.

The biplane is intended to use the same engines as the monoplane, for which Mr Bowers does not recommend anything heavier than the Continental O-200. Since some biplane builders have desired to use the 93 kW (125 hp) Textron Lycoming O-290, a modification has been authorised for the biplane, whereby the wing sweep is decreased by 5° for CG reasons.

TYPE: Single-seat homebuilt biplane.
DIMENSIONS, EXTERNAL:

Wing span	6.71 m (22 ft 0 in)
Height overall	2.08 m (6 ft 10 in)

AREA:

Wings, gross	13.94 m² (150.0 sq ft)

WEIGHTS:

Weight empty	295 kg (651 lb)
Max T-O weight	440 kg (972 lb)

PERFORMANCE (at max T-O weight):

Cruising speed	75 knots (140 km/h; 87 mph)
Max rate of climb at S/L	267 m (875 ft)/min

BRISTOL
URIEL BRISTOL
PO Box 6093, Sunny Isle, St Croix, Virgin Islands 00820

BRISTOL BX-200

First flown as a prototype on 14 July 1986, the BX-200 has the general appearance of an enlarged Cassutt but is an original design. Plans are available and kits were expected to be marketed by the close of 1988. Assembly time for the kit is under 1,000 working hours.
TYPE: Side by side two-seat cross-country homebuilt.

AIRFRAME: All-wood wings, with NACA 2300 laminar flow section. Remainder of airframe has welded steel tube structure, Ceconite covered except for glassfibre forward fuselage skins, engine cowling and canopy frame. Non-retractable tailwheel landing gear.

POWER PLANT: One 134 kW (180 hp) Textron Lycoming O-360-A4A. Fuel capacity 102 litres (27 US gallons; 22.5 Imp gallons).

DIMENSIONS, EXTERNAL:

Wing span	6.10 m (20 ft 0 in)
Length overall	5.31 m (17 ft 5 in)
Height overall	1.50 m (4 ft 11 in)

WEIGHTS:

Weight empty	363 kg (800 lb)
Baggage capacity	22.7 kg (50 lb)
Max T-O weight	612 kg (1,350 lb)

PERFORMANCE:

Max level speed at 610 m (2,000 ft)	
	195 knots (361 km/h; 224 mph) IAS
Max rate of climb at S/L	610 m (2,000 ft)/min
T-O and landing run	457 m (1,500 ft)

BROCK

KEN BROCK MANUFACTURING INC
(Division of Santa Ana Metal Stamping)
11852 Western Avenue, Stanton, California 90680
Telephone: (714) 898 4366

KEN BROCK KB-2 FREEDOM MACHINE

The KB-2 prototype flew in 1970. Manufacture of kits began in 1979; several hundred have been sold.

The KB-2 is built from eight kits of parts. Assembly of the basic airframe takes approximately 1½ hours, and the KB-2 can be assembled ready for testing in unpowered form in one weekend.

TYPE: Single-seat homebuilt autogyro.

ROTOR SYSTEM: Single two-blade semi-rigid rotor, of all-metal construction. Blade section modified Clark Y.

AIRFRAME: All-aluminium alloy construction, but with alternative wooden tail unit. Non-retractable tricycle landing gear.

POWER PLANT: One 53.7 kW (72 hp) McCulloch 4318A or Volkswagen modified motorcar engine (max power rating 74.5 kW; 100 hp). Patented seat/fuel tank, capacity 33.7 litres (8.9 US gallons; 7.4 Imp gallons).

DIMENSIONS, EXTERNAL:

Rotor diameter	6.70 m (22 ft 0 in)
Length of fuselage	3.43 m (11 ft 3 in)
Max height	2.03 m (6 ft 8 in)
Propeller diameter	1.22 m (4 ft 0 in)

AREA:

Rotor disc	35.32 m² (380.1 sq ft)

WEIGHTS:

Weight empty	109 kg (240 lb)
Max T-O weight	272 kg (600 lb)

PERFORMANCE (at max T-O weight):

Max level speed	78 knots (145 km/h; 90 mph)
Econ cruising speed	52 knots (97 km/h; 60 mph)
Min level speed	22 knots (40 km/h; 25 mph)
Max rate of climb at S/L	366 m (1,200 ft)/min
Service ceiling	3,050 m (10,000 ft)
T-O run	61 m (200 ft)
Landing run	3 m (10 ft)
Range with max fuel	130 nm (241 km; 150 miles)
Endurance	2 h

KEN BROCK KB-3

The KB-3 is a microlight development of the KB-2 and is available in kit form. The tail unit comprises a rudder only, the mast is 25 cm (1 ft) taller, and a 90° pre-rotator is fitted to the rotor to eliminate the need for a gearbox.

TYPE: Single-seat microlight autogyro; conforms to FAR Pt 103.

POWER PLANT: One 48.5 kW (65 hp) Rotax 532. Fuel capacity 19 litres (5 US gallons; 4.2 Imp gallons).

DIMENSIONS, EXTERNAL:

Rotor diameter	6.70 m (22 ft 0 in)
Length of fuselage	3.35 m (11 ft 0 in)
Propeller diameter	1.52 m (5 ft 0 in)

WEIGHTS:

Weight empty	113 kg (250 lb)
Max T-O weight	272 kg (600 lb)

PERFORMANCE:

Max level speed	55 knots (101 km/h; 63 mph)
Cruising speed	48 knots (89 km/h; 55 mph)
Min level speed	22 knots (40 km/h; 25 mph)
Max rate of climb at S/L	152 m (500 ft)/min
T-O run	31-46 m (100-150 ft)
Landing run	0-1.5 m (0-5 ft)
Range	65 nm (120 km; 75 miles)

KEN BROCK AVION

The Avion was designed by the late Mr Bob Lovejoy. Construction time from a Ken Brock kit is up to 30 working hours.

TYPE: Single-seat microlight; conforms to FAR Pt 103 and AC 103-7.

AIRFRAME: Aluminium alloy airframe, double surface Dacron covered wings and tail surfaces. Three-axis control. Non-retractable tricycle landing gear.

POWER PLANT: One 20 kW (27 hp) Rotax 277. Fuel capacity 19 litres (5 US gallons; 4.2 Imp gallons) in patented seat fuel tank.

DIMENSIONS, EXTERNAL:

Wing span	8.84 m (29 ft 0 in)
Length overall	4.72 m (15 ft 6 in)
Height overall	2.08 m (6 ft 10 in)
Propeller diameter	1.22 m (4 ft 0 in)

AREA:

Wings, gross	13.47 m² (145.0 sq ft)

WEIGHTS:

Weight empty	109 kg (240 lb)
Pilot weight range	59-95 kg (130-210 lb)
Max T-O weight	227 kg (500 lb)

PERFORMANCE:

Max level speed	45 knots (84 km/h; 52 mph)
Econ cruising speed	39 knots (72 km/h; 45 mph)
Stalling speed: power on and power off	24 knots (44 km/h; 27 mph)
Max rate of climb at S/L	213 m (700 ft)/min
Service ceiling	3,050 m (10,000 ft)
T-O run	55 m (180 ft)
Landing run	46 m (150 ft)
Range with standard fuel	121 nm (225 km; 140 miles)
Endurance with standard fuel	more than 4 h
g limits	+6/−4

BROKAW

BROKAW AVIATION INC
2625 Johnson Point, Leesburg, Florida 32748
Telephone: (904) 787 2329

Full details of the Brokaw Bullet two-seat high-speed homebuilt aircraft, and an illustration, can be found in the 1987-88 *Jane's*.

BROWN

MICHAEL BROWN
c/o Climber Aviation, 800 West Third Street, Dayton, Ohio 45407
Telephone: (513) 223 8780

BROWN ASCENT I

In 1984 design rights for the Super 2 (2+2) and four-seat versions of the Imp were purchased from Aerocar Inc by Mr Brown, including the prototype then under construction in St Louis. Thereafter the Imp became known as the Ascent I. The prototype was completed by Mr Brown in two-seat form. Development continues, currently to reduce the weight of the Ascent I Super 2 by 113 kg (250 lb) before plans are made available. Eventually the Ascent I will be tested in the originally planned full four-seat form, with a more powerful engine and increased fuel capacity.

The data that follow refer to the Ascent I as detailed on current information sheets.

TYPE: Two-plus-two (Super 2) or four-seat homebuilt.

AIRFRAME: All-metal construction, except for glassfibre shells used on wing leading-edges and forward fuselage. Wing section GA(PC)-1. Retractable tricycle landing gear.

POWER PLANT: Prototype in Super 2 configuration currently fitted with 97 kW (130 hp) Franklin. Four-seat Ascent I will have a 149 kW (200 hp) Textron Lycoming. Super 2 prototype has fuel capacity of 106 litres (28 US gallons; 23.4 Imp gallons). Four-seater will have fuel capacity of 170 litres (45 US gallons; 37.5 Imp gallons).

DIMENSIONS, EXTERNAL:

Wing span	8.84 m (29 ft 0 in)
Length overall	6.86 m (22 ft 6 in)
Height overall	2.29 m (7 ft 6 in)
Propeller diameter: two-blade	1.83 m (6 ft 0 in)
four-blade	1.52 m (5 ft 0 in)

AREA:

Wings, gross	10.41 m² (112.0 sq ft)

WEIGHTS (A: Super 2, actual; B: Four-seat, estimated):

Weight empty: A	590 kg (1,300 lb)
B	567 kg (1,250 lb)
Baggage: A	77 kg (170 lb)
B	91 kg (200 lb)
Design max T-O weight: A	816 kg (1,800 lb)
B	998 kg (2,200 lb)

PERFORMANCE (prototype, estimated):

Max level speed	156 knots (290 km/h; 180 mph)
Stalling speed	58 knots (107 km/h; 66 mph)
Max rate of climb at S/L	309 m (1,013 ft)/min
T-O to 15 m (50 ft)	457 m (1,500 ft)

BUSHBY

BUSHBY AIRCRAFT INC
674 Route 52, Minooka, Illinois 60447
Telephone: (815) 467 2346

The Midget Mustang and M-II Mustang II are available in plans and kit forms.

BUSHBY/LONG MM-1 MIDGET MUSTANG

The prototype Midget Mustang was completed in 1948 by David Long. Two basic versions were developed by Robert Bushby from the original design, as follows:

MM-1-85. Powered by 63.5 kW (85 hp) Continental C85-8FJ or -12 engine. Flew for the first time on 9 September 1959.

MM-1-125. Powered by 101 kW (135 hp) Textron Lycoming O-290-D2 engine. Flew for first time in July 1963.

Approximately 360 Midget Mustangs had been completed by early 1988, with 1,100 more under construction throughout the world.

TYPE: Single-seat fully aerobatic sporting homebuilt.

AIRFRAME: All-aluminium alloy flush riveted construction. Wing section NACA 64A212 at root, NACA 64A210 at tip. Non-retractable tailwheel landing gear. Some examples built with retractable gear.

POWER PLANT: See model listing. Several Midget Mustangs flying with 112 kW (150 hp) Textron Lycoming O-320. MM-1-85 fuel capacity 57 litres (15 US gallons; 12.5 Imp gallons). Optional integral wing fuel tanks, each with capacity of 57 litres (15 US gallons; 12.5 Imp gallons). Optional wingtip tanks, each with capacity of 13 litres (3.5 US gallons; 2.9 Imp gallons). MM-1-125 fuel capacity 57 litres (15 US gallons; 12.5 Imp gallons). No provision for wingtip tanks.

DIMENSIONS, EXTERNAL:

Wing span, without tip tanks	5.64 m (18 ft 6 in)
Length overall	5.00 m (16 ft 5 in)
Height overall	1.37 m (4 ft 6 in)

AREA:

Wings, gross	6.32 m² (68.0 sq ft)

WEIGHTS:

Weight empty: MM-1-85	261 kg (575 lb)
MM-1-125	268 kg (590 lb)
Baggage capacity	5.5 kg (12 lb)
Max T-O and landing weight:	
MM-1-85	397 kg (875 lb)
MM-1-125	408 kg (900 lb)

PERFORMANCE (at max T-O weight):

Max level speed at S/L:	
MM-1-85	165 knots (306 km/h; 190 mph)
MM-1-125	195 knots (362 km/h; 225 mph)
Econ cruising speed:	
MM-1-85	129 knots (238 km/h; 148 mph)
MM-1-125	143 knots (265 km/h; 165 mph)
Stalling speed, flaps down:	
MM-1-85	50 knots (92 km/h; 57 mph)
MM-1-125	53 knots (97 km/h; 60 mph)
Max rate of climb at S/L:	
MM-1-85	533 m (1,750 ft)/min
MM-1-125	670 m (2,200 ft)/min
Service ceiling: MM-1-85	over 4,875 m (16,000 ft)
MM-1-125	5,790 m (19,000 ft)
T-O run: MM-1-85	137 m (450 ft)
MM-1-125	122 m (400 ft)
Landing run	152 m (500 ft)
Range with max fuel:	
MM-1-85	347 nm (640 km; 400 miles)
MM-1-125	325 nm (603 km; 375 miles)
Range with max fuel and tip tanks:	
MM-1-85	651 nm (1,200 km; 750 miles)

BUSHBY M-II MUSTANG II

This side by side two-seat derivative of the Midget Mustang flew for the first time on 9 July 1966. About 1,200 Mustang IIs were being built by amateurs in early 1988, at which time 300 had been completed.

The description applies to the de luxe model, which is stressed for +6g. The empty weight quoted includes IFR instrumentation and nav/com equipment. The M-II can also be operated as an aerobatic aircraft in what Bushby Aircraft calls the 'Sport' configuration. This is identical to the de luxe model except that the electrical system, radio, additional IFR instrumentation, soundproofing and upholstery, wheel fairings, and some baggage capacity are deleted. The 'Sport' model has an empty weight of 340 kg (750 lb), T-O weight of 567 kg (1,250 lb) and is stressed for +9g.

TYPE: Two-seat, dual-control sporting homebuilt.

AIRFRAME: All-aluminium alloy flush riveted construction. Wing section NACA 64A212 at root, NACA 64A210 at tip. Standard version has non-retractable tailwheel landing gear. Alternative non-retractable tricycle gear.

POWER PLANT: Normally one 119 kW (160 hp) Textron Lycoming O-320. Provision for other engines including a 93 kW (125 hp) Textron Lycoming O-290. Fuel capacity 94.6 litres (25 US gallons; 21 Imp gallons). Optional integral wing fuel tanks, each with a capacity of 45 litres (12 US gallons; 10 Imp gallons). Provision for wingtip tanks.

DIMENSIONS, EXTERNAL:

Wing span	7.37 m (24 ft 2 in)
Length overall	5.94 m (19 ft 6 in)
Height overall	1.60 m (5 ft 3 in)
Propeller diameter: 93 kW (125 hp)	1.73 m (5 ft 8 in)
119 kW (160 hp)	1.83 m (6 ft 0 in)

AREA:

Wings, gross	9.02 m² (97.12 sq ft)

WEIGHTS:

Weight empty, equipped, 119 kW (160 hp) engine and tailwheel landing gear	420 kg (927 lb)
Baggage capacity	34 kg (75 lb)
*Max T-O weight	680 kg (1,500 lb)

*Except for countries that restrict max wing loading to 73.2 kg/m² (15 lb/sq ft), where T-O weight of 658 kg (1,450 lb) applies

Ken Brock KB-2 Freedom Machine

Ken Brock Avion single-seat three-axis microlight (third prototype)

Bushby/Long MM-1 Midget Mustang owned by Mr James Speas of Reno, Nevada *(John Wegg)*

Bushby M-II Mustang II built by Mr Paul Cox of Louisville, Kentucky (149 kW; 200 hp Textron Lycoming engine)

Brown Ascent I Super 2 prototype (97 kW; 130 hp Franklin engine)

Carlson Aircraft Sparrow light aircraft *(Geoffrey P. Jones)*

PERFORMANCE (119 kW; 160 hp engine, tailwheel landing gear, at max T-O weight):
Max level speed at S/L   200 knots (370 km/h; 230 mph)
Max cruising speed at 2,285 m (7,500 ft)
                        181 knots (335 km/h; 208 mph)

Stalling speed: flaps down   51 knots (94 km/h; 58 mph)
                flaps up   53 knots (96 km/h; 60 mph)
Max rate of climb at S/L   670 m (2,200 ft)/min
Service ceiling   6,400 m (21,000 ft)
T-O run   137 m (450 ft)

Landing run   168 m (550 ft)
Range with standard fuel (75% power)
                            373 nm (692 km; 430 miles)
Range with optional wingtip tanks
                            542 nm (1,005 km; 625 miles)

BUTTERWORTH
G. N. BUTTERWORTH
Richmond Airport, Heaton Orchard Road, West Kingston, Rhode Island 02892
Telephone: (401) 789 0384

Details and an illustration of Mr Butterworth's Westland Whirlwind Mark II ⅔-scale replica fighter can be found in the 1987-88 *Jane's*.

CARLSON
CARLSON AIRCRAFT INC
51012 State Route 14, East Palestine, Ohio 44413
Telephone: (216) 426 3934
PRESIDENT: Ernest W. Carlson

CARLSON SPARROW
The Sparrow is marketed in materials kit and quick build kit forms, the latter with all welding and machining completed.
TYPE: Single-seat light aircraft; conforms to FAR Pt 103.
AIRFRAME: All-metal structure, Dacron covered except for glassfibre engine cowling. Göttingen wing section. Three-axis control. Non-retractable tricycle landing gear.
POWER PLANT: One 20 kW (27 hp) Rotax 277. Fuel capacity 19 litres (5 US gallons; 4.2 Imp gallons).

DIMENSIONS, EXTERNAL:
Wing span   9.21 m (30 ft 2⅜ in)
Length overall   5.11 m (16 ft 9 in)
Height overall   2.06 m (6 ft 9 in)
AREA:
Wings, gross   11.15 m² (120.0 sq ft)
WEIGHTS:
Weight empty   115 kg (254 lb)
Max T-O weight   229 kg (504 lb)
PERFORMANCE (77 kg; 170 lb pilot; no wind):
Max level speed   55 knots (101 km/h; 63 mph)
Cruising speed   50 knots (93 km/h; 58 mph)
Stalling speed   23 knots (42 km/h; 26 mph)
Max rate of climb at S/L   229 m (750 ft)/min
T-O run   43 m (140 ft)
Landing run   59 m (195 ft)
Range at cruising speed   173 nm (321 km; 200 miles)

CARLSON SPARROW SPORT SPECIAL
This Experimental category homebuilt derivative of the Sparrow design uses the same form of wing, fuselage, tail unit and landing gear structures as the basic version but is considerably heavier, due mainly to the use of a larger engine and an increase in fuel capacity. It is available in materials kit and quick build kit forms.
TYPE: Single-seat homebuilt.
POWER PLANT: One 38.8 kW (52 hp) Rotax 503. Fuel capacity 30 litres (8 US gallons; 6.66 Imp gallons).
WEIGHTS:
Weight empty   134 kg (295 lb)
Max T-O weight   272 kg (600 lb)
PERFORMANCE:
Max level speed   87 knots (161 km/h; 100 mph)
Cruising speed   74 knots (137 km/h; 85 mph)
Stalling speed   26 knots (48 km/h; 30 mph)

Max rate of climb at S/L	274 m (900 ft)/min
T-O run	30 m (99 ft)
Landing run	46 m (149 ft)
Range at cruising speed	260 nm (482 km; 300 miles)

CARLSON SPARROW II

This is basically an enlarged side by side two-seat derivative of the Sparrow Sport Special, offering dual controls, short field performance, 38 litre (10 US gallon; 8.3 Imp gallon) fuel capacity, and a baggage compartment with a 9 kg (20 lb) capacity. Options will include different engines (after testing), and ski and float landing gears. Although it is planned to offer kits, consideration is being given to certificating the aircraft for factory-built status.

TYPE: Side by side two-seat homebuilt.

DIMENSIONS, EXTERNAL:

Wing span	9.75 m (32 ft 0 in)
Length overall	5.49 m (18 ft 0 in)
Height overall	2.13 m (7 ft 0 in)
AREA:	
Wings, gross	13.38 m² (144.0 sq ft)
WEIGHTS (48.5 kW; 65 hp engine):	
Weight empty	177 kg (390 lb)
Max T-O weight	395 kg (870 lb)
PERFORMANCE (48.5 kW; 65 hp engine):	
Max level speed	82 knots (153 km/h; 95 mph)
Cruising speed	74 knots (137 km/h; 85 mph)
Stalling speed	26 knots (47 km/h; 29 mph)
Max rate of climb at S/L	305 m (1,000 ft)/min
T-O and landing run	61 m (200 ft)
Range at cruising speed	260 nm (483 km; 300 miles)

CARLSON SKYCYCLE '87

Designed and built by Mr Neal K. Carlson, the original Skycycle first appeared in 1945. The fuselage was constructed from a Second World War drop tank. Only the prototype was built (with a 41 kW; 55 hp Textron Lycoming O-145A engine) and this was destroyed in a fire in about 1946.

The much refined Skycycle '87 will be available only in ready assembled form once prototype testing has been completed. The basic structure will be of welded steel tubing, with glassfibre skins and a Plexiglas bubble canopy. Anticipated empty weight is 134 kg (295 lb) with a 44.7 kW (60 hp) engine installed.

The following dimensions refer to the original Skycycle, but are likely to be close to those for the Skycycle '87 as Carlson Aircraft has stated its intention to duplicate as near as possible for size the original design parameters:

DIMENSIONS, EXTERNAL (original Skycycle prototype):

Wing span	6.10 m (20 ft 0 in)
Length overall	4.83 m (15 ft 10 in)

CASCADE

CASCADE ULTRALITES INC

4700 188th Street North-East, Arlington, Washington 98223

Telephone: (206) 435 8614

PRESIDENT: Steven J. Grossruck

CASCADE KASPERWING 1-80

Design of the Kasperwing was begun in order to flight test the theories of Mr Witold Kasper regarding what he described as 'vortex lift'. Mr Kasper believes that it is possible to develop a wing configuration which, at angles of attack of 30° or more, can induce a spanwise vortex that will produce enough lift to bring about drastic reductions in aircraft stalling speed and rate of sink.

Four versions are believed to be available, as follows:

1-80B. Basic version, without fuselage pod and powered by a 17.2 kW (23 hp) Zenoah 242 cc engine.

1-80BX. As 1-80B, but having as standard a fully enclosed glassfibre pod for the pilot, 19 litre (5 US gallon; 4.2 Imp gallon) fuel tank, and other refinements, any or all of which are optional with the standard 1-80 model. In addition, the BX can be supplied with a more powerful Kawasaki 440 engine.

1-80C. As 1-80BX, but with three-axis control, 20 kW (27 hp) Rotax 277 engine as standard and other refinements. Aircraft illustrated has Rotax 503 engine.

1-80CR. As 1-80C, but with 35 kW (47 hp) Rotax 503 engine. Does not comply with FAR Pt 103.

TYPE: Single-seat microlight; all except 1-80CR conform to FAR Pt 103.

AIRFRAME: Aluminium alloy main frame. Semi-rigid wing, with ribs, covered in single thickness Dacron. Two-axis control system standard on B/BX (weight shift, reflexed wingtips, and endplate fins and rudders); three-axis control optional on B/BX, standard on C/CR. Non-retractable tricycle landing gear. Floats optional.

POWER PLANT: One piston engine, as shown under model listings. Fuel capacity 9.5 litres (2.5 US gallons; 2.1 Imp gallons) standard on B; 19 litre (5 US gallon; 4.2 Imp gallon) tank optional on B, standard on BX/C/CR.

DIMENSIONS, EXTERNAL (all versions):

Wing span	10.67 m (35 ft 0 in)
Length overall	3.86 m (12 ft 8 in)
Height overall	2.29 m (7 ft 6 in)
Propeller diameter: B, BX	1.37 m (4 ft 6 in)
C	1.52 m (5 ft 0 in)
AREA (all versions):	
Wings, gross	16.72 m² (180.0 sq ft)
WEIGHTS:	
Weight empty: B	72.5 kg (160 lb)
BX	86 kg (190 lb)
C	111 kg (245 lb)

Pilot weight range: B, BX	59-100 kg (130-220 lb)
C	45-113 kg (100-250 lb)
Max T-O weight: B	172 kg (380 lb)
BX	190.5 kg (420 lb)
C	238 kg (525 lb)
PERFORMANCE (with 68 kg; 150 lb pilot):	
Max level speed: B, BX	48 knots (89 km/h; 55 mph)
C	52 knots (96 km/h; 60 mph)
Econ cruising speed: B	30 knots (56 km/h; 35 mph)
BX, C	39 knots (72 km/h; 45 mph)
Stalling speed (all versions):	
power on	20 knots (36 km/h; 22 mph)
power off	16 knots (29 km/h; 18 mph)
Max rate of climb at S/L: B	183-244 m (600-800 ft)/min
BX	183 m (600 ft)/min
C	244 m (800 ft)/min
Service ceiling (all versions)	4,575 m (15,000 ft)
T-O run (all versions)	15-23 m (50-75 ft)
Landing run (all versions)	15 m (50 ft)
Range with standard fuel: B	74 nm (137 km; 85 miles)
BX	173 nm (322 km; 200 miles)
C	130 nm (241 km; 150 miles)
Endurance with standard fuel: B	2 h 15 min
BX	5 h
C	3 h 30 min
g limits: B	+7/–4 ultimate
C	+9/–6 ultimate

CASSUTT

MANUFACTURED/DISTRIBUTED by: National Aeronautics and Manufacturing Co Inc, 1741 River Drive, Watertown Municipal Airport, Hangar 6, Watertown, Wisconsin 53094

Telephone: (414) 261 4662

Plans, parts and kits of parts of the original Cassutt Special I design, and plans of a sporting version with a larger cockpit, are available from the National Aeronautics and Manufacturing Co Inc. About 2,000 sets of plans have been sold; more than 125 Cassutt Specials are believed to be flying.

CASSUTT SPECIAL I

The following description applies to the Cassutt Special I as offered in Continental and Sport versions by the National Aeronautics and Manufacturing Co Inc. The Sport model, for sport flying and aerobatics, is essentially the same as the Continental racing model, except for having a greater wing span and area, slightly raised seat for the pilot, and alternative open or enclosed cockpit.

TYPE: Single-seat racing homebuilt.

AIRFRAME: Wooden wings, with plywood skin and overall fabric covering. Wing section Cassutt 1107. Ailerons, fuselage and tail unit of welded steel tube construction, fabric covered. No flaps as standard, but a few constructors have added flaps. Non-retractable tailwheel landing gear.

POWER PLANT: One Continental engine in the 63.5-74.5 kW (85-100 hp) range. Fuel capacity 55 litres (14.5 US gallons; 12.1 Imp gallons).

DIMENSIONS, EXTERNAL (A: Continental, B: Sport):

Wing span: A	4.57 m (15 ft 0 in)
B	5.18 m (17 ft 0 in)
Length overall: A, B	4.88 m (16 ft 0 in)
Height overall: A, B	1.22 m (4 ft 0 in)
AREAS:	
Wings, gross: A	6.27 m² (67.5 sq ft)
B	7.11 m² (76.5 sq ft)
WEIGHTS:	
Weight empty: A, B	227 kg (500 lb)
Max T-O weight: A, B	363 kg (800 lb)
PERFORMANCE (63.5 kW; 85 hp engine):	
Max level speed:	
A, B	more than 174 knots (322 km/h; 200 mph)
Max cruising speed:	
A, B	more than 156 knots (290 km/h; 180 mph)
Max rate of climb at S/L: A	457 m (1,500 ft)/min
B	914 m (3,000 ft)/min

Range: A, B	425 nm (788 km; 490 miles)
g limit: A, B	+6.5

CASSUTT SPECIAL II

TYPE: Single-seat racing homebuilt.

AIRFRAME: Similar construction and landing gear to Special I. Wing section Cassutt 13106.

POWER PLANT: As for Cassutt Special I.

DIMENSIONS, EXTERNAL:

Wing span	4.16 m (13 ft 8 in)
Length overall	4.88 m (16 ft 0 in)
Height overall	1.16 m (3 ft 10 in)
AREA:	
Wings, gross	6.13 m² (66.0 sq ft)
WEIGHTS:	
Weight empty	196 kg (433 lb)
Max T-O weight	363 kg (800 lb)
PERFORMANCE (at max T-O weight):	
Max level speed at S/L	204 knots (378 km/h; 235 mph)
Max cruising speed	174 knots (322 km/h; 200 mph)
Stalling speed	54 knots (100 km/h; 62 mph)
Max rate of climb at S/L	915 m (3,000 ft)/min
Endurance with max fuel	3 h

CGS
CGS AVIATION INC

The address for this company given in the 1987-88 *Jane's* is no longer current. Full details of the CGS Hawk can be found in that edition, together with an illustration of the AG Hawk cropspraying version.

CHRISTEN

CHRISTEN INDUSTRIES INC

PO Box 547, Afton, Wyoming 83110

Telephone: (307) 886 3151

MARKETING DEPARTMENT: Edmond A. Heinbockel

CHRISTEN EAGLE II

The Eagle II flew for the first time in February 1977. By January 1986, construction of more than 600 Eagle IIs had started and over 250 were known to have been completed by amateur builders. Each aircraft is built from 25 parts kits, requiring 1,400-1,600 working hours to assemble.

TYPE: Two-seat unlimited class homebuilt aerobatic biplane.

AIRFRAME: Wooden wing spars and ribs; metal leading- and trailing-edges, polyester fabric covered. Symmetrical wing section. Ailerons on upper and lower wings, of similar construction to wings. Welded steel tube fuselage, covered with removable light alloy panels from firewall to back of rear seat and fabric over rear fuselage. Welded steel tube tail unit, fabric covered. Non-retractable tailwheel landing gear.

POWER PLANT: One 149 kW (200 hp) Textron Lycoming AEIO-360-A1D. Fuel capacity 98.4 litres (26 US gallons; 21.6 Imp gallons). Fuel system allows unlimited inverted flight.

DIMENSIONS, EXTERNAL:

Wing span	6.07 m (19 ft 11 in)
Length overall	5.64 m (18 ft 6 in)
Height overall	1.98 m (6 ft 6 in)
Propeller diameter	1.93 m (6 ft 4 in)
AREA:	
Wings, gross	11.61 m² (125.0 sq ft)
WEIGHTS:	
Weight empty	465 kg (1,025 lb)
Baggage capacity	13.6 kg (30 lb)
Max T-O and landing weight	725 kg (1,600 lb)
PERFORMANCE:	
Max level speed at S/L	160 knots (296 km/h; 184 mph)
Econ cruising speed at 1,825 m (6,000 ft)	
	137 knots (254 km/h; 158 mph)
Stalling speed	51 knots (94 km/h; 58 mph)
Max rate of climb at S/L	645 m (2,120 ft)/min
Service ceiling	5,180 m (17,000 ft)
T-O run	244 m (800 ft)
Landing from 15 m (50 ft)	480 m (1,575 ft)
Range with max fuel and max payload	
	330 nm (611 km; 380 miles)
g limits	+9/–6

Cascade Kasperwing 1-80C, with Rotax 503 engine *(Peter M. Bowers)*

Chuck's Aircraft Texan Chuck Bird *(Geoffrey P. Jones)*

Cassutt Special Continental owned by Mr S. C. Thompson of the UK
(R. Kunert)

Cirrus Design Corporation Cirrus VK30 four/five-seat homebuilt aircraft
(Geoffrey P. Jones)

Christen Industries Eagle II two-seat aerobatic biplane built by Mr B. H.
Grant McKay and Mr Bob Petryk of Calgary, Alberta, Canada
(Neil A. Macdougall)

Collins Aero W-7 Dipper amphibious flying-boat *(Howard Levy)*

CHUCK's
CHUCK's AIRCRAFT COMPANY
11845 Loop 107, Adkins, Texas 78101
Telephone: (512) 649 1727
PROPRIETOR: Chuck Beeson

CHUCK's AIRCRAFT TEXAN CHUCK BIRD
Shown in an accompanying illustration, this strut braced parasol monoplane appears to be a three-axis control microlight, powered by a 30 kW (40 hp) Chaparral engine. It is available in ready assembled form or as a series of kits.

The only known details follow:
DIMENSIONS, EXTERNAL:
Wing span	7.77 m (25 ft 6 in)
Length of fuselage	4.57 m (16 ft 0 in)

CIRRUS
CIRRUS DESIGN CORPORATION
Baraboo-Dells Airport, S3440A Highway 12, Baraboo, Wisconsin 53913
Telephone: (608) 356 3460

CIRRUS DESIGN CIRRUS VK30
First flown on 11 February 1988, the Cirrus will be made available in prefabricated kit form once flight testing has been completed. Major design features include new laminar flow wing sections, large Fowler flaps, and a tail mounted pusher propeller.
TYPE: Four/five-seat high-performance homebuilt.

AIRFRAME: Constructed of vacuum-bagged vinylester resin/ glassfibre sandwich with polyurethane foam core; Kevlar and PVC foam used in selected areas for weight reduction. Wing sections based on NASA NLF(1)-0414F. Retractable tricycle landing gear.
POWER PLANT: Prototype fitted with 216 kW (290 hp) Textron Lycoming IO-540-G1A5. Fuel capacity 360 litres (95 US gallons; 79 Imp gallons). Engine options will be researched at a later date.
DIMENSIONS, EXTERNAL:
Wing span	11.79 m (38 ft 8 in)
Length overall	7.92 m (26 ft 0 in)
Height overall	3.25 m (10 ft 8 in)
Propeller diameter	1.88 m (6 ft 2 in)

AREA:
Wings, gross	11.15 m² (120.0 sq ft)

WEIGHTS (prototype):
Weight empty	998 kg (2,200 lb)
Max T-O weight	1,565 kg (3,450 lb)

PERFORMANCE (prototype, estimated):
Cruising speed	more than 217 knots (402 km/h; 250 mph)
Stalling speed	57 knots (105 km/h; 65 mph)
Max rate of climb at S/L	549 m (1,800 ft)/min
T-O run	366 m (1,200 ft)
Range, 75% power, with reserves	1,129 nm (2,092 km; 1,300 miles)

CLUTTON-TABENOR
ERIC CLUTTON
913 Cedar Lane, Tullahoma, Tennessee 37388

Details of the Fred Series 3, and an illustration of the Fred Series 2, can be found in the 1987-88 *Jane's*.

COLLINS
COLLINS AERO
386 Fairville Road RD1, Chadds Ford, Pennsylvania 19317
Telephone: (215) 388 2393
OWNER: Willard C. Collins

COLLINS AERO W-7 DIPPER
The Dipper prototype made its first flight on 24 August

1982. An information brochure and plans are available to amateur constructors.
TYPE: Side by side two-seat homebuilt amphibious flying-boat.
AIRFRAME: Uses aluminium alloy wings from a Cessna 150, with floats added close to wingtips. Modified Cessna 150 basic fuselage, with instrument panel and windscreen moved forward by 0.91 m (3 ft 0 in) and glassfibre

two-step boat hull and nose cowling added for water operations. Basic Cessna 150 tail unit, but with fin of increased height and tailplane raised by 0.46 m (1 ft 6 in). Dorsal fin added. Retractable tricycle landing gear.

POWER PLANT: One 134 kW (180 hp) Textron Lycoming O-360. Fuel capacity 148 litres (39 US gallons; 32.5 Imp gallons).

DIMENSIONS, EXTERNAL:	
Wing span	10.16 m (33 ft 4 in)
Length overall	7.72 m (25 ft 4 in)
Height overall	2.84 m (9 ft 4 in)
Propeller diameter	1.88 m (6 ft 2 in)
AREA:	
Wings, gross	14.86 m² (160.0 sq ft)

WEIGHTS:	
Weight empty, equipped	481 kg (1,060 lb)
Max T-O weight	798 kg (1,760 lb)
PERFORMANCE:	
Max level speed at 2,135 m (7,000 ft)	
	130 knots (241 km/h; 150 mph)
Econ cruising speed	100 knots (185 km/h; 115 mph)

Stalling speed	45 knots (84 km/h; 52 mph)
Max rate of climb at S/L	427 m (1,400 ft)/min
Service ceiling	5,485 m (18,000 ft)
T-O run	122 m (400 ft)
Landing run	152 m (500 ft)
Range with max fuel	500 nm (926 km; 575 miles)

COUNTRY AIR
COUNTRY AIR INC
1230 Shepherd Street, Hendersonville, North Carolina 28739
Telephone: (704) 692 7784
OWNER: Jesse D. Anglin

COUNTRY AIR J-6 KARATOO

Kits are available to amateur constructors. The following details are based on the Grover J-6 Karatoo, from which the Country Air model was derived.
TYPE: Side by side two-seat homebuilt.
AIRFRAME: Fabric covered airframe. Non-retractable tailwheel landing gear.
POWER PLANT: Powered normally by a 39 kW (52 hp) Rotax 503. A 48.5 kW (65 hp) Volkswagen engine is optional.

DIMENSIONS, EXTERNAL:	
Wing span	9.91 m (32 ft 6 in)
Length overall	6.10 m (20 ft 0 in)
Height overall	1.68 m (5 ft 6 in)

AREA:	
Wings, gross	13.56 m² (146.0 sq ft)
WEIGHTS (Rotax engine):	
Weight empty	172 kg (380 lb)
Max T-O weight	408 kg (900 lb)
PERFORMANCE (Rotax engine):	
Max level speed	74 knots (137 km/h; 85 mph)
Cruising speed	65 knots (120 km/h; 75 mph)
Max rate of climb at S/L	228 m (750 ft)/min
T-O run	46 m (150 ft)

COUNTRY AIR SPACE WALKER

The Space Walker is designed to look like Ryan monoplanes of the late 1930s and early 1940s but is built of modern materials and uses a modern engine. Drawings and component parts are available to amateur constructors. A ready assembled microlight version was to follow.
TYPE: Single-seat homebuilt.
AIRFRAME: Fabric covered wooden wings. Welded chrome-molybdenum steel tube fuselage and wire braced tail unit,

also fabric covered. Non-retractable tailwheel landing gear.
POWER PLANT: One 48.5-63 kW (65-85 hp) Continental. Fuel capacity 38 litres (10 US gallons; 8.3 Imp gallons).

DIMENSIONS, EXTERNAL:	
Wing span	7.93 m (26 ft 0 in)
Length overall	5.49 m (18 ft 0 in)
Height overall	1.60 m (5 ft 3 in)
AREA:	
Wings, gross	10.87 m² (117.0 sq ft)
WEIGHTS (48.5 kW; 65 hp Continental):	
Weight empty	245 kg (540 lb)
Max T-O weight	385 kg (850 lb)
PERFORMANCE (48.5 kW; 65 hp Continental):	
Max level speed at S/L	108 knots (201 km/h; 125 mph)
Cruising speed	97 knots (180 km/h; 112 mph)
Stalling speed: power off	37 knots (68 km/h; 42 mph)
power on	33 knots (61 km/h; 38 mph)
Max rate of climb at S/L	259 m (850 ft)/min
g limits	+6/−5

Co Z
Co Z EUROPE
Ahornstrasse 10A, D-8901 Ried, German Federal Republic
Design rights to the Cozy side by side two-seat development of the Rutan Long-EZ were sold in 1987 to this West German company by Co Z Development Corporation of Arizona, USA. The new owner continues to sell plans worldwide, except in the USA.

Co Z EUROPE COZY

The prototype Cozy flew for the first time on 19 July 1982. The following details refer specifically to this prototype:
TYPE: Two/three-seat sporting homebuilt.
AIRFRAME: Wing and foreplane structures of unidirectional

glassfibre with rigid foam core. Eppler wing section. Composite fuselage comprising large sheets of rigid urethane foam, with wood strips as corner fillers, and internal and external covering of unidirectional glassfibre. Light alloy extrusion used for engine mount. Tricycle landing gear, with retractable nosewheel.
POWER PLANT: One 88 kW (118 hp) Textron Lycoming O-235-L2C.

DIMENSIONS, EXTERNAL:	
Wing span	7.96 m (26 ft 1¼ in)
Length overall	5.12 m (16 ft 9½ in)
Height overall	2.30 m (7 ft 6½ in)
Propeller diameter	1.60 m (5 ft 3 in)
AREA:	
Wings, gross	8.88 m² (95.6 sq ft)

WEIGHTS:	
Weight empty, basic	386 kg (850 lb)
Max T-O weight	680 kg (1,500 lb)
PERFORMANCE:	
Max level speed at S/L	165 knots (306 km/h; 190 mph)
Econ cruising speed at 3,660 m (12,000 ft)	
	124 knots (230 km/h; 143 mph)
Stalling speed	53 knots (97 km/h; 60 mph)
Max rate of climb at S/L	457 m (1,500 ft)/min
Service ceiling	6,100 m (20,000 ft)
T-O run	213 m (700 ft)
Landing run	183 m (600 ft)
Range with max fuel, at 122 knots (225 km/h; 140 mph) at 3,660 m (12,000 ft), with 1½ h reserves	
	1,563 nm (2,896 km; 1,800 miles)

CVJETKOVIC
ANTON CVJETKOVIC
5324 West 121 Street, Hawthorne, California 90250
Telephone: (213) 643 6931

CVJETKOVIC CA-61/-61R MINI ACE

The CA-61 can be built as a single-seat or side by side two-seat light aircraft, with any Continental engine of between 48.5 and 63.5 kW (65 and 85 hp), and with non-retractable tailwheel landing gear or retractable gear (as the **CA-61R**). Alternatively, the single-seater can be fitted with a modified Volkswagen engine. Plans are available. Construction takes less than 1,000 h.
The following details refer specifically to the single-seat CA-61 prototype:
TYPE: Single-seat homebuilt.
AIRFRAME: All-wood construction, with fabric only over wings and ailerons. Wing section NACA 4415. Landing gear as detailed above.
POWER PLANT: Engine options as detailed above. Fuel capacity 64 litres (17 US gallons; 14.2 Imp gallons).

DIMENSIONS, EXTERNAL:	
Wing span	8.38 m (27 ft 6 in)
Length overall	5.77 m (18 ft 11 in)
Height overall (in flying position)	2.08 m (6 ft 10 in)
AREA:	
Wings, gross	11.75 m² (126.5 sq ft)
WEIGHTS:	
Weight empty: single-seat	275 kg (606 lb)
two-seat	363 kg (800 lb)
Max T-O weight: single-seat	430 kg (950 lb)
two-seat	590 kg (1,300 lb)

PERFORMANCE:	
Max level speed at S/L	104 knots (193 km/h; 120 mph)
Normal cruising speed	87 knots (161 km/h; 100 mph)
Min flying speed:	
single-seat	37 knots (68 km/h; 42 mph)
two-seat	44 knots (81 km/h; 50 mph)
Range with max fuel:	
single-seat	369 nm (685 km; 425 miles)
two-seat	321 nm (595 km; 370 miles)

CVJETKOVIC CA-65

The prototype CA-65 flew for the first time in July 1965. Plans are available.
TYPE: Two-seat, dual-control homebuilt.
AIRFRAME: All-wood construction, with fabric covering only on ailerons, elevators and rudder. Modified NACA 4415 wing section. Retractable tailwheel landing gear.
POWER PLANT: One 93 kW (125 hp) Textron Lycoming O-290-G. Other Textron Lycoming engines of 80.5-112 kW; 108-150 hp can be fitted. Fuel capacity 106 litres (28 US gallons; 23.3 Imp gallons).

DIMENSIONS, EXTERNAL:	
Wing span	7.62 m (25 ft 0 in)
Length overall	5.79 m (19 ft 0 in)
Height overall (in flying position)	2.24 m (7 ft 4 in)
Propeller diameter	1.73 m (5 ft 8 in)
AREA:	
Wings, gross	10.03 m² (108.0 sq ft)
WEIGHTS:	
Weight empty	408 kg (900 lb)
Max T-O weight	680 kg (1,500 lb)

CVJETKOVIC CA-65A

This is an all-metal version of the wooden CA-65.
POWER PLANT: Structure is designed to accommodate a Textron Lycoming engine of 80.5-112 kW (108-150 hp).

DIMENSIONS, EXTERNAL: As for Model CA-65 except:	
Wing span	7.75 m (25 ft 5 in)
Length overall	5.99 m (19 ft 8 in)
Height overall	2.29 m (7 ft 6 in)
AREA:	
Wings, gross	10.16 m² (109.4 sq ft)
PERFORMANCE (112 kW; 150 hp engine):	
Max level speed	151 knots (280 km/h; 174 mph)
Normal cruising speed	130 knots (241 km/h; 150 mph)
Stalling speed	48 knots (89 km/h; 55 mph)
Max rate of climb at S/L	466 m (1,530 ft)/min
Service ceiling	4,570 m (15,000 ft)
T-O run	99 m (325 ft)
Landing run	183 m (600 ft)
Range with max fuel	460 nm (853 km; 530 miles)
g limits	+9/−6 ultimate

PERFORMANCE (at max T-O weight):

Max level speed	156 knots (290 km/h; 180 mph)
Normal cruising speed	135 knots (249 km/h; 155 mph)
Stalling speed	48 knots (89 km/h; 55 mph)
Max rate of climb at S/L	305 m (1,000 ft)/min
Service ceiling	4,575 m (15,000 ft)
T-O run	137 m (450 ft)
Landing run	183 m (600 ft)
Range with max fuel	434 nm (804 km; 500 miles)
g limits	+9/−6 ultimate

D 2
D 2 INC
PO Box 265, Bend, Oregon 97709
PROPRIETOR: Sidney L. Ellis
D 2 Inc acquired the designs of the Davis DA-2A and DA-5A and the Aerosport Quail, and is remarketing them.

D 2 (DAVIS) DA-2A

This two-seat homebuilt was flown for the first time on 21 May 1966. D 2 Inc offers both plans and kits of the DA-2A. The DA-2A is of all-metal construction, with a V tail and non-retractable tricycle landing gear. Power plant in the prototype was a 48.5 kW (65 hp) Continental A65-8, but the DA-2A is stressed for engines of up to 74.5 kW (100 hp). Fuel capacity is 75 litres (20 US gallons; 16.7 Imp gallons).
There is baggage space aft of the side by side seats or, alternatively, a child's seat may be located in this position.

DIMENSIONS, EXTERNAL:	
Wing span	5.86 m (19 ft 2¾ in)
Length overall	5.44 m (17 ft 10¼ in)
Height overall	1.65 m (5 ft 5 in)
AREA:	
Wings, gross	7.66 m² (82.5 sq ft)
WEIGHTS (A65-8 engine):	
Weight empty	277 kg (610 lb)
Max T-O weight	510 kg (1,125 lb)
PERFORMANCE (A65-8 engine):	
Max level speed at S/L	104 knots (193 km/h; 120 mph)
Cruising speed	100 knots (185 km/h; 115 mph)
Range with max fuel	390 nm (725 km; 450 miles)

D 2 (DAVIS) DA-5A

The first flight of the DA-5A was made on 22 July 1974. Plans are available to amateur constructors.

TYPE: Single-seat homebuilt aircraft.
AIRFRAME: All-metal stressed-skin construction with a V tail. Wing section Clark Y. Non-retractable tricycle landing gear.
POWER PLANT: One 48.5 kW (65 hp) Continental A65. Fuel capacity 64.3 litres (17 US gallons; 14.2 Imp gallons).

DIMENSIONS, EXTERNAL:	
Wing span	4.76 m (15 ft 7¼ in)
Length overall	4.80 m (15 ft 9 in)
Height overall	1.35 m (4 ft 5¼ in)
Propeller diameter	1.52 m (5 ft 0 in)
AREA:	
Wings, gross	5.31 m² (57.2 sq ft)
WEIGHTS:	
Weight empty	208 kg (460 lb)
Max T-O weight	351 kg (775 lb)

Country Air Space Walker homebuilt (*Howard Levy*)

Country Air J-6 Karatoo (*J. M. G. Gradidge*)

First plans-built Co Z Cozy, built by Uli and Linda Wolters (*Howard Levy*)

Cvjetkovic CA-65, with extended propeller shaft and landing gear doors

The single-seat Cvjetkovic CA-61R (Continental A65 engine)

D 2 (Davis) DA-2A built by Mr Wade Hammer of Augusta, Georgia
(*Geoffrey P. Jones*)

D2 (Davis) DA-5A single-seat homebuilt sporting aircraft

D 2 (Aerosport) Quail single-seat homebuilt aircraft

PERFORMANCE (at max T-O weight):
Max level speed at S/L   139 knots (257 km/h; 160 mph)
Econ cruising speed at S/L
                     104 knots (193 km/h; 120 mph)
Stalling speed   52 knots (97 km/h; 60 mph)
Max rate of climb at S/L   244 m (800 ft)/min
Service ceiling   4,420 m (14,500 ft)
T-O run   183 m (600 ft)
Landing run   183 m (600 ft)
Range with max fuel   390 nm (724 km; 450 miles)

D 2 (AEROSPORT) QUAIL

The Quail, designed by Aerosport Inc. flew for the first time in December 1971. Plans and kits are now available from D 2 Inc.

TYPE: Single-seat homebuilt.

AIRFRAME: All-metal construction. Wing section NACA 23015. Non-retractable tricycle landing gear.

POWER PLANT: One 1,600 cc modified Volkswagen motorcar engine. Provision for other Volkswagen engines from 1,500 cc to 1,800 cc capacity. Fuel capacity 38 litres (10 US gallons; 8.3 Imp gallons).

DIMENSIONS, EXTERNAL:
Wing span   7.32 m (24 ft 0 in)
Length overall   4.85 m (15 ft 11 in)
Height overall   1.69 m (5 ft 6½ in)
Propeller diameter   1.37 m (4 ft 6 in)
AREA:
Wings, gross   7.8 m² (84.0 sq ft)

WEIGHTS:
Weight empty   242 kg (534 lb)
Baggage capacity   9 kg (20 lb)
Normal T-O weight   345 kg (762 lb)
Max T-O weight   359 kg (792 lb)
PERFORMANCE (at max T-O weight):
Max level speed at S/L   113 knots (209 km/h; 130 mph)
Econ cruising speed   96 knots (177 km/h; 110 mph)
Stalling speed, flaps down   42 knots (78 km/h; 48 mph)
Max rate of climb at S/L   259 m (850 ft)/min
Service ceiling (estimated)   3,660 m (12,000 ft)
T-O run   91 m (300 ft)
Landing run   122 m (400 ft)
Range with max fuel, no reserves
                     200 nm (370 km; 230 miles)

D'APUZZO

NICHOLAS E. D'APUZZO
102 Blue Rock Lane, Blue Bell, Pennsylvania 19422
Telephone: (215) 646 4792

D'APUZZO D-201 SPORTWING

The D-201 is a development of the earlier PJ-260/D-260 Senior Aero Sport series, of which at least 32 amateur built examples were flown, with others still under construction. Plans and partial kits of the D-201 are available.

TYPE: Tandem two-seat homebuilt sporting biplane.

AIRFRAME: All-metal construction, except for fabric covering of the rear fuselage. Wing section NACA M-12 (modified). Non-retractable tailwheel landing gear.

POWER PLANT: One 119 kW (160 hp) Textron Lycoming IO-320-B1A. Design suitable for any Textron Lycoming engine from the 93 kW (125 hp) O-235 to the 149 kW (200 hp) O-360.

DIMENSIONS, EXTERNAL:
Wing span: upper   8.23 m (27 ft 0 in)
lower   7.86 m (25 ft 9½ in)
Length overall, tail up   6.59 m (21 ft 7½ in)
Height overall, tail down   2.34 m (7 ft 8 in)
AREA:
Wings, gross   17.14 m² (184.5 sq ft)

WEIGHTS:
Weight empty   591 kg (1,303 lb)
Design max T-O weight   862 kg (1,900 lb)
PERFORMANCE (at max T-O weight):
Max level speed at 2,135 m (7,000 ft)
                     115 knots (212 km/h; 132 mph)
Max cruising speed at 2,135 m (7,000 ft)
                     106 knots (196 km/h; 122 mph)
Stalling speed   41 knots (76 km/h; 47 mph)
Max rate of climb at S/L   320 m (1,050 ft)/min
T-O run   128 m (420 ft)
Landing run   168 m (550 ft)
Range with max fuel   313 nm (579 km; 360 miles)

DAVIS

LEEON D. DAVIS

PLANS AND PARTS: Joe Gauthier, GFG Enterprises, 9 Kowal Drive, Cromwell, Connecticut 06416
Telephone: (203) 635 4058

DAVIS DA-7

The side by side two-seat DA-7 is intended for certification in the proposed Primary Aircraft category and subsequent commercial production in ready to fly form. It is of conventional light alloy construction, with a V tail. Wing section is USA 35B, and power is provided by an 86 kW (115 hp) Textron Lycoming O-235-L2C engine.

DIMENSIONS, EXTERNAL:
Wing span	6.25 m (20 ft 6 in)
Length overall	5.84 m (19 ft 2 in)

AREA:
Wings, gross	8.33 m² (89.7 sq ft)

WEIGHTS:
Weight empty	327 kg (720 lb)
Max T-O weight	576 kg (1,270 lb)

PERFORMANCE:
Max cruising speed (75% power)	
	126 knots (233 km/h; 145 mph)
Stalling speed	51 knots (94 km/h; 58 mph)

DAVIS

DAVIS WING LTD

PO Box 1103, Nampa, Idaho 83653-1103
PRESIDENT: Gilbert E. Davis

DAVIS WING STARSHIP GEMINI

The single-seat prototype Davis Wing, known as *Starship Alpha*, was flown for the first time on 10 June 1986. Kits are to be offered for a two-seat version, the Starship Gemini.
TYPE: Two-seat homebuilt flying wing.
AIRFRAME: Majority of airframe built of pre-moulded composites, including glassfibre, Nomex honeycomb, aramid fibres, graphite fibres and various foams. Other materials include 4130 steel tubing, stainless steel and aluminium alloy. Retractable tricycle landing gear.

POWER PLANT: Standard engine is 48.5 kW (65 hp) Rotax 532. Fuel capacity 120 litres (31.7 US gallons; 26.4 Imp gallons). Optional engine is a Textron Lycoming O-235, requiring fuselage nose ballast.

DIMENSIONS, EXTERNAL:
Wing span	12.19 m (40 ft 0 in)
Length overall	3.66 m (12 ft 0 in)
Height to top of canopy	1.62 m (5 ft 3½ in)
Propeller diameter	1.53 m (5 ft 0 in)

AREA:
Wings, gross	22.30 m² (240.0 sq ft)

WEIGHTS:
Weight empty	272 kg (600 lb)
Max T-O weight	590 kg (1,300 lb)

PERFORMANCE:
Max level speed at S/L	130 knots (240 km/h; 150 mph)
Stalling speed	36 knots (67 km/h; 42 mph)
Max rate of climb at S/L	426 m (1,400 ft)/min
Max operating height	7,620 m (25,000 ft)
T-O run at max T-O weight	54 m (175 ft)
Range at 70% power and 116 knots (215 km/h; 133 mph), at max T-O weight	868 nm (1,609 km; 1,000 miles)
Max range at 50% power and 100 knots (185 km/h; 115 mph), at max T-O weight	
	1,302 nm (2,414 km; 1,500 miles)
g limits, normal T-O weight	+6/−3

DELTA TECHNOLOGY — *See Magnum Industries*

DENNEY

DENNEY AEROCRAFT COMPANY

Nampa Airport, 100 North Kings Road, Nampa, Idaho 83651
Telephone: (208) 466 1711

DENNEY AEROCRAFT KITFOX

The Kitfox was designed to have exceptional short-field performance. It is marketed in kit form, and 210 kits had been sold by February 1988, of which 70 had been assembled. In addition, Philippine Aircraft Company in the Philippines has received a licence to produce ready assembled aircraft, and orders for 36 have already been received from Philippine provincial governments. A specially equipped version has been delivered for police duties.
TYPE: Side by side two-seat, dual-control homebuilt.

AIRFRAME: Wings have extruded spars of aluminium alloy tubing, plywood ribs and drooped glassfibre tips, with Stits Poly-Fiber covering overall. Steel tube fuselage and tail unit, with Poly-Fiber covering. Non-retractable tailwheel landing gear. Optional floats, skis and under-fuselage cargo pod.
POWER PLANT: One 38.8 kW (52 hp) Rotax 503, 47.7 kW (64 hp) Rotax 532 or 46 kW (62 hp) KFM 112. Fuel capacity 37 litres (9.75 US gallons; 8.1 Imp gallons) standard. Two wing tanks optional; total capacity 45 litres (12 US gallons; 10 Imp gallons).

DIMENSIONS, EXTERNAL:
Wing span	9.55 m (31 ft 4 in)
Length overall	5.21 m (17 ft 1 in)
Height overall	1.70 m (5 ft 7 in)
Propeller diameter	1.63 m (5 ft 4 in)

AREA:
Wings, gross	11.92 m² (128.3 sq ft)

WEIGHTS:
Weight empty	177 kg (390 lb)
Pilot weight range	68-113 kg (150-250 lb)
Max recommended pilot and passenger weight	
	181 kg (400 lb)
Max T-O weight	431 kg (950 lb)

PERFORMANCE (two crew, Rotax 503 engine, at 385 kg; 850 lb AUW unless stated otherwise):
Cruising speed	65-69 knots (121-129 km/h; 75-80 mph)
Stalling speed	28 knots (52 km/h; 32 mph)
Max rate of climb at S/L	302 m (990 ft)/min
Service ceiling	6,100 m (20,000 ft)
T-O run	61-69 m (200-225 ft)
Landing run	46-61 m (150-200 ft)
Range with max fuel, 70% power, pilot only	
	239 nm (442 km; 275 miles)
Endurance, pilot only	approx 3 h
g limits, pilot only	+6/−3

DIEHL

DIEHL AERO-NAUTICAL

1855 North Elm, Jenks, Oklahoma 74037
Telephone: (918) 299 4445
PRESIDENT: Dan Diehl

DIEHL XTC HYDROLIGHT

The prototype XTC flew for the first time in March 1982. Production of kits began a year later.
TYPE: Single-seat microlight or homebuilt landplane or amphibian; conforms to FAR Pt 103 as microlight.
AIRFRAME: Wings, foreplane, fins and rudders of graphite and epoxy, with Mylar, Tedlar or fabric covering. Stabilising floats integral with wingtips. Glassfibre fuselage. Optional cockpit enclosure. Three-axis control. Retractable tricycle landing gear.
POWER PLANT: One 18.6 kW (25 hp) 294 cc KFM 107ER, 20 kW (27 hp) Rotax 277 or 32 kW (43 hp) Rotax 447. Fuel capacity 19 litres (5 US gallons; 4.2 Imp gallons); 38 litres (10 US gallons; 8.3 Imp gallons) optional.

DIMENSIONS, EXTERNAL:
Wing span	9.75 m (32 ft 0 in)
Length overall	4.62 m (15 ft 2 in)
Height overall	1.45 m (4 ft 9 in)
Propeller diameter	1.32 m (4 ft 4 in)

AREA:
Wings, gross	13.66 m² (147.0 sq ft)

WEIGHTS:
Weight empty	136 kg (300 lb)
Pilot weight range	45-90 kg (100-200 lb)
Baggage capacity	4.5 kg (10 lb)
Max T-O weight	254 kg (560 lb)

PERFORMANCE (KFM 107 engine, unless otherwise stated):
Max level speed	52 knots (97 km/h; 60 mph)
Econ cruising speed	39 knots (72 km/h; 45 mph)
Stalling speed	24 knots (44 km/h; 27 mph)
Max rate of climb at S/L	152 m (500 ft)/min
Service ceiling	3,110 m (10,200 ft)
T-O and landing distance:	
land and water	61 m (200 ft)
Range with standard fuel	130 nm (241 km; 150 miles)
Endurance with standard fuel	2 h 30 min
g limits	±4

DURAND

DURAND ASSOCIATES INC

84th and McKinley Road, Omaha, Nebraska 68122
Telephone: (402) 571 7058

DURAND Mk V

The prototype Durand Mk V flew for the first time on 28 June 1978. Plans are available to amateur builders, and 79 sets had been sold by early 1988.
TYPE: Two-seat, dual-control homebuilt biplane.
AIRFRAME: All-metal (light alloy) construction, with negative wing stagger. Wing section NACA 23012. Non-retractable tricycle landing gear.

POWER PLANT: One 112 kW (150 hp) Textron Lycoming O-320-E2A. Fuel capacity 93 litres (24.5 US gallons; 20.4 Imp gallons). Two auxiliary wing tanks optional, each 15 litres (4 US gallons; 3.33 Imp gallons).

DIMENSIONS, EXTERNAL:
Wing span, both	7.47 m (24 ft 6 in)
Length overall	6.17 m (20 ft 3 in)
Height overall	2.03 m (6 ft 8 in)
Propeller diameter	1.83 m (6 ft 0 in)

AREA:
Wings, gross	13.38 m² (144.0 sq ft)

WEIGHTS:
Weight empty	549 kg (1,210 lb)
Baggage capacity	58 kg (128 lb)
Max T-O weight	834 kg (1,840 lb)

PERFORMANCE (at max T-O weight):
Max cruising speed at 2,285 m (7,500 ft)	
	117 knots (217 km/h; 135 mph)
Econ cruising speed at 2,285 m (7,500 ft)	
	109 knots (201 km/h; 125 mph)
Max rate of climb at S/L	366 m (1,200 ft)/min
Absolute ceiling, estimated	4,575 m (15,000 ft)
T-O run	168 m (550 ft)
Landing run	137 m (450 ft)
Range, no reserves:	
standard fuel	347 nm (644 km; 400 miles)
max optional fuel	451 nm (837 km; 520 miles)

DYKE

DYKE AIRCRAFT

2840 Old Yellow Springs Road, Fairborn, Ohio 45324
Telephone: (513) 878 9832
DESIGNER: John W. Dyke

DYKE AIRCRAFT JD-2 DELTA

Plans of the JD-2 are available to amateur constructors, and a total of about 360 were thought to be under construction in early 1988. Hardware and tubing kits are available.
TYPE: Delta-winged four-seat homebuilt.
AIRFRAME: Delta wing of modified NACA 63012 and 66015 section. Wings, fuselage and tail unit have welded steel tube structures. Wings use stainless steel capstrips to which laminated glassfibre skins are secured by pop rivets (optional aluminium skins). Fuselage similar except for steel tube capstrips and Poly-Fiber covering on undersurface. Elevons and tail unit Poly-Fiber covered. Optional all-moving T tail of all-metal construction for improved low-speed trim with heavier engine. Retractable tricycle landing gear.
POWER PLANT: Prototype has one 134 kW (180 hp) Textron Lycoming O-360. 149 kW (200 hp) engine installation optional. Fuel capacity 178 litres (47 US gallons; 39.1 Imp gallons), with pilot and two passengers. Fuel capacity reduced to 117 litres (31 US gallons; 26 Imp gallons) as a four-seat aircraft.

DIMENSIONS, EXTERNAL:
Wing span	6.87 m (22 ft 2½ in)
Length overall	5.79 m (19 ft 0 in)
Height overall	1.68 m (5 ft 6 in)
Propeller diameter	1.88 m (6 ft 2 in)

AREA:
Wings, gross	16.07 m² (173.0 sq ft)

WEIGHTS (with 134 kW; 180 hp or 149 kW; 200 hp engine):
Weight empty: basic equipped	481 kg (1,060 lb)
IFR equipped	490 kg (1,080 lb)
Baggage capacity	45.4 kg (100 lb)
Max T-O weight	884 kg (1,950 lb)

PERFORMANCE (at max T-O weight with 134 kW; 180 hp engine, except where indicated):

Prototype D'Apuzzo D-201 Sportwing, built by Mr Larry Stangil of Ferndale, Pennsylvania

Diehl XTC Hydrolight *(Ernest Koppe)*

Davis DA-7, intended for FAA certification *(Howard Levy)*

Durand Mk V all-metal two-seat biplane *(Howard Levy)*

Davis Wing *Starship Alpha* flying wing *(Jim Borchers)*

Modified Dyke Delta built by Mr Bernie Schaknowski (Textron Lycoming O-360 engine) *(Peter M. Bowers)*

Denney Kitfox with Rotax 532 engine and twin floats

Unfinished prototype of the Eagle Wings Jaeger *(Howard Levy)*

Max level speed at 2,285 m (7,500 ft), constant-speed propeller	174 knots (322 km/h; 200 mph)	Max rate of climb at S/L	610 m (2,000 ft)/min	Range: with max fuel and pilot only, at 66% power

Max level speed at 2,285 m (7,500 ft), constant-speed propeller   174 knots (322 km/h; 200 mph)
Econ cruising speed at 2,285 m (7,500 ft)   135 knots (249 km/h; 155 mph)

Max rate of climb at S/L   610 m (2,000 ft)/min
Service ceiling   4,420 m (14,500 ft)
T-O run   213 m (700 ft)
Landing run   244-305 m (800-1,000 ft)

Range: with max fuel and pilot only, at 66% power   755 nm (1,400 km; 870 miles)
with max payload   576 nm (1,067 km; 663 miles)

EAGLE WINGS
EAGLE WINGS AIRCRAFT CORPORATION
3939 Perimeter Road, Boca Raton, Florida 33431
Telephone: (305) 391 4895

EAGLE WINGS JAEGER
The Jaeger offers performances ranging from high speed to motor gliding. This is achieved by the use of plug-in wing

extensions, enabling a 7.32 m (24 ft) 'docile' wing to be used by inexperienced pilots, a 4.88 m (16 ft) wing by those wishing to achieve high performance, and a 9.75 m (32 ft) wing for motor gliding. Kits will become available.
TYPE: Single-seat homebuilt/motor glider.
AIRFRAME: All-aluminium alloy wings, except for glassfibre tips. Wing section Wortmann FX 67-K 170. Wing extensions 'plug in' between standard wing centre-section

and wingtips. Welded steel tube mounting within the composites fuselage supports wings and engine. Folding twin-boom tail unit. Non-retractable tricycle landing gear.
POWER PLANT: One 48.5 kW (65 hp) Rotax 532LC. Fuel capacity 64 litres (17 US gallons; 14.2 Imp gallons).
DIMENSIONS, EXTERNAL (A: 16 ft span, B: 24 ft span, C: 32 ft span motor glider):

Wing span: A	4.88 m (16 ft 0 in)	WEIGHTS (A, B, C as above):	Cruising speed: A	188 knots (349 km/h; 217 mph)
B	7.32 m (24 ft 0 in)	Weight empty: A	125 kg (275 lb)	B	166 knots (307 km/h; 191 mph)
C	9.75 m (32 ft 0 in)	B	134 kg (295 lb)	C	150 knots (278 km/h; 173 mph)
Length overall: A, B, C	3.92 m (12 ft 10½ in)	C	143 kg (315 lb)	Stalling speed: A	59 knots (110 km/h; 68 mph)
Height overall: A, B, C	1.19 m (3 ft 11 in)	Max T-O weight: A, B, C	261 kg (575 lb)	B	48 knots (89 km/h; 55 mph)
AREAS (A, B, C as above):		PERFORMANCE (A, B, C as above, calculated):	C	42 knots (78 km/h; 48 mph)
Wings, gross: A	2.87 m² (30.9 sq ft)	Max level speed: A	206 knots (381 km/h; 237 mph)	g limits: A	+ 15
B	4.38 m² (47.125 sq ft)	B	181 knots (336 km/h; 209 mph)	B	+ 9
C	5.86 m² (63.125 sq ft)	C	166 knots (307 km/h; 191 mph)	C	+ 6

EARTHSTAR
EARTHSTAR AIRCRAFT INC
1615-JA Parkhill Road, Santa Margarita, California 93453
Telephone: (805) 438 5235
DESIGNER AND PRESIDENT: Mark H. Beierle

EARTHSTAR LAUGHING GULL and LAUGHING GULL II
The first of five prototype Laughing Gulls flew in 1976. The single-seat model is available in ready assembled **LG1** form with a Rotax 277 engine, or as an **LG1H** microlight or homebuilt kit with engine options of up to 30 kW (40 hp). The two-seat **T2** Laughing Gull II is fitted with dual controls as a trainer, and **T2H** homebuilt kits are available with engine options of up to 47 kW (63 hp). A cropduster model is also available. Construction time is estimated at 160-190 working hours for the LG1H, and 180-250 for the T2H.

TYPES: Single-seat (Laughing Gull) and two-seat (Laughing Gull II) single-engined microlight and homebuilt aircraft; conform to FAR Pt 103/7 in LG1 and T2 forms and FAA Experimental requirements in LG1H and T2H homebuilt forms.

AIRFRAME: Welded steel tube fuselage; fully enclosed cockpit with glassfibre nosecone. Airframe structure, other than fuselage, of aluminium alloy. Double surface wings with Dacron covering. Three-axis control. Non-retractable tricycle, or optionally tailwheel, landing gear.

POWER PLANT: *Laughing Gull:* standard engine is 20 kW (27 hp) Rotax 277. Homebuilt version can have engine of up to 30 kW (40 hp). Fuel capacity 38 litres (10 US gallons; 8.3 Imp gallons). *Laughing Gull II:* standard engine is 47 kW (63 hp) Rotax 532. *Homebuilt version* can have engine of up to 47 kW (63 hp). Optional engines include a conversion of the Honda Civic motorcar engine, or a Chevrolet Sprint. Fuel capacity 38 litres (10 US gallons; 8.3 Imp gallons).

DIMENSIONS, EXTERNAL (A: LG1 and B: T2):
Wing span: A	9.14 m (30 ft 0 in)
B	9.75 m (32 ft 0 in)
Length overall: A	5.72 m (18 ft 9 in)
B	6.10 m (20 ft 0 in)
Height overall: A	2.13 m (7 ft 0 in)
B	2.29 m (7 ft 6 in)
Propeller diameter: A	1.52 m (5 ft 0 in)

AREAS (A and B as above):
Wings, gross: A	13.94 m² (150.0 sq ft)
B	14.86 m² (160.0 sq ft)

WEIGHTS (A and B as above):
Weight empty: A	113 kg (250 lb)
B	156.5 kg (345 lb)
Max T-O weight: A	227 kg (500 lb)
B	363 kg (800 lb)

PERFORMANCE (A: LG1, B: T2H, unless stated otherwise):
Max level speed: A	55 knots (101 km/h; 63 mph)
B	91 knots (169 km/h; 105 mph)
Cruising speed:	
A	48-52 knots (89-97 km/h; 55-60 mph)
B	74-78 knots (137-145 km/h; 85-90 mph)
Stalling speed: A	22 knots (41 km/h; 25 mph)
B	28 knots (52 km/h; 32 mph)
Max rate of climb at S/L: A	274 m (900 ft)/min
B	244 m (800 ft)/min
Service ceiling: A, B	4,420 m (14,500 ft)
T-O run: A	30 m (100 ft)
B	55 m (180 ft)
Landing run: A	30 m (100 ft)
B	61 m (200 ft)
Range with max fuel: A	132 nm (244 km; 152 miles)
g limits: A, B	+6/-4
Laughing Gull homebuilt	+7/-5
Laughing Gull II	+5.5/-3.8

EARTHSTAR ULTRA GULL
The Ultra Gull has a special arrangement of high lift devices allowing it to be so small that no rigging is necessary before flying (as it is trailered fully assembled). The tandem wing and vertical stabiliser arrangement controls the wingtip vortices, giving the aircraft extra stability and better performance.

Two versions are available: the basic ready assembled Ultra Gull **U1** microlight, with conventional three-axis control and a 20 kW (27 hp) Rotax 277 engine; and the kit-built Ultra Gull Homebuilt **U1H** with any Rotax engine of 20-44.7 kW (27-60 hp).

TYPES: U1: Single-seat microlight. U1H: Single-seat homebuilt.

AIRFRAME: Aluminium skinned wings, with tubular spar and foam core. Welded steel fuselage. Three-axis control. Landing gear as for Laughing Gull.

POWER PLANT: See introduction. U1 fuel capacity 19 litres (5 US gallons; 4.2 Imp gallons); U1H 38 litres (10 US gallons; 8.4 Imp gallons).

DIMENSIONS, EXTERNAL (A: U1, B: U1H):
Wing span: A	7.32 m (24 ft 0 in)
B	6.10 m (20 ft 0 in)
Length overall: A, B	3.20 m (10 ft 6 in)
Height overall: A, B	1.83 m (6 ft 0 in)
Propeller diameter: A	1.52 m (5 ft 0 in)
B	1.47 m (4 ft 10 in)

AREAS (A: U1, B: U1H):
Wings, gross: A	11.15 m² (120.0 sq ft)
B	9.29 m² (100.0 sq ft)

WEIGHTS (A: U1, B: U1H):
Weight empty: A	102 kg (225 lb)
B	more than 105 kg (232 lb)
Max pilot weight: A, B	100 kg (220 lb)
Max T-O weight: A, B	227 kg (500 lb)

PERFORMANCE (A: U1, B: U1H with 44.7 kW; 60 hp engine):
Max level speed: A	55 knots (101 km/h; 63 mph)
B	130 knots (241 km/h; 150 mph)
Cruising speed: A	52 knots (97 km/h; 60 mph)
B	122 knots (225 km/h; 140 mph)
Stalling speed: A	24 knots (44 km/h; 27 mph)
B	28 knots (52 km/h; 32 mph)
Max rate of climb at S/L: A	274 m (900 ft)/min
B	472 m (1,550 ft)/min
Service ceiling: A, B	4,420 m (14,500 ft)
T-O run: A	31 m (100 ft)
B	43 m (140 ft)
Landing run: A	37 m (120 ft)
B	40 m (130 ft)
Range with max fuel:	
A	over 147 nm (273 km; 170 miles)
B	over 260 nm (482 km; 300 miles)
g limits: A, B	±6

EBERSHOFF
EBERSHOFF AND COMPANY
Irongate IV, 777 South Wadsworth Boulevard, Suite 206, Lakewood, Colorado 80226
Telephone: (303) 980 8686

EBERSHOFF-STEEN SKYBOLT
Plans for this modified version of the Steen Skybolt are available to amateur constructors, and many thousands have been sold.

TYPE: Tandem two-seat aerobatic homebuilt biplane.

AIRFRAME: Fabric covered wooden symmetrical wings and ailerons (upper and lower wings). Wing sections: upper NACA 63₂A015, lower NACA 0012. Welded steel tube fuselage and tail unit, with fabric covering. Non-retractable tailwheel landing gear.

POWER PLANT: One 268.5 kW (360 hp) Textron Lycoming IO-540-C. Fuel capacity 110 litres (29 US gallons; 24.1 Imp gallons). Optional tank of 37.8 litres (10 US gallons; 8.3 Imp gallons) capacity in centre-section of upper wing.

DIMENSIONS, EXTERNAL:
Wing span: upper	7.32 m (24 ft 0 in)
lower	7.01 m (23 ft 0 in)
Length overall	5.79 m (19 ft 0 in)
Height overall	2.13 m (7 ft 0 in)
Propeller diameter	2.13 m (7 ft 0 in)

AREA:
Wings, gross	14.2 m² (152.7 sq ft)

WEIGHTS:
Weight empty	612 kg (1,350 lb)
Baggage capacity	13.6 kg (30 lb)
Max T-O weight	907 kg (2,000 lb)

PERFORMANCE (at max T-O weight):
Max level speed	191 knots (354 km/h; 220 mph)
Cruising speed	143 knots (265 km/h; 165 mph)
Max rate of climb at S/L	975 m (3,200 ft)/min
T-O run	134 m (440 ft)
Range with max fuel	325 nm (603 km; 375 miles)
g limits	±12

EICH
JAMES P. EICH
1820 W Grand Avenue, Alhambra, California 91801
Telephone: (818) 289 1983

EICH JE-2 GYROPLANE
The prototype JE-2 first flew in 1977. Detailed drawings and instructions for building the aircraft are available from: Tech Man Company, 8525 E Duarte Road, San Gabriel, California 91775. At least 40 sets of plans have been sold.

The following details apply specifically to the prototype:

TYPE: Tandem two-seat, dual-control light autogyro.

ROTOR SYSTEM: Two-blade aluminium teetering rotor, with pre-rotation system.

AIRFRAME: Square section welded steel-tube girder fuselage, covered with Dacron. Dacron fin integral with fuselage covering. Stabiliser and rudder of sheet aluminium. Non-retractable tricycle landing gear.

POWER PLANT: One 63.5 kW (85 hp) Continental C85 engine. Optional engines from A65 to O-200. Fuel capacity 64.5 litres (17 US gallons; 14.2 Imp gallons).

DIMENSIONS, EXTERNAL:
Main rotor diameter	7.92 m (26 ft 0 in)
Length of fuselage	4.27 m (14 ft 0 in)
Height overall	2.59 m (8 ft 6 in)
Propeller diameter	1.78 m (5 ft 10 in)

WEIGHTS:
Weight empty	211 kg (465 lb)
Max T-O weight	417 kg (920 lb)

PERFORMANCE (with current rotor blades):
Max level speed at 915 m (3,000 ft)	70 knots (129 km/h; 80 mph)
Econ cruising speed at 915 m (3,000 ft)	48 knots (89 km/h; 55 mph)
Min flying speed (no stall)	39 knots (73 km/h; 45 mph)
Max rate of climb at 915 m (3,000 ft)	91.5 m (300 ft)/min
T-O run with pre-rotation	153 m (500 ft)
Landing run	15 m (50 ft)
Range with max fuel and max payload	156 nm (290 km; 180 miles)

EIPPER
EIPPER INDUSTRIES
PO Box 1572, 42143 Avenita Alvarado, Temecula, California 92390
Telephone: (714) 676 6886
Telex: 499 0565
PRESIDENT: Lyle Byrum

EIPPER QUICKSILVER
The most recent known variants of the Quicksilver are as follows:

Quicksilver MXL. Three-axis microlight, introduced in 1983.

Quicksilver MXL II. Side by side two-seat version of MXL. Wing area increased to 15.42 m² (166 sq ft).

The following data apply to the MXL.

TYPE: Single-seat microlight; conforms to FAR Pt 103 and FAI requirements.

AIRFRAME: Framework of anodised aluminium alloy tubing. Dacron covered wings (double surface), elevator and rudder. Non-retractable tricycle landing gear. Skis, floats, amphibious gear and nose fairing optional.

POWER PLANT: One 26 kW (35 hp) Rotax 337. Fuel capacity 19 litres (5 US gallons; 4.2 Imp gallons).

DIMENSIONS, EXTERNAL:
Wing span	9.14 m (30 ft 0 in)
Length overall	5.51 m (18 ft 1 in)
Height overall	2.95 m (9 ft 8 in)
Propeller diameter	1.32 m (4 ft 4 in)

Earthstar Laughing Gull II built by Mr Danny Romo *(John Wegg)*

Eich JE-2 Gyroplane (Continental C85 engine) with pre-rotation gear fitted

Earthstar Ultra Gull microlight aircraft

Ebershoff-Steen Skybolt with a rear cockpit canopy *(Dr Dean Hall)*

Eipper Quicksilver GT with optional cockpit enclosure *(Geoffrey P. Jones)*

Eipper Quicksilver MXL with optional pilot fairing and wheel fairings

AREAS:
Wings, gross: MXL	13.94 m² (150.0 sq ft)
MXL II	15.42 m² (166.0 sq ft)

WEIGHTS:
Weight empty	112 kg (247 lb)
Pilot weight range	54-109 kg (120-240 lb)
Max T-O weight	249 kg (550 lb)

PERFORMANCE (with 79.5 kg; 175 lb pilot):
Max level speed	53 knots (98 km/h; 61 mph)
Econ cruising speed	36 knots (66 km/h; 41 mph)
Stalling speed, power off	24 knots (44 km/h; 27 mph)
Max rate of climb at S/L	259 m (850 ft)/min
Service ceiling	3,050 m (10,000 ft)
T-O and landing run	23 m (75 ft)
Range with max fuel	99 nm (183 km; 114 miles)
Endurance with max fuel	2 h 43 min
g limits	+6/-3.8

EIPPER QUICKSILVER GT

The Quicksilver GT, despite its name, is an entirely new aircraft that was introduced in 1984. The current **GT400** model is available in 'C' and 'S' forms, with cable or strut bracing respectively. It has Dacron covered wings, with ailerons and four-position flaps. The single-boom fuselage is a two-piece 13 cm (5 in) diameter aluminium tube. A glassfibre nose 'bullet' is standard; options include a wraparound fuselage pod or a full cockpit enclosure. The GT400C and S are available in kit and ready assembled forms. Kit assembly time is approximately 70-80 hours.

The following data apply to the GT400S:

POWER PLANT: One 38 kW (51 hp) Rotax 462. Fuel capacity 19 litres (5 US gallons; 4.2 Imp gallons).

DIMENSIONS, EXTERNAL:
Wing span	9.14 m (30 ft 0 in)
Length overall	6.20 m (20 ft 4 in)
Height overall	2.39 m (7 ft 10 in)
Propeller diameter	1.52 m (5 ft 0 in)

AREA:
Wings, gross	13.56 m² (146.0 sq ft)

WEIGHTS:
Weight empty	139 kg (306 lb)
Max T-O weight	259 kg (570 lb)

PERFORMANCE:
Max level speed	51 knots (96 km/h; 60 mph)
Max cruising speed	48 knots (88 km/h; 55 mph)
Stalling speed, flaps down, power off	24 knots (44 km/h; 27 mph)
Max rate of climb at S/L	305 m (1,000 ft)/min
g limits	+4/-2 design

EVANS

EVANS AIRCRAFT

PO Box 744, La Jolla, California 92037

Designed for easy building and safety to fly, the single-seat Evans VP-1 and two-seat VP-2 are available in plans form. Approximately 4,000 sets of drawings had been sold by early 1988. Those for European customers are supplied through the Popular Flying Association (PFA) in the UK (which see).

EVANS VP-1

TYPE: Single-seat homebuilt.

AIRFRAME: Virtually all-wood structure, with fabric covered wings and tail unit, and plywood covered fuselage with glassfibre fairing aft of pilot's seat. Wing section NACA 4412. Non-retractable tailskid landing gear. Enclosed cockpit optional.

POWER PLANT: One 30 kW, 39.5 kW or 44.5 kW (40 hp, 53 hp or 60 hp) modified Volkswagen motorcar engine. Fuel capacity 30 litres (8 US gallons; 6.7 Imp gallons).

DIMENSIONS, EXTERNAL:
Wing span	7.32 m (24 ft 0 in)
Length overall	5.49 m (18 ft 0 in)
Height overall	1.56 m (5 ft 1½ in)
Propeller diameter	1.37 m (4 ft 6 in)

AREA:
Wings, gross	9.29 m² (100.0 sq ft)

WEIGHTS:
Weight empty	200 kg (440 lb)
Max T-O weight	340 kg (750 lb)

PERFORMANCE (30 kW; 40 hp engine, at T-O weight of 295 kg; 650 lb):

Cruising speed	65 knots (121 km/h; 75 mph)
Stalling speed	35 knots (65 km/h; 40 mph)
Max rate of climb at S/L	122 m (400 ft)/min
T-O run (average breeze)	137 m (450 ft)
Landing run (average breeze)	61 m (200 ft)

EVANS VP-2

Except for an increase in overall dimensions, two seats side by side, and adoption of a higher rated Volkswagen engine as standard, the basic VP-2 is generally similar to the VP-1.
TYPE: Two-seat homebuilt.
AIRFRAME: NACA 4415 wing section. Fuselage width increased by 0.305 m (1 ft 0 in).
POWER PLANT: One 44.5 kW (60 hp) 1,834 cc or 48.5 kW (65 hp) 2,100 cc modified Volkswagen motorcar engine. Fuel capacity 53 litres (14 US gallons; 11.7 Imp gallons).
DIMENSIONS, EXTERNAL:

Wing span	8.23 m (27 ft 0 in)
Length overall	5.87 m (19 ft 3 in)
Propeller diameter	1.52 m (5 ft 0 in)

AREA:

Wings, gross	12.08 m² (130.0 sq ft)

WEIGHTS:

Weight empty	290 kg (640 lb)
Max T-O weight	471 kg (1,040 lb)

PERFORMANCE (44.5 kW; 60 hp engine, at max T-O weight):

Max level speed	87 knots (161 km/h; 100 mph)
Max cruising speed	65 knots (121 km/h; 75 mph)
Stalling speed	35 knots (65 km/h; 40 mph)
Max rate of climb at S/L:	
pilot only	213 m (700 ft)/min
pilot and passenger	122 m (400 ft)/min

FIRST STRIKE
FIRST STRIKE AVIATION INC
4 Wade Avenue, Piggott, Arkansas 72454
Telephone: (501) 598 5126
PRESIDENT: Bobby Baker

FIRST STRIKE BOBCAT and SUPER CAT
The first flight of the prototype Bobcat was achieved in May 1984. Kits and plans are available, together with those for the Experimental and stronger Super Cat. Estimated building time of a Bobcat and Super Cat is 150-200 and 300 working hours respectively. Individual component parts are available to builders using plans only.
TYPES: Single-seat microlight (Bobcat) and homebuilt (Super Cat) aircraft.
AIRFRAME: Fuselage uses spruce longerons and plywood bulkheads, the wings have spruce capped foam ribs with plywood D section leading-edges, all Ceconite 7600 fabric covered. Glassfibre engine cowling. Non-retractable tailwheel landing gear.
POWER PLANT: *Bobcat:* one 20 kW (27 hp) Rotax 277. *Super Cat:* one 26 kW (35 hp) Rotax 377; optional Rotax 447. Fuel capacity 19 litres (5 US gallons; 4.2 Imp gallons) in Bobcat, 30 litres (8 US gallons; 6.66 Imp gallons) in Super Cat.
DIMENSIONS, EXTERNAL:

Wing span	8.43 m (27 ft 8 in)
Length overall	4.65 m (15 ft 3 in)
Height overall	1.83 m (6 ft 0 in)
Propeller diameter: Bobcat	1.52 m (5 ft 0 in)
Super Cat	1.73 m (5 ft 8 in)

AREAS:

Wings, gross: Bobcat	10.41 m² (112.0 sq ft)
Super Cat	11.15 m² (120.0 sq ft)

WEIGHTS (A: Bobcat, B: Super Cat):

Weight empty: A	114 kg (251 lb)
B	150 kg (330 lb)

Max T-O weight: A	226 kg (500 lb)
B	283 kg (625 lb)

PERFORMANCE (A: Bobcat, B: Super Cat):

Max level speed: A	55 knots (101 km/h; 63 mph)
B	74 knots (137 km/h; 85 mph)
Max cruising speed:	
A	39-43 knots (72-80 km/h; 45-50 mph)
B	56 knots (105 km/h; 65 mph)
Stalling speed: A	24 knots (44 km/h; 27 mph)
B	32 knots (60 km/h; 37 mph)
Max rate of climb at S/L: A	213 m (700 ft)/min
B	259 m (850 ft)/min
T-O run: A	38 m (125 ft)
B	23 m (75 ft)
Landing run: A	61 m (200 ft)
g limits: A	±4
B	+5.5/−4.5

FISHER
FISHER FLYING PRODUCTS INC
Route 2, Box 282, South Webster, Ohio 45682
Telephone: (614) 778 3185
PRESIDENT: Michael E. Fisher

Fisher Flying Products markets full and partial kits and prefabricated subassemblies for each aircraft listed except the Culex, which is marketed by its Aero Visions International subsidiary. All use geodetic construction except the Culex.

FISHER FLYING PRODUCTS FP-101
First flown in mid-1982, the FP-101 kit takes 200-250 working hours to assemble.
TYPE: Single-seat microlight; conforms to FAR Pt 103.
AIRFRAME: Moulded glassfibre engine cowling. Rest of structure of geodetic wood construction, covered with doped Stits Poly-Fiber fabric (double surface on wings). Three-axis control. Non-retractable tailwheel landing gear.
POWER PLANT: One 20 kW (27 hp) Rotax 277. Fuel capacity 19 litres (5 US gallons; 4.2 Imp gallons).
DIMENSIONS, EXTERNAL:

Wing span	8.79 m (28 ft 10 in)
Length overall	5.03 m (16 ft 6 in)
Height overall	1.73 m (5 ft 8 in)
Propeller diameter	1.52 m (5 ft 0 in)

AREA:

Wings, gross	10.78 m² (116.0 sq ft)

WEIGHTS:

Weight empty	109-113 kg (240-250 lb)
Pilot weight range	45.5-100 kg (100-220 lb)
Max T-O weight	227 kg (500 lb)

PERFORMANCE (Rotax 277 engine):

Max level speed	52 knots (97 km/h; 60 mph)
Econ cruising speed	43 knots (80 km/h; 50 mph)
Stalling speed	23 knots (42 km/h; 26 mph)
Max rate of climb at S/L	183-213 m (600-700 ft)/min
T-O run	46 m (150 ft)
Landing run	38 m (125 ft)
Range with max fuel	130 nm (241 km; 150 miles)
Endurance with max fuel	3 h
g limits	+4.6/−2.3

FISHER FLYING PRODUCTS FP-202 KOALA
Except for having rounded tail surfaces and wing flaps, the FP-202 Koala is generally similar to the FP-101. In addition to kits, it is available in ready assembled form.
The FP-202 can, optionally, be completed with a pre-welded steel tube fuselage. In other respects, the description of the FP-101 applies equally to the FP-202. Assembly time, depending on the form of construction chosen, is 125-300 working hours.
DIMENSIONS, EXTERNAL:

Wing span	8.84 m (29 ft 10 in)
Length overall	5.41 m (17 ft 9 in)
Height overall	1.70 m (5 ft 7 in)

AREA:

Wings, gross	11.15 m² (120.0 sq ft)

WEIGHTS:

Weight empty	109-113 kg (240-250 lb)
Max T-O weight	227 kg (500 lb)

PERFORMANCE:

Max cruising speed	52 knots (97 km/h; 60 mph)
Econ cruising speed	48 knots (89 km/h; 55 mph)
Stalling speed:	
power on	23 knots (42 km/h; 26 mph)
power off	21 knots (39 km/h; 24 mph)
Max rate of climb at S/L	213-244 m (700-800 ft)/min
T-O run	46 m (150 ft)
Landing run	38 m (125 ft)
Range with max fuel	143 nm (265 km; 165 miles)
Endurance with max fuel	3 h
g limits	+4.6/−2.3

FISHER FLYING PRODUCTS SUPER KOALA
This larger and higher-powered two-seat variant of the Koala flew for the first time in the Spring of 1984. The standard kit takes about 400 working hours to complete; a quick-build kit requires only 150-200 working hours due to the large number of factory prefabricated components. Like the FP-202, the Super Koala can be fitted optionally with a pre-welded chrome-molybdenum steel tube fuselage.
The description of the FP-101 applies generally to the Super Koala, except as follows:
TYPE: Side by side two-seat, dual-control STOL microlight; has training exemption to FAR Pt 103 and conforms to Canadian regulations.
AIRFRAME: High-lift wing with flaps, and wider fuselage.
POWER PLANT: One 38.8 kW (52 hp) Rotax 503 or, optionally, one 47.7 kW; 64 hp Rotax 532. Fuel capacity 30 litres (8 US gallons; 6.66 Imp gallons). Auxiliary tank can be carried, of up to 19 litres (5 US gallons; 4.2 Imp gallons) capacity.
DIMENSIONS, EXTERNAL:

Wing span	9.45 m (31 ft 0 in)
Length overall	5.51 m (18 ft 1 in)
Height overall	1.70 m (5 ft 7 in)
Propeller diameter	1.83 m (6 ft 0 in)

AREA:

Wings, gross	13.0 m² (140.0 sq ft)

WEIGHTS:

Weight empty	147-152 kg (325-335 lb)
Pilot weight range	45.5-163 kg (100-360 lb)
Max T-O weight	335 kg (740 lb)

PERFORMANCE:

Max level speed	69 knots (129 km/h; 80 mph)
Econ cruising speed	48 knots (88 km/h; 55 mph)
Stalling speed: power on	26 knots (49 km/h; 30 mph)
power off	28 knots (52 km/h; 32 mph)
Max rate of climb at S/L	244 m (800 ft)/min
T-O run	61 m (200 ft)
Landing run	76 m (250 ft)
Range with max standard fuel	126 nm (233 km; 145 miles)
Endurance	2 h
g limits	+4.6/−2.3

FISHER FLYING PRODUCTS FP-303
The FP-303 first flew in January 1984.
TYPE: Single-seat low-wing microlight; conforms to FAR Pt 103 and FAI/CAA regulations.
AIRFRAME: Dacron covered wooden structure, with geodetic rear fuselage. Three-axis control, plus flaps. Non-retractable tailwheel landing gear.
POWER PLANT: One 20 kW (27 hp) Rotax 277. Fuel capacity 9.5 litres (2.5 US gallons; 2.1 Imp gallons). Optional 9.5 litre (2.5 US gallon; 2.1 Imp gallon) auxiliary tank.
DIMENSIONS, EXTERNAL:

Wing span	8.43 m (27 ft 8 in)
Length overall	5.03 m (16 ft 6 in)
Height overall	1.57 m (5 ft 2 in)
Propeller diameter	1.52 m (5 ft 0 in)

AREA:

Wings, gross	10.3 m² (111.0 sq ft)

WEIGHTS:

Weight empty	104-109 kg (230-240 lb)
Pilot weight range	45.5-95 kg (100-210 lb)
Max T-O weight	204 kg (450 lb)

PERFORMANCE:

Max cruising speed	52 knots (97 km/h; 60 mph)
Econ cruising speed	48 knots (89 km/h; 55 mph)
Stalling speed, flaps down	22 knots (41 km/h; 25 mph)
Max rate of climb at S/L	213-244 m (700-800 ft)/min
Service ceiling	3,350 m (11,000 ft)
T-O run	38 m (125 ft)
Landing run	40 m (130 ft)
Range with max standard fuel	72 nm (133 km; 83 miles)
Endurance	1 h 30 min
g limits	+4.6/−2.3

FISHER FLYING PRODUCTS FP-404 CLASSIC
This single-seat biplane has a geodetic wooden fuselage and wings (semi-symmetrical section), all fabric covered, three-axis control, and tailwheel landing gear. Either a 35.8 kW (48 hp) Rotax 503 or a 47.7 kW (64 hp) Rotax 532 engine can be fitted to the homebuilt version, or a 20 kW (27 hp) Rotax 277 to the microlight model. All use a 19 litre (5 US gallon; 4.2 Imp gallon) fuel tank. Construction takes 250-300 working hours.
DIMENSIONS, EXTERNAL:

Wing span	5.49 m (18 ft 0 in)
Length overall	4.42 m (14 ft 6 in)
Height overall	1.65 m (5 ft 5 in)

AREA:

Wings, gross	11.15 m² (120.0 sq ft)

WEIGHTS (A: microlight, B: homebuilt):

Weight empty: A	104-109 kg (230-240 lb)
B	122-127 kg (270-280 lb)
Max T-O weight: A	213 kg (470 lb)
B	245 kg (540 lb)

PERFORMANCE (A and B as above):

Max cruising speed: A	52 knots (97 km/h; 60 mph)
B	70 knots (128 km/h; 80 mph)
Econ cruising speed: A	48 knots (89 km/h; 55 mph)
B	52 knots (97 km/h; 60 mph)
Stalling speed: A	24 knots (44 km/h; 27 mph)
B	26 knots (49 km/h; 30 mph)
Max rate of climb at S/L:	
A	107-137 m (350-450 ft)/min
B	213-274 m (700-900 ft)/min
T-O run: A	54 m (175 ft)
B	38 m (125 ft)
g limits: A	+4/−2
B	+6/−3

Evans VP-2 built by Mr John Reinschmidt of Puyallup, Washington
(Peter M. Bowers)

Fisher Flying Products Classic II biplane *(Howard Levy)*

First Strike Super Cat homebuilt cabin monoplane *(Geoffrey P. Jones)*

Fisher Flying Products FP-606 Sky Baby prototype *(Howard Levy)*

Fisher Flying Products Culite *(J. M. G. Gradidge)*

Fisher Flying Products FP-101 single-seat microlight

Fisher Flying Products FP-505 Skeeter parasol microlight *(Howard Levy)*

Fisher Flying Products FP-303 low-wing microlight aircraft

FISHER FLYING PRODUCTS CLASSIC II

This is a tandem two-seat derivative of the FP-404 Classic, first flown on 25 March 1987. The prototype uses a 47.7 kW (64 hp) Rotax 532 engine but, alternatively, a 35.8 kW (48 hp) Rotax 503 can be fitted to kit-built aircraft.

DIMENSIONS, EXTERNAL:
Wing span	6.71 m (22 ft 0 in)
Length overall	5.33 m (17 ft 6 in)
Height overall	1.88 m (6 ft 2 in)

WEIGHTS:
Weight empty	181 kg (400 lb)
Max T-O weight	386 kg (850 lb)

PERFORMANCE (Rotax 532 engine):
Cruising speed	65 knots (121 km/h; 75 mph)
Max rate of climb at S/L	275 m (900 ft)/min
T-O run	54 m (175 ft)
Landing run, without brakes	76 m (250 ft)
g limits	+6.5/–3.5

FISHER FLYING PRODUCTS FP-505 SKEETER

The FP-505 single-seat parasol-wing microlight uses an FP-101/202 type wing and FP-202 landing gear, and has the usual Fisher type of fabric covered geodetic wood fuselage. Construction time from kits is estimated at 200-250 hours.

TYPE: Single-seat microlight aircraft.

POWER PLANT: One 20 kW (27 hp) Rotax 277. Fuel capacity 19 litres (5 US gallons; 4.2 Imp gallons).

DIMENSIONS, EXTERNAL:
Wing span	8.53 m (28 ft 0 in)
Length overall	5.03 m (16 ft 6 in)

AREA:
Wings, gross	10.41 m² (112.0 sq ft)

WEIGHTS:
Weight empty	109-113 kg (240-250 lb)
Max T-O weight	227 kg (500 lb)

PERFORMANCE:
Cruising speed	48-52 knots (89-97 km/h; 55-60 mph)
Stalling speed	23 knots (42 km/h; 26 mph)
Max rate of climb at S/L	213-244 m (700-800 ft)/min
T-O run	46 m (150 ft)
g limits	+4.6/–2.3

FISHER FLYING PRODUCTS FP-606 SKY BABY

The Sky Baby resembles the larger Cessna 150 and is the first Fisher Flying Products aircraft with a non-retractable tricycle landing gear. A 20 kW (27 hp) Rotax 277 engine is standard, but larger engines up to the 35.8 kW (48 hp) Rotax 503 can be fitted. Fuel capacity is 19 litres (5 US gallons; 4.2 Imp gallons) in microlight form, or 30 litres (8 US gallons; 6.7 Imp gallons) in homebuilt form. It is to be made available in both kit and ready to fly forms.

DIMENSIONS, EXTERNAL:
Wing span	8.79 m (28 ft 10 in)
Length overall	5.28 m (17 ft 4 in)
Height overall	1.80 m (5 ft 11 in)

WEIGHTS:
Weight empty	113 kg (250 lb)
Max T-O weight	227 kg (500 lb)

PERFORMANCE:
Max level speed	approx 56 knots (105 km/h; 65 mph)
Cruising speed	48-52 knots (89-97 km/h; 55-60 mph)
Stalling speed	23 knots (42 km/h; 26 mph)
Max rate of climb at S/L	213-244 m (700-800 ft)/min
T-O and landing run	46 m (150 ft)
Range	113 nm (209 km; 130 miles)
g limits	+4/-2.5

FISHER FLYING PRODUCTS CULITE

The Culite is a development of the Culex, designed to use high power-to-weight ratio Rotax engines and a lighter airframe, with fabric covered wooden geodetic fuselage. Unlike the Culex, the Culite is available only with a non-retractable tricycle landing gear.

POWER PLANT: Two 35.8 kW (48 hp) Rotax 503s. Fuel capacity 60.5 litres (16 US gallons; 13.3 Imp gallons).

Optional tankage of 121 litres (32 US gallons; 26.6 Imp gallons).

DIMENSIONS, EXTERNAL:
As for Culex, except:
Wing span	8.53 m (28 ft 0 in)

AREA:
Wings, gross	13.00 m² (140.0 sq ft)

WEIGHTS:
Weight empty	249 kg (550 lb)
Max T-O weight	522 kg (1,150 lb)

PERFORMANCE (estimated):
Cruising speed (75% power)	104 knots (193 km/h; 120 mph)
Stalling speed: flaps up	37 knots (68 km/h; 42 mph)
flaps down	30 knots (55 km/h; 34 mph)
Max rate of climb at S/L	366 m (1,200 ft)/min
T-O run	76 m (250 ft)
Landing run	107 m (350 ft)

FISHER FLYING PRODUCTS CULEX

The Culex is powered by two 59.6 kW (80 hp) Limbach L2000 engines, and has a fuel capacity of 174 litres (46 US gallons; 38.3 Imp gallons). Airframe is an all-wood semi-monocoque structure, plywood skinned. A choice of landing gears is offered: non-retractable tailwheel or tricycle, or retractable tailwheel type.

The Culex is offered in plans form, as partial or complete

airframe kits, or in a number of separate prefabricated subassembly kits.

TYPE: Tandem two-seat homebuilt.

DIMENSIONS, EXTERNAL:
Wing span	9.40 m (30 ft 0 in)
Length overall	6.20 m (20 ft 4 in)
Height overall	1.93 m (6 ft 4 in)
Propeller diameter	1.60 m (5 ft 3 in)

AREA:
Wings, gross	13.94 m² (150.0 sq ft)

WEIGHTS:
Weight empty	454 kg (1,000 lb)
Payload with max fuel	215 kg (474 lb)
Max T-O weight: aerobatic	680 kg (1,500 lb)
utility	794 kg (1,750 lb)

PERFORMANCE (estimated at utility T-O weight):
Max level speed	130 knots (241 km/h; 150 mph)
Cruising speed (75% power)	121 knots (225 km/h; 140 mph)
Stalling speed: 'clean'	52 knots (97 km/h; 60 mph)
wheels and flaps down	42 knots (77 km/h; 48 mph)
Max rate of climb at S/L	457 m (1,500 ft)/min
Rate of climb at S/L, one engine out	107 m (350 ft)/min
T-O run	92-107 m (300-350 ft)
Landing run	76-92 m (250-300 ft)
Range with max fuel	651 nm (1,207 km; 750 miles)
g limits	+6.5/-3

FISHERCRAFT
FISHERCRAFT INC
7887 Lester Drive, Painesville, Ohio 44077
Telephone: (216) 254 4802
PRESIDENT: Ed Fisher

FISHERCRAFT ZIPPY SPORT

The prototype Zippy Sport flew for the first time on 9 October 1982. Plans are available.

TYPE: Single-seat cabin homebuilt.

AIRFRAME: Wooden wing spars and duralumin ribs, fabric covered. Near full span ailerons of aluminium alloy construction. Wing section NACA 4412. Steel tube

fuselage and tail unit, fabric covered. Non-retractable tailwheel landing gear.

POWER PLANT: One 22.4 kW (30 hp) Cuyuna 430 RR, 1,200 cc Volkswagen or 34 kW (45.6 hp) Rotax 503. Fuel capacity 19 litres (5 US gallons; 4.2 Imp gallons).

DIMENSIONS, EXTERNAL:
Wing span	8.03 m (26 ft 4 in)
Length overall	5.44 m (17 ft 10 in)
Height overall	1.52 m (5 ft 0 in)
Propeller diameter	1.42-1.52 m (4 ft 8 in-5 ft 0 in)

AREA:
Wings, gross	9.34 m² (100.5 sq ft)

WEIGHTS (Cuyuna engine):
Weight empty	156.5 kg (345 lb)
Max T-O weight	272 kg (600 lb)

PERFORMANCE (Cuyuna engine):
Max level speed at 305 m (1,000 ft)	102 knots (190 km/h; 118 mph)
Econ cruising speed at 305 m (1,000 ft)	69 knots (129 km/h; 80 mph)
Stalling speed, power off	33 knots (62 km/h; 38 mph)
Max rate of climb at S/L	229 m (750 ft)/min
Service ceiling	3,050 m (10,000 ft)
T-O run	107 m (350 ft)
Landing run	107 m (350 ft)
Range with 1.9 litre (0.5 US gallon; 0.42 Imp gallon) reserves	173 nm (322 km; 200 miles)
g limits	+4.4/-3.1

FLIGHTWORKS
FLIGHTWORKS CORPORATION
311-D East St Elmo Road, Austin, Texas 78745
Telephone: (512) 441 8844

FLIGHTWORKS CAPELLA

Kits are being marketed to construct the Capella. Two wing spans are available, offering high manoeuvrability or short-field operation.

TYPE: Single-seat homebuilt; conforms to FAR Pt 23.

AIRFRAME: All-aluminium alloy wing. Welded steel tube fuselage structure, the upper portion covered with aluminium alloy skins and the remainder with Dacron.

Non-retractable tricycle or tailwheel landing gear. Floats optional.

POWER PLANT: One 30 kW (40 hp) Rotax 447. Fuel capacity 26.5 litres (7 US gallons; 5.8 Imp gallons).

DIMENSIONS, EXTERNAL:
Wing span:	
long span	9.52 m (31 ft 3 in)
short span	8.31 m (27 ft 3 in)
Length overall	5.28 m (17 ft 4 in)
Height overall	1.73 m (5 ft 8 in)

AREAS:
Wings, gross:	
long span	11.52 m² (124.0 sq ft)
short span	10.03 m² (108.0 sq ft)

WEIGHTS (short span wings):
Weight empty	151 kg (332 lb)
Max T-O weight	261 kg (575 lb)

PERFORMANCE (short span wings):
Max level speed	80 knots (148 km/h; 92 mph)
Cruising speed, 75% power	71 knots (132 km/h; 82 mph)
Stalling speed: flaps up	33 knots (61 km/h; 38 mph)
flaps down	27 knots (50 km/h; 31 mph)
Max rate of climb at S/L	244 m (800 ft)/min
T-O run	46 m (150 ft)
Landing run	31 m (100 ft)

FLSZ
FLIGHT LEVEL SIX-ZERO INC
PO Box 9980, Colorado Springs, Colorado 80932

FLSZ DER KRICKET DK-1

The prototype Der Kricket DK-1 first flew on 19 September 1978. Plans are available.

TYPE: Single-seat homebuilt sporting biplane.

AIRFRAME: Wing section NACA 4412. Wings and tail surfaces have light alloy structure, with pop riveted light alloy skins. Tips of Styrofoam covered with glassfibre. Ailerons on lower wings only. Basic fuselage structure of bolted and riveted light alloy angle, covered by light alloy skins. Non-retractable tailwheel landing gear.

POWER PLANT: Modified Volkswagen motorcar engine of 37.3-48.5 kW (50-65 hp). Fuel capacity 30.3 litres (8 US gallons; 6.66 Imp gallons).

DIMENSIONS, EXTERNAL:
Wing span (both)	4.88 m (16 ft 0 in)
Length overall	4.88 m (16 ft 0 in)
Height overall	1.68 m (5 ft 6 in)
Propeller diameter	1.37 m (4 ft 6 in)

AREA:
Wings, gross	8.92 m² (96.0 sq ft)

WEIGHTS:
Weight empty	249 kg (550 lb)
Max T-O weight	354 kg (780 lb)

PERFORMANCE (at max T-O weight):
Max level speed	91 knots (169 km/h; 105 mph)
Econ cruising speed	74 knots (137 km/h; 85 mph)
Stalling speed, power off	46 knots (84 km/h; 52 mph)
Max rate of climb at S/L	229 m (750 ft)/min
Absolute ceiling	3,660 m (12,000 ft)
T-O run	213 m (700 ft)
Landing run	198 m (650 ft)
Range with max fuel	173 nm (322 km; 200 miles)

FLSZ VAGRANT II

This new side by side two-seat monoplane will use the same pop riveted light alloy form of construction as Der Kricket, and can be powered by either an 1,835 cc (or larger) Volkswagen modified motorcar engine or a standard aircraft engine of up to 85.75 kW (115 hp).

In configuration the Vagrant II is a cantilever low-wing cabin monoplane, with a GAW-2 wing section and conventional control surfaces. The landing gear is of non-retractable tailwheel type. The prototype was expected to fly in early 1988, but no news has been received.

The following data apply to the Vagrant II with an 1,835 cc VW engine:

DIMENSIONS, EXTERNAL:
Wing span	6.40 m (21 ft 0 in)
Length overall	5.03 m (16 ft 6 in)

AREA:
Wings, gross	8.73 m² (94.0 sq ft)

WEIGHTS:
Weight empty	227 kg (500 lb)
Max T-O weight	431-454 kg (950-1,000 lb)

PERFORMANCE (estimated):
Max level speed	122 knots (225 km/h; 140 mph)
Cruising speed	113 knots (209 km/h; 130 mph)
Stalling speed: flaps down	44 knots (81 km/h; 50 mph)
flaps up	48 knots (89 km/h; 55 mph)
Max rate of climb at S/L	244 m (800 ft)/min

FREEDOM FLIERS
FREEDOM FLIERS INC
The address given for this company in the 1987-88 *Jane's*

is no longer current. Details and illustrations of the Freedom Fliers Ascender microlights and Buckeye para-wing can be found in that edition.

FREEDOM MASTER
FREEDOM MASTER CORPORATION
700B South Plumosa, Merritt Island, Florida 32952
Telephone: (305) 453 4678
PRESIDENT: Ronald A. Lueck

FREEDOM MASTER FM-2 AIR SHARK I

The prototype Air Shark flew for the first time on 5 April 1985. Kits of pre-moulded parts are available, and by February 1988 twenty-four kits had been delivered. By that date two kit-built Air Shark Is had flown.

TYPE: Four-seat homebuilt sporting amphibian.

AIRFRAME: Wing section NASA NLF-0215-F. Wing spar caps of S-2 glassfibre or Kevlar rovings. All aerofoils are vacuum moulded. Wing upper shell and upper fuselage of glassfibre/epoxy and Clark foam plastics sandwich construction, with wing lower surfaces of Kevlar/epoxy. Hull and control surfaces of Kevlar/epoxy with Nomex

Fishercraft Zippy Sport

Unfinished Flightworks Capella prototype at 1988 Sun 'n Fun
(Geoffrey P. Jones)

Freedom Master Air Shark I four-seat homebuilt amphibian *(Joel Rieman)*

Free Spirit two-seat homebuilt aircraft *(J. M. G. Gradidge)*

Grega GN-1 Aircamper (Continental A80 engine) built by Dr Samuel
Meredith of West Memphis, Arkansas

FLSZ Der Kricket DK-1 single-seat sporting biplane

honeycomb cores. Winglets of glassfibre/epoxy. Tail unit construction similar to wings. Retractable tricycle landing gear.

POWER PLANT: One 149 kW (200 hp) Textron Lycoming IO-360C1C. Alternative Porsche PFM 3200 Allison C250-B17 or Continental IO-360 engine. Fuel capacity 227 litres (60 US gallons; 50 Imp gallons).

ARMAMENT: Hardpoints for weapons and other stores optional.

DIMENSIONS, EXTERNAL:

Wing span	9.96 m (32 ft 8 in)
Length overall	6.93 m (22 ft 9 in)
Height overall	2.49 m (8 ft 2 in)
Propeller diameter	1.83 m (6 ft 0 in)

AREA:

Wings, gross	12.31 m² (132.5 sq ft)

WEIGHTS:

Weight empty	680 kg (1,500 lb)
Baggage capacity	54 kg (120 lb)
Max T-O weight	1,270 kg (2,800 lb)

PERFORMANCE (at max T-O weight):

Max level speed at 2,285 m (7,500 ft)	178 knots (330 km/h; 205 mph)
Econ cruising speed at 2,285 m (7,500 ft)	148 knots (274 km/h; 170 mph)
Stalling speed: power off	55 knots (102 km/h; 63 mph)
Max rate of climb at S/L	380 m (1,250 ft)/min
Service ceiling	5,640 m (18,500 ft)
T-O run	488 m (1,600 ft)
Landing run	305 m (1,000 ft)
Range	1,736 nm (3,218 km; 2,000 miles)
Endurance	11 h 48 min
g limits	+10/–4

FREE SPIRIT

FREE SPIRIT AIRCRAFT COMPANY, INC

c/o SOTAAP Inc. 21622 Kanakoa Lane, Huntington Beach, California 92646
Telephone: (714) 968 3571
DESIGNER: Richard Cabrinha

FREE SPIRIT RC 412-II

The RC 412D prototype flew for the first time in July 1986. By February 1988 twenty-six kits to build the RC 412-II 'production' version had been ordered.

TYPE: Side by side two-seat, dual-control homebuilt.

AIRFRAME: Glassfibre, graphite and honeycomb composites construction. Wing section NASA 0215. Retractable tricycle landing gear.

POWER PLANT: One 127 kW (170 hp) Textron Lycoming IO-320. Fuel capacity 151.5 litres (40 US gallons; 33.3 Imp gallons). Provision for auxiliary tank of 57 litres (15 US gallons; 12.5 Imp gallons) capacity.

DIMENSIONS, EXTERNAL:

Wing span	8.23 m (27 ft 0 in)
Length overall	6.25 m (20 ft 6 in)
Height overall	2.13 m (7 ft 0 in)
Propeller diameter	1.83 m (6 ft 0 in)

AREA:

Wings, gross	7.25 m² (78.0 sq ft)

WEIGHTS:

Weight empty	397 kg (875 lb)
Baggage capacity:	
without auxiliary fuel tank	90 kg (200 lb)
with auxiliary fuel tank	50 kg (110 lb)
Max T-O weight	816 kg (1,800 lb)

PERFORMANCE:

Max level speed	230 knots (426 km/h; 265 mph)
Econ cruising speed at 3,660 m (12,000 ft)	195 knots (360 km/h; 224 mph)
Stalling speed: clean, solo	48 knots (89 km/h; 55 mph)
flaps and landing gear down, cowl flap open	39 knots (73 km/h; 45 mph)
Max rate of climb at S/L, solo	845 m (2,775 ft)/min
Service ceiling	6,400 m (21,000 ft)
T-O run, solo	99 m (325 ft)
Landing run	91 m (300 ft)
Range with max standard fuel	1,467 nm (2,719 km; 1,690 miles)
Range with auxiliary fuel	2,032 nm (3,765 km; 2,340 miles)
Endurance	8 h 40 min
g limits	+9/–6

GREGA

JOHN W. GREGA

355 Grand Boulevard, Bedford, Ohio 44146

In addition to the standard Aircamper design, of which plans are available from Mr Don Pietenpol (see under 'Pietenpol'), a modernised version has been developed by Mr John Grega. Plans of this are available to homebuilders, and by 1988 about 1,400 sets had been sold.

GN-1 AIRCAMPER

The prototype GN-1 Aircamper flew for the first time in November 1965. Builders can choose wood or steel tube fuselage construction.

TYPE: Tandem two-seat homebuilt.

POWER PLANT: One 48.5 kW (65 hp) Continental A65-8. Other engines of up to 63.5 kW (85 hp) can be installed. Fuel capacity 68 litres (18 US gallons; 15 Imp gallons).

DIMENSIONS, EXTERNAL:		WEIGHT:		Max rate of climb at S/L	152 m (500 ft)/min
Wing span	8.84 m (29 ft 0 in)	Max T-O weight	499 kg (1,100 lb)	T-O run	122 m (400 ft)
Length overall	5.51 m (18 ft 1 in)	PERFORMANCE (at max T-O weight):		Landing run	76 m (250 ft)
Height overall	2.06 m (6 ft 9 in)	Max level speed at S/L	100 knots (185 km/h; 115 mph)	Range with max fuel	347 nm (640 km; 400 miles)
AREA:		Max cruising speed at S/L	78 knots (145 km/h; 90 mph)		
Wings, gross	13.94 m² (150.0 sq ft)	Stalling speed	31 knots (56 km/h; 35 mph)		

GROVE
GROVE AIRCRAFT COMPANY

Plans are no longer available to construct the Grove GR-2 Whisper. Full details of this aircraft and an illustration can be found in the 1987-88 *Jane's*.

GYRO
GYRO 2000

1416 4th Street, Santa Fe, New Mexico 87501
Telephone: (505) 988 7188
PROPRIETOR: David Gittens

The 1987-88 *Jane's* described and illustrated the Wind Dancer proof of concept gyroplane. The same company, now known as Gyro 2000, has developed the DAKI 530Z/Ikenga.

GYRO 2000 DAKI 530Z/IKENGA

First flown in February 1988, this gyroplane will be made available in kit form for light utility, commuter/courier and recreational uses. Under development are a full cockpit enclosure, cargo pod, crop spraying equipment and

provision for additional passengers. The present pre-rotator is to be superseded by a 'jump' capability rotor head. The pilot sits astride the fuel tank, as on a motorcycle.
TYPE: Single-seat autogyro.
ROTOR SYSTEM: Two-blade Skywheels composites rotor. Eagle performance rotor head and Wunderlich pre-rotator on prototype. Parsons jump capability rotor head to be fitted.
AIRFRAME: Structure of aluminium alloy and steel tubing. Glassfibre cockpit fairing.
POWER PLANT: One 71 kW (95 hp) Suzuki engine, driving an MTH tractor propeller. Fuel capacity 57 litres (15 US gallons; 12.5 Imp gallons)

DIMENSIONS, EXTERNAL:	
Rotor diameter	7.01 m (23 ft 0 in)

Length overall	3.33 m (10 ft 11 in)
Height overall	2.13 m (7 ft 0 in)
Propeller diameter	1.52 m (5 ft 0 in)
WEIGHTS:	
Useful load	125 kg (275 lb)
Max T-O weight	238 kg (525 lb)
PERFORMANCE (estimated):	
Cruising speed	78-82 knots (145-153 km/h; 90-95 mph)
Min level speed	13 knots (24 km/h; 15 mph)
Max rate of climb at S/L	457 m (1,500 ft)/min
Service ceiling	4,420 m (14,500 ft)
T-O run	91 m (300 ft)
T-O run with pre-rotator	23 m (75 ft)
Range	260 nm (482 km; 300 miles)

HAMILTON
HAMILTON AEROSPACE

San Antonio, Texas

This ·company is developing a two-seat cross-country homebuilt as the HX-321. Configured to look like a pusher-engined fighter, it will be offered in kit form. Other aircraft under development (see main Aircraft section) are the H-1 advanced trainer powered by a 20 kN (4,500 lb st) Garrett TFE731-5 turbofan engine, and a close support aircraft, both using similar basic structures to the homebuilt. The HX-321 and H-1 were expected to fly in prototype form in the Summer of 1988.

HAMILTON HX-321

TYPE: Tandem two-seat, dual-control cross-country homebuilt.
AIRFRAME: Vacuum bagged moulded structure of carbon-

fibre, epoxy, foam and Hexcel core sandwich construction. Wing section NACA 6400 modified. Optional cranked wings of double the area. Accommodation can be pressurised. Retractable tricycle landing gear.
POWER PLANT: One 224 kW (300 hp) Textron Lycoming IO-540. TSIO-540 recommended with cranked wing. Optional 373 kW (500 hp) Allison 250-C20 turboprop. Fuel capacity 568 litres (150 US gallons; 125 Imp gallons); doubled fuel capacity in cranked wing.

DIMENSIONS, EXTERNAL:	
Wing span	8.53 m (28 ft 0 in)
Length overall	10.06 m (33 ft 0 in)
Height overall	3.35 m (11 ft 0 in)
AREA:	
Wings, gross (standard)	11.15 m² (120.0 sq ft)
WEIGHTS:	
Weight empty	671 kg (1,480 lb)

Baggage and equipment capacity	454 kg (1,000 lb)
Max T-O weight	1,497 kg (3,300 lb)
PERFORMANCE:	
Max level speed at S/L	304 knots (563 km/h; 350 mph)
Cruising speed at 2,440 m (8,000 ft), 78% power	
	215 knots (399 km/h; 248 mph)
Stalling speed, flaps down	52 knots (97 km/h; 60 mph)
Max rate of climb at S/L	670-792 m (2,200-2,600 ft)/min
Service ceiling: IO-540 engine	7,620 m (25,000 ft)
TSIO-540 engine	9,150 m (30,000 ft)
T-O run	275 m (900 ft)
Landing run	336 m (1,100 ft)
Range	2,431 nm (4,506 km; 2,800 miles)
Endurance	9 h
g limits	±12

HAPI
HAPI ENGINES INC

Eloy Municipal Airport, RR 1 Box 1000, Eloy, Arizona 85231
Telephone: (602) 466 9244

In October 1983 HAPI Engines acquired the rights to market Captain A. M. Sisler's Cygnet SF-2A. Plans and pre-welded airframe kits are available. Also, in 1987, HAPI purchased the rights in the former INAV Sonerai, which it is marketing. It is a dealer for the Viking Dragonfly, quick-assembly 'Snap' Dragonfly, and Corby CJ-1 Starlet.

CYGNET SF-2A

TYPE: Two-seat homebuilt.
AIRFRAME: Wooden geodetic wing structure, with overall Dacron covering. Wing section NACA 3413. Welded chrome molybdenum steel tube fuselage and strut braced tail unit, Dacron covered. Non-retractable tailwheel landing gear. A float gear is under development.
POWER PLANT: One 44.7 kW (60 hp) 1,834 cc HAPI converted Volkswagen motorcar engine. Fuel capacity 57 litres (15 US gallons; 12.5 Imp gallons).

DIMENSIONS, EXTERNAL:	
Wing span	9.14 m (30 ft 0 in)
Length overall	5.79 m (19 ft 0 in)
Height overall	1.78 m (5 ft 10 in)
Propeller diameter	1.47 m (4 ft 10 in)
AREA:	
Wings, gross	11.60 m² (124.8 sq ft)
WEIGHTS:	
Weight empty	265 kg (585 lb)
Baggage capacity	23 kg (50 lb)
Max T-O weight	499 kg (1,100 lb)
PERFORMANCE (at max T-O weight):	
Max level speed	94 knots (174 km/h; 108 mph)
Cruising speed at 2,440 m (8,000 ft)	
	87 knots (161 km/h; 100 mph)
Stalling speed: power off	42 knots (78 km/h; 48 mph)
power on	37 knots (68 km/h; 42 mph)
Max rate of climb at S/L	177 m (580 ft)/min
Service ceiling	3,660 m (12,000 ft)
T-O to 15 m (50 ft)	213 m (700 ft)
Landing from 15 m (50 ft)	213 m (700 ft)
Range	304 nm (563 km; 350 miles)
g limit	+4

HAPI SONERAI I

The first flight by the prototype Sonerai was made in July 1971. Plans and certain components are available to amateur constructors, and the estimated building time is 800 working hours when a pre-welded fuselage is not used. More than 400 Sonerai Is are under construction or flying.
TYPE: Single-seat homebuilt Formula V racing aircraft.
AIRFRAME: Wings of aluminium alloy construction, with NACA 64212 section. Full span aluminium alloy ailerons. Welded steel tube fuselage and tail unit, fabric covered except for glassfibre engine cowlings. Non-retractable tailwheel landing gear.
POWER PLANT: One 44.7 kW (60 hp) Volkswagen 1,600 cc modified motorcar engine. Alternative Volkswagen engines of up to 2,180 cc may be fitted. Fuel capacity 38 litres (10 US gallons; 8.3 Imp gallons).

DIMENSIONS, EXTERNAL:	
Wing span	5.08 m (16 ft 8 in)
Length overall	5.08 m (16 ft 8 in)
Height overall	1.52 m (5 ft 0 in)
Propeller diameter	1.27 m (4 ft 2 in)
AREA:	
Wings, gross	6.97 m² (75.0 sq ft)
WEIGHTS:	
Weight empty	199 kg (440 lb)
Max pilot weight	113 kg (250 lb)
Utility max T-O weight	340 kg (750 lb)
Max T-O weight	454 kg (1,000 lb)
PERFORMANCE (at max T-O weight):	
Max level speed at S/L	
	148 knots (273 km/h; 170 mph)
Econ cruising speed	109 knots (201 km/h; 125 mph)
Stalling speed	35 knots (65 km/h; 40 mph)
Max rate of climb at S/L	305 m (1,000 ft)
T-O and landing run	183 m (600 ft)
Range, with reserves	
	217-260 nm (402-482 km; 250-300 miles)
g limits	±6g

HAPI SONERAI II, IIL, II-LT and II-LTS

The prototype of the tandem two-seat Sonerai II made its first flight in July 1973 and at least 500 have since been built and flown. Many components, complete kits for fuselage and wings, and materials, are available to amateur

constructors. Estimated building time is 850 working hours.
One variant, first flown in June 1980, is the **Sonerai IIL**, with low-wing instead of mid-wing configuration and 3° of dihedral. Another variant, first flown in January 1983, is the **Sonerai II-LT**, which is similar to the Sonerai IIL but has a 2,180 cc VW engine as standard, a tricycle landing gear and larger front cockpit for a taller pilot. A retrofit kit has been produced to allow existing Sonerais to be fitted with the tricycle gear. The latest variant is the **Sonerai II-LTS**, which is basically a 'stretched' version of the Sonerai II-LT, first flown in June 1984.

The description of the Sonerai I applies also to Sonerai II, IIL, II-LT and II-LTS except as follows:
TYPE: Two-seat, dual-control sporting homebuilt.
POWER PLANT: One 1,700 cc Volkswagen modified motorcar engine, developing 48.5-52.2 kW (65-70 hp). Alternative Volkswagen engines of 1,600 to 2,180 cc may be fitted, and the 2,180 cc version is standard for the Sonerai II-LT and II-LTS. Fuel capacity 38 litres (10 US gallons; 8.3 Imp gallons) for all versions except Sonerai II-LTS, which has standard capacity of 68 litres (18 US gallons; 15 Imp gallons).

DIMENSIONS, EXTERNAL: As Sonerai I, except:	
Wing span	5.69 m (18 ft 8 in)
Length overall:	
all except Sonerai II-LTS	5.74 m (18 ft 10 in)
Sonerai II-LTS	6.20 m (20 ft 4 in)
Propeller diameter	1.32-1.37 m (4 ft 4 in to 4 ft 6 in)
AREA:	
Wings, gross	7.80 m² (84.0 sq ft)
WEIGHTS (Sonerai II):	
Weight empty	227 kg (500 lb)
Utility max T-O weight	431 kg (950 lb)
Max T-O weight	521 kg (1,150 lb)
PERFORMANCE (Sonerai II/IIL with 1,700 cc engine):	
Max level speed at S/L	139 knots (257 km/h; 160 mph)
Econ cruising speed at S/L	
	113 knots (209 km/h; 130 mph)
Stalling speed	38 knots (71 km/h; 44 mph)
Max rate of climb at S/L	152 m (500 ft)/min
T-O run, ISA	274 m (900 ft)
Landing run	152 m (500 ft)
Range, with reserves	304 nm (563 km; 350 miles)
g limits: pilot only, aerobatic	±6
max T-O weight, utility	±4.4

Gyro 2000 DAKI 530Z/Ikenga single-seat autogyro

Sonerai II-LT alongside the component parts available from HAPI for construction of the Sonerai II series

Hatz CB-1 homebuilt biplane *(Howard Levy)*

Engineering mockup of the Hamilton HX-321 homebuilt *(Howard Levy)*

Cygnet SF-2A, designed by Captain A. M. Sisler and marketed by HAPI Engines *(J. M. G. Gradidge)*

Headberg (Flaglor) Sky Scooter light sporting monoplane *(Peter M. Bowers)*

HATZ
HATZ AIRPLANE SHOP
Route 2, Gleason, Wisconsin 54435
INFORMATION: Dudley Kelly, Rt 4, Versailles, Kentucky 40383

HATZ CB-1 BIPLANE
The prototype CB-1 first flew on 19 April 1968. Plans have been marketed, and Weldtech of Benton City, Washington, made airframe components available.
TYPE: Two-seat homebuilt biplane.
AIRFRAME: Wooden wings and ailerons, fabric covered. Wing section Clark Y. Fuselage and wire braced tail unit of welded steel tube, with fabric covering. Non-retractable tailwheel landing gear.
POWER PLANT: One 86 kW (115 hp) Textron Lycoming O-235. Fuel capacity 68 litres (18 US gallons; 15 Imp gallons).
DIMENSIONS, EXTERNAL:

Wing span (both)	7.72 m (25 ft 4 in)
Length overall	5.79 m (19 ft 0 in)
Height overall	2.39 m (7 ft 10 in)
Propeller diameter	1.78 m (5 ft 10 in)

AREA:

Wings, gross	16.54 m² (178.0 sq ft)

WEIGHTS:

Weight empty	397 kg (875 lb)
Max T-O weight	726 kg (1,600 lb)

PERFORMANCE (at max T-O weight):

Max cruising speed	78 knots (145 km/h; 90 mph)
Stalling speed	35 knots (65 km/h; 40 mph)
Max rate of climb at S/L	244 m (800 ft)/min
T-O run	approx 122 m (400 ft)
Range with max fuel, 30 min reserves	174 nm (322 km; 200 miles)

HEADBERG
HEADBERG AVIATION INC
265 Needles Trail, Longwood, Florida 32750
Telephone: (305) 788 0471

HEADBERG (FLAGLOR) SKY SCOOTER
Designed by Mr Ken Flaglor, the Sky Scooter first flew in June 1967. Plans are available, and construction requires about 500 working hours.
TYPE: Single-seat homebuilt.
AIRFRAME: Wing section NACA 23012. All wooden structure, except for aluminium alloy wing leading-edge, steel tube centre-section and engine mounting, and Ceconite covering on wings, ailerons and rear fuselage. Non-retractable tailwheel landing gear.
POWER PLANT: One 30 kW (40 hp) Volkswagen 1,500 cc flat-four engine. Fuel capacity 19 litres (5 US gallons; 4.2 Imp gallons).
DIMENSIONS, EXTERNAL:

Wing span	8.48 m (27 ft 10 in)
Length overall	4.72 m (15 ft 6 in)
Height overall	2.13 m (7 ft 0 in)

AREA:

Wings, gross	10.68 m² (115.0 sq ft)

WEIGHTS:

Weight empty	177 kg (390 lb)
Max T-O and landing weight	283 kg (625 lb)

PERFORMANCE:

Max level speed	69 knots (129 km/h; 80 mph)
Econ cruising speed	56 knots (105 km/h; 65 mph)
Stalling speed	30 knots (55 km/h; 34 mph)
Max rate of climb at S/L	183 m (600 ft)/min
T-O and landing run	76 m (250 ft)
Range with max fuel, no reserves	152 nm (282 km; 175 miles)

HOLCOMB

JERRY HOLCOMB

Perigee Associates, 1010 NE 122nd Avenue, Vancouver, Washington 98684
Telephone: (206) 892 7732

HOLCOMB PERIGEE

The Perigee (originally Ultra Imp) was conceived as a single-seat tail-pusher aircraft, utilising the TPG form of construction described under the Aerocar heading in this section. The prototype flew for the first time on 4 April 1987.

The Perigee is offered for amateur construction in plans form, supported by the availability of component parts, and 22 sets of plans had been sold by February 1988.

TYPE: Single-seat sporting homebuilt.

AIRFRAME: Wing section GA(PC)-1 modified. Composite wings with riveted aluminium alloy and TPG main I beam spar, spruce/TPG rear spar, wooden main ribs, TPG nose ribs, glassfibre D section leading-edge, and fabric covering aft of the leading-edge. Full span flaperons, constructed of aluminium alloy sheet over a polystyrene foam core. Streamline semi-monocoque composites fuselage, with spruce longerons, TPG bulkheads, cockpit floor, tailcone and side skins, detachable glassfibre nose, and some aluminium alloy components. Fixed tail surfaces have TPG spars and ribs, with aluminium alloy spar doublers, pre-moulded glassfibre leading-edges and fabric aft. Elevators are all-TPG. Non-retractable tailwheel landing gear. Optional skis.

POWER PLANT: One 26 kW (35 hp) Cuyuna 430. Fuel capacity 26.5 litres (7 US gallons; 5.8 Imp gallons). Optional Rotax 447, 503 and 532 engines.

DIMENSIONS, EXTERNAL:

Wing span	8.53 m (28 ft 0 in)
Length overall	4.78 m (15 ft 8 in)
Height overall	1.57 m (5 ft 2 in)
Propeller diameter (max)	1.32 m (4 ft 4 in)

AREA:

Wings, gross	7.53 m² (81.0 sq ft)

WEIGHTS:

Weight empty	172 kg (380 lb)
Max design T-O weight	326 kg (720 lb)

PERFORMANCE (at max T-O weight):

Max level speed	104 knots (193 km/h; 120 mph)
Econ cruising speed	84 knots (156 km/h; 97 mph)
Stalling speed, flaps down, power on	33 knots (61 km/h; 38 mph)
Max rate of climb at S/L	213 m (700 ft)/min
Service ceiling	3,810 m (12,500 ft)
T-O run	122 m (400 ft)
Landing run	122-213 m (400-700 ft)
Range	173 nm (322 km; 200 miles)
Endurance	2 h
g limits	+6/−4 design

HOVEY

ROBERT W. HOVEY

Aircraft Specialties Co, PO Box 1074, Canyon Country, California 91351
Telephone: (805) 252 4054

HOVEY WHING DING II (WD-II)

The Whing Ding II was first flown in February 1971. Over 15,000 sets of plans have been sold and many Whing Dings are under construction or flying.

TYPE: Single-seat microlight biplane; conforms to FAR Pt 103.

AIRFRAME: Wooden fabric-covered wings with ribs and wingtip bows of light alloy tube. Leading-edge faired in with rigid urethane foam. Wing warping control. No ailerons, or flaps. Fuselage is a plywood box, filled with urethane foam. Aluminium tube tailboom, reinforced by high strength alloy sheet at forward end, bonded with epoxy resin and filled with free-foam urethane. Fabric covered wooden tail surfaces. Non-retractable tailwheel landing gear.

POWER PLANT: One 10.5 kW (14 hp) McCulloch MC-101A. Fuel capacity 1.9 litres (0.5 US gallon; 0.4 Imp gallon).

DIMENSIONS, EXTERNAL:

Wing span (both)	5.69 m (18 ft 8 in)
Length overall	4.27 m (14 ft 0 in)
Height overall	1.68 m (5 ft 6 in)
Propeller diameter	1.22 m (4 ft 0 in)

AREA:

Wings, gross	9.85 m² (106.0 sq ft)

WEIGHTS:

Weight empty, incl fuel	55 kg (120 lb)
Max pilot weight	84 kg (185 lb)
Max T-O weight	140 kg (310 lb)

PERFORMANCE (at max T-O weight):

Max level speed at S/L	43 knots (80 km/h; 50 mph)
Econ cruising speed at S/L	35 knots (64 km/h; 40 mph)
Stalling speed	23 knots (42 km/h; 26 mph)
Service ceiling	1,220 m (4,000 ft)
T-O run	76 m (250 ft)
Landing run	46 m (150 ft)
Range	17 nm (32 km; 20 miles)

HOVEY BETA BIRD

The Beta Bird (originally Bushwacker) is basically a monoplane version of the Whing Ding II. The prototype was first flown in April 1979. Plans are available.

TYPE: Single-seat microlight.

AIRFRAME: Fabric covered wings have wooden spars and aluminium alloy tube ribs. Wing section Hovey BB-14. Full span ailerons can be drooped to a maximum of 16° to reduce take-off and landing runs. Fuselage and tailboom construction as for Whing Ding II. Wire braced tail unit of aluminium tube, fabric covered. Non-retractable tailwheel landing gear.

POWER PLANT: One 33.5 kW (45 hp) Volkswagen 1,385 cc modified motorcar engine. Fuel capacity 28.4 litres (7.5 US gallons; 6.2 Imp gallons).

DIMENSIONS, EXTERNAL:

Wing span	7.77 m (25 ft 6 in)
Length overall	5.03 m (16 ft 6 in)
Height overall	1.83 m (6 ft 0 in)
Propeller diameter	1.37 m (4 ft 6 in)

AREA:

Wings, gross	8.08 m² (87.0 sq ft)

WEIGHTS:

Weight empty	184 kg (405 lb)
Max fuel weight	20.4 kg (45 lb)
Max T-O weight	295 kg (650 lb)

PERFORMANCE (at max T-O weight):

Max level speed at 915 m (3,000 ft)	74 knots (137 km/h; 85 mph)
Max cruising speed	69 knots (129 km/h; 80 mph)
Stalling speed	39 knots (73 km/h; 45 mph)
Max rate of climb at S/L	over 122 m (400 ft)/min
T-O and landing run	76 m (250 ft)
Range with max fuel, no reserves	113 nm (209 km; 130 miles)

HOVEY DELTA BIRD

The Delta Bird first flew in January 1981. Plans and instructional manuals are available, as well as many parts, kits and assemblies.

TYPE: Single-seat microlight biplane; conforms to FAR Pt 103.

AIRFRAME: Aluminium tube structure, with fabric covering. Full span ailerons on upper wings only. Three-axis control. Non-retractable tailwheel landing gear.

POWER PLANT: One 22.5 kW (30 hp) Cuyuna 430R. Fuel capacity 11.4 litres (3 US gallons; 2.5 Imp gallons).

DIMENSIONS, EXTERNAL:

Wing span: upper	7.32 m (24 ft 0 in)
lower	6.15 m (20 ft 2 in)
Length overall	4.60 m (15 ft 1 in)
Height overall	1.78 m (5 ft 10 in)
Propeller diameter	1.42 m (4 ft 8 in)

AREA:

Wings, gross	14.86 m² (160.0 sq ft)

WEIGHTS:

Weight empty	99 kg (218 lb)
Max pilot weight	95 kg (210 lb)
Max T-O weight	209.5 kg (462 lb)

PERFORMANCE (at max T-O weight):

Max level speed at S/L	48 knots (88 km/h; 55 mph)
Econ cruising speed at S/L	35 knots (64 km/h; 40 mph)
Stalling speed	24 knots (44 km/h; 27 mph)
Max rate of climb at S/L	122 m (400 ft)/min
Service ceiling	2,440 m (8,000 ft)
T-O and landing run	76 m (250 ft)
Range with max fuel	61 nm (112 km; 70 miles)
g limits	+3.0 normal
	+4.5 ultimate

HOVEY DELTA HAWK and SUPER HAWK

In 1983 Mr Hovey introduced the **Delta Hawk** which has a new power plant and fuselage allied to the wings, tail, landing gear and control system of the Delta Bird. By early 1988 at least 190 sets of plans for this aircraft had been sold. The Delta Hawk is also available in ready to fly form.

The following description applies to the Delta Hawk. The **Super Hawk**, introduced in 1985, has identical dimensions and performance, but has a Rotax engine, pop riveted all-metal fuselage skin, and an empty weight of 113 kg (250 lb).

TYPE: Single-seat, single-engined microlight biplane; conforms to FAR Pt 103-7 requirements.

AIRFRAME: Aluminium alloy structure. Double surface Dacron covered wings. Three-axis control. Non-retractable tailwheel landing gear.

POWER PLANT: One 28.7 kW (38.5 hp) 440 cc Kawasaki 440. Fuel capacity 13.25 litres (3.5 US gallons; 2.9 Imp gallons).

DIMENSIONS, EXTERNAL:

Wing span	7.32 m (24 ft 0 in)
Length overall	4.75 m (15 ft 7 in)
Height overall	1.83 m (6 ft 0 in)
Propeller diameter	1.52 m (5 ft 0 in)

AREA:

Wings, gross	14.12 m² (152.0 sq ft)

WEIGHTS:

Weight empty	112 kg (248 lb)
Pilot weight range	54-100 kg (120-220 lb)
Max T-O weight	202 kg (446 lb)

PERFORMANCE:

Max level speed	55 knots (101 km/h; 63 mph)
Econ cruising speed	43 knots (80 km/h; 50 mph)
Stalling speed	24 knots (44 km/h; 27 mph)
Max rate of climb at S/L	213 m (700 ft)/min
T-O and landing run	61 m (200 ft)
Range with max fuel	65 nm (120 km; 75 miles)
g limits	±6

HUMMEL

HUMMEL AIRCRAFT

509 East Butler Street, Bryan, Ohio 43506
Telephone: (419) 636 3390
DESIGNER: Morry Hummel

HUMMEL AIRCRAFT HUMMEL BIRD

The Hummel Bird is a modified Watson Windwagon, with a fully enclosed cockpit, a choice of engines, and tricycle or tailwheel type landing gear. The prototype first flew in June 1981.

By early 1988 a total of about 600 sets of plans of the Hummel Bird had been sold; these cover modifications that have to be made to the basic Windwagon plans, which must be purchased first from Gary Watson (see entry in this section). About 1,000 sets of plans for a 29 kW (39 hp) 1,050 cc half Volkswagen engine to power the aircraft have also been sold, and a kit of parts for this engine is available. For microlight aircraft, the half Volkswagen can be built using aluminium finned cylinders and a lightweight propeller hub from Mosler Motors, with 041 racing heads and big valves.

Under construction are removable wingtip extensions to convert the prototype into a motor glider. With the 0.91 m (3 ft) extensions fitted, the wing area will increase to 6.60 m² (71.0 sq ft).

TYPE: Single-seat homebuilt.

AIRFRAME: Airframe of pop riveted aluminium alloy. Wing section Clark Y. Non-retractable tailwheel or tricycle landing gear.

POWER PLANT: Prototype fitted with half Volkswagen modified motorcar engine, rated at 22.4 kW (30 hp). A half Volkswagen engine of 24, 27.6 or 29 kW (32, 37 or 39 hp), or Mosler Motors engine can be fitted to homebuilt Hummel Birds. Fuel capacity 21 litres (5.5 US gallons; 4.6 Imp gallons). Wing tanks available.

DIMENSIONS, EXTERNAL:

Wing span	5.49 m (18 ft 0 in)
Length overall	4.06 m (13 ft 4 in)
Height overall	1.37 m (4 ft 6 in)
Propeller diameter	1.14 m (3 ft 9 in)

AREA:

Wings, gross	5.30 m² (57.0 sq ft)

WEIGHTS (prototype):

Weight empty	122 kg (268 lb)
Baggage capacity	18 kg (40 lb)
Max T-O weight	248 kg (548 lb)

PERFORMANCE (22.4 kW; 30 hp half Volkswagen engine):

Max level speed	104 knots (193 km/h; 120 mph)
Econ cruising speed	82 knots (153 km/h; 95 mph)
Stalling speed	39 knots (73 km/h; 45 mph)
Max rate of climb at S/L	213 m (700 ft)/min
T-O run	122 m (400 ft)
Landing run	183 m (600 ft)
Range	260 nm (483 km; 300 miles)

HUTCHINSON

HUTCHINSON AIRCRAFT COMPANY

PO Box 169, Bay St Louis, Mississippi 39520
Telephone: (601) 467 2707 or 467 2743

PRESIDENT AND DESIGNER: Jack Hutchinson

HUTCHINSON AG MASTER

The AG Master can produce a swath width of 13.75 m (45 ft), with an application of 0.9 litre (0.25 US gallon; 0.21 Imp gallon) of chemicals per acre, which (allowing for a ten minute turnaround time) could allow 60 hectares (150 acres) to be sprayed in an hour.

Hovey Delta Hawk microlight biplane

Holcomb Perigee single-seat homebuilt pusher monoplane (*Peter M. Bowers*)

Hovey Whing Ding II built by Mr Lin Bruty of Mt Emu Farm, Australia
(*The Herald & Weekly Times, Melbourne*)

Hummel Aircraft Hummel Bird, fitted with half of a Volkswagen engine and tailwheel landing gear

Hutchinson AG Master homebuilt agricultural aircraft (*J. M. G. Gradidge*)

Hovey Beta Bird lightweight monoplane (1,385 cc Volkswagen engine)

Javelin Wichawk built by Mr Bill Taylor of Sydney, Australia (*Qantas*)

The AG Master is available as a kit, reportedly taking about 50 working hours to construct.

TYPE: Single-seat homebuilt ULV agricultural aircraft.

AIRFRAME: Airframe constructed of steel tubing, covered with Surfkote (heat shrunk Mylar and Dacron sandwich material) that is pre-sewn into envelopes. Non-retractable tailwheel landing gear. Broyhill Aero SprA spraybooms, and removable aerodynamic 76 litre (20 US gallon; 16.66 Imp gallon) chemical hopper between mainwheel legs.

POWER PLANT: Engine of unspecified type. One 38 litre (10 US gallon; 8.33 Imp gallon) fuel tank.

DIMENSIONS, EXTERNAL:
Wing span	8.74 m (28 ft 8 in)
Length overall	5.33 m (17 ft 6 in)
Height overall	2.01 m (6 ft 7 in)

AREA:
Wings, gross	13.54 m² (145.7 sq ft)

WEIGHTS:
Weight empty	204 kg (450 lb)
Max T-O weight	454 kg (1,000 lb)

PERFORMANCE (at max T-O weight):
Design manoeuvring speed	45 knots (83 km/h; 52 mph)
Min approach speed	40 knots (74 km/h; 46 mph)
Max rate of climb at S/L	91 m (300 ft)/min
T-O run	137 m (450 ft)
Landing from 15 m (50 ft)	152 m (500 ft)

JAVELIN
JAVELIN AIRCRAFT COMPANY INC
Municipal Airport, Augusta, Kansas 67010
Telephone: (316) 733 1011
PRESIDENT AND CHIEF ENGINEER: David D. Blanton

JAVELIN WICHAWK
The prototype Wichawk first flew on 24 May 1971. Plans and some components are available.

TYPE: Two/three-seat, dual-control homebuilt sporting biplane.

AIRFRAME: Wing section NACA 23015. Each wing has two wooden spars and light alloy ribs, fabric covered. Ailerons on lower wings only. Welded fuselage and tail unit of steel tube, with light alloy tubular fuselage stringers, fabric covered. Non-retractable tailwheel landing gear.

POWER PLANT: Prototype has 134 kW (180 hp) Textron Lycoming O-360. Provision for alternative horizontally opposed or radial engines from 112 kW (150 hp) to 224 kW (300 hp). Fuel capacity 151.5 litres (40 US gallons; 33.5 Imp gallons).

DIMENSIONS, EXTERNAL:
Wing span (upper)	7.32 m (24 ft 0 in)
Length overall	5.87 m (19 ft 3 in)
Height overall	2.18 m (7 ft 2 in)
Propeller diameter	1.93 m (6 ft 4 in)

AREA:
Wings, gross	17.2 m² (185.0 sq ft)

WEIGHTS (A: prototype with 134 kW; 180 hp engine. B: three-seat version with six-cylinder engine):

Weight empty: A	582.5 kg (1,284.5 lb)
B	635 kg (1,400 lb)
Baggage capacity	54.4 kg (120 lb)

*Max T-O weight: A	907 kg (2,000 lb)
B	978 kg (2,156 lb)

*Max T-O weight is increased to 998 kg (2,200 lb) with high-powered engines

PERFORMANCE (prototype with 134 kW; 180 hp engine):

Max level speed at S/L	121 knots (225 km/h; 140 mph)
Max cruising speed	110 knots (204 km/h; 127 mph)
Stalling speed	50 knots (92 km/h; 57 mph) IAS
Max rate of climb at S/L	518 m (1,700 ft)/min
T-O run	46 m (150 ft)
g limits	+12/−6

KELLY
DUDLEY R. KELLY
Route 4, Versailles, Kentucky 40383
Telephone: (606) 873 5253

KELLY-D
The prototype Kelly-D first flew on 20 December 1981. Plans are available.
TYPE: Tandem two-seat homebuilt aerobatic biplane.
AIRFRAME: Wing section NACA 4412. Wooden wings, with wooden ailerons on lower wings only. Welded steel tube fuselage and wire braced tail unit. All fabric covered. Non-retractable tailwheel landing gear.
POWER PLANT: One 86 kW (115 hp) Textron Lycoming O-235. Fuel capacity 91 litres (24 US gallons; 20 Imp gallons).

DIMENSIONS, EXTERNAL:

Wing span (both)	8.03 m (26 ft 4 in)
Length overall	5.87 m (19 ft 3 in)
Height overall	2.36 m (7 ft 9 in)
Propeller diameter	1.88 m (6 ft 2 in)

AREA:

Wings, gross	19.54 m² (210.38 sq ft)

WEIGHTS:

Basic operating weight empty	431 kg (950 lb)
Baggage capacity	18 kg (40 lb)
Max T-O and landing weight	726 kg (1,600 lb)

PERFORMANCE:

Cruising speed	78 knots (145 km/h; 90 mph)
Stalling speed	39 knots (73 km/h; 45 mph)
Max rate of climb at S/L, pilot only	274 m (900 ft)/min
Range with max fuel, 20 min reserves	243 nm (450 km; 280 miles)

KELLY-DII
At Sun 'n Fun, held in Lakeland, Florida, in March 1987 was exhibited the new Kelly-DII, for which a complete kit is marketed by Rogers Aircraft of 1642 Hangar Road, Building 145, Sanford, Florida 32771. Similar in appearance to the Kelly-D except for its engine cowling, it is lighter and lower powered.

TYPE: Two-seat lightweight homebuilt aerobatic biplane.
AIRFRAME: Structure similar to Kelly-D, with Ceconite covering. Sheet metal firewall and cowling.
POWER PLANT: One 34.3 kW (46 hp) Rotax 503. Fuel capacity 23 litres (6 US gallons; 5 Imp gallons).

DIMENSIONS, EXTERNAL:

Wing span, both	7.01 m (23 ft 0 in)
Length overall	5.79 m (19 ft 0 in)
Height overall	2.03 m (6 ft 8 in)

WEIGHTS:

Weight empty	206 kg (455 lb)
Baggage capacity	11.3 kg (25 lb)
Max T-O weight	388 kg (855 lb)

PERFORMANCE:

Cruising speed	65 knots (121 km/h; 75 mph)
Stalling speed	31 knots (57 km/h; 35 mph)
Range, with 20 min reserves	173 nm (321 km; 200 miles)

KENNEDY
KENNEDY AIRCRAFT COMPANY INC
2405 North Coolidge Street, Orlando, Florida 32804
PRESIDENT: Edward Kennedy

KENNEDY SKYCYCLE and FLYCYCLE
First flown as a prototype in 1960, the developed Skycycle autogyro is now marketed in plans and kit forms, in single and tandem two-seat versions. A lightweight variant is also available as the Flycycle. All are covered under Experimental regulations, while the Flycycle can also meet microlight requirements.
ROTOR SYSTEM: Rotor of aluminium alloy construction, with two McCutchin Sky Wheel blades for Skycycles. Lightweight Rotordyne rotor for Flycycle. Pre-rotator fitted.
AIRFRAME: Basic structure of bolted square light alloy tubing, with plywood fairing on single-seat Skycycle, aluminium on two-seater, and no fairing on Flycycle. Non-retractable tricycle landing gear.
POWER PLANT: Skycycle single-seater and Flycycle have 35 kW (47 hp) Rotax 503. Fuel capacity 19 litres (5 US gallons; 4.2 Imp gallons). Skycycle two-seater has 48.5 kW (65 hp) Rotax 532. Fuel capacity 23 litres (6 US gallons; 5 Imp gallons) standard; 49 litres (13 US gallons; 10.8 Imp gallons) optional.

DIMENSIONS, EXTERNAL:

Rotor diameter: Single-seaters	7.01 m (23 ft 0 in)
Two-seater	7.62 m (25 ft 0 in)
Length of fuselage: Single-seat Skycycle	3.35 m (11 ft 0 in)
Two-seater	3.66 m (12 ft 0 in)
Height overall	2.13 m (7 ft 0 in)

WEIGHTS:

Weight empty: Single-seat Skycycle	121 kg (267 lb)
Two-seater	141 kg (310 lb)
Max pilot weight: Single-seaters	113 kg (250 lb)
Max T-O weight: Two-seat Skycycle	317 kg (700 lb)

PERFORMANCE:

Max level speed: Single-seat Skycycle	69 knots (129 km/h; 80 mph)
Two-seater	100 knots (185 km/h; 115 mph)
Cruising speed: Two-seater	61-65 knots (113-121 km/h; 70-75 mph)
Min forward speed: Single-seaters	7-9 knots (13-16 km/h; 8-10 mph)
T-O run, with pre-rotator: Single-seaters	30.5-61 m (100-200 ft)
Endurance with standard fuel: Two-seater	2 h

KIMBREL
MICHAEL G. KIMBREL
1333 Garrard Creek Road, Oakville, Washington 98568
Telephone: (206) 273 9203
Mr Michael Kimbrel also markets Sorrell SNS-2 Guppy plans.

KIMBREL DORMOY BATHTUB Mk 1
Based on the Dormoy Bathtub of 1924, the Kimbrel prototype first flew on 29 April 1978. Drawings are available.
TYPE: Single-seat homebuilt.
AIRFRAME: Wooden wings, Dacron covered. Clark Y wing section. Fuselage consists of Dacron-covered steel tube nacelle, with wire braced steel tubes to support a tail unit of similar construction. Non-retractable tailwheel landing gear.
POWER PLANT: Prototype has 30 kW (40 hp) 1,200 cc Volkswagen modified motorcar engine. Other Bathtubs have flown with 27 kW (36 hp) Volkswagen, 45 kW (60 hp) Franklin and 30 kW (40 hp) Continental engines. Fuel capacity 21.5 litres (5.7 US gallons; 4.75 Imp gallons).

DIMENSIONS, EXTERNAL:

Wing span	7.29 m (23 ft 11 in)
Length overall	4.14 m (13 ft 7 in)
Height overall	2.03 m (6 ft 8 in)

AREA:

Wings, gross	7.80 m² (84.0 sq ft)

WEIGHTS (prototype):

Weight empty	137 kg (302 lb)
Max T-O weight	245 kg (540 lb)

PERFORMANCE (prototype):

Max level speed	56 knots (105 km/h; 65 mph)
Cruising speed	48 knots (88 km/h; 55 mph)
Stalling speed	31 knots (57 km/h; 35 mph)
Max rate of climb at S/L	122 m (400 ft)/min
Absolute ceiling	1,980 m (6,500 ft)
T-O run	152 m (500 ft)
Landing run	91 m (300 ft)
Range with max fuel	87 nm (161 km; 100 miles)

KIMBREL BUTTERFLY
Designed as an ARV, plans of the Butterfly are available. Construction requires about 500 working hours.
TYPE: Single-seat microlight; conforms to FAR Pt 103.
AIRFRAME: Fuselage boom consists of 7.6 cm (3 in) diameter aluminium irrigation tube, with aluminium tubing in the cockpit area, bolted and pop riveted. Spruce/plywood wings with aluminium leading-edges and double surface Stits fabric covering. Aerofoil section USA35B (modified). Three-axis control. Non-retractable two-wheel landing gear, with tailskid.
POWER PLANT: One 20 kW (27 hp) Rotax 277. Fuel capacity 19 litres (5 US gallons; 4.2 Imp gallons).

DIMENSIONS, EXTERNAL:

Wing span	11.13 m (36 ft 6 in)
Length overall	6.55 m (21 ft 6 in)
Propeller diameter	1.27 m (4 ft 2 in)

AREA:

Wings, gross	13.66 m² (147.0 sq ft)

WEIGHTS:

Weight empty	90 kg (198 lb)
Max pilot weight	93 kg (205 lb)
Max T-O weight	195 kg (430 lb)

PERFORMANCE:

Cruising speed	39 knots (72 km/h; 45 mph)
Min speed: power on	19 knots (36 km/h; 22 mph)
power off	22 knots (41 km/h; 25 mph)

Max rate of climb at S/L	more than 137 m (450 ft)
Service ceiling	more than 2,440 m (8,000 ft)
T-O run	40 m (130 ft)
Landing run	61 m (200 ft)
Range with max standard fuel	78 nm (145 km; 90 miles)
Endurance with standard fuel	2 h 30 min
g limits	+4/−2 design

KIMBREL BANTY
The simple low-cost Banty microlight is offered in plans form for amateur construction. Building takes an estimated 500 working hours. The prototype flew for the first time on 9 June 1985.
TYPE: Single-seat non-aerobatic microlight.
AIRFRAME: Fabric covered all-wood construction, except for aluminium alloy tubing for cabane and lift struts. Modified USA35B wing section. Three-axis control. Non-retractable tailskid landing gear.
POWER PLANT: One 20 kW (27 hp) Rotax 277. Fuel capacity 19 litres (5 US gallons; 4.2 Imp gallons).

DIMENSIONS, EXTERNAL:

Wing span	9.75 m (32 ft 0 in)
Length overall	5.74 m (18 ft 10 in)
Height overall	1.83 m (6 ft 0 in)
Propeller diameter	1.52 m (5 ft 0 in)

WEIGHTS:

Weight empty	108 kg (237 lb)
Pilot weight range	50-102 kg (110-225 lb)
Max T-O weight	227 kg (500 lb)

PERFORMANCE:

Cruising speed	43 knots (80 km/h; 50 mph)
T-O run, 10° flap	67 m (220 ft)
g limit	+6

KOLB
KOLB COMPANY INC
RD 3, Box 38, Phoenixville, Pennsylvania 19460
Telephone: (215) 948 4136
PRESIDENT: Homer Kolb

KOLB ULTRASTAR
The UltraStar appeared in March 1982 and is offered in kit form.
TYPE: Single-seat microlight; conforms to FAR Pt 103.
AIRFRAME: Welded steel cage fuselage with aluminium tailboom. Dacron covered aluminium alloy wings. Three-axis control. Non-retractable tailwheel landing gear. Optional floats and skis.
POWER PLANT: One 26 kW (35 hp) Cuyuna ULII-02; 26 kW (35 hp) Rotax 377 optional. Two fuel tanks, each with capacity of 6.6 litres (1.75 US gallons; 1.46 Imp gallons).

DIMENSIONS, EXTERNAL:

Wing span	8.38 m (27 ft 6 in)
Length overall	6.40 m (21 ft 0 in)
Height overall	1.83 m (6 ft 0 in)
Propeller diameter	1.27 m (4 ft 2 in)

AREA:

Wings, gross	13.47 m² (145.0 sq ft)

WEIGHTS:

Weight empty	114 kg (252 lb)
Pilot weight range	54.5-106.5 kg (120-235 lb)
Max T-O weight	229 kg (505 lb)

PERFORMANCE (at max T-O weight):

Max level speed	55 knots (101 km/h; 63 mph)
Econ cruising speed	39 knots (72 km/h; 45 mph)
Stalling speed, power on	22 knots (41 km/h; 25 mph)
Max rate of climb at S/L	244 m (800 ft)/min

Kelly-D two-seat aerobatic biplane

Kennedy Skycycle autogyro in single- and two-seat forms *(Geoffrey P. Jones)*

Kimbrel Butterfly microlight prototype

Kimbrel Dormoy Bathtub Mk 1 (Continental A40 engine) built by Mr Harley Dahler of Nokomis, Illinois

Kimbrel Banty single-seat amateur-built microlight

Kolb UltraStar microlight *(Brian M. Service)*

Kolb TwinStar Mark II *(Howard Levy)*

T-O and landing run	31 m (100 ft)
g limits	+4/−2

KOLB TWINSTAR MARK II

The original TwinStar first flew as a prototype in August 1984. The current model is the Mark II, differing mainly in having a wider FireStar type enclosed cockpit and canopy. By February 1988, 115 kits had been delivered of 138 ordered.

TYPE: Side by side two-seat homebuilt.

AIRFRAME: Welded steel cage structure and aluminium boom. Wings have aluminium tube spar with aluminium ribs, double surface Stits Dacron covered. Three-axis control. Non-retractable tailwheel landing gear. Options include ballistic recovery parachute, floats and skis.

POWER PLANT: One 35 kW (47 hp) Rotax 503. Fuel capacity 19 litres (5 US gallons; 4.2 Imp gallons).

DIMENSIONS, EXTERNAL:

Wing span	9.15 m (30 ft 0 in)
Length overall	6.71 m (22 ft 0 in)
Height overall	1.75 m (5 ft 9 in)
Propeller diameter	1.68 m (5 ft 6 in)

AREA:

Wings, gross	14.86 m² (160.0 sq ft)

WEIGHTS:

Weight empty, without fairing	145 kg (320 lb)
Max T-O weight	340 kg (750 lb)

PERFORMANCE (at max T-O weight):

Max level speed	63 knots (118 km/h; 73 mph)
Econ cruising speed at S/L	48 knots (89 km/h; 55 mph)
Stalling speed at S/L	26 knots (49 km/h; 30 mph)
Max rate of climb at S/L	213 m (700 ft)/min
Service ceiling	3,660 m (12,000 ft)
T-O run, on grass	92 m (300 ft)
Landing run with brakes	37 m (120 ft)
Range	61 nm (112 km; 70 miles)
Endurance	1 h 30 min
g limits	+4/−2

KOLB FIRESTAR

The prototype FireStar first flew in May 1984. It was the first in the Kolb range to incorporate a semi-enclosed cockpit rather than the previous open position or optional nose fairing. By February 1988, 149 kits had been delivered.

TYPE: Single-seat microlight; conforms to FAR Pt 103-7.

AIRFRAME: Pre-welded steel tube and aluminium alloy construction, with fabric covered wings and tail unit. Three-axis control. Non-retractable tailwheel landing gear. Optional recovery parachute.

POWER PLANT: One 26 kW (35 hp) Rotax 377. Fuel capacity 19 litres (5 US gallons; 4.2 Imp gallons).

DIMENSIONS, EXTERNAL:

Wing span	8.43 m (27 ft 8 in)
Length overall	6.17 m (20 ft 3 in)
Height overall	1.75 m (5 ft 9 in)
Propeller diameter	1.68 m (5 ft 6 in)

AREA:

Wings, gross	13.84 m² (149.0 sq ft)

WEIGHTS:
Weight empty · 120 kg (264 lb)
Pilot weight range · 64-118 kg (140-260 lb)
Max T-O weight · 252 kg (555 lb)
PERFORMANCE:
Max level speed · 61 knots (113 km/h; 70 mph)

Econ cruising speed at S/L · 39 knots (72 km/h; 45 mph)
Stalling speed · 24 knots (44 km/h; 27 mph)
Max rate of climb at S/L · 366 m (1,200 ft)/min
Service ceiling · 4,875 m (16,000 ft)
T-O and landing run, on grass · 31 m (100 ft)
Range · 95 nm (177 km; 110 miles)

Endurance · 2 h 30 min
g limits · +4/−2

LACO

LACO
PO Box 415, Desert Hot Springs, California 92240
Telephone: (619) 329 9354

LACO-125 and LACO-145

The original **LACO-125** prototype first flew on 29 May 1977. It was followed by the more powerful **LACO-145**. Plans for both models are available.
TYPE: Two-seat homebuilt biplane.
AIRFRAME: Wing section NACA 2412. Wing structure has wooden spars and ribs, aluminium leading- and trailing-edges, and steel fittings. Modified Frise ailerons

on lower wings only. Welded Warren truss fuselage of steel tubing, with wooden formers and stringers. Braced tail unit of welded steel tubing. Entire airframe fabric covered. Non-retractable tailwheel landing gear.
POWER PLANT: LACO-125: One 93 kW (125 hp) Continental C-125-2. LACO-145: One 108 kW (145 hp) Continental C145. Fuel capacity 91 litres (24 US gallons; 20 Imp gallons).
DIMENSIONS, EXTERNAL:
Wing span: upper · 6.93 m (22 ft 8¾ in)
lower · 6.29 m (20 ft 7½ in)
Length overall · 5.94 m (19 ft 6 in)
Height overall · 2.18 m (7 ft 2 in)
Propeller diameter: LACO-125 · 1.83 m (6 ft 0 in)
LACO-145 · 1.93 m (6 ft 4 in)

AREA:
Wings, gross · 13.94 m² (150.0 sq ft)
WEIGHTS:
Weight empty · 390 kg (860 lb)
Max T-O weight · 635 kg (1,400 lb)
PERFORMANCE (LACO-125):
Max level speed · 108 knots (200 km/h; 124 mph)
Max cruising speed · 98 knots (182 km/h; 113 mph)
Stalling speed: power off · 49 knots (90 km/h; 56 mph)
power on · 44 knots (81 km/h; 50 mph)
Max rate of climb at S/L · 274 m (900 ft)/min
Range with max fuel · 282 nm (523 km; 325 miles)

LEADER'S

LEADER'S INTERNATIONAL INC
212 North Mecklenburg Avenue, South Hill, Virginia 23970
Telephone: (804) 447 4919
PRESIDENT: Dr Rolf Brand

LEADER'S INTERNATIONAL JB-1000

The JB-1000 is available in plan, kit and ready assembled forms.
TYPE: Single-seat microlight; conforms to FAR Pt 103.
AIRFRAME: Constructed of carbonfibre and Kevlar. Three-axis control. Non-retractable tailwheel landing gear.

POWER PLANT: One 20 kW (27 hp) Rotax 277. Fuel capacity 19 litres (5 US gallons; 4.2 Imp gallons).
DIMENSIONS, EXTERNAL:
Wing span · 9.14 m (30 ft 0 in)
Length overall · 6.10 m (20 ft 0 in)
Height overall · 1.78 m (5 ft 10 in)
Propeller diameter · 1.52 m (5 ft 0 in)
AREA:
Wings, gross · 13.47 m² (145.0 sq ft)
WEIGHTS:
Weight empty · 113 kg (250 lb)
Pilot weight range · 63.5-100 kg (140-220 lb)
Max T-O weight · 238 kg (525 lb)
PERFORMANCE:
Max level speed · 52 knots (97 km/h; 60 mph)

Econ cruising speed · 36 knots (68 km/h; 42 mph)
Stalling speed: power on · 22 knots (41 km/h; 25 mph)
power off · 24 knots (44 km/h; 27 mph)
Max rate of climb at S/L · 122 m (400 ft)/min
Service ceiling · 3,660 m (12,000 ft)
T-O run · 29 m (95 ft)
Landing run · 30 m (100 ft)
g limits · +4/−2

LEADER'S INTERNATIONAL AM-DSII

This single-seat military aircraft was described and illustrated in the 1987-88 *Jane's*.

LIGHT AERO

LIGHT AERO INC
PO Box 728, 4823 Aviation Way, Caldwell, Idaho 83606
Telephone: (208) 454 2600
PRESIDENT: Dean Wilson

LIGHT AERO AVID FLYER

The Avid Flyer takes from 200 to 400 working hours to assemble. It is available as a single kit, or as six separate kits to spread the cost of purchase. Military operators include the Peruvian Air Force (see under Peru in main Aircraft section).

The Avid Flyer features two forms of interchangeable wings: the original high-lift STOL wings with unique near full span auxiliary aerofoil flaperons and shorter span 'speed' wings using a new wing section. With the 'speed' wings fitted, cruising speed is increased to 95 knots (177 km/h; 110 mph) and stalling speed becomes 35 knots (65 km/h; 40 mph) at max T-O weight.
TYPE: Side by side two-seat, dual-control homebuilt.
AIRFRAME: Aluminium wing spars and plywood ribs, covered with heat shrunk Dacron. Welded fuselage, rudder, tailplane and elevators of steel tubing, Dacron covered except for fuselage nose which has pre-moulded glassfibre cowlings. Fin integral with fuselage. Non-retractable nosewheel or tailwheel landing gear. Optional floats, skis and wheel-skis.
POWER PLANT: One 48.5 kW (65 hp) Rotax 532. Fuel capacity 34 litres (9 US gallons; 7.5 Imp gallons). Optional 40 litre (10.5 US gallon; 8.75 Imp gallon) wing tanks.
DIMENSIONS, EXTERNAL:
Wing span: STOL wings · 9.11 m (29 ft 10½ in)

'Speed' wings · 7.30 m (23 ft 11½ in)
Length overall · 5.18 m (17 ft 0 in)
Height overall · 1.70 m (5 ft 7 in)
Propeller diameter · 1.83 m (6 ft 0 in)
AREAS:
Wings, gross: STOL wings · 11.38 m² (122.5 sq ft)
'Speed' wings · 9.04 m² (97.31 sq ft)
WEIGHTS:
Weight empty: STOL wings · 154-172 kg (340-380 lb)
'Speed' wings · 150-168 kg (330-370 lb)
Max T-O weight · 385 kg (850 lb)
PERFORMANCE (A: STOL wings, B: 'Speed' wings, both at 385 kg; 850 lb AUW):
Max cruising speed: A · 74 knots (137 km/h; 85 mph)
B · 95 knots (177 km/h; 110 mph)
Stalling speed: A · 28 knots (52 km/h; 32 mph)
B · 35 knots (65 km/h; 40 mph)
Max rate of climb at S/L: A · 427 m (1,400 ft)/min
B · 419 m (1,375 ft)/min
Service ceiling: A · 5,335 m (17,500 ft)
B · 4,575 m (15,000 ft)
T-O run: A · 43 m (140 ft)
B · 92 m (300 ft)
T-O to 15 m (50 ft): A · 104 m (340 ft)
B · 152 m (500 ft)
Landing run: A · 46 m (150 ft)
B · 183 m (600 ft)
Range with max fuel · 260 nm (483 km; 300 miles)
g limits · +3.8 (+5.7 ultimate)

LIGHT AERO AVID AMPHIBIAN

The Avid Amphibian first flew on 12 July 1985. Kits are available. It can be built optionally for land operation only.

TYPE: Three-seat homebuilt amphibian or landplane.
AIRFRAME: Original high lift wing section. Wing structure comprises aluminium alloy tube spars, plywood ribs, and aluminium and steel drag tubes, covered with Ceconite. Downward canted wingtips serve as stabilising floats on water. Full span trailing-edge flaperons of auxiliary aerofoil type, of similar construction to wings. Single-step flying-boat hull, with structure of steel tube, covered with glassfibre shells back to step and Ceconite over rear fuselage. Wire braced tail unit of steel tube covered with Ceconite. Retractable tailwheel landing gear.
POWER PLANT: One 48.5 kW (65 hp) Rotax 532. Fuel capacity 66 litres (17.5 US gallons; 14.6 Imp gallons).
DIMENSIONS, EXTERNAL:
Wing span · 10.97 m (36 ft 0 in)
Length overall · 5.92 m (19 ft 5 in)
Height overall · 1.75 m (5 ft 9 in)
Propeller diameter · 1.91 m (6 ft 3 in)
AREA:
Wings, gross · 13.94 m² (150.0 sq ft)
WEIGHTS:
Weight empty · 254 kg (560 lb)
Max T-O weight · 544 kg (1,200 lb)
PERFORMANCE (at max T-O weight):
Max cruising speed · 65 knots (120 km/h; 75 mph)
Stalling speed · 29 knots (53 km/h; 33 mph)
Max rate of climb at S/L · 286 m (940 ft)/min
Service ceiling · 3,580 m (11,750 ft)
T-O run: on land · 92 m (300 ft)
on water · 230 m (756 ft)
Landing run: on land · 183 m (600 ft)
on water · 84 m (275 ft)

LIGHT MINIATURE

LIGHT MINIATURE AIRCRAFT INC
Building 411, Opa-Locka Airport, Opa-Locka, Florida 33054
Telephone: (305) 681 4068
PRESIDENT: Fred F. McCallum

LIGHT MINIATURE AIRCRAFT LM-1

This is basically a single-seat three-quarter scale Piper J-3 Cub replica. The prototype first flew on 15 July 1983.
Plans for the LM-1 are available. Estimated building time from plans is 600 working hours. Complete kits, partial kits and component parts for the LM-1 are available from Wicks Aircraft Supply, Highland, Illinois 62249.
TYPE: Single-seat homebuilt.
AIRFRAME: Wing section NACA 4412 modified. Dacron-covered all-wood airframe, except for aluminium alloy wing and aileron ribs. Non-retractable tailwheel landing gear.

POWER PLANT: One 22.4 kW (30 hp) Cuyuna 430RR. Fuel capacity 21 litres (5.5 US gallons; 4.6 Imp gallons).
DIMENSIONS, EXTERNAL:
Wing span · 8.23 m (27 ft 0 in)
Length overall · 5.38 m (17 ft 8 in)
Height overall · 1.70 m (5 ft 7 in)
Propeller diameter · 1.27 m (4 ft 2 in)
AREA:
Wings, gross · 11.29 m² (121.5 sq ft)
WEIGHTS:
Weight empty · 156 kg (345 lb)
Max T-O and landing weight · 272 kg (600 lb)
PERFORMANCE:
Max level speed and max cruising speed at 610 m (2,000 ft) · 56 knots (105 km/h; 65 mph)
Econ cruising speed · 43 knots (80 km/h; 50 mph)
Stalling speed, engine idling · 21 knots (39 km/h; 24 mph)
Max rate of climb at S/L · 137 m (450 ft)/min
T-O run · 61 m (200 ft)

Landing run · 91-107 m (300-350 ft)
Range with 30 min reserves · 139 nm (257 km; 160 miles)

LIGHT MINIATURE AIRCRAFT LM-1U and LM-1X

The prototype **LM-1U** microlight variant of the LM-1 flew for the first time on 7 April 1985. Kits are available, together with kits of an Experimental category homebuilt version, known as the **LM-1X**, which is identical except for having a 26 kW (35 hp) Rotax 377 engine and increased empty weight.
The following details refer to the LM-1U:
TYPE: Single-seat microlight; conforms to FAR Pt 103.
AIRFRAME: Wing section Göttingen 387 modified. Aluminium alloy airframe, except for wooden wing spars and overall Dacron covering. Three-axis control. Non-retractable tailwheel landing gear. Ballistic parachute and floats optional.
POWER PLANT: One 20 kW (27 hp) Rotax 277. Fuel capacity 20.4 litres (5.4 US gallons; 4.5 Imp gallons).

LACO-145 two-seat light biplane

Prototype three-seat Light Aero Avid Amphibian

Light Aero Avid Flyer fitted with optional twin floats

Light Miniature Aircraft LM-1U microlight

Light Miniature Aircraft LM-3X homebuilt aircraft

Leader's International JB-1000 microlight aircraft

DIMENSIONS, EXTERNAL:
Wing span	9.14 m (30 ft 0 in)
Length overall	5.44 m (17 ft 10 in)
Height overall	1.70 m (5 ft 7 in)
Propeller diameter	1.52 m (5 ft 0 in)

AREA:
Wings, gross	10.87 m² (117.0 sq ft)

WEIGHTS (LM-1U):
Weight empty	114 kg (252 lb)
Pilot weight range	62-102 kg (135-225 lb)
Max baggage capacity	11.3 kg (25 lb)
Max T-O weight	238 kg (525 lb)

PERFORMANCE (LM-1U):
Max level speed at 305 m (1,000 ft)
61 knots (113 km/h; 70 mph)
Econ cruising speed at 305 m (1,000 ft)
47 knots (87 km/h; 54 mph)
Stalling speed, engine idling
23 knots (42 km/h; 26 mph)
Max rate of climb at S/L	168 m (550 ft)/min
T-O run	61 m (200 ft)
Landing run	91 m (300 ft)

Range, with 15 min reserves
156 nm (289 km; 180 miles)

LIGHT MINIATURE AIRCRAFT LM-3U and LM-3X

Identical except for engine and empty weight, the microlight **LM-3U** and Experimental category homebuilt **LM-3X** are three-quarter scale representations of the Aeronca 7AC Champ light aircraft. Kits to build the LM-3U and LM-3X include the appropriate Rotax engine. The prototype LM-3 flew for the first time in July 1986.

TYPES: Single-seat microlight (LM-3U) and homebuilt (LM-3X); LM-3U conforms to FAR Pt 103 and LM-3X to Experimental category regulations.

AIRFRAME: Wing section Göttingen 387. Ceconite covered wings, with wooden spars, stamped aluminium ribs and glassfibre leading-edges. Aluminium alloy fuselage longerons, uprights and cross members, with wooden formers and stringers, Ceconite covered. Glassfibre engine cowling. Three-axis control. Non-retractable tailwheel landing gear. Optional floats and recovery parachute.

POWER PLANT: LM-3U: One 20 kW (27 hp) Rotax 277. LM-3X: One 26 kW (35 hp) Rotax 377. Fuel capacity 19 litres (5 US gallons; 4.2 Imp gallons). LM-3X has option of two 20.4 litre (5.4 US gallon; 4.5 Imp gallon) auxiliary fuel tanks fitted in wingroots.

AVIONICS: Hand-held radio.

DIMENSIONS, EXTERNAL:
Wing span	9.14 m (30 ft 0 in)
Length overall	5.33 m (17 ft 6 in)
Height overall	1.70 m (5 ft 7 in)
Propeller diameter: LM-3U	1.52 m (5 ft 0 in)
LM-3X	1.63 m (5 ft 4 in)

AREA:
Wings, gross: both	11.15 m² (120.0 sq ft)

WEIGHTS (A: LM-3U, B: LM-3X):
Weight empty: A	114 kg (252 lb)
B	147 kg (325 lb)
Pilot weight range: A, B	61.5-102 kg (135-225 lb)
Baggage capacity	11.3 kg (25 lb)
Max T-O weight: A	249 kg (550 lb)
B	272 kg (600 lb)

PERFORMANCE (A and B as above):
Max level speed: A, B	65 knots (121 km/h; 75 mph)
Econ cruising speed: A, B	48 knots (89 km/h; 55 mph)

Stalling speed:
A, B
19-24 knots (36-44 km/h; 22-27 mph)
Max rate of climb at S/L: A	168 m (550 ft)/min
B	183 m (600 ft)/min
T-O run: A, B	46-61 m (150-200 ft)
Landing from 15 m (50 ft): A, B	76-91 m (250-300 ft)

Range, standard fuel, with reserves:
A	130 nm (241 km; 150 miles)
B	95 nm (177 km; 110 miles)
Endurance: A	3 h
B	2 h
g limits: A, B	+5/−4.5

LOEHLE
LOEHLE ENTERPRISES

'The Aviation Valley', Shipmans Creek Road, Wartrace, Tennessee 37183

Telephone: (615) 857 3419

PRESIDENT: Michael Loehle

RITZ STANDARD MODEL A

The Ritz Aircraft company, owned by Mr Michael Loehle, continues to market the Standard Model A from the above address.

TYPE: Single-seat microlight; conforms to FAR Pt 103.

AIRFRAME: Wings and tail unit have wooden structures, with 'geodetic' cross bracing. Fuselage is 'geodetic' structure, with steel frame and plywood box cockpit/nose section. Complete airframe is Dacron covered. Non-retractable tailwheel landing gear.

POWER PLANT: One 16.5 kW (22 hp) Zenoah. Fuel capacity 19 litres (5 US gallons; 4.2 Imp gallons).

DIMENSIONS, EXTERNAL:
Wing span	10.97 m (36 ft 0 in)
Length overall	5.49 m (18 ft 0 in)

Height overall 1.68 m (5 ft 6 in)
Propeller diameter 1.37 m (4 ft 6 in)

AREA:
Wings, gross 13.01 m² (140.0 sq ft)

WEIGHTS:
Weight empty 91 kg (200 lb)
Pilot weight range 57-125 kg (125-275 lb)
Max T-O weight 227 kg (500 lb)

PERFORMANCE:
Max level speed 52 knots (97 km/h; 60 mph)
Max cruising speed 48 knots (88 km/h; 55 mph)
Stalling speed:
power on 14 knots (26 km/h; 16 mph)
power off 16 knots (29 km/h; 18 mph)
Max rate of climb at S/L more than 122 m (400 ft)/min
T-O run (concrete) 30 m (100 ft)
Landing run approx 61 m (200 ft)
Range with max fuel 217 nm (402 km; 250 miles)
Endurance with max fuel 5 h
g limits +4.5/–2

UFM of KY AEROPLANE XP

Kits are available from Mr Loehle's UFM of Ky Inc, at Loehle Enterprises' address.

TYPE: Single-seat microlight biplane.

AIRFRAME: Construction is of aluminium alloy, with double thickness Dacron covering on wings, an underslung 'trike' unit, and conventional tail surfaces. Floats optional.

POWER PLANT: One 26 kW (35 hp) Cuyuna ULII-02. Fuel capacity 19 litres (5 US gallons; 4.2 Imp gallons).

DIMENSIONS, EXTERNAL:
Wing span 8.53 m (28 ft 0 in)
Length overall 3.51 m (11 ft 6 in)
Height overall 2.34 m (7 ft 8 in)
Propeller diameter 1.37 m (4 ft 6 in)

AREA:
Wings, gross 16.17 m² (174.0 sq ft)

WEIGHTS:
Weight empty 111 kg (244 lb)
Max T-O weight 227 kg (500 lb)

PERFORMANCE:
Max level speed 52 knots (97 km/h; 60 mph)
Max cruising speed 43 knots (80 km/h; 50 mph)
Stalling speed 19 knots (34 km/h; 21 mph)
Max rate of climb at S/L 305 m (1,000 ft)/min
g limits +9/–5 ultimate

LOEHLE AVIATION THE FUN MACHINE

The first aircraft from Loehle Aviation Inc was The Fun Machine, available for purchase as a bolt-together kit.

TYPE: Single-seat microlight biplane; conforms to FAR Pt 103.

AIRFRAME: Structure of aluminium alloy, with double surface Mylar laminated Dacron on wings and boom-mounted tail unit. Three-axis control. Non-retractable tricycle landing gear. Optional floats or skis.

POWER PLANT: One 26 kW (35 hp) Cuyuna ULII-02. Fuel capacity 19 litres (5 US gallons; 4.2 Imp gallons).

DIMENSIONS, EXTERNAL:
Wing span 8.53 m (28 ft 0 in)
Length overall 3.51 m (11 ft 6 in)
Height overall 2.34 m (7 ft 8 in)
Propeller diameter 1.37 m (4 ft 6 in)

AREA:
Wings, gross 16.16 m² (174.0 sq ft)

WEIGHTS:
Weight empty 110 kg (244 lb)
Pilot weight range 50-113 kg (110-250 lb)
Max T-O weight 227 kg (500 lb)

PERFORMANCE:
Max level speed 52 knots (97 km/h; 60 mph)
Econ cruising speed 39 knots (72 km/h; 45 mph)
Stalling speed: power on 16 knots (29 km/h; 18 mph)
power off 19 knots (34 km/h; 21 mph)
Max rate of climb at S/L 305 m (1,000 ft)/min
Service ceiling more than 5,485 m (18,000 ft)
T-O and landing run 31 m (100 ft)
Range with max fuel 108 nm (201 km; 125 miles)

LOEHLE AVIATION 5151 MUSTANG

Mr Michael Loehle's approximate $^3/_4$-scale representation of a Second World War P-51 Mustang fighter is offered in kit form under Experimental category regulations. Construction time is approximately 300-400 working hours.

The prototype, which flew for the first time on 30 January 1986, is a single seater constructed primarily of wood, with both conventional and geodetic structures. The whole assembly is glued together, using T-88 epoxy, and is fabric covered. Power is provided by a 34 kW (46 hp) Rotax 503. Fuel capacity is 19 litres (5 US gallons; 4.2 Imp gallons), with optional 38 or 57 litre (10 or 15 US gallon; 8.3 or 12.5 Imp gallon) tanks available as alternatives on kit-built aircraft. A non-retractable tailwheel type landing gear is standard, but retractable gear is available as an option.

DIMENSIONS, EXTERNAL:
Wing span 8.36 m (27 ft 5 in)
Length overall 6.96 m (22 ft 10 in)

AREA:
Wings, gross 12.54 m² (135.0 sq ft)

WEIGHTS:
Weight empty little over 181 kg (400 lb)
Max T-O weight 317 kg (700 lb)

PERFORMANCE:
Cruising speed 61-65 knots (113-121 km/h; 70-75 mph)
Stalling speed 24-25 knots (44-45 km/h; 27-28 mph)
Max rate of climb at S/L 244-305 m (800-1,000 ft)/min
T-O run 46 m (150 ft)
Landing run 61 m (200 ft)
Range with standard fuel 108 nm (201 km; 125 miles)
g limits for wings +4/–2

LUNDY

BRIAN LUNDY

1257 East Shadowridge Drive 11J, Midvale, Utah 84047

GRAFLITE

Mr Brian Lundy and Mr Steve Kotula, both mechanical engineers in composite construction, designed the Graflite with the first-time builder in mind. The prototype first flew on 11 July 1987 and kits became available in late 1988. An aerobatic version is optional.

The following details refer to the prototype. The kit-built version has as standard a Textron Lycoming O-360 engine and fuel capacity of 170 litres (45 US gallons; 37.5 Imp gallons).

TYPE: Side by side two-seat homebuilt.

AIRFRAME: Moulded and vacuum bagged components of graphite/epoxy/core sandwich construction. Wing section NACA 64212.5. Winglets standard. Retractable tricycle landing gear.

POWER PLANT: One 112 kW (150 hp) Textron Lycoming O-320-A2B. Fuel capacity 129 litres (34 US gallons; 28.3 Imp gallons).

DIMENSIONS, EXTERNAL:
Wing span over winglets 7.67 m (25 ft 2 in)
Length overall 6.32 m (20 ft 9 in)
Height overall 1.88 m (6 ft 2 in)
Propeller diameter 1.70 m (5 ft 7 in)

WEIGHTS:
Weight empty 449 kg (989 lb)
Max crew weight 154 kg (340 lb)
Baggage weight 41 kg (90 lb)
Max T-O weight 726 kg (1,600 lb)

PERFORMANCE:
Max level speed at S/L 180 knots (333 km/h; 207 mph)
Econ cruising speed at 2,440 m (8,000 ft) 156 knots (290 km/h; 180 mph)
Stalling speed, engine idling 56 knots (103 km/h; 64 mph)
Max rate of climb at S/L 457 m (1,500 ft)/min
Service ceiling 5,790 m (19,000 ft)
Range with max fuel 547 nm (1,014 km; 630 miles)
Endurance 3 h 30 min
g limits +4.4/–3

MACFAM

MACFAM

Box 788, Great Falls, Montana 59403-0788

Readopting an earlier name, MacFam (formerly McAsco) continues to offer plans for its Cavalier range of homebuilts, plus the Jungsters designed by Mr Rim Kaminskas.

MACFAM SA 102.5 CAVALIER

The prototype SA 102.5 Cavalier is currently being reworked and refurbished in an effort to reduce empty weight from the original 477 kg (1,051 lb) to 408 kg (900 lb). Fitted with a Continental O-200 engine and a new wooden propeller, it is anticipated that a true air speed of 139 knots (257 km/h; 160 mph) will be achieved at 2,450 rpm, at a maximum weight of about 658-680 kg (1,450-1,500 lb).

TYPE: Side by side two-seat homebuilt.

AIRFRAME: All-wood airframe except for Dacron covered outer wing panels, rear top decking and tail unit, plus glassfibre cockpit canopy frame and doors. Wing section NACA 23015 at root, NACA 23012 at tip. Non-retractable tricycle landing gear, with optional floats or skis.

POWER PLANT: Wide choice of four-cylinder engines, including 63.5, 67 or 74.5 kW (85, 90 or 100 hp) Continental, 93-97 kW (125-130 hp) Franklin Sport 4A, 80.5 or 86 kW (108 or 115 hp) Textron Lycoming O-235, or 93 or 101 kW (125 or 135 hp) Textron Lycoming O-290. Wingtip fuel tanks, total capacity 151 litres (40 US gallons; 33.5 Imp gallons).

DIMENSIONS, EXTERNAL:
Wing span over tip tanks 8.33 m (27 ft 4 in)
Length overall 6.71 m (22 ft 0 in)
Height overall 2.23 m (7 ft 4 in)
Propeller diameter see under 'Power Plant'

AREA:
Wings, gross 10.87 m² (117.0 sq ft)

WEIGHTS:
Basic operating weight empty 408 kg (900 lb)
Baggage weight 56 kg (125 lb)
Max T-O weight 680 kg (1,500 lb)

PERFORMANCE (at max T-O weight, 93 kW; 125 hp Textron Lycoming engine):
Max level speed at 2,135 m (7,000 ft) 160 knots (297 km/h; 185 mph)
Econ cruising speed 134 knots (249 km/h; 155 mph)
Stalling speed:
flaps up 44 knots (81 km/h; 50 mph) IAS
flaps down 35 knots (65 km/h; 40 mph) IAS
Max rate of climb at S/L over 518 m (1,700 ft)/min
Service ceiling 4,875 m (16,000 ft)
T-O run 107 m (350 ft)
Landing run 183 m (600 ft)
Max range, no reserves 720 nm (1,335 km; 830 miles)

MACFAM SA 105 SUPER CAVALIER

Although similar in general configuration to the SA 102.5, except for its retractable landing gear, the SA 105 was an entirely new design. Plans were being revised in 1988 to incorporate structural simplification and weight reductions.

The following description applies to the current standard SA 105 built to MacFam plans:

TYPE: Two-seat dual control homebuilt.

AIRFRAME: All-wood airframe except for fabric covering on wings aft of main spar, rear fuselage, top decking and control surfaces; and glassfibre canted wingtip tanks, cockpit roof, side window/door frames and engine cowling. Wing section NACA 23015 at root, NACA 23010 at tip. Retractable tricycle landing gear.

POWER PLANT: Recommended are 112-119 kW (150-160 hp) Textron Lycoming O-320/IO-320. Min recommended power plant is 93 kW (125 hp) Franklin 4A-235 or Textron Lycoming O-290/O-290-D2/O-290-G. Max recommended is the Javelin Aircraft Company's Ford Model 230 motorcar engine conversion, or 149 kW (200 hp) Textron Lycoming O-360/IO-360. Total fuel capacity 127 litres (33.6 US gallons; 28 Imp gallons). Optional sump tanks (with engines over 112 kW; 150 hp) raise capacity to 152.75 litres (40.3 US gallons; 33.6 Imp gallons).

DIMENSIONS, EXTERNAL:
Wing span over tip tanks 8.42 m (27 ft 7$\frac{3}{8}$ in)
Length overall (nominal) 7.25 m (23 ft 9$\frac{1}{2}$ in)
Propeller diameter 1.83 m (6 ft 0 in)

AREA:
Wings, gross 11.00 m² (118.5 sq ft)

WEIGHTS:
Weight empty 431-454 kg (950-1,000 lb)
Baggage capacity 172 kg (379 lb)
Max T-O weight (dependent on engine) up to 885 kg (1,950 lb)

PERFORMANCE (estimated at AUW of 816 kg; 1,800 lb, with 112 kW; 150 hp engine):
Cruising speed 152-156 knots (281-289 km/h; 175-180 mph)
Stalling speed:
flaps up 52-61 knots (97-105 km/h; 60-65 mph) IAS
15° flap 48-52 knots (89-97 km/h; 55-60 mph) IAS
Max rate of climb at S/L 274-305 m (900-1,000 ft)/min
T-O run 244 m (800 ft)

MACFAM JUNGSTER I

The primary design requirements of this aircraft were to duplicate as closely as possible the performance and flight characteristics of the Bücker Jungmeister. The prototype flew for the first time in October 1962. Sets of plans have been available to amateur constructors for many years, with several hundred sets sold.

TYPE: Single-seat sporting homebuilt.

AIRFRAME: Braced biplane with wood structure, plywood and fabric covered except for aluminium alloy engine cowling. Wing section NACA 4413. Non-retractable tailwheel landing gear.

POWER PLANT: Options include 63.4-74.5 kW (85-100 hp) Continental C85, C90 or O-200; 93-97 kW (125-130 hp) Franklin Sport 4, 4A or 4B; 80.5-86 kW (108-115 hp) Textron Lycoming O-235-C or -C1; 93-100.6 kW (125-135 hp) Textron Lycoming O-290-D or -D2; 104.5-112 kW (140-150 hp) Textron Lycoming O-320; or European engines in the same weight/power class. Fuel capacity 62 litres (16.5 US gallons; 13.7 Imp gallons); optional 26 litre (7 US gallon; 5.8 Imp gallon) tank in upper wing centre-section, increasing total capacity to 88 litres (23.5 US gallons; 19.4 Imp gallons).

DIMENSIONS, EXTERNAL (prototype):
Wing span 5.08 m (16 ft 8 in)

Jungster II monoplane owned by Mr Ed Sullivan of Fresno, California
(John Wegg)

Lundy Graflite all-composites homebuilt aircraft

Loehle Ritz Standard Model A *(Howard Levy)*

MacFam marketed Jungster I built by Mr Dave Clark of Renton, Washington

Loehle Aviation 5151 Mustang homebuilt aircraft

Loehle Aviation The Fun Machine

MacFam SA 102.5 Cavalier two-seat homebuilt aircraft *(Geoffrey P. Jones)*

Length overall	4.88 m (16 ft 0 in)
Propeller diameter	1.73 m (5 ft 8 in)
AREA:	
Wings, gross	7.43 m² (80.0 sq ft)
WEIGHTS:	
Weight empty	275 kg (606 lb)
T-O weight, aerobatic	385 kg (850 lb)
Max T-O weight	455 kg (1,000 lb)

PERFORMANCE (prototype, at max T-O weight, Textron Lycoming O-235 engine):

Max level speed at S/L
109 knots (201 km/h; 125 mph) IAS

Max cruising speed at S/L
103 knots (192 km/h; 119 mph)

Stalling speed	45 knots (84 km/h; 52 mph) IAS
Max rate of climb at S/L	455 m (1,500 ft)/min
Service ceiling	3,960 m (13,000 ft)
T-O run	91 m (300 ft)
Landing run	152 m (500 ft)

Range with max fuel (incl centre-section tank)
260 nm (482 km; 300 miles)

g limits +9/–6

MACFAM JUNGSTER II

The prototype of this strut braced parasol monoplane flew for the first time in March 1966. Plans are available.

TYPE: Single-seat sporting homebuilt.

AIRFRAME: All-wood structure, plywood and fabric covered. Wing section NACA 2412. Non-retractable tailwheel landing gear.

POWER PLANT (prototype): One 134 kW (180 hp) Textron Lycoming O-360. Fuel capacity 75 litres (20 US gallons; 16.7 Imp gallons). Other engines available optionally include those listed under Jungster I description, plus 119 kW (160 hp) Textron Lycoming O-320 and 134 kW (180 hp) Textron Lycoming O-360.

DIMENSIONS, EXTERNAL:

Wing span	6.81 m (22 ft 4 in)
Length overall (tail up)	5.16 m (16 ft 11 in)
Height to top of wings (tail up)	2.06 m (6 ft 9 in)
Propeller diameter	1.68 m (5 ft 6 in)

AREA:		
Wings, gross	7.80 m² (84.0 sq ft)	

WEIGHTS (original 134 kW; 180 hp version):
Weight empty 335 kg (739 lb)
Max T-O weight 517 kg (1,139 lb)

PERFORMANCE (original 134 kW; 180 hp version, at max T-O weight):
Max level speed at S/L
139 knots (257 km/h; 160 mph)
Max cruising speed up to 3,050 m (10,000 ft)
135 knots (249 km/h; 155 mph)

Stalling speed 48 knots (89 km/h; 55 mph) IAS
Max rate of climb at S/L 1,065 m (3,500 ft)/min

MAGNUM
MAGNUM INDUSTRIES
9815 Lemona Avenue, Sepulveda, California 91343
Telephone: (818) 893 9240
GENERAL MANAGER: Rodney E. Gage

In June 1987 Magnum Industries acquired from Delta Technology all assets related to the Nomad and Honcho series of microlights. An expanded manufacturing facility is being established at Palmdale, California.

Magnum intends to produce one or more enclosed cabin versions of these microlights, although aircraft in existing forms can be built against orders. In the meantime, the company is supplying parts and retrofit kits for all models to existing owners. Future plans may include offering licensed manufacture to foreign companies.

The details below refer to the microlights in present open form.

MAGNUM NOMAD II
TYPE: Single-seat microlight.
AIRFRAME: All-aluminium frame, assembled with bolts and pop rivets. Wing section NACA 4415. All flying surfaces covered with Ceconite. Three-axis control. Non-retractable tricycle landing gear.
POWER PLANT: One 20 kW (27 hp) Rotax 277. Fuel capacity 19 litres (5 US gallons; 4.2 Imp gallons).
DIMENSIONS, EXTERNAL:
Wing span 11.00 m (36 ft 1 in)
Length overall 5.75 m (18 ft 10½ in)

Height overall 2.87 m (9 ft 5 in)
Propeller diameter 1.22 m (4 ft 0 in)
AREA:
Wings, gross 13.69 m² (147.34 sq ft)
WEIGHTS:
Weight empty 97 kg (214 lb)
Max T-O weight 200.5 kg (442 lb)
PERFORMANCE (at max T-O weight):
Max level speed 49 knots (90 km/h; 56 mph) CAS
Max cruising speed 42 knots (77 km/h; 48 mph) CAS
Stalling speed 20 knots (37 km/h; 23 mph) CAS
Max rate of climb at S/L 201 m (660 ft)/min
Absolute power ceiling 4,575 m (15,000 ft)
T-O run, firm ground 31 m (100 ft)
Range with max fuel 139 nm (257 km; 160 miles)
Endurance with max fuel 4 h 6 min
g limits +6.67/-2.5

MAGNUM HONCHO II and SUPER-HONCHO
Generally similar to the Nomad, except for a shorter fuselage and shorter span wings, the Honcho II retains the 20 kW (27 hp) engine. The Super-Honcho has a 37.3 kW (50 hp) Rotax 503.
DIMENSIONS, EXTERNAL (A: Honcho II, B: Super-Honcho):
Wing span: A, B 9.80 m (32 ft 2 in)
Length overall: A 5.35 m (17 ft 6½ in)
B 5.46 m (17 ft 11 in)
Height overall: A 2.87 m (9 ft 5 in)
B 3.02 m (9 ft 11 in)

Propeller diameter: A 1.22 m (4 ft 0 in)
B 1.37 m (4 ft 6 in)
AREA:
Wings, gross: A, B 12.20 m² (131.35 sq ft)
WEIGHTS:
Weight empty: A 108 kg (239 lb)
B 110 kg (243 lb)
Max T-O weight: A 190.5 kg (420 lb)
B 238 kg (525 lb)
PERFORMANCE (at max T-O weight):
Max level speed: A 50 knots (93 km/h; 58 mph) CAS
B 55 knots (101 km/h; 63 mph) CAS
Max cruising speed:
A 43 knots (80 km/h; 50 mph) CAS
B 50 knots (93 km/h; 58 mph) CAS
Stalling speed: A 22 knots (41 km/h; 25 mph) CAS
B 24 knots (44 km/h; 27 mph) CAS
Max rate of climb at S/L: A 213 m (700 ft)/min
B 481 m (1,580 ft)/min
Absolute power ceiling: A 3,810 m (12,500 ft)
B 5,335 m (17,500 ft)
T-O run, firm ground: A 29 m (95 ft)
B 18.5 m (60 ft)
Range with max fuel: A 139 nm (257 km; 160 miles)
B 121 nm (225 km; 140 miles)
Endurance with max fuel: A 3 h 36 min
B 2 h 24 min
g limits: A +6.67/-2.5
B +6.67/-3.5

MARQUART
ED MARQUART
PO Box 3032, Riverside, California 92519
Telephone: (714) 683 9582

MARQUART MA-4 LANCER
Available in plans form only, the Lancer is a single-seat biplane powered by an engine in the 48.5-93.2 kW (65-125 hp) range. Construction is of wood, steel tube and fabric.
DIMENSIONS, EXTERNAL:
Wing span 6.10 m (20 ft 0 in)
Length overall 5.03 m (16 ft 6 in)
Height overall 1.98 m (6 ft 6 in)
AREA:
Wings, gross 10.78 m² (116.0 sq ft)
WEIGHTS:
Weight empty 295 kg (650 lb)
Max T-O weight 454 kg (1,000 lb)

PERFORMANCE (93.2 kW; 125 hp engine):
Max level speed 113 knots (209 km/h; 130 mph)
Cruising speed 104 knots (193 km/h; 120 mph)
Stalling speed 48 knots (89 km/h; 55 mph)
Max rate of climb at S/L 488 m (1,600 ft)/min
Service ceiling 3,050 m (10,000 ft)
T-O run 91 m (300 ft)
Landing run 244 m (800 ft)
Range 325 nm (603 km; 375 miles)

MARQUART MA-5 CHARGER
Plans and component parts of this popular homebuilt biplane are available.
TYPE: Two-seat homebuilt sporting biplane.
AIRFRAME: Wooden wings and steel tube fuselage, all fabric covered. Non-retractable tailwheel landing gear.
POWER PLANT: One engine of 74.6-134 kW (100-180 hp); typically, a 134 kW (180 hp) Textron Lycoming O-360-A1G6. Fuel capacity 98.4 litres (26 US gallons; 21.6 Imp gallons).

DIMENSIONS, EXTERNAL:
Wing span 7.32 m (24 ft 0 in)
Length overall 5.94 m (19 ft 6 in)
Height overall 2.29 m (7 ft 6 in)
AREA:
Wings, gross 15.8 m² (170.0 sq ft)
WEIGHTS:
Weight empty 454 kg (1,000 lb)
Baggage capacity 11.3 kg (25 lb)
Max T-O weight 703 kg (1,550 lb)
PERFORMANCE (134 kW; 180 hp engine):
Max level speed 126 knots (233 km/h; 145 mph)
Max cruising speed 117 knots (217 km/h; 135 mph)
Stalling speed 37 knots (68 km/h; 42 mph)
Max rate of climb at S/L 549 m (1,800 ft)/min
Service ceiling 4,260 m (14,000 ft)
T-O run 122 m (400 ft)
Landing run 244 m (800 ft)
Range with max fuel 390 nm (724 km; 450 miles)

MAXAIR
MAXAIR AIRCRAFT CORPORATION
3855 Highway 27 North, Lake Wales, Florida 33853
Telephone: (813) 676 0771
Telex: 4996511
DIRECTOR OF MARKETING AND SALES: Phillip Lockwood

MAXAIR DRIFTER SERIES
In addition to the five versions of the Drifter of which details follow, new strut-braced models of the XP503 and MU532 became available in August 1988. Each has a single chrome molybdenum steel tube strut each side and stamped aluminium alloy ribs, plus full-span flaperons for STOL performance. Kits of all models are available.

DR277. Original single-seat model with Rotax 277 engine, introduced in early 1983 and the only version available also in ready assembled form. Conforms to FAR Pt 103 requirements.

DR377. More powerful single-seater with Rotax 377 engine.

XP503. Tandem two-seat, dual control version of the basic Drifter. Higher weight makes it an Experimental category homebuilt aircraft.

MU532. Tandem two-seat, dual control utility counterpart of XP503, suitable for heavy duty applications such as floatplane operation and agricultural spraying. Strengthened wings and landing gear permit a 245 kg (540 lb) useful load. Rotax 532 engine.

DR532. High-performance single-seat version with Rotax 532 engine, shorter wing span and wide-chord full span ailerons for quick roll response. Classed as Experimental category homebuilt.

TYPES: DR277 and DR377 conform to FAR Pt 103, other models to FAA Experimental requirements.
AIRFRAME: Braced mainframe of steel and aluminium alloy tube. Wings and tail surfaces have double surface Dacron covering. Three-axis control. Non-retractable tailwheel landing gear. Options include floats, amphibious gear and nose fairings.
POWER PLANT: DR277: One 20 kW (27 hp) Rotax 277. DR377: One 26 kW (35 hp) Rotax 377. XP503: One 34 kW (46 hp) Rotax 503. MU532 and DR532: One 47.7 kW (64 hp) Rotax 532. Fuel capacity 19 litres (5 US gallons; 4.2 Imp gallons) standard; 38 litres (10 US gallons; 8.3 Imp gallons) optional.
DIMENSIONS, EXTERNAL (A: DR277, B: XP503, C: MU532, and D: DR532):
Wing span: A, B, C 9.14 m (30 ft 0 in)
D 7.01 m (23 ft 0 in)
Length overall: A, B, C, D 5.79 m (19 ft 0 in)
Height overall: A 2.67 m (8 ft 9 in)
B, C 2.82 m (9 ft 3 in)
D 2.79 m (9 ft 2 in)
Propeller diameter: A, B, C, D 1.52 m (5 ft 0 in)
AREAS:
Wings, gross: A, B, C 14.12 m² (152.0 sq ft)
D 10.87 m² (117.0 sq ft)
WEIGHTS (A, B, C and D as above):
Weight empty: A 109 kg (240 lb)
B 152 kg (335 lb)
C 163 kg (360 lb)
D 141 kg (310 lb)
Max pilot weight: A 104 kg (230 lb)
B, C 109 kg (240 lb)
D 106 kg (235 lb)

Max T-O weight: A 227 kg (500 lb)
B 356 kg (785 lb)
C 408 kg (900 lb)
D 258 kg (570 lb)
PERFORMANCE (A and D with 79 kg; 175 lb pilot, B and C with two 79 kg; 175 lb crew):
Max level speed: A 55 knots (101 km/h; 63 mph)
B, C 65 knots (120 km/h; 75 mph)
D 74 knots (137 km/h; 85 mph)
Econ cruising speed: A 35 knots (64 km/h; 40 mph)
Stalling speed: A 23 knots (42 km/h; 26 mph)
B 27 knots (50 km/h; 31 mph)
C 32 knots (58 km/h; 36 mph)
D 30 knots (55 km/h; 34 mph)
Max rate of climb at S/L: A, B 183 m (600 ft)/min
C 244 m (800 ft)/min
D 396 m (1,300 ft)/min
Service ceiling: A 3,050 m (10,000 ft)
T-O run: A 46-84 m (150-275 ft)
B, C 76-107 m (250-350 ft)
D 79 m (260 ft)
Landing run with brakes: A 69 m (225 ft)
B, D 91 m (300 ft)
C 98 m (320 ft)
Range, 65% power: A 104 nm (193 km; 120 miles)
B 87 nm (161 km; 100 miles)
C 74 nm (136 km; 85 miles)
D 69 nm (129 km; 80 miles)
Endurance with max fuel: A 2 h 30 min
g limits: A +6/-3.3
B +4.2 limit
B +6/-3 ultimate

Two-seat Maxair Drifter XP503 *(Phillip Lockwood)*

Magnum Nomad II with retrofit cockpit pod and door *(Peter M. Bowers)*

Marquart MA-5 Charger sporting biplane *(J. M. G. Gradidge)*

Single-seat Maxair Drifter with Lotus Mono-Hull amphibious landing gear
(Howard Levy)

Mirage Celerity (Textron Lycoming O-320 engine) *(Peter M. Bowers)*

MERGANSER
MERGANSER AIRCRAFT CORPORATION

PO Box 8, Annapolis, Maryland 21404

The Merganser Aircraft Corporation's Merganser two-seat amphibious flying-boat is still under development. Details and an illustration can be found in the 1987-88 *Jane's*.

MILLER
MILLER AIR SPORTS INC

Boerne Stage Airfield, Route 3, Box 3452, Boerne, Texas 78006

Telephone: (512) 755 8702

MILLER TEXAS GEM 260

Mr Jim Miller's Texas Gem 260 pusher-engined racer is now available in kit form for amateur construction. It is a tandem two-seater, with rear-mounted wings and a uniquely styled T tail. Construction is of glassfibre and carbonfibre. Power is provided by a 74.5 kW (100 hp) Continental O-200 racing specification engine. The main units of the tricycle landing gear are faired and non-retractable. A photograph of the Texas Gem 260 can be found in the 1985-86 *Jane's*.

PERFORMANCE:
Max level speed	226 knots (418 km/h; 260 mph)
Cruising speed	204 knots (378 km/h; 235 mph)

MINER
EARL L. MINER
Box 466, Marshfield, Missouri 65706

Details and an illustration of the Miner Tragonfly cargo carrying autogyro can be found in the 1987-88 *Jane's*. Its development is continuing.

MIRAGE
MIRAGE AIRCRAFT INC
3936 Austin Street, Klamath Falls, Oregon 97603
Telephone: (503) 884 4011
PRESIDENT: Larry Burton

MIRAGE CELERITY

The prototype Celerity flew for the first time on 18 May 1985. It has since undergone considerable development, and now has retractable landing gear, as shown on plans available from Mirage Aircraft. An inexperienced builder could take more than 3,000 working hours to build a Celerity from plans. Various kits and upholstery patterns to cut working time are available via Wicks Aircraft Supply (410 Pine Street, Highland, Illinois 62249).

TYPE: Side by side two-seat homebuilt.
AIRFRAME: Wing section NACA 23015 at root, NACA 23010 at tip. Airframe structure of wood, with composite skins of foam, glassfibre and epoxy resin. Retractable tailwheel landing gear.
POWER PLANT: One 119 kW (160 hp) Textron Lycoming O-320-B1A. Fuel capacity 114 litres (30 US gallons; 25 Imp gallons). Two auxiliary tip tanks, each of 38 litres (10 US gallons; 8.3 Imp gallons) capacity. Engines of 74.6-134 kW (100-180 hp) optional.
DIMENSIONS, EXTERNAL:
Wing span over tip tanks	7.01 m (23 ft 0 in)
Length overall	6.55 m (21 ft 6 in)
Height overall	1.68 m (5 ft 6 in)
Propeller diameter	1.93 m (6 ft 4 in)

AREA:
Wings, gross	8.36 m² (90.0 sq ft)

WEIGHTS:
Weight empty	530 kg (1,169 lb)
Baggage capacity	27 kg (60 lb)
Max T-O weight	828 kg (1,825 lb)

PERFORMANCE (at max T-O weight):
Econ cruising speed	165 knots (306 km/h; 190 mph)
Stalling speed	46 knots (86 km/h; 53 mph)
Max rate of climb at S/L	549 m (1,800 ft)/min
T-O run	244 m (800 ft)
Landing run	305 m (1,000 ft)
Range with max standard fuel	
	781-868 nm (1,448-1,609 km; 900-1,000 miles)

MITCHELL WING
MITCHELL AEROSPACE COMPANY
1900 S. Newcomb, Porterville, California 93257
Telephone: (209) 781 8100
DIRECTOR: James M. Meade

MITCHELL WING B-10

The B-10 flew for the first time in 1976, powered by a 9 kW (12 hp) McCulloch MC-101 engine. The two current models available in plans, kit and ready assembled forms, use a basic hang glider rigid wing:

B-10F. Foot-launch powered version, with a tubular frame structure that serves as fuselage, engine mounting, and open cockpit for the pilot. Two mainwheels only.

B-10. Powered version with tricycle landing gear.

TYPE: Single-seat microlight; conforms to FAR Pt 103. Two-seat version available.

AIRFRAME: Wing structure of wood and Dacron, with foam ribs. Wing section NACA 23015. Mitchell patented trailing-edge 'stabilators'. Rudders, mounted above each wingtip, operated conventionally for yaw control; can also be actuated differentially as airbrakes. Braced fuselage framework of aluminium tube. Optional 'podule' glassfibre cockpit module.

POWER PLANT: One 15 kW (20 hp) Honda. Fuel capacity 5.7 litres (1.5 US gallons; 1.25 Imp gallons); auxiliary tanks optional.

DIMENSIONS, EXTERNAL:
Wing span	10.36 m (34 ft 0 in)
Height overall	1.22 m (4 ft 0 in)
Propeller diameter	1.22 m (4 ft 0 in)

AREA:
Wings, gross	12.63 m² (136.0 sq ft)

WEIGHTS:
Weight empty	91 kg (200 lb)
Max pilot weight	136 kg (300 lb)
Max T-O weight: standard	238 kg (525 lb)
restricted	329 kg (725 lb)

PERFORMANCE (B-10 at max standard T-O weight):
Max level speed	56 knots (105 km/h; 65 mph)
Econ cruising speed at S/L	31 knots (58 km/h; 36 mph)
Stalling speed	21 knots (39 km/h; 24 mph)
Max rate of climb at S/L	122 m (400 ft)/min
Service ceiling	3,660 m (12,000 ft)
T-O run	61 m (200 ft)
Landing run	30 m (100 ft)
Range with max standard fuel and max payload	35 nm (64 km; 40 miles)
Range with auxiliary fuel	434 nm (805 km; 500 miles)
g limits	±6

MITCHELL WING U-2 SUPERWING

The prototype U-2 Superwing first flew during 1979. Plans and kits are available.

TYPE: Single-seat microlight; does not conform to FAR Pt 103.

AIRFRAME: Wings generally similar to those of B-10, except for modified Wortmann section and combined fin and rudder assemblies at the wingtips. Fuselage structure of wood and steel tube within wing centre-section. Retractable tricycle landing gear. Optional non-retractable gear.

POWER PLANT: As described for B-10. Fuel capacity 5.7 litres (1.5 US gallons; 1.25 Imp gallons). Auxiliary tanks optional.

DIMENSIONS, EXTERNAL: As for B-10 except:
Length overall	2.84 m (9 ft 4 in)
Height overall	0.91 m (3 ft 0 in)

WEIGHTS:
Weight empty	136 kg (300 lb)
Max pilot weight	136 kg (300 lb)
Max standard T-O weight	272 kg (600 lb)

PERFORMANCE (at max standard T-O weight):
Max level speed at S/L	74 knots (137 km/h; 85 mph)
Max cruising speed at S/L	56 knots (105 km/h; 65 mph)
Stalling speed	26 knots (47 km/h; 29 mph)
Max rate of climb at S/L	152 m (500 ft)/min
Service ceiling	3,660 m (12,000 ft)
T-O run	61 m (200 ft)
Landing run	38 m (125 ft)
Range with max standard fuel and max payload	39 nm (72 km; 45 miles)
Range with auxiliary fuel	434 nm (805 km; 500 miles)
g limits	±10

MITCHELL WING P-38 LIGHTNING

The P-38 was designed to be assembled by four people in one day. It flew for the first time in late 1980 and is available in plans and kit forms. Assembly time for the kit is quoted as 100 man-hours.

An **AG-38A Terrier** agricultural version, with a 12V battery, 53 litre (14 US gallon; 11.7 Imp gallon) ULV spraytank, two Beeco Mist sprayheads and an electric spraypump, is also available.

The following description applies to the standard P-38:

TYPE: Single-seat microlight; does not conform to FAR Pt 103.

AIRFRAME: Main structure of aluminium, with quick-fit ribs and Dacron covered wing and tail surfaces. Wing section NACA 23015. Three-axis control. Non-retractable tricycle landing gear. Optional cockpit 'podule', floats and skis.

POWER PLANT: One 22 kW (30 hp) 250 cc Cuyuna 430. Fuel capacity 5.7 litres (1.5 US gallons; 1.25 Imp gallons). Options include 15 litre (4 US gallon; 3.33 Imp gallon) auxiliary fuel tank.

DIMENSIONS, EXTERNAL:
Wing span	8.53 m (28 ft 0 in)
Length overall	5.49 m (18 ft 0 in)
Height overall	1.52 m (5 ft 0 in)

AREA:
Wings, gross	11.52 m² (124.0 sq ft)

WEIGHTS:
Weight empty	136 kg (300 lb)
Max pilot weight	136 kg (300 lb)
Max T-O weight: standard	249 kg (550 lb)
restricted	340 kg (750 lb)

PERFORMANCE (at max standard T-O weight):
Max level speed	52 knots (97 km/h; 60 mph)
Max cruising speed	48 knots (88 km/h; 55 mph)
Stalling speed	28 knots (51 km/h; 32 mph)
Max rate of climb at S/L	76-91 m (250-300 ft)/min
T-O run	68 m (225 ft)
Landing run	61 m (200 ft)
Range with max standard fuel	43 nm (80 km; 50 miles)
Range with auxiliary fuel	434 nm (805 km; 500 miles)
g limits	±6

MITCHELL WING AG-38-A WAR EAGLE

The AG-38-A War Eagle is an enlarged military version of the P-38/AG-38 series, with a more powerful engine, increased fuel and provision for a variety of operational equipment. An illustration appeared in the 1987-88 *Jane's*.

POWER PLANT: One 29.4 kW (39.4 hp) Rotax 447. Standard fuel capacity 24 litres (6.5 US gallons; 5.4 Imp gallons). Optional long-range fuel tank, capacity 151 litres (40 US gallons; 33.3 Imp gallons).

OPERATIONAL EQUIPMENT: Optional items include two M60 machine-gun mounts; four Strem 89 rocket mounts; wind-driven agricultural spraypump with full-span 25 nozzle spray system and 151 litre (40 US gallon; 33.3 Imp gallon) hopper capacity; ballistic parachute; radios; video camera, transmitter and antenna; Kevlar pilot protection and night vision goggles.

DIMENSIONS, EXTERNAL:
Wing span	10.36 m (34 ft 0 in)
Length overall	5.79 m (19 ft 0 in)
Height overall	2.11 m (6 ft 11 in)
Propeller diameter	1.47 m (4 ft 10 in)

AREA:
Wings, gross	14.86 m² (160.0 sq ft)

WEIGHTS:
Weight empty	168 kg (370 lb)
Max pilot weight	104 kg (230 lb)
Max T-O weight: Normal	363 kg (800 lb)
Restricted category	476 kg (1,050 lb)

PERFORMANCE (Normal category, 77 kg; 170 lb pilot):
Best cruising speed	60 knots (111 km/h; 69 mph)
Stalling speed, power off	30 knots (56 km/h; 35 mph)
Max rate of climb at S/L	152 m (500 ft)/min
T-O run	61 m (200 ft)
Endurance with max fuel	1 h 40 min

MITCHELL WING A-10 SILVER EAGLE

Based on the B-10, but of mainly aluminium construction, the A-10 was designed to conform to all FAA ultralight (microlight) regulations, including FAR Pt 103, and is produced in ready to fly form only. A two-seat model is designated **TU-10 Double Eagle.**

TYPE (A-10): Single-seat microlight; conforms to FAR Pt 103.

AIRFRAME: Wing section NACA 23015. Wings formed by process based on honeycomb, using injections of NASA developed SP502 foam. All skins of Alclad aluminium sheet; all fuselage tubing and spar caps of aircraft aluminium; aerodynamic fairings of pre-moulded glassfibre. Non-retractable tricycle landing gear. Floats optional.

POWER PLANT: One 17.2 kW (23 hp) Zenoah in A-10; fuel capacity 11.4 litres (3 US gallons; 2.5 Imp gallons). TU-10 has a 29.4 kW (39.4 hp) Rotax 447 and 22.7 litres (6 US gallons; 5 Imp gallons) of fuel.

DIMENSIONS, EXTERNAL (A-10):
Wing span	10.46 m (34 ft 4 in)
Length overall	2.59 m (8 ft 6 in)
Height overall	1.88 m (6 ft 2 in)

AREA (A-10):
Wings, gross	12.45 m² (134.0 sq ft)

WEIGHTS:
Weight empty	113 kg (250 lb)
Pilot weight range	54.5-129 kg (120-285 lb)
Max T-O weight	251 kg (553 lb)

PERFORMANCE (A-10 prototype with full fuel and 75 kg; 165 lb pilot):
Max level speed	55 knots (101 km/h; 63 mph)
Max cruising speed, 75% power	50 knots (93 km/h; 58 mph)
Stalling speed, power off	24 knots (44 km/h; 27 mph)
Max rate of climb at S/L	195 m (640 ft)/min
Service ceiling	3,660 m (12,000 ft)
T-O run	69 m (225 ft)
Landing run	61 m (200 ft)
Range with max fuel, 75% power, no reserves	131 nm (243 km; 151 miles)
Endurance, conditions as above	2 h 24 min
g limits	±5.5

MOSLER
MOSLER MOTORS INC
140 Ashwood Road, Hendersonville, North Carolina 28739
Telephone: (704) 692 7713
PRESIDENT: John W. Martin

Mosler Motors has taken over the products of Nostalgair and Global Machine Tools. The only aircraft currently available are the N3 Pup and Super Pup.

MOSLER MOTORS N3 PUP and SUPER PUP

Mosler's N3 Pup is a microlight representation of the Piper Cub, available in ready to fly and kit forms. Average construction time is 200 working hours. The Super Pup conforms to Experimental and ARV regulations and has clipped wings, wheel fairings, brakes, a 45.5 litre (12 US gallon; 10 Imp gallon) fuel capacity and higher cruising speed. The following details refer to the Pup microlight.

TYPE: Single-seat microlight; conforms to FAR Pt 103.

AIRFRAME: Strut braced, with stamped aluminium alloy wing ribs, aluminium alloy spars, welded steel tube fuselage and overall Stits Dacron covering. Glassfibre engine cowling. Three-axis control. Non-retractable tailwheel landing gear. Options include floats, skis and ballistic parachute.

POWER PLANT: One 26 kW (35 hp) Mosler MM Series engine. Fuel capacity 15.9 litres (4.2 US gallons; 3.5 Imp gallons).

DIMENSIONS, EXTERNAL:
Wing span	9.14 m (30 ft 0 in)
Length overall	5.08 m (16 ft 8 in)
Height overall	1.57 m (5 ft 2 in)
Propeller diameter	1.42 m (4 ft 8 in)

AREA:
Wings, gross	11.43 m² (123.0 sq ft)

WEIGHTS:
Weight empty	112 kg (248 lb)
Max T-O weight	242 kg (535 lb)

PERFORMANCE:
Max level speed	55 knots (101 km/h; 63 mph)
Max cruising speed	50 knots (93 km/h; 58 mph)
Stalling speed	22 knots (41 km/h; 25 mph)
Max rate of climb at S/L	198 m (650 ft)/min
Service ceiling	1,525 m (5,000 ft)
T-O run	38 m (125 ft)
Landing run	61 m (200 ft)
Range with max fuel	173 nm (322 km; 200 miles)
Endurance with max fuel	3 h
g limits	+6/-3

MOSLER MOTORS QUESTOR

The Questor is not currently in production. Details and an illustration can be found in the 1987-88 *Jane's* under the former Nostalgair heading.

NEICO
NEICO AVIATION INC
403 South Ojai Street, Santa Paula, California 93060
Telephone: (805) 933 2747

NEICO AVIATION LANCAIR 200 and 235

The prototype Lancair 200 first flew in June 1984.

Current advertisements show the **Lancair 235** which, apart from having an 88 kW (118 hp) O-235 engine, has a 0.40 m³ (14.0 cu ft) baggage area. Cruising speed is increased to more than 174 knots (322 km/h; 200 mph). Kits of pre-moulded and pre-welded components to build the Lancair are available.

The following details refer mainly to the Lancair 200:

TYPE: Side by side two-seat sporting and cross-country homebuilt.

AIRFRAME: Wing section NLF 0215F. Composite airframe of glassfibre, Nomex honeycomb, Polyimide Rohacell foam and epoxy resin. Retractable tricycle landing gear.

POWER PLANT: Originally one 74.6 kW (100 hp) Continental O-200. Currently advertised with 88 kW (118 hp) O-235.

Mitchell Wing U-2 built by Mr Art Johnson, with a 28 kW (38 hp) Kawasaki TA 440B engine *(John Wegg)*

Mosler Motors N3 Pup *(Geoffrey P. Jones)*

Demonstration of Mitchell Wing AG-38 cropsprayer in China

Neico Aviation Lancair 235 *(John Wegg)*

Mitchell Wing A-10 Silver Eagle

NuWaco T-10 taperwing three-seat homebuilt biplane

Fuel capacity 106-114 litres (28-30 US gallons; 23.3-25 Imp gallons).

DIMENSIONS, EXTERNAL:

Wing span	7.16 m (23 ft 6 in)
Length overall	5.99 m (19 ft 8 in)
Width, wings folded	2.54 m (8 ft 4 in)
Height overall	1.85 m (6 ft 1 in)
Propeller diameter	1.47-1.52 m (4 ft 10 in-5 ft 0 in)

AREA:

Wings, gross	7.06 m² (76.0 sq ft)

WEIGHTS:

Weight empty	295 kg (650 lb)
Max T-O weight	578 kg (1,275 lb)

PERFORMANCE (100 hp engine):

Max level speed at S/L	185 knots (343 km/h; 213 mph)
Econ cruising speed	165 knots (306 km/h; 190 mph)

Stalling speed, engine idling

	48 knots (89 km/h; 55 mph)
Max rate of climb at S/L	457 m (1,500 ft)/min
Service ceiling	5,485-6,100 m (18,000-20,000 ft)
T-O and landing run	183 m (600 ft)
Range with max fuel	868 nm (1,609 km; 1,000 miles)

NUWACO
NUWACO AIRCRAFT COMPANY INC
PO Box 427, Calhan, Colorado 80808
Telephone: (719) 347 2325
PRESIDENT: Ernest A. Bode

NUWACO T-10
NuWaco markets plans and kits of this modernised version of the pre-war Waco 10-T taperwing biplane. The prototype made its first flight on 5 May 1984.

TYPE: Three-seat homebuilt replica biplane.

AIRFRAME: Welded steel tube fuselage and wire-braced tail unit, and braced wooden wings, all fabric covered. Wing section M-6. Non-retractable tailwheel landing gear. Options include floats and cockpit canopy.

POWER PLANT: Suited to engines of 164-336 kW (220-450 hp). Prototype fitted with 205 kW (275 hp) Jacobs R-755-B2 radial. Optional engines include Continental W-670, Pratt & Whitney R-985, Wright R-975 or J5, and Jacobs R-755-A2. Fuel capacity 227 litres (60 US gallons; 50 Imp gallons). Two auxiliary fuel tanks in upper wing centre section optional, each with capacity of 64.4 litres (17 US gallons; 14.2 Imp gallons).

DIMENSIONS, EXTERNAL:

Wing span	9.22 m (30 ft 3 in)
Length overall	6.86 m (22 ft 6 in)
Height overall	2.74 m (9 ft 0 in)
Propeller diameter: standard	2.74 m (9 ft 0 in)
optional	2.59 m (8 ft 6 in)

AREA:

Wings, gross	21.09 m² (227.0 sq ft)

WEIGHTS:

Weight empty	798 kg (1,760 lb)
Baggage capacity	18 kg (40 lb)
Max T-O weight	1,179 kg (2,600 lb)

PERFORMANCE (at max T-O weight):

Max level speed at 2,440 m (8,000 ft)
139 knots (257 km/h; 160 mph)

Econ cruising speed at 2,440 m (8,000 ft)
113 knots (209 km/h; 130 mph)

Stalling speed, power off	44 knots (81 km/h; 50 mph)
Service ceiling	6,400 m (21,000 ft)
T-O run	83 m (270 ft)
Landing run	244 m (800 ft)
Range	564 nm (1,046 km; 650 miles)
Endurance with max standard fuel	5 h
g limits	+10/-7

OSPREY
OSPREY AIRCRAFT
3741 El Ricon Way, Sacramento, California 95864
Telephone: (916) 483 3004

PEREIRA GP3 OSPREY II
Developed from the Osprey I flying boat, the prototype Osprey II amphibian first flew from water in April 1973. Sets of plans, as well as material and component kits, are available to amateur constructors. By early 1988, more than 1,000 sets of plans had been sold to potential builders in 48 countries, and at least 35 Ospreys had flown.

TYPE: Side by side two-seat, dual-control homebuilt amphibian.

AIRFRAME: Wing section NACA 23012. All-wood wings, except for fabric covering aft of spar. Wingtip stabilising floats of polyurethane foam covered with glassfibre. All-wood hull covered with marine plywood. Hull undersurface contours formed from sculptured polyurethane foam, protected by several layers of glassfibre cloth bonded with resin. All-wood tail unit. Water rudder. Retractable tricycle landing gear.

POWER PLANT: One 112 kW (150 hp) Textron Lycoming O-320. Usable fuel capacity 98.4 litres (26 US gallons; 21.6 Imp gallons). Wing tanks available to replace standard fuselage tank, allowing increased baggage area.

DIMENSIONS, EXTERNAL:

Wing span	7.92 m (26 ft 0 in)
Length overall	6.25 m (20 ft 6 in)
Height overall (wheels down)	1.83 m (6 ft 0 in)
Propeller diameter	1.68 m (5 ft 6 in)

AREA:

Wings, gross	12.08 m² (130.0 sq ft)

WEIGHTS:

Weight empty	440 kg (970 lb)
Baggage capacity	41 kg (90 lb)
Max T-O weight	707 kg (1,560 lb)

PERFORMANCE (at max T-O weight except where indicated):

Max cruising speed at 75% power
113 knots (209 km/h; 130 mph)

Econ cruising speed at 55% power
94 knots (175 km/h; 109 mph)
Stalling speed   53 knots (97 km/h; 60 mph)
Max rate of climb at S/L, with pilot only
365 m (1,200 ft)/min
Rate of climb at S/L   305 m (1,000 ft)/min
T-O run: land   122 m (400 ft)
water   159 m (520 ft)
Range with wing tanks   313 nm (579 km; 360 miles)

PEREIRA GP4

This aircraft flew for the first time in 1984. Plans to construct the GP4 are available. In addition, pre-welded fittings and a wood kit will be made available to reduce construction time.

TYPE: Two-seat cross-country homebuilt.
AIRFRAME: All-wood construction except for foam and glassfibre used in cowling and fairings. Wing section Laminar 63 series. Retractable tricycle landing gear.
POWER PLANT: One 149 kW (200 hp) Textron Lycoming IO-360. Fuel capacity 204 litres (54 US gallons; 45 Imp gallons).
DIMENSIONS, EXTERNAL:
Wing span   7.52 m (24 ft 8 in)
Length overall   6.55 m (21 ft 6 in)
Propeller diameter   1.83 m (6 ft 0 in)
AREA:
Wings, gross   9.66 m² (104.0 sq ft)
WEIGHTS:
Weight empty   566 kg (1,248 lb)

Baggage capacity   34 kg (75 lb)
Max T-O weight   900 kg (1,985 lb)
PERFORMANCE (initial tests):
Cruising speed, 75% power
208 knots (386 km/h; 240 mph)
Stalling speed, 'clean'   57 knots (105 km/h; 65 mph)
Max rate of climb at S/L:
2 crew, 50% fuel   670 m (2,200 ft)/min
max T-O weight   457 m (1,500 ft)/min
Range: 75% power   955 nm (1,770 km; 1,100 miles)
60% power (195 knots; 362 km/h; 225 mph)
1,085 nm (2,011 km; 1,250 miles)
g limits   +8/-6

PARAPLANE

PARAPLANE CORPORATION

5801 Magnolia Avenue, Pennsauken, New Jersey 08109
Telephone: (609) 663 2234
PRESIDENT: Steve Snyder

PARAPLANE

The ParaPlane utilises a sport parachute as its 'wing', attached to a 'powered trike' airframe. The aerofoil section parachute can be held open by two ground assistants before ground roll begins, though this is not necessary. It takes about five seconds to deploy as the lifting surface. Recreational flying is not recommended in winds in excess of 13 knots (24 km/h; 15 mph). Many hundreds have been sold.

TYPE: Single-seat microlight.
AIRFRAME: Aircraft's 'wing' is an inherently stable ram air sport parachute, made of F-111 ripstop nylon and having single-axis control through steering lines. Airframe consists of a T frame of aluminium alloy. Non-retractable tricycle landing gear.
POWER PLANT: Two 11.2 kW (15 hp) Solo 210 cc engines, driving counter-rotating pusher propellers on concentric shafts. Fuel capacity 17 litres (4.5 US gallons; 3.75 Imp gallons).
DIMENSIONS, EXTERNAL:
Parachute span   9.30 m (36 ft 6 in)
Airframe length   1.73 m (5 ft 8 in)
Airframe height   1.70 m (5 ft 7 in)
Propeller diameter (each)   1.29 m (4 ft 3 in)

AREA:
Parachute   37.16 m² (400.0 sq ft)
WEIGHTS:
Weight empty   69 kg (153 lb)
Max pilot weight   84 kg (185 lb)
Max T-O weight   170 kg (375 lb)
PERFORMANCE:
Max level and cruising speed
22 knots (41 km/h; 26 mph)
Glide speed, engine idling   18 knots (34 km/h; 21 mph)
Max rate of climb   150 m (495 ft)/min
Service ceiling   more than 1,525 m (5,000 ft)
T-O run   30-46 m (100-150 ft)
Range   43 nm (80 km; 50 miles)
Endurance   1 h 30 min

PARKER

CALVIN Y. PARKER

PO Box 625, Coolidge, Arizona 85228-0625
Telephone: (602) 723 5660

PARKER TEENIE TWO

Mr Parker's original aim in starting work on the Teenie series was to build an aircraft specifically to utilise the Volkswagen motorcar engine and, at the same time, to produce an all-metal design that would present few constructional problems to homebuilders with virtually no metal-working experience. This was achieved, and no special tools or jigs are needed beyond a tool to close and form the cadmium plated steel pop rivets that are used for practically all assembly. One gauge of aluminium sheet and one size of light alloy angle section are used for almost all of the structure, except for steel tube and sheet which are required for construction of the landing gear and control

actuation tubes respectively. For simplicity and economy, push/pull tubes are used for all flying controls.

Plans, including details of modifications for the Volkswagen engine, and complete kits of parts, are available to amateur constructors, and approximately 3,600 sets of plans have been sold. Well over 300 Teenie Twos have been built from plans.
TYPE: Single-seat homebuilt.
AIRFRAME: Pop-riveted all-metal airframe, mostly of light alloy, including skins. Wing section NACA 4415. Non-retractable tricycle landing gear.
POWER PLANT: One 31.5 kW (42 hp) 1,600 cc, or 30 kW (40 hp) 1,500 cc, or 48.5 kW (65 hp) Volkswagen modified motorcar engine (conversion parts sold by Parker). Standard fuel capacity 34 litres (9 US gallons; 7.5 Imp gallons). A 45.5 litre (12 US gallon; 10 Imp gallon) fuel tank can be installed if the pilot is under 1.83 m (6 ft) tall. Optional cockpit canopy.

DIMENSIONS, EXTERNAL:
Wing span   5.49 m (18 ft 0 in)
Length overall   3.91 m (12 ft 10 in)
WEIGHTS:
Weight empty   140 kg (310 lb)
Max T-O weight   267 kg (590 lb)
PERFORMANCE (at max T-O weight, 1,600 cc engine):
Max level speed   104 knots (193 km/h; 120 mph)
Max cruising speed (75% power)
95 knots (177 km/h; 110 mph)
Landing speed   44 knots (81 km/h; 50 mph)
Max rate of climb at S/L:
standard propeller   244 m (800 ft)/min
52 × 37 propeller   up to 457 m (1,500 ft)/min
Service ceiling   4,575 m (15,000 ft)
Range   347 nm (643 km; 400 miles)

PARSONS

BILL PARSONS

PO Box 532, Lake Monroe, Florida 32747
Telephone: (305) 323 9440

PARSONS TANDEM TRAINER

Kits are available for a tandem two-seat, dual-control autogyro known simply as the Tandem Trainer. It is of conventional configuration and metal tube construction,

with a two-blade glassfibre rotor, a three-blade pusher propeller powered by a Rotax 532 or McCulloch engine, and a non-retractable tricycle landing gear.

PAZMANY

PAZMANY AIRCRAFT CORPORATION

PO Box 80051, San Diego, California 92138
Telephone: (714) 276 0424
PROPRIETOR: Ladislao Pazmany

PAZMANY PL-2

The PL-2 was developed from the Pl-1 (see 1979-80 *Jane's*), first flying on 4 April 1969. Plans are available. Aircraft built and flown include several examples for evaluation and use by foreign military training centres.
TYPE: Side by side two-seat, dual-control homebuilt.
AIRFRAME: All-aluminium alloy construction, except for glassfibre wingtips (including wingtip fuel tanks), wing fillets, tailcone, engine cowling, and the tips of the fin and tailplane. Wing section NACA 63₂615. Semi-monocoque fuselage has only flat or single-curvature skins. Non-retractable tricycle landing gear.
POWER PLANT: Recommended Textron Lycoming power plants include the 80.5 kW (108 hp) O-235-C1, 93 kW (125 hp) O-290-G (ground power unit), 101 kW (135 hp) O-290-D2B or 112 kW (150 hp) O-320-A. Some PL-2s are fitted with O-360 engines. Fuel capacity 95 litres (25 US gallons; 20.8 Imp gallons). Some PL-2s built with additional integral wing tanks, total capacity 94 litres (25 US gallons; 21 Imp gallons).
DIMENSIONS, EXTERNAL:
Wing span   8.53 m (28 ft 0 in)
Length overall   5.90 m (19 ft 3½ in)
Height overall   2.44 m (8 ft 0 in)

AREA:
Wings, gross   10.78 m² (116.0 sq ft)
WEIGHTS (with 93 kW; 125 hp engine):
Weight empty   408 kg (900 lb)
Baggage capacity   18 kg (40 lb)
Max T-O weight   655 kg (1,445 lb)
PERFORMANCE (with 93 kW; 125 hp engine, at max T-O weight):
Max level speed at S/L   125 knots (232 km/h; 144 mph)
Econ cruising speed   111 knots (206 km/h; 128 mph)
Stalling speed (flaps down) 47 knots (87 km/h; 54 mph)
Max rate of climb at S/L   457 m (1,500 ft)/min
Range at econ cruising speed 422 nm (780 km; 486 miles)
Endurance   4 h 6 min

PAZMANY PL-3 GURI

This is to be a type certificated production version of the PL-2, prepared by students of Argentina's ENET technical school.

PAZMANY PL-4A

The prototype of this economical single-seater flew for the first time on 12 July 1972. Sets of plans, kits of prefabricated components, glassfibre wingtips and fuel tank, and transparent cockpit canopy are available to amateur constructors.
TYPE: Single-seat sporting homebuilt.
AIRFRAME: All-aluminium alloy construction, except for glassfibre cambered wingtips, fairings, engine cowling, spinner, elevator trim kit and fuel tank. Wing section NACA 63₃418. Non-retractable tailwheel landing gear.

POWER PLANT: One 1,600 cc modified Volkswagen motorcar engine, developing approximately 37.5 kW (50 hp). Optional Volkswagen engine conversions from Revmaster, Limbach and others, of up to 2,100 cc, or Continental A65 or C80. Fuel capacity 45 litres (12 US gallons; 10 Imp gallons).
DIMENSIONS, EXTERNAL:
Wing span   8.13 m (26 ft 8 in)
Length overall   5.04 m (16 ft 6½ in)
Height overall   1.73 m (5 ft 8 in)
Propeller diameter   1.73 m (5 ft 8 in)
AREA:
Wings, gross   8.27 m² (89.0 sq ft)
WEIGHTS:
Weight empty   262 kg (578 lb)
Baggage capacity   9 kg (20 lb)
Max T-O and landing weight   385 kg (850 lb)
PERFORMANCE (37.5 kW; 50 hp engine, at max T-O weight):
Max level speed at S/L   109 knots (201 km/h; 125 mph)
Econ cruising speed at S/L
78 knots (145 km/h; 90 mph)
Stalling speed:
power on   40 knots (74 km/h; 46 mph)
power off   42 knots (78 km/h; 48 mph)
Max rate of climb at S/L   198 m (650 ft)/min
Service ceiling   3,960 m (13,000 ft)
T-O run   148 m (486 ft)
Landing run   133 m (436 ft)
Range with max fuel, no allowances
295 nm (545 km; 340 miles)
Endurance   3 h 48 min

PHANTOM SPORT

PHANTOM SPORT AIRPLANE CORPORATION

Box 145, Southern Pines, North Carolina 28387
Telephone: (919) 692 7554

PRESIDENT: Michael Holden

Phantom Sport Airplane Corporation acquired the assets of Ultralight Flight Inc in 1987 and continue to market the Phantom microlight.

PHANTOM SPORT AIRPLANE PHANTOM

Available in kit form, several thousand Phantoms have been built. A two-seat variant, known as the Phantom II, has been developed. The following details refer to the single-seat Phantom:

UK registered Pereira Osprey II two-seat amphibian (*Peter J. Bish*)

Pereira GP4 prototype two-seat homebuilt cross-country aircraft
(*Scott Kemper*)

Pazmany PL-4A built by Mr Michael Dorey of Orillia, Ontario, Canada
(*Neil A. Macdougall*)

Phantom Sport Airplane single-seat Phantom

Parker Teenie Two built by Mr L. Flagg of Fort Scott, Kansas

Pazmany PL-2 built in Sweden by Mr Hans Nielsen

ParaPlane in flight (*Howard Levy*)

TYPE: Single-seat microlight; conforms to FAR Pt 103.
AIRFRAME: Wing has aluminium spars and ribs, with double surface Dacron covering. Libek thin-section aerofoil, with double camber. Mainframe of aluminium alloy tube, with 10 cm (4 in) diameter tubular tailboom. Three-axis control. Non-retractable tricycle landing gear. Optional floats and skis.
POWER PLANT: One 26 kW (35 hp) Rotax 377. Other engines of up to 48 kW (64 hp) may be fitted. Fuel capacity 19 litres (5 US gallons; 4.2 Imp gallons).
DIMENSIONS, EXTERNAL:
Wing span — 8.69 m (28 ft 6 in)

Length overall	5.11 m (16 ft 9 in)	
Height overall	2.21 m (7 ft 3 in)	
Propeller diameter	1.47 m (4 ft 10 in)	
AREA:		
Wings, gross	13.19 m² (142.0 sq ft)	
WEIGHTS:		
Weight empty	114 kg (252 lb)	
Pilot weight range	41-97 kg (90-215 lb)	
Max T-O weight	231 kg (510 lb)	
PERFORMANCE:		
Max level speed	54 knots (100 km/h; 62 mph)	
Econ cruising speed	39 knots (72 km/h; 45 mph)	

Stalling speed, power on	23 knots (42 km/h; 26 mph)
Max rate of climb at S/L	244 m (800 ft)/min
Service ceiling	4,420 m (14,500 ft)
T-O run	30.5 m (100 ft)
Landing run	12-46 m (40-150 ft)
Range with max fuel	126 nm (233 km; 145 miles)
Endurance with max fuel	2 h
g limits	+6/−4 design
	+9.9/−6.6 ultimate

PHOENIX
PHOENIX AVIATION INC
304 Via Del Norte, Oceanside, California 92054
Telephone: (619) 931 9055
PRESIDENT: Paul A. McShane

PHOENIX AVIATION PHOENIX
The tandem two-seat Phoenix is marketed in kit form, requiring about 100 working hours to assemble. A pre-built wing is among available options. It has three-axis control; the landing gear is non-retractable tricycle type.

Power plant is a 38.8 kW (52 hp) Rotax 503; fuel capacity 57 litres (15 US gallons; 12.5 Imp gallons). Available options include a ballistic recovery parachute and dual controls.
DIMENSIONS, EXTERNAL:
Wing span	10.36 m (34 ft 0 in)
Length overall	5.49 m (18 ft 0 in)
Height overall	2.74 m (9 ft 0 in)
WEIGHTS:	
Weight empty	238 kg (525 lb)
Max T-O weight	499 kg (1,100 lb)

PERFORMANCE (pilot and passenger with combined weight of 158.8 kg; 350 lb, full fuel, no wind, 59°F at S/L):
Cruising speed	97 knots (180 km/h; 112 mph)
Max rate of climb at 52 knots (97 km/h; 60 mph)	
	213 m (700 ft)/min
Service ceiling	3,660 m (12,000 ft)
T-O run	91 m (300 ft)
Landing run	107 m (350 ft)
Range at cruising speed	390 nm (724 km; 450 miles)
g limits	+6/−2.8

PIETENPOL
DONALD PIETENPOL
215, 21st Street SE, Rochester, Minnesota 55904

PIETENPOL B4 AIRCAMPER
The prototype of Mr Bernard H. Pietenpol's Aircamper two-seat parasol monoplane flew for the first time in 1929, powered by a 30 kW (40 hp) Ford Model A engine. Plans were published in the magazine *Modern Mechanics and Inventions* in the following year and large numbers of Aircampers, with a wide variety of power plants, were built by amateurs, either from the magazine plans or from kits of parts marketed by Mr Pietenpol. Plans continue to be available. (See also Grega.)

The original Aircamper was of all-wood construction, with fabric covering, but some examples completed recently, or currently being built, have a steel tube fuselage and tail unit.

TYPE: Single-seat homebuilt (design makes provision for second seat).

AIRFRAME: Parasol monoplane, with Pietenpol special wing section. Fabric covered all-wood construction standard, except for plywood fuselage skins forward of rear cockpit and steel tubes used in tail unit structure. Non-retractable tailwheel landing gear.

POWER PLANT: One 45 kW (60 hp) Chevrolet Corvair converted motorcar engine, or other engine of similar rating. Fuel capacity 30 litres (8 US gallons; 6.66 Imp gallons).

DIMENSIONS, EXTERNAL:
Wing span	8.84 m (29 ft 0 in)
Propeller diameter	1.52 m (5 ft 0 in)

AREA:
Wings, gross	13.47 m² (145.0 sq ft)

WEIGHT:
Weight empty	282 kg (622 lb)

PERFORMANCE:
Max level speed	95 knots (177 km/h; 110 mph)
Econ cruising speed	69 knots (129 km/h; 80 mph)
Stalling speed	33 knots (62 km/h; 38 mph)
Max rate of climb at S/L	152 m (500 ft)/min
T-O and landing run	76 m (250 ft)
Range, 30 min reserves	330 nm (611 km; 380 miles)

PINAIRE
PINAIRE ENGINEERING INC
1313 Newton Avenue, Evansville, Indiana 47715
Telephone: (812) 477 9818
PRESIDENT: Lon Pinaire

It is believed that the two-seat Ultra-Aire II is not being marketed (see 1987-88 *Jane's*).

PINAIRE ULTRA-AIRE I
Pinaire offers the single-seat Ultra-Aire I in kit and ready assembled forms. Assembly is said to require approximately 40 working hours.

TYPE: Single-seat microlight; conforms to FAR Pt 103.

AIRFRAME: Mainframe, wings and foreplane of aluminium tube, steel, and single surface Dacron construction, with endplate fins and rudders on wings. Three-axis control. Non-retractable tricycle landing gear. Options include cockpit fairing, windscreen and floats.

POWER PLANT: One 26 kW (35 hp) Cuyuna ULII-02. Fuel capacity 11.4 litres (3 US gallons; 2.5 Imp gallons) standard; 19 litres (5 US gallons; 4.2 Imp gallons) optional.

DIMENSIONS, EXTERNAL:
Wing span	7.92 m (26 ft 0 in)
Foreplane span	3.05 m (10 ft 0 in)
Length overall	4.32 m (14 ft 2 in)
Height overall	2.11 m (6 ft 11 in)
Propeller diameter	1.37 m (4 ft 6 in)

AREAS:
Wings, gross	12.08 m² (130.0 sq ft)
Foreplane, gross	1.86 m² (20.0 sq ft)

WEIGHTS:
Weight empty	109 kg (240 lb)
Max T-O weight	249 kg (550 lb)

PERFORMANCE:
Max level speed	55 knots (101 km/h; 63 mph)
Cruising speed, at 50% power	35 knots (64 km/h; 40 mph)
Max rate of climb at S/L	183 m (600 ft)/min
T-O run	34 m (110 ft)
Landing from 15 m (50 ft)	55 m (180 ft)
g limits	+6/-4

PITTS — *see Christen Industries in main Aircraft section*

POLLIWAGEN
POLLIWAGEN INC
40940 Eleanora Way, PO Box 860, Murrieta, California 92362
Telephone: (714) 677 7877
PRESIDENT: Joseph P. Alvarez

POLLIWAGEN
The Polliwagen flew for the first time in July 1977. Plans were made available, together with a wide range of component parts, including a prefabricated fuselage, elevator, spars and wing skins.

TYPE: Side by side two-seat aerobatic homebuilt.

AIRFRAME: Made entirely of glassfibre epoxy composite, pre-moulded in female moulds. NL(S)-0715F wing section. Wingtip tanks increase effective span by reducing drag. Retractable tricycle landing gear. Optional non-retractable gear.

POWER PLANT: One 56 kW (75 hp) Revmaster 2100 D Turbo. Alternative installation of 74.5 kW (100 hp) Continental O-200, 86 kW (115 hp) Textron Lycoming O-235 and 112 kW (150 hp) Textron Lycoming O-320 engines. Fuel capacity 132 litres (35 US gallons; 29 Imp gallons).

DIMENSIONS, EXTERNAL:
Wing span over tip tanks	7.92 m (26 ft 0 in)
Length overall	4.88 m (16 ft 0 in)
Height overall	1.70 m (5 ft 7 in)
Propeller diameter	1.45 m (4 ft 9 in)

AREA:
Wings, gross	8.36 m² (90.0 sq ft)

WEIGHTS (Revmaster engine):
Weight empty	295 kg (650 lb)
Baggage capacity	18 kg (40 lb)
Max T-O weight	567 kg (1,250 lb)

PERFORMANCE (Revmaster engine):
Max level speed	174 knots (322 km/h; 200 mph)
Cruising speed (75% power) at 2,600 m (8,500 ft)	146 knots (270 km/h; 168 mph)
Stalling speed, flaps and landing gear down	45 knots (82 km/h; 51 mph)
Max rate of climb at S/L	over 213 m (700 ft)/min
T-O and landing run	152 m (500 ft)
Range with max fuel (75% power), 45 min reserves	1,320 nm (2,446 km; 1,520 miles)
g limits at 500 kg (1,100 lb) AUW	+9/-6

PRESCOTT
PRESCOTT AERONAUTICAL CORPORATION
1006 West 53rd Street North, PO Box 4590, Wichita, Kansas 67204
Telephone: (316) 832 1400
CHAIRMAN: Linden Blue

PRESCOTT PUSHER
The prototype Pusher first flew on 9 July 1985. Currently, the aircraft is offered in kit form only, as a complete airframe with retractable landing gear, including the hydraulic system and components for the landing gear and flaps. The kit includes basic instruments, but not avionics, interior, engine and propeller. The first kit-built Pusher flew on 8 April 1988.

TYPE: Four-seat homebuilt.

AIRFRAME: Wings, ailerons and flaps of aluminium alloy construction; cambered glassfibre wingtips. Wing section NLF(1)-0215. Fuselage of welded square-section steel tubing, covered by non-structural glassfibre shells in two parts plus a nose section. T tail of aluminium alloy construction. Retractable tricycle landing gear, with tailskid to protect propeller in tail-down attitude.

POWER PLANT: One 134 kW (180 hp) Textron Lycoming O-360-A2A, driving a tail-mounted propeller. Fuel capacity 214 litres (56.5 US gallons; 47 Imp gallons).

DIMENSIONS, EXTERNAL:
Wing span	8.94 m (29 ft 4 in)
Length overall	6.18 m (20 ft 3¼ in)
Height overall	2.67 m (8 ft 9 in)
Propeller diameter (max)	1.57 m (5 ft 2 in)

AREA:
Wings, gross	10.29 m² (110.8 sq ft)

WEIGHTS:
Weight empty	703 kg (1,550 lb)
Baggage capacity	45 kg (100 lb)
Max T-O weight	1,088 kg (2,400 lb)

PERFORMANCE (O-360 engine):
Max level speed at S/L	184 knots (340 km/h; 212 mph)
Max cruising speed at S/L	174 knots (322 km/h; 200 mph)
Stalling speed: flaps up	63 knots (116 km/h; 72 mph)
flaps down	58 knots (106 km/h; 66 mph)
Max rate of climb at S/L	290 m (950 ft)/min
Service ceiling	5,485 m (18,000 ft)
T-O to 15 m (50 ft)	526 m (1,725 ft)
Landing from 15 m (50 ft)	473 m (1,550 ft)
Range: with max fuel	869 nm (1,609 km; 1,000 miles)
with max payload	738 nm (1,368 km; 850 miles)

PROWLER
PROWLER AVIATION INC
Auto Aviation Development Company, 3641 Soquel Drive, Soquel, California 95073
Telephone: (408) 462 5321
PRESIDENT: George Morse

PROWLER
The prototype Prowler, reminiscent of a Supermarine Spitfire, made its first flight on 17 March 1985. Prowler Aviation offers kits to allow amateur construction of the aircraft.

TYPE: Tandem two-seat high-performance homebuilt.

AIRFRAME: Aluminium alloy construction. Wing section NACA 64A212 at roots, NACA 64A210 at tips. Retractable tailwheel landing gear.

POWER PLANT: One 168 kW (225 hp) Auto Aviation modified Oldsmobile F-85 motorcar engine. Fuel capacity 136 litres (36 US gallons; 30 Imp gallons). Two 45 litre (12 US gallon; 10 Imp gallon) auxiliary fuel tanks offer total possible fuel capacity of 227 litres (60 US gallons; 50 Imp gallons).

DIMENSIONS, EXTERNAL:
Wing span	7.62 m (25 ft 0 in)
Length overall	6.40 m (21 ft 0 in)
Height overall	2.21 m (7 ft 3 in)
Propeller diameter	1.98 m (6 ft 6 in)

AREA:
Wings, gross	9.66 m² (104.0 sq ft)

WEIGHTS:
Weight empty	618 kg (1,362 lb)
Baggage capacity	16 kg (35 lb)
Max T-O weight	975 kg (2,150 lb)

PERFORMANCE (at max T-O weight):
Max level speed at S/L	191 knots (354 km/h; 220 mph) IAS
Econ cruising speed at 2,135 m (7,000 ft)	148 knots (274 km/h; 170 mph)
Stalling speed, flaps up, power off	48 knots (89 km/h; 55 mph) IAS
Max rate of climb at S/L	549 m (1,800 ft)/min
Service ceiling	5,180 m (17,000 ft)
T-O and landing run	457 m (1,500 ft)
Landing from 15 m (50 ft)	610 m (2,000 ft)
Range:	
with max standard fuel	1,042 nm (1,931 km; 1,200 miles)
with auxiliary fuel	1,302 nm (2,414 km; 1,500 miles)

Phoenix Aviation Phoenix two-seat light aircraft

ProTech PT-2 Sassy two-seat homebuilt aircraft *(J. M. G. Gradidge)*

Prowler Aviation Prowler all-metal two-seat homebuilt aircraft

Polliwagen two-seat light sporting aircraft *(Roland Eichenberger)*

Second 'frozen design' prototype of the Prescott Pusher

Pinaire Ultra-Aire I with float landing gear

Two-seat Pietenpol Aircamper (Continental C90 engine) *(J. M. G. Gradidge)*

PT
PROTECH AIRCRAFT INC
11903 Westheimer Road, Houston, Texas 77077
Telephone: (713) 589 0628

PROTECH PT-2 SASSY
The ProTech PT-2 is available in kit form, requiring about 300 working hours to assemble.

TYPE: Side by side two-seat, dual control homebuilt STOL aircraft.

AIRFRAME: Wings have preformed aluminium alloy ribs, spars and skins. Glassfibre wingtips, wingroot fillets, rear cabin fairing and engine cowlings. Steel tube and aluminium flaperons. Welded steel tube fuselage and tail surfaces, Ceconite covered. Non-retractable tailwheel landing gear.

POWER PLANT: One 56 kW (75 hp) Revmaster. Standard fuel capacity 53 litres (14 US gallons; 11.7 Imp gallons). Optional auxiliary fuel tanks of similar capacity.

DIMENSIONS, EXTERNAL:
Wing span   9.68 m (31 ft 9 in)
Length overall   5.33 m (17 ft 6 in)
Propeller diameter   1.52 m (5 ft 0 in)
AREA:
Wings, gross   13.75 m² (148.0 sq ft)

WEIGHTS:
Weight empty   295 kg (650 lb)
Baggage weight   27 kg (60 lb)
Max T-O weight   569 kg (1,254 lb)
PERFORMANCE (pilot only):
Max level speed   100 knots (185 km/h; 115 mph)
Cruising speed   91 knots (169 km/h; 105 mph)
Stalling speed   26 knots (47 km/h; 29 mph)
T-O and landing run   61 m (200 ft)
Normal range at cruising speed, no reserves
    364 nm (675 km; 420 miles)
g limits   +6–4 computer evaluated

QUAD CITY
QUAD CITY ULTRALIGHT AIRCRAFT CORPORATION
3610 Coaltown Road, Moline, Illinois 61265
Telephone: (309) 764 3515
Telex: 468556 WJ BOWMAN MOLI
PRESIDENT: Dave Goulet

QUAD CITY CHALLENGER and CHALLENGER II
The Challenger prototype first flew in November 1982. Kits for this and the two-seat Challenger II are available, requiring 40-60 working hours to assemble. With the Rotax 277 engine installed, the Challenger falls within FAR Pt 103 for microlights. With larger engines it comes within the FAA's Experimental aircraft regulations for homebuilts. The Challenger II is a microlight trainer and Experimental category aircraft.

TYPE: Single-seat microlight (Challenger) and tandem two-seat dual control microlight trainer (Challenger II); conform to FAR Pt 103 and FAA Experimental category for homebuilts.

AIRFRAME: Mainframe constructed from aluminium alloy and steel, with Dacron covering on fuselage and double surface wings and tail unit. Three-axis control, with optional 'flaperons'. Non-retractable tricycle landing gear. Options include agricultural spray equipment (for Challenger II only), floats, skis and amphibious floats.

POWER PLANT: *Challenger:* One 20 kW (27 hp) Rotax 277. Optional Rotax 337, 447 and 503 engines. *Challenger II:* One 31.3 kW (42 hp) Rotax 447 or, optionally, Rotax 503. Fuel capacity 19 litres (5 US gallons; 4.15 Imp gallons). Optional 38 litre (10 US gallon; 8.3 Imp gallon) tank.

DIMENSIONS, EXTERNAL (A: Challenger, B: Challenger II):

Wing span: A, B	9.60 m (31 ft 6 in)
Length overall: A	5.64 m (18 ft 6 in)
B	6.10 m (20 ft 0 in)
Height overall: A, B	1.83 m (6 ft 0 in)
Propeller diameter: A, B	1.32 m (4 ft 4 in)

AREAS:

Wings, gross: A	13.19 m² (142.0 sq ft)
B	16.07 m² (173.0 sq ft)

WEIGHTS (A: Challenger, B: Challenger II):

Weight empty: A	107 kg (235 lb)
B	132 kg (290 lb)
Pilot weight range: B	68-136 kg (150-300 lb)
Max T-O weight: A	227 kg (500 lb)
B	358 kg (790 lb)

PERFORMANCE (A: Challenger, B: Challenger II):

Max level speed: A	55 knots (101 km/h; 63 mph)
B	69 knots (128 km/h; 80 mph)
Econ cruising speed: A	43 knots (80 km/h; 50 mph)
B	49 knots (92 km/h; 57 mph)
Stalling speed: A	22 knots (41 km/h; 25 mph)
B, pilot only	22 knots (41 km/h; 25 mph)
B, pilot and passenger	31 knots (57 km/h; 35 mph)

Max rate of climb at S/L: A	213 m (700 ft)/min
B, pilot only	305 m (1,000 ft)/min
B, pilot and passenger	183 m (600 ft)/min
Service ceiling: A	3,810 m (12,500 ft)
B, pilot only	4,265 m (14,000 ft)
B, pilot and passenger	3,350 m (11,000 ft)
T-O run: A	46 m (150 ft)
B, pilot only	31 m (100 ft)
B, pilot and passenger	91 m (300 ft)
Landing run: A	46 m (150 ft)
B, pilot only	46 m (150 ft)
B, pilot and passenger	61 m (200 ft)

Range with max standard fuel:

A	130 nm (241 km; 150 miles)
B, pilot only	139 nm (257 km; 160 miles)
B, pilot and passenger	121 nm (225 km; 140 miles)
Endurance: A	2 h 30 min
B	2 h 10 min
g limits: A	+6/–3 tested
B	+4/–3

QUAD CITY CHALLENGER SPECIAL and CHALLENGER II SPECIAL

These are higher performing versions of the Challenger and Challenger II, with streamline wing struts, and landing gears, shortened wings covered with Stits Poly-Fiber or Ceconite, flaperons, Lexan door kits, and higher-powered Rotax engines as standard, to give a higher cruising speed and improved rate of roll. Kits are available. Construction time for the Challenger II Special is 150 working hours.

TYPE: Single-seat (Challenger Special) and tandem two-seat (Challenger II Special) homebuilts.

POWER PLANT: Challenger Special: One 31.3 kW (42 hp) Rotax 447, with 19 litres (5 US gallons; 4.2 Imp gallons) fuel. Challenger II Special: One 38.8 kW (52 hp) Rotax 503, with 38 litres (10 US gallons; 8.3 Imp gallons) fuel.

DIMENSIONS, EXTERNAL: As for Challenger, except:

Wing span	7.92 m (26 ft 0 in)
Length overall, Challenger II Special	
	6.32 m (20 ft 9 in)
Propeller diameter: Challenger Special	
	1.35 m (4 ft 5 in)
Challenger II Special	1.37 m (4 ft 6 in)

AREAS (A: Challenger Special, B: Challenger II Special):

Wings, gross: A	11.15 m² (120.0 sq ft)
B	13.29 m² (143.0 sq ft)

WEIGHTS (A and B as above):

Weight empty: A	118 kg (260 lb)
B	158 kg (350 lb)
Pilot weight range: A	63.5-104 kg (140-230 lb)
Max T-O weight: A	245 kg (540 lb)
B	385 kg (850 lb)

PERFORMANCE (A and B as above):

Max level speed: A	78 knots (145 km/h; 90 mph)
B	82 knots (153 km/h; 95 mph)
Cruising speed: A	69 knots (129 km/h; 80 mph)
B	74 knots (137 km/h; 85 mph)
Stalling speed: A, flaperons up	29 knots (53 km/h; 33 mph)
B, flaperons up	32 knots (60 km/h; 37 mph)
A, flaperons down	24 knots (44 km/h; 27 mph)
B, flaperons down	28 knots (52 km/h; 32 mph)
Max rate of climb at S/L: A, B	305 m (1,000 ft)/min
Service ceiling: A, B	3,660 m (12,000 ft)
T-O and landing run: A	46 m (150 ft)
B	61 m (200 ft)
Range with max fuel: A	130 nm (241 km; 150 miles)
B	191 nm (354 km; 220 miles)
Endurance: A	1 h 45 min
g limits: A	+7/–4
B	+6/–4

QUESTAIR

QUESTAIR INC

PO Box 18946, 7700 Airline Road, Greensboro, North Carolina 27419
Telephone: (919) 668 7890 or (800) 852 3889
PRESIDENT: James E. Griswold

QUESTAIR VENTURE

The prototype Venture flew for the first time on 1 July 1987. The aircraft is now available for purchase in a series of four kits of component parts, which include the engine and propeller.

TYPE: Side by side two-seat, dual-control sporting and cross-country homebuilt.

AIRFRAME: All-metal construction. Retractable tricycle landing gear.

POWER PLANT: One 224 kW (300 hp) Continental IO-550. Fuel capacity 197 litres (52 US gallons; 43.3 Imp gallons).

DIMENSIONS, EXTERNAL:

Wing span	8.38 m (27 ft 6 in)
Length overall	4.95 m (16 ft 3 in)
Height overall	2.35 m (7 ft 8½ in)

AREA:

Wings, gross	6.76 m² (72.75 sq ft)

WEIGHTS:

Weight empty	544 kg (1,200 lb)
Max T-O weight	862 kg (1,900 lb)

PERFORMANCE:

Max cruising speed at S/L	250 knots (463 km/h; 288 mph)
Stalling speed	61 knots (113 km/h; 71 mph)
Max rate of climb at S/L	762 m (2,500 ft)/min
T-O to 15 m (50 ft)	305 m (1,000 ft)
Landing from 15 m (50 ft)	488 m (1,600 ft)

Range at 205 knots (380 km/h; 236 mph), at 3,660 m (12,000 ft), 45 min reserves

	1,000 nm (1,853 km; 1,151 miles)
g limits: solo	+6/–3
at max T-O weight	+5/–2.5

RAND ROBINSON

RAND ROBINSON ENGINEERING INC

5395-A Industrial Drive, Huntington Beach, California 92649
Telephone: (714) 898 3811

RAND ROBINSON KR-1

The KR-1 prototype flew for the first time in February 1972. Plans are available to amateur constructors; many thousands of sets have been sold and at least 200 KR-1s are known to be flying.

TYPE: Single-seat sporting homebuilt.

AIRFRAME: Wings have wooden spars and polyurethane foam ribs, polyurethane foam slab filling between ribs and Dynel reinforced epoxy covering. Wing section RAF 48. Ailerons of polyurethane foam, with Dynel reinforced epoxy covering; tail unit similar, with wooden spars. Lower half of fuselage of wooden construction, upper surface of carved Styrofoam covered with Dynel epoxy. Retractable (optionally non-retractable) tailwheel landing gear.

POWER PLANT: One Volkswagen modified motorcar engine. Prototype has a Rajay turbocharged 67 kW (90 hp) 2,074 cc VW. Fuel capacity with this engine is 190 litres (50 US gallons; 41.6 Imp gallons).

DIMENSIONS, EXTERNAL:

Wing span	5.18 m (17 ft 0 in)
Length overall	3.89 m (12 ft 9 in)
Height overall	1.07 m (3 ft 6 in)
Propeller diameter	1.35 m (4 ft 5 in)

AREA:

Wings, gross	5.76 m² (62.0 sq ft)

WEIGHTS (67 kW; 90 hp VW engine):

Weight empty, equipped	218 kg (480 lb)
Max T-O weight	408 kg (900 lb)

PERFORMANCE (67 kW; 90 hp VW engine, at max T-O weight):

Max level speed at S/L	191 knots (354 km/h; 220 mph)

Econ cruising speed at 5,485 m (18,000 ft)

	217 knots (402 km/h; 250 mph)
Stalling speed	39 knots (73 km/h; 45 mph)
Max rate of climb at S/L	457 m (1,500 ft)/min
Service ceiling	9,145 m (30,000 ft)
T-O run	122 m (400 ft)
Landing run	152 m (500 ft)
Range with max fuel	2,600 nm (4,825 km; 3,000 miles)

RAND ROBINSON KR-2

The KR-2 is a slightly larger side by side two-seat version of the KR-1, to which it is generally similar in construction. The prototype flew for the first time in July 1974. More than 7,000 sets of plans and a great many kits have been sold; at least 350 KR-2s are known to be flying.

TYPE: Side by side two-seat sporting homebuilt.

POWER PLANT: Airframe designed to accept Volkswagen modified motorcar engines of 1,600 to 2,200 cc. Fuel capacity 144 litres (38 US gallons; 31.6 Imp gallons).

DIMENSIONS, EXTERNAL:

Wing span	6.30 m (20 ft 8 in)
Length overall	4.42 m (14 ft 6 in)
Height overall	1.07 m (3 ft 6 in)
Propeller diameter	1.32 m (4 ft 4 in)

AREA:

Wings, gross	7.43 m² (80.0 sq ft)

WEIGHTS (prototype, with turbocharger):

Weight empty, equipped with IFR and electrics	263 kg (580 lb)
Max T-O and landing weight	499 kg (1,100 lb)

PERFORMANCE (prototype, with turbocharger):

Max level speed at S/L	161 knots (298 km/h; 185 mph)

Max cruising speed at 5,485 m (18,000 ft)

	191 knots (354 km/h; 220 mph)

Stalling speed, prototype without turbocharger

	39 knots (73 km/h; 45 mph)

Max rate of climb at 5,485 m (18,000 ft)

	244 m (800 ft)/min
Service ceiling	7,925 m (26,000 ft)
T-O run	122 m (400 ft)
Landing run	152 m (500 ft)
Range with max fuel	1,735 nm (3,215 km; 2,000 miles)

RAND ROBINSON KR-100

This is an entirely new single-seater of wood, foam and glassfibre construction, with a non-retractable tailwheel landing gear and powered by a Continental O-200 engine in prototype form. Kits are to be made available, containing mostly moulded components of composites sandwich construction. The prototype KR-100 was nearing completion in mid-1988.

DIMENSIONS, EXTERNAL:

Wing span	5.79 m (19 ft 0 in)
Length overall	4.72 m (15 ft 6 in)

WEIGHT (estimated):

Weight empty	249 kg (550 lb)

PERFORMANCE (estimated):

Max level speed	208 knots (386 km/h; 240 mph)
Cruising speed	182 knots (338 km/h; 210 mph)
Stalling speed, flaps down	45 knots (84 km/h; 52 mph)

RANS

RANS COMPANY

1104 East Highway 40 By-Pass, Hays, Kansas 67601
Telephone: (913) 625 6346
PROPRIETOR: Randy Schlitter

RANS S-4 COYOTE

The Coyote first flew in March 1983. It is available as a ready to fly microlight or as a homebuilt in kit form.

TYPE: Single-seat aircraft; conforms to FAR Pt 103-7 as a microlight and to Experimental regulations as a homebuilt.

AIRFRAME: Wing spars, ribs and fuselage structure of aluminium alloy tubing; Dacron/Ceconite covering on entire airframe. Three-axis control. Microlight version has non-retractable tricycle landing gear. Other models have non-retractable tailwheel landing gear. Optional floats, skis and side doors.

POWER PLANT: One 20 kW (27 hp) Rotax 277 (microlight), 26 kW (34.9 hp) Rotax 377 or 31.3 kW (42 hp) Rotax 447. Fuel capacity 19 litres (5 US gallons; 4.2 Imp gallons). Optional fuel capacity up to 42 litres (11 US gallons; 9.2 Imp gallons).

DIMENSIONS, EXTERNAL:

Wing span	8.99 m (29 ft 6 in)
Length overall	5.18 m (17 ft 0 in)

Single-seat Quad City Challenger with Rotax 503 engine *(Peter M. Bowers)*

Rand Robinson KR-2 operated in the UK *(R. Kunert)*

Questair Venture sporting and cross-country monoplane *(Howard Levy)*

RANS Coyote without cabin doors

RANS S-7 Courier homebuilt aircraft

Rand Robinson KR-1 (44.75 kW; 60 hp HAPI 1,835 cc engine) built by Mr George Q. Johnson of Graham, Washington *(Peter M. Bowers)*

Height overall: tailwheel gear	1.78 m (5 ft 10 in)
tricycle gear	2.26 m (7 ft 5 in)
Propeller diameter: Rotax 277	1.52 m (5 ft 0 in)
Rotax 377/447	1.63 m (5 ft 4 in)

AREA:

Wings, gross	11.80 m² (127.0 sq ft)

WEIGHTS (A; with Rotax 277, B: Rotax 447 engine):

Weight empty: A	113 kg (250 lb)
B	125 kg (276 lb)
Max T-O weight: A	243 kg (535 lb)
B	266 kg (587 lb)

PERFORMANCE (A and B as above):

Max level speed: A, B	55 knots (101 km/h; 63 mph)
Cruising speed, 75% power:	
A	39 knots (72 km/h; 45 mph)
B	48 knots (89 km/h; 55 mph)
Stalling speed:	
A, flaps down, power on	16 knots (29 km/h; 18 mph)
A, flaps up, power on	14 knots (26 km/h; 16 mph)
B, flaps down, power on	15 knots (28 km/h; 17 mph)
B, flaps up, power on	11 knots (20 km/h; 12 mph)
Max rate of climb at S/L: A	183 m (600 ft)/min
B	366 m (1,200 ft)/min
Service ceiling: A	4,265 m (14,000 ft)
B	4,875 m (16,000 ft)
T-O run: A	31 m (100 ft)
B	12 m (40 ft)
Landing run: A, B, with brakes	18 m (60 ft)
g limits: A, B	+6/−3

RANS S-7 COURIER

RANS is offering standard kits (300-500 working hours to assemble) or a quick-build kit (150 working hours, approximately) for the Courier. Following the general configuration of the Coyote, the Courier is fitted with dual controls and is therefore suited to training, in addition to recreational flying and such utility tasks as agricultural spraying. The prototype first flew in October 1985.

TYPE: Two-seat STOL homebuilt aircraft.

AIRFRAME: Fabric covered structure, with aluminium alloy wings, and welded steel fuselage and tail unit. Glassfibre engine cowling. Non-retractable tailwheel landing gear. Optional floats and skis.

POWER PLANT: One 48.5 kW (65 hp) Rotax 532. Fuel capacity 49 litres (13 US gallons; 10.8 Imp gallons).

DIMENSIONS, EXTERNAL:

Wing span	8.92 m (29 ft 3 in)
Length overall	6.40 m (21 ft 0 in)
Height overall	1.91 m (6 ft 3 in)
Propeller diameter	1.73 m (5 ft 8 in)

AREA:

Wings, gross	14.03 m² (151.0 sq ft)

WEIGHTS:

Weight empty, equipped	181 kg (400 lb)
Max T-O weight	420 kg (925 lb)

PERFORMANCE (two persons at 381 kg; 840 lb AUW):

Cruising speed	69 knots (129 km/h; 80 mph)
Stalling speed:	
power off, flaps up	31 knots (57 km/h; 35 mph)
power off, flaps down	26 knots (49 km/h; 30 mph)

Max rate of climb at S/L	229 m (750 ft)/min
Service ceiling	4,115 m (13,500 ft)
T-O run	49 m (160 ft)
Landing run to safe turn speed	93 m (303 ft)
Range	208 nm (386 km; 240 miles)
Endurance	3 h
g limits	+6/−3

RANS S-9

The S-9 is offered in microlight and Experimental category versions. Construction from the kits is estimated to take 200-300 working hours.

TYPE: Single-seat aerobatic microlight and homebuilt aircraft; microlight designed to conform to FAR Pt 103.

AIRFRAME: Aluminium alloy wings, and pre-welded steel tube fuselage and tail unit, Cooper Super-Flite fabric covered. Pre-moulded engine cowling. Three-axis control. Non-retractable tailwheel landing gear.

POWER PLANT: Microlight version has 31.3 kW (42 hp) Rotax 447; homebuilt version has 35 kW (47 hp) Rotax 503 or 48.5 kW (65 hp) Rotax 532. Fuel capacity 19 litres (5 US gallons; 4.2 Imp gallons) for microlight, 25 litres (6.5 US gallons; 5.4 Imp gallons) for homebuilt.

DIMENSIONS, EXTERNAL:

Wing span	6.71 m (22 ft 0 in)
Length overall	4.78 m (15 ft 8 in)
Height overall	1.47 m (4 ft 10 in)
Propeller diameter	1.63 m (5 ft 4 in)

AREA:

Wings, gross	8.50 m² (91.5 sq ft)

WEIGHTS (A: microlight, B: homebuilt with Rotax 503):

Weight empty: A	115 kg (254 lb)
B	129 kg (285 lb)
Max T-O weight: A	240 kg (530 lb)
B	259 kg (570 lb)

PERFORMANCE (A and B as above):

Cruising speed:	
A, full power	55 knots (101 km/h; 63 mph)
A, 50% power	43 knots (80 km/h; 50 mph)
B, full power	89 knots (166 km/h; 103 mph)
B, 50% power	61 knots (113 km/h; 70 mph)
Stalling speed:	
A, power on	18 knots (33 km/h; 20 mph)
A, power off	21 knots (39 km/h; 24 mph)
B, power off	26 knots (47 km/h; 29 mph)
Max rate of climb at S/L: A	274 m (900 ft)/min
B	366 m (1,200 ft)/min
Service ceiling: A, B	4,725 m (15,500 ft)
T-O run: A	76 m (250 ft)
B	61 m (200 ft)

Landing run, no brakes: A, B	122 m (400 ft)
Endurance:	
A	1 h 30 min
B	2 h
g limits: A	+9/−3
B	+9/−6

RANS S-10

The S-10 is basically a larger two-seat derivative of the S-9, with a 'roll-up' canopy. Construction and features are generally as those detailed for the Experimental category homebuilt version of the S-9. In addition to the kit, options available include flaperons and glassfibre wingtips.

TYPE: Side by side two-seat homebuilt.

POWER PLANT: One 35 kW (47 hp) Rotax 503 or 48.5 kW (65 hp) Rotax 532. Fuel capacity 49 litres (13 US gallons; 10.8 Imp gallons).

DIMENSIONS, EXTERNAL:

Wing span	7.01 m (23 ft 0 in)
Length overall	5.44 m (17 ft 10 in)

Height overall	1.47 m (4 ft 10 in)
Propeller diameter	1.63 m (5 ft 4 in)
AREA:	
Wings, gross	8.83 m² (95.0 sq ft)
WEIGHTS (503 engine):	
Weight empty	170 kg (375 lb)
Max T-O weight	372 kg (820 lb)

PERFORMANCE (503 engine):

Cruising speed:	
full power	87 knots (161 km/h; 100 mph)
50% power	52 knots (97 km/h; 60 mph)
Stalling speed:	
power off	25 knots (45 km/h; 28 mph)
power on	23 knots (42 km/h; 26 mph)
Max rate of climb at S/L	244 m (800 ft)/min
T-O run	107 m (350 ft)
Landing run, no brakes	152 m (500 ft)
g limits	+6/−3

R.D.

R.D. AIRCRAFT

PO Box 211, Mayville, New York 14757
Telephone: (716) 753 2111
PRESIDENT: Robert G. Dart
ENGINEER: Emerson W. Stevens

R.D. SKYCYCLE and SKYCYCLE II

The Skycycle first flew in early 1982 and is marketed in plans, prefabricated kit, component and ready assembled forms. A larger microlight trainer version with dual controls is known as the **Skycycle II**.

TYPES: Single-seat (Skycycle) and side by side two-seat, dual control training (Skycycle II) microlights; conform to FAR Pt 103 requirements.

AIRFRAME: Mainframe and tail surfaces of welded steel tube. Wings have wooden spars, foam/wood ribs and double surface Dacron/Ceconite covering. Wing section (Skycycle) RAF-6 modified; (Skycycle II) USA-35B. Three-axis control. Non-retractable tailwheel type landing gear. Optional floats and skis.

POWER PLANT: One 15 kW (20 hp) Snowmobile (or similar) engine for Skycycle, and 26 kW (35 hp) Cuyuna ULII-02 for Skycycle II. Alternative engines for the Skycycle are 15 kW (20 hp) Zenoah, 16.4 kW (22 hp) Yamaha 246 cc, 15 kW (20 hp) CGS Powerhawk and 18.6 kW (25 hp) KFM 107SR. Optional engines for the Skycycle II are 28.3 kW (38 hp) Kawasaki TA440 and 26 kW (35 hp) Rotax 377. Fuel capacity 19 litres (5 US gallons; 4.2 Imp gallons).

DIMENSIONS, EXTERNAL (Skycycle):

Wing span	9.65 m (31 ft 8 in)
Length overall	5.99 m (19 ft 8 in)
Height overall	1.98 m (6 ft 6 in)
Propeller diameter	1.37 m (4 ft 6 in)
AREA (Skycycle):	
Wings, gross	14.21 m² (153.0 sq ft)
WEIGHTS (Skycycle):	
Weight empty	112.5 kg (248 lb)
Pilot weight range	50-118 kg (110-260 lb)
Max T-O weight	227 kg (500 lb)

PERFORMANCE (Skycycle at max T-O weight except where indicated):

Max level speed	48 knots (90 km/h; 56 mph)
Econ cruising speed	30 knots (56 km/h; 35 mph)
Stalling speed: power on	21 knots (39 km/h; 24 mph)
power off	24 knots (44 km/h; 27 mph)
Max rate of climb at S/L	244 m (800 ft)/min
Service ceiling	3,660 m (12,000 ft)
T-O run (68 kg; 150 lb pilot)	18 m (60 ft)
Landing run (without brakes)	30 m (100 ft)

Range with max fuel	174 nm (322 km; 200 miles)
Endurance	4 h
g limits	+3.5/−2

R.D. SKYCYCLE GYPSY SERIES

This series encompasses five individual aircraft. The basic model is the **Skycycle Gypsy** single-seat microlight, conforming to FAR Pt 103 and derived directly from the Skycycle, but with changes including an optional 20 kW (27 hp) Rotax 277. The prototype Skycycle Gypsy flew for the first time in early 1984, and this model is available in the form of plans, kits, components and ready assembled aircraft.

The single-seat **Skycycle Gypsy II** differs from the Skycycle Gypsy only in having its wings braced with tubular aluminium alloy V struts each side, instead of by means of a kingpost.

The **Skycycle Cabin Gypsy** is similar to the Gypsy II but with slightly smaller dimensions, a fully enclosed cabin and standard use of a 20 kW (27 hp) Rotax 277 engine.

The fourth aircraft in the series is the **Gypsy Trainer**, the only two-seat model, with an enclosed cabin and a 30 kW (40 hp) Rotax 447. Fuel capacity is increased to 30 litres (8 US gallons; 6.7 Imp gallons). The prototype was due to fly for the first time in 1988.

The fifth aircraft is the **Wood Gypsy**, intended for builders who prefer working with wood rather than welding. Because of its likely weight, it has been designed to FAR Pt 23 as a sporting aircraft. It is to be offered in plan and kit forms. Wing section is RAF-6 modified. Power plant is a Rotax 277, with 19 litres (5 US gallons; 4.2 Imp gallons) of fuel.

DIMENSIONS, EXTERNAL (A: Gypsy, B: Gypsy Trainer):

Wing span: A	9.65 m (31 ft 8 in)
B	9.35 m (30 ft 8 in)
Length overall: A	6.20 m (20 ft 4 in)
B	6.17 m (20 ft 3 in)
Height overall: A	2.08 m (6 ft 10 in)
B	1.80 m (5 ft 11 in)
Propeller diameter: A	1.37 m (4 ft 6 in)
B	1.73 m (5 ft 8 in)
AREAS (A and B as above):	
Wings, gross: A	14.21 m² (153.0 sq ft)
B	14.12 m² (152.0 sq ft)
WEIGHTS (A and B as above):	
Weight empty: A	112 kg (246 lb)
B	159 kg (350 lb)
Pilot weight range: A	50-118 kg (110-260 lb)
B	55-154 kg (120-340 lb)
Max T-O weight: A	227 kg (500 lb)
B	363 kg (800 lb)

PERFORMANCE (A and B as above):

Max level speed: A	49 knots (90 km/h; 56 mph)
B	61 knots (113 km/h; 70 mph)
Econ cruising speed: A	32 knots (60 km/h; 37 mph)
B	39 knots (72 km/h; 45 mph)
Stalling speed:	
A, power on	21 knots (39 km/h; 24 mph)
A, power off	28 knots (52 km/h; 32 mph)
B, power off	31 knots (57 km/h; 35 mph)
Max rate of climb at S/L: A, B	244 m (800 ft)/min
Service ceiling: A, B	3,660 m (12,000 ft)
T-O run (68 kg; 150 lb pilot): A	18 m (60 ft)
B, solo	37 m (120 ft)
Landing run (without brakes): A	30 m (100 ft)
B	46 m (150 ft)
Range with max fuel:	
A, B	174 nm (322 km; 200 miles)
g limits: A	+3.5/−2
B	+3.8/−1.9

R.D. LITTLE DIPPER REPLICA

Construction of a prototype of this reproduction of the Lockheed Little Dipper (illustrated in 1947 *Jane's*) began in February 1988.

TYPE: Single-seat ARV and homebuilt; conforms to FAR Pt 23.

AIRFRAME: Aluminium alloy construction, with some use of glassfibre. Wing section NACA 4415. Three-axis control, plus flaps. Non-retractable tricycle landing gear. Options will include cockpit canopy.

POWER PLANT: One 30 kW (40 hp) Rotax 447FA. Fuel capacity 30 litres (8 US gallons; 6.7 Imp gallons). Rotax 503 optional.

DIMENSIONS, EXTERNAL:

Wing span	7.42 m (24 ft 4 in)
Length overall	5.49 m (18 ft 0 in)
Height overall	2.21 m (7 ft 7¼ in)
Propeller diameter	1.73 m (5 ft 8 in)
AREA:	
Wings, gross	9.48 m² (102.0 sq ft)
WEIGHTS:	
Weight empty	201 kg (443 lb)
Max T-O weight	300 kg (661 lb)

PERFORMANCE:

Max level speed at S/L	87 knots (161 km/h; 100 mph)
Stalling speed, power off	32 knots (58 km/h; 36 mph)
Max rate of climb at S/L	229 m (750 ft)/min
T-O run	76 m (250 ft)
Range	456 nm (845 km; 525 miles)
g limits	+4.6/−2.6

ROBERTS

ROBERTS SPORT AIRCRAFT

PO Box 9217, Yakima, Washington 98909
Telephone: (509) 457 4377

The first prototype Sceptre I flew in November 1983. Ready assembled and kit Sceptres are believed to be available, including the two-seat Sceptre II version.

ROBERTS SCEPTRE I

TYPE: Single-seat homebuilt.

AIRFRAME: Constructed of glassfibre, pre-impregnated with epoxy resin, and glassfibre/Nomex honeycomb sandwich. Non-retractable tricycle landing gear.

POWER PLANT: One 39 kW (52 hp) Rotax 503. Watercooled 48 kW (65 hp) Rotax engine optional. Fuel capacity 76 litres (20 US gallons; 16.7 Imp gallons).

DIMENSIONS, EXTERNAL:

Wing span	8.05 m (26 ft 5 in)
Length overall	5.92 m (19 ft 5 in)
Height overall	1.50 m (4 ft 11 in)
Propeller diameter	1.63 m (5 ft 4 in)
AREA:	
Wings, gross	10.36 m² (111.5 sq ft)
WEIGHTS:	
Weight empty	304 kg (670 lb)
Max T-O weight	474 kg (1,045 lb)

PERFORMANCE (52 hp engine):

Max level speed at S/L	100 knots (185 km/h; 115 mph)
Stalling speed	39 knots (73 km/h; 45 mph)
Max rate of climb at S/L	198 m (650 ft)/min
Service ceiling	4,265 m (14,000 ft)
T-O run	122 m (400 ft)
Landing run	92 m (300 ft)
g limits	+4.4/−1.7

ROBERTS SCEPTRE II

The Sceptre II is generally identical to the Sceptre I, except that the fuselage is widened to accommodate two persons side by side; a 63.4 kW (85 hp) Limbach engine is standard. First flown in late 1985.

ROTEC

ROTEC ENGINEERING INC

PO Box 380220, Duncanville, Texas 75138
Telephone: (214) 298 2505
Telex: 288777 ROTEC DCVL
Fax: (214) 296 9614
PRESIDENT: William W. Adaska

Rotec's aircraft are available in kit and/or ready to fly forms. Details of its military Ground Troop Army Trainers can be found in the 1987-88 *Jane's*.

ROTEC RALLY 2B

TYPE: Single-seat microlight; conforms to FAR Pt 103.

AIRFRAME: Mainframe of anodised aluminium tubing, with single thickness Dacron covered wing and tail surfaces.

Three-axis control. Non-retractable tailwheel landing gear. Options include wing endplates, windscreen, agricultural spray kit, skis and glassfibre floats.

POWER PLANT: One 28.3 kW (38 hp) Rotax 377. Fuel capacity 13.25 litres (3.5 US gallons; 2.9 Imp gallons) standard.

DIMENSIONS, EXTERNAL:

Wing span	9.45 m (31 ft 0 in)

RANS S-9 in homebuilt form

R.D. Aircraft Skycycle single-seat microlight

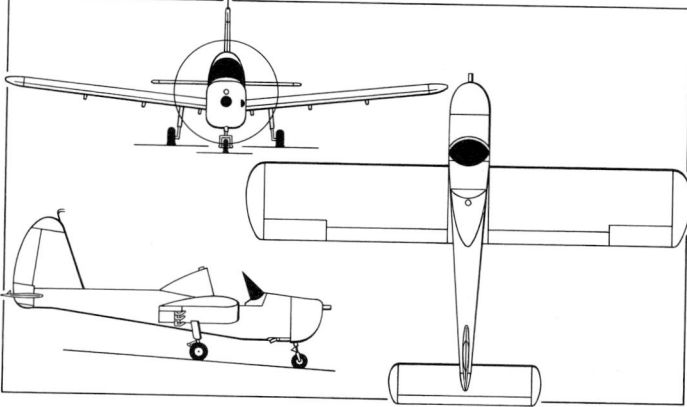

R.D. Little Dipper Replica *(Jane's/Mike Keep)*

R.D. Aircraft Skycycle Cabin Gypsy microlight aircraft

Rotec Rally 2B amphibian

Roberts Sceptre I single-seat homebuilt aircraft *(Howard Levy)*

Length overall	5.13 m (16 ft 10 in)
Height overall	3.15 m (10 ft 4 in)
Propeller diameter	1.37 m (4 ft 6 in)
AREA:	
Wings, gross	14.40 m² (155.0 sq ft)
WEIGHTS:	
Weight empty	98 kg (216 lb)
Max pilot weight	100 kg (220 lb)
Max T-O weight	208 kg (460 lb)

PERFORMANCE (with 79.5 kg; 175 lb pilot, 75% power except where indicated):

Max cruising speed	35 knots (64 km/h; 40 mph)
Stalling speed: full power	13 knots (25 km/h; 15 mph)
power off	16 knots (29 km/h; 18 mph)
Max rate of climb at S/L	152 m (500 ft)/min
Service ceiling	above 3,050 m (10,000 ft)
T-O run, full power	23 m (75 ft)
Landing run	15 m (50 ft)
Range with max fuel	73 nm (135 km; 84 miles)
Endurance with max fuel	2 h 6 min
g limits	+3/−1.5

ROTEC RALLY 3

The Rally 3, introduced in 1981, is a larger, side by side two-seat version of the 2B, to which it is otherwise basically similar except in having a 35.8 kW (48 hp) 497 cc Rotax engine, horn balanced rudder and elevators, and a new patent-pending rough field landing gear with swing arms and optional 4 in 'tundra tyres'. Dual controls are standard, and wheel, float or ski landing gear can be fitted. Options include a glassfibre cockpit pod and agricultural spraygear. The Rally 3 is also suited to other utility tasks, such as ranching, aerial photography and security surveillance.

DIMENSIONS, EXTERNAL:

Wing span	11.58 m (38 ft 0 in)
Length overall	5.28 m (17 ft 4 in)
Height overall	3.25 m (10 ft 8 in)
AREA:	
Wings, gross	17.65 m² (190.0 sq ft)
WEIGHTS:	
Weight empty	129 kg (285 lb)
Pilot and passenger (max)	195 kg (430 lb)

PERFORMANCE (with 159 kg; 350 lb useful load, 75% power, full fuel, except where indicated):

Max cruising speed	35 knots (64 km/h; 40 mph)
Stalling speed: full power	18 knots (33 km/h; 20 mph)
power off	20 knots (36 km/h; 22 mph)
Max rate of climb at S/L, full power	137 m (450 ft)/min
Service ceiling	above 3,050 m (10,000 ft)
T-O run, full power	30 m (100 ft)
Landing run	25 m (80 ft)
Range with max standard fuel	
	87 nm (161 km; 100 miles)
Endurance with max standard fuel	2 h 30 min

ROTEC RALLY SPORT

The Rally Sport was designed to withstand flight manual approved aerobatic manoeuvres, and is the *only* Rally approved for this type of flying. A parachute is required during aerobatics, and at least five hours of aerobatic flight time in a certificated aircraft is recommended before attempting aerobatics in the Rally Sport.

AIRFRAME: Similar construction to Rally 2B. Glassfibre cockpit pod and wing endplates optional.

POWER PLANT: One 35.8 kW (48 hp) 496 cc Rotax 503. Fuel capacity 13.25 litres (3.5 US gallons; 2.9 Imp gallons).

DIMENSIONS, EXTERNAL:

Wing span	8.23 m (27 ft 0 in)
Length overall	5.05 m (16 ft 7 in)
Height overall	3.15 m (10 ft 4 in)
Propeller diameter	1.52 m (5 ft 0 in)
AREA:	
Wings, gross	12.54 m² (135.0 sq ft)
WEIGHTS:	
Weight empty	112 kg (248 lb)
Pilot weight range (incl parachute)	
	45.5-100 kg (100-220 lb)

PERFORMANCE (with 79.5 kg; 175 lb pilot, 75% power and full fuel, except where indicated):

Max level speed	52 knots (96 km/h; 60 mph)
Econ cruising speed	30 knots (56 km/h; 35 mph)
Stalling speed: full power	18 knots (33 km/h; 20 mph)
power off	20 knots (37 km/h; 23 mph)
Max rate of climb at S/L, full power	
	more than 305 m (1,000 ft)/min
Service ceiling	above 3,050 m (10,000 ft)
T-O run, full power	21 m (70 ft)
Landing run	23 m (75 ft)
Range with max fuel	72 nm (133 km; 83 miles)
Endurance with max fuel	1 h 30 min
g limits	+6/−3

ROTEC RALLY CHAMP

The Rally Champ is a lower-powered, low-cost version of the Rally 2B. Options include wing endplates and a cockpit pod.

POWER PLANT: One 20 kW (27 hp) Rotax 277. Fuel capacity 13.25 litres (3.5 US gallons; 2.9 Imp gallons).

DIMENSIONS, EXTERNAL:

Wing span	9.45 m (31 ft 0 in)
Length overall	5.13 m (16 ft 10 in)
Height overall	3.15 m (10 ft 4 in)
Propeller diameter	1.37 m (4 ft 6 in)

AREA:

Wings, gross	14.40 m² (155.0 sq ft)

WEIGHTS:

Weight empty	92 kg (202 lb)
Pilot weight range	55-91 kg (120-200 lb)
Max T-O weight	192 kg (424 lb)

PERFORMANCE (at 75% power except where indicated, with 79 kg; 175 lb pilot):

Max cruising speed	35 knots (64 km/h; 40 mph)
Econ cruising speed	30 knots (56 km/h; 35 mph)
Stalling speed: full power	16 knots (30 km/h; 18 mph)
power off	18 knots (33 km/h; 20 mph)
Max rate of climb at S/L, full power	137 m (450 ft)/min
Service ceiling	3,050 m (10,000 ft)
T-O run, full power	30 m (100 ft)
Landing run, zero wind	15 m (50 ft)
Range with max fuel	74 nm (136 km; 85 miles)
Endurance with max fuel	2 h 20 min
g limits	+3.5/−1.5

ROTEC PANTHER

TYPE: Single-seat cabin microlight.

AIRFRAME: Mainframe of aluminium alloy, with double surface Dacron covered wings and tail surfaces. Three-axis control. Non-retractable tailwheel landing gear. Optional floats and skis.

POWER PLANT: One 20 kW (27 hp) Rotax 277. Rotax 377 and 447 engines optional. Fuel capacity 19 litres (5 US gallons; 4.2 Imp gallons).

DIMENSIONS, EXTERNAL:

Wing span	10.36 m (34 ft 0 in)
Length overall	4.88 m (16 ft 10 in)
Height overall	1.91 m (6 ft 3 in)
Propeller diameter	1.37 m (4 ft 6 in)

AREA:

Wings, gross	13.75 m² (148.0 sq ft)

WEIGHTS:

Weight empty	113 kg (250 lb)
Pilot weight range	45-91 kg (100-200 lb)

PERFORMANCE (with 79 kg; 175 lb pilot, 75% power and full fuel, except where indicated):

Max cruising speed	50 knots (93 km/h; 58 mph)
Stalling speed: full power	19 knots (36 km/h; 22 mph)
power off	21 knots (39 km/h; 24 mph)
Max rate of climb at S/L, full power	122 m (400 ft)/min
Service ceiling	3,050 m (10,000 ft)
T-O run, full power	37 m (120 ft)
Landing run, zero wind	23 m (75 ft)
Range with max standard fuel	149 nm (277 km; 172 miles)
g limits	+4/−1.9

ROTEC PANTHER PLUS and SEA PANTHER

Rotec's follow-on aircraft to the Panther, the Panther Plus, is not a microlight but is covered by the FAA's Experimental homebuilt category. Construction from the optional kit takes about 40 hours.

The standard **Panther Plus** employs many features of the Panther, but has a fully enclosed cabin and a 31.3 kW (42 hp) Rotax 447. A twin-float variant of the Panther Plus is the **Sea Panther**, with foam core glassfibre floats of 3.45 m (11 ft 4 in) length. The Sea Panther has a maximum speed of 69 knots (129 km/h; 80 mph), a cruising speed of 65 knots (121 km/h; 75 mph), a range of 152 nm (281 km; 175 miles), and a useful load of 152 kg (335 lb). Military versions of the Panther have been proposed.

The description of the Panther applies also to the Panther Plus, except as detailed above and below.

AIRFRAME: As Panther but with fully enclosed cabin.

DIMENSIONS, EXTERNAL:

Wing span	10.36 m (34 ft 0 in)
Length overall	4.88 m (16 ft 10 in)
Height overall	2.06 m (6 ft 9 in)
Propeller diameter	1.52 m (5 ft 0 in)

AREA:

Wings, gross	13.75 m² (148.0 sq ft)

WEIGHTS:

Weight empty	134 kg (295 lb)
Pilot weight range	63.5-111 kg (140-245 lb)
Baggage capacity	18 kg (40 lb)
Max T-O weight	286 kg (630 lb)

PERFORMANCE:

Max level speed	65 knots (121 km/h; 75 mph)
Econ cruising speed	52 knots (97 km/h; 60 mph)
Stalling speed: full power	19 knots (34 km/h; 21 mph)
power off	23 knots (42 km/h; 26 mph)
Max rate of climb at S/L	244 m (800 ft)/min
Service ceiling	more than 3,050 m (10,000 ft)
T-O run	28 m (90 ft)
Landing run	23 m (75 ft)
Range with max fuel	152 nm (281 km; 175 miles)
Endurance	2 h 30 min
g limits	+3.5/−1.5

ROTEC PANTHER 2 PLUS

The Panther 2 Plus is basically a Panther Plus with a lengthened cabin to provide tandem seating for a pilot and passenger. The Rotax 447 engine remains the standard power plant; options are the 35.8 kW (48 hp) Rotax 503 and a 48.5 kW (65 hp) Rotax. An auxiliary 13.25 litre (3.5 US gallon; 2.9 Imp gallon) fuel tank is offered to supplement the standard 19 litre (5 US gallon; 4.2 Imp gallon) tank. Options include floats (**as Sea Panther 2 Plus**), skis, wheel fairings, dual controls and agricultural spraying equipment.

TYPE: Tandem two-seat cabin homebuilt; conforms to FAA Experimental category.

DIMENSIONS, EXTERNAL:

Wing span	10.36 m (34 ft 0 in)
Length overall	5.59 m (18 ft 4 in)
Height overall	2.13 m (7 ft 0 in)
Propeller diameter	1.65 m (5 ft 5 in)

AREA:

Wings, gross	17.09 m² (184.0 sq ft)

WEIGHTS:

Weight empty	179 kg (395 lb)
Pilot and passenger weight range (combined)	136-208 kg (300-460 lb)
Max T-O weight	422 kg (930 lb)

PERFORMANCE (standard aircraft, except where indicated):

Max level speed	69 knots (129 km/h; 80 mph)
Econ cruising speed	56 knots (105 km/h; 65 mph)
Stalling speed: power on	21 knots (39 km/h; 24 mph)
power off	25 knots (47 km/h; 29 mph)
Max rate of climb at S/L: 2 crew	167 m (550 ft)/min
pilot only	more than 274 m (900 ft)/min
Sea Panther	152 m (500 ft)/min
Service ceiling	more than 3,050 m (10,000 ft)
T-O run	54 m (175 ft)
T-O run, Sea Panther	106 m (350 ft)
Landing run	38 m (125 ft)
Range with max fuel	173 nm (322 km; 200 miles)
Endurance	2 h 30 min
g limits	+3.5/−1.5

ROTORWAY

ROTORWAY AIRCRAFT INC

7411 West Galveston, Chandler, Arizona 85226
Telephone: (602) 961 1001
Telex: 683 5059
Fax: (602) 961 1158

ROTORWAY EXEC

RotorWay currently offers Exec component kits for construction by amateur builders, as well as the RW-152-D engine, and a training programme for the constructor/pilot. All new Execs have as standard the latest 'hi-lift blade system' with asymmetrical aerofoil rotor blades.

In Thailand, the International Aircraft Co Ltd (IAC) has requested government support to produce the Exec for domestic and export markets, thereby establishing the nation's first helicopter assembly line.

TYPE: Side by side two-seat homebuilt helicopter.

ROTOR SYSTEM: Asymmetrical section two-blade main rotor. All-metal aluminium alloy blades are attached to aluminium alloy teetering rotor hub by retention straps. Teetering tail rotor, with two blades each comprising a steel spar and aluminium alloy skin. Swashplate for cyclic pitch control. Cable through rotor shaft to blades for collective pitch control. Optional elastomeric rotor hub.

AIRFRAME: Basic steel tube structure for fuselage pod. Monocoque tailboom of aluminium alloy. Twin skid landing gear standard. Options include ground handling wheels, floats (including Full Lotus inflatable type), dual controls and agricultural spraygear.

POWER PLANT: One 113.3 kW (152 hp) RotorWay RW-152-D. Standard fuel capacity 64.4 litres (17 US gallons; 14.2 Imp gallons).

DIMENSIONS, EXTERNAL:

Main rotor diameter	7.72 m (25 ft 4 in)
Length of fuselage	6.55 m (21 ft 6 in)
Height to top of main rotor	2.39 m (7 ft 10 in)

WEIGHTS:

Weight empty	376 kg (830 lb)
Max T-O weight	599 kg (1,320 lb)

PERFORMANCE (at max T-O weight):

Max level speed	100 knots (185 km/h; 115 mph)
Normal cruising speed	82 knots (153 km/h; 95 mph)
Max rate of climb at S/L	366 m (1,200 ft)/min

Hovering ceiling, with two persons:

IGE	2,285 m (7,500 ft)
OGE	1,370 m (4,500 ft)

Range with max fuel at optimum cruising power

174 nm (323 km; 201 miles)

SANDS

RON SANDS INC

RD 1, Box 341, Mertztown, Pennsylvania 19539-9611
Telephone: (215) 682 6788
VICE-PRESIDENT: Ron Sands

Ron Sands Inc has available plans and kits to construct a full-size reproduction of the Fokker Dr. I First World War fighter. The company also offers fully or partially assembled aircraft to special order. Currently under development is a Fokker D.VIII Parasol replica, the prototype of which is expected to be completed in early 1989.

RON SANDS FOKKER Dr. I REPLICA TRIPLANE

TYPE: Single-seat homebuilt replica triplane.
AIRFRAME: Wooden wings and welded steel tube fuselage and tail unit, fabric covered. Göttingen wing section. Ailerons on upper wing only. Non-retractable tailskid landing gear.

POWER PLANT: Engines recommended are: 112-134 kW (150-180 hp) Textron Lycoming O-320/O-360; 108, 123 or 138 kW (145, 165 or 185 hp) Warner seven-cylinder radial; or 82 or 89.5 kW (110 or 120 hp) Le Rhône nine-cylinder rotary. Fuel capacity 85 litres (22.5 US gallons; 18.7 Imp gallons). Two optional auxiliary tanks, each of 11.4 litres (3 US gallons; 2.5 Imp gallons).

DIMENSIONS, EXTERNAL:

Wing span: upper	6.73 m (22 ft 1 in)
centre	6.25 m (20 ft 6 in)
lower	5.77 m (18 ft 11 in)
Length overall	5.80 m (19 ft 0¼ in)
Height overall	2.87 m (9 ft 5 in)

AREA:

Wings, gross	18.75 m² (201.84 sq ft)

WEIGHTS:

Weight empty	544 kg (1,200 lb)
Pilot weight range	50-102 kg (110-225 lb)
Baggage capacity	9 kg (20 lb)
Max T-O weight	726 kg (1,600 lb)

PERFORMANCE (at max T-O weight):

Max level speed at 3,050 m (10,000 ft)	104 knots (193 km/h; 120 mph)
Econ cruising speed at 3,050 m (10,000 ft)	78 knots (145 km/h; 90 mph)
Stalling speed: power off	31 knots (57 km/h; 35 mph)
Max rate of climb at S/L	549 m (1,800 ft)/min
Service ceiling	4,575 m (15,000 ft)
T-O run	91 m (300 ft)
Landing run	61 m (200 ft)
Range	217 nm (402 km; 250 miles)
Endurance	2 h 30 min

SEQUOIA

SEQUOIA AIRCRAFT CORPORATION

2000 Tomlynn Street, PO Box 6861, Richmond, Virginia 23230

Telephone: (804) 353 1713

PRESIDENT: Alfred P. Scott

MODEL 300 SEQUOIA

This aircraft is available in plan and kit forms.
TYPE: Side by side two-seat utility and aerobatic homebuilt.
AIRFRAME: Wing section NACA 64₂A215 at root, NACA 64A210 at tip. Wings, ailerons, slotted flaps and tail unit of flush riveted aluminium alloy construction. Wings have glassfibre tips. Welded steel tube fuselage, covered entirely with lightweight shell of glassfibre/PVC foam/glassfibre sandwich, attached to tubing with glassfibre and epoxy resin. Retractable tricycle landing gear.

POWER PLANT: One 224 kW (300 hp) Textron Lycoming TIO-540-S1AD. Other Textron Lycoming engines of 175-224 kW (235-300 hp) may be used. Fuel capacity 291.5 litres (77 US gallons; 64 Imp gallons). Provision for tip tanks of approximately 75 litres (20 US gallons; 16.7 Imp gallons) capacity each; and two underwing

Rotec Panther 2 Plus (*Geoffrey P. Jones*)

Rotec Panther Plus in military guise (*Howard Levy*)

Ron Sands Fokker Dr. I Triplane replica (Warner radial engine)

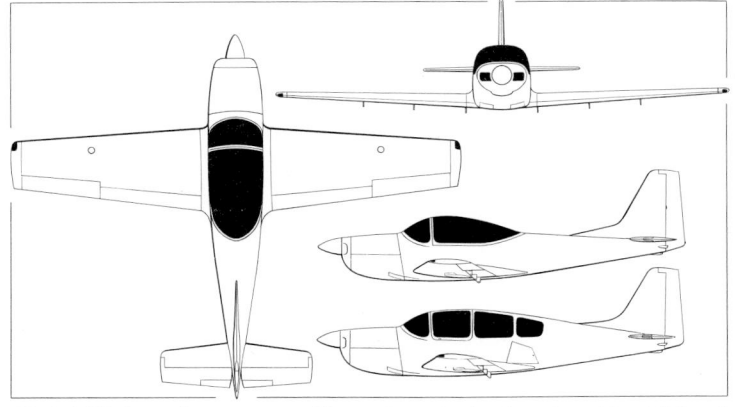

Model 300 Sequoia two-seat utility and aerobatic aircraft, with additional (lower) side view of Model 302 Kodiak (*Pilot Press*)

RotorWay Exec with Full Lotus inflatable floats

Sequoia Falco F.8L homebuilt aircraft

attachment points for additional fuel tanks, radar or stores of up to 272 kg (600 lb) combined weight.

DIMENSIONS, EXTERNAL:

Wing span	9.14 m (30 ft 0 in)
Length overall	7.62 m (25 ft 0 in)
Height overall	2.90 m (9 ft 6 in)
Propeller diameter	2.03 m (6 ft 8 in)

AREA:

Wings, gross	12.08 m² (130.0 sq ft)

WEIGHTS:

Weight empty	816 kg (1,800 lb)
Baggage capacity	45 kg (100 lb)
Max T-O weight: utility	1,270 kg (2,800 lb)
aerobatic	1,088 kg (2,400 lb)

PERFORMANCE (estimated):

Max level speed at S/L	195 knots (362 km/h; 225 mph)
Max cruising speed at 2,440 m (8,000 ft)	
	185 knots (343 km/h; 213 mph)
Stalling speed: 'clean'	75 knots (139 km/h; 86 mph)
flaps and wheels down	60 knots (111 km/h; 69 mph)
Max rate of climb at S/L	664 m (2,180 ft)/min
Service ceiling	7,620 m (25,000 ft)
T-O run	457 m (1,500 ft)
Landing run	548 m (1,800 ft)
Range at max cruising speed, with 45 min reserves	
	868 nm (1,609 km; 1,000 miles)

SEQUOIA MODEL 302 KODIAK

The Kodiak is a four-seat development of the Model 300 Sequoia with gull-wing doors to provide access to the enclosed cabin. It was designed to be fully aerobatic and is available in plan and kit forms (latter does not include prepared fuselage).

Power plant is in the 186-224 kW (250-300 hp) Textron Lycoming IO-540/TIO-540-S1AD range. Empty weight will be 839 kg (1,850 lb); max T-O weight 1,451 kg (3,200 lb); fuel capacity 341 litres (90 US gallons; 75 Imp gallons).

SEQUOIA FALCO F.8L

Sequoia Aircraft markets plans and kits to build an improved version of the Falco F.8L high-performance monoplane, designed in Italy by Ing Stelio Frati of General Avia and first flown on 15 June 1955. By February 1988, a total of 532 sets of plans had been sold and fifteen Falcos had flown.

TYPE: Side by side two-seat, dual control homebuilt. Provision for child's seat in baggage space.

AIRFRAME: Entire airframe has plywood covered wood structure, with overall fabric covering and glassfibre wing fillets. Optional metal control surfaces. NACA 64₂212.5 wing section at root, NACA 64₂210 at tip. Retractable tricycle landing gear.

POWER PLANT: One 119 kW (160 hp) Textron Lycoming IO-320-B1A is standard for kit-built aircraft. Optional engines for which Sequoia offers installation kits are the 112 kW (150 hp) IO-320-A1A and 134 kW (180 hp) IO-360-B1E. Fuel capacity 151 litres (40 US gallons; 33.3 Imp gallons). Optional 7.6 litre (2 US gallon; 1.7 Imp gallon) header tank to permit inverted flight.

DIMENSIONS, EXTERNAL:

Wing span	8.00 m (26 ft 3 in)
Length overall	6.50 m (21 ft 4 in)
Height overall	2.29 m (7 ft 6 in)

AREA:

Wings, gross	10.00 m² (107.6 sq ft)

WEIGHTS (119 kW; 160 hp engine):

Weight empty	550 kg (1,212 lb)
Payload with max fuel	194 kg (428 lb)
Baggage capacity	40 kg (88 lb)
Max aerobatic weight	748 kg (1,650 lb)
Max T-O weight	853 kg (1,880 lb)

PERFORMANCE (119 kW; 160 hp engine):

Max level speed at S/L	184 knots (341 km/h; 212 mph)
Cruising speed at 1,830 m (6,000 ft), 75% power	
	165 knots (306 km/h; 190 mph)
Stalling speed, flaps and wheels down	
	54 knots (100 km/h; 62 mph)
Max rate of climb at S/L	347 m (1,140 ft)/min
Service ceiling	5,790 m (19,000 ft)
Range at econ cruising speed	
	868 nm (1,609 km; 1,000 miles)

SILHOUETTE

SILHOUETTE AIRCRAFT INC
(Division of Task Research Incorporated)
848 East Santa Maria Street, Santa Paula Airport, Santa
Paula, California 93060
Telephone: (805) 525 4545
Fax: (805) 525 3164

SILHOUETTE AIRCRAFT SA-60
SILHOUETTE I
The prototype Silhouette flew for the first time on 3 July
1984. Kits are available, and numerous aircraft have been
assembled and flown. Bolt-on wingtip extensions allow for
the Silhouette's use as a motor glider.
TYPE: Single-seat sport/recreational homebuilt and motor
glider; designed and tested to FAR Pt 23 standards.

AIRFRAME: Wings have glassfibre spars, pre-cut foam cores,
glassfibre skins and pre-moulded wingtips. Basic wings
have half span ailerons of composite construction.
Provision for bolt-on wingtip extensions for use as motor
glider. Centreline dive brake optional. Fuselage of
glassfibre and Nomex honeycomb, pre-moulded in
halves with integral tail fin. Tail surfaces of foam and
glassfibre. Non-retractable tricycle landing gear.
POWER PLANT: One 30 kW (40 hp) Rotax 447. Fuel capacity
38 litres (10 US gallons; 8.3 Imp gallons).
DIMENSIONS, EXTERNAL:

Wing span: standard	9.75 m (32 ft 0 in)
with optional wing extensions	12.50 m (41 ft 0 in)
Length overall	5.87 m (19 ft 3 in)
Height overall	2.03 m (6 ft 8 in)
Propeller diameter	1.47 m (4 ft 10 in)

AREAS:

Wings, gross: standard	7.06 m² (76.0 sq ft)
with extensions	8.36 m² (90.0 sq ft)

WEIGHTS:

Weight empty: standard wings	223 kg (490 lb)
Max T-O weight	351 kg (775 lb)

PERFORMANCE (standard wings):

Max level speed	117 knots (217 km/h; 135 mph)
Econ cruising speed	96 knots (177 km/h; 110 mph)
Stalling speed	42 knots (77 km/h; 48 mph)
Max rate of climb at S/L	244 m (800 ft)/min
Service ceiling	4,575 m (15,000 ft)
T-O run	244 m (800 ft)
Landing run	152 m (500 ft)
Range with max fuel	more than 434 nm (804 km; 500 miles)

SMYTH

JERRY SMYTH
ADDRESS FOR PLANS: Wicks Aircraft Supply, 410 Pine Street,
Highland, Illinois 62249
Telephone: (618) 654 7447
Fax: (618) 654 6253

SMYTH MODEL 'S' SIDEWINDER
The prototype Sidewinder first flew on 21 February 1969.
Plans and component parts are available. The following
description applies to the prototype:
TYPE: Side by side two-seat limited aerobatic homebuilt.
AIRFRAME: Aluminium alloy wings, ailerons and tail unit;
wings filled with epoxy. Wing section NACA 64-612 at
root, NACA 64-210 at tip. Welded steel tube fuselage,
with aluminium formers and skin. Electrically operated
speed brake may be fitted on lower fuselage. Non-

retractable tricycle landing gear. Aircraft have been
completed with retractable landing gear (see 1975-76
Jane's) and tailwheel type landing gear (see 1980-81
Jane's).
POWER PLANT: Provision for installation of engines from 67
to 134 kW (90-180 hp). Prototype has a 93 kW (125 hp)
Textron Lycoming O-290-G. Fuel capacity 66.2 litres
(17.5 US gallons; 14.6 Imp gallons). Provision for wingtip
tanks.
DIMENSIONS, EXTERNAL:

Wing span	7.57 m (24 ft 10 in)
Length overall	5.89 m (19 ft 4 in)
Height overall	1.66 m (5 ft 5½ in)
Propeller diameter	1.70 m (5 ft 7 in)

AREA:

Wings, gross	8.92 m² (96.0 sq ft)

WEIGHTS:

Weight empty	393 kg (867 lb)
Baggage capacity	41 kg (90 lb)
Max T-O and landing weight	657 kg (1,450 lb)

PERFORMANCE (at max T-O weight):

Max level speed at 610 m (2,000 ft)	161 knots (298 km/h; 185 mph)
Max cruising speed, 75% power at 610 m (2,000 ft)	139 knots (257 km/h; 160 mph)
Stalling speed	48 knots (89 km/h; 55 mph)
Max rate of climb at S/L: at 0°C	366 m (1,200 ft)/min
at 24°C	274 m (900 ft)/min
Service ceiling	4,575 m (15,000 ft)
T-O run	244 m (800 ft)
Landing run	457 m (1,500 ft)
Range with max fuel, no reserves	369 nm (684 km; 425 miles)
g limit	+9 design

SORRELL

SORRELL AIRCRAFT COMPANY LTD
16525 Tilley Road S, Tenino, Washington 98589
Telephone: (206) 264 2866

SORRELL SNS-2 GUPPY
In 1967 the late Mr Hobie Sorrell flew his SNS-2 Guppy
cabin biplane for the first time, powered by a 13.5 kW (18
hp) OMC Cushman Model 200 engine. Plans for this 'back
staggered' non-aerobatic single-seater are available from
Sorrell Aircraft Company and/or from Mr Michael
Kimbrel (which see). Sorrell is also believed to offer a kit of
component parts which includes a Rotax 377 engine.
TYPE: Single-seat homebuilt cabin biplane.
AIRFRAME: Modified Grant X wing section. Wooden wings
and fuselage, except for steel tube wingtips, aluminium
fittings and wing drag member; Dacron covered. Full
span ailerons on lower wings only, of aluminium tubing
with riveted aluminium skins. Steel tube engine mounting,
interplane struts and Dacron covered tail unit. Non-
retractable tailwheel landing gear.
POWER PLANT: Engines of up to 27 kW (36 hp) can be fitted,
including Volkswagen modified motorcar engines. Sorrell
kit includes 24 kW (32 hp) Rotax 377. Fuel capacity 23
litres (6.5 US gallons; 5.4 Imp gallons).
DIMENSIONS, EXTERNAL:

Wing span	6.48 m (21 ft 3 in)
Length overall	4.70 m (15 ft 5 in)
Height overall	1.57 m (5 ft 2 in)

AREA:

Wings, gross	11.98 m² (129.0 sq ft)

WEIGHTS (prototype with Cushman engine):

Weight empty	159 kg (350 lb)
Max T-O weight	272 kg (600 lb)

PERFORMANCE (prototype with Cushman engine):

Max level speed	69 knots (129 km/h; 80 mph)
Cruising speed	61 knots (113 km/h; 70 mph)
Stalling speed, power off	26 knots (49 km/h; 30 mph)
Max rate of climb at S/L	91 m (300 ft)/min
Absolute ceiling	3.110 m (10,200 ft)
T-O run	91 m (300 ft)
Landing from 15 m (50 ft)	91 m (300 ft)
Range	182 nm (338 km; 210 miles)
g limit	+4 recommended

SORRELL SNS-7 HIPERBIPE
The Hiperbipe made its initial flight as the SNS-6
prototype in March 1973. According to reports, the SNS-7
version is on sale in plans form, with component parts
available upon request.
TYPE: Side by side two-seat, dual control homebuilt
aerobatic biplane.
AIRFRAME: Modified NACA 0012 wing sections. Welded
steel interplane struts. Fabric-covered all-wood back-
staggered wings, but with centre-section of upper wing
skinned with transparent plastics to allow improved view
for aerobatics. Cambered wingtips. Four full span

flaperons of pop-riveted aluminium alloy. Fuselage and
tail unit of welded steel tube, fabric covered. Glassfibre
engine cowling. Non-retractable tailwheel landing gear.
POWER PLANT: One 134 kW (180 hp) Textron Lycoming
IO-360-B1E. Fuel capacity 147.5 litres (39 US gallons;
32.5 Imp gallons).
DIMENSIONS, EXTERNAL:

Wing span	6.96 m (22 ft 10 in)
Length overall	6.35 m (20 ft 10 in)
Height overall	1.80 m (5 ft 10¾ in)
Propeller diameter	1.93 m (6 ft 4 in)

AREA:

Wings, gross (projected)	13.9 m² (150.0 sq ft)

WEIGHTS:

Weight empty	561 kg (1,236 lb)
Baggage capacity	36 kg (80 lb)
Max T-O weight: aerobatic	766 kg (1,690 lb)
normal	867 kg (1,911 lb)

PERFORMANCE (at max T-O weight):

Max level speed at S/L	149 knots (277 km/h; 172 mph)
Econ cruising speed	130 knots (241 km/h; 150 mph)
Stalling speed:	
flaperons down	43 knots (79 km/h; 49 mph)
flaperons up	51 knots (94 km/h; 58 mph)
Max rate of climb at S/L	457 m (1,500 ft)/min
Service ceiling, estimated	6,100 m (20,000 ft)
T-O run	122 m (400 ft)
Landing run	181 m (595 ft)
Range	436 nm (807 km; 502 miles)

SORRELL SNS-8 HIPERLIGHT and HIPERLIGHT EXP
The **Hiperlight** is claimed to be capable of limited
aerobatics. It was first flown in 1983, and kits became
available soon after this.
The **Hiperlight EXP**, although generally similar to the
basic version, has a more powerful Rotax 377 engine, basic
instrumentation and hydraulic disc brakes as standard and
Stits Poly-Fiber airframe covering. The EXP airframe
requires only 75-100 working hours to complete from the
kit.
TYPE: Single-seat microlight biplane; conforms to FAR Pt
103.
AIRFRAME: Wing framework and ribs, rear fuselage and tail
unit are of welded aluminium alloy tube, with Dacron
covering. Cockpit/centre-fuselage structure of welded
steel tube, also Dacron covered. Three-axis control.
Non-retractable tailwheel landing gear. Optional floats
and skis.
POWER PLANT: One 20 kW (27 hp) Rotax 277 (Hiperlight) or
26.8 kW (36 hp) Rotax 377 (Hiperlight EXP). Fuel
capacity 19 litres (5 US gallons; 4.2 Imp gallons).
DIMENSIONS, EXTERNAL:

Wing span	6.71 m (22 ft 0 in)
Length overall	4.72 m (15 ft 6 in)
Height overall	1.60 m (5 ft 3 in)
Propeller diameter	1.52 m (5 ft 0 in)

AREA:

Wings, gross	13.01 m² (140.0 sq ft)

WEIGHTS (Hiperlight):

Weight empty	111.5 kg (246 lb)
Max pilot weight	104 kg (230 lb)
Max T-O weight	227 kg (500 lb)

PERFORMANCE (Hiperlight with 77 kg; 170 lb pilot):

Max level speed	55 knots (101 km/h; 63 mph)
Max cruising speed	52 knots (96 km/h; 60 mph)
Stalling speed, power off	24 knots (44 km/h; 27 mph)
Max rate of climb at S/L	183 m (600 ft)/min
Service ceiling	3,660 m (12,000 ft)
T-O run	46 m (150 ft)
Landing run	53 m (175 ft)
Range with max fuel	174 nm (322 km; 200 miles)
Endurance with max fuel	3 h
g limits at max T-O weight	+6/-4

SORRELL SNS-9 EXP II
First flown on 22 May 1985, the SNS-9 EXP II is a side by
side two-seat sport/trainer, with dual controls and basic
instrumentation as standard. Like other recent Sorrell
designs, it is a small back-staggered biplane. The wings are
made of pop riveted aluminium alloy, covered with Stits
Poly-Fiber. The welded steel tube fuselage is also Poly-Fiber
covered. Power for the prototype is provided by a 31.3 kW
(42 hp) Rotax 447. Standard fuel capacity is 34 litres (9 US
gallons; 7.5 Imp gallons). Assembly from pre-welded
component kits is said to require 300 hours of work.
TYPE: Two-seat homebuilt cabin biplane.
DIMENSIONS, EXTERNAL:

Wing span	7.11 m (23 ft 4 in)
Length overall	5.49 m (18 ft 0 in)
Height overall	1.63 m (5 ft 4 in)

AREA:

Wings, gross	13.75 m² (148.0 sq ft)

WEIGHTS:

Weight empty	162 kg (356 lb)
Max T-O weight	367 kg (810 lb)

PERFORMANCE (estimated at max T-O weight):

Max cruising speed	74 knots (136 km/h; 85 mph)
Stalling speed	34 knots (63 km/h; 39 mph)
Max rate of climb at S/L	183 m (600 ft)/min
T-O and landing run on grass	92 m (300 ft)
Range with max standard fuel	221 nm (410 km; 255 miles)
g limits	+3.8/-1.9

SORRELL SNS-10 INTRUDER
This single-seater is thought to be basically a strengthened
version of the Hiperlight for limited aerobatics. It is not
known whether kits are available.
DIMENSION, EXTERNAL:

Wing span	4.57 m (15 ft 0 in)

WEIGHT:

Max T-O weight	159 kg (350 lb)

Long-wing Silhouette Aircraft SA-60 Silhouette I motor glider (foreground) and version with standard wings (rear) *(Howard Levy)*

Sorrell SNS-7 Hiperbipe two-seat aerobatic biplane *(Geoffrey P. Jones)*

Smyth Sidewinder (Textron Lycoming IO-320 engine) built 20% oversize by Mr G. Walker of Renton, Washington *(Peter M. Bowers)*

Sorrel SNS-2 Guppy built to plans

Sorrell SNS-9 EXP II sport/trainer *(Peter M. Bowers)*

Spencer Amphibian Air Car four-seat amphibian

Sport Aircraft S-18 built by the late Mr Luther D. Sunderland

SPENCER

SPENCER AMPHIBIAN AIR CAR INC
11019-A Glenoaks Boulevard, Pacoima, California 91331
Telephone: (818) 899 1010

SPENCER AMPHIBIAN AIR CAR Sr MODEL S-12-E
This latest version of the S-12 series is available in plan and kit forms, while plans and certain glassfibre mouldings and metal assemblies for the differently powered and earlier S-12-D are also available.

TYPE: Four-seat, dual control homebuilt amphibian.
AIRFRAME: Specially designed STOL (modified NACA 4415) wing section. Wing structure of wood, steel and glassfibre. Wooden ailerons and trailing-edge flaps. Glassfibre stabilising float on strut beneath each wing. Single-stepped hull with wood frames, longerons and

skin, sheathed in glassfibre and Kevlar. Welded steel tube structure to provide wing and engine mountings and attachment points for the retractable tricycle landing gear. Retractable water rudder.

POWER PLANT: One 224 kW (300 hp) Teledyne Continental Tiara 6-285. Also recommended is 224 kW (300 hp) Teledyne Continental IO-520. Development under way in 1988 to install a Ford 351-W converted motorcar engine. Fuel capacity 360 litres (95 US gallons; 79 Imp gallons).

DIMENSIONS, EXTERNAL:
Wing span	11.38 m (37 ft 4 in)
Length overall	7.92 m (26 ft 0 in)
Height overall, landing gear down	3.58 m (11 ft 9 in)
Propeller diameter	2.13 m (7 ft 0 in)

AREA:
Wings, gross	17.1 m² (184.0 sq ft)

WEIGHTS:
Weight empty	993 kg (2,190 lb)
Max T-O weight	1,451 kg (3,200 lb)

PERFORMANCE (at max T-O weight):
Max level speed at 2,440 m (8,000 ft)
  135 knots (249 km/h; 155 mph)
Econ cruising speed at 3,050 m (10,000 ft)
  109 knots (201 km/h; 125 mph)
Stalling speed, flaps down, power off
  39 knots (73 km/h; 45 mph)
Max rate of climb at S/L 320 m (1,050 ft)/min
Service ceiling 4,875 m (16,000 ft)
T-O run from calm water 213 m (700 ft)
Landing run 213 m (700 ft)
Range, 65% power at 2,315 m (7,600 ft), 20 min reserves 695 nm (1,285 km; 800 miles)
Endurance 7 h

SPORT

SPORT AIRCRAFT INC
104 East Avenue, K4 Unit G, Lancaster, California 93535
Telephone: (805) 949 2312

SPORT AIRCRAFT (SUNDERLAND) S-18
Originating from the Thorp T-18 Tiger, the modified S-18 was offered in plans form by Sunderland Aircraft, while Sport Aircraft Inc made kits and prefabricated

components available. Following the closure of Sunderland Aircraft, Sport Aircraft has taken over the sale of plans also. More than 1,400 sets have been sold, and over 500 T-18s and S-18s have flown.

TYPE: Side by side two-seat, dual-control homebuilt; provision for child's jump seat.
AIRFRAME: Aluminium alloy construction. Wing section LDS-4-212. Non-retractable tailwheel landing gear.
POWER PLANT: One Textron Lycoming engine in 100-134 kW (135-180 hp) category. Optional Ford V6 motorcar

engine modification by Blanton. Fuel capacity 110 litres (29 US gallons; 24.1 Imp gallons). Optional integral tank in wing leading-edge.

DIMENSIONS, EXTERNAL:
Wing span	6.35 m (20 ft 10 in)
Length overall	5.77 m (18 ft 11 in)
Height overall	1.55 m (5 ft 1 in)
Propeller diameter	1.68 m (5 ft 6 in)

AREA:
Wings, gross	8.0 m² (86.0 sq ft)

WEIGHTS (104.4 kW; 140 hp engine):
Weight empty	390 kg (860 lb)
Max T-O weight	670 kg (1,478 lb)

PERFORMANCE (112 kW; 150 hp Textron Lycoming):

Max level speed at S/L	174 knots (322 km/h; 200 mph)
Max cruising speed (75% power) at 2,590 m (8,500 ft)	
	166 knots (307 km/h; 191 mph)
Stalling speed	53 knots (97 km/h; 60 mph)

Max rate of climb at S/L	366 m (1,200 ft)/min
Service ceiling	6,100 m (20,000 ft)
Range with max fuel	460 nm (853 km; 530 miles)
Endurance	3 h 45 min

SPORT FLIGHT

SPORT FLIGHT ENGINEERING INC

PO Box 2164, Grand Junction, Colorado 81502
Telephone: (303) 245 3899
PRESIDENT: Stephen K. Wood

SPORT FLIGHT SKY PUP

Average construction time of the Sky Pup from plans varies between 350 and 450 working hours. By early 1988, a total of about 2,000 sets of plans had been sold.

TYPE: Single-seat microlight; conforms to FAR Pt 103.

AIRFRAME: Wood and foam construction, with Dacron double surface covering on wings. NACA 43018 wing section. Two-axis control. Non-retractable tailskid landing gear.

POWER PLANT: One 20 kW (27 hp) Rotax 277. Wide variety of other engines in 13.5-20 kW (18-27 hp) class being fitted by homebuilders. Fuel capacity 9.5 litres (2.5 US gallons; 2.1 Imp gallons).

DIMENSIONS, EXTERNAL:
Wing span	9.45 m (31 ft 0 in)
Length overall	4.85 m (15 ft 11 in)
Height overall	1.32 m (4 ft 4 in)
Propeller diameter	1.52 m (5 ft 0 in)

AREA:
Wings, gross	12.08 m² (130.0 sq ft)

WEIGHTS:
Weight empty	91 kg (200 lb)
Max pilot weight	86 kg (190 lb)
Max T-O weight	182 kg (400 lb)

PERFORMANCE:
Max level speed	53 knots (98 km/h; 61 mph)
Econ cruising speed	45 knots (84 km/h; 52 mph)
Stalling speed	23 knots (42 km/h; 26 mph)
Max rate of climb at S/L	244 m (800 ft)/min
Service ceiling	6,100 m (20,000 ft)
T-O run	46 m (150 ft)
Landing run	76 m (250 ft)
Range with max fuel	104 nm (193 km; 120 miles)
Endurance with max fuel	2 h
g limits	+3.8/−1.9 design
	+6/−3 ultimate

SQUADRON

SQUADRON AVIATION INC

1300 South Columbus Airport Road, Columbus, Ohio 43207
PRESIDENT: W. G. McDermitt

This company markets kits of scale representations of single-seat First World War aircraft, including the Fokker D.VII, S.E.5A and Spad S.XIII. Ready to fly versions are also available. These can operate as homebuilt aircraft, or as microlights under FAR Pt 103 if built within regulations. The following description applies to the Fokker D.VII, which is typical of the series.

SQUADRON AVIATION FOKKER D.VII

AIRFRAME: Built of aluminium alloy, with Dacron covering.

Three-axis control. Non-retractable tailskid landing gear.

POWER PLANT: One 26 kW (35 hp) Cuyuna ULII-02. Fuel capacity 19 litres (5 US gallons; 4.2 Imp gallons). Optional Rotax 377 engine.

DIMENSIONS, EXTERNAL:
Wing span	7.31 m (24 ft 0 in)
Length overall	4.88 m (16 ft 0 in)
Height overall	1.93 m (6 ft 4 in)
Propeller diameter	1.83 m (6 ft 0 in)

AREA:
Wings, gross	15.61 m² (168.0 sq ft)

WEIGHTS:
Weight empty	113 kg (250 lb)

Max pilot weight	102 kg (225 lb)
Max T-O weight	238 kg (525 lb)

PERFORMANCE:
Max level speed	54 knots (101 km/h; 63 mph)
Max and econ cruising speed	
	45 knots (84 km/h; 52 mph)
Stalling speed	16 knots (29 km/h; 18 mph)
Max rate of climb at S/L	305 m (1,000 ft)/min
Service ceiling	3,810 m (12,500 ft)
T-O run	15 m (50 ft)
Landing run	46 m (150 ft)
Range	86.5-173 nm (161-322 km; 100-200 miles)
g limits	+4/−2

STARFIRE

STARFIRE AVIATION INC

910 S Hohokam Drive, Suite 107, Tempe, Arizona 85281
Telephone: (602) 968 2556
PRESIDENT: H. G. McKenzie

FIREBOLT CONVERTIBLE

First flown on 15 May 1987, the Firebolt Convertible incorporates Skybolt features but is longer to give more cockpit room. Plans and material kits are available, and by April 1988 sixteen kits had been sold; two aircraft had, by then, also been built from plans.

TYPE: Tandem two-seat aerobatic homebuilt biplane.

AIRFRAME: Wooden wings, steel tube fuselage with aluminium alloy stringers, and steel tube tail unit, all Stits

Poly-Fiber covered. Wing section NACA 63₂A015 on upper wing; NACA 0012 on lower wings. Non-retractable tailwheel landing gear.

POWER PLANT: One 134 kW (180 hp) Textron Lycoming IO-360-B1B. Fuel capacity 151 litres (40 US gallons; 33.3 Imp gallons). Optional 224 kW (300 hp) Textron Lycoming IO-540-K1A5 engine.

DIMENSIONS, EXTERNAL:
Wing span, both	7.32 m (24 ft 0 in)
Length overall	6.10 m (20 ft 0 in)
Height overall	2.18 m (7 ft 2 in)
Propeller diameter	1.88 m (6 ft 2 in)

AREA:
Wings, gross	13.94 m² (150.0 sq ft)

WEIGHTS:
Weight empty	583 kg (1,285 lb)

Pilot weight range	68-113 kg (150-250 lb)
Baggage capacity	9 kg (20 lb)
Max T-O weight	885 kg (1,950 lb)

PERFORMANCE:
Max level speed at S/L	195 knots (362 km/h; 225 mph)
Econ cruising speed	
	109 knots (201 km/h; 125 mph) IAS
Stalling speed, power off	51 knots (94 km/h; 58 mph)
Max rate of climb at S/L	548 m (1,800 ft)/min
Service ceiling	5,790 m (19,000 ft)
T-O run	183 m (600 ft)
Landing run	259 m (850 ft)
Range with max standard fuel	
	521 nm (965 km; 600 miles)
Endurance	4 h 35 min
g limits	±6

STAR FLIGHT

STAR FLIGHT AIRCRAFT

Liberty Landing Airport, Route 3, Box 197, Liberty, Missouri 64066
Telephone: (816) 781 2250
PRESIDENT: Richard Turner

STAR FLIGHT XC SERIES

The **XC 280 Stiletto**, the basic model of the XC range with a Rotax 377 engine and smallest wing span, was flown at the Sun 'n Fun Fly-in in 1984. With a greater wing area (15.33 m²; 165.0 sq ft) the aircraft becomes the **XC 320**. The **XC 2000** combines the larger wing area of the XC 320 with a more powerful Rotax 447 engine, a heavier airframe and tandem two-seat accommodation. Options for all versions include a glassfibre cockpit pod. Options for the XC 2000 include cropspraying equipment, with which the aircraft is known as the XC 2000 **AgLite** and is flown as a single-seater, and dual controls.

Each aircraft of the XC series is believed to be available in plans form, as component parts, or as a kit. The XC 2000 kit is approved by the FAA for amateur built 'Experimental' status.

TYPE: Single- and two-seat microlights; conform to FAR Pt 103.

AIRFRAME: Mainframe of aluminium alloy tubing. Single surface Dacron covering on wings and tail unit. Three-axis control. Non-retractable tricycle landing gear. Optional floats.

POWER PLANT: XC 280 and XC 320: One 24 kW (32 hp) Rotax 377; 20 kW (27 hp) Rotax 277 optional. XC 2000: One 30 kW (40 hp) Rotax 447. Fuel capacity 19 litres (5 US gallons; 4.2 Imp gallons).

DIMENSIONS, EXTERNAL (XC 280):
Wing span	8.69 m (28 ft 6 in)
Length overall	5.18 m (17 ft 0 in)
Height overall	2.44 m (8 ft 0 in)
Propeller diameter	1.52 m (5 ft 0 in)

AREA (XC 280):
Wings, gross	13.66 m² (147.0 sq ft)

WEIGHTS (XC 280):
Weight empty	107 kg (235 lb)
Pilot weight range	59-113 kg (130-250 lb)
Max T-O weight	227 kg (500 lb)

PERFORMANCE (XC 280):
Max level speed	42 knots (77 km/h; 48 mph)
Stalling speed: power on	20 knots (37 km/h; 23 mph)
power off	23 knots (42 km/h; 26 mph)
Max rate of climb at S/L	183 m (600 ft)/min
Service ceiling	4,575 m (15,000 ft)
T-O and Landing run	61 m (200 ft)
Range with max fuel	78 nm (145 km; 90 miles)
g limits	+6/−4 ultimate

STAR-LITE

STAR-LITE AIRCRAFT INC

2219 Orange Blossom, San Antonio, Texas 78247
Telephone: (512) 494 9812
PRESIDENT: Mark D. Brown

STAR-LITE AIRCRAFT STAR-LITE SL-1

The prototype Star-Lite SL-1 flew for the first time on 17 May 1983. The Star-Lite is now offered to amateur constructors in three separate kits, of which construction time averages about 400 working hours. By February 1988 a total of at least 120 complete kits had been ordered, and 35 Star-Lites had already been assembled and flown.

A side by side two-seat version of the Star-Lite was scheduled to fly for the first time in 1988.

TYPE: Single-seat sporting homebuilt.

AIRFRAME: Wing section NACA 2415. Mostly wooden wing

structure, but with polystyrene ribs. Long span Frise flaperons of aluminium construction. Monocoque fuselage and tail unit of pre-moulded composite construction, using sandwich of pre-impregnated epoxy-glassfibre with PVC foam core. Non-retractable tailwheel or tricycle landing gear.

POWER PLANT: One 30 kW (40 hp) Rotax 447. Fuel capacity 30 litres (8 US gallons; 6.7 Imp gallons).

DIMENSIONS, EXTERNAL:
Wing span	6.55 m (21 ft 6 in)
Length overall	4.99 m (16 ft 4¾ in)
Height overall	1.22 m (4 ft 0 in)
Propeller diameter	1.27 m (4 ft 2 in)

AREA:
Wings, gross	5.30 m² (57.0 sq ft)

WEIGHTS:
Weight empty	113 kg (250 lb)

Pilot weight range	41-91 kg (90-200 lb)
Baggage capacity	13.5-27 kg (30-60 lb)
Max T-O weight	227 kg (500 lb)

PERFORMANCE:
Max level speed at 915 m (3,000 ft)	
	121 knots (225 km/h; 140 mph)
Econ cruising speed at 915 m (3,000 ft)	
	87 knots (161 km/h; 100 mph)
Stalling speed, flaps down, engine idling	
	37 knots (68 km/h; 42 mph)
Max rate of climb at S/L	366 m (1,200 ft)/min
Service ceiling	4,570 m (15,000 ft)
T-O and landing run	91 m (300 ft)
Range	347 nm (643 km; 400 miles)
g limits	+6/−4

Sport Flight Sky Pup single-seat microlight aircraft

Squadron Aviation Fokker D.VII (*Neil A. Macdougall*)

Star Flight XC 280 Stiletto microlight aircraft

Firebolt Convertible two-seat aerobatic homebuilt

Star-Lite Aircraft Star-Lite SL-1s with tricycle and tailwheel landing gears

Stewart S-51D ⁷⁄₁₀th-scale P-51D Mustang representation

STEWART

STEWART AIRCRAFT CORPORATION
615 Paulina Road, Jupiter, Florida 33477-5038
Telephone: (305) 744 1704
PRESIDENT: Jim D. Stewart

STEWART S-51D

The S-51D is a ⁷⁄₁₀th-scale representation of a North American P-51D Mustang fighter of the Second World War. The first example to be completed was an all-metal version, first flown in May 1985. It was followed by an all-wood example. Plans are available for the standard all-metal version, and 150 sets had been sold by February 1988. Eight plans-built S-51Ds have been completed, in addition to five aircraft built by Stewart Aircraft Corporation.

TYPE: Single- or tandem two-seat ⁷⁄₁₀th-scale homebuilt fighter representation.
AIRFRAME: All riveted aluminium alloy construction. Wing section 66-215(216). Retractable tailwheel landing gear.
POWER PLANT: One 224 kW (300 hp) GMC V-350 converted motorcar engine. Two wing fuel tanks, each with capacity of 95 litres (25 US gallons; 20.8 Imp gallons). Two optional external tanks, each 76 litres (20 US gallons; 16.7 Imp gallons) capacity.
DIMENSIONS, EXTERNAL:

Wing span	7.92 m (26 ft 0 in)
Length overall	6.71 m (22 ft 0 in)
Height overall	1.91 m (6 ft 3 in)
Propeller diameter	2.18 m (7 ft 2 in)
AREA:	
Wings, gross	10.87 m² (117.0 sq ft)

WEIGHTS:

Weight empty	912 kg (2,010 lb)
Max T-O weight	1,188 kg (2,620 lb)
PERFORMANCE:	
Max level speed at 2,440 m (8,000 ft)	
	230 knots (426 km/h; 265 mph)
Cruising speed	205 knots (380 km/h; 236 mph)
Stalling speed, flaps down and engine idling	
	57 knots (105 km/h; 65 mph)
Max rate of climb at S/L	610 m (2,000 ft)/min
T-O run	305 m (1,000 ft)
Landing run	457 m (1,500 ft)
Range	694 nm (1,287 km; 800 miles)
Endurance	3 h 8 min
g limits	+9/−4.5

STODDARD-HAMILTON

STODDARD-HAMILTON AIRCRAFT INC
18701 58th Avenue NE, Arlington, Washington 98223
Telephone: (206) 435 8533
Fax: (206) 435 9644
PRESIDENT: Theodore E. Setzer

STODDARD-HAMILTON GLASAIR TD and FT

The original **Glasair TD** (taildragger) prototype first flew in 1979. Stoddard-Hamilton offers kits of parts to build this model, as well as the **Glasair FT** (non-retractable tricycle gear), and **Glasair RG** (retractable gear, described separately). Approximately 900 kits had been sold by early 1988, and production continues at a rate of 10-12 kits per month, all intended to utilise a 112-134 kW (150-180 hp) Textron Lycoming engine. By early 1988, 875 kits had been delivered and some 200 Glasairs were then flying. On average 1,500 working hours are needed to complete a Glasair.

All versions of the basic Glasair are being superseded by the Glasair II and III, described separately.
TYPE: Side by side two-seat, dual control homebuilt.
AIRFRAME: Glassfibre and foam composite construction, coated with Gelcoat. Wing section NASA LS(1)-0413. Optional detachable wingtip extensions, or 'wet' wingtip extensions containing auxiliary fuel. Non-retractable tailwheel landing gear (TD) or non-retractable tricycle type (FT). Tricycle gear retrofittable to existing TDs.
POWER PLANT: Almost any Textron Lycoming O-320 or IO-320 engine of 112 or 119 kW (150 or 160 hp) can be fitted (with the exception of the O-320-H series) or a 134 kW (180 hp) IO-360. IO-360 is usual engine choice. Fuel capacity 159 litres (42 US gallons; 35 Imp gallons). Capacity increased to 208 litres (55 US gallons; 45.8 Imp gallons) when 'wet' extended wingtips installed.
DIMENSIONS, EXTERNAL:

Wing span: standard wingtips	7.09 m (23 ft 3 in)
with wingtip extensions	8.31 m (27 ft 3 in)
Length overall	5.66 m (18 ft 7 in)
Height overall	2.18 m (7 ft 2 in)
Propeller diameter	1.73-1.83 m (5 ft 8 in-6 ft 0 in)
AREAS:	
Wings, gross: standard	7.55 m² (81.3 sq ft)
with wingtip extensions	8.51 m² (91.6 sq ft)
WEIGHTS (TD with 119 kW; 160 hp engine):	
Weight empty	420 kg (925 lb)
Baggage capacity	36-45.5 kg (80-100 lb)
Max T-O weight	726 kg (1,600 lb)
PERFORMANCE (TD with 119 kW; 160 hp engine, standard wingtips):	
Max level speed at S/L	200 knots (370 km/h; 230 mph)
Max cruising speed (75% power at S/L)	
	180 knots (335 km/h; 208 mph)
Econ cruising speed (55% power at 2,440 m; 8,000 ft)	
	156 knots (290 km/h; 180 mph)
Stalling speed: pilot only, flaps up	
	55 knots (102 km/h; 63 mph)
max T-O weight, flaps down	
	54 knots (100 km/h; 62 mph)

Max rate of climb at S/L, at max T-O weight
426 m (1,400 ft)/min
Service ceiling over 6,100 m (20,000 ft)
T-O run 241 m (790 ft)
Landing run 168 m (550 ft)
Range with max standard fuel (55% power)
868 nm (1,609 km; 1,000 miles)
Range with wingtip tanks
1,215 nm (2,253 km; 1,400 miles)
g limits at 726 kg (1,600 lb) AUW +6/–4 limit
+9/–6 ultimate

STODDARD-HAMILTON GLASAIR RG

The prototype of this version of the Glasair with retractable landing gear was flown for the first time on 13 July 1982, and kits for the Glasair RG became available in the following year. Approximately 300 kits have been sold; this model is being superseded by the Glasair II & III (which see). Maximum speed of the Glasair RG is 222 knots (412 km/h; 256 mph) with a 134 kW (180 hp) Textron Lycoming IO-360 engine. Full details can be found in the 1987-88 *Jane's*.

STODDARD-HAMILTON GLASAIR II

The Glasair II is available in TD, FT and RG forms to supersede the basic Glasair series. Powered by the same 160 and 180 hp engines, the Glasair II has been redesigned to have short wingtips with upswept Hoerner style trailing-edges, a larger rudder with pre-moulded faired socket for a tail light, and a slightly larger cabin. It is supplied in kit form with more pre-formed/moulded components to cut estimated building time by more than 500 working hours, and the airframe parts are lighter, stronger, more accurate, and easier to assemble, being based on new tooling techniques. Deliveries of TD and FT kits began in September 1986. Fuel capacities for all versions (usable) are 129 litres (34 US gallons; 28.3 Imp gallons) in the wings, 23 litres (6 US gallons; 5 Imp gallons) in a header tank, and 42 litres (11 US gallons; 9.2 Imp gallons) in optional wingtip extensions.

DIMENSIONS, EXTERNAL:
Wing span, standard 7.09 m (23 ft 3 in)
Length overall 5.74 m (18 ft 10 in)
Height overall 2.13 m (7 ft 0 in)
AREA:
Wings, gross 7.55 m² (81.3 sq ft)
WEIGHTS (A: RG, B: FT, C: TD):
Weight empty: A 499 kg (1,100 lb)
B 454 kg (1,000 lb)
C 431 kg (950 lb)
Baggage capacity 36 kg (80 lb)
Max T-O weight: A 816 kg (1,800 lb)
B 771 kg (1,700 lb)
C 726 kg (1,600 lb)
PERFORMANCE (A: RG with 180 hp engine, B: FT with 160 hp, C: TD with 180 hp):
Max level speed at S/L:
A 222 knots (412 km/h; 256 mph)
B 196 knots (364 km/h; 226 mph)
C 209 knots (388 km/h; 241 mph)
Cruising speed (55% power) at 2,440 m (8,000 ft):
A 173 knots (320 km/h; 199 mph)
B 154 knots (285 km/h; 177 mph)
C 164 knots (304 km/h; 189 mph)
Stalling speed:
A, pilot only, flaps and wheels up
56 knots (103 km/h; 64 mph)
A, pilot only, flaps and wheels down
52 knots (95 km/h; 59 mph)
A, flaps and wheels down, max T-O weight
55 knots (102 km/h; 63 mph)
B, C, pilot only, flaps up
55 knots (102 km/h; 63 mph)
B, C, pilot only, flaps down
51 knots (94 km/h; 58 mph)
B, C, flaps down, max T-O weight
54 knots (100 km/h; 62 mph)
Service ceiling: all versions approx 5,790 m (19,000 ft)
Max rate of climb at S/L:
A 518 m (1,700 ft)/min
B 427 m (1,400 ft)/min
C, pilot only 838 m (2,750 ft)/min
Range at 55% power (approx):
A, B 911 nm (1,690 km; 1,050 miles)
A, B, with tip tanks 1,172 nm (2,172 km; 1,350 miles)
C 868 nm (1,609 km; 1,000 miles)
C, with tip tanks 1,129 nm (2,092 km; 1,300 miles)
g limits at AUW of 726 kg (1,600 lb):
all versions +6/–4 limit
+9/–6 ultimate

STODDARD-HAMILTON GLASAIR III

The Glasair III is a completely new addition to the company's range, retaining a similar configuration to the earlier models but designed to offer exceptional performance, constructional simplicity and economical kit price. The landing gear is retractable. Construction takes approximately 1,800 working hours.

The Glasair III has a longer and wider fuselage for increased baggage space, payload capacity and comfort, also improving the longitudinal and directional stability and thereby making it a better cross-country and IFR aircraft. It features a thicker windscreen to improve protection against bird strikes at its higher speeds, and has additional glassfibre laminates, integral longerons, and a lay-up schedule which provides a structurally stronger and torsionally stiffer fuselage. The Glasair III wing uses the LS(I)-0413 section, is strengthened, and carries more fuel than previous models. NACA style air vents provide cabin ventilation.

A prototype was displayed at Oshkosh '86. By early 1988 more than 110 Glasair IIIs had been sold.

POWER PLANT: One 224 kW (300 hp) Textron Lycoming IO-540-K1H5. Fuel capacity in wings 208 litres (55 US gallons; 45.8 Imp gallons). Fuselage header tank, capacity 38 litres (10 US gallons; 8.3 Imp gallons). Optional tanks in wingtip extensions, total capacity 49 litres (13 US gallons; 10.8 Imp gallons). Optional engine installation may be a 194 kW (260 hp) IO-540 eventually.

DIMENSIONS, EXTERNAL:
Wing span, standard 7.09 m (23 ft 3 in)
Length overall 6.50 m (21 ft 4 in)
Height overall 2.18 m (7 ft 2 in)
AREA:
Wings, gross 7.55 m² (81.3 sq ft)
WEIGHTS:
Weight empty 703 kg (1,550 lb)
Baggage capacity 45 kg (100 lb)
Max T-O weight 1,089 kg (2,400 lb)
PERFORMANCE (standard wings, except where indicated):
Max level speed at S/L 252 knots (467 km/h; 290 mph)
Cruising speed: 75% power at 2,440 m (8,000 ft)
245 knots (454 km/h; 282 mph)
50% power at 5,335 m (17,500 ft)
219 knots (406 km/h; 252 mph)
Stalling speed: pilot only, flaps and wheels up
65 knots (119 km/h; 74 mph)
flaps and wheels down, max T-O weight
68 knots (126 km/h; 78 mph)
Service ceiling approx 7,315 m (24,000 ft)
Max rate of climb at S/L 732 m (2,400 ft)/min
Range at 55% power:
standard fuel 1,129 nm (2,092 km; 1,300 miles)
with tip tanks 1,302 nm (2,414 km; 1,500 miles)
g limits at AUW of 862 kg (1,900 lb) +6/–4 limit
+9/–6 ultimate

AROCET AT-9

In association with Arocet Inc, Stoddard-Hamilton is developing a low-cost military trainer version of the Glasair III, powered by an Allison turboprop engine. Details can be found in the main Aircraft section of this edition.

STOLP

STOLP STARDUSTER CORPORATION

4301 Twining Flabob Airport, Riverside, California 92509
Telephone: (714) 686 7943
PRESIDENT AND GENERAL MANAGER: William C. Clouse Jr

Stolp Starduster Corporation continues to market plans, kits and materials for the two-seat Starduster Too (well over 2,000 sets of plans sold), single-seat Starlet, aerobatic V-Star, and Acroduster Too. The latest biplane is known as the Super Starduster.

Stolp has also taken over design and marketing rights for the Steen Skybolt, of which a new Mk II version has been developed.

STOLP SA-300 STARDUSTER TOO

TYPE: Tandem two-seat homebuilt sporting biplane.
AIRFRAME: Wing section M-6 modified. All-wood wing and aileron structures, fabric covered. Welded steel tube fuselage and tail unit, with fabric covering. Glassfibre turtleback. Non-retractable tailwheel landing gear.
POWER PLANT: Prototype has a 134 kW (180 hp) Textron Lycoming O-360-A1A. Horizontally opposed or radial engines of 93-194 kW (125-260 hp) may be fitted.
DIMENSIONS, EXTERNAL:
Wing span: upper 7.32 m (24 ft 0 in)
Length overall 6.63 m (21 ft 9 in)
Height overall 2.21 m (7 ft 3 in)
WEIGHTS (typical; with 149 kW; 200 hp engine):
Weight empty 517 kg (1,139 lb)
Max T-O weight 907 kg (2,000 lb)
PERFORMANCE (typical; with 149 kW; 200 hp engine):
Max level speed 174 knots (322 km/h; 200 mph)
Econ cruising speed 100 knots (185 km/h; 115 mph)
Stalling speed 51 knots (94 km/h; 58 mph)
Sustained rate of climb, with pilot only
548 m (1,800 ft)/min

STOLP SA-500 STARLET

The prototype Starlet flew for the first time on 1 June 1969.

TYPE: Single-seat parasol wing homebuilt.
AIRFRAME: Dacron covered all-wood wings. Clark YH wing section. Welded steel tube fuselage and tail unit structures, Dacron covered. Non-retractable tailwheel landing gear.
POWER PLANT: Prototype has 1,500 cc Volkswagen converted motorcar engine. Other engines of 63.5-93 kW (85-125 hp) may be fitted, the 80.5 kW (108 hp) Textron Lycoming being recommended.
DIMENSIONS, EXTERNAL:
Wing span 7.62 m (25 ft 0 in)
Length overall 5.18 m (17 ft 0 in)
Height overall 2.03 m (6 ft 8 in)
AREA:
Wings, gross 7.71 m² (83.0 sq ft)
WEIGHT (prototype):
Max T-O weight 340 kg (750 lb)
PERFORMANCE (prototype, at max T-O weight):
Cruising speed 78 knots (145 km/h; 90 mph)
Landing speed 48-52 knots (89-97 km/h; 55-60 mph)

STOLP SA-750 ACRODUSTER TOO

The SA-750 is a two-seat aerobatic biplane generally similar to the Starduster Too. It has symmetrical wings. A 149 kW (200 hp) Textron Lycoming IO-360 engine is fitted to the prototype. The front cockpit is open and has a small windscreen, while the bubble canopy for the rear cockpit is faired to the turtledeck.

DIMENSIONS, EXTERNAL:
Wing span: upper 6.53 m (21 ft 5 in)
Length overall 5.64 m (18 ft 6 in)
Height overall 2.08 m (6 ft 10 in)
AREA:
Wings, gross 12.1 m² (130.0 sq ft)
PERFORMANCE (at max T-O weight):
Cruising speed 139 knots (257 km/h; 160 mph)
Stalling speed 61 knots (113 km/h; 70 mph)
Max rate of climb at S/L 701 m (2,300 ft)/min
g limits ±9

STOLP SA-900 V-STAR

To meet the demand for low cost, low horsepower aircraft with aerobatic capability, Stolp introduced the SA-900 V-Star, which is essentially a biplane version of the SA-500 Starlet. The prototype has a 48.5 kW (65 hp) Continental engine, but engines of 44.5-93 kW (60-125 hp) may be installed.

DIMENSIONS, EXTERNAL:
Wing span: upper 7.01 m (23 ft 0 in)
Length overall 5.23 m (17 ft 2 in)
Height overall 2.26 m (7 ft 5 in)
AREA:
Wings, gross 13.1 m² (141.0 sq ft)
PERFORMANCE (prototype, at max T-O weight):
Cruising speed 65 knots (121 km/h; 75 mph)
Stalling speed 31 knots (57 km/h; 35 mph)
Max rate of climb at S/L 183 m (600 ft)/min
g limits ±9

STOLP SUPER STARDUSTER

The Super Starduster is the first of a new series of special aerobatic aircraft for unlimited class aerobatic competition. The prototype, first flown on 1 April 1983, features a unique linkage between the ailerons and flaps, allowing the former to serve as flaps (down) with stick back, or flaps (up) with stick forward for outside loops.

TYPE: Single-seat homebuilt aerobatic biplane.
AIRFRAME: Osborne A-1 symmetrical wing section (modified). Dacron covered wooden wings and ailerons, the latter (on upper and lower wings) serving also as flaps during normal and inverted flight. Welded steel tube fuselage and tail unit, the former covered with fabric, aluminium alloy and glassfibre, and the latter with fabric. Non-retractable tailwheel landing gear.
POWER PLANT: One 149 kW (200 hp) Textron Lycoming IO-360-A1A. Fuel capacity 113.5 litres (30 US gallons; 25 Imp gallons).
DIMENSIONS, EXTERNAL:
Wing span 5.94 m (19 ft 6 in)
Length overall 4.88 m (16 ft 0 in)
Height overall 2.13 m (7 ft 0 in)
Propeller diameter 1.88 m (6 ft 2 in)
AREA:
Wings, gross 9.75 m² (105.0 sq ft)
WEIGHTS:
Basic operating weight empty 426 kg (940 lb)
Max T-O weight 680 kg (1,500 lb)
PERFORMANCE:
Max level speed at 2,440 m (8,000 ft)
156 knots (289 km/h; 180 mph) IAS
Econ cruising speed at 2,440 m (8,000 ft)
122 knots (225 km/h; 140 mph) IAS
Stalling speed, power off
48 knots (89 km/h; 55 mph) IAS
Max rate of climb at S/L 914 m (3,000 ft)/min
Service ceiling 3,810 m (12,500 ft)
T-O run 61 m (200 ft)
Landing run 335 m (1,100 ft)
Range with max fuel 440 nm (816 km; 507 miles)

STOLP (STEEN) SKYBOLT

Mr Lamar Steen designed a two-seat fully aerobatic biplane named Skybolt, which was built as a class project in

Stolp Starduster Too two-seat sporting biplane *(John Wegg)*

Top to bottom: **Stoddard-Hamilton Glasair TD, FT, RG and Glasair III**
(Jim Larsen)

Stolp SA-900 V-Star **(Textron Lycoming O-290-D2 engine)** *(Howard Levy)*

Stolp (Steen) Super Skybolt two-seat aerobatic biplane *(J. M. G. Gradidge)*

Stolp Super Starduster special aerobatic biplane built for Mr Dick Green
(Don Dwiggins)

Stolp SA-500 Starlet built in England by Mr S. S. Miles *(PFA)*

---

a school. Simplicity of construction was a primary aim. The prototype first flew in October 1970. Plans are available, together with fuselage and wing kits; more than 3,500 sets of plans had been sold before the design was taken over by Stolp.

The following description applies to the original prototype with a 134 kW (180 hp) Textron Lycoming engine:

TYPE: Two-seat homebuilt aerobatic biplane.

AIRFRAME: Fabric covered wooden wings and ailerons (on upper and lower wings). Wing sections: upper wing NACA 63₂A015, lower wings NACA 0012. Welded steel tube fuselage and tail unit, with fabric covering. Non-retractable tailwheel landing gear.

POWER PLANT: One 134 kW (180 hp) Textron Lycoming HO-360-B1B. Provision for alternative engines of 93-194 kW (125-260 hp). Fuel capacity 110 litres (29 US gallons; 24 Imp gallons). Optional tank of 38 litres (10 US gallons; 8.3 Imp gallons) capacity can be installed in centre-section of upper wing.

DIMENSIONS, EXTERNAL:

Wing span: upper	7.32 m (24 ft 0 in)
lower	7.01 m (23 ft 0 in)
Length overall	5.79 m (19 ft 0 in)
Height overall	2.13 m (7 ft 0 in)
Propeller diameter	1.88 m (6 ft 2 in)

AREA:

Wings, gross	14.2 m² (152.7 sq ft)

WEIGHTS:

Weight empty	490 kg (1,080 lb)
Baggage capacity	13.6 kg (30 lb)
Max T-O weight	748 kg (1,650 lb)

PERFORMANCE (at max T-O weight):

Max level speed	126 knots (233 km/h; 145 mph)
Cruising speed	113 knots (209 km/h; 130 mph)
Max rate of climb at S/L	762 m (2,500 ft)/min
Service ceiling	5,500 m (18,000 ft)
T-O run	122 m (400 ft)
Range with max fuel	390 nm (720 km; 450 miles)
g limits	+12/-10

STOLP SUPER SKYBOLT

Mr William Clouse Jr and Mr Eric Shilling have developed a refined version of the Skybolt biplane (see accompanying illustration). Brief details can be found in the 1987-88 *Jane's*.

STRIPLIN

STRIPLIN AIRCRAFT CORPORATION

PO Box 2001, Lancaster, California 93539-2001
Telephone: (805) 256 2270
PRESIDENT: Kenneth Striplin

STRIPLIN LONE RANGER and SKY RANGER SERIES

The only microlight in this series is the single-seat **Lone Ranger Ultralight**; the remaining versions of the Lone Ranger and the **Sky Ranger** are Experimental homebuilt aircraft offered in **Silver Cloud STOL** form, with a tricycle landing gear; non-STOL **Silver Cloud X** form, with a tricycle landing gear and conventional inset ailerons, for higher-speed cross-country flying; and **Silver Cloud Husky STOL** form, with a tailwheel landing gear.

TYPES: Single-seat microlight and homebuilt (Lone Ranger) or two-seat homebuilt (Sky Ranger).

AIRFRAME: Wings constructed of wood, glassfibre and foam, with glassfibre skin on leading-edge and Dacron covering overall. NASA wing section. Full span flaperons on trailing-edges, of glassfibre/foam construction on all versions except the Silver Cloud X, which has in-wing ailerons. Pod and boom fuselage, the forward portion having base frame of unidirectional glassfibre, impregnated with epoxy resin, with moulded outer shell of glassfibre. At top of pod is U shaped channel, in which is buried a lightweight metal tube to which the wings are bolted and which also supports rear fuselage and tail unit. Tailboom is triangular section glassfibre and foam sandwich structure; tail surfaces of similar construction to wings. Removable fuselage side panels optional. Recovery parachute standard on all models. Non-retractable tricycle landing gear on all models except Husky which has tailwheel type. Tailwheel, float and ski landing gears optional on all models.

POWER PLANT: *Lone Ranger Ultralight:* One 20 kW (27 hp) Rotax 277. Fuel capacity 19 litres (5 US gallons; 4.2 Imp gallons). *Lone Ranger Silver Cloud X* and *Husky STOL* have One 33.6 kW (45 hp) Rotax 503, 48.5 kW (65 hp) Rotax 532 or 48.5 kW (65 hp) Volkswagen 1,834 cc modified motorcar engine. *Lone Ranger Silver Cloud X* and *Husky STOL* have similar options to Silver Cloud STOL but with addition of 56 kW (75 hp) Volkswagen engine. *Sky Ranger* series all have same engine options as for Lone Ranger Silver Cloud STOL, plus 41 kW (55 hp) Volkswagen 1,600 cc engine. Fuel capacity for Lone Rangers (other than Ultralight) and Sky Rangers 38 litres (10 US gallons; 8.3 Imp gallons).

DIMENSIONS, EXTERNAL (A: Lone Ranger Ultralight, B: Lone Ranger STOL with Rotax 503, C: Lone Ranger Husky STOL with 75 hp VW, D: Sky Ranger Silver Cloud X with Rotax 532):

Wing span: A, B, C	10.36 m (34 ft 0 in)
D	10.67 m (35 ft 0 in)
Length overall: A, B, C	4.78 m (15 ft 8 in)
D	4.88 m (16 ft 0 in)
Height overall: D	2.13 m (7 ft 0 in)

AREAS (A, B, C, D as above):

Wings, gross: A, B, C	12.45 m² (134.0 sq ft)
D	10.22 m² (110.0 sq ft)

WEIGHTS (A, B, C, D as above):

Weight empty: A with parachute	125 kg (275 lb)
B	163 kg (360 lb)
C	200 kg (440 lb)
D	222 kg (490 lb)
Max T-O weight: A	272 kg (600 lb)
B	363 kg (800 lb)
C, D	454 kg (1,000 lb)

PERFORMANCE (A, B, C, D as above):

Max level speed: A	54 knots (100 km/h; 62 mph)
B	73 knots (135 km/h; 84 mph)
C	89 knots (164 km/h; 102 mph)
D	95 knots (177 km/h; 110 mph)
Cruising speed: A	48 knots (89 km/h; 55 mph)
B	65 knots (121 km/h; 75 mph)
C	78 knots (145 km/h; 90 mph)
D	87 knots (161 km/h; 100 mph)
Stalling speed:	
A, flaps down	22 knots (41 km/h; 25 mph)
A, flaps up	26 knots (49 km/h; 30 mph)
B, flaps down	25 knots (45 km/h; 28 mph)
B, flaps up	30 knots (55 km/h; 34 mph)
C, flaps down	25 knots (47 km/h; 29 mph)
C, flaps up	32 knots (58 km/h; 36 mph)
D, flaps down	37 knots (68 km/h; 42 mph)
D, flaps up	42 knots (78 km/h; 48 mph)
Max rate of climb at S/L: A	183 m (600 ft)/min
B	305 m (1,000 ft)/min
C	427 m (1,400 ft)/min
D	244 m (800 ft)/min
Service ceiling: A	2,895 m (9,500 ft)
B	3,505 m (11,500 ft)
C	4,265 m (14,000 ft)
D	3,810 m (12,500 ft)
T-O run: A	54 m (175 ft)
B	46 m (150 ft)
C	34 m (110 ft)
D	191 m (625 ft)
Range, no reserves:	
A, B, C	217 nm (402 km; 250 miles)
D	234 nm (434 km; 270 miles)

SUN AEROSPACE
SUN AEROSPACE GROUP INC
PO Box 317, Nappanee, Indiana 46550
Telephone: (219) 773 3220
PRESIDENT: Russell A. McDonald

SUN AEROSPACE SUN RAY 100
The prototype of the **Sun Ray 100** made its first flight on 4 September 1983. Kits available for purchase are estimated to take 500 working hours to assemble. Thought to be under development are an amphibious version and a two-seat model known as the **Sun Ray 200**.
TYPE: Single-seat homebuilt.
AIRFRAME: Wings are spruce reinforced, with a pre-moulded glassfibre leading-edge, aluminium alloy trailing-edge, and glassfibre wrapped ribs, covered overall with Ceconite or Stits Poly-Fiber. Wing section Roncz 1104. Aluminium alloy ailerons. Twin fins and rudders of aluminium alloy tubing. Foreplane with pre-moulded skins has Roncz 1104 section. Full span elevators of similar construction on foreplane. Fuselage structure of welded aluminium alloy tubing, over which are fitted three pre-moulded glassfibre shells. Non-retractable tricycle landing gear.
POWER PLANT: One 38.8 kW (52 hp) Rotax 503. Fuel capacity 45 litres (12 US gallons; 10 Imp gallons).

DIMENSIONS, EXTERNAL:

Wing span	9.75 m (32 ft 0 in)
Length overall	3.96 m (13 ft 0 in)
Height overall	1.83 m (6 ft 0 in)
Propeller diameter	1.52 m (5 ft 0 in)

AREA:

Wings, gross (incl foreplane)	14.59 m² (157.0 sq ft)

WEIGHTS:

Weight empty	249 kg (550 lb)
Pilot weight range	46-92 kg (100-200 lb)
Baggage capacity	9 kg (20 lb)
Max T-O weight	386 kg (850 lb)

PERFORMANCE (estimated):

Max level speed	87 knots (161 km/h; 100 mph)
Econ cruising speed	74 knots (136 km/h; 85 mph)
Stalling speed	39 knots (71 km/h; 44 mph)
Max rate of climb at S/L	244 m (800 ft)/min
Service ceiling	4,115 m (13,500 ft)
T-O run	92 m (300 ft)
Landing run	46 m (150 ft)
Range	369 nm (684 km; 425 miles)
g limit	+4

SUNRISE
SUNRISE ULTRALIGHT MANUFACTURING COMPANY
Rt 4, Box 336, New Caney, Texas 77357
Telephone: (713) 354 1348
PRESIDENT: Kim A. Zorzi

SUNRISE ULTRALIGHT SPITFIRE I and SONIC SPITFIRE
The **Spitfire I** is the standard microlight version, available as a bolt-together kit requiring 40 working hours to assemble. The **Sonic Spitfire**, available in similar form, uses a dual carburettor Rotax 503 engine and has a 38 litre (10 US gallon; 8.3 Imp gallon) fuel capacity. Maximum speed of the Sonic Spitfire is 78 knots (145 km/h; 90 mph). An optional engine is the Rotax 532.

The following details refer to the Spitfire I:
TYPE: Single-seat microlight; conforms to FAR Pt 103.
AIRFRAME: Mainframe of aluminium alloy; wings and tail unit double surfaced with Dacron. Three-axis control, with flaps. Non-retractable tricycle landing gear. Optional floats, skis, cockpit fairing and ballistic parachute.
POWER PLANT: One 30 kW (40 hp) Rotax 447. Options are Rotax 377 and Rotax 503. Some aircraft are fitted with Kawasaki 440 engine. Fuel capacity 19 litres (5 US gallons; 4.2 Imp gallons).

DIMENSIONS, EXTERNAL:

Wing span	9.14 m (30 ft 0 in)
Length overall	5.44 m (17 ft 10 in)
Height overall	2.34 m (7 ft 8 in)
Propeller diameter	1.73 m (5 ft 8 in)

AREA:

Wings, gross	14.31 m² (154.0 sq ft)

WEIGHTS:

Weight empty	115 kg (253 lb)
Pilot weight range	45-136 kg (100-300 lb)
Max T-O weight	251 kg (553 lb)

PERFORMANCE:

Max level speed	55 knots (101 km/h; 63 mph)
Econ cruising speed	43 knots (80 km/h; 50 mph)
Stalling speed: power on, flaps down	17 knots (31 km/h; 19 mph)
power off	19 knots (36 km/h; 22 mph)
Max rate of climb at S/L	259 m (850 ft)/min
Service ceiling	3,810 m (12,500 ft)
T-O run	30 m (100 ft)
Landing run, flaps down	54 m (175 ft)
Range with max fuel	112 nm (209 km; 130 miles)
Endurance	2 h 30 min
g limits	+9/-6

SUNRISE ULTRALIGHT SPITFIRE II
This is basically a two-seat homebuilt version of the Spitfire I. Construction from the kit takes 50-60 working hours. Details, where they differ are as follows:
TYPE: Side by side two-seat homebuilt; conforms to FAI/CAA Experimental aircraft category.
AIRFRAME: Wider optional cockpit fairing. Agricultural cropspraying equipment and ballistic parachute optional.
POWER PLANT: One 35.8 kW (48 hp) Rotax 503. Alternative 37.3 kW (50 hp) liquid-cooled Rotax engine.

DIMENSION, EXTERNAL:

Height overall	2.41 m (7 ft 11 in)

WEIGHTS:

Weight empty	159 kg (350 lb)
Max T-O weight	358 kg (790 lb)

PERFORMANCE:

Max level speed	74 knots (137 km/h; 85 mph)
Econ cruising speed	52 knots (97 km/h; 60 mph)
Stalling speed, power on, flaps down	39 knots (73 km/h; 45 mph)
Max rate of climb at S/L	152 m (500 ft)/min
Service ceiling	3,660 m (12,000 ft)
T-O run	23-38 m (75-125 ft)
Range with max fuel	95 nm (177 km; 110 miles)
Endurance	2 h
g limits	+6/-4

SUNRISE ULTRALIGHT CLIPPER SERIES
The Clipper I is a microlight of conventional aeroplane configuration. It is available as a bolt-together kit, requiring about 40 working hours to assemble. A two-seat version was expected to become available in late 1988. A third version has Sonic Spitfire wings and a Rotax 503 or 532 engine, allowing a maximum speed in excess of 87 knots (161 km/h; 100 mph). This model will be registered as a microlight in Europe and as an Experimental aircraft in the USA.

The following details refer to the single-seat Clipper I:
TYPE: Single-seat microlight; conforms to FAR Pt 103.
AIRFRAME: Mainframe of welded steel tubing and aluminium alloy, Dacron covered. Three-axis control with flaps. Non-retractable tailwheel landing gear. Floats, skis and ballistic parachute optional.
POWER PLANT: One 30 kW (40 hp) Rotax 447. Some Clippers built with 71 kW (95 hp) Suzuki engine. Fuel capacity 19 litres (5 US gallons; 4.2 Imp gallons). Auxiliary tank optional, capacity 38 litres (10 US gallons; 8.3 Imp gallons).

DIMENSIONS, EXTERNAL:

Wing span	9.14 m (30 ft 0 in)
Length overall	5.28 m (17 ft 4 in)
Height overall	2.29 m (7 ft 6 in)
Propeller diameter	1.73 m (5 ft 8 in)

AREA:

Wings, gross	14.12 m² (152.0 sq ft)

WEIGHTS:

Weight empty	114 kg (252 lb)
Pilot weight range	50-158 kg (110-350 lb)
Max T-O weight	263 kg (580 lb)

PERFORMANCE:

Max level speed	55 knots (101 km/h; 63 mph)
Econ cruising speed	48 knots (89 km/h; 55 mph)
Stalling speed, flaps down	18 knots (32 km/h; 20 mph)
Max rate of climb at S/L	152 m (500 ft)/min
Service ceiling	4,265 m (14,000 ft)
T-O run	30 m (100 ft)
Landing run, with brakes	46 m (150 ft)
Range with max standard fuel	87 nm (161 km; 100 miles)
Endurance	2 h 20 min
g limits	+6/-4

SWEARINGEN — *See main US Aircraft section*

TAYLOR
TAYLOR AERO INC
5855 State Route 40, Tipp City, Ohio 45371
Telephone: (513) 845 1226
PRESIDENT: Col Robert H. Taylor

TAYLOR TA-2/3 BIRD
Plans and additional data are available to homebuilders, who can complete the Taylor Bird in **TA-2** form, with non-retractable tailwheel landing gear, or **TA-3** form, with non-retractable tricycle gear. Optional floats and skis. By January 1988, about 90 sets of plans had been sold. Construction of 12 aircraft is known to have been undertaken, with two completed. Partial assembly kits are also available to amateur builders (fin, rudder, tailplane and elevators); difficult to fabricate components, such as the main load-bearing member and pre-formed glassfibre fairings, can be purchased. Engine and propeller reduction drawings are available as a set of separate plans, plus a propeller reduction kit and plans for constructing a clamp-on towbar.
TYPE: Tandem two-seat homebuilt.
AIRFRAME: Wings have aluminium alloy structure, with pop riveted Alclad T3 skin and plastics composite root section. Wing section NACA 23015. Full span slotted metal ailerons. Main load-bearing member of fuselage comprises a 150 mm (6 in) diameter aluminium alloy tube, to which are bolted two pylons for the cabin/landing gear/engine/wing group and the tail unit assembly.

Striplin Lone Ranger (flying), with Husky and Sky Ranger Silver Cloud X (left and right on ground)

Sun Aerospace Group Sun Ray 100 *(Howard Levy)*

Sunrise Ultralight Clipper I single-seat microlight

Taylor TA-2 Bird with nose fairing door slid forward

Sunrise Ultralight Spitfire I

All fairings, including cabin enclosures, of glassfibre. Cantilever T tail has aluminium alloy spars and ribs, covered with Alclad T-3 skins.
POWER PLANT: One 53.7 or 84.3 kW (72 or 113 hp) watercooled Subaru 1,600 cc or 1,800 cc converted motorcar engine. Optional Volkswagen modified motorcar engine. Fuel capacity 57 litres (15 US gallons; 12.5 Imp gallons).
DIMENSIONS, EXTERNAL:

Wing span	7.92 m (26 ft 0 in)
Length overall	5.59 m (18 ft 4 in)
Height overall	1.68 m (5 ft 6 in)
Propeller diameter	1.52 m (5 ft 0 in)

AREA:

Wings, gross	10.07 m² (108.42 sq ft)

WEIGHTS:

Weight empty	277 kg (610 lb)
Max T-O weight	526 kg (1,160 lb)

PERFORMANCE:

Max level speed	113 knots (209 km/h; 130 mph)
Econ cruising speed	82 knots (153 km/h; 95 mph)
Stalling speed	39 knots (73 km/h; 45 mph)
Service ceiling	4,265 m (14,000 ft)
T-O run	137 m (450 ft)
Landing run	122 m (400 ft)
Range, with max fuel, no reserves	295 nm (547 km; 340 miles)

T.E.A.M.
TENNESSEE ENGINEERING AND MANUFACTURING INC
State Route 53 and Ivy Bluff Road, Route 1, Box 338C, Bradyville, Tennessee 37026
Telephone: (615) 765 5397
DESIGNER: Wayne Ison

T.E.A.M. MINIMAX
The first prototype miniMAX flew for the first time in February 1985. The miniMAX is available as a kit; alternatively, the airframe and plans can be purchased separately. By early 1988 a total of 250 kits and 275 sets of plans had been sold.
TYPE: Single-seat microlight and homebuilt; conforms to FAR Pt 103 (microlight) and Experimental regulations.

AIRFRAME: Airframe of wooden Warren truss construction, fabric covered. Wing section NACA 4415. Three-axis control. Non-retractable tailwheel landing gear.
POWER PLANT: One 20 kW (27 hp) Rotax 277. Fuel capacity 19 litres (5 US gallons; 4.2 Imp gallons). Optional Rotax 377 and 447 engines.
DIMENSIONS, EXTERNAL:

Wing span	7.62 m (25 ft 0 in)
Length overall	4.72 m (15 ft 6 in)
Height overall	1.60 m (5 ft 3 in)
Propeller diameter	1.52 m (5 ft 0 in)

AREA:

Wings, gross	10.45 m² (112.5 sq ft)

WEIGHTS:

Weight empty	109 kg (240 lb)
Max pilot weight	104 kg (230 lb)
Baggage capacity	2.3 kg (5 lb)
Max T-O weight	218 kg (480 lb)

PERFORMANCE:

Max level speed at S/L	52 knots (97 km/h; 60 mph)
Econ cruising speed at S/L	43 knots (80 km/h; 50 mph)
Stalling speed, engine idling:	
flaps up	23 knots (42 km/h; 26 mph)
20° flap	19 knots (36 km/h; 22 mph)
Max rate of climb at S/L	244 m (800 ft)/min
Service ceiling	3,050 m (10,000 ft)
T-O run	46 m (150 ft)
Landing run	55 m (180 ft)
Range	95.5 nm (177 km; 110 miles)
Endurance	2 h 30 min
g limits	+4.4/-2.2

T.E.A.M. HI-MAX

The Hi-MAX is basically an enclosed cabin version of the miniMAX, with a strut braced high-mounted wing and choice of tailwheel or tricycle landing gear.

The general structural description and specification of the miniMAX apply also to the Hi-MAX, except as follows:

WEIGHTS:
Weight empty	113 kg (250 lb)
Recommended useful load	118 kg (260 lb)

PERFORMANCE:
Max level speed at S/L	52 knots (97 km/h; 60 mph)
Max cruising speed at S/L	48 knots (89 km/h; 55 mph)
Stalling speed, engine idling	
	23 knots (42 km/h; 26 mph)

Max rate of climb at S/L	198 m (650 ft)/min
T-O run (from grass)	46 m (150 ft)
Landing run (on grass)	55 m (180 ft)

T.E.A.M. EZE-MAX

The EZE-Max is a 'profile' development of the miniMax, in which the pilot sits astride the narrow fuselage. Other changes can be gleaned from the accompanying illustration. The prototype first flew in 1987 and kits are available. Construction is of wood and fabric.

POWER PLANT: Prototype has one 20 kW (27 hp) Rotax 277. Other engines of 16.4-28.3 kW (22-38 hp) can be fitted.

DIMENSIONS, EXTERNAL:
Wing span	7.32 m (24 ft 0 in)

Length overall	4.72 m (15 ft 6 in)
Height overall	1.37 m (4 ft 6 in)

WEIGHTS:
Weight empty	91 kg (200 lb)
Max T-O weight	200 kg (440 lb)

PERFORMANCE (20 kW; 27 hp Rotax 277 engine):
Cruising speed	55 knots (101 km/h; 63 mph)
Max rate of climb at S/L	229 m (750 ft)/min
T-O run	23 m (75 ft)

TERATORN

TERATORN AIRCRAFT INC

1604 South Shore Drive, Clear Lake, Iowa, 50428
Telephone: (515) 357 7161
Fax: (515) 357 7592
PRESIDENT: Dale Kjellsen

TERATORN TIERRA I

The Tierra can be converted to a two-seater (operated in the US Experimental category), with the centrally positioned single-pilot seat moved sideways to accommodate the second occupant.

Three models are currently offered, using Rotax 277, 377 and 447 engines. In other respects they are almost identical.

TYPE: Single-seat microlight; conforms to FAR Pt 103.

AIRFRAME: Aluminium alloy and Mylar coated Dacron construction, with double surface covering. Three-axis control. Non-retractable tailwheel landing gear. Optional floats, skis, amphibious gear combining floats with retractable wheels, and semi-enclosed or fully enclosed cockpit.

POWER PLANT: Three engine choices: 20 kW (27 hp) Rotax 277 with 19 litre (5 US gallon; 4.2 Imp gallon) fuel capacity; 26 kW (35 hp) Rotax 377 with 23 litres (6 US gallons; 5 Imp gallons) fuel; or 29.4 kW (39.4 hp) Rotax 447 with 23 litres (6 US gallons; 5 Imp gallons) of fuel.

DIMENSIONS, EXTERNAL:
Wing span	9.45 m (31 ft 0 in)
Length overall	5.49 m (18 ft 0 in)
Height overall	1.68 m (5 ft 6 in)

AREA:
Wings, gross	14.31 m² (154.0 sq ft)

WEIGHTS (Rotax 377 engine):
Weight empty	125 kg (275 lb)
Pilot weight range	55-113 kg (120-250 lb)
Max T-O weight	238 kg (525 lb)

PERFORMANCE (engine as above):
Max level speed at 762 m (2,500 ft)
	61 knots (113 km/h; 70 mph)

Econ cruising speed at 762 m (2,500 ft)
	52 knots (97 km/h; 60 mph)
Stalling speed	25 knots (45 km/h; 28 mph)
Max rate of climb at S/L	244 m (800 ft)/min
Service ceiling	3,050 m (10,000 ft)
T-O run	23 m (75 ft)
Landing run	46 m (150 ft)
Range with max fuel	104 nm (193 km; 120 miles)

TERATORN TIERRA II

This is a two-seat Tierra, with a Rotax 532 engine, wing flaps, enclosed cabin with rigid Lexan doors, and breakaway steerable tailwheel. Options include floats, skis and agricultural spraying equipment.

TYPE: Side by side two-seat, dual-control homebuilt; conforms to Experimental regulations.

POWER PLANT: One 48.5 kW (65 hp) Rotax 532. Fuel capacity 45.4 litres (12 US gallons; 10 Imp gallons).

DIMENSIONS, EXTERNAL:
Wing span	11.20 m (36 ft 9 in)
Length overall	5.69 m (18 ft 8 in)
Height overall	1.85 m (6 ft 1 in)
Propeller diameter	1.78 m (5 ft 10 in)

AREA:
Wings, gross	17.65 m² (190.0 sq ft)

WEIGHTS:
No data received, except:
Crew weight range	55-204 kg (120-450 lb)

PERFORMANCE:
Max level speed at 762 m (2,500 ft)
	61 knots (113 km/h; 70 mph)

Econ cruising speed at 762 m (2,500 ft)
	48 knots (89 km/h; 55 mph)
Stalling speed	27 knots (50 km/h; 31 mph)
Max rate of climb at S/L	183 m (600 ft)/min
Service ceiling	3,050 m (10,000 ft)
T-O run	38 m (125 ft)
Landing run	54 m (175 ft)
Range with max fuel	208 nm (386 km; 240 miles)

THOMPSON

THOMPSON AIRCRAFT

336 Fitzwater Street, Philadelphia, Pennsylvania 19147

Details and an illustration of the Thompson Boxmoth can be found in the 1987-88 and previous editions of *Jane's*.

THUNDER WINGS

THUNDER WINGS (a division of Thunder Development Inc)

14631 North Scottsdale Road, Suite 100, Scottsdale, Arizona 85254
Telephone: (602) 991 5531
PRESIDENT: David A. Bratset

This company intended to sell 100 kits of each of its reproductions of Second World War combat aircraft. However, it was reported in 1987 that Mr Wolfe Nottelman of Thunder Aircraft of Canada (4360 Canterbury Crescent, North Vancouver, British Columbia V7R 3N6) was negotiating to take over marketing and production of the kits. No more recent news has been received.

The Thunder Group has also been involved in development of the Venga TG-10 jet trainer, described in the main Canadian Aircraft section of this edition, and in government contracting.

THUNDER WINGS CURTISS P-40C

TYPE: Single-seat or tandem two-seat ⁸⁄₁₀th scale homebuilt fighter replica.

AIRFRAME: Wing section NACA 23015. Wing, aileron and tail unit spars and ribs of moulded sandwich composite material. Preformed skins attached by structural bonding. Monocoque fuselage of composite material, covered by preformed half-shells. Retractable tailwheel landing gear.

POWER PLANT: One 224 kW (300 hp) Lightning Merlin V-12. Fuel capacity 170 litres (45 US gallons; 37.5 Imp gallons). Long-range tanks of 265 litre (70 US gallon; 58.3 Imp gallon) combined capacity optional.

DIMENSIONS, EXTERNAL:
Wing span	9.14 m (30 ft 0 in)
Length overall	7.62 m (25 ft 0 in)
Height overall	3.05 m (10 ft 0 in)

AREA:
Wings, gross	14.03 m² (151.0 sq ft)

WEIGHTS:
*Weight empty, equipped	1,064 kg (2,345 lb)
Max T-O weight	1,324 kg (2,919 lb)

Includes optional avionics and equipment

PERFORMANCE (at max T-O weight, flown solo):
Cruising speed	174 knots (322 km/h; 200 mph)
Range: with standard fuel	434 nm (805 km; 500 miles)
with optional long-range fuel	
	651 nm (1,207 km; 750 miles)
g limits	±6

THUNDER WINGS FOCKE-WULF Fw 190A

The Fw 190A is offered in wood and steel structural form only.

TYPE: Single-seat ⁸⁄₁₀th scale homebuilt fighter replica.

AIRFRAME: Construction of wings and tail unit similar to P-40C. Welded steel tube fuselage, covered with pre-moulded skins.

POWER PLANT: One 179 kW (240 hp) Continental W670 radial engine. Fuel capacity 189.25 litres (50 US gallons; 41.6 Imp gallons).

DIMENSIONS, EXTERNAL:
Wing span	8.53 m (28 ft 0 in)
Length overall	7.01 m (23 ft 0 in)
Height overall	2.44 m (8 ft 0 in)

AREA:
Wings, gross	12.26 m² (132.0 sq ft)

WEIGHTS:
*Weight empty, equipped	897 kg (1,978 lb)
Baggage capacity	18 kg (40 lb)
Max T-O weight	1,168 kg (2,575 lb)

Includes optional avionics, equipment and systems

PERFORMANCE (at max T-O weight):
Cruising speed	161 knots (298 km/h; 185 mph)
Range	544 nm (1,009 km; 627 miles)
g limits	±6

THUNDER WINGS SUPERMARINE SPITFIRE Mk IX

Details of the Spitfire Mk IX are generally similar to those of the P-40C except as follows:

TYPE: Single-seat ⁸⁄₁₀th scale homebuilt fighter replica.

POWER PLANT: Fuel capacity 246 litres (65 US gallons; 54 Imp gallons).

DIMENSIONS, EXTERNAL:
Wing span	8.23 m (27 ft 0 in)
Length overall	7.01 m (23 ft 0 in)
Height overall	2.74 m (9 ft 0 in)

AREA:
Wings, gross	11.89 m² (128.0 sq ft)

WEIGHTS:
*Weight empty, equipped	751 kg (1,655 lb)
Baggage capacity	13.6 kg (30 lb)
Max T-O weight	1,023 kg (2,255 lb)

Includes optional avionics, equipment and systems

PERFORMANCE (at max T-O weight):
Cruising speed	195 knots (362 km/h; 225 mph)
Range	705 nm (1,306 km; 812 miles)
g limits	±6

THURSTON

THURSTON AEROMARINE CORPORATION

24 Ledge Road, Cumberland Foreside, Maine 04110
Telephone: (207) 829 6108
PRESIDENT: David B. Thurston

THURSTON TA16 TROJAN

The TA16 Trojan four-seat amphibian was conceived originally for the homebuilt market and plans are available only from Thurston Aeromarine. A production version became the TA16 Seafire. The Trojan and Seafire are identical and the details of the Seafire given under the International Aeromarine Corporation entry in the main Aircraft section of this edition apply equally to the Trojan.

TRI Q

TRI Q DEVELOPMENT COMPANY

PO Box 519, Vandalia, Ohio 45377

TRI Q QUICKIE Q2 MODIFICATION

A modification to the Quickie Q2, primarily to provide a tricycle landing gear, is available from Tri Q Development Co. The prototype flew for the first time on 13 March 1985, and by early 1988 about 170 kits had been sold. Tri Q is also reportedly developing a retractable landing gear conversion for the Velocity (which see).

Thunder Wings scale replica of a Curtiss P-40C

The two-seat Teratorn Tierra II homebuilt aircraft *(Geoffrey P. Jones)*

T.E.A.M. miniMAX single-seat microlight and homebuilt aircraft

T.E.A.M. Hi-MAX prototype *(Howard Levy)*

T.E.A.M. EZE-Max single-seat microlight *(Howard Levy)*

Production prototype Turner T-100D Mariah microlight

TUBE WORKS
TUBE WORKS INC
6352 Sashabaw Road, Clarkston, Michigan 48016
Telephone: (313) 625 1500

Tube Works produces aluminium alloy tube and fabric microlights, known as the Phoenix, Phoenix II and Phoenix Laser. Brief details and an illustration can be found in the 1987-88 *Jane's*.

TURNER
TURNER AIRCRAFT INC
Route 4, Box 115AB3, Grandview, Texas 76050
PRESIDENT: E. L. Gene Turner

The original Turner T-40 first flew on 3 April 1961. Plans of the T-40, T-40A and Super T-40A are available to homebuilders; many hundreds of sets have been sold. The T-40B design (see 1976-77 *Jane's*) is to be modified and updated, and kits may be made available at a later date. In the meantime, development of the **T-77**, latest derivative of the basic T-40, continues. The prototype, now fitted with a foreplane, made its first flight in this form on 30 July 1987. Full details of the T-77 can be found in the 1987-88 *Jane's*.

In addition to the T-40/T-77 series, Turner has developed a microlight aircraft known as the T-100D Mariah and a high-performance derivative as the T-110.

TURNER T-100D MARIAH
The first flight of the prototype T-100 was made on 19

December 1982. Plans and ready assembled aircraft are thought to be available in 'production' form. Kits of the T-100D will become available if sufficient demand is established.
TYPE: Single-seat microlight; conforms to FAR Pt 103.
AIRFRAME: Constructed from either wood or composite materials. Three-axis control. Non-retractable tricycle landing gear. Options include cockpit side windows.
POWER PLANT: Prototype powered by a 15 kW (20 hp) Cuyuna 215. Production model powered by a KFM 105ER or Ultra engine. Fuel capacity 19 litres (5 US gallons; 4.2 Imp gallons).
DIMENSIONS, EXTERNAL:
Wing span	9.75 m (32 ft 0 in)
Length overall	5.18 m (17 ft 0 in)
Height overall	1.70 m (5 ft 7 in)
Propeller diameter	1.07 m (3 ft 6 in)

AREA:
Wings, gross	13.14 m² (141.4 sq ft)

WEIGHTS:
Weight empty	114 kg (251 lb)
Max pilot weight	100 kg (220 lb)
Max T-O and landing weight	228 kg (504 lb)

PERFORMANCE:
Max level speed	53 knots (98 km/h; 61 mph)
Econ cruising speed	43 knots (80 km/h; 50 mph)
Stalling speed:	
power on	18 knots (34 km/h; 21 mph)
power off	23 knots (44 km/h; 27 mph)
Range with max fuel	125 nm (231 km; 144 miles)
Endurance with max fuel	3 h 25 min
g limits	+5.8/−2.9

TURNER T-110
This high-performance derivative of the T-100D is powered by a 32 kW (43 hp) engine. A prototype has been flight tested. Brief details and an illustration can be found in the 1987-88 *Jane's*.

TWO WINGS
TWO WINGS AVIATION
821 3rd Street, Farmington, Minnesota 55024
Telephone: (612) 463 2808
DESIGNER: Larry Seivert

TWO WINGS FURY
The Fury is available as a microlight in ready assembled and kit forms, with a 29.4 kW (39.4 hp) Rotax 447 engine, or as a ready assembled homebuilt aircraft powered by a 38 kW (51 hp) Rotax. Structure is of aluminium alloy, with metal skin on the underfuselage nose and turtledeck, and the entire airframe is Ceconite covered. Three-axis control is provided, and the landing gear is of non-retractable tailwheel type.

DIMENSIONS, EXTERNAL:
Wing span	8.64 m (28 ft 4 in)
Length overall	3.96 m (13 ft 0 in)
Height overall	2.36 m (7 ft 9 in)

PERFORMANCE:
Cruising speed	more than 52 knots (97 km/h; 60 mph)
Max rate of climb at S/L	305 m (1,000 ft)/min

ULTRA EFFICIENT PRODUCTS
ULTRA EFFICIENT PRODUCTS INC
1637 7th Street, Sarasota, Florida 34236
Telephone: (813) 955 0710
PRESIDENT: Nicholas R. Leichty

ULTRA EFFICIENT PRODUCTS INVADER Mk III-B
The Invader Mk III made its debut in 1982. Plans and some prefabricated parts are available, including a prefabricated fuselage structure. The current version is designated Invader Mk III-B. Construction from plans takes about 600 working hours.

TYPE: Single-seat microlight; conforms to FAR Pt 103.

AIRFRAME: Wings have wood and foam plastics/Styrofoam structure, Mylar or Dacron covered. Welded aluminium alloy fuselage pod, Dacron covered; 10 cm (4 in) diameter aluminium alloy tailboom. 'Ruddervators' of similar construction to wings, except for aluminium alloy tubular spar. Three-axis control. Non-retractable tricycle landing gear.

POWER PLANT: One 20 kW (27 hp) Rotax 277. Fuel capacity 19 litres (5 US gallons; 4.2 Imp gallons).

DIMENSIONS, EXTERNAL:
Wing span	9.45 m (31 ft 0 in)
Length overall	5.49 m (18 ft 0 in)
Height overall	1.22 m (4 ft 0 in)
Propeller diameter	1.12 m (3 ft 8 in)

AREA:
Wings, gross	13.38 m² (144.0 sq ft)

WEIGHTS:
Weight empty	111 kg (245 lb)
Pilot weight range	59-91 kg (130-200 lb)
Max T-O weight	215 kg (475 lb)

PERFORMANCE:
Max level speed	52 knots (97 km/h; 60 mph)
Cruising speed, 75% power	43 knots (80 km/h; 50 mph)
Stalling speed	24 knots (44 km/h; 27 mph)
Max rate of climb at S/L	228 m (750 ft)/min
Service ceiling	2,440 m (8,000 ft)
T-O run (grass)	46 m (150 ft)
Landing run	31 m (100 ft)
Range	217 nm (402 km; 250 miles)
g limits (at 165 kg; 365 lb AUW)	±6

ULTRA EFFICIENT PRODUCTS PENETRATER
Shown at the 1985 Sun 'n Fun meeting, this microlight is being marketed by Ultra Efficient products in plans form.

TYPE: Single-seat microlight.

AIRFRAME: Wooden wing spars and foam ribs, plywood covered foam D-cell leading-edge and aluminium trailing-edge, Mylar double surface covered. Ailerons and optional flaps. Fuselage boom of 4 in aluminium alloy tube, supporting V tail with all-moving 'ruddervators' of similar construction to wings, except for aluminium alloy tubular spar. Three-axis control. Non-retractable tricycle landing gear.

POWER PLANT: One 15 kW (20 hp) Zenoah G25B. Fuel capacity 19 litres (5 US gallons; 4.2 Imp gallons).

DIMENSIONS, EXTERNAL:
Wing span	7.32 m (24 ft 0 in)
Length overall	4.88 m (16 ft 0 in)
Height overall	1.83 m (6 ft 0 in)
Propeller diameter	1.42 m (4 ft 8 in)

AREA:
Wings, gross	10.03 m² (108.0 sq ft)

WEIGHTS:
Weight empty	79.5 kg (175 lb)
Max T-O weight	181 kg (400 lb)

PERFORMANCE (at max T-O weight):
Max level speed at S/L	52 knots (97 km/h; 60 mph)
Stalling speed	21 knots (39 km/h; 24 mph)
Max rate of climb at S/L	290 m (950 ft)/min
Service ceiling	2,440 m (8,000 ft)
T-O run	23 m (75 ft)
Landing run	15 m (50 ft)
Range at cruising speed	217 nm (402 km; 250 miles)
g limits	±6

ULTRA EFFICIENT PRODUCTS DEMOISELLE
Designed to resemble Alberto Santos-Dumont's Demoiselle of 1909-10, this microlight has its aluminium alloy tube fuselage structure painted a shade of tan and 'ringed' to give the tubes the appearance of bamboo, from which the original was constructed. The wooden wings and aluminium alloy tube tail surfaces are fabric covered.

Available in plans form only, supported by some prefabricated component parts, the single-seat Demoiselle is said to take approximately 600 working hours to build. Power is provided by a 15 kW (20 hp) Zenoah G25B engine, and fuel capacity is 11.4 litres (3 US gallons; 2.5 Imp gallons).

DIMENSIONS, EXTERNAL:
Wing span	8.23 m (27 ft 0 in)
Length overall	6.40 m (21 ft 0 in)
Height overall	2.13 m (7 ft 0 in)
Propeller diameter	1.52 m (5 ft 0 in)

AREA:
Wings, gross	13.94 m² (150.0 sq ft)

WEIGHTS:
Weight empty	111 kg (245 lb)
Max T-O weight	215 kg (475 lb)

PERFORMANCE (at max T-O weight):
Max level speed at S/L	43 knots (80 km/h; 50 mph)
Cruising speed, 50% power	35 knots (65 km/h; 40 mph)
Stalling speed	21 knots (39 km/h; 24 mph)
Max rate of climb at S/L	152 m (500 ft)/min
Service ceiling	1,220 m (4,000 ft)
T-O run	46 m (150 ft)
Landing run	31 m (100 ft)
Range at cruising speed	86 nm (161 km; 100 miles)
g limits	+4/−3

ULTRA SAIL
ULTRA SAIL INC
225 East Side Avenue, Mattituck, New York, 11952
Telephone: (516) 298 8055
PRESIDENT: Erwin Rodger

ULTRA SAIL CLOUD DANCER
The Cloud Dancer is marketed as prefabricated parts or in flyaway form. Construction time is only 16 hours. Although qualified as a microlight, the Cloud Dancer is intended primarily for power-off soaring.

TYPE: Single-seat microlight motor glider; conforms to FAR Pt 103.

AIRFRAME: Aluminium alloy construction, except for Kevlar nose fairing with windscreen, and Dacron wing and tail unit covering. Three-axis control by spoilers and 'ruddervators'. Non-retractable tailwheel landing gear. Optional inflatable floats and ballistic parachute.

POWER PLANT: One 20 kW (27 hp) Rotax 277. Fuel capacity 19 litres (5 US gallons; 4.2 Imp gallons).

DIMENSIONS, EXTERNAL:
Wing span	12.19 m (40 ft 0 in)
Length overall	5.41 m (17 ft 9 in)
Height overall	1.41 m (4 ft 7½ in)
Propeller diameter	1.22 m (4 ft 0 in)

AREA:
Wings, gross	12.22 m² (131.5 sq ft)

WEIGHTS:
Weight empty	115 kg (253 lb)
Pilot weight range	50-100 kg (110-220 lb)
Baggage capacity with 77 kg (170 lb) pilot	20-30 kg (45-67 lb)
Max T-O weight	236 kg (520 lb)

PERFORMANCE:
Max level speed	55 knots (101 km/h; 63 mph)
Econ cruising speed	35 knots (64 km/h; 40 mph)
Stalling speed: power on	22 knots (41 km/h; 25 mph)
power off	24 knots (44 km/h; 27 mph)
Max rate of climb at S/L	183 m (600 ft)/min
Service ceiling	4,575 m (15,000 ft)
T-O run (on grass)	37 m (120 ft)
Landing run (on grass)	52 m (170 ft)
Range, at 36 knots (68 km/h; 42 mph)	173 nm (322 km; 200 miles)
Max endurance	6 h 30 min
g limits	±4.5

V-8 SPECIAL
PLANS AND KITS FROM: Mizell Enterprises, 15749 Harvest Mile Road, Brighton, Colorado 80601
Telephone: (303) 654 0049

The V-8 Special was first flown on 22 September 1978. Following the death of its designer, Mr Chris Beachner, rights in the aircraft were purchased by Mr Bill Mizell, who currently offers plans, kits, engine conversion plans and ready converted V-8 engines. Mr Mizell is also offering plans and kits of the **V-8 Special SXS**, a side by side seating model with optional non-retractable tricycle or tailwheel landing gear, or fully retractable gear.

The following details apply to the standard V-8 Special:

V-8 SPECIAL
TYPE: Tandem two-seat sporting homebuilt.

AIRFRAME: Wings, ailerons and tail unit of glassfibre/epoxy resin and polyurethane foam construction. Welded steel tube fuselage structure, covered with a shell of glassfibre/epoxy over a polyurethane foam core. Non-retractable or retractable tailwheel landing gear.

POWER PLANT: One 93.2 kW (125 hp) modified Buick watercooled motorcar engine. Alternatively, other engines in 93.2-186.4 kW (125-250 hp) range. Fuel capacity 132.5 litres (35 US gallons; 29 Imp gallons).

DIMENSIONS, EXTERNAL:
Wing span	7.32 m (24 ft 0 in)
Length overall	5.64 m (18 ft 6 in)
Propeller diameter	1.45 m (4 ft 9 in)

AREA:
Wings, gross	8.92 m² (96.0 sq ft)

WEIGHTS:
Weight empty	381 kg (840 lb)
Baggage capacity	18 kg (40 lb)
Max T-O weight	588 kg (1,296 lb)

PERFORMANCE:
Max cruising speed	more than 174 knots (322 km/h; 200 mph)
Cruising speed (50% power)	128 knots (238 km/h; 148 mph) IAS
Stalling speed: landing gear and flaps up	56 knots (103 km/h; 64 mph) IAS
flaps down	35 knots (65 km/h; 40 mph)
*Max rate of climb at S/L	over 762 m (2,500 ft)/min

*Depending on engine rating

VANCRAFT
VANCRAFT COPTERS
7246 North Mohawk Avenue, Portland, Oregon 97203
Telephone: (503) 286 5462

VANCRAFT COPTERS VANCRAFT
Kits to build this autogyro are available.

TYPE: Tandem two-seat autogyro.

ROTOR SYSTEM: Two-blade rotor, with steel spar, wooden core, and bonded and riveted aluminium alloy skins. Patented rotor head with no springs. Hydraulic pre-rotator.

AIRFRAME: Basic structure of 2 in square steel tubing, bolted and welded. Small horizontal stabiliser, fin, large-area rudder and mast supports constructed of circular-section tubing. Glassfibre cabin shell. Non-retractable tricycle landing gear.

POWER PLANT: One 74.6 kW (100 hp) SCAT modified Volkswagen 2,180 cc motorcar engine. Fuel capacity 34 litres (9 US gallons; 7.5 Imp gallons).

DIMENSIONS, EXTERNAL:
Rotor diameter	8.53 m (28 ft 0 in)
Length overall	3.96 m (13 ft 0 in)
Height overall	2.29 m (7 ft 6 in)
Propeller diameter	1.42 m (4 ft 8 in)

WEIGHTS:
Weight empty	204 kg (450 lb)
Payload	159-181 kg (350-400 lb)

PERFORMANCE:
Max level speed	87 knots (161 km/h; 100 mph)
Cruising speed	56-65 knots (105-121 km/h; 65-75 mph)
Max rate of climb at S/L	366 m (1,200 ft)/min
T-O run	15-61 m (50-200 ft)
Range	261-304 nm (483-563 km; 300-350 miles)
Endurance	3 h 30 min

Two Wings Fury in microlight form *(J. M. G. Gradidge)*

Ultra Efficient Products Penetrater single-seat microlight

Ultra Efficient Products Invader Mk III-B

Tandem two-seat V-8 Special *(Howard Levy)*

Ultra Efficient Products Demoiselle single-seat microlight

Vancraft Rotor Lightning Sport Copter microlight autogyro

Ultra Sail Cloud Dancer microlight powered glider

VANCRAFT ROTOR LIGHTNING SPORT COPTER

This autogyro first flew in 1985.

TYPE: Single-seat microlight autogyro; conforms to FAR Pt 103.

ROTOR SYSTEM: As for Vancraft, except optional pre-rotator.

AIRFRAME: Basic structure of circular-section steel tubing, with some use of aluminium alloy. Glassfibre cabin shell. Tail unit as for Vancraft, with rudder skins of moulded glassfibre. Non-retractable tricycle landing gear. Optional floats.

POWER PLANT: One 34.3 kW (46 hp) Rotax 503.

DIMENSIONS, EXTERNAL:
Rotor diameter   7.01 or 8.53 m (23 ft 0 in or 28 ft 0 in)
Length overall   3.63 m (11 ft 11 in)
Height overall   2.46 m (8 ft 1 in)
Propeller diameter   1.63 m (5 ft 4 in)

WEIGHTS:
Weight empty   114 kg (252 lb)
Pilot weight range   68-100 kg (150-220 lb)
PERFORMANCE:
Max level speed   54 knots (101 km/h; 63 mph)
Minimum speed   4.5-9 knots (8-16 km/h; 5-10 mph)
Max rate of climb at S/L   over 305 m (1,000 ft)/min
T-O run   0-61 m (0-200 ft)
Landing run   0-6 m (0-20 ft)
Range   69-95 nm (128-177 km; 80-110 miles)

VAN'S

VAN'S AIRCRAFT INC

PO Box 160, North Plains, Oregon 97133
Telephone: (503) 647 5117
PRESIDENT: Richard VanGrunsven

VAN'S RV-3

More than 1,100 sets of plans of the RV-3 have been sold, with at least 200 aircraft under construction and over 140 RV-3s flying by early 1988.

TYPE: Single-seat sporting homebuilt.

AIRFRAME: Built of light alloy, with glassfibre wing and tail unit tips and engine cowling. Wing section NACA 23012. Non-retractable tailwheel landing gear.

POWER PLANT: One 93 kW (125 hp) Textron Lycoming O-290-G (GPU). Fuel capacity 91 litres (24 US gallons; 20 Imp gallons).

DIMENSIONS, EXTERNAL:
Wing span   6.07 m (19 ft 11 in)
Length overall   5.79 m (19 ft 0 in)
Height overall   1.55 m (5 ft 1 in)
Propeller diameter   1.73 m (5 ft 8 in)

AREA:
Wings, gross   8.36 m² (90.0 sq ft)
WEIGHTS:
Weight empty   315 kg (695 lb)
Max T-O weight   476 kg (1,050 lb)
PERFORMANCE (at max T-O weight):
Max level speed at S/L   169 knots (314 km/h; 195 mph)
Econ cruising speed at 3,050 m (10,000 ft)
   139 knots (257 km/h; 160 mph)
Stalling speed: flaps up   46 knots (84 km/h; 52 mph)
flaps down   42 knots (78 km/h; 48 mph)

Max rate of climb at S/L	579 m (1,900 ft)/min
Service ceiling	6,400 m (21,000 ft)
T-O run	61 m (200 ft)
Landing run	91 m (300 ft)
Range, no reserves	520 nm (965 km; 600 miles)

VAN'S RV-4

The two-seat RV-4 is some 20 per cent larger than the RV-3 and there is no commonality of airframe components, although the configuration is unchanged. The first flight of the prototype was made on 21 August 1979. Plans and kits are available to homebuilders. By early 1988, a total of 2,000 sets of plans had been sold, with about 900 aircraft under construction and more than 150 RV-4s flying.

TYPE: Tandem two-seat sporting homebuilt.

AIRFRAME: As for RV-3, except wing section Van's Aircraft 135.

POWER PLANT: One 112 kW (150 hp) Textron Lycoming O-320-E1F. Fuel capacity 121 litres (32 US gallons; 26.6 Imp gallons).

DIMENSIONS, EXTERNAL:

Wing span	7.01 m (23 ft 0 in)
Length overall	6.21 m (20 ft 4½ in)
Height overall	1.60 m (5 ft 3 in)
Propeller diameter	1.73 m (5 ft 8 in)

AREA:

Wings, gross	10.22 m² (110.0 sq ft)

WEIGHTS:

Weight empty	404 kg (890 lb)
Baggage capacity	13.6 kg (30 lb)
Max T-O weight	680 kg (1,500 lb)

PERFORMANCE (at max T-O weight, and prior to prototype's aerodynamic clean-up):

Max level speed at S/L	175 knots (323 km/h; 201 mph)
Econ cruising speed (55% power at 2,440 m; 8,000 ft)	142 knots (264 km/h; 164 mph)
Stalling speed	47 knots (87 km/h; 54 mph)
Max rate of climb at S/L	503 m (1,650 ft)/min
Service ceiling	5,945 m (19,500 ft)
T-O run	137 m (450 ft)
Landing run	130 m (425 ft)
Range with max fuel (55% power)	695 nm (1,287 km; 800 miles)

VAN'S RV-6

This is basically a side by side two-seat derivative of the RV-4. The prototype first flew in June 1986. Plans and kits are available. One has been purchased by AIEP of Nigeria (see main Aircraft section) as the prototype Air Beetle military trainer.

TYPE: Side by side two-seat sporting homebuilt.

AIRFRAME: Similar to RV-4.

POWER PLANT: One 119.3 kW (160 hp) Textron Lycoming O-320. Fuel capacity 140 litres (37 US gallons; 30.8 Imp gallons).

DIMENSIONS, EXTERNAL:

Wing span	7.01 m (23 ft 0 in)
Length overall	6.16 m (20 ft 2½ in)
Height overall	1.60 m (5 ft 3 in)
Propeller diameter	1.73 m (5 ft 8 in)

AREA:

Wings, gross	10.22 m² (110.0 sq ft)

WEIGHTS:

Weight empty	431 kg (950 lb)
Baggage capacity	27.2 kg (60 lb)
Max T-O weight	726 kg (1,600 lb)

PERFORMANCE (at max T-O weight):

Max level speed at S/L	175 knots (323 km/h; 201 mph)
Econ cruising speed (55% power) at 2,440 m (8,000 ft)	146 knots (270 km/h; 168 mph)
Stalling speed	47 knots (87 km/h; 54 mph)
Max rate of climb at S/L	503 m (1,650 ft)/min
Service ceiling	5,945 m (19,500 ft)
T-O run	160 m (525 ft)
Landing run	153 m (500 ft)
Range with max fuel (55% power)	803 nm (1,488 km; 925 miles)

VELOCITY

VELOCITY AIRCRAFT

200 West Airport Drive, Sebastian, Florida 32958

VELOCITY AIRCRAFT VELOCITY

The prototype Velocity made its debut at the 1985 Sun 'n Fun meeting. Velocity Aircraft offers it in kit form, with the glassfibre components pre-moulded.

TYPE: Two-plus-two homebuilt.

AIRFRAME: Built of foam cores, unidirectional/biaxial-triaxial glassfibre and epoxy resin. Rear mounted wings use modified Eppler aerofoil section. Three Roncz 'vortillons' under leading-edge of each wing. Endplate fins and rudders. Speed brake under fuselage. Foreplanes on nose, of original section and with near full-span elevators. Non-retractable main landing gear. Retractable nosewheel.

POWER PLANT: Any Textron Lycoming engine of 112 to 149 kW (150 to 200 hp) or Continental IO-360. Prototype has one 134 kW (180 hp) Textron Lycoming HIO-360. Fuel capacity of 277 litres (73 US gallons; 60.8 Imp gallons).

DIMENSIONS, EXTERNAL:

Wing span	8.72 m (28 ft 7½ in)
Length overall	5.49 m (18 ft 0 in)
Height overall	2.44 m (8 ft 0 in)
Propeller diameter	1.73 m (5 ft 8 in)

AREA:

Wings, gross	8.92 m² (96.0 sq ft)

WEIGHTS:

Weight empty	499 kg (1,100 lb)
Max T-O weight	1,020 kg (2,250 lb)

PERFORMANCE (prototype, at max T-O weight):

Max cruising speed at 610 m (2,000 ft)	191 knots (354 km/h; 220 mph)
Max rate of climb at S/L	305 m (1,000 ft)/min
Range with max fuel	1,736 nm (3,218 km; 2,000 miles)

VIKING

VIKING AIRCRAFT LTD

RR No. 1, PO Box 1000V, Eloy, Arizona 85231
Telephone: (602) 466 7538
PRESIDENT: Rex Taylor

VIKING DRAGONFLY

The prototype Dragonfly first flew on 16 June 1980. Plans are available, together with a pre-formed engine cowling and canopy. Also, kits of prefabricated component parts, requiring no complex jigging or tooling, are available. In this form the aircraft is known as the 'Snap' Dragonfly. It is estimated that the kits save the builder more than 700 working hours.

In its original configuration, with the non-retractable mainwheels at the tips of the foreplane, the aircraft was designated **Dragonfly Mark I.** In parallel production, for operation from unprepared strips and narrow taxiways, was the **Dragonfly Mark II.** This has its main landing gear in the form of short non-retractable cantilever units under the wings, with individual hydraulic toe brakes, and increased foreplane and elevator areas. In 1985, a **Dragonfly Mark III** version, with non-retractable tricycle landing gear, underwent flight trials.

TYPE: Side by side two-seat, dual control sporting homebuilt.

AIRFRAME: Composites wing, foreplane and tail unit structures of styrene foam, glassfibre, carbonfibre and epoxy. Wing section Eppler 1213. Foreplane of GU25 section. Semi-monocoque fuselage, formed (not carved) from 12.5 mm (½ in) thick urethane foam, with strips of 18 mm (¾ in) foam bonded along edges to allow large-radius external corners. Fuselage covered with glassfibre inside and out. (See introduction for landing gears.)

POWER PLANT: One 44.5 kW (60 hp) HAPI 1,835 cc modified Volkswagen motorcar engine; 1,600 cc engine, rated at 33.5 kW (45 hp), optional. Fuel capacity 56.8 litres (15 US gallons; 12.5 Imp gallons).

DIMENSIONS, EXTERNAL:

Wing span	6.71 m (22 ft 0 in)
Length overall	5.79 m (19 ft 0 in)
Height overall: Mk I	1.22 m (4 ft 0 in)
Propeller diameter	1.32 m (4 ft 4 in)

AREA:

Wings, gross	4.51 m² (48.5 sq ft)

WEIGHTS (Dragonfly Mk I with 1,835 cc engine):

Weight empty	274 kg (605 lb)
Max payload	184 kg (405 lb)
Max T-O weight	488 kg (1,075 lb)

PERFORMANCE (Dragonfly Mk I with 1,835 cc engine):

Max level speed at S/L	146 knots (270 km/h; 168 mph) IAS
Econ cruising speed at 2,285 m (7,500 ft)	121 knots (225 km/h; 140 mph)
Stalling speed, power on	39 knots (73 km/h; 45 mph) IAS
Max rate of climb at S/L	259 m (850 ft)/min
Service ceiling	5,640 m (18,500 ft)
T-O run	137 m (450 ft)
Landing run	213 m (700 ft)
Range with max fuel, 30 min reserves	434 nm (804 km; 500 miles)
g limits	+4.4/-2

VOLMER

VOLMER AIRCRAFT

Box 5222, Glendale, California 91201
Telephone: (818) 247 8718
PRESIDENT: Volmer Jensen

VOLMER VJ-22 SPORTSMAN

The prototype Sportsman flew for the first time on 22 December 1958. Plans are available to amateur constructors. Over 800 sets had been sold by early 1988 and more than 100 Sportsman amphibians are flying. Some have tractor propellers, but this modification is not recommended by Mr Jensen.

TYPE: Side by side two-seat, dual control homebuilt amphibian.

AIRFRAME: Wings are standard Aeronca Chief or Champion assemblies with wooden spars, light alloy ribs and fabric covering, and carry stabilising floats under the tips. Plans of specially designed wing, with wooden ribs and spars, available. Flying-boat hull of wooden construction, coated with glassfibre. Steel tube tail unit, fabric covered. Retractable tailwheel landing gear. Water rudder.

POWER PLANT: One 63.5 kW (85 hp) Continental C85, 67 kW (90 hp) or 74.5 kW (100 hp) Continental O-200-B. Fuel capacity 76 litres (20 US gallons; 16.7 Imp gallons).

DIMENSIONS, EXTERNAL:

Wing span	11.12 m (36 ft 6 in)
Length overall	7.32 m (24 ft 0 in)
Height overall	2.44 m (8 ft 0 in)

AREA:

Wings, gross	16.3 m² (175.0 sq ft)

WEIGHTS (63.5 kW; 85 hp):

Weight empty	454 kg (1,000 lb)
Max T-O weight	680 kg (1,500 lb)

PERFORMANCE (63.5 kW; 85 hp, at max T-O weight):

Max level speed at S/L	83 knots (153 km/h; 95 mph)
Max cruising speed	74 knots (137 km/h; 85 mph)
Stalling speed	39 knots (72 km/h; 45 mph)
Max rate of climb at S/L	183 m (600 ft)/min
Service ceiling	3,960 m (13,000 ft)
Range with max fuel, no reserves	260 nm (480 km; 300 miles)

VOLMER VJ-23E SWINGWING

Drawings for the pilot-only **VJ-23E** powered version of the VJ-23 Swingwing hang glider (fuel capacity 3.75 litres; 1 US gallon; 0.8 Imp gallon) are available.

AIRFRAME: Constructed of steel tube and wood, with double surface Dacron or other fabric covering. Three-axis control. Mainwheels only for ground handling.

POWER PLANT: One small engine carried above wing on pylon structure (see 1981-82 *Jane's* for details of David Cook's installation).

DIMENSIONS, EXTERNAL:

Wing span	9.93 m (32 ft 7 in)
Length overall	5.31 m (17 ft 5 in)
Height overall	1.83 m (6 ft 0 in)

AREA:

Wings, gross	16.63 m² (179.0 sq ft)

WEIGHTS:

Weight empty	54.5 kg (120 lb)
Pilot weight range	45.5-91 kg (100-200 lb)

VOLMER VJ-24W SUNFUN

The **VJ-24E** is a powered version of the aluminium tube/fabric VJ-24 hang glider (itself developed from the VJ-23) with a 7.5 kW (10 hp) McCulloch go-kart engine driving a pusher propeller, and a fuel capacity of 3.8 litres (1 US gallon; 0.8 Imp gallon).

The **VJ-24W** has an 11.2 kW (15 hp) Yamaha engine driving a tractor propeller, a 5.7 litre (1.5 US gallon; 1.25 Imp gallon) fuel tank, two-wheel landing gear, and cockpit pod with windscreen.

Plans of all versions of the VJ-24 are available from Volmer Aircraft.

The following details apply to the VJ-24W:

DIMENSIONS, EXTERNAL:

Wing span	11.13 m (36 ft 6 in)
Length overall	5.64 m (18 ft 6 in)
Height overall	1.75 m (5 ft 9 in)

AREA:

Wings, gross	15.14 m² (163.0 sq ft)

WEIGHTS:

Weight empty	95 kg (210 lb)
Max T-O weight	156 kg (345 lb)

PERFORMANCE:

Cruising speed	24 knots (45 km/h; 28 mph)
Stalling speed	13 knots (25 km/h; 15 mph)

Van's RV-4 built by Mr Claudio Tennini and used for a return flight between Marlboro, New Jersey (USA), and São Paulo (Brazil) *(Howard Levy)*

Viking Aircraft Dragonfly Mark I built in West Germany as the Schneider TC-1 Dragonfly *(Geoffrey P. Jones)*

Van's RV-6 side by side two-seat homebuilt aircraft *(Howard Levy)*

Second prototype of Velocity all-composites four-seat homebuilt aircraft *(Geoffrey P. Jones)*

Volmer VJ-22 Sportsman two-seat homebuilt amphibian

Wag-Aero Sport Trainer built by Placerville, California, chapter of EAA *(John Wegg)*

Mr Volmer Jensen flying a VJ-24W Sunfun microlight aircraft

WAG-AERO

WAG-AERO INC
PO Box 181, 1216 North Road, Lyons, Wisconsin 53148
Telephone: (414) 763 9586
PRESIDENT: Richard H. Wagner
MARKETING SUPERVISOR: Mary Pat Henningfield

WAG-AERO SPORT TRAINER

Wag-Aero plans and kits offer homebuilders the choice of four different modern versions of the Piper J-3.

Known as the **Sport Trainer**, the basic two-seat sporting aircraft follows the original design, but the wing has a wooden main spar and ribs, light alloy leading-edge and fabric covering. The fuselage and tail unit are of welded steel tube with fabric covering. The Sport Trainer can be powered by any flat-four Continental, Franklin or Textron Lycoming engine of between 48.5 and 93 kW (65 and 125 hp).

Also available are the **Acro Trainer**, which differs from the standard version by having a strengthened fuselage, shortened wings (8.23 m; 27 ft), modified lift struts, improved wing fittings and rib spacing, and a new leading-edge; the **Observer**, which is a replica L-4 military liaison aircraft; and the **Super Sport**, with structural modifications to accept engines of up to 112 kW (150 hp), making it suitable for glider towing, bush operations, or for operation as a floatplane.

The Sport Trainer first flew on 12 March 1975. The following details refer to this version.

DIMENSIONS, EXTERNAL:
Wing span	10.73 m (35 ft 2½ in)
Length overall	6.82 m (22 ft 4½ in)
Height overall	2.03 m (6 ft 8 in)

AREA:
Wings, gross	16.58 m² (178.5 sq ft)

WEIGHTS:
Weight empty	327 kg (720 lb)
Max T-O weight	635 kg (1,400 lb)

PERFORMANCE (at max T-O weight):
Max level speed at S/L	89 knots (164 km/h; 102 mph)
Cruising speed	82 knots (151 km/h; 94 mph)
Stalling speed	34 knots (63 km/h; 39 mph)
Max rate of climb at S/L	149 m (490 ft)/min
Service ceiling	over 3,660 m (12,000 ft)
T-O run	114 m (375 ft)
Range at cruising speed with standard fuel (45.5 litres; 12 US gallons; 10 Imp gallons)	191 nm (354 km; 220 miles)
Range with auxiliary fuel (98.5 litres; 26 US gallons; 21.6 Imp gallons)	395 nm (732 km; 455 miles)

WAG-AERO WAG-A-BOND

The name Wag-A-Bond applies to a replica of the Piper PA-15 Vagabond, known as the **Classic**, and the **Traveler**. The latter is a modified and updated version of the Piper Vagabond with port and starboard doors, overhead skylight window, extended sleeping deck (conversion from aircraft to camper interior taking about two minutes and accommodating two persons), extended baggage area, engine of up to 85.7 kW (115 hp), and provision for a full electrical system.

The prototype Wag-A-Bond was completed by Wag-Aero in May 1978. The following details apply to both versions, unless stated otherwise:

TYPE: Side by side two-seat homebuilt.

AIRFRAME: All-wood wing and aluminium alloy aileron structures. Welded steel tube and flat plate fuselage structure, and steel tube tail unit. Complete airframe is fabric covered. Non-retractable tailwheel landing gear. Optional skis.

POWER PLANT: Traveler can be powered by a Textron Lycoming engine of 80.5-85.7 kW (108-115 hp). Classic can be powered by a Continental engine of 48.5-74.5 kW (65-100 hp). Fuel capacity: Traveler 98.5 litres (26 US gallons; 21.6 Imp gallons), Classic 45.5 litres (12 US gallons; 10 Imp gallons).

DIMENSIONS, EXTERNAL:
Wing span	8.32 m (29 ft 3½ in)
Length overall	5.66 m (18 ft 7 in)
Height overall	1.83 m (6 ft 0 in)

AREA:	
Wings, gross	13.70 m² (147.5 sq ft)

WEIGHTS (A: Traveler, B: Classic):

Weight empty: A	329 kg (725 lb)
B	290 kg (640 lb)
Baggage capacity:	
A	27 kg (60 lb)
B	18 kg (40 lb)
Max T-O weight: A	658 kg (1,450 lb)
B	567 kg (1,250 lb)

PERFORMANCE (A: Traveler, B: Classic):

Max level speed: A	118 knots (219 km/h; 136 mph)
B	91 knots (169 km/h; 105 mph)
Cruising speed: A	108 knots (200 km/h; 124 mph)
B	83 knots (153 km/h; 95 mph)
Stalling speed: A, B	39 knots (73 km/h; 45 mph)
Max rate of climb at S/L: A	259 m (850 ft)/min
B	190 m (625 ft)/min

WAG-AERO 2+2 SPORTSMAN

The 2 + 2 Sportsman is based on the Piper PA-14 Family Cruiser. It is a true four-seater, with the option of a hinged rear fuselage decking to provide access to the baggage and rear seat areas. The rear seat itself can be removed so that cargo or a stretcher can be carried.

Plans and material kits are available for the 2+2 Sportsman. A pre-welded fuselage structure is also available.

TYPE: Four-seat homebuilt.

AIRFRAME: Similar construction to Wag-A-Bond, with glassfibre tips. Alternatively, drawings and materials provided to modify standard PA-12, PA-14 or PA-18 wings. Upper and lower spoilers.

POWER PLANT: Engine of 93-149 kW (125-200 hp). Usable fuel capacity 148 litres (39 US gallons; 32.5 Imp gallons).

DIMENSIONS, EXTERNAL:

Wing span	10.90 m (35 ft 9 in)
Length overall	7.12 m (23 ft 4½ in)
Height overall	2.02 m (6 ft 7½ in)

AREA:	
Wings, gross	16.18 m² (174.12 sq ft)

WEIGHTS:	
Weight empty	490 kg (1,080 lb)
Max T-O weight	998 kg (2,200 lb)

PERFORMANCE (typical; actual data depend on engine fitted):

Max level speed	112 knots (207 km/h; 129 mph)
Cruising speed	108 knots (200 km/h; 124 mph)
Stalling speed	33 knots (62 km/h; 38 mph)
Max rate of climb at S/L	244 m (800 ft)/min
Service ceiling	4,510 m (14,800 ft)
Range at cruising speed	582 nm (1,078 km; 670 miles)

WAR

WAR AIRCRAFT REPLICAS

348 South Eighth Street, Santa Paula, California 93060
Telephone: (805) 525 8212
PRESIDENT: James McKeehan

War Aircraft Replicas markets plans and kits for a series of half-scale reproductions of Second World War aircraft, using a common wooden fuselage box and spar structure.

WAR AIRCRAFT REPLICAS FOCKE-WULF 190

TYPE: Single-seat ½-scale homebuilt fighter representation.
AIRFRAME: Wing section NACA 23015 at root, 23012 at tip. Basic airframe structure of wood, with polyurethane foam used for ribs and to achieve aerofoil and fuselage contours. Laminating fabric and epoxy resin used for covering, and for internal strengthening. Retractable tailwheel landing gear.
POWER PLANT: One 74.6 kW (100 hp) Continental O-200, or Textron Lycoming or Volkswagen engine of similar power. Fuel capacity 38 litres (10 US gallons; 8.3 Imp gallons).

DIMENSIONS, EXTERNAL:

Wing span	6.10 m (20 ft 0 in)
Length overall	5.05 m (16 ft 7 in)
Height overall	2.13 m (7 ft 0 in)
Propeller diameter	1.52 m (5 ft 0 in)

AREA:	
Wings, gross	6.50 m² (70.0 sq ft)

WEIGHTS (O-200 engine):

Weight empty	286 kg (630 lb)
Max T-O weight	408 kg (900 lb)

PERFORMANCE (O-200 engine, at max T-O weight):

Max level speed at 1,065 m (3,500 ft)	169 knots (314 km/h; 195 mph)
Econ cruising speed at 1,065 m (3,500 ft)	108 knots (201 km/h; 125 mph)
Stalling speed	48 knots (89 km/h; 55 mph)
Max rate of climb at S/L	305 m (1,000 ft)/min
Service ceiling	3,810 m (12,500 ft)
T-O run	305 m (1,000 ft)
Landing run	366 m (1,200 ft)
Range with max fuel	347 nm (643 km; 400 miles)
g limits	±6

WAR AIRCRAFT REPLICAS F4U CORSAIR

The ½-scale F4U Corsair replica can be built from plans. Construction is as described for the WAR Focke-Wulf 190, and the aircraft is powered by a 74.6 kW (100 hp) Continental O-200-A engine.

DIMENSIONS, EXTERNAL:

Wing span	6.10 m (20 ft 0 in)
Length overall	5.03 m (16 ft 6 in)
Height overall	1.52 m (5 ft 0 in)
Propeller diameter	1.52 m (5 ft 0 in)

WEIGHTS:

Weight empty	418 kg (921 lb)
Max T-O weight	544 kg (1,200 lb)

PERFORMANCE (at max T-O weight):

Max level speed	147 knots (273 km/h; 170 mph)
Max cruising speed	121 knots (225 km/h; 140 mph)
Max rate of climb at S/L	426 m (1,400 ft)/min
T-O run	305 m (1,000 ft)
Landing run	457 m (1,500 ft)
Range with max fuel	347 nm (643 km; 400 miles)

WAR AIRCRAFT REPLICAS P-47 THUNDERBOLT

Construction is as described for the WAR Focke-Wulf 190, and the aircraft is powered by a 52-74.6 kW (70-100 hp) geared Volkswagen or 74.5 kW (100 hp) Continental O-200-A engine. The P-47 can be built with either a high turtledeck rear fuselage and early type canopy or a bubble canopy.

DIMENSIONS, EXTERNAL:

Wing span	6.10 m (20 ft 0 in)
Length overall	5.18 m (17 ft 0 in)
Propeller diameter	1.52 m (5 ft 0 in)

WAR AIRCRAFT REPLICAS HAWKER SEA FURY

Construction is as described for the WAR Focke-Wulf 190, and the aircraft is powered by a 74.6 kW (100 hp) Continental O-200-A engine. The first replica Sea Fury (G-BLTG) was flown on 24 February 1986.

DIMENSIONS, EXTERNAL:

Wing span	6.10 m (20 ft 0 in)
Length overall	5.11 m (16 ft 9 in)
Propeller diameter	1.52 m (5 ft 0 in)

WAR AIRCRAFT REPLICAS MITSUBISHI A6M5 ZERO (ZEKE 52)

Construction is as described for the WAR Focke-Wulf 190, and power is provided by a 74.6 kW (100 hp) Continental O-200-A or similar engine.

DIMENSIONS, EXTERNAL:

Wing span	6.40 m (21 ft 0 in)
Length overall	5.03 m (16 ft 6 in)
Propeller diameter	1.52 m (5 ft 0 in)

WARNER

WARNER AVIATION INC

Thunderhill Aerodrome, Route 4, Box 501, Covington, Louisiana 70433
Telephone: (504) 892 3721
PRESIDENT: Richard M. Warner

ANDERSON EA-1 KINGFISHER

The prototype EA-1 Kingfisher amphibian was designed and built by Mr Earl Anderson. The first flight was made on 24 April 1969. Plans were made available to amateur constructors via Anderson Aircraft Corporation; all rights to the Kingfisher have since been transferred to Warner Aviation. By February 1988 a total of 232 sets of plans had been sold, and about 75 Kingfishers are flying.

Homebuilders are discouraged from installing engines more powerful than 86 kW (115 hp).
TYPE: Side by side two-seat homebuilt amphibian.
AIRFRAME: Standard J3, PA-11, PA-12 Piper Cub or homebuilt wing with aluminium alloy spars and ribs, and fabric covering. Wing section USA 35B modified. Wing stabilising floats and flying-boat hull of wooden construction, covered with plywood and coated with glassfibre. Strut braced tail unit of steel tubing, fabric covered. Retractable tailwheel landing gear.
POWER PLANT: One 86 kW (115 hp) Textron Lycoming O-235-C1 recommended. Fuel capacity 76 litres (20 US gallons; 16.7 Imp gallons).

DIMENSIONS, EXTERNAL:

Wing span	11.00 m (36 ft 1 in)
Length overall	7.16 m (23 ft 6 in)
Height overall	2.44 m (8 ft 0 in)
Propeller diameter	1.83 m (6 ft 0 in)

AREA:	
Wings, gross	17.19 m² (185.0 sq ft)

WEIGHTS (O-235 engine):

Weight empty	494 kg (1,090 lb)
Baggage capacity	22.7 kg (50 lb)
Max T-O weight	726 kg (1,600 lb)

PERFORMANCE (with O-235 engine, at max T-O weight):

Max level speed	104 knots (193 km/h; 120 mph)
Econ cruising speed	69 knots (129 km/h; 80 mph)
Stalling speed	37-39 knots (68-73 km/h; 42-45 mph)
Max rate of climb at S/L	183-274 m (600-900 ft)/min
Service ceiling	3,050 m (10,000 ft)
Range	226 nm (418 km; 260 miles)
Endurance	3 h 15 min

WATSON

WATSON WINDWAGON COMPANY

Route 1, Box 51, Newcastle, Texas 76372
Telephone: (817) 862 5615
OWNER: Gary Watson

WATSON GW-1 WINDWAGON

The prototype Windwagon first flew on 19 April 1977. Plans to build the Windwagon are available to amateur builders, and more than 1,025 sets have been sold (including details for modifying the VW engine).

TYPE: Single-seat homebuilt.

AIRFRAME: Pop riveted aluminium alloy construction. Wing section Clark Y. Non-retractable tricycle landing gear.
POWER PLANT: One 22.4 kW (30 hp) 900 cc half-Volkswagen modified motorcar engine. Fuel capacity 15.1 litres (4 US gallons; 3.3 Imp gallons).

DIMENSIONS, EXTERNAL:

Wing span	5.49 m (18 ft 0 in)
Length overall	3.96 m (13 ft 0 in)
Height overall	1.07 m (3 ft 6 in)
Propeller diameter	1.22 m (4 ft 0 in)

AREA:	
Wings, gross	5.02 m² (54.0 sq ft)

WEIGHTS:

Weight empty	124 kg (273 lb)
Baggage capacity	9 kg (20 lb)
Max T-O weight	220 kg (485 lb)

PERFORMANCE:

Max level speed	117 knots (217 km/h; 135 mph)
Cruising speed	over 87 knots (161 km/h; 100 mph)
Stalling speed	35 knots (65 km/h; 40 mph)
Max rate of climb at S/L	137 m (450 ft)/min
Service ceiling	3,660 m (12,000 ft)
T-O run	76 m (250 ft)
Landing run	91 m (300 ft)
Range	260 nm (483 km; 300 miles)

WHATLEY

VASCOE WHATLEY Jr

PO Box 474, Allendale, South Carolina 29810
Telephone: (803) 584 2691

WHATLEY SPECIAL

The prototype Whatley Special flew for the first time on 23 June 1981. Plans are available to amateur builders.

TYPE: Single-seat homebuilt biplane.
AIRFRAME: Wing section NACA 4412 (modified). Dacron covered all-wood structure, with steel tube cabane struts. Ailerons on lower wings only. Non-retractable tailwheel landing gear.
POWER PLANT: One Volkswagen 2,232 cc modified motorcar engine. Fuel capacity 34 litres (9 US gallons; 7.5 Imp gallons).

DIMENSIONS, EXTERNAL:

Wing span: upper	6.22 m (20 ft 5 in)
lower	5.82 m (19 ft 1 in)

WEIGHTS:

Weight empty	222 kg (490 lb)
Max T-O weight	336 kg (740 lb)

PERFORMANCE:

Cruising speed	65 knots (121 km/h; 75 mph)

WAR half-scale replica of a Hawker Sea Fury (Textron Lycoming O-235 engine), built by Mr Roger Haver of British Columbia, Canada
(Peter M. Bowers)

Whatley Special single-seat light biplane

Prototype Wheeler Express four-seat homebuilt cabin monoplane

Warner (Anderson) EA-1 Kingfisher amphibian *(Geoffrey P. Jones)*

White Der Jäger D.IX without wheel fairings, built by Mr B. W. Salyer
(J. M. G. Gradidge)

Watson GW-1 Windwagon (half an 1,800 cc Volkswagen modified motorcar engine)

WHEELER
WHEELER AIRCRAFT COMPANY
Dept 27, Tacoma Narrows Airport, Gig Harbor, Washington 98335
Telephone: (206) 851 5793
PRESIDENT: Ken Wheeler

WHEELER EXPRESS
The Express was CAD designed as a high speed cross-country kitplane, with the unusual seating arrangement of one forward and one aft facing seat in the rear, behind two front seats with dual controls. The prototype, built from a kit of pre-moulded parts, flew for the first time on 28 July 1987.
TYPE: Four-seat, dual-control cross-country homebuilt; conforms to FAR Pt 23.
AIRFRAME: Constructed of composites sandwich material,

comprising polyurethane foam core, glassfibre, unidirectional glassfibre tape and vinylester resin. Wing section NASA NFL 0215-F (laminar flow). Non-retractable tricycle landing gear. Retractable gear optional.
POWER PLANT: Prototype fitted with 149 kW (200 hp) Textron Lycoming IO-360-C1D6; 119 or 134 kW (160 or 180 hp) Textron Lycoming engine optional. Fuel capacity (usable) 193 litres (51 US gallons; 42.5 Imp gallons).
DIMENSIONS, EXTERNAL:

Wing span	9.45 m (31 ft 0 in)
Length overall	7.62 m (25 ft 0 in)
Height overall	2.13 m (7 ft 0 in)

AREA:

Wings, gross	11.71 m² (126.0 sq ft)

WEIGHTS:

Weight empty	567 kg (1,250 lb)

Baggage capacity, with four

77 kg (170 lb) persons	29 kg (64 lb)
Max T-O weight	1,043 kg (2,300 lb)

PERFORMANCE (149 kW; 200 hp engine, retractable landing gear):
Max level speed at S/L 204 knots (378 km/h; 235 mph)
Max cruising speed at S/L (75% power)
182 knots (338 km/h; 210 mph)
Stalling speed at max T-O weight:

flaps up	55 knots (101 km/h; 63 mph)
flaps down	50 knots (92 km/h; 57 mph)

Max rate of climb at S/L 488 m (1,600 ft)/min
Range at 55% power, no reserves
1,042 nm (1,931 km; 1,200 miles)

g limits	+4.4/–2.2
	+8.8/–4.4 ultimate

WHITE
E. MARSHALL WHITE
Meadowlark Airport, 5141 Warner Avenue, Huntington Beach, California 92649
Telephone: (714) 846 2409

WHITE WW-1 DER JÄGER D.IX
The Der Jäger D.IX prototype first flew on 7 September 1969. Plans, kits and some components have been made available.
The following details apply to the prototype in its original form. It has since been re-engined with a 112 kW (150 hp) Textron Lycoming.
TYPE: Single-seat homebuilt biplane.

AIRFRAME: Wings of M-6 aerofoil section, with wood spars and ribs, fabric covered. Internal steel tube bracing. Ailerons in both top and bottom wings. Welded steel tube fuselage and tail unit, fabric covered. Wood or glassfibre fuselage turtleback. Aluminium engine cowling. Tail unit has sheet metal ribs. Non-retractable tailwheel landing gear.
POWER PLANT: One 86 kW (115 hp) Textron Lycoming O-235-C1. Structure suitable for alternative power plants from 1,600 cc Volkswagen up to 112 kW (150 hp). Fuel capacity 91 litres (24 US gallons; 20 Imp gallons).

DIMENSIONS, EXTERNAL:

Wing span: upper	6.10 m (20 ft 0 in)
lower	4.88 m (16 ft 0 in)
Length overall	5.18 m (17 ft 0 in)
Propeller diameter	1.68 m (5 ft 6 in)

AREA:

Wings, gross	10.68 m² (115.0 sq ft)

WEIGHTS:

Weight empty	242 kg (534 lb)
Max T-O weight	403 kg (888 lb)

PERFORMANCE (at max T-O weight):
Max level speed at 610 m (2,000 ft)
126 knots (233 km/h; 145 mph)
Max cruising speed at 610 m (2,000 ft)
116 knots (214 km/h; i33 mph)

Stalling speed	47 knots (87 km/h; 54 mph)
Max rate of climb at S/L	732 m (2,400 ft)/min
T-O run	46 m (150 ft)

WHITE LIGHTNING
WHITE LIGHTNING AIRCRAFT CORPORATION

Box 497, Walterboro, South Carolina 29488
Telephone: (803) 538 3999
PRESIDENT: Nick Jones

WHITE LIGHTNING AIRCRAFT WHITE LIGHTNING

The first prototype White Lightning flew initially on 8 March 1986. In the same year it established several world speed records in Classes C1b and C1c.

Kits are available, and 16 had been delivered by February 1988. Construction takes under 1,000 working hours.

TYPE: Four-seat homebuilt.

AIRFRAME: Wing section NACA 66₂-215. Wings have graphite tubular 'wet' main spar, and glassfibre front and rear spars and ribs, all pre-cast in the lower glassfibre skin. Fowler flaps. Glassfibre/epoxy fuselage moulded in upper and lower halves. Tail unit has spars and ribs of fin and tailplane pre-cast into one skin of each. Retractable tricycle landing gear.

POWER PLANT: Prototype has 156.6 kW (210 hp) Continental IO-360 CB. Fuel capacity 257 litres (68 US gallons; 56.6 Imp gallons).

DIMENSIONS, EXTERNAL:
Wing span	8.43 m (27 ft 8 in)
Length overall	7.11 m (23 ft 4 in)
Height overall	2.18 m (7 ft 2 in)
Propeller diameter	1.85 m (6 ft 1 in)

AREA:
Wings, gross	8.27 m² (89.0 sq ft)

WEIGHTS:
Weight empty	635 kg (1,400 lb)
Max baggage capacity	154 kg (340 lb)
Max T-O weight	1,088 kg (2,400 lb)

PERFORMANCE (at max T-O weight):
Max level speed at S/L	243 knots (450 km/h; 280 mph)
Econ cruising speed at 3,350 m (11,000 ft)	221 knots (410 km/h; 255 mph)
Stalling speed: flaps up	78 knots (145 km/h; 90 mph)
flaps down	58 knots (108 km/h; 67 mph)
Max rate of climb at S/L	579 m (1,900 ft)/min
Service ceiling	7,010 m (23,000 ft)
T-O run, full flaps	381 m (1,250 ft)
Landing run	397 m (1,300 ft)
Range with max fuel	1,389 nm (2,575 km; 1,600 miles)
Endurance	6 h 10 min
g limits	+6/−4 aerobatic

WIND DANCER — *See Gyro 2000*

WINDRYDER
WINDRYDER ENGINEERING INC

555 Alter Street, No. 15, Broomfield, Colorado, 80020
Telephone: (303) 466 6669
Fax: (303) 442 4131
PRESIDENT: Jim McCutchen

WINDRYDER ENGINEERING WINDRYDER

The first of four prototype WindRyder autogyros flew initially in July 1986. Kits are available, and by March 1988 three had been ordered. The first kit had been delivered, assembled and flown by then. Construction takes about 100 working hours.

The WindRyder was demonstrated to the US Army, in Florida, in April 1987.

TYPE: Single-seat autogyro.

ROTOR SYSTEM: Skywheels two-blade rotor of 8H12 section, constructed of unwoven bi-directional S-glass in a vinylester matrix, with an extruded aluminium alloy spar bonded inside the leading-edge. Unwoven bi-directional S-glass pylon, manufactured in two halves, with tubular D section forward half carrying most loads. 'Tilt spindle' rotor head. Pre-rotator.

AIRFRAME: Monocoque fuselage of pre-moulded inner and outer shells, factory bonded, using bi-directional unwoven S-glass and graphite in a polyester resin matrix, completed by installation of composite seat/fuel tank. Dihedral tailplane, three fins and large central rudder. Tail surfaces have NACA 0012 section. Non-retractable tricycle landing gear.

POWER PLANT: One 47.7 kW (64 hp) Rotax 532. Fuel capacity in seat tank 66 litres (17.5 US gallons; 14.6 Imp gallons). Optional 82 kW (110 hp) Hirth F30 engine.

DIMENSIONS, EXTERNAL:
Rotor diameter	8.84 m (29 ft 0 in)
Length overall (excl rotor)	4.06 m (13 ft 4 in)
Height overall	2.54 m (8 ft 4 in)
Propeller diameter	1.63 m (5 ft 4 in)

AREA:
Rotor disc	61.3 m² (660.0 sq ft)

WEIGHTS:
Weight empty	204 kg (450 lb)
Pilot weight range	45-136 kg (100-300 lb)
Max T-O weight	363 kg (800 lb)

PERFORMANCE:
Max level speed	100 knots (185 km/h; 115 mph)
Econ cruising speed	69 knots (129 km/h; 80 mph)
Max rate of climb at S/L	305 m (1,000 ft)/min
Service ceiling	3,050 m (10,000 ft)
T-O run	61 m (200 ft)
Landing run	0-15 m (0-50 ft)
Range	173 nm (322 km; 200 miles)
Endurance	2 h
g limits	+3/−0

WITTMAN
S. J. WITTMAN

7200 SE 85th Lane, Ocala, Florida 32672

WITTMAN TAILWIND MODEL W-8

The prototype W-8 was built in 1952-53. Sets of plans and prefabricated components are available, and more than 350 Tailwinds have flown. Some Tailwinds have been built with tricycle landing gear, retractable mainwheels and other design changes.

TYPE: Side by side two-seat cabin homebuilt.

AIRFRAME: Wing section is a combination of NACA 4309 (upper surface) and NACA 0006 (lower surface). Wooden wing structure with plywood and fabric covering. Ailerons, flaps and tail unit of steel and stainless steel construction. Steel tube fuselage, fabric covered. Non-retractable tailwheel landing gear standard.

POWER PLANT: Normally one 67 kW (90 hp) Continental C90-12F. Alternative engines include the 63.5 kW (85 hp) Continental C85, 74.5 kW (100 hp) Continental O-200, 86 kW (115 hp) Textron Lycoming O-235 and 104.5 kW (140 hp) Textron Lycoming O-290. Fuel capacity 94.5-132.5 litres (25-35 US gallons; 20.8-29.1 Imp gallons).

DIMENSIONS, EXTERNAL:
Wing span	6.86 m (22 ft 6 in)
Length overall	5.87 m (19 ft 3 in)
Height overall	1.73 m (5 ft 8 in)
Propeller diameter	1.63 m (5 ft 4 in)

AREA:
Wings, gross	8.36 m² (90.0 sq ft)

WEIGHTS (74.5 kW; 100 hp Continental O-200 engine):
Weight empty	318 kg (700 lb)
Baggage capacity	27 kg (60 lb)
Max T-O weight	590 kg (1,300 lb)

PERFORMANCE (74.5 kW; 100 hp Continental O-200 engine at max T-O weight):
Max level speed at S/L	143 knots (265 km/h; 165 mph)
Econ cruising speed	113 knots (209 km/h; 130 mph)
Landing speed: flaps down	48 knots (89 km/h; 55 mph)
flaps up	57 knots (105 km/h; 65 mph)
Max rate of climb at S/L	275 m (900 ft)/min
Service ceiling	more than 4,875 m (16,000 ft)
T-O run	245 m (800 ft)
Landing run	183 m (600 ft)
Range with max payload at 3,050 m (10,000 ft), no reserves:	
at 139 knots (257 km/h; 160 mph)	521 nm (965 km; 600 miles)
at 122 knots (225 km/h; 140 mph)	607 nm (1,125 km; 700 miles)

WITTMAN TAILWIND MODEL W-10

Recent revisions to the Tailwind plans (available as a separate package) have produced a new version known as the Model W-10. This is basically a W-8 with a 112 kW (150 hp) Textron Lycoming O-320, 108 kW (145 hp) Continental, or aluminium block Oldsmobile F85 or Buick V-8 engine. Fuel capacity is 114 litres (30 US gallons; 25 Imp gallons). Airframe improvements include a new and more efficient wingtip design and round spring steel landing gear legs with wood and fabric fairings. Empty and max T-O weights of this version, with Continental O-300 engine, are 413 kg (910 lb) and 680 kg (1,500 lb) respectively.

PERFORMANCE (Continental O-300 engine):
Max level speed at S/L	182 knots (338 km/h; 210 mph)
Econ cruising speed	156 knots (290 km/h; 180 mph)
Stalling speed: flaps up	38 knots (70 km/h; 43 mph)
flaps down	35 knots (65 km/h; 40 mph)
Service ceiling	4,875 m (16,000 ft)
T-O run	366 m (1,200 ft)

WOLF
DONALD S. WOLF

17 Chestnut Street, Huntington, New York 11743
Telephone: (516) 427 9678

The prototype Boredom Fighter flew initially on 30 August 1979. Plans are available to amateur constructors, and 150 Boredom Fighters were under construction in early 1988.

WOLF W-11 BOREDOM FIGHTER

TYPE: Single-seat homebuilt biplane.

AIRFRAME: Wing section NACA 4412. Wooden wing and tail unit structure, fabric covered. Ailerons on lower wings, of similar construction to wings. Spruce Warren truss fuselage, with plywood covering in cockpit area; fabric covered rear fuselage. Non-retractable tailwheel landing gear.

POWER PLANT: One 48.5 kW (65 hp) Continental A65 engine recommended; other engines of 37.5-74.5 kW (50-100 hp) can be fitted. Fuel capacity 56.8 litres (15 US gallons; 12.5 Imp gallons).

DIMENSIONS, EXTERNAL:
Wing span, both	6.10 m (20 ft 0 in)
Length overall	4.79 m (15 ft 8½ in)
Height overall	1.83 m (6 ft 0 in)
Propeller diameter	1.83 m (6 ft 0 in)

AREA:
Wings, gross	9.06 m² (97.5 sq ft)

WEIGHTS:
Weight empty, equipped	214.5 kg (473 lb)
Baggage capacity	3.6 kg (8 lb)
Max T-O weight	349 kg (770 lb)

PERFORMANCE:
Max level speed at 610 m (2,000 ft)	102 knots (190 km/h; 118 mph)
Econ cruising speed at 610 m (2,000 ft)	87 knots (161 km/h; 100 mph)
Stalling speed, engine idling	37 knots (68 km/h; 42 mph)
Max rate of climb at S/L	366 m (1,200 ft)/min
Service ceiling	approx 4,875 m (16,000 ft)
T-O run on grass	46 m (150 ft)
Landing run on grass	91 m (300 ft)
Range with max fuel, 20 min reserves	404 nm (750 km; 466 miles)

WOOD WING
WOOD WING SPECIALTY

PO Box 1258, Tehachapi, California 93561

PLUMB CJ-3D CRACKER JACK

The prototype Cracker Jack made its first flight on 6 October 1982. In addition to plans, Wood Wing Specialty offers four prefabricated components, comprising a glassfibre nose cowling, wingtips, windscreen and propeller.

TYPE: Single-seat homebuilt.

AIRFRAME: Fabric covered all-wood airframe structure, except for aluminium alloy tubing used for elevator and rudder curves. Wing section NACA 4413. Glassfibre nose cowling. Non-retractable tailwheel landing gear. Optional cockpit side windows.

POWER PLANT: One 28.3 kW (38 hp) Aero-DAF 95 950 cc converted motorcar engine. Main fuel tank capacity 17 litres (4.5 US gallons; 3.7 Imp gallons), plus header tank of 3.8 litres (1 US gallon; 0.83 Imp gallon) capacity. Optional half-Volkswagen converted motorcar engine (950-1,000 cc).

DIMENSIONS, EXTERNAL:
Wing span	8.53 m (28 ft 0 in)
Length overall	5.33 m (17 ft 6 in)
Propeller diameter	1.32 m (4 ft 4 in)

AREA:
Wings, gross	9.29 m² (100.0 sq ft)

WEIGHTS:
Weight empty	159 kg (350 lb)

First prototype White Lightning Aircraft White Lightning four-seat composites homebuilt *(Howard Levy)*

Wittman Tailwind W-10 (inverted 93 kW; 125 hp 3,500 cc Oldsmobile F85 engine)

Wolf W-11 Boredom Fighter

WindRyder Engineering WindRyder single-seat composites autogyro in latest configuration

Wood Wing Specialty CJ-3D Cracker Jack

Recommended max pilot weight	91 kg (200 lb)	Max and econ cruising speed at S/L	Range	173 nm (321 km; 200 miles)
Baggage capacity	9 kg (20 lb)	65 knots (121 km/h; 75 mph)	Endurance	2 h 42 min
Max T-O weight	272 kg (600 lb)	Stalling speed 34 knots (63 km/h; 39 mph)	g limits	+6/−4
PERFORMANCE:		Max rate of climb at S/L 244 m (800 ft)/min		
Max level speed at S/L	74 knots (137 km/h; 85 mph)	Service ceiling 3,050 m (10,000 ft)		
		T-O and landing run 91 m (300 ft)		

SAILPLANES

AUSTRALIA

LYNCH
JOHN F. LYNCH
RMB 161, Tocumwal, NSW 2714
Telephone: 058742594

LYNCH (PILATUS) B4M1
Mr Lynch has motorised two examples of the Pilatus B4-PC11A sailplane which, in early 1988, were still awaiting delivery of redesigned 17.9 kW (24 hp) König SC 430

engines to allow further flight testing and full certification under JAR 22 (Normal category). Further details of this project, and an illustration, can be found in the 1987-88 *Jane's.*

SCHNEIDER
EDMUND SCHNEIDER PTY LTD
Two Wells Road (Aerodrome), Gawler, South Australia 5118
Telephone: 085 22 2978
CHIEF DESIGNER: Harry Schneider

Edmund Schneider Pty Ltd was instrumental in the development of gliding in Australia, having designed and built the ES 52 Kookaburra two-seater used by most clubs in the 1950s and 1960s, the ES 57 Kingfisher, ES 60 Boomerang, and other well known types.

In the 1970s, after shelving the projected ES 63 two-seat sailplane (1977-78 *Jane's*), the company continued to import Grob and Schempp-Hirth glassfibre sailplanes, as well as providing a repair, maintenance and spare parts service. Its latest design is the ES 65.

SCHNEIDER ES 65 PLATYPUS
The ES 65 Platypus is a development of the ES 63, designed in response to a Gliding Federation of Australia requirement for a two-seat sailplane suitable for the full GFA training syllabus, including spinning. It made its first flight in 1984.

Features include side by side seating (for ergonomic and instructional advantages and to eliminate need for duplicating instruments), and construction entirely of epoxy/glassfibre and epoxy/carbonfibre composites. It is claimed to have outstanding handling characteristics, resembling modern high-performance single-seaters, with particular emphasis on classic stall and spin characteristics (the latter throughout the full CG range); very good slow speed handling, stability and manoeuvrability; and better ground handling and rigging features than most other available two-seaters. The cockpit is designed for maximum crash protection.

No other technical details were available at the time of going to press, but the general appearance of the ES 65 can be seen in the accompanying photograph. In early 1988 efforts were under way to acquire the necessary funding for tooling up, type approval and the start of production.

AUSTRIA

HB
HB-AIRCRAFT INDUSTRIES LUFTFAHRZEUG AG
Postfach 27, Dr Adolf-Schärf-Strasse 42, A-4053 Haid
Telephone: (07229) 88375/87680
Telex: 21909
DIRECTORS:
Ing Heino Brditschka
Heribert Katzenberger

HB-AIRCRAFT HB-23 HOBBYLINER and SCANLINER
The following versions of this motor glider were in production in 1988:

HB-23/2400 Hobbyliner. Basic side by side two-seat motor glider; 30 built by January 1988. Certificated in Austria, West Germany, Italy, Switzerland and the USA.

HB-23/2400 Scanliner. Version of HB-23 with bubble canopy to provide optimum air to ground forward view. Suitable for oil and powerline inspection, coastal and border patrol, policing, observation, survey, fish spotting, polution control, and communications platform roles. Provision for hardpoint under each wing, on which can be carried a miniature FLIR or SLAR pod, LLL TV, searchlight or other stores. In production, with ten built by January 1988. Certificated in Austria, Italy, Spain and the USA.

TYPE: Two-seat motor glider.
AIRFRAME: Cantilever high-wing monoplane. Wortmann wing sections: FX-61-184 at root, FX-60-126 at tip. Dihedral 2° on outer panels. Incidence 3°. No sweep. Single main box spar of PhBu 7 (laminated beechwood) and plywood, wooden ribs, and overall plywood covering. All-wood ailerons. Spoilers on upper surface. Main fuselage pod has a welded steel tube frame with glassfibre skin; rear fuselage comprises upper and lower tailbooms, covered in plywood except for triangular cutout in area of propeller arc. Plywood covered wooden tail unit comprises fin, rudder, fixed incidence T tailplane, and elevators. Trim tab in starboard elevator. Non-retractable tricycle landing gear. Mainwheels have self-sprung cantilever glassfibre legs, size 5.00-5 or 6.00-6 tyres (pressure 2.5 bars; 36.3 lb/sq in). Steerable nosewheel, with size 3.00-4, 3.50 or 4.00-4 tyre. Fully enclosed cabin for two persons, on side by side adjustable seats; 0.23 m³ (8.1 cu ft) of baggage space aft of seats. One-piece fixed canopy forward, aft of which are twin window/doors hinged on centreline and opening upward. VFR instrumentation standard, IFR panel optional.
POWER PLANT: One 74.2 kW (98 hp) 2,400 cc Porsche modified Volkswagen G/2 four-cylinder motorcar engine, mounted aft of cabin with rubber belt drive to a Mühlbauer MT 172LD 130 2C or Hoffmann HO-14C/172 130LD two-blade fixed-pitch pusher propeller (variable-pitch three-blade propeller optional). Single fuel tank in wing centre-section, capacity 76 litres (20 US gallons; 16.7 Imp gallons) in Hobbyliner, 106 litres (28 US gallons; 23.3 Imp gallons) in Scanliner.

DIMENSIONS, EXTERNAL:

Wing span	16.40 m (53 ft 9¾ in)
Wing chord: at root	1.538 m (5 ft 0½ in)
at tip	0.60 m (1 ft 11½ in)
Wing aspect ratio	14.1
Width, outer wing panels removed	7.15 m (23 ft 5½ in)
Length overall: Hobbyliner	8.00 m (26 ft 3 in)
Scanliner	7.35 m (24 ft 1½ in)
Height overall	2.45 m (8 ft 0½ in)
Wheel track	1.80 m (5 ft 11 in)
Wheelbase	2.46 m (8 ft 1 in)

AREA:

Wings, gross	19.067 m² (205.2 sq ft)

WEIGHTS AND LOADINGS:

Weight empty, equipped: both versions	560 kg (1,234 lb)
Max T-O weight: Hobbyliner	760 kg (1,676 lb)
Scanliner	850 kg (1,874 lb)
Max wing loading:	
Hobbyliner	39.86 kg/m² (8.16 lb/sq ft)
Scanliner	44.58 kg/m² (9.13 lb/sq ft)
Max power loading:	
Hobbyliner	10.24 kg/kW (17.10 lb/hp)
Scanliner	11.46 kg/kW (19.12 lb/hp)

PERFORMANCE, UNPOWERED:

Best glide ratio at 53 knots (98 km/h; 61 mph):	
Hobbyliner	22
Scanliner	19
Min rate of sink at 50 knots (92 km/h; 57 mph):	
Hobbyliner	1.20 m (3.94 ft)/s
Scanliner	1.40 m (4.59 ft)/s
Stalling speed	41 knots (75 km/h; 47 mph)
g limits:	
(both versions) (semi-aerobatic, up to T-O weight of 750 kg; 1,653 lb)	+5.3/-3
(both versions) (Utility category)	+4.4/-3

PERFORMANCE, POWERED:

Never-exceed speed:	
both versions	108 knots (200 km/h; 124 mph) IAS
Max cruising speed (75% power):	
both versions	97 knots (180 km/h; 112 mph)
Min patrol speed:	
both versions	54 knots (100 km/h; 62 mph)
Stalling speed:	
both versions	43 knots (80 km/h; 50 mph)
Max rate of climb at S/L:	
Hobbyliner	228 m (748 ft)/min
Scanliner	216 m (709 ft)/min
Service ceiling: both versions	5,000 m (16,400 ft)
T-O to 15 m (50 ft):	
Hobbyliner	160 m (525 ft)
Scanliner	290 m (950 ft)
Landing run: both versions	210 m (689 ft)
Range with max fuel, no reserves:	
Hobbyliner	432 nm (800 km; 497 miles)
Scanliner	693 nm (1,285 km; 798 miles)
Endurance: Hobbyliner	6 h
Scanliner	10 h

BELGIUM

ARPLAM
ALL REINFORCED PLASTIC MOULDINGS
Sint-Eloois-Winkel, Flanders

ARPLAM LEUVENSE L-1
Two flying prototypes and a ground test airframe of the L-1 are being built by Arplam, with first flight scheduled for early 1988. With a configuration reminiscent of the Polish SZD-45 Ogar or, more recently, the French Aérostructure Lutin 80, the L-1 was designed by students of the Leuvense University Aero Club, and its construction has been assisted financially by the Flemish regional government and the Belgian Department of Science.

TYPE: Tandem two-seat motor glider.
AIRFRAME: Cantilever low/mid-wing monoplane, with pod and boom fuselage and T tail unit. Construction is of laminated epoxy material, with tailboom and other areas reinforced in Kevlar. Non-retractable semi-recessed monowheel, tailwheel, and balancer wheel at each downturned wingtip.
POWER PLANT: One 29.8 kW (40 hp) modified Citroën Visa motorcar engine, mounted aft of rear cockpit and driving a Poincelet two-blade pusher propeller with spinner.

DIMENSIONS, EXTERNAL:

Wing span	12.20 m (40 ft 0¼ in)
Length overall	6.80 m (22 ft 3¾ in)

WEIGHT:

Max T-O weight	430 kg (948 lb)

PERFORMANCE (estimated):

Never-exceed speed	135 knots (250 km/h; 155 mph)
Max cruising speed	75 knots (140 km/h; 87 mph)
Stalling speed	39 knots (72 km/h; 45 mph)
Max rate of climb at S/L	120 m (394 ft)/min
Range at max cruising speed	432 nm (800 km; 497 miles)
Best glide ratio	24

Prototype of the Edmund Schneider ES 65 Platypus two-seat training sailplane

HB-Aircraft HB-23/2400 Scanliner

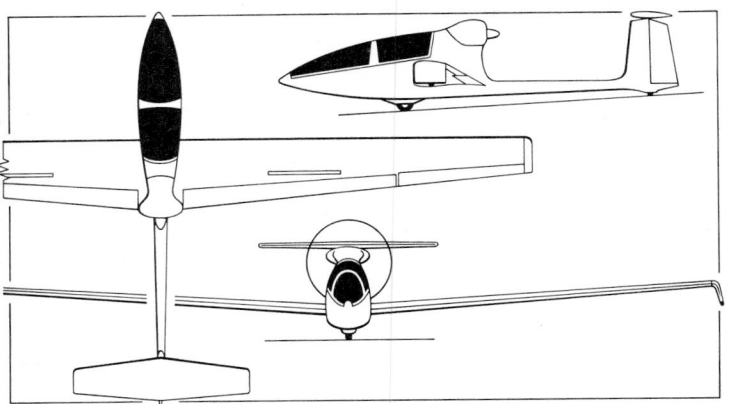

HB-Aircraft HB-23/2400 Hobbyliner two-seat motor glider

Arplam Leuvense L-1 tandem two-seat motor glider *(Jane's/Mike Keep)*

BRAZIL

AEROMOT
AERONAVES E MOTORES SA
Caixa Postal 8031, Aeroporto Internacional Salgado Filho,
90201, Porto Alegre, RS
Telephone: (0512) 42 3344
Telex: (051) 1991 AEMT
PRESIDENT: Claudio Miguel Barreto Viana
OPERATIONAL AND SPECIAL PROGRAMMES MANAGER:
Sílvio Barreto Viana

AEROMOT AMT-100 XIMANGO
The Ximango is the current production version of the French Aérostructure (Fournier) RF-10 motor glider.

First flown on 6 March 1981, the original RF-10 was generally similar to the Fournier RF-9 (1981-82 *Jane's*) but of plastics construction and having a carbonfibre main spar. A more powerful engine was fitted, fuel capacity increased, all control surfaces balanced, and the main landing gear had larger wheels. Two prototypes were built by Fournier Aviation in 1981, with low-set tailplanes, but a T tail was adopted for the production version, which first flew on 10 May 1984.

By the time French certification was granted on 23 October 1984 a total of 11 RF-10s had been completed, and by early 1985 orders from French production totalled 30, of which 13 had been delivered to customers in Brazil, France and Portugal.

The French company sold all production rights to Aeromot in July 1985. Brazilian CTA certification was granted on 5 June 1986, and series production is under way,

the Aeromot aircraft being known as the AMT-100 Ximango.

The Civilian Aeronautical Department ordered 100 Ximangos. One of the first two produced was certificated with a Brazilian Retimotor RM-2000A version of the Limbach/Volkswagen engine. Other sales and deliveries of the AMT-100 have been made, to private customers in Brazil and Argentina.

TYPE: Side by side two-seat training and sporting motor glider.

AIRFRAME: Cantilever low-wing monoplane, of glassfibre construction with a carbonfibre main spar. NACA 64₃618 section unswept wings, with 2° 30' dihedral from roots. Ailerons of GRP; light alloy Schempp-Hirth upper surface airbrakes. Wings can be detached from fuselage for transportation; outer portion of each wing can be folded inward for stowage, without disconnecting aileron controls. Semi-monocoque glassfibre fuselage, slightly swept fin and rudder, and fixed incidence T tailplane with elevator. Entire tail unit of GRP. Mechanically retractable mainwheels (tyre size 330 × 130), with hydraulic suspension and JPX hydraulic disc brakes; steerable tailwheel with size 210 × 65 tyre. One-piece cockpit canopy opens upward and rearward. Dual controls standard.

POWER PLANT: One 59.5 kW (80 hp) Limbach L 2000 EO1 flat-four engine, driving a Hoffmann two-blade three-position variable-pitch propeller. Fuel in two main tanks in wings, combined capacity 90 litres (23.8 US gallons; 19.75 Imp gallons). Electric starter and 12V 30A alternator.

DIMENSIONS, EXTERNAL:
Wing span	17.47 m (57 ft 3¾ in)
Wing aspect ratio	16.3
Width, wings folded	10.15 m (33 ft 3½ in)
Length overall	7.89 m (25 ft 10¾ in)
Height over tail	1.93 m (6 ft 4 in)

AREA:
Wings, gross	18.70 m² (201.3 sq ft)

WEIGHTS AND LOADINGS:
Weight empty	600 kg (1,323 lb)
Max T-O weight	800 kg (1,764 lb)
Max wing loading	42.78 kg/m² (8.77 lb/sq ft)
Max power loading	13.42 kg/kW (22.05 lb/hp)

PERFORMANCE, UNPOWERED (at max T-O weight):
Best glide ratio at 54 knots (100 km/h; 62 mph)	30
Min rate of sink at 49 knots (90 km/h; 56 mph)	0.96 m (3.15 ft)/s
Stalling speed	39 knots (72 km/h; 45 mph)
Max speed (smooth air)	133 knots (245 km/h; 153 mph)
Max speed (rough air)	97 knots (180 km/h; 112 mph)
g limits	+5.3/−2.65

PERFORMANCE, POWERED (at max T-O weight):
Max cruising speed	108 knots (200 km/h; 124 mph)
Econ cruising speed	97 knots (180 km/h; 112 mph)
Stalling speed	39 knots (72 km/h; 45 mph)
Max rate of climb at S/L	150 m (492 ft)/min
Service ceiling	5,000 m (16,400 ft)
Range with max fuel	728 nm (1,350 km; 839 miles)
Max endurance	7 h 30 min

IPE
INDÚSTRIA PARANAENSE DE ESTRUTURAS
Caixa Postal 7931, Rua J. Durski 357, 80.000 Curitiba, Paraná State
MANAGER: Eng J. C. Boscardin

IPE KW 1 b 2 QUERO QUERO II
Brazilian Air Force designation: Z-16
Four prototypes of the Quero Quero were built (first flight 1 October 1972), followed by 154 production

examples. Series production was halted in mid-1986, after an unsuccessful attempt to gain US certification. Sales were made to Brazilian flying clubs, the Brazilian Air Force Academy (16) and private owners.

In 1987 it was anticipated that IPE would rebuild between 10 and 30 of these aircraft damaged during intensive use.

TYPE: Single-seat training glider.

AIRFRAME: Cantilever high-wing monoplane, with Scheibe Spatz wing section, built of wood and plywood (Brazilian pine). Upper/lower surface spoilers. Non-retractable monowheel and tailwheel. One-piece canopy.

DIMENSIONS, EXTERNAL:
Wing span	15.00 m (49 ft 2½ in)
Wing aspect ratio	19.2
Length overall	6.47 m (21 ft 2¾ in)
Height overall	1.34 m (4 ft 4¾ in)

AREA:
Wings, gross	11.70 m² (125.9 sq ft)

WEIGHTS AND LOADING:
Weight empty	170 kg (374 lb)
Max T-O weight	270 kg (595 lb)
Max wing loading	21.3 kg/m² (4.36 lb/sq ft)

Chengdu X-7 Jian Fan two-seat glassfibre training glider (*Charles M. Gyenes*)

Shenyang X-9 two-seat training glider, with enclosed cockpits
(*Charles M. Gyenes*)

Aeromot AMT-100 Ximango side by side two-seat motor gliders

IPE 02b Nhapecan II two-seat training sailplanes for the Brazilian Air Force
Academy

Shenyang X-10 Qian Jin single-seat sailplane

PERFORMANCE (at max T-O weight):
Best glide ratio at 39 knots (73 km/h; 45 mph)   28
Min rate of sink at 33 knots (62 km/h; 39 mph)
  0.64 m (2.10 ft)/s
Stalling speed   33 knots (60 km/h; 38 mph)
Max speed (rough and smooth air)
  81 knots (150 km/h; 93 mph)
Max aero-tow speed   65 knots (120 km/h; 75 mph)
Max winch-launching speed   not applicable
g limit   +8

IPE KW 1 GB
This 15 metre Class version of the Quero Quero was constructed of wood and glassfibre. Two examples were built (one with water ballast). Further brief details can be found in the 1987-88 *Jane's*.

IPE 02b NHAPECAN II
Brazilian Air Force designation: TZ-14
The IPE 02 Nhapecan I first prototype (PP-ZQL) flew for the first time on 24 May 1979, and was described and illustrated in the 1983-84 *Jane's*.

The second prototype, known as the IPE 02b Nhapecan II, was considerably redesigned, with different dimensions and a more modern wing section based on the work of the Brazilian engineer Francisco Leme Galvão. As a result, performance was noticeably improved, and initial certification was followed by delivery of 15 to the Brazilian Air Force Academy. These were subsequently retrofitted with rudder and elevator mass balances. Final certification was granted and production resumed, with 12 delivered to Brazilian aero clubs by June 1987 and the 32nd aircraft then in final assembly. A large clubs contract for up to 72 Nhapecan IIs was anticipated in the Autumn of 1987. No more recent news has been received.

TYPE: Tandem two-seat training sailplane.

AIRFRAME: Shoulder-wing monoplane with Galvão BR-JKNA 3511/04 wing section. Ailerons and upper/lower surface spoilers. Wooden wings and tail surfaces; steel tube (4130) fuselage with glassfibre skin. Non-retractable monowheel, in streamline fairing, and tailwheel.

DIMENSIONS, EXTERNAL:
Wing span   16.60 m (54 ft 5½ in)
Wing aspect ratio   16.0
Length overall   8.54 m (28 ft 0¼ in)
Height over tail   1.90 m (6 ft 2¾ in)
AREA:
Wings, gross   17.20 m² (185.1 sq ft)
WEIGHTS AND LOADING:
Weight empty   340 kg (749 lb)
Max T-O weight   560 kg (1,234 lb)
Max wing loading   32.56 kg/m² (6.67 lb/sq ft)
PERFORMANCE (at max T-O weight):
Best glide ratio at 48 knots (88 km/h; 55 mph)
  better than 32
Min rate of sink at 38 knots (70 km/h; 43 mph):
  single-seat   0.65 m (2.13 ft)/s
  two-seat   0.75 m (2.46 ft)/s
Stalling speed   37 knots (68 km/h; 43 mph)
Max speed (smooth air)
  108 knots (200 km/h; 124 mph)

CISKEI

CISKEI AIRCRAFT INDUSTRIES (PTY) LTD
PO Box 1, Kidds Beach, Bisho 5264
Telephone: (04323) 694 02 or (011) 802 4342
The CAI, at a newly built factory at Bisho's Bulembu

Airport, was scheduled to begin production in November 1987 of the Austrian **HB-Aircraft Hobbyliner and Scanliner**. First orders, from the Wonderboom Flying School in Pretoria, South Africa, were received in mid-1987,

and deliveries were due to begin before the end of that year. No more recent news has been received.

CHINA
(PEOPLE'S REPUBLIC)

NATIONAL AIRCRAFT FACTORIES
WORKS: see Aircraft section
Sailplane development in China began in 1958, when a number of Polish gliding instructors were invited into the country to train air force cadets. Since that time the Chinese industry has manufactured more than 1,000 gliders of various types. The X prefix in designations stands for Xiangji, the Chinese word for glider.

CHENGDU X-7 JIAN FAN (SWORD POINT)
Built at the Chengdu sailplane factory in Sichuan Province, the X-7 was flown for the first time in October 1966. A total of 130 had been built by the beginning of 1980; present production status is not known.
TYPE: Tandem two-seat basic training glider.
AIRFRAME: High-wing monoplane, braced by single I strut on each side. Wing section Göttingen 535 (modified). Dihedral from roots. Single-spar constant chord wings, comprising a glassfibre/honeycomb/epoxy sandwich torsion box, fabric covered aft of spar. Glassfibre ailerons

and upper surface airbrakes. Semi-monocoque glassfibre pod and boom fuselage, moulded in two halves and joined at centreline. Fabric covered glassfibre cruciform tail unit; fin built integrally with fuselage. Non-retractable monowheel, nose-skid and tailskid. Tandem open cockpits, with windscreen.
DIMENSIONS, EXTERNAL:
Wing span   13.07 m (42 ft 10½ in)
Wing aspect ratio   9.5
Length overall   7.06 m (23 ft 2 in)
Height over tail   1.60 m (5 ft 3 in)
AREA:
Wings, gross   18.00 m² (193.75 sq ft)
WEIGHTS AND LOADING:
Weight empty   220 kg (485 lb)
Max T-O weight   370 kg (816 lb)
Max wing loading   20.55 kg/m² (4.21 lb/sq ft)
PERFORMANCE (at max T-O weight):
Best glide ratio at 30 knots (55 km/h; 34 mph)   12
Min rate of sink at 29 knots (53 km/h; 33 mph)
  1.40 m (4.59 ft)/s
Stalling speed   25 knots (45 km/h; 28 mph)

Max speed (smooth air)   81 knots (150 km/h; 93 mph)
Max speed (rough air)   54 knots (100 km/h; 62 mph)
Max winch-launching speed
  43 knots (80 km/h; 50 mph)
g limits   +4/−2

SHENYANG X-9
Used extensively in the Chinese People's Republic, the X-9 is a tandem two-seat training glider, said to have flying characteristics similar to those of the Schweizer SGS 2-33 (see US section). It is a braced high-wing monoplane, of wood and aluminium construction. Design and first flight took place in 1977, and approx 150 had been built by the Autumn of 1980. The X-9 is thought still to be in production.
DIMENSIONS, EXTERNAL:
Wing span   14.42 m (47 ft 3¾ in)
Wing aspect ratio   11.0
Length overall   7.335 m (24 ft 0¾ in)
Height over tail   2.32 m (7 ft 7¼ in)

AREA:

Wings, gross	18.90 m² (203.4 sq ft)

WEIGHTS AND LOADING:

Weight empty	230 kg (507 lb)
Max T-O weight	380 kg (837 lb)
Max wing loading	20.10 kg/m² (4.12 lb/sq ft)

PERFORMANCE (at max T-O weight):

Best glide ratio at 32 knots (60 km/h; 37 mph)	17
Min rate of sink at 30 knots (55 km/h; 34 mph)	
	0.96 m (3.15 ft)/s
Stalling speed	24 knots (43 km/h; 27 mph)
Max speed (smooth air)	81 knots (150 km/h; 93 mph)
Max speed (rough air)	54 knots (100 km/h; 62 mph)
Max aero-tow speed	65 knots (120 km/h; 75 mph)
Max winch-launching speed	
	54 knots (100 km/h; 62 mph)

SHENYANG X-10 QIAN JIN (FORWARD)

This single-seat high performance sailplane is a licence built version of the Polish SZD-8/14 Jaskolka, modernised to utilise both wood and glassfibre construction. It has been built in large numbers, and is probably the most widely used single-seater in China. Production status is unknown, although production was reportedly continuing in 1985.

DIMENSIONS, EXTERNAL:

Wing span	16.00 m (52 ft 6 in)
Wing aspect ratio	18.3
Length overall	7.625 m (25 ft 0¼ in)
Height over tail	1.605 m (5 ft 3¼ in)

AREA:

Wings, gross	14.00 m² (150.7 sq ft)

WEIGHTS AND LOADING:

Weight empty	264 kg (582 lb)
Max T-O weight	354 kg (780 lb)
Max wing loading	25.3 kg/m² (5.18 lb/sq ft)

PERFORMANCE (at max T-O weight):

Best glide ratio at 38 knots (70 km/h; 43 mph)	26
Min rate of sink at 37 knots (68 km/h; 42 mph)	
	0.75 m (2.46 ft)/s
Stalling speed	33 knots (60 km/h; 38 mph)
Max speed (smooth air)	135 knots (250 km/h; 155 mph)
Max speed (rough air)	97 knots (180 km/h; 112 mph)
Max aero-tow speed	81 knots (150 km/h; 93 mph)
Max winch-launching speed	
	59 knots (110 km/h; 68 mph)

CZECHOSLOVAKIA

AEROTECHNIK

AEROTECHNIK

Letiste Kunovice, 68604 Uh. Hradiste
Telephone: Uh. Hradiste 5510 and 5511
Telex: 60380
HEAD OF TECHNICAL DEPARTMENT: Ing J. Valný.

In addition to the overhaul and re-engining of Zlin 226s and 326s, Aerotechnik is producing for Czech aeroclubs the L-13SW Vivat, a motor glider version of the Let L-13 Blanik.

AEROTECHNIK L-13SW VIVAT

Design of the L-13SW began in the Summer of 1976, and construction of three prototypes started in the Autumn of the following year. The first of these (OK-068) made its initial flight on 10 May 1978. Aerotechnik is manufacturing 200 of these aircraft for use by Czech aeroclubs. The first production example flew for the first time in November 1983, and more than 55 had been completed by early 1988, in which year Aerotechnik expected to produce a further 25.

The Vivat, which features side by side seating instead of the tandem layout of the Blaník sailplane on which it is based, has been optimised for both elementary and advanced training. Authorised manoeuvres include sharp turns and stalls up to 60°, slips, skids, and unlimited spinning.

The following description applies to the initial production version:

TYPE: Side by side two-seat motor glider.
AIRFRAME: Cantilever mid-wing monoplane. NACA wing sections: 63₂A615 at root, 63₂A612 at tip. Dihedral 3°. Incidence 4° at root, 1° at tip. Sweepforward 5° at quarter-chord. All-metal single-spar wings, with light alloy riveted skin and wingtip 'salmons'. Fabric covered light alloy ailerons and slotted area-increasing flaps. DFS type light alloy airbrakes in upper and lower surfaces. Oval section fuselage, forward portion being a welded metal tube structure with glassfibre skin, rear portion a riveted light alloy semi-monocoque. Light alloy fin and fixed incidence tailplane; fabric covered rudder and elevators. Trim tab in each elevator. Horizontal tail surfaces fold upward for transportation. Mechanically semi-retractable rubber sprung monowheel, with size 350 × 135-125 mm tyre (pressure 3.2 bars; 46.4 lb/sq in); non-retractable rubber sprung controllable tailwheel, with size 200 × 50-90 mm tyre (pressure 1.2 bars; 17.4 lb/sq in); and retractable outrigger wheels in wingtip 'salmons'. Moravan NP mechanical brake on monowheel. One-piece Plexiglas bubble canopy, raised upwards and rearwards on struts to permit access to cockpit. Tesla LS 5 VHF com radio and standard VFR instrumentation.

POWER PLANT: One 48.5 kW (65 hp) Aerotechnik (formerly Walter) Mikron III S (A) inline engine, driving an Aeron Brno V 208 fixed-pitch or Hoffmann HO-V-62R two-blade wooden propeller with spinner. Welded light alloy fuel tank in centre-fuselage, max capacity 50 litres (13.2 US gallons; 11 Imp gallons).

DIMENSIONS, EXTERNAL:

Wing span	16.705 m (54 ft 9¾ in)
Wing aspect ratio	13.8
Length overall	8.30 m (27 ft 2¾ in)
Height overall	2.30 m (7 ft 6½ in)

AREA:

Wings, gross	20.20 m² (217.4 sq ft)

WEIGHTS AND LOADINGS:

Weight empty, equipped	463 kg (1,021 lb)
Max T-O weight	670 kg (1,477 lb)
Max wing loading	33.17 kg/m² (6.79 lb/sq ft)
Max power loading	13.8 kg/kW (22.72 lb/hp)

PERFORMANCE, UNPOWERED (at max T-O weight with propeller feathered. A: V 208, B: HO-V-62R):

Best glide ratio:

A at 48 knots (90 km/h; 56 mph)	21
B at 53 knots (98 km/h; 61 mph)	24

Min rate of sink:

A at 43 knots (80 km/h; 50 mph)	1.20 m (3.94 ft)/s
B at 46 knots (85 km/h; 53 mph)	1.05 m (3.44 ft)/s
Stalling speed: A, B	34 knots (62 km/h; 39 mph)

Max speed (smooth air):

A, B	124 knots (230 km/h; 143 mph)

Max speed (rough air):

A, B	86 knots (160 km/h; 99 mph)
g limits: A, B	+5.3/-2.6

PERFORMANCE, POWERED (at max T-O weight; A and B as above):

Max cruising speed:

A	94 knots (175 km/h; 109 mph)
B	100 knots (185 km/h; 115 mph)
Econ cruising speed: A	84 knots (155 km/h; 96 mph)
B	86 knots (160 km/h; 99 mph)
Stalling speed: A, B	33 knots (60 km/h; 37 mph)
Max rate of climb at S/L: A	140 m (460 ft)/min
B	198 m (650 ft)/min
Service ceiling: A, B	4,000 m (13,125 ft)
T-O run: A	200 m (655 ft)
B	110 m (361 ft)
T-O to 15 m (50 ft): A	430 m (1,410 ft)
B	370 m (1,214 ft)
Landing from 15 m (50 ft): A, B	370 m (1,214 ft)
Landing run: A, B	110 m (361 ft)

Range (depending on weight of crew):

A, B, 30 litres (7.9 US gallons; 6.6 Imp gallons) fuel
205 nm (380 km; 236 miles)
A, B, 50 litres (13.2 US gallons; 11 Imp gallons) fuel
345 nm (640 km; 398 miles)

LET

LET NÁRODNÍ PODNIK (Let National Corporation)

Uherské Hradiste-Kunovice
Telephone: Kunovice 411111
Telex: 060387 and 060388
OFFICERS: see Aircraft section

LET L-23 BLANÍK

Well known as the source of the L-13 Blaník sailplane (1984-85 and earlier *Jane's*), Let designed the L-23 version to meet the requirements of OSTIV 1986 and the Utility category of JAR 22. Construction of a prototype began in July 1986, and this aircraft (OK-8621) made its first flight in mid-1987. Production was planned to begin in 1988.

More than 2,600 examples of the L-13 were built. Major design changes in the L-23 include improved cockpit comfort and view, and the introduction of a T tail unit.

TYPE: Tandem two-seat training and performance soaring sailplane.
AIRFRAME: Cantilever shoulder-wing monoplane. NACA wing sections: 63₂A-615 at root, 63₂A-612 at tip. Dihedral 3°. Incidence 4°. Sweepforward 5° at quarter-chord. All-metal wings, with three-bolt attachment to fuselage each side. Single main spar forms rigid torsion box with leading-edge. Ailerons and Fowler trailing-edge slotted flaps are of fabric covered light alloy. DFS type upper and lower surface airbrakes. Downturned wingtips are of polyester FRP. All-metal semi-monocoque oval section fuselage, forward portion comprising a frame of longerons and bulkheads with stressed skin; rear portion consists of two semi-monocoque halves, riveted to reinforcing bulkheads. Sweptback fin and rudder; non-swept, fixed incidence T tailplane with elevators. Fin (integral with fuselage) and tailplane are all-metal; rudder and elevators are of fabric covered light alloy. Trim tab in each elevator. Single mainwheel, with Let oleo-pneumatic shock absorber and mechanical drum brake, is fitted with Rudy Rijen Otrokovice Barum tyre, size 350 × 135 mm, pressure 2.5 bars (36 lb/sq in), and can be semi-retracted manually by lever mechanism. Non-retractable rubber sprung tailwheel is fully castoring and spring centred. Small undernose skid. Aero-tow hook forward of this, ahead of first fuselage bulkhead; CG towing hook optional. Winch towing coupling each side at fourth fuselage bulkhead. Tandem seating for one or two occupants, with dual controls, upholstered seat cushions, GRP backrests and four-point harnesses standard. Forward backrest adjustable for length and inclination; both backrests shaped for back type parachutes. Space for 20 kg (44 lb) of baggage. Separate Plexiglas canopies, the forward one (which is jettisonable from either seat) opening sideways to starboard; rear canopy is hinged at rear and opens upward. Both cockpits are ventilated, and have provision for radio, oxygen equipment and an artificial horizon.

DIMENSIONS, EXTERNAL:

Wing span	16.20 m (53 ft 1¾ in)
Wing aspect ratio	13.7
Length overall	8.50 m (27 ft 10¾ in)
Height over tail	1.90 m (6 ft 2¾ in)

AREA:

Wings, gross	19.15 m² (206.1 sq ft)

WEIGHTS AND LOADINGS (A: single-seat, B: two-seat):

Weight empty: A, B	310 kg (683 lb)
Max T-O weight: A	420 kg (926 lb)
B	510 kg (1,124 lb)
Max wing loading: A	21.93 kg/m² (4.49 lb/sq ft)
B	26.63 kg/m² (5.45 lb/sq ft)

PERFORMANCE (estimated at max T-O weight, A and B as above):

Best glide ratio:

A at 38 knots (70 km/h; 44 mph)	28
B at 49 knots (90 km/h; 56 mph)	28

Min rate of sink:

A at 38 knots (70 km/h; 44 mph)	0.73 m (2.40 ft)/s
B at 43 knots (80 km/h; 50 mph)	0.82 m (2.69 ft)/s
Stalling speed: A	28 knots (51 km/h; 32 mph)
B	31 knots (56 km/h; 35 mph)

Max speed (smooth air):

A, B	138 knots (255 km/h; 158 mph)

Max speed (rough air):

A, B	86 knots (160 km/h; 99 mph)

Max aero-tow speed:

A, B	81 knots (150 km/h; 93 mph)

Max winch-launching speed:

A, B	64 knots (120 km/h; 74 mph)

Max speed for flap extension:

A, B	70 knots (130 km/h; 81 mph)
g limits: A	+6/-3
B	+5.3/-1.5

VSO

VYVOJOVÁ SKUPINA ORLICAN

c/o Orlican Národní Podnik, 56537 Chocen
Telephone: Chocen 952
Telex: 0 196 210

DESIGNER: Dipl Ing Paval Tomaua

This group was formed by members of the former VSB (1973-74 *Jane's*) and some of the design staff of the Orlican National Works. Its first product is the VSO 10.

VSO 10 GRADIENT

Design of the VSO 10 began in March 1972. Construction of three prototypes (one for structural test and two for flight test) began in 1975, and the first flight took place on 26 October 1976. Series production began in December 1978.

Aerotechnik L-13SW Vivat, a powered version of the original Blaník sailplane

VSO 10C Gradient single-seat Club Class sailplane (Adolf Wilsch)

Prototype of the Let L-23 Blaník two-seat training sailplane

Centrair Pégase B single-seat Standard Class sailplane (Peter F. Selinger)

By the beginning of 1988 a total of 184 had been delivered to Czechoslovak aeroclubs, including 12 of the VSO 10C Club Class version with non-retractable monowheel.

TYPE: Single-seat Standard and Club Class sailplane.

AIRFRAME: Cantilever shoulder-wing monoplane, with Wortmann wing sections: FX-61-163 at root, FX-60-126 at tip. Dihedral 3°. All-wood single-spar forward-swept wings with glassfibre sandwich skin. All-metal DFS airbrakes on upper surfaces. All-wood slotted ailerons. Glassfibre monocoque front and centre fuselage sections, latter reinforced by steel tube frame. Monocoque rear fuselage of aluminium alloy sheet. Metal T tail with fabric covered elevators and rudder. Fixed incidence tailplane. Retractable rubber sprung monowheel (tyre pressure approx 2.45 bars; 35.5 lb/sq in), with drum brake.

Semi-recessed unsprung tailwheel. Detachable cockpit canopy. Provision for 56 litres (14.8 US gallons; 12.3 Imp gallons) water ballast.

DIMENSIONS, EXTERNAL:
Wing span	15.00 m (49 ft 2½ in)
Wing aspect ratio	18.75
Length overall	7.00 m (22 ft 11¾ in)
Height over tail	1.38 m (4 ft 6¼ in)

AREA:
Wings, gross	12.00 m² (129.2 sq ft)

WEIGHTS AND LOADING (both versions):
Weight empty	250 kg (551 lb)
Max T-O weight	380 kg (837 lb)
Max wing loading	31.67 kg/m² (6.49 lb/sq ft)

PERFORMANCE (at max T-O weight):
Best glide ratio:		
10 at 49 knots (90 km/h; 56 mph)		36
10C at 51 knots (95 km/h; 59 mph)		34
Min rate of sink:		
10 at 39 knots (73 km/h; 45 mph)	0.64 m (2.10 ft)/s	
10C at 43 knots (79 km/h; 49 mph)	0.72 m (2.36 ft)/s	
Stalling speed: 10	37 knots (68 km/h; 43 mph)	
10C	38 knots (70 km/h; 44 mph)	
Max speed (smooth air):		
10, 10C	135 knots (250 km/h; 155 mph)	
Max speed (rough air), and max aero-tow speed:		
10, 10C	86 knots (160 km/h; 99 mph)	
Max winch-launching speed:		
10, 10C	65 knots (120 km/h; 75 mph)	
g limits: 10, 10C	+5.3/-3.5	

FRANCE

CENTRAIR
SA CENTRAIR
Aérodrome Le Blanc, BP 44, 36300 Le Blanc
Telephone: (54) 37 06 91 and 37 07 96
Telex: 750272 F
PRESIDENT/DIRECTOR GENERAL: Marc Ranjon

Centrair was founded in January 1970 by M Marc Ranjon, an ex-Aéronavale pilot and a flying and gliding instructor. It had a 1987 workforce of 89 people, with another 21 at its Chauvigny subsidiary, Composites Aéronautiques Avancés (CA2). These two companies specialise in constructions using carbonfibre, glassfibre and Kevlar. Centrair has a covered factory space of 7,000 m² (75,347 sq ft) spread over nine locations. CA2 has 500 m² (5,382 sq ft) spread over nine locations. The two companies have their own research and development department, and are major subcontractors for Aérospatiale, Dassault-Breguet, Matra and other French aerospace companies (see main Aircraft section).

CENTRAIR 101 and PÉGASE
Of all-French design, the Centrair 101 was available in 1988 in the following versions:

101 Club. Basic version, with non-retractable monowheel, no water ballast and no instrumentation. First flown November 1981, certificated June 1982. Total of 38 delivered by early 1988.

Pégase A. As 101, but with retractable monowheel. Prototype (F-WFRA), first flown on 20 November 1981,

was of this version. Certificated June 1982; winglet version first flown May 1982. Total of 312 built by early 1988.

Pégase B. Identical to Pégase A except standard water ballast capacity of 160 litres (42.3 US gallons; 35.2 Imp gallons). First flown May 1984. Total of 30 delivered by early 1988.

Pégase D. Definitive competition version, embodying experience gained with Pégase BC. Certificated by DGAC on 3 November 1986; total of 32 delivered by early 1988.

TYPE: Single-seat Standard or Club Class sailplane.

AIRFRAME: Cantilever shoulder-wing monoplane, constructed of Conticell sandwich and epoxy resin, with glassfibre roving spar. Onera wing sections: COAP 1 at root, COAP 2 at tip. Dihedral 2° 18′. Double plate upper surface airbrakes. Turned-down wingtips. Glassfibre/epoxy resin monocoque fuselage (reinforced with carbonfibre on all except 101). Cantilever T tailplane, with elevator. All control surfaces mass balanced. Retractable (all Pégase variants) or non-retractable (101 Club) unsprung monowheel (size 5.00-5, pressure 3.5 bars; 50.75 lb/sq in), with drum brake (hydraulic disc brake on Pégase B from September 1985); rubber tail bumper, with metal skid or recessed wheel. Nosewheel on 101 Club. Nose or CG towing hook. One-piece cockpit canopy, hinged at front and opening upward. Pégase B and D have two 80 litre (21.1 US gallon; 17.6 Imp gallon) leading-edge water ballast tanks as standard.

DIMENSIONS, EXTERNAL (all versions):
Wing span	15.00 m (49 ft 2½ in)
Wing aspect ratio	21.4
Length overall	6.82 m (22 ft 4½ in)
Height over tail	1.42 m (4 ft 8 in)

AREA:
Wings, gross (all versions)	10.50 m² (113.0 sq ft)

WEIGHTS AND LOADINGS:
Weight empty, equipped: 101	245 kg (540 lb)
Pégase A	251 kg (553 lb)
Pégase B	256 kg (564 lb)
Pégase D	252 kg (556 lb)
Max T-O weight: 101, Pégase A	455 kg (1,003 lb)
Pégase B, D	505 kg (1,113 lb)
Max wing loading:	
101, Pégase A	43.3 kg/m² (8.87 lb/sq ft)
Pégase B, D	48.1 kg/m² (9.86 lb/sq ft)

PERFORMANCE (at max T-O weight):
Best glide ratio:		
101 at 50 knots (92 km/h; 57 mph)		38
Pégase A at 53 knots (98 km/h; 61 mph)		40
Pégase B at 55 knots (102 km/h; 63 mph)		40
Pégase D at 57 knots (105 km/h; 65 mph)		42.5
Min rate of sink:		
101 at 39 knots (72 km/h; 45 mph)	0.65 m (2.13 ft)/s	
Pégase A at 43 knots (80 km/h; 50 mph)		
	0.67 m (2.20 ft)/s	

Pégase B at 45 knots (83 km/h; 51 mph)
0.65 m (2.13 ft)/s
Pégase D at 46 knots (85 km/h; 53 mph)
0.62 m (2.03 ft)/s
Max speed (smooth air):
all versions 135 knots (250 km/h; 155 mph)
Max speed (rough air):
all versions 97 knots (180 km/h; 112 mph)
Max aero-tow and max winch-launching speed:
all versions 86 knots (160 km/h; 99 mph)

CENTRAIR 2001 MARIANNE

The Marianne is a tandem two-seat sailplane for training and aerobatics. All structural calculations were made by Dassault-Breguet, and the programme receives financial assistance from the French government. The Marianne was the winner of an FFVV competition, and 250 are expected to be acquired for use by French aero clubs.

First flight by prototype F-WGMA was made on 19 September 1985. Certification was granted on 29 January 1987; by early 1988, Centrair had delivered 71 production examples.

AIRFRAME: Cantilever shoulder-wing monoplane. Onera laminar flow aerofoil sections: COAP 1 at root, COAP 2 at tip. Laminated wings, of Klégécel/glassfibre/epoxy resin construction with glassfibre roving spar. Dihedral 3°. Ailerons of similar construction. No flaps. Double

plate aluminium upper surface airbrakes. Laminated fuselage of Klégécel, glassfibre, carbonfibre and epoxy. Cantilever T tailplane, with elevator; construction of glassfibre and epoxy. Non-retractable 5.00-5 monowheel, tyre pressure 3.5 bars (50.75 lb/sq in), with hydraulic disc brake; non-retractable 3.00-3 nosewheel. Two seats in tandem under separate canopies: front canopy opens forward, rear canopy sideways to starboard. No water ballast. Aero-tow and winch-launching hooks.

DIMENSIONS, EXTERNAL:
Wing span	18.55 m (60 ft 10¼ in)
Wing aspect ratio	19.9
Length overall	9.00 m (29 ft 6½ in)
Height over tail	1.55 m (5 ft 1 in)

AREA:
Wings, gross	17.185 m² (185.0 sq ft)

WEIGHTS AND LOADING:
Weight empty, equipped	430 kg (948 lb)
Max T-O weight	650 kg (1,433 lb)
Max wing loading	37.82 kg/m² (7.75 lb/sq ft)

PERFORMANCE (at max T-O weight):
Best glide ratio at 57 knots (105 km/h; 65 mph)	40
Min rate of sink at 46 knots (85 km/h; 53 mph)	0.65 m (2.13 ft)/s
Stalling speed	37 knots (67 km/h; 42 mph)
Max speed (smooth air)	135 knots (250 km/h; 155 mph)
Max speed (rough air), and max aero-tow speed	92 knots (170 km/h; 105 mph)

Max winch-launching speed
70 knots (130 km/h; 81 mph)
g limits +4.3/-1.5 ultimate

CENTRAIR 2001M MARIANNE M

Centrair has received 23 orders for this powered version of the Marianne, and hoped to fly a prototype by the close of 1988. Airframe is identical to the sailplane but has underwing balancer wheels for take-off and landing.

POWER PLANT: One 45 kW (60 hp) Volkswagen engine (JPX modification), driving a two-blade fixed-pitch propeller and mounted in a detachable pod which also accommodates a 15 litre (4 US gallon; 3.3 Imp gallon) fuel tank.

WEIGHTS AND LOADINGS:
Weight empty, equipped	500 kg (1,102 lb)
Max T-O weight	725 kg (1,598 lb)
Max wing loading	42.15 kg/m² (8.64 lb/sq ft)
Max power loading	16.21 kg/kW (26.64 lb/hp)

PERFORMANCE, POWERED (estimated at max T-O weight):
Max cruising speed	108 knots (200 km/h; 124 mph)
Econ cruising speed	84 knots (155 km/h; 96 mph)
Stalling speed	49 knots (90 km/h; 56 mph)
Best glide ratio at 54 knots (100 km/h; 62 mph)	31
Min rate of sink at 52 knots (96 km/h; 60 mph)	1.00 m (3.28 ft)/s

FOURNIER
AVIONS RENÉ FOURNIER
Aérodrome d'Athée-Nitray, 37270 Montlouis-sur-Loire
Telephone: 47 50 68 30
Telex: 751 236 F
DIRECTOR: René Fournier
PRODUCTION: Coparavia SA, Beas de Segura (Jaen), Andalucia, Spain

M René Fournier re-established this company to put back into series production his RF 5 motor glider, of which more than 200 were delivered to customers in about 30 countries. All manufacturing and assembly is now done by partner company Coparavia SA in Spain, with the French company acting solely as marketer and distributor for the aircraft. New production began in May 1987, and the RF 5 is available in both kit form and ready to fly. The co-production agreement provides also for re-introduction of the Fournier RF 4.

FOURNIER RF 5
TYPE: Tandem two-seat motor glider.
AIRFRAME: Cantilever low-wing monoplane. NACA wing sections: 23015 at root, 23012 at tip. Dihedral 3° 15' at main spar centreline. Incidence 4° at root, 0° at tip. No sweepback. All-wood single-spar wings, with plywood

and fabric covering. Fabric covered wooden ailerons. Three-section metal skinned spoilers on each upper surface. Outer wing panels fold inward for transportation and storage. All-wood oval section fuselage of bulkheads and stringers, plywood and fabric covered. Conventional all-wood tail unit, plywood and fabric covered, is detachable for transportation. Fixed incidence tailplane; Flettner tab in port elevator. Spring assisted, manually retractable Tost monowheel, with twin oleo-pneumatic shock absorbers. Dunlop tyre, size 6.00-6, pressure 1.96 bars (28.4 lb/sq in). Manually operated mainwheel brake. Tailwheel, also with shock absorber, is steerable by rudder pedals. Outrigger wheel beneath each wing just inboard of fold line. Adjustable tandem seats for pilot and passenger, with dual controls, under one-piece sideways opening canopy. Adjustable rudder pedals and canopy emergency release standard. Space for 10 kg (22 lb) of baggage aft of rear seat. Cockpits heated and ventilated.

POWER PLANT: One 59 kW (80 hp) Limbach L 2000 EOI flat-four engine, driving a Hoffmann HO-V-62-R/160 two-blade fixed-pitch propeller with spinner. Fuel in two wingroot leading-edge metal tanks, total capacity 60 litres (15.9 US gallons; 13.2 Imp gallons). Refuelling point on top of port wing.

DIMENSIONS, EXTERNAL:
Wing span	13.74 m (45 ft 1 in)
Width, wings folded	8.60 m (28 ft 2½ in)
Wing aspect ratio	12.5
Length overall	7.80 m (25 ft 7¼ in)
Height overall, tail down	1.96 m (6 ft 5 in)

AREA:
Wings, gross	15.12 m² (162.8 sq ft)

WEIGHTS AND LOADINGS:
Weight empty	420 kg (926 lb)
Max T-O weight	650 kg (1,433 lb)
Max wing loading	42.8 kg/m² (8.77 lb/sq ft)
Max power loading	10.9 kg/kW (17.91 lb/hp)

PERFORMANCE (at max T-O weight):
Never-exceed speed	135 knots (250 km/h; 155 mph)
Max cruising speed	113 knots (210 km/h; 130 mph)
Stalling speed, 'clean' configuration	43 knots (78 km/h; 49 mph)
Max rate of climb at S/L	195 m (640 ft)/min
T-O and landing run	200 m (655 ft)
Range with max fuel	378-485 nm (700-900 km; 435-559 miles)
Best glide ratio	20
g limits	+6/-3

ISSOIRE
ISSOIRE-AVIATION SA (Groupe Siren)
Aérodrome d'Issoire-le-Broc (Puy-de-Dôme), BP No.1, 63501 Issoire Cédex
Telephone: (73) 89 01 54
Telex: 990 185 F ISSAVIA
PRESIDENT/DIRECTOR GENERAL: Xavier Laguette
TECHNICAL DIRECTOR: Xavier Lauras

This company is one of three forming the Siren group, the others being Siren SA (which see) and Aéro Berry. Issoire is responsible for the PIK-20E2F and PIK-30 self-launching sailplanes.

ISSOIRE PIK-20E2F
Details of the PIK-20 sailplane can be found under the Eiri heading in the Finnish sections of the 1979-80 and previous editions of *Jane's*.

The prototype of the PIK-20E powered version flew for the first time on 2 October 1976 and was described in the 1977-78 *Jane's*. The production prototype made its first powered flight on 18 March 1978, and series production began in late 1978. Approx 50 were delivered by Eiri before production in Finland ended in 1980. A description can be found in the 1980-81 *Jane's*.

The French built version has a Rotax 505 (instead of 501) engine and is designated PIK-20E2F. By January 1987, when the last figures were provided, a total of 129 PIK-20s had been delivered, including Eiri production.

As part of a programme to collect airflow data on flight at low Reynolds numbers, NASA's Dryden Research Center is using a PIK-20 as a testbed to develop wing profiles appropriate to high-altitude low-speed flight. Such flight characteristics are of interest to researchers investigating possible designs for high-altitude unmanned aircraft which could serve as long term communications relays, using solar power and beamed microwave energy for electric propulsion.

For initial testing, a hot-wire anemometer and tape recorder are attached to the PIK-20's wing. The recorded sound registers distinct differences as the airflow changes from laminar (a smooth, soft sound) to transitional (a

hissing noise) to turbulent (a roar). The pilot, using a cockpit microphone, gives a simultaneous voice record of his flight profile, and the airflow changes are demonstrated visually by coating the wing with dark oil, which forms distinctive patterns as the flow changes. Later testing is expected to include installing experimental aerofoil glove sections on the aircraft's wings.

The following description applies to the standard production PIK-20E2F:

TYPE: Single-seat self-launching 15 metre Class sailplane.

AIRFRAME: Cantilever shoulder-wing monoplane with T tail. Wortmann wing sections: FX-67-K-170 at root, FX-67-K-150 at tip. Dihedral 3°. Sweepback 1° 21.6'. Glassfibre/epoxy/PVC foam sandwich wings. Spars of carbonfibre reinforced epoxy. Schempp-Hirth airbrakes standard. Plain flaps ('flaperons') function as both flaps and ailerons. Provision for 80 litres (21.1 US gallons; 17.5 Imp gallons) of water ballast. Glassfibre/epoxy monocoque fuselage, reinforced with ribs and carbonfibre. T tail of similar construction to wings. Fixed incidence tailplane, with one-piece elevator. Retractable sprung Tost monowheel with drum brake. Steerable rubber sprung tailwheel. Non-retractable wingtip wheels. Forward hinged one-piece cockpit canopy. Optional Tost towing hook.

POWER PLANT: One 32 kW (43 hp) Rotax 505 two-cylinder two-stroke engine, with reduction drive to a Hoffmann two-blade fixed-pitch wooden propeller and retracting manually into fuselage aft of cockpit when not in use. Electric starter. Kevlar fuel tank, capacity 30 litres (7.9 US gallons; 6.6 Imp gallons).

DIMENSIONS, EXTERNAL:
Wing span	15.00 m (49 ft 2½ in)
Wing aspect ratio	22.5
Length overall	6.53 m (21 ft 5 in)
Height over tail	1.47 m (4 ft 10 in)

AREA:
Wings, gross	10.00 m² (107.6 sq ft)

WEIGHTS AND LOADINGS:
Weight empty	310 kg (683 lb)
Max water ballast	80 kg (176 lb)
Max T-O weight	470 kg (1,036 lb)
Max wing loading	47.0 kg/m² (9.63 lb/sq ft)
Max power loading	14.62 kg/kW (24.03 lb/hp)

PERFORMANCE, UNPOWERED (at max T-O weight, engine retracted):
Best glide ratio at 63 knots (117 km/h; 73 mph)	41
Min rate of sink at 47 knots (88 km/h; 55 mph)	0.70 m (2.30 ft)/s
Stalling speed	41 knots (75 km/h; 47 mph)
Max speed (smooth air)	154 knots (285 km/h; 177 mph)
Max speed (rough air)	119 knots (220 km/h; 136 mph)
Max aero-tow speed	105 knots (195 km/h; 121 mph)
Max winch-launching speed	67 knots (125 km/h; 78 mph)

PERFORMANCE, POWERED (at max T-O weight except where indicated):
Cruising speed (75% power) at 370 kg (816 lb) AUW	73 knots (135 km/h; 84 mph)
Stalling speed	41 knots (75 km/h; 47 mph)
Max rate of climb at S/L	162 m (531 ft)/min
Service ceiling	5,200 m (17,050 ft)
T-O to 15 m (50 ft)	less than 500 m (1,640 ft)
Landing run	300 m (985 ft)
Range with max fuel	156 nm (290 km; 180 miles)

ISSOIRE PIK-30
Construction of this aircraft, which is basically a 17 metre Open Class version of the PIK-20E2F, started in 1983. The prototype first flew in April 1984, followed by a second aircraft, to production standard, in December 1984. French certification was awarded in September 1985. Thirty PIK-30s had been ordered by February 1988, including one for evaluation by the French Air Force and others for customers in France, New Zealand, UK and USA. Production is at the rate of one per month.

The PIK-30 incorporates removable, 1 metre long, glassfibre wingtips, enabling it to qualify also in the FAI 15 m Class if desired.

Prototype Centrair Marianne two-seat training and aerobatic sailplane

Issoire built PIK-30 self-launching sailplane, with power plant extended

Fournier RF 5 tandem two-seat motor glider

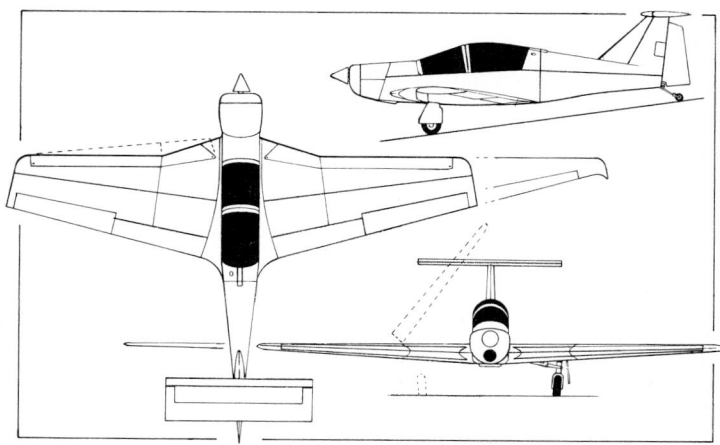

Lucas L6-7 sport aircraft, with extended-wing motor glider version shown in broken line *(Michael A. Badrocke)*

POWER PLANT: As for PIK-20E2F, plus automatic system for vertical positioning of propeller when engine is stopped. Fuel capacity 29 litres (7.7 US gallons; 6.4 Imp gallons).
DIMENSIONS, EXTERNAL: As PIK-20E2F except:
Wing span	17.00 m (55 ft 9¼ in)
Wing aspect ratio	27.2
AREA:
Wings, gross	10.63 m² (114.42 sq ft)
WEIGHTS AND LOADINGS:
Weight empty	310 kg (683 lb)
Max T-O weight	460 kg (1,014 lb)

Max wing loading	43.27 kg/m² (8.86 lb/sq ft)
Max power loading	14.38 kg/kW (23.58 lb/hp)

PERFORMANCE, UNPOWERED (at max T-O weight):
Best glide ratio at 59 knots (110 km/h; 68 mph)	45
Min rate of sink at 41 knots (75 km/h; 47 mph)	0.54 m (1.77 ft)/s
Stalling speed	38 knots (70 km/h; 44 mph)
Never-exceed speed	140 knots (260 km/h; 162 mph)
Max speed (rough air), and max aero-tow speed	102 knots (190 km/h; 118 mph)

Max winch-launching speed	67 knots (125 km/h; 78 mph)
g limits	+5.3/−2.65
PERFORMANCE, POWERED (at max T-O weight):
Max cruising speed	73 knots (135 km/h; 84 mph)
Econ cruising speed	65 knots (120 km/h; 75 mph)
Stalling speed	38 knots (70 km/h; 44 mph)
Max rate of climb at S/L	240 m (785 ft)/min
T-O run	280 m (920 ft)
Landing run	300 m (985 ft)
Range with max fuel	162 nm (300 km; 186 miles)

LUCAS
EMILE LUCAS
Corbonod, 01420 Seyssel
Telephone: (1) 50 59 27 54
In addition to marketing plans of his L5 light aircraft (see Sport Aircraft section), Mr Lucas has built the prototype of a new aircraft, the L6-7, which can be operated as a motor glider. The first flight of the prototype L6-7 had been expected to take place in 1987.

LUCAS L6-7
The L6-7 has been designed as a sporting aircraft in its basic form, capable of conversion to a motor glider by the addition of a 2 m (6 ft 6¾ in) extension panel to each outer wing. Power plant is a 62 kW (83 hp) Limbach flat-four engine, driving a two-blade variable-pitch propeller.

Standard fuel capacity is 50 litres (13.2 US gallons; 11 Imp gallons), in a fuselage tank aft of the rear cockpit, but this can be increased in the motor glider by a further 260 litres (68.7 US gallons; 57.2 Imp gallons) carried in four tanks in the wings.
The following details apply to the motor glider version:
DIMENSIONS, EXTERNAL:
Wing span	13.50 m (44 ft 3½ in)
Wing aspect ratio	11.4
AREA:
Wings, gross	16.00 m² (172.2 sq ft)
WEIGHTS AND LOADINGS:
Weight empty	485 kg (1,069 lb)
Normal T-O weight (fuselage fuel only)	690 kg (1,521 lb)

Max T-O weight (fuselage and wing fuel)	905 kg (1,995 lb)
Wing loading:
at normal T-O weight	43.12 kg/m² (8.84 lb/sq ft)
at max T-O weight	56.56 kg/m² (11.59 lb/sq ft)
Power loading:
at normal T-O weight	11.16 kg/kW (18.33 lb/hp)
at max T-O weight	14.63 kg/kW (24.04 lb/hp)
PERFORMANCE (estimated, at normal T-O weight except where indicated):
Max cruising speed	195 knots (361 km/h; 224 mph)
Econ cruising speed	165 knots (306 km/h; 190 mph)
Max rate of climb at S/L	195 m (640 ft)/min
Service ceiling	5,500 m (18,045 ft)
T-O run	360 m (1,181 ft)
Landing run	200 m (656 ft)

SIREN — *See Issoire*

STRALPES AÉRO
STRALPES AÉRO SARL
BP 14, Aérodrome RN6, 73190 Challes-les-Eaux
Telephone: (79) 70 49 27
DIRECTOR: Christian Brondel
STRALPES Aéro (Société de Traitement, Réparation, Approvisionnement, Livraison de Pièces En Stratifié) was formed in March 1979. It is a distributor and maintenance centre for Glaser-Dirks sailplanes, and developed the ST-11 and other designs of its own.

STRALPES AÉRO ST-11
Objective of the ST-11's designers was to produce a low cost sailplane for club and personal use, with a wing span of

less than 15 m and built of composite materials. The prototype (F-WBCB) made its first flight on 29 August 1982. General appearance is shown in the accompanying photograph. An **ST-11M** powered version was also designed (see 1986-87 edition).

TYPE: Single-seat Club Class sailplane.

AIRFRAME: Cantilever mid-wing monoplane, with cruciform tail unit, non-retractable semi-recessed monowheel and tailskid. Wings have a STRALPES Aéro (modified Wortmann) section, with thickness/chord ratio of 15% at root and 12.6% at tip. Carbonfibre main spar, upper surface airbrakes, and glassfibre/epoxy sandwich skin. One-piece cockpit canopy. No water ballast.

DIMENSIONS, EXTERNAL:
Wing span	11.60 m (38 ft 0¾ in)
Wing aspect ratio	20.6
Length overall	5.55 m (18 ft 2½ in)
Height over tail	1.135 m (3 ft 8¾ in)
AREA:
Wings, gross	6.54 m² (70.4 sq ft)
WEIGHTS AND LOADING:
Weight empty	110 kg (243 lb)
Max T-O weight	230 kg (507 lb)
Max wing loading	35.17 kg/m² (7.20 lb/sq ft)
PERFORMANCE (at wing loading of 29 kg/m²; 5.94 lb/sq ft):
Best glide ratio at 54 knots (100 km/h; 62 mph)	35

Min rate of sink at 43 knots (80 km/h; 50 mph)
                                    0.65 m (2.13 ft)/s
Stalling speed   37 knots (68 km/h; 42 mph)
Max speed (rough and smooth air)
                            124 knots (230 km/h; 143 mph)
Max aero-tow speed   89 knots (165 km/h; 102 mph)
Max winch-launching speed
                            70 knots (130 km/h; 80 mph)

g limits (JAR 22)   +5.3/−2.65

STRALPES AÉRO ST-15

The prototype of this 15 metre Class sailplane (F-WBCD) flew for the first time on 23 August 1986. It has a

Horstmann-Quast wing section, aspect ratio of 22.9 and best glide ratio of 41.5. No other details are known.

WEIGHTS:
Weight empty   240 kg (529 lb)
Max T-O weight:
    without water ballast   350 kg (772 lb)
    with water ballast   440 kg (970 lb)

GERMANY

(FEDERAL REPUBLIC)

AKAFLIEG BERLIN
AKADEMISCHE FLIEGERGRUPPE BERLIN eV

Technische Universität Berlin, Strasse des 17 Juni 135,1000 Berlin 30
Telephone: (030) 314 24995
INFORMATION: Holm Friedrich

Akaflieg Berlin comprises a group of students concerned with the development and construction of sailplanes. The current B 12T represents the earlier, damaged, B 12 now given a T tail (see 1978-79 *Jane's*), while the B 13 is an entirely new design. Flying is done from an airfield at Ehlershausen-Grosses Moor, near Celle, where four other sailplanes are also flown by the group.

AKAFLIEG BERLIN B 12T

The original B 12 (D-7612) first flew on 27 July 1977. In 1986 it was damaged while being transported by road, including shearing off of the tail unit. A new T tail has been constructed for the B 12, which is now redesignated B 12T. This tail unit is similar to that of the B 13 but not so tall. The first flight of the B 12T was achieved on 11 August 1987. It is said to have slightly improved handling, although its best glide ratio is not quite as good as for the B 12 configuration. No other B 12Ts are planned.
TYPE: Two-seat Open Class sailplane.
AIRFRAME: Cantilever shoulder-wing monoplane, with a T tail. Wings of Schempp-Hirth Janus type with 2° forward sweep; wing section FX-67-K-170. Dihedral 2°. Incidence 10°. Complete airframe constructed of GFRP, except for CFRP used also in fuselage and AFRP used to construct rudder. Trailing-edge flaps. Retractable mainwheel on AFRP/GFRP spring leg, with tyre size 380 x 150; pressure 4 bars (58 lb/sq in). Tailwheel tyre size 210 x 65; pressure 2 bars (29 lb/sq in). Mainwheel brakes. Tandem seating under removable one-piece canopy.

DIMENSIONS, EXTERNAL:
Wing span   18.20 m (59 ft 8½ in)
Wing aspect ratio   20
Length overall   8.865 m (29 ft 1 in)
Height overall   1.65 m (5 ft 5 in)

AREA:
Wings, gross   16.58 m² (178.47 sq ft)

WEIGHTS:
Weight empty, equipped   438.5 kg (967 lb)
Max T-O weight   620 kg (1,367 lb)

PERFORMANCE:
Best glide ratio at 59 knots (110 km/h; 68 mph)   40.5
Min rate of sink at 49 knots (90 km/h; 56 mph)
                                    0.68 m (2.23 ft)/s
Stalling speed   39 knots (72 km/h; 45 mph)
Max speed (smooth air)   135 knots (250 km/h; 155 mph)
Max speed (rough air)   97 knots (180 km/h; 112 mph)
Max aero-tow speed   81 knots (150 km/h; 93 mph)
Max winch-launching speed 70 knots (130 km/h; 81 mph)
g limits   +6/−4

AKAFLIEG BERLIN B 13

The B 13 is a motor glider but without self-launching capability. The Rotax engine is carried within the front of the fuselage and is fixed, driving a five-blade folding propeller developed by Professor Claus Oehler (a member of Akaflieg Berlin) via a belt-driven shaft.

Design of the B 13 began in 1982, with construction of the prototype starting in the following year. By February 1988 the wings were almost completed, with cockpit assembly, tailplane mating and power plant installation then making good progress. It was then anticipated that the first flight would be made in early 1989.

TYPE: Side by side two-seat Open class motor glider.

AIRFRAME: Cantilever mid-wing monoplane with a T tail. Wings of Stemme S 10 type, designed by Akaflieg Berlin and modified to have wider carry-through structure in fuselage. Wing section HQ 41. Dihedral 1° 18′. Incidence 0°. Wings constructed of CFRP. Ailerons of CFRP, coupled to flaps of similar construction. Schempp-Hirth airbrakes, constructed of aluminium alloy and GFRP. Water ballast in wings, capacity 160 litres (42.2 US gallons; 35.2 Imp gallons). Fuselage of CFRP/AFRP sandwich construction, with stringers. T tail of similar materials to fuselage, with rudder and elevators. Landing gear similar to that of B 12T. Two seats side by side under front-hinged one-piece canopy.

POWER PLANT: One 24 kW (32 hp) Rotax 377 two-cylinder piston engine, driving an Oehler folding five-blade propeller. One fuel tank, capacity 25 litres (6.6 US gallons; 5.5 Imp gallons).
DIMENSIONS, EXTERNAL:
Wing span   23.20 m (76 ft 1½ in)
Wing aspect ratio   28.5
Length overall   8.30 m (27 ft 2¾ in)
Height overall   1.90 m (6 ft 2¾ in)
Propeller diameter   0.86 m (2 ft 10 in)
AREA:
Wings, gross   18.90 m² (203.44 sq ft)
WEIGHTS AND LOADINGS: Not yet available
PERFORMANCE, UNPOWERED (calculated):
Best glide ratio at 57 knots (105 km/h; 65 mph)   49
Min rate of sink at 40 knots (75 km/h; 47 mph)
                                    0.55 m (1.80 ft)/s
Stalling speed   38 knots (70 km/h; 44 mph)
Max speed (smooth air)   151 knots (280 km/h; 174 mph)
Max speed (rough air)   108 knots (200 km/h; 124 mph)
Max aero-tow speed   75 knots (140 km/h; 87 mph)
Max winch-launching speed
                            64 knots (120 km/h; 74 mph)
g limits   +5.3/−2.65

AKAFLIEG BRAUNSCHWEIG
AKADEMISCHE FLIEGERGRUPPE BRAUNSCHWEIG eV

Flughafen Akafliegheim, 3300 Braunschweig
Telephone: 0531 3952149

AKAFLIEG BRAUNSCHWEIG SB-13

Construction of the prototype SB-13 began in 1985, and the first flight was made on 18 March 1988.

TYPE: Standard Class sailplane.

AIRFRAME: Cantilever mid-wing 'flying wing' monoplane with Horstmann-Quast HQ-34N aerofoil section at root, HQ-36K at tip. Dihedral 4°. Incidence −1° 48′ at mid span, −0° 48′ at tip. Wings have compound sweepback (15° max, 12° mean, at quarter-chord), are turned up at tips to form winglets/fins and rudders, and are built of

carbonfibre (HT and HM) reinforced plastics, with two tanks in each wing for a total of 115 litres (30.4 US gallons; 25.3 Imp gallons) of water ballast. Two carbonfibre elevons on each trailing-edge, carbon/metal Schempp-Hirth airbrakes in upper surface. Fuselage is a load-bearing shell of GFRP. Size 300 × 100 mm sprung monowheel, tyre pressure 3.2 bars (46 lb/sq in), and 260 × 85 mm non-steerable nosewheel, tyre pressure 2.6 bars (38 lb/sq in), both fully retractable; brake on monowheel. Single seat under one-piece Plexiglas canopy which opens sideways to starboard. Rescue system comprising three parachutes, allowing a descent rate of 180 m (590 ft)/min.
DIMENSIONS, EXTERNAL:
Wing span   15.00 m (49 ft 2½ in)
Wing aspect ratio   19.4
Length of fuselage   3.02 m (9 ft 11 in)
Height over tail   1.96 m (6 ft 5¼ in)

AREA:
Wings, gross   11.60 m² (124.86 sq ft)

WEIGHTS AND LOADING:
Weight empty, including rescue system   270 kg (595 lb)
Max T-O weight   435 kg (959 lb)
Max wing loading   37.5 kg/m² (7.68 lb/sq ft)

PERFORMANCE (estimated at wing loading of 27 kg/m²; 5.53 lb/sq ft):
Stalling speed at AUW of 350 kg (770 lb)
                            38 knots (70 km/h; 44 mph)
Max speed (rough and smooth air)
                     above 113 knots (210 km/h; 130 mph)
Max aero-tow speed   91 knots (170 km/h; 105 mph)
Max winch-launching speed
                            81 knots (150 km/h; 93 mph)
g limits (JAR 22)   +5.3/−2.65

AKAFLIEG DARMSTADT
AKADEMISCHE FLIEGERGRUPPE DARMSTADT eV

Technische Hochschule, Magdalenenstrasse 8, 6100 Darmstadt
Telephone: 06151 24720

The Fliegergruppe of Darmstadt University has been designing, building and flying sailplanes since 1920. Its postwar products have been described in several previous editions of *Jane's*. Latest of them is the D-40 single-seat 15 metre Class sailplane, of which details can be found in the 1987-88 edition.

AKAFLIEG HANNOVER
AKADEMISCHE FLIEGERGRUPPE HANNOVER ev

Welfengarten 1a, 3000 Hannover 1
Telephone: (041051 1) 762 6422 or 70 30 32
PROJECT MANAGER: AFH 24: Manfred Hüser
PUBLIC RELATIONS MANAGER: Jörg Burmeister

AKAFLIEG HANNOVER AFH 24

Features of the AFH 24 single-seat Standard Class sailplane include a forward-sliding nose section for cockpit access instead of a hinged canopy. General configuration is

that of a shoulder-wing monoplane, with a minimal diameter rear fuselage supporting a T tail; landing gear comprises a retractable monowheel and tail bumper. The wings, fitted with upper surface spoilers, are essentially those of a Glaser-Dirks DG-300, but have a modified HQ (Horstmann-Quast) aerofoil section. Construction is mainly of GFRP, CFRP and AFRP composites.

Design of the AFH 24 began in October 1982; the first flight is planned for early 1989.

DIMENSIONS, EXTERNAL:
Wing span   15.00 m (49 ft 2½ in)
Wing aspect ratio   21.8

Fuselage: Max width   0.64 m (2 ft 1¼ in)
          Max depth   0.81 m (2 ft 8 in)

AREA:
Wings, gross   10.30 m² (110.9 sq ft)

WEIGHTS AND LOADING:
Weight empty   240 kg (529 lb)
Max T-O weight   500 kg (1,102 lb)
Max wing loading   48.5 kg/m² (9.94 lb/sq ft)

PERFORMANCE (estimated):
Max speed (smooth air)   162 knots (300 km/h; 186 mph)

STRALPES Aéro ST-11 prototype Club Class sailplane

Akaflieg Braunschweig SB-13 prototype prior to making its first flight

Akaflieg Berlin B 12T, the B 12 with a new T-tail

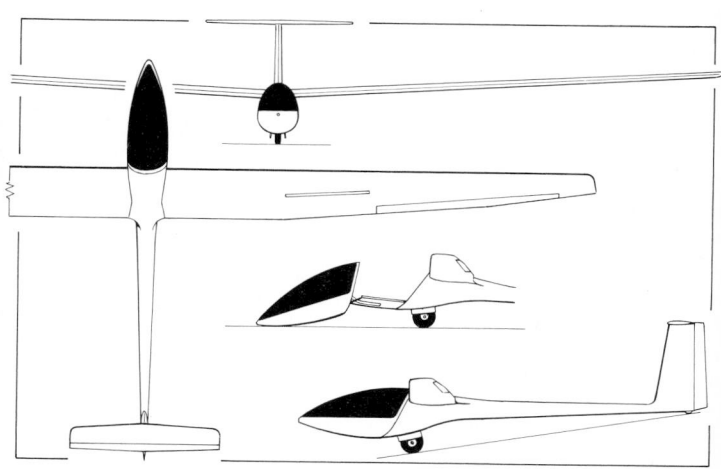

Akaflieg Hannover's Standard Class AFH 24, with scrap view illustrating forward sliding nose *(Michael A. Badrocke)*

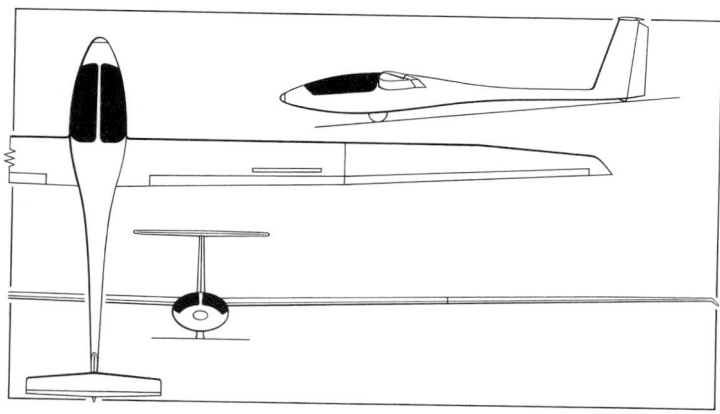

Akaflieg Berlin B 13 side by side two-seat Open Class motor glider
(Jane's/Mike Keep)

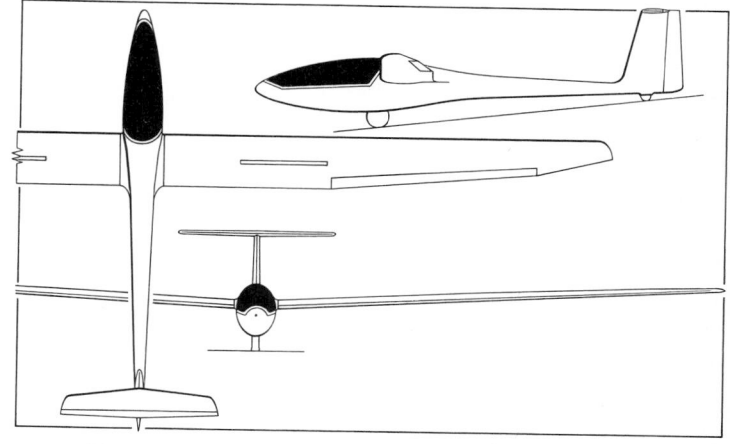

Akaflieg Karlsruhe AK-5 all-plastics Standard Class sailplane
(Jane's/Mike Keep)

AKAFLIEG KARLSRUHE
AKADEMISCHE FLIEGERGRUPPE KARLSRUHE eV

Akademische Fliegergruppe an der Universität Karlsruhe eV, Kaiserstrasse 12, 7500 Karlsruhe 1
Telephone: 0721 608 2044
SECRETARY: Wolfgang Lieff

AKAFLIEG KARLSRUHE AK-5

Design of this single-seat FAI Standard Class sailplane began in August 1984, with the objective of providing group members with experience in designing and building sailplanes using composite materials. The AK-5 is expected to have a performance comparable with such other German types as the Glaser-Dirks DG-300, Rolladen-Schneider LS4, Schempp-Hirth Discus and Streifeneder Falcon.

General appearance of the AK-5 can be seen in an accompanying three-view drawing. First flight was planned for Summer 1988.

TYPE: Single-seat Standard Class sailplane.

AIRFRAME: Cantilever mid-wing monoplane with T tailplane and separate elevator. Horstmann-Quast HQ-21 wing section from root to tip. Dihedral 3°. Incidence 1°. Sweepforward approx 0° 18′ at quarter-chord. Entire airframe built of GFRP composites. Schempp-Hirth airbrakes in upper surface. Tanks in wings for 160 litres (42.3 US gallons; 35.2 Imp gallons) of water ballast; trim tank for 7 litres (1.85 US gallons; 1.54 Imp gallons) of water in tail. Retractable monowheel, with brake; non-retractable tailwheel. Canopy hinged at front, opening upward.

DIMENSIONS, EXTERNAL:
Wing span	15.00 m (49 ft 2½ in)
Wing aspect ratio	21.1
Length overall	6.80 m (22 ft 3¾ in)
Height over tail	1.45 m (4 ft 9 in)

AREA:
Wings, gross	10.656 m² (114.7 sq ft)

WEIGHTS AND LOADING:
Weight empty, equipped	245 kg (540 lb)
Max water ballast	160 kg (353 lb)
Max T-O weight	485 kg (1,069 lb)
Max wing loading	45.51 kg/m² (9.32 lb/sq ft)

PERFORMANCE (calculated at wing loading of 35 kg/m²; 7.17 lb/sq ft):
Best glide ratio at 51 knots (95 km/h; 59 mph)	41
Min rate of sink at 45 knots (84 km/h; 52 mph)	0.60 m (1.97 ft)/s
Stalling speed	38 knots (70 km/h; 44 mph)
Max speed (smooth air)	146 knots (270 km/h; 168 mph)
Max speed (rough air), and max aero-tow speed	105 knots (195 km/h; 121 mph)
Max winch-launching speed	81 knots (150 km/h; 93 mph)
g limits	+5.3/−2.65

AKAFLIEG STUTTGART
AKADEMISCHE FLIEGERGRUPPE STUTTGART eV

Pfaffenwaldring 35, 7000 Stuttgart 80
Telephone: 0711 685 2443
PRESIDENT: Steffen Rollev

AKAFLIEG STUTTGART FS-32

This new single-seat 15 metre Class sailplane is under construction, and building is planned to continue into 1989. General appearance is shown in an accompanying three-view drawing.

Main features of the FS-32 are the Fowler type high lift slotted flaps, which are in two segments on each wing. With the ailerons, they occupy the entire trailing-edge. The wings, which are of Wortmann FX-81-K-144/20 section, will be constructed of carbonfibre and other composite materials, and will have upper surface airbrakes. Dihedral angle is 3°. The carbon/aramid/glassfibre fuselage is modified from that of a Schempp-Hirth Ventus b, and has an improved version of the Ventus T tail. Landing gear comprises a flapped wings are expected to permit a reduction in stalling speed compared with other 15 m Class sailplanes, and to bring about a considerable improvement in all-round handling and performance.

DIMENSIONS, EXTERNAL:

Wing span	15.00 m (49 ft 2½ in)
Wing aspect ratio	22.6

Length overall	6.53 m (21 ft 5 in)

AREA:

Wings, gross	9.94 m² (107.0 sq ft)

WEIGHTS (estimated):

Weight empty	260 kg (573 lb)
Max T-O weight	500 kg (1,102 lb)

PERFORMANCE (estimated):

Best glide ratio at 57 knots (105 km/h; 65 mph)	43
Min rate of sink at 46 knots (85 km/h; 53 mph)	
	0.60 m (1.97 ft)/s
Stalling speed	approx 33 knots (60 km/h; 38 mph)
Max speed (smooth air)	135 knots (250 km/h; 155 mph)

DOKTOR FIBERGLAS

DOKTOR FIBERGLAS (URSULA HÄNLE)

Postfach 1112, 5438 Westerburg
Telephone: 02663 3420
DIRECTOR: Ursula Hänle

HÄNLE H 101 SALTO

This single-seat Standard and Club Class sailplane was produced originally by the Start + Flug company, which delivered 60 before its closure in the Spring of 1978.

The Salto is based on the Glasflügel Standard Libelle, from which it differs chiefly in having a V tail. It first flew in 1971, and is certificated by the LBA and FAA for both Utility and Aerobatic category flying. In the latter category it is fitted with the standard span (13.30 m; 43 ft 7½ in) wings; in the Utility category it is available either with 13.30 m wings or with detachable tips which extend the span to 15.50 m (50 ft 10¼ in).

TYPE: Single-seat Standard and Club Class sailplane.

AIRFRAME: Cantilever mid-wing monoplane. Wings have Conticell sandwich shell and HH type glassfibre spar caps, and detachable tip extensions (except in Aerobatic category). Dihedral 3° from roots. Glassfibre ailerons and four flush-fitting airbrakes on trailing-edges. Glass-fibre monocoque fuselage. Cantilever V tail (included angle 99°), with glassfibre fixed surfaces and glassfibre/honeycomb sandwich balanced 'ruddervators'. Non-retractable semi-recessed monowheel, size 300 × 100 mm, with glassfibre shock absorption and internally expanding brake. Non-retractable semi-recessed tail-wheel. Brake parachute attachment standard on all versions. Canopy opens sideways to starboard.

DIMENSIONS, EXTERNAL (A: Aerobatic, U: Utility):

Wing span: A	13.30 m (43 ft 7½ in)
U (optional)	15.50 m (50 ft 10¼ in)
Wing aspect ratio: A	20.6
U (optional)	26.4
Length overall	5.70 m (18 ft 8½ in)
Height over tail	0.80 m (2 ft 7½ in)

AREAS:

Wings, gross: A	8.58 m² (92.4 sq ft)
U (optional)	9.10 m² (98.0 sq ft)

WEIGHTS AND LOADINGS:

Weight empty: A	182 kg (401 lb)
U	187 kg (412 lb)
Max T-O weight: A	280 kg (617 lb)
U	310 kg (683 lb)

Max wing loading: A	32.6 kg/m² (6.68 lb/sq ft)
U (13.3 m)	36.1 kg/m² (7.40 lb/sq ft)
U (15.5 m)	34.0 kg/m² (6.97 lb/sq ft)

PERFORMANCE (at max T-O weight except where indicated):

Best glide ratio at 51 knots (94 km/h; 58 mph):	
A	34.5
U	37
Min rate of sink at 39 knots (72 km/h; 45 mph):	
A, U (15.5 m), at AUW of 280 kg (617 lb)	
	0.70 m (2.30 ft)/s
A, U (15.5 m), at AUW of 250 kg (551 lb)	
	0.60 m (1.97 ft)/s
U (13.3 m), at AUW of 250 kg (551 lb)	
	0.55 m (1.80 ft)/s
Stalling speed: A	38 knots (70 km/h; 44 mph)
U	34 knots (62 km/h; 39 mph)
Max speed (rough and smooth air):	
A	151 knots (280 km/h; 174 mph)
U	135 knots (250 km/h; 155 mph)
Max aero-tow speed:	
A, U	81 knots (150 km/h; 93 mph)
Max winch-launching speed:	
A, U	70 knots (130 km/h; 81 mph)
g limits: A	+7/–4.9

GLASER-DIRKS

GLASER-DIRKS FLUGZEUGBAU GmbH

Im Schollengarten 19-20, Postfach 41 47, 7520 Bruchsal 4
Telephone: 07257 89 01
Telex: 7822410 GL DG D
DIRECTORS: Gerhard Glaser and Dipl-Ing Wilhelm Dirks

Glaser-Dirks was formed in 1973; its 1,000th aircraft (including Elan licence production) was completed in 1987. The company designed, and remains the type certificate holder for, the DG-101 and DG-300 sailplanes, now manufactured by Elan in Yugoslavia (which see). Glaser-Dirks' main current activity concerns production of the DG-400 and DG-500, and development of the new DG-600.

GLASER-DIRKS DG-400

The DG-400 is a self-launching development of the DG-202 (1984-85 *Jane's*), from which it differs principally in having a slightly deeper rear fuselage to accommodate the power plant when retracted. As with the unpowered versions, the DG-400 has 15 m span wings with add-on tips which increase the span to 17 m. The prototype (D-KOLL) flew for the first time on 1 May 1981. Deliveries began in June 1982; a total of 225 had been built by 1 January 1988, of 250 then on order.

TYPE: Single-seat self-launching sailplane.

AIRFRAME: Cantilever shoulder-wing monoplane. Wing section Wortmann FX-67-K-170-17 at root, FX-67-K-170 (15 m span) or FX-60-K-126 (17 m span) at tip. Dihedral 3° from roots. Incidence –1°. Carbonfibre roving main spar, wing skin, flaps and ailerons. Schempp-Hirth aluminium airbrakes on upper surfaces. All-glassfibre semi-monocoque fuselage, fin and rudder. Glassfibre/foam sandwich T tailplane, with carbonfibre elevator. Manually retractable monowheel, size 5.00-5, tyre pressure 3.0 bars (43.5 lb/sq in), with Tost drum brake; size 200 × 50 tailwheel, tyre pressure 2.0 bars (29 lb/sq in). One-piece cockpit canopy, hinged at front to open upwards. Water ballast tank in each wing, combined capacity 90 litres (23.8 US gallons; 19.8 Imp gallons).

POWER PLANT: One 32 kW (43 hp) Rotax 505 two-stroke engine, pylon-mounted on fuselage aft of wing trailing-edge and driving a Hoffmann two-blade fixed-pitch propeller. Installation retracts, electrically, rearward into fuselage when not in use. Single fuselage fuel tank standard, capacity 20 litres (5.3 US gallons; 4.4 Imp gallons). Optional 15 litre (4 US gallon; 3.3 Imp gallon) tank in each wing, in lieu of water ballast, raising total fuel capacity to 50 litres (13.2 US gallons; 11 Imp gallons).

DIMENSIONS, EXTERNAL:

Wing span: 15 m	15.00 m (49 ft 2½ in)
17 m	17.00 m (55 ft 9¼ in)
Wing aspect ratio: 15 m	22.5
17 m	27.3
Length overall	7.00 m (22 ft 11¾ in)
Height over tail	1.40 m (4 ft 7 in)
Propeller diameter	1.29 m (4 ft 2¾ in)

AREAS:

Wings, gross: 15 m	10.00 m² (107.6 sq ft)
17 m	10.57 m² (113.8 sq ft)

WEIGHTS AND LOADINGS:

Weight empty	305 kg (672 lb)
Max T-O weight: 15 m	480 kg (1,058 lb)
17 m	460 kg (1,014 lb)
Max wing loading: 15 m	48.0 kg/m² (9.84 lb/sq ft)
17 m	43.5 kg/m² (8.91 lb/sq ft)
Max power loading: 15 m	14.9 kg/kW (24.6 lb/hp)
17 m	14.0 kg/kW (23.1 lb/hp)

PERFORMANCE, UNPOWERED (at max T-O weight):

Best glide ratio at 59 knots (110 km/h; 68 mph):	
15 m	45
17 m	47
Min rate of sink at 43 knots (80 km/h; 50 mph):	
15 m	0.60 m (1.97 ft)/s
17 m	0.50 m (1.64 ft)/s
Stalling speed: 15 m	35 knots (65 km/h; 41 mph)
17 m	34 knots (63 km/h; 40 mph)
Max speed (smooth air)	
	146 knots (270 km/h; 168 mph)
Max speed (rough air), and max aero-tow speed	
	102 knots (190 km/h; 118 mph)
Max winch-launching speed	
	70 knots (130 km/h; 81 mph)
g limits	+6/–4

PERFORMANCE, POWERED (at max T-O weight):

Max cruising speed	76 knots (140 km/h; 87 mph)
Econ cruising speed	70 knots (130 km/h; 81 mph)
Stalling speed: 15 m	35 knots (65 km/h; 41 mph)
17 m	34 knots (63 km/h; 40 mph)
Max rate of climb at S/L	234 m (768 ft)/min
Service ceiling	5,000 m (16,400 ft)
T-O run at 15°C	170 m (558 ft)
Landing run	50 m (164 ft)
Range with max fuel:	
level cruise	215 nm (400 km; 248 miles)
'saw-tooth' cruise/soar	404 nm (750 km; 466 miles)

GLASER-DIRKS DG-500

The DG-500 is a two-seat sailplane/motor glider, produced by Glaser-Dirks, with airframe components manufactured by Elan in Yugoslavia. The **DG-500M** motor glider prototype (D-KMDG) made its first flight on 19 March 1987, with a Rotax 535C power plant installation similar to that of the DG-400 but uprated to 44.7 kW (60 hp). Production of the DG-500M began in Spring 1988. The other production versions are the **DG-500/22** and **DG-500 Elan Trainer**, both generally similar to the DG-500M but without the engine. Max T-O weight of the DG-500/22 is 750 kg (1,653 lb).

The Elan Trainer has a reduced wing span, no flaps, choice of retractable or non-retractable main wheel, glassfibre wings with carbonfibre spar caps, and full controls in each cockpit. The prototype Elan Trainer was scheduled to fly for the first time in June 1988. It is to be certificated for all aerobatic manoeuvres necessary to obtain an aerobatic licence.

The following details refer to the DG-500M prototype, unless stated otherwise:

TYPE: Open Class two-seat sailplane.

AIRFRAME: Cantilever mid-wing monoplane. Wortmann wing sections: FX-73-K-170/20 at root, -170/22 at tip. Dihedral 3°. Incidence 0°. Sweepforward 0° 36' at quarter-chord. Four-piece wings built entirely of CFRP, including interconnected ailerons and trailing-edge flaps. Schempp-Hirth two-plate upper surface airbrakes. Fuselage of GFRP, the rear boom being of sandwich construction. T tail unit, with fixed incidence tailplane, is also all-GFRP. Fully retractable bungee sprung monowheel (tyre size 380 x 150.5, pressure 3.0 bars; 43.5 lb/sq in), with brake; semi-recessed 260 x 85 steerable nosewheel and 200 x 50 tailwheel. Tanks for 160 litres (43.2 US gallons; 35.2 Imp gallons) of water ballast in wings. Tandem seats for two persons; canopies open sideways to starboard.

POWER PLANT: One 44.7 kW (60 hp) Rotax 535C two-cylinder two-stroke engine, mounted on pylon aft of rear cockpit and driving a Hoffmann HO-11H-HM two-blade fixed-pitch propeller. Installation retracts into fuselage when not in use. Single 40 litre (10.6 US gallon; 8.8 Imp gallon) fuselage fuel tank standard; optional 20 litre (5.3 US gallon; 4.4 Imp gallon) tank in each wing, raising total fuel capacity to 80 litres (21.1 US gallons; 17.6 Imp gallons).

DIMENSIONS, EXTERNAL (A: prototype, B: Elan Trainer):

Wing span: A	22.00 m (72 ft 2 in)
B	18.00 m (59 ft 0¾ in)
Wing aspect ratio: A	26.4
B	19.52
Length overall: A, B	8.66 m (28 ft 5 in)
Height overall: A	1.80 m (5 ft 11 in)
B	1.665 m (5 ft 5½ in)
Propeller diameter: A	1.58 m (5 ft 2¼ in)

AREAS (A and B as above):

Wings, gross: A	18.30 m² (197.0 sq ft)
B	16.60 m² (178.7 sq ft)

WEIGHTS AND LOADINGS (A and B as above):

Weight empty: A	510 kg (1,124 lb)
B	390 kg (860 lb)
Max water ballast: A	160 kg (353 lb)
Max T-O weight: A	825 kg (1,819 lb)
B	630 kg (1,389 lb)
Max wing loading: A	45.08 kg/m² (9.23 lb/sq ft)
B	37.95 kg/m² (7.77 lb/sq ft)
Max power loading: A	18.45 kg/kW (30.31 lb/hp)

PERFORMANCE, UNPOWERED (A and B as above):

Stalling speed: A	46.5 knots (85.5 km/h; 53.5 mph)
B at 470 kg (1,036 lb) AUW	
	35 knots (65 km/h; 41 mph)
Max speed (smooth air):	
A, B	145 knots (270 km/h; 167 mph)
Max speed (rough air), and max aero-tow speed:	
A, B	106 knots (197 km/h; 122 mph)
Max winch-launching speed:	
A	75 knots (140 km/h; 87 mph)
g limits: A	+5.3/–2.65

GLASER-DIRKS DG-600

The prototype DG-600 (D-8600) made its first flight on 15 April 1987, design having started some two years earlier. It is intended for the 15 metre Class, but there is the option of add-on wingtip panels to extend the span to 17 m.

Features include a new thin-section wing, with construction similar to that of the earlier DG-202; a fuselage based on that of the DG-400, but with a slimmer tailboom; a DG-300/400 one-piece canopy; and a new horizontal tail.

Production of the DG-600 began in 1988, against early orders for 80 aircraft.

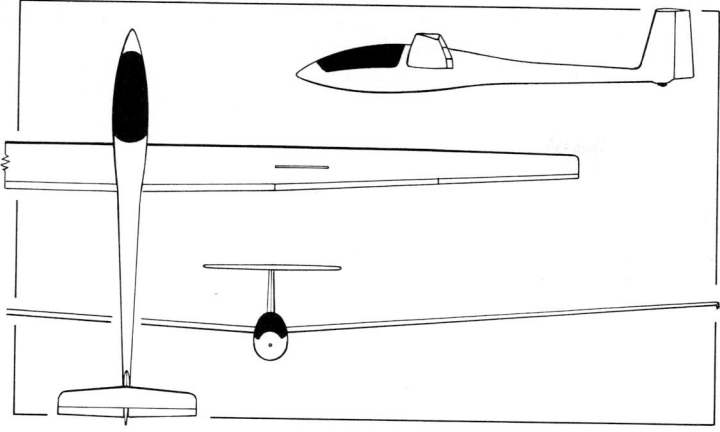

The 15 metre Class Akaflieg Stuttgart FS-32 *(Michael A. Badrocke)*

Glaser-Dirks DG-400 self-launching sailplane

The motorised DG-500M prototype for the DG-500 series *(Peter F. Selinger)*

Hänle (Doktor Fiberglas) H 101 Salto *(Peter F. Selinger)*

Prototype of the Glaser-Dirks DG-600 *(Peter F. Selinger)*

TYPE: 15 metre Class sailplane.

AIRFRAME: Cantilever mid-wing monoplane with T tail. Wing sections HQ-35 at root, HQ-37 at tip. Dihedral 2° 30′. Incidence −1°. Sweepforward 0° 5′ 24″ at quarter-chord. Wings, and full span 'flaperons', are all-composites sandwich structures of CFRP and PVC foam, except for their Schempp-Hirth aluminium upper surface airbrakes. Fuselage is a GRP shell; tail unit is similarly constructed, but with elevator and rudder of GRP and PVC foam sandwich. Single retractable steel-sprung mainwheel (tyre size 5.00-5, pressure 3.3 bars; 48 lb/sq in), with brake. Fixed tailwheel, tyre size 200 × 50 mm, pressure 2.0 bars (29 lb/sq in). Single seat under one-piece canopy which is hinged at front and opens upward. Wing tanks for 180 litres (47.6 US gallons; 39.6 Imp gallons) of water ballast, plus small amount in vertical fin.

DIMENSIONS, EXTERNAL:

Wing span: 15 m	15.00 m (49 ft 2½ in)
17 m	17.00 m (55 ft 9¼ in)
Wing aspect ratio: 15 m	20.5
17 m	24.9
Length overall	6.83 m (22 ft 5 in)
Height over tail	1.35 m (4 ft 5¼ in)

AREAS:

Wings, gross: 15 m	10.95 m² (117.9 sq ft)
17 m	11.59 m² (124.75 sq ft)

WEIGHTS AND LOADINGS:

Weight empty, equipped: 15 m	255 kg (562 lb)
17 m	260 kg (573 lb)
Max water ballast (both): wings	180 kg (397 lb)
vertical fin	7 kg (15.4 lb)

Max T-O weight (both)	525 kg (1,157 lb)
Max wing loading: 15 m	47.94 kg/m² (9.82 lb/sq ft)
17 m	45.30 kg/m² (9.28 lb/sq ft)

PERFORMANCE (estimated at max T-O weight):

Best glide ratio: 15 m	46
17 m	50
Min rate of sink: 15 m	0.56 m (1.84 ft)/s
17 m	0.50 m (1.64 ft)/s
Stalling speed	35 knots (64 km/h; 40 mph)
Max speed (smooth air)	146 knots (270 km/h; 168 mph)
Max rough air and aero-tow speed	108 knots (200 km/h; 124 mph)
Max winch-launching speed	81 knots (150 km/h; 93 mph)
g limits	+5.8/−3.8

GROB

BURKHART GROB FLUGZEUGBAU (Subsidiary of Grob-Werke GmbH & Co KG)

Postfach 150, 8948 Mindelheim
DIRECTOR: Dipl-Ing Burkhart Grob

This company built 200 Schempp-Hirth Standard Cirrus under licence between 1972 and 1975, before concentrating on composites sailplanes and motor gliders of its own design, all meeting JAR 22 European airworthiness requirements. However, having sold a total of approximately 3,000 aircraft, no gliders or motor gliders have been built for some time, although production could resume if demand merits it. In the meantime, the company continues to produce its G 115 and G 116 lightplanes (see main Aircraft section) and has the GF 200 in the initial study stage.

Details and illustrations of the Grob G 102 Series III, G 103C Twin III and G 109B can be found in the 1987-88 *Jane's*.

HOFFMANN

WOLF HOFFMANN FLUGZEUGBAU KG

Sportflugplatz, 8870 Günzburg/Ulm
Telephone: 08221 1417
Telex: 531625 HOFBG D
DIRECTOR: Dipl-Ing Wolf D. Hoffmann

In addition to production of its aircraft in West Germany, including the H-40 (see main Aircraft section), the Dimona has been built by Hoffmann Aircraft Flugzeugproduktion und Entwicklung GmbH, Postfach 100, A-1214 Vienna, Austria. *Telephone:* (0043) 222 253691. *Telex:* 112820 HAC.

HOFFMANN H-36 DIMONA Mk II

The prototype of this two-seat motor glider flew for the first time on 9 October 1980, and was followed by two further prototypes. The Dimona was awarded LBA type certification on 30 March 1982, and also has a British C of

A. By February 1988 a total of more than 220 had been delivered.

Current version is the **Dimona Mk II**, which has strengthened main landing gear, a sprung tailwheel, modified engine cowling, improved propeller pitch control, better cockpit heating and ventilation, a redesigned instrument panel and other refinements.

TYPE: Side by side two-seat motor glider; positive aerobatics permissible.

AIRFRAME: Cantilever low/mid-wing monoplane, constructed of GFRP. Wing section Wortmann FX-63-137. Upper surface airbrakes. Wings are attached independently to fuselage by bolts, and can be folded back alongside fuselage for transportation and storage. Fuselage sidewalls and frames are strengthened with extensive GFRP rovings. Double shell in cockpit area. Cantilever T tail. Non-retractable tailwheel type landing gear, with 6 in mainwheels and sprung, steerable

tailwheel. Cantilever GFRP mainwheel legs. Fairings on main legs and wheels. Cockpit canopy hinged at rear to open upward. Baggage space aft of seats.

POWER PLANT: One 59.7 kW (80 hp) Limbach L 2000 EBI engine, driving a Hoffmann HO-V62/160 two-blade three-position propeller. Fuel tank capacity 80 litres (21.1 US gallons; 17.5 Imp gallons).

DIMENSIONS, EXTERNAL:

Wing span	16.00 m (52 ft 6 in)
Wing aspect ratio	16.8
Width, wings folded	2.10 m (6 ft 10¾ in)
Length overall	6.85 m (22 ft 5¾ in)
Length, wings folded	9.30 m (30 ft 6¼ in)
Height over tail	1.625 m (5 ft 4 in)
Propeller diameter	1.60 m (5 ft 3 in)

AREA:

Wings, gross	15.20 m² (163.6 sq ft)

WEIGHTS AND LOADINGS:

Weight empty	560 kg (1,234 lb)
Max T-O weight	770 kg (1,697 lb)
Max wing loading	50.7 kg/m² (10.38 lb/sq ft)
Max power loading	12.91 kg/kW (21.21 lb/hp)

PERFORMANCE, UNPOWERED (at max T-O weight):

Best glide ratio at 56 knots (105 km/h; 65 mph)		27
Min rate of sink at 43 knots (80 km/h; 50 mph)		
		1.06 m (3.48 ft)/s
Stalling speed	39 knots (72 km/h; 45 mph)	
Max speed (smooth air)	148 knots (275 km/h; 171 mph)	
Max speed (rough air)	113 knots (210 km/h; 130 mph)	
g limits:	+5.3/−2.65 permissible	
	+9.3 ultimate	

PERFORMANCE, POWERED (at max T-O weight):

Max cruising speed	97 knots (180 km/h; 112 mph)
Econ cruising speed	92 knots (170 km/h; 106 mph)
Stalling speed	39 knots (72 km/h; 45 mph)
Max rate of climb at S/L	210 m (689 ft)/min
Service ceiling	6,000 m (19,675 ft)
T-O run	180 m (590 ft)
Landing run	150 m (492 ft)
Range with max fuel	540 nm (1,000 km; 621 miles)

HOFFMANN H-36D

The H-36D is a development of the H-36, incorporating several modifications without changing the basic design. It is to be produced only in West Germany.

Compared to the H-36 Dimona, the H-36D has the fuselage of the H-40 lightplane, a 67 kW (90 hp) Limbach L 2400 EB engine with optional dual ignition and driving a Muehlbauer MTV constant-speed fully-feathering propeller, better access to the engine and control system by the use of completely removable cowlings, a carbonfibre wing spar and main bulkhead, increased elevator chord and trim tab for improved longitudinal stability, improved spin characteristics resulting from a modified inboard wing leading-edge and the CG range moved forward, an improved airbrake mechanism, a reinforced main landing gear with removable fairings, an improved sprung tailwheel, and a new larger canopy with new mechanism. Certain aerobatic manoeuvres are permissible. Maximum take-off weight has been increased.

DIMENSIONS, EXTERNAL:

Wing span	16.00 m (52 ft 6 in)
Wing aspect ratio	16.8
Length overall	6.99 m (22 ft 11¼ in)
Length, wings folded	9.30 m (30 ft 6¼ in)

AREA:

Wings, gross	15.2 m² (163.61 sq ft)

WEIGHTS AND LOADINGS:

Weight empty	580 kg (1,279 lb)
Max T-O weight	850 kg (1,874 lb)
Max wing loading	55.92 kg/m² (11.45 lb/sq ft)
Max power loading	12.69 kg/kW (20.82 lb/hp)

PERFORMANCE, POWERED:

Never-exceed speed	148 knots (275 km/h; 171 mph)
Max level speed	116 knots (215 km/h; 134 mph)
Stalling speed	41 knots (75 km/h; 47 mph)
Max rate of climb at S/L	240 m (787 ft)/min
T-O run	180 m (590 ft)
Range	539 nm (1,000 km; 621 miles)
Best glide ratio at 57 knots (105 km/h; 65 mph)	27

HOFFMANN H-38 OBSERVER

Development of the H-38 Observer ended in early 1987. Details and an illustration can be found in the 1987-88 *Jane's*.

JUBI

JUBI GmbH SPORTFLUGZEUGBAU

Flugplatz 2, 4811 Oerlinghausen
Telephone: 05202 3422

Jubi is currently the sole production source for the Schleicher ASK 13 two-seat sailplane.

JUBI (SCHLEICHER) ASK 13

This tandem-seat sailplane was developed by Schleicher from the K 7, which is in worldwide use by gliding clubs. The prototype first flew in July 1966.

Production by Schleicher has ended, but the ASK 13 is still manufactured, under licence, by Jubi.

TYPE: Tandem two-seat training and high-performance sailplane.

AIRFRAME: Cantilever mid-wing monoplane. Wing section developed from Göttingen 535 and 549. Sweepforward at quarter-chord 6°. Dihedral 5°. Single-spar wooden wings, with fabric covering. Wooden ailerons, with plywood covering; Schempp-Hirth metal airbrakes above and below each wing. Welded steel tube fuselage with spruce formers and fabric main covering. Nose made of glassfibre. Turtledeck aft of canopy is plywood shell. Cantilever wooden tail unit, plywood covered except for fabric covered rear portion of rudder and elevators. Flettner tab in starboard elevator. Non-retractable sprung monowheel, with Tost drum brake; skid in front of wheel; steel tailskid. Canopy opens sideways to starboard.

DIMENSIONS, EXTERNAL:

Wing span	16.00 m (52 ft 6 in)
Wing aspect ratio	14.6
Length overall	8.18 m (26 ft 9½ in)
Height over tail	1.60 m (5 ft 3 in)

AREA:

Wings, gross	17.50 m² (188.4 sq ft)

WEIGHTS AND LOADING:

Weight empty	290 kg (640 lb)
Max T-O weight	480 kg (1,060 lb)
Max wing loading	26.8 kg/m² (5.49 lb/sq ft)

PERFORMANCE (at 470 kg; 1,036 lb T-O weight):

Best glide ratio at 49 knots (90 km/h; 56 mph)		28
Min rate of sink at 38 knots (70 km/h; 43 mph)		
		0.80 m (2.62 ft)/s
Stalling speed	33 knots (61 km/h; 38 mph)	
Max speed (smooth air)	108 knots (200 km/h; 124 mph)	
Max speed (rough air), and max aero-tow speed		
	76 knots (140 km/h; 87 mph)	
Max winch-launching speed		
	54 knots (100 km/h; 62 mph)	
g limit (safety factor of 2)		+4

ROLLADEN-SCHNEIDER

ROLLADEN-SCHNEIDER FLUGZEUGBAU GmbH

Postfach 1130, Mühlstrasse 10, 6073 Egelsbach/Hessen
Telephone: 06103 4126

OFFICERS: Walter Schneider and Dipl-Ing Wolf Lemke

Current activities are concerned with continuing manufacture of the LS4 and development of the LS6. Rolladen-Schneider's 1,000th sailplane, an LS4, was completed in 1981.

ROLLADEN-SCHNEIDER LS4

Design of this Standard Class sailplane began in the Winter of 1979/80, and the prototype (D-6680) flew for the first time on 28 March 1980. In the 1983 World Championships at Hobbs, New Mexico, USA, LS4s took 13 of the first 15 places in the Standard Class, including all of the first six places.

The LS4 utilises a modified LS3-a fuselage combined with a new, thin-section wing, mid-mounted on the fuselage. The **LS4-a** is identical except for an additional rubber spring on the monowheel (introduced also on the LS4 from mid-1983), and twin water ballast bag tanks in each wing, increasing the volume to 80-85 litres (21.1-22.4 US gallons; 17.6-18.7 Imp gallons) per wing.

A total of at least 640 LS4s and LS4-as had been built by February 1988.

TYPE: Single-seat Standard Class sailplane.

AIRFRAME: Cantilever mid-wing monoplane, of glassfibre/Conticell foam construction. Wings have thickness/chord ratio of 15% at root and 13% at tip (modified Wortmann sections), 3° 30′ dihedral, and 0° incidence. Schempp-Hirth upper surface airbrakes. No flaps. Provision for 140 litres (37 US gallons; 30.8 Imp gallons) water ballast in wings on LS4, 160-170 litres (42.3-44.9 US gallons; 35.2-37.4 Imp gallons) on LS4-a. Semi-monocoque fuselage. Cantilever T tailplane, with elevator. Entire structure of GFRP sandwich. Retractable Tost rubber sprung monowheel, tyre pressure 2.94 bars (43 lb/sq in); tailskid standard, 200 mm tailwheel optional. Tost Kobold brake on mainwheel. Canopy hinged at front to open upward.

DIMENSIONS, EXTERNAL:

Wing span	15.00 m (49 ft 2½ in)
Wing aspect ratio	21.4
Length overall	6.83 m (22 ft 5 in)
Height over tail	1.26 m (4 ft 1½ in)

AREA:

Wings, gross	10.50 m² (113.0 sq ft)

WEIGHTS AND LOADINGS (A: LS4, B: LS4-a):

Weight empty: A		238 kg (525 lb)
B		240 kg (529 lb)
Max T-O weight: A		472 kg (1,040 lb)
B		525 kg (1,157 lb)
Max wing loading: A		44.9 kg/m² (9.21 lb/sq ft)
B		50.0 kg/m² (10.25 lb/sq ft)

PERFORMANCE (at max T-O weight):

Best glide ratio at 54 knots (100 km/h; 62 mph)		40.5
Min rate of sink at 40 knots (75 km/h; 47 mph)		
		0.60 m (1.97 ft)/s
Stalling speed	37 knots (68 km/h; 43 mph)	
Max speed (smooth air):		
A	146 knots (270 km/h; 168 mph)	
B	151 knots (280 km/h; 174 mph)	
Max speed (rough air) and max aero-tow speed:		
A	97 knots (180 km/h; 112 mph)	
B	102 knots (190 km/h; 118 mph)	
Max winch-launching speed:		
A	70 knots (130 km/h; 81 mph)	
B	75 knots (140 km/h; 87 mph)	
g limits:		
at 97 knots (180 km/h; 112 mph)		+5.3/−2.65
at 146 knots (270 km/h; 168 mph)		+4/−1.5

ROLLADEN-SCHNEIDER LS6

The LS6 is a successor to the LS3. Development had been started by the beginning of 1982, and the prototype (D-0662) flew for the first time on 1 December 1983. Series production began in August 1984, and at least 130 LS6s had been built by January 1988. LS6s gained first, second and sixth places in the 1985 World Championships, held in Italy.

An **LS6-a** version is available with a 5.5 litre (1.45 US gallon; 1.2 Imp gallon) water tank in the fin; the **LS6-b** has carbonfibre wings, with the fin water tank as an optional extra.

TYPE: 15 metre Class single-seat sailplane.

AIRFRAME: Cantilever mid-wing monoplane, constructed mainly of PVC foam and glassfibre. Wings have modified Wortmann sections, 4° dihedral, no sweep (forward or back), and carbonfibre spar caps. Ailerons and flaps are of Kevlar, glassfibre and Rohacell foam sandwich. Schempp-Hirth upper surface airbrakes. Water ballast tanks in wings. Glassfibre monocoque fuselage, with integral fin of PVC foam sandwich; Kevlar rudder. Fixed incidence T tailplane with elevator, built of PVC foam sandwich, carbonfibre and glassfibre. Rubber sprung (three element) Tost monowheel, as on LS4 but with new folding-strut retraction mechanism; choice of tailskid or 200 mm tailwheel. Tost Kobold mainwheel brake. One-piece Plexiglas canopy, hinged at front and opening upward; instrument panel opens with canopy.

DIMENSIONS, EXTERNAL:

Wing span	15.00 m (49 ft 2½ in)
Wing aspect ratio	21.4
Length overall	6.65 m (21 ft 9¾ in)
Height over tail (with tailwheel)	1.30 m (4 ft 3¼ in)

AREA:

Wings, gross	10.50 m² (113.0 sq ft)

WEIGHTS AND LOADING:

Weight empty	250 kg (551 lb)
Max water ballast	180 kg (397 lb)
Max T-O weight	525 kg (1,157 lb)
Max wing loading	50.0 kg/m² (10.25 lb/sq ft)

PERFORMANCE:

Best glide ratio	more than 40
Min rate of sink	less than 0.60 m (1.97 ft)/s
Max speed (smooth air)	
	146 knots (270 km/h; 168 mph)
Stalling speed	36 knots (65 km/h; 41 mph)

SCHEIBE

SCHEIBE FLUGZEUGBAU GmbH

HEAD OFFICE AND WORKS: August-Pfaltz-Strasse 23, Postfach 1829, 8060 Dachau, near Munich
Telephone: 08131 72083 and 72084
Telex: 05 26 650

MANAGERS: Dipl-Ing Egon Scheibe and Ing Christian Gad

Scheibe Flugzeugbau GmbH was founded at the end of 1951 by Dipl-Ing Scheibe; its first type produced in quantity was the Mü-13E Bergfalke I.

Subsequently, Scheibe has built many new types of sailplane, and since 1957 has been a major producer of motor gliders in the Federal Republic of Germany.

Principal production model in 1988 continued to be the SF-25C/C-2000 Falke; the SF-25E Super-Falke, SF-28A Tandem-Falke and SF-36 motor gliders, and the SF-34 sailplane, remain available, although production in recent years has been minimal.

Scheibe has built more than 2,000 aircraft of various types, in addition to many kits for home construction by

Hoffmann H-36 Dimona Mk II two-seat motor glider (*Peter F. Selinger*)

Schleicher ASK 13, still in production by Jubi at Oerlinghausen
(*Peter F. Selinger*)

Rolladen-Schneider LS4 Standard Class sailplane (*Avio Data*)

15 m Class Rolladen-Schneider LS6 (*Martin Fricke*)

Scheibe SF-25C-2000 two-seat motor glider

amateurs. Gliders of Scheibe design are built under licence by gliding clubs as well as by foreign companies.

SCHEIBE SF-25C FALKE 88 (FALCON)

The SF-25C is an improved version of the SF-25B Falke, to which it is structurally similar. The primary difference is the use of a more powerful engine, giving an enhanced performance. Type certification was granted in September 1972.

By January 1988 a total of 434 SF-25C Falkes had been built by Scheibe; a further 50 were built under licence by Sportavia in Germany. Scheibe also produced 20 **SF-25C-S**, with Hoffmann feathering propellers, as detailed in earlier editions of *Jane's*.

Current models, known as **SF-25C Falke 88**, have the design improvements listed in the 1977-78 *Jane's*. With optional 59.5 kW (80 hp) Limbach engine, they are known as **SF-25C-2000**. Optional features include an additional exhaust outlet and a slower-turning propeller. With this installation the nominal noise level is reduced to less than 60 dB.

TYPE: Side by side two-seat motor glider, particularly suitable for basic and advanced training.

AIRFRAME: Cantilever low-wing monoplane. Forward swept wooden wings, with airbrakes and aerodynamically balanced ailerons. Fully folding wings optional. Fabric covered welded steel tube fuselage; forward section coated with laminated glassfibre. Wooden tail unit. Non-retractable rubber sprung monowheel with brake and aerodynamic fairing; steerable tailwheel; sprung outrigger stabilising wheel under each wing. Alternative twin-wheel main gear available optionally, with streamline wheel fairings.

POWER PLANT: One 48.5 kW (65 hp) Limbach SL 1700 EA modified Volkswagen engine (59.5 kW; 80 hp L 2000 EA in SF-25C-2000), driving a two-blade propeller. Feathering propeller optional. Electric starter. Fuel in single fuselage tank, capacity 55 litres (14.5 US gallons; 12.1 Imp gallons) standard, 80 litres (21.1 US gallons; 17.6 Imp gallons) optional.

SYSTEM: 12V electrical system.

DIMENSIONS, EXTERNAL:

Wing span	15.30 m (50 ft 2½ in)
Wing aspect ratio	12.9
Length overall	7.60 m (24 ft 11¼ in)
Height over tail	1.85 m (6 ft 0¾ in)

AREA:

Wings, gross	18.20 m² (195.9 sq ft)

WEIGHTS AND LOADINGS:

Weight empty	approx 400 kg (882 lb)
Max T-O weight	650 kg (1,433 lb)
Max wing loading	35.71 kg/m² (7.32 lb/sq ft)
Max power loading: C	13.41 kg/kW (22.05 lb/hp)
C-2000	10.89 kg/kW (17.91 lb/hp)

PERFORMANCE, UNPOWERED (at max T-O weight):

Best glide ratio	23-24
Min rate of sink	approx 1.00 m (3.28 ft)/s

PERFORMANCE, POWERED (at max T-O weight):

Max level speed: C	97 knots (180 km/h; 112 mph)
C-2000	102 knots (190 km/h; 118 mph)
Max cruising speed: C	86 knots (160 km/h; 99 mph)
C-2000	92 knots (170 km/h; 106 mph)
Stalling speed (both)	36 knots (65 km/h; 41 mph)
Max rate of climb at S/L: C	138 m (453 ft)/min
C-2000	192 m (630 ft)/min
Service ceiling: C	5,000 m (16,400 ft)
T-O run: C	approx 180 m (590 ft)
C-2000	approx 100 m (328 ft)
Landing run: C	100 m (328 ft)
Range with max fuel (both)	approx 378 nm (700 km; 435 miles)

SCHEIBE SF-25E SUPER-FALKE

Developed from the SF-25C-S, the Super-Falke has increased wing span and a rubber sprung monowheel; a cabin heater is standard. Production aircraft have a tailwheel and upper surface Schempp-Hirth airbrakes.

A 48.5 kW (65 hp) Limbach SL 1700 EA I engine is fitted, with a 12V battery and alternator for electric engine starting. Fuel capacity is 45 litres (11.9 US gallons; 9.9 Imp gallons).

The Super-Falke was flown for the first time in the Summer of 1974; 60 had been delivered by January 1983, but only four more are known to have been completed. Details of the SF-25E can be found in the 1985-86 and earlier editions of *Jane's*.

SCHEIBE SF-28A TANDEM-FALKE

The Tandem-Falke, as its name implies, is a further development of the Falke series of motor gliders in which the two seats are arranged in tandem. Design began in 1970, and the prototype (D-KAFJ) flew for the first time in May

1971, powered by a 33.5 kW (45 hp) Stamo MS 1500 engine. Details of the production version have appeared in the 1985-86 and earlier editions of *Jane's*. Production had totalled 118 by January 1983, but only two more examples have been completed since that time.

SCHEIBE SF-34

Design of the SF-34 sailplane began in 1978, and the prototype flew for the first time on 28 October that year. Production takes place, under licence, in Hungary; a total of 30 had been built by January 1988. Brauchle Segelflugzeugbau und Charter GmbH of Lindenberg in West Germany currently advertises an SF-34B version, which appears to be identical to the details given below for the SF-34.

TYPE: Tandem two-seat training and sporting sailplane.

AIRFRAME: Cantilever mid-wing monoplane. Wortmann wing sections: FX-61-184 at root, FX-60-126 at tip. Glassfibre roving main spar. Wings and tail unit of GFRP honeycomb sandwich; fuselage is a GFRP shell. Schempp-Hirth airbrake in upper surface of each wing. Non-retractable semi-exposed monowheel and nosewheel, tyre sizes 5.00-5 and 260 × 85 respectively; tailskid. Tandem seats under frameless one-piece sideways opening flush canopy. Towing hooks under nose and at CG.

DIMENSIONS, EXTERNAL:

Wing span	15.80 m (51 ft 10 in)
Wing aspect ratio	16.9
Length overall	7.50 m (24 ft 7¼ in)
Height over tail	1.40 m (4 ft 7 in)

AREA:

Wings, gross	14.80 m² (159.3 sq ft)

WEIGHTS AND LOADING:

Weight empty	approx 320 kg (705 lb)
Max T-O weight	540 kg (1,190 lb)
Max wing loading	36.5 kg/m² (7.48 lb/sq ft)

PERFORMANCE (at max T-O weight):

Best glide ratio at 51 knots (95 km/h; 59 mph)	35
Min rate of sink at 41 knots (75 km/h; 47 mph)	0.70 m (2.30 ft)/s
Stalling speed	38 knots (70 km/h; 44 mph)
Max speed (rough and smooth air)	135 knots (250 km/h; 155 mph)
Max aero-tow speed	86 knots (160 km/h; 99 mph)
Max winch-launching speed	67 knots (125 km/h; 78 mph)

SCHEIBE SF-36

A prototype of this two-seat motor glider (D-KOOP) was flown for the first time in the Summer of 1980; production began in January 1981, and five had been completed by January 1983. Only one further example has been built since then. Further details can be found in the 1987-88 *Jane's*.

SCHEMPP-HIRTH

SCHEMPP-HIRTH FLUGZEUGBAU GmbH

Krebenstrasse 25, Postfach 14 43, 7312 Kirchheim unter Teck

Telephone: 07021 2441 and 45007

Telex: 7267817 HATE D

DIRECTOR: Dipl-Ing Klaus Holighaus

Schempp-Hirth specialises in the production of high-performance Open Class, FAI 15 m Class, Standard Class and two-seat sailplanes and powered sailplanes. Dipl-Ing Klaus Holighaus is 100% shareholder.

Production of the Schempp-Hirth Standard Cirrus was undertaken by Jastreb in Yugoslavia (see 1987-88 *Jane's*).

The 'Oehler system' power plant installation, described under the Ventus heading, is also available for the Janus and Nimbus series.

SCHEMPP-HIRTH NIMBUS 3

The prototype Nimbus 3 (D-2111) flew for the first time on 21 February 1981. Production versions are the basic **Nimbus 3** and the **Nimbus 3/24.5** with add-on wingtip extensions. Nimbus 3s fitted with the Oehler power plant system (see Ventus entry) are designated **Nimbus 3T** (for Turbo). The two-seat **Nimbus 3D** versions are described separately. A total of nearly 100 of all versions had been built by early 1988.

TYPE: Single-seat Open Class sailplane and powered sailplane.

AIRFRAME: Cantilever mid-wing monoplane. Four-piece (six on 3/24.5), thin section (Wortmann/Holighaus) wings, with 14% thickness/chord ratio, fitted with spoilerons, trailing-edge flaps and interconnected Schempp-Hirth upper surface airbrakes, and inboard/outboard leading-edge tanks for up to 280 litres (74 US gallons; 61.5 Imp gallons) of water ballast. Turned-down wingtips. Cantilever T tailplane, with elevators. Forward fuselage is a glassfibre shell; rear fuselage of carbonfibre, reinforced by GFRP/foam sandwich webs. Wing shells of carbonfibre/foam sandwich, with carbonfibre spar caps and GFRP/foam sandwich shear webs. Carbonfibre/GFRP/foam sandwich tailplane, with CF/GFRP elevators; CF/foam sandwich fin, with GFRP/foam sandwich rudder. Fully retractable monowheel, with shock absorption; tail bumper. One-piece canopy, opening sideways.

DIMENSIONS. EXTERNAL:

Wing span: 3	22.90 m (75 ft 1½ in)
3/24.5	24.50 m (80 ft 4½ in)
Wing aspect ratio: 3	32.2
3/24.5	35.9
Length overall	7.63 m (25 ft 0½ in)
Height over tail	1.55 m (5 ft 1 in)

AREAS:

Wings, gross: 3	16.30 m² (175.45 sq ft)
3/24.5	16.70 m² (179.76 sq ft)

WEIGHTS AND LOADINGS:

Weight empty: 3	392 kg (864 lb)
3/24.5	396 kg (873 lb)
Max T-O weight: 3, 3/24.5	750 kg (1,653 lb)
Max wing loading: 3	46.0 kg/m² (9.43 lb/sq ft)
3/24.5	44.9 kg/m² (9.19 lb/sq ft)

PERFORMANCE (at max T-O weight except where indicated):
Best glide ratio at 51 knots (95 km/h, 59 mph), wing loading of 29 kg/m² (5.94 lb/sq ft):

3	55
3/24.5	58

Min rate of sink at 40 knots (75 km/h; 47 mph):

3	0.44 m (1.44 ft)/s
3/24.5	0.41 m (1.35 ft)/s
Stalling speed: 3	33 knots (60 km/h; 38 mph)
3/24.5	32 knots (59 km/h; 37 mph)
Max speed (smooth air)	146 knots (270 km/h; 168 mph)

Max speed (rough air):

3	108 knots (200 km/h; 124 mph)
3/24.5	102 knots (190 km/h; 118 mph)
Max aero-tow speed	97 knots (180 km/h; 112 mph)
Max winch-launching speed	81 knots (150 km/h; 93 mph)
g limits at design manoeuvring speed	+5.3/−2.65

SCHEMPP-HIRTH NIMBUS 3D

A prototype of this Open Class two-seater (D-KCJC) flew for the first time on 2 May 1986. It combines a modified Janus fuselage with the long-span Nimbus 3/24.5 wing, a new wing mounting structure and a reinforced main spar, has 1° 30′ of forward sweep at the leading-edge and a small nosewheel. Two powered versions are also available which use the Oehler power plant system, namely the **3DT** with the 'Turbo' retrieve system based on a Solo engine, and the **3DM** offering full self-launching capability using a Rotax engine. The prototype 3DM flew for the first time on 17 March 1988. About ten Nimbus 3Ds and 3DTs had been completed by early 1988.

TYPE: Open Class two-seat sailplane (3DT powered sailplane and 3DM self-launching sailplane).

AIRFRAME: Cantilever mid-wing monoplane. Wortmann wing sections: FX-79-K-143/17 at root, FX-77-135/20 at tip. Dihedral 3°. Incidence 1° 30′. Wings, fuselage and tail unit otherwise generally as described for Nimbus 3, except that fuselage is constructed of carbonfibre for the centre and aft sections (including fin) and carbon/Kevlar for the forward section, fairings are used at the wing-fuselage junctures, water ballast tanks (each of 84 litres; 22.2 US gallons; 18.5 Imp gallons capacity) are in outer wing panels only, and wingtips are not turned down. Retractable unsprung monowheel (tyre size 5.00-5, pressure 4.5 bars; 65 lb/sq in), with brake, plus tailskid and mini nosewheel bumper. Two seats in tandem, under one-piece canopy which opens sideways to starboard.

POWER PLANT: *Nimbus 3DT:* One 19.4 kW (26 hp) Solo 2350 auxiliary engine, installed in retractable mounting aft of cockpit and driving an OE-FL 5.88/83 propeller with five foldable blades. Retraction method as for Janus CM; extension takes 15 seconds, with an altitude loss of 80 m (265 ft). Fuel in single fuselage tank, capacity 16 litres (4.2 US gallons; 3.5 Imp gallons). *Nimbus 3DM:* One 44.7 kW (60 hp) Rotax 535C two-cylinder two-stroke engine, with 3:1 tooth belt reduction to a two-blade composites propeller, the installation retracting as for the 3DT. Fuel capacity 50 litres (13.2 US gallons; 11 Imp gallons).

DIMENSIONS, EXTERNAL:

Wing span	24.60 m (80 ft 8½ in)
Wing aspect ratio	35.9
Length overall	8.70 m (28 ft 6½ in)
Height over tail	1.39 m (4 ft 6¾ in)
Propeller diameter	0.88 m (2 ft 10¾ in)

AREA:

Wings, gross	16.85 m² (181.4 sq ft)

WEIGHTS AND LOADINGS (A: 3D, B: 3DT, C: 3DM):

Weight empty: A	485 kg (1,069 lb)
B	530 kg (1,168 lb)
C	575 kg (1,268 lb)
Max water ballast: A	168 kg (370 lb)
Max crew weight (each)	100-110 kg (220-243 lb)
Max T-O weight: A	750 kg (1,653 lb)
B, C	800 kg (1,764 lb)
Max wing loading: A	44.51 kg/m² (9.12 lb/sq ft)
B	47.48 kg/m² (9.73 lb/sq ft)
Max power loading: B	41.24 kg/kW (67.83 lb/hp)
C	17.90 kg/kW (29.4 lb/hp)

PERFORMANCE, UNPOWERED (at max T-O weight):

Best glide ratio at 57 knots (105 km/h; 65 mph)	57
Min rate of sink at 43 knots (80 km/h; 50 mph)	
	0.45 m (1.48 ft)/s
Stalling speed	42 knots (77 km/h; 48 mph)
Max speed (smooth air)	148 knots (275 km/h; 171 mph)
Max speed (rough air)	102 knots (190 km/h; 118 mph)
Max aero-tow speed	97 knots (180 km/h; 112 mph)
Max winch-launching speed	81 knots (150 km/h; 93 mph)
g limits	+5.4/−3.4

PERFORMANCE, POWERED (B and C as above at max T-O weight):

Never-exceed speed:	
B, C	148 knots (275 km/h; 171 mph)
C, under power	100 knots (185 km/h; 115 mph)
Max cruising speed: B	67 knots (125 km/h; 78 mph)
C, at 65% power	80 knots (148 km/h; 92 mph)
Stalling speed: B	43 knots (80 km/h; 50 mph)
Max rate of climb at S/L: B	33 m (108 ft)/min
C	132 m (433 ft)/min
T-O run: C	270 m (885 ft)
T-O to 15 m (50 ft): C	399 m (1,310 ft)
Range: C, cruising	190 nm (352 km; 218 miles)
C, 'sawtooth method'	280 nm (518 km; 322 miles)
Min rate of sink at 43 knots (80 km/h; 50 mph):	
B	29 m (95 ft)/min
C	31 m (102 ft)/min

SCHEMPP-HIRTH JANUS

The Janus design was started by Dipl-Ing Holighaus in 1969, and the prototype made its first flight in the Spring of 1974.

Production began in January 1975 with the second, improved aircraft; a **Janus B** version became available in March 1978, with fixed incidence tailplane; the **Janus C** has 20 m span carbonfibre wings and a carbonfibre tailplane. At the end of 1985 Janus C sailplanes held FAI records for distance in a straight line, distance to a fixed goal, out and return distance to a goal, and speed around triangular courses of 100 km and 300 km.

The **Janus CM** self-launching version of the C, first flown in 1978, has the same Rotax engine installation as the Nimbus 3DM, pylon mounted aft of the cockpit and retracting rearward into the top of the fuselage when not in use by means of an electric spindle drive (also used on Nimbus 3DM). Empty and max T-O weights are 480 kg (1,058 lb) and 700 kg (1,543 lb) respectively. This version holds world records in FAI Class DM-2 for multi-seat motor gliders for out and return distance to a goal, and speed over triangular courses of 300 and 500 km. The **Janus CT** powered retrieve system version is similar, but has the Oehler installation described under the Ventus entry.

By early 1988 production totalled 240 Janus, Janus B, Janus C, Janus CM and Janus CT, including 30 of the CM version.

The following description applies to the standard Janus B, except where indicated:

TYPE: Tandem two-seat high-performance training sailplane.

AIRFRAME: Cantilever mid-wing monoplane. Wortmann wing sections: FX-67-K-170 at root, FX-67-K-15 at tip. Dihedral 4°. Sweepforward 2° on leading-edge. Glassfibre/foam sandwich wings, with glassfibre monocoque ailerons, trailing-edge flaps and Schempp-Hirth upper surface airbrakes. Ailerons and flaps interconnected. Glassfibre fuselage shell, with bonded-in foam bulkheads, on a welded steel tube central frame. Cantilever glassfibre/foam sandwich fixed incidence T tailplane, with elevator. Non-retractable semi-recessed monowheel (diameter 380 mm) and nosewheel. Continental tyres: pressure 2.69 bars (39 lb/sq in) on mainwheel; pressure 0.79 bars (11.5 lb/sq in) on nosewheel. Tost drum brake on mainwheel. Bumper under rear fuselage. Jettisonable tail drag-chute. One-piece canopy opens sideways to starboard. Provision for 200 kg (440 lb) of water ballast.

DIMENSIONS, EXTERNAL:

Wing span: B	18.20 m (59 ft 8½ in)
C	20.00 m (65 ft 7½ in)
Wing aspect ratio: B	20.0
C	23.0
Length overall	8.62 m (28 ft 3¼ in)
Height over tail	1.45 m (4 ft 9 in)

AREAS:

Wings, gross: B	16.60 m² (178.7 sq ft)
C	17.40 m² (187.3 sq ft)

WEIGHTS AND LOADINGS:

Weight empty: B	365 kg (805 lb)
C	355 kg (783 lb)
Max T-O weight: B	620 kg (1,366 lb)
C	700 kg (1,543 lb)
Max wing loading: B	37.0 kg/m² (7.58 lb/sq ft)
C	40.0 kg/m² (8.20 lb/sq ft)

PERFORMANCE (at max T-O weight except where indicated):
Best glide ratio at wing loading of 36.5 kg/m² (7.48 lb/sq ft) and speed of 59 knots (110 km/h; 68 mph):

B	39.5
C	43.5

Min rate of sink at above wing loading and speed of 49 knots (90 km/h; 56 mph):

B	0.70 m (2.30 ft)/s
C	0.60 m (1.97 ft)/s
Stalling speed at above wing loading:	
B, C	38 knots (70 km/h; 43 mph)
Max speed (rough and smooth air):	
B	118 knots (220 km/h; 136 mph)
C	135 knots (250 km/h; 155 mph)
Max aero-tow speed:	
B	91 knots (170 km/h; 105 mph)
C	97 knots (180 km/h; 112 mph)
Max winch-launching speed:	
B	65 knots (120 km/h; 75 mph)
C	81 knots (150 km/h; 93 mph)
g limits: B, C	+5.3/−2.65

SCHEMPP-HIRTH VENTUS

First flown on 3 May 1980, the Ventus (Latin for wind) features a thin section carbonfibre wing. It became available with a choice of two fuselages, the Ventus b having a slightly larger cockpit for pilots more than 1.75 m (5 ft 9 in) tall.

In 1982 Schempp-Hirth introduced the **Ventus b/16.6**, with detachable CFRP/GfK wingtip extensions, for Open Class competition.

An Oehler retractable power plant, using a 13.5 kW (18 hp) Solo engine and 15 litre (4.0 US gallon; 3.3 Imp gallon) fuel tank, became available in 1982 on the Ventus b/16.6, which is then known as the **Ventus bT**. Engine and wingtips are readily removable for reversion to 15 metre Class flying. This installation provides a retrieve system.

In late 1987 the **Ventus c** was introduced to the range. Wingtip extensions can be fitted to the standard 15.00 m wings to provide optional spans of 16.60 m (54 ft 5½ in) or 17.60 m (57 ft 9 in). The Ventus c also has flaps that can act as additional inboard ailerons, Schempp-Hirth airbrakes, a 5 litre (1.32 US gallon; 1.1 Imp gallon) water ballast tank in the tail fin, the options of a sprung landing gear and swing-up instrument panel, and drag-reducing wing/fuselage fairings. Mini winglets are an option for the 15.00 m wings. Two fuselage sizes are available for the Ventus c.

First SF-34 to be completed by Hungarian workers at Scheibe's factory
(Peter F. Selinger)

Schempp-Hirth Janus B *(Peter F. Selinger)*

Schempp-Hirth Nimbus 3/24-5 *(Peter F. Selinger)*

Ventus b/T with Webra engine *(Peter F. Selinger)*

Schempp-Hirth Ventus cM self-launching sailplane *(Peter F. Selinger)*

Schempp-Hirth Nimbus 3DM *(Peter F. Selinger)*

A 15.3 kW (20.5 hp) Solo-engined 'Turbo' retrieve version is the **Ventus cT**, with 17.60 m (57 ft 9 in) span. By removing the engine, battery, propeller, fuel tank and wingtip extensions, the aircraft returns to Ventus c configuration. Fuel capacity is 16 litres (4.2 US gallons; 3.5 Imp gallons).

A self-launching version of the Ventus c is also available, as the **Ventus cM**. First flown on 18 February 1988, it too has wingtip extensions to provide the full 17.60 m span. The Solo power plant is uprated to give 18.6-20 kW (25-27 hp) and is fitted with 2.3:1 belt reduction drive. The fuselage is constructed of carbonfibre/Kevlar except for aramid fibre in the cockpit area. Removal of the power plant can be performed quickly. Fuel capacity is 22 litres (5.8 US gallons; 4.8 Imp gallons).

Ventus production (all versions) totalled 370 by early 1988.

TYPE: Single-seat 15 metre Class sailplane (Ventus cT powered sailplane and cM self-launching sailplane).

AIRFRAME: *Ventus a and b:* Cantilever mid-wing monoplane, with newly developed Wortmann/Holighaus/Althaus thin-section wings of all-carbonfibre construction, including skins. Two-segment ailerons. Schempp-Hirth upper surface airbrakes. Fuselage centre frame of steel tube to carry main wing and landing gear loads. Cantilever fixed incidence T tailplane, with elevator; rudder area increased on Ventus b. Retractable monowheel; tail bumper. One-piece cockpit canopy, opening sideways to starboard. Provision for 150 kg (331 lb) of water ballast. *Ventus c, cT and cM:* See introductory paragraphs.

DIMENSIONS, EXTERNAL (A: a, B: b, C: b/16.6, D: bT, E: c, F: cT, and G: cM):

Wing span: A, B, E	15.00 m (49 ft 2½ in)
C, D, E optional	16.60 m (54 ft 5¼ in)
E optional, F, G	17.60 m (57 ft 9 in)
Wing aspect ratio: A, B, E	23.7
C, D, E with 16.60 m span	27.7
E with 17.60 m span, F, G	30.2
Length overall: A	6.35 m (20 ft 10 in)
all other versions	6.58 m (21 ft 7 in)
Height overall: all versions	1.27 m (4 ft 2 in)

AREAS:

Wings, gross: A, B, E	9.51 m² (102.4 sq ft)
C, D, E with 16.60 m span	9.96 m² (107.2 sq ft)
E with 17.60 m span, F, G	10.15 m² (109.25 sq ft)

WEIGHTS AND LOADINGS (A, B, C, D, E, F, G as above):

Weight empty: A, B, E	approx 240 kg (529 lb)
C	243 kg (535 lb)
E with 17.60 m span	244 kg (538 lb)
F	289 kg (637 lb)
G	300 kg (661 lb)
Max T-O weight: A, B, E	525 kg (1,157 lb)
C, F, G	430 kg (948 lb)
E with 17.60 m span	500 kg (1,102 lb)
Max wing loading:	
A, B, E	55.2 kg/m² (11.31 lb/sq ft)
C	43.2 kg/m² (8.85 lb/sq ft)
E with 17.60 m span, G	49.3 kg/m² (10.10 lb/sq ft)
F	42.4 kg/m² (8.68 lb/sq ft)
Max power loading:	
F	28.10 kg/kW (46.24 lb/hp)
G	9.62 kg/kW (15.80 lb/hp)

PERFORMANCE, UNPOWERED (at max T-O weight except where indicated; A, B, C, E, G as above):

Best glide ratio at wing loading of 35 kg/m² (7.17 lb/sq ft):	
A, B, E at 56 knots (105 km/h; 65 mph)	43.5
C at 51 knots (95 km/h; 59 mph)	46.5
E with 17.60 m span	49
G at 56 knots (105 km/h; 65 mph)	48-49
Min rate of sink at 41 knots (75 km/h; 47 mph):	
A, B	0.58 m (1.90 ft)/s
C	0.59 m (1.94 ft)/s
G, power plant retracted	approx 0.68 m (2.23 ft)/s
Stalling speed: A, B	36 knots (65 km/h; 41 mph)
C	35 knots (64 km/h; 40 mph)
Max speed (smooth air):	
A, B, C	135 knots (250 km/h; 155 mph)
E	145 knots (270 km/h; 167 mph)
Max speed (rough air):	
A, B, C	108 knots (200 km/h; 124 mph)
Max aero-tow speed:	
A, B, C	97 knots (180 km/h; 112 mph)
Max winch-launching speed:	
A, B, C	81 knots (150 km/h; 93 mph)
g limits at design manoeuvring speed:	
A, B, C	+5.3/-2.65

PERFORMANCE, POWERED (at max T-O weight; D and G as above):

Max speed:	
G, power plant retracted	146 knots (270 km/h; 168 mph)
G, power on	97 knots (180 km/h; 112 mph)
Cruising speed:	
D	approx 70 knots (130 km/h; 81 mph)
G	approx 76 knots (140 km/h; 87 mph)

Min speed: G 41 knots (75 km/h; 47 mph)
Max rate of climb: G 120 m (394 ft)/min
Rate of climb (depending upon altitude and ambient temperature):
D 38-68 m (125-225 ft)/min
T-O run: G approx 280 m (919 ft)
T-O to 15 m (50 ft): G approx 420 m (1,378 ft)
Range (combining powered climbs and engine-off glides in 'sawtooth' method):
D more than 108 nm (201 km; 125 miles)
G approx 270 nm (500 km; 310 miles)
Range in cruise: G approx 172 nm (320 km; 199 miles)
Max endurance: G 2 h

SCHEMPP-HIRTH DISCUS

A total of 210 production examples of this Standard Class sailplane had been built by early 1988, in two versions. The first prototype, **Discus a** (D-6111), flew for the first time on 21 April 1984 and the second prototype, **Discus b** (D-8111), made its initial flight on 17 May 1984. The Discus a utilises the fuselage and tail unit of the 15 metre Class Ventus a. The Discus b has the longer fuselage of the Ventus b, incorporating a roomier cockpit.

Discus sailplanes of both versions took five of the first six places at the 1985 World Championships held at Rieti, Italy; first ten places at the 1986 US National Championships; first place at the Australian, Finnish, West German, Italian, Swedish and Swiss nationals in 1986; and first six places at the 1987 World Championships.

A new version flew for the first time on 18 November 1987 as the aerobatic **Discus K**. Production aircraft will be delivered from late 1988. It is capable of negative g manoeuvres.

The Discus K has new wingtip extensions of different geometry in aerobatic configuration, offering a span of only 13.7 m (44 ft 11½ in) but with the size of the ailerons remaining unchanged. These wingtips give a higher standard of manoeuvrability about the longitudinal axis. Best glide ratio remains nearly 38, and the min rate of sink is less than 0.7 m (2.30 ft)/s. Max speed is limited at present to 146 knots (270 km/h; 168 mph). g limits are +7/–5.

The following details refer to the Discus a and b:
TYPE: Single-seat Standard Class sailplane.
AIRFRAME: Cantilever mid-wing monoplane, with 3° dihedral. No details have been released of the wing aerofoil section. Boundary layer control is achieved with lower surface turbulator strips. Kinked, sweptback leading-edges on outer sections. Centre-section is unswept, with constant chord. The wings are of GFRP with a carbonfibre main spar, and have ailerons of GFRP, plus Schempp-Hirth upper surface airbrakes. Fuselage and tail unit as described for Ventus a/b. Retractable rubber sprung monowheel (tyre size 4.00-4, pressure 4.41 bars; 64 lb/sq in), with drum brake; fixed rubber tailskid.

Provision for 180 litres (47.6 US gallons; 39.6 Imp gallons) of water ballast.

DIMENSIONS, EXTERNAL:
Wing span (a, b) 15.00 m (49 ft 2½ in)
Wing aspect ratio (a, b) 21.3
Length overall: a 6.35 m (20 ft 10 in)
b 6.58 m (21 ft 7 in)
Height over tail (a, b) 1.27 m (4 ft 2 in)
AREA:
Wings, gross (a, b) 10.58 m² (113.9 sq ft)
WEIGHTS AND LOADING:
Weight empty: a 228 kg (503 lb)
b 233 kg (514 lb)
Max T-O weight (a, b) 525 kg (1,157 lb)
Max wing loading (a, b) 49.62 kg/m² (10.16 lb/sq ft)
PERFORMANCE (a, b, at max T-O weight):
Best glide ratio at 54 knots (100 km/h; 62 mph) 42.2
Min rate of sink at 42 knots (78 km/h; 49 mph) 0.59 m (1.94 ft)/s
Stalling speed 36 knots (66 km/h; 41 mph)
Max speed (smooth air) 135 knots (250 km/h; 155 mph)
Max speed (rough air) 108 knots (200 km/h; 124 mph)
Max aero-tow speed 97 knots (180 km/h; 112 mph)
Max winch-launching speed 81 knots (150 km/h; 93 mph)
g limits +5.3/–2.65

SCHLEICHER
ALEXANDER SCHLEICHER GmbH & Co

HEAD OFFICE AND WORKS: Postfach 60, 6416 Poppenhausen/ Wasserkuppe
Telephone: 06658 225

This company is one of the oldest manufacturers of sailplanes in the world. Since its formation in 1927, Schleicher and its licencees have built approximately 5,200 wood/metal gliders and over 2,000 composites sailplanes and motor gliders. Those in its current range designed by Ing Rudolf Kaiser are prefixed ASK; those with ASW designations are designed by Ing Gerhard Waibel. An ASH prefix indicates the work of Schleicher's youngest designer, Martin Heide. Schleicher also manufactures and markets spare parts, constructional materials, and dust- and weatherproof covers for sailplanes.

SCHLEICHER ASK 13

Production of the ASK 13 by Schleicher, which totalled 603, has ended, but the ASK 13 is still being manufactured, under licence, by Jubi GmbH (which see).

SCHLEICHER ASW 20 B and 20 C

The ASW 20 was designed to take advantage of the March 1975 CIVV regulations for unlimited 15 metre sailplanes, and is fitted with trailing-edge flaps as well as large upper surface spoilers. It has an additional high-drag flap range incorporating a special mechanism to eliminate pitch and airspeed changes when changing flap position.

The prototype ASW 20 made its first flight on 29 January 1977, and a total of 762 of various models had been built by Schleicher, plus 100 more under licence, by mid-1988, including the ASW 20 BL and 20 CL, which are described separately. Current basic production models are designated **ASW 20 B** and **ASW 20 C**, the former having a reinforced wing structure enabling it to carry more water ballast in good soaring conditions. The B and C models differ from the original ASW 20 in having a modified wing undersurface with lower drag and DFVLR patented 'turbulators' (see ASW 22 entry for description) which smooth out the airflow in the area of the flap hinges. Other improvements include metal foil sealing of the wing control surfaces (optional), automatic elevator connection, disc (instead of drum) brake, and instrument panel hinged to open with the canopy. These modifications also apply to the BL and CL models.

The following details apply to the ASW 20 B and C:
TYPE: Single-seat 15 metre Class sailplane.
AIRFRAME: Cantilever mid-wing monoplane. Wing sections Wortmann FX-63-131-K (modified DFVLR/ Horstmann-Quast) at root, Wortmann FX-60-126 at tip. Dihedral 2° 20′. No sweepforward at quarter-chord. Glassfibre roving wing main spar. Wings of GFRP/hard foam sandwich, with leading-edge bag tanks for water ballast. Schempp-Hirth metal airbrakes in upper surface. GFRP monocoque fuselage. Cantilever T tail and elevator, with new Wortmann aerofoil sections. Five-position trailing-edge wing flaps (travel –12° to +40°). Ailerons are linked with flaps, and are automatically deflected upward when 'flaps down' is selected for landing. All control surfaces are of aramid/GFRP, and are partly mass balanced. Retractable sprung monowheel, size 5.00-5, with hydraulic disc brake. Rubber tailskid with wear plate is standard; optional fit of tailskid with polyamid roller, or fixed 210 × 65 mm tailwheel with pneumatic tyre and fairing. One-piece Plexiglas canopy, hinged at front and opening upward, can be jettisoned in emergency. Tost towing hook at CG. Options include oxygen bottle, barograph, battery and headrest.

DIMENSIONS, EXTERNAL:
Wing span 15.00 m (49 ft 2½ in)
Wing aspect ratio 21.4
Length overall 6.82 m (22 ft 4½ in)
Height over tail 1.45 m (4 ft 9 in)
AREA:
Wings, gross 10.50 m² (113.0 sq ft)
WEIGHTS AND LOADINGS:
Weight empty: B 260 kg (573 lb)
C 250 kg (551 lb)
Max water ballast: B 160 kg (352 lb)
C 120 kg (264 lb)
Max T-O weight with water ballast:
B 525 kg (1,157 lb)
C 454 kg (1,001 lb)
Max wing loading: B 50.00 kg/m² (10.25 lb/sq ft)
C 43.24 kg/m² (8.86 lb/sq ft)
PERFORMANCE (at max T-O weight except where indicated):
Best glide ratio:
B (without ballast) at 54 knots (100 km/h; 62 mph) 42.5
B (with ballast) at 65 knots (120 km/h; 75 mph) 43
C (without ballast) at 48 knots (90 km/h; 56 mph) 43
C (with ballast) at 62 knots (115 km/h; 71 mph) 42
Min rate of sink:
B (without ballast) at 45 knots (84 km/h; 52 mph) 0.59 m (1.93 ft)/s
C (without ballast) at 47 knots (87 km/h; 54 mph) 0.57 m (1.87 ft)/s
C (with ballast) at 52 knots (96 km/h; 60 mph) 0.68 m (2.23 ft)/s
Stalling speed (without ballast):
B, C 35 knots (65 km/h; 41 mph)
Max speed (smooth air):
B 151 knots (280 km/h; 174 mph)
C 143 knots (265 km/h; 165 mph)
Max speed (rough air):
B 103 knots (191 km/h; 118 mph)
C 143 knots (265 km/h; 165 mph)
Max aero-tow speed:
B 103 knots (191 km/h; 118 mph)
C 97 knots (180 km/h; 112 mph)
Max winch-launching speed:
B 70 knots (129 km/h; 80 mph)
C 67 knots (125 km/h; 78 mph)
g limits:
B at 103 knots (191 km/h; 118 mph), C (without ballast) at 94 knots (174 km/h; 108 mph) +5.3/–2.65
B at 151 knots (280 km/h; 174 mph), C (without ballast) at 143 knots (265 km/h; 165 mph) +4/–1.5

SCHLEICHER ASW 20 BL and 20 CL

The ASW 20 L (for Lang: long), first flown in May 1977, is a version of the ASW 20 with detachable outer wing panels, increasing the span to 16.59 m (54 ft 5¼ in) for Open Class competition. Production began in late 1978. Current models are the ASW 20 BL and CL, to which the following data apply:
TYPE: Single-seat Open Class sailplane.
AIRFRAME: Generally as for ASW 20 B and C except for wings, which have detachable span-increasing outer panels. Reduced water ballast in BL, no provision for water ballast in CL.
DIMENSIONS, EXTERNAL: As ASW 20 B and C except:
Wing span 16.59 m (54 ft 5¼ in)
Wing aspect ratio 24.9
AREA:
Wings, gross 11.05 m² (118.9 sq ft)

WEIGHTS AND LOADINGS:
Weight empty: BL 265 kg (584 lb)
CL 255 kg (562 lb)
Max water ballast: BL 50 kg (110 lb)
Max T-O weight: BL 430 kg (948 lb)
CL 380 kg (837 lb)
Max wing loading: BL 38.91 kg/m² (7.97 lb/sq ft)
CL 34.39 kg/m² (7.05 lb/sq ft)
PERFORMANCE (at max T-O weight except where indicated):
Best glide ratio:
BL (without ballast) at 48 knots (90 km/h; 56 mph) 45
CL at 49 knots (91 km/h; 57 mph) 46
Min rate of sink:
BL (without ballast) at 43 knots (80 km/h; 50 mph) 0.56 m (1.83 ft)/s
CL at 45 knots (84 km/h; 52 mph) 0.53 m (1.74 ft)/s
Stalling speed:
BL (without ballast) and CL 35 knots (64 km/h; 40 mph)
Max speed (smooth air):
BL, CL 135 knots (250 km/h; 155 mph)
Max speed (rough air):
BL 97 knots (180 km/h; 112 mph)
CL 89 knots (165 km/h; 103 mph)
Max aero-tow speed:
BL 89 knots (165 km/h; 103 mph)
CL 86 knots (160 km/h; 99 mph)
Max winch-launching speed:
BL 70 knots (130 km/h; 80 mph)
CL 65 knots (120 km/h; 75 mph)
g limits:
BL at 97 knots (180 km/h; 112 mph) +5.3/–2.65
CL at 89 knots (165 km/h; 103 mph) +5.3/–2.65

SCHLEICHER ASK 21

Designed by Ing Kaiser, the ASK 21 prototype flew for the first time on 6 February 1979; it received LBA certification on 18 April 1980. A total of 385 had been built by mid-1988, including ten in 1983 for the UK Air Cadets, by whom they are known as the **Vanguard**.

TYPE: Tandem two-seat competition and training sailplane.
AIRFRAME: Cantilever mid-wing monoplane. Two-piece wings, primarily of GFRP/foam sandwich construction with GFRP roving spar. Wortmann wing sections: FX-S-02-196 from root to inboard of ailerons, FX-60-126 at tip. Dihedral 4°. Sweepforward at quarter-chord 1° 30′. Schempp-Hirth upper surface metal airbrakes. GFRP/honeycomb sandwich fuselage. Fixed T tailplane and separate elevator; rudder and elevator partly mass-balanced. Non-retractable semi-recessed nosewheel (size 4.00-4) and rubber sprung monowheel (size 5.00-5), the latter with hydraulic disc brake; steel shod rubber tailskid standard, pneumatic tailwheel (210 × 65 mm) optional. Front and rear canopies hinged at front and rear respectively, both opening upward.

DIMENSIONS, EXTERNAL:
Wing span 17.00 m (55 ft 9¼ in)
Wing aspect ratio 16.1
Length overall 8.35 m (27 ft 4¾ in)
Height over tail 1.55 m (5 ft 1 in)
AREA:
Wings, gross 17.95 m² (193.2 sq ft)
WEIGHTS AND LOADING:
Weight empty 360 kg (794 lb)
Max T-O weight 600 kg (1,323 lb)
Max wing loading 33.4 kg/m² (6.84 lb/sq ft)

Schempp-Hirth Discus b Standard Class sailplane *(Peter F. Selinger)*

Schleicher ASK 21 tandem two-seat sailplane *(Avio Data)*

Schleicher ASW 22 BE motor glider *(Peter F. Selinger)*

Schleicher ASW 20 C Open Class sailplane *(Peter F. Selinger)*

Schleicher ASK 23 training and performance sailplane

PERFORMANCE (carrying pilot only):
Best glide ratio at 46 knots (85 km/h; 53 mph)	35
Min rate of sink at 36 knots (67 km/h; 42 mph)	
	0.65 m (2.13 ft)/s
Stalling speed	34 knots (62 km/h; 39 mph)
Max speed (smooth air)	151 knots (280 km/h; 174 mph)
Max speed (rough air)	135 knots (250 km/h; 155 mph)
Max aero-tow speed	94 knots (175 km/h; 109 mph)
Max winch-launching speed	
	70 knots (130 km/h; 81 mph)
g limits at 97 knots (180 km/h; 112 mph)	+6.5/−4

SCHLEICHER ASW 22 B

Extensive use is made of composite materials in the construction of this Open Class sailplane, which has combined flaps/airbrakes similar to those fitted to the ASW 20. A special feature of the wing design is the provision of about 1,000 tubular apertures ('turbulators') in the underside, over 17 m (55 ft 9¼ in) of the span, through which air can be vented to provide a form of boundary layer control and improve performance at the upper end of the speed range.

Design of the ASW 22 began in 1979, and the prototype (D-7122) flew for the first time on 4 July 1981. Production ended in July 1985, a total of 39 having been completed, all with 22 m (72 ft 2¼ in) span wings. A description can be found in the 1985-86 *Jane's*.

In January 1986 Schleicher began building a prototype of the ASW 22 B version, with wing span increased from 22 to 25 metres and other improvements including a new HQ-17 aerofoil section on the inner wings. This replaced the original model in production, and three had been built by mid-1988. The description which follows applies to the ASW 22 B:

TYPE: Single-seat Open Class sailplane.
AIRFRAME: Cantilever mid-wing monoplane. Wing sections DFVLR-HQ-17 at root, Delft University DU84-132 V3 at tip. Dihedral 3° 30′. Incidence 5°. Sweepback 0° 48′ on outer panels only. Main wing structure of carbonfibre/epoxy (90 per cent) and GFRP (10 per cent). Trailing-edge flaps and ailerons are of Kevlar construction. Schempp-Hirth aluminium upper surface airbrakes. Monocoque fuselage of carbon/aramid/GFRP. Cantilever T tail with carbonfibre/epoxy sandwich tailplane, AFRP sandwich fin, and Kevlar sandwich elevator and rudder. Main landing gear is a twin-wheel (size 5.00-5) retractable unit, both with rubber shock absorption and one with Cleveland hydraulic disc brake. Foam rubber tailskid, with wear plate, is standard;

non-retractable tailwheel (size 210 × 65 mm) is optional. Tost CG towing hook, covered in flight by landing gear doors. Two 60 litre (15.8 US gallon; 13.2 Imp gallon) and two 50 litre (13.2 US gallon; 11 Imp gallon) water ballast tanks in wing leading-edges. One-piece jettisonable canopy, hinged at front to open upward.

DIMENSIONS, EXTERNAL:
Wing span	25.00 m (82 ft 0¼ in)
Wing aspect ratio	38.3
Length overall	8.10 m (26 ft 7 in)
Height over tail	1.66 m (5 ft 5½ in)

AREA:
Wings, gross	16.31 m² (175.6 sq ft)

WEIGHTS AND LOADING:
Weight empty, equipped	450 kg (992 lb)
Max water ballast	235 kg (518 lb)
Max T-O weight	750 kg (1,653 lb)
Max wing loading	45.98 kg/m² (9.42 lb/sq ft)

PERFORMANCE (estimated):
*Best glide ratio at 51 knots (95 km/h; 59 mph)	60
*Min rate of sink at 43 knots (80 km/h; 50 mph)	
	0.41 m (1.35 ft)/s
*Stalling speed	35 knots (65 km/h; 41 mph)
Max speed (smooth air)	151 knots (280 km/h; 174 mph)
Max speed (rough air), and max aero-tow speed	
	102 knots (190 km/h; 118 mph)
Max winch-launching speed	
	75 knots (140 km/h; 87 mph)
g limits	+5.3/−2.65

*without ballast

SCHLEICHER ASW 22 BE

Construction of prototypes of this motor glider version of the ASW 22 B started in November 1985. First flight, by D-KKJP, took place on 22 March 1986, and a total of eight ASW 22 BEs had been built by mid-1988.

AIRFRAME: As for ASW 22 B except for changes necessary to accommodate power plant, and two (instead of four) 60 litre (15.8 US gallon; 13.2 Imp gallon) water ballast tanks in wings.

POWER PLANT: One 31.6 kW (42.4 hp) Bombardier Rotax 505 engine, driving a two-blade propeller. Fuel in one fuselage and two inboard wing tanks, combined capacity 70 litres (18.5 US gallons; 15.4 Imp gallons).

DIMENSIONS, EXTERNAL: As ASW 22 B, plus:
Propeller diameter	1.58 m (5 ft 2¼ in)

WEIGHTS AND LOADINGS:
Weight empty, equipped	510 kg (1,124 lb)
Max water ballast	120 kg (264 lb)
Max T-O weight	750 kg (1,653 lb)
Max wing loading	45.98 kg/m² (9.42 lb/sq ft)
Max power loading	23.73 kg/kW (38.99 lb/hp)

PERFORMANCE, UNPOWERED (estimated): As ASW 22 B, except:
*Best glide ratio at 59 knots (110 km/h; 68 mph)	60
*Min rate of sink at 46 knots (85 km/h; 53 mph)	
	0.46 m (1.51 ft)/s
*Stalling speed	41 knots (76 km/h; 48 mph)

*without ballast

PERFORMANCE, POWERED (estimated):
Max cruising speed	92 knots (170 km/h; 106 mph)
Econ cruising speed (alternate climbing/gliding profile)	
	49 knots (90 km/h; 56 mph)
Stalling speed	44 knots (80 km/h; 51 mph)
Max rate of climb at S/L	132 m (433 ft)/min
T-O run	200 m (656 ft)
Range with max fuel	431 nm (800 km; 497 miles)

SCHLEICHER ASK 23

Announced in the Spring of 1981, the ASK 23 is essentially a successor to the K 8 as a single-seat training and club glider, but making use of GFRP constructional materials. Design began in November 1980; production started in October 1983.

Schleicher also manufactures the **ASK 23 B**, suitable for cloud flying and aerobatic manoeuvres in accordance with JAR 22 Category U. This has empty and max T-O weights of 235 kg (518 lb) and 360 kg (793 lb); speeds and other performance data are as for the original ASK 23. A total of 108 of both models had been built by mid-1988. The following description applies to the ASK 23:

TYPE: Single-seat training and performance sailplane.
AIRFRAME: Cantilever shoulder-wing monoplane. Wortmann wing sections FX-61-168 at root, FX-60-126 at tip. Dihedral 2° 40′. Sweepback 0° 53′ 24″ at quarter-chord. Construction of GFRP/foam sandwich, with glassfibre roving main spar and aluminium upper surface airbrakes. GFRP honeycomb sandwich fuselage shell. Cantilever T tail, of similar construction to wings, with separate elevator. Landing gear comprises a 260 × 85 mm nosewheel, non-retractable rubber sprung 5.00-5 mainwheel (with Tost drum brake), and rubber sprung tailskid. One-piece forward opening Plexiglas canopy, with emergency jettison. Nose and CG towing hooks standard.

DIMENSIONS, EXTERNAL:
Wing span	15.00 m (49 ft 2½ in)
Wing aspect ratio	17.4
Length overall	7.10 m (23 ft 3½ in)
Height over tail	1.40 m (4 ft 7 in)

AREA:
Wings, gross	12.90 m² (138.8 sq ft)

WEIGHTS AND LOADING:
Weight empty	230 kg (507 lb)
Max T-O weight	380 kg (837 lb)
Max wing loading	29.5 kg/m² (6.04 lb/sq ft)

PERFORMANCE (at 340 kg; 750 lb T-O weight):
Best glide ratio at 43 knots (80 km/h; 50 mph)	34
Min rate of sink at 40 knots (74 km/h; 46 mph)	
	0.62 m (2.03 ft)/s
Stalling speed	33 knots (60 km/h; 38 mph)
Max speed (smooth air)	118 knots (220 km/h; 137 mph)
Max speed (rough air), and max aero-tow speed	
	80 knots (148 km/h; 92 mph)
Max winch-launching speed	
	67 knots (125 km/h; 77 mph)
g limits at 80 knots (148 km/h; 92 mph)	+5.3/-2.65

SCHLEICHER ASW 24 and 24 E

The ASW 24, the prototype of which flew in 1986, was intended as a successor to the ASW 19. An all-new design, it incorporates a wing aerofoil section developed by the Department of Aerospace Engineering at Delft University of Technology in the Netherlands. Eleven had been built by mid-1988, plus a single example of a motor glider version designated **ASW 24 E**, of which no details have been received. Production of the 24 E will begin in 1989.

TYPE: Standard Class sailplane.

AIRFRAME: Cantilever mid-wing monoplane, with Delft University DU84-158 aerofoil section from root to tip. Dihedral 3°. Incidence 4°. Two-piece wing, of glass/aramid fibre and hard foam sandwich construction, with carbonfibre spar caps; ailerons of aramid/foam sandwich. Double-panelled aluminium airbrakes in upper wing surface, with spring loaded GFRP cover plates. Fuselage is a carbon/aramid/GFRP monocoque. Cantilever T tail, with elevator, is of carbon/aramid/GFRP and hard foam sandwich. Retractable rubber sprung monowheel (tyre size 5.00-5), with hydraulic disc brake, plus tailskid. Canopy hinged at front, opening upward. Wing tanks for 170 litres (44.9 US gallons; 37.4 Imp gallons) of water ballast. CG towing hook standard. Options include nose towing hook, tailwheel with 210 × 65 mm pneumatic tyre, oxygen bottle and battery.

DIMENSIONS, EXTERNAL:
Wing span	15.00 m (49 ft 2½ in)
Wing aspect ratio	22.5
Length overall	6.55 m (21 ft 6 in)
Height over tail	1.30 m (4 ft 3¼ in)

AREA:
Wings, gross	10.00 m² (107.6 sq ft)

WEIGHTS AND LOADING:
Weight empty, equipped	225 kg (496 lb)
Max water ballast	170 kg (375 lb)
Max T-O weight	500 kg (1,102 lb)
Max wing loading	50.0 kg/m² (10.24 lb/sq ft)

PERFORMANCE (estimated, at max T-O weight except where indicated):
*Best glide ratio at 57 knots (105 km/h; 65 mph)	43
Min rate of sink at 38 knots (70 km/h; 44 mph)	
	0.58 m (1.90 ft)/s
*Stalling speed	38 knots (69 km/h; 43 mph)
Max speed (smooth air)	145 knots (270 km/h; 168 mph)
Max speed (rough air) and max aero-tow speed	
	110 knots (205 km/h; 127 mph)
Max winch-launching speed	
	75 knots (140 km/h; 87 mph)
g limits	+5.3/-2.65

*at AUW of 315 kg (694 lb)

SCHLEICHER ASH 25

Prototype construction of the ASH 25 (D-1025) started in January 1986, a year after design, by Martin Heide, began. The AS 22-2 (see 1985-86 and 1986-87 *Jane's*) was used as the basis of the design, with some fuselage modifications. First flight was made on 11 May 1986. During December 1986 and January 1987, in Australia, ASH 25s set five records for speed over triangular courses varying from 300 km to 1,380 km, the fifth and fastest being a 300 km circuit by H. W. and W. Grosse at a speed of 85.31 knots (158.0 km/h; 98.17 mph). Thirty-five had been built by mid-1988, plus 13 **ASH 25 E** motor gliders of which no details have been received.

TYPE: Open Class tandem two-seat sailplane.

AIRFRAME: Wings and tail unit as for AS 22-2, but two 60 litre (15.8 US gallon; 13.2 Imp gallon) water ballast tanks only (in outer panels). Fuselage is a hybrid carbon/aramid FRP monocoque. Retractable rubber sprung monowheel, tyre size 380 × 150 mm, pressure 3.5 bars (51 lb/sq in), with brake; retractable tailwheel, tyre size 210 × 65 mm, pressure 2.5 bars (36 lb/sq in). Canopies similar to those of ASK 21.

DIMENSIONS, EXTERNAL:
Wing span	25.00 m (82 ft 0¼ in)
Wing aspect ratio	38.3
Length overall	9.00 m (29 ft 6¼ in)
Height over tail	1.67 m (5 ft 5¾ in)

AREA:
Wings, gross	16.31 m² (175.6 sq ft)

WEIGHTS AND LOADING:
Weight empty, equipped	approx 470 kg (1,036 lb)
Max water ballast	220 kg (485 lb)
Max T-O weight	750 kg (1,653 lb)
Max wing loading	45.98 kg/m² (9.42 lb/sq ft)

PERFORMANCE (estimated, at max T-O weight):
Best glide ratio at 51 knots (95 km/h; 59 mph)	58
Min rate of sink at 43 knots (80 km/h; 50 mph)	
	0.45 m (1.48 ft)/s
Stalling speed	42-45 knots (77-84 km/h; 48-52 mph)
Max speed (smooth air)	151 knots (280 km/h; 174 mph)
Max speed (rough air) and max aero-tow speed	
	103 knots (190 km/h; 118 mph)
Max winch-launching speed	
	75 knots (140 km/h; 87 mph)

SCHLEICHER ASH 25 MB

First flown (D-KOWB) on 28 March 1986, the ASH 25 MB combines the wings of the ASW 22 B/BE with a carbonfibre/balsa sandwich fuselage, an ASW 22 tail unit and the Rotax 505 engine of the ASW 22 BE. Weight empty (equipped) is 501 kg (1,104 lb). No production is envisaged.

STEMME

STEMME GmbH & Co KG

Gustav Meyer Allee 25, 1000 Berlin 65
Telephone: (030) 4634071
MANAGING DIRECTOR: Dr Reiner Stemme
SALES OFFICE: Flughafen Lilienthalplatz, 3300 Braunschweig
Telephone: (0531) 351705
SALES MANAGER: Ingo Andresen
UK AGENTS:
Michael Jefferyes
Hermann Sommersell
15 Sycamore Way, Chelmsford, Essex, CM2 9LZ
Telephone: (0245) 261145

Stemme GmbH & Co KG was formed in Berlin in November 1984 to develop a high performance two-seat motor glider designated the S 10. Its power plant is based on the concept invented by Dr Reiner Stemme.

STEMME S 10

Claimed by Stemme to be the first sailplane to incorporate a fully effective propulsion system without suffering aerodynamic penalties, the first S 10 prototype (D-KKST) made its first flight at Braunschweig on 6 July 1986. During powered phases, only the propeller blades are extended outside the aircraft, instead of the pylon structure associated with most other retractable power plant installations.

Known originally as the HMS (Hochleistungs Motor Segelflugzeug: high performance motor glider), the S 10 was flown solo in initial flight trials, due mainly to load-bearing limitations of the interim wings, which were essentially those of a Glaser-Dirks DG-500. The production wings use the new HQ-41 section developed from the HQ-17 to enable the S 10 to realise its full two-seat performance potential. The first delivery of an S 10 to a customer took place in February 1988.

TYPE: Side by side two-seat high performance motor glider.

AIRFRAME: Cantilever shoulder-wing monoplane with T tail. High aspect ratio wings, with tapered outer panels. Wing section Horstmann & Quast HQ-41/14.35. Long-span flaps and ailerons on trailing-edges; Schempp-Hirth upper surface airbrakes. Wings are built of CFRP, in four sections, with integral fuel and water ballast tanks. Inboard sections can be folded on to fuselage. Modular fuselage comprises three sections bolted together. The central load-bearing mainframe is of welded steel tube, with GFRP cladding. The cockpit is of CFRP with Kevlar lining, and the rear fuselage is also of CFRP. Tail unit incorporates a damped elevator. Landing gear comprises twin 348 × 122 mm mainwheels on steel tube legs, each sprung and fully retractable into its own bay, and a partially recessed 210 × 65 mm steerable tailwheel. Side by side seats, with dual controls, under one-piece canopy which is hinged at front and opens upward. 12V 44Ah battery for engine starting.

POWER PLANT: One 67 kW (90 hp) Limbach L 2400 four-cylinder four-stroke engine, mounted in centre-fuselage aft of seats and beneath wings, close to CG. Propeller, at front of fuselage, consists of a hub and two hinged blades and is driven via a carbon shaft in a Kevlar tunnel between the two seats, and a five-belt gearbox, power transmission occurring, via a centrifugal clutch. Start-up is achieved by extending the nosecone forward (on the ground or in flight, by control in cockpit) with no change to trim; the propeller blades deploy by centrifugal force. For gliding flight, the engine is stopped and the propeller blades fold in sideways by spring loading. Once aligned the blades are concealed within fuselage by returning the nosecone to its 'glider' position to restore an aerodynamically clean nose contour. Fuel (mogas) in two integral wing tanks with combined capacity of 80 litres (21.1 US gallons; 17.6 Imp gallons) or, optionally, 120 litres (31.7 US gallons; 26.4 Imp gallons).

DIMENSIONS, EXTERNAL:
Wing span	23.00 m (75 ft 5½ in)
Wing aspect ratio	28.22
Length overall	8.42 m (27 ft 7½ in)
Height over tail	1.81 m (5 ft 11¼ in)
Wheel track	1.15 m (3 ft 9¼ in)
Wheelbase	5.40 m (17 ft 8½ in)
Propeller diameter	1.58 m (5 ft 2¼ in)

AREAS:
Wings, gross	18.74 m² (201.7 sq ft)
Ailerons (total)	1.37 m² (14.75 sq ft)
Flaps (total)	1.50 m² (16.15 sq ft)
Airbrakes (total)	0.44 m² (4.74 sq ft)
Vertical tail surfaces (total)	1.48 m² (15.93 sq ft)
Horizontal tail surfaces (total)	1.46 m² (15.72 sq ft)

WEIGHTS AND LOADINGS:
Weight empty	approx 635 kg (1,400 lb)
Max T-O weight	850 kg (1,874 lb)
Max wing loading	45.36 kg/m² (9.29 lb/sq ft)
Max power loading	12.69 kg/kW (20.82 lb/hp)

PERFORMANCE, UNPOWERED (at AUW of 710 kg; 1,565 lb, ISA):
Best glide ratio at 57 knots (105 km/h; 65 mph)	51
Min rate of sink	0.55 m (1.80 ft)/s
Stalling speed	38 knots (69 km/h; 43 mph)
Max speed (smooth air)	151 knots (280 km/h; 174 mph)
Max speed (rough air)	102 knots (190 km/h; 118 mph)

PERFORMANCE, POWERED (at AUW of 710 kg; 1,565 lb, ISA):
Max cruising speed	108 knots (200 km/h; 124 mph)
Max rate of climb at S/L	210 m (689 ft)/min
Service ceiling	5,600 m (18,375 ft)
T-O run	195 m (640 ft)
T-O to 15 m (50 ft)	325 m (1,066 ft)
Landing from 15 m (50 ft)	370 m (1,214 ft)
Landing run	205 m (673 ft)
Range with max fuel at 108 knots (200 km/h; 124 mph)	
	1,176 nm (2,180 km; 1,354 miles)

VALENTIN

VALENTIN FLUGZEUGBAU GmbH

Flugplatzstrasse 18 (Postfach 26), 8728 Hassfurt
Telephone: (09521) 4730
MANAGING DIRECTOR:
Dipl-Ing Bernard Valentin
SALES MANAGER: Dipl-Ing Rudolf Neumann
HEAD OFFICE AND OTHER WORKS: Germanenstrasse 2 (Postfach 1165), 8901 Königsbrunn
Telephone: (08231) 4033/4

This company is producing the Taifun two-seat motor glider and Kiwi sailplane. In July 1981 it took over the former MFB company (see 1981-82 *Jane's*), and became responsible for producing that company's Mistral-C sailplane. Development work and construction of metal components takes place at Königsbrunn; production of GFRP components, and final assembly, are undertaken at Hassfurt.

VALENTIN TAIFUN 17E (TYPHOON)

The Taifun motor glider was proposed originally in two versions, the 15 m span Taifun 15E and 17 m span Taifun 17E, as detailed in the 1983-84 and previous editions of *Jane's*. Construction of the first prototype, to Taifun 17E configuration, began in July 1979, and this aircraft (D-KONO) made its first flight on 28 February 1981. A second prototype was used for extended trials and development of the mechanical (instead of the original electrical) undercarriage retraction gear, a shock absorbing engine mounting, and other improvements.

In 1982, due to lack of sufficient interest in the smaller version, it was decided to begin production only of the Taifun 17E. German certification of this version, with a 59 kW (80 hp) Limbach L 2000 EB engine, was awarded on 29 April 1983, and series manufacture began in mid-year. At least 80 had been built by early 1988. The current version, to which the following description applies, has a more powerful engine.

A reduced span variant, the **Taifun 12E**, developed for the lightplane market, was described in the main Aircraft section of the 1987-88 *Jane's*.

TYPE: Two-seat motor glider.

AIRFRAME: Cantilever low-wing monoplane with T tail. Wortmann FX-67-K-170/17 wing section. Dihedral 3°. Incidence 0° 48'. Sweepforward 0° 38' 24" at quarter-chord. Wings and ailerons of glassfibre/foam sandwich, with double T section glassfibre roving main spar booms. All-glassfibre cambered trailing-edge flaps, interconnected with ailerons at 8° setting only. Schempp-Hirth upper surface airbrakes. Wings fold back alongside

Schleicher ASW 24 Standard Class sailplane

ASH 25, designed by Schleicher's Martin Heide (*Peter F. Selinger*)

Stemme S 10 self launching sailplane and motor glider

Valentin Taifun 17E two-seat motor glider (*Wolfgang Wagner*)

Valentin Mistral-C single-seat Club Class sailplane (*Peter F. Selinger*)

fuselage for transportation and storage. Fuselage is a stressed skin structure of glassfibre and foam sandwich, reinforced with carbonfibre in the cockpit area. Fixed incidence T tailplane, with horn balanced elevator, of similar construction to wings. Flettner tab in port half of elevator. Mechanically retractable tricycle landing gear, with hydraulically damped pneumatic shock absorbers, Goodyear 5 in mainwheel tyres, pressure 2.5 bars (36 lb/sq in), and Cleveland type hydraulic mainwheel disc brakes. Single nosewheel or tailwheel. Cockpit seats two persons side by side under rearward sliding canopy.

POWER PLANT: One 67 kW (90 hp) Limbach L 2400 EB four-cylinder four-stroke engine, driving a Mühlbauer MTV-1-A two-blade variable-pitch feathering propeller. Fuel in two wing tanks, total capacity 90 litres (23.8 US gallons; 19.8 Imp gallons).

DIMENSIONS, EXTERNAL:
Wing span	17.00 m (55 ft 9¼ in)
Wing aspect ratio	16.4
Length overall	7.782 m (25 ft 6½ in)
Height over tail	2.48 m (8 ft 1½ in)
Tailplane span	3.30 m (10 ft 10 in)
Wheel track	2.36 m (7 ft 9 in)
Wheelbase	1.75 m (5 ft 9 in)
Propeller diameter	1.60 m (5 ft 3 in)

AREA:
Wings, gross	17.60 m² (189.4 sq ft)

WEIGHTS AND LOADINGS:
Weight empty	610 kg (1,345 lb)
Max T-O weight	850 kg (1,874 lb)
Max wing loading	48.30 kg/m² (9.90 lb/sq ft)
Max power loading	12.67 kg/kW (20.82 lb/hp)

PERFORMANCE, UNPOWERED (at max T-O weight):
Best glide ratio at 57 knots (105 km/h; 65 mph)	30
Min rate of sink at 46 knots (85 km/h; 53 mph)	
	0.95 m (3.12 ft)/s
Stalling speed	39 knots (72 km/h; 45 mph)
Max speed (smooth air)	135 knots (250 km/h; 155 mph)
Max speed (rough air)	100 knots (185 km/h; 115 mph)
g limits	+5.3/−2.65

PERFORMANCE, POWERED (at max T-O weight):
Max cruising speed	119 knots (220 km/h; 137 mph)
Stalling speed	39 knots (72 km/h; 45 mph)
Max rate of climb at S/L	192 m (630 ft)/min
Service ceiling	5,000 m (16,400 ft)
T-O run	250 m (820 ft)
Landing run	200 m (655 ft)
Range with max fuel	675 nm (1,250 km; 777 miles)

VALENTIN MISTRAL-C

The original Mistral was described and illustrated under the Strauber heading in the 1976-77 *Jane's*. The Mistral-C made its first flight on 21 October 1976, and 25 of this model had been completed by the beginning of 1980.

A new Mistral-Flugzeugbau (MFB) production facility was completed in 1980, which from January 1981 continued manufacture of the Mistral-C at the rate of five per month. On 1 July 1981 MFB was taken over by Valentin, to continue production of the Mistral-C. Valentin had built 70 Mistrals by the beginning of 1985, but has not advised since then whether the type continues in production.

TYPE: Single-seat Club Class sailplane.

AIRFRAME: Cantilever shoulder-wing monoplane with T tail. Wortmann wing sections: FX-61-163 at root, FX-60-126 at tip. Dihedral 4° 12'. Sweepforward 1° at quarter-chord. Main wings and tail of GFRP/foam/Conticell CC60 sandwich, ailerons of GFRP. Schempp-Hirth aluminium airbrakes on upper surfaces. GFRP monocoque fuselage, with one-piece sideways hinged canopy. Fixed incidence tailplane, with spring trim. Non-retractable monowheel, tyre pressure 2.5 bars (36.25 lb/sq in), with Tost brake; tailskid.

DIMENSIONS, EXTERNAL:
Wing span	15.00 m (49 ft 2½ in)
Wing aspect ratio	20.7
Length overall	6.73 m (22 ft 1 in)
Height over tail	1.42 m (4 ft 8 in)

AREA:
Wings, gross	10.85 m² (116.8 sq ft)

WEIGHTS AND LOADING:
Weight empty	approx 225 kg (496 lb)
Max T-O weight	350 kg (771 lb)
Max wing loading	32.3 kg/m² (6.62 lb/sq ft)

PERFORMANCE (at max T-O weight except where indicated):
Best glide ratio at 51 knots (95 km/h; 59 mph)	37.5
Min rate of sink at 43 knots (80 km/h; 50 mph)	
	0.66 m (2.17 ft)/s
Stalling speed at AUW of 295 kg (650 lb)	
	35 knots (65 km/h; 41 mph)
Max speed (smooth air)	135 knots (250 km/h; 155 mph)
Max speed (rough air) and max aero-tow speed	
	86 knots (160 km/h; 99 mph)
Max winch-launching speed	
	70 knots (130 km/h; 81 mph)

g limits:
at 135 knots (250 km/h; 155 mph)	+4/−1.5
at 86 knots (160 km/h; 99 mph) (JAR 22)	
	+5.3/−2.65

VALENTIN KIWI

Expected to become available in 1988, the Kiwi has an optional retractable engine package to provide self-launch capability and auxiliary power for short periods of flying. The prototype (D-KELT) flew for the first time in August 1986.

TYPE: Single-seat (optionally self-launching) sailplane.

AIRFRAME: Cantilever mid-wing monoplane, with Wortmann FX-61-163 wing section. Wings are of glassfibre and PVC rigid foam sandwich construction, over an I spar with carbonfibre spar caps, and are bolted to fuselage. Airbrakes on upper surface only. Fuselage comprises an all-GFRP shell at front, with a tailboom and T tail unit of glassfibre and PVC rigid foam. Non-retractable sprung monowheel, with drum brake, plus tailwheel. Cockpit has bonded-in glassfibre seat pan, and is enclosed by a one-piece, front-hinged upward opening canopy.

POWER PLANT (optional): Fully retractable F & E Fischer 'TOP' installation, comprising a 17.9 kW (24 hp) König SC 430 three-cylinder two-stroke engine driving a three-blade folding pusher propeller via a toothed belt reduction gear. Fuel tank capacity 10 litres (2.6 US gallons; 2.2 Imp gallons).

DIMENSIONS, EXTERNAL:
Wing span	15.00 m (49 ft 2½ in)
Wing aspect ratio	20.4
Length overall	6.80 m (22 ft 3¾ in)
Height over tail	1.46 m (4 ft 9½ in)
Propeller diameter	1.30 m (4 ft 3¼ in)

AREA:
Wings, gross	11.03 m² (118.7 sq ft)

WEIGHTS AND LOADINGS (A: without/B: with engine):
Weight empty: A	210 kg (463 lb)
B	250 kg (551 lb)
Max T-O weight: A	300 kg (661 lb)
B	380 kg (838 lb)
Max wing loading: A	27.2 kg/m² (5.57 lb/sq ft)
B	34.4 kg/m² (7.05 lb/sq ft)

PERFORMANCE (at max T-O weight):
Best glide ratio: A	37
B	35
Min rate of sink: A	0.75 m (2.46 ft)/s
Max cruising speed:	
B	124 knots (230 km/h; 143 mph)
Stalling speed: A, B	40 knots (74 km/h; 46 mph)
Max rate of climb at S/L: B	84 m (275 ft)/min
T-O run: B	300 m (985 ft)

HUNGARY

AUTO-AERO
AUTO-AERO KÖZLEKEDÉSTECHNIKAI VÁLLALAT (Automobile and Aeronautical Technical Establishment)
Szombathely, H-9700 Zanati u. 4
Telephone: 36 94 11341
SOLE EXPORTER: **Technika Hungarian Foreign Trading Company**, PO Box 125, H-1475 Budapest
Telephone: 338 305 and 340 149
Telex: 225 765

AUTO-AERO GÓBÉ R-26S
The first of two R-26 prototypes made its initial flight on 6 May 1961, and 120 of the original version were put into production in the mid-1960s, as last described in the 1965-66 *Jane's*. The current version, to which the following details apply, is designated R-26S. This entered production by Auto-Aero (formerly Aviatechnika) in 1983, and 48 had been completed by 1 January 1987. No revised figure has been received.

TYPE: Two-seat training sailplane.
AIRFRAME: Cantilever shoulder-wing monoplane. Constant chord wings of Göttingen 549 (modified) section, having 3° dihedral and 1° 30′ of forward sweep. Single-spar wings, with leading-edge torsion box covered by riveted metal skin; fabric covering aft of 35 per cent chord line. Schempp-Hirth perforated metal airbrakes in upper and lower surfaces. Frise type slotted ailerons, of fabric covered metal construction. Metal-frame fuselage, with metal and fabric covering. Conventional fabric covered metal tail surfaces, with tailplane mounted at intersection of fin and dorsal fin. Balanced rudder; ground adjustable tab on port elevator. Non-retractable, partly recessed rubber sprung monowheel, with brake; faired tailskid under rear fuselage. Towing hook/cable release under front fuselage, forward of monowheel. Two seats in tandem under one-piece framed canopy which opens sideways to starboard.

DIMENSIONS, EXTERNAL:
Wing span	14.00 m (45 ft 11¼ in)
Wing aspect ratio	10.9
Length overall	9.00 m (29 ft 6⅓ in)
Height over tail	1.96 m (6 ft 5¼ in)

AREA:
Wings, gross	18.00 m² (193.75 sq ft)

WEIGHTS AND LOADING:
Weight empty	220-240 kg (485-529 lb)
Max T-O weight	440 kg (970 lb)
Max wing loading	24.4 kg/m² (5.00 lb/sq ft)

PERFORMANCE (at max T-O weight):
Best glide ratio at 44 knots (81 km/h; 50 mph)	23.7
Min rate of sink at 44 knots (81 km/h; 50 mph)	0.97 m (3.18 ft)/s
Max speed (smooth air)	113 knots (210 km/h; 130 mph)
Max speed (rough air)	77 knots (143 km/h; 89 mph)
Max aero-tow speed	70 knots (130 km/h; 81 mph)
Max winch-launching speed	59 knots (110 km/h; 68 mph)
g limits	+5.3/−2.65

INDIA

CIVIL AVIATION DEPARTMENT
TECHNICAL CENTRE, CIVIL AVIATION DEPARTMENT
Civil Aviation Department, Opp. Safdarjung Airport, New Delhi 110003
WORKS: Technical Centre, opposite Safdarjung Airport, New Delhi 110003
Telephone: 611504
Telex: 31 66407 NAA
DIRECTOR GENERAL: P. C. Sen
DIRECTOR (R & D): Y. P. Bawa

Since 1950 the Technical Centre of the Indian Civil Aviation Department has undertaken design and development of gliders utilising predominantly indigenous materials. The first of these gliders was flown in November 1950. Since then the Centre has built nine types for use at gliding clubs and centres in India, as listed in previous editions of *Jane's*. Of these, six have been original designs.

The Technical Centre does not undertake quantity production of gliders. Drawings of designs developed at the Centre are supplied to interested organisations with permission to manufacture them in series.

ATS-1 ARDHRA
This two-seat training sailplane was designed by the team responsible earlier for the Mrigasheer, last described in the 1980-81 *Jane's*. The Ardhra prototype (VT-GEJ) made its first flight on 5 March 1979 and was certificated by the Indian DGCA on 2 November of that year.

The Ardhra has been approved for use by the National Cadet Corps and civil gliding clubs, and is now in production at the Kanpur Division of Hindustan Aeronautics Ltd. A second prototype (VT-GEN), flown for the first time on 28 June 1981, was representative of the production version, of which 50 were ordered by the Indian Air Force. All had been delivered by the end of 1987. A substantial number were fitted with enlarged canopies. (Illustration in 1985-86 *Jane's*).

TYPE: Tandem two-seat advanced training sailplane.

AIRFRAME: Cantilever shoulder-wing monoplane. Wortmann FX-61-184 wing section from root to tip. Dihedral 3°. Incidence 3° at root. Sweepforward 3° at leading-edge; 2° washout on outer half of each wing. Two-spar wooden wings, plywood covered on leading- and trailing-edges; plain wood ailerons; wood airbrakes in upper and lower wing surfaces. Tail unit of similar construction, but with rear portions of rudder and elevator fabric covered. Horn balanced rudder; mass and horn balanced elevator. Plywood covered tab in starboard elevator. Semi-monocoque wood fuselage, with plywood covering. Nosecone of glassfibre. Non-retractable unsprung monowheel, tyre size 6.00-4. Rubber sprung nose-skid, with replaceable steel shoe, and rubber sprung tailskid.

DIMENSIONS, EXTERNAL:
Wing span	16.50 m (54 ft 1½ in)
Wing aspect ratio	12.5
Length overall	8.61 m (28 ft 3 in)
Height over tail	2.464 m (8 ft 1 in)

AREA:
Wings, gross	21.83 m² (235.0 sq ft)

WEIGHTS AND LOADING:
Weight empty	328 kg (723 lb)
Max T-O weight	508 kg (1,120 lb)
Max wing loading	23.28 kg/m² (4.77 lb/sq ft)

PERFORMANCE (at max T-O weight):
Best glide ratio at 47 knots (87 km/h; 54 mph)	26
Min rate of sink at 39 knots (72 km/h; 45 mph)	0.78 m (2.56 ft)/s
Stalling speed	33 knots (61 km/h; 38 mph)
Max speed (smooth air)	113 knots (210 km/h; 130 mph)
Max speed (rough air)	69 knots (127 km/h; 79 mph)
Max aero-tow and max winch-launching speed	59 knots (110 km/h; 68 mph)
g limits	+5.3/−2.65

POLAND

PW
POLITECHNIKA WARSZAWSKA (Warsaw University of Technology)
Research Group for Aircraft Composite Structures Technology, ul. Nowowiejska 22/24, 00-665 Warszawa
Telephone: 21007 965
Telex: 8133076 PW PL
DIRECTOR: Dr Roman Switkiewicz

PW-2 GAPA
The PW-2 Gapa is the productionised version of the ULS (Ultralekkiego Szybowca: ultralight sailplane), which flew for the first time on 27 September 1981 and was described and illustrated in the 1984-85 *Jane's*.

Construction of three PW-2 prototypes (including one for ground tests) began in September 1984, and the first flight was made on 25 July 1985. Designed for basic training and recreation, the Gapa can be winch or bungee launched, or tow launched by an aircraft or motorcar. Its light glassfibre structure meets all requirements of JAR 22, and a novel feature are the wing strut fairings, which are hinged and can be pivoted for use as airbrakes.

The PW-2 is available in plans or kit form, as well as ready to fly. Manufacture of 15 production examples was under way by early 1987, when the last information was received.

TYPE: Single-seat ultra-lightweight sailplane.
AIRFRAME: Braced high-wing monoplane. Constant chord wings, of NACA 4415 constant section from root to tip. Dihedral 1°. Incidence 3°. No sweep. Single-spar wings, spar and D nose section forming a glassfibre torsion box; fabric covered glassfibre structure aft of spar. Glassfibre ailerons, projecting aft of trailing-edge. No spoilers. Fairing behind each bracing strut pivots to act as airbrake. Keel type fuselage, of glassfibre laminate. Conventional unbraced tail unit, of similar construction to rear portion of wings. Non-retractable rubber sprung monowheel, tyre size 255 × 110 mm, pressure 1.8 bars (26 lb/sq in); no brake. Nose-skid and small tailskid. Single seat in open cockpit with windscreen.

DIMENSIONS, EXTERNAL:
Wing span	11.00 m (36 ft 1 in)
Wing aspect ratio	9.5
Length overall	5.50 m (18 ft 0¾ in)
Height over tail	2.45 m (8 ft 0½ in)

AREA:
Wings, gross	12.70 m² (136.7 sq ft)

WEIGHTS AND LOADING:
Weight empty, equipped	110 kg (243 lb)
Max T-O weight	220 kg (485 lb)
Max wing loading	17.32 kg/m² (3.55 lb/sq ft)

PERFORMANCE (at max T-O weight):
Best glide ratio at 37 knots (69 km/h; 43 mph)	16
Min rate of sink at 31 knots (58 km/h; 36 mph)	1.00 m (3.28 ft)/s
Stalling speed	27 knots (50 km/h; 31 mph)
Max speed (smooth air)	81 knots (150 km/h; 93 mph)
Max speed (rough air) and max aero-tow speed	64 knots (120 km/h; 74 mph)
Max winch-launching speed	54 knots (100 km/h; 62 mph)
g limits	+5.3/−2.65

PW-3 BAKCYL and PW-4
These are progressive developments of the PW-2, the two-seat PW-3 having inset ailerons and an enclosed cabin, increasing the empty weight and improving the best glide ratio. The PW-4 will be a powered version, with a nose mounted engine and non-retractable tricycle landing gear. Empty weight of the PW-4 is estimated at 250 kg (551 lb), max and stalling speeds at 81 knots (150 km/h; 93 mph) and 30 knots (55 km/h; 35 mph) respectively.

The PW-4 is expected to appear in the 1988-90 period. The following data apply to the PW-3, which had been due to appear in 1987:

TYPE: Two-seat training glider.

DIMENSIONS, EXTERNAL:
Wing span	14.60 m (47 ft 10¾ in)
Wing aspect ratio	12.0
Length overall	7.25 m (23 ft 9½ in)
Height overall	2.45 m (8 ft 0½ in)

AREA:
Wings, gross	17.80 m² (191.6 sq ft)

WEIGHTS:
Weight empty	190 kg (419 lb)
Max T-O weight	400 kg (882 lb)

PERFORMANCE (estimated):
Best glide ratio	22
Min rate of sink	0.90 m (2.95 ft)/s
Stalling speed	28 knots (52 km/h; 33 mph)
Max speed (smooth air)	97 knots (180 km/h; 112 mph)
g limits	+5.3/−2.65

Auto-Aero Góbé R-26S two-seat training sailplane *(Peter J. Bish)*

Politechnika Warszawska PW-2 Gapa lightweight single-seater

Indian Civil Aviation Dept ATS-1 Ardhra two-seat training sailplane in Indian Air Force markings

SZD-42-2 Jantar 2B Open Class sailplane

SZD

PRZEDSIEBIORSTWO DOŚWIADCZALNO-PRODUKCYJNE SZYBOWNICTWA (Experimental and Production Concern for Gliders) PZL-BIELSKO

HEAD OFFICE AND WORKS: Ulica Cieszyńska 325, 43-300 Bielsko-Biala 1
Telephone: 250 21 to 250 23
Telex: 035259 PZL PL
-DIRECTOR: Ing Jerzy Cieśla
TECHNICAL DIRECTOR: Jerzy Smielkiewicz MSc
SALES REPRESENTATIVE: Pezetel, 61 Aleja Stanow Zjednoczonych (PO Box 6), 00-991 Warszawa 44
Telephone: 10 80 01
Telex: 813314

The Instytut Szybownictwa (Gliding Institute), formed officially in January 1946 at Bielsko-Biala, has since undergone several changes of name, as detailed in the *1977-78 Jane's*. The change to the present title took place in July 1975, but the well known designation initials SZD are retained. This organisation is responsible for the design and development of nearly all Polish sailplanes. Production plants are at Bielsko-Biala, Wroclaw and Jezów.

Between 1947 and 1 January 1988 the Polish aircraft industry produced 4,713 gliders of more than 115 different types, and SZD sailplanes have been exported all over the world in substantial numbers.

SZD-42-2 JANTAR 2B (AMBER 2B)

Designed by Dipl-Ing Adam Kurbiel, the SZD-42-2 Open Class sailplane is based on the SZD-42-1. The prototype flew for the first time on 13 March 1978, and 120 Jantar 2Bs had been built by 1 January 1988.

A 22/24 m (72 ft 2¼ in/78 ft 9 in) Open Class Jantar, with detachable wingtips, was planned as a developed version of the SZD-42-2 Jantar 2B. However, initial studies revealed some disadvantages of the design and the project was abandoned.

TYPE: Single-seat Open Class sailplane.

AIRFRAME: Cantilever shoulder-wing monoplane. Wortmann wing sections: FX-67-K-150 at root, FX-67-K-170 at tip. Dihedral 2°. Sweepback 0° at quarter-chord. Single-spar four-part ribless wings with foam filled glassfibre/epoxy resin sandwich skin. Two-part hinged ailerons; top-hinged 'elastic' flaps. Light alloy DFS type airbrakes. All-glassfibre/epoxy resin shell fuselage; centre portion has a steel tube frame coupling together the wings, fuselage and landing gear. Cantilever cruciform tail unit of glassfibre/epoxy resin. Monowheel, diameter 400 mm, with two rubber shock absorbers and disc brake. Tailwheel diameter 200 mm. Water ballast provision 167 litres (44.1 US gallons; 36.7 Imp gallons). Improvements

made to elevator spring trim, monowheel retraction system and cockpit comfort. Hinged canopy and provision for CG tow hook.

DIMENSIONS, EXTERNAL:
Wing span	20.50 m (67 ft 3 in)
Wing aspect ratio	29.5
Length overall	7.18 m (23 ft 6¾ in)
Height over tail	1.76 m (5 ft 9¼ in)

AREA:
Wings, gross	14.25 m² (153.4 sq ft)

WEIGHTS AND LOADING:
Weight empty	362 kg (798 lb)
Max T-O weight:	
without water ballast	458 kg (1,010 lb)
with water ballast	649 kg (1,430 lb)
Max wing loading	45.6 kg/m² (9.28 lb/sq ft)

PERFORMANCE (at max T-O weight):
Best glide ratio at 56 knots (103 km/h; 64 mph)	50.3
Min rate of sink at 44 knots (80 km/h; 50 mph)	
	0.46 m (1.51 ft)/s
Stalling speed	43 knots (79 km/h; 49 mph)
Max speed (smooth air)	135 knots (250 km/h; 155 mph)
Max speed (rough air)	108 knots (200 km/h; 124 mph)
Max aero-tow speed	76 knots (140 km/h; 87 mph)
Max winch-launching speed	
	62 knots (115 km/h; 71 mph)
g limits	+5.3/-2.65

SZD-48-3 JANTAR STANDARD 3

This Standard Class sailplane is the current version of the SZD-48-1 and SZD-48-2 Jantar Standard 2, which were described in the 1983-84 *Jane's*. Production of these versions, which totalled 313, ended in March 1983.

The prototype SZD-48-3 Jantar Standard 3 was flown for the first time on 9 February 1983, and 233 of this version had been built by 1 January 1988.

TYPE: Single-seat Standard Class sailplane.

AIRFRAME: Cantilever shoulder-wing monoplane, with NN-8 wing section. Dihedral 1° 30′. Single glassfibre roving main spar, with glassfibre/foam/glassfibre moulded skins (no ribs) and plain ailerons. Glassfibre upper/lower surface airbrakes. Glassfibre fuselage, with steel tube central support structure, rear portion stiffened by half-frames and fin ribs. Cantilever T tail of similar construction to wings. Fin integral with fuselage; mass balanced rudder, with upward angled lower edge to avoid damage in tail-down landing. Mass balanced elevator, with spring trim. Retractable unsprung monowheel, tyre size 350 × 135 mm, with disc brake; semi-recessed tailwheel, diameter 200 mm. One-piece canopy, hinged at front and opening upward. Optional CG towing hook on mainwheel fork. Provision for 150 litres (39.6 US gallons; 33 Imp gallons) water ballast.

DIMENSIONS, EXTERNAL:
Wing span	15.00 m (49 ft 2½ in)
Wing aspect ratio	21.1
Length overall	6.85 m (22 ft 5¾ in)
Height over tail	1.51 m (4 ft 11½ in)

AREA:
Wings, gross	10.66 m² (114.7 sq ft)

WEIGHTS AND LOADING:
Weight empty	274 kg (604 lb)
Max T-O weight:	
without water ballast	390 kg (860 lb)
with water ballast	540 kg (1,190 lb)
Max wing loading	50.7 kg/m² (10.38 lb/sq ft)

PERFORMANCE (at max T-O weight):
Best glide ratio at 66 knots (123 km/h; 76 mph)	40
Min rate of sink at 52 knots (97 km/h; 60 mph)	
	0.77 m (2.53 ft)/s
Stalling speed	45 knots (82 km/h; 51 mph)
Max speed (smooth air)	154 knots (285 km/h; 177 mph)
Max speed (rough air)	108 knots (200 km/h; 124 mph)
Max aero-tow speed	81 knots (150 km/h; 93 mph)
Max winch-launching speed	
	67 knots (125 km/h; 77 mph)
g limits	+5.3/-2.65

SZD-50-3 PUCHACZ (EAGLE OWL)

The Puchacz, designed by Dipl-Ing Adam Meus, is a high performance sailplane intended particularly for training and performance flying. It was modified and developed from a prototype, designated SZD-50-1 Dromader, which first flew on 21 December 1976.

A second prototype made its initial flight on 20 December 1977, and the first production SZD-50-2 Puchacz (SP-3151) followed on 13 April 1979. A total of 178 had been built by 1 January 1988, with exports made to Argentina, Austria, Canada, China, Denmark, Finland, East and West Germany, Greece, Sweden, Switzerland, Turkey, the UK and the USSR. The current version of the Puchacz, designated SZD-50-3, has a larger horizontal tail situated 30 cm (11¾ in) higher on the fin, an enlarged rudder, and a fairing over the mainwheel. Inverted flight and extended aerobatic manoeuvres became permissible in 1986.

TYPE: Tandem two-seat high performance training sailplane.

AIRFRAME: Cantilever mid-wing monoplane, mainly of glassfibre sandwich construction. Wortmann wing sections. Plain ailerons. Upper/lower surface airbrakes. Glassfibre fuselage, supported in central portion by two wooden frames, with integral fin. Glassfibre sandwich cruciform tail unit, with fabric covered glassfibre rudder. Non-retractable semi-recessed nosewheel (size 255 × 110 mm) and sprung monowheel (size 350 × 135 mm, with disc brake), and tailskid. One-piece canopy opens sideways.

DIMENSIONS, EXTERNAL:

Wing span	16.67 m (54 ft 8¼ in)
Wing aspect ratio	15.3
Length overall	8.38 m (27 ft 6 in)
Height over tail	2.04 m (6 ft 8¼ in)

AREA:

Wings, gross	18.16 m² (195.5 sq ft)

WEIGHTS AND LOADING:

Weight empty	360 kg (794 lb)
Max T-O weight	570 kg (1,256 lb)
Max wing loading	31.4 kg/m² (6.43 lb/sq ft)

PERFORMANCE (at max T-O weight):

Best glide ratio at 46 knots (85 km/h; 53 mph)	30
Min rate of sink at 40 knots (75 km/h; 47 mph)	0.70 m (2.30 ft)/s
Stalling speed	33 knots (60 km/h; 38 mph)
Max speed (smooth air)	116 knots (215 km/h; 133 mph)
Max speed (rough air)	86 knots (160 km/h; 99 mph)
Max aero-tow speed	81 knots (150 km/h; 93 mph)
Max winch-launching speed	59 knots (110 km/h; 68 mph)
g limits	+5.3/−2.65

SZD-51-1 JUNIOR

Designed in 1979 by Dipl-Ing Stanislaw Zientek, and first flown in SZD-51-0 prototype form on 31 December 1980, the Junior is a single-seat Club Class sailplane of GFRP construction. Production began at Wroclaw in 1984, and 92 Juniors had been completed by 1 January 1988.

TYPE: Single-seat Club Class sailplane.

AIRFRAME: Cantilever shoulder-wing monoplane, with FX-S-02-196 (root) and FX-S-02/1-158 (tip) wing sections. Dihedral 3° from roots. Incidence 1° 30'. No sweep. Single glassfibre I section roving main spar, with glassfibre/foam/glassfibre sandwich moulded skins (no ribs). Schempp-Hirth duralumin upper surface airbrakes. Airbrake boxes and airbrakes, and aileron pushrod control system, suspended on main spar. Glassfibre fuselage, with steel tube central support structure; rear portion stiffened by PVC foam half-frames and foam ribs. Fin, which carries VHF aerial, is integral with fuselage; rudder fabric covered. Cantilever T tail unit, of similar construction to wings; elevators have mass balance and spring trim. Non-retractable unsprung monowheel (tyre size 350 × 135 mm), with SZD disc brake; semi-recessed tailwheel, tyre size 200 × 50 mm; auxiliary front skid. Nose and CG towing hooks.

One-piece Mecaplex canopy, opening sideways to starboard.

DIMENSIONS, EXTERNAL:

Wing span	15.00 m (49 ft 2½ in)
Wing aspect ratio	18.0
Length overall	6.69 m (21 ft 11½ in)
Height over tail	1.54 m (5 ft 0⅔ in)

AREA:

Wings, gross	12.51 m² (134.7 sq ft)

WEIGHTS AND LOADING:

Weight empty	242 kg (533 lb)
Max T-O weight	355 kg (783 lb)
Max wing loading	28.4 kg/m² (5.81 lb/sq ft)

PERFORMANCE (at wing loading of 26 kg/m²; 5.33 lb/sq ft):

Best glide ratio at 43 knots (80 km/h; 50 mph)	35
Min rate of sink at 39 knots (72 km/h; 45 mph)	0.59 m (1.94 ft)/s
Stalling speed	33 knots (60 km/h; 38 mph)
Max speed (smooth air)	119 knots (220 km/h; 137 mph)
Max speed (rough air)	81 knots (150 km/h; 93 mph)
Max aero-tow speed	75 knots (140 km/h; 87 mph)
Max winch-launching speed	69 knots (128 km/h; 79 mph)
g limits	+5.3/−2.65

WSK PZL-KROSNO

WYTWÓRNIA SPRZETU KOMUNIKACYJNEGO PZL-KROSNO (Transport Equipment Manufacturing Centre, Krosno)

38-400 Krosno n. Wislokiem
Telephone: 229 11
Telex: 065247 or 065263
GENERAL MANAGER: Ing Jan Czerniecki
CHIEF DESIGNER: Ing Eugeniusz Pelczar

WSK PZL-Krosno has designed a two-seat training glider intended for widespread use by Polish aeroclubs. Known as the KR-03A Puchatek, it is Krosno's first glider design for more than 20 years.

PZL-KROSNO KR-03A PUCHATEK ('POOH')

Polish aeroclubs (Aeroklub PRL) are suffering a shortage of two-seat sailplanes suitable for basic and advanced training. Only dozens remain of the Bocian, the most popular type for more than 25 years, plus a handful of the earlier Czaplas. Their place was intended to be taken by the SZD-50 Puchacz (which see), but supplies of this aircraft have been slow, due mainly to a reliance on imported composite materials which require hard currency payments and have made the cost of the Puchacz unacceptably high.

In an attempt to remedy this deficiency, PZL-Krosno designed the Puchatek ('Pooh', after A. A. Milne's famous Winnie-the-Pooh) in response to a specification issued in June 1982. This meets Aeroklub PRL requirements in terms of cost, materials and ease of maintenance, as well as providing adequate performance.

Preliminary design work, under the leadership of Eng Jerzy Krawczyk, started in March 1983, and construction of a static test aircraft began in mid-1984. The **KR-03** first flying prototype (SP-P336), using the second airframe, flew for the first time on 1 August 1985. The second Puchatek prototype, which flew for the first time on 20 November 1986, differed slightly in construction and was designated **KR-03A**. Polish certification (JAR-22) was awarded on 19 December 1987, and the first five initial production KR-03A Puchateks first flew in February 1988. The head of Aeroklub PRL has said that up to 600 Puchateks may be built to meet present and future requirements. After basic training on the Puchatek, students will graduate to the SZD-51-1 Junior (which see).

TYPE: Tandem two-seat basic training sailplane.

AIRFRAME: Cantilever mid-wing monoplane. Constant chord wings of Wortmann FX-S-02-158 section, set at incidence of 5°. Sweepforward 3°. Dihedral 4° from roots. Conventional structure of PA-7 duralumin main and auxiliary spars and ribs, each wing being attached to fuselage by three bolts. Forward portion of each wing is duralumin skinned, rear portion fabric covered. Two-segment slotted ailerons on each wing, of fabric covered metal construction. Ailerons, and Schempp-Hirth upper/lower surface airbrakes at mid span, actuated by pushrods. Fuselage is an all-metal semi-monocoque, reinforced with nine frames but having no longitudinal stiffening. Forward (cockpit) section consists of two riveted halves of PA-2 duralumin sheet; rear section comprises two conical sections of PA-7 duralumin sheet. Conventional T tail surfaces, fin (integral with fuselage) and fixed incidence tailplane being all-metal (PA-2/PA-7), rudder and elevators (incorporating spring trim) of fabric covered metal construction. Non-retractable 350 × 135 mm sprung monowheel, with oleo-pneumatic shock absorber and brake; rubber sprung tailskid; and rubber sprung ash nose-skid. Tandem seats for instructor (at rear) and pupil. One-piece canopy, opening sideways to starboard. Dual controls and radio standard.

DIMENSIONS, EXTERNAL:

Wing span	16.40 m (53 ft 9¾ in)
Wing chord, constant	1.20 m (3 ft 11¼ in)
Wing aspect ratio	13.8
Length overall	8.62 m (28 ft 3½ in)
Height over tail	1.55 m (5 ft 1 in)

AREA:

Wings, gross	19.44 m² (209.25 sq ft)

WEIGHTS AND LOADING:

Weight empty	345 kg (761 lb)
Max T-O weight	540 kg (1,190 lb)
Max wing loading	27.78 kg/m² (5.69 lb/sq ft)

PERFORMANCE:

Best glide ratio	27
Min rate of sink	0.78 m (2.56 ft)/s
Stalling speed	32 knots (59 km/h; 37 mph)
Max speed (smooth air)	105 knots (195 km/h; 121 mph)
g limits	+5.3/−2.65

ROMANIA

ICA

INTREPRINDEREA DE CONSTRUCTII AERONAUTICE (Aeronautical Construction Enterprise)

Str. Aeroportului 1, Căsuta Postală 198, 2200 Brasov
Telephone: 16719 and 16720
Telex: 61266
DIRECTOR: Eng Ion Georgescu

As detailed in the Aircraft section, the current activities of the Romanian aircraft industry are divided between four main centres: IAv Bucuresti, IAv Bacau, IAv Craiova and ICA Brasov. In addition to its work on powered aircraft (which see), the ICA is responsible for all sailplane development and production. The principal Romanian designer of sailplanes was Dipl Ing Iosif Silimon, who died in February 1981. His designs are prefixed with the letters IS. Details of his earlier sailplanes have appeared in many previous editions of *Jane's*.

IS-28B2

This high performance sailplane was developed from the IS-28B (1975-76 *Jane's*), which made its first flight on 26 April 1973, and the IS-28B1 (1976-77 edition). Standard version since 1976, of which more than 380 had been built by early 1988, is the IS-28B2, with Hütter (instead of DFS type) airbrakes and trailing-edge split flaps. Production is continuing, and exports have been made to about 20 countries which include Argentina, Australia, Botswana, Canada, China, Colombia, France, West Germany, Hungary, India, Norway, the UK and the USA.

TYPE: Tandem two-seat training and aerobatic sailplane.

AIRFRAME: Cantilever shoulder-wing monoplane. Wortmann wing sections: FX-61-163 at root, FX-60-126 at tip. Forward swept all-metal wings, with L section main spar booms and dural web, dural auxiliary spar, and dural ribs. Upper surface Hütter metal airbrakes. Ailerons and split trailing-edge flaps fabric covered. No tabs. All-metal semi-monocoque forward and centre fuselage. Rear fuselage is duralumin monocoque. Cantilever T tail, with moderate tailplane dihedral. Elevator trailing-edges and rudder fabric covered. Trim tab in each elevator. Semi-retractable monowheel with oleo-pneumatic shock absorber and shoe brake; non-retractable tailwheel. Canopy opens sideways (to starboard) and can be jettisoned in flight. Dual controls standard. Nose towing hook, with Tost cable release, is standard; CG towing hook optional.

DIMENSIONS, EXTERNAL:

Wing span	17.00 m (55 ft 9¼ in)
Wing aspect ratio	15.8
Length overall	8.45 m (27 ft 8¾ in)
Height over tail	1.87 m (6 ft 1½ in)

AREA:

Wings, gross	18.24 m² (196.3 sq ft)

WEIGHTS AND LOADINGS:

Weight empty	400 kg (882 lb)
Max T-O weight: single-seat	520 kg (1,146 lb)
two-seat	590 kg (1,300 lb)
Max wing loading:	
single-seat	28.51 kg/m² (5.84 lb/sq ft)
two-seat	32.34 kg/m² (6.62 lb/sq ft)

PERFORMANCE (at max T-O weight except where indicated):

Best glide ratio:		
single-seat at 51 knots (94 km/h; 58 mph)		33
two-seat at 54 knots (100 km/h; 62 mph)		33
Min rate of sink:		
single-seat at 43 knots (80 km/h; 50 mph)		0.74 m (2.43 ft)/s
two-seat at 46 knots (85 km/h; 53 mph)		0.78 m (2.56 ft)/s
Stalling speed: single-seat	37 knots (67 km/h; 42 mph)	
two-seat	39 knots (72 km/h; 45 mph)	
Max speed (smooth air)	124 knots (230 km/h; 143 mph)	

Max speed (rough air)	91 knots (169 km/h; 105 mph)
Max aero-tow speed	76 knots (140 km/h; 87 mph)
Max winch-launching speed	59 knots (110 km/h; 68 mph)
g limits:	+6.5/−4 single-seat
	+5.3/−2.65 two-seat

IS-28M2A

Two motor glider versions of the IS-28B2 were developed initially, with tandem (IS-28M1) and side by side seating (IS-28M2). The former was described in the 1981-82, the latter in 1984-85 and earlier editions of *Jane's*. The IS-28M1 has since been redesignated IAR-34.

The rear fuselage is essentially the same as that of the IS-28B2, but the powered version is of low-wing configuration and has a redesigned forward fuselage, cockpit canopy and main landing gear.

The prototype (YR-1013) flew for the first time on 26 June 1976; production continues. All since c/n 41 are fitted with reinforced wings and are designated IS-28M2A. The aircraft is certificated in Australia, Japan, Norway, Portugal and the UK, and has been supplied to customers in Argentina, Australia, Canada, Denmark, Hungary, India, Israel, Norway, the Philippines, Spain, Sweden, Switzerland, the UK and the USA.

TYPE: Two-seat motor glider.

AIRFRAME: Cantilever low-wing monoplane, of mainly metal construction. Wortmann wing sections: FX-61-163 at root, FX-60-126 at tip. Dihedral 2°. Sweepforward 2° 30' at quarter-chord. Single-spar wings, with aluminium ribs and skin, fabric covered metal ailerons and (optionally) all-metal split flaps on trailing-edges. Flaps can be set to a negative position. All-metal two-section Hütter airbrakes on upper surfaces. Conventional fuselage, in three parts: metal front portion, built up on two longerons and cross-frames and having glassfibre fairings and engine cowling panels; aluminium alloy

SZD-48-3 Jantar Standard 3 single-seat sailplane

SZD-50-3 Puchacz two-seat training sailplane

SZD-51-1 Junior Club Class sailplane

First prototype WSK PZL-Krosno KR-03 Puchatek two-seat training sailplane

IS-28B2 tandem two-seat high performance training sailplane
(Peter F. Selinger)

IS-28M2A two-seat motor glider

IS-29D2 single-seat sailplane (Peter F. Selinger)

monocoque centre portion; and rear portion of aluminium alloy frames and skin. Cantilever aluminium alloy T tail, with dihedral tailplane. Rudder and elevator trailing-edges fabric covered. Trim tab in each elevator. Two retractable mainwheels, with rubber disc shock absorbers and mechanically operated drum brakes, side by side under fuselage centre-section; steerable tailwheel, also with shock absorber. Side by side seats under rearward sliding canopy. Dual controls standard.

POWER PLANT: One 50.7 kW (68 hp) Limbach SL 1700 EI (optionally a 59.5 kW; 80 hp Limbach L 2000 EOI) flat-four engine, driving a Hoffmann HO-V-62R/L160T two-blade adjustable-pitch fully-feathering propeller with spinner. Single fuel tank aft of cockpit, capacity 40 litres (10.6 US gallons; 8.8 Imp gallons) standard, 60 litres (15.8 US gallons; 13.2 Imp gallons) optional.

DIMENSIONS, EXTERNAL: As IS-28B2 except:

Length overall	7.00 m (22 ft 11½ in)
Height over tail	2.15 m (7 ft 0¾ in)
Wheel track	1.36 m (4 ft 5½ in)

WEIGHTS AND LOADINGS:

Weight empty	560 kg (1,234 lb)
Max T-O weight	760 kg (1,675 lb)
Max wing loading	41.7 kg/m² (8.54 lb/sq ft)
Max power loading: 68 hp	14.7 kg/kW (24.1 lb/hp)
80 hp	12.7 kg/kW (20.9 lb/hp)

PERFORMANCE, UNPOWERED (at max T-O weight):

Best glide ratio at 54 knots (100 km/h; 62 mph)	27
Min rate of sink at 43 knots (80 km/h; 50 mph)	
	1.20 m (3.94 ft)/s
Stalling speed, flaps down	36 knots (66 km/h; 41 mph)
Max speed (smooth air)	113 knots (210 km/h; 130 mph)
Max speed (rough air)	95 knots (177 km/h; 110 mph)
g limits	+5.3/−2.65

PERFORMANCE, POWERED (at max T-O weight):

Never-exceed speed	113 knots (210 km/h; 130 mph)
Max level speed: 68 hp	97 knots (180 km/h; 112 mph)
80 hp	100 knots (185 km/h; 115 mph)
Max cruising speed	92 knots (170 km/h; 106 mph)
Econ cruising speed	70 knots (130 km/h; 81 mph)
Stalling speed	36 knots (65 km/h; 41 mph)
Max rate of climb at S/L: 68 hp	120 m (394 ft)/min
80 hp	138 m (453 ft)/min
Service ceiling: 68 hp	4,700 m (15,420 ft)
80 hp	5,000 m (16,400 ft)
T-O run (grass)	250 m (820 ft)
T-O to 15 m (50 ft) (grass): 68 hp	593 m (1,945 ft)
80 hp	430 m (1,410 ft)
Landing run	90 m (295 ft)
Range with max fuel, no reserves	
	243 nm (450 km; 280 miles)
g limits	+5.3/−2.65

IS-29D2

Descriptions can be found in the 1980-81 and earlier editions of *Jane's* of the IS-29B, D, D3, D4, E, E4, G, and IS-31(E3). None of these versions is now in production. Models current in 1988 were as follows:

IS-29D2. Current Standard Class version, with improved cockpit and controls, Hütter airbrakes, separate tailplane and elevator, and improved rigging system. Certificated in Australia, Canada, China, West Germany, Hungary, Switzerland, Turkey, the USA and elsewhere. More than 210 built; in production.

IS-29D2 Club. Club Class version of D2, with flaps deleted and non-retractable monowheel. Certification granted. Small number built, including some for Australia; further orders placed.

The following description applies to the IS-29D2, except where indicated:

TYPE: Single-seat Standard Class (Club class) sailplane.

AIRFRAME: Cantilever shoulder-wing monoplane, with T tail. Wortmann wing sections: FX-61-163 at root, FX-61-126 at tip. All-metal wings, with main spar, false rear spar and riveted dural skin. Full span trailing-edge flaps and ailerons coupled to operate in unison, but can be disconnected for separate operation during landing. Hütter airbrake in upper surface of each wing. All-metal semi-monocoque fuselage. Detachable glassfibre nose-cap. Cantilever all-metal T tail, with full span elevator. Retractable sprung monowheel, with brake; non-retractable tailwheel. Canopy hinges sideways to starboard and can be jettisoned in flight.

DIMENSIONS, EXTERNAL:

Wing span	15.00 m (49 ft 2½ in)
Wing aspect ratio	21.6
Length overall	7.30 m (23 ft 11½ in)
Height over tail	1.68 m (5 ft 6¼ in)

AREA:

Wings, gross	10.40 m² (111.9 sq ft)

WEIGHTS AND LOADING:

Weight empty	240 kg (529 lb)
Max T-O weight	360 kg (793 lb)
Max wing loading	34.62 kg/m² (7.09 lb/sq ft)

PERFORMANCE (at max T-O weight):

Best glide ratio at 50 knots (93 km/h; 58 mph): D2	37
D2 Club	36
Min rate of sink at 42 knots (78 km/h; 48 mph)	
	0.65 m (2.13 ft)/s
Stalling speed:	
D2 (flaps down)	36 knots (65 km/h; 41 mph)
D2 Club	41 knots (75 km/h; 47 mph)

Max speed (smooth air)   121 knots (225 km/h; 140 mph)
Max speed (rough air)   93 knots (172 km/h; 107 mph)
Max aero-tow speed   76 knots (140 km/h; 87 mph)
Max winch-launching speed
70 knots (130 km/h; 81 mph)
g limits   +5.3/−2.65

IS-30

The IS-30, which underwent flight testing in the Spring of 1978, is based on the IS-28B2. Two prototypes were built, followed by a small number of production aircraft; further orders placed.

TYPE: Tandem two-seat sailplane.

AIRFRAME: All-metal cantilever shoulder-wing monoplane. Wortmann wing sections: FX-61-163 at root, FX-60-126 at tip. Dihedral 2°. Incidence 4°. No sweep on leading-edge. Hütter two-plate upper and lower surface metal airbrakes. All-metal ailerons; flaps optional. All-metal semi-monocoque fuselage, generally similar to IS-28B2. All-metal cantilever T tail, with full span elevator. Standard landing gear comprises a non-retractable rubber sprung 5 in Tost monowheel and 210 × 65 mm tailwheel; a semi-retractable 6 in monowheel and 280 × 85 mm nosewheel are available optionally. One-piece canopy opens sideways to starboard, and can be jettisoned in flight. Dual controls standard; fully equipped front and rear instrument panels optional. Nose towing hook, with Tost cable release, standard; CG towing hook optional. No provision for water ballast.

DIMENSIONS, EXTERNAL, AND WING AREA: As IS-28B2 except:
Height over tail   2.27 m (7 ft 5½ in)
WEIGHTS AND LOADINGS: As IS-28B2
PERFORMANCE (at max T-O weight): As IS-28B2 except:
Stalling speed: single-seat   38 knots (70 km/h; 43 mph)
two-seat   41 knots (75 km/h; 47 mph)
Max speed (smooth air):
single-seat   135 knots (250 km/h; 155 mph)
two-seat   121 knots (225 km/h; 140 mph)
Max speed (rough air)   86 knots (160 km/h; 99 mph)
Max winch-launching speed
67 knots (125 km/h; 78 mph)

IS-32

First shown publicly at the Paris Air Show in June 1977, the IS-32 tandem two-seat Open Class sailplane was developed from the IS-28B2. Certification is to BCAR Section E.

Fifteen IS-32s had been built by 1988, and small scale production is continuing. Customers to date have been from Australia, China, the UK and the USA.

TYPE: Tandem two-seat Open Class sailplane.

AIRFRAME: All-metal cantilever shoulder-wing monoplane. Wortmann wing sections: FX-67-K-170 at root, FX-67-K-150 at tip. Dihedral 2° 30′. Incidence 2°. Sweepforward 2° on leading-edge. Hütter two-plate upper and lower surface metal airbrakes. All-metal interconnected flaps and ailerons. All-metal semi-monocoque fuselage, generally similar to IS-28B2 and IS-30. All-metal cantilever T tail, with full span elevator. Mechanically retractable Tost monowheel, size 5.00-5, with Tost double shoe brake and oleo-pneumatic shock absorber; semi-recessed 210 × 65 mm tailwheel. One-piece jettisonable canopy, opening sideways to starboard; tinted canopy optional. Dual controls standard; fully equipped front and rear instrument panels optional. Nose towing hook, with Tost cable release. No provision for water ballast.

DIMENSIONS, EXTERNAL:
Wing span   20.00 m (65 ft 7½ in)
Wing aspect ratio   27.25
Length overall   8.36 m (27 ft 5¼ in)
Height over tail   2.27 m (7 ft 5½ in)
AREA:
Wings, gross   14.68 m² (158.0 sq ft)
WEIGHTS AND LOADING:
Weight empty   400 kg (882 lb)
Max T-O weight   590 kg (1,300 lb)
Max wing loading   40.2 kg/m² (8.23 lb/sq ft)
PERFORMANCE (at max T-O weight):
Best glide ratio at 59 knots (110 km/h; 68 mph)   44.5
Min rate of sink at 49 knots (90 km/h; 56 mph)
0.62 m (2.03 ft)/s
Stalling speed   43 knots (78 km/h; 49 mph)
Max speed (smooth air)   105 knots (195 km/h; 121 mph)
Max speed (rough air)   87 knots (161 km/h; 100 mph)
Max aero-tow speed   76 knots (140 km/h; 87 mph)
Max winch-launching speed
59 knots (110 km/h; 68 mph)
g limits   +4/−1.5

IAR-35

The IAR-35 is a single-seat all-metal glider designed to JAR 22 requirements, essentially for aerobatics but also for general purpose use. Design began in 1984, and the prototype (illustrated) made its first flight in May 1986.

TYPE: Single-seat aerobatic sailplane.

AIRFRAME: Cantilever shoulder-wing monoplane, with constant chord non-swept centre-section (NACA 64-015) and tapered outer panels. Dihedral 0° on centre-section, 2° on outer panels. Incidence 1°. Three-spar wing structure, with ribs and adhesive-bonded metal-to-metal stiffened skins, each wing being attached to fuselage by two fittings each side. All-metal statically balanced ailerons occupy entire trailing-edge. Automatic and aerodynamic trim tab in each aileron. All-metal DFS type upper and lower surface airbrakes. Metal endplate, with sprung rubber balancer wheel, at each wingtip. Fuselage has all-metal semi-monocoque structure, with aluminium alloy frames and longerons, covered with duralumin skins. Sweptback fin and statically balanced rudder; fixed incidence, strut braced tailplane with statically balanced elevators. Trim tab in each elevator. Ailerons, airbrakes and elevators are actuated by pushrods; rudder and elevator tabs are cable actuated. Mechanically retractable 340 × 125 mm monowheel, with brake; semi-recessed, non-retractable 210 × 65 mm tailwheel. Single seat for pilot (adjustable for height and inclination), under one-piece detachable Plexiglas canopy.

DIMENSIONS, EXTERNAL:
Wing span   12.00 m (39 ft 4½ in)
Wing aspect ratio   13.3
Length overall   6.47 m (21 ft 2¾ in)
Height over tail   1.72 m (5 ft 7¾ in)
AREA:
Wings, gross   10.80 m² (116.2 sq ft)
WEIGHTS AND LOADING:
Weight empty   250-270 kg (551-595 lb)
Max T-O weight   380 kg (838 lb)
Max wing loading   35.19 kg/m² (7.21 lb/sq ft)
PERFORMANCE (estimated):
Best glide ratio at 51 knots (95 km/h; 59 mph)   28
Min rate of sink at 43 knots (80 km/h; 50 mph)
0.85 m (2.79 ft)/s
Stalling speed   41 knots (75 km/h; 47 mph)
Max speed (smooth air)   205 knots (380 km/h; 236 mph)
Max speed (rough air) and design manoeuvring speed
(V_A)   109 knots (202 km/h; 125 mph)
g limits   +7.4/−7

SWEDEN

RADAB
AB RADAB
PO Box 81054, S-104 81 Stockholm
Telephone: (46) 8 440610
Telex: 124 43 FOTEX S Att WINDEXRADAB
MANAGING DIRECTOR: Harald Undén
TECHNICAL DIRECTOR: Sven Olof Ridder

RADAB WINDEX 1200

This small single-seat motor glider was designed in 1981 to meet the requirements of JAR 22 (Aerobatic category). Construction of the Windex 1100 prototype (SE-XSD) started in January 1982, and this made its first flight, unpowered, on 15 March 1985. Test flying with a 16.4 kW (22 hp) Limbach engine started in the Summer of 1985, but production aircraft will be slightly higher powered with a new engine comprising three chain-saw cylinders in line and offering 18.6 kW (25 hp). The first prototype had hot-wire shaped wings of 11.00 m (36 ft 1 in) span, but production kit aircraft, designated Windex 1200, have Nomex honeycomb moulded wings of increased span, though the wing area remains unchanged. The tailplane, originally mounted halfway up the fin, has been raised to a T configuration to simplify rudder geometry and improve elevator efficiency.

The first prototype was described and illustrated in the 1985-86 *Jane's*. Three production prototypes were built in 1987, at which time Radab had orders for about 40 kits. No update has been received.

TYPE: Single-seat homebuilt motor glider.

AIRFRAME: Cantilever mid-wing monoplane, with KTH-FFA (Stockholm Royal Institute of Technology) laminar flow wing section having 17% thickness/chord ratio from root to tip. Dihedral 3° 30′ from roots. Incidence 2° 35′ 24″. No sweep. Wings have a single spar of unidirectional glassfibre, with glassfibre/epoxy/Nomex honeycomb sandwich skin, and are detachable for transportation and storage. Bottom-hinged plain flaps/airbrakes, top-hinged balanced ailerons, and downswept winglets at tips, are all of similar construction, as are the fuselage, sweptback fin and rudder, and non-swept T tailplane and one-piece elevator. The engine cowling is part aluminium. Non-retractable, partially enclosed unsprung 12 in monowheel with drum brake. Landing skid forward of monowheel. Fixed tailwheel. Single moulded, reclined bucket seat under two-piece canopy, rear portion of which opens upward. Ballistic parachute and water ballast tanks optional.

POWER PLANT: One 18.6 kW (25 hp) Windex 300 three-cylinder aircooled two-stroke inline engine, with V belt reduction drive to a Radab propeller which has mechanically operated variable pitch and feathering and two Kevlar/epoxy blades. Engine is mounted halfway up fin. Single aluminium fuel tank below wing spar central joint, capacity approx 20 litres (5.3 US gallons; 4.4 Imp gallons).

DIMENSIONS, EXTERNAL:
Wing span   12.10 m (39 ft 8½ in)
Wing aspect ratio   19.75
Length overall   4.92 m (16 ft 1¾ in)
Height over tail   1.14 m (3 ft 9 in)
Propeller diameter   1.05 m (3 ft 5½ in)
AREA:
Wings, gross   7.41 m² (79.8 sq ft)
WEIGHTS AND LOADINGS:
Weight empty   120 kg (264 lb)
Max T-O weight: Aerobatic   250 kg (551 lb)
Utility   300 kg (661 lb)
Max wing loading:
Aerobatic   33.74 kg/m² (6.91 lb/sq ft)
Utility   40.48 kg/m² (8.29 lb/sq ft)
Max power loading:
Aerobatic   13.44 kg/kW (22.05 lb/hp)
Utility   16.10 kg/kW (26.45 lb/hp)
PERFORMANCE (estimated at 230 kg; 507 lb T-O weight):
Best glide ratio at 54 knots (100 km/h; 62 mph)   38
Min rate of sink at 41 knots (75 km/h; 47 mph)
0.61 m (2.00 ft)/s
Stalling speed   35 knots (65 km/h; 41 mph)
Max speed (rough air)   109 knots (202 km/h; 125 mph)
g limits   +7/−5
PERFORMANCE, POWERED (estimated at 230 kg; 507 lb T-O weight):
Never-exceed speed   170 knots (316 km/h; 196 mph)
Max level speed   146 knots (270 km/h; 168 mph)
Cruising speed (50% power)
113 knots (210 km/h; 130 mph)
Stalling speed   35 knots (65 km/h; 41 mph)
Max rate of climb at S/L   264 m (865 ft)/min
T-O run (grass)   110 m (360 ft)
T-O to 10 m (33 ft)   250 m (820 ft)
Range with max fuel, no reserves
485 nm (900 km; 559 miles)

SWITZERLAND

CANARD
CANARD AVIATION AG
(Division of H. Bucher Leichtbau)
Sagenrainstrasse 4, CH-8636 Wald
Telephone: (055) 952055
Telex: 828 429 BUFA

CANARD AVIATION CANARD SC

The Canard SC is based on the Canard-2 FL foot launched sailplane designed by Dipl-Ing Hans U. Farner, which was described and illustrated in the 1982-83 and earlier editions of *Jane's*. A prototype of the Canard SC was first flown on 23 July 1983, and made 40 flights, totalling about 20 hours, in its first year. To accelerate the flight test programme, it was given self-launch capability by mounting a 15 kW (11.2 hp) König three-cylinder two-stroke engine, with a foldable propeller, on a pylon between the V struts and main wing.

Flight tests of the powered SC proved so successful that after registration of the glider version, expected in 1988, it is intended to obtain certification, to JAR 22, of a powered sailplane variant. It is planned to build a small pre-production batch after Swiss certification has been obtained.

Designated **Canard SCM**, the powered version will have a 15 to 18 kW (11.2 to 13.4 hp) three-cylinder two-stroke engine with a special low-noise propeller/exhaust system. It will be possible to convert Canard SC sailplanes into Canard SCMs by installing the power modification kit.

Danish registered IS-30 two-seat sailplane (*Peter F. Selinger*)

Prototype of the aerobatic single-seat IAR-35

ICA-Brasov IS-32 Open Class sailplane (*Air Photo Supply*)

Self-launch prototype of the Canard SC sailplane

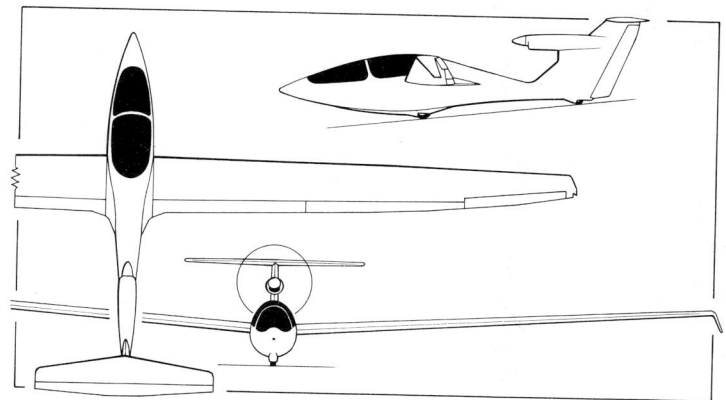

Radab Windex 1200 powered sailplane (*Michael A. Badrocke*)

LAK-11 Nida single-seat 15 metre Class sailplane

TYPE: Single-seat sailplane (SC) or motor glider (SCM).

AIRFRAME: 'Parasol monoplane' configuration, with single-spar anhedral main wing at rear supported by V-form pylons which act as both lifting surfaces and 'vertical' fins; fixed incidence foreplane, with elevator. Aerofoil sections: Wortmann FX-63-137 (main wings and V struts), Eppler E 1232 (foreplane), and Clark Y (11.7% thickness/chord ratio) (winglets). Wings have ailerons; trailing-edges of V tail pylons movable to act as spoilers. Construction is of glassfibre, Kevlar and carbonfibre rovings, CIBA XB 3052 epoxy and Rohacell foam plastics. Three-axis control by ailerons, forward elevator, and dependent winglet/rudder at each wingtip. Non-retractable semi-recessed bungee sprung steerable monowheel, size 260 × 85 mm, with brake; semi-recessed fixed tailwheel, size 200 × 50 mm. Pre-series aircraft under construction in January 1985 have revised, sideways opening, canopy.

POWER PLANT (SCM): One 11.2 to 13.4 kW (15 to 18 hp) three-cylinder two-stroke radial engine with reduction

drive to a two-blade pusher propeller with foldable Kevlar blades. Single fuel tank, capacity 10 litres (2.6 US gallons; 2.2 Imp gallons). Entire engine unit (but not fuel tank) can be removed for normal soaring flights.

DIMENSIONS, EXTERNAL:

Wing span	13.50 m (44 ft 3½ in)
Foreplane span	3.80 m (12 ft 5½ in)
Wing aspect ratio	21.2
Foreplane aspect ratio	6.0
Length overall	4.75 m (15 ft 7 in)
Height overall	2.23 m (7 ft 3¾ in)
Propeller diameter (SC prototype)	1.10 m (3 ft 7¼ in)

AREAS:

Wings, gross	8.60 m² (92.57 sq ft)
Foreplane, gross	2.40 m² (25.83 sq ft)

WEIGHTS AND LOADINGS:

Weight empty: SC (without engine)	130 kg (287 lb)
SCM	150 kg (331 lb)

Max T-O weight: SC	240 kg (529 lb)
SCM	270 kg (595 lb)
Max wing/foreplane loading:	
SC	21.8 kg/m² (4.46 lb/sq ft)
SCM	24.5 kg/m² (5.02 lb/sq ft)

PERFORMANCE, UNPOWERED (SC, estimated at max T-O weight):

Best glide ratio at 39 knots (72 km/h; 45 mph)	25-30
Min rate of sink at 33 knots (62 km/h; 38 mph)	
	0.60-0.70 m (1.97-2.30 ft)/s
Max speed (smooth air)	97 knots (180 km/h; 112 mph)
Max speed (rough air)	68 knots (126 km/h; 78 mph)
Stalling speed: SC	28 knots (51 km/h; 32 mph)
SCM	30 knots (55 km/h; 35 mph)

PERFORMANCE, POWERED (SCM, estimated at max T-O weight):

Max rate of climb at S/L	90-120 m (295-395 ft)/min
T-O distance (on concrete)	80-100 m (265-330 ft)

UNION OF SOVIET SOCIALIST REPUBLICS

ESAG and SSAKTB
EKSPERIMENTINE SPORTINES AVIACIJOS GAMYKLA (Experimental Sport Aviation Plant)
Pociūnai, Prienai, Lietuvos TSR (Lithuania)
DIRECTOR: Aleksandras Jonušas
CHIEF ENGINEER: Algimantas Zadavičius
HEAD OF PRODUCTION: Algimantas Pauža
CHIEF TEST PILOT: Algirdas Virbickas

SPECIALUS SPORTINES AVIACIJOS KONSTRAVIMO — TECHNOLOGINIS BIURAS
(Special Sport Aviation Design and Technology Bureau)
DIRECTOR: Klemas Juočas
DEPUTY DIRECTOR: Vytautas Mekšriūnas
CHIEF ENGINEER: Julius Armonaitis
CHIEF DESIGNERS:
Jonas Bankauskas

Gintaras Sabaliauskas
Vilhelmas Gerlichas
TEST PILOTS:
Gintautas Nekrašius
Vytautas Sabeckis
ESAG originated in 1969, with the objective of developing a plastics-construction sailplane. Its first (and the first Soviet) plastics sailplane, designed by Mr Boleslovas Karvelis, was the BK-7 Lietuva, which was first flown on 8 December 1972 and was described and illustrated in the 1975-76 *Jane's*. This has undergone progressive development, the latest version being the LAK-12.

In July 1986 ESAG was divided into two sections, ESAG itself and SSAKTB (at the same address). ESAG is charged with manufacture and repair, in a new building, while SSAKTB is concerned with research and design. The initials LAK, designating products of ESAG and SSAKTB, stand for Lietuviška Aviacine Konstrukcija (Lithuanian Aviation Construction).

Current products of ESAG are the LAK-12 Lietuva and LAK-16 sailplanes, the LAK-T3 trailer/hangar and LAK-T4 universal trailer/hangar (1988 design), and the LAK-RE-303 electronic variometer. The LAK-16 was conceived by SSAKTB, as was the SL-2P flying laboratory twin-fuselage sailplane that is used for aerofoil research.

ESAG is the sole overhaul centre in the USSR for the LAK-12 and Czechoslovak L-13 Blaník sailplanes. Repairs have also been undertaken of Polish Cobra-15, German MBB Phoebus and Schleicher ASW 15 plastics sailplanes.

LAK-5 NEMUNAS
Three LAK-5 side by side two-seat motor gliders had been built when production was terminated in 1983. Details and an illustration appeared in the 1987-88 *Jane's*. The designer was Mr K Juočas, and not as stated in that edition.

LAK-11 NIDA
This single-seat 15 metre Class sailplane, named after a resort in Lithuania, was designed by Mr Jonas Bankauskas

and flew for the first time on 6 July 1982. Seven LAK-11s had been built when production ended in 1986. The following newly-received data correct information given in the 1987-88 *Jane's*:

DIMENSION, EXTERNAL:
Length overall   6.69 m (21 ft 11½ in)
PERFORMANCE (A: at 330 kg; 727 lb, B: at 480 kg; 1,058 lb AUW):
Max speed (rough air):
  A, B   102 knots (190 km/h; 118 mph)
  Max aero-tow speed: A   86 knots (160 km/h; 99 mph)
  B   75 knots (140 km/h; 87 mph)
g limits   +6/–3.3

LAK-12 LIETUVA (LITHUANIA)

The Lietuva was the first all-plastics sailplane produced in the USSR, and in its latest known form is designated LAK-12. Development began in 1969; details of the BK-7/7A/7V/7S, LAK-9/9M and LAK-10 early versions can be found in the 1982-83 *Jane's*.

The LAK-12 is the sixth and latest production version. Compared with the earlier versions originated by Mr Boleslovas Karvelis, it was considerably redesigned under the leadership of Mr Kęstutis Gečas. It is intended as a training aircraft for high class glider pilots participating in all-Soviet and international events, and for record attempts. Compared with the LAK-10 it has a more comfortable cockpit, with improved instrument layout, a better positioned control column, and a one-piece canopy. Streamlining of the airframe is enhanced, the wings are lowered to a mid position, the fuselage and horizontal tail surfaces are of completely new design, and construction makes extensive use of composite materials, including carbonfibre for the wing spars and other components.

First flight of the LAK-12 took place on 21 December 1979. Flight testing was completed in 1980, and deliveries of production aircraft began later that year. A total of 144 Lietuvas had been delivered by early 1988, including 110 LAK-12s.

TYPE: Single-seat Open Class sailplane.
AIRFRAME: Cantilever mid-wing monoplane. Wortmann wing sections: FX-67-K-170 from root to junction with outer panels, then tapering to FX-67-K-150 at tip. No wing fillets. Main wing spar is a carbonfibre T beam. Trailing-edge flaps and interconnected ailerons are attached to auxiliary rear spar. Airbrakes on upper surfaces only. Wings, split flaps and ailerons have a skin of three-ply glasscloth, with foam plastics infill between each layer; carbonfibre tape is used to reinforce flap construction. Fuselage, and integral fin, are of glassfibre construction, reinforced with carbonfibre tape. Slightly swept fin and rudder, and non-swept low-mounted tailplane and elevators (all of Wortmann FX-71-L-150/25 section), are of similar construction to wings. Rudder and elevators are mass balanced. Retractable monowheel, with mechanical brake and oleo-pneumatic shock absorber; non-retractable shock absorbing tail bumper. One-piece cockpit canopy. Provision for 190 litres (50 US gallons; 41.8 Imp gallons) water ballast in wing leading-edge tanks.

DIMENSIONS, EXTERNAL:
Wing span   20.42 m (67 ft 0 in)

Wing aspect ratio   28.5
Length overall   7.23 m (23 ft 8½ in)
Height over tail   1.92 m (6 ft 3½ in)
AREA:
Wings, gross   14.63 m² (157.5 sq ft)
WEIGHTS AND LOADING:
Weight empty   340 kg (749 lb)
Max T-O weight:
  without water ballast   430 kg (948 lb)
  with water ballast   650 kg (1,433 lb)
Max wing loading   44.42 kg/m² (9.10 lb/sq ft)
PERFORMANCE (at max T-O weight except where indicated):
Best glide ratio at 62 knots (115 km/h; 71 mph)   48
Min rate of sink at 40 knots (75 km/h; 47 mph), at 430 kg
  (948 lb) AUW   0.48 m (1.57 ft)/s
Stalling speed   36 knots (65 km/h; 41 mph)
Max speed (smooth air)   135 knots (250 km/h; 155 mph)
Max aero-tow speed   75 knots (140 km/h; 87 mph)
g limits   +6/–3

LAK-12 LIETUVA 2R

The LAK-12 Lietuva 2R is a two-seat Open Class version of the Lietuva, designed by Mr Antanas Rukas and Mr Algimantas Jonušas. Construction of the prototype began in 1985, and this first flew in April 1986. By March 1988, a second aircraft had been completed. Compared with the single-seater, the Lietuva 2R has a reinforced fuselage structure with a modified control system, a modified and reinforced retractable landing gear with a brake and bungee suspension, 100 litres (26.4 US gallons; 22 Imp gallons) of water ballast in wing tanks, and tandem seats in the longer fuselage.

DIMENSION, EXTERNAL:
Length overall   7.73 m (25 ft 4¼ in)
WEIGHTS AND LOADING:
Weight empty   400 kg (882 lb)
Max water ballast   100 kg (220 lb)
Max T-O weight, with water ballast   690 kg (1,521 lb)
Max wing loading   47.16 kg/m² (9.66 lb/sq ft)
PERFORMANCE:
Best glide ratio at 62 knots (115 km/h; 71 mph)   48
Min rate of sink at 43 knots (80 km/h; 50 mph)
                                     0.50 m (1.64 ft)/s
Stalling speed   38 knots (70 km/h; 44 mph)
Max speed (smooth air)   135 knots (250 km/h; 155 mph)
Max speed (rough air)   94 knots (175 km/h; 108 mph)
Max aero-tow speed   75 knots (140 km/h; 87 mph)
g limits   +4/–2

LAK-16

Designed by Mr Gintaras Sabaliauskas and Mr Kestutis Leonavičius as a successor to the LAK-14 Strazdas, the LAK-16 first prototype was flown initially on 6 September 1986 with a LAK-14 wooden wing. Production aircraft have a higher aspect ratio wing, with inset ailerons, constructed initially of fabric covered GFRP. A metal framed wing will be introduced later, for added strength. The LAK-16 is said to be less costly to produce than the Strazdas, and capable of wider application, having provisions for the future addition of such features as wing spoilers, ski landing gear and a power plant if required. It is believed that production began in 1987.

TYPE: Single-seat primary training glider.
AIRFRAME: Strut braced high-wing monoplane. Wings have an R-IIIA-15 aerofoil section, with dihedral from roots, and are constructed initially from a GFRP spar, ribs and leading-edge with fabric covering. Ailerons are of fabric covered duralumin tube. All bracing wires are covered in translucent PVC sleeves, and (with the aileron controls) can be disconnected, enabling the entire wing to pivot and align with the fuselage for transportation and storage. Open frame fuselage is of steel tube at front, riveted duralumin tube at rear. Tail unit is of fabric covered duralumin tube, with cable controlled elevators and rudder. Tailplane strut (but not control cables) can be disconnected to stow horizontal surfaces for transportation and storage. Landing gear comprises twin mainwheels on self sprung GFRP legs, a self sprung GFRP nose-skid, and a self-centring tailwheel. Pilot sits on a GFRP seat (adjustable fore and aft) attached at three points to the lower and rear steel fuselage members, and is provided with a seat belt and headrest.

DIMENSIONS, EXTERNAL:
Wing span   9.60 m (31 ft 6 in)
Wing aspect ratio   8.5
Length overall   5.45 m (17 ft 10½ in)
AREA:
Wings, gross   10.90 m² (117.3 sq ft)
WEIGHTS:
Weight empty   75 kg (165 lb)
Pilot weight range   40-80 kg (88-176 lb)
PERFORMANCE:
Best glide ratio at 27 knots (50 km/h; 31 mph)   10
Max speed (smooth air)   43 knots (80 km/h; 50 mph)
Max landing speed with 80 kg pilot
                           24 knots (45 km/h; 28 mph)

SSAKTB SL-2P

First flown on 25 June 1987, the SL-2P is a flying laboratory for aerofoil research. The single example has been constructed by joining two standard L-13 Blaník sailplanes, using an SSAKTB-designed centre wing and centre tailplane. The starboard fuselage has had its cockpit canopy blanked off, and a structure for carrying the aerofoil test specimen is mounted above the centre wing. The two crew are accommodated in tandem in the port cockpits.

DIMENSIONS, EXTERNAL:
Wing span   18.82 m (61 ft 9 in)
Wing aspect ratio   15.07
Length overall   8.40 m (27 ft 6¾ in)
Height overall   4.66 m (15 ft 3½ in)
AREA:
Wings, gross   23.51 m² (253.06 sq ft)
WEIGHTS AND LOADING:
Weight empty   789 kg (1,739 lb)
Max T-O weight   950 kg (2,094 lb)
Max wing loading   40.41 kg/m² (8.28 lb/sq ft)
PERFORMANCE:
Stalling speed   43 knots (80 km/h; 50 mph)
Max speed (smooth air)   108 knots (200 km/h; 124 mph)
Max speed (rough air) and max aero-tow speed
                           75 knots (140 km/h; 87 mph)
g limits   +3.7/–1.7

OŠKINIS

OŠKINIS BRO-23KR GARNYS (STORK)

Designed in 1981, the BRO-23KR is a single-seat open-cockpit primary training glider, designed to provide a successor to the BRO-11M/LAK-2, of which production was completed in 1979. Mr Oškinis was assisted in its design by pilots Ch. Kišonas and K. Rinkevičius of the Kaunas hang gliding club. Production is believed to have started in about 1983 or 1984.

AIRFRAME: Strut and steel cable braced high-wing monoplane. Constant chord slotted wings have a GA(W)-1 aerofoil section, 16% thickness/chord ratio, dihedral from roots, full span ailerons and turned-down tips. Ribs and spar are of woven glassfibre, with three-ply glasscloth skin forward of main spar. Spaces between ends of ribs filled with flat plates made of two layers of glasscloth. Trailing fixed portion of wings is cast with epoxy filler,

using longitudinal glassfibre, and covered with glasscloth. Entire ribbed surface is then covered with Lavsan film, glued in position and heat-shrunk to fit. Ailerons are of similar construction. Wingtips of textolite. GRP fuselage, including cockpit, is built in two halves. T tail unit is of similar construction to wings. Five rubber blocks provide main landing shock absorption, to which can be fitted a wide GRP snow skid for Winter flying; the same skid with a wheel attached for Summer use; a tricycle undercarriage for 'aeroplane landing' training; or floats for waterborne operation. Self-sprung tail bumper of glassfibre reinforced resin. Aircraft has been tested also with a small nosewheel. Open cockpit, lined with polyurethane and fitted with windscreen and foam plastics reclining seat.

DIMENSIONS, EXTERNAL:
Wing span   8.20 m (26 ft 10¾ in)
Wing aspect ratio   6.5
Length overall   6.40 m (21 ft 0 in)
Height over tail   2.20 m (7 ft 2½ in)

AREA:
Wings, gross   10.40 m² (111.9 sq ft)

WEIGHTS AND LOADING:
Weight empty   83.5 kg (184 lb)
Max T-O weight   158.5 kg (349 lb)
Max wing loading   15.2 kg/m² (3.11 lb/sq ft)

PERFORMANCE:
Best glide ratio   15
Min rate of sink   1.00 m (3.28 ft)/s
Stalling speed   23 knots (42 km/h; 27 mph)
Max speed (smooth air)   54 knots (100 km/h; 62 mph)

UNITED KINGDOM

LIGHTWING

LIGHTWING RESEARCH

68 Timberleys, Littlehampton, West Sussex BN17 6QB
Telephone: (0903) 722578
DESIGNER/BUILDER: John M. Lee

Lightwing has been in existence for more than ten years, designing and building aircraft for slow-speed flight research. Its L6FS Mouse (see 1987-88 *Jane's*) was conceived specifically to investigate the suitability of its wing section, configuration and handling qualities for a subsequent lightweight sailplane. It was the designer's aim to reintroduce inexpensive glider flying to the UK.

LIGHTWING CT6 COMPANION

Mr Lee began designing this lightweight training glider in January 1984, prototype construction being started in 1986. First flight was made in Spring 1987. It is intended to have a small power unit available as an option.

TYPE: Tandem two-seat training glider.
AIRFRAME: Cantilever high-wing monoplane. Wings have Göttingen 535 root and tip sections, 0° dihedral, 0° sweepback at one-third chord, 0° washout, and 3° incidence. They, and the ailerons, are semi-monocoque shells of epoxy foam and glassfibre, laminated with other composite materials. No flaps, but airbrake to become available later. Moulded semi-monocoque composites fuselage, of pod and boom configuration. Conventional

cruciform tail surfaces, with large rudder and one-piece elevator. Underfuselage ash landing skid, aft of which is a wheel with balloon tyre adjacent to the CG. Seats for two persons in tandem in open cockpit, with provision for full wraparound soft plastics transparency. Recovery parachute optional.

DIMENSIONS, EXTERNAL:
Wing span   12.19 m (40 ft 0 in)
Wing aspect ratio   9.6
Length overall   6.71 m (22 ft 0 in)
Height over tail   1.37 m (4 ft 6 in)
AREA:
Wings, gross   15.51 m² (167.0 sq ft)

LAK-12 Lietuva 2R two-seat sailplane

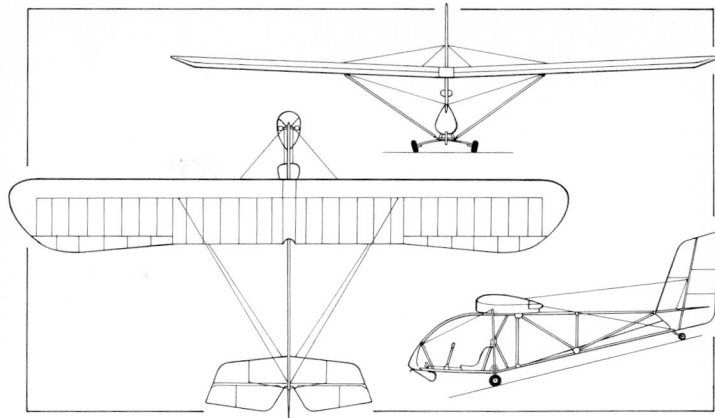

LAK-16 single-seat training glider *(Michael A. Badrocke)*

SSAKTB SL-2P twin-fuselage flying laboratory for aerofoil research

Lightwing CT6 Companion training glider

Oškinis BRO-23KR primary training glider (reproduced from *Krilya Rodini*)

Prototype Advanced Aviation Sierra single-seat sailplane *(Howard Levy)*

WEIGHTS AND LOADING:
Weight empty	109 kg (240 lb)
Max T-O weight (two persons)	286 kg (630 lb)
Wing loading (solo)	10.74 kg/m² (2.20 lb/sq ft)

PERFORMANCE:
Best glide ratio (solo) at 17 knots (32 km/h; 20 mph)	20
Min rate of sink	0.91 m (3.0 ft)/s
Stalling speed (solo)	16 knots (29 km/h; 18 mph)

Max speed (rough air)	61 knots (112 km/h; 70 mph)
Max aero-tow speed	52 knots (96 km/h; 60 mph)
Max winch-launching speed	43 knots (80 km/h; 50 mph)

UNITED STATES OF AMERICA

ADVANCED AVIATION
ADVANCED AVIATION INC
323 North Ivey Lane, Orlando, Florida 32811

Advanced Aviation is best known for its range of microlight and Experimental aeroplanes and amphibians (see Sport Aircraft section). It has now added to its range a low-cost, lightweight sailplane known as the Sierra.

ADVANCED AVIATION SIERRA
The Sierra was first flown in prototype form on 25 March 1988. In June that year it became available as a bolt-together kit, requiring approximately 60 working hours to assemble, and in ready assembled form. The prototype differed from 'production' aircraft only in having an aluminium cockpit pod instead of the now standard moulded pod. The Sierra can be air-towed, auto-towed, winch or bungee launched, and the company's King Cobra and Caribou have already been used as towing aircraft.

TYPE: Single-seat lightweight sailplane.

AIRFRAME: Strut-braced high-wing monoplane. Bolted aluminium alloy tubular structure, with Dacron covering. Moulded composites cockpit pod. Three-axis control (via ailerons, rudder and elevators). Monowheel landing gear with tailskid. Set up time 20 mins.

DIMENSIONS, EXTERNAL:
Wing span	11.87 m (38 ft 11½ in)
Length overall	6.57 m (21 ft 6½ in)

AREA:
Wings, gross	12.17 m² (131.0 sq ft)

WEIGHTS AND LOADING:
Weight empty	70 kg (155 lb)
Max T-O weight	181 kg (400 lb)
Max wing loading	14.89 kg/m² (3.05 lb/sq ft)

PERFORMANCE (calculated; 77 kg; 170 lb pilot, ISA):
Best glide ratio	approx 20
Min rate of sink	0.86 m (2.83 ft)/s
Best glide speed	30 knots (56 km/h; 35 mph)
Stalling speed	23 knots (42 km/h; 26 mph)

INAV
INAV LTD

INAV Ltd ceased trading in 1987. HAPI Engines Inc took over the company's sport aircraft (see Sport Aircraft section). Full details of the Monerai sailplane and Moni motor glider, and illustrations, can be found in the 1987-88 *Jane's*. It is worth noting also that on 23 October 1987 Mr David Green flew a Moni to a new world speed record over a 3 km course in FAI Class C1, achieving 97.76 knots (181.16 km/h; 112.56 mph), subject to confirmation.

MARSKE

MARSKE AIRCRAFT CORPORATION

130 Crestwood Drive, Michigan City, Indiana 46360
Telephone: (219) 879 7039
PRESIDENT: James J. Marske

MARSKE MONARCH

The Monarch was designed and built by Mr Jim Marske, and made its first flight on 4 July 1974. Plans and kits are available, and 106 sets of drawings had been sold by the beginning of 1988, from which eight Monarchs had been completed.

In 1976 Mr Marske successfully test flew the Monarch prototype in self-launching form, with a 9 kW (12 hp) McCulloch engine installed behind the pilot's seat, driving a 0.635 m (2 ft 1 in) diameter pusher propeller. This did not provide sufficient power, but is expected to be adequate for the Monarch E which is at least 9.1 kg (20 lb) lighter. The company's own Monarch E has not yet been flown in powered form.

The earlier Monarch B was described in the 1977-78 *Jane's*; the following description applies to the Monarch C and subsequent versions, including the D (longer span ailerons) and E (revised spoiler location, overhead window and larger rudder).

TYPE: Single-seat ultralight homebuilt glider.

AIRFRAME: Braced high-wing monoplane, with single extruded aluminium strut each side. Wing section NACA 43012A, reflexed at 75 per cent chord. Dihedral 2°. Sweepforward 3° at quarter-chord. Moulded glassfibre D leading-edge, with glassfibre front spar web and booms, corrugated glassfibre web ribs with wooden capstrips, wooden rear spar and trailing-edge, and Dacron covering. Inset transparency in centre of leading-edge on Monarch E. Ailerons (outboard) and elevators (inboard) each have single Sitka spruce spar and glassfibre/wood ribs. Fixed tab on each elevator. All control surfaces Dacron covered. Aluminium spoiler above each wing. Simple minimal beam type fuselage of laminated glassfibre, moulded in two halves and joined at centreline. Forward section supports pilot's seat, with nose fairing over instrument panel; rear section forms integral fin leading-edge. CG tow hook on each side of nose fairing. Fin and rudder, above and below level of wings. Glassfibre leading-edge (fin), wooden trailing-edge (rudder), glassfibre/wood ribs and fabric covering. No horizontal tail surfaces. Reinforced underfuselage landing skid. Single landing wheel, below and slightly behind pilot's open seat. Conventional floor-mounted control column.

DIMENSIONS, EXTERNAL:

Wing span	12.80 m (42 ft 0 in)
Wing aspect ratio	9.5
Length overall	3.71 m (12 ft 2 in)
Height over tail	2.39 m (7 ft 10 in)

AREA:

Wings, gross	17.19 m² (185.0 sq ft)

WEIGHTS AND LOADING:

Weight empty: C, D, E	100 kg (220 lb)
Pilot weight range	45-104 kg (100-230 lb)
Max T-O weight	204 kg (450 lb)
Max wing loading	11.72 kg/m² (2.40 lb/sq ft)

PERFORMANCE:

Best glide ratio at 35 knots (64 km/h; 40 mph)	19
Min rate of sink at 26 knots (48 km/h; 30 mph)	0.82 m (2.70 ft)/s
Stalling speed	21 knots (39 km/h; 24 mph)
Max speed (smooth air)	61 knots (113 km/h; 70 mph)
Max speed (rough air), max aero-tow and max winch-launching speed	43 knots (80 km/h; 50 mph)
T-O and landing run	12 m (40 ft) or less
*g limits	+5.3/−2.6

*Has been static loaded to +9.6g without failure

MARSKE PIONEER II

Designed some years ago as a simple, high performance sailplane for amateur construction, the Pioneer I prototype first flew in 1971. From it were developed the initial Pioneer IA, and then the smaller and lighter Pioneer II which made its first flight in July 1972.

The Pioneer II-A featured NACA 23012R/23010R wing sections and short bubble canopy, these being changed in the Pioneer II-B to a longer canopy and NACA 33012R/33010R wing sections which considerably improved low-speed performance. Improvements in the current **Pioneer II-C**, to which the following description applies, include a further refinement of the wing aerofoil section, closer spacing of the wing nose ribs, a simplified fuselage structure with lighter and more comfortable glassfibre bucket seat, reduction of 51 mm (2 in) in cockpit height and 102 mm (4 in) lower top line to the nose to improve forward view. Like the Monarch, the Pioneer is highly resistant to stalls and spins. The **Pioneer II-D** is similar to the II-C except for a sweptback tail and a modified upper surface in the wing leading-edge D tube.

By early 1988 Marske had sold 96 sets of Pioneer drawings, and 16 of these aircraft had been flown. These have accumulated more than 2,000 flying hours without a single reported accident.

TYPE: Single-seat homebuilt sailplane.

AIRFRAME: Cantilever mid-wing monoplane. Dihedral 4° 30′. Incidence 6°. Sweepforward 2° at quarter-chord. Modified NACA 33012/33010 wing sections in II-C and II-D. Wings have a single I-section spruce main spar, plywood ribs and D-tube skins; remainder fabric covered. Ailerons and inboard mounted elevators have spruce ribs and spars, with fabric covering. Upper and lower surface spoilers each consist of aluminium plate hinged at forward edge. Short, stubby fuselage has a welded steel tube frame and two-part outer shell of moulded glassfibre/epoxy. Upper half, including top-decking and fin, incorporates all necessary ribs and stiffeners bonded into place; lower half is supplied with all bulkheads bonded in. Rudder is of fabric covered wood construction. Single 30.5 cm (12 in) mainwheel, with drag brake, slightly aft of CG; 2 in castoring tailwheel. Towing hook on each side of fuselage under wing leading-edge, near CG. One-piece removable cockpit canopy.

DIMENSIONS, EXTERNAL:

Wing span	12.98 m (42 ft 7 in)
Wing aspect ratio	12.6
Length overall	3.81 m (12 ft 6 in)
Height over tail	1.98 m (6 ft 6 in)

AREA:

Wings, gross	13.38 m² (144.0 sq ft)

WEIGHTS AND LOADINGS:

Weight empty: II-C	163 kg (360 lb)
II-D	159 kg (380 lb)
Pilot weight range	57-104 kg (125-230 lb)
Max T-O weight: II-C	295 kg (650 lb)
II-D	286 kg (630 lb)
Max wing loading: II-C	22.0 kg/m² (4.51 lb/sq ft)
II-D	21.4 kg/m² (4.38 lb/sq ft)

PERFORMANCE (at max T-O weight):

Best glide ratio at 52 knots (97 km/h; 60 mph)	35
Min rate of sink at 39 knots (72 km/h; 45 mph)	0.70 m (2.30 ft)/s
Stalling speed	31 knots (57 km/h; 35 mph)
Max speed (rough and smooth air)	113 knots (209 km/h; 130 mph)
Max aero-tow speed	87 knots (161 km/h; 100 mph)
Max winch-launching speed	61 knots (113 km/h; 70 mph)
g limits	+5.3/−2.65

MAUPIN

JIM MAUPIN

Star Route 3, Box 430037, Tehachapi, California 93561-9803

MAUPIN WOODSTOCK ONE

The Woodstock One was flown for the first time in early 1970. It has been flight tested to include spins (four turns) and stalls; and has been dived at 110 per cent of its never-exceed speed.

Plans, including an instructional booklet, have been available to amateur constructors, and by early 1988 more than 450 sets of plans had been sold, in the USA and 20 other countries. Homebuilders' kits are no longer available.

TYPE: Single-seat homebuilt sailplane.

AIRFRAME: Cantilever shoulder-wing monoplane, of Douglas fir and birch construction with some fabric covering. Culver wing sections (thickness/chord ratio 18% at root, 13% at tip). Airbrakes on upper wing surfaces. Non-retractable semi-recessed monowheel. Undernose towing hook. Plans depict both open and enclosed cockpits, and a powered version with a non-retractable pylon mounted power plant aft of the cockpit.

DIMENSIONS, EXTERNAL:

Wing span	11.89 m (39 ft 0 in)
Wing aspect ratio	14.5
Length overall	5.87 m (19 ft 3 in)
Height over tail	1.30 m (4 ft 3 in)

AREA:

Wings, gross	9.73 m² (104.7 sq ft)

WEIGHTS AND LOADING:

Weight empty	106.5 kg (235 lb)
Max T-O weight	204 kg (450 lb)
Max wing loading	20.9 kg/m² (4.29 lb/sq ft)

PERFORMANCE (at max T-O weight):

Best glide ratio at 39 knots (72 km/h; 45 mph)	24
Min rate of sink at 35 knots (64 km/h; 40 mph)	0.79 m (2.60 ft)/s
Stalling speed	28 knots (52 km/h; 32 mph)
Max speed (smooth air)	87 knots (161 km/h; 100 mph)
Max speed (rough air)	68 knots (125 km/h; 78 mph)
Max aero-tow and max winch-launching speed	56 knots (105 km/h; 65 mph)
g limit	+5

MAUPIN WINDROSE

The Windrose self-launching sailplane, first flown in 1983, was made available in plans form (more than 100 sets sold by early 1988, in the USA and ten other countries), with instruction book. It was intended that the sailplane would be marketed as a complete kit for homebuilding, or partial kit (eg hardware, moulded fuselage pod). Its general appearance is shown in an accompanying photograph.

The first prototype was sold to a Japanese buyer, and a second, with a 30 kW (40 hp) Rotax engine, was built in 1986. The following description applies to the lower powered first prototype with a Cuyuna engine.

TYPE: Single-seat self-launching sailplane.

AIRFRAME: Cantilever shoulder-wing monoplane, of pod and boom configuration. Wings each made of five blocks of plastics foam, hot wire cut with rib pattern at each end; each piece is notched top and bottom to take spar cap, and dowel is pushed into foam between spar caps and glued in position. Unidirectional glassfibre spar caps are laid into notches in foam blocks before skinning. 'Flaperons' (interchangeable left/right) on inboard trailing-edges. Delta shaped spoiler on wing centre-section. Basic fuselage formed by two plywood boxes, one forming tailboom, the other extending forward under pilot, joined by two boxed-in plywood slabs. One-piece balanced elevator; one-piece balanced rudder, with small ventral fin. Enclosed cockpit. Towing hook.

POWER PLANT: One 24.6 kW (33 hp) Cuyuna ULII-02 two-cylinder two-stroke engine, driving a pusher propeller. Fuel capacity 19 litres (5 US gallons; 4.2 Imp gallons).

DIMENSIONS, EXTERNAL:

Wing span	12.65 m (41 ft 6 in)
Wing aspect ratio	17.9
Length overall	6.58 m (21 ft 7 in)
Height overall	1.68 m (5 ft 6 in)
Propeller diameter	0.81 m (2 ft 8 in)

AREA:

Wings, gross	8.92 m² (96.0 sq ft)

WEIGHTS AND LOADINGS:

Weight empty	232 kg (512 lb)
Normal T-O weight	317 kg (700 lb)
Max T-O weight	335 kg (740 lb)
Wing loading:	
at normal T-O weight	35.59 kg/m² (7.29 lb/sq ft)
at max T-O weight	37.64 kg/m² (7.71 lb/sq ft)
Power loading:	
at normal T-O weight	12.89 kg/kW (21.2 lb/hp)
at max T-O weight	13.62 kg/kW (22.4 lb/hp)

PERFORMANCE, UNPOWERED (A: at normal T-O weight, B: at max T-O weight):

Best glide ratio at 45 knots (84 km/h; 52 mph): A, B	29
Min rate of sink:	
A, B at 40 knots (74 km/h; 46 mph)	0.70 m (2.30 ft)/s

Max speed (smooth air):	
A	114 knots (212 km/h; 132 mph)
B	110 knots (204 km/h; 127 mph)
Max speed (rough air):	
A	87 knots (161 km/h; 100 mph)
B	83 knots (154 km/h; 96 mph)
Manoeuvring speed: A	76 knots (142 km/h; 88 mph)
B	73 knots (135 km/h; 84 mph)

PERFORMANCE, POWERED (Cuyuna engine):

Max rate of climb at S/L	152 m (500 ft)/min
Ceiling	3,960 m (13,000 ft)
T-O run at S/L, ISA	213 m (700 ft)

MAUPIN CARBON DRAGON

The prototype of this foot launchable homebuilt glider is believed to have made its first flight in the Spring of 1987. Two other examples were then under construction. The design objective was to bring foot launch soaring performance up into the lower performance range of sailplanes.

TYPE: Foot launchable homebuilt glider.

AIRFRAME: Cantilever high-wing monoplane, with pod and boom fuselage and conventional tail unit. Wings have a Culver aerofoil section and are fitted with full span 'flaperons' which occupy 30 per cent of the total chord, being operable from −5° to +15° as flaps and differentially from −5° to +25° as ailerons. They are actuated by two vertical pushrods inside the fuselage. Rudder is cable actuated from foot pedals. Pilot pod is constructed from two triangular torque boxes, faired to an overall oval cross-section, and has a 1.52 × 0.46 m (5 ft 0 in × 1 ft 6 in) side-hinged 'landing gear' door in its floor for the pilot's legs. This door is closable after foot launch, with landing made on a skid on the door's underside. (Provision to re-open door for optional foot landing is under study.) One-piece Lexan canopy.

DIMENSIONS, EXTERNAL:

Wing span	13.41 m (44 ft 0 in)
Wing aspect ratio	12.9
Length overall	approx 6.10 m (20 ft 0 in)

AREA:

Wings, gross	13.94 m² (150.0 sq ft)

WEIGHTS:

Weight empty	54.5 kg (120 lb)
Max T-O weight	136 kg (300 lb)

PERFORMANCE (estimated):

Best glide ratio	25
Min rate of sink	0.51 m (1.67 ft)/s

Marske Monarch single-seat homebuilt glider

Maupin Woodstock One homebuilt sailplane

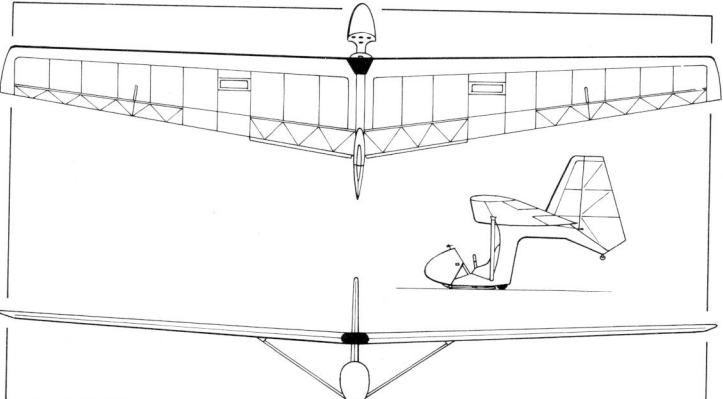

Marske Monarch E single-seat ultralight glider *(Michael A. Badrocke)*

Rotax engined Maupin Windrose self-launching sailplane flying in Indonesia

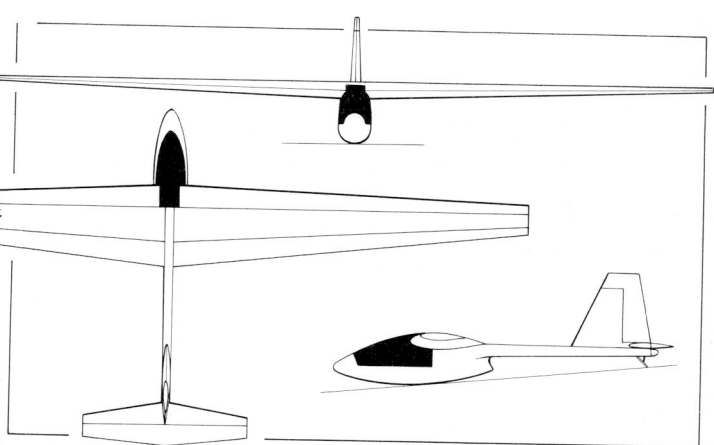

Maupin Carbon Dragon foot launchable homebuilt glider
(Michael A. Badrocke)

Marske Pioneer II-C homebuilt sailplane

Schweizer SGS 2-33A two-seat general purpose sailplane
(Neil A. Macdougall)

SCHWEIZER
SCHWEIZER AIRCRAFT CORPORATION
PO Box 147, Elmira-Corning Regional Airport, Elmira, New York 14902
Telephone: (607) 739 3821
Telex: 932459
OFFICERS: see Aircraft section

Schweizer Aircraft Corporation has long been the leading American designer and manufacturer of sailplanes. Its current types include the SGS 2-33A, SGS 1-36 Sprite and SGM 2-37.

Schweizer also owns all rights to the (originally Grumman) Ag-Cat series of agricultural aircraft and (formerly McDonnell Douglas) Model 300C light helicopter series, and undertakes a variety of aircraft subcontract manufacturing. Further details of these activities can be found under the Schweizer heading in the main Aircraft section.

SCHWEIZER SGS 2-33A
The SGS 2-33 was developed to meet the demand for a medium priced two-seat sailplane for training and general family soaring. The prototype was first flown in the Autumn of 1966 and received FAA type approval in February 1967. Production began in January 1967, and 85 of the original **2-33** model were built. These were superseded by the **2-33A** production version, and the **2-33AK** kit version for amateur construction. Sales of the 2-33A and 2-33AK by January 1985 totalled 470 and 20 respectively. No further sales had been notified by April 1988, but the aircraft continues to be available. A more comprehensive description can be found in the 1987-88 *Jane's*.

TYPE: Tandem two-seat training sailplane.
DIMENSIONS, EXTERNAL:
Wing span	15.54 m (51 ft 0 in)
Length overall	7.85 m (25 ft 9 in)
Height over tail	2.83 m (9 ft 3½ in)

AREA:
Wings, gross	20.39 m² (219.48 sq ft)

WEIGHTS AND LOADING:
Weight empty	272 kg (600 lb)
Max T-O weight	472 kg (1,040 lb)
Max wing loading	23.14 kg/m² (4.74 lb/sq ft)

PERFORMANCE (at max T-O weight except where indicated):
Best glide ratio at 45 knots (84 km/h; 52 mph) dual, 39 knots (72 km/h; 45 mph) solo   22.25
Min rate of sink: dual at 37 knots (68 km/h; 42 mph)
    0.95 m (3.10 ft)/s
    solo at 33 knots (61 km/h; 38 mph)   0.79 m (2.60 ft)/s

Stalling speed: dual 31 knots (57 km/h; 35 mph)
      solo 27 knots (50 km/h; 31 mph)
Max speed (rough and smooth air), and max aero-tow
    speed 85 knots (158 km/h; 98 mph)
Max winch-launching speed
    60 knots (111 km/h; 69 mph)
g limits $+4.67/-2.56$

SCHWEIZER SGS 1-36 SPRITE

The Sprite was designed to offer modern performance, handling and appearance to up to 99 per cent of the solo glider pilots in the USA and overseas as a personal, school or club sailplane. Although a new design, it utilises some components of the 1-34 and 1-35 in its construction. The Sprite is, however, aimed at a different market from these earlier types, and is a 'one-design' class, as was the 1-26. The Sprite is also intended to fulfil a worldwide need for a single-seat Club Class sailplane.

Two versions are available:

36903-1. With forward-positioned monowheel, sprung tailwheel, and no nose-skid. One example of this version, used by NASA's Dryden Research Center, was fitted with a pivoting tailplane for flight research into aircraft controllability problems, particularly those involving deep stall situations. This tailplane can be set at approx 60° nose down.

36903-3. With monowheel further aft, unsprung tailwheel, and aluminium nose-skid. This version is recommended for school and club operation, where sturdiness and ease of ground handling are important considerations.

The prototype flew for the first time on 2 August 1979. FAA certification was received in September 1980, and by January 1985 a total of 43 had been sold. No further sales notified since that time, but the aircraft remained available in 1988. A more comprehensive description can be found in the 1987-88 *Jane's*.

TYPE: Single-seat multi-purpose sailplane.

DIMENSIONS, EXTERNAL:
Wing span 14.07 m (46 ft 2 in)
Length overall 6.27 m (20 ft 7 in)
Height over tail 1.45 m (4 ft 9 in)
AREA:
Wings, gross 13.07 m² (140.72 sq ft)
WEIGHTS AND LOADING:
Weight empty 215 kg (475 lb)
Max T-O weight 322 kg (710 lb)
Max wing loading 24.64 kg/m² (5.05 lb/sq ft)
PERFORMANCE (at max T-O weight):
Best glide ratio at 46 knots (85 km/h; 53 mph) 31
Min rate of sink at 36 knots (68 km/h; 42 mph)
    0.68 m (2.25 ft)/s
Stalling speed 31 knots (57 km/h; 35 mph)
Max speed (rough and smooth air), and max aero-tow
    speed 105 knots (195 km/h; 121 mph)
Max winch-launching speed
    68 knots (126 km/h; 78 mph)
g limits $+5.33/-2.67$

SCHWEIZER SGM 2-37
US Air Force designation: TG-7A

First details of this two-seat motor glider were announced in early 1982. The prototype (N36221) flew for the first time on 21 September 1982, and certification was received in the following February. Eight TG-7As were delivered to the USAF Academy at Colorado Springs for sailplane flight training duties. Modified versions for other roles are being studied, including the more powerful **SA 2-37A** (see main Aircraft section).

TYPE: Two-seat motor glider.

AIRFRAME: Cantilever low-wing monoplane, of all-metal construction. Wortmann wing sections: FX-61-163 from root to station 246, FX-60-126 at tip. Dihedral 3° 30′ on outer panels. Leading-edges have extended chord on portions of outer panels to improve stall characteristics. Incidence 1° at root, 0° at tip. No sweepback. Aluminium airbrake in upper and lower surface of each outer panel. Aluminium alloy top-hinged ailerons; no flaps. Semi-monocoque fuselage of aluminium alloy. Slightly swept fin and rudder; non-swept all-moving tailplane, with anti-servo tab. Non-retractable mainwheels, with cantilever legs, urethane block shock absorbers, Cleveland disc brakes and 14 × 5 × 5 in tyres, pressure 2.41 bars (35 lb/sq in); non-retractable and castoring Scott tailwheel, with 6 × 2 × 3 in solid tyre (USAF aircraft have 5.00-5 mainwheels for operation from hard runways). Two seats side by side under rearward sliding canopy, with dual controls. Baggage compartment aft of seats, max capacity 45 kg (100 lb).

POWER PLANT: One 83 kW (112 hp) Textron Lycoming O-235-L2C flat-four engine, driving a Sensenich 72CK-0-50 two-blade fixed-pitch metal propeller. Optional engines include 112 kW (150 hp) Textron Lycoming O-320-E26 and 134 kW (180 hp) Textron Lycoming O-360-A series, with choice of McCauley fixed-pitch climb propeller for glider towing or Hoffmann HO-V-72 constant-speed feathering propeller for soaring. Single fuel tank in port wing standard, capacity 59 litres (15.5 US gallons; 12.9 Imp gallons), of which 54 litres (14.2 US gallons; 11.8 Imp gallons) are usable. Provision for optional similar tank, in starboard wing, increasing total capacity to 118 litres (31 US gallons; 25.8 Imp gallons).

DIMENSIONS, EXTERNAL:
Wing span 18.14 m (59 ft 6 in)
Wing aspect ratio 18.1
Length overall 8.36 m (27 ft 5 in)
Height over tail 2.37 m (7 ft 9½ in)
Wheel track 2.79 m (9 ft 2 in)
Wheelbase 5.74 m (18 ft 10 in)
Propeller diameter 1.83 m (6 ft 0 in)
DIMENSIONS, INTERNAL:
Cockpit: Max width 1.14 m (3 ft 9 in)
Baggage compartment volume 0.76 m³ (27 cu ft)
AREA:
Wings, gross 18.18 m² (195.71 sq ft)
WEIGHTS AND LOADINGS:
Weight empty 572 kg (1,260 lb)
Max T-O weight 839 kg (1,850 lb)
Max wing loading 46.14 kg/m² (9.45 lb/sq ft)
Max power loading 10.11 kg/kW (16.5 lb/hp)
PERFORMANCE, UNPOWERED (at max T-O weight):
Best glide ratio at 52 knots (97 km/h; 60 mph) 22
Min rate of sink at 49 knots (90 km/h; 56 mph)
    1.13 m (3.70 ft)/s
Stalling speed 42 knots (78 km/h; 48 mph)
Max speed (smooth air) 115 knots (214 km/h; 133 mph)
Max speed (rough air) 88 knots (162 km/h; 101 mph)
g limits $+5.3/-2.67$
PERFORMANCE, POWERED (at max T-O weight):
Max cruising speed at 2,285 m (7,500 ft), 75% power
    99 knots (183 km/h; 114 mph)
Econ cruising speed 82 knots (153 km/h; 95 mph)
Stalling speed 42 knots (78 km/h; 48 mph)
Max rate of climb at S/L 328 m (1,075 ft)/min
Service ceiling above 7,315 m (24,000 ft)
T-O run (grass) 152 m (500 ft)
T-O to 15 m (50 ft) (grass) 310 m (1,018 ft)
Landing from 15 m (50 ft) (grass) 386 m (1,266 ft)
Landing run 126 m (412 ft)
Range with standard fuel, 75% power, no reserves
    213 nm (396 km; 246 miles)
Range with max optional fuel
    520 nm (963 km; 598 miles)
Endurance at 50% power, no reserves 3 h 30 min
g limits $+5.3/-2.67$

SILHOUETTE
SILHOUETTE AIRCRAFT INC

848 East Santa Maria Street, Santa Paula Airport, Santa Paula, California 93060
Telephone: (805) 525 4545

SILHOUETTE AIRCRAFT SILHOUETTE

As explained in the Sport Aircraft section, the Silhouette is produced in kit form in two versions, the aerobatic sport aircraft being convertible to a Utility category motor glider by the addition of bolt-on wing extensions. These result in the following changes:

TYPE: Single-seat motor glider.

AIRFRAME: As described in Sport Aircraft section, plus bolt-on wing extension panels comprising stub spars, pre-shaped polystyrene cores and materials for glassfibre/epoxy skin. No washout in extensions.

POWER PLANT: Engine and standard fuel capacity details as for Sport Aircraft version. Motor glider has option for variable-pitch feathering propeller, but no option for larger fuel tank.

DIMENSIONS, EXTERNAL:
Wing span 12.50 m (41 ft 0 in)
Wing chord at tip 0.39 m (1 ft 3½ in)
Wing aspect ratio 19.3
AREA:
Wings, gross 8.08 m² (87.0 sq ft)
WEIGHTS AND LOADING:
Weight empty 231 kg (510 lb)
Max T-O weight 351 kg (775 lb)
Max wing loading 43.5 kg/m² (8.91 lb/sq ft)
PERFORMANCE (motor glider at max T-O weight):
Never-exceed speed 104 knots (193 km/h; 120 mph) IAS
Max cruising speed 87 knots (161 km/h; 100 mph) IAS
Econ cruising speed 57 knots (105 km/h; 65 mph) IAS
Stalling speed:
    power on 40 knots (74 km/h; 46 mph) IAS
    power off 44 knots (80 km/h; 50 mph) IAS
Max rate of climb at S/L 229 m (750 ft)/min
T-O run 244 m (800 ft)
Landing run 168 m (550 ft)
Endurance at max cruising speed 4 h 6 min
g limits $+4.4/-2$
Best glide ratio 25

STROJNIK
PROF ALEX STROJNIK

2337 East Manhatton Drive, Tempe, Arizona 85282
Telephone: (602) 838 1832

Mr Strojnik, a Professor of Physics at Arizona State University, has designed a homebuilt motor glider known as the S-2A.

STROJNIK S-2A

The S-2A is a single-seat motor glider, design and construction of which began in September 1977. The S-2 prototype (N8037X) was flown for the first time in November 1980, and plans for the slightly lighter S-2A are now available. A total of 65 sets of plans and partial kits had been sold by April 1987, and three S-2As were expected to fly during that year. No further update has been received.

On 25 July 1985 the prototype S-2 flew a controlled 300 km triangle, earning its pilot/designer a completed FAI Gold Badge with one Diamond. Mr Strojnik believes this to be the first ever Gold + Diamond achieved in a homebuilt motor glider.

TYPE: Single-seat motor glider.

AIRFRAME: Cantilever shoulder-wing monoplane, with Wortmann wing sections. Dihedral 2° on outer panels. Incidence 0°. No sweep. Carbonfibre and aluminium main spar; wing skin, ailerons and trailing-edge flaps of glassfibre. No airbrakes. Pod and boom fuselage: pod has a glassfibre skin and plywood bulkheads, boom is an aluminium tube. Glassfibre tail unit, with elevators on low-set tailplane. Non-retractable unsprung twin mainwheels in tandem, each with tyre size 10 × 3.75 in, pressure 31.86 bars (56 lb/sq in), with friction brakes. One-piece Plexiglas canopy, opening sideways to starboard. Standard sailplane instrumentation and radio. No provision for water ballast.

POWER PLANT: One 21 kW (28 hp) Kohler K 340-2AX piston engine, mounted aft of cockpit and driving a Farrington two-blade (foldable) fixed-pitch wooden pusher propeller with spinner. Single fuselage fuel tank, capacity 7.5 litres (2 US gallons; 1.7 Imp gallons).

DIMENSIONS, EXTERNAL:
Wing span 15.00 m (49 ft 2½ in)
Wing aspect ratio 19.1
Length overall 6.88 m (22 ft 7 in)
Height over tail 1.65 m (5 ft 5 in)
Propeller diameter 0.94 m (3 ft 1 in)
AREA:
Wings, gross 11.80 m² (127.0 sq ft)
WEIGHTS AND LOADINGS (S-2):
Weight empty 280 kg (617 lb)
Max T-O weight 444 kg (980 lb)
Max wing loading 37.7 kg/m² (7.72 lb/sq ft)
Max power loading 21.14 kg/kW (35.0 lb/hp)
PERFORMANCE, UNPOWERED (S-2 at max T-O weight):
Best glide ratio at 48 knots (88 km/h; 55 mph) 34
Min rate of sink at 35 knots (64 km/h; 40 mph)
    0.67 m (2.20 ft)/s
Stalling speed, flaps down 33 knots (62 km/h; 38 mph)
Max speed (smooth air) 129 knots (240 km/h; 149 mph)
Max speed (rough air) 87 knots (161 km/h; 100 mph)
g limits $+5.3/-4.2$
PERFORMANCE, POWERED (S-2 at max T-O weight):
Max cruising speed 78 knots (145 km/h; 90 mph)
Econ cruising speed 43 knots (80 km/h; 50 mph)
Stalling speed 33 knots (62 km/h; 38 mph)
Max rate of climb at S/L 107 m (350 ft)/min
T-O run 610 m (2,000 ft)
Landing run 91 m (300 ft)
Range with max fuel 87 nm (161 km; 100 miles)

Schweizer TG-7A (SGM 2-37) in service with the US Air Force Academy

Schweizer SGS 1-36 Sprite training and club sailplane (36903-3 version)

Strojnik S-2 prototype for the S-2A homebuilt motor glider

DG-101G Elan Standard Class sailplane (*Air Photo Supply*)

Elan/Glaser-Dirks DG-300 Club Elan Standard Class sailplane
(*Peter F. Selinger*)

YUGOSLAVIA

ELAN
ELAN TOVARNA ŠPORTNEGAORODJA N.SOL.O
Begunje St 1, 64275 Begunje na Gorenjskem
Telephone: (064) 75 010, 75 218 and 75 560
Telex: 34518
MANAGER, SAILPLANES DIVISION: Dipl Ing Tone Čerin

Formed in 1944 by a group of 10 workers to make skis for Yugoslavia's partisan fighters, Elan is now well known as a manufacturer of sports equipment, glassfibre pleasure and fishing craft, and gliders. Since 1979 it has been associated with Glaser-Dirks of the Federal German Republic (which see), and is now the sole production centre for that company's DG-101 series of Standard Class sailplanes. It is responsible also for production of the jointly designed DG-300 Elan, including the latest DG-300 Club Elan version. The DG-500 Elan, stated to be a product of Elan in the 1987-88 *Jane's*, is actually a Glaser-Dirks sailplane (which see).

ELAN (GLASER-DIRKS) DG-101 ELAN
The basic DG-100 was a modified and lighter-weight development of the Akaflieg Darmstadt D-38. By the end of 1978 Glaser-Dirks had completed 105 DG-100s, including 16 DG-100Gs. From early 1979 production was transferred to Elan, which introduced the improved DG-101 models on to the line from c/n E58 in early 1981. By March 1987 Elan had produced 207 of these sailplanes (173 DG-100G/101G and 34 DG-100/101). No further update has been received.

Improvements in the 101 models include a one-piece cockpit canopy, roomier cockpit (as in the DG-202), new instrument console, more efficient water ballast valves, and a sprung monowheel.

Three versions are available, as follows:
DG-101 Elan. Standard Class version. All-moving T tailplane, fitted with full span anti-Flettner tab, and provision for 100 kg (220 lb) of water ballast.
DG-101G Elan. As DG-101 Elan, but with conventional fixed incidence tailplane and spring-trim elevator.
DG-101(G) Club Elan. Club version, with non-retractable monowheel, and choice of all-moving or conventional tailplane. No water ballast. Convertible to Standard Class DG-101 Elan.

TYPE: Single-seat Standard or Club Class sailplane.
AIRFRAME: Cantilever shoulder-wing monoplane. Wortmann wing sections: FX-61-184 at centreline, FX-60-126 at tip. Dihedral 3° from roots. Sweepforward 0° 48′ at quarter-chord. Glassfibre roving main spar. Glassfibre/Conticell/foam sandwich wings, ailerons and T tailplane; all glassfibre semi-monocoque fuselage, fin and rudder. Automatic self-connecting elevator on DG-101G Elan. Schempp-Hirth duralumin airbrakes on wing upper surfaces. Water ballast tank in each wing (except on Club Elan), combined capacity 100 kg (220 lb). Manually retractable sprung monowheel (non-retractable on Club version), with Tost drum brake, and tailwheel. Tyre size 361 × 126-127 mm, pressure 2.5 bars (36.25 lb/sq in), on monowheel; tailwheel tyre size 200 × 50-100 mm, pressure 2.0 bars (29 lb/sq in). One-piece cockpit canopy, hinged at nose and opening upward.

DIMENSIONS, EXTERNAL:
Wing span	15.00 m (49 ft 2½ in)
Wing aspect ratio	20.5
Length overall	7.00 m (22 ft 11¾ in)
Height over tail	1.40 m (4 ft 7 in)

AREA:
Wings, gross	11.00 m² (118.4 sq ft)

WEIGHTS AND LOADINGS (A: DG-101, B: DG-101G, C: DG-101 (G) Club version):
Weight empty, equipped: A	235 kg (518 lb)
B	230 kg (507 lb)
C	225 kg (496 lb)
Max T-O weight:	
A and B (with water ballast)	418 kg (921 lb)
C	385 kg (849 lb)
Max wing loading:	
A and B (with water ballast)	38.0 kg/m² (7.78 lb/sq ft)
C	35.0 kg/m² (7.17 lb/sq ft)

PERFORMANCE (at max T-O weight):
Best glide ratio:	
A, B, at 57 knots (105 km/h; 65 mph)	39
C at 49 knots (90 km/h; 56 mph)	36
Min rate of sink at 40 knots (74 km/h; 46 mph):	
A, B	0.59 m (1.94 ft)/s
C	0.60 m (1.97 ft)/s

Stalling speed: A, B, C   33 knots (60 km/h; 38 mph)
Max speed (rough and smooth air):
A, B, C   140 knots (260 km/h; 161 mph)
Max aero-tow speed:
A, B, C   89 knots (165 km/h; 103 mph)
Max winch-launching speed:
A, B, C   70 knots (130 km/h; 81 mph)
g limit: A, B, C   +6.1

ELAN/GLASER-DIRKS DG-300 ELAN
This Standard Class design, first flown on 27 April 1983, is a joint venture by Elan and Glaser-Dirks, and is a developed version of the DG-101G, which it resembles closely. Design began in July 1982, and five pre-series aircraft were built by Elan. Series production began in December 1983, at which time 110 had been ordered; including the pre-series examples, Elan had completed 235 DG-300s by March 1987. No more recent figure has been received.

Principal differences from the DG-101G include a new low-drag, laminar flow wing section, developed by engineers of the German DFVLR, which incorporates a tubular boundary layer distribution system for optimum lift; larger airbrakes; location of the wings slightly further aft, with an improved wing/fuselage junction; a 20 cm (7.9 in) reduction in fuselage length; improved directional stability, resulting from an improved fin aerofoil section and reduced rudder depth; a 2 cm (0.79 in) wider and more comfortable cockpit; automatically connecting controls; and provision for an auxiliary water ballast tank in the fin.

The latest version is the **DG-300 Club Elan**, which has been in series production since January 1988. Like the DG-101(G) Club Elan version of the DG-101, the DG-300 Club Elan has a non-retractable monowheel, no water ballast and no boundary layer distribution system.

The following data apply to the standard DG-300 Elan:
TYPE: Single-seat Standard Class sailplane.
AIRFRAME: Cantilever shoulder-wing monoplane, with Horstmann-Quast 300 G-D (Mod 2) aerofoil section. Incidence 3°. Sweepforward 0° 30′ at quarter-chord. Glassfibre/Conticell/foam sandwich wings, with Schempp-Hirth duralumin airbrakes in upper surface. All-glassfibre semi-monocoque fuselage. Cantilever T tailplane, with elevator; tail unit construction as described

Jastreb Standard Cirrus G/81, developed from the 75-VTC

Jastreb VUK-T all-plastics training sailplane

for DG-101G. Landing gear and cockpit canopy as for DG-101G. Standard provision for 130 or 190 litres (34.3 or 50.2 US gallons; 28.6 or 41.8 Imp gallons) of water ballast in wings; optional tank in fin has max capacity of 5.5 litres (1.5 US gallons; 1.2 Imp gallons).

DIMENSIONS, EXTERNAL:

Wing span	15.00 m (49 ft 2½ in)
Wing aspect ratio	21.9
Length overall	6.80 m (22 ft 3¾ in)
Height over tail	1.40 m (4 ft 7 in)

AREA:

Wings, gross	10.27 m² (110.5 sq ft)

WEIGHTS AND LOADING:

Weight empty	245 kg (540 lb)
Max T-O weight	525 kg (1,157 lb)
Max wing loading	51.1 kg/m² (10.47 lb/sq ft)

PERFORMANCE (at max T-O weight except where indicated):

Best glide ratio:
at wing loading of 32 kg/m² (6.55 lb/sq ft) and speed of 54 knots (100 km/h; 62 mph)   41
at wing loading of 50 kg/m² (10.24 lb/sq ft) and speed of 66 knots (122 km/h; 76 mph)   42

Min rate of sink:
at wing loading of 32 kg/m² (6.55 lb/sq ft) and speed of 39 knots (72 km/h; 45 mph)   0.59 m (1.94 ft)/s
at wing loading of 50 kg/m² (10.24 lb/sq ft) and speed of 48 knots (88 km/h; 55 mph)   0.68 m (2.23 ft)/s

Stalling speed at wing loading of 32 kg/m² (6.55 lb/sq ft)   35 knots (65 km/h; 41 mph)

Max speed (smooth air)   147 knots (270 km/h; 168 mph)
Max speed (rough air), and max aero-tow speed   108 knots (200 km/h; 124 mph)
Max winch-launching speed   70 knots (130 km/h; 80 mph)

g limits: +5.3/−2.65 (at VA)   +4/−1.5 (at VNE)

JASTREB

JASTREB FABRIKA AVIONA I JEDRILICA (Jastreb Aircraft and Sailplanes Factory)

ul. Podrvsanska 17, 26300 Vrsac
Telephone: (013) 813 639
Telex: 13193 YU JASTREB
MANAGER: Zec Predrag

Jastreb, known formerly as VTC, is the production centre for two versions of the Standard Cirrus sailplane, designed originally by Schempp-Hirth in West Germany and built subsequently under licence by VTC at Vrsac (see 1981-82 *Jane's*). It also manufactures the VUK-T, designed at the University of Belgrade, and has built a two-seat motor glider known as the SOLE-77.

JASTREB (SCHEMPP-HIRTH) STANDARD CIRRUS 75-VTC

Designed by Dipl-Ing Klaus Holighaus of Schempp-Hirth, this Standard Class version of the Cirrus entered production in Germany in the Summer of 1969, following its first flight in March 1969. By April 1977, when West German production ended, a total of 700 Standard Cirrus had been built, including 200 under licence by Grob Flugzeugbau.

Licence manufacture has been undertaken since January 1979 by VTC (now Jastreb) in Yugoslavia. Production by Jastreb totalled 83 by 1 January 1987, when the last update was received.

TYPE: Single-seat Standard and Club Class sailplane.

AIRFRAME: Cantilever mid-wing monoplane. Wortmann wing section. Dihedral 3°. Sweepback 1° 18' at leading-edge. Glassfibre/foam sandwich wings, ailerons and tail surfaces. Schempp-Hirth glassfibre airbrakes on upper surfaces. Glassfibre fuselage shell, stiffened with bonded-in foam rings. All-moving T tailplane. Retractable monowheel standard; non-retractable faired monowheel optional. Tost wheel with drum brake and Continental tyre, pressure 3.45 bars (50 lb/sq in). Canopy opens sideways to starboard. Provision for 60 kg (132 lb) of water ballast.

DIMENSIONS, EXTERNAL:

Wing span	15.00 m (49 ft 2½ in)
Wing aspect ratio	22.5
Length overall	6.41 m (21 ft 8½ in)
Height over tail	1.32 m (4 ft 4¾ in)

AREA:

Wings, gross	10.00 m² (107.6 sq ft)

WEIGHTS AND LOADINGS:

Weight empty	220 kg (485 lb)

Max T-O weight:
without water ballast   330 kg (727 lb)
with water ballast   390 kg (860 lb)

Max wing loading:
without water ballast   33.0 kg/m² (6.76 lb/sq ft)
with water ballast   39.0 kg/m² (7.99 lb/sq ft)

PERFORMANCE (at max T-O weight):

Best glide ratio at 49 knots (90 km/h; 56 mph)   38.5
Min rate of sink at 38 knots (70 km/h; 44 mph)   0.57 m (1.87 ft)/s
Stalling speed   34 knots (62 km/h; 39 mph)
Max speed (rough and smooth air)   119 knots (220 km/h; 137 mph)
Max aero-tow speed   81 knots (150 km/h; 93 mph)
Max winch-launching speed   65 knots (120 km/h; 75 mph)
g limit   +10

JASTREB STANDARD CIRRUS G/81

The Standard Cirrus G/81 was developed by Jastreb from the Standard Cirrus 75-VTC, and differs from it in the following respects. Jastreb had built 18 of this version by 1 January 1987, when the last update was received.

AIRFRAME: As 75-VTC except for lack of option for non-retractable monowheel; new canopy, based on that of Schempp-Hirth Mini-Nimbus, opening sideways to starboard; roomier cockpit, able to accommodate a larger pilot; and a variable incidence T tailplane with separate elevator. CG tow hook standard, nose hook optional.

DATA: As for Cirrus 75-VTC

JASTREB VUK-T

The prototype of this single-seat all-plastics sailplane was designed and built at Belgrade University in 1976, and made its first flight in 1977. Production, started by Jastreb in January 1979, totalled 75 by 1 January 1987. No further update has been received.

Chief features of the VUK-T are the use of plastics stressed-skin construction and a supercritical wing section. The sailplane is designed to OSTIV airworthiness requirements, and is cleared for cloud flying, aerobatics and spinning.

TYPE: Single-seat advanced training sailplane.

AIRFRAME: Cantilever mid-wing monoplane. NASA GAW-1 supercritical wing section from root to tip, with no twist. Thickness/chord ratio 17%. Dihedral 3°. Glassfibre roving main spar, integral with the upper and lower wing skins, which are of glassfibre/Conticell foam sandwich. Auxiliary rear spar carries the top-hinged plain ailerons. Schempp-Hirth airbrakes in upper surfaces at 50 per cent chord. Fuselage is of glassfibre sandwich construction forward, glassfibre monocoque aft. Cantilever T tailplane, with separate elevator, of similar construction to wings. Retractable sprung monowheel, with brake, and non-retractable tailwheel. Semi-reclining seat under one-piece flush-fitting jettisonable canopy which opens sideways to starboard. No water ballast provision.

DIMENSIONS, EXTERNAL:

Wing span	15.00 m (49 ft 2½ in)
Wing aspect ratio	15.0
Length overall	6.50 m (21 ft 4 in)
Height over tail	1.35 m (4 ft 5¼ in)

AREA:

Wings, gross	15.00 m² (161.5 sq ft)

WEIGHTS AND LOADING:

Weight empty	245 kg (540 lb)
Max T-O weight	355 kg (782 lb)
Max wing loading	23.67 kg/m² (4.85 lb/sq ft)

PERFORMANCE (at max T-O weight):

Best glide ratio at 51 knots (95 km/h; 59 mph)   37.5
Min rate of sink at 42 knots (78 km/h; 49 mph)   0.65 m (2.13 ft)/s
Stalling speed   32 knots (59 km/h; 37 mph)
Max speed (smooth air)   129 knots (240 km/h; 149 mph)
Max speed (rough air)   81 knots (150 km/h; 93 mph)
Max aero-tow speed   70 knots (130 km/h; 80 mph)
Max winch-launching speed   65 knots (120 km/h; 75 mph)
g limits (safety factor 1.5)   +5.3/−2.65

SOKO

SOUR VAZDUHOPLOVNA INDUSTRIJA SOKO

88000 Mostar
Telephone: (088) 22-121, 33-831, 35-244, 35-541, 37-943 and 55-120
Telex: 46 180 YU SOKOMO

PRESIDENT: Dipl Ing Milenko Pjescić
VICE-PRESIDENT, RESEARCH AND DEVELOPMENT:
Dipl Ing Mladen Zadro

SOKO SL-40 LISKA

Construction of the prototype Liska single-seat motor glider began at the end of 1975, and it flew for the first time on 19 February 1981. The flight test programme is running behind schedule, due to the flight test department's high workload on other projects. Full details of the Liska can be found in the 1987-88 and previous editions of *Jane's*.

HANG GLIDERS

Country	Company	Address	Telephone/Telex/Fax
Australia	Moyes Delta Gliders Pty Ltd	173 Bronte Road, Waverley, Sydney, NSW 2024	Tel: (02) 387 5114 Telex: 10101 INTSY AA Fax: 61 2 3874472
Austria	Steinbach-Delta	Gewerbecenter, A-6382 Kirchdorf, Tyrol	Tel: 05352 3383
France	SARL La Mouette	1 rue de la Petite Fin, 21121 Fontaine les Dijon	Tel: (80) 56 66 47 Telex: 350 053 F
Germany (Federal Republic)	Drachen Studio Kecur GmbH	Obschwarzbach 8, 5603 Wülfrath	Tel: 02058 3000
	Finsterwalder Drachenflug GmbH	Pagodenburgstrasse 8, 8000 Munich 60	Tel: 811 65 28
	Firebird Schweiger & Jehle KG	Postfach 28, Hitzleriederstrasse 15, 8959 Seeg	Tel: (08364) 8282 1078 Telex: 541412
	Günter Rochelt	Josef-Schwarz-Weg 11, 8000 Munich 71	Tel: (089) 791 4646
Italy	Polaris Srl	Via Flaminia 208, 06021 Costacciaro (Perugia)	Tel: (075) 917 01 86/917 04 92 Telex: 564006 POLARE I
Poland	Akademicki Ośrodek Konstrukcyjny (Academic Design Centre)	Wydzial Doświadczalny Kompozytów Polimerowych ('Kompol'), Instytut Inżynierii Materiałowej Politechniki Warszawskiej, ul. Narbutta 85, 02-524 Warszawa	Tel: 25 06 33
	Instytut Lotnictwa (Aviation Institute)	Al. Krakowska 110/114, 02-256 Warszawa-Okecie	Tel: Warszawa 460011 and 460801 Telex: 813537
Switzerland	Swiss Aerolight	PO Box 22, Pt Lancy 1, CH-1213 Geneva	Tel: (022) 93 37 22
Union of Soviet Socialist Republics	O. K. Antonov Design Bureau	Kiev	
United Kingdom	Airwave Gliders Ltd	Elm Lane, Shalfleet, Newport, Isle of Wight PO30 4JY	Tel: 0983 78611 Telex: 869188 GLIDER G
	Pegasus Transport Systems Ltd/ Solar Wings Ltd	56 George Lane, Marlborough, Wiltshire SN8 4BY	Tel: 0672 54414
United States of America	Delta Wing Aviation	PO Box 483, Van Nuys, California 91408	Tel: (818) 787 6000 Telex: 65-1425
	Pacific Windcraft Ltd	PO Box 4384, Salinas, California 93912	Tel: (408) 422 2299
	Seedwings	5760 Thornwood Drive No. 3, Santa Barbara, California 93117	Tel: (805) 967 4848
	UP Inc (Ultralite Products)	PO Box 659, Temecula, California 92390	Tel: (714) 676 5652 Telex: 910 332 1306
	Volmer Aircraft	PO Box 5222, Glendale, California 91201	Tel: (818) 247 8718
	Wills Wing Inc	1208-H, East Walnut, Santa Ana, California 92701	Tel: (714) 547 1344/6366

RIGID AND FLEXIBLE WING DATA

Manufacturer and Model	Rigid: R Flexwing: F	FAI or other class	Span: m/ft-in	Leading-edge (flexwing): m/ft-in	Length (rigid); Keel (flexwing): m/ft-in	Nose/Billow angle (flexwing): degrees
AUSTRALIA						
Moyes Delta						
Mars 150	F	1	8.84/29-0	5.10/16-9	2.54/8-4	125/0.5
Mars 170	F	1	9.45/31-0	5.51/18-1	2.62/8-7	125/0.5
Mars 190	F	1	10.06/33-0	5.87/19-3	2.74/9-0	125/0.5
GTR 148	F	1	9.75/32-0	4.80/15-9	1.98/6-6	130/0-1.5
GTR 162	F	1	10.36/34-0	5.14/16-10½	3.57/11-8½	130/0-1.5
GTR 175	F	1	10.97/36-0	5.49/18-0	2.13/7-0	130/0-1.5
GTR 210	F	1	10.97/36-0	5.49/18-0	2.90/9-6	130/0-1.5
Mission 170	F	1	9.55/31-4	5.51/18-1	2.62/8-7	125/0.5
AUSTRIA						
Steinbach-Delta						
Condor	F	n.k.	8.10/26-7	n.k.	3.10/10-2	n.k.
Para Fun1	F	n.k.	9.10/29-10¼	n.k.	3.35/11	n.k.
Para Fun	F	n.k.	n.k.	n.k.	n.k.	n.k.
Para Safe	F	n.k.	n.k.	n.k.	n.k.	n.k.
SP	F	n.k.	10.40/34-1½	n.k.	n.k.	128/n.k.
SP Vario	F	n.k.	10.50/34-5½	n.k.	n.k.	126-130/n.k.
FRANCE						
La Mouette						
Atlas 14	F	1	9.30/30-6¼	5.36/17-7	3.50/11-5¾	120/0.5
Atlas 16	F	1	9.90/32-5¾	5.70/18-8½	3.50/11-5¾	120/0.5
Atlas 18	F	1	10.50/34-5½	6.10/20-0	3.50/11-5¾	120/0.5
Hermes 13	F	1	10.60/34-9¼	5.10/16-9	n.k.	130/n.k.
Hermes 14	F	1	10.60/34-9¼	5.90/19-4¼	n.k.	130/n.k.
Hermes 15	F	1	10.60/34-9¼	5.90/19-4¼	n.k.	130/n.k.
Hermes 16	F	1	10.60/34-9¼	5.90/19-4¼	n.k.	130/n.k.
Profil 15	F	1	10.00/32-9¾	5.80/19-0¼	3.50/11-5¾	120/0
Profil 17	F	1	10.50/34-5½	6.20/20-4	3.50/11-5¾	120/0
GERMANY						
Drachen						
Tropi 16	F	n.k.	10.60/34-9¼	n.k.	n.k.	130/n.k.
Tropi 17	F	n.k.	10.60/34-9¼	n.k.	n.k.	130/n.k.
Finsterwalder						
Funfex	F	1 & 2 (DHV)	9.60/31-6	5.60/18-4½	2.40/7-10	120/0
Minifex II	F	2 (DHV)	9.00/29-6¼	n.k.	n.k.	130/0
Topfex	F	2 & 3 (DHV)	10.40/34-1½	5.80/19-0¼	2.00/6-6¾	130/0
Firebird						
Uno	F	1 & 2 (DHV)	9.95/32-7¾	5.75/18-10½	n.k.	125/n.k.
Uno Piccolo	F	1 & 2 (DHV)	9.35/30-8	5.40/17-8½	n.k.	125/n.k.
Quattro	F	1 & 2 (DHV)	9.95/32-7¾	5.75/18-10½	n.k.	125/n.k.
Quattro-S	F	2 & 3 (DHV)	9.95/32-7¾	5.75/18-10½	n.k.	125/n.k.
Spirit	F	3 (DHV)	10.90/35-9	5.80/19-0¼	n.k.	130-133/n.k.
Rochelt						
Schneid Air	F	n.k.	9.00/29-6⅓	n.k.	n.k.	n.k.
ITALY						
Polaris						
FR 16	F	1	10.85/35-7¼	5.60/18-4½	3.60/11-9¾	132/0
*Ares	F	1	11.15/36-7	5.50/18-0½	3.30/10-10	130/0
*Gryps	F	1	10.60/34-9¼	5.50/18-0½	3.30/10-10	130/0
*Spit	Semi-R	1	10.60/34-9¼	5.50/18-0½	3.30/10-10	130/0
Touring 13	F	1	9.60/31-6	5.23/17-2	3.50/11-5¾	120/0
Touring 15	F	1	9.60/31-6	5.23/17-2	3.50/11-5¾	120/0

*Ares, Gryps and Spit are specifically for powered flying,
using trikes or other attachable units (single- or two-seat).

Manufacturer and Model	Rigid: R Flexwing: F	FAI or other class	Span: m/ft-in	Leading-edge (flexwing): m/ft-in	Length (rigid); Keel (flexwing): m/ft-in	Nose/Billow angle (flexwing): degrees
POLAND						
AOK						
SB-1 WARS	F	1	9.50/31-2	6.00/19-8¼	4.20/13-9¼	105/0
Stratus E-2C I	F	1	10.60/34-9¼	6.10/20-0¼	3.60/11-9¾	126/variable
Stratus E-2C II	F	1	11.10/36-5	6.40/21-0	3.80/12-5½	126/variable
Stratus E-3C I	F	1	10.20/33-5½	5.90/19-4¼	3.60/11-9¾	126/variable
Stratus E-3C II	F	1	10.70/35-1¼	6.15/20-2¼	3.80/12-5½	126/variable
Stratus E-4 C	F	1	9.80/32-1¾	5.65/18-6½	3.60/11-9¾	126/0
Instytut Lotnictwa						
Zeta-87	Semi-R	1	11.60/38-0¾	6.00/19-8¼	3.60/11-9¾	134/-2
SWITZERLAND						
Swiss Aerolight						
Nimbus	R	n.k.	12.50/41-0¼	n.k.	n.k.	—
UNION OF SOVIET SOCIALIST REPUBLICS						
Antonov						
Slavutitch-UT	F	n.k.	8.80/28-10½	5.72/18-9¼	4.235/13-10¾	104/1.0
UNITED KINGDOM						
Airwave						
Calypso	F	1	9.30/30-6¼	5.30/17-4½	n.k.	120/0
Magic IV 133	F	1	8.95/29-4½	5.20/17-0¾	n.k.	n.k.
Magic IV 150	F	1	9.50/31-2	5.53/18-1¾	n.k.	n.k.
Magic IV 155	F	1	9.99/32-9¼	5.89/19-4	3.66/12-0	120/n.k.
Magic IV 166	F	1	10.40/34-1½	5.99/19-8	3.66/12-0	120/n.k.
Magic IV 177	F	1	10.64/34-11	6.21/20-4½	3.66/12-0	120/n.k.
Magic Kiss	F	1	10.40/34-1½	n.k.	n.k.	132/0

n.k. = not known

Wing area: m²/sq ft	Wing aspect ratio	Weight: kg/lb	Glide ratio	Sink rate: m/ft per min	Pilot weight: kg (lb)	Stalling speed: knots (km/h; mph)	g limits
13.94/150.0	5.6	23.6/52	8.5	61/200	41-82 (90-180)	19 (34; 21)	+6/-4
15.98/172.0	5.6	28.1/62	8	61/200	57-109 (125-240)	23 (42; 26)	+6/-4
17.65/190.0	5.7	30/66.1	8	55/180	68-113 (150-250)	12 (21; 13)	+6/-4
13.75/148.0	6.9	30/66.1	10	61/200	54-100 (120-220)	14 (26; 16)	n.k.
15.05/162.0	7.2	30.8/68	10	55/180	59-104 (130-230)	15 (28; 18)	n.k.
16.26/175.0	7.4	35/77.2	10	55/180	68-113 (150-250)	13 (23; 14)	n.k.
19.51/210.0	6.2	40/88.2	10	55/180	73-118 (160-260)	11 (20; 12)	n.k.
16.16/174.0	5.8	29/63.9	9	58/190	59-95 (130-210)	11 (20; 12)	+6/-4
26.00/279.9	n.k.	28/61.7	n.k.	n.k.	60-90 (132-198)	n.k.	n.k.
31.00/333.0	n.k.	32/70.5	n.k.	n.k.	60-100 (132-220)	n.k.	n.k.
29.00/312.2	n.k.	n.k.	n.k.	n.k.	n.k.	n.k.	n.k.
26.00/279.9	n.k.	n.k.	n.k.	n.k.	n.k.	n.k.	n.k.
15.80/170.1	6.85	29/63.9	n.k.	n.k.	n.k.	n.k.	n.k.
15.80/170.1	6.98	33/72.8	n.k.	n.k.	n.k.	n.k.	n.k.
13.80/148.5	6.3	24.5/54	9	60/197	50-75 (110-165)	14 (25; 16)	+6/-4
15.80/170.0	6.2	25/55.1	9	60/197	65-95 (143-209)	14 (25; 16)	+6/-4
18.00/193.8	6.1	29/63.9	9	60/197	90-140 (198-308)	14 (25; 16)	+6/-4
13.30/143.2	8.4	29.8/65.7	12	n.k.	55-70 (121-154)	n.k.	n.k.
13.80/148.5	8.1	30/66.1	12	n.k.	55-75 (121-165)	n.k.	n.k.
14.80/159.3	7.6	31/68.3	12	n.k.	60-80 (132-176)	n.k.	n.k.
15.80/170.0	7.1	31.5/69.4	12	n.k.	75-100 (165-220)	n.k.	n.k.
15.00/161.5	6.7	27/59.5	11	54/177	50-80 (110-176)	14 (25; 16)	n.k.
16.30/175.5	6.8	29/63.9	11	54/177	65-100 (143-220)	13 (23; 15)	n.k.
15.30/164.7	7.3	30/66.1	n.k.	n.k.	50-110 (110-242)	11 (20; 12)	n.k.
16.30/175.5	6.9	32/70.5	n.k.	n.k.	65-110 (143-242)	11 (20; 12)	n.k.
16.50/177.6	5.6	22/48.5	11	52/171	60-95 (132-209)	15 (28; 18)	n.k.
14.20/152.8	5.7	22/48.5	11	54/177	45-65 (99-143)	15 (28; 18)	n.k.
16.10/173.3	6.7	29/63.9	12	54/177	65-110 (143-242)	18 (32; 20)	n.k.
15.50/166.8	6.4	25.5/56.2	8.5	n.k.	50-100 (110-220)	12 (22; 14)	+6/-3
14.00/150.7	6.2	19.5/43.0	n.k.	n.k.	75 (165) max	12 (22; 14)	+6/-3
15.50/166.8	6.4	26.5/58.4	10	n.k.	50-125 (110-275)	14 (25; 16)	+6/-3
15.80/170.1	6.4	26.5/58.4	n.k.	n.k.	60-118 (132-260)	14 (25; 16)	+6/-3
16.00/172.2	7.4	34/75	n.k.	n.k.	60-110 (132-242)	17 (30; 19)	n.k.
n.k.	n.k.	19/42	n.k.	n.k.	n.k.	n.k.	n.k.
15.60/167.9	7.5	32/70.5	12	n.k.	80-95 (176-209)	14 (25; 16)	n.k.
20.50/220.7	6	42/92.6	8	n.k.	240 (529) max	15 (28; 18)	n.k.
18.50/199.1	6	42/92.6	9	n.k.	240 (529)	15 (28; 18)	n.k.
13.50/145.3	8.3	43/94.8	8	n.k.	240 (529)	15 (28; 18)	n.k.
13.50/145.3	6.8	23/50.7	10	54/177	55-72 (121-159)	14 (25; 16)	n.k.
15.00/161.5	6.14	24/52.9	10	54/177	68-86 (150-189)	14 (25; 16)	n.k.
18.90/203.4	4.8	25/55.1	8	75/246	50-110 (110-242)	16 (29; 19)	+6/-3
15.30/164.7	7.34	30/66	11	54/177	55-90 (121-198)	27 (50; 31)	n.k.
16.90/181.9	7.29	33/72.8	11	54/177	75-105 (165-231)	27 (50; 31)	n.k.
15.00/162.5	6.94	29/63.9	10	57/187	55-85 (121-187)	26 (48; 30)	n.k.
16.60/178.7	6.90	31/68.3	10	57/187	70-100 (154-220)	26 (48; 30)	n.k.
15.50/166.8	6.20	27/60	8.5	66/217	55-90 (121-198)	25 (47; 29)	n.k.
14-19/151-205	7-9	30-35/66-77	11-14	48-54/157-177	50-120 (110-264)	n.k.	+6/-3
16.20/174.4	n.k.	38/84	18	45/148	50-100 (110-220)	16 (28; 18)	+8/-6
17.60/189.4	4.4	25/55	7	78/256	n.k.	14 (25; 16)	n.k.
15.80/170.0	5.5	28/61.7	n.k.	n.k.	55-105 (121-231)	15 (28; 18) estimated	+6/-3
12.36/133.0	6.6	26/57.3	n.k.	n.k.	45-60 (100-132)	n.k.	n.k.
13.94/150.0	6.3	26/57.3	n.k.	n.k.	52-64 (115-160)	n.k.	n.k.
14.49/156.0	6.7	29/64	11	52/171	64-73 (140-160)	16 (29; 18)	n.k.
15.79/170.0	6.8	29.9/66	11	52/171	70-79 (155-175)	16 (29; 18)	n.k.
16.54/178.0	6.8	32.2/71	11	54/177	79-91 (175-200)	16 (29; 18)	n.k.
14.40/155.0	7.4	31/68.3	n.k.	n.k.	95 (209) max	15 (28; 18) estimated	+6/-3

RIGID AND FLEXIBLE WING DATA *(continued)*

Manufacturer and Model	Rigid: R Flexwing: F	FAI or other class	Span: m/ft-in	Leading-edge (flexwing): m/ft-in	Length (rigid); Keel (flexwing): m/ft-in	Nose/Billow angle (flexwing): degrees
UNITED KINGDOM *Contd.*						
Pegasus/Solar Wings						
Ace/Ace RX (small)	F	1	9.60/31-6	n.k.	n.k.	122/variable
Ace/Ace RX (medium)	F	1	9.91/32-6	n.k.	n.k.	122/variable
Ace/Ace RX (large)	F	1	10.36/34-0	n.k.	n.k.	122/variable
UNITED STATES OF AMERICA						
Delta Wing						
Dream 165	F	1	9.55/31-4	n.k.	n.k.	124/1.0
Dream 175	F	1	n.k.	n.k.	n.k.	n.k.
Dream 185	F	1	10.31/33-10	n.k.	n.k.	124/1.0
Mystic 155	F	n.k.	9.96/32-8	n.k.	n.k.	n.k.
Mystic 166	F	n.k.	10.39/34-1	n.k.	n.k.	n.k.
Mystic 177	F	n.k.	10.57/34-8	n.k.	n.k.	n.k.
Streak 130	F	1	8.84/29-0	n.k.	n.k.	133/0
Streak 160	F	1	10.62/34-10	5.56/18-3	3.35/11-0	133/0
Streak 180	F	1	11.38/37-4	n.k.	n.k.	133/0
Pacific Windcraft						
Vision 148	F	n.k.	n.k.	n.k.	n.k.	122/n.k.
Vision 175	F	n.k.	n.k.	n.k.	n.k.	122/n.k.
Vision 194	F	n.k.	n.k.	n.k.	n.k.	122/n.k.
Vision Eclipse 17	F	n.k.	9.27/30-5	n.k.	n.k.	122/n.k.
Vision Eclipse 19	F	n.k.	9.75/32-0	n.k.	n.k.	122/n.k.
Seedwings						
Sensor 510-160 VG	F	n.k.	10.57/34-8	n.k.	n.k.	n.k.
Sensor 510-165	F	n.k.	10.67/35-0	5.18/17-0	n.k.	n.k.
UP						
Comet 2B 165	F	1	9.96/32-8	5.86/19-2¾	2.49/8-2	120/0
Comet 2B 185	F	1	10.57/34-8	6.22/20-4¾	2.62/8-7	120/0
Gemini M 134	F	1	8.78/28-9½	5.22/17-1½	2.18/7-2	120/1.0
Gemini M 164	F	1	9.91/32-6	5.86/19-2¾	2.49/8-2	120/1.0
Gemini M 184	F	1	10.49/34-5	6.22/20-4¾	2.62/8-7	120/1.0
Glidezilla 155	F	1	10.36/34-0	5.87/19-3	2.06/6-9	126/0
Volmer						
VJ-23 Swingwing	R	n.k.	9.93/32-7	9.93/32-7	5.31/17-5	—
VJ-24 Sunfun	R	n.k.	11.13/36-6	11.13/36-6	5.54/18-2	—
Wills Wing						
Skyhawk 168	F	1	9.19/30-2	5.49/18-0	3.66/12-0	115/0
Skyhawk 188	F	1	10.01/32-10	5.94/19-6	3.66/12-0	115/0
Sport 150	F	1	9.60/31-6	5.54/18-2	3.45/11-4	124/0
Sport 167	F	1	10.21/33-6	5.94/19-6	3.45/11-4	124/0
Sport American 167	F	1	10.21/33-6	5.94/19-6	3.45/11-4	124/0
HP II	F	1	10.46/34-4	5.92/19-5	3.45/11-4	128/0

n.k. = not known

Wing area: m²/sq ft	Wing aspect ratio	Weight: kg/lb	Glide ratio	Sink rate: m/ft per min	Pilot weight: kg (lb)	Stalling speed: knots (km/h; mph)	g limits
13.94/150.0	6.6	28.6/63	n.k.	n.k.	51-83 (113-183)	n.k.	n.k.
14.86/160.0	6.6	31.8/70	n.k.	n.k.	70-89 (154-196)	n.k.	n.k.
15.79/170.0	6.8	33.6/74	n.k.	n.k.	83-100 (183-220)	n.k.	n.k.
15.33/165.0	6.4	28.1/62	n.k.	n.k.	59-91 (130-200)	n.k.	n.k.
16.26/175.0	n.k.	n.k.	n.k.	n.k.	n.k.	n.k.	n.k.
17.19/185.0	6.2	30.8/68	n.k.	n.k.	n.k.	n.k.	n.k.
14.49/156.0	6.7	29/64	n.k.	n.k.	45-77 (100-170)	n.k.	n.k.
15.42/166.0	6.8	29.9/66	n.k.	n.k.	64-95 (140-210)	n.k.	n.k.
16.26/175.0	6.8	32.2/71	n.k.	n.k.	77-109 (170-240)	n.k.	n.k.
12.08/130.0	6.6	24.9/55	n.k.	50/165	n.k.	n.k.	+8.5/-5
14.68/158.0	7.5	32.7/72	n.k.	50/165	59-100 (130-220)	n.k.	+8.5/-5
16.72/180.0	7.6	37.2/82	n.k.	50/165	n.k.	n.k.	+8.5/-5
13.75/148.0	5.7	23.6/52	n.k.	n.k.	45-113 (100-250)	n.k.	n.k.
16.26/175.0	5.7	26.8/59	n.k.	45-113 (100-250)	n.k.	n.k.	n.k.
18.02/194.0	5.5	29/64	n.k.	n.k.	45-113 (100-250)	n.k.	n.k.
15.89/171.0	5.4	27.2/60	n.k.	n.k.	32-64 (70-140)	n.k.	n.k.
17.19/185.0	5.5	29/64	n.k.	n.k.	39-84 (86-186)	n.k.	n.k.
14.96/161.0	7.5	29.9/66	n.k.	n.k.	n.k.	n.k.	n.k.
15.33/165.0	7.4	29.9/66	n.k.	n.k.	n.k.	n.k.	n.k.
15.33/165.0	6.5	29/64	10+	55/180	59-104 (130-230)	13.5 (25; 15) IAS	+6.5/-3.5
17.19/185.0	6.6	35.4/78	10+	55/180	68-113 (150-250)	13.5 (25; 15) IAS	+6.5/-3.5
12.45/134.0	6.2	24.9/55	8.5	64/210	43-75 (95-165)	12.5 (23; 14) IAS	n.k.
15.24/164.0	6.4	28.6/63	8.5	64/210	57-91 (125-200)	12.5 (23; 14) IAS	n.k.
17.09/184.0	6.4	34/75	8.5	64/210	68-104 (150-230)	12.5 (23; 14) IAS	n.k.
14.31/154.0	7.5	32.7/72	12.5	52/170	64-104 (140-230)	13 (24; 15)	+6.5/-3.5
16.63/179.0	5.9	45.5/100	9	n.k.	45.5-91 (100-200)	13 (24; 15)	+2.57 normal +3.87 ultimate
15.14/163.0	8.2	50/110	9	n.k.	91 (200) max	n.k.	n.k.
15.42/166.0	5.5	24.5/54	8.5	69/225	52-75 (115-165)	19 (36; 22)	+6/-3
17.47/188.0	5.7	29/64	8.5	69/225	66-88 (145-195)	19 (36; 22)	+6/-3
13.94/150.0	6.6	24.5/54	9	73/240	56.7-95.3 (125-210)	19 (36; 22)	n.k.
15.51/167.0	6.7	26.8/59	9	73/240	64-95 (140-210)	18 (33; 20)	n.k.
15.51/167.0	6.7	29.9/66	9	n.k.	n.k.	n.k.	n.k.
15.61/168.0	7.0	31.8/70	10+	76/250	68-113 (150-250)	22 (41; 25)	+10/-5.6 estimated

LIGHTER THAN AIR: AIRSHIPS

AUSTRALIA

ADA

AIRSHIP DEVELOPMENTS AUSTRALIA PTY LTD

96 Rankins Road, Kensington, Victoria 3031
Telephone: (03) 376 2450
DESIGNER: Bruce N. Blake

Nearly a decade ago Mr Bruce Blake, then a newly graduated aeronautical engineer, contributed to the design and construction of Australia's first airship, the non-rigid *Ardath*. In the interim, after working at the Department of Aviation, Government Aircraft Factories and Australian Aircraft Consortium, he initiated a series of airship designs under the name of his Airship Developments Australia company. These include a pair of drones, a single- and two-seat non-rigid, a twin-engined, four/six-seat light utility airship, and a 50-passenger tourist craft. The single-seat project was terminated at mockup stage when studies indicated that resources were better committed to refinement of the LUA (light utility airship) design. As the means of demonstrating the airworthiness of this design, at minimal cost, while generating revenue, a scaled-down drone version of the LUA, named Albatross, was funded and built during 1985.

ADA ALBATROSS

First flown on 6 November 1986, the Albatross RPMB (remotely piloted mini-blimp) is intended to prove several innovative features, including a lifting outrigger with blown flap similar to one wind-tunnel tested in the USA for the GZ-16 non-rigid of the 1950s. Revenue will be generated at outdoor displays and other promotional opportunities. The ability to carry a small TV camera system may improve market access, as well as pave the way for more advanced guidance and piloting technology. The full scale version of the LUA, for which preliminary design work has been completed, is known as the **ADA-1200**. News of venture capital for the ADA-1200 was expected in mid-1988.

Initial flight testing of the Albatross has demonstrated most of the expected performance characteristics of the full scale design. The airship can be taxied in light winds, and has shown very short take-off and landing performance. Successful flights at more than 20 per cent heaviness have been made; hands-off stability appears to be excellent, combining positive pitch stability with weathercocking yaw stability. No pitch or yaw oscillations have been observed, and roll damping is satisfactory.

The following description relates to the Albatross one-third scale prototype:
ENVELOPE: The envelope is a two-skin type, the inner (gas cell) being made from metallised laminated nylon film while the outer (load carrying) skin is of stabilised polyester fabric. Seams of the outer skin are double sewn, with heat-sealed tapes to attain full fabric strength across the seams. The inner skin, which is highly plastic and roughing tolerant, conforms to the shape of the outer skin as it stretches with use. A single spherical ballonet (volume 8.0 m³; 283 cu ft) is provided, constructed from nylon film. Automatic pressure control is achieved by the use of a pressure switch, an electric centrifugal blower (with a one-way flow valve) and an outflow valve. An overpressure valve is provided to vent helium, should envelope pressure exceed safe limits. Additionally, a remotely controlled dump valve will enable the initiation of a controlled descent in an emergency. The Albatross has an X-fin tail unit, each fin being fitted with two

The ADA Albatross remotely controlled airship, a scale prototype for the ADA-1200

'ruddervators' for redundancy, actuated by servos, with electronic mixing, to provide control in pitch and yaw. The fins are constructed from balsa wood and covered with a heat-shrunk polyester film.
POWER PLANT: Two 2.6 kW (3.5 hp) Robin EY15D single-cylinder four-stroke engines, lightened in weight and each fitted with an electric starter/generator. Engines are mounted on stub-wings, each with direct drive to a two-blade wooden propeller with spinner. Single fuel tank in spine fairing, max capacity 15 litres (4 US gallons; 3.3 Imp gallons).
GONDOLA, SPINE AND WING: The cabin/spine unit is of scale size, and is an innovation of the LUA design. Past non-rigids have generally relied upon cables and catenary curtains fitted into the upper envelope to support the gondola, but by elongating the cabin/spine it is entirely practicable, with modern materials, to introduce vertical loading into the lower envelope surface. In addition, the cabin/spine configuration leads to improved stiffness, in pitch and roll, between it and the envelope, and allows the installation of tricycle landing gear, essential for ground manoeuvring. The Albatross prototype is not entirely representative of the full size ADA-1200, since the CG of the cabin/spine is aft of the appropriate position, and the two-skin envelope precludes a conventional internal suspension system. Instead, cords at the wingtips provide the missing support. Materials used in the cabin/spine are hand laid glass/epoxy/PVC foam sandwich, with aircraft plywood structural reinforcing. The wing, lifting outrigger or lift plane, attached to the rear of the spine, is constructed from light gauge aluminium alloy sheet and provides structural attachment for the engines and main landing gear units. The trailing-edge is formed by a 30% chord flap, servo actuated to $\pm 40°$ deflection. This provides a useful increment of aerodynamic lift control. Landing gear has gas strut shock absorption and twin wheels, with 5½ in pneumatic tyres, on each unit.

GUIDANCE AND CONTROL: A standard FM radio control unit is used for line-of-sight operation. Minor modification was made to enable the use of a large external battery for the transmitter, with a similar improvement at the receiver. Control is provided for throttles, 'ruddervators', flaps and dump valve; three channels remain unused. The system provides an electronic discriminator for 'fail-safe' operation in the event of signal interference. Advanced RPV television based guidance is a possibility for future out-of-sight operations.

DIMENSIONS, OVERALL:
Length	12.00 m (39 ft 4½ in)
Height	4.40 m (14 ft 5¼ in)
Width	3.60 m (11 ft 9¾ in)

DIMENSIONS, ENVELOPE:
Length	12.00 m (39 ft 4½ in)
Max diameter	3.20 m (10 ft 6 in)
Volume	76.5 m³ (2,702 cu ft)

DIMENSIONS, GONDOLA/WING:
Gondola: Length	3.90 m (12 ft 9½ in)
Height (incl landing gear)	1.00 m (3 ft 3¼ in)
Wing span	2.10 m (6 ft 10¾ in)
Wing chord	0.60 m (1 ft 11½ in)
Wheel track	2.00 m (6 ft 6¾ in)
Wheelbase	2.50 m (8 ft 2½ in)
Propeller diameter	0.76 m (2 ft 6 in)

WEIGHTS:
Weight empty	64 kg (141 lb)
Max fuel	11 kg (24 lb)
Max payload	11 kg (24 lb)

PERFORMANCE:
Max level speed:	
neutral buoyancy	34 knots (63 km/h; 39 mph)
18% heavy	30 knots (55 km/h; 34.5 mph)
Min flying speed, 20% heavy	7 knots (13 km/h; 8.1 mph)
Max operating height	305 m (1,000 ft)

CANADA

HYSTAR

HYSTAR AEROSPACE DEVELOPMENT CORPORATION

5455 Airport Road South, Richmond, British Columbia V7B 1B5
Telephone: (604) 278 0107
Fax: (604) 278 7238
VICE-PRESIDENT: John Pearson

HYSTAR 103

The Hystar 103 is a lenticular hybrid design of toroidal (doughnut) shape, developed by Mr George Ninkovich and designed for use by the Canadian forestry industry. Radio controlled models, one of which was demonstrated during the 1986 Expo 86 World Fair in Vancouver, can vary in size from 4.5 to 17 m (14.76 to 55.77 ft) in length. Piloted versions can be produced varying in length from 17 to 35 m

(55.77 to 114.83 ft), with lifting capacities of up to 6,800 kg (14,990 lb) and speeds of up to 56 knots (105 km/h; 65 mph). The first piloted Hystar 103 was due to make its first flight in the Summer of 1987, but no confirmation of this has been received.

MAGNUS

MAGNUS AEROSPACE CORPORATION

Place de Ville, 330 Sparks Street, Suite 2910, Tower 'C', Ottawa, Ontario K1R 7R9
POSTAL ADDRESS: PO Box 599, Station 'B', Ottawa, Ontario K1P 5P7
Telephone: (613) 236 4798
Fax: (613) 236 6279
DIRECTOR, COMMUNICATIONS: Horace M. MacBean

Conceived as a heavy lift craft for short to medium ranges, in conditions and locations normally inaccessible to conventional airships, the Magnus project was initiated by Van Dusen Commercial Development (Canada) Ltd (now Magnus Aerospace Corporation) in February 1978. Eight months of market research resulted in a design concept using modern materials to overcome traditional airship problems of ballasting, controllability and changing buoyancy resulting from variations in temperature and altitude. The helium filled lifting envelope is a pressurised

sphere made from a high strength Kevlar material, and is able to withstand a sufficiently high internal pressure to maintain constant volume and shape over a wide range of pressure, temperature and wind conditions. The LTA vehicle uses this superpressure balloon concept in conjunction with the so-called Magnus effect, which generates additional lift from rotation of the spherical balloon. (Magnus effect is a force which will raise the flight path of a spinning ball, and was named after the 19th century German physicist who first noted it.)

MAGNUS MANNED DEMONSTRATOR VEHICLE

Magnus has finalised the design of a manned demonstrator of its LTA concept. It will utilise constructional methods and materials that are current state of the art, with much of the structure completed in composites, and will be capable of all the manoeuvres required of the full scale LTA, including precision hover. The demonstrator will be powered by two 373 kW (500 shp) turboshaft engines, each driving a 1.22 m (4 ft 0 in) diameter ducted fan, and will be flown by a crew of two.

DIMENSION, ENVELOPE:
Diameter	16.76 m (55 ft 0 in)

WEIGHTS:
Weight empty	1,905 kg (4,200 lb)
Max payload	907 kg (2,000 lb)
Gross buoyancy	2,222 kg (4,900 lb)

PERFORMANCE (estimated):
Cruising speed	43 knots (80 km/h; 50 mph)
Max range	121 nm (225 km; 140 miles)

MAGNUS LTA 20-1

Under this designation, Magnus is designing a commercial version of its new airship. This heavy lift craft is intended for short- and medium-range transport of oversize loads to remote or normally inaccessible locations.

In 1984, contracts were awarded to prepare the first stage engineering definition of the LTA 20-1 production craft, including hardware options for the propulsion system, control systems, structure, vehicle dynamics, and weight and cost estimates. Its configuration will be generally similar to that of the drone scale model (see 1983-84 *Jane's*). VTOL capability will be provided by internal ballasting and engine thrust, enabling the craft to take off and land unassisted. Sphere rotation allows de-icing of the entire envelope surface from the gondola. The airship will be powered by four 2,610 kW (3,500 shp) engines, two being mounted at each end of the horizontal axle and each able to rotate independently through 90° to vector thrust from a vertical take-off mode to a horizontal cruising position.

The gondola, suspended from the horizontal axle, will accommodate two or three operators, utilising controls similar to those of a helicopter, and will carry payload within its cargo hold or as a slung load beneath the gondola. Additional lift will be generated by the vertical thrust of the engines during take-off and by the large Magnus force in horizontal cruising flight. After the payload has been offloaded, neutral buoyancy will be achieved by stopping sphere rotation to eliminate Magnus lift, reducing buoyant volume by expansion of the inner ballonet, and by taking in ballast as required.

DIMENSIONS, ENVELOPE:
Diameter	60.96 m (200 ft 0 in)
Volume, gross	118,613 m³ (4,188,790 cu ft)

Artist's impression of the heavy lift Magnus LTA 20-1 in a typical application

DIMENSIONS, GONDOLA (A: excluding/B: including arms and engines):
Length overall	59.44 m (195 ft 0 in)
Width: A	31.70 m (104 ft 0 in)
B	79.55 m (261 ft 0 in)
Height: A	4.27 m (14 ft 0 in)
B	41.45 m (136 ft 0 in)

WEIGHTS:
Max payload capacity	54,430 kg (120,000 lb)
Max T-O weight	124,285 kg (274,000 lb)

PERFORMANCE (estimated):
Max level speed	52 knots (96 km/h; 60 mph)
Cruising speed	43 knots (80 km/h; 50 mph)
Range with max payload at 43 knots (80 km/h; 50 mph), ISA	698 nm (804 km; 500 miles)

MAGNUS HAPP

The HAPP (high-altitude powered platform) is a variant of the LTA 20-1, modified for high-altitude endurance station-keeping capability and remote pilot operation. The design incorporates a high capacity ballonet within the main sphere; three smaller towed spheres, kept neutrally buoyant, contain supplemental fuel and solar concentrators for the electric power plant.

DIMENSIONS, ENVELOPE:
Diameter: main sphere	45.72 m (150 ft 0 in)
towed spheres (each)	30.48 m (100 ft 0 in)

WEIGHT:
Net payload	2,000 kg (4,409 lb)

PERFORMANCE (estimated):
Dash speed	70 knots (130 km/h; 81 mph)
Cruising speed	45 knots (83 km/h; 52 mph)
Endurance	more than 100 days

CHINA
(PEOPLE'S REPUBLIC)

BIAA
BEIJING INSTITUTE OF AERONAUTICS AND ASTRONAUTICS (Light Aircraft Design and Research Section)

37 Xue Yun Road, Beijing 100083
Telephone: 2017251
Telex: 22036 BIAAT CN
DIRECTOR AND SENIOR RESEARCH ENGINEER: Hu Jizhong

BIAA MIFENG-6 (BEE-6)

Following a number of microlight aircraft (see Sport Aircraft section), the BIAA's sixth Mifeng (Bee) design, started in September 1985, is a four-place hot-air airship. It has an envelope of lightweight high-strength nylon which, in its carrying bag, occupies only 1.5 m³ (53 cu ft) of space. There are two vertical fins, each with a rudder for yaw control, and two horizontal stabilisers (without elevators). The gondola/car has a mainframe of chrome molybdenum steel tube, covered with sheet aluminium. The envelope is inflated by the propulsion engine, two gas burners providing heat for buoyancy control. Propulsion is provided by a 31.3 kW (42 hp) Rotax 447 two-stroke engine driving a BIAA three-blade fixed pitch pusher propeller. Fuel tank capacity is 50 litres (13.2 US gallons; 11.0 Imp gallons).

The prototype, which first flew on 20 December 1985, utilised a modified hot-air balloon envelope. Two production Mifeng-6s had been completed by early 1988, and the airship had already been used for aerial photography, cinema film photography, scientific experiment flights and sightseeing. One example assisted in erecting power transmission lines for the Ge-Zhou hydro-electric power station, successfully lifting the 500,000V ultra-high-voltage lead cable in this mountainous area.

DIMENSIONS:
Length overall	33.70 m (110 ft 6¾ in)
Length of gondola	3.60 m (11 ft 9¾ in)

Production example of the BIAA Mifeng-6 hot-air airship

Envelope diameter (max)	13.30 m (43 ft 7½ in)	WEIGHTS:	
Height overall, incl car	16.40 m (53 ft 9¾ in)	Weight empty	325 kg (716 lb)
Tailplane span	15.00 m (49 ft 2½ in)	Max T-O weight	740 kg (1,631 lb)
Wheel track	1.20 m (3 ft 11¼ in)	PERFORMANCE:	
Propeller diameter	1.28 m (4 ft 2½ in)	Max level speed at S-L	19 knots (35 km/h; 22 mph)
Envelope volume, gross	2,983 m³ (105,344 cu ft)	Cruising speed at S-L	13.5 knots (25 km/h; 15.5 mph)

Gondola of the Mifeng-6

Max rate of climb at S-L, 15°C	120 m (394 ft)/min
Min turning radius	50 m (164 ft)
Design ceiling	3,000 m (9,840 ft)
Range with max fuel	16 nm (30 km; 18.5 miles)

BIAA/HONGWEI TIANZHOU 1

In conjunction with the Hongwei Aircraft Factory, the BIAA has developed and flown a hot-air airship known as the **Tianzhou 1** or **TZ-1**, the name meaning 'Skyship' in English. No other details are known.

BIAA/Hongwei Tianzhou 1 hot-air airship

HACDC
HANGZHOU AIRSHIP COMPREHENSIVE DEVELOPMENT COMPANY

c/o Lin An Physico-Chemical Research Institute, Hangzhou, Lin An County, Zhejiang Province

HACDC XIHU-1 (WEST LAKE 1)

All known details of this 20-passenger airship, together with a photograph, can be found in the 1987-88 *Jane's*. No recent news of the Xihu-1 has been received.

FRANCE

AERAZUR
AERAZUR (Member company of the Groupe Zodiac)
Division Equipements Aéronautiques
58 boulevard Galliéni, 92137 Issy-les-Moulineaux
Telephone: (1) 45 54 92 80
Telex: 270 887 F
Fax: (1) 45 57 99 85
CHIEF EXECUTIVE OFFICER: Jean Louis Gerondeau
INTERNATIONAL MARKETING MANAGER: Jean-Pierre Fetu

Aerazur began building lighter than air craft before the Second World War, and in the 1960s manufactured the world's largest non-rigid kite balloons (up to 15,000 m³; 529,720 cu ft), which were used for tests in the atmosphere of French nuclear weapons. It has made a series of small Vénus balloons for the French space agency CNES, as well as very large stratosphere research balloons of up to 1 million m³ (35,314,720 cu ft) in volume. Recent programmes have included development of a surveillance balloon carrying a Thomson-CSF radar, and barrage balloons for anti-aircraft defence. Aerazur designs and manufactures envelopes for the Airship Industries Skyship 500 and 600 series, and is associated in designing the envelope for the Sentinel airship for the US Navy.

AERAZUR DINOSAURE

Designed in 1975, originally for meteorological applications, the Dinosaure is a twin hulled 'catamaran' airship (hydrogen or helium filled). The two hulls each have internal air ballonets, a gondola, separate cruciform tail surfaces, and are joined together in 'Siamese twin' fashion by a rigid central structure. A single engine mounted at the rear, between the hulls, drives a pusher propeller.

Details of the small scale Dino 3 test model can be found in the 1987-88 and earlier editions. The full size Dinosaure, of which no details were received, did not proceed beyond the prototype stage.

GERMANY
(FEDERAL REPUBLIC)

GEFA-FLUG
GEFA-FLUG GmbH
Königstrasse 29, 5100 Aachen
Telephone: 0241 36202
Telex: 8 329 756 ABAC D
MANAGING DIRECTOR: Karl Ludwig Busemeyer

Gefa-Flug has been operating advertising, filming and passenger-carrying balloons and airships since 1975. It has provided camera platforms for BBC television in the UK, and for various archaeological research projects in Germany, Italy, Oman, Pakistan, Syria and Turkey. The company currently operates the only Thunder & Colt AS 42 single-seat hot-air airship in West Germany, and its passenger and advertising craft include half a dozen Thunder & Colt hot-air balloons. A leading part of Gefa-Flug's activities consists of aerial photogrammetry of archaeological sites, to obtain photographs from which accurate measurements can be calculated by computer.

GEFA-FLUG KENWOOD

The Kenwood (see accompanying photograph) is a small, unmanned semi-rigid airship remotely controlled by a Microprop seven-channel PCM radio transmitter. It has an envelope of polyester foil, is powered by two 75W (0.1 hp) electric motors, and carries a small stills camera. Other data are as follows:

DIMENSIONS:
Length	6.00 m (19 ft 8¼ in)
Max diameter	1.50 m (4 ft 11 in)
Envelope volume	6.00 m³ (212 cu ft)

WEIGHTS:
Payload	0.5 kg (1.1 lb)
Gross lift	6 kg (13.2 lb)

Gefa-Flug Kenwood electrically powered, remotely controlled mini-airship

PERFORMANCE:
Max level speed	14 knots (26 km/h; 16 mph)
Max endurance	1 h

GEFA-FLUG HOT-AIR AIRSHIP

This unmanned, radio controlled craft, illustrated in an accompanying photograph, is used primarily for aerial photogrammetry work, for which it carries a 6 × 6 Rolleiflex SLX camera. A slightly larger version is under development.

DIMENSIONS:
Length	14.00 m (45 ft 11¼ in)
Max diameter	6.00 m (19 ft 8¼ in)
Envelope volume	200.0 m³ (7,063 cu ft)

WEIGHTS:
Max payload	20 kg (44 lb)
Gross lift	70 kg (154 lb)

PERFORMANCE:
Max operating height	300 m (985 ft)
Max endurance	2 h

Gefa-Flug hot-air airship used for aerial photogrammetry

ITALY

BONANNO
PAOLO LETTERIO BONANNO

Via Volo 3/A, 12036 Revello (CN)
Telephone: (0175) 75666
Fax: (0175) 759313

Mr Bonanno's AX-8 class hot-air balloon I-PAAM (see tables at end of this section) is being used as a testbed for a new Mk 4 double burner, with hydraulic remote control and manifold valve, which he has developed for Cameron Balloons Ltd of the UK.

In addition, Mr Bonanno was building in 1988 the prototype of an **RBX-7** racing hot-air airship which he hoped to have ready in time for the first world hot-air airship championships to be held in Luxembourg in August 1988. The RBX-7 is a two-place craft, with an envelope volume of 2,200 m³ (77,692 cu ft).

MEXICO

SPACIAL
SERVICIOS PUBLICITARIOS AÉREOS CONSTRUCCIÓN E INGENIERÍA DE AERONAVES LIGERAS SA de CV

Margaritas 312-8, Colonia Florida, Mexico DF 01030
Telephone: 524 7262
CHAIRMAN: Lic Ramón González Parra
DIRECTOR GENERAL: Ing Mario Sánchez Roldán
CONSTRUCTION MANAGER: Marco Antonio Renteria

SPACIAL MLA-32-A TOLUCA

Research, development and design work on this unusual rigid airship (MLA is an abbreviation of the Spanish for 'lighter than air') began in 1973. The MLA-24-A prototype was nearing completion in the Spring of 1985 but was destroyed in a tornado before it could make its first flight. Details and illustrations of the MLA-24-A were published in the 1985-86 *Jane's*.

By early 1986 construction of the larger MLA-32-A(XB-RGP) had begun on a new site at Toluca, 64 km (40 miles) south-west of Mexico City where the first flight was originally set for 19 December 1986. This was delayed by sabotage, but the repaired craft was ready to begin test flying in mid-March 1987, only to be damaged again by hurricane winds. The first take-off was eventually made on 12 February 1988, inadvertently, due to the Toluca breaking free from its mooring mast while final adjustments for a crewed first flight were being made to the port engine. Fortunately, damage was confined to the gondola and one split gas cell, and the company hoped to repair the airship and refit a new gondola in time for a genuine first flight in October 1988. It will then be fitted with a spoiler and have radio control on board.

The envelope/hull of the MLA-32-A consists of an ellipsoid frame of 6063-T6 aluminium tube and steel, with an aluminium box structure at the equator and glassfibre 'stars' connecting the tubular intersections. The hull is covered with a protective layer of foam plastics and an outer skin of polyester fabric, and is of NACA 0012 aerofoil section. Inside the frame are six helium cells each made of four layers of Mylar, nylon and polyethylene, and the water ballast tanks. At the rear is a wide span tailplane, with a centrally mounted fin and rudder above and below it. Kevlar cables connect the hull to the gondola, which is constructed of aluminium, Styrofoam and acrylic materials with an inner and outer skin of Kevlar. The gondola has accommodation for a pilot and five passengers, a

Spacial MLA-32-A Toluca elliptical hull airship, due to fly in late 1988

Gondola and power plant of the Spacial MLA-32-A Toluca, named after the state capital where it was built

bulletproof floor, and provision for carrying an aerial camera.

Power plant comprises a pair of 67 kW (90 hp) McCulloch two-stroke engines, which can be swivelled through 140° (120° down/20° up) to provide thrust vectoring for manoeuvring. A computer-coupled Sperry digital inclinometer is installed to trim the airship automatically.

DIMENSIONS, EXTERNAL:

Hull diameter	32.0 m (105 ft 0 in)
Hull depth (max)	10.67 m (35 ft 0 in)

Hull volume	5,944 m³ (209,910 cu ft)
Height overall (incl gondola and wheel)	
	13.87 m (45 ft 6 in)

WEIGHTS:

Gondola, incl control and ballast system	387 kg (853 lb)
Water ballast	400 kg (882 lb)
Total weight empty (excl ballast)	3,420 kg (7,540 lb)
Max T-O weight (calculated)	5,788 kg (12,760 lb)

LIFT:

Dynamic lift (thrust)	879 kg (1,938 lb)

Useful lift (static) at 305 m (1,000 ft)	
	2,150 kg (4,740 lb)
Total vertical lift	3,422 kg (7,544 lb)
Gross lift at 4,591 m³ (162,130 cu ft) inflation	
	4,581 kg (10,099 lb)

PERFORMANCE (estimated):

Cruising speed	60 knots (111 km/h; 69 mph)
Rate of sink, power off	0.20 m (0.66 ft)/s

NEW ZEALAND

NEW ZEALAND AIRSHIPS LTD — *See Advanced Airship (UK)*

UNION OF SOVIET SOCIALIST REPUBLICS

MAI (YEGER) AIRSHIP

A large cargo airship, possibly lenticular in shape, is reportedly being designed at the Moscow Aviation Institute under the leadership of Sergei Yeger. It is said to have a diameter of 150 m (492.13 ft), and to be capable of payloads up to 300 tonnes (661,387 lb) and ranges of up to 2,160 nm (4,000 km; 2,485 miles). The helium lift will be supplemented by heated air to help prevent icing during cold weather operations. No other details were known at the time of going to press.

UNITED KINGDOM

ADVANCED AIRSHIP

ADVANCED AIRSHIP CORPORATION

Meadows Court, West Street, Ramsey, Isle of Man
Telephone: (0624) 812894
Telex: 627835 AIRSHP G
TECHNICAL DIRECTOR: P. W. C. Monk
MARKETING MANAGER: Ian Alexander

Advanced Airship Corporation is the new name of the former Wren Skyships Ltd. Work on the Wren RS.1 rigid airship project (1987-88 *Jane's*) has been suspended, but is continuing on the non-rigid ANR. Advanced Airship Corporation has also taken over the NZ-1 project from New Zealand Airships Ltd, of which it was the parent company, and NZA Ltd has been discontinued.

ADVANCED AIRSHIP ANR

The ANR (advanced non-rigid), under construction in 1987-88, is a 20/30-seat passenger airship which can also operate as a maritime patrol airship having an on-station endurance in excess of 24 hours at a patrol speed of 40 knots (74 km/h; 46 mph). The envelope is manufactured by Thunder & Colt. First flight was scheduled for December 1988.

TYPE: Non-rigid helium filled airship.

ENVELOPE: Conventional non-rigid ellipsoidal structure, manufactured from polyester fabric coated on the exterior with titanium oxide filled polyurethane and internally with a PVC film. Two catenary curtains, 12 catenary cables and five gondola attachment points each side. Nosecone stiffened internally with 16 battens. One ballonet in nose and one in rear of hull, each supplied by a single-stage axial flow fan capable of delivering 160 m³ (5,650 cu ft)/min. Four equally spaced tail-fins, in X configuration, all four being used for both pitch and yaw control.

POWER PLANT: Two 313 kW (420 shp) Allison 250-B17C turboprops, mounted on stub-wing attached to gondola and each driving a three-blade ducted propeller. Entire wing/propulsion unit can rotate nacelle to 75° up, 30° down, to vector thrust for climb and descent. Single flap on wing trailing-edge can deflect propeller slipstream to increase effective tilt up to 90°. Standard fuel capacity 1,432 litres (378 US gallons; 315 Imp gallons).

ACCOMMODATION: Crew of two on gondola flight deck. Main cabin can accommodate a variety of passenger layouts, ranging from 14 in a 7-pair 'twin dining alcove' arrangement to 30 in a four-abreast layout, all with a central aisle, plus provision for one or two cabin attendants. Toilet and galley installations to customer's requirements. Large baggage hold at rear of gondola. All-cargo interior available optionally.

DIMENSIONS, EXTERNAL:

Length overall	60.96 m (200 ft 0 in)
Height overall, incl gondola	18.90 m (62 ft 0 in)
Envelope: Max diameter	15.24 m (50 ft 0 in)
Volume	7,270 m³ (256,724 cu ft)
Ballonet volume (two, total)	1,753 m³ (61,922 cu ft)
Fin area (total, net)	116.8 m² (1,257 sq ft)

General appearance of the Advanced Airship ANR, under construction in 1987-88

Gondola: Length	13.66 m (44 ft 9½ in)
Max width	2.84 m (9 ft 4 in)
Max height	2.35 m (7 ft 8½ in)
Propeller diameter	2.44 m (8 ft 0 in)

DIMENSIONS, INTERNAL:

Gondola passenger cabin:

Length of seating area	6.71 m (22 ft 0 in)
Max width	2.67 m (8 ft 9 in)
Min height	1.98 m (6 ft 6 in)

WEIGHTS:

Weight empty	3,371 kg (7,432 lb)
Fuel: (standard)	1,134 kg (2,500 lb)
minimum	590 kg (1,300 lb)
Payload (typical):	
26 passengers, cabin attendant and baggage	
	3,052 kg (6,728 lb)
cargo, with min fuel	3,052 kg (6,728 lb)
Max T-O weight	7,167 kg (15,800 lb)

PERFORMANCE (estimated, standard fuel, at 915 m; 3,000 ft, ISA):

Max level speed	80 knots (148 km/h; 92 mph)
Max cruising speed	78 knots (144 km/h; 90 mph)
Lower limit speed at max heaviness	
	24 knots (45 km/h; 28 mph)
Max rate of climb	610 m (2,000 ft)/min
Pressure ceiling: commercial	1,525 m (5,000 ft)
coastal patrol	1,830 m (6,000 ft)
Range:	
at 50 knots (93 km/h; 58 mph)	
	714 nm (1,323 km; 822 miles)
at 70 knots (130 km/h; 81 mph)	
	481 nm (891 km; 554 miles)
Endurance:	
at 50 knots (93 km/h; 58 mph)	14 h 18 min
at 70 knots (130 km/h; 81 mph)	6 h 54 min

AIRSHIP INDUSTRIES

AIRSHIP INDUSTRIES (UK) LTD (Associate of Bond Corporation)

Bond House, 347-353 Chiswick High Road, London W4 4HS

Telephone: (01) 995 7811
Telex: 299964 SKYSHP G
MANAGING DIRECTOR: Michael Hoffman
TECHNICAL DIRECTOR: Roger Munk
HEAD OF MARKETING: Ian Matheson

MANAGER, PUBLIC RELATIONS: Claire Baker

Airship Industries is a CAA approved company for the design and manufacture of non-rigid airships. Skyship 500 and 600 are intended to satisfy requirements in the civil and paramilitary fields. The prime civil applications are for aerial advertising and promotional and pleasure flight operations.

The paramilitary roles are essentially surveillance activities, reinforced by the airship's ability to lower a boarding boat/party for inspection or prosecution. General coastguard activities, EEZ (exclusive economic zone) patrol, fishery protection, and search and rescue, are logical applications. In all of these roles the extended endurance, low noise and vibration levels, spacious cabin and attractive operating costs render the airship a cost-effective and viable platform.

Due to the high payload volume of the gondola, which can house a thorough and sophisticated communications, navigation and sensor system, and the large dimensions of the envelope for mounting internal antennae, the airship also has considerable potential in such roles as airborne early warning, electronic warfare and mine countermeasures.

AIRSHIP INDUSTRIES SKYSHIP 500

The first production Skyship 500 (G-BIHN, c/n 02) made its first flight, at RAE Cardington, Bedfordshire, on 28 September 1981. Four more Skyship 500s had been completed by mid-1988, as detailed in the 1987-88 *Jane's*. Operation was under a British CAA 'aerial work' C of A initially, but a full transport category certificate—the first since the 1930s—was awarded on 21 November 1984, and on 23 April 1986 Skyship 500-02 inaugurated the first scheduled airship passenger service for 49 years when it took off from Leavesden Airport for the first of four daily sightseeing flights over central London. The service continued to run until 15 June 1986, and proved so successful that it was repeated, from 6 May to 16 October 1987, using the larger Skyship 600-01.

The envelope of the Skyship 500 is manufactured, by the Zodiac division of Aerazur in France, from a strong-in-weft single ply polyester fabric, coated with a titanium dioxide loaded polyurethane to reduce ultraviolet degradation, and with a polyvinylidene chloride film bonded on the inside to minimise loss of helium gas. The nose structure consists of a domed disc, moulded from GRP and carrying the fitting by which the airship is moored to its mast. Two ballonets, which together comprise 26 per cent of the envelope volume, are installed fore and aft, so that differential inflation will provide static fore and aft trim. There is a ballonet air intake aft of each propulsor unit. Four catenary curtains carry 12 main cables of Kevlar within the envelope for suspension of the gondola. The tail unit is of conventional cruciform layout, each surface being attached to the envelope at its root and braced by four wires on each side. All four surfaces are constructed from interlocking ribs and spars of Fibrelam and have GRP skins: their hinged rudder and elevator control surfaces are cable operated, and each has a spring tab.

The gondola is a one-piece moulding of Kevlar reinforced plastics, with flooring and bulkheads of Fibrelam panels; those which form the engine compartment at the rear of the gondola are faced with titanium for fire protection. There is accommodation for a pilot and co-pilot, with dual controls, although the airship is designed to be flown by a single pilot. The standard civil configuration seats passengers on five individual seats and a three-person bunk seat at the rear. Ballast in the form of lead shot is contained in a box situated below the crew seats, and disposable water ballast up to a maximum of 513 kg (1,130 lb) is contained in tanks at the rear of the gondola. On the ground, the airship rests on a single wheel, with double tyres, mounted beneath the rear part of the gondola.

Power plant comprises two 152 kW (204 hp) Porsche 930/10 six-cylinder aircooled piston engines mounted in the rear of the gondola. Each drives, via a modified Lynx helicopter tail rotor gearbox and a lateral driveshaft, a ducted propulsor consisting of a Hoffmann five-blade reversible-pitch propeller rotating within an annular duct constructed of GRP, reinforced with carbonfibre. Each propulsor can be rotated about its pylon attachment to the gondola through an arc of 210°: 90° upward and 120° downward. The vectored thrust available gives the airship a V/STOL capability, as well as in-flight hovering ability. A

The first Skyship 500, G-BIHN, at its Cardington base

fuel tank, capacity 545 litres (144 US gallons; 120 Imp gallons), is mounted at the rear of the engine compartment. Engine modifications include provision of automatic mixture control, fuel injection and electronic ignition. The 28V electrical system is supplied by engine driven alternators. Avionics include King Silver Crown series dual nav/com, ADF, Omega, VOR/ILS and weather radar.

DIMENSIONS, ENVELOPE:

Length overall	52.00 m (170 ft 7¼ in)
Max diameter	14.00 m (45 ft 11¼ in)
Height overall	18.66 m (61 ft 2½ in)
Tail fin span	17.00 m (55 ft 9 in)
Volume: gross	5,153 m³ (181,977 cu ft)
ballonets (total)	1,334 m³ (47,102 cu ft)

DIMENSIONS, GONDOLA:

Length overall	9.24 m (30 ft 3½ in)
Max width	2.41 m (7 ft 10¾ in)
Cabin: Length	4.20 m (13 ft 9½ in)
Height	1.96 m (6 ft 5 in)

WEIGHT:

Gross disposable load	1,260 kg (2,778 lb)

PERFORMANCE:

Max level speed	55 knots (101 km/h; 63 mph)
Cruising speed (50% power)	
	47 knots (87 km/h; 54 mph)
Pressure ceiling	3,050 m (10,000 ft)
Still air range at 40 knots (74 km/h; 46 mph)	
	470 nm (870 km; 541 miles)
Endurance	12 h

AIRSHIP INDUSTRIES SKYSHIP 500 HL

The 500 HL is a heavy lift airship currently under development. It combines the gondola of 500-04 with a new Skyship 600 envelope, and has a gross disposable load of 2,076 kg (4,578 lb). First flight was made on 30 July 1987. After this prototype has been certificated, 500-02 is due to be similarly converted.

PERFORMANCE:
Not yet available

AIRSHIP INDUSTRIES SKYSHIP 600

The Skyship 600 is a 'stretched' version of the Skyship 500, with accommodation for up to 13 passengers. The increased volume of the envelope provides approximately 740 kg (1,631 lb) more payload capability, and the lengthened gondola has a usable floor area of 12.0 m² (130.0 sq ft). The addition of turbochargers to the Porsche engines increases the available power to 190 kW (255 hp) per engine, fuel capacity is increased to 682 litres (180 US gallons; 150 Imp gallons), and auxiliary fuel tanks are available as

optional equipment. A special category C of A was awarded to Skyship 600 by the UK CAA on 1 September 1984. Aerial work certification was received in the Spring of 1986, and on 8 January 1987 the Skyship 600 received its certification for full passenger carriage. As a result of this award, the company started its Skycruise service, an aerial sightseeing tour, over the cities of London, San Francisco and Sydney, in May 1987. A Paris Skycruise began on 7 April 1988.

Developed to meet the needs of operators who require greater payload and/or endurance than are provided by the Skyship 500, the 600 is considered to be suited to roles which require long endurance patrols or extended time on station. The large cabin permits a high degree of crew comfort and efficiency. Equipment installed for evaluations in this role have included an MEL Marec 2 search radar, Tracor Omega navigation system, and a Zodiac two-man inflatable high-speed launch. As a major assistance to handling the Skyship 600 during prolonged sorties, a fly by light (fibre optics) flight control system, developed by GEC Avionics, has been purchased by Airship Industries and is currently being further developed and tested for use in the Skyship 600.

The prototype (G-SKSC, c/n 01), which made its first flight on 6 March 1984, continues to be based at Cardington, Bedfordshire. The second and sixth (VH-HAA and VH-HAN) are based at Sydney, Australia. Skyships 600-03, -04 and -05 (G-SKSG, G-SKSF and G-SKSJ respectively) are currently based in the USA at Weeksville, North Carolina. Skyship 600-07 was delivered to Japan in 1987. Sales of two more Skyship 600s, one to South Korea (for Olympic Games coverage) and one to Japan Airship Services, were announced in the Spring of 1988, with first flights (after assembly in those countries) scheduled for May and June 1988 respectively.

DIMENSIONS, ENVELOPE:

Length overall	59.00 m (193 ft 7 in)
Max diameter	15.20 m (49 ft 10½ in)
Height overall	20.30 m (66 ft 7¼ in)
Tail fin span	19.20 m (63 ft 0 in)
Volume: gross	6,666 m³ (235,400 cu ft)
ballonets (total)	1,733 m³ (61,200 cu ft)

DIMENSIONS, GONDOLA:

Length overall	11.67 m (38 ft 3½ in)
Max width	2.56 m (8 ft 4¾ in)
Cabin: Length	6.89 m (22 ft 7¼ in)
Height	1.92 m (6 ft 3½ in)

WEIGHT (design):

Gross disposable load	2,343 kg (5,165 lb)

PERFORMANCE:

Max level speed	58 knots (107 km/h; 67 mph)
Cruising speed (70% power)	
	52 knots (96 km/h; 60 mph)
Pressure ceiling	3,050 m (10,000 ft)
Still air range at 40 knots (74 km/h; 46 mph), without	
auxiliary tanks	550 nm (1,019 km; 633 miles)

AIRSHIP INDUSTRIES SENTINEL 5000
US Navy designation: YEZ-2A

Six-month study contracts were placed in mid-1985 by the Lighter Than Air Project Office of the US Naval Air Systems Command with three US companies (Boeing Military Airplanes, Goodyear and Westinghouse), to investigate the suitability of airships for use by the US Navy in an independent airborne early warning role.

The Navy's interest lies in development of an independent airborne early warning system capable of operating with surface attack groups anywhere in the world. Primary functions were described by the Naval Air Development Center as "detection, classification, identification and tracking of surface and airborne targets, particularly those of low radar cross-section, flying at low altitude and high speed in a sea clutter environment, and communications connectivity between surface ships in a battle group". The

Airship Industries Skyship 600-01, which gained the type's full passenger carrying C of A in January 1987

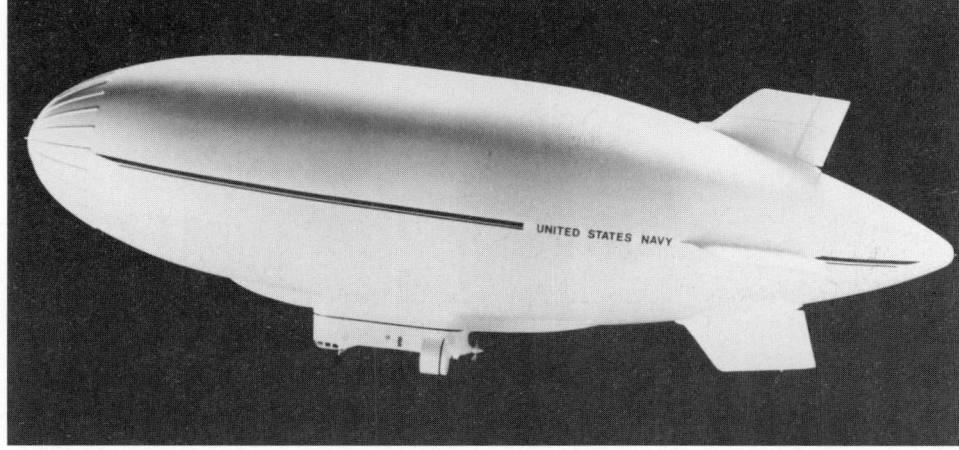

General configuration of the Sentinel 5000 and its three-deck control car. The latter will have a cross-sectional area comparable with that of a Boeing 747

surveillance system would warn surface ships of threats beyond the range of shipboard radars, including long-range sea-skimming cruise missiles.

Because of the independent operations required of the surveillance systems, and the long endurance required to accompany a naval force, an airship was considered the only feasible solution. The airship would be equipped with a large, long-range radar carried internally, the size of which largely dictated the size of the airship.

All three study contractors responded initially to the USN request for proposals issued in August 1986, but Boeing (whose design was the only rigid airship submitted) subsequently withdrew, leaving Goodyear and the Westinghouse/Airship Industries partnership as the final contenders. Award of a $168.9 million contract to WAI for an operational development model (ODM) airship, based on the Airship Industries Sentinel 5000 design, was announced by NASC on 5 June 1987. Using the avionics suite of the Grumman E-2C Hawkeye, and operating in the 1,525-3,050 m (5,000-10,000 ft) altitude range, this vehicle will have an unrefuelled endurance of 2-3 days; by refuelling and replenishing from surface units within a task force, a mission capability of some 30 days is intended. Designated USN missions are surveillance and targeting, airborne early warning, and communications.

The NASC contract included options for up to five additional airships, and the potential production programme could involve up to 50 of these craft. Defence budget cuts led to termination of the naval airship programme in early 1988, but in May continued development was reinstated with limited FY 1989 funding of $1.2 million. First flight of the ODM prototype is now planned for 1991, with full scale engineering development towards a fully operational vehicle anticipated after an 18-month period of flight test and evaluation. Final assembly and

initial flight testing of the Sentinel 5000 will take place in the USA.

Based on earlier Airship Industries studies for very large airships, the Sentinel 5000 as originally proposed will be the largest non-rigid ever constructed, and will carry a crew of 10-15 in a multi-deck, wide-bodied and fully pressurised gondola, the primary structure of which will be built of glassfibre and other composites. The upper deck will provide living accommodation for the crew, including double cabins, showers, separate wardroom galley, and a small gymnasium. Mission avionics, control information centre, galley, replenishment stores and refuelling equipment will occupy the lower deck. Below these two is a smaller flight deck containing the flight controls and instrumentation. The envelope will be made of a single-ply Dacron weave material, laminated with Tedlar and Mylar and bonded with Hytrel, and will carry a conventional cruciform tail unit with two control surfaces per fin, each control surface having two actuators and triple hinges.

An unpressurised engine room aft contains a CODAG (combined diesel and gas turbine) propulsion system, comprising an internally mounted pair of 1,342 kW (1,800 hp) ducted propulsion diesel units, with propeller thrust vectoring, plus a 1,342 kW (1,800 shp) class General Electric T700 turboprop, mounted on the gondola centreline at the rear, to provide additional power when a higher 'dash' speed is required. A substantial winching bay is located between the engine room aft and pressurised accommodation section forward, from where refuelling, re-storing and personnel transfers will be conducted through a large opening in the base of the gondola.

The choice of radar for the ODM has not yet been finalised, but the most likely candidate system is a modified version of the AN/APS-139 used in the Grumman E-2C, with an enlarged 12.19 m (40 ft) antenna. The flight control

system on the Sentinel 5000 will have full autostabilisation and autopilot provided by GEC Avionics 'fly by light' (computer controlled, optically signalled) control actuation. The latter system, using two MIL-STD-1750A standard computers and a MIL-STD-1553B databus, will provide redundant fail-safe actuation of the movable tail surfaces via fibre-optic signalling, automatic stability and good handling characteristics throughout the flight regime, hands-off autopilot control for cruising, hovering and mooring, and automatic speed control.

A preliminary design review of the ODM programme was due in September 1988.

DIMENSIONS, ENVELOPE:

Length overall	129.54 m (425 ft 0 in)
Max diameter	32.00 m (105 ft 0 in)
Height overall	45.70 m (150 ft 0 in)
Tail fin span	41.60 m (136 ft 6 in)
Volume, gross	70,864 m³ (2,502,540 cu ft)

DIMENSIONS, GONDOLA:

Length	24.60 m (80 ft 8½ in)
Max width	4.80 m (15 ft 9 in)
Max height	7.32 m (24 ft 0 in)
Upper deck floor area	130.0 m² (1,400 sq ft)

PERFORMANCE (estimated):

Max level speed (3 engines)	more than 80 knots (148 km/h; 92 mph)
Operating height range	S/L to 3,050 m (10,000 ft)
Pressure ceiling	4,270 m (14,000 ft)
Max unrefuelled endurance at 40 knots (74 km/h; 46 mph) at 1,525 m (5,000 ft):	
E-2C avionics	61 h 20 min
TPS-63 avionics	77 h 30 min
Mission capability	30 days

CAMERON
CAMERON BALLOONS LTD

St John's Street, Bedminster, Bristol BS3 4NH

Telephone: (0272) 637216

Fax: (0272) 661168

MANAGING DIRECTOR:
D. A. Cameron, BSc (Aero Eng), MIE, MRAeS
SALES DIRECTOR: Philip Dunnington, BA

Cameron began manufacturing hot-air balloons since 1968 and holds CAA, FAA, French CNT and West German Musterzulassungsschein type certificates for its balloons. By January 1988 it had produced some 1,700 balloons at two UK factories (Bristol and Harrogate), plus about 300 more under licence in the USA by its factory at Dexter, Michigan. Output includes more than 70 specially shaped balloons for advertising purposes. In 1986-87 the O-120, N-133, and N-145 new models were introduced to cater for increasing demand for passenger carrying balloons, and in August 1987 the N-850, with a double-deck basket, achieved a new world record of 45 passengers carried in a balloon. Cameron balloons hold all three absolute records for hot-air balloons, including an altitude record of 16,805 m (55,137 ft) set by Julian Nott in an A-375. The company also developed the ULD-1 helium filled pressure balloon for Mr Nott (see 'Endeavour' entry in the 1987-88 *Jane's*), and is making the envelope for the full size *Endeavour*. Cameron's current range of commercial balloons is listed in the tables at the end of this section.

Cameron Balloons Ltd also designs and produces hot-air airships, being the first company to develop a craft of this type. Production hot-air airships now include an improved two/three-seat D-96, the single-seat D-50, and the pressurised DP Skystar series. Helium filled airships are also available: a DG-19 single-seater and DG-25 two-seater.

Cameron DP 60 pressurised hot-air airship for a customer in Luxembourg *(Peter J. Bish)*

CAMERON DP SKYSTAR SERIES

First flown in April 1986, the Skystar prototype (G-BMEZ) was the first of a new generation of pressurised hot-air airships, differing from earlier airships of this kind in utilising a single engine (a 570 cc four-cylinder König

driving a three-blade shrouded pusher propeller) for both propulsion and pressure control. In the event of an engine failure the DP series can be flown unpressurised, and landed like a hot-air balloon. Twin silencers are fitted, to minimise the engine noise level. The DP 50 has a new, specially designed aluminium gondola, and is equipped with an ergonomically designed single-seat cockpit and a unique Cameron self-regulating pressure control system. The larger DP 60 and DP 70 can carry one or two persons.

By 1 January 1988 Cameron had completed, in addition to the DP 50 prototype, one DP 60 and five DP 70s; two more DP 70s were then on order, and customer countries comprised Belgium, Luxembourg, Switzerland, the USA and Venezuela. Figures in the designations indicate envelope volume in thousands of cubic feet. All three models utilise the same gondola, and carry 9 litres (2.4 US gallons; 2 Imp gallons) of petrol/oil and two propane cylinders.

DIMENSIONS, ENVELOPE:
Length overall: DP 50	29.00 m (95 ft 1¾ in)
DP 60	28.00 m (91 ft 10½ in)
Height: DP 60	11.00 m (36 ft 1 in)
Max diameter: DP 60	13.00 m (42 ft 7¾ in)
Volume, gross: DP 50	1,415.8 m³ (50,000 cu ft)
DP 60	1,699.0 m³ (60,000 cu ft)
DP 70	1,982.2 m³ (70,000 cu ft)

WEIGHTS:
Gondola (all models)	195 kg (430 lb)
Envelope: DP 60	146 kg (322 lb)
Max T-O weight: DP 50	452 kg (997 lb)
DP 60, one person	469 kg (1,034 lb)
DP 60, two persons	546 kg (1,204 lb)
DP 70, one person	485 kg (1,069 lb)
DP 70, two persons	562 kg (1,239 lb)

PERFORMANCE:
Max speed: DP 50	19 knots (35 km/h; 22 mph)
DP 60	15 knots (28 km/h; 17 mph)
Endurance: DP 50	1 h 30 min

Cameron DP 70 one/two-person airship for delivery to a Swiss customer

CAMERON D-96

First flight of the prototype D-96 (G-BAMK), the world's first hot-air airship, was made at Wantage, Berkshire, on 7 January 1973. The envelope is made from a light but high strength nylon fabric. A lightweight gondola carries the propane burner, gas supply, pilot and power plant. A pilot and two passengers can be accommodated. Power plant is a 33.5 kW (45 hp) 1,600 cc Volkswagen modified motorcar engine, driving a large-diameter semi-shrouded pusher propeller.

The first production D-96 airship was completed for a customer in the USA. A total of 19 had been completed by 1 January 1988, for customers in Australia, Belgium, Canada, Chile, Colombia, France, Japan, Netherlands, Spain, Sweden and the UK.

DIMENSIONS, ENVELOPE:
Length overall	34.14 m (112 ft 0 in)
Max diameter	13.72 m (45 ft 0 in)
Volume, gross	2,917 m³ (103,000 cu ft)

WEIGHTS:
Envelope	89 kg (196 lb)
Gondola, empty	91 kg (200 lb)
Propane fuel	23.6 kg (52 lb)

PERFORMANCE:
Max speed	13 knots (24 km/h; 15 mph)
Turning radius at 9 knots (16 km/h; 10 mph)	
	30.5 m (100 ft)
Endurance	2 h

CAMERON D-38

The prototype D-38 flew for the first time on 25 September 1980, and was followed by three production examples by early 1985. A description and illustration can be found in the 1987-88 *Jane's*.

CAMERON D-50

Early testing showed that the single-seat D-38 hot-air airship was too small for use in high-altitude/high-temperature locations, so Cameron developed the larger single-seat D-50. It introduced also a revised form of tail unit, shown in the accompanying illustration, which is now applied to Cameron hot-air airships of all sizes. First flight was made on 2 September 1981, and 14 D-50s had been completed by 1 January 1988.

DIMENSIONS, ENVELOPE:
Length overall	25.00 m (82 ft 0¼ in)
Height, incl gondola	16.80 m (55 ft 1½ in)

Spanish registered Cameron D-50 hot-air airship

Max diameter	10.90 m (35 ft 9 in)
Volume, gross	1,416 m³ (50,000 cu ft)

DIMENSIONS, GONDOLA:
Length	1.65 m (5 ft 5 in)
Propeller diameter	1.32 m (4 ft 4 in)

WEIGHTS:
Envelope	105 kg (231 lb)
Gondola, empty	91 kg (200 lb)
Propane fuel	23.6 kg (52 lb)

PERFORMANCE:
Not available

CAMERON HELIUM FILLED AIRSHIPS

Tests of the two-man helium filled **DG-19** prototype (G-BKIK) during the Summer of 1983 convinced Cameron Balloons that the design offered a new formula for a 'minimum' low-cost airship.

Two DG-19s have been built, plus one example of the 708 m³ (25,000 cu ft) **DG-25**. Data for the DG-19 were given in the 1986-87 *Jane's*, and dimensions of the DG-25 in the 1987-88 edition. Weights and performance data are not available.

THUNDER & COLT
THUNDER & COLT LTD

Maesbury Road, Oswestry, Shropshire SY10 8HA
Telephone: (0691) 652216
Telex: 35503 COLT G
Fax: (0691) 656540
MANAGING DIRECTOR: Per Lindstrand
TECHNICAL DIRECTOR: Mark Broome
SALES AND MARKETING DIRECTOR: Chris Kirby

In addition to its current range of hot-air and helium airships described in this entry, Thunder & Colt was constructing in 1988 the envelope of the Wren ANR airship described under the Advanced Airship Corporation heading in this section. Thunder & Colt also manufactures an extensive range of hot-air balloons (see details in tables at the end of this section), of which the 300A is currently the

world's largest passenger-carrying balloon for regular operation. Current output totals more than 200 hot-air balloons and airships per year, of which over 80 per cent are exported. The 1987 *Virgin Atlantic Flyer*, at 60,315 m³ (2.13 million cu ft) the largest hot-air balloon ever manufactured, was described in the 1987-88 *Jane's*. In a new 16,990 m³ (600,000 cu ft) high altitude balloon named *Stratoquest* the company's managing director, Mr Per Lindstrand reached approx 19,812 m (65,000 ft) after take-off from Laredo, Texas, on 1 June 1988, and has submitted this for ratification as a new world altitude record.

COLT AS 76

The AS 76 is Thunder & Colt's largest hot-air airship at present in production. It is a new design that draws on the experience from the previous twin-crew hot-air airships, the

AS 80, AS 90, (1985-86 *Jane's*) and AS 105 (1987-88 edition), in its design. By changing the power plant to a lighter unit and incorporating a more sophisticated envelope pressurisation system, it has been possible to lower the all-up weight of the gondola which, in turn, has meant a decrease in envelope volume. These changes have made ground handling easier and reduced pilot workload.

The envelope of the AS 76 is manufactured in HTN90K high-tenacity and high temperature resistant fabric. It has a fineness ratio of 2.5, and four inflated fins in a cruciform configuration. Steering is by a single rudder on the bottom fin, operated by ropes connecting it to the gondola. The twin catenary load suspension system distributes the loads of gondola weight and power plant forces evenly into the gondola. The gondola is a stainless steel tubular spaceframe with tricycle landing gear; pilot and passenger sit in tandem.

If operated in single-seat configuration, the passenger seat is exchanged for an extra fuel tank. The windscreen is made from polycarbonate sheet, and is fastened into a composite sheet construction forming a partially enclosed cockpit.

The power plant is a 38.8 kW (52 hp) Rotax 462 watercooled engine driving a pusher propeller. The engine also drives a generator supplying an electric pressurising fan used to pressurise the envelope. Additional air for pressurisation of the envelope is taken from a scoop situated in the propeller slipstream. The burners are situated inside the envelope and operated electrically with a manual override. Pilot lights are fitted with electric spark ignition and are specially modified to operate directly underneath the inflating fan without blowing out. Standard instrumentation comprises an altimeter, variometer, envelope temperature and pressure gauges, propane volume gauge, petrol level gauge, voltmeter, engine CHT and water temperature and engine rpm gauge. A 720-channel VHF com transceiver option, with pilot-passenger intercom, is available.

DIMENSIONS, ENVELOPE:	
Length overall	31.00 m (101 ft 8½ in)
Max diameter	12.40 m (40 ft 8¼ in)
Volume	2,123.8 m³ (75,000 cu ft)
DIMENSIONS, GONDOLA:	
Length overall	4.00 m (13 ft 1½ in)
Max width	1.60 m (5 ft 3 in)
Height overall	1.80 m (5 ft 11 in)
WEIGHTS:	
Envelope	190 kg (419 lb)
Gondola, empty	160 kg (353 lb)
Gross lift	600 kg (1,323 lb)
PERFORMANCE:	
Max level speed	20 knots (37 km/h; 23 mph)
Max endurance	3 h

Colt AS 56 single-place thermal airship

COLT AS 56

The AS 56 is the one-man hot-air airship available from Thunder & Colt. Construction largely follows the same lines as that of AS 76, with a stainless steel tubular spaceframe and tricycle landing gear. The envelope is also of similar construction, with twin catenary curtains and cruciform tail surfaces. The power plant is an 18 kW (24 hp) König SC430 engine driving a pusher propeller.

Recently, the AS 56 envelope pressurisation system has been modified, and now incorporates a similar system to that used in the AS 76, with electric fan and automatic pressure relief system.

DIMENSIONS, ENVELOPE:	
Length overall	28.00 m (91 ft 10½ in)
Max diameter	11.20 m (36 ft 9 in)
Volume	1,585.75 m³ (56,000 cu ft)
DIMENSIONS, GONDOLA:	
Length overall	2.75 m (9 ft 0¼ in)
Max width	1.40 m (4 ft 7 in)
Height overall	1.50 m (4 ft 11 in)
WEIGHTS:	
Envelope	120 kg (265 lb)
Gondola	100 kg (220 lb)
Max T-O weight	365 kg (805 lb)
PERFORMANCE:	
Max level speed	20 knots (37 km/h; 23 mph)
Max endurance	3 h

COLT GA 42

This helium filled dirigible is a project in which Thunder & Colt co-operates with its sister company Airborne Industries of Southend on Sea. Thunder & Colt undertook design and production of the gondola and design of the envelope; Airborne Industries was responsible for envelope manufacture.

The GA 42 has twin ballonets, a gross lift of 980 kg (2,160 lb), and features rigid control surfaces. The aluminium monocoque gondola offers fully enclosed accommodation

Prototype (G-MATS) of the new GA 42 helium airship, which first flew in September 1987

for two crew. The power plant is a 74.5 kW (100 hp) Teledyne Continental O-200-B engine driving a pusher propeller. The design is to be certificated to BCAR CAP 471 Section Q in the Aerial Work category. The prototype (G-MATS) made its first flight on 2 September 1987. Three further GA 42s were due to be completed by the Spring of 1988. These have a slightly modified fin assembly compared with the prototype.

DIMENSIONS, ENVELOPE:	
Length	27.50 m (90 ft 2¾ in)
Max diameter	9.20 m (30 ft 2¼ in)
Volume	1,200 m³ (42,377 cu ft)
WEIGHT:	
Gross lift	980 kg (2,160 lb)
PERFORMANCE (estimated):	
Max level speed	35 knots (65 km/h; 40 mph)

WREN — *See Advanced Airship*

UNITED STATES OF AMERICA

AEROLIFT
AEROLIFT INC
4105 Blimp Boulevard, Tillamook, Oregon 97141-9694

Telephone: (503) 842 8891

PRESIDENT AND CHIEF EXECUTIVE OFFICER:
W. Larry Mahaffey

VICE-PRESIDENT, ENGINEERING:
Wilfred J. Eggington

EXECUTIVE ASSISTANT TO THE PRESIDENT: Mary Priss

AeroLift was founded in 1980, and merged on 6 March 1984 with the gas and oil properties company Western Adera Ltd. Its operations are based in a Second World War airship hangar at Tillamook, Oregon, which is one of the world's largest timber structures. Originally funded by five major Canadian logging companies, it is now publicly owned and is licensed under exclusive patents to develop a

hybrid (aerostatic/aerodynamic) heavy lift vehicle known as the Cyclo-Crane.

AEROLIFT CYCLO-CRANE
The Cyclo-Crane introduced a new concept for a lighter than air craft, combining fixed-wing and rotating-wing techniques. As can be seen in the accompanying illustrations, it has a helium filled centrebody resembling the envelope of a conventional airship. Structure within the envelope supports four external aerofoil surfaces, known as blades. These are attached at 90° intervals around its circumference, which enables them to rotate and so vary their angle of attack in relation to airflow past the vehicle. An articulated symmetrical wing surface is mounted in T form at the outer end of each blade. On the outer side of each of two opposing wings is a pylon mounted pod containing a 112 kW (150 hp) Textron Lycoming AEIO-320 engine, driving a four-blade tractor propeller.

The entire centrebody rotates at a max 13 rpm about a shaft which passes longitudinally through its axis. This rotation allows an airflow over the wings of 52 knots (96 km/h; 60 mph), creating the required lift necessary for manoeuvring. At the forward end of the shaft is a cylindrical housing for control equipment; at the rear are stabilising surfaces in the form of a multi-faceted annular structure. A pilot's cabin is suspended by cables attached at each end to outer race bearings on the central shaft. The load to be airlifted is slung on cables beneath this cabin.

The structure is so designed that the net aerostatic lift of the helium is equal to the sum of all structural weight, fuel, crew, and 50 per cent of the intended sling load. The balance of lift for the sling load, and thrust for control and translation, are created by the external aerofoils.

When the Cyclo-Crane is in a hover mode *(Fig. a)*, the wings are positioned parallel to the shaft on which the centrebody rotates, providing lift via cyclic control enabling

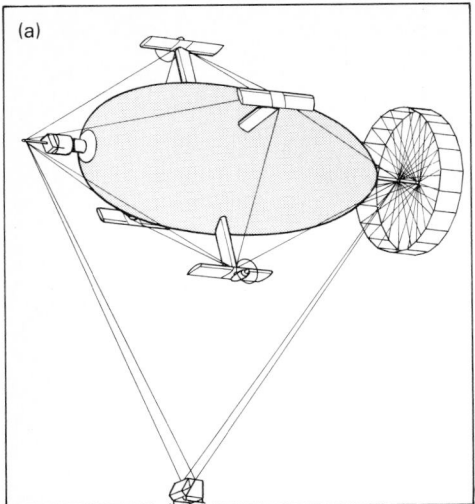
(a)

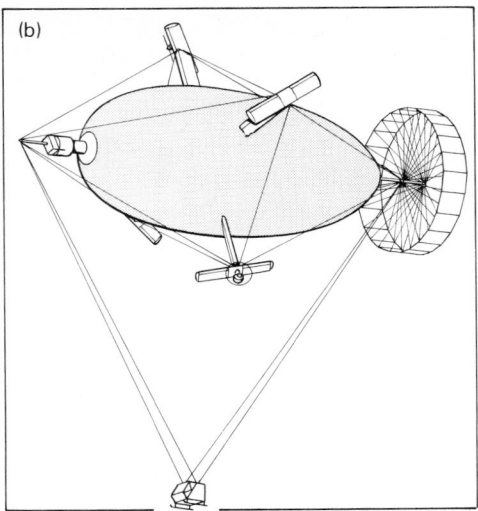
(b)

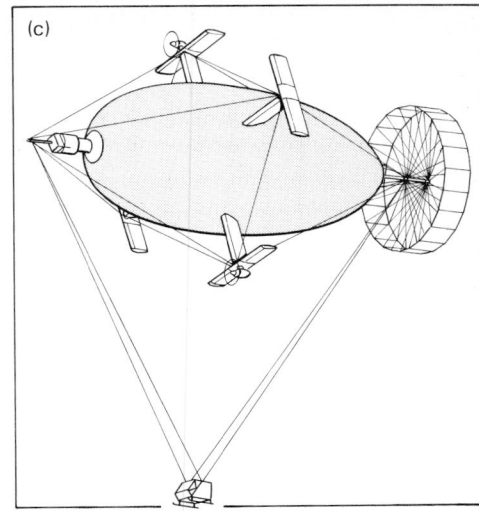
(c)

Figure a: **Cyclo-Crane in hover mode, with wings parallel to the horizontal axis of rotation. For forward (or reverse) movement, the blade aerofoils are used to generate forces in line with the horizontal axis by turning the entire wing/blade assemblies.** *Figure b:* **The wing/blade assemblies continue to turn as the Cyclo-Crane accelerates.** *Figure c:* **At maximum forward speed, aerofoils and engines are all aligned directly with the direction of flight, and the centrebody**

the Cyclo-Crane to ascend and descend vertically as well as laterally. The blade aerofoils have both cyclic and collective control systems. The cyclic system allows the aircraft to pitch and yaw; the collective system allows it to move short distances forward and backward. The wing and blade control systems, while rotating, allow the Cyclo-Crane to maintain a position over the ground or over a load. Non-rotating forward flight is accomplished by turning the entire wing/blade assemblies. The wing/blade assemblies continue to turn as the vehicle accelerates *(Fig. b)*. When optimum forward speed is reached, all aerofoil surfaces and engines are aligned with the direction of flight *(Fig. c)* and the centrebody ceases to rotate. Cruising speed is expected to be similar to that of a helicopter hauling a comparable external load.

The proof-of-concept vehicle has a two-ton sling load capacity. Unmanned testing in its current modified form began in August 1984, followed by initial manned test flights starting on 23 October 1984. Flight testing has ended, and data and dynamic computer model analysis have verified earlier Princeton University studies indicating that a Cyclo-Crane should offer controllability equal to that of a helicopter of similar external lift capacity under gust and direct side wind conditions. It can be mast moored and can be designed to float hundreds of feet above the ground on a single line tether. When major storms are predicted, standard aircraft procedures would be followed and the vehicle flown out of the area of danger. The eventual full scale version is intended primarily for logging use worldwide, and its preliminary development was partially supported by the US Forest Service and the Defense Advanced Research Projects Agency (DARPA). It is, however, suitable for other ultra-heavy vertical lift applications where precision lifting and placement of heavy and outsize cargo are required. Commercial use of Cyclo-Cranes, initially on Vancouver Island, is expected to start in the 1990s, as soon as larger capacity vehicles have been built and certificated. Each of these is likely to have a sling load capacity of 16 tons; but AeroLift emphasises that the Cyclo-Rotor concept is valid for sling loads of up to at least 100 tons.

In 1987 AeroLift developed, under contract to the US Army Aviation Systems Command, a preliminary design of a 31.75-40.8 tonne (35-45 US ton) heavy lift Cyclo-Crane for over-the-shore logistics and other missions. A contract for further work towards the development of a production prototype was anticipated in 1988. In addition, AeroLift conducted an evaluation of the application of Cyclo-Crane technology to high endurance surveillance platforms, as part of the US Strategic Defense Initiative programme during 1987. A contract for further work to develop Cyclo-Crane surveillance platforms was also expected in 1988.

The following data apply to the present proof-of-concept Cyclo-Crane:

DIMENSIONS:
Length overall	54.25 m (178 ft 0 in)
Height overall, top centre engine nacelle to payload hook	77.73 m (255 ft 0 in)
Aerostat diameter (max)	20.73 m (68 ft 0 in)
Aerostat length	41.45 m (136 ft 0 in)
Helium volume (nominal)	9,345 m³ (330,000 cu ft)

WEIGHTS (design):
Operating weight empty (buoyant)	680 kg (1,500 lb)
Max gross weight (allowing for combined aerostatic and aerodynamic lift)	1,451 kg (3,200 lb)

Cyclo-Crane proof-of-concept prototype

AEROTEK
AEROTEK CORPORATION
Blimp Boulevard, Tillamook, Oregon 97141

Originally known as Grace Aircraft Corporation, and later (1985) as US Airship Corporation, this company began designing its first commercial airship in January 1983, and its Eugene engineering facility became operational by the end of that year. Major components of the USA 100 prototype were built at Eugene; final assembly took place in the former US Navy airship hangars at Tillamook, Oregon.

AEROTEK USA 100
The USA 100 (previously designated GAC-20) is intended for commercial advertising, and as a testbed for further engineering and development of airships and airship systems. It is designed and built in accordance with new FAA airworthiness standards for airships, in the definition of which the company has been actively involved. First flight was made on 28 October 1987. The airship was slightly damaged in its hangar after completing 52 hours flying, but has since been repaired.

HULL: Non-rigid envelope of ellipsoidal configuration, made of polyurethane coated Dacron with a non-woven material laminated on the inside for bias stability. Seams are heat-sealed inside and out. Nose is stiffened by 16 battens to permit higher airspeeds and distribute mooring loads. Weight of gondola is supported by cables attached to four internal catenary curtains which hang from upper quarter of envelope over half of its length. Side loads and thrust from car are transmitted to envelope via the car catenary, a fabric doubler extending away from car perimeter in all directions to ensure uniform load distribution to envelope. Two air-filled ballonets within

Model of the Aerotek USA 100

helium compartment, to compensate for variations in hull pressure and adjust in-flight trim, are made of heat sealed urethane coated nylon. Air is supplied to ballonets via ram air duct aft of propeller, with mechanically controlled valves to duct air to front or rear ballonet as required. A passive pressure relief valve is fitted to each ballonet and in the helium compartment to control and prevent accidental envelope overpressure. Manual cable control permits controlled venting of helium or air if required. Inverted Y tail unit, comprising three identical aluminium fins, covered with doped fabric; each fin is attached to envelope with 13 fan patches at its base and supported by three guy wires on each side.

GONDOLA: Control car is shaped as an ellipsoidal hyperbola with a circular end section, and has an exterior shell of glassfibre epoxy sandwich construction with a foam core, over a welded steel tube frame. Windows of Plexiglas. The cabin seats eight persons, including the crew, in pairs, and is separated acoustically from the engine compartment at the rear; it is heated (by exhaust heat exchanger) and ventilated. The single-wheel landing gear is of trailing link type, pivoting about a vertical axis.

POWER PLANT: One 224 kW (300 hp) Textron Lycoming IO-540-K1A5 flat-six engine, mounted aft of control car on a 4130 steel tube frame and driving a Hartzell HC-3YR-7LF three-blade constant-speed reversible-pitch pusher propeller within an annular duct. Fuel tanks at rear of car, combined capacity 439 litres (116 US gallons; 96.6 Imp gallons).

SYSTEMS: Electrical system is a standard light aircraft 28V 70A negative ground type, powered by an engine driven alternator. While moored, onboard system is powered by a ground based generator for automatic monitoring and control of envelope pressurisation. Flight control is cable driven and hydraulically boosted, using a conventional stick with pushrods in combination with an adjustable friction damper, hydraulic boost system and mechanical mixer for the tail surfaces. System can be flown manually in the event of hydraulic failure.

AVIONICS AND EQUIPMENT: Avionics include dual nav/com radios with VOR/ILS, Loran, ADF, transponder, marker beacon receivers, and optional autopilot. Standard instrumentation includes ASI, VSI, attitude indicator, barometric and radar altimeters, turn co-ordinator, directional gyro, magnetic compass, engine and fuel system instruments, inside and outside air temperature gauges, ballonet and helium envelope manometers, hydraulic system temperature and pressure gauges, and clock.

DIMENSIONS, OVERALL:

Length	48.77 m (160 ft 0 in)
Width	12.80 m (42 ft 0 in)
Height	17.37 m (57 ft 0 in)
Envelope volume	3,908 m³ (138,000 cu ft)

DIMENSIONS, GONDOLA:
External:

Length: incl power plant	6.55 m (21 ft 6 in)
excl power plant	approx 5.79 m (19 ft 0 in)
Max width	approx 1.83 m (6 ft 0 in)
Max height	approx 2.74 m (9 ft 0 in)

Internal (cabin):

Length	4.07 m (13 ft 4¼ in)
Max width: at floor	1.65 m (5 ft 4¾ in)
at ceiling	1.77 m (5 ft 9½ in)
Max height	1.93 m (6 ft 4 in)

WEIGHTS:

Control car, empty	approx 907 kg (2,000 lb)
Max fuel	239 kg (528 lb)
Gross weight	4,048 kg (8,925 lb)

PERFORMANCE (estimated):

Max cruising speed	39 knots (72 km/h; 45 mph)

With max fuel, cruising at 25 knots (46 km/h; 29 mph):

Range	400 nm (741 km; 460 miles)
Endurance	17 h

BOLAND

BOLAND BALLOON

Pine Drive, RFD 2, Burlington, Connecticut 06013
Telephone: (203) 673 1307
PROPRIETOR: Brian J. Boland

Mr Brian Boland has designed and built 45 hot-air balloons (see tables at the end of this section), as well as a hot-air airship named *Albatross*. A description of *Albatross* can be found in the 1985-86 and earlier editions of *Jane's*. Manufacture of a second airship, named *Rover*, began in early 1982.

BOLAND A-2 ROVER

Work to manufacture the envelope of *Rover* began in early 1982. It consists of 10 gores and 311 panels, is fabricated from 1.4 oz polyurethane coated ripstop nylon for the main body, with similar material of 1.0 to 1.4 oz for the nose and tail sections. The deflation system consists of a mechanically safety-locked panel of Velcro, approx 6.10 m (20 ft) wide and 7.92 m (26 ft) long, that can be peeled back to create a rectangular opening on top of the envelope. There are four pressurised inflatable fins at the rear in a cruciform arrangement, with a single 10.97 m (36 ft) tall inflatable rudder running the full height of the vertical pair. The envelope was first inflated outdoors, at Farmington, Connecticut, on 24 November 1985 and made its first free flight on 8 September 1986.

The gondola, which was being built in the Spring of 1987, carries a crew of two seated side by side, and is suspended from exterior load tapes. It is hoped to use the 30 kW (40 hp) Rockwell JLO engine from the A-1 *Albatross* eventually, with a 0.91 m (3 ft 0 in) diameter propeller, but *Rover* will probably be powered initially by a lighter-weight 15 kW (20 hp) Xenoah with belt reduction drive to a slower-turning 1.22 m (4 ft 0 in) propeller. Fuel will consist of 151.4 litres (40 US gallons; 33.3 Imp gallons) of liquid propane gas, contained in one 75.7 litre (20 US gallon; 16.6 Imp gallon) stainless steel tank and two 37.9 litre (10 US gallon; 8.3 Imp

Envelope of the Boland A-2 hot-air airship *Rover*

gallon) aluminium cylinders. The two smaller cylinders can be replaced easily with full cylinders from a 'chase' vehicle for flights of longer duration.

DIMENSIONS, ENVELOPE:

Length	30.48 m (100 ft 0 in)
Volume	2,265 m³ (80,000 cu ft)

WEIGHTS (estimated):

Weight empty (excl fuel)	204 kg (450 lb)
Operating weight empty	363 kg (800 lb)
Max T-O weight	590 kg (1,300 lb)
Max theoretical gross weight	726 kg (1,600 lb)

PERFORMANCE (estimated, with 151.4 litres; 40 US gallons; 33.3 Imp gallons of propane):

Range	17.5 nm (32.2 km; 20 miles)
Endurance	2 h

GOODYEAR

THE GOODYEAR TIRE & RUBBER COMPANY

1144 East Market Street, Akron, Ohio 44316-0001
Telephone: (216) 796 2995
Telex: 640550
MANAGER, AIRSHIP PUBLIC RELATIONS: Richard F. Sailer

During the past 76 years Goodyear has built over 310 airships, more than any other company in the world. Of these, over 250 were constructed under contract for the US Army and Navy.

In March 1987 Goodyear's aircraft and aerospace subsidiary for more than 60 years, Goodyear Aerospace Corporation, was sold to Loral Corporation, and continues to operate as Loral Systems Group. It is expected to continue providing airship manufacturing services and support to the Goodyear airship programme. Loral also

continues development of the new Goodyear GZ-22 airship.

Goodyear currently operates three GZ-20A non-rigid airships in the USA for public relations and sales promotion activities: *America* (N3A), *Columbia* (N10A) and *Enterprise* (N1A). Details of the most recently constructed *Columbia* were given in the 1987-88 *Jane's*. In size, equipment and performance it is generally the same as the two other airships in the fleet.

GOODYEAR GZ-22

This new airship, which flew for the first time on 9 October 1987, has a conventional envelope of typical Goodyear construction (a sandwich of Neoprene between two layers of rubber coated polyester fabric), with tail fins set in an X configuration. It is powered by two 313 kW (420 shp) Allison 250-B17C turboprops, each driving a three-blade Hartzell propeller turning within an annular

duct which can be swivelled to vector the thrust. The gondola, built by Advanced Technology and Research Inc of Clearwater, Florida, is of composite construction, with AFRP honeycomb and fabric covering over a steel frame. It has dual controls for one or two pilots, and the airship has an electronic fly by wire control system with a mechanical backup.

The GZ-22, registered N4A and named *Spirit of Akron*, is larger than the current Goodyear airships, and the first to be powered by turbine engines. Vectoring of the ducted fans provides more precise control during very slow speed and ground handling manoeuvres. The cabin is larger, with larger windows, and seats nine passengers; an improved night sign, with truer colours and greater resolution, is mounted on the envelope and is made up of 8,064 lamps. After certification the GZ-22 is to be based at Pompano Beach (Florida).

DIMENSIONS, ENVELOPE:

Length overall	62.64 m (205 ft 6 in)
Height	18.34 m (60 ft 2 in)
Max diameter	14.33 m (47 ft 0 in)
Volume (helium)	7,017 m³ (247,800 cu ft)

DIMENSIONS, GONDOLA:

Length	9.75 m (32 ft 0 in)
Max width	2.44 m (8 ft 0 in)
Max depth	2.44 m (8 ft 0 in)
Propeller diameter	2.08 m (6 ft 10 in)

WEIGHTS:

Gondola	181.5 kg (400 lb)
Max payload	998 kg (2,200 lb)
Useful load	1,996 kg (4,400 lb)
Max gross weight	6,804 kg (15,000 lb)

PERFORMANCE (estimated):

Max speed	56 knots (105 km/h; 65 mph)
Normal cruising speed	30-35 knots (56-64 km/h; 35-40 mph)
Operating altitude	305-915 m (1,000-3,000 ft)
Pressure ceiling	3,050 m (10,000 ft)

Model of the Goodyear Aerospace Corporation GZ-22, first flown in October 1987

MEMPHIS
MEMPHIS AIRSHIPS INC
Isle-A-Port Airport, 1720 Harbor, PO Box 13114, Memphis, Tennessee 38113

Memphis Airships was formed in 1981 as a producer of small unmanned advertising airships and fan supported inflatables. From 1982 it was involved with the research and development of a small air recreation vehicle known as the Ultrablimp, designed by Mr Steve Garner. Details and a photograph of the one-off Dreamfinder non-rigid single-place airship appeared in the 1986-87 *Jane's*.

A prototype of the Ultrablimp was flown at the 1985 Sun 'n Fun and Oshkosh meetings, and was described and illustrated in the 1987-88 *Jane's*. No details of the company's activities have been received since early 1986, although a new EXP-11 two-seat advertising airship was reported in mid-1988.

PIASECKI
PIASECKI AIRCRAFT CORPORATION
2nd Street West, Essington, Pennsylvania 19029
Telephone: (215) 521 5700
PRESIDENT: Frank N. Piasecki
VICE-PRESIDENT, ENGINEERING: Donald N. Meyers

Details of this company's Model 16H-3 Pathfinder compound helicopter programme can be found in the main Aircraft section. Latest news follows here of the Heli-Stat Concept.

PIASECKI HELI-STAT
A Heli-Stat is a hybrid VTOL vehicle which links the envelope of a lighter than air craft with a helicopter type power system. The aerostat provides static lift to support approximately the full empty weight of the entire assembly. Rotors furnish the lift to support the payload, as well as providing propulsion and control.

Details of an early Heli-Stat project can be found in the 1977-78 *Jane's*; a full description and photographs of the logging demonstrator **Model 97-34J** were published in the 1986-87 edition. This craft was destroyed on 1 July 1986 after about 15 successful untethered flights. It was accelerating along the ground when all four landing gear assemblies began to shimmy, causing the rotors to oscillate in resonance and leading all four SH-34J helicopter 'modules' to tear free from the fuselage frame structure, resulting in the death of one occupant of the port forward helicopter.

Artist's impression of the Piasecki Heli-Stat II

Current activity is focused on a proposed **Heli-Stat II** which would employ a rigid-envelope buoyancy lift aerostat with compartmented construction, thrust being provided by four six-blade 'tiltable thrusters', each of 24.1 m (79 ft) diameter.

THOMPSON
JAMES THOMPSON, AIAA
1700 Citizens Plaza, Louisville, Kentucky 40202
Telephone: (502) 589 0130
Telex: 204335

THOMPSON AIRSHIP
Progress with this small, two-person sport and advertising airship was continuing in 1988, and completion and first flight were expected by the end of the year.

The airship has a helium filled envelope, inside which are two 56.6 m³ (2,000 cu ft) capacity air ballonets that will be filled unequally to provide pitch trim. The tail unit is a fabric covered aluminium tube inverted Y structure (all three angles 120°), the elevators of which operate differentially to control rolling moment. There are no catenary curtains: cables attached to five finger patches on each side of the envelope suspend the gondola slightly forward of the centre of buoyancy, to compensate for pitch-up. The gondola itself has a steel tube frame, with glassfibre and urethane foam skin panels, and accommodates the crew, power plant and two water ballast tanks. Propulsion is provided by a 1,200 cc Honda liquid-cooled engine, with 2.2:1 toothed-belt reduction drive to a two-blade shrouded wooden pusher propeller. The gondola is stabilised by three cables attached to the propeller shroud.

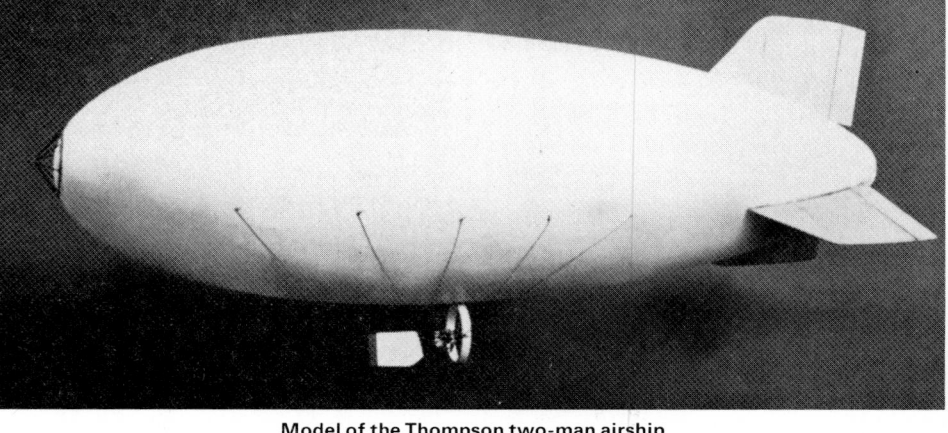

Model of the Thompson two-man airship

DIMENSIONS, ENVELOPE:

Length overall	24.91 m (81 ft 9 in)		
Max diameter	7.91 m (25 ft 11¼ in)		
Volume: helium	695.0 m³ (24,544 cu ft)		
ballonets	97.9 m³ (3,456 cu ft)	Gondola	187 kg (412 lb)
design total	792.9 m³ (28,000 cu ft)	Water ballast	81.5 kg (180 lb)
Fineness ratio	3.15	Max T-O weight	696 kg (1,534 lb)
WEIGHTS:		PERFORMANCE (estimated):	
Envelope	244 kg (538 lb)	Design speed	30 knots (55 km/h; 34 mph)

ULITA
ULITA INDUSTRIES INC (Manufacturing Division)
PO Box 412, Sheboygan, Wisconsin 53082-0412
Telephone: (414) 458 2842
PRESIDENT AND TECHNICAL ADVISER: Thomas S. Berger
VICE-PRESIDENT, MARKETING: Mark R. Forss

Ulita has three current light utility airship programmes: the UM20 and UM10, of which prototypes are under construction, and the UM30, which is in the design stage.

ULITA UM10
Optimised for the ARV (air recreational vehicle) category, the UM10 was conceived and designed by Mr T. S. Berger, President and Technical Adviser of Ulita Industries Inc. It is intended as a low-cost light utility airship, and will be Ulita's initial lighter than air product. It is hoped that it will appeal to a broad range of markets that larger contemporary airships cannot satisfy.

Prototype construction of the control car was continuing in Spring 1988. Envelope construction was due to begin later that year, and completion of the airship was expected by the end of 1988.

ENVELOPE: Non-rigid helium filled hull, of identical design to UM20 but with only one ballonet. Tail unit is of inverted U configuration, with vertical fin and rudder at end of each U leg and a central tailplane and elevator spanning gap between fins. One landing wheel at base of each fin.
GONDOLA: Generally similar in configuration to UM20, with side by side seats for pilot and one passenger. Two landing wheels, mounted on outriggers. Accommodation ventilated, but not heated.
POWER PLANT: Two 18 kW (24 hp) König SC430 three-cylinder two-stroke engines, each driving a 1.07 m (3 ft 6 in) diameter three-blade fixed-pitch ducted propeller, mounted on an outrigger from gondola and capable of rotation to provide horizontal or vertical thrust. Fuel tank on each outrigger, combined capacity 38 litres (10 US gallons; 8.3 Imp gallons).
ELECTRICAL SYSTEM: As for UM20.

DIMENSIONS, OVERALL:

Length	23.93 m (78 ft 6 in)
Width	7.10 m (23 ft 3.4 in)
Height	8.72 m (28 ft 7.3 in)

DIMENSIONS, ENVELOPE:

Length	23.47 m (77 ft 0 in)
Max diameter	6.52 m (21 ft 4.7 in)
Volume: ballonet	117.3 m³ (4,141 cu ft)
total	547.4 m³ (19,331 cu ft)

DIMENSIONS, GONDOLA:

Length	3.12 m (10 ft 3 in)
Max width (excl propulsors)	1.32 m (4 ft 4 in)
Max height (incl landing gear)	2.13 m (7 ft 0 in)

WEIGHTS:

Weight empty	340.5 kg (751 lb)
Fuel (standard)	27 kg (60 lb)
Total gross lift	549 kg (1,211 lb)

PERFORMANCE (estimated):

Max level speed	42 knots (78 km/h; 48 mph)
Max cruising speed	26 knots (48 km/h; 30 mph)
Pressure ceiling	2,440 m (8,000 ft)

ULITA UM20
Details of the UM20 (formerly LUA-1) were released in 1981, and a prototype has been partially completed. The control car was 90 per cent complete in Spring 1988, with the envelope and tail unit still to be built. Work will be resumed in 1989. After flight testing and certification, it is intended to use the prototype for aerial advertising within the USA, with production UM20s being leased for similar work or training by the company's Airship Operations Division.

ENVELOPE: Non-rigid helium filled airship, with two ballonets. Tail unit, of inverted Y configuration, is a riveted aluminium truss structure with lightweight fabric covering. Trim tab on rudder and each elevator.
GONDOLA: Primary structure is a welded 4130 steel tube truss, with a skin of light gauge aluminium sheet riveted to aluminium angle and channel. It is fitted with a single non-retractable landing gear unit, carrying twin fully

castoring and bungee sprung wheels of 9.6 in diameter, and has side by side seats for a pilot and one passenger. Storage space behind seats. Forward opening door on each side. Accommodation is heated and ventilated.

POWER PLANT: One 85.75 kW (115 hp) Textron Lycoming O-235-1E flat-four engine, driving a two-blade reversible-pitch pusher propeller. Single 98 litre (26 US gallon; 21.6 Imp gallon) fuel tank standard; 76 litre (20 US gallon; 16.6 Imp gallon) auxiliary tank optional.

ELECTRICAL SYSTEM: 12V DC battery and alternator.

DIMENSIONS, OVERALL:

Length	35.73 m (117 ft 2.9 in)
Width	11.09 m (36 ft 4.4 in)
Height	14.41 m (47 ft 3.4 in)

DIMENSIONS, ENVELOPE:

Length	35.05 m (115 ft 0 in)
Max diameter	9.74 m (31 ft 11.3 in)
Volume: ballonets (two)	510.6 m³ (18,033 cu ft)
total	1,823.7 m³ (64,404 cu ft)

DIMENSIONS, GONDOLA:

Length	4.20 m (13 ft 9½ in)
Max width	1.07 m (3 ft 6 in)
Max height	2.01 m (6 ft 7¼ in)
Volume	2.41 m³ (85 cu ft)

WEIGHTS (estimated):

Weight empty	1,088 kg (2,400 lb)
Fuel (standard)	72.5 kg (160 lb)
Payload	272 kg (600 lb)
Total gross lift	1,510 kg (3,330 lb)

PERFORMANCE (estimated):

Max level speed	43 knots (80 km/h; 50 mph)
Max cruising speed	26 knots (48 km/h; 30 mph)
Pressure ceiling	3,350 m (11,000 ft)

Model of the Ulita UM10 air recreation vehicle airship

ULITA UM30

Still in the design stage, the UM30 (originally LUA-2) is a 'second-generation' vehicle intended to offer greater payload capacity and in-flight endurance than the UM20, opening up the market to such applications as harbour patrol, rescue/casevac and short-range maritime surveillance. Features will include vectored thrust propulsion, tricycle landing gear for improved ground handling, gondola accommodation for a pilot and three passengers, composite construction, and a fly by light control system with automated flight control capabilities.

Construction is not anticipated in the near future, and a detailed description is therefore inappropriate, but general parameters include a 41.45 m (136 ft) long envelope with a volume of 2,022 m³ (71,413 cu ft), empty weight of 1,386 kg (3,055 lb), power plant of one 149 kW (200 hp) Textron Lycoming IO-360 engine driving twin ducted fans, max cruising speed of 48 knots (90 km/h; 56 mph), pressure ceiling of 2,135 m (7,000 ft) and a max endurance with auxiliary fuel of 12 hours.

WAI
WESTINGHOUSE-AIRSHIP INDUSTRIES INC

PO Box 17193, Baltimore, Maryland 21203, USA
Telephone: (301) 379 2303
Fax: (301) 379 2310
PRESIDENT: Edward J. Hogan Jr
EXECUTIVE DIRECTOR: J. W. Phipps
EXECUTIVE ASSISTANT: Louis L. Foltzer III

ARLINGTON OFFICE:
Telephone: (703) 685 7908
Fax: (703) 685 7928

SENTINEL 5000

As recorded under the US Navy entry in the 1986-87 *Jane's*, a Naval Airship Program (NAP) was initiated by Naval Air Systems Command in 1985 to investigate the suitability of airships in the AEW role. A request for proposals, issued in August 1986, was followed in June 1987 by the award of a contract to WAI selecting the Sentinel 5000 as the basis for an operational development model (ODM) airship. A description and illustrations of the Sentinel 5000 can be found under the Airship Industries heading in the UK part of this section.

LIGHTER THAN AIR: BALLOONS

CONTRACTORS' ADDRESSES:

Country	Company	Address	Telephone/Telex/Fax
Australia	Kavanagh Balloons Pty Ltd	13/10 Pioneer Avenue, Thornleigh, NSW 2120	Tel: (02) 484 3193
Czechoslovakia	Aerotechnik	Letiste Kunovice, 68604 Uherské Hradiště	Tel: 5510 and 5511 Telex: 60380
France	Ballons Chaize	48 rue Balay, 42000 Saint-Étienne	Tel: (77) 33 43 76
Germany (Federal Republic)	Ballonfabrik See- und Luftausrüstung GmbH & Co KG	Postfach 101327, Austrasse 35, 8900 Augsburg 1	Tel: (0821) 41 50 41 Telex: 17/821810
Hungary	MÉM Repülőgépes Szolgálat	PO Box 56, Koérberki út 36, H 1112 Budapest XI	Tel: 851 344 Telex: 22-5187
Italy	Paolo Letterio Bonanno	Via Volo 3/A, 12036 Revello (CN)	Tel: (0175) 75666 Fax: (0175) 759313
South Africa	Flamboyant Balloons (Pty) Ltd	PO Box 149, Lanseria 1748, Transvaal	Tel: (011) 659 1370
United Kingdom	Cameron Balloons Ltd	St John's Street, Bedminster, Bristol BS3 4NH	Tel: (0272) 637216 Telex: 444825 GASBAG G Fax: (0272) 661168
	Thunder & Colt Ltd	Maesbury Road, Oswestry, Shropshire SY10 8HA	Tel: (0691) 652216 Telex: 35503 COLT G Fax: (0691) 656540
United States of America	Adams Balloon Loft Inc	Building 27, Dekalb Peachtree Airport, Atlanta, Georgia 30341	Tel: (404) 452 8066
	Avian Balloon Company	South 3722 Ridgeview Drive, Spokane, Washington 99206	Tel: (509) 928 6847
	The Balloon Works	PO Box 827, 810 Salisbury Road, Statesville, North Carolina 28677	Tel: (704) 878 9501
	Boland Balloon	Pine Drive, RFD 2, Burlington, Connecticut 06013	Tel: (203) 673 1307
	Galaxy Balloons Inc	820 Salisbury Road, Statesville, North Carolina 28677	Tel: (704) 878 9147
	Raven Industries Inc	Box 1007, Sioux Falls, South Dakota 57117	Tel: (605) 336 2750
	Solo System Inc	265 Front Street, Mattawan, Michigan 49071	Tel: (616) 668 4228

HOT-AIR (AX) AND GAS BALLOON (AA) DATA

Country	Company	Model	Volume m³/cu ft	Diameter m/ft	Height m/ft	Crew	Basket	Fuel Cylinders	Burners
FAI CLASS AA/AX-2 (250-400 m³; 8,829-14,126 cu ft)									
UK	Thunder & Colt	Cloudhopper Junior	396.4/14,000	8.53/28	8.53/28	1	Harness seat	1	1
USA	Raven	MG-300	300/10,595	8.78/28.8	8.23/27	1	Mixed structure	NA	NA
FAI CLASS AA/AX-3 (400-600 m³; 14,126-21,189 cu ft)									
West Germany	Ballonfabrik	K 630/1-Ri	630/22,248	10.64/34.91	18.0/59	3-4	Rattan	NA	NA
UK	Cameron	Viva-20	566.3/20,000	9.14/30	9.75/32	1	Harness seat	1	1
UK	Thunder & Colt	Cloudhopper Midi	481.4/17,000	9.45/31	9.45/31	1	Harness seat	1	1
UK	Thunder & Colt	Cloudhopper Super	594.7/21,000	10.06/33	10.67/35	1	Harness seat	1	1
FAI CLASS AA/AX-4 (600-900 m³; 21,189-31,783 cu ft)									
West Germany	Ballonfabrik	K 780/2-Ri	780/27,545	11.5/37.73	19.81/65	4	Rattan	NA	NA
West Germany	Ballonfabrik	B 800/2-Ri	800/28,252	11.5/37.73	20.12/66	4	Rattan	NA	NA
West Germany	Ballonfabrik	K 945/2-Ri	945/33,372	12.17/39.93	20.42/67	5-6	Rattan	NA	NA
Hungary	MÉM RSZ	RSZ-06	896/31,642	12.5/41	15.5/50.9	1	Rattan	1	1
UK	Cameron	N-31	890/31,430	12.5/41	14.63/48	1	Willow/Cane	2	1
UK	Cameron	O-31	890/31,430	12.5/41	14.63/48	1	Willow/Cane	2	1
UK	Cameron	Viva-31	890/31,430	12.5/41	14.63/48	1	Willow/Cane	2	1
UK	Thunder & Colt	31Z	890/31,430	12.19/40	14.63/48	1	Wicker/Cane	2	1
USA	Boland	Ultralight	899.5/31,765	11.58/38	?	1	?	2	1
USA	Boland	Ultralight	879/31,044	?	?	1	?	2	1
USA	Boland	Football	718.5/25,373	11.13/36.5	?	1	?	1	1
USA	Raven	S-40	900/31,783	12.19/40	16.76/55	1	Aluminium chair	1	1
USA	Solo	SS-103	793/28,000	9.14/30	10.67/35	1	Plastics	1	1
FAI CLASS AA/AX-5 (900-1,200 m³; 31,783-42,378 cu ft)									
West Germany	Ballonfabrik	K 1050/3-Ri	1,050/37,080	12.6/41.3	20.7/67.9	5-6	Rattan	NA	NA
West Germany	Ballonfabrik	K 1260/3-Ri	1,260/44,496	13.4/44	22.25/73	6	Rattan	NA	NA
South Africa	Flamboyant	AX5-40M	1,132/40,000	12.9/42.32	14.0/45.93	1	Rattan	1	1
UK	Cameron	O-42	1,190/42,024	14.26/46.8	12.07/39.6	2	Willow/Cane	2	1
UK	Thunder & Colt	42 Series 1	1,190/42,024	13.59/44.6	14.30/46.9	2	Wicker/Cane	2	1
UK	Thunder & Colt	42A	1,190/42,024	13.69/44.9	14.50/47.6	2	Wicker/Cane	2	1
USA	Adams	LD	964/34,029	12.95/42.5	15.54/51	1	Rattan	1/2	1
USA	Adams	LD-S	1,104/38,978	12.95/42.5	16.46/54	1-2	Rattan	1/2	1
USA	Avian	Sparrow	1,189/42,000	13.41/44	16.46/54	1	Wicker	2	1
USA	Balloon Works	FireFly 42	1,182/41,740	14.02/46	14.63/48	1-2	Wicker	3	2
USA	Boland	Puppy Chow	906/32,000	?	?	1-2	?	1-4	1
USA	Raven	MG-1000	1,047/36,959	13.34/43.76	12.72/41.72	1-3	Rattan	NA	NA
FAI CLASS AA/AX-6 (1,200-1,600 m³; 42,378-56,503 cu ft)									
France	Chaize	CS.1600	1,600/56,503	14.0/45.93	22.5/73.82	2	Rattan	2	1
West Germany	Ballonfabrik	K1360/4-Ri	1,360/48,028	13.75/45.11	25.0/82.02	6	Rattan	NA	NA
West Germany	Ballonfabrik	K1680/4-Ri	1,680/59,329	14.78/48.5	24.4/80	6	Rattan	NA	NA
South Africa	Flamboyant	AX6-56	1,586/56,000	15.0/49.2	18.0/59.0	2	Rattan	2	1
South Africa	Flamboyant	AX6-56M	1,586/56,000	15.0/49.2	18.0/59.0	2	Rattan	2	1
UK	Cameron	O-56	1,590/56,150	15.24/50	17.07/56	3	Willow/Cane	2	1
UK	Cameron	Viva-56	1,590/56,150	15.24/50	17.07/56	3	Willow/Cane	2	1
UK	Cameron	N-56	1,590/56,150	15.24/50	17.07/56	3	Willow/Cane	2	1
UK	Thunder & Colt	56 Series 1	1,590/56,150	15.39/50.5	16.31/53.5	3	Wicker/Cane	2-3	1
UK	Thunder & Colt	56A	1,590/56,150	15.61/51.2	16.40/53.8	3	Wicker/Cane	2-3	1
USA	Adams	A50	1,557/54,985	15.24/50	17.68/58	2	Rattan	1-4	1
USA	Balloon Works	GadFly 56	1,576/55,660	15.3/50.1	16.1/52.8	3	Wicker	3	1
USA	Balloon Works	GadFly 560	1,576/55,660	15.24/50	16.46/54	1-3	Wicker	3	1
USA	Balloon Works	DragonFly 56	1,576/55,660	15.24/50	15.85/52	1-3	Wicker	3	1
USA	Balloon Works	DragonFly 560	1,576/55,660	15.24/50	15.85/52	1-3	Wicker	3	1
USA	Boland	Baby Snake	1,359/48,000	13.72/45	?	2-3	Wicker/Aluminium	2	1
USA	Boland	Rainbow-Stars	1,444/51,000	14.02/46	?	2	?	1-4	1
USA	Raven	S-50A	1,597/56,400	15.24/50	17.68/58	2-4	Wicker	3	1
USA	Raven	RX-6	1,597/56,400	15.24/50	17.68/58	2-3	Wicker	2	1
FAI CLASS AA/AX-7 (1,600-2,200 m³; 56,503-77,692 cu ft)									
Czechoslovakia	Aerotechnik	AB-2	2,180/76,986	16.0/52.49	20.0/65.62	4	Wicker/GFRP	2	2
France	Chaize	CS.1800	1,800/63,566	15.0/49.2	22.5/73.8	2-3	Rattan	3	1
France	Chaize	CS. 2000	2,000/70,629	16.5/54.1	22.5/73.8	3	Rattan	3	1
France	Chaize	CS. 2200	2,200/77,692	18.0/59	22.5/73.8	3-4	Rattan	4	2
Hungary	MÉM RSZ	RSZ-05	2,200/77,692	17.0/55.77	20.7/68	1-3	Rattan	2-4	2
South Africa	Flamboyant	AX7-65	1,840/65,000	16.0/52.5	20.0/65.6	3	Rattan	2	1
South Africa	Flamboyant	AX7-77M	2,180/77,000	16.0/52.5	20.0/65.6	3	Rattan	2	1
UK	Cameron	Viva-65	1,840/64,980	16.15/53	18.0/59	3	Willow/Cane	3	1
UK	Cameron	O-65	1,840/64,980	16.15/53	18.0/59	3	Willow/Cane	3	1
UK	Cameron	N-65	1,840/64,980	16.15/53	18.0/59	3	Willow/Cane	2	1
UK	Cameron	Viva-77	2,190/77,339	17.07/56	18.9/62	4	Willow/Cane	4	1
UK	Cameron	O-77	2,190/77,339	17.07/56	18.9/62	4	Willow/Cane	4	1
UK	Cameron	N-77	2,190/77,339	17.07/56	18.9/62	4	Willow/Cane	4	1
UK	Thunder & Colt	65 Series 1	1,840/64,980	16.18/53.1	17.19/56.4	3	Wicker/Cane	2-3	1
UK	Thunder & Colt	69A	1,954/69,000	16.31/53.5	17.31/56.8	3	Wicker/Cane	2-3	1
UK	Thunder & Colt	77 Series 1	2,190/77,339	16.79/55.1	18.11/59.4	4	Wicker/Cane	2-3	1-2
UK	Thunder & Colt	77A	2,190/77,339	17.01/55.8	18.29/60	4	Wicker/Cane	2-3	1-2
USA	Adams	A50S	1,755/61,977	15.24/50	18.59/61	3	Rattan	1-4	1
USA	Adams	A55	2,123/74,973	16.76/55	19.51/64	3	Rattan	1-4	1
USA	Avian	Falcon II	1,699/60,000	15.54/51	18.59/61	1-3	Wicker	2	1
USA	Balloon Works	DragonFly 65	1,840/65,000	17.07/56	17.68/58	3-4	Wicker	3	1
USA	Balloon Works	DragonFly 650	1,840/65,000	7.07/56	17.68/58	3-4	Wicker	3	1
USA	Balloon Works	DragonFly 77	2,167/76,520	17.07/56	17.68/58	3-4	Wicker	3	1

NA: Not applicable (gas balloon)

HOT-AIR (AX) AND GAS BALLOON (AA) DATA *(continued)*

Country	Company	Model	Volume m³/cu ft	Diameter m/ft	Height m/ft	Crew	Basket	Fuel Cylinders	Burners
FAI CLASS AA/AX-7 (1,600-2,200 m³; 56,503-77,692 cu ft) *(continued)*									
USA	Balloon Works	DragonFly 770	2,167/76,520	17.07/56	17.68/58	3-4	Wicker	3	1
USA	Balloon Works	FireFly 65	1,840/65,000	17.07/56	17.68/58	3-4	Wicker	3	1
USA	Balloon Works	FireFly 650	1,840/65,000	17.07/56	17.68/58	3-4	Wicker	3	1
USA	Balloon Works	FireFly 77	2,167/76,520	17.07/56	17.68/58	3-4	Wicker	3	1
USA	Balloon Works	FireFly 770	2,167/76,520	17.07/56	17.68/58	3-4	Wicker	3	1
USA	Boland	*MIA-POW*	1,736/61,304	14.63/48	?	2-3	Rattan/Plywood	2-4	1
USA	Boland	*Mrs Snake*	1,869/66,000	15.24/50	?	3-4	Wicker/Aluminium	2-4	1
USA	Galaxy	Galaxy 7	2,170/76,633	17.07/56	17.68/58	3-4	Rattan/Wicker	4	1-2
USA	Raven	S-55-A	2,195/77,500	16.76/55	19.2/63	3-4	Wicker	3	1
USA	Raven	RX-7	2,195/77,500	16.76/55	19.2/63	3	Wicker	3	1
FAI CLASS AX-8 (2,200-3,000 m³; 77,692-105,944 cu ft)									
France	Chaize	CS.3000	3,000/105,944	19.44/63.8	25.0/82	5-6	Rattan	5	2
Hungary	MÉM RSZ	RSZ-03/1	3,000/105,944	18.70/61.35	22.90/75.13	3-4	Rattan	3-4	2
Italy	Bonanno	I-PAAM	2,950/104,178	19.0/62.34	22.0/72.18	4	?	4	2
South Africa	Flamboyant	AX8-85	2,407/85,000	18.0/59	20.0/65.6	4	Rattan	2	1
South Africa	Flamboyant	AX8-105	2,973/105,000	19.0/62.3	21.0/68.9	6	Rattan	3	2
UK	Cameron	O-84	2,380/84,047	17.68/58	19.5/64	4	Willow/Cane	4	1
UK	Cameron	N-90	2,548/90,000	17.98/59	19.81/65	.4-5	Wicker	6	2
UK	Cameron	A-105	2,970/104,885	18.9/62	20.73/68	6	Willow/Cane	6	2
UK	Cameron	N-105	2,970/104,885	18.9/62	20.73/68	6	Willow/Cane	6	2
UK	Cameron	O-105	2,970/104,885	18.9/62	20.73/68	6	Willow/Cane	6	2
UK	Thunder & Colt	84 Series 1	2,380/84,047	17.3/56.8	18.41/60.4	4	Wicker/Cane	2-3	1-2
UK	Thunder & Colt	90A	2,550/90,050	17.5/57.5	17.5/57.5	5	Wicker/Cane	2-4	2
UK	Thunder & Colt	90 Series 2	2,550/90,050	17.50/57.4	18.59/61	5	Wicker/Cane	2-4	2
UK	Thunder & Colt	105 Series 1	2,970/104,885	18.44/60.5	18.44/60.5	6	Wicker/Cane	2-6	2
UK	Thunder & Colt	105A	2,970/104,885	18.90/62	19.90/65.3	6	Wicker/Cane	2-6	2
UK	Thunder & Colt	105 Series 2	2,970/104,885	18.84/61.8	19.78/64.9	6	Wicker/Cane	2-6	2
USA	Adams	A55S	2,350/82,990	16.76/55	20.42/67	4	Rattan	1-4	1
USA	Adams	A60	2,973/105,000	18.59/61	22.25/73	5	Rattan	4	1-2
USA	Avian	Skyhawk	2,265/80,000	16.76/55	20.12/66	1-4	Wicker	2	1
USA	Avian	Turbo 8	2,973/105,000	18.29/60	21.33/70	1-6	Wicker	4	2
USA	Balloon Works	DragonFly 90	2,600/91,818	17.98/59	18.75/61.5	3-4	Wicker	3	1
USA	Balloon Works	DragonFly 105	2,957/104,440	18.90/62	19.51/64	4-5	Wicker	6	2
USA	Balloon Works	DragonFly 900	2,600/91,818	17.98/59	18.75/61.5	3-4	Wicker	3	1
USA	Balloon Works	DragonFly 1050	2,957/104,440	18.90/62	19.51/64	4-5	Wicker	6	2
USA	Balloon Works	FireFly 90	2,600/91,818	17.98/59	18.75/61.5	3-4	Wicker	3	1
USA	Balloon Works	FireFly 105	2,957/104,440	18.90/62	19.51/64	4-5	Wicker	6	2
USA	Balloon Works	FireFly 900	2,600/91,818	17.98/59	18.75/61.5	3-4	Wicker	3	1
USA	Balloon Works	FireFly 1050	2,957/104,440	18.90/62	19.51/64	4-5	Wicker	6	2
USA	Boland	*Levity*	2,563/90,500	?	?	4	Rattan/Plywood	4	2
USA	Raven	S-60A	2,973/105,000	18.29/60	21.03/69	3-4	Wicker	3	2
FAI CLASS AX-9 (3,000-4,000 m³; 105,944-141,259 cu ft)									
France	Chaize	CS.4000	4,000/141,259	22.0/72.2	27.5/90.2	8	Rattan	6	2
Hungary	MÉM RSZ	RSZ-04/1	4,000/141,259	20.6/67.6	24.7/81.0	3-6	Rattan	3-6	2
UK	Cameron	A-120	3,398/120,000	19.02/62.4	18.29/60	7	Willow/Cane	6	2
UK	Cameron	O-120	3,398/120,000	20.24/66.4	17.07/56	7	Willow/Cane	6	2
UK	Cameron	N-133	3,766/133,000	19.90/65.3	18.59/61	7	Willow/Cane	6	2
UK	Cameron	A-140	3,960/139,846	20.73/68	21.95/72	8	Willow/Cane	6	2
UK	Thunder & Colt	120A	3,398/120,000	19.51/64	21.03/69	?	Wicker/Cane	2-6	2
UK	Thunder & Colt	140	3,965/140,023	20.36/66.8	20.36/66.8	8	Stainless steel/Cane*	2-6	2
USA	Adams	A60S	3,370/119,000	18.59/61	22.86/75	5-6	Rattan	4	2
USA	Adams	AB	3,540/125,000	19.51/64	23.16/76	6	Rattan	6	2
USA	Avian	Magnum IX	3,964/140,000	20.12/66	23.16/76	1-8	Wicker	4	2
USA	Balloon Works	FireFly 140	3,964/140,000	20.12/66	22.86/75	5-6	Wicker	6-9	2
USA	Boland	*Tour d'Argent*	3,693/130,400	19.66/64.5	?	7	Rattan	6	2
USA	Raven	S-66A	4,000/141,259	20.12/66	22.86/75	8	Wicker	6	2
FAI CLASS AX-10 (4,000-6,000 m³; 141,259-211,888 cu ft)									
South Africa	Flamboyant	AX10-150	4,248/150,000	21.0/68.9	22.0/72.2	8	Rattan	4	2
UK	Cameron	N-145	4,106/145,000	20.54/67.4	19.20/63	8	Willow/Cane	6	2
UK	Cameron	O-160	4,530/160,000	21.0/69	22.25/73	8	Willow/Cane	6	2
UK	Cameron	N-180	5,097/180,000	27.13/89	29.57/97	9	Willow/Cane	8	3
UK	Cameron	A-210	5,947/210,000	23.77/78	24.99/82	12	Willow/Cane	8	4
UK	Thunder & Colt	160 Series 1	4,530/159,976	21.61/70.9	22.71/74.5	9	Stainless steel/Cane*	2-8	3
UK	Thunder & Colt	160A	4,530/159,976	21.70/71.2	23.01/75.5	9	Stainless steel/Cane*	2-8	3
UK	Thunder & Colt	180A	5,097/180,000	23.0/75.46	24.0/78.74	10	Stainless steel/Cane*	2-9	3
USA	Boland	*Red Baron*	4,814/170,000	19.66/64.5	27.43/90	8	Rattan/Plywood	6	2
USA	Raven	S-77A	6,000/211,888	23.47/77	25.3/83	8	Wicker	6	2
FAI CLASS AX-11 (6,000-9,000 m³; 211,888-317,832 cu ft)									
UK	Cameron	A-250	7,079/250,000	24.32/79.8	23.41/76.8	15	Willow/Cane	8	3
UK	Cameron	A-300	8,495/300,000	25.85/84.8	24.81/81.4	20	Willow/Cane	8	3-4
UK	Thunder & Colt	240A	6,796/240,000	24.51/80.4	25.79/84.6	12	Stainless steel/Cane*	2-10	3-4
UK	Thunder & Colt	300A	8,495/300,000	26.46/86.8	27.19/89.2	12	Stainless steel/Cane*	?	?
USA	Boland	*Mr Gunsnook*	6,513/230,000	22.25/73	30.48/100	13	?	6	3
FAI CLASS AX-12 (9,000-12,000 m³; 317,832-423,776 cu ft)									
UK	Thunder & Colt	400A	11,327/400,000	29.11/95.5	29.99/98.4	16	Stainless steel/Cane*	?	?
FAI CLASS AX-13 (12,000-16,000 m³; 423,776-565,035 cu ft)									
UK	Cameron	A-530	15,008/530,000	31.21/102.4	29.99/98.4	30	Willow/Cane	10	3-4
FAI CLASS AX-15 (22,000 m³; 776,924 cu ft and above)									
UK	Cameron	N-850	24,069/850,000	37.49/123	35.05/115	50	Willow/Cane	12	6

*T-partition format

Aerotechnik AB-2 (AX-7 class)

Chaize CS.4000 (AX-9 class)

Bonanno AX-8

MÉM RSZ-03/1 (AX-9 class)

Flamboyant AX8-85

Cameron special shape hot-air balloon for Canada

Cameron Air Chair for one/two-seat balloons

Thunder & Colt 2,973m³ (105,000 cu ft) special shape

Thunder & Colt 69A (AX-7 class)

Cameron V-65 (AX-7 class)

Avian Turbo 8 (AX-8 class)

Galaxy 7 (AX-7 class)

Balloon Works FireFly 77 (AX-7)

Group of balloons made by Raven Industries; largest is the S-77A

Boland 4,814 m³ (170,000 cu ft) *Red Baron*

Boland 899.5 m³ (31,765 cu ft) AX-4 class ultralight

AERO ENGINES

> This section includes all available details of engines of manned aircraft, including microlights, and aerospacecraft. Rocket engines and other propulsion systems used purely for RPVs, targets, missiles and unmanned spaceflight are no longer included. Readers are referred for these subjects to *Jane's Weapon Systems, World Unmanned Aircraft* by Kenneth Munson, and *Jane's Spaceflight Directory*.

AUSTRALIA

HDHV
HAWKER DE HAVILLAND VICTORIA LTD
Box 779H, GPO Melbourne, Victoria 3001
Telephone: (03) 647 6111
Telex: AA 30721
Fax: (03) 646 3431
OFFICERS: See HDH entry in Aircraft section

HDHV makes components for engines and airframes. It makes F404 blades and seals, and assembles and tests engines for the RAAF. It makes CF6-50 and -80 rings for GE, and CMF56 rings, and supports RAAF Atar 9C and Viper engines.

AUSTRIA

ROTAX
BOMBARDIER-ROTAX GmbH
Postfach 5, A-4623 Gunskirchen
Telephone: (07246) 271-0
Telex: 25 546 BRG K A
Fax: (07246) 271286
PRODUCT MANAGER: Rudolf Krinninger

This company is one of the world's largest producers of light piston engines. Those listed for light aircraft, microlights and gliders use 1:50 mix of oil with petrol (gasoline) of not below MON 83 or RON 90 grade. Customers have many options, including rewind manual or electric starter.

Rotax 912 four-cylinder four-stroke
(53 kW; 71 hp)

ROTAX LIGHT AIRCRAFT ENGINES

Engine Model	277	377	447	503	503.2V	462	508	532	912
Layout	1 cylinder (4,7) Piston port	2 cylinder (4,7) Piston port	2 cylinder (4,7) Piston port	2 cylinder (4,7) Piston port	2 cylinder (4,7) Piston port	2 cylinder (5,7) Rotary valve	2 cylinder (4,8) Overhead valve	2 cylinder (5,7) Rotary valve	4 cylinder (6,8) Overhead valve
Bore/stroke mm (in)	72.0/66.0 (2.83/2.60)	62.0/61.0 (2.44/2.40)	67.5/61.0 (2.66/2.40)	72.0/61.0 (2.83/2.40)	72.0/61.0 (2.83/2.40)	69.5/61.0 (2.74/2.40)	71.0/64.0 (2.79/2.52)	72.0/64.0 (2.83/2.52)	79.5/61.0 (3.13/2.40)
Capacity cc (cu in)	268.7 (16.397)	368.3 (22.475)	436.5 (26.637)	496.7 (30.310)	496.7 (30.310)	462.8 (28.242)	507.0 (30.8)	521.1 (31.799)	1,211.2 (73.912)
Weight, Dry (1) kg (lb)	19.0 (41.9)	27.5 (60.6)	27.5 (60.6)	30.2 (66.6)	30.2 (66.6)	27.0 (59.5)	38.0 (83.7)	28.0 (61.7)	—
Weight, Dry (2) kg (lb)	24.0 (52.9)	32.5 (71.6)	32.5 (71.6)	36.2 (79.8)	36.2 (79.8)	32.0 (70.5)	48.5 (106.9)	33.0 (72.8)	59.9 (132.0)
Rating (3) kW (hp)	19 (25.5) 6,500 rpm	26 (34.9) 6,500 rpm	29.4 (39.4) 6,500 rpm	34 (45.6) 6,500 rpm	38 (51.0) 6,500 rpm	38 (51.0) 6,500 rpm	31.0 (41.6) 7,800 rpm	47 (63.0) 6,500 rpm	53 (71) 5,500 rpm

Notes: 1, Bare, unequipped; 2, with carburettor (503.2V, twin carburettors), intake silencer and exhaust system; 3, standard bare engine; 4, aircooled; 5, liquid cooled; 6, liquid cooled heads, aircooled barrels; 7, two-stroke; 8, four-stroke.

WESTERMAYER
OSKAR WESTERMAYER
Hauptstrasse 11, A-2161 Poysbrunn
Telephone: (02554) 405
Telex: 73379

This engineer has developed a piston engine with aircooled barrels but liquid-cooled heads. He claims that, compared with the Continental O-200 which was the basis for the engine, fuel consumption is reduced by 25 per cent. Compression ratio is raised to 8.6.

WESTERMAYER W 5/33
This flat-four engine has cylinder heads of cast aluminium alloy, cooled by pure ethylene glycol. The coolant pump feeds via a separate pipe to each head, and the return line passes through an air radiator. By the beginning of 1987, running on 100, 100LL or Mogas fuel, a total of 1,688 flight hours had been recorded since 1985 on seven engines installed in Westermayer WE 04 autogyros (see 1981-82 *Jane's*) and a Cessna 150, plus 826 hours on the bench. Certification to FAR 33 was completed in December 1986.
DIMENSIONS:
Length   730 mm (28.7 in)

The 74.6 kW (100 hp) Westermayer W 5/33

Width   790 mm (31.1 in)
Height: carburettor   625 mm (24.6 in)
      airbox   700 mm (27.6 in)
WEIGHT, DRY:
   Bare   85 kg (187 lb)
   With starter, alternator and silencer   102 kg (225 lb)

Westermayer W 5/33 engine installation in Cessna 150

PERFORMANCE RATING:
   T-O   74.6 kW (100 hp) at 2,750 rpm
FUEL CONSUMPTION:
   T-O   25.5 litres (6.7 US gallons; 5.6 Imp gallons)/h
SPECIFIC FUEL CONSUMPTION:
   T-O   71 µg/J (0.42 lb/h/hp)

BELGIUM

FN

FABRIQUE NATIONALE HERSTAL SA
Voie de Liège 33, B-4400 Herstal
Telephone: 041 640800
FN Moteurs
ENGINE DIVISION: Route de Liers 121, B-4411 Milmort
 (Herstal)
Telephone: 3241 784671
Telex: B 42075 MONAT
Fax: 3241 785207
VICE-PRESIDENT AND DIVISION MANAGER: R. Boulanger

With long experience of work on aircraft piston engines, FN began jet engine production in 1949. Its current major activity is centred on the Pratt & Whitney F100, with responsibility for the fan and core modules and assembly and test. FN Moteurs has signed a co-operation agreement with Turbomeca for critical parts of the TM333. It is a member of the consortium (RR, MTU, SNECMA, FN) building the Tyne engine for the Atlantic and the Transall, produces parts for the Pratt & Whitney JT9D-7R4, and has a 3 per cent share in the PW4000 series.

FN is associated with SNECMA on the CFM56. The lubrication modules for the CFM56-2 and CFM56-3 were developed by FN and are in production. FN Moteurs has increased its participation up to 10 per cent of the SNECMA share (5 per cent overall) in future versions, starting with the CFM56-5, including endurance testing of engines.

BRAZIL

CELMA

CELMA-CIA ELECTROMECANICA
Rue Alice Hervê 356, PO Box 90341, 25600 Petropolis, RJ
Telephone: (0242) 43 4962

PRESIDENT: Edivio Caldas Sanctos
TECHNICAL DIRECTOR: Carlos A. R. Pereira
 This company of 1,400 people has facilities totalling 35,000 m² (376,736 sq ft) in which it overhauls many kinds

of jet engine and accessories. It now shares in the production of components for the Rolls-Royce Spey 807 turbofan which powers the AMX attack aircraft produced jointly by Italy and Brazil.

IMAER

INDÚSTRIA MECÂNICA E AERONÁUTICA LTDA
HEAD OFFICE AND WORKS: Aeroporto de Botucatú, PO Box 301, 18600 Botucatú SP
Telephone: (0149) 22 1908 and 22 5938
 IMAER, formerly Retimotor, manufactures four-stroke reciprocating engines for light aircraft, ultralights and powered gliders.

IMAER 2000

This engine is available in two models: the **2000 M1**, with single ignition, JAR 22 certificated, and the **ME1**, with dual ignition, being certificated in 1988.
TYPE: Four-cylinder horizontally-opposed aircooled.
CYLINDERS: Bore 90.4 mm (3.56 in). Stroke 78.4 mm (3.09 in). Swept Volume 2,017 cc (123.08 cu in). Compression ratio 8.7.
INDUCTION: Stromberg-Zenith 150 CD or Marvel-Schebler MA 3PA carburettor.

FUEL GRADE: Avgas 100/130.
IGNITION: Slick 4230 or Bendix S4RN21 magneto and/or Bosch electronic.
DIMENSIONS:

Length	590 mm (23.23 in)
Width	764 mm (30.08 in)
Height	447 mm (17.60 in)
WEIGHT:	78-81 kg (172-178.6 lb)
PERFORMANCE RATING:	59.7 kW (80 hp) at 3,400 rpm

IMAER 1000

Again these are two models: The **1000 M1**, with magneto single ignition, not certificated, and the **1000 E1**, with electronic single ignition, not certificated.
TYPE: Two-cylinder horizontally-opposed aircooled.
DIMENSIONS:

Length	370 mm (14.57 in)
Width	764 mm (30.08 in)
Height	410 mm (16.14 in)
WEIGHT:	39 kg (86.0 lb)
PERFORMANCE RATING:	47.6 kW (63.8 hp) at 3,600 rpm.

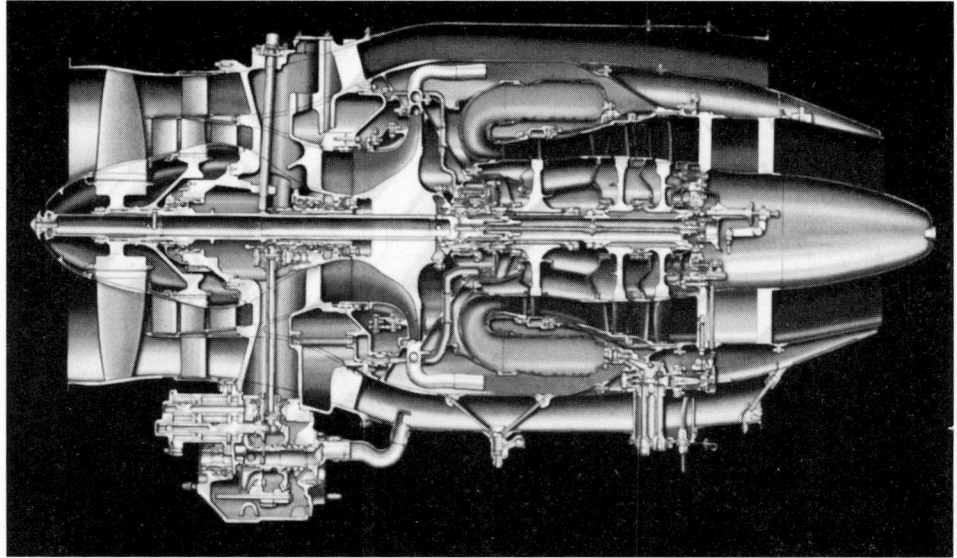

IMAER 2000 M1 (59.7 kW; 80 hp)

RETIMOTOR — see *IMAER*

CANADA

ORENDA

HAWKER SIDDELEY CANADA INC (Orenda Division)
PO Box 6001, Toronto AMF, Ontario L5P 1B3

Telephone: (416) 677 3250
Telex: 06-968727
GENERAL MANAGER: R. J. Munro

Orenda has a 67,262 m² (724,000 sq ft) facility close to Toronto International Airport. It meets the maintenance needs of the Canadian Forces for General Electric J85 and F404 engines, and makes engine parts under subcontract.

P&WC

PRATT & WHITNEY CANADA (Subsidiary of United Technologies Corporation)
1000 Marine Victoria, Longueuil, Quebec J4G 1A1
Telephone: (514) 677 9411
PRESIDENT AND CHIEF EXECUTIVE OFFICER: L. D. Caplan
SENIOR VICE-PRESIDENT: G. P. Ouimet (Marketing and Product Support)
VICE-PRESIDENTS:
 P. Henry (Communications)
 C. B. Wrong (Engineering)
 Pratt & Whitney Canada is owned 97 per cent by United Technologies Corporation, Connecticut, USA, and is the P&W Group member responsible for engines for general aviation and regional transport. P&WC occupies more than 224,000 m² (2.4 million sq ft) of space and employs 8,700 persons. By 1 January 1988 P&WC had delivered 30,535 engines.

P&WC JT15D

Designed to power business aircraft, small transports and training aircraft, the JT15D first ran on 23 September 1967.
 Initial application was the twin-engined Cessna Citation. Up to 1976 Cessna used the **JT15D-1**. Late that year it announced the Citation I powered by the **JT15D-1A** and the Citation II powered by the **JT15D-4**. During 1983 the D-1A was replaced by the **D-1B**.
 Other twin-engined business jets powered by the JT15D-4 are the Aérospatiale Corvette and Mitsubishi Diamond I. TBO is 3,500 h for the JT15D-1/D-1A, and 3,000 h for the JT15D-4.
 The **JT15D-4B** is an altitude optimised variant for the Citation S/II.

Longitudinal section of the P&WC JT15D-5 turbofan (12.89 kN; 2,900 lb st)

The **JT15D-4C** has an aerobatic oil system for sustained inverted flight, and an electronic fuel control. Selected for SIAI-Marchetti S.211.
 The **JT15D-4D** is flat rated for improved hot/high performance for the Diamond IA.
 The **JT15D-5** is a growth version. A new fan with higher pressure ratio and flow, plus an improved boost stage and

HP compressor, are combined to produce 25 per cent more altitude cruise thrust, with a 3 per cent improvement in sfc. HP turbine blades and electronic fuel control are also improved. Powers Cessna T-47A and Diamond II.
 The **JT15D-5A** has a hydromechanical fuel control. Selected for Citation V. By 1988 total deliveries of all JT15D engines had reached 3,397. Operating time was 9,106,053 h.

The following description relates to the JT15D-1B:
TYPE: Two-shaft turbofan.
FAN: Single-stage axial with 28 solid titanium blades with part-span shrouds. Mass flow, 34 kg (75 lb)/s; bypass ratio about 3.3; fan pressure ratio 1.5.
COMPRESSOR: Single stage titanium centrifugal. Overall pressure ratio about 10:1. (D-4 and D-5 have axial boost stage between fan and compressor.)
COMBUSTION CHAMBER: Annular reverse flow type. Spark igniters at 5 and 7 o'clock (viewed from rear).
FUEL SYSTEM: Pump delivering at 44.8 bars (650 lb/sq in). D-1, 4, 4B, 5A have DP-L2 hydromechanical control; 4C, 4D and 5 have JFC 118 or 119 electronic system.
FUEL GRADES: JP-1, JP-4, JP-5 to CPW 204.
TURBINE: Single-stage HP with 71 solid blades; two-stage LP, first stage cast integrally with 61 blades and second carrying 55 blades in fir tree roots.
LUBRICATION SYSTEM: Integral oil system, with gear type pump delivering at up to 5.52 bars (80 lb/sq in). Capacity, 9.0 litres (2.4 US gallons; 2.0 Imp gallons).
OIL SPECIFICATION: PWA521 Type II, CPW 202.
STARTING: Air turbine starter or electric starter/generator.
DIMENSIONS:

Diameter: JT15D-1		691 mm (27.2 in)
JT15D-4		686 mm (27.0 in)
Length overall: JT15D-1		1,506 mm (59.3 in)
JT15D-4		1,600 mm (63.0 in)

WEIGHT, DRY:

JT15D-1, -1A	232.5 kg (514 lb)
JT15D-1B	235 kg (519 lb)
JT15D-4	253 kg (557 lb)
JT15D-4B	258 kg (568 lb)
JT15D-4C	261 kg (575 lb)
JT15D-4D	255 kg (560 lb)
JT15D-5	291.5 kg (632 lb)

PERFORMANCE RATINGS:

T-O: JT15D-1, -1A, -1B	9.8 kN (2,200 lb st)
JT15D-4, -4B, -4C, -4D	11.12 kN (2,500 lb st)
JT15D-5	12.89 kN (2,900 lb st)
Max continuous:	
JT15D-1, -1A, -1B	9.3 kN (2,090 lb st)
JT15D-4, -4B, -4D	10.56 kN (2,375 lb st)
JT15D-4C	9.45 kN (2,125 lb st)
JT15D-5	12.89 kN (2,900 lb st)

SPECIFIC FUEL CONSUMPTION (T-O):

JT15D-1, -1A, -1B	15.30 mg/Ns (0.540 lb/h/lb st)
JT15D-4, -4C	15.92 mg/Ns (0.562 lb/h/lb st)
JT15D-5	15.61 mg/Ns (0.551 lb/h/lb st)

P&WC PW300

Planned for corporate aircraft of the 1990s, this engine is aimed at US coast-to-coast flights at Mach 0.75 at 14,325 m (47,000 ft). MTU of West Germany will be responsible for the LP turbine section, as a partner sharing 25 per cent of the estimated development cost of $Can 500 million.
Certification is due in 1990. The PW300/3 is a projected uprated growth version.
TYPE: Two-shaft turbofan.
FAN: Single-stage, overhung ahead of front bearing. Pointed rotating spinner. Bypass ratio 4.5.
COMPRESSOR: Four axial stages followed by one centrifugal. Core pressure ratio 15.
COMBUSTION CHAMBER: Annular, fed around periphery by ring of separate curved pipes ducting air from diffuser case of centrifugal compressor.
CONTROL SYSTEM: Hamilton Standard full-authority digital, with dual channels.
HP TURBINE: Two axial stages, the first having aircooled blades.
LP TURBINE: Three axial stages joined via centre stage disc to fan shaft. Two main shaft bearings.
DIMENSIONS (estimated):

Diameter	890 mm (35.0 in)
Length	1,650 mm (65.0 in)

WEIGHT, DRY (estimated): 400 kg (880 lb)

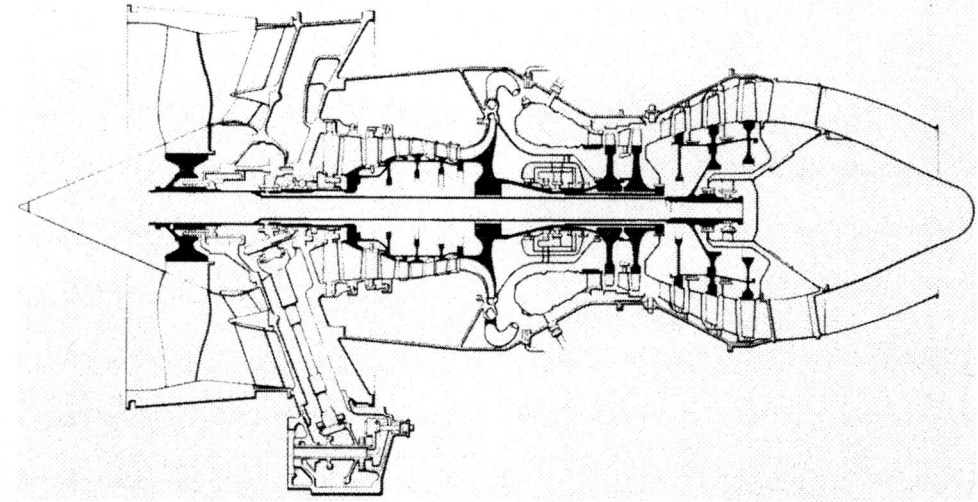
Section through the P&WC PW300/1 turbofan

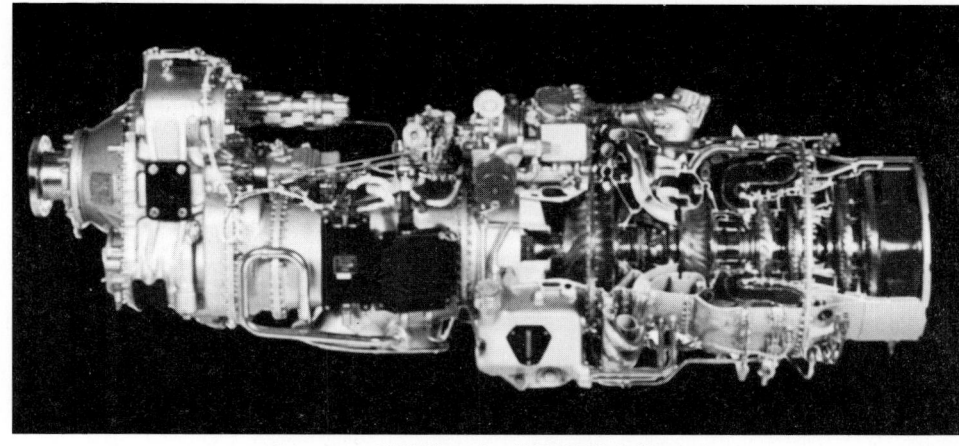
A cutaway PW124 engine (1,790 kW; 2,400 shp)

PERFORMANCE RATINGS (ISA, estimated):

T-O, S/L	23.29 kN (5,236 lb st) or flat rated at 21.13 kN (4,750 lb st) to 25°C
Cruise Mach 0.8 at 12,200 m (40,000 ft)	4.95 kN (1,113 lb)

SPECIFIC FUEL CONSUMPTION (estimate):

T-O as above	11.50 mg/Ns (0.406 lb/h/lb st)
Cruise as above	19.12 mg/Ns (0.675 lb/h/lb)

P&WC PW100

The PW100 is a free turbine turboprop consisting of turbomachine and reduction gearbox modules connected by a torque-measuring driveshaft and integrated structural intake case.
Flight development of the PW100 began in February 1982. Principal versions are as follows:
PW115. T-O rated at 1,256 ekW; 1,193 kW (1,685 ehp; 1,600 shp) at 1,300 propeller rpm to 44°C. Selected for Embraer EMB-120 Brasilia. Certificated December 1983.
PW118. T-O rated at 1,411 ekW; 1,342 kW (1,892 ehp; 1,800 shp) at 1,300 propeller rpm to 33°C. Selected for EMB-120 Brasilia.
PW120. T-O rated at 1,566 ekW; 1,491 kW (2,100 ehp; 2,000 shp) at 1,200 propeller rpm to 27.7°C. Selected for Boeing Canada Dash 8-100 and Aérospatiale/Aeritalia ATR 42. Certificated December 1983.
PW120A. T-O rated at 1,566 ekW; 1,491 kW (2,100 ehp; 2,000 shp) at 1,200 propeller rpm to 29°C. Selected for Dash 8.
PW121. T-O rated at 1,679 ekW; 1,603 kW (2,252 ehp; 2,150 shp) at 1,200 propeller rpm to 26°C.
PW123. T-O rated at 1,866 ekW; 1,775 kW (2,502 ehp; 2,380 shp) at 1,200 propeller rpm to 35°C. Selected for Dash 8-300.
PW124. Growth version, with T-O rating of 1,880 ekW; 1,790 kW (2,522 ehp; 2,400 shp) to 34.4°C. Powers BAe ATP and Fokker 50. PW124A is identical but has higher max continuous power rating. Selected for BAe ATP.
PW124B. PW124 with PW123 turbomachinery to suit four-blade propeller. Selected for ATR 72.
PW125B. Growth PW124 with T-O rating of 2,095 ekW; 1,864 kW (2,810 ehp; 2,500 shp) at 1,200 propeller rpm to 30°C.
PW126. Growth engine, max contingency 2,216 ekW; 1,945 kW (2,972 ehp; 2,609 shp) at 1,200 propeller rpm to 32.4°C.
By 1988 deliveries of engines of the PW100 family had reached 719. Operating time was 1,017,210 h.
The following description applies to all PW100 series engines:
TYPE: Free turbine turboprop.

PROPELLER DRIVE: Twin-layshaft gearbox with propeller shaft offset above turbomachine. Max propeller speeds 1,300 rpm (PW115) and 1,200 rpm (PW120).
AIR INTAKE: S-bend duct. A secondary duct forms a flowing bypass to prevent foreign object ingestion.
COMPRESSOR: Two centrifugal impellers in series, each driven by its own turbine. Air guided through ring of curved pipes from LP diffuser to HP entry.
COMBUSTION CHAMBER: Annular reverse flow type, with 14 air blast fuel nozzles around periphery and two spark igniters.
FUEL SYSTEM: Hydromechanical control and electronic power management.
FUEL GRADES: JP-1, JP-4, JP-5 to PWA Spec 522.
TURBINES: Single-stage HP with 47 aircooled blades. Single-stage LP with 53 solid blades. Two-stage power turbine, first with 68 blades and second with 74, all with shrouded tips.
ACCESSORY DRIVES: Pads driven by HP compressor, for starter/generator, hydromechanical fuel control and hand turning. Pads on reduction gearbox for alternator, hydraulic pump, propeller control module, overspeed governor and electric auxiliary pump. Electric torque signal and auto power augmentation.
LUBRICATION SYSTEM: One pressure pump and two scavenge pumps, all driven off HP rotor. Integral tank, capacity 9.44 litres (2.5 US gallons, 2.08 Imp gallons).
OIL SPECIFICATION: CPW202 or PWA521 Type II.
STARTING: Electric starter/generator.
DIMENSIONS:

Length: PW115, 118	2,057 mm (81 in)
PW120, 123, 124, 124A	2,134 mm (84 in)
Width: PW115, 118, 120, 120A, 121	635 mm (25 in)
others	660 mm (26 in)
Height: all	787 mm (31 in)

WEIGHT, DRY:

PW115, 118	391 kg (861 lb)
PW120	417.8 kg (921 lb)
PW120A	423 kg (933 lb)
PW121	425 kg (936 lb)
PW123	450 kg (992 lb)
PW124, 125, 126 models	481 kg (1,060 lb)

PERFORMANCE RATINGS (S/L, static):
T-O: See under model listings
Max continuous:

PW115	1,256 ekW; 1,193 kW (1,685 ehp; 1,600 shp) at 1,300 rpm to 44°C
PW118	1,411 ekW; 1,342 kW (1,892 ehp; 1,800 shp) at 1,300 rpm to 33°C
PW120	1,333 ekW; 1,268 kW (1,787 ehp; 1,700 shp) at 1,200 rpm to 32.7°C
PW120A	1,411 ekW; 1,342 kW (1,892 ehp; 1,800 shp) at 1,200 rpm to 33°C
PW121	1,524 ekW; 1,454 kW (2,044 ehp; 1,950 shp) at 1,200 rpm to 28°C
PW123, 124	1,686 ekW; 1,603 kW (2,261 ehp; 2,150 shp) at 1,200 rpm to 45°C
PW124A	1,749 ekW; 1,663 kW (2,345 ehp; 2,230 shp) at 1,200 rpm to 42°C
PW125B	2,095 ekW; 1,603 kW (2,810 ehp; 2,150 shp) at 1,200 rpm to 45°C
PW126	1,879 ekW; 1,627 kW (2,520 ehp; 2,182 shp) at 1,200 rpm to 27.9°C

Max cruise:

PW115	1,178 ekW; 1,119 kW (1,580 ehp; 1,500 shp) at 1,300 rpm to 20°C
PW118	1,188 ekW; 1,128 kW (1,593 ehp; 1,512 shp) at 1,300 rpm to 20°C
PW120	1,271 ekW; 1,207 kW (1,704 ehp; 1,619 shp) at 1,200 rpm to 15°C
PW120A	1,296 ekW; 1,231 kW (1,738 ehp; 1,651 shp) at 1,200 rpm to 15°C
PW121	1,330 ekW; 1,268 kW (1,784 ehp; 1,700 shp) at 1,200 rpm to 15°C
PW123, 124, 124A	1,593 ekW; 1,514 kW (2,136 ehp; 2,030 shp) at 1,200 rpm to 22.2°C
PW125B	1,623 ekW; 1,513 kW (2,203 ehp; 2,030 shp) at 1,200 rpm to 22.2°C

PW126   1,749 ekW; 1,536 kW
           (2,346 ehp; 2,060 shp) at 1,200 rpm to 26.3°C
SPECIFIC FUEL CONSUMPTION:
  T-O rating:
  PW115   87.2 μg/J (0.516 lb/h/ehp)
  PW118   84.2 μg/J (0.498 lb/h/ehp)
  PW120, 120A   82.0 μg/J (0.485 lb/h/ehp)
  PW121   80.4 μg/J (0.476 lb/h/ehp)
  PW123   79.4 μg/J (0.470 lb/h/ehp)
  PW124, 124A   79.1 μg/J (0.468 lb/h/ehp)
  PW125B, 126   78.2 μg/J (0.463 lb/h/ehp)

P&WC PT6A

US military designations: T74 (separate entry) and **T101** (PT6A-45R)

The PT6A is a free turbine turboprop, built in many versions since November 1959. By 1988 a total of 20,675 had logged 120,975,054 h in 9,274 aircraft of 4,205 customers.

Current versions of the PT6A are as follows:

PT6A-11. Flat rated at 394 ekW; 373 kW (528 ehp; 500 shp) at 2,200 propeller rpm to 42°C. Fitted to Piper Cheyenne I and IA, T-1040, original Claudius Dornier Seastar and Harbin Y-12 II.

PT6A-110. Flat rated at 374 ekW; 354 kW (502 ehp; 475 shp) at 1,900 propeller rpm to 38°C. Fitted to Dornier 128-6.

PT6A-11AG. Flat rated at 394 ekW; 373 kW (528 ehp; 500 shp) at 2,200 propeller rpm to 42°C. Can use diesel fuel. Fitted to Ayres Turbo-Thrush, Schweizer Turbo Ag-Cat and Weatherly 620 TP.

PT6A-112. Flat rated at 394 ekW; 373 kW (528 ehp; 500 shp) at 1,900 propeller rpm to 56°C. Fitted to Cessna Conquest I, Reims-Cessna F 406 Caravan II, Claudius Dornier Seastar CD2 and AAC Turbine P-210 conversion.

PT6A-114. Flat rated at 471 ekW; 447 kW (632 ehp; 600 shp) at 1,900 propeller rpm to 54.4°C. Fitted to Cessna Caravan I, with single exhaust.

PT6A-15AG. Flat rated at 533 ekW; 507 kW (715 ehp; 680 shp) at 2,200 propeller rpm to 22°C. Can use diesel fuel. Fitted to Ayres Turbo-Thrush, Frakes Turbo-Cat, Schweizer Turbo Ag-Cat D, Air Tractor AT-400, and prototypes of ICA Brasov IAR-827TP and IAR-825TP Triumf.

PT6A-21. Flat rated at 432.5 ekW; 410 kW (580 ehp; 550 shp) at 2,200 propeller rpm to 33°C. Mates A-27 power unit with A-20A gearbox. Fitted to Beechcraft King Air C90.

PT6A-25. Flat rated at 432.5 ekW; 410 kW (580 ehp; 550 shp) at 2,200 propeller rpm to 33°C. Oil system for sustained inverted flight. Fitted to Beechcraft T-34C and Norman Firecracker.

PT6A-25A. Some castings of magnesium alloy instead of aluminium alloy. Fitted to Pilatus PC-7.

PT6A-25C. Flat rated at 584 ekW; 559 kW (783 ehp; 750 shp) at 2,200 propeller rpm to 31°C. A-25 with A-34 hot end and A-27 first stage reduction gearing. Fitted to Embraer EMB-312. Selected for production IAR-825TP Triumf.

PT6A-27. Flat rated at 553 ekW; 507 kW (715 ehp; 680 shp) at 2,200 propeller rpm to 22°C, attained by increase in mass flow, at lower turbine temperatures than in PT6A-20. Hamilton Westwind II/III (Beech 18) conversions, Beechcraft 99 and 99A, and U-21A and U-21D, DHC-6 Twin Otter 300, Pilatus/Fairchild Industries PC-6/B2-H2 Porter, Frakes Aviation (Grumman) Mallard conversion, Let L-410A Turbolet, Saunders ST-27A conversion, Embraer EMB-110 Bandeirante (early), Harbin Y-12 II, SAC Spectrum-One, and Schafer Comanchero 500B/Neiva Carajá.

PT6A-28. Similar to PT6A-27 this has an additional cruise rating of 419 ekW (562 ehp) available to 21°C and max cruise up to 33°C. Beechcraft King Air E90 and A100, and 99A, Piper Cheyenne II, Avtek 400 and Embraer Xingu I.

PT6A-34. Flat rated at 584 ekW; 559 kW (783 ehp; 750 shp) at 2,200 propeller rpm to 31°C, this version has aircooled nozzle guide vanes. IAI 102/201 Arava, Saunders ST-28, Frakes Aviation (Grumman) Mallard conversion, Airmaster Avalon 680, Omni Turbo Titan, Spectrum-One, Embraer EMB-110P1/P2 and EMB-111, and Carajá.

PT6A-34B. Aluminium alloy replaces magnesium in major castings. Fitted to Beechcraft T-44A.

PT6A-34AG. Agricultural certificated on diesel fuel. Frakes conversion of Ag-Cat and Ayres Turbo-Thrush. Selected for PZL-106AT/BT Turbo-Kruk, Schweizer Turbo Ag-Cat and Norman Fieldmaster.

PT6A-135. Flat rated at 587 ekW; 559 kW (787 ehp; 750 shp) at 1,900 rpm. Changed drive ratio to reduce noise; higher cycle temperatures. JetCrafters Taurus, Beechcraft King Air F90 (-135A), Embraer 121A1 Xingu II, Piper Cheyenne IIXL, AAC Regent 1500 (Riley Turbine Eagle 421), Airmaster Avalon 680, and Schafer Comanchero/Comanchero 750 conversions.

PT6A-135A. Higher thermodynamic ratings. Avtek 400, Beech F90-1 and OMAC Laser 300.

PT6A-36. Flat rated at 586 ekW; 559 kW (786 ehp; 750 shp) at 2,200 propeller rpm to 36°C. Similar to -34 but higher rating. Fitted to IAI 101B/202 Arava and Beechcraft C99.

PT6A-41. Higher mass flow, aircooled nozzle guide vanes and two-stage free turbine. T-O rating of 673 ekW; 634 kW (903 ehp; 850 shp) at 2,000 propeller rpm, to 41°C. Thermodynamic power 812 ekW (1,089 ehp). Beechcraft Super King Air 200 and C-12, and Piper Cheyenne III.

PT6A-41AG. For agricultural aviation. Frakes Turbo-Cat and Schweizer Turbo Ag-Cat.

PT6A-42. A-41 with increase in cruise performance. Beechcraft Super King Air B200.

PT6A-45A. A-41 with gearbox to transmit higher powers at reduced speeds. Rated at 916 ekW; 875 kW (1,229 ehp; 1,173 shp) at 1,700 rpm to 8°C, or to 21°C with water injection. Shorts 330 and Mohawk 298.

PT6A-45B. A-45A with increased water injection.

PT6A-45R. A-45B with reserve power rating and deleted water system.

T101-CP-100. A-45R for Shorts C-23A.

PT6A-50. A-41 with higher ratio reduction gear for quieter operation. T-O 875.5 ekW; 835 kW (1,174 ehp; 1,120 shp) with water up to 34°C at 1,210 propeller rpm. DHC-7.

PT6A-60A. A-45B with jet flap intake and increased mass flow for high altitude cruise. Rated at 830 ekW; 783 kW (1,113 ehp; 1,050 shp) at 1,700 rpm to 25°C. Beech Super King Air 300.

PT6A-61. A-60 gas generator matched with A-41 power section with 2,000 rpm gearbox. T-O rating 673 ekW; 634 kW (903 ehp; 850 shp) to 46°C. Cheyenne IIIA.

PT6A-62. Flat rated to 708 kW (950 shp). Pilatus PC-9.

PT6A-65B. A-65R without reserve rating. Flat rated at 875.5 ekW; 820 kW (1,174 ehp; 1,100 shp) at 1,700 rpm to 51°C. Beechcraft 1900 and C-12 J.

PT6A-65R. A-45R with four-stage compressor with jet flap intake, fuel control and fuel dump. Improved hot end and exhaust duct. Reserve power 1,087 ekW; 1,026 kW (1,459 ehp; 1,376 shp) at 1,700 rpm to 28°C. Alternative T-O at 975 ekW; 917 kW (1,308 ehp; 1,230 shp) at 1,700 rpm to 24°C. Shorts 360.

PT6A-65AR. Reserve power 1,125 ekW; 1,062 kW (1,509 ehp; 1,424 shp) at 1,700 rpm to 27.7°C. Shorts 360 and AMI DC-3.

PT6A-66. Flat rated at 674 ekW; 534 kW (905 ehp; 850 shp) at 2,000 rpm to 62.2°C. Piaggio Avanti with opposed rotation gearbox.

PT6A-67. Flat rated at 870 ekW; 820 kW (1,167 ehp; 1,100 shp) at 1,700 rpm to 60°C. Beechcraft Starship 2000 and RC-12K.

PT6A-67A. Flat rated at 948 ekW; 894 kW (1,272 ehp; 1,200 shp) at 1,700 rpm to 51°C. Powers Beech Starship 1.

PT6A-67AF. Flat rated at 1,125 ekW; 1,061 kW (1,509 ehp; 1,424 shp) at 1,700 rpm to 37.2°C. Powers Conair/IMP Turbo Firecat.

PT6A-67R. A-67 with reserve power rating for commuter aircraft.

PT6A-67R. Flat rated at 1,125 ekW; 1,061 kW (1,509 ehp; 1,424 shp) at 1,700 rpm to 37.2°C. Powers Shorts 360-300.

The following data apply generally to the PT6A series:
TYPE: Free turbine axial-plus-centrifugal turboprop.
PROPELLER DRIVE (all models up to and including PT6A-41): Two-stage planetary. Ratio 15. Higher ratio gears for A-45R, -50, -60, -65 and -67.

AIR INTAKE: Annular at rear with screen. Aircraft-supplied alcohol or inertial anti-icing.
COMPRESSOR: Three axial stages, plus single centrifugal (-65 series, four axial stages). PT6A-27: pressure ratio 6.7, mass flow 3.1 kg (6.8 lb/s). PT6A-65: pressure ratio 10, mass flow 4.3 kg (9.5 lb/s).
COMBUSTION CHAMBER: Annular reverse flow, with 14 simplex burners. Versions up to A-34 have two glow plug igniters with option of two spark igniters; A-38 onwards, two spark igniters.
FUEL SYSTEM: Bendix DP-F2 pneumatic automatic fuel control. A-50 has DP-F3 with starting spill valve and motive flow systems; A-60 series (except -62) have Woodward 83212 hydromechanical system.
FUEL GRADE: JP-1, JP-4, JP-5, MIL-J-5624. Gasolines (MIL-G-5572) grades 80/87, 91/98, 100/130 and 115/145 for up to 150 h during any overhaul period. Agricultural use, diesel.
TURBINES: Up to A-34 two single-stage axial; HP (58 blades) drives compressor, and LP (41 shrouded blades) drives output shaft. A-41 onward have two-stage LP turbine. All blades have fir tree root.
ACCESSORIES: Pads on accessory case (rear of engine) for starter/generator, hydraulic pump, aircraft accessory drive, vacuum pump and tachometer generator. Pad on reduction gear for propeller governor, constant speed unit and tachometer.
LUBRICATION SYSTEM: One pressure and four scavenge elements driven by gas generator. Integral oil tank 8.75 litres (2.3 US gallons).
OIL SPECIFICATION: CPW202, PWA521 Type II (7.5 cs vis) (MIL-L-23699, MIL-L-7808 for military engines).
STARTING: Electric starter/generator on accessory case.
DIMENSIONS:

Max diameter	483 mm (19 in)
Length, excl accessories:	
PT6A-11 to -36	1,575 mm (62 in)
PT6A-41, 42, 61	1,701 mm (67 in)
PT6A-45, 60A	1,829 mm (72 in)
PT6A-50	2,133 mm (84 in)
PT6A-62, -66	1,778 mm (70 in)
PT6A-65B, -67	1,880 mm (74 in)
PT6A-65R, -65AR	1,905 mm (75 in)

WEIGHT, DRY:

PT6A-11	142.4 kg (314 lb)
PT6A-11AG	145.6 kg (321 lb)
PT6A-110	148.3 kg (327 lb)
PT6A-112	147.8 kg (326 lb)
PT6A-114	156.5 kg (345 lb)
PT6A-15AG	144.7 kg (319 lb)
PT6A-21	143.3 kg (316 lb)
PT6A-25	154.6 kg (341 lb)
PT6A-25A	150.1 kg (331 lb)
PT6A-25C	151.9 kg (335 lb)
PT6A-27, -28	142.4 kg (314 lb)
PT6A-34, -36	145.1 kg (320 lb)
PT6A-34B, -135, -135A	149.7 kg (330 lb)
PT6A-34AG	143.8 kg (317 lb)
PT6A-41, -42	177.3 kg (391 lb)
PT6A-41AG	181.4 kg (400 lb)
PT6A-45A	196.8 kg (434 lb)
PT6A-45R	197.7 kg (436 lb)
PT6A-50	275.3 kg (607 lb)
PT6A-60A	210.9 kg (465 lb)
PT6A-61	193.2 kg (426 lb)
PT6A-62	205.9 kg (454 lb)
PT6A-65B, -65R	218.2 kg (481 lb)
PT6A-65AR	220.4 kg (486 lb)
PT6A-66	216.4 kg (477 lb)
PT6A-67, -67A	229.5 kg (506 lb)
PT6A-67AF	241.0 kg (532 lb)
PT6A-67R	233.5 kg (515 lb)

PERFORMANCE RATINGS (S/L, static):
  T-O: See under model listings
  Max continuous:

PT6A-110	374 ekW; 354 kW (502 ehp; 475 shp) at 1,900 rpm (to 38°C)
PT6A-11, 11AG	394 ekW; 373 kW (528 ehp; 500 shp) at 2,200 rpm (to 42°C)
PT6A-112	394 ekW; 373 kW (528 ehp; 500 shp) at 1,900 rpm (to 56°C)
PT6A-114	471 ekW; 447 kW (632 ehp; 600 shp) at 1,900 rpm (to 54.4°C)
PT6A-15AG, -27, -28	533 ekW; 507 kW (715 ehp; 680 shp) at 2,200 rpm (to 22°C)
PT6A-21	432.5 ekW; 410 kW (580 ehp; 550 shp) at 2,200 rpm (to 33°C)
PT6A-25, -25A	432.5 ekW; 410 kW (580 ehp; 550 shp) at 2,200 rpm (to 33°C)
PT6A-25C	584 ekW; 559 kW (783 ehp; 750 shp) at 2,200 rpm (to 31°C)
PT6A-34	584 ekW; 559 kW (783 ehp; 750 shp) at 2,200 rpm (to 30°C)
PT6A-135	587 ekW; 559 kW (787 ehp; 750 shp) at 1,900 rpm (-135 to 29°C, -135A to 34°C)
PT6A-36	586 ekW; 559 kW (786 ehp; 750 shp) at 2,200 rpm (to 36°C)
PT6A-41	673 ekW; 634 kW (903 ehp; 850 shp) at 2,000 rpm (to 41°C)
PT6A-42	674 ekW; 634 kW (904 ehp; 850 shp) at 2,000 rpm (to 41°C)

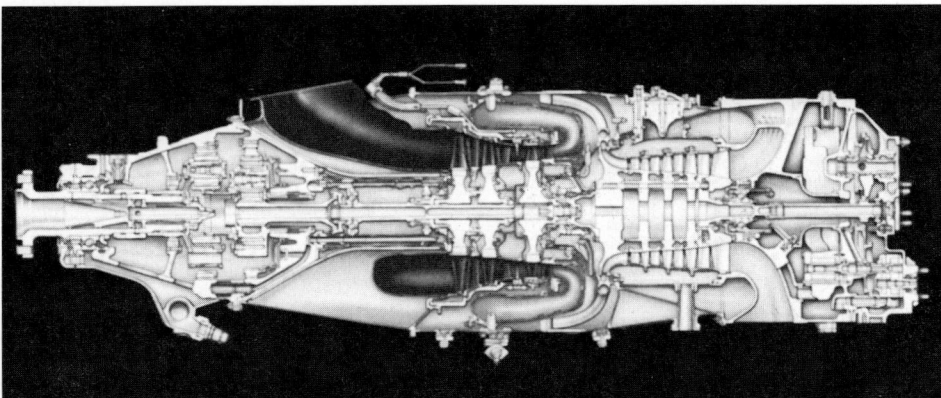

Longitudinal section through PT6A-67 turboprop (870 ekW; 1,167 ehp)

PT6A-45A, -45B, -45R   798 ekW; 761 kW (1,070 ehp;
                        1,020 shp) at 1,700 rpm
        (to: -45A, 26.7°C; -45B, 29°C; -45R, 33°C)
PT6A-50   762 ekW; 725.5 kW
        (1,022 ehp; 973 shp) at 1,210 rpm (to 32°C)
PT6A-60A   830 ekW; 783 kW
        (1,113 ehp; 1,050 shp) at 1,700 rpm (to 25°C)
PT6A-61   673 ekW; 634 kW (902 ehp; 850 shp)
                        at 2,000 rpm (to 46°C)
PT6A-62   751 ekW; 708 kW
        (1,008 ehp; 950 shp) at 2,000 rpm (to 37°C)
PT6A-65B   875 ekW; 820 kW
        (1,174 ehp; 1,100 shp) at 1,700 rpm (to 45°C)
PT6A-65R   931 ekW; 875 kW
        (1,249 ehp; 1,173 shp) at 1,700 rpm (to 38°C)
PT6A-66   675 ekW; 634 kW
        (905 ehp; 850 shp) at 2,000 rpm (to 62°C)
PT6A-67   870 ekW; 820 kW
        (1,167 ehp; 1,100 shp) at 1,700 rpm (to 54.4°C)
PT6A-67R   965 ekW; 910 kW
        (1,294 ehp; 1,220 shp) at 1,700 rpm (to 48°C)
Max cruise rating:
PT6A-110   374 ekW; 354 kW (502 ehp; 475 shp)
                        at 1,900 rpm (to 19°C)
PT6A-11   394 ekW; 373 kW (528 ehp; 500 shp)
                        at 2,200 rpm (to 37°C)
PT6A-11AG   394 ekW; 373 kW (528 ehp; 500 shp)
                        at 2,200 rpm (to 36°C)
PT6A-112   394 ekW; 373 kW (528 ehp; 500 shp)
                        at 1,900 rpm (to 48°C)
PT6A-114   471 ekW; 447 kW (632 ehp; 600 shp)
                        at 1,900 rpm (to 31.1°C)
PT6A-15AG   as PT6A-27
PT6A-21, -25, -25A
               432.5 ekW; 410 kW (580 ehp; 550 shp)
        at 2,200 rpm (to 47.2°C; 33°C; 33°C)
PT6A-25C   545 ekW; 522 kW (731 ehp; 700 shp)
                        at 2,200 rpm (to 19°C)
PT6A-27   486 ekW; 462 kW (652 ehp; 620 shp)
                        at 2,200 rpm (to 21°C)
PT6A-28   486 ekW; 462 kW (652 ehp; 620 shp)
                        at 2,200 rpm (to 33°C)
PT6A-34   545 ekW; 522 kW (731 ehp; 700 shp)
                        at 2,200 rpm (to 19°C)
PT6A-135   548 ekW; 522 kW (735 ehp; 700 shp)
        at 1,900 rpm (-135 to 37°C, -135A to 41°C)
PT6A-36   548 ekW; 522 kW (735 ehp; 700 shp)
                        at 2,200 rpm (to 19°C)
PT6A-41   673 ekW; 634 kW (903 ehp; 850 shp)
                        at 2,000 rpm (to 28°C)
PT6A-42   674 ekW; 634 kW (904 ehp; 850 shp)
                        at 2,000 rpm (to 33°C)
PT6A-45   749 ekW; 713 kW
        (1,004 ehp; 956 shp) at 1,425 rpm (to 15°C)
PT6A-50   706 ekW; 671 kW (947 ehp; 900 shp)
                        at 1,020-1,160 rpm (to 23°C)
PT6A-60A   791 ekW; 746 kW
        (1,061 ehp; 1,000 shp) at 1,700 rpm (to 28°C)
PT6A-61   as max continuous but to 43.8°C
PT6A-62   712 ekW; 671 kW
        (955 ehp; 900 shp) at 2,000 rpm (to 32°C)
PT6A-65B, -65R   762 ekW; 713 kW
        (1,022 ehp; 956 shp) at 1,425 rpm (to 27°C)
PT6A-65AR   762 ekW; 713 kW
        (1,022 ehp; 956 shp) at 1,425 rpm (to 29°C)
PT6A-66   675 ekW; 634 kW
        (905 ehp; 850 shp) at 2,000 rpm (to 56°C)
PT6A-67, -67A   792 ekW; 746 kW
        (1,062 ehp; 1,000 shp) at 1,700 rpm (to 50°C)
PT6A-67AF   808 ekW; 760 kW
        (1,083 ehp; 1,020 shp) at 1,700 rpm (to 37°C)
PT6A-67R   808 ekW; 761 kW
        (1,083 ehp; 1,020 shp) at 1,425 rpm (to 35°C)
SPECIFIC FUEL CONSUMPTION:
At T-O rating:
PT6A-110   111.0 µg/J (0.657 lb/h/ehp)
PT6A-11, -11AG   109.4 µg/J (0.647 lb/h/ehp)
PT6A-112   107.6 µg/J (0.637 lb/h/ehp)
PT6A-114   108.2 µg/J (0.640 lb/h/ehp)
PT6A-15AG, -27, -28   101.8 µg/J (0.602 lb/h/ehp)
PT6A-21, -25, -25A   106.5 µg/J (0.630 lb/h/ehp)
PT6A-25C, -34, -34B, -34AG
                        100.6 µg/J (0.595 lb/h/ehp)
PT6A-135, -135A   98.9 µg/J (0.585 lb/h/ehp)
PT6A-36   99.7 µg/J (0.590 lb/h/ehp)
PT6A-41, -61   99.9 µg/J (0.591 lb/h/ehp)
PT6A-42   101.5 µg/J (0.601 lb/h/ehp)
PT6A-45A, -45B   93.5 µg/J (0.554 lb/h/ehp)
PT6A-45R   93.4 µg/J (0.553 lb/h/ehp)
PT6A-50   94.6 µg/J (0.560 lb/h/ehp)
PT6A-60A   92.6 µg/J (0.548 lb/h/ehp)
PT6A-62   95.8 µg/J (0.567 lb/h/ehp)
PT6A-65B   90.6 µg/J (0.536 lb/h/ehp)
PT6A-65R   86.5 µg/J (0.512 lb/h/ehp)
PT6A-65AR   86.0 µg/J (0.509 lb/h/ehp)
PT6A-66   104.8 µg/J (0.620 lb/h/ehp)
PT6A-67   92.4 µg/J (0.547 lb/h/ehp)
PT6A-67R   92.8 µg/J (0.549 lb/h/ehp)
PT6A-67AF, -67R   87.9 µg/J (0.520 lb/h/ehp)
OIL CONSUMPTION:
Max   0.091 kg (0.20 lb)/h

The P&WC PT6B-36, with contingency rating of 760 kW (1,020 shp)

P&WC T74

T74 is a US designation for military versions of the PT6A turboprop and PT6B turboshaft.

T74-CP-700. US Army PT6A-20. More than 300 delivered to Beechcraft for 129 U-21A. Inertial separator system.

T74-CP-702. Rated at 580 ekW (778 ehp) and retrofitted in Beechcraft U-21.

P&WC PT6B/PT6C

The PT6B is the commercial turboshaft version of the PT6A and has a lower ratio reduction gear. Current versions are:

PT6B-36. Reverse drive 6,409 rpm gearbox. T-O rating 732 kW (981 shp) to 15°C, with 2½-min contingency 770 kW (1,033 shp) to 15°C. Sikorsky S-76B.

PT6B-36A. Identical to -36 but with different ratings.

PT6C. Direct drive from the power turbine.

DIMENSIONS:
Max diameter: PT6B-36, -36A   495 mm (19.5 in)
Length, excl accessories:
PT6B-36, -36A,   1,504 mm (59.2 in)
WEIGHT, DRY:
PT6B-36   169 kg (372 lb)
PT6B-36A   171 kg (378 lb)
PERFORMANCE RATINGS:
T-O: See under model listings
Max cruise, continuous:
PT6B-36   640 kW (870 shp) to 15°C
PT6B-36A   652 kW (887 shp) to 15°C
SPECIFIC FUEL CONSUMPTION:
At T-O rating:
PT6B-36   100.5 µg/J (0.594 lb/h/shp)
PT6B-36A   98.2 µg/J (0.581 lb/h/shp)
OIL CONSUMPTION:
Max   0.091 kg (0.20 lb)/h

P&WC PT6T TWIN-PAC
US military designation: T400 (separate entry)

First run in July 1968, the Twin-Pac comprises two PT6 turboshaft engines side by side and driving a combining gearbox.

PT6T-3. T-O rating 1,342 kW (1,800 shp). For Bell and Agusta Bell 212 and S-58T.

In these applications, shaft power is limited by the transmission. In the Model 212 the 1,342 kW (1,800 shp) PT6T-3 is restricted to a T-O rating of 962 kW (1,290 shp) and 843 kW (1,130 shp) for continuous power. In the S-58T the limits are 1,122 kW (1,505 shp) at T-O and 935 kW (1,254 shp) for continuous operation.

PT6T-3B. PT6T-3 with some T-6 hardware and improved single-engine performance. Bell 212 and 412.

PT6T-6. Improved compressor-turbine nozzle guide vanes and rotor blades. S-58T and AB 212. By 1988 16,750,000 equivalent PT6 hours had been flown by PT6T engines in 2,004 helicopters in 82 countries.

The following features differ from the PT6:
TYPE: Coupled free turbine turboshaft.
SHAFT DRIVE: Combining gearbox comprises three separate gear trains, two input and one output, each contained within an individual sealed compartment and all interconnected by drive shafts. Overall reduction ratio 5.
AIR INTAKES: Additional inertial particle separator to reduce ingestion. High frequency compressor noise suppressed.
FUEL SYSTEM: As PT6 with manual backup, and dual manifold for cool starts. Automatic power sharing and torque limiting.
FUEL GRADES: JP-1, JP-4 and JP-5.
ACCESSORIES: Starter/generator and tachogenerator on accessory case at front of each power section. Other drives on gearbox, including power turbine governors and tachogenerators, and provision for blowers and aircraft accessories.

OIL SPECIFICATION: PWA Spec 521. For military engines, MIL-L-7808 and -23699.
STARTING: Electrical, with cold weather starting down to −54°C.
DIMENSIONS:
Length   1,702 mm (67.0 in)
Width   1,118 mm (44.0 in)
Height   838 mm (33.0 in)
WEIGHT, DRY (standard equipment):
PT6T-3   292 kg (645 lb)
PT6T-3B, -6   298 kg (657 lb)
PERFORMANCE RATINGS:
T-O (5 min):
Total output, at 6,600 rpm:
PT6T-3, -3B   1,342 kW (1,800 shp)
PT6T-6   1,398 kW (1,875 shp) (to 21°C)
Single power section only, at 6,600 rpm:
PT6T-3, -3B   671 kW (900 shp)
PT6T-6, -3B (2½ min) 764 kW (1,025 shp)
30 min power (single power section), at 6,600 rpm:
PT6T-3B, -6   723 kW (970 shp)
Cruise A:
Total output, at 6,600 rpm:
PT6T-3, -3B   932 kW (1,250 shp)
PT6T-6   1,014 kW (1,360 shp)
Single power section only, at 6,600 rpm:
PT6T-3, -3B   466 kW (625 shp)
PT6T-6   500 kW (670 shp)
Cruise B:
Total output, at 6,600 rpm:
PT6T-3, -3B   820 kW (1,100 shp)
PT6T-6   891 kW (1,195 shp)
Single power section only, at 6,600 rpm:
PT6T-3, -3B   410 kW (550 shp)
PT6T-6   440 kW (590 shp)
Ground idle, at 2,200 rpm   44.7 kW (60 shp) max
SPECIFIC FUEL CONSUMPTION:
At 2½-min rating (single power section):
PT6T-3B   100.7 µg/J (0.596 lb/h/shp)
PT6T-6   101.6 µg/J (0.602 lb/h/shp)
OIL CONSUMPTION:
Max (for both gas generators)   0.18 kg (0.4 lb)/h

P&WC T400

Military version of the PT6T Twin-Pac; castings of aluminium instead of magnesium and minimum infra-red signature. Produced since March 1970 for Bell UH-1N, AH-1J and CH-135. Deliveries totalled 799 engines.

The T400-WV-402 is the military PT6T-6 and is used in the AH-1T; 524 were delivered.

DIMENSIONS (CP-400 and WV-402):
Length   1,659 mm (65.3 in)
Width   1,115 mm (43.5 in)
Height   828 mm (32.6 in)
WEIGHT, DRY:
T400-CP-400   324 kg (714 lb)
T400-WV-402   338 kg (745 lb)
PERFORMANCE RATINGS:
Intermediate:
T400-CP-400   1,342 kW (1,800 shp) at 6,600 rpm
T400-WV-402   1,469 kW (1,970 shp) at 6,600 rpm
Max continuous:
T400-CP-400   1,141 kW (1,530 shp) at 6,600 rpm
T400-WV-402   1,248 kW (1,673 shp) at 6,600 rpm
SPECIFIC FUEL CONSUMPTION (Intermediate rating):
T400-CP-400   100.4 µg/J (0.594 lb/h/shp)
T400-WV-402   99.9 µg/J (0.591 lb/h/shp)

P&WC PW200

In 1983 P&WC announced the development of this new engine series. The basic design is flexible and is planned to permit increased power and reduced sfc without dimensional change. The first model in the series is the

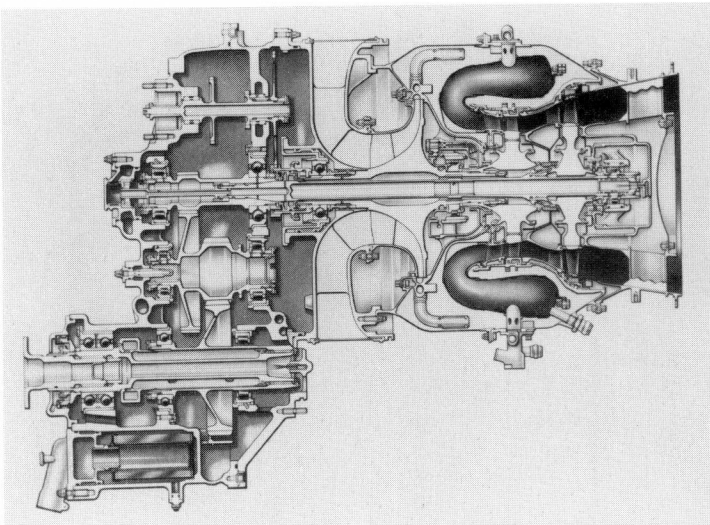

Cutaway drawing and photograph of the P&WC PW205B free-turbine turboshaft (466 kW; 625 shp)

PW205B. The power section contains fewer than half as many parts as in previous engines. Certification is due in January 1990. The first application is the MBB BO 105LS B-1.

TYPE: Free-turbine turboshaft.

AIR INTAKE: Inwards amidships through mesh screen, with integral scroll.

COMPRESSOR: Single-stage centrifugal of machined titanium. Pressure ratio 8.

COMBUSTION CHAMBER: Reverse-flow annular with 12 air blast nozzles. Two capacitor discharge igniters.

FUEL SYSTEM: Hydromechanical with digital electronics powered by dedicated alternator.
FUEL GRADE: Any turbine type of diesel A or AA.
TURBINES: Single-stage axial compressor and power turbines with blades held in dovetail slots. Cold junction temperature sensing.
GEARBOX: Front mounted combined reduction and accessory gearbox with 6,000 rpm output. Includes phase shift torquemeter and drives for starter/generator, hydraulic pump and alternator.
DIMENSIONS:
Length   907 mm (35.7 in)

Width	566 mm (22.3 in)
Height	483 mm (19 in)
PERFORMANCE RATINGS:	
2½ min	466 kW (625 shp)
30 min and T-O	440 kW (590 shp)
Max continuous	358 kW (480 shp)
SPECIFIC FUEL CONSUMPTIONS:	
2½ min	93.8 µg/J (0.555 lb/h/ehp)
30 min and T-O	93.9 µg/J (0.556 lb/h/ehp)
Max continuous	96.8 µg/J (0.573 lb/h/ehp)

CHINA
(PEOPLE'S REPUBLIC)

CATIC
CHINA AERO-TECHNOLOGY IMPORT AND EXPORT CORPORATION
ADDRESS: PO Box 1671, Beijing
Telephone: 442 444
Telex: 22318 AEROT CN
Cable: CAID Beijing

NATIONAL AIRCRAFT ENGINE FACTORIES
LOCATIONS: Shenyang, Xian, Harbin, Chengdu, Liyang, Zuzhou and Shanghai

PISTON ENGINES
The first aircraft engine made in numbers in the People's Republic of China was the Soviet M-11 radial. In 1958 licences were obtained for two additional Soviet engines, the Ivchenko AI-14R and Shvetsov ASh-62IR (both described under Poland), fitted respectively to the locally built Jinge (Chinko) No. 1 (Yak-12) and Y-5 (An-2). Both of these aircraft and their engines were built in large numbers, the engines being known as the HS-6A and HS-5 (Huosai-6A and -5) respectively. By 1959 the 1,268 kW (1,700 shp) Shvetsov ASh-82V 14-cylinder radial and the Czech M 332 were also being produced.

Production is continuing on the Huosai-6A (based now on the Vedeneyev AI-14RF) for the CJ-6 trainer and Y-11 STOL transport.

GAS TURBINE ENGINES
In 1959 the first Chinese J-5 (F-5), a licence built MiG-17F, began a production run of more than 1,000 aircraft, all powered by Chinese built WP-5 (Klimov VK-1F) turbojets rated at 33.2 kN (7,452 lb st). The non-afterburning WP-5D (VK-1A) version powers the JJ-5 trainer and all versions of the H-5 (Chinese Il-28).

Plans to build the Tu-16 bomber and its Mikulin AM-3M engines were drawn up in 1958. The bomber and all spare parts remain in production at Xian, together with Wopen-8 (RD-3M) engines.

In February 1959 the Chinese obtained a licence for the MiG-19 fighter. Soon afterwards the relationship with the Soviet Union was severed; but the Chinese, working alone, managed to fly a locally built J-6 (F-6) (MiG-19) in 1961, and have since produced this fighter in very large numbers. Thus, several thousand WP-6 (R-9BF-811) engines have been made at Shenyang.

In 1975 a licence was obtained for manufacture of the Rolls-Royce Spey 202. Engines were produced and qualified, but full production was not undertaken at that period. In 1988 the prototype of a Spey-powered military aircraft was expected to fly, and the Xian factory is

Yuhe YH 280 piston engine

preparing for full production, not only of the Mk 202 but also of Speys for surface applications.

Turboprops manufactured in China include the WJ-5A-1 (Wojiang 5A-1), the Ivchenko AI-24A; the WJ-6 (Ivchenko AI-20K); and a modified WJ-5, the WZ-5 (Wozhou-5), for the Z-6 helicopter. In May 1986 China signed an agreement for licence assembly and testing of the P&WC PT6A used in the Chinese Y-12, and orders for the A310, MD-82 and Challenger civil transports may lead to renewed interest in other P&W engines. Chinese factories also undertake licence production of the Turbomeca Arriel turboshaft, for the Harbin Z-9 (Aérospatiale Dauphin 2) helicopter, as the WZ-8.

SHENYANG WP-6
This engine is the Chinese version of the Soviet Tumansky RD-9BF-811. Several thousand have been made for J-6 and JJ-6 fighter and training aircraft. From it the Shenyang factory developed the **WP-6A**, which differs in having variable inlet stators, a redesigned first-stage compressor, completely revised hot section with improved materials, and a new afterburner stabiliser giving a wider stable combustion range with reduced loss. The following is a description of the WP-6A which powers the Q-5 (A-5).
INLET: Cast assembly with four de-iced radial struts, one housing drive to accessory section above and projecting ahead of inlet. Central fixed bullet and front bearing.
COMPRESSOR: Welded ring construction with one row of variable inlet stators and nine rows of rotor blades. T-O airflow 46.2 kg (101.85 lb)/s. Pressure ratio 7.44.
COMBUSTION CHAMBER: Can-annular type with 12 flame tubes, each terminating in a section of turbine inlet periphery. Spill type burners. Two igniters fed from starting tank.

TURBINE: Two-stage type with blades inserted into large flat discs, driving compressor via tubular shaft.
AFTERBURNER: Constant diameter type with main starting burner in turbine rear cone and single ring of fuel nozzles and gutter flameholders around rear of cone. Ten adjustable nozzle flaps positioned by four rams.
DIMENSIONS:

Length	5,483 mm (215.9 in)
Max height	950 mm (37.4 in)
Diameter	668 mm (26.3 in)
WEIGHT, DRY:	725 kg (1,598 lb)
PERFORMANCE RATINGS (S/L, static):	
Afterburner	36.78 kN (8,267 lb st)
Max dry	29.42 kN (6,614 lb st)
Normal	24.03 kN (5,401 lb st)
SPECIFIC FUEL CONSUMPTION:	
Afterburner	0.163 kg/h/N (45.24 mg/Ns; 1.597 lb/h/lb st)
Max	0.1 kg/h/N (27.76 mg/Ns; 0.980 lb/h/lb st)
Normal	0.099 kg/h/N (27.48 mg/Ns; 0.970 lb/h/lb st)

CHENGDU WP-7
Chengdu was entrusted with modifying the Soviet Tumansky R-11 turbojet and putting it into production for the F-7 (MiG-21F) as the WP-7. This engine is no longer in production. The **WP-7BM**, needing no separate gasoline starting tank, is in production for the F-7M Airguard. The following details relate to the WP-7BM:
TYPE: Two-shaft turbojet with afterburner.
INLET: No inlet guide vanes, first LP compressor stage overhung ahead of front roller bearing.
COMPRESSOR: Three-stage LP compressor with pressure ratio of 2.74. Three-stage HP compressor giving overall pressure ratio of 8.1. All blades inserted into discs carried on short tubular shafts.
COMBUSTION CHAMBER: Can-annular, with ten flame tubes, Nos. 1 and 6 being of a different pattern and incorporating torch igniters.
TURBINES: Single-stage HP with 96 inserted shrouded blades. Single-stage LP with shrouded blades. Outlet gas temperature 1,083°K (810°C).
AFTERBURNER: Multiple gutters and double-wall liner. Multi-flap nozzle driven by four hydraulic rams. Up to 40 h operation permitted in each 200 h overhaul period.
PERFORMANCE RATINGS (S/L, static):

Max afterburner	59.82 kN (13,448 lb st)
Max dry	43.15 kN (9,700 lb st)
SPECIFIC FUEL CONSUMPTION (as above):	
Max afterburner	56.37 mg/Ns (1.99 lb/h/lb st)
Max dry	28.61 mg/Ns (1.01 lb/h/lb st)

LIYANG WP-13

This engine is derived from the WP-7. The compressor work per stage and airflow are both increased. The HP compressor has five stages, the casing being titanium. There are many other modifications, aimed mainly at increasing service life (see data). The derived WP-13A II, made at the Liyang Machinery Co, has a longer afterburner and is the power unit of the J-8 II twin-engined fighter.

DIMENSIONS:
Length overall:
WP-13   4,600 mm (181.1 in)
WP-13A II   5,150 mm (202.75 in)
Diameter: both   907 mm (35.71 in)
Max height: WP-13   1,085 mm (42.72 in)

WEIGHT, DRY:
WP-13   1,211 kg (2,670 lb)
WP-13A II   1,201 kg (2,648 lb)
PERFORMANCE RATINGS (S/L, static):
Max afterburner:
WP-13   64.73 kN (14,550 lb st) at 11,156 LP rpm
WP-13A II   65.9 kN (14,815 lb st)
Max dry:
WP-13   40.21 kN (9,039 lb st) at 11,156 LP rpm
WP-13A II   42.7 kN (9,590 lb st)
SPECIFIC FUEL CONSUMPTION (as above):
Max afterburner:
WP-13   63.73 mg/Ns (2.25 lb/h/lb st)
WP-13A II   62.32 mg/Ns (2.20 lb/h/lb st)

Max dry:
WP-13   27.19 mg/Ns (0.96 lb/h/lb st)
WP-13A II   28.04 mg/Ns (0.99 lb/h/lb st)
OVERHAUL LIFE:
WP-13   500 h (total service life 1,500 h)
WP-13A II   300 h (including up to 90 h in afterburner)

SHENYANG WS-6

This two-spool afterburning turbofan, in the 122 kN (27,500 lb st) class, has reportedly been tested to British military engine standards, and may be the intended power plant of the new (H-7?) bomber.

The WP-6A afterburning turbojet

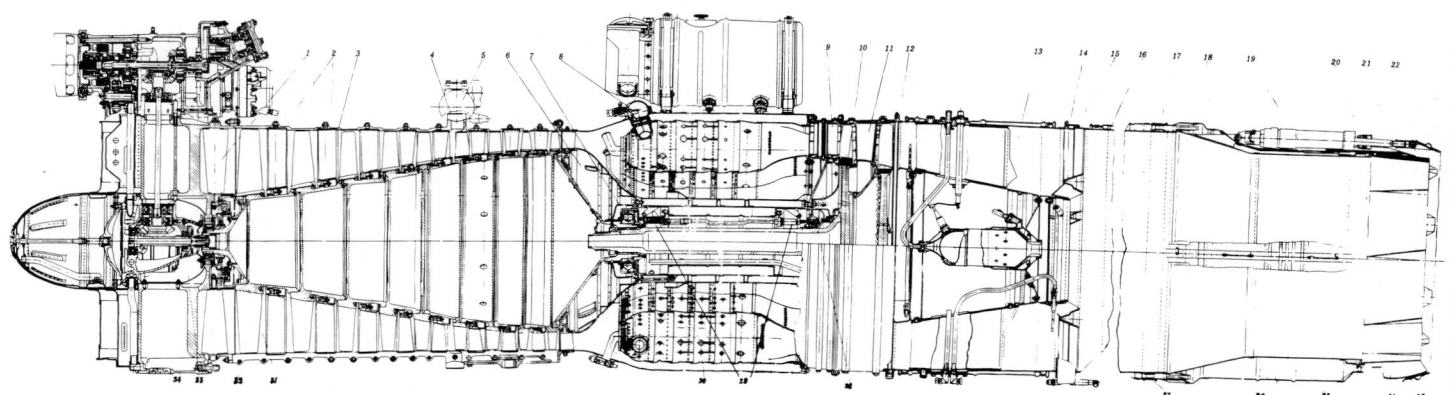

Longitudinal section through WP-6A turbojet
1 variable inlet stator, 2 stator vanes, 3 compressor case, 4 air bleed band, 5 bleed actuating cylinder, 6 rear load relief cavity, 7 centre bearing, 8 starting igniter, 9 stage 1 nozzle, 10 turbine rotor, 11 stage 2 nozzle, 12 quick-release ring, 13 diffuser, 14 quick-release ring, 15 front flange, 16 case, 17 shroud, 18 bracket, 19 actuating cylinder, 20 adjustable flap flange, 21 actuator and rod heat shield, 22 nozzle adjusting ring , 23 copper plate, 24 flap, 25 centring pin, 26 cylinder cowl, 27 clamp strip, 28 rear bearing, 29 oil jet, 30 flame tube, 31 compressor, 32 front load relief cavity, 33 front bearing, 34 front case

CHINESE AERO ENGINES

Class	Factory	Engine	Derivation	Max rating	Application
Piston (Huosai)	Zhuzhou	HS-5	ASh-62IR	746 kW (1,000 hp)	Y-5
	Harbin	HS-5A	ASh-82V	1,268 kW (1,700 hp)	Z-5
	Zhuzhou	HS-6A	AI-14RF	213 kW (285 hp)	CJ-6, Y-11, Haiyan (257 kW; 345 hp)
	?	HS-26	Chinese design?	19.4 kW (26 hp)	?
Turboprop (Wojiang)	Harbin	WJ-5A-1	AI-24A	1,901 ekW (2,550 ehp)	Y-7, Y7-100, Y-14, SH-5 (2,349 kW; 3,150 ehp)
	Shanghai	WJ-6	AI-20K	3,169 ekW (4,250 ehp)	Y-8
Turboshaft (Wozhou)	Shanghai	WZ-5	WJ-5A	about 1,790 kW (2,400 shp)	Z-6
	?	WZ-6	?	about 1,118 kW (1,500 shp)	Z-8
	Harbin	WZ-8	Arriel 1C/1C1	about 520 kW (698 shp)	Z-9/9A
Turbojet (Wopen)	Harbin	WP-2	RD-45	22.24 kN (5,000 lb st)	MiG-15, MiG-15UTI
	Harbin	WP-5	VK-1F	33.15 kN (7,452 lb st)*	J-5
	Harbin	WP-5D	VK-1A	26.48 kN (5,952 lb st)	JJ-5, H-5, HJ-5, HZ-5
	Shenyang	WP-6	RD-9BF-811	31.87 kN (7,165 lb st)*	J-6 and variants, Q-5/A-5
	Shenyang	WP-6A	WP-6	36.78 kN (8,267 lb st)*	Q-5M/A-5M
	Chengdu	WP-7A	R-11	50.01 kN (11,243 lb st)*	Early J-7/F-7
	Chengdu	WP-7B	WP-7A (improved afterburner)	59.82 kN (13,448 lb st)*	Current J-7/F-7, J-8/F-8 I
	Chengdu	WP-7B (BM)	WP-7B (kerosene instead of gasoline starting)	59.82 kN (13,448 lb st)*	F-7M, JJ-7
	Xian	WP-8	RD-3M	93.17 kN (20,944 lb st)	H-6
	Liyang	WP-13A II	R-13-300	65.9 kN (14,815 lb st)*	J-8 II
Turbofan (Woshan)	Shenyang	WS-6	?	122 kN (27,500 lb st)*	H-7?
	?	WS-9	?	?	?

*With afterburning

WS-9

The accompanying photograph, revealed in 1986, is all that was available on this augmented turbofan by mid-1988. It appears to have an overhung first fan stage with 31 or 32 blades with part-span shrouds, and several features suggest kinship with Tumansky engines and also with the small Pratt & Whitney Canada JT15D.

WP-7BM afterburning turbojet for the F-7M Airguard fighter

The Liyang WP-13A II turbojet (afterburner not fitted)

The first illustration of the Woshan-9 augmented turbofan

CZECHOSLOVAKIA

OMNIPOL

OMNIPOL FOREIGN TRADE CORPORATION
Nekázanka 11, 112 21 Prague 1
Telephone: (02) 2140 111

Omnipol is responsible for exporting products of the Czechoslovak aviation industry and for supplying information on those products which are available for export.

AEROTECHNIK

68604 Uherské Hradiste 4, Kunovice
Telephone: 5122
Telex: 60380
TECHNICAL DEPT: Ing J. Valný

This company is now producing the long established inverted four-cylinder Walter Mikron piston engine, of 2,180 cc (133 cu in) capacity. The factory at Mor. Trebová calls it the **Mikron IIIS (A)**. It is rated at 48.5 kW (65 hp) and powers the Aerotechnik L-13SW Vivat motor glider.

AVIA

AVIA OBOROVÝ PODNIK
199 03 Prague 9, Letňany
Telephone: Prague 89 51 21

Telex: Prague AVIA C 121 475

This company is at present engaged in series production of piston engines, propellers and spare parts.

AVIA M 137 A

Designed to power light aerobatic aircraft, the 134 kW (180 hp) M 137 A piston engine is a modification of the M 337 with fuel and oil systems for aerobatic operation and without a supercharger. It powers the Zlin 42 M and Z 526 F. The **M 137 AZ** is a modified version, with the air intake port at the rear so that a dust filter can be incorporated. Details are as M 337, with the following differences:

CRANKSHAFT: No oil holes for propeller control.
FUEL SYSTEM: Type LUN 5150 pump; system designed for sustained aerobatics.
STARTER: LUN 2131 electric.
DIMENSIONS:

Length	1,344 mm (52.9 in)
Width	443 mm (17.44 in)
Height	630 mm (24.80 in)
WEIGHT (incl starter):	141.5 kg (312 lb)

PERFORMANCE RATINGS:

T-O	134 kW (180 hp) at 2,750 rpm
Max continuous	119 kW (160 hp) at 2,680 rpm
Max cruise	104.5 kW (140 hp) at 2,580 rpm

SPECIFIC FUEL CONSUMPTION:

At T-O rating	91.26 μg/J (0.540 lb/h/hp)
At max cruise rating	81.96 μg/J (0.485 lb/h/hp)

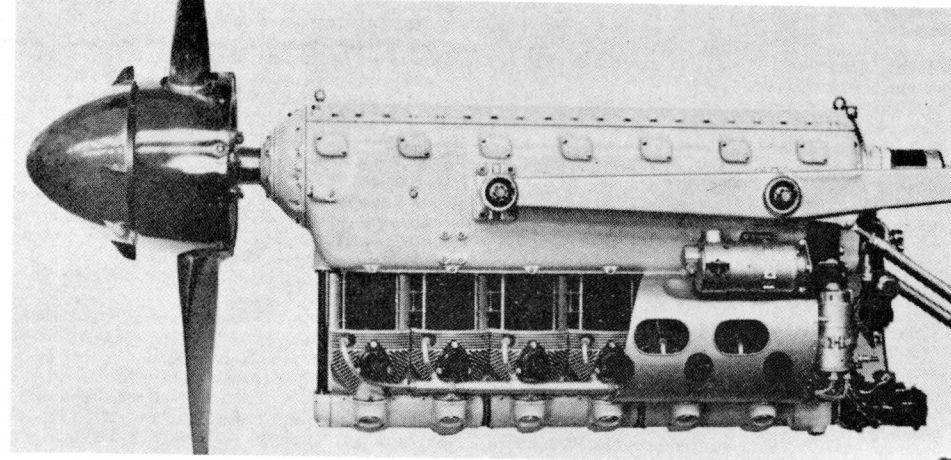

The 134 kW (180 hp) Avia M 137 A six-cylinder aircooled piston engine

AVIA M 337 A

The M 337 A six-cylinder aircooled supercharged engine powers several types of light aircraft that were built in Czechoslovakia, including the L-200D Morava, Zlin 43 and Zlin 726K. It can be supplied with hubs for fixed-pitch or controllable-pitch propellers. The **M 337 AK** is fitted to the Zlin 142.

TYPE: Six-cylinder inverted in-line aircooled, ungeared, supercharged and with direct fuel injection.
CYLINDERS: Bore 105 mm (4.13 in). Stroke 115 mm (4.53 in). Swept volume 5.97 litres (364.31 cu in). Compression ratio 6.3 : 1. Steel cylinders with cooling fins machined from solid. Cylinder bores nitrided. Detachable cylinder heads are aluminium alloy castings.
PISTONS: Aluminium alloy with graphited surfaces.
CONNECTING RODS: Two split big ends bolted together.
CRANKSHAFT: Forged from chrome vanadium steel, machined all over. Nitrided crankpins.

CRANKCASE: Heat treated magnesium alloy (Elektron).
IGNITION: Shielded type. Two plugs per cylinder.
LUBRICATION: Dry sump pressure feed type. The M 337 AK has a system for sustained inverted operation.
SUPERCHARGER: Centrifugal, ratio 7.4 : 1.
FUEL SYSTEM: Low pressure injection system with nozzles in front of inlet valves. The M 337 A has a unified fuel injection pump.
FUEL GRADE: Minimum 72-78 octane.
STARTING: Electric, engaged by an electromagnet.
ACCESSORIES: One 600W 28V dynamo. Electric tachometer. Propeller control unit. Mechanical tachometer on oil pump. Hydraulic pump to special order.
PROPELLER DRIVE: Direct left hand tractor.

DIMENSIONS:

Length, excl propeller boss	1,410 mm (55.51 in)
Width	472 mm (18.58 in)
Height	628 mm (24.72 in)
WEIGHT, DRY:	148 kg (326.3 lb)

PERFORMANCE RATINGS:

T-O	157 kW (210 hp) at 2,750 rpm
Max cruise at 1,200 m (3,940 ft)	112 kW (150 hp) at 2,400 rpm

SPECIFIC FUEL CONSUMPTION:

At T-O rating	100.6 μg/J (0.595 lb/h/hp)
At max cruise rating at 1,200 m (3,940 ft)	72.7 μg/J (0.430 lb/h/hp)

MOTORLET
MOTORLET NC, ZÁVOD JANA SVERMY
Prague-Jinonice
Telephone: Prague 520714
GENERAL MANAGER: Zdenek Horcik

Motorlet National Corporation operates the main aero engine establishment in Czechoslovakia, based on the former Walter factory at Jinonice, previously well known for its piston engines. The Walter name continues as a trademark for Motorlet engines. Motorlet started turbine engine manufacture in 1952 with licensed production of the Soviet RD-45 turbojet.

WALTER M 601
The M 601 was designed to power the L-410 transport. It drives an Avia V 508 propeller.

The first version, rated at 550 ehp, ran in October 1967. Development of the **M 601B**, of increased diameter, started during 1968. The Let L-410M powered by M 601B engines was in Aeroflot service by early 1979. The M 601B powers the L-410UVP. In 1982 a third variant, the **M 601D**, entered production. This gives increased power and can be operated for longer TBO.

By 1985 the **M 601Z** had entered production to power the Z 37T agricultural aircraft. It drives an auxiliary blower for the spraying/dusting installation. TBO is 1,000 h. The **M 601E** powers the current L-410UVP-E, and has been developed to a TBO of 2,000 h. It drives a VJ 8.508E five-blade propeller, and an alternator for anti-icing windshields and propeller blades.

TYPE: Free turbine turboprop.
PROPELLER DRIVE: Reduction gear at front of engine with drive from free turbine. Reduction ratio 14.9.
COMPRESSOR: Two axial stages of stainless steel, plus single centrifugal stage of titanium. Pressure ratio (601B) 6.4, (601D) 6.55, (601 E) 6.65, at 36,660 rpm gas generator speed. Air mass flow (601B) 3.25 kg (7.17 lb)/s, (601D) 3.55 kg (7.83 lb)/s, (601E) 3.6 kg (7.94 lb)/s.

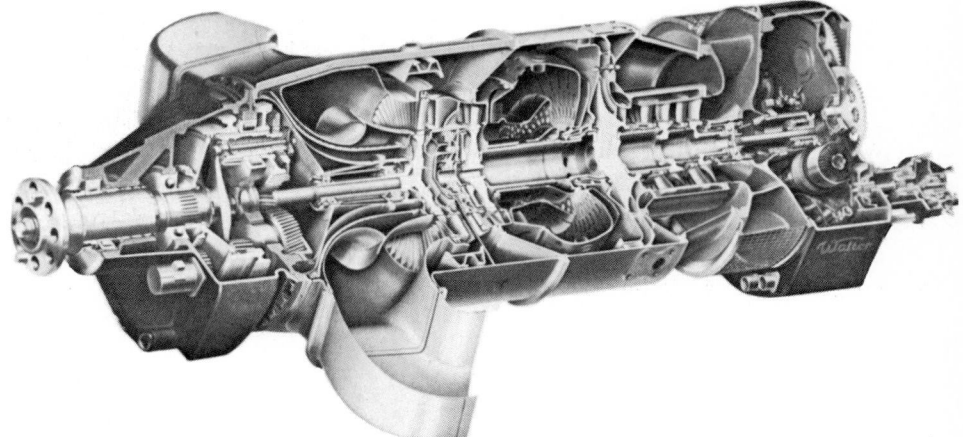

Cutaway drawing of the Walter M 601 E turboprop (560 kW; 751 shp)

COMBUSTION CHAMBER: Annular combustor with rotary fuel injection and low-voltage ignition.
COMPRESSOR TURBINE: Single stage; inlet temperature 952°C.
POWER TURBINE: Single stage.
FUEL SYSTEM: Low pressure regulator, providing gas generator and power turbine speed controls.
FUEL GRADE: PL4, PL5 kerosene.
LUBRICATION SYSTEM: Pressure gear-pump circulation. Integral oil tank and cooler.
OIL SPECIFICATION: B3V synthetic oil.
STARTING: LUN 2132-8 8kW electric starter/generator.
DIMENSIONS:

Length: 601D	1,658 mm (65.27 in)
601B, E, Z	1,675 mm (65.94 in)
Width	590 mm (23.23 in)
Height	650 mm (25.59 in)

WEIGHT, DRY:

601B, D, E	193 kg (425.5 lb)
601Z	197 kg (434.3 lb)

PERFORMANCE RATINGS (T-O):

601B	515 kW (691 shp)
601D	540 kW (724 shp)
601E	560 kW (751 shp)
601Z	360 kW (483 shp)

SPECIFIC FUEL CONSUMPTION (T-O):

601B	109.55 μg/J (0.648 lb/h/ehp)
601D	109.4 μg/J (0.647 lb/h/ehp)

EGYPT

AOI
AOI ENGINE FACTORY (135)
PO Box 12, Helwan
Telephone: 745090, 747984 and 781088
Telex: 92135 ENFAC UN

CHAIRMAN: Hassan El Gebali

Among other work, about 3,500 people are employed in assembly and test of the Larzac 04 and PT6A-25E, delivery of the first PT6 having been made in 1985. Following selection of a new fighter for the Egyptian Air Force, the factory is expected to assemble either the F100, F404 or M53-P2. Since 1980 AOI/EF has carried out complete overhaul, repair and test of Soviet APUs and the SNECMA Atar 9C and Larzac, GE T64 and Allison T56.

FRANCE

FAM
FRANCE AÉRO MOTEURS SARL
Roanne

CONTACT: Avions Pierre Robin (see Aircraft section)

This company, inaugurated on 29 April 1985, was formed on a 50/50 basis by Avions Pierre Robin and the Motorop division of Besson-Moteurs Sopart, to develop an aircraft version of the PRV (Peugeot-Renault-Volvo) V6 car engine. It is still in the development phase.

JPX

ATELIERS JPX

Z.I. Nord, BP 13, 72320 Vibraye
Telephone: 43 93 61 74
Telex: 722151 F
Fax: 43 93 62 71

PUL 212

The PUL 212 is a single-cylinder low cost two-stroke, with bore of 66 mm (2.6 in), stroke of 62 mm (2.44 in) and capacity of 212 cc. Weighing 7.9 kg (17.42 lb) with pull cord inertia starter, it gives 11 kW (15 hp) at 6,000 rpm and is cleared to run at up to 6,500 rpm.

PUL 425

This is an opposed engine with two cylinders of the same size as in the PUL 212. Dry weight is 14.5 kg (32 lb), or 16.7 kg (36.8 lb) with silencer. Rated power is 16.4 kW (22 hp) at 4,600 rpm. With 0.5 reduction gear weight is 21 kg (46 lb).

JPX 4T60/A

Unlike previous JPX engines this is a four-stroke, with four opposed aircooled cylinders with bore 93.0 mm (3.66 in) and stroke 75.4 mm (2.97 in). Capacity 2,050 cc (125 cu in). Compression ratio 8.2. Overall length 650 mm (25.6 in). Width 805 mm (31.7 in). Weight, dry (without propeller hub) 73.0 kg (161 lb). Developed from the Volkswagen VW126A of smaller capacity, the 4T60/A has an electric starter and alternator, and is rated at 47.8 kW (65 hp) at 3,200 rpm, and 42.0 kW (57 hp) at 2,500 rpm. Using 4-star motor fuel or 100LL fuel, this engine was certificated by the DGAC on 9 January 1985, ready for production for the Robin ATL. The **4T60/AES** for ultralight aircraft weighs 61 kg (134 lb).

The lightweight JPX 4T60/AES

MICROTURBO

MICROTURBO SA

Chemin du Pont de Rupé, BP 2089, 31019 Toulouse Cédex
Telephone: (61) 70 11 27
Telex: 531442
Fax: (61) 70 75 40
MANAGEMENT:
  A. Halna du Fretay
  P. Calmels (General Manager)
  L. Pech (Deputy General Manager)

Microturbo operates as the gas turbine division of the Labinal group, in conjunction with Ames Industrial Ltd (Microturbo UK) of Fareham, England, Microturbo North America of Bohemia, NY, USA, and Electromecanismes RFB in Paris. Total staff of the Division is 800.

Details of Microturbo engines for missiles, RPVs and target drones can be found in the 1987-88 *Jane's*.

MICROTURBO TRB

Development of the TRB 13 and TRB 19 turbojets began in 1986. The former has a diameter of 230 mm (9.06 in), length of 480 mm (18.90 in), weight of 16 kg (35.3 lb) and thrust rating of 0.81 kN (182 lb st) with sfc of 32.5 mg/Ns (1.15 lb/h/lb st). The TRB 19 has a diameter of 280 mm (11.02 in), length of 580 mm (22.85 in), weight of 28 kg (61.7 lb) and thrust rating of 1.2 kN (270 lb st) with sfc of 33.0 mg/Ns (1.17 lb/h/lb st)

MICROTURBO TRS 18

This single-shaft turbojet is of modular construction. The forward module incorporates the intake, gearbox, electronic governing and start sequencing. The starter/generator is in the nose bullet. The oil tank, with submerged pump, is on the underside, and includes provision for inverted flight.

The turbine module comprises: the one-piece centrifugal compressor, with diffuser and straightener vanes; the axial turbine rotor and nozzle diaphragm; and the main frame. The aft module comprises: the turbine backplate, carrying the annular folded combustion chamber; 10 spill burners; two igniter plugs, and jetpipe.

The fuel pump is driven electrically. The lubrication system is a closed circuit, with pressure supply. The engine can be shut down and restarted in flight, and incorporates automatic fault and protection systems.

The following are current versions for piloted aircraft:
TRS 18 Model 046. Powers Bede BD-5J and various prototypes. 28V starter/generator up to 600W.
TRS 18 Model 046-1. Powers Microjet 90, A-21SI Calif, NASA/Ames AD-1, Fairchild scaled NGT and other prototypes. 28V starter/generator up to 900W.
TRS 18-1 Models 081 and 083. Powers Microjet 200B and Caproni C-22J.

TRS 18-1 Model 202. For Caproni C-22J.

DIMENSIONS:	
Length: TRS 18	578 mm (22.75 in)
TRS 18-1	564 mm (22.20 in)
Width: TRS 18, 18-1	306 mm (12.05 in)
Height: TRS 18	349 mm (13.74 in)
TRS 18-1	339.5 mm (13.36 in)
WEIGHT, DRY:	
TRS 18	37.0 kg (81.5 lb)
TRS 18-1	38.5 kg (84.9 lb)
PERFORMANCE RATINGS (T-O, ISA, S/L):	
TRS 18	1.00 kN (225 lb st)
TRS 18-1	1.45 kN (326 lb st)
SPECIFIC FUEL CONSUMPTION (as above):	
TRS 18	34.5 mg/Ns (1.22 lb/h/lb st)
TRS 18-1	33.4 mg/Ns (1.18 lb/h/lb st)

MICROTURBO TFA

Two simple turbofans have been under study since 1986. The TFA 66, with a diameter of 350 mm (13.78 in) and length of 1,000 mm (39.37 in), will be rated at 3.60 kN (810 lb st) with sfc of 25.28 mg/Ns (0.892 lb/h/lb st). The TFA 130, with a diameter of 440 mm (17.32 in) and length of 975 mm (38.39 in), will be rated at 3.57 kN (802 lb st) with sfc of 17.48 mg/Ns (0.617 lb/h/lb st). Projected weight for each of these engines is approx 60 kg (132 lb).

MUDRY

MOTEURS MUDRY-BUCHOUX (AVIONS MUDRY et CIE)

Aérodrome de Bernay, BP 47, 27300 Bernay
Telephone: (32) 43 47 34
DIRECTOR: Auguste Mudry

MUDRY MB-4-80

This aircooled four-stroke flat-four incorporates some parts, such as piston rings, rocker arms, valves and springs, of standard auto industry type. Development is continuing.
CYLINDERS: Cast in pairs in light alloy with cast iron liners. Bore 93 mm (3.7 in). Stroke 92 mm (3.6 in). Capacity 2,498 cc (152.4 cu in).
VALVES: Flat cylinder heads with twin vertical overhead valves operated by pushrods.
PISTONS: Hypersilicate alloy, forming chamber in head. Three rings including U-Flex scraper.
CRANKCASE: AS7G-06 alloy divided on vertical centreline.

FUEL GRADE: 100LL or automobile gasoline.
ACCESSORIES: Generator, starter and alternator. Two 32 mm carburettors. Bendix dual ignition.

DIMENSIONS:	
Length	730 mm (28.7 in)
Width	710 mm (28.0 in)
Height	420 mm (16.5 in)
WEIGHT, DRY (equipped):	83 kg (183 lb)
PERFORMANCE RATING (S/L):	
Max T-O	59.7 kW (80 hp) at 2,750 rpm

RECTIMO

RECTIMO AVIATION SA

Aérodrome de Chambéry, 73420 Savoie
Telephone: (79) 54 40 06
Telex: 980 202
DIRECTOR: André Rosselot

Rectimo has manufactured more than 500 **Type 4 AR 1200** single ignition derivatives of the Volkswagen four-cylinder aircooled car engine, which together with the larger 4 AR 1600 are used in the Sportavia RF4D motor glider and various lightweight aircraft. The 30 kW (40 hp) 4 AR 1200 engine has a 1,192 cc cubic capacity, 7 : 1 compression ratio and weighs 61.5 kg (136 lb). Fuel consumption under cruise conditions is 11 litres (2.9 US gallons; 2.4 Imp gal)/h. The 4 AR 1600 produces 45.5 kW (61 hp) at T-O and has a cubic capacity of 1,600 cc and an 8 : 1 compression ratio. Weight is 64 kg (141 lb). Both engines have a maximum speed of 3,600 rpm.

Rectimo 4 AR 1200 piston engine of 30 kW (40 hp)

SCOMA

SCOMA-ÉNERGIE

OFFICE: 11-13 Rue Forest, 75018 Paris
Telephone: (1) 43 87 55 79
WORKS: 58 Rue de la Fosse aux Anglais, 77190 Dammarie-les-Lys (Melun)
Telephone: (1) 64 37 46 17

This company, which specialises in diesel research and applications, has been flying a Cessna L-19 since June 1987 equipped with a GMA 140 TK geared diesel. This is a four-inline liquid cooled engine of 2,068 cc (126 cu in) capacity, with turbocharger and geared drive. Installed weight is 180 kg (397 lb), and T-O power is 96 kW (136 hp) at 2,660 propeller rpm. At economic cruise of 2,300 propeller rpm the power is 65 kW (88 hp) and fuel consumption less than 22 litres (5.8 US gallons; 4.8 Imp gallons)/h. The engine has multi-fuel capability and is run mainly on Jet 1 or light diesel oil. Experience with this engine is being used to assist the design of a new range of engines called Comete (Comet), which are 170° V type engines with 1, 4, 6, 8, 12 or 16 cylinders each of 94 mm (3.7 in) bore and stroke. All are turbocharged and liquid cooled geared units, with ratings from 30 kW (40 hp) to 480 kW (653 hp).

The Cessna L-19 powered by a SCOMA GMA 140 TK diesel engine

SNECMA

SOCIÉTÉ NATIONALE D'ÉTUDE ET DE CONSTRUCTION DE MOTEURS D'AVIATION

2 boulevard Victor, 75724 Paris Cédex 15
Telephone: 40 60 80 80
Telex: 202 834 MOTAV
CHAIRMAN AND CHIEF EXECUTIVE: Bernard Capillon
SENIOR VICE-PRESIDENT:
  Pierre Alesi (Engineering and Production)
VICE-PRESIDENTS:
  Jean-Louis Bonnet (Military Programmes and Marketing)

Dominique Paris (Commercial Programme Management and Marketing)
COMMUNICATION ADVISER: Vonick Morel

More than 5,200 Atar turbojets have been produced for Mirage fighters. SNECMA is now producing the M53 turbojet and developing the M88. It is also participating in international collaborative programmes, as described hereunder.

Today, SNECMA heads about 26,000 persons formed around its major subsidiaries: SEP (rocket motors, remote sensing and composites), Hispano-Suiza (aeronautical equipment, nuclear and robotic equipment), Messier-Hispano-Bugatti (landing gears) and Sochata SNECMA (engine repair).

SNECMA ATAR 9K50

The Atar is a single-shaft military turbojet first run in 1946 and subsequently developed and cleared for flight at Mach numbers greater than 2. The current version is the Atar 9K50, which powers all production Mirage F1 versions and the Mirage 50.

DIMENSIONS:
Diameter	1,020 mm (40.2 in)
Length overall	5,944 mm (234 in)

WEIGHTS:
Dry, complete with all accessories	1,582 kg (3,487 lb)

PERFORMANCE RATINGS:
With afterburner	70.6 kN (15,870 lb st) at 8,400 rpm
Without afterburner	49.2 kN (11,055 lb st)

SPECIFIC FUEL CONSUMPTION:
With afterburner	55.5 mg/Ns (1.96 lb/h/lb st)
Without afterburner	27.5 mg/Ns (0.97 lb/h/lb st)

OIL CONSUMPTION: 1.5 litres (3.2 US pints; 2.64 Imp pints)/h

SNECMA Atar 9K50 turbojet of 70.6 kN (15,870 lb st) with afterburning

SNECMA M53

The M53 is a single-shaft turbofan capable of propelling fighter aircraft to Mach 2.5, without any throttle limitations over the flight envelope. Its modular construction allows easier maintenance.

It includes a three-stage fan, five-stage compressor, annular combustion chamber, two-stage turbine and an after-burner equipped with a multi-flap variable nozzle. The control system is monitored by an ELECMA electronic computer. The following versions are in service.

M53-5. Produced in 1980-85 as the initial engine of the Mirage 2000.

M53-P2. Designed to power the Mirage 2000 from 1985; current production version.

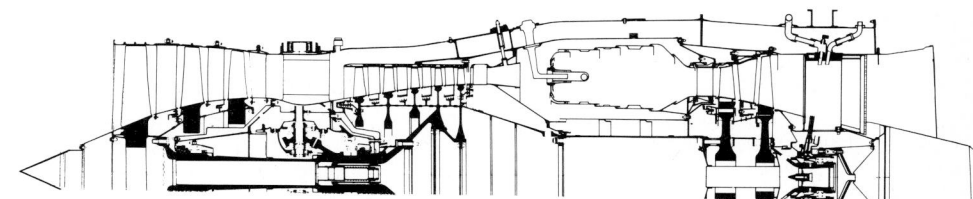

Longitudinal section through the SNECMA M53 showing LP and HP sections on single shaft (pressure ratio, 9.3 at 10,500 rpm) and bypass duct

DIMENSIONS:
Length, overall	5,070 mm (199.6 in)
Max diameter	1,055 mm (41.5 in)

WEIGHT, DRY:
M53-5	1,470 kg (3,240 lb)
M53-P2	1,500 kg (3,307 lb)

PERFORMANCE RATINGS:
Max with afterburner:
M53-5	88.2 kN (19,830 lb st)
M53-P2	95.0 kN (21,355 lb st)

Max without afterburner:
M53-5	54.4 kN (12,230 lb st)
M53-P2	64.3 kN (14,455 lb st)

SPECIFIC FUEL CONSUMPTION (without afterburner):
M53-5	24.64 mg/Ns (0.87 lb/h/lb st)
M53-P2	25.55 mg/Ns (0.90 lb/h/lb st)

SNECMA M53-P2 augmented bypass turbojet of 95.0 kN (21,360 lb st)

SNECMA M88

The M88-2 is an advanced augmented turbofan, under development for the future Rafale aircraft of the French Air Force. Manufacture of nine development engines began in 1987, the first test is planned for the beginning of 1989 and the first flight for 1990.

The M88-2 is the outcome of a six-year demonstration programme in which two complete engines have been run since 1984 and an uprated core with 1,850°K turbine entry temperature completed its first simulated altitude tests in February 1987.

The M88-2 core can lead to derivative fighter engines of up to 105 kN (23,600 lb st). SNECMA is currently proposing an 85 kN (19,100 lb st) version, the **M88-3**, that uses 90 per cent of the parts of the M88-2 and will fit in light combat aircraft as planned by Yugoslavia and other countries.

The following relates to the basic M88-2:

TYPE: Two-shaft augmented turbofan.
COMPRESSOR: Variable inlet guide vanes, three stage LP (fan), six-stage HP.
COMBUSTOR: Annular.
TURBINES: Single-stage HP, single-stage LP.
ACCESSORIES: Digital control system.

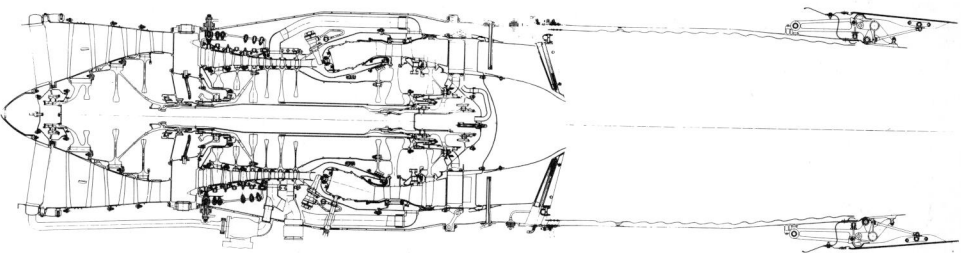

Longitudinal section through SNECMA M88 augmented turbofan

DIMENSION:
Length:	3,526 mm (138.8 in)

WEIGHT, DRY:
	877 kg (1,933 lb)

PERFORMANCE RATINGS:
With afterburner	74.9 kN (16,840 lb st)
Without afterburner	49.9 kN (11,220 lb st)

SPECIFIC FUEL CONSUMPTION:
With afterburner	49.9 mg/Ns (1.76 lb/h/lb st)
Without afterburner	24.8 mg/Ns (0.875 lb/h/lb st)

GE/SNECMA/MTU/VOLVO/FIAT CF6

As a continuation of the CF6-50 and CF6-80A programmes, SNECMA participates in the General Electric CF6-80C2 programme for all applications with a share on a cost basis of 10 per cent.

CFM INTERNATIONAL CFM56

This programme is covered under CFM in the International part of this section.

SNECMA M88-15 demonstrator (74.9 kN; 16,840 lb st)

GE/SNECMA GE36

SNECMA has a 35 per cent share in the GE36 UDF (unducted fan) programme, and was in charge of acoustic measurement during flight testing on a Boeing 727. SNECMA participated in development of an improved engine for flight test on an MD-80. Jointly with GE, SNECMA is now developing a very advanced gas generator, and is in charge of the HP compressor, combustor, structural casings, fuel systems and nacelle.

SNECMA/TURBOMECA LARZAC

This appears under Turbomeca-SNECMA GRTS.

RR/SNECMA/MTU/FN TYNE

Under Rolls-Royce licence, the Tyne 22 turboprop for the Transall C-160, was put back into production in October 1977. The similar Tyne 21 has been ordered to power the Dassault-Breguet Atlantique 2. These 4,549 kW (6,100 ehp) engines were last described in the 1975-76 *Jane's*.

TURBOMECA
SOCIÉTÉ TURBOMECA

Bordes, 64320 Bizanos
Telephone: (59) 32 84 37
Telex: 560928
Fax: 59 53 15 12
PARIS OFFICE: 1 rue Beaujon, 75008 Paris
Telephone: (33/1) 45 61 48 95
Telex: 650347
Fax: (33/1) 45 63 51 76
CHAIRMAN: Joseph R. Szydlowski
CHIEF EXECUTIVE OFFICERS:
  Sonia Meton
  A. H. du Fretay
PRESS RELATIONS MANAGER: Jacques Millepied

By 1 January 1988 more than 25,500 Turbomeca engines for fixed and rotating-wing applications and aircraft auxiliary duties had been delivered to customers in 115 countries. Of these, some 570 were manufactured in 1987. Approximately 14,000 more engines have been built under licence by what are today Rolls-Royce plc in the UK, Teledyne CAE in the USA, ENMASA in Spain, Hindustan Aeronautics in India, Bet-Shemesh in Israel, HAMC in China and state factories in Romania and Yugoslavia.

A European Small Engines Co-operation Agreement signed in April 1985 joins Turbomeca, MTU of West Germany and Rolls-Royce of the UK in promoting three complementary new engines: the Turbomeca TM 333, MTU-Turbomeca RR MTR 390 and Rolls-Royce Turbomeca RTM 322. Other European small engine makers may join the collaboration, in which each partner may share in engines sold to its own government.

Total covered floor area for Turbomeca's three plants at Bordes, Mézières and Tarnos is 136,487 m² (1,469,134 sq ft). The company employs about 4,260 people.

ROLLS-ROYCE TURBOMECA ADOUR

This turbofan appears in the International part of this section.

TURBOMECA-SNECMA LARZAC

This turbofan appears under Turbomeca-SNECMA GRTS.

TURBOMECA ARRIEL

This turboshaft powers the single-engined AS 350 Ecureuil, twin-engined SA 365 Dauphin, Agusta A 109K and Sikorsky S-76A Plus.

The Arriel has modular construction, and is expected to form the basis for a turboprop and a turbofan in the 4.90 kN (1,100 lb st) class. The first complete engine ran on 7 August 1974.

There are four production versions, differing essentially only in power rating:

Arriel 1A, 1B. Intermediate contingency rating 478 kW (641 shp); powers AS 350B and SA 365C.
Arriel 1C. Intermediate contingency rating 492 kW (660 shp); powers SA 365N.
Arriel 1D. Intermediate contingency rating 510 kW (684 shp); powers AS 350B and L₁.
Arriel 1C1, 1M, 1K, 1S. All have intermediate contingency rating of 522 kW (700 shp); power SA 365C, F and N, A 109K and S-76A Plus.

By 1 January 1988 a total of 1,813 Arriels had been delivered, with production continuing at the rate of 250 per year. These engines had then flown 1.8 million hours in 69 countries. These totals do not include engines produced under licence in China.

TYPE: Single-shaft free turbine turboshaft.

Turbomeca Arriel turboshaft (478 kW; 641 shp)

Turbomeca Astazou XX turboshaft, rated at 749 kW (1,005 shp)

COMPRESSOR: Single-stage axial and supersonic centrifugal. Pressure ratio 9.
COMBUSTION CHAMBER: Annular, with flow radially outwards and then inwards. Centrifugal fuel injection.
GAS-GENERATOR TURBINE: Two integral cast axial stages with solid blades.
POWER TURBINE: Single axial stage with inserted blades.
REDUCTION GEAR: Light alloy gearbox, containing two stages of helical gears, giving drive at 6,000 rpm to front and rear. Hydraulic torquemeter.
ACCESSORY DRIVES: Main pad provides for optional 12,000 rpm alternator; other drives for oil pumps, tachometer generator, governor and starter.
LUBRICATION SYSTEM: Independent circuit through gear pump and metallic cartridge filter.
OIL SPECIFICATION: AIR 3512 or 3513A.
STARTING: Electric starter or starter/generator.
DIMENSIONS:

Length, excl accessories	1,090 mm (42.91 in)
Height overall	569 mm (22.40 in)
Width	430 mm (16.93 in)

WEIGHT, DRY:

With all engine accessories	109 kg (240 lb)

PERFORMANCE RATINGS (Arriel 1A, 1B):

Max contingency	520 kW (698 shp)
Max contingency, later	544 kW (730 shp)
T-O and intermediate contingency	478 kW (641 shp)
Max continuous	441 kW (592 shp)

SPECIFIC FUEL CONSUMPTION:

Max contingency	93.1 µg/J (0.551 lb/h/shp)
Intermediate contingency	96.8 µg/J (0.573 lb/h/shp)

TURBOMECA ASTAZOU TURBOPROP

The Astazou turboprop is in production in its 761 kW (1,020 ehp) Astazou XVI (AZ16) version. The XVIG, equipped for sustained inverted flight, powers the Argentine IA 58 Pucará. By 1988 deliveries of all XVI versions totalled 367, against orders for 440.

The following data refer to the XVIG:
DIMENSIONS:

Diameter over intake cowl	546 mm (21.5 in)
Overall length, incl propeller	2,047 mm (80.6 in)

WEIGHT, DRY:

	228 kg (502 lb)

PERFORMANCE RATINGS:

T-O	761 ekW; 720 kW
	(1,020 ehp; 965 shp) at 43,000 rpm
Max continuous	696 ekW; 654 kW
	(934 ehp; 877 shp) at 43,000 rpm

SPECIFIC FUEL CONSUMPTION:

At T-O rating	88.7 µg/J (0.525 lb/h/shp)

TURBOMECA ASTAZOU TURBOSHAFT

This turboshaft series is derived from the Astazou II turboprop. Variants are:
Astazou IIA. Rated at 390 kW (523 shp) for SA 318C. Total of 615 built.
Astazou IIIA. Derived from IIA but with revised turbine to match power needs of SA 341G. Produced jointly by Turbomeca and Rolls-Royce, with 1,008 delivered.
Astazou XIVB and XIVF. For SA 319B; XIVB is civil and XIVF military. Flat rated to 441 kW (591 shp) (1 h) up to 4,000 m (13,125 ft) or +55°C.
Astazou XIVH. For SA 342J/L, to remove altitude and temperature limitations; 1,146 delivered.
Astazou XVIIIA. Higher gas temperature. Powers SA 360C.
Astazou XX. Fourth axial compressor stage added. Designed for operation in hot and high countries.

The following description relates to the Astazou IIIN except where indicated:
TYPE: Single-shaft axial-plus-centrifugal turboshaft.
REDUCTION GEAR: Two stage epicyclic having helical primary and straight secondary gears. Ratio 7.039 : 1 (XIVB/F, 7.345; XVIIIA, 7.375).
COMPRESSOR: Single-stage axial (IIA, IIN, IIIN), two-stage axial (XIV, XVIII) or three stage-axial (XX) followed by single-stage centrifugal. Mass flow 2.5 kg (5.5 lb)/s.
COMBUSTION CHAMBER: Reverse flow annular with centrifugal injector using rotary atomiser. Two ventilated torch igniters.
TURBINE: Three-stage axial with blades integral with discs.
ACCESSORIES: Five drive pads on casing forming rear of air intake.
FUEL SYSTEM: Automatic constant speed control.
LUBRICATION SYSTEM: Pressure type with gear type pumps. Oil tank of 8 litre (14 Imp pint) capacity.
STARTING: Electrical, automatic.
DIMENSIONS:

Length overall: Astazou IIA	1,272 mm (50.0 in)
Astazou III, XIVB/F	1,433 mm (56.3 in)
Astazou XIVH	1,470 mm (57.9 in)
Astazou XVIIIA	1,327 mm (52.2 in)
Astazou XX	1,529 mm (60.22 in)
Height: Astazou IIA	458 mm (18 in)
Astazou III, XIVH	460 mm (18.1 in)
Astazou XVIIIA	698 mm (27.48 in)
Astazou XX	721 mm (28.4 in)
Width: Astazou IIA	480 mm (18.8 in)
Astazou III, XIVH	460 mm (18.1 in)

WEIGHTS:

Equipped: Astazou III	147 kg (324 lb)
Astazou III (suffix 2)	150 kg (330 lb)
Astazou XIVB/F	166 kg (366 lb)
Astazou XIVH	160 kg (353 lb)
Astazou XVIIIA	155 kg (341 lb)
Astazou XX	195 kg (430 lb)

PERFORMANCE RATINGS:

Max power: Astazou IIA	390 kW (523 shp)
Astazou III	441 kW (592 shp)
Astazou III (suffix 2)	481 kW (645 shp)
Astazou XX	749 kW (1,005 shp)
One hour: Astazou XIVB/F	441 kW (591 shp)
Astazou XVIIIA	651 kW (873 shp)
	maintained at sea level to 40°C
Max continuous: Astazou IIA	353 kW (473 shp)
Astazou III	390 kW (523 shp)
Astazou III (suffix 2)	441 kW (592 shp)
Astazou XIVB/F	405 kW (543 shp)

Astazou XIVH   flat rated in SA 341 at 440.7 kW
      (591 shp) to 55°C or 4,000 m (13,125 ft)
Astazou XVIIIA   600 kW (805 shp)
Astazou XX   675 kW (905 shp)

SPECIFIC FUEL CONSUMPTION:

At max power rating:

Astazou IIA	105.3 μg/J (0.623 lb/h/shp)
Astazou III	108.7 μg/J (0.643 lb/h/shp)
Astazou III (suffix 2)	109.9 μg/J (0.650 lb/h/shp)
Astazou XIVB/F	105.5 μg/J (0.624 lb/h/shp)
Astazou XVIIIA	91.3 μg/J (0.540 lb/h/shp)
Astazou XX	85.9 μg/J (0.508 lb/h/shp)

TURBOMECA ARTOUSTE III

The Artouste IIIB is a single-shaft turboshaft with two-stage axial-centrifugal compressor and three-stage turbine. Pressure ratio 5.2. Mass flow 4.3 kg/s (9.5 lb/s) at 33,300 rpm. Built under licence in India by Hindustan Aeronautics.

The IIIB powers the SA 315B and SA 316B/C. The uprated IIID has a reduction gear giving 5,864 rpm at the driveshaft (instead of 5,773) and in revised equipment. The IIID powers the SA 316C; data are for this version. A total of 2,525 Artouste III engines had been built by 1988.

DIMENSIONS:

Length	1,815 mm (71.46 in)
Height	627 mm (24.68 in)
Width	507 mm (19.96 in)

WEIGHT, DRY: 178 kg (392 lb)

PERFORMANCE RATING (T-O, maintained up to 55°C at S/L or up to 4,000 m; 13,125 ft):   440 kW (590 shp)

SPECIFIC FUEL CONSUMPTION: 126.2 μg/J (0.747 lb/h/shp)

MTU-TURBOMECA RR MTR 390

This appears in the International part of this section.

TURBOMECA TM 333

This turboshaft was launched in July 1979 to power the SA 365 and other helicopters in the 4,000 kg (8,800 lb) class including the Indian ALH. French certification was obtained on 11 July 1986.

TM 333 1A. Basic version, composed of a gas generator module, free turbine module and reduction gear module.

TM 333 1M. For military SA 365M.

TM 333 2B. Growth version with aircooled HP turbine, giving T-O rating of 747 kW (1,001 shp). First run 6 November 1984. Selected for HAL (India) ALH.

The TM 333 is one of three new engines included in the European Small Engines Co-operation Agreement. Data are for the 1A.

TYPE: Free turbine turboshaft.

COMPRESSOR: Variable inlet guide vanes, two stage axial compressor, single stage centrifugal.

COMBUSTION CHAMBER: Annular, reverse flow.

GAS GENERATOR TURBINE: Single-stage with uncooled inserted blades.

POWER TURBINE: Single-stage axial with uncooled inserted blades.

GEARBOX: Two stages to give drive at 6,000 rpm to front output shaft.

LUBRICATION: Independent system. Oil passes through gear pump and metallic cartridge filter.

FUEL SYSTEM: Microprocessor numerical control.

DIMENSIONS:

Length, including accessories	943 mm (37.1 in)
Height overall	557 mm (21.9 in)
Width	415 mm (16.3 in)

WEIGHT, DRY: 140 kg (308 lb)

PERFORMANCE RATINGS:

Max contingency	680 kW (912 shp)
T-O	625 kW (838 shp)
Max continuous	560 kW (751 shp)

SPECIFIC FUEL CONSUMPTION:

Max contingency	88 μg/J (0.523 lb/h/shp)
T-O	89.4 μg/J (0.529 lb/h/shp)
Max continuous	91.7 μg/J (0.543 lb/h/shp)

TURBOMECA TM 319

This turboshaft is compact, there being no axial compressor. Initial rating is 340 kW (456 shp). The first TM 319 was run on the bench on 21 February 1983. Full authority digital electronic control is supplied by Elecma. By 1 January 1988, 16 engines had run over 9,900 h including 1,000 in flight. Production deliveries for the AS 355 began in 1987, and were continuing in 1988 at the rate of 50 per year. Certification was due in late 1988. The same gas generator is used in the TP 319 turboprop, and is under study as an APU.

DIMENSIONS:

Length	782 mm (30.78 in)
Width	360 mm (14.2 in)
Height	540 mm (21.26 in)

WEIGHT, DRY: 87 kg (192 lb)

PERFORMANCE RATINGS (ISA, S/L):

Max contingency	380 kW (509 shp)
Max T-O	340 kW (456 shp)
Max continuous	295 kW (395 shp)

TURBOMECA TP 319

The turboprop version is fully aerobatic. The gas generator and power turbine modules are identical with

The 625 kW (838 shp) Turbomeca TM 333 turboshaft

The 313 kW (420 shp) Turbomeca TP 319 turboprop

those of the TM 319. The first TP 319 ran on 11 September 1985. Flight testing in an Epsilon began in November 1985, followed by a Valmet L-90TP in December 1987. Certification was due in 1988.

DIMENSIONS:

Length	826 mm (32.52 in)
Width	476 mm (18.74 in)
Height	590 mm (23.22 in)

WEIGHT, DRY (bare):   111 kg (245 lb)

PERFORMANCE RATINGS (ISA, S/L):

Twin T-O contingency	343 kW (460 shp)
T-O	313 kW (420 shp)
Cruise (6,100 m, 20,000 ft)	179 kW (240 shp)

TURBOMECA TURMO

The Turmo free turbine engine is in service in both turboshaft and turboprop versions.

Current variants are as follows:

Turmo IIIC₅, IIIC₆, IIIC₇. For SA 321F/G/H/Ja. Total production 549.

Turmo IIIE₆. Higher turbine temperature.

Turmo IVA. Civil engine derived from IIIC₄, with contingency rating of 1,057 kW (1,417 shp). The IVB is a military version.

TYPE: Free turbine turboshaft.

REDUCTION GEAR: $IIIC_3$, C_5 and E_3 fitted with rear mounted reduction gear; $IIIC_4$ direct drive.

COMPRESSOR: Single-stage axial followed by single-stage centrifugal. Pressure ratio 5.9 on $IIIC_3$. Mass flow 5.9 kg (13 lb)/s.

COMBUSTION CHAMBER: Reverse flow annular with centrifugal fuel injector using rotary atomiser. Two ventilated torch igniters.

GAS GENERATOR TURBINE: Two-stage axial.

POWER TURBINE: Two-stage axial unit in $IIIC_3$, C_5 and E_3, and single stage in $IIIC_4$.

ACCESSORIES: Pads for oil pump, fuel control, electric starter, tacho-generator and, on $IIIC_4$, oil cooler fan.

FUEL SYSTEM: Fuel control for gas generator on $IIIC_3$, C_5 and E_3, with speed limiter for power turbine on E_3. Constant-speed system on $IIIC_4$ power turbine.

FUEL GRADE: AIR 3405 for $IIIC_4$.

LUBRICATION SYSTEM: Pressure type with oil cooler and 13 litre (23 Imp pint) tank.

OIL SPECIFICATION: AIR 3155A, or AIR 3513, for $IIIC_4$.

STARTING: Automatic system with electric starter motor.

DIMENSIONS:

Length:

Turmo $IIIC_3$, C_5 and E_3	1,975.7 mm (78.0 in)
Turmo $IIIC_4$	2,184 mm (85.5 in)
Turmo $IIID_3$	1,868 mm (73.6 in)

Width:

Turmo $IIIC_3$, C_5 and E_3	693 mm (27.3 in)
Turmo $IIIC_4$	637 mm (25.1 in)
Turmo $IIID_3$	934 mm (36.8 in)

Height:

Turmo $IIIC_3$, C_5 and E_3	716.5 mm (28.2 in)
Turmo $IIIC_4$	719 mm (28.3 in)
Turmo $IIID_3$	926 mm (36.5 in)

WEIGHT, DRY:

Turmo $IIIC_3$ and E_3, fully equipped	297 kg (655 lb)
Turmo $IIIC_5$, $IIIC_6$ and $IIIC_7$	325 kg (716 lb)
Turmo $IIIC_4$, equipped engine	225 kg (496 lb)
Turmo $IIID_3$, basic engine	365 kg (805 lb)

PERFORMANCE RATINGS:

T-O: Turmo $IIIC_3$, D_3 and E_3	1,104 kW (1,480 shp)
Turmo $IIIE_6$	1,181 kW (1,584 shp)

Max contingency:

Turmo $IIIC_4$ at 33,800 gas generator rpm	1,032 kW (1,384 shp)
Turmo $IIIC_6$ at 33,550 gas generator rpm	1,156 kW (1,550 shp)
Turmo $IIIC_7$ at 33,800 gas generator rpm	1,200 kW (1,610 shp)
Turmo IVA at 33,950 gas generator rpm	1,057 kW (1,417 shp)
Turmo IVC at 33,800 gas generator rpm	1,163 kW (1,560 shp)

T-O and intermediate contingency:

Turmo $IIIC_5$	1,050 kW (1,408 shp)

SPECIFIC FUEL CONSUMPTION:

At T-O rating:

Turmo $IIIC_3$ and E_3	101.9 μg/J (0.603 lb/h/shp)
Turmo $IIID_3$	104.1 μg/J (0.616 lb/h/shp)

At max contingency rating:

Turmo $IIIC_4$, C_5, C_6, C_7 and IV	106.8 μg/J (0.632 lb/h/shp)
Turmo IVA	106.3 μg/J (0.629 lb/h/shp)

ROLLS-ROYCE TURBOMECA RTM 322

See International part of this section.

TURBOMECA MAKILA

This turboshaft powers the SA 332. Derived partly

from the Turmo, it incorporates rapid-strip modular construction; three axial stages of compression plus one centrifugal; centrifugal atomiser; two-stage gas generator turbine with cooled blades; two-stage free power turbine; and lateral exhaust.

The Makila 1A was certificated in 1980, and the 1A1 followed in 1984. By 1988 deliveries reached 717, and TBO was 3,000 h. Production was at the rate of 140 engines per year in 1988.

DIMENSIONS:
Length, intake face to rear face	1,395 mm (54.94 in)
Max diameter	514 mm (20.25 in)

WEIGHT, DRY: Basic 210 kg (463 lb)
Equipped 243 kg (535 lb)

PERFORMANCE RATINGS (ISA, S/L):
Max contingency:
1A
  1,310 kW (1,757 shp) at 36,300 gas generator rpm
1A1
  1,400 kW (1,877 shp) at 36,300 gas generator rpm
Cruise: 1A, 1A1 700 kW (939 shp)

SPECIFIC FUEL CONSUMPTION:
Max contingency: 1A 83.9 µg/J (0.496 lb/h/hp)
1A1 81.4 µg/J (0.481 lb/h/hp)

Turbomeca Makila IA free turbine turboshaft, with initial ratings up to 1,398 kW (1,875 shp)

Cruise: 1A 97.7 µg/J (0.578 lb/h/hp)
1A1 95.0 µg/J (0.562 lb/h/hp)

TURBOMECA-SNECMA
GROUPEMENT TURBOMECA-SNECMA (GRTS)
1 rue Beaujon, BP 37-08, 75362 Paris Cédex 08
Telephone: 49 24 18 61

Groupement Turbomeca-SNECMA is a company formed jointly by Société Turbomeca and SNECMA to manage the Larzac turbofan launched in 1968. GRTS has no capital and comprises primarily a joint management organisation.

TURBOMECA-SNECMA LARZAC
In February 1972 the **Larzac 04** turbofan was selected for a joint Franco-German programme to provide propulsion for the Alpha Jet (see under Alpha Jet in International part of Aircraft section). In addition to the two French partners, two West German companies, MTU and KHD, are sharing in production and development. Complete engines were assembled in both countries.

Latest versions are as follows:

Larzac 04-C6. Two-stage fan, four-stage HP compressor, annular combustion chamber, single-stage HP turbine with cooled blades and single-stage LP turbine. Maximum airflow 28 kg (62 lb)/s, pressure ratio 10.6 and BPR 1.13. First production delivery September 1977.

Larzac 04-C20. Growth version with increased mass flow compressor and higher temperature HP turbine. Thrust increased by 7 to 15 per cent according to speed and altitude. First run March 1982; first flight December 1982; production deliveries from September 1984.

DIMENSIONS:
Overall length of basic engine	1,179 mm (46.4 in)
Overall diameter	602 mm (23.7 in)

WEIGHT, DRY: 290 kg (640 lb)

Turbomeca-SNECMA Larzac 04-C20 two-shaft turbofan, rated at 14.12 kN (3,175 lb st)

T-O THRUST (S/L, static):
Larzac 04-C6 13.19 kN (2,966 lb)
Larzac 04-C20 14.12 kN (3,175 lb)

SPECIFIC FUEL CONSUMPTION:
Larzac 04 20.1 mg/Ns (0.71 lb/h/lb st)

GERMANY
(FEDERAL REPUBLIC)

HIRTH
GÖBLER HIRTHMOTOREN GmbH
Postfach 20, Max Eyth Strasse 10, 7141 Benningen
Telephone: 07144 6074
Telex: 7 264 530 GHIR D

This company produces small piston engines for microlights and other aircraft. Except for the F30, all are two-cylinder upright in-line two-strokes with carburettor, Bosch magneto ignition and direct drive.

HIRTH F 263 R 53
Cylinders 66 mm (2.598 in) bore and 56 mm (2.205 in) stroke, giving capacity of 383 cc (23.37 cu in). Compression ratio 9.5, using 25:1 fuel mix. Weight with electric starter 24.0 kg (52.8 lb), silencer adding 2.5 kg (5.5 lb). Max power 16.2 kW (22 hp) at 3,900 rpm.

HIRTH F 22
Cylinders as F263. Weight with electric starter 20.0 kg (44 lb), silencer adding 3 kg (6.6 lb). Max power 17 kW (23 hp) at 5,000 rpm.

HIRTH F 23A
Cylinders 72 mm (2.835 in) bore and 64 mm (2.52 in) stroke, giving capacity of 521 cc (31.79 cu in). Compression ratio 10.5, using 50:1 fuel mix. Equipped weight 24.0 kg (52 lb), silencer adding 4.5 kg (10 lb). Max power 30 kW (40 hp) at 5,500 rpm.

HIRTH 2701 R 03
Cylinders 70 mm (2.756 in) bore and 64 mm (2.52 in) stroke, giving capacity of 493 cc (30.08 cu in). Compression ratio 11, using 50:1 fuel mix. Weight with fan and recoil starter 32.8 kg (72.5 lb). Max power 32 kW (43 hp) at 6,750 rpm.

HIRTH 2702 R 03
Cylinders as F 23A. Weight with fan and recoil starter 35.0 kg (77 lb). Max power 26.5 kW (36 hp) at 5,500 rpm.

HIRTH F30
Four-cylinder engine tested in two sizes, the smaller (1,042 cc) being a twinned 2702 but lighter. Both can have direct or geared drive, data being for the former.

1,042 cc (63.58 cu in) version: Weight dry 36.0 kg (79.4 lb). Max power 48.5 kW (65 hp) at 4,500 rpm, 82 kW (110 hp) at 6,500 rpm.

The Hirth F30 flat-four engine

1,270 cc (77.50 cu in) version. Weight dry 35.0 kg (77 lb). Max power 59.5 kW (80 hp) at 4,500 rpm, 97 kW (130 hp) at 6,500 rpm.

KHD
KHD LUFTFAHRTTECHNIK GmbH
Hohemark Str 60-70, Postfach 1246, D-6370 Oberursel
Telephone: (06171) 500-1
Telex: 410727

Fax: 06171 500485

KHD Luftfahrttechnik GmbH produces small gas turbine engines and aircraft gearboxes. A major programme is the Tornado secondary power system, driven by the T 312 APU. A new SPS for future fighters is under development.

The T 117 has entered series production for the Canadair/ Dornier CL-289 RPV. Collaborative programmes include the CFM56-5, Larzac, and the joint development with Rolls-Royce and Williams International of the engine for the Modular Stand-Off Weapon (MSOW).

KÖNIG

KÖNIG MOTORENBAU

Friedrich-Olbricht Damm 72, 1000 Berlin 13
Telephone: 030 344 3071

This company produces small two-stroke piston engines for microlights and other aircraft. All except the SF 930 have radial cylinders of 66 mm (2.598 in) bore and 42 mm (1.654 in) stroke, with natural air cooling. A 33:1 fuel mix is used, aspirated through a single bowl carburettor and with capacitor discharge ignition. The SC 430 and SD 570 have an electric starter and are available with direct drive or with 1.75:1 Powergrip belt.

KÖNIG SC 430

This engine has three cylinders spaced at 120°, giving a capacity of 430 cc (26.24 cu in). Weight with full equipment is 16 kg (35.3 lb) and max power 18 kW (24 hp) at 4,000-4,200 rpm.

KÖNIG SD 570

This engine has four cylinders spaced at 90°, giving a capacity of 570 cc (34.78 cu in). Weight with full equipment is 18.5 kg (41 lb) and max power 21 kW (28 hp) at 4,000-4,200 rpm.

KÖNIG SF 930

Production of this larger four-cylinder radial began in April 1985. Bore and stroke are respectively 70 and 60 mm (2.756 and 2.362 in), giving a capacity of 930 cc (56.75 cu in); equipped weight is 36 kg (79.4 lb) and maximum power 35.8 kW (48 hp) at 4,000-4,200 rpm.

The 35.8 kW (48 hp) König SF 930 driving a four-blade propeller

---

LIMBACH

LIMBACH FLUGMOTOREN GmbH

Kotthausener Strasse 5, 5330 Königswinter 21,Sassenberg
Telephone: (02244) 2322 and 3031
Telex: 889574 plm d
PRESIDENT: Peter Limbach Sen

This company manufactures four-stroke and two-stroke piston engines for very light aeroplanes and powered gliders.

LIMBACH SL 1700

Several variants have been certificated by the LBA.
Limbach SL 1700D. Dual ignition. Not certificated. Fitted to Sportavia RF7.
Sportavia-Limbach SL 1700E. Fitted to Sportavia RF5 and RF5B.
Limbach SL 1700EA. Front-end starter and different induction system. Fitted to Scheibe SF-25C Falke.
Limbach SL 1700EAI. Hoffmann variable-pitch propeller. Fitted to Scheibe SF-28.
Limbach SL 1700EC. E with carburettor intake heating box.
Limbach SL 1700 ECI. EC equipped to drive Hoffmann propeller.
Sportavia-Limbach SL 1700EI. E equipped to drive Hoffmann propeller. Optional for Sportavia RF5B.

Unless otherwise stated, the following description refers to the SL 1700E:
TYPE: Four-cylinder opposed aircooled four-stroke piston engine.
CYLINDERS: Bore 88 mm (3.46 in). Stroke 69 mm (2.71 in). Capacity 1,680 cc (102.51 cu in). Compression ratio 8.
INDUCTION: Stromberg-Zenith 150CD carburettor.
FUEL GRADE: 90 octane.
IGNITION: Single Slick 4230 magneto feeding one Bosch WB 240 ERT 1 plug in each cylinder.
STARTING: One Fiat 0.37 kW (0.5 hp) starter (EA, EAI, one Bosch 0.3 kW; 0.4 hp).
ACCESSORIES: Ducellier 250W alternator; APG 17.09.001 fuel pump (EA,EAI, 17.09.001A).
DIMENSIONS:

Length overall: SL 1700D	649 mm (25.6 in)	
SL 1700EA, EAI	558 mm (22.0 in)	
SL 1700E, EI, EC, ECI	618 mm (24.3 in)	
Width overall: SL 1700D	800 mm (31.5 in)	
SL 1700EA, EAI	770 mm (30.3 in)	
other variants	764 mm (30.1 in)	
Height overall: SL 1700D	451 mm (17.8 in)	
SL 1700EA, EAI	392 mm (15.4 in)	
other variants	368 mm (14.5 in)	

WEIGHT, DRY:

SL 1700E, EI	73 kg (161 lb)
SL 1700EA, EAI	70 kg (154 lb)
SL 1700EC, ECI	74 kg (164 lb)

PERFORMANCE RATINGS:

T-O: SL 1700D	48.5 kW (65 hp) at 3,600 rpm
SL 1700E, EI, EC, ECI	51 kW (68 hp) at 3,600 rpm
SL 1700EA, EAI	44.7 kW (60 hp) at 3,550 rpm
Continuous: SL 1700E, EI, EC, ECI	45.5 kW (61 hp) at 3,200 rpm
SL 1700EA, EAI	41.7 kW (56 hp) at 3,300 rpm

Sportavia-Limbach SL 1700E flat-four four-stroke engine, rated at 51 kW (68 hp)

Limbach SL 1700EA flat-four four-stroke engine, rated at 44.7 kW (60 hp)

LIMBACH L 2000

This family is based on the SL 1700 with increased bore and stroke:
Limbach L 2000EOI. As 1700EI. Installed in Fournier RF-9 and Valentin Taifun.
Limbach L 2000EAI. As 1700EAI. Installed in Scheibe SF-25C Falke 2000 and SF-36.
Limbach L 2000EBI. As 1700EBI. Installed in Grob G109 and Hoffmann Dimona.

Details as for SL 1700, except for following:
CYLINDERS: Bore 90 mm (3.54 in). Stroke 78.4 mm (3.09 in). Capacity 1,994 cc (120.26 cu in). Compression ratio 8.7 (EAI, 8.9).
FUEL GRADE: 100L.
WEIGHT, DRY (with all accessories):

L 2000EOI	70 kg (154 lb)
L 2000EAI	69 kg (152 lb)
L 2000EBI	71.5 kg (157.5 lb)

PERFORMANCE RATINGS:

T-O: all models	59 kW (80 hp) at 3,400 rpm
Continuous:	
L 2000EOI, EAI	52 kW (70 hp) at 3,000 rpm
L 2000EBI	53 kW (72 hp) at 3,000 rpm

Limbach L 275E two-stroke for microlight aircraft and RPV applications, rated at 18 kW (24 hp)

LIMBACH L 2400

Similar to L 2000 but has further increased dimensions.
CYLINDERS: Bore 97 mm (3.82 in). Stroke 82 mm (3.23 in). Capacity 2,424 cc (147.91 cu in). Compression ratio 8.5.
INDUCTION: Twin Stromberg-Zenith 150 CD-3 carburettors.
FUEL GRADE: Minimum 96 RON.
IGNITION: Slick 4230 or Bendix S4RN21 magneto feeding single Bosch WB 240 ERT 1 plugs.
ACCESSORIES: 1.4 kW starter, 14-V 33 or 55 A generator, fuel pump and tachometer. Provision for Hoffmann or Mühlbauer variable-pitch propeller.
WEIGHT, DRY: 82 kg (181 lb)
PERFORMANCE RATINGS:

T-O (5 min)	65 kW (87 hp) at 3,200 rpm
Continuous	63 kW (84.5 hp) at 3,000 rpm

LIMBACH L 275E

This engine is intended for low cost propulsion of RPVs and microlight aircraft.
TYPE: Two-cylinder horizontally opposed two-stroke aircooled piston engine.
CYLINDERS: Cast aluminium alloy with Nicasil liner. Bore 66 mm (2.6 in). Stroke 40 mm (1.57 in). Capacity 274 cc (16.72 cu in).
INDUCTION: Two all-attitude diaphragm carburettors.
FUEL GRADE: 90 octane, mixed 25:1 with two-stroke oil.
IGNITION: 12V Bosch transistorised, one Bosch WK 175T6 plug per cylinder.
ACCESSORIES: Leistritz type turbo silencer (muffler).
DIMENSIONS:

Length overall	226 mm (8.89 in)
Width overall	390 mm (15.35 in)
Height overall	187 mm (7.36 in)

WEIGHT (with silencer): 7.5 kg (16.5 lb)
PERFORMANCE RATING: 18 kW (24 hp) at 7,300 rpm

LIMBACH L 550E

This is a four-cylinder version of the two-stroke L 275E. Capacity is thus 548 cc (33.5 cu in).
WEIGHT, DRY: 15.5 kg (34 lb)
PERFORMANCE RATING: 32 kW (43 hp) at 7,300 rpm

MTU

MOTOREN- UND TURBINEN-UNION MÜNCHEN GmbH

Dachauer Str 655, Munich-Allach, (postal address, Postfach 500640, 8000 Munich 50)
Telephone: (089) 1489 1

Telex: 529 500-15 MT D
Fax: (089) 1502621

MTU München, owned by Daimler-Benz AG, is Germany's largest aero engine company. It produces engines for all classes of aircraft. The following are major programmes:

GENERAL ELECTRIC CF6

MTU has approximately a 12 per cent share in the manufacture of the CF6-50 for the A300, approximately an 8 per cent share of the CF6-80A/A1 for the A310 and 767 and a 7 per cent share of the CF6-80C2 for the A300-600, 747 and 767. MTU makes HP turbine parts.

PRATT & WHITNEY PW2000

MTU is a partner, with Fiat of Italy, in the PW2037 and 2040. It is responsible for the LP turbine, under an 11.2 per cent share.

IAE V 2500

MTU has a 12.1 per cent share in IAE (see International part of this section).

PRATT & WHITNEY JT8D-200

MTU has a 12.5 per cent share, being largely responsible for the LP turbine.

EUROJET EJ200

MTU has a 33 per cent share in this engine, described in the International part of this section.

TURBOMECA-SNECMA LARZAC

MTU has a 23 per cent share (see under France).

TURBO-UNION RB199

MTU has a 40 per cent share in this engine, described in the International part of this section.

ROLLS-ROYCE TYNE

MTU has a 28 per cent share in about 170 Tyne turboprops for the Transall. MTU supports all Tyne 21 engines (Atlantique) and Tyne 22 (Transall), as well as Tynes used by civil operators.

ALLISON 250-C20B

MTU licence built more than 700 engines, designated 250-MTU-C20B, for the PAH-1 and VBH (see MBB in Aircraft section). MTU is converting C20Bs into C20Rs and is supporting engines used by civil operators.

ALLISON T406

MTU is collaborating with Allison in developing a propfan based on the T406 core. It is intended to power the MBB/CATIC MPC 75.

MTU-TURBOMECA RR MTR 390

Brief details of this three-nation helicopter engine are given in the International part of this section.

P&WC PW300

MTU has a 25 per cent share in this Canadian turbofan. One of its responsibilities will be the LP turbine.

PARODI
PARODI MOTORSEGLERTECHNIK
Hauptstrasse 70, 7895 Klettgau-Erzingen
Telephone: 07742 7689

DIRECTOR: Roland Parodi

This company has developed a family of piston engines for ultralight aircraft and motor gliders. With various designations in the HP 45 and HP 60 series, these are derived from a Honda design, with a new crankcase and lubrication system.

Details were given in the 1984-85 *Jane's* of the HP 60 series engines of 44.7 kW (60 hp). These have been uprated to the 59.7 kW (80 hp) class, and are being used to support later engines for two-seat aircraft. Parodi hopes to produce two definitive engines: one with variable turbo pressure for 74.6 kW (100 hp), cruising at 55.9 kW (75 hp); and the other for 96.9 kW (130 hp), cruising at 74.6 kW (100 hp).

PIEPER
PIEPER MOTORENBAU GmbH
Postfach 1229, D-4950 Minden, Viktoriastrasse, 50
Telephone: (0571) 34088

STAMO MS 1500

Pieper manufactures the 33.5 kW (45 hp) Stamo MS 1500-1 modified Volkswagen four-cylinder aircooled piston engine, applications for which have included the Scheibe SF-25B Falke two-seat motor glider. Capacity 1,500 cc, compression ratio 7.2 : 1, length 640 mm (25 in), width 745 mm (29.3 in), height 395 mm (15.5 in) and dry weight 52 kg (115 lb). The MS 1500-1 operates on 80/86 or 90 octane fuel, and is started by a pull-cord. The MS 1500-2, has electric starter and generator. This increases weight to 60 kg (132 lb). By 1986 well over 600 engines had been delivered, and the period between complete overhauls had been extended to 1,000 h.

Pieper built Stamo MS 1500-1 four-cylinder four-stroke engine, rated at 33.5 kW (45 hp)

PORSCHE
DR ING h c F. PORSCHE AG
Postfach 1140, 7251 Weissach
Telephone: 07044 35 2743
Telex: 7 263 771
Fax: 07044 35 2555
MANAGER, DEVELOPMENT AIRCRAFT ENGINE:
  Dipl Ing Heinz Dorsch

PORSCHE PFM 3200

Developed from the well known 911 sports car engine, this piston engine is the first since 1955 designed for aircraft (standard 911S engines power the Airship Industries Skyships). A four-stroke flat-six, the PFM 3200 is aircooled, with a fan, and has a capacity of 3.2 litres (195 cu in). Dry sump lubrication makes the engine fully aerobatic; it has a geared drive of 0.442 ratio, single-lever control, and electronic ignition. Rated at 156 kW (212 hp), the PFM can burn Avgas or Mogas, or any mixture, and has fuel consumption 10-20 per cent lower than competitor engines.

Certification was completed in September 1984 by the LBA and in August 1985 by the FAA. Pilot production was initiated in August 1985.

The following versions have been announced:

N00. Derated N01, lower compression, unleaded Mogas.
N01. Basic model.
N02. N01 with oil cooler and thermostat and oil filter.
N03. Uprated, higher compression, 100LL only.
T03. N03 with lower compression, different pistons, Garrett density controlled turbocharger.
T33. T03 for helicopters with belt drive and second cooling fan for oil and intercooling.

Series production started in April 1987. The first turbocharged version, rated at 179 kW (240 hp), was being flight tested at that time, ready for series production in September 1989.

CYLINDERS: Bore 95.0 mm (3.74 in). Stroke 74.4 mm (2.93 in). Capacity 3,164 cc (193 cu in). Compression ratio N01, 02, 9.2; N03, 10.5; N00, T03, T33, 8.5.

FUEL SUPPLY: K-Jetronic direct injection, two electrical pumps; fuel grade 100LL or Mogas.

ACCESSORIES: Magneti Marelli electronic ignition, power/speed proportional fan cooling, two 28V alternators, two vacuum pumps, drive for hydraulic pump.

DIMENSIONS:

Length	973 mm (38.3 in)
Width	855 mm (33.7 in)
Height (excluding exhaust system)	610 mm (24.0 in)

WEIGHT, DRY:

Bare engine	181 kg (399 lb)
N01, 02, 03 equipped	200 kg (441 lb)
T03	220 kg (480 lb)

PERFORMANCE RATING (S/L):

T-O:	
N01, 02	156 kW (209 hp) at 5,300 rpm
N03	162 kW (217 hp) at 5,300 rpm
T03	180 kW (241 hp) to 5,500 m (18,000 ft)

Econ cruise:	
N01, 02	109 kW (146 hp) at 4,550 rpm
N03	113 kW (151.5 hp) at 4,550 rpm
T03	126 kW (169 hp) to 5,500 m (18,000 ft)

SPECIFIC FUEL CONSUMPTION (econ cruise):

N01, 02	73.5 μg/J (0.435 lb/h/hp)
N03	70.3 μg/J (0.416 lb/h/hp)
T03	74.7 μg/J (0.442 lb/h/hp)

The 156 kW (212 hp) Porsche PFM 3200 piston engine

SAUER

SAUER MOTORENBAU GmbH

6501 Ober Olm, Nieder-Olmer Str 16
Telephone: 0 6136/8 9377

This company is marketing two sizes of four-cylinder four-stroke piston engine. The larger is the **ST 2500 H1S**, of approximately 2,500 cc (152 cu in) capacity. Details are available of the smaller engine.

SAUER SS 2100 H1S

This engine can have dual Slick 4230 magnetos and runs on 100LL Avgas or Mogas. It has twin Bing 64/32 carburettors, a 12V starter and 15A alternator.

CYLINDERS: Bore 90 mm (3.54 in). Stroke 84 mm (3.31 in). Capacity 2,135 cc (130.3 cu in). Compression ratio 9.5.

WEIGHT, DRY: 76 kg (168 lb)

PERFORMANCE RATING: 59.5 kW (80 hp) at 3,000 rpm

Sauer SS 2100 H1S piston engine
(Wolfgang Wagner)

ZOCHE

MICHAEL ZOCHE

Keferstrasse 13, 8000 Munich 40
Telephone: (089) 34 45 91
Telex: 523 402 ZOCHE D

This company's diesel aero engines incorporate the latest cylinder technology as well as such refinements as tungsten counterweights and full aerobatic pressure lubrication. Both engines have a propeller governor and four accessory drive pads. The weights given include starter, alternator, governor, vacuum pump and turbocharger.

ZOCHE ZO 01A

CYLINDERS: Four, arranged at 90°. Bore 92 mm (3.62in). Stroke 94 mm (3.70 in). Capacity 2,500 cc (153 cu in). Compression ratio 17.

FUEL GRADES: Diesel No 2, JP-4 or Jet A.

DIMENSIONS:
Length	720 mm (28 in)
Height or width	530 mm (20.9 in)
Diameter	640 mm (25.2 in)

WEIGHT, DRY: 89 kg (196 lb)

PERFORMANCE RATING: 110 kW (150 hp) at 2,500 rpm

SPECIFIC FUEL CONSUMPTION (above rating): 65.0 µg/J (0.385 lb/h/hp)

ZOCHE ZO 02A

This is a double-row eight-cylinder engine using 01A cylinders. It is 825 mm (32.5 in) long, weighs under 130 kg (286 lb) and has a T-O rating of 220 kW (300 hp).

Zoche ZO 01A four-cylinder diesel engine
(Howard Levy)

INDIA

GTRE

GAS TURBINE RESEARCH ESTABLISHMENT

Suranjan Das Road, Post Bag 7577, Bangalore, 560075
Telephone: 570698
Telex: 0845438 GTRE
DIRECTOR: A. Prasad

Established in 1956, the GTRE is one of 42 R&D facilities administered by the DRDO (Defence Research and Development Organisation). By far its biggest challenge is the design of a new fighter engine.

GTRE GTX-35

This engine is planned as the production powerplant of the HAL LCA (Light Combat Aircraft). Although influenced by existing engines, the GTX-35 is a completely Indian project, and no attempt has been made to find a foreign partner.

GTX-37-14U. This afterburning turbojet was the first designed in India. First run in 1977, it had a three-stage LP compressor and seven-stage HP compressor, both driven by single-stage turbines, and it was flat rated to 30°C at 44.5 kN (10,000 lb st) dry and 64 kN (14,385 lb st) with full reheat. Several will continue running to support later engines.

GTX-37-14UB. Turbofan version with bypass ratio of 0.2. Maximum thrust 89 kN (20,000 lb st), but frontal area too great.

GTX-35. Advanced turbojet with five-stage variable-capacity HP compressor, new annular combustor and increased turbine temperature. Offered correct thrusts for LCA but excessive fuel consumption.

GTX-35VS. Improved turbofan planned as engine for LCA. Core to run in 1988-89, engine in 1990.

LP COMPRESSOR: Three stages, with transonic blading. Pressure ratio 3.23.

HP COMPRESSOR: Five stages with some variable stators. Overall pressure ratio 21.

COMBUSTION CHAMBER: Annular, with air-blast atomisers.

HP TURBINE: Heavily loaded single stage with DS cooled blades. Entry gas temperature over 1,127°C. Later to have thermal barrier coating, followed by single-crystal blades.

LP TURBINE: Single stage.

CONTROL SYSTEM: FADEC, developed in collaboration with DSIC Ltd by HAL Lucknow Division.

PERFORMANCE RATINGS (S/L, T-O, maintained to 30°C):
Max: dry	44.62 kN (10,030 lb st)
with afterburning	86.30 kN (19,400 lb st)

HAL

HINDUSTAN AERONAUTICS LTD

Indian Express Building, Dr Ambedkar Veedhi, PO Box 5150, Bangalore 560 017
Telephone: 76091
OFFICERS: see Aircraft section

The Bangalore Engine and Koraput Divisions of HAL constitute the main aero engine manufacturing elements of the Indian aircraft industry.

BANGALORE COMPLEX (Engine Division)

Adour 811 engines are manufactured under Rolls-Royce Turbomeca licence. The Orpheus 701 and Dart 536-2T are manufactured under licence from Rolls-Royce. The Artouste IIIB is made under licence from Turbomeca.

Bangalore is developing the 3.43 kN (771 lb st) PTAE-7 short-life turbojet (Pilotless Target Aircraft Engine 7) for the ADE PTA. On 2 July 1984, DSIC (Dowty & Smiths Industries Controls) announced its first run. The engine nosecone contains a DSIC integrated digital control system complete with fuel pumps, valves, electronics and alternator.

KORAPUT DIVISION

This Division was established to manufacture under Soviet government licence the Tumansky R-11 afterburning turbojet. With help from the Soviet Union, the first engine was run on the bench (which it was used to calibrate) in early 1969. In 1977 production switched to the R-25 for the MiG-21 bis, followed in 1984 by the R-29B for the MiG-27M.

HAL PTAE-7 short-life turbojet *(Brian M. Service)*

INTERNATIONAL PROGRAMMES

ALLISON/MTU

ALLISON see under USA
MTU see under Germany (Federal Republic)

On 6 May 1988 these companies signed an MoU under the terms of which they are collaborating on a propfan to power the MBB/CATIC MPC 75 twin-engined transport.

The engine core will be based on the Allison T406 in the 4,476 kW (6,000 shp) class.

CFM

CFM INTERNATIONAL SA

2 boulevard Victor, 75015 Paris, France
Telephone: (1) 40 60 8189
CHAIRMAN AND CHIEF EXECUTIVE: J. Bilien

CFM International, a joint company, was formed by SNECMA (France) and General Electric (USA) in 1974 to provide management for the CFM56 programme and a single customer interface.

GE is responsible for design integration, the core engine and the main engine control. The core engine is derived from that of the F101 turbofan developed for the US military. SNECMA is responsible for the low-pressure system, gearbox, accessory integration and engine installation.

CFM INTERNATIONAL CFM56

US military designation: F108

In the late 1960s SNECMA and General Electric concluded that a large market existed for a high bypass ratio engine in the ten ton class (97.9-106.8 kN; 22,000-24,000 lb st). The first CFM56 demonstrator ran at GE's Evendale plant on 20 June 1974.

The CFM56 designation covers a family of engines from 89.0 to 138.7 kN (20,000-31,200 lb st). By April 1988 a total of 2,500 engines had been delivered, against orders for 4,100. The following are current versions:

CFM56-2. Certificated 8 November 1979, under FAR Pt 33 and JAR-E, at 106.8 kN (24,000 lb st); but several applications use only a 97.9 kN (22,000 lb) T-O rating. CFM56-2 production was launched in 1979 to re-engine the DC-8-60 to Super 70 standard. Scheduled operations began on 24 April 1982. 110 aircraft are in service with 18 operators and have logged more than 4,000,000 engine flight hours. Engine-caused shop visit rate is 0.12 and the dispatch reliability is 99.85 per cent. The CMF56-2 exists in several variants, differing by their ratings or configuration details.

CFM56-2A. Certificated 6 June 1985 at 106.8 kN (24,000 lb st), flat rated to 35°C (95°F), the CFM56-2A-2 powers the US Navy E-6 communications aircraft and the Royal Saudi Air Force E-3 advanced warning aircraft and KE-3 tanker, and will power the E-3s for the UK and France and, when funded, the USAF Joint-STARS 707. These applications require long duration oil tank, integral reverser and gearbox for two high capacity integrated drive generators.

CFM56-2-B. Certificated 25 June 1984 at 97.9 kN (22,000 lb st), flat rated to 32°C (90°F), the CFM56-2-B1 was selected by the US Air Force for its KC-135A tanker re-engining programme on 22 January 1980. First flight of a KC-135R took place on 4 August 1982 and production F108-CF-100 engines power KC-135R and KC-135C aircraft delivered from late 1983; 256 ordered by May 1988. CFM56-2-B1 also retrofits C-135FR tankers of the French Armée de l'Air.

CFM56-2C. Version of CFM56-2 for re-engining DC-8; T-O thrust of 99.79 kN (22,000 lb st), with flat rating at 30°C (86°F) to 41°C (106°F) in -2-C1 to -2-C6 subvariants.

CFM56-3-B1. Derivative of CFM56-2, rated at 89.00 kN (20,000 lb st), flat rated to 30°C (86°F), with smaller fan based on CF6-80. Powers 737-300. First ran in March 1982. US and French certification granted 12 January 1984. Entered airline service November 1984.

CFM56-3B-2. Certificated to 97.90 kN (22,000 lb st), flat rated to 30°C (86°F), on 20 June 1984. For 737-300 and 737-400 with improved payload/range from short, hot, high airfields.

CFM56-3C-1. Rated at 104.5 kN (23,500 lb st) for 737-400. Certificated December 1986.

By December 1987 more than 50 customers/operators had ordered 1,764 CFM56-35s. The 343 737-300s in service had logged more than 3,000,000 engine flight hours. Engine-caused shop visit (12 month rolling averages) was 0.074, and dispatch reliability 99.95.

CFM56-5-A1. Launched September 1984, for A320. Has fan diameter of –2, with improved aerodynamics in all LP and HP components, advanced clearance control features and full authority digital engine control. With nominal rating of 111.21 kN (25,000 lb st), flat rated to 30°C (86°F) and growth potential, it is being modified to achieve the specified fuel saving of 17 per cent compared with the CFM56-2C-1. Certificated 27 August 1987.

CFM56-5C-2. With a T-O rating of 138.7 kN (31,200 lb st), this is the advanced version of the -5 selected by Airbus Industrie as the launch engine of the A340.

TYPE: Two-shaft subsonic turbofan.

FAN: Single-stage axial. Forged titanium disc holding (CFM56-2) 44 titanium blades, each with a tip shroud to form a continuous ring; (CFM56-3) 38 titanium blades, each with part-span shroud. (CFM56-5) 36 titanium blades, each with part-span shroud. Max airflow (-2A-2) 370 kg (817 lb)/s, (-3B-2) 312 kg (688 lb)/s, (-5-A1) 386 kg (852 lb)/s. Bypass ratio (-2) 6, (-3) 5, (-5) 6, (-5C) 6.7.

LP COMPRESSOR: Three axial stages (4 on -5C-2), on titanium drum bolted to fan disc. A ring of bleed doors allows core airflow to escape into fan duct at low power settings.

HP COMPRESSOR: Nine-stage rotor with three stages of titanium blades and remainder of steel. Stator vanes are steel, with first four stators variable. Overall pressure ratio 25:1 class (-3, 22.6; -5, 26.5; -5C, climb, 37.5).

COMBUSTION CHAMBER: Machined ring, fully annular, with advanced film cooling. Based upon F101 but modified for reduced emission.

HP TURBINE: Single-stage with aircooled stator and rotor airfoils, directionally solidified on -5. Entry gas temperature in 1,260°C class. HP system carried in two bearings (-5, three bearings).

LP TURBINE: Four-stage (4½ on -5-A1, 5 on -5C-2) axial with tip shrouds.

EXHAUST UNIT (FAN): Constant diameter duct of sound-absorbent construction. Outer cowl and engine cowl form convergent plug nozzle, with airframe mounted reverser.

EXHAUST UNIT (CORE): Fixed-area with convergent plug nozzle, mixer on -5C-2.

ACCESSORY DRIVE: (CFM56-2 and -5) Gearbox in front sump transmits drive from front of HP spool to transfer gearbox on underside of fan case. Air starter at transfer gearbox (-2) or accessory gearbox (-5). (CFM56-3) Side mounted accessory drive gearbox with transfer gearbox; air starter pad on accessory gearbox.

CONTROL SYSTEM: Hydromechanical with electronic trim (-2, -3). Full authority digital engine control (-5).

LUBRICATION: Non-pressure-regulated system.

DIMENSIONS:

Length, excl spinner:

CFM56-2	2,430 mm (95.7 in)
CFM56-3	2,360 mm (93.0 in)
CFM56-5-A1	2,422 mm (95.4 in)
CFM56-5C-2	2,667 mm (105 in)

Fan diameter:

CFM56-2	1,733 mm (68.2 in)
CFM56-3	1,522 mm (60.0 in)
CFM56-5-A1	1,733 mm (68.2 in)
CFM56-5C-2	1,836 mm (72.3 in)

WEIGHT, DRY:

CFM56-2A-2	2,185 kg (4,817 lb)
CFM56-2B-1	2,093 kg (4,614 lb)
CFM56-2C series	2,101 kg (4,632 lb)
CFM56-3-B1	1,939 kg (4,275 lb)
CFM56-3B-2, -3C	1,950 kg (4,299 lb)
CFM56-5-A1	2,204 kg (4,859 lb)
CFM56-5C-2	2,492 kg (5,494 lb)

PERFORMANCE RATINGS:

Max T-O: see under model listings

Cruise, installed, 10,670 m (35,000 ft), Mach 0.8, ISA:

CFM56-2A-2	25.60 kN (5,755 lb)
CFM56-2B-1	22.10 kN (4,970 lb)
CFM56-2C series	22.14 kN (4,970 lb)
CFM56-3-B1	20.67 kN (4,650 lb)
CFM56-3B-2	22.40 kN (5,035 lb)
CFM56-3C	23.27 kN (5,230 lb)
CFM56-5-A1	22.23 kN (5,000 lb)
CFM56-5C-2 (with mixer)	28.00 kN (6,300 lb)

SPECIFIC FUEL CONSUMPTION (cruise, as above):

CFM56-2A-2	18.83 mg/Ns (0.665 lb/h/lb)
CFM56-2B-1	18.57 mg/Ns (0.656 lb/h/lb)
CFM56-2C series	19.00 mg/Ns (0.671 lb/h/lb)
CFM56-3-B1, -3B-2	18.80 mg/Ns (0.664 lb/h/lb)
CFM56-3C	18.54 mg/Ns (0.655 lb/h/lb)
CFM56-5-A1	16.87 mg/Ns (0.596 lb/h/lb)
CFM56-5C-2 (with mixer)	15.45 mg/Ns (0.545 lb/h/lb)

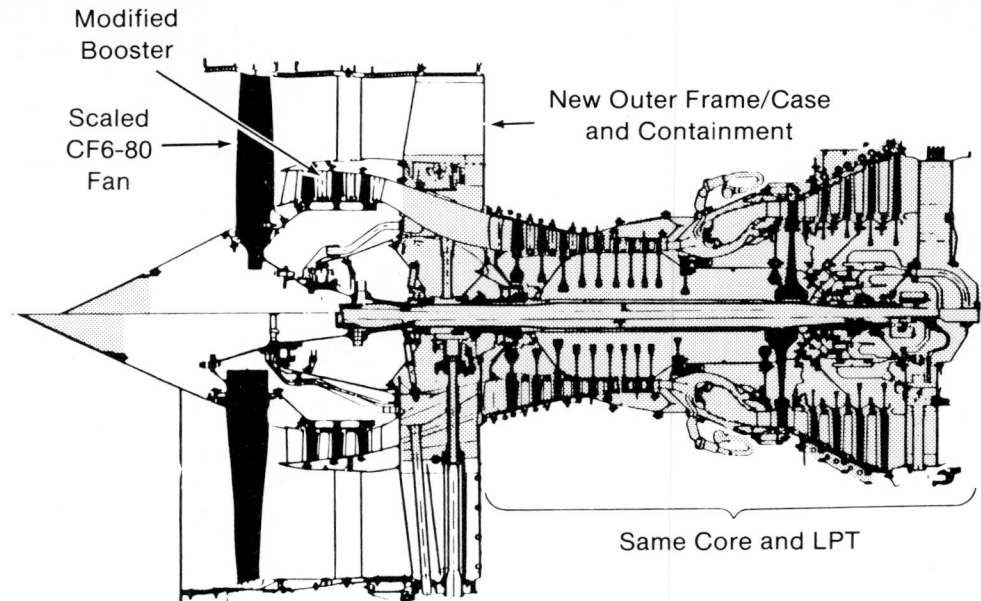

Modified Booster

Scaled CF6-80 Fan

New Outer Frame/Case and Containment

Same Core and LPT

Comparative sections of the CFM56-2 (lower half) and -3 (upper)

The CFM56-5A-1 turbofan (111.25 kN; 25,000 lb st)

EUROJET

EUROJET TURBO GmbH

Arabellastrasse 13, D-8000 Munich 81, Federal Republic of Germany
Telephone: (089) 9210050
Telex: 5212124 EJET D
Fax: (089) 912100539
MANAGING DIRECTOR: Colin H. Green

Formed in August 1986 by a consortium of Fiat Aviazione of Italy, MTU-München GmbH of West Germany, Rolls-Royce of the UK and Sener of Spain, this company became operational on 1 January 1987 as EUROJET Turbo GmbH. It was established to coordinate the design, development and manufacture of the EJ200 engine for the European Fighter Aircraft.

The workshare is proportional to the expected aircraft requirements of the four nations, and has been agreed as follows. Fiat (21 per cent), LP turbine and shaft, interstage support, reheat system, gearbox, oil system, and participation in the intermediate casing. MTU (33 per cent), LP compressor, HP compressor, participation in HP turbine, and FADEC (full authority digital electronic control) design responsibility. Rolls-Royce (33 per cent), combustion system, HP turbine, intermediate casing, and participation in LP and HP compressors, LP turbine, interstage support, reheat system and nozzle. SENER (13 per cent), nozzle, jetpipe, exhaust diffuser and bypass duct.

Engine build and test during development and production will be at each partner's facilities. Each partner will provide comprehensive support for engines of its own national air force. The initial requirement of the four nations is for nearly 800 aircraft, including about 2,000 engines. The formal go-ahead was signed on 16 May 1988.

EUROJET EJ200

This engine will be an advanced turbofan designed for Mach numbers of about 2. It is fully modular, and allows for on-condition maintenance with built-in engine health monitoring and test equipment. Low maintenance and life-cycle cost along with high reliability have been prime design criteria. The total number of aerofoils is only approximately 60 per cent of those used in the RB199. First run is scheduled for 18 months from go-ahead, with flight clearance approximately two years later. Entry into service is expected to be in 1995.

TYPE: Two-shaft augmented turbofan.
LP COMPRESSOR: Three-stages, with 3-D transonic blades of robust large-chord section. No inlet guide vanes. Third stage blisks. Overhung ahead of high-capacity ball bearing and forward roller bearing. Bypass ratio about 0.4. Pressure ratio 4-plus.
HP COMPRESSOR: Five stages, with first-stage variable inlet guide vanes and blisk rotor stage. Shaft supported between front ball and rear roller bearings. Overall pressure ratio more than 25.

Full scale model of the EUROJET EJ200 *(Brian M. Service)*

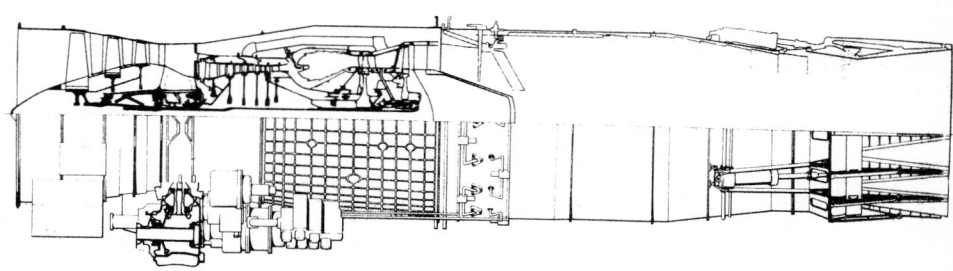

Longitudinal section through the EUROJET EJ200 two-shaft augmented turbofan

COMBUSTOR: Fully annular, with vaporising burners.
HP TURBINE: Single-stage, with powder metallurgy disc and low density aircooled single crystal blades.
LP TURBINE: Single-stage, with powder metallurgy disc and single crystal blades. Both turbine bearings in single interstage support frame.
EXHAUST SYSTEM: High efficiency augmentor of burn-then-mix type, with fully variable convergent-divergent nozzle.

ACCESSORIES: Central gearbox driven via tower shaft in interstage support. Full authority digital electronic control. Integrated health monitoring system. Rotating-tank oil system to give artificial positive gravity at all times.
DIMENSIONS: Smaller throughout than RB199.
WEIGHT: In 1,000 kg (2,000 lb) class.
PERFORMANCE RATING: In 90 kN (20,000 lb st) class.

IAE

INTERNATIONAL AERO ENGINES AG

OFFICES: 287 Main Street, East Hartford, Connecticut 06108, USA
Telephone: (203) 280 1800
Telex: 4436031 INTLAERO
Fax: (203) 525 1586/4966
ENGINEERING FACILITY: Eastgate House, Nottingham Road, Derby DE1 3QL, England
Telephone: 0332 40811
Telex: 378260 IAEAG G
PRESIDENT AND CHIEF EXECUTIVE OFFICER:
Nicholas R. Tomassetti
PUBLIC RELATIONS MANAGER: Alan C. Brothers

IAE stems from an agreement signed by five aero engine companies in Derby, England, on 11 March 1983, to develop an advanced technology turbofan for future 150-passenger airliners. The five companies were Rolls-Royce (UK), United Technologies' Pratt & Whitney (USA), The Japanese Aero Engines Corporation, MTU (West Germany) and Fiat Aviazione of Italy. JAEC comprises IHI, KHI and MHI (see under Japan).

The company was registered on 15 December 1983 in Zurich, Switzerland. IAE members announced a 30-year commitment to produce engines in the thrust range 80.1-133.4 kN (18,000-30,000 lb st). The engine, the V2500, was officially launched on 1 January 1984. The V of the designation is intended to be read as the Roman numeral five, for the five companies in five nations which are the shareholders, and the 2500 denotes the 25,000 lb thrust (111.25 kN) rating of the baseline engine.

IAE V2500

The V2500 meets the power requirements for the 72 tonne version of the Airbus A320. By 1988, it had been selected to power A320s ordered by five airlines. It is a candidate engine for Boeing projects, for the KC-135 re-engining programme and for the MD-80/90 family.

Pratt & Whitney and Rolls-Royce each have 30 per cent workshares in the V2500, Japanese Aero Engines has 23 per cent, MTU 11 per cent and Fiat Aviazione six per cent. IAE directs the design, development and manufacture of the V2500 at the shareholders' facilities. The company is

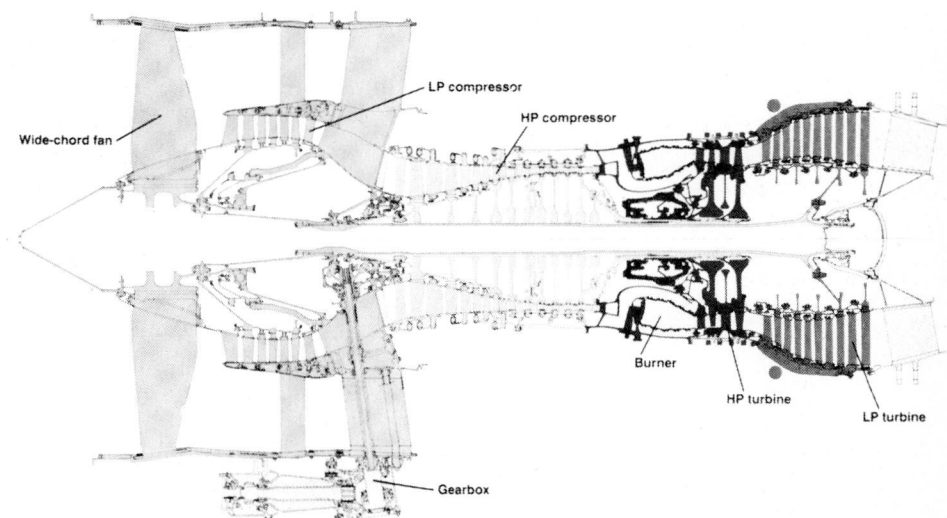

Cross-section of the IAE V2500 turbofan in its latest configuration with three-stage LP booster

responsible for marketing the engine, for providing product support, and keeping close financial controls on the whole project.

JAEC holds responsibility for the fan and LP compressor; Rolls-Royce for the HP compressor; Pratt & Whitney for the combustor and HP turbine; MTU for the LP turbine; and Fiat for the accessory gearbox and turbine exhaust case. Design integration is under the direction of the IAE engineering group at Pratt & Whitney.

While the fan is a derivative of that of the Rolls-Royce 535E4, the HP compressor is derived from the HP compressor research programme by Rolls-Royce which also formed the basis for the HP compressor on the RB401 and RJ500 engines. The turbines, gearbox and electronic engine control are derived from the PW2037 developed by

Pratt & Whitney in conjunction with MTU, Fiat and Hamilton Standard.

IAE is offering a complete propulsion system package, including the nacelle (by Rohr/Shorts). Testing of the engine began in December 1985. Difficulties have been experienced with the HP compressor as a result of which Pratt & Whitney has assumed the role of technical manager. In Spring 1987 the engine was reconfigured, the fan being recambered and moved forward and the LP booster upgraded from one to three stages, relieving stage loading on the HP spool. Modified engines began running in November 1987, and 12 had run 4,400 h by June 1988. A flight programme on a Boeing 720B in Canada was completed in 35 h in Spring 1988, and every ingestion and fan-blade-off test was passed first time (believed an industry record). The first pair of propulsion systems was delivered to Airbus Industrie in March 1988, and the V2500 was certificated to the requirements of the FAA, and the airworthiness authorities in the UK, Japan, West Germany and Italy, in June 1988.

The primary design features of the V2500 are as follows:

TYPE: Two-spool subsonic turbofan.

FAN: Single-stage with wide-chord shroudless blading. Diameter 1,600 mm (63.0 in). Pressure ratio 1.70. Bypass ratio 5.42. T-O airflow 355 kg (783 lb)/s.

LP COMPRESSOR: Three stages, bolted to rear of fan to boost inlet to core.

HP COMPRESSOR: Ten stages of blading supported by a drum rotor. End bend and controlled diffusion aerodynamic improvements are incorporated. Inlet guide and first three vane stages variable. Overall pressure ratio 29.4.

EIS (1989) blading has revised profile for higher efficiency.

COMBUSTOR: Annular segmented construction eliminates hoop stresses and provides low emissions and uniform exit temperatures.

HP TURBINE: Two stages of aircooled single-crystal blading in powder metallurgy discs. Active tip clearance control.

LP TURBINE: Five stages of uncooled blading in welded and bolted rotor. Active clearance control.

GEARBOX: Modular unit, fan-case mounted.

CONTROL SYSTEM: Full authority digital electronic control (FADEC) to provide command outputs for engine fuel flow, stator vane angle, bleed modulation, turbine and exhaust case cooling, oil cooling, ignition and reverser functions. Supplied by Hamilton Standard.

NACELLE: Full length nacelle comprising inlet, fan cowl doors, fan ducts, reverser, common nozzle, engine mounts and engine build unit. Cowl load sharing to minimise case deflections. Acoustically treated. Supplied by Rohr/Shorts.

DIMENSIONS:
Length (flange to flange) 3,200 mm (126 in)
Fan diameter 1,600 mm (63 in)

WEIGHT, DRY (with original single-stage LP compressor):
Bare engine 2,242 kg (4,942 lb)
Complete power plant, incl nacelle 3,311 kg (7,300 lb)

PERFORMANCE RATINGS (installed):
T-O, S/L, ISA 111.25 kN (25,000 lb st) to ISA + 15°C
Cruise Mach 0.8, 10,670 m (35,000 ft): 21.6 kN (4,850 lb)

SPECIFIC FUEL CONSUMPTION (cruise Mach 0.8, 10,670 m;
35,000 ft, installed): 16.29 mg/Ns (0.575 lb/h/lb)

MTR
MTU-TURBOMECA-RR GmbH

Postfach 500640, 8000 Munich 50, Federal Republic of Germany
Telephone: (089) 1489 1
Telex: 529 500-15 MT D
Fax: (089) 1502621

MTU-TURBOMECA-RR MTR 390

This turboshaft engine is being developed by MTR GmbH, a joint company owned equally by MTU, Turbomeca and Rolls-Royce. First application will be in the Eurocopter Franco-German helicopters. The direct-drive MTR 390T is a candidate for the JEH Tonal derivative of the Agusta A 129. All models are covered by the European Small Engines Co-operation Agreement described in the introduction to Turbomeca of France. First run is due in

1989, and flight in a Dauphin testbed is to follow in 1990.

COMPRESSOR: Two centrifugal stages. Mass flow 3.2 kg (7.05 lb)/s. Pressure ratio 13.

COMBUSTION CHAMBER: Reverse flow annular.

TURBINES: Single-stage cooled gas generator turbine. Two-stage free power turbine.

CONTROL SYSTEM: Full authority digital.

DIMENSIONS:
Length 1,070 mm (42.1 in)
Width 432 mm (17.0 in)
Height 659 mm (25.9 in)

WEIGHT: 180 kg (397 lb)

RATINGS:
Emergency (30 s) 1,138 kW (1,526 hp)
T-O (5 min) 958 kW (1,285 hp)
Max continuous 873 kW (1,171 hp)

SPECIFIC FUEL CONSUMPTION:
T-O 75.8 µg/J (0.448 lb/h/hp)

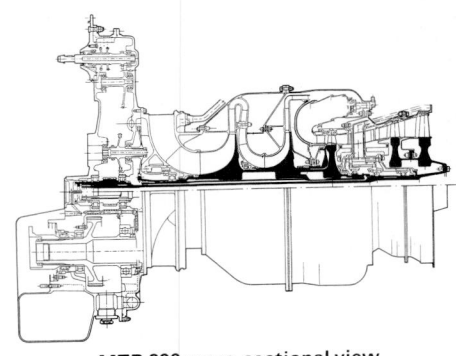

MTR 390 cross-sectional view

ROLLS-ROYCE TURBOMECA
ROLLS-ROYCE TURBOMECA LIMITED

4/5 Grosvenor Place, London SW1X 7HH, England
Telephone: 01 235 3641
Telex: 918944
Fax: 01 245 6385

This joint company was formed in June 1966 to control design, development and production programmes for the Adour two-shaft turbofan.

In 1980 Rolls-Royce Turbomeca launched the RTM 321 turboshaft demonstrator, leading to the RTM 322.

ROLLS-ROYCE TURBOMECA ADOUR
US military designation: F405

The Adour was designed for the SEPECAT Jaguar. The whole engine is simple and robust and of modular design.

Bench testing began at Derby on 9 May 1967. Engines for Jaguars were assembled at Derby (R-R) and Tarnos (Turbomeca) from parts made at single sources in Britain and France. Turbomeca makes the compressors, casings and external pipework (to preserve Anglo-French parity the afterburner is subcontracted to SNECMA); Rolls-Royce makes the remainder.

Following selection of the Adour for the Mitsubishi T-2 trainer and F-1 fighter/support aircraft, Ishikawajima-Harima Heavy Industries has been producing the Adour since 1970 under a licence agreement. In 1972 a non-afterburning Adour was selected to power the British Aerospace Hawk advanced trainer. More than 2,200 engines have been produced, including licence manufacture in Japan, India and Finland. Flight hours exceed 2.75 million.

Current versions of the engine are as follows:

Mk 102. Original production engine for Jaguars in service with RAF and Armee de l'Air. Qualified in 1972.

Mk 104. Uprated RT172-26 version similar to Mk 804; RAF Mk 102 engines were converted to this standard.

Mk 151. Non-afterburning version for Hawk. Internal components and certification temperatures identical to Mk 102 and Mk 801A. Qualified in 1975.

Mk 801A. Japanese designation TF40-IHI-801A. For Mitsubishi T-2 and F-1. Qualified in 1972. (See Ishikawajima-Harima in Japanese section.)

Mk 804. Uprated engine for Jaguar International. Rating with full afterburner at Mach 0.9 at S/L, ISA, increased by 27 per cent. Qualified in 1976.

Mk 811. Uprated version for Jaguar International. Revised compressor aerodynamics and hot-end improvements. Assembled by Hindustan Aeronautics, with increasing Indian manufactured content.

Mk 815C. Mk 804 uprated to Mk 811 performance level by conversion at overhaul.

Mk 851. Non-afterburning version of Mk 804 for export Hawk.

Mk 861. Non-afterburning version of Mk 811, first deliveries 1981.

Mk 861-49. US designation **F405-RR-400.** Derated version of Mk 861, for McDD/BAe T-45A Goshawk for US Navy. Certificated 1988.

Mk 871. Uprated version for BAe Hawk Series 100 and 200. Certification scheduled for 1989.

Rolls-Royce Turbomeca Adour Mk 151 for British Aerospace Hawk T. Mk 1, rated at 23.1 kN (5,200 lb st)

TYPE: Two-shaft turbofan for subsonic aircraft.

FAN: Two-stage. Full length bypass duct leading to afterburner. Bypass ratio, 0.75-0.80.

COMPRESSOR: Five stages. Overall pressure ratio 11 : 1.

COMBUSTION CHAMBER: Annular, with 18 air spray fuel nozzles and two igniter plugs. Engine fuel system by Lucas.

HP TURBINE: Single-stage, aircooled.

LP TURBINE: Single-stage. Squeeze-film bearings.

DIMENSIONS:
Length:
Mks 102, 801A, 804, 811 2,970 mm (117 in)
Mks 151, 851, 861, 861-49, 871 1,956 mm (77 in)
Inlet diameter (all) 559 mm (22 in)
Max width (all) 762 mm (30 in)
Max height (all) 1,041 mm (41 in)

WEIGHT, DRY:
Mk 102, 801A 704 kg (1,552 lb)
Mk 104, 804 713 kg (1,571 lb)
Mk 151 553 kg (1,220 lb)
Mk 851 568 kg (1,252 lb)
Mk 861 577 kg (1,273 lb)
Mk 811 738 kg (1,627 lb)
Mk 871 603 kg (1,330 lb)

PERFORMANCE RATINGS (S/L T-O):
Mk 102, 801A 32.5 kN (7,305 lb st)*
Mk 104 35.1 kN (7,900 lb st)*
Mk 151, 851 23.1 kN (5,200 lb st)
Mk 804 35.8 kN (8,040 lb st)*

Mk 861 25.4 kN (5,700 lb st)
Mk 861-49 24.2 kN (5,450 lb st)
Mk 811 37.4 kN (8,400 lb st)*
Mk 871 26.0 kN (5,845 lb st)
With afterburner

SPECIFIC FUEL CONSUMPTION (Mk 102):
S/L static, dry 21 mg/Ns (0.74 lb/h/lb st)
Mach 0.8, 11,890 m (39,000 ft)
27 mg/Ns (0.955 lb/h/lb st)

ROLLS-ROYCE TURBOMECA RTM 322

RTM 322 technology is derived from existing engine programmes and research projects. Since 1986 Piaggio of Italy has shared in development and production for markets outside North America.

The launch engine is the **RTM 322-01** turboshaft, which is conservatively rated at 1,566 kW (2,100 shp) with growth potential to 2,240 kW (3,000 shp).

The family, which will include turboprop and turbofan derivatives, is configured to combine simple design, reliability, low fuel consumption, light weight and low cost of ownership.

The turboshaft itself has full authority digital electronic control, availability of different output drive configurations, a choice of three starting systems, and options for an inlet particle separator and infra-red suppressor. Combined with engine mounts configured for compatability with certain existing airframes, these give the unit a wide range of potential civil and military applications in the 7 to 15 tonne class. Examples are: EH 101, Sikorsky Black Hawk and Sea Hawk series, Westland WS-70, AH-64 Apache, JEH Tonal and European NH 90. The engine has been studied by the US Army as a potential growth power plant for the Black Hawk and Apache, and during 1987 the US Navy carried out an operability study in an SH-60B with a view to future purchases of this and the SH-60F. In November 1986 Pratt & Whitney confirmed its licence rights for marketing and manufacture of the RTM 322 for sales to the US and Canadian Governments after an initial agreement made in 1985, but in May 1988 a major Pentagon decision was taken in favour of the all-American T700.

The first complete RTM 322-01 ran on 4 February 1985, and by the end of that year design verification had been completed. Over 1,790 kW (2,400 shp) had been demonstrated with good reliability and low spares, and exhibited good starting usage, and power response. The first flight was on 14 June 1986 in an S-70C. Accelerated mission testing began in July 1986, and a total of 7,000 hours running is scheduled in this programme. Certification was due in early 1988.

Rolls-Royce Turbomeca is studying a turboprop that uses the RTM 322-01 core. This would produce 1,193-1,490 kW (1,600-2000 shp), with potential for growth to 2,090 kW (2,800 shp). It is therefore suitable for aircraft in the 35-70 seat range.

The following particulars apply to the RTM 322-01 turboshaft:

COMPRESSOR: Three-stage axial and single-stage centrifugal.

COMBUSTOR: Annular reverse flow. Ignition by Lucas Aerospace exciter.

Rolls-Royce Turbomeca RTM 322-01 turboshaft

TURBINES: Two-stage gas generator turbine. Cooling is applied to the 1st and 2nd stage stators and 1st stage rotor. The 2nd stage rotor is made of single crystal material and is uncooled. Two-stage power turbine with drive to front or rear.

DIMENSIONS:
Length overall	1,171 mm (46 in)
Diameter	604 mm (23.8 in)

WEIGHT, DRY: 240 kg (538 lb)
PERFORMANCE RATINGS (S/L):
Max contingency	1,724 kW (2,312 shp)
Max T-O	1,566 kW (2,100 shp)
Typical cruise	940 kW (1,260 shp)

SPECIFIC FUEL CONSUMPTION:
Cruise (as above)	81 μg/J (0.48 lb/shp/h)

TURBO-UNION
TURBO-UNION LTD
PO Box 3, Filton, Bristol BS12 7QE, England
Telephone: 0272 791234
Telex: 44185 RR BSLG
MUNICH OFFICE: Arabellastrasse 13, D-8000 Munich 81, Federal Republic of Germany
Telephone: (089) 9242 1
Telex: 524151 TUD
CHAIRMAN: Dr G. C. Boffetta
MANAGING DIRECTOR: Kurt Münzenmaier

Formed in 1969 as a European engine consortium comprising Rolls-Royce plc (40%) of the United Kingdom, MTU Motoren- und Turbinen-Union München GmbH (40%) of the Federal Republic of Germany and Fiat Aviazione SpA (20%) of Italy. The consortium was established to design, develop, manufacture and support the RB199 turbofan for the Panavia Tornado aircraft.

TURBO-UNION RB199
The RB199 is a three-spool turbofan offering low fuel consumption for long-range dry cruise and approximately 100 per cent thrust augmentation with full afterburner for combat manoeuvre and supersonic acceleration. It features an integral thrust reverser system for installation in the Tornado, but is available for other applications without it. The present engine family comprises:

Mk 103. Standard production engine for Tornado IDS. In-service experience at low level in the most arduous conditions has proven the RB199's high resilience to FOD and birdstrike, a direct result of the three-spool layout incorporating short, rigid rotating assemblies held between small bearing spans.

Mk 104. Identical to Mk 103 but incorporates a jetpipe extended by 360 mm (14 in) to provide thrust increases up to 10 per cent as well as reduced sfc. The Mk 104 also features full authority digital engine control (FADEC) and was the first military engine in the world to feature this without a hydromechanical back-up. (FADEC is now available on Mk 103 engines). The 104 is the standard production engine for the Tornado ADV F.3. The **104D** powers the BAe EAP. The main difference is absence of the reverser, which reduces weight by 10 per cent.

Mk 105. The Tornado ECR is powered by the Mk 105, for delivery to the Luftwaffe in 1989. Similar to the 103, it includes an increased pressure ratio and mass flow LP compressor, providing thrust increase of 10 per cent, as well as significant life-cycle cost reductions. Single-crystal HP turbine blades. This represents a major step towards an enhanced engine in early 1990. This will have the 105 features as well as improved IP and HP compressors, turbine NGVs and single-crystal IP turbine blades. Thrust improvements of over 20 per cent will be available, together with significant LCC reductions.

The RB199 passed one million flying hours in Summer 1988. Firm orders exist for over 2,400 engines, guaranteeing new engine production into the 1990s.

The following refers to the first production engine, the Mk 101:

TYPE: Three-shaft turbofan with afterburner and reverser.
LP COMPRESSOR: Three-stage axial of titanium alloy. Casing of three bolted sections. Rotor of three discs welded together. Rotor blades secured by dovetail roots, all with snubbers. Mass flow approx 70 kg (154 lb)/s. Bypass ratio about 1:1.

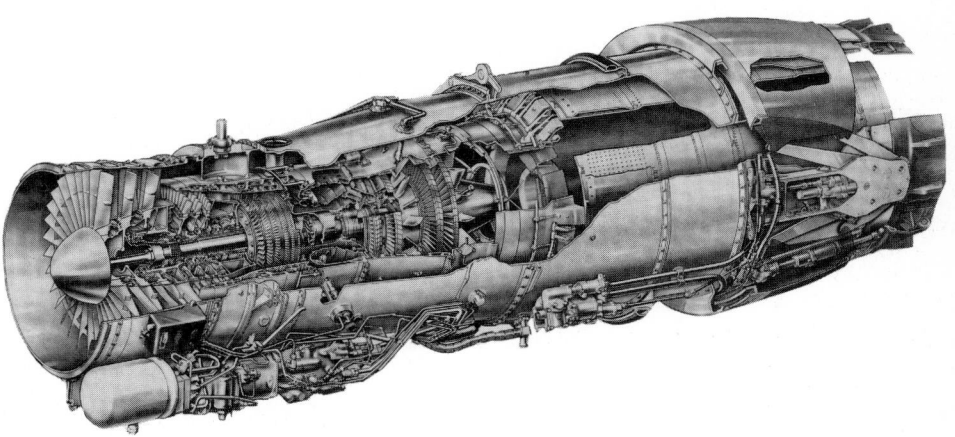

Cutaway drawing of Turbo-Union RB199 Mk 104, the current production engine for Tornado ADV aircraft

Turbo-Union RB199 Mk 104D engine of EAP

IP COMPRESSOR: Three stages of titanium alloy. Rotor has welded discs in which blades are secured by dovetails.

HP COMPRESSOR: Six-stage; material changes from titanium at front to heat resisting alloy at rear, except stator blades are heat resisting steel throughout. Rotor discs secured by ten through-bolts, carrying blades by dovetail roots. Bevel drive to gearbox. Overall pressure ratio greater than 23.

BYPASS DUCT: Fabricated in titanium.

COMBUSTION CHAMBER: Annular flame tube fabricated from nickel alloy, bolted at rear end between outer casing, forged and chemically milled in nickel-iron alloy, and inner casing of nickel alloy. Carries 13 double-headed fuel vaporisers which give combustion without visible smoke. Two igniter plugs. Hot-streak injector for afterburner ignition.

HP TURBINE: Shrouded single stage. Entry temperature over 1,327°C. Rotor blades and stator vanes aircooled.

IP TURBINE: Shrouded single stage. Aircooled stator vanes and rotor blades.

LP TURBINE: Two-stage with shrouded hollow uncooled rotor blades.

AFTERBURNER: Front end of titanium fabricated jetpipe carries afterburner in which bypass air and core gas burn concurrently, without a mixing section. For core flow, two gutter flameholders fed by upstream atomisers. For bypass flow, reverse colander with radial extensions, each containing vaporising primary burner, between which multiple jets inject remainder of afterburner fuel. Fully modulated augmentation.

NOZZLE: Variable area, short petal, convergent nozzle operated by shroud actuated by four screwjacks, driven by fourth stage HP air motor via flexible shafting. Each of 14 master and 14 secondary petals is precision casting in cobalt alloy which minimises friction.

REVERSER: External two bucket type driven via flexible shafts by motor using HP air. In stowed position outer skins form aircraft profile. Deployment takes 1 s at any thrust setting from idle to max dry.

ACCESSORY DRIVES: Accessory gearbox on underside of intermediate casing (quick attach/detach coupling) carries hydromechanical portions of main and afterburner fuel systems, oil tank and pump, and output shaft to aircraft gearbox carrying KHD gas turbine starter/APU.

FUEL SYSTEM: Electronic main engine control unit uses signals from pilot's lever and power plant sensors. Afterburner fuel from engine driven vapour core pump.

DIMENSIONS:

Length overall	3,230 mm (127 in)
Max diameter	870 mm (34.25 in)

WEIGHT, DRY:

Excl reverser	approx 900 kg (1,980 lb)
Incl reverser	1,084 kg (2,390 lb)

PERFORMANCE RATINGS (Mk 103, S/L, ISA):

Max dry	42.95 kN (9,656 lb st)
Max afterburning	75.26 kN (16,920 lb st)

ISRAEL

BET-SHEMESH
BET-SHEMESH ENGINES LTD
Mobile Post Haela, Bet-Shemesh 99000
Telephone: 02 911661-6
Telex: 25290

Bet-Shemesh Engines is owned by the Israeli government. The manufacturing plant was based on the Turbomeca factory at Tarnos. On 1 January 1977 a change in management took place. Over the subsequent year the number of employees increased from 550 to about 1,300, and plant area increased to 22,500 m² (242,000 sq ft). At first Bet-Shemesh manufactured on behalf of Turbomeca. By 1973 complete Marboré VI turbojets were being produced. As the centralised source for all aircraft gas turbine manufacture in Israel, it makes portions of the J79 (see IAI entry) and F100, and provides support for the

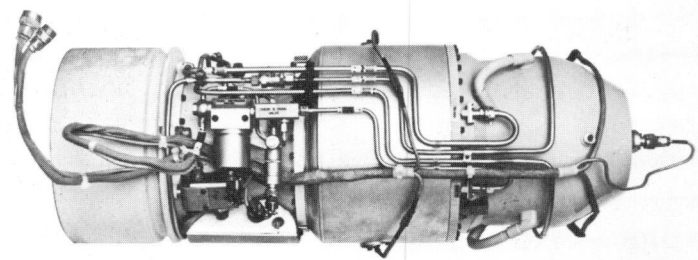

**Bet-Shemesh Sorek 4
expendable turbojet**

Allison 250-C20. It was prime contractor for the PW1120 for the IAI Lavi. With Reshef Systems it is developing a FADEC.

IAI
ISRAEL AIRCRAFT INDUSTRIES LTD
Ben-Gurion International Airport, 70100
Telephone: 03 97131111
Telex: ISRAV-IL 371133
Fax: 03 972290

The Engine Overhaul Plant is part of IAI's Bedek Aviation Division. It produces J79 engines and performs extensive overhaul and maintenance of civil and military engines.

J79-IAI-J1E
The J79-IAI-J1E powers the IAI Kfir and is produced by IAI under GE licence. It is a J79-GE-19 incorporating 102 per cent engine speed at high aircraft Mach number, smokeless combustors, and a T_5 reset for fast acceleration. Accessories and gearboxes are relocated, and a titanium heatshield covers the afterburner. A Combat Plus system increases T-O thrust from 78.9 kN (17,750 lb) to 83.4 kN (18,750 lb).

Details of the J79 can be found in the 1978-79 edition of *Jane's*.

Data for the J1E include:

MASS FLOW:	77.1 kg (170 lb)/s
PRESSURE RATIO:	12.4
DIMENSIONS:	
Max diameter	995.7 mm (39.2 in)
Length	5,283 mm (208 in)
WEIGHT:	1,699 kg (3,746 lb)
MAX RATINGS (T-O, S/L):	
With augmentation	83.4 kN (18,750 lb st)
Dry	49.4 kN (11,110 lb st)

ITALY

ALFA ROMEO AVIO
ALFA ROMEO AVIO SpA
80038 Pomigliano D'Arco, Naples
Telephone: 081 8430111
Telex: 710083 ARAVIO
CHAIRMAN: Gen Fulvio Ristori
MANAGING DIRECTOR: Ing Filippo De Luca

Alfa Romeo Avio was prime contractor for the manufacture, under General Electric licence, of the J85, J79 and T58. It manufactures CF6 combustors and JT9D components, and assembles PT6T engines for the AB 212. Under GE licence it is responsible for the hot section of the T64-P4D, co-produced with Fiat, and participates in the RB199. The company is a partner in Italian production of the Rolls-Royce Spey 807.

In February 1986 it began deliveries of GE T700-401 engines for EH 101 prototypes. It supplies components for T700 engines fitted to American helicopters and is developing new versions. It is also involved, with Fiat, in the development of the GE CT7-6, aimed at the EH 101, NH 90 and a new version of the A 129.

ALFA ROMEO AVIO AR.318
Alfa Romeo Avio is developing this simple turboprop to cover powers from 298 to 596 kW (400-800 shp). The programme draws upon Rolls-Royce under a contract for technical support. RAI (Italian civil) certification was achieved in April 1985, and production engines with FAA certification are now available.

TYPE: Single-shaft turboprop.

REDUCTION GEAR: Epicyclic, driven by muff coupling from compressor forward shaft. Accessory gear train driven from first reduction stage. Phase displacement torque-meter and torque/speed sensing unit.

COMPRESSOR: Single-stage centrifugal. Pressure ratio 5.4.

COMBUSTION CHAMBER: Annular reverse flow type, with eight T shape vaporiser tubes. Two igniters and three starter spray nozzles.

The 453 kW (608 shp) Alfa Romeo Avio AR.318 turboprop

TURBINE: Two-stage axial. Each IGV row is a one-piece investment casting. Rotors and blades are integral solid castings, joined by a curvic coupling.

OIL SYSTEM: One pressure and two scavenge pumps. Provision for engine mounted tank, fuel heater and temperature/pressure transducers.

FUEL SYSTEM: Single assembly of filters, pumps, metering and overspeed protection. Optional beta control, top temperature and torque limiting, and autofeather.

FUEL GRADE: JP-1, JP-4.

DIMENSIONS:
Length	1,061 mm (41.8 in)
Width	534 mm (21.0 in)
Height	658 mm (25.9 in)

WEIGHT, DRY: 140.6 kg (310 lb)

PERFORMANCE RATINGS (S/L, ISA):
T-O (no time limit)	453 kW (608 shp)
Max continuous	420 kW (564 shp)
Cruise	394 kW (529 shp)

SPECIFIC FUEL CONSUMPTION:
T-O	97.7 µg/J (0.578 lb/h/shp)
Max continuous	99.2 µg/J (0.587 lb/h/shp)
Cruise	102.4 µg/J (0.606 lb/h/shp)

ARROW

ARROW snc

Via Badiaschi 25, 29100 Piacenza
Telephone: 0523 41932
Telex: 530112 CC PC1
Fax: 0523 34367
CHAIRMAN: Tullio Osellini
ENGINEERING MANAGER: G. Polidoro

This company produces modular aircooled piston engines for microlights and homebuilts. In 1985 Arrow won the French ULM championship and the Grande Course for two-seat microlights.

ARROW GT250

Single-cylinder geared two-stroke. Cast light alloy cylinder with ceramic coated interior. Bore 74.6 mm (2.94 in). Stroke 57.0 mm (2.24 in). Capacity 250 cc (15.25 cu in). Induction through 36 mm Dell'Orto carburettor of 100 grade fuel mixed with 2 per cent oil. Electric starter and 12 V electronic ignition with one or two plugs. Planetary reduction gear of 0.335 ratio.

DIMENSIONS:
Length	460 mm (18.12 in)
Width	370 mm (14.60 in)
Height	380 mm (15.0 in)

WEIGHT, READY TO RUN: 26.0 kg (57.26 lb)
PERFORMANCE RATING: 25.33 kW (34 hp) at 6,800 rpm
FUEL CONSUMPTION:
4 to 6 litres (1.06-1.58 US gallons; 0.88-1.32 Imp gallons)/h

ARROW GT500

This is the opposed-twin version of the GT250. A 38 mm carburettor is used.

DIMENSIONS:
Length	500 mm (19.65 in)
Width	500 mm (19.65 in)
Height	451 mm (17.70 in)

WEIGHT, READY TO RUN: 36.0 kg (79.3 lb)
PERFORMANCE RATING: 48.5 kW (65 hp) at 6,800 rpm
FUEL CONSUMPTION:
6 to 10 litres (1.58-2.64 US gallons; 1.32-2.20 Imp gallons)/h

ARROW GT1000

This is the flat-four version, using the same cylinders as in the foregoing engines. Two 38 mm carburettors are fitted.

DIMENSIONS:
Length	521 mm (20.45 in)
Width	500 mm (19.65 in)
Height	451 mm (17.70 in)

Arrow GT250 single-cylinder engine

Arrow GT1000 four-cylinder engine

Arrow GT500 two-cylinder engine

Arrow GT654 V-twin engine

WEIGHT, READY TO RUN: 54.0 kg (119 lb)
PERFORMANCE RATING: 82 kW (110 hp) at 6,200 rpm
FUEL CONSUMPTION:
8 to 14 litres (2.11-3.70 US gallons; 1.76-3.08 Imp gallons)/h

ARROW GT654

This is a 90° V twin four-stroke based on the Moto Guzzi V65 motorcycle engine. The light alloy cylinders have Nicasil liners. Bore 80.0 mm (3.15 in). Stroke 64.0 mm (2.52 in). Capacity 650 cc (39.66 cu in). Fuel is 100 mogas fed through twin 30 mm Dell'Orto carburettors. A 12V starter is fitted, and the planetary geared drive has a ratio of 0.335.

DIMENSIONS:
Length	702 mm (27.6 in)
Width	431 mm (17.0 in)
Height	460 mm (18.12 in)

WEIGHT, READY TO RUN: 60.0 kg (132 lb)
PERFORMANCE RATING: 41.0 kW (55 hp) at 6,500 rpm
FUEL CONSUMPTION:
4 to 6 litres (1.06-1.58 US gallons; 0.88-1.32 Imp gallons)/h

FIAT

FIAT AVIAZIONE SpA

Via Nizza 312, 10127 Turin

Telephone: (011) 69311

Telex: 221320 FIATAV

MANAGING DIRECTOR: G. C. Boffetta

Fiat's main aircraft engine programmes now concern the IAE V2500, Turbo-Union RB199, Rolls-Royce Spey 807 and Viper 600, Pratt & Whitney PW2037 and General Electric CF6 (including CF6-80C2), CT7 and T64. In addition the company produced the J79-19 under General Electric licence and participated in the licence production by Alfa Romeo of the J85-GE-13A. It is a partner in EUROJET Turbo.

Fiat assisted Pratt & Whitney Canada and Sikorsky in mating the PT6B-36 turboshaft to the S-76 helicopter. An engine was tested at Sangone, sandwiched between Fiat reduction and power gearboxes, and a testbed aircraft was flown for the first time on 22 June 1984.

TURBO-UNION RB199

Fiat holds 20% of the shares of Turbo-Union Ltd. Its responsibility is the LP turbine and shaft, exhaust diffuser, jetpipe and nozzle.

IAE V2500

The V2500 is being developed by the IAE consortium. Fiat is responsible for the accessory gearbox, oil tank and pumps, exhaust case and No 5 bearing compartment.

ROLLS-ROYCE SPEY 807

This turbofan is produced under a Rolls-Royce licence to the Italian government, by Fiat (prime contractor in Italy) and CELMA (prime contractor in Brazil). The engine underwent type testing in the first half of 1987. Fiat carries out bench testing in support of the prototype aircraft, and rig testing of the engine Group-A parts.

PRATT & WHITNEY PW2037

Since 1974 Fiat has been responsible for design and development of the accessory drive gearbox for the Pratt & Whitney PW2037.

GENERAL ELECTRIC CF6

Fiat produces components for the CF6 for GE and SNECMA. For GE the company supplies accessory gearboxes, transfer gearboxes, inlet gearboxes and shafts. SNECMA is supplied with gearbox components and shafts for CF6-50 engines. Fiat is collaborating with GE on CF6-80C/C2 engines.

GENERAL ELECTRIC T64-P4D

This turboprop powers the Aeritalia G222. Under a licence agreement between GE and the Italian government, the engine is manufactured in Italy, with Fiat as prime contractor.

ROLLS-ROYCE VIPER 600

Development of this turbojet was undertaken in collaboration with Rolls-Royce. For most versions, components rearward of the compressor (except turbine discs and blades) are Fiat's responsibility. However, the Mk 632-43 is licensed to Piaggio.

IAME

ITAL-AMERICAN MOTOR ENGINEERING

Via Lisbona 15, 24040 Zingonia
Telephone: (035) 883022
Telex: 301205
Fax: (035) 885744

IAME light piston engines are known as KFM (Komet Flight Motors). They were launched in 1981, the chief market being US homebuilders and microlight aircraft manufacturers.

KFM 107 MAXI

Two-cylinder two-stroke engine for microlights, motor gliders, RPVs and similar uses. Available as: **107E**, direct drive, with electric starter and alternator; and **107ER**, with V belt reduction gear (2 : 1).
CYLINDERS: Bore 64 mm (2.52 in). Stroke 52 mm (2.05 in).
Capacity 334 cc (20.38 cu in).

KFM 107E Maxi two-stroke piston engine

KFM 112 flat-four piston engine

DIMENSIONS:

Length	435 mm (17.13 in)
Width (over plugs)	440 mm (17.32 in)
Height	253 mm (9.96 in)

WEIGHT, DRY:

Maxi 107E	19.0 kg (41.8 lb)
Maxi 107ER	22.5 kg (49.6 lb)

PERFORMANCE RATINGS:

Max T-O	22.4 kW (30 hp) at 6,300 rpm
Max continuous	20.1 kW (27 hp) at 6,080 rpm

FUEL CONSUMPTION:

Cruise	8.3 litres (2.19 US gallons; 1.83 Imp gallons)/h

PIAGGIO

INDUSTRIE AERONAUTICHE E MECCANICHE RINALDO PIAGGIO SpA

Via Cibrario 4, 16154, Genoa
Telephone: (10) 600 41
Telex: 270695
WORKS AND OFFICERS: see Aircraft section

KFM 112

This is the only KFM four-stroke engine currently in production.
CYLINDERS: Bore 90 mm (3.54 in). Stroke 64 mm (2.52 in)
Capacity 1,628.6 cc (99.4 cu in)
DIMENSIONS:

Length	583 mm (22.95 in)
Width	603 mm (23.74 in)
Height	380 mm (14.96 in)

WEIGHT, DRY (with starter and dual ignition):

	54 kg (119 lb)

The Aero Engine Division of Piaggio manufactures the following engines under licence agreements: Rolls-Royce Viper 11, 526, 540 and 632-43 turbojets to power the Aermacchi MB-326 and 339 (a sublicence for manufacture of the Viper 11 and 540 was issued to Atlas Aircraft to power South African built MB-326 aircraft); Textron Lycoming T53-L-13 turboshafts for various Bell and Agusta-Bell helicopters; Textron Lycoming T55-L-11 and

PERFORMANCE RATINGS:

Max T-O	44.16 kW (60 hp)
Max continuous	39.74 kW (54 hp)

FUEL CONSUMPTION:

Max continuous	
	16.35 litres (4.3 US gallons; 3.6 Imp gallons)/h
70 per cent cruise	
	11.25 litres (2.97 US gallons; 2.47 Imp gallons)/h

-712 and derivatives for CH-47 Chinook helicopters; and Rolls-Royce Gem 1004 turboshafts for the Agusta A 129 anti-tank helicopter. Piaggio also participates in co-production under licence of the Rolls-Royce Spey 807 turbofan. Following a 1986 agreement, Piaggio has joined Rolls-Royce Turbomeca in development and production of the RTM 322-01 turboshaft.

JAPAN

IHI

ISHIKAWAJIMA-HARIMA JUKOGYO KABUSHIKI KAISHA
(Ishikawajima-Harima Heavy Industries Co Ltd)

Shin Ohtemachi Bldg 2-1, Ohtemachi 2-chome, Chiyoda-ku, Tokyo 100, Japan
AERO-ENGINE AND SPACE OPERATIONS (ASO):
ADDRESS: As above
Telephone: 03 244 5331
Telex: 22232 IHIHQT J
GENERAL MANAGER, ASO: Masami Hamanaka
GENERAL MANAGER, BUSINESS PLANNING & PUBLIC RELATIONS:
Koichi Ichida

In February 1960 IHI began licence production of the General Electric J79-IHI-11A turbojet for the F-104J, followed by the J79-IHI-17 for the F-4EJ. IHI delivered 610 J79s, ending in 1980.

Under further licensing agreements with GE, IHI is producing the T58 turboshaft and T64 turboprop, and under agreement with Allison it produces the T56 turboprop. By March 1988 deliveries totalled 800 T58s, 391 T64s and 190 T56s. Under licence from RR Turbomeca, IHI delivered 426 Adour turbofans designated TF40-IHI-801A.

IHI is participating in development of the V2500, described under IAE in the International part of this section. It is responsible for the fan.

IHI was nominated in 1978 as prime contractor of the Pratt & Whitney F100 for the F-15J; by March 1988 IHI had delivered 249 F100s.

IHI produced 247 J3 turbojets, and helped to develop the XJ11 liftjet, as well as the JR100 and JR200 built under supervision of the NAL. In collaboration with Mitsubishi and Kawasaki, IHI built prototypes of the FJR710 (see NAL entry).

IHI F3

Development of this turbofan began in 1976, with funding by the JDA's Technical Research & Development Institute. The Phase 1 **XF3-1** form has a single-stage fan with bypass ratio of 1.9, five-stage transonic compressor,

The 16.37 kN (3,680 lb st) class F3-IHI-30 turbofan

12-burner combustor and single-stage HP and LP turbines. Rating is 11.79 kN (2,650 lb st).

In 1977 JDA contracted with IHI for the **XF3-20**, with reduced bypass ratio and higher turbine temperature to give a rating of 16.28 kN (3,660 lb st). This was followed by the **XF3-30**, which in 1982 was selected by the JASDF as the engine for the XT-4 trainer. XF3-30 qualification was completed in March 1986. The engine is now redesignated **F3-IHI-30**, and the first production engine was delivered to JDA on 17 December 1987.
TYPE: Two-shaft turbofan.
FAN: Two-stage axial. No inlet guide vanes. Airflow 34 kg (75 lb)/s. Pressure ratio 2.6. Bypass ratio 0.9.
COMPRESSOR: Five stages. First two stators variable. Overall pressure ratio 11.
COMBUSTION CHAMBER: Annular, with 12 duplex fuel nozzles.
HP TURBINE: Single-stage, aircooled rotor blades.
LP TURBINE: Two-stage, tip shrouded.
FUEL SYSTEM: Hydromechanical, with electronic supervisor.
DIMENSIONS:

Length	1,340 mm (52.76 in)
Inlet diameter	560 mm (22.0 in)

WEIGHT, DRY:

	340 kg (750 lb)

PERFORMANCE RATING (T-O, S/L):

	16.37 kN (3,680 lb st) class

SPECIFIC FUEL CONSUMPTION:

	19.83 mg/Ns (0.7 lb/h/lb st)

IHI ITS 90

News of this pioneer all-Japanese helicopter turboshaft engine was received in May 1988. It was then stated that a prototype had run successfully and that IHI was investing 10⁹ Yen in the programme. The second prototype is hoped to weigh only 130 kg (287 lb).
COMPRESSOR: Axial stage followed by centrifugal.
COMBUSTION CHAMBER: Annular reverse flow.
TURBINES: Axial, on single shaft.
FUEL SYSTEM: FADEC control being developed.
DIMENSIONS:

Length	900 mm (35.4 in)
Diameter	600 mm (23.6 in)

WEIGHT, DRY:

	150 kg (331 lb)

PERFORMANCE RATING:

	746 kW (1,000 shp)

KAWASAKI

KAWASAKI JUKOGYO KABUSHIKI KAISHA
(Kawasaki Heavy Industries Ltd)

1-18 Nakamachi-dori 2-chome, Chuo-ku, Kobe 650-91
Telephone: Kobe (078) 341 7731
JET ENGINE DIVISION: 1-1 Kawasaki-cho, Akashi 673
Telephone: (078) 923 1313
Telex: 5628 951 to 953
OFFICERS: see Aircraft section

In 1967 KHI started manufacturing T53 turboshafts. Deliveries of the resulting KT5311A, KT5313B and T53-K-13B engines totalled 285 by 1986. KHI now licence-builds the T53-K-703 for AH-1S HueyCobras and T55-K-712 for CH-47J Chinooks. Kawasaki shares in parts manufacturing for the Adour, F100 and JT8D and IHI-assembled T56. It is a member of the IAE consortium (see under International heading).

KAWASAKI KJ12

This simple low cost turbojet has been developed as the core of various future engine programmes. In its present form it is suited to RPVs and sporting aircraft. Component testing began in 1979 and the first KJ12 ran in early 1981. It has a centrifugal compressor driven by a single-stage axial turbine; the combustion chamber is annular and the control system of the electronic type.
DIMENSIONS:

Length	653 mm (25.71 in)
Max diameter	314 mm (12.36 in)

WEIGHT, DRY:

	40 kg (88.2 lb)

PERFORMANCE RATINGS:

T-O	1.47 kN (331 lb st)
Cruise (9,145 m; 30,000 ft at Mach 0.9)	715 N (161 lb)

Full scale display model of Kawasaki KJ12 turbojet

MITSUBISHI

MITSUBISHI JUKOGYO KABUSHIKI KAISHA (Mitsubishi Heavy Industries Ltd)

HEAD OFFICE: 5-1, Marunouchi 2 chome, Chiyoda-ku, Tokyo 100
ENGINE WORKS: Komaki North Plant, Nagoya Aircraft Works, 1200, Higashi-Tanaka, Komaki-Shi, Aichi 485
Telephone: (0568) 79 2111

OFFICERS: see Aircraft section

In 1967 Mitsubishi Heavy Industries (MHI) began production of the CT63 turboshaft to power Hughes 369HM helicopters for the JGSDF, under a licence agreement with Allison. A total of 217 engines was delivered by March 1978. Between January 1973 and June 1981, under licence agreement with Pratt & Whitney, MHI delivered 72 JT8D-M-9 turbofans.

In collaboration with IHI and Kawasaki, MHI participates in the V2500 (see IAE in the International part of this section).

NAL
NATIONAL AEROSPACE LABORATORY
7-44-1 Jindaijihigashi-machi, Chofu City, Tokyo 182
Telephone: 0422 47 5911
DIRECTOR: Hideo Nagasu
HEAD OF AERO-ENGINE DIVISION: Hiroyuki Nouse

The NAL is a government establishment responsible for research and development. In 1971 the Ministry of International Trade and Industry (MITI) funded a high bypass ratio turbofan development programme.

MITI/NAL FJR710
NAL manages the design of the FJR710. Manufacture of development engines was contracted to IHI, Kawasaki and Mitsubishi. The first engine ran in May 1973.

Phase 2 of the programme began in 1976, and the first of three FJR710/600s had been completed by December 1978. This version was followed by the lower-rated FJR710/600S, rated at 47 kN (10,582 lb st), which powers the experimental Asuka QSTOL aircraft. By the end of 1987 total FJR710 running time had reached 6,300 h. The following description applies to the /600 engine:

TYPE: Two-shaft turbofan.
FAN: Single-stage, with inserted titanium blades with part span shrouds. Bypass ratio 6.5.
COMPRESSOR: Twelve-stage axial with inserted blades of titanium and high nickel alloy. Five rows of variable stator blades.
COMBUSTION CHAMBER: Smokeless annular type.
TURBINE: Two-stage HP with cooled blades; gas temperature 1,250°C. Four-stage LP.
DIMENSIONS (approx):
Length (flange to flange)	2,350 mm (93 in)
Diameter (inlet)	1,240 mm (49 in)
WEIGHT, DRY:	980 kg (2,160 lb)

The FJR710/600S turbofan (47 kN; 10,582 lb st)

PERFORMANCE RATINGS (ISA):
T-O	50 kN (11,243 lb st)
Cruise at 7,600 m (25,000 ft) at Mach 0.75	13.24 kN (2,976 lb)

SPECIFIC FUEL CONSUMPTION:
T-O	10.5 mg/Ns (0.370 lb/h/lb st)
Cruise, as above	19.3 mg/Ns (0.680 lb/h/lb st)

POLAND

PZL
POLSKIE ZAKŁADY LOTNICZE
ul. Miodowa 5, 00251 Warsaw
Telephone: Warsaw 261441
Telex: 814281

PEZETEL Foreign Trade Enterprise Co:
00-991 Warsaw 44, Al. Stanów Zjednoczonych 61, PO Box 6
Telephone: 108001
Telex: 813314

The Polish aircraft and diesel engine industry is managed by the association of aviation and engine producers 'PZL'. Pezetel handles all exports of Polish aeronautical material and diesel engines.

IL
INSTYTUT LOTNICTWA (Aviation Institute)
HEADQUARTERS: Al. Krakowska 110/114, 02-256 Warsaw-Okecie
Telephone: Warsaw 460993
MANAGING DIRECTOR: Ing Marian Piłat
CHIEF CONSULTANT FOR SCIENTIFIC AND TECHNICAL CO-OPERATION: Dipl Ing Jerzy Grzegorzewski
CHIEF OF SCIENTIFIC, TECHNICAL AND ECONOMIC INFORMATION DIVISION: Dr Ing Tadeusz Kostia

The Aviation Institute is concerned with aeronautical research and testing. It can construct prototypes to its own design.

IL SO-1
The Aviation Institute designed the SO-1 turbojet to power the TS-11 trainer. Guaranteed overhaul life is 200 h. Production was handled by the WSK-Rzeszów, as noted in that organisation's entry.

TYPE: Single-shaft axial-flow turbojet.
COMPRESSOR: Seven-stage axial, all-steel. Stator blades bonded with resin into slots in carrier rings. Pressure ratio 4.8.
COMBUSTION CHAMBER: Annular with 24 vaporisers.
FUEL SYSTEM: Starting system has six injectors. Main system has 12 twin injectors with outlets towards the vaporisers.
FUEL SPECIFICATION: Kerosene P-2 or TS-1.
TURBINE: Single-stage axial.
LUBRICATION SYSTEM: Open type for rear compressor and turbine bearings. Closed type for all other points.
OIL SPECIFICATION: Type AP-26 (synthetic).
ACCESSORY DRIVES: Gearbox at bottom of air intake casing and driven by bevel shaft.
STARTING: 27V starter/generator.

IL SO-3B turbojet rated at 10.8 kN (2,425 lb st)

DIMENSIONS:
Length overall	2,151 mm (84.7 in)
Width	707 mm (27.8 in)
Height	764 mm (30.1 in)
WEIGHT, DRY:	303 kg (668 lb)

PERFORMANCE RATINGS:
T-O	9.8 kN (2,205 lb st) at 15,600 rpm
Max continuous	8.7 kN (1,958 lb st) at 15,100 rpm

SPECIFIC FUEL CONSUMPTION:
At T-O rating	29.6 mg/Ns (1.045 lb/h/lb st)

OIL CONSUMPTION: 0.8 litres (1.7 US pints; 1.4 Imp pints)/h

IL SO-3
This improved SO-1 replaced the earlier type in production. Intended for tropical use, it incorporates minor changes in compressor, combustion chamber and turbine, data remaining the same as for the SO-1. The **SO-3B** is now the standard TS-11 engine, with TBO of 400h. It also powers the PZL I-22, with the designation SO-3W22. A revised vaporising burner and flame tube result in more uniform gas temperature entering the turbine. Data are as for the SO-1 except:

OIL SPECIFICATION: AW-30 synthetic.
WEIGHT, DRY:	321 kg (708 lb)

PERFORMANCE RATINGS:
T-O	10.8 kN (2,425 lb st) at 15,600 rpm
Max continuous	9.8 kN (2,205 lb st) at 15,100 rpm

OIL CONSUMPTION: 1.0-1.2 litres (2.1-2.5 US pints; 1.7-2.1 Imp pints)/h

REFRIGERATION EQUIPMENT
REFRIGERATION EQUIPMENT WORKS
ul. Metalowców 25, 39-200 Debica
Telephone: Debica 2031
Telex: 066617 WUCH PL

PZL-F ENGINES
In 1975 Pezetel acquired rights to manufacture and market the entire range of aircooled piston engines formerly produced by the Franklin Engine Company (Aircooled Motors) of the USA. These engines, known as PZL-F, are being produced in Poland for light aircraft and motor

PZL-F 4A-235B (93 kW; 125 hp)

gliders. Previously manufactured by WSK-PZL Rzeszów, they were transferred in 1985 to the Debica works.

Current applications include the SZD-45-2 Ogar F motor glider (2A-120C), PZL-110 Koliber (4A-235B3), and PZL Mielec M-20 Mewa (6A-350C). The 2A-120C, 4A-235B3 and 6A-350C each have a Polish CACA certificate.

All models are of the horizontally opposed type, with cylinders of 117.48 mm (4.625 in) bore and 88.9 mm (3.5 in) stroke. All have direct drive and operate on 100/130 grade fuel. Accessories normally include electric starter, alternator and fuel pump. Other details are tabulated:

PZL-F 2A-120C (45 kW; 60 hp)

PZL-F 6A-350 six-cylinder aircooled piston engine

PZL-F ENGINES

Engine model	Cylinder arrangement	Capacity cc (cu in)	Compression ratio	Max T-O rating at S/L kW (hp) at rpm	Overall dimensions mm (in)			Weight, dry kg (lb)
					length	width	height	
2A-120C	2 horiz	1,916 (117)	8.5	45 (60) at 3,200	581 (22.9)	795 (31.3)	515 (20.3)	75.8 (167)
4A-235B	4 horiz	3,850 (235)	8.5	93 (125) at 2,800	774 (30.5)	795 (31.3)	637 (25.1)	117.6 (259)
6A-350C	6 horiz	5,735 (350)	10.5	164 (220) at 2,800	952 (37.5)	795 (31.3)	641 (25.25)	167 (367)

WSK-PZL KALISZ
WYTWÓRNIA SPRZETU KOMUNIKACYJNEGO-PZL KALISZ

ul. Czestochowska 140, 62-800 Kalisz
Telephone: 77351
Telex: 046 384
GENERAL MANAGER: Dipl Ing Jan Kolodziej

In 1952 the Soviet Union transferred responsibility for manufacture and service support of Soviet aircooled radial piston engines to the WSK (transport equipment manufacturing centre) at Kalisz. Current production is centred on the following, plus the TVD-10B turboprop described under WSK-PZL Rzeszów.

PZL (IVCHENKO) AI-14R

The original 260 hp AI-14R version of this nine-cylinder aircooled radial engine was produced in very large quantities, in the Soviet Union, China and Poland. Subsequent versions are:

AI-14RA. Rated at 191 kW (256 hp). Piston compressor drive and pneumatic starter. For Yak-12, Yak-18, PZL-101A Gawron and PZL-104 Wilga 35.

AI-14RA-KAF. RA with carburettor further aft, for Wilga 80.

AI-14RD. Rated at 206 kW (276 hp). Electric starter. For PZL-104 Wilga.

AI-14RDP. With pneumatic starter. For PZL-104 Wilga.

K8-AA. Direct drive and pneumatic starter. Aerobatic. For PZL-130 Orlik (Vedeneyev M-14Pm).

The following description refers to the AI-14RA:
TYPE: Nine-cylinder aircooled radial.
CYLINDERS: Bore 105 mm (4.125 in). Stroke 130 mm (5.125 in). Capacity 10.16 litres (620 cu in). Compression ratio 5.9.
FUEL GRADE: 91 to 100 octane.
PROPELLER DRIVE: Planetary gears, ratio 0.787.
DIMENSIONS:
Length   956 mm (37.63 in)
Diameter   985 mm (38.78 in)
WEIGHT, DRY: 200 kg (441 lb)
PERFORMANCE RATINGS:
T-O   191 kW (256 hp) at 2,350 rpm
Rated   162 kW (217 hp) at 2,050 rpm
SPECIFIC FUEL CONSUMPTION:
T-O   95-104.3 µg/J (0.562-0.617 lb/h/hp)

PZL K8-AA (M-14Pm) piston engine (206 kW; 276 hp)

PZL (SHVETSOV) ASz-62R

Power plant of the An-2 transport biplane, the ASz-62R was developed in the Soviet Union as the ASh-62. Current versions are:

ASz-62IR-16. Centrifugal oil filter. For An-2 and PZL-106 Kruk.

ASz-62IR-M18. Hydraulic airframe pump drive. For PZL M-18 Dromader.

ASz-62IR-M18/DHC-3. As M18 plus vacuum pump. For DHC-3 Otter.

K9-AA. Uprated engine designed at Kalisz, 860 kW (1,170 hp) at 2,300 rpm. Electric starter and hydraulic airframe pump. For PZL M-24 Super Dromader.
TYPE: Nine-cylinder aircooled radial.
CYLINDERS: Bore 155 mm (6.10 in). Stroke 174 mm (6.85 in). Capacity 29.87 litres (1,823 cu in). Compression ratio 6.4.
FUEL GRADE: 91 to 100 octane.
PROPELLER DRIVE: Planetary gears, ratio 0.687.

PZL ASz-62IR piston engine

The following relates to the IR-16:
DIMENSIONS:
Length overall   1,130 mm (44.50 in)
Diameter   1,375 mm (54.13 in)
WEIGHT, DRY:
Without power take-off 579 kg (1,276 lb)
PERFORMANCE RATINGS:
T-O   735 kW (985 hp) at 2,200 rpm
Rated power   603 kW (809 hp) at 2,100 rpm
SPECIFIC FUEL CONSUMPTION:
T-O   112 µg/J (0.661 lb/h/hp)

WSK-PZL RZESZÓW
WYTWÓRNIA SPRZETU KOMUNIKACYJNEGO-PZL RZESZÓW

ul. Obrońców Stalingradu 120, 35-078 Rzeszów, PO Box 340
Telephone: 46100
Telex: 0632411
GENERAL MANAGER: Ing Henryk Trzesicki

Current production at WSK Rzeszów is centred on the TVD-10 turboprop and turboshaft, and GTD-350 turboshaft, together with WR-2 reduction gear for Mi-2 helicopters; the tropicalised SO-3 turbojet for the TS-11 Iskra trainer; and the PZL-3S piston engine for agricultural aircraft. The SO-3 is described under the IL heading.

TVD-10B

The Soviet designed Glushenkov TVD-10B turboprop engine, rated at 716 kW (960 shp), is made under licence in Poland for the An-28 STOL light transport built at WSK-PZL Mielec.

Glushenkov TVD-10B licensed to PZL Rzeszów

TYPE: Free turbine turboprop.

AIR INTAKE: Three radial struts, inlet guide vanes and starter de-iced by bleed air from combustion chamber.

COMPRESSOR: Six axial stages and one centrifugal. Stage 1 has front bearing journal, bolted to stages 2 to 6 which are pinched by compressor shaft used as tie bolt. Blades in dovetail roots. Pressure ratio 7.4. Mass flow 4.6 kg (10.14 lb)/s at 29,600 rpm.

COMPRESSOR CASING: Forward upper and lower halves in titanium; rear section welded from sheet steel and containing anti-surge bleed valve and radial diffuser.

COMBUSTION CHAMBER: Annular with centrifugal burner, and two starting units each with semiconductor igniter and auxiliary burner.

FUEL SYSTEM: Comprises supply pump, filter, pump governor, acceleration control, signalling block and thermocorrector.

FUEL GRADE: T-1, T-2, TS-1 or RT.

COMPRESSOR TURBINE: Two-stage axial. Blades held by fir tree roots. Inlet guide vanes of hollow sheet with air cooling. Casing has ceramic liner.

POWER TURBINE: Single-stage axial, blades with fir tree roots, held in front roller and rear ball bearing.

REDUCTION GEARS: Single-stage spur high speed gear to accessory box and propeller gear; under the high speed gear is the feathering pump oil tank. Accessory box drives 16kW alternator, propeller tachometer and reduction gear oil pump, with propeller brake. Upper driveshaft to single-stage planetary reduction gear.

ENGINE ACCESSORIES: Box contains oil centrifuge; and drives tachometer, oil pump, fuel pump and pump governor. The starter is on the front with a claw clutch.

OIL SYSTEM: Closed and pressurised. Gas generator and reduction gear pumps. Oil tank capacity 16 litres (3.5 Imp gallons).

OIL GRADE: Oil mixture: 25 per cent MK-22 or MS-20, 75 per cent MK-8 or MS-8p.

DIMENSIONS:

Length without airframe jetpipe	2,060 mm (81.1 in)
Width	555 mm (21.9 in)
Height	900 mm (35.4 in)

WEIGHT, DRY:

Complete engine	230 kg (507 lb) 295 kg (650 lb)

PERFORMANCE RATINGS:

T-O	754 kW (1,011 shp)
Nominal	613 kW (823 shp)
Max cruise	547 kW (739 shp)

SPECIFIC FUEL CONSUMPTION (T-O):

95.8 µg/J (0.567 lb/h/shp)

PZL-10W

This is the helicopter version of the TVD-10B, two of which power the PZL Swidnik Sokól. It uses the same gas generator, with the following differences:

TYPE: Free turbine turboshaft engine.

FUEL SYSTEM: Pump governor provides automatic operation at selected constant helicopter rotor speeds, as well as control of anti-surge bleed valve, maintaining constant fuel flow in starting cycle, limiting shaft speed and gas temperature and automatic switch-off of faulty engine and selection of emergency power on remaining unit.

POWER TURBINE: Single-stage axial, with blades held in fir tree roots. Speed maintained at 22,490 rpm.

OIL SYSTEM: Closed and pressurised, with one delivery and four-section scavenge pump. Oil tank airframe-mounted, normal capacity 14 litres (3.08 Imp gallons).

OIL GRADE: B-3W synthetic.

ACCESSORIES: Integral cast box drives 5kW starter, starter unit, electronic temperature limiter, vibration sensor, tachometer generator, oil pumps and centrifuge, phase torquemeter, de-icing valve, power-turbine speed limiter and operation time counter.

DIMENSIONS:

Length with jetpipe	1,875 mm (73.8 in)

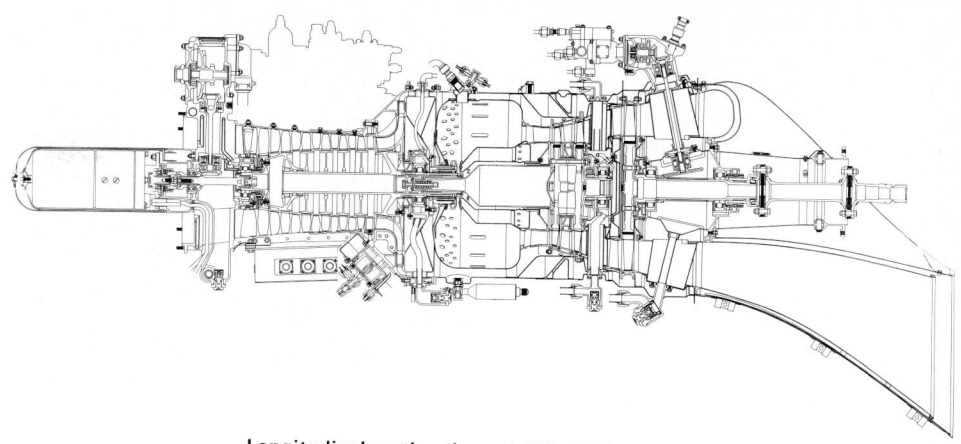

Longitudinal section through PZL-10W turboshaft

Width	740 mm (29.0 in)

WEIGHT, DRY:

	141 kg (310 lb)

PERFORMANCE, RATINGS (ISA):

T-O	662 kW (900 shp)
Max contingency	858 kW (1,150 shp)
Max cruise	522 kW (700 shp)

SPECIFIC FUEL CONSUMPTION:

T-O	97 µg/J (0.575 lb/h/hp)

PZL GTD-350

The **GTD-350** is a helicopter turboshaft. In the Mi-2, the drive is taken from the rear. Though developed by the Isotov bureau in the Soviet Union, it is in production only in Poland. PZL Rzeszów has developed a new version rated at 331 kW (444 shp) and designated **GTD-350P**. TBO of the GTD-350 is 4,000 h.

TYPE: Axial/centrifugal-flow free turbine turboshaft.

AIR INTAKE: Stainless steel. Automatic de-icing of inlet guide vanes and bullet by air bleed.

COMPRESSOR: Seven axial stages and one centrifugal, all of steel. Pressure ratio 6.05. Mass flow 2.19 kg (4.83 lb)/s at 45,000 rpm.

COMBUSTION CHAMBER: Reverse-flow type with air supply through two tubes. Centrifugal duplex single-nozzle burner. Semiconductor igniter plug.

FUEL SYSTEM: NR-40TA pump governor; RO-40TA power turbine governor, DS-40 controlling bleed valves; and electromagnetic starting valve.

FUEL GRADE: TS-1, TS-2 or Jet A-1.

COMPRESSOR TURBINE: Single stage. Shrouded blades with fir tree roots. Temperature before turbine 940°C (GTD-350P, 985°C).

POWER TURBINE: Two-stage constant speed (24,000 rpm). Shrouded blades with fir tree roots. Discs bolted together. Turbine stators integrally cast.

REDUCTION GEARING: Two sets of gears, with ratio of 0.246 : 1, in magnesium alloy casing. Output speed 5,900 rpm.

LUBRICATION SYSTEM: Closed type. Gear type pump with one pressure and four scavenge units. Cooler and tank, capacity 12.5 litres (2.75 Imp gallons).

OIL GRADE: B3-W (synthetic) or Shell Turbine Oil-500.

ACCESSORIES: STG3 3kW starter/generator, NR-40TA governor pump, D1 tachometer and oil pumps driven by gas generator. RO-40TA speed governor, D1 tachometer and centrifugal breather driven by power turbine.

STARTING: STG3 starter/generator suitable for operation at up to 4,000 m (13,125 ft) altitude.

DIMENSIONS:

Length overall	1,385 mm (54.53 in)
Max width	520 mm (20.47 in)
Width (with jetpipes)	626 mm (24.65 in)

Max height	630 mm (24.80 in)
Height (with jetpipes)	760 mm (29.9 in)

WEIGHT, DRY:

Less jetpipes and accessories	139.5 kg (307 lb)

PERFORMANCE RATINGS:

T-O rating (6 min) at 96% max gas generator rpm:

GTD-350	298 kW (400 shp)
GTD-350P	331 kW (444 shp)

Nominal rating (1 h) at 90% gas generator rpm:

GTD-350	238.5 kW (320 shp)
GTD-350P	261 kW (350 shp)

Cruise rating (I)

212.5 kW (285 shp) at 87.5% gas-generator rpm

Cruise rating (II)

175 kW (235 shp) at 84.5% gas-generator rpm

SPECIFIC FUEL CONSUMPTION:

T-O	136 µg/J (0.805 lb/h/shp)
Nominal	146 µg/J (0.861 lb/h/shp)
Cruise (I)	154 µg/J (0.913 lb/h/shp)
Cruise (II)	165 µg/J (0.978 lb/h/shp)

OIL CONSUMPTION:

Max	0.3 litres (0.63 US pints; 0.53 Imp pints)/h

PZL-3S

Derived from Soviet AI-26W via LiT-3. Applications include PZL-106A Kruk, IAR-827A and conversions of Grumman/Schweizer Ag-Cat A, B and C, Thrush Commander, DHC-2 Beaver and DHC-3 Otter.

TYPE: Seven-cylinder aircooled radial.

CYLINDERS: Bore 155.5 mm (6.12 in). Stroke 155 mm (6.1 in). Capacity 20.6 litres (1,265 cu in). Comp ratio 6.4.

PISTONS: Forged aluminium.

INDUCTION SYSTEM: Float type carburettor. Mechanically driven supercharger.

FUEL GRADE: Aviation gasoline, minimum 91 octane.

LUBRICATION: Gear type oil pump. Oil grade Aero Shell 100 or other to MIL-L-6082.

PROPELLER DRIVE: Direct. Provision for constant-speed US-132000A propeller.

ACCESSORIES: ANG 6423 Prestolite alternator and two output shafts, one 20 kW (27 hp) (26 kW; 35 hp max) for spraying pump and the other 3.7 kW (5 hp).

STARTING: Electric.

DIMENSIONS:

Diameter	1,267 mm (49.88 in)
Length	1,110 mm (43.72 in)

WEIGHT, DRY:

	411 kg (906 lb)

PERFORMANCE RATINGS:

Max T-O	447 kW (600 hp) at 2,200 rpm
Max continuous	410 kW (550 hp) at 2,050 rpm
Cruise (75 per cent)	310 kW (415 hp) at 2,000 rpm

PZL (Isotov) GTD-350 turboshaft engine (298 kW; 400 shp)

Cutaway PZL-3S seven-cylinder radial

SPECIFIC FUEL CONSUMPTION:
T-O, max continuous   105 μg/J (0.61 lb/h/hp)
Cruise   86 μg/J (0.51 lb/h/hp)

PZL-3SR

This is the geared version of the PZL-3S. Applications include the PZL-106AR and BR and M-21. The following are the main differences:

PROPELLER DRIVE: Planetary gear of 0.7 ratio. Provision for constant-speed propeller, Type US-133000.
DIMENSION:
Length   1,271 mm (50.06 in)
WEIGHT, DRY: 446 kg (983 lb)

ROMANIA

TURBOMECANICA

INTREPRINDEREA TURBOMECANICA BUCURESTI

c/o Centrul National Aeronautic, Bulevardul Dacia 13, Casuta Postala 22-149, R-70185 Bucharest
Telephone: 12 08 78
Telex: 10660 CNAER

This factory produces under licence the Rolls-Royce Spey 511-14W and Viper 632/633, and the Turbomeca Turmo IVC.

SINGAPORE

SAI

SINGAPORE AIRCRAFT INDUSTRIES
3 Lim Teck Kim Rd, 09.01 STC Building, Singapore 0208

Telephone: 2257977
Telex: RS43255
SAI manufactures engine parts for General Electric and

Turbomeca. It has 2 per cent of the PW4000 programme and will be sole source of eleven high-precision parts, mainly in the compressor section.

SOUTH AFRICA

ATLAS

ATLAS AIRCRAFT CORPORATION OF SOUTH AFRICA (PTY) LTD

PO Box 11, Atlas Road, Kempton Park 1620, Transvaal
Atlas is manufacturing the Rolls-Royce Viper 540

turbojet under sublicence from Piaggio of Italy, for use in Atlas Impala attack trainers.

SPAIN

SENER

SENER-INGENIERIA Y SISTEMAS SA
Raimundo Fernández Villaverde 65 Madrid 28003
Telephone: (1) 456 7062

AEROSPACE MANAGER: A. Azcarraga
SENER, engaged in NATO programmes and ESA space activities, is the Spanish partner in the consortium that will

build the engine of the future Eurofighter EFA. This is briefly referred to under the EUROJET entry in the International part of this section.

SWEDEN

FLYGMOTOR

VOLVO FLYGMOTOR AB
S-461 81 Trollhättan
Telephone: 0520 94000
Telex: 420 40 VOLFA S
Fax: 0520 34010

Volvo Flygmotor produces turbofans, ramjets and rockets. Since 1980 it has been a risk and revenue sharing partner with General Electric on the CF6-80A and -80C for the Boeing 747-300 and 767, and Airbus A300-600 and A310. Volvo Flygmotor also participates in development and production of the Garrett TFE731-5 turbofan. The company also entered into a risk- and revenue-sharing collaboration with Pratt & Whitney on the JT8D-200.

FLYGMOTOR RM8

The RM8 is a Swedish military version of the Pratt & Whitney JT8D turbofan which Flygmotor developed to power the Saab 37 Viggen. Following the **RM8A** for the AJ 37, SF 37, SH 37 and SK 37, the **RM8B** was developed for the JA 37. The major change to improve functional stability at high altitude involved replacing the first stage of the LP compressor by a third stage on the fan. To increase thrust the RM8B has a four-nozzle burner combustion system and a new HP turbine. Delivery of RM8B engines was due for completion in 1988.

The following description refers to the RM8A:

TYPE: Two-spool turbofan with modulated afterburner.

FAN: Two-stage front fan. Titanium blades.

LP COMPRESSOR: Four-stage integral with fan.

HP COMPRESSOR: Seven-stages. Overall pressure ratio 16.5. Bypass ratio approximately 1. Mass flow 145 kg (320 lb)/s.

COMBUSTION CHAMBER: Cannular with nine flame tubes. Two spark plugs, each with its own igniter.

HP TURBINE: Single-stage with cast aircooled blades.

LP TURBINE: Three-stage axial flow, with cast blades.

AFTERBURNER: One hot streak igniter. Hydraulically (fuel) actuated nozzle.

CONTROL SYSTEMS: Bendix hydromechanical controls for gas generator and for afterburner and nozzle.

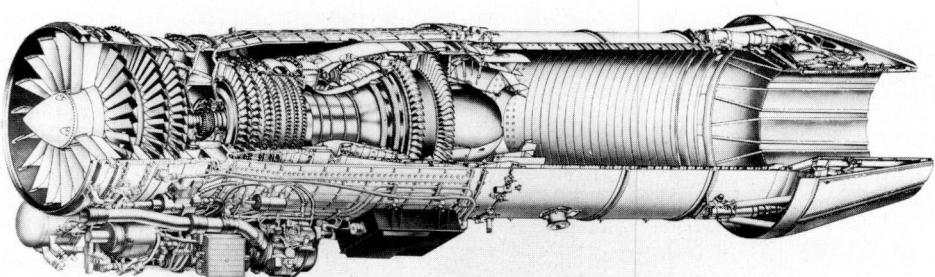

Cutaway drawing of Flygmotor RM12 (80.5 kN; 18,100 lb st)

ACCESSORY DRIVE: Via gearbox driven from HP shaft.

DIMENSIONS:
Length overall: RM8A   6,197 mm (244 in)
                RM8B   6,279 mm (247.2 in)
Max diameter (both versions)   1,397 mm (55 in)
Inlet diameter (both)   1,030 mm (40.55 in)

WEIGHT, DRY:
RM8A   2,100 kg (4,630 lb)
RM8B   2,250 kg (4,960 lb)

PERFORMANCE RATINGS (ISA, S/L):
Max T-O, augmented:
RM8A   115.6 kN (25,990 lb st)
RM8B   125 kN (28,110 lb st)
Max T-O, dry:
RM8A   65.6 kN (14,750 lb st)
RM8B   72.1 kN (16,200 lb st)

SPECIFIC FUEL CONSUMPTION:
Max augmented:
RM8A   70.0 mg/Ns (2.47 lb/h/lb st)
RM8B   71.4 mg/Ns (2.52 lb/h/lb st)
Max dry:
RM8A   17.8 mg/Ns (0.63 lb/h/lb st)
RM8B   18.1 mg/Ns (0.64 lb/h/lb st)
Max continuous (both)   17.3 mg/Ns (0.61 lb/h/lb st)

FLYGMOTOR RM12

The RM12 is a version of the F404 developed jointly by General Electric and Volvo Flygmotor to power the JAS 39 Gripen. General Electric retains all rights to the design and engineering policy and supplies approximately 60 per cent by value of parts.

Volvo Flygmotor is a 20 per cent partner in all F404 single-engine applications. Volvo Flygmotor will supply parts to General Electric similar to those parts that it manufactures for the RM12.

The RM12 thrust improvement has been achieved by increasing the turbine inlet temperature by up to 105°C and by increasing fan airflow. The fan meets more stringent bird strike requirements, and this has required changes to the control system, with built-in redundancy to ensure get-home power. Increased temperature and pressure have required changes to hot section materials. RM12 testing started at GE in June 1984. Production deliveries are due in 1991.

The following are changes from the F404:

FAN: Variable first-stage stator. Airflow 68 kg (150 lb)/s. Bypass ratio 0.28.

WEIGHT, DRY: 1,050 kg (2,315 lb)

PERFORMANCE RATINGS:
Max T-O: dry   54 kN (12,140 lb st)
         augmented   80.5 kN (18,100 lb st)

TURKEY

TEI

TUSAS ENGINE INDUSTRIES
Muttalip Mevkii Mrk, PK 610 Eskisehir

MANAGING DIRECTOR: F. Monsipapa

This is the new Turkish aero engine industry, to be located at a factory near Eskisehir airbase. It is to build the

F110 fighter engine under licence from US General Electric. The latter also has a 7% holding in the TAI aircraft company.

UNION OF SOVIET SOCIALIST REPUBLICS

GLUSHENKOV

In 1969 this design bureau was responsible for the TVD-10 turboprops of the Be-30. Since then it has produced turboprop and turboshaft engines.

GLUSHENKOV TVD-10

This free turbine engine was developed to power the Kamov Ka-25 helicopter, and received the military designation **GTD-3**. The civil turboshaft was licensed to Poland for production, and a description appears under WSK-PZL Rzeszów. Ka-25 engines were made in the Soviet Union, the GTD-3 being rated at 671 kW (900 shp) and the **GTD-3BM** at 738 kW (990 shp).

The **TVD-10B** is the turboprop version selected to power the An-28. This engine is produced in Poland as the **TVD-10S**, as described under WSK-PZL Rzeszów.

GLUSHENKOV TVD-20

This turboprop is fitted to the An-3. Its rating of 1,081 kW (1,450 hp) is sufficiently greater than that of TVD-10 to conclude that it has a new gas generator. In the An-3 the gearbox has a particularly large reduction ratio to drive a slow-turning propeller. The exhaust stack is at the front, confirming the same back-to-front layout as in the TVD-10B.

ISOTOV

This bureau, headed by S. P. Isotov until his death in 1983, was responsible for the GTD-350 turboshaft which powers Mil Mi-2 helicopters. It is in production in Poland, and is described under WSK-PZL Rzeszów.

ISOTOV TV2-117A

The power plant of the Mi-8 comprises two TV2-117A engines coupled through a VR-8A gearbox. The complete package incorporates a control system (separate from the control system of each gas generator) which maintains desired rotor speed, synchronises the power of both engines, and increases the power of the remaining engine if the other should fail.

TYPE: Free turbine helicopter turboshaft.

COMPRESSOR: Ten-stage axial. Inlet guide vanes and stators of stages 1, 2 and 3 are variable. Pressure ratio 6.6 at 21,200 rpm.

COMBUSTION CHAMBER: Annular, with eight burner cones.

FUEL GRADE: T-1 or TS-1 to GOST 10227-62 specification (Western equivalents, DERD.2494, MIL-F-5616).

TURBINE: Two-stage axial compressor turbine with solid blades. Two-stage free power turbine.

OUTPUT SHAFT: Conveys torque from the free turbine to the overrunning clutch of the main gearbox (VR-8A) and also to the speed governor. Max output speed 12,000 rpm; main rotor speed 192 rpm.

ACCESSORIES: Engine control system includes fuel, hydraulic, anti-icing, gas temperature restriction, engine electric supply and starting, and monitoring systems. Up to 1.8 per cent of the mass flow can be used to heat the intake and other parts liable to icing. Fire extinguishant can be released by the pilot.

LUBRICATION: Pressure circulation type. Oil is scavenged from the five main bearings by the lower pump, returned through the air/oil heat exchanger and thence to the tank.

Isotov TV2-117A turboshaft (1,267 kW; 1,700 shp)

OIL GRADE: Synthetic, Grade B-3V to MRTU 38-1-157-65 (nearest foreign substitute Castrol 98 to DERD.2487).

STARTING: The SP3-15 system comprises DC starter/ generator, six storage batteries, control panel, ground supply receptacle, and control switches and relays; airframe mounted except the GS-18TP starter/generator. The ignition unit comprises a control box, two plugs, solenoid valve, and switch. The starting fuel system comprises an automatic unit on the NR-40V pump, constant-pressure valve, and two igniters.

DIMENSIONS:

Length overall	2,835 mm (111.5 in)
Width	547 mm (21.5 in)
Height	745 mm (29.25 in)

WEIGHT, DRY:

Engine, without generator, etc	330 kg (727 lb)
VR-8A gearbox, less entrapped oil	745 kg (1,642 lb)

PERFORMANCE RATINGS:

Max	1,267 kW (1,700 shp)
T-O (S/L, static)	1,118 kW (1,500 shp)
Max continuous	895 kW (1,200 shp)

Cruise (122 knots; 225 km/h; 140 mph at 500 m; 1,640 ft) 746 kW (1,000 shp)

SPECIFIC FUEL CONSUMPTION:

T-O, as above	102.4 µg/J (0.606 lb/h/shp)
Cruise, as above	115.4 µg/J (0.683 lb/h/shp)

ISOTOV TV3-117

The A-10 (Mi-24) helicopter in which G. Karapetyan set a speed record for helicopters in 1978 was powered by two TV3-117 turboshafts, each rated at 1,640 kW (2,200 shp). Similar engines power the Mi-14, Mi-17, Mi-24 and Ka-27/32. They may also power the Kamov 'Hokum' and Mil Mi-28 'Havoc'.

The Mi-17 is powered by the **TV3-117MT**, with a normal T-O rating of 1,417 kW (1,900 shp) and emergency 2½ min rating of 1,640 kW (2,200 shp). Pneumatic (air turbine) starters are fitted. The Ka-27 and Ka-32 are each powered by two **TV3-117V** engines, rated at 1,660 kW (2,225 shp).

The engine's designation and applications suggest that the TV3-117 is an uprated version of the TV2-117, but no other details are available.

IVCHENKO

GENERAL DESIGNER IN CHARGE OF BUREAU: Vladimir Lotarev

The collective at Zaporozhye, headed by A. G. Ivchenko until his death in 1968, is now headed by V. Lotarev, who has his own entry later.

The first Ivchenko engine was the 41 kW (55 hp) AI-4G piston engine used in the Ka-10 helicopter. He progressed, via the AI-14 and AI-26 piston engines, to become a leading producer of gas turbine engines. Since 1952 Soviet piston engines have been assigned to Poland (see under WSK-PZL Kalisz). Ivchenko turboprops are also produced in China (which see).

IVCHENKO AI-20

This turboprop was developed as the NK-4 at the Kuznetsov bureau in 1947-52, with the assistance of German engineers. Eventually preferred to the VK-2, the Zaporozhye collective was charged with refinement and production. Redesignated AI-20, it was produced from 1955.

AI-20K. Rated at 2,942 ekW (3,945 ehp). Used in Il-18V, An-10A and An-12. Produced at Shanghai as WJ-6.

AI-20M. Initial T-O rating of 3,124 ekW (4,190 ehp), later increased to 3,169 ekW (4,250 ehp). Fitted to An-12 and Il-18/20/22/38.

AI-20D. Rated at 3,124 ekW (4,190 ehp); navalised engine fitted to Beriev M-12.

AI-20DM. Rated at 3,862 ekW (5,180 ehp). Fitted to An-32. In 1985 this engine was reported to the FAI as the **AM-20**.

The AI-20 was designed to operate from −60°C to +55°C. The rotor speed is at 12,300 rpm by automatic variation of propeller pitch. TBO of the AI-20K was 4,000 h in the Spring of 1966; the same life was reached by the -20M in 1968.

The following description refers to the AI-20M:

TYPE: Single-shaft turboprop.

COMPRESSOR: Ten-stages. Magnesium alloy stator casing in upper and lower halves. Pressure ratio 9.2 under altitude cruise conditions. Air mass flow 20.7 kg (45.6 lb)/s.

COMBUSTION CHAMBER: Annular with ten burner cones. Pilot burners and ignition plugs at top of casing.

FUEL GRADE: T-1 or TS-1 to GOST-10227-62 (DERD.2492, JP-1 to MIL-F-5616).

TURBINE: Three stages. Rotor blades shrouded at inner and outer ends and installed in pairs in slots in aircooled discs.

Ivchenko AI-20M turboprop of 3,169 ekW (4,250 ehp) *(courtesy of Aviation Magazine International, Paris)*

REDUCTION GEAR: Planetary type, incorporating six-cylinder torquemeter and negative-thrust transmitter (type IKM), for autofeathering AV-68I propeller. Ratio 0.08732 (input speed 12,300 rpm except ground-idle 10,400 rpm).

LUBRICATION: Pressure-feed type with full recirculation.

OIL GRADE: 75 per cent GOST 982-56 or MK-8 to GOST 6457-66 (DERD.2490 or MIL-O-6081B) and 25 per cent MS-20 or MK-22 to GOST 1013-49 (DERD.2472 or MIL-O-6082B).

STARTING: Two electric starter/generators, Type STG-12 TMO-1000, supplied from ground or TG-16 APU.

DIMENSIONS:

Length	3,096 mm (121.89 in)
Width	842 mm (33.15 in)
Height	1,180 mm (46.46 in)

WEIGHT, DRY: 1,040 kg (2,292 lb)

PERFORMANCE RATINGS:

T-O	3,169 ekW (4,250 ehp)
Cruise (350 knots; 650 km/h; 404 mph at 8,000 m; 26,000ft)	2,013 ekW (2,700 ehp)

SPECIFIC FUEL CONSUMPTION:

T-O	104.3 µg/J (0.617 lb/h/ehp)
Cruise, as above	73.3 µg/J (0.434 lb/h/ehp)

IVCHENKO AI-24

This turboprop powers the An-24 and its derivatives. Production began in 1960 and the following data refer to engines of the second series, which were in production by the Spring of 1966.

The **AI-24** of 1,875 ekW (2,515 ehp) powered the An-24V Series I, and was followed by the **AI-24A** with provision for water injection; produced at Harbin as the Wojiang-5A.

The **AI-24T** of 2,103 ekW (2,820 ehp) with water injection is used in the An-26 and An-30. Vibration monitoring, automatic relief of overloads and gas temperature and autofeathering. From 1980, designated **AI-24VT**; ratings unchanged.

The AI-24 is maintained at 15,100 rpm by automatic variation of propeller pitch. The engine is flat rated to 3,500 m (11,500 ft). TBO was 3,000 h in the Spring of 1966; by 1968 the AI-24T had reached 4,000 h.

Following the flight testing of propellers with eight blades on an AI-24, a research programme has been under way on propfans, with emphasis on contra-rotating configurations. Two full scale examples have been run with an AI-24 engine. Typical configurations have 6+6, 7+7 and 8+8 blades.

TYPE: Single-shaft turboprop.

COMPRESSOR: Ten-stage axial. Pressure ratio (max continuous) 7.85. Air mass flow 14.4 kg (31.7 lb)/s.

COMBUSTION CHAMBER: Annular, with eight simplex burners and two starting units, each comprising a body, pilot burner and igniter plug.

FUEL GRADE: T-1, TS-1 to GOST 10227-62 (DERD.2494 or MIL-F-5616).

TURBINE: Three-stage axial with solid blades. Rotor/stator sealing effected by soft inserts mounted in grooves in nozzle assemblies. Peak exhaust temperature during starting 750°C.

REDUCTION GEAR: Planetary type, incorporating hydraulic torquemeter and electromagnetic negative thrust transmitter for propeller autofeathering. Type AV-72 propeller (AI-24T drives AV-72T propeller). Ratio 0.08255.

LUBRICATION: Pressure circulation system.

OIL GRADE: 75 per cent GOST 982-56 or MK-8 (DERD.2490 or MIL-O-6081B) and 25 per cent MS-20 or MK-22 (DERD.2472 or MIL-O-6082B).

ACCESSORIES: Mounted on front casing are starter/generator, alternator, aerodynamic probe, ice detector, negative-thrust feathering valve, torque transmitter, oil filter, propeller speed governor and centrifugal breather. Below casing are oil unit, air separator, LP and HP fuel pumps and drives to hydraulic pump and tachometer generators.

STARTING: Electric STG-18TMO starter/generator supplied from ground power or from TG-16 APU.

DIMENSIONS:

Length overall	2,346 mm (92.36 in)
Width	677 mm (26.65 in)
Height	1,075 mm (42.32 in)

WEIGHT, DRY: 600 kg (1,323 lb)

PERFORMANCE RATINGS:

T-O: AI-24A	1,875 ekW (2,515 ehp)
AI-24T	2,103 ekW (2,820 ehp)

Cruise rating at 243 knots (450 km/h; 280 mph) at 6,000 m (18,300 ft):

AI-24A	1,156 ekW (1,550 ehp)
AI-24T	1,178 ekW (1,580 ehp)

SPECIFIC FUEL CONSUMPTION:

At cruise rating: AI-24A	91.3 µg/J (0.540 lb/h/ehp)
AI-24T	90.1 µg/J (0.533 lb/h/ehp)

OIL CONSUMPTION: 0.85 kg (1.87 lb)/h

The 1,875 ekW (2,515 ehp) Ivchenko AI-24 turboprop *(courtesy of Aviation Magazine International, Paris)*

IVCHENKO AI-25

This turbofan powers the Yak-40. Yak-40Bs of the Soviet Air Force have an AI-25 with an aircooled HP turbine and rating of 17.13 kN (3,850 lb st). The AI-25TL powers the Czech L-39 trainer. The AI-25 was selected for the Semurg light transport by MAI and the Tashkent High School.

TYPE: Two-shaft turbofan.

FAN: Three-stage axial. Drum/disc construction with pin-jointed blades. Casing and fan duct of magnesium alloy. Pressure ratio, 1.695 at 10,750 rpm. Bypass ratio 2.

COMPRESSOR: Eight-stage axial. Drum/disc construction of titanium, with aluminium and magnesium casing. Dovetailed blades. Peak pressure ratio, 4.68 at 16,640 rpm. Overall pressure ratio, 8.

COMBUSTION CHAMBER: Annular. Inner and outer casings joined upstream to 12 burner heads with stabilisers.

FUEL GRADE: T-1, TS-1 to GOST 10227-62 (DERD.2494, MIL-F-5616).

TURBINE: Single-stage HP turbine; two-stage LP turbine. Shrouded solid rotor blades held by fir tree roots in cooled discs.

LUBRICATION: Self-contained, pressure circulating.

OIL GRADE: MK-8 to GOST 6457-66 or MK-6 to GOST 10328-63 (Western equivalents, DERD.2490 or MIL-O-6081B). Consumption 0.3 litres (0.53 Imp pints)/h.

ACCESSORIES: All mounted on gearbox driven off HP spool. Equipment includes automatic fire extinguishing (agent can be supplied into oil-contacted labyrinth cavities), ice protection, automatic starting and control system, oil system chip detector and casing vibration monitor.

Ivchenko AI-25TL turbofan (14.71 kN; 3,307 lb st), which powers the Czechoslovak Aero L-39

STARTING: Pneumatic. Air starter type SV-25 is supplied from ground hose or AI-9 APU or an operating engine bleed.

DIMENSIONS:

Length overall	1,993 mm (78.46 in)
Width overall	820 mm (32.28 in)
Height overall	895 mm (35.24 in)

WEIGHT, DRY:

Without accessories	290 kg (639 lb)

PERFORMANCE RATINGS:

T-O	14.71 kN (3,307 lb st)

Long-range cruise rating, 6,000 m (20,000 ft) and 296 knots (550 km/h; 342 mph)   3.49 kN (785 lb st)

SPECIFIC FUEL CONSUMPTION:

T-O	15.86 mg/Ns (0.56 lb/h/lb st)
Cruise, as above	23.71 mg/Ns (0.837 lb/h/lb st)

KOLIESOV

It is reported that this design bureau took over the assets of that of V. A. Dobrynin in the 1950s, and has since concentrated on powerful afterburning turbojets.

KOLIESOV VD-7

This large single-shaft turbojet was fitted to at least the final Myasishchev M-50 supersonic bomber (NATO reporting name 'Bounder'), with afterburners on the inner

engines. Maximum thrust estimated in the 137.3 kN (30,865 lb st; 14 tonne) class. It is commonly supposed that a derived version powers the Tu-22 (NATO 'Blinder') family.

KOLIESOV Tu-144D ENGINE

In 1973 an American journalist was told that the Koliesov bureau was developing a variable geometry engine capable of operating as a turbofan in the subsonic regime and as an augmented turbojet in supersonic flight. In 1979 the engines of the Tu-144D were said to be "50 per cent more

economical" than the NK-144s originally fitted. The large bomber called 'Blackjack' by NATO may be powered by similar engines.

KOLIESOV LIFT JET

The Koliesov bureau has been reported as responsible for the lift engines of the Yak-38 (NATO 'Forger'). See 'Engines of Unknown Design' at the end of Soviet entries.

KUZNETSOV

GENERAL DESIGNER IN CHARGE OF BUREAU:
Nikolai Dmitrievich Kuznetsov

Kuznetsov was deputy to General V. Ya. Klimov during the Second World War. In the late 1940s his own bureau at Kuibyshev developed large turboprops and turbofans. The NK-4 was transferred to Ivchenko, and is described under that collective's heading, as the AI-20. Later engines are described here.

KUZNETSOV NK-8

The NK-8 was developed through a number of variants, the most powerful of which is the NK-144. Basic versions are the 99.1 kN (22,273 lb st) **NK-8-4**, later uprated to 103 kN (23,150 lb st), which originally powered the Il-62, and the 93.2 kN (20,950 lb) **NK-8-2** which was the original engine of the Tu-154. The NK-8-4 remains in service with several Il-62 (not Il-62M) operators, including LOT. It led to the NK-86 described later.

TYPE: Two-shaft turbofan.

FAN: Two-stage axial, with anti-flutter sweptback blades on first rotor stage. Pressure ratio 2.15 at 5,350 rpm. Bypass ratio 1.02 (NK-8-2, 1.00).

COMPRESSOR: Two IP stages on fan shaft. Six-stage HP compressor. Construction almost wholly of titanium. Core pressure ratio, 10.8 at 6,950 HP rpm (NK-8-2, 10 at 6,835 rpm).

COMBUSTION CHAMBER: Annular, with 139 burners.

FUEL GRADE: T-1 and TS-1 to GOST 10227-62 or T-7 to GOST 12308-66 (equivalent to Avtur 50).

TURBINE: Single-stage HP turbine, two-stage LP turbine, all with shrouded rotor blades, aircooled discs and hollow nozzle blades (stators). Gas temperature, not over 870°C (1,143°K) ahead of turbine, not over 670°C (NK-8-2, 650°C) downstream.

JETPIPE: Mixer leads bypass flow into common jetpipe which may be fitted with blocker/cascade type reverser giving up to 48 per cent (NK-8-2, 45 per cent) reverse thrust, and noise suppressor.

LUBRICATION: Continuous pressure feed and recirculation. Pressure not less than 2.28 bars (33 lb/sq in).

OIL GRADE: Mineral oil MK-8 or MK-8P to GOST 6457-66 (DERD.2490 or MIL-O-6081B).

ACCESSORIES: These include automatic flight deck warning of vibration, ice and fire. All grouped beneath fan duct casing. RTA-26-9-1 turbine temperature controller by Smiths Industries.

STARTING: HP spool driven by constant-speed drive type PPO-62M, or started pneumatically by air from TA-6 APU from ground hose or by air bleed (NK-8-2, pneumatic only).

DIMENSIONS:

NK-8-4: Length, no reverser	5,100 mm (201 in)
NK-8-2: Length, with reverser	5,288 mm (208.19 in)
Length, no reverser	4,762 mm (187.48 in)
Diameter	1,442 mm (56.8 in)

WEIGHT, DRY:

NK-8-4: No reverser	2,100 kg (4,629 lb)
With reverser	2,400 kg (5,291 lb)
NK-8-2: No reverser	2,100 kg (4,629 lb) max
With reverser	2,350 kg (5,180 lb) max

PERFORMANCE RATINGS:
NK-8-4: T-O rating   103.0 kN (23,150 lb st)
Cruise rating at 11,000 m (36,000 ft) and 458 knots (850 km/h; 530 mph)   27.0 kN (6,063 lb)
NK-8-2: T-O rating   93.2 kN (20,950 lb st)
NK-8-2U: T-O rating   103.0 kN (23,150 lb st)
SPECIFIC FUEL CONSUMPTION:
At cruise rating at 11,000 m (36,000 ft) and 458 knots (850 km/h; 530 mph):
NK-8-4   22.1 mg/Ns (0.78 lb/h/lb st)
NK-8-2   21.53 mg/Ns (0.76 lb/h/lb st)

KUZNETSOV NK-86

Though described by the Ilyushin aircraft bureau as a new engine, this turbofan of 127.5 kN (28,660 lb st) is closely related to the NK-8 series. Four power the Il-86 with combined reversers and noise attenuators.

KUZNETSOV NK-88

Almost certainly another derivative of the NK-8 series, the NK-88 is the engine fitted to the Tu-155 (Tu-154 development) fuelled by liquid hydrogen, which first flew on 15 April 1988. No major modification is needed for the cryogenic fuel (other than to the aircraft and engine fuel systems), nor to burn LNG (liquefied natural gas) which was expected to be used in 1988 in the same aircraft. Engine performance is unlikely to differ materially from the NK-8-2U.

KUZNETSOV NK-144

This augmented turbofan was derived from the NK-8 to power the Tu-144 SST. A version of the NK-144 is believed to be the engine of at least the first subtype of the Tupolev Tu-26 supersonic bomber known to NATO as 'Backfire'.

The NK-144 is reported to have a two-stage titanium fan, three-stage IP compressor, eleven-stage HP compressor, annular combustion chamber, single stage HP turbine and two-stage LP turbine. Aircooled blades are used in the HP turbine, and titanium is used extensively in construction of the engine. Bypass ratio is reported to be 1 : 1, maximum mass flow 250 kg (551 lb)/s, and pressure ratio 15 : 1. The jetpipe incorporates an afterburner, with hydraulically actuated variable area nozzle. Gas temperature at turbine entry is 1,050°C.

DIMENSIONS:
Length overall   5,200 mm (204.7 in)
Diameter   1,500 mm (59 in)
WEIGHT:
Without jetpipe, but with afterburner
    2,850 kg (6,283 lb)
PERFORMANCE RATINGS:
Max: without afterburning   127.5 kN (28,660 lb st)
with afterburning   196.1 kN (44,090 lb st)

KUZNETSOV NK-12M

Designed at Kuibyshev in 1947-52 under N. D. Kuznetsov and former German engineers, the NK-12M is the most powerful turboprop in the world. The **NK-12M** developed 8,948 ekW (12,000 ehp). The **NK-12MV** is rated at 11,033 ekW (14,795 ehp) and powered the Tu-114, driving four-blade contra-rotating propellers of 5.6 m (18 ft 4 in) diameter. As the **NK-12MA**, rated at 11,185 kW (15,000 shp), it powers the An-22, with propellers of 6.2 m (20 ft 4 in) diameter. A further application is in the Tupolev Tu-95/-142 bomber and its derivatives, and Tu-126, both believed to be powered by the NK-12MV.

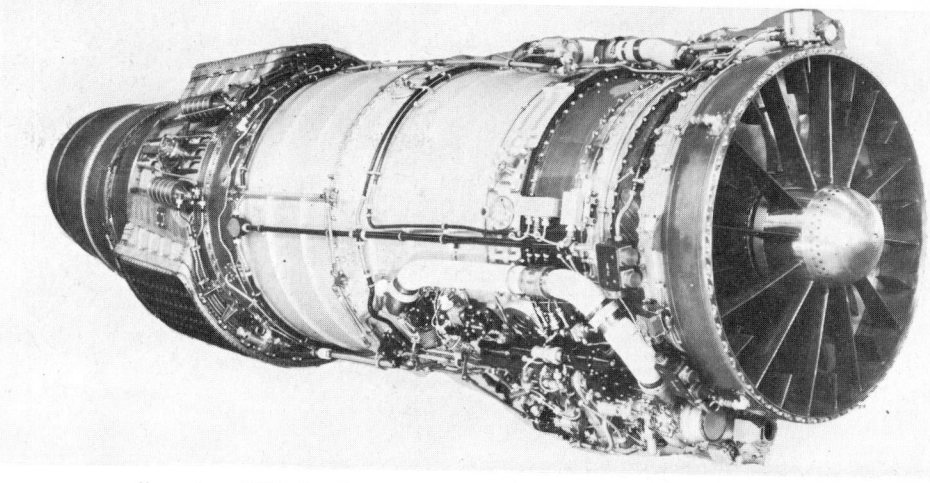

Kuznetsov NK-8-2 turbofan with thrust reverser (93.2 kN; 20,950 lb st)

Kuznetsov NK-12MV single-shaft turboprop of 11,033 ekW (14,795 ehp)
(courtesy of Aviation Magazine International, Paris)

The NK-12M has a 14-stage axial-flow compressor. Pressure ratio varies from 9 to 13 according to altitude, and variable inlet vanes and blow-off valves are necessary. A cannular type combustion system is used: each flame tube is mounted centrally on a downstream injector, but all tubes merge at their maximum diameter to form an annular secondary region. The single turbine is a five-stage axial. Mass flow is 65 kg (143 lb)/s.

The casing is made in four portions, from sheet steel, precision welded. An electric control for variation of propeller pitch is incorporated, to maintain constant speed.

DIMENSIONS:
Length   6,000 mm (236.2 in)
Diameter   1,150 mm (45.3 in)
WEIGHT, DRY: 2,350 kg (5,181 lb)
PERFORMANCE RATINGS (NK-12MV):
T-O   11,033 ekW (14,795 ehp)
Nominal power
    8,826 ekW (11,836 ehp) at 8,300 rpm
Idling speed   6,600 rpm

LOTAREV

GENERAL DESIGNER IN CHARGE OF BUREAU:
Vladimir A. Lotarev
DEPUTY CHIEF DESIGNER: Fedor Muravtchyenko

LOTAREV D-36

As successor to Ivchenko at Zaporozhye, Lotarev has developed the turbofan that powers the An-72, An-74 and Yak-42. Bench testing was in progress by September 1973. Also see D-436.
TYPE: Three-shaft turbofan.
FAN: Single-stage; 29 inserted titanium blades with part-span shrouds (snubbers). Bypass ratio 5.6.
LP COMPRESSOR: Multi-stage axial with variable inlet vanes.
HP COMPRESSOR: Multi-stage axial. Overall engine pressure ratio at T-O, S/L ISA static, 20.
COMBUSTION CHAMBER: Annular, with 28 burners and with integral inlet guide vanes to HP turbine.
HP TURBINE: Single-stage; aircooled blades. Max inlet temperature 1,177°C (1,450°K).
LP TURBINE: Single-stage. (Called IP in Western engines.)
FAN TURBINE: Two-stage. (Called LP in Western engines.)
BYPASS DUCT: Short-length, comprising forward module (fan contravane) and rear module (intermediate case). Contravane contains 49 vanes to remove twist. Provision for reverser downstream of intermediate case.
ACCESSORIES: Shaft driven units mounted on gearbox mounted around underside of intermediate case.
DIMENSIONS: Not disclosed
WEIGHT, DRY: 1,100 kg (2,425 lb)
PERFORMANCE RATINGS (ISA):
T-O static   63.74 kN (14,330 lb st)

Max continuous   49.0 kN (11,025 lb st)
Max cruise at 8,000 m (26,250 ft) at Mach 0.75
    15.7 kN (3,527 lb)
SPECIFIC FUEL CONSUMPTION:
T-O   10.195 mg/Ns (0.360 lb/h/lb st)
At max cont rating   9.83 mg/Ns (0.347 lb/h/lb st)
Max cruise as above   18.4 mg/Ns (0.65 lb/h/lb)

LOTAREV D-18T

For many years the main gap in the spectrum of available Soviet engines was a large HBPR (high bypass ratio) turbofan. In the 1970s the Lotarev bureau produced such engines in two sizes, the smaller (D-36) to an earlier timescale. The linear scale is about 2 : 1; so, in terms of airflow and thrust, the ratio is about 4 : 1.

The bigger engine is more advanced than the small one, its pressure ratio and turbine entry temperature being higher. The D-18T also has an integral fan duct reverser. Four were fitted to the An-124 prototype which made its first flight on 26 December 1982.
TYPE: Three-shaft turbofan for large subsonic aircraft.
FAN: Single-stage with 33 inserted titanium blades with part-span shrouds. Bypass ratio 5.7 at ISA S/L static.
IP COMPRESSOR: Seven-stage axial with variable inlet vanes.
HP COMPRESSOR: Seven-stage axial. Overall engine pressure ratio 27.5.
COMBUSTION CHAMBER: Annular, with forged and machined outer case and 28 vaporising burners.
FUEL GRADE: T-1, TS-1 or T-7 (Avtur equivalent).
HP TURBINE: Single-stage with aircooled directionally solidified blades with tip shrouds and raised root

platforms. Max inlet temperature 1,327°C (1,600°K); temperature at cruise (as below) 1,080°C (1,353°K).
IP TURBINE: Single-stage with aircooled blades with tip shrouds.
LP TURBINE: Four stages with tip shrouded blades.
BYPASS DUCT: Comprises forward module, called contravane, with inserted blades (vanes) to remove twist from flow, followed by rear case with six large radial struts carrying pipes and shaft drives.
REVERSER: Attached to rear fan duct case, with multiple blocker doors pulled inwards by axial movement of translating cowl section, which simultaneously opens peripheral cascade rings directing expelled air forwards.
ACCESSORIES: Oil tank and all shaft driven accessories are grouped around lower half of rear fan case.
DIMENSION:
Fan diameter   2,330 mm (91.73 in)
WEIGHT, DRY: 4,100 kg (9,039 lb)
PERFORMANCE RATINGS:
T-O (S/L, ISA + 13°C)   229.77 kN (51,655 lb st)
Max cruise (11,000 m; 36,100 ft, Mach 0.75, ISA)
    47.66 kN (10,715 lb)
SPECIFIC FUEL CONSUMPTION:
T-O   10.195 mg/Ns (0.360 lb/h/lb st)
Cruise as above   16.142 mg/Ns (0.570 lb/h/lb)

LOTAREV D-136

This turboshaft is fitted to the Mi-26 helicopter. It is of modular construction, and Aviaexport stresses its background of over 20,000 h running prior to certification to standards which included FAR and BCAR.
TYPE: Two-spool free turbine turboshaft.

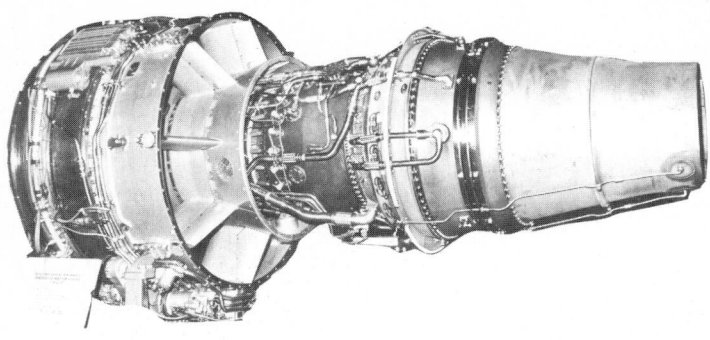

Lotarev D-36 turbofan, rated at 63.74 kN (14,330 lb st)
(Brian M. Service)

Lotarev D-136 free turbine turboshaft, rated at 8,500 kW (11,400 shp)
(Brian M. Service)

Lotarev D-18T turbofan with reverser fitted *(Brian M. Service)*

**Sixteen-blade advanced technology contra-prop
for the Lotarev D-236 turboprop**
(Flight International)

LP COMPRESSOR: Six stages, with one row of variable inlet guide vanes. Faces for bleed ducts for anti-icing the Mi-26 air inlets.

HP COMPRESSOR: Six stages, in casing with large bleed pipes and carrying main gearbox and mounting points. Overall pressure ratio 18.3.

COMBUSTION CHAMBER: Annular, with 28 burners and incorporating inlet guide vanes for HP turbine.

HP TURBINE: Single-stage with aircooled blades. Max inlet temperature 1,205°C (1,478°K).

LP TURBINE: Single-stage, separated from HP rotor by large intermediate case with 26 guide vanes (stators).

POWER TURBINE: Two stages forming separate module; casing with 12 long-chord radial struts.

DRIVE SHAFT: Flexibly mounted shaft at rear.
ACCESSORIES: Mounted on gearbox above HP compressor.
DIMENSIONS: Not disclosed
WEIGHT, DRY: 1,050 kg (2,315 lb)
PERFORMANCE RATINGS (ISA, S/L):
Max T-O at 8,300 rpm 8,500 kW (11,400 shp)
Max cont at 7,500 output rpm 8,280 kW (11,100 shp)
SPECIFIC FUEL CONSUMPTION:
Max T-O 73.8 µg/J (0.4365 lb/h/shp)

LOTAREV D-236
This engine uses a core similar to that of the D-136 turboshaft, but it incorporates a reduction gearbox to drive a contra-rotating propfan. As exhibited in 1987, the front

propeller only, with eight composite blades, weighed 380 kg (838 lb). Rotational speed is 960 rpm, propulsive efficiency is 87 per cent at Mach 0.7, and both propellers have reverse-pitch capability. Diameter is 4.2 m (13 ft 10 in). The D-236 was scheduled to begin flight test (initially without propellers) in December 1987. The Antonov Bureau is designing a transport aircraft for this engine.

LOTAREV D-436
No details of this engine are available beyond its max T-O rating of 73.6 kN (16,550 lb st). It powers the stretched Yak-42M. It is assumed to be an uprated version of the D-36.

LYULKA
During the late 1930s A. M. Lyulka, who died in June 1984, worked on an axial turbojet that became an early war casualty. Brief details of his subsequent work have appeared in previous editions of *Jane's*. His first major success was achieved with the AL-7.

LYULKA AL-7
Service designation: TRD-31
The first AL-7 ran on the bench in late 1952 and the first production version was cleared for use in 1954 at a design rating of 63.74 kN (14,330 lb st). By 1963 production had been transferred to an uprated afterburning version designated **AL-7F-1**, of which details follow:
TYPE: Single-shaft turbojet, with or without afterburner.
COMPRESSOR: Nine-stage axial (eight stages in original AL-7 design). First two stages widely separated axially, with

variable stators ahead of second stage. Pressure ratio about 8 : 1.
COMBUSTION CHAMBER: Annular type with perforated inner flame tube. Multiple downstream fuel injectors inserted through cups in forward face of liner.
TURBINE: Two-stage axial-flow type. Both wheels overhung behind rear bearing; front disc bolted to flange on hollow tubular driveshaft.
AFTERBURNER (AL-7F): Comprises upstream diffuser and downstream combustion section. Pilot combustor includes single nozzle ring and flame holder; main spray ring and gutter flame holder assembly downstream at greater radius. Refractory liner in combustion section. Variable-area nozzle, with multiple hinged flaps.
ACCESSORIES: Fuel pump and control unit, oil pumps, hydraulic pump, electric generator, tachometer and other items grouped into quickly replaceable packages beneath compressor casing.

PERFORMANCE RATINGS:
Max rating:
AL-7F, unaugmented	63.0 kN (14,250 lb st)
AL-7F, afterburning	88.25 kN (19,840 lb st)
AL-7RV	63.74 kN (14,330 lb st)
AL-7F-1, unaugmented	68.65 kN (15,432 lb st)
AL-7F-1, afterburning	98.1 kN (22,046 lb st)

LYULKA AL-21
The AL-21 resembles the AL-7 closely, and may be installationally interchangeable, but has significant improvements to the compressor and other components. One production version is the **AL-21F-3**, for the Su-17 variable geometry tactical aircraft ('Fitter-C to K'). It also powers the Su-24, and an unaugmented vectored thrust version is believed to be fitted as main engine to the Yak-38.
PERFORMANCE RATINGS:
Max S/L: unaugmented 76.5 kN (17,200 lb st)
afterburning 110 kN (24,700 lb st)

MIKULIN
A. A. Mikulin was a leading designer of engines from 1916. The large turbojet described here was designed immediately after the Second World War.

MIKULIN AM-3
Service designation: TRD-3
The AM-3M single-spool turbojet was developed under the leadership of P. F. Zubets from the Mikulin M-209 (civil

RD-3 or AM-3) which powers the Tu-16 and early M-4 bombers and was adapted for the USSR's first jet transport, the Tu-104. Current M-4s are believed to have the AM-3D; while the usual engine of Tu-16s is the AM-3M. This engine is produced at the Xian factory in China as the Wopen-8.

It has a simple configuration, with an eight-stage compressor, annular combustion system with 14 flame tubes, and a two-stage turbine. The compressor casing is made in front, centre and rear portions, the front casing housing a row of inlet guide vanes. The inlet bullet houses

an S-300M gas turbine starter, developing 75 kW (100 hp) at 31,000-35,000 rpm. Pressure ratio is 6.4; temperature after turbine 720°C.
DIMENSIONS:
Length overall 5,340 mm (210.23 in)
Diameter 1,400 mm (55.12 in)
PERFORMANCE RATINGS (T-O):
AM-3 85.8 kN (19,285 lb st)
AM-3D 85.3 kN (19,180 lb st)
AM-3M, RD-3M 93.19 kN (20,950 lb st)

SHVETSOV

FOUNDER OF BUREAU: Arkadiya Dmitrievich Shvetsov

A. D. Shvetsov was responsible for the M-11 five-cylinder aircooled radial engines made in enormous numbers in 1928-59 at powers from 74.6 kW (100 hp) to 149 kW (200 hp). He later developed larger radials, the most important

being the ASh-82, which at ratings up to 1,491 kW (2,000 hp) powered Lavochkin fighters, the Tu-2 and Tu-4 bombers, Il-12 and -14 transports and Mi-4 and Yak-24 helicopters. The ASh-62 was made in large numbers at ratings in the 750 kW (1,000 hp) class for the Li-2 and An-2. The ASh-62M agricultural version, developed by Vedeneyev, and all An-2 engines after 1952, were transferred

to Poland (see WSK-PZL Kalisz and WSK-PZL Rzeszów). Another important engine was the 545 kW (730 hp) ASh-21, fitted to the Yak-11. All these have been described in earlier editions. The ASh-62 and ASh-82 have been produced under licence in China, as described in the Chinese entry in this section.

SOLOVIEV

GENERAL DESIGNER IN CHARGE OF BUREAU: P. A. Soloviev

Engines for which Soloviev's design team is responsible include the turbofans fitted in the Il-62M, Il-76, Il-96-300, Tu-124, Tu-134, Tu-154M and Tu-204 transport aircraft, and the turboshafts which power the Mi-6 and Mi-10 helicopters.

SOLOVIEV D-15

This engine was first reported, in 1959, as that fitted to the Type 201-M which gained world records for speed and altitude. This aircraft was a special Myasishchev M-4, and the engine was standard in some versions of this aircraft. Details of the D-15 are still unknown in the West, but it is probably a two-shaft turbojet. It laid the foundation upon which Soloviev's bureau produced the civil D-20 and D-30.

PERFORMANCE RATING:
T-O   128.6 kN (28,660 lb st)

SOLOVIEV D-25V

D-25V is the Soloviev designation for the turboshaft which powers the Mi-6 and Mi-10 helicopters. It is usually referred to by its official designation of **TV-2BM**.

The helicopter power plant comprises two D-25V engines, identical except for handed jetpipes, and an R-7 gearbox. The latter has four stages of large gearwheels providing an overall ratio of 69.2. The R-7 is 2,795 mm (110.04 in) high, 1,551 mm (61.06 in) wide and 1,852 mm (72.91 in) long. Its dry weight is 3,200 kg (7,054 lb).

The D-25V is flat rated to maintain rated power to 3,000 m (10,000 ft) or to temperatures up to 40°C at sea level.

The **D-25VF** is uprated to 4,847 kW (6,500 shp). These engines are believed to incorporate a zero stage on the compressor and to operate at higher turbine gas temperatures. They power the Mi-10K crane helicopter.

The following details apply to the basic D-25V:

TYPE: Single-shaft turboshaft with free power turbine.
COMPRESSOR: Nine-stage axial, with fixed inlet guide vanes and blow-off valves. Pressure ratio 5.6 at T-O power, 10,530 rpm.
COMBUSTION CHAMBER: Can-annular with 12 flame tubes.
FUEL GRADE: T-1, TS-1 to GOST 10227-62 (DERD.2494, MIL-F-5616)
TURBINE: Single-stage compressor turbine, overhung behind rear roller bearing. Two-stage power turbine, overhung on end of rear output shaft. Normal power turbine rpm, 7,800-8,300; maximum 9,000.
LUBRICATION: Pressure circulation at 3.45-4.41 bars (50-64 lb/sq in). Separate systems for gas generator and for power turbine, transmission and gearbox.
OIL GRADE: Gas generator, MK-8 to GOST 6457-66 or GOST 982-56. Power turbine and gearbox, mixture (75-25 Summer, 50-50 Winter) of MK-22 or MS-20 to GOST 1013-49 and MK-8 or 982-56.
ACCESSORIES: SP3-12TV electric supply and starting system; fuel supply to separate LP and HP systems; airframe accessories driven off upper and lower gearboxes.
STARTING: The SP3-12TV comprises an STG-12TM starter/generator on each engine, igniter unit, two spark plugs with cooling shrouds, two contactors, solenoid air valve, pressure warning, PSG-12V control panel and electro-hydraulic cutout switch of the TsP-23A centrifugal governor.
DIMENSIONS:
Length overall, bare   2,737 mm (107.75 in)
Length overall with transmission shaft
                                    5,537 mm (218.0 in)
Width   1,086 mm (42.76 in)
Height   1,158 mm (45.59 in)
WEIGHT, DRY:
With engine mounted accessories   1,325 kg (2,921 lb)
PERFORMANCE RATINGS:
T-O   4,101 kW (5,500 shp)
Rated power   3,504 kW (4,700 shp)
Cruise (1,000 m; 3,280 ft, 135 knots; 250 km/h; 155 mph)   2,983 kW (4,000 shp)
SPECIFIC FUEL CONSUMPTION:
T-O, as above   108 µg/J (0.639 lb/h/shp)
Cruise, as above   118.1 µg/J (0.699 lb/h/shp)

SOLOVIEV D-30

Since about 1972 the standard engine of the Tu-134A has been the **D-30-II**, with reverser. One Tu-134 was flown with D-30 engines with a zero stage on the LP compressor; the existing ratings were obtained at reduced gas temperature and maintained to ISA + 25°C.

TYPE: Two-shaft turbofan (bypass turbojet).
FAN: Four-stage axial (LP compressor). First stage has shrouded titanium blades held in disc by pinned joints. Pressure ratio (T-O rating), 7,700 rpm, S/L, static), 2.65. Mass flow 125 kg (265 lb)/s. Bypass ratio 1.

The 4,101 kW (5,500 shp) Soloviev D-25V turboshaft

Soloviev D-30 Series II turbofan (66.68 kN; 14,990 lb st) with thrust reverser

Soloviev D-30KU turbofan (108 kN; 24,250 lb st) complete with external dressing, tankage and reverser

COMPRESSOR: Ten-stage axial (HP compressor). Drum and disc construction, largely of titanium. Pressure ratio (T-O rating, 11,600 rpm, S/L, static), 7.1. Overall pressure ratio, 17.4.
COMBUSTION CHAMBER: Can-annular, with 12 flame tubes fitted with duplex burners.
FUEL GRADE: T-1 and TS-1 to GOST 10227-62 (equivalent to DERD.2494 or MIL-F-5616).
TURBINE: Two-stage HP turbine. First stage has cooled blades in both stator and rotor. LP turbine also has two stages. All blades shrouded and bearings shock mounted.
JETPIPE: Main and bypass mixer with curvilinear ducts. D-30-II engine of Tu-134A fitted with twin-clamshell reverser.
LUBRICATION: Open type, with oil returned to tank.
OIL GRADE: Mineral oil MK-8 or MK-8P to GOST 6457-66 (equivalent to DERD.2490 or MIL-O-6081B).
ACCESSORIES: Automatic ice protection system, fire extinguishing for core and bypass flows, vibration detectors on casings, oil chip detectors and automatic limitation of exhaust gas temperature to 620°C at take-off or when starting and to 630°C in flight (5 min limit). Shaft driven accessories driven via radial bevel gear shafts in centre casing, mainly off HP spool. D-30-II carries constant speed drives for alternators.
STARTING: Electric DC starting system incorporating STG-12TVMO starter/generators.
DIMENSIONS:
Overall length   3,983 mm (156.8 in)
Base diameter of inlet casing   1,050 mm (41.3 in)
WEIGHT, DRY: 1,550 kg (3,417 lb)
PERFORMANCE RATINGS:
T-O   66.68 kN (14,990 lb st)
Long-range cruise rating, 11,000 m (36,000 ft) and Mach 0.75   12.75 kN (2,866 lb st)

SPECIFIC FUEL CONSUMPTION:
T-O   17.56 mg/Ns (0.62 lb/h/lb st)
Cruise, as above   21.81 mg/Ns (0.77 lb/h/lb st)

SOLOVIEV D-30K

Despite its designation, this turbofan is much larger and more powerful than the D-30. The basic **D-30KU**, to which the specification details apply, replaced the NK-8-4 as power plant of the Il-62M. The **D-30KU-154-II** is configured to suit the Tu-154M and is derated to 104 kN (23,380 lb st). The **D-30KP**, rated at 117.7 kN (26,455 lb st), powers the Il-76. Clamshell reversers are fitted to all four engines of this aircraft, and to the outer engines of the Il-62M. These reversers are airframe assemblies incorporated in the nacelle.

TYPE: Two-shaft turbofan, with mixer and reverser.
FAN (LP COMPRESSOR): Three stages, mainly of titanium alloy. First-stage rotor blades with part-span snubbers. Mass flow, 269 kg (593 lb)/s at 4,730 rpm (87.9 per cent), with bypass ratio of 2.42.
HP COMPRESSOR: Eleven stages, first two having part-span snubbers. Guide vanes over 7,900-9,600 rpm, while air is bled from fifth and sixth stages. Overall pressure ratio (S/L, static) 20 at HP speed of 10,460 rpm (96 per cent).
COMBUSTION CHAMBER: Cannular type with 12 flame tubes. Each tube comprises hemispherical head and eight short sections welded with gaps for dilution air. Single swirl type main/pilot burner centred in each tube. Igniter plugs in two tubes.
FUEL GRADE: T-1, TS-1, GOST-10227-62, A-1 (D1655/63t), DERD.2494 or 2498, Air 3405/B or 3-GP-23e.
TURBINES: Two-stage HP turbine with cooled blades in both stages. Second-stage rotor blades tip shrouded. Max gas temperature 1,122°C. Four-stage LP turbine with shrouded blades.

LUBRICATION: Closed type. Fuel/oil heat exchanger and centrifugal air separator with particle warning.
OIL GRADE: MK-8 or MK-8P to GOST 6467-66 (mineral) or BNII NP-50-1-4F to GOST 13076-67 (synthetic).
ACCESSORIES: Front and rear drive boxes under engine carry all shaft driven accessories. Differential constant speed drive to alternator and air turbine starter.
STARTING: Pneumatic starter fed by ground supply, APU or cross-bleed.
DIMENSIONS:

Length with reverser	5,700 mm (224 in)
Inlet diameter	1,464 mm (57.6 in)
Maximum diameter of casing	1,560 mm (61.4 in)

WEIGHT, DRY:

With reverser	2,650 kg (5,842 lb)
Without reverser	2,300 kg (5,071 lb)

PERFORMANCE RATINGS (ISA):

T-O	108 kN (24,250 lb st) to 21°C
Cruise at 11,000 m (36,000 ft) and Mach 0.8	
	27 kN (6,063 lb st)

SPECIFIC FUEL CONSUMPTION:

At T-O rating	13.88 mg/Ns (0.49 lb/h/lb st)
Cruise, as above	19.83 mg/Ns (0.70 lb/h/lb)

SOLOVIEV PS-90A(D-90A)

This high bypass ratio turbofan is not derived from any existing engine. It is assembled from 11 modules, and is designed for long life, high reliability and low fuel burn.

Bench testing began in 1985. Flight testing was in progress in 1987 with an engine replacing a D-30KP in an Il-76. Certification is due in early 1989. The PS-90A will power the Il-96-300, followed into service by the Tu-204. Prototypes of both aircraft were to fly before the end of 1988.

TYPE: Two-shaft turbofan with mixer and fan reverser.
FAN: Single-stage, with 28 wide-chord titanium blades, without snubbers or shrouds. Bypass ratio (cruise) 4.8.
LP COMPRESSOR: Two-stage booster bolted to rear of fan.
HP COMPRESSOR: 13-stage spool with some variable inlet guide vanes. Overall pressure ratio (cruise) 35.5.
COMBUSTION CHAMBER: Fully annular with multiple burners and two igniters.
HP TURBINE: Two stages, with advanced aircooled blades. Entry gas temperature 1,565°K (1,292°C).
LP TURBINE: Four stages.
REVERSER: Multiple blocker doors close off fan duct as

Soloviev PS-90A turbofan (157.1 kN; 35,275 lb st) *(Brian M. Service)*

translating mid-section of cowl moves to rear, to uncover all-round reverser cascades. No core reverser.
DIMENSIONS:

Fan diameter	1,900 mm (74.8 in)
Overall length	5,329 mm (209.8 in)

WEIGHT, DRY: 2,800 kg (6,173 lb)

PERFORMANCE RATINGS (ISA):

T-O, S/L	157.1 kN (35,275 lb st) to 30°C
Cruise at 11,000 m (36,000 ft) and Mach 0.8	
	34.36 kN (7,716 lb)

SPECIFIC FUEL CONSUMPTION:

Cruise, as above	16.43 mg/Ns (0.58 lb/h/lb)

TUMANSKY

Academician Sergei Konstantinovich Tumansky, who died in 1973, was a noted designer of piston engines. His RD-9 axial turbojet went into production in 1953. On Mikulin's disgrace in 1956, Tumansky was appointed head of the bureau. Production of his subsequent engines easily exceeds that of any other family of aircraft gas turbines in the post-1955 era.

TUMANSKY RD-9

First axial turbojet of wholly Soviet design to be placed in production, this engine was designed under Tumansky in the Mikulin bureau in 1950-51 and received the TsIAM designation **AM-5**. The afterburning **AM-5F** was selected for the MiG-19 and the unaugmented engine for the Yak-25. After Mikulin's removal in 1956 the engine was redesignated **RD-9**, the afterburning type being called **RD-9B**. In 1957 the **RD-9BM** entered production, with a hydraulically actuated three-step nozzle. All variants have a nine-stage compressor, can-annular combustor and two-stage turbine; pressure ratio at take-off is 7.14. Production in the Soviet Union tapered off in 1958 in favour of the R-11. In China, production of the RD-9BM began in 1960 and has continued for the J-6 and Q-5. Diameter of all models is 813 mm (32.0 in). Maximum T-O rating of the BM is 32.36 kN (7,275 lb st).

A detailed description and drawing will be found under the designation WP-6 in the Chinese part of this section.

TUMANSKY R-11
Service designation: TRD-37.

The first R-11 turbojets (known as the R-37 series by the armed forces) ran in 1953 and entered production in 1956. The R-11 is a two-spool engine, with accessories grouped on the underside of the compressor. It was one of the first engines to have an overhung first rotor stage without inlet guide vanes. Other features include a can-annular combustion chamber with ten flame tubes, which in some versions provides large air bleed couplings for flap blowing, and, in most installations, a large afterburner with multi-flap variable nozzle. All early versions (but not the Chinese derivative) are started on petrol (gasoline) fed from a separate tank, and gaseous oxygen can be fed to the burners to increase relight altitude from 8 to 11.9 km (26,250 to 39,000 ft). Considerably more than 20,000 of all versions have been delivered from Soviet plants, to power many types of aircraft including versions of the MiG-21 and Yak-28. Many more have been produced by Hindustan Aeronautics in India, and by the Chinese as the Chengdu WP-7. Known Soviet versions are:

R-11. Initial production series, rated at 38.25 kN (8,600 lb st) dry and 50.0 kN (11,240 lb st) with afterburner. Three-stage transonic LP compressor and three-stage HP, each driven by single-stage turbine.

Tumansky R-11F2S-300 built under licence by HAL in India

R-11-300. Fitted with enlarged afterburner and new nozzle. Powered speed-record Ye-66 in 1959. Dry thrust unchanged but maximum increased to 58.4 kN (13,120 lb st).

R-11F. Original engine uprated, with small afterburner; dry thrust unchanged, maximum 56.4 kN (12,676 lb st).

R-11FS, F2S. Suffix S signifies provision for flap blowing. Final version was the **R-11F2S-300**, with maximum rating of 60.8 kN (13,668 lb st). This is believed to be still in production in India and China. Details will be found in the entry on the Chinese WP-7.

TUMANSKY R-13

This two-spool turbojet supplanted the R-11 as the MiG-21 engine in the late 1960s, before giving way to the R-25. It has an advanced afterburner, and a new five-stage HP compressor handling a greater airflow. It is also fitted in

the Su-15 and an unaugmented version powers the Su-25. The **PDM** fitted to the record breaking Ye-66B of 1974 may have been an R-13. The standard ratings for the R-13-300 are 41.55 kN (9,340 lb st) dry and 64.73 kN (14,550 lb st) with afterburner. Fuller details will be found in the entry on the Chinese WP-13.

TUMANSKY RU-19
Service designation: TRD-29

This single-shaft turbojet has been used to power aircraft and as an APU and emergency booster (in the An-26). When used as an APU its thrust is reduced depending upon the shaft power extracted. The fully rated **RU-19-300** has a thrust of 8.83 kN (1,985 lb st). This is installed in the An-24RV and An-24RT. The **RU-19A-300** is rated at 7.85 kN (1,765 lb st) and is installed in the An-26 and An-30. When providing full electrical power the residual thrust is only 2.16 kN (485 lb st). An RU-19 was selected as the APU/booster for the MAI-Tashkent Semurg, the rating in this application being 3.1 kN (697 lb st). Another RU-19, equipped as a turbojet and fully rated, powers the La-17 target (see RPVs and Targets in 1977-78 *Jane's*). The RU-19 powered the Yak-30 and Yak-32 jet trainers.

TUMANSKY R-25

This two-spool turbojet was a new design, and its compressor of high pressure ratio confers a markedly lower sfc than the R-13. The R-25 has redesigned accessory systems but is installationally interchangeable with the R-13. The first LP compressor stage has 21 titanium blades of large chord. The afterburner has two stages (the R-11 and R-13 having one) and so can be used in combat at high altitudes. Maximum S/L thrust is 73.6 kN (16,535 lb st). No longer made, except under licence by HAL of India for MiG-21 bis.

TUMANSKY R-266/R-31

The R-26 sub-type 6 is a single-shaft afterburning turbojet designed for the MiG-25. It stemmed from the P-166 fitted to the Ye-166 which set a world speed record in 1962. The P-166 had a thrust with afterburner of 98.06 kN (22,046 lb st). This was also the thrust of the original R-266, announced under its service designation of **R-31** as being fitted to prototypes of the MiG-25 (designated Ye-266).

Constructed mainly of steel, the R-266 has a five-stage compressor with T-O pressure ratio of about 7, driven by a single-stage turbine with uncooled blades. Special T-6 fuel is used, with freezing point of –62.2°C and flash point of 54.4°C. In the MiG-25, water/methanol is injected into the variable inlet duct at supersonic speeds. At Mach 3 most of the thrust is generated by the three-ring afterburner and multi-flap variable nozzle. Ratings are 91.18 kN (20,500 lb st) dry and 120 kN (27,010 lb st) with afterburner.

RD-F. This is an uprated R-266 fitted to the Ye-266M (MiG-25 variant) which set time-to-height records in 1975. A military engine, probably designated **R-31F**, powers the MiG-25E, with the same maximum rating of 137.3 kN (30,865 lb st). It is assumed that an advanced version also powers the MiG-31 'Foxhound'.

TUMANSKY R-27

Using a core similar to that of the R-25, this simple and efficient turbojet was developed for the MiG-23 family. Rated at 68.65 kN (15,430 lb st) dry and 100 kN (22,485 lb st) with afterburner and water injection, the R-27 was produced in modest numbers for early ('Flogger-B') versions of the MiG-23, as well as for MiG-23U trainer versions and some export models. Basic features are similar to those of the higher-rated R-29B.

TUMANSKY R-29

One of the most important engines in the Soviet inventory, this augmented turbojet is simpler than the corresponding American F100, with fewer compressor stages and a lower pressure ratio; but it is more powerful and costs much less. Different subtypes are fitted to all current MiG-23 and MiG-27 versions for Warsaw Pact

Tumansky R-25 turbojet built by HAL in India for the licence built MiG-21 bis

front-line use, and to the Su-22. In all these aircraft water injection is used on take-off, the MiG-23MF water tank having a capacity of 28 litres (7.4 US gallons; 6.2 Imp gallons).

The following versions have been identified:

R-29B. Original full-rated production engine for MiG-23MF and related versions.

R-29PN. This replaced the R-29B as the standard engine of non-export MiG-23 aircraft.

R-29-300. Simplified engine with small afterburner and short two-position nozzle for subsonic low-level operation. Fitted to all MiG-27 versions, with fixed or variable inlet ducts.

The following data refer to the R-29B:

COMPRESSOR: Five-stage LP, six-stage HP. Overall pressure ratio 12.4. Maximum airflow 105 kg (235 lb)/s.
COMBUSTION CHAMBER: Annular, vaporising burners.
TURBINES: HP has single stage with aircooled blades. LP unknown.
AFTERBURNER: Fuel rings with separate light-up give modulated fully variable augmentation. Fully variable nozzles differ in different installations.
WEIGHT, DRY: 1,760 kg (3,880 lb)

PERFORMANCE RATINGS:
Max S/L unaugmented	78.45 kN (17,635 lb st)
Min with afterburner	97.1 kN (21,825 lb st)
Max T-O, wet (R-29-300)	112.8 kN (25,350 lb st)
Max T-O, wet (MiG-23MF)	122.0 kN (27,500 lb st)

TUMANSKY R-32

R-32 is the Soviet service designation of the turbofans fitted to the Sukhoi P-42 fighter that set four time-to-height records in November and December 1986. The aircraft is believed to be a specially prepared Su-27. Engine rating was given as 133.25 kN (29,955 lb st) with afterburning.

TUMANSKY R-33

Designation of the Tumansky turbofans used in the MiG-29 is reported to be R-33D. No details are known, except for the following ratings:

PERFORMANCE RATINGS:
Max S/L unaugmented	50.0 kN (11,245 lb st)
Max T-O with afterburner	81.4 kN (18,300 lb st)

VEDENEYEV

GENERAL DESIGNER IN CHARGE OF BUREAU:
Ivan M. Vedeneyev

This designer was responsible for improvement of the AI-14 piston engine designed by the Ivchenko bureau. He also developed the ASh-62M, produced in Poland as the ASz-62M, from Shvetsov's ASh-62IR.

M-14V-26

Derived from the AI-14 engines for fixed-wing aircraft, the M-14V-26 powers the Ka-26 helicopter. In this installation the stub wing carries an engine on each tip. Beneath the rotor an R-26 gearbox combines the power of the engines and distributes it equally between the two coaxial main rotors. The same engine in a revised installation powers the Mi-34 helicopter.

The engine has forced cooling by an axial fan driven via a friction clutch and extension shaft ahead of the main output bevel box at 1.452 times crankshaft speed. The planetary gearbox has a ratio of 0.309 and incorporates friction and ratchet clutches. The central R-26 gearbox has a ratio of 0.34; it also drives the generator, hydraulic pump, oil pump and tachometer generator.

DIMENSIONS:
Length	1,145 mm (45.08 in)
Diameter	985 mm (38.78 in)

WEIGHT, DRY: 245 kg (540 lb)

PERFORMANCE RATINGS:
T-O	242 kW; 325 hp at 2,800 rpm
Max continuous I	205 kW; 275 hp at 2,450 rpm
Max continuous II	142 kW; 190 hp at 2,350 rpm
Cruise I	142 kW; 190 hp at 2,350 rpm
Cruise II	108 kW; 145 hp at 2,350 rpm

SPECIFIC FUEL CONSUMPTION:
At cruise ratings   77.7 µg/J (0.46 lb/h/hp)

VEDENEYEV M-14P

For fixed-wing applications, the M-14P was used with direct drive in the original version of the OSKB-1-3PM Kwant, at a T-O rating of 242 kW (325 hp). Currently, the Kwant has an M-14 II of 268 kW (360 hp). The same rating is quoted for the M-14P fitted to the Yak-18T, -50, 52, 53 and 55 and Su-26, all of which have a controllable-pitch propeller.

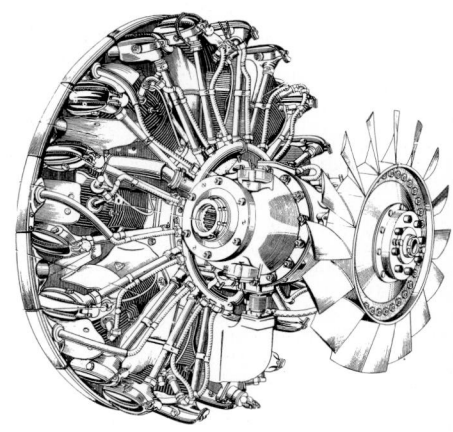

Vedeneyev M-14V-26 radial piston engine, with cooling fan, for Kamov Ka-26 helicopter

SOVIET ENGINES OF UNKNOWN DESIGN

1. Liftjet. Soviet design bureaux conducted extensive research into jet lift from the late 1950s. At a 1967 air show three liftjet V/STOL research aircraft were displayed. A modified MiG-21 had two liftjets in the mid-fuselage. A larger MiG had a similar arrangement, differing in design of the dorsal door. A modified Su-15 had three lift engines fed by two upper doors. All these installations had large open slots in the dorsal doors (which were hinged at the rear) and transverse louvres filling the ventral jet aperture (probably

hinged and under pilot control to give variable forward thrust). Photographs of these aircraft last appeared in the 1971-72 *Jane's*. The two liftjets used in the Yak-38 are probably developments of the same engines, though details are not known. The inlet door has open louvres. Thrust is estimated at 35.5 kN (8,000 lb). A Czechoslovak magazine in 1984 described them as Koliesov type ZM.

2. Il-114 engine. This transport is powered by twin turboprops rated at 1,839 kW (2,466 shp). Specific fuel consumption is given, unusually for a propeller engine, as 0.18 kg/h/kg thrust. It is not possible readily to translate this figure into sfc per unit of shaft power.

UNITED KINGDOM

EMDAIR
EMDAIR LTD
Harbour Road, Rye, E Sussex TN31 7TH
Telephone: 0797 223460
Telex: 957116 FOR EMDAIR
Fax: (0797) 224615

Activities centre on lightweight four-stroke flat-twin engines. These aircooled engines run on Mogas and have four-valve heads, dual electronic ignition with central and side spark plugs, direct injection, alternator and electric starter. They are intended to combine high specific output at low rpm with low sfc, low costs and long life. Each engine is available in A (direct drive) and B (geared, torsional damping and extension shaft) versions.

EMDAIR CF 077A
Crankshaft rotation counterclockwise, seen from the front. An exhaust muffler (silencer) is optional.
CYLINDERS: Bore 95.0 mm (3.74 in). Stroke 88.9 mm (3.50 in). Capacity 1,261 cc (76.91 cu in). Compression ratio 9.5.

DIMENSIONS:
Length	400 mm (15.75 in)
Width	698 mm (27.5 in)
Height	447 mm (17.75 in)
WEIGHT, DRY (with starter):	47.27 kg (104 lb)

PERFORMANCE RATINGS:
Max	44.8 kW (60 hp) at 3,600 rpm
Max cruise	33.6 kW (45 hp) at 3,090 rpm

FUEL CONSUMPTION:
Max cruise 11.8 litres (3.1 US gallons; 2.6 Imp gallons)/h

EMDAIR CF 077B
This version powers the De Vore Sunbird, designed to

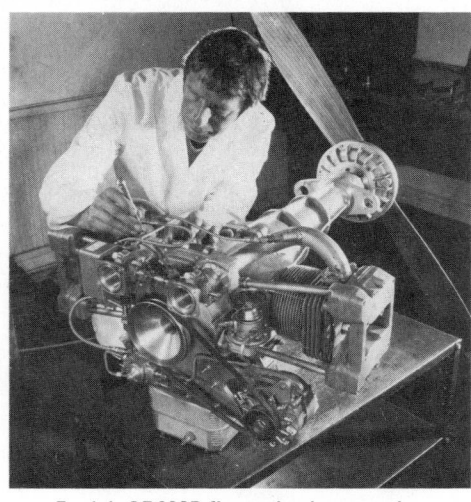

Emdair CF 092B flat-twin piston engine

FAR Pt 23. Geared output with torsional vibration damping, reducing propeller speed to 2,600 rpm.

EMDAIR CF 092A
CYLINDERS: Bore 104.0 mm (4.094 in). Stroke 88.9 mm (3.50 in). Capacity 1,511 cc (92.17 cu in). Compression ratio 9.5.

DIMENSIONS:
Length	401 mm (15.8 in)

DIMENSIONS:
Width	698 mm (27.5 in)
Height	447 mm (17.75 in)
WEIGHT, DRY (with starter):	51.0 kg (112 lb)

PERFORMANCE RATINGS:
Max	52.2 kW (70 hp) at 3,600 rpm
75 per cent cruise	39.1 kW (52.5 hp) at 3,075 rpm

EMDAIR CF 100A
CYLINDERS: Bore 101.6 mm (4.0 in). Stroke 99.06 mm (3.9 in). Capacity 1,606 cc (98.0 cu in). Compression ratio 9.5.

DIMENSIONS:
Length	400 mm (15.75 in)
Width	701 mm (27.6 in)
Height	447 mm (17.75 in)
WEIGHT, DRY (with starter):	53 kg (115 lb)

PERFORMANCE RATINGS:
Max	56 kW (75 hp) at 3,400 rpm
Alternative (medium speed)	
	46 kW (62 hp) at 2,800 rpm

EMDAIR CF 112
The 112B has an epicyclic gearbox giving a propeller speed of 2,500 rpm at a crankshaft speed of 3,600 rpm. The following relates to the 112A:
CYLINDERS: Bore 110 mm (4.35 in). Stroke 96.0 mm (3.78 in). Capacity 1,834 cc (112 cu in). Compression ratio 9.5.

DIMENSIONS:
Length	412.75 mm (16.25 in)
Width	711.2 mm (28.0 in)
Height	425 mm (16.75 in)
WEIGHT, DRY (with starter):	57.28 kg (128 lb)

PERFORMANCE RATINGS:
Max	63.4 kW (85.0 hp) at 3,600 rpm
75 per cent cruise	47.5 kW (63.75 hp) at 3,270 rpm

NORTON
NORTON MOTORS LTD
Lynn Lane, Shenstone, Lichfield, Staffs WS14 0EA
Telephone: 0543 480101
Telex: 335998 NORTON G
Fax: 0543 481128
MANAGING DIRECTOR: Philippe Le Roux
DIRECTOR OF ENGINEERING: David W. Garside
DIRECTOR OF MARKETING: Jon H. Skofic

Norton designs and manufactures gasoline-fuelled Wankel-type rotary engines from 22 to 90 kW (30 to 120

hp). Norton claims these engines offer a power-to-weight ratio superior to a two-stroke. With sfc competitive with a four-stroke, the rotary is capable of longer missions or carrying greater payload than a two-stroke. Radial vibration is eliminated and torsional vibration has been brought down to give a smoother ride for the pilot or a sensitive electronic payload. The rotary's low maintenance requirement approaches that of a gas turbine.

In addition to the engine described below, Norton has developed an important range of rotary engines for RPV/target applications, including the P63, P73 and P80.

NORTON AEROTOR 90
This engine is based on the twin-rotor technology used in the Norton rotary motorcycle. It is rated at 67 kW (90 hp) and, complete with 3:1 reduction gearbox, weighs 54.5 kg (120 lb). It is suitable for light and ultralight aircraft and for larger surveillance drones. It complies with BCAR Section C, and went into production in 1988 with an initial TBO of 500 h. Teledyne Continental's designation is **R-36**.

NPT
NOEL PENNY TURBINES LTD
Siskin Drive, Toll Bar End, Coventry CV3 4FE
Telephone: 0203 301528
Telex: 312285 PENNY G
Fax: 0203 307765
CHAIRMAN AND MANAGING DIRECTOR: R. N. Penny

NPT specialises in turbojets for low-cost manufacture. New products range from a 0.22 kN (50 lb st) turbojet, for ultra low-cost production to replace a rocket, to a 4.0 kN (900 lb st) two-shaft turbofan. NPT also produces industrial and aerospace gas turbines rated at up to 1,865 kW (2,500 shp) and 6.67 kN (1,500 lb st). Details of engines for unmanned applications can be found in the 1987-88 *Jane's*.

NPT 301
The 301 family was developed for re-usable drones and target vehicles requiring thrusts in the range 1.3 to 2 kN (300 to 450 lb st) at up to 13,850 m (45,000 ft). One version has a manned aircraft application.

Versions are as follows:

NPT 301-1. For ten one-hour missions with zero-length launch and sea water recovery.

NPT 301-2. For ten 90 min missions with carousel launch and parachute and ground impact recovery.

NPT 301-3/4. Experimental application to prototype CMC Leopard light business aircraft.

NPT 301-5. For ten three-hour missions with zero-length, helicopter and underwing air launch and parachute and sea water recovery. NPT digital electronic control unit.

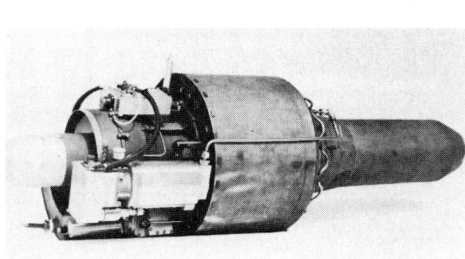

NPT 301-1 turbojet

NPT 301-6. Instrumented laboratory model for research and instruction.
TYPE: Single shaft turbojet.
COMPRESSOR: Centrifugal, aluminium alloy. Air mass flow 2.27 kg (5.0 lb)/s. Pressure ratio 4.5.
COMBUSTION CHAMBER: Reverse flow annular, with vaporising burners.
FUEL SYSTEM: LP pressurised inlet electric pump. Analog or digital electronic control.
FUEL GRADES: Jet A-1, JP-5.
TURBINE: Single-stage axial with integral blades.

STARTING: External air source impingement on compressor.
ACCESSORY DRIVE: Alternator, currently 2.5 kW.
LUBRICATION: Total loss pulsed oil flow.
DIMENSIONS:
Length	1,000 mm (39.6 in)
Diameter	343 mm (13.5 in)

WEIGHT, DRY:
301-1, -2	40.37 kg (89 lb)
301-5	45.4 kg (100 lb)

PERFORMANCE RATING (S/L):
301-1	1.334 kN (300 lb st)
301-2	1.40 kN (315 lb st)
301-5	1.47 kN (330 lb st)
SPECIFIC FUEL CONSUMPTION:	30.6 mg/Ns (1.08 lb/h/lb st)

NPT 401B
Based on the NPT 301-5, the NPT-401B is to power an extended-range airframe. It differs in the following characteristics:
COMPRESSOR: Air mass flow 2.62 kg (5.77 lb)/s. Pressure ratio 4.8.
STARTING: Integral starter, or external air impingement.
ACCESSORY DRIVE: 1.8 kW alternator.
DIMENSION:
Length	1,082 mm (42.6 in)
WEIGHT, DRY:	45.4 kg (100 lb)

PERFORMANCE RATING (S/L):
Max	1.779 kN (400 lb st)
SPECIFIC FUEL CONSUMPTION:	33.4 mg/Ns (1.18 lb/h/lb st)

ROLLS-ROYCE
ROLLS-ROYCE plc
65 Buckingham Gate, London SW1E 6AT
Telephone: 01 222 9020
Telex: 918091
MAIN LOCATIONS:
PO Box 31, Moor Lane, Derby DE2 8BJ
Telephone: 0332 242424
PO Box 3, Filton, Bristol BS12 7QE
Telephone: 0272 791234
Leavesden, Watford WD2 7BZ
Telephone: 0923 674000
CHAIRMAN: Sir Francis Tombs
MANAGING DIRECTOR: Sir Ralph Robins

More than 278 million hours have been accumulated with Rolls-Royce civil and military gas turbines, which are used by over 270 airlines, over 110 armed forces and more than 700 executive customers.

The main activities are at Derby, Glasgow, Bristol, Coventry and Leavesden, where aircraft gas turbines are produced, and at Ansty, where aircraft gas turbine techniques are applied to industrial and marine uses. Employees total 41,500.

In April 1985 Rolls-Royce joined with Turbomeca and MTU in the European Small Engines Co-operation Agreement. This involves the Rolls-Royce Turbomeca RTM 322, MTU-Turbomeca RR-MTR 390, and Turbomeca TM 333. Further details are given under Turbomeca

(France) and in the International part of this section. The company is a partner in IAE, EUROJET, Turbo-Union and Rolls-Royce Turbomeca.

In 1983 Rolls-Royce announced that it was engaged in a broad study programme on possible future engines to drive advanced propellers for aircraft speeds of about Mach 0.8.

ROLLS-ROYCE TURBOMECA ADOUR
See the International part of this section.

TURBO-UNION RB199
See the International part of this section.

EUROJET EJ 200
See the International part of this section.

IAE V2500
See the International part of this section.

ROLLS-ROYCE RB211

The designation RB211 applies to a family of three-shaft turbofans of high bypass ratio and high pressure ratio, with thrusts from 166 kN (37,400 lb) to 330 kN (74,000 lb). The engine was selected by Lockheed in March 1968 to power the L-1011 TriStar, and later by Boeing as an alternative option on the 747 and 767.

For all announced applications Rolls-Royce retains responsibility for the complete propulsion system, comprising the engine, fan airflow reverser, pod cowlings and related systems, and noise attenuation for the intake, fan cowl and turbine exhaust duct. The engine is built up of seven modules, each changed easily.

The **RB211-22B**, fitted to the L-1011-1 and -100 TriStar, is flat rated at 187 kN (42,000 lb st) to 28.9°C. Certificated in February 1973 by the CAA and in April 1973 by the FAA. Production ceased in 1982 when over 670 engines had been delivered. By 1988 engine flight hours in service were nearly 16 million.

The **RB211-524** series of engines was developed from the RB211-22B and covers a range of thrusts from 222 kN (50,000 lb) to 330 kN (74,000 lb). The -524 entered airline service in 1977 with the L-1011 and 747. By the beginning of 1988 more than 660 engines had been delivered, and service experience of nearly 10.5 million hours achieved.

The **RB211-524B**, which powers the L-1011-200, L-1011-500 and 747, is certificated at 222 kN (50,000 lb) to 28.9°C. Further developments at the same thrust but offering better fuel consumption include the **RB211-524B3**, giving a 3.5 per cent improvement over the -524B, and which entered service in May 1980; and the **RB211-524B4**, which offers up to 4.8 per cent better sfc than the 524B and entered service in February 1981. Further savings are obtained from the **524B4 Improved** and the **524B4-B**, which incorporate additional sfc and component life improvements. These engines can be installed new or by modifying existing engines in the L-1011-250.

The **RB211-524C** offers increased thrust ratings for the 747. It entered service in April 1980 with a rating of 229 kN (51,000 lb).

The **RB211-524D4** is an improved engine rated at 236 kN (53,000 lb) for the 747, and offering a 4.8 per cent better fuel consumption relative to the -524B. Certification was followed by entry into service in November 1981.

The **RB211-524D4 Upgrade** offers 2.6 per cent lower sfc than the D4 and is rated at 236 kN (53,000 lb) for the 747. This engine entered service in 1984. Variants entering service from 1987 increased the sfc improvements to around 5 per cent.

The **RB211-524G** incorporates advanced features proven on the 535E4, such as the wide-chord fan, 3-D aerodynamics, directionally solidified HP and IP turbine blades and integrated mixer nozzle. Another new feature is a digital control system. It is rated at 258 kN (58,000 lb st), with sfc 8.8 per cent lower than the D4, and was certificated in early 1988 for the 747-400. It will enter service in early 1989.

The **RB211-524H**, rated at 270 kN (60,600 lb st) will enter service with the Boeing 767 in late 1989, and is mechanically identical to the 524G.

A higher thrust variant, the **RB211-524L**, is being developed to provide thrusts between 290-330 kN (65-74,000 lb st) for the latest generation of wide-body airliners such as the McDonnell Douglas MD-11, Airbus Industrie A330, and developments of the Boeing 767 and 747. It will feature a 2.4 m (95 in) diameter wide-chord fan, an increased flow IP compressor, an increased efficiency HP compressor, a four-stage LP turbine, and a full authority digital electronic control (FADEC). It will incorporate substantial weight-saving features. Specific fuel consumption will be at least 2 per cent better than the 524G and 524H. On 10 June 1988 MoUs were signed that enable this engine to be offered on the A330 and MD-11. Service entry is planned for Summer 1994.

The following description relates to the RB211-524G:

TYPE: Three-shaft axial turbofan. Overall pressure ratio 33.

FAN: Single-stage overhung, driven by LP turbine. Composite nosecone, 24 hollow wide-chord blades in titanium alloy, supercritical outlet guide vanes. Aluminium casing, with Armco containment ring. Total airflow 728 kg (1,604 lb)/s. Bypass ratio 4.3.

IP COMPRESSOR: Seven-stage, driven by IP turbine. Two drums, one of titanium discs welded together and the other of welded steel discs, bolted to form one rotor, carrying titanium blades. Aluminium and steel casings carry steel stator blades. Single-stage titanium variable inlet guide vanes.

HP COMPRESSOR: Six-stage, driven by HP turbine. Welded titanium discs, single steel disc and welded nickel alloy discs bolted together carrying titanium, steel and nickel alloy blades. Steel casing carries steel and Nimonic stator blades.

COMBUSTION CHAMBER: Fully annular, with steel outer casings and nickel alloy combustor. Downstream fuel injection by 18 airspray burners with annular atomisers. High energy igniter plugs in Nos 8 and 12 burners.

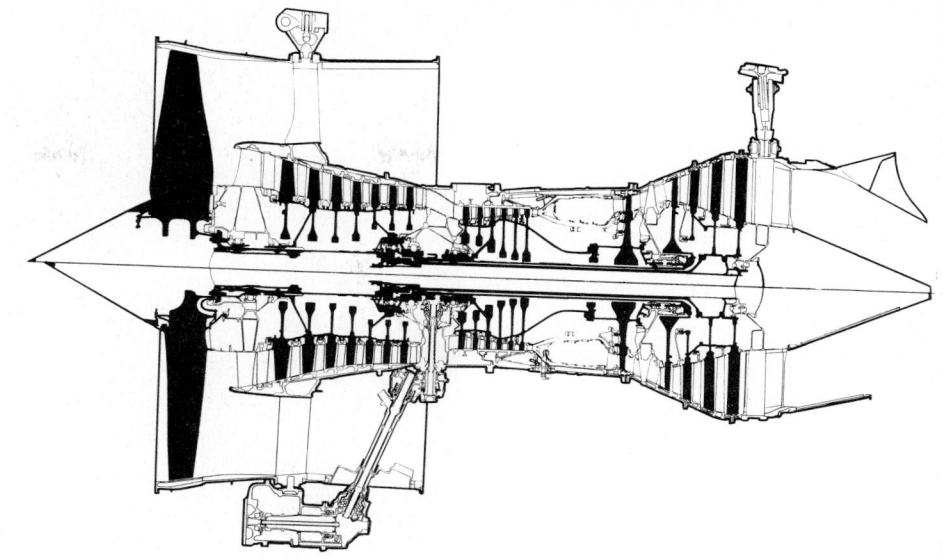

Cross-sections of the Rolls-Royce RB211-524G (upper half) and RB211-524D4 Upgrade (lower)

HP TURBINE: Single-stage, with directionally solidified nickel alloy rotor blades, both convection and film cooled, mounted in nickel alloy disc by fir tree roots.

IP TURBINE: Single-stage, with directionally solidified nickel alloy rotor blades fir tree mounted in nickel alloy disc.

LP TURBINE: Three-stage, with nickel alloy rotor blades fir tree mounted in steel discs.

EXHAUST NOZZLE: Integrated nozzle with deep-chute forced mixer.

ACCESSORY DRIVES: Radial drive from HP shaft to gearbox on fan casing. Accessories include integrated drive generator and aircraft hydraulic pumps.

LUBRICATION SYSTEM: Continuous circulation dry sump system supplying oil to four bearing chambers with a combination of ball and roller bearings. 27 litre (48 Imp pint) oil tank integral with gearbox.

DIMENSIONS:
Length overall:

RB211-22B, -524C2	3,033 mm (119.4 in)
RB211-524B4, -524D4	3,106 mm (122.3 in)
RB211-524G, -524H	3,175 mm (125.0 in)

Fan diameter:

RB211-22B, -524C2	2,154 mm (84.8 in)
RB211-524B4, -524D4	2,180 mm (85.8 in)
RB211-524G, -524H	2,192 mm (86.3 in)

WEIGHT, DRY:

RB211-22B	4,171 kg (9,195 lb)
RB211-524B4, B4 Improved	4,452 kg (9,814 lb)
RB211-524C2	4,472 kg (9,859 lb)
RB211-524D4, D4 Upgrade, -524G/H	4,479 kg (9,874 lb)

PERFORMANCE RATINGS:
T-O: see model listings
Cruise at 10,670 m (35,000 ft) and Mach 0.85 (uninstalled):

RB211-22B	42.2 kN (9,495 lb)
RB211-524B4, B4 Improved	48.9 kN (11,000 lb)
RB211-524C2	51.1 kN (11,490 lb)
RB211-524D4 (all models)	50.0 kN (11,230 lb)
RB211-524G, -524H	49.4 kN (11,100 lb)

SPECIFIC FUEL CONSUMPTION (cruise):

RB211-22B	17.79 mg/Ns (0.628 lb/h/lb)
RB211-524B4	17.56 mg/Ns (0.620 lb/h/lb)
RB211-524B4 Improved	17.16 mg/Ns (0.606 lb/h/lb)
RB211-524C2	18.21 mg/Ns (0.642 lb/h/lb)
RB211-524D4	17.48 mg/Ns (0.617 lb/h/lb)
RB211-524D4 Upgrade (1987)	16.68 mg/Ns (0.589 lb/h/lb)
RB211-524G, -524H	15.95 mg/Ns (0.563 lb/h/lb)

ROLLS-ROYCE 535

The **535C** was launch engine for the Boeing 757. It has an HP module based on the RB211-22B, six-stage IP compressor without variable stator vanes, and a scaled down -524 fan. Fan airflow is 18 per cent lower than that of the -22B, and core airflow 12 per cent lower. The engine runs at moderate temperatures, pressures and velocities, resulting in low noise and optimisation for short-haul operation. The 535C entered service on 1 January 1983. In the first five years of service the total engine-caused removal rate was 0.063 per 1,000 h.

The **535E4** is an advanced version offering increased thrust, together with about 10 per cent reduction in fuel consumption relative to the 535C. These stem from a new wide chord fan blade without snubbers, together with advanced compressor and turbine blading and an integrated nozzle. CAA certification was achieved in November 1983, at a T-O rating of 178 kN (40,100 lb), and revenue service began in October 1984. The E4 reliability rates are similar to those of its predecessor. In the first three years of service the total engine-caused removal rate was 0.05 per 1,000 h. The 757 with this engine is the quietest civil aircraft with more than 100 seats. The E4 allowed 757s powered by it to be cleared for extended-range operations (EROPS) in December 1986.

The following description relates to the 535E4:

TYPE: Three-shaft turbofan.

FAN: Single-stage, with only 22 wide chord blades, without snubbers, each of accelerated diffusion bonded titanium skins on titanium honeycomb core. Fan case of Rohrbond with Kevlar containment. Fan airflow 522 kg (1,150 lb)/s. Bypass ratio 4.1 (535C, 4.4).

IP COMPRESSOR: Six stages of controlled diffusion design. No variable vanes.

HP COMPRESSOR: Six stages of end-bend blading, with stage -4, -5 and -6 discs in titanium super alloy. Low expansion

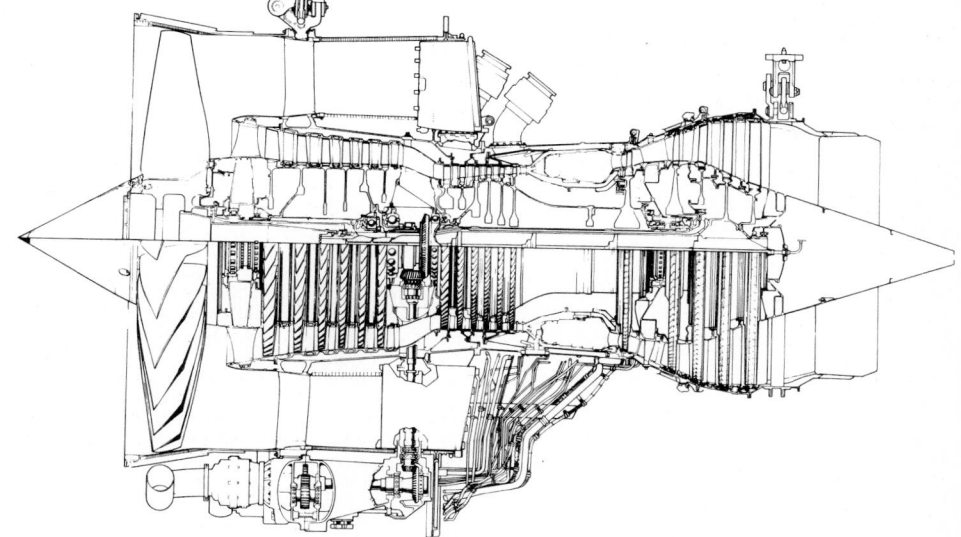

Comparative cross-sections of Rolls-Royce 535C (upper) and 535E4 (lower)

casing for improved tip clearance control. Overall engine pressure ratio 28.5 (535C, 21.2).

COMBUSTION CHAMBER: Annular, 18 airspray nozzles, flexible liner mountings, heatshields and thermal barrier coatings.

HP TURBINE: Single-stage. Rotor blades, directionally solidified, cast with HP leading-edge cooling, HP and LP internal cooling passages both with triple pass system. Nozzle guide vanes with curved stacking, highly cooled and with thermal barrier coating on platforms.

IP TURBINE: Single stage. Cooled NGVs with multi-lean stacking for improved airflow onto high aspect ratio blades.

LP TURBINE: Three stages. All turbine casings double wall and cooled.

JETPIPE: Core and bypass flows mixed in integrated nozzle.

REVERSER: Fan reverser only. Jacks move translating cowl to rear, blocker deals seal fan duct and uncover cascade vanes. Over expansion reduces core thrust.

GEARBOX: Mounted under fan case, driven from HP spool.

DIMENSIONS:

Length: 535C	3,010 mm (118.5 in)
535E4	2,995 mm (117.9 in)
Inlet diameter: 535C	1,877 mm (73.9 in)
535E4	1,892 mm (74.5 in)

WEIGHT, DRY:

535C	3,309 kg (7,294 lb)
535E4	3,295 kg (7,264 lb)

PERFORMANCE RATINGS (note: flexible T-O ratings involving considerable derating are used in operation):

T-O (S/L, ISA): 535C	166.4 kN (37,400 lb st)
535E4	178.4 kN (40,100 lb st)
Max climb (10,670 m; 35,000 ft, Mach 0.80):	
535C	40.1 kN (9,023 lb)
535E4	41.4 kN (9,300 lb)
Max cruise (10,670 m; 35,000 ft, Mach 0.80):	
535C	37.6 kN (8,453 lb)
535E4	38.7 kN (8,700 lb)

SPECIFIC FUEL CONSUMPTION (cruise, as above):

535C	17.33 mg/Ns (0.612 lb/h/lb)
535E4	16.09 mg/Ns (0.568 lb/h/lb)

ROLLS-ROYCE RB163 CIVIL SPEY
US military designation: F113

Design of the Spey began in September 1959. The first engine ran at the end of December 1960. Civil Speys are the subject of a collaborative production programme between Rolls-Royce and the government of Romania. The **F113-RR-100** is the Mk 511-8 which powers the Gulfstream C-20A C-SAM aircraft.

The following details refer to the Spey Mk 512-14DW, as fitted to the BAe and Rombac One-Eleven Series 500, except where indicated:

TYPE: Two-spool turbofan.

COMPRESSOR: Two spools. Five-stage (four-stage on Mks 505 and 506) low pressure (LP) and 12-stage high pressure (HP). First-stage HP stator vanes variable incidence. Pressure ratio 21.2. Air mass flow 94.4 kg (208 lb)/s. Bypass ratio 0.64.

COMBUSTION CHAMBER: Tubo-annular with 10 Nimonic sheet liners. Duplex downstream burners, one per chamber. High energy igniters in chambers 4 and 8.

FUEL SYSTEM: Plessey LP pump feeding through fuel cooled oil cooler and Marston Excelsior fuel heater to LP filter at inlet to Lucas GD pump.

FUEL GRADE: DERD.2482 or 2486.

WATER INJECTION SYSTEM (engines bearing 'W' suffix): Water supplied by Lucas air turbopump to injector passages in fuel spray nozzles.

TURBINES: Two two-stage. First HP aircooled. Nickel alloy blades attached by fir tree roots.

REVERSER AND SUPPRESSOR: Normally internal clamshell (Gulfstream II and III target type). Five- or six-chute silencing nozzles available.

ACCESSORY DRIVES: Port gearbox, driven from LP rotor, carries LP governor and LP tacho. Starboard gearbox, driven from HP rotor, carries LP and HP fuel pumps, fuel regulator, main oil pumps, airflow control rpm signal transmitter, starter and HP tacho. Provision in starboard gearbox for aircraft ancillaries.

LUBRICATION SYSTEM: Self-contained continuous circulation. Tank capacity 6.8 litres (12 Imp pints). Normal pressure 2.41-3.45 bars (35-50 lb/sq in).

OIL SPECIFICATION: DERD.2487.

STARTING: Plessey 220 air turbine starter.

DIMENSIONS:

Length, less tailpipe	2,911 mm (114.6 in)
Diameter	942 mm (37.1 in)

WEIGHT, DRY:

	1,168 kg (2,574 lb)

PERFORMANCE RATINGS:

Max T-O	55.8 kN (12,550 lb st)
Max continuous	
	51.5 kN (11,580 lb st) at 12,450 rpm
Typical cruise rating at 450 knots (834 km/h; 518 mph) at	
9,750 m (32,000 ft)	13.7 kN (3,070 lb)

SPECIFIC FUEL CONSUMPTION (cruise as above)

	22.7 mg/Ns (0.800 lb/h/lb)

OIL CONSUMPTION:

Max (all Marks)	0.42 litres (0.89 US pints; 0.75 Imp pints)/h

Rolls-Royce 535E4 three-shaft turbofan

ROLLS-ROYCE RB183

Developed for the Fokker F28, this derivative engine has a similar configuration to the Spey but has a four-stage LP compressor. Pressure ratio 15.4, mass flow 90.27 kg (199 lb)/s and bypass ratio 1. The following versions are in use:

Mk 555-15. Basic model, rated at 43.8 kN (9,850 lb st).

Mk 555-15H. Hot-day version, flat rated at 44.0 kN (9,900 lb st) to 29.7°C. Entered service 1973.

Mk 555-15N. Mk 555-15 with 10-lobe mixer.

Mk 555-15P. More fuel-efficient -15H with 10-lobe mixer. Entered service 1982.

The following data refer to the 555-15P:

DIMENSIONS:

Length	2,553 mm (100.5 in)
Diameter	940 mm (37.0 in)

WEIGHT, DRY:

	1,024 kg (2,257 lb)

PERFORMANCE RATINGS:

T-O: see model listings	
Cruise at 7,620 m (25,000 ft) at 440 knots (815 km/h; 507 mph)	16.59 kN (3,730 lb)

SPECIFIC FUEL CONSUMPTION:

T-O	15.9 mg/Ns (0.560 lb/h/lb st)
Cruise (as above)	22.7 mg/Ns (0.800 lb/h/lb)

ROLLS-ROYCE RB168 SPEY

The RB168 military versions of the Spey are as follow:

Mk 101. Basic engine, but with air offtake for BLC. Fitted to BAe Buccaneer.

Mk 202. Augmented engine for supersonic aircraft, with shaft/disc LP compressor and fully modulated afterburner. Fitted to Phantom FGR.2 (F-4M) and licensed to China. Phantom FG.1 (F-4K) has **Mk 203**.

Mk 250. Fully navalised. Fitted to BAe Nimrod MR.1, R.1 and MR.2.

Mk 807. Mk 101 rotors within RB183 structure, with BLC deleted and fitted with manual emergency fuel control. Produced under licence in Italy with Brazilian participation for AMX aircraft.

DIMENSIONS:

Length: Mk 101	2,911 mm (114.6 in)
Mk 202	5,204 mm (204.9 in)
Mk 250, 251	2,972 mm (117.0 in)
Mk 807	2,456 mm (96.7 in)
Diameter	825 mm (32.5 in)

WEIGHT, DRY:

Mk 101	1,121 kg (2,471 lb)
Mk 202	1,857 kg (4,093 lb)
Mk 250, 251	1,243 kg (2,740 lb)
Mk 807	1,083 kg (2,388 lb)

PERFORMANCE RATINGS (max T-O):

Mk 101, 807	49.1 kN (11,030 lb st)
Mk 202: dry	54.5 kN (12,250 lb st)
augmented	91.2 kN (20,515 lb st)
Mk 250, 251	53.3 kN (11,995 lb st)

ROLLS-ROYCE TAY

The Tay turbofan is designed around the core and external gearbox of the RB183 Mk 555. The LP system has been tailored to complement this by maintaining core inlet and outlet conditions similar to those of the original engine. The wide-chord fan and three-stage IP compressor are driven by a three-stage LP turbine which uses the latest proven technology. The cold bypass air and hot exhaust are

Rolls-Royce Spey Mk 807 turbofan for the Italian/Brazilian AMX combat aircraft

combined in a forced mixer. The bypass duct is carbonfibre composite.

The initial production versions are the **Tay 610** and **620**. The **Tay 650** gives a 9 per cent increase in maximum take-off thrust and a 15 per cent increase in maximum continuous, climb, and cruise thrusts, achieved by a small increase in fan diameter and an advanced HP turbine.

The Tay 610 and 620 engines received certification from the CAA in June 1986, with certification of the Tay 650 engine achieved ahead of schedule in June 1988. More than 630 Tays had been ordered in advance of the engine's entry into service in the Spring of 1987.

The Tay easily meets all current emission standards, and enable the Fokker 100, Gulfstream IV and re-engined BAe One-Eleven to comply with FAR Pt 36 stage 3 noise requirements. The engine is a strong contender for re-engining other 100-seat short-haul aircraft.

Tay 610-8. Selected for Gulfstream IV. Certificated on 26 June 1986. Now replaced by **Tay 611**.

Tay 620-15. Selected for Fokker 100. Entered service early 1988.

Tay 650-14. Selected to re-engine BAe One-Eleven.

Tay 650-15. Specified for heavier versions of Fokker 100.

Tay 670. Proposed version of 77.84 kN (17,500 lb st) to re-engine aircraft in 100-130 seat class.

TYPE: Two-shaft turbofan.

FAN: Single-stage with wide chord blades.

LP COMPRESSOR: New design with three stages on fan shaft.

HP COMPRESSOR: 12-stage axial (RB183 Mk 555).

COMBUSTION CHAMBER: Tubo-annular with 10 flame tubes, each with one duplex burner.

FUEL SYSTEM: As RB183 Mk 555 but with improved fuel control unit.

HP TURBINE: All Mks except 650, two stages as RB183 Mk 555. Mk 650, advanced two-stage design.

LP TURBINE: New design with three stages.

MIXER: Forced deep chute type with 12 lobes.

DIMENSIONS:
Length	2,405 mm (94.7 in)
Inlet diameter: Tay 610/620	1,118 mm (44.0 in)
Tay 650	1,138 mm (44.8 in)

PERFORMANCE RATING (T-O):
Tay 610-8	55.24 kN (12,420 lb st) to 37°C
Tay 611, 620-15	61.61 kN (13,850 lb st) to 30°C
Tay 650	67.17 kN (15,100 lb st) to 30°C

SPECIFIC FUEL CONSUMPTION (cruise):
Tay 610 (13,100 m; 43,000 ft, Mach 0.8)	
	20.1 mg/Ns (0.709 lb/h/lb)
Tay 620 and 650 (9,145 m; 30,000 ft, Mach 0.73)	
	19.5 mg/Ns (0.69 lb/h/lb)

ROLLS-ROYCE RB550

The RB550 is a projected new turboprop which incorporates the technology of the core of the Rolls-Royce Turbomeca RTM 322 turboshaft mated with reduction gear technology from the latest Rolls-Royce Dart engine. It will enable the company to exploit commercial opportunities in the 60/80-passenger aircraft market.

The RB550 would have greater mass flow than the RTM 322. By adopting an in-line configuration the engine has several advantages over turboprops which have a flexible chin intake duct, including much lighter and simpler mounting, improved airflow, simpler anti-icing and oil cooling, less external drag and reduced noise. For ease of maintenance the engine is intended to be assembled from seven modules.

ROLLS-ROYCE TYNE

The 4,549 ekW (6,100 ehp) Tyne two-shaft turboprop is being produced by a consortium comprising SNECMA and MTU (prime contractors carrying out assembly and test), Rolls-Royce and FN. The Mk 21 engine powers the Atlantique and the Mk 22 the Transall.

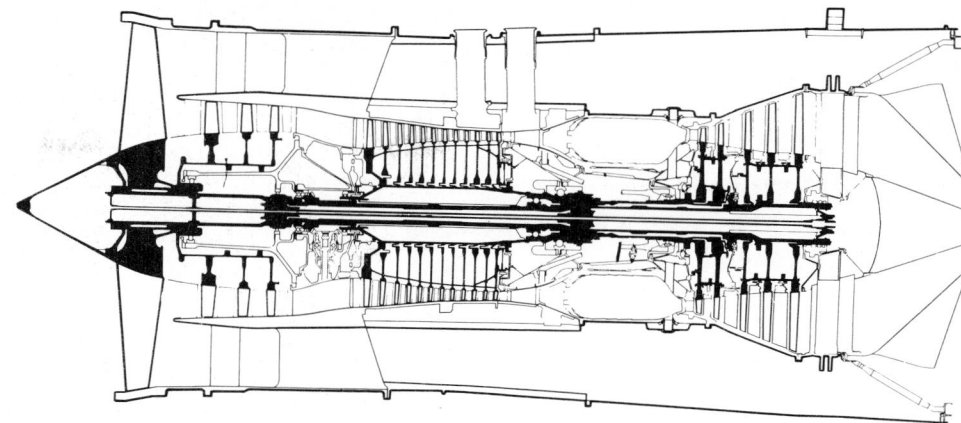

Cross-section of Rolls-Royce Tay turbofan

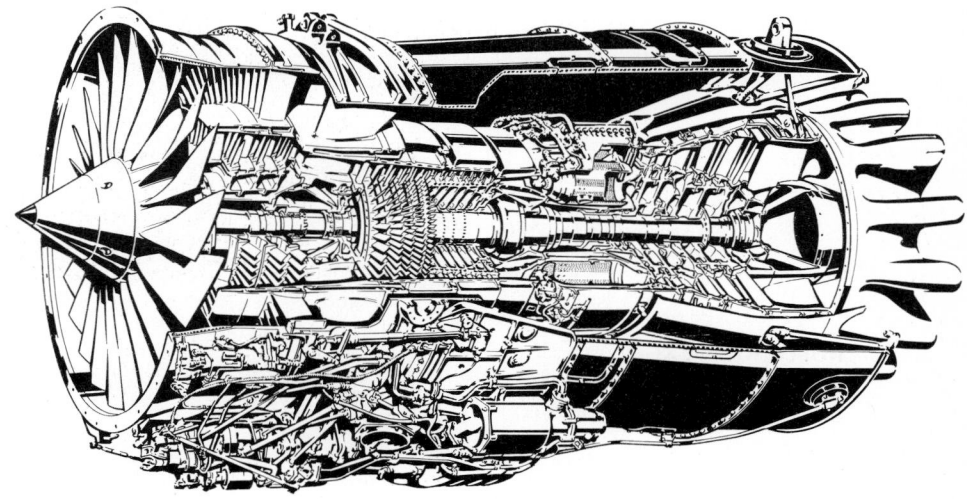

Cutaway drawing of the Rolls-Royce Tay turbofan

ROLLS-ROYCE RB545

Under this designation, project design studies are in hand at Bristol on the unique combined air-breathing and rocket propulsion system for the BAe HOTOL. During the first nine minutes of flight the engine will use oxygen from the atmosphere, thereafter switching to on-board liquid oxygen. Rig testing of critical components began early in 1986 at the company's facility at Ansty, Coventry, as part of a two-year proof of concept study.

ROLLS-ROYCE VIPER

This turbojet remains in production. More than 5,000 are in operation in 29 countries.

Current versions are as follows:

Viper 11 (Mk 200 Series). Single-shaft seven-stage axial compressor driven by single-stage turbine. Mass flow 20 kg (44 lb)/s. Type tested at 11.12 kN (2,500 lb st) and powers Jindivik Mk 3 drone, Jet Provost T.4 and 5, SOKO Galeb and HJT-16 Kiran Mk I/IA.

A Viper 11 version, the 22-1, was built under licence in Italy by Piaggio for the Aermacchi MB-326 and by Atlas of South Africa and HDHV of Australia.

Viper 500 Series. Development with zero stage on compressor. Major applications include early HS 125 (Mks 521, 522) and PD-808 executive aircraft (Mk 526) and Strikemaster (Mk 535), MB-326GB (Mk 540) and Jastreb

(Mk 531) training and light combat aircraft. Mk 540 built under licence by Piaggio and Atlas.

Viper 600 Series. Eight-stage compressor driven by two-stage turbine; annular vaporising combustion chamber. Take-off rating 16.7 kN (3,750 lb st) civil and 17.8 kN (4,000 lb st) military. Agreement signed with Fiat (Italy) in July 1969 for technical collaboration (see Fiat).

The civil Viper 601 powers the BAe 125-600; the military 632 is fitted to the G-4 Super Galeb, MB-326K and MB-339. The 632-41 powers the Orao/IAR-93A and IAR-99. The 632 is built under licence in Italy, Romania and Yugoslavia. The 633 has an afterburner of the two-gutter type, with hot streak ignition; rating 22.3 kN (5,000 lb).

The **Viper 680** is in production for the MB-339. It produces up to 15 per cent more thrust than the Viper 632.

The following details apply to the Viper 600 series:

TYPE: Single-shaft axial turbojet.

COMPRESSOR: Eight-stage. Steel drum type rotor with disc assemblies. Magnesium alloy casing with blow-off valve. Pressure ratio 5.8 : 1. Mass flow 26.5 kg (58.4 lb)/s.

COMBUSTION CHAMBER: Short annular type with 24 vaporising burners and six starting atomisers. Electric ignition.

FUEL SYSTEM: Hydromechanical, with pump, barometric control and air/fuel control.

FUEL GRADE: JP-1 or JP-4.

TURBINE: Two-stage axial. Shrouded blades attached to discs by fir tree roots and locking strips.

ACCESSORY DRIVES: Gearbox driven from front of compressor by bevel gear.

LUBRICATION SYSTEM: Self contained recirculatory system. Military version fully aerobatic.

OIL SPECIFICATION: Mobil Jet 2, Shell ASTO 500 and Castrol 98.

STARTING: 24V starter/generator.

DIMENSIONS:
Length (flange to flange):	
Viper 11	1,626 mm (64.0 in)
Viper 531, 535, 540, 632	1,806 mm (71.1 in)
Max casing diameter:	
all versions	622 mm (24.5 in)

WEIGHT, DRY:
Viper 11	284 kg (625 lb)
Viper 531	345 kg (760 lb)
Viper 535	331 kg (730 lb)
Viper 540	342 kg (755 lb)
Viper 601, 632 and 680	358 kg (790 lb)

PERFORMANCE RATINGS (T-O):
Viper 11	11.12 kN (2,500 lb st)
Viper 531	13.9 kN (3,120 lb st)
Viper 535, 540	14.9 kN (3,360 lb st)
Viper 601	16.7 kN (3,750 lb st)

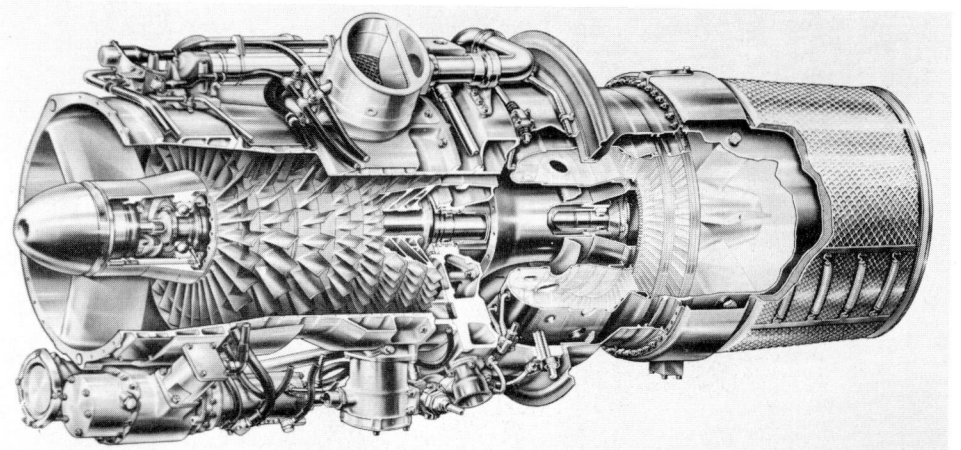

Cutaway drawing of the Rolls-Royce Viper 632 single-shaft turbojet (take-off rating 17.8 kN; 4,000 lb st)

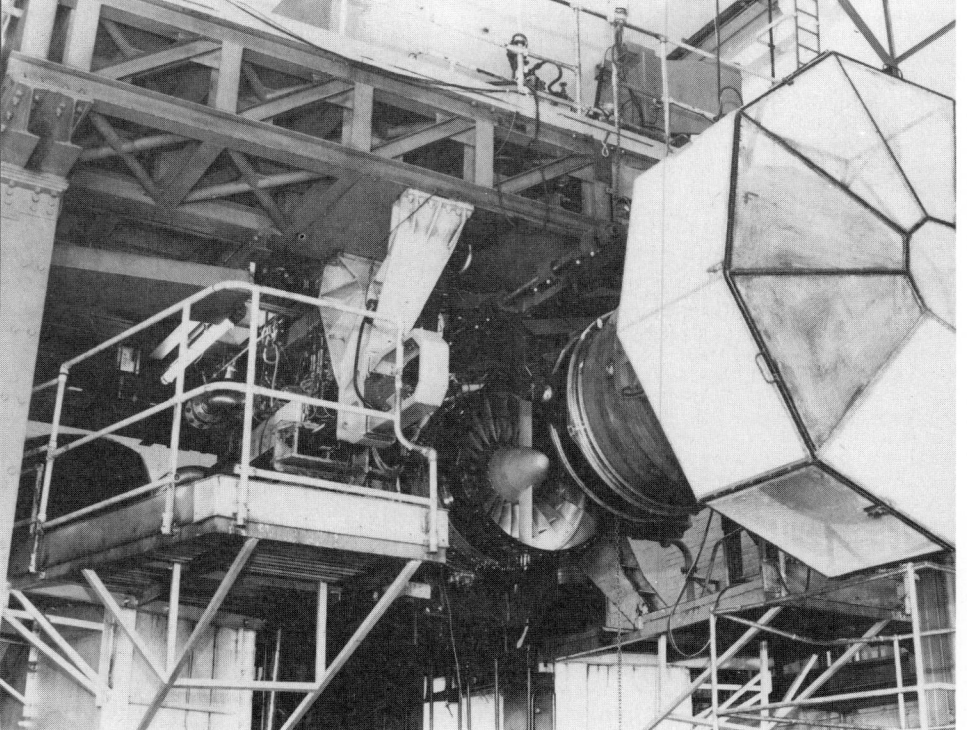

Longitudinal section drawing through the Rolls-Royce XG40 (90 kN; 20,234 lb st class)

Viper 632	17.8 kN (4,000 lb st)
Viper 680	19.8 kN (4,450 lb st)

SPECIFIC FUEL CONSUMPTION (T-O):

Viper 11	30.3 mg/Ns (1.07 lb/h/lb st)
Viper 500 series	28.3 mg/Ns (1.00 lb/h/lb st)
Viper 601	26.6 mg/Ns (0.94 lb/h/lb st)
Viper 632	27.5 mg/Ns (0.97 lb/h/lb st)

OIL CONSUMPTION (max):

all versions	0.71 litres (1.5 US pints; 1.25 Imp pints)/h

ROLLS-ROYCE XG40

XG40 is a technology programme which encompasses rig testing, core engine running and two demonstrator engines. Launched in 1983, the programme is centred at Bristol and funded jointly by the company and MoD. Its purpose is to demonstrate the technology required for an advanced fighter engine. It will provide a solid background for Rolls-Royce to contribute its share of the collaborative EUROJET EJ200 (which see in International section).

Each XG40 engine module was extensively tested in rig form, and in March 1986 the core engine first ran. The first complete demonstrator engine ran on 23 December 1986, and the second was to enter the programme in 1987.

ROLLS-ROYCE PEGASUS

The Pegasus is a turbofan for STOVL applications. It has two main rotating systems which rotate in opposite directions, thus minimising gyroscopic effects. Thrust vectoring is achieved by four rotatable nozzles simultaneously operated and symmetrically positioned on each side of the engine. The total thrust is divided between the four nozzles, and the resultant thrust passes through a fixed point irrespective of nozzle angle, thus minimising aircraft control problems. HP bleed air is used for aircraft stabilisation.

The Pegasus ran in August 1959. The engine entered service in the BAe Harrier in 1969 as the **Pegasus 11 Mk 103**, (US designation **F402-RR-402**), rated at 95.64 kN (21,500 lb st).

A maritime version of the Mk 103 is designated **Mk 104**. Developed for the Sea Harrier, it embodies material changes to the LP and intermediate casings, sacrificial protective coatings on ferrous components, and an increased capacity gearbox.

The **Pegasus 11-21** developed for the McDonnell Douglas/BAe Harrier II has the US designation **F402-RR-406** and UK designation **Mk 105**; it includes improved HP turbine cooling, a new shrouded LP turbine, revised swan-neck intermediate casing and changes to suit the revised airframe. Delivery of 96.75 kN (21,750 lb st) development batch Mk 105 engines began in December 1984. Since 1986 production engines for the AV-8B (designated **F402-RR-406A**) and Harrier GR.5 have been fitted with FADEC (full authority digital engine control), replacing the previous hydromechanical system.

To enhance the Harrier II's hot-day vertical landing capability, and to cater for future growth, an uprating programme began in 1983. This programme, designated **XG15**, is funded by the company and MoD. On 22 October 1986 the full-performance demonstrator engine first ran. It has the fan pressure ratio raised from 2.3 to 2.6, a new combustor and improved cooling with single-crystal turbine blades. The engine is running at thrust levels higher than those of the **Pegasus 11-61**, the version scheduled for production, which provides 15 per cent more thrust than the 11-21, together with improved reliability and maintainability, and lower life-cycle costs.

Work is continuing on thrust augmentation by plenum chamber burning (PCB). Testing has demonstrated a thrust increase at the front nozzles of over 100 per cent, equivalent to about 50 per cent overall. High altitude PCB tests have indicated that handling and ignition are compatible with

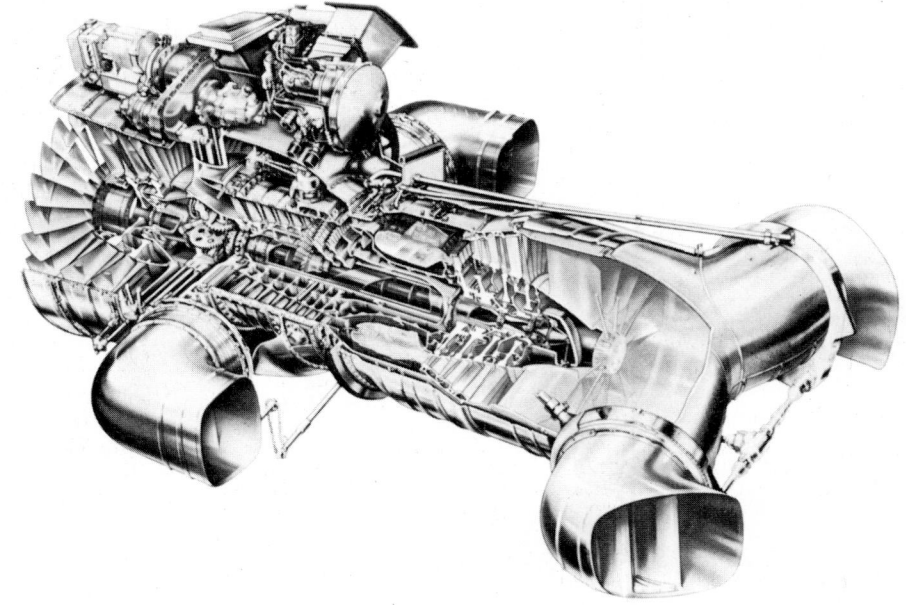

Rolls-Royce XG15 vectored thrust demonstrator

Cutaway drawing of the Rolls-Royce Pegasus 11-21 (F402-RR-406A, Mk 105) turbofan (96.75 kN; 21,750 lb st)

future supersonic V/STOL aircraft. A Pegasus 11 with PCB would have a thrust of 120 kN (27,000 lb st).

For future combat aircraft Rolls-Royce is studying vectored-thrust engines (with and without PCB) together with other advanced V/STOL systems such as a hybrid fan, remote augmented lift and ejector lift. The company is also studying lift fan engines for advanced transports and RPVs.

The following data apply specifically to the Pegasus 11-21 (-406A, Mk 105):

TYPE: Two-shaft vectored thrust turbofan.

FAN: Three-stage, overhung ahead of front bearing. Titanium blades with part-span snubbers. Mass flow 196 kg (432 lb)/s. Pressure ratio 2.3. Bypass ratio 1.4.

HP COMPRESSOR: Eight-stage with titanium rotor blades. Overall pressure ratio 14.

COMBUSTION SYSTEM: Annular, with LP vaporising burners.

FUEL SYSTEM: DSIC duplicated digital electronic control with emergency manual backup.

TURBINES: Two-stage HP with cooled blades and two-stage LP.

THRUST NOZZLES: Two steel zero-scarf cold nozzles and two Nimonic hot nozzles, actuated by duplicated air motors through shafts and chains under pilot command.

LUBRICATION SYSTEM: Self contained, with fuel cooled oil cooler.

STARTING: Gas turbine starter/APU on intermediate casing.

DIMENSIONS:

Length, without nozzles	2,510 mm (98.83 in)
Length, with nozzles	3,485 mm (137.2 in)
Diameter, fan casing	1,220 mm (48.05 in)

WEIGHT, DRY (without nozzles):

Mk 103	1,412 kg (3,113 lb)
Mk 104	1,442 kg (3,179 lb)
Mk 105	1,470 kg (3,240 lb)

PERFORMANCE RATINGS:
See under subtype descriptions

ROLLS-ROYCE TURBOMECA RTM 322
See the International part of this section.

MTU-TURBOMECA RR-MTR 390
See the International part of this section.

ROLLS-ROYCE GEM
The Gem was developed at Leavesden, for the Westland Lynx helicopter. Subsequent applications are the Westland 30, Westland Lynx 3 and Agusta A 129. The Gem 41 and 60 have been civil certificated.

Choice of a two-spool gas generator gives fast response to power demand without the need for a complex control system. There are seven major modules, each assembled, tested and released as an interchangeable unit.

Provision is made for in-flight and on-ground condition monitoring systems. Features include access ports for intrascope inspection of each LP compressor stage, HP compressor, combustor, LP turbine and power turbine, and mountings for vibration pickups.

The following versions have been announced:

Gem Mk 1001. Engine change unit for Lynx of British services and French Navy. Rated at 671 kW (900 shp).

Gem 2. Export military, rated at 671 kW (900 shp).

RR 1004. For Agusta A 129. Direct drive in place of reduction gearbox and electronic instead of hydromechanical control. Production under licence by Piaggio.

Gem 41 series. Modified compressor to increase mass flow by about 10 per cent plus small increase in TET. In production for Lynx and Westland 30.

Gem Mk 1020. Engine change unit of Gem 41 for uprated Lynx of British and French Navies.

Gem 42 series. Same ratings as Gem 41, but improved reliability and power retention.

Gem Mk 510. Civil Gem 41 for Westland 30.

Gem 60 series. Further increase in mass flow of approximately 26 per cent over Gem 41, derived from LP compressor incorporating new blades; TET also increased.

Gem Mk 531. Civil Gem 60 for Westland 30.

The following description relates to the Gem Mk 1001:

TYPE: Free turbine turboshaft.

SHAFT DRIVE: Single-stage double-helical reduction gear with rotating planet cage carried by ball bearing at front and roller bearing at rear. Alternative of direct drive output at 27,000 rpm or gearbox giving governed output speed of 6,000 rpm.

LP COMPRESSOR: Four-stage axial.

Cutaway drawing of the Rolls-Royce Gem 60 free turbine turboshaft

HP COMPRESSOR: Single-stage centrifugal, alternate inducer and radial vanes. Overall pressure ratio 12.0.

COMBUSTION CHAMBER: Annular reverse flow with air atomiser fuel sprays. High energy ignition.

HP TURBINE: Single-stage close-coupled to HP impeller.

LP TURBINE: Single-stage with shrouded blades.

POWER TURBINE: Two-stage axial with shrouded blades.

ACCESSORY DRIVES: Bevel gear on front of HP shaft drives starter/generator, fuel pump, oil cooler fan and other accessories.

FUEL SYSTEM: Plessey fluidics automatic control, and power matching for multi-engine installation. Hamilton Standard electronic control fitted to RR 1004 and Gem 60.

LUBRICATION SYSTEM: Engine mounted oil tank and cooler. Magnetic chip detectors. Oil filter in accessory wheelcase.

DIMENSIONS:

Length overall	1,099 mm (43.2 in)
Width overall	575 mm (22.6 in)
Height overall	596 mm (23.5 in)

WEIGHT, DRY:

Gem 1001, 2	150 kg (330 lb)
Gem 41, 42	156 kg (343 lb)
RR 1004	140 kg (309 lb)
Gem 60	155 kg (342 lb)

PERFORMANCE RATINGS: see table

SPECIFIC FUEL CONSUMPTION:
50 per cent max T-O:

Except Gem 60	110 µg/J (0.65 lb/h/shp)
Gem 60	103 µg/J (0.61 lb/h/shp)

ROLLS-ROYCE GNOME
Gnome is the name given to the General Electric T58 turboshaft which Rolls-Royce manufactures. More than 2,300 have been delivered in the following versions:

H.1000. Initial version, rated at 783 kW (1,050 shp) for Whirlwind and Agusta-Bell 204B.

H.1200. Rated at 932 kW (1,250 shp). Used in Agusta-Bell 204B, Boeing 107 and some Kawasaki KV107-II-5s. Coupled version for Wessex comprises two H.1200s driving through a coupling gearbox.

H.1400. Rated at 1,044 kW (1,400 shp). Based on the H.1200, with modified compressor to increase airflow.

H.1400-1. Rated at 1,145 kW (1,535 shp). Increased gas generator speed and improved gas generator turbine blades. In production for Sea King and Commando.

H.1400-1T. Tropical model; turbine nozzle adjusted for better high ambient performance.

The following description refers to the H.1400-1:

TYPE: Free turbine turboshaft.

COMPRESSOR: Ten-stage axial. Variable inlet guide vanes and first three stator rows. Mass flow 6.26 kg (13.8 lb)/s.

COMBUSTION CHAMBER: Annular with 16 Simplex injectors, eight on each of two sets of manifolds. One Lodge high energy igniter.

FUEL SYSTEM: Lucas hydromechanical controlled by BAeD computer.

FUEL GRADE: DERD.2452, 2453, 2454, 2486, 2494 and 2498 (NATO F44, F34, F40, F35 and F43).

GAS-PRODUCER TURBINE: Two-stage.

POWER TURBINE: Single-stage free turbine.

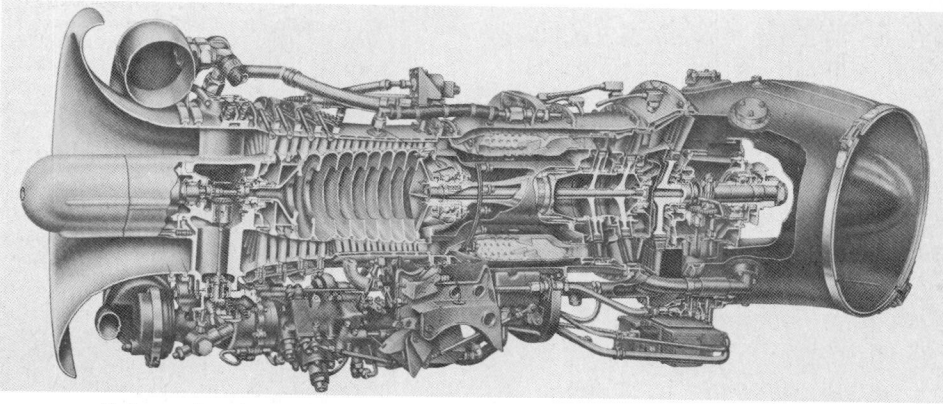

Cutaway drawing of the Rolls-Royce Gnome H. 1400-1 free turbine turboshaft

GEM ENGINE RATINGS, kW (shp) ISA S/L STATIC

| Designation | Date In Service | Emergency (20 s) | One Engine Inoperative | | | Normal Twin Operation | | |
			Max Contingency (2½ min)	Intermediate Contingency (60 min)	Max (T-O) (30 min)	Max (T-O) (5 min)	Max Continuous
Gem 2, Mk 1001	1976	N/A	671 (900)	619 (830)	N/A	619 (830)	559 (750)
RR 1004	1988	772 (1,035)	710 (952)	667.5 (895)	667.5 (895)	N/A	608 (815)
Gem 41-1, Mk 1014	1978	N/A	835 (1,120)	790.5 (1,060)	N/A	746 (1,000)	664 (890)
Gem 42, Mk 1017	1987	N/A	835 (1,120)	790.5 (1,060)	N/A	746 (1,000)	664 (890)
Gem 60-3/1 Mk 530	1983	N/A	897 (1,203)	844 (1,132)	N/A	844 (1,132)	821.75 (1,102)
Gem 60-3/3 Mk 531	1983	N/A	897 (1,203)	844 (1,132)	N/A	821.75(1,102)	821.75 (1,102)

N/A: Not applicable

REDUCTION GEAR: Optional double helical gear providing reduction from nominal 19,500 rpm power turbine speed to 6,600 rpm at left or right output shaft.

ACCESSORY DRIVES: Fuel and lubrication systems mounted beneath compressor casing. Power take-off shaft up to 100 shp.

LUBRICATION: Scavenged gear pumps. Serck oil cooler.

STARTING: Rotax electric starter in nose bullet.

DIMENSIONS:

Length: H.1400-1   1,392 mm (54.8 in)

Max height: H.1400-1	549 mm (21.6 in)
Max width: H.1400-1 (ungeared)	577 mm (22.7 in)

WEIGHT, DRY:

H.1400-1 (ungeared)	148 kg (326 lb)
Reduction gearbox	52.6 kg (116 lb)

PERFORMANCE RATINGS (at power turbine shaft):

Max contingency (2½ min; multi-engine aircraft only):

H.1400-1	1,238 kW (1,660 shp)
H.1400-1T	1,092 kW (1,465 shp) to 45°C

Max one-hour (single engine):

H.1400-1	1,145 kW (1,535 shp)
H.1400-1T	1,030 kW (1,380 shp) to 45°C

Max continuous:

H.1400-1	932 kW (1,250 shp)
H.1400-1T	783 kW (1,050 shp) to 45°C

SPECIFIC FUEL CONSUMPTION:

At max contingency rating:

H.1400-1	102.75 µg/J (0.608 lb/h/shp)
H.1400-1T (30°C)	105.8 µg/J (0.626 lb/h/shp)

UNITED STATES OF AMERICA

AEROJET

AEROJET-GENERAL CORPORATION
(Subsidiary of GenCorp Inc)

10300 N Torrey Pines Road, La Jolla, California 92037

Telephone: (619) 455 8500

PRESIDENT: G. W. Leisz

VICE-PRESIDENT, PUBLIC AFFAIRS: Tom Sprague

Aerojet is a major aerospace and defence contractor with expertise in solid and liquid rocket propulsion, electronics and ordnance.

AEROJET SOLID PROPULSION CO

Development and production of motors for Peacekeeper, Minuteman, Improved Hawk, Sparrow, Sky Flash, Standard Missile, Sidewinder, Shrike, Improved Shrike and Skipper, and booster for Harpoon. In development, motors for AMRAAM and SRAM II. Data for many spacecraft motors and other rocket products were given in the 1981-82 *Jane's*.

AEROJET TECHSYSTEMS CO

Sacramento, California: Development and manufacture of all liquid fuel engines for the US Air Force's Titan family of vehicles; second stage propulsion for the Japanese Space Agency (NASDA) N-II launch vehicles; and Orbiter Manoeuvring System (OMS) engines for the Space Shuttle.

AEROJET SPACE SHUTTLE OMS ENGINE

The Space Shuttle Orbiter has two Orbiter Manoeuvring System (OMS) engines, in pods each side of the vertical stabiliser (fin). They provide thrust for orbit insertion, circularisation and plane change, rendezvous and de-orbit manoeuvres. The propellants are monomethylhydrazine (MMH) and nitrogen tetroxide. At launch the basic system carries 4,087 kg (9,010 lb) of usable MMH and 6,743 kg (14,866 lb) of usable oxidiser. Fully qualified OMS engines have flown on all Shuttle missions to date. The following are chief characteristics:

THRUST (in vacuo):	26.7 kN (6,000 lb)
CHAMBER PRESSURE (in vacuo):	8.62 bars (125 lb/sq in)
SPECIFIC IMPULSE:	316 s
MIXTURE RATIO:	1.65 : 1
NOZZLE AREA RATIO (flight):	55 : 1
WEIGHT, DRY:	118 kg (260 lb)
THRUST VECTOR LIMITS:	±7°
STORAGE LIFE:	10 years
FIRING LIFE (100 missions):	15 h
NUMBER OF STARTS:	500
LONGEST SINGLE FIRING:	1,250 s

Aerojet Space Shuttle OMS engine

ALLISON

ALLISON GAS TURBINE DIVISION, GENERAL MOTORS CORPORATION

Indianapolis, Indiana 46206-0420

Telephone: (317) 230 5000

GENERAL MANAGER: Dr F. Blake Wallace

Allison Gas Turbine Division has 7,500 employees producing gas turbine engines and components for aircraft, vehicular and industrial/marine applications.

Collaboration on the T800 engine with Garrett is described under LHTEC on a later page. Collaboration with MTU is reported under the International heading.

ALLISON MODEL 250
US military designations: T63 and T703

The Model 250 is a small turboshaft/turboprop. Deliveries exceed 21,000.

A development contract for the T63 military version was received by Allison in June 1958. Details of early versions last appeared in the 1978-79 *Jane's*; the following are current models:

T63-A-720. Military engine with hot-end improvements, increasing T-O rating to 313 kW (420 shp), for the Bell OH-58C.

T703-A-700. Military engine corresponding to 250-C30R, for Bell OH-58D.

250-B17. Uprated version of B15 turboprop. The **B17B** operates at 17°C higher turbine gas temperature with hot-end improvements which maintain full power at high ambient temperatures. Produced from 1974 for Turbostar 402 conversions, Turbostar 414, ASTA Nomad N22 and 24, SIAI-Marchetti SM.1019E and various agricultural aircraft. **B17C** introduced improved gearbox allowing use of 313 kW (420 shp) on T-O. Produced for Nomad N22 and 24, SIAI-Marchetti SF.260TP and 600TP, Turbostar 402, Pilatus Britten-Norman BN-2T Turbine Islander, Windecker Eagle and Partenavia Viator. **B17F**, with new compressor as in -C20R for increased T-O power, introduced in 1985.

250-C20B. Introduced 1974, and rated at 313 kW (420 shp). For Bell and Agusta-Bell 206B JetRanger and 206L LongRanger, MBB BO 105 C, Agusta A 109A and A 109A Mk II, MD 500D and E, PZL Kania, Hiller Aviation FH-1100 and UH-12E conversion, Soloy C20B turboprop and Bell 47G conversions.

250-C20F. For AS 355 Ecureuil 2/Twinstar.

250-C20J. For Bell and Agusta-Bell 206B JetRanger III.

250-C20R. Derivative of C20B with new axial-centrifugal compressor. **C20R/1** with redundant overspeed system for twin-engine applications certificated September 1986. **C20R/2** for single-engine helicopters certificated early 1987.

250-C20S. For Soloy Turbine Pac conversions of Cessna 185, 206 and 207.

250-C28. Major redesign with single centrifugal compressor only, with increased airflow. Reduced noise and emissions, and minimal infra-red signature. New main gearbox. Certificated December 1977.

250-C28B. With particle separator; 2½-min rating of 410 kW (550 shp). Powers Bell LongRanger I.

250-C28C. Improved model with plain inlet; 2½-min rating of 410 kW (550 shp). Powers MBB BO 105 LS.

250-C30. Advanced single-stage compressor and dual ignition. Initial rating 485 kW (650 shp), with a 2½ min rating of 522 kW (700 shp). Certification completed March 1978. C30L, M, P (Bell LongRanger III), R and S (Sikorsky

The 313 kW (420 shp) Allison Model 250-B17C turboprop engine

The 335 kW (450 shp) Allison Model 250-C20R turboshaft engine

S-76 Mk II) variants are detailed in the descriptive text.
C30R, with digital control, powers AHIP Bell OH-58D.

250-C34. C30 with single-stage gas generator turbine allowing increased gas temperatures for higher T-O power. Certification due 1989.

TYPE: Light turboshaft or turboprop.

COMPRESSOR: C20, C20B and B17B have six axial stages and one centrifugal. B17F and C20R have four axial stages and one centrifugal. Other models have single-stage centrifugal compressor only. Pressure ratio: C20, 7.0; C20B, B17, 7.2: C28B/C, C30, C34, 8.4. Air mass flow: C20, 1.5 kg (3.4 lb)/s; C20B, B17C, 1.56 kg (3.45 lb)/s; C28B/C, 2.02 kg (4.45 lb)/s; C30, C34, 2.54 kg (5.6 lb)/s.

COMBUSTION CHAMBER: Single can type at rear. Single duplex fuel nozzle in rear face. One igniter on C20, C20B, B17C, C28B/C and C30L/M/P/R. Dual igniters on C30, C30S and C34; optional on C28B/C.

TURBINES: Two-stage (C34, new single-stage) gas producer turbine and two-stage free power turbine. Integrally cast rotor blades and wheels.

CONTROL SYSTEM: Pneumatic-mechanical system (B17C, hydromechanical; C20B, C28, C30/30M/P/S, pneumatic-mechanical; C30L, C30R, C34, supervisory electronic).

FUEL: Primary fuels are ASTM-A or A-1 (Model 250-C20, ASTM D-1655) and MIL-T-5624, JP-4, JP-5 and diesel fuel.

LUBRICATION: Dry sump.

OIL SPECIFICATION: MIL-L-7808 and MIL-L-23699.

DIMENSIONS:

Length: B17C	1,143 mm (45.0 in)
C20B, R	985 mm (38.8 in)
C28C	1,201 mm (47.3 in)
C30	1,041 mm (41.0 in)
C34	1,097 mm (43.3 in)
Width: B17C, C20B	483 mm (19.0 in)
C28, C30, C34	557 mm (21.94 in)
Height: B17C	572 mm (22.5 in)
C20B	589 mm (23.2 in)
C28, C30, C34	638 mm (25.13 in)

WEIGHT, DRY:

B17C	88.4 kg (195 lb)
C20B	71.5 kg (158 lb)
C20R	76.0 kg (168 lb)
C28	99.3 kg (219 lb)
C28B, C	104 kg (230 lb)
C30	109.3 kg (240 lb)
C34	118.9 kg (262 lb)

PERFORMANCE RATINGS (S/L, ISA):

T-O: B17C, C20B (5 min), C20J, C20S	313 kW (420 shp)
B17F, C20R (5 min, to 26.7°C)	335 kW (450 shp)
C20F	317 kW (425 shp)
C28, 28B, 28C (30 min)	373 kW (500 shp)
C30 (2½ min)	522 kW (700 shp) to 32.2°C
C34	548 kW (735 shp)
Max continuous: B17C (cruise)	275 kW (369 shp)
C20B	298 kW (400 shp)
C20R	283 kW (380 shp)
C28	373 kW (500 shp)
C30	485 kW (650 shp)
C34	469 kW (629 shp)
Cruise B (75 per cent): B17C	206 kW (277 shp)
C20B	207 kW (278 shp)
C20R	236 kW (317 shp)
C28	274 kW (367 shp)
C30	312 kW (418 shp)
C34	352 kW (472 shp)

SPECIFIC FUEL CONSUMPTION:

At T-O rating: B17C	111 µg/J (0.657 lb/h/shp)
C20B	110 µg/J (0.650 lb/h/shp)
C20R	103 µg/J (0.608 lb/h/shp)
C28	102.5 µg/J (0.606 lb/h/shp)
C30	100 µg/J (0.592 lb/h/shp)
C34	100.7 µg/J (0.596 lb/h/shp)
At cruise B rating: B17C	120.8 µg/J (0.715 lb/h/shp)
C20B	120 µg/J (0.709 lb/h/shp)
C20R	112.5 µg/J (0.666 lb/h/shp)
C28	112 µg/J (0.664 lb/h/shp)
C30, C34	111 µg/J (0.657 lb/h/shp)

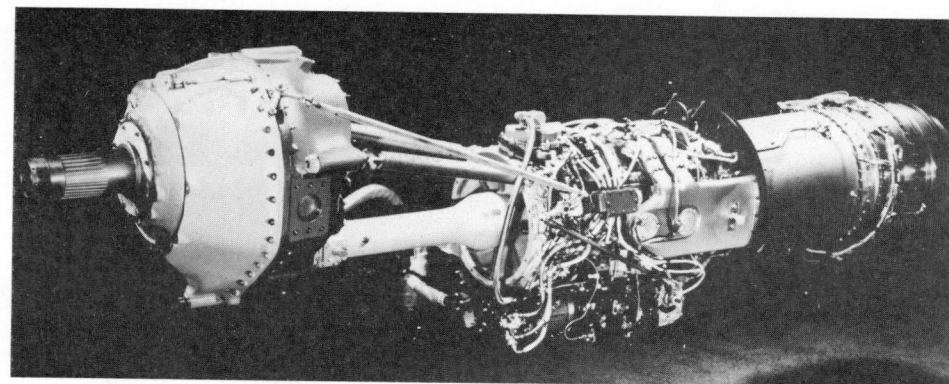

The 3,915 kW (5,250 shp) Allison T56-A-427 turboprop engine which powers late versions of the Grumman E-2C Hawkeye

Allison T406-AD-400 free turbine engine for the V-22 Osprey

ALLISON MODEL 225

The Model 225 is a derivative of the Model 250, available as the 225-B10 turboprop (derived from the 250-B17C) and the 225-C10 turboshaft (derived from the 250-C20B).

The objective of the programme is to provide worldwide a low-cost multifuel tolerant engine for general aviation. Parts are predominantly sourced in Asia. Initial assembly, test and distribution will be in North America. Allison plans later to transition to Asian assembly, test and distribution.

BASIC DESCRIPTION: As for Model 250. Compressor pressure ratio 7.2. Mass flow (B10) 1.62 kg (3.57 lb)/s, (C10) 1.59 kg (3.51 lb)/s.

DIMENSIONS:

Length: B10	1,143 mm (45.0 in)
C10	985 mm (38.8 in)
Width; B10, C10	483 mm (19.0 in)
Height: B10	572 mm (22.5 in)
C10	589 mm (23.2 in)

WEIGHT, DRY:

B10	90.7 kg (200 lb)
C10	73.9 kg (163 lb)

PERFORMANCE RATINGS (both, S/L, ISA):

T-O (5 min) and max continuous	261 kW (350 shp)
Normal cruise	212.5 kW (285 shp)

ALLISON T56 and MODEL 501

US Military designation: T56 and T406

Current versions of the T56 are as follows:

T56-A-14. Rated at 3,661 ekW (4,910 ehp). Generally similar to T56-A-15, but seven-point suspension and detail changes. Powers the P-3B and C Orion.

T56-A-15. Rated at 3,661 ekW (4,910 ehp). Introduced aircooled turbine blades. Powers current C-130.

T56-A-423 and **A-16.** Rated at 3,661 ekW (4,910 ehp). Powers US Navy versions of the C-130.

T56-A-425. Rated at 3,661 ekW (4,910 ehp). Powers E-2C Hawkeye and C-2A Greyhound.

T56-A-427. Rated at 3,915 kW (5,250 shp), this engine provides increase in power and 13 per cent improvement in specific fuel consumption compared with the T56-A-425. It features a digital electronic supervisory control and a modified propeller drive to maintain the 1,106 rpm output with 14,239 power section rpm.

Model 501-D22A. Rated at 3,490 ekW (4,680 ehp). Commercial version of T56-A-15. Powers Lockheed L-100.

Model 501-D39. Commercial derivative of T56-A-427 with modified propeller drive to provide 1,020 rpm output with 14,239 power section rpm.

Model 501-M78. Turboprop version of YT701 incorporating modified T56-A-14 gearbox for NASA-sponsored propfan flight testing at Mach numbers to 0.8. One M78, driving a single-rotation tractor propfan, is mounted on the port wing of a Gulfstream II.

T406-AD-400 (company designation 501-M80). Free turbine front drive 4,476 kW (6,000 shp) class engine, incorporating aerodynamic features of T56-A-427 and free-turbine arrangement of T701. Six rows of variable stators, full authority digital electronic control and oil system capable of operation in vertical attitude. For JVX (V-22 Osprey). Full qualification scheduled for September 1990. Second source, Pratt & Whitney, will receive about 45 per cent of the first four production lots of 629 engines.

T406-PF. As yet undesignated, a propfan based on the core of the Allison 501-M80 will be developed jointly with MTU of West Germany, an MoU being signed on 6 May 1988. It will power the MBB/CATIC MPC 75 (see Aircraft section, International).

Including the Model 501 commercial engines, production of these engines reached 14,830 by 1 January 1986.

The following details apply to the T56-A-15:

TYPE: Axial-flow turboprop.

Allison 501-M78 for PTA (Propfan Test Assessment) programme

PROPELLER DRIVE: Combination spur/planetary gear type. Overall gear ratio 13.54. Power section rpm 13,820. Weight of gearbox approximately 249 kg (550 lb) with pads on rear face for accessory mounting.
COMPRESSOR: Fourteen-stage axial flow. Pressure ratio 9.5. Air mass flow 14.70 kg (32.4 lb)/s. Constant speed 13,820 rpm.
COMBUSTION CHAMBER: Six stainless steel cannular type perforated combustion liners within one-piece stainless steel outer casing. Two ignitors in diametrically opposite combustors.
FUEL SYSTEM: High pressure type. Bendix control system. Water/alcohol augmentation system available.
FUEL GRADE: MIL-J-5624, JP-4 or JP-5.
TURBINE: Four-stage. Rotor assembly consists of four stainless steel discs, with first stage having hollow aircooled blades, secured by fir tree roots. Gas temperature before turbine 1,076°C.
ACCESSORY DRIVES: Accessory pads on rear face of reduction gear housing at front end of engine.
LUBRICATION SYSTEM: Low pressure. Dry sump. Pesco dual-element oil pump. Normal oil supply pressure 3.8 bars (55 lb/sq in).
OIL SPECIFICATION: MIL-L-7808.
MOUNTING: Three-point suspension.
STARTING: Air turbine, gearbox mounted.
DIMENSIONS:

Length (all current versions)	3,708 mm (146 in)
Width (all current versions)	686 mm (27 in)
Height: A-15, A-16, A-425, D-22A	991 mm (39 in)
A-14	1,118 mm (44 in)

WEIGHT, DRY: A-14 ... 855 kg (1,885 lb)

A-15	828 kg (1,825 lb)
A-16	835 kg (1,841 lb)
A-425	860 kg (1,895 lb)
D22A	832 kg (1,834 lb)

PERFORMANCE RATINGS (S/L, ISA, static):
T-O: A-14, A-15, A-16, A-425
    3,661 ekW; 3,424 kW (4,910 ehp; 4,591 shp)
501-D22A   3,490 ekW (4,680 ehp)
Normal: A-14, A-15, A-16, A-425, D22A
    3,255 ekW; 3,028 kW (4,365 ehp; 4,061 shp)
SPECIFIC FUEL CONSUMPTION:
At max rating:
A-14, A-15, D22A   84.67 μg/J (0.501 lb/h/ehp)
At normal rating:
A-14, A-15   87.4 μg/J (0.517 lb/h/ehp)
OIL CONSUMPTION:
A-14, A-15
    1.3 litres (0.35 US gallons; 0.29 Imp gallons)/h

ALLISON 501-M62
US military designation: T701-AD-700
Developed from the T56, the T701 is a free turbine turboshaft of modular construction and handling substantially greater airflow. It has served as the basis for the T406 engine for the JVX (V-22 Osprey).

The 6,025 kW (8,079 shp) Allison XT701-AD-700 turboshaft engine

TYPE: Free-turbine turboshaft.
COMPRESSOR: Thirteen-stage axial, with variable inlet guide vanes and first five stator rows. Longitudinally jointed casing incorporates large bleed manifold for 10th stage air. Pressure ratio 12.8. Mass flow 20.1 kg (44.3 lb)/s.
COMBUSTION CHAMBER: Annular, with 16 burners disposed around inner wall of flame tube fed with primary air through narrow annular gap at upstream end of snout section. Smoke-free combustion.
FUEL GRADE: MIL-T-5624 grades JP-4, JP-5.
TURBINE: Gas-generator turbine has two axial stages with aircooled blades, both stages cantilevered behind rear roller bearing. Power turbine also has two axial stages.
OUTPUT: Power turbine forward shaft is splined to central driveshaft, incorporating torque sensing assembly. Rated speed 11,500 rpm.
ACCESSORY DRIVES: Main accessory gearcase beneath air intake. Drives on front for starter/generator and tachometer, and at rear face for fuel pump and control.
LUBRICATION SYSTEM: Self-contained integral oil system with external tank on left side of compressor casing.
OIL SPECIFICATION: MIL-L-23699, MIL-L-7808.
DIMENSIONS:
Length (intake face to jetpipe exit)
    1,633 mm (64.3 in)

Length overall	1,880 mm (74.0 in)
Intake diameter	516 mm (20.3 in)
Jetpipe diameter	714 mm (28.1 in)
Width	767 mm (30.2 in)
Height	935 mm (36.8 in)

WEIGHT, DRY: ... 534 kg (1,179 lb)
PERFORMANCE RATINGS (ISA, S/L, static at gas generator speed of 15,049 rpm):

Intermediate (30 min)	6,025 kW (8,079 shp)
Max continuous	5,447 kW (7,305 shp)
75%	4,085 kW (5,478 shp)
50%	2,720 kW (3,648 shp)
25%	1,362 kW (1,827 shp)

SPECIFIC FUEL CONSUMPTION (conditions as above):

Intermediate	79.6 μg/J (0.471 lb/h/ehp)
Max continuous	78.1 μg/J (0.462 lb/h/ehp)
75%	79.1 μg/J (0.468 lb/h/ehp)
50%	85.5 μg/J (0.506 lb/h/ehp)
25%	107.7 μg/J (0.637 lb/h/ehp)

ALLISON MODEL 578
This is described later under the entry for PW-Allison Engines.

ALTURDYNE
ALTURDYNE
8050 Armour Street, San Diego, California 92111
Telephone: (619) 565 2131
Telex: (910) 335-2000
Fax: (619) 279 4296
PRESIDENT: Frank Verbeke

This company has developed small gas turbines for RPVs and very light aircraft. It was formed in 1970 and employs 100 people.
At present it purchases the basic gas generator and incorporates this into a complete engine for various purposes. The two main products are of 112 kW (150 hp) and 157 kW (210 hp). These are based upon the Solar T62 Titan single-shaft gas turbine (last described in the 1975-76

Jane's). A company funded lightweight rotary combustion aircraft engine is under development in two sizes up to 186.5 kW (250 hp). The first engines were tested in December 1984 and were exhibited at the EAA Oshkosh meet in 1985. Tests in 1986 were conducted with a reduction gearbox. A diesel unit is now being developed.

AMI
AEROMOTION INC
This company has produced a light two-cylinder opposed piston engine tailored to light aircraft. It uses some off the shelf automotive parts. The first AeroMotion Twin ran in April 1982 and has shown high reliability since then. Pre-production engines flew in a Heath Parasol in March 1984 and in a Ken Brock autogyro a month later.

AEROMOTION TWIN
TYPE: Two-cylinder opposed four-stroke aircooled piston engine.

CYLINDERS: Bore 104.8 mm (4.125 in). Stroke 95.25 mm (3.75 in). Capacity 1,650 cc (100 cu in).
IGNITION: Twin Slick magnetos, dual plugs.
DIMENSIONS:

Length	451 mm (17.75 in)
Width	787 mm (31.0 in)
Height	470 mm (18.5 in)

WEIGHT, DRY (equipped): ... 45 kg (100 lb)
PERFORMANCE RATING (S/L):
    37-39.5 kW (50-53 hp) at 3,100 rpm

AeroMotion Twin piston engine

CFE
CFE COMPANY
111 S 34th St, PO Box 5217, Phoenix, Arizona 85010
Telephone: (602) 231 2029
This company was formed jointly by Garrett Turbine Engine Co and General Electric in June 1987. It is managing all phases of the development, manufacture and marketing of the CFE738 turbofan.

CFE738
This turbofan is being developed to power large business jet aircraft required to fly 3,000 nm (5,560 km; 3,456 miles)

at Mach 0.8 against any headwind. GE and Garrett estimate about 2,000 such aircraft will be produced in 1991-2010. The CFE738 is being designed to the latest airline standard technology, with modular construction for 'on wing' maintenance. Its core is essentially that of the GE27, developed under the US Army's MTDE (Modern Technology Demonstrator Engine) programme since 1983. This core is designed to have an initial time between overhauls of 5,000 hours. Cores will be shipped to Garrett complete with the engine control system. Garrett is responsible for the new fan and LP turbine, and for engine assembly and test. Complete engine testing for certification

programmes will be shared equally by the two partners. Deliveries of the first version, CFE738-1, are due in 1991 after 6,000 hours of testing.
The following data relate to the CFE738-1. Growth versions are planned with thrust ratings exceeding 31.1 kN (7,000 lb).
TYPE: Two-shaft subsonic turbofan.
FAN: Single stage with 30 inserted titanium blades with part-span snubbers and rotating pointed spinner. Front end of LP shaft held in large-capacity ball bearing. Fan airflow 109 kg (240 lb)/s. Pressure ratio 1.7. Bypass ratio 5.3.

HP COMPRESSOR: Five axial stages followed by one centrifugal. First three stator stages variable. Overall pressure ratio 30.

COMBUSTION CHAMBER: Centrifugal diffuser leads into annular chamber with 16 burners.

HP TURBINE: Two stages with cooled blades.

LP TURBINE: Three stages.

JETPIPE: Fixed mixer assembly with 14 chutes for combining the hot and cold flows from core and bypass duct. Provision for reverser.

DIMENSIONS:

Overall diameter	889 mm (35 in)
Length	1,552 mm (61 in)

WEIGHT, DRY: 490 kg (1,080 lb)

PERFORMANCE RATINGS (ISA, ideal installation):

S/L, T-O	24.87 kN (5,600 lb st)
Cruise, 12,190 m (40,000 ft), Mach 0.8	
	5.79 kN (1,300 lb)

SPECIFIC FUEL CONSUMPTION:

S/L, T-O	10.54 mg/Ns (0.372 lb/h/lb st)
Cruise (as above)	18.27 mg/Ns (0.645 lb/h/lb)

The CFE738 turbofan for large business aircraft, under joint development by Garrett and General Electric (*Brian M. Service*)

CSD

CHEMICAL SYSTEMS DIVISION (A division of United Technologies Corporation)

PO Box 49028, San Jose, California 95161-9028
Telephone: (408) 281 1122
DIVISION EXECUTIVE VICE-PRESIDENT AND GENERAL MANAGER: David E. Lee

In 1986 CSD joined the Booster Production Company (BPC) and a newly formed unit, Space Flight Systems (SFS), to create Space Transportation Systems, an operating unit of UTC's Defense & Space Group. CSD is formed into four units: Strategic and SDI Booster Systems; Space Launch Booster Systems; Space Maneuvering Systems; and Tactical Systems; as well as an Advanced Propulsion Technology group. Many of its activities are now covered by other *Jane's* publications.

CSD IUS

In October 1976 the US Air Force awarded the Boeing/CSD team a contract to develop the Inertial Upper Stage (IUS) for the Space Shuttle and the Titan 34D space launch vehicle. The propulsion system for the two-stage IUS consists of two solid motors: a 2.31 m (91 in) aft motor, designated SRM-1, containing 9,707 kg (21,400 lb) of propellant, and a 1.6 m (63 in) forward stage motor, designated SRM-2, with 2,722 kg (6,000 lb) of propellant. Further details appeared in the 1986-87 *Jane's*.

The SRM-1 has been selected to power a new Shuttle upper stage being developed by Orbital Sciences and Martin Marietta, and a spin-stabilised derivative has been developed to place the Hughes Intelsat VI comsats in transfer orbit.

CSD AIR-BREATHING PROPULSION

CSD spearheads the efforts of its parent, United Technologies Corporation, in the research and development of ramjet propulsion systems. In 1973 it was awarded a contract by the US Navy to develop an integral rocket/ramjet (IRR) which operates as a solid rocket booster until it reaches supersonic speeds. At that point, through a series of mechanical changes, it becomes a ramjet. These changes involve the opening of air inlets, an increase in the nozzle diameter and a switch to the burning of liquid fuel and air in the combustion chamber within a common system.

CSD small IUS, motor type SRM-2, showing the EEC (extendible exit cone) in the nested position

EMG

EMG ENGINEERING COMPANY

PO Box 1368, Hesperia, California 92345
Telephone: (714) 247 8519

Eugene M. Gluhareff, a pioneer of ultra-lightweight rotorcraft, has been developing a simple air-breathing jet engine for rotor tip drive. The first model was the G8-2, which was designed in 1955 and developed for tip drive or sailplane auxiliary propulsion. Production has been hard pressed to keep up with demand, a fast growing market being radio controlled flight vehicles. Manned platforms, hang gliders and small helicopters are also proving to be a large market for EMG engines.

GLUHAREFF G8-2

The design is based on propane. Tank pressure delivers the fuel, via a needle valve throttle, to the burner. The fuel is vaporised in a heat exchanger. Vapour passes to the injector where its residual pressure is converted to kinetic energy. The high velocity gas jet induces air through three 'supercharger' intakes, each synchronised to the internal flow, which gives the correct fuel/air ratio for the combustion chamber. Here the mixture is initially ignited by a spark plug and thereafter burns continuously.

Since 1979 three more models have been available, the G8-2-20, -80 and -130, rated respectively at 0.09, 0.36 and 0.58 kN (20, 80 and 130 lb st). A G8-2-250 (1.1 kN, 250 lb st) was then on bench test. The best sfc has been reduced dramatically from 170 mg/Ns (6 lb/h/lb st) to only 21.8 mg/Ns (0.77 lb/h/lb st).

The units are manufactured by Gluhareff's subsidiary EMG Engineering Co. Customers have the option of buying plans, a construction package, an assembly kit or finished engine.

GARRETT

GARRETT ENGINE DIVISION (a division of Allied Signal Aerospace Company)

Sky Harbor Airport, 111 S 34th St, PO Box 5217, Phoenix, Arizona 85010
Telephone: (602) 231 1000
PRESIDENT: Malcolm E. Craig

Garrett Engine Division has been called the world's largest producer of small gas turbines.

At the end of 1984 Garrett announced its collaboration with Allison on the T800-LHT-800 turboshaft for the LHX helicopter programme. This is mentioned under LHTEC.

The CFE738 turbofan, being developed jointly by Garrett and General Electric, is to be found under CFE.

GARRETT ATF3
US military designation: F104-GA-100

The ATF3 was the first engine to combine three-spool design with a reverse-flow combustion system and turbines, and mixed-flow exhaust.

The arrangement of components allows the fan design to be determined largely independently of the gas generator, and permits operation at optimum fan speed. Omission of inlet guide vanes, mixing of the exhaust with the fan airflow,

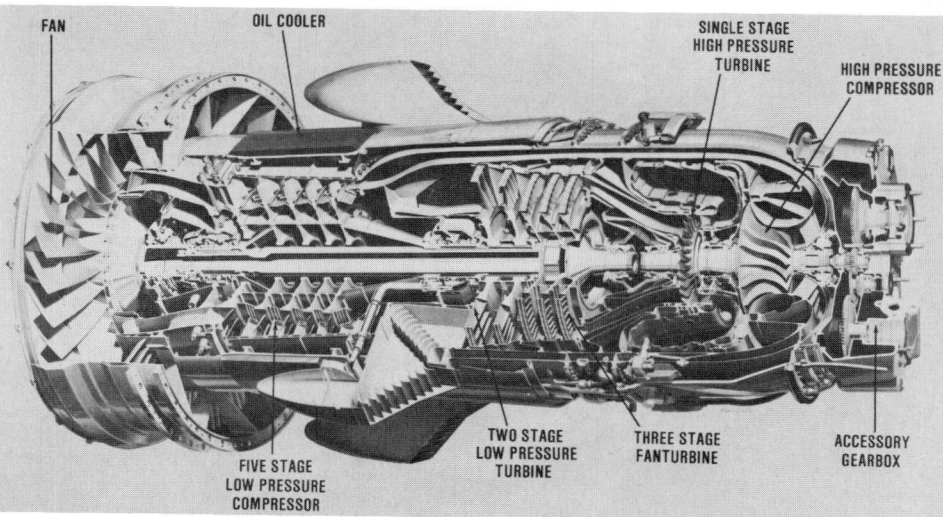

Cutaway of the Garrett ATF3-6A three-shaft turbofan (24.20 kN; 5,440 lb st)

In May 1976 it was announced that the **ATF3-6A** had been selected by Dassault-Breguet to power the Falcon 200 business jet. FAA certification was achieved on 24 December 1981, and Falcon 200 deliveries began in 1983. The ATF3-6A is offered under a retrofit programme for Falcon 20 aircraft. It also powers the HU-25A Guardian.

TYPE: Three-shaft axial-flow turbofan.

LOW PRESSURE (FAN) SYSTEM: Single-stage titanium fan, driven by three-stage IP turbine. Bypass ratio 2.8 at take-off. Total airflow 73.5 kg (162 lb)/s.

INTERMEDIATE PRESSURE SYSTEM: Five-stage titanium compressor, driven by two-stage LP turbine. Airflow is delivered to rearward facing HP compressor via eight tubes feeding into annular duct. Core airflow 18.15 kg (40 lb)/s.

HIGH PRESSURE SYSTEM: Single titanium centrifugal compressor, driven by single-stage HP turbine. IP airflow enters the impeller from the rear. Overall pressure ratio (T-O) 21, (high altitude cruise) 25.

COMBUSTION SYSTEM: Reverse-flow annular type.

TURBINES: Single-stage HP, three-stage IP and two-stage LP turbines drive, respectively, the HP, fan (LP) and IP compressors. IP and LP turbines have shrouded blades. Aircooled HP rotor blades. Exhaust gases turned 180° through eight sets of cascades to mix with fan bypass flow.

FUEL SYSTEM: Electromechanical, incorporating solid state computer. Manual emergency backup system.

ACCESSORY DRIVES: Three drive pads on rear-mounted gearbox driven by HP shaft, providing for hydraulic pump, starter/generator and one spare.

EXHAUST SYSTEM: Mixed fan and turbine exhaust discharged via annular nozzle surrounding combustion section.

LUBRICATION SYSTEM: Hot tank integral with gearbox.

STARTING: Electric or pneumatic.

DIMENSIONS:

Length	2,591 mm (102.0 in)
Max diameter	853 mm (33.6 in)

WEIGHT, DRY: 510 kg (1,125 lb)

PERFORMANCE RATINGS (uninstalled):

T-O (ISA, S/L, static)	24.20 kN (5,440 lb st)
Cruise (12,200 m; 40,000 ft at Mach 0.8)	
	4.69 kN (1,055 lb)

SPECIFIC FUEL CONSUMPTION:

At T-O rating (S/L, ISA static)	
	14.33 mg/Ns (0.506 lb/h/lb st)
At cruise (as above)	23.51 mg/Ns (0.83 lb/h/lb)

GARRETT TFE76
US military designation: F109-GA-100

Based on the core of the T76/TPE331 turboprops, with performance improvements, this turbofan was selected in July 1982 as the engine of the US Air Force's Fairchild T-46A. This was subsequently cancelled, but the TFE76 is now flying in the Promavia Jet Squalus.

The core of the F109 is used in the ATE109 helicopter engine, described under LHTEC.

TYPE: Two-shaft turbofan.

FAN: Single-stage, with 28 blades with part span shrouds (snubbers) inserted in self-de-icing rotating spinner.

COMPRESSER: Tandem two-stage centrifugal with titanium impellers. LP and HP bleeds.

COMBUSTION CHAMBER: Annular reverse flow type, with piloted air blast nozzles for low emissions.

HP TURBINE: Two-stage axial with single pass cooling.

LP TURBINE: Two-stage axial, with tip shrouds.

CONTROL SYSTEM: Digital with hydromechanical backup.

ACCESSORIES: Mounted on one-piece gearbox, under intermediate case, with drive from HP shaft taken through one of five main aerofoil struts spaced at 72°.

DIMENSIONS:

Length	942 mm (37.1 in)
Diameter	523 mm (20.6 in)

WEIGHT, DRY: 182 kg (400 lb)

PERFORMANCE RATINGS (ISA):

T-O	5.92 kN (1,330 lb st)

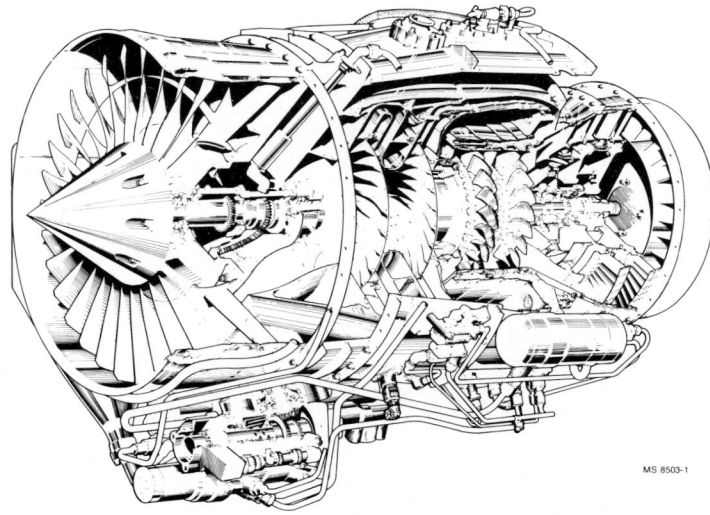

Cutaway drawing of the Garrett F109-GA-100 turbofan (5.92 kN; 1,330 lb st)

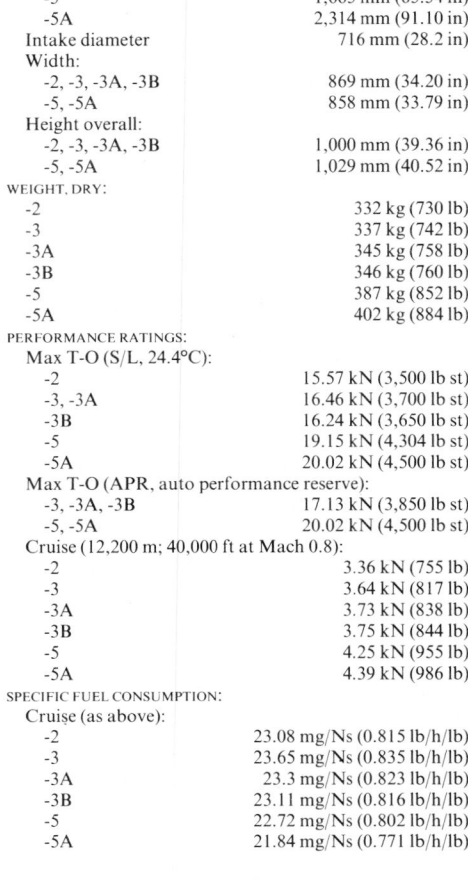

Section of the TFE731-5 (top half) and TFE731-3 (bottom half)

731-5

731-3

Max continuous (9,145 m; 30,000 ft, Mach 0.5)	
	1.78 kN (400 lb)

SPECIFIC FUEL CONSUMPTION:

Max T-O as above	11.10 mg/Ns (0.392 lb/h/lb st)

GARRETT TFE731

Announced in April 1969, the TFE731 is a two-spool geared turbofan designed for business jet aircraft. Use of a geared fan confers flexibility in operation and yields optimum performance at up to 15,545 m (51,000 ft).

Deliveries for the Falcon 10 took place in August 1972, and for the JetStar II in 1974. The **TFE731-3** was also selected for the Learjet 35/36, Cessna Citation III, Dassault-Breguet Falcon 50, BAe 125-700, IAI Westwind 1 and 2 and Astra, Rockwell International's Sabreliner 65A, CASA C-101 and Argentine IA 63 trainer and light attack aircraft and Learjet 54/56.

In 1980 the **731-5** was announced, to offer higher thrust and reduced noise, while maintaining low smoke characteristics. The -5 has a higher bypass ratio fan driven by a new LP turbine.

This version was certificated in November 1983. Its first applications are the BAe 125-800 and the CASA C-101. The **TFE731-5A**, with a mixer nozzle reducing sfc and raising standard thrust to that of the APR rating, was certificated in December 1984. It powers the Dassault-Breguet Falcon 900, and is offered as a retrofit for the Falcon 20. Volvo Flygmotor has a 5.6 per cent share of the 731-5 production programme.

TYPE: Turbofan with two shafts and geared front fan.

FAN: Single-stage axial titanium fan, with inserted blades. The fan shaft is connected directly to the planetary gearbox ring gear. Max fan airflow, sea level static, TFE731-2, 51.25 kg (113 lb)/s; -3, 53.7 kg (118.3 lb)/s; -5, 64.86 kg (143 lb)/s. Bypass ratio, -2, 2.66; -3, 2.80; -5, 3.48.

COMPRESSOR: Four-stage LP, followed by centrifugal HP on separate shaft running at higher speeds. Overall pressure ratio (S/L, static): -2, 14.0; -3, 14.6.

COMBUSTION CHAMBER: Annular reverse flow type, with 12 nozzles injecting tangentially. Meets EPA/FAA emission requirements.

FUEL SYSTEM: Hydro-electronic, with single lever control.

TURBINES: Single-stage HP and three-stage LP. Average HP inlet gas temperature, S/L, max T-O, -2, 860°C; -3, 907°C; -5, 952°C.

ACCESSORY DRIVES: Pads provided for hydraulic pump, starter/generator or starter motor and alternators. Pads on back side of drive fuel control and oil pump.

DIMENSIONS:

Length overall:	
-2, -3	1,520 mm (59.83 in)
-3A, -3B	1,440 mm (59.7 in)
-5	1,665 mm (65.54 in)
-5A	2,314 mm (91.10 in)
Intake diameter	716 mm (28.2 in)
Width:	
-2, -3, -3A, -3B	869 mm (34.20 in)
-5, -5A	858 mm (33.79 in)
Height overall:	
-2, -3, -3A, -3B	1,000 mm (39.36 in)
-5, -5A	1,029 mm (40.52 in)

WEIGHT, DRY:

-2	332 kg (730 lb)
-3	337 kg (742 lb)
-3A	345 kg (758 lb)
-3B	346 kg (760 lb)
-5	387 kg (852 lb)
-5A	402 kg (884 lb)

PERFORMANCE RATINGS:

Max T-O (S/L, 24.4°C):	
-2	15.57 kN (3,500 lb st)
-3, -3A	16.46 kN (3,700 lb st)
-3B	16.24 kN (3,650 lb st)
-5	19.15 kN (4,304 lb st)
-5A	20.02 kN (4,500 lb st)
Max T-O (APR, auto performance reserve):	
-3, -3A, -3B	17.13 kN (3,850 lb st)
-5, -5A	20.02 kN (4,500 lb st)
Cruise (12,200 m; 40,000 ft at Mach 0.8):	
-2	3.36 kN (755 lb)
-3	3.64 kN (817 lb)
-3A	3.73 kN (838 lb)
-3B	3.75 kN (844 lb)
-5	4.25 kN (955 lb)
-5A	4.39 kN (986 lb)

SPECIFIC FUEL CONSUMPTION:

Cruise (as above):	
-2	23.08 mg/Ns (0.815 lb/h/lb)
-3	23.65 mg/Ns (0.835 lb/h/lb)
-3A	23.3 mg/Ns (0.823 lb/h/lb)
-3B	23.11 mg/Ns (0.816 lb/h/lb)
-5	22.72 mg/Ns (0.802 lb/h/lb)
-5A	21.84 mg/Ns (0.771 lb/h/lb)

GARRETT TPE331
US military designation: T76

Based upon experience with APUs, this was the first Garrett engine for aircraft propulsion. By January 1988 deliveries of all versions had passed 11,000.

The following are major versions:

TPE331 series I, II. FAA certificated in February 1965. Rated at 451 ekW; 429 kW plus 0.33 kN (605 ehp; 575 shp plus 75 lb st). Redesignated **TPE331-25/61** and **-25/71** and produced until 1970. Powers MU-2 (A to E models), Porter, Jet Liner, Super Turbo 18, FU-24, Hawk Commander and 680, and Turbo Beaver.

TPE331-1 series. Certificated December 1967 at 526 ekW; 496 kW plus 0.44 kN (705 ehp; 665 shp plus 100 lb st). Powers MU-2 (F and G), Turbo-Porter and AU-23A Peacemaker, CJ600, Turboliner, Interceptor 400, Turbo Commander and (customer option) Thrush Commander, Merlin IIB and Fletcher 1284, Turbo Thrush and Turbo Ag-Cat.

TPE331-2 series. Certificated in December 1967 at 563 ekW; 533 kW plus 0.45 kN (755 ehp; 715 shp plus 102 lb st). Powers Skyvan, CASA 212 pre-series and Turbo Goose and Turbo Beaver.

TPE331-3 series. Certificated in March 1970 at 674 ekW; 626 kW plus 0.71 kN (904 ehp; 840 shp plus 159 lb st). Uprated gas generator with increased airflow and pressure ratio, but same turbine temperature as in original TPE 331. Powers Merlin III, IV and Metro, and Jetstream III.

TPE331-5/6 series. The -5 was certificated in March 1970; this matches the gas generator of the -3 with the 715 shp gearbox, and is flat rated to 2,134 m (7,000 ft). Powers MU-2, King Air B100 (-6), CASA 212 (-5), D228 (-5), and

Commander 840/900. The -5 designation indicates output speed of 1,591 rpm; the -6 has an output speed of 2,000 rpm.

TPE331-8. Matches compressor and gearbox of -3 with new turbine section. Thermodynamic power of 676 ekW; 645 kW (905 ehp; 865 shp) plus 0.47 kN (105 lb st), but flat rated at 533 kW (715 shp) to 36°C. Certification was received in November 1976. Powers Conquest II.

TPE331-9. Thermodynamic rating 645 kW (865 shp).

TPE331-10. Rated at 746 kW (1,000 shp). Certificated January 1978. Powers Marquise and Solitaire, Commander 980/1000, Merlin IIIC, CASA 212-200 and Jetstream 31.

TPE331-11. Certificated 1979. Higher gearbox limit; wet rating 820 kW (1,100 shp). Powers Metro III.

TPE331-12. Same size as -10 but offers 834 kW (1,119 shp). Certificated December 1984. Powers Jetstream Super 31 and Metro V. The **TPE331-12B**, powers the Shorts Tucano. Rolls-Royce makes 30 per cent by value of engines for Shorts, and supports RAF engines in service.

TPE331-14/15. Scaled-up models, with thermodynamic power in the 1,227 kW (1,645 shp) class. The -14 was certificated in April 1984 and is flat rated at 746 kW (1,000 shp) for the Cheyenne 400. In the Metro VI it is rated at 932 kW (1,250 shp).

T76. Military engine, with gas generator similar to TPE331-1 but with front end inverted, to give inlet above spinner. All models power OV-10 Bronco.

Except for the TPE331-14, all versions are of similar frame size, and the following data apply generally to all:

TYPE: Single-shaft turboprop.

PROPELLER DRIVE: Two-stage reduction gear, one helical spur and one planetary, with overall ratio of 20.865 or 26.3.

COMPRESSOR: Tandem two-stage centrifugal made from titanium. Mass flow, 2.61 kg (5.78 lb)/s for 25/61, 25/71, 2.81 kg (6.2 lb)/s for -1, 2.80 kg (6.17 lb)/s for -2 and T76, 3.52 kg (7.75 lb)/s for -251 and 3.54 kg (7.8 lb)/s for -3. Pressure ratio 8.0 for 25/61, 25/71, 8.34 for -1, 8.54 for -2 and T76, 10.37 for -251 and -3.

COMBUSTION CHAMBER: Annular, with capacitor discharge igniter plug on turbine plenum.

FUEL SYSTEM: Woodward or Bendix control with Beta propeller control. Max fuel pressure 41.4 bars (600 lb/sq in).

FUEL GRADE (TPE331): ASTM designation D1655-64T types Jet A, Jet B and Jet A-1; MIL-F-5616-1, Grade JP-1.

TURBINE: Three-stage axial. In early models, blades cast integrally with disc. In -10, -11, -12 first-stage disc with inserted blades. In -14/-15 inserted blades in all three stages. Inlet gas temperature, 987°C for 25/61, 25/71, 993°C, 1,005°C for all other models.

ACCESSORIES: AND 20005 Type XV-B tachometer generator, AND 20002 Type XII-D starter/generator, AND

Cutaway drawing of Garrett TPE331-14 turboprop (932 kW; 1,250 shp, or flat rated at 746 kW; 1,000 shp)

20010 Type XX-A propeller governor and AND 20001 Type XI-B hydraulic pump.

LUBRICATION SYSTEM: Medium pressure dry sump system. Normal oil supply pressure 6.90 bars (100 lb/sq in).

OIL SPECIFICATION: MIL-L-23699-(1) or MIL-L-7808.

STARTING: Pad for 399A starter/generator.

DIMENSIONS (approx):

Length overall:	
TPE331	1,092 to 1,333 mm (43-52.5 in)
T76	1,118 mm (44 in)
Width: TPE331	533 mm (21 in)
T76	483 mm (19 in)
Height: TPE331	660 mm (26 in)
T76	686 mm (27 in)

WEIGHT, DRY:

TPE331-25/61, 71	152 kg (335 lb)
TPE331-1, -2	152.5 kg (336 lb)
T76	155 kg (341 lb)
TPE331-3	161 kg (355 lb)
TPE331-5	163 kg (360 lb)
TPE331-8	168 kg (370 lb)
TPE331-10	172 kg (380 lb)
TPE331-11	182 kg (400 lb)
TPE331-12	176 kg (387 lb)
TPE331-14/15	256 kg (565 lb)

PERFORMANCE RATINGS:

T-O	see under model listings
Military (30 min): T76-G-410/411	
	533 kW; 563 ekW (715 shp; 755 ehp)
Normal: T76-G-410/411	
	485 kW; 514.5 ekW (650 shp; 690 ehp)
Max cruise (ISA, 3,050 m; 10,000 ft and 250 knots; 463 km/h; 288 mph):	
TPE331-25/61, 71	332 kW (445 shp)
TPE331-1	404 kW (542 shp)
TPE331-2, T76	430 kW (577 shp)
TPE331-3, -5	530 kW (710 shp)

SPECIFIC FUEL CONSUMPTION:
At T-O rating:

TPE331-25/61, 71	111.5 µg/J (0.66 lb/h/shp)
TPE331-1	102.2 µg/J (0.605 lb/h/shp)
TPE331-2	99.4 µg/J (0.588 lb/h/shp)
TPE331-3	99.7 µg/J (0.59 lb/h/shp)
TPE331-5	105.8 µg/J (0.626 lb/h/shp)
TPE331-8	96.7 µg/J (0.572 lb/h/shp)
TPE331-10	94.6 µg/J (0.560 lb/h/shp)
TPE331-11	94.3 µg/J (0.558 lb/h/shp)
TPE331-12	92.8 µg/J (0.549 lb/h/shp)
TPE331-14/-15	84.8 µg/J (0.502 lb/h/shp)
T76-G-410/411	101.4 µg/J (0.60 lb/h/shp)

OIL CONSUMPTION:

Max	0.009 kg (0.02 lb)/h

GENERAL ELECTRIC
GE AIRCRAFT ENGINES

Neumann Way, Evendale, Ohio 45215
Telephone: (513) 243 2000
SENIOR VICE-PRESIDENT AND GROUP EXECUTIVE: B. H. Rowe

Current products of GE Aircraft Engines include the F103, F110, F120, F404, GE38, T58, T64, T700, TF34 and TF39 for military use, and the CF6, CF34, CT7, CT58 and GE36 for the commercial and general aviation market. A new turbofan is being developed in partnership with Garrett and appears under CFE. In partnership with SNECMA of France a company was formed to develop and market the CFM56 turbofan, as described in the International part of this section under CFM International.

Details of the F101, J79, J85, CJ610 and CF700 engines, which are no longer in production, can be found in the 1986-87 and earlier editions of *Jane's*.

GENERAL ELECTRIC F404

The F404 is an augmented turbofan rated at 71.2-89 kN (16,000-20,000 lb st). In May 1975 the US Navy selected the McDonnell Douglas/Northrop team to develop its F/A-18 Hornet, powered by two F404-GE-400 engines.

First F404 engine test took place in December 1976. Preliminary flight rating test took place in May 1978, first F/A-18 flight in November 1978 and MQT (model qualification test) in July 1979. The first production delivery took place in December 1979 and 1,650 had been delivered by May 1988.

The following are current versions of the F404:

F404-GE-400. Original production engine for F/A-18A, F/A-18B and CF-18. Also powers the Grumman X-29A and Dassault-Breguet Rafale. Deliveries by mid-1987 exceeded 1,500.

F404-GE-400D. Unaugmented version of Dash-400 rated at 48.0 kN (10,800 lb st). Powered Grumman A-6F. A basically similar engine powers the Lockheed reconnaissance/attack stealth aircraft.

F404-GE-100. Version of Dash-100A uprated to 80.0 kN (18,000 lb st). Developed for F-20A, candidate for Japanese FSX and Yugoslav 'Novi Avion'.

F404-GE-100D. Unaugmented version similar to Dash-400D, with new control system as fitted to Dash-100A

General Electric F404-GE-100A augmented turbofan (75.6 kN; 17,000 lb st)

and RM12. To be rated at 48.9 kN (11,000 lb st) for Singapore A-4S-1.

F404/RM12. Fan handles 10 per cent greater airflow and has increased resistance to foreign-object damage. Increased turbine inlet temperature provides operating margin for lower right corner of flight envelope. Modified control system for single-engined JAS 39 Gripen. Interim engine for Indian LCA and proposed for re-engining Chinese F-7. Rated at 80.5 kN (18,100 lb st). See Volvo Flygmotor, Sweden.

The following description applies to the F404-GE-400, except where otherwise noted:

TYPE: Two-shaft augmented low ratio turbofan (turbojet with continuous bypass bleed).

FAN: Three-stage. Bypass ratio 0.34. Airflow 64.4 kg (142 lb)/s.

HP COMPRESSOR: Seven-stage. Overall pressure ratio, 25 : 1 class.

COMBUSTION CHAMBER: Single-piece annular.

HP TURBINE: Single-stage with aircooled blades.

LP TURBINE: Single-stage.

EXHAUST SYSTEM: Close coupled afterburner. Convergent-divergent exhaust nozzle with hydraulic actuation.

CONTROL SYSTEM: Electrical-hydromechanical.

DIMENSIONS:

Length overall	4,030 mm (158.8 in)
Max diameter	880 mm (34.8 in)

WEIGHT, DRY:

	989 kg (2,180 lb)

PERFORMANCE RATING:

Max T-O	71.2 kN (16,000 lb st)

GENERAL ELECTRIC TF34

This turbofan won a 1965 US Navy competition. In August 1972 the **TF34-GE-2**, the initial variant for the Lockheed S-3A Viking, completed its model qualification test (MQT) and entered fleet service in February 1974. In January 1975 GE began shipment of the **TF34-GE-400A**, which replaced the GE-2 as S-3A engine. In 1970 the TF34 was selected to power the A-10A attack aircraft as the **TF34-GE-100**, with a long fan duct and side mountings.

In 1974 a third version was selected to provide auxiliary (thrust) power for the Sikorsky S-72 research aircraft.

TYPE: Two-shaft high bypass ratio turbofan.

General Electric CF34-3A turbofan of 41.0 kN (9,220 lb st)

FAN: Single-stage fan has blades forged in titanium. Mass flow 153 kg (338 lb)/s at 7,365 rpm with pressure ratio 1.5. Bypass ratio 6.2.

COMPRESSOR: 14-stage axial on HP shaft. Inlet guide vanes and first five stators variable. First nine rotor stages titanium, remainder high nickel alloy. Performance at max S/L rating, core airflow 21.3 kg (47 lb)/s at 17,900 rpm with pressure ratio 14 : 1, overall pressure ratio 21.

COMBUSTION CHAMBER: Annular Hastelloy liner and front dome, with 18 carburetting burners.

TURBINE: Two-stage HP; four-stage LP with tip-shrouded blades. EGT 1,225°C maximum.

FUEL SYSTEM: Hydromechanical with electronic amplifier. Fuel grade JP-4 or JP-5.

DIMENSIONS:
Max diameter:

TF34-GE-400A	1,321 mm (52.0 in)
TF34-GE-100	1,245 mm (49.0 in)
Basic length (both)	2,540 mm (100.0 in)

WEIGHT, DRY:

TF34-GE-400A	670 kg (1,478 lb)
TF34-GE-100	653 kg (1,440 lb)

PERFORMANCE RATING: Max T-O (S/L, static):

TF34-GE-400A	41.3 kN (9,275 lb st)
TF34-GE-100	40.3 kN (9,065 lb st)

SPECIFIC FUEL CONSUMPTION: Max T-O (S/L, static):

TF34-GE-400A	10.3 mg/Ns (0.363 lb/h/lb st)
TF34-GE-100	10.5 mg/Ns (0.370 lb/h/lb st)

GENERAL ELECTRIC CF34

The CF34-3A is a commercial adaptation of the TF34-GE-100. Total airflow at take-off power with automatic power reserve (APR) is 151 kg (332 lb)/s. Bypass ratio is 6.3. Certificated in January 1980, the CF34 powers the Challenger 601.

DIMENSIONS:

Length (overall)	2,616 mm (103.0 in)
Max diameter (at mounts)	1,245 mm (49.0 in)

WEIGHT, DRY: 739 kg (1,625 lb)

PERFORMANCE RATINGS (S/L, static):

T-O (APR)	41.0 kN (9,220 lb st)
T-O (Normal)	38.8 kN (8,729 lb st)

SPECIFIC FUEL CONSUMPTION (as above):

T-O (APR)	10.35 mg/Ns (0.365 lb/h/lb st)
T-O (Normal)	10.21 mg/Ns (0.360 lb/h/lb st)

GENERAL ELECTRIC TF39

This turbofan was designed to power the C-5A; it entered service with Military Airlift Command in 1970. The **TF39-GE-1C** is an improved model demonstrating improved durability and performance retention. The -1C powers the C-5A and C-5B.

TYPE: Two-shaft high bypass ratio turbofan.

FAN: '1½-stage', with two stages in the inner flowpath and one in the outer. Bypass ratio 8. Mass flow 700 kg (1,541 lb)/s.

COMPRESSOR: 16-stage axial; IGVs and first six stator stages variable. Overall pressure ratio 22.

COMBUSTOR: High efficiency annular, virtually eliminating visual emissions.

HP TURBINE: Two-stage, with TET approx 1,316°C.

LP TURBINE: Six-stage, with uncooled shrouded blades; inlet temperature approx 871°C.

REVERSER: Fan thrust reverser consists of a support assembly, translating cowl, blocker doors, fixed forward fan cowl, inner splitter, and inner cowl assembly, supported from the engine.

DIMENSIONS:

Max diameter	2,540 mm (100 in)
Length, flange to flange	4,801 mm (189 in)
Length overall	6,880 mm (271 in)

WEIGHT, DRY: 3,583 kg (7,900 lb)

PERFORMANCE RATING (T-O, S/L, ISA):
Flat rated to 27.5°C   191.3 kN (43,000 lb st)

GENERAL ELECTRIC CF6
US military designation (CF6-50E): F103-GE-100

On 11 September 1967 General Electric announced the commitment of corporate funding for development of the CF6 turbofan for wide-body transports. The CF6-6D for the DC-10-10 was selected by United and American on 25 April 1968. Details of this and other early versions appeared in the 1987-88 *Jane's*. The following are current versions:

CF6-50C2/E2. Rated 233.5 kN (52,500 lb st) to 30°C. Certification 1978. Military -50C2 powers KC-10; -50E2 powers Boeing E-4.

CF6-80A/A3. Improved sfc and performance retention, with length and weight reduced by elimination of turbine mid frame and reduction in combustor and diffuser length. Engine rated at 213.5 kN (48,000 lb) as the -80A/A1, and 222.4 kN (50,000 lb) as the -80A2/A3. Fitted to 767 and A310. Programme launched November 1977, first engine ran October 1979 and certification October 1981. About 9 per cent built by Volvo Flygmotor.

CF6-80C2. Described separately.

The following data relate to the with CF6-50C2/E2, with -80 differences noted:

TYPE: Two-shaft high bypass ratio turbofan.

FAN: Single-stage with three-stage LP compressor both driven by LP turbine. The 38 fan rotor blades have anti-vibration shrouds at two-thirds span. Blades, discs, spool of titanium; exit guide vanes of aluminium; fan frame and shaft of steel; spinner and fan case of aluminium alloy. Total airflow 591 kg (1,303 lb)/s, bypass ratio 5.7. CF6-80A/A1 has better efficiency and bird strike resistance, with Kevlar containment in fan case. Fan diameter 2,195 mm (86.4 in). Total airflow 658 kg (1,450 lb)/s; bypass ratio 4.3. CF6-80A/A1, 651 kg (1,433 lb)/s; -80A2/A3, 663 kg (1,460 lb)/s. Bypass ratio, -80A/A1, 4.7; -80A2/A3, 4.6.

LP COMPRESSOR: Three core booster stages; 12 bypass doors maintain flow matching between fan/LP and core by opening at low power settings, closed during take-off and cruise.

HP COMPRESSOR: Fourteen-stage with inlet guide vanes and first six stator rows having variable incidence. Core airflow 125 kg (276 lb)/s. CF6-80A series incorporate bore cooling for blade/casing clearance control, and one-piece steel casing with insulated aft stages and short diffuser section. Overall pressure ratio (T-O), 29.13 (-50C), 30.1 (-50E), 28.0 (-80A/A1), 29.0 (-80A2/A3).

COMBUSTOR: Fully annular. CF6-80A has rolled ring combustor, 152 mm (6.0 in) shorter, mounted at aft flange.

HP TURBINE: Two-stage aircooled, TET 1,330°C. CF6-80A has no turbine mid-frame and eliminates one main bearing, and HP case has active clearance control.

LP TURBINE: Four-stage constant tip diameter with nominal 871°C inlet temperature. Rotor blades tip-shrouded and not aircooled. CF6-80A, new turbine with active clearance control.

THRUST REVERSER (FAN): Rear portion of fan outer cowl translates aft on rotating ballscrews to uncover cascade vanes. Blocker doors (16) flush-mounted in cowl on link arms hinged in inner cowl, rotate inwards to expose cascade vanes and block fan duct. CF6-80A1/A3 (A310) similar; 767 reverser by Boeing.

ACCESSORY DRIVE: Inlet gearbox in forward sump transfers energy from the core. Transfer gearbox on bottom of fan frame with starter, fuel pump, main engine control, lubrication pump and tachometer. Pads for aircraft hydraulic pumps, constant speed drive and alternator. CF6-80A gearbox in environmental enclosure on core; -80A1 on fan case.

FUEL SYSTEM: Hydromechanical, schedules acceleration and deceleration fuel flow, variable stator vane position and LP compressor variable bypass doors. CF6-80, electronic trimming.

FUEL GRADES: Fuels conforming to ASTM-1655-65T, Jet A, Jet A1 and Jet B, and MIL-T-5624G2 grades JP-4 or JP-5 are authorised, but Jet A is primary specification.

LUBRICATION SYSTEM: Dry sump centre-vented nominal pressure is 2.07-6.21 bars (30-90 lb/sq in).

STARTING: Air turbine starter mounted on the front of the accessory gearbox at the through shaft.

NOISE SUPPRESSION: Acoustic panels integrated with fan casing, fan front frame and thrust reverser.

DIMENSIONS:
Max height (over gearbox)   2,675 mm (105.3 in)
Length overall (cold):

CF6-50 series	4,394 mm (173.0 in)
CF6-80A	3,998 mm (157.4 in)

WEIGHT, DRY:
Basic engine:

CF6-50C2	3,960 kg (8,731 lb)
CF6-50E, -E1	3,851 kg (8,490 lb)
CF6-50E2	3,977 kg (8,768 lb)
CF6-80A	3,826 kg (8,435 lb)
CF6-80A1	3,769 kg (8,310 lb)

Reverser:

CF6-50E	962 kg (2,121 lb)

PERFORMANCE RATINGS:
Max T-O, uninstalled, ideal nozzle: See under model listings
Max cruise thrust at 10,670 m (35,000 ft), Mach 0.85, flat rated to ISA + 10°C, uninstalled, real nozzle:

CF6-50C2, -E2	50.3 kN (11,300 lb)
CF6-80A, -80A1	45.9 kN (10,320 lb)

SPECIFIC FUEL CONSUMPTION:
At T-O thrust, as above:

CF6-50E	10.65 mg/Ns (0.376 lb/h/lb st)
CF6-50C2, -E2	10.51 mg/Ns (0.371 lb/h/lb st)
CF6-80A	9.74 mg/Ns (0.344 lb/h/lb st)

OIL CONSUMPTION: 0.9 kg (2.0 lb)/h

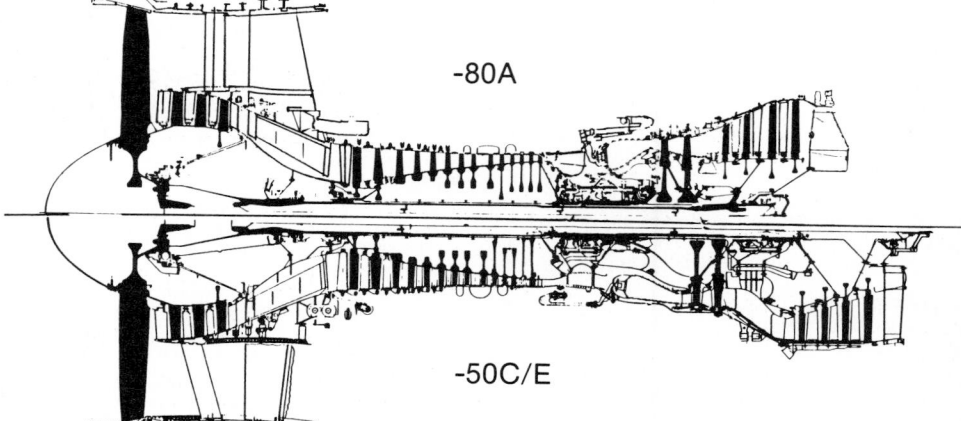

-80A

-50C/E

Features of the General Electric CF6-80A (upper half of drawing) compared with the CF6-50C/E (lower half)

GENERAL ELECTRIC CF6-80C2

This engine is a major redesign for higher thrust and improved sfc, based on the CF6-80A1/A3 but with a 2,362 mm (93 in) diameter fan. It has a four-stage LP compressor and LP turbine redesigned aerodynamically with 5½ stages. The first CF6-80C2 ran in May 1982, and exceeded 276 kN (62,000 lb) corrected thrust. Flight test on an A300 took place between August and December 1984, leading to certification on 28 June 1985. The engine entered revenue service on 5 October 1985.

Programme sharing agreements have been signed with SNECMA of France, MTU of Germany, Volvo Flygmotor of Sweden and Fiat Aviazione of Italy. Applications are as follows:

The CF6-80C2 differs from earlier CF6 engines in the following features:

FAN: Single-stage, with integrally mounted four-stage booster (LP compressor). Mainly titanium except for steel mid-fan shaft, aluminium spinner and blade-containment shroud of layers of Kevlar around aluminium case. Eighty composite exit guide vanes canted for better aerodynamic efficiency. Total mass airflow 796 kg (1,754 lb)/s; bypass ratio 5.2.

LP COMPRESSOR: Four stages with blades and vanes mounted orthogonally, with dovetail offset from centre of pressure to reduce bending.

HP COMPRESSOR: 14-stage, with inlet guide vanes and first five stator rows with variable incidence. Blades in stages 1-5 titanium, 6-14 steel; vanes all steel. One-piece steel casing with insulated aft stages. Core airflow 154 kg (340 lb)/s. Overall pressure ratio 30.4.

COMBUSTOR: Annular, rolled ring construction, aft-mounted with film cooling.

HP TURBINE: Two-stage. Stage one blades directionally solidified. Casing with active and passive clearance control. No midframe.

LP TURBINE: Five stages, with cambered struts in rear frame to reduce exit swirl, effectively producing another half-stage. Rear hub heated by exhaust gas to reduce thermal stress.

FUEL SYSTEM: Hydromechanical fan speed control with electronic supervision; one throttle position corresponds to each engine rating in all flight conditions. FADEC available from 1988.

DIMENSION:
Length   4,087 mm (160.9 in)
WEIGHT, DRY: 4,058 kg (8,946 lb)
PERFORMANCE RATINGS (uninstalled, ideal nozzle):
Max T-O   See table
Max cruise (10,670 m; 35,000 ft, Mach 0.85)
                          50.4 kN (11,330 lb)
SPECIFIC FUEL CONSUMPTION:
T-O, as above   9.32 mg/Ns (0.329 lb/h/lb st)

GENERAL ELECTRIC F110

The F110 (previously F101 DFE) is a fighter engine derivative of the F101. The first ran in late 1979. In early 1984 the USAF selected the F110 to power future F-16 aircraft.

The initial USAF contract was for 126 F110-GE-100 engines. Follow-on contracts for 638 engines have since been announced. Israel announced selection of 100 F110 engines, and Turkey is buying 177 engines. Other orders have been received from Bahrain, Egypt and Greece. Delivery of production F-16C/D aircraft with F110 engines began in mid-1986. The US Navy selected the Dash-100 to power its F-16Ns for the adversary role. Under test in 1987 was the F110-GE-129, which has demonstrated more than 129 kN (29,000 lb st) and is a candidate for future F-15s and F-16s. The F110-GE-400 powers F-14A (Plus) and F-14D Tomcats for the US Navy.

FAN: Inlet guide vanes with variable trailing-edge flaps. Three fan stages, a scaled-up F404 design, with solid titanium blades. Pressure ratio over 3. Airflow 113-122 kg (250-270 lb)/s. Bypass ratio 0.87.

HIGH PRESSURE COMPRESSOR: Nine stages.
COMBUSTOR: Annular, dual cone nozzles.
HP TURBINE: Single-stage aircooled.
LP TURBINE: Two stages.
AUGMENTOR: Scaled F101. Flows mix in plane of flameholder, and 90 per cent of core flow is completely burned before fuelling of any bypass air is initiated.
EXHAUST NOZZLE: Scaled-up version of F404 design.
DIMENSIONS:
Length   4,620 mm (181.9 in)
Diameter   1,181 mm (46.5 in)
PERFORMANCE RATING:
T-O   122.8 kN (27,600 lb st)

GENERAL ELECTRIC GE36 (UDF)

Using thin scimitar-like blades with a diameter of 3.57 m (140 in), the UDF (unducted fan) engine has a bypass ratio of 36. The proof-of-concept demonstrator used an F404 core and was rated in the 111.2 kN (25,000 lb st) class. Flight testing on a Boeing 727 started on 20 August 1986, and was completed in February 1987. Flight testing on an MD-80 began on 18 May 1987 and was completed in March 1987.

After accomplishing all flight objectives, GE started development of the product engine, which is expected to be in commercial service in the 1990s. GE considers it suitable

CF6-80C2 MODELS

Model	Thrust Ideal nozzle	Real nozzle	Application
CF6-80C2A2	238 kN (53,500 lb)	233.5 kN (52,460 lb) to 43.9°C	A310-200, -300
CF6-80C2A3	268 kN (60,200 lb)	262 kN (58,950 lb) to 30°C	A300-600
CF6-80C2A5	273.5 kN (61,500 lb)	267.5 kN (60,100 lb) to 30°C	A300-600R
CF6-80C2A6F	285 kN (64,000 lb)	280.5 kN (63,000 lb)	A330
CF6-80C2B1	252 kN (56,700 lb)	247.5 kN (55,640 lb) to 30°C	747-200, -300
CF6-80C2B1F	257.5 kN (57,900 lb)	253 kN (56,850 lb) to 32.2°C	747-400
CF6-80C2B2	233.5 kN (52,500 lb)	229.5 kN (51,570 lb) to 32.2°C	767-200
CF6-80C2B2F	234 kN (52,700 lb)	231 kN (52,010 lb) to 32.2°C	767-300ER
CF6-80C2B4	257.5 kN (57,900 lb)	253 kN (56,850 lb) to 32.2°C	767-300ER
CF6-80C2B4F	258 kN (58,100 lb)	255 kN (57,280 lb) to 32.2°C	767-300ER
CF6-80C2B6	273.5 kN (61,500 lb)	267 kN (60,070 lb) to 30°C	767-300ER (400 K)
CF6-80C2B6F	270 kN (60,800 lb)	267 kN (60,030 lb) to 32.2°C	767-300ER
CF6-80C2D1F	273.5 kN (61,500 lb)	267 kN (60,070 lb) to 30°C	MD-11

Thrusts are S/L static ISA, full ram recovery, no bleed or extraction

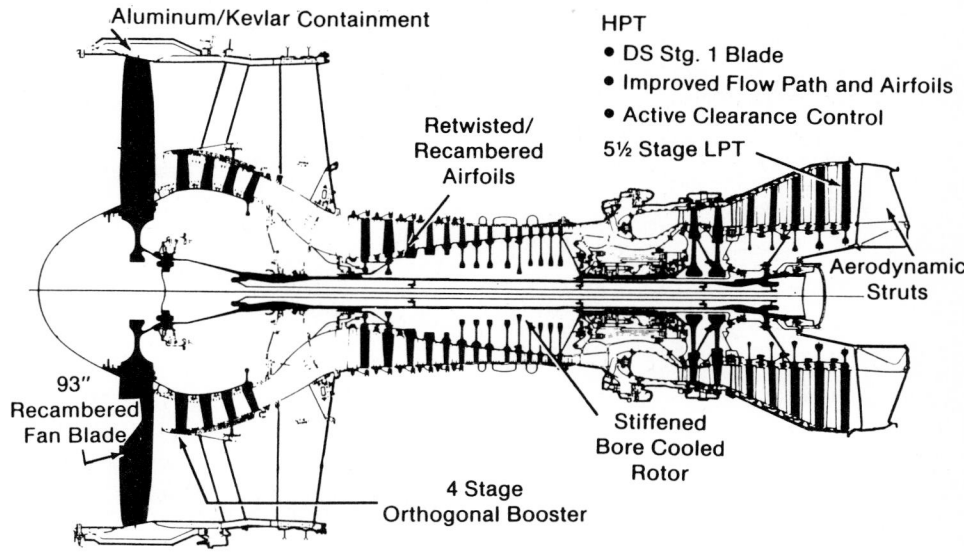

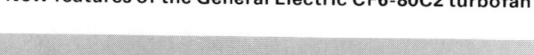

New features of the General Electric CF6-80C2 turbofan

General Electric CF6-80C2 turbofan, rated at up to 285 kN (64,000 lb st)

for use on the MD-91, MD-92 and 7J7. On 30 May 1985 GE and SNECMA signed an agreement assigning to the French company a 35 per cent share of the UDF programme. SNECMA participated in the proof-of-concept demonstration, and is currently involved in the design and development of major portions of the product engine.

The key to the light weight and low fuel consumption of the UDF lies in elimination of a drive gearbox. Instead, the gas from the core passes through large multi-stage contra-rotating turbines downstream. This substitutes rotor blades for what would normally be the turbine stators, and the visible propeller blades are mounted directly on the two rotors of the power turbine. Blade loading for the LP power turbines is normal, but speed is low and the resulting

'insignificant' stress levels allow the unique construction at low risk.

The external propulsor blades are designed using techniques established with fan blades, the hub radius ratio of more than 0.45 being more than twice that common for propellers. The composite blades change pitch from flight settings through feather to reverse, and the pitch is set to control speed and power output.

GENERAL ELECTRIC GE37
US military designation: F120

This advanced augmented turbofan is one of the candidate engines for the USAF Advanced Tactical Fighter. Prototypes of the rival ATFs, the Lockheed

YF-22A and Northrop YF-23A, are to fly with both the YF120 and the competing Pratt & Whitney YF119.

GENERAL ELECTRIC GE38

The GE38 is to be a related family of shaft-power and jet engines derived from the GE27 (see next entry). Like the CFE738 (see entry under CFE), the GE38 versions use the GE27 core, which has five axial plus one centrifugal compressor stages, a short annular combustor and two-stage turbine. This core is in the 4,475 kW (6,000 shp) class. There will be turboshaft and turboprop versions, and also a UDF (unducted fan) rated at 26.7-40 kN (6,000-9,000 lb st).

GE has announced three partners on the GE38. Textron Lycoming participates in the management, development and production of turboshaft and turboprop versions. Bendix Corporation, already involved in the GE27, is responsible for a FADEC for the whole GE38/CFE738 family. Ruston Gas Turbines of the UK (a subsidiary of the totally unconnected British General Electric plc) is working on compressor- and power-turbine parts.

GENERAL ELECTRIC GE27

In March 1983 the Department of Defense, on behalf of the US Army, placed a contract to design and build this MTDE (modular turboshaft demonstrator engine) in the 3,730 kW (5,000 shp) class. It has an inlet particle separator, compressor with five axial and one centrifugal stages, short annular combustor, two-stage compressor turbine and three-stage power turbine. A power:weight ratio of 6.5 is claimed, together with an sfc 15 to 30 per cent better than existing engines. The core engine first ran in December 1983, and the full engine in late 1984. Anticipated full scale development would make production engines available in the 1990s. A family comprising turboshaft, turboprop and turbofan engines is planned. Applications could include maritime patrol aircraft, medium/heavy-lift helicopters, tilt-rotors and business jets.

GENERAL ELECTRIC T58

The T58 turboshaft was developed for helicopter propulsion for the US Navy Bureau of Weapons. A civil version, the CT58, was awarded a Type Certificate on 1 July 1959 and is described separately. Rolls-Royce produces modified versions under licence as the Gnome. The T58 is also licensed for manufacture in Italy and Japan.

Versions currently in service or in production are as follows:

T58-GE-3. Five-minute rating of 988 kW (1,325 shp). Powers UH-1F.

T58-GE-5. Five-minute rating of 1,119 kW (1,500 shp). Powers CH-3E, HH-3E/F and NASA RSRA (S-72).

T58-GE-8E, F. Rated at 1,007 kW (1,350 shp). Powers CH-46A, SH-2, SH-3A/G and HH-52A.

T58-GE-10. Rated at 1,044 kW (1,400 shp). Powers SH-3D/H, and CH-46D/F.

T58-GE-16. Rated at 1,394 kW (1,870 shp). Powers CH-46E.

T58-GE-100. Uprated T58-GE-5. Ten-minute rating 1,119 kW (1,500 shp) to 15°C or 1,100 kW (1,475 shp) to 26°C. Powers selected CH/HH-3E. Qualified 1976.

TYPE: Free turbine turboshaft.

COMPRESSOR: Ten-stage axial. Variable inlet guide vanes and first three stator rows. Pressure ratio 8.4. Air mass flow 5.62 kg (12.4 lb)/s in T58-GE-3 and -8E, 6.21 kg (13.7 lb)/s in -5, -10 and -100, 6.30 kg (13.9 lb)/s in -16.

COMBUSTION CHAMBER: Annular type. Sixteen fuel nozzles (eight on each of two manifolds).

GAS GENERATOR TURBINE: Two-stage. T58-GE-16 has aircooled first-stage blades.

POWER TURBINE: Single-stage (two-stage in T58-GE-16). Operated nominally at 19,500 rpm.

GEARBOX (optional except on -16): Reduces power speed to 6,000 rpm. Includes integral torque sensing.

CONTROLS (except -10 and -16): Free turbine constant speed control. Hydromechanical controls.

CONTROLS (-10, -16): Integrated hydromechanical/electrical power control system for isochronous speed governing and twin-engine load sharing.

DIMENSIONS:
Max width:
except T58-GE-16	526 mm (20.7 in)
T58-GE-16	607 mm (23.9 in)

Length overall:
except T58-GE-16	1,499 mm (59.0 in)
T58-GE-16	1,626 mm (64.0 in)

WEIGHT, DRY:
T58-GE-3	140 kg (309 lb)
T58-GE-5, -100	152 kg (335 lb)
T58-GE-8E, F	138 kg (305 lb)
T58-GE-10	159 kg (350 lb)
T58-GE-16	201 kg (443 lb)

PERFORMANCE RATINGS:
Five-minute: See under model listings
Military:
T58-GE-3	988 kW (1,325 shp) at 20,960 rpm
T58-GE-5, 10	1,044 kW (1,400 shp) at 19,500 rpm
T58-GE-8E, F	1,007 kW (1,350 shp) at 19,500 rpm
T58-GE-16	1,394 kW (1,870 shp) at 19,500 rpm
T58-GE-100	1,119 kW (1,500 shp) at 19,500 rpm

The General Electric F101-GE-102 augmented turbofan (133 kN; 30,000 lb st class), the power plant for the Rockwell International B-1B strategic bomber. It was described in the 1987-88 edition, and was also the starting point for the F118 engine to power the Northrop B-2 advanced technology bomber

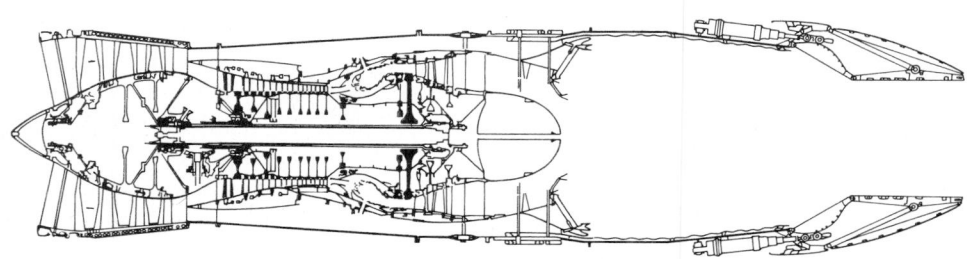

Longitudinal section through the General Electric F110 fighter engine (122.8 kN; 27,600 lb st)

General Electric F110 augmented turbofan (122.8 kN; 27,600 lb st)

General Electric GE36 UDF engine installed on MD-80 (cowling removed)

Cruise:

T58-GE-3	798 kW (1,070 shp)
T58-GE-5, 10	932 kW (1,250 shp)
T58-GE-8E, F	857.5 kW (1,150 shp)
T58-GE-16	1,320 kW (1,770 shp)
T58-GE-100	1,015 kW (1,360 shp) at 19,500 rpm

SPECIFIC FUEL CONSUMPTION:
At cruise rating:

T58-GE-3	106.5 µg/J (0.63 lb/h/shp)
T58-GE-5, 100	103 µg/J (0.61 lb/h/shp)
T58-GE-8E, F	105 µg/J (0.62 lb/h/shp)
T58-GE-10	105 µg/J (0.62 lb/h/shp)
T58-GE-16	91 µg/J (0.54 lb/h/shp)

GENERAL ELECTRIC CT58

The commercial version of the T58 was the first US helicopter turbine to receive FAA certification.

Current versions are as follows:

CT58-110. Rated at 932 kW; 1,250 shp (1,007 kW; 1,350 shp for 2½ min) at 19,500 rpm. Air mass flow 5.67 kg (12.7 lb)/s. Pressure ratio 8.2.

CT58-140. Rated at 1,044 kW; 1,400 shp (1,119 kW; 1,500 shp for 2½ min) at 19,500 rpm. Air mass flow 6.21 kg (13.7 lb)/s. Pressure ratio 8.4.

The CT58 powers the Sikorsky S-61 and S-62 and Boeing 107 Model II.

DIMENSIONS:

Max width	406 mm (16.0 in)
Length overall	1,500 mm (59.0 in)

WEIGHT, DRY:

CT58-110	143 kg (315 lb)
CT58-140	154 kg (340 lb)

PERFORMANCE RATINGS:
2½ min and normal T-O: See under model listings
Cruise:

CT58-110	783 kW (1,050 shp)
CT58-140	932 kW (1,250 shp)

SPECIFIC FUEL CONSUMPTION:

At normal T-O rating	103 µg/J (0.61 lb/h/shp)

At cruise rating:

CT58-110	108 µg/J (0.64 lb/h/shp)
CT58-140	105 µg/J (0.62 lb/h/shp)

GENERAL ELECTRIC T64

The T64 was developed initially for the US Navy. The basic T64 turboshaft becomes a turboprop with the addition of a reduction gearbox.

Current versions include:

T64-GE-7. Turboshaft rated at 2,928 kW (3,925 shp). Powers CH-53B, CH-53C and HH-53C. Produced under licence by MTU for VFW built CH-53D/G.

T64-GE-7A. Turboshaft flat rated at 2,935 kW (3,936 shp) to 28°C. Powers S-65.

T64-GE-10. Turboprop with gearbox above centreline. Rated at 2,215 kW (2,970 shp). Produced under licence by IHI for PS-1 and US-1 and P-2J.

T64-GE-100. (T64-T4C2). Flat rated at 3,229 kW (4,330 shp) to 29.4°C. Powers S-65C.

T64-GE-413A. Turboshaft rated at 2,935 kW (3,936 shp). Powers US Navy CH-53D.

T64-GE-415. Improved combustion liner and turbine cooling. Max rating 3,266 kW (4,380 shp). Powers RH-53D.

T64-GE-416. As -415; powers CH-53E.

T64-GE-419. As -416 with improved turbine, and integral fuel/oil heat exchanger. Max rating 3,542 kW (4,750 shp). To power CH-53E and MH-53E from 1990.

CT64-GE-820. CT64-820-1, -2 and -3 turboprops based on early turboshaft versions power DHC-5C Buffalo. CT64-820-4 has improved components of T64-415 and is flat rated at 2,336 kW (3,133 shp) to 38°C for DHC-5D.

T64-P4D. Turboprop flat rated at 2,535 kW (3,400 shp) to 45°C for G222. Production by Fiat, supported by Alfa Romeo Avio, from 1975.

All T64s are qualified to operate from 100° nose-up to 45° nose-down. Current engines rated at 3,266 kW (4,380 shp) have aircooled first-stage gas generator turbine. The addition of aircooling to the second stage provides growth beyond 3,729 kW (5,000 shp).

TYPE: Free turbine turboshaft/turboprop engine.

COMPRESSOR: Fourteen-stage axial-flow. Single-spool steel rotor for -10 and -820-1/2/3. Titanium and steel compressor for -7A, -413A, -415, -P4D and CT64-820-4. Inlet guide vanes and first four stages of stator blades variable. Air mass flow per second: -10, 11.6 kg (25.5 lb); -7A, -413A, 12.8 kg (28.3 lb); -415, 13.3 kg (29.4 lb); -820-4, 11.9 kg (26.2 lb); P4D, 12.2 kg (27.0 lb). Pressure ratio: -10, -820-4, 12.5; -7A, -413A, 14.1; -415/-416, 14.0; P4D, 13.0.

COMBUSTION CHAMBER: Annular type. Double fuel manifold feeds twelve duplex type fuel nozzles.

GAS GENERATOR TURBINE: Two-stage, coupled directly to compressor rotor by spline connection.

POWER TURBINE: Two-stage, mechanically independent of gas generator turbine.

REDUCTION GEAR: Remotely mounted basic reduction gear for turboprop versions is offset and accessible for inspection and replacement. Propeller gear ratio 13.44 : 1.

STARTING: Mechanical, airframe supplied.

DIMENSIONS:
Length:

T64-GE-7A, -413A, -415, -416	2,006 mm (79 in)

General Electric GE27 turboshaft demonstrator engine

The 1,394 kW (1,870 shp) General Electric T58-GE-16 turboshaft

The 2,935 kW (3,936 shp) General Electric T64-GE-413A turboshaft

T64-GE-10, -P4D	2,793 mm (110 in)
CT64-820	2,870 mm (113 in)
Width:	
T64-GE-7A, -413A, -415, -416	660 mm (26.0 in)
T64-GE-10, -P4D, -820	683 mm (26.9 in)
Height:	
T64-GE-7A, -413A, -415, -416	825 mm (32.5 in)
T64-GE-10, -P4D	1,168 mm (46 in)
CT64-820	1,026 mm (40.4 in)
WEIGHT, DRY:	
T64-GE-7A, -415, -416	327 kg (720 lb)
T64-GE-10	529 kg (1,167 lb)
T64-GE-413A	325 kg (716 lb)
CT64-820-1	513 kg (1,130 lb)
CT64-820-2, -4	520 kg (1,145 lb)
CT64-820-3	518 kg (1,140 lb)
T64-P4D	538 kg (1,188 lb)
PERFORMANCE RATINGS:	
Max rating (S/L):	
T64-GE-7A, -413A	2,935 kW (3,936 shp)
T64-GE-10	
	2,215 kW (2,970 shp) at 1,160 output rpm
T64-GE-415, -416	3,266 kW (4,380 shp)
CT64-820-4	2,336 kW (3,133 shp)
T64-P4D	2,535 kW (3,400 shp)
SPECIFIC FUEL CONSUMPTION (S/L):	
At max rating:	
T64-GE-7A, -415, -416	79.4 µg/J (0.47 lb/h/shp)
T64-GE-10	84.5 µg/J (0.50 lb/h/shp)
T64-GE-413A, -P4D	81 µg/J (0.48 lb/h/shp)
CT64-820-4	82.8 µg/J (0.49 lb/h/shp)

General Electric T700-401 turboshaft engine for SH-60B

GENERAL ELECTRIC T700

The T700 was selected in 1971 to power the US Army's utility tactical transport aircraft system (UTTAS) helicopter. The first T700 was tested in February 1973.

The following are current T700 versions:

T700-GE-700. First production model delivered from early 1978. Following description refers to this version, except where otherwise noted. Powers UH-60A Black Hawk.

T700-GE-701. Upgrade of 10 per cent. In production for AH-64A Apache.

T700-GE-401. Navalised and upgraded version with over 95 per cent commonality. Powers SH-60B Seahawk, SH-2G Seasprite and AH-1W SuperCobra.

T700-GE-401C/701C. Models suitable for tri-service application. Being qualified at powers 20 per cent higher than Dash-700. Selected for future Hawk series helicopters.

A further growth plan utilising new aerodynamics, materials and manufacturing processes, as well as a compressor booster stage, will result in power about 70 per cent greater than the T700-700.

TYPE: Ungeared free turbine turboshaft engine.

INTAKE: Annular, with anti-iced separator designed to remove 95 per cent of sand, dust and foreign object ingestion. Extracted matter discharged by blower driven from accessory gearbox.

COMPRESSOR: Combined axial/centrifugal. Five axial stages and single centrifugal stage mounted on same shaft. Each axial stage is one-piece 'blisk' (blades plus disc) in AM355 steel highly resistant to erosion. Inlet guide vanes and first two stator stages variable. Pressure ratio, about 15 : 1. Airflow about 4.5 kg (10 lb)/s at 44,720 rpm.

COMBUSTION CHAMBER: Fully annular. Central fuel injection to maximise acceptance of contaminated fuel and give minimal smoke generation. Ignition power from separate winding on engine mounted alternator serves dual plugs.

General Electric CT7 turboprop (typical of all models)

TURBINE: Two stage gas generator (HP) turbine operates at gas temperatures exceeding 1,100°C. First stage nozzle investment cast in X40. Second stage nozzle investment cast in two-vane segments in R80. Rated speed (S/L, ISA, max T-O), 44,720 rpm. Two stage free power turbine, with tip shrouded blades and segmented nozzles. Power turbine inlet temperature at intermediate power, 827°C. Output speed, 21,000 rpm.

CONTROLS: Hydromechanical control can be replaced in less than 12 minutes. Electrical control provides twin-engine speed and torque matching.

ACCESSORIES: Grouped at top of engine, together with engine control system. Integral oil tank, plus emergency mist lubrication. Torque sensor provides signal to electrical control.

DIMENSIONS:
Length overall   1,168 mm (46.0 in)

Width	635 mm (25 in)
Height overall	584 mm (23 in)
WEIGHT, DRY (with particle separator):	
T700-700	198 kg (437 lb)
T700-401	197 kg (434 lb)
PERFORMANCE RATINGS (ISA, S/L, static):	
T700-700:	
intermediate	1,210 kW (1,622 shp)
continuous	987 kW (1,324 shp)
T700-401:	
contingency	1,285 kW (1,723 shp)
intermediate	1,260 kW (1,690 shp)
continuous	1,072 kW (1,437 shp)
SPECIFIC FUEL CONSUMPTION (ISA, S/L, static):	
T700-700:	
continuous	79.41 µg/J (0.470 lb/h/shp)
T700-401:	
intermediate	78.40 µg/J (0.464 lb/h/shp)

GENERAL ELECTRIC CT7

Commercial engine based on the T700. Certification April 1977. The **CT7-2A** powers the Bell 214ST and the **CT7-2B** the Westland 30-300.

The **CT7-6** has been developed in partnership with Alfa Romeo Avio and Fiat Aviazione to power the EH 101 and other helicopters such as the NH-90. First delivery for the EH 101 took place on the 26 April 1988. The marinised -6A will power the Italian naval EH 101. Certification was due in June 1988, with production to follow in 1991.

The same core is used in the CT7 turboprop, which has a remote propeller gearbox. This engine received FAA certification in August 1983 and is in production as the **CT7-5A2** for the Saab 340 and the **CT7-7A** for the Airtech CN-235.

CT7 growth engines include the **CT7-9**, to be flat rated at 1,395 kW (1,870 shp). Increased power is obtained by improvements in aerodynamics, materials and turbine cooling. The Dash-9 has been selected for the Airtech CN-235-100, Saab 340B and Bromon Aircraft BR-2000.

GE is also discussing a compact Dash-9 flat rated at 1,119 kW (1,500 shp). This **CT7-3** would have a Hamilton Standard gearbox located on the front of the engine, saving 660 mm (26 in) in length and 56.7 kg (125 lb) in weight.

Data below are for the current turboshaft versions:

DIMENSIONS:
Length	1,168 mm (46.0 in)
Diameter (max envelope)	635 mm (25.0 in)

WEIGHT, DRY:
CT7-2A	202 kg (444 lb)

Full scale model of the General Electric CT7-6 turboshaft *(Brian M. Service)*

| CT7-2D/2B | 201 kg (442 lb) |
| CT7-6 | 209 kg (460 lb) |

PERFORMANCE RATINGS (S/L, static, 15°C):
Contingency (2½ min OEI):

| CT7-2A, 2B, -2D | 1,287 kW (1,725 shp) |
| CT7-6 | 1,491 kW (2,000 shp) |

T-O (5 min) and en route contingency (30 min):

| CT7-2A, 2B, -2D | 1,211 kW (1,623 shp) |

| CT7-2B | 1,212 kW (1,625 shp) |
| CT7-6 | 1,491 kW (2,000 shp) |

SPECIFIC FUEL CONSUMPTION:
Max continuous:

CT7-2A, -2B	79.9 µg/J (0.473 lb/h/shp)
CT7-6 (15°C)	77.4 µg/J (0.458 lb/h/shp)
CT7-6 (35°C)	82.8 µg/J (0.490 lb/h/shp)

Data below are for the current turboprop versions:

DIMENSIONS:

| Length | 2,438 mm (96.0 in) |
| Height overall | 737 mm (29.0 in) |

WEIGHT, DRY: 351 kg (773 lb)

PERFORMANCE RATINGS (S/L, static):

| T-O: CT7-5A2, -7A | 1,293 ekW (1,735 ehp) to 34°C |

Max continuous:

| CT7-5A2 | 1,192 kW (1,600 shp) to 35°C |
| CT7-7A | 1,267 kW (1,700 shp) to 30°C |

IN-TECH

IN-TECH INTERNATIONAL, INC

West 7510 Hall Avenue, Spokane, Washington 99204-5708
Telephone: (509) 455 6116
Fax: (509) 747 1701

In September 1985 In-Tech International acquired the Merlyn engine (see Machen in 1985-86 *Jane's*). Due to product liability exposure, the Merlyn will be available for aircraft only after experience shows that the risk can be minimised.

IN-TECH MERLYN

Research shows a need for a new piston engine in the 373-522 kW (500-700 hp) class, with liquid cooling. Design goals included a power: weight ratio better than 0.34 kg/kW (1 lb/hp); ability to use multifuels (Jet A, JP-4, JP-5, Nos. 1 and 2 diesel); an sfc 20 per cent lower than small turboprops; low frontal area and drag; and at least six accessory pads.
TYPE: Three-cylinder inline two-stroke diesel.
CYLINDERS: Bore 130 mm (5.125 in). Stroke 86 mm (3.388 in). Capacity 3.47 litres (210 cu in). Twin overhead camshaft and four exhaust valves per cylinder. Offset crankshaft.
DIMENSIONS:

Length	1,283 mm (50.5 in)
Width	457 mm (18.0 in)
Height	648 mm (25.5 in)

WEIGHT, DRY: 263 kg (580 lb)

In-Tech Merlyn
two-stroke diesel
(485 kW; 650 hp)

PERFORMANCE RATINGS:

| T-O | 485 kW (650 hp) at 4,800 rpm |
| Max continuous | 448 kW (600 hp) |

JAVELIN

JAVELIN AIRCRAFT COMPANY INC

Municipal Airport, Augusta, Kansas 67010
Telephone: (316) 733 1011

Javelin has a long-term programme to produce liquid cooled aircraft engines. Extensive work has been done on the Javelin Ford 140 (cu in capacity). A completely engineered power plant with turbocharger was flight tested in a Cessna 172. The 140T continues in demand for replica fighters, but most homebuilders need the smaller Ford Escort/Lynx 98 of 1,607 cc (98 cu in). Six Ford 98s are on test, one being a 'hi-drive' for amphibians with the engine and radiator inside the hull and propeller above. The conventional installation weighs about 129 kg (285 lb) with toothed belt drive. By early 1982 one 98-size engine was flying in a Cessna 150, held to 93 kW (125 hp) and cruising at 44.8 kW (60 hp) with sfc of 62 µg/J (0.37 lb/h/hp). In 1983

intensive flight development was in progress on the Ford 230 (Windsor) V-6, with a continuous rating of 149 kW (200 hp) for a weight, with reduction gear and all accessories, of 176 kg (387 lb).

Javelin Ford 230 V-6 (149 kW; 200 hp)

LHTEC

LIGHT HELICOPTER TURBINE ENGINE COMPANY

MEMBER COMPANIES: **Allison Gas Turbine Division**
PO Box 420, Indianapolis 46206
Garrett Engine Division
Phoenix, Arizona 85010

These two companies have combined their resources to develop the T800-LHT-800 895 kW (1,200 shp) class turboshaft engine for the multi-service LHX programme.

T800-LHT-800

This helicopter engine stems from programmes that the two partners started prior to 1983. The Garrett TSE109 used a core based on the F109 turbofan and did extensive running before leading to the T800 technology prototypes, incorporating Allison technology, which exceeded 940 kW (1,260 shp) in December 1984 with lower than the required fuel consumption. The initial flight evaluation of the adaptive fuel control was completed in January 1985. Chandler Evans and AiResearch Electronic System Division are teamed to develop the control system. Flight development of prototype engines began on 7 March 1985. By mid-1988 prototype engines had run more than 3,500 h, including sand and ice ingestion and loss of oil demonstrations.

Cutaway of the
T800-LHT-800 turbo-
shaft engine in the
895 kW (1,200 shp)
class

MARQUARDT

THE MARQUARDT COMPANY (subsidiary of International Signal and Control Group)

16555 Saticoy Street, Van Nuys, California 91409
Telephone: (818) 989 6400
Telex: (910) 4951710
PRESIDENT: F. X. Marshall

Marquardt's main business continues to be advanced aerospace propulsion and the supply of ram air turbine power systems. Marquardt is developing composite rocket/air breathing propulsion systems for the US Air Force and Navy. Marquardt has developed bipropellant rockets for spacecraft since 1959, as described in the 1984-85 and earlier editions of *Jane's*.

MARQUARDT RAMJETS

Marquardt continues to be a principal developer of advanced ramjet systems. This activity has included the development of an integral rocket/ramjet for an advanced strategic air launched missile, the development of fixed and variable flow ducted rockets and small scale integral rocket/ramjets for air-launched missile applications.

MARQUARDT MA-196

This dual-mode scramjet is designed to operate in both subsonic and supersonic combustion modes as a function of vehicle flight speed. Below Mach 4 the engine operates as a conventional ramjet, and transitions to the supersonic combustion mode above approximately Mach 5. Engine performance in each mode has been demonstrated with both liquid hydrogen and conventional hydrocarbon fuels.

DIMENSIONS:
Length overall	2,794 mm (110 in)
Cross section	622.62 cm² (96.5 sq in)

PERFORMANCE (net thrust at dynamic pressure 4,882 kg/m²; 1,000 lb/sq ft)
Subsonic combustion	3.34 kN (750 lb) at Mach 4
Supersonic combustion	1.20 kN (270 lb) at Mach 8

SPECIFIC IMPULSE:
Subsonic combustion	3,000 s at Mach 4
Supersonic combustion	1,800 s at Mach 8

MARQUARDT ROCKETS

Precision bipropellant rocket engines are available in the thrust sizes of 0.004, 0.02, 0.04, 0.06, 0.11, 0.22, 0.44, 0.89 and 4 kN (1, 5, 10, 15, 25, 50, 100, 200 and 900 lb). Thrust sizes to 8 kN (1,800 lb) can be made available on request.

MARQUARDT R-40A

This precision control rocket was developed and qualified for the Shuttle Orbiter and is being used as an orbit insertion engine for the US Navy's Shuttle Launch Dispenser.

TYPE: Liquid propellant reaction control rocket.
PROPELLANTS: Nitrogen tetroxide and monomethyl hydrazine.
THRUST CHAMBER ASSEMBLY: Single chamber. Area ratio 20. Made of silicide coated columbium, with welded-on orthogonal and scarfed nozzle extension in same material. Internal film cooling. Multiple doublet injector with hypergolic ignition.
PROPELLANT FEED SYSTEM: Pressurised tanks, with feed of 0.526 kg (1.16 lb)/s fuel and 0.838 kg (1.85 lb)/s oxidant at 16.4 bars (238 lb/sq in abs).

DIMENSIONS:
Length overall	472 mm (18.6 in)
Nozzle exit diameter	267 mm (10.5 in)
WEIGHT, DRY:	9.5 kg (21.0 lb)

Marquardt MA-196 dual-mode scramjet

Marquardt R-40A reaction control rocket

PERFORMANCE RATINGS:
Max thrust (vacuum)	3.87 kN (870 lb)
Chamber pressure	10.5 bars (152 lb/sq in)
Specific impulse: area ratio 20	281
area ratio 120	306

MARQUARDT R-1E

This small high performance rocket was qualified as the vernier for the Shuttle Orbiter.

TYPE: Liquid bipropellant rocket for use in space.
PROPELLANTS: Nitrogen tetroxide and monomethyl hydrazine.

Marquardt R-1E vernier long scarf thruster

THRUST CHAMBER: Single chamber. Minimum area ratio 26 with orthogonal and scarfed nozzles. Made of silicide coated columbium. Insulated for buried installation. Single doublet injector with hypergolic ignition.
PROPELLANT FEED SYSTEM: Pressurised tank. Flow rate 0.016 kg (0.0354 lb)/s fuel and 0.0256 kg (0.565 lb)/s oxidant.

DIMENSIONS:
Length overall	279 mm (11.0 in)
Width	147 mm (5.8 in)
Height (depth)	145 mm (5.7 in)
WEIGHT, DRY:	3.7 kg (8.2 lb)

PERFORMANCE RATINGS:
Max thrust (vacuum)	0.11 kN (25.0 lb)
Chamber pressure	7.45 bars (108 lb/sq in)
Specific impulse (area ratio 100)	290

MNA
MICROTURBO NORTH AMERICA INC

55 Orville Drive, Bohemia, NY 11716

Telephone: (516) 567 3780
Telex: (510) 228 7320
Facsimile: (516) 567 3763
PRESIDENT: Robert P. Schiller

This company was established in 1970 as the US subsidiary of Microturbo (see under France). It makes, overhauls and repairs Microturbo turbojets, APUs and other products.

MORTON THIOKOL
MORTON THIOKOL INC

3340 Airport Rd, Ogden, Utah 84405
Telephone: (801) 625 4996
SOLID PROPELLANT ROCKET MOTOR PLANTS: Elkton, Maryland; Huntsville, Alabama; Marshall, Texas; Brigham City, Utah
PRESIDENT, AEROSPACE GROUP: U. E. Garrison

In 1943, the discovery by Thiokol of liquid polymer, a new type of synthetic rubber, paved the way for the 'case-bonded' rocket. The company's polysulphide liquid polymer proved to be the catalyst for production of efficient solid motors.

MORTON THIOKOL SHUTTLE RSRM

Each Space Shuttle solid rocket motor **(SRM)** is cast in four segments, stacked vertically in pairs as part of the solid

rocket booster system. Thrust vector control for each SRM is provided by a flexible bearing movable nozzle driven by two hydraulic actuators. After burnout, the two boosters are separated and fall back into the atmosphere, where parachutes control impact velocity into the ocean. The boosters are then towed back to a recovery site. In its original form, the SRM was the largest solid rocket propulsion system to reach operational status. It was also the first to be qualified for manned flight, and the first to demonstrate reusability of major components. A high performance motor (HPM) became standard from the eighth flight in August 1983. Development was also begun on a graphite epoxy case expected to increase into-orbit payload by 2,087 kg (4,600 lb).

As a result of the loss of STS-S.1 (Challenger) in January 1986, the SRM has been redesigned, and the **RSRM** (redesigned SRM) was to be used in resumed flights in 1988. The following HPM data will apply almost exactly to the RSRM:

DIMENSIONS:
Length	38.47 m (126.2 ft)
Diameter	3,708 mm (146 in)

WEIGHTS:
Propellant	503,487 kg (1,110,000 lb)
Loaded motor	569,893 kg (1,256,400 lb)

THRUST:
Average vacuum	11,521 kN (2,590,000 lb)

BURN TIME: 123 s

MORTON THIOKOL SPACE MOTORS

Morton Thiokol produces a wide variety of space motors for satellite orbit insertion. These range in size from 330 mm (13 in) to 1,590 mm (63 in) in diameter with weights up to 3,505 kg (7,711 lb). The largest motor flown is the STAR-63D, which provides propulsion for the McDonnell Douglas PAM-D II Spinning Solid Upper Stage and is used for both Expendable Launch Vehicles (Atlas and Delta) and Space Shuttle payloads.

NELSON
NELSON AIRCRAFT CORPORATION

PO Box 454, 8075 Pennsylvania Ave, Irwin, Pennsylvania 15642
Telephone: (412) 863 5900
PRESIDENT: Charles R. Rhoades
DEVELOPMENT DEPARTMENT: 420 Harbor Drive, Naples, Florida 33940
Telephone: (813) 261 1670

Nelson Aircraft Corporation, among its many industrial activities, produces to order the Nelson H-63 four-cylinder two-cycle aircooled engine, which is certificated by the FAA as a power unit for single-seat helicopters, and is also available as a power plant for propeller driven aircraft. These engines are capable of sustained inverted flight. Recommended overhaul period is 800 h.

The affiliated Sport Plane Power Inc in Naples, Florida, is the subject of a separate entry.

NELSON H-63
US military designation: YO-65

Developed originally as a power unit for single-seat

helicopters, the H-63 is now available in two versions, as follows:

H-63C. Basic helicopter power unit for vertical installation. Battery/electronic ignition and direct drive. Certificated by FAA. Supplied as complete power package, including clutch, cooling fan and shroud.

H-63CP. Basically as H-63C, but without clutch, fan and shroud. Intended primarily for installation in horizontal position, with direct drive to propeller. FAA certificated.

Nelson has developed a 1.07 m (42 in) wooden propeller with glassfibre covering for use with the H-63. It is suitable for either tractor or pusher installation.

TYPE: Four-cylinder horizontally opposed aircooled, two-stroke.
CYLINDERS: Bore 68.3 mm (2¹¹⁄₁₆ in). Stroke 70 mm (2¾ in). Total capacity 1.03 litres (63 cu in). Compression ratio 8 : 1.
PISTONS: Aluminium alloy casting. Two piston rings. Two needle roller bearings pressed in boss.
CONNECTING RODS: Alloy steel forging. Caged roller bearing at big-end.

The 32 kW (43 hp) Nelson H-63C four-cylinder two-stroke engine

CRANKSHAFT: Four-throw. Nitralloy shaft on ball and roller bearings.
CRANKCASE: Two-piece magnesium alloy cast case divided on horizontal centreline.
INDUCTION: Nelson diaphragm type all-angle fuel control carburettor. Fuel/oil mixture valves from crankcase through rotary valve driven by crankshaft. Intake to and exhaust from cylinders through ports.
FUEL: 80/87 octane gasoline and SAE 30 ash-free-base oil in 16 : 1 mixture.
IGNITION: Battery/electronic dual ignition with two Champion D-9 or 5 COM spark plugs per cylinder.
LUBRICATION: See under 'Fuel'.
POWER TAKE-OFF (H-63C): Hollow shaft extension from Salisbury centrifugal clutch output drive.
STARTING: 12V DC Autolite electric motor and Bendix drive.
COOLING: (H-63C): Centrifugal aluminium fan and two-piece glassfibre shrouding for FAA hot day of 37.8°C. (H-63CP): by propeller slipstream.
DIMENSIONS (H-63C):
Length 508 mm (20.0 in)
Height 376 mm (14.8 in)
Width 605 mm (23.8 in)
WEIGHT, DRY (with accessories):
H-63C 34.5 kg (76 lb)
H-63CP 30.8 kg (68 lb)

POWER RATINGS:
T-O:
H-63C 32 kW (43 hp) at 4,000 rpm
H-63CP 35.8 kW (48 hp) at 4,400 rpm
Max continuous:
H-63C 32 kW (43 hp) at 4,000 rpm
H-63CP 33.6 kW (45 hp) at 4,000 rpm

The 35.8 kW (48 hp) Nelson H-63CP for fixed-wing aircraft

PRATT & WHITNEY
UNITED TECHNOLOGIES PRATT & WHITNEY
HEADQUARTERS: East Hartford, Connecticut 06108
Telephone: (203) 565 4321
PRESIDENT: Arthur E. Wegner

Pratt & Whitney Aircraft was formed in 1925. Today Pratt & Whitney is the world's largest producer of gas turbine engines. Excluding P & W Canada (which see) it had by 1988 delivered 70,000 aircraft gas turbines, including 25,000 airline jet engines.

PRATT & WHITNEY JT8
US military designation: J52

The J52 is a two-spool turbojet, with 12 compressor stages, a 'cannular' combustion system fed by 36 dual orifice injectors and single-stage HP and LP turbines. The P-408 has two-position inlet guide vanes and aircooled first-stage turbine vanes and blades. P-8 and P-408 can be upgraded to P-409 by field retrofit.
J52-P-6A, 6B, 8A, 8B. Rated at 37.8 kN (8,500 lb st) (6A, 6B) or 41.4 kN (9,300 lb st) (8A, 8B). Powers A-4, and A-6.
J52-P-408. Rated at 49.8 kN (11,200 lb st). Powers A-4F, A-4M, some export A-4 versions, EA-6B.
J52-P-409. Rated at 53.4 kN (12,000 lb st).
Data below are for the P-408:
DIMENSIONS:
Diameter 814.3 mm (32.06 in)
Length 3,020 mm (118.9 in)
WEIGHT, DRY: 1,052 kg (2,318 lb)

PRATT & WHITNEY JT8D
This turbofan was developed to power the Boeing 727. Military versions have been developed in Sweden by Volvo Flygmotor (see RM8 in that company's entry).
The JT8D entered commercial service on 1 February 1964. It has since become the most widely used commercial jet engine, almost 12,000 having logged more than 400 million flight hours by January 1988.
The following are current versions:
JT8D-9, -9A. Develops 64.5 kN (14,500 lb st) to 28.9°C at S/L. Specified for 727-100, -100C and -200, 737-200, -200C and T-43A, DC-9-20, -30, -40, C-9A, C-9B and VC-9C, Caravelle 12 and Kawasaki C-1. Produced under licence in Japan (see Mitsubishi).
JT8D-11. Develops 66.7 kN (15,000 lb st) to 28.9°C at S/L. Specified for DC-9-20, -30 and -40.
JT8D-15. Develops 69 kN (15,500 lb st) to 28.9°C. Powers Mercure, Advanced 727 and 737, and DC-9.
JT8D-15A. In 1982 new components in the Dash-15 resulted in a 5.5 per cent reduction in cruise fuel consumption. The same parts in the Dash-17 produce the **JT8D-17A**, and when fitted to the Dash-17R the **JT8D-17AR**.
JT8D-17. Develops 71.2 kN (16,000 lb st) to 28.9°C. Powers Advanced Boeing 727 and 737, and DC-9.
JT8D-17R. Normal T-O rating 72.95 kN (16,400 lb st) but has capability of providing 4.448 kN (1,000 lb) additional thrust in the event of significant thrust loss on any other engine.
JT8D-200 Series. Described separately.
Since February 1970 all new JT8D engines have incorporated smoke reduction hardware, and conversion kits are available. Two noise reduction options are also available.
TYPE: Two-spool turbofan.
FAN: Two-stage front fan. Airflow: -9, -9A, 145 kg (319 lb)/s; -11, -15, 146 kg (322 lb)/s; -17, 147 kg (324 lb)/s; -17R, 148 kg (326 lb)/s. Bypass ratio: -9, -9A, 1.04; -11, 1.05; -15, 1.03; -17, 1.02; -17R, 1.00.

Pratt & Whitney J52-P-408 two-shaft turbojet rated at 49.8 kN (11,200 lb st)

LP COMPRESSOR: Six-stage, integral with fan.
HP COMPRESSOR: Seven-stage. Overall pressure ratio: -9, -9A, 15.9; -11, 16.2; -15, 16.5; -17, 16.9; -17R, 17.3.
COMBUSTION CHAMBER: Cannular type with nine cylindrical flame tubes, each with a single Duplex burner.
HP TURBINE: Single-stage. Solid blades in -9, aircooled in -11 and later.
LP TURBINE: Three-stage.
DIMENSIONS:
Diameter 1,080 mm (42.5 in)
Length 3,137 mm (123.5 in)
WEIGHT, DRY:
JT8D-9, -9A 1,532 kg (3,377 lb)
JT8D-11 1,537 kg (3,389 lb)

JT8D-15,	
-15A	1,549 kg (3,414 lb)
	1,576 kg (3,474 lb)
JT8D-17,	1,556 kg (3,430 lb)
-17A	1,577 kg (3,475 lb)
JT8D-17R,	1,585 kg (3,495 lb)
-17AR	1,588 kg (3,500 lb)

PERFORMANCE RATINGS:
T-O thrust (S/L, static) see model descriptions Max cruise thrust (10,670 m; 35,000 ft at Mach 0.8):
JT8D-9, -9A 18.2 kN (4,100 lb)
JT8D-11 17.6 kN (3,950 lb)
JT8D-15, -15A 18.2 kN (4,100 lb)
JT8D-17, -17R, -17A, -17AR 18.9 kN (4,240 lb)
SPECIFIC FUEL CONSUMPTION:
T-O rating:
JT8D-9, 9A 16.85 mg/Ns (0.595 lb/h/lb st)

Pratt & Whitney JT8D-219 turbofan rated at 93.4 kN (21,000 lb st)

JT8D-11	17.56 mg/Ns (0.620 lb/h/lb st)
JT8D-15	17.84 mg/Ns (0.630 lb/h/lb st)
-15A	16.63 mg/Ns (0.587 lb/h/lb st)
JT8D-17	18.27 mg/Ns (0.645 lb/h/lb st)
-17A	17.05 mg/Ns (0.602 lb/h/lb st)
JT8D-17R	18.55 mg/Ns (0.655 lb/h/lb st)
-17AR	17.31 mg/Ns (0.611 lb/h/lb st)

Max cruise rating, as above:

JT8D-9, -9A	22.86 mg/Ns (0.807 lb/h/lb)
JT8D-11	23.14 mg/Ns (0.817 lb/h/lb)
JT8D-15	22.97 mg/Ns (0.811 lb/h/lb)
JT8D-17, -17R	23.37 mg/Ns (0.825 lb/h/lb)

PRATT & WHITNEY JT8D-200 SERIES

This reduced noise derivative of the JT8D combines the HP compressor, HP turbine spool and combustion section of the JT8D-9 with advanced LP technology. It offers increased thrust with reduced noise and specific fuel consumption. The fan has increased diameter. The new six-stage LP compressor, integral with the fan, offers increased pressure ratio. The LP turbine has 20 per cent greater annular area and achieves a higher efficiency. Surrounding the engine is a new bypass duct. The exhaust system includes a 12 lobe mixer. FAA certification of the JT8D-209 was awarded in June 1979. Volvo Flygmotor has a 9 per cent share of the programme, delivering components and spares for the -209, -217 and -219.

The following are current models:

JT8D-209. Rated at 82.2 kN (18,500 lb st) to 25°C, and 85.6 kN (19,250 lb st) following loss of thrust on any other engine. Entered service in October 1980, powering the MD-81.

JT8D-217. Rated at 88.96 kN (20,000 lb st), and 92.75 kN (20,850 lb st) following loss of thrust on any other engine. Powers MD-82.

JT8D-217A. T-O thrust available to 28.9°C or up to 1,525 m (5,000 ft). Powers MD-82.

JT8D-217C. Incorporates JT8D-219 performance improvements to reduce sfc. Powers MD-82 and -87.

JT8D-219. Rated at 93.4 kN (21,000 lb st), with a reserve power of 96.5 kN (21,700 lb st). Powers MD-83 and other MD-80 aircraft.

TYPE: Two-spool turbofan.
FAN: Single-stage front fan has 34 titanium blades, with part-span shrouds. Airflow: at normal T-O rating: -209, 213 kg (469 lb)/s; -217 (all), 219 kg (483 lb)/s; -219, 221 kg (488 lb)/s. Bypass ratio: -209, 1.78; -217 (all), 1.73; -219, 1.77.
LP COMPRESSOR: Six-stage axial, integral with fan.
HP COMPRESSOR: Seven-stage axial. Overall pressure ratio: -209, 17.1; -217 (all), 18.6; -219, 19.2.
COMBUSTION CHAMBER: Nine cannular low-emissions burners with aerating fuel nozzles.
HP TURBINE: Single-stage. Aircooled blades in -217 and -219.
LP TURBINE: Three-stage.
DIMENSIONS:

Diameter	1,250 mm (49.2 in)
Length	3,911 mm (154 in)

WEIGHT, DRY:

JT8D-209	2,012 kg (4,435 lb)
JT8D-217, -217A	2,028 kg (4,470 lb)
JT8D-217C, -219	2,048 kg (4,515 lb)

PERFORMANCE RATINGS:
T-O (S/L static): see model descriptions
Max cruise thrust (10,670 m; 35,000 ft at Mach 0.8):

JT8D-209	22.0 kN (4,945 lb)
JT8D-217, -217A, -217C	23.31 kN (5,240 lb)
JT8D-219	23.35 kN (5,250 lb)

SPECIFIC FUEL CONSUMPTION:
Max cruise rating, as above:

JT8D-209	20.50 mg/Ns (0.724 lb/h/lb)
JT8D-217, -217A	21.32 mg/Ns (0.753 lb/h/lb)
JT8D-217C	20.84 mg/Ns (0.736 lb/h/lb)
JT8D-219	20.87 mg/Ns (0.737 lb/h/lb)

PRATT & WHITNEY PW4000

The PW4000 is a third generation turbofan for wide-body transports. Ratings range from 213.5 kN (48,000 lb) to 275.8 kN (62,000 lb). The first engine achieved 275 kN (61,800 lb) thrust during initial testing in April 1984. First flight test on an A300B took place on 31 July 1985. Certificated July 1986 at 249 kN (56,000 lb st) and in 1988 at 275.8 kN (62,000 lb st). Entered service on Pan Am A310 on 20 June 1987. The last two numbers denote thrust (thus, the initially certificated 56,000 lb st engine is the PW4056). Programme sharing agreements have been signed with FN (Belgium), Fiat (Italy), Norske Jet Motors (Norway), Kawasaki (Japan), Samsung (South Korea), Eldim (Netherlands) and Singapore Aircraft Industries.

Fuel consumption is reduced seven per cent compared with the JT9D-7R4. There are about half as many parts, promising reductions in maintenance cost exceeding 25 per cent. HP compressor pressure ratio is increased by 10 per cent and the HP rotor operates at 27 per cent higher speed.

The PW4000 incorporates single-crystal turbine blades, aerodynamically enhanced aerofoils, an efficiency improving Thermatic rotor, and a full authority electronic engine control. It fits into existing -7R4 nacelles with minimum changes.

TYPE: Two-shaft turbofan.
FAN: Single stage. Titanium alloy hub retains 38 titanium alloy blades with aft part-span shrouds. Diameter 2,373

The Pratt & Whitney PW4000 turbofan engine

PW4000 MODELS

Model	Thrust (ideal nozzle)	Application
PW4152	231.3 kN (52,000 lb) to 42.2°C	A310-300
PW4156	249.1 kN (56,000 lb) to 30°C	A300-600
PW4158	258.0 kN (58,000 lb) to 30°C	A300-600R
PW4052	232.2 kN (52,200 lb) to 33.3°C	767-200/200ER
PW4056	252.4 kN (56,750 lb) to 33.3°C	767-300/-300ER/747-400
PW4060	266.9 kN (60,000 lb) to 30°C	767-300ER/747-400
PW4360	266.9 kN (60,000 lb) to 30°C	MD-11

Ratings are S/L static, no bleed or power extraction

mm (93.44 in). Data for 249 kN (56,000 lb st) rating: airflow 773 kg (1,705 lb)/s. Fan pressure ratio 1.7. Bypass ratio 4.85.
LP COMPRESSOR: Four stages with controlled diffusion aerofoils.
HP COMPRESSOR: Eleven stages with first four vane rows variable. Clearance control accomplished via rotor response to ventilation air temperature. Overall pressure ratio at 249 kN rating, 29.7.
COMBUSTOR: Annular, forged nickel alloy roll-ring with double-pass cooling. 24 air-blast anti-coking injectors.
HP TURBINE: Two stages with aircooled blades cast as single crystal (PWA 1480) in first row and directional crystal (PWA 1422) in second row, retained in double-hub nickel alloy rotor with active clearance control. Vane aerofoils thermal barrier coated.
LP TURBINE: Four stages with active clearance control.
CONTROL SYSTEM: Full authority digital electronic with dual channel computer.
DIMENSIONS:

Length	3,371 mm (132.7 in)
Fan case diameter	2,463 mm (96.98 in)
Exhaust case diameter	1,467 mm (57.76 in)

WEIGHT, DRY:

Basic engine	4,173 kg (9,200 lb)

RATINGS: See table.
SPECIFIC FUEL CONSUMPTION (ISA, ideal nozzle, Mach 0.8, 10,670 m/35,000 ft): 15.21 mg/Ns (0.537 lb/h/lb)

PRATT & WHITNEY JT9D

This was the first of the new era of large, high bypass ratio turbofans on which the design of wide-body commercial transports rests. First run was in December 1966. The first flight of the Boeing 747 was on 9 February 1969.

Current versions include:

JT9D-3A. Water injection rating of 200.8 kN (45,150 lb) to 26.7°C. Powers 747-100 and -200B.

JT9D-7. Higher thrust version; powers 747-200B, C, F and SR.

JT9D-7A. Aerodynamic improvements; powers 747-200 and 747SP.

JT9D-7F, -7J. Directionally solidified turbine blades; -7J also has improved cooling, giving -7F T-O rating without water injection.

JT9D-7Q, -7R. Described later.

JT9D-20, -20J. D-7A and D-7J with accessory gearbox under fan case.

JT9D-59A, -70A. Fan diameter approximately 25.4 mm (one inch) larger, with re-profiled blades; LP compressor has zero (fourth) stage and is redesigned; burners recontoured, HP turbine carbon seal added, HP blades directionally solidified, and HP annulus larger. Both configured for common nacelle for 747 (-70A) or DC-10 and A300B (-59A). The **-59D** and **-70D** are higher thrust versions.

JT9D-7Q Series. As -59A and -70A but configured like -7 for 747-200 nacelle. Thrust 236-249 kN (53,000-56,000 lb).

JT9D-7R4 Series. Seven models (7R4D to 7R4H), with larger fan with wide chord blades, zero stage on LP compressor, improved combustor, single crystal HP turbine blades, increased diameter LP turbine, supervisory electronic fuel control and many smaller changes. 7R4D, 7R4E and 7R4E4 for Boeing 767; 7R4D1 and 7R4E1 for A310; -7R4G2 for 747; -7R4H1 for the A300B-600.

Deliveries exceed 3,150 and flight time in early 1988 was in excess of 80 million h.

The following applies to early versions, with later models in parentheses:

TYPE: Two-shaft turbofan of high bypass ratio.

FAN: Single stage, with 46 titanium blades of 4.6 aspect ratio (-7R4, 40 blades of 4.0 a.r.) and two part-span shrouds (-7R4, one shroud) dovetailed in titanium LP rotor. Nominal airflow 684 kg (1,509 lb)/s at 3,650 rpm (-7, 698 kg; 1,540 lb/s at 3,750 rpm; -59A, -70A, -7Q 744 kg; 1,640 lb/s at 3,430 rpm; -7R4G/H, 769 kg; 1,695 lb/s at 3,530 rpm). Pressure ratio typically 1.6 : 1. Bypass ratio: -3A, 5.17; -7, 5.15; -59A, -70A, 4.9; -7R4D, E, 5.0; -7R4G2, H1, 4.8.

LP COMPRESSOR: Three stages (JT9D-59A, -70A, -7Q, -7R4, four stages), rotating with fan. Rotor stages have 104, 132 and 130 (-7Q, -59A, -70, -7R4, 108, 120, 112, 100) dovetailed blades of titanium alloy. Core airflow typically 118 kg (260 lb)/s (all versions).

HP COMPRESSOR: Eleven stages. Rotor stages have 60, 84, 102, 100, 110, 108, 104, 94 and 100 dovetailed titanium blades and 102 and 90 nickel alloy blades. First three stator stages are variable, plus intermediate IGV stage. Max HP speed: -3A, 7,850 rpm; -7, 8,000 rpm; -7R4E4/G/H, 8,080 rpm. Overall pressure ratio: -3A, 21.5; -7, 22.2; -7Q, -59A, -70, 24.5; -7R4D, D1, 23.4; -7R4E/E1/E4, 24.2; -7R4G2, 26.3; -7R4H1, 26.7.

COMBUSTION CHAMBER: Annular, nickel alloy. Ignition by dual AC 4-joule capacitor system serving two plugs.

FUEL SYSTEM: Hydraulic control operating at up to 76 bars (1,100 lb/sq in). (-7R4 except G2 has digital electronic system to control hydromechanical control; engine is operational with or without electronic system functioning.) Water injection adds 18.1 kg (40 lb) to weight (not fitted to -7R4).

FUEL GRADE: P&W specification PWA 522.

HP TURBINE: Two stages. First has 116 aircooled blades and second has 138 solid blades (aircooled in -D7 and subsequent; -7R4, single crystal in first-stage blades to 222.4 kN, 50,000 lb st, and in first and second blades and second stator (vane) for higher-thrust models.) Turbine inlet temperature (-3A, max T-O), typically 1,243°C (-59A, -70A, 1,350-1,370°C, -7R4 1,200-1,300°C).

LP TURBINE: Four stages. Solid nickel alloy blades held in fir tree roots in discs of nickel alloy (fifth disc, iron alloy). In 1982 an improved LP turbine was introduced to -7R4 production.

REVERSER: Fan reverser comprises a translating sleeve which moves aft, causing links to close blocker doors and simultaneously pulling aft the cascade vanes. Primary (core) reverser, uses fixed cascades uncovered by aft movement of translating sleeves. No primary reverser on -59A, -70A, -7Q or -7R4.

ACCESSORY DRIVES: Main accessory gearbox driven from front of HP spool and mounted under central diffuser case (-20, -59A, -70A, under fan discharge case). Accessories include CSD (IDG on -7R4 except G2) fuel pump and control, starter, hydraulic pump, alternator and N_2 tachometer; Boeing 747 includes primary reverser motor and DC-10-40 a second hydraulic pump and fuel boost pump.

LUBRICATION SYSTEM: Pressure feed through fuel/oil cooler to four main bearings and return to 18.8-37.6 litre (5-10 US; 4.16-8.32 Imp gallon) tank.

OIL GRADE: PWA 521C.

STARTING: Pneumatic, by HamStan PS 700 or AiResearch ATS100-384 (DC-10, PS 700 only).

DIMENSIONS:
JT9D-3A, -7, -7A, -7F, -7J, -20:
  Diameter   2,427 mm (95.56 in)
  Length (flange to flange)   3,255 mm (128.15 in)
JT9D-59A, -70A, -7Q:
  Diameter   2,464 mm (97.0 in)
  Length   3,358 mm (132.2 in)
JT9D-7R4D to H:
  Diameter   2,463 mm (96.98 in)
  Length   3,371 mm (132.7 in)

WEIGHT, DRY:
Guaranteed, including standard equipment:
JT9D-3A   3,905 kg (8,608 lb)
JT9D-7, -7A, -7F, -7J   4,014 kg (8,850 lb)
JT9D-20   3,833 kg (8,450 lb)

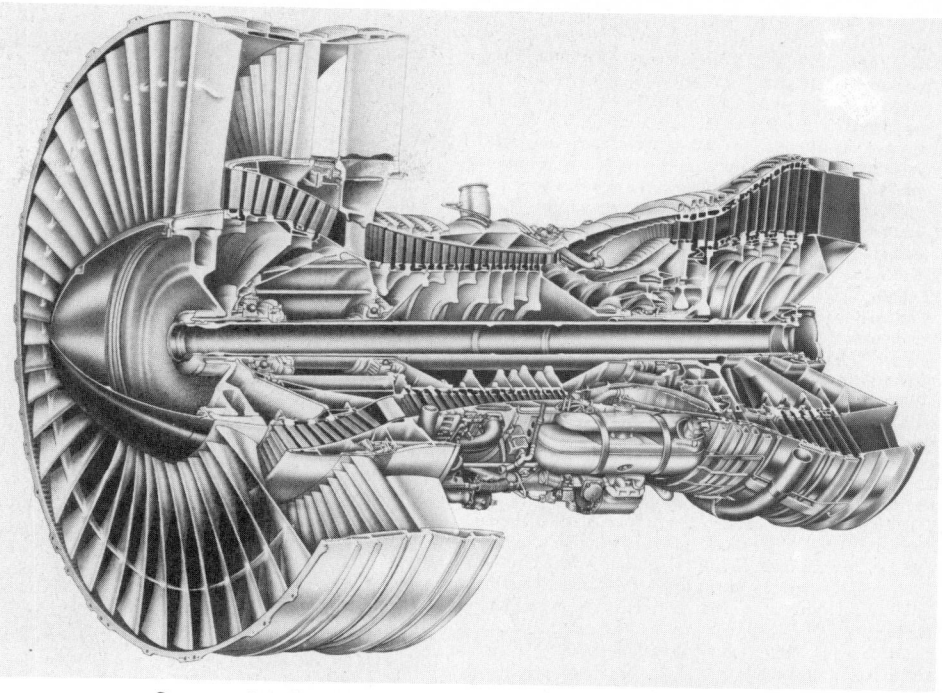

Cutaway drawing of JT9D-7R4 (213.5-249 kN; 48,000-56,000 lb st)

JTRD-20J	3,883 kg (8,560 lb)
JT9D-59A	4,146 kg (9,140 lb)
JT9D-70A	4,153 kg (9,155 lb)
JT9D-7Q	4,216 kg (9,295 lb)
JT9D-7R4D, E, E4	4,039 kg (8,905 lb)
JT9D-7R4D1, E1	4,029 kg (8,885 lb)
JT9D-7R4G2	4,143 kg (9,135 lb)
JT9D-7R4H1	4,029 kg (8,885 lb)

PERFORMANCE RATINGS (ideal nozzle):
T-O, dry:

JT9D-3A	193.9 kN (43,600 lb st) to 26.7°C
JT9D-7	202.8 kN (45,600 lb st) to 26.7°C
JT9D-7A	205.7 kN (46,250 lb st) to 26.7°C
JT9D-7F	213.5 kN (48,000 lb st) to 26.7°C
JT9D-7J, -20J	222.4 kN (50,000 lb st) to 30°C
JT9D-20	206.0 kN (46,300 lb st) to 28.9°C
JT9D-59A, -70A, -7Q	236.0 kN (53,000 lb st) to 30°C
JT9D-7R4D, D1	213.5 kN (48,000 lb st) to 33°C
JT9D-7R4E, E1	222.4 kN (50,000 lb st) to 33°C
JT9D-7R4E4	222.4 kN (50,000 lb st) to 45.6°C
JT9D-7R4G2	243.4 kN (54,750 lb st) to 30°C
JT9D-7R4H1	249.0 kN (56,000 lb st) to 30°C

T-O, wet:

JT9D-3A	200.8 kN (45,150 lb st) to 26.7°C
JT9D-7	210.0 kN (47,200 lb st) to 30°C
JT9D-7A	212.4 kN (47,750 lb st) to 30°C
JT9D-7F	222.4 kN (50,000 lb st) to 30°C
JT9D-20	220.0 kN (49,400 lb st) to 30°C

Max cruise, 10,670 m (35,000 ft) at Mach 0.85:

JT9D-3A, -7	45.4 kN (10,200 lb)
JT9D-7F, -7J	48.2 kN (10,830 lb)
JT9D-20, -20J	49.2 kN (11,050 lb)
JT9D-59A, -70A, -7Q	47.5 kN (10,680 lb)
JT9D-7R4D, D1	53.2 kN (11,950 lb)
JT9D-7R4E, E1	50.0 kN (11,250 lb)
JT9D-7R4G2, H1	52.0 kN (11,700 lb)
	54.5 kN (12,250 lb)

SPECIFIC FUEL CONSUMPTION (ideal nozzle):
Max cruise, ISA + 10°C. Mach 0.85 at 10,670 m (35,000 ft):

JT9D-3A	17.67 mg/Ns (0.624 lb/h/lb)
JT9D-7	17.55 mg/Ns (0.620 lb/h/lb)
JT9D-7A	17.69 mg/Ns (0.625 lb/h/lb)
JT9D-7F, -7Q, -59A, -70A	17.87 mg/Ns (0.631 lb/h/lb)
JT9D-20, -20J	17.67 mg/Ns (0.624 lb/h/lb)
JT9D-7R4D, D1	17.42 mg/Ns (0.615 lb/h/lb)
JT9D-7R4E, E1	17.55 mg/Ns (0.620 lb/h/lb)
JT9D-7R4G2	18.10 mg/Ns (0.639 lb/h/lb)
JT9D-7R4H1	17.79 mg/Ns (0.628 lb/h/lb)

PRATT & WHITNEY PW2000
US military designation: F117

The PW2000 is a third generation turbofan upon which major changes have been made since 1972. In mid-1980 it was scaled up to be compatible with the Boeing 757-200, at 170.1 kN (38,250 lb st). The first model was given the designation **PW2037**, the last two digits denoting thrust in thousands of pounds. The first engine test run took place in December 1981. FAA certification was achieved in December 1983, and the first flight was made on the prototype 757 on 14 March 1984.

Companies participating are MTU of Federal Germany and Fiat of Italy. Pratt & Whitney bears 84.8 per cent of the programme, MTU 11.2 per cent and Fiat 4 per cent. A collaboration agreement between these companies was signed in July 1977.

Current applications are in versions of the Boeing 757 and McDonnell Douglas C-17. The PW2037-powered 757 was certificated on 25 October 1984 and entered revenue service on 1 December. An uprated engine, the **PW2040**, was certificated in January 1987 and entered service in September 1987 powering the 757PF. The C-17 will be powered by four **F117-PW-100** engines similar to the commercial engine.

The PW2000 engine family is expected to consist ultimately of a series of models which will span a take-off thrust range of 133.4 to 195.7 kN (30,000 to 44,000 lb).

TYPE: Two-shaft turbofan of high bypass ratio.

FAN: Single-stage. Titanium forged hub, with 36 inserted titanium alloy blades with part-span shrouds. Tip diameter 1,994 mm (78.5 in). Max airflow 608 kg (1,340 lb)/s. Pressure ratio 1.7. Bypass ratio 6.0.

LP COMPRESSOR: Four stages, with controlled diffusion aerofoils with thick leading- and trailing-edges.

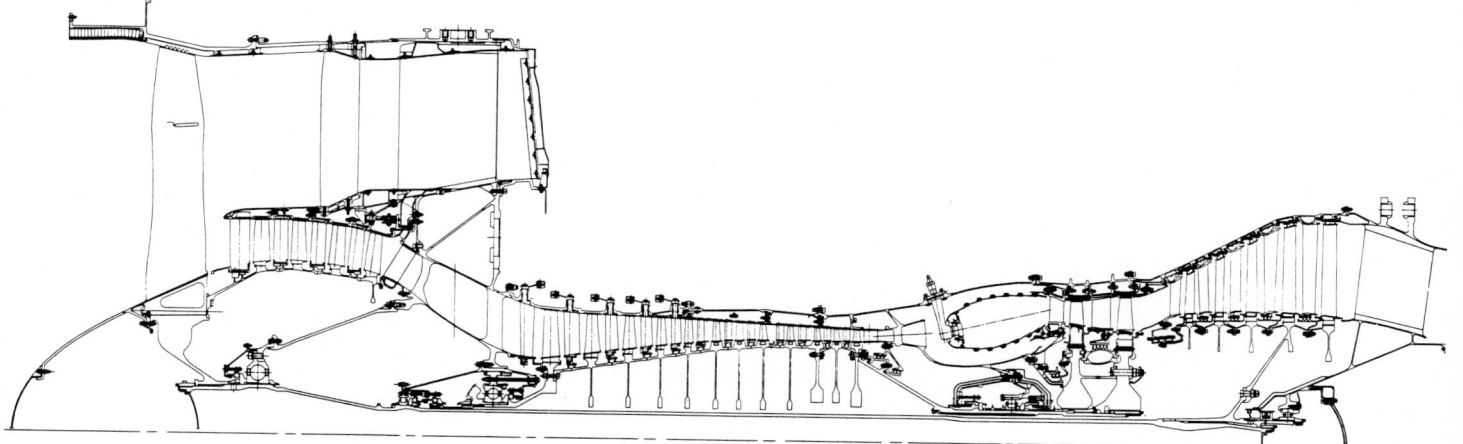

Longitudinal cross-section through Pratt & Whitney PW2037, rated at 170.1 kN (38,250 lb st)

HP COMPRESSOR: Twelve stages, with controlled diffusion aerofoils. Variable vanes on first five stages and active clearance control on last eight stages. Overall cruise pressure ratio 31.8.

COMBUSTION CHAMBER: Annular, with flame tube fabricated in nickel alloy. Single-pipe fuel nozzles.

HP TURBINE: Two stages with aircooled blades cast as single crystals in PW 1480 alloy. Rotors with active clearance control. Both discs of PW1100 nickel based powder.

LP TURBINE: Five stages, with active clearance control.

CONTROL SYSTEM: Full authority digital electronic with two redundant computers.

DIMENSIONS:

Length	3,591 mm (141.4 in)
Fan case diameter	2,154 mm (84.8 in)

WEIGHT, DRY: 3,248 kg (7,160 lb)

PERFORMANCE RATING (T-O, S/L):

PW2037	170.1 kN (38,250 lb st)
PW2040	185.5 kN (41,700 lb st)

SPECIFIC FUEL CONSUMPTION (ideal nozzle, cruise at Mach 0.8 at 10,670 m; 35,000 ft): 15.95 mg/Ns (0.563 lb/h/lb)

PRATT & WHITNEY JTF10A
US military designation: TF30

Development of this military engine began in 1958. It was chosen as the power plant for the F-111 and A-7A.

A third application is the F-14A Tomcat, powered by the **TF30-P-414**, since converted to **-414A** standard which significantly improves engine stability and extends overhaul interval to 2,400 h.

The following description refers to the P-414A:

TYPE: Two-shaft turbofan.

FAN: Three stages. Rotor and stator and casings all of titanium, except for steel containment case.

LP COMPRESSOR: Six stages integral with fan. Titanium, except steel stator blades.

HP COMPRESSOR: Seven stages, mainly nickel alloy.

COMBUSTION CHAMBER: Can-annular, with eight Hastelloy combustors, each with four dual-orifice burners.

FUEL SYSTEM: HP system (above 69 bars; 1,000 lb/sq in), with conventional hydromechanical control.

FUEL GRADES: JP-4, JP-5, JP-8.

HP TURBINE: Single stage, with 40 aircooled nozzle guide vanes (stators) of single-crystal nickel based material and aircooled rotor blades of nickel-based alloy.

LP TURBINE: Three stages of nickel based alloys.

AFTERBURNER: Double wall outer duct and inner liner carrying five-zone combustion system. Ignition by auxiliary squirt, coupled with main squirt in No. 4 burner can which produces hot streak through turbine. Max gas temperature 1,677°C.

NOZZLE: Primary nozzle has six hinged segments actuated by fuel rams. Ejector nozzle has 18 iris segments.

ACCESSORY DRIVES: Main gearbox under compressor, driven by bevel shaft from HP spool.

LUBRICATION SYSTEM: Self contained dry sump system.

OIL GRADE: MIL-L-7808, MIL-L-23699.

STARTING: Air turbine starter on left forward drive pad.

DIMENSIONS:

Max diameter	1,293 mm (50.9 in)
Length overall	5,987 mm (235.7 in)

WEIGHT, DRY: 1,905 kg (4,201 lb)

PERFORMANCE RATING:

T-O, S/L	93 kN (20,900 lb st)

SPECIFIC FUEL CONSUMPTION (T-O): 78.75 mg/Ns (2.78 lb/h/lb st)

Pratt & Whitney PW2037 turbofan engine

PRATT & WHITNEY JTF22
US military designation: F100

The JTF22 is a military turbofan with afterburner for supersonic applications. In February 1970 the decision was taken to use the JTF22 core engine as the basis for the **F100-PW-100** (JTF22A-25A) to power the F-15 Eagle. Subsequently, the F100 was adopted for the F-16, early versions of which are powered by the **F100-PW-200**, with a backup fuel control. By 1988 more than 4,600 engines had flown nearly 5 million hours.

In mid-1985 the improved **F100-PW-220** was qualified for the F-15C and F-16C (see 'CONTROL SYSTEM' below).

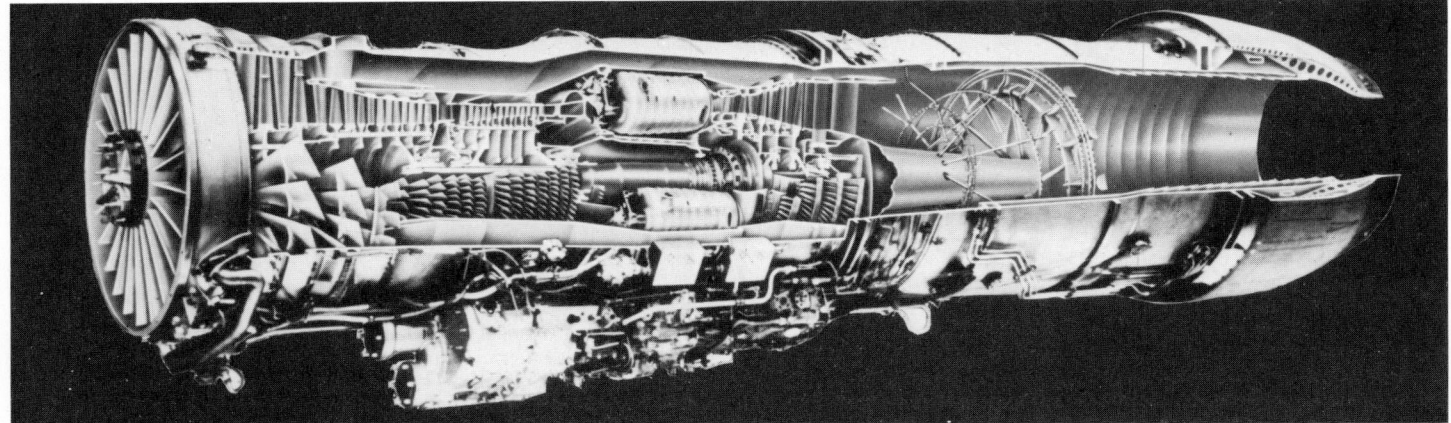

Cutaway drawing of TF30-P-414A, rated at 93 kN (20,900 lb st)

Cutaway drawing of the F100-PW-220, rated at 104.3 kN (23,450 lb st)

Cutaway drawing of the Pratt & Whitney PW1120 afterburning turbojet (91.7 kN; 20,620 lb st)

Upgrade packages are available for PW-100 and -200 engines to give engines equivalent to the -220. Further in the future is the **F100-PW-229** (see PW1129).

TYPE: Two-shaft turbofan with afterburner.

FAN: Three stages. Fan blades have part-span shrouds. Entry diameter 928 mm (36.5 in). Bypass ratio 0.7.

COMPRESSOR: Ten-stage axial, on HP shaft. First three stages have variable stators. Pressure ratio 8. Overall pressure ratio 25.

COMBUSTION CHAMBER: Annular. Cobalt based alloy with film cooling. Air blast fuel nozzles. Capacitor-discharge ignition.

HP TURBINE: Two stages. Discs forged IN-100. Blades and vanes directionally solidified Mar M200/Hf alloy with aluminide coating; first rotor transpiration convectively cooled, second with HP bleed only. Max gas temperature 1,399°C. Maximum speed 13,450 rpm.

LP TURBINE: Two stages. Discs forged IN-100. Blades, uncooled, cast in IN-100 with aluminide coating. Max speed 10,400 rpm.

AFTERBURNER: Five spray rings in flow from core and two downstream in bypass airflow. Flameholder downstream with high energy ignition to give modulated light-up.

NOZZLE: Multi-flap balanced beam articulated nozzle.

CONTROL SYSTEM: Unified hydromechanical fuel and nozzle area control, with electronic supervisory control. Dash-220 includes a digital electronic control, gear type main fuel pump, and ILC (increased life core) with a 4,000 cycle depot refurbishment interval.

DIMENSIONS:

Overall diameter	1,181 mm (46.5 in)
Length:	
F100-PW-100, excl bullet	4,855 mm (191.2 in)
F100-PW-220	5,280 mm (208 in)

WEIGHT, DRY:

F100-PW-100	1,375 kg (3,033 lb)
F100-PW-200	1,400 kg (3,087 lb)
F100-PW-220	1,444 kg (3,184 lb)

PERFORMANCE RATINGS (S/L, ISA):

Max T-O, dry:	
F100-PW-100	65.2 kN (14,670 lb st)
F100-PW-220	63.9 kN (14,370 lb st)
Max T-O, augmented:	
F100-PW-100	106.0 kN (23,830 lb st)
F100-PW-220	104.3 kN (23,450 lb st)

PRATT & WHITNEY PW1120

The PW1120 is a turbojet derivative of the F100. Its development was initiated in June 1980. It retains the F100 core module, gearbox, fuel pump and forward ducts, as well as the F100 digital electronic control, with only minor modifications.

Unique PW1120 components include a wide chord LP

Mockup of Pratt & Whitney F119, with 2D (two-dimensional) nozzle with limited thrust vectoring

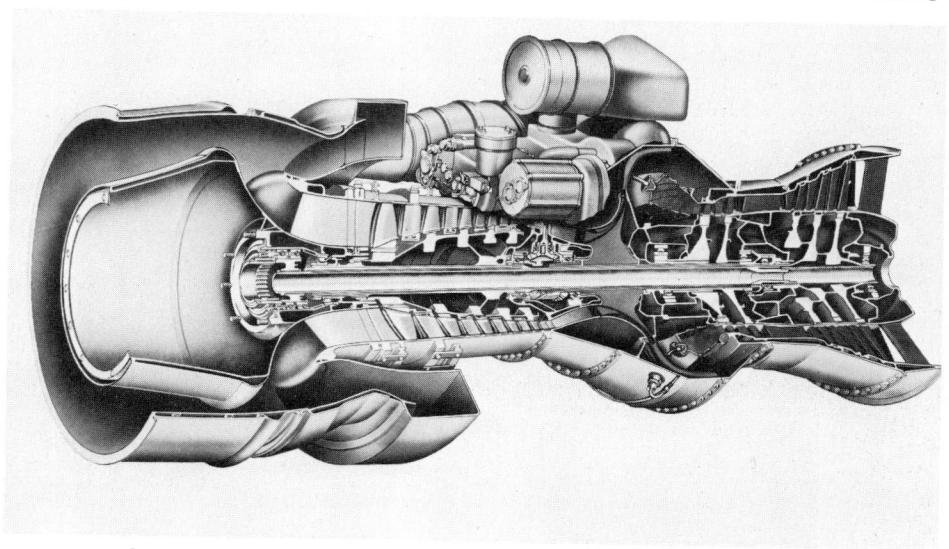

Cutaway of the Pratt & Whitney PW3005 turboshaft (4,993 kW; 6,693 shp)

compressor, single-stage uncooled LP turbine, simplified single stream augmentor, and a lightweight convergent/divergent nozzle. Mass flow is 80.9 kg (178 lb)/s and pressure ratio 26.8.

Full scale testing was initiated in June 1982, and the engine completed flight clearance testing in August 1984. The PW1120 was selected to power the Israeli Lavi, later cancelled. Flight demonstration in an F-4 began on 30 July 1986. The engine is a candidate for F-4 re-engining as well as for other fighter projects.

DIMENSIONS:

Max diameter	1,021 mm (40.2 in)
Length	4,110 mm (161.8 in)

WEIGHT, DRY: 1,292 kg (2,848 lb)

PERFORMANCE RATINGS (S/L, ISA):

Max T-O	91.7 kN (20,620 lb st)
Intermediate	60.3 kN (13,550 lb st)

SPECIFIC FUEL CONSUMPTION:

Maximum	52.65 mg/Ns (1.86 lb/h/lb)
Intermediate	22.7 mg/Ns (0.8 lb/h/lb)

Cutaway drawing of the Pratt & Whitney PW1129 augmented turbofan (129 kN; 29,000 lb st)

PRATT & WHITNEY PW1129
US military designation: F100-PW-229

The PW1129 has been designed as a bolt-in replacement for the F100 in F-15s and F-16s. Using components of the F100-PW-220 and PW1128 EMD (see 1984-85 *Jane's*), it has many new features including an improved compressor and Float-wall combustor. The first engine ran in late 1986, and the first flight was due in mid-1988. Production engines will be available in 1989.

DIMENSIONS:

Length	5,280 mm (208 in)
Diameter	1,180 mm (46.5 in)

WEIGHT, DRY: 1,651 kg (3,640 lb)

PERFORMANCE RATINGS (S/L, ISA):

Max T-O	129 kN (29,000 lb st)
Intermediate	80.1 kN (18,000 lb st)

SPECIFIC FUEL CONSUMPTION:

Max T-O	58.07 mg/Ns (2.05 lb/h/lb)
Intermediate	20.96 mg/Ns (0.74 lb/h/lb)

PRATT & WHITNEY PW5000
US military designation: F119

This advanced augmented turbofan is competing against the General Electric GE37 as the ATF (advanced tactical fighter) engine for the period after 1995. The F119 will provide supersonic persistence, without afterburner. It has roughly 40 per cent fewer parts than predecessor fighter engines, and should have much greater durability. A demonstrator began sea-level testing in mid-1986. Flight test of F119 prototypes is planned for the early 1990s, with operational introduction due in the mid to late 1990s. Development is continuing on advanced exhaust nozzles that could incorporate reversing and limited vectoring features.

PRATT & WHITNEY PW3000

In June 1981 Pratt & Whitney announced this family of shaft drive engines in the power range 2,984-5,968 kW (4,000-8,000 shp). The 3000 series engines are planned in turboshaft and turboprop versions for helicopters and fixed-wing aircraft. The same core can be mated with a fan to yield a turbofan. The first member of the family is the PW3005, rated at 4,993 kW (6,693 shp) as a turboshaft.
The following data are estimates:

DIMENSIONS:

Length: Turboshaft with inlet particle separator	2,017 mm (79.4 in)
Turboprop	1,580 mm (62.2 in)
Diameter: Turboshaft with IPS	787 mm (31 in)
Turboprop	655 mm (25.8 in)

WEIGHT, DRY:

Turboshaft with IPS	429 kg (946 lb)
Turboprop	385 kg (850 lb)

PERFORMANCE RATINGS (ISA, S/L, static, max power):

Turboshaft	4,993 kW (6,693 shp) to 15°C
Turboprop	3,790 kW (5,080 shp) to 39.5°C

PW-ALLISON

MEMBER COMPANIES:
Allison Gas Turbine Division, GMC
Indianapolis, Indiana 46206
Pratt & Whitney, UTC
East Hartford, Connecticut 06108

United Technologies' Pratt & Whitney and General Motors' Allison Gas Turbine Division formed a joint partnership in February 1987 to develop propfan propulsion systems. The partnership has the backing of propfan pioneer Hamilton Standard.

PW-ALLISON MODEL 578DX

PW-Allison is developing the Model 578 geared counter-rotation propfan propulsion system for 100/190-passenger commercial transport aircraft. The initial flight test demonstrator is the 578DX, rated at 7,460 kW (10,000 shp). This incorporates a three-stage LP compressor, modified Allison 571 core engine, and an advanced technology 9,698 kW (13,000 shp) differential planetary gear system. The latter drives two 3.5 m (11 ft 6 in) six-blade Hamilton Standard propfans. A modified Pratt & Whitney PW2037 full authority digital electronic engine control regulates fuel flow, variable compressor stators and propfan blade angles. The 578DX was to be demonstrated on an MD-80 aircraft by the third quarter of 1988.

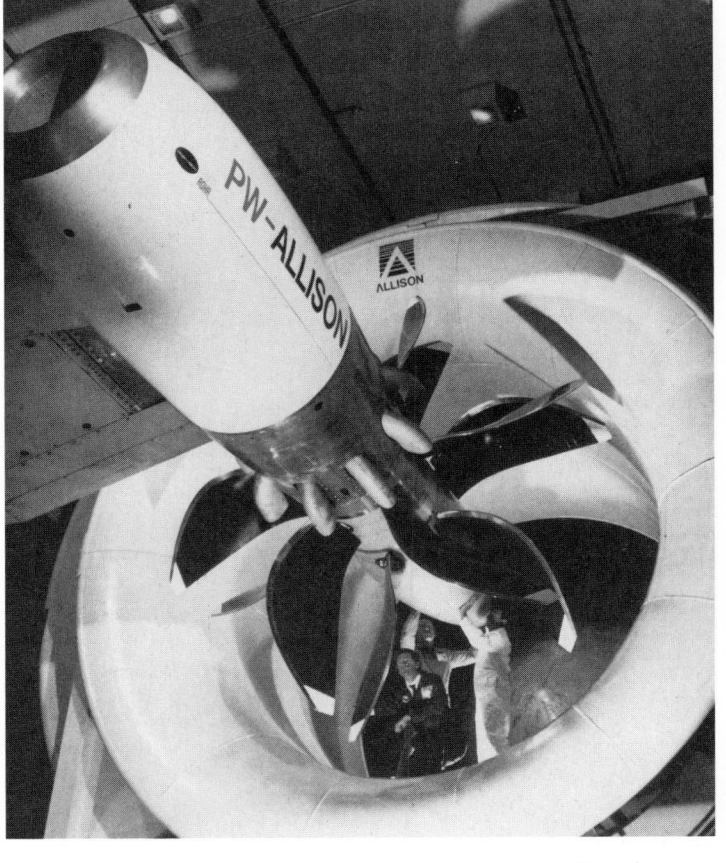

PW-Allison Model 578DX on preliminary flight rating test

ROCKETDYNE
ROCKETDYNE DIVISION OF ROCKWELL INTERNATIONAL

6633 Canoga Avenue, Canoga Park, California 91303
Telephone: (818) 710 6300
Telex: 698478
PRESIDENT: R. Schwartz

Rocketdyne is devoted primarily to rocket engines for the US Air Force and the National Aeronautics and Space Administration. It was established as a separate division in November 1955. Rocketdyne liquid propellant engines have powered more than three-quarters of all large US space vehicle stages.

ROCKETDYNE SSME

On 13 July 1971 Rocketdyne was selected by NASA to develop the main engine for the Shuttle Orbiter. Three of these engines provide a total of 6,833 kN (1,536,000 lb) vacuum thrust, and power the vehicle to near orbit.

The SSME was designed for high reliability, reusability, multiple re-start capability and low cost. It is designed for 7½ h of burn time, accrued during 55 flights.

The design combines the merits of high pressure operation, an optimum bell nozzle, and a regeneratively cooled thrust chamber, capable of 11° gimballing. The chamber wall is cooled to 567°C, although the combustion temperature is about 3,300°C. No propellants are wasted in the cooling process. The combustion chamber wall is made of slotted metal, rather than tubes, using Rocketdyne developed NARloy-Z, copper alloy.

The SSME is controlled by a unique system incorporating dual redundant digital computers. This system monitors engine parameters such as pressure and flow rate, and the engine is adjusted automatically to operate at the required thrust and mixture ratio. The system also develops a record of engine operating history for maintenance purposes.

Flight certification was achieved in December 1980. Another cycle in the FPL (full power level) certification programme was completed in April 1983. Certification required four test series of 5,000 s each, involving engine

SSME undergoing FPL test

power levels of 104, 105, 109 and 111 per cent. This testing provided flight readiness certification for engine sets for the *Challenger*, *Columbia*, *Discovery* and *Atlantis* orbiters.

The Shuttle programme began its operational phase with the STS-5 launch of the *Columbia* on 11 November 1982. On 4 April 1983 a second vehicle, *Challenger*, powered by SSMEs rated at 104 per cent thrust, was launched on STS-6. The third Orbiter, *Discovery*, was launched on 30 August 1984. A total of 24 launches, all successful, had been accomplished prior to the loss of *Challenger* on 28 January 1986. Excellent flight-to-flight performance repeatability had been achieved.

Certification extension testing up to 20 equivalent flights has been accomplished on one engine, while another has run 15 equivalent flights at 104 per cent power level. Testing is being continued to extend the life of the HP turbomachinery, increase performance margin by reducing flow losses and investigate other modifications that could allow uprating or life extension.

COMBUSTION CHAMBER: Channel wall construction with regenerative cooling by the hydrogen fuel. Concentric element injector.

TURBOPUMPS: Two low pressure pumps boost the inlet pressures for two high pressure pumps. Dual pre-burners provide turbine drive gases to power the high-pressure pumps. Hydrogen pump discharge pressure is 485.4 bars (7,040 lb/sq in) at 37,250 rpm; it develops 57,650 kW (77,310 hp).

CONTROLLER: Honeywell digital computer provides closed loop control, in addition to data processing and signal conditioning for control, checkout, monitoring engine status, and maintenance data acquisition.

CONTROLS: Hydraulic actuation. Dual redundant self-monitoring servo actuators respond to signals from the controller to position the ball valves. A pneumatic system provides backup for engine cut-off.

MAINTENANCE: Airline type maintenance procedure for on-the-vehicle servicing. Planned life between overhauls 40 flights.

DIMENSIONS:
Length 4,242 mm (167 in)
Diameter at nozzle exit 2,388 mm (94 in)

PERFORMANCE:
S/L thrust (one engine) 1,856 kN (417,300 lb)
Vacuum thrust 2,277 kN (512,000 lb)
Specific impulse 455 s
Chamber pressure 224.8 bars (3,260 lb/sq in)

Throttling ratio 1.67
Expansion ratio 77.5

ROTORWAY
ROTORWAY AIRCRAFT INC
7411 W Galveston, Chandler, Arizona 85226
Telephone: (602) 961 1001
Telex: 683 5059

RotorWay produces helicopters for amateur assembly (see Sport Aircraft section). Since 1974 it has been developing its own power plants.

ROTORWAY RW152-D
This engine was designed to power the RotorWay Exec light helicopter.

TYPE: Horizontally opposed, water-cooled, four-cylinder four-stroke piston engine. Crankshaft vertical or horizontal.

CYLINDERS: Offset left and right for plain connecting rods side by side. Capacity 2.65 litres (162 cu in). Compression ratio 9.6.

INDUCTION: Dual downdraught carburettors with heating. Overhead valves.

IGNITION: High voltage distributor coil.

LUBRICATION: Dry sump. Oil temperature 82°-99°C. Oil pressure 2.72-4.1 bars (40-60 lb/sq in).

COOLING: Closed water system, operating temperature 85-100°C.

WEIGHT, DRY (with starter): 77.1 kg (170 lb)
PERFORMANCE RATING: 113 kW (152 hp)

RotorWay RW152-D helicopter engine

SOLOY
SOLOY CONVERSIONS LTD
450 Pat Kennedy Way SW, Olympia, Washington 98502
Telephone: (206) 754 7000
Fax: (206) 943 7659
PRESIDENT: Joe I. Soloy

Soloy has developed Turbine Pac installations for the Allison 250 turboprop. The initial application, the Cessna 206, has the 250-C20S rated at 313 kW (420 shp). Features include aft facing inlet, downward inclined exhaust (with cabin heat provision without power loss), a remote gearbox mounted on the airframe, and a 1,810 rpm propeller drive with autofeather. The package is suited to Model 250 engines of 298-548 kW (400-735 shp). The Turbine Pac was

FAA certificated in May 1984. Applications include the Cessna 206, 207, 210 and 185, and Beechcraft A36 Bonanza (with B17C basic gas generator) with or without tip fuel pods.

Further details can be found in the US Aircraft section.

The Soloy 206 Turbine Pac, based on the Allison 250-C20S turboprop of 313 kW (420 shp)

SOLOY
SOLOY DUAL PAC INC
450 Pat Kennedy Way SW, Olympia, Washington 98502
Telephone: (206) 754 7000
Fax: (206) 943 7659

SOLOY DUAL PAC
This research and development company is collaborating with Teledyne Continental Motors in the development of a turboprop installation which combines two of the latter company's TP-500 power sections into a single gearbox and propeller drive. Complete redundancy is maintained throughout the power train, lubrication and governing systems to enable single-propeller aircraft to qualify under FAA Part 135 for IFR passenger operation. Each power section can be started separately. The jetpipes can be turned outboard to avoid penetration of the firewall. Flight demonstrations were planned for late 1988.

Soloy Dual Pac incorporating twin TP-500 power sections (with original jetpipes)

SPP
SPORT PLANE POWER INC
3659 Arnold Avenue, Naples, Florida 33942
Telephone: (813) 775 2214

This company is an associate of Nelson (see entry in this section). Its first product is the K-100A.

SPORT PLANE POWER K-100A
A four-cylinder four-stroke piston engine, the K-100A is an automotive derived high performance unit with liquid cooling, altitude compensation, overhead camshafts, electronic control and speed reducing drive, allowed for in the figure for weight.

WEIGHT, WET: 88.5 kg (195 lb)
PERFORMANCE RATING: 74.6 kW (100 hp)

The Sport Plane Power K-100A piston engine

TCM
TELEDYNE CONTINENTAL MOTORS
(Aircraft Products Division)
PO Box 90, Mobile, Alabama 36601
Telephone: (205) 438 3411
Telex: 505519
PRESIDENT: D. G. Bigler
MANAGER, PUBLIC RELATIONS: Susan Brane

At the Paris Air Show in 1985 TCM (as the company now abbreviates itself) unveiled new developments. One is a line of liquid-cooled engines, the first of which (Voyager 200 and 300) are described briefly. A second is a family of rotary (or rotating-combustion) engines, also described (R-18 and GR-36) and further mentioned under Norton in the UK part of this section. In 1988 a turboprop was introduced.

CONTINENTAL O-200 SERIES
The O-200-A is a four-cylinder horizontally opposed aircooled engine. It is fitted with a single updraught carburettor, dual magnetos and starter and generator. The O-200-B is designed for pusher installation.

For other details see table.

Teledyne Continental Voyager 200 four-cylinder liquid-cooled engine

Teledyne Continental GR-18 single-rotor engine

Teledyne Continental Voyager 550 six-cylinder liquid-cooled engine

Teledyne Continental GR-36 twin-rotor engine

The 149 kW (200 hp) Continental TSIO-360-E

TELEDYNE CONTINENTAL VOYAGER 200

This is the first of the company's liquid-cooled engines. Derived from the familiar O-200, it has a high-compression (11.4) cylinder with combustion chamber improvements aimed at minimising fuel consumption. The 60 per cent ethylene glycol coolant can operate at 121°C. The engine is more powerful than the aircooled predecessor (see table), and is claimed to offer improved cooling, reduced wear, reduced drag, longer life and TBO, and higher altitude capability. An sfc of 63.38 µg/J (0.375 lb/h/bhp) can be maintained across a broad operating range. A Voyager 200 powered the Voyager aircraft on its unique nonstop journey round the world.

TELEDYNE CONTINENTAL VOYAGER 300

This six-cylinder liquid-cooled engine uses the same high-turbulence high-compression cylinder as the 200. The turbocharged version has demonstrated sfc well below 62.5 µg/J (0.37 lb/h/bhp) at altitude. The weight given in the table includes magnetos, plugs, fuel injection system, coolant pump, alternator and starter.

CONTINENTAL IO-360 SERIES

Newest members of this family of flat-six engines include the TSIO and LTSIO-360-E, EB and KB. These are counter-rotating engines for the Piper Seneca II and III.

CONTINENTAL O-470 SERIES

Engines in the O-470 series (including the E-185 and E-225) are all basically similar. Engines prefixed 'IO' have direct injection.

CONTINENTAL IO-520 SERIES

These engines are basically similar to the IO-470, but with cylinders of larger bore. They are fitted with an alternator driven either by a belt or by a face gear on the crankshaft. The TSIO-520 series are turbocharged. In 1981 TCM announced a lightweight series of engines with magnesium replacing aluminium in some areas, modified camshaft and cylinder heads (with parallel valves or inclined valves of larger diameter), and a range of turbocharging options. The first production models are the TSIO-520-AE and LTSIO-520-AE for the Cessna Crusader, with initial TBO

of 2,000 h. The TSIO-520BE, for the Piper Malibu, has a top intake, dual turbos and two aftercoolers. The GTSIO-520 series are geared and uprated. For other details see table.

TELEDYNE CONTINENTAL VOYAGER 550

Largest of the new range of liquid-cooled engines, the Voyager 550 offers the same advantages as its smaller predecessors.

CONTINENTAL IO-550

In 1984 this series of fuel-injected engines was introduced, similar to the IO-520 but with greater stroke. Initial applications are the Beechcraft Baron and Bonanza.

TELEDYNE CONTINENTAL GR-18

This single-rotor engine is the first of the TCM rotaries (rotating-combustion, popularly called Wankel-type engines). Under development for several years, it is aimed at air and surface applications, chiefly in general aviation and RPVs. Design features include a rotor cooled by the oil/air mixture entering the engine, liquid-cooled housings, reduction gear, rolling-element bearings, carburettor or direct fuel injection, dual capacitive-discharge electronic ignition, total loss metered oil-injection system, 12V starter and provision for alternator up to 2.5kW. Compression ratio is 9, and the carburettor type fuel system was in 1985 running on automotive or aviation petrol (gasoline) but in future will have multifuel capability, including JP-5 and DF-2. This engine was flown in a SkyEye R4E-50 RPV in November 1986 and is currently in production. It is readily adaptable to turbocharging.

ROTOR: Single multilobe with rolling element bearings.
Capacity 294 cc (17.9 cu in).
DIMENSIONS:

Length	536.2 mm (21.11 in)
Width	232.2 mm (9.14 in)
Height	254 mm (10 in)

WEIGHT, DRY (equipped): 22.7 kg (50 lb)
PERFORMANCE RATING (S/L): 33.5 kW (45 hp) at 7,500 rpm

TELEDYNE CONTINENTAL GR-36

This twin-rotor engine is virtually a double GR-18, and is available for RPV applications with or without reduction gear. It may be offered later for general aviation applications. It runs slightly slower than the single-rotor machine, at 6,900 rpm, giving a propeller speed of 2,300 rpm. Capacity is 588 cc (35.8 cu in). The GR-36 has the same features as the GR-18 but drives a 27A alternator. TCM claims for its rotary engines compactness, light weight, extremely low vibration and simple construction with few moving parts.

DIMENSIONS:
Length	678 mm (26.70 in)
Width (with coolant pipe)	298 mm (11.75 in)
Height	244 mm (9.60 in)

WEIGHT, DRY: 50 kg (110 lb)
PERFORMANCE RATINGS (S/L): 63.5 kW (85 hp) at 6,900 rpm
67 kW (90 hp) at 7,500 rpm

TELEDYNE CONTINENTAL TP-500

After prolonged development this simple turboprop is now being marketed for general aviation. It first flew in a Cheyenne II on 29 September 1982. Soloy (which see) is developing a twinned version.

COMPRESSOR: Single centrifugal, titanium. Airflow 1.91 kg (4.21 lb)/s and pressure ratio 8 at 50,000 rpm.
COMBUSTION CHAMBER: Folded annular, reverse flow, ten burners.
TURBINE: Two-stage axial. Max inlet temperature 1,027°C. Stud/nut attachment.
FUEL SYSTEM: Supervisory electronic control. Grade Jet A, A-1, B, JP-4.
PROPELLER DRIVE: Two-stage coupled planetary giving 2,014 rpm output. Modular design in cast casings with integral torquemeter.
ACCESSORY DRIVES: Two tower shafts in reduction gearcase drive fuel control, propeller governor, starter generator and tachometer generator. Optional belt drive for freon compressor or secondary alternator.

DIMENSIONS:
Length	1,325 mm (52.18 in)
Width	599 mm (23.57 in)
Height	542 mm (21.34 in)

WEIGHT, DRY: 146 kg (322 lb)
PERFORMANCE RATINGS (ISA):
T-O, S/L: 380 kW (510 shp)

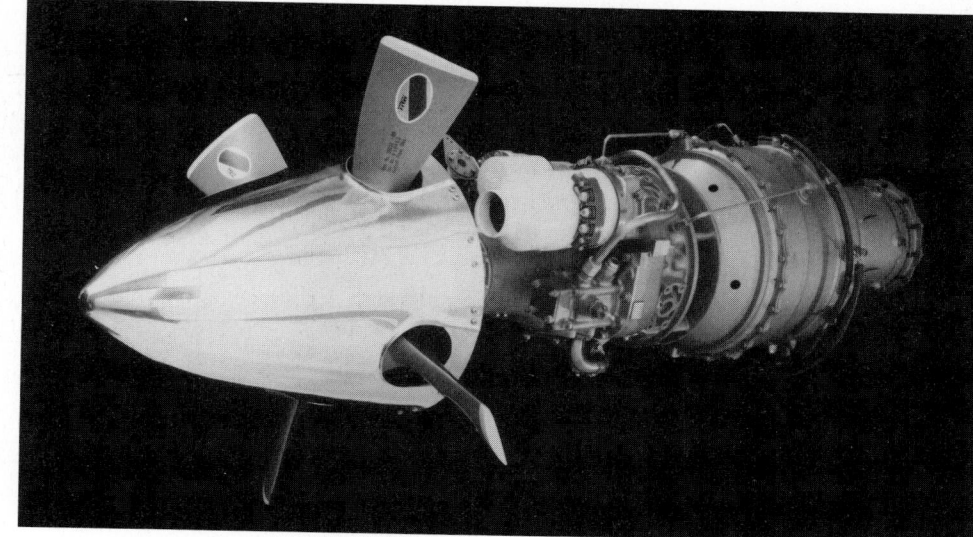

Teledyne Continental TP-500 turboprop (with cropped-blade display propeller)

T-O, 3,048 m (10,000 ft): 298 kW (400 shp)
Cruise 97% at 4,575 m (15,000 ft): 220 kW (295 shp)
Cruise 97% alt limit 7,620 m (25,000 ft): 149 kW (200 shp)
FUEL FLOW (uninstalled, no power extraction):
T-O, S/L: 136 kg (299 lb)/h
Cruise 7,620 m (25,000 ft): 60 kg (131 lb)/h

REPRESENTATIVE TCM HORIZONTALLY OPPOSED ENGINES

Engine Model	No. of Cylinders	Bore and Stroke mm (in)	Capacity litres (cu in)	Power Ratings kW (hp) at rpm Take-off	M.E.T.O.	Comp. Ratio	Dry Weight* kg (lb)	Length mm (in)	Width mm (in)	Height mm (in)	Octane Rating
O-200-A	4	103.2 × 98.4 (4¹/₁₆ × 3⅞)	3.28 (201)	74.5 (100) at 2,750	74.5 (100) at 2,750	7.0	99.8 (220)	725 (28.53)	802 (31.56)	589 (23.18)	80/87
Voyager 200	4	103.2 × 98.4 (4¹/₁₆ × 3⅞)	3.28 (201)	81.95 (110) at 2,750	81.95 (110) at 2,750	11.4	88.0 (194)	708 (27.86)	819 (32.25)	588 (23.16)	100/100LL
Voyager 300	6	103.2 × 98.4 (4¹/₁₆ × 3⅞)	4.93 (301)	127 (170) at 2,700	127 (170) at 2,700	11.4	132 (291)	864 (34.0)	819 (32.25)	533 (21.0)	100/100LL
IO-360-D	6	112.7 × 98.4 (4⁷/₁₆ × 3⅞)	5.9 (360)	157 (210) at 2,800	157 (210) at 2,800	8.5	148.3 (327)	877 (34.53)	798 (31.40)	618 (24.33)	100/130
IO-360-KB	6	112.7 × 98.4 (4⁷/₁₆ × 3⅞)	5.9 (360)	145.5 (195) at 2,600	145.5 (195) at 2,600	8.5	148.3 (327)	864 (34.03)	841 (33.11)	781 (30.74)	100/130
TSIO-360-C, D	6	112.7 × 98.4 (4⁷/₁₆ × 3⅞)	5.9 (360)	168 (225) at 2,800	168 (225) at 2,800	7.5	136 (300)	910† (35.84)	838 (33.03)	603 (23.75)	100/130
LTSIO-360-EB TSIO-360-FB	6	112.7 × 98.4 (4⁷/₁₆ × 3⅞)	5.9 (360)	149 (200) at 2,575	149 (200) at 2,575	7.5	175 (385)	1,437¼ (56.58)	795 (31.30)	671 (26.44)	100/130
TSIO-360-LB	6	112.7 × 98.4 (4⁷/₁₆ × 3⅞)	5.9 (360)	156.5 (210) at 2,700	156.5 (210) at 2,700	7.5	175 (386)	902 (35.52)	795 (31.30)	699 (27.53)	100/130
LTSIO-360-KB	6	112.7 × 98.4 (4⁷/₁₆ × 3⅞)	5.9 (360)	164 (220) at 2,800	164 (220) at 2,800	7.5	178 (392)	1,437 (56.58)	795 (31.30)	672 (26.44)	100/130
TSIO-360-LB	6	112.7 × 98.4 (4⁷/₁₆ × 3⅞)	5.9 (360)	156.5 (210) at 2,700	156.5 (210) at 2,700	7.5	180.5 (401)	1,087 (42.78)	860 (33.88)	822 (32.34)	100LL
IO-470-H	6	127 × 101.6 (5 × 4)	7.7 (471)	194 (260) at 2,625	194 (260) at 2,625	8.6	202.5 (446.5)	1,100 (43.31)	852 (33.56)	502 (19.75)	100/130
IO-470-L	6	127 × 101.6 (5 × 4)	7.7 (471)	194 (260) at 2,625	194 (260) at 2,625	8.6	215.4 (474.9)	1,100 (43.31)	852 (33.56)	678 (26.71)	100/130
O-470-R, S	6	127 × 101.6 (5 × 4)	7.7 (471)	172 (230) at 2,600	172 (230) at 2,600	7.0	193.2 (426)	915 (36.03)	852 (33.56)	723 (28.42)	80/87
O-470-U	6	127 × 101.6 (5 × 4)	7.7 (471)	171.5 (230) at 2,400	171.5 (230) at 2,400	8.6	176.4 (388.9)	915 (36.03)	852 (33.56)	732 (28.42)	100LL
IO-520-A	6	133 × 101.6 (5¼ × 4)	8.5 (520)	212.5 (285) at 2,700	212.5 (285) at 2,700	8.5	215.9 (476)	1,053 (41.41)	852 (33.56)	502 (19.75)	100/130
IO-520-BA, -BB	6	133 × 101.6 (5¼ × 4)	8.5 (520)	212.5 (285) at 2,700	212.5 (285) at 2,700	8.5	207.3 (457)	1,009 (39.71)	853 (33.58)	678 (26.71)	100/130
IO-520-CB	6	133 × 101.6 (5¼ × 4)	8.5 (520)	212.5 (285) at 2,700	212.5 (285) at 2,700	8.5	204.7 (451.3)	1,087 (42.81)	852 (33.56)	502 (19.78)	100/130
IO-520-D	6	133 × 101.6 (5¼ × 4)	8.5 (520)	224 (300) at 2,850	212.5 (285) at 2,700	8.5	208.2 (459)	949 (37.36)	901 (35.46)	604 (23.79)	100/130
IO-520-L	6	133 × 101.6 (5¼ × 4)	8.5 (520)	224 (300) at 2,850	212.5 (285) at 2,700	8.5	211.7 (466.7)	1,039 (40.91)	852 (33.56)	591 (23.25)	100/130
IO-520-M, -MB	6	133 × 101.6 (5¼ × 4)	8.5 (520)	212.5 (285) at 2,700	212.5 (285) at 2,700	8.5	188 (415)	1,189 (46.80)	852 (33.56)	518 (20.41)	100/130
TSIO-520-C	6	133 × 101.6 (5¼ × 4)	8.5 (520)	212.5 (285) at 2,700	212.5 (285) at 2,700	7.5	208 (458)	1,040† (40.91)	852 (33.56)	509 (20.04)	100/130
TSIO-520-E, -EB	6	133 × 101.6 (5¼ × 4)	8.5 (520)	224 (300) at 2,700	224 (300) at 2,700	7.5	219 (483)	1,010† (39.75)	852 (33.56)	527 (20.74)	100/130
TSIO-520-J, N, -JB, -NB	6	133 × 101.6 (5¼ × 4)	8.5 (520)	231 (310) at 2,700	231 (310) at 2,700	7.5	221.3 (487.8)	997 (39.25)	852 (33.56)	516 (20.32)	100/130

REPRESENTATIVE TCM HORIZONTALLY OPPOSED ENGINES (continued)

Engine Model	No. of Cylinders	Bore and Stroke mm (in)	Capacity litres (cu in)	Power Ratings kW (hp) at rpm		Comp. Ratio	Dry Weight* kg (lb)	Dimensions			Octane Rating
				Take-off	M.E.T.O.			Length mm (in)	Width mm (in)	Height mm (in)	
TSIO-520-L, -LB	6	133 × 101.6 (5¼ × 4)	8.5 (520)	231 (310) at 2,700	231 (310) at 2,700	7.5	244.5 (539)	1,286 (50.62)	852 (33.56)	508 (20.02)	100/130
TSIO-520-M, R	6	133 × 101.6 (5¼ × 4)	8.5 (520)	231 (310) at 2,700	212.5 (285) at 2,600	7.5	198 (436)	1,040† (40.91)	852 (33.56)	598 (23.54)	100/130
TSIO-520-T	6	133 × 101.6 (5¼ × 4)	8.5 (520)	231 (310) at 2,700	231 (310) at 2,700	7.5	193.4 (426.3)	970 (38.2)	852 (33.56)	819 (32.26)	100/130
TSIO-520-VB	6	133 × 101.6 (5¼ × 4)	8.5 (520)	242.5 (325) at 2,700	242.5 (325) at 2,700	7.5	207.2 (456.7)	997 (39.25)	852 (33.56)	518 (20.41)	100/130
TSIO-520-UB	6	133 × 101.6 (5¼ × 4)	8.5 (520)	224 (300) at 2,700	224 (300) at 2,700	7.5	191.6 (422.5)	1,136 (44.5)	852 (33.56)	733 (28.86)	100/130
TSIO-520-WB	6	133 × 101.6 (5¼ × 4)	8.5 (520)	242.5 (325) at 2,700	242.5 (325) at 2,700	7.5	188.75 (416.1)	1,286 (50.62)	852 (33.56)	509 (20.02)	100/130
GTSIO-520-C	6	133 × 101.6 (5¼ × 4)	8.5 (520)	254 (340) at 3,200	254 (340) at 3,200	7.5	252.7 (557)	1,081 (42.56)	880 (34.04)	587 (23.1)	100/130
GTSIO-520-D, H	6	133 × 101.6 (5¼ × 4)	8.5 (520)	280 (375) at 3,400	280 (375) at 3,400	7.5	250 (550.4)	1,081 (42.56)	880 (34.04)	680 (26.78)	100/130
GTSIO-520-F, K	6	133 × 101.6 (5¼ × 4)	8.5 (520)	324 (435) at 3,400	324 (435) at 3,400	7.5	272.0 (600)	1,426 (56.12)	880 (34.04)	664 (26.15)	100/130
GTSIO-520-L, M, N	6	133 × 101.6 (5¼ × 4)	8.5 (520)	280 (375) at 3,350	280 (375) at 3,350	7.5	228 (502)‡	1,114 (43.87)	880 (34.04)	671 (26.41)	100/130
LTSIO-520-AE	6	133 × 101.6 (5¼ × 4)	8.5 (520)	186.5 (250) at 2,400	186.5 (250) at 2,400	8.5	172.2 (379.6)	967 (38.07)	846 (33.29)	543 (21.38)	100/130
TSIO-520-AF	6	133 × 101.6 (5¼ × 4)	8.5 (520)	231 (210) at 2,700	212.5 (285) at 2,600	7.5	197.8 (436.15)	1,039 (40.91)	852 (33.56)	598 (23.54)	100/130
TSIO-520-B, -BB	6	133 × 101.6 (5¼ × 4)	8.5 (520)	213 (285) at 2,700	213 (285) at 2,700	7.5	219 (483)	1,490 (58.67)	852 (33.56)	516 (20.32)	100/130
TSIO-520-BE	6	133 × 101.6 (5¼ × 4)	8.5 (520)	231 (310) at 2,600	231 (310) at 2,600	7.5	?	1,083 (42.64)	1,079 (42.5)	851 (33.5)	100LL
TSIO-520-CE	6	133 × 101.6 (5¼ × 4)	8.5 (520)	242.5 (325) at 2,700	242.5 (325) at 2,700	7.5	237 (527)	1,039 (40.91)	852 (33.56)	597 (23.54)	100LL
Voyager 550	6	133 × 108 (5¼ × 4¼)	9.0 (550)	261 (350) at 2,700	261 (350) at 2,700	7.5	228.6 (504)				100/ 100LL
IO-550-B	6	133 × 108 (5¼ × 4¼)	9.0 (550)	224 (300) at 2,700	224 (300) at 2,700	8.5	207.9 (462)	964 (37.97)	852 (33.56)	694 (27.32)	100LL
IO-550-C	6	133 × 108 (5¼ × 4¼)	9.0 (550)	224 (300) at 2,700	224 (300) at 2,700	8.5	211.95 (471)	1,100.1 (43.31)	852 (33.56)	502 (19.78)	100LL

*With accessories; †Not including turbocharger;
‡N weight 220 kg (486 lb)

TELEDYNE CAE
TELEDYNE CAE DIVISION OF TELEDYNE INC
1330 Laskey Road, Toledo, Ohio 43612-0971
Telephone: (419) 470 3000
Telex: EASYLINK 6 288 4828
Fax: (419) 470 3386
PRESIDENT: Robert R. Schwanhausser
Teledyne CAE produces small gas turbine engines for training aircraft, missiles and RPVs. See 1987-88 *Jane's* for further details.

TELEDYNE CAE 352 and 356
US military designation: J69
Four versions of this simple turbojet are available.
J69-T-25 (Teledyne CAE Model 352-5A). Long life version; powers Cessna T-37B.
J69-T-29 (Teledyne CAE Model 356-7A). Powers Teledyne Ryan BQM-34A target. Operational ceiling is 18,300 m (60,000 ft). Single-stage transonic axial compressor supercharging centrifugal stage.
J69-T-41A (Teledyne CAE Model 356-29A). Transonic axial and revised centrifugal compressor handling airflow of 13.5 kg (29.8 lb)/s with pressure ratio of 5.45. Operational ceiling in excess of 21,030 m (69,000 ft).

Teledyne CAE J69-T-29 turbojet of 7.56 kN (1,700 lb st)

YJ69-T-406 (Teledyne CAE Model 356-34A). Produced for BQM-34E and BQM-34F supersonic RPVs.

DIMENSIONS (nominal):
Length overall:
J69-T-25   899 mm (35.39 in)
YJ69-T-406, J69-T-41A and J69-T-29
                                            1,138 mm (44.8 in)
Width:
J69-T-25   566 mm (22.30 in)

J69-T-41A, J69-T-29   568 mm (22.36 in)
YJ69-T-406   572 mm (22.52 in)
WEIGHT, DRY:
J69-T-25   165 kg (364 lb)
J69-T-29   154 kg (341 lb)
J69-T-41A   159 kg (350 lb)
YJ69-T-406   163 kg (360 lb)
PERFORMANCE RATINGS:
Max T-O thrust:
J69-T-25   4.56 kN (1,025 lb) at 21,730 rpm

J69-T-29   7.56 kN (1,700 lb) at 22,000 rpm
J69-T-41A   8.54 kN (1,920 lb) at 22,000 rpm
YJ69-T-406   8.54 kN (1,920 lb) at 22,150 rpm
SPECIFIC FUEL CONSUMPTION (max T-O):
J69-T-25   32.30 mg/Ns (1.14 lb/h/lb st)
J69-T-41A, T-29   31.16 mg/Ns (1.10 lb/h/lb st)
YJ69-T-406   31.44 mg/Ns (1.11 lb/h/lb st)

TEXTRON LYCOMING
TEXTRON LYCOMING
550 Main Street, Stratford, Connecticut 06497
Telephone: (203) 385 2000
PRESIDENT: J. R. Myers

Textron Lycoming produces several families of engines, including the T53, T55, ALF 502 and LT101, with turboshaft, turboprop, turbofan, vehicular and marine variants. The Company has teamed with Pratt & Whitney to develop the T800-APW-800 (see later entry). In June 1987 Textron Lycoming and General Electric agreed joint development of gas turbines for aero and ground applications. The aero engine is the GE38, described under General Electric.

TEXTRON LYCOMING ALF 502
The ALF 502 was launched in 1969, primarily for commercial and executive aircraft. The core is the T55, and construction is modular.

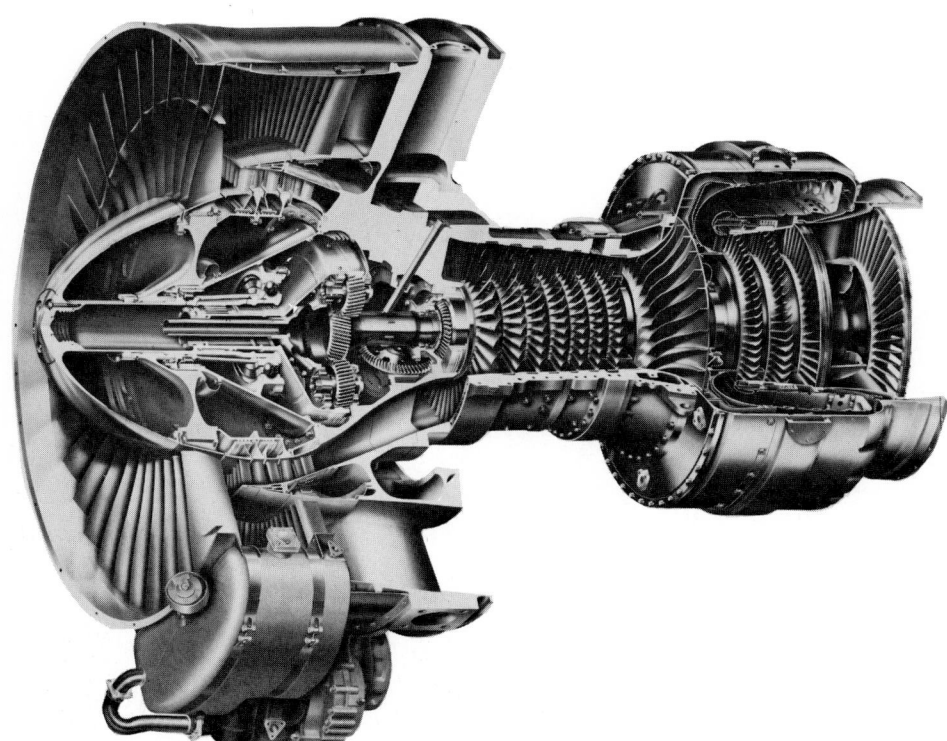

Current versions are as follows:
ALF 502L. First commercial version, FAA certificated in February 1980. Powers Canadair Challenger 600 in ALF 502L-2 form. L-2A, L-2C and L-3 certificated 1982-3.
ALF 502R. Reduced rating, FAA certificated January 1981 as R-3 to power BAe 146. Improved R-3A, R-4 and R-5 certificated 1982-3. R-6 certificated 1984.
By 1988 a total of 184 engines had flown 250,000 h in the Challenger, while another 419 had flown 1,500,000 h in the BAe 146. TBO was 4,000 h, but the ALF 502 is usually operated on-condition.

TYPE: High bypass ratio, two-shaft geared turbofan.

FAN MODULE: Cast frame includes four engine mounts 90° apart, and may carry reverser. Fan rotor blades are base and part-span shrouded. Mounted directly behind rotor (6,700 lb st engines) is a single or (7,500 lb st engines) two stages of compression. Anti-icing of LP compressor inlet by bleed air. Accessory gearbox on fan frame takes HP

shaft power. Reduction gear couples LP turbine to fan. Bypass ratio: 502R-3, 5.71; 502R-5, 5.6; 502L, 5.0.
COMPRESSOR: HP compressor has seven stages and single centrifugal. Acceleration bleed between stages 6 and 7 operated by main fuel control. Overall pressure ratio: R-3, 11.6; R-5, 12.0; L-2, 13.6.
TURBINE: HP has two aircooled stages. LP has two stages. All rotor blades base shrouded: LP tip shrouded.
COMBUSTION CHAMBER: One-piece annular combustor wraps around turbine. Atomising nozzles inserted through outer chamber at rear. Disconnecting permits removal of combustor/turbine module, providing access to HP turbine.
ACCESSORY DRIVES: Accessory gearbox carries main fuel control, oil pump and filter, tachometer (if required) and provisions for customer accessories.
DATA: See table.

TEXTRON LYCOMING LTC1
US military designation: T53
The T53 was developed under a joint US Air Force/Army contract. More than 19,000 have logged over 41 million hours since 1956.

Licences for manufacture of the T53 are held by Klöckner-Humboldt-Deutz in the Federal Republic of Germany, Piaggio in Italy, Kawasaki in Japan, and in Taiwan.

Current versions are as follows:
T53-L-13. Uprated L-11. Redesigned 'hot end' and initial stages of compressor. Four turbine stages, compared with two in earlier models, and variable inlet guide vanes combined with redesigned first two compressor stages. Atomising combustor to facilitate operation on a wider range of fuels. Powers Bell UH-1M and UH-1H and AH-1G HueyCobra. The **T5313A** commercial version has been superseded by the **T5313B.**
T53-L-701. Turboprop incorporating 'split power' reduction gear.
T53-L-703. Improved durability L-13. Flat rated.
LTC1K-4K. Direct drive L-13 suitable for operation from 105° nose up to 90° nose down.
T5317A. Improvements over L-13 include improved cooling of first gas producer turbine nozzle plus aircooled blades in first turbine rotor.
The following details apply to the T53-L-13 and L-701:
TYPE: Free turbine turboshaft.
COMPRESSOR: Five axial stages followed by single centrifugal stage. Variable inlet guide vanes. Pressure ratio 7.2. Mass flow 5.53 kg (12.2 lb)/s at 25,150 gas producer rpm.
COMBUSTION CHAMBER: Annular reverse flow, with 22 atomising injectors.
FUEL CONTROL SYSTEM: Chandler Evans TA-2S system with one dual fuel pump, 41.4 bars (600 lb/sq in). Interstage air bleed control.
FUEL GRADE: ASTM A-1, MIL-J-5624, MIL-F-26005A, JP-1, JP-4, JP-5, CITE.

Textron Lycoming ALF 502L geared turbofan rated at 33.36 kN (7,500 lb st)

TEXTRON LYCOMING ALF 502, LTC1/T53 and LTC4/T55 ENGINES

Manufacturer's and civil designation	Military designation	Type*	T-O Rating kN (lb st) or max kW (hp)	SFC µg/J; ‡ mg/Ns (lb/h/hp; ‡lb/h/lb st)	Weight, Dry less tailpipe kg (lb)	Max diameter mm(in)	Length overall mm (in)	Remarks
T5311A	—	ACFS	820 kW (1,100 shp)	115 (0.68)	225 (496)	584 (23)	1,209 (47.6)	Bell 204B
T5313B	—	ACFS	1,044 kW (1,400 shp)	98 (0.58)	245 (540)	584 (23)	1,209(47.6)	Bell 205A
T5317A	—	ACFS	1,119 kW (1,500 shp)	99.7 (0.59)	256 (564)	584 (23)	1,209(47.6)	
—	T53-L-13B	ACFS	1,044 kW (1,400 shp)	98 (0.58)	245 (540)	584 (23)	1,209 (47.6)	Advanced UH-1H, AH-1G
—	T53-L-703	ACFS	1,106 kW (1,485 shp)	101.4 (0.60)	247 (545)	584 (23)	1,209 (47.6)	Bell AH-1S TOW/Cobra
LTC1K-4K	—	ACFS	1,156 kW (1,550 shp)	98.7 (0.584)	234 (515)	584 (23)	1,209 (47.6)	Bell XV-15
—	T53-L-701	ACFP	1,082 ekW (1,451 ehp)	101.4 (0.60)	312 (688)	584 (23)	1,483 (58.4)	Grumman OV-1D, AIDC (Taiwan) T-CH-1
—	YT55-L-9	ACFP	1,887 ekW (2,529 ehp)	102.7 (0.608)	363 (799)	615 (24.2)	1,580 (62.2)	Piper Enforcer
—	T55-L-7C	ACFS	2,125 kW (2,850 shp)	101.4 (0.60)	267 (590)	615 (24.2)	1,118 (44)	
T5508D (LTC4B-8D)	—	ACFS	2,186 kW (2,930 shp) flat rated at 1,678 kW (2,250 shp)	100.1 (0.592) 106.0 (0.628)	274 (605)	610 (24)	1,118 (44)	Bell 214A, 214B
—	T55-L-712†	ACFS	2,796 kW (3,750 shp)	89.6 (0.53)	340 (750)	615 (24.2)	1,181 (46.5)	Boeing CH-47D
AL5512	—	ACFS	3,039 kW (4,075 shp)	89.6 (0.53)	355 (780)	615 (24.2)	1,118 (44)	Boeing 234
ALF 502R-3	—	ACFF	29.8 kN (6,700 lb)	‡11.64 (‡0.411)	576 (1,270)	1,059 (41.7)	1,443 (56.8)	BAe 146
ALF 502R-3A	—	ACFF	31.0 kN (6,968 lb)	‡11.55 (‡0.408)	576 (1,270)	1,059 (41.7)	1,443 (56.8)	
ALF 502R-5	—	ACFF	31.0 kN (6,968 lb)	‡11.55 (‡0.408)	583 (1,283)	1,059 (41.7)	1,443 (56.8)	BAe 146-200 and -300
ALF 502R-6	—	ACFF	33.36 kN (7,500 lb)	‡11.73 (‡0.415)	589 (1,298)	1,059 (41.7)	1,487 (58.56)	BAe 146-300
ALF 502R-7	—	ACFF	33.36 kN (7,500 lb)	‡11.73 (‡0.415)	623 (1,370)	1,059 (41.7)	1,487 (58.56)	BAe 146-300
ALF 502L/L-2	—	ACFF	33.36 kN (7,500 lb)	‡12.1 (‡0.428)	589 (1,298)	1,059 (41.7)	1,487 (58.56)	Canadair Challenger 600
ALF 502L-2A	—	ACFF	33.36 kN (7,500 lb)	‡11.70 (‡0.414)	589 (1,298)	1,059 (41.7)	1,487 (58.56)	
ALF 502L-3	—	ACFF	34.74 kN (7,800 lb)	‡11.73 (‡0.415)	589 (1,298)	1,059 (41.7)	1,487 (58.56)	

*ACFS = axial plus centrifugal, free-turbine shaft; ACFP = axial plus centrifugal, free-turbine propeller; ACFF = axial plus centrifugal, free-turbine fan
†Applies to T55-L-11A, C**, D, E** and 712**, those designated ** having 2½ min contingency rating of 3,357 kW (4,500 shp).

TURBINE: First two stages, driving compressor, use hollow aircooled stator vanes and cored-out cast steel rotor blades. Second two stages, driving reduction gearing, have solid steel blades.

ACCESSORIES: Electric starter or starter/generator. Bendix-Scintilla TGLN high energy ignition unit.

LUBRICATION: Recirculating system, with gear pump, 4.83 bars (70 lb/sq in).

OIL GRADE: MIL-L-7808, MIL-L-23699.

DATA: See table.

TEXTRON LYCOMING LTC4
US military designation: T55

This engine is based on the T53 with higher mass flow. Total operating time by early 1988 on more than 3,900 engines was over 5.0 million hours.

Current versions are as follows:

LTC4B-8D. Modified T55-L-7C.

T5508D. Commercial version of LTC4B-8D.

T55-L-11 (LTC4B-11B) series. Uprated L-7, with variable inlet guide vanes and two-stage compressor turbine.

T55-L-712. Improved L-11D. Wide chord compressor blades without inlet guide vanes, and one-piece rotor.

AL5512. Commercial L-712, with engine out contingency rating of 3,250 kW (4,355 shp).

LTC4B-12. Proposed growth version with 3,430 kW (4,600 shp) maximum power rating, 3,258 kW (4,370 shp) on hot day. Higher turbine entry temperature.

YT55-L-9A. Turboprop version of L-7C using split-power reduction gears.

The following description applies to the T55-L-11:

TYPE: Free turbine turboshaft.

COMPRESSOR: Seven axial stages followed by single centrifugal stage. Variable inlet guide vanes. Late models have wide chord blades in first two stages and no inlet guide vanes. Pressure ratio 8.2. Air mass flow 12.25 kg (27 lb)/s.

COMBUSTION CHAMBER: Annular reverse flow. Twenty-eight downstream burners.

FUEL SYSTEM: Hamilton Standard JFC 31 fuel control. Gear type pump, with gas producer and power shaft governors.

FUEL GRADE: MIL-J-5624 grade JP-4, JP-5, MIL-F-46005A or CITE.

TURBINE: Gas generator turbine has two stages with cored-out cast steel blades. Two-stage power turbine has solid steel blades.

ACCESSORIES: Electric starter or starter/generator, or air or hydraulic starter. Bendix-Scintilla TGLN high energy ignition unit. Four igniter plugs.

LUBRICATION: Recirculating. Integral tank and cooler.

OIL GRADE: MIL-L-7808, MIL-L-23699.

DATA: See table.

TEXTRON LYCOMING LT 101
US military designation: YT702-LD-700

The LT 101 is designed for low life cycle costs. Each engine comprises an accessory reduction gearbox, gas generator and combustor/power turbine module. The engine has a single axial compressor stage followed by a single centrifugal stage, a reverse flow annular combustor, a single-stage gas generator turbine, and a single-stage power turbine. Front gearboxes provide output speeds of 1,925, 6,000 or 9,545 rpm. The 6,000 rpm gearbox has both forward and aft drives. The engine has either a scroll or radial inlet, each with an optional particle separator. Mass flow is 2.03 kg (4.8 lb)/s, and pressure ratio 8.5.

Current production versions include turboshaft (LTS) and turboprop (LTP) models, with max power in the 459 to 548 kW (615 to 735 shp) range. All are certificated under FAR Pt 33 for 2,400 h TBO or on-condition maintenance. LT 101 operating experience now totals more than 1 million h.

TEXTRON LYCOMING LTS 101

The **LTS 101-600A-2** is a 6,000 rpm power plant for the Aérospatiale AS 350D Astar. The **650C-2/C-3** is a 9,545 rpm power plant for the Bell 222. The **650B-1**, a 6,000 rpm engine with a radial inlet for the MBB/Kawasaki BK 117. The **600A-3** powers the AS 350D Mk 3. A growth version, the **750C-1**, powers the Bell 222B and 222UT. The **750B-2**, with radial inlet, powers the SA 366 and HH-65A Dolphin.

DATA: See table.

Cutaway drawing of the 1,044 kW (1,400 shp) Textron Lycoming T53-L-13B turboshaft engine

Textron Lycoming T55-L-712 (military) or AL5512 (commercial) turboshaft

TEXTRON LYCOMING LTS 101 ENGINES

Engine Model	Performance Rating (T-O, S/L) kW (shp)	SFC µg/J (lb/h/shp)	Weight, Dry kg (lb)	Length mm (in)	Diameter mm (in)
LTS 101-600A/600B	441.5 (592)	96.5 (0.571)	109.5 (241)	785 (30.9)	472 (18.6)
LTS 101-600A-2/650A-2	459 (615)	96.5 (0.571)	115 (253)	785 (30.9)	599 (23.6)
LTS 101-600A-3	459 (615)	98.4 (0.582)	120 (265)	785 (30.9)	599 (23.6)
LTS 101-650B-1	410 (550)	95.5 (0.565)	120.5 (266)	790 (31.1)	645 (25.4)
LTS 101-650C-2/C-3/C-3A	447 (600)	96.7 (0.572)	109.5 (241)	787 (31.0)	574 (22.6)
LTS 101-750B-2	461 (618)	96.3 (0.570)	123 (271)	822 (32.36)	627 (24.7)
LTS 101-750C-1	510 (684)	97.5 (0.577)	110.5 (244)	790 (31.1)	574 (22.6)

Textron Lycoming turbine engines in the 600 shp class (left to right): LTS 101-650B-1, LTP 101-700A-1A and LTS 101-750C-1

TEXTRON LYCOMING LTP 101

The LTP 101 turboprop incorporates a free power turbine, provisions for tractor or pusher installation, hydraulic propeller governor, radial screened inlet and anti-icing protection. Output speed is 1,700-1,950 rpm. The **LTP 101-600** has been selected for the P.166-DL3, Turbo Tractor and Fletcher agricultural aircraft, Riley Cessna 421 and Page Turbo Thrush and Ag-Cat. It has flown in Piper Brave, Turbo-Islander and Dornier 128-6 prototypes. The **LTP 101-700** was certificated in July 1980. An aerobatic version is under development.

DIMENSIONS:
Length	914 mm (36.0 in)
Diameter	533 mm (21.0 in)

WEIGHT, DRY:	152 kg (335 lb)
PERFORMANCE RATINGS (T-O, S/L):	
LTP 101-600	462 ekW (620 ehp)
LTP 101-700	522 ekW (700 ehp)
SPECIFIC FUEL CONSUMPTION (T-O, S/L):	
LTP 101-600, -700	93 μg/J (0.55 lb/h/ehp)

WILLIAMSPORT

652 Oliver St, Williamsport, Pennsylvania 17701
Telephone: (717) 327 7058
Williamsport is the world's largest producer of piston engines for general aviation.

TEXTRON LYCOMING O-235 SERIES

Four cylinders of 111 mm (4⅜ in) bore and 98.4 mm (3⅞ in) stroke. The high compression O-235-N is the most recent production version of the O-235, used in several trainers. It requires 100 octane fuel.

TEXTRON LYCOMING O-320 and IO-320 SERIES

Cylinder bore increased to 130 mm (5⅛ in). The O-320 is an engine in the 112-119 kW (150-160 hp) class. Both carburetted and fuel injected versions are produced in low and high compression models for use with 80/87 or 100 octane minimum grade fuels, respectively. Fully aerobatic models are available.

TEXTRON LYCOMING O-360 and IO-360 SERIES

The O-360 series is basically the same as the O-320 except for an increase in stroke to 111 mm (4⅜ in). Like the O-320, this engine is manufactured with low or high compression, with carburettor or fuel injection. The various models include aerobatic capability, a specific design for helicopters and a turbocharged version. The IO-360-A has fuel injection, tuned induction and high output cylinders, while the IO-360-B has continuous flow port injection and standard cylinders. In the TIO-360-C the turbocharger is pilot controlled.

TEXTRON LYCOMING O-540 and IO-540 SERIES

The O-540 is a direct drive, six-cylinder version of the four-cylinder O-360. It is available in low and high compression versions, and the VO-540 is a helicopter power plant with crankshaft vertical. Fuel injected IO-540 models are manufactured with ratings of 186-224 kW (250-300 hp). An aerobatic version is available.

TEXTRON LYCOMING TIO-540 SERIES

This is a turbocharged version of the fuel injected IO-540, with tuned induction. It is manufactured for unpressurised Piper Navajo and turbocharged Saratoga aircraft. The turbo can be auto-controlled or, in the 540-S, governed directly by throttle lever position. The V2AD has an intercooler and downdraught cooling.

TEXTRON LYCOMING TIO-541 SERIES

Although the displacement of this turbocharged, six-cylinder series is the same as that of the TIO-540, the TIO-541 and geared TIGO-541 are totally redesigned. The TIO-541-E is rated at 283 kW (380 hp) and the geared TIGO-541-E at 317 kW (425 hp). A double scroll blower is available to provide cabin pressurisation.

TEXTRON LYCOMING IO-720 SERIES

This eight-cylinder version of the IO-540 is used at ratings from 280 to 298 kW (375 to 400 hp).

Textron Lycoming IO-360, typically 134 kW (180 hp)

Textron Lycoming TIO-540-V rated at 269 kW (360 hp)

Textron Lycoming O-540 six-cylinder engine

The 298 kW (400 hp) Textron Lycoming IO-720 flat-eight engine

TEXTRON LYCOMING HORIZONTALLY OPPOSED PISTON ENGINES

Engine Model*	No. of Cylinders	Rated output at Sea Level kW (hp) at rpm	capacity litres (cu in)	Compression Ratio	Fuel grade Minimum	Weight Dry kg (lb)	Length Overall mm (in)	Width Overall mm (in)	Height Overall mm (in)	Gear Ratio†
O-235-C	4	86 (115) at 2,800	3.85 (233)	6.75	80/87	97.5 (215)	751 (29.56)	812 (32.00)	569 (22.40)	D
O-235-L	4	86 (115) at 2,700 78 (105) at 2,400	3.85 (233)	8.5	100	98 (218)	738 (29.05)	812 (32.00)	569 (22.40)	D
O-235-N, P	4	87 (116) at 2,800	3.85 (233)	8.1	100	98 (218)	738 (29.05)	812 (32.00)	569 (22.40)	D
O-320-A	4	112 (150) at 2,700	5.2 (319.8)	7.0	80/87	110 (243)	751 (29.56)	819 (32.24)	584 (22.99)	D
O-320-D	4	119 (160) at 2,700	5.2 (319.8)	8.5	91/96	114 (253)	808 (31.82)	819 (32.24)	488 (19.22)	D
AEIO-320-D	4	119 (160) at 2,700	5.2 (319.8)	8.5	100	123 (271)	780 (30.70)	819 (32.24)	589 (23.18)	D
O-320-E	4	112 (150) at 2,700	5.2 (319.8)	7.0	80/87	113 (249)	738 (29.05)	819 (32.24)	584 (22.99)	D

TEXTRON LYCOMING HORIZONTALLY OPPOSED PISTON ENGINES

Engine Model*	No. of Cylinders	Rated output at Sea Level kW (hp) at rpm	capacity litres (cu in)	Compression Ratio	Fuel grade Minimum	Weight Dry kg (lb)	Length Overall mm (in)	Width Overall mm (in)	Height Overall mm (in)	Gear Ratio†
O-320-H	4	119 (160) at 2,700	5.2 (319.8)	9.0	100	115 (253)	819 (32.26)	830 (32.68)	621 (24.46)	D
O-360-A	4	134 (180) at 2,700	5.92 (361)	8.5	91/96	118 (260)	808 (31.82)	848 (33.37)	488 (19.22)	D
LO-360-A	4	134 (180) at 2,700	5.92 (361)	8.5	91/96	120 (266)	808 (31.82)	848 (33.37)	488 (19.22)	D
O-360-F	4	134 (180) at 2,700	5.92 (361)	8.5	100	122 (269)	808 (31.81)	859 (33.38)	507 (19.96)	D
TO-360-C, F	4	157 (210) at 2,575 to 3,050 m (10,000 ft)	5.92 (361)	7.3	100	154 (343)	876 (34.50)	921 (36.25)	534 (21.02)	D
IO-360-A	4	149 (200) at 2,700	5.92 (361)	8.7	100	133 (293)	757 (29.81)	870 (34.25)	491 (19.35)	D
IO-360-B	4	134 (180) at 2,700	5.92 (361)	8.5	100	122 (268)	757 (29.81)	848 (33.37)	631 (24.84)	D
IO-360-C	4	149 (200) at 2,700	5.92 (361)	8.7	100	134 (298)	855 (33.65)	870 (34.25)	495 (19.48)	D
TIO-360-C	4	210 (282) at 2,575 to 3,050 m (10,000 ft)	5.92 (361)	7.3	100	158 (348)	910 (35.82)	921 (36.25)	550 (21.65)	D
HIO-360-D	4	142 (190) at 3,200 to 1,280 m (4,200 ft)	5.92 (361)	10.0	100	132 (290)	894 (35.23)	904 (35.62)	495 (19.48)	D
HIO-360-E	4	142 (190) at 2,900	5.92 (361)	8.0	100	132 (290)	797 (31.36)	870 (34.25)	507 (19.97)	D
HIO-360-F	4	142 (190) at 3,050	5.92 (361)	8.0	100	133 (293)	797 (31.36)	870 (34.25)	507 (19.97)	D
AEIO-360-A	4	149 (200) at 2,700	5.92 (361)	8.7	100	139 (307)	780 (30.70)	870 (34.25)	492 (19.35)	D
AEIO-360-B	4	134 (180) at 2,700	5.92 (361)	8.5	91/96	125 (277)	738 (29.05)	848 (33.37)	631 (24.84)	D
O-540-B	6	175 (235) at 2,575	8.86 (541.5)	7.2	80/87	166 (366)	945 (37.22)	848 (33.37)	624 (24.56)	D
O-540-E	6	194 (260) at 2,700	8.86 (541.5)	8.5	91/96	167 (368)	976 (38.42)	848 (33.37)	624 (24.56)	D
O-540-G	6	194 (260) at 2,700	8.86 (541.5)	8.5	91/96	174 (386)	999 (39.34)	848 (33.37)	624 (24.56)	D
O-540-J	6	175 (235) at 2,400	8.86 (541.5)	8.5	100	162 (357)	989 (38.93)	848 (33.37)	519 (20.43)	D
VO-540-B	6	227 (305) at 3,200	8.86 (541.5)	7.3	80/87	202 (446)	882 (34.73)	880 (34.70)	617 (24.29)	D V
VO-540-C	6	227 (305) at 3,200 to 915 m (3,000 ft)	8.86 (541.5)	8.7	100	200 (441)	882 (34.73)	880 (34.70)	649 (25.57)	D V
IO-540-C	6	186 (250) at 2,575	8.86 (541.5)	8.5	91/96	170 (375)	976 (38.42)	848 (33.37)	622 (24.46)	D
IO-540-K	6	224 (300) at 2,700	8.86 (541.5)	8.7	100	201 (443)	999 (39.34)	870 (34.25)	498 (19.60)	D
IO-540-W	6	175 (235) at 2,400	8.86 (541.5)	8.5	100	166 (367)	989 (38.93)	848 (33.37)	492 (19.35)	D
AEIO-540-D	6	194 (260) at 2,700	8.86 (541.5)	8.5	91/96	174 (386)	999 (39.34)	848 (33.37)	621 (24.46)	D
AEIO-540-L	6	224 (300) at 2,700	8.86 (541.5)	8.7	100	202 (445)	989 (38.93)	870 (34.25)	622 (24.46)	D
TIO-540-A	6	231 (310) at 2,575 to 4,575 m (15,000 ft)	8.86 (541.5)	7.3	100	232 (511)	1,304 (51.34)	870 (34.25)	577 (22.71)	D
TIO-540-AE2A	6	261 (350) at 2,600	8.86 (541.5)	7.3	100	249 (549)				D
TIO-540-C	6	186 (250) at 2,575 to 4,575 m (15,000 ft)	8.86 (541.5)	7.2	100	205 (456)	1,026 (40.38)	848 (33.37)	770 (30.33)	D
TIO/LTIO-540-F	6	242 (325) at 2,575 to 4,575 m (15,000 ft)	8.86 (541.5)	7.3	100	233 (514)	1,304 (51.34)	870 (34.25)	570 (22.42)	D
TIO/LTIO-540-J	6	261 (350) at 2,575 to 4,575 m (15,000 ft)	8.86 (541.5)	7.3	100	235 (518)	1,308 (51.50)	870 (34.25)	573 (22.56)	D
TIO-540-S	6	224 (300) at 2,700 to 3,660 m (12,000 ft)	8.86 (541.5)	7.3	100	228 (502)	1,004 (39.56)	915 (36.02)	667 (26.28)	D
TIO/LTIO-540-U	6	261 (350) at 2,500 to 4,575 m (15,000 ft)	8.86 (541.5)	7.3	100	248 (547)	1,204 (47.40)	870 (34.25)	574 (22.59)	D
TIO/LTIO-540-V	6	269 (360) at 2,600 to 5,486 m (18,000 ft)	8.86 (541.5)	7.3	100	248 (547)	1,352 (53.21)	886 (34.88)	621 (24.44)	D
TIO-541-E	6	283 (380) at 2,900 to 4,575 m (15,000 ft)	8.86 (541.5)	7.3	100	270 (596)	1,282 (50.70)	905 (35.66)	640 (25.17)	D
TIGO-541-E	6	317 (425) at 3,200 to 4,575 m (15,000 ft)	8.86 (541.5)	7.3	100	319 (704)	1,462 (57.57)	885 (34.86)	575 (22.65)	0.667
IO-720-A	8	298 (400) at 2,650	11.84 (722)	8.7	100	257 (567)	1,179 (46.41)	870 (34.25)	573 (22.53)	D
IO-720-B	8	298 (400) at 2,650	11.84 (722)	8.7	100	252 (556)	1,218 (47.97)	870 (34.25)	530 (20.88)	D
IO-720-D	8	298 (400) at 2,650	11.84 (722)	8.7	100	259 (570)	1,189 (46.80)	870 (34.25)	562 (22.11)	D

*Model designation code: A, Aerobatic; AE, Aerobatic engine; G, Geared; H, Helicopter; I, Fuel injected; L, Left-hand rotation crankshaft; O, Opposed cylinders; S, Supercharged; T, Turbocharged; V, Vertical mounting; †D, Direct drive; V, Vertical mounting

---

TEXTRON LYCOMING/PRATT & WHITNEY

TEXTRON LYCOMING
Stratford, Connecticut 06497

UNITED TECHNOLOGIES PRATT & WHITNEY
East Hartford, Connecticut 06108

These companies joined forces in August 1984 to submit a proposal for joint development of a new turboshaft to power the US Army's LHX next-generation helicopter. In July 1985 the Textron Lycoming and Pratt & Whitney team received one of two competitive development contracts.

T800-APW-800
This 895 kW (1,200 shp class) turboshaft is based on the PLT34 (Advanced Technology Demonstrator Engine), enhanced by PW high-temperature technology. The first engine ran in 1986. A decision on which T800 team to select was due in September 1988.
TYPE: Free-turbine turboshaft.
COMPRESSOR: Two axial stages, with two variable stators, and one centrifugal. Intermediate power mass flow 3.9 kg (8.6 lb)/s and pressure ratio 15.
COMBUSTION CHAMBER: Folded annular reverse-flow.

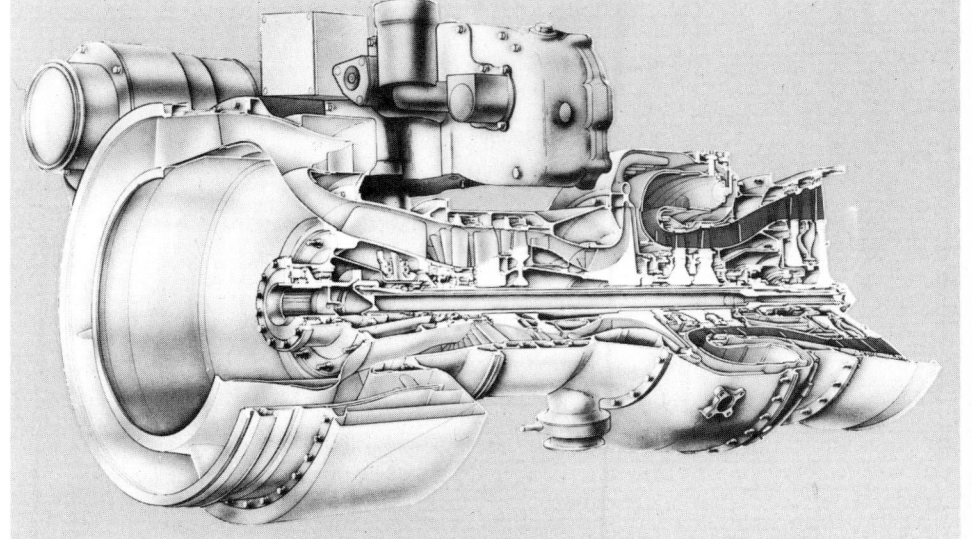

Cutaway of the Textron Lycoming/Pratt & Whitney T800-APW-800 turboshaft

TURBINES: Two-stage gas generator turbine with single-crystal aircooled blades. Two-stage power turbine with uncooled blades.

GEARCASE: Tower shaft takes drive vertically to grouped accessories above engine. All parts combat tolerant.

CONTROL SYSTEM: Dual redundant digital electronic control.

Hamilton Standard is teamed with Lucas Aerospace to develop the integrated engine management system.

DIMENSIONS:
Length	986 mm (38.8 in)
Basic diameter	470 mm (18.5 in)

WEIGHT, DRY: 185.0 kg (298.0 lb)

PERFORMANCE RATING (S/L, ISA):
T-O	895 kW (1,200 shp)

SPECIFIC FUEL CONSUMPTION:
At T-O	78.6 μg/J (0.465 lb/h/shp)

THERMO-JET

THERMO-JET STANDARD INC

PO Box 55976, Houston, Texas 77055
Telephone: (713) 465 5735
MANAGER: John A. Melenric

This company specialises in valveless pulsejet units for RPVs and the homebuilt market. These engines are devoid of moving parts and are characterised by multiple reverse flow air inlets to a combustion chamber in which is burned propane, butane or compressed natural gas. Intermittent combustion and expulsion takes place at a cycle frequency determined by the chamber size and geometry and combustion pressure.

Thermo-Jet offers six sizes of unit, the J3-200 (0.0179 kN, 4 lb st at S/L), J5-200 (0.045 kN, 10 lb st at S/L), J7-300 (0.09 kN, 21 lb st at S/L), J8-200 (0.045 kN, 10 lb st at S/L), J10-200 (0.244 kN, 55 lb st at S/L), and J13-202 (0.4 kN, 90 lb st at S/L). Further details were given in the 1979-80 *Jane's.*

Thermo-Jet J10-200 on test stand

UP

UP INC

PO Box 659, Temecula, California 92390

Peter Brock of this company states that the Arrow P-4 (see Sport Aircraft section of 1987-88 edition) has not been put into production because UP is not satisfied with available engines. Accordingly the company has run the prototype of a six-cylinder radial of 1,800 cc (110.9 cu in), weighing 18 kg (40 lb) and rated at 29.8 kW (40 hp), as well as a single cylinder of a proposed V-8 of 1,600 cc (98.5 cu in), to weigh 14.5 kg (32 lb) and be rated at 23.9 kW (32 hp). Production was planned for late 1988.

WILLIAMS

WILLIAMS INTERNATIONAL

2280 West Maple Road, PO Box 200, Walled Lake, Michigan 48088
Telephone: (313) 624 5200
PRESIDENT: Sam Williams
VICE-PRESIDENT, PUBLIC RELATIONS: David C. Jolivette

Details of the engines manufactured by Williams for unmanned applications can be found in the 1987-88 *Jane's.*

WILLIAMS FJ44

Development of this turbofan began in 1971. It was chosen at a rating of 3.78 kN (850 lb st) for the proposed Foxjet, but was subsequently redesigned to incorporate F107 technology, with bypass ratio of 3.24, resulting in increased thrust and reduced fuel consumption.

The first FJ44, built to meet FAR.33 requirements, achieved design thrust at "a very modest turbine inlet temperature" on its first build. Scaled Composites has built a proof of concept light business jet powered by twin-FJ44 engines, and Swearingen is also developing a twin-FJ44 aircraft.

DIMENSIONS:
Length (with tailpipe)	1,227 mm (48.3 in)
Max diameter	602 mm (23.7 in)

WEIGHT, DRY: 190 kg (420 lb)

PERFORMANCE RATINGS:
T-O (S/L) to 24°C	8.0 kN (1,800 lb st)
Max cruise (11,000 m; 36,090 ft, Mach 0.6)	1.96 kN (440 lb)

SPECIFIC FUEL CONSUMPTION:
T-O (S/L)	12.69 mg/Ns (0.448 lb/h/lb st)
Max cruise (as above)	19.83 mg/Ns (0.70 lb/h/lb)

Williams FJ44 turbofan (8 kN; 1,800 lb st)

YUGOSLAVIA

ORAO

ORAO AIR FORCE DEPOT

Federal Directorate of Supply and Procurement
9 Nemanjina St, 11005 Belgrade 9

Telephone: 11 621522

Telex: 11360, 11541, 11591, 11821
Fax: 11 324981

The depot was established in 1944. Today its main task is licence manufacture of the Rolls-Royce Viper 632-41 and 632-46, and the latest afterburning 633-41, used in most of the Orao twin-engined combat aircraft at present flying.

The Orao works has built up a design and development team which, in collaboration with Turbomecanica of Romania, has been developing the afterburning Viper Mk 633-47 engine for production IAR-93s and Oraos. The first afterburning engines were overweight, but an Orao 2 flew with afterburning engines on 20 October 1983.

ADDENDA

AIRCRAFT

BRAZIL

EMBRAER (page 10)

EMBRAER MFT/LF

Following submission of a concept to the Brazilian Air Force in 1987, Embraer has begun project design of a tandem two-seat aircraft provisionally designated MFT/LF

(modern fighter trainer/light fighter). The intention is to develop it in the former category first, but to make the same design the basis for an advanced light fighter. The MFT would be a replacement for the EMB-326 Xavante in the Brazilian Air Force, and the LF a successor to its Mirages and Northrop F-5s.

Initial design parameters include a conventional con-

figuration, a top speed of about Mach 1.8 with a 40 kN (9,000 lb st) class afterburning engine, extensive use of advanced composites, low gross weight, and high agility. The Brazilian requirement is reportedly for 60-70 trainers and 70-80 light fighters. Development with an international partner is under consideration.

CHINA (PEOPLE'S REPUBLIC)

NAMC (page 39)

The French manufacturer Marmande Aéronautique announced in May 1988 that negotiations with CATIC were expected to result shortly in the signing of an agreement under which the **Microjet 200** (which see) lightweight jet trainer would be built under licence in China by the Nanchang factory. The Microjet was evaluated by Chinese military pilots in November 1986, and the PLA Air Force and Naval Air Force are said to have an initial requirement for 300 aircraft of this type.

XAC (page 44)

XAC H-7

This new multi-role combat aircraft, of Chinese design, was first shown in model form in September 1988 at the Farnborough Air Show. In the same class as the Soviet Su-24 'Fencer', the H-7 is being developed as an interdictor/strike aircraft for the PLA Air Force and in maritime attack form for the Naval Air Force. The first of two prototypes, each with twin 91.2 kN (20,515 lb st) Rolls-Royce Spey Mk 202 augmented turbofans, was rolled out in August 1988 and was scheduled to fly in November. Production H-7s are expected to be powered by two Chinese WS-6 afterburning turbofans, each rated at 122 kN (27,500 lb st), giving them a maximum speed of Mach 1.8 at height.

The general appearance of the H-7 is shown in the accompanying three-view drawing. It is a shoulder-wing monoplane, with compound-swept wings, lateral engine air intakes, and tandem seating for the crew of two on HTY-4 ejection seats suitable for use at speeds from zero to 540 knots (1,000 km/h; 621 mph) and heights from sea level to 20,000 m (65,600 ft). The wings are fitted with leading-edge slats. The large fin is supplemented by a single ventral fin. On the model, the four underwing stores pylons were shown with two C801 anti-shipping missiles inboard and external fuel tanks outboard. A 23 mm twin-barrel gun in the nose, and close-range air-to-air missile on each wingtip, are claimed to give the H-7 a secondary air-to-air capability. Terrain following radar and avionics on the prototypes are claimed to be of Chinese design and manufacture.

DIMENSIONS (estimated):

Wing span	12.65 m (41 ft 6 in)
Length overall, incl probe	18.60 m (61 ft 0 in)

XAC Y-14

Xian Aircraft Company is developing, under the designation Y-14, its own derivative of the Soviet Antonov An-26 medium-range military transport for both domestic use and export. A prototype was expected to be completed by the end of 1988.

The Y-14 will have as much commonality as possible with the Y-7, including the wings (with added winglets), forward fuselage, twin 'military versions' of the WJ-5A turboprop (each driving a J16-G10 four-blade constant-speed metal propeller), and a turbojet APU for take-off assistance in 'hot and high' conditions. It will carry a crew of five (pilot, co-pilot, navigator, flight engineer and radio operator) and have accommodation for up to 38 fully equipped troops or 39 paratroops, or 24 stretcher cases and one medical attendant in a medevac role. Up to 2,000 kg (4,409 lb) of external stores, such as weapons or supply containers, can be carried on fuselage attachment points. The fuselage, like that of the An-26, has a rear-loading ramp/door in the underside. Other features include a nose mounted weather radar, rough-field landing gear, enlarged flight deck windows, and modern avionics comprising navaids, an AHRS and autopilot.

DIMENSIONS, EXTERNAL:

Wing span	29.20 m (95 ft 9½ in)
Length overall	23.98 m (78 ft 8 in)

CANADA

BOEING CANADA (page 21)

Newly completed and unpainted Boeing Canada CT-142 navigation trainer version of the DHC-8 Dash 8M, described briefly on page 24 *(D. W. H. Godfrey)*

STAF (Page 43)

Model of STAF Y-8, illustrating its ability to carry underwing two Chinese RPVs similar in appearance to the US Teledyne Ryan 147 *(Brian M. Service)*

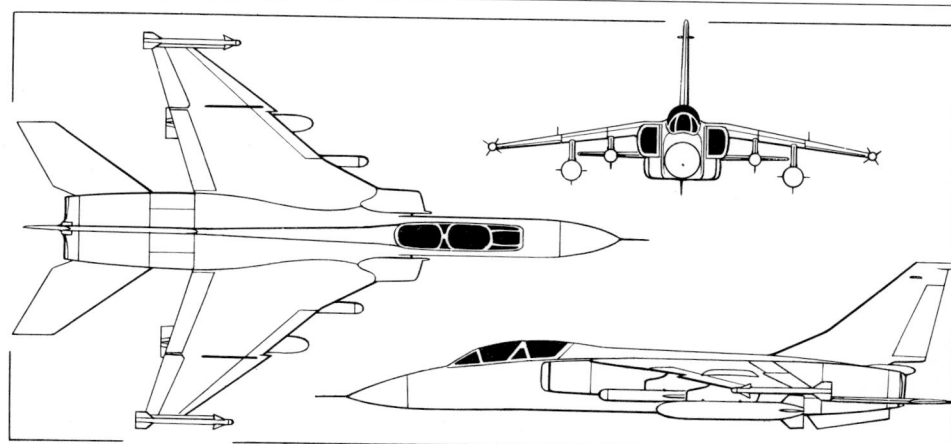

Provisional three-view of XAC H-7 in maritime attack form *(Pilot Press)*

Height overall	8.89 m (29 ft 2 in)	Width	2.78 m (9 ft 1½ in)
Wheel track	7.90 m (25 ft 11 in)	Height	1.91 m (6 ft 3¼ in)
Wheelbase	8.03 m (26 ft 4¼ in)	AREA:	
Crew door: Height	1.40 m (4 ft 7 in)	Wings, gross	74.98 m² (807.08 sq ft)
Width*	0.60 m (1 ft 11½ in)	WEIGHTS:	
DIMENSIONS, INTERNAL:		Operating weight empty	15,400 kg (33,950 lb)
Cargo hold: Length	11.10 m (36 ft 5 in)	Max fuel weight	5,500 kg (12,125 lb)

Max payload	5,500 kg (12,125 lb)
Max ramp weight	24,230 kg (53,420 lb)
Max T-O and landing weight	24,000 kg (52,910 lb)

PERFORMANCE (estimated at max T-O weight, except where indicated):

Max cruising speed at 6,000 m (19,685 ft) at AUW of 22,500 kg (49,600 lb)	240 knots (445 km/h; 276 mph)
Max rate of climb at S/L	480 m (1,575 ft)/min
Rate of climb at S/L, one engine out	144 m (472 ft)/min
Service ceiling	8,200 m (26,900 ft)
Service ceiling, one engine out	3,800 m (12,465 ft)
T-O run	857 m (2,812 ft)
Landing run	634 m (2,080 ft)
Range at 236 knots (438 km/h; 272 mph) at 6,000 m (19,685 ft):	
with max payload	560 nm (1,038 km; 645 miles)
with 3,300 kg (7,275 lb) payload	1,187 nm (2,200 km; 1,367 miles)
Max endurance	5 h 23 min

Model of XAC Y-14 medium-range military transport (*Brian M. Service*)

GERMANY (FEDERAL REPUBLIC)

DORNIER (page 87)

DORNIER 328

On 3 August 1988, the partners of Dornier GmbH took the decision to resume full development of the Dornier 328 twin-turboprop pressurised regional transport. This aircraft is intended to offer take-off, climb and landing characteristics comparable to those of the company's earlier utility and commuter aircraft, including the capability to operate from STOLports and rough unprepared airstrips. Other criteria include a 78 dBA noise level in 75 per cent of the passenger cabin, 'stand-up' cabin height, and a seat width per passenger better than that in the average Boeing 727 or 737.

The basic TNT wing profile of the Dornier 228 is retained, with an enlarged centre-section housing more fuel, and a new flap system incorporating ground and flight spoilers. This is combined with a new and enlarged circular-section fuselage, developed using data from the Federal Ministry of Research and Technology's NRT (Neue Rumpf-technologien: new fuselage technologies) programme, and a T tail unit of new design. Much use will be made in the structure of various composites materials and some aluminium-lithium alloy.

The company expects to begin flight testing the first of three development aircraft in late 1990 or early 1991. LBA certification to FAR Pts 25 and 135 standards is planned for mid-1992, with deliveries beginning shortly after this and FAA type approval following in Autumn 1992.

TYPE: Twin-turboprop pressurised regional transport.

WINGS: Cantilever high-wing monoplane, essentially scaled up from that of Dornier 228 by enlarging centre-section, enabling it to accommodate an additional fuel tank. Flight spoiler (outboard) and two ground spoilers added forward of trailing-edge flaps on each wing. Wing skins of aluminium alloy forward, Kevlar/CFRP sandwich at rear. Flaps, ailerons and wingtips of CFRP.

FUSELAGE: Circular-section semi-monocoque pressurised structure, with conical nosecone and tailcone. Primary structure is of aluminium alloy, with aluminium-lithium used for longerons, stringers, window frames and skin panels. Rear fuselage of CFRP, tailcone of Kevlar/CFRP sandwich; nosecone of CFRP sandwich. Doors of superplastic formed aluminium alloy. Long Kevlar/CFRP wing/fuselage fairing, offering space for systems installation outside main pressure shell.

TAIL UNIT: Cantilever T tail, comprising sweptback fin and rudder and tapered, non-swept horizontal surfaces. Entire structure of CFRP except for dorsal fin (Kevlar/CFRP sandwich) and tailplane leading-edge (aluminium alloy). Trim tab in rudder and each elevator.

LANDING GEAR: Retractable tricycle type, with twin wheels on each unit. Nose unit retracts forward, main units into long Kevlar/CFRP sandwich unpressurised fairings on fuselage sides. Tyre pressures 3.72 bars (54 lb/sq in) on nose unit, 6.55 bars (95 lb/sq in) on main units.

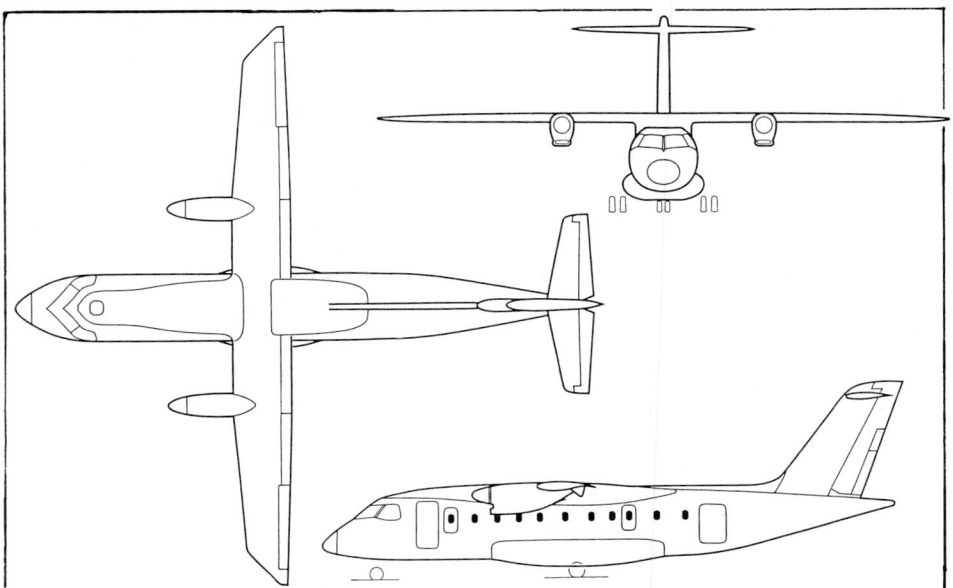

Dornier three-view of the Dornier 328 twin-turboprop regional transport

POWER PLANT: Two 1,268 kW (1,700 shp) class turboprops, each driving a four-blade propeller with synchrophasing. Nacelles of superplastic formed aluminium-lithium alloy. All fuel in wing tanks, total capacity approx 500 kg (1,102 lb) greater than that of Dornier 228.

ACCOMMODATION: Flight crew and cabin attendant(s). Main cabin seats up to 30 passengers, three-abreast at 79 cm (31 in) pitch, with single aisle. Galley to rear of passenger seats; wardrobe and toilet at front of cabin. Large baggage hold between passenger cabin and rear pressure bulkhead, with access from cabin and externally via baggage door in port side. Additional overhead and underseat baggage stowage in main cabin. Crew/passenger airstair door at front on port side, with Type III emergency exit opposite; Type III emergency exit on port side at rear of cabin, with service door/Type II exit at rear on starboard side.

SYSTEMS: Air-conditioning and pressurisation systems standard (max differential 0.45 bar; 6.53 lb/sq in). Hydraulic and electrical systems housed in main landing gear fairings.

AVIONICS: To customer's requirements.

DIMENSIONS, EXTERNAL (provisional):

Wing span	20.00 m (65 ft 7½ in)
Wing aspect ratio	10.3
Length overall	21.08 m (69 ft 2 in)
Fuselage: Max diameter	2.415 m (7 ft 11 in)
Height overall	7.02 m (23 ft 0½ in)
Propeller diameter	3.20 m (10 ft 6 in)
Propeller/fuselage clearance	0.80 m (2 ft 7½ in)

DIMENSIONS, INTERNAL:

Cabin: Max width	2.18 m (7 ft 2 in)
Width at floor	1.84 m (6 ft 0½ in)
Max height	1.86 m (6 ft 1¼ in)
Baggage hold volume	6.0 m³ (211.9 cu ft)

DESIGN WEIGHTS:

Max payload	3,450 kg (7,605 lb)
Max T-O weight	11,600 kg (25,573 lb)
Max zero-fuel weight	11,000 kg (24,250 lb)
Max landing weight	11,370 kg (25,066 lb)

DESIGN PERFORMANCE:

Max cruising speed at 7,620 m (25,000 ft)	350 knots (648 km/h; 402 mph)
Max rate of climb at S/L	802 m (2,630 ft)/min
Required runway length	1,005 m (3,298 ft)
Range with 30 passengers, with reserves	701 nm (1,300 km; 808 miles)

HUNGARY

GANZAVIA (page 97)

The following details amend or augment those given in the main section of this edition.

GANZAVIA GAK-22 DINO

The proof of concept aircraft HA-XAD was built by the Aerofa enterprise in Budapest in 1985-86. Design of the Dino began at the end of 1986, prototype construction started in the first half of 1987, and construction of a second (pre-production) GAK-22 was due to start in the second half of 1988, after the first prototype had flown. The GAK-22 is envisaged as a possible agricultural aircraft in addition to its use for club and sport flying.

WINGS: Wing sections are NACA 23018 on constant chord portion, NACA 23012 at tapered tip. Wingtips are sweptback 30° and have 1° 12′ dihedral. There is no dihedral or anhedral on the main portion of either wing; these are set at incidence angles of 4° (upper) and 3° (lower), and are of single-spar construction using AlZuMgCu, a high strength corrosion resistant aluminium alloy.

TAIL UNIT: Fixed surfaces are of single-spar duralumin construction; rudder and elevators are fabric covered. Tailplane has mechanically variable incidence.

LANDING GEAR: All three units have self-sprung cantilever legs of carbon/glassfibre composites; nosewheel fitted additionally with a polyurethane shimmy damper. Mechanical brakes on mainwheels.

POWER PLANT: Propeller type is MT 178R 117-2C. Fuel tank is located in lower fuselage, at CG, with refuelling point in fuselage side. Oil capacity 6.8 litres (1.8 US gallons; 1.5 Imp gallons).

ACCOMMODATION: Side by side seats are fully adjustable, and have space for 30 kg (66 lb) of baggage at rear. 'Gull wing' cabin window/doors, hinged on centreline and opening upward. Cabin heated and ventilated.

AVIONICS AND EQUIPMENT: FSG 70 radio standard. Provision for 200 litre (53 US gallon; 44 Imp gallon) chemical tank in fuselage for agricultural operations.

DIMENSIONS, EXTERNAL:
Wing chord: at tip   0.25 m (9.8 in)
Wing aspect ratio (each)   4.1
Fuselage: Max depth   1.25 m (4 ft 1¼ in)
DIMENSIONS, INTERNAL:
Cabin: Length   1.40 m (4 ft 7 in)
Max width   1.13 m (3 ft 8½ in)
Max height   1.00 m (3 ft 3¼ in)
Baggage compartment volume   0.1 m³ (3.53 cu ft)
AREAS:
Flaperons, total   1.37 m² (14.75 sq ft)

Rudder   0.88 m² (9.47 sq ft)
Tailplane   1.80 m² (19.38 sq ft)
Elevators, total   1.27 m² (13.67 sq ft)
WEIGHTS AND LOADINGS (estimated. A: Aerobatic. B:
agricultural version)
Weight empty, equipped: A   360 kg (794 lb)
B   385 kg (849 lb)
Max fuel weight: A   80 kg (176 lb)
B   35 kg (77 lb)
Max T-O weight: A   650 kg (1,433 lb)
B   710 kg (1,565 lb)

Max wing loading: A   46.3 kg/m² (9.49 lb/sq ft)
B   50.6 kg/m² (10.36 lb/sq ft)
Max power loading: A   7.58 kg/kW (12.46 lb/hp)
B   8.28 kg/kW (13.61 lb/hp)
PERFORMANCE (at max T-O weight):
Never-exceed speed   188 knots (350 km/h; 217 mph)
Econ cruising speed at S/L
     96 knots (177 km/h; 110 mph)
Stalling speed, flaperons up, power off
     45 knots (83 km/h; 52 mph)

INTERNATIONAL

ATR (page 112)

Photograph of the unpainted prototype ATR 72 twin-turboprop transport, taken in Summer 1988

JAPAN

MITSUBISHI (page 169)

MITSUBISHI SX-3

Under the former programme title FS-X, now redesignated SX-3, the Japan Defence Agency has for some time been examining alternative options for a successor to the Mitsubishi F-1 close support fighter. In the final stages, derivatives of the F-15 and F-18, and a proposal to develop a wholly indigenous Japanese design, were rejected in October 1987 in favour of a derivative of the General Dynamics F-16 Fighting Falcon.

Due to begin a three-year flight test programme in 1993, the SX-3 will be developed jointly by GD and a Japanese industry team headed by Mitsubishi as prime contractor, and will be "significantly modified" from the standard F-16, probably employing a cranked-arrow wing similar to that flown experimentally on GD's own F-16XL. Japanese airframe companies involved are expected to include Kawasaki (centre and rear fuselage sections) and Fuji (all-composites control surfaces), with Mitsubishi building the front fuselage and having overall responsibility for design and integration. A Mitsubishi Electric/Nippon Electric/Fujitsu team will develop the radar, nav/attack computer and ECM. Japan will be totally responsible for the SX-3 programme, including all funding, and will subcontract approx 35-45 per cent of the work to US companies. The JASDF has a requirement for up to 130 production SX-3s, with deliveries to begin at the end of 1997 and continue until 2001.

POLAND

WSK-PZL MIELEC (page 182)

First photograph of a Polish built Antonov An-28 in Polish Air Force insignia (*Andrzej Glass*)

PZL Mielec M-18AS two-seat dual-control training version of the Dromader, first flown on 21 March 1988 (*Andrzej Glass*)

The second prototype of the PZL Mielec M-24
Dromader Super has a cowled engine
(Andrzej Glass)

Mockup of PZL Mielec M-18 Dromader Turbo
(Pratt & Whitney Canada PT6A-65AG turboprop)
(Andrzej Glass)

PZL Mielec M-26 01 Iskierka second prototype
with Textron Lycoming AEIO-540 engine
(Andrzej Glass)

WSK-PZL WARSZAWA-OKECIE (page 190)

**PZL-130 Orlik in production form, with one-piece
canopy** *(Andrzej Glass)*

FFV AEROTECH
S-73281 Arboga
Telephone: 46 589 800
Telex: 732 46 FFVA S

This entry supersedes the short item on the BA-14 under the MFI heading in the Sport Aircraft section.

FFV AEROTECH BA-14 STARLING
First flown on 25 August 1988, the BA-14 Starling is a two-seat light aircraft built primarily from composites. Development, to a design by Mr Björn Andreasson, was a joint venture by Malmo Forsknings & Innovations AB (MFI) and FFV Aerotech. Following certification to FAR Pt 23 standards, the Starling will be marketed in basic two-seat touring and training form, with optional instrumentation and radio for IFR training, and optional 119 kW (160 hp) engine driving a constant-speed propeller; as a reconnaissance aircraft carrying cameras, video equipment and other special sensors; as a light transport with optional stretcher installation and hardpoints for airdrop containers; and as an agricultural sprayplane, with a chemical hopper behind the cockpit, and sprayboom with atomisers under the wings.

TYPE: Two-seat multi-purpose light aircraft.

WINGS: Shoulder-wing monoplane, with single bracing strut each side. No dihedral. Sweepforward 3°. GFRP composite construction; spar caps reinforced with carbonfibre pultruded bars. Welded steel tube wing carry-through structure. Detachable wingtips. Conventional ailerons. Junkers type auxiliary aerofoil flaps aft of wing trailing-edge.

FUSELAGE: Semi-monocoque pod and boom structure of GFRP composites. Downward hinged hatch for access to baggage/freight compartment in upswept portion of centre-fuselage.

TAIL UNIT: V tail, comprising fixed surfaces with large horn balanced control surfaces, of sheet metal construction. Small ventral fin carrying tailskid.

LANDING GEAR: Non-retractable tricycle type. Mainwheels carried on an arched GFRP leafspring.

POWER PLANT: One 85.75 kW (115 hp) Textron Lycoming O-235 flat-four engine standard, driving a two-blade fixed-pitch propeller. A 119 kW (160 hp) Textron Lycoming O-320 engine is optional for Utility and Normal category operation, standard for Restricted category operation. Welded steel tube engine mounting.

ACCOMMODATION: Two persons side by side under large one-piece transparent canopy. Baggage compartment aft of seats. All flying controls operated through pushrods. Safety harness standard for both occupants.

DIMENSIONS, EXTERNAL:
Wing span	11.38 m (37 ft 4 in)
Length overall	6.56 m (21 ft 6¼ in)
Height overall	2.70 m (8 ft 10¼ in)
Wheel track	2.26 m (7 ft 5 in)
Wheelbase	1.65 m (5 ft 5 in)

WEIGHTS: (U, Utility category; N, Normal category; R, Restricted category):
Weight empty: U, N	480 kg (1,059 lb)
R	505 kg (1,114 lb)

SWEDEN

Prototype of the FFV BA-14 Starling two-seat light aircraft

Standard fuel	60 kg (132 lb)	
Max T-O weight: U	710 kg (1,565 lb)	
N	815 kg (1,796 lb)	
R	950 kg (2,094 lb)	
PERFORMANCE (estimated):		
Max level speed at S/L:		
U	130 knots (240 km/h; 150 mph)	
N	125 knots (231 km/h; 144 mph)	

R	150 knots (278 km/h; 172 mph)
Max rate of climb at S/L: U	213 m (700 ft)/min
N	183 m (600 ft)/min
R	274 m (900 ft)/min
T-O to 15 m (50 ft): U	330 m (1,083 ft)
N	425 m (1,395 ft)
R	390 m (1,280 ft)

SAAB-SCANIA (page 221)

First prototype of the Saab JAS 39 Gripen undergoing final tests before its first flight

---

UNION OF SOVIET SOCIALIST REPUBLICS

ANTONOV (page 220)

ANTONOV An-72
In the illustration on page 226, in which 'Madcap' is visible in the background, the aircraft in the foreground is incribed 'An-72A'. This is a standard production version, with uprated D-36 turbofans, each giving 1,000 kg (2,205 lb) greater thrust than the engines fitted to the original An-72 and An-74.

Additional and amended weight and performance data have become available for the version with 63.74 kN (14,330 lb st) engines, which can now be equipped to carry 68 passengers on side and removable central seats, some on the ramp:

WEIGHTS:
Max T-O weight:
on 1,500 m (4,922 ft) runway	33,000 kg (72,750 lb)
on 1,000 m (3,280 ft) runway	27,500 kg (60,625 lb)

PERFORMANCE (at max T-O weight, except where indicated):
T-O run	820 m (2,690 ft)
T-O to 10.5 m (35 ft)	1,100 m (3,610 ft)
Landing from 15 m (50 ft)	800 m (2,625 ft)
Landing run	400 m (1,313 ft)

Range, with fuel reserves for one hour:
with 10,000 kg (22,045 lb) payload	
	464 nm (860 km; 534 miles)
with 7,500 kg (16,535 lb) payload	
	1,080 nm (2,000 km; 1,242 miles)
with max fuel	2,700 nm (5,000 km; 3,106 miles)

ILYUSHIN (page 229)

ILYUSHIN Il-78
The designation of the flight refuelling tanker version of the Il-76 is now known to be Il-78 (NATO 'Midas'). It has a flight refuelling pod under each outer wing. The third hose and drogue are streamed from a box type pod mounted on the port side of the rear fuselage.

TUPOLEV (page 263)

NEW TUPOLEV BOMBER (NATO 'Blackjack')
Additional information on the Soviet bomber known to NATO as 'Blackjack' has become available since the US Defense Secretary, Mr Frank C. Carlucci, was invited to inspect an example, with the number '12' stencilled on the nosewheel doors and fin, on 2 August 1988. It is suggested that the aircraft's designation is Tu-160, and that the first operational unit had been formed by the date of Mr Carlucci's visit. Standard weapon loads are now known to include short-range attack missiles as well as ALCMs, confirming the aircraft's suitability for a low-altitude penetration role in addition to its mission as a high-altitude standoff cruise missile launch vehicle.

The following data supplement or correct those given on page 269.

MIL (page 248)

MIL Mi-34
The performance data given for the Mi-34 are now stated by Aviaexport to apply to the helicopter at its current increased max take-off weight of 1,300 kg (2,866 lb), except for the ranges which are at a take-off weight of 1,250 kg (2,755 lb). For aerobatic flying, at a take-off weight of 1,020 kg (2,249 lb), max rearward speed is 70 knots (130 km/h; 80 mph). *g* limits are as stated.

WINGS: Sweep is selected manually, from 20° fully spread to 65° fully swept.

TAIL UNIT: The one-piece all-moving upper fin pivots on the fixed lower portion some distance above the all-moving horizontal surfaces. There is a conical fairing aft of the trailing edge of the fin/tailplane intersection.

LANDING GEAR: Twin nosewheels retract rearward. The main gear comprises two bogies, each with three pairs of wheels. The two forward pairs of wheels on each bogie are farther apart than the two rear pairs. Retraction is very like that on the Tu-154 airliner. As each leg pivots rearward, the bogie rotates through 90° around the axis of the centre pair of wheels, to lie parallel with the retracted leg. The gear retracts into the thickest part of the wing, between the fuselage and inboard engine on each side; so the track is relatively small.

ACCOMMODATION: The four crew members are seated in pairs, as in the B-1B, on individual ejection seats. One window on each side of the flight deck can be moved inward and rearward for ventilation on the ground. Flying controls utilise fighter type sticks rather than yokes or wheels. Crew enter the aircraft via the nosewheel bay.

AVIONICS: Radar in turned-up nose reminiscent of that of 'Backfire-C', claimed to provide terrain following capability. Fairing with flat glazed front panel under front fuselage, as on 'Backfire', is assumed to be for a video camera to provide visual assistance for weapon aiming. No head-up display on flight deck. Single CRT, apparently for caution and warning data. Vertical tape engine instrumentation on centre console.

ARMAMENT: Two large weapon bays in tandem, in fuselage, each house a rotary launcher able to carry six air-launched cruise missiles or twelve short-range attack missiles, assumed to be similar to USAF's XAGM-131A SRAM II.

WEIGHT:
Max T-O weight   267,625 kg (590,000 lb)

UNITED KINGDOM

MoD
MINISTRY OF DEFENCE
Whitehall, London SW1Y 2HB

ASTOR (AIRBORNE STAND-OFF RADAR) PROGRAMME

The MoD's ASTOR requirement calls for the development of long-range battlefield surveillance and reconnaissance radars that will provide information on the buildup and movement of forces behind enemy lines. Some additional details of earlier stages of the programme are given in the entry for the ASTOR Defender under the Pilatus Britten-Norman heading in the main UK section. ASTOR will be designed to be interoperable with both the US JSTARS system (see entry for the Boeing E-8A) and the French Orchidée system, some details of which are given in the French section in the entry referring to the Aérospatiale Puma demonstrator.

To fulfil its ASTOR requirement, the MoD has contracted Thorn EMI Electronics' Radar Division to pursue the parallel development of two technology demonstrators, to investigate what is achievable with two alternative types of radar: a synthetic aperture radar (SAR) for imaging static targets, and a coherent radar with moving target indication (MTI) for detecting moving vehicles. Other objectives include evaluating the possibility of incorporating MTI capability into the SAR installation.

The SAR programme, an extension of the work already undertaken by the Royal Signals and Radar Establishment (RSRE) and Thorn EMI, will demonstrate the capabilities of SAR at long ranges and low grazing angles. The SAR system testbed is an RSRE Canberra B. Mk 6 (WT327), fitted with a Thorn EMI Searchwater transmitter and Skymaster hardware, and is being used to assess the ASTOR concept at high altitudes. Improved motion compensation and a new electrically driven antenna will enhance the detail and resolution of the SAR display; using the same antenna, transmitter and display facilities, additional signal processing will enable an MTI capability to be demonstrated in conjunction with the SAR imagery.

The low-level demonstrator programme is based on the use of a Pilatus Britten-Norman Turbine Defender (G-TEMI), equipped with an MTI radar based on the Thorn EMI Skymaster multirole I-band radar and optimised for battlefield surveillance operation at altitudes up to 3,050 m (10,000 ft). Also using the new electrically driven antenna and additional signal processing techniques, the Skymaster has been adapted to provide the requisite detection and azimuth resolution of slow-moving targets against a ground clutter background. Due to fly in the Defender demonstrator in the latter part of 1988, it will undergo a full programme of trials during 1989, during which a data link will be installed to evaluate the system's interoperability with JSTARS.

The eventual choice of radar/aircraft will decide which service will operate the ASTOR system. Any high level platform (which would be a more modern type of transonic jet aircraft than the Canberra) will be operated by the RAF; if the Defender proves to have a sufficiently high ceiling for optimum functioning of the system, it would be operated by the Army Air Corps.

ORCA AIRCRAFT LTD
ORCA SAH-1

Following takeover of the former Trago Mills Ltd (see page 311) by a new management team, of whom the principal financial backer is Mr Norman Whale, the company has been renamed Orca Aircraft Ltd (orca being Latin for 'whale'). The Chief Designer Mr Sydney A. Holloway and other senior members of the team which developed the SAH-1 trainer remain with the new company. Production of the SAH-1 is under way, at Bodmin, with substantial grant assistance from the Department of Trade and Industry.

PILATUS BRITTEN-NORMAN (page 301)

PILATUS BRITTEN-NORMAN ELINT DEFENDER

In a programme funded jointly with Racal Radar Defence Systems Ltd, Pilatus Britten-Norman has proposed the Turbine Defender as an economically viable electronic warfare platform, and in the Summer of 1988 a BN-2T was being fitted with a Racal Kestrel lightweight EW avionics suite to serve as an Elint Defender demonstrator.

The Kestrel system provides the ability to compile a comprehensive library of electronic intelligence which can be constantly updated. The data can be used to establish peacetime orders of battle, and subsequent changes in deployment which may be the first warnings of hostile action; to provide information on the tactical deployment of forces in neighbouring areas, and their degree of alertness; and to provide the basis on which the defensive systems of own forces can be programmed. Kestrel can offer total radar band coverage, with real-time onboard analysis and/or data recording for ground replay and analysis, and the aircraft will be suitable for use either in a peacetime strategic intelligence role or for tactical elint in an active environment.

RSRE Canberra high-altitude ASTOR demonstrator, with underfuselage synthetic aperture radar

Pilatus Britten-Norman Turbine Defender, with nose mounted ASTOR (Skymaster) radar

Artist's impression of the Pilatus Britten-Norman Elint Defender

UNITED STATES OF AMERICA

AROCET (page 326)

Prototype Arocet AT-9 tactical trainer, based on the Glasair airframe (*J. M. G. Gradidge*)

JAFFE AIRCRAFT CORPORATION

1770 Sky Place Boulevard, San Antonio, Texas 78216
Telephone: (512) 821 6301
Telex: 767438 COMTRAN UD
Fax: (512) 822 7766

JAFFE SA-32T TURBO TRAINER

As noted on page 491, the SA-32T is a turboprop military trainer based on the Swearingen SX300 high-performance homebuilt. A piston-engined prototype embodying some of the changes proposed for the SA-32T, such as a one-piece transparent canopy, was exhibited at the 1988 Sun 'n Fun meeting. A mockup of the fully developed Turbo Trainer was displayed at the 1988 Farnborough Air Show.

The SA-32T will be generally as described in the Swearingen entry. Compared with the SX300, it will have larger wheels, tyres and brakes, and the skin thickness will be increased to cater for higher performance. The canopy will be jettisonable, and the crew will be provided with either a rocket extraction system or Martin Baker lightweight

GRUMMAN (page 393)

GRUMMAN (DASSAULT-BREGUET) NIGHT STALKER

To meet a US Coast Guard requirement, Grumman has modified eight of the Service's HU-25A Guardians (based on the Dassault-Breguet Mystère-Falcon 20) into aircraft capable of intercepting airborne drug smugglers. Known as Night Stalkers, each Guardian has been equipped with a version of the Westinghouse AN/APG-66 radar installed in the F-16 fighter, and an all-weather day/night sensor package. Other modifications made by Grumman include the installation of search windows, airdrop hatches, camera doors and auxiliary fuel tanks, together with a WF-360 FLIR and HF, UHF and VHF-FM secure communications. Delivery of all eight aircraft to bases at Mobile, Alabama, and Miami, Florida, was expected before the end of 1988.

ejection seats. The NASA designed laminar-flow wing section is claimed to produce the handling characteristics of a jet aircraft, and Jaffe is considering development of a single-seat anti-helicopter combat version with increased performance.

The following additional data became available at Farnborough:

PERFORMANCE (estimated):
Never-exceed speed   348 knots (644 km/h; 400 mph)
Max manoeuvring speed 207 knots (383 km/h; 238 mph)
Max gear extraction speed
           170 knots (315 km/h; 195 mph)
Max speed for full flap extension
           135 knots (250 km/h; 155 mph)
g limits   ±6

Modified SX300, with piston engine, built by Jaffe Aircraft (*Geoffrey P. Jones*)

Mockup of the Jaffe SA-32T Turbo Trainer (*Air Portraits*)

NASA (Page 446)

Artist's impression of the NASA/US Navy F-8 oblique-wing demonstrator

SPORT AIRCRAFT

AUSTRALIA

Skytek Maverick aerobatic aircraft, described briefly on page 505
(*Greg Meggs*)

SAILPLANES

POLAND

PW (page 636)

PW-3 BAKCYL

The prototype of this two-seat sailplane (SP-P500) is now known to have flown for the first time on 14 August 1988. Amended data are as follows:

DIMENSIONS, EXTERNAL:
  Wing span   14.65 m (48 ft 0¾ in)
  Height overall   2.50 m (8 ft 2½ in)
AREA:
  Wings, gross   17.50 m² (188.4 sq ft)
WEIGHTS:
  Weight empty   220 kg (485 lb)
  Max T-O weight   420 kg (925 lb)

Prototype of the PW-3 Bakcyl two-seat sailplane

Production version of the PZL-Krosno KR-03A Puchatek sailplane
(Andrzej Glass)

LIGHTER THAN AIR: AIRSHIPS

UNITED STATES OF AMERICA

SKYRIDER
SKYRIDER AIRSHIPS INC
2840 Wilderness Place (Suite E), PO Box 1158, Boulder, Colorado 80306
Telephone: (303) 449 2190
Fax: (303) 449 2074
PRESIDENT: Frank E. Rider

RIDER BA-3
Built in 14 months, the BA-3 prototype (N25FR) was flown for the first time on 11 May 1988. A single-passenger, non-rigid helium airship, it is powered by two small engines but can be free ballooned in the event of engine failure. It can be kept safely at its mooring mast in winds of more than 35 knots (64 km/h; 40 mph), and requires a ground crew of four or five when away from the mast.

ENVELOPE: Main envelope made of 6.5 oz methane coated nylon. Two ballonets (one forward, one aft), occupying 18 per cent of total volume and filled by onboard blowers. Three valves (air and helium), operated by automatic pressure switching system with manual backup. Tail surfaces are of fabric covered welded chromoly steel.

GONDOLA: Welded chromoly structure, with composites skin panels and Lexan windscreen, suspended from envelope by internal catenary curtains.

POWER PLANT: Two 21 kW (28 hp) Rotax 277FA flat-twin engines, each driving a 1.14 m (3 ft 9 in) diameter GSC Systems three-blade ground adjustable propeller and mounted on an electrically actuated shaft permitting thrust to be vectored between 90° up and 45° down.

AVIONICS AND EQUIPMENT: 720-channel nav/com. Instrument panel includes standard flight instruments, JPI engine temperature scanner and Dwyer photohelic pressure gauge. Onboard water ballast.

Prototype of the Rider BA-3 single-passenger airship

DIMENSIONS, OVERALL:	
Length	29.26 m (96 ft 0 in)
Width	8.23 m (27 ft 0 in)
Height	9.75 m (32 ft 0 in)
DIMENSIONS, ENVELOPE:	
Length	29.26 m (96 ft 0 in)
Max diameter	7.32 m (24 ft 0 in)
Volume	849.5 m³ (30,000 cu ft)
WEIGHTS:	
Weight empty	612 kg (1,350 lb)
Max T-O weight at S/L	907 kg (2,000 lb)

PERFORMANCE:	
Max level speed	30 knots (56 km/h; 35 mph) IAS
Cruising speed	17-22 knots (32-40 km/h; 20-25 mph) IAS
Landing speed	4.3 knots (8 km/h; 5 mph)
Pressure ceiling	approx 1,070 m (3,500 ft)
Typical T-O run	15-30 m (50-100 ft)
Typical landing run	less than 15 m (50 ft)
Endurance, with reserves	4 h

AERO ENGINES

AUSTRIA

ROTAX (page 675)

ROTAX 912
Until now Rotax has produced about 6,500 aircraft engines per year, all derived from motorcycle or snowmobile engines. To meet a demand, the company has now developed the Model 912 specifically for aircraft, partly for new aircraft such as the Robin ATL (was to evaluate a 912 in July 1988) and partly as a replacement for older (eg Continental) engines.

TYPE: Four-cylinder, four-stroke piston engine.
CYLINDERS: Aircooled barrels, water-cooled heads. Total capacity 1,200 cc (73.2 cu in).

LUBRICATION: Dry sump.
WEIGHT: With accessories and exhaust 60 kg (132 lb).
PERFORMANCE RATING: T-O   60 kW (79 hp)
FUEL CONSUMPTION: 75% power   15 litres (4 US gal)/h

POLAND

IL (page 699)

IL K-15
This turbojet was announced in Summer 1988.
TYPE: Single-shaft turbojet.
COMPRESSOR: Six stages. Rotor blades and shrouded stator blades of stainless steel. Two blow-off valves. Pressure ratio 5.3. Mass flow 23 kg (50.7 lb)/s.
COMBUSTION CHAMBER: Short annular type, with 18 vaporising burners and six starting atomisers. Electric ignition.
FUEL SYSTEM: Hydromechanical, with electronic blow-off valve control and overspeed and overtemperature limiters.
FUEL GRADE: Kerosene PSM-2 or TS-1.
TURBINE: Single stage. Disc attached by Hirth coupling.

LUBRICATION SYSTEM: Self-contained recirculatory system. Fully aerobatic.
OIL SPECIFICATION: Type SDF synthetic.
ACCESSORY DRIVES: Gearbox at bottom of intake casing driven by bevel gear from front of compressor.
STARTING: 27V starter/generator in nose bullet.

DIMENSIONS:	
Length overall	1,560 mm (61.42 in)
Width	725 mm (28.54 in)
Height	892 mm (35.12 in)
WEIGHT, DRY:	350 kg (772 lb)

PERFORMANCE RATINGS:	
T-O	14.7 kN (3,305 lb st) at 15,900 rpm
Max continuous	11.5 kN (2,585 lb st) at 15,025 rpm
SPECIFIC FUEL CONSUMPTION:	
At T-O rating	28.49 mg/Ns (1,006 lb/h/lb/st)

An IL K-15 turbojet on the testbed

INDEXES

(Items in italics refer to the ten previous editions)

AIRCRAFT (including homebuilt aircraft)

A

A-1 (AMX International) 111
A1 Flamingo-Trainer (FUS) (1983-84) 86
A-1 Husky (Christen) 380
A1 Mk 2 (Cranfield) (1980-81) 239
A2F-1 Intruder (Grumman) 395
A-3 (Cranfield) (1987-88) 314
A-4 conversions (SAI) (1987-88) 215
A-4S-1 Super Skyhawk (SAI) 203
A-4 Skyhawk (Douglas) (1981-82) 413
A-4PTM Skyhawk (Grumman/McDonnell Douglas) (1986-87) 424
A-4S Skyhawk Conversion (LAS/McDonnell Douglas) (1978-79) 358
A-5 (NAMC) 39
A-5/F-6bis (China) (1980-81) 34
A-5M (NAMC) 41
A-6 Intruder (Grumman) (1987-88) 427
A-6E Intruder (Grumman) 395
A-6E/TRAM (Grumman) 395
A-6F Intruder (Grumman) 396
A-7 Corsair II (LTV) 420
A-9B-M Quail (AAMSA) (983-84) 161
A-10A (Fairchild Republic) (1987-88) 414
A10B (HDH) (1986-87) 7
A-12 (General Dynamics/McDonnell Douglas) 393
A20 (AAC) (1985-86) 6
A 20 (Saab) (1979-80) 169
A-22 (Sadler) 468
A36 Bonanza (Beechcraft) 331
A36 Halcón (CASA) 207
A-36 Halcón (ENAER) 33
A36TC Bonanza (Beechcraft))1981-82) 282
A-37 (Cessna) (1978-79) 311
A100 King Air (Beechcraft) (1982-83) 299
A 109A (Agusta) (1981-82) 124
A 109A (Military, Naval & Police versions) (Agusta) (1981-82) 125
A 109A Mk II (Agusta) 147
A 109A Mk II (Military, Naval & Police versions) (Agusta) 148
A 109 EOA (Agusta) 149
A 109K (Agusta) 149
A-122A Uirapuru (Aerotec) (1980-81) 10
A-122B Uirapuru (Aerotec) (1980-81) 10
A 129 developed versions (Agusta) 151
A 129, Lah Tonal (JEH) 123
A 129 Mangusta (Agusta) 150
A-132 Tangará (Aerotec) (1983-84) 10
A-135 Tangará II (Aerotec) 9
A150 Aerobat (Cessna) (1978-79) 299
A300 (Airbus) (1984-85) 99
A300B2-600 (Airbus) (1983-84) 101
A300-600 (Airbus) 103
A300-600 Convertible (Airbus) 105
A300C (Airbus) (1986-87) 105
A300C4/F4 (Airbus) (1983-84) 102
A300F (Airbus) (1986-87) 105
A310 (Airbus) 105
A320 (Airbus) 107
A330 (Airbus) 108
A340 (Airbus) 108
A340-300 Combi (Airbus) 109
A-750 (Airmaster) (1986-87) 331
A-1200 (Airmaster) 322
AA-1C (Gulfstream American) (1979-80) 352
AA-5A (Gulfstream American) (1980-81) 355
AA-5B (Gulfstream American) (1980-81) 355
AAC (see Hawker de Havilland Ltd) (1985-86) 7
AAI (see American Aviation Industries) 319
AAMSA (see Aeronautica Agricola Mexicana SA) (1984-85) 164
AB 115 (Aero Boero) 1
AB 115 BS (Aero Boero) (1983-84) 1
AB 115/150 (Aero Boero) (1983-84) 1
AB 150 Ag (Aero Boero) (1983-84) 1
AB 150 RV (Aero Boero) (1983-84) 1
AB 180 Ag (Aero Boero) 1
AB 180 RV (Aero Boero) 1
AB 180 RVR (Aero Boero) 1
AB 180 SP (Aero Boero) 1
AB 260 Ag (Aero Boero) 2
ABHC (see Arab British Helicopter Company) (1980-81) 45
AC-4 (Super Rotor) 16
AC-130 (Lockheed) 415
AC-130U Spectre (Rockwell/Lockheed) 465
ACAP, Model D292 (Bell) 347
ACA/EAP (BAe) 292
ACAP programme (Sikorsky/US Army) (1986-87) 512
A.C.E. (see A.C.E. International) 55
ACLG (Bell) (1979-80) 277
ACS (see Aero-Club Der Schweiz) (1985-86) 205
ACT (Dassault-Breguet) (1984-85) 65
ACT Jaguar (BAe) (1985-86) 126
ACX (Dassault-Breguet) (1984-85) 65
AD-1 (Ames) (1980-81) 261
AD-1 Oblique-wing aircraft (NASA) (1983-84) 445
ADAL (see Aeronautical Development Associates Ltd) (1983-84) 248
ADDAX/LCRV (Williams) (1985-86) 315
ADOCS programme (Boeing Vertol) (1986-87) 386
AERO (see Aero Vodochody Narodni Podnik) 47
AEW Defender (Pilatus Britten-Norman) 304
AEW/MR Defender (Pilatus Britten-Norman) 304
AFTI/F-16 (General Dynamics) (1986-87) 413
AG 04 Pigeon (Gatard) (1980-81) 476
AG 05 Mésange (Gatard) (1978-79) 475
AH-1E HueyCobra (Bell) 344
AH-1F HueyCobra (Bell) 344
AH-1G HueyCobra (Bell) 343
AH-1J SeaCobra (Bell) 343
AH-1P HueyCobra (Bell) 344
AH-1Q HueyCobra (Bell) 343
AH-1R HueyCobra (Bell) 343
AH-1S (Fuji-Bell) 167
AH-1S HueyCobra (Bell) 344
AH-1T SeaCobra (Bell) 343
AH-1W SeaCobra (Bell) 343
AH-58D Warrier (Bell) 342
AH-64A Apache (McDonnell Douglas) 439
AHIP Army Helicopter Improvement Program (Bell) 342
AIC (see Ames Industrial Corporation) (1984-85) 300
AICSA (see Aero Industrial Colombiana SA) 46
AIDC (see Aero Industry Development Center) 217
AIEP (see Aeronautical Industrial Engineering and Project Management Co. Ltd) 179
AIM (see Aerospace Industries of Malaysia) 174
AIRTECH (see Aircraft Technology Industries) 109
AISA (see Aeronautica Industrial SA) 205
AJ-2 (Smith) (1982-83) 569
AJ 37 Viggen (Saab) (1984-85) 196
AJEP (see AJEP Developments) (1978-79) 213
AJI (see American Jet Industries Inc) (1979-80) 259
ALR (see Arbeitsgruppe für Luft- und Raumfahrt) (1987-88) 227
AM (see École Nationale Supérieure d'Arts et Métiers) (1978-79) 470
AM-C 111 (Air-Metal) (1978-79) 65
AMIN (see Aero Maroc Industries) (1984-85) 165
AMIT Fouga (AIA) 142
AMST (Boeing) (1979-80) 301
An-2 (Antonov) 220
An-2 Antek (WSK PZL-Mielec) 182
An-3 (Antonov) 220
An 3M (WSK-PZL Warszawa-Okecie/Antonov) (1986-87) 193
An-12 (Antonov) 220
An-14 Pchelka (Antonov) (1980-81) 179
An-22 (Antonov) 221
An-24 (Antonov) 222
An-26 (Antonov) 222
An-28 (Antonov) 223
An-28 (WSK PZL-Mielec) 183
An-30 (Antonov) 223
An-32 (Antonov) 224
An-32 (HAL/Antonov) (1981-82) 90
An-40 (Antonov) (1979-80) 181
An-72 (Antonov) 225
An-74 (Antonov) 225
An-74 Variant (Antonov) 226
AN-100 (Neukom) (1980-81) 492
An-124 (Antonov) 226
An-400 (Antonov) (1984-85) 211
AOI (see Arab Organisation for Industrialisation) 53
AP 68B (Partenavia) (1981-82) 138
AP 68TP (Partenavia) (1982-83) 129, 144
AP 68TP Series 100 (Aeritalia) (1982-83) 129, 144
AP 68TP-300 (Partenavia) 162
AP 68TP-600 (Partenavia) 163
AR 404 (Ahrens) (1981-82) 273
ARDC OF NZ (see Aeronautical Research and Development Company of New Zealand) (1981-82) 498
ARIA, EC-18B (Boeing) 370
ARTI (Bell) 348
ARTB (Lockheed) 418
ARTI (Boeing) (1986-87) 386
ARV (see Island Aircraft Ltd) 279
ARV-1 (Island Aircraft) 279
AS-27 (Starck) (1978-79) 483
AS-32T Turbo Trainer (FFA) (1983-84) 192
AS-37 (Starck) (1982-83) 510
AS-61 (Agusta-Sikorsky) 153
AS-61A-4 (Agusta-Sikorsky) (1980-81) 124
AS-61N1 (Agusta-Sikorsky) 154
AS-61R (Agusta-Sikorsky) 154
AS-90 Super New Look (Starck) (1979-80) 484
AS 202 Bravo (FFA) (1986-87) 214
AS 202/18A Bravo (FFA) 213
AS 332, Super Puma (Aérospatiale) 57
AS 350 Ecureuil/Astar (Aérospatiale) 60
AS 351 (Aérospatiale) (1984-85) 56
AS 355 Ecureuil 2/Twinstar (Aérospatiale) 61
AS 365F Dauphin 2 (Aérospatiale) (1981-82) 54
AS 365M Dauphin 2 (Nurtanio-Aérospatiale) (1981-82) 54
AS 365N, Dauphin 2 (Aérospatiale) (1981-82) 53
AS 366G Dauphin 2 (Aérospatiale) (1981-82) 55
ASF, air-superiority fighter (USSR) 277
ASH-3H (Agusta-Sikorsky) 153
ASP-XJ (Baldwin) 328
ASTEC (see Advanced Systems Technology Inc) (1981-82) 275
ASTOR Defender (Pilatus Britten-Norman) 303
ASTOVL programme (NASA) 447
ASTRA Hawk (Cranfield) 296
ASW/ASV Maritime Defender (Pilatus Britten-Norman) 304
AT-3 (AIDC) 218
AT-9 (Avocet) 326
AT-19 (Greenapples) (1982-83) 544
AT-26 (Embraer) (1982-83) 17
AT-46A (Fairchild Republic) (1986-87) 403
AT-301/301B Air Tractor (Air Tractor) 322
AT-302 Air Tractor (Air Tractor) (1985-86) 320
AT-400 (Air Tractor) 323
AT-400A (Air Tractor) 323
AT-401 (Air Tractor) 323
AT-500 (Air Tractor) (1985-86) 320
AT-501 (Air Tractor) 324
AT-502 (Air Tractor) 324
AT-503 (Air Tractor) 324
ATA (General Dynamics/McDonnell Douglas) 393
ATAC (see Advanced Technology Aircraft Co Inc) (1986-87) 335
ATB (Northrop) (1987-88) 479
ATCA (Douglas) (1979-80) 391
ATF (Lockheed) 411
ATF (McDonnell Douglas/Northrop) 429
ATF (USAF) 494
ATF 580S Turbo Flagship (Allison) (1987-88) 346
ATI-2 Fantrainer (RFB) (1984-85) 90
ATL (FMA) (1985-86) 5
ATL (Robin) 83
ATL, AIRCRAFT TECHNOLOGY LTD (China) (1987-88) 38
ATL2, Atlantique (Dassault-Breguet) 71
ATM 42L (ATR) 114
ATOPS (NASA) 447
ATP (BAe) 283
ATR (see Avions de Transport Régional) 112
ATR-42 (ATR) 112
ATR 72 (ATR) 114
AT-TC-3 (AIDC) (1984-85) 203
AUH-76 (Sikorsky) (1984-85) 504
AV-8A (BAe) 290
AV-8B (McDonnell Douglas/BAe) 124
AV-8C Harrier (BAe/McDonnell) (1982-83) 416
AV-8S (BAe) 290
AV.44 (Fauvel) (1979-80) 474
AV.50(61) Lutin (Fauvel) (1979-80) 474
AVEX (see Asociacion Argentina de Constructores de Aviones Experimentales) (1979-80) 465
AWACS (Boeing) (1979-80) 300
AWI-2, Fantrainer (RFB) (1984-85) 90
ABE, KEIICHI (Japan) (1982-83) 514
ABELS, L. GALE (USA) (1980-81) 500
ACA INDUSTRIES INC (USA) 320
ACE AIRCRAFT MANUFACTURING CO (USA) (1984-85) 554
A.C.E. INTERNATIONAL (France) 55
Acey Deucy Mk II Biplane (Powell) (1984-85) 591
Acro Z-CH 150 (Zenair) (1980-81) 470
Acrobin (Robin) (1979-80) 68
Acroduster 1 (Stolp) (1982-83) 575
Acro-Sport I (EAA) (1983-84) 555
Acro-Sport II (EAA) (1983-84) 555
ADAMS INDUSTRIES INC (USA) (1983-84) 292
Advanced Airborne Command Post (Boeing) (1985-86) 363
ADVANCED AIRCRAFT CORPORATION (USA) 320
Advanced Harrier (McDonnell) (1980-81) 383
Advanced Hercules (Lockheed) (1979-80) 376
Advanced Light Helicopter (HAL/MBB) 99
ADVANCED SYSTEMS TECHNOLOGY INC (USA) (1981-82) 275
Advanced Tactical Fighter (General Dynamics/McDonnell Douglas) 393
Advanced Tactical Fighter ATF (USAF) 494
ADVANCED TECHNOLOGY AIRCRAFT CO INC (USA) (1986-87) 335
Advanced Technology Tactical Transport (Beechcraft) 340
Advanced Transport Systems Research Vehicle (NASA) (1986-87) 469
Advanced TriStar (Lockheed) (1982-83) 405
Advanced Wild Weasel F-4G (McDonnell) (1980-81) 380
AERITALIA/AERMACCHI/EMBRAER (International) (1986-87) 101
AERITALIA—SOCIETÀ AEROSPAZIALE ITALIANA SpA (Italy) 142
AERMACCHI SpA (Italy) 145
Aerobat (Reims/Cessna) (1986-87) 78
Aerobat Model 152 (Cessna) (1984-85) 359
AERO BOERO SA (Argentina) 1
Aerobot (Moller) 442
AERO-CLUB DER SCHWEIZ (Switzerland) (1985-86) 205
AÉRO CLUBE DE RIO CLARO (Brazil) (1986-87) 17
AEROCOM INC (USA) (1978-79) 249
AERO DESIGN ASSOCIATES (USA) (1980-81) 502
AERODYNE SYSTEMS ENGINEERING LTD (USA) (1987-88) 341
AEROFAN AIRCRAFT MANUFACTURING CO (USA) (1986-87) 329
Aerofoilcraft, X-114 (RFB) (1978-79) 70
AERO GARE (USA) (1984-85) 558
AERO INDUSTRIAL COLOMBIANA SA (Colombia) 46
AERO INDUSTRY DEVELOPMENT CENTER (Taiwan) 217
Aero Knight Twister (Payne) (1985-86) 607
AERO MAROC INDUSTRIE (Morocco) (1984-85) 165
AERO MERCANTIL (Colombia) 46
Aero Model A (Meyer) (1982-83) 554
AERO MOD GENERAL (USA) (1987-88) 342

AERONAUTICA AGRICOLA MEXICANA SA (Mexico) (1984-85) 164
AERONAUTICA INDUSTRIAL SA (Spain) 205
AERONAUTICAL INDUSTRIAL ENGINEERING AND PROJECT MANAGEMENT CO LTD (Nigeria) 179
AERONAUTICAL DEVELOPMENT ASSOCIATES LTD (UK) (1983-84) 248
AERONAUTICA MACCHI SpA (Italy) 145
AERONAUTICAL RESEARCH AND DEVELOPMENT COMPANY OF NEW ZEALAND (New Zealand) (1981-82) 498
AERONCA INC (USA) (1979-80) 257
AERONEERING INC (USA) (1979-80) 503
AERONICS (PTY) LTD (South Africa) (1981-82) 171
AEROSPACE (see New Zealand Aerospace Industries Ltd) (1982-83) 160
AEROSPACE GENERAL COMPANY (USA) (1980-81) 259
AEROSPACE INDUSTRIES OF MALAYSIA (Malaysia) 174
Aero-Space Plane (NASA) 446
AEROSPACE TECHNOLOGIES OF AUSTRALIA PTY LTD (Australia) 4
AÉROSPATIALE/ASTA/CATIC 103
AÉROSPATIALE SNI (France) 55
AÉROSPATIALE/AERITALIA (International) (1981-82) 92
Aero Sportster (Moser) (1985-86) 604
Aerostar 600A (Piper) (1984-85) 478
Aerostar 602P (Piper) (1985-86) 488
Aerostar 700P (Piper) (1985-86) 488
Aero Subaru (Fuji) (1986-87) 166
AERO-TECH (USA) (1985-86) 575
AEROTEC S/A INDUSTRIA AERONAUTICA (Brazil) (1984-85) 10
AEROTECHNIK (Czechoslovakia) (1984-85) 44
AEROTEC S/A INDUSTRIA AERONAUTICA (Brazil) 9
AERO TRADER LTD (New Zealand) 178
AERO UNION CORPORATION (USA) 321
AERO VODOCHODY NARODNI PODNIK (Czechoslovakia) 47
AGcarryall (Cessna) (1980-81) 313
Ag-Cat B-Plus (Schweizer) (1983-84) 482
Ag-Cat G-164/R-1820 (Serv-Aero) (1979-80) 440
Ag-Cat/Leonides (Serv-Aero) (1979-80) 439
Ag-Cat Super B (Schweizer) 471
Ag-Cat Super B Turbine (EAC) 53
Ag-Cat Turbine (Schweizer) 471
Ag Husky (Cessna) 374
Agile Falcon (General Dynamics) 391
AgMaster (Frontier) (1981-82) 355
AGRICOPTEROS LTDA (Colombia) (1984-85) 42
Agricultural aircraft (NASA) (1981-82) 418
Agro-Turbo, Zlin 37T (Moravan) (1983-84) 47
Agro Turbo, Z37T (Zlin) 52
AGRUPACION AVIONES-DEPARTAMENTO INGENIERIA, GUARNICION AEREA CORDOBA (Argentina) (1979-80) 3
AgTrainer, Cessna (Aviones de Colombia) 46
Ag Truck (Cessna) 374
AGUSTA SpA 147
Ag Wagon (Cessna) (1981-82) 330
AHRENS AIRCRAFT CORPORATION (USA) (1981-82) 273
AHRENS AIRCRAFT INC (USA) (1981-82) 273
Aiglon, R 1180 (Robin) (1984-85) 77
Aileron-rudder interconnect programme (NASA) (1986-87) 469
AIR AMERICA INC (USA) (1986-87) 330
Air Beetle (AIEP) 179
Air Breathing Fan (Sadlier) 6
Airborne Laser Laboratory (USAF/Boeing) (1982-83) 330
Airbuggy (WHE) (1984-85) 299
Airbuggy, VoWi 10 (Airconcept) (1980-81) 77
AIRBUS INDUSTRIE (International) 103
AIRCONCEPT FLUGZEUG UND GERÄTEBAU GmbH und Co KG (West Germany) (1981-82) 76
Aircraft 101 (Tupolev) (1985-86) 262
AIRCRAFT DESIGNS (BEMBRIDGE) LTD (UK) (1984-85) 256
AIRCRAFT GROUP, ROCKWELL INTERNATIONAL (USA) (1981-82) 452
Aircraft noise monitoring programme (NASA) (1980-81) 396
AIRCRAFT TECHNOLOGY INDUSTRIES (International) 109
Air Cushion Landing Gear (Bell) (1979-80) 277
AIRESEARCH AVIATION COMPANY (USA) (1986-87) 330
Air Force One (Boeing) 370
Airfox, IAR-317 (ICA) 201
Airguard, F-7M (CAC) 35
Airkart, MW3 (Whittaker) (1979-80) 500
Airlifter CV-880 (GACC) (1981-82) 355
AIRMASTER INC (USA) 322
AIR-METAL FLUGZEUGBAU UND ENTWICKLUNGS GmbH & CO BETRIEBS-KG (West Germany) (1978-79) 65
AIRPLANE ALLEY (USA) (1982-83) 526
AIR-PLANE CO LTD (UK) (1982-83) 518
Air Sentry (Fairchild) (1985-86) 401
AIRTECH CANADA (Canda) 17
Air Tractor (Air Tractor) 322, 323
AIR TRACTOR INC (USA) 322
Airtrainer CT4A (Aerospace) (1981-82) 155
Airtrainer CT4C/CR/D (PAC) 179
Airtruk (PL-12 (Transavia) (1987-88) 9
Airtruk T-320 (Transavia) (1979-80) 8
Ajeet (HAL) (1984-85) 93
Ajeet Trainer (HAL) 98
AJEP DEVELOPMENTS (UK) (1978-79) 213
AKASAMITRA HOMEBUILT AIRCRAFT ASSOCIATION (Indonesia) (1986-87) 100
Akro (Stephens) (1981-82) 554
Albatros L-39 (AERO) 47
Albatross, G-111 (Grumman/Resorts International) (1986-87) 416
Albatross Tanker conversion (Aero Union) 321
Alizé (Breguet) (1985-86) 67
ALLISON GAS TURBINE DIVISION GMC (USA) 324
Alouette III (Aérospatiale) 57
Alouette III, IAR-316B (ICA) 201
Alouette III, SA 316B (HAL/Aérospatiale). (1987-88) 106
Alpha (Robinson) (1985-86) 493
Alpha Jet (Dassault-Breguet/Dornier) 115
ALPHA JET (International) (1982-83) 104
Alpha series (Robin) (1984-85) 76
Alpha Sport (Robin) (1983-84) 76
Alpine Commander (Rockwell International) (1980-81) 431
Alpha XH-1 (ATLAS) (1987-88) 216
ALVAREZ, JOSEPH P. (USA) (1978-79) 504
AMERICAN AIR RACING INC (USA) ... (1978-79) 504
AMERICAN AVIATION INDUSTRIES (USA) 319
AMERICAN JET INDUSTRIES INC (USA) (1979-80) 259
AMES INDUSTRIAL CORPORATION (USA) (1984-85) 300
Ami Pou, GL02 (Landray) (1982-83) 504
Amphibian Air Car Jr (Spencer) (1984-85) 600
AMS/OIL (USA) (1984-85) 559
AMX INTERNATIONAL (International) 111
ANAHUAC, FABRICA DE AVIONES, SA (Mexico) (1981-82) 150
Analogue (Mikoyan) (1979-80) 192
ANDERSON AIRCRAFT CORPORATION (USA) (1984-85) 560
Andorinha (Super Rotor) 16
Angel (King's) 405
Antek, An-2 (WSK PZL-Mielec) 182
Antheus (Antonov) 221
ANTONOV, OLEG, DESIGN BUREAU K (USSR) 220
Apache (McDonnell Douglas) 439
Apache, sea-going (McDonnell Douglas) 441
APOLLO HELICOPTER SERVICES (USA) (1987-88) 347
Apollo Jetstream (ADAL) (1982-83) 243, 245
ARAB BRITISH HELICOPTER COMPANY (Egypt) (1980-81) 45
ARAB ORGANISATION FOR INDUSTRIALISATION 53
Araguaia (EMBRAER) (1978-79) 14
Arapaho (Piper) (1980-81) 416
Arava (IAI) 139
ARBEITSGEMEINSCHAFT TRANSALL (International) 136
ARBEITSGRUPPE FÜR LUFT- UND RAUMFAHRT (Switzerland) (1987-88) 227
Archer II (Piper) 452
ARCTIC AIRCRAFT COMPANY (USA) 325
Arctic Tern (Arctic) 325
Aries T-250 (Bellanca) (1980-81) 287
AROCET INC (USA) 326
Arrow IV (Piper) (1982-83) 437
ARTOMOV, MIKHAIL (USSR) (1982-83) 517
ARV AVIATION LTD (UK) (1987-88) 294
ARVIN/CALSPAN ADVANCED TECHNOLOGY CENTER (USA) (1983-84) 349
ASOCIACION ARGENTINA DE CONSTRUCTORES DE AVIONES EXPERIMENTALES (Argentina) (1979-80) 465
Astar AS 350 (Aérospatiale) 60
Astra, 1125 (IAI) 140
Asuka (Kawasaki) 167
Asuka (NAL) 171
Atlantic 1 Modernisation (Aeritalia) 144
Atlantic 1 Modernisation Programme (Dornier) 89
Atlantique 2 (Dassault-Breguet) 71
Atlantic KWS Br.1150 (Dornier/Breguet) ... (1982-83) 85
ATLAS AIRCRAFT CORPORATION OF SOUTH AFRICA (PTY) LIMITED (South Africa) 203
Attack Helicopter (Cardoen) (1987-88) 35
ATTAS (MBB) 94
Aucán (ENAER) 33
Augmentor wing jet STOL research aircraft (NASA/DITC) (1980-81) 25
Aurora (Lockheed) 412
Aurora (MTC) 445
AUSTRALIAN AIRCRAFT CONSORTIUM PTY LTD (Australia) (1985-86) 6
AUSTRALIAN AUTOGYRO CO, THE (Australia) 4
Australian basic trainer (AAC) (1983-84) 6
Australian F/A-18A (McDonnell Douglas) .. (1986-87) 452
Autogyro (Everett) 297
Auto-Gyrocopter, W.S.9 (Seremet) (1980-81) 471
Auxiliary Fuel System C130 (Aero Union) 321
Avalon 680 (Airmaster) (1986-87) 331
AVALON AVIATION (Canada) 18
Avalon Twin Star 800 (Airmaster) (1985-86) 319
Avalon Twin Star 1000 (Airmaster) 322
Avianti (Piaggio) 163
Avenger (Marchetti) (1982-83) 552
Aviocar, C-212 Series 200 (CASA) (1987-88) 217
Aviocar, C-212 Series 300 (CASA) 205
Aviocar ASW and Maritime Patrol (CSA) 206
Aviocar ELINT/ECM (CASA) 207
Aviocar, NC-212 (IPTN) 102
Aviojet, C-101 (CASA) 207
AVIOLIGHT (Italy) 160
AVIONES DE COLOMBIA SA (Colombia) 46
Avion Liviano (ENAER) 33
AVIONS DE TRANSPORT RÉGIONAL (International) 112
AVIONS MARCEL DASSAULT/BREGUET AVIATION (France) 65
AVIONS MUDRY ET CIE (France) 78
AVIONS PIERRE ROBIN (France) 81
AVIONS PIERRE ROBIN INC (Canada). (1985-86) 29
AVTEK CORPORATION (USA) 326
AYRES CORPORATION (USA) 327
Ayres Thrush modification (Serv-Aero) (1984-85) 497
Aztec (Piper) (1982-83) 435

B

B-1, Sylkie One (Wayne) (1979-80) 506
B-1-A (Drews) (1979-80) 516
B-1B (Rockwell) 463
B-2 (Northrop) 448
B-2B (Brantly-Hynes) (1983-84) 347
B-2B Brantly (Naras) 100
B3LA (Saab) (1978-79) 157
B-6 (XAC) 44
B-8HD (Bensen) (1981-82) 512
B-8MH Hover-Gyro (Bensen) (1980-81) 506
B-8MJ (Bensen) (1983-84) 543
B-10 (Mitchell) (1980-81) 531
B-18 Hover-Gyro (Bensen) (1984-85) 561
B36TC, Turbo Bonanza (Beechcraft) 331
B-52 Stratofortress (Boeing) 368
B60 Duke (Beechcraft) (1983-84) 305
B80 Queen Air (Beechcraft) (1979-80) 271
B80 Queen Airliner (Beechcraft) (1979-80) 271
B99 Airliner (Beechcraft) (1978-79) 267
B100 King Air (Beechcraft) (1983-84) 308
B200 Super King Air (Beechcraft) 333
B200T Maritime Patrol (Beechcraft) 334
BA-4B (Crosby/Andreasson) (1980-81) 494
BA-11 (Andreasson) (1982-83) 515
BAC 1-11 (Dee Howard) 384
BAC 111-400 (Dee Howard) (1986-87) 398
BAC 167 Strikemaster (BAe) (1981-82) 245
BAe (see British Aerospace PLC) 279
BAe 125 Series 700 (BAe) (1983-84) 251
BAe 125 Series 800 (BAe) 282
BAe 146 (BAe) 284
BAe 146 Series 100 (BAe) 284
BAe 146 Series 200 (BAe) 284
BAe 146 Series 300 (BAe) 284
BAe 146 Series 350 (BAe) 285
BAe 146 CC Mk 2 (BAe) 284
BAe 146MSL (BAe) 286
BAe 146MT (BAe) 286
BAe 146-QT Quiet Trader (BAe) 285
BAe 146STA (BAe) 285
BAe 246M (BAe) 286
BAe 748 Coastguarder (BAe) (1984-85) 261
BAe 748 Series 2B (BAe) (1983-84) 253
BAe 748 Series 2B Super (BAe) (1983-84) 254
BAe 748 (AEW) (HAL) (1987-88) 107
BAe 748(M) (HAL) (1984-85) 94
BAe 748 Water Bomber Conversion (Cranfield) (1987-88) 314
BD-8 (Bede-Huffmann) (1982-83) 526
Be-12 Tchaika (Beriev) 228
BGA (see British Gliding Association) (1982-83) 260
BGP1 Biplane (Plumb) (1983-84) 536
Bi 20 (Binder) (1980-81) 486
BK 117 (Nurtanio/MBB) (1983-84) 97
BK 117 A-3 (MBB/Kawasaki) 123
BK 117A-3M (MBB/Kawasaki) (1987-88) 130
BK 117A-4 (MBB/Kawasaki) 123
BK 117 Improvement Programme (MBB/Kawasaki) (1984-85) 113
BK 117M (MBB) 94
BN-2A Mk III Tri-Commutair (IAC/Pilatus Britten-Norman) (1984-85) 424
BN-2A Mk III Trislander (Pilatus Britten-Norman) (1982-83) 268
BN-2B Islander (Pilatus Britten-Norman) 301
BN-2T Turbine Islander (Britten-Norman) 302
BN 109 (NTT) 128
BO 105 (MBB) 92
BO 105 (PADC/MBB) 180
BO 105 Executaire (Boeing Vertol) (1979-80) 306
BO 105 LS (MBB Helicopter Canada) 30
BO 108 (MBB) 94
BO 108 (MBB) (1984-85) 89
Br.1150 Atlantic KWS (Dornier/Breguet) ... (1982-83) 85
BR2000 (Bromon) 372
BX-50A (Berger-Helicopter) (1984-85) 549
BX-110 (Berger-Helicopter) (1983-84) 531
BX-110A (Berger) (1984-85) 549
Baby Ace Model D (Ace Aircraft) (1982-83) 523
Baaz (MiG) 245
Backfire (Tupolev) 268
Badger (XAC) 44
Badger (Tupolev) 263
Bahadur (HAL) 100, 243
BAKENG AIRCRAFT (USA) (1979-80) 504
BALDWIN AIRCRAFT INTERNATIONAL (USA) 328
BALL-BARTOE AIRCRAFT CORPORATION (USA) (1979-80) 261
Bamboo Aircraft (PATS/NSDB) (1980-81) 153
B & B AVIATION (USA) (1983-84) 296
Bandeirante (EMBRAER) 10
Bandit (Practavia) (1979-80) 498
BARNEY OLDFIELD AIRCRAFT CO (USA) (1985-86) 578
Baron 58 (Beechcraft) 331
Baron 58 (RAM/Beech) 461
Baron 58P (Beechcraft) (1987-88) 354
Baron 58TC (Beechcraft) (1985-86) 328
Baron Model 95-B55 (Beechcraft) (1983-84) 303
Baron Model E55 (Beechcraft) (1984-85) 311
Barracuda (Jeffair) (1982-83) 548
BARRETT AIRCRAFT CORPORATION (USA) (1982-83) 528
BARTON, WAYNE (USA) (1980-81) 504
Basant, HA-31 Mk II (Hal) (1982-83) 95
Bayern II (Maiss) (1985-86) 562
Bazant (WSK-PZL Swidnik/Mil) (1985-86) 183
BEACHNER, CHRIS (USA) (1985-86) 576

Beagle H-5 (Harbin) ... *(1986-87)* 34
Bear (Tupolev) ... 264
Beaver, DHC-2 (Modern Wing) ... 31
Beaver, DHC-2/PZL-3S (Airtech) ... 17
BECKER, HORST (West Germany) ... *(1979-80)* 484
BEDE AIRCRAFT, INC (USA) ... *(1979-80)* 506
Bede-Huffman BD-8 (Airplane Alley) ... *(1982-83)* 526
BEECH AIRCRAFT CORPORATION (USA) ... 329
Beechcraft 99 conversions (ENAER Chile) .. *(1987-88)* 37
Beechjet (Beechcraft) ... 339
Beech Research & Development Projects (Beechcraft) 340
BEETS, GLENN (USA) ... *(1983-84)* 560
Belfast conversion (Marshall) ... *(1985-86)* 292
BELL AEROSPACE TEXTRON (USA) .. *(1980-81)* 278
BELL HELICOPTER CANADA (Canada) ... *(1987-88)* 21
BELL HELICOPTER TEXTRON (Canada) ... 18
BELL HELICOPTER TEXTRON INC (USA) ... 341
BELLANCA AIRCRAFT CORPORATION (USA) ... *(1981-82)* 303
BELLANCA AIRCRAFT ENGINEERING INC (USA) ... *(1985-86)* 348
BELLANCA INC (USA) ... 350
Belphegor, M-15 (WSK-PZL Mielec) ... *(1982-83)* 167
BEN-AIR LTD (UK) ... *(1983-84)* 267
Bengali, HN 500 (Nicollier) ... *(1983-84)* 521
Bergwind (Van Aswegen) ... *(1979-80)* 490
BERIEV (USSR) ... 228
Beta Bird (Hovey) ... *(1985-86)* 595
Beta, R22 (Robinson) ... 462
Beta, XTP-1 (Atlas) ... *(1987-88)* 204
BEZZOLA, GION (Switzerland) ... *(1983-84)* 531
'Big Bird' (Quickie) ... *(1981-82)* 544
BigLifter (Bell) ... *(1982-83)* 311
Big Wing Harrier (BAe) ... *(1980-81)* 235
BINDER, HELLMUTH (West Germany) . *(1980-81)* 486
Bionic Bat (MacReady) ... *(1985-86)* 444
Bird (Taylor) ... *(1985-86)* 626
BIRDMAN INC (USA) ... *(1980-81)* 506
Bison (Myasishchev) ... 256
'Blackbirds' (Lockheed) ... *(1983-84)* 417
Black Hawk (Sikorsky) ... 480
BLACKHOLE INVESTMENTS LTD (Canada) ... 21
Blackjack (Tupolev) ... 269
Blinder (Tupolev) ... 267
BOB ANDERSON SPORT AIRCRAFT (USA) ... *(1982-83)* 530
Boeing 707/720 conversions (IAI) ... 142
Boeing 747 combi conversions (IAI) ... 142
BOEING AEROSPACE (USA) ... 350
BOEING COMMERCIAL AIRPLANES (USA) ... 352
BOEING COMPANY, THE (USA) ... 350
BOEING FABRICATION AND SERVICES COMPANY OF CANADA (Canada) ... *(1986-87)* 20
BOEING HELICOPTERS (USA) ... 364
BOEING MILITARY AIRPLANES (USA) ... 368
BOEING OF CANADA LTD (Canada) ... 21
BOEING OF CANADA LTD (VERTOL DIVISION) (Canada) ... *(1982-83)* 21
BOEING VERTOL COMPANY (USA) .... *(1986-87)* 381
BOEING WICHITA COMPANY (USA) .. *(1979-80)* 301
BOLEN INC, RALPH (USA) ... *(1982-83)* 335
BÖLKOW (see Messerschmitt-Bölkow-Blohm (GmbH) ... *(1981-82)* 82
Bonanza 400 (Smith) ... 488
Bonanza A36 (Beechcraft) ... 331
Bonanza B36TC (Beechcraft) ... 331
Bonanza F33A/C (Beechcraft) ... 330
Bonanza V35B (Beechcraft) ... *(1986-87)* 338
BOND, JOHN (USA) ... *(1984-85)* 562
Boomerang (Rotor Master) ... *(1979-80)* 538
BORCHERS, LOWELL J (USA) ... *(1981-82)* 512
BORG, RICHARD R (USA) ... *(1981-82)* 513
BOUNSALL, EDDIE (USA) ... *(1984-85)* 562
Boxer, LDA-500 (Lockspeiser) ... *(1986-87)* 298
Boxer, LDA-1000 (Lockspeiser) ... *(1986-87)* 299
Boxmoth (Thompson) ... *(1981-82)* 557
BOYD, GARY (USA) ... *(1982-83)* 532
BOYETTE, ERNIE (USA) ... *(1983-84)* 544
BRANSON AIRCRAFT CORPORATION (USA) .. 371
BRANTLY-HYNES HELICOPTER INC (USA) ... *(1983-84)* 347
Brasilia, EMB-120 (EMBRAER) ... 12
Brave (Piper) ... *(1982-83)* 446
Bravo, AS 202 (FFA) ... *(1986-87)* 214
Bravo, ADS202/18A (FFA) ... 213
BREDANARDI COSTRUZIONI AERONAUTICHE SpA (Italy) ... 160
Breezy Model RLU-1 (RLU) ... *(1983-84)* 578
Brewer (Yakovlev) ... 273
BRISTOL AEROSPACE LTD (Canada) ... 24
Bristol F.2B Fighter replica (Ohmert) ... *(1980-81)* 534
BRITISH AEROSPACE AIRCRAFT GROUP (UK) ... *(1984-85)* 256
BRITISH AEROSPACE DYNAMICS GROUP (UK) ... *(1984-85)* 257
BRITISH AEROSPACE PUBLIC LIMITED COMPANY (UK) ... 279
BRITISH GLIDING ASSOCIATION (UK) ... *(1982-83)* 260
BRITTEN-NORMAN (BEMBRIDGE) LTD (UK) ... *(1978-79)* 231
BROMON AIRCRAFT COMPANY (USA) ... 372
Bronco (Rockwell) ... *(1987-88)* 495
BROOKLANDS AIRCRAFT LIMITED (UK) ... 294
Buccaneer (BAe) ... *(1979-80)* 237
Buccaneer update (BAe) ... 287
Buckeye (Rockwell) ... *(1982-83)* 461
Buffalo, DHC-5D (Boeing Canada) ... 21
Bulldog, SA-3-120 Series 120 (BAe) ... *(1983-84)* 258
Bulldog Series 200 (BAe) ... *(1978-79)* 223
Bull Thrush S2R-R1820/510 (Ayres) ... 327
BURKHART GROB FLUGZEUGBAU (West Germany) ... 90
BUSH CONVERSIONS INC (USA) ... 372
Businessliner (Cessna) ... *(1985-86)* 383

C

C-1 modifications (Kawasaki) ... 167
C-2A Greyhound (Grumman) ... 394
C4M Kudu (Atlas) ... *(1983-84)* 184
C-5 Galaxy (Lockheed) ... 418
C-8A Buffalo (DH Canada) ... *(1983-84)* 26
C-9A Nightingale (Douglas) ... *(1985-86)* 454
C-9B Skytrain II (Douglas) ... *(1985-86)* 454
C-12 (Beeccraft) ... 335
C-12J (Beechcraft) ... 337
C.14 (Dassault Breguet) ... 67
C-15 (McDonnell Douglas) ... 427
C-17 (McDonnell Douglas) ... *(1985-86)* 459
C-17A (McDonnell Douglas) ... 436
C-18A (Boeing) ... *(1986-87)* 380
C-19A (Boeing) ... 371
C-20 Gulfstream III (Gulfstream Aerospace) (1987-88) 432
C-21A (Learjet) ... 407
C22J (Caproni Vizzola) ... 159
C22R (Caproni Vizzola) ... *(1985-86)* 154
C-23A Sherpa (Shorts) ... 306
C-25A (Boeing) ... *(1986-87)* 380
C-26A (Fairchild Aircraft) ... 386
C-27 (USAF) ... 495
C-29A (BAe) ... 282
C90A King Air (Beechcraft) ... 332
C-95 (EMBRAER) ... *(1981-82)* 10
C-95A (EMBRAER) ... *(1981-82)* 10
C-95 (EMBRAER) ... 10
C99 Airliner (Beechcraft) ... *(1987-88)* 360
C100 King Air (Beechcraft) ... *(1978-79)* 269
C-101 Aviojet (CASA) ... 207
C-101BB Aviojet (Indaer Chile/CASA) ... *(1983-84)* 33
C-102 (CASA) ... *(1982-83)* 181
C-112 (CASA) ... *(1978-79)* 155
C-122S (Chadwick) ... 379
C-123T (Mancro/Fairchild) ... *(1983-84)* 428
C-130 AEW (Lockheed) ... *(1986-87)* 442
C-130 (Lockheed) ... 415
C-130 Auxiliary Fuel System (Aero Union) ... 321
C130 Conversions (IAI) ... 142
C-130 Conversion (Lockheed) ... 420
C-141 StarLifter (Lockheed) ... *(1983-84)* 423
C-160 (Maritime versions) (Transall) ... *(1982-83)* 120
C-160 (Second series) (Transall) ... 136
C-160S (Transall) ... *(1984-85)* 126
C-160SE (Transall) ... *(1984-85)* 126
C-212-5 Aviocar (CASA) ... *(1981-82)* 173
C-212 Series 200 Aviocar (CASA) ... *(1987-88)* 217
C-212 Series 200 Aviocar ASW and Maritime Patrol (CASA) ... 206
C-212 Aviocar ELINT/ECM version (CASA) ... 207
C-212 Series 300 Aviocar (CASA) ... 205
CAC (see Chengdu Aircraft Corporation) ... 35
CAC (see Commuter Aircraft Corporation). *(1983-84)* 348
CAC-100 (CAC) ... *(1982-83)* 336
CAF, counter-air fighter (USSR) ... 277
CAI (see Composites Aircraft Industries) .... *(1987-88)* 217
CAMC (see Changhe Aircraft Manufacturing Corporation) ... 36
CAP (see Club Aviazione Popolare) ... *(1983-84)* 528
CAP 10 B (Mudry) ... 78
CAP 20 (C.A.A.R.P./Mudry) ... *(1978-79)* 49
CAP 20L (Mudry) ... *(1982-83)* 73
CAP 21 (Mudry) ... 79
CAP 230 (Mudry) ... 79
CAP X (Mudry) ... *(1987-88)* 84
CASA (see Construcciones Aeronáuticas SA) ... 205
CASI (see Canadian Aeronautics and Space Institute) ... *(1978-79)* 467
CASTOR Islander (Pilatus Britten Norman) ... *(1986-87)* 307
CATIC, CHINA NATIONAL AERO-TECHNOLOGY IMPORT AND EXPORT CORPORATION (China) ... 34
CBA-123 (Embraer/Fama) ... 119
CBA-123 (FAMA) ... 2
CC-115 Buffalo (DH Canada) ... *(1981-82)* 22
CC-130 Hercules (Lockheed) ... 415
CC-132 (DH Canada) ... *(1986-87)* 25
CC-138 (Boeing Canada) ... 21
CC-142 (Boeing Canada) ... 22, 24
CC-144 (Canadair) ... 25
CCE-208 (Colani/Composite Engineering) ... 86
CCV YF-16 (General Dynamics) ... *(1978-79)* 336
CCW A-6A (Grumman) ... *(1979-80)* 346
CD2 Seastar (Claudius Dornier) ... 86
CE.15 (McDonnell Douglas) ... 427
CERVA (G.I.E.) (see Consortium Européen de Réalisation et de Ventes d'Avions) (Groupement d'Intérêts Économiques) ... *(1978-79)* 45
CF-5 (Northrop) ... *(1978-79)* 392
CF-5A, Upgrade programme (Bristol Aerospace) ... 24
CF-18 Hornet (McDonnell Douglas) ... *(1983-84)* 433
CF-18A/B (McDonnell Douglas) ... 427
CH-3 (Sikorsky) ... *(1983-84)* 485
CH-34 SuperPuma (Aérospatiale) ... 57
CH-46 Sea Knight (Boeing) ... 364
CH-47 Chinook (Boeing) ... 364
CH-47 Chinook (Kawasaki/Boeing) ... 169
CH-47C (EM/Boeing) ... 155
CH-47D Chinook (Boeing) ... 364
CH-47J Chinook (Kawasaki/Boeing) ... 169
CH-50 Esquilo (Aérospatiale) ... 60
CH 50 Mini Z (Zenair) ... *(1984-85)* 526
CH-53 Sea Stallion (Sikorsky) ... *(1982-83)* 472
CH-53E (Sikorsky) ... 478
CH-54 (Sikorsky) ... *(1978-79)* 433
CH-55 (Aérospatiale) ... 61
CH-60 (Zenair) ... *(1985-86)* 543
CH-100, Mono Z (Zenair) ... *(1983-84)* 510
CH-113 Labrador (Boeing of Canada) ... *(1985-86)* 19
CH-113A Voyageur (Boeing of Canada) ... *(1985-86)* 19
CH-118 Iroquois (Bell) ... 341
CH-124 (Sikorsky) ... *(1983-84)* 485
CH-135 (Bell) ... 19
CH-136 (Bell) ... *(1987-88)* 365
CH-147 (Boeing) ... 364
CH 400 (Zenair) ... *(1985-86)* 30
CIAR (see Centrala Industriala Aeronautica Romania) ... *(1979-80)* 159
CJ-5 (China) ... *(1982-83)* 37
CJ-6 (NAMC) ... 41
C.K.1 (Cicaré) ... *(1979-80)* 3
CL-1 Zipper (Cleary) ... *(1985-86)* 394
CL-215 (Canadair) ... 26
CL-215T (Canadair) ... 27
CL-600 Challenger (Canadair) ... *(1983-84)* 21
CL-601 Challenger (Canadair) ... *(1983-84)* 21
CL-601 RJ (Canadair) ... 26
CL-610 Challenger E (Canadair) ... *(1981-82)* 20
CMC (see Chichester-Miles Consultants Ltd) ... 295
CN-235 Series 100 (AIRTECH) ... 109
CNA (see Centrul National Aeronautic) ... 197
CNIAR (see Centrul National al Industriei Aeronautice Române) ... 196
CNPSL-PZL-WARSZAWA (see Centrum Naukowo-Produkcyjne Samolotow Lekkich PZL-Warszawa) ... *(1981-82)* 158
CP-140 Aurora (Lockheed) ... 412
CP 301, Mistral (Becker) ... *(1979-80)* 484
C.P.500 (Piel) ... *(1982-83)* 508
C-SAM Gulfstream III (Gulfstream Aerospace) ... *(1984-85)* 412
CSIR (see Council for Scientific and Industrial Research) ... *(1981-82)* 172
CT4A, Airtrainer (Aerospace) ... *(1981-82)* 155
CT4C, CR and D Airtrainer (PAC) ... 179
CT-39 Sabreliner (Rockwell) ... *(1978-79)* 424
CT-134A Musketeer II (Beechcraft) ... *(1984-85)* 306
CT-142 (D Boeing H Canada) ... 22, 24
CTA (see Centro Técnico Aerospacial) ... 10
CTDC (see Zaidan Hozin Minkan Yusooki Kaihatsu Kyokai) ... *(1979-80)* 127
CTN Twin Navion (Camair) ... *(1980-81)* 306
CUH-IH (Bell) ... *(1978-79)* 272
CUH-IN (Bell) ... *(1978-79)* 276
CV-880 Airlifter (GACC) ... *(1981-82)* 355
CX (McDonnell) ... *(1981-82)* 413
Cadet (Robin) ... 81
Cadet (Piper) ... 452
CAGNY, RAMOND DE (France) ... 65
CALIFORNIA HELICOPTER INTERNATIONAL INC (USA) ... 373
CALIFORNIA POLYTECHNIC STATE UNIVERSITY (USA) ... *(1979-80)* 307
Cali, T-610 (PAF/AJI) ... *(1981-82)* 157
CAL POLY (see California Polytechnic State University) ... *(1979-80)* 307
CALSPAN ADVANCED TECHNOLOGY CENTER (USA) ... *(1981-82)* 323
CALSPAN CORPORATION (see Arvin Calspan Advanced Technology Center) ... *(1983-84)* 349
CALYPSO AIRWAYS (USA) ... *(1985-86)* 373
CAMAIR AIRCRAFT CORPORATION (USA) ... *(1980-81)* 306
Camber (Ilyushin) ... 234
CAMMACORP (USA) ... *(1986-87)* 387
CAM Special (Carothers) ... *(1985-86)* 583
CANADAIR, INC (Canada) ... 25
CANADIAN AERONAUTICS AND SPACE INSTITUTE (Canada) ... *(1978-79)* 467
Canary Hawk (Karp) ... *(1983-84)* 564
Candid (Ilyushin) ... 232
Canguro, F.600 (General Avia) ... *(1980-81)* 133
Canguro, SF.600 TP (SIAI-Marchetti) ... 158
Canso/Turbo-Canso water bomber (Avalon) *(1983-84)* 20
CAPRONI VIZZOLA COSTRUZIONI AERONAUTICHE SpA (Italy) ... 159
Captain (Russell) ... *(1985-86)* 616
Carajá (EMBRAER/Piper) ... 15
Carajá (NEIVA) ... 16
Caravan I (Cessna) ... 374
Caravan II, F406 (Reims/Cessna) ... 79
Cardinal RG (Cessna) ... *(1979-80)* 310
Cardinal RG II (Cessna) ... *(1979-80)* 310
Cardinal Classic (Cessna) ... *(1979-80)* 310
CARDOEN, INDUSTRIAS LTDA (Chile) ... 32
Careless (Tupolev) ... 270
Cargo aircraft ground mobility system (Boeing) ... 371
Cargo Commuterliner (IAI) ... *(1982-83)* 123
CargoLifter (Bensen) ... *(1985-86)* 350
Cargoliner (Cavenaugh) ... 373
Carioca (EMBRAER/Piper) ... *(1983-84)* 18
Carioquinha, EMB-712 (EMBRAER) ... *(1978-79)* 16
CARMICHAEL, BOX (USA) ... *(1981-82)* 516
CAROTHERS, CHUCK (USA) ... *(1985-86)* 583
Cash (Antonov) ... 223
Cash (WSK-PZL-Mielec) ... 183
Castor Islander (Pilatus Britten-Norman) ... *(1986-87)* 307
CATH (Eurocopter) ... *(1987-88)* 126
CAUCHY, ALAIN (France) ... *(1981-82)* 482
CAVENAUGH AVIATION INC (USA) ... 373
CENTRAIR SA (France) ... 65
CENTRALA INDUSTRIALA AERONAUTICA ROMANA (Romania) ... *(1979-80)* 159
CENTRE DE RECHERCHES JEAN ST-GERMAIN INC (Canada) ... *(1982-83)* 490
CENTRO TÉCNICO AEROESPACIAL (Brazil) ... 10
CENTRUL NATIONAL AERONAUTIC (Romania) ... 197
CENTRUL NATIONAL AL INDUSTRIEI AERONAUTICE ROMANE (Romania) ... 196
CENTRUM NAUKOWO-PRODUKCYJNE SAMOLOTOW LEKKICH PZL-WARSZAWA (Poland) ... *(1981-82)* 158

Centurion (Cessna) 376
Centurion conversion (Air America) (1984-85) 300
Century V Eagle (Sierra) 474
Century 600 (Colemill) (1985-86) 394
CENTURY AIRCRAFT CORPORATION (USA) (1978-79) 299
CEPPATELLI, GIANFRANCO (Italy) (1984-85) 546
Cessna 210 landing gear door modification (Sierra) 473
Cessna 340/340A (Air America) (1986-87) 330
CESSNA AIRCRAFT COMPANY (USA) 373
Cessna auxiliary fuel systems (Sierra) 473
CHADWICK HELICOPTERS INC (USA) 379
CHAGNES, LÉO (France) (1980-81) 472
Challenger 600 (Canadair) 25
Challenger 601 (Canadair) 25
Challenger E, CL-610 (Canadair) (1981-82) 20
CHANGHE AIRCRAFT MANUFACTURING CORPORATION (China) 36
CHAMPION AIRCRAFT COMPANY INC (USA) (1986-87) 395
Chancellor (Cessna) 376
Chandra, RTAF-4 (RTAF) (1983-84) 196
Charger (Tupolev) (1983-84) 241
Charlie, P.66C-160 (Partenavia) (1984-85) 153
Charlie Trainer P.66T (Partenavia) (1984-85) 153
CHASLE, YVES (France) (1979-80) 470
Cheetah (Aérospatiale) 57
Cheetah (Atlas) 204
Cheetah (Gulfstream American) (1980-81) 355
Cheetah (HAL/Aérospatiale) (1987-88) 106
Chegoong-Ho (KA) (1986-87) 174
Chegoong-Ho (KA) 174
Cheney 1 (Cheney) (1982-83) 819
CHENGDU AIRCRAFT CORPORATION (China) 35
Cherokee Arrow Trainer (Chincul/Piper) (1983-84) 2
Cherokee Chief TG180,Piper (Rays) (1985-86) 615
Cherokee PA-28 conversion (Isham/Piper) (1984-85) 426
Cherokee Pathfinder (Piper) (1979-80) 408
Cherokee SIX (Piper) (1978-79) 400
Chetak (Aérospatiale) (1982-83) 51
Chetak (HAL/Aérospatiale) (1987-88) 106
Chevalier, DR 400/160 (Robin) (1979-80) 67
Cheyenne I (Piper) (1983-84) 458
Cheyenne IA (Piper) (1986-87) 483
Cheyenne II (Piper) (1983-84) 459
Cheyenne IIXL, (Piper) (1986-87) 484
Cheyenne IIIA (Piper) 455
Cheyenne IV (Piper) (1983-84) 461
Cheyenne 400 (Piper) 456
CHICHESTER-MILES CONSULTANTS LTD (UK) 295
Chieftain (Piper) (1986-87) 481
CHINCUL S.A.C.A.I.F.I. (Argentina) 2
Chinook Commercial (Boeing) 367
Chinook CH-47C (Boeing/EM) 155
Chinook CH-47 (Kawasaki/Boeing) 169
Chinook CH-47D Weights and performance (Boeing) 365
Chinook HC MkI (Boeing) 364
Chiricahua (Pilatus) 214
CHRISTEN INDUSTRIES INC (USA) 380
Chrysalis (MIT) (1981-82) 413
Chrysalis, DHR G-1 (Wood) (1983-84) 509
Chujiao-6 (NAMC) 41
Chuji Jiaolianji-6 (NAMC) 41
Chung Cheng (AIDC) (1987-88) 232
CICARÉ AERONÁUTICA SC (Argentina) (1980-81) 4
Citabria (Champion) (1985-86) 390
Citabria (Bellanca/Champion) (1980-81) 287
Citation, Air ambulance equipment (Branson) 372
Citation, Extended width cargo door (Branson) 372
Citation, Extended range fuel system (Branson) 371
Citation I (Cessna) (1984-85) 376
Citation I/SP Model 501 (Cessna) (1984-85) 377
Citation II (Cessna) 376
Citation III (Cessna) 378
Citation V (Cessna) 377
Citation Eagle (ASTEC) (1978-79) 253
Citation S/II (Cessna) 376
CITROËN-MARCHETTI (France) (1978-79) 45
CIVIL AVIATION DEPARTMENT, TECHNICAL CENTRE (India) (1978-79) 72
Clank (Antonov) 223
CLASSIC AIRCRAFT CORPORATION (USA) 381
Classic, Il-62 (Ilyushin) 231
Classic, IP-62M/MK (Ilyushin) 232
CLAUDIUS DORNIER SEASTAR GmbH & Co KG (West Germany) 86
CLEARY AIRCRAFT CORPORATION (USA) (1985-86) 394
Cline (Antonov) 224
Cline (HAL) (1981-82) 90
Clobber (Yakovlev) 275
Clod (Antonov) (1980-81) 179
CLUB AVIAZIONE POPOLARE (Italy) (1983-84) 528
CLUTTON, ERIC (UK) (1983-84) 532
Coaler (Antonov) 225
Coastguarder (BAe) (1984-85) 260
Cobra 2000 (Bell) (1983-84) 321
Cobra, F-3 (Forbes) (1978-79) 520
Cochise (Beechcraft) (1982-83) 293
Cock (Antonov) 221
Codling (Yakovlev) (1983-84) 245
Coke (Antonov) 222
Coke (XAC) 44
COLANI/COMPOSITE ENGINEERING (West Germany) 86
COLEMILL ENTERPRISES INC (USA) 382
Collegiate (Rankin) (1987-88) 493
Colt (Antonov) 220
Colt (HMP) 39
Colt (WSK-PZL-Mielec) 182
Comanchero (Schafer) 469
Comanchero 500 (Schafer) 469
Comanchero 750 (Schafer) 470
Commander 112 (Rockwell) (1978-79) 426
Commander 114 (Rockwell) (1978-79) 427
Commander 700 (Rockwell) (1980-81) 432
Commander 710 (Rockwell) (1980-81) 432
COMMANDER AIRCRAFT COMPANY (USA) 383
Commander Jetprop 840 (Gulfstream Aerospace) (1984-85) 413
Commander Jetprop 900 (Gulfstream Aerospace) (1984-85) 414
Commander Jetprop Special Mission Aircraft (Gulfstream Aerospace) (1984-85) 415
Commander Jetprop 980 (Gulfstream Aerospace) (1984-85) 414
Commander Jetprop 1000 (Gulfstream Aerospace) (1984-85) 414
Commander Jetprop 1200 (Gulfstream Aerospace) (1984-85) 415
Commando (Westland) 316
Commercial Chinook (Boeing) 367
Commercial Hercules (Lockheed) 448
COMMONWEALTH AIRCRAFT CORPORATION LIMITED (Australia) (1985-86) 6
Commuter (Reims) (1978-79) 57
Commuter IIA/IIB (International Helicopters) (1983-84) 562
Commuter 1900 (Beechcraft) (1982-83) 299
Commuter C99 (Beechcraft) (1982-83) 298
COMMUTER AIRCRAFT CORPORATION (USA) (1983-84) 348
Commuter, Model 340 (SAAB/Fairchild) (1982-83) 114
Competitor, VM-7 (Murphy) (1981-82) 537
COMPOSITE AIRCRAFT CORPORATION (USA) (1987-88) 409
COMPOSITE AIRCRAFT INDUSTRIES (South Africa) (1987-88) 217
COMPOSITE INDUSTRIES LTD (Australia) (1987-88) 7
COMTRAN LTD (USA) 383
CONAIR AVIATION LTD (Canada) 28
Concorde (Concorde) (1981-82) 101
CONCORDE SUPERSONIC TRANSPORT (International) (1981-82) 101
Condor (Antonov) 226
Condor (Hollmann) (1982-83) 546
Condor F.20 TP (General Avia) 161
Condor, Type 526 AFM (Aerotechnik/Zlin) (1984-85) 44
Condor, Zlin 526 AFM (Morovan) (1982-83) 47
CONDOR AERO INC (USA) (1983-84) 550
Conquest I (Cessna) 376
Conquest II (Cessna) 376
CONSORTIUM EUROPÉEN DE RÉALISATION ET DE VENTES D'AVIONS (GROUPEMENT D'INTÉRETS ÉCONOMIQUES) (France) (1978-79) 45
CONSTRUCCIONES AERONÁUTICAS SA (Spain) 205
CONTINENTAL COPTERS, INC (USA) (1981-82) 347
Coot-A (Ilyushin) 229
Coot-B (Ilyushin) 230
Corisco (EMBRAER/Piper) (1984-85) 17
Corisco Turbo (EMBRAER/Piper) 15
Cormoran (Colani/composite Engineering) 86
Cormorano, S.700 (SIAI/Marchetti) (1984-85) 151
Corporate 77-32 (Boeing) (1987-88) 376
Corporate 77-33 (Boeing) (1987-88) 378
Corporate 77-43 (Boeing) (1986-87) 369
Corporate 77-52 (Boeing) (1987-88) 384
Corporate 77-62 (Boeing) (1987-88) 385
Corsair (Cessna) (1982-83) 352
Corsair, modified (Riley) (1983-84) 472
Corsair Update Programmes (LTV) 421
Corsair II (LTV) 420
Corsair II² (Vought) (1980-81) 453
Corvette (Aérospatiale) (1978-79) 37
COSTRUZIONI AERONAUTICHE GIOVANNI AGUSTA SpA (Italy) 147
Cougar (EAA) (1979-80) 519
Cougar (Gulfstream American) (1980-81) 355
COUNCIL FOR SCIENTIC AND INDUSTRIAL RESEARCH (South Africa) (1981-82) 172
Coupe RSH-1A (Rotor Sport) (1982-83) 566
Courier 700 and 800 (Helio) (1987-88) 435
COX AIRCRAFT CORPORATION (USA) (1983-84) 372
COX AIR RESOURCES LTD (Canada) (1980-81) 23
CRANFIELD AERONAUTICAL SERVICES LIMITED (UK) 296
CRANFIELD INSTITUTE OF TECHNOLOGY (UK) (1982-83) 260
CRANFIELD INSTITUTE OF TECHNOLOGY, COLLEGE OF AERONAUTICS (UK) 296
Credible Hawk (Sikorsky) (1987-88) 513
Cresco 08-600 (PAC) 179
Cresco 600 (Aerospace) (1981-82) 156
Cricri, MC 10 (Colomban) (1981-82) 480
Crici, MC 12 (Colomban) (1982-83) 496
CROSBY AVIATION LTD (UK) (1980-81) 494
Crusader (Cessna) 376
Crusty (Tupolev) (1984-85) 248
CRUTCHLEY, S (South Africa) (1979-80) 489
Cub (Antonov) 220
Cub (STAF) 43
CUBy (Wag-Aero) (1982-83) 581
Curl (Antonov) 222
Cutlass (Cessna) (1984-85) 360
Cutlass RG (Cessna) 374
Cygnet, SF-2A (Sisler) (1983-84) 580

D

D.1 (Jones) (1981-82) 475
D-1 Derringer (Wing) (1982-83) 486
D-2M (Derringer) (1982-83) 487
D2 Special, 100 (Denight) (1984-85) 571
D.92 Bébé (Jodel) (1985-86) 551
D-200 Freshman (D'Apuzzo) (1982-83) 537
D-260/D295 Senior Aerosport (D'Apuzzo) (1983-84) 552
D292 (ACAP) (Bell) 347
D-3300 (McDonnell Douglas) (1983-84) 442
DA-2A (Davis) (1985-86) 588
DA-3 (Davis) (1980-81) 514
DA-5A (Davis) (1983-84) 552
DA-6 (Davis) (1983-84) 553
DAL-1 Tuholer (Spezio) (1982-83) 572
DC-1 (Delmontez-Cauchy) (1981-82) 482
DC-3 Spraying System (Aero Union) (1984-85) 300
DC-3 Turbo Express (USAC) (1987-88) 528
DC-3-65TP (Schafer) 470
DC-3/2000 (Airtech Canada) 18
DC-8 freighter conversion (Aeritalia) 144
DC-8 Super 71/72/73 (Cammacorp) (1986-87) 387
DC-8 Series 71/72/73 (McDonnell Douglas) (1983-84) 435
DC-9 (McDonnell Douglas) (1985-86) 454
DC-9 Super 80 (Douglas) (1982-83) 419
DC-10 (McDonnell Douglas) 432
DC-10 Series 30CF (Douglas) 433
DC-10 Series 30F (McDonnell Douglas) 433
DC-130 (Lockheed) 415
DC-XX (McDonnell) (1981-82) 413
DF-4B Phantom II (McDonnell) (1980-81) 380
DG-1 (Aero Design) (1980-81) 502
DHC-2 Beaver (Modern Wing) 31
DHC-2 Mk III Turbo-Beaver (DH Canada) (1984-85) 24
DHC-2/PZL-3S Beaver (Airtech) 17
DHC-3 Otter (DH Canada) (1983-84) 24
DHC-3/1000 Otter (Airtech) 17
DHC-3/PZL-3S Otter (Airtech) (1983-84) 20
DHC-3-T(Cox) (1983-84) 372
DHC-5 Buffalo (DH Canada) (1983-84) 24
DHC-5/C-8A augmentor wing jet/STOL research aircraft (DH Canada) (1983-84) 26
DHC-5D Buffalo (Boeing Canada) 21
DHC-5E Transporter (DH Canada) (1984-85) 24
DHC-6 Twin Otter Series 300 (Boeing Canada) 21
DHC-6 Twin Otter Series 300M (DH Canada) (1985-86) 25
DH-6-300 MR Military Twin Otter (DH Canada) (1985-86) 25
DHC-7 Dash 7 (Boeing Canada) 21
DHC-7 Dash 7R (DH Canada) (1984-85) 29
DHC-7 Dash 7IR (Boeing Canada) 21
DHC-8 Dash 8 Series 100 (Boeing Canada) 22
DHC-8 Dash 8 Series 200 (DH Canada) 30, 32
DHC-8 Dash 8 Series 300 (Boeing Canada) 24
DHC-8 Dash 8 Series 400 (Boeing Canada) 24
DHC-8 Dash 8M (Boeing Canada) 24
DHR G-1 Chrysalis (Wood) (1983-84) 509
D.L.5 (Livesey) (1979-80) 496
Do 24A (Dornier) (1978-79) 67
Do 24TT (Dornier) (1985-86) 87
Do 28 D-2 Skyservant (Dornier) (1987-88) 93
Do 128 Skyservant (Dornier) (1981-82) 77
Do 128-6 Turbo-Skyservant (Dornier) (1981-82) 78
Do 228 (Dornier) (1981-82) 78
DR 400/100 Cadet (Robin) 81
DR 400/100 2 + 2 (Robin) (1980-81) 71
DR 400/120 Dauphin (Robin) 81
DR 400/140B Major (Robin) (1979-80) 66
DR 400/160 Major (Robin) 81
DR 400/180 Régent (Robin) 81
DR 400/180R Remorqueur (Robin) 81
DSA-1 Miniplane (Smith) (1981-82) 550
DSK-1 Hawk (DSK Airmotive) (1980-81) 515
DSK-2 Golden Hawk (DSK Airmotive) (1980-81) 515
DAEDALUS RESEARCH INC (USA) 383
Dakota (Piper) 453
Dash 7, DHC-7 (Boeing Canada) 21
Dash 7IR, DHC-7 (Boeing Canada) 21
Dash 7R, DHC-7 (DH Canada) (1984-85) 29
Dash 8, Series 100 DHC-8 (Boeing Canada) 22
Dash 8 200, DHC-8 (DH Canada) (1987-88) 30, 32
Dash 8 Series 300, DHC-8 (Boeing Canada) 24
Dash 8 Series 400, DHC-8 (Boeing Canada) 24
Dash 8M, DHC-8 (Boeing Canada) 24
Dash X (DH Canada) (1979-80) 26
DASSAULT-BREGUET AVIATION, AVIONS MARCEL (France) 65
DASSAULT-BREGUET/DORNIER (International) 115
DATWYLER, MDC MAX, AG (Switzerland) 212
Dauntless, SBD-3 (Roberts) (1979-80) 538
Dauphin, DR 400/120 (Robin) 81
Dauphin, SA 360C (Aérospatiale) (1984-85) 57
Dauphin, SA 361H/HCL (Aérospatiale) (1979-80) 49
Dauphin 2, SA 365C (Aérospatiale) (1982-83) 57
Dauphin 2, SA 365F/AS.15TT (Aérospatiale) 62
Dauphin 2, SA 365M (Aérospatiale) (1985-86) 57
Dauphin 2, SA 365N (Aérospatiale) 63
Dauphin 2, SA 366 (Aérospatiale) 63
Decathlon (Champion) (1985-86) 391
Decathlon (Bellanca/Champion) (1980-81) 287
DEE HOWARD COMPANY, THE (USA) 383
Defender (Pilatus Britten-Norman) 302
Defender (McDonnell Douglas) 438
Defiant (Rutan) (1985-86) 613
DE HAVILLAND AIRCRAFT OF CANADA LTD., THE (Canada) (1987-88) 28
DELEMONTEZ-CAUCHY (see Cauchy, Alain) (1981-82) 482
Delta Bird (Hovey) (1981-82) 529
Delta-Ente (Richter) (1982-83) 511
Delta Stingray (Borchers) (1981-82) 512
DENIGHT, RONALD A (USA) (1984-85) 571
Der Donnerschlag (Harmon) (1978-79) 521
DeRic DE 13P Delta-Ente (Richter) (1982-83) 511
Derringer, D-1 (Wing) (1982-83) 486
DEUTSCHE AIRBUS GmbH (West Germany) (1987-88) 93
DE VORE AVIATION CORPORATION (USA) (1986-87) 399
DEWEY, JIM (USA) (1982-83) 538

Diablo 1200, MA-1B (Emair) (1980-81) 333
Diamond I (MAI) (1983-84) 427
Diamond I Long-range tank (Branson) 371
Diamond IA (MAI) (1985-86) 446
Diamond II (MAI) (1985-86) 447
DIETRICK SALES & SERVICE (USA) (1981-82) 347
Digital Fly-By-Wire system (NASA) (1978-79) 389
Dino (Ganzavia) 97
Dolphin, HH-65A (Aérospatiale) 63
Dolphinair (Omnionics) (1980-81) 401
DOMINION AIRCRAFT CORPORATION LTD (USA) (1979-80) 330
Don Kichot, J-1B (Janowski) (1979-80) 488
Doppelraab, RE 2 (Ehmann) (1984-85) 544
DORNIER GmbH (West Germany) 87
Dornier 128-6 (Dornier) (1985-86) 85
Dornier 228 (Dornier) 87
Dornier 228 (HAL) 99
Dornier 228 Maritime Patrol (Dornier) 89
Dornier 328 (Dornier) (1987-88) 95
Dos Equis Challenger (Statler) (1982-83) 572
Double Duce (Bakeng) (1979-80) 505
Double Teenie (Parker) (1979-80) 532
DOUGLAS AIRCRAFT COMPANY (USA) 429
Drake (Frizzle) (1979-80) 466
Draken J35J (Saab-Scania) 212
Dragon (Phalanx) (1987-88) 482
Dragonfly, Model 318E (Cessna) (1981-82) 336
Dreadnought (Sanders) (1984-85) 493
DREWS, JOHN (USA) (1979-80) 516
Dromader Water Bomber (Melex) 442
Dromader, M-18 (WSK-PZL Mielec) 184
Dromader, M-18A (WSK-PZL-Mielec) 185
Dromader Mikro (WSK-PZL-Mielec) (1983-84) 176
Dromader Mini, M-21 (WSK-PZL-Mielec) 186
Dromader Super, M-24 (WSK-PZL-Mielec) 186
DSK AIRMOTIVE (USA) (1980-81) 515
Duce (Bakeng) (1979-80) 504
Duchess 76 (Beechcraft) (1984-85) 310
Duet (Knowles) (1980-81) 495
Duke (Beechcraft) (1983-84) 305
Dyna-cam engine project (Piper) 459

E

E-2 Hawkeye (Grumman) 393
E-2B (Grumman) 393
E-2C (Grumman) 393
E-3 Sentry (Boeing) 350
E-4 (Boeing) (1985-86) 363
E-6A Tacamo (Boeing) 351
E-6A (Boeing) 352
E-8A (Boeing) 352, 370
E-9A (Boeing Canada) 24
E.25 Mirlo (CASA) 207
E.26 Tamiz (CASA) 208
E.26 Tamiz (ENAER) 32
E-33 (Mikoyan) (1982-83) 207
E47 Elf (Ward) (1985-86) 571
E55 Baron (Beechcraft) (1984-85) 311
E-66 (Mikoyan) (1982-83) 207
E-76 (Mikoyan) (1982-83) 207
E90 King Air (Beechcraft) (1982-83) 297
E-133 (Mikoyan) (1982-83) 211
E-266 (MiG) (1987-88) 259
E-266M (Mikoyan) (1984-85) 227
E400 (Gyroflug) 91
E401 (Gyroflug) (1987-88) 98
EA-6 Intruder (Grumman) (1987-88) 427
EA-6A Intruder (Grumman) 395
EA-6B Prowler (Grumman) 396
EA7 Optica (Edgley) (1985-86) 289
EA230 Ultimate (ACS) (1985-86) 205
EAA (see Eagle Aircraft Australia) 5
EAA (see Experimental Aircraft Association, Inc) (1984-85) 572
EAA Biplane (EAA) (1983-84) 555
EAC (see Ethiopian Airlines Corporation) 53
EAP (BAe) 292
EAV-8B (McDonnell Douglas/BAe) (1986-87) 120
EBI Rotor Buggy (Boyette) (1983-84) 544
E.C.2 Easy Too (Clutton-Tabenor) (1983-84) 550
EC-18B (Boeing) 370
EC-18C (Boeing) 370
EC-18D (Boeing) 370
EC-20F (Grumman Aerospace) 400
EC-24A (Electrospace Systems) 384
EC-95 (EMBRAER) (1981-82) 10
EC-130 (Lockheed) 415
EC-130 ARE (LAS) (1981-82) 803
EC-137D (Boeing) (1987-88) 388
EF-4 Phantom II (McDonnell) (1980-81) 380
EF-111A (General Dynamics) (1982-83) 369
EF-111A (Grumman/General Dynamics) 398
EFA (see European Fighter Aircraft) 121
EFA/JF-90 (Eurofighter) 121
EFM-Enhanced Fighter Manoeuvrability) 132
EGHS (see Eau Gallie High School) (1985-86) 590
EH-1H Iroquois (Bell) 341
EH-60A Black Hawk (Sikorsky) 480
EH 101 (EHI) 117
EHI (see EH Industries) 117
EM (see Elicotteri Meridionali Spa) 155
EMB-110 Bandeirante (EMBRAER) 10
EMB-110K1 (EMBRAER) (1980-81) 12
EMB-110P (EMBRAER) (1980-81) 12
EMB-110P1 (EMBRAER) (1984-85) 10
EMB-110P1/41 (EMBRAER) (1984-85) 11
EMB-110P1SAR (EMBRAER) (1983-84) 11
EMB-110P2 (EMBRAER) (1984-85) 11
EMB-110P2/41 (EMBRAER) (1984-85) 11
EMB-110P3 (EMBRAER) (1983-84) 11
EMB-111 (EMBRAER) 11
EMB-120 Brasilia (EMBRAER) 12
EMB-121A Xingu I (EMBRAER) (1983-84) 15
EMB-121A1 Xingu II (EMBRAER) (1987-88) 16
EMB-121B Xingu III (EMBRAER) (1987-88) 17
EMB-123 (EMBRAER) (1987-88) 17
EMB-123 Tapajos (EMBRAER) (1978-79) 14
EMB-201A Ipanema (EMBRAER) 14
EMB-201R (EMBRAER) (1980-81) 17
EMB 312 Tucano (Aol) 53
EMB-312 Tucano (EMBRAER) 13
EMB-326GB Xavante (EMBRAER/Aermacchi) (1984-85) 15
EMB-710 Carioca (EMBRAER/Piper) (1983-84) 18
EMB-711T Corisco (EMBRAER/Piper) (1984-85) 17
EMB-711 ST Corsico Turbo (EMBRAER/Piper) 15
EMB-712 Tupi (EMBRAER/Piper) 15
EMB-720 Minuano (EMBRAER/Piper) 15
EMB-721 Sertanejo (EMBRAER/Piper) (1985-86) 16
EMB-810 Senaca III (EMBRAER/Piper) 15
EMB-820 Navajo (EMBRAER/Piper) 15
EMB N-821 (EMBRAER/Piper) (1985-86) 16
EMBRAER (see Empresa Brasileira de Aeronáutica SA) 10
ENAER (see Empresa Nacional de Aeronáuticade Chile) 32
EOS/SFA (Frederick-Ames) (1984-85) 575
EUROFAR-European Future Advanced Rotorcraft 121
ER-2 (Lockheed) 411
ER-2 (NASA/Lockheed) (1982-83) 429
EX101 Firefly (Nutting) (1985-86) 605
Eagle (ASTEC/Cessna) (1981-82) 276
Eagle (Composite) (1985-86) 395
Eagle (Eagle) (1979-80) 331
Eagle (Eagle Aircraft) (1983-84) 372
Eagle (Enstrom) (1978-79) 325
Eagle I (Christen) (1984-85) 568
Eagle I/II/III (Composite/Windecker) (1985-86) 395
Eagle II (ASTEC/Grumman) (1980-81) 262
Eagle II (Composite) (1980-81) 331
Eagle II (Eagle Helicopter) (1981-82) 524
Eagle 220 (Eagle) (1983-84) 372
Eagle 300 (Eagle) (1983-84) 372
Eagle DW-1 (Eagle) (1980-81) 332
Eagle/Eagle SP (Sierra) 474
Eagle, F-15 (McDonnell Douglas) 424
Eagle, F-15DJ (Mitsubishi) 170
Eagle, F-15E (McDonnell Douglas) 426
Eagle, F-15J (Mitsubishi) 170
Eagle H-76 (Sikorsky) 485
Eagle SP (ASTEC/Cessna) (1981-82) 276
Eagle, Model 480 (Enstrom) (1980-81) 334
Eagle, Windecker (Composite) (1983-84) 371
Eagle X (Composite Industries) (1987-88) 7
Eagle X (EAA) 5
EAGLE AIRCRAFT AUSTRALIA (Australia) 5
EAGLE AIRCRAFT COMPANY (USA) (1984-85) 386
EAGLE HELICOPTER CORPORATION (USA) (1981-82) 524
Easy Too, E.C.2 (Clutton-Tabenor) (1983-84) 550
EAU GALLIE HIGH SCHOOL (USA) (1985-86) 590
EBERSHOFF AIRPLANE COMPANY (USA) (1984-85) 573
ÉCOLE NATIONALE SUPÉRIEURE D'ARTS ET MÉTIERS (France) (1978-79) 470
ECTOR AIRCRAFT COMPANY INC (USA) 384
Ecureuil/Astar (Aérospatiale) 60
Ecureuil 2/Twinstar (Aérospatiale) 61
EDGLEY AIRCRAFT LTD (UK) (1985-86) 289
EDWARDS, WILLIAM (USA) (1983-84) 583
Egrett-1 (Egreet) 116
EGREET (International) 116
EH INDUSTRIES (International) 117
EHMANN, ROLF (Germany) (1984-85) 544
EIDGENÖSSISCHES FLUGZEUGWERK (Switzerland) 217
EKIN (ENGINEERING) CO. LTD., W.H. (UK) (1984-85) 299
Electrically-powered light aircraft (NASA) (1980-81) 396
ELECTROSPACE SYSTEMS INC (USA) 384
Elf, E47 (Ward) (1985-86) 571
ELICOTTERI MERIDIONALI SpA (Italy) 155
El Tomcat (Continental) (1980-81) 331, 332
EMAIR (USA) (1981-82) 349
EMBRAER/FAMA (International) 119
EMPRESA BRASILEIRA DE AERONÁUTICA SA (Brazil) 10
EMPRESA NACIONAL DE AERONAUTICA DE CHILE (Chile) 32
Enforcer (Piper) (1985-86) 488
Enhanced Eagle, F-15E (McDonnell Douglas) (1983-84) 432
ENSTROM HELICOPTER CORPORATION, THE (USA) 385
Epsilon (Aérospatiale) 56
Epsilon, TB 30 (SOCATA) (1980-81) 76
Equator (Equator) (1985-86) 87
Equator, P-300/-350/-400/-420/-450/550 (Equator) (1984-85) 85
EQUATOR AIRCRAFT GESELLSCHAFT FÜR FLUGZEUGBAU mbH ULM (West Germany) (1987-88) 96
ESCOLA ENGENHARIA DE SAO CARLOS (Brazil) (1986-87) 17
Esqualo-180 (Moura) (1983-84) 505
Esquilo, CH-50 (Aérospatiale) 60
Esquilo, HB 350B (Helibras) 16
ETHIOPIAN AIRLINES CORPORATION (Ethiopia) 53
EUROCOPTER GIE (International) 120
Eurofighter (Eurofighter) 121
EUROFIGHTER JAGDFLUGZEUG GmbH (International) 121
European Fighter Aircraft (Eurofighter) 121
Evader (Skytrader) 487
EVERETT R. J. ENGINEERING LTD (UK) 297
EVERGREEN AIR CENTER INC (USA) (1987-88) 413
EXCALIBUR AVIATION COMPANY (USA) 386
Excalibur (Excalibur) (1979-80) 334
Excalibur 800 (Excalibur) (1979-80) 334
Executaire (Boeing Vertol) (1979-80) 305
Executive (Mooney) (1978-79) 388
Executive 600 (Colemill) 383
Executive commuter Mark III (JetCraft) 403
Executive Mark I (JetCraft) 403
Expediter (Fairchild Aircraft) 386
EXPERIMENTAL AIRCRAFT ASSOCIATION, INC. (USA) (1984-85) 572
Extender (McDonnell Douglas) 433
Extra 230 (Extra) 89
EXTRA-FLUGZEUGBAU (West Germany) 89

F

F-1 (Mitsubishi) 170
F1 Mirage (Dassault-Breguet) 67
F-2 (China) (1978-79) 27
F.2B Fighter replica (Ohmert) (1980-81) 534
F-3 Cobra (Forbes) (1978-79) 520
F-4 Cobra (China) (1978-79) 27
F-4 Phantom, modernised (Boeing/McDonnell Douglas) (1986-87) 380
F-4 Phantom II (McDonnell) (1981-82) 403
F-4 Phantom II (McDonnell Douglas) 424
F4B-2/P-12C Fighter repica (Aero Tech) (1985-86) 575
F-4CCV (McDonnell) (1979-80) 382
F-4EJKai (Mitsubishi) 170
F4F Ice Programme (MBB) 94
F-4G Advanced Wild Weasel (McDonnell) (1980-81) 380
F-5 (Frebel) (1979-80) 484
F-5 (Northrop) (1978-79) 392
F-5 Waco Classic (Classic) 381
F-5E Tiger II (KA) 174
F-5F Tiger II (KA) 174
F-5E Tiger II (Northrop) (1986-87) 470
F-5F Tiger II (Northrop) (1986-87) 470
F-5G Tigershark (Northrop) (1986-87) 472
F-5T (China) (1983-84) 33
F-6 (Shenyang) (1987-88) 46
F-6bis (China) (1980-81) 34
F-7 (CAC) 35
F-7B (CAC) 35
F-7M (CAC) 35
F-8 (Shenyang) (1987-88) 46
F-811 (SAC) 42
F-8 oblique-wing demonstrator (NASA) 447
F-9 (China) (1980-81) 35
F-14 airflow experiments (NASA) (1986-87) 469
F-14 Tomcat (Grumman) 397
F-14/TARPS (Grumman) (1978-79) 341
F-15 Eagle (McDonnell Douglas) 424
F-15 Advanced Technology Eagle (McDonnell Douglas) (1984-85) 449
F-15, HIDEC (NASA) 447
F-15 Strike Eagle (McDonnell) (1981-82) 404
F-15DJ (Mitsubishi) 170
F-15E Eagle (McDonnell Douglas) 426
F15E Picchio (Procaer) (1982-83) 146
F15F (Procaer/General Avia) (1985-86) 161
F-15J (Mitsubishi) 170
F-15S/MTD (McDonnell Douglas) 427
F-16 Fighting Falcon (General Dynamics) 390
F-16/79 (General Dynamics) (1986-87) 413
F-16/101 (General Dynamics) (1983-84) 385
F-16E (General Dynamics) (1983-84) 386
F-16XL (General Dynamics) (1986-87) 415
F-19 (Lockheed) (1986-87) 435
F-19 Sportsman 100 (Taylorcraft) (1979-80) 451
F.20 Pegaso (General Avia) (1981-82) 136
F-20 Tigershark (Northrop) (1986-87) 472
F.20 TP Condor (General Avia) 161
F-21 (Taylorcraft) (1987-88) 525
F-21A Kfir (IAI) 137
F-21A (Taylorcraft) (1984-85) 510
F-21B (Taylorcraft) 492
F-22 (Taylorcraft) 492
F27 Firefighter (Conair) 29
F.27 Firefighting, Fokker (Conair) (1986-87) 24
F.27 Friendship (Fokker) (1987-88) 185
F27 Maritime (Fokker) (1985-86) 171
F-28 Falcon (Enstrom) 385
F.28 Fellowship (Fokker) (1987-88) 187
F29 (Fokker) (1980-81) 149
F33A/C Bonanza (Beechcraft) 330
F90 King Air (Beechcraft) (1983-84) 307
F90-1, King Air (Beechcraft) (1987-88) 356
F-104CCV (MBB) (1985-86) 92
F-104RB Starfighter (Red Baron/Greenamyer) (1978-79) 535
F-104S (Aeritalia/Lockheed) (1984-85) 134
F-104S ASA (Aeritalia/Lockheed) 144
F-106B storm hazards tests (NASA) (1987-88) 478
F-110 Phantom II (McDonnell) (1979-80) 381
F-111 (General Dynamics) (1982-83) 369
F 150 Aerobat (Reims) (1978-79) 57
F 150 Commuter (Reims) (1978-79) 57
F 152 Aerobat (Reims) (1986-87) 78
F 172 Skyhawk/100 (Reims) (1986-87) 78
F 177RG (Reims) (1978-79) 58
F 182 (Reims) (1981-82) 70
F-337 (Reims) (1980-81) 70
F406 Caravan II (Reims) 79
F.600 (Foxjet) (1980-81) 338
F.600 Canguro (General Avia) (1980-81) 133
F.1300 Squalo (General Avia) (1985-86) 156
F1300 NGT Jet Squalus (General Avia) (1986-87) 158
F1300 NGT Jet Squalus (Promavia) 8
F.3500 Sparverio (General Avia) (1986-87) 160
F/A-18 high-alpha research (NASA) 447
F/A-18A Hornet (McDonnell Douglas) 427
F/A-18L (McDonnell Douglas) (1985-86) 454
FA 152 Aerobat (Reims) (1986-87) 78
FA-200 Aero Subaru (Fuji) (1986-87) 166

FA-300/Model 700 (Fuji) (1980-81) 136
FA-300/Model 710 (Fuji) (1981-82) 142
FAC (see Fuerza Aérea Chilena) (1983-84) 32
FAMA (see Fabrica Argentina de Materials Aeroespaciales) 2
FB-111 (General Dynamics) (1980-81) 345
FBW Jaguar (International) (1982-83) 117
FFA-2000 (FFA) 214
FH-1100A/B (Hiller) (1983-84) 402
FH-1100C (Hiller) (1984-85) 417
FIMA (Future International Military/Civil Airlifter) 122
FJX (Shorts) 308
FLAC (Striplin) (1980-81) 552
FR 172 Hawk XP (Reims) (1982-83) 74
FR 182 RG (Reims) (1981-82) 70
FRA 150 Aerobat (Reims) (1978-79) 57
FRC 225 (Fairchild) (1983-84) 378
FRS. Mk 1/2 (BAe) 291
FRS. Mk 51 (BAe) 291
FSW demonstrator (Grumman) 399
FT-5 (China) (1983-84) 33
FT-6 (State Aircraft Factories) (1984-85) 35
FT-7 (GAIGC) 37
FT 337P (Reims) (1980-81) 70
FTB 337 (Reims/Cessna) (1982-83) 75
FU-24-954 (Aerospace/Fletcher) (1981-82) 155
FU24-954, Fletcher (PAC) 178
FUS (see Flugzeug-Union-Süd GmbH) (1984-85) 86
F + W (see Swiss Federal Aircraft Factory) 217
FABRICA DE AVIONES ANAHUAC SA (Mexico) (1981-82) 150
FABRICA FEDERALE D'AEROPLANI (Switzerland) 217
FÁBRICA ARGENTINA DE MATERIALES AEROESPACIALES (Argentina) 2
FABRIQUE FEDERALE D'AVIONS (Switzerland) 217
FAIRCHILD AIRCRAFT CORPORATION (USA) 386
FAIRCHILD INDUSTRIES INC (USA) (1987-88) 413
FAIRCHILD REPUBLIC COMPANY (USA) (1987-88) 413
FAIRCHILD SWEARINGEN CORPORATION (USA) (1982-83) 364
Fajr (IRGC) 136
Falcon (Enstrom) (1978-79) 325
Falcon (National Dynamics/Reed) (1979-80) 163
Falcon 10 (Dassault) (1979-80) 59
Falcon 20/Mystère (Dassault) (1979-80) 59
Falcon 20 Re-engining Programme (Garrett) 389
Falcon 50 (AOI) 53
Falcon A (Munninghoff) (1985-86) 604
Falcon, F-28F (Enstrom) 385
Falcon ST (Dassault-Breguet) (1982-83) 68
Falcon Cargo Jet (Dassault) (1982-83) 69
Falcon Guardian (Dassault) (1979-80) 59
Fan Commander (American Aviation) (1985-86) 321
Fanliner (RFB/Grumman American) (1978-79) 70
Fanstar (AAI) 319
Fantan (NAMC) 39
Fantrainer 400/600 (RFB) 95
Fantrainer 400/600 (RTAF) 218
Fantrainer 1000 (RFB) 95
Fantrainer AWI-2 (RFB) (1979-80) 79
Farmer-C (Shenyang) (1987-88) 46
Farmer-D (Shenyang) (1987-88) 46
Faucon, PMB-78 (Milon) (1980-81) 481
FAUVEL, CHARLES (France) (1980-81) 475
Fellowship, F28 (Fokker) (1987-88) 187
Fencer (Sukhoi) 259
FFA FLUGZEUGWERKE ALTENRHEIN AG (Switzerland) 213
FIBRA AB (Sweden) (1987-88) 221
Fibra 8 (Fibra) (1986-87) 207
Fiddler (Tupolev) 270
Fieldmaster (NAC) 299
Fighter (AIDC) 218
Fighting Falcon, F-16 (General Dynamics) 390
FIKE, WILLIAM J. (USA) (1980-81) 519
Finback (SAC) 42
Finesse, S-1275 (Schapel) (1983-84) 482
Firebar (Yakovlev) 273
Firecat (Conair) 28
Firecracker (NAC) 298
Firecracker, NDN 1 (NDN) (1983-84) 272
Firefighter (Britten-Norman) (1978-79) 232
Firefighter (Conair) 29
Firefly, EX 101 (Nutting) (1985-86) 605
Firefly 160, T67M (Slingsby) 310
Firefly T67M200 (Slingsby) 310
Fishbed (China) (1981-82) 32
Fishbed (HAL) (1983-84) 96
Fishbed (CAC) 35
Fishbed (MiG) 240
Fishbed (XAC) 35
Fishbed-N (HAL) 108
FISHER, DICK AND VAN NORMAN, CHARLES (USA) (1980-81) 520
FISHER-VAN NORMAN (see Fisher, Dick and Van Norman, Charles) (1980-81) 520
Fishpot (Sukhoi) (1983-84) 230
Fitter-A (Sukhoi) 257
Fitter-C, D, E, F, G, H, J and K (Sukhoi) 258
Fixed-wing aircraft prototype (PADC/NSDB) (1981-82) 157
FLAGLOR AIRCRAFT (USA) (1980-81) 520
FLAGLOR, K (USA) (1985-86) 592
Flaglor Sky Scooter (Headberg) (1985-86) 594
Flagon (Sukhoi) 257
Flamingo-Trainer (FUS) (1984-85) 86
Flanker (Sukhoi) 262
Fletcher Cresco (Aerospace) (1978-79) 136
FLIGHT ENGINEERS LTD (New Zealand) (1980-81) 152
FLIGHT INVERT LTD-CRANFIELD (UK) (1978-79) 235
FLIGHT REFUELLING LTD (UK) (1985-86) 290
Floatmaster (GAF) (1985-86) 7
Flogger (HAL) (1981-82) 90
Flogger-A, B, C, E, F, G, H and K (MiG) 241
Flogger-D/J (MiG) 243
Flogger-J (HAL) 100
FLUG- und FAHRZEUGWERKE AG (Switzerland) (1986-87) 214
FLUGZEUG-UNION-SÜD GmbH (West Germany) (1984-85) 86
FLUGZEUGWERKE ALTENRHEIN AG (Switzerland) (1982-83) 183
Flying Bathtub (MaHugh) (1980-81) 529
Flyray (Flyray) (1980-81) 520
FLYRAY (USA) (1980-81) 520
Fly Rod (Miller) (1982-83) 820
Fokker 50 (Fokker) 174
Fokker 50 Maritime and Surveillance versions (Fokker) 176
Fokker 100 (Fokker) 177
FOKKER, NV KONINKLIJKE NEDERLANDSE VLIEGTUIGFABRIEK (Netherlands) 174
FOKKER-VFW BV (Netherlands) (1979-80) 141
Foo Fighter (Stewart) (1984-85) 602
FORBES, DAVID (USA) (1983-84) 602
FORBES ENTERPRISES (USA) (1978-79) 520
Forger (Yakovlev) 273
Forward Swept Wing Demonstrator (Grumman) 399
Fouga 90 (Aérospatiale) (1980-81) 46
FOURNIER AVIATION (France) (1981-82) 67
Four Runner (Wood) (1982-83) 820
Fourtouna, M.J.14 (Jurca) (1982-83) 503
Foxbat (MiG) 244
Foxhound (MiG) 247
FOXJET INTERNATIONAL INC (USA) (1981-82) 355
Foxstar Baron (Colemill) 383
FRAKES AVIATION INC (USA) 389
FRAKES AVIATION INC. (USA) (1978-79) 329
FREBEL, HERMANN (West Germany) (1979-80) 484
FREDERICK-AMES RESEARCH CORPORATION (USA) (1984-85) 575
Fred Series 2 (Clutton-Tabenor) (1982-83) 518
Free Enterprise (Quickie) (1982-83) 564
Freelance (NAC) 300
Frégate (Aérospatiale) (1978-79) 36
Freshman, D-200 (D'Apuzzo) (1982-83) 537
FR GROUP PLC (UK) (1986-87) 298
Friendship, F27 (Fokker) (1987-88) 185
FRIZZLE, JAMES R. (Canada) (1980-81) 466
Frogfoot (Sukhoi) 260
FRONTIER-AEROSPACE INC (USA) (1982-83) 367
FUERZA AÉREA CHILENA (Chile) (1983-84) 32
FUERZA AÉREA PERUANA (Peru) (1981-82) 801
FUJI HEAVY INDUSTRIES LTD (Japan) 166
Fulcrum (MiG) 245
FUS (see Flugzeug-Union-Süd GmbH) (1984-85) 86

G

G2-A Galeb (Soko) (1982-83) 487
G-4 Super Galeb (Soko) 498
G 11 Moto-Delta (Geiser) (1980-81) 68
G 20 Moto-Delta (Geiser) (1980-81) 69
G-21 Turbo-Goose (McKinnon-Viking) (1980-81) 29
G 110 (Grob) (1984-85) 86
G 111 (Grob) (1983-84) 87
G-111 Albatross (Grumman/Resorts International) (1986-87) 416
G 112 (Grob) (1985-86) 88
G 115 (Grob) 90
G 116 (Grob) 90
G159C Gulfstream I-C (Gulfstream Aerospace) (1983-84) 395
G-164 C-T Turbo Cat (Marsh) 422
G-164F Turbo Ag-Cat D (Gulfstream American) (1980-81) 356
G222 (Aeritalia) 143
G.801 Orion (Grinvalds) (1982-83) 500
G.802 Orion (Grinvalds) (1983-84) 516
G1159C (Grumman Aerospace) 400
GA-7 (Gulfstream American) (1980-81) 355
GAB (see Grupul Aeronautic Bucuresti) (1979-80) 159
GAC 159-C Gulfstream I Commuter (Gulfstream American) (1980-81) 353
GACC (see Gulfstream American Corporation of California) (1981-82) 355
GAC COMMANDER (see Gulfstream Aerospace Corporation, Commander Division) (1983-84) 399
GAF (see Government Aircraft Factories) (1986-87) 6
GAIGC (see Guizhou Aviation Industry Group Company) 37
GAK-22 (Ganzavia) 97
G.B.1 (Boyd) (1982-83) 532
G/B Special (Beets) (1982-83) 543
GB-1 Luftibus (Bezzola) (1978-79) 490
GB-2 Retro (Bezzola) (1983-84) 531
GF 200 (Grob) 91
GJ-1 (Pietsch) (1982-83) 820
GLO1 (Landray) (1982-83) 503
GLO2 Ami Pou (Laundray) (1982-83) 504
GLO3 (Landray) (1982-83) 504
GL-1 (Laudray) (1980-81) 480
GN, Autogyro (AISA) (1983-84) 185
GOHL (see Guangzhou Orlando Helicopters Ltd) 37
GP-180 (Gates/Piaggio) (1985-86) 114
GROB (see Burkhart Grob Flugzeugbau) 90
GTP-350 Gemini (Daedalus) (1987-88) 410
GV-1 Hercules (Lockheed) (1981-82) 395
GY-201 Minicab (Ord-Hume) (1979-80) 497
Gabier (SOCATA) (1985-86) 81
GafHawk 125 (Hawk) 402
Gaillard (SOCATA) (1981-82) 73
Gajaraj (Ilyushin) 232
Galaxy, C-5 (Lockheed) 418
Galeb G2-A (Soko) (1982-83) 487
Galérien (SOCATA) (1983-84) 78
Galopin (SOCATA) (1983-84) 78
Ganagobie 05 (ARDC of NZ) (1981-82) 498
GANZAVIA (Hungary) 97
Gardian (Dassault-Breguet) (1986-87) 71
Gardian 2 (Dassault-Breguet) 74
Gardian 50 (Dassault-Breguet) 76
Garnement (SOCATA) (1981-82) 73
GARRETT GENERAL AVIATION SERVICES COMPANY (USA) 389
Gasior (WSK-PZL Warszawa-Okecie) 193
GATES LEARJET CORPORATION (USA) (1987-88) 418
GATES/PIAGGIO (International) (1985-86) 114
Gaucho (SOCATA) (1981-82) 74, 75
Gavião, (Helibras) 15
Gavilan (Aero Mercantil) 46
Gazelle (Aérospatiale) 59
G/B AIRCRAFT (USA) (1983-84) 560
Gee Bee Model Z Super Sportster (Turner) (1982-83) 579
Gee Bee Y Replica (Flaglor) (1985-86) 592
GEIDE, RICHARD F (USA) (1982-83) 543
GEISER, JEAN MARC (France) (1980-81) 68
Gem-260 (Miller) (1985-86) 601
Gemini GTP-350 (Daedalus) (1987-88) 410
GENERAL AVIA COSTRUZIONI AERONAUTICHE SRL (Italy) 161
GENERAL AVIATION DIVISION, ROCKWELL CORPORATION (USA) (1980-81) 431
General Aviation stall/spin flight research (NASA) (1987-88) 478
GENERAL DYNAMICS CORPORATION (USA) 390
GENERAL DYNAMICS/MCDONNELL DOUGLAS (USA) 393
General purpose airborne simulator (NASA) (1979-80) 397
Gepal Mk IV 550 (AMIN) (1983-84) 161
Geronimo (Seguin) 473
Ghinassi helicopter (AVEX) (1979-80) 465
Golden Eagle (Cessna) 376
Golden Hawk (DSK Airmotive) (1980-81) 515
GOODE, RICHARD (UK) (1983-84) 534
Goshawk (BAe) 287
Goshawk T-45A (McDonnell Douglas/BAe) 126
Gossamer Albatross (MacCready) (1981-82) 398
Gossamer Albatross (NASA/MacCready) (1981-82) 419
Gossamer Condor (MacCready) (1979-80) 528
GOVERNMENT AIRCRAFT FACTORIES (Australia) (1986-87) 6
GRADY, MELVIN (USA) (1981-82) 526
Gran Turismo Commander (Rockwell International) (1981-82) 431
GREAT LAKES AIRCRAFT COMPANY INC (USA) 393
GREENAPPLES AIRCRAFT (USA) (1982-83) 544
Greyhound, C-2A (Grumman) 394
Griffon (Agusta-Bell) 152
Grillon 120 (Sellet/Pelletier) 84
GRINVALDS, JEAN (France) (1983-84) 516
Gripen (Saab-Scania) 210
Grizzly, Model 72 (Rutan) (1985-86) 503
GRUMMAN AEROSPACE CORPORATION (USA) (1985-86) 413
GRUMMAN CORPORATION (USA) 393
Grumman/Rand Monoplane (Grady) (1981-82) 526
GRUPUL AERONAUTIC BUCURESTI (Romania) (1979-80) 159
GUANGZHOU ORLANDO HELICOPTERS LTD (China) 37
Guardian (Dassault-Breguet) (1978-79) 52
Guardian A-750 (Airmaster) (1986-87) 331
Guardian A-1200 (Airmaster) 322
Guardian, HU-25A (Dassault-Breguet) (1985-86) 69
Guerrier (SOCATA) (1987-88) 84
GUEX, JEAN-CLAUDE (Switzerland) (1979-80) 492
GUIZHOU AVIATION INDUSTRY GROUP COMPANY (China) 37
GULFSTREAM AMERICAN CORPORATION (USA) (1982-83) 381
GULFSTREAM AEROSPACE CORPORATION (USA) 400
GULFSTREAM AMERICAN CORPORATION, COMMANDER DIVISION (USA) (1982-83) 384
GULFSTREAM AEROSPACE CORPORATION, COMMANDER DIVISION (USA) (1983-84) 399
GULFSTREAM AEROSPACE TECHNOLOGIES (USA) 401
GULFSTREAM AMERICAN CORPORATION OF CALIFORNIA (USA) (1981-82) 355
Gulfstream I-C, G159C (Gulfstream Aerospace) (1983-84) 395
Gulfstream II-B (Gulfstream Aerospace) (1986-87) 424
Gulfstream III (Gulfstream Aerospace) (1987-88) 432
Gulfstream III C-SAM (Gulfstream Aerospace) (1984-85) 412
Gulfstream III Maritime (Gulfstream Aerospace) (1984-85) 412
Gulfstream III Special Mission Versions (Gulfstream Aerospace) (1987-88) 432
Gulfstream IV (Gulfstream Aerospace) 400
Gulfstream IV-B (Gulfstream Aerospace) (1986-87) 426
Gulfstream SRA-1 (Gulfstream Aerospace) (1984-85) 412
Gull (EGHS) (1985-86) 590
Gyracar (Barrett) (1982-83) 528
GYROFLUG INGENIEURSGESELLSCHAFT mbH (West Germany) 91

H

H-1 (Hamilton) 401
H-2 (Hynes) (1987-88) 436
H-5 (Hynes) (1987-88) 436
H-5 (HAMC) 39
H-5 (Harbin) (1986-87) 34
H-6 (XAC) 44
H-40 (Hoffmann) 92
H-53E (Sikorsky) 478

H-76 (Sikorsky) ... 485
H-76N (Sikorsky) ... 486
HA-2M Sportster (Hollmann) ... (1985-86) 595
HA-31 Mk II Basant (HAL) ... (1982-83) 95
HAC (Eurocopter) ... 120
HAFFS (See Heliborne Aerial FireFighting System) .. 321
HAI (see Hellenic Aerospace Industry) ... 97
HAL (see Hindustan Aeronautics Limited) ... 97
HAMC (see Harbin Aircraft Manufacturing Corporation) ... 37
HAP/PAH-2/HAC-3G (Eurocopter) ... (1986-87) 116
HAP (Eurocopter) ... 120
HB 315B Gaviao (Helibras) ... 15
HB 350 Esquilo (Helibras) ... 15
HB 355F2 Esquilo (Helibras) ... 15
HC-130 (Lockheed) ... 415
HDH (see Hawker de Havilland Ltd) ... 5
HEFFS (see Helicopter Emergency Fire Fighting System) ... (1987-88) 342
HELIBRAS (see Helicopteros do Brasil SA) ... 15
HF-24 Marut (HAL) ... (1979-80) 81
HFB 320 Hansa Jet (MBB) ... (1980-81) 83
HH-1 Hawker Hurricane (Sindlinger) ... (1981-82) 549
HH-1 Zipper (Hammer-Hunt ... (1980-81) 358
HH-1H Iroquois (Bell) ... 341
HH-2 Seasprite (Kaman) ... 404
HH-3 (Sikorsky) ... (1983-84) 485
HH-3A (Sikorsky) ... (1983-84) 485
HH-3F (Agusta/Sikorsky) ... 154
HH-53 (Sikorsky) ... (1981-82) 460
HH-60 Night Hawk (Sikorsky) ... (1987-88) 513
HH-60D Night Hawk (Sikorsky) ... (1983-84) 488
HH-60H (Sikorsky) ... 481
HH-60J (Mitsubishi) ... 171
HH-60J (Sikorsky) ... 481
HH-65A Dolphin (Aérospatiale) ... 63
HHC helicopter (McDonnell Douglas) ... (1985-86) 463
HIDEC F-15 (NASA) ... 447
HJ-5 (Harbin) ... (1986-87) 34
HJT-16 Mk I Kiran (HAL) ... (1983-84) 93
HJT-16 Kiran Mk II (HAL) ... 98
HKP 10 (Aerospatiale) ... 57
HKP-4C (Kawasaki-Boeing) ... (1984-85) 159
HMP(see Huabei Machinery Plant) ... 39
HN 500 Bengali (Nicollier) ... (1983-84) 521
HOTOL (BAe) ... 293
HPA (see Hertfordshire Pedal Aeronauts) .. (1979-80) 494
HPA 1 (Kiceniuk) ... (1978-79) 524
HPT-32 (HAL) ... 100
HR 100/4 + 2 (Robin) ... (1979-80) 68
HR 100/250TR President (Robin) ... (1980-81) 72
HR 100/285 Tiara (Robin) ... (1978-79) 60
HS 9 Biplane (Schoenenberg) ... (1983-84) 526
HS 125 Series 700 (BAe) ... (1983-84) 251
HS 146 (BAe) ... (1978-79) 219
HS 747 (BAe) ... (1978-79) 217
HS 748 (HAL BAe) ... (1984-85) 94
HS 748 (BAe 748) Coastguarder (BAe) ... (1984-85) 261
HS 748 Military Transport (BAe) ... (1983-84) 254
HS 748 Series 2B (BAe) ... (1983-84) 253
HS 748 (BAe 748) Super (BAe) ... (1986-87) 282
HSS-2 Sea King (Sikorsky) ... (1982-83) 470
HSX-3 (Schilling) ... (1979-80) 485
HT.17 (Boeing) ... 364
HTH (see Helitrans Hybrid-Flugzeugbau GmbH) ... (1985-86) 89
HT-L (HAL) ... (1982-83) 94
HTT-34 (HAL) ... (1986-87) 99
HTTB (Lockheed) ... 418
HU-1H (Fuji-Bell) ... 166
HU2K-1 Seasprite (Kaman) ... (1981-82) 386
HU-16B Albatross Tanker conversion (Aero Union).. 321
HU-25A Guardian (Dassault-Breguet) ... (1985-86) 69
HVS (see Hutter/Villinger/Schule) ... (1984-85) 544
HVS (HVS) ... (1984-85) 544
HW 03 (Hellbach) ... (1979-80) 485
HZ-5 (Harbin) ... (1986-87) 34
Haitun (HAMC) ... 39
Haiyan (NAMC) ... 41
Halcón, T-36 (CASA) ... 207
Halcón, T-36 (ENAER) ... 33
HALLOCK, BRUCE (USA) ... (1982-83) 544
Halo (MIL) ... 254
HAMAO, Y (Japan) ... (1978-79) 485
Hamao Shiokaratombo (JAA) ... (1980-81) 488
HAMILTON AEROSPACE (USA) ... 401
HAMILTON AVIATION (USA) ... (1982-83) 386
HAMMER, ROBERT AND HUNT, RICHARD (USA) ... (1980-81) 358
HAMMER-HUNT (see Hammer, Robert and Hunt, Richard) ... (1980-81) 358
HAN JIN GROUP, THE (South Korea) .... (1978-79) 128
Hansa Jet, HFB 320 (MBB) ... (1980-81) 83
Harbin Y-11T (China) ... (1982-83) 40
Harbin (Aérospatiale) SA 365N Dauphin 2 (China) ... (1982-83) 37
HARBIN AIRCRAFT MANUFACTURING CORPORATION (China) ... 37
Harbin/Nanchang (Mil) Mi-8 (State Aircraft Factories) ... (1984-85) 38
Harke (MIL) ... 250
Harrier (BAe) ... 290
Harrier II, AV-8B (McDonnell Douglas/BAe) ... 124
Harrier II Plus (McDonnell Douglas/BAe) ... 126
Harrier III (McDonnell Douglas/BAe) ... (1987-88) 132
Harrier GR Mk 3 (BAe) ... 290
Harrier GR Mk 5 (McDonnell Douglas/BAe) ... 124
Harrier GR Mk 7 (McDonnell Douglas/BAe) ... 125
Harrier T Mk 4/4A (BAe) ... 290
Hauler (Rogerson Hiller) ... 467
Havoc (MIL) ... 255
Hawk (Enstrom) ... (1982-83) 361
Hawk 200 Series (BAe) ... 289
Hawk, DSK-1 (DSK Airmotive) ... (1980-81) 515
Hawk T. Mk 1 (BAe) ... 287
Hawk, two-seat versions (BAe) ... 287
Hawk VTXTS (McDonnell Douglas/BAe).. (1984-85) 450
Hawk, US Navy (McDonnell Douglas/BAe) (1984-85) 116
Hawk XP (Cessna) ... (1982-83) 338
Hawk XP/II (Cessna981-88326
Hawk XP, FR 172K (Reims) ... (1982-83) 74
HAWK INTERNATIONAL (USA) ... 401
Hawker 731 (Airesearch) ... (1986-87) 330
HAWKER DE HAVILLAND LTD (Australia) ... 5
HAWKER DE HAVILLAND VICTORIA LTD (Australia) ... 5
Hawker Hurricane, HH-1 (Sindlinger) ... (1981-82) 549
HAWKER SIDDELEY CANADA INC (Canada) ... (1982-83) 30
Hawkeye (Grumman) ... 393
HAYES INTERNATIONAL CORPORATION (USA) ... 402
Haze (MIL) ... 251
Headwind (Stewart) ... (1984-85) 602
Heintz Zenith-CH 200 (Zenair) ... (1980-81) 468
Heintz Zenith-CH 400 (Zenair) ... (1985-86) 30
Heliborne Aerial Fire Fighting System (Aero Union) . 321
Heli-Camper (Orlando) ... 449
HELICOP-JET (France) ... (1982-83) 71
HELICOP-JET PROJECT MANAGEMENT (Canada) ... 30
Helicop-Jet (Helicop-Jet. Canada) ... 30
HELICOP-JET PROJECT MANAGEMENT (France) ... (1986-87) 75
Helicopter Emergency Fire Fighting System (Aero Union) ... (1987-88) 342
HELICOPTEROS DO BRASIL S/A (Brazil) ... 15
HELI-EUROPE INDUSTRIES LTD (International) ... (1978-79) 84
HELIGYRO CORPORATION (USA) ... (1978-79) 522
HELIO AIRCRAFT LTD (USA) ... (1987-88) 435
HELIO COURIER LTD (USA) ... (1979-80) 358
Heli-Stat (Piasecki) See Lighter Than Air Section
Helitankers (Conair) ... 29
HELITEC CORPORATION (USA) ... (1979-80) 358
HELITRANS HYBRID-FLUGZEUGBAU GmbH (West Germany) ... (1985-86) 89
Helitruck (HTH) ... (1985-86) 89
Helix-A, B and D (Kamov) ... 238
Helix-C (Kamov) ... 239
HELLBACH, WALTER (West Germany) . (1979-80) 485
HELLENIC AEROSPACE INDUSTRY (Greece) ... 97
HELWAN (Egypt) ... (1983-84) 48
Hercules (Lockheed) ... 415
Hercules, commercial (Lockheed) ... 417
Hercules C Mk1, W Mk2 and C Mk3 (Lockheed) ... 415
Hercules C.Mk IK Tanker (Marshall) ... 297
Hercules C.Mk IP/3P ... 297
Hercules conversions (IAI) ... 142
Hercules conversions (Marshall) ... (1987-88) 315
Hercules Regional Airfreighter (Lockheed) . (1980-81) 377
Hermes Aerospacecraft (Aérospatiale) ... 65, 77
Hermit (MIL) ... 256
HERTFORDSHIRE PEDAL AERONAUTS (UK) ... (1979-80) 494
HIBBARD AVIATION (USA) ... (1984-85) 417
High-alpha research F/A-18 (NASA) ... 447
HILL, KLAUS (USA) ... (1979-80) 523
HILLER AVIATION INC (USA) ... (1983-84) 402
HILLER HELICOPTERS (USA) ... (1985-86) 425
HILLMAN HELICOPTER ASSOCIATES (USA) ... (1984-85) 419
Hind (MIL) ... 252, 254
Hind look-alike (Orlando) ... 449
HINDUSTAN AERONAUTICS LIMITED (iNDIA) ... 97
Hip (State Aircraft Factories) ... (1983-84) 38
Hip (MIL) ... 248
Hip-H (MIL) ... 251
HOFFMANN, WOLF, FLUGZEUGBAU KG (West Germany) ... 92
Hokum (Kamov) ... 240
Holiday Knight Twister SKT-1250 (Payne). (1985-86) 608
HOLLMANN (See Winther-Hollmann Aircraft Inc) ... (1982-83) 546
HOLLMANN TECHNOLOGIES INC (USA) ... (1985-86) 595
Homer (Mil ... (1978-79) 190
Honeybee (Sinfield) ... (1979-80) 542
Hong-5 (Harbin) ... (1986-87) 34
Hong-6 (XAC) ... 44
Hongzhaji-5 (Harbin) ... (1986-87) 34
Hongzhaji Jiaolianji-5 (Harbin) ... (1986-87) 34
Hongzhaji-6(XAC) ... 44
Hongzhaji Zhenchaji-5 (Harbin) ... (1986-87) 34
Hongzhen-5 (Harbin) ... (1986-87) 34
Hoodlum-A (Kamov) ... 237
Hoodlum-B (Kamov) ... 240
Hook (MIL) ... 248
Hoplite (WSK-PZL Swidnik) ... 187, 248
Hormone (Kamov) ... 237
Hornet, F/A-18A (McDonnell-Douglas) ... 427
Hornet, M79 (Aerodyne) ... (1987-88) 341
Hornet RH-1199M (Hiller) ... 467
Hornisse (Wallerkowski) ... (1981-82) 495
Hound (State Aircraft Factories, China) ... (1985-86) 38
Hound (Mil) ... (1982-83) 213
Hover-Gyro, B-18 (Bensen) ... (1984-85) 561
HUABEI MACHINERY PLANT (China) ... 39
HueyCobra (Bell) ... 343
HueyCobra, Modernised Version (Bell) ... 344
HUGHES (see McDonnell-Douglas) ... 424
Humbug (Sky Sports) ... (1980-81) 441
Humlan 2 (Elkström) ... (1983-84) 530
Hummer (Hummer) ... (1980-81) 524
HUMMER (USA) ... (1980-81) 524
Hummingbird (Jonas) ... (1980-81) 526
Hunter Mk 8M (BAe) ... (1979-80) 237
HUNTING FIRECRACKER AIRCRAFT LTD (UK) ... (1985-86) 290
Husky (Christen) ... 380
Hustler Model 400 (AJI) ... (1978-79) 252
Hustler 500 (GACC) ... (1981-82) 355
HUTTER/VILLINGER/SCHULE (West Germany) ... (1984-85) 544
HYNES HELICOPTER INC (USA) ... 402

I

I-22 (IL) ... 181
I-122 (AISA) ... (1981-82) 173
I-124 (AISA) ... (1981-82) 173
IA 58 Pucará (FAMA) ... 2
IA 58C Pucará Charlie (FAMA) ... 3
IA 63 Pampa (FAMA) ... 3
IA 66 (FAMA) ... 2
IA 80 Piranha (Issoire) ... (1980-81) 67
IAC (see International Aeromarine Corporation) ... 402
IAC (see International Aircraft Company) ... 218
IAC (see International Aircraft Corporation) ... (1987-88) 437
IAE (see Instituto de Atividades Espaciais).. (1982-83) 11
IAI (see Israel Aircraft Industries) ... 136
IAI-101 Arava (IAI) ... (1984-85) 130
IAI-101B (IAI) ... (1986-87) 135
IAI-102 Arava (IAI) ... (1986-87) 135
IAI-201 Arava (IAI) ... (1986-87) 135
IAI-202 Arava (IAI) ... (1986-87) 135
IAI 1123 Westwind (IAI) ... (1978-79) 103
IAI 1124 Westwind (IAI) ... (1986-87) 136
IAI 1124 Westwind I (IAI) ... (1986-87) 136
IAI 1124A Westwind 2 (IAI) ... 140
IAI 1124N Sea Scan (IAI) ... (1986-87) 136
IAI 1125 Astra (IAI) ... 140
IAR-28MA (ICA) ... 199
IAR-93/Orao (SOKO/CNIAR) ... 134
IAR-99 Soim (IAv Craiova) ... 199
IAR-316B Alouette III (ICA) ... 201
IAR-317 Airfox (ICA) ... 201
IAR-330L Puma (ICA) ... 202
IAR-822 (ICA-Brasov) ... (1979-80) 160
IAR-822B (ICA-Brasov) ... (1979-80) 160
IAR-823 (ICA) ... 199
IAR-824 (ICA) ... (1980-81) 164
IAR-825TP Triumf (ICA) ... 200
IAR-826 (ICA-Brasov) ... (1979-80) 160
IAR-827A (ICA) ... 200
IAR-827TP (ICA) ... (1983-84) 183
IAR-828TP (ICA) ... 200
OAR-831 Pelican (ICA) ... 201
IAv BACAU (see Intreprinderea de Avionane Bacau) 197
IAv BUCURESTI (see Intreprinderea de Avioane Bucuresti) ... 197
IAv CRAIOVA (see Intreprinderea de Avioane Craiova) ... 199
ICA (see Intreprindera de Constructii Aeronautice) ... 199
ICE Programme (MBB) ... 94
IEP (see Instituto de Ensaios e Padroes) ... (1978-79) 10
IFI (see Instituto de Fomento e Coordenacão Industrial) ... (1982-83) 11
IHI (see Iranian Helicopter Industry) ... (1980-81) 101
IL (see Instytut Lotnictwa) ... 181
Il-18 (Ilyushin) ... (1983-84) 205
IL-18 DORR (Ilyushin) ... 229
Il-20 (Ilyushin) ... 229
Il-22 (Ilyushin) ... 230
Il-28 (China) ... (1982-83) 36
Il-38 (Ilyushin) ... 230
Il-62 (Ilyushin) ... 231
Il-62M (Ilyushin) ... 232
Il-62MK (Ilyushin) ... 232
Il-76 (Ilyushin) ... 232
Il-76 AEW&C (Ilyushin) ... 234
Il-76 Refuelling tanker (Ilyushin) ... 234
Il-86 (Ilyushin) ... 234
Il-96 Twin-engined version (Ilyushin) ... 236
Il-96-300 (Ilyushin) ... 235
Il-114 (Ilyushin) ... 236
IPAI-26 Tuca (São Carlos) ... (1984-85) 19
IPAI-27 Jipe Voador (São Carlos) ... (1983-84) 19
IPAI-28 Super Surubim (Rio Claro) ... (1984-85) 18
IPAI-29 Tira Prosa (São Carlos) ... (1983-84) 19
IPAI-30 (São Carlos) ... (1984-85) 19
IPD (see Instituto de Pesquisas e Desenvolvimento) ... (1982-83) 11
IPE (see Industria Paranaensede Estruturas) ... 16
IPE 04 (IPE) ... 16
IPT-16 Surubim Modificado (Rio Claro/IPT) ... (1979-80) 17
IPTN (see Indusri Pesawatterbang Nusantara) ... 101
IRGC (see Islamic Revolutionary Guards Corps) ... 136
ITA (see Instituto Technológico de Aeronáutica) ... (1982-83) 11
Ibis, A, NM-77 (Nihon) ... (1979-80) 486
ICX AVIATION INC (USA) ... (1980-81) 364
ILYUSHIN (USSR) ... 229
IML GROUP (New Zealand) ... (1984-85) 171
Impala Mk 2 (Atlas) ... (1986-87) 203
Imperial Knight Twister M6 (Payne) ... (1982-83) 559
Improved Fouga (IAI) ... (1985-86) 130
Improved SeaCobra (Bell) ... (1985-86) 341
INDAER CHILE (see Industria Aeronautica de Chile) ... (1983-84) 32
INDAER-PERU (Peru) ... (1985-86) 177
INDUSTRIA AERONAUTICA DE CHILE (Chile) ... (1983-84) 32
INDUSTRIA AERONÁUTICA NEIVA S/A (Brazil) ... 16
INDUSTRIA PARANAENSE DE ESTRUTURAS (Brazil) ... 16
INDUSTRIE AERONAUTICHE E MECCANICHE RINALDO PIAGGIO (Italy) ... 163
INDUSTRI PESAWATTERBANG NUSANTARA (Indonesia) ... 101

INGENIEURBURO PROF. DIPLING C DORNIER JR (West Germany) (1983-84) 87
INSTITUTO DE ATIVIDADES ESPACIAIS (Brazil) (1982-83) 11
INSTITUTO DE ENSAIOS E PADROES (Brazil) (1978-79) 10
INSTITUTO DE FOMENTO E COORDENACÁO INDUSTRIAL (Brazil) (1982-83) 11
INSTITUTO DE PESQUISAS E DESENVOLVIMENTO (Brazil) (1982-83) 11
INSTITUTO TECHNOLÓGICO DE AERONÁUTICA (Brazil) (1982-83) 11
INSTYTUT LOTNICTWA (Poland) 181
Interceptor 400A (Prop-Jets) (1985-86) 490
INTERCEPTOR COMPANY (USA) (1979-80) 363
Intercity 748 (BAe) (1983-84) 253
INTERNATIONAL AEROMARINE CORPORATION (USA) 402
INTERNATIONAL AIRCRAFT COMPANY (Thailand) 218
INTERNATIONAL AIRCRAFT CORPORATION (USA) (1987-88) 437
INTERNATIONAL HELICOPTERS INC (USA) (1983-84) 562
Interstate S1B2 (Arctic) 325
INTRAN USA INC (USA) (1984-85) 425
INTREPRINDEREA DE AVIOANE BACAU (Romania) 197
INTREPRINDEREA DE AVIOANE BUCURESTI (Romania) 197
INTREPRINDEREA DE AVIOANE CRAIOVA (Romania) 199
INTREPRINDEREA DE CONSTRUCTII AERONAUTICE (Romania) 199
Intruder (Grumman) 395
Intruder II (Grumman) 396
Ipanema (EMBRAER) 14
IRANIAN HELICOPTER INDUSTRY (Iran) (1979-80) 101
Iroquois (Bell) 341
Iryd (IL) 181
Isfahan, Model 214A (Bell) (1978-79) 277
ISHAM AIRCRAFT (USA) (1984-85) 426
Iskierka, M-26 (WSK-PZL Mielec) 186
Iskra-bis, TS-11 (WSK-PZL Mielec) 184
ISLAMIC REVOLUTIONARY GUARDS CORPS (Iran) 136
ISLAND AIRCRAFT LTD (UK) 279
Islander (IAv Bucuresti) 199
Islander (PADC/Pilatus Britten-Norman) 180
Islander BN-2B (Pilatus Britten-Norman) 301
ISRAEL AIRCRAFT INDUSTRIES LTD (Israel) 136
ISSOIRE-AVIATION, SOCIÉTÉ (France) (1980-81) 67

J

J-? (SAC) 42
J-1/RJ-1 Jastreb (SOKO) (1980-81) 455
J-1 Martin Fierro (RRA) (1981-82) 4
J-1B Don Kichot (Janowski) (1979-80) 488
J-2 Polonez (Janowski) (1979-80) 589
J-5, Janowski (Marko-Elektronik) (1984-85) 547
J-6 (Shenyang) (1987-88) 46
J-7 (CAC) 35
J-7 III (SAC) 42
J-8 (Shenyang) (1987-88) 46
J-8 II (SAC) 42
J-9 (CATIC) 34
J-10 (Jackson) (1984-85) 579
J-22 (SOKO/CNIAR) 134
J32E Lansen (Saab-Scania) (1987-88) 225
J35J (Draken (Saab-Scania) 212
JA 37 Viggen (Sab-Scania) 211
JAS 39 Gripen (Saab-Scania) 210
JC-1 Jet Cat (Continental Copters) (1980-81) 331
JC-2D Tri-Coupé (Coupé-Aviation) (1983-84) 514
JC-24 Weedhopper (Weedhopper) (1980-81) 558
JC-130 (Lockheed) 415
JD_1HW 1.7 Headwind (Stewart) (1984-85) 602
JD_2FF Foo Fighter (Stewart) (1984-85) 602
JEH (see Joint European Helicopter Srl) 123
JET (see Joint European Transort) (1979-80) 93
JJ-5 (China) (1983-84) 33
JJ-6 (State Aircraft Factories) (1984-85) 35
JJ-7 (GAIGC) 37
JP001 Wild Turkey (American Air Racing) (1978-79) 504
JS-1 (Anger/Selcher) (1985-86) 616
J-STARS (Boeing) 370
Ju 87B-2 Replica (Langhurst) (1981-82) 533
JVX (Bell/Boeing Vertol) (1987-88) 398
JW-1 Jetwing (Ball-Bartoe) (1978-79) 254
JW-1 (ACA) 320
JW-2 (ACA) 320
JW-3 (ACA) 320
JZ-6 (Shenyang) (1986-87) 39
JACKSON, L. A. (USA) (1984-85) 579
JACOBS JETS INC (USA) (1983-84) 410
Jaguar Development (SEPECAT) (1982-83) 117
Jaguar International (HAL/SEPECAT) 97
Jaguar International (SEPECAT) 133
JAMES-DENNIS ENTERPRISES INC (USA) (1980-81) 524
Janowski J-5 (Marko-Electronik) (1984-85) 547
JANOWSKI, JAROSLAW (Poland) (1979-80) 488
JAPAN AMATEUR BUILT AIRCRAFT LEAGUE (Japan) (1984-85) 547
JARZAB, KAZIMIERZ (Poland) (1981-82) 498
JAS (JAS) (1981-82) 176
JAS, INDUSTRI GRUPPEN (Sweden) (1981-82) 176
Jastreb (Soko) (1980-81) 455
Jastreb Trainer 9Soko) (1980-81) 455
JAVELIN AIRCRAFT COMPANY INC (USA) (1987-88) 437
Javelin, Cessna P210 (Air America) (1986-87) 330
JEAN ST-GERMAIN INC, CENTRE DE RECHERCHES (Canada) (1981-82) 474
JEFFAIR CORPORATION (USA) (1982-83) 548
Jet Craft JC-1 (Continental Copters) (1980-82) 331
JETCRAFT (USA) 403
JETCRAFTERS INCORPORATED (USA) (1982-83) 397
Jet Cruiser, Mark II (Jetcraft) 403
Jet Prop 340 (Riley) (1979-80) 423
Jet Prop 421 (Riley) (1978-79) 415
Jet Provost (B.A.C.) (1978-79) 177
JetRanger II (Agusta-Bell) (1978-79) 104
JetRanger III (Agusta-Bell) 151
JetRanger III (Bell Helicopter Textron) 18, 342
Jet Squalus (General Avia) (1986-87) 158
Jet Squalus, F1300 NGT (Promavia) 8
JetStar II (Lockheed) (1980-81) 377
JetStar laminar flow control (NASA) (1986-87) 469
Jetstream III (Volpar/Century) (1980-81) 451
Jetstream 31 (BAe) 280
Jetstream Series 200 (BAe) (1979-80) 225
Jetstream Super 31 (BAe) 282
Jetstream 41 (BAe) 282
Jetstream T.Mk 3 (BAe) 280
Jet Wasp II (Texas Helicopter) (1983-84) 496
Jetwing, JW-1 (Ball-Bartoe) (1978-79) 254
Jian-6 (Shenyang) (1987-88) 46
Jian-7 (CAC) 35
Jian-8 (Shenyang) (1987-88) 46
Jian-8 II (SAC) 42
Jianjiao-5 (China) (1983-84) 33
Jianjiao-6 (China) (1984-85) 35
Jianjiao-7 (GAIGC) 37
Jianjiji-6 (Shenyang) (1987-88) 46
Jianjiji-7 (CAC) 35
Jianjiji-8 (Shenyang) (1987-88) 46
Jianjiji-8 II (SAC) 42
Jianjiji Jiaolianji-6 (China) (1984-85) 35
Jianjiji Jiaolianji-7 (GAIGC) 37
Jipe Voador, IPAI-27 (São Carlos) (1983-84) 19
JOINT EUROPEAN HELICOPTER Srl (International) 123
JOINT EUROPEAN TRANSPORT (International) (1979-80) 93
Jolly Green Giant (Sikorsky) (1983-84) 485
JONAS, GERALD (USA) (1980-81) 526
JONES, DANIEL G. (Canada) (1981-82) 475
JONES, STANLEY (USA) (1983-84) 563
JOSES, CHARLES RUPERT (Brazil) (1983-84) 505
Junior Ace Model E (Ace Aircraft) (1982-83) 523

K

K-1 Flamingo-Trainer (FUS) (1983-84) 86
K-1 Super Fli (Kraft) (1982-83) 550
KA (see Korean Air) 173
KA-6 (Grumman) (1987-88) 427
KA-6D (Grumman) 395
KA-7 Corsair II (Vought) (1981-82) 469
Ka-25 (Kamov) 237
Ka-25K (Kamov) (1981-82) 199
Ka-26 (Kamov) 237
Ka-27 (Kamov) 238
Ka-28 (Kamov) 239
Ka-32 (Kamov) 239
Ka-126 (ICA) 202
Ka-126 (Kamov) 240
Ka-?, Hokum (Kamov) 240
KA-840 (Kawasaki) (1980-81) 138
KA-850 (Kawasaki) (1981-82) 144
KBHC (see Korea Bell Helicopter Company) 174
KC-3 Skylark (Larkin) (1980-81) 528
KC-10A (McDonnell Douglas) 433
KC-130 (Lockheed) 415
KC-135 winglet tests (NASA/USAF) (1982-83) 428
KC-135A Stratotanker (Boeing) 369
KE-3A (Boeing) 370
KM-2 (Fuji) (1982-83) 148
KM-2B (Fuji) (1982-83) 148
KM-2D (Fuji) 166
KM-180 (SACAB) (1987-88) 226
KM C-180 (SACAB) (1987-88) 226
KF-02 (WSK-PZL Krosno) 182
KR-3 (Rand Robinson) (1979-80) 534
KS-3A Viking (Lockheed) (1986-87) 439
KT-75 Knight Twister Junior (Payne) (1980-81) 536
KV-107II (Kawasaki/Boeing) (1984-85) 159
KV-107IIA (Kawasaki) 168
Kachina, Model 2150A-TG (Hibbard/Varga) (1983-84) 402
Kachina, Model 2150A (Varga) (1983-84) 497
Kachina, Model 2180 (Varga) (1983-84) 498
KAKO, TERUO (Japan) (1979-80) 486
KAMAN AEROSPACE CORPORATION (USA) 403
KAMOV (USSR) 237
Kania (WSK-PZL-Swidnik) 188
Kania Model (WSK-PZL-Swidnik) 188
Karakorum 8 (NAMC) 41
KARP, LARRY (USA) (1983-84) 564
KAWASAKI JUKOGYO KABUSHIKI KAISHA (Japan) 167
Kawka, PZL-107 (WSK-PZL Warszawa-Okecie) (1983-84) 171
KELEHER, JAMES J. (USA) (1984-85) 580
KENDALL, DR RIDLEY (UK) (1982-83) 520
Kfir (IAI) 137
KICENIUK JR, TARAS (USA) (1978-79) 524
Kiddy Hawk (Calypso) (1985-86) 373
King Air A100 (Beechcraft) (1982-83) 299
King Air B100 (Beechcraft) (1983-84) 308
King Air C90A (Beechcraft) 332
King Air C100 (Beechcraft) (1978-79) 269
King Air conversion (Frakes) 389
King Air E90 (Beechcraft) (1982-83) 297
King Air Exec-Liner (Beechcraft) (1987-88) 360
King Air F90 (Beechcraft) (1983-84) 307
King Air F90-1 (Beechcraft) (1987-88) 356
Kingbird, F27 (Fokker) (1985-86) 171
King Cat (Mid-Continent) 442
KING'S ENGINEERING FELLOWSHIP, THE (USA) 405
KINMAN, DUANE (USA) (1982-83) 550
Kiowa (Bell) (1987-88) 365
Kiran Mk I/IA (HAL) (1983-84) 93
Kiran Mk II (HAL) 98
Kitty Hawk (WSK-PZL Swidnik) 189
Kittiwake I (Mitchell-Procter) (1978-79) 498
Klos (Jarzab) (1981-82) 498
K-Meyer Aero Model A (Meyer) (1981-82) 535
Knight Twister Junior KT-85 (Payne) (1980-81) 536
Knight Twister KT-85 (Payne) (1980-81) 536
KNOWLES, GP CAPT A.S. (UK) (1980-81) 495
KOENIG, M (France) (1980-81) 479
Koliber (WSK PZL Warszawa Okecie) 193
KOREA BELL HELICOPTER COMPANY (Korea) 174
KOREAN AIR (Korea) 173
KOVACH, KIM (USA) (1981-82) 532
KRAFT, PHIL (USA) (1982-83) 550
KRAFT SYSTEMS INC (USA) (1982-82) 532
Kruk (WSK PZL-Warszawa-Okecie) 192
KUYBYSHEV POLYTECHNIC (USSR) (1981-82) 172
Kudu (Atlas) (1982-84) 184

L

L-5 (SSVV) (1980-81) 135
L-8 (NAMC) 41
L-19 (Ector) (1983-84) 373
L-39 (AERO) 47
L-70 Militrainer (Valmet) 55
L-80 TP (Valmet) (1985-86) 50
L-90TP (Valmet) 54
L-100 conversions (IAI) 142
L-100 series (Lockheed) 417
L 100-50 Hercules (Lockheed) (1980-81) 377
L 400 Twin Hercules (Lockheed) (1980-81) 377
L-410 UVP-E (LET) 48
L-602 (Let) (1983-84) 46
L-610 (LET) 49
L-1011 conversions (Lockheed) 420
L-1011 (Lockheed) 415
L-1011F (Hayes-Lockheed) 402
LA-4-200 Amphibian (Lake) 405
LA-250 Renegade (Lake) 406
LA-250 Turbo Renegrade (Lake) 406
LAPAN (see Lembaga Penerbagan dan Antariska Nasional) (1981-82) 90
LAS (see Lockheed Aircraft Service Company) (1986-87) 434
LBH Light Battlefield Helicopter (Augusta) 151
LC-3, X-Avia (Lewis) (1981-82) 388
LC-10 Criquet (Croses) (1981-82) 481
LC-130 Hercules (Lockheed) 415
LCRA (NAL) 100
LD 261 (Midgy) (1980-81) 481
LDA-01 (Lockspeiser) (1981-82) 253
LDA-500 Boxer (Lockspeiser) (1986-87) 298
LDA-1000 Boxer (Lockspeiser) (1986-87) 299
LET (see Let Národni Podnik) 48
LHX (Bell) 348
LIPNUR (see Nurtanio P.T.) (1978-79) 77
LT-200 (LIPNUR) (1978-79) 77
LTA (Dornier) (1979-80) 74
LTV (see LTV Aircraft Products Group) 420
Labrador, CH-113 (Boeing Canada) (1985-86) 19
Lah Tonal (JEH) 123
LAKE AIRCRAFT INC (USA) 405
LAKE AMPHIBIAN INC (USA) (1985-86) 431
Lama (Aérospatiale) 57
Lama, SA 315B (HAL/Aérospatiale) (1987-88) 106
Laminar (Pazmany) (1980-81) 536
Laminar flow aircraft (NASA) (1982-83) 428
Lance II (Piper) (1980-81) 408
Lansen J32E (Saab-Scania) (1987-88) 225
LANDRAY, GILBERT (France) (1982-83) 503
Lapwing (Snipe) (1985-86) 305
Lark 1B (Keleher) (1984-85) 580
LARKIN AIRCRAFT COMPANY (USA) (1980-81) 528
Laser 200 (Carmichael) (1981-82) 516
Laser 300 (Omac) 448
Laser Jet (Machen) (1985-86) 445
LASHER, C. W. (USA) (1983-84) 366
Lasta (Ulva) 500
Lavi (IAI) 137
LAVORINI, NEDO (Italy) (1982-83) 512
LEAR FAN CORPORATION (USA) (1981-82) 387
Lear Fan 2100 (Lear Fan) (1984-85) 276, 429
LEAR FAN LIMITED (USA) (1985-86) 433
LEAR FAN LTD (UK) (1984-85) 276
Learjet (Arvin/Calspan) (1982-83) 285
Learjet 24E/R (Gates Learjet) (1981-82) 357
Learjet 25D (Gates Learjet) (1986-87) 406
Learjet 25F (Gates Learjet) (1979-80) 332
Learjet 25G (Dee Howard/Gates) (1986-87) 398
Learjet 25G (Gates Learjet) (1986-87) 407
Learjet 28/29 Longhorn (Gates Learjet) (1982-83) 367
Learjet 31 (Learjet) 408
Learjet 35A/36A (Learjet) 407
Learjet 35A/36A Special missions versions (Learjet) 408
Learjet 55 (Gates Learjet) (1986-87) 409
Learjet 55 Long-range tanks (Branson) 371
Learjet 55B (Gates Learjet) (1987-88) 419
Learjet 55C (Learjet) 409
LEG-AIR CORPORATION (USA) (1985-86) 599
LEICHTFLUGZEUGE-ENTWICKLUNGEN DIPL ING HERMANN MYLIUS (West Germany) (1985-86) 92
LEISURE SPORT LTD (UK) (1980-81) 196
Leko-70 (Valmet) (1978-79) 35

LEMBAGA PENERBANGAN DAN ANTARISKA NASIONAL (Indonesia) (1981-82) 90
Leonardo, M.B.3 (Militi) (1983-84) 528
Leopard (CMC) 295
LET NÁRODNÍ PODNIK (Czechoslovakia) 48
LEWIS AIRCRAFT CORPORATION (USA) (1981-82) 388
Lift Activator Disc (VTOL Aircraft) (1987-88) 10
Light Combat Aircraft (HAL) 97
Lightning Model 38P (Beechcraft) (1984-85) 309
Lightning Model 400 (Smith) (1982-83) 478
Lil Quickie, OR-71 (Vin-Del/Owl) (1981-82) 539
Lil Rascal (Aeroneering) (1979-80) 503
LIVESEY, DAVID M. (UK) (1979-80) 496
LIVINGSTON, GENE (USA) (1982-83) 552
LOBET-DE-ROUVRAY AVIATION PTLTD. (New Zealand) (1978-79) 487
LOCK HAVEN RE-MAN CENTER (USA) (1987-88) 441
Lockheed F-104/Shuttle Insulation Tests (NASA) *(1983-84)* 445
LOCKHEED AERONAUTICAL SYSTEMS COMPANY (USA) 411
LOCKHEED AIRCRAFT SERVICE COMPANY (USA) (1986-87) 434
LOCKHEED-CALIFORNIA COMPANY (USA) (1986-87) 435
LOCKHEED CORPORATION (USA) 410
LOCKHEED-GEORGIA COMPANY (USA) (1986-87) 439
LOCKSPEISER AIRCRAFT LTD (UK) .. (1981-82) 253
LOCKSPEISER AIRCRAFT LTD (UK) .. (1987-88) 314
Long-EZ, RAF Model 61 (Rutan) (1985-86) 613
Longhorn (Gates Learjet) (1982-83)) 367, 368
Long Ranger (Agusta-Bell) (1979-80) 114
Long Ranger II (Bell) (1983-84) 317
Long Ranger III (Bell Helicopter Textron) 19, 342
Longwing (Sierra) 474
LTV AIRCRAFT PRODUCTS GROUP (USA) 420
LTV AEROSPACE AND DEFENCE COMPANY (USA) (1986-87) 444
LUDWIG, HARRY (USA) (1981-82) 533
Luftibus, GB-1 (Bezzola) (1978-79) 490
Lunar Rocket (Maule) (1985-86) 448
LUSCOMBE AIRCRAFT LTD (UK) (1987-88) 315
Lutin (Fauvel) (1979-80) 474
Lynx (ABHC/Westland) (1980-81) 45
Lynx (Gulfstream American) (1979-80) 352
Lynx (Westland) 316
Lynx-3 (Westland) (1987-88) 337

M

M-1 (Super Rotor) 16
M-4 (Myasischev) 256
M-5 Lunar Rocket (Maule) (1985-86) 448
M6, Imperial Knight Twister (Payne) (1982-83) 559
M-6 Super Rocket (Maule) (1983-84) 429
M-7 Super Rocket (Maule) 423
M-12 Tchaika (Beriev) 228
M-15 Belphegor (WSK-PZL Mielec) (1982-83) 167
M-17 (WSK-Mielec) (1979-80) 156
M-18 Dromader (WSK-PZL Mielec) 184
M-18A Fromader (WSK-PZL Mielec) 185
M-20 Mewa (WSK-PZL Mielec) 185
M20J (Mooney) (1985-86) 467
M20K (Mooney) (1985-86) 468
M20L Pegasus (Mooney) 445
M-21 Dromader Mini (WSK-PZL Mielec) 186
M-24 Dromader Super (WSK-PZL Mielec) 186
M-26 Iskierka (WSK-PZL Mielec) 186
M-30 (Mooney) (1982-83) 428
M-74 Wasp (Texas Helicopter) (1982-83) 480
M79 Hornet (Aerodyne) (1987-88) 341
M79 Wasp II (Texas Helicopter) (1982-83) 480
M102 Scorchy (Mace) (1981-82) 534
MA-1B Diablo 1200 (Emair) (1980-81) 333
MA-3 Maverick (Marquart) (1982-83) 552
MAFFS (see Modular Airborne Fire Fighting System (Aero Union) 321
MAI (see Mitsubishi Aircraft International) (1986-87) 446
MAI (see Moscow Aviation Institute) (1985-86) 233
MARS (see Mission Aviation Related Services) (1981-82) 804
MB-3 (Brügger) (1980-81) 492
M.B.3 Leonardo (Militi) (1983-84) 528
M.B.4 (Militi) (1983-84) 528
M.B.326 (Aermacchi) (1981-82) 122
M.B.339 Uprated version (Aermacchi) (1984-85) 139
M.B.339A (Aermacchi) 145
MB-339B (Aermacchi) 146
MB-339C (Aermacchi) 146
MB-339D (Aermacchi) 146
MB-339K (Aermacchi) 146
MB-339AN (Aermacchi) 145
MB-339RM (Aermacchi) 145
MBB (see Messerschmitt-Bölkow-Blohm GmbH) 92
MC-8 Mini-Copter (Aerospace General) (1978-79) 250
MC 10 Cricri (Colomban) (1981-82) 480
MC 12 Cricri (Colomban) (1982-83) 496
MC-130 Hercules (Lockheed) 415
MD-3 (Datwyler) 212
MD-9XX (McDonnell Douglas) 431
MD-11 (McDonnell Douglas) 434
MD-11X (McDonnell Douglas) (1985-86) 459
MD-80 Series (McDonnell Douglas) 429
MD-81 (McDonnell Douglas) 429
MD-82 (McDonnell Douglas) 429
MD-82 (SAIC McDonnell Douglas) 43
MD-83 (McDonnell Douglas) 430
MD-87 (McDonnell Douglas) 430
MD-88 (McDonnell Douglas) 430
MD-89 (McDonnell Douglas) (1985-86) 455
MD-90 (McDonnell Douglas) (1983-84) 437
MD-90 UHB (McDonnell Douglas) 431
MD-91 (McDonnell Douglas) 431
MD-92 (McDonnell Douglas) 431
MD-94X (McDonnell Douglas) (1987-88) 463
MD-100 (McDonnell Douglas) (1984-85) 455
MD-500/520/530 civil conversions (McDonnell Douglas) 437
MD 520N NOTOR (McDonnell Douglas) 439
MDF-100 (McDonnell/Fokker) (1981-82) 111
MDX (McDonnell Douglas) 439
MF-85 P-RG (Ruschmeyer) 96
MFI (see Malmo Forsknings & Innovations AB) (1985-86) 202
MFI-18 (MFI) (1985-86) 202
MH-6A (McDonnell Douglas) 438
MH-53E (Sikorsky) 478
MH-53J (Sikorsky) 486
MH-60G (Sikorsky) 480
MH-60K (Sikorsky) 480
Mi-2 (MIL) 248
Mi-2 Mil (WSK-PZL Swidnik) 187
Mi-2B (WSK-PZL Swidnik) 188
Mi-2R (WSK-PZL Swidnik/Mil) (1984-85) 179
Mi-4 (Mil) (1982-83) 213
Mi-6 (MIL) 248
Mi-8 Harbin/Nanchang (1984-85) 38
Mi-8 (MIL) 248
Mi-10 (MIL) 250
Mi-10K (MIL) 250
Mi-12 (MIL) (1978-79) 190
Mi-14 (MIL) 251
Mi-17 (Mil) 251
Mi-18 (Mil) (1983-84) 225
Mi-24 (MIL) 252
Mi-25 (MIL) 254
Mi-26 (MIL) 254
Mi-28 (MIL) 255
Mi-34 (MIL) 256
MiG (formerly Mikoyan) (USSR) 240
MiG-19PF (China) (1981-82) 29
MiG-19SF (China) (1981-82) 29
MiG-21 (MiG) 240
MiG-21bis (HAL) (1987-88) 108
MiG-21M (HAL) (1982-83) 95
MiG-21MF (HAL) (1982-83) 95
MiG-23 (HAL) (1981-82) 90
MiG-23 (MiG) 241
MiG-25 (MiG) 244
MiG-27 (MiG) 243
MiG-27M (HAL) 100
MiG-29 (MiG) 245
MiG-31 (MiG) 247
MIT (see Massachusetts Institute of Technology) (1985-86) 466
M.J.14 Fourtouna (Jurca) (1982-83) 503
M.J.20 Tempête (Jurca) (1983-84) 518
ML74 Wasp (Aerodyne) 341
ML79 Hornet (Aerodyne) *(1987-88)* 341
MP-18 Dragon (Phalanx) (1987-88) 482
MP.205 Busard (Lefebvre) (1985-86) 555
MPC 75 (MBB/CATIC) 127
MPC-75 GmbH (International) 127
MRCA (Panavia) *(1982-83)* 111
MT20 Military Trainer (Mooney) (1985-86) 468
MTC (see MOSHIER TECHNOLOGIES CORPORATION) (USA) 445
MT-X (Kawasaki) (1982-83) 150
MU-2 (Mitsubishi) (1986-87) 170
MU-2 (MAI) (1985-86) 445
MU-2 Express conversions (MU-2) 446
MU-2 MODIFICATIONS INC (USA) 446
MU-300 (Mitsubishi) (1987-88) 181
MW3 Airkart (Whittaker) (1979-80) 500
MY 102 Tornado (Mylius) (1985-86) 92
MY 103 Mistral (Mylius) (1980-81) 84
MY 104 Passatt (Mylius) (1980-81) 84
MACE AIRCRAFT (USA) (1981-82) 534
MacCREADY, DR PAUL B. (USA) (1985-86) 444
MacDONALD AIRCRAFT CO 9USA0 (1979-80) 528
MACERA, SILVANO (Italy) (1984-85) 546
MACFAM WORLD TRADERS (Canada) (1984-85) 524
MACHEN INC (USA) 421
Madcap (Antonov) 226
Maestro (Yakovlev) 273
Magnum (O'Neill) (1986-87) 475
MAHUGH, G. IRVIN (U.S.A.) (1980-81) 529
Maiden (Sukhoi) (1983-84) 230
Mail (Beriev) 228
Mainstay (Ilyushin) 234
MAISS, ULRICH (Germany) (1985-86) 562
Major, DR 400/140B (Robin) (1979-80) 66
Major, DR 400/160 (Robin) 81
Malibu (Piper) 458
MALMO FORSKNINGS & INNOVATIONS AB (Sweden) (1985-86) 202
MANCRO AIRCRAFT COMPANY (USA) (1983-84) 428
Mangusta, A 129 (Agusta) 150
MARCHETTI, FRANK (USA) (1982-83) 552
Marimo, TK-1 (Kako) (1978-79) 486
Mariner (Robinson) 462
Maritime, F27 (Fokker) (1985-86) 171
Maritime Defender (Pilatus Britten-Norman) 302
Maritime Defender, AEW, AEW/MR, and ASW/ASV (Pilatus Britten-Norman) 304
Maritime Enforcer, F27 (Fokker) (1985-86) 171
Maritime Patrol B200T (Beechcraft) 334
Mark I (Spitfire) (1984-85) 508
Mark II (Merkel) (1978-79) 527
Mark II (Spitfire) (1984-85) 508
Mark II System (Howard/Raisbeck) (1980-81) 420
Mark IV (Spitfire) (1983-84) 494
Mark IV System (Raisbeck) (1980-81) 421
Mark IV System (Raisbeck/Western) (1983-84) 469
Mark V System (Rockwell/Raisbeck) (1980-81) 421
Mark VI System (Raisbeck) 459
Mark VII System (Raisbeck) 460
Mark Five System (Rockwell/Raisbeck) (1980-81) 421
Mark Four Learjet Century III Impovements (Raisbeck) (1980-81) 421
MARKO-ELEKTRONIK COMPANY (Poland) (1984-85) 547
Marlin, TSC-1A3 (TAC) (1979-80) 27
MARMANDE AÉRONAUTIQUE (France) (1985-86)) 74
Marquise (MAI) (1985-86) 445
MARSH AVIATION COMPANY (USA) 422
MARSHALL OF CAMBRIDGE (ENGINEERING) LTD. (UK) 297
Martin Fierro, J-1 (RRA) (1981-82) 4
Marut (HAL) (1979-80) 81
Mascot, HJ-5 (Harbin) (1986-87) 34
MASSACHUSETTS INSTITUTE OF TECHNOLOGY (USA) (1985-86) 466
*MASTER-MEHRZWECKFLUGZEUG-*ENTWICKLUNGS GmbH & CO KG (West Germany) *(1978-79)* 67
Matador (BAe) 290
MAULE AIR INC (USA) 423
Maverick, MA-3 (Marquart) (1982-83) 552
Mavi Isik 78-XA (THvK/KIBM) (1983-84) 197
Mavi Isik-B (THvK/KIBM) (1983-84) 197
Mavi Isik-G (THvK/KIBM) (1983-84) 197
Max (China) (1980-81) 37
Maxi Cat (Aero Mod) (1984-85) 300
May (Ilyushin) 230
Mayfly (Kendall) (1982-83) 520
MBB/AÉROSPATIALE (International) (1983-84) 110
MBB/CATIC (International) (1987-88) 128
MBB HELICOPTER CANADA LTD (Canada) 30
MBB HELICOPTER CORPORATION (USA) 424
MBB/KAWASAKI (International) 123
McCARLEY, MRS CHARLES E. (USA). (1982-83) 552
MCDONNELL DOUGLAS/BAe (International) 124
MCDONNELL AIRCRAFT COMPANY (USA) 424
MCDONNELL DOUGLAS CORPORATION (USA) 424
MCDONNELL DOUGLAS HELICOPTER COMPANY (USA) 437
MCDONNELL DOUGLAS/FOKKER (International) (1982-83) 111
McKINNON-VIKING ENTERPRISES (Canada) (1981-82) 27
M COMPANY (USA) (1979-80) 529
MELEX USA (USA) 442
Merganser (Van Dine) (1982-83) 579
MERIDIONALI SpA ELICOTTERI (Italy) (1985-86) 150
MERKEL AIRPLANE COMPANY (USA) (1978-79) 527
MERLYN PRODUCTS INC (USA) 442
Merlin IIIC, SA227-TT (Fairchild) (1983-84) 379
Merlin IVC, SA227-AT (Fairchild Aircraft) 388
Merlin V (Fairchild) 389
Merlin 200 Aerobot (Moller) (1987-88) 474
Merlin 300, SA227 TT/41 (Fairchild Aircraft) 388
Merlin 300 Aerobot (Moller) 443
Merlin 400SP (Fairchild) (1987-88) 416
Merlin maritime surveillance aircraft (Swearingen) (1980-81) 445
Merlin SM (Swearingen) (1980-81) 445
Méange (Gatard) (1978-79) 475
Mescalero (Cessna) (1980-81) 308
MESSERSCHMITT-BÖLKOW-BLOHM GmbH (West Germany) 92
Metal Hurlant (Thompson) (1979-80) 552
Meteorite (Wallis) (1986-87) 317
Meteorite 2 (Wallis) (1987-88) 331
Metro II (Swearingen) (1980-81) 443
Metro IIA (Swearingen) (1980-81) 444
Metro III (Fairchild Aircraft) 386
Metro IIIA (Fairchild) (1986-87) 404
Metro V (Fairchild) 389
Metro VI (Fairchild) (1987-88) 416
Mewa, M-20 (WSK-PZL Mielec) 185
MEYER, CLAIR O (USA) (1983-84) 567
MEYER, LES K. (USA) (1982-83) 554
MEYERS AIRCRAFT MANUFACTURING COMPANY (USA) (1980-81) 391
Microjet 200B (Microjet) 77
MICROJET SA (France) 77
Microjet 200 (Microturbo) (1982-83) 72
Microstar (Chagnes) (1980-81) 472
MICROTURBO SA (France) (1982-83) 72
Midas (Ilyushin) 234
MID-CONTINENT AIRCRAFT CORPORATION (USA) 442
MIDGY, M (France) (1980-81) 481
MiG (USSR) 240
MIL (USSR) 248
MILITI, BRUNO (Italy) (1983-84) 528
MILLER, J. W. AVIATION INC (USA)... (1985-86) 601
MILLER, WILLIAM Y. (USA) (1985-86) 602
MILLICER, HENRY K. (Australia) (1978-79) 466
MILON, PIERRE (France) (1980-81) 481
Miltrainer, L-70 (Valmet) 55
Minicab (Ord-Hume) (1979-80) 497
Mini Z, CH 50 (Zenair) (1984-85) 526
Mini-Cap (Mudry) (1982-83) 74
Mini-Copter (Aerospace General) (1978-79) 249
Mini-Coupe (Bob Anderson) (1982-83) 530
Mini Coupe (Sport Air Craft) (1981-82) 552
Mini Coupe TD (Sport Air Craft) (1980-81) 548
Mini-Dromader, M-21 (WSK PZL-Mielec) (1982-83) 168
Mini-Esqualo (Brazil) (1985-86) 538
MiniHawk (Hawk) (1980-81) 358
MINI-HAWK INTERNATIONAL INC. (USA) (1981-82) 536
Mini-Mac (McCarley) (1982-83) 552
Mini-Moni (Monnett) (1982-83) 555
Miniplane (Smith) (1981-82) 463

Mini-Swat, S-350 (Schapel) (1983-84) 481
Minor (Ord-Hume) (1979-80) 497
MINTY, E. R. (Australia) (1983-84) 9
Minuano (EMBRAER/Piper) 15
Mirage III (Dassault-Breguet) 65
Mirage III/5 upgrade (IAI) 141
Mirage 3 NG (Dassault-Breguet) 66
Mirage IV-P (Dassault) 66
Mirage 5 (Dassault-Breguet) 65
Mirage 50 (Dassault-Breguet) 65
Mirage 50 Upgrade (ENAER) 33
Mirage 50M (Dassault-Breguet) 66
Mirage 2000 (AOI) 53
Mirage 2000 (Dassault-Breguet) 68
Mirage 4000 (Dassault-Breguet) 70
Mirage F1 (Dassault-Breguet) 67
Mirage advanced technology update programme (Dassault-Breguet) 66
Mirage Improvement Programme (F + W) 217
Mirage modifications (IAI) (1987-88) 144
Mirlo (CASA) 207
Mission adaptive wing (NASA/USAF/Boeing) 371
MISSION AVIATION RELATED SERVICES (USA) (1981-82) 804
Missionmaster (GAF) (1985-86) 7
Mistral CP 301 (Becker) (1979-80) 484
Mistral, MY 103 (Mylius) (1980-81) 84
MITCHELL AIRCRAFT CORPORATION (USA) (1980-81) 531
Mitchell Wing (M Company) (1979-80) 529
MITSUBISHI AIRCRAFT INTERNATIONAL INC (USA) (1986-87) 446
MITSUBISHI JUKOGYO KABUSHIKI KAISHA (Japan) 169
Mizzet No III (Abe) (1981-82) 496
Mod AH-1S (Bell) (1984-85) 328
Model 1-A (Bowers) (1982-83) 530
Model 1-B (Bowers) (1982-83) 531
Model 1-Nine-O (Jurca) (1979-80) 477
Model 2 Super Sportster (Turner) (1980-81) 554
Model 2T-1A-2 Sport Trainer (Great Lakes) (1987-88) 424
Model 7ECA/7GCAA/7GCBCJ Citabria (Bellanca) (1979-80) 287
Model 8GCBC Scout (Bellanca) (1980-81) 287
Model 8GCBC Scout (Champion) (1985-86) 392
Model 8KCAB Decathlon (Bellanca/Champion) (1980-81) 287
Model 16H-3 (Piasecki) 450
Model 17-30A (Bellanca) (1980-81) 287
Model 17-31A (Bellanca) (1979-80) 286
Model 17-31ATC (Bellanca) (1979-80) 286
Model 18 (Volpar/Beechcraft) (1982-83) 483
Model 19-25 Skyrocket II (Bellanca) (1980-81) 288
Model 21A (Helio) (1987-88) 435
Model 24 (Gates Learjet) (1981-82) 357
Model 25 (Gates Learjet) (1982-83) 367
Model 25 (Bellanca) (1985-86) 348
Model 27 (RAF) (1985-86) 612
Model 28/29 Longhorn (Gates Learjet) (1982-83) 367
Model 31 (RAF) (1985-86) 612
Model 31 (Learjet) 408
Model 32 (RAF) (1985-86) 612
Model 33 (RAF) (1985-86) 612
Model 35A/36A (Learjet) 407
Model 35A/36A special missions versions (Learjet) 408
Model 38P, Lightning (Beechcraft) (1984-85) 309
Model 40 Defiant (Rutan) (1985-86) 613
Model 44, Angel (King's) 405
Model 55 (Gates Learjet) (1986-87) 409
Model 55C (Learjet) 409
Model 58 Baron (Beechcraft) 331
Model 58P Baron (Beechcraft) (1987-88) 354
Model 58TC (Beechcraft) (1984-85) 342
Model 59 Predator (Rutan) (1983-84) 481
Model 60 Duke (Beechcraft) (1982-83) 296
Model 61 (RAF) (1985-86) 613
Model 72 Grizzly (Rutan) (1985-86) 503
Model 74 (Rutan) (1983-84) 480
Model 77 Apache (McDonnell Douglas) 439
Model 77 Skipper (Beechcraft) (1984-85) 306
Model 85 Orion (Lockheed) (1982-83) 402
Model 85 (Sabreliner) (1987-88) 501
Model 95-B55 (Beechcraft) (1983-84) 303
Model 99 Airliner (Beechcraft) (1979-80) 273
Model 100 (De Vore) (1986-87) 399
Model 100 King Air (Beechcraft) (1983-84) 308
Model 100 Sunbird (Verilite) 495
Model 105 (Spratt) (1980-81) 546
Model 107 (Boeing) 364
Model 107 (Spratt) (1983-84) 583
Model 114 (Boeing) 364
Model 122 Uirapuru (Aerotec) (1980-81) 10
Model 142 (Zlin) 50
Model 150 (Cessna) (1978-79) 299
Model 152 (Cessna) 374
Model 152 Aerobat (Cessna) (1984-85) 359
Model 172 (RAM/Cessna) 460
Model 180 (Cessna) (1982-83) 338
Model 185 Orion (Lockheed) 412
Model 185 Skywagon (Cessna) (1986-87) 388
Model 200D (Meyers) (1979-80) 392
Model 200T (Beechcraft) 333
Model 200X (Moller) 442
Model 201 (Mooney) (1985-86) 467
Model 201C (Weatherley) (1979-80) 459
Model 201 (Mooney) 443
Model 204B (Fuji/Bell) (1984-85) 157
Model 204B-2 (Fuji/Bell) 166
Model 205 (Agusta-Bell) 151
Model 205 (Bell) 341
Model 205 (Mooney) 444
Model 205 A-1 (Bell) (1982-83) 304
Model 205 A-1/UH-1H (Fuji/Bell) (1982-83) 148
Model 206, Cessna, turbine PAC (Soloy) 489
Model 206B Jet Ranger III (Agusta-Bell) 151
Model 206B Jet Ranger III (Bell Helicopter Textron) 18, 342
Model 206L Texas Ranger (Bell) (1985-86) 341
Model 206L-1 Long Ranger II (Bell) (1983-84) 317
Model 206L-3 Long Ranger III (Bell Helicopter Textron) 19, 342
Model 207, Cessna, turbine PAC (Soloy) 489
Model 208 Caravan I (Cessna) 374
Model 209 HueyCobra (Bell) 343
Model 209 HueyCobra (Modernised version) 344
Model 209 SeaCobra (Bell) 343
Model 209 SuperCobra (Bell) 343
Model 212 (Agusta-Bell) 151
Model 212 (China) (1981-82) 34
Model 212ASW (Agusta-Bell) 152
Model 212 Twin Two-Twelve (Bell) 370
Model 212 Twin Two-Twelve (Bell Helicoper Textron) 19
Model 214A (Agusta-Bell) (1978-79) 105
Model 214A/C (Bell) (1980-81) 283
Model 214B BigLifter (Bell) (1982-83) 311
Model 214ST Super Transport (Bell) 345
Model 222 (Bell) 346
Model 231 (Mooney) (1985-86) 468
Model 234 (Boeing) 367
Model 235CA, Rallye (SOCATA) (1978-79) 63
Model 235G, Rallye (SOCATA) (1978-79) 63
Model 249 HueyCobra (Bell) (1983-84) 320
Model 252TSE (Mooney) 444
Model 280 (Enstrom) 385
Model 285 Orion (Lockheed) 412
Model 298 (Mohawk) (1978-79) 329
Models 300 and 301 (Aeronics/Sequoia) (1980-81) 165
Model 300 Tauro (Anahuac) (1980-81) 140
Model 300 Viking (Bellanca) (1979-80) 286
Model 300C (Hughes) (1984-85) 419
Model 300C (Schweizer) 472
Model 300CQ (Hughes) (1982-83) 390
Model 301 (Bell) 347
Model 301 (Mooney) (1985-86) 469
Model 301 (Sequoia) (1980-81) 544
Model 303 (Cessna) (1985-86) 382
Models 305 (Brantly-Hynes) (1981-82) 322
Model 305 Brantly (Navas) 101
Model 310 (Cessna) (1982-83) 347
Model 310 II (Cessna) (1982-83) 347
Model 318 (Cessna) (1978-79) 311
Model 318E Dragonfly (Cessna) (1981-82) 336
Model 330 (Shorts) 304
Model 330 Sky Night (Schweizer) 473
Model 335/335 II (Cessna) (1981-82) 336
Model 337 Skymaster/Skymaster II (Cessna) (1981-82) 336
Model 337 Skymaster (Reims/Cessna) (1980-81) 70
Model 340A/340A II/340A III (Cessna) (1984-85) 370
Model 340/340A (RAM/Cessna) 460
Model 360 (Boeing) 368
Model 360 (Hillman) (1983-84) 404
Model 360 (Shorts) (1986-87) 311
Model 360 Advanced (Shorts) (1987-88) 324
Model 360-300 (Shorts) 306
Model 369 (Kawasaki/Hughes) (1981-82) 145
Model 369D (Kawasaki/Hughes) (1984-85) 160
Model 380-L (Lederlin) (1982-83) 504
Model 382 Hercules (Lockheed) 415
Model 385 TriStar (Lockheed) 415
Model 400 (Avtek) (1986-87) 335
Model 400 (Interceptor) (1978-79) 354
Model 400 Beechjet (Beechcraft) 338
Model 400 Combat Twin (Bell, Canada) (1987-88) 22
Model 400 Hustler (AJI) (1978-79) 252
Model 400 Hustler (GACC) (1980-81) 339
Model 400 Lightning (Smith) (1982-83) 478
Model 400 TwinRanger (Bell) (1985-86) 340
Model 400A (Avtek) 326
Model 400A (Bell, Canada) 22
Model 400A Interceptor (Prop-Jets) (1985-86) 490
Model 400C Aurora (MTC) 445
Model 400M Aurora (MTC) (1987-88) 477
Model 401/402A/402B/402C/ (RAM)/Cessna) 460
Model 402/402C (Cessna) 376
Model 406-5 (Reims-Cessna) (1984-85) 75, 372
Model 406-6 (Reims-Cessna) (1982-83) 75
Model 406 AHIP (Bell) 342
Model 406 CS (Bell) 343
Model 406LM Long Ranger (Bell) (1985-86) 340
Model 410 (Teledyne Ryan) 493
Model 412 (Agusta-Bell) (1986-87) 151
Model 412 SP (Agusta-Bell) 152
Model 412 (Bell) (1986-87) 370
Model 412 (Bell Helicopter Textron) 20
Model 412 (China) (1981-82) 34
Model 412 (Nurtanio/Bell) (1985-86) 99
Model 414 (Boeing) 364
Model 414/414A (RAM/Cessna) 460
Model 414A Chancellor (Cessna) 376
Model 414A (RAM/Cessna) 460
Model 421 Golden Eagle (Cessna) 376
Model 421/421CW (RAM/Cessna) 460
Model 425 Corsair (Cessna) (1982-83) 352
Model 425 Conquest I (Cessna) 376
Model 440 (Bell/Canada) (1987-88) 22
Model 441 Conquest II (Cessna) 376
Model 440E Commuter (Moller) (1986-87) 467
Model 480 (Advanced Technology) (1985-86) 321
Model 480 Eagle (Enstrom) (1980-81) 334
Model 480 Predator (ATAC) (1986-87) 335
Model 500 Hustler (Gulfstream American) (1980-81) 339
Models 500/530, McDonnell Douglas (KA) 174
Model 500 (Kawasaki/Hughes) (1982-83) 151
Model 500C (Kawasaki/Hughes) (1982-83) 151
Model 500 Citation (Cessna) (1984-85) 376
Model 500D (Kawasaki/McDonnell Douglas) 169
Model 500/530 Defender (McDonnell Douglas) 438
Model 500MD/ASW Defender (McDonnell Douglas) (1985-86) 461
Model 500ME (Hughes) (1983-84) 406
Model 500MF (Hughes) (1983-84) 406
Model 501 Citation I/SP (Cessna) (1984-85) 377
Model 550 Citation II (Cessna) 376
Model 560 Citation V (Cessna) 377
Model 600A (Piper) (1984-85) 478
Model 600X (Hughes) (1982-83) 393
Model 602P (Piper) (1985-86) 488
Model 620 (Weatherley) (1982-83) 486
Model 650 Citation III (Cessna) 378
Model 680 Rotor (Bell) 348
Model 700/FA-300 (Fuji) (1980-81) 136
Model 700P (Piper) (1985-86) 488
Model 700R (Aeofan) (1986-87) 329
Model 707 (Boeing) 352
Model 707 Tanker/Transport (Boeing) 370
Model 710/FA-300 (Fuji) (1981-82) 142
Model 712 (Grumman) 399
Model 727 (Boeing) (1983-84) 327
Model 727, Boeing, conversion (Lockheed) (1987-88) 451
Model 737 (Boeing) (1983-84) 328
Model 737-200 (Boeing) 353
Model 737-300 (Boeing) 354
Model 737-400 (Boeing) 355
Model 737-500 (Boeing) 355
Model 747 (Boeing) 356
Model 747 CRAF (Boeing) 371
Model 747 EUD (Boeing) (1982-83) 323
Model 747SP (Boeing) 358
Model 747-123 Space Shuttle Orbiter Carrier (Boeing/NASA) (1979-80) 298
Model 747-200F Freighter (Boeing) 357
Model 747-300 (Boeing) 358
Model 747-400 (Boeing) 359
Model 757 (Boeing) 360
Model 757 LRAACA (Boeing) 371
Model 767 (Boeing) 361
Model 767-200ER (Boeing) 362
Model 767-300 (Boeing) 362
Model 767-300-ER (Boeing) 362
Model 767 AOA (Boeing) 352
Model 7J7 (Boeing) 364
Model 777 (Boeing) (1979-80) 300
Model 800 Skytrader (Dominion) (1979-80) 330
Model 800J (Aerofan) (1986-87) 329
Model 800/8800 (Excalibur) 386
Model 1300 (Beechcraft) (1979-80) 273
Model 1300 Commuter (Beechcraft) 336
Model 1329-25 JetStar II (Lockheed) (1980-81) 377
Model 1400 Commuterliner (Skytrader) 488
Model 1900 Exec-Liner (Beechcraft) 337
Model 1900C Airliner (Beechcraft) 337
Model 2000 Starship (Beechcraft) 338
Model 2000C (Morrisey) 445
Model 2100 (Lear Fan) (1984-85) 429
Model 2150A Kachina (Varga) (1983-84) 497
Model 2150A-TG, Kachina (Hibbard/Varga) (1983-84) 402
Model 2180 Kachina (Varga) (1984-84) 498
Model A Sport (Geide) (1982-83) 543
Model A36 (Beechcraft) 331
Model A36TC (Beechcraft) (1982-83) 291
Model AT-301 (Air Tractor) 322
Model AT-302 (Air Tractor) (1985-86) 320
Model AT-400 (Air Tractor) 323
Model AT-400A (Air Tractor) 323
Model AT-401 (Air Tractor) 323
Model AT-500 (Air Tractor) (1985-86) 320
Model AT-501 (Air Tractor) 324
Model AT-502 (Air Tractor) 324
Model AT-503 (Air Tractor) 324
Model B, Scamp (Agricopteros/Aerosport) (1984-85) 42
Model B-1, Sylkie One (Wayne) (1980-81) 504
Model B-2B (Brantly-Hynes) (1984-84) 347
Model B36TC (Beechcraft) 331
Model B-10 (Mitchell) (1980-81) 531
Model C90A King Air (Beechcraft) 332
Model D (Ace Aircraft) (1982-83) 523
Model D (Fike) (1979-80) 520
Model D292, ACAP (Bell) 347
Model E (Ace Aircraft) (1982-83) 523
Model "E" (Fike) (1979-80) 520
Model E55, Baron (Beechcraft) (1984-85) 311
Model F-21 (Taylorcraft) (1987-88) 525
Model F-21B (Taylorcraft) 492
Model F-22 (Taylorcraft) 492
Model F-28 (Enstrom) 385
Model F33A/C Bonanza (Beechcraft) 330
Model F90, King Air (Beechcraft) (1983-84) 307
Model F90-1, King Air (Beechcraft) (1987-88) 356
Model F406 (Reims/Cessna) 79
Model G-164D Turbo Ag-Cat D (Schweizer) (1981-82) 457
Model H (Navion) (1978-79) 391
Model H-295 (Helio Courier) (1978-79) 348
Model HT-295 (Helio Courier) (1978-79) 348
Model J Magnum (O'Neill) (1986-87) 475
Model P-210, Cessna Centurion conversion (Air America) (1986-87) 330
Model P337 Pressurised Skymaster (Cessna) (1980-81) 320
Model R22 Alpha (Robertson) (1984-85) 489
Model R22 Beta (Robinson) 462
Model R22HP (Robertson) (1983-84) 477
Model R172 Hawk XP (Cessna) (1982-83) 338
Model S-2A Pitts (Christen) (1987-88) 407
Model S-2B Pits (Christen) 381
Model S-2S Pitts (Christen) 381
Model S-325 Mini-Swat (Schapel) (1982-82) 455
Model S550 Citation S/11 (Cessna) 376
Model S-1080 Thunderbolt (Schapel) (1983-84) 481
Model SA227-AC Metro III (Fairchild) 386

Model SA227-AC Metro III (Fairchild Swearingen) .... *(1982-83)* 364
Model T-34C (Beechcraft) 329
Model T303 Crusader (Cessna) .... *(1985-86)* 382
Model T206/210 (RAM Cessna) 460
Model T310/320D-F (RAM Cessna) 460
Model T310/T310 II (Cessna) .... *(1981-82)* 335
Model V35 Bonanza (Beechcraft) .... *(1986-87)* 338
Model XM-4 (Moller) 442
Model Z Super Sportster (Turner) .... *(1982-83)* 579
MODERN WING AIRCRAFT LTD (Canada) 31
MOD SQUAD, THE, INC (USA) 442
Modular Airborne Fire Fighting System (Aero Union) 321
Mohawk (Grumman) .... *(1983-84)* 391
Mohawk, modified (PIA) 450
Mohawk OV-1/RV-1 (Grumman) 398
Mohawk 298 (Frakes) .... *(1978-79)* 329
MOHAWK AIR SERVICES (USA) .... *(1978-79)* 355
Mojave (Piper) .... *(1986-87)* 482
MOLLER INTERNATIONAL (USA) 442
MONARCH AVIATION INC (USA) .... *(1987-88)* 474
Monarch B (MIT) .... *(1985-86)* 466
Monex (Monnett) .... *(1983-84)* 568
MONG/MORTENSEN (USA) .... *(1985-86)* 602
Mong/Mortensen Biplane .... *(1985-86)* 602
Mongol (MiG) 240
Moni (Monnett) .... *(1982-83)* 555
MONNETT EXPERIMENTAL AIRCRAFT INC. (USA) .... *(1985-86)* 602
Montalvá (Super Rotor) 16
MOONEY AIRCRAFT CORPORATION (USA) 443
Mooney Mite (Mooney Mite) .... *(1979-80)* 531
MORAVAN NÁRODNÍ PODNIK (Czechoslovakia) 50
MORRISSEY AIRCRAFT COMPANY (USA) 445
MORRISSEY COMPANY, THE (USA) .... *(1984-85)* 585
MORTENSEN, DAN (see Mong/Mortensen) .... *(1985-86)* 602
MOSCOW AVIATION INSTITUTE (USSR) .... *(1985-86)* 233
MOSER, E. H., AIRCRAFT COMPANY (USA) .... *(1985-86)* 604
MOSHIER TECHNOLOGIES CORPORATION (USA) 445
Mosquito (Aviolight) 160
Moss (Tupolev) 266
MOTO-DELTA (see Geiser, Jean Marc) .... *(1980-81)* 68
Moto-Delta G 11 (Geiser) .... *(1980-81)* 68
Moujik (Sukhoi) 257
Mountaineer (Ector) 384
Mrówka (WSK-PZL Warszawa-Okecie) 194
Mr Smoothie (Sawano) .... *(1980-81)* 489
MUDRY AVIATION LTD (USA) .... *(1982-83)* 72
MUDRY et CIE, AVIONS (France) 78
MUKAI, ISAO (Japan) .... *(1982-83)* 514
MUNNINGHOFF, IVAN (USA) .... *(1985-86)* 604
MURPHY, R. L. (USA) .... *(1981-82)* 537
Mushshak (PAC) 180
Musketeer II, CT-134A (Beechcraft) .... *(1984-85)* 306
MUSSO, PAUL (USA) .... *(1981-82)* 538
Mustang (Venture Aviation) .... *(1984-85)* 611
Mustang 2 (Timofeyev) .... *(1982-83)* 518
MYASISHCHEV (USSR) 256
MYLIUS (see Leichtflugzeuge-Entwicklungen Dip Ing Hermann Mylius) .... *(1985-86)* 92
Mystère-Falcon 10MER (Dassault) .... *(1984-85)* 70
Mystère-Falcon 20 Series F (Dassault-Breguet) .... *(1982-83)* 67
Mystère-Falcon 20 G (Dassault-Breguet) .... *(1985-86)* 69
Mystère-Falcon 20-5 (Dassault-Breguet) 73
Mystère-Falcon 50 (Dassault-Breguet) 75
Mystère-Falcon 100 (Dassault-Breguet) 74
Mystère-Falcon 200 (Dassault-Breguet) 73
Mystère-Falcon 900 (Dassault-Breguet) 76
Mystery S replica (Younkin) .... *(1980-81)* 560

N

N22C Nomad (GAF) .... *(1986-87)* 6
N24 Nomad (GAF) .... *(1985-86)* 7
N-228 (IPTN) 102
N262 (Aérospatiale .... *(1978-79)* 36
N-260 (IPTN) 102
N-621 Universal (Neiva) .... *(1981-82)* 17
N-622 Universal (Neiva) .... *(1981-82)* 17
N-821 Corajá (EMBRAER/Piper) .... *(1985-86)* 16
N-821 Corajá (NEIVA) .... *(1985-86)* 17
NAC (see Norman Aeroplane Company Ltd, The) 298
NAC 1 (NAC) 300
NAC 6 (NAC) 299
NACI, Freelance (NDN) .... *(1984-85)* 280
NAL (see National Aeronautical Laboratory 100
NAL (see National Aerospace Laboratory) 171
NAL (see National Aircraft Leasing Ltd) .... *(1978-79)* 388
NAM (see National Aero Manufacturing Corporation) .... *(1981-82)* 157
NAMC (see Nanchang Aircraft Manufacturing Company) 39
NAMC (see National Aero Manufacturing Corporation) .... *(1979-80)* 147
NAMC (see Nihon Kokuki Seizo Kabushiki Kaisha) .... *(1979-80)* 137
NAS-332 Super Puma (IPTN) 102
NASA (see National Aeronautics and Space Administration) 446
NBELL-412 (IPTN) 102
NBO 105 (IPTN) 102
NBK-117 (IPTN) 102
NC-212 Aviocar (IPTN) 102
NDN (see NDN Aircraft Ltd) .... *(1984-85)* 279
NDN 1 Firecracker (NDN) .... *(1983-84)* 272
NDN 1T Turbo Firecracker (NDN) .... *(1983-84)* 272
NDN 6 Fieldmaster (NDN) .... *(1984-85)* 279
NE-821 Carajá (EMBRAER) 15
NE-821 Carajá (NEIVA) 16
NEIVA (see Industria Aeronáutica Neiva S/A) 16
NF-5 (Northrop) .... *(1978-79)* 392
NFH 90 (NH90) 128
NGT (Next Generation Trainer) (Fairchild) (1987-88) 414
NH 90 (International) 128
NIPPI (see Nihon Hikoki Kabushiki Kaisha) 172
NKC-135 ALL (USAF/Boeing) .... *(1982-83)* 330
NM-77 Ibis A (Nihon) .... *(1978-79)* 486
NOTAR helicopter (McDonnell Douglas) 439
NSA-300 Puma (Nurtanio) .... *(1984-85)* 97
NT-33A (Arvin/Calspan) .... *(1982-83)* 285
NTT (see New Transport Technologies Ltd) 128
NWI (see Northwest Industries Limited) 31
Nammer (IAI) 139
Namu II (Bowers) .... *(1978-79)* 509
Nanchang (Yakovlev) CJ-5 (China) .... *(1982-83)* 37
NANCHANG AIRCRAFT MANUFACTURING COMPANY (China) 39
NARAS AVIATION PVT LTD (India) 100
NASH AIRCRAFT LTD (UK) 300
NATIONAL AERO MANUFACTURING CORPORATION (Philippines) .... *(1981-82)* 157
NATIONAL AERONAUTICAL LABORATORY (India) 100
NATIONAL AERONAUTICS AND SPACE ADMINISTRATION (USA) 446
NATIONAL AEROSPACE LABORATORY (Japan) 171
National Aero-Space Plane (NASA) 446
NATIONAL AIRCRAFT FACTORIES (China) 34
NATIONAL AIRCRAFT LEASING LTD (USA) .... *(1978-79)* 388
NATIONAL DYNAMICS (PTY) LTD (South Africa) .... *(1979-80)* 163
Navajo (EMBRAER/Piper) 15
Navajo (Piper) .... *(1983-84)* 455
Navajo C/R (Piper) .... *(1984-85)* 471
Navajo, Panther (Colemill) 382
Naval helicopter (Mil) .... *(1981-82)* 214
NAVION RANGEMASTER AIRCRAFT CORPORATION (USA) .... *(1979-80)* 397
NDN AIRCRAFT LTD (UK) .... *(1984-85)* 279
Nesher (IAI) .... *(1980-81)* 110
Nesmith Cougar (EAA) .... *(1979-80)* 519
NEUMANN, EVERETT (USA) .... *(1980-81)* 534
New Brave, PA-36 (WTA/Piper) 497
NEW TRANSPORT TECHNOLOGIES LTD (International) 128
New heavy bomber (Tupolev) .... *(1980-81)* 213
NEWMAN, HARLEY (Australia) .... *(1982-83)* 489
New Technology Wing (TNT) testbed aircraft (Dornier) .... *(1982-83)* 82
New Tupolev Bomber (Tupolev) 269
NEW ZEALAND AEROSPACE INDUSTRIES LTD (New Zealand) .... *(1982-83)* 160
Next Generation Trainer (NGT) (Fairchild) (1987-88) 414
N-Flyer (Cal Poly) .... *(1979-80)* 307
NICOLLIER, HENRI (France) .... *(1984-85)* 539
NIEMII, LEONARD (USA) .... *(1980-81)* 534
Night/Adverse Weather A-10 (Fairchild Republic) .... *(1981-82)* 352
Nightfox (McDonnell Douglas) 438
Night Hawk (Sikorsky) .... *(1987-88)* 513
NIKON HIKOKI KABUSHIKI KAISHA (Japan) 172
NIHON KOKUKI SEIZO KABUSHIKI KAISHA (Japan) .... *(1979-80)* 137
NIHON UNIVERSITY, COLLEGE OF SCIENCE AND TECHNOLOGY (Japan) .... *(1981-82)* 497
Nimrod (BAe) 293
Nimrod AEW Mk 3 (BAe) .... *(1987-88)* 310
Nite Hawk (Olsen) .... *(1982-83)* 556
Nite Star (Olsen) .... *(1982-83)* 556
Nite-Writer (Orlando) 449
Nomad (ASTA) 4
Nomad N22/24 (GAF) .... *(1985-86)* 6
Nomad N22C (GAF) .... *(1986-87)* 6
NORMAN AEROPLANE COMPANY LTD, THE (UK) 298
NORTH AMERICAN (see Rockwell International Corporation) .... *(1979-80)* 429
NORTH AMERICAN AEROSPACE OPERATIONS (USA) .... *(1981-82)* 452
NORTH AMERICAN AIRCRAFT (USA) 463
NORTH AMERICAN SPACE OPERATIONS (USA) 465
NORTHROP CORPORATION (USA) 447
NORTHWEST INDUSTRIES LIMITED (Canada). 31
Novi Avion (Soko) 499
Nuri (Sikorsky) .... *(1980-81)* 435
NUTTING, D. (USA) .... *(1985-86)* 605
NYGE-AERO AB (Sweden) .... *(1987-88)* 221

O

O-2 (Cessna) .... *(1981-82)* 336
O2-337 Sentry (Summit) 489
O-2ST (Robertson/Brico) .... *(1984-85)* 485
OA-4M Skyhawk (Douglas) .... *(1980-81)* 390
OA7 (Optica) .... *(1986-87)* 304
OA-46A (Fairchild Republic) .... *(1986-87)* 403
OGMA (see Oficinas Gerais de Material Aeronáutico) 196
O-H4B Minor (Ord-Hume) .... *(1979-80)* 497
OH-6D (Kawasaki/McDonnell Douglas) 169
OH-6J (Kawasaki/Hughes) .... *(1981-82)* 145
OH-58 (Bell) .... *(1987-88)* 365
OH-58D (Bell) 342
OR-71 Lil Quickie (Vin-Del/Owl) .... *(1981-82)* 539
OV-1 (Grumman) .... *(1983-84)* 391
OV-1/RV-1 (Grumman) 398
OV-1A modified (PIA) 450
OV-10 (Rockwell) .... *(1987-88)* 495
Oblique-wing demonstrator F-8 (NASA) 447
Observer (Partenavia) .... *(1982-83)* 145
Observer P.68 (Partenavia) 162
Ocean Hawk (Sikorsky) 481
OFICINAS GERAIS DE MATERIAL AERONÁUTICO (Portugal) 196
OHMERT, VERNON R (USA) .... *(1980-81)* 534
Olive No. 2 (Mukai) .... *(1981-82)* 496
Olive SMG III (Mukai) .... *(1982-83)* 514
OLSEN, GORDON L (USA) .... *(1982-83)* 556
OMAC 1 (Omac) .... *(1983-84)* 450
OMAC INC (USA) 448
OMNIONICS (USA) .... *(1981-82)* 424
OMNIPOL FOREIGN TRADE CORPORATION (Czechoslovakia) 47
OMNI TITAN CORPORATION (USA) ... *(1987-88)* 486
OMNI WELD (USA) .... *(1985-86)* 605
One-Eleven (BAe) .... *(1984-85)* 264
One-Eleven (IAv Bucuresti) 208, 302
One-Eleven, Auxiliary Fuel System (Cranfield) 296
One-Eleven, Tay (BAe) 287
O'NEILL AIRPLANE COMPANY (USA) (1987-88) 480
ONISHI, MR (Japan) .... *(1978-79)* 486
OPTICA AVIATION (UK) .... *(1986-87)* 304
Optica, EA7 (Edgley) .... *(1985-86)* 289
Optica (Optica) .... *(1986-87)* 304
Optica Scout (Brooklands) .... *(1987-88)* 311
Optica Scout Mk II (Brooklands) 294
Orao J22 (SOKO/CNIAR) 134
ORD-HUME, ARTHUR W. J. G. (UK) ... *(1979-80)* 497
Orion (Kawasaki) 167
Orion (Lockheed) 412
Orion, G.801 (Grinvalds) .... *(1982-83)* 500
Orion, Lockheed P-3B, upgrade (Boeing) ... *(1985-86)* 364
Orion, operation ability modified (Cranfield) 296
ORLANDO HELICOPTER AIRWAYS INC (USA) 449
Orlik (WSK-PZL Warszawa-Okecie) 194
Osprey (Bell/Boeing) 348
Otter, DHC-3/1000 (Airtech) 17
OWL, GEORGE JR (USA) .... *(1981-82)* 539

P

P1 Bandeirante (EMBRAER) .... *(1984-85)* 11
P2 Bandeirante (EMBRAER) .... *(1984-85)* 12
P-2J (Kawasaki) .... *(1980-81)* 137
P2V-5 Tanker conversion (Evergreen) .... *(1987-88)* 413
P2V-7 (P-2H) VSA (Kawasaki) .... *(1981-82)* 143
P-3 (Lockheed) 412
P3 Rattler (Luscombe) .... *(1985-86)* 291
P-3A conversions (Lockheed) 420
P3B Viper (Luscombe) .... *(1985-86)* 291
P-3B Orion uprgrade (Boeing) .... *(1985-86)* 364
P-3C Orion (Kawasaki) 167
P-9D (McDonnell Douglas) 431
P-51B Mustang scale replica (Meyer) .... *(1983-84)* 567
P-51D Mustang Replica (Fisher-Van Norman) .... *(1980-81)* 520
P.66C-160 Charlie (Partenavia) .... *(1984-85)* 153
P.66T Charlie Trainer (Partenavia) .... *(1984-85)* 153
P.68 Floatplane/amphibian (Partenavia) .... *(1981-82)* 137
P.68 (Partenavia) 161
P.68B Victor (Partenavia) .... *(1981-82)* 137
P.68C Observer (Partenavia) 162
P.68C-R (Partenavia) .... *(1981-82)* 137
P.68R (Partenavia) .... *(1981-82)* 138
P.68RTC (Partenavia) .... *(1980-81)* 127
P.68WB (Partenavia) .... *(1980-81)* 127
P.70 Acey Deucy (Powell) .... *(1985-86)* 610
P.78 (Aeritalia) .... *(1981-82)* 121
P.78 (Partenavia) .... *(1982-83)* 145
P.86 (Aviolight) 160
P.95 (EMBRAER) 11
P120 (CATIC) .... *(1987-88)* 38
P.166-DL2 (Piaggio) .... *(1978-79)* 110
P.166-DL3 (Piaggio) 165
P.166-DL3-MAR (Piaggio) .... *(1983-84)* 152
P.180 (Piaggio) 163
P.210 Centurion Conversion (Air America) . *(1986-87)* 330
P.210 Rocket (Riley) 461
P.210 Turbine (Advanced Aircraft) 320
P-300 Equator (Equator) .... *(1984-85)* 85
P337 Pressurised Skymaster (Cessna) .... *(1980-81)* 320
P-350 Equator (Equator) .... *(1984-85)* 85
P-400 Equator (Equator) .... *(1984-85)* 85
P-420 Turbo Equator (Equator) .... *(1984-85)* 85
P.450 Equator (Equator) .... *(1984-85)* 85
P-550 Turbo Equator (Equator) .... *(1984-85)* 85
PA-18-150 Super Cub (Piper) 451
PA-18-150 Super Cub (WTA/Piper) .... *(1987-88)* 532
PA-23-250 Aztec (Piper) .... *(1982-83)* 435
PA-23T-250 Turbo Aztec (Piper) .... *(1982-83)* 435
PA-25-235 Pawnee D (Piper) .... *(1982-83)* 435
PA-28 Cherokee conversion (Isham/Piper) .. *(1984-85)* 426
PA-28-140/-151 (RAM/Piper) 460
PA-28-161 Cadet (Piper) 452
PA-28-161 Warrior II (Piper) 451
PA-28-181 Archer II (Piper) 452
PA-28-201T Turbo Dakota (Piper) .... *(1981-82)* 430
PA-28-236 Dakota (Piper) 453
PA-28R-201 Arrow III (Piper) .... *(1978-79)* 399
PA-28R-300 Pillan (Indaer Chile/Piper) .... *(1983-84)* 32
PA-28R-300XBT (Piper) .... *(1985-86)* 480
PA-28RT-201 Arrow IV (Piper) .... *(1982-83)* 437
PA-28RT-201T Turbo Arrow IV (Piper) 452
PA-31 Navajo (Piper) .... *(1983-84)* 455
PA-31-325 Navajo C/R (Piper) .... *(1984-85)* 471
PA-31-350 Chieftain (Piper) .... *(1986-87)* 481
PA-31-350 T-1020 (Piper) .... *(1985-86)* 488
PA-31P-350 Mojave (Piper) .... *(1986-87)* 482
PA-31T Cheyenne II (Piper) .... *(1984-85)* 474
PA-31T-1 Cheyenne IA (Piper) .... *(1986-87)* 483
PA-31T-2 Cheyenne IIXL (Piper) .... *(1986-87)* 484
PA-31T-3 T-1040 (Piper) .... *(1985-86)* 489
PA-32-300 SIX 300 (Piper) .... *(1979-80)* 408
PA-32RT-300 Lance II (Piper) .... *(1980-81)* 408
PA-32RT-300T Turbo Lance II (Piper) .... *(1980-81)* 408
PA-32-301 Saratoga (Piper) 453
PA-32-301T Turbo Saratoga (Piper) .... *(1984-85)* 469

PA-32R-301 Saratoga SP (Piper) 454
PA-32R-301T Turbo Saratoga SP (Piper) 454
PA-34-220T Seneca III (Piper) 457
PA-36 Brave (Piper) (1982-83) 446
PA-36 New Brave (WTA/Piper) 497
PA-38-112 Tomahawk II (Piper) (1984-85) 477
PA-40 Arapaho (Piper) (1980-81) 416
PA-42-720 Cheyenne IIIA (Piper) 455
PA-42-1000 Cheyenne 400 (Piper) 456
PA-44-180 Seminole (Piper) (1983-84) 463
PA-44-180T Turbo Seminole (Piper) (1982-83) 447
PA-46-310P Malibu (Piper) 458
PA-48 Enforcer (Piper) (1985-86) 488
PA-60 Aerostar 600A (Piper) (1984-85) 478
PA-60-700P Aerostar 700P (Piper) (1985-86) 488
PAC (see Pacific Aerospace Corporation Limited) 178
PAC (see Pakistan Aeronautical Complex) 179
PAC (see Philippine Aircraft Company) 180
PACE (see Goode, Richard) (1983-84) 534
PADC (see Philippine Aerospace Development Corporation) 180
PAF (see Philippine Air Force) (1982-83) 161
PAH-2 (Eurocopter) 120
PAH-2/HAC (MBB/Aérospatiale) (1983-84) 110
PAT (see Piper Advanced Technology Inc) (1981-82) 805
PAT-1 (PAT) (1981-82) 805
PATS/NSDB (see Philippine Air Transport & Training Services Inc/National Science Development Board) (1980-81) 153
PC-6 Turbo-Porter (Pilatus) 214
PC-6 Turbo-Porter Agricultural (Pilatus) (1986-87) 216
PC-7 Turbo-Trainer (Pilatus) 215
PC-7/CH Turbo-Trainer (Pilatus) 215
PC-9 (Pilatus) 216
PC-9/A Pilatus (HDH) 5
PC-12 (Pilatus) 217
PD-808 (Piaggio) (1978-79) 111
PDQ (see PDQ Aircraft Products) (1983-84) 574
PDQ-2 (PDQ) (1982-83) 560
PFM (Mooney) 445
PIA (see Pittsburgh Institute of Aeronautics) 450
PIK (see Polyteknikkojen Ilmailukerho) (1982-83) 496
PIK-21 Super Sytky (PIK) (1982-83) 496
PIK-23 Towmaster (Valmet) (1985-86) 50
PL-1 Laminar (Pazmany) (1979-80) 534
PL-1B (Pazmany) (1979-80) 534
PL-12 550T (Transavia) (1986-87) 8
PL-12 M300 (Transavia) (1985-86) 8
PL-12 Airtruk (Transavia) 7
PMB-78 Faucon (Milon) (1980-81) 481
PR-01 Pond Racer (Sealed Composites) 469
PRC (Aérospatiale) SA 365N Dauphin 2 (China) (1981-82) 34
PRC-105 (Lockheed) (1987-88) 445
PROCAER (see Progetti Costruzioni Aeronautiche) (1983-84) 153
PS-1 (Shin Meiwa) (1980-81) 142
PS-5 (HAMC) 37
PT-6 (NAMC) 41
PT NURTANIO (see PT Industri Pesawat Terbang Nurtanio) (1985-86) 98
PZL (see Zrzeszinie Wytworcow Sprzetu Lotniczegol Silnikowego PZL) 181
PZL-104 Wilga (WSK PZL-Okecie) 190
PZL-105 (WSK PZL-Warszawa-Okecie) 191
PZL-106B Kruk (WSK PZL-Warszawa-Okecie) 192
PZL-106AT Turbo-Kruk (WSK PZL-Okecie) (1985-86) 187
PZL-106BT Turbo-Kruk (WSK PZL Warszawa-Okecie) 193
PZL-107 Kawaka (WSK PZL-Warszawa-Okecie) (1983-84) 171
PZL-110 Koliber (WSK PZL-Warszawa-Okecie) 193
PZL-112 M-20 Mewa (Pezetel) (1978-79) 138
PZL-118 Mewa (WSK PZL-Mielec) (1986-87) 184
PZL-126 (WSK PZL-Warszawa-Okecie) 194
PZL-130 Orlik (WSK PZL-Warszawa-Okecie) 194
PZL-130T (WSK-PZL Warszawa—Okecie) (1986-87) 193
PZL-140 Gasior (WSK-PZL Warszawa-Okecie) 193
PACIFIC AEROSPACE CORPORATION LIMITED (New Zealand) 178
PAGE, LEONARD (USA) (1982-83) 558
PAKISTAN AERONAUTICAL COMPLEX (Pakistan) 179
Palomino (Palomino) (1984-85) 587
PALOMINO AIRCRAFT ASSOCIATES (USA) (1985-86) 606
Pampa, IA 63 (FAMA) 3
Pamela (Tucker) (1983-84) 590
PANAVIA AIRCRAFT GmbH (International) 129
Panda (GOHL) 37
Panther II (Colemill) 382
Panther Navajo (Colemill) 382
Panther Navajo/winglets (Colemill) (1985-86) 394
Panther SA 365M (Aérospatiale) 64
Paris Jet IV (Jacobs Jets) (1983-84) 572
Parkot Biplane (Parkot) (1985-86) 564
PARKOT, ROMAN (Poland) (1985-86) 564
PARTENAVIA COSTRUZIONI AERONAUTICHE SpA (Italy) 161
Passatt, MY 104 (Mylius) (1980-81) 84
Pathfinder (Piasecki) 450
Patroller (Maule) (1985-86) 448
Paulistinha 56 (CTA) 10
Pave Hawk (Sikorsky) 480
Pawnee D (Piper) (1982-83) 435
Pawnee conversion (Chincul/Piper) (1983-84) 3
Payloader, S-61 (Sikorsky) (1979-80) 441
Pchelka (Antonov) (1980-81) 179
PDQ AIRCRAFT PRODUCTS (USA) (1983-84) 574
PEACOCK AIRCRAFT LEASE & OVERHAUL LTD (Canada) (1983-84) 31
Pegaso, F.20 (General Avia) (1981-82) 136
Pegasus I (Frontier) (1981-82) 355
Pegasus II (Frontier) (1981-82) 355
Pegasus, M20L (Mooney) (1987-88) 476
Pegasus programme (Aérospatiale) (1979-80) 41
Pelican (Sikorsky) (1981-82) 459
Pelican, IAR-831 (ICA) 201
Perco Wasp (1982-83) 558
Peregrine (Gulfstream Aerospace) (1984-85) 415
Pereraca (Weber) (1982-83) 490
Performance 2000 (Cagny) 65
Petit Prince, DR 400/120 (Robin) (1979-80) 66
Petrel (Nash) 300
PEZETEL FOREIGN TRADE ENTERPRISE CO LTD (Poland) 181
Pezetel Thrush S2R-R3S (Ayres) (1984-85) 304
PFLUMM, MANFRED (Germany) (1981-82) 494
PHALANX ORGANISATION INC (USA) 450
Phantom, new wing (BAe) 287
Phantom II (McDonnell) (1981-82) 403
Phantom II, new windscreen (McDonnell Douglas) 424
Phantom F-4, modernised (Boeing/McDonnell Douglas) (1986-87) 380
Phantom 2000 (IAI) 141
PHILIPPINE AERONAUTICS TRAINING SCHOOL/NATIONAL SCIENCE DEVELOPMENT BOARD (Philippines) (1978-79) 137
PHILIPPINE AEROSPACE DEVELOPMENT CORPORATION (Philippines) 180
PHILIPPINE AIRCRAFT COMPANY (Philippines) 180
PHILIPPINE AIR FORCE (Philippines) (1982-83) 161
PHILIPPINE AIR TRANSPORT & TRAINING SERVICES INC/NATIONAL SCIENCE DEVELOPMENT BOARD (Philippines) (1980-81) 153
Phillicopter Mk 1 (VTOL Aircraft) 7
Phillips Phillicopter Mk 1 (VTOL) (1979-80) 9
Phoenix (Air-Plane) (1982-83) 518
Phoenix (Javelin/Mullens) (1982-83) 548
Phoenix F-22 (Taylorcraft) 492
Phoenix man-powered aircraft (To) (1982-83) 273
PIAGGIO SpA, INDUSTRIE AERONAUTICHE E MECCANICHE, RINALDO (Italy) 163
PIASECKI AIRCRAFT CORPORATION (USA) 450
Picchio, F15E (PROCAER) (1982-83) 146
PIETENPOL, BERNARD H. (USA) (1978-79) 532
Pigeon (Gatard) (1980-81) 476
PILATUS BRITTEN-NORMAN LTD (UK) 301
PILATUS FLUGZEUGWERKE A.G. (Switzerland) 214
Pillan (Enaer) 32
Pillan, PA-28R-300 (Indaer Chile) (1983-84) 32
Pillan (Piper) (1985-86) 480
Pillan, T35C (CASA/Enaer) (1985-86) 202
PIPER ADVANCED TECHNOLOGY INC (USA) (1981-82) 805
PIPER AIRCRAFT CORPORATION (USA) 451
Piranha 6 (ALR) (1987-88) 227
Piranha, IA 80 (Issoire) (1980-81) 67
PITTS AEROBATICS (USA) (1983-84) 467, 574
PITTSBURGH INSTITUTE OF AERONAUTICS (USA) 450
PLUMB, BARRY G (UK) (1983-84) 536
Pober P-9 Pixie (EAA) (1983-84) 556
Police R22 (Robinson) 462
Polonez, J-2 (Janowski) (1979-80) 489
POLSKIE ZAKLADY LOTNICZE (Poland) (1980-81) 153
POLYTEKNIKKOJEN ILMAILUKERHO (Finland) (1982-83) 496
Pond Racer (Scaled composites) 469
PORSCHE AVIATION PRODUCTS INC (USA) 459
Pouss Pou, GL03 (Landray) (1982-83) 504
POWELL, JOHN C. (USA) (1985-86) 610
PRACTAVIA LTD (UK) (1982-83) 268, 522
Predator, Model 59 (Rutan) (1983-84) 481
Predator, Model 480 (ATAC) (1986-87) 335
President 600 (Colemill) 383
President, HR 100/250TR (Robin) (1980-81) 72
Pressurised Centurion (Cessna) 376
Pressurised Skymaster (Reims) (1978-79) 58
Pressurised Skymaster I/II (Cessna) (1980-81) 320
PROCAER (see Progetti Costruzioni Aeronautiche Srl) (1985-86) 161
PROCTOR (see Procter Aircraft Associates Ltd.) (1980-81) 498
PROCTER AIRCRAFT ASSOCIATES LTD. (UK) (1980-81) 498
PROGETTI COSTRUZIONI AERONAUTICHE Srl (Italy) (1985-86) 161
Project 7307 En (PATS/NSBDB) (1978-79) 137
Protector (BAe) (1982-83) 246
'Project Stealth' (Lockheed) (1983-84) 415
PROMAVIA SA (Belgium) 8
Propfan (NASA/Lockheed) 420
Propfan test assessment programme (NASA) 447
Prop-Jet, XP-99 (Smith) (1985-86) 518
PROP-JETS INC (USA) (1986-87) 488
Prowler (Grumman) 396
Pterodactyl (Hallock) (1982-83) 544
PT INDUSTRI PESAWAT TERBANG NURTANIO (Indonesia) (1985-86) 98
Pucará IA58 (FAMA) 2
Pucará Charlie IA58C (FAMA) 3
Pucará IA66 (FAMA) 2
Pulsar (Partenavia) (1984-85) 156
Puma (Aérospatiale) 57
Puma (Nurtanio/Aérospatiale) (1984-85) 97
Puma, IAR-330L (ICA) 202
Pure Air Machine (Ludwig) (1981-82) 533
PÜTZER (see Sportavia-Pützer) (1980-81) 86

Q

Q-5 (NAMC) 39
Q-5M (NAMC) 41
QF-4B Phantom II (McDonnell) (1980-81) 380
QSRA (DH Canada) (1980-81) 25
QSRA (NASA/Boeing) (1981-82) 417
Qiang-5 (NAMC) 39
Qiangjiji-5 (NAMC) 39
Quail (Aerosport) (1983-84) 539
Quail A9B-M (AAMSA) (1983-84) 161
QUASAR, P. JEAN and P. MONTEL (France) (1985-86) 561
Quaser 200 (Quaser) (1985-86) 561
Queen Air B80 (Beechcraft) (1979-80) 271
Queenaire 800/8800 (Excalibur) 386
Queen Airliner B80 (Beechcraft) (1979-80) 271
Questor (Omni) (1985-86) 605
Quiet 727 (Valsan) 495
Quiet Short-Haul Research Aircraft (DH Canada) (1980-81) 25
Quiet Trader, BAe 146 (BAe) 285
Quiet turbofan propeller system (Raisbeck) 460

R

R-1 (Rivers) (1985-86) 615
R-11 (Joses) (1983-84) 505
R22 Alpha (Robertson) (1985-86) 493
R22 Beta (Robertson) 462
R22HP (Robinson) (1983-84) 477
R44 (Robinson) 463
R-95 (EMBRAER) (1981-82) 10
R172E (Cessna) (1981-82) 325
R172 Hawk XP (Cessna) (1982-83) 338
R172K Skyhawk conversions (Isham/Cessna) (1984-85) 426
R 235 Gabier (SOCATA) (1985-86) 81
R 235 Guerrier (SOCATA) 84
R 1180 Aiglon (Robin) (1984-85) 77
R 2000 Alpha series (Robin) (1984-85) 77
R 2112 Alpha (Robin) (1983-84) 76
R 2160 Alpha Sport (Robin) (1983-84) 76
P 3000 series (Robin) 82
RA-7E Corsair II (Vought) (1979-80) 457
RA-20 (Newman) (1982-83) 489
RA 110 (Reims Aviation) (1982-83) 74
RACA (see Representaciones Aero Commerciales Argentinas) SA (1984-85) 5
RAF (see Rutan Aircraft Factory) (1985-86) 612
RC-130 Hercules (Lockheed) 415
RE 2 Doppelraab (Ehmann) (1984-85) 544
REP-2 (Replogle) (1979-80) 538
RF-4 Phantom II (McDonnell) (1981-82) 403
RF-5E Tigereye (Northrop) (1986-87) 472
RF6 Sportsman (Sportavia) (1979-80) 79
RF6-180 Sportsman (Sportavia) (1979-80) 79
RF-6B (Fournier) (1981-82) 67
RF-19 (Lockheed) 411
RF-110 Phantom II (McDonnell) (1980-81) 380
RF-111C (General Dynamics) (1980-81) 345
RFB (see Rhein-Flugzeugbau GmbH) 95
RH-3 Sea King (Sikorsky) (1981-82) 458
RH-53 (Sikorsky) (1979-80) 443
RH-53D (Sikorsky) (1979-80) 443
RH-1100 (Hiller) (1985-86) 426
RH-1100 (Rogerson Hiller) 467
RJ-1 (Jastreb) (1979-80) 460
RLU (see Charles Roloff, Robert Liposky and Carl Unger) (1983-84) 578
RLU-1 Breezy (RLU) (1983-84) 578
RP-3D Orion (Lockheed) (1981-82) 390
R.R.1 Special (Rosebrugh) (1982-83) 492
RRA (see Ronchetti Razzetti Aviación SA) (1981-82) 4
RS 180 Sportsman (RFB) (1981-82) 86
RSH-1A, Coupe (Rotor Sport) (1982-83) 566
RTAF (SWDC) (see Royal Thai Air Force) 218
RTAF-4 Chandra (RTAF) (1983-84) 196
RTAF-5 (RTAF) (1987-88) 233
RU-21J (Beechcraft) (1985-86) 330
RV-1D (Grumman) (1983-84) 391
RV-5 Swinger (Van's) (1979-80) 550
Racer (Mortensen/Rutan) (1982-83) 556
Racer (Statler/Beck) (1983-84) 584
Rafale A (Dassault-Breguet) 70
Rafale B (Dassault-Breguet) (1986-87) 69
Rafale D (Dassault-Breguet) 71
Rafale M (Dassault-Breguet) 71
Rafale, R 2160 A (Robin) (1979-80) 68
Rail Mk II (Aerosport) (1982-83) 525
RAISBECK ENGINEERING INC (USA) 459
RAISBECK GROUP, THE (USA) (1980-81) 420
Rallye series (Socata) (1985-86) 81
RAM AIRCRAFT CORPORATION (USA) 460
RAM AIRCRAFT MODIFICATIONS INC (USA) (1983-84) 469
Ram air recovery system (Raisbeck) 460
Ram-M (USSR) 277
Rangemaster Model H (Navion) (1978-79) 391
Ranger (Grob) (1985-86) 88
Ranger (Luscombe) (1986-87) 299
Ranger (Mooney) (1980-81) 393
Ranger (UAT) 311
Ranger, DHC-7R (DH Canada) (1981-82) 25
RANKIN AIRCRAFT (USA) (1987-88) 493
Rat'ler (Helio) (1987-88) 435
Rattler, P3 (Luscombe) (1985-86) 291
Raven (Grumman/General Dynamics) 398
RAY'S AVIATION (USA) (1985-86) 615
Raz-Mut (St-Germain) (1981-82) 474
Real Sporty (Musso) (1981-82) 538
RED BARON FLYING SERVICE (USA) (1978-79) 535
Redigo (Valmet) 54
Red Wing Black Bird (Wallis) (1981-82) 562
Regent 1500 (Advanced Aircraft) 321
Régent, DR 400/180 (Robin) 81
Regianne 2000, scale (Tesori) (1983-84) 508
REIMS AVIATION SA (France) 79
Rekcub (Guex) (1979-80) 492
Remorqueur, DR 400/180R (Robin) 81
Renegade (Lake) 406
Renegade 1 (Lasher) (1983-84) 566

REPAIR AG ALTENRHEIN (Switzerland) (1980-81) 174
Replica Ike (Kovach) (1981-82) 532
Replica P-51D Mustang (Fisher-Van Norman) (1980-81) 520
REPLOGLE, E. H. (USA) (1979-80) 538
REPRESENTACIONES AEROCOMMERCIALES ARGENTINAS SA (Argentina) (1984-85) 5
Research Projects (PATA/NSDB (1979-80) 149
Retro, GB-2 (Bezzola) (1983-84) 531
Reusable Space Plane (USSR) 277
Revathi Mk II (India) (1978-79) 72
RHEIN-FLUGZEUGBAU GmbH (West Germany) 95
RICHTER, KLAUS J (Germany) (1982-83) 511
RILEY AIRCRAFT MANUFACTURING (USA) (1983-84) 470
RILEY INTERNATIONAL CORPORATION (USA) 461
Ring fin anti-torque device (Bell) (1982-83) 303
RIO CLARO, AÉRO CLUBE DE (Brazil) (1986-87) 17
RIVERS (see STONE, C. RIVERS) (1985-86) 615
ROBERTS, DON (USA) (1979-80) 538
ROBERTSON AIRCRAFT CORPORATION (USA) (1984-85) 484
ROBIN, AVIONS PIERRE (France) 81
ROBINSON HELICOPTER COMPANY INC (USA) 462
Rocket 340 (Riley) (1983-84) 471
Rocket P-210 (Riley) 461
Rocket Power 414 (Riley) (1983-84) 471
Rocket Powered 421 (Riley) (1978-79) 415
ROCKWELL INTERNATIONAL CORPORATION (USA) 463
ROCKWELL INTERNATIONAL/MBB (International) 132
ROGERSON HILLER CORPORATION (USA) 467
ROLOFF, CHARLES, ROBERT LIPOSKY & CARL UMGER (USA) (1983-84) 578
Rombac 1-11 (IAv Bucuresti) 197
RONCHETTI, RAZZETTI AVIACION SA (Argentina) (1981-82) 4
ROSEBRUGH, ROY H (Canada) (1982-83) 492
Rose Parakeet Replica (Borg) (1981-82) 513
Rotor Buggy, EBI (Boyette) (1983-84) 544
ROTOR MASTER AIRCRAFT (USA) (1979-80) 538
ROTOR SPORT HELICOPTERS INC (USA) (1982-83) 566
ROYAL THAI AIR FORCE (Thailand) 218
R/STOL SYSTEMS (USA) (1986-87) 499
RUSCHMEYER LUFTFAHRTTECHNIK (West Germany) 96
RUSSELL, Michael (USA) (1985-86) 616
Rutan 68 (Ams/Oil) (1984-85) 559
RUTAN AIRCRAFT FACTORY INC (USA) (1985-86) 503, 612

S

S-1 Pitts Special (Christen) (1987-88) 407
S1 Solar Wind (Venture) (1985-86) 542
S1B2 Arctic Tern (Arctic) 325
S-1D Pitts Special (Christen) (1987-88) 407
S-1E Special (Pitts) (1983-84) 574
S-1T Pitts Special (Christen) 381
S-2 (Sheppard) (1980-81) 544
S-2 Turbo Conversion (Marsh/Grumman) 422
S-2A Pitts Special (Christen) (1987-88) 407
S-2B Pitts (Christen) 381
S-2E (Pitts) (1983-84) 574
S2R Turbo Thrush (Ayres) 328
S2R-600 Thrush (Ayres) 327
S2R-R1820/510 Bull Thrush (Ayres) 327
S2R-T Turbo-Thrush (Marsh) 422
S-2S Pitts (Christen) 381
S-2T (Grumman) 400
S-3 Viking (Lockheed) 414
S.5 replica (Leisure Sport) (1979-80) 496
S-20 (MacDonald) (1979-80) 528
S-21 (MacDonald) (1979-80) 528
S25X Mr Smoothie (Sawano) (1980-81) 489
S25X II Tandem Smoothie (Sawano) (1980-81) 489
S-52 civil conversion (Orlando) 449
S-52-3 (VAT) 495
S-55/H-19 (Orlando) 449
S-55T (Helitec/Sikorsky) (1978-79) 349
S-58/H-34 (Orlando) 450
S-58T (California Helicopter) 373
S-58T (Sikorsky) (1978-79) 431
S-61 (Mitsubishi) 171
S-61A-4 (Agusta-Sikorsky) (1979-80) 115
S-61A-4 Nuri (Sikorsky) (1980-81) 435
S-61A/B (Sikorsky) (1983-84) 485
S-61D-4 (Sikorsky) (1980-81) 436
S-61L/N (Sikorsky) (1980-81) 435
S-61R (Sikorsky) (1983-84) 485
S-61R (Agusta-Sikorsky) (1986-87) 152
S-61/SH-3 Sea King (Sikorsky) 478
S-64 Skycrane (Sikorsky) (1978-79) 433
S-65A (Sikorsky) (1981-82) 460
S-65 (MCM (Sikorsky) (1978-79) 435
S-65-Oe (Sikorsky) (1978-79) 434
S-69 (Sikorsky) (1983-84) 486
S-70A (Sikorsky) 480
S-70B (Sikorsky) 481
S-70C (Sikorsky) 483
S-72 (RSRA) (Sikorsky) (1980-81) 440
S-72XI Wing project (Sikorsky) 486
S-75 ACAP (Sikorsky/US Army) (1986-87) 512
S-76 (Sikorsky) 486
S-76 Mark II (Sikorsky) 484
S-76B (Sikorsky) 485
S-80 (Sikorsky) 482
S-185 (Schapel) (1986-87) 505
S.205 AC (SIAI-Marchetti) (1980-81) 132
S.205/20R (SIAI-Marchetti) (1982-83) 139
S.208A (SIAI-Marchetti) (1982-83) 139
S.211 (SIAI-Marchetti) 157
S.226 (SIAI-Marchetti) (1983-84) 148
S 312 Tucano (Shorts) 308
S-325 Mini-Swat (Schapel) (1981-82) 455
S-350 Mini-Swat (Schapel) (1983-84) 481
S-525 Super Swat (Schapel) (1983-84) 481
S.700 Cormorano (SIAI/Marchetti) (1984-85) 151
S-1080 Thunderbolt (Schapel) (1983-84) 481
S-1275 Finesse (Schapel) (1983-84) 482
SA (Airbus) (1980-81) 97
S.A. III Swalesong (Coates) (1985-86) 568
SA 2-37A (Schweizer) 470
SA-3-120 Bulldog Series 120 (BAe) (1984-85) 264
SA-3-200 Bulldog (BAe) (1978-79) 223
SA30 Fanjet (Swearingen) 491
SA-32T (Swearingen) 491
SA-226TC Metro II (Swearingen) (1980-81) 443
SA227-AC Metro III (Fairchild Aircraft) 386
SA227-AT (Fairchild Aircraft) 388
SA227-AT Merlin IVC (Fairchild) (1983-84) 380
SA227-TT Merlin IIIC (Fairchild) (1983-84) 379
SA227 TT/41 (Fairchild Aircraft) 388
SA 315B Lama (Aérospatiale) 57
SA 315B Lama (HAL/Aérospatiale) (1987-88) 106
SA 316B Alouette III (Aéospatiale) 57
SA 316B Alouette III (HAL/Aérospatiale) (1987-88) 106
SA 319B Aloutte III (Aérospatiale) 57
SA 321 Super Frelon (Aérospatiale) (1983-84) 52
SA 330 Puma (Aérospatiale) 57
SA 330 Puma (Nurtanio/Aérospatiale) (1983-84) 97
SA 341 Gazelle (Aérospatiale/Westland) (1984-85) 54
SA 342 Gazelle (Aérospatiale/Westland) 59
SA 349-2 (Aérospatiale) (1978-79) 42
SA 360 Dauphin (Aérospatiale) (1984-85) 57
SA 360 C Dauphin (Aérospatiale) (1984-85) 57
SA 361H/HCL Dauphin (Aérospatiale) (1979-80) 49
SA 365C Dauphin 2 (Aérospatiale) (1982-83) 57
SA 365F/AS.15TT Dauphin 2 (Aérospatiale) 62
SA 365M Dauphin 2 (Aérospatiale) (1985-86) 57
SA 365M Panther (Aérospatiale) 64
SA 365N Dauphin 2 (Aérospatiale) 63
SA 366 Dauphin 2 (Aérospatiale) 63
SA-550 Spectrum-One (Spectrum) (1984-85) 493
SA-700 Acroduster 1 (Stolp) (1982-83) 575
SA-882 Flying Wing (Schapel) (1986-87) 505
SA-981 Swat (Schapel) (1983-84) 481
SABCA (see Société Anonyme Belge de Constructions Aéronautiques) 9
SAC (see Shenyang Aircraft Company) 42
SAC (see Spectrum Aircraft Corporation) (1984-85) 493
SACAB (see Scandinavian Aircraft Construction AB (Sweden) 212
SADLIER (see VTOL Industries Australia Ltd) 6
SAH-1 (Trago Mills) 311
SAI (see Singapore Aircraft Industries) 203
SAIC (see Shanghai Aviation Industrial Corporation) 43
SARA II (CSIR) (1978-79) 151
SARA III (CSIR) (1980-81) 166
SB-4 (Seabird) 6
SBD-3 Dauntless (Roberts) (1979-80) 538
SC.7 Skyvan Series 3 (Shorts) (1987-88) 307
SC.7 Skyvan Series 3M (Shorts) 307
SC-95B (EMBRAER) 10
SC 01 Speed Canard (Gyroflug) (1987-88) 97
SC01B Speed Canard (Gyroflug) 91
SD3-M (Shorts) (1980-81) 247
SD3-MR Seeker (Shorts) (1980-81) 247
SE-86 (CAI) (1987-88) 217
SE 3160 Alouette III (Aérospatiale) (1981-82) 45
SEPECAT (see Société Européenne de Production de l'Avion ECAT) 133
SF-2A Cygnet (Sisler) (1983-84) 580
SF-5A/B (Northrop) (1978-79) 392
SF 37 Viggen (Saab) (1984-85) 196
SF.260A (SIAI-Marchetti) (1980-81) 132
SF.260D (SIAI-Marchetti) 155
SF 260M (SIAI-Marchetti) 155
SF.260SW Sea Warrior (SIAI-Marchetti) 155
SF.260TP (SIAI-Marchetti) 156
SF.260W Warrier (SIAI—Marchetti) 155
SF 340A (Saab-Scania) (1986-87) 208
SF.600 Canguro (SIAI-Marchetti) (1982-83) 139
SF.600TP Canguro (SIAI-Marchetti) 158
SH-2 (Kaman) 404
SH-2D LAMPS (Kaman) (1982-83) 397
SH-3 Sea King (Sikorsky) (1983-84) 485
SH-3D (Agusta-Sikorsky) (1984-85) 145
SH-3D/TS (Agusta-Sikorsky) 153
SH-3H (Agusta-Sikorsky) 153
SH-5 (HAMC) 37
SH 37 Viggen (Saab) (1984-85) 196
SH-60B (Sikorsky) 481
SH-60F (Sikorsky) 481
SH-60J (Mitsubishi) 171
SH-200 (Silvercraft) (1978-79) 115
SK-1 Trempik (Simunek/Kamaryt) (1982-83) 495
SK 37 Viggen (Saab) (1984-85) 196
SKT-125 Sunday Knight Twister (Payne) (1979-80) 533
SKT-1250, Holiday Knight Twister (Payne) (1985-86) 608
SM.1019E (SIAI-Marchetti) (1982-83) 140
SN 601 Corvette (Aérospatiale) (1978-79) 37
SOCATA (see Société de Construction d'Avions de Tourisme et d'Affaires) 84
SOKO (see Sour Vazduhoplovna Industrija Soko) 498
SONACA (see Société Nationale de Construction Aérospatiale SA) 9
SRA-4 (Gulfstream/Aerospace) 401
SS-1 (Scholz-Schmitz) (1979-80) 485
SS-2 (Shin Meiwa) (1981-82) 148
SS-2A (Shin Meiwa) 172
SSVV (see Sezione Sperimentale Volo a Vela) (1980-81) 135
ST-220 (Akasamitra) (1985-86) 98
ST-600-S/8 (Foxjet) (1979-80) 337
ST 1700 Conestoga (Skytrader) 487
ST 1700 MD Evader (Skytrader) 487
STAF (see Shaanxi Transport Aircraft Factory) 43
STOL improvements (Seaplane Flying) (1979-80) 439
STOVL programme (NASA) 447
Su-7B (Sukhoi) 257
Su-9 (Sukhoi) (1983-84) 230
Su-11 (Sukhoi) (1983-84) 230
Su-15 (Sukhoi) 257
Su-17 (Sukhoi) 258
Su-19 (Sukhoi) (1979-80) 207
Su-20 (Sukhoi) 258
Su-21 (Sukhoi) (1987-88) 274
Su-22 (Sukhoi) 258
Su-24 (Sukhoi) 259
Su-25 (Sukhoi) 260
Su-26 (Sukhoi) (1985-86) 253
Su-26M (Sukhoi) 261
Su-27 (Sukhoi) 262
SW-4 (WSK-PZL Swidnik) 190
SWL (Rockwell) (1978-79) 422
WS 70 (Sikorsky-Westland) (1987-88) 338
SY Motor Glider (Yamato) (1980-81) 490
SAAB/FAIRCHILD AIRCRAFT (International) (1985-86) 124
SAAB-SCANIA AKTIEBOLAG (Sweden) 208
Saab 35 (Saab-Scania) 212
Saab 37X (Saab) (1981-82) 177
Saab 105 (Saab-Scania) 212
Saab-114 (Sab) (1983-84) 190
Saab 340A (Saab-Scania) 208
Saab 340B (Saab-Scania) 209
Saab 2110 Gripen (Saab) (1983-84) 189
Sabre 2 (CAC) 36
Sabreliner 40R (Rockwell) (1982-83) 464
Sabreliner 60 (Rockwell) (1979-80) 432
Sabreliner 60A (Rockwell) (1978-79) 425
Sabreliner 65 (Rockwell) (1982-83) 464
Sabreliner 75A (Rockwell) (1979-80) 432
Sabreliner 80A (Rockwell) (1978-79) 426
Sabreliner 85 (Rockwell) (1979-80) 434
SABRELINER CORPORATION (USA) 468
SABRELINER DIVISION, ROCKWELL INTERNATIONAL (USA) (1983-84) 480
Sabre Super Searcher (Sabreliner) (1987-88) 501
SADLER AIRCRAFT COMPANY (USA) 468
SADLIER (Australia) 6
Safari (Saab) (1981-82) 178
Safari TS (Saab) (1981-82) 178
Salon, Mi-8 (Mil) (1983-84) 223
Samurai 350 (Merlyn) 442
SANDBERG, JOHN (USA) (1984-85) 596
SANDERS AIRCRAFT INC (USA) (1984-85) 493
Saratoga (Piper) 453
Saratoga SP (Piper) 454
SAO CARLOS (see Escola De Engenharia de São Carlos) (1986-87) 17
SARCUP programme (Boeing Canada/CAF) (1985-86) 19
SAWANO, SHIRO (Japan) (1980-81) 489
SAWYER, RALPH (USA) (1978-79) 538
Scale NGT (Fairchild/Ames) (1982-83) 364
Scale Regianne 2000 (Tesori) (1983-84) 508
SCALED COMPOSITES INC (USA) 469
Scamp Model B (Agricopteros/Aerosport) (1984-85) 42
SCANDINAVIAN AIRCRAFT CONSTRUCTION AB (Sweden) 212
SCENIC AIRLINES INC (USA) (1987-88) 502
SCENIC AVIATION SERVICES (USA) (1980-81) 433
SCHAFER AIRCRAFT MODIFICATIONS INC (USA) 469
SCHAPEL AIRCRAFT COMPANY (USA) (1986-87) 505
SCHILLING, ING HORST (West Germany) (1979-80) 485
SCHOENENBERG, HEINRICH (Germany) (1984-85) 544
SCHOLZ, MANFRED (West Germany) (1979-80) 485
SCHOLZ-SCHMITZ (see Scholz, Manfred) (1979-80) 485
SCHWEIZER AIRCRAFT CORPORATION (USA) 470
Scooter (Flaglor) (1979-80) 521
Scorchy, M-102 (Mace) (1981-82) 534
Scorpion 133 (RotorWay) (1984-85) 596
Scout, 8GCBC (Champion) (1985-86) 392
Scout (Bellanca/Champion) (1980-81) 287
Scout (Skycraft) (1980-81) 8
Scout A (Skytrader) 488
Scout Defender (Hughes) (1985-86) 461
Scout STOL (Skytrader) 487
SEABIRD AVIATION AUSTRALIA PTY LTD (Australia) 6
SeaCobra (Bell) 343
Sea Dragon (Sikorsky) 478
Seafire, TA16 (IAC) 402
Sea Harrier (BAe) 291
Sea Hawk (Aero Gare) (1984-85) 558
Seahawk SH-60B (Sikorsky) 481
Sea Hawker (Leg Air) (1985-86) 599
Sea King (Sikorsky) (1982-83) 470
Sea King (Westland) 314
Sea Knight (Boeing) 364
Sea Patrol (Gates Learjet) 81-82
SEAPLANES INC (USA) (1985-86) 507
SeaRanger, TH-57 (Bell) 342
Searchmaster (GAF) (1985-86) 7
Sea Scan (IAI) (1986-87) 136
Seasprite (Flight Dynamics) (1984-85) 574
Seasprite (Kaman) 404
Sea Stallion (Sikorsky) (1982-83) 472
Seastar (Claudius Dornier) 86
Seastar (Ingenieurburo Dornier) (1983-84) 88
Sea Thrush (Speciality Aircraft Sales) (1985-86) 30
Sea Warrior (SIAI-Marchetti) 155

Seawolf (Lake)		406
Seeker, SD3-MR (Shorts)	*(1979-80)*	248
SEGUIN AVIATION INC (USA)		473
SÉGUIN, M (France)	*(1980-81)*	486
Séguin/Adams-Wilson Helicopter (Séguin)	*(1980-81)*	486
SELCHER, JOHN L. (USA)	*(1985-86)*	616
SELLET/PELLETIER HELICOPTÈRE (France)		84
Seminole (Piper)	*(1983-84)*	463
Semurg (MAI)	*(1984-85)*	222
Seneca II (EMBRAER/Piper)	*(1982-83)*	18
Seneca III (EMBRAER/Piper)		18
Seneca III, PA-34-220T (Piper)		457
Senior Aero Sport (D'Apuzzo)	*(1983-84)*	552
Sentinel, F-27 (Fokker)	*(1985-86)*	171
Sentinel, SB-4 (Seabird)		6
Sentry AEW Mk I (Boeing)		350
Sentry, E-3 (Boeing)		350
Sentry 02-337 (Summit)		489
SEPECAT (see Société Européenne de Production de l'avion E.C.A.T.)		133
SEREMET W. VINCENT (Denmark)	*(1980-81)*	471
Series 12X (EMBRAER)	*(1978-79)*	14
Sertanejo (EMBRAER/Piper)	*(1985-86)*	16
SERV-AERO ENGINEERING INC (USA)	*(1984-85)*	497
SEZIONE SPERIMENTALE VOL A VELA (Italy)	*(1980-81)*	135
SHAANXI TRANSPORT FACTORY (China)		43
Shadow (Sikorsky)		486
Shama (Wells)	*(1985-86)*	634
SHANGHAI AVIATION INDUSTRIAL CORPORATION (China)		43
Shark (Enstrom)	*(1985-86)*	396
Shennong-1 (CATIC)		34
SHENYANG AIRCRAFT COMPANY (China)		42
Shenyang JJ-5 (China)	*(1983-84)*	33
Shenyang/Tianjin JJ-6 (State Aircraft Factories)	*(1984-85)*	35
Sherpa (Shorts)		306
SHEPPARD, H. GORDON (USA)	*(1980-81)*	544
Sheriff (Aircraft Designs/Britten)	*(1983-84)*	248
SHESTAVIN, STANISLAV (USSR)	*(1984-85)*	550
SHIN MEIWA INDUSTRY CO., LTD. (Japan)		172
Shiokaratombo (Hamao)	*(1979-80)*	486
Shoestring (Condor)	*(1983-84)*	550
SHORT BROTHERS PLC (UK)		304
Short-field enhancement system (Raisbeck)		460
SHOWA HIKOKI KOGYO KABUSHIKI KAISHA (Japan)	*(1983-84)*	160
Shrike Commander 500S (Rockwell International)	*(1980-81)*	431
Shui Hong (China)	*(1983-84)*	38
Shuihong-5 (HAMC)		37
Shuishang Hongzhaji (HAMC)		37
Shuttle Carrier Aircraft (NASA/Boeing)	*(1979-80)*	395
Shuttle Orbiter (USSR)		277
Shuttle Spacecraft (Rockwell International)		466
Shuttle Training Aircraft (NASA)	*(1980-81)*	395
SIAI-MARCHETTI SpA (Italy)		155
Sierra 200 (Beechcraft)	*(1984-85)*	306
SIERRA INDUSTRIES INC (USA)		473
SIKORSKY AIRCRAFT, DIVISION OF UNITED TECHNOLOGIES CORPORATION (USA)		478
Silver (Agusta-Sikorsky)		154
SILVERCRAFT SpA (Italy)	*(1979-80)*	126
SIMUNEK, JAN & KAMARÝT, JAROSLAV (Czechoslovakia)	*(1982-83)*	495
Simurg (Artomov)	*(1982-83)*	517
SINDLINGER AIRCRAFT (USA)	*(1982-83)*	568
SINFIELD, ROLAND A (USA)	*(1979-80)*	539
SINGAPORE AIRCRAFT INDUSTRIES PTL LTD (Singapore)		203
SingleTwin (Aerofan)	*(1986-87)*	329
SISLER AIRCRAFT COMPANY (USA)	*(1983-84)*	580
Skipper, Model 77 (Beechcraft)	*(1984-85)*	306
SKYCRAFT PTY LTD (Australia)	*(1980-81)*	8
Skycrane (Sikorsky)	*(1978-79)*	433
Skycycle (Todhunter)	*(1980-81)*	465
Sky Dancer (Bond)	*(1984-85)*	562
Skyfarmer (Transavia)		7
Skyfox (Boeing)	*(1987-88)*	393
SKYFOX CORPORATION (USA)	*(1985-86)*	517
Skyhawk (Cessna)		374
Skyhawk (Douglas)	*(1980-81)*	390
Skyhawk/100 (Reims)	*(1978-79)*	57
Skyhawk/100 (Reims/Cessna)	*(1982-83)*	74
Skyhawk/100, F172 (Reims/Cessna)	*(1986-87)*	78
Skyhawk A-4PTM (Grumman/McDonnell Douglas)	*(1986-87)*	424
Skyhawk R172K conversions (Isham/Cessna)	*(1984-85)*	426
Skyhawk Conversion (LAS/McDonnell Douglas)	*(1978-79)*	358
Skyhawk upgrade (IAI)		141
Skyhook (Australian Autogyro)		4
Skyhook Mini Chopper (Minty)	*(1983-84)*	9
Skyjacket II (Sawyer)	*(1978-79)*	538
Sky Knight (Hughes)	*(1982-83)*	390
Skylane (Cessna)		374
Skylane RG (Cessna)		374
Skylark (Larkin)	*(1980-81)*	528
Skyliner (Shorts)	*(1980-81)*	248
Skymaster (Cessna)	*(1981-82)*	336
Skymaster (Reims/Cessna)	*(1980-81)*	70
Skymaster II (Cessna)	*(1981-82)*	336
Sky Knight (Schweizer)		473
Sky-Rider (Kimberley)	*(1980-81)*	465
Skyrocket (Bellanca)	*(1985-86)*	348
Skyrocket II (Bellanca)	*(1980-81)*	288
Skyservant, Do 28 D2 (Dornier)	*(1987-88)*	93
Skyservant (Dornier)	*(1981-82)*	77
SKY SPORTS INTERNATIONAL (USA)	*(1980-81)*	441
SKYTRADER CORPORATION (USA)		487
Skytrader 800 (Dominion)	*(1979-80)*	330
Skyvan SC.7 Series 3	*(1987-88)*	325

SMITH, MRS. FRANK W. (DOROTHY) (USA) (1982-83) 570
SMITH AERO INC, MIKE (USA) 488
SNIPE AIRCRAFT DEVELOPMENTS LTD (UK) (1985-86) 305
SOCATA/MOONEY (International) (1987-88) 140
SOCIEDADE CONSTRUCTORA AERONAUTICA NEIVA, LTDA. (Brazil) (1979-80) 16
SOCIÉTÉ ANONYME BELGE DE CONSTRUCTIONS AÉRONAUTIQUES (Belgium) 9
SOCIÉTÉ DE CONSTRUCTION D'AVIONS DE TOURISME ET D'AFFAIRES (France) 84
SOCIÉTÉ EUROPÉENNE DE PRODUCTION DE L'AVION E.C.A.T. (International) 133
SOCIÉTÉ ISSOIRE-AVIATION (France) (1980-81) 67
SOCIÉTÉ NATIONALE DE CONSTRUCTION AÉROSPATIALE SA (Belgium) 9
SOCIÉTÉ NATIONALE INDUSTRIELLE AÉROSPATIALE (France) (1981-82) 43
SOCIÉTÉ NOUVELLE WASSMER AVIATION (France) (1978-79) 64
Soim, IAR-99 (IAv Craoiva) 199
SOKO/CNIAR (International) 134
Sokol W-3 (WSK-PZL Swednik) 189
Solar Challenger (MacCready) (1982-83) 410
Solar One (To) (1980-81) 249
SOLAR-POWERED AIRCRAFT DEVELOPMENTS (UK) (1982-83) 273
Solar Riser (UFM) (1980-81) 555
Solar Wind (Venture) (1985-86) 542
Solitaire (MAI) (1985-86) 445
SOLOY CONVERSIONS LTD (USA) 488
Solution (Weeks) (1982-83) 582
SOUR VAZDUHOPLOVNA INDUSTRIJA SOKO (Yugoslavia) 498
SOUTHERN CLASSIC AEROPLANES (USA) (1985-86) 620
Southern Classic Biplane (Southern Classic) (1985-86) 620
Spaceplane studies (NAL) 172
Space Shuttle Orbiter Carrier (Boeing) (1979-80) 298
Space transportation system (Rockwell) 465
Sparrow (Nyge-Aero) (1986-87) 208
Sparrow Hawk (Aero Dynamics) (1985-86) 574
Sparrowhawk 12/35 (Ben-Air) (1982-83) 812
Spartacus, AP 68TP-300 (Partenavia) 162
Spartacus, Maritime Patrol Version (Partenavia) (1984-85) 156
Spartacus Series 300 (Partenavia) (1984-85) 155
Sparviero (Macera) (1984-85) 546
Sparviero, F.3500 (General Avia) (1986-87) 160
Special (Denight) (1984-85) 571
Special (Weeks) (1982-83) 582
Special Mission Aircraft (Fairchild Aircraft) 387
Special, R.R.1 (Rosebrugh) (1982-83) 492
Special S-1, Pitts (Christen) 407
Special S-1 (Pitts) (1983-84) 467
Special, S-1D/-1E (Pitts) (1983-84) 574
Special S-1T Pitts (Christen) 407
Special S-2A, Pitts (Christen) 407
Special S-2A (Pitts) (1983-84) 468
Special S-2B Pitts (Christen) 407
Special, S-2E/-2S (Pitts) (1983-84) 574
SPECIALISED AIRCRAFT CO (USA) (1978-79) 439
Special-Missions/Sea Patrol Version (Gates Learjet) (1981-82) 359
SPECIALTY AIRCRAFT SALES (Canada) (1986-87) 30
Spectre, AC-130U (Rockwell/Lockheed) 465
SPECTRUM AIRCRAFT CORPORATION (USA) (1984-85) 493
Spectrum-One (Spectrum) (1984-85) 493
Speed-Canard SC01 (Gyroflug) (1987-88) 88
Speed Canard (Gyroflug) 91
SPEZIO (USA) (1983-84) 583
Spirit (Pace) (1983-84) 534
Spirit 750 (Advanced Aircraft) (1985-86) 316
Spirit S-76 (Sikorsky) (1981-82) 463
SPITFIRE HELICOPTER COMPANY LTD (USA) (1986-87) 519
SPITFIRE HELICOPTERS INTERNATIONAL (Spain) (1985-86) 202
Spitfire Mark I (Spitfire) (1984-85) 508
Spitfire Mark II (Spitfire) (1984-85) 508
Spitfire Mark IV (Spitfire) (1983-84) 494
Sport 150 (Beechcraft) (1978-79) 257
Sport (Geide) (1982-83) 543
SPORT AIR CRAFT INTERNATIONAL (USA) (1981-82) 552
SPORTAVIA (see Sportavia-Pützer) (1980-81) 86
SPORTAVIA-PÜTZER GmbH ü CO KG (West Germany) (1980-81) 86
Sportsman, RS 180 (RFB) (1981-82) 86
Sportsman 100 (Taylorcraft) (1980-81) 451
Sportster, HA-2M (Hollmann) (1985-86) 595
Sport Trainer (Great Lakes) (1987-88) 424
SPRATT & COMPANY INC (USA) (1983-84) 583
Sprinter (Niemi) (1980-81) 534
Sprite (Practavia) (1981-82) 259, 505
Squalo, F.1300 (General Avia) (1985-86) 156
Stallion (Helio) (1987-88) 435
STARCK, ANDRE (France) (1982-83) 510
Starcraft (Maule) 424
Starfighter (Aeritalia/Lockheed) (1984-85) 134
Starfighter, F-104RB (Red Baron/Greenamyer) (1978-79) 535
Starfire Bonanza (Colemill) 383
StarLifter, C-141 (Lockheed) (1983-84) 423
Starship I (Beechcraft) 338
Star Rocket (Maule) 423
STATE AIRCRAFT FACTORIES (China) (1986-87) 33
Statesman (BAe) 285
Stationair (Cessna) (1978-79) 306
Stationair 6 (Cessna) 374
Stationair 8 (Cessna) (1984-85) 365
Statoplan AG 04 Pigeon (Gatard) (1989-81) 476
Statoplan AG 05 Mésange (Gatard) (1978-79) 475
Stellux 3esse3 Trenzo (Stellux) 165
STELLUX AIRCRAFT CORPORATION (Italy) 165
STEPHENS AIRCRAFT (USA) (1982-83) 573
STEWART AIRCRAFT CORPORATION (USA) (1985-86) 623
ST-GERMAIN, JEAN (see Centre de Recherches Jean St-Germain Inc) (1982-83) 490
Stinson 108-3 (Univair) (1987-88) 528
Stinson L-5 (SSVV) (1980-81) 135
STONE C. RIVERS (USA) (1985-86) 615
Strategic Reconnaissance Aircraft (USAF) 495
Stratofortress (Boeing) 368
Stratotanker, KC-135A (Boeing) 369
Strekoza (Kuybyshev) (1981-82) 500
Stretched Gazelle (Aérospatiale) (1984-85) 54
Strike Eagle, F-15 (McDonnell) (1981-82) 404
Strikemaster (BAe) (1981-82) 245
Strikemaster, total sales (BAe) 287
STRIPLIN AIRCRAFT CORPORATION (USA) (1981-82) 552
SUKHOI (USSR) 257
SUMMIT AVIATION INC (USA) 489
Sunbird (De Vore) (1986-87) 399
Sunbird (Verlite) 495
Sunday Knight Twister SKT-125 (Payne) (1980-81) 536
Sundowner 180 (Beechcraft) (1984-85) 306
Sup' Air (Centrair) (1987-88) 70
Super2 (Island Aircraft) 279
Super 71, 72, 73 (McDonnell Douglas) (1986-87) 453
Super 80 (Douglas) (1982-83) 419
Super 80 SF (Douglas) (1978-79) 380
Super 310 (Riley) 461
Super 340 (Riley) 461
SUPER 580 AIRCRAFT COMPANY (USA) 490
Super 580 (Super 580 Aircraft) 490
Super 580 Falcon (Super 580 Aircraft) 490
Super 580 ST (Super 580 Aircraft) 490
Super 748 (BAe) 283
Super BA-4B (Crosby/Andreasson) (1980-81) 494
Super F28 (VFW-Fokker) (1979-80) 146
Super T-40A (Turner) (1982-83) 578
Super Ag-Cat (Gulfstream American) (1981-82) 374
Super Ag-Cat B/450 (Schweizer) (1981-82) 456
Super Ag-Cat C/600 (Schweizer) (1981-82) 456
Super Ag Max (Aero Mod) (1987-88) 342
Super Beaver (Wipaire) 497
Super Bug (Bensen) (1983-84) 542
Super Courier Model H-295 (Helio Courier) (1978-79) 348
Super Cub (Piper) 451
Super Cub, PA-18-150 (WTA/Piper) (1987-88) 532
SuperCobra (Bell) 343
Super Decathlon (Bellanca) (1979-80) 288
Super Decathlon (Champion) (1985-86) 391
Super Etendard (Dassault-Breguet) 70
Super Fli, K-1 (Kraft) (1982-83) 550
Super Foxbat (MiG) (1981-82) 206
Super Frelon (Aérospatiale) (1983-84) 52
Super Galeb (Soko) 498
Super Guppy (Airbus) (1982-83) 104
Super Gyro-Copter (Bensen) (1985-86) 578
Super Hornet (McDonnell Douglas) (1987-88) 460
Super Interceptor (Smith) (1980-81) 441
Super King Air B200 (Beechcraft) 333
Super King Air 200/B200 Military versions (Beechcraft) 335
Super King Air 300 (Beechcraft) (1987-88) 359
Super King Air A100 (Beechcraft) (1980-81) 274
Super King Air F90 (Beechcraft) (1981-82) 288
Super Lynx (Westland) 316
Super Mirage 4000 (Dassault-Breguet) (1986-87) 68
Super Mountaineer (Ector) (1985-86) 396
Supermunk (BGA) (1982-83) 260
Super Mystère B-2 (IAI/Dassault) (1980-81) 102
Super New Look (Starck) (1982-83) 510
Super Phantom (IAI) 142
Super Puma (A01) 53
Super Puma AS 332 (IPTN) 102
Super Puma AS 332 (Aérospatiale) 57
Super Puma Mk II (Aérospatiale) 59
Super Q (Comtran) 383
Super Quickie Q2 (Quickie) (1982-83) 563
Super Ranger (Luscombe) (1986-87) 300
Super Ranger (UAT) 312
Super Rocket (Maule) 423
SUPER ROTOR INDUSTRIA AERONAUTIC LTDA, M.M. (Brazil) 16
Super Seasprite (Kaman) 404
Super Simple I (Kinman) (1982-83) 550
Super Skyhawk (SAI) 203
Super Sportster (Turner) (1982-83) 579
Super Surubim, IPAI-28 (Rio Claro) (1984-85) 18
Super Stallion (Sikorsky) 478
Superstar I (Machen) (1985-86) 444
Superstar II (Machen) (1985-86) 444
Superstar III (Machen) (1985-86) 445
Superstar 650 (Machen) 421
Superstar 680 (Machen) 422
Super Swat S-525 (Schapel) (1983-84) 481
SuperTransport, Model 214ST (Bell) 345
Super Viking 300 (Bellanca) (1980-81) 287
Super Widgeon (McKinnon-Viking) (1980-81) 30
Supporter (Saab) (1979-80) 169
Surubim Modificado, IPT-16 (Rio Claro/IPT) (1979-80) 17
Surveiller (Boeing) (1987-88) 376
"SURVOL" CHARLES FAUVEL (France) (1979-80) 474
Sutlej (Antonov) 224
Swalesong (Coates) (1985-86) 568
Swat, SA-981 (Schapel) (1983-84) 481
SWEARINGEN ENGINEERING AND TECHNOLOGY INC. (USA) 490
SWEARINGEN AVIATION CORPORATION (USA) (1980-81) 443
Swinger (Van's) (1978-79) 550
SWISS FEDERAL AIRCRAFT FACTORY (F + W) (Switzerland) 217
Swiss Trainer (Dätwyler) 212
Sylkie One Model B-1 (Wayne) (1980-81) 504
Syuan Fen (China) (1980-81) 37
Szmiel (Kuybyshev) (1981-82) 500

T

T1 Flamingo-Trainer (FUS) (1983-84) 86
T-2 (Mitsubishi) 170
T-2CCV (Mitsubishi) (1986-87) 171
T-2 Buckeye (Rockwell) (1982-83) 461
T-3 (Fuji) (1982-83) 148
T-4 (Kawasaki) 167
T-12B (CASA) (1979-80) 165
T-17 (Saab) (1978-79) 159
T-18 Tiger (Thorp) (1985-86) 627
T-23 (Aerotec) (1979-80) 9
T-25 (Neiva) (1981-82) 17
T-25B (Neiva) (1980-81) 19
T-27 Tucano (EMBRAER) 13
T-34 Turbo Mentor (Marsh) (1983-84) 429
T-34C (Beechcraft) 329
T-34C, Laminar Flow Jetstar (NASA) (1986-87) 469
T-34V Turbotrainer (Volpar/Beechcraft) (1980-81) 451
T-35 (ENAER) 32
T-35C (CASA Enaer) (1985-86) 200
T-35T (ENAER) 33
T-35TX (ENAER Chile) (1987-88) 36
T-36 (CASA) 207
T-36 (ENAER) 33
T-37 (Cessna) (1978-79) 311
T-39 Sabreliner (Rockwell) (1979-80) 432
T-40A (Turner) (1982-83) 578
T-40A, Super (Turner) (1982-83) 578
T-40C (TEDDE) (1979-80) 550
T-41A Mescalero (Cessna) (1978-79) 300
T-41B/C/D Mescalero (Cessna) (1980-81) 308
T-42A Cochise (Beechcraft) (1982-83) 293
T-43A (Boeing) 353
T-44A (Beechcraft) (1982-83) 298
T-45 (McDonnell Douglas/BAe) (1984-85) 116, 450
T-45 Goshawk (McDonnell Douglas/BAe) 126, 287
T45 Turbine Dromader (Melex) 442
T45 Turbine Dromader (WSK-PZL Mielec) 184
T-45TS (McDonnell Douglas/BAe) (1987-88) 132
T-46A (Fairchild) (1987-88) 414
T-47A Citation S/II (Cessna) 376
T67 (Slingsby) 309
T67M Firefly 160 (Slingsby) 310
T67M200 Firefly (Slingsby) 310
T68 (Slingsby) (1983-84) 282
T69 (Slingsby) (1983-84) 282
T-80 Texas Tern (Turner) (1982-83) 577
T200 (Javelin) (1982-83) 548
T200A (Javelin) (1982-83) 820
T206/210 (RAM/Cessna) 460
T207 (RAM/Cessna) (1985-86) 491
T211 (Adams/Thorp) (1983-84) 292
T211 (Thorp) 493
T-250 Aries (Bellanca) (1980-81) 287
T-300 Skyfarmer (Transavia) (1981-82) 8
T-300A Skyfarmer (Transavia) (1981-82) 8
T303 Crusader (Cessna) 376
T310/320D-F (RAM/Cessna) 460
T-320 Airtruk (Transavia) (1979-80) 8
T-400 Skyfarmer (Transavia) 7
T-619 Cali (Super Pinto) (PAF/AJI) (1981-82) 157
T-1020 (Piper) (1985-86) 488
T-1040 (Piper) (1985-86) 489
TA-4 Skyhawk (Douglas) (1980-81) 390
TA-4S Skyhawk conversion (LAS) (1978-79) 358
TA-7 Corsair II, Vought (LTV) 420
TA9 (Airbus) (1982-83) 103
TA11 (Airbus) (1982-83) 104
TA12 (Airbus) (1982-83) 104
TA16 Seafire (IAC) 402
TAC (see Teal Aircraft Corporation) (1979-80) 27
TACAMO, E-6 (Boeing) 351
Tag-D (Berier) 229
TAI (see Tusas Aerospace Industries Inc) 219
TAI (see Tusas Havacilik ve Uzay Sanayii As) (1987-88) 234
TAP (see Thompson Aero Products) 492
TAV-8A (BAe) 290
TAV-8B (McDonnell Douglas/BAe) 124
TAV-8S (BAe) 290
TB 9 Tampico (SOCATA) 84
TB 10 Tobago (SOCATA) 84
TB 11 Tobago (SOCATA) (1983-84) 78
TB 16 (Socata) (1985-86) 83
TB 20/21 Trinidad (SOCATA) 85
TB 30 Epsilon (SOCATA) (1980-81) 76
TBM 700 (TBM) 135
TBN CORPORATION (International) 135
T-CH-1 (AIDC) 217
TE-2C Hawkeye (Grumman) 393
TEDDE (see Turner Educational Development Enterprises) (1979-80) 549
TF-1 Tomcat (Tru-Flite) (1978-79) 548
TF-6 (China) (1979-80) 29
TF-25 (Robertson) (1984-85) 486
TG-01 (Tsilefski) (1983-84) 526
TG-10 (Venga) 31
TG 180 Piper Cherokee Chief (Ray's) (1985-86) 615
TH-1S HueyCobra (Bell) 344
TH-57 SeaRanger (Bell) 342
TH.E.01 Tiger-Hawk (Mini-Hawk) (1981-82) 536
THvK (1984-85) 205
TIFS (Arvin/Calspan) (1982-83) 285
TJ-1 Jastreb Trainer (Soko) (1979-80) 460

TK-1 (Kako) (1979-80) 486
TL-1 (Fuji) (1982-83) 148
TL-1A (Birdman) (1980-81) 506
TM (see TM Aircraft) (1985-86) 628
TM-5 (TM) (1985-86) 628
TNT (New Technology Wing) testbed aircraft (Dornier) (1983-84) 82
TO (see Solar-Powered Aircraft Developments) (1982-83) 273
Tp 88 (Fairchild Aircraft) 386
Tp89 (CASA) 206
TR-1 (Lockheed) 411
TR-1 Trigull (Trident) (1981-82) 27
TR.12A (Casa) (1979-80) 165
TRANSAVIA (see Transfield Pty Ltd) 7
TS-11 Iskra-bis (WSK-PZL Mielec) 184
TSC-1 Teal (TAC) (1979-80) 27
TSC-1A3 Marlin (TAC) (1979-80) 27
TSW (Turner) (1980-81) 499
TSz-1 (Shestavin) (1984-85) 550
TT30 (Westland) (1987-88) 337
TT300 (Westland) (1987-88) 337
TTH90 (NH90) 128
TTTS (see Tanker/Transport Training System) 495
Tu-16 (Tupolev) 263
Tu-22 (Tupolev) 267
Tu-22M (Tupolev) 268
Tu-26 (Tupolev) (1982-83) 231
Tu-26 (Tupolev) 268
Tu-28P (Tupolev) 270
Tu-95 (Tupolev) 264
Tu-104A (Meteorological) (Tupolev) (1982-83) 233
Tu-126 (Tupolev) 266
Tu-128 (Tupolev) 270
Tu-134 (Tupolev) (1984-85) 248
Tu-142 (Tupolev) 264
Tu-144 (Tupolev) (1983-84) 241
Tu-144D (Tupolev) (1983-84) 142
Tu-154 (Tupolev) 270
Tu-154A/B (Tupolev) (1985-86) 263
Tu-154C (Tupolev) 271
Tu-154M (Tupolev) 270
Tu-155 (Tupolev) 271
Tu-164 (Tupolev) (1984-85) 250
Tu-204 (Tupolev) 272
TUSAS (see Türk Ucak Sanayii Anonim Ortakligi) (1985-86) 213
TX-1 (Mooney) (1985-86) 468
Taifun 11S (Valentin) 96
Taifun 12E (Valentin) (1987-88) 103
Taildragger' conversions (Bush/Bolen) 372
Tailwind (AJEP/Wittman) (1978-79) 213
Tailwind Model W-9 (Wittman) (1979-80) 553
Tamiz, E.26 (CASA) 208
Tamiz, E.26 (ENAER) 32
Tampico, TB 9 (SOCATA) 84
Tandem Smoothie (Sawano) (1980-81) 489
Tangará, A-132 (Aerotec) (1983-84) 10
Tangará II (Aerotec) 9
Tanker/Transport Training System (USAF) 495
Tapajos (EMBRAER) (1978-79) 14
Tarhe (Sikorsky) (1978-79) 433
TaskMaster (Frontier) (1981-82) 355
Tauro 300 (Anahuac) (1980-81) 145
Tauro 350 (Anahuac) (1981-82) 150
Taurus (Spitfire/WSK-PZL Swidnik) (1984-85) 508
Taurus (WSK-PZL Swidnik) (1985-86) 184
Taurus modification (Swearingen) 490
TAYLOR, C. GILBERT (USA) (1980-81) 552
TAYLOR, MRS. JOHN F. (UK) (1985-86) 570
TAYLORCRAFT AVIATION CORPORATION (USA) 492
T-cat (Gulfstream American) (1979-80) 352
Tchaika (Beriev) 228
Teal (TAC) (1979-80) 27
TEAL AIRCRAFT CORPORATION (Canada) (1979-80) 27
TEAL AIRCRAFT CORPORATION (USA) (1979-80) 451
TELEDYNE RYAN AERONAUTICAL (USA) 493
TENSA SA (Argentina) (1981-82) 4
Terr-Mar Turbo Sea Thrush (Ayres) 328
TESORI, ROBERT (Canada) (1983-84) 508
Texas Gem (Miller) (1985-86) 601
TEXAS HELICOPTER CORPORATION (USA) (1984-85) 510
Texas Ranger, Model 206L (Bell) (1984-85) 326
Texas Tern, T-80 (Turner) (1982-83) 577
THOMPSON AERO PRODUCTS (USA) 492
THOMPSON, DR NORMAN (USA) (1979-80) 552
THOMPSON, JOHN A. (USA) (1979-80) 551
THORP ENGINEERING COMPANY (USA) (1985-86) 627
Thorp T211 (Adams/Thorp) (1982-83) 283
Thorpe T211 (Intran) (1984-85) 425
THORP T211 AIRCRAFT INC (USA) 493
Thrush (Ayres) 327
Thrush, Ayres conversion (Aero Mod) (1987-88) 342
Thrush-600 (Ayres) (1981-82) 276
Thrush Commander (Ayres) (1978-79) 253
Thrush Commander-600 (Rockwell) (1978-79) 429
Thrush Commander-800 (Rockwell) (1978-79) 429
Thrush Commander/PT6 (Serv-Aero) (1978-79) 430
Thrush Commander/R-1820 (Serv-Aero) (1984-85) 497
Thrush Commander S-2R/Pezetal PZL-3 (Serv-Aero (1978-79) 430
Thrush modification (Serv-Aero/Ayres) (1984-85) 497
Thrush S2R-600 (Ayres) 327
Thunderbird 211 (Mod Squad) 442
Thunderbolt, S-1080 (Schapel) (1983-84) 481
Thunderbolt II (Fairchild Republic) (1987-88) 414
Tiara, HR 100/285 (Robin) (1979-80) 60
Tiger, AS332 (Aerospatiale) 57
Tiger (Gulfstream American) (1980-81) 355
Tiger (Thorp) (1985-86) 627
Tiger II (KA) 174
Tiger II (Northrop) 448
Tigereye, RF-5E (Northrop) (1986-87) 472
Tiger Hawk (Mini-Hawk) (1981-82) 536
Tigershark, F-20 (Northrop) (1986-87) 472
Tilt-rotor (Agusta) (1987-88) 161
Tilt-rotor aircraft (USSR) 277
TIMOFEYEV, VIKTOR (USSR) (1982-83) 518
Tira Prosa, IPAI-29 (São Carlos) (1983-84) 19
Titan Ambassador/II/III (Cessna) (1982-83) 353
Titan Courier/II (Cessna) (1982-83) 353
Titan Freighter/II (Cessna) (1982-83) 353
TM AIRCRAFT (USA) (1985-86) 628
Togago TB 10 (SOCATA) 84
Tobago, TB 11 (SOCATA) (1983-84) 78
TODHUNTER, R. W. (Australia) (1979-80) 465
Tomahawk (Piper) (1981-82) 415
Tomahawk II, PA-38-112 (Piper) (1984-85) 477
Tomahawk SP (Aero Boero/Piper) (1985-86) 1
Tomcat (Grumman) 397
Tom-Pouss (Koenig) (1980-81) 479
Tomcat, TF-1 (Tru-Flite) (1978-79) 548
Tonal,A129 (JEH) 123
Tonopah Low (Forbes) (1983-84) 558
Tornado ADV (Panavia) 131
Tornado ECR (Panavia) 131
Tornado F Mk 2/2A/3 (Panavia) 131
Tornado GR Mk 1 (Panavia) 129
Tornado IDS (Panavia) 129
Tornado Mid-Life improvement programme (Panavia) 131
Tornado, MY 102 (Mylius) (1985-86) 92
Toucan Mk II (HPA) (1979-80) 494
Tourbillon (Chasle) (1979-80) 470
Towmaster PIK-23 (Valmet) (1985-86) 50
TRAGO MILLS LTD(UK) 311
Trainer (Skyfox) (1985-86) 517
TRANSFIELD PTY LTD, TRANSFIELD DIVISION (AUSTRALIA) 7
TRANSALL, ARBEITSGEMEINSCHAFT (International) 136
Transonic Aircraft Technology (NASA) (1979-80) 396
Transporter, DHC-5E (Canada) (1984-85) 24
Travel Air Mystery S replica (Younkin) (1980-81) 560
Trempik, SK-1 (Simunek/Kamaryt) (1982-83) 495
Trenzo 3esse3 (Stellux) 165
Tri-Commutair, BN-2A Mk III (IAC/Pilatus Britten-Norman) (1984-85) 424
TriCoupé, JC-2D (Coupé Aviation) (1983-84) 514
Trident (VAe) (1979-80) 233
TRIDENT AIRCRAFT LTD (Canada) (1981-82) 27
Trigear Courier Model HT-295 (Helio Courier) (1978-79) 348
Trigull, TR-1 (Trident) (1981-82) 27
Trinidad (SOCATA) 85
Trislander, BN-2A Mk III (Pilatus Britten-Norman) (1982-83) 268
TriStar (Lockheed) 415
TriStar modification, civil (Marshall) 298
TriStar tanker conversion (Marshall) (1987-88) 315
Tri-Tail Bonanza (Smith) (1987-88) 522
Tri Turbo 3 (Tri-Turbo) (1979-80) 452
TRI-TURBO CORPORATION (USA) (1980-81) 447
Triumf, IAR-825TP (ICA) 200
TRU-FLITE (USA) (1978-79) 548
TSILEFSKI, G (France) (1983-84) 526
Tsunami (Sandberg) (1984-85) 596
Tuca, IPAI-26 (São Carlos) (1984-85) 19
Tucano, EMB312 (AOI) 53
Tucano, EMB-312 (EMBRAER) 13
Tucano (Shorts) 308
Tucano T Mk I (Shorts) 308
TUCKER, L. G. (USA) (1983-84) 590
Tuholer (Spezio) (1982-83) 572
Tupi, EMB-712 (EMBRAER)/Piper) 15
TUPOLEV (USSR) 263
Turbine 404 (Riley) (1983-84) 471
Turbine Bonanza (Allison) 324
Turbine Chancellor (Riley) (1984-85) 484
Turbine Defender (Pilatus Britten Norman) 302
Turbine Dromader (Melex) 442
Turbine Dromader (WSK-PZL Mielec) 184
Turbine Eagle 421 (Riley) (1983-84) 472
Turbine Islander (Pilatus Britten-Norman) 302
Turbine Malibu (Piper) 458
Turbine Malibu (Riley) (1984-85) 484
Turbine Mentor (Allison) 325
Turbine Mentor 34C (Beechcraft) 329
Turbine P-210 (Advanced Aircraft) 320
Turbine P-210 (Riley) (1983-84) 470
Turbine Pac conversions (Soloy) 488
Turbine Rocket 421 (Riley) 462
Turbo 18 (Volpar/Beechcraft) (1982-83) 483
Turbo 350 Bonanza (Machen) (1985-86) 445
Turbo Ag-Cat D (Gulfstream American) (1980-81) 356
Turbo Ag-Cat (Schweizer) (1981-82) 457
Turbo Air Tractor (Air Tractor) 344
Turbo-Albatros (Frakes) (1987-88) 417
Turbo Arrow IV (Piper) 452
Turbo Aztec (Piper) (1981-82) 426
Turbo-Beaver, DHC-2 Mk III (de Havilland Canada) (1984-85) 24
Turbo Bonanza, Model B36 TC (Beechcraft) 331
Turbo-Canso (Avalon) 18
Turbo-Cat (Frakes/Grumman) (1978-79) 329
Turbo Cat, G-162 C-T (Marsh) 422
Turbo Centurion (Cessna) 376
Turbo Commander 690B (Rockwell) (1979-80) 435
Turbo Dakota (Piper) (1981-82) 430
Turbo Equator (Equator) (1985-86) 87
Turbo Express, DC-3 (USAC) 528
Turbo Firecat (Conair) 29
Turbo Flagship ATF 580S (Allison) (1987-88) 346
Turbo-Goose, G-21G (McKinnon-Viking) (1980-81) 28
Turbo-Kruk (WSK-PZL Warszawa-Okecie) 193
Turbo Lance II (Piper) (1980-81) 408
Turbolet L-410UVP (Let) (1985-86) 44
Turbolet L-410UVP-E (LET) 48
Turboliner (Volpar/Beechcraft) (1982-83) 484
Turboliner II (Volpar/Beechcraft) (1982-83) 484
Turbo Mentor, T-34 (Marsh) (1983-84) 429
Turbo Mooney 231 (Mooney) (1984-85) 457
Turbo Orlik, PZL (Airtech Canada) 18
Turbo Orlik (WSK-PZL Warszawa-Okecie) 195
Turbo Otter (Cox) (1983-84) 372
Turbo-Panda, Y-12 (China) (1984-85) 41
Turbo Pillan (Enaer Chile) (1985-86) 32
Turbo-Porter (Pilatus) 214
Turbo-Porter Agricultural (Pilatus) (1986-87) 216
Turboprop Goose Conversion (McKinnon-Viking) (1980-81) 30
Turbo Renegade (Lake) 406
Turbo Saratoga (Piper) (1984-85) 469
Turbo Saratoga SP (Piper) 454
Turbo Sea Thrush (Ayres) 328
Turbo Seminole (Piper) (1982-83) 447
Turbo Single Otter (Cox) (1978-79) 21
Turbo Skylane (Cessna) (1984-85) 361
Turbo Skylane RG (Cessna) 374
Turbo-Skymaster/Skymaster II (Cessna) (1980-81) 319
Turbo-Skyservant, Do 128-6 (Dornier) (1981-82) 78
Turbo Star 402 (Scenic/AJI) (1979-80) 438
Turbo-Stationair 6 (Cessna) 374
Turbo-Stationair 8 (Cessna) (1984-85) 365
Turbo T310/T310 II (Cessna) (1981-82) 335
TURBOTECH IN (USA) 494
Turbo-Thrush S-2R (Ayres) 328
Turbo-Thrush, S2R-T (Marsh) 422
Turbo Titan (OMNI) (1987-88) 480
Turbo Tracker (Grumman) 400
Turbotrainer (Volpar/Beechcraft) (1980-81) 451
Turbo Trainer, AS 32T (FFA) (1983-84) 192
Turbo-trainer, PC-7 (Pilatus) 215
Turbo Trigull (Trident) (1980-81) 31
Turbo Viking (Bellanca) (1979-80) 286
TÜRK HAVA KUVVETLERI, KAYSERI HAVA IKMAL BAKIM MERKEZI KOMÜTANLIGI (Turkey) (1984-85) 205
TURKISH AIR FORCE (Turkey) (1984-85) 205
TURK UCcAK SANAYII ANONIM ORTAKLIGI (Turkey) (1985-86) 213
TURNER, BILL (USA) (1982-83) 579
TURNER, CHRISTOPHER (UK) (1980-81) 499
TURNER EDUCATIONAL DEVELOPMENT ENTERPRISES (USA) (1979-80) 549
TUSAS AEROSPACE INDUSTRIES INC (Turkey) 219
TUSAS HAVACILIK VE UZAY SANAYII AS (Turkey) (1987-88) 234
Twin Cat (Gulfstream American/Twin Cat) (1980-81) 447
TWIN CAT CORPORATION (USA) (1980-81) 447
Twin Equator (Equator) (1985-86) 87
Twin Hercules (Lockheed) (1980-81) 377
Twin Navion (Camair) (1980-81) 306
Twin Otter Series 300, DHC-6 (Boeing Canada) 21
TwinRanger (Bell) (1985-86) 340
TwinRanger (Bell Helicopter Textron) 20
TwinRanger (Luscombe) (1986-87) 300
Twin Ranger (UAT) 312
Twinstar (Aérospatiale) 61
Twin Star 1000 (Airmaster) 322
Twin Two-Twelve (Bell) (1987-88) 370
Twin Two-Twelve (Bell Helicopter Textron) 19
Type 02-337 Sentry (Summit) (1982-83) 479
Type 05-Ganagobie (ARDC of NZ) (1981-82) 498
Type 2 + 2, DR 400/100 (Robin) (1980-81) 66
Type 10A (Jones) (1983-84) 563
Type 30 (Westland) (1987-88) 337
Type 66-400 (HAL) (1982-83) 95
Type 66-600 (HAL) (1982-83) 95
Type 74 (HAL) (1982-83) 95
Type 75 (HAL) (1982-83) 95
Type 75 (UTVA) (1987-88) 534
Type 76 (HAL) (1982-83) 95
Type 77 (HAL) (1982-83) 95
Type 78 (UTVA) (1985-86) 529
Type 96 (HAL) (1982-83) 95
Type 101 (Tupolev) (1985-86) 262
Type 128-2 (Dornier) (1983-84) 81
Type 128-6 (Dornier) (1987-88) 93
Type 201 (Mooney) 443
Type 205 (Mooney) 444
Type 228 (Dornier) 87
Type 228 Maritime Patrol (Dornier) 89
Type 231 (Mooney) (1985-86) 468
Type 252TSE (Mooney) 444
Type 300 (Fairchild) (1985-86) 402
Type 301 (Mooney) (1985-86) 469
Type 328 (Dornier) (1987-88) 95
Type 330 (Shorts) 304
Type 330-200 (Shorts) 305
Type 330-UTT (Shorts) 306
Type 340 (Saab-Fairchild) (1985-86) 124
Type 360 Advanced (Shorts) (1987-88) 324
Type 360-300 (Shorts) 306
Type 360-30F (Shorts) 307
Type 400 (Fairchild) (1984-85) 394
Type 440 (Saab-Fairchild) (1985-86) 125
Type 460P (Wren) 497
Type 526 AFM Condor (Aerotechnik/Zlin) (1984-85) 44
Type 748(M) (HAL/BAe) (1984-85) 94
Type 731 Hawker (Garrett) (1987-88) 417
Type 731 Hawker (Airesearch) (1986-87) 330
Type 1000 (Rockwell) (1980-81) 433
Tzukit (IAI) 142

U

U-2 (Lockheed) (1983-84) 415
U-2 (Mitchell) (1980-81) 531
U-2 (NASA/Lockheed) (1983-84) 445

U-2R (Lockheed) 401
U-3 (Cessna) (1978-79) 310
U-19 (EMBRAER) (1980-81) 17
U-21F (Beechcraft) (1982-83) 299
U-26A (Cessna) 374
U-36A Learjet (Gates Lerjet) (1986-87) 407
UAT (see United Aerospace Technologies Ltd) 311
UCA-1 (James-Dennis) (1979-80) 524
UFM (see Ultralight Flying Machines) (1980-81) 555
UH-1D/H/V (Bell) 341
UH-1H (Fuji-Bel) 166
UH-1N (Bell) 19
UH-2 Seasprite (Kaman) (1984-85) 427
UH-12 (Hiller) (1985-86) 426
UH-12E Hauler (Rogerson Hiller) 467
UH-46 (Boeing) 364
UH-60A Black Hawk (Sikorsky) 480
UHB MD90 Programme (McDonnell Douglas) 431
UP-2J (Kawasaki) (1982-83) 149
US-1A (Shin Meiwa) 172
USAC (see United States Aircraft Corporation) (1987-88) 528
USAF (see United States Air Force Systems Command) 494
UTC (see United Technologies Corporation. (1980-81) 448
UV-18A (Boeing Canada) 21
UV-18B (Boeing Canada) 21
UV-20A Chiricahua (Pilatus) 214
Uirapuru (Aerotec) (1980-81) 10
Uirapuru II, A-132 (Aerotec) (1980-81) 10
Ultimate EA 230 (ACS) (1985-86) 205
Ultra Imp (Aerocar) (1983-84) 539
ULTRALIGHT FLYING MACHINES (USA) (1980-81) 555
Ultralite Test Vehicle (Flight Dynamics) (1985-86) 403
UNITED AEROSPACE TECHNOLOGIES LTD (UK) 311
UNITED STATES AIRCRAFT CORPORATION (USA) (1987-88) 528
UNITED STATES AIR FORCE SYSTEMS COMMAND (USA) 494
UNITED TECHNOLOGIES CORPORATION (USA) (1980-81) 448
UNIVAR AIRCRAFT CORPORATION (USA) 494
Universal (Neiva) (1981-82) 17
Universal, Z 726 (Moravan) (1978-79) 35
Universal II, Model 622 (Nieva) (1981-82) 17
Up-gun AH-1S (Bell) (1987-88) 369
URDANETA Y GALVEZ LTDA (Colombia) (1978-79) 30
UTVA-SOUR METALNE INDUSTRIJE, RO FABRIKA AVIONA (Yugoslavia) 499
Utva-75A11 (Utva) 500
Utva-75A21 (Utva) 499
Utva-75A41 (Utva) 500
Utva-78 (Utva) (1985-86) 529

V

V-2 (Mil) 248
V-8 (Mil) 248
V-8 Special (Beachner) (1985-86) 576
V-10 (Mil) (1982-83) 215
V-12 (Mil) (1978-79) 190
V-14 (Mil) 251
V-22 Osprey (Bell/Boeing) 348
V35B Bonanza (Beechcraft) (1986-87) 338
V-529D (Vought) (1979-80) 458
V-530 (Vought) (1978-79) 449
V-539 Eaglet (MBB) (1981-82) 83
VAAC Harrier (Cranfield) (1987-88) 314
VAT (see Vertical Aviation Technoogy) 495
VC.1A (McDonnell Douglas/BAe) 124
VC-6B King Air (Beechcraft) (1982-83) 297
VC-9C (McDonnell Douglas) (1985-86) 454
VC10 K.Mk 2/Mk 3 Tankers (BAe) 293
VC-11A (Gulfstream American) (1980-81) 354
VC-25A (Boeing) 370
VC-97 Brasilia (Embraer) 12
VC-137 (Boeing) 352
VCA-1 (James-Dennis) (1980-81) 524
VFW 614 VFW-Fokker) (1978-79) 72
VFW 614 ATTAS (MBB) 94
VH-3 (Sikorsky) (1983-84) 485
VH-55 (Aerospatiale) 61
VH-60A (Sikorsky) 480
V-Jet (Williams) (1986-87) 525
VLA-1 (Nyge-Aero) (1986-87) 208
VN-7 Competitor (Murphy) (1981-82) 537
VoWi 10 Airbuggy (Airconcept) (1980-81) 77
VP-1 (Yamazaki) (1979-80) 488
VSA (Kawasaki) (1981-82) 143
VU-9 (EMBRAER) (1984-85) 15
VZLU (see Vyzkumny a Zkusebni Letecky Ustav) (1983-84) 46
Vajra (Dassault-Breguet) 68
VALENTIN FLUGZEUGBAU GmbH (West Germany) 96
Valiant (Luscombe) (1985-86) 290
VALMET AVIATION INDUSTRIES (Finland) 54
VALSAN PARTNERS (USA) 495
VAN ASWEGEN, C. H. J. (South Africa) (1981-82) 498
VAN DINE, PETER D (USA) (1982-83) 579
Vansin (Van Aswegen) (1981-82) 498
VARGA AIRCRAFT CORPORATION (USA) (1984-85) 511
Variable Stability Aircraft (Kawasaki) (1981-82) 143
VariEze, RAF Model 31/33 (Rutan) (1985-86) 612
VariViggen, RAF Model 27/32 (Rutan) (1985-86) 612
Veltro 2 (Aermacchi) (1987-88) 156
VENGA AIRCRAFT INC (Canada) 31
Venom Mk 2 (Wallis) (1987-88) 331
Ventura, C22J (Caproni Vizzola) 159
VENTURE AVIA (1984-85) 611
VEREINIGTE FLUGTECHNISCHE WERKE-FOKKER GmbH (West Germany) (1981-82) 86
VERILITE AIRCRAFT COMPANY INC (USA) 495
VERTICAL AVIATION TECHNOLOGY (USA) 495
VFW-FOKKER GmbH (West Germany) (1979-80) 80
Viator (Partenavia) 163
Victor (Partenavia) (1984-85) 153
Viggen (Saab-Scania) 211
Viking (Bellanca) (1986-87) 363
Viking (Lockheed) 414
VIKING AVIATION (USA) (1982-83) 483
Viking series (Bellanca) (1979-80) 286
VIN-DEL AIRCRAFT (USA) (1981-82) 539
Vindicator (Wallis) (1987-88) 331
Vink (Valmet) 55
VINTEN LTD, W (UK) (1986-87) 316
VINTEN/WALLIS (see W. Vinten Ltd) (1983-84) 282
Viper, P3B (Luscombe) (1985-86) 291
Viper I (Thunder Wings) (1984-85) 608
Vistaliner (Scenic) (1987-88) 502
Vistaplane (Orlando) 449
Vliôm (Vliôm Development) (1979-80) 163
VLIÔM DEVELOPMENT CO (PTY) LTD (South Africa) (1979-80) 163
VOLPAR AIRCRAFT CORPORATION (USA) (1987-88) 529
VOUGHT CORPORATION (USA) (1983-84) 498
Voyager (Voyager) (1987-88) 529
VOYAGER AIRCRAFT INC (USA) (1987-88) 529
Voyageur, CH-113A (Boeing Canada) (1985-86) 19
VTOL AIRCRAFT PTY LTD (Australia) 7
VTOL INDUSTRIES AUSTRALIA LTD (Australia) 6
Vulcan (BAe) (1982-83) 260
VYZKUMNY A ZKUSEBNI LETECKY USTAV (Czechoslovakia) (1983-84) 46

W

W-3 Sokol (WSK-PZL-Swednik) 189
WA-116 (Wallis) 313
WA-116-T (Wallis) 313
WA-116 Venom (Wallis) (1987-88) 331
WA-116X (Wallis) 313
WA-116/W (Wallis) (1983-84) 283
WA-117/R-R (Wallis) (1986-87) 317
WA-118/M Meteorite (Wallis) (1986-87) 317
WA-120/R-R (Wallis) (1987-88) 331
WA-121 (Wallis) 314
WA-121/M Meteorite 2 (Wallis) (1987-88) 331
WA-122/R-R (Wallis) (1987-88) 332
WA-201 (Wallis) 314
WC-130 (Lockheed) 446
WD-II (Hovey) (1981-82) 528
WE 01 (Westermayer) (1980-81) 465
WE 02 (Westermayer) (1980-81) 465
WE 03 (Westermayer) (1980-81) 465
WE 04 (Westermayer) (1981-82) 473
WG-30 (Westland) (1981-82) 271
WG-34 (Westland) (1979-80) 251
WHE (see Ekin, W. H. (Engineering) Co Ltd) (1984-85) 299
WM-2 (Miller) (1985-86) 602
WP-3 Orion (Lockheed) (1981-82) 390
W.S.8 (Seremet) (1978-79) 470
W.S.9 Auto-Gyrocopter (Seremet) (1980-81) 471
W.S.12 (Seremet) (1980-81) 471
WS-70 (Westland/Sikorsky) 319
WSK-PZL KROSNO (Poland) 182
WSK-PZL MIELEC (see Wytwornia Sprzetu Komunikacyj-nego-PZL Mielec) 182
WSK-PZL SWIDNIK (see Wytwornia Sprzetu Komunikacyj-nego Im. Zygmunta Pulawskiego-PZL Swidnik) 187
WSK PZL-WARSZAWA-OKECIE (see Wytwornia Sprzetu Komunikacyjnego PZL-Warszawa-Okecie) 190
WU-2 (Lockheed) (1980-81) 369
Waco Classic F5 (Classic) 381
Waco Meteor (SIAI-Marchetti) (1980-81) 132
Wallbro monoplane replica (Wallis) (1978-79) 242
WALLERKOWSKI, HEINZ (West Germany) (1981-82) 495
WALLIS, STANLEY B (USA) (1981-82) 562
WALLIS AUTOGYROS LTD (UK) 313
WARD, M. (UK) (1985-86) 571
Warrier (Bell) 342
Warrior (SIAI-Marchetti) 165
Warrior II (Piper) 451
Wasp ML74 (Aerodyne) (1987-88) 341
Wasp (Texas Helicopter) (1983-84) 496
Wasp II (Texas Helicopter) (1983-84) 496
Wasp II (Williams) (1985-86) 524
WASSMER AVIATION, SOCIÉTÉ NOUVELLE (France) (1978-79) 64
WATSON, GARY (USA) (1979-80) 554
WEATHERLEY AVIATION COMPANY INC (USA) (1983-84) 500
WEBER, WILLIBALD (Brazil) (1982-83) 490
Weedhopper, JC-24 (Weedhopper) (1980-81) 558
WEEDHOPPER OF UTAH INC (USA) (1980-81) 558
WEEKS, KERMIT (USA) (1982-83) 582
WELLS, EUGENE W. (USA) (1985-86) 634
Westair 204 (Western) (1985-86) 634
WESTERMAYER, OSKAR (Austria) (1981-82) 473
WESTERN AIRCRAFT CORPORATION (USA) (1985-86) 634
WESTERN WINGS (USA) (1987-88) 530
Westland 30 (Westland) (1987-88) 317
WESTLAND PLC (UK) 314
WESTLAND HELICOPTERS LIMITED (UK) 314
Westwind I (IAI) (1986-87) 136
Westwind 2, 1124A (IAI) 140
Westwind IISTD (Hamilton) (1981-82) 376
Westwind III (Hamilton) (1981-82) 375
Westwind IV (Hamilton) (1980-81) 358
Whing Ding II (Hovey) (1981-82) 528
Whisper Jet, Mark III (JetCraft) (1987-88) 438
WHITTAKER, MICHAEL W. J. (UK) (1979-80) 500
WILDEN, ING HELMUT (West Germany) (1978-79) 72
Wildfire (Statler/Beck) (1984-85) 602
Wild Turkey, JP001 (American Air Racing) (1978-79) 504
Wilga 35, PZL-104 (WSK-PZL Warszawa-Okecie) 190
Wilga 80, PZL-104 (WSK-PZL Warszawa-Okecie) 190
WILLIAMS, DAVID (UK) (1985-86) 315
WILLIAMS INTERNATIONAL (USA) (1987-88) 530
WINDSTAR (USA) (1978-79) 552
WING AIRCRAFT COMPANY (USA) (1983-84) 500
Wingtip sails (Cranfield) (1980-81) 239
Wingtip vortex turbine research (NASA) 447
WINTHER-HOLLMANN AIRCRAFT INC (USA) (1982-83) 546
WIPAIRE (USA) 497
WIPLINE INC (USA) (1985-86) 524
WOOD, THOMAS M (Canada) (1983-84) 509
Woody Pusher (Aerosport) (1978-79) 502
WREN AIRCRAFT INC (USA) 496
WTA INC (USA) 497
WYTWORNIA SPRZETU KOMUNIKACYJNEGO-PZL KROSNO (Poland) 182
WYTWORNIA SPRZETU KOMUNIKACYJNEGO-PZL MIELEC (Poland) 182
WYTWORNIA SPRZETU KOMUNIKACYJNEGO-PZL WARSZAWA-OKECIE (Poland) 190
WYTWORNIA SPRZETU KOMUNIKACYJNEGO IM. ZYGMUNTA PULAWSKIEGO-PZL SWIDNIK (Poland) 187

X

X.001 (Xausa) (1984-85) 546
X-22A (Arvin/Calspan) (1982-83) 285
X-29A (Grumman) 399
X-30 (NASA) 446
X-31A EFM (Rockwell International/MBB) 132
X-114 Aerofoilcraft (RFB) (1978-79) 70
XAC (see Xian Aircraft Company) 44
XC-2 (AIDC) (1982-83) 187
XCH-62 (Boeing) (1986-87) 381
XF4H-1 Phantom II (McDonnell) (1980-81) 380
XFV-12A (Rockwell) (1981-82) 454
XH-1 (Atlas) (1987-88) 216
XH-59 (Sikorsky) (1983-84) 486
X-Jet (Williams) (1986-87) 525
XP-99 Prop-Jet (Smith) (1985-86) 518
XR Learjet (Dee Howard) 383
XSH-60J (Mitsubishi-Sikorsky) (1987-88) 182
XST (Lockheed) 411
XT-001 (PAF) (1979-80) 148
XT-4 (Kawasaki) (1985-86) 162
XT-400 (LAPAN) (1981-82) 90
XTP-1 (Atlas) 204
XV-15 (Bell) 347
XAUSA, RENATO (Italy) (1984-85) 546
Xavante (EMBRAER/Aermacchi) (1984-85) 15
X-Avia LC-3 (Lewis) (1981-82) 388
XIAN AIRCRAFT COMPANY (China) 44
Xian (Antonov) Y-5 (China) (1982-83) 38
Xingu II (EMBRAER) (1987-88) 16
Xingu III (EMBRAER) (1987-88) 17
Xuanfeng (China) (1985-86) 38
X-Wing project (Sikorsky) 486
X-wing rotor (Lockheed) (1982-83) 406

Y

Y-5, Antonov (HMP) 39
Y-7 (XAC) 44
Y7-100 (XAC) 44
Y-8, Antonov (STAF) 43
Y-9 (State Aircraft Factories) (1983-84) 39
Y-10 (Shanghai) (1987-88) 45
Y-11 (Harbin) (1986-87) 34
Y-11T (China) (1982-83) 40
Y-12 (HAMC) 38
YA-7 Corsair II (Vought) (1981-82) 469
YA-7E Corsair II$_2$ (Vought) (1980-81) 453
YAH-64 (McDonnell Douglas) (1985-86) 463
Yak-18T (Yakovlev) 272
Yak-28 (Yakovlev) 273
Yak-36MP (Yakovlev) 273
Yak-38 (Yakovlev) 273
Yak-40 (Yakovlev) (1983-84) 245
Yak-41 (Yakovlev) 274
Yak-42 (Yakovlev) 275
Yak-42M (Yakovlev) 276
Yak-50 (Yakovlev) 276
Yak-52 (IAv Bacau) 197
Yak-52 (Yakovlev) 276
Yak-53 (Yakovlev) 276
Yak-55 (Yakovlev) 277
YC-12 Tourbillon (Chasle) (1979-80) 470
YC-14 (Boeing) (1979-80) 301
YC-15 (Douglas) (1979-80) 392
YC-121 (Chasle) (1979-80) 470
YC-122 (Chasle) (1979-80) 470
YC-123 (Chasle) (1979-80) 470
YCH-47D Chinook (Boeing Vertol) (1981-82) 318
YCH-54A (Sikorsky) (1978-79) 433
Ye-133 (Mikoyan) (1987-88) 259
Ye-266M (Mikoyan) 244
YF-12 Programme (NASA) (1979-80) 395
YF-22A (USAF) 411, 494
YF-23A (USAF) 494
YF-80 (Windstar) (1978-79) 552
YF-111A (General Dynamics) (1980-81) 345
YOV-10 (Rockwell) (1980-81) 429

YSH-3J (Sikorsky)	(1978-79)	431
YT-17 (Aerotec)	(1983-84)	10
YT-25B (Neiv)	(1981-82)	17
YX Programme (CTDC)	(1979-80)	127
YAKOVLEV (USSR)		272
YAMATO, SAWAZO (Japan)	(1980-81)	490
YAMAZAKI, TAKASHI (Japan)	(1979-80)	488
YOUNKIN, JIM (USA)	(1980-81)	560
Yun-5 (HMP)		39
Yun-7 (XAC)		44
Yun-8 (STAF)		43
Yun-10 (Shanghai)	(1987-88)	45
Yun-11 (Harbin)	(1986-87)	34
Yun-12 (HAMC)		38
Yunshuji-5 (HMP)		39
Yunshuji-7 (XAC)		44
Yunshuji-8 (STAF)		43
Yunshuji-10 (Shanghai)	(1987-88)	45
Yunshuji-11 (Harbin)	(1986-87)	34
Yunshuji-12 (HAMC)		38

Z

Z-5 (State Aircraft Factories)	(1985-86)	38
Z-6 (HAMC)		39
Z-8 (CAMC)		36
Z-9 Aérospatiale (HAMC)		39
Z-14 (Bell)	(1980-81)	280
Z-16 (Bell)	(1979-80)	280
Z-37T Omelák (Let)	(1982-83)	45
X 37T (Zlin)		52
Z 50 L (Moravan)	(1982-83)	46
Z 50L (Zlin)		51
Z 50 LS (Zlin)	(1986-87)	49
Z 50M (Zlin)		52
Z 726 Universal (Moravan)	(1978-79)	35
ZLIN (see Moravan Národni Podnik)		50
ZAIDAN HOZIN MINKAN YUSOOKI KAIHATSU KYOKAI (Japan)	(1979-80)	127
Zef, C.P.80 (Piel)	(1979-80)	480
ZENAIR LTD (Canada)	(1986-87)	31

ZENTRALGESELLSCHAFT VFW-FOKKER mbH (International)	(1979-80)	101
Zhi-5 (State Aircraft Factories)	(1985-86)	38
Zhi-6 (Harbin)	(1986-87)	34
Zhi-8 (CMC)		36
Zhi-9 (HAMC)		39
Zhishengji-5 (State Aircraft Factories)	(1985-86)	38
Zhishengji-6 (Harbin)	(1986-87)	35
Zhishengji-8 (CAMC)		36
Zhishengji-9 (HAMC)		39
Zipper (Cleary)	(1985-86)	394
Zipper HH-1 (Hammer-Hunt)	(1980-81)	358
ZRZESZINIE WYTWÓRCÓW SPRZETU LOTNICZEGO I SILNIKOWEGO PZL (Poland)		181
Zlin 42 M (Moravan)	(1981-82)	40
Zlin 42 MU (Moravan)	(1981-82)	40
Zlin 43 (Moravan)	(1978-79)	34
Zlin 142 (Zlin)		50
Zlin 526 AFM (Condor (Moravan)	(1982-83)	47

SPORT AIRCRAFT

A

A-2-S Barracuda (Hobbystica) 537
A-2-2 Barracuda (Hobbystica) 538
A-5 (Aeroprakt) (1987-88) 611
A-6 (Byelyi) (1987-88) 612
A6M5 Zero (WAR) 612
A-10 Silver Eagle (Mitchell Wing) 586
A-11M (Aeroprakt) (1986-87) 610
ACE (see Aircraft Composite Engineering) (1985-86) 639
ACT (see Aircraft Composite Technology) (1983-84) 652
AD-100, Traveller (NAI) (1987-88) 563
AFC (see Adventure Flight Centres Inc) (1982-83) 624
AFG (see Allgäuer UL-Flugzeugbau GmbH) (1987-88) 592
AG-7 (IAC) (1986-87) 674
AG-38 Falcon (Mitchell Wing) (1984-85) 706
AG Bearcat (Aerolites) 554
AG Bearcat (Litecraft) (1986-87) 682
AG Master (Hutchinson) 576
AG Zipper (Zenair) (1987-88) 561
AG 02 (Gatard) (1987-88) 574
AG 02 Sp (Gatard) 522
AG-38-A (Mitchell Wing) 586
AILE (see Air Industrie Loisir Engineering) (1986-87) 563
A.I.R.'SSA (see Air International Services) 518
AJS 2000 (Sky-Craft) (1986-87) 609
AM-DSI (Leader's) (1986-87) 679
AM-DSII (Leader's) (1987-88) 676
AN-20 (Neukom) (1983-84) 646
AN-20B (Neukom) (1984-85) 674
AN-20B (Richter) (1983-84) 643
AN-20K, Piccolo (Borowski) (1987-88) 594
AN-21R (Neukom) (1984-85) 674
AN-22 (Albatros) (1987-88) 593
AN-22 (Neukom) (1984-85) 674
AN-22 (Point) (1985-86) 660
ASA 200 (Feugray) (1986-87) 574
ASL 18 (ASL) 518
ASL (see Club d'Avions Supers Léger du Cher) 518
AT-9 (Stoddard Hamilton) 602
ATOI (Terrade) (1987-88) 590
AUI (see Aviazione Ultraleggera Italiana) 536
ABE, KEIICHI (Japan) (1984-85) 673
ABERNATHY, BOB (USA) (1986-87) 622
Acapella (Option Air Reno) (1986-87) 692
Accipiter II (Pagen) (1984-85) 728
ACE AIRCRAFT COMPANY (USA) 549
Acey Deucy, Powell P.70 (Acey Deucy) (1986-87) 622
ACEY DEUCY SPORT AIRCRAFT INC (USA) (1986-87) 622
Acroduster Too (Stolp) 602
Acro Sport I (Acro Sport) 549
Acro Sport II (Acro Sport) 550
ACRO SPORT INC (USA) 549
Acro X (Catto) (1986-87) 648
Acro Zenith CH 150 (Zenair) 514
ADVANCED AVIATION INC (USA) 550
ADVANCED COMPOSITE TECHNOLOGY (USA) (1987-88) 628
Adventure (Mead Engineering) (1986-87) 685
ADVENTURE FLIGHT CENTRES INC (Canada) (1982-83) 624
Aeolus (Aeolus) (1985-86) 665
AEOLUS AVIATION (UK) (1985-86) 665
Aeolus (Poisestar) (1983-84) 650
AERMAS (see Automobiles Martini) 517
Aermas 386 (Aermas) 517
Aero (Bowen) (1984-85) 718
AEROCAR INC (USA) 552
AERO COMPOSITE TECHNOLOGY INC (USA) 552
AÉRO DELTA SERVICE (France) (1986-87) 562
AERO DESIGNS INC (USA) 552
AERODIS, SARL (France) 518
AERO DYNAMICS LTD (USA) 553
AERODYNE SYSTEMS INC (USA) (1985-86) 674
Aero-Fox (Lite-Flite) (1987-88) 679
AERO INNOVATIONS INC (USA) (1987-88) 631
AÉROKART, SOCIÉTÉ (France) (1986-87) 562
Aerokart 4315 (Aerokart) (1986-87) 562
Aerokart 4320 (Aerokart) (1986-87) 563
AEROLIGHT FLIGHT DEVELOPMENT INC (USA) (1984-85) 686
AEROLITES INC (USA) 554
AERO MIRAGE (USA) 554
AERONAUTIC 2000 (France) 518
Aeroplane XP (UFM of Kentucky) (1984-85) 718
AÉROPLUM (France) (1986-87) 563
Aeropower 28 (Hughes) 503
AEROPRAKT (USSR) (1987-88) 611
AEROSERVICE ITALIANA SRL (Italy) 536
AEROSPORT LTD (USA) 554
Aerostar (Goldwing) (1986-87) 667
Aerostat 340 (Aerolight) (1983-84) 652
AÉROSTRUCTURE (France) (1984-85) 663
AERO TECH AVIATION LTD (Canada) (1983-84) 633
AEROTECH DYNAMICS CORPORATION (USA) (1986-87) 631
AEROTECH INTERNATIONAL LTD (UK) 543
AEROTIQUE AVIATION INC (USA) (1986-87) 631
AERO VENTURES (USA) (1985-86) 674
AERO VISIONS INTERNATIONAL (USA) (1987-88) 633
AG Master (Hutchinson) 576
Agricol (ULAC) (1985-86) 664
Agri-Delta (Agri-Delta) (1983-84) 638
AGRI-PLANE (see La Culture de l'An 2000 SA) (1986-87) 563
Aiglon (Danis) (1982-83) 628
AILES DE K, L DE KALBERMATTEN (Switzerland) (1985-86) 663
AILE VOLANTE B. DANIS (France) (1987-88) 572
AIRBORNE WING DESIGN (USA) (1984-85) 686
Aircamper GN-1 (Grega) 573
Aircamper (Pietenpol) 590
Air Car Sr (Spencer) 599
AIR-CEFELEC AÉRONAUTIQUE (France) (1983-84) 638
AIR COMMAND MANUFACTURING INC (USA) 554
AIRCRAFT COMPOSITE ENGINEERING (Australia) (1985-86) 639
AIRCRAFT COMPOSITE TECHNOLOGY (USA) (1983-84) 652
AIRCRAFT DESIGNS INC (USA) 555
AIRCRAFT DEVELOPMENT INC (USA) 556
AIR CREATION SARL (France) 518
Aircross (Distri) 522
Air Cub (Chuck's) (1987-88) 650
Air-Dinghy (Polaris Motor) 538
Air-Dinghy 1 + 1 (Polaris Motor) 538
AIR INDUSTRIE LOSIER ENGINEERING SA (France) (1986-87) 563
AIR INTERNATIONAL SERVICE SA (France) 518
AIRMASS—CIRRUS INDUSTRIES (USA) (1983-84) 653
AIRPLANE FACTORY INC, THE (USA) 556
Airplume (Croses, Emilien) (1984-85) 666
Airplume (Croses, Yves) (1986-87) 570
Air Shark I (Freedom Master) 572
AIRTECH CANADA (Canada) 507
AKAFLIEG MÜNCHEN (see Flugtechnische Forschungsgruppe an der Technischen Universität München) 531
Akro Model Z (Laser) 504
ALBARDE (France) (1986-87) 564
Albatross (Vulcan Ul-Aviation) 534
ALBATROS ULTRA FLIGHT GmbH (West Germany) (1987-88) 592
Albertan (Ultimate Aircraft) (1987-88) 554
ALDERFER GYROCHOPPER AIRCRAFT CORPORATION (USA) 556
Alex-I (Parmesani) (1987-88) 604
ALIFERRARI (Italy) 536
Allegro (A.I.R'S) 518
ALLGÄUER UL-FLUGZEUGBAU GmbH (West Germany) (1987-88) 592
ALPAIR ULM (Italy) (1987-88) 602
Alto 833 (ULM Aérotechnic) (1983-84) 641
Alto-Stratus (Stratus) (1983-84) 690
American (American Air Jet) 556
AMERICAN AEROLIGHTS INC (USA) (1983-84) 653
AMERICAN AIRCRAFT INC (USA) 556
AMERICANAIR JET INC (USA) 556
AMERICAN AIR TECHNOLOGY (USA) (1987-88) 638
AMERICAN MICROFLIGHT INC (USA) (1986-87) 634
AMF MICROFLIGHT LTD (UK) 543
ANDERSON EARL (USA) (1987-88) 639
ANDREASSON, BJÖRN (Sweden) 540
ANGLIN SPECIAL AERO PLANES INC (USA) (1984-85) 688
ANTONOV (USSR) 542
Antares (Soyer/Barritault) 520
Aolus (Spectra) (1982-83) 652, 658
APCO AVIATION (West Germany) (1987-88) 593
Apollo (Product MZ) (1987-88) 600
Aquitain 2 + 2 (Lanot) (1983-84) 640
Aquitain (Lanot) (1986-87) 580
Ara, PM-2 (MDK Krakow) (1983-84) 644
Arco (Reuter) (1986-87) 596
Ariete (Tesori) (1987-88) 553
Arrow, P-3 (UP) (1987-88) 726
Arthur (Dohet) (1987-88) 573
Ascender (Freedom Fliers) (1987-88) 665
Ascender (Pterodactyl) (1983-84) 670
Ascent I (Brown) 560
Asterix (Michel) (1987-88) 582
Astra (Astra International) (1983-84) 654
ASTRA INTERNATIONAL (USA) (1983-84) 654
ATLANTIS AVIATION INC (USA) (1984-85) 688
Atlas (Birdman) (1983-84) 634
AUSTIN AEROSPACE CORPORATION (USA) (1987-88) 640
AUSTRALIAN AEROLITE (Australia (1985-86) 639
Austrostrike (Steinbach-Delta) (1987-88) 543
AUTOMOBILES MARTINI SA (France) 517
Avenger (Airborne Wing) (1983-84) 653
AVIASUD ENGINEERING SA (France) 519
AVIATION COMPOSITES (UK) 544
AVIAZIONE ULTRALEGGERA ITALIANA (Italy) 536
Avid Amphibian (Light Aero) 580
Avid Flyer (Light Aero) 580
Avion (Avion) (1983-84) 655
Avion (Brock) 560
AVIONS A. GATARD (France) 522
AVIONS JODEL SA (France) 523
AVIONS MUDRY ET CIE (France) (1983-84) 641
AVIONS YVES GARDAN (France) (1986-87) 575

B

B1-RD (Robertson) (1984-85) 712
B1-RD Instructor (Robertson) (1984-85) 712
B2-RD (Robertson) (1983-84) 672
B4 Aircamper (Pietenpol) 590
B-8 Gyro Glider (Bensen) (1986-87) 638
B-8M Gyro Copter (Bensen) (1986-87) 638
B-8MW Hydro-Copter (Bensen) (1986-87) 638
B-8V Gyro Copter (Bensen) (1986-87) 638
B-8W Hydro Glider (Bensen) (1986-87) 638
B-10 (Mitchell Wing) 586
B-80 Gyro Glider (Bensen) (1986-87) 639
B-80D Gyro Glider (Bensen) (1986-87) 639
B-85 Rotax (Bensen) (1986-87) 640
B-532 King Cobra B (Advanced Aviation) 550
BA-4B (Andreasson) 540
BA-12 Slandan Andreasson, (MFI) 542
BA-14 (MFI) 542
BA83 (Binder) 532
BAC (see Brutsche Aircraft Corporation) 557
BD-4 Modification (Ward) (1987-88) 732
B-EC-9 Paras-Cargo (Croses) (1986-87) 570
BF-3 (Cup) 537
BG-1 (Bredelet and Gros) (1987-88) 568
BIAA (see Beijing Institute of Aeronautics and Astronautics) 516
BOAC (see Barney Oldfield Aircraft Company) (USA) 558
BX-2 Cherry (Brändli) 542
BX-111 Giro-Hili (Berger) (1987-88) 610
BX200 (Bristol) 559
Baby Ace Model D (ACE Aircraft) 549
Baby Bird (Stitts) (1987-88) 712
'Baby' Lakes (BOAC) 558
Balade (Stern) 530
Balans (Kolodziej) (1984-85) 725, 730
Balerit (Mignet) 527
Banchee (International Ultralite) (1985-86) 692
B & B AIRCRAFT COMPANY (USA) (1984-85) 689
B & G AIRCRAFT COMPANY INC (USA) (1985-86) 678
Banty (Kimbrel) 578
BARBERO (France) (1986-87) 565
BARDOU, ROBERT (France) (1986-87) 565
BARNETT ROTORCRAFT (USA) 558
BARNEY OLDFIELD AIRCRAFT COMPANY (USA) 558
Barnstormer (Fisher) (1983-84) 660
Barracuda (Barracuda) 558
BARRACUDA (see Bueth Enterprises Inc) 558
Barracuda A-2-S (Hobbystica) 537
Barracuda A-2-2 (Hobbystica) 538
Baroudeux (Aéronautic 2000) 518
Baroudeur, (Aéronautic 2000) 518
Bathtub Mk I (Kimbrel/Dormoy) 578
BEACHY, ERNEST (USA) (1986-87) 637
Bearcat (Aerolites) 554
Bearcat (Litecraft) (1986-87) 682
Bearcat (Ultra Classics) (1984-85) 719
BEARD, ROBERT (USA) (1987-88) 641
BEAUJON AIRCRAFT CO (USA) (1986-87) 637
BEAUJON ULTRALIGHTS (USA) (1983-84) 656
Beaver RX-28 (Spectrum) 510
Beaver RX-35 (Spectrum) 510
Beaver RX-35 Floater (Spectrum) 510
Beaver RX-550 Series (Spectrum) 511
Bébé Series (Jodel) 523
BEDSON (see GORDON BEDSON AND ASSOCIATES) (1986-87) 537
BEIJING INSTITUTE OF AERONAUTICS AND ASTRONAUTICS (China) 516
BELL, F.M. ULTRALITE AIRCRAFT INC (USA) (1986-87) 637
BENSEN AIRCRAFT CORPORATION (USA) (1986-87) 638
BERGER-HELICOPTER (Switzerland) (1987-88) 610
Beryl (Piel) 528
Beta Bird (Hovey) 576
BEZZOLA-VILS, GION (Switzerland) (1987-88) 610
Bidulm 44 (Cosmos) (1987-88) 570
Bifly (Lascaud) 526
BINDER AVIATIK GmbH (West Germany) 532
Biplane (Ostrowski) (1985-86) 662
Biplum (Guerpont) 522
Bird (Taylor) 604
BIRDMAN AIRCRAFT INTERNATIONAL (USA) (1985-86) 679
BIRDMAN ENTERPRISES 1986 LTD (Canada) 507
BIRDMAN INC (USA) (1982-83) 639
BIRDMAN SPORTS LTD (UK) (1983-84) 688
Blackbird (Black) (1987-88) 642
BLACK, FRANK E. (USA) (1987-88) 642
BLACK, JAMES G. (USA) (1983-84) 656
BLALOCK, KEN (USA) (1987-88) 642
BLUE MAX ULTRALIGHT (Australia) 503
Blue Max (Blue Max) 503
Bobcat (First Strike) 570
Boomerang (Fisher) (1983-84) 660
BOROWSKI, LTB (West Germany) (1987-88) 594
Boredom Fighter (Wolf) 614
BOUDEAU, MICHEL (France) (1986-87) 566
BOUNSALL AIRCRAFT (USA) (1987-88) 642
Bouvreuil (Pottier) 530
BOWEN AERO (USA) (1984-85) 726
Bowen Aero (Bowen Aero) (1984-85) 726
BOWERS, PETER M. (USA) 558
Boxmoth (Thomson) (1983-84) 678
Boxmoth B (Thomson) (1986-87) 724
Bravo OM-1 (Morrisey) (1987-88) 686
BRÄNDLI, MAX (Switzerland) 542
BREDELET AND GROS (France) (1987-88) 568
BREEN AVIATION (UK) (1983-84) 646
Breezer (Beachy) (1986-87) 637
BRIFFAUD, GEORGES (France) (1986-87) 566
BRISTOL, URIEL (Bristol) 559
BROC ENTERPRISE, BERNARD (France) 520
BROCK, KEN, MANUFACTURING (USA) 560
Brok-1M (LAK) 543
BROKAW AVIATION (USA) (1987-88) 645
BROWN, MICHAEL (USA) 560
Bronco (Thalhofer) (1987-88) 598
BRÜGGER MAX (Switzerland) 542

BRUTSCHE AIRCRAFT CORPORATION (USA) 557
BRYAN, COURTNEY (USA) (1986-87) 644
Buccaneer (Advanced Aviation) 550
Buccaneer SX (Advanced Aviation) 551
Buccaneer II, XA/650 (Highcraft/Advanced Aviation) 551
BUCK SPORT AIRCRAFT INC (USA) (1987-88) 646
Buckeye (Freedom Fliers) (1987-88) 666
'Buddy Baby' Lakes (BOAC) 558
BUETHE ENTERPRISES W. B. INC (USA) 558
Bull (Windryder) (1987-88) 735
Bullet (Brokaw) (1987-88) 645
Bumble Bee (Aircraft Designs) 555
BURKE AIRCRAFT (USA) (1987-88) 646
Busard (Lefebvre) (1985-86) 555
Bushbird (Fletcher) (1987-88) 548
BUSHBY AIRCRAFT INC (USA) 560
Bushmaster (Sylvaire) (1987-88) 553
Bushmaster II (Morgan) (1986-87) 690
Bushranger (Seabird) (1986-87) 540
BUTTERFLY COMPANY (Belgium) (1985-86) 642
Butterfly (Butterfly) (1984-85) 659
Butterfly (Kimbrel) 578
BUTTERWORTH, G. N. (USA) 561
BYELYI (USSR) (1987-88) 612

C

CA-05 (Elmwood) 508
CA-15 (Goldwing) (1981-82) 620
CA-61/-61R Mini Ace (Cvjetkovic) 564
CA-65 (Cvjetkovic) 564
CA-65A (Cvjetkovic) 564
CB-1 Biplane (Hatz) 575
CC-01 (Chudzik) (1987-88) 568
C.C.C. (Mathews) (1986-87) 684
CFM (see Cook Flying Machines) 544
CGS (see CGS Aviation Inc) (1987-88) 650
CH-8 (Elmwood) 508
CH 150 (Zenair) 514
CH 180 (Zenair) 514
CH 200 (Zenair) 514
CH 250 (Zenair) 514
CH 600 (Zenair) 514
CH 701 (Zenair) 514
CH 2000 (Zenair) 515
CIVL (see Commission Internationale de Vol Libre) (1982-83) 623
CJ-1 (Corby) 503
CJ-3D Cracker Jack (Wood Wing) 614
CJC.01 (Chaboud) (1987-88) 568
CL-1 Ersatz Junkers (Haigh) (1986-87) 669
CMV (see Construction Machines Volantes) (1987-88) 569
CP-16 (Goldwing) (1982-83) 644
C.P. 70/750/751 Beryl (Piel) 528
C.P. 80 (Piel) 529
C.P. 90 Pinocchio (Piel) 529
C.P. 150 Onyx (Piel) 530
C.P. 300 series, Emeraude (Piel) 528
C.P. 600 series, Super Diamant (Piel) 528
C.P. 1320 (Piel) 528
CSRI-01 Tse Tse (Souquet) (1987-88) 589
CUP (see Centro Ultraleggeri Partenopeo) 536
CX-901 (Command-Aire) (1984-85) 692
Calao 2000 (Agri-Plane) (1982-83) 628
CALDER (USA) (1984-85) 690
CALVEL PLASTIQUE AERONAUTIQUE, JACQUES (France) (1984-85) 664
CAMPBELL-JONES, MICHAEL (UK) (1983-84) 646
CANA AIRCRAFT COMPANY (Singapore) (1987-88) 607
Canadian Skyrider (Aero Tech) (1983-84) 633
Canadian Skyseeker (AFC) (1982-83) 624
CANAERO DYNAMICS AIRCRAFT INC (Canada) 508
Canard-2 FL (Canard) (1982-83) 633
CANARD AVIATION (Switzerland) (1982-83) 633
Capella (Flightworks) 572
Capena (Pena) (1987-88) 584
CARLSON AIRCRAFT INC (USA) 561
CAROTHERS, CHUCK AIR SHOW (USA) (1986-87) 646
Carrera (Advanced Aviation) (1987-88) 628
CASCADE ULTRALIGHTS INC (USA) 562
CASSUTT (USA) 562
Catfish (Eaves) (1987-88) 660
CATTO AIRCRAFT (USA) (1986-87) 648
Cavalier (Macfam) 582
CAVU Flyer (Peters) (1985-86) 702
Celerity (Mirage Aircraft) 585
CENTRAIR SA (France) 520
CENTRO ULTRALEGGERI PARTENOPEO (Italy) 536
Centurion (Sport Aviation) (1983-84) 690
CGS AVIATION INC (USA) (1987-88) 650
CHABOUD, CLAUDE (France) (1987-88) 568
Challenger (Quad City) 591
Challenger 11 (Quad City) 591
Challenger (Sunbird) (1982-83) 653
Challenger (Ulm Pyrénées) (1986-87) 591
Challender Special (Quad City) 592
Challenger 11 Special (Quad City) 592
Channel Wing (Smith) (1986-87) 710
Charger (Marquart) 584
CHARGUS GLIDING CO (UK) (1984-85) 676
CHASLE, YVES (France) 520
Cherokee (Birdman) (1982-83) 634
Cherry (Brändli) 542
Chevvron 2-32 (AMF) 543
Chicken Hawk (Atlantis) (1984-85) 688
Chinook 1-S (Birdman) 507
Chinook 2-S (Birdman) 508
Chinook, WT-11 (Birdman) (1986-87) 544
Chotia Gypsy (Weedhopper) (1981-82) 629
Chouca 2045 (Agri-Plane) (1982-83) 628
Choucas (Bardou) (1986-87) 565
Christavia Mk 1 (Elmwood) 508
Christavia Mk 4 (Elmwood) 508
CHRISTEN INDUSTRIES INC (USA) 562
CHUCK'S AIRCRAFT CO (USA) 563
CHUDZIK (France) (1987-88) 568
CIESLAR, MARIAN AND SWIGON, PIOTR (Poland) (1981-82) 612, 632
CIESLAR/SWIGÔN (see Cieslar, Marian and Świgón, Piotr) (1981-82) 612, 632
CIRCA REPRODUCTIONS (Canada) 508
Cirrus VK 30 (Cirrus) 563
CIRRUS DESIGN CORPORATION (USA) 563
Classic (Fisher) (1986-87) 664
Classic 11 (Fisher) 571
Classic FP-404 (Fisher) 570
Clipper (Bell, F.M.) (1986-87) 638
Clipper (Worldwide Ultralite) (1984-85) 722
Clipper series (Sunrise) 604
Cloudbuster (Cloudbuster) (1985-86) 681
Cloudbuster (Kubasek) (1981-82) 622
CLOUDBUSTER ULTRALIGHTS INC (USA) (1985-86) 681
Cloud Dancer (Rodger) (1984-85) 712
Cloud Dancer (Ultra Sail) 608
CLOUD DANCER AEROPLANE WORKS INC (USA) (1987-88) 651
CLUB D'AVIONS SUPERS LEGERS DU CHER (France) 518
Club (Jodel) 524
CLUTTON-TABENOR, Eric Clutton (USA) (1987-88) 651
COATES, J. R. (UK) (1986-87) 612
Cobra (Advanced Aviation) 550
Cobra Carrera (Advanced Aviation) 551
Cobra HP (Advanced Aviation) (1983-84) 652
Cobra Mk 1 (Romain) 548
COLANI, LUIGI (Switzerland) (1986-87) 608
Colibri 2 (Brügger) 542
COLLINS AERO (USA) 563
COLOMBAN, MICHEL (France) 520
COLUMBIA PLASTICS INC (USA) (1983-84) 658
Comet (UP) (1984-85) 728
Comet 135 (UP) (1983-84) 690, 694
Comet 165 (UP) (1984-85) 730
Comet 185 (UP) (1984-85) 730
COMMAND-AIRE AIRCRAFT (USA) (1985-86) 682
Commander 447 (Air Command) 554
Commander 503 (Air Command) 554
Commander Elite 532 (Air Command) 554
Commander 532 Two-seater (Air Command) 554
COMMISSION INTERNATIONALE DE VOL LIBRE (France) (1983-84) 623
Commuter IIA (Tamarind) (1986-87) 721
Commuter IIB (Tamarind) (1986-87) 721
COMPETITION AIRCRAFT (USA) (1983-84) 658
COMPOSITE INDUSTRIES LTD (Australia) (1987-88) 537
Condor II (Condor) (1985-86) 682
Condor III (Condor) (1985-86) 682
Condor III + 2 (Condor) (1985-86) 682
Condor 2090 (Agri-Plane) (1986-87) 563
CONDOR AIRCRAFT (USA) (1985-86) 682
CONTROT (France) (1986-87) 568
COOK, DAVID (UK) (1981-82) 614
COOK FLYING MACHINES (UK) 544
CONSTRUCTION MACHINES VOLANTES (France) (1987-88) 569
Corben Jr Ace (Acro Sport) 626
CORBY, JOHN C. (Australia) 503
Cormorano (Aliferrari) 536
Corsair F4U (WAR) 612
Cosmagri (Cosmos) (1987-88) 571
COSMOS SARL (France) (1987-88) 570
Cosmos (Skylines) (1984-85) 714
Cosmos Dragster (Skylines) (1986-87) 709
Cougar Model 1 (Acro Sport) 550
COUNTRY AIR INC (USA) 564
Country Eagle XL (Aeroservice Italiana) (1987-88) 601
COUPE-AVIATION (France) 521
Courier (Rans) 593
Coyote (Advanced Aviation) (1983-84) 652
Coyote (Rans) 592
Co Z DEVELOPMENT CORPORATION (USA) (1987-88) 652
Co Z EUROPE (West Germany) 564
Cozy (Co Z) 564
COZZA/SCHOLL AIRCRAFT INC (USA) (1984-85) 692
Cracker Jack (Wood Wing) 614
Crechet (Leningrad Central) (1982-83) 634
Cricket (Winton) (1982-83) 624
Cricri MC 15 (Colomban) 515
Criquet (Croses) 522
Crossbow (Cunion) (1984-85) 726
CROSES, EMILIEN (France) (1984-85) 532, 666
CROSES, EMILIEN (France) 522
CROSES, YVES (France) (1986-87) 570
Cross-Country (Polaris Motor) 538
ČS Flash (Mainair Sports) (1987-88) 616
Cuby I (Magal) 509
Cuby II (Magal) 509
CUELLAR, JESSE (USA) (1986-87) 651
Cuellar Monoplane (Cuellar) (1986-87) 651
Culex (Fisher) (1986-87) 664
Culex (Fisher) 572
Culite (Fisher) 572
Currie Wot (PFA) 546
Curtiss P-40C (Thunder Wings) 606
CUSTOM AIRCRAFT CONVERSIONS (USA) (1984-85) 692
Cutlass (Skyhook) (1984-85) 688, 692
CUVEILIER, ROLAND (France) (1986-87) 571
CVJETKOVIC, ANTON (USA) 564
Cygnet (Australia) (1982-83) 623
Cygnet (Hapi) 574

D

D-01, Ibis (Delemontez) (1986-87) 572
D 2 INC (USA) 564
D.2 (Jones, Mason) (1986-87) 546
D.9 Bébé (Jodel) 523
D.11 (Jodel) 524
D.18 (Jodel) 524
D.19 (Jodel) 524
D31 (PFA) 547
D.112 Club (Jodel 524
D.113 (Jodel) 524
D.119 (Jodel) 524
D-201 (D'Apuzzo) 565
DA-2A (Davis (D2) 564
DA-5A (Davis) (D2) 564
DA-7 (Davis) 566
DD-100 (Delmotte) (1987-88) 573
DD-200 (Delmotte) (1987-88) 573
DK-1 (FLSZ) 572
DK-3 (Janowski) 540
DL 260 (Lesage) (1986-87) 582
DP01 (Prost) (1984-85) 671
DS-26 Nomad (Delta) (1982-83) 640
DS-27A Honcho (Delta) (1982-83) 640
DS-27B Honcho II (Delta) (1982-83) 640
DS-27C Super Honcho (Delta) (1982-83) 640
DS-28A Super Honcho (Delta) (1981-82) 617
DX-1 (Davis Wing) (1986-87) 654
DAHU PLANE (ÉTABLISSEMENTS NOIN AÉRONAUTIQUE) (France) (1981-82) 608
Daki 530Z/Ikenga (Gyro 2000) 574
DALLACH FLUGZEUGE GmbH (West Germany) 532
D'APUZZO, NICHOLAS E (USA) 565
DANIS (see Aile Volante B. Danis) (1987-88) 572
Dart (Jurca) (1987-88) 577
Das Ultralighterfighter (Airplane Factory) 556
DAVENPORT, BRAD (USA) (1986-87) 653
DAVIS, LEEON D (USA) 566
DAVIS WING LTD (USA) 566
DECHOW, CURT (USA) (1981-82) 617
DEDALUS Srl (Italy) 537
DEGRAW, RICHARD R (USA) (1986-87) 654
DELEMONTEZ-DESJARDINS (France) (1986-87) 572
DELMOTTE (France) (1987-88) 573
Delta Bird (Hovey) 576
Delta Hawk (Hovey) 576
Delta JD-2 (Dyke) 566
DELTA SAILPLANE CORPORATION (USA) (1982-83) 640
DELTA TECHNOLOGY (USA) (1987-88) 656
DELTA WING KITES AND GLIDERS INC (USA) (1982-83) 641
Demoiselle (Ultra Efficient Products) 608
DENNEY AEROCRAFT COMPANY (USA) 566
Der Jäger D.IX (White) 613
Der Kricket, DK-1 (FLSZ) 572
DESIGNABILITY (1984-85) 678
DESIGNABILITY LTD (UK) (1983-84) 647
Diamant (Franz) (1987-88) 594
Diana (Hoffmann) (1986-87) 595
DIEHL AERO-NAUTICAL (USA) 566
DiMASCIO (USA) (1986-87) 656
Dipper (Collins Aero) 563
DISTRI SNAP SARL (France) 522
Djins 300 (Ulm Technic Acromarine) (1984-85) 668
DJURIC, VLADIMIR (West Germany) (1986-87) 594
DMITRIYEV, V (1987-88) 612
DOBROCINSKI, TADEUSZ (Poland) (1984-85) 673
DOHET, RAMOND (France) (1987-88) 573
DOUBLE EAGLE AIRCRAFT (USA) (1986-87) 656
Double Eagle (Mitchell Wing) 586
Doublequick (Eipper) (1982-83) 641
Doublestar (Starflight) (1983-84) 676
Dragon (Dragon) (1984-85) 678
Dragonfly (Viking) 610
DRAGON LIGHT AIRCRAFT CO LTD (UK) (1985-86) 666
Dragoon (Pegasus) (1987-88) 620
Dragster (La Mouette) (1982-83) 628
Dragster 25 (Cosmos) (1987-88) 570
Dragster 25 (Skylines/Cosmos) (1986-87) 709
Dragster 34 (Cosmos) (1987-88) 570
Dragster 34 (Skylines/Cosmos) (1986-87) 709
Dream (NAC) (1986-87) 690
Drifter Series (Maxair) 584
DRIGGERS, MICHAEL (USA) (1987-88) 658
Druine D31 Turbulent (PFA) 547
Dual (American Air) (1987-88) 638
Dual Striker Trike (Flexi-Form) (1986-87) 612
Dual Star (Pioneer) (1985-86) 702
Dual Trainer Raven (Hornet) (1986-87) 614
Duet (Designability) (1983-84) 647
Duet (Jordan Aviation) (1984-85) 680
DURAND ASSOCIATES INC (USA) 566
Durand Mk 5 (Durand) 566
DURUBLE, ROLAND (France) (1986-87) 572
DYKE AIRCRAFT (USA) 566
Dynamic Trick (Polaris) 538

E

EA-1 King Fisher (Anderson) (1986-87) 636
EA-1 Kingfisher (Anderson-Warner) 612
EAC-3 Pouplume (Croses) 522
EC-6 Cricket (Croses) 522
EC-8 Tourisme (Croses) 522
EEL (see Entwicklung und Erprobung von Leichtflugzeugen) (1982-83) 629
EZ-1 (Aircraft Development) 556
EZE-Max (T.E.A.M.) 606
Eagle (American Aerolights) (1983-84) 653
Eagle (Ultrasport) (1984-85) 672
Eagle 1 (American Aerolights) (1982-83) 638
Eagle 2 (American Aerolights) (1982-83) 638
Eagle 2-PLC (Aeroservice Italiana) 536

Eagle 2-PLC (Ultrasport) (1986-87) 603
Eagle II (Christen) 562
EAGLE WINGS AIRCRAFT CORPORATION (USA) 567
Eagle X (Composite Industries) (1987-88) 537
Eagle XL (Aeroservice Italiana) 536
Eagle XL (American Aerolights) (1983-84) 653
Eagle XL (Ultrasport) (1986-87) 602
Eagle XL 2-place (American Aerolights) (1983-84) 653
Eagle (Sky Sports) (1981-82) 625, 632
EARTHSTAR AIRCRAFT INC (USA) 568
EASTERN ULTRALIGHTS INC (USA) (1984-85) 694
EASTWOOD AIRCRAFT PTY LTD (Australia) 503
Easy Riser (UFM) (1982-83) 654
Easy Riser Arrow (UFM) (1981-82) 628
EAVES, LEONARD (USA) (1987-88) 660
EBERSCHOFF AND COMPANY (USA) 568
Eclair VI (CMV) (1985-86) 652
Eclipse (Phase III) (1984-85) 710
ECLIPSE (UK) (1981-82) 614
Ecnelight (Columbia Plastics) (1983-84) 658
Edelweiss (Duruble) (1986-87) 572
Edelweiss 150 (Duruble) (1986-87) 572
EGRETTE, Association (France) (1986-87) 573
EICH, JAMES P (USA) 568
EIPPER-FORMANCE INC (USA) (1982-83) 641
EIPPER INDUSTRIES (USA) 568
EKSTRÖM, STAFFAN W (Sweden) 541
Electric Powered Glider (Gigax) (1984-85) 674
El Moscardon (Farge) (1987-88) 537
ELMWOOD AVIATION (Canada) 508
EMC2 AVIONICS (Belgium) (1982-83) 624
Emeraude (Piel) 528
Epsilon (Distri) 522
Ersatz Junkers CL-1 (Haigh) (1986-87) 669
ENTWICKLUNG UND ERPROBUNG VON LEICHTFLUGZEUGEN (West Germany) (1982-83) 629
ERPALS INDUSTRIE (see Etudes et réalisations de prototypes pour l'aviation légère et sportive) (1986-87) 574
Esqualo II (MIM) (1987-88) 544
ETS NOIN AÉRONAUTIQUES (France) 528
ETUDES ET RÉALISATIONS DE PROTOTYPES POUR L'AVIATION LÉGÈRE ET SPORTIVE (France) (1986-87) 574
EURO WING (UK) (1983-84) 648
EVANS AIRCRAFT (USA) 569
EVERGREEN ULTRALITE INC (USA) (1986-87) 661
Excel (Alpair) (1987-88) 602
Excelsior (St Croix) (1984-85) 714
Exec (Rotorway) 596
Executive (Hornet) (1987-88) 614
Express (Wheeler) 613
Exp-Spirito (UFM) (1983-84) 680

F

F2-Foxcat (Aeroservice Italiana) 536
F2-Foxcat 2 PLC (Aeroservice Italiana) 536
F2 Foxcat (Ultrasport) (1986-87) 603
F2 Twin Foxcat (Ultrasport) (1986-87) 603
F3 (Cup) 536
F.3 (Féré) (1986-87) 574
F4U Corsair (WAR) 612
F.8L Falco (Sequoia) 597
FA-1 (Fulton) 544
FB-1 (Tirith) (1986-87) 621
FB-2 (Tirith) (1986-87) 621
FD-1 (Flight Designs) (1982-83) 642
FK6 (MBB) (1987-88) 596
FLSZ (see Flight Level Six-Zero) 572
FM-2 (Freedom Master) 572
FP-101 (Fisher) (1987-88) 570
FP-101 (Fisher) (1986-87) 662
FP-202 (Fisher) (1986-87) 662
FP-202 Koala (Fisher) (1987-88) 570
FP-303 (Fisher) (1987-88) 570
FP-303 (Fisher) (1986-87) 663
FP-404 Classic (Fisher) (1987-88) 570
FP-404 (Fisher) (1986-87) 664
FP-505 Skeeter (Fisher) (1987-88) 571
FP-505 (Fisher) (1986-87) 664
FP-606 (Fisher) (1987-88) 571
FSRW-1 (Smith) (1987-88) 541
Fw 190A Focke-Wulf (Thunder Wings) 606
Fair-Fax Trikes (Riemann) (1987-88) 596
Falco (Sequoia) 597
Falcon (American Aerolights) (1983-84) 654
Falcon (American Aircraft) 556
Falcon (Blalock) (1987-88) 642
Falcon XP (American Aircraft) (1987-88) 639
Falcon I (Birdman) (1982-83) 625, 656
Falcon II (Birdman) (1982-83) 625, 656
Falcon V (CGS) (1981-82) 616, 632
Falcon 5 + (CGS) (1981-82) 616, 632
Falcon, AG-38 (Mitchell Wing) (1985-86) 698
FARGE, JUAN DE LA (Argentina) (1987-88) 537
Farmate (SV Aircraft) 506
Faucheux (Danis) (1987-88) 572
Feiyan (Beijing) (1982-83) 626
FÉRÉ, RENÉ (France) (1986-87) 574
FEUGRAY, G (France) (1986-87) 574
Fiesta (Aero Innovations) (1987-88) 631
Firebird FB-1 (Tirith) (1986-87) 621
Firebird FB-2 (Tirith) (1986-87) 621
FIREBIRD LEICHTFLUGZEUGBAU GmbH (West Germany) (1984-85) 669
FIREBIRD SCHWIEGER & JEHLE (West Germany) (1986-87) 594
Firebolt (Starfire) (1987-88) 710
Firebolt convertible (Starfire) 600
Firefly (Payne) (1987-88) 690
Firefly (Statler) (1986-87) 715
Firestar (Kolb) 579
FIRST STRIKE INC (USA) 570
Firebird Flyer (Competition Aircraft) (1983-84) 658
FISHERCRAFT INC (USA) 572
FISHER FLYING PRODUCTS INC (USA) 570
Flamingon (Kolodziej) (1983-84) 692
Flash (Pegasus) (1987-88) 618
Flash-3 (Wolff) 539
FLETCHER, DANIEL & RICHARD (Canada) (1987-88) 548
FLEXI-FORM SKYSAILS (UK) (1986-87) 612
FLICK AVIATION (USA) (1987-88) 664
Flick Monoplane (Flick Aviation) (1987-88) 664
FLIGHT 95 (Australia) (1987-88) 538
FLIGHT DYNAMICS INC (USA) (1986-87) 664
FLIGHT LEVEL SIX-ZERO INC (USA) 572
FLIGHT RESEARCH (UK) (1986-87) 612
FlightStar (Pioneer) (1985-86) 703
FLIGHTWORKS CORPORATION (USA) 572
Floater, Beaver (Spectrum) 510
FLUGTECHNISCHE FORSCHUNGSGRUPPE an der TECHNISCHEN UNIVERSITÄT MÜNCHEN (Germany) 531
Fly Baby 1A (Bowers) 558
Fly Baby 1B (Bowers) 559
Flycycle (Kennedy Aircraft) 578
Flyer (Kolb) (1983-84) 665
Flying-Boat (Polaris Motor) (1987-88) 605
FLYLITE (UK) (1986-87) 613
Focke-Wulf 190 (WAR) 612
Focke-Wulf Fw 190 (Thunder Wings) 606
Fokker D.VII (Squadron Aviation) 600
Fokker Dr 1 Replica Triplane (Sands) 596
Fokker D.VII Replica (Iseman) (1986-87) 675
Fokker-Lite (Tact-Avia) (1986-87) 720
Forger (Chargus) (1984-85) 677
Forger (Pegasus) (1987-88) 618
FORSGREN, LYLE (USA) (1987-88) 665
Fox (Gigax) (1984-85) 674
Fox-C22 (Ikarus Deutschland Comco) 533
Fox-D (Ikarus Deutschland Comco) 533
FoxBat Fledge (Manta) (1982-83) 647
Foxbat (Manta) (1987-88) 680
Foxcat (Ultrasport) (1986-87) 603
FRANCE AÉROLIGHTS SA (France) (1987-88) 574
FRANZ (see Ul-Bau-Franz) (1987-88) 594
Fred Series 3 (Clutton-Tabenor) (1987-88) 651
Freedom 28 (BAC) 557
Freedom 48 (BAC) 558
FREEDOM FLIERS INC (USA) 572
Freedom Machine (Brock) 560
FREEDOM MASTER CORPORATION (USA) 572
FREE FLIGHT AVIATION PTY LTD (Australia) (1986-87) 538
FREE SPIRIT AIRCRAFT COMPANY LTD (USA) 573
FRIEBE LUFTFAHRT-BEDARF (West Germany) (1983-84) 642
Frolov Monoplane (1987-88) 612
FROLOV, V (USSR) (1987-88) 612
FULMAR (France) (1983-84) 640
FULMAR ULTRALIGHT DIFFUSION (Belgium) (1985-86) 642
FULTON AIRCRAFT LTD (UK) 544
FUM (Australia) (1987-88) 538
Fun Fly (Swiss Aerolight) 542
Fun Javelin (1986-87) 538
Fury (Two Wings) 607
Fury II (Isaacs) 544

G

G11 (Moto-Delta) (1983-84) 640
G20 (Moto-Delta) (1982-83) 628
G-802 (Aerodis) 518
GB-3 Vetro (Bezzola) (1987-88) 610
G.B.10 Pou-Push (Briffaud) (1986-87) 566
GL06 (Landray) (1987-88) 579
GMD 330 (Goodwin) (1985-86) 667
GN-1 Aircamper (Grega) 573
GP3 Pereira (Osprey Aircraft) 587
GP4 Pereira (Osprey Aircraft) 588
GR-2 Whisper (Grove) (1987-88) 668
GQ-01 Monogast (Quaissard) (1986-87) 590
GT, Quicksilver (Eipper) 569
GW-1 Windwagon (Watson) 612
GY-120 (Gardan) (1986-87) 575
Gambit (Scicraft) 535
GANZER, DAVID, W (USA) (1987-88) 666
GARDAN (see Avions Yves Gardan) (1986-87) 575
GARDNER, DEGA APPLIED TECHNOLOGY (UK) (1987-88) 614
Garnis (LAK) 543
GATARD (see Avions A. Gatard) 522
GEISER, JEAN MARC (France) (1984-85) 668
Gemini (Ganzer) (1987-88) 666
Gemini (Thruster Aircraft) (1987-88) 542
Gemini 2 (Mainair Sports) (1987-88) 616
Gemini Flash 2 (Mainair Sports) (1987-88) 616
Gemini Flash 2 Alpha (Mainair Sports) 544
GEMINI INTERNATIONAL INC (USA) (1985-86) 688
Gidra (Aeroprakt) (1986-87) 610
GIGAX, HANS (Switzerland) (1985-86) 663
Gil (Kolodziej) (1984-85) 692
Giro-Heli (Berger) (1987-88) 610
GLA INC (USA) (1982-83) 644
Glasair II (Stoddard-Hamilton) 602
Glasair III (Stoddard-Hamilton) 603
Glasair FT (Stoddard-Hamilton) 601
Glasair RG (Stoddard-Hamilton) 602
Glasair TD (Stoddard-Hamilton) 601
Gnatsum (Jurca) 524
Gold Duster (Goldwing) (1982-83) 644
GOLDEN AGE AIRCRAFT COMPANY (USA) (1985-86) 688
Goldwing (Goldwing) (1986-87) 667
GOLDWING LTD (USA) (1986-87) 667
GOODWIN PROPELLERS (UK) (1985-86) 667
GORDON BEDSON AND ASSOCIATES (Australia) (1986-87) 537
Goshawk (Highster) (1981-82) 620
Grach (Leningrad Central) (1982-83) 634
Graflite (Lundy) 582
Grasshopper (Winton) (1982-83) 624
GREENWOOD AIRCRAFT INC (USA) (1986-87) 668
GREGA, JOHN W (USA) 573
Ground Troop Army Trainers (Rotec) (1987-88) 703
GROVE AIRCRAFT COMPANY (USA) (1987-88) 668
GROVER AIRCRAFT CORPORATION (USA) (1986-87) 669
GUERPONT (France) 522
Guri (Pazmany) 588
Gypsy, Chotia (Weedhopper) (1981-82) 629
GYRO 2000 (USA) 574
Gyrochopper II (Alderfer) 556
Gyrochopper III (Alderfer) 556
Gyro Copter (Bensen) (1986-87) 638
Gyro Glider (Bensen) (1986-87) 638
Gyroplane, JE-2 (Eich) 568

H

H-39 Diana (Hoffmann) (1986-87) 595
HA-2M Sportster (Aircraft Designs) 555
HFL-UL (Höhenflug) (1984-85) 670
H.M.81 Tomcat (Waspair) (1983-84) 683
H.M.81 (Midwest) (1985-86) 697
HM 1000 (Mignet) 527
HN 433 Menestral (Nicollier) 528
HN 434 Super Menestral (Nicollier) 528
HN 600 Week-End (Nicollier) 528
HP.IV (High Perspective) (1981-82) 607
HX-321 (Hamilton) 574
HAIGH, JOSEPH (USA) (1986-87) 669
Half Pint (Medway Microlights) 546
HALL, LARRY (USA) (1981-82) 620
HALLMARK AIRCRAFT CORPORATION (USA) (1984-85) 700
HAMILTON AEROSPACE (USA) 574
Hamlet (Aeroprakt) (1986-87) 610
HAPI ENGINES INC (USA) 574
HARMON (USA) (1987-88) 668
Harrier (Wills Wing) (1982-83) 657
HATZ AIRPLANE SHOP (USA) 575
Hawk (Austin) (1986-87) 636
Hawk (CGS) (1987-88) 650
HEADBERG AVIATION INC (USA) 575
Helios (Aéro Delta) (1986-87) 562
Heron (Fulmar) (1984-85) 659
HEWA-TECHNICS (West Germany) 532
HFL-FLUGZEUGBAU GmbH (West Germany) 532
Hidra (Aeroprakt) (1987-88) 611
HIGHCRAFT AERO-MARINE (USA) (1986-87) 670
HIGH PERSPECTIVE INC (Canada) (1981-82) 607
Highster (Highster) (1981-82) 620
HIGHSTER AIRCRAFT INC (USA) (1981-82) 620
Hi-Max (T.E.A.M.) 606
Hi-Nuski (Lafayette) (1981-82) 622
Hi-Nuski Huski (Advanced Aviation) (1983-84) 652
Hiperbipe (Sorrell) 598
Hiperlight (Sorrell) 598
Hiperlight EXB (Sorrell) 598
Hirondelle (Chasle) 520
Hirondelle, PGK-1 (Western Aircraft) 513
HIRTH GmbH, WOLF (West Germany) (1981-82) 610
Hitchiker (Labahan) 504
HIWAY HANG GLIDERS LTD (UK) (1984-85) 726
HOBBYSTICA AVIO (Italy) 537
HOFFMANN FLUGZEUGBAU KG, WOLF (West Germany) (1986-87) 595
HOLCOMB, JERRY (USA) 576
Hollman Bumble Bee (Aircraft Designs) 555
Hollman Sportster (Aircraft Designs) 555
Honcho, DS-27A (Delta) (1982-83) 640
Honcho, DS-28A (Delta) (1981-82) 617
Honcho II (Magnum) 584
HONGXING MACHINERY FACTORY (China) (1985-86) 650
Hornet (Free Flight) (1986-87) 538
Hornet (SR-1) (1985-86) 709
Hornet 130S (Free Flight) (1983-84) 633
HORNET MICROLIGHTS (TEMPLEWARD LTD) (UK) (1987-88) 614
HOSKINS, CRAIG (USA) (1986-87) 671
HOVEY, ROBERT W. (USA) 576
HOWARD HUGHES ENGINEERING PTY LTD (Australia) 503
HOWATHERM GmbH & Co KG (West Germany) (1986-87) 596
HUABEI MACHINERY FACTORY (China) (1987-88) 562
Huber 101-1 Aero (Huber) (1985-86) 690
HUBER, JAMES M (USA) (1985-86) 690
HUDSON, SANDY (USA) (1982-83) 646
HUGHES (see Howard Hughes Engineering) 503
HUMBERT (France) (1987-88) 574
Humlan (Ekström) 541
HUMMEL AIRCRAFT (USA) 576
Hummel Bird (Hummel) 576
Hummer (Maxair) (1985-86) 696
Hummingbird (Degraw) (1986-87) 654
Hummingbird (Gemini) (1984-85) 698
HUNTAIR LTD (UK) (1985-86) 667
HUTCHINSON AIRCRAFT COMPANY (USA) 576
Hybred 440R (Medway Microlights) 545
Hydro-Copter (Bensen) (1986-87) 638
Hydro-Glider (Bensen) (1986-87) 638
Hydrolight (Diehl) 566
HYDROPLUM (Sarl) 522
Hydroplum (Tisserand/Hydroplum) 522
Hydroplum II/Petrel (Tisserand/Hydroplum) 522

I

I-66L San Francesco (Iannotta) 538
IAC (see International Aeromarine Corporation) ... *(1986-87)* 674
IAC (see International Aircraft Corporation) ... *(1986-87)* 674
Iannotta 940 Zefiro (Iannotta) 538
IANNOTTA DOTT ING ORLANDO (Italy) 538
Ibis (ACT) ... *(1982-83)* 638
Ibis (Delemontez) ... *(1986-87)* 572
Ibis (Junqua) ... *(1987-88)* 576
IKARUS-COMCO (West Germany) ... *(1984-85)* 670
IKARUS DEUTSCHLAND COMCO GmbH (West Germany) 532
Imp (Aerocar/Brown) ... *(1986-87)* 643
INAV Ltd (USA) ... *(1986-87)* 674
Instructor (Robertson) ... *(1984-85)* 712
Intermezzo (Aéroplum) ... *(1986-87)* 563
INTERNATIONAL AEROMARINE CORPORATION (USA) ... *(1986-87)* 674
INTERNATIONAL AIRCRAFT CORPORATION (USA) ... *(1986-87)* 674
INTERNATIONAL ULTRALIGHTS INC (USA) ... *(1985-86)* 692
INTERNATIONAL ULTRALITE AVIATION INC (USA) ... *(1985-86)* 692
Intruder (Sorrell) 598
Invader (Hornet) ... *(1986-87)* 614
Invader Updated (Hornet) ... *(1986-87)* 614
Invader Mk III-B (Ultra Efficient Products) 608
ISAACS, JOHN O (UK) 544
ISEMAN BOB (USA) ... *(1986-87)* 675
ITALZAIR (see Nike Aeronautica) ... *(1986-87)* 602
Italzair (Italzair) ... *(1986-87)* 602
Italzair (Nike Aeronautica) 538

J

J-2 Polonez (Janowski) 540
J2G2 (Black) ... *(1983-84)* 656
J-3 Kitten (Anglin) ... *(1984-85)* 688
J-3 Kitten (Grover) ... *(1985-86)* 689
J-4 Sportster (Grover) ... *(1985-86)* 689
J 4B (Barnett Rotorcraft) 558
J 4B-2 (Barnett Rotorcraft) 558
J-5 Janowski (Marko-Elektronik) ... *(1986-87)* 605
J-5 Marco (Hewa-Technics) 532
J-5 Marco (Marko-Elektronik) ... *(1986-87)* 605
J-6 Karatoo (Country Air) 564
JB-1000 (Leader's) 580
JC-01 (Coupé-Aviation) 521
JC-2 (Coupé-Aviation) 521
JC-3 (Coupé-Aviation) 521
JC-24B Weedhopper (Weedhopper) ... *(1981-82)* 629
JC-24BL Weedhopper II (Weedhopper) ... *(1981-82)* 629
JC-24C Weedhopper C (Weedhopper) ... *(1983-84)* 683
JC-31C (Weedhopper) ... *(1982-83)* 657
JD-2 Delta (Dyke) 566
JD3 Puffin (Stewart) ... *(1981-82)* 625
JE-2 Gyroplane (Eich) 568
J.H.03 Le Courlis (Erpals Industrie) ... *(1986-87)* 574
J.T.1 Monplane (Taylor) 548
J.T.2 Titch (Taylor) 548
JT-5 (Tervamaki) 516
Ju 87B2 replica (Langhurst) ... *(1987-88)* 676
Jackeroo (Winton) ... *(1986-87)* 543
Jaeger (Eagle Wings) 567
JAEGER, JIM (USA) ... *(1982-83)* 646
JANOWSKI, JAROSLOW (Poland) 540
Javelin (Flight 95) ... *(1987-88)* 538
JAVELIN AIRCRAFT COMPANY INC (USA) 577
J-Bird (Jaeger) ... *(1982-83)* 646
Jeep (Fum) ... *(1987-88)* 538
Jenny (Cloud Dancer) ... *(1987-88)* 651
Jet Hawk II (Saunders) ... *(1987-88)* 704
Jet Wing ATV (Flight Designs) ... *(1984-85)* 696
JINZHOU MICROLIGHT HELICOPTER COMPANY (China) ... *(1986-87)* 560
Johan SH-1 (LADAS) ... *(1981-82)* 630
JONES, MASON (Canada) ... *(1986-87)* 546
JORDAN AVIATION LTD (UK) ... *(1985-86)* 668
JODEL (see Avions Jodel SA) 523
Jr Ace, Corben (Acro Sport) 550
Junior Ace Model E (ACE Aircraft) 549
Juno (Thor) 512
Junster I (Macfam) 582
Junster II (Macfam) 582
JUNQUA/ANDREAZZA, ROGER and JEAN-YVES (France) ... *(1986-87)* 576
JUNQUA, ROGER (France) ... *(1987-88)* 576
JURCA, MARCEL (France) 524

K

KB-2 (Brock) 560
KB-3 (Brock) 560
KDA (see Kany, Dreyer and Aupy) ... *(1983-84)* 640
Kh-14A (Dmitriev) ... *(1987-88)* 612
KR-1 (Rand Robinson) 592
KR-2 (Rand Robinson) 592
KR-100 (Rand Robinson) 592
KNL (see Kolo Naukowe Lotnikow, Politechnika Warszawska) ... *(1982-83)* 632
KX 400 (Kolb) ... *(1985-86)* 692
KALER CORPORATION, THE (USA) ... *(1985-86)* 692
Kanion (Sznapki) ... *(1983-84)* 687, 692
KANY, DREYER and AUPY (France) ... *(1983-84)* 640
Karatoo (Country Air) 564
Kasia DK-3 (Marganski) 540
Kasperwing 1-80 (Cascade) 562
KAZUROV/POLUSHKIN/RUSAKOV (USSR) ... *(1982-83)* 634
KELLY, DUDLEY R (USA) 578
Kelly-D (Kelly) 578
Kelly-D11 (Kelly) 578
KENNEDY AIRCRAFT COMPANY INC (USA) 578
Kestrel Hawk (Sun Fun) ... *(1987-88)* 552
KICENIUK JR, TARAS (USA) ... *(1981-82)* 621
KIMBERLEY, GARETH J. (Australia) 503
KIMBREL, MICHAEL G. (USA) 578
King Cobra (Advanced Aviation) ... *(1985-86)* 673
King Cobra B (Advanced Aviation) 550
Kitfox (Denny Aerocraft) 566
Kitten (Anglin) ... *(1984-85)* 688
Kitten (Grover) ... *(1985-86)* 689
King Fisher (Anderson) ... *(1986-87)* 636
Kingfisher (Anderson-Warner) 612
KITTY HAWK KITES INC (USA) ... *(1982-83)* 646
Knight Twister (Payne) ... *(1985-86)* 607
Koala (Fisher) ... *(1986-87)* 662
Koala FP-202 (Fisher) 570
Kobuz (Korola) ... *(1982-83)* 632
Kodiak (Sequoia) 597
KOLB COMPANY INC (USA) 578
Kolibri (AFG) ... *(1987-88)* 592
KOLODZIEJ, ZDZISLAW (Poland) ... *(1984-85)* 725, 730
KOLO NAUKOWE LOTNIKOW, POLITECHNIKA WARSZAWSKA (Poland) ... *(1982-83)* 632
KONSUPROD GmbH & Co KG (Germany) 534
KOROLA, J (Poland) ... *(1982-83)* 632
KOROLEV, Y (USSR) ... *(1987-88)* 612
Kricket DK 1 (FLSZ) 572
KUBASEK, JOHN W (USA) ... *(1981-82)* 622

L

L5 (Lucas) 526
L6-7 (Lucas) 527
L.A4a Luton Minor (PFA) 547
LAK (see Litovskaya Aviatsionnaya Konstruktsiya) 543
LF-1 (Forsgren) ... *(1987-88)* 665
LG 150 (Leglaive-Gautier) ... *(1987-88)* 580
LM-1 (Light Miniature) 580
LM-1U (Light Miniature) 580
LM-1X (Light Miniature) 580
LM-3U (Light Miniature) 581
LM-3X (Light Miniature) 581
LNB 11 (Cuvelier) ... *(1986-87)* 571
LO-120 (Vogt) 534
LP-1 Sibylle (Lendepergt) 526
LABAHAN, ROBERT (Australia) 504
LADAS (see Liga Argentina de Aerodeslizadores Superlivianos) ... *(1981-82)* 605
Lady Bug (McAsco) ... *(1987-88)* 549
Lala 1 (Djuric) ... *(1986-87)* 594
LEAF (see Leading Edge Air Foils Inc) ... *(1984-85)* 702
LEE, G, CIRCA REPRODUCTIONS (Canada) ... *(1985-86)* 644
LACO (USA) 580
Laco-125 (Laco) 580
Laco-145 (Laco) 580
Lacroix 2L12 (Cuvelier) ... *(1986-87)* 571
Lacroix LNB-11 (Cuvelier) ... *(1986-87)* 571
Ladybird (Campbell-Jones) ... *(1983-84)* 646
LAFAYETTE AVIATION AND AIRCRAFT (USA) ... *(1981-82)* 622
Lancair 200 (Neico Aviation) 586
Lancair 235 (Neico Aviation) 586
Lancer IVL (Flight Designs) ... *(1981-82)* 618, 632
Lancer IVS (Flight Designs) ... *(1981-82)* 618, 632
Lancer MA-4 (Marquart) 584
Lancer Mk IV (Pacific Kites) ... *(1984-85)* 686
LANDRAY, GILBERT (France) ... *(1987-88)* 579
LANGHURST, LOUIS F. (USA) ... *(1987-88)* 676
LANOT-AVIATION (France) ... *(1986-87)* 580
LASCAUD, ETS D (France) 526
LASER AEROBATICS (Australia) 504
LATÉCOÈRE (see Société Industrielle Latécoère SA) ... *(1986-87)* 580
Latécoère 225 (Latécoère) ... *(1986-87)* 580
Laughing Gull (Earthstar) 568
Laughing Gull II (Earthstar) 568
LAVORINI, NEDO (Italy) ... *(1987-88)* 604
Lazair (Ultraflight) 512
Lazair II (Ultraflight) 512
LEADER'S INTERNATIONAL INC (USA) 580
LEADING EDGE AIR FOILS INC (USA) ... *(1984-85)* 702
Le Courlis (Erpals Industrie) ... *(1986-87)* 574
LEDERLIN, FRANÇOIS (France) 526
Lederlin 380-L (Lederlin) 526
LEFEBVRE, ROBERT (France) ... *(1986-87)* 581
LEGLAIVE-GAUTIER (France) ... *(1987-88)* 580
LEICHTFLUGZEUG GmbH & Co KG (Germany) 534
LENDEPERGT, PATRICK (France) 526
LENINGRAD CENTRAL NII (USSR) ... *(1982-83)* 634
Leone (Aui) 536
Le Pelican (Ultravia) 513
LESAGE, CHRISTIAN ... *(1986-87)* 582
Le Solitaire (Cuvelier) 571
Lespace (Proust/Sigur) ... *(1986-87)* 589
LIGA ARGENTINA DE AERODESLIZADORES SUPERLIVIANOS (Argentina) ... *(1981-82)* 605
LIGETI AERO-NAUTICAL PTY LTD (Australia) 505
LIGHT AERO INC (USA) 580
Light Flyer (Pterodactyl) ... *(1983-84)* 672
Light Flyer (Freedom Fliers) ... *(1984-85)* 698
LIGHT MINIATURE AIRCRAFT INC (USA) 580
Lightning DS (Ultra Sports) ... *(1984-85)* 684
Lightning P-38 (Mitchell Wing) 586
LightWing Aeropower 28 (Hughes) 503
LightWing R 55 (Hughes) 503
Lion Cub (MFS) ... *(1987-88)* 608
LITECRAFT INC (USA) ... *(1986-87)* 682
LITE-FLITE INC (USA) ... *(1987-88)* 679
LITOVSKAYA AVIATSIONNAYA KONSTRUKTSIYA (USSR) 543
LITTLE AIRPLANE COMPANY, THE (USA) ... *(1985-86)* 694
Little Bi (Simpson Midwest) ... *(1986-87)* 709
Little Dipper replica (R.D. Aircraft) 594
LOEHLE ENTERPRISES (USA) 581
Lone Ranger (Striplin) ... *(1983-84)* 677
Lone Ranger (Striplin) 603
LONG, JIM (USA) ... *(1983-84)* 666
Longnose Pelican (Ultravia) 513
LOPRESTI BROTHERS AIRCRAFT INC (USA) ... *(1987-88)* 680
Lotus 15 (La Mouette) ... *(1981-82)* 609, 630
Lotus 17 (La Mouette) ... *(1981-82)* 609, 630
LOTUS CARS LTD (UK) ... *(1985-86)* 668
Lotus Microlight (Lotus) ... *(1985-86)* 668
LUCANT, MOTO (France) ... *(1987-88)* 580
LUCAS, EMILE (France) 526
Lucky (T.E.D.A.) 538
LUNDY, BRIAN (USA) 582
Luton L.A.4a Minor (PFA) 547

M

M1 (Antonov) 542
M1 (Firebird) ... *(1986-87)* 594
M 11 (Bushby) 560
MA-4 (Marquart) 584
MA-5 (Marquart) 584
MAC Mattison (see Hallmark) ... *(1984-85)* 703
MB-2 Colibri 2 (Brügger) 542
MB.10 (Boudeau) ... *(1986-87)* 566
MBA (see Micro Biplane Aviation) ... *(1985-86)* 669
MBB (see Messerschmitt-Bölkow-Blohm GmbH) ... *(1987-88)* 596
MC 15 Cricri (Colomban) 520
MEA (see Micro Engineering (Aviation) Ltd) ... *(1982-83)* 636
MFI (see Malmo Forsknings & Innovations AB) 542
MFI-9 HB (Andreasson) 540
MFS (see Microlight Flight Systems Pty Ltd) 540
MIM (see Moura, Maurice Impelizieri) ... *(1987-88)* 544
MIT (see Massachusetts Institute of Technology) ... *(1987-88)* 684
M.J.2 Tempête (Jurca) 524
M.J.3H Dart (Jurca) ... *(1987-88)* 577
MJ-5 (Birdman) ... *(1982-83)* 625, 656
M.J.5 Sirocco (Jurca) 524
M.J.5 Sirocco Sport Wing (Jurca) 524
MJ-6 (Birdman) ... *(1982-83)* 625, 656
M.J.7 Gnatsum (Jurca) 524
M.J.7S Solo (Jurca) ... *(1987-88)* 578
M.J.8 (Jurca) 525
M.J.9 One-Oh-Nine (Jurca) 526
M.J.10 Spit (Jurca) 526
M.J.12 Pee-40 (Jurca) 526
M.J.22 Tempête (Jurca) 524
M.J.51 Sperocco (Jurca) 524
M.J.52 Zephyr (Jurca) 524
M.J.70 (Jurca) 525
M.J.77 Gnatsum (Jurca) 524
M.J.80 1-Nine-Oh (Jurca) 525
M.J.90 (Jurca) 526
M.J.100 (Jurca) 526
MM-1 (Bushby) 560
MP-16 (Fulmar) ... *(1984-85)* 659
M.P. Unik (Pomergau) ... *(1987-88)* 550
MT5 (VPM SnC) ... *(1986-87)* 604
MT7 (VPM SnC) ... *(1986-87)* 604
Mü 30 (Akaflieg München) 531
MW4 (Whittaker) ... *(1983-84)* 651
MW5 Sorcerer (Whittaker) 548
MW5, Whittaker (Aerotech) ... *(1986-87)* 612
MW6 Merlin (Whittaker) 548
MACAIR INDUSTRIES INC (Canada) 509
MACFAM (USA) 582
Mach .07 (Beaujon) ... *(1986-87)* 637
Mach 01 (France Aérolights) ... *(1986-87)* 574
Mach 20 (France Aérolights) ... *(1986-87)* 574
Maestro (A.I.R's) 518
MAGAL HOLDINGS LTD (Canada) 509
MAGNUM INDUSTRIES (USA) 584
MAINAIR SPORTS LTD (UK) 544
MALMO FORSKNINGS & INNOVATIONS AB (Sweden) 542
MANTA PRODUCTS INC (USA) ... *(1987-88)* 680
Marco J-5 (Hewa-Technics) 532
MARGANSKI, EDWARD (Poland) 540
MARKO-ELEKTRONIK COMPANY (Poland) ... *(1986-87)* 605
Mariah, T-100A (Turner) ... *(1983-84)* 680
Mariah, T-100B (Turner) ... *(1985-86)* 712
Mariah, T-100D (Turner) 607
MARQUART, ED (USA) 584
MARQUIOND R (France) ... *(1987-88)* 582
Mars-Beryl, WT-10 (Talanchuk) ... *(1981-82)* 607, 630
Mars-Marta, WT-9 (Talanchuk) ... *(1981-82)* 607, 630
MARSHALL, FRANK (UK) ... *(1981-82)* 614
MARSKE AIRCRAFT CORPORATION (USA) ... *(1982-83)* 648
MASSACHUSETTS INSTITUTE OF TECHNOLOGY (USA) ... *(1987-88)* 684
MATTHEWS, LYLE (USA) ... *(1986-87)* 684
MATTISON AIRCRAFT COMPANY (USA) ... *(1983-84)* 666
Maverick (Skytek) 505
MAXAIR AIRCRAFT CORPORATION (USA) 584
Maxi Stinger Mark III (Moyes) ... *(1982-83)* 623, 656
Maxi Stinger Mark IV (Moyes) ... *(1982-83)* 624
Maxi Stinger SP (Moyes) ... *(1982-83)* 624, 656
Maya (Percy) 505
McASCO AIRCRAFT DIVISION (Canada) 548
MDK KRAKOW-NOWA HUTA (Poland) ... *(1983-84)* 644
MEAD ENGINEERING COMPANY (USA) ... *(1986-87)* 685
Meadowlark (Meadowlark) ... *(1986-87)* 686
MEADOWLARK ULTRALIGHT CORPORATION (USA) ... *(1986-87)* 686
MEDWAY MICROLIGHTS (UK) 545
Mega Major (Moyes) ... *(1982-83)* 624, 656

Mega Mark II (Moyes) (1982-83) 624, 656
Mega Mark III (Moyes) (1982-83) 624, 656
Menestrel (Nicollier) 528
Mercure (Danis) (1987-88) 572
Mercury (Aviation Composites) 544
Mercury (Inav/Aviation Composites) (1986-87) 675
MERGANSER AIRCRAFT CORPORATION (USA) 585
Merganser (Merganser) (1987-88) 682
Merlin (Macair) 509
Merlin (Mainair) (1985-86) 668
Merlin (Whittaker) 548
MESSERSCHMITT-BÖLKOW-BLOHM GmbH (West Germany) (1987-88) 596
Météor (Danis) (1982-83) 628
MICHEL (France) (1987-88) 582
Michelob Light Eagle (MIT) (1987-88) 684
Micro-Bipe (MBA) (1982-83) 636
MICRO BIPLANE AVIATION (UK) (1985-86) 669
MICRO FLIGHT AIRCRAFT LTD (UK) 546
MICRO ENGINEERING (AVIATION) LTD (UK) (1982-83) 636
Micro-Imp (Aerocar) 552
MICROLIGHT FLIGHT SYSTEMS PTY LTD (South Africa) 540
Microlight (Lotus) (1985-86) 668
MICROLITE SYSTEMS INC (USA) (1982-83) 648
Micro-Star (Friebe) (1983-84) 642
Micro Star (Gygax) (1983-84) 646
Microtug Tow Trike (Mainair) (1985-86) 669
Midget IV (Abe) (1982-83) 631
Midget V (Abe) (1983-84) 644
Midget 6 (Abe) (1984-85) 673
Midget Mustang (Bushby) 560
MIDLAND ULTRALIGHTS LTD (UK) (1987-88) 617
MIDWEST MICROLIGHTS (USA) (1985-86) 696
Mifeng-2 (BIAA) 516
Mifeng-3 (BIAA) 516
Mifeng-4 and 4A (BIAA) 516
Mifeng-5 (BIAA) 516
MIGNET (see Société d'exploitation des Aéronefs Henri Mignet) 527
Mignet (Lavorini) (1987-88) 604
Mikro-2M (Shcheglov) (1987-88) 612
Milan (Howatherm) (1986-87) 596
MILLER SPORTS INC (USA) 585
MINER, EARL L (USA) 682
Mini Ace (Cvjetkovic) 564
Minibat (GLA) (1982-83) 644
Mini Coupe (Buck Sport) (1986-87) 644
Mini-Imp (Aerocar) 552
Mini-Jumbo (Say, Maxwell) (1986-87) 549
MiniMax (T.E.A.M.) 605
MINIMAX T.E.A.M. (USA) (1985-86) 697
Minimum (NST) (1987-88) 596
Minimum-Trike (NST) (1987-88) 596
Mini-Spit (Ailes de K) (1985-86) 663
Ministar (NST) (1987-88) 596
Minor, L.A. 4a (PFA) 547
Mirac (Mainair) (1985-86) 669
Mirage II (Mirage) (1987-88) 684
MIRAGE AIRCRAFT INC (MASS) (USA) 585
MIRAGE AIRCRAFT INC (OREGON) (USA) (1987-88) 683
Mirage (Ultralight Flight) (1983-84) 681
MIRA SLOVAK AVIATION (USA) (1987-88) 684
Missile (Moyes) (1984-85) 724, 730
Mister America (Harmon) (1987-88) 668
Mistral (Aviasud) 519
Mistral II, BA83 (Binder) 532
Mistral 503 (Aviasud) 520
Mistral Trainer (MEA) (1982-83) 636
MITCHELL AEROSPACE COMPANY (USA) 586
MITCHELL AIRCRAFT CORPORATION (USA) (1983-84) 667
MITCHELL WING (see Mitchell Aerospace Company) 586
Mobycoptère (Pauchard) (1987-88) 584
Model II (Monarch) (1982-83) 649
Model V (Stratus) (1981-82) 626, 632
Model 75 Gemini (Ganzer) (1987-88) 666
Model 300 Sequoia (Sequoia) 596
Model 302 Kodiak (Sequoia) 597
Model A (Partnerships) (1984-85) 708
Model A, Standard Ritz (Loehle) 581
Model C (Meadowlark) (1986-87) 686
Model D, Baby Ace (ACE Aircraft) 549
Model E, Junior Ace (ACE Aircraft) 549
Model RF (Double Eagle) (1986-87) 656
Model 'S' Sidewinder (Smyth) 598
Model S-12-E Sr (Spencer) 599
Model W-8 Tailwind (Wittman) 614
Model W-10 Tailwind (Wittman) 614
Model T (Worldwide Ultralite) (1984-85) 722
Model XA/350 Buccaneer (Advanced Aviation) 550
Model Z (Laser Aerobatics) 504
Mohawk (Warpath) (1983-84) 682
Monarch II (Monarch) (1982-83) 649, 658
Monarch C (Marske) (1981-82) 622
Monarch D (Marske) (1982-83) 648, 658
MONARCH PRODUCTS INC (USA) (1982-83) 649
Mono-Fly (Teman) (1982-83) 653
Monogast (Quaissard) (1986-87) 590
Monoplane (Frolov) (1987-88) 612
Monoplane (Lucant) (1987-88) 580
Monoplane, J.T.1 (Taylor) 548
Mono Z-CH 100 (Zenair) 514
MOONEY MITE AIRCRAFT CORPORATION (USA) (1986-87) 689
Mooney Mite (Mooney Mite) (1986-87) 689
MORGAN AIRCRAFT (USA) (1986-87) 690
MORRISEY AIRCRAFT CORPORATION (USA) (1987-88) 686
Moskito (Konsuprod) 534
MOSLER MOTORS INC (USA) 586
MOTO-DELTA (see Geiser, Jean Marc) (1984-85) 668
Moto du Cicl (Humbert) (1987-88) 574
MOTOPLANE (France) (1983-84) 641
MOTORIZED GLIDERS OF IOWA (USA) (1982-83) 649
Mouette (La Mouette) (1981-82) 609, 630
MOURA, MAURICIO IMPELIZIERI P (Brazil) (1987-88) 544
Mouse (Nostalgair) (1987-88) 687
Mr East (Mathews) (1986-87) 684
MUDRY ET CIE, AVIONS (France) (1983-84) 641
MURPHY, A (Ireland) (1986-87) 599
MURPHY AVIATION LTD (Canada) 510
Mustang (Ulm Progress) (1987-88) 590
Mustang 11 (Bushby) 560
Mustang 5151 (Loehle) 582

N

N2 Mouse (Nostalgair) (1987-88) 687
N3 Pup (Mosler Motors) 586
N3 Pup (Nostalgair) (1987-88) 688
NAC (see National Aircraft Corporation) (1986-87) 690
NAI (see Nanjing Aeronautical Institute) 516
NF.001 (Michel) (1987-88) 582
NFL (Pterodactyl) (1981-82) 624
NST (see Norbert Schwarze Maschinenbau) (1987-88) 596
NANJING AERONAUTICAL INSTITUTE (China) 516
NASH, PAUL L (USA) (1984-85) 707
NATIONAL AIRCRAFT CORPORATION (USA) (1986-87) 690
NEICO AVIATION INC (USA) 586
NELSON, ROBERT (USA) (1984-85) 707
NEUKOM SEGELFLUGZEUGBAU, ALBERT (Switzerland) (1985-86) 663
Nexus (Goldwing) (1984-85) 688
NICOLLIER, AVIONS H (France) 528
Nieuport 11 (Circa Reproductions) 508
Nieuport 12 (Circa Reproductions) 508
Nighthawk (Theis) (1981-82) 627
NIKE AERONAUTICA SRL (Italy) 538
Nimbus Minimot (APCO Aviation) (1987-88) 593
Ninja series (CMV) (1987-88) 569
NIPPER KITS AND COMPONENTS LTD (UK) 546
Nipper Mk IIIb (Nipper) 546
NOBLE HARDMAN AVIATION LTD (UK) 546
NOIN (see Ets Noin Aéronautiques) 528
Nomad, DS-26 (Delta) (1982-83) 640
Nomad (Flight Research) (1985-86) 666
Nomad II (Magnum) 584
Nomad 425 (Flight Research) (1986-87) 612
Nomad Tribe (Flight Research) (1986-87) 612
NORBERT SCHWARZE MASCHINENBAU (West Germany) (1987-88) 596
NORTHSTAR LTD (USA) (1986-87) 690
NOSTALGAIR INC (USA) (1987-88) 687
Nova (Sunbird) (1981-82) 627, 632
Nova 2000 (Nova Air) (1985-86) 701
NOVA AIR INC (USA) (1985-86) 701
NUWACO AIRCRAFT COMPANY (USA) 587
Nugget (Davenport) (1986-87) 653

O

O&O Special (Wittman) (1987-88) 735
OM-1 (Morrisey) (1987-88) 686
ODYSSEY INC (USA) (1981-82) 624
OMNI-WELD INC (USA) (1984-85) 708
One-Nine-Oh (Jurca) 525
One-Oh-Nine (Jurca) 526
Onyx (Piel) 530
Opteryx III (Opteryx) (1986-87) 692
Opteryx (South and Rogers) (1983-84) 675
OPTERYX ULTRALIGHT AIRCRAFT (USA) (1986-87) 692
OPTION AIR RENO (USA) (1986-87) 692
Orion (Aerodis) 518
Orion (Skyhook Sailwings) (1984-85) 682
Orlik (Orlinski) 540
ORLINSKI, ROMAN (Poland) 540
Oscar (La Mouette) (1982-83) 628, 658
Osprey II (Osprey Aircraft) 587
OSPREY AIRCRAFT (USA) 587
Ostrowski Biplane (Ostrowski) (1985-86) 662
OSTROWSKI, JERZY (Poland) (1985-86) 662

P

P-3 (Up) (1987-88) 726
P-4 (Up) (1987-88) 726
P-9 Pixie (Acro Sport) 550
P-38 Lightning (Mitchell Wing) 586
P-40 Curtiss (Thunder Wing) 606
P-40 (DiMasco) (1986-87) 656
P-47 Thunderbolt (WAR) 612
P.50 Bouvreuil (Pottier) 530
P.70 Powell Acey Deucy (Acey Deucy) (1986-87) 622
P.70S (Pottier) 530
P.80S (Pottier) (1987-88) 588
P.100TS (Pottier) (1987-88) 588
P.105TS (Pottier) (1987-88) 588
P.110TS (Pottier) (1987-88) 588
P.170TS (Pottier) 530
P.180S (Pottier) 530
P.A.8 (Parmesani) (1987-88) 604
PFA (see Popular Flying Association) 546
PGK-1 (Western Aircraft) 513
PL.2 (Pazmany) 588
PL.3 (Pazmany) 588
PL.4A (Pazmany) 588
PM-2 Ara (MDK Krakow) (1983-84) 644
PT2 (Protech Aircraft) 591
P.U.P. (Matthews) (1986-87) 684
PW (see Politechniki Warszawskiej) (1981-82) 612
PX-2000 (Aile) (1986-87) 564
PACIFIC GULL (USA) (1981-82) 624
PACIFIC KITES (New Zealand) (1984-85) 686
Padre (Morrisey) (1987-88) 686
PAGEN, DENNIS (USA) (1984-85) 728
Panther (Rotec) 596
Panther 2 Plus (Rotec) 596
Panther Plus (Rotec) 596
Panther (Ultra Sports) (1984-85) 684
Panther XL (Pegasus) (1987-88) 619
Panther XL (Ultra Sports) (1984-85) 684
Papillon (Broc) 520
Papillon (Brugger) (1984-85) 674
Papillon (Paup) (1982-83) 650
Parafan (Centrair) 520
Parafan II (Centrair) 520
Paraplane (Paraplane) 588
PARAPLANE CORPORATION (USA) 588
Paras-Cargo, B-EC-9 (Croses) (1986-87) 570
Parasol (Aerotique) (1986-87) 631
PARKER, CALVIN Y (USA) 588
PARMESANI SANDRO (Italy) (1987-88) 604
PARSONS, DON (USA) 588
PARTNERSHIPS LIMITED INC (USA) (1985-86) 702
Pathfinder II (Huntair) (1984-85) 679
Patrilor 3 (Aile) (1986-87) 563
PAUCHARD, GIRONEF (France) (1987-88) 584
PAUP AIRCRAFT (USA) (1984-85) 708
PAYNE, VERNON W (USA) (1987-88) 690
PAZMANY AIRCRAFT CORPORATION (USA) 588
P-Craft (Paup) (1984-85) 708
Pee-40 (Jurca) 526
Pegasus (Those Flying Machines) (1983-84) 679
Pegasus II (TFM) (1986-87) 723
Pegasus Supra (TFM) (1986-87) 723
Pegasus Titan (TFM) (1986-87) 724
PEGASUS TRANSPORT SYSTEMS LTD (UK) 546
Peregrine (Sky Sports) (1981-82) 625
Pelican Club (Ultravia) 513
PENA, LOUIS (France) (1987-88) 584
Penetrater (Ultra Efficient Products) 608
PERCY, GRAHAM J (Australia) 505
Perigee (Holcomb) 576
PERSONAL PLANES INC (USA) (1983-84) 670
PETERS, WILLIAM R (USA) (1985-86) 702
Petit Breezy (Matthews) (1983-84) 666
PFLUMM, MANFRED (West Germany) (1981-82) 610
Phantom (Motoplane) (1983-84) 641
Phantom (Phantom Sport) 588
Phantom (Ultralight Flight) (1987-88) 725
PHANTOM SPORT AIRPLANE CORPORATION (USA) 588
PHASE III INC (USA) (1984-85) 710
Phoenix 6D (Delta Wing) (1982-83) 641, 658
Phoenix (Nova Air) (1985-86) 701
Phoenix (Phoenix Aviation) 599
Phoenix (Phoenix Development) (1986-87) 695
Phoenix (Soleair) (1983-84) 651
PHOENIX AVIATION (USA) 599
PHOENIX DEVELOPMENT & SPECIALITIES INC (USA) (1986-87) 695
Phoenix Lazor (Delta Wing) (1982-83) 641, 658
Phoenix SG-1 (Westwind) (1987-88) 623
Phoenix SL (Bryan) (1986-87) 644
Phoenix (Tube Works) (1987-88) 722
Phoenix Viper (Delta Wing) (1982-83) 641, 658
Phoenix X Series (Delta Wing) (1982-83) 641
Photon (Pegasus) (1987-88) 620
Piccolo (Technoflug) 534
Piccolo, AN-20K, (Borowski) (1987-88) 594
PIEL, AVIONS CLAUDE (France) 528
PIETENPOL, DONALD (USA) 590
PINAIRE ENGINEERING INC (USA) 590
Pintail (Little Airplane) (1985-86) 694
Pinocchio (Piel) 529
PIONEER INTERNATIONAL AIRCRAFT INC (USA) (1985-86) 703
Pipistrelle 2B (Southdown Aerostructure) (1986-87) 620
Pipistrelle 2C (Southdown Aerostructure) (1987-88) 622
PITTS (see Christen Industries Inc) (1987-88) 650
Pixie (Skyhook Sailwings) (1984-85) 682
Pixie, P-9 Pober (Acro Sport) 550
PLETNYOV (USSR) (1982-83) 634
Plumb Cracker Jack (Wood Wing) 614
Pober P-9 Pixie (Acro Sport) 550
POLARIS MOTOR SRL (Italy) 538
POINT AVIATION FLUGZEUGBAU GmbH (West Germany) (1985-86) 660
POISESTAR LTD (UK) (1983-84) 650
POLITECHNIKI WARSZAWSKIEJ (Poland) (1981-82) 612
Polliwagen (Polliwagen) 590
POLLIWAGEN INC (USA) 590
Polonez (Janowski) 540
POLTERGEIST AIRCRAFT DIVISION (USA) 1986-87) 697
POMERGAU, MICHAEL (Canada) (1987-88) 550
Pontresina (Colani) (1986-87) 608
Pony (Tesori Aircraft) (1986-87) 552
Poppy (Dedalus) 537
POPULAR FLYING ASSOCIATION, THE (UK) 546
POTTIER, JEAN (France) 530
Pou (Controt) (1986-87) 568
Pouplume (Croses) 522
POUR LE MERITE ULTRALIGHTS (Australia) (1987-88) 540
Pou-Push (Briffaud) (1986-87) 566
Poussin AG02 (Gatard) (1987-88) 574
Poussin AG 02Sp (Gatard) 522
Powergyro (Bensen) (1986-87) 640
PRESCOTT AERONAUTICAL CORPORATION (USA) 590
PREVOT (France) (1986-87) 589
PRODUCT MZ (Hungary) (1987-88) 600
Project 102 (Windsoar) (Birdman) (1983-84) 634
Prop-Copter (Driggers) (1985-86) 683
PROST, D (West Germany) (1984-85) 670

Prospector (Bounsall) (1987-88) 642
PROTECH AIRCRAFT INC (USA) 591
PROUST, CHRISTIAN/SIGUR (France). (1986-87) 589
PROWLER AVIATION LTD (USA) 590
Prowler (Prowler Aviation 590
PTERODACTYL (USA) (1984-85) 710
PTERODACTYL LTD (USA) (1983-84) 670
Ptiger (Freedom Fliers) (1984-85) 697
Ptraveler (Freedom Fliers) (1984-85) 696
Puffin JD3 (Stewart) (1981-82) 626
Pulsar (Aero Designs) 552
Puma (Ultrasports) (1983-84) 651
Pup (Mosler Motors) 586
Pup (Nostalgair) (1987-88) 688
Pusher (Prescott) 590

Q

Q (Pegasus) 546
Q2 Quickie (Quickie Aircraft) (1986-87) 700
Q-2, Quicksilver (Eipper) (1982-83) 642
Q-200 Quickie (Quickie Aircraft) (1986-87) 700
QM-1, Quicksilver (Eipper) (1984-85) 694
QM-2, Quicksilver (Eipper) (1984-85) 694
Qingting 5 (Shijiazhuang) 516
Qingting 6 (Shijiazhuang) 516
QUAD CITY ULTRALIGHT AIRCRAFT CORPORATION (USA) 591
QUAD CITY ULTRALIGHTS (USA) (1983-84) 672
QUAISSARD, G (France) (1986-87) 590
Quail (Aerosport) (D 2) 565
QUESTAIR INC (USA) 592
QUESTOR (MOSLER MOTORS) 586
Questor (Nostalgair) (1987-88) 688
Questor (Omni-Weld) (1984-85) 708
Quickie (Quickie Aircraft) (1986-87) 699
QUICKIE AIRCRAFT CORPORATION (USA) (1986-87) 699
Quickie Q2 (Quickie Aircraft) (1986-87) 700
Quickie Q2 Modification (Tri Q) 606
Quickie Q-200 (Quickie Aircraft) (1986-87) 700
Quicksilver (Eipper) 568
Quicksilver GT (Eipper) 569
Quicksilver MXL (Eipper) 568
Quicksilver Q-2 (Eipper) (1982-83) 642
Quicksilver QM-1 (Eipper) (1984-85) 694
Quicksilver QM-2 (Eipper) (1984-85) 694

R

RB-1 (Birdman) (1984-85) 690
RB-1 Lightning (Ultra Sports) (1984-85) 684
RB 60 (Barbero) (1986-87) 565
RC 412-11 (Free Spirit) 573
RD-02A Edelweiss (Duruble) (1986-87) 572
RD-03 Edelweiss 150 (Duruble) (1986-87) 572
RD-30V (Vidor) (1987-88) 606
RD-95 (Vidor) (1987-88) 606
Re 2002 ¾ scale (Tesori) (1987-88) 553
RJ-02 (Junqua) (1987-88) 576
RJ-03 (Junqua) (1987-88) 576
RM-02 (Marquoind) (1987-88) 582
RO-7 (Orlinski) 540
RV-3 (Van's Aircraft) 609
RV-4 (Van's Aircraft) 610
RV-6 (Van's Aircraft) 610
RX-28 (Spectrum) 510
RX-35 (Spectrum) 510
RX-550 (Spectrum) 511
RFC (see Recreational Flight Centres Inc) (1982-83) 626
Racer (Air Creation) 518
Rally 2B (Rotec) 594
Rally 2 Series (Rotec) (1982-83) 650
Rally 3 (Rotec) 595
Rally Champ (Rotec) 595
Rally Marine (Rotec) (1982-83) 650
Rally Sport (Rotec) 595
RAM AIRCRAFT COMPANY (Costa Rica) (1987-88) 564
RAND ROBINSON ENGINEERING INC (USA) 592
RANGER (1984-85) 710
Ranger (T.E.D.A) 538
RANGER AVIATION (USA) (1983-84) 672
RANS COMPANY (USA) 592
Rapier (Mainair) *(1985-86)* 668
Raven II (Custom Aircraft Conversions) (1984-85) 692
Raven (Hornet) (1987-88) 614
Raven (Wills Wing) (1981-82) 629, 632
R. D. AIRCRAFT (USA) 594
RECREATIONAL FLIGHT CENTRES INC (Canada) (1982-83) 626
Redtail Stinger (Moyes) (1982-83) 624, 656
REIMANN (see Ul-Bau Reimann) (1987-88) 596
Renegade II (Murphy) 510
Renegade Spirit (Murphy) 510
Replica Junkers Ju 87B-2 'Stuka' (Langhurst) (1987-88) 676
REPLICA PLANS (Canada) 510
Resurgam (Bedson) (1986-87) 537
REUTER, DIPL-ING ADOLF K (West Germany) (1986-87) 596
RICHTER INGENIEURBÜRO, KLAUS J (West Germany) (1983-84) 642
RITZ AIRCRAFT CO (USA) (1984-85) 712
ROBERTS SPORTS AIRCRAFT (USA) 594
ROBERTSON AIRCRAFT CORPORATION (USA) (1985-86) 705
ROCHELT, GÜNTER (West Germany) (1983-84) 644
ROCOURT, MICHAEL (Belgium) (1987-88) 544
RODGER, ERWIN (USA) (1984-85) 712
ROMAIN, J AND SONS (UK) 548
Romibutter (Rocourt) (1987-88) 544
Ronair (Taylor) (1982-83) 653
Rotax Gyro-Copter (Bensen) (1986-87) 640
ROTEC ENGINEERING INC (USA) 594
Rotor Lightning Sport Copter (Vancraft) 609
ROTORWAY AIRCRAFT INC (USA) 596
Rouseabout (Seabird) (1985-86) 640
Rouseabout Mk 5 (Seabird) (1986-87) 540
Royal (Ulm Pyrénées) (1986-87) 591
RUTAN AIRCRAFT FACTORY INC (USA) (1985-86) 503
Ruty (Albarde) (1986-87) 564

S

S-1 series (Pitts) (1986-87) 696
S-2 series (Pitts) (1986-87) 696
S-2B Upside-Down Pitts (Hoskins) (1986-87) 671
S-4 Saunders (1985-86) 616
S-4 Coyote (Rans) 592
S-4A Jet Hawk II (Saunders) (1987-88) 704
S-6 Supermarine Replica (Flight Dynamics) (1986-87) 664
S-7 Courier (Rans) 593
S-9 (Rans) 593
S 10 (Free Flight) (1986-87) 538
S-10 (Rans) 594
S-18 (Sunderland/Sport Aircraft) 599
S-18 T (Sunderland) (1987-88) 718
S-18 T-18C-W (Thorp) (1986-87) 724
S-51D (Stewart) 601
SA-60 (Silhouette) 598
SA 102.5 (Macfam) 582
SA 103 (McAsco) (1986-87) 547
SA 104 (McAsco) (1986-87) 547
SA 105 (Macfam) 582
SA 106 (McAsco) (1987-88) 549
SA-300 (Stolp) 602
SA-500 (Stolp) 602
SA-750 (Stolp) 602
SA-900 (Stolp) 602
SB1 Antares (Soyer/Barritault) 530
SB-1 (Seabird) (1986-87) 540
SB-2 (Seabird) (1986-87) 540
SB-3 (Seabird) (1986-87) 540
SCWAL SA (Belgium) 507
SCWAL 101 (SCWAL) 507
S.E.5A (Replica Plans) 510
SF-2A (Hapi) 574
SG-1 Phoenix (Westwind) (1987-88) 623
SL-1 (Nelson) (1984-85) 707
SL-1 Star-Lite (Star-lite) 600
SL 180 (Flight Designs) (1981-82) 618, 632
SL 200 (Flight Designs) (1981-82) 618, 632
SL 220 (Flight Designs) (1981-82) 618, 632
SNS-2 Guppy (Sorrell) 598
SNS-7 Hiperbipe (Sorrell) 598
SNS-8 Hiperlight (Sorrell) 598
SNS-9 Exp II (Sorrell) 598
SNS-10 Intruder (Sorrell) 598
SP (see Sinaya Ptitsa Klub Deltaplaneristov Rostov-Don) (1985-86) 665
SP-1 (SP) (1982-83) 634
SP-2 (SP) (1982-83) 634
SP-3 (SP) (1982-83) 634
SP-8UT (SP) (1984-85) 676
SPM (SP) (1983-84) 646
SR-1 (SR-1) (1985-86) 709
SR-1 ULTRA SPORT AVIATION (USA) (1985-86) 709
SR-10 (Mitchell Wing) (1987-88) 684
ST 80 Balade (Stern) 530
STOL CH 701 (Zenair) 514
SV-1 (Skywise) 505
SV-2 (Skywise) 505
SV-8 (Veenstra) (1984-85) 658
SV9 (Veenstra) (1985-86) 642
SV 11B (SV Aircraft) 506
SV 14 (SV Aircraft) 506
SV AIRCRAFT PTY LTD (Australia) 506
SVCIAF (American Microflight) (1986-87) 635
SX-300 (Swearingen) (1987-88) 718
SXS (V-8 Special) 608
SY-5S (Beijing) (1982-83) 626
SOFREC 'VELIPLANE' (see Société Francaise de Représentation et d'Exchanges Commerciaux) (1982-83) 628
SVAZARM (see Svazu pro spolupráci s Armádou) (1982-83) 626
Sabre (Danis) (1983-84) 640
Sabre (Skyhook) (1982-83) 637
Sabre 1K (Pour le Merite) (1987-88) 540
Sabre 1R (Pour le Merite) (1987-88) 540
Sabre 170 (Flight Designs) (1982-83) 642, 658
Sabre 205 (Flight Designs) (1982-83) 642, 658
Sabre A (Skyhook) (1983-84) 688, 692
Sabre B (Skyhook) (1983-84) 688, 692
Sabre C (Skyhook) (1983-84) 688, 692
Sadler Vampire (American Microflight) (1986-87) 634
Sadler Vampire (Skywise) 505
Sadler Vampire Trainer (American Microflight) (1986-87) 635
Safari G-TB1 (Air Creation) 518
Samourai (Aéronautic 2000) (1983-84) 637
Samson Replica (Pitts) (Wolf) (1986-87) 737
SANDBERG, JOHN R (USA) (1987-88) 704
SANDER VEENSTRA (Australia) (1985-86) 642
Sand Piper (B & B) (1984-85) 689
SANDS, RON INC (USA) 596
San Francesco (Iannotto) 538
Sapphire (Winten) 506
SARL LA MOUETTE (France) (1983-84) 686
SAUNDERS, DON (USA) (1987-88) 704
Sauterelle (EMC2) (1982-83) 624
SAY, MAXWELL A (Canada) (1986-87) 549
Scamp A (Aero Sport) 554
Sceptre I (Roberts Sport) 594
Sceptre II (Roberts Sport) 594
SCHEIBE FLUGZEUGBAU GmbH (West Germany) (1984-85) 671
Schlacro (Akaflieg München 531
SCHLITTER, RANDY (USA) (1984-85) 711
SCHÜRMANN, WERNER (West Germany) (1981-82) 611
SCICRAFT (Israel) 535
Scorcher (Mainair Sports) 544
Scorpion (Cozza/Scholl) (1984-85) 692
Scorpion (Southern Aero Sports) (1982-83) 637
Scout (Wheeler) (1982-83) 624
Scout (Gardner) (1987-88) 614
Scout (Topa) (1986-87) 725
Scout Mk III (Wheeler) 506
SEABIRD AVIATION PTY LTD (Australia) (1987-88) 540
SEABIRD ULTRALIGHT AIRCRAFT (Australia) (1985-86) 640
Sea Fury, Hawker (WAR) 612
Sea Hawker (Aero composite) 552
Sea Panther (Rotec) 596
Seaquick (Eipper) (1982-83) 641
Seawind 2000 (Seawind) 510
SEAWIND INTERNATIONAL INC (Canada) 510
Sequoia (Sequoia) 596
SEQUOIA AIRCRAFT CORPORATION (USA) 596
SEVILLE AIRCRAFT INC (Canada) 510
Seville Two Place (Seville) 510
Shadow (CFM) 544
Shadow (MFS) 540
Shadow I 377 (Evergreen) (1986-87) 661
Shadow II 503 (Evergreen) (1986-87) 661
Sharkfire (Lopresti) (1987-88) 680
SHAW, IVAN (UK) (1987-88) 622
SHCHEGLOV, V (USSR) (1987-88) 612
SHENYANG AVIATION SCHOOL (China) (1982-83) 626
Sherpa I (Ikarus Deutschland Comco) 532
Sherpa II (Ikarus Deutschland Comco) 532
SHIJIAZHUANG AIRCRAFT PLANT (China) 516
Shrike (Kaler) (1985-86) 692
Shtyvnoplat (Kazurov/Polushkin/Rusakov). (1982-83) 634
Sibylle (Lendepergt) 526
Sidewinder (International Ultralights) (1985-86) 692
Sidewinder, Model S (Smyth) 598
Sierra Whitehawk 185 (Beck Productions) (1984-85) 726, 730
SILHOUETTE AIRCRAFT INC (USA) 598
Silhouette I (Silhouette) 598
Silhouette (Skyhook Sailwings) (1984-85) 682
Silver Eagle (Mitchell Wing) 586
Silver Cloud (Ranger) (1983-84) 672
SIMPSON MIDWEST ULTRALIGHTS (USA) (1986-87) 709
SINAYA PTITSA KLUB DELTAPLANERISTOVE ROSTOV-DON (USSR) (1985-86) 665
SIRIO SRL (Italy) (1986-87) 602
Sirio 2 (Sirio) (1986-87) 602
Sirius (Noin) 528
Sirocco (Aviasud) 519
Sirocco (Jurca) 524
Sirocco Sport Wing (Jurca) 524
Sirocco III (Sky Sports) (1981-82) 625
Sirocco 377GB (Midland Ultralights) (1987-88) 617
Skeeter (Aero Ventures) (1985-86) 674
Skeeter (Fisher) (1986-87) 664
Skeeter FP505 (Fisher) 571
Skybaby (Skyhigh) (1986-87) 709
Skybaby (Stits) (1987-88) 712
Skybaby FP606 (Fisher) 571
Skybolt (Ebershoff) 568
Skybolt (Steen) (1986-87) 716
Skybolt Steen (Stolp) 602
Skybolt Mk II (Stolp) (1987-88) 716
SKY-CRAFT SA (Switzerland) (1986-87) 609
Skycycle (R.D. Aircraft) 594
Skycycle (Kennedy Aircraft) 578
Skycycle II (R.D.Aircraft) 594
Skycycle '87 (Carlson) 562
Skycycle Gipsy series (R. D. Aircraft) 594
SKYE TRECK (Canada) (1983-84) 634
SKYHIGH ULTRALIGHTS INC (USA). (1986-87) 709
SKYHOOK SAILWINGS LTD (UK). (1984-85) 682, 726
SKY KING INTERNATIONAL (Canada) (1985-86) 644
Skylark (Airtech) 507
SKYLINES ENTERPRISES (USA) (1986-87) 709
SKYOTE AEROMARINE LTD (USA) (1986-87) 709
Skyote (Skyote) (1986-87) 709
Sky Pup (Sport Flight) 600
Skyraider (Worldwide Ultralite) (1984-85) 722
Sky Ranger (Striplin) (1983-84) 677
Sky Ranger series (Striplin) 603
Sky-Rider (Kimberley) 503
Skyrider (RFC) (1982-83) 626
Sky Scooter (Flaglor/Headberg) 575
Skyseeker I/III (Skye Treck) (1983-84) 634
SKYSEEKER AIRCRAFT CORPORATION (Canada) (1985-86) 645
Skyseeker Mk III (Skyseeker) (1985-86) 645
SKY SPORTS INC (USA) (1981-82) 625
SKYTEX AUSTRALIA PTY LTD (Australia) 505
Skytrike (Hiway) (1982-83) 636
Skywalker (Leichtflugzeug) (1987-88) 596
Skywalker (Leichtflugzeug) 534
Sky Walker (Sterner) (1984-85) 716
SKYWISE ULTRAFLIGHT PTE LTD (Australia) 505
Slandan BA-12 (MFI) 542
Slavutitch M-1 (Antonov) 542
SMITH, ALLAN C, DEVELOPMENTS (Australia) (1987-88) 506
SMITH, WILLIAM M (USA) (1986-87) 710
SMYTH, JERRY 598
Snoop (Eastern) (1984-85) 694
Snowbird Mk III (Noble Hardman) (1987-88) 618
Snowbird Mi IV (Noble Hardman) 546
SOCIÉTÉ AÉROKART (France) (1986-87) 562
SOCIÉTÉ D'EXPLOITATION DES AÉRONEFS HENRI MIGNET (France) 527

SOCIÉTÉ FRANCAISE DE REPRÉSENTATION ET D'ÉXCHANGES COMMERCIAUX (France) (1982-83) 628
SOCIÉTÉ INDUSTRIELLE LATÉCOÈRE SA (France) (1986-87) 580
SOCIETE MAVIC (France) (1986-87) 582
Sojourn I (Dechow) (1981-82) 617
Sokol 3 (Leningrad Central) (1982-83) 634
Solair I (Rochelt) (1983-84) 644
Solar Riser (UFM) (1982-83) 654
SOLEAIR AVIATION (UK) (1983-84) 651
Solo (American Air) (1987-88) 638
Solo M.J. 7S (Jurca) (1987-88) 578
Somethin' Special (Ultralite Soaring) (1984-85) 721
Sonic (Spectra) (1983-84) 690
Sonic Spitfire (Sunrise) 604
Sonerai (Hapi) 574
Sonerai I (Inav) (1986-87) 674
Sonerai II, IIL, II-LT, II-LTS (Hapi) 574
Sonerai II, III, II-LT and II-LTS (Inav) (1986-87) 674
Sooper-Coot Model A (Aerocar) 552
Sophie (Egrette) (1986-87) 573
Sopwith Triplane (Circa Reproductions) 508
Sorcerer Aerotech (Whittaker) (1986-87) 624
Sorcerer MW5 (Whittaker) 548
SORRELL AIRCRAFT COMPANY LTD (USA) 598
SOUQUET (France) (1987-88) 589
SOUTH COAST AIR CENTRE PTY LTD (Australia) (1985-86) 640
SOUTH, DON AND ROGERS, TOM (USA) (1983-84) 675
SOUTHDOWN AEROSTRUCTURE (UK) 548
SOUTHERN AERO SPORTS (UK) (1983-84) 651
SOUTH/RODGERS (USA) (1984-85) 715
SOYER/BARRITAULT, Claude/Jean (France) 530
Space Walker (Country Air) 564
Sparrow (B & G) (1985-86) 678
Sparrow (Carlson) 561
Sparrow II (Carlson) 562
Sparrow Hawk (Aero Dynamics) (1985-86) 574
Sparrow Hawk Mk II (Aero Dynamics) 553
Sparrow Sport Special (Carlson) 561
Special (Pitts) (1986-87) 696
Special (Pitts-Ultimate Aircraft) 512
Special (Whatley) 612
Special I (Cassutt) 562
Special II (Cassutt) 562
Special O & O (Wittman) (1987-88) 735
SPECTRA AIRCRAFT CORPORATION (USA) (1983-84) 690
Spectrum (Microflight Aircraft) 546
SPECTRUM AIRCRAFT INC (Canada) 510
SPENCER AMPHIBIAN AIR CAR INC (USA) 599
Sperocco (Jurca) 524
Spirit (Ultralite Soaring) (1984-85) 720
Spirit 1 (Spirit One) (1986-87) 712
SPIRIT ONE CORPORATION (USA) (1986-87) 712
Spit (Jurca) 526
Spitfire (Isaacs) 544
Spitfire (Worldwide Ultralite) (1984-85) 722
Spitfire I (Bell, F.M.) (1986-87) 637
Spitfire I (Sunrise) 604
Spitfire II (Bell, F.M.) (1986-87) 638
Spitfire II (Sunrise) 604
Spitfire II (Worldwide Ultralite) (1984-85) 722
Spitfire Mk IX (Thunder Wings) 606
Split Tail (Nash) (1984-85) 707
Sport (Partnerships) (1984-85) 708
Sport (Ulm Pyrénées) (1986-87) 591
SPORT AIRCRAFT INC (USA) 599
SPORT AVIATION (USA) (1983-84) 690
SPORT FLIGHT ENGINEERING INC (USA) 600
Sportsman (Volmer) 610
Sportsman 2 + 2 (Wag-Aero) 612
Sportsman (Winton) (1986-87) 543
Sportster (Grover) (1985-86) 689
Sportster (Poltergeist) (1986-87) 697
Sportster HA-2M (Aircraft Designs) 555
Sport Trainer (Wag-Aero) 611
Sportwing (D'Apuzzo) 565
Sprite (Murphy) (1986-87) 599
SQUADRON AVIATION INC (USA) 600
Staggerbipe Mk I (WAACO) (1987-88) 542
Stallion, CX-901 (Command-Aire) (1984-85) 692
Standard (Hornet) (1987-88) 614
Standard Model A Ritz (Loehle) 581
Starduster Too (Stolp) 602
STARFIRE AVIATION INC (USA) 600
STAR FLIGHT AIRCRAFT (USA) 600
STARFLIGHT MANUFACTURING (USA) (1984-85) 676
Star Lance I (Nelson) (1984-85) 707
Starlet (Corby) 503
Starlet (Stolp) 602
STAR-LITE AIRCRAFT INC (USA) 600
Star-Lite SL-1 (Star-Lite) 600
Starship (Ultimate Hi) (1981-82) 628, 632
Starship Gemini (Davis Wing) 566
S.T.A.R.-Trike (Wisch & Nist) (1987-88) 599
Statoplan Poussin (Gatard) 522
STATLER, WILLIAM H (USA) (1986-87) 714
ST CROIX PROPELLERS (USA) (1984-85) 714
ST CROIX ULTRALIGHTS (USA) (1982-83) 652
STEEN AERO LAB INC (USA) (1986-87) 716
STEINBACH DELTA (Austria) (1987-88) 543
STERN, RÊNE (France) 530
STERNER AIRCRAFT (USA) (1984-85) 716
STEWART AIRCRAFT CORPORATION (USA) (1982-83) 652
STEWART AIRCRAFT CORPORATION (USA) 601
Stimul-10 (Korolyev) (1987-88) 612
Stinger (SR-1) (1983-84) 675
Stingray (Ace) (1985-86) 639
Sting Ray (Eaves) (1986-87) 659
STITS, DON (USA) (1987-88) 712
STODDARD-HAMILTON AIRCRAFT INC (USA) 601
STOLP STARDUSTER CORPORATION (USA) 602
Stratos (HFL) (1986-87) 594
Stratos (Ligeti Aero-Nautical) 505
Stratos II (HFL) 532
Stratos (Stratos) (1984-85) 716
STRATOS AVIATION (USA) (1984-85) 716
STRATUS UNLIMITED INC (USA) (1983-84) 690
Streaker (Abernathy) (1986-87) 622
Striker (Flexi-Form) (1985-86) 666
Strikr Tri-Flyer (Mainair) (1985-86) 668
STRIPLIN AIRCRAFT CORPORATION (USA) 603
SUMMIT AIRCRAFT CORPORATION (USA) (1987-88) 716
SUN AEROSPACE GROUP INC (USA) 604
SUN AEROSPACE CORPORATION (USA) (1983-84) 677
SUNBIRD ULTRALIGHT GLIDERS (USA) (1982-83) 653
Sunburst (Airmass) (1983-84) 653
SUNDERLAND AIRCRAFT (USA) (1987-88) 718
Sundowner Convertible (Ultra-Fab) (1985-86) 713
SUN FUN ULTRALIGHT AVIATION (Canada) (1987-88) 552
Sunfun VJ-24W (Volmer) 610
Sun Ray 100 (Sun Aerospace) 604
Sun Ray 200 (Sun Aerospace) 604
Sun Ray (Sun Aerospace) (1983-84) 677
Sunrise (Personal Planes) (1983-84) 670
Sunrise II (Dallach Flugzeuge) 532
SUNRISE ULTRALIGHT MANUFACTURING COMPANY (USA) 604
Super Acro Sport (Acro Sport) 550
Super Acro-Zenith CH180 (Zenair) 514
'Super Baby' Lakes (BOAC) 558
Super Cat (First Strike) 570
Super Cavalier (Macfam) 582
Super Diamant (Piel) 528
Super Emeraude (Piel) 528
Super Eagle (Eclipse) (1981-82) 614
Super FLAC (Striplin) (1981-82) 626
Super Hawk (Hovey) 576
Super Honcho (Magnum) 584
Super Kitten (Grover) (1985-86) 689
Super Koala (Fisher) (1986-87) 662
Super Koala (Fisher) 570
Super Lancer 180 (Flight Designs) (1982-83) 642, 658
Supermarine S.6 Replica (Flight Dynamics) (1986-87) 664
Supermarine Spitfire Mk IX (Thunder Wings) 606
Super Menestral (Nicollier) 528
Super Mono-Fly (Teman) (1984-85) 717
Super Pelican (Ultravia) 513
Super Prospector (Bounsall) (1987-88) 643
Super Pup (Mosler Motors) 586
Super Scout (Flylite) (1986-87) 613
Super Skybolt (Stolp) 603
Super-Sport (ULM Pyrénées) (1986-87) 591
Super Star (Starflight) (1983-84) 676
Super Starduster (Stolp) 602
Superwing (Mitchell Wing) 586
Super Zodiac (Zenair) (1986-87) 558
Supra 200 (LEAF) (1982-83) 647, 658
Supreme (Hornet) (1984-85) 678
SV AIRCRAFT PTY LTD (Australia) 506
SVAZU PRO SPOLUPRÁCIS ARMÁDOU (Czechoslovakia) (1982-83) 626
Swallow A (Swallow) (1985-86) 711
SWALLOW AEROPLANE COMPANY, THE (USA) (1985-86) 710
Swallow B (Swallow) (1985-86) 710
SWEARINGEN AIRCRAFT CORPORATION (USA) (1987-88) 718
Swingwing VJ-23E (Volmer) 610
SWISS AEROLIGHT (Switzerland) 542
SYLVAIRE MANUFACTURING LTD (Canada) (1987-88) 553
SZNAPKI, ZDZISLAW (Poland) (1983-84) 687

T

T-1 (Thor) 512
T-2 (Thor) 512
T-IV (Canaero Dynamics) (1986-87) 544
T7 Leone (Aui) 536
T8 Leone (Aui) 536
T.10 (Nuwaco Aircraft) 587
T-77 (Turner) (1987-88) 723
T-100A Mariah (Turner) (1983-84) 680
T-100B Mariah (Turner) (1985-86) 712
T-100D Mariah (Turner) 607
T-110 (Turner) 607
T.250, Vortex (Chargus) (1984-85) 677
T.440, Forger (Chargus) (1984-85) 677
T.440, Titan (Chargus) (1984-85) 676
T.503 (Pegasus) (1987-88) 618
TA (Teratorn) (1984-85) 718
TA-2/3 Bird (Taylor) 604
TA16 (IAC) (1986-87) 674
TA16 Trojan (Thurstan) 606
TC-2 (Aero Mirage) 554
TD-13 Wazka (Dobrocinski) (1984-85) 673
T.E.D.A. (see Tecnologia Europea Divisione Aeronoutica) 538
T.E.A.M. (see Tennessee Engineering Manufacturing Inc) 605
TE-F3 (Temple-Wing) (1984-85) 672
TE-F3A (Temple Wing) (1987-88) 598
TFM (see Those Flying Machines) (1986-87) 723
TL-1A (Birdman) (1982-83) 639
T-M Scout (Gardner) (1987-88) 614
TM-5 (TM Aircraft) (1985-86) 628
TR-7 (IAC) (1986-87) 674
TR 260 (Feugray) (1986-87) 574
TST (Thruster) 506
TU-10 (Mitchell Wing) 586
TX1000 (Starflight) (1984-85) 716
TACT-AVIA CORPORATION (USA) (1986-87) 720
Tailwind (Wittman) 614
TALANCHUK, VLADIMIR (Canada) (1982-83) 626
Talon (LEAF) (1982-83) 647, 658
TAMARIND INTERNATIONAL LTD (USA) (1986-87) 721
Tandem Trainer (Parsons) 588
TAYLOR AERO INC (USA) 604
Taylor Bullet 2100 (Aerocar) 552
TAYLOR, RON (USA) (1982-83) 678
TAYLOR, T (UK) 548
TECHNOFLUG LEICHTFLUGZEUBAU GmbH (West Germany) 534
TECNOLOGIA EUROPEA DIVISIONE AERONAUTICA (Italy) 538
Teenie Two (Parker) 588
TEMAN AIRCRAFT INC (USA) (1984-85) 717
TEMPLE, PROF DIPL-ING BERNHARD E.R.J. DE (West Germany) (1987-88) 598
Tempête (Jurca) 524
Temple-Wing TE-F1 (Temple) (1982-83) 630
Temple-Wing TE-F2 (Temple) (1982-83) 630
Ten Series (Ultimate Aircraft) (1986-87) 552
TENNESSEE ENGINEERING AND MANUFACTURING INC (USA) 605
Teratorn (Motorized Gliders) (1982-83) 649
TERATORN AIRCRAFT INC (USA) 606
TERRADE, A (France) (1987-88) 300
TERVAMÄKI, JUKKA (Finland) 516
TESORI AIRCRAFT LTD (Canada) (1986-87) 552
TESORI, ROBERT (Canada) (1987-88) 553
Texan Chuckbird (Chuck's) 563
Texan Gem 260 (Miller) 585
TFM INC (see Those Flying Machines) (1983-84) 679
THALHOFER LUDWIG (West Germany) (1987-88) 598
The Fun Machine (Loehle) 582
THOMPSON AIRCRAFT (USA) (1987-88) 721
THOR AIR (Canada) 512
Thor T-1 (Thor Air) 512
THORP (USA) (1986-87) 724
THOSE FLYING MACHINES, TFM, INC (USA) (1986-87) 723
Thunderbolt (WAR) 612
THUNDER WINGS (USA) 606
THURSTON AEROMARINE CORPORATION (USA) 606
THRUSTER AIRCRAFT (AUSTRALIA) PTY LTD (Australia) 506
Thruster (Thruster Aircraft) (1986-87) 542
Thruster 447 (Thruster) (1985-86) 641
Thruster TST (Thruster) (1985-86) 641
Thruster Utility (Thruster) (1985-86) 641
Thruster (Ultralight) (1984-85) 658
Tierra (Teratorn) (1983-84) 678
Tierra I (Teratorn) 606
Tierra II (Teratorn) 606
Tierra UL (Teratorn) (1986-87) 722
Tiger Cub (MBA) (1984-85) 682
TI-Ram (Ram) (1987-88) 564
TIRITH MICROPLANE LTD (UK) (1987-88) 622
TISSERAND, CLAUDE (France) (1987-88) 590
Titan (Chargus) (1984-85) 676
Titan T.440 (Pegasus) (1985-86) 670
Titch (Taylor) 548
TM AIRCRAFT (USA) (1985-86) 628
Tomcat (Midwest) (1985-86) 697
Tomcat (Waspair) (1983-84) 682
TOPA AIRCRAFT COMPANY (USA) (1986-87) 725
Toucan Series II (Canaero Dynamics) 508
Toucan T-IV (Canaero Dynamics) (1986-87) 544
Toucan (Earthstar) (1985-86) 684
Toucan (Long) (1983-84) 666
Tourisme (Croses) 522
Tragonfly (Miner) (1987-88) 682
Traveller (NAI) (1987-88) 563
Traveller WH-1 (Wendt) (1986-87) 734
TriCX (Firebird) (1986-87) 594
Trident T-3 (Summit) 604
Tri-Flyer 330 (Mainair) (1985-86) 668
Tri-Flyer Sprint (Mainair) (1985-86) 668
Trike (Delta Wing) (1984-85) 726, 730
Trike (LEAF) (1984-85) 702
Trike (Skyhook Sailwings) (1983-84) 688
Tri-Pacer (Ultrasports) (1983-84) 651
TRI Q DEVELOPMENT COMPANY (USA) 606
Tri-Star (Starflight) (1983-84) 676
Tri-Z CH 300 (Zenair) 514
Trojan (IAC) (1986-87) 674
Trojan (Thurston) 606
Trolslandon BA-12, Andreasson (MFI) (1985-86) 662
Tse Tse (Souquet) (1987-88) 589
Tsunami (Sandberg) (1987-88) 704
TUBE WORKS (USA) (1987-88) 722
Tug (Pegasus) (1987-88) 619
Turbulent D31 (PFA) 547
TURNER AIRCRAFT INC (USA) 607
Twin Foxcat (Ultrasport) (1986-87) 603
TwinStar (Kolb) (1987-88) 674
TwinStar Mark II (Kolb) 579
Twin-Varieze (Shaw) (1987-88) 622
Two Easy (Beard) (1987-88) 641
Two Place (Seville) 510
TWO WINGS AVIATION (USA) 607
Type II (Monarch) (1982-83) 649, 658
Type 200/300/400 (MAC) (1983-84) 666
Type 610 (Vector) (1982-83) 655
Type 2000 (Agri-Plane) (1982-83) 627
Type 4315 (Aérokart) (1986-87) 562
Type 4320 (Aérokart) (1986-87) 563
Type 4320-A83 (Aérokart (1983-84) 636
Tyro (South Coast) (1984-85) 657
Tyro Mk II (Eastwood Aircraft) 503

U

U-2 Superwing (Mitchell Wing) 586
U76 (Brugger) (1984-85) 674
UAC (see Ultralight Aviation Centre) (1981-82) 615
UFM (see Ultralight Flying Machines) (1983-84) 680
UFM (see Ultralight Flying Machines of Wisconsin) (1982-83) 654
ULF-1 (EEL) (1982-83) 629
ULM 811 (Air Cefelec) (1983-84) 638
ULM 812 (Air Cefelec) (1983-84) 638
ULM (see Ultra Léger Motorisé SARL) (1981-82) 610
ULS (NKL) (1982-83) 632
UP (see UP Sports Ultralite Products) (1986-87) 728
UR-1 (Mira Slovak) (1987-88) 684
UW-7 (Weller) (1986-87) 598
UL-BAU-FRANZ (Germany) (1987-88) 594
UL-BAU-REIMANN (Germany) (1987-88) 596
UFM OF KENTUCKY (USA) (1984-85) 718
ULAC (see Ultra Light Aircraft Corporation) (1985-86) 664
Uli (Scheibe) (1984-85) 671
Ulm (Prevot) (1986-87) 589
Ulm-1B (Konsuprod) 534
ULM AÉROTECHNIC (France) (1983-84) 641
Ulm Leduc 104 (Ulm Leduc) (1985-86) 656
ULM LEDUC (France) (1985-86) 656
ULM PROGRESS (France) (1987-88) 590
ULM PYRÉNÉES (France) (1986-87) 591
ULM TECHNIC AEROMARINE SARL (France) (1984-85) 668
ULTAVIA AIRCRAFT LTD (USA) (1984-85) 719
Ultavia (Ultavia) (1984-85) 719
ULTIMATE AIRCRAFT (Canada) 512
Ultimate Aircraft 10 Dash 100/300 (Ultimate Aircraft) 512
Ultimate Aircraft 20 Dash 300 (Ultimate Aircraft) 512
ULTIMATE HI (USA) (1984-85) 719
ULTRA-FAB (USA) (1985-86) 713
Ultra (Scheibe) (1984-85) 671
Ultra-Airel (Pinaire) 590
Ultra-Aire II (Pinaire) (1987-88) 692
ULTRAVIA AERO INC (Canada) 513
ULTRA CLASSICS (USA) (1984-85) 719
ULTRA EFFICIENT PRODUCTS INC (USA) 608
ULTRAFLIGHT SALES LTD (Canada) 512
Ultra Gull (Earthstar) 568
ULTRALEICHT-FLUGGERÄTEBAU GmbH (West Germany) 534
ULTRA LÉGER MOTORISÉ SARL (France) (1981-82) 610
ULTRA LIGHT AIRCRAFT CORPORATION (Switzerland) (1985-86) 664
ULTRALIGHT AIRCRAFT INDUSTRIES (AUST) PTY LTD (Australia) (1985-86) 641
ULTRALIGHT AVIATION (Australia) (1984-85) 658
ULTRALIGHT AVIATION CENTRE LTD (UK) (1982-83) 615
ULTRALIGHT FLIGHT INC (USA) (1987-88) 725
ULTRALIGHT FLYING MACHINES OF WISCONSIN (USA) (1982-83) 654
ULTRALITE SOARING INC (USA) (1985-86) 714
Ultramental (Burke) (1986-87) 644
ULTRA SAIL INC (USA) 608
Ultrastar (Kolb) 578
ULTRASPORT SRL (Italy) (1986-87) 602
ULTRA SPORTS LTD (UK) (1984-85) 683
ULTRAVIA AERO INC (Canada) 513
Unik (Pomergau) (1987-88) 550
UP INC (USA) (1987-88) 726
UP SPORTS (ULTRALITE PRODUCTS) (USA) (1986-87) 728
Upside-Down Pitts S-2B (Hoskins) (1986-87) 671
US MOYES INC (USA) (1984-85) 728

V

V-8 SPECIAL (USA) 608
V-8 Special (V-8 Special) 608
VJ-22 Sportsman (Volmer) 610
VJ-23E Swingwing (Volmer) 610
VJ-24W (Volmer) 610
VK30 (Cirrus) 650
VP-1 (Evans) 569
VP-2 (Evans) 570
V-Star (Stolp) 602
VTOL (BIAA) (1987-88) 562
Vagrant II (FLSZ) 572
Vampyr (Odyssey) (1981-82) 624
Vampire (Skywise) 505
VAN LITH, JEAN (France) (1987-88) 591
Van Lith VIII (Van Lith) (1987-88) 591
VAN'S AIRCRAFT (USA) 609
Vancraft (Vanek) (1986-87) 729
Vancraft (Vancraft) 608
VANCRAFT COPTERS (USA) 608
VANEK, CHUCK (USA) (1986-87) 729
VECTOR (1984-85) 721
VECTOR AIRCRAFT CORPORATION (USA) (1982-83) 655
Vector 600 (Sky Sports) (1981-82) 625
Vector 610 (Aerodyne Systems) (1984-85) 685
Vector 610 (Sky King) (1985-86) 644
Vector 627 (Aerodyne Systems) (1984-85) 685
Vector 627 (Sky King) (1985-86) 644
VEENSTRA (see Sander Veenstra) (1985-86) 642
Vega SST-A (Wierzbowski) (1982-83) 632, 658
Vega SST-B (Wierzbowski) (1982-83) 632, 658
Vega Star (Wierzbowski) (1982-83) 632, 658
Velocity (Velocity Aircraft) 610
VELOCITY AIRCRAFT (USA) 610
Venture (Questair) 592
VENTURE FLIGHT DESIGN INC (Canada) (1986-87) 554
VERNER, VLADA (Czechoslovakia) (1987-88) 564
Vert-X (Driggers) (1987-88) 658
Vetro (Bezzola) (1987-88) 610
VIDOR, GUISEPPE (Italy) (1987-88) 606
Viking (Northstar) (1986-87) 690
VIKING, AIRCRAFT LTD (USA) 610
Viper II (Microlite) (1982-83) 648
VOGT, HELMUT (West Germany) 534
VOLMER AIRCRAFT (USA) 610
Volucelle (Junqua) (1987-88) 576
Vortex (Chargus) (1984-85) 677
Vortex T.250 (Pegasus) (1985-86) 670
VPM Sn C (Italy) (1986-87) 604
VULCAN UL-AVIATION (West Germany) 534

W

W-02 (Verner) (1987-88) 564
W-7 Dipper (Collins Aero) 563
W8 Tailwind (Wittman) 614
W10 Tailwind (Wittman) 614
W-11 Boredom Fighter (Wolf) 614
WAACO (see West Australian Aircraft Company) 506
WAC (see Wolfe Aviation Company) (1984-85) 721
Waco II (Golden Age) (1985-86) 688
WAR (see War Aircraft Replicas) 612
WAT (WAC) (1984-85) 721
WH-1 Traveller (Wendt) (1986-87) 734
WSK-PZL WARSZAWA-OKECIE (see Wytwornia Sprzetu Komunikacyjnego-PZL Warszawa-Okecie) (1983-84) 687
WT-9 Mars-Marta (Talanchuk) (1981-82) 607, 630
WT-10 Mars-Beryl (Talanchuk) (1981-82) 607, 630
WT-11 Chinook (Birdman) (1986-87) 544
WT-11 Chinook 2S (Birdman) (1985-86) 644
WW-1 Der Jager D IX (White) 613
Wag-a-Bond (Wag-Aero) 611
WAG-AERO INC (USA) 611
WAR AIRCRAFT REPLICAS (USA) 612
WARD, RAY (USA) (1987-88) 732
War Eagle (Mitchell Wing) 586
WARNER AVIATION INC (USA) 612
WARPATH AVIATION (USA) (1983-84) 682
WASPAIR (see Midwest) (1984-85) 722
WASPAIR CORPORATION (USA) (1983-84) 682
WATSON WINDWAGON COMPANY (USA) 612
Wazka TD-13 (Dobrocinski) (1984-85) 673
WEEDHOPPER (see Nova Air) (1984-85) 722
Weedhopper C, JC-24C (Weedhopper) (1983-84) 683
WEEDHOPPER OF UTAH INC (USA) (1983-84) 683
Week-end (Nicollier) 528
Wel-1 (Wiweko) (1986-87) 598
WELLER, ROMAN (West Germany) (1986-87) 598
WENDT AIRCRAFT ENGINEERING (USA) (1986-87) 734
Westair 204 (Western) (1985-86) 634
WEST AUSTRALIAN AIRCRAFT COMPANY (Australia) 506
WESTERN AIRCRAFT CORPORATION (USA) (1985-86) 634
WESTERN AIRCRAFT SUPPLIES (Canada) 513
Westland Whirlwind Mark II (Butterworth) (1987-88) 648
WESTWIND CORPORATION LTD (UK) 548
WHATLEY, VASCOE Jr (USA) 612
WHEELER AIRCRAFT (SALES) PTY LTD, RON (Australia) 506
WHEELER AIRCRAFT COMPANY (Hovey) 613
Whing Ding II (WD-11) (Hovey) 576
Whisper (Grove) (1987-88) 668
Whitehawk 185 (Beck) (1983-84) 688
WHITE, MARSHALL E (USA) 613
White Lightning (White Lightning) 614
WHITE LIGHTNING AIRCRAFT CORPORATION (USA) 614
WHITTAKER, MICHAEL W. J. (UK) 548
Wichawk (Javelin) 577
WIERZBOWSKI, PAWEL (Poland) (1983-84) 687
Wildente (Ultraleicht) 534
Wildente 2 (Ultraleicht) 534
WIND DANCER (USA) (1987-88) 734
Wind Dancer (Wind Dancer) (1987-88) 734
Wind Rider (Aerotech) (1986-87) 631
WindRyder (WindRyder) 614
WINDRYDER ENGINEERING INC (USA) 614
Windwagon (Watson) 612
WINTON, SCOTT (Australia) 506
WINTON AIRCRAFT (Australia) (1986-87) 543
WISCH & NIST GmbH (West Germany) (1987-88) 599
Witch (Greenwood) (1986-87) 668
WITTMAN, S. J. (USA) 614
WIWEKO, SOEPONO (Indonesia) (1986-87) 598
Wizard (Schürmann) (1981-82) 611
Wizard (Ultralite Soaring) (1984-85) 720
WOLF, DONALD S (USA) 614
WOLF, STEVE (USA) (1986-87) 737
WOLF, WILLIAM H (USA) (1981-82) 629
WOLFE AVIATION COMPANY (USA) (1984-85) 721
WOLFF, ATELIES PAUL (Luxembourg) 539
WONDER MUDRY AVIATION (France) (1984-85) 668
WOOD WING SPECIALITY (USA) 614
WORLD WIDE RACING SERVICES (UK) (1986-87) 622
WORLDWIDE ULTRALITE INDUSTRIES INC (USA) (1984-85) 722
Wren (Advanced Composite) (1987-88) 628
WREN AVIATION INC (USA) (1985-86) 715
Wren (Calder) (1983-84) 656
Wren (Wren) (1985-86) 715

X

X99 (Ulac) (1985-86) 664
XA/650 Buccaneer II (Advanced Aviation) 551
XC (Birdman) (1981-82) 607, 630
XC 280 (Starflight) (1984-85) 716
XC Series (Star Flight) 600
XL (Pegasus) 546
XL Panther (Pegasus) (1987-88) 619
XL Panther (Ultra Sports) (1984-85) 684
XP Aeroplane, UFM of Ky (Loehle) 582
XP Falcon (American Aircraft) (1987-88) 639
XTC Hydrolight (Diehl) 566
X-Ray 14 (La Mouette) (1982-83) 628, 658
X-Ray 16 (La Mouette) (1982-83) 628, 658
X-Ray 18 (La Mouette) (1982-83) 628, 658

Y

YC-100 Series (Chasle) 520
YC-210 (Chasle) (1987-88) 568
Yunhe No 1 (Jinzhou) (1986-87) 560

Z

Z-CH 100 (Zenair) 514
Zk-1 (SVAZARM) (1982-83) 626
Zk-2 (SVAZARM) (1982-83) 626
Zarus (Kolodziej) (1983-84) 692
Zeffir (Calvel) (1984-85) 664
Zefivo (Iannotta) 538
ZENAIR LTD (Canada) 514
ZENITH-AVIATION (France) (1987-88) 592
Zenith-CH 200 (Zenair) 514
Zenith-CH 250 (Zenair) 514
Zenith CH2000 (Zenair) 515
Zéphyr (Jurca) 524
Zephyr II (Euro Wing) (1983-84) 648
Zero, Mitsubishi (WAR) 612
Zhuravlic (1982-83) 634
Zipper (Mainair Sports) (1987-88) 616
Zipper (Zenair) (1987-88) 560
Zipper II (Zenair) (1987-88) 561
Zipper RX (Zenair) (1987-88) 560
Zippy Sport (Fishercraft) 572
ZMIEJ AERO CLUB (Bulgaria) (1982-83) 624
Zodiac CH 600 (Zenair) 514
Zmiej-4 (Zmiej) (1982-83) 624, 656

SAILPLANES

A

A-21S (Caproni Vizzola) (1984-85) 639
A-21SJ (Caproni Vizzola) (1984-85) 639
AA FLIGHT SYSTEMS (USA) (1979-80) 599
AEROMOT (see Aeronaves E Motores SA) 618
AFH 22 (Akaflieg Hannover) (1984-85) 628
AFH 24 (Akaflieg Hannover) 624
AK-2 (Akaflieg Karlsruhe) (1985-86) 735
AK-5 (Akaflieg Karlsruhe) 625
ALPLA (see Alpla-Werke Alwin Lechner OHG) (1979-80) 554
AMT-100 (Aeromot) 618
AN-21 (Neukom) (1980-81) 580
AN-66C (Neukom) (1979-80) 577, 590
ANB (KAPU) (1986-87) 765
AR 124 (Ahrens) (1978-79) 576, 586
ARPLAM (see All Reinforced Plastic Mouldings) 617
AS (see Aero Saladillo) (1979-80) 557
ASH 25 (Schleicher) 634
ASH 25 MB (Schleicher) 634
ASK 13 (Jubi/Schleicher) 628
ASK 13 (Schleicher) 632
ASK 21 (Schleicher) 632
ASK 23 (Schleicher) 633
ASK 23B (Schleicher) 633
ASW 15 B (Schleicher) (1978-79) 567
ASW 17 Super Orchidee (Schleicher) (1978-79) 567
ASW 19 (Schleicher) (1986-87) 756
ASW 19 Club (Schleicher) (1985-86) 742
ASW 19B (Schleicher) (1985-86) 742
ASW 20 (Schleicher) (1986-87) 756
ASW 20 B (Schleicher) 632
ASW 20 BL (Schleicher) 632
ASW 20 C (Schleicher) 632
ASW 20 CL (Schleicher) 632
ASW 20F (Centrair/Schleicher) (1982-83) 591
ASW 20 L (Schleicher) (1986-87) 756
ASW 22 (Schleicher) (1986-87) 756
ASW 22-2 (Schleicher) (1985-86) 744
ASW 22 B (Schleicher) 633
ASW 22 BE (Schleicher) 633
ASW 24 (Schleicher) 634
ASW 24E (Schleicher) 634
ATS-1 Ardhra (Civil Aviation Department) 636
AV.45 (Fauvel) (1979-80) 561, 586
AV.222 (Fauvel) (1979-80) 561, 586
AV.361 (Fauvel) (1979-80) 561
AV 451 (Fauvel) (1979-80) 561
AV.451 (Gross/Fauvel) (1981-82) 574, 598, 604
AVEX (see Asociacion Argentina de Constructores de Aviones Experimentales) (1978-79) 554

AVO 68V Samburo (Alpla) (1979-80) 557
Acroracer (Glaser-Dirks) (1982-83) 596
ADVANCED AVIATION (USA) 643
AERO CLUBE DE RIO CLARO (Brazil) (1986-87) 740
AERONAVES E MOTORES SA (Brazil) 618
AERO SALADILLO (Argentina) (1979-80) 557
AEROSTRUCTURE SARL (France) (1987-88) 744
AEROTECHNIK (Czechoslovakia) 620
AERO TEK (USA) (1979-80) 578
AHRENS AIRCRAFT CORPORATION (USA) (1979-80) 578
Aiglon J.P. 15-36 A/AR (CARMAM) (1983-84) 602
AKADEMISCHE FLIEGERGRUPPE BERLIN eV (West Germany) 624
AKADEMISCHE FLIEGERGRUPPE BRAUNSCHWEIG eV (West Germany) 624
AKADEMISCHE FLIEGERGRUPPE DARMSTADT eV (West Germany) 624
AKADEMISCHE FLIEGERGRUPPE ESSLINGEN eV (West Germany) (1985-85) 734
AKADEMISCHE FLIEGERGRUPPE HANNOVER eV (West Germany) 624
AKADEMISCHE FLIEGERGRUPPE KARLSRUHE eV (West Germany) 625
AKADEMISCHE FLIEGERGRUPPE MÜNCHEN eV (West Germany) (1983-84) 606
AKADEMISCHE FLIEGERGRUPPE STUTTGART eV (West Germany) 625
AKAFLIEG BERLIN (see Akademische Fliegergruppe Berlin eV) 624
AKAFLIEG BRAUNSCHWEIG (see Akademische Fliegergruppe Braunschweig eV) 624
AKAFLIEG DARMSTADT (see Akademische Fliegergruppe Darmstadt eV) 624
AKAFLIEG ESSLINGEN (see Akademische Fliegergruppe Esslingen eV) (1985-86) 734
AKAFLIEG HANNOVER (see Akademische Fliegergruppe Hannover eV) 624
AKAFLIEG KARLSRUHE (see Akademische Fliegergruppe Karlsruhe eV) 625
AKAFLIEG MÜNCHEN (see Flugtechnische Forschungsgruppe eV) (1986-87) 748
AKAFLIEG STUTTGART (see Akademische Fliegergruppe Stuttgart eV) 625
ALANNE, PENTTI (Finland) (1985-86) 730
Albatross, NP-100A (Nippi) (1982-83) 604
ALL REINFORCED PLASTICS MOULDINGS (Belgium) 617
ALPLA-WERKE ALWIN LECHNER OHG (Austria) (1979-80) 557
AmEAGLE CORPORATION (U.S.A.) (1982-83) 608
American Eaglet (AmEagle) (1982-83) 608, 618
Antares, SB-11 (Akaflieg Braunschweig) (1979-80) 563, 586
APPLEBAY INC (USA) (1985-86) 753
Aqua Glider (Explorer) (1983-84) 624
Araponga (Rio Claro) (1986-87) 740
Ardhra, ATS-1 (Civil Aviation Department) 636
Arrow (Muller-Kites) (1978-79) 596
Arrow (UP Sports) (1984-85) 652
ASOCIACION ARGENTINA DE CONSTRUCTORES DE AVIONES EXPERIMENTALES (Argentina) (1978-79) 554
Astir (Grob) (1983-84) 608
Astir II (Grob) (1983-84) 608
Astir IIB (Grob) (1982-83) 596, 616
AUTO-AERO KÖZLEKEDÉSTECHNIKAI VALLALAT (Hungary) 636
AVIAFIBER AG (Switzerland) (1980-81) 578
AVIATECHNIKA (Hungary) (1986-87) 759
AVIONS RENÉ FOURNIER (France) 622
AVIONS POTTIER (France) (1987-88) 746

B

B4M1 (Pilatus-Lynch) 617
B4-PC11AF (Nippi/Pilatus) (1984-85) 640
B-12 (Akaflieg Berlin) (1978-79) 560, 582
B 12T (Akaflieg Berlin) 624
B-13 (Akaflieg Berlin) 624
BF IV-BIMO (LVD) (1978-79) 564, 584
BIAA (see Beijing Institute of Aeronautics & Astronautics) (1984-85) 621
BJ-1b Duster (DSK) (1982-83) 610, 620
BK-7 Lietuva (LAK) (1983-84) 623
BMW-1 (Wilkes) (1984-85) 652
Bro-11M Zile (LAK/Oshkinis) (1985-86) 752
Bro-16 (LAK/Oshkinis) (1984-85) 644
Bro-17U Utochka (LAK/Oshkinis) (1984-85) 644
BRO-20 Pukyalis (LAK) (1984-85) 644
BRO-21 Vituris (LAK) (1984-85) 644
Bro-21 Trener (LAK/Oshkinis) (1982-83) 608
BRO-23KR Garnis (Esag and Ssaktb) 642
Batso (Kiceniuk) (1979-80) 599, 604
Bakcyl (PW) 636
BEDE AIRCRAFT INC (USA) (1977-78) 612
BEIJING INSTITUTE OF AERONAUTICS & ASTRONAUTICS (China) (1984-85) 621
Bergfalke-IV (Scheibe) (1982-82) 580, 598
BETTERIDGE, DAVID (Australia) (1981-82) 567
Blanik (LET) 620
Blanik, L-13A (Let) (1984-85) 622
Blanik, L-13J (Let) (1979-80) 558
BLESSING, GERHARD (West Germany) (1982-83) 594
Blue Wren, T-5 (Todhunter) (1987-88) 739
Bocian IE (SZD) (1978-79) 571
BOULAY-FERRIER (see Boulay, Jacques and Ferrier, Hubert) (1984-85) 624
BOULAY, JACQUES AND FERRIER, HUBERT (France) (1984-85) 624
Brawo, SZD-48-3M (SZD) (1986-87) 761
BRDITSCHKA HB, GmbH & CO KG (Austria) (1987-88) 739
BRIEGLEB (see Sailplane Corporation of America) (1978-79) 577
BRYAN AIRCRAFT INC (USA) (1985-86) 753
BUCHANAN, JOHN (Australia) (1982-83) 587
BURKHART GROB FLUGZEUGBAU (West Germany) 627
BYTTEBIER, JOHAN F (Argentina) (1979-80) 596

C

C.38 (CARMAM) (1983-84) 602
C.40 (CARMAM) (1982-83) 591
CA-14 (WBAC) (1979-80) 601
CB-2/B Minuano (EEUFMG-CEA) (1981-82) 568, 596
CB-3 (Ultralight Flight Systems) (1979-80) 602
CERVA (see Consortium Européen de Réalisation et de Ventes d'Avions, Groupement d'Intérêts Économiques (1978-79) 558
CT6 (Lightwing) 642
CTA (see Centro Tecnico Aeroespacial) (1984-85) 619
CVT (see Centro di Volo a Vela del Politecnico di Torino) (1977-78) 603
Calif Series (caproni Vizzola) (1984-85) 639
CALVEL, JACQUES (France) (1984-85) 624
Canard-2 FL (Aviafiber) (1980-81) 578, 592
CANARD AVIATION AG (Switzerland) 640
Canard SC (Canard) 640
CAPRONI VIZZOLA COSTRUZIONI AERONAUTICHE SpA (Italy) (1984-85) 639
Carbon Dragon (Maupin) 644
CARMAM (France) (1984-85) 624
CASES, FRANCISCO (Spain) (1982-83) 606
CENTRAIR, SA (France) 621
CENTRO TECNICO AEROESPACIAL (Brazil) (1984-85) 619
C-Falke '80 (Scheibe) (1982-83) 598, 616, 622
Chanute biplane glider (1896) (Spurgeon) (1979-80) 600
CHUCK'S GLIDER SUPPLIES (USA) (1979-80) 599
Cirrus (VTC/Schempp-Hirth) (1981-82) 596, 602
Cirrus 17-VTC (Jastreb/Schempp-Hirth) (1982-83) 613
Cirrus 78L (SCAP) (1981-82) 574, 598
Cirrus G/81 (Jastreb/Schempp-Hirth) (1984-85) 654
CISKEI AIRCRAFT INDUSTRIES (PTY) LTD (China) 619
CIVIL AVIATION DEPARTMENT (India) 636
Cloudster, ST-100 (Ryson) (1984-85) 650
Club III, G102 (Grob) (1984-85) 630
Club IIIb, G102 (Grob) (1987-88) 750
Club, ASW 19 (Schleicher) (1982-83) 600, 618
Club Astir II (Grob) (1982-83) 596
Club Elan, DG-100 (ELAN) (1979-80) 582, 592
Club Elan, DG-100 (Elan/Glaser-Dirks) (1982-83) 613, 620
Club Libelle (Glasflügel) (1978-79) 562
Club-Spatz (Scheibe) (1978-79) 566
Colibri 1 SL (Farner) (1981-82) 588
Compact (GEPAS) (1980-81) 566, 588
Companion (Lightwing) 642
Condor (Boulay-Ferrier) (1984-85) 624
Condor (Ferrier) (1981-82) 572, 598, 604
Condor (Hollmann) (1984-85) 647
Condor (Hollmann/Klepeis) (1981-82) 592, 602, 604
Condor (Up Inc) (1979-80) 600, 604
Condor, MG3-15L (Maggi) (1981-82) 584, 600
CONSORTIUM EUROPÉEN DE RÉALISATION ET DE VENTES D'AVIONS (GROUPEMENT D'INTÉRÊTS ÉCONOMIQUES) (France) (1978-79) 558
Cuervo, FS-25 F (ENSMA) (1982-83) 592
Cuervo, FS-26 (ENSMA) (1978-79) 558
Cumulus (Eipper-Formance) (1978-79) 598
Cumulus III (Dahu Plane) (1978-79) 596

D

D-39 (Akaflieg Darmstadt) (1981-82) 575, 598, 604
D-39b (Akaflieg Darmstadt) (1985-86) 734
D-40 (Akaflieg Darmstadt) 1987-88) 747
D 77 Iris (Issoire) (1984-85) 626
D 177 Iris (Issoire) (1978-79) 560, 582
DG-100 (Glaser-Dirks) (1982-83) 594
DG-100 Club Elan (Elan) (1979-80) 582, 592
DG-100 Club Elan (Elan/Glaser Dirks) (1982-83) 613, 620
DG-100 Elan (Elan/Glaser-Dirks) (1982-83) 612, 620
DG-101 Elan (Elan/Glaser-Dirks) 647
DG-101 (Glaser-Dirks) (1985-86) 736
DG-101 (G) (Elan) (1982-83) 613
DG-200 (Glaser-Dirks) (1985-86) 736
DG-202 (Glaser-Dirks) (1985-86) 736
DG-300 Elan (Elan/Glaser-Dirks) 647
DG-300 Elan (Glaser-Dirks) (1985-86) 736
DG-400 (Glaser-Dirks) 626
DG-500 (Glaser-Dirks) (1984-85) 630
DG-500 Elan (Elan/Glaser-Dirks) (1987-88) 772
DG-500M (Glaser-Dirks) 626
DG-600 (Glaser-Dirks) 626
DANIS, BERNARD (France) (1979-80) 597
Delphin, HB-1340 (Mahrer) (1979-80) 576, 590
Delphin, SF-34 (Scheibe) (1986-87) 753
Demoisel (MAV) (1979-80) 597, 603
Dimona Mk II H-36 (Hoffmann) 627
Discus (Schempp-Hirth) 632
DIVISAO DE AERONAVES (Brazil) (1982-83) 587
DOKTOR FIBERGLAS (URSULA HÄNLE) (West Germany) 626
Dophin (Projekt 8) (1982-83) 590
Dolphin M2 (Projekt 8) (1982-83) 590
Drag-N-Fly (Volpar/Spencer) (1980-81) 585, 592
Drifter (DSK) 1979-80) 599
DSK AIRCRAFT CORPORATION (USA) 1983-84) 624
DSK (DUSTER SAILPLANE KITS) (USA) (1979-80) 599
Duster, BJ-lb (DSK) (1982-83) 610, 620

E

E-14 (Akaflieg Esslingen) (1985-86) 734
E-14 (FAG Esslingen) (1987-88) 748
E 75 Silène (Issoire) (1978-79) 559, 582
E 78 Silène (Issoire) (1985-86) 732
ES 65 (Schneider) 617
EEL (see Entwicklung und Erprobung von Leichflugzeugen) (1987-88) 748
EEUFMG (CEA) (see Escola de Engenharia da Universidade Federal de Minas Gerais: Centro de Estudos Aeronáuticos) (1981-82) 568
EFF (see Entwicklungsgemeinschaft für Flugzeugbau) (1982-83) 606
EIRI (see Eino Rühela KV) (1981-82) 571
ENSAE (see École Nationale Supérieure de l'Aéronautique et de l'Espace) (1979-80) 560
ENSMA (see École Nationale Supérieure de Mécanique et d'Aérotechnique) (1983-84) 603
Eaglet (AmEagle) (1980-81) 581, 592
ÉCOLE NATIONALE SUPÉRIEURE DE L'AÉRONAUTIQUE ET DE L'ESPACE (France) (1979-80) 560
ÉCOLE NATIONALE SUPÉRIEURE DE MÉCANIQUE ET D'AÉROTECHNIQUE (France) (1983-84) 603
Eden (MAV) (1979-80) 597, 603
EINO RIIHELA KV (Finland) (1980-81) 564
EKSPERIMENTINE SPORTINES AVIACIJOS GAMYKLA (USSR) 641
ELAN TOVARNA ŠPORTNEGAORODJA N.SOL.O (Yugoslavia) 647
Elan, DG-100 (Elan/Glaser-Dirks) (1982-83) 612, 620
Elan, DG-101 (Elan/Glaser-Dirks) 647
Elan, DG-300 (Elan/Glaser-Dirks) 647
Elan, DG-500 (Elan/Glaser-Dirks) (1987-88) 772
Elastic Wing Z-77 (Wolf) (1979-80) 598, 603
Elektra (Farrelly) (1979-80) 602
Elfe 15 (Neukom) (1981-82) 588, 602
Elfe 17 (Neukom) (1982-83) 606, 618
Elfe M 17 (Parodi) (1985-86) 739
ENTWICKLUNGSGEMEINSCHAFT FÜR FLUGZEUGBAU (Switzerland) (1982-83) 606
ENTWICKLUNG UND ERPROBUNG VON LEICHFLUGZEUGEN (West Germany) (1987-88) 748
ESAG and SSAKTB (see Eksperimentine Sportines Aviacijos Gamykla) 641
ESCOLA DE ENGENHARIA DA UNIVERSIDADE FEDERAL DE MINAS GERAIS: CENTRO DE ESTUDOS AERONAUTICOS (Brazil) (1981-82) 568
Espadon, WA 28 (Wassmer) (1977-78) 585
Exo 7 (La Mouette) (1978-79) 597
EXPLORER AIRCRAFT COMPANY INC (USA) (1983-84) 624

F

FS-25 F Cuervo (ENSMA) (1982-83) 592
FS-26 Cuervo (ENSMA) (1978-79) 558
FS-31 (Akaflieg Stuttgart) (1984-85) 628
FS-32 (Akaflieg Stuttgart) 625
FVA (see Flugwissenschaftliche Vereinigung Aachen (1920) EV) (1983-84) 608
FVA-20 F.B. Schmetz (FVA) (1983-84) 608
FAG ESSLINGEN (see Flugtechnische Arbeitsgemeinschaft) (1987-88) 748
Falcon (Chuck's Glider Supplies) (1979-80) 599, 604
Falcon (Streifeneder) (1982-83) 602, 618
Falcon (Waspair) (1979-80) 598, 603
Falcon V (Waspair) (1979-80) 599, 603
Falcon 15 m (Wright) (1982-83) 608
Falke (Scheibe) (1985-86) 740
Falke 80 (Scheibe) (1982-83) 598, 616, 622
Falke 82 (Scheibe) (1984-85) 634
Falke 85 SF-25C (Scheibe) (1985-86) 740
Falke 86 SF-25C (Scheibe) (1986-87) 752
Falke 87 SF-25C (Scheibe) (1987-88) 753
Falke 88 SF-25C (Scheibe) 629
Falke, T.61G (Slingsby) (1982-83) 608
Faltente (Pflumm & Richter) (1980-81) 570, 594
Fantail (Marshall) (1978-79) 597
Farfelu (ENSAE) (1978-79) 558, 582
FARNER, DIPL-ING ETH HANS ULRICH (Switzerland) (1981-82) 588
FARRELLY HANG GLIDERS (Australia) (1979-80) 596
FAUVEL, CHARLES (France) (1980-81) 566
FERRIER, HUBERT (France) (1981-82) 572
Firefly (UP Inc) (1979-80) 600, 604
Flatlander (DSK) (1979-80) 599
Fledgling (Manta) (1979-80) 599
Flexi-Flier (Eipper-Formance) (1978-79) 598
Flexi-Floater (Eipper-Formance) (1978-79) 598
FLIGHT DYNAMICS INC (USA) (1984-85) 647
Flying Circus (High Perspective) (1978-79) 596
FLUGTECHNISCHE ARBEITSGEMEINSCHAFT (West Germany) (1987-88) 748
FLUGTECHNISCHE FORSCHUNGSGRUPPE (West Germany) (1986-87) 748
FLUGWISSENSCHAFTLICHE VEREINIGUNG AACHEN (1920) EV (West Germany) (1983-84) 608
FOURNIER AVIONS, RENÉ (France) 622
FOURNIER AVIATION (France) (1983-84) 603
Foxbat (Solar Wings) 1978-79) 597
FREE FLIGHT AVIATION PTY LTD (Australia) (1982-83) 587
FREE FLIGHT HANG GLIDERS (Australia) (1979-80) 596
Frelon (Calvel) (1982-83) 590, 616, 622

G

G 102 Series III (Grob) (1987-88) 750
G 103 Twin II (Grob) (1987-88) 750
G 109 (Grob) (1983-84) 609
G 109B (Grob) (1987-88) 750

G160, Gryphon (Waspair) (1979-80) 599, 603
G180, Gryphon (Waspair) (1979-80) 599, 603
Gapa, PW-2 (PW) 636
GEP (see Groupe d'Études Georges Payre) (1979-80) 562
GEPAS (see Groupe d'Études Pour l'Aviation Sportive) (1980-81) 566
Garnis, BRO-23KR, Oshkinis (Esag and Ssaktb) 642
Gemini (Marsden) (1981-82) 568
GLASER-DIRKS FLUGZEUGBAU GmbH (West Germany) 626
GLASFASER ITALIANA SrL (Italy) (1983-84) 618
GLASFLÜGEL GmbH & Co KG (West Germany) (1982-83) 596
Globetrotter, H 121 (Start + Flug) (1978-79) 568, 584
Gobé, R-26S (Auto-Aero) 636
Gradient, VSO 10 (VSO) 620
GROB (see Burkhart Grob Flugzeugbau) (West Germany) 627
GROSS, FRANCOIS AND RIGER (France) (1981-82) 574
GROUPE D'ETUDES GEORGES PAYRE (France) (1979-80) 562
GROUPE D'ETUDES POUR L'AVIATION SPORTIVE (France) (1980-81) 566
Gryphon (Miles Wings) (1979-80) 598
Gryphon G160 (Waspair) (1979-80) 599, 603
Gryphon G180 (Waspair) (1979-80) 599, 603
Gullwing (Solar Wings) (1978-79) 597

H

H-36 Dimona Mk II (Hoffmann) 627
H-36D (Hoffmann) 628
H-38 Observer (Hoffmann) (1987-88) 752
H 101 Salto (Hänle) (Doktor Fiberglas) 626
H 101 Salto (Start + Flug) (1978-79) 568, 584
H 121 Globetrotter (Start + Flug) (1978-79) 568, 584
HA-18 (Pacific Gull) (1978-79) 598
HA-19 (Pacific Gull) (1978-79) 598
HA-20 (Pacific Gull) (1978-79) 598
HB (see HB Aircraft Industries Luftfahrzeug AG) 617
HB-21 (Brditschka) (1981-82) 567, 596, 604
HB-21 Hobbyliner (Brditschka) (1985-86) 727
HB-21/2400 Hobbylifter (Brditschka) (1985-86) 727
HB-22 (Brditschka) (1981-82) 567, 596, 604
HB-22 Hobbyliner (Brditschka) (1983-84) 597
HB-22/2400 Hobbylifter (Brditschka) (1983-84) 597
HB-23 Hobbyliner (HB-Aircraft) 617
HB-23/2000 Hobbyliner (Brditschka) (1985-86) 727
HB-23/2400 Hobbyliner (HB-Aircraft) 617
HB-23/2400 Scanliner (HB-Aircraft) 617
HB-1340 Delphin (Mahrer) (1979-80) 576, 590
HF Colibri 1 SL (Farner) (1981-82) 588
HP-18 (Bryan/Schreder) (1985-86) 754
HP-19 (Bryan/Schreder) (1983-84) 624
HP-20 (Bryan/Schreder) (1983-84) 624
HP-21 (Bryan/Schreder) (1985-86) 754
HS-11 Mrigasheer (India) (1981-82) 584
HS-7 Mini-Nimbus (Schempp-Hirth) (1981-82) 582, 600
HS-7 Mini-Nimbus C (Schempp-Hirth) (1982-83) 599
HANG GLIDERS PTY LTD (Australia) (1979-80) 596
HÄNLE, URSULA (West Germany) (1981-82) 578
Happy Duck (United Hang Gliders) (1978-79) 597
Hawk (Muller Kites) (1978-79) 596
HAWKSWORTH SKYSPORTS LTD (UK) (1978-79) 593
HB-AIRCRAFT INDUSTRIES LUFTFAHRZEUG AG (Austria) 617
Hippie (Start + Flug) (1979-80) 568, 584
Hirondelle Club (Véliplane) (1978-79) 597
Hobbyliner, (HB-Aircraft) 617
HOFFMAN FLUGZEUGBAU KG, WOLF (West Germany) 627
HOLIGHAUS & HILLENBRAND GmbH & Co KG (West Germany) (1979-80) 564
HOLLMANN (USA) (1984-85) 647
Hornet (Glasflügel) (1981-82) 578, 598
Hornet 130S (Free Flight) (1982-83) 587, 614, 622
Hornet C (Glasflügel) (1981-82) 578, 598
HUFNAGEL, BERNHARD (West Germany) (1981-82) 579

I

I 79 (Issore) (1980-81) 566
IAR-35 (ICA) 640
ICA (see Intreprinderea de Constructii Aeronautice) 638
IPE (see Industria Paranaense de Estruturas) 618
IPE 02 Nhapecam (IPE) (1983-84) 598
IPE 02b Nhapecam II (IPE) (1985-86) 728
IPE 03 (IPE) (1985-86) 728
IS-28B2 (ICA) 638
IS-28M (ICA) (1981-82) 586, 600, 604
IS-28M2 (ICA) (1984-85) 642
IS-28M2A (ICA) 638
IS-28MA (ICA) (1983-84) 620
IS-29 (ICA) (1982-83) 606
IS-29D2 (ICA) 639
IS-29DM (ICA) (1982-83) 606
IS-29EM (ICA) (1982-83) 606
IS-30 (ICA) 640
IS-30A (ICA) (1984-85) 643
IS-31 (ICA) (1980-81) 590
IS-32 (ICA) 640
IS-33 (ICA) (1982-83) 606
ISF (see Ingenieur-Büro Dipl-Ing Strauber-Frommhold GmbH & Co KG) (1980-81) 570
INAV LTD (USA) 643
INDUSTRIA PARANAENSE DE ESTRUTURAS (Brazil) 618
INGENIEUR-BÜRO DIPL-ING STRAUBER-FROMMHOLD GmbH & Co KG (West Germany) (1980-81) 570
INTREPRINDEREA DE CONSTRUCTII AERONAUTICE (Romania) 638
Iris, D 77 (Issoire) (1984-85) 626
Iris, D 177 (Issoire) (1978-79) 560, 582
ISSOIRE-AVIATION SA (France) 622

J

J5 Janowski (Marco-Elektronik Company) (1985-86) 746
JEAA (Japan) (1979-1980) 597
J.P.15-36A Aiglon (CARMAM) (1983-84) 602
J.P.15-36 A R Aiglon (CARMAM) (1983-84) 602
Jantar 2, SZD-42-1 (SZD) (1981-82) 586
Jantar 2B (SZD) 637
Jantar 15, SZD-52 (SZD) (1986-87) 762
Jantar K, SZD-49 (SZD) (1981-82) 586
Jantar Standard, SZD-41A (SZD) (1981-82) 586
Jantar Standard 2, SZD-48 (SZD) (1983-84) 619
Jantar Standard 3 (SZD) 637
Janus (Schempp-Hirth) 630
JASTREB FABRICA AVIONA I JEDRILICA (Yugoslavia) 648
Javelin (Wings) (1979-80) 602
Jet (La Mouette) (1978-79) 597
Jian Fan, X-7 (National Aircraft Factories) 619
Jiefang-3 (China) (1982-83) 614
João Grande (Sidou) (1982-83) 588
Johan 087 (Byttebier) (1979-80) 602
JUBI GmbH SPORTFLUGZEUGBAU (West Germany) 628
Junior (SZD) 638

K

KAI (see Kazan Aviation Institute) (1984-85) 644
KAI-50 (KAI) (1984-85) 644
KN-1 (Knechtel) (1985-86) 738
KR-1B (Rand Robinson) (1984-85) 650
KR-03A Puchatek (WSK PZL-Krosno) 638
KS-II Kartik (India) (1977-78) 602
KW 1 b 2 Quero Quero II (IPE) 618
KW 1 GB (IPE) 619
KW 162 Quero Quero II (IPE) (1982-83) 588
KAPU (see Kuibyshevski Aviation Institute and Production Unit) (1987-88) 766
KAZAN AVIATION INSTITUTE (USSR) (1984-85) 644
Kestrel 17 (Glasflügel) (1979-80) 564, 586
Kestrel 22 Srs 2, T.58H (Vickers-Slingsby/Glasflügel) (1978-79) 576, 586
K-Falke '80 (Scheibe) (1981-82) 580, 600, 604
Kit-Club 14-34 (Pottier) (1984-85) 626
Kit-Club 15-34 (CARMAM/Pottier) (1982-83) 591
Kit-Club 15-34 (Pottier) (1986-87) 745
Kiwi (Valentin) 635
KNECHTEL, ING WILHELM (West Germany) (1985-86) 738
KONDOR KITE CO (USA) (1978-79) 593
Kora I (Kortenbach & Rauh) (1980-81) 570
KORTENBACH & RAUH (West Germany) (1980-81) 570
Kosava-2-S (Jastreb) (1985-86) 760
Krokus, SZD-52 (SZD) (1986-87) 762
KUFFNER (see Leichtflugzeugbau Werner Kuffner) (1987-88) 752
KUIBYSHEVSKI AVIATION INSTITUTE AND PRODUCTION UNIT (1987-88) 766

L

L-1 (Arplam) 617
L6-7 (Lucas) 623
L6FS Mouse (Lightwing) (1987-88) 767
L-13 Wankel (Let) (1979-80) 558
L-13A Blanik (Let) (1984-85) 622
L-13J Blanik (Let) (1979-80) 558
L-13SW Vivat (Aerotechnik) 620
L-13SW (Let) (1980-81) 564
L-13-2M (Let) (1979-80) 558
L-23 (LET) 620
L190, Laser (Waspair) (1979-80) 599, 603
LA—11 Topaze (Loravia) (1979-80) 562
LAK (see Litovskaya Aviatsionnaya Konstruktsiya) (1987-88) 766
LAK-2 (LAK) (1985-86) 752
LAK-5 Nyamunas (Esag and Ssaktb) 641
LAK-6 (Let) (1979-80) 558
LAK-9 Lietuva (LAK) (1983-84) 623
LAK-10 Lietuva (Esag and Ssaktb) (1983-84) 623
LAK-11 Nida (Esag and Ssaktb) 641
LAK-12 Lietuva (Esag and Ssaktb) 642
LAK-12 Lietuva 2R (Esag and Ssaktb) 642
LAK-14 Strazdas (LAK) (1987-88) 767
LAK-16 (Esag and Ssaktb) 642
LCF (see Luftsportclub der Zeppelinstadt Friedrichshafen) (1979-80) 566
LCF II (LCF) (1979-80) 566
LO 170 (Stähls) (1982-83) 602
LSI-f (Rolladen-Schneider) (1978-79) 564
LS3 (Rolladen-Schneider) (1981-82) 580
LS3-a (Rolladen-Schneider (1981-82) 580, 598
LS3-17 (Rolladen-Schneider) (1981-82) 580
LS4 (Rolladen-Schneider) 628
LS5 (Rolladen-Schneider) (1981-82) 580
LS6 (Rolladen-Schneider) 628
LVD (see Schülerfluggemeinschaft der Luftsportverein Detmold EV) (1979-80) 566
LAISTER SAILPLANES INC (USA) (1979-80) 578
LANAVERRE INDUSTRIE (France) (1978-79) 560
Lanzalone Aulanz (AVEX) (1978-79) 554, 588
Laser L190 (Waspair) (1979-80) 599, 603
LEICHTFLUGZEUGBAU WERNER KUFFNER (West Germany) (1987-88) 752
Lenticular 15 S (AS) (1979-80) 557
LET NÁRODNI PODNIK (Czechoslovakia) 620
Leuvense (Arplam) 617
Libel-lula (Cases) (1981-82) 588
Lietuva 2R, LAK 12 (Esag and Ssaktb) 642
Lietuva, Lak-9 (LAK) (1982-84) 623
Lietuva, LAK-10 (LAK) (1983-84) 623
Lietuva LAK-12 (Esag and Ssaktb) 642
Lietuva 2R LAK-12 (Esag and Ssaktb) 642
LIGHTER THAN AIR PRODUCTS (USA) (1978-79) 593
LIGHTWING RESEACH (UK) 642
Lilienthal monoplane glider (1895) (Spurgeon) (1979-80) 600
LINDNER GmbH & Co KG, FIBERGLAS-TECHNIK RUDOLF (West Germany) (1982-83) 597
Liska, SL-40 (Soko) 648
LITOVSKAYA AVIATSIONNAYA KONSTRUKTSIYA (USSR) (1987-88) 766
LORAVIA (see Lorraine Aviation) (1979-80) 562
LORRAINE AVAIATION (France) (1978-80) 562
LUCAS, EMILE (France) 623
LUFTSPORTCLUB DER ZEPPELINSTADT FRIEDRICHSHAFEN (West Germany) (1979-80) 566
Lutin 80 (Aerostructure) (1987-88) 744
LYNCH, JOHN F. (Australia) 617
Lynx (Wings) (1979-80) 602
Lynx B (McBroom) (1978-79) 598

M

M2, Dolphin (Projekt 8) (1982-83) 590
M2, Milomei (Meier) (1983-84) 610
MAV (see Manufacture d'Ailes Volantes) (1979-80) 597
MF (see Masinski Fakultet) (1982-83) 614
MFB (see Mistral Flugzeugbau) (1982-83) 598
MG-1 (Civil Aviation Department) (1986-87) 760
MG3-15L Condor (Maggi) (1981-82) 585, 600
MJ-4 (Birdman Enterprises) (1978-79) 596
Mü 27 (Akaflieg München) (1981-82) 576, 598
Mü 28 (Akaflieg München) (1985-86) 736
MAGGI, ANGELO (Italy) (1981-82) 585
MAHRER, FRITZ (Switzerland) (1979-80) 576
MANUFACTURE D'AILES VOLANTES (France) (1979-80) 597
MARCO-ELEKTRONIK COMPANY (Poland) (1985-86) 760
Marauder (Muller Kites) (1978-79) 596
Marianne, Type 201 (Centrair) (1984-85) 625
Marianne, Type 2001 (Centrair) 622
Marianne M, Type 2001 M (Centrair) 622
MARSDEN, DR DAVID J (Canada) (1984-85) 620
MARSHALL, FRANK (South Africa) (1979-80) 598
MARSKE AIRCRAFT CORPORATION (USA) 644
MASINSKI FAKULTET (Yugoslavia) (1982-83) 614
MAUPIN, JIM (USA) 644
Maxi Strato (Sunbird) (1978-79) 599
McBROOM SAILWINGS LTD (UK) (1978-79) 593
MEIER, MICHEL-LORENZ (West Germany) (1983-84) 610
Micro Stinger (Moyes) (1979-80) 596, 602
Midas (Chargus) (1978-79) 597
Midi-Stinger (Moyes) (1978-79) 596
MILES WINGS (ENGINEERS) LTD (UK) (1979-80) 598
Milomei M2 (Meier) (1983-84) 610
Mini-Moni (Monnett) (1985-86) 756
Mini-Nimbus C (Schempp-Hirth) (1981-82) 582, 600
Minimus, ST-11 (Stralpes Aero) (1983-84) 605
Mini-Nimbus, HS-7 (Schempp-Hirth) (1981-82) 582, 600
Mini-Stinger (Moyes) (1979-80) 596, 602
Mini Strato (Sunbird) (1978-79) 599
Minuano, CB-2/B (EEUFMG/CEA) (1981-82) 568, 596
Mistral-C (Valentin) 635
Mistral-C, Model 2 (ISF) (1980-81) 570, 588
Mistral C, Model 2 (MFB) (1981-82) 580
MISTRAL FLUGZEUGBAU (DIPL-ING STRAUBER GmbH & Co KG) (West Germany) (1982-83) 598
Mita III (Tainan) (1979-80) 572, 588
Moba 2C (Sunderland) (1982-83) 587, 614
Moba 3 Virago (Sunderland) (1982-83) 587
Model II (LCF) (1978-79) 564, 584
Model 2 Mistral-C (ISF) (1980-81) 570, 588
Model 2 Mistral C (MFB) (1981-82) 580
Model 2-32 (Schweizer) (1978-79) 580, 586
Model 10 (VSO) (1985-86) 730
Model 77 Solitaire (Rutan) (1983-84) 628
Model 77-6 Solitaire (Rutan) (1985-86) 756
Model 1616 (Muller Kites) (1978-79) 596
Model 1718 (Muller Kites) (1978-79) 596
Model 1820 (Muller Kites) (1978-79) 596
Modified FS-25 Cuervo (ENSMA) (1979-80) 560
Monarch (Marske) 644
Monerai (INAV) (1987-88) 768
Monerai P (Monnett) (1985-86) 756
Monerai S (Monnett) (1985-86) 755
Monerai-Max (Monnett) (1985-86) 756
Moni (INAV) (1987-88) 768
Moni (Monnett) (1985-86) 756
MONNETT EXPERIMENTAL AIRCRAFT INC (USA) (1985-86) 755
Montgomery monoplane glider (1883) (Spurgeon) (1979-80) 600
Moonraker 78 (Birdman Sports) (1978-79) 597
Mosquito (Glasflügel) (1979-80) 565, 588
Mosquito B (Glasflügel) (1981-82) 578, 598
Motorblanik (Alanne) (1983-84) 601
Motorlerche (Alanne) (1984-85) 623
Mouse, L6FS (Lightwing) (1987-88) 767
Mrigasheer (India) (1981-82) 584
MULLER KITES LTD (Canada) (1979-80) 596
Mustang (Muller Kites) (1978-79) 596

N

NIPPI (see Nihon Hikoki Kabushiki Kaisha) (1984-85) 640
No. II My Wing (JEAA) (1979-80) 597
NP-100A Albatross (Nippi) (1982-83) 604
NATIONAL AIRCRAFT FACTORIES (China) 619
NEUOM SEGELFLUGZEUGBAU, ALBERT (Switzerland) (1982-83) 606
Nhapecam, IPE 02 (IPE) (1983-84) 598
Nhapecan II, 02B (IPE) 619
Nida (Esag and Ssaktb) 641
NIHON HIKOKI KABUSHIKI KAISHA (Japan) (1984-85) 640
Nimbus 2C (Schempp-Hirth) (1983-84) 612
Nimbus 3 (Schempp-Hirth) 630
Nimbus 3D (Schempp-Hirth) 630
Nyamunas, (Esag and Ssaktb) 641

O

O2 (IPE) (1978-79) 555, 582
O2b (IPE) (1985-86) 728
O2b Nhapecan II (IPE) 619
O3 (IPE) (1986-87) 740
O-3 (Oldershaw) (1979-80) 581
Observer (Hoffmann) (1987-88) 752
Odyssée (Favul) (1979-80) 597, 602
Ogar, SZD-45A (SZD) (1980-81)576, 590, 594
OLDERSHAW, VERNON W (USA) (1979-80) 581
OMNIPOL FOREIGN TRADE CORPORATION (Czechoslovakia) (1985-86) 730

P

PAR (see Divisao de Aeronaves) (1982-83) 587
PATS/NSDB (see Philippine Aeronautics Training School/National Science Development Board) (1978-79) 570
PE-80367 Urubu (CTA) (1983-84) 598
PG-1 Aqua Glider (Explorer) (1983-84) 624
PIK-20E (Siren/EIRI) (1981-82)574, 598, 604
PIK-20E2F (Issoire) 622
PIK-20E2F (17-metre version) (Issoire) (1984-85) 626
PIK-30 (Issoire) 622
PW (see Politechnika Warszawaska) 636
PW-2 GAPA (PW) 636
PW-3 (PW) 636
PW-4 (PW) 636
PARODI MOTORSEGLERTECHNIK (West Germany) (1985-86) 739
Pathfinder (Electra) (1985-86) 739
PAYRE, GROUPE D'ETUDES GEORGE (France) (1979-80) 562
Pégase (Centrair) 621
Pégase (Centrair) 621
Pégase B (Centrair) 621
Pégase BC (Centrair) (1986-87) 743
Pégase C (Centrair) (1986-87) 743
Pégase CC (Centrair) (1986-87) 743
Pégase D (Centrair) 621
Pégase P (Centrair) (1984-85) 625
Pégase Club (Centrair) (1985-86) 732
Belzner biplane glider (1920/21) (Spurgeon) (1979-80) 600
PENNER, HELMUTH (West Germany) (1978-79) 592
PELUMM, MANFRED and RICHTER, K.J. (West Germany) (1980-81) 570
PHILIPPINE AERONAUTICS TRAINING SCHOOL/NATIONAL SCIENCE DEVELOPMENT BOARD (Philippines) (1978-79) 570
Phoebus B 3 (Lindner) (1982-83) 597
Phoenix (Delta Wing) (1978-79) 598
Pilatus B4-PC11AF (Nippi) (1984-85) 640
PILATUS FLUGZEUGWERKE AG (Switzerland) (1978-79) 574
Pioneer II (Marske) 644
Pirat, SZD-30C (SZD) (1980-81) 576, 590
Platypus (Schneider) 617
POLITECHNIKA WARSZAWSKA (Poland) 636
PONSOT, BERNARD (France) (1981-82) 574
POTTIER, AVIONS (France) (1987-88) 746
PROJEKT 8 I/S (Denmark) (1982-83) 590
Prometheus (EFF) (1982-83) 606, 618, 622
PRZEDSIEBIORSTWO DOSWIADCZALNO-PRODUKCYJNE SZYBOWNICTWA (Poland) 637
Puchacz (SZD) 637
Puchatek KR-03 (WSK PZL-Krosno) 638
Pukyalis, BRO-20 (LAK) (1984-85) 644

Q

Qian Jin, Z-10 (National Aircraft Factories) 620
Quero Quero II (IPE) (1980-81) 562
Quero Quero II, KW 162 (IPE) (1982-83) 588
Quero Quero II, KW 1 b 2 (IPE) 618

R

R-26S Gobé (Auto-Aero) 636
RF 5 (Fournier) 622
RF5 (Sportavia/Avion Planeur) (1979-80)570, 588, 594
RF5B Sperber (Sportavia) (1980-81) 573
RF-9 (Fournier) (1982-83)592, 616, 622
RF-10 (Aerostructure) (1986-87) 742
RS-15 (Bryan) (1985-86) 753
RADAB AB (Sweden) 640
Raider (Birdman Enterprises) (1978-79) 596
RAND ROBINSON ENGINEERING INC (USA) (1984-85) 650
Ranger (Wings) (1979-80) 602
Rebell (Blessing) (1980-81) 568
RILEY & CO (SPORTAVIA) (Australia), (1983-84) 597
Rhönlerche IIM (Knechtel) (1982-83)596, 616, 622
Ricochet (Buchanan) (1982-83) 587
Ridgemaster (Electra) (1978-79) 598
RIO CLARO (see Aéro Clube de Rio Claro) (1986-87) 740
ROLLADEN-SCHNEIDER FLUGZEUGBAU GmbH (West Germany) 628
Rooster (Lightwing) (1985-86) 753
RUTAN AIRCRAFT FACTORY INC (USA) (1986-87) 769
RYSON AVIATION CORPORATION (USA) (1985-86) 756

S

S-2A (Strojnik) 646
S-4A Elfe 15 (Neukom) (1981-82) 588, 602
S 10 (Stemme) 634
SB-11 (Akaflieg Braunschweig) (1979-80) 563, 586
SB-12 (Akaflieg Braunschweig) (1981-82) 575, 598
SB-13 (Akaflieg Braunschweig) 624
SC Canrad (1985-86) 750
SCAP (see Société de Commercialisation Aéronautiques du Plessis, SaRL) (1981-82) 574
SCM (Canrad) (1985-86) 750
SD3-15T (Swales) (1982-83) 608
SD3-15V (Swales) (1978-79) 575, 586
SF-25C 2000 (Scheibe) (1985-86) 740
SF-25C Falke (Scheibe) (1982-83)598, 616, 622
SF-25C Falke 82 (Scheibe) (1984-85) 634
SF-25C Falke 86 (Scheibe) (1985-86) 740
SF-25C Falke 86 (Scheibe) (1986-87) 752
SF-25C Falke 87 (Scheibe) (1987-88) 753
SF-25C Falke 88 (Scheibe) 629
SF-25C-S Falke '76 (Scheibe) (1979-80)568, 588, 594
SF-25C-S Falke '82 (Scheibe) (1982-83) 598
SF-25E Super-Falke (Scheibe) 629
SF-28A Tandem-Falke (Scheibe) 629
SF-30 Club-Spatz (Scheibe) (1978-79) 566
SF-32 (Scheibe) (1978-79) 566
SF-34 (Scheibe) 629
SF-36 (Scheibe) (1987-88) 754
SF-33 Trainer (Scheibe) (1978-79)566, 584, 588
SGM 2-37 (Schweizer) 646
SGS 1-26E (Schweizer) (1981-82) 594
SGS 1-34B (Schweizer) (1979-80) 582, 592
SGS 1-35 (Schweizer) (1982-83) 612
SGS 1-36 Sprite (Schweizer) 646
SGS 2-32 (Schweizer) (1979-80) 582, 592
SGS 2-33A (Schweizer) 645
SK 1 (Danis) (1979-80) 597
SK 2 (Danis) (1979-80) 597
SK 3 (Danis) (1979-80) 597
SL-2 (SCAP-Lanaverre) (1980-81) 567, 588
SL-2P (Esag and Ssaktb) 642
SL-40 Liska (Soko) 648
SOKO (see Sour Soko Vazduhoplovna Industrija) 648
SST (Hawksworth) (1978-79) 598
ST-11 (Stralpes Aero) 623
ST-12 (Stralpes Aero) (1986-87) 746
ST-14 (Stralpes Aero) (1986-87) 746
ST-15 (Stralpes Aero) 623
ST-100 Cloudster (Ryson) (1984-85) 650
SY-5S (BIAA) (1984-85) 621
SZD (see Przedsiebiorstow Doswiadczalno-Produkcyjne Szybownictwa) 637
SZD-9 bis Bocian IE (SZD) (1978-79) 571
SZD-30C Pirat (SZD) (1980-81) 576, 590
SZD-36A Cobra 15 (SZD) (1978-79) 571, 584
SZD-38 Jantar-1 (SZD) (1977-78) 605
SZD-41A Jantar Standard (SZD) (1982-82) 586
SZD-42-1 Jantar 2 (SZD) (1981-82) 586
SZD-42-2 Jantar 2B (SZD) 637
SZD-45A Ogar (SZD) (1980-81)576, 590, 594
SZD-48-1 Jantar Standard 2 (SZD) (1983-84) 619
SZD-48-2 Jantar Standard 2 (SZD) (1983-84) 619
SZD-48-3 Jantar Standard 3 (SZD) 637
SZD-48-3M Brawo (SZD) (1986-87) 761
SZD-49 Jantar K (SZD) (1981-82) 586
SZD-50-3 Pushacz (SZD) 637
SZD-51-1 Junior (SZD) 638
SZD-51-3 Junior (SZD) (1985-86) 748
SZD-52 Jantar 15 (SZD) (1986-87) 762
SZD-52 Krokus (SZD) (1986-87) 762
SAILPLANE CORPORATION OF AMERICA (USA) (1978-79) 577
SAILWINGS (SCOTLAND) LTD (UK) (1979-80) 598
Salto H 101 (Hänle) (Doktor Fiberglas) 626
Salto, H 101 (Start + Flug) (1978-79) 568, 584
Samburo, Avo 68V (Alpla) (1979-80) 557
Saturn IV (Free Flight) (1979-80) 602
Scanliner (HB Aircraft) 617
SCHEIBE FLUGZEUGBAU GmbH (West Germany) 628
SCHEMPP-HIRTH FLUGZEUGBAU GmbH & Co KG (West Germany) 630
SCHLEICHER GmbH & Co, ALEXANDER (West Germany) 632
SCHNEIDER PTY LTD, EDMUND (Australia) 617
SCHÜLERFLUGGEMEINSCHAFT DER LUFTSPORTVEREIN DETMOLD EV (West Germany) (1979-80) 566
SCHWEIZER AIRCRAFT CORPORATION (USA) 645
SCOT-KITES (UK) (1979-80) 598
Seagull (Seagull) (1979-80) 600, 604
Seasprite (Flight Dynamics) (1982-83) 610, 620
Shadow (Birdman Enterprises) (1978-79) 596
SIDOU, ENG ANTONIO MENEZE (Brazil) (1982-83) 588
Sierra (Advanced Aviation) 643
Silène, E 78 (Issoire) (1985-86) 732
Silhouette (Silhouette) 646
SILHOUETTE AIRCRAFT INC (USA) 646
SIREN, SA (France) (1987-88) 746
Skydart (Ultralight Flight Systems) (1979-80) 602
Skyhook (Ultralight Flight Systems) (1979-80) 602
Skytrek (Delta Wing) (1978-79) 598
SLINGSBY ENGINEERING LTD (UK) (1982-83) 608
SOBIESZCZANSKI, WITOLD (Poland) (1978-79) 592
SOCIÉTÉ DE COMMERCIALISATION AÉRONAUTIQUE DU PLESSIS, SàRL (France) (1981-82) 572
SOCIÉTÉ NOUVELLE WASSMER AVIATION (France) (1977-78) 585
SOKO VAZDUHOPLOVNA INDUSTRIJA RADNA ORGANIZACIJA VAZDUHOPLOVSTVO (Yugoslavia) (1985-86) 760
SOLAR WINGS (South Africa) (1979-80) 598
SOLE-77 (Jastreb) (1987-88) 774
Solitaire, Model 77 (Rutan) (1985-86) 756
SOUR VAZDUKOPLOVNA INDUSTRUJA SOKA (Yugoslavia) 648
Speed Astir II (Grob) (1982-83) 596, 616
Sperber (Sportavia) (1980-81) 573
Spitfire (Chuck's Glider Supplies) (1979-80) 599, 604
SPORTAVIA-PÜTZER GmbH u Co KG (West Germany) (1980-81) 573
SPORT KITES INC (USA) (1978-79) 594
Sport Vega, T.65C (Slingsby) (1982-83) 608
Spring Wing Z-76 (Wolf) (1979-80) 598, 603
Sprite, SGS 1-36 (Schweizer) 646
SPURGEON, JIM (USA) (1979-80) 600
Spyder (UP Inc) (1979-80) 600, 604
Staff Rebel (Blessing) (1981-82)576, 598, 604
STAHLS, BODO (West Germany) (1982-83) 602
Standard III, G102 (Grob) (1985-86) 737
Standard Astir (Grob) (1979-80) 566, 588
Standard Astir II (Grob) (1983-84) 608
Standard Cirrus (Lanaverre) (1978-79) 560, 582
Standard Cirrus (Schempp-Hirth) (1978-79) 566
Standard Cirrus G (Jastreb) (1985-86) 760
Standard Cirrus 75-VTC (Jastreb/Schempp-Hirth) 648
Standard Cirrus 75-VTC (VCT/Schempp-Hirth) (1981-82) 597, 602
Standard Cirrus G/81 (Jastreb) 648
Standard Strato (Sunbird) (1978-79) 599
Star (Favul) (1979-80) 597, 602
START + FLUG GmbH (West Germany) (1978-79) 568
STEMME GmbH & Co KG (West Germany) 634
Sterne (Véliplane) (1978-79) 597
Stinger (Moyes) (1979-80) 596, 602
STRALPES AÉRO SARL (France) 623
Strazdas, LAK-14 (LAK) (1987-88) 767
Streaker (AA Flight) (1979-80) 599, 604
STROJNIK, PROF. ALEX (USA) 646
SUNDERLAND, GARY (Australia) (1983-84) 597
Sunspot (Skyhooks Sailwings) (1979-80) 599
Super Elfe AN-66C (Neukom) (1979-80) 577, 590
Super-Falke SF-25E (Scheibe) 629
Super Lynx (McBroom) (1978-79) 567
Super Orchidee, ASW 17 (Schleicher) (1978-79) 598
Super Strato (Sunbird) (1978-79) 599
Super Swallowtail (Sport Kites) (1978-79) 599
SWALES SAILPLANES (UK) (1982-83) 608

T

T-5 Blue Wren (Todhunter) (1987-88) 739
T.59H Kestrel 22 Srs 2 (Vickers-Slingsby/Glasflügel) (1978-79) 576, 586
T.61F Venture (Slingsby) (1982-83) 608
T.61G Falke (Slingsby) (1982-83) 608
T.65C Sport Vega (Slingsby) (1982-83) 608
TCV-03 Trucavaysse (GEP) (1979-80) 562
TCV-04 (GEP) (1978-79) 558
TG-7A (Schweizer) 646
TN-1 (Tainan) (1980-81) 576, 590
TZ-14 (IPE) 619
Taifun (Valentin) (1983-84) 616
Taifun 17E (Valentin) 634
Taifun 17E-90 (Valentin) (1986-87) 758
TAINAN INDUSTRY CO LTD (Japan) (1981-82) 586
Tandem-Falke SF-28A (Scheibe) 629
Tantal Sinusöide (MAV) (1979-80) 597, 603
TECHNICAL CENTRE, CIVIL AVIATION DEPARTMENT (India) (1987-88) 636
TODHUNTER, R. W. (Australia) 739
Topaze, LA-11 (Loravia) (1979-80) 562
Tornado (United Hang Gliders) (1978-79) 597
Trainer, SF-33 (Scheibe) (1978-79)566, 584, 588
Trener (VTC) (1978-79) 580, 588
Trener, Bro-21 (LAK/Oshkinis) (1982-83) 608
Trucavaysse (GEP) (1979-80) 562
Twin II, G 103 (Grob) (1986-87) 750
Twin III G 103C (Grob) (1987-88) 750
Twin-Astir (Grob) (1980-81) 570
Twin-Astir Trainer (Grob) (1979-80) 566, 588
Twister V (Free Flight) (1979-80) 602
Type 01 Compact (GEPAS) (1980-81) 566, 588
Type 03 (IPE) (1980-81) 562
Type 101 (Centrair) 621
Type 101 Club (Centrair) 621
Type 201, Marianne (Centrair) (1984-85) 625
Type 205 Club Libelle (Glasflügel) (1978-79) 562
Type 206 Hornet (Glasflügel) (1978-79) 562, 584
Type 303 Mosquito (Glasflügel) (1978-79) 562
Type 304 (Glasflügel) (1981-82) 578, 598
Type 402 (Glasflügel) (1981-82) 578, 598
Type 1100 Windex (Radab) (1985-86) 750
Type 2001 Marianne (Centrair) 622
Type 2001M Marianne M (Centrair) 622

U

ULF-1 (EEL) (1987-88) 748
ULS (PW) (1985-86) 746
UP SPORTS (see Ultralite Products) (1984-85) 652
Uavg-15 (Marsden) (1984-85) 620
ULTRALIGHT FLIGHT SYSTEMS (Australia) (1979-80) 596

ULTRALITE PRODUCTS (USA) (1984-85) 652
UNITED HANG GLIDERS (South Africa) (1979-80) 598
Upstart (UP Inc) (1978-79) 599
Urubu, PE-80367 (CTA) (1983-84) 598
Utochka, Bro-17U (LAK/Oshkinis) (1984-85) 644

V

VSO (see Vyvojová Skupina Orlican) 620
VSO 10 Gradient (VSO) 620
VTC (see Vazduhoplovno Tehnicki Centar-VRSAC) (1981-82) 596
VUK-T (Jastreb) 648
VALENTIN FLUGZEUGBAU GmbH (West Germany) 634
VALENTIN GmbH GERÄTE UND MASCHINENBAU (West Germany) (1985-86) 744
Valiant (Schleicher) (1985-86) 742
Vanguard (Schleicher) 632
VAZDUHOPLOVNO TEHNICKI CENTAR-VRSAC (Yugoslavia) (1981-82) 596
Vega (Slingsby) (1982-83) 608
Vega (Vickers-Slingsby) (1979-80) 578, 590
Vega II (Chargus) (1978-79) 597
VELIPLANE (France) (1978-79) 591
Venture, T.61F (Slingsby) (1982-83) 608
Ventus (Schempp-Hirth) 630
VICKERS-SLINGSBY, A DIVISION OF VICKERS LIMITED OFFSHORE ENGINEERING GROUP (U.K.) (1979-80) 578
Viking (Favul) (1979-80) 597, 602
Viking TX Mk 1 (Grob) (1986-87) 750
Virago, Moba 3 (Sunderland) (1982-83) 587
Vituris, BRO-21 (LAK) (1984-85) 644
Vivat L-13SW (Aerotechnik) 620
VOLPAR INC (U.S.A.) (1981-82) 594
VYVOJOVÁ SKUPINA ORLICAN (Czechoslovakia) 620

W

WBAC (see Wright Brothers Aeroplane Co, The) (1979-80) 601
WK-1 (Kuffner) (1984-85) 652
WK-1b (Kuffner) (1987-88) 752
WM 1 (WWS) (1982-83) 602, 618
WM-1 (Wiegand) (1981-82) 584, 600
WSK PZL-KROSWO (see Wytwornia Sprzetu Komunikacyjnego Pzl-Krosno) 638
WWS (see Wiegand und Wisser Sportflugzeugbau GmbH & Co KG) (1982-83) 602
WASPAIR LTD (UK) (1979-80) 599
Waterman & Seagull Flyer (Seagull) (1979-80) 600
WIEGAND, HEINZ (West Germany) (1981-82) 584
WIEGAND UND WISSER SPORTFLUGZEGUBAU GmbH & Co KG (West Germany) (1982-83) 602
WILKES, RAYMOND S. (USA) (1984-85) 652
Windex 1100 (Radab) (1985-86) 750
Windex 1200 (Radab) 640
Windrose (Maupin) 641
Windspiel (Penner) (1978-79) 592
WINGS (Australia) (1979-80) 596
WINTHER-HOLLMANN AIRCRAFT INC (USA) (1982-83) 610
Woodstock One (Maupin) 644
WRIGHT, PETER W (UK) (1982-83) 608
WRIGHT BROTHERS AEROPLANE CO. THE (USA) (1979-80) 601
WYTWORNIA SPRZETU KOMUNIKACYJNEGO PZL-KROSNO (Poland) 638

X

X-5A (State Aircraft Factories) (1985-86) 728
X-7 Jian Fan (National Aircraft Factories) 619
X 9 (Danis) (1979-80) 597
X-9 (National Aircraft Factories) 619
X-10 (National Aircraft Factories) 620
X-11 (State Aircraft Factories) (1984-85) 622
XL-13M (Let) (1979-80) 558
XL-13T (Let) (1979-80) 558
XG-001 (PATS/NSDB) (1979-80) 570
Ximango (Aeromot) 618

Z

Z-16 (IPE) 618
Z-75 (Wolf) (1978-79) 592
Z-75-7 (Wolf) (1978-79) 592
Z-76, Spring Wing (Wolf) (1979-80) 598, 603
Z-77, Elastic Wing (Wolf) (1979-80) 598, 603
Zamberle (Hufnagel) (1981-82) 579
Zia (Applebay) (1985-86) 753
Zile, Bro-11M (LAK/Oshkinis) (1985-86) 752
Zuni (Applebay) (1980-81) 582, 592
Zuni, Model V (Aero Tek) (1979-80) 578, 592

HANG GLIDERS

A

AOK (See Akademicki Osrodek Konstrukcyjny) 649
Ace (Pegasus) (1987-88) 778, 782
Ace/Ace RX (small) (Pegasus) 650
Ace/Ace RX (medium) (Pegasus) 650
Ace/Ace RX (large) (Pegasus) 650
AIRWAVE GLIDERS LTD (UK) 649
AKADEMICKI OSRODEK KONSTRUKCYJNY (Poland) 649
ANTONOV (see O.K. Antonov Design Bureau) 649
Ares (Polaris) 650
Atlas (La Mouette) (1987-88) 776
Atlas 14 (La Mouette) 650
Atlas 16 (La Mouette) 650
Atlas 18 (La Mouette) 650
Attack Duck (Wills Wing) (1986-87) 779
Azur (La Mouette) (1985-86) 716

B

BECK PRODUCTIONS, CRAIG (USA) (1985-86) 718
Blade (Pegasus) (1987-88) 778
Breez (Progressive) (1985-86) 720

C

Calyso (Airwave) 650
Comet 2B (UP) (1987-88) 780
Comet 2B 165 (UP) 652
Comet 2B 185 (UP) 652
Condor (Steinbach) 650
CUNION, EVERARD (UK) (1986-87) 776

D

Delta (Polaris) (1986-87) 774
Delta 13 (Polaris) (1986-87) 778
Delta 16 (Polaris) (1986-87) 778
Delta 19 (Polaris) (1986-87) 778
Delta 21 (Polaris) (1986-87) 778
DELTA WING AVIATION (USA) 649
Demon (Flight Designs) (1985-86) 718
DRACHEN STUDIO KECURE GmbH (West Germany) 649
Dream (Delta Wing) (1987-88) 779
Dream 165 (Delta Wing) 652
Dream 175 (Delta Wing) 652
Dream 185 (Delta Wing) 652
Duck (Wills Wing) (1986-87) 779
Duck 160 (Wills Wing) (1986-87) 780
Duck 180 (Wills Wing) (1986-87) 780

E

E-2C (AOK) 650
E-3C (AOK) 650
E-4 (AOK) (1987-88) 782
E-4C (AOK) 650

F

FR 16 (Polaris) 650
FINSTERWALDER, DRACHENFLUG (West Germany) 649
FIREBIRD, SCHWEIGER & JEHLE KG (West Germany) 649
Fledge III (Manta) (1986-87) 777
FLIGHT DESIGNS INC (USA) (1985-86) 718
FREE FLIGHT MICROLIGHTS AND HANG GLIDERS NZ (New Zealand) (1986-87) 775
Funfex (Finisterwalder) 650

G

GTR (Moyes) (1987-88) 776
GTR 148 (Moyes) 650
GTR 162 (Moyes) 650
GTR 175 (Moyes) 650
GTR 210 (Moyes) 650
Gamma 177 (Polaris) (1986-87) 774,778
Gemini (UP) (1987-88) 780
Gemini M 134 (UP) 652
Gemini M 164 (UP) 652
Gemini M 184 (UP) 652
Glidezilla 155 (UP) 652
Grypes (Polaris) 650

H

HP 11 (Wills Wing) 652
HP 170 (Wills Wing) (1986-87) 779, 780
Hermes (La Mouette) (1987-88) 776
Hermes 13 (La Mouette) 650
Hermes 14 (La Mouette) 650
Hermes 15 (La Mouette) 650
Hermes 16 (La Mouette) 650

I

IL (see Instytut Lotnictwa) 649
IKARUSFLUG BODENSEE (West Germany) (1985-86) 716
INSTYTUT LOTNICTWA (Poland) 649

K

KOLECKI NEW AVIATION ENGINEERING (Sweden) (1987-88) 778

L

LA MOUETTE, SARL (France) 649
Lancer Mk IV (Free Flight) (1985-86) 717

M

Magic IV (Airwave) (1987-88) 778
Magic IV 133 (Airwave) 650
Magic IV 150 (Airwave) 650
Magic IV 155 (Airwave) 650
Magic IV 166 (Airwave) 650
Magic IV 177 (Airwave) 650
Magic IV FR (Airwave) (1987-88) 778
Magic Kiss (Airwave) 650
MANTA PRODUCTS INC (USA) (1986-87) 777
Mars (Moyes) (1987-88) 776
Mars 150 (Moyes) 650
Mars 170 (Moyes) 650
Mars 190 (Moyes) 650
Minifex II (Finsterwalder) 650
Mission 170 (Moyes) 650
Motolotnia 80 White Eagle (Kolecki) (1987-88) 778
MOYES DELTA GLIDERS PTY LTD (Australia) 649
Mystic (Delta Wing) (1987-88) 779
Mystic 155 (Delta Wing) 652
Mystic 166 (Delta Wing) 652
Mystic 177 (Delta Wing) 652

N

Nimbus (Swiss Aerolight) 650
O.K. Antonov Design Bureau (USSR) 649

O

O.K. Antonov Design Bureau (USSR) 649

P

PACIFIC WINDCRAFT LTD (USA) 649
Parafun (Steinbach) 650
Parafunl (Steinbach) 650
Parasafe (Steinbach) 650
PEGASUS TRANSPORT SYSTEMS LTD/SOLAR WINGS LTD (UK) 649
Phoenix Dream (Delta Wing) (1985-86) 718
Phoenix Streak (Delta Wing) (1985-86) 718
POLARIS SRL (Italy) 649
Proair (Progressive) (1985-86) 720
Profil (La Mouette) (1987-88) 776
Profil 15 (La Mouette) 650
Profil 17 (La Mouette) 650
PROGRESSIVE AIRCRAFT COMPANY (USA) (1986-87) 777
Prostar II (Progressive) (1985-86) 720

Q

Quattro (Firebird) 650
Quattro-S (Firebird) 650
Quattro-Spiccolo (Firebird) (1987-88) 777

R

R-10 Stratus (Warsaw Technical University) (1986-87) 775
R-11 Stratus (Warsaw Technical University) (1986-87) 775
R-12 Stratus (Warsaw Technical University) (1986-87) 775
R-15 Stratus (Warsaw Technical University) (1986-87) 775
Racer GP (Pegasus) (1987-88) 778
ROCHELT, GÜNTER (West Germany) 649
Robert Schneid Air (Firebird) 650

S

S4-Plus (Pegasus) (1987-88) 778
S4-Racer (Pegasus) (1987-88) 778
SB-1 (AOK) (1987-88) 778, 782
SB-1 WARS (AOK) 650
SP (Steinbach) 650
SEEDWINGS (USA) 649
Sensor 510-B (Seedwings) (1987-88) 780
Sensor 510-160 VG (Seedwings) 652
Sensor 510-165 (Seedwings) 652
Shadow (Flight Designs) (1985-86) 718
Sierra (Firebird) (1986-87) 774
Sierra 155 (Firebird) (1986-87) 778
Sierra 175 (Firebird) (1986-87) 778
Skyhawk (Wills Wing) (1987-88) 780
Skyhawk 168 (Wills Wing) 652
Skyhawk 188 (Wills Wing) 652
Slavutitch-UT (Antonov) 650
Solar Ace (Pegasus) (1987-88) 778
Solar Storm (Pegasus) (1987-88) 778
Spirit (Firebird) 650
Spirit New Wave (Firebird) (1987-88) 777
Spit (Polaris) 650
Sport 150 (Wills Wing) 652
Sport 167 (Wills Wing) 652
Sport American 167 (Wills Wing) 652
STEINBACH-DELTA (Austria) 649
Stratus (Warsaw Technical University) (1986-87) 775
Stratus E Series (AOK) 650
Streak (Delta Wing) (1987-88) 779
Streak 130 (Delta Wing) 652
Streak 160 (Delta Wing) 652
Streak 180 (Delta Wing) 652

Sunfun, VJ-24 (Volmer) 652
Super 13 (Polaris) .... *(1987-88)* 782
Super 16 (Polaris) .... *(1987-88)* 782
Swingwing, VJ-23 (Volmer) 652
SWISS AEROLIGHT (Switzerland) 649

T

Tempest (Pegasus) .... *(1987-88)* 778
Topfex (Finsterwalder) 650
Touring 13 (Polaris) 650
Touring 15 (Polaris) 650
Tropi (Drachen) .... *(1987-88)* 776
Tropi 16 (Drachen) 650
Tropi 17 (Drachen) 650
Typhoon (Pegasus) .... *(1987-88)* 778

U

Uno (Firebird) 650
Uno Piccolo (Firebird) 650
UP Inc (ULTRALITE PRODUCTS) (USA) 649
US MOYES INC (USA) .... *(1985-86)* 720

V

VJ-23 Swingwing (Volmer) 652
VJ-24 Sunfun (Volmer) 652
Vampyre Mk II (Free Flight) .... *(1985-86)* 717
Vision (Pacific Windcraft) .... *(1987-88)* 779
Vision 148 (Pacific Windcraft) 652
Vision 175 (Pacific Windcraft) 652
Vision 194 (Pacific Windcraft) 652
Vision Eclipse (Pacific Windcraft) .... *(1987-88)* 782
Vision Eclipse 17 (Pacific Windcraft) 652
Vision Eclipse 19 (Pacific Windcraft) 652
VOLMER AIRCRAFT (USA) 649

W

Wars (AOK) .... *(1987-88)* 778
WARSAW TECHNICAL UNIVERSITY (Poland) .... *(1986-87)* 775
WILLS WING INC (USA) 649
Windspiel 2 (Ikarusflug) .... *(1985-86)* 716
World Cup 90-5 School Glider (Firebird) .... *(1986-87)* 774, 778
WSK-PZL WARSZAW A-OKECIE (Poland) .... *(1985-86)* 717

Z

Zeta-80B (IL) .... *(1987-88)* 778
Zeta-84 (IL) .... *(1987-88)* 778, 782
Zeta 87 (IL) 650

LIGHTER-THAN-AIR

A

A-1 Albatross (Boland) .... *(1985-86)* 770
A-1 (Aviatik Brno) .... *(1987-88)* 786
A-2 Rover (Boland) 665
A-3 (Piccard) .... *(1983-84)* 705
A-4 (Piccard) .... *(1983-84)* 705
A-5 (Piccard) .... *(1983-84)* 705
A50 (Adams) 670
A50S (Adams) 670
A55 (Adams) 670
A55S (Adams) 671
A60 (Adams) 671
A60S (Adams) 671
A-105 (Cameron) 671
A-120 (Cameron) 671
A-140 (Cameron) 671
A-210 (Cameron) 671
A-250 (Cameron) 671
A-300 (Cameron) 671
A-530 (Cameron) 671
AB (Adams) 671
AB-1 (Aviatik Brno) .... *(1987-88)* 800
AB-2 (Aerotechnik) 670
ABC (see American Balloon Comany) .... *(1986-87)* 801
AD-500 (Airship Industries) .... *(1981-82)* 635
ADA (see Airship Developments Australia) 655
ADA-1200 (ADA) 655
AG-60 (ILC) .... *(1987-88)* 807
ANR (Advanced Airship) 659
ANR (Wren) .... *(1987-88)* 793
AS-42 Colt (Thunder and Colt) .... *(1985-86)* 768
AS 42 Mk II, Colt (Thunder & Colt) .... *(1987-88)* 792
AS 56 (Thunder & Colt) 663
AS 76 (Colt) 662
A.S.80 (Thunder and Colt) .... *(1982-83)* 662
AS-90 Colt (Thunder and Colt) .... *(1985-86)* 767
AS-105 Colt (Thunder & Colt) .... *(1987-88)* 792
AV-1 (Aviatik Brno) .... *(1987-88)* 786
AX-4 (Hare) .... *(1979-80)* 612
AX-5 (Boland) .... *(1987-88)* 806
AX-5 (Hare) .... *(1979-80)* 612
AX5-40M (Flamboyant) 670
AX-6 (Boland) 670
AX-6 (Hare) .... *(1979-80)* 613
AX6-56 (Flamboyant) .... *(1987-88)* 810
AX6-56M (Flamboyant) 670
AX-7 (Boland) .... *(1987-88)* 806
AX-7 (Hare) .... *(1979-80)* 613
AX7-65 (Flamboyant) 670
AX7-77M (Flamboyant) 670
AX-8 (Boland) .... *(1987-88)* 806
AX-8 (Bonanno) 672
AX-8 (Hare) .... *(1979-80)* 613
AX8-85 (Flamboyant) 671
AX8-105 (Flamboyant) 671
AX-9 (Boland) .... *(1987-88)* 806
AX-9 (Hare) .... *(1979-80)* 613
AX9-140 (Flamboyant Balloons) .... *(1982-83)* 670
AX-10 (Boland) .... *(1987-88)* 806
AX10-150 (Flamboyant) 671
AX-11 (Boland) .... *(1987-88)* 806
ADAMS' BALLOON LOFT INC (USA) 669
ADVANCED AIRSHIP CORPORATION (UK) 659
AÉRAZUR (France) 657
AEROLIFT INC (USA) 663
Aero-Ship Model 500 (Fuji) .... *(1981-82)* 635
AEROSPACE DEVELOPMENTS (LONDON) LTD (UK) .... *(1979-80)* 606
Aerostat, 56,000 cu ft, sea-based (RCA) .... *(1987-88)* 808
Aerostat, 250,000 cu ft (ILC) .... *(1987-88)* 807
AEROSYSTEMS INC (see California Airships) (USA) 796
AEROTECHNIK (Czechoslovakia) 669
AEROTEK CORPORATION (USA) 664
Air Chair (Thunder & Colt) .... *(1985-86)* 781
AIRBORNE INDUSTRIES LIMITED (UK) .. *(1987-88)* 802
Airship (Thompson) 666
AIRSHIP DEVELOPMENTS AUSTRALIA PTY LTD (Australia) 655
AIRSHIP INDUSTRIES (UK) LTD 659
Albatross (ADA) 655
AIRSHIP USA INC (USA) .... *(1986-87)* 655
Albatross, A-1 (Boland) .... *(1985-86)* 770
America GZ-20A (Goodyear) .... *(1987-88)* 796
America N3A (Goodyear .... *(1984-85)* 738
Americana (ABC) .... *(1986-87)* 801, 807
AMERICAN BALLOON COMPANY (USA) .... *(1986-87)* 801
Angren-84 (USSR) 788
AVIAN BALLOON COMPANY (USA) 669
AVIATIK CLUB BRNO (Czechoslovakia) .... *(1987-88)* 786, 800

B

B 800/2-Ri (Ballonfabrik) 670
BIAA (see Beijing Institute of Aeronautics and Astronautics) 656
Baby Snake (Boland) 670
BALLONFABRIK SEE-UND LUFT-AUSRÜSTUNG GmbH und Co KG (West Germany) 669
BALLOON WORKS, THE (USA) 669
BALLONS CHAIZE (France) 669
BEIJING INSTITUTE OF AERONAUTICS AND ASTRONAUTICS (China) 656
BOLAND BALLOON (USA) 665, 669
BONANNO, PAOLO LETTERIO (Italy) 658, 669
Bumerang (USSR) .... *(1985-86)* 765

C

CAC (see Commercial Airship Company) ... *(1987-88)* 788
CS.1600 (Chaize) 670
CS.1800 (Chaize) 670
CS.2000 (Chaize) 670
CS.2200 (Chaize) 670
CS.3000 (Chaize) 671
CS.4000 (Chaize) 671
Calibre, 32 (Avian) .... *(1986-87)* 802
CALIFORNIA AIRSHIPS (USA) .... *(1987-88)* 796
CAMERON BALLOONS LTD (UK) 661, 669
CHAIZE (see Balloons Chaize) 669
Challenger (Semco) .... *(1979-80)* 613
Circus Maximus (Boland) .... *(1987-88)* 805
Cloudhopper Junior (Thunder & Colt) 670
Cloudhopper Midi (Thunder & Colt) 670
Cloudhopper Super (Thunder & Colt) 670
COLT BALLOONS LTD (UK) .... *(1984-85)* 736
Columbia, GZ 20A (Goodyear) .... *(1987-88)* 796
COMMERCIAL AIRSHIP COMPANY (New Zealand) .... *(1987-88)* 788
CONRAD AIRSHIP CORPORATION (USA) .... *(1979-80)* 608
Cyclo-crane (Aerolift) 663

D

D-38 (Cameron) .... *(1987-88)* 791
D-50 (Cameron) 662
DP Skystar series (Cameron) 661
D-96 (Cameron) 662
DG-14 (Cameron) .... *(1986-87)* 788
DG-19 (Cameron) .... *(1986-87)* 788
DG-25 (Cameron) .... *(1987-88)* 792
Desert Fox (Boland) .... *(1987-88)* 805
Dimples (Boland) .... *(1987-88)* 805
Dino 3 (Aérazur) .... *(1986-87)* 784
DragonFly 56 (Balloon Works) 670
DragonFly 65 (Balloon Works) 670
DragonFly 77 (Balloon Works) 670
DragonFly 90 (Balloon Works) 671
DragonFly 105 (Balloon Works) 671
DragonFly 560 (Balloon Works) 670
DragonFly 650 (Balloon Works) 670
DragonFly 770 (Balloon Works) 671
DragonFly 900 (Balloon Works) 671
DragonFly 1050 (Balloon Works) 671
Dreamfinder (Memphis) .... *(1986-87)* 794
Drifter (Hoverair) .... *(1986-87)* 803, 806
Dino 3 (Aérazur) .... *(1987-88)* 786
Dinosaure (Aérazur) 657

E

Eagle (Avian) .... *(1979-80)* 613
ENDEAVOUR (UK) .... *(1987-88)* 802
Enterprise (Goodyear) .... *(1981-82)* 638

F

Falcon II (Avian) 670
FireFly 5 (Balloon Works) .... *(1983-84)* 705
FireFly 6 (Balloon Works) .... *(1983-84)* 706
FireFly 6B (Balloon Works) .... *(1983-84)* 706
FireFly 7 (Balloon Works) .... *(1983-84)* 706
FireFly 8 (Balloon Works) .... *(1983-84)* 706
FireFly 42 (Balloon Works) 670
FireFly 56 (Balloon Works) .... *(1983-84)* 706
FireFly 65 (Balloon Works) 671
FireFly 77 (Balloon Works) 671
FireFly 90 (Balloon Works) 671
FireFly 105 (Balloon Works) 671
FireFly 140 (Balloon Works) 671
FireFly 650 (Balloon Works) 671
FireFly 770 (Balloon Works) 671
FireFly 900 (Balloon Works) 671
FireFly 1050 (Balloon Works) 671
Fitzgerald (Boland) .... *(1987-88)* 805
FLAMBOYANT BALLOONS (PTY) LTD (South Africa) 669
Fred II (Boland) .... *(1983-84)* 705
Football (Boland) 670
FUJI MANUFACTURING CO LTD (JAPAN) .... *(1982-83)* 661

G

GA 42 (Thunder & Colt) 663
GAC-20 (Grace) .... *(1985-86)* 772
GB55 (Yost) .... *(1985-86)* 780
GZ-20A America (Goodyear) .... *(1986-87)* 792
GZ-20A Columbia (Goodyear) .... *(1987-88)* 796
GZ-22 (Goodyear Aerospace) 665
GadFly 56 (Balloon Works 670
Gadfly 560 (Balloon Works) 670
GALAXY BALLOONS INC (USA) 669
Galaxy 7 (Galaxy) 671
GEFA-FLUG GmbH (West Germany) 657
GENERAL BALLOON CORPORATION (USA) .... *(1982-83)* 668
GOODYEAR AEROSPACE CORPORATION (USA) .... *(1986-87)* 792
GOODYEAR TIRE & RUBBER COMPANY, THE (USA) 665
GOODYEAR TIRE & RUBBER COMPANY — AIRSHIP OPERATIONS (USA) .... *(1985-86)* 771
GRACE (see US Airship) .... *(1986-87)* 796
GRACE AIRCRAFT CORPORATION (USA) .... *(1985-86)* 772

H

HACDC (see Hangzhou Airship Comprehensive Development Company) 657
HAPP (Magnus) 656
HI-SPOT (LMSC) .... *(1983-84)* 701
HX-1 (Hov-Air-Ship) .... *(1982-83)* 664
HANGZHOU AIRSHIP COMPREHENSIVE DEVELOPMENT COMPANY (China) 657
HARE BALLOONS (USA) .... *(1979-80)* 611
Heli-Stat (Piasecki) 666
Helium filled airships (Cameron) 662
High Altitude Platforms (ILC) .... *(1986-87)* 793
High Altitude System (RCA) .... *(1987-88)* 808
High Fred (Boland) .... *(1985-86)* 781
Hot-Air Airship (Gefa-Flug) 658
Hot-Air Airship (MEM RSZ) .... *(1987-88)* 787
Hybrid heavy-lift vehicles (ILC) .... *(1986-87)* 793
HYSTAR (Canada) 655
Hystar 103 (Hystar) 655
HOV-AIR-SHIP INC (USA) .... *(1982-83)* 664
HOVERAIR LTD (USA) .... *(1986-87)* 803

I

ILC DOVER (USA) .... *(1987-88)* 797, 807
I-PAAM (Bonanno) 658, 671

K

K 630/1-Ri (Ballonfabrik) 670
K 780/2-Ri (Ballonfabrik) 670

K 945/2-Ri (Ballonfabrik) 670
K 1050/3-Ri (Ballonfabrik) 670
K 1260/3-Ri (Ballonfabrik) 670
K 1360/4-Ri (Ballonfabrik) 670
K 1680/4-Ri (Ballonfabrik) 670
KAVANAGH BALLOONS PTY LTD (Australia) 669
Kenwood (Gefa-Flug) 657

L

LD (Adams) 670
LD-S (Adams) 670
LMSC (see Lockheed Missiles & Space Company) (1983-84) 701
LTA (Magnus) (1986-87) 783
LTA 20-01 (Van Dusen) (1983-84) 696
LTA 20-1 (Magnus) 656
LTA 20-1 (Van Dusen) (1983-84) 696
LTA 20-16 (Magnus) (1986-87) 783
LTA 20-16 (Van Dusen) (1984-85) 732
LTA 20-60 (Van Dusen) (1984-85) 732
LUA (ADA) (1986-87) 782
LUA-1 (Ulita) (1987-88) 798
LUA-2 (Ulita) (1987-88) 799
LUA-6 (ADA) (1985-86) 762
Large-volume aerostat (ILC Dover) (1983-84) 701
Le Mans (General) (1982-83) 670
LETTERIO BONANNO (Italy) 658
Levity (Boland) 671
Lightning 33 (General) (1982-83) 669
Lightning 45 (General) (1982-83) 669
LIN HA SCIENCE INSTITUTE (China) (1985-86) 762
LOCKHEED MISSILES & SPACE COMPANY INC (a subsidiary of Lockheed Corporation) (U.S.A.) (1983-84) 701
LTA SYSTEMS LTD (Canada) (1983-84) 697

M

MA-1 (Mantainer) (1979-80) 606
Mark VII-S (TCOM) (1987-88) 809
MEM RSZ (see Mém Repülógépes Szologát 669
MG-300 (Raven) 670
MG-1000 (Raven) 670
MLA-24-A (Spacial) (1985-86) 764
MLA-32-A (Spacial) 658
Magnum IX (Avian) 671
MAGNUS AEROSPACE CORPORATION (Canada) 655
Mai (USSR) 659
Manned Demonstrator Vehicle (Magnus) 656
MAINTAINER PTY LTD (Australia) (1979-80 606
Mayflower (Goodyear) (1979-80) 608
MÉM REPÜLÓGÉPES SZOLOGAT (Hungary) 669
MEMPHIS AIRSHIPS INC (USA) 666
Mia Pow (Boland) 671
Mifeng-6 (BIAA) 656
MIKE ADAMS BALLOON LOFT INC (USA) (1985-86) 777
Model 97-34J (Piasecki) 666
Model 500 Aero-Ship (Fuji) (1981-82) 635
Model 4060 (Airship Industries) (1981-82) 636
Model T (Semco) (1979-80) 613
Mr. Gunsnook (Boland) 671
Mr Snake (Boland) (1986-87) 802
Mrs Snake (Boland) 671

N

N-31 (Cameron) 670
N-56 (Cameron) 670
N-65 (Cameron) 670
N-77 (Cameron) 670
N-90 (Cameron) 671
N-105 (Cameron) 671
N-133 (Cameron) 671
N-145 (Cameron) 671
N-180 (Cameron) 671
N-850 (Cameron) 671
NCS ULD 1 (Endeavour) (1987-88) 802
NZ-1 (NZA) (1987-88) 788
NZA (see New Zealand Airships Ltd) (1987-88) 788
NAVAL AIR SYSTEMS COMMAND (USA) (1986-87) 796
Naval Airship Program (US Navy) (1986-87) 796
Newport (General) (1982-83) 670
NEW ZEALAND AIRSHIPS LTD (1987-88) 788

O

O-20 (Cameron) (1980-81) 614
O-31 (Cameron) 670
O-42 (Cameron) 670
O-56 (Cameron) 670
O-65 (Cameron) 670
O-77 (Cameron) 670
O-84 (Cameron) 671
O-105 (Cameron) 671
O-120 (Cameron) 671
O-160 (Cameron) 671

P

PTB 50 (Airborne) (1986-87) 799
Peaches (Boland) (1987-88) 805
PIASECKI AIRCRAFT CORPORATION (USA) 666
Piccard (General) (1982-83) 669
Piccard (Piccard) (1983-84) 705
Piccard A-3 (General) (1982-83) 669
Piccard A-4 (General) (1982-83) 669
Piccard A-5 (General) (1982-83) 669
PICCARD BALLOONS (USA) (1980-81) 614
PICCARD BALLOONS LTD, DON (USA) (1983-84) 704
Piccolo (Boland) (1983-84) 705
Piccup-3 (General) (1982-83) 669
Puppy Chow (Boland) 670

R

R-225 (Cameron) (1987-88) 802
RBX-7 (Bonanno) 658
RS-1 (Wren) (1987-88) 793
RS_3-03 (MÉM RS_3) (1983-84) 702, 706
RS_3-04 (MÉM RS_3) (1983-84) 702
RSZ-03 (MÉM RSZ) (1987-88) 811
RSZ-03/1 (MÉM RS) 671
RSZ-04 (MÉM RSZ) (1987-88) 811
RSZ-04/1 (MÉM RS) 671
RSZ-05 (MÉM RSZ) 670
RSZ-06 (MÉM RSZ) 670
RX-6 (Raven) 670
RX-7 (Raven) 671
Rainbow-Stars (Boland) 670
RAVEN INDUSTRIES INC (USA) 669
RCA SERVICE COMPANY (USA) (1987-88) 808
Red Baron (Boland) 671
Riff-Raff (Boland) (1987-88) 805
Rover, A-2 (Boland) 665

S

S-40 (Raven) 670
S-50A (Raven) 670
S-55A (Raven) 671
S-60A (Raven) 671
S-66A (Raven) 671
S-77A (Raven) 671
SPACIAL (see Servicios Publicitarios Aereos Construccion e Ingenieria de Aeronaves Ligeras SA de CV) (Mexico) 658
SS-103 (Solo) 670
SSP-6000 (ILC) (1987-88) 807
SEMCO BALLOON (USA) (1979-80) 612
Sentinel 5000 (Airship Industries) 660, 667
Sentinel 5000 (WAI) 667
SERVICIOS PUBLICITARIOS AEREOS CONSTRUCCION E INGENIERIA DE AERONAVES LIGERAS SA de CV (Mexico) 658
Silver Hawk, TX-1 (Tucker) (1981-82) 639
Sky Chariot (Maxi) (ThunderColt) (1985-86) 781
Sky Chariot (Midi) (ThunderColt) (1985-86) 781
Sky Chariot (Mini) (ThunderColt) (1985-86) 780
Skyhawk (Avian) 671
Skyship 500 (Airship Industries) 660
Skyship 500HL (Airship Industries) 660
Skyship 600 (Airship Industries) 660
Skyship 7000 (Airship Industries) (1985-86) 766
Skystar (Cameron) 661
Sparrow (Avian) 670
Spirit of Lake Garda (Boland) (1987-88) 805
SOLO SYSTEM INC (USA) 669
Stars (TCOM Corporation) (1987-88) 808
Stretch (General) (1982-83) 670

T

TC-4 (Semco) (1979-80) 613
TCOM 25M (TCOM) (1987-88) 808
TCOM 365B/H (TCOM) (1987-88) 809
TCOM CORPORTION (USA) (1987-88) 808
TX-1 Silver Hawk (Tucker) (1981-82) 639
Thompson Airship (Thompson) 666
THOMPSON, JAMES, AIAA (USA) 666
THUNDER & COLT LTD (UK) 662, 669
THUNDER BALLOONS (UK) (1984-85) 740
THUNDERCOLT BALLOONS LTD (UK) (1983-84) 662, 667
Tianzhou 1 (BIAA/Hongwei) 657
Toluca (Spacial) 658
Tour d'Argent (Boland) 671
TUCKER AIRSHIP COMPANY (USA) (1982-83) 665
Turbo 8 (Avian) 671
Type 25M (TCOM Corporation) (1987-88) 808
Type 30-AL (Semco) (1979-80) 612
Type 31Z (Thunder and Colt) 670
Type 32 calibre (Avian) (1986-87) 806
Type 42 (ThunderColt) (1985-86) 781
Type 42 Series 1 (Thunder & Colt) 670
Type 42A (Thunder & Colt) 670
Type 56 (ThunderColt) (1985-86) 781
Type 56 Series 1 (Thunder & Colt) 670
Type 56A (Thunder & Colt) 670
Type 65 (ThunderColt) (1985-86) 782
Type 65 Series 1 (Thunder & Colt) 670
Type 69A (Thunder & Colt) 670
Type 77 (ThunderColt) (1985-86) 782
Type 77 series 1 (Thunder & Colt) 670
Type 77A (Thunder & Colt) 670
Type 84 (ThunderColt) (1985-86) 782
Type 84 Series 1 (Thunder & Colt) 671
Type 90 (ThunderColt) (1985-86) 782
Type 90 Series 2 (Thunder & Colt) 671
Type 90A (Thunder & Colt) 671
Type 105 (ThunderColt) (1985-86) 782
Type 105 Series 1 (Thunder & Colt) 671
Type 105 Series 2 (Thunder & Colt) 671
Type 105A (Thunder & Colt) 671
Type 120A (Thunder & Colt) 671
Type 140 (Thunder & Colt) 671
Type 160 Series 1 (Thunder & Colt) 671
Type 160A (Thunder & Colt) 671
Type 180A (Thunder & Colt) 671
Type 200A (Thunder & Colt) 671
Type 240A (Thunder & Colt) 671
Type 280A (Thunder & Colt) (1987-88) 811
Type 300A (Thunder & Colt) 671
Type 365B/H (TCOM Corporation) (1987-88) 809
Type 400A (Thunder & Colt) 671

U

ULD-1 (Cameron) (1987-88) 802
ULD-1 (Endeavour) (1987-88) 802
UM-10 (Ulita) 666
UM20 (Upita) 666
UM30 (Upita) 667
USA 100 (Aerotek) 664
ULITA INDUSTRIES INC (USA) 666
ULITA MANUFACTURING INC (USA) (1985-86) 773
Ultrablimp (Memphis) (1987-88) 797
Ultralight (Boland) 670
Ural-3 (USSR) (1983-84) 697
US AIRSHIP CORPORATION (USA) (1986-87) 796

V

VAN DUSEN COMMERCIAL DEVELOPMENT (CANADA) LTD (Canada) (1984-85) 732
Virgin Atlantic Flyer (Thunder & Colt) (1987-88) 803
Viva-20 (Cameron) 670
Viva-31 (Cameron) 670
Viva-56 (Cameron) 670
Viva-65 (Cameron) 670
Viva-77 (Cameron) (1987-88) 810

W

WAI (see Westinghouse-Airship Industries) (1987-88) 667
WATSON MODEL WORKS (USA) (1987-88) 796
WESTINGHOUSE-AIRSHIP INDUSTRIES INC (USA) 667
White Dwarf (California Airships) (1986-87) 792
WREN SKYSHIPS LTD 793

X

X-8 (Bonanno) (1987-88) 801
Xihu (Lin Hai) (1985-86) 762
Xihu-1 (HACDC) (1987-88) 786
XXUS (Boland) (1985-86) 780

Y

YEZ-2A (Airship Industries) 660
Yankee Doodle (ABC) (1986-87) 801, 806
YOST, ED (USA) (1985-86) 780

AERO-ENGINES

A

AEIO-320 (Textron Lycoming) 741
AEIO-360 (Textron Lycoming) 742
AEIO-540 (Textron Lycoming) 742
AGM-88 A (Thiokol) (1982-83) 800
AI-14R (WSK-PZL Kalisz) 700
AI-20 (Ivchenko) 703
AI-24 (Ivchenko) 703
AI-25 (Ivchenko) 704
AIC (see Ames Industrial Corporation) (1985-86) 888
AL-7 (Lyulka) 706
AL-21 (Lyulka) 706
ALF 101 (Avco Lycoming) (1982-83) 771
ALF 502 (Textron Lycoming) 739
AM-3 (Mikulin) 706
AM-5 (Tumansky) 708
AMI (see Aeromotion Inc) 718
APW34 (AVCO/P & W) (1985-86) 895
AR.318 (Alfa Romeo Avio) 696
ARC (see Atlantic Research Corporation) (1984-85) 859
ARTJ 140 (Alfa Romeo) (1985-86) 862
ASz-62R (WSK-PZL Kalisz) 700
ASz-621 R (PZL) (1983-84) 787
ATF-3 (Garrett) 719
AVCO/P & W (USA) (1985-86) 895
AZ 14 (Turboméca) (1982-83) 730
AZ 16 (Turboméca) (1982-83) 730
Adour (Rolls-Royce/Turboméca) 694
Advanced Apogee Motor (CSD/SEP) (1984-85) 865
AERO BONNER LTD.(UK) (1985-86) 878
AEROJET-GENERAL CORPORATION (USA) 716

AEROJET LIQUID ROCKET COMPANY (USA) (1983-84) 808
AEROJET SOLID PROPULSION COMPANY (USA) (1981-82) 758
AEROJET STRATEGIC PROPULSION COMPANY (USA) (1985-86) 887
AEROJET TACTICAL SYSTEMS COMPANY (USA) (1985-86) 887, 888
AEROJET TECHSYSTEMS CO (USA) 716
AEROMOTION INC (USA) 718
Aeromotion Twin (Aeromotion) 718
AEROTECHNIK (Czechoslovakia) 682
Aerotor 90 (Norton) 710
Agena engine (Bell) (1982-83) 773
Air breathing propulsion (CSD) 719
AIRESEARCH MANUFACTURING COMPANY OF ARIZONA (USA) (1980-81) 747
Alcor 1 B (Aerojet) (1981-82) 760
ALFA ROMEO AVIO SpA (Italy) 696
Algol III (CSD) (1984-85) 864
ALLISON GAS TURBINE DIVISION, GENERAL MOTORS CORPORATION 716
ALLISON/MTU (International) 691
Altair III (Morton Thiokol) (1984-85) 879
ALTURDYNE (USA) 718
AMES INDUSTRIAL CORPORATION (USA) (1985-86) 888
Antares III (Morton Thiokol) (1984-85) 879
AOI ENGINE FACTORY (135) (Egypt) 683
Apache (Thiokol) (1981-82) 795
Arbizon (Turboméca) (1984-85) 815
Arc (SEP) (1980-81) 695
Ardem Mk X (Rollason) (1982-83) 759
Ardem Mk XI (Rollason) (1982-83) 759
Arriel (Turboméca) 686
ARROW snc (Italy) 697
Artouse III (Turobméca) 687
Astafan (Turboméca) (1981-82) 723
Astazou Turboprop (Turboméca) 686
Astazou Turboshaft (Turboméca) 686
Astrobee F (Aerojet) (1983-84) 809
Atar (SNECMA) (1986-87) 886
Atar 9K50 (SNECMA) 685
ATELIERS JPX (France) 684
ATLANTIC RESEARCH CORPORATION (USA) (1984-85) 859
ATLAS AIRCRAFT CORPORATION OF SOUTH AFRICA (PTY) LTD. (South Africa) 702
AVCO LYCOMING/PRATT & WHITNEY (USA) (1987-88) 945
AVCO LYCOMING TEXTRON STRATFORD DIVISION (USA) (1987-88) 941
AVCO LYCOMING WILLIAMSPORT DIVISION (USA) (1987-88) 943
AVIA NARODNI PODNIK (Czechoslovakia) (1986-87) 883
AVIA OBOROVY PODNIK (Czechoslovakia) 682

B

Baby Mamba (Dreher) (1983-84) 818
BAJ VICKERS LTD (UK) (1984-85) 846
Ball (SEP) (1980-81) 695
Bastan (Turboméca) (1980-81) 700
BELL AEROSPACE TEXTRON (USA) (1984-85) 863
BET-SHEMESH ENGINES LTD (Israel) 696
BONNER (see Aero Bonner Ltd) (1985-86) 878
BOMBARDIER-ROTAX GmbH (Austria) 675
Booster separation motor (CSD) (1987-88) 946
BORZECKI, JOZEF (Poland) (1986-87) 903
BPD SETTORE DIFESA E SPAZIO (Italy) (1984-85) 828
BRISTOL AEROJET LIMITED (UK) (1979-80) 719
Butalane (SNPE) (1985-86) 830
Butalite (SNPE) (1984-85) 815

C

C90 (Continental) (1978-79) 755
C90 (Rolls-Royce/Continental) (1980-81) 733
CAC (see Commonwealth Aircraft Corporation Ltd) (1986-87) 876
CATIC (see China Aero-Technology Import and Export Corporation) 680
CF 077A (Emdair) 710
CF 077B (Emdair) 710
CF6 (Fiat) 697
CF6 (General Electric) 722
CF6 (GE/MTU/VOLVO/FIAT (SNECMA)) 685, 689
CF6-32 (GE/SNECMA/Alfa Romeo/Volvo) (1980-81) 696
CF6-50E (General Electric) 722
CF6-80C2 (General Electric) 723
CF34 (General Electric) 722
CF 100A (Emdair) 710
CF 112 (Emdair) 710
CF-150A (Emdair) (1986-87) 916
CF700 (General Electric) (1986-87) 940
CFE738 (CFE) 718
CFJ 810 (IHI) (1979-80) 706
CFM56 (CFM International) 691
CJ610 (General Electric) (1986-87) 940
CSD (see Chemical Systems Division) 719
CSTM (see Centro Studi Trasporti Missilistici) (1984-85) 828
CT7 (General Electric) 726
CT58 (General Electric) 725
CT 3201 (Lucas) (1980-81) 726
Castor II (Morton Thiokol) (1984-85) 878
Castor IV (Morton Thiokol) (1984-85) 878
CELMA-CIA ELECTROMECANICA (Brazil) 676
CFE COMPANY (USA) 718
CENTRO STUDI TRASPORTI MISSILISTICI (Italy) (1984-85) 828
CFM INTERNATIONAL SA (International) 691
CHEMICAL SYSTEMS DIVISION (USA) 719
CHINA AERO-TECHNOLOGY IMPORT AND EXPORT CORPORATION (China) 680
CHOTIA (see Weedhopper of Utah Inc) (1984-85) 863
CICARÉ AERONAUTICA SC (Argentina) (1980-81) 687
Ciron (SEP) (1980-81) 695
Civil Spey RB163 (Rolls-Royce) 712
COMMONWEALTH AIRCRAFT CORPORATION LIMITED (Australia) (1986-87) 876
CONTINENTAL (see Teledyne Continental Motors) (1985-86) 918
Couguar (Microturbo) (1980-81) 693
CURTISS-WRIGHT CORPORATION WOOD-RIDGE FACILITY (USA) (1985-86) 896
CUYUNA ENGINE CO (USA) (1987-88) 947

D

D-15 (Soloviev) 707
D-18T (Lotarev) 705
D-20P (Soloviev) (1987-88) 923
D-25V (Soloviev) 707
D-30 (Soloviev) 707
D-30K (Soloviev) 707
D-36 (Lotarev) 705
D-90A (Soloviev) 708
D-136 (Lotarev) 705
D-236 (Lotarev) 706
D-236T (Lotarev) (1986-87) 911
D-436 (Lotarev) 706
DSI (see Developmental Sciences Inc) (1979-80) 741
Dart (Rolls-Royce) (1987-88) 933
Delta (TRW) (1984-85) 892
DETROIT DIESEL ALLISON DIVISION, GENERAL MOTORS CORPORATION (USA) (1983-84) 810
DEVELOPMENTAL SCIENCES INC. (USA) (1979-80) 741
DIFESA E SPAZIO SpA (Italy) (1982-83) 742
Double Turmastazou (Turboméca) (1979-80) 697
DOWTY ROTOL LTD (UK) (1982-83) 758
DRAGON ENGINE CORPORATION (USA) (1987-88) 974
DREHER ENGINEERING COMPANY (USA) (1984-85) 866
Dropt (SEP) (1980-81) 695
Ducted Propulsor (Dowty Rotol) (1982-83) 758
Ducted rocket (Marquardt) (1982-83) 786

E

EJ-200 (Eurojet) 693
ETJ1081 (Garrett) (1987-88) 948
ÉCOLE NATIONAL DES INGÉNIEURS DE SAINT-ETIENNE (France) (1985-86) 847
ENISE (see École National des Ingénieurs de Saint-Etienne) (France) (1985-86) 847
ETJ131 (Garrett-AiResearch) (1980-81) 748
EX-104 (Morton Thiokol) (1984-85) 878
EHMANN, ROLF (West Germany) (1984-85) 818
EMDAIR LTD (UK) 710
EMG ENGINEERING COMPANY (USA) 719
Epictete (SNPE) (1985-86) 850
ERNO RAUMFAHRTTECHNIK GmbH (West Germany) (1982-83) 733
EUROJET TURBO GmbH (International) 693

F

F3 (IHI) 698
F22 (Hirth) 688
F23A (Hirth) 688
F30 (Hirth) 688
F100 (Pratt & Whitney) 732
F100 EMD (Pratt & Whitney) (1984-85) 885
F100-PW-229 (Pratt & Whitney) 734
F101 (General Electric) (1987-88) 953
F101-DFE (General Electric) (1982-83) 783
F103-GE-100 (General Electric) 722
F104-GA-100 (Garrett) 719
F105-PW-100 (Pratt & Whitney) (1982-83) 790
F107 (Williams) (1987-88) 974
F108 (CFM International) 691
F109-GA-100 (Garrett) 720
F110 (General Electric) 723
F112 (Williams) (1987-88) 974
F113 (Rolls-Royce) 712
F117 (Pratt & Whitney) 731
F119 (Pratt & Whitney) 734
F120 (General Electric) 723
F263 R53 (Hirth) 688
F401 (Pratt & Whitney) (1979-80) 757
F404 (General Electric) 721
F404J (Flygmotor/General Electric) (1983-84) 790
F405 (Rolls-Royce Turbomeca) 694
FA150 (Fiat) (1985-86) 863
FAM (see France Aéro Moteurs) 683
FE.260AG (Fieldhouse) (1987-88) 927
FE.525A(F) (Fieldhouse) (1987-88) 927
FE.525AG (Fieldhouse) (1987-88) 927
FJ44 (Williams) 743
FJR710 (NAL) 699
FN (see Fabrique Nationale Herstal SA) 676
FW-5 (CSD) (1983-84) 817
FABRIQUE NATIONALE HERSTAL SA (Belgium) 676
FIAT AVIAZIONE SpA (Italy) 697
FIELDHOUSE ENGINES LTD (UK) (1987-88) 927
Firebrand booster (Thiokol) (1982-83) 799
Firebrand ramjet (Marquardt) (1982-83) 786
FLYGMOTOR (see Volvo Flygmotor AB) 702
FRANCE AÉROMOTEURS SARL (France) 683

G

G2P (see Groupement pour les Gros Propulseurs à Poudre) (1984-85) 810
G8-2 (Gluhareff-EMG) 719
G25B (Zenoah) (1986-87) 902
G72C-C (Zenoah) (1982-83) 744
GDL (USSR) (1984-85) 836
GE27 (General Electric) 724
GE36 (General Electric) 685, 723
GE37 (General Electric) 723
GE38 (General Electric) 724
GK (SECA) (1987-88) 885
GMA 140 TK (Scoma) 684
GMA 200 (Allison) (1982-83) 768
GMA 300 (Allison) (1981-82) 761
GMA 500 (Allison) (1984-85) 858
GPS motor (CSD) (1978-79) 731
GR-18 (TCM/Continental) 736
GR-36 (TCM/Continental) 737
GT250 (Arrow) 697
GT500 (Arrow) 697
GT654 (Arrow) 697
GT1000 (Arrow) 697
GTD-3 (Glushenkov) 703
GTD-3BM (Glushenkov) 703
GTD-350 (WSK-PZL-Rzeszów) 701
GTRE (see Gas Turbine Research Establishment) 691
GTSIO-520 (TCM/Continental) 738
GTX-35 (GTRE) 691
GARRETT ENGINE DIVISION (USA) 719
GARRETT/VOLVO FLYGMOTOR (International) (1982-83) 737
Gas turbine engines (CATIC) 680
GAS TURBINE RESEARCH ESTABLISHMENT (India) 691
GE AIRCRAFT ENGINES (USA) 721
Gem (Rolls-Royce) 715
GENERAL ELECTRIC (USA) 721
GESCHWENDER AEROMOTIVE INC (USA) (1981-1982) 779
GLUHAREFF (see EMG Engineering Company) 719
GLUSHENKOV (USSR) 703
Gnome (Rolls-Royce) 715
GROUPEMENT POUR LES GROS PROPULSEURS A POUDRE (France) (1984-85) 810
GROUPEMENT TURBOMÉCA -SNECMA (GRTS) (France) 688

H

H-63 (Nelson) 728
H.1000 Gnome (Rolls-Royce) 715
H.1200 Gnome (Rolls-Royce) 715
H.1400 Gnome (Rolls-Royce) 715
HAL (see Hindustan Aeronautics Ltd.) 691
HARM TU-780 (Morton Thiokol) (1987-88) 960
HDHV (see Hawker de Havilland Victoria Ltd) 675
HIO-360 (Textron Lycoming) 742
HM4 (SEP) (1979-80) 689
HM7 (SEP) (1984-85) 813
HP 60Z (Parodi) (1984-85) 821
HS-5 (CATIC) 681
HS-6 (CATIC) 681
HS-26 (CATIC) 681
HS.260A (Fieldhouse) (1987-88) 927
HS.525A (Fieldhouse) (1987-88) 927
HARKER & ASSOCIATES (UK) (1981-1982) 751
Harpoon (Morton Thiokol) (1984-85) 878
Harpoon booster motor (Aerojet) (1984-85) 856
HAWKER SIDDELEY CANADA INC (Canada) 676
Hawk motor (Aerojet) (1984-1985) 856
HAWKER DE HAVILLAND VICTORIA LTD (Australia) 675
Hellfire, TX 657 (Morton Thiokol) (1987-88) 960
Hellfire, TX 773 (Morton Thiokol) (1987-88) 960
HELWAN (Egypt) (1985-86) 847
HINDUSTAN AERONAUTICS LTD (India) 691
HIRTH MOTOREN, GÖBLER, GmbH (West Germany) 688
Huosai-16 (CATIC) (1987-88) 890
Hybrid propulsion (CSD) (1987-88) 946
Hydrazine Thruster (SEP) (1984-85) 813

I

IAE (see International Aero Engines AG) 693
IAI (see Israel Aircraft Industries Ltd) 696
IAME (see Ital-American Industries Ltd) 697
IHI (see Ishikawajima-Harima Jukogyo Kabushiki Kaisha) 698
IL (see Instytut Lotnictwa) 699
IL-144 engine (USSR) 709
IMAER (see Indústria Mecânica E Aeronautica Ltda) 676
IO-320 (Textron Lycoming) 741
IO-360 (TCM/Continental) 736, 737
IO-360 (Textron Lycoming) 741
IO-360 (Rolls-Royce/Continental) (1980-81) 733
IO-368 (Continental) (1982-83) 797
IO-368 (Rolls-Royce/Continental) (1980-81) 733
IO-470 (TCM/Continental) 737
IO-520 (TCM/Continental) 736, 737
IO-540 (Textron Lycoming) 741
IO-550 (TCM/Continental) 736, 738
IO-720 (Textron Lycoming) 741, 742
IOL-200 (TCM) (1986-87) 959, 960
IOL-300 (TCM) (1986-87) 959, 960
IPSM-II (Morton Thiokol) (1984-1985) 878
ISM (CSD) (1984-85) 865
ITS-90 (IHI) 698
IUS (CSD) 719
INDÚSTRIA MEĈANICA E AERONAUTICA LTDA (Brazil) 676
INSTYTUT LOTNICTWA (Poland) 699
IN-TECH INTERNATIONAL, INC (USA) 727

INTERNATIONAL AERO ENGINES AG (International) 693
INTREPRINDEREA TURBOMECANICA BUCURESTI (Romania) 702
Ion Thruster (SEP) (1979-1980) 691
ISAYEV (USSR) (1984-85) 837
ISHIKAWAJIMA-HARIMA JUKOGYO KABUSHIKI KAISHA (Japan) 698
Isolane (SNPE) (1985-86) 850
ISOTOV (USSR) 703
ISRAEL AIRCRAFT INDUSTRIES LTD (Israel) 696
ITAL-AMERICAN MOTOR ENGINEERING (Italy) 697
IVCHENKO (USSR) 703

J

J3 (IHI) (1981-82) 737
J7-300 (Thermo-Jet) (1980-81) 770
J8-200 (Thermo-Jet) (1980-81) 770
J10-200 (Thermo-Jet) (1980-81) 770
J13-202 (Thermo-Jet) (1980-81) 770
J52 (Pratt & Whitney) 729
J60 (Pratt & Whitney) (1978-79) 745
J69 (Teledyne CAE) *(1987-88)* 738
J75 (Pratt & Whitney) *(1987-88)* 961
J79 (General Electric) (1986-87) 939
J79 (MTU) (1978-79) 691
J79-IAI-J1E (IAI) 696
J85 (General Electric) (1986-87) 939
J85-13 (Fiat/General Electric) (1981-82) 736
J100-CA-100 (Teledyne CAE) (1981-82) 791
J100-CA-101 (Teledyne CAE) (1981-82) 791
J400 (Williams) *(1987-88)* 974
J402-CA-400 (Teledyne CAE) *(1987-88)* 970
J402-CA-401 (Teledyne CAE) *(1987-88—* 970
J402-CA-700 (Teledyne CAE) *(1987-88)* 970
J402-CA-702 (Teledyne CAE) *(1987-88)* 970
J403-MT-400 (Microturbo) *(1987-88)* 895
JB 2 × 250 (Borzecki) (1986-87) 903
JPX (see Ateliers JPX) 684
JPX 4T60/A (JPX) 684
JR 200 (IHI/NAL) (1982-83) 744
JR 220 (IHI/NAL) (1982-83) 744
JT3D (Pratt & Whitney) *(1987-88)* 961
JT4 (Pratt & Whitney) *(1987-88)* 961
JT8 (Pratt & Whitney) 729
JT8D (Pratt & Whitney) 729
JT8D-200 series (Pratt & Whitney) 730
JT9D (Pratt & Whitney) 730
JT10D (Pratt & Whitney) (1980-81) 703, 710, 762
JT12 (Pratt & Whitney) (1978-79) 745
JT15D (P&WC) 676
JTF10A (Pratt & Whitney) 732
JTF22 (Pratt & Whitney) 732
JVX (General Electric) (1983-84) 827
JACOBS (see Page Industries Inc) (1981-82) 779
JACOBS SERVICE COMPANY (USA) (1982-83) 786
JANOWSKI, JAROSLAW (Poland) *(1987-88)* 914
JAVELIN AIRCRAFT COMPANY INC (USA) 727

K

K-5 (WSK-Kalisz) (1978-79) 701
K-100A (SPP) 735
KFM 104 (IAME) (1986-87) 900
KFM 105 (IAME) (1986-87) 900
KFM 107 (IAME) (1984-85) 829
KFM 107 Maxi (IAME) 697
KFM 112 (IAME) 698
KJ12 (Kawasaki) 698
KHD (see Klöckner-Humboldt-Deutz AG) (1980-81) 701
KAWASAKI JUKOGYO KABUSHIKI KAISHA (Japan) 698
KHD LUFTFAHRTTECHNIK GmbH (West Germany) 688
KLÖCKNER-HUMBOLDT-DEUTZ AG (West Germany) (1980-81) 701
KOLIESOV (USSR) 704
KOMATSU ZENOAH COMPANY (Japan) (1986-87) 902
KONIG MOTORENBEAU (West Germany) 689
KOSBERG (USSR) (1984-85) 840
KUZNETSOV (USSR) 704

L

L 275E (Limbach) 689
L 550E (Limbach) 689
L 2000 (Limbach) 689
L 2400 (Limbach) 689
LAPAN (see Lembaga Penerbangen dan Antariska Nasional) (1982-83) 736
LE-5 (Mitsubishi) (1985-86) 830
LHTEC (Allison Gas Turbine Division) (1985-86) 908
LHTEC (see Light Helicopters Turbine Engine Company) 727
LJ95 (Teledyne CAE) (1985-86) 918
LO-360 (Avco Lycoming) *(1987-88)* 944
LR89-NA-5 (Rocketdyne) (1984-85) 887
LR101-NA-7 (Rocketdyne) (1984-85) 887
LR105-NA-5 (Rocketdyne) (1984-85) 887
LT101 (Textron Lycoming) 740
LTC1 (Textron Lycoming) 739
LTC4 (Textron Lycoming) 739, 740
LTP 101 (Textron Lycoming) 741
LTS 101 (Textron Lycoming) 740
LTSIO-360 (TCM) *(1987-88)* 972
LTSIO-520 (TCM) 738
LVRJ (Vought (1979-80) 767
Larzac (Turboméca/SNECMA) 688
LEMBAGA PENERBANGAN DAN ANTARISKA NASIONAL (Indonesia) (1982-83) 736
LEONIDES (see Harker & Associates) (1981-82) 751
Liftjet (Koliesov) 704
Liftjet (USSR) 709
LIGHT HELICOPTER TURBINE ENGINE COMPANY (USA) 727
LIMBACH FLUGMOTOREN GmbH (West Germany) 689
LIMBACH MOTORENBAU (West Germany) (1985-86) 855
LOTAREV (USSR) 705
LOTUS CARS LTD (UK) *(1987-88)* 927
LTV AEROSPACE AND DEFENCE (USA) (1984-85)
LUCAS AEROSPACE LTD. (UK) (1982-83) 758
LYCOMING (see Avco Lycoming) (1985-86) 893
LYULKA (USSR) 706

M

M-14P (Vedeneyev) 709
M-14V-26 (Vedeneyev) 709
M45 Series (Rolls-Royce/SNECMA) (1979-80) 723
M45H (Rolls-Royce/SNECMA) (1979-80) 723
M45S-11 (Rolls-Royce/SNECMA) (1978-79) 694
M45SD-02 (Rolls-Royce/SNECMA) (1979-80) 703, 724
M49 Larzac (SNECMA/Turboméca) (1985-86) 772, 775, 777
M53 (SNECMA) 685
M-55 (Thiokol) (1979-80) 765
M88 (SNECMA) 685
M 137 (Avia) (1985-86) 846
M 137A (Avia) 682
M 337 (Avia) (1985-86) 846
M 337A (Avia) 683
M 462RF (Avia) (1978-79) 679
M 601 (Motorlet) 683
M 701 (Motorlet) (1978-79) 680
MA-3 (Rocketdyne) (1984-85) 887
MA-5 (Rocketdyne) (1984-85) 887
MA-196 (Marquardt) 728
MA210/212 (Marquardt) (1982-83) 787
MA-225XAA (Marquardt) (1985-86) 908
MB-4-80 (Mudry) 684
MNA (see Microturbo North America Inc) 728
MTM 385 (MTU) (1984-85) 821
MBB (see MBB/ERNO Space Division) (1984-85) 820
MiG-23 engine (Tumansky) (1980-81) 723
Mig-25 engine (Tumansky) (1978-79) 710
Mk 36 Mod 9 (Morton Thiokol) (1985-86) 909
MS-1500 (Pieper) 690
MTM (see MTU-Turboméca-RR) 694
MTM 380 (MTU/Turboméca) (1982-83) 731
MTM 385-R (MTU/Turboméca) *(1987-88)* 907
MTM 390 (MTM) 694
MTU (see Motoren-und Turbinen-Union München GmbH 689
MX Stage-II motor (Aerojet) (1982-83) 766
MACHEN INC (USA) (1985-86) 908
Mage (SEP) (1984-85) 613
Makila (Turboméca) 687
Malemute (Morton Thiokol) (1984-85) 878
Marboré (Turboméca) (1982-83) 730
MARQUARDT COMPANY, THE (USA) 727
Maverick Motor (Aerojet) *(1987-88)* 937
Maverick, TX-481 (Morton Thiokol) *(1987-88)* 960
Maverick, TX-633 (Morton Thiokol) *(1987-88)* 960
MBB (West Germany) (1984-85) 820
MBB/ERNO SPACE DIVISION (West Germany) (1984-85) 820
Merlyn (Intech) 727
Merlyn (Machen) (1985-86) 908
Mikron IIIS (Aerotechnik) 682
MICROTURBO NORTH AMERICA INC (USA) 728
MICROTURBO SA (France) 684
Mikron IIIS (A) (Aerotechnik) 682
MIKULIN (USSR) 706
Military Spey (Rolls-Royce) 712
Minuteman first-stage motor (Thiokol) (1979-1980) 765
Minuteman motor (Aerojet) (1984-85) 856
Minuteman third-stage motor (Thiokol) (1979-80) 765
MITSUBISHI JUKOGYO KABUSHIKI KAISHA (Japan) 698
Model 2RB (Borzecki) (1980-81) 713
Model 4C2T (Cicaré) (1979-80) 683
Model 4T60/A (JPX) 684
Model 225 (Allison) 717
Model 250 (Allison) 716
Model 250-C20B Allison (MTU) 690
Model 280 (Allison) (1986-87) 928
Model 352 (Teledyne CAE) 738
Model 356 (Teledyne CAE) 738
Model 356-28A (Teledyne CAE) (1981-82) 791
Model 356-28E (Teledyne) (1979-80) 761
Model 356-28F (Teledyne CAE) (1982-83) 796
Model 365 (Teledyne CAE) (1985-86) 918
Model 370 (Teledyne CAE) *(1987-88)* 970
Model 370-1 (Teledyne CAE) *(1987-88)* 970
Model 372-2 (Teledyne CAE) *(1987-88)* 970
Model 372-11A (Teledyne CAE) *(1987-88)* 960
Model 373 (Teledyne CAE) *(1987-88)* 970
Model 401A (NPT) (1979-80) 720
Model 440/555 (Teledyne CAE) (1983-4) 839
Model 455 (Teledyne CAE) *(1987-88)* 970
Model 471 (Teledyne) (1978-79) 755
Model 501 (Allison) 717
Model 501-M62 (Allison) 718
Model 535 (Rolls-Royce) 711
Model 578 (Allison) 718
Model 578DX (PW-Allison) 734
Model 912-B46 and B51 (Rolls-Royce/Allison) (1984-85) 824
Model 912-B52 (Allison) *(1987-88)* 941
Model 1000 (IMAER) 676
Model 2000 (IMAER) 676
Model 4318F (Northrop) *(1987-88)* 960
Model 8096 Agena engine (Bell) (1984-85) 863
Monopropellant engines (MBB) (1978-79) 690
Monopropellant gas-generators (MBB) (1982-83) 734
MORTON THIOKOL INC (USA) 728
MOTEURS MUDRY-BUCHOUX (AVIONS MUDRY et CIE) (France) 684
MOTOREN-UND TURBINEN-UNION MÜNCHEN GmbH (West Germany) 689
MOTORLET NC, ZAVOD JANA SVERMY (Czechoslovakia) 683
MTU/MOTOREN-UND TURBINEN-UNION MÜNCHEN GmbH (West Germany) (1985-86) 892
MTU/TURBOMÉCA GmbH (International) 907
MTU/TURBOMÉCA-RR GmbH (International) 694
MTU/TURBOMÉCA SARL (International) (1985-86) 858
MUDRY (see Moteurs Mudry Buchoux; Avions Mudry et Cie 684

N

NAL (see National Aerospace Laboratory) 699
NGL (see Normalair-Garrett Ltd) *(1987-88)* 928
NK-8 (Kuznetsov) 704
NK-12M (Kuznetsov) 705
NK-86 (Kuznetsov) 705
NK-88 (Kuzetsov) 705
NK-144 (Kuznetsov) 705
NPT (see Noel Penny Turbines Ltd) 710
NATIONAL AEROSPACE LABORATORIES (Japan) 699
NATIONAL AIRCRAFT ENGINE FACTORY (China) *(1982-83)* 723
NATIONAL AIRCRAFT ENGINE FACTORIES (China) 680
NELSON AIRCRAFT CORPORATION (USA) 728
Nitramite (SNPE) (1985-86) 850
NOEL PENNY TURBINES LTD (UK) 710
NORMALAIR-GARRETT LIMITED (UK) *(1987-88)* 928
NORTHROP CORPORATION, VENTURA DIVISION (USA) *(1987-88)* 960
NORTON MOTORS LTD (UK) 710

O

O22 Couguar (Microturbo) (1980-81) 693
O-100-3 (Northrop) *(1987-88)* 960
O-160 (Avco Lycoming) (1986-87) 933
O-200 (TCM Continental) 735
O-200-A (Rolls-Royce/Continental) (1980-81) 733
O-235 (Textron Lycoming) 741
O-240-A (Rolls-Royce/Continental) (1980-81) 733
O-300 (Rolls-Royce/Continental) (1980-81) 733
O-320 (Textron Lycoming) 741,742
O-360 (Textron Lycoming) 741,742
O-470 (TCM/Continental) 736
O-540 (Textron Lycoming) 742
OMS (Aerojet) 716
Odin (Rolls-Royce) (1984-85) 853
Olympus (Rolls-Royce) (1979-80) 725
Olympus 593 (Rolls-Royce/SNECMA) (1980-81) 696, 707
OMNIPOL FOREIGN TRADE CORPORATION (Czechoslovakia) 682
ORAO AIR FORCE DEPOT (Yugoslavia) 743
ORENDA (see Hawker Siddeley Canada Inc) 676
Orpheus (Rolls-Royce) (1981-82) 755

P

P4 (SEP) (1980-81) 694
P8E-9 (Rocketdyne) (1980-81) 766
P41 (Norton) *(1987-88)* 928
P60 (Norton) *(1987-88)* 928
P64 (Norton) *(1987-88)* 928
P.80 (Piper) *(1987-88)* 929
P.80 (Piper TTL) (1984-85) 854
P80/2 (Piper) *(1987-88)* 929
P.80/2 (Piper TTL) (1984-85) 855
P.100 (Piper) *(1987-88)* 930
P.100 (Piper TTL) (1984-85) 855
P.200 (Piper) *(1987-88)* 930
P.200 (Piper TTL) (1984-85) 855
P&WC (see Pratt & Whitney Canada) 676
PAL 640 (JPX) *(1987-88)* 894
PAL 1300 (JPX) *(1987-88)* 894
PDM (Tumansky) (1985-86) 877
PFM 3200 (Porsche) 690
PLT-27 (Avco Lycoming) (1979-80) 735
PLT34 (Avco Lycoming) *(1987-88)* 943
PRV V6 (FAM) *(1987-88)* 894
PS-90A (Sopoylev) 708
PT6Γ Twin-Pac (P8WC) *(1987-88)* 889
PT6A (P&WC) 678
PT6B/PT6C (P&WC) 679
PT6T Twin-Pac (P&WC) 679
PUL 212 (JPX) 684
PUL 425 (JPX) 684
PW11XX (Pratt & Whitney) (1985-86) 916
PW100 (P&WC) 677
PW200 (P&WC) 679
PW205B (P&WC) *(1987-88)* 890
PW209T (P&WC) *(1987-88)* 890
PW300 (P&WC) 677
PW400 (P&WC) *(1987-88)* 887
PW1120 (Pratt & Whitney) 733
PW1128 (Pratt & Whitney) (1984-85) 885
PW1129 (Pratt & Whitney) 734
PW1130 (Pratt & Whitney) *(1982-83)* 793
PW2000 (Pratt & Whitney) 731
PW2037 (Pratt & Whitney) 731
PW3000 (Pratt & Whitney) 734
PW4000 (Pratt & Whitney) 730
PW5000 (Pratt & Whitney) 734
PZL (see Polskie Zaklady Lotnicze) 699

PZL-3R (WSK-PZL-Rzeszów) (1985-86) 868
PZL-3S (WSK-PZL-Rzeszów) 701
PZL-3SR (WSK-PZL-Rzeszów) 702
PZL-10 (WSK-PZL-Rzeszów) 1983-84) 788
PZL-10S (WSK-PZL-Rzeszów) (1984-85) 833
PZL-10W (WSK-PZL-Rzeszów) 701
PZL-F engines (Refrigeration Equipment) 699
PZL TVD-10S (WSK-PZL Rzeszów) (1985-86) 867
PAGE INDUSTRIES INC (USA) 1981-82) 779
PARODI, MOTORESEGLERTECHNIK (West Germany) 690
Patriot (Morton Thiokol) (1984-85) 878
Pave Tiger (Cuyuna) (1987-88) 947
Peacekeeper motors (Aerojet) (1984-85) 856
Peacekeeper Stage-I (Morton Thiokol) (1984-85) 878
Pedro (Morton Thiokol) (1984-85) 879
Pegasus (Rolls-Royce) 714
PIAGGIO, INDUSTRIE AERONAUTICHE E MECCANICHE RINALDO SpA (Italy) 698
PIEPER MOTORENBAU GmbH (West Germany) 690
PIPER FM LTD (UK) (1987-88) 929
PIPER LTD (UK) (1985-86) 880
PIPER-TARGET TECHNOLOGY LTD (UK) (1984-85) 854
Piston engines (CATIC) 680
Polaris A3R motor (Aerojet) (1984-85) 856
POLSKIE ZAKLADY LOTNICZE (Poland) 699
PORSCHE, DR ING h c F, PORSCHE AG (West Germany) 690
Poseidon first stage motor (Thiokol) (1980-81) 771
PRATT & WHITNEY: UNITED TECHNOLOGIES PRATT & WHITNEY (USA) 729
PRATT & WHITNEY CANADA (Canada) 676
PULCH, OTTO (West Germany) (1984-85) 822
PUSAT TEKNOLOGI DIRGANTARA (Indonesia) (1982-83) 736
PW-ALLISON (USA) 734

R

R-1E (Marquardt) 728
R-4D (Marquardt) (1984-85) 877
R-6C (Marquardt) (1984-85) 877
R-11 (Tumansky) 708
R-13 (Tumansky) 708
R-18 (TCM) (1986-87) 961
R-25 (Tumansky) 709
R-27 (Tumansky) 709
R-29 (Tumansky) 709
R-30 (Marquardt) (1984-85) 877
R-32 (Tumansky) 709
R-33 (Tumansky) 709
R-36 (Norton) 710
R-40A (Marquardt) 728
R-266 (Tumansky) (1984-85) 845
R-266/R-31 (Tumansky) 709
R-755 (Jacobs) (1980-81) 756
RB.162 (Rolls-Royce) (1978-79) 713
RB.163 Civil Spey (Rolls-Royce) 712
RB.168 Military Spey (Rolls-Royce) 712
RB.168-62 and -66 Spey (Rolls-Royce/Allison) (1984-85) 824
RB 183 (Rolls-Royce) 712
RB.183 Civil Spey (Rolls-Royce) (1979-80) 723
RB.199 (Turbo-Union) 695
RB.211 (Rolls-Royce) 711
RB.318 (Rolls-Royce/Alfa Romeo) (1981-82) 736, 754
RB.401 (Rolls-Royce) (1984-85) 852
RB.410D-2 (Rolls-Royce/SNECMA) (1979-80) 703
RB.410-11 (Rolls-Royce/SNECMA) (1979-80) 703
RB.432 (Rolls-Royce) (1979-80) 722
RB545 (Rolls-Royce) 713
RB550 (Rolls-Royce) 713
RC engines (Avco Lycoming) (1986-87) 932
RC engines (Wright) (1981-82) 770
RC2-60 (Wright) (1981-82) 770
RC2-75 (Wright) (1981-82) 770
RC2-90 (Wright) (1981-82) 770
RC-741 (LAPAN) (1982-83) 736
RD-3M-500 (Mikulin) (1986-87) 912
RD-9 (Tumansky) 708
RD-100/101/103/107/108/111 (GDL) (1984-85) 836
RD-119/214/216/219/253 (GDL) (1984-85) 837
RFB (see Rhein-Flugzeugbau GmbH) (1984-85) 822
RJ500 (Rolls-Royce) (1984-85) 801
RJ.500 (RRJAEL) (1982-83) 738, 761
RL10 (Pratt & Whitney) (1984-85) 886
RM8 (Flygmotor) 702
RM12 (Flygmotor) 702
RM-1000-A (Retimotor) (1987-88) 885
RM-2000 (Retimotor) (1987-88) 885
RRJAEL (see Rolls-Royce and Japanese Aero Engines Ltd) (1982-83) 738
RRX1 (Flygmotor) (1984-85) 836
RRX5 (Flygmotor) (1984-85) 836
RS-27 (Rocketdyne) (1984-85) 887
RS-34 (Rocketdyne) (1984-85) 887
RT.172 (Rolls-Royce/Turboméca) (1979-80) 703
RTM 321 (Rolls-Royce/Turboméca) (1983-84) 774, 781, 806
RTM 322 (Rolls-Royce/Turboméca) 694
RU-19 (Tumansky) 708
RW-100 (Rotor Way) (1984-85) 888
RW-133 (Rotor Way) (1983-84) 838
RW152-D (Rotor Way) 735
Ramjets (Marquardt) 727
Ram rocket (MBB) (1984-85) 820
RECTIMO AVIATION SA (France) 684
REFRIGERATION EQUIPMENT WORKS (Poland) 699
Resonating ramjet (DSI) (1979-80) 741
RETIMOTOR ENGENHARIA LTDA (Brazil) (1987-88) 885
RHEIN-FLUGZEUGBAU GmbH (West Germany) (1984-85) 822
Rita II (SEP) (1984-85) 813
ROCKETDYNE DIVISION OF ROCKWELL INTERNATIONAL (USA) 734
Rockets (Marquardt) 728
ROLLASON AIRCRAFT & ENGINES LTD (UK) (1983-84) 801
ROLLS-ROYCE & JAPANESE AERO ENGINES LTD (International) (1982-83) 738
ROLLS-ROYCE plc (UK) 710
ROLLS-ROYCE/ALLISON (International) (1984-85) 824
ROLLS-ROYCE MOTORS LTD (UK) (1982-83) 765
ROLLS-ROYCE/SNECMA (International) (1980-81) 707
ROLLS-ROYCE TURBOMÉCA LIMITED (International) 694
ROTAX (see Bombardier-Rotax) 675
ROTORWAY INC (USA) 735

S

SACMA (France) (1985-86) 849
SAI (see Singapore Aircraft Industries) 702
SARV retro (Morton Thiokol) (1985-86) 879
SC 430 (König) 689
SD 570 (König) 689
SD (SNPE) (1985-86) 850
SECA (see Société d'Entreprises Commerciales et Aéronautiques SA) (1987-88) 885
SEP (see Société Européenne de Propulsion) (1984-85) 812
SEP 163 (SEP) (1980-81) 695
SEP 299 (SEP) (1980-81) 695
SEP 300 (SEP) (1980-81) 695
SEP 6854 (SEP) (1980-81) 695
SEP 7342 (SEP) (1980-81) 695
SEP 7382 (SEP) (1980-81) 695
SEP 7392 (SEP) (1980-81) 695
SETE (Curtiss-Wright) (1982-83) 776
SF 930 (König) 689
SG 85 (RFB) (1981-82) 704
SG 95 (RFB) (1984-85) 822
SL 1700 (Limbach) 689
SM 160 (Valmet) (1981-82) 718
SNECMA (see Société Nationale d'Étude et de Construction de Moteurs d'Aviation) 684
SNIA BPD SpA (Italy) (1985-86) 863
SNPE (see Société Nationale des Poudres et Explosifs) (1987-88) 897
SO-1 (IL) 699
SO-3 (IL) 699
SP-440 (Alturdyne) (1981-82) 762
SPP (see Sport Plane Power Inc) 735
SR49-TC-1 (Thiokol) (1982-83) 800
SR73-AJ-1 (Thiokol) (1979-80) 765
SR-114-TC-1 (Morton Thiokol) (1987-88) 960
SRM (Morton Thiokol) 728
SS 2100 HIS (Sauer) 691
SSME (Rocketdyne) 734
SS-RPV (Microturbo/Turboméca) (1984-85) 811
SSUS-A motor (Morton Thiokol) (1987-88) 959
STAR-6 (Thiokol) (1981-82) 795
STAR-6B (Morton Thiokol) (1984-85) 879
STAR-13 (Morton Thiokol) (1984-85) 879
STAR-13A (Thiokol) (1982-83) 800
STAR-17 (Morton Thiokol) (1984-85) 879
STAR-17A (Morton Thiokol) (1984-85) 879
STAR-20 (Morton Thiokol) (1984-85) 879
STAR-24 (Morton Thiokol) (1984-85) 879
STAR-26B (Thiokol) (1981-82) 795
STAR-27 (Morton Thiokol) (1984-85) 879
STAR-30 (Morton Thiokol) (1984-85) 879
STAR-31 (Morton Thiokol) (1984-85) 879
STAR-37 (Morton Thiokol) (1984-85) 879
STAR-37FM (Morton Thiokol) (1984-85) 879
STAR-37X (Thiokol) (1982-83) 801
STAR-37XF (Morton Thiokol) (1984-85) 879
STAR-48 (Morton Thiokol) (1984-85) 879
STM (Vought) (1983-84) 844
Su-15 (Lyulka) (1987-88) 922
SVM (Aerojet) (1979-80) 730
Sandhawk (Thiokol) (1981-82) 795
Satellite engines (Aerojet) (1984-85) 856
Saturn 500 (Janowski) (1987-88) 914
SAUER MOTORENBAU GmbH (West Germany) 691
SCOMA-ÉNERGIE (France) 684
Segmented motor (CSD) (1984-85) 863
SENER-INGENIERIA Y SISTEMAS SA (Spain) 702
SHVETSOV (USSR) 707
Sidewinder motor (Aerojet) (1987-88) 937
SINGAPORE AIRCRAFT INDUSTRIES (Singapore) 702
Slat (LTV) (1984-85) 876
SNIA VISCOSA (Italy) (1980-81) 711
SOCIETA PER AZIONI ALFA-ROMEO (Italy) (1982-83) 742
SOCIÉTÉ D'ENTREPRISES COMMERCIALES ET AÉRONAUTIQUES SA (Belgium) (1987-88) 885
SOCIÉTÉ EUROPÉENNE DE PROPULSION (France) (1984-85) 812
SOCIÉTÉ NATIONALE DES POUDRES ET EXPLOSIFS (France) (1987-88) 897
SOCIÉTÉ NATIONALE D'ÉTUDE ET DE CONSTRUCTION DE MOTEURS D'AVIATION (France) 684
SOCIÉTÉ TURBOMÉCA (France) 686
SOLOY CONVERSIONS LTD (USA) 735
SOLOY DUAL PAC INC (USA) 735
SOLOVIEV (USSR) 707
Sorek 4 (Bet-Shemesh) 696
Space Shuttle OMS engine (Aerojet) 716
Space Shuttle RSRM (Morton Thiokol) 728
Space Shuttle SRM (Morton Thiokol) 728
Space Shuttle SSME (Rocketdyne) 734
Space Vehicle Motors (SVM) (Aerojet) (1979-80) 730
Sparrow/Shrike Skipper motors (Aerojet) (1987-88) 937
Spey (Rolls-Royce) 712
Spey 807 (Fiat) 697
Spin/despin motors (Thiokol) (1979-80) 767
SPORT PLANE POWER INC (USA) 735
Stamo 1000 (Pieper) (1985-86) 856
Stamo MS 1500 (Pieper) 690
Standard missile motor (Aerojet) (1984-85) 856
STATE AIRCRAFT ENGINE FACTORIES (China) (1987-88) 890
Statolite (SNPE) (1985-86) 850
Styx (SEP) (1984-85) 813
Super Sapphire (Bonner) (1985-86) 878

T

T53 (Textron Lycoming) 739
T55 (Textron Lycoming) 740
T56 (Allison) 717
T58 (General Electric) 724
T63 (Allison) 716
T64 (General Electric) 725
T64-P4D (Fiat) 697
T64-P4D (General Electric) (1982-83) 742, 784
T70 (TTL) (1987-88) 937
T74 (P&WC) 679
T76 (Garrett) 720
T101 (P&WC) (1985-86) 842
T117 (KHD) (1987-88) 901
T317 (KHD) (1984-85) 819
T400 (P&WC) 679
T406 (Allison) 717
T405 (Avco Lycoming) (1979-80) 735
T700 (General electric) 726
T701-AD-700 (Allison) 718
T703 (Allison) 716
T800-APW-800 (Textron Lycoming/Pratt & Whitney) 742
T800-LHT-800 (LHTEC) 727
TCM (see Teledyne Continental Motors) 735
TE-260G (Thiokol) (1980-81) 771
TE495-TC700 (Thunder) (1986-87) 962
TE-M-29-8 (Morton Thiokol) (1984-85) 879
TE-M-236 (Morton Thiokol) (1984-85) 879
TE-M-307 Apache (Thiokol) (1981-82) 795
TE-M-364 (Morton Thiokol) (1984-85) 879
TE-M-416 Tomahawk (Morton Thiokol) (1984-85) 878
TE-M-442-1 (Thiokol) (1981-82) 795
TE-M-458 (Morton Thiokol) (1984-85) 879
TE-M-473 Sandhawk (Thiokol) (1981-82) 795
TE-M-479 (Morton Thiokol) (1984-85) 879
TE-M-516 (Thiokol) (1982-83) 800
TE-M-521 (Morton Thiokol) (1984-85) 879
TE-M-541/542 (Thiokol) (1981-82) 795
TE-M-604 (Morton Thiokol) (1984-85) 879
TE-M-616 (Morton Thiokol) (1984-85) 879
TE-M-640 Altair III (Morton Thiokol) (1984-85) 879
TE-M-696 (Morton Thiokol) (1984-85) 879
TE-M-697 (Morton Thiokol) (1984-85) 879
TE-M-700 (Morton Thiokol) (1984-85) 879
TE-M-707 (Morton Thiokol) (1984-85) 878
TE-M-711 (Morton Thiokol) (1984-85) 879
TE-M-714 (Morton Thiokol) (1984-85) 879
TE-M-762 Antares III (Morton Thiokol) (1984-85) 879
TE-M-764 (Morton Thiokol) (1984-85) 879
TE-M-783 (Morton Thiokol) (1984-85) 879
TE-M-790 (Morton Thiokol) (1984-85) 879
TEI (see Tusas Engine Industries) 702
TF30 (Pratt & Whitney) 732
TF33 (Pratt & Whitney) (1987-88) 961
TF34 (General Electric) 721
TF39 (General Electric) 722
TF40-IHI-801A (IHI) (1981-82) 737
TF41 Spey (Rolls-Royce/Allison) (1984-85) 824
TFA (Microturbo) 684
TFE76 (Garrett) 720
TFE731 (Garrett) 720
TFE1042 (Garrett/Volvo Flygmotor) (1985-86) 898
TIGO-541 (Textron Lycoming) 742
TIO-360 (Textron Lycoming) 742
TIO-540 (Textron Lycoming) 741, 742
TIO-541 (Textron Lycoming) 741, 742
TIO/LTIO-540 (Textron Lycoming) 742
TJD-76C Baby Mamba (Dreher) (1983-84) 818
TJD-76D and E (Dreher) (1983-84) 818
TJE 341 (Garrett-AiResearch) (1980-81) 748
TM 319 (Turboméca) 687
TM 333 (Turboméca). 687
TO-360 (Avco Lycoming) (1987-88) 944
TP 319 (Turboméca) 687
TP-500 (Teledyne Continental) 737
TPE331 (Garrett) 720
TR-201 (TRW) (1984-85) 892
TR 281 (Turboméca) (1978-79) 685
TRB (Microturbo) 684
TRD-3 (Mikulin) 706
TRD-29 (Tumansky) 708
TRD-31 (Lyulka) 706
TRD-37 (Tumansky) 708
TRI 60 (Microturbo) (1987-88) 895
TRI 80 (Microturbo) (1987-88) 895
TRS 18 (Microturbo) 684
TRS 18-046 (Microturbo) (1986-87) 885
TRS 18-056 (Microturbo) (1984-85) 811
TRS 18-075 (Microturbo) (1984-85) 811
TRS 18-076 (Microturbo) (1984-85) 811
TRS 20/22 (Microturbo) (1984-85) 811
TRW (see TRW Defense and Space Systems Group) (1984-85) 892
TSE 331-3U (Garrett-AiResearch) (1980-81) 749
TSIO-360 (TCM) (1987-88) 972
TS10-520 (TCM/Continental) 737, 738

TSIO-520 (TCM) 737
TTL (see Piper Target Technology) (1984-85) 854
TTL (see Target Technology Ltd) (1987-88) 937
TU-122 (Thiokol) (1978-79) 757
TU-289 (Thiokol) (1982-83) 800
TU-758 (Morton Thiokol) (1984-85) 842
TU-780 (Morton Thiokol) (1987-88) 960
TU-876 (Morton Thiokol) (1984-85) 878
TV-2BM (Soloviev) (1980-81) 722
TV2-117A (Isotov) 703
TV3-117 (Isotov) 703
TVD-10 (Glushenkov) 703
TVD-10B (Glushenkov) 703
TVD-10B (WSK-PZL Rzeszów) 700
TVD-20 (Glushenkov) 703
TVD-850 (Isotov) (1987-88) 918
TX-30 (Thiokol) (1979-80) 765
TX-174 (Thiokol) (1982-83) 800
TX-175 (Thiokol) (1982-83) 800
TX-261 (Thiokol) (1979-80) 765
TX-306 (Thiokol) (1979-80) 765
TX-354 Castor II (Morton Thiokol) (1984-85) 878
TX-481 (Morton Thiokol) (1987-88) 960
TX-486 (Morton Thiokol) (1984-85) 878
TX-526 Castor IV (Morton Thiokol) (1984-85) 878
TX-581 (Thiokol) (1981-82) 794
TX-632 (Morton Thiokol) (1987-88) 960
TX-633 (Morton Thiokol) (1987-88) 960
TX-657 (Morton Thiokol) (1987-88) 960
TX-683 (Morton Thiokol) (1987-88) 960
TX-690 (Thiokol) (1982-83) 799
TX-732 (Thiokol) (1981-82) 795
TX 773 (Morton Thiokol) (1987-88) 960
TACTICAL SYSTEMS CO (ATSC) (1987-88) 937
TARGET TECHNOLOGY LTD (UK) (1987-88) 937
Tay (Rolls-Royce) 712
TELEDYNE CAE DIVISION OF TELEDYNE INC (USA) 734
TELEDYNE CONTINENTAL MOTORS (USA) 735
TEXTRON LYCOMING (USA) 739
TEXTRON LYCOMING/PRATT & WHITNEY (USA) 742
THERMO-JET STANDARD INC (USA) 743
THIOKOL CORPORATION (see Morton Thiokol) 959
Three cylinder (Pulch) (1984-85) 822
THUNDER ENGINES INC (1986-87) 962
Tiara Series (Continental) (1978-79) 756
Titan III engines (Aerojet) (1984-85) 855
Tomahawk (CSD) (1984-85) 865
Tomahawk (Morton Thiokol) (1984-85) 878
Trap (SEP) (1980-81) 695
Trident motors (Morton Thiokol) (1984-85) 878
TRW DEFENSE AND SPACE SYSTEMS GROUP (USA) (1984-85) 892
Tu-144D engine (Koliesov) 704
TUMANSKY (USSR) 708
TUMSAS (Turkey) (1987-88) 917
TURBOMECANICA (see Intreprinderea Turbomecanica Bucuresti) 702
TURBOMECA-SNECMA GROUPEMENT GRTS (France) 688
TURBOMÉCA, SOCIÉTÉ (France) 686
TURBO-UNION LTD (International) 695
Turmastazou (Turboméca) (1979-80) 697
Turmo (Turboméca) 687
TUSAS ENGINE INDUSTRIES (Turkey) 702
Twin (AMI) 718
Twin-Pac PT6T (P&WC) (1987-88) 889
Tyne (Rolls-Royce) 713
Tyne (RR/SNECMA/MTU/FN) 685, 690
Type 003 (Pulch) (1984-85) 822
Type 060 (Weslake) (1978-79) 720
Type 1.7-50 (Dragon) (1987-88) 947
Type 2RB (Borzecki) (1979-80) 708
Type 4C2T (Cicaré) (1979-80) 683
Type 4T60/A (JPX) 684
Type 57 (USSR) (1986-87) 915
Type 116 (Weslake) (1981-82) 757
Type 151 (NPT) (1987-88) 929
Type 171 (NPT) (1987-88) 929
Type 200 (Weslake) (1981-82) 757
Type 215 (Cuyuna) (1987-88) 947
Type 225 (Lotus) (1987-88) 927
Type 250-C20B (MTU/Allison) 902
Type 251 (NPT) (1980-81) 726
Type 274 (Weslake) (1981-82) 757
Type 301 (NPT) 710
Type 331 (NPT) (1987-88) 929
Type 342 (Weslake) (1981-82) 757
Type 352 (Teledyne CAE) 738
Type 356 (Teledyne CAE) 738
Type 356-28A (Teledyne CAE) (1981-82) 791
Type 356-28F (Teledyne CAE) (1981-82) 791
Type 365 (Teledyne CAE) (1985-86) 918
Type 370 (Teledyne CAE) (1987-88) 970
Type 370-1 (Teledyne CAE) (1987-88) 970
Type 372-2 (Teledyne CAE) (1987-88) 970
Type 372-11A (Teledyne CAE) (1987-88) 970
Type 373 (Teledyne CAE) (1987-88) 970
Type 401 (SEP) (1984-85) 813
Type 401A (NPT) (1980-81) 726
Type 401B (NPT) 710
Type 402 (SEP) (1984-85) 813
Type 403 (SEP) (1984-85) 813
Type 430 (Cuyana) (1987-88) 947
Type 430 (Westlake) (1981-82) 757
Type 440/555 (Teledyne CAE) (1983-84) 839
Type 450 (Lotus) (1987-88) 927
Type 455 (Teledyne CAE) (1987-88) 970
Type 460 (Chotia) (1984-85) 863
Type 490 (Teledyne CAE) (1983-84) 839
Type 501-M62 (Allison) 718
Type 535 (Rolls-Royce) 711
Type 548 (Weslake) (1981-82) 757
Type 600N WAEL (NGL) (1987-88) 928
Type 860 (Westlake) (1981-82) 757
Type 902 (SEP) (1984-85) 889
Type 904 (SEP) (1984-85) 889
Type 1527 (Westlake) (1981-82) 757
Type 2701 R 03 (Hirth) 688
Type 2702 R 03 (Hirth) 688

U

UL11-02 (Cuyuna) *(1987-88)* 947
UP INC (USA) 743
USINE DE SAINT MÉDARD (France) (1977-78) 759

V

V2500 (IAE) 693
VD-7 (Koliesov) 704
VO-540 (Textron Lycoming) 742
VR-35 (Flygmotor) (1984-85) 836
VALMET OY (Finland) (1982-83) 724
VEDENEYEV (USSR) 709
Viking (SEP) (1984-85) 812
Viper (Rolls-Royce) 713
Viper 600 (Fiat/Rolls-Royce) 697
VOLVO FLYGMOTOR AB (Sweden) 702
VOUGHT CORPORATION (USA) (1983-84) 844
Voyager 200 (TCM) 736, 737
Voyager 300 (TCM) 736, 737
Voyager 500 (TCM) 736, 738

W

W 5/33 (Westmayer) 675
W40/50; 42/55; 65/80; 70/85 (Weslake) (1984-85) 855
WAEL 342 (NGL) (1987-88) 928
WAEL 600N (NGL) (1987-88) 928
WAM 274 (NGL) (1985-86) 879
WAM 342 (NGL) (1985-86) 880
WAM 684 (NGL) (1983-84) 800
WJ-5 (CATIC) 681
WJ-6 (CATIC) 681
WP-2 (CATIC) 681
WP-5 (CATIC) 681
WP-6 (CATIC) 680
WP-7 (CATIC) 680
WP-8 (CATIC) 681
WP-13 (CATIC) 681
WR2 (Williams) (1987-88) 974
WR19 (Williams) 974
WR19-A7 (Williams) (1987-88) 974
WR24 (Williams) (1987-88) 974
WR34 (Williams) (1985-86) 922
WR44 (Williams) (1984-85) 893
WS-6 (CATIC) 681
WS-9 (CATIC) 682
WSK-PZL-KALISZ (see Wytwórnia Sprzetu Komunikacyjnego-PZL-Kalisz) 700
WSK-PZL-RZESZOW (see Wytwórnia Sprzetu Komunikacyjnego-PZL-Rzeszów) 700
WTS34 (Williams) (1986-87) 963
WTS34-16 (Williams) *(1987-88)* 974
WZ-5 (CATIC) 681
WZ-6 (CATIC) 681
WZ-8 (CATIC) 681
Walter M 601 (Motorlet) 683
WEEDHOPPER OF UTAH INC (USA) (1984-85) 863
WESLAKE AEROMARINE ENGINES LTD (UK) (1982-83) 765
WESLAKE & COMPANY (UK) (1985-86) 887
WESTERMAYER, OSKAR (Austria) 675
WILLIAMS INTERNATIONAL (USA) 743
WYTWÓRNIA SPRZETU KOMUNI-KACYJNEGO-PZL-KALISZ (Poland) 700
WYTWÓRNIA SPREZETU KOMUNIKACYJNEGO-PZL-RZESZÓW (Poland) 700

X

XAGM-88A (Thiokol) (1981-82) 795
XF3 (IHI) (1986-87) 901
XG-40 (Rolls-Royce) 714
XG50C (Zenoah) *(1986-87)* 902
XJ11 (IHI) *(1978-79)* 698

Y

YH 280 (CATIC) *(1987-88)* 890
YJ69-Y-406 (Teledyne CAE) 739
YLR89-NA-7 (Rocketdyne) (1984-85) 887
YLR101-NA-15 (Rocketdyne) (1984-85) 887
YLR105-NA-7 (Rocketdyne) (1984-85) 887
YO-65 (Nelson) 728
YT702-LD-700 (Textron Lycoming) 740

Z

ZO 01A (Zoche) 691
ZO 02A (Zoche) 691
ZENOAH (see Komatsu Zenoah Company) (1986-87) 902
ZOCHE, MICHAEL (West Germany) 691